Peterson's® Four-Year Colleges 2019

© 2018 Peterson's

Previous editions published as *Peterson's Annual Guide to Undergraduate Study* © 1970, 1971, 1972, 1973, 1974, 1975, 1976, 1977, 1978, 1979, 1980, 1981, 1982 and as *Peterson's Four-Year Colleges* © 1983, 1984, 1985, 1986, 1987, 1988, 1989, 1990, 1991, 1992, 1993, 1994, 1995, 1996, 1997, 1998, 1999, 2000, 2001, 2002, 2003, 2004, 2005, 2006, 2007, 2008, 2009, 2010, 2011, 2012, 2013, 2014, 2015. 2016, 2017

ISSN 1544-2330
ISBN 978-0-7689-4124-1

Printed in the United States of America

10 9 8 7 6 5 4 3 2 1   20 19 18

Forty-ninth Edition

Contents

A Note from the Peterson's® Editors   v

THE ADVICE CENTER

College Admissions Countdown Calendar   2

Choosing Your Top Ten Colleges   4

Surviving Standardized Tests   7

Planning is Essential on the Road to College   10

The Whys and Whats of College Visits   11

Honors Programs and Colleges: Smart Choices for an Undergraduate Education   15

Public and Private Colleges and Universities—How to Choose   18

Distance Education—It's Closer Than You Think   22

Why Not Women's Colleges?   27

Applying 101   31

The "Early Decision" Decision   33

Coming to America: Tips for International Students Considering Study in the U.S.   38

Financial Aid Countdown Calendar   41

Who's Paying for This? Financial Aid Basics   43

How to Use This Guide   46

Institutional Changes Since Peterson's® Four-Year Colleges 2018   51

PROFILES

United States and U.S. Territories   55

Canada   1191

International   1214

COLLEGE CLOSE-UPS

Featured Schools   1228

INDEXES

Majors   1513

Entrance Difficulty   1661

Cost Ranges   1667

Advertisers Index   1671

Alphabetical Listing of Colleges and Universities   1673

Geographic Listing of Close-Ups   1689

A Note from the Peterson's® Editors

For over fifty years, Peterson's® has given students and parents the most comprehensive, up-to-date information on undergraduate institutions in the United States and Canada. *Peterson's® Four-Year Colleges 2019* features advice and tips on the college search and selection process, such as how to consider the factors that truly make a difference during your search, how to understand the application process, and how to get financial aid. Each year, Peterson's® researches the data published in *Peterson's® Four-Year Colleges*. The information is furnished by the colleges and is accurate at the time of publishing.

Opportunities abound for students, and this guide can help you find what you want in a number of ways:

- For application and admissions advice and guidance, just head to **THE ADVICE CENTER.** The "College Admissions Countdown Calendar" outlines pertinent month-by-month milestones. "Choosing Your Top Ten Colleges" gets you started on putting together the most important Top Ten list you have ever made. You'll find some excellent advice in the article, "Planning is Essential on the Road to College," by Sarah E. Gibbs, Director of Admissions at Grove City College. Next, "Surviving Standardized Tests" describes frequently used tests and what you need to know to succeed on them. Of course, part of the college selection process involves visiting the schools themselves, and "The Whys and Whats of College Visits" is the planner you need to make those trips well worth your while. Be sure to check out the articles on specific institutions and programs that may be just right for you, including "Honors Programs and Colleges: Smart Choices for an Undergraduate Education," "Public and Private Colleges and Universities—How to Choose," "Distance Education—It's Closer than You Think," and "Why Not Women's Colleges?" Next, "Applying 101" provides advice on how best to approach the application phase of the process. If you can't make sense out of the early decision/early action conundrum, "The 'Early Decision' Decision" may help clarify it for you. The article "Coming to America: Tips for International Students Considering Study in the U.S." offers helpful information and expert tips from professionals who work with international students at colleges and universities throughout the United States. For essential information on how to meet your education expenses, you'll find the "Financial Aid Countdown Calendar" followed by the articles "Who's Paying for This? Financial Aid Basics" and "Middle Income Families: Making the Financial Aid Process Work." Finally, you'll want to read through the "How to Use This Guide" section, which explains the information presented for each individual college, how Peterson's collects its data, and how Peterson's determines eligibility for inclusion in this guide.

- Next up is the **PROFILES** section. Here you'll find our unparalleled college profiles, arranged alphabetically by state, U.S. territories, and by country. They provide need-to-know information about accredited four-year colleges—including entrance difficulty, campus setting, total enrollment, student-faculty ratio, application deadlines, expenses, most frequently chosen baccalaureate fields, and academic programs. The contact information appears at the conclusion of each college profile. Display ads, which appear near some of the institutions' profiles, have been provided and paid for by those colleges or universities that wished to supplement their profile data with additional information about their institution. A star ★ next to the name of a school signifies that the school also has an expanded profile on Peterson's website at www.petersons.com.

- Nearly 200 two-page narrative descriptions appear as **COLLEGE CLOSE-UPS**—descriptions written by admissions or college officials that provide great detail about each school. They are edited to provide a consistent format across entries for your ease of comparison.

- If you already have specifics in mind, such as a particular major or institution, turn to the **INDEXES** section. Here you can search for a school based on major, entrance difficulty, cost ranges, and geography. If you already have colleges in mind that pique your interest, you can use the "Alphabetical Listing of Colleges and Universities" to search for these schools. Page numbers referring to all information presented about a college are conveniently referenced.

Peterson's® publishes a full line of books—college and grad guides, education exploration, test preparation, financial aid, and career preparation. Peterson's® publications can be found at high school guidance offices, college libraries and career centers, and your local bookstore and library. Peterson's® books are also available at www.petersonsbooks.com.

We welcome any comments or suggestions you may have about this publication. Your feedback will help us make educational dreams possible for you—and others like you.

Colleges will be pleased to know that Peterson's® helped you in your selection. Admissions staff members are more than happy to answer questions, address specific problems, and help in any way they can. The editors at Peterson's® wish you great success in your college search!

A Note from the Peterson's® Editors

The Advice Center

College Admissions Countdown Calendar

This practical month-by-month calendar is designed to help you stay on top of the process of applying to college. For most students, the process begins in September of the junior year of high school and ends in June of the senior year. You may want to begin considering financial aid options, reviewing your academic schedule, and attending college fairs before your junior year.

JUNIOR YEAR

September

- Check with your counselor to make sure your course credits will meet college requirements.
- Be sure you are involved in one or two extracurricular activities.
- Begin building your personal list of colleges.

October

- Register for and take the PSAT/NMSQT®.

November

- Strive to get the best grades you can. A serious effort will provide you with the most options during the application process.

December

- Get involved in a community service activity.
- Begin to read newspapers, reputable online news sources, and news magazines.
- Buy *Peterson's® SAT® Prep Guide*, or *Peterson's ACT® Prep Guide* and begin to study for the tests.

January

- With your school counselor, decide when to take the ACT®, SAT®, and SAT Subject Tests™ (and which Subject Tests to take). If English is not your primary language and you are planning on attending a college in North America, decide when to take the TOEFL®.
- Keep your grades up!

February

- Plan a challenging schedule of classes for your senior year.
- Think about which teachers you will ask to write recommendations.
- Check www.nacacnet.org/ and click on "College Fairs" for up-to-date schedules and locations of college fairs.

March

- Register for the tests you will take in the spring (ACT®, SAT®, SAT Subject Tests™, or the TOEFL®).
- Meet with your school counselor to discuss college choices.
- Review your transcript and test scores with your counselor to determine how competitive your range of choices should be.
- Develop a preliminary list of fifteen to twenty colleges and universities.
- Start scheduling campus visits. The best time is when school is in session (but never during final exams). Summers are OK but will not show you what the college is really like. If possible, save your top college choices for the fall. Be aware, however, that fall is the busiest visit season, and you will need advance planning. Don't forget to write thank you letters to your interviewers.

April

- Take any standardized tests for which you have registered.
- Create a list of your potential college choices and begin to record personal and academic information that can be transferred later to your college applications.

May

- Plan college visits and make appointments.
- Structure your summer plans to include advanced academic work, travel, volunteer work, or a job.
- Confirm your academic schedule for the fall.

Summer

- Write to any colleges on your list that do not accept the Common Application to request application forms.
- Begin working on your application essays.

SENIOR YEAR

September

❏ Register for the ACT®, SAT®, SAT Subject Tests™, or the TOEFL®, as necessary.

❏ Check with your school counselor for the fall visiting schedule of college reps.

❏ Ask appropriate teachers if they would write recommendations for you. Don't forget to write thank you letters when they accept.

❏ Meet with your counselor to compile your final list of colleges.

October

❏ Prepare the Free Application for Federal Student Aid (FAFSA®), available at www.fafsa.ed.gov or through your school counseling office. An estimated income tax statement (which can be corrected later) can be used. The sooner you apply for financial aid, the better your chances. For academic year 2018–2019, the FAFSA® application window opens October 1, 2017, and closes June 30, 2019.

❏ Mail or send early applications electronically after carefully checking them to be sure they are completely filled out.

❏ Photocopy or print extra copies of your applications to use as a backup.

❏ Take the tests for which you have registered.

❏ Don't be late! Keep track of all deadlines for transcripts, recommendations, financial aid, etc.

November

❏ Be sure that you have requested your ACT® and SAT® scores be sent to your colleges of choice.

❏ Complete and submit all applications. Print or photocopy an extra copy for your records.

December

❏ Take any necessary tests: ACT®, SAT®, SAT Subject Tests™, or the TOEFL®.

❏ Meet with your counselor to verify that all is in order and that transcripts were sent to colleges.

February

❏ Submit your FAFSA® either online or via U.S. mail.

❏ Be sure your midyear report has gone out to the colleges to which you've applied.

❏ Let colleges know of any new honors or accomplishments that were not in your original application.

March

❏ Register for any Advanced Placement® (AP®) tests you might take.

❏ Be sure you have received a FAFSA® acknowledgment.

April

❏ Review the acceptances and financial aid offers you receive.

❏ Go back to visit one or two of your top-choice colleges.

❏ Notify your college of choice that you have accepted its offer (and send in a deposit by May 1).

❏ Notify the colleges you have chosen not to attend of your decision.

May

❏ Take AP® tests.

June

❏ Graduate! Congratulations and best of luck.

Choosing Your Top Ten Colleges

By using all the information in the various sections of this guide, you will find colleges worthy of the most important top-ten list on the planet—yours.

The first thing you will need to do is decide what type of institution of higher learning you want to attend. Each of the thousands of four-year colleges and universities in the United States is as unique as the people applying to it. Although listening to the voices and media hype around you can make it sound as though there are only a few elite schools worth attending, this simply is not true. By considering some of the following criteria, you will soon find that the large pool of interesting colleges can be narrowed down to a more reasonable number.

SIZE AND CATEGORY

Schools come in all shapes and sizes, from tiny rural colleges of 400 students to massive state university systems serving 100,000 students or more. If you are coming from a small high school, a college with 3,500 students may seem large to you. If you are currently attending a high school with 3,000 students, selecting a college of a similar size may not feel like a new enough experience. Some students coming from very large impersonal high schools are looking for a place where they will be recognized from the beginning and offered a more personal approach. If you don't have a clue about what size might feel right to you, try visiting a couple of nearby colleges of varying sizes. You do not have to be seriously interested in them; just feel what impact the number of students on campus has on you.

Large Universities

Large universities offer a wide range of educational, athletic, and social experiences. Universities offer a full scope of undergraduate majors and award master's and doctoral degrees as well. Universities are usually composed of several smaller colleges. Depending on your interest in a major field or area of study, you would likely apply to a specific college within the university. Each college has the flexibility to set its own standards for admission, which may differ from the overall average of the university. The colleges within a university system also set their own course requirements for earning a degree.

Universities may be public or private. Some large private universities, such as Harvard, Yale, Princeton, University of Pennsylvania, New York University, Northwestern, and Stanford, are well-known for their high entrance standards, the excellence of their education, and the success rates of their graduates. These institutions place a great deal of emphasis on research and compete aggressively for grants from the federal government to fund these projects. Large public universities,

such as the State University of New York (SUNY) System, University of Michigan, University of Texas, University of Illinois, University of Washington, and University of North Carolina, also support excellent educational programs, compete for and win research funding, and have successful graduates. Public universities usually offer substantially lower tuition rates to in-state students, although their tuition rates for out-of-state residents are often comparable to those of private institutions.

At many large universities, sports play a major role on campus. Athletics can dominate the calendar and set the tone year-round at some schools. Alumni travel from far and wide to attend their alma mater's football or basketball games, and the campus—and frequently the entire town—grinds to a halt when there is a home game. Athletes are heroes and dominate campus social life.

What are some other features of life on a university campus? Every kind of club imaginable, from literature to bioengineering and chorus to politics, can be found on most college campuses. You will be able to play the intramural version of almost every sport in which the university fields interscholastic teams and join fraternities, sororities, and groups dedicated to social action. You can become a member of a band, an orchestra, or perhaps a chamber music group or work on the newspaper, the literary magazine, or the website. The list can go on and on. You may want to try out a new interest or two or pursue what you have always been interested in and make like-minded friends along the way.

Take a look at the size of the classrooms in the larger universities and envision yourself sitting in that atmosphere. Would this offer a learning environment that would benefit you?

Liberal Arts Colleges

If you have considered large universities and come to the conclusion that all that action could be a distraction, a small liberal arts college might be right for you. Ideally tucked away on a picture-perfect campus, a liberal arts college generally has fewer than 5,000 students. The mission of most liberal arts schools is learning for the sake of learning, with a strong emphasis on creating lifelong learners who will be able to apply their education to any number of careers. This contrasts with objectives of the profession-based preparation of specialized colleges.

Liberal arts colleges cannot offer the breadth of courses provided by the large universities. As a result, liberal arts colleges try to create a niche for themselves. For instance, a college may place its emphasis on its humanities departments, whose professors are all well-known published authors and international presenters in their areas of expertise. A college may highlight its science departments by providing state-of-the-art facilities where undergraduates conduct research side by side with top-notch professors and copublish their findings in the most prestigious scientific journals in the country. The personal approach is very important at liberal arts colleges. Whether in advisement, course selection, athletic programs tailored to students' interests, or dinner with the department head at her home, liberal arts colleges emphasize that they get to know their students.

If they are so perfect, why doesn't everyone choose a liberal arts college? Well, the small size limits options. Fewer people may mean less diversity. The fact that many of these colleges encourage a study-abroad option (a student elects to spend a semester or a year studying in another country) reduces the number of students on campus even further. Some liberal arts colleges have a certain reputation that does not appeal to some students. You should ask yourself questions about the campus life that most appeals to you. Will you fit in with the campus culture? Will the small size mean that you go through your social options quickly? Check out the activities listed on the Student Center bulletin board. Does the student body look diverse enough for you? Will what is happening keep you busy and interested? Do the students have input into decision making? Do they create the social climate of the school?

Small Universities

Smaller universities often combine stringent admissions policies, handpicked faculty members, and attractive scholarship packages. These institutions generally have undergraduate enrollments of about 4,000 students. Some are more famous for their graduate and professional schools but have also established strong undergraduate colleges. Smaller universities balance the great majors options of large universities with a smaller campus community. They offer choices but not to the same extent as large universities. On the other hand, by limiting admissions and enrollment, they manage to cultivate some of the characteristics of a liberal arts college. Like a liberal arts college, a small university may emphasize a particular program and go out of its way to draw strong candidates in a specific area, such as premed, to its campus. Universities such as The Johns Hopkins University, University of Notre Dame, Vanderbilt University, Washington University in St. Louis, and Wesleyan University in Connecticut are a few examples of this category.

Technical or Specialized Colleges

Another alternative to the liberal arts college or large university is the technical or otherwise specialized college. Its goal is to offer a specialized and saturated experience in a particular field of study. Such an institution might limit its course offerings to engineering and science, the performing or fine arts, or business. Schools such as California Institute of Technology, Carnegie Mellon University, Massachusetts Institute of Technology, and Rensselaer Polytechnic Institute concentrate on attracting the finest math and science students in the country. At other schools, like Bentley College in Massachusetts or Bryant College in Rhode Island, students eat, sleep, and breathe business. These institutions are purists at heart and strong believers in the necessity of focused, specialized study to produce excellence in their graduates' achievements. If you are certain about your chosen path in life and want to immerse yourself in subjects such as math, music, or business, you will fit right in.

Religious Colleges

Many private colleges have religious origins, and many of these have become secular institutions with virtually no trace of their religious roots. Others remain dedicated to a religious way of education. What sets religious colleges apart is the way they combine faith, learning, and student life. Faculty members and administrators are hired with faith as a criterion as much as their academic credentials.

Single-Gender Colleges

There are strong arguments that being able to pursue one's education without the distraction, competition, and stress caused by the presence of the opposite sex helps a student evolve a stronger sense of her or his self-worth; achieve more academically; have a more fulfilling, less pressured social schedule; and achieve more later in life. For various historic, social, and psychological reasons, there are many more all-women than all-men colleges. A strict single-sex environment is rare. Even though the undergraduate day college adheres to an all-female or all-male admissions policy, coeducational evening classes or graduate programs and coordinate facilities and classes shared with nearby coed or opposite-sex institutions can result in a good number of students of the opposite sex being found on campus. If you want to concentrate on your studies and hone your leadership qualities, a single-gender school is an option.

LOCATION

Location and distance from home are two other important considerations. If you have always lived in the suburbs, choosing an urban campus can be an adventure, but after a week of the urban experience, will you long for a grassy campus and open space? On the other hand, if you choose a college in a rural area, will you run screaming into the Student Center some night looking for noise, lights, and people? The location—urban, rural, or suburban—can directly affect how easy or how difficult adjusting to college life will be for you.

Don't forget to factor in distance from home. Everyone going off to college wants to think he or she won't be homesick, but sometimes it's nice to get a home-cooked meal or to do the laundry in a place that does not require quarters. Even your kid sister may seem like less of a nuisance after a couple of months away.

Here are some questions you might ask yourself as you go through the selection process: In what part of the country do I want to be? How far away from home do I want to be? What is the cost of returning home? Do I need to be close to a city? How close? How large of a city? Would city life distract me? Would I concentrate better in a setting that is more rural or more suburban?

ENTRANCE DIFFICULTY

Many students will look at a college's entrance difficulty as an indicator of whether or not they will be admitted. For instance, if you have an excellent academic record, you might wish to primarily consider those colleges that are highly competitive. Although entrance difficulty does not translate directly to quality of education, it indicates which colleges are attracting large numbers of high-achieving students. A high-achieving student body usually translates into prestige for the college and its graduates. Prestige has some advantages but should definitely be viewed as a secondary factor that might tip the scales when all the other important factors are equal. Never base your decision on prestige alone!

The other principle to keep in mind when considering this factor is to not sell yourself short. If everything else tells you that a college might be right for you, but your numbers just miss that college's average range, apply there anyway. Your numbers—grades and test scores—are undeniably important in the admissions decision, but there are other considerations. First, lower grades in honors or AP® courses will impress colleges more than top grades in regular-track courses because they demonstrate that you are the kind of student willing to accept challenges. Second, admissions directors are looking for different qualities in students that can be combined to create a multifaceted class. For example, if you did poorly in

your freshman and sophomore years but made a great improvement in your grades in later years, this usually will impress a college. If you are likely to contribute to your class because of your special personal qualities, a strong sense of commitment and purpose, unusual and valuable experiences, or special interests and talents, these factors can outweigh numbers that are weaker than average. Nevertheless, be practical. Overreach yourself in a few applications, but put the bulk of your effort into gaining admission to colleges where you have a realistic chance for admission.

THE PRICE OF AN EDUCATION

The price tag for higher education continues to rise, and it has become an increasingly important factor for people. While it is necessary to consider your family's resources when choosing a list of colleges to which you might apply, never eliminate a college solely because of cost. There are many ways to pay for college, including loans, and a college education will never depreciate in value, unlike other purchases. It is an investment in yourself and will pay back the expense many times over in your lifetime.

Surviving Standardized Tests

WHAT ARE STANDARDIZED TESTS?

Colleges and universities in the United States use tests to help evaluate applicants' readiness for admission or to place them in appropriate courses. The tests that are most frequently used by colleges are the ACT® Exam and the College Board's SAT® Exam. In addition, the Educational Testing Service (ETS) offers the TOEFL® test, which evaluates the English-language proficiency of nonnative speakers. The tests are offered at designated testing centers located at high schools and colleges throughout the United States and U.S. territories and at testing centers in various countries throughout the world.

Upon request, special accommodations for students with documented visual, hearing, physical, or learning disabilities are available. Examples of special accommodations include tests in Braille or large print and such aids as a reader, recorder, magnifying glass, or sign language interpreter. Additional testing time may be allowed in some instances. Contact the appropriate testing program or your guidance counselor for details on how to request special accommodations.

THE ACT® Exam

The ACT® exam is a standardized college entrance examination that measures knowledge and skills in English, mathematics, reading comprehension, and science reasoning and the application of these skills to future academic tasks. The ACT® exam consists of four multiple-choice tests. The four tests and the content covered in each is as follows:

English Test (75 questions; 45 minutes)
- Usage and mechanics
- Rhetorical skills

Mathematics Test (60 questions; 60 minutes)
- Pre-algebra
- Elementary algebra
- Intermediate algebra
- Coordinate geometry
- Plane geometry
- Trigonometry

Reading Test (40 questions; 35 minutes)
- Literary narrative/Prose fiction
- Humanities
- Social studies
- Natural sciences

Science (40 questions; 35 minutes)
- Data representation
- Research summaries
- Conflicting viewpoints

Each section is scored from 1 to 36 and is scaled for slight variations in difficulty. Students are not penalized for incorrect responses. The composite score is the average of the four scaled scores. The ACT® Plus Writing includes the four multiple-choice tests and the 40-minute Writing Test, which measures writing skills emphasized in high school English classes and in entry-level college composition courses.

To prepare for the ACT® Exam, ask your guidance counselor for a free guidebook, *Preparing for the ACT® Test*, or download it at www.act.org/content/dam/act/unsecured/documents/Preparing-for-the-ACT.pdf. Besides providing general test-preparation information and additional test-taking strategies, this guidebook provides a full-length practice exam including the Writing Test, instructions for taking the Writing Test, test-preparation strategies, and what to expect on test day.

DON'T FORGET TO . . .

- ❏ Take the SAT® Exam or ACT® Exam before application deadlines.
- ❏ Note that test registration deadlines precede test dates by about six weeks.
- ❏ Register to take the TOEFL® test if English is not your native language and you are planning on studying at a North American college.
- ❏ Contact the College Board or ACT, Inc., in advance if you need special accommodations when taking tests.

The SAT® has these sections: Evidence-Based Reading and Writing, Math, and the SAT® Essay. It is based on 1600 points—the top scores for the Math section and the Evidence-Based Reading and Writing section will be 800, and the SAT® Essay score is reported separately.

Reading Test (52 questions; 65 minutes)
Passages in U.S. and world literature, history/social studies, and science are used to test the following skills:
- Command of Evidence
- Words in Context
- Analysis in History/Social Studies and in Science

Writing and Language Test (44 questions; 35 minutes)
Passages in careers, history/social studies, humanities, and science are used to test the following skills:
- Command of Evidence
- Words in Context
- Analysis in History/Social Studies and in Science
- Expression of ideas
- Standard English conventions

Math Test (58 questions; 80 minutes)

This test is divided into two sections: the no-calculator section (25 minutes) and the calculator section (55 minutes).

- Content includes algebra, problem solving and data analysis, advanced math, area and volume calculations, trigonometric functions, and lines, triangles, and circles using theorems.

SAT® Essay (Optional)

* 50 minutes

- Argument passage written for a general audience

- Analysis of argument in passage using text evidence

- Score: 3–12 (Reading: 1–4 scale, Analysis: 1–4 scale, Writing: 1–4 scale)

According to the College Board's website, the following are the "Key Content Features" of the SAT® exam:

- **Relevant Words in Context:** Students need to interpret the meaning of words based on the context of the passage in which they appear. The focus is on "relevant" words—not obscure ones.

- **Command of Evidence:** In addition to demonstrating writing skills, students need to show that they're able to interpret, synthesize, and use evidence found in a wide range of sources.

- **Essay Analyzing a Source:** Students read a passage and explain how the author builds an argument, and supports their claims with actual data from the passage.

- **Math Focused on Three Key Areas:** Problem Solving and Data Analysis (using ratios, percentages, and proportional reasoning to solve problems in science, social science, and career contexts), the Heart of Algebra (mastery of linear equations and systems), and Passport to Advanced Math (more complex equations and the manipulation they require).

- **Problems Grounded in Real-World Contexts:** All of the questions are grounded in the real world, directly related to work performed in college.

- **Analysis in Science and in Social Studies:** Students need to apply reading, writing, language, and math skills to answer questions in contexts of science, history, and social studies.

- **Founding Documents and Great Global Conversation:** Students will find an excerpt from one of the Founding Documents—such as the Declaration of Independence, the Constitution, and the Bill of Rights—or a text from the "Great Global Conversation" about freedom, justice, and human dignity.

- **No Penalty for Wrong Answers:** Students earn points for the questions they answer correctly.

Check out the College Board's website at https://collegereadiness.collegeboard.org/sat-subject-tests/about/at-a-glance for the most up-to-date information.

Top 10 Ways NOT to Take the Test

1. Cramming the night before the test.
2. Not becoming familiar with the directions before you take the test.
3. Not becoming familiar with the format of the test before you take it.
4. Not knowing how the test is graded.
5. Spending too much time on any one question.
6. Second-guessing yourself.
7. Not checking spelling, grammar, and sentence structure in essays.
8. Writing a one-paragraph essay.
9. Forgetting to take a deep breath—
10. and finally—Don't lose it!

SAT SUBJECT TESTS™

SAT Subject Tests™ are required by some institutions for admission and/or placement in freshman-level courses. Each Subject Test measures one's knowledge of a specific subject and the ability to apply that knowledge. Students should check with each institution for its specific requirements. In general, students are required to take three Subject Tests (one English, one mathematics, and one of their choice).

Subject Tests are given in the following areas: biology, chemistry, Chinese, French, German, Italian, Japanese, Korean, Latin, literature, mathematics, modern Hebrew, physics, Spanish, U.S. history, and world history. These tests are 1 hour long and are primarily multiple-choice tests. Three Subject Tests may be taken on one test date.

On the subject tests, students gain a point for each correct answer and lose a fraction of a point for each incorrect answer. The raw scores are then converted to scaled scores that range from 200 to 800 For more details about SAT Subject Tests™, visit https://collegereadiness.collegeboard.org/sat-subject-tests/about/at-a-glance.

THE TOEFL (IBT)® INTERNET-BASED TEST

The Test of English as a Foreign Language Internet-Based Test (TOEFL iBT®) is designed to help assess a student's grasp of English if it is not the student's first language. Performance on the TOEFL® test may help interpret scores on the critical reading sections of the SAT® exam. The test consists of four integrated sections: speaking, listening, reading, and writing. The TOEFL iBT® emphasizes integrated skills. The paper-based versions of the TOEFL® test will continue to be administered in certain countries where the Internet-based version has not yet been introduced. For further information, visit www.ets.org/toefl.

WHAT OTHER TESTS SHOULD I KNOW ABOUT?

The AP® Program

The AP® program allows high school students to try college-level work and build valuable skills and study habits in the process. Subject matter is explored in more depth in AP courses than in other high school classes. A qualifying score on an AP test—which varies from school to school—can earn you college credit or advanced placement. Getting qualifying grades on enough exams can even earn you a full year's credit and sophomore standing at more than 1,500 higher-education institutions. There are more than thirty AP courses across multiple subject areas, including art history, biology, and computer science. Speak to your guidance counselor for information about your school's offerings. For more information about the AP® program, visit www.apstudent. collegeboard.org/home.

College-Level Examination Program (CLEP®)

The CLEP® exam enables students to earn college credit for what they already know, whether it was learned in school, through independent study, or through other experiences outside of the classroom. More than 2,900 colleges and universities now award credit for qualifying scores on one or more of the 33 CLEP exams. The exams, which are 90 minutes in length and are primarily multiple choice, are administered at participating colleges and universities.
For more information, check out the website at www.clep.collegeboard.org.

WHAT CAN I DO TO PREPARE FOR THESE TESTS?

Know what to expect. Get familiar with how the tests are structured, how much time is allowed, and the directions for each type of question. Get plenty of rest the night before the test and eat breakfast that morning.

There are a variety of products, from books to software to videos, available to help you prepare for most standardized tests. Find the learning style that suits you best. As for which products to buy, there are two major categories—those created by the test-makers and those created by private companies. The best approach is to talk to someone who has been through the process and find out which product or products he or she recommends.

Some students report significant increases in scores after participating in coaching programs. Longer-term programs (40 hours) seem to raise scores more than short-term programs (20 hours), but beyond 40 hours, score gains are minor. Math scores appear to benefit more from coaching than critical reading scores.

Resources

There is a variety of ways to prepare for standardized tests—find a method that fits your schedule and your budget—but you should definitely prepare. Far too many students walk into these tests cold, either because they find standardized tests frightening or annoying or they just haven't found the time to study. The key is that these exams are standardized. That means these tests are largely the same from administration to administration; they always test the same concepts. They have to, or else you couldn't compare the scores of people who took the tests on different dates. The numbers or words may change, but the underlying content doesn't.

So how do you prepare? At the very least, you should review relevant material, such as math formulas and commonly used vocabulary words, and know the directions for each question type or test section. You should take at least one practice test and review your mistakes so you don't make them again on the test day. Beyond that, you know best how much preparation you need. You'll also find lots of material in libraries or bookstores to help you: books and software from the test-makers and from other publishers (including Peterson's) or live courses that range from national test-preparation companies to teachers at your high school who offer classes.

Planning is Essential on the Road to College

Sarah E. Gibbs, Director of Admissions
Grove City College

The road to college is much like an expedition. It can appear overwhelming, exciting, and at times too far away to be tangible. However, much like planning a trip out of town or across the globe, there is preparation involved, and it is always best to start that planning early. First, you must figure out where you want to go, then how you want to get there, and finally, what you want to do once you arrive. Each decision will require a different route—a route that may or may not look the same as that of your friends.

The same is true when considering college planning. If you start early—making short-term and long-term goals—it will help you determine your next steps. For instance, if you start your freshman year determining you want to graduate with a certain GPA, that decision will dictate your next steps, like studying, choosing to take harder curriculum, and prioritizing your involvement in activities.

Once you establish your short-term and long-term goals, you need to make wise decisions about those goals. For instance, if you do not do well in a certain class, don't make a rash decision to withdraw from that subject area. You may want to continue in that subject knowing that you may need to seek out help or tutors to help you achieve your goal.

In addition to thinking through your academic goals, you must also consider your personal interests and activities. Your interests may determine the type of college you would like to attend. Decide early on what your passion(s) are, and invest your time wisely in those pursuits. If you know those activities are ones you want to pursue in college, then visit college campuses that fulfill your desire to march in the band, compete in a varsity or intramural sport, or participate in a service organization.

Ask yourself the question that most students do not: Am I ready for college? If the answer is no, then ask yourself what you need to do to be ready, and work towards that goal.

When looking at applicants, most private colleges will look holistically at the student, taking into consideration his or her commitment, dedication, and character. These attributes, along with academic performance and specific major pursuit, indicate whether the student may succeed at a campus. Also, make sure you participate in any interview process through an admissions office. Interviewing with an Admission Counselor allows him/her to get to know you and become your advocate.

Ultimately, the sooner you start planning, the better prepared you will be for the journey you are about to take. Not only will you be prepared for the college planning process, you will be well equipped for attending college and achieving your goals and dreams for a successful future.

Sarah E. Gibbs has spent seventeen years serving families in higher education. She is currently the Director of Admission at Grove City College in Grove City, Pennsylvania.

The Whys and Whats of College Visits

Dawn B. Sova, Ph.D.

The campus visit should not be a passive activity for you and your parents. Take the initiative and gather information beyond that provided in the official tour. You will see many important indicators during your visit that will tell you more about the true character of a college and its students than the tour guide will reveal. Know what to look for and how to assess the importance of such indicators.

WHAT SHOULD YOU ASK AND WHAT SHOULD YOU LOOK FOR?

Your first stop on a campus visit is the visitor center or admissions office, where you will probably have to wait to meet with a counselor. Colleges usually plan to greet visitors later than the appointed time in order to give them the opportunity to review some of the campus information that is liberally scattered throughout the visitor waiting room. Take advantage of the time to become even more familiar with the college by arriving 15 to 30 minutes before your appointment to observe the behavior of staff members and to browse through the yearbooks and student newspapers that will be available.

If you prepare in advance, you will have already reviewed the college catalog and map of the campus. These materials familiarize you with the academic offerings and the physical layout of the campus, but the true character of the college and its students emerges in other ways.

Begin your investigation with the visitor center staff members. As a student's first official contact with the college, they should make every effort to welcome prospective students and project a friendly image.

- How do they treat you and other prospective students who are waiting? Are they friendly and willing to speak with you, or do they try their hardest to avoid eye contact and conversation?

- Are they friendly with each other and with students who enter the office, or are they curt and unwilling to help?

- Does the waiting room have a friendly feeling or is it cold and sterile?

If the visitor center staff members seem indifferent to prospective students, there is little reason to believe that they will be warm and welcoming to current students. View such behavior as a warning to watch very carefully the interaction of others with you during the tour. An indifferent or unfriendly reception in the admissions office may be simply the first of many signs that attending this college will not be a pleasant experience.

Look through several yearbooks and see the types of activities that are actually photographed, as opposed to the activities that colleges promise in their promotional literature. Some questions are impossible to answer if the college is very large, but for small and moderately sized colleges the yearbook is a good indicator of campus activity.

- Has the number of clubs and organizations increased or decreased in the past five years?

- Do the same students appear repeatedly in activities?

- Do sororities and fraternities dominate campus activities?

- Are participants limited to one sex or one ethnic group, or is there diversity?

- Are all activities limited to the campus, or are students involved in activities in the community?

Use what you observe in the yearbooks as a means of forming a more complete understanding of the college, but don't base your entire impression on just one facet. If time permits, look through several copies of the school newspaper, which should reflect the major concerns and interests of the students. The paper is also a good way to learn about the campus social life.

- Does the paper contain a mix of national and local news?

- What products or services are advertised?

- How assertive are the editorials?

- With what topics are the columnists concerned?

- Are movies and concerts that meet your tastes advertised or reviewed?

- What types of ads appear in the classified section?

The newspaper should be a public forum for students, and, as such, should reflect the character of the campus and of the student body. A paper that deals only with seemingly safe and well-edited topics on the editorial page and in regular feature columns might indicate administrative censorship. A lack of ads for restaurants might indicate either a lack of good places to eat or that area restaurants do not welcome student business. A limited mention of movies, concerts, or other entertainment might reveal a severely limited campus social life. Even if ads and reviews are included, you should still balance how such activities reflect your tastes.

You will have only a limited amount of time to ask questions during your initial meeting with the admissions counselor, for very few schools include a formal interview in the initial campus visit or tour. Instead, this brief meeting is often just a nicety that allows the admissions office to begin a file for the student and to record some initial impressions. Save your questions for the tour guide and for students on campus you meet along the way.

HOW CAN YOU ASSESS THE TRUE CHARACTER OF A COLLEGE AND ITS STUDENTS?

Colleges do not train their tour guides to deceive prospective students, but they do caution guides to avoid unflattering topics and campus sites. Does this mean that you will see only a sugarcoated version of life on a particular college campus? Not at all, especially not if you are observant.

Most organized campus visits include such campus facilities as dormitories, dining halls, libraries, student activity and recreation centers, and the health and student services centers. Some may only be pointed out, while you will walk through others. Either way, you will find that many signs of the true character of the college emerge if you keep your eyes open.

Bulletin boards in dormitories and student centers contain a wealth of information about campus activities, student concerns, and campus groups. Read the posters, notices, and messages to learn what *really* interests students. Unlike ads in the school newspaper, posters put up by students advertise both on-and off-campus events, so they will give you an idea of what is also available in the surrounding community.

Review the notices, which may cover either campuswide events or events that concern only small groups of students. The catalog may not mention a performance group, but an individual dormitory with its own small theater may offer regular productions. Poetry readings, jam sessions, writers' groups, and other activities may be announced and show diversity of student interests.

Even the brief bulletin board messages offering objects for sale and noting objects that people want to purchase reveal a lot about a campus. Are most of the items computer-related? Or do the messages specify audio equipment or musical instruments? Are offers to trade goods or services posted? Don't ignore the "ride wanted" messages. Students who want to share rides home during a break may specify widely diverse geographical locations. If so, then you know that the student body is not limited to only the immediate area or one locale. Other messages can also enhance your knowledge of the true character of the campus and its students.

As you walk through various buildings, examine their condition carefully.

- Is the paint peeling, and do the exteriors look worn?

- Are the exteriors and interiors of the building clean?

- Is the equipment in the classrooms up-to-date or outdated?

Pay particular attention to the residence halls, especially to factors that might affect your safety. Observe the appearance of the structure, and ask about the security measures in and around the residence halls.

- Are the residence halls noisy or quiet?

- Do they seem crowded?

- How good is the lighting around each residence hall?

- Are the residence halls spread throughout the campus or are they clustered in one main area?

- Who has access to the residence halls in addition to students?

- How secure are the means by which students enter and leave the residence hall?

While you are on the subject of dormitory safety, you should also ask about campus safety. Don't expect that the guide will rattle off a list of crimes that have been committed in the past year. To obtain that information, access the recent year of issues of *The Chronicle of Higher Education* and locate its yearly report on campus crime. Also ask the guide about safety measures that the campus police take and those that students have initiated.

- Can students request escorts to their residences late at night?

- Do campus shuttle buses run at frequent intervals all night?

- Are "blue-light" telephones liberally placed throughout the campus for students to use to call for help?

- Do the campus police patrol the campus regularly?

If the guide does not answer your questions satisfactorily, wait until after the tour to contact the campus police or traffic office for answers.

Campus tours usually just point out the health services center without taking the time to walk through. Even if you don't see the inside of the building, you should take a close look at the location of the health services center and ask the guide questions about services.

- How far is the health center from the residence halls?

- Is a doctor always on call?

- Does the campus transport sick students from their dormitories or must they walk?

- What are the operating hours of the health center?

- Does the health center refer students to a nearby hospital?

If the guide can't answer your questions, visit the health center later and ask someone there.

Most campus tours take pride in showing students their activities centers, which may contain snack bars, game rooms, workout facilities, and other means of entertainment. Should you scrutinize this building as carefully as the rest? Of course. Outdated and poorly maintained activity equipment contributes to your total impression of the college. You should also ask about the hours, availability, and cost (no, the activities are usually not free) of using the bowling alleys, pool tables, air hockey tables, and other amenities.

As you walk through campus with the tour, also look carefully at the appearance of the students who pass. The way in which both men and women groom themselves, the way they dress, and even their physical bearing communicate a lot more than any guidebook can. If everyone seems to conform to the same look, you might feel that you would be uncomfortable at the college, however nonconformist that look might be. On the other hand, you might not feel comfortable on a campus that stresses diversity of dress and behavior, and your observations now can save you discomfort later.

- Does every student seem to wear a sorority or fraternity t-shirt or jacket?

- Is everyone of your sex sporting the latest fad haircut?

- Do all of the men or the women seem to be wearing expensive name-brand clothes?

- Do most of the students seem to be working hard to look outrageous with regards to clothing, hair color, and body art?

- Would you feel uncomfortable in a room full of these students?

Is appearance important to you? If it is, then you should consider very seriously if you answer *yes* to any of the questions above. You don't have to be the same as everyone else on campus, but standing out too much may make you unhappy.

As you observe the physical appearance of the students, also listen to their conversations as you pass them. What are they talking about? How are they speaking? Are their voices and accents all the same, or do you hear diversity in their speech? Are you offended by their language? Think how you will feel if surrounded by the same speech habits and patterns for four years.

WHERE SHOULD YOU VISIT ON YOUR OWN?

Your campus visit is not over when the tour ends because you will probably have many questions yet to be answered and many places to still be seen. Where you go depends upon the extent to which the organized tour covers the campus. Your tour should take you to view residential halls, health and student services centers, the gymnasium or field house, dining halls, the library, and recreational centers. If any of the facilities on this list have been omitted, visit them on your own and ask questions of the students and staff members you meet. In addition, you should step off campus and gain an impression of the surrounding community. You will probably become bored with life on campus and spend at least some time off campus. Make certain that you know what the surrounding area is like.

The campus tour leaves little time to ask impromptu questions of current students, but you can do so after the tour. Eat lunch in one of the dining halls. Most will allow visitors to pay cash to experience a typical student meal. Food may not be important to you now while you are living at home and can simply take anything you want from the refrigerator at any time, but it will be when you are away at college with only a meal ticket to feed you.

- How clean is the dining hall? Consider serving tables, floors, and seating.

- What is the quality of the food?

- How big are the portions?

- How much variety do students have at each meal?

- How healthy are the food choices?

While you are eating, try to strike up a conversation with students and tell them that you are considering attending their college. Their reactions and advice can be eye-opening. Ask them questions about the academic atmosphere and the professors.

- Are the classes large or small?

- Do the majority of the professors only lecture or are tutorials and seminars common?

- Is the emphasis of the faculty career-oriented or abstract?

- Are the teaching methods innovative and stimulating or boring and dull?

- Is the academic atmosphere pressured, lax, or somewhere in between?

- Which are the strong majors? The weak majors?

- Is the emphasis on grades or social life or a mix of both at the college?

- How hard do students have to work to receive high grades?

Current students can also give you the inside line on the true nature of the college social life. You may gain some idea through looking in the yearbook, in the newspaper, and on the bulletin boards, but students will reveal the true highs and lows of campus life. Ask them about drug use, partying, dating, drinking, and anything else that may affect your life as a student.

- Which are the most popular club activities?

- What do students do on weekends? Do most go home?

- How frequently do concerts occur on campus? Who has recently performed?

- How can you become involved in specific activities (name them)?

- How strictly are campus rules enforced and how severe are penalties?

- What counseling services are available?

- Are academic tutoring services available?

- Do they feel that the faculty really cares about students, especially freshmen?

You will receive the most valuable information from current students, but you will only be able to speak with them after the tour is over. And you might have to risk rejection as you try to initiate conversations with students who might not want to reveal how they feel about the campus. Still, the value of this information is worth the chance.

If you have the time, you should also visit the library to see just how accessible research materials are and to observe the physical layout. The catalog usually specifies the days and hours of operation, as well as the number of volumes contained in the library and the number of periodicals to which it subscribes. A library also requires accessibility, good lighting, an adequate number of study carrels, and lounge areas for students. Many colleges have created 24-hour study lounges for students who find the residence halls too noisy for studying, although most colleges claim that they designate areas of the residences as "quiet study" areas. You may not be interested in any of this information, but when you are a student you will have to make frequent use of the campus library so you should know what is available. You should at least ask how extensive their holdings are in your proposed major area. If they have virtually nothing, you will have to spend a lot of time ordering items via interlibrary loan or making copies, which can become expensive. The ready answer of students that they will obtain their information from the Internet is unpleasantly countered by professors who demand journal articles with documentation.

Make a point of at least driving through the community surrounding the college because you will be spending time there shopping, dining, working in a part-time job, or attending events. Even the largest and best-stocked campus will not meet all of your social and personal needs. If you can spare the time, stop in several stores to see if they welcome college students.

- Is the surrounding community suburban, urban, or rural?

- Does the community offer stores of interest, such as bookstores, craft shops, and boutiques?

- Do the businesses employ college students?

- Does the community have a movie or stage theater?

- Are there several types of interesting restaurants?

- Do there seem to be any clubs that court a college clientele?

- Is the center of activity easy to walk to, or do you need other transportation?

You might feel that a day is not enough to answer all of your questions, but even answering some questions will provide you with a stronger basis for choosing a college. Many students visit a college campus several times before making their decision. Keep in mind that for the rest of your life you will be associated with the college that you attend. You will spend four years of your life at this college. The effort of spending several days to obtain the information to make your decision is worthwhile.

———————

Dawn B. Sova, Ph.D., is a former newspaper reporter and columnist, as well as the author of more than eight books and numerous magazine articles. She teaches creative and research writing, as well as scientific and technical writing, newswriting, and journalism.

Honors Programs and Colleges: Smart Choices for an Undergraduate Education

Dr. Joan Digby

In general, students and their parents are guided toward a narrow selection of colleges and universities based on reputation, conversations with friends, or promotional material. Few people think to approach the college search focused on honors opportunities. As a result, students with extraordinary talents and interests miss out on a rich variety of untapped financial resources and exciting college experiences.

The smarter approach is to seek out a distinctive education that caters to students' great diversity of intellectual and creative strengths. If you are a strong student filled with ideas, longing for creative expression and ready to take on career-shaping challenges, then an honors education is just for you. Honors programs and colleges offer some of the finest undergraduate degrees available at U.S. colleges and do it with students in mind. The essence of honors is personal attention, top faculty, enlightening seminars, illuminating study-travel experiences, research options, and career-building internships—all designed to enhance a classic education and prepare you for life achievements. And here is an eye-opening bonus: Honors programs and colleges may reward your past academic performance by giving you scholarships that will help you pay for your higher education!

Take your choice of institutions: community college, state or private, two- or four-year, college or large research university. There are honors opportunities in each. What they share is an unqualified commitment to academic excellence. Honors education teaches students to think and write clearly, be excited by ideas, and become independent, creative, self-confident learners. It prepares exceptional students for professional choices in every imaginable sphere of life: arts and sciences, engineering, business, health, education, medicine, theater, music, film, journalism, media, law, politics—invent your own professional goal and honors will guide you to it! Whichever honors program or college you choose, you can be sure to enjoy an extraordinarily fulfilling undergraduate education.

WHO ARE HONORS STUDENTS?

Who are you? Perhaps a high school junior filling out your first college application, a community college student seeking to transfer to a four-year college, or possibly a four-year college student doing better than you had expected. You might be an international student, a varsity athlete, captain of the debate team, or second violin in the orchestra. Whether you are the first person in your family to attend college or an adult with a grown family seeking a new career, honors might well be right for you. Honors programs admit students with every imaginable background and educational goal.

How does honors satisfy students and give them something special? Read what students in some honors programs and colleges say. Although they refer to particular honors colleges or programs, their experiences are typical of what students find exciting about honors education on hundreds of campuses around the country.

"Being an honors program student has been a life-changing experience for me. I have gained tremendously in knowledge, experience, and self-esteem. I have learned so much more in the program than any textbook could teach about the value of encouraging support and positive thinking."

—*Cheri, Mount Wachusett Community College*

"I've been in a healing ceremony in Ecuador and have performed music on stage. I've guided my peers and Navajo children, hiked the Grand Canyon, and so much more. Sometimes, experience speaks for itself; always, it creates paths, opens eyes, and helps us find our places. Thanks to my honors program, I've experienced these wonders and accomplishments. Now I know that there are no greater lessons than how to learn and love discovery."

—*April, University of North Florida*

"The Honors College has been my home away from home. In the midst of a diverse, fairly large university, it has provided me with the intimacy that I needed... My freshman-year living situation on the honors floor... allowed me to find like-minded students early in my college career."

—*Brian, Davidson Honors College, University of Montana*

"I was able to transition from an honors program at a two-year institution into an honors program at a four-year institution without any reservations or tribulations."

—*Rachel, Harrisburg Area Community College*

"Every single professor is in love with what they do and it shows in their research, their amazing teaching, and their interaction with students outside of the classroom. The undergraduate journey can be very difficult at times, but as an Honors College student, you're sure to have plenty of support every step of the way."

—*Walteria, Wilkes Honors College, Florida Atlantic University*

"The class size is perfect and I've been able to make some of my closest relationships with students and teachers through the program. The majority of honors faculty I have encountered have been overwhelmingly helpful... and my favorite courses have been honors classes."

—*Ellen, Eastern Illinois University*

"Our professor met us at a local restaurant the last evening of class, and we shared a wonderful dinner. It had such a familiar feel to it because these are students I have known throughout my four years in the program."

—*Betsy, University of La Verne*

"For the last two years, I have investigated new synthetic methods under the direction of a professor emeritus. Through the University Honors College, I am able to pursue this interest in chemistry and other academic endeavors... that have allowed me to develop my academic potential and contribute to the scientific body of knowledge."

—*Justin, University of Pittsburgh*

"The most rewarding part of being a member of the honors program is the joy of doing creative, meaningful projects with faculty I love."

—*Meleia, Hartwick College*

"I would... like to add a word of praise for the way the curriculum is structured. It has deepened and enriched my thinking and helped me develop tools to negotiate the complex world we live in."

—*Monideepa, Southeastern Louisiana University*

"We have a better time... our discussions get rather heated. In a lot of classes, only one or two students will speak up, but in the honors classes, it's a free-for-all."

—*Jonathan, Reinhardt College*

"My internship at a major international bank gave me an in-depth look into the world of investment and accounting. Funded by the Honors College, I was able to study business and culture in Shanghai, China, for a month. These valuable experiences are helping me to develop professionally, academically, and personally."

—*Jenny, Honors College, The College of Staten Island, CUNY*

"The honors thesis was the key factor during the selection process at my future employer.... It helped me to get the job and have an advantage over others. It is a lot of work but, in the end, it is worth it."

—*Olgierd, Lee Honors College, Western Michigan University*

These portraits don't tell the whole story, but they should give you a sense of what it means to be part of an honors program or college. One of the great strengths of honors programs and colleges is that they are nurturing environments that encourage students to be well-rounded and help students make life choices.

WHAT IS AN HONORS PROGRAM?

An honors program is a sequence of courses designed specifically to encourage independent and creative learning. For more than half a century, honors education—given definition by the National Collegiate Honors Council—has been an institution on U.S. campuses. Although honors programs have many different designs, there are typical components. At two-year colleges, the programs often concentrate on special versions of general education courses and may have individual capstone projects that come out of students' special interests. At four-year colleges and universities, honors programs are generally designed for students of almost every major in every college on campus. In growing numbers, they are given additional prominence as honors colleges. Whether a program or a college, honors often includes a general education or "core" component followed by advanced courses (often called colloquia or seminars). Some programs have honors contracts that shape existing courses into honors components to suit the needs of individual students. Many have interdisciplinary or collaborative seminars that bring students of different majors together to discuss a complex topic with faculty members from different disciplines. A good number have final thesis, capstone, or creative projects, which may or may not be in the departmental major. Almost always, honors curriculum is incorporated within whatever number of credits is required of every student for graduation. Honors very rarely requires students to take additional credits. Students who complete an honors program or honors college curriculum frequently receive transcript and diploma notations as well as certificates, medallions, or other citations at graduation ceremonies.

In every case, catering to the student as an individual plays a central role in honors course design. Most honors classes are small (fewer than 20 students); most are discussion-oriented, giving students a chance to present their own interpretations of ideas and even teach a part of the course. Many classes are interdisciplinary, which means they are taught by faculty members from two or more departments, providing different perspectives on a subject. All honors classes help students develop and articulate their own perspectives by cultivating both verbal and written style. They help students mature intellectually, preparing them to engage in their own explorations and research. Some programs even extend the options for self-growth to study abroad and internships in science, government, the arts, or business related to the major. Other programs encourage or require community service as part of the honors experience. In every case, honors is an experiential education that deepens classroom learning and extends far beyond.

Despite their individual differences, all honors programs and honors colleges rely on faculty members who enjoy working with bright, independent students. The ideal honors faculty members are open-minded, encouraging master teachers. They want to see their students achieve at their highest capacity and are glad to spend time with students in discussions and laboratories, on field trips and at conferences, or online in e-mail. They often influence career decisions, are inspiring role models, and remain friends long after they have served as thesis advisers.

WHERE ARE HONORS PROGRAMS AND HONORS COLLEGES LOCATED?

Because honors programs and honors colleges include students from many different departments or colleges, they usually have their own offices and space on campus. Some have their own buildings. Most programs have honors centers or lounges, where students gather together for informal conversations, luncheons, discussions, lectures, and special projects.

Many honors students have cultivated strong personal interests that have nothing to do with classes. They may be multilingual; they may be fine artists or poets, musicians or racing car enthusiasts, mothers or fathers. Some volunteer in hospitals or do landscape gardening to pay for college. Many work in retail stores and in catering. Some are avid sports enthusiasts, while others collect antiques. When they get together in honors lounges, there is always an interesting mixture of ideas!

In the honors center, you will also find the honors director or dean. The honors director often serves as a personal adviser to all of the students in the program. Many programs also have peer counselors and mentors who are upperclass honors students and know the ropes from a student's perspective and experience. Some have specially assigned honors advisers who guide honors students through their degrees, assist in registration, and answer every imaginable question. The honors office area usually is a good place to meet people, ask questions, and solve problems.

In general, honors provides an environment in which students feel free to talk about their passionate interests and ideas knowing that they will find good listeners and, sometimes, even arguers. There is no end to conversations among honors students. Like many students in honors, you may feel a great relief in finding a sympathetic group that respects your intelligence and creativity. In honors, you can be eccentric; you can be yourself! Some lifelong friendships, even marriages, are the result of social relationships developed in honors programs.

ARE YOU READY FOR HONORS?

Admission to honors programs and honors colleges is generally based on a combination of several factors: high school or previous college grades, experience taking AP or IB courses, SAT or ACT scores, personal essay, and extracurricular achievements. To stay in honors, students need to maintain a certain grade point average (GPA) and show progress toward the completion of the specific honors program or college requirements. Since you have probably exceeded admissions standards all along, maintaining your GPA will not be as big a problem as it sounds. Your professors and your honors director are there to help you succeed in the program. Most honors programs have very low attrition rates because students enjoy classes and do well.

Of course, you must be careful about how you budget your time for studying. Honors encourages well-rounded, diversified students, so you should play a sport, work at the radio station, join clubs of interest, or pledge a sorority or fraternity. You might find a job in the student center or library that will help you pay for your car expenses and that also is reasonable. But remember, each activity takes time, and you must strike the balance that leaves you enough time to do your homework, write papers, prepare for seminar discussions, do your research, and do well on exams. Choose the jobs and activities that attract you, but never let them overshadow your primary purpose—which is to be a student.

Sometimes even the very best students who apply for admission into an honors program or college are frightened by the thought of speaking in front of a group, giving seminar papers, or writing a thesis. But if you understand how the programs work, you will see that there is nothing to fear. The basis of honors is confidence in the student and building the student's self-confidence. Admittance to an honors program means you have already demonstrated your academic achievement in high school or college classes. Once in the honors environment, you learn how to formulate and structure ideas so that you can apply critical judgment to sets of facts and opinions. In small seminar classes, you practice discussion and arguments, so by the time you come to the senior thesis or project, the method is second nature. For most honors students, the senior thesis, performance, or portfolio presentation is the project that gives them the greatest fulfillment and pride. In many honors programs and colleges, students present their work either to other students or to faculty members in their major departments. Students often present their work at regional and national honors conferences. Some students even publish their work jointly with their faculty mentors. These are great achievements, and they come naturally with the training. There is nothing to fear. Honors will prepare you for life.

Dr. Joan Digby is Director of the Honors Program and Professor of English at Long Island University, C.W. Post Campus. She was also President of the National Collegiate Honors Council from 1999 to 2000.

Public and Private Colleges and Universities— How to Choose

Debra Humphreys

As you survey the thousands of four-year colleges in the country and weigh the options before you, it is important to be aware of how colleges differ and what kind of educational experience each college offers you. In every state in the country, you will find both public and private colleges and universities. What are the differences between public and private colleges, and how should you approach the decision to attend one or the other? What are some common misconceptions regarding both public and private colleges that you should know about before you eliminate an entire category of institution from your list of prospective schools?

WHAT ARE THE BASIC CHARACTERISTICS OF PUBLIC AND PRIVATE INSTITUTIONS?

Over the course of the nation's history, what began as a small group of mostly church-affiliated colleges has grown in both size and complexity. Over the years, education in the United States became increasingly democratized, and more and more state-sponsored institutions and state systems of higher education emerged. These included small colleges, sometimes called "normal schools," designed to train school teachers for the expanding public school system; land-grant colleges and universities brought into existence with federal support in the mid-nineteenth century in order to prepare workers to expand the nation's agricultural and technological capacity; and large state systems that evolved in the twentieth century and now include two-year colleges, basic four-year institutions, and large research universities, all supported at least in part by state revenues.

While there are some clear distinctions to be made, even some of the core characteristics of public and private colleges vary from state to state. In general, a public institution receives at least part of its operating budget from state tax revenues, operates with a mandate and mission from the state where it is located, and is accountable to the elected officials of that state. Most private colleges and universities are independent, not-for-profit institutions. They operate with revenues from tuition; income from endowments; private gifts and bequests; and federal, private, or corporate foundation grants. These institutions are primarily accountable to a board of trustees, usually made up of local or national business and community leaders and esteemed alumni.

There are also a small but growing number of for-profit colleges whose operating revenues include tuition dollars but also might include investor financing. Some of these colleges are owned and operated by publicly traded corporations. Most of the following generalizations about private institutions however refer to the more familiar not-for-profit independent college previously described.

While the distinction between public and private institutions might seem clear at first, these two kinds of colleges and universities actually share many characteristics. All accredited colleges and universities in the country—whether public or private, for profit or not—are entitled to receive public funds from the federal government in the form of direct grants and loans for eligible students, support for student work-study programs, and competitive grants to support research or campus programs. In exchange for this federal support, all schools undergo a peer-reviewed accreditation process by a regional accreditor authorized by the federal government's Department of Education.

Whether a college is public or private, you should know if it is accredited and therefore an institution whose students are eligible for all available federal financial aid. Accreditation status also provides you with assurance that the school operates in a fiscally responsible manner and that its academic programs have been deemed sound by an outside group of educators from its peer institutions.

HOW ARE PUBLIC AND PRIVATE COLLEGES AND UNIVERSITIES RUN?

In many ways, your experience as a student will not differ significantly based on what type of governance system a college or university uses. However, some knowledge of this might be useful in making choices among the various options. Private colleges and universities tend to have more independence and autonomy in how they are run, with boards of trustees that oversee financial and other programs and life on campus at these schools. Public colleges and universities often have more complex governing structures with boards of regents or other types of oversight committees made up of politically appointed or elected officials exercising more or less oversight and intrusion into their day-to-day operations. New York, for instance, has a board of regents that oversees the system's campuses and is more actively involved in reviewing and revising curricular requirements that apply to institutions throughout the system. Other states have multiple public colleges, each with its own board overseeing each campus' operations with more or less intrusion into day-to-day operations.

Whether an institution is public or private, you will want to ask lots of questions about campus climate and academic programs in order to help you determine if a school is right for you. Being aware of some facts about public and private institutions will help you frame these questions to get truly useful answers.

ARE ALL PUBLIC COLLEGES AND UNIVERSITIES BIG AND IMPERSONAL?

Like private institutions, public colleges come in all shapes and sizes. Some are large institutions offering multiple degrees and majors to both undergraduate and graduate students alike. These institutions offer students many curricular options as well as access to leading scholars and an environment where cutting-edge academic research is conducted. While an institution of this size and scope might seem intimidating at first, remember that there are large institutions that do take very seriously their undergraduate programs. While you may receive less customized attention at a larger institution, many large public and private research universities offer options such as smaller honors programs, academic learning communities with smaller cohorts of students, or theme residence halls that can minimize the potential that you will get lost in the crowd.

If you are considering a large research institution—whether it is public or private—you should ask questions about the undergraduate program. What is the student-faculty ratio for undergraduates? What is the average class size, especially for introductory first-year courses? How many courses are taught by graduate students, and what sort of teacher training do those students receive? Are there opportunities for undergraduate students to participate in research projects with university faculty members?

In addition to the large, public research universities, there are many other smaller, state-funded regional institutions that still offer a wide range of both liberal arts and sciences fields as well as professional fields of study. Many states also offer small, public liberal arts colleges that share many of the defining characteristics of traditional, private liberal arts colleges. In 1987, some of these institutions formed the Council of Public Liberal Arts Colleges (COPLAC). COPLAC schools pride themselves on providing students of high ability and from all backgrounds access to a quality liberal education. These colleges and universities have been nationally recognized as outstanding in many ways. They offer small classes, innovations in teaching, personal interactions with faculty members, opportunities for faculty-supervised research, and supportive atmospheres. Most of them are located on campuses in rural or small-town settings. In addition to offering

rigorous and well-integrated undergraduate programs, these institutions often charge far less tuition than many private colleges do. More information can be found at www.coplac.org.

These public liberal arts colleges, along with more traditional private liberal arts institutions, do offer unique learning environments that research suggests often lead to higher levels of student achievement. Liberal arts colleges tend to offer a high degree of student-faculty interaction, high levels of student engagement with both in-class and out-of-class experiences, and lots of opportunities for collaborative and innovative learning practices. Businesses are also increasingly asking for exactly the set of skills and capacities that a liberal education provides, whether offered in a traditional liberal arts college setting or within a larger university that grants degrees in both liberal arts and other fields. Many public liberal arts and more comprehensive colleges and universities also now offer students a rigorous liberal education while integrating liberal learning into professional degree programs, for instance in health sciences, engineering, or education.

ARE PUBLIC COLLEGES CHEAPER THAN PRIVATE COLLEGES?

The cost of college is not easy to calculate and is not limited simply to the advertised price of tuition. It is absolutely not the case that attending a public college will always cost a student less money than attending a private institution. It is true that the basic tuition for in-state or out-of-state students attending public colleges is on average less expensive than the advertised tuition rate at private institutions. It is very important, however, to note that many private colleges and universities offer significant amounts of financial aid—often beyond the basic federal loans and grants available to all students. Many, but not all, private colleges have large endowments that allow them to effectively discount the standard, published tuition rates for a great number of their students. The National Association of College and University Business Officers sampled a small group of private colleges and discovered that only 10 percent of entering students were paying the full, advertised tuition. Ninety percent of their students received price discounts in the form of scholarships or financial aid. In other words, don't write off a college simply because its tuition looks extremely high relative to other institutions.

Both private and public institutions, however, have been fiscally stressed in recent years because of declining values of stock portfolios in endowments or because of declining state revenues. It is safe to say that for many students in the coming years, it will become increasingly difficult to get large amounts of financial aid. Many institutions, however, remain committed to widening access to more students from less economically privileged backgrounds. In addition, students demonstrating high levels of academic achievement are being rewarded at both private and public institutions—both in terms of admission and financial aid.

It is important to look carefully at the tuition and the financial aid requirements and availability at each school you are considering, private or public. In-state and out-of-state tuitions and the difference between them varies substantially from state to state. Out-of-state tuition also varies from state to state but still tends to be lower than average private tuition levels.

Policies vary as well for determining state residency status. In many states, the policy for dependent students requires that their parents must have lived in the state for at least twelve months prior to attendance in order to qualify for in-state tuition. For independent students, the requirement of twelve months residence prior to enrollment applies to the student. Independent status must be verified and generally entails proof that a student receives no support from parents or other relatives living in or out of the state in question. As budgets have increasingly tightened, states have over the past several years made it increasingly difficult to establish in-state residence after matriculating at a school. Exceptions are sometimes made, however, for students from migrant, refugee, or military families.

IS IT EASIER TO GAIN ADMISSION TO A PUBLIC INSTITUTION ESPECIALLY AS A STATE RESIDENT?

Few public colleges and universities automatically admit students who graduate from a public high school in their state. Many, however, give preference in admissions and financial assistance to in-state residents. Moreover, some states have implemented policies that guarantee admission to at least one of the state's public institutions for all students graduating in a top percentage of their high school classes.

There are, indeed, more highly selective private than public institutions. Many public colleges and universities, however, do admit very few applicants. These highly selective institutions might draw their students from a national pool of applicants and can be among the most selective in the country. However, the national universities and liberal arts colleges with the lowest acceptance rates in the country are mostly all private institutions.

While some public institutions offer virtually open admissions to state residents, it is important for all prospective students to realize that even an open-admission institution will require incoming students to meet certain academic standards before being admitted to credit-bearing courses. In most cases, public and private institutions give incoming students a series of placement exams that determines at what level the student can begin his or her course work. Depending on the results of these exams, a student may be required to take and pass one or more remedial courses before being admitted to courses that will actually count towards a degree.

Since each state's requirements are different and shift often, you should not assume that, regardless of your academic background, admission is automatic to your local state college. In the current climate—with costs rising and competition across systems tightening—admission rates are dropping at many public institutions.

IS THE CLIMATE ON A PUBLIC COLLEGE CAMPUS SIGNIFICANTLY DIFFERENT THAN THAT ON A PRIVATE COLLEGE CAMPUS?

The social and academic climate at colleges and universities varies substantially, and public institutions do not necessarily offer a distinctively different climate than private institutions do. You can find, at some public institutions, the small, residential environment traditionally associated with private liberal arts colleges. You will also find the presence of fraternities and sororities at both public and private institutions. You should look carefully at whether a school in which you are interested has fraternities and sororities and how much influence the Greek system has on college life. At some institutions, fraternities and sororities dominate the entire social life of the campus.

One campus environment that can only be found at a private institution is a highly religious environment. Many early colleges and universities were founded by churches or religious orders. Some of these institutions no longer retain a strong affiliation with one church or denomination. Others do retain a strong affiliation, and church traditions can heavily influence the climate of these institutions. Usually, these campuses will admit a student from any religious background, but they may require students to attend chapel services and/or take religion or theology courses to graduate. In addition, some college missions and curricula are influenced by their religious affiliations. For instance, many Catholic institutions have a strong commitment to community service and social justice. Students may find, at these institutions, curricula related to social justice issues and requirements that they complete a community-service learning activity or course to graduate. Institutions with a strong mission are also often able to develop more coherent, cohesive, and innovative curricula for their students.

Finally, other important climate factors to consider include whether a college or university is in an urban or rural setting; what the diversity of the student body is in terms of geographic, religious, or racial/ethnic background; if most students live on campus or commute from home; and finally if the college dominates the life of the community in which it is located. Each of these options has advantages and disadvantages you will want to weigh in making your decisions.

ARE PRIVATE COLLEGES MORE ACADEMICALLY RIGOROUS THAN PUBLIC COLLEGES?

Private colleges and universities are not necessarily more academically rigorous than public institutions. You will find rigorous, intellectually challenging, and innovative academic programs at both private and public institutions. There is also a common misconception that schools that are more highly selective have the most effective or engaging academic programs. Research suggests that there is no connection between the selectivity of an institution and the presence of effective or innovative teaching and learning practices. There is, however, preliminary research that suggests that the academic quality of

Questions to Ask as You Evaluate Prospective Colleges and Universities

- Does the college offer a distinctive first-year experience?
- Does the college offer a small-size freshman seminar for all students?
- Are all students required to complete a senior project or assignment that allows them to integrate all that they have learned and demonstrate acquired skills and knowledge?
- Are students encouraged or required to complete internships and/or service learning courses?
- Are students encouraged to study abroad? Is support for study abroad provided to all students and are study abroad experiences integrated into a student's overall curricula?
- Does the college offer learning communities, especially in the student's early years?
- Are students required to complete rigorous writing courses not only in the freshman year but also across the curriculum in whatever major he or she chooses to pursue?
- Are there opportunities for students to pursue independent research or creative projects under the supervision of a senior faculty member?

one's peers does seem to have an impact on the grade point averages of fellow students.

Nothing could be more important in your decision-making process than evaluating the nature of academic programs at prospective colleges or universities. Across both public and private institutions, there have been exciting and important changes in how colleges and universities are organizing undergraduate curricula. Many promising programs have been

proven to result in higher levels of student retention, graduation, satisfaction, and academic achievement.

Many colleges and universities also now participate in the National Survey of Student Engagement. This survey asks students in both their first and last years about a series of effective educational practices and the degree to which they are engaged in the academic life of their school. Issues that are examined in the survey include the level of academic challenge, active and collaborative learning opportunities, the nature of student-faculty interactions, the number of enriching educational experiences available, and the supportive nature of the campus environment. Ask if the school you are considering participates in this survey and if you can see the results from recent classes of students.

THE PRIVATE/PUBLIC CHOICE

While there are distinct differences between public and private colleges and universities you should not limit your choice—whatever your background—to only one type of institution. There are wonderful opportunities at many different kinds of schools. The availability of many kinds of financial aid may bring private institutions with high-tuition levels within reach for you, whatever your financial background. Whether a school is highly selective or has open admissions, you should also be able to find a college or university that will challenge you academically and provide you with a supportive environment in which to live, learn, and pursue a college degree of lasting value.

Debra Humphreys is Senior Vice President for Academic Planning and Public Engagement for the Association of American Colleges and Universities.

Distance Education—
It's Closer Than You Think

You may not realize it, but as an incoming college student, you are joining a revolution that is radically changing education. It's called distance learning. From kindergarten up to postgraduate degrees, distance learning is fast becoming an essential teaching tool. Most of the colleges and universities you are considering for a bachelor's degree offer distance learning in one form or another. Most likely you will be a distance learner at some point, whether during college or graduate school or throughout your career.

In case you're not familiar with distance learning—or asynchronous learning, online learning, or distance education—it means you don't sit in a classroom facing a teacher. You can be hundreds of miles or minutes from the teacher and other students. Most often you connect through the Internet to the teacher, fellow students, and study materials. However, increasingly sophisticated technologies, such as virtual laboratories, simulations, and interactive multimedia, are also used. You may run across the term "blended learning." Many institutions incorporate online learning into their face-to-face classes. In fact, a number of colleges require that a part of all classes is online.

FROM SNAIL-MAIL COURSES TO LEADING-EDGE TECHNOLOGY

Talk about change. Distance education began in the late 1800s, when schools mailed correspondence courses to farmers who wanted to learn how to grow better crops. Since technology came along, distance learning has become accessible and widespread. At first educators were skeptical, but as name-plate universities began to incorporate it into their teaching methodology, distance education became accepted.

When brick-and-mortar colleges and universities first considered distance education, the goal was to make it as good as face-to-face education. Now, says Ray Schroeder, Professor Emeritus of Communication and Director of the Center for Online Learning, Research, and Service (COLRS), at the University of Illinois at Springfield, "Field research shows that online learning technologies are better than face-to-face learning in a number of ways." Having taught online, he has seen firsthand how students participate more in discussions and learn from one another. Peg Miller, Ph.D., former Coordinator of Academic Support for Distributed Learning, University of Central Florida, cites a survey she conducted every other semester that compares face-to-face and distance learners at her institution. She has found that students from face-to-face and online classes were almost identical in the grades they earned and in their satisfaction with the classes.

ON THE UPSWING

Many reasons have caused the phenomenal growth of distance education. It's convenient and user-friendly, plus the scope of classes is stunning. Not that you'll likely begin your college years with classes in forensics or grading diamonds, but they are offered and indicate the enormous variety of courses. Along with many others in education, Michael P. Lambert, former executive director of the Distance Education Training Council, feels that online learning has transformed how people learn. "You no longer sit in a box with 35 other people where you might never raise your hand," he says. Adds Gerald Heeger, former President of the University of Maryland University College (UMUC), "Online learning gets rid of the limitations of geography and time. And as bandwidth increases, we will do more and more."

PROCEED WITH CAUTION

Now that you're convinced that distance education sounds great, and you're ready to say "sign me up," it's only fair to warn you that perhaps you shouldn't start your bachelor's degree totally online. Distance learning changes how you study, respond to your teachers, participate in class discussions, and take exams. If you're not prepared for the differences, you can easily fall behind and even fail. Though the age of online students continues to drop, most are older, have had some life experience since graduating from high school, and have the self-discipline, maturity, and self-motivation, that distance education demands. The average age of distance students is in the mid-30s, and 95 percent of them work full-time. They know what they want from college and are willing to meet the rigors of online learning, which are considerable.

Of course, some students straight from high school do successfully start college as distance learners because they've already had some online learning experience. Some take online classes in high school or advanced-placement and college courses. At Stevens Institute of Technology's Web Campus, incoming freshmen brush up on math and precalculus online before their first fall semester. At first, Nathan Kahl, former instructor for the Euclid Program at Stevens Institute of Technology Web Campus, was skeptical that high school graduates could succeed in the online courses he taught, but he saw that "everyone quickly got into the swing of things." He admits that he underestimated the students' ability to learn online. Heeger agrees "There's no reason why a bright junior in high school who is ready to take college freshmen courses can't do it."

The University of Phoenix Online (parent company: Apollo Group, Inc.) has developed a bachelor's degree program specifically for incoming freshmen of any age—including those just out of high school. In today's job market, a college education is a necessity, yet many students have life situations that prevent them from attending. Notes former president of Apollo Group, Inc., Brian Mueller about the accommodations their program makes for students who are new to higher education, "It is our experience that if you create an online classroom, it must have all the features that incoming students need, which are small, highly interactive, and collaborative classes." Their freshman classes average 15 and require that the instructor has consistent contact with the students. New freshmen also get a tremendous amount of support in writing, math, and online research skills and have the help of an academic counselor who closely tracks them for ten weeks into their first semester. "We think there are more students coming out of high school who must have jobs, so we took the model for working adults and created an environment for traditional students that combines education and work," says Mueller.

However, not all educators have the same experience with incoming freshmen. Jimmy Reeves, Ph.D., Professor of Chemistry and Coordinator of the Tablet PC Initiative at the University of North Carolina at Wilmington, teaches both online and face-to-face classes and knows how students can react. Freshmen who fail his face-to-face class sometimes ask to take his class online. He says no because the discipline required is rare among 19-year-old students. "Junior and senior college students do well, but it has more to do with their level of maturity and the reasons why they're in college," he says, referring to the fact that many incoming college students want to experiment or come because their parents demand it. "Without any real desire to learn or sense of why they're in college, it's easy to get distracted in online classes," he notes. You can't hide in the back of a lecture hall half asleep on Monday morning and hope for the best on multiple-choice questions. In online classes, your active participation is noticed and taken into account for final grades.

Attending college isn't just about acquiring knowledge in a particular field in order to get a job. It's also about learning social skills and meeting people with different ideas from diverse backgrounds. "If you want to live in a dorm and have bull sessions on the meaning of life with the kids down the hall, then being a fully online freshman student isn't for you," advises Cynthia Davis, Acting Vice Provost and Dean of the Undergraduate School at the University of Maryland University College (UMUC). She adds that sometimes students mistakenly think getting a bachelor's degree online will take less time than physically attending classes or won't require as much work. But as she points out, online classes demand the same amount of effort, if not more, than face-to-face classes.

WHAT'S IT GOING TO BE LIKE?

Blended learning or mixed-mode classes, combining face-to-face and online instruction, are becoming a permanent fixture in higher education. Students might sit in a classroom on Monday but take the remaining two classes for that week online. Professors routinely post the syllabus, class calendar, or PowerPoint lectures. Reeves says that it's rare to see college classes without some Web-based materials. Davis comments that UMUC routinely Web-enhances all of its face-to-face classes with companion Web classrooms. Students can have optional online discussions or print copies of class materials.

"We find more students use online technology to enhance their studies and get better grades," comments Schroeder. Educators see a trend of students enrolling in one university and taking courses from other institutions. For instance, say you're in an art class but want to study German cathedral architecture, which your university doesn't have but another one offers online. It's only a matter of time before this will be a standard option for college students.

LOTS TO LOOK FOR, LOTS TO AVOID, LOTS TO ASK

Though much of distance education depends on the Internet, you can't just type in "distance education" and see what comes up in a search for a college. You must seriously research and do background checks to make sure a diploma mill doesn't hand you a bachelor's degree that isn't credible. There are plenty of places to get information. Petersons.com offers a database of colleges and universities that have online courses, as well as totally online distance education providers. "You have to be a good consumer," recommends Heeger. "It's no different from getting a loan. You don't borrow money from people you never heard of. You shouldn't get degrees from people you never heard of." Schroeder suggests checking the course completion of online programs, their enrollment, and growth of programs. "Just as one checks with friends and colleagues about the quality of consumer services, such as computers and cars, one should check with students who are enrolled in online programs," he advises.

Is the Institution Accredited by a Valid Accrediting Body?

There are several kinds of accrediting organizations:

- The six regional accrediting agencies recognized by the U.S. Department of Education
- The Council for Higher Education Accreditation (www.chea.org)
- Other institutional accrediting agencies, such as the Accrediting Council for Independent Colleges and Schools and the Distance Education and Training Council
- Specialized accrediting agencies that cover schools offering everything from acupuncture to veterinary medicine
- Other discipline-based accrediting organizations, such as those for law and business schools

Can You Transfer Credits Received Online from One Institution to Another?

Policies vary greatly among universities and colleges. Though distance education is widely accepted, there are so many places where students can take bogus online courses that institutions are justifiably cautious. If students do decide they want to get a bachelor's degree completely online, they need to be sure the campus-based program and distance education program offer the same degree. At most institutions, both on-campus and online degrees are the same, but others do differentiate in the degrees conferred, and it will show up on your diploma.

Test-Drive an Online Class

Just like face-to-face instruction, online classes are different, depending on the course material and how each teacher chooses to structure the course, but here's a typical scenario of what it's like to be a distance learner.

Getting started. First you'll want to get to the general information page for the class, which you'll visit often. The professor's contact information, the class calendar, the syllabus, and announcements on quizzes and tests or links to other pages on which you'll find posted discussion questions may be found here. Some teachers will ask you to tell something about yourself to the other students in the class. Be sure to read the syllabus, which will outline the course and tell you when assignments are due and how grades are determined.

Responding to discussion questions. Those students who never raised their hands will get a shock in online courses. Responding with thoughtful answers to online discussion groups is mandatory. Usually the teacher will assign reading material and then post a discussion question. The material might be from your textbook or websites. You must respond to the question and possibly to the postings of other students in the class. Teachers will gauge your participation in the class and how well you learn the material.

Interacting with fellow students and your teacher. Ray Schroeder, Professor Emeritus of Communication and Director of the Center for Online Learning, Research, and Service (COLRS) at the University of Illinois at Springfield, gives talks about distance education. Often he'll ask his audience to recall their favorite class from elementary school up to college and what made it so memorable. Was it the textbook? The actual classroom? The view out the window? When he asks if it was the interaction among students and with the teacher, the audience realizes that's what made the class good. "Both in person and online, learning takes place in the interaction," says Schroeder. "Otherwise, we would do just as well to read a book or watch a video to learn." In online classes, interaction between you and the professor and other students is an enormous part of your success.

Nathan Kahl, former instructor for the Euclid Program at Stevens Institute of Technology Web Campus, explains, "Distance students expect that their teachers will be online at least as much as they are." The level of interaction expected from you will vary by school and course, but you should know that in online courses, you must be an active participant. On the flip side, teachers carefully monitor discussions to make sure the more talkative students don't dominate. Keith W. Miller, Professor of Computer Science at the University of Illinois at Springfield, interacts with his students in a variety of ways. "I make announcements to the whole class on the homepage. I send e-mails to the whole class. I enter into the electronic discussions on the bulletin board forums, and post daily reminders and assignments to the course calendar. The students interact with me using e-mail, notes in their assignments, and via the bulletin boards. Now and then someone calls me at my office on the phone, but that's rare." He likes to answer his e-mails at least once a day, which means that his students get much more feedback than they would if he were physically in a classroom with them.

As do most online teachers, Cynthia Davis, Associate Dean of Academic Affairs in the School of Undergraduate Studies at the University of Maryland University College, gets students to participate with a weekly discussion topic. "If we're reading a novel," she says, "I ask them to discuss the role of the narrator or analyze a passage. The students respond individually and then respond to other students' comments."

Attending virtual lectures. Some online courses allow you to hear and see the professor or other guest speakers who are also online. If you want to ask a question, there's a button to indicate you want to speak. Everyone else can hear you as if you all were in the same room. Other professors add voice to PowerPoint lectures, which you can view when you want to, not at some prearranged time.

Taking quizzes and tests. No more waiting weeks to get your tests back. Online technology in some courses instantly zaps back the corrected test and notes that you missed question six and need to study page 54 of the textbook. Just like in face-to-face classes, you have an allotted amount of time to take the quiz. Some online courses may have automated components, such as instant quizzes and animated and interactive practice sessions. Others have mandatory proctored exams at a nearby community college or learning center for students who are off campus.

What Kind of Refund Policy Does the University Have for Distance Learners?

It might become painfully apparent for students that online learning is not for them, and they want to drop out. Find out ahead of time about the refund policy for online classes. What happens if you're ill during an online class? How can you make up the work? Even before taking any classes, you should find out if you're suited for online learning. Many institutions offer self-assessment tests on their websites.

What Online Services Does the College Provide?

Is the dorm wired? Can you get an e-mail address from the university? What about browsers and computer compatibility? Ask how the Internet is part of face-to-face classes. To what extent is the library online, and is it available 24/7 for research? Ask about writing and math labs and help-desk support. Look for online tutorials that show students how to use the school's specific software. Is there a tech fee?

IF YOU'RE LEARNING ONLINE, YOU BETTER HAVE THESE

Since online learning is part of college, it's helpful to know what to expect ahead of time, rather than three weeks into the class, when you feel like throwing your laptop out the window and would happily settle for sitting in the back row of the nearest classroom. Here are the five skills and abilities that successful online students must have:

1. You must have the self-discipline to do things you don't want to do when you don't want to do them.

If you're a procrastinator, you'll find the catch-up tactics that served you well in face-to-face classes won't work online. "Students get the idea they can whiz by without studying, or they came from high schools where they weren't pushed," cautions Heeger. "Maybe they never got Fs in high school, but they do here." That's because they don't realize they're responsible for learning the material on their own. The burden is on you to keep up with the homework. It doesn't take long to fall far behind in online classes.

Typically, students in face-to-face and online classes need 2 hours for work outside of class for every hour in class. But online students often forget to add that hour. For every hour they would have to sit in a traditional classroom, they should be listening, studying, thinking, writing, responding to discussions, and getting ready for tests, plus the 2 hours outside of class. Three classes a week—that's 9 to 10 hours for one class. Online teachers keep students on track with weekly quizzes and homework assignments. If students start lagging, they're likely to get an e-mail from the professor asking what's going on. Claudine SchWeber, Ph.D., Chair of the Doctor of Management Program at the University of Maryland University College, has taught online for years and states, "My classes are structured by weekly readings, activities, and discussions. Students can't decide to get around to doing the work when they feel like it. It must be done at the instructor's pace. The first shot of online can be a shock to their system."

2. You must have the ability to manage your time without anyone telling you do your homework NOW.

In high school, students usually can put off studying until the weekend. "That doesn't work in college. You can't write complex papers the night before," says Karen L. Kirkendall, Ph.D., Associate Professor of Liberal and Integrative Studies and Director of the Capitol Scholars Honors Program at the University of Illinois at Springfield. She teaches both online and face-to-face classes and has seen first-time online students who have never failed before start to slip and suddenly realize they are in big trouble. "My online classes are extraordinarily structured so I pretty much know when students aren't engaged, which I monitor by seeing how much they participate in online discussions," she notes.

3. You must have the skills to communicate your thoughts in writing.

"Online participation in class discussions isn't instant messaging. You are what you write in online classes," advises SchWeber. Most of the work in online classes is written,

Distance Learning Myths

As distance education becomes more accepted, people will readily discard some of the myths on this list. But for now, they persist.

Distance learning is for people on ranches 200 miles from the nearest freeway. Geography is not a factor. Many distance learners who are located across the campus or a few miles away just don't want to deal with the commute or have a work schedule that conflicts with being in a class at a certain time. They appreciate the flexibility that distance education gives them.

Distance learning is easier than face-to-face classes. Once you start an online class, you'll knock that myth off the list. Still, some students think it will be easier. When they realize they must not only respond to discussion questions but also comment on the responses from other students, they wonder why they ever thought distance education was going to be easy. Online teachers normally keep track of how their students progress with frequent monitoring and quizzes.

I'll get a better education in face-to-face classes. Much research has been conducted comparing the two and consistently, online learning is equivalent or better. Teachers of online courses now have plenty of precedents to follow, training and research to help them teach better, and technology to prepare for classes and keep up with their students' progress.

I'll talk to a computer all day. Yes, you are in front of a computer as a distance learner, but you also interact with professors and other students much more than you ever would in a core freshman class of 200. Teachers have sophisticated software to facilitate interaction. Even though you don't physically see your teachers, they put a great deal of effort into class preparation and reading e-mails. Some get as many as 3,000 e-mails in a ten-week class. Distance learners often get to know fellow students much more easily online than they would walking in and out of a class.

I need to be a computer geek. If you can handle the simplest maneuvers around a computer, such as attaching documents to e-mails or going to a specified Web address, you can be a distance learner. And you'll have tech support to help out if you run into problems.

Distance education is cheaper than face-to-face. Too bad this is a myth. It costs the same as a traditional college if you attend a recognized institution. Most students pay for distance education through student loans.

whether it's participation in discussions, homework, quizzes, papers, or tests.

Since you'll communicate by e-mail and post your thoughts, netiquette is essential. You need to think differently online than when speaking on the phone or face-to-face. "You can't write a report that sounds like you are hanging out with friends," advises SchWeber. "When you are totally online, the only image people (including your professor) have of you is how you write." Kirkendall has reprimanded students who sent e-mails showing disrespect to the teacher because they were upset about something. Probably they would never respond that way if face-to-face. "Never hit the submit button when you're angry," Kirkendall cautions.

4. You must have the ability to research worthwhile information on the Web.

You need to know what's junk and what's reliable. In addition, professors take plagiarism very seriously, especially because it's so easy to do.

5. You must have some computer skills and know some computer-speak.

Those who design the software and set up how a distance learning class is taught are careful to make sure the technology

doesn't get in the way of learning; however, you should know the basics. "In some classes, certain downloads are required, such as Adobe Acrobat, but in general, the skills are not beyond the abilities used daily by most elementary school children," says Schroeder, pointing out that if distance programs use expensive or exotic technology, they defeat the purpose. He reports that most computers that are five years old have the speed, memory, and capability to support online learning. Some classes might require a microphone. You should be familiar with some of the computer jargon so that if you're asked to post something or use a drop box, add an attachment, or take part in a threaded discussion, you'll know what you need to do. Just about every distance learning provider has online tutorials to familiarize you with their particular online software. If you run into technical problems, help-desk support is available.

Why Not Women's Colleges?

Before we start talking about the many advantages that women's colleges offer, let's get some myths out of the way. It is almost certain that the minute you hear "women's colleges" in the same sentence with "choosing colleges" you immediately think: no boys, no fun, no way!

Maybe that is why some girls who visit Joan Jaffe's office at Mills College in San Francisco, California, rush in to tell her that they just saw some guys on the campus of this women's college. Jaffe, Associate Dean of Admission, frequently gets this reaction from the young women who visit the campus. That's because many think that if they go to a women's college they are never going to see a guy within 2 miles of the campus gates, which, by the way, will clang shut behind them, leaving them secluded inside a heavily guarded male-free zone.

KISS MYTH NUMBER ONE GOOD-BYE

Forget iron gates. The first myth to get rid of is the one that assumes attending a women's college means kissing your social life good-bye. In fact, as Patricia Gibbs, Vice President for Student Affairs, Dean of Students at Wesleyan College in Macon, Georgia, points out, "If you were a guy looking for a date, where would you go?" Not only that, the majority of women's colleges are near, if not next to, coed campuses. Most share activities with other colleges and universities, and many have reciprocal agreements so that guys can take classes at the women's college and vice versa.

When it comes to dating, women's colleges offer the best of both worlds. You can hang out with guys when you want to and then retreat to your own lovely environment (women's dorms usually are beautiful) and hang out with the girls. Julie Binder, who transferred from the University of Wisconsin to all-women's Barnard College in New York City, notes that there is open registration with Columbia University, which just happens to be right next door. "Campus life is shared. Sports are shared," she says.

As you dig deeper into this myth, you will find that attending a women's college is not about isolation, it's about options. You get to choose if you want to be in classes, clubs, and organizations only with women or mingle with the men.

SCRATCH MYTH NUMBER TWO

Myth Number Two: Women's colleges are just a bunch of catty, competitive females waiting for the right moment to claw each other's eyes out. Scratch that myth, too. Instead, women's colleges cultivate an environment of sisterhood— women who look out for one another. Most women's colleges encourage women in the upper-level classes to help their younger classmates. Talking to their "big sisters," newcomers can find out what classes to take and which professors are best, and they find a sympathetic ear for the problems that most first-year college students face.

The Rich Traditions in Women's Colleges

Tradition plays an important part of the experience women have in women's colleges. They run the gamut from solemn ceremonies of passing along the bond of sisterhood to the fun of secret surprises. "Women's colleges have a strong sense of tradition," says Amy Shaver, former Academic Dean at Stephens College in Columbia, Missouri. It's also a wonderful way to help women from all social, economic, religious, and ethnic backgrounds to share a common experience and pass it on to the next generation of students. "Traditions bond women over the generations," says Jennifer Rickard, former Dean of Admissions and Financial Aid at Bryn Mawr College, who notes that it's not unusual at all to have students today singing songs and participating in ceremonies that the class of 1945 did and which will be the same when today's students have their twenty-year reunion.

Here's a sampling of the many traditions you'll find on women's college campuses:

Lantern Night At Bryn Mawr's Lantern Night, women gather around a fountain on campus. Each woman is given a lantern as a symbol of knowledge and learning. Each class has a color, and as the lanterns are passed from the sophomores to the first-year students, songs are sung in Greek that are the same as the ones sung 100 years ago around the same fountain.

Senior Paint Night Mills College seniors get the okay to paint the campus in their class color. Along with brushes and cans of paint, they are given a few guidelines as to what can and cannot be painted, but the rest is up to them.

The Crossing of the Bridge As women students come to Stephens to begin their college education, they cross over a bridge on campus in a ceremony symbolizing their entrance into the world of academia. At graduation, they cross over another bridge on campus and are welcomed into the alumnae society.

Candlelight Induction Ceremony Spelman students dressed in white dresses and black shoes light candles and hear the charge to be the best they can be. While the candles are still lit, they sing the Spelman hymn.

Midnight Breakfast At Barnard, the night before finals, the president of the college, deans, and professors make breakfast for the students.

"The sense of community is very strong at women's colleges," observes Fran Samuels, former Director of College Counseling at The Master's School in Dobbs Ferry, New York. "The myth is that a women's college will be cliquish. In truth, the women are supportive of each other." The strong bonds of sisterhood that naturally develop connect students to their college, its history, and its students—past, present, and future. Many women's colleges designate a rotating color for each incoming class. For example, if the freshman class you enter is dubbed the golden hearts, by the time you graduate, you are connected to all the golden hearts who graduated ahead of you and all the golden hearts who will graduate after you.

TOSS MYTH NUMBER THREE

Another myth that should be tossed out is that women's colleges don't prepare you for the "real world." Well, try saying that to the 12 women members of Congress who graduated from women's colleges. Or to the 15 women on *Business Week*'s list of the rising stars in corporate America. Although you are not in a totally coed situation, on the other hand you are in an environment in which you can gain skills to think critically and learn to meet challenges. Becky Marsh, Director of Communications and Marketing at Whitfield School, in St. Louis, Missouri, points out that when you first ride a bike, training wheels allow you to learn how to balance. Once you are ready to race down the street, you take them off. Same with women's colleges. The focus is on your education and your strengths, and who you are. You graduate ready to take on the obstacles of the real world. "In high school, I had the feeling that boys were given more opportunities to share their knowledge. It was harder and more intimidating for me to share my opinions in a coed class," says Brittany Johnson, from Spelman College in Atlanta, Georgia. "Now I feel like I can do anything."

Graduates of women's colleges feel empowered and willing to confront any limits to their abilities. While in college, they have many opportunities to assume leadership roles and see women in leadership positions as professors and deans. "They don't doubt whether they can do anything. Instead, they ask, 'Why can't I do it now?'" reports Amy Shaver, former Academic Dean at Stephens College in Columbia, Missouri. Women can find their own voices and establish their own ways of approaching things that will ultimately make them successful in a male-dominated world. They learn from seeing other women students and professors engaged in the intellectual process.

THE ADVANTAGES

As more young women find out about the advantages that women's colleges offer them, they like what they see. Maybe that is why attendance at women's colleges is growing. Learning leadership skills tops the list of advantages. Says Shaver, "Women in a same-sex environment are more likely to take risks and speak up in class. They are more willing to stand up and voice an opinion." If you think about it, students get plenty of practice at a women's college because all the leadership roles go to women. From day one, you will see women leading the entire college or involved in interesting and significant research. You get more exposure to what leadership is and what to expect as a leader. "Leadership becomes ingrained," notes Jennifer Fondiller, Dean of Enrollment Management at Barnard College in New York City.

You might not realize it, but women react differently in classrooms with all women. They tend to speak up with confidence and test their ideas more readily when they are not competing with men. Researchers find that even as early as the fifth grade, girls are taught differently than boys. Teachers call on boys more frequently and don't ask girls the more thought-provoking questions or to critically analyze problems. In coed situations, the more aggressive and competitive guys take over, whereas in all-female classes, research indicates there is much more give-and-take and exchange of ideas.

Coming from a coed public school, Johnson realized that more attention was given to the guys in her classes, but at Spelman, she says, "Everyone is on the same path." Arlene Cash, former Vice President for Enrollment Management at Spelman, notes that women don't have to vie for attention or retreat into the intellectual background in all-women classes. In a coed class, the environment becomes more adversarial. "Women feel they have to perform. In women's colleges they become more academically involved and interact with faculty members more frequently," says Debbie Greenberg, former College Counselor at Whitfield School. Speaking of the rich interaction that occurs in her classes at Barnard, Binder says, "The diversity of experience around the discussion table is unparalleled."

YOU CAN SUCCEED

Shaver characterizes the environment in women's colleges as one in which there is no fear of failing when the social pressures and dynamics of men and women are removed from the classroom. Women's colleges give women the opportunity to explore different avenues without the fear of failing. "We challenge them to become what they want to become," says Gibbs from Wesleyan. "No one says, 'You can't do that because you are a woman.'" At the same time, you are interacting with other women who have the same goals as you, which reinforces who you are. Or, as Jennifer Rickard, former Dean of Admissions and Financial Aid at Bryn Mawr College, in Bryn Mawr, Pennsylvania, points out, women are not just sitting in classes to do well on exams and get good grades. They also are figuring out what they want to do with their education. "There's less expectation to conform to an external measure," she says.

Many women's colleges foster self-government and give their students responsibilities they might not find in a coed institution. At Bryn Mawr, for instance, students pay a self-government association fee as part of their tuition. This is put into a fund that is controlled by a student government that takes ownership of how the students want to govern themselves. "This isn't student government making only recommendations to the administration as to how to allocate the budget to the different student groups vying for funds," notes Rickard. "You have students dealing with real-world management issues, such as resource allocation."

Since women's colleges are smaller than big coed universities, women receive all the benefits that students get from a small liberal arts college in addition to the advantages that only a women's college offers. A big plus is interaction with professors and staff, which is hard to achieve when you are one of 200 students in a lecture hall taught by a graduate student. Women's colleges tend to foster seminar-style classes taught by full professors, many of them women. "You have an expert

What Made You Choose a Women's College?

When she got to the point of choosing which college to attend, Wisambi Loundu had plenty of options. Coming from San Diego, the California universities were a logical choice. Women's colleges were not on her list. In fact, she hardly knew they existed. Her first thought when someone suggested a women's college to her was, "I'm not going to a school full of girls minus boys." Her second thought was just as negative. "If it's all girls, they will always be fighting." The third and fourth thoughts assumed that a women's college wouldn't prepare her for the real world, plus she would be isolated.

But then her math teacher's daughter told her about Bryn Mawr, and as Wisambi started exploring the possibility, the advantages of a women's college started lining up. However, it wasn't until she visited Bryn Mawr that she really began to see herself there. "I fell in love with the campus," says Wisambi. "It was like nothing I'd ever seen before." Her stay in the dorm added to her steadily growing thoughts that Bryn Mawr might be it. "The girls I stayed with in the dorm were so friendly. At first I was suspicious, but I saw it was not a front. Plus, there were girls from all over the world."

But Wisambi didn't make her final decision just yet. She decided to look at other schools, like Wellesley and the University of California schools, as well as Stanford. Meanwhile, her friend told her more about Bryn Mawr. "She said I'd make lasting friends and she talked about how the academics would train me for the outside world even if there were no men on campus. Bryn Mawr would build my identity as a woman."

She still wasn't convinced and made a second visit, along with visits to Wellesley and Stanford, which she says were nice, but too big. It would be too hard to make friends there, she thought. When the time came to make her final selection, she chose Bryn Mawr.

Now at Bryn Mawr, how does Wisambi feel about her choice? The academics are more challenging than she anticipated but doable, and she is excited about the internships she will be able to access. She also finds that the staff and teachers at Bryn Mawr go out of their way to make her feel at home. "They match us up with a mentor and professor," she says.

How about dating? Since Bryn Mawr is part of a tri-college community, guys are around, though Wisambi says you have to make an effort to meet people on other campuses.

Talking to seniors who are getting ready to head out to the "real world," Wisambi can see that they are full of confidence and don't think for a minute that they won't do well. "And that's a positive," she says.

teaching you," says Gibbs. Faculty members get to know their students and can challenge them intellectually on an individual basis. "Within two days, all my teachers knew my name," recalls Johnson, who says she was given each professor's e-mail address, home phone number, and all the contact information she needed and was encouraged to reach out to them.

Women are encouraged to achieve their intellectual goals. Professors often will point out specific programs that they know suit the student's interests. Add to this the opportunities to conduct research with a professor, and in many cases actually present research findings to a professional society, and you can see why women graduate with a terrific resume before they even start their careers. Rickard mentions the opportunity that Bryn Mawr students have to work on funded projects with professors during the summer and then present the results along with them at conferences. "It's a window into the academic world and the world of the intellectual," she notes. It's no surprise that women in women's colleges major in math and science at a higher national average than women in coed institutions.

Paid and unpaid internships, too, are more available for women at women's colleges, mainly because of the network of women graduates in business and industry who want to help their "sisters" at their alma maters. "I'm getting my professional edge now," says Binder, who is interested in TV production and had a paid internship as a production assistant while a sophomore at Barnard. "You will have an amazing resume by the time you graduate," she says.

Peggy Hock, Ph.D., former College Counselor at Notre Dame High School in San Jose, California, points out that colleges naturally rely on their alumni to come forward with networking opportunities for students; however, the alumnae of women's colleges tend to be more loyal and willing to give of their time. This translates into many more opportunities for internships, mentoring, and job possibilities. At Barnard, for example, the career office has an alumna mentor network. Students can call, ask questions, and get advice about career choices. At alumnae events, current students mix with the graduates. Binder takes full advantage of the Web log of women who are working all over the world and willing to spend time online with Barnard students. She applied for a job at a public relations firm in New York after contacting a fellow Barnard graduate working there. She met with her and subsequently got a letter of recommendation.

HOW TO CHOOSE

Choosing a women's college isn't any different from choosing a coed college. You should definitely visit the campus and don't be afraid to ask lots of questions—even the ones that might make you uncomfortable. Because women's colleges are similar to small coed liberal arts colleges, make sure that you don't compare a women's campus to a big university.

Janet Ashley, former Interim Director for Admissions at Spelman College, advises high school women to ask what a women's college can give them academically. "Their choice depends on what their goals are," she says.

Why Not Women's Colleges?

If you're worried about the dating scene, ask about the levels of interaction with guys and how close the relationships are with neighboring institutions.

"Look at the individuality of each women's college," suggests Rickard, "because each has its own personality."

Look at the school before looking at the fact that it's a women's college, and on the flip side, don't rule out a school just because it is a women's college. "So many students make quick decisions about where to apply," warns Fondiller, noting that sometimes the decision hinges on what schools a friend is applying to rather than if that institution really fits the student. Many women's colleges specialize in certain fields like science, math, or theater.

Famous Firsts from Women's Colleges

Do you know which college the first woman to be named Secretary of State graduated from? Or the woman scientist who identified the Hong Kong flu? Or the first woman executive vice president of the American Stock Exchange? Here's a big clue. They were all graduates of women's colleges.

SENATOR
- Barbara Mikulski (MD)—Mount Saint Agnes College

REPRESENTATIVES (Current and Former)
- Tammy Baldwin (WI)—Smith College
- Donna Christian-Christensen (VI)—St. Mary's College
- Rosa DeLauro (CT)—Marymount College
- Jane Harman (CA)—Smith College
- Gabrielle Giffords (AZ, 2007–12)—Scripps College
- Eddie Bernice Johnson (TX)—Saint Mary's College
- Barbara Lee (CA)—Mills College
- Nita Lowey (NY)—Mount Holyoke College
- Betty McCollum (MN)—College of Saint Catherine
- Nancy Pelosi (CA), first woman elected as Speaker of the House of Representatives—Trinity College
- Allyson Schwartz (PA)—Simmons College

FORMER SECRETARY OF STATE
- Hillary Rodham Clinton (NY)—Wellesley College

OTHER FAMOUS WOMEN FIRSTS
- Madeleine Albright, first woman to be named Secretary of State in the United States, appointed in 1997—Wellesley College
- Jane Amsterdam, first woman editor, the New York Post—Cedar Crest College
- Emily Green Balch, first woman to receive the Nobel Peace Prize in 1946—Bryn Mawr College
- Catherine Brewer Benson, first woman to receive a college bachelor's degree—Wesleyan College
- Earla Biekert, first scientist to identify the Hong Kong flu virus—Wesleyan College
- Cathleen Black, first woman leader of the American Newspaper Publishers Association—Trinity Washington University
- Sarah Porter Boehmler, first woman executive vice president of American Stock Exchange—Sweet Briar College
- Jane Matilda Bolin, first African American woman judge in the United States—Wellesley College
- Dorothy L. Brown, first African American woman general surgeon in the South—Bennett College for Women
- Pearl S. Buck, first American woman to win the Nobel Prize in Literature—Randolph-Macon Woman's College
- Ila Burdett, Georgia's first female Rhodes Scholar—Agnes Scott College
- Dorothy Vredenburgh Bush, first woman secretary of the Democratic National Party—Mississippi University for Women
- Hon. Audrey J. S. Carrion, first Hispanic woman judge Circuit Court for Baltimore City—College of Notre Dame of Maryland
- Rachel Carson, first environmentalist who awakened public consciousness through her book, *Silent Spring*—Chatham University
- Barbara Cassani, first woman CEO of a commercial airline—Mount Holyoke College
- Elaine L. Chao, U.S. Secretary of Labor, 2001; First Asian American woman appointed to a President's cabinet—Mount Holyoke College

Adapted from the website of the Women's College Coalition at http://www.womenscolleges.org.

Applying 101

The words "applying yourself" have several important meanings in the college application process. One meaning refers to the fact that you need to keep focused during this important time in your life, keep your priorities straight, and know the dates that your applications are due so you can apply on time. The phrase might also refer to the person who is really responsible for your application—you.

You are the only person who should compile your college application. You need to take ownership of this process. The guidance counselor is not responsible for completing your applications, and neither are your parents. College applications must be completed in addition to your normal workload at school, college visits, and SAT®, ACT®, or TOEFL® testing.

THE APPLICATION

The application is your way of introducing yourself to a college admissions office. As with any introduction, you want to make a good first impression. The first thing you should do in presenting your application is to find out what the college or university needs from you. Read the application carefully to find out the application fee and deadline, required standardized tests, number of essays, interview requirements, and anything else you can do or submit to help improve your chances for acceptance.

FOLLOW THESE TIPS WHEN FILLING OUT YOUR APPLICATIONS

- **Follow the directions to the letter.** You don't want to be in a position to ask an admissions officer for exceptions due to your inattentiveness.
- **Proofread all parts of your application,** including your essay. Again, the final product indicates to the admissions staff how meticulous and careful you are in your work.
- **Submit your application as early as possible,** provided all of the pieces are available. If there is a problem with your application, this will allow you to work through it with the admissions staff in plenty of time. If you wait until the last minute, it not only takes away that cushion but also reflects poorly on your sense of priorities.
- **Keep a copy of the completed application,** whether it is a photocopy or a copy saved on your computer.
  (For more hands-on help with your application essays, pair up with a professional editor who can provide you with proofreading services as well as full critiques: www.essayedge.com)

Completing college applications yourself helps you learn more about the schools to which you are applying. The information a college asks for in its application can tell you much about the school. State university applications often tell you how they are going to view their applicants. Usually, they select students based on GPAs and test scores. Colleges that request an interview, ask you to respond to a few open-ended questions, or require an essay are interested in a more personal approach to the application process and may be looking for different types of students than those sought by a state school.

In addition to submitting the actual application, there are several other items that are commonly required. You will be responsible for ensuring that your standardized test scores and your high school transcript arrive at the colleges to which you apply. Most colleges will ask that you submit teacher recommendations as well. Select teachers who know you and your abilities well and allow them plenty of time to complete the recommendations. When all portions of the application have been completed and sent in, whether electronically or by mail, make sure you follow up with the college to ensure their receipt.

THE APPLICATION ESSAY

Whereas the other portions of your application—your transcript, test scores, and involvement in extracurricular activities—are a reflection of what you've accomplished up to this point, your application essay is an opportunity to present yourself in the here and now. The essay shows your originality and verbal skills and how you approach a topic or problem and express your opinion.

Some colleges may request one essay or a combination of essays and short-answer topics to learn more about who you are and how well you can communicate your thoughts. Common essay topics cover such simple themes as writing about yourself and your experiences or why you want to attend that particular school. Other colleges will ask that you show your imaginative or creative side by writing about a favorite author, for instance, or commenting on a hypothetical situation. In such cases, they will be looking at your thought processes and level of creativity.

Admissions officers, particularly those at small or mid-size colleges, use the essay to determine how you, as a student, will fit into life at that college. The essay, therefore, is a critical component of the application process. Here are some tips for writing a winning essay:

- Colleges are looking for an honest representation of who you are and what you think. Make sure that the tone of the essay reflects enthusiasm, maturity, creativity, the ability to communicate, talent, and your leadership skills.
- Be sure you set aside enough time to write the essay, revise it, and revise it *again*. Running "spell check" will only

detect a fraction of the errors you probably made on your first pass at writing it. Take a break and then come back to it and reread it. You will probably notice other style, content, and grammar problems—and ways that you can improve the essay overall.

- Always answer the question that is being asked, making sure that you are specific, clear, and true to your personality.

- Enlist the help of reviewers who know you well— friends, parents, teachers—since they are likely to be the most honest and will keep you on track in the presentation of your true self.

THE PERSONAL INTERVIEW

Although it is relatively rare that a personal interview is required, many colleges recommend that you take this opportunity for a face-to-face discussion with a member of the admissions staff. Read through the application materials to determine whether or not a college places great emphasis on the interview. If they strongly recommend that you have one, it may work against you to forego it.

In contrast to a group interview and some alumni interviews, which are intended to provide information about a college, the personal interview is viewed both as an information session and as further evaluation of your skills and strengths. You will meet with a member of the admissions staff who will be assessing your personal qualities, high school preparation, and your capacity to contribute to undergraduate life at the institution. On average, these meetings last about 45 minutes—a relatively short amount of time in which to gather information and leave the desired impression—so here are some suggestions on how to make the most of it.

Scheduling Your Visit

Generally, students choose to visit campuses in the summer or fall of their senior year. Both times have their advantages. A summer visit, when the campus is not in session, generally allows for a less hectic visit and interview. Visiting in the fall, on the other hand, provides the opportunity to see what campus life is like in full swing. If you choose the fall, consider arranging an overnight trip so that you can stay in one of the college dormitories. At the very least, you should make your way around campus to take part in classes, athletic events, and social activities. Always make an appointment and avoid scheduling more than two college interviews on any given day. Multiple interviews in a single day hinder your chances of making a good impression, and your impressions of the colleges will blur into each other as you hurriedly make your way from place to place.

Preparation

Know the basics about the college before going for your interview. Read the college catalog and website in addition to this guide. You will be better prepared to ask questions that are not answered in the literature and that will give you a better understanding of what the college has to offer. You should also spend some time thinking about your strengths and weak-

nesses and, in particular, what you are looking for in a college education. You will find that as you get a few interviews under your belt, they will get easier. You might consider starting with a college that is not a top contender on your list, so that the stakes are not as high.

Asking Questions

Inevitably, your interviewer will ask you, "Do you have any questions?" Not having one may suggest that you're unprepared or, even worse, not interested. When you do ask questions, make sure that they are ones that matter to you and that have a bearing on your decision about whether or not to attend that college. The questions that you ask will give the interviewer some insight into your personality and priorities. Avoid asking questions that are answered in the college literature—again, a sign of unpreparedness. Although the interviewer will undoubtedly pose questions to you, the interview should not be viewed merely as a question-and-answer session. If a conversation evolves out of a particular question, so much the better. Your interviewer can learn a great deal about you from how you sustain a conversation. Similarly, you will be able to learn a great deal about the college in a conversational format.

Separate the Interview from the Interviewer

Many students base their feelings about a college solely on their impressions of the interviewer. Try not to characterize a college based only on your personal reaction, however, since your impressions can be skewed by whether you and your interviewer hit it off. Pay lots of attention to everything else that you see, hear, and learn about a college. Once on campus, you may never see your interviewer again.

In the end, remember to relax and be yourself. Your interviewer will expect you to be somewhat nervous, which will relieve some of the pressure. Don't drink jitters-producing caffeinated beverages prior to the interview, and suppress nervous fidgets like leg-wagging, finger-drumming, or bracelet jangling. Consider your interview an opportunity to put forth your best effort and to enhance everything that the college knows about you up to this point.

THE FINAL DECISION

Once you have received your acceptance letters, it is time to go back and look at the whole picture. Provided you received more than one acceptance, you are now in a position to compare your options. The best way to do this is to compare your original list of important college-ranking criteria with what you've discovered about each college along the way. In addition, you and your family will need to factor in the financial aid component. You will need to look beyond these cost issues and the quantifiable pros and cons of each college, however, and know that you have a good feeling about your final choice. Before sending off your acceptance letter, you need to feel confident that the college will feel like home for the next four years. Once the choice is made, the only hard part will be waiting for an entire summer before heading off to college!

The "Early Decision" Decision

Maybe a senior you knew last year didn't get into the college he wanted. He said it was because he didn't apply "early decision." Maybe your friend's mom told your mom that unless students apply early decision, their chances of getting into top schools are slim to none, even though they have great grades and spectacular essays. Maybe you figure you'd better get in on the early decision action.

All of the above are true—well, sort of—because many students applying to college get the term "early decision" backwards. High school guidance and college counselors run into this kind of thinking all the time and suggest putting "decision" before "early"—as in making a wise decision about committing to a college before applying early. For some students, early decision is a great option. For others, early decision is loaded with pitfalls and dangers.

"When students come back in the fall of their senior year, I often hear 'I know I want to apply early. Can you help me choose the school?'" says Kathy Cleaver, Co-Director of College Counseling at Durham Academy in Durham, North Carolina. She compares that to saying, "I know I want to get married, please help me pick the man." Continues Cleaver, "First you have to fall in love with the school and know it's your first choice and then join the circus for early decision." She's referring to the media hype flying around high school halls about early decision—it's easy to fall prey to the early decision madness. Hot competition to get into "top" schools creates early decision anxiety. Michael "Mickey" Gilbert, Guidance Counselor at Passaic High School in Passaic, New Jersey, throws out some scary numbers that confirm that, yes, the competition for admittance to top schools is white-hot. There are about 30,000 high schools in the United States, and although the majority of high school seniors apply to institutions in their own states, there are still limited spaces in the "top" schools and the eight Ivy League schools. "No wonder kids think that early decision is the way to go," speculates Gilbert. Early decision panic sets in because students are convinced that if they get their applications in early, they have an edge. Sometimes early decision might make the difference, but there are many issues to consider before taking the early decision leap.

EARLY THIS, EARLY THAT

With all the buzz about early decision, do you really know what it means along with all the other early options, such as early action and early notification? And what about the variations of early decision? Each institution can have its own version of early decision, meaning that deadlines and criteria are different. There's the early decision that notifies students by December, there's the early decision round two, and then there is the early action/single choice.

Seeing the confusion, the National Association for College Admission Counseling (NACAC) developed a standard set of definitions. NACAC is an education association of secondary school counselors, college and university admissions and financial aid officers, counselors, and other individuals who work with students as they transition from high school to college. While each institution has its own variations of each early option, an understanding of the basic differences can help. The list that follows was adapted from the definitions found on the NACAC website (www.nacacnet.org).

Early Decision

- Early decision is the application process in which students make a commitment to a first-choice institution where, if admitted, they definitely will enroll. Should a student who applies for financial aid not be offered an award that makes attendance possible, the student may decline the offer of admission and be released from the early decision commitment.

- While pursuing admission under an early decision plan, students may apply to other institutions, but may have only one early decision application pending at any time.

- The institution must notify the applicant of the decision within a reasonable and clearly stated period of time after the early decision deadline. Usually, a nonrefundable deposit must be made well in advance of May 1.

- A student applying for financial aid must adhere to institutional early decision aid application deadlines.

- The institution will respond to an application for financial aid at or near the time of an offer of admission.

- The early decision application supercedes all other applications. Immediately upon acceptance of an offer of admission, a student must withdraw all other applications and make no subsequent applications.

- The application form will include a request for a parent and a counselor signature, in addition to the student's signature, indicating an understanding of the early decision commitment and agreement to abide by its terms.

Early Action

- Early action is the application process in which students make application to an institution of preference and receive a decision well in advance of the institution's regular response date. Students who are admitted under early action are not obligated to accept the institution's offer of admission or to submit a deposit until the regular reply date (not prior to May 1).

The "Early Decision" Decision

- A student may apply to other colleges without restriction.

- The institution must notify the applicant of the decision within a reasonable and clearly stated period of time after the early action deadline.

- A student applying for financial aid must adhere to institutional aid application deadlines.

- A student admitted under an early action plan may not be required to make a commitment prior to May 1, but may be encouraged to do so as soon as a final college choice is made. Colleges that solicit commitments to offers of early action admission and/or financial assistance prior to May 1 may do so provided those offers include a clear statement that written requests for extensions until May 1 will be granted, and that such requests will not jeopardize a student's status for admission or financial aid.

Regular Decision

- Regular decision is the application process in which a student submits an application to an institution by a specified date and receives a decision within a reasonable and clearly stated period of time, but not later than April 15.

- A student may apply to other colleges without restriction.

- The institution will state a deadline for completion of applications and will respond to completed applications by a specified date.

- A student applying for financial aid must adhere to institutional aid application deadlines.

- A student admitted under a regular decision plan may not be required to make a commitment prior to May 1, but may be encouraged to do so as soon as a final college choice is made. Colleges that solicit commitments to offers of admission and/or financial assistance prior to May 1 may do so provided those offers include a clear statement that written requests for extensions until May 1 will be granted, and that such requests will not jeopardize a student's status for admission or financial aid.

Rolling Admission

- Rolling admission is the application process in which an institution reviews applications as they are completed and renders admission decisions to students throughout the admission cycle.

- A student may apply to other colleges without restriction.

- The institution will respond to completed applications in a timely manner.

- A student applying for financial aid must adhere to institutional aid application deadlines.

- A student admitted under a rolling admission plan may not be required to make a commitment prior to May 1, but may be encouraged to do so as soon as a final college choice is made. Colleges that solicit commitments to offers of admission and/or financial assistance prior to May 1 may do so provided those offers include a clear statement that

written requests for extensions until May 1 will be granted, and that such requests will not jeopardize a student's status for admission or financial aid.

Wait List

- Wait list is an admission decision option utilized by institutions to protect against shortfalls in enrollment. Wait lists are sometimes made necessary because of the uncertainty of the admission process, as students submit applications for admission to multiple institutions and may receive several offers of admission. By placing a student on the wait list, an institution does not initially offer or deny admission, but extends to a candidate the possibility of admission in the future before the institution's admission cycle is concluded.

- The institution will ensure that a wait list, if necessary, is of reasonable length and is maintained for a reasonable period of time, but never later than August 1.

- In the letter offering a wait list position, the institution should provide a past wait list history, which describes the number of students placed on the wait list(s), the number offered admission from the wait list, and the availability of financial aid. Students should be given an indication of when they can expect to be notified of a final admission decision.

- An institution must resolve final status and notify wait list candidates as soon after May 1 as possible.

- The institution will not require students to submit deposits to remain on a wait list or pressure students for a commitment to enroll prior to sending an official offer of admission in writing.

There is one more option, called early action/single choice (EASC), that some highly selective schools such as Harvard, Yale, Princeton, and Stanford have begun using. Early action/single choice is a nonbinding early admission option for freshman applicants that replaces early decision. With this change, students learn about their admission decision in December without being required to reply until May 1. This option allows students to apply to as many colleges as they want under a regular admission time frame. The difference is that the early action/single choice option does not allow a candidate to apply to other schools under any type of early action, early decision, or early notification program. Students are asked to sign a statement in their application agreeing to file only one early application.

Each of these options has variations, depending on the institution using them. Some schools have a November 1 deadline for early decision round one. Smaller schools have a deadline of November 15, while others have a December 1 deadline. Then there's an early decision round two. To make matters even more complicated, some schools with early decision say that students can't apply to other institutions if they've sent in an early decision application to their admissions office. Others say it's okay to apply to other schools at the same time you're applying early decision to them, but if they send you an acceptance, you must withdraw the other applications.

PARENTS, SOME ADVICE FOR YOU

Though guidance counselors stress that high school students should make the final decision about which college to attend, they also say that parents are a very important part of the decision equation. Parents can help as organizers of all the information and provide the support needed to make a good choice. "Little things like setting up file folders and keeping track of deadlines can keep a student on track," advises David Gibson, former College Advisor at St. Mary's Parish in Annapolis, Maryland.

Along with their children, parents also need to understand the basics of early option terminology as it applies to each institution being considered. Five different colleges might have five different early decision criteria. Read the fine print, and make note of deadlines.

What really will help—you, your child, and your wallet—is to understand the basics about financial aid. Says Shawn Leftwich, Director of Undergraduate Admissions at Wheaton College in Illinois, "Have an in-depth discussion with the financial aid officer so that you are aware of the ramifications, restrictions, and implications of the financial aid offer."

If possible, make an appointment to visit with a financial aid officer at the college while your child is visiting the campus. Bring your tax forms and discuss the prospects of financial aid. "Financial aid people are straight shooters. It's not in their best interest to tell you one thing to get your foot in the door and then turn around and pull the rug out from under you," says Bill McClintick, Dean of College Relations and Outreach at Mercerburg Academy. "Parents might not like the answer they get from the financial aid officer, but they will get a candid assessment of their eligibility for financial aid."

Leftwich suggests having an honest discussion with your child early in the college selection process. Talk about what you can realistically afford, what colleges will appropriately challenge him or her, if location is a factor, and what kind of environment best suits your child. Whichever option your child uses to apply, you both will know the decision is an informed one.

Just because two institutions have an application process called early decision or early action doesn't mean that their policies are identical. "There is no common terminology, even among the colleges that have early decision," says Christoph Guttentag, Dean of Undergraduate Admissions at Duke University in Durham, North Carolina. He also points out that just when you think you've got the definitions figured out, institutions change them. "Colleges are always balancing the needs of their institution and the needs of students," he comments.

EARLY DECISION: A MATCHMAKING TOOL OR A CLEVER STRATEGY?

Despite the differences in what actually constitutes early decision, it has become more of a strategy than a matchmaking tool, according to Bill McClintick, Director of College Relations and Outreach at Mercersburg Academy in Mercersburg, Pennsylvania. He also chairs the national steering committee on admissions standards for NACAC. The focus of early decision used to be on matching the student with the college and letting the admissions office know that that institution is where the student wants to be above all others. Today, early decision is misunderstood and misused. High school seniors think that they must use the early decision tactic to get an edge. The result, says McClintick is "at many of the top places, early decision applications have gone through the roof."

Though high school students may have exaggerated ideas of how much early decision can really help them, it is true that it does give a small segment of students applying at highly selective schools an advantage. Generally, the more selective the institution, the more small differences matter. "Even if it's a small increase, you need everything you can get," states John Latting, Ph.D., Emory University's Assistant Vice Provost for Undergraduate Enrollment and Dean of Admission.

"Remember," cautions McClintick, "we're only talking about a small slice of kids in the grand scheme of things." He mentions 5 percent of high school seniors nationally who aspire to the "top" institutions. State colleges and universities fill a much lower percentage of their freshman class with early decision applications. "I don't believe that more kids are chasing the same number of spots," says Jon Reider, Director of College Counseling at San Francisco University High School in San Francisco, California. "Students are applying to more and more schools, even with the early decision option on the side. This is inflating the selectivity of some colleges beyond what it used to be." In reality, 90 percent of students apply regular admission. Interest in early decision comes from a relatively small segment of the college applicant pool.

THE BENEFITS OF EARLY DECISION

There are clear benefits for students who apply for early decision. Aside from the fact that early decision does play a role in acceptance rates for a relatively small percentage of students at a small number of schools, early decision is a good option. The caveat is that students must know, without a shred of doubt, that one institution, above all others, is the best match for their goals and their likes and dislikes, and that based on grades and test scores, they solidly match the institution's criteria for admission. The option to go early decision should be taken after extensive research, multiple visits to the campus, and talking to a lot of people. "Early decision is for those who can put their hearts and souls into one application," advises Cleaver.

There are other advantages. You have to make only one choice, and you will know by December if you've been accepted. You have to fill out only one application. You are not chewing your nails over your list of possibilities during the winter break. Instead, you know where you're going and can sit back and enjoy the rest of your senior year, while others in your class are madly filling out applications, writing essays, and agonizing over the thin envelopes that arrive in the mail. Says Guttentag, "The advantage of having that challenging process over with is not insignificant."

Early decision is helpful for admissions officers at selective colleges because it allows them to make decisions between well-qualified students and select those who really want to be at their institution. As Shawn Leftwich, Director of Undergraduate Admissions at Wheaton College in Illinois, points out, early decision is for the students who are strongly committed. "We like you. You like us. We know you're coming, and we can fill our freshman class." However, on the flip side, she adds that some students aren't so sure about which college they want to attend, and early decision only makes the process more stressful.

Before you decide to go with early decision, consider early action. Many high school counselors lean toward early action, which is another good option. With early action you're able to apply later in the process. This means you will be able to take the SATs again. Your first-semester grades and AP classes taken in the first semester of your senior year can be used to evaluate your eligibility. You have September and October to visit several campuses while they are in session and plenty of time to do the research to put more than one school on your list.

THE PITFALLS OF EARLY DECISION

Though early decision has benefits, before you jump into it, look at the ramifications of that option. Advises Gilbert, "Early decision might give you an edge, but the tradeoff is not so great."

Perhaps the most compelling reason why students should seriously examine early decision before jumping at it is because they are bound by an agreement to attend that school if accepted. Students sign a pledge to attend that institution and are required to withdraw applications from all other schools. They also are obligated to accept the financial aid award that the institution gives them. An early decision is a binding decision. "Regardless," advises David Gibson, of David Gibson College Advising, LLC, in Annapolis, Maryland, "students don't learn about their financial aid awards until March or April, and if the award funding is not at all acceptable because the family's financial need was not met, they need to decline the offer and begin searching for a new college. March or April is not a good time to start applying to new colleges."

How binding is binding? Though no school can force a student to attend if they've signed an early decision agreement, students who decide not to attend that school hurt others with that decision. High school counselors have to sign the binding agreement, along with parents, and must state that they will not send out transcripts to other institutions. Many institutions will not accept the application of a student who applied early decision elsewhere and backed out of the agreement. Admissions officers may find out in May that an

QUESTIONS TO ASK YOURSELF BEFORE APPLYING EARLY DECISION

What if you don't get accepted early decision—then what? Speaking from the experience of seeing students deal with early decision rejection letters, Reider says, "Some of your friends are getting acceptance letters, and you get one thin envelope and the pain of rejection. You've given the early decision institution your best shot and you lost." Cleaver has seen kids in her high school end up thinking they won't get in anywhere. "This is the first time they've faced a big rejection and news they don't want to hear," she says, noting that because of the timetable of early decision, letters often come right around exam time in December.

When students apply regular decision, meaning they wait until well into their senior year and apply to several different institutions, it's "all or some," quips Latting. "With early decision, it's all or nothing." Many application deadlines for regular decision are in January. If you get that rejection letter from the school you were counting on, that doesn't give you much time to apply to other schools, much less visit them.

Are you ready to make such a drastic decision so early in your senior year? A lot can change in how you think about your future between the beginning of your senior year and graduation. With six or seven months behind you as a senior, you might be in a better position to compare colleges in April than you were back in September. Think about it—you're making the decision about where you want to spend the next four years of your life in early October of your senior year!

Have you given yourself enough time to pick one college above all others? If you want to apply early decision, you should start making plans to do so in your junior year. In order to apply early decision, you must have your ACTs or SATs taken, campus visits done, a final choice made, a dynamite essay written, a stellar application filled out, and teacher recommendation letters collected. That's a lot to cram into the end of your junior year and a few months into your senior year.

Have you given an admissions office enough information to make a decision about you? The more information the admissions office has about grades and classes you took and activities and leadership positions you held, the better they can decide if you're a good match for them. Do you really want decisions being made about you based on sophomore and junior grades and activities? What happens to that AP English class you finally felt ready to take the beginning of your senior year? What about that calculus class you aced in the first semester of your senior year? Admissions won't be able to assess that on an early decision application.

early decision student is not coming, so they'll call the counselor and ask if the student applied to another school. If so, often a phone call to the other institution is made and acceptance denied. Sometimes the counselor loses a good reputation with that institution, putting applicants who follow in subsequent years at a disadvantage.

After the consequences of signing a binding agreement, the financial aspect of early decision is the next biggest pitfall. "You can't compare financial aid offers," says Latting. "You have only one offer." Students won't know if they're eligible for Pell grants or merit scholarships. Government FAFSA forms are not submitted until January, and students might not find out how much aid they can get until March or April, long after the early decision agreement was signed and sealed. "This means that if they are accepted, they are then obligated to a college that might not fund them to the level of their financial need," says Gibson. Students who apply early action or regular decision are in a better position to negotiate financial aid packages.

EARLY DECISION REJECTION

In case you haven't heard, "fat" is good, "thin" is bad. Thin envelopes from college admissions offices usually mean a single-page letter saying good luck, we wish you the best, but you're not going to be attending our school next fall. However stated, it's hard to be rejected, especially when you've applied early decision, which states to the college and to yourself that this is the college you've decided is the only one you really, really want to attend above all others.

But thin envelopes don't mean the end of the world. Cleaver advises to not let early decision get control of you. "There are too many choices of colleges for you not to get into college. You might not get into Princeton, but there are many other wonderful schools if you do the research to look for a good match. Early decision is a tool to use to apply, but it is not always the best tool."

Objecting to the term "perfect match," Reider asks, "Does it really matter what kind of car you drive? There are twenty different colleges that can get you where you want to go. You'll be successful in most places."

HOW TO DO EARLY DECISION THE RIGHT WAY

Taking the early decision option requires more than gathering information, filling out an application, writing an essay, and waiting for an envelope to come in the mail or an e-mail to hit your Inbox. If you're going to be serious about early decision, the time to start is in your junior year.

Research the institutions at the top of your list. Think through what you want out of college—not just in terms of a future

career, but also factors such as location, size, distance from home, sports, and other activities. Think about who you want to be. "It has to be a love connection," says Cleaver. Tune out all the early decision talk and do your homework about each college. Then ask yourself if one stands out above all the others you've researched. Is this the one to which you can commit to a binding agreement? Are you in the competition to be admitted? Will you have the funds to attend this college?

"Admissions can tell if your application is from the heart," Cleaver cautions. Students ask her how to make their applications "look like they want to go there." She replies that what they put on an application and in an essay has to pour out of their hearts. Students who visit the campus and sit in on a class or a campus organization have the edge if something really clicked with them. They will write a convincing application. Perhaps they'll tell about how exciting the professor they heard was or how wonderful it is that the college has a chess club. Cleaver observes that kids usually write about an institution's sports team or about the ivy-covered walls of the campus on their application essay instead of writing about some interesting aspect of the university that spoke to them, which takes research, time, and reflection. "Don't make the mistake of chasing a name and not being a good consumer," cautions McClintick. Part of being a good consumer is to make sure you are a reasonably competitive applicant. This means looking at the school's admission criteria and statistics. What percentage of the freshman class is filled with early decision and early action students? If it's a high percentage, then you might want to reconsider where that school falls on your wish list. How many students return for their sophomore year? If more than 10 percent leave after their freshman year, that should tell you something about student satisfaction—and ultimately yours.

One of the most important ways to choose the right school is to visit the campus, perhaps multiple times and preferably with students on campus. "Campus visits are a critical time to talk with undergraduates and to find out what the academic, social, and physical climate is like," advises Guttentag. If you're staying in a dorm on Tuesday night during a visit, you can tell how serious kids are about their work. What kinds of conversations are they having? "Are these the kind of kids you want to spend four years of your life with?" asks McClintick.

After you've thoroughly investigated all the aspects of a college and decided it's at the absolute top of your list, after you are familiar with the early decision requirements at that institution, and after you've determined that you have a good chance of getting into that institution, then you can say early decision is for you. For those who are not so sure, fortunately, colleges and universities have plenty of other options for admission.

Coming to America: Tips for International Students Considering Study in the U.S.

Introduction:
Why Study in the United States?

Are you thinking about going to a college or university in the United States? If you're looking at this book, you probably are! All around the world, students like you who are pursuing high education are considering that possibility. They envision themselves on modern, high-tech campuses in well-known cities, surrounded by American students, taking classes and having fun. A degree from a U.S. school would certainly lead to success and fortune, either back in your home country or perhaps even in the United States, wouldn't it?

It can be done—but becoming a student at a college or university in the U.S. requires academic talent, planning, time, effort, and money. While there may be only a small number of institutions of higher learning in your country, there are more than 2,900 four-year colleges and universities in the United States. Choosing one, being accepted, and then traveling and becoming a student in America is a big undertaking.

If this is your dream, here is some helpful information and expert tips from professionals who work with international students at colleges and universities throughout the United States.

Timing and Planning

The journey to a college or university in the U.S. often starts years in advance. Most international students choose to study in the U.S. because of the high quality of academics. Your family may also have a lot of input on this decision, too.

"We always tell students they should be looking in the sophomore year, visiting in the junior year, and applying in the senior year," says Father Francis E. Chambers, OSA, D.Min., Associate Director of International Admission at Villanova University. He stresses that prospective students need to be taking challenging courses in the years leading up to college. "We want to see academic rigor. Most admission decisions are based on the first six semesters—senior year is too late."

Heidi Gregori-Gahan, Assistant Provost for International Programs at the University of Southern Indiana agrees that it's important to start early. "Plan ahead and do your homework. There is so much to choose from—so many schools, programs, degrees, and experiences. It can be overwhelming."

While students in some countries may pay an agent to help them get into a school in the United States, Gregori-Gahan often directs potential international students to EducationUSA (http://educationusa.state.gov), a U.S. State Department network of over 400 international student advising centers in more than 170 countries. "They are there to provide unbiased information about studying in the United States and help you understand the process and what you need to do."

Two to three years of advance planning is also recommended by Daphne Durham, who has been an international student adviser at Harvard, Suffolk University, Valdosta State University, and the University of Georgia. She points out that the academic schedule in other countries is often different than that of the United States, so you need to synchronize your calendar accordingly.

You will have to take several tests in order to gain admission to a U.S. school, so it's important to know when those tests are given in your country, then register and take them so your scores will be available when you apply. Even if you have taken English in school, you will probably have to take The Test of English as a Foreign Language (TOEFL®), but some schools also accept the International English Language Testing Sytem (IELTS). You will probably also have to take the SAT® or ACT® tests, which are achievement or aptitude tests, and are usually required of all students applying for admission, not just international students.

"Make sure you understand how the international admissions process works at the school or schools you want to attend," says Durham. "What test scores are needed and when? Does the school have a fixed calendar or rolling admissions?" Those are just some of the many factors that can impact your application and could make a difference in when you are able to start school.

"Every university is unique in what's required and what they need to do. Even navigating each school's different website can be challenging," explains Gregori-Gahan.

Searching for Schools

This book contains information on thousands of four-year colleges and universities, and it will be a valuable resource for you in your search and application process. But with so many options, how do you decide which school you should attend?

"Where I find a big difference with international students is if their parents don't recognize the school, they don't apply to the school," says Fr. Chambers. "They could be overlooking a lot of great schools. They have to look outside the box."

The school Gregori-Gahan represents is in Evansville, Indiana, and it probably isn't familiar to students abroad. "Not many people have heard of anything beyond New York and California and maybe Florida. I like to tell students that this is 'real America.' But happy international students on our campus have recruited others to come here."

She points out that Internet technology has made a huge difference in the search process for international students. Websites full of information, live chat, webinars, virtual tours, and admission interviews via Skype have made it easier for potential students to connect with U.S. institutions, get more information, and be better able to visualize the campus.

One thing that will help narrow your search for a school is knowing specifically what you want to study. You need to know what the course of study is called in the United States, what it means, and what is required in order to study that subject. You also need to consider your future plans. What are your goals and objectives? What do you plan to do after earning your degree?

"If you're going to overcome the hurdles and get to a U.S. school, you have to have a directed path chosen," says Durham.

The other thing that could help your search process is finding a school that is a good fit.

Fit Is Important

You want your clothing and shoes to fit you properly and be comfortable, so a place where you will spend four or more years of your life studying should also be comfortable and appropriate for you. So how can you determine if a particular school is a good fit?

"We really recommend international students visit first. Yes, there are websites and virtual tours, but there's still nothing that beats an in-person visit," says Fr. Chambers. He estimates that 50 to 60 percent of Villanova's international students visited the campus before enrolling.

"It can be hard to get a sense of a place—you're so far away and you're probably not going to set foot on campus until you arrive," says Gregori-Gahan. "There is a high potential for culture shock."

You need to ask yourself what is important to you in a campus environment, then do some homework to ensure that the schools you are considering meet those needs. Here are some things to consider when it comes to fit:

- **Location:** Is it important for you to be in a well-known city or is a part of the United States that is unfamiliar a possibility? "Look at geographic areas, but also cost of living," recommends Durham. "Be sure to factor in transportation costs also, especially if you plan to return to your home country regularly."
- **Student population:** Some small schools have 1,000 students while larger ones may have 30,000 students or more.
- **Familiar faces:** Is it important for you to be at a school with others from your home nation or region?

- **Climate:** Some students want a climate similar to where they live now, but others are open and curious about seasons and weather conditions they may not have ever experienced. "We do have four seasons here," says Gregori-Gahan. "Sometimes students who come here from tropical regions are concerned about the winters. The first snow is so exciting, but after that, students may not be aware of how cold it really is."
- **Amenities:** Do you want to find your own housing or choose a school where the majority of students live on campus? Is there public transportation available or is it necessary to walk or have a bicycle or car? Does the school or community have access to things that are important to you culturally and meet the traditions you want to follow?
- **Campus size:** Some campuses are tightly compacted into a few city blocks, but others cover hundreds of acres of land. "International students are amazed by how green and spacious our campus is, with blooming flowers, trees, and lots of grass," says Gregori-Gahan.
- **Academic offerings:** Does this school offer the program you want to study? Can you complete it in four years or perhaps sooner? What sort of internship and career services are available?
- **Finances:** Can you afford to attend this school? Is there any sort of financial assistance available for international students?
- **Support services:** Durham suggests students look carefully at each school's offerings for international students. "Does the school have online guidance for getting your visa? Is ESL tutoring available? Does the school offer host family or community friend programs?" She also suggests you look for campus support groups for students from your country or region.

Looking at the listings and reading the in-depth descriptions in this book can help you search for a school that is a good fit for you.

Government Requirements

The one thing that every international student must have in order to study in the United States is a student visa. Having accurate advice and following all the necessary steps regarding the visa process is essential to being able to enter this country and start school.

As you schedule your tests and application deadlines, you must also consider how long it will take to get your visa. This varies depending on where you live; in some countries, extensive background checks are required. The subject you plan to study can also impact your visa status; it does help to have a major rather than be undeclared. The U.S. State Department website,https://travel.state.gov/content/travel/en/us-visas/study.html, can give you an idea of how long it will take.

In addition to the visa, you will also need a Form I-20, which is a U.S. government immigration form. You must have this form when you get to the United States.

"It's very different from being a tourist. You need to be prepared to meet with an immigration officer and be interviewed about your college," explains Durham. "Where you are going, why you are going, where the school is located, what you are studying, and so on."

You also need to keep in mind that there are reporting requirements once you are a student in the United States. Every semester, your adviser has to report to the government to confirm that you are enrolled in and attending school in order for you to stay.

Finances

Part of the visa process includes having the funds to pay for the cost of your schooling and support yourself. Finances are a huge hurdle in the process of becoming a college student in the United States.

"It's crucial. So many foreign systems offer 'free' higher education to students. How is your family going to handle the ongoing expense of attending college for four years or longer in the United States?" Durham reiterates that planning ahead is key because there are so many details. Student loans require a U.S.-based cosigner. Each school has its own financial aid deadlines. You have to factor in your own government's requirements, such currency exchange and fund transfers.

The notion that abundant funds are available to assist international students is not true. Sometimes state schools may offer diversity waivers or there may be special scholarship opportunities for international students. But attending school in the U.S. is still a costly venture.

"We do offer financial aid to international students, but they still have to be able to handle a large portion of the costs. Full-need scholarships are not likely," explained Fr. Chambers. "Sometimes students think that once they get here, it will all work out and the funds will be there. But the scenario for the first year has to be repeated each year they are on campus."

Once You Arrive…

You've taken your tests, researched schools, found a good fit, applied, got accepted, arranged the financing, gotten your visa and I-20, and made it to the campus in the United States. Now what?

You can expect the school where you have enrolled to be welcoming and helpful, but within reason. If you arrive on a weekend, or at a time outside of the time when international students are scheduled to arrive, the assistance you need may not be available to you.

Every school offers different levels of assistance to international students. For instance, Villanova offers a full-service office that can assist students with everything from visas, to employment, to finding a place for students to stay over breaks.

Fr. Chambers attends the international student orientation session to greet the students he's worked with through the recruitment and application process. "But I rarely see an international student after that. I think that bodes well for them being integrated into the entire university."

"Those of us who work with international students are really working to help them adjust," says Gregori-Gahan. "International students get here well before school starts so they can get over jet lag. We have orientation sessions and pair them with peer advisers who help them navigate the first few days, and we assure them that we are there for them."

Students should be open to their new setting, but they should be prepared that things may not be at all how they had envisioned during their planning and searching process. "While you may think you'll meet lots of Americans, don't underestimate the importance of community with your traditional home culture and people," says Durham.

Don't Make These Mistakes

The journey to college attendance in the United States is a long one, with many steps. Experts warn about avoiding common mistakes along the way and offer the following helpful advice:

"Not reading through everything thoroughly and not understanding what the program of study really is and what will it cost. You have to be really clear on the important details," says Gregori-Gahan.

"Every school does things differently," cautions Fr. Chambers. "International students must be aware of that as they are applying."

Durham stresses that going to school in the United States is too big a decision to leave to someone else. "Students need to know about their school—they have to be in charge of their application."

"It involves a lot of work to be successful and happy and not surprised by too many things," Gregori-Gahan says.

Hopefully now, you are more informed and better prepared to pursue your dream of studying at a college or university in the United States.

Financial Aid Countdown Calendar

JUNIOR YEAR

Fall

Now is the time to get serious about the colleges in which you are interested. Meet with your guidance counselor to help you narrow down your choices. Hopefully by the spring, your list will have five to ten solid choices. College visits are always a great idea—remember this will be the place you will call home for four years, so start your campus visits soon!

❏ Register for the PSAT/NMSQT®.

❏ Check out local financial aid nights in the area. Be sure to attend these valuable sessions, especially if this is the first time your family is sending someone off to college. Try to become familiar with common financial aid terms. Start reviewing the literature available and begin to familiarize yourself with the various programs. A good booklet is published by the U.S. Department of Education, "2018-2019 Do you Need Money for College? The Guide to Federal Student Aid" and is available at any financial aid office or on the web at https://studentaid.ed.gov/sa/resources.

❏ In October, take the PSAT/NMSQT®.

❏ Do some web browsing! There are many free scholarship search engines, such as Petersons.com. Also, head to the bookstore or library and pick up a copy of *Peterson's® Scholarships, Grants & Prizes,* which features details on aid from private sources, or *Best Scholarships for the Best Students,* which offers great info on scholarships, fellowships, and experiential learning programs for top students.

❏ Ask your parents to contact their employers, unions, and any religious and fraternal organizations with which they have a connection to learn about possible scholarship opportunities.

❏ Check with your high school guidance counselor for the qualifications and deadlines of local scholarship awards. Many guidance counselors report that there are few applicants for these awards.

Winter

❏ Keep checking for scholarships! Remember that this is the one area over which you have control. The harder you work, the better your chances for success!

❏ Register and study for the ACT® or SAT® and SAT Subject Tests™.

Spring

❏ Spring Break—a great time to visit colleges. Remember your top ten list? Time to start narrowing it down.

❏ Review the requirements for local scholarships. What can you do now and over the summer to improve your chances?

❏ Take the ACT® or SAT®. Good luck!

❏ Look for a summer job, especially one that ties in with your college plans. For example, if you want to major in premed, why not try to get a job at a hospital or with a laboratory?

Summer

❏ College visit time! Ask: Is this where I see myself getting my undergraduate degree? Can I adjust to the seasons, the town surrounding the campus, the distance from home, the college size? Does this school feel right for me?

❏ Why not get a jump on college (and maybe save some money!) and enroll for a college course at the local community college? Or, better yet, do some extra prep work for the ACT® or SAT®!

SENIOR YEAR

Fall

How's the college list coming? Can you get your list down to five or six choices? Your guidance counselor can help with this process. Once you have your top choices, make a list of what each college requires for admission and financial aid. Be sure your list includes all deadlines. Attend a financial aid night presentation with your parents. Some of these sessions offer help in completing forms; others offer a broader view of the process. Contact the presenter (usually a local college financial aid professional) to be sure you are getting the information you need.

❏ Do any of these colleges require the CSS/Financial Aid PROFILE® financial aid application? Many private colleges use this form for institutional aid. You need to file this comprehensive form in late September or early October. For more information or to find out which colleges use this supplemental form, go to https://cssprofile.collegeboard.org/. (Website registration is free; however, PROFILE® is a fee-based application).

❏ If you are planning on applying for federal student aid, you should complete and submit your FAFSA® Application as soon as possible. The application can be submitted as early as October 1 every year.

❏ Don't falter now in your scholarship search. Get the applications filed by the published deadlines.

❏ Register now if you are planning to retake the SAT®.

❏ Most important, start completing your college applications—the earlier, the better! If you are interested in early decision or early action, now is the time! Remember, accuracy and completeness are a must!

Winter

❏ Ensure all college applications are completed.

❏ Do you have questions? Call the local financial aid office. Many states have special toll-free call-in programs in January and February (Financial Aid Awareness Month). Be sure that you have completed each school's required forms.

❏ As the letters of admission start to arrive, the financial aid award letters should be right behind them. Important question for parents: What is the bottom line? Remember, aid at a lower-cost state school will be less than a higher-cost private college. But what will you be required to pay? This can be confusing, so consider gift aid (scholarships and grants), student loans, and parent loans. The school with the lowest sticker price (tuition, fees, and room and board) might not be the best bargain when you look at the overall financial aid package.

Spring

❏ Still not sure where to go? The financial aid package at your top choice just not enough? Call the financial aid office and the admissions office. Talk it over. While schools don't like to bargain, they are usually willing to take a second look. Is there something unusual about your family's financial situation that might impact your parents' ability to pay?

❏ By May 1, you must make your final decision. Notify your chosen college and find out what you need to do next. Tell the other colleges you are not accepting their offers of admission and financial aid.

Summer

❏ Time to crunch the numbers. Parents, get information from the college on the total charges for the coming fall term. Deduct the aid package and then plan for how the balance will be paid. Contact the college financial aid office for the best parental loan program. If you want to arrange for a payment plan, contact the business office for further information. Most schools have deferred payment plans available for a nominal fee.

Congratulations! Remember that you need to reapply for aid every year!

Who's Paying for This? Financial Aid Basics

A college education can be expensive—costing more than $150,000 for four years at some of the higher priced private colleges and universities. Even at the lower-cost state colleges and universities, the cost of a four-year education can approach $60,000. Determining how you and your family will come up with the necessary funds to pay for your education requires planning, perseverance, and learning as much as you can about the options that are available to you. But before you get discouraged, College Board statistics show that 53 percent of full-time students attend four-year public and private colleges with tuition and fees less than $9,000, while 20 percent attend colleges that have tuition and fees more than $36,000. College costs tend to be less in the western states and higher in New England.

Paying for college should not be looked at as a four-year financial commitment. For many families, paying the total cost of a student's college education out of current income and savings is usually not realistic. For families that have planned ahead and have financial savings established for higher education, the burden is a lot easier. But for most, meeting the cost of college requires the pooling of current income and assets and investing in longer-term loan options. These family resources, together with financial assistance from state, federal, and institutional sources, enable millions of students each year to attend the institution of their choice.

FINANCIAL AID PROGRAMS

There are three types of financial aid:

1. Gift-aid—Scholarships and grants are funds that do not have to be repaid.

2. Loans—Loans must be repaid, usually after graduation; the amount you have to pay back is the total you've borrowed plus any accrued interest. This is considered a source of self-help aid.

3. Student employment—Student employment is a job arranged for you by the financial aid office. This is another source of self-help aid.

The federal government has four major grant programs—the Federal Pell Grant, the Federal Supplemental Educational Opportunity Grant, Academic Competitiveness Grants (ACG), and National SMART (Science and Mathematics Access to Retain Talent) grants. ACG and SMART grants are limited to students who qualify for a Pell Grant and are awarded to a select group of students. Overall, these grants are targeted to low-to-moderate income families with significant financial need. The federal government also sponsors a student employment program called the Federal Work-Study Program, which offers jobs both on and off campus, and several loan programs, including those for students and for parents of undergraduate students.

There are two types of student loan programs: subsidized and unsubsidized. The subsidized Federal Direct Loan and the Federal Perkins Loan are need-based, government-subsidized loans. Students who borrow through these programs do not have to pay interest on the loan until after they graduate or leave school. The unsubsidized Federal Direct Loan and the Federal Direct PLUS Loan Program are not based on need, and borrowers are responsible for the interest while the student is in school. These loans are administered by different methods. Once you choose your college, the financial aid office will guide you through this process.

After you've submitted your financial aid application and you've been accepted for admission, each college will send you a letter describing your financial aid award. Most award letters show estimated college costs, how much you and your family are expected to contribute, and the amount and types of aid you have been awarded. Most students are awarded aid from a combination of sources and programs. Hence, your award is often called a financial aid "package."

SOURCES OF FINANCIAL AID

Millions of students and families apply for financial aid each year. Financial aid from all sources exceeds $143 billion per year. The largest single source of aid is the federal government, which will award more than $100 billion this year.

The next largest source of financial aid is found in the college and university community. Most of this aid is awarded to students who have a demonstrated need based on the Federal Methodology. Some institutions use a different formula, the Institutional Methodology (IM), to award their own funds in conjunction with other forms of aid. Institutional aid may be either need-based or non-need based. Aid that is not based on need is usually awarded for a student's academic performance (merit awards), specific talents or abilities, or to attract the type of students a college seeks to enroll.

Another source of financial aid is from state government. All states offer grant and/or scholarship aid, most of which is need-based. However, more and more states are offering substantial merit-based aid programs. Most state programs award aid only to students attending college in their home state.

Other sources of financial aid include:

- Private agencies
- Foundations
- Corporations
- Clubs
- Fraternal and service organizations

- Civic associations
- Unions
- Religious groups that award grants, scholarships, and low-interest loans
- Employers that provide tuition reimbursement benefits for employees and their children

More information about these different sources of aid is available from high school guidance offices, public libraries, college financial aid offices, directly from the sponsoring organizations, and online at www.petersons.com/college-search/scholarship-search.aspx.

HOW NEED-BASED FINANCIAL AID IS AWARDED

When you apply for aid, your family's financial situation is analyzed using a government-approved formula called the Federal Methodology. This formula looks at five items:

1. Demographic information of the family
2. Income of the parents
3. Assets of the parents
4. Income of the student
5. Assets of the student

This analysis determines the amount you and your family are expected to contribute toward your college expenses, called your Expected Family Contribution, or EFC. If the EFC is equal to or more than the cost of attendance at a particular college, then you do not demonstrate financial need. However, even if you don't have financial need, you may still qualify for aid, as there are grants, scholarships, and loan programs that are not need-based.

If the cost of your education is greater than your EFC, then you do demonstrate financial need and qualify for assistance. The amount of your financial need that can be met varies from school to school. Some are able to meet your full need, while others can only cover a certain percentage of need. Here's the formula:

> Cost of Attendance
> − Expected Family Contribution
> = Financial Need

The EFC remains constant, but your need will vary according to the costs of attendance at a particular college. In general, the higher the tuition and fees at a particular college, the higher the cost of attendance will be. Expenses for books and supplies, room and board, transportation, and other miscellaneous items are included in the overall cost of attendance. It is important to remember that you do not have to be low-income to qualify for financial aid. Many middle and upper-middle income families qualify for need-based financial aid.

APPLYING FOR FINANCIAL AID

Every student must complete the Free Application for Federal Student Aid (FAFSA) to be considered for financial aid. The FAFSA is available from your high school guidance office, many public libraries, colleges in your area, or directly from the U.S. Department of Education.

Students are encouraged to apply for federal student aid on the Web. The electronic version of the FAFSA can be accessed at http://www.fafsa.ed.gov.

The NEW Federal Student Aid ID

In order for a student to complete the online FAFSA®, he or she will need a Federal Student Aid (FSA) ID. You can get this online at https://fsaid.ed.gov/npas/index.htm. Since May 2015, the FSA ID has replaced the previously used PIN system. Parents of dependent students also need to obtain their own FSA ID in order to sign their child's FAFSA® electronically online.

The FSA ID can be used to access several federal aid-related websites, including FAFSA.gov and StudentLoans.gov. It consists of a username and password and can be used to electronically sign Federal Student Aid documents, access your personal records, and make binding legal obligations. The FSA ID is beneficial in several ways:

- It removes your personal identifiable information (PII), such as your Social Security number, from your log-in credentials.
- It creates a more secure and efficient way to verify your information when you log in to access to your federal student aid information online.
- It gives you the ability to easily update your personal information.
- It allows you to easily retrieve your username and password by requesting a secure code be sent to your e-mail address or by answering challenge questions.

It's relatively simple to create an FSA ID and should only take a few minutes. In addition, you will have an opportunity to link your current Federal Student Aid PIN (if you already have one) to your FSA ID. The final step is to confirm your e-mail address. You will receive a secure code to the e-mail address you provided when you set up your FSA ID. Once you retrieve the code from your e-mail account and enter it—to confirm your e-mail address is valid—you will be able to use this e-mail address instead of your username to log in to any of the federal aid-related websites, making the log-in process EVEN simpler for you and your parents.

When you initially create your FSA ID, your information will need to be verified with the Social Security Administration. This process can take anywhere from one to three days. For that reason, it's a good idea to take care of setting up your FSA ID as early as possible, so it will be all set when you are ready to begin completing your FAFSA.

IMPORTANT NOTE: Since your FSA ID provides access to your personal information and is used to sign online documents, it's imperative that you protect this ID. Don't share it with *anyone* or write it down in an insecure location—you could place yourself at great risk for identify theft.

If Every College You're Applying to for Fall 2019 Requires the FAFSA

. . . then it's pretty simple: Complete the FAFSA after October 1, 2018, being certain to send it in before any college-imposed deadlines. Students will be required to report income infor-

Who's Paying for This? Financial Aid Basics

THE ADVICE CENTER

mation from an earlier tax year. For example, on the 2018-19 FAFSA, students (and parents, as appropriate) will report their 2017 income information, rather than their 2018 income information.

After you send in your FAFSA, you'll receive a Student Aid Report (SAR) that includes all of the information you reported and shows your EFC. If you provided an e-mail address, the SAR is sent to you electronically; otherwise, you will receive a SAR or SAR Acknowledgment in the mail, which lists your FAFSA information but may require you to make any corrections on the FAFSA website. Be sure to review the SAR, checking to see if the information you reported is accurately represented. If you used estimated numbers to complete the FAFSA, you may have to resubmit the SAR with any corrections to the data. The college(s) you have designated on the FAFSA will receive the information you reported and will use that data to make their decision.

The CSS/Financial Aid PROFILE®

To award their own funds, some colleges require an additional application, the CSS/Financial Aid PROFILE® form. The PROFILE asks supplemental questions that some colleges and awarding agencies feel provide a more accurate assessment of the family's ability to pay for college. It is up to the college to decide whether it will use only the FAFSA or both the FAFSA and the PROFILE. PROFILE applications are available from the high school guidance office and on the Web. Both the paper application and the website list those colleges and programs that require the PROFILE application.

If a College Requires the PROFILE

Step 1: Register for the CSS/Financial Aid PROFILE in the fall of your senior year in high school. You can apply for the PROFILE online at https://cssprofile.collegeboard.org/. Registration information with a list of the colleges that require the PROFILE is available in most high school guidance offices. There is a fee for using the Financial Aid PROFILE application ($25 for the first college, which includes the $9 application fee, and $16 for each additional college). You must pay for the service by credit card when you register. If you do not have a credit card, you will be billed. A limited number of fee waivers are automatically granted to first-time applicants based on the financial information provided on the PROFILE.

Step 2: Fill out your customized CSS/Financial Aid PROFILE. Once you register, your application will be immediately available online and will have questions that all students must complete, questions which must be completed by the student's parents (unless the student is independent and the colleges or programs selected do not require parental information), and *may* have supplemental questions needed by one or more of your schools or programs. If required, those will be found in Section Q of the application.

In addition to the PROFILE application you complete online, you may also be required to complete a Business/ Farm Supplement via traditional paper format. Completion of this form is not a part of the online process. If this form is required, instructions on how to download and print the supplemental form are provided. If your biological or adoptive parents are separated or divorced and your colleges and programs require it, your noncustodial parent may be asked to complete the Noncustodial PROFILE.

Once you complete and submit your PROFILE application, it will be processed and sent directly to your requested colleges and programs.

IF YOU DON'T QUALIFY FOR NEED-BASED AID

If you are not eligible for need-based aid, you can still find ways to lessen your burden.

Here are some suggestions:

- Search for merit scholarships. You can start at the initial stages of your application process. College merit awards are increasingly important as more and more colleges award these to students they especially want to attract. As a result, applying to a college at which your qualifications put you at the top of the entering class may give you a larger merit award. Another source of aid to look for is private scholarships that are given for special skills and talents. Additional information can be found at www.finaid.org.

- Seek employment during the summer and the academic year. The student employment office at your college can help you locate a school-year job. Many colleges and local businesses have vacancies remaining after they have hired students who are receiving Federal Work-Study Program financial aid.

- Borrow through the unsubsidized Federal Direct Loan program. This is generally available to all students. The terms and conditions are similar to the subsidized loans. The biggest difference is that the borrower is responsible for the interest while still in college, although the government permits students to delay paying the interest right away and add the accrued interest to the total amount owed. You must file the FAFSA to be considered.

- After you've secured what you can through scholarships, working, and borrowing, you and your parents will be expected to meet your share of the college bill (the Expected Family Contribution). Many colleges offer monthly payment plans that spread the cost over the academic year. If the monthly payments are too high, parents can borrow through the Federal Direct PLUS Loan Program, through one of the many private education loan programs available, or through home equity loans and lines of credit. Families seeking assistance in financing college expenses should inquire at the financial aid office about what programs are available at the college. Some families seek the advice of professional financial advisers and tax consultants.

How to Use This Guide

PROFILES

The **PROFILES** section contains basic data in capsule form for quick review and comparison. Organized by state, more than 2,700 colleges and universities are listed alphabetically, followed by their city and state and website URL. Those schools that offer a special, detailed listing at www.petersons.com, will also have a ★ next to their name.

The following outline of the format shows the section headings and the items that each section covers. Any item that does not apply to a particular college or for which no information was supplied is omitted from that college's listing. Display ads, which appear near some of the institutions' profiles, have been provided and paid for by those colleges and universities that chose to supplement their profile with additional information.

Category Overviews

Type of Institution

Private institutions are designated as *independent* (nonprofit), *proprietary* (profit-making), or *independent with a specific religious denomination or affiliation*. Nondenominational or interdenominational religious orientation is possible and would be indicated. Public institutions are designated by the source of funding. Designations include *federal, state, province, commonwealth* (Puerto Rico), *territory* (U.S. territories), *county, district* (an educational administrative unit often having boundaries different from units of local government), *city, state and local* (local may refer to county, district, or city), or *state-related* (funded primarily by the state but administratively autonomous). *Religious affiliation* may follow, along with year founded. Each institution is classified as one of the following:

- Primarily two-year: Awards baccalaureate degrees but majority of students are enrolled in two-year programs.

- Four-year: Awards baccalaureate degrees; may also award associate degrees; does not award graduate (postbaccalaureate) degrees.

- Five-year: Awards a five-year baccalaureate in a professional field such as architecture or pharmacy; does not award graduate degrees.

- Upper-level: Awards baccalaureate degrees, but entering students must have at least two years of previous college-level credit; may also offer graduate degrees.

- Comprehensive: Awards baccalaureate degrees; may also award associate degrees; offers graduate degree programs, primarily at the master's, specialist's, or professional level, although one or two doctoral programs may be offered.

- University: Offers four years of undergraduate work, plus graduate degrees through the doctorate in more than two academic or professional fields.

Setting

Designated as *urban* (located within a major city), *suburban* (a residential area within commuting distance of a major city), *small town* (a small but compactly settled area not within commuting distance of a major city), or *rural* (a remote and sparsely populated area).

Endowment

The total dollar value of funds and/or property donated to the institution or the multicampus educational system of which the institution is a part.

Student Body

An institution is *coed* (coeducational—admits men and women), *primarily* (80 percent or more) *women, primarily men, women only,* or *men only*. A few schools are designated as *undergraduate: women only; graduate: coed* or *undergraduate: men only; graduate: coed.*

Entrance

The five levels of entrance difficulty *(most difficult, very difficult, moderately difficult, minimally difficult,* and *noncompetitive)* are based on the percentage of applicants who were accepted for fall 2017 freshman admission (or, in the case of upper-level schools, for entering-class admission) and on the high school class rank and standardized test scores of the accepted freshmen who actually enrolled in fall 2017. The colleges were asked to select the level that most closely corresponds to their entrance difficulty, according to these guidelines.

UNDERGRAD STUDENTS

Number of full-time or part-time undergraduates. Number of states and territories that students come from; percentages of undergraduates who are out-of state; live on campus; Black or African American, non-Hispanic/Latino; Hispanic/Latino; Asian, non-Hispanic/Latino; Native Hawaiian or other Pacific Islander, non-Hispanic/Latino; American Indian or Alaska Native, non-Hispanic/Latino American Indian or Alaska Native, non-Hispanic/Latino; two or more races, non-Hispanic/Latino; race/ethnicity unknown; international; and percentage of students who transferred in are given.

Freshmen

Admission: Figures are given for the number of students who applied for fall 2017 admission, the number of those who were admitted, and the number who enrolled. *Average high school GPA:* Freshman statistics include the average high school GPA. *Test scores:* Percentage of freshmen who took the SAT® (not the Redesigned SAT) and received critical reading, math, and writing scores above 500, above 600, and above 700; as well as percentage of freshmen taking the ACT® who received a composite score of 18 or higher, 24 or higher, and 30 or higher.

Retention: The percentage of full-time freshmen who returned the following year for the fall semester/term.

FACULTY

Total: The total number of faculty members; percentage of full-time faculty members as of fall 2017; and percentage of total faculty members who hold terminal degrees. *Student/faculty ratio:* School's estimate of the ratio of matriculated undergraduate students to faculty members teaching undergraduate courses.

ACADEMICS

Calendar: Most colleges indicate one of the following: 4-1-4, 4-4-1, or a similar arrangement (two terms of equal length plus an abbreviated winter or spring term, with the numbers referring to months); semesters; trimesters; quarters; 3-3 (three courses for each of three terms); modular (the academic year is divided into small blocks of time; courses of varying lengths are assembled according to individual programs); or standard year (for most Canadian institutions). *Degrees:* This names the full range of levels of certificates, diplomas, and degrees, including prebaccalaureate, baccalaureate, graduate, and professional, that are offered by this institution.

Special study options: Details on study options available at each college, such as accelerated degree program, academic remediation for entering students, Advanced Placement credit, cooperative education programs, distance learning, double majors, English as a second language (ESL), and external degree programs. *ROTC:* Army, Naval, or Air Force Reserve Officers' Training Corps programs offered either on campus, at a branch campus [designated by a (b)], or at a cooperating host institution [designated by (c)].

Unusual degree programs: Information is offered here on any unique programs at the institution, such as 3-2 engineering, computer science, or business administration programs.

Computers: Information is provided on the numbers of computers/terminals available on campus for general student use, what computer technology is accessible to students, and availability of a campuswide network and wireless campus network.

STUDENT LIFE

Housing options: Institution's policy about whether students are permitted to live off-campus or are required to live on campus for a specified period; whether freshmen only, coed, single-sex, cooperative, and disabled student housing options are available; whether campus housing is leased by the school and/or provided by a third party; whether freshman applicants are given priority for college housing. "College housing not available" indicates that no college-owned or -operated housing facilities are provided for undergraduates and that noncommuting students must arrange for their own accommodations.

Activities and organizations: Information on clubs and organizations, including sororities and fraternities.

Athletics: Membership in one or more of the following athletic associations is indicated by initials: NCAA: National Collegiate Athletic Association; NAIA: National Association of Intercollegiate Athletics; NCCAA: National Christian College Athletic Association; USCAA: United States Colle-giate Athletic Association; and CIS: Canadian Interuniversity Sport. The overall NCAA division in which all or most intercollegiate teams compete is designated by I, II, or III. All teams that do not compete in this division are listed as exceptions.

Sports offered by the college are divided into two groups: *Intercollegiate* ("M" or "W" following the name of each sport indicates that it is offered for men or women) and *Intramural.* An "s" in parentheses following an "M" or "W" for an intercollegiate sport indicates that athletic scholarships (or grants-in-aid) are offered for men or women in that sport, and a "c" indicates a club team as opposed to a varsity team.

Campus security: Campus safety measures including 24-hour emergency response devices (phones and alarms) and patrols by trained security personnel, student patrols, late-night transport-escort service, and controlled dormitory access (key, security card, etc.).

Student services: Information indicates services offered to students by the college, such as legal services, health clinics, personal-psychological counseling, and women's centers.

COSTS & FINANCIAL AID

Costs: Costs are given for the 2018–19 academic year or for the 2017–18 academic year if 2018–19 figures were not yet available. *Tuition:* Annual expenses may be expressed as a comprehensive fee (including full-time tuition, mandatory fees, and college room and board) or as separate figures for full-time tuition, fees, room and board, or room only. For public institutions where tuition differs according to residence, separate figures are given for area or state residents and for nonresidents. Part-time tuition is expressed in terms of a per-unit rate (per credit, per semester hour, etc.).

The tuition structure at some institutions is complex in that freshmen and sophomores may be charged a different rate from that for juniors and seniors, a professional or vocational division may have a different fee structure from the liberal arts division of the same institution, or part-time tuition may be prorated on a sliding scale according to the number of credit hours taken. Tuition and fees may vary according to academic program, campus/location, class time (day, evening, weekend), course/credit load, course level, degree level, reciprocity agreements, and student level. *Room and board* charges are reported as an average for one academic year and may vary according to the board plan selected, campus/location, type of housing facility, or student level. *Payment plans* may include tuition prepayment, installment payments, and deferred payment. A tuition prepayment plan gives a student the option of locking in the current tuition rate for the entire term of enrollment by paying the full amount in advance rather than year by year. *Waivers:* availability of full or partial undergraduate tuition waivers to minority students, children of alumni, employees or their children, adult students, and senior citizens may be listed.

Financial Aid: This information represents aid awarded to undergraduates for the available academic year. Figures are given for the number of undergraduates who applied for aid, the number who were judged to have need, and the number who had their need met. The number of Federal Work-Study Programs and/or part-time jobs and average earnings are listed, as well as the number of non-need-based awards. The *Average percent of need met* for those determined to have need, *Average financial aid package* awarded to undergraduates (the amount of scholarships, grants, work-study payments, or loans in the institutionally administered financial aid package divided by the number of students who received any financial aid-amounts used to pay the officially designated Expected Family Contribution (EFC), *Average need-based loan, Average need-based gift aid,* and *Average non-need-based aid* are given. *Average indebtedness upon graduation,* which is the average per-borrower indebtedness of the last graduating undergraduate class from amounts borrowed at this institution through any loan programs, excluding parent loans, is listed last.

APPLYING

Standardized Tests

The most commonly required standardized tests are the ACT®, SAT®, and SAT Subject Tests™. These and other standardized tests may be used for selective admission, as a basis for counseling or course placement, or for both purposes. This section notes if a test is used for admission or placement and whether it is required, required for some, or recommended. In addition to the ACT and SAT, the following standardized entrance and placement examinations are referred to by their initials: ABLE (Adult Basic Learning Examination); ACT ASSET (ACT Assessment of Skills for Successful Entry and Transfer); ACT PEP (ACT Proficiency Examination Program); CAT (California Achievement Tests); CELT (Comprehensive English Language Test); CPAt (Career Programs Assessment); CPT (Computerized Placement Test); DAT (Differential Aptitude Test); LSAT (Law School Admission Test); MAPS (Multiple Assessment Program Service); MCAT (Medical College Admission Test); MMPI (Minnesota Multiphasic Personality Inventory); OAT (Optometry Admission Test); PAA (Prueba de Aptitud Académica—Spanish-language version of SAT); PCAT (Pharmacy College Admission Test); PSAT/NMSQT® (Preliminary SAT/National Merit Scholarship Qualifying Test); SCAT (Scholastic College Aptitude Test); TABE (Test of Adult Basic Education); TASP (Texas Académic Skills Program); TOEFL® (Test of English as a Foreign Language); WPCT (Washington Pre-College Test).

Options: This includes the following: Early admission—(highly qualified students may matriculate before graduating from high school); Early action—admission plan that allows students to apply and be notified of an admission decision well in advance of the regular notification dates (if accepted, the candidate is not committed to enroll; students may reply to the offer under the college's regular reply policy); Deferred entrance—practice of permitting accepted students to postpone enrollment, usually for a period of one academic term or year; Early decision deadline—plan that permits students to apply and be notified of an admission decision (and financial aid offer, if applicable) well in advance of the regular notification date, and applicants agree to accept an offer of admission and to withdraw their applications from other colleges.

Application fee: The fee required with an application is noted.

Required, Required for some, and Recommended: Other application requirements are grouped into three categories and may include an essay, standardized test scores, a high school transcript, a minimum high school grade point average (expressed as a number on a scale of 0 to 4.0, where 4.0 equals A, 3.0 equals B, etc.), letters of recommendation, an interview on campus or with local alumni, and, for certain types of schools or programs, special requirements such as a musical audition or an art portfolio.

Application deadlines and notification: Admission application deadlines and dates for notification of acceptance or rejection are given either as specific dates or as rolling and continuous. Rolling means that applications are processed as they are received, and qualified students are accepted as long as there are openings. Continuous means that applicants are notified of acceptance or rejection as applications are processed up until the date indicated or the actual beginning of classes. The application deadline and the notification date for transfers are given if they differ from the dates for freshmen. Early decision and early action application deadlines and notification dates are also indicated when relevant.

CONTACT

The name, title, mailing address, and phone number of the person to contact for further information are given at the end of the profile. The fax number and e-mail address may also be provided.

Additional Information

Each school that has a College Close-Up and a half-page display in this guide will have a cross-reference with the page numbers of the half-page display and Close-Up.

COLLEGE CLOSE-UPS

The nearly 175 two-page descriptions provide an inside look at colleges and universities. The descriptions provide a wealth of information that is crucial in the college decision-making process—components such as tuition, financial aid, and major fields of study. Prepared exclusively by college officials, the descriptions are designed to help give students a better sense of the individuality of each institution, in terms that include campus environment, student activities, and lifestyle. The absence of any college or university does not constitute an editorial decision on the part of Peterson's. In essence, these descriptions are an open forum for colleges and universities, on a voluntary basis, to communicate their particular message to prospective college students. The colleges included have paid a fee to Peterson's to provide this information. The College Close-Ups are edited to provide a consistent format across entries for your ease of comparison.

INDEXES

Here you'll find easy-to-use breakdowns of schools' majors, entrance difficulty, and cost ranges. In addition, you'll find an "Advertisers Index," a "Geographical Listing of College Close-Ups," and an "Alphabetical Listing of Colleges and Universities."

Majors

This listing presents hundreds of undergraduate fields of study that are currently offered, according to the colleges' responses on *Peterson's® Annual Survey of Undergraduate Institutions*. The majors appear in alphabetical order, each followed by an alphabetical list of the schools that offer a bachelor's-level program in that particular field. Liberal Arts and Sciences/ Liberal Studies indicates a general program with no specified major.

The terms used are those of the U.S. Department of Education Classification of Instructional Programs (CIP). Many institutions, however, use different terms. Although the term major is used in this guide, some colleges may use other terms, such as concentration, program of study, or field.

Entrance Difficulty

This listing groups colleges by their own assessment of their entrance difficulty level. The colleges were asked to select the level that most closely corresponds to their entrance difficulty. Institutions for which high school class rank and/or standardized test scores do not apply as admission criteria were asked to select the level that best indicates their entrance difficulty as compared to other institutions.

Cost Ranges

Colleges are grouped into ten price ranges, from under $2,000 to $30,000 and over.

DATA COLLECTION PROCEDURES

The data contained in the **PROFILES** and **INDEXES** sections were researched between winter 2017 and spring 2018 through *Peterson's® Annual Survey of Undergraduate Institutions*. Questionnaires were sent to the more than 4,500 colleges and universities that met the outlined inclusion criteria. All data included in this edition have been submitted by officials (usually admissions and financial aid officers, registrars, or institutional research personnel) at the colleges. Some of the institutions that submitted data were contacted directly by the Peterson's research staff to verify unusual figures, resolve discrepancies, or obtain additional data. All usable information received in time for publication has been included. The omission of any particular item from the **PROFILES** and **INDEXES** sections signifies that the information is either not applicable to that institution or not available. Because of Peterson's comprehensive editorial review and because all material comes directly from college officials, we believe that the information presented is accurate. You should check with a specific college or university at the time of application to verify such figures as tuition and fees, which may have changed since this guide's publication.

CRITERIA FOR INCLUSION IN THIS BOOK

The term "four-year college" is the commonly used designation for institutions that grant the baccalaureate degree. Four years is the expected amount of time required to earn this degree, although some bachelor's degree programs may be completed in three years, others require five years, and part-time programs may take considerably longer. Upper-level institutions offer only the junior and senior years and accept only students with two years of college-level credit. Therefore, "four-year college" is a conventional term that accurately describes most of the institutions included in this guide, but should not be taken literally in all cases.

To be included in this guide, an institution must have full accreditation or be a candidate for accreditation (preaccreditation) status by an institutional or specialized accrediting body recognized by the U.S. Department of Education or the Council for Higher Education Accreditation (CHEA). Institutional accrediting bodies, which review each institution as a whole, include the six regional associations of schools and colleges (Middle States, New England, North Central, Northwest, Southern, and Western), each of which is responsible for a specified portion of the United States and its territories. Other institutional accrediting bodies are national in scope and accredit specific kinds of institutions (e.g., Bible colleges, independent colleges, and rabbinical and Talmudic schools). Program registration by the New York State Board of Regents is considered to be the equivalent of institutional accreditation, since the board requires that all programs offered by an institution meet its standards before recognition is granted. A Canadian institution must be chartered and authorized to grant degrees by the provincial government, affiliated with a chartered institution, or accredited by a recognized U.S. accrediting body. This guide also includes institutions outside the United States that are accredited by these U.S. accrediting bodies. There are recognized specialized or professional accrediting bodies in more than forty different fields, each of which is authorized to accredit institutions or specific programs in its particular field. For specialized institutions that offer programs in one field only, we designate this to be the equivalent of institutional accreditation. A full explanation of the accrediting process and complete information on recognized, institutional (regional and national) and specialized accrediting bodies can be found online at www.chea.org or at www2.ed.gov/admins/finaid/accred/index.html.

Institutional Changes Since *Peterson's®* *Four-Year Colleges* 2018

The following is an alphabetical listing of institutions that have closed, merged with other institutions, or changed their names or status since *Peterson's® Four-Year Colleges 2018*.

Alliant International University–México City (Mexico City, Mexico): *closed.*

Allied American University (Laguna Hills, CA): *closed.*

American National University (Canton, OH): *closed.*

American National University (Cincinnati, OH): *closed.*

American National University (Cleveland, OH): *closed.*

American National University (Columbus, OH): *closed.*

American National University (Stow, OH): *closed.*

Argosy University, Washington DC (Arlington, VA): *name changed to Argosy University, Northern Virginia.*

The Art Institute of Charlotte, a campus of South University (Charlotte, NC): *name changed to The Art Institute of Charlotte, a branch of Miami International University of Art & Design.*

The Art Institute of Dallas, a campus of South University (Dallas, TX): *name changed to The Art Institute of Dallas, a branch of Miami International University of Art & Design.*

The Art Institute of Raleigh-Durham, a campus of South University (Durham, NC): *name changed to The Art Institute of Raleigh-Durham, a branch of Miami International University of Art & Design.*

The Art Institutes International Minnesota (Minneapolis, MN): *closed.*

Berkeley College (Woodland Park, NJ): *name changed to Berkeley College–Woodland Park Campus.*

Blessing-Rieman College of Nursing (Quincy, IL): *name changed to Blessing-Rieman College of Nursing & Health Sciences.*

Broadview University–Boise (Meridian, ID): *closed.*

Broadview University–Layton (Layton, UT): *closed.*

Brooks Institute (Ventura, CA): *closed.*

Brown Mackie College–Birmingham (Birmingham, AL): *closed.*

Brown Mackie College–Dallas/Ft. Worth (Bedford, TX): *closed.*

Brown Mackie College–San Antonio (San Antonio, TX): *closed.*

Burlington College (Burlington, VT): *closed.*

Cabrini College (Radnor, PA): *name changed to Cabrini University.*

California Maritime Academy (Vallejo, CA): *name changed to California State University Maritime Academy.*

Calvary Bible College and Theological Seminary (Kansas City, MO): *name changed to Calvary University.*

Career Point College (San Antonio, TX): *closed.*

Castleton State College (Castleton, VT): *name changed to Castleton University.*

Centenary College (Hackettstown, NJ): *name changed to Centenary University.*

Colorado Heights University (Denver, CO): *closed.*

Colorado Technical University Denver South (Aurora, CO): *name changed to Colorado Technical University Aurora.*

The Criswell College (Dallas, TX): *name changed to Criswell College.*

Daniel Webster College (Nashua, NH): *merged into Southern New Hampshire University (Manchester, NH).*

DeVry College of New York (New York, NY): *name changed to DeVry College of New York–Midtown Manhattan Campus.*

DeVry University (Mesa, AZ): *now a DeVry University center and no longer profiled separately.*

DeVry University (Phoenix, AZ): *name changed to DeVry University–Phoenix Campus.*

DeVry University (Alhambra, CA): *closed.*

DeVry University (Anaheim, CA): *now a DeVry University center and no longer profiled separately.*

DeVry University (Bakersfield, CA): *now a DeVry University center and no longer profiled separately.*

DeVry University (Fremont, CA): *name changed to DeVry University–Fremont Campus.*

DeVry University (Long Beach, CA): *name changed to DeVry University–Long Beach Campus.*

DeVry University (Oakland, CA): *now a DeVry University center and no longer profiled separately.*

DeVry University (Oxnard, CA): *closed.*

DeVry University (Palmdale, CA): *now a DeVry University center and no longer profiled separately.*

DeVry University (Pomona, CA): *name changed to DeVry University–Pomona Campus.*

DeVry University (San Diego, CA): *name changed to DeVry University–San Diego Campus.*

DeVry University (Sherman Oaks, CA): *name changed to DeVry University–Sherman Oaks Campus.*

DeVry University (Colorado Springs, CO): *now a DeVry University center and no longer profiled separately.*

DeVry University (Westminster, CO): *name changed to DeVry University–Westminster Campus.*

DeVry University (Jacksonville, FL): *name changed to DeVry University–Jacksonville Campus.*

DeVry University (Miramar, FL): *name changed to DeVry University–Miramar Campus.*

DeVry University (Orlando, FL): *name changed to DeVry University–Orlando Campus.*

DeVry University (Alpharetta, GA): *name changed to DeVry University–Alpharetta Campus.*

DeVry University (Atlanta, GA): *now a DeVry University center and no longer profiled separately.*

DeVry University (Decatur, GA): *name changed to DeVry University–Decatur Campus.*

DeVry University (Duluth, GA): *now a DeVry University center and no longer profiled separately.*

DeVry University (Addison, IL): *name changed to DeVry University–Addison Campus.*

DeVry University (Chicago, IL): *name changed to DeVry University–Chicago Campus.*

DeVry University (Downers Grove, IL): *now a DeVry University center and no longer profiled separately.*

DeVry University (Elgin, IL): *now a DeVry University center and no longer profiled separately.*

DeVry University (Gurnee, IL): *now a DeVry University center and no longer profiled separately.*

DeVry University (Naperville, IL): *now a DeVry University center and no longer profiled separately.*

DeVry University (Tinley Park, IL): *name changed to DeVry University–Tinley Park Campus.*

DeVry University (Merrillville, IN): *now a DeVry University center and no longer profiled separately.*

DeVry University (Bethesda, MD): *closed.*

DeVry University (Kansas City, MO): *name changed to DeVry University–Kansas City Campus.*

DeVry University (Charlotte, NC): *name changed to DeVry University–Charlotte Campus.*

DeVry University (North Brunswick, NJ): *name changed to DeVry University–North Brunswick Campus.*

DeVry University (Paramus, NJ): *now a DeVry University center and no longer profiled separately.*

DeVry University (Henderson, NV): *name changed to DeVry University–Henderson Campus.*

DeVry University (Columbus, OH): *name changed to DeVry University–Columbus Campus.*

DeVry University (Seven Hills, OH): *name changed to DeVry University–Seven Hills Campus.*

DeVry University (Oklahoma City, OK): *name changed to DeVry University–Oklahoma City Campus.*

DeVry University (Fort Washington, PA): *name changed to DeVry University–Ft. Washington Campus.*

DeVry University (King of Prussia, PA): *closed.*

DeVry University (Philadelphia, PA): *now a DeVry University center and no longer profiled separately.*

DeVry University (Nashville, TN): *name changed to DeVry University–Nashville Campus.*

DeVry University (Austin, TX): *name changed to DeVry University–Austin Campus.*

DeVry University (Irving, TX): *name changed to DeVry University–Irving Campus.*

DeVry University (San Antonio, TX): *name changed to DeVry University–San Antonio Campus.*

DeVry University (Sandy, UT): *closed.*

DeVry University (Arlington, VA): *name changed to DeVry University–Arlington Campus.*

DeVry University (Chesapeake, VA): *name changed to DeVry University–Chesapeake Campus.*

DeVry University (Manassas, VA): *closed.*

Doane College (Crete, NE): *name changed to Doane University.*

Dowling College (Oakdale, NY): *closed.*

ECPI University (Lake Mary, FL): *merged into a single entry for ECPI University (Virginia Beach, VA).*

ECPI University (Raleigh, NC): *merged into a single entry for ECPI University (Virginia Beach, VA).*

ECPI University (Glen Allen, VA): *merged into a single entry for ECPI University (Virginia Beach, VA).*

ECPI University (Manassas, VA): *merged into a single entry for ECPI University (Virginia Beach, VA).*

ECPI University (Newport News, VA): *merged into a single entry for ECPI University (Virginia Beach, VA).*

Ellis University (Oakbrook Terrace, IL): *closed.*

Everest University (Jacksonville, FL): *closed.*

Everest University (Lakeland, FL): *closed.*

Everest University (Largo, FL): *closed.*

Everest University (Melbourne, FL): *closed.*

Everest University (Orlando, FL): *closed.*

Everest University (Pompano Beach, FL): *closed.*

Ex'pression College for Digital Arts (Emeryville, CA): *name changed to SAE Expression College.*

Globe Institute of Technology (New York, NY): *closed.*

Globe University–Appleton (Grand Chute, WI): *closed.*

Globe University–Eau Claire (Eau Claire, WI): *closed.*

Globe University–Green Bay (Bellevue, WI): *closed.*

Globe University–La Crosse (Onalaska, WI): *closed.*

Globe University–Madison East (Madison, WI): *closed.*

Globe University–Madison West (Middleton, WI): *closed.*

Globe University–Sioux Falls (Sioux Falls, SD): *closed.*

Globe University–Wausau (Rothschild, WI): *closed.*

Hillsdale Free Will Baptist College (Moore, OK): *name changed to Randall University.*

Iowa Wesleyan College (Mount Pleasant, IA): *name changed to Iowa Wesleyan University.*

ITT Technical Institute (Tempe, AZ): *closed.*

ITT Technical Institute (Clovis, CA): *closed.*

ITT Technical Institute (Concord, CA): *closed.*

ITT Technical Institute (Corona, CA): *closed.*

ITT Technical Institute (Deerfield Beach, FL): *closed.*

ITT Technical Institute (West Palm Beach, FL): *closed.*

ITT Technical Institute (Douglasville, GA): *closed.*

ITT Technical Institute (Springfield, IL): *closed.* ITT Technical Institute (Indianapolis, IN): *closed.*

ITT Technical Institute (Lexington, KY): *closed.*

ITT Technical Institute (Hanover, MD): *closed.*

ITT Technical Institute (Madison, MS): *closed.*

ITT Technical Institute (Charlotte, NC): *closed.*

ITT Technical Institute (Durham, NC): *closed.*

ITT Technical Institute (Oklahoma City, OK): *closed.*

ITT Technical Institute (Salem, OR): *closed.*

Lakehead University–Orillia (Orillia, ON, Canada): *merged into a single entry for Lakehead University (Thunder Bay, ON) by request from the institution.*

Lakeland College (Sheboygan, WI): *name changed to Lakeland University.*

Laurel University (High Point, NC): *name changed to John Wesley University.*

Mary Baldwin College (Staunton, VA): *name changed to Mary Baldwin University.*

The Master's College and Seminary (Santa Clarita, CA): *name changed to The Master's University.*

Mater Ecclesiae College (Greenville, RI): *closed.*

Minnesota School of Business–Blaine (Blaine, MN): *closed.*

Minnesota School of Business–Elk River (Elk River, MN): *closed.*

Minnesota School of Business–Lakeville (Lakeville, MN): *closed.*

Minnesota School of Business–Richfield (Richfield, MN): *closed.*

Minnesota School of Business–Rochester (Rochester, MN): *closed.*

Minnesota School of Business–St. Cloud (Waite Park, MN): *closed.*

National American University (Denver, CO): *closed.*

Northwood University, Texas Campus (Cedar Hill, TX): *merged into a single entry for Northwood University, Michigan Campus (Midland, MI) by request from the institution.*

Oregon College of Art & Craft (Portland, OR): *name changed to Oregon College of Art and Craft.*

Our Lady of Holy Cross College (New Orleans, LA): *name changed to University of Holy Cross.*

Pioneer Pacific College–Eugene/Springfield Branch (Springfield, OR): *merged into a single entry for Pioneer Pacific College (Wilsonville, OR).*

Purdue University Northwest (Westville, IN): *merged into a single entry for Purdue University Northwest (Hammond, IN) by request from the institution.*

Rasmussen College Appleton (Appleton, WI): *merged into Rasmussen College Green Bay (Green Bay, WI).*

St. Catharine College (St. Catharine, KY): *closed.*

Saint Joseph's College (Rensselaer, IN): *closed.*

Santa Fe University of Art and Design (Santa Fe, NM): *closed.*

School of the Museum of Fine Arts, Boston (Boston, MA): *merged as a unit into Tufts University (Medford, MA).*

Skyline College (Roanoke, VA): *closed.*

Summit University (Clarks Summit, PA): *name changed to Clarks Summit University.*

Tennessee Wesleyan College (Athens, TN): *name changed to Tennessee Wesleyan University.*

Truett-McConnell College (Cleveland, GA): *name changed to Truett McConnell University.*

The University of Montana (Missoula, MT): *name changed to University of Montana.*

Waldorf College (Forest City, IA): *name changed to Waldorf University.*

Profiles

A ★ *indicates that the school has detailed information with a Premium Profile on Petersons.com.*

U.S. AND U.S. TERRITORIES

ALABAMA

Alabama Agricultural and Mechanical University
Huntsville, Alabama
http://www.aamu.edu/

CONTACT
Dr. Evelyn Ellis, Interim Director of Admissions, Alabama Agricultural and Mechanical University, 4900 Meridian Street, Huntsville, AL 35811. *Phone:* 256-372-5245. *Toll-free phone:* 800-553-0816. *Fax:* 256-851-9747.

Alabama State University
Montgomery, Alabama
http://www.alasu.edu/
- **State-supported** comprehensive, founded 1867, part of Alabama Commission on Higher Education
- **Urban** 172-acre campus
- **Endowment** $89.3 million
- **Coed** 4,208 undergraduate students, 92% full-time, 62% women, 38% men
- **Minimally difficult** entrance level, 98% of applicants were admitted

UNDERGRAD STUDENTS
3,866 full-time, 342 part-time. Students come from 40 states and territories; 24 other countries; 34% are from out of state; 94% Black or African American, non-Hispanic/Latino; 1% Hispanic/Latino; 0.3% Asian, non-Hispanic/Latino; 0.1% Native Hawaiian or other Pacific Islander, non-Hispanic/Latino; 0.2% American Indian or Alaska Native, non-Hispanic/Latino; 1% Two or more races, non-Hispanic/Latino; 1% Race/ethnicity unknown; 1% international; 2% transferred in; 34% live on campus.

Freshmen:
Admission: 6,842 applied, 6,696 admitted, 967 enrolled. *Average high school GPA:* 2.9. *Test scores:* SAT evidence-based reading and writing scores over 500: 38%; SAT math scores over 500: 31%; ACT scores over 18: 42%; SAT evidence-based reading and writing scores over 600: 3%; SAT math scores over 600: 2%; ACT scores over 24: 5%; SAT math scores over 700: 1%.
Retention: 59% of full-time freshmen returned.

FACULTY
Total: 445, 52% full-time, 42% with terminal degrees.
Student/faculty ratio: 17:1.

ACADEMICS
Calendar: semesters. *Degrees:* certificates, bachelor's, master's, doctoral, post-master's, and postbachelor's certificates.
Special study options: academic remediation for entering students, advanced placement credit, cooperative education, distance learning, double majors, freshman honors college, honors programs, independent study, internships, part-time degree program, student-designed majors, summer session for credit. *ROTC:* Army (c), Air Force (b).
Computers: 805 computers/terminals and 805 ports are available on campus for general student use. Students can access the following: computer help desk, free student e-mail accounts, online (class) grades, online (class) registration, online (class) schedules. Campuswide network is available. 100% of college-owned or -operated housing units are wired for high-speed Internet access. Wireless service is available via entire campus.
Library: Levi Watkins Learning Center plus 1 other. *Books:* 436,536 (physical), 69,784 (digital/electronic); *Serial titles:* 1,607 (physical), 4,340 (digital/electronic); *Databases:* 182. Weekly public service hours: 78; study areas open 24 hours, 5–7 days a week; students can reserve study rooms.

STUDENT LIFE
Housing options: men-only, women-only, special housing for students with disabilities. Campus housing is university owned.
Activities and organizations: drama/theater group, student-run newspaper, radio station, choral group, marching band, Alpha Kappa Alpha Sorority Inc., Empower Ministry, Nu Alpha Nu Service Fraternity Inc., Gamma Sigma Sigma National Service Sorority Inc., Delta Sigma Theta Sorority Inc, national fraternities, national sororities.
Athletics Member NCAA. All Division I. *Intercollegiate sports:* baseball M(s), basketball M(s)/W(s), bowling W(s), cheerleading M(s)/W(s), cross-country running M(s)/W(s), football M(s), golf M(s)/W(s), soccer W(s), softball W(s), tennis M(s)/W(s), track and field M(s)/W(s), volleyball W(s). *Intramural sports:* basketball M, football M.
Campus security: 24-hour emergency response devices and patrols, late-night transport/escort service, self-defense education, well-lit campus.
Student services: health clinic, personal/psychological counseling.

COSTS & FINANCIAL AID
Costs (2018–19) *One-time required fee:* $150. *Tuition:* state resident $8328 full-time, $347 per credit hour part-time; nonresident $16,656 full-time, $694 per credit hour part-time. Full-time tuition and fees vary according to class time, course level, course load, degree level, program, and student level. Part-time tuition and fees vary according to class time, course level, course load, degree level, program, and student level. *Required fees:* $2740 full-time, $446 per credit hour part-time. *Room and board:* $6050. Room and board charges vary according to board plan and housing facility. *Payment plan:* deferred payment. *Waivers:* employees or children of employees.
Financial Aid Of all full-time matriculated undergraduates who enrolled in 2017, 3,722 applied for aid, 3,643 were judged to have need, 1,687 had their need fully met. 530 Federal Work-Study jobs (averaging $1687). 480 state and other part-time jobs (averaging $620). In 2017, 61 non-need-based awards were made. *Average percent of need met:* 79. *Average financial aid package:* $16,124. *Average need-based loan:* $3809. *Average need-based gift aid:* $5368. *Average non-need-based aid:* $9364. *Average indebtedness upon graduation:* $34,691.

APPLYING
Standardized Tests *Required:* SAT or ACT (for admission).
Options: electronic application, early admission, deferred entrance.
Application fee: $25.
Required: high school transcript, minimum 2.0 GPA. *Recommended:* essay or personal statement, interview.
Application deadlines: 7/31 (freshmen), 7/31 (transfers).
Notification: continuous (freshmen), continuous (transfers).
CONTACT
Mr. Freddie Williams, Director of Admissions and Recruitment, Alabama State University, 915 South Jackson Street, Montgomery, AL 36101-0271. *Phone:* 334-229-4291. *Toll-free phone:* 800-253-5037. *Fax:* 334-229-4984. *E-mail:* fwilliams@alasu.edu.

Amridge University
Montgomery, Alabama
http://www.amridgeuniversity.edu/
- **Independent** university, founded 1967, affiliated with Church of Christ
- **Urban** 10-acre campus
- **Endowment** $2.1 million
- **Coed** 318 undergraduate students, 46% full-time, 63% women, 37% men
- **Minimally difficult** entrance level

UNDERGRAD STUDENTS
145 full-time, 173 part-time. Students come from 48 states and territories; 46% are from out of state; 41% Black or African American, non-Hispanic/Latino; 0.3% Hispanic/Latino; 0.3% Native Hawaiian or other Pacific Islander, non-Hispanic/Latino; 0.6% American Indian or Alaska Native, non-Hispanic/Latino; 26% Race/ethnicity unknown.

Freshmen:
Admission: 4 enrolled.

FACULTY
Total: 55, 58% full-time, 65% with terminal degrees.
Student/faculty ratio: 12:1.

ACADEMICS
Calendar: semesters. *Degrees:* associate, bachelor's, master's, and doctoral.

Special study options: academic remediation for entering students, accelerated degree program, adult/continuing education programs, advanced placement credit, distance learning, double majors, external degree program, independent study, internships, part-time degree program, services for LD students, summer session for credit.

Computers: 5 computers/terminals are available on campus for general student use. Students can access the following: computer help desk, free student e-mail accounts, online (class) grades, online (class) registration, online (class) schedules. Campuswide network is available. Wireless service is available via entire campus.
Library: Southern Christian University Library. Weekly public service hours: 50.

STUDENT LIFE
Housing options: college housing not available.

Activities and organizations: Amridge University Student Advisory Committee.

Campus security: 24-hour emergency response devices, security guards.

COSTS & FINANCIAL AID
Costs (2017–18) *Tuition:* $9000 full-time, $6880 per term part-time. Full-time tuition and fees vary according to course load, program, and student level. Part-time tuition and fees vary according to course load, program, and student level. No tuition increase for student's term of enrollment. *Required fees:* $900 full-time, $450 per term part-time. *Payment plans:* tuition prepayment, installment. *Waivers:* employees or children of employees.

Financial Aid Of all full-time matriculated undergraduates who enrolled in 2016, 131 applied for aid, 129 were judged to have need, 96 had their need fully met. *Average financial aid package:* $9097. *Average need-based loan:* $5280. *Average need-based gift aid:* $2804. *Average indebtedness upon graduation:* $11,179.

APPLYING
Standardized Tests *Required for some:* SAT or ACT (for admission).
Options: electronic application, early admission.
Application fee: $50.
Required: high school transcript, minimum 2.0 GPA.
Application deadlines: rolling (freshmen), rolling (transfers).

CONTACT
Amridge University, 1200 Taylor Road, Montgomery, AL 36117. *Phone:* 334-387-3877 Ext. 7528. *Toll-free phone:* 888-790-8080.

Athens State University

Athens, Alabama
http://www.athens.edu/
- **State-supported** upper-level, founded 1822
- **Small-town** 45-acre campus
- **Coed** 2,969 undergraduate students, 41% full-time, 67% women, 33% men
- **Noncompetitive** entrance level

UNDERGRAD STUDENTS
1,210 full-time, 1,759 part-time. Students come from 18 states and territories; 2 other countries; 4% are from out of state; 13% Black or African American, non-Hispanic/Latino; 3% Hispanic/Latino; 0.9% Asian, non-Hispanic/Latino; 0.1% Native Hawaiian or other Pacific Islander, non-Hispanic/Latino; 2% American Indian or Alaska Native, non-Hispanic/Latino; 2% Two or more races, non-Hispanic/Latino; 3% Race/ethnicity unknown; 21% transferred in.

FACULTY
Total: 196, 41% full-time, 49% with terminal degrees.
Student/faculty ratio: 17:1.

ACADEMICS
Calendar: semesters. *Degrees:* certificates, bachelor's, and master's.
Special study options: adult/continuing education programs, advanced placement credit, cooperative education, distance learning, double majors, independent study, internships, off-campus study, part-time degree program, study abroad, summer session for credit.

Computers: 210 computers/terminals are available on campus for general student use. Students can access the following: computer help desk, free student e-mail accounts, online (class) grades, online (class) registration, online (class) schedules, transcripts, e-mail. Campuswide network is available. Wireless service is available via entire campus.
Library: Athens State University Library. *Books:* 83,092 (physical), 255,950 (digital/electronic); *Serial titles:* 289 (physical), 296,023 (digital/electronic); *Databases:* 23,955. Students can reserve study rooms.

STUDENT LIFE
Housing options: college housing not available.

Activities and organizations: drama/theater group, student-run newspaper, SGA, Accounting, Art, PE.

Campus security: 24-hour emergency response devices and patrols.

Student services: personal/psychological counseling.

COSTS & FINANCIAL AID
Costs (2017–18) *Tuition:* state resident $5940 full-time; nonresident $11,880 full-time. *Required fees:* $750 full-time. *Payment plan:* installment. *Waivers:* senior citizens and employees or children of employees.

Financial Aid Of all full-time matriculated undergraduates who enrolled in 2016, 1,003 applied for aid, 909 were judged to have need, 27 had their need fully met. In 2016, 11 non-need-based awards were made. *Average percent of need met:* 47. *Average financial aid package:* $10,201. *Average need-based loan:* $3326. *Average need-based gift aid:* $4110. *Average non-need-based aid:* $2603.

APPLYING
Options: electronic application, deferred entrance.
Application fee: $30.
Notification: continuous (transfers).

CONTACT
Athens State University, 300 North Beaty Street, Athens, AL 35611. *Phone:* 256-233-8151. *Toll-free phone:* 800-522-0272.

Auburn University

Auburn University, Alabama
http://www.auburn.edu/
- **State-supported** university, founded 1856
- **Small-town** 1875-acre campus with easy access to Atlanta, Birmingham
- **Endowment** $718.0 million
- **Coed** 23,964 undergraduate students, 91% full-time, 49% women, 51% men
- **Moderately difficult** entrance level, 84% of applicants were admitted

UNDERGRAD STUDENTS
21,762 full-time, 2,202 part-time. Students come from 52 states and territories; 59 other countries; 35% are from out of state; 6% Black or African American, non-Hispanic/Latino; 3% Hispanic/Latino; 2% Asian, non-Hispanic/Latino; 0.4% American Indian or Alaska Native, non-Hispanic/Latino; 2% Two or more races, non-Hispanic/Latino; 0.4% Race/ethnicity unknown; 6% international; 5% transferred in; 19% live on campus.

Freshmen:
Admission: 18,072 applied, 15,168 admitted, 4,836 enrolled. *Average high school GPA:* 3.9. *Test scores:* SAT evidence-based reading and writing scores over 500: 97%; SAT math scores over 500: 98%; ACT scores over 18: 100%; SAT evidence-based reading and writing scores over 600: 59%; SAT math scores over 600: 55%; ACT scores over 24: 83%; SAT evidence-based reading and writing scores over 700: 10%; SAT math scores over 700: 14%; ACT scores over 30: 30%.
Retention: 92% of full-time freshmen returned.

FACULTY
Total: 1,555, 86% full-time, 84% with terminal degrees.
Student/faculty ratio: 19:1.

ACADEMICS
Calendar: semesters. *Degrees:* bachelor's, master's, doctoral, post-master's, and postbachelor's certificates.

Special study options: accelerated degree program, adult/continuing education programs, advanced placement credit, cooperative education, distance learning, double majors, English as a second language, freshman honors college, honors programs, independent study, internships, off-campus study, part-time degree program, services for LD students, study abroad, summer session for credit. *ROTC:* Army (b), Navy (b), Air Force (b).

Unusual degree programs: 3-2 engineering.

Computers: 1,722 computers/terminals are available on campus for general student use. Students can access the following: computer help desk, free student e-mail accounts, online (class) grades, online (class) registration, bursar payments, course materials. Campuswide network is available. 100% of college-owned or -operated housing units are wired for high-speed Internet access. Wireless service is available via entire campus.
Library: R. B. Draughon Library plus 3 others. *Books:* 4.6 million (physical), 1.0 million (digital/electronic); *Serial titles:* 76,272 (physical), 83,255 (digital/electronic); *Databases:* 253. Study areas open 24 hours, 5–7 days a week.

STUDENT LIFE
Housing options: coed, men-only, women-only, special housing for students with disabilities. Campus housing is university owned.

Activities and organizations: drama/theater group, student-run newspaper, radio and television station, choral group, marching band, Student Government Association, University Program Council, IMPACT (volunteer opportunities), International Student Organization, student media (AU Plainsman newspaper, WEGL radio, Glomerata yearbook, Eagle Eye television, AU Circle literary journal), national fraternities, national sororities.

Athletics Member NCAA. All Division I except football (Division I-A). *Intercollegiate sports:* baseball M(s), basketball M(s)/W(s), cheerleading M/W, cross-country running M(s)/W(s), equestrian sports W(s), golf M(s)/W(s), gymnastics W(s), soccer W(s), softball W(s), swimming and diving M(s)/W(s), tennis M(s)/W(s), track and field M(s)/W(s), volleyball W(s). *Intramural sports:* basketball M/W, crew M(c)/W(c), football M, golf M/W, ice hockey M(c)/W(c), lacrosse M(c)/W(c), racquetball M/W, rugby M(c), sailing M(c)/W(c), sand volleyball M(c)/W(c), skiing (downhill) M(c)/W(c), soccer M/W, softball M/W, swimming and diving M/W, table tennis M/W, tennis M/W, track and field M/W, ultimate Frisbee M/W, volleyball M/W, water polo M(c)/W(c), wrestling M(c)/W(c).

Campus security: 24-hour emergency response devices and patrols, late-night transport/escort service, controlled dormitory access.

Student services: health clinic, personal/psychological counseling.

COSTS & FINANCIAL AID
Costs (2017–18) *Tuition:* state resident $9336 full-time, $389 per semester hour part-time; nonresident $28,008 full-time, $1167 per semester hour part-time. Full-time tuition and fees vary according to program and reciprocity agreements. Part-time tuition and fees vary according to course load, program, and reciprocity agreements. *Required fees:* $1632 full-time, $816 per term part-time. *Room and board:* $13,332; room only: $7860. Room and board charges vary according to board plan and housing facility. *Payment plan:* installment. *Waivers:* employees or children of employees.

Financial Aid Of all full-time matriculated undergraduates who enrolled in 2016, 13,335 applied for aid, 7,246 were judged to have need, 972 had their need fully met. 175 Federal Work-Study jobs (averaging $4202). In 2016, 4487 non-need-based awards were made. *Average percent of need met:* 45. *Average financial aid package:* $10,829. *Average need-based loan:* $4529. *Average need-based gift aid:* $7847. *Average non-need-based aid:* $7249. *Average indebtedness upon graduation:* $29,295.

APPLYING
Standardized Tests *Required:* SAT or ACT (for admission).
Options: electronic application, early admission, early action.
Application fee: $50.

Required: essay or personal statement, high school transcript, minimum 2.0 GPA. *Required for some:* minimum 3.0 GPA. *Recommended:* minimum 3.0 GPA.
Application deadlines: 1/15 (freshmen), 6/1 (transfers), 10/1 (early action).
Notification: 2/1 (freshmen), 2/1 (out-of-state freshmen), continuous (transfers), 10/15 (early action).

CONTACT
Auburn University, Auburn University, AL 36849. *Toll-free phone:* 800-AUBURN9.

Auburn University at Montgomery
Montgomery, Alabama
http://www.aum.edu/
- **State-supported** comprehensive, founded 1967, part of Auburn University
- **Urban** 500-acre campus
- **Coed** 4,313 undergraduate students, 75% full-time, 64% women, 36% men
- **Moderately difficult** entrance level, 83% of applicants were admitted

UNDERGRAD STUDENTS
3,239 full-time, 1,074 part-time. 6% are from out of state; 38% Black or African American, non-Hispanic/Latino; 1% Hispanic/Latino; 3% Asian, non-Hispanic/Latino; 0.1% Native Hawaiian or other Pacific Islander, non-Hispanic/Latino; 0.5% American Indian or Alaska Native, non-Hispanic/Latino; 3% Two or more races, non-Hispanic/Latino; 0.5% Race/ethnicity unknown; 4% international; 11% transferred in; 23% live on campus.

Freshmen:
Admission: 2,474 applied, 2,042 admitted, 673 enrolled. *Average high school GPA:* 3.3. *Test scores:* SAT evidence-based reading and writing scores over 500: 65%; SAT math scores over 500: 69%; ACT scores over 18: 100%; SAT evidence-based reading and writing scores over 600: 8%; SAT math scores over 600: 8%; ACT scores over 24: 26%; SAT math scores over 700: 4%; ACT scores over 30: 1%.
Retention: 68% of full-time freshmen returned.

FACULTY
Total: 363, 57% full-time, 66% with terminal degrees.
Student/faculty ratio: 15:1.

ACADEMICS
Calendar: semesters. *Degrees:* bachelor's, master's, doctoral, and post-master's certificates.

Special study options: academic remediation for entering students, advanced placement credit, cooperative education, distance learning, double majors, English as a second language, honors programs, independent study, internships, off-campus study, part-time degree program, services for LD students, study abroad, summer session for credit. *ROTC:* Army (b), Air Force (c).

Computers: 500 computers/terminals are available on campus for general student use. Students can access the following: computer help desk, free student e-mail accounts, online (class) grades, online (class) registration, online (class) schedules. Campuswide network is available. 100% of college-owned or -operated housing units are wired for high-speed Internet access. Wireless service is available via entire campus.
Library: Auburn University at Montgomery Library. *Books:* 502,246 (physical), 722,903 (digital/electronic). Weekly public service hours: 84; students can reserve study rooms.

STUDENT LIFE
Housing options: coed, special housing for students with disabilities. Campus housing is university owned.

Activities and organizations: drama/theater group, student-run newspaper, television station, choral group, Student Government Association, Campus Activities Board, Panhellenic Association, Accounting Club, national fraternities, national sororities.

Athletics Member NCAA. All Division II. *Intercollegiate sports:* baseball M(s), basketball M(s)/W(s), cheerleading M(s)/W(s), cross-country running M(s)/W(s), soccer M(s)/W(s), softball W(s), tennis

M(s)/W(s). *Intramural sports:* badminton M/W, golf M(c)/W(c), table tennis M/W, tennis M/W, ultimate Frisbee M/W, volleyball M/W.

Campus security: 24-hour emergency response devices and patrols, student patrols, late-night transport/escort service, controlled dormitory access, personal safety and emergency preparedness seminars.

Student services: health clinic, personal/psychological counseling.

COSTS & FINANCIAL AID

Costs (2018–19) *One-time required fee:* $125. *Tuition:* state resident $7536 full-time, $314 per credit hour part-time; nonresident $16,994 full-time, $706 per credit hour part-time. Full-time tuition and fees vary according to course load and degree level. Part-time tuition and fees vary according to course load and degree level. *Required fees:* $700 full-time. *Room and board:* $6980; room only: $4580. Room and board charges vary according to housing facility. *Payment plan:* installment. *Waivers:* senior citizens and employees or children of employees.

Financial Aid Of all full-time matriculated undergraduates who enrolled in 2016, 2,369 applied for aid, 2,073 were judged to have need, 183 had their need fully met. 52 Federal Work-Study jobs (averaging $3798). In 2016, 297 non-need-based awards were made. *Average percent of need met:* 58. *Average financial aid package:* $8263. *Average need-based loan:* $3463. *Average need-based gift aid:* $4672. *Average non-need-based aid:* $3798. *Average indebtedness upon graduation:* $27,007.

APPLYING

Standardized Tests *Required:* SAT or ACT (for admission).

Options: electronic application, early admission.

Required: high school transcript, minimum 2.3 GPA.

Application deadlines: 8/1 (freshmen), rolling (transfers).

Notification: continuous (freshmen), continuous (out-of-state freshmen), continuous (transfers).

CONTACT

Director of Admissions and Recruiting, Auburn University at Montgomery, PO Box 244023, Montgomery, AL 36124. *Phone:* 334-244-3615. *Toll-free phone:* 800-227-2649. *Fax:* 334-244-3795. *E-mail:* admissions@aum.edu.

Birmingham-Southern College

Birmingham, Alabama

http://www.bsc.edu/

- **Independent Methodist** 4-year, founded 1856
- **Urban** 196-acre campus with easy access to Birmingham
- **Endowment** $51.7 million
- **Coed** 1,231 undergraduate students, 98% full-time, 47% women, 53% men
- **Moderately difficult** entrance level, 65% of applicants were admitted

UNDERGRAD STUDENTS

1,208 full-time, 23 part-time. Students come from 33 states and territories; 18 other countries; 41% are from out of state; 8% Black or African American, non-Hispanic/Latino; 3% Hispanic/Latino; 4% Asian, non-Hispanic/Latino; 0.9% American Indian or Alaska Native, non-Hispanic/Latino; 0.6% Two or more races, non-Hispanic/Latino; 0.9% Race/ethnicity unknown; 2% transferred in; 85% live on campus.

Freshmen:

Admission: 1,846 applied, 1,202 admitted, 327 enrolled. *Average high school GPA:* 3.5. *Test scores:* ACT scores over 18: 100%; ACT scores over 24: 73%; ACT scores over 30: 20%.

Retention: 85% of full-time freshmen returned.

FACULTY

Total: 114, 75% full-time, 76% with terminal degrees.

Student/faculty ratio: 13:1.

ACADEMICS

Calendar: 4-1-4. *Degree:* bachelor's.

Special study options: advanced placement credit, cooperative education, double majors, honors programs, independent study, internships, off-campus study, part-time degree program, student-designed majors, study abroad, summer session for credit. *ROTC:* Army (c), Air Force (c).

Unusual degree programs: 3-2 engineering with Auburn University, Columbia University, Washington University in St. Louis, University of Alabama at Birmingham; nursing with University of Alabama at Birmingham; environmental studies with Duke University, law with Cumberland School of Law.

Computers: 306 computers/terminals and 306 ports are available on campus for general student use. Students can access the following: campus intranet, computer help desk, free student e-mail accounts, online (class) grades, online (class) registration, online (class) schedules. Campuswide network is available. 100% of college-owned or -operated housing units are wired for high-speed Internet access. Wireless service is available via entire campus.

Library: Charles Andrew Rush Learning Center/N. E. Miles Library. Students can reserve study rooms.

STUDENT LIFE

Housing options: on-campus residence required for freshman year; coed, men-only, women-only, special housing for students with disabilities. Campus housing is university owned. Freshman campus housing is guaranteed.

Activities and organizations: drama/theater group, student-run newspaper, choral group, marching band, Student Government Association, Quest II Event Programming, Black Student Union, Multi-Cultural Awareness Organization, Reformed University Fellowship, national fraternities, national sororities.

Athletics Member NCAA. All Division III. *Intercollegiate sports:* baseball M, basketball M/W, cheerleading M/W, cross-country running M/W, football M, golf M/W, lacrosse M/W, soccer M/W, softball W, swimming and diving M/W, tennis M/W, track and field M/W, volleyball W. *Intramural sports:* basketball M/W, football M/W, racquetball M/W, soccer M/W, softball M, table tennis M/W, tennis M/W, ultimate Frisbee M/W, volleyball M/W, water polo M/W.

Campus security: 24-hour emergency response devices and patrols, late-night transport/escort service, controlled dormitory access, vehicle safety inspections for students, emergency phone stations throughout campus.

Student services: health clinic, personal/psychological counseling.

COSTS & FINANCIAL AID

Costs (2018–19) *One-time required fee:* $300. *Comprehensive fee:* $29,950 includes full-time tuition ($16,353), mandatory fees ($1297), and room and board ($12,300). *College room only:* $6950. Room and board charges vary according to board plan, housing facility, and location. *Waivers:* employees or children of employees.

Financial Aid Of all full-time matriculated undergraduates who enrolled in 2017, 876 applied for aid, 747 were judged to have need, 230 had their need fully met. In 2017, 521 non-need-based awards were made. *Average percent of need met:* 74. *Average financial aid package:* $32,882. *Average need-based loan:* $4218. *Average need-based gift aid:* $6431. *Average non-need-based aid:* $21,770. *Average indebtedness upon graduation:* $30,084.

APPLYING

Standardized Tests *Recommended:* SAT or ACT (for admission).

Options: electronic application, early admission, early decision, early action, deferred entrance.

Application fee: $50.

Required: high school transcript, minimum 2.5 GPA, 1 letter of recommendation. *Required for some:* interview. *Recommended:* essay or personal statement, interview.

Notification: 3/1 (freshmen), 12/15 (early action).

CONTACT

Birmingham-Southern College, 900 Arkadelphia Road, Birmingham, AL 35254. *Toll-free phone:* 800-523-5793.

Columbia Southern University

Orange Beach, Alabama

http://www.columbiasouthern.edu/

- **Proprietary** comprehensive, founded 1993
- **Small-town** campus
- **Coed** 15,050 undergraduate students, 57% full-time, 37% women, 63% men
- **Noncompetitive** entrance level

UNDERGRAD STUDENTS
8,567 full-time, 6,483 part-time. Students come from 49 states and territories; 8 other countries; 94% are from out of state; 20% Black or African American, non-Hispanic/Latino; 7% Hispanic/Latino; 2% Asian, non-Hispanic/Latino; 0.2% Native Hawaiian or other Pacific Islander, non-Hispanic/Latino; 1% American Indian or Alaska Native, non-Hispanic/Latino; 3% Two or more races, non-Hispanic/Latino; 5% Race/ethnicity unknown; 0.1% international; 13% transferred in.

Freshmen:
Admission: 371 enrolled.

FACULTY
Total: 475, 30% full-time, 66% with terminal degrees.
Student/faculty ratio: 70:1.

ACADEMICS
Calendar: Non-standard Term: 9-weeks of instruction, LifePace Learning: 10-week courses that are self-paced. *Degrees:* certificates, associate, bachelor's, master's, doctoral, and postbachelor's certificates (offers only distance learning degree programs).
Special study options: academic remediation for entering students, adult/continuing education programs, distance learning, off-campus study, part-time degree program, services for LD students.
Computers: Students can access the following: computer help desk, online (class) grades, online (class) registration, online (class) schedules, student portals for learning modules, policy updates, and other institutional information. Wireless service is available via entire campus.
Library: CSU Online Library.

STUDENT LIFE
Housing options: college housing not available.
Activities and organizations: Student Veteran Association, American Criminal Justice Association, Delta Epsilon Tou (DET) - Alumni Honor Society.
Campus security: 24-hour emergency response devices.

COSTS
Costs (2018–19) *One-time required fee:* $135. *Tuition:* $5400 full-time, $225 per credit hour part-time. Full-time tuition and fees vary according to course load and degree level. Part-time tuition and fees vary according to course load and degree level. *Payment plan:* installment. *Waivers:* employees or children of employees.

APPLYING
Options: electronic application.
Required for some: high school transcript.
Application deadlines: rolling (freshmen), rolling (transfers).

CONTACT
Director of Admissions, Columbia Southern University, 21982 University Lane, Orange Beach, AL 36561. *Phone:* 251-981-3771. *Toll-free phone:* 800-977-8449. *Fax:* 251-224-0540. *E-mail:* admissions@columbiasouthern.edu.

Faulkner University
Montgomery, Alabama
http://www.faulkner.edu/
- **Independent** university, founded 1942, affiliated with Church of Christ
- **Urban** 75-acre campus with easy access to Montgomery
- **Endowment** $18.9 million
- **Coed**
- **Minimally difficult** entrance level

FACULTY
Student/faculty ratio: 11:1.

ACADEMICS
Calendar: semesters. *Degrees:* associate, bachelor's, master's, and doctoral.
Library: Gus Nichols Library System plus 4 others. *Books:* 282,460 (physical), 223,809 (digital/electronic); *Serial titles:* 1,563 (physical); *Databases:* 128. Weekly public service hours: 74.

STUDENT LIFE
Housing options: on-campus residence required through junior year; men-only, women-only, special housing for students with disabilities. Campus housing is university owned. Freshman campus housing is guaranteed.
Activities and organizations: drama/theater group, student-run newspaper, choral group, marching band, Student Government, Marching Band, Dinner Theatre, A cappella Chorus, Phi Lambda/Kappa Social Clubs.
Athletics Member NAIA.
Campus security: 24-hour emergency response devices and patrols, late-night transport/escort service, controlled dormitory access.
Student services: health clinic, personal/psychological counseling.

COSTS & FINANCIAL AID
Costs (2017–18) *Comprehensive fee:* $28,370 includes full-time tuition ($19,160), mandatory fees ($1810), and room and board ($7400). Full-time tuition and fees vary according to class time, course load, location, and program. Part-time tuition: $650 per semester hour. Part-time tuition and fees vary according to class time, course load, location, and program. *Required fees:* $320 per term part-time. *College room only:* $3500. Room and board charges vary according to board plan and housing facility. *Payment plans:* installment, deferred payment.
Financial Aid Of all full-time matriculated undergraduates who enrolled in 2015, 253 applied for aid, 236 were judged to have need, 27 had their need fully met. In 2015, 24 non-need-based awards were made. *Average percent of need met:* 61. *Average financial aid package:* $14,006. *Average need-based loan:* $3064. *Average need-based gift aid:* $11,587. *Average non-need-based aid:* $6113. *Average indebtedness upon graduation:* $29,000. *Financial aid deadline:* 8/1.

APPLYING
Standardized Tests *Required for some:* SAT or ACT (for admission).
Options: electronic application, early admission, deferred entrance.
Required: high school transcript, minimum 2.0 GPA. *Recommended:* essay or personal statement, 2 letters of recommendation, interview.

CONTACT
Mr. Neil Scott, Director of Admissions, Faulkner University, 5345 Atlanta Highway, Montgomery, AL 36109-3398. *Phone:* 334-386-7200. *Toll-free phone:* 800-879-9816. *Fax:* 334-386-7137. *E-mail:* nscott@faulkner.edu.

Heritage Christian University
Florence, Alabama
http://www.hcu.edu/

CONTACT
Mr. Brad McKinnon, Dean of Students, Heritage Christian University, PO Box HCU, Florence, AL 35630. *Phone:* 256-766-6610 Ext. 305. *Toll-free phone:* 800-367-3565. *Fax:* 256-766-9289. *E-mail:* bmckinnon@hcu.edu.

Herzing University
Birmingham, Alabama
http://www.herzing.edu/birmingham/

CONTACT
Ms. Tess Anderson, Admissions Coordinator, Herzing University, 280 West Valley Avenue, Birmingham, AL 35209. *Phone:* 205-916-2800. *Toll-free phone:* 800-596-0724. *E-mail:* admiss@bhm.herzing.edu.

Huntingdon College
Montgomery, Alabama
http://www.huntingdon.edu/
- **Independent United Methodist** 4-year, founded 1854
- **Suburban** 70-acre campus with easy access to Birmingham
- **Endowment** $48.2 million
- **Coed** 1,102 undergraduate students, 80% full-time, 52% women, 48% men

UNDERGRAD STUDENTS
878 full-time, 224 part-time. Students come from 22 states and territories; 4 other countries; 30% are from out of state; 21% Black or African

American, non-Hispanic/Latino; 6% Hispanic/Latino; 0.5% Asian, non-Hispanic/Latino; 0.3% Native Hawaiian or other Pacific Islander, non-Hispanic/Latino; 0.5% American Indian or Alaska Native, non-Hispanic/Latino; 5% Two or more races, non-Hispanic/Latino; 3% Race/ethnicity unknown; 0.1% international; 9% transferred in; 68% live on campus.

Freshmen:
Admission: 294 enrolled. *Average high school GPA:* 3.4. *Test scores:* SAT evidence-based reading and writing scores over 500: 73%; SAT math scores over 500: 78%; ACT scores over 18: 90%; SAT evidence-based reading and writing scores over 600: 25%; SAT math scores over 600: 19%; ACT scores over 24: 28%; SAT evidence-based reading and writing scores over 700: 3%; ACT scores over 30: 1%.
Retention: 65% of full-time freshmen returned.

FACULTY
Total: 101, 47% full-time, 57% with terminal degrees.
Student/faculty ratio: 15:1.

ACADEMICS
Calendar: semesters. *Degree:* bachelor's.
Special study options: adult/continuing education programs, advanced placement credit, distance learning, double majors, freshman honors college, honors programs, independent study, internships, off-campus study, part-time degree program, services for LD students, student-designed majors, study abroad, summer session for credit. *ROTC:* Army (c), Air Force (c).
Computers: 9 computers/terminals are available on campus for general student use. Students can access the following: computer help desk, free student e-mail accounts, online (class) grades, online (class) registration, online (class) schedules. Campuswide network is available. 100% of college-owned or -operated housing units are wired for high-speed Internet access. Wireless service is available via dorm rooms, libraries.
Library: Houghton Memorial Library. *Books:* 91,034 (physical), 103,891 (digital/electronic); *Serial titles:* 187 (physical), 41,336 (digital/electronic); *Databases:* 114. Students can reserve study rooms.

STUDENT LIFE
Housing options: on-campus residence required through junior year; coed, men-only, women-only, special housing for students with disabilities. Campus housing is university owned. Freshman campus housing is guaranteed.
Activities and organizations: drama/theater group, student-run newspaper, choral group, marching band, Student Government Association, Campus Activities Board, Voice of Justice, Freshman Forum, Exchange Club, national fraternities, national sororities.
Athletics Member NCAA. All Division III. *Intercollegiate sports:* baseball M, basketball M/W, cross-country running M/W, football M, golf M/W, lacrosse M/W, sand volleyball W, soccer M/W, softball W, tennis M/W, volleyball W, wrestling M. *Intramural sports:* baseball W(c), basketball M/W, cheerleading M(c)/W(c), football M/W, sand volleyball M/W, soccer M/W, softball M/W, table tennis M/W, tennis M/W, ultimate Frisbee M(c)/W(c), volleyball M/W.
Campus security: 24-hour emergency response devices and patrols, late-night transport/escort service, controlled dormitory access, electronic video surveillance, weather alert broadcasts.
Student services: health clinic, personal/psychological counseling.

COSTS & FINANCIAL AID
Costs (2017–18) *Comprehensive fee:* $35,900 includes full-time tuition ($24,900), mandatory fees ($1500), and room and board ($9500). Full-time tuition and fees vary according to course load and program. Part-time tuition: $1040 per credit hour. Part-time tuition and fees vary according to course load and program. *Room and board:* Room and board charges vary according to housing facility. *Payment plan:* installment. *Waivers:* employees or children of employees.
Financial Aid Of all full-time matriculated undergraduates who enrolled in 2017, 755 applied for aid, 675 were judged to have need, 87 had their need fully met. 149 Federal Work-Study jobs (averaging $910). In 2017, 191 non-need-based awards were made. *Average percent of need met:* 67. *Average financial aid package:* $19,156. *Average need-based loan:* $4197. *Average need-based gift aid:* $15,593. *Average non-need-based aid:* $11,673. *Average indebtedness upon graduation:* $32,201.

APPLYING
Standardized Tests *Required:* SAT or ACT (for admission).
Required: high school transcript. *Required for some:* essay or personal statement, 3 letters of recommendation, interview, audition required for music majors; portfolio recommended for art majors.

CONTACT
Office of Admission, Huntingdon College, 1500 East Fairview Avenue, Montgomery, AL 36106-2148. *Phone:* 334-833-4497. *Toll-free phone:* 800-763-0313. *Fax:* 334-833-4347. *E-mail:* admiss@hawks.huntingdon.edu.

Huntsville Bible College
Huntsville, Alabama
http://www.huntsvillebiblecollege.org/

CONTACT
Huntsville Bible College, 904 Oakwood Avenue, Huntsville, AL 35811-1632.

Jacksonville State University
Jacksonville, Alabama
http://www.jsu.edu/
- **State-supported** comprehensive, founded 1883
- **Small-town** 459-acre campus with easy access to Birmingham
- **Coed**
- **Moderately difficult** entrance level

FACULTY
Student/faculty ratio: 18:1.

ACADEMICS
Calendar: semesters. *Degrees:* bachelor's, master's, doctoral, post-master's, and postbachelor's certificates.
Library: Houston Cole Library. *Books:* 711,815 (physical), 32,128 (digital/electronic); *Databases:* 307. Weekly public service hours: 87.

STUDENT LIFE
Housing options: on-campus residence required for freshman year; coed, men-only, women-only, special housing for students with disabilities. Campus housing is university owned.
Activities and organizations: drama/theater group, student-run newspaper, radio and television station, choral group, marching band, Student Government Association, Archaeology Club, Campus Fellowship Clubs, Computer Science Club, Biology Club, national fraternities, national sororities.
Athletics Member NCAA. All Division I except football (Division I-AA).
Campus security: 24-hour emergency response devices and patrols, student patrols, late-night transport/escort service, controlled dormitory access, night security officer in female residence halls.
Student services: health clinic, personal/psychological counseling.

COSTS & FINANCIAL AID
Costs (2017–18) *Tuition:* state resident $9270 full-time, $309 per credit hour part-time; nonresident $18,540 full-time, $618 per credit hour part-time. *Required fees:* $750 full-time, $750 per year part-time. *Room and board:* $7898. Room and board charges vary according to board plan and housing facility.
Financial Aid Of all full-time matriculated undergraduates who enrolled in 2015, 4,849 applied for aid, 4,761 were judged to have need. *Average financial aid package:* $9592. *Average need-based loan:* $992. *Average need-based gift aid:* $4558.

APPLYING
Standardized Tests *Required:* SAT or ACT (for admission).
Options: electronic application, early admission, deferred entrance.
Application fee: $35.
Required: high school transcript.

CONTACT
Mr. Andrew Green, Director of Admission, Jacksonville State University, 700 Pelham Road North, Jacksonville, AL 36265. *Phone:* 256-782-5363. *Toll-free phone:* 800-231-5291. *Fax:* 256-782-5291. *E-mail:* info@jsu.edu.

Judson College
Marion, Alabama
http://www.judson.edu/

CONTACT
Ms. Layne Hoggle, Executive Director of Enrollment Services, Judson College, 302 Bibb Street, Marion, AL 36756. *Phone:* 334-683-5110. *Toll-free phone:* 800-447-9472. *Fax:* 334-683-5282. *E-mail:* admissions@judson.edu.

Miles College
Fairfield, Alabama
http://www.miles.edu/

CONTACT
Mr. Christopher Robertson, Director of Admissions and Recruitment, Miles College, 5500 Myron Massey Boulevard, Bell Building, Fairfield, AL 35064. *Phone:* 205-929-1657. *Toll-free phone:* 800-445-0708. *Fax:* 205-929-1627. *E-mail:* admissions@miles.edu.

Oakwood University
Huntsville, Alabama
http://www.oakwood.edu/

CONTACT
Mr. Jason McCracken, Director of Enrollment Management, Oakwood University, 7000 Adventist Boulevard, NW, Huntsville, AL 35896. *Phone:* 256-726-7354. *Toll-free phone:* 800-824-5312. *Fax:* 256-726-7154. *E-mail:* admission@oakwood.edu.

Remington College–Mobile Campus
Mobile, Alabama
http://www.remingtoncollege.edu/

CONTACT
Remington College–Mobile Campus, 828 Downtowner Loop West, Mobile, AL 36609. *Phone:* 251-343-8200. *Toll-free phone:* 800-323-8122.

Samford University
Birmingham, Alabama
http://www.samford.edu/

- **Independent Baptist** university, founded 1841
- **Suburban** 212-acre campus
- **Endowment** $292.2 million
- **Coed** 3,373 undergraduate students, 97% full-time, 66% women, 34% men
- **Moderately difficult** entrance level, 83% of applicants were admitted

UNDERGRAD STUDENTS
3,266 full-time, 107 part-time. Students come from 38 states and territories; 26 other countries; 67% are from out of state; 7% Black or African American, non-Hispanic/Latino; 3% Hispanic/Latino; 1% Asian, non-Hispanic/Latino; 0.2% American Indian or Alaska Native, non-Hispanic/Latino; 2% Two or more races, non-Hispanic/Latino; 0.6% Race/ethnicity unknown; 2% international; 4% transferred in; 68% live on campus.

Freshmen:
Admission: 3,808 applied, 3,168 admitted, 857 enrolled. *Average high school GPA:* 3.7. *Test scores:* SAT evidence-based reading and writing scores over 500: 95%; SAT math scores over 500: 89%; ACT scores over 18: 100%; SAT evidence-based reading and writing scores over 600: 56%; SAT math scores over 600: 40%; ACT scores over 24: 75%; SAT evidence-based reading and writing scores over 700: 11%; SAT math scores over 700: 4%; ACT scores over 30: 20%.

Retention: 87% of full-time freshmen returned.

FACULTY
Total: 547, 65% full-time, 73% with terminal degrees.
Student/faculty ratio: 12:1.

ACADEMICS
Calendar: 4-1-4. *Degrees:* certificates, bachelor's, master's, doctoral, post-master's, and postbachelor's certificates.

Special study options: accelerated degree program, adult/continuing education programs, distance learning, double majors, honors programs, independent study, internships, off-campus study, part-time degree program, services for LD students, study abroad, summer session for credit. *ROTC:* Army (c), Air Force (b).

Unusual degree programs: 3-2 engineering with The University of Alabama at Birmingham, Auburn University, Mercer University.

Computers: 330 computers/terminals and 400 ports are available on campus for general student use. Students can access the following: campus intranet, computer help desk, free student e-mail accounts, online (class) grades, online (class) registration, online (class) schedules, free online storage and tech support. Campuswide network is available. 100% of college-owned or -operated housing units are wired for high-speed Internet access. Wireless service is available via entire campus.
Library: University Library plus 2 others. *Books:* 635,009 (physical), 212,093 (digital/electronic); *Serial titles:* 6,055 (physical), 113,159 (digital/electronic); *Databases:* 307. Weekly public service hours: 99; students can reserve study rooms.

STUDENT LIFE
Housing options: on-campus residence required through sophomore year; men-only, women-only. Campus housing is university owned. Freshman campus housing is guaranteed.

Activities and organizations: drama/theater group, student-run newspaper, radio station, choral group, marching band, Student Government Association, Greek Chapters and councils, Campus Ministries, national fraternities, national sororities.

Athletics Member NCAA. All Division I except football (Division I-AA). *Intercollegiate sports:* baseball M(s), basketball M(s)/W(s), cross-country running M(s)/W(s), golf M(s)/W(s), soccer W(s), softball W(s), tennis M(s)/W(s), track and field M(s)/W(s), volleyball W(s). *Intramural sports:* basketball M/W, crew M(c)/W(c), football M/W, golf M(c)/W(c), lacrosse W(c), rugby M(c), sand volleyball M/W, soccer M/W, softball M/W, table tennis M/W, ultimate Frisbee M/W, volleyball M/W.

Campus security: 24-hour emergency response devices and patrols, late-night transport/escort service, blue-light emergency phones, lighted sidewalks, nighttime campus access control gate.

Student services: health clinic, personal/psychological counseling.

COSTS & FINANCIAL AID
Costs (2018–19) *Comprehensive fee:* $42,200 includes full-time tuition ($30,800), mandatory fees ($850), and room and board ($10,550). Full-time tuition and fees vary according to course load and program. Part-time tuition: $1030 per credit hour. Part-time tuition and fees vary according to course load and program. *Required fees:* $355 per term part-time. *College room only:* $5686. Room and board charges vary according to board plan and housing facility. *Payment plan:* installment. *Waivers:* employees or children of employees.

Financial Aid Of all full-time matriculated undergraduates who enrolled in 2016, 1,828 applied for aid, 1,282 were judged to have need, 271 had their need fully met. 412 Federal Work-Study jobs (averaging $2091). 715 state and other part-time jobs (averaging $1535). In 2016, 1504 non-need-based awards were made. *Average percent of need met:* 69. *Average financial aid package:* $19,523. *Average need-based loan:* $3936. *Average need-based gift aid:* $15,859. *Average non-need-based aid:* $10,848. *Average indebtedness upon graduation:* $27,539.

APPLYING
Standardized Tests *Required:* SAT or ACT (for admission).

Options: electronic application, early admission, deferred entrance.

Application fee: $40.

Required: essay or personal statement, high school transcript, 1 letter of recommendation. *Required for some:* interview.

Notification: continuous until 11/1 (freshmen).

CONTACT
Mr. Brian L. Kennedy, Director of Recruitment, Samford University, 800 Lakeshore Drive, Samford Hall, Birmingham, AL 35229-0002. *Phone:* 205-726-4176. *Toll-free phone:* 800-888-7218. *E-mail:* blkenned@samford.edu.

Selma University

Selma, Alabama

http://www.selmauniversity.edu/

CONTACT
Selma University, 1501 Lapsley Street, Selma, AL 36701-5299. *Phone:* 334-872-2533 Ext. 116.

South University

Montgomery, Alabama

http://www.southuniversity.edu/montgomery/

CONTACT
South University, 5355 Vaughn Road, Montgomery, AL 36116-1120. *Phone:* 334-395-8800. *Toll-free phone:* 866-629-2962.

Spring Hill College

Mobile, Alabama

http://www.shc.edu/

- **Independent Roman Catholic (Jesuit)** comprehensive, founded 1830
- **Suburban** 450-acre campus
- **Coed** 1,393 undergraduate students, 99% full-time, 63% women, 37% men
- **Moderately difficult** entrance level, 46% of applicants were admitted

UNDERGRAD STUDENTS
1,379 full-time, 14 part-time. Students come from 34 states and territories; 23 other countries; 58% are from out of state; 16% Black or African American, non-Hispanic/Latino; 2% Hispanic/Latino; 1% Asian, non-Hispanic/Latino; 0.2% Native Hawaiian or other Pacific Islander, non-Hispanic/Latino; 0.6% American Indian or Alaska Native, non-Hispanic/Latino; 5% Two or more races, non-Hispanic/Latino; 3% Race/ethnicity unknown; 4% international; 3% transferred in; 71% live on campus.

Freshmen:
Admission: 8,544 applied, 3,903 admitted, 393 enrolled. *Average high school GPA:* 3.6. *Test scores:* SAT evidence-based reading and writing scores over 500: 85%; SAT math scores over 500: 85%; ACT scores over 18: 95%; SAT evidence-based reading and writing scores over 600: 27%; SAT math scores over 600: 19%; ACT scores over 24: 42%; SAT evidence-based reading and writing scores over 700: 8%; ACT scores over 30: 6%.

Retention: 79% of full-time freshmen returned.

FACULTY
Total: 126, 68% full-time, 78% with terminal degrees.

Student/faculty ratio: 14:1.

ACADEMICS
Calendar: semesters. *Degrees:* certificates, bachelor's, master's, post-master's, and postbachelor's certificates.

Special study options: academic remediation for entering students, accelerated degree program, adult/continuing education programs, advanced placement credit, distance learning, double majors, honors programs, independent study, internships, off-campus study, part-time degree program, services for LD students, student-designed majors, study abroad, summer session for credit. *ROTC:* Army (c), Air Force (c).

Unusual degree programs: 3-2 engineering with Marquette University, University of Alabama at Birmingham, University of Florida, Auburn University, Texas A&M University, University of South Alabama.

Computers: Students can access the following: campus intranet, computer help desk, free student e-mail accounts, online (class) grades, online (class) registration, online (class) schedules. Campuswide network is available. 100% of college-owned or -operated housing units are wired for high-speed Internet access. Wireless service is available via computer centers, computer labs, dorm rooms, libraries, student centers.
Library: Marnie and John Burke Memorial Library plus 1 other.

STUDENT LIFE
Housing options: on-campus residence required through senior year; coed. Campus housing is university owned. Freshman campus housing is guaranteed.

Activities and organizations: drama/theater group, student-run newspaper, choral group, Fraternities and sororities, SHAPe, National Society of Leadership and Success, Peer One Project, Chemistry Club, national fraternities, national sororities.

Athletics Member NCAA. All Division II. *Intercollegiate sports:* baseball M(s), basketball M(s)/W(s), cross-country running M(s)/W(s), golf M(s)/W(s), soccer M(s)/W(s), softball W(s), tennis M(s)/W(s), track and field M(s)/W(s), volleyball W(s). *Intramural sports:* basketball M/W, bowling M(c)/W(c), football M/W, racquetball M/W, rugby M(c)/W(c), soccer M/W, ultimate Frisbee M/W, volleyball M/W.

Campus security: 24-hour emergency response devices and patrols, late-night transport/escort service, controlled dormitory access.

Student services: health clinic, personal/psychological counseling.

COSTS & FINANCIAL AID
Costs (2017–18) *Comprehensive fee:* $50,654 includes full-time tuition ($35,312), mandatory fees ($2272), and room and board ($13,070). Full-time tuition and fees vary according to course load. Part-time tuition: $1104 per credit hour. Part-time tuition and fees vary according to course load. *Required fees:* $57 per credit hour part-time. *College room only:* $6900. Room and board charges vary according to board plan and housing facility. *Payment plan:* installment. *Waivers:* employees or children of employees.

Financial Aid Of all full-time matriculated undergraduates who enrolled in 2017, 1,090 applied for aid, 951 were judged to have need, 228 had their need fully met. In 2017, 343 non-need-based awards were made. *Average percent of need met:* 82. *Average financial aid package:* $33,589. *Average need-based loan:* $4418. *Average need-based gift aid:* $8275. *Average non-need-based aid:* $23,594.

APPLYING
Standardized Tests *Required:* SAT or ACT (for admission).

Options: electronic application, early admission, deferred entrance.

Application fee: $25.

Required: essay or personal statement, high school transcript, 1 letter of recommendation. *Recommended:* minimum 2.5 GPA, interview.

Application deadlines: 7/15 (freshmen), rolling (transfers).

Notification: continuous (freshmen), continuous (out-of-state freshmen), continuous (transfers).

CONTACT
Ms. Britney Finley, Admissions Counselor, Spring Hill College, 4000 Dauphin Street, Mobile, AL 36608-1791. *Phone:* 251-380-3032. *Toll-free phone:* 800-SHC-6704. *Fax:* 251-460-2186. *E-mail:* bfinley@shc.edu.

Stillman College

Tuscaloosa, Alabama

http://www.stillman.edu/

CONTACT
Stillman College, PO Drawer 1430, 3600 Stillman Boulevard, Tuscaloosa, AL 35403-9990. *Phone:* 205-366-8837. *Toll-free phone:* 800-841-5722.

Strayer University–Birmingham Campus

Birmingham, Alabama

http://www.strayer.edu/alabama/birmingham/

CONTACT
Strayer University–Birmingham Campus, 3570 Grandview Parkway, Suite 200, Birmingham, AL 35243. *Toll-free phone:* 888-311-0355.

Strayer University–Huntsville Campus

Huntsville, Alabama

http://www.strayer.edu/alabama/huntsville/

CONTACT
Strayer University–Huntsville Campus, 4955 Corporate Drive, NW, Suite 200, Huntsville, AL 35805. *Toll-free phone:* 888-311-0355.

Talladega College

Talladega, Alabama
http://www.talladega.edu/
- **Independent** 4-year, founded 1867
- **Small-town** 130-acre campus with easy access to Birmingham
- **Endowment** $3.3 million
- **Coed** 780 undergraduate students, 97% full-time, 47% women, 53% men
- **Moderately difficult** entrance level, 15% of applicants were admitted

UNDERGRAD STUDENTS
760 full-time, 20 part-time. Students come from 30 states and territories; 3 other countries; 39% are from out of state; 87% Black or African American, non-Hispanic/Latino; 5% Hispanic/Latino; 0.1% American Indian or Alaska Native, non-Hispanic/Latino; 3% Two or more races, non-Hispanic/Latino; 0.8% Race/ethnicity unknown; 2% international; 9% transferred in; 65% live on campus.

Freshmen:
Admission: 2,047 applied, 312 admitted, 158 enrolled. *Average high school GPA:* 2.4.
Retention: 59% of full-time freshmen returned.

FACULTY
Total: 64, 61% full-time, 47% with terminal degrees.
Student/faculty ratio: 20:1.

ACADEMICS
Calendar: semesters. *Degrees:* associate and bachelor's.
Special study options: accelerated degree program, adult/continuing education programs, distance learning, double majors, English as a second language, independent study, internships, off-campus study, part-time degree program, services for LD students, study abroad, summer session for credit.
Computers: 186 computers/terminals and 240 ports are available on campus for general student use. Students can access the following: computer help desk, free student e-mail accounts, online (class) grades, online (class) registration, online (class) schedules. Campuswide network is available. 100% of college-owned or -operated housing units are wired for high-speed Internet access. Wireless service is available via entire campus.
Library: Savery Library. *Books:* 100,000 (physical); *Serial titles:* 1,922 (digital/electronic); *Databases:* 244. Weekly public service hours: 77; students can reserve study rooms.

STUDENT LIFE
Housing options: men-only, women-only. Campus housing is university owned. Freshman campus housing is guaranteed.
Activities and organizations: choral group, marching band, Student Government Association, Crimson Ambassadors, Students in Free Enterprise (SIFE), Talladega College Choir, Social Work Club, national fraternities, national sororities.
Athletics Member NAIA. *Intercollegiate sports:* baseball M, basketball M, golf M, softball W, tennis W. *Intramural sports:* baseball M, basketball M/W, cheerleading M/W, football M, tennis M/W, volleyball W.
Campus security: 24-hour patrols, late-night transport/escort service, campus police.
Student services: health clinic, personal/psychological counseling.

COSTS & FINANCIAL AID
Costs (2017–18) *One-time required fee:* $125. *Comprehensive fee:* $19,044 includes full-time tuition ($11,192), mandatory fees ($1148), and room and board ($6704). Full-time tuition and fees vary according to course load. Part-time tuition: $466 per credit hour. *Required fees:* $574 per credit hour part-time. *College room only:* $3200. *Payment plans:* tuition prepayment, installment. *Waivers:* employees or children of employees.
Financial Aid Of all full-time matriculated undergraduates who enrolled in 2003, 407 applied for aid, 375 were judged to have need, 100 had their need fully met. 141 Federal Work-Study jobs (averaging $691). *Average percent of need met:* 90. *Average financial aid package:* $5000. *Average need-based loan:* $5335. *Average need-based gift aid:* $3025. *Average non-need-based aid:* $5774. *Average indebtedness upon graduation:* $12,790. *Financial aid deadline:* 6/30.

APPLYING
Standardized Tests *Required:* SAT or ACT (for admission).
Options: electronic application, early admission.
Application fee: $25.
Required: high school transcript, minimum 2.0 GPA.
Application deadlines: rolling (freshmen), rolling (transfers), rolling (early action).
Notification: continuous (freshmen), continuous (transfers).

CONTACT
Talladega College, 627 West Battle Street, Talladega, AL 35160-2354. *Phone:* 256-761-6175. *Toll-free phone:* 866-540-3956.

Troy University

Troy, Alabama
http://www.troy.edu/
- **State-supported** comprehensive, founded 1887, part of Troy University System
- **Small-town** 906-acre campus
- **Endowment** $104.4 million
- **Coed** 14,000 undergraduate students, 68% full-time, 60% women, 40% men
- **90%** of applicants were admitted

UNDERGRAD STUDENTS
9,491 full-time, 4,509 part-time. Students come from 48 states and territories; 61 other countries; 31% are from out of state; 30% Black or African American, non-Hispanic/Latino; 4% Hispanic/Latino; 0.9% Asian, non-Hispanic/Latino; 0.1% Native Hawaiian or other Pacific Islander, non-Hispanic/Latino; 0.5% American Indian or Alaska Native, non-Hispanic/Latino; 3% Two or more races, non-Hispanic/Latino; 4% Race/ethnicity unknown; 5% international; 11% transferred in; 16% live on campus.

Freshmen:
Admission: 6,565 applied, 5,938 admitted, 2,160 enrolled. *Average high school GPA:* 3.4. *Test scores:* SAT evidence-based reading and writing scores over 500: 49%; ACT scores over 18: 83%; SAT evidence-based reading and writing scores over 600: 18%; ACT scores over 24: 31%; SAT evidence-based reading and writing scores over 700: 10%; ACT scores over 30: 5%.
Retention: 70% of full-time freshmen returned.

FACULTY
Total: 1,079, 49% full-time, 31% with terminal degrees.
Student/faculty ratio: 15:1.

ACADEMICS
Calendar: semesters. *Degrees:* certificates, associate, bachelor's, master's, doctoral, post-master's, and postbachelor's certificates.
Special study options: academic remediation for entering students, accelerated degree program, advanced placement credit, distance learning, double majors, English as a second language, honors programs, independent study, internships, part-time degree program, services for LD students, study abroad, summer session for credit. *ROTC:* Army (b), Air Force (b).
Computers: 1,935 computers/terminals and 21,221 ports are available on campus for general student use. Students can access the following: campus intranet, computer help desk, free student e-mail accounts, online (class) grades, online (class) registration, online (class) schedules. Campuswide network is available. Wireless service is available via classrooms, dorm rooms, libraries.
Library: Lurleen B. Wallace Library (Troy Campus) plus 2 others. *Books:* 603,904 (physical), 277,690 (digital/electronic); *Serial titles:* 213 (physical), 134,396 (digital/electronic); *Databases:* 261.

STUDENT LIFE
Housing options: on-campus residence required for freshman year; coed, men-only, women-only. Campus housing is university owned. Freshman campus housing is guaranteed.
Activities and organizations: drama/theater group, student-run newspaper, television station, choral group, marching band, T-Day/Athletic Events

(Homecoming), Activities Council, Pep Rallies, national fraternities, national sororities.

Athletics Member NCAA. All Division I except football (Division I-A). *Intercollegiate sports:* baseball M(s), basketball M(s)/W(s), cross-country running M(s)/W(s), golf M(s)/W(s), soccer W(s), softball W(s), tennis M(s)/W(s), track and field M(s)/W(s), volleyball W(s). *Intramural sports:* basketball M/W, bowling M/W, cross-country running M/W, football M, golf M/W, soccer W, softball W, tennis M/W, track and field M/W, volleyball W.

Campus security: 24-hour emergency response devices and patrols, student patrols, late-night transport/escort service, controlled dormitory access.

Student services: health clinic, personal/psychological counseling.

COSTS & FINANCIAL AID
Costs (2017–18) *Tuition:* state resident $10,112 full-time, $316 per credit hour part-time; nonresident $20,224 full-time, $632 per credit hour part-time. Full-time tuition and fees vary according to location and program. Part-time tuition and fees vary according to location and program. *Required fees:* $2043 full-time, $39 per credit hour part-time, $50 per term part-time. *Room and board:* $7946; room only: $4458. Room and board charges vary according to board plan and housing facility. *Payment plan:* installment. *Waivers:* employees or children of employees.

Financial Aid Of all full-time matriculated undergraduates who enrolled in 2017, 6,534 applied for aid, 6,465 were judged to have need. In 2017, 2126 non-need-based awards were made. *Average financial aid package:* $4356. *Average need-based loan:* $4245. *Average need-based gift aid:* $4757. *Average non-need-based aid:* $7439.

APPLYING
Standardized Tests *Required:* SAT or ACT (for admission).

Options: electronic application, deferred entrance.

Application fee: $30.

Required: high school transcript, rigor of secondary school record.

Application deadlines: rolling (freshmen), rolling (transfers).

CONTACT
Mr. Buddy Starling, Associate Vice Chancellor for Enrollment Management, Troy University, University Avenue, Troy, AL 36082. *Phone:* 334-670-3243. *Toll-free phone:* 800-551-9716. *Fax:* 334-670-3733. *E-mail:* bstar@troy.edu.

Tuskegee University
Tuskegee, Alabama
http://www.tuskegee.edu/

CONTACT
Hon. Courtney L. Griffin, Executive Director of Enrollment Management, Tuskegee University, 1200 Old Montgomery Road, Margaret Murray Hall, Admissions, Tuskegee, AL 36088. *Phone:* 334-724-4828. *Toll-free phone:* 800-622-6531. *Fax:* 334-727-5750. *E-mail:* cgriffin@mytu.tuskegee.edu.

United States Sports Academy
Daphne, Alabama
http://www.ussa.edu/
- **Independent** upper-level, founded 1972
- **Suburban** 10-acre campus
- **Coed** 124 undergraduate students, 31% full-time, 18% women, 82% men

UNDERGRAD STUDENTS
39 full-time, 85 part-time. 96% are from out of state; 11% Black or African American, non-Hispanic/Latino; 10% Hispanic/Latino; 2% Asian, non-Hispanic/Latino; 0.8% American Indian or Alaska Native, non-Hispanic/Latino; 2% Two or more races, non-Hispanic/Latino; 6% Race/ethnicity unknown.

FACULTY
Total: 24, 25% full-time, 100% with terminal degrees.

Student/faculty ratio: 41:1.

ACADEMICS
Calendar: continuous. *Degrees:* bachelor's, master's, and doctoral.

Special study options: distance learning, part-time degree program.

Computers: Students can access the following: computer help desk, free student e-mail accounts, online (class) grades, online (class) registration, online (class) schedules. Campuswide network is available.

Library: United States Sports Academy Library plus 1 other. Weekly public service hours: 5.

STUDENT LIFE
Activities and organizations: Alumni Association.

Campus security: Electronically operated building entrances.

COSTS & FINANCIAL AID
Costs (2018–19) *Tuition:* $14,652 full-time, $407 per credit hour part-time. *Required fees:* $1320 full-time. *Payment plan:* installment. *Waivers:* employees or children of employees.

Financial Aid Of all full-time matriculated undergraduates who enrolled in 2016, 31 applied for aid, 31 were judged to have need, 25 had their need fully met. *Average percent of need met:* 29. *Average financial aid package:* $4748. *Average need-based loan:* $4758. *Average need-based gift aid:* $3978.

APPLYING
Options: electronic application.

Notification: continuous (transfers).

CONTACT
United States Sports Academy, One Academy Drive, Daphne, AL 36526-7055. *Phone:* 251-626-3303 Ext. 7147. *Toll-free phone:* 800-223-2668.

The University of Alabama
Tuscaloosa, Alabama
http://www.ua.edu/
- **State-supported** university, founded 1831, part of University of Alabama System
- **Suburban** 1026-acre campus with easy access to Birmingham
- **Endowment** $683.2 million
- **Coed** 33,305 undergraduate students, 90% full-time, 56% women, 44% men
- **Moderately difficult** entrance level, 53% of applicants were admitted

UNDERGRAD STUDENTS
29,923 full-time, 3,382 part-time. Students come from 51 states and territories; 60 other countries; 60% are from out of state; 10% Black or African American, non-Hispanic/Latino; 5% Hispanic/Latino; 1% Asian, non-Hispanic/Latino; 0.1% Native Hawaiian or other Pacific Islander, non-Hispanic/Latino; 0.3% American Indian or Alaska Native, non-Hispanic/Latino; 3% Two or more races, non-Hispanic/Latino; 0.4% Race/ethnicity unknown; 2% international; 5% transferred in; 24% live on campus.

Freshmen:
Admission: 38,129 applied, 20,321 admitted, 7,407 enrolled. *Average high school GPA:* 3.7. *Test scores:* SAT evidence-based reading and writing scores over 500: 93%; SAT math scores over 500: 89%; ACT scores over 18: 100%; SAT evidence-based reading and writing scores over 600: 43%; SAT math scores over 600: 37%; ACT scores over 24: 71%; SAT evidence-based reading and writing scores over 700: 13%; SAT math scores over 700: 15%; ACT scores over 30: 40%.

Retention: 87% of full-time freshmen returned.

FACULTY
Total: 1,898, 73% full-time, 71% with terminal degrees.

Student/faculty ratio: 23:1.

ACADEMICS
Calendar: semesters. *Degrees:* bachelor's, master's, doctoral, and post-master's certificates.

Special study options: academic remediation for entering students, accelerated degree program, adult/continuing education programs, advanced placement credit, cooperative education, distance learning, double majors, English as a second language, external degree program, freshman honors college, honors programs, independent study, internships, off-campus study, part-time degree program, services for LD students, student-designed majors, study abroad, summer session for credit. *ROTC:* Army (b), Air Force (b).

Computers: 2,500 computers/terminals and 12,000 ports are available on campus for general student use. Students can access the following: campus intranet, computer help desk, free student e-mail accounts, online (class) grades, online (class) registration, online (class) schedules. Campuswide network is available. 100% of college-owned or -operated housing units are wired for high-speed Internet access. Wireless service is available via entire campus.

Library: Amelia Gayle Gorgas Library plus 8 others. *Books:* 3.3 million (physical), 1.5 million (digital/electronic); *Serial titles:* 419 (physical), 199,096 (digital/electronic); *Databases:* 589. Weekly public service hours: 146; study areas open 24 hours, 5–7 days a week; students can reserve study rooms.

STUDENT LIFE

Housing options: on-campus residence required for freshman year; coed, men-only, women-only, special housing for students with disabilities. Campus housing is university owned and leased by the school. Freshman campus housing is guaranteed.

Activities and organizations: drama/theater group, student-run newspaper, radio station, choral group, marching band, ABXY Gaming Network, Residence Hall Association, International Student Association, Student Government Association, Black Student Union, national fraternities, national sororities.

Athletics Member NCAA. All Division I except football (Division I-A). *Intercollegiate sports:* badminton M(c)/W(c), baseball M(s), basketball M(s)/W(s), bowling M(c)/W(c), cheerleading M(s)/W(s), crew M(c)/W(s), cross-country running M(s)/W(s), equestrian sports M(c)/W(c), field hockey W(c), golf M(s)/W(s), gymnastics W(s), ice hockey M(c), lacrosse M(c)/W(c), racquetball M(c)/W(c), rugby M(c)/W(s), soccer M(c)/W(s), softball W(s), swimming and diving M(s)/W(s), table tennis M(c)/W(c), tennis M(s)/W(s), track and field M(s)/W(s), triathlon M(c)/W(c), ultimate Frisbee M(c)/W(c), volleyball M(c)/W(s), water polo M(c), wrestling M(c). *Intramural sports:* basketball M/W, soccer M/W, tennis M/W, ultimate Frisbee M/W, volleyball M/W.

Campus security: 24-hour emergency response devices and patrols, late-night transport/escort service, controlled dormitory access, 24-hour patrols by University of Alabama Police (UAPD), certified law enforcement personnel.

Student services: health clinic, personal/psychological counseling, women's center, legal services.

COSTS & FINANCIAL AID

Costs (2017–18) *Tuition:* state resident $10,780 full-time; nonresident $28,100 full-time. Full-time tuition and fees vary according to course load. Part-time tuition and fees vary according to course load. *Room and board:* $9974; room only: $6300. Room and board charges vary according to board plan, housing facility, and location. *Payment plans:* installment, deferred payment. *Waivers:* employees or children of employees.

Financial Aid Of all full-time matriculated undergraduates who enrolled in 2016, 15,985 applied for aid, 12,599 were judged to have need, 2,597 had their need fully met. 681 Federal Work-Study jobs (averaging $2702). In 2016, 7532 non-need-based awards were made. *Average percent of need met:* 54. *Average financial aid package:* $14,459. *Average need-based loan:* $4303. *Average need-based gift aid:* $12,730. *Average non-need-based aid:* $15,945. *Average indebtedness upon graduation:* $34,305.

APPLYING

Standardized Tests *Required:* SAT or ACT (for admission).

Options: electronic application, early admission.

Application fee: $40.

Required: high school transcript, minimum 3.0 GPA. *Required for some:* essay or personal statement, 2 letters of recommendation, interview.

Application deadlines: 5/1 (freshmen), 3/1 (transfers).

Notification: continuous (freshmen), continuous (transfers).

CONTACT

Dr. Rick Barth, Assistant Vice President for Enrollment Management, The University of Alabama, Box 870132, Tuscaloosa, AL 35487. *Phone:* 205-348-8666. *Toll-free phone:* 800-933-BAMA. *Fax:* 205-348-9046. *E-mail:* admissions@ua.edu.

The University of Alabama at Birmingham

Birmingham, Alabama

http://www.uab.edu/

- **State-supported** university, founded 1969, part of University of Alabama System
- **Urban** 323-acre campus with easy access to Birmingham
- **Endowment** $424.5 million
- **Coed** 13,134 undergraduate students, 74% full-time, 59% women, 41% men
- **Moderately difficult** entrance level, 92% of applicants were admitted

UNDERGRAD STUDENTS

9,677 full-time, 3,457 part-time. Students come from 45 states and territories; 50 other countries; 13% are from out of state; 26% Black or African American, non-Hispanic/Latino; 3% Hispanic/Latino; 6% Asian, non-Hispanic/Latino; 0.3% American Indian or Alaska Native, non-Hispanic/Latino; 4% Two or more races, non-Hispanic/Latino; 0.7% Race/ethnicity unknown; 2% international; 12% transferred in; 22% live on campus.

Freshmen:

Admission: 7,555 applied, 6,936 admitted, 2,299 enrolled. *Average high school GPA:* 3.7. *Test scores:* ACT scores over 18: 100%; ACT scores over 24: 59%; ACT scores over 30: 18%.

Retention: 84% of full-time freshmen returned.

FACULTY

Total: 975, 90% full-time, 85% with terminal degrees.

ACADEMICS

Calendar: semesters. *Degrees:* certificates, bachelor's, master's, doctoral, post-master's, and postbachelor's certificates.

Special study options: academic remediation for entering students, accelerated degree program, adult/continuing education programs, advanced placement credit, cooperative education, distance learning, double majors, English as a second language, freshman honors college, honors programs, independent study, internships, off-campus study, part-time degree program, services for LD students, student-designed majors, study abroad, summer session for credit. *ROTC:* Army (b), Air Force (c).

Unusual degree programs: 3-2 engineering; biology, computer science.

Computers: Students can access the following: campus intranet, computer help desk, free student e-mail accounts, online (class) grades, online (class) registration, online (class) schedules, transcript requests. Campuswide network is available. 100% of college-owned or -operated housing units are wired for high-speed Internet access. Wireless service is available via classrooms, computer centers, computer labs, dorm rooms, learning centers, libraries, student centers.

Library: Mervyn Sterne Library plus 2 others. *Books:* 1.3 million (physical). Students can reserve study rooms.

STUDENT LIFE

Housing options: coed, special housing for students with disabilities. Campus housing is university owned and is provided by a third party. Freshman applicants given priority for college housing.

Activities and organizations: drama/theater group, student-run newspaper, radio station, choral group, marching band, campus ministries, service-oriented groups, sports-affiliated groups, national fraternities, national sororities.

Athletics Member NCAA. All Division I. *Intercollegiate sports:* baseball M(s), basketball M(s)/W(s), bowling W(s), cross-country running W(s), football M(s), golf M(s)/W(s), riflery W(s), soccer M(s)/W(s), softball W(s), tennis M(s)/W(s), track and field W(s), volleyball W(s). *Intramural sports:* badminton M(c)/W(c), basketball M/W, football M/W, lacrosse M(c)/W(c), rugby M(c), soccer M/W, softball M/W, table tennis M(c)/W(c), tennis M(c)/W(c), ultimate Frisbee M/W, wrestling M(c).

Campus security: 24-hour emergency response devices and patrols, late-night transport/escort service, controlled dormitory access.

Student services: health clinic, personal/psychological counseling, women's center.

COSTS & FINANCIAL AID

Costs (2017–18) *Tuition:* state resident $10,410 full-time, $347 per semester hour part-time; nonresident $23,790 full-time, $793 per semester hour part-time. Full-time tuition and fees vary according to course load, degree level, program, and reciprocity agreements. Part-time tuition and fees vary according to course load, degree level, program, and reciprocity agreements. *Required fees:* $225 full-time. *Room and board:* $11,682; room only: $6200. Room and board charges vary according to board plan and housing facility. *Payment plan:* installment. *Waivers:* employees or children of employees.

Financial Aid Of all full-time matriculated undergraduates who enrolled in 2017, 7,091 applied for aid, 5,880 were judged to have need, 625 had their need fully met. In 2017, 1996 non-need-based awards were made. *Average percent of need met:* 50. *Average financial aid package:* $10,787. *Average need-based loan:* $4370. *Average need-based gift aid:* $5250. *Average non-need-based aid:* $7651. *Average indebtedness upon graduation:* $34,872.

APPLYING

Standardized Tests *Required:* SAT or ACT (for admission).

Options: electronic application, early admission, deferred entrance.

Application fee: $30.

Required: high school transcript.

Application deadlines: 6/1 (freshmen), 6/1 (transfers).

Notification: continuous (freshmen), continuous (transfers).

CONTACT

The University of Alabama at Birmingham, 1720 2nd Avenue South, Birmingham, AL 35294. *Toll-free phone:* 800-421-8743.

The University of Alabama in Huntsville

Huntsville, Alabama

http://www.uah.edu/

- **State-supported** university, founded 1950, part of University of Alabama System
- **Suburban** 400-acre campus
- **Endowment** $66.9 million
- **Coed**
- **Moderately difficult** entrance level

FACULTY

Student/faculty ratio: 17:1.

ACADEMICS

Calendar: semesters. *Degrees:* certificates, bachelor's, master's, doctoral, post-master's, and postbachelor's certificates.
Library: Louis Salmon Library. *Books:* 239,503 (physical), 387,481 (digital/electronic); *Serial titles:* 3,441 (physical), 42,868 (digital/electronic); *Databases:* 133.

STUDENT LIFE

Housing options: on-campus residence required through sophomore year; coed, cooperative, special housing for students with disabilities. Campus housing is university owned. Freshman campus housing is guaranteed.

Activities and organizations: drama/theater group, student-run newspaper, choral group, Student Government Association, Student Run Sports, International Student Association, CRU, Blue Crew, national fraternities, national sororities.

Athletics Member NCAA. All Division II except ice hockey (Division I).

Campus security: 24-hour emergency response devices and patrols, late-night transport/escort service, controlled dormitory access, 24/7 dispatch center, community policing efforts.

Student services: health clinic, personal/psychological counseling.

COSTS & FINANCIAL AID

Costs (2017–18) *Tuition:* state resident $9356 full-time, $411 per credit hour part-time; nonresident $20,556 full-time, $908 per credit hour part-time. Full-time tuition and fees vary according to course load and program. Part-time tuition and fees vary according to course load and program. *Required fees:* $924 full-time. *Room and board:* $9748; room only: $6608. Room and board charges vary according to board plan and housing facility.

Financial Aid Of all full-time matriculated undergraduates who enrolled in 2016, 5,231 applied for aid, 2,650 were judged to have need, 456 had their need fully met. 66 Federal Work-Study jobs (averaging $3904). In 2016, 1403 non-need-based awards were made. *Average percent of need met:* 61. *Average financial aid package:* $10,713. *Average need-based loan:* $7218. *Average need-based gift aid:* $7486. *Average non-need-based aid:* $8507. *Average indebtedness upon graduation:* $35,009. *Financial aid deadline:* 7/31.

APPLYING

Standardized Tests *Required:* SAT or ACT (for admission).

Options: electronic application, deferred entrance.

Application fee: $30.

Required: high school transcript.

CONTACT

Ms. Peggy Masters, Director of Undergraduate Admissions, The University of Alabama in Huntsville, Enrollment Services, 301 Sparkman Drive, Huntsville, AL 35899. *Phone:* 256-824-2771. *Toll-free phone:* 800-UAH-CALL. *Fax:* 256-824-4539. *E-mail:* uahadmissions@uah.edu.

University of Mobile

Mobile, Alabama

http://www.umobile.edu/

- **Independent Southern Baptist** comprehensive, founded 1961
- **Suburban** 880-acre campus
- **Endowment** $23.2 million
- **Coed** 1,443 undergraduate students, 80% full-time, 64% women, 36% men
- **Moderately difficult** entrance level, 62% of applicants were admitted

UNDERGRAD STUDENTS

1,152 full-time, 291 part-time. Students come from 30 states and territories; 21 other countries; 18% are from out of state; 19% Black or African American, non-Hispanic/Latino; 2% Hispanic/Latino; 1% Asian, non-Hispanic/Latino; 0.1% Native Hawaiian or other Pacific Islander, non-Hispanic/Latino; 1% American Indian or Alaska Native, non-Hispanic/Latino; 3% Two or more races, non-Hispanic/Latino; 12% Race/ethnicity unknown; 3% international; 7% transferred in; 45% live on campus.

Freshmen:

Admission: 935 applied, 579 admitted, 228 enrolled. *Average high school GPA:* 3.6. *Test scores:* SAT evidence-based reading and writing scores over 500: 64%; SAT math scores over 500: 50%; ACT scores over 18: 95%; SAT evidence-based reading and writing scores over 600: 10%; SAT math scores over 600: 18%; ACT scores over 24: 37%; SAT evidence-based reading and writing scores over 700: 5%; ACT scores over 30: 7%.

Retention: 69% of full-time freshmen returned.

FACULTY

Total: 172, 42% full-time, 41% with terminal degrees.

Student/faculty ratio: 14:1.

ACADEMICS

Calendar: semesters. *Degrees:* associate, bachelor's, and master's.

Special study options: academic remediation for entering students, accelerated degree program, adult/continuing education programs, advanced placement credit, distance learning, double majors, honors programs, independent study, internships, part-time degree program, services for LD students, summer session for credit. *ROTC:* Army (c), Air Force (c).

Unusual degree programs: 3-2 engineering with University of South Alabama.

Computers: 100 computers/terminals are available on campus for general student use. Students can access the following: campus intranet, computer help desk, free student e-mail accounts, online (class) grades, online (class) registration, online (class) schedules. Campuswide network is available. 100% of college-owned or -operated housing units are wired for high-speed Internet access. Wireless service is available via entire campus.
Library: J. L. Bedsole Library. *Books:* 66,089 (physical), 157,420 (digital/electronic); *Serial titles:* 153 (physical), 151,115 (digital/electronic); *Databases:* 80.

STUDENT LIFE

Housing options: on-campus residence required through sophomore year; men-only, women-only. Campus housing is university owned. Freshman campus housing is guaranteed.

Activities and organizations: drama/theater group, choral group, Campus Activity Board, Campus Ministry, Student Government Association, Student Nurse Organization.

Athletics Member NAIA. *Intercollegiate sports:* baseball M(s), basketball M(s)/W(s), cheerleading M/W(s), cross-country running M(s)/W(s), golf M(s)/W(s), soccer M(s)/W(s), softball W(s), tennis M(s)/W(s), track and field M(s)/W(s), volleyball W(s). *Intramural sports:* basketball M/W, golf M/W, soccer M/W, softball M/W, tennis M/W, track and field M/W, volleyball M/W.

Campus security: 24-hour emergency response devices and patrols, controlled dormitory access, text alerts.

Student services: personal/psychological counseling.

COSTS & FINANCIAL AID

Costs (2017–18) *Comprehensive fee:* $31,810 includes full-time tuition ($21,010), mandatory fees ($1200), and room and board ($9600). Full-time tuition and fees vary according to course load and program. Part-time tuition: $750 per credit hour. Part-time tuition and fees vary according to course load and program. *Required fees:* $400 per credit hour part-time. *College room only:* $5400. Room and board charges vary according to board plan and housing facility. *Payment plan:* installment. *Waivers:* employees or children of employees.

Financial Aid Of all full-time matriculated undergraduates who enrolled in 2016, 970 applied for aid, 888 were judged to have need, 887 had their need fully met. 55 Federal Work-Study jobs (averaging $1575). In 2016, 163 non-need-based awards were made. *Average percent of need met:* 66. *Average financial aid package:* $17,739. *Average need-based loan:* $2175. *Average need-based gift aid:* $5279. *Average non-need-based aid:* $10,158. *Average indebtedness upon graduation:* $30,029.

APPLYING

Standardized Tests *Required:* SAT or ACT (for admission).

Options: electronic application, deferred entrance.

Application fee: $25.

Required: high school transcript, minimum 2.8 GPA.

Application deadlines: rolling (freshmen), rolling (transfers).

Notification: continuous (freshmen), continuous (transfers).

CONTACT

Mrs. Hali Givens, Director of Enrollment, University of Mobile, 5735 College Parkway, Mobile, AL 36613-2842. *Phone:* 251-442-2222. *Toll-free phone:* 800-946-7267. *E-mail:* hgivens@umobile.edu.

University of Montevallo

Montevallo, Alabama

http://www.montevallo.edu/

- **State-supported** comprehensive, founded 1896
- **Small-town** 160-acre campus with easy access to Birmingham
- **Endowment** $19.1 million
- **Coed** 2,346 undergraduate students, 90% full-time, 67% women, 33% men
- **Moderately difficult** entrance level, 67% of applicants were admitted

UNDERGRAD STUDENTS

2,101 full-time, 245 part-time. Students come from 33 states and territories; 29 other countries; 16% Black or African American, non-Hispanic/Latino; 5% Hispanic/Latino; 0.9% Asian, non-Hispanic/Latino; 0.3% American Indian or Alaska Native, non-Hispanic/Latino; 3% Two or more races, non-Hispanic/Latino; 3% Race/ethnicity unknown; 2% international; 48% live on campus.

Freshmen:

Admission: 1,868 applied, 1,245 admitted, 487 enrolled. *Average high school GPA:* 3.4. *Test scores:* ACT scores over 18: 98%; ACT scores over 24: 48%; ACT scores over 30: 10%.

Retention: 78% of full-time freshmen returned.

FACULTY

Total: 221, 69% full-time, 73% with terminal degrees.

Student/faculty ratio: 14:1.

ACADEMICS

Calendar: semesters. *Degrees:* bachelor's, master's, and post-master's certificates.

Special study options: academic remediation for entering students, accelerated degree program, advanced placement credit, distance learning, double majors, honors programs, independent study, internships, part-time degree program, services for LD students, study abroad, summer session for credit. *ROTC:* Army (c), Air Force (c).

Unusual degree programs: 3-2 engineering with Auburn University, University of Alabama at Birmingham.

Computers: 340 computers/terminals are available on campus for general student use. Students can access the following: campus intranet, computer help desk, free student e-mail accounts, online (class) grades, online (class) registration, online (class) schedules. Campuswide network is available. 100% of college-owned or -operated housing units are wired for high-speed Internet access. Wireless service is available via classrooms, computer centers, computer labs, dorm rooms, libraries, student centers. **Library:** Carmichael Library. Students can reserve study rooms.

STUDENT LIFE

Housing options: on-campus residence required for freshman year; coed, men-only, women-only. Campus housing is university owned. Freshman campus housing is guaranteed.

Activities and organizations: drama/theater group, student-run newspaper, television station, choral group, Student Government Association, University Programming Council, Campus Ministries, Greek Life, Environmental Club, national fraternities, national sororities.

Athletics Member NCAA. All Division II. *Intercollegiate sports:* baseball M(s), basketball M(s)/W(s), cheerleading W, cross-country running M/W, golf M(s)/W(s), lacrosse M/W, soccer M(s)/W(s), softball W, tennis M/W(s), track and field M/W, volleyball W(s). *Intramural sports:* basketball M/W, bowling M, football M, golf M, tennis M/W, volleyball M/W.

Campus security: 24-hour emergency response devices and patrols, late-night transport/escort service, controlled dormitory access.

Student services: health clinic, personal/psychological counseling.

COSTS & FINANCIAL AID

Costs (2017–18) *Tuition:* state resident $11,730 full-time, $391 per credit hour part-time; nonresident $24,360 full-time, $812 per credit hour part-time. *Required fees:* $670 full-time. *Room and board:* $7512; room only: $4762. Room and board charges vary according to housing facility. *Payment plan:* installment. *Waivers:* employees or children of employees.

Financial Aid Of all full-time matriculated undergraduates who enrolled in 2017, 1,630 applied for aid, 1,422 were judged to have need, 253 had their need fully met. 111 Federal Work-Study jobs (averaging $1828). In 2017, 488 non-need-based awards were made. *Average percent of need met:* 57. *Average financial aid package:* $12,058. *Average need-based loan:* $3993. *Average need-based gift aid:* $9413. *Average non-need-based aid:* $11,534. *Average indebtedness upon graduation:* $34,408.

APPLYING

Standardized Tests *Required:* SAT or ACT (for admission).

Options: electronic application, early admission, deferred entrance.

Application fee: $30.

Required: high school transcript, minimum 2.0 GPA. *Recommended:* interview.

Application deadlines: 8/15 (freshmen), rolling (transfers).

Notification: 9/1 (freshmen).

CONTACT

Audrey Crawford, Director of Admissions, University of Montevallo, University of Montevallo, Office of Admissions, Station 6030, Montevallo, AL 35115-6030. *Phone:* 205-665-6030. *Toll-free phone:* 800-292-4349. *Fax:* 205-665-6032. *E-mail:* admissions@montevallo.edu.

University of North Alabama
Florence, Alabama
http://www.una.edu/

- **State-supported** comprehensive, founded 1830
- **Urban** 200-acre campus with easy access to Huntsville
- **Endowment** $32.6 million
- **Coed** 6,221 undergraduate students, 83% full-time, 59% women, 41% men
- **Minimally difficult** entrance level, 70% of applicants were admitted

UNDERGRAD STUDENTS
5,150 full-time, 1,071 part-time. Students come from 42 states and territories; 38 other countries; 17% are from out of state; 15% Black or African American, non-Hispanic/Latino; 3% Hispanic/Latino; 0.6% Asian, non-Hispanic/Latino; 0.1% Native Hawaiian or other Pacific Islander, non-Hispanic/Latino; 0.9% American Indian or Alaska Native, non-Hispanic/Latino; 3% Two or more races, non-Hispanic/Latino; 2% Race/ethnicity unknown; 3% international; 10% transferred in; 29% live on campus.

Freshmen:
Admission: 3,969 applied, 2,787 admitted, 1,128 enrolled. *Average high school GPA:* 3.4. *Test scores:* SAT evidence-based reading and writing scores over 500: 80%; SAT math scores over 500: 44%; ACT scores over 18: 87%; SAT evidence-based reading and writing scores over 600: 36%; SAT math scores over 600: 16%; ACT scores over 24: 35%; SAT math scores over 700: 4%; ACT scores over 30: 5%.
Retention: 76% of full-time freshmen returned.

FACULTY
Total: 429, 62% full-time, 58% with terminal degrees.
Student/faculty ratio: 19:1.

ACADEMICS
Calendar: semesters. *Degrees:* bachelor's, master's, post-master's, and postbachelor's certificates.

Special study options: academic remediation for entering students, accelerated degree program, advanced placement credit, cooperative education, distance learning, double majors, English as a second language, external degree program, honors programs, independent study, internships, off-campus study, part-time degree program, services for LD students, student-designed majors, study abroad, summer session for credit. *ROTC:* Army (b).

Unusual degree programs: 3-2 business administration; engineering with The University of Alabama; nursing; social work.

Computers: 925 computers/terminals are available on campus for general student use. Students can access the following: campus intranet, computer help desk, free student e-mail accounts, online (class) grades, online (class) registration, online (class) schedules. Campuswide network is available. 100% of college-owned or -operated housing units are wired for high-speed Internet access. Wireless service is available via entire campus.

Library: Collier Library plus 3 others. *Books:* 225,076 (physical), 469,260 (digital/electronic); *Serial titles:* 4,070 (physical), 55,929 (digital/electronic); *Databases:* 182. Weekly public service hours: 98; students can reserve study rooms.

STUDENT LIFE
Housing options: on-campus residence required for freshman year; coed, men-only, women-only. Campus housing is university owned and is provided by a third party. Freshman campus housing is guaranteed.

Activities and organizations: drama/theater group, student-run newspaper, choral group, marching band, Phi Mu, Alpha Gamma Delta, Zeta Tau Alpha, Alpha Delta Pi, Student Government Association, national fraternities, national sororities.

Athletics Member NCAA. All Division II. *Intercollegiate sports:* baseball M(s), basketball M(s)/W(s), cheerleading M(s)/W(s), cross-country running M(s)/W(s), football M(s), golf M(s), soccer W(s), softball W(s), tennis M(s)/W(s), track and field W(s), volleyball W(s). *Intramural sports:* badminton M/W, basketball M/W, bowling M/W, equestrian sports W, football M/W, rugby M, soccer M/W, swimming and diving M/W, table tennis M/W, ultimate Frisbee M/W, volleyball M/W, weight lifting M/W.

Campus security: 24-hour emergency response devices and patrols, student patrols, late-night transport/escort service, controlled dormitory access.

Student services: health clinic, personal/psychological counseling, women's center.

COSTS & FINANCIAL AID
Costs (2017–18) *Tuition:* state resident $8310 full-time, $277 per credit hour part-time; nonresident $16,620 full-time, $554 per credit hour part-time. Full-time tuition and fees vary according to course load, program, and student level. Part-time tuition and fees vary according to course load and program. *Required fees:* $2060 full-time, $238 per credit hour part-time. *Room and board:* $7684. Room and board charges vary according to board plan, housing facility, and student level. *Payment plan:* installment. *Waivers:* senior citizens and employees or children of employees.

Financial Aid Of all full-time matriculated undergraduates who enrolled in 2017, 3,958 applied for aid, 3,911 were judged to have need, 144 had their need fully met. In 2017, 427 non-need-based awards were made. *Average percent of need met:* 50. *Average financial aid package:* $8629. *Average need-based loan:* $3852. *Average need-based gift aid:* $3677. *Average non-need-based aid:* $2870.

APPLYING
Standardized Tests *Required:* SAT or ACT (for admission).

Options: electronic application, early admission, deferred entrance.

Application fee: $35.

Required: high school transcript, minimum 2.0 GPA, 13 approved units from high school academic core.

Application deadlines: rolling (freshmen), rolling (transfers).

Notification: continuous (freshmen), continuous (transfers).

CONTACT
Mrs. Julie Taylor, Interim Director of Admissions, University of North Alabama, One Harrison Plaza, Florence, AL 35632-0001. *Phone:* 256-765-4680. *Toll-free phone:* 800-TALK-UNA. *Fax:* 256-765-4329. *E-mail:* admissions@una.edu.

University of South Alabama
Mobile, Alabama
http://www.southalabama.edu/

- **State-supported** university, founded 1963
- **Suburban** 1225-acre campus
- **Endowment** $147.1 million
- **Coed** 10,988 undergraduate students, 83% full-time, 57% women, 43% men
- **Moderately difficult** entrance level, 81% of applicants were admitted

UNDERGRAD STUDENTS
9,090 full-time, 1,898 part-time. Students come from 42 states and territories; 69 other countries; 18% are from out of state; 22% Black or African American, non-Hispanic/Latino; 3% Hispanic/Latino; 3% Asian, non-Hispanic/Latino; 0.1% Native Hawaiian or other Pacific Islander, non-Hispanic/Latino; 0.7% American Indian or Alaska Native, non-Hispanic/Latino; 3% Two or more races, non-Hispanic/Latino; 2% Race/ethnicity unknown; 6% international; 6% transferred in; 29% live on campus.

Freshmen:
Admission: 6,035 applied, 4,911 admitted, 1,886 enrolled. *Average high school GPA:* 3.6. *Test scores:* SAT math scores over 500: 76%; ACT scores over 18: 99%; SAT math scores over 600: 21%; ACT scores over 24: 45%; SAT math scores over 700: 3%; ACT scores over 30: 9%.
Retention: 78% of full-time freshmen returned.

FACULTY
Total: 1,033, 58% full-time, 60% with terminal degrees.
Student/faculty ratio: 18:1.

ACADEMICS
Calendar: semesters. *Degrees:* certificates, bachelor's, master's, doctoral, post-master's, and postbachelor's certificates.

Special study options: academic remediation for entering students, accelerated degree program, adult/continuing education programs, advanced placement credit, cooperative education, distance learning, double majors, English as a second language, freshman honors college, honors programs, independent study, internships, part-time degree program, services for LD students, student-designed majors, study abroad, summer session for credit. *ROTC:* Army (b), Air Force (b).

Computers: Students can access the following: campus intranet, computer help desk, free student e-mail accounts, online (class) grades, online (class) registration, online (class) schedules. Campuswide network is available. 100% of college-owned or -operated housing units are wired for high-speed Internet access. Wireless service is available via entire campus.

Library: Marx Library plus 5 others. *Books:* 690,889 (physical), 40,397 (digital/electronic); *Serial titles:* 4,343 (physical), 1.2 million (digital/electronic); *Databases:* 669.

STUDENT LIFE

Housing options: coed, special housing for students with disabilities. Campus housing is university owned and is provided by a third party.

Activities and organizations: drama/theater group, student-run newspaper, radio and television station, choral group, marching band, Student Government Association, African American Student Association, Council of International Student Organizations, Alpha Epsilon Delta Pre-Health Professions, Panhellenic Council, national fraternities, national sororities.

Athletics Member NCAA. All Division I. *Intercollegiate sports:* baseball M(s), basketball M(s)/W(s), cross-country running M(s)/W(s), football M(s), golf M(s)/W(s), soccer W(s), softball W(s), tennis M(s)/W(s), track and field M(s)/W(s), volleyball W(s). *Intramural sports:* basketball M/W, cheerleading M(c)/W(c), football M(c)/W(c), rock climbing M(c)/W(c), rugby M(c)/W(c), sailing M(c)/W(c), sand volleyball M(c)/W(c), soccer M/W, softball M/W, ultimate Frisbee M(c)/W(c), volleyball M/W, water polo M/W.

Campus security: 24-hour emergency response devices and patrols, late-night transport/escort service.

Student services: health clinic, personal/psychological counseling, women's center, legal services.

COSTS & FINANCIAL AID

Costs (2017–18) *Tuition:* state resident $9390 full-time, $313 per credit hour part-time; nonresident $18,780 full-time, $626 per credit hour part-time. Full-time tuition and fees vary according to course load and program. Part-time tuition and fees vary according to course load and program. *Room and board:* $7490; room only: $3980. Room and board charges vary according to board plan and housing facility. *Payment plan:* installment. *Waivers:* employees or children of employees.

Financial Aid Of all full-time matriculated undergraduates who enrolled in 2015, 7,167 applied for aid, 5,829 were judged to have need, 487 had their need fully met. In 2015, 1146 non-need-based awards were made. *Average percent of need met:* 50. *Average financial aid package:* $9708. *Average need-based loan:* $4348. *Average need-based gift aid:* $6606. *Average non-need-based aid:* $5321.

APPLYING

Standardized Tests *Required for some:* SAT or ACT (for admission).

Options: electronic application, early admission, deferred entrance.

Application fee: $45.

Required: high school transcript. *Required for some:* essay or personal statement, minimum 3.5 GPA, 1 letter of recommendation, minimum high school GPA of 3.0 for Accelerated College Enrollment Program, minimum high school GPA of 3.5 for Early Admission. *Recommended:* minimum 2.5 GPA.

Application deadlines: 7/15 (freshmen), 7/15 (transfers).

Notification: continuous (freshmen), continuous (out-of-state freshmen), continuous (transfers).

CONTACT

Ms. Kristin Odom, Director, New Student Recruitment, University of South Alabama, 390 Alumni Circle, 2500 Meisler Hall, Mobile, AL 36688-0002. *Phone:* 251-460-7834. *Toll-free phone:* 800-872-5247. *Fax:* 251-460-7876. *E-mail:* recruitment@southalabama.edu.

The University of West Alabama
Livingston, Alabama
http://www.uwa.edu/

- **State-supported** comprehensive, founded 1835
- **Small-town** 514-acre campus
- **Endowment** $43,733
- **Coed** 2,111 undergraduate students, 87% full-time, 55% women, 45% men
- **Minimally difficult** entrance level, 28% of applicants were admitted

UNDERGRAD STUDENTS

1,843 full-time, 268 part-time. Students come from 30 states and territories; 28 other countries; 20% are from out of state; 44% Black or African American, non-Hispanic/Latino; 2% Hispanic/Latino; 0.2% Asian, non-Hispanic/Latino; 0.3% American Indian or Alaska Native, non-Hispanic/Latino; 3% Two or more races, non-Hispanic/Latino; 3% Race/ethnicity unknown; 5% international; 13% transferred in; 43% live on campus.

Freshmen:
Admission: 7,388 applied, 2,084 admitted, 461 enrolled. *Test scores:* ACT scores over 18: 79%; ACT scores over 24: 19%; ACT scores over 30: 1%.
Retention: 67% of full-time freshmen returned.

FACULTY
Total: 277, 47% full-time, 62% with terminal degrees.
Student/faculty ratio: 13:1.

ACADEMICS

Calendar: semesters. *Degrees:* certificates, associate, bachelor's, master's, and post-master's certificates.

Special study options: academic remediation for entering students, accelerated degree program, advanced placement credit, cooperative education, distance learning, double majors, English as a second language, freshman honors college, honors programs, independent study, internships, part-time degree program, services for LD students, student-designed majors, study abroad, summer session for credit. *ROTC:* Air Force (c).

Unusual degree programs: 3-2 engineering with Auburn University, The University of Alabama at Birmingham, Mississippi State University, The University of Alabama; forestry with Auburn University; social work with University of Alabama; wildlife with Auburn University.

Computers: 600 computers/terminals are available on campus for general student use. Students can access the following: campus intranet, computer help desk, free student e-mail accounts, online (class) grades, online (class) registration, online (class) schedules. Campuswide network is available. 100% of college-owned or -operated housing units are wired for high-speed Internet access. Wireless service is available via entire campus.

Library: Julia Tutwiler Library plus 1 other. *Books:* 201,627 (physical), 2,121 (digital/electronic); *Serial titles:* 2,093 (physical), 108,952 (digital/electronic); *Databases:* 174. Weekly public service hours: 94; students can reserve study rooms.

STUDENT LIFE

Housing options: on-campus residence required for freshman year; coed. Campus housing is university owned. Freshman campus housing is guaranteed.

Activities and organizations: drama/theater group, student-run newspaper, television station, choral group, marching band, The UWA Band, The Student Government Association, UWA Ambassadors, Phi Mu, Blue Key, national fraternities, national sororities.

Athletics Member NCAA. All Division II. *Intercollegiate sports:* baseball M(s), basketball M(s)/W(s), cross-country running M(s)/W(s), football M(s), golf M(s)/W(s), soccer M(s)/W(s), softball W(s), tennis M(s)/W(s), track and field M(s)/W(s), triathlon W(s), volleyball W(s). *Intramural sports:* badminton M/W, football M/W, soccer M/W, table tennis M/W, tennis M/W, ultimate Frisbee M/W, volleyball M/W.

Campus security: 24-hour emergency response devices and patrols, student patrols, late-night transport/escort service, controlled dormitory access.

Student services: health clinic, personal/psychological counseling.

COSTS & FINANCIAL AID

Costs (2017–18) *Tuition:* state resident $7614 full-time, $324 per hour part-time; nonresident $15,228 full-time, $648 per hour part-time. Full-time tuition and fees vary according to course load. Part-time tuition and fees vary according to course load. *Required fees:* $1590 full-time. *Room and board:* $7080; room only: $4480. Room and board charges vary according to board plan, housing facility, and student level. *Payment plan:* installment. *Waivers:* employees or children of employees.

Financial Aid Of all full-time matriculated undergraduates who enrolled in 2016, 1,490 applied for aid, 1,297 were judged to have need, 97 had their need fully met. 73 Federal Work-Study jobs (averaging $3338). In 2016, 70 non-need-based awards were made. *Average percent of need met:* 21. *Average financial aid package:* $10,427. *Average need-based gift aid:* $4812. *Average non-need-based aid:* $5456. *Average indebtedness upon graduation:* $25,114.

APPLYING

Standardized Tests *Required:* SAT or ACT (for admission).

Options: electronic application, deferred entrance.

Application fee: $40.

Required: high school transcript, minimum 2.0 GPA.

Application deadlines: rolling (freshmen), rolling (transfers).

Notification: continuous (freshmen), continuous (transfers).

CONTACT

Mrs. Brenda Edwards, Coordinator of Admissions Operations, The University of West Alabama, Station 4, Livingston, AL 35470. *Phone:* 205-652-3699. *Toll-free phone:* 888-636-8800. *Fax:* 205-652-3881. *E-mail:* belliott@uwa.edu.

Virginia College in Birmingham

Birmingham, Alabama

http://www.vc.edu/

CONTACT

Director of Admissions, Virginia College in Birmingham, 488 Palisades Boulevard, Birmingham, AL 35209. *Phone:* 205-802-1200.

Virginia College in Huntsville

Huntsville, Alabama

http://www.vc.edu/

CONTACT

Director of Admission, Virginia College in Huntsville, 2021 Drake Avenue SW, Huntsville, AL 35801. *Phone:* 256-533-7387. *Fax:* 256-533-7785.

ALASKA

Alaska Bible College

Palmer, Alaska

http://www.akbible.edu/

- **Independent nondenominational** 4-year, founded 1966
- **Small-town** 2-acre campus with easy access to Anchorage, AK
- **Coed** 50 undergraduate students, 58% full-time, 32% women, 68% men
- **Minimally difficult** entrance level

UNDERGRAD STUDENTS

29 full-time, 21 part-time. Students come from 7 states and territories; 2 other countries; 10% are from out of state; 2% Black or African American, non-Hispanic/Latino; 4% Hispanic/Latino; 4% American Indian or Alaska Native, non-Hispanic/Latino; 4% Two or more races, non-Hispanic/Latino; 40% transferred in; 25% live on campus.

Freshmen:

Admission: 6 enrolled.

Retention: 20% of full-time freshmen returned.

FACULTY

Total: 12, 25% full-time, 8% with terminal degrees.

Student/faculty ratio: 4:1.

ACADEMICS

Calendar: semesters. *Degrees:* certificates, associate, and bachelor's.

Special study options: academic remediation for entering students, advanced placement credit, distance learning, double majors, independent study, internships, off-campus study, part-time degree program.

Computers: 2 computers/terminals are available on campus for general student use. Students can access the following: campus intranet, computer help desk, free student e-mail accounts, online (class) grades, online (class) registration, online (class) schedules. Campuswide network is available. 4% of college-owned or -operated housing units are wired for high-speed Internet access. Wireless service is available via entire campus. **Library:** Alaska Bible College Ball Memorial Library. *Books:* 32,000 (physical); *Serial titles:* 46 (physical). Weekly public service hours: 40.

STUDENT LIFE

Housing options: men-only, women-only. Campus housing is university owned. Freshman applicants given priority for college housing.

COSTS

Costs (2018–19) *Comprehensive fee:* $15,300 includes full-time tuition ($9000), mandatory fees ($600), and room and board ($5700). Part-time tuition: $375 per credit hour. *Required fees:* $50 per term part-time. *Payment plan:* installment. *Waivers:* employees or children of employees.

APPLYING

Standardized Tests *Required:* SAT or ACT (for admission).

Options: electronic application, deferred entrance.

Application fee: $35.

Required: essay or personal statement, high school transcript, minimum 2.0 GPA, 3 letters of recommendation.

Application deadlines: 7/1 (freshmen), 7/1 (transfers).

Notification: continuous until 7/15 (freshmen), continuous until 7/15 (transfers).

CONTACT

Justin Archuletta, Director of Admissions, Alaska Bible College, 248 E. Elmwood Avenue, Palmer, AK 99645. *Phone:* 907-745-3201 Ext. 111. *Toll-free phone:* 800-478-7884. *Fax:* 907-745-3210. *E-mail:* admissions@akbible.edu.

Alaska Pacific University

Anchorage, Alaska

http://www.alaskapacific.edu/

- **Independent** comprehensive, founded 1959
- **Urban** 170-acre campus
- **Coed** 294 undergraduate students, 71% full-time, 63% women, 37% men
- **Minimally difficult** entrance level, 55% of applicants were admitted

UNDERGRAD STUDENTS

209 full-time, 85 part-time. Students come from 2 other countries; 4% Black or African American, non-Hispanic/Latino; 1% Hispanic/Latino; 3% Asian, non-Hispanic/Latino; 0.7% Native Hawaiian or other Pacific Islander, non-Hispanic/Latino; 14% American Indian or Alaska Native, non-Hispanic/Latino; 12% Two or more races, non-Hispanic/Latino; 10% Race/ethnicity unknown; 19% transferred in; 26% live on campus.

Freshmen:

Admission: 474 applied, 261 admitted, 41 enrolled. *Average high school GPA:* 3.2.

Retention: 46% of full-time freshmen returned.

FACULTY

Total: 82, 34% full-time, 34% with terminal degrees.

Student/faculty ratio: 10:1.

ACADEMICS

Calendar: semesters. *Degrees:* certificates, associate, bachelor's, master's, doctoral, and postbachelor's certificates.

Special study options: academic remediation for entering students, accelerated degree program, adult/continuing education programs, advanced placement credit, distance learning, double majors, independent study, internships, part-time degree program, services for LD students, student-designed majors, study abroad, summer session for credit. *ROTC:* Air Force (c).

Unusual degree programs: 3-2 environmental science.

Computers: 105 computers/terminals and 480 ports are available on campus for general student use. Students can access the following: campus intranet, computer help desk, free student e-mail accounts, online (class) grades, online (class) registration, online (class) schedules. Campuswide network is available. 100% of college-owned or -operated housing units are wired for high-speed Internet access. Wireless service is available via entire campus.

Library: Consortium Library. Students can reserve study rooms.

STUDENT LIFE

Housing options: on-campus residence required through sophomore year; coed. Campus housing is university owned. Freshman campus housing is guaranteed.

Activities and organizations: drama/theater group, student-run newspaper, choral group, ASAPU (Associated Students of Alaska Pacific University), Photography Club, Dive Club, Basketball club, Spectrum Club.

Athletics *Intramural sports:* basketball M/W, skiing (cross-country) M/W, soccer M/W, volleyball M/W.

Campus security: 24-hour emergency response devices, student patrols, late-night transport/escort service, controlled dormitory access.

Student services: personal/psychological counseling.

COSTS & FINANCIAL AID

Costs (2018–19) *Comprehensive fee:* $29,060 includes full-time tuition ($20,350), mandatory fees ($480), and room and board ($8230). Full-time tuition and fees vary according to course load, degree level, program, and reciprocity agreements. Part-time tuition and fees vary according to course load, degree level, and program. *Room and board:* Room and board charges vary according to board plan and housing facility. *Payment plans:* installment, deferred payment. *Waivers:* employees or children of employees.

Financial Aid Of all full-time matriculated undergraduates who enrolled in 2015, 147 applied for aid, 129 were judged to have need, 30 had their need fully met. In 2015, 36 non-need-based awards were made. *Average percent of need met:* 39. *Average financial aid package:* $10,522. *Average need-based loan:* $4128. *Average need-based gift aid:* $5973. *Average non-need-based aid:* $4635. *Average indebtedness upon graduation:* $8922.

APPLYING

Options: electronic application, deferred entrance.

Application fee: $25.

Required: high school transcript, minimum 2.5 GPA.

Application deadlines: 8/1 (freshmen), 8/1 (transfers).

Notification: continuous (freshmen), continuous (out-of-state freshmen), continuous (transfers).

CONTACT

Alaska Pacific University, 4101 University Drive, Anchorage, AK 99508-4672. *Toll-free phone:* 800-252-7528.

Charter College

Anchorage, Alaska

http://www.chartercollege.edu/

CONTACT

Ms. Lily Sirianni, Vice President, Charter College, 2221 East Northern Lights Boulevard, Suite 120, Anchorage, AK 99508. *Phone:* 907-277-1000. *Toll-free phone:* 888-200-9942.

University of Alaska Anchorage

Anchorage, Alaska

http://www.uaa.alaska.edu/

CONTACT

Enrollment Services, University of Alaska Anchorage, PO Box 141629, 3901 Old Seward Highway, Anchorage, AK 99508-8046. *Phone:* 907-786-1480. *Fax:* 907-786-4888. *E-mail:* enroll@uaa.alaska.edu.

University of Alaska Anchorage, Kenai Peninsula College

Soldotna, Alaska

http://www.kpc.alaska.edu/

CONTACT

Mrs. Julie Cotterell, Admission and Student Records Coordinator, University of Alaska Anchorage, Kenai Peninsula College, 156 College Road, Soldotna, AK 99669-9798. *Phone:* 907-262-0311. *Toll-free phone:* 877-262-0330. *E-mail:* jmcotterell@kpc.alaska.edu.

University of Alaska Fairbanks

Fairbanks, Alaska

http://www.uaf.edu/

- **State-supported** university, founded 1917, part of University of Alaska System
- **Small-town** 2250-acre campus
- **Endowment** $98.9 million
- **Coed** 6,718 undergraduate students, 45% full-time, 58% women, 42% men
- **Minimally difficult** entrance level, 77% of applicants were admitted

UNDERGRAD STUDENTS

3,022 full-time, 3,696 part-time. Students come from 51 states and territories; 32 other countries; 14% are from out of state; 3% Black or African American, non-Hispanic/Latino; 7% Hispanic/Latino; 2% Asian, non-Hispanic/Latino; 0.5% Native Hawaiian or other Pacific Islander, non-Hispanic/Latino; 14% American Indian or Alaska Native, non-Hispanic/Latino; 8% Two or more races, non-Hispanic/Latino; 15% Race/ethnicity unknown; 1% international; 5% transferred in; 36% live on campus.

Freshmen:

Admission: 1,631 applied, 1,251 admitted, 804 enrolled. *Average high school GPA:* 3.3. *Test scores:* SAT evidence-based reading and writing scores over 500: 80%; SAT math scores over 500: 83%; ACT scores over 18: 75%; SAT evidence-based reading and writing scores over 600: 47%; SAT math scores over 600: 38%; ACT scores over 24: 36%; SAT evidence-based reading and writing scores over 700: 11%; SAT math scores over 700: 8%; ACT scores over 30: 8%.

Retention: 77% of full-time freshmen returned.

FACULTY

Total: 831, 58% full-time, 54% with terminal degrees.

Student/faculty ratio: 8:1.

ACADEMICS

Calendar: semesters. *Degrees:* certificates, associate, bachelor's, master's, doctoral, and postbachelor's certificates.

Special study options: academic remediation for entering students, accelerated degree program, advanced placement credit, cooperative education, distance learning, double majors, English as a second language, external degree program, honors programs, independent study, internships, off-campus study, part-time degree program, services for LD students, student-designed majors, study abroad, summer session for credit. *ROTC:* Army (b).

Unusual degree programs: 3-2 engineering; computer science.

Computers: 125 computers/terminals and 22 ports are available on campus for general student use. Students can access the following: campus intranet, computer help desk, free student e-mail accounts, online (class) grades, online (class) registration, online (class) schedules, university portal. Campuswide network is available. 100% of college-owned or -operated housing units are wired for high-speed Internet access. Wireless service is available via entire campus.

Library: Rasmuson Library plus 1 other. *Books:* 533,679 (physical), 324,260 (digital/electronic); *Serial titles:* 222,847 (physical), 30,490 (digital/electronic); *Databases:* 175. Weekly public service hours: 87; students can reserve study rooms.

STUDENT LIFE

Housing options: coed, special housing for students with disabilities. Campus housing is university owned. Freshman applicants given priority for college housing.

Activities and organizations: drama/theater group, student-run newspaper, radio station, choral group, Chi Alpha, Yoga Club, Aurora Aerial Arts, Festival of Native Arts, Gender and Sexuality Alliance.

Athletics Member NCAA. All Division II except ice hockey (Division I). *Intercollegiate sports:* basketball M(s)/W(s), cross-country running M(s)/W(s), ice hockey M(s), riflery M(s)/W(s), skiing (cross-country) M(s)/W(s), swimming and diving W(s), volleyball W(s). *Intramural sports:* badminton M(c)/W(c), basketball M/W, cross-country running M(c)/W(c), fencing M(c)/W(c), ice hockey M/W, soccer M/W, ultimate Frisbee M/W, volleyball M/W.

Campus security: 24-hour emergency response devices and patrols, student patrols, late-night transport/escort service, controlled dormitory access, ID check at door of residence halls, crime prevention and safety workshops.

Student services: health clinic, personal/psychological counseling, legal services.

COSTS & FINANCIAL AID

Costs (2018–19) *Tuition:* state resident $7020 full-time, $212 per credit hour part-time; nonresident $23,190 full-time, $751 per credit hour part-time. Full-time tuition and fees vary according to course level, course load, location, program, and reciprocity agreements. Part-time tuition and fees vary according to course level, course load, location, program, and reciprocity agreements. *Required fees:* $1780 full-time. *Room and board:* $8930; room only: $4200. Room and board charges vary according to board plan, housing facility, and location. *Payment plans:* installment, deferred payment. *Waivers:* senior citizens and employees or children of employees.

Financial Aid Of all full-time matriculated undergraduates who enrolled in 2016, 2,554 applied for aid, 1,669 were judged to have need, 254 had their need fully met. 33 Federal Work-Study jobs (averaging $4765). In 2016, 432 non-need-based awards were made. *Average percent of need met:* 54. *Average financial aid package:* $8233. *Average need-based loan:* $3809. *Average need-based gift aid:* $7056. *Average non-need-based aid:* $3653. *Average indebtedness upon graduation:* $22,155. *Financial aid deadline:* 7/1.

APPLYING

Standardized Tests *Required:* SAT or ACT (for admission).

Options: electronic application, deferred entrance.

Application fee: $50.

Required: high school transcript, minimum 2.5 GPA.

Application deadlines: 6/15 (freshmen), 6/15 (transfers).

Notification: continuous (freshmen), continuous (out-of-state freshmen), continuous (transfers).

CONTACT
University of Alaska Fairbanks, PO Box 757500, Fairbanks, AK 99775-7520. *Toll-free phone:* 800-478-1823.

See below for display ad and page 1452 for the College Close-Up.

University of Alaska Southeast
Juneau, Alaska
http://www.uas.alaska.edu/

CONTACT
Ms. Deema Ferguson, Admissions Clerk, University of Alaska Southeast, 11120 Glacier Highway, Juneau, AK 99801-8625. *Phone:* 907-796-6294 Ext. 6100. *Toll-free phone:* 877-465-4827. *Fax:* 907-796-6365. *E-mail:* admissions@uas.alaska.edu.

University of Alaska Southeast, Sitka Campus
Sitka, Alaska
http://www.uas.alaska.edu/

CONTACT
Ms. Teal Gordon, Admissions Representative, University of Alaska Southeast, Sitka Campus, UAS Sitka, 1332 Seward Avenue, Sitka, AK 99835. *Phone:* 907-747-7726. *Toll-free phone:* 800-478-6653. *Fax:* 907-747-7731. *E-mail:* ktgordon@uas.alaska.edu.

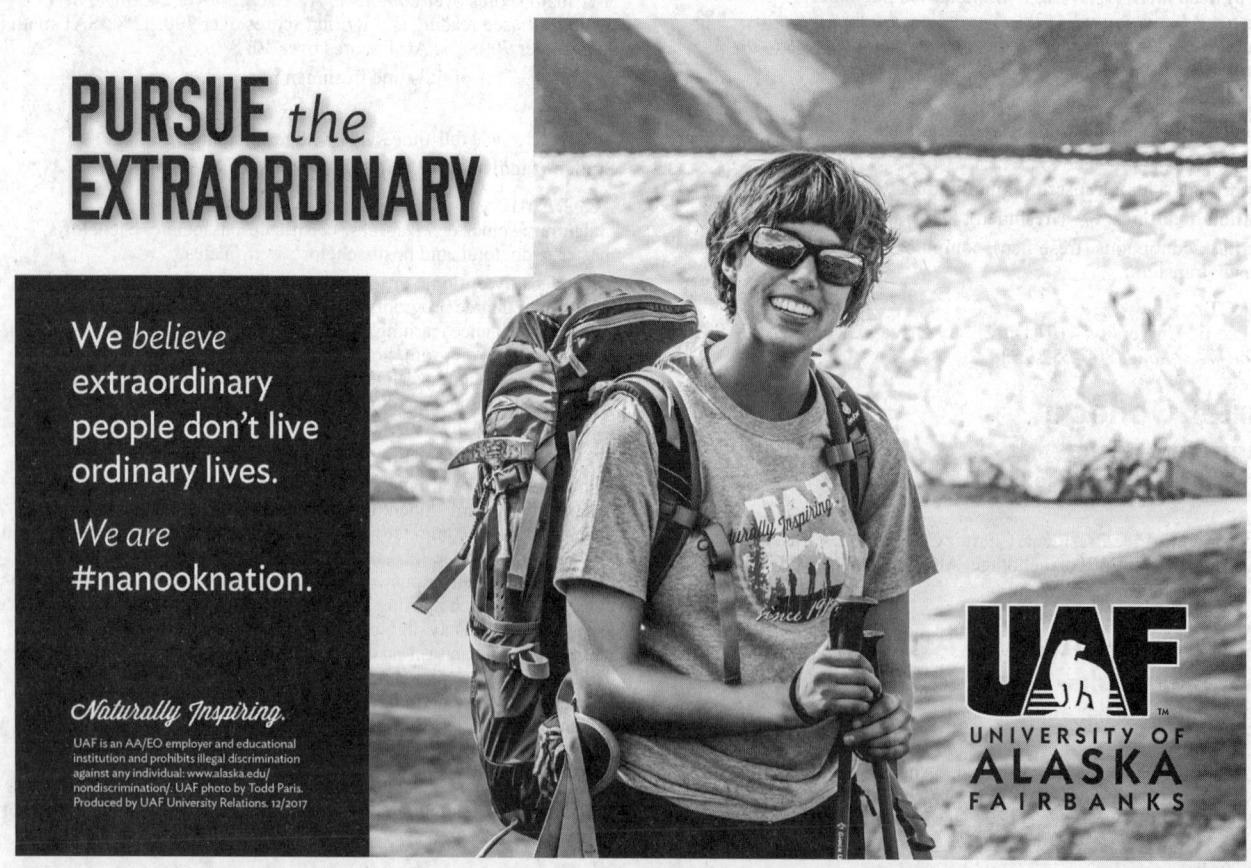

ARIZONA

Argosy University, Phoenix

Phoenix, Arizona

http://www.argosy.edu/phoenix-arizona/default.aspx

CONTACT

Argosy University, Phoenix, 2233 West Dunlap Avenue, Phoenix, AZ 85021. *Phone:* 602-216-2600. *Toll-free phone:* 866-216-2777.

Arizona Christian University

Phoenix, Arizona

http://arizonachristian.edu/

- **Independent Conservative Baptist** 4-year, founded 1960
- **Urban** 19-acre campus with easy access to Phoenix
- **Coed** 700 undergraduate students, 92% full-time, 36% women, 64% men

UNDERGRAD STUDENTS

643 full-time, 57 part-time. 29% are from out of state; 15% Black or African American, non-Hispanic/Latino; 22% Hispanic/Latino; 0.7% Asian, non-Hispanic/Latino; 0.3% Native Hawaiian or other Pacific Islander, non-Hispanic/Latino; 1% American Indian or Alaska Native, non-Hispanic/Latino; 6% Two or more races, non-Hispanic/Latino; 2% Race/ethnicity unknown; 4% international; 32% live on campus.

Freshmen:

Admission: 153 enrolled. *Test scores:* SAT evidence-based reading and writing scores over 500: 53%; SAT math scores over 500: 58%; ACT scores over 18: 63%; SAT evidence-based reading and writing scores over 600: 15%; SAT math scores over 600: 11%; ACT scores over 24: 20%; SAT math scores over 700: 1%; ACT scores over 30: 1%.

FACULTY

Total: 88, 19% full-time, 10% with terminal degrees.

Student/faculty ratio: 16:1.

ACADEMICS

Calendar: semesters. *Degrees:* associate and bachelor's.

Special study options: academic remediation for entering students, adult/continuing education programs, advanced placement credit, distance learning, double majors, independent study, internships, part-time degree program, services for LD students, study abroad, summer session for credit. *ROTC:* Air Force (c).

Computers: 37 computers/terminals are available on campus for general student use. Students can access the following: free student e-mail accounts, online (class) grades, online (class) registration, online (class) schedules. 100% of college-owned or -operated housing units are wired for high-speed Internet access. Wireless service is available via entire campus.

Library: R. S. Beal Library. *Books:* 28,496 (physical), 19,581 (digital/electronic); *Serial titles:* 471 (physical), 32 (digital/electronic); *Databases:* 18. Weekly public service hours: 76.

STUDENT LIFE

Housing options: on-campus residence required through sophomore year; coed. Campus housing is university owned. Freshman campus housing is guaranteed.

Activities and organizations: choral group, Joseph Story Pre-Law Society, International Student Association, Pre-Medicine Club, Flock Council and Flock Leaders, Reason and Religion.

Athletics Member NAIA, NCCAA. *Intercollegiate sports:* baseball M(s), basketball M(s)/W(s), cross-country running M(s)/W(s), football M(s), golf M(s)/W(s), soccer M(s)/W(s), softball W(s), swimming and diving W(s), tennis M(s)/W(s), track and field M(s)/W(s), volleyball W(s). *Intramural sports:* basketball M/W, bowling M(c)/W(c), cheerleading W(c), soccer M/W, table tennis M/W, volleyball M/W.

Campus security: 24-hour emergency response devices, student patrols, late-night transport/escort service, controlled dormitory access, 20-hour patrol with a guard on call on weekdays, 24-hour patrol by trained security personnel on weekends.

Student services: personal/psychological counseling.

COSTS & FINANCIAL AID

Costs (2018–19) *Comprehensive fee:* $13,220 includes full-time tuition ($2546) and room and board ($10,674). Full-time tuition and fees vary according to class time, course load, and program. Part-time tuition: $1062 per credit hour. Part-time tuition and fees vary according to class time, course load, and program. *College room only:* $5400. Room and board charges vary according to board plan. *Payment plan:* installment. *Waivers:* employees or children of employees.

Financial Aid Of all full-time matriculated undergraduates who enrolled in 2014, 503 applied for aid, 446 were judged to have need. In 2014, 52 non-need-based awards were made. *Average financial aid package:* $15,811. *Average need-based loan:* $3705. *Average need-based gift aid:* $13,195. *Average non-need-based aid:* $5414. *Average indebtedness upon graduation:* $26,228. *Financial aid deadline:* 6/5.

APPLYING

Standardized Tests *Required:* SAT or ACT (for admission).

Required: essay or personal statement, high school transcript, minimum 2.0 GPA, 1 letter of recommendation.

CONTACT

Lambert Cruz, Registrar and Asst Dir Enrollment Mgmt, Arizona Christian University, 2625 E. Cactus Road, Phoenix, AZ 85032. *Phone:* 602-386-4160. *Toll-free phone:* 800-247-2697. *Fax:* 602-4042159. *E-mail:* lambert.cruz@arizonachristian.edu.

Arizona College–Mesa

Mesa, Arizona

http://www.arizonacollege.edu/

CONTACT

Arizona College–Mesa, 163 N Dobson Road, Mesa, AZ 85201.

Arizona State University at the Downtown Phoenix campus

Phoenix, Arizona

http://campus.asu.edu/downtown/

- **State-supported** university, founded 2006
- **Urban** 18-acre campus with easy access to Phoenix
- **Coed** 8,902 undergraduate students, 89% full-time, 68% women, 32% men
- **Moderately difficult** entrance level, 77% of applicants were admitted

UNDERGRAD STUDENTS

7,956 full-time, 946 part-time. Students come from 36 other countries; 27% are from out of state; 6% Black or African American, non-Hispanic/Latino; 31% Hispanic/Latino; 5% Asian, non-Hispanic/Latino; 0.2% Native Hawaiian or other Pacific Islander, non-Hispanic/Latino; 2% American Indian or Alaska Native, non-Hispanic/Latino; 4% Two or more races, non-Hispanic/Latino; 0.6% Race/ethnicity unknown; 2% international; 10% transferred in; 17% live on campus.

Freshmen:

Admission: 5,340 applied, 4,123 admitted, 1,301 enrolled. *Average high school GPA:* 3.6. *Test scores:* SAT evidence-based reading and writing scores over 500: 91%; SAT math scores over 500: 88%; ACT scores over 18: 93%; SAT evidence-based reading and writing scores over 600: 49%; SAT math scores over 600: 38%; ACT scores over 24: 51%; SAT evidence-based reading and writing scores over 700: 6%; SAT math scores over 700: 6%; ACT scores over 30: 8%.

Retention: 86% of full-time freshmen returned.

FACULTY

Total: 635, 87% full-time, 69% with terminal degrees.

Student/faculty ratio: 19:1.

ACADEMICS

Calendar: semesters. *Degrees:* certificates, bachelor's, master's, doctoral, post-master's, and postbachelor's certificates.

Special study options: accelerated degree program, advanced placement credit, cooperative education, distance learning, double majors, freshman honors college, honors programs, independent study, internships, off-campus study, part-time degree program, services for LD students, student-designed majors, study abroad, summer session for credit. *ROTC:* Army (c), Navy (c), Air Force (c).

Computers: 486 computers/terminals are available on campus for general student use. Students can access the following: campus intranet, computer help desk, free student e-mail accounts, online (class) grades, online (class) registration, online (class) schedules. Campuswide network is available. 100% of college-owned or -operated housing units are wired for high-speed Internet access. Wireless service is available via classrooms, computer centers, computer labs, dorm rooms, learning centers, libraries, student centers.

Library: Downtown Phoenix campus Library. *Books:* 3.9 million (physical), 963,136 (digital/electronic); *Serial titles:* 72,649 (physical), 73,043 (digital/electronic); *Databases:* 650. Weekly public service hours: 149; study areas open 24 hours, 5–7 days a week; students can reserve study rooms.

STUDENT LIFE

Housing options: on-campus residence required for freshman year; coed, special housing for students with disabilities. Campus housing is leased by the school and is provided by a third party. Freshman campus housing is guaranteed.

Activities and organizations: drama/theater group, student-run newspaper, radio and television station, Student Nurses Association, American Medical Student Association, Exercise and Wellness Organization, Student Nutrition Council, Physical Therapy Club.

Athletics Member NCAA. All Division I. *Intercollegiate sports:* baseball M(s), basketball M(s)/W(s), cross-country running M(s)/W(s), football M(s), golf M(s)/W(s), gymnastics W(s), ice hockey M(s), lacrosse W(s), sand volleyball W(s), soccer W(s), softball W(s), swimming and diving M(s)/W(s), tennis M(s)/W(s), track and field M(s)/W(s), triathlon W(s), volleyball W(s), water polo W(s), wrestling M(s). *Intramural sports:* baseball M(c), basketball M/W, cheerleading M(c)/W(c), crew M(c), equestrian sports M(c)/W(c), fencing M(c)/W(c), golf M(c)/W(c), gymnastics M(c)/W(c), ice hockey M(c)/W(c), lacrosse M(c)/W(c), racquetball M(c)/W(c), rowing M(c)/W(c), rugby M(c)/W(c), sailing M(c)/W(c), soccer M(c)/W(c), softball M/W, tennis M(c)/W(c), triathlon M(c)/W(c), ultimate Frisbee M(c)/W(c), volleyball M(c)/W(c), water polo M(c)/W(c), weight lifting M(c)/W(c).

Campus security: 24-hour emergency response devices and patrols, late-night transport/escort service, controlled dormitory access, LiveSafe smart phone application, surveillance camera in some residence halls.

Student services: health clinic, personal/psychological counseling.

FINANCIAL AID

Financial Aid Of all full-time matriculated undergraduates who enrolled in 2016, 6,691 applied for aid, 5,766 were judged to have need, 1,011 had their need fully met. 431 Federal Work-Study jobs (averaging $2689). 1,321 state and other part-time jobs (averaging $3390). In 2016, 1181 non-need-based awards were made. *Average percent of need met:* 58. *Average financial aid package:* $14,667. *Average need-based loan:* $4030. *Average need-based gift aid:* $10,233. *Average non-need-based aid:* $8125. *Average indebtedness upon graduation:* $24,368.

APPLYING

Standardized Tests *Required for some:* SAT or ACT (for admission), SAT Subject Tests (for admission). *Recommended:* SAT or ACT (for admission).

Options: electronic application, deferred entrance.

Application fee: $50.

Required: high school transcript, minimum 3.0 GPA. *Required for some:* essay or personal statement, letters of recommendation, additional requirements for Honors College and certain majors.

Application deadlines: rolling (freshmen), rolling (out-of-state freshmen), rolling (transfers).

Notification: continuous until 9/1 (freshmen), continuous until 9/1 (out-of-state freshmen), continuous (transfers).

CONTACT

Admission Services, Arizona State University at the Downtown Phoenix campus, PO Box 870112, Tempe, AZ 85287-0112. *Phone:* 480-965-7788. *Fax:* 480-965-3610. *E-mail:* admissions@asu.edu.

Arizona State University at the Polytechnic campus
Mesa, Arizona
http://campus.asu.edu/polytechnic

- **State-supported** university, founded 1996
- **Suburban** 575-acre campus with easy access to Phoenix
- **Coed** 4,239 undergraduate students, 87% full-time, 31% women, 69% men
- **Moderately difficult** entrance level, 76% of applicants were admitted

UNDERGRAD STUDENTS

3,683 full-time, 556 part-time. Students come from 52 other countries; 22% are from out of state; 5% Black or African American, non-Hispanic/Latino; 21% Hispanic/Latino; 6% Asian, non-Hispanic/Latino; 0.6% Native Hawaiian or other Pacific Islander, non-Hispanic/Latino; 1% American Indian or Alaska Native, non-Hispanic/Latino; 5% Two or more races, non-Hispanic/Latino; 0.5% Race/ethnicity unknown; 8% international; 12% transferred in; 23% live on campus.

Freshmen:
Admission: 2,483 applied, 1,894 admitted, 581 enrolled. *Average high school GPA:* 3.4. *Test scores:* SAT evidence-based reading and writing scores over 500: 93%; SAT math scores over 500: 93%; ACT scores over 18: 98%; SAT evidence-based reading and writing scores over 600: 48%; SAT math scores over 600: 51%; ACT scores over 24: 54%; SAT evidence-based reading and writing scores over 700: 7%; SAT math scores over 700: 14%; ACT scores over 30: 15%.

Retention: 85% of full-time freshmen returned.

FACULTY

Total: 219, 93% full-time, 79% with terminal degrees.

Student/faculty ratio: 21:1.

ACADEMICS

Calendar: semesters. *Degrees:* certificates, bachelor's, master's, and doctoral.

Special study options: accelerated degree program, advanced placement credit, cooperative education, distance learning, double majors, freshman honors college, honors programs, independent study, internships, off-campus study, part-time degree program, services for LD students, student-designed majors, study abroad, summer session for credit. *ROTC:* Army (c), Navy (c), Air Force (c).

Computers: 535 computers/terminals are available on campus for general student use. Students can access the following: campus intranet, computer help desk, free student e-mail accounts, online (class) grades, online (class) registration, online (class) schedules. Campuswide network is available. 100% of college-owned or -operated housing units are wired for high-speed Internet access. Wireless service is available via classrooms, computer centers, computer labs, dorm rooms, learning centers, libraries, student centers.

Library: Polytechnic campus Library. *Books:* 3.9 million (physical), 963,136 (digital/electronic); *Serial titles:* 72,649 (physical), 73,043 (digital/electronic); *Databases:* 650. Weekly public service hours: 149; study areas open 24 hours, 5–7 days a week; students can reserve study rooms.

STUDENT LIFE

Housing options: on-campus residence required for freshman year; coed, special housing for students with disabilities. Campus housing is university owned and is provided by a third party. Freshman campus housing is guaranteed.

Activities and organizations: drama/theater group, student-run newspaper, Pre-Health Club, AIGA Polytechnic, Environmental Resource Management Club, Computer Science, Disc Golf Club.

Athletics Member NCAA. All Division I. *Intercollegiate sports:* baseball M(s), basketball M(s)/W(s), cross-country running M(s)/W(s), football M(s), golf M(s)/W(s), gymnastics W(s), ice hockey M(s), lacrosse W(s), sand volleyball W(s), soccer W(s), softball W(s), swimming and diving M(s)/W(s), tennis M(s)/W(s), track and field M(s)/W(s), triathlon W(s), volleyball W(s), water polo W(s), wrestling M(s). *Intramural sports:* baseball M(c), basketball M/W, cheerleading M(c)/W(c), equestrian sports M(c)/W(c), fencing M(c)/W(c), golf M(c)/W(c), gymnastics M(c)/W(c), ice hockey M(c)/W(c), lacrosse M(c)/W(c), racquetball M(c)/W(c), rowing M(c)/W(c), rugby M(c)/W(c), sailing M(c)/W(c), sand volleyball M/W, soccer M(c)/W(c), softball M/W, table tennis M/W, tennis M(c)/W(c), triathlon M(c)/W(c), ultimate Frisbee M(c)/W(c), volleyball M(c)/W(c), water polo M(c)/W(c), weight lifting M(c)/W(c), wrestling M(c)/W(c).

Campus security: 24-hour emergency response devices and patrols, late-night transport/escort service, controlled dormitory access, LiveSafe smart phone application, surveillance camera in some residence halls.

Student services: health clinic, personal/psychological counseling.

FINANCIAL AID
Financial Aid Of all full-time matriculated undergraduates who enrolled in 2016, 2,491 applied for aid, 2,102 were judged to have need, 414 had their need fully met. 197 Federal Work-Study jobs (averaging $2581). 777 state and other part-time jobs (averaging $3900). In 2016, 435 non-need-based awards were made. *Average percent of need met:* 58. *Average financial aid package:* $13,973. *Average need-based loan:* $4155. *Average need-based gift aid:* $9309. *Average non-need-based aid:* $6948. *Average indebtedness upon graduation:* $26,797.

APPLYING
Standardized Tests *Required for some:* SAT or ACT (for admission), SAT Subject Tests (for admission). *Recommended:* SAT or ACT (for admission).

Options: electronic application, deferred entrance.

Application fee: $50.

Required: high school transcript, minimum 3.0 GPA. *Required for some:* essay or personal statement, letters of recommendation, additional requirements for Honors College and certain majors.

Application deadlines: rolling (freshmen), rolling (out-of-state freshmen), rolling (transfers).

Notification: continuous until 9/1 (freshmen), continuous until 9/1 (out-of-state freshmen), continuous (transfers).

CONTACT
Admission Services, Arizona State University at the Polytechnic campus, PO Box 870112, Tempe, AZ 85287-0112. *Phone:* 480-965-7788. *Fax:* 480-965-3610. *E-mail:* admissions@asu.edu.

Arizona State University at the Tempe campus
Tempe, Arizona
http://www.asu.edu/
- **State-supported** university, founded 1885
- **Urban** 661-acre campus with easy access to Phoenix
- **Coed** 42,427 undergraduate students, 91% full-time, 43% women, 57% men
- **Moderately difficult** entrance level, 84% of applicants were admitted

UNDERGRAD STUDENTS
38,814 full-time, 3,613 part-time. Students come from 116 other countries; 25% are from out of state; 4% Black or African American, non-Hispanic/Latino; 21% Hispanic/Latino; 7% Asian, non-Hispanic/Latino; 0.2% Native Hawaiian or other Pacific Islander, non-Hispanic/Latino; 1% American Indian or Alaska Native, non-Hispanic/Latino; 4% Two or more races, non-Hispanic/Latino; 0.5% Race/ethnicity unknown; 13% international; 7% transferred in; 22% live on campus.

Freshmen:
Admission: 24,127 applied, 20,302 admitted, 7,874 enrolled. *Average high school GPA:* 3.5. *Test scores:* SAT evidence-based reading and writing scores over 500: 94%; SAT math scores over 500: 95%; ACT scores over 18: 97%; SAT evidence-based reading and writing scores over 600: 59%; SAT math scores over 600: 60%; ACT scores over 24: 67%; SAT evidence-based reading and writing scores over 700: 14%; SAT math scores over 700: 18%; ACT scores over 30: 20%.
Retention: 87% of full-time freshmen returned.

FACULTY
Total: 2,283, 94% full-time, 88% with terminal degrees.
Student/faculty ratio: 22:1.

ACADEMICS
Calendar: semesters. *Degrees:* certificates, bachelor's, master's, doctoral, post-master's, and postbachelor's certificates (profile includes data for the West, Polytechnic and Downtown Phoenix campuses).

Special study options: accelerated degree program, advanced placement credit, cooperative education, distance learning, double majors, English as a second language, freshman honors college, honors programs, independent study, internships, off-campus study, part-time degree program, services for LD students, student-designed majors, study abroad, summer session for credit. *ROTC:* Army (b), Navy (b), Air Force (b).

Computers: 2,421 computers/terminals are available on campus for general student use. Students can access the following: campus intranet, computer help desk, free student e-mail accounts, online (class) grades, online (class) registration, online (class) schedules. Campuswide network is available. 100% of college-owned or -operated housing units are wired for high-speed Internet access. Wireless service is available via classrooms, computer centers, computer labs, dorm rooms, learning centers, libraries, student centers.

Library: Hayden Library plus 3 others. *Books:* 3.9 million (physical), 963,136 (digital/electronic); *Serial titles:* 72,649 (physical), 73,043 (digital/electronic); *Databases:* 650. Weekly public service hours: 149; study areas open 24 hours, 5–7 days a week; students can reserve study rooms.

STUDENT LIFE
Housing options: on-campus residence required for freshman year; coed, special housing for students with disabilities. Campus housing is university owned, leased by the school and is provided by a third party. Freshman campus housing is guaranteed.

Activities and organizations: drama/theater group, student-run newspaper, choral group, marching band, Sun Devil Ski Club, Residence Hall Association, Alpha Epsilon Delta, American Medical Student Association, Software Developers Association, national fraternities, national sororities.

Athletics Member NCAA. All Division I. *Intercollegiate sports:* baseball M(s), basketball M(s)/W(s), cross-country running M(s)/W(s), football M(s), golf M(s)/W(s), gymnastics W(s), ice hockey M(s), lacrosse W(s), sand volleyball W(s), soccer W(s), softball W(s), swimming and diving M(s)/W(s), tennis M(s)/W(s), track and field M(s)/W(s), triathlon W(s), volleyball W(s), water polo W(s), wrestling M(s). *Intramural sports:* badminton M/W, baseball M(c), basketball M/W, cheerleading M(c)/W(c), equestrian sports M(c)/W(c), fencing M(c)/W(c), golf M(c)/W(c), gymnastics M(c)/W(c), ice hockey M(c)/W(c), lacrosse M(c)/W(c), racquetball M(c)/W(c), rowing M(c)/W(c), rugby M(c)/W(c), sailing M(c)/W(c), sand volleyball M/W, soccer M(c)/W(c), softball M/W, table tennis M/W, tennis M(c)/W(c), triathlon M(c)/W(c), ultimate Frisbee M(c)/W(c), volleyball M(c)/W(c), water polo M(c)/W(c), weight lifting M(c)/W(c), wrestling M(c)/W(c).

Campus security: 24-hour emergency response devices and patrols, late-night transport/escort service, controlled dormitory access, LiveSafe smart phone application, surveillance cameras in some residence halls.

Student services: health clinic, personal/psychological counseling.

COSTS & FINANCIAL AID
Costs (2017–18) *Tuition:* state resident $9834 full-time, $702 per credit hour part-time; nonresident $26,684 full-time, $1112 per credit hour part-time. *Required fees:* $688 full-time, $196 per term part-time. *Room and board:* Room and board charges vary according to board plan and housing facility. *Payment plan:* installment. *Waivers:* employees or children of employees.

Financial Aid Of all full-time matriculated undergraduates who enrolled in 2016, 25,918 applied for aid, 20,975 were judged to have need, 4,088 had their need fully met. 1,136 Federal Work-Study jobs (averaging $2470). 6,382 state and other part-time jobs (averaging $3322). In 2016, 8547 non-need-based awards were made. *Average percent of need met:* 62. *Average financial aid package:* $14,940. *Average need-based loan:* $4004. *Average need-based gift aid:* $10,528. *Average non-need-based aid:* $8329. *Average indebtedness upon graduation:* $23,237.

APPLYING
Standardized Tests *Required for some:* SAT or ACT (for admission), SAT Subject Tests (for admission). *Recommended:* SAT or ACT (for admission).

Options: electronic application, deferred entrance.

Application fee: $50.

Required: high school transcript, minimum 3.0 GPA. *Required for some:* essay or personal statement, letters of recommendation, additional requirements for Honors College and certain majors.

Application deadlines: rolling (freshmen), rolling (out-of-state freshmen), rolling (transfers).

Notification: continuous until 9/1 (freshmen), continuous until 9/1 (out-of-state freshmen), continuous (transfers).

CONTACT
Admission Services, Arizona State University at the Tempe campus, PO Box 870112, Tempe, AZ 85287-0112. *Phone:* 480-965-7788. *Fax:* 480-965-3610. *E-mail:* admissions@asu.edu.

Arizona State University at the West campus

Glendale, Arizona

http://campus.asu.edu/west

- **State-supported** comprehensive, founded 1984
- **Urban** 278-acre campus with easy access to Phoenix
- **Coed** 3,630 undergraduate students, 85% full-time, 59% women, 41% men
- **Moderately difficult** entrance level, 80% of applicants were admitted

UNDERGRAD STUDENTS

3,078 full-time, 552 part-time. Students come from 30 other countries; 14% are from out of state; 5% Black or African American, non-Hispanic/Latino; 32% Hispanic/Latino; 5% Asian, non-Hispanic/Latino; 0.3% Native Hawaiian or other Pacific Islander, non-Hispanic/Latino; 1% American Indian or Alaska Native, non-Hispanic/Latino; 4% Two or more races, non-Hispanic/Latino; 0.6% Race/ethnicity unknown; 6% international; 17% transferred in; 14% live on campus.

Freshmen:

Admission: 2,231 applied, 1,777 admitted, 522 enrolled. *Average high school GPA:* 3.5. *Test scores:* SAT evidence-based reading and writing scores over 500: 86%; SAT math scores over 500: 81%; ACT scores over 18: 90%; SAT evidence-based reading and writing scores over 600: 42%; SAT math scores over 600: 33%; ACT scores over 24: 37%; SAT evidence-based reading and writing scores over 700: 5%; SAT math scores over 700: 3%; ACT scores over 30: 5%.

Retention: 88% of full-time freshmen returned.

FACULTY

Total: 292, 93% full-time, 78% with terminal degrees.
Student/faculty ratio: 14:1.

ACADEMICS

Calendar: semesters. *Degrees:* certificates, bachelor's, master's, doctoral, and postbachelor's certificates.

Special study options: accelerated degree program, advanced placement credit, cooperative education, distance learning, double majors, English as a second language, freshman honors college, honors programs, independent study, internships, off-campus study, part-time degree program, services for LD students, student-designed majors, study abroad, summer session for credit. *ROTC:* Army (c), Navy (c), Air Force (c).

Computers: 612 computers/terminals are available on campus for general student use. Students can access the following: campus intranet, computer help desk, free student e-mail accounts, online (class) grades, online (class) registration, online (class) schedules. Campuswide network is available. 100% of college-owned or -operated housing units are wired for high-speed Internet access. Wireless service is available via classrooms, computer centers, computer labs, dorm rooms, learning centers, libraries, student centers.

Library: Fletcher Library at the West campus. *Books:* 3.9 million (physical), 963,136 (digital/electronic); *Serial titles:* 72,649 (physical), 73,043 (digital/electronic); *Databases:* 650. Weekly public service hours: 149; study areas open 24 hours, 5–7 days a week; students can reserve study rooms.

STUDENT LIFE

Housing options: on-campus residence required for freshman year; coed, special housing for students with disabilities. Campus housing is university owned and is provided by a third party. Freshman campus housing is guaranteed.

Activities and organizations: drama/theater group, student-run newspaper, choral group, Hispanic Honor Society, Teachers of the Future, Business to Business, W. P. Carey MBA Association, American Medical Student Association.

Athletics Member NCAA. All Division I. *Intercollegiate sports:* baseball M(s), basketball M(s)/W(s), cross-country running M(s)/W(s), football M(s), golf M(s)/W(s), gymnastics W(s), ice hockey M(s), lacrosse W(s), sand volleyball W(s), soccer W(s), softball W(s), swimming and diving M(s)/W(s), tennis M(s)/W(s), track and field M(s)/W(s), triathlon W(s), volleyball W(s), water polo W(s), wrestling M(s). *Intramural sports:* baseball M(c), basketball M/W, cheerleading M(c)/W(c), equestrian sports M(c)/W(c), fencing M(c)/W(c), golf M(c)/W(c), gymnastics M(c)/W(c), ice hockey M(c)/W(c), lacrosse M(c)/W(c), racquetball M(c)/W(c), rowing M(c)/W(c), rugby M(c)/W(c), sailing M(c)/W(c), soccer M(c)/W(c), softball M/W, table tennis M/W, tennis M(c)/W(c), triathlon M(c)/W(c), ultimate Frisbee M(c)/W(c), volleyball M(c)/W(c), water polo M(c)/W(c), weight lifting M(c)/W(c).

Campus security: 24-hour emergency response devices and patrols, late-night transport/escort service, controlled dormitory access, LiveSafe smart phone application, surveillance camera in some residence halls.

Student services: health clinic, personal/psychological counseling.

FINANCIAL AID

Financial Aid Of all full-time matriculated undergraduates who enrolled in 2016, 2,238 applied for aid, 1,981 were judged to have need, 293 had their need fully met. 169 Federal Work-Study jobs (averaging $2277). 506 state and other part-time jobs (averaging $3380). In 2016, 234 non-need-based awards were made. *Average percent of need met:* 59. *Average financial aid package:* $12,895. *Average need-based loan:* $4137. *Average need-based gift aid:* $9034. *Average non-need-based aid:* $6743. *Average indebtedness upon graduation:* $24,498.

APPLYING

Standardized Tests *Required for some:* SAT or ACT (for admission), SAT Subject Tests (for admission). *Recommended:* SAT or ACT (for admission).

Options: electronic application, deferred entrance.

Application fee: $50.

Required: high school transcript, minimum 3.0 GPA. *Required for some:* essay or personal statement, letters of recommendation, additional requirements for Honors College and certain majors.

Application deadlines: rolling (freshmen), rolling (out-of-state freshmen), rolling (transfers).

Notification: continuous until 9/1 (freshmen), continuous until 9/1 (out-of-state freshmen), continuous (transfers).

CONTACT
Arizona State University at the West campus, PO Box 870112, Tempe, AZ 85287-0112. *Phone:* 480-965-7788. *Fax:* 480-965-3610. *E-mail:* admissions@asu.edu.

The Art Institute of Phoenix

Phoenix, Arizona

http://www.artinstitutes.edu/phoenix/

CONTACT
The Art Institute of Phoenix, 2233 West Dunlap Avenue, Phoenix, AZ 85021-2859. *Phone:* 602-331-7500. *Toll-free phone:* 800-474-2479.

Brookline College

Phoenix, Arizona

http://brooklinecollege.edu/

CONTACT
Ms. Theresa Dean, Director of Admissions, Brookline College, 2445 West Dunlap Avenue, Suite 100, Phoenix, AZ 85021. *Phone:* 602-242-6265. *Toll-free phone:* 800-793-2428. *Fax:* 602-973-2572. *E-mail:* tdean@brooklinecollege.edu.

Brookline College

Tempe, Arizona

http://brooklinecollege.edu/

CONTACT
Ms. Cheryl Kindred, Campus Director, Brookline College, 1140-1150 South Priest Drive, Tempe, AZ 85281. *Phone:* 480-545-8755. *Toll-free phone:* 888-886-2428. *Fax:* 480-926-1371. *E-mail:* ckindred@brooklinecollege.edu.

Brookline College

Tucson, Arizona

http://brooklinecollege.edu/

CONTACT
Ms. Leigh Anne Pechota, Campus Director, Brookline College, 5441 East 22nd Street, Suite 125, Tucson, AZ 85711. *Phone:* 520-748-9799. *Toll-free phone:* 888-292-2428. *Fax:* 520-748-9355. *E-mail:* lpechota@brooklinecollege.edu.

Chamberlain College of Nursing

Phoenix, Arizona

http://www.chamberlain.edu/

CONTACT
Admissions, Chamberlain College of Nursing, 2149 West Dunlap Avenue, Phoenix, AZ 85021. *Phone:* 602-331-2720. *Toll-free phone:* 877-751-5783.

CollegeAmerica–Flagstaff

Flagstaff, Arizona

http://www.collegeamerica.edu/

CONTACT
CollegeAmerica–Flagstaff, 399 South Malpais Lane, Flagstaff, AZ 86001. *Phone:* 928-213-6060 Ext. 1402. *Toll-free phone:* 800-622-2894.

CollegeAmerica–Phoenix

Phoenix, Arizona

http://www.collegeamerica.edu/

CONTACT
CollegeAmerica–Phoenix, 9801 North Metro Parkway East, Phoenix, AZ 85051. *Toll-free phone:* 800-622-2894.

DeVry University–Phoenix Campus

Phoenix, Arizona

http://www.devry.edu/

- **Proprietary** comprehensive, founded 1967, part of DeVry University
- **Urban** campus
- **Coed**
- **Minimally difficult** entrance level

FACULTY
Student/faculty ratio: 11:1.

ACADEMICS
Calendar: semesters. *Degrees:* associate, bachelor's, master's, and postbachelor's certificates.
Library: Learning Resource Center.

STUDENT LIFE
Housing options: college housing not available.

COSTS
Costs (2017–18) *Tuition:* $14,252 full-time. *Required fees:* $500 full-time.

APPLYING
Options: deferred entrance.
Application fee: $30.
Required: high school transcript, interview.

CONTACT
DeVry University–Phoenix Campus, 2149 West Dunlap Avenue, Phoenix, AZ 85021. *Phone:* 602-870-9222. *Toll-free phone:* 866-338-7934.

Dunlap-Stone University

Phoenix, Arizona

http://www.dunlap-stone.edu/

CONTACT
Dunlap-Stone University, 19820 North 7th Street, Suite #100, Phoenix, AZ 85024. *Phone:* 602-648-5750. *Toll-free phone:* 800-474-8013.

Embry-Riddle Aeronautical University–Prescott

Prescott, Arizona

http://www.prescott.erau.edu/

- **Independent** comprehensive, founded 1978
- **Small-town** 547-acre campus with easy access to Phoenix
- **Endowment** $111.2 million
- **Coed**
- **Moderately difficult** entrance level

FACULTY
Student/faculty ratio: 17:1.

ACADEMICS
Calendar: semesters. *Degrees:* bachelor's, master's, and doctoral.
Library: Christine & Steven F. Udvar-Hazy Library & Learning Center. *Books:* 30,076 (physical), 179,675 (digital/electronic); *Serial titles:* 149 (physical), 51,589 (digital/electronic); *Databases:* 101. Students can reserve study rooms.

STUDENT LIFE
Housing options: on-campus residence required for freshman year; coed. Campus housing is university owned. Freshman campus housing is guaranteed.

Activities and organizations: student-run newspaper, choral group, Hawaii Club, Strike Eagles, Theta XI, American Institute of Aeronautics and Astronautics (AIAA), Arnold Air Society, national fraternities, national sororities.

Athletics Member NCAA, NAIA. All NCAA Division II.

Campus security: 24-hour emergency response devices and patrols, student patrols, late-night transport/escort service, controlled dormitory access.

Student services: health clinic, personal/psychological counseling, women's center.

COSTS & FINANCIAL AID
Costs (2017–18) *Comprehensive fee:* $45,130 includes full-time tuition ($33,408), mandatory fees ($1254), and room and board ($10,468). Full-time tuition and fees vary according to course load. Part-time tuition: $1392 per credit hour. Part-time tuition and fees vary according to course load. *Required fees:* $627 per term part-time. *College room only:* $5860. Room and board charges vary according to board plan, housing facility, location, and student level.

Financial Aid Of all full-time matriculated undergraduates who enrolled in 2017, 1,656 applied for aid, 1,513 were judged to have need. 30 Federal Work-Study jobs (averaging $2503). 607 state and other part-time jobs (averaging $2643). In 2017, 506 non-need-based awards were made. *Average financial aid package:* $16,671. *Average need-based loan:* $4307. *Average need-based gift aid:* $14,902. *Average non-need-based aid:* $11,347.

APPLYING
Standardized Tests *Recommended:* SAT or ACT (for admission), SAT and SAT Subject Tests or ACT (for admission).

Options: electronic application, deferred entrance.

Application fee: $50.

Required: high school transcript, minimum 2.0 GPA, 2 letters of recommendation, medical examination for flight students.
Recommended: essay or personal statement, minimum 3.0 GPA, interview.

A ★ *indicates that the school has detailed information with a Premium Profile on Petersons.com.*

EXPLORE. FLY. DESIGN. BUILD. PREDICT. PROTECT.

▶ No. 1 in Aeronautical/Aerospace Engineering

▶ Nation's 1st College of Security and Intelligence

▶ 11-time National Champion Flight Team

▶ 97% Job Placement Rate

Embry-Riddle's Prescott Campus — A mile high in the Bradshaw Mountains of central Arizona where flying conditions are pristine and the land's natural beauty is spectacular. There's peacefulness here. But just listen and you'll hear the buzz of remote-controlled planes students are flying at RSP Field; or the roar of a new turbine engine prototype that students are testing in one of our massive wind tunnels. *National Geographic* named Prescott one of America's best adventure towns, with some of the best mountain biking in the country.

EMBRY-RIDDLE
Aeronautical University
PRESCOTT, ARIZONA

Explore more! prescott.erau.edu | f 🐦 📷 v 👻

CONTACT
Prescott Campus Admissions, Embry-Riddle Aeronautical University–Prescott, 3700 Willow Creek Road, Prescott, AZ 863013720. *Phone:* 800-888-3728. *Toll-free phone:* 800-888-3728. *Fax:* 928-777-6606. *E-mail:* prescott@erau.edu.

See this page for display ad and page 1284 for the College Close-Up.

Grand Canyon University
Phoenix, Arizona
http://www.gcu.edu/

CONTACT
Enrollment, Grand Canyon University, 3300 West Camelback Road, PO Box 11097, Phoenix, AZ 86017-3030. *Phone:* 800-486-7085. *Toll-free phone:* 800-800-9776. *E-mail:* admissionsonline@gcu.edu.

Harrison Middleton University
Tempe, Arizona
http://www.hmu.edu/
- **Independent** comprehensive, founded 1998
- **Suburban** campus with easy access to Phoenix
- **Coed** 10 undergraduate students, 70% full-time, 40% women, 30% men

UNDERGRAD STUDENTS
7 full-time. 100% are from out of state.

FACULTY
Total: 23, 74% full-time, 43% with terminal degrees.
Student/faculty ratio: 1:1.

ACADEMICS
Calendar: continuous. *Degree:* diplomas, master's, and doctoral.
Special study options: advanced placement credit, distance learning, double majors, independent study, student-designed majors, summer session for credit.
Library: William Speight Harrison Athenaeum Online LIbrary.

STUDENT LIFE
Housing options: college housing not available.

COSTS
Costs (2017–18) *One-time required fee:* $400. *Tuition:* $3600 full-time, $300 per credit hour part-time. *Payment plan:* installment.

APPLYING
Options: electronic application.
Application fee: $50.
Required: high school transcript, interview.
Application deadlines: rolling (freshmen), rolling (transfers).
Notification: continuous (freshmen), continuous (transfers).

CONTACT
Harrison Middleton University, 1105 East Broadway, Tempe, AZ 85282. *Phone:* 877-248-6724. *Toll-free phone:* 877-248-6724.

International Baptist College and Seminary
Chandler, Arizona
http://www.ibcs.edu/

CONTACT
Director of Admissions, International Baptist College and Seminary, 2211 West Germann Road, Chandler, AZ 85286. *Phone:* 480-245-7970. *Toll-free phone:* 800-422-4858. *E-mail:* admissions@ibconline.edu.

National Paralegal College
Phoenix, Arizona
http://nationalparalegal.edu/
- **Proprietary** comprehensive, founded 2003
- **Coed** 776 undergraduate students, 97% full-time, 89% women, 11% men
- 85% of applicants were admitted

UNDERGRAD STUDENTS

752 full-time, 24 part-time. Students come from 51 states and territories; 4 other countries; 96% are from out of state; 7% Black or African American, non-Hispanic/Latino; 5% Hispanic/Latino; 1% Asian, non-Hispanic/Latino; 0.6% Native Hawaiian or other Pacific Islander, non-Hispanic/Latino; 0.4% American Indian or Alaska Native, non-Hispanic/Latino; 0.1% Two or more races, non-Hispanic/Latino; 56% Race/ethnicity unknown; 15% transferred in.

Freshmen:

Admission: 2,331 applied, 1,979 admitted, 91 enrolled.

Retention: 58% of full-time freshmen returned.

FACULTY

Total: 33, 15% full-time, 97% with terminal degrees.

Student/faculty ratio: 28:1.

ACADEMICS

Calendar: continuous new session each month. *Degrees:* certificates, associate, bachelor's, and master's.

Special study options: academic remediation for entering students, accelerated degree program, distance learning, part-time degree program, summer session for credit.

Unusual degree programs: legal and paralegal studies, taxation studies.

Computers: Students can access the following: online (class) grades, online (class) registration, online (class) schedules.

Library: Jones eGlobal Library. *Books:* 27,803 (digital/electronic); *Databases:* 56. Weekly public service hours: 168.

COSTS

Costs (2018–19) *One-time required fee:* $195. *Tuition:* $7800 full-time, $325 per credit part-time. Full-time tuition and fees vary according to course load. Part-time tuition and fees vary according to course load. No tuition increase for student's term of enrollment. *Payment plans:* tuition prepayment, installment. *Waivers:* employees or children of employees.

APPLYING

Options: electronic application.

Required for some: high school transcript. *Recommended:* essay or personal statement, interview.

Application deadlines: rolling (freshmen), rolling (out-of-state freshmen), rolling (transfers).

Notification: continuous (freshmen), continuous (out-of-state freshmen), continuous (transfers).

CONTACT

Admissions Office, National Paralegal College, 717 E Maryland Ave, Phoenix, AZ 85104. *Phone:* 845-371-9101 Ext. 0. *Toll-free phone:* 800-371-6105. *Fax:* 866-347-2744. *E-mail:* info@nationalparalegal.edu.

★ **Northern Arizona University**

Flagstaff, Arizona

http://www.nau.edu/

- **State-supported** university, founded 1899, part of Arizona University System
- **Small-town** 683-acre campus
- **Endowment** $30.5 million
- **Coed** 27,086 undergraduate students, 81% full-time, 60% women, 40% men
- **Moderately difficult** entrance level, 81% of applicants were admitted

UNDERGRAD STUDENTS

21,990 full-time, 5,096 part-time. Students come from 50 states and territories; 70 other countries; 28% are from out of state; 3% Black or African American, non-Hispanic/Latino; 24% Hispanic/Latino; 2% Asian, non-Hispanic/Latino; 0.3% Native Hawaiian or other Pacific Islander, non-Hispanic/Latino; 3% American Indian or Alaska Native, non-Hispanic/Latino; 6% Two or more races, non-Hispanic/Latino; 1% Race/ethnicity unknown; 4% international; 10% transferred in; 35% live on campus.

Freshmen:

Admission: 36,875 applied, 29,812 admitted, 5,900 enrolled. *Average high school GPA:* 3.6. *Test scores:* SAT evidence-based reading and writing scores over 500: 85%; SAT math scores over 500: 83%; ACT scores over 18: 91%; SAT evidence-based reading and writing scores over

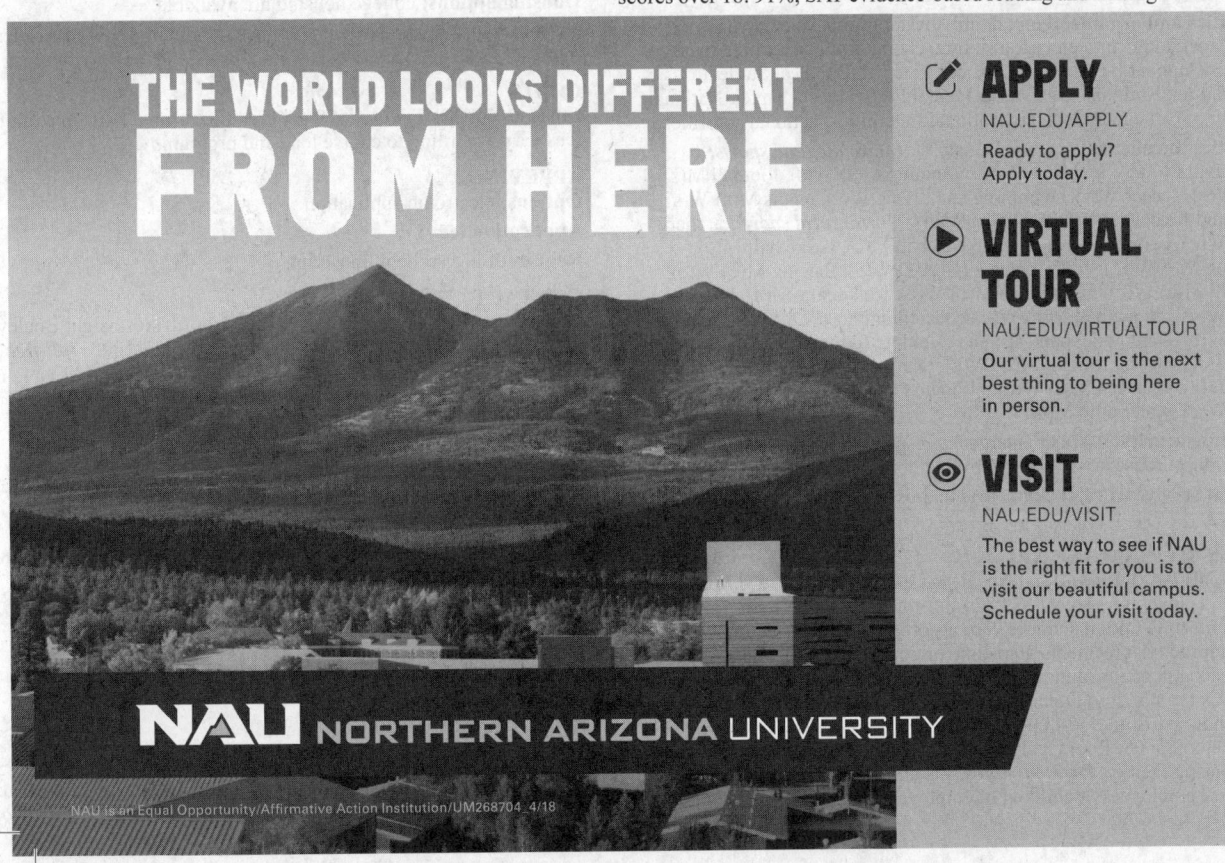

THE WORLD LOOKS DIFFERENT FROM HERE

NAU NORTHERN ARIZONA UNIVERSITY

APPLY
NAU.EDU/APPLY
Ready to apply?
Apply today.

VIRTUAL TOUR
NAU.EDU/VIRTUALTOUR
Our virtual tour is the next best thing to being here in person.

VISIT
NAU.EDU/VISIT
The best way to see if NAU is the right fit for you is to visit our beautiful campus. Schedule your visit today.

NAU is an Equal Opportunity/Affirmative Action Institution/UM268704_4/18

A ★ *indicates that the school has detailed information with a Premium Profile on Petersons.com.*

600: 34%; SAT math scores over 600: 31%; ACT scores over 24: 38%; SAT evidence-based reading and writing scores over 700: 3%; SAT math scores over 700: 4%; ACT scores over 30: 4%.

Retention: 76% of full-time freshmen returned.

FACULTY
Total: 1,725, 66% full-time.
Student/faculty ratio: 19:1.

ACADEMICS
Calendar: semesters. *Degrees:* certificates, bachelor's, master's, doctoral, post-master's, and postbachelor's certificates.

Special study options: accelerated degree program, advanced placement credit, cooperative education, distance learning, double majors, English as a second language, freshman honors college, honors programs, independent study, internships, off-campus study, part-time degree program, services for LD students, study abroad, summer session for credit. *ROTC:* Army (b), Air Force (b).

Unusual degree programs: 3-2 business administration; engineering; forestry; social work; athletic training, sustainable communities, criminology, climate science solutions, career and technical education, applied geospatial sciences, psychological sciences, forestry, English teaching; law with The University of Arizona.

Computers: 294 computers/terminals and 2,000 ports are available on campus for general student use. Students can access the following: campus intranet, computer help desk, free student e-mail accounts, online (class) grades, online (class) registration, online (class) schedules, computer repair service available on campus. Campuswide network is available. 100% of college-owned or -operated housing units are wired for high-speed Internet access. Wireless service is available via entire campus.
Library: Cline Library plus 1 other. *Books:* 574,711 (physical), 237,606 (digital/electronic); *Serial titles:* 6,264 (physical), 93,756 (digital/electronic); *Databases:* 146. Weekly public service hours: 117; students can reserve study rooms.

STUDENT LIFE
Housing options: coed, special housing for students with disabilities. Campus housing is university owned and is provided by a third party. Freshman campus housing is guaranteed.

Activities and organizations: drama/theater group, student-run newspaper, radio and television station, choral group, marching band, Louie's Cupboard, Feral Cat Alliance, American Medical Student Association, National Alliance on Mental Illness local chapter, National Society of Collegiate Scholars, national fraternities, national sororities.

Athletics Member NCAA. All Division I. *Intercollegiate sports:* basketball M(s)/W(s), cross-country running M(s)/W(s), football M(s), golf W(s), soccer W(s), swimming and diving W(s), tennis M(s)/W(s), track and field M(s)/W(s), volleyball W(s). *Intramural sports:* archery M(c)/W(c), badminton M(c)/W(c), baseball M(c), basketball M(c), bowling M(c)/W(c), equestrian sports M(c)/W(c), fencing M(c)/W(c), football M(c)/W(c), gymnastics M(c)/W(c), ice hockey M(c), lacrosse M(c)/W(c), racquetball M(c)/W(c), rock climbing M(c)/W(c), rugby M(c)/W(c), sand volleyball M(c)/W(c), skiing (downhill) M(c)/W(c), soccer M(c)/W(c), softball M(c)/W(c), tennis M(c)/W(c), track and field M(c)/W(c), triathlon M(c)/W(c), ultimate Frisbee M(c)/W(c), volleyball M(c)/W(c), water polo M(c).

Campus security: 24-hour emergency response devices and patrols, late-night transport/escort service, controlled dormitory access.

Student services: health clinic, personal/psychological counseling, legal services.

COSTS & FINANCIAL AID
Costs (2017–18) *Tuition:* state resident $10,038 full-time, $717 per credit hour part-time; nonresident $23,820 full-time, $993 per credit hour part-time. Full-time tuition and fees vary according to course load, location, and reciprocity agreements. Part-time tuition and fees vary according to course load, location, and reciprocity agreements. No tuition increase for student's term of enrollment. *Required fees:* $1022 full-time, $14 per credit hour part-time, $343 per term part-time. *Room and board:* $9944; room only: $5408. Room and board charges vary according to board plan and housing facility. *Payment plans:* installment, deferred payment. *Waivers:* employees or children of employees.

Financial Aid Of all full-time matriculated undergraduates who enrolled in 2016, 16,002 applied for aid, 13,207 were judged to have need, 1,441 had their need fully met. In 2016, 3576 non-need-based awards were made. *Average percent of need met:* 61. *Average financial aid package:* $12,003. *Average need-based loan:* $4237. *Average need-based gift aid:* $6941. *Average non-need-based aid:* $6610. *Average indebtedness upon graduation:* $24,413.

APPLYING
Standardized Tests *Recommended:* SAT (for admission), SAT Subject Tests (for admission).

Options: electronic application, deferred entrance.

Application fee: $25.

Required: high school transcript, minimum 2.5 GPA, 16 college preparatory courses with minimum 2.0 in each subject area.

Application deadlines: rolling (freshmen), rolling (out-of-state freshmen), rolling (transfers).

Notification: continuous (freshmen), continuous (out-of-state freshmen), continuous (transfers).

CONTACT
Undergraduate Admissions, Northern Arizona University, Box 4084, Flagstaff, AZ 86011. *Phone:* 928-523-5511. *Toll-free phone:* 888-628-2968. *Fax:* 928-523-6023. *E-mail:* admissions@nau.edu.

See previous page for display ad and page 1368 for the College Close-Up.

Penn Foster College
Scottsdale, Arizona
http://www.pennfostercollege.edu/
- **Proprietary** primarily 2-year
- **Coed**

ACADEMICS
Calendar: continuous. *Degrees:* certificates, associate, and bachelor's.
Library: Penn Foster College Online Library.

STUDENT LIFE
Housing options: college housing not available.

Activities and organizations: Online Community-Hosted Academic Interest Groups.

COSTS
Costs (2017–18) *Tuition:* $79 per credit part-time. Part-time tuition and fees vary according to course load and program.

APPLYING
Options: electronic application.

Application fee: $75.

Required: high school transcript.

CONTACT
Admissions, Penn Foster College, 14300 North Northsight Boulevard, Suite 120, Scottsdale, AZ 85260. *Phone:* 888-427-1000. *Toll-free phone:* 800-471-3232.

Pima Medical Institute
Mesa, Arizona
http://www.pmi.edu/

CONTACT
Admissions Office, Pima Medical Institute, 957 South Dobson Road, Mesa, AZ 85202. *Phone:* 480-644-0267 Ext. 225. *Toll-free phone:* 800-477-PIMA.

Pima Medical Institute
Tucson, Arizona
http://www.pmi.edu/

CONTACT
Admissions Office, Pima Medical Institute, 3350 East Grant Road, Tucson, AZ 85716. *Phone:* 520-326-1600 Ext. 5112. *Toll-free phone:* 800-477-PIMA.

Prescott College

Prescott, Arizona

http://www.prescott.edu/

- **Independent** comprehensive, founded 1966
- **Small-town** 13-acre campus
- **Endowment** $1.5 million
- **Coed**
- **Moderately difficult** entrance level

FACULTY

Student/faculty ratio: 9:1.

ACADEMICS

Calendar: semesters (4-week blocks followed by 10-week terms for each quarter). *Degrees:* bachelor's, master's, doctoral, post-master's, and postbachelor's certificates.

Library: Prescott College Library.

STUDENT LIFE

Housing options: on-campus residence required for freshman year; coed. Campus housing is university owned. Freshman campus housing is guaranteed.

Activities and organizations: drama/theater group, choral group, Student Union, Catalyst, WEB (Women's Empowerment Breakthrough), HUB (Helping Understand Bikes), Aztlan Center.

Campus security: 24-hour emergency response devices, late-night transport/escort service, controlled dormitory access.

Student services: personal/psychological counseling.

COSTS & FINANCIAL AID

Costs (2017–18) *One-time required fee:* $1075. *Comprehensive fee:* $37,266 includes full-time tuition ($28,976), mandatory fees ($590), and room and board ($7700). Full-time tuition and fees vary according to course load. Part-time tuition and fees vary according to course load. *College room only:* $6900. Room and board charges vary according to board plan and housing facility.

Financial Aid Of all full-time matriculated undergraduates who enrolled in 2016, 218 applied for aid, 187 were judged to have need, 16 had their need fully met. In 2016, 76 non-need-based awards were made. *Average percent of need met:* 64. *Average financial aid package:* $20,132. *Average need-based loan:* $4576. *Average need-based gift aid:* $15,202. *Average non-need-based aid:* $6575. *Average indebtedness upon graduation:* $27,130.

APPLYING

Standardized Tests *Required:* SAT or ACT (for admission).

Options: electronic application, early decision, deferred entrance.

Required: essay or personal statement, high school transcript, 1 letter of recommendation. *Required for some:* interview.

CONTACT

Nancy Simmons, Admissions Coordinator, Prescott College, 220 Grove Avenue, Prescott, AZ 86301. *Phone:* 928-350-2100. *Toll-free phone:* 877-350-2100. *Fax:* 928-776-5242. *E-mail:* admissions@prescott.edu.

Southwest University of Visual Arts

Tucson, Arizona

http://www.suva.edu/

CONTACT

Robert Mairs, Director of Admissions, Southwest University of Visual Arts, 2525 North Country Club Road, Tucson, AZ 85716-2505. *Phone:* 520-325-0123. *Toll-free phone:* 800-825-8753. *Fax:* 520-325-5535.

University of Advancing Technology

Tempe, Arizona

http://www.uat.edu/

- **Proprietary** comprehensive, founded 1983
- **Urban** campus with easy access to Phoenix, AZ
- **Coed, primarily men**

FACULTY

Student/faculty ratio: 13:1.

ACADEMICS

Calendar: semesters. *Degrees:* associate, bachelor's, and master's.

Library: University of Advancing Computer Technology Library.

STUDENT LIFE

Housing options: on-campus residence required for freshman year; coed. Campus housing is university owned, leased by the school and is provided by a third party.

Activities and organizations: student-run newspaper, television station, Web Club, Gaming Club, Animation Club, Video Club, Student Government.

Campus security: 24-hour patrols.

FINANCIAL AID

Financial Aid Of all full-time matriculated undergraduates who enrolled in 2010, 799 applied for aid, 747 were judged to have need. *Average financial aid package:* $10,343. *Average need-based loan:* $5512. *Average need-based gift aid:* $6767.

APPLYING

Standardized Tests *Required for some:* SAT or ACT (for admission).

Options: electronic application.

Required: essay or personal statement, high school transcript. *Required for some:* minimum 2.5 GPA.

CONTACT

Admissions Office, University of Advancing Technology, 2625 West Baseline Road, Tempe, AZ 85283-1042. *Phone:* 602-383-8228. *Toll-free phone:* 800-658-5744. *Fax:* 602-383-8222. *E-mail:* admissions@uat.edu.

The University of Arizona

Tucson, Arizona

http://www.arizona.edu/

- **State-supported** university, founded 1885, part of Arizona Board of Regents
- **Urban** 392-acre campus
- **Endowment** $754.4 million
- **Coed** 35,123 undergraduate students, 85% full-time, 52% women, 48% men
- **Moderately difficult** entrance level, 84% of applicants were admitted

UNDERGRAD STUDENTS

29,783 full-time, 5,340 part-time. Students come from 53 states and territories; 112 other countries; 31% are from out of state; 4% Black or African American, non-Hispanic/Latino; 27% Hispanic/Latino; 5% Asian, non-Hispanic/Latino; 0.3% Native Hawaiian or other Pacific Islander, non-Hispanic/Latino; 1% American Indian or Alaska Native, non-Hispanic/Latino; 5% Two or more races, non-Hispanic/Latino; 0.7% Race/ethnicity unknown; 8% international; 7% transferred in; 20% live on campus.

Freshmen:

Admission: 33,608 applied, 28,089 admitted, 7,362 enrolled. *Average high school GPA:* 3.3. *Test scores:* SAT evidence-based reading and writing scores over 500: 87%; SAT math scores over 500: 90%; ACT scores over 18: 92%; SAT evidence-based reading and writing scores over 600: 50%; SAT math scores over 600: 49%; ACT scores over 24: 57%; SAT evidence-based reading and writing scores over 700: 10%; SAT math scores over 700: 12%; ACT scores over 30: 15%.

Retention: 83% of full-time freshmen returned.

FACULTY

Total: 2,347, 85% full-time, 91% with terminal degrees.

Student/faculty ratio: 15:1.

ACADEMICS

Calendar: semesters. *Degrees:* certificates, bachelor's, master's, doctoral, post-master's, and postbachelor's certificates.

Special study options: accelerated degree program, adult/continuing education programs, advanced placement credit, cooperative education, distance learning, double majors, English as a second language, external degree program, freshman honors college, honors programs, independent study, internships, off-campus study, part-time degree program, services for LD students, student-designed majors, study abroad, summer session for credit. *ROTC:* Army (b), Navy (b), Air Force (b).

Computers: 514 computers/terminals are available on campus for general student use. Students can access the following: campus intranet, computer help desk, free student e-mail accounts, online (class) grades, online (class) registration, online (class) schedules. Campuswide network is available. 100% of college-owned or -operated housing units are wired for high-speed Internet access. Wireless service is available via entire campus.

Library: University of Arizona Main Library plus 4 others. *Books:* 3.1 million (physical), 1.8 million (digital/electronic); *Serial titles:* 6.3 million (physical), 101,171 (digital/electronic); *Databases:* 835. Weekly public service hours: 94; study areas open 24 hours, 5–7 days a week; students can reserve study rooms.

STUDENT LIFE
Housing options: coed, women-only, special housing for students with disabilities. Campus housing is university owned and leased by the school. Freshman applicants given priority for college housing.

Activities and organizations: drama/theater group, student-run newspaper, radio and television station, choral group, marching band, Alpha Epsilon Delta, Wildcats Committed to Animal Rescue and Education, Physiology, Psi Chi Chapter, Investments Club, national fraternities, national sororities.

Athletics Member NCAA. All Division I.

Campus security: 24-hour patrols, student patrols, late-night transport/escort service, controlled dormitory access, emergency telephones.

Student services: health clinic, personal/psychological counseling, women's center, legal services.

COSTS & FINANCIAL AID
Costs (2017–18) *Tuition:* state resident $12,200 full-time; nonresident $35,700 full-time. Full-time tuition and fees vary according to class time, course level, course load, degree level, location, program, reciprocity agreements, and student level. Part-time tuition and fees vary according to class time, course level, course load, degree level, location, program, reciprocity agreements, and student level. No tuition increase for student's term of enrollment. *Room and board:* $12,550. Room and board charges vary according to board plan and housing facility. *Payment plan:* installment. *Waivers:* employees or children of employees.

Financial Aid Of all full-time matriculated undergraduates who enrolled in 2016, 18,155 applied for aid, 14,902 were judged to have need, 1,578 had their need fully met. 1,117 Federal Work-Study jobs (averaging $2581). 7,384 state and other part-time jobs (averaging $2892). In 2016, 6555 non-need-based awards were made. *Average percent of need met:* 58. *Average financial aid package:* $13,288. *Average need-based loan:* $5160. *Average need-based gift aid:* $10,555. *Average non-need-based aid:* $7974. *Average indebtedness upon graduation:* $23,956.

APPLYING
Standardized Tests *Recommended:* SAT or ACT (for admission).
Options: electronic application, deferred entrance.
Application fee: $50.
Required: high school transcript. *Required for some:* minimum 3.0 GPA. *Recommended:* essay or personal statement, interview.
Application deadlines: 5/1 (freshmen), rolling (transfers).
Notification: continuous (freshmen).

CONTACT
The University of Arizona, Tucson, AZ 85721. *Phone:* 520-621-3705.

University of Phoenix–Online Campus
Phoenix, Arizona
http://www.phoenix.edu/

CONTACT
Marc Booker, Sr. Director, Office of Admissions and Evaluation, University of Phoenix–Online Campus, 4035 South Riverpoint Parkway, Mail Stop CF-L101, Phoenix, AZ 85040. *Phone:* 602-557-4609. *Toll-free phone:* 866-766-0766. *Fax:* 480-643-1156.

University of Phoenix–Phoenix Campus
Tempe, Arizona
http://www.phoenix.edu/

CONTACT
Marc Booker, Sr. Director, Office of Admissions and Evaluation, University of Phoenix–Phoenix Campus, 4035 South Riverpoint Parkway, Mail Stop CF-L101, Phoenix, AZ 85040. *Phone:* 602-557-4609. *Toll-free phone:* 866-766-0766. *Fax:* 480-643-1156.

ARKANSAS

Arkansas Baptist College
Little Rock, Arkansas
http://www.arkansasbaptist.edu/

CONTACT
Arkansas Baptist College, 1621 Dr. Martin Luther King, Jr. Drive, Little Rock, AR 72202-6067. *Phone:* 501-244-5104 Ext. 5124.

Arkansas State University
Jonesboro, Arkansas
http://www.astate.edu/

CONTACT
Ms. Tracy Finch, Director of Admissions, Records, and Registration, Arkansas State University, PO Box 1570, State University, AR 72467. *Phone:* 870-972-2031. *Toll-free phone:* 800-382-3030. *Fax:* 870-972-3406. *E-mail:* admissions@astate.edu.

Arkansas Tech University
Russellville, Arkansas
http://www.atu.edu/

- **State-supported** comprehensive, founded 1909
- **Small-town** 559-acre campus
- **Endowment** $33.3 million
- **Coed** 10,781 undergraduate students, 62% full-time, 54% women, 46% men
- **Moderately difficult** entrance level, 95% of applicants were admitted

UNDERGRAD STUDENTS
6,729 full-time, 4,052 part-time. Students come from 40 states and territories; 38 other countries; 4% are from out of state; 8% Black or African American, non-Hispanic/Latino; 7% Hispanic/Latino; 1% Asian, non-Hispanic/Latino; 0.8% American Indian or Alaska Native, non-Hispanic/Latino; 3% Two or more races, non-Hispanic/Latino; 4% international; 4% transferred in; 31% live on campus.

Freshmen:
Admission: 5,006 applied, 4,743 admitted, 1,846 enrolled. *Average high school GPA:* 3.3. *Test scores:* SAT evidence-based reading and writing scores over 500: 17%; SAT math scores over 500: 33%; ACT scores over 18: 84%; ACT scores over 24: 40%; ACT scores over 30: 6%.
Retention: 72% of full-time freshmen returned.

FACULTY
Total: 623, 59% full-time, 47% with terminal degrees.
Student/faculty ratio: 19:1.

ACADEMICS
Calendar: semesters. *Degrees:* certificates, associate, bachelor's, master's, doctoral, and post-master's certificates.

Special study options: academic remediation for entering students, accelerated degree program, adult/continuing education programs, advanced placement credit, distance learning, double majors, English as a second language, honors programs, independent study, internships, off-campus study, part-time degree program, services for LD students, study abroad, summer session for credit. *ROTC:* Army (c).

Computers: 1,124 computers/terminals are available on campus for general student use. Students can access the following: campus intranet, computer help desk, free student e-mail accounts, online (class) grades, online (class) registration, online (class) schedules. Campuswide network is available. 100% of college-owned or -operated housing units are wired for high-speed Internet access. Wireless service is available via classrooms, computer centers, computer labs, dorm rooms, learning centers, libraries, student centers.

Library: Ross Pendergraft Library and Technology Center. *Books:* 313,011 (physical), 47,410 (digital/electronic); *Serial titles:* 265 (physical), 151 (digital/electronic); *Databases:* 262. Students can reserve study rooms.

STUDENT LIFE

Housing options: on-campus residence required through sophomore year; coed, men-only, women-only, special housing for students with disabilities. Campus housing is university owned. Freshman campus housing is guaranteed.

Activities and organizations: drama/theater group, student-run newspaper, radio and television station, choral group, marching band, national fraternities, national sororities.

Athletics Member NCAA. All Division II. *Intercollegiate sports:* baseball M(s), basketball M(s)/W(s), cheerleading M(s)/W(s), cross-country running W(s), football M(s), golf M(s)/W(s), softball W(s), tennis W(s), volleyball W(s). *Intramural sports:* basketball M/W, bowling M/W, golf M(c)/W(c), racquetball M/W, soccer M/W, softball M/W, table tennis M/W, tennis M/W, ultimate Frisbee M/W, volleyball M/W.

Campus security: 24-hour emergency response devices and patrols, student patrols, late-night transport/escort service, controlled dormitory access.

Student services: health clinic, personal/psychological counseling.

COSTS & FINANCIAL AID

Costs (2017–18) *Tuition:* state resident $6780 full-time, $226 per credit hour part-time; nonresident $13,560 full-time, $452 per credit hour part-time. Full-time tuition and fees vary according to course load and location. Part-time tuition and fees vary according to course load and location. *Required fees:* $2100 full-time, $70 per credit hour part-time. *Room and board:* $7338; room only: $4412. Room and board charges vary according to board plan, housing facility, and location. *Payment plans:* installment, deferred payment. *Waivers:* senior citizens and employees or children of employees.

Financial Aid Of all full-time matriculated undergraduates who enrolled in 2016, 6,107 applied for aid, 4,670 were judged to have need, 401 had their need fully met. In 2016, 897 non-need-based awards were made. *Average percent of need met:* 59. *Average financial aid package:* $9538. *Average need-based loan:* $3601. *Average need-based gift aid:* $4554. *Average non-need-based aid:* $6650. *Average indebtedness upon graduation:* $24,816.

APPLYING

Standardized Tests *Required:* SAT or ACT (for admission).

Options: electronic application, early action, deferred entrance.

Required: high school transcript, minimum 2.0 GPA.

Notification: continuous (freshmen), continuous (out-of-state freshmen), continuous (transfers).

CONTACT

Ms. Jessica Brock, Interim Director of Admissions, Arkansas Tech University, Brown Hall, Suite 104, 105 West O Street, Russellville, AR 72801. *Phone:* 479-968-0343. *Toll-free phone:* 800-582-6953. *Fax:* 479-964-0522. *E-mail:* tech.enroll@atu.edu.

Central Baptist College

Conway, Arkansas

http://www.cbc.edu/
- **Independent Baptist** 4-year, founded 1952
- **Small-town** 11-acre campus
- **Coed**
- **Minimally difficult** entrance level

FACULTY

Student/faculty ratio: 12:1.

ACADEMICS

Calendar: semesters. *Degrees:* associate and bachelor's.
Library: Story Library. Students can reserve study rooms.

STUDENT LIFE

Housing options: on-campus residence required through senior year; coed.

Activities and organizations: drama/theater group, student-run newspaper, radio station, choral group.

Athletics Member NCCAA.

Campus security: controlled dormitory access.

Student services: personal/psychological counseling.

COSTS

Costs (2017–18) *Comprehensive fee:* $23,250 includes full-time tuition ($14,250), mandatory fees ($1500), and room and board ($7500). Full-time tuition and fees vary according to course load. Part-time tuition: $475 per credit hour. Part-time tuition and fees vary according to course load. *Required fees:* $1500 per year part-time. *Room and board:* Room and board charges vary according to board plan and housing facility.

APPLYING

Standardized Tests *Required:* SAT or ACT (for admission).

Options: electronic application, early admission.

Required: high school transcript.

CONTACT

Central Baptist College, 1501 College Avenue, Conway, AR 72032. *Toll-free phone:* 800-205-6872.

Crowley's Ridge College

Paragould, Arkansas

http://www.crc.edu/
- **Independent** 4-year, founded 1964, affiliated with Church of Christ
- **Small-town** 150-acre campus
- **Coed** 189 undergraduate students
- **Noncompetitive** entrance level

ACADEMICS

Calendar: semesters. *Degrees:* associate and bachelor's.

Special study options: academic remediation for entering students, distance learning, honors programs, independent study, part-time degree program, summer session for credit.

Computers: Campuswide network is available.
Library: Learning Center.

STUDENT LIFE

Housing options: on-campus residence required through sophomore year; men-only, women-only. Campus housing is university owned.

Activities and organizations: drama/theater group, choral group.

Athletics Member NAIA. *Intercollegiate sports:* baseball M, basketball M(s)/W(s), cross-country running M(s)/W(s), golf M(s), softball W(s), volleyball W(s).

COSTS & FINANCIAL AID

Costs (2018–19) *Comprehensive fee:* $17,600 includes full-time tuition ($11,250) and room and board ($6350). Part-time tuition and fees vary according to course load. *College room only:* $2800. Room and board charges vary according to board plan and housing facility. *Payment plan:* installment. *Waivers:* employees or children of employees.

Financial Aid Of all full-time matriculated undergraduates who enrolled in 2016, 78 Federal Work-Study jobs (averaging $500).

APPLYING

Options: electronic application.

Required: high school transcript, recommendation form filled out by high school. *Required for some:* interview.

CONTACT

Crowley's Ridge College, 100 College Drive, Paragould, AR 72450-9731. *Toll-free phone:* 800-264-1096.

COLLEGES AT-A-GLANCE

Ecclesia College

Springdale, Arkansas
http://www.ecollege.edu/

- **Independent Christian** comprehensive, founded 1995
- **Small-town** 200-acre campus with easy access to Northwest Arkansas
- **Coed**
- **Noncompetitive** entrance level

FACULTY
Student/faculty ratio: 10:1.

ACADEMICS
Calendar: semesters. *Degrees:* associate, bachelor's, and master's.
Library: Ecclesia College Library.

STUDENT LIFE
Housing options: on-campus residence required through senior year; men-only, women-only. Campus housing is university owned. Freshman campus housing is guaranteed.

Activities and organizations: drama/theater group, choral group, Service Learning, Student Council, Worship Team, Missions.

Athletics Member NCCAA.

Campus security: student patrols.

Student services: personal/psychological counseling.

COSTS
Costs (2017–18) *Comprehensive fee:* $20,150 includes full-time tuition ($14,250), mandatory fees ($890), and room and board ($5010). Full-time tuition and fees vary according to course load and degree level. Part-time tuition: $475 per credit hour. Part-time tuition and fees vary according to course load and degree level. *Required fees:* $40 per credit hour part-time. *Room and board:* Room and board charges vary according to housing facility.

APPLYING
Standardized Tests *Required:* SAT or ACT (for admission).
Options: electronic application.
Application fee: $35.
Required: essay or personal statement, high school transcript, minimum 2.0 GPA, 1 letter of recommendation, interview.

CONTACT
Ecclesia College, 9653 Nations Drive, Springdale, AR 72762. *Phone:* 479-248-7236 Ext. 223.

 # Harding University

Searcy, Arkansas
http://www.harding.edu/

- **Independent** university, founded 1924, affiliated with Church of Christ
- **Small-town** 350-acre campus with easy access to Little Rock
- **Endowment** $128.7 million
- **Coed** 4,182 undergraduate students, 94% full-time, 55% women, 45% men
- **Moderately difficult** entrance level, 72% of applicants were admitted

UNDERGRAD STUDENTS
3,945 full-time, 237 part-time. Students come from 54 states and territories; 49 other countries; 71% are from out of state; 4% Black or African American, non-Hispanic/Latino; 3% Hispanic/Latino; 0.7% Asian, non-Hispanic/Latino; 0.5% American Indian or Alaska Native, non-Hispanic/Latino; 3% Two or more races, non-Hispanic/Latino; 7% international; 3% transferred in; 90% live on campus.

Freshmen:
Admission: 2,023 applied, 1,461 admitted, 945 enrolled. *Average high school GPA:* 3.7. *Test scores:* SAT evidence-based reading and writing scores over 500: 91%; SAT math scores over 500: 91%; ACT scores over 18: 98%; SAT evidence-based reading and writing scores over 600: 48%; SAT math scores over 600: 39%; ACT scores over 24: 61%; SAT evidence-based reading and writing scores over 700: 14%; SAT math scores over 700: 11%; ACT scores over 30: 19%.
Retention: 83% of full-time freshmen returned.

FACULTY
Total: 415, 73% full-time, 60% with terminal degrees.
Student/faculty ratio: 14:1.

ACADEMICS
Calendar: semesters. *Degrees:* bachelor's, master's, doctoral, and post-master's certificates.

Special study options: academic remediation for entering students, accelerated degree program, adult/continuing education programs, advanced placement credit, cooperative education, distance learning, double majors, English as a second language, freshman honors college, honors programs, independent study, internships, part-time degree program, services for LD students, student-designed majors, study abroad, summer session for credit. *ROTC:* Army (c).

Computers: 512 computers/terminals and 3,200 ports are available on campus for general student use. Students can access the following: campus intranet, computer help desk, free student e-mail accounts, online (class) grades, online (class) registration, online (class) schedules. Campuswide network is available. 100% of college-owned or -operated housing units are wired for high-speed Internet access. Wireless service is available via entire campus.

Library: Brackett Library plus 1 other. *Books:* 187,048 (physical), 286,079 (digital/electronic); *Serial titles:* 959 (physical), 78,392 (digital/electronic); *Databases:* 178. Students can reserve study rooms.

STUDENT LIFE
Housing options: on-campus residence required through senior year; men-only, women-only, special housing for students with disabilities. Campus housing is university owned. Freshman campus housing is guaranteed.

Activities and organizations: drama/theater group, student-run newspaper, radio and television station, choral group, marching band, Bisons for Christ, Harding in Action, Spring Break Campaigns, HUmanity.

Athletics Member NCAA. All Division II. *Intercollegiate sports:* baseball M(s), basketball M(s)/W(s), cheerleading W, cross-country running M(s)/W(s), football M(s), golf M(s)/W(s), lacrosse M(c), rugby M(c), soccer M(s)/W(s), tennis M(s)/W(s), track and field M(s)/W(s), ultimate Frisbee M(c)/W(c), volleyball W(s). *Intramural sports:* basketball M/W, cross-country running M/W, football M/W, golf M/W, racquetball M/W, soccer M/W, softball M/W, swimming and diving M/W, table tennis M/W, tennis M/W, track and field M/W, ultimate Frisbee M/W, volleyball M/W, weight lifting M/W.

Campus security: 24-hour emergency response devices and patrols, student patrols, late-night transport/escort service, controlled dormitory access.

Student services: health clinic, personal/psychological counseling.

COSTS & FINANCIAL AID
Costs (2017–18) *Comprehensive fee:* $26,084 includes full-time tuition ($18,690), mandatory fees ($500), and room and board ($6894). Full-time tuition and fees vary according to course load. Part-time tuition: $623 per credit hour. Part-time tuition and fees vary according to course load. *Required fees:* $25 per credit hour part-time. *College room only:* $3592. Room and board charges vary according to board plan and housing facility. *Payment plans:* tuition prepayment, installment. *Waivers:* senior citizens and employees or children of employees.

Financial Aid Of all full-time matriculated undergraduates who enrolled in 2016, 3,177 applied for aid, 2,561 were judged to have need, 407 had their need fully met. 600 Federal Work-Study jobs (averaging $929). 1,455 state and other part-time jobs (averaging $1281). In 2016, 1230 non-need-based awards were made. *Average percent of need met:* 78. *Average financial aid package:* $12,882. *Average need-based loan:* $5204. *Average need-based gift aid:* $9508. *Average non-need-based aid:* $7000. *Average indebtedness upon graduation:* $31,007.

APPLYING
Standardized Tests *Required:* SAT or ACT (for admission).
Options: electronic application, early admission, early action, deferred entrance.
Application fee: $50.
Required: essay or personal statement, high school transcript, 3 letters of recommendation.
Application deadlines: rolling (freshmen), rolling (transfers).

Notification: continuous (freshmen), continuous (transfers).

CONTACT
Mr. Glenn Dillard, Assistant Vice President for Enrollment Management, Harding University, 915 E. Market Avenue, Box 12255, Searcy, AR 72149-5615. *Phone:* 501-279-4407. *Toll-free phone:* 800-477-4407. *Fax:* 501-279-4129. *E-mail:* admissions@harding.edu.

See this page for display ad and page 1304 for the College Close-Up.

Henderson State University
Arkadelphia, Arkansas
http://www.hsu.edu/
- **State-supported** comprehensive, founded 1890
- **Small-town** 151-acre campus with easy access to Little Rock
- **Coed**
- **Moderately difficult** entrance level

FACULTY
Student/faculty ratio: 15:1.

ACADEMICS
Calendar: semesters. *Degrees:* certificates, bachelor's, master's, post-master's, and postbachelor's certificates.
Library: Huie Library plus 1 other. *Books:* 225,859 (physical), 142,000 (digital/electronic); *Databases:* 223. Weekly public service hours: 80; students can reserve study rooms.

STUDENT LIFE
Housing options: on-campus residence required through sophomore year; coed, men-only, women-only. Campus housing is university owned and is provided by a third party. Freshman applicants given priority for college housing.
Activities and organizations: drama/theater group, student-run newspaper, radio and television station, choral group, marching band, Heart and Key, Student Government Association, Residence Hall Association, national fraternities, national sororities.
Athletics Member NCAA. All Division II.
Campus security: 24-hour emergency response devices and patrols, late-night transport/escort service, controlled dormitory access, Reddie Rides offered at night.
Student services: health clinic, personal/psychological counseling.

COSTS & FINANCIAL AID
Costs (2017–18) *Tuition:* state resident $6630 full-time, $221 per credit hour part-time; nonresident $8280 full-time, $276 per credit hour part-time. Full-time tuition and fees vary according to course load. Part-time tuition and fees vary according to course load. *Required fees:* $1681 full-time. *Room and board:* $7320. Room and board charges vary according to board plan and housing facility.
Financial Aid Of all full-time matriculated undergraduates who enrolled in 2014, 2,703 applied for aid, 2,424 were judged to have need, 265 had their need fully met. In 2014, 138 non-need-based awards were made. *Average percent of need met:* 57. *Average financial aid package:* $11,778. *Average need-based loan:* $3714. *Average need-based gift aid:* $4572. *Average non-need-based aid:* $5730. *Average indebtedness upon graduation:* $23,641.

APPLYING
Standardized Tests *Required:* SAT or ACT (for admission). *Recommended:* ACT (for admission).
Options: electronic application, deferred entrance.
Required: high school transcript. *Required for some:* essay or personal statement, 3 letters of recommendation. *Recommended:* minimum 2.5 GPA.

CONTACT
Dr. Brandie Benton, Associate Provost Enrollment Services and Admissions, Henderson State University, 1100 Henderson Street, PO Box 7560, Arkadelphia, AR 71999-0001. *Phone:* 870-230-5203. *Toll-free phone:* 800-228-7333. *Fax:* 870-230-5066. *E-mail:* bentonb@hsu.edu.

Hendrix College
Conway, Arkansas
http://www.hendrix.edu/

- **Independent United Methodist** comprehensive, founded 1876
- **Suburban** 180-acre campus with easy access to Little Rock
- **Endowment** $185.5 million
- **Coed** 1,238 undergraduate students, 99% full-time, 52% women, 48% men
- **Very difficult** entrance level, 80% of applicants were admitted

UNDERGRAD STUDENTS
1,228 full-time, 10 part-time. 7% Black or African American, non-Hispanic/Latino; 6% Hispanic/Latino; 5% Asian, non-Hispanic/Latino; 0.8% American Indian or Alaska Native, non-Hispanic/Latino; 4% Two or more races, non-Hispanic/Latino; 5% Race/ethnicity unknown; 2% international; 1% transferred in.

Freshmen:
Admission: 1,465 applied, 1,169 admitted, 338 enrolled. *Average high school GPA:* 3.9. *Test scores:* SAT evidence-based reading and writing scores over 500: 95%; SAT math scores over 500: 91%; ACT scores over 18: 100%; SAT evidence-based reading and writing scores over 600: 66%; SAT math scores over 600: 58%; ACT scores over 24: 82%; SAT evidence-based reading and writing scores over 700: 30%; SAT math scores over 700: 26%; ACT scores over 30: 36%.

Retention: 83% of full-time freshmen returned.

FACULTY
Total: 136, 76% full-time, 87% with terminal degrees.
Student/faculty ratio: 11:1.

ACADEMICS
Calendar: semesters. *Degrees:* bachelor's and master's.

Special study options: advanced placement credit, cooperative education, double majors, English as a second language, independent study, internships, off-campus study, services for LD students, student-designed majors, study abroad. *ROTC:* Army (c).

Unusual degree programs: 3-2 engineering with Columbia University, Vanderbilt University, Washington University in St. Louis; public health with University of Arkansas.

Computers: Students can access the following: campus intranet, computer help desk, free student e-mail accounts, online (class) grades, online (class) registration, online (class) schedules. Campuswide network is available. 100% of college-owned or -operated housing units are wired for high-speed Internet access. Wireless service is available via entire campus.

Library: Olin C. and Marjorie H. Bailey Library plus 1 other. Weekly public service hours: 83; study areas open 24 hours, 5–7 days a week.

STUDENT LIFE
Housing options: on-campus residence required through senior year; coed, men-only, women-only, special housing for students with disabilities. Campus housing is university owned. Freshman campus housing is guaranteed.

Activities and organizations: drama/theater group, student-run newspaper, radio station, choral group.

Athletics Member NCAA. All Division III. *Intercollegiate sports:* baseball M, basketball M/W, cross-country running M/W, field hockey W, football M, golf M/W, lacrosse M/W, soccer M/W, softball W, swimming and diving M/W, tennis M/W, track and field M/W, volleyball W. *Intramural sports:* basketball M/W, cheerleading M/W, football M/W, racquetball M/W, soccer M/W, softball M/W, table tennis M/W, tennis M/W, ultimate Frisbee M/W.

Campus security: 24-hour emergency response devices and patrols, late-night transport/escort service, controlled dormitory access.

Student services: health clinic, personal/psychological counseling.

COSTS & FINANCIAL AID
Costs (2018–19) *Comprehensive fee:* $58,074 includes full-time tuition ($45,440), mandatory fees ($350), and room and board ($12,284). Full-time tuition and fees vary according to course load. Part-time tuition: $5466 per course. Part-time tuition and fees vary according to course load. *College room only:* $6324. Room and board charges vary according to board plan and housing facility. *Payment plan:* installment. *Waivers:* employees or children of employees.

Financial Aid Of all full-time matriculated undergraduates who enrolled in 2016, 1,099 applied for aid, 902 were judged to have need, 355 had their need fully met. 579 Federal Work-Study jobs (averaging $1911). 328 state and other part-time jobs (averaging $1684). In 2016, 378 non-need-based awards were made. *Average percent of need met:* 85. *Average financial aid package:* $35,223. *Average need-based loan:* $3675. *Average need-based gift aid:* $31,309. *Average non-need-based aid:* $25,907. *Average indebtedness upon graduation:* $30,213.

APPLYING
Standardized Tests *Required:* SAT or ACT (for admission).

Options: electronic application, early action.

Application fee: $40.

Required: essay or personal statement, high school transcript. *Required for some:* interview. *Recommended:* 1 letter of recommendation.

Application deadlines: 6/1 (freshmen), 11/15 (early action).

Notification: continuous (freshmen), 12/15 (early action).

CONTACT
Hendrix College, 1600 Washington Avenue, Conway, AR 72032. *Phone:* 501-450-1362. *Toll-free phone:* 800-277-9017. *Fax:* 501-450-3843. *E-mail:* adm@hendrix.edu.

John Brown University
Siloam Springs, Arkansas
http://www.jbu.edu/

- **Independent interdenominational** comprehensive, founded 1919
- **Small-town** 200-acre campus
- **Endowment** $113.3 million
- **Coed** 1,972 undergraduate students, 76% full-time, 57% women, 43% men
- **Moderately difficult** entrance level, 76% of applicants were admitted

UNDERGRAD STUDENTS
1,490 full-time, 482 part-time. Students come from 41 states and territories; 50 other countries; 49% are from out of state; 2% Black or African American, non-Hispanic/Latino; 6% Hispanic/Latino; 2% Asian, non-Hispanic/Latino; 0.1% Native Hawaiian or other Pacific Islander, non-Hispanic/Latino; 2% American Indian or Alaska Native, non-Hispanic/Latino; 4% Two or more races, non-Hispanic/Latino; 4% Race/ethnicity unknown; 5% international; 7% transferred in; 58% live on campus.

Freshmen:
Admission: 1,198 applied, 908 admitted, 326 enrolled. *Average high school GPA:* 3.7. *Test scores:* SAT evidence-based reading and writing scores over 500: 89%; SAT math scores over 500: 92%; ACT scores over 18: 99%; SAT evidence-based reading and writing scores over 600: 64%; SAT math scores over 600: 43%; ACT scores over 24: 76%; SAT evidence-based reading and writing scores over 700: 21%; SAT math scores over 700: 8%; ACT scores over 30: 24%.

Retention: 82% of full-time freshmen returned.

FACULTY
Total: 239, 36% full-time, 50% with terminal degrees.
Student/faculty ratio: 14:1.

ACADEMICS
Calendar: semesters. *Degrees:* associate, bachelor's, master's, and post-master's certificates.

Special study options: academic remediation for entering students, accelerated degree program, adult/continuing education programs, cooperative education, distance learning, double majors, English as a second language, external degree program, honors programs, independent study, internships, part-time degree program, services for LD students, student-designed majors, study abroad. *ROTC:* Army (c), Air Force (c).

Computers: 250 computers/terminals are available on campus for general student use. Students can access the following: campus intranet, computer help desk, free student e-mail accounts, online (class) grades, online (class) registration, online (class) schedules. Campuswide network is available. 100% of college-owned or -operated housing units are wired for

high-speed Internet access. Wireless service is available via entire campus.

Library: Arutunoff Learning Resource Center plus 4 others. *Books:* 105,116 (physical), 329,913 (digital/electronic); *Serial titles:* 1,032 (physical), 67,078 (digital/electronic); *Databases:* 144. Weekly public service hours: 110; students can reserve study rooms.

STUDENT LIFE

Housing options: on-campus residence required through junior year; coed, men-only, women-only, special housing for students with disabilities. Campus housing is university owned. Freshman campus housing is guaranteed.

Activities and organizations: drama/theater group, student-run newspaper, radio and television station, choral group, Student Government Association, Student Ministries Organization, Student Activities Club, Student Missionary Fellowship, Enactus.

Athletics Member NAIA. *Intercollegiate sports:* basketball M(s)/W(s), cross-country running M(s)/W(s), rugby M(c)/W(c), soccer M(s)/W(s), tennis M(s)/W(s), ultimate Frisbee M(c)/W(c), volleyball W(s). *Intramural sports:* basketball M/W, football M/W, soccer M/W, softball M/W, volleyball M/W.

Campus security: 24-hour emergency response devices and patrols, late-night transport/escort service, controlled dormitory access.

Student services: health clinic, personal/psychological counseling.

COSTS & FINANCIAL AID

Costs (2018–19) *Comprehensive fee:* $36,152 includes full-time tuition ($25,750), mandatory fees ($1178), and room and board ($9224). Full-time tuition and fees vary according to course load and degree level. Part-time tuition: $833 per credit hour. Part-time tuition and fees vary according to course load and degree level. *Required fees:* $286 per term part-time. *College room only:* $4424. Room and board charges vary according to board plan and housing facility. *Payment plan:* installment. *Waivers:* employees or children of employees.

Financial Aid Of all full-time matriculated undergraduates who enrolled in 2016, 1,217 applied for aid, 1,050 were judged to have need, 172 had their need fully met. In 2016, 768 non-need-based awards were made. *Average percent of need met:* 67. *Average financial aid package:* $19,535. *Average need-based loan:* $4582. *Average need-based gift aid:* $14,636. *Average non-need-based aid:* $15,114. *Average indebtedness upon graduation:* $24,467.

APPLYING

Standardized Tests *Required for some:* SAT or ACT (for admission).

Options: electronic application, deferred entrance.

Application fee: $25.

Required: essay or personal statement, high school transcript, minimum 2.5 GPA, 2 letters of recommendation. *Recommended:* interview.

Application deadlines: rolling (freshmen), rolling (transfers).

Notification: continuous (freshmen), continuous (transfers).

CONTACT

Mr. Jared Burgess, Director of Visitation Program, John Brown University, 2000 West University, Siloam Springs, AR 72761. *Phone:* 479-524-7190. *Toll-free phone:* 877-JBU-INFO. *Fax:* 479-524-4196. *E-mail:* jburgess@jbu.edu.

Lyon College

Batesville, Arkansas

http://www.lyon.edu/

- **Independent Presbyterian** 4-year, founded 1872
- **Small-town** 136-acre campus
- **Coed** 672 undergraduate students, 97% full-time, 45% women, 55% men
- **Moderately difficult** entrance level, 64% of applicants were admitted

UNDERGRAD STUDENTS

652 full-time, 20 part-time. 32% are from out of state; 7% Black or African American, non-Hispanic/Latino; 8% Hispanic/Latino; 3% Asian, non-Hispanic/Latino; 2% American Indian or Alaska Native, non-Hispanic/Latino; 6% Race/ethnicity unknown; 4% international; 7% transferred in; 70% live on campus.

Freshmen:

Admission: 1,652 applied, 1,062 admitted, 190 enrolled. *Average high school GPA:* 3.6. *Test scores:* SAT evidence-based reading and writing scores over 500: 83%; SAT math scores over 500: 93%; ACT scores over 18: 98%; SAT evidence-based reading and writing scores over 600: 37%; SAT math scores over 600: 47%; ACT scores over 24: 61%; SAT evidence-based reading and writing scores over 700: 7%; ACT scores over 30: 20%.

Retention: 62% of full-time freshmen returned.

FACULTY

Total: 57, 75% full-time, 82% with terminal degrees.

Student/faculty ratio: 14:1.

ACADEMICS

Calendar: semesters. *Degree:* bachelor's.

Special study options: accelerated degree program, advanced placement credit, double majors, independent study, internships, off-campus study, part-time degree program, student-designed majors, study abroad, summer session for credit.

Unusual degree programs: 3-2 engineering with Missouri University of Science and Technology, University of Arkansas, University of Minnesota.

Computers: Students can access the following: campus intranet, computer help desk, free student e-mail accounts, online (class) grades, online (class) registration, online (class) schedules. Campuswide network is available. 100% of college-owned or -operated housing units are wired for high-speed Internet access. Wireless service is available via entire campus.

Library: Mabee-Simpson Library.

STUDENT LIFE

Housing options: on-campus residence required through junior year; coed. Campus housing is university owned. Freshman campus housing is guaranteed.

Activities and organizations: drama/theater group, student-run newspaper, choral group, Wesley Fellowship, Gay-Straight Alliance, Alpha Xi Delta Sorority, Fellowship of Christian Athletes, Young Democrats/Japanese Culture Club, national fraternities, national sororities.

Athletics Member NAIA. *Intercollegiate sports:* baseball M(s), basketball M(s)/W(s), cross-country running M(s)/W(s), football M(s), golf M(s)/W(s), soccer M(s)/W(s), softball W(s), volleyball W(s), wrestling M(s)/W(s). *Intramural sports:* badminton M/W, basketball M/W, football M/W, softball M/W, table tennis M/W, tennis M/W, ultimate Frisbee M/W, volleyball M/W.

Campus security: 24-hour patrols, late-night transport/escort service, controlled dormitory access.

Student services: health clinic, personal/psychological counseling.

COSTS & FINANCIAL AID

Costs (2017–18) *Comprehensive fee:* $36,120 includes full-time tuition ($27,100), mandatory fees ($240), and room and board ($8780). Full-time tuition and fees vary according to course load. Part-time tuition: $895 per credit hour. *Required fees:* $450 per credit hour part-time. *College room only:* $2499. Room and board charges vary according to board plan and housing facility. *Payment plan:* installment. *Waivers:* employees or children of employees.

Financial Aid Of all full-time matriculated undergraduates who enrolled in 2016, 569 applied for aid, 507 were judged to have need, 115 had their need fully met. 142 Federal Work-Study jobs (averaging $963). 7 state and other part-time jobs (averaging $857). In 2016, 101 non-need-based awards were made. *Average percent of need met:* 71. *Average financial aid package:* $21,210. *Average need-based loan:* $3992. *Average need-based gift aid:* $18,345. *Average non-need-based aid:* $14,205. *Average indebtedness upon graduation:* $22,321.

APPLYING

Standardized Tests *Required:* SAT or ACT (for admission).

Options: electronic application, early admission, early action, deferred entrance.

Required: high school transcript, minimum 2.5 GPA. *Required for some:* essay or personal statement, 2 letters of recommendation.

Application deadlines: rolling (freshmen), rolling (transfers).

Notification: continuous (freshmen), continuous (transfers).

CONTACT
Office of Enrollment Services, Lyon College, 2300 Highland Road, Batesville, AR 72501. *Phone:* 870-307-7250. *Toll-free phone:* 800-423-2542. *Fax:* 870-307-7542. *E-mail:* admissions@lyon.edu.

Ouachita Baptist University
Arkadelphia, Arkansas
http://www.obu.edu/
- **Independent Baptist** 4-year, founded 1886
- **Small-town** 200-acre campus with easy access to Little Rock
- **Endowment** $108.2 million
- **Coed** 1,545 undergraduate students, 97% full-time, 55% women, 45% men
- **Moderately difficult** entrance level, 71% of applicants were admitted

UNDERGRAD STUDENTS
1,500 full-time, 45 part-time. Students come from 28 states and territories; 28 other countries; 31% are from out of state; 8% Black or African American, non-Hispanic/Latino; 5% Hispanic/Latino; 0.5% Asian, non-Hispanic/Latino; 0.2% Native Hawaiian or other Pacific Islander, non-Hispanic/Latino; 0.4% American Indian or Alaska Native, non-Hispanic/Latino; 2% Two or more races, non-Hispanic/Latino; 3% international; 2% transferred in; 96% live on campus.

Freshmen:
Admission: 1,786 applied, 1,267 admitted, 468 enrolled. *Average high school GPA:* 3.6. *Test scores:* SAT evidence-based reading and writing scores over 500: 87%; SAT math scores over 500: 72%; ACT scores over 18: 96%; SAT evidence-based reading and writing scores over 600: 40%; SAT math scores over 600: 36%; ACT scores over 24: 56%; SAT evidence-based reading and writing scores over 700: 10%; SAT math scores over 700: 2%; ACT scores over 30: 16%.
Retention: 79% of full-time freshmen returned.

FACULTY
Total: 177, 56% full-time, 63% with terminal degrees.
Student/faculty ratio: 12:1.

ACADEMICS
Calendar: semesters. *Degrees:* associate and bachelor's.
Special study options: academic remediation for entering students, accelerated degree program, adult/continuing education programs, advanced placement credit, cooperative education, distance learning, double majors, English as a second language, honors programs, independent study, internships, off-campus study, part-time degree program, study abroad, summer session for credit. *ROTC:* Army (b).
Unusual degree programs: 3-2 engineering with University of Arkansas.
Computers: 275 computers/terminals and 1,375 ports are available on campus for general student use. Students can access the following: campus intranet, computer help desk, free student e-mail accounts, online (class) grades, online (class) schedules, student Web portal. Campuswide network is available. 100% of college-owned or -operated housing units are wired for high-speed Internet access. Wireless service is available via entire campus.
Library: Riley-Hickingbotham Library plus 2 others. *Books:* 176,669 (physical), 5,279 (digital/electronic). Weekly public service hours: 80; students can reserve study rooms.

STUDENT LIFE
Housing options: on-campus residence required through senior year; men-only, women-only, special housing for students with disabilities. Campus housing is university owned and leased by the school. Freshman campus housing is guaranteed.
Activities and organizations: drama/theater group, student-run newspaper, television station, choral group, marching band, Phi Beta Lambda, Student Foundation, Student Education Association, Campus Activities Board, International Club.
Athletics Member NCAA. All Division II. *Intercollegiate sports:* baseball M(s), basketball M(s)/W(s), cheerleading M/W, cross-country running W(s), football M(s), soccer M(s)/W(s), softball W(s), swimming and diving M(s)/W(s), tennis M(s)/W(s), volleyball W(s), wrestling M(s). *Intramural sports:* basketball M/W, football M/W, soccer M, softball M/W, table tennis M/W.

Campus security: 24-hour emergency response devices and patrols, controlled dormitory access.
Student services: health clinic, personal/psychological counseling.

COSTS & FINANCIAL AID
Costs (2018–19) *Comprehensive fee:* $34,670 includes full-time tuition ($26,200), mandatory fees ($590), and room and board ($7880). Full-time tuition and fees vary according to degree level and location. Part-time tuition: $725 per semester hour. Part-time tuition and fees vary according to degree level and location. *Room and board:* Room and board charges vary according to housing facility. *Payment plans:* installment, deferred payment. *Waivers:* employees or children of employees.
Financial Aid Of all full-time matriculated undergraduates who enrolled in 2017, 1,198 applied for aid, 995 were judged to have need, 359 had their need fully met. In 2017, 450 non-need-based awards were made. *Average percent of need met:* 85. *Average financial aid package:* $23,850. *Average need-based loan:* $4024. *Average need-based gift aid:* $16,576. *Average non-need-based aid:* $13,091. *Average indebtedness upon graduation:* $28,406. *Financial aid deadline:* 5/1.

APPLYING
Standardized Tests *Required:* SAT or ACT (for admission).
Options: deferred entrance.
Required: high school transcript, minimum 2.8 GPA. *Recommended:* interview.
Application deadlines: 8/15 (freshmen), 8/15 (transfers).
Notification: continuous (freshmen), continuous (transfers).

CONTACT
Mrs. Lori Motl, Director of Admissions Counseling, Ouachita Baptist University, OBU Box 3776, Arkadelphia, AR 71998-0001. *Phone:* 870-245-5110. *Toll-free phone:* 800-342-5628. *Fax:* 870-245-5500. *E-mail:* motll@obu.edu.

Philander Smith College
Little Rock, Arkansas
http://www.philander.edu/
- **Independent United Methodist** 4-year, founded 1877
- **Urban** 25-acre campus
- **Coed**
- **Minimally difficult** entrance level

FACULTY
Student/faculty ratio: 16:1.

ACADEMICS
Calendar: semesters. *Degree:* bachelor's.
Library: D. W. Reynolds Library & Technology Center. *Books:* 74,152 (physical), 20,575 (digital/electronic); *Serial titles:* 190 (physical), 166 (digital/electronic); *Databases:* 47. Weekly public service hours: 81; students can reserve study rooms.

STUDENT LIFE
Housing options: on-campus residence required for freshman year; coed. Campus housing is university owned. Freshman campus housing is guaranteed.
Activities and organizations: drama/theater group, choral group, Student Government Association, Panther Programming Council, Panther Dolls, Panther Newscast, Religious Life Council, national fraternities, national sororities.
Athletics Member NAIA.
Campus security: 24-hour emergency response devices and patrols, student patrols, controlled dormitory access.
Student services: health clinic, personal/psychological counseling.

COSTS & FINANCIAL AID
Costs (2017–18) *One-time required fee:* $235. *Comprehensive fee:* $17,906 includes full-time tuition ($11,804), mandatory fees ($910), and room and board ($5192). Full-time tuition and fees vary according to program. Part-time tuition: $245 per credit hour. Part-time tuition and fees vary according to course load. *Required fees:* $910 per year part-time, $405 per term part-time. *College room only:* $3058. Room and board charges vary according to board plan and housing facility. *Payment plans:* installment, deferred payment.

Financial Aid Of all full-time matriculated undergraduates who enrolled in 2016, 690 applied for aid, 668 were judged to have need, 36 had their need fully met. 88 Federal Work-Study jobs (averaging $2600). In 2016, 31 non-need-based awards were made. *Average percent of need met:* 51. *Average financial aid package:* $13,134. *Average need-based loan:* $3653. *Average need-based gift aid:* $9917. *Average non-need-based aid:* $13,673. *Average indebtedness upon graduation:* $46,965.

APPLYING
Standardized Tests *Required:* SAT or ACT (for admission).

Options: electronic application, deferred entrance.

Application fee: $25.

Required: high school transcript.

CONTACT
Mr. Maurice Osbourne, Director of Admissions, Philander Smith College, 900 West Daisy Bates Drive, Little Rock, AR 72202. *Phone:* 501-370-5221. *Toll-free phone:* 800-446-6772. *Fax:* 501-370-5225.

Southern Arkansas University–Magnolia
Magnolia, Arkansas
http://www.saumag.edu/

- **State-supported** comprehensive, founded 1909, part of Southern Arkansas University System
- **Small-town** 1390-acre campus
- **Endowment** $33.9 million
- **Coed** 3,475 undergraduate students, 84% full-time, 55% women, 45% men
- **Moderately difficult** entrance level, 69% of applicants were admitted

UNDERGRAD STUDENTS
2,924 full-time, 551 part-time. Students come from 26 states and territories; 19 other countries; 23% are from out of state; 27% Black or African American, non-Hispanic/Latino; 4% Hispanic/Latino; 1% Asian, non-Hispanic/Latino; 0.4% Native Hawaiian or other Pacific Islander, non-Hispanic/Latino; 0.7% American Indian or Alaska Native, non-Hispanic/Latino; 2% international; 6% transferred in; 52% live on campus.

Freshmen:
Admission: 3,604 applied, 2,503 admitted, 870 enrolled. *Average high school GPA:* 3.3. *Test scores:* SAT evidence-based reading and writing scores over 500: 68%; SAT math scores over 500: 73%; ACT scores over 18: 84%; SAT evidence-based reading and writing scores over 600: 15%; SAT math scores over 600: 18%; ACT scores over 24: 35%; ACT scores over 30: 4%.

Retention: 66% of full-time freshmen returned.

FACULTY
Total: 282, 56% full-time, 47% with terminal degrees.

Student/faculty ratio: 18:1.

ACADEMICS
Calendar: semesters. *Degrees:* certificates, associate, bachelor's, and master's.

Special study options: academic remediation for entering students, accelerated degree program, adult/continuing education programs, advanced placement credit, distance learning, double majors, English as a second language, freshman honors college, honors programs, independent study, internships, part-time degree program, services for LD students, study abroad, summer session for credit.

Computers: 199 computers/terminals and 199 ports are available on campus for general student use. Students can access the following: campus intranet, computer help desk, free student e-mail accounts, online (class) grades, online (class) registration, online (class) schedules. Campuswide network is available. 100% of college-owned or -operated housing units are wired for high-speed Internet access. Wireless service is available via computer centers, computer labs, dorm rooms, libraries, student centers.

Library: Magale Library. *Books:* 143,395 (physical), 10,521 (digital/electronic); *Serial titles:* 145 (physical), 75 (digital/electronic); *Databases:* 186. Weekly public service hours: 87.

STUDENT LIFE
Housing options: on-campus residence required through sophomore year; coed, men-only, women-only. Campus housing is university owned and is provided by a third party. Freshman campus housing is guaranteed.

Activities and organizations: drama/theater group, student-run newspaper, radio station, choral group, marching band, Student Government Association, Student Activities Board, Resident Hall Association, Residential College, International Student Association, national fraternities, national sororities.

Athletics Member NCAA. All Division II. *Intercollegiate sports:* baseball M(s), basketball M(s)/W(s), cheerleading M(s)(c)/W(s)(c), cross-country running M(s)/W(s), football M(s), golf M/W, softball W(s), tennis W(s), track and field M(s)/W(s), volleyball W(s). *Intramural sports:* badminton M/W, basketball M/W, football M, golf M/W, soccer M/W, softball M/W, swimming and diving M/W, table tennis M/W, tennis M/W, ultimate Frisbee M/W, volleyball M/W.

Campus security: 24-hour emergency response devices, student patrols, late-night transport/escort service, controlled dormitory access.

Student services: health clinic, personal/psychological counseling.

COSTS & FINANCIAL AID
Costs (2017–18) *Tuition:* state resident $6840 full-time, $228 per credit hour part-time; nonresident $10,650 full-time, $355 per credit hour part-time. Full-time tuition and fees vary according to course load. Part-time tuition and fees vary according to course load. *Required fees:* $1506 full-time. *Room and board:* $6028; room only: $2988. Room and board charges vary according to board plan and housing facility. *Payment plan:* installment. *Waivers:* children of alumni, senior citizens, and employees or children of employees.

Financial Aid Of all full-time matriculated undergraduates who enrolled in 2016, 2,547 applied for aid, 2,244 were judged to have need, 890 had their need fully met. 548 Federal Work-Study jobs (averaging $1716). 474 state and other part-time jobs (averaging $3015). In 2016, 459 non-need-based awards were made. *Average percent of need met:* 56. *Average financial aid package:* $12,305. *Average need-based loan:* $3796. *Average need-based gift aid:* $4705. *Average non-need-based aid:* $5286. *Average indebtedness upon graduation:* $22,616.

APPLYING
Standardized Tests *Required:* SAT or ACT (for admission). *Recommended:* ACT (for admission).

Options: electronic application, early admission, deferred entrance.

Required: high school transcript. *Required for some:* interview.

Application deadlines: 8/27 (freshmen), 8/27 (transfers).

CONTACT
Southern Arkansas University–Magnolia, 100 East University, Magnolia, AR 71753. *Phone:* 870-235-4040. *Toll-free phone:* 800-332-7286.

Strayer University–Little Rock Campus
Little Rock, Arkansas
http://www.strayer.edu/arkansas/little-rock/

CONTACT
Strayer University–Little Rock Campus, 10825 Financial Centre Parkway, Suite 400, Little Rock, AR 72211. *Toll-free phone:* 888-311-0355.

University of Arkansas
Fayetteville, Arkansas
http://www.uark.edu/

- **State-supported** university, founded 1871, part of University of Arkansas System
- **Urban** 718-acre campus
- **Coed** 23,044 undergraduate students, 89% full-time, 53% women, 47% men
- **Moderately difficult** entrance level, 66% of applicants were admitted

UNDERGRAD STUDENTS
20,464 full-time, 2,580 part-time. Students come from 47 states and territories; 84 other countries; 45% are from out of state; 4% Black or African American, non-Hispanic/Latino; 9% Hispanic/Latino; 2% Asian,

non-Hispanic/Latino; 0.1% Native Hawaiian or other Pacific Islander, non-Hispanic/Latino; 0.9% American Indian or Alaska Native, non-Hispanic/Latino; 4% Two or more races, non-Hispanic/Latino; 0.5% Race/ethnicity unknown; 3% international; 6% transferred in; 25% live on campus.

Freshmen:

Admission: 21,715 applied, 14,324 admitted, 5,065 enrolled. *Average high school GPA:* 3.7. *Test scores:* SAT evidence-based reading and writing scores over 500: 96%; SAT math scores over 500: 95%; ACT scores over 18: 100%; SAT evidence-based reading and writing scores over 600: 55%; SAT math scores over 600: 48%; ACT scores over 24: 75%; SAT evidence-based reading and writing scores over 700: 9%; SAT math scores over 700: 9%; ACT scores over 30: 22%.

Retention: 82% of full-time freshmen returned.

FACULTY

Total: 1,384, 86% full-time, 79% with terminal degrees.

Student/faculty ratio: 19:1.

ACADEMICS

Calendar: semesters. *Degrees:* certificates, bachelor's, master's, doctoral, post-master's, and postbachelor's certificates.

Special study options: academic remediation for entering students, accelerated degree program, advanced placement credit, cooperative education, distance learning, double majors, English as a second language, freshman honors college, honors programs, independent study, internships, off-campus study, part-time degree program, services for LD students, student-designed majors, study abroad, summer session for credit. *ROTC:* Army (b), Air Force (b).

Unusual degree programs: 3-2 business administration; law.

Computers: 675 computers/terminals and 24 ports are available on campus for general student use. Students can access the following: computer help desk, free student e-mail accounts, online (class) grades, online (class) registration, online (class) schedules. Campuswide network is available. 100% of college-owned or -operated housing units are wired for high-speed Internet access. Wireless service is available via entire campus.

Library: David W. Mullins Library plus 4 others. *Books:* 1.7 million (physical), 659,516 (digital/electronic); *Serial titles:* 3,154 (physical), 92,699 (digital/electronic); *Databases:* 332. Weekly public service hours: 109; students can reserve study rooms.

STUDENT LIFE

Housing options: on-campus residence required for freshman year; coed, women-only, special housing for students with disabilities. Campus housing is university owned. Freshman campus housing is guaranteed.

Activities and organizations: drama/theater group, student-run newspaper, radio and television station, choral group, marching band, Associated Student Government, Catholic Campus Ministry, Chinese Students and Scholars, Alpha Lambda Delta, Student Alumni Association, national fraternities, national sororities.

Athletics Member NCAA. All Division I except football (Division I-A). *Intercollegiate sports:* baseball M(s), basketball M(s)/W(s), cross-country running M(s)/W(s), golf M(s)/W(s), gymnastics W(s), soccer W(s), softball W(s), swimming and diving W(s), tennis M(s)/W(s), track and field M(s)/W(s), volleyball W(s). *Intramural sports:* badminton M/W, baseball M(c), basketball M/W, bowling M/W, golf M/W, ice hockey M(c), lacrosse M(c)/W(c), racquetball M/W, riflery M(c)/W(c), rugby M(c)/W(c), sand volleyball M/W, soccer M/W, softball M/W, swimming and diving M(c)/W(c), table tennis M/W, tennis M/W, track and field M/W, triathlon M(c)/W(c), ultimate Frisbee M(c)/W(c), volleyball M/W.

Campus security: 24-hour emergency response devices and patrols, student patrols, late-night transport/escort service, controlled dormitory access, RAD (Rape Aggression Defense program); tornado siren; self-defense seminars; Defibrillators; 24 hr police dispatch, Smart 911.

Student services: health clinic, personal/psychological counseling, women's center, legal services.

COSTS & FINANCIAL AID

Costs (2017–18) *Tuition:* state resident $7384 full-time, $246 per credit hour part-time; nonresident $22,630 full-time, $754 per credit hour part-time. Full-time tuition and fees vary according to course load, location, and program. Part-time tuition and fees vary according to course load, location, and program. *Required fees:* $1678 full-time, $56 per credit

hour part-time. *Room and board:* $10,704; room only: $6884. Room and board charges vary according to board plan and housing facility. *Payment plan:* installment. *Waivers:* senior citizens and employees or children of employees.

Financial Aid Of all full-time matriculated undergraduates who enrolled in 2017, 13,111 applied for aid, 8,755 were judged to have need, 1,080 had their need fully met. 1,004 Federal Work-Study jobs (averaging $2638). In 2017, 3086 non-need-based awards were made. *Average percent of need met:* 57. *Average financial aid package:* $9830. *Average need-based loan:* $5249. *Average need-based gift aid:* $7650. *Average non-need-based aid:* $5273. *Average indebtedness upon graduation:* $26,242.

APPLYING

Standardized Tests *Required:* SAT or ACT (for admission).

Options: electronic application, early action.

Application fee: $40.

Required: high school transcript, minimum 3.0 GPA, minimum ACT Composite score of 20 or SAT total (math and EBRW only) of 1020, completion of 16 core academic units. *Required for some:* essay or personal statement.

Application deadlines: 8/1 (freshmen), 8/1 (transfers), 11/1 (early action).

Notification: continuous until 9/1 (freshmen), continuous (transfers), 12/15 (early action).

CONTACT

Wendy Stouffer, Associate Vice Provost for Enrollment Services and Assistant Dean of Admissions and Financial Aid, University of Arkansas, 232 Silas H. Hunt Hall, Office of Admissions, Fayetteville, AR 72701-1201. *Phone:* 479-575-3806. *Toll-free phone:* 800-377-8632. *Fax:* 479-575-7515. *E-mail:* uofa@uark.edu.

University of Arkansas at Little Rock
Little Rock, Arkansas
http://www.ualr.edu/

CONTACT

Ms. Tammy Harrison, Director of Admissions, University of Arkansas at Little Rock, 2801 South University Avenue, Little Rock, AR 72204-1099. *Phone:* 501-569-3127. *Toll-free phone:* 800-482-8892. *Fax:* 501-569-8956. *E-mail:* twharrison@ualn.edu.

University of Arkansas at Monticello
Monticello, Arkansas
http://www.uamont.edu/

CONTACT

Ms. Mary Whiting, Director of Admissions, University of Arkansas at Monticello, 346 University Drive, Monticello, AR 71656. *Phone:* 870-460-1026. *Toll-free phone:* 800-844-1826. *E-mail:* admissions@uamont.edu.

University of Arkansas at Pine Bluff
Pine Bluff, Arkansas
http://www.uapb.edu/

CONTACT

University of Arkansas at Pine Bluff, 1200 North University Drive, Pine Bluff, AR 71601-2799. *Phone:* 870-575-8492. *Toll-free phone:* 800-264-6585.

University of Arkansas for Medical Sciences
Little Rock, Arkansas
http://www.uams.edu/

- **State-supported** university, founded 1879, part of University of Arkansas System
- **Urban** 10-acre campus with easy access to Little Rock
- **Endowment** $317.3 million
- **Coed**

FACULTY
Student/faculty ratio: 7:1.

ACADEMICS
Calendar: semesters. *Degrees:* certificates, associate, bachelor's, master's, doctoral, and postbachelor's certificates (bachelor's degree is upper-level).
Library: Medical Sciences Library. *Books:* 27,764 (physical), 2,356 (digital/electronic); *Serial titles:* 96,524 (physical), 62,819 (digital/electronic); *Databases:* 120. Weekly public service hours: 87; study areas open 24 hours, 5–7 days a week.

STUDENT LIFE
Housing options: coed. Campus housing is university owned.
Campus security: 24-hour emergency response devices and patrols, late-night transport/escort service, controlled dormitory access.
Student services: health clinic, personal/psychological counseling.

COSTS & FINANCIAL AID
Costs (2017–18) *Tuition:* state resident $6540 full-time, $273 per hour part-time; nonresident $14,316 full-time, $597 per hour part-time. Full-time tuition and fees vary according to course load, location, program, and reciprocity agreements. Part-time tuition and fees vary according to course load, location, program, and reciprocity agreements. *Required fees:* $1607 full-time. *Room only:* $7560. Room and board charges vary according to housing facility.
Financial Aid *Average indebtedness upon graduation:* $7000.

APPLYING
Options: electronic application.
Application fee: $50.
Required: high school transcript, . *Required for some:* essay or personal statement, interview, national entrance exam scores.

CONTACT
University of Arkansas for Medical Sciences, 4301 West Markham, Little Rock, AR 72205-7199.

University of Arkansas–Fort Smith
Fort Smith, Arkansas
http://uafs.edu/

CONTACT
Ms. Kelly Westeen, Director of Admissions, University of Arkansas–Fort Smith, 5210 Grand Avenue, PO Box 3649, Fort Smith, AR 72913-3649. *Phone:* 479-788-7106. *Toll-free phone:* 888-512-5466. *Fax:* 479-424-6106. *E-mail:* kelly.westeen@uafortsmith.edu.

University of Central Arkansas
Conway, Arkansas
http://www.uca.edu/
- **State-supported** university, founded 1907
- **Small-town** 356-acre campus
- **Coed** 9,542 undergraduate students, 85% full-time, 59% women, 41% men
- **Moderately difficult** entrance level, 90% of applicants were admitted

UNDERGRAD STUDENTS
8,064 full-time, 1,478 part-time. Students come from 43 states and territories; 73 other countries; 9% are from out of state; 16% Black or African American, non-Hispanic/Latino; 5% Hispanic/Latino; 2% Asian, non-Hispanic/Latino; 0.1% Native Hawaiian or other Pacific Islander, non-Hispanic/Latino; 0.5% American Indian or Alaska Native, non-Hispanic/Latino; 4% Two or more races, non-Hispanic/Latino; 0.3% Race/ethnicity unknown; 5% international; 8% transferred in.

Freshmen:
Admission: 5,362 applied, 4,823 admitted, 1,937 enrolled. *Average high school GPA:* 3.5. *Test scores:* ACT scores over 18: 97%; ACT scores over 24: 54%; ACT scores over 30: 13%.
Retention: 72% of full-time freshmen returned.

FACULTY
Total: 726, 74% full-time.
Student/faculty ratio: 16:1.

ACADEMICS
Calendar: semesters. *Degrees:* certificates, bachelor's, master's, doctoral, post-master's, and postbachelor's certificates.
Special study options: academic remediation for entering students, accelerated degree program, advanced placement credit, cooperative education, distance learning, double majors, English as a second language, freshman honors college, honors programs, independent study, internships, part-time degree program, services for LD students, study abroad, summer session for credit. *ROTC:* Army (b).
Unusual degree programs: 3-2 engineering with Arkansas Tech University.
Computers: 610 computers/terminals are available on campus for general student use. Students can access the following: campus intranet, computer help desk, free student e-mail accounts, online (class) grades, online (class) registration, online (class) schedules. Campuswide network is available. 100% of college-owned or -operated housing units are wired for high-speed Internet access. Wireless service is available via entire campus.
Library: Torreyson Library plus 1 other. *Books:* 334,487 (physical), 16,056 (digital/electronic); *Serial titles:* 2,979 (physical), 55,507 (digital/electronic); *Databases:* 125. Study areas open 24 hours, 5–7 days a week; students can reserve study rooms.

STUDENT LIFE
Housing options: on-campus residence required for freshman year; coed, men-only, women-only, special housing for students with disabilities. Campus housing is university owned and leased by the school. Freshman campus housing is guaranteed.
Activities and organizations: drama/theater group, student-run newspaper, radio and television station, choral group, marching band, Bears Den, Greek Organizations, national fraternities, national sororities.
Athletics Member NCAA. All Division I. *Intercollegiate sports:* baseball M(s), basketball M(s)/W(s), cheerleading M(s)(c)/W(s)(c), cross-country running M(s)/W(s), football M(s), golf M(s)/W(s), soccer M(s)/W(s), softball W(s), tennis W(s), track and field M(s)/W(s), volleyball W(s). *Intramural sports:* basketball M/W, soccer M/W, softball M/W, tennis W, track and field M/W, volleyball M/W.
Campus security: 24-hour emergency response devices and patrols, student patrols, late-night transport/escort service, controlled dormitory access.
Student services: health clinic, personal/psychological counseling, women's center.

COSTS & FINANCIAL AID
Costs (2017–18) *Tuition:* state resident $6523 full-time, $217 per credit hour part-time; nonresident $13,046 full-time, $435 per credit hour part-time. Full-time tuition and fees vary according to course load. Part-time tuition and fees vary according to course load. *Required fees:* $2001 full-time. *Room and board:* $6518. Room and board charges vary according to board plan and housing facility. *Payment plan:* installment. *Waivers:* senior citizens and employees or children of employees.
Financial Aid *Financial aid deadline:* 7/1.

APPLYING
Standardized Tests *Required:* SAT or ACT (for admission).
Options: electronic application, early admission, deferred entrance.
Application fee: $25.
Required: high school transcript. *Required for some:* minimum 2.75 GPA, minimum ACT score of 21 or SAT score of 1450.
Application deadlines: rolling (freshmen), rolling (transfers).
Notification: continuous (freshmen), continuous (transfers).

CONTACT
Admissions Office, University of Central Arkansas, 201 Donaghey Avenue, Bernard 100, Conway, AR 72035. *Phone:* 501-450-3120. *Toll-free phone:* 800-243-8245. *Fax:* 501-450-5228. *E-mail:* admissions@uca.edu.

University of the Ozarks
Clarksville, Arkansas
http://www.ozarks.edu/

CONTACT
Ms. Jana Hart, Dean of Admission and Financial Aid, University of the Ozarks, 415 North College Avenue, Clarksville, AR 72830-2880. *Phone:* 479-979-1227. *Toll-free phone:* 800-264-8636. *Fax:* 479-979-1417. *E-mail:* admiss@ozarks.edu.

Williams Baptist College
Walnut Ridge, Arkansas
http://www.wbcoll.edu/

- **Independent Southern Baptist** comprehensive, founded 1941
- **Rural** 180-acre campus
- **Coed**
- **Minimally difficult** entrance level

FACULTY
Student/faculty ratio: 14:1.

ACADEMICS
Calendar: semesters. *Degrees:* associate, bachelor's, and master's.
Library: Felix Goodson Library plus 1 other. *Books:* 60,000 (physical), 100,000 (digital/electronic); *Serial titles:* 17 (physical), 5 (digital/electronic); *Databases:* 102. Weekly public service hours: 87; students can reserve study rooms.

STUDENT LIFE
Housing options: on-campus residence required through sophomore year; men-only, women-only. Campus housing is university owned. Freshman campus housing is guaranteed.

Activities and organizations: drama/theater group, choral group, Student Government, Student Activities Board, Bancroft Society, Cultural Awareness, International Student Society.

Athletics Member NAIA.

Campus security: 24-hour emergency response devices and patrols, student patrols, late-night transport/escort service, controlled dormitory access.

Student services: health clinic, personal/psychological counseling.

COSTS & FINANCIAL AID
Costs (2017–18) *Comprehensive fee:* $24,920 includes full-time tuition ($16,200), mandatory fees ($1120), and room and board ($7600). Part-time tuition: $675 per credit hour. Part-time tuition and fees vary according to course load. *Required fees:* $81 per term part-time. *Room and board:* Room and board charges vary according to board plan.

Financial Aid Of all full-time matriculated undergraduates who enrolled in 2016, 370 applied for aid, 285 were judged to have need. 169 Federal Work-Study jobs (averaging $1580). 21 state and other part-time jobs (averaging $1597). *Average financial aid package:* $17,498. *Average need-based loan:* $3915. *Average need-based gift aid:* $4856. *Average indebtedness upon graduation:* $22,747.

APPLYING
Standardized Tests *Required:* SAT or ACT (for admission).

Options: electronic application, early admission.

Required: high school transcript, minimum 2.6 GPA. *Required for some:* essay or personal statement, 2 letters of recommendation, interview.

CONTACT
Mr. Andrew Watson, Director of Admissions, Williams Baptist College, PO Box 3737, Walnut Ridge, AR 72476. *Phone:* 870-759-4118. *Toll-free phone:* 800-722-4434. *Fax:* 870-759-4163. *E-mail:* awatson@wbcoll.edu.

CALIFORNIA

Academy of Art University
San Francisco, California
http://www.academyart.edu/

- **Proprietary** comprehensive, founded 1929
- **Urban** 3-acre campus
- **Coed** 7,652 undergraduate students, 58% full-time, 57% women, 43% men
- **Noncompetitive** entrance level, 100% of applicants were admitted

UNDERGRAD STUDENTS
4,422 full-time, 3,230 part-time. Students come from 50 states and territories; 103 other countries; 44% are from out of state; 7% Black or African American, non-Hispanic/Latino; 11% Hispanic/Latino; 6% Asian, non-Hispanic/Latino; 0.7% Native Hawaiian or other Pacific Islander, non-Hispanic/Latino; 0.5% American Indian or Alaska Native, non-Hispanic/Latino; 3% Two or more races, non-Hispanic/Latino; 25% Race/ethnicity unknown; 29% international; 12% transferred in; 15% live on campus.

Freshmen:
Admission: 2,529 applied, 2,529 admitted, 813 enrolled.
Retention: 76% of full-time freshmen returned.

FACULTY
Total: 1,292, 21% full-time, 19% with terminal degrees.
Student/faculty ratio: 14:1.

ACADEMICS
Calendar: semesters. *Degrees:* certificates, associate, bachelor's, master's, and postbachelor's certificates.

Special study options: academic remediation for entering students, adult/continuing education programs, distance learning, English as a second language, independent study, internships, part-time degree program, services for LD students, study abroad, summer session for credit. *ROTC:* Army (c).

Computers: 900 computers/terminals are available on campus for general student use. Students can access the following: free student e-mail accounts, online (class) grades, online (class) registration, online (class) schedules, support for students taking online courses. Campuswide network is available. 100% of college-owned or -operated housing units are wired for high-speed Internet access. Wireless service is available via entire campus.

Library: Academy of Art University Library. *Books:* 35,255 (physical), 10,238 (digital/electronic); *Serial titles:* 197 (physical), 400,000 (digital/electronic); *Databases:* 20. Weekly public service hours: 83; students can reserve study rooms.

STUDENT LIFE
Housing options: coed, men-only, women-only. Campus housing is university owned and leased by the school. Freshman campus housing is guaranteed.

Activities and organizations: drama/theater group, student-run newspaper, radio and television station, choral group, Tea Time Animation, Beyond the Front Row, Children's Book Club, Comic Book Club, Empower, national fraternities, national sororities.

Athletics Member NCAA. All Division II. *Intercollegiate sports:* baseball M(s), basketball M(s)/W(s), cross-country running M(s)/W(s), golf M(s)/W(s), soccer M(s)/W(s), softball W(s), tennis W(s), track and field M(s)/W(s), volleyball W(s).

Campus security: 24-hour emergency response devices and patrols, late-night transport/escort service, controlled dormitory access, ID check at all buildings.

COSTS & FINANCIAL AID
Costs (2018–19) *Comprehensive fee:* $44,458 includes full-time tuition ($27,510), mandatory fees ($300), and room and board ($16,648). Full-time tuition and fees vary according to course load. Part-time tuition: $917 per unit. Part-time tuition and fees vary according to course load. *Room and board:* Room and board charges vary according to board plan and housing facility. *Payment plan:* installment.

Financial Aid Of all full-time matriculated undergraduates who enrolled in 2016, 2,115 applied for aid, 1,978 were judged to have need, 51 had their need fully met. 100 Federal Work-Study jobs (averaging $4940). In 2016, 69 non-need-based awards were made. *Average percent of need met:* 34. *Average financial aid package:* $11,828. *Average need-based loan:* $3948. *Average need-based gift aid:* $10,925. *Average non-need-based aid:* $7290. *Average indebtedness upon graduation:* $35,862.

APPLYING
Options: electronic application, early admission, deferred entrance.
Application fee: $50.
Required: high school transcript. *Recommended:* interview.
Application deadlines: rolling (freshmen), rolling (transfers).
Notification: continuous (freshmen), continuous (transfers).

CONTACT
Admissions, Academy of Art University, 79 New Montgomery Street, San Francisco, CA 94105. *Phone:* 800-544-2787. *Toll-free phone:* 800-544-ARTS. *Fax:* 415-618-6287. *E-mail:* info@academyart.edu.

See below for display ad and page 1228 for the College Close-Up.

Alliant International University–San Diego

San Diego, California
http://www.alliant.edu/
- **Independent** university, founded 1952, part of Alliant International University
- **Suburban** 60-acre campus with easy access to San Diego
- **Coed** 168 undergraduate students, 73% full-time, 69% women, 31% men
- **Minimally difficult** entrance level

UNDERGRAD STUDENTS
123 full-time, 45 part-time. Students come from 7 states and territories; 12 other countries; 10% are from out of state.

FACULTY
Total: 520.

Student/faculty ratio: 15:1.

ACADEMICS
Calendar: semesters. *Degrees:* certificates, bachelor's, master's, doctoral, and postbachelor's certificates.

Special study options: academic remediation for entering students, advanced placement credit, distance learning, English as a second language, internships, part-time degree program, services for LD students, summer session for credit.

Computers: 100 computers/terminals are available on campus for general student use. Students can access the following: campus intranet, computer help desk, free student e-mail accounts, online (class) grades, online (class) registration, online (class) schedules, degree completion status. Campuswide network is available. Wireless service is available via entire campus.
Library: Walter Library.

STUDENT LIFE
Housing options: college housing not available.

Activities and organizations: Residence Hall Association, Latino Students Association, Finance Club, Student Government, Sigma Iota Epsilon.

Campus security: 24-hour patrols.

Student services: health clinic, personal/psychological counseling.

COSTS & FINANCIAL AID
Costs (2017–18) *Tuition:* $17,250 full-time, $575 per credit hour part-time. *Required fees:* $260 full-time. *Payment plan:* deferred payment. *Waivers:* children of alumni and employees or children of employees.

Financial Aid Of all full-time matriculated undergraduates who enrolled in 2016, 103 applied for aid, 103 were judged to have need, 3 had their need fully met. 27 Federal Work-Study jobs (averaging $4000). In 2016, 103 non-need-based awards were made. *Average percent of need met:* 64. *Average financial aid package:* $14,450. *Average need-based loan:* $5000. *Average need-based gift aid:* $9590. *Average non-need-based aid:* $4000.

APPLYING
Options: electronic application, deferred entrance.

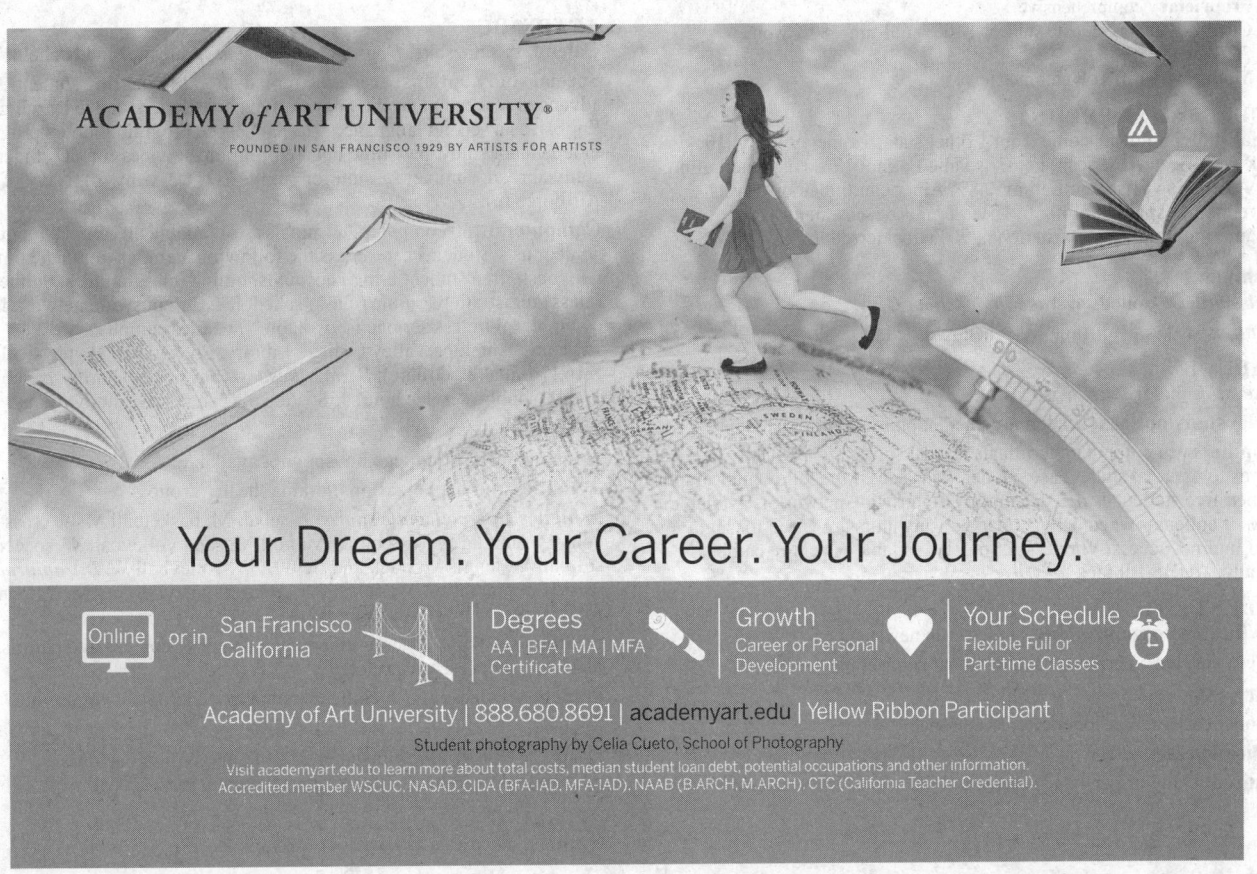

Application fee: $65.
Required: high school transcript, minimum 2.0 GPA.
Notification: continuous (transfers).

CONTACT
Ms. Ashley Carter, Director of Admissions, Alliant International University–San Diego, 10455 Pomerado Road, San Diego, CA 92131-1799. *Phone:* 866-825-5426. *Toll-free phone:* 866-825-5426. *E-mail:* admissions@alliant.edu.

American Jewish University
Bel Air, California
http://www.aju.edu/

CONTACT
Mr. Yosef Funke, Director of Undergraduate Admissions, American Jewish University, Familian Campus, 15600 Mulholland Drive, Los Angeles, CA 90077-1599. *Phone:* 310-440-1250. *Toll-free phone:* 888-853-6763. *Fax:* 310-471-3657. *E-mail:* admissions@aju.edu.

American Musical and Dramatic Academy, Los Angeles
Los Angeles, California
http://www.amda.edu/

CONTACT
Ms. Karen Jackson, Director of Admission, American Musical and Dramatic Academy, Los Angeles, 6305 Yucca Street, Los Angeles, CA 90028. *Phone:* 323-469-3300. *Toll-free phone:* 888-474-9444. *Fax:* 323-469-5246. *E-mail:* kjackson@amda.edu.

American University of Health Sciences
Signal Hill, California
http://www.auhs.edu/
- **Proprietary** comprehensive
- **Coed** 249 undergraduate students, 100% full-time, 80% women, 20% men
- **Moderately difficult** entrance level

UNDERGRAD STUDENTS
249 full-time. Students come from 1 other state; 1 other country; 10% Black or African American, non-Hispanic/Latino; 17% Hispanic/Latino; 60% Asian, non-Hispanic/Latino; 0.8% American Indian or Alaska Native, non-Hispanic/Latino; 6% Two or more races, non-Hispanic/Latino; 0.4% international; 20% transferred in.

Freshmen:
Admission: 2 enrolled. *Average high school GPA:* 2.5.
Retention: 83% of full-time freshmen returned.

ACADEMICS
Degrees: bachelor's and master's.
Special study options: academic remediation for entering students.
Computers: 20 computers/terminals and 100 ports are available on campus for general student use. Students can access the following: campus intranet, free student e-mail accounts. Campuswide network is available. 100% of college-owned or -operated housing units are wired for high-speed Internet access. Wireless service is available via entire campus.
Library: AUHS LIbrary.

STUDENT LIFE
Activities and organizations: student-run newspaper.
Student services: personal/psychological counseling.

APPLYING
Options: early admission, deferred entrance.
Application fee: $80.
Required: essay or personal statement, high school transcript, interview.

CONTACT
American University of Health Sciences, 1600 East Hill Street, Building #1, Signal Hill, CA 90755.

Angeles College
Los Angeles, California
http://www.angelescollege.edu/

CONTACT
Angeles College, 3440 Wilshire Boulevard, Suite 310, Los Angeles, CA 90010.

Antelope Valley College
Lancaster, California
http://www.avc.edu/
- **District-supported** primarily 2-year, founded 1929, part of California Community College System
- **Suburban** 135-acre campus with easy access to Los Angeles
- **Endowment** $4.6 million
- **Coed** 14,125 undergraduate students, 29% full-time, 59% women, 41% men
- **Noncompetitive** entrance level, 100% of applicants were admitted

UNDERGRAD STUDENTS
4,031 full-time, 10,094 part-time. Students come from 10 states and territories; 1 other country; 16% Black or African American, non-Hispanic/Latino; 53% Hispanic/Latino; 4% Asian, non-Hispanic/Latino; 0.2% Native Hawaiian or other Pacific Islander, non-Hispanic/Latino; 0.3% American Indian or Alaska Native, non-Hispanic/Latino; 5% Two or more races, non-Hispanic/Latino; 0.8% Race/ethnicity unknown; 0.1% international.

Freshmen:
Admission: 2,105 applied, 2,105 admitted, 2,105 enrolled.

FACULTY
Total: 622, 28% full-time, 8% with terminal degrees.
Student/faculty ratio: 24:1.

ACADEMICS
Calendar: semesters. *Degrees:* certificates, associate, and bachelor's.
Special study options: academic remediation for entering students, advanced placement credit, cooperative education, distance learning, English as a second language, external degree program, honors programs, independent study, part-time degree program, services for LD students, study abroad, summer session for credit. *ROTC:* Army (c), Navy (c), Air Force (c).
Computers: 160 computers/terminals are available on campus for general student use. Students can access the following: campus intranet, computer help desk, free student e-mail accounts, online (class) grades, online (class) registration, online (class) schedules. Campuswide network is available. Wireless service is available via entire campus.
Library: Antelope Valley College Library. *Books:* 54,721 (physical), 8,152 (digital/electronic); *Serial titles:* 10 (physical); *Databases:* 65. Weekly public service hours: 58; students can reserve study rooms.

STUDENT LIFE
Housing options: college housing not available.
Activities and organizations: drama/theater group.
Athletics *Intercollegiate sports:* baseball M, basketball M/W, cross-country running M/W, football M, golf M, sand volleyball W, soccer W, softball W, tennis W, track and field M/W, volleyball W. *Intramural sports:* basketball M/W, golf M/W, swimming and diving M/W, tennis M/W, volleyball M/W, weight lifting M/W.
Campus security: 24-hour emergency response devices and patrols, late-night transport/escort service.
Student services: health clinic, personal/psychological counseling.

COSTS
Costs (2018–19) *Tuition:* state resident $46 per unit part-time; nonresident $295 per unit part-time. *Payment plan:* installment.

APPLYING
Options: electronic application, early admission.

Application deadlines: rolling (freshmen), rolling (transfers).
Notification: continuous (freshmen), continuous (transfers).

CONTACT
Welcome Center, Antelope Valley College, 3041 West Avenue K, SSV Building, Lancaster, CA 93536. *Phone:* 661-722-6300 Ext. 6331.

Antioch University Los Angeles
Culver City, California
http://www.antioch.edu/los-angeles/
- **Independent** upper-level, founded 1972, part of Antioch University
- **Urban** 1-acre campus with easy access to Los Angeles
- **Coed** 252 undergraduate students, 33% full-time, 56% women, 43% men
- **Moderately difficult** entrance level

UNDERGRAD STUDENTS
83 full-time, 167 part-time. Students come from 13 states and territories; 3 other countries; 1% are from out of state.

ACADEMICS
Calendar: quarters. *Degrees:* bachelor's, master's, doctoral, post-master's, and postbachelor's certificates.

Special study options: academic remediation for entering students, accelerated degree program, adult/continuing education programs, advanced placement credit, cooperative education, distance learning, double majors, independent study, internships, part-time degree program, services for LD students, student-designed majors, summer session for credit.

Computers: Students can access the following: computer help desk, free student e-mail accounts, online (class) registration. Campuswide network is available. Wireless service is available via classrooms, computer labs, libraries.

STUDENT LIFE
Housing options: college housing not available.
Activities and organizations: student-run newspaper, radio and television station.
Campus security: 24-hour emergency response devices, late-night transport/escort service.
Student services: personal/psychological counseling.

COSTS
Costs (2017–18) *Tuition:* $27,160 full-time, $679 per credit hour part-time. Full-time tuition and fees vary according to course load and program. Part-time tuition and fees vary according to course load and program. *Required fees:* $400 full-time. *Payment plan:* installment. *Waivers:* employees or children of employees.

APPLYING
Options: electronic application, deferred entrance.
Application fee: $60.
Notification: continuous until 10/1 (transfers).

CONTACT
Admissions, Antioch University Los Angeles, 400 Corporate Pointe, Culver City, CA 90230. *Phone:* 310-578-1080 Ext. 100. *Toll-free phone:* 800-726-8462. *Fax:* 310-822-4824. *E-mail:* admissions@antiochla.edu.

Antioch University Santa Barbara
Santa Barbara, California
http://www.antioch.edu/santa-barbara/
- **Independent** upper-level, founded 1977, part of Antioch University
- **Urban** campus
- **Coed** 104 undergraduate students, 57% full-time, 65% women, 35% men
- **Moderately difficult** entrance level

UNDERGRAD STUDENTS
59 full-time, 45 part-time. Students come from 10 states and territories; 3 other countries; 1% are from out of state; 4% Black or African American, non-Hispanic/Latino; 24% Hispanic/Latino; 3% Asian, non-Hispanic/Latino; 3% Two or more races, non-Hispanic/Latino; 12% Race/ethnicity unknown; 9% international.

FACULTY
Total: 78, 12% full-time.

ACADEMICS
Calendar: quarters. *Degrees:* certificates, bachelor's, master's, and doctoral.

Special study options: academic remediation for entering students, accelerated degree program, cooperative education, distance learning, external degree program, independent study, internships, off-campus study, part-time degree program, services for LD students, student-designed majors, summer session for credit.

Computers: 16 computers/terminals are available on campus for general student use. Students can access the following: computer help desk, free student e-mail accounts, online (class) grades, online (class) registration, online (class) schedules. Campuswide network is available. Wireless service is available via entire campus.
Library: Sage Library.

STUDENT LIFE
Housing options: college housing not available.
Activities and organizations: student-run newspaper.
Campus security: late-night transport/escort service.

COSTS
Costs (2017–18) *Tuition:* $17,820 full-time, $495 per credit part-time. Full-time tuition and fees vary according to course load, degree level, and program. Part-time tuition and fees vary according to course load, degree level, and program. *Required fees:* $400 full-time. *Payment plan:* installment. *Waivers:* employees or children of employees.

APPLYING
Standardized Tests *Required for some:* TOEFL for international students.
Options: electronic application, deferred entrance.
Application fee: $60.
Notification: continuous (transfers).

CONTACT
Jessica Grater, Research Analyst, Antioch University Santa Barbara, 602 Anacapa Street, Santa Barbara, CA 93101-1581. *Phone:* 407-967-6547. *Toll-free phone:* 866-526-8462. *E-mail:* jgrater@antioch.edu.

Argosy University, Inland Empire
Ontario, California
http://www.argosy.edu/locations/inland-empire/

CONTACT
Argosy University, Inland Empire, 3401 Centre Lake Drive, Suite 200, Ontario, CA 91761. *Phone:* 909-472-0800. *Toll-free phone:* 866-217-9075.

Argosy University, Los Angeles
Los Angeles, California
http://www.argosy.edu/locations/los-angeles/

CONTACT
Argosy University, Los Angeles, 5230 Pacific Concourse, Suite 200, Los Angeles, CA 90045. *Phone:* 310-531-9700. *Toll-free phone:* 866-505-0332.

Argosy University, Orange County
Orange, California
http://www.argosy.edu/locations/los-angeles-orange-county/

CONTACT
Argosy University, Orange County, 601 South Lewis Street, Orange, CA 92868. *Phone:* 714-620-3700. *Toll-free phone:* 800-716-9598.

Argosy University, San Diego

San Diego, California

http://www.argosy.edu/locations/san-diego/

CONTACT
Argosy University, San Diego, 1615 Murray Canyon Road, Suite 100, San Diego, CA 92108. *Phone:* 619-321-3000. *Toll-free phone:* 866-505-0333.

Argosy University, San Francisco Bay Area

Alameda, California

http://www.argosy.edu/locations/san-francisco/

CONTACT
Argosy University, San Francisco Bay Area, 1005 Atlantic Avenue, Alameda, CA 94501. *Phone:* 510-217-4700. *Toll-free phone:* 866-215-2777.

ArtCenter College of Design

Pasadena, California

http://www.artcenter.edu/

- **Independent** comprehensive, founded 1930
- **Suburban** 163-acre campus with easy access to Los Angeles
- **Coed** 2,005 undergraduate students, 86% full-time, 54% women, 46% men
- **Very difficult** entrance level

UNDERGRAD STUDENTS
1,717 full-time, 288 part-time. Students come from 51 other countries; 32% are from out of state; 1% Black or African American, non-Hispanic/Latino; 12% Hispanic/Latino; 33% Asian, non-Hispanic/Latino; 0.3% Native Hawaiian or other Pacific Islander, non-Hispanic/Latino; 0.2% American Indian or Alaska Native, non-Hispanic/Latino; 4% Two or more races, non-Hispanic/Latino; 0.6% Race/ethnicity unknown; 32% international; 9% transferred in.

Freshmen:
Admission: 223 enrolled.

ACADEMICS
Calendar: semesters. *Degrees:* bachelor's and master's.

Special study options: advanced placement credit, independent study, internships, off-campus study, services for LD students, study abroad, summer session for credit.

Computers: 470 computers/terminals and 502 ports are available on campus for general student use. Students can access the following: campus intranet, computer help desk, free student e-mail accounts, online (class) grades, online (class) registration, online (class) schedules. Campuswide network is available. Wireless service is available via entire campus.

Library: James Lemont Fogg Memorial Library plus 1 other. *Books:* 101,955 (physical), 1.0 million (digital/electronic); *Serial titles:* 592 (physical), 36,738 (digital/electronic); *Databases:* 46. Weekly public service hours: 63.

STUDENT LIFE
Housing options: college housing not available.

Activities and organizations: ACSG, Christian Fellowship, Stop Motion Club, Art Center Business Club, Fine Art Society.

Campus security: 24-hour emergency response devices and patrols, late-night transport/escort service.

Student services: personal/psychological counseling.

COSTS & FINANCIAL AID
Costs (2017–18) *Tuition:* $41,408 full-time, $1726 per credit part-time. *Required fees:* $600 full-time.

Financial Aid *Average financial aid package:* $17,803. *Average need-based loan:* $10,169. *Average need-based gift aid:* $14,627.

APPLYING
Standardized Tests *Required for some:* SAT (for admission), ACT (for admission), SAT or ACT (for admission).

Options: electronic application, deferred entrance.
Application fee: $50.
Required: essay or personal statement, portfolio. *Required for some:* high school transcript.

CONTACT
Ms. Kit Baron, Vice President, Admissions and Enrollment Management, ArtCenter College of Design, 1700 Lida Street, Pasadena, CA 91103. *Phone:* 626-396-2322. *Fax:* 626-795-0578. *E-mail:* kit.baron@artcenter.edu.

The Art Institute of California–Hollywood, a campus of Argosy University

North Hollywood, California

http://www.artinstitutes.edu/hollywood/

CONTACT
The Art Institute of California–Hollywood, a campus of Argosy University, 5250 Lankershim Boulevard, North Hollywood, CA 91601. *Phone:* 818-299-5100. *Toll-free phone:* 877-468-6232.

The Art Institute of California–Inland Empire, a campus of Argosy University

San Bernardino, California

http://www.artinstitutes.edu/inlandempire/

CONTACT
The Art Institute of California–Inland Empire, a campus of Argosy University, 674 East Brier Drive, San Bernardino, CA 92408. *Phone:* 909-915-2100. *Toll-free phone:* 800-353-0812.

The Art Institute of California–Orange County, a campus of Argosy University

Santa Ana, California

http://www.artinstitutes.edu/orangecounty/

CONTACT
The Art Institute of California–Orange County, a campus of Argosy University, 3601 West Sunflower Avenue, Santa Ana, CA 92704. *Phone:* 714-830-0200. *Toll-free phone:* 888-549-3055.

The Art Institute of California–Sacramento, a campus of Argosy University

Sacramento, California

http://www.artinstitutes.edu/sacramento/

CONTACT
The Art Institute of California–Sacramento, a campus of Argosy University, 2850 Gateway Oaks Drive, Suite 100, Sacramento, CA 95833. *Phone:* 916-830-6320. *Toll-free phone:* 800-477-1957.

The Art Institute of California–San Diego, a campus of Argosy University

San Diego, California

http://www.artinstitutes.edu/sandiego/

CONTACT
The Art Institute of California–San Diego, a campus of Argosy University, 7650 Mission Valley Road, San Diego, CA 92108. *Phone:* 858-598-1200. *Toll-free phone:* 866-275-2422.

The Art Institute of California–San Francisco, a campus of Argosy University

San Francisco, California
http://www.artinstitutes.edu/sanfrancisco/

CONTACT
The Art Institute of California–San Francisco, a campus of Argosy University, 10 United Nations Plaza, San Francisco, CA 94102-4928. *Phone:* 415-865-0198. *Toll-free phone:* 888-493-3261.

Ashford University

San Diego, California
http://www.ashford.edu/

CONTACT
Ms. Waunita M. Sullivan, Director of Enrollment, Ashford University, 8620 Spectrum Center Boulevard, San Diego, CA 92123. *Phone:* 563-242-4023 Ext. 3401. *Toll-free phone:* 866-711-1700. *E-mail:* admissns@tfu.edu.

Azusa Pacific University

Azusa, California
http://www.apu.edu/

- **Independent nondenominational** university, founded 1899
- **Suburban** 60-acre campus with easy access to Los Angeles
- **Coed** 5,671 undergraduate students, 89% full-time, 66% women, 34% men
- **Moderately difficult** entrance level, 60% of applicants were admitted

UNDERGRAD STUDENTS
5,075 full-time, 596 part-time. 20% are from out of state; 5% Black or African American, non-Hispanic/Latino; 32% Hispanic/Latino; 10% Asian, non-Hispanic/Latino; 1% Native Hawaiian or other Pacific Islander, non-Hispanic/Latino; 0.2% American Indian or Alaska Native, non-Hispanic/Latino; 8% Two or more races, non-Hispanic/Latino; 2% Race/ethnicity unknown; 3% international; 6% transferred in.

Freshmen:
Admission: 8,939 applied, 5,374 admitted, 1,005 enrolled. *Average high school GPA:* 3.7. *Test scores:* ACT scores over 18: 94%; ACT scores over 24: 52%; ACT scores over 30: 10%.
Retention: 83% of full-time freshmen returned.

FACULTY
Total: 1,511, 32% full-time, 19% with terminal degrees.
Student/faculty ratio: 10:1.

ACADEMICS
Calendar: semesters. *Degrees:* certificates, bachelor's, master's, doctoral, post-master's, and postbachelor's certificates.
Special study options: academic remediation for entering students, accelerated degree program, adult/continuing education programs, advanced placement credit, cooperative education, distance learning, double majors, English as a second language, freshman honors college, honors programs, independent study, internships, off-campus study, part-time degree program, services for LD students, study abroad, summer session for credit. *ROTC:* Army (b), Air Force (c).
Unusual degree programs: 3-2 business administration; engineering; nursing; social work.
Computers: Students can access the following: campus intranet, computer help desk, free student e-mail accounts, online (class) grades, online (class) registration, online (class) schedules. Campuswide network is available. Wireless service is available via entire campus.
Library: Marshburn Memorial Library plus 3 others. Study areas open 24 hours, 5–7 days a week; students can reserve study rooms.

STUDENT LIFE
Housing options: on-campus residence required through sophomore year; coed, men-only, women-only. Campus housing is university owned and leased by the school. Freshman applicants given priority for college housing.

Activities and organizations: drama/theater group, student-run newspaper, radio and television station, choral group, marching band.
Athletics Member NCAA, NAIA. All NCAA Division II. *Intercollegiate sports:* baseball M(s), basketball M(s)/W(s), cross-country running M(s)/W(s), football M(s), gymnastics W(s), soccer M(s)/W(s), softball W(s), swimming and diving W(s), tennis M(s)/W(s), track and field M(s)/W(s), volleyball W(s), water polo W. *Intramural sports:* basketball M/W, cheerleading W(c), rugby M(c), skiing (downhill) M/W, soccer M/W, softball M/W, tennis M/W, ultimate Frisbee M/W, volleyball M/W.
Campus security: 24-hour emergency response devices and patrols, student patrols, late-night transport/escort service, controlled dormitory access.
Student services: health clinic, personal/psychological counseling, women's center.

COSTS & FINANCIAL AID
Costs (2018–19) *Tuition:* $36,926 full-time, $1596 per unit part-time. Full-time tuition and fees vary according to course load and degree level. Part-time tuition and fees vary according to course load and degree level. *Required fees:* $580 full-time. *Room only:* $5770. Room and board charges vary according to board plan and housing facility. *Payment plan:* installment. *Waivers:* employees or children of employees.
Financial Aid Of all full-time matriculated undergraduates who enrolled in 2016, 5,101 applied for aid, 3,910 were judged to have need, 541 had their need fully met. In 2016, 1070 non-need-based awards were made. *Average percent of need met:* 36. *Average financial aid package:* $24,503. *Average need-based loan:* $4759. *Average need-based gift aid:* $11,242. *Average non-need-based aid:* $11,349. *Average indebtedness upon graduation:* $31,277.

APPLYING
Standardized Tests *Required:* SAT or ACT (for admission).
Options: electronic application, early action.
Required: essay or personal statement, high school transcript, minimum 3.0 GPA, 1 letter of recommendation, SAT composite of 990 (writing excluded) or ACT composite 19. *Required for some:* interview.
Application deadlines: 6/1 (freshmen), 7/1 (transfers), 11/15 (early action).
Notification: continuous until 10/1 (freshmen), continuous (transfers), 1/15 (early action).

CONTACT
Ms. Lynnette Barnes, Processing Coordinator, Azusa Pacific University, 901 East Alosta Avenue, PO Box 7000, Undergraduate Admissions, 7221, Azusa, CA 91702-7000. *Phone:* 626-815-6000 Ext. 3419. *Toll-free phone:* 800-TALK-APU. *E-mail:* admissions@apu.edu.

Bergin University of Canine Studies

Rohnert Park, California
http://www.berginu.edu/

CONTACT
Bergin University of Canine Studies, 5860 Labath Avenue, Rohnert Park, CA 94928.

Bethesda University

Anaheim, California
http://www.buc.edu/

CONTACT
Jacquie Ha, Director of Admission, Bethesda University, 730 North Euclid Street, Anaheim, CA 92801. *Phone:* 714-517-1945. *Fax:* 714-517-1948. *E-mail:* admission@bcu.edu.

Beverly Hills Design Institute

Beverly Hills, California
http://www.bhdi.edu/

CONTACT
Beverly Hills Design Institute, 8484 Wilshire Boulevard, Suite 730, Beverly Hills, CA 90211. *Phone:* 310-360-8888.

Biola University

La Mirada, California

http://www.biola.edu/

- **Independent interdenominational** university, founded 1908
- **Suburban** 95-acre campus with easy access to Los Angeles
- **Coed** 4,091 undergraduate students, 96% full-time, 64% women, 36% men
- **Moderately difficult** entrance level, 69% of applicants were admitted

UNDERGRAD STUDENTS

3,947 full-time, 144 part-time. 26% are from out of state; 2% Black or African American, non-Hispanic/Latino; 20% Hispanic/Latino; 17% Asian, non-Hispanic/Latino; 0.3% Native Hawaiian or other Pacific Islander, non-Hispanic/Latino; 0.2% American Indian or Alaska Native, non-Hispanic/Latino; 6% Two or more races, non-Hispanic/Latino; 3% Race/ethnicity unknown; 3% international; 6% transferred in; 65% live on campus.

Freshmen:
Admission: 3,926 applied, 2,706 admitted, 872 enrolled. *Average high school GPA:* 3.3. *Test scores:* SAT evidence-based reading and writing scores over 500: 81%; SAT math scores over 500: 82%; ACT scores over 18: 97%; SAT evidence-based reading and writing scores over 600: 40%; SAT math scores over 600: 43%; ACT scores over 24: 56%; SAT evidence-based reading and writing scores over 700: 8%; SAT math scores over 700: 6%; ACT scores over 30: 12%.
Retention: 84% of full-time freshmen returned.

FACULTY

Total: 536, 51% full-time, 43% with terminal degrees.
Student/faculty ratio: 15:1.

ACADEMICS

Calendar: 4-1-4. *Degrees:* diplomas, bachelor's, master's, doctoral, post-master's, and postbachelor's certificates.

Special study options: adult/continuing education programs, advanced placement credit, cooperative education, distance learning, double majors, English as a second language, honors programs, independent study, internships, off-campus study, part-time degree program, services for LD students, study abroad, summer session for credit. *ROTC:* Army (c), Air Force (c).

Unusual degree programs: 3-2 engineering.

Computers: Students can access the following: campus intranet, computer help desk, free student e-mail accounts, online (class) grades, online (class) registration, online (class) schedules. Campuswide network is available. 100% of college-owned or -operated housing units are wired for high-speed Internet access. Wireless service is available via entire campus.

Library: Biola University Library plus 1 other. *Books:* 550,000 (physical); *Databases:* 259. Weekly public service hours: 100; students can reserve study rooms.

STUDENT LIFE

Housing options: coed, women-only, special housing for students with disabilities. Campus housing is university owned. Freshman campus housing is guaranteed.

Activities and organizations: drama/theater group, student-run newspaper, radio and television station, choral group, Adventure Club, Guerilla Film Society, Biola Cross-Fit, Xopoc Dance Team, Lacrosse Club.

Athletics Member NCAA, NAIA. All NCAA Division II. *Intercollegiate sports:* baseball M(s), basketball M(s)/W(s), cross-country running M(s)/W(s), golf M(s)/W(s), soccer M(s)/W(s), softball W(s), swimming and diving M(s)/W(s), tennis M(s)/W(s), track and field M(s)/W(s), volleyball W(s). *Intramural sports:* archery M(c)/W(c), basketball M/W, bowling M/W, cheerleading W(c), football M/W, lacrosse M(c)/W(c), rugby M(c), soccer M/W, softball M/W, tennis M/W, ultimate Frisbee M/W, volleyball M(c)/W, water polo M(c)/W(c).

Campus security: 24-hour emergency response devices and patrols, late-night transport/escort service, controlled dormitory access.

Student services: health clinic, personal/psychological counseling.

COSTS & FINANCIAL AID

Costs (2017–18) *One-time required fee:* $60. *Comprehensive fee:* $49,420 includes full-time tuition ($38,448) and room and board ($10,972). Full-time tuition and fees vary according to course load and degree level. Part-time tuition: $1602 per credit hour. Part-time tuition and fees vary according to course load and degree level. *College room only:* $6500. Room and board charges vary according to board plan and housing facility. *Payment plan:* installment. *Waivers:* employees or children of employees.

Financial Aid Of all full-time matriculated undergraduates who enrolled in 2016, 2,984 applied for aid, 2,646 were judged to have need, 241 had their need fully met. In 2016, 1200 non-need-based awards were made. *Average percent of need met:* 52. *Average financial aid package:* $21,694. *Average need-based loan:* $3564. *Average need-based gift aid:* $15,750. *Average non-need-based aid:* $8465. *Average indebtedness upon graduation:* $35,489.

APPLYING

Standardized Tests *Required:* SAT or ACT (for admission).

Options: electronic application, early decision, early action, deferred entrance.

Application fee: $45.

Required: essay or personal statement, high school transcript. *Required for some:* interview. *Recommended:* minimum 3.0 GPA.

Application deadlines: 3/1 (freshmen), 3/1 (transfers), 11/15 (early action).
Notification: 4/1 (freshmen), 4/1 (out-of-state freshmen), 4/1 (transfers), 1/15 (early action).

CONTACT

Mrs. Michelle Reider, Associate Director of Undergraduate Freshman Admissions, Biola University, 13800 Biola Avenue, La Mirada, CA 90639. *Phone:* 562-903-4752. *Toll-free phone:* 800-652-4652. *E-mail:* admissions@biola.edu.

Brandman University

Irvine, California

http://www.brandman.edu/

- **Independent** comprehensive, founded 1958
- **Suburban** campus with easy access to Greater Los Angeles Area
- **Coed** 3,677 undergraduate students, 28% full-time, 61% women, 39% men

UNDERGRAD STUDENTS

1,033 full-time, 2,644 part-time. Students come from 49 states and territories; 1 other country; 22% are from out of state; 10% Black or African American, non-Hispanic/Latino; 16% Hispanic/Latino; 4% Asian, non-Hispanic/Latino; 2% Native Hawaiian or other Pacific Islander, non-Hispanic/Latino; 0.9% American Indian or Alaska Native, non-Hispanic/Latino; 2% Two or more races, non-Hispanic/Latino; 13% Race/ethnicity unknown; 19% transferred in.

Freshmen:
Admission: 50 enrolled.

FACULTY

Student/faculty ratio: 15:1.

ACADEMICS

Calendar: trimesters. *Degrees:* certificates, associate, bachelor's, master's, doctoral, post-master's, and postbachelor's certificates.

Special study options: academic remediation for entering students, accelerated degree program, adult/continuing education programs, advanced placement credit, cooperative education, distance learning, double majors, independent study, internships, off-campus study, part-time degree program, services for LD students, summer session for credit.

Computers: 837 computers/terminals and 837 ports are available on campus for general student use. Students can access the following: campus intranet, computer help desk, free student e-mail accounts, online (class) grades, online (class) registration, online (class) schedules. Campuswide network is available. Wireless service is available via entire campus.

Library: Leatherby Library plus 1 other. Weekly public service hours: 65; study areas open 24 hours, 5–7 days a week; students can reserve study rooms.

STUDENT LIFE

Housing options: college housing not available.

Activities and organizations: Social Work Student Association, Society for Human Resource Management, Nursing Honor Society, American Holistic Nurses Association.

Campus security: late-night transport/escort service.

Student services: personal/psychological counseling.

COSTS

Costs (2017–18) *Tuition:* $15,000 full-time, $500 per credit hour part-time. *Required fees:* $360 full-time, $90 per term part-time. *Payment plan:* deferred payment. *Waivers:* employees or children of employees.

APPLYING

Required: high school transcript, minimum 2.0 GPA. *Required for some:* 3 letters of recommendation, 3 letters of recommendation, CPR certification, immunizations, professional liability insurance, RN licensure, and prerequisite coursework for RN-BSN program.

CONTACT

Admissions Office, Brandman University, 16355 Laguna Canyon Drive, Irvine, CA 92618. *Phone:* 800-7460082 Ext. 39847. *Toll-free phone:* 800-746-0082. *E-mail:* apply@brandman.edu.

California Baptist University

Riverside, California

http://www.calbaptist.edu/

- **Independent Southern Baptist** comprehensive, founded 1950
- **Suburban** 160-acre campus with easy access to Los Angeles
- **Endowment** $41.8 million
- **Coed** 7,414 undergraduate students, 86% full-time, 63% women, 37% men
- **Moderately difficult** entrance level, 77% of applicants were admitted

UNDERGRAD STUDENTS

6,367 full-time, 1,047 part-time. Students come from 47 states and territories; 31 other countries; 8% are from out of state; 7% Black or African American, non-Hispanic/Latino; 36% Hispanic/Latino; 5% Asian, non-Hispanic/Latino; 1% Native Hawaiian or other Pacific Islander, non-Hispanic/Latino; 0.6% American Indian or Alaska Native, non-Hispanic/Latino; 6% Two or more races, non-Hispanic/Latino; 4% Race/ethnicity unknown; 2% international; 11% transferred in; 40% live on campus.

Freshmen:
Admission: 5,039 applied, 3,884 admitted, 1,413 enrolled. *Average high school GPA:* 3.6. *Test scores:* SAT evidence-based reading and writing scores over 500: 76%; SAT math scores over 500: 69%; ACT scores over 18: 84%; SAT evidence-based reading and writing scores over 600: 26%; SAT math scores over 600: 20%; ACT scores over 24: 32%; SAT evidence-based reading and writing scores over 700: 3%; SAT math scores over 700: 3%; ACT scores over 30: 4%.
Retention: 77% of full-time freshmen returned.

FACULTY

Total: 872, 39% full-time, 46% with terminal degrees.
Student/faculty ratio: 17:1.

ACADEMICS

Calendar: 2-4-4-2. *Degrees:* associate, bachelor's, master's, and doctoral.

Special study options: academic remediation for entering students, accelerated degree program, adult/continuing education programs, advanced placement credit, distance learning, double majors, English as a second language, honors programs, internships, off-campus study, part-time degree program, services for LD students, study abroad, summer session for credit. *ROTC:* Army (b), Air Force (c).

Computers: 279 computers/terminals are available on campus for general student use. Students can access the following: campus intranet, computer help desk, free student e-mail accounts, online (class) grades, online (class) registration, online (class) schedules, online course evaluations. Campuswide network is available. 70% of college-owned or -operated housing units are wired for high-speed Internet access. Wireless service is available via entire campus.

Library: Annie Gabriel Library. *Books:* 130,837 (physical), 190,918 (digital/electronic); *Serial titles:* 59,915 (physical), 21,548 (digital/electronic); *Databases:* 83. Weekly public service hours: 101; students can reserve study rooms.

STUDENT LIFE

Housing options: on-campus residence required for freshman year; men-only, women-only. Campus housing is university owned. Freshman applicants given priority for college housing.

Activities and organizations: drama/theater group, student-run newspaper, choral group, International Service Projects, United States Service Projects, CBU Crazies (Campus Spirit), Summer of Service, Associated Students of California Baptist University (government and leadership).

Athletics Member NCAA. All Division II. *Intercollegiate sports:* baseball M(s), basketball M(s)/W(s), cheerleading W(s), cross-country running M(s)/W(s), golf M(s)/W(s), soccer M(s)/W(s), softball W(s), swimming and diving M(s)/W(s), track and field M(s)/W(s), volleyball M(s)/W(s), water polo M(s)/W(s), wrestling M(s). *Intramural sports:* basketball M/W, bowling M/W, football M/W, golf M/W, rock climbing M/W, sand volleyball M/W, soccer M/W, table tennis M/W, ultimate Frisbee M/W, volleyball M/W.

Campus security: 24-hour emergency response devices and patrols, late-night transport/escort service, controlled dormitory access.

Student services: health clinic, personal/psychological counseling.

COSTS & FINANCIAL AID

Costs (2018–19) *One-time required fee:* $310. *Comprehensive fee:* $45,638 includes full-time tuition ($31,668), mandatory fees ($1810), and room and board ($12,160). Full-time tuition and fees vary according to course load, location, and program. Part-time tuition: $1218 per unit. Part-time tuition and fees vary according to course load, location, and program. *Required fees:* $175 per term part-time. *College room only:* $5860. Room and board charges vary according to board plan and housing facility. *Payment plan:* installment. *Waivers:* employees or children of employees.

Financial Aid Of all full-time matriculated undergraduates who enrolled in 2017, 5,713 applied for aid, 5,143 were judged to have need, 823 had their need fully met. 359 Federal Work-Study jobs (averaging $893). In 2017, 351 non-need-based awards were made. *Average percent of need met:* 57. *Average financial aid package:* $20,693. *Average need-based loan:* $4622. *Average need-based gift aid:* $16,706. *Average non-need-based aid:* $10,684. *Average indebtedness upon graduation:* $38,324.

APPLYING

Standardized Tests *Required:* SAT or ACT (for admission). *Recommended:* SAT and SAT Subject Tests or ACT (for admission).

Options: electronic application, early action, deferred entrance.

Application fee: $45.

Required: essay or personal statement, minimum 2.0 GPA. *Required for some:* high school transcript.

Application deadlines: rolling (freshmen), rolling (transfers).

Notification: continuous (freshmen), continuous (transfers).

CONTACT

Mr. Dustin Lowe, Director of Undergraduate Admissions, California Baptist University, 8432 Magnolia Avenue, Riverside, CA 92504-3297. *Phone:* 951-343-4477. *Toll-free phone:* 877-228-8866. *Fax:* 951-343-4525. *E-mail:* admissions@calbaptist.edu.

California Christian College

Fresno, California

http://www.calchristiancollege.edu/

- **Independent Free Will Baptist** 4-year
- **Urban** campus
- **Endowment** $166,018
- **Coed** 16 undergraduate students, 44% full-time, 25% women, 75% men
- **Noncompetitive** entrance level, 100% of applicants were admitted

UNDERGRAD STUDENTS

7 full-time, 9 part-time. Students come from 2 states and territories; 0.2% are from out of state; 19% Black or African American, non-Hispanic/Latino; 44% Hispanic/Latino; 6% American Indian or Alaska Native, non-Hispanic/Latino; 13% transferred in; 19% live on campus.

COLLEGES AT-A-GLANCE

Freshmen:
Admission: 3 applied, 3 admitted, 3 enrolled.

FACULTY
Total: 7, 14% full-time, 43% with terminal degrees.

ACADEMICS
Calendar: semesters. *Degrees:* associate and bachelor's.

Special study options: academic remediation for entering students, cooperative education, distance learning, independent study, part-time degree program.

Computers: 12 computers/terminals and 5 ports are available on campus for general student use. Students can access the following: free student e-mail accounts, online (class) grades. Campuswide network is available. 100% of college-owned or -operated housing units are wired for high-speed Internet access. Wireless service is available via entire campus.
Library: Cortese Library. *Books:* 17,572 (physical); *Serial titles:* 12 (physical). Weekly public service hours: 15.

STUDENT LIFE
Housing options: men-only, women-only. Campus housing is leased by the school.

Student services: personal/psychological counseling.

COSTS & FINANCIAL AID
Costs (2017–18) *Tuition:* $8640 full-time, $360 per credit hour part-time. *Required fees:* $690 full-time. *Room only:* $4950. *Payment plan:* installment.

Financial Aid Of all full-time matriculated undergraduates who enrolled in 2016, 13 applied for aid, 13 were judged to have need. 3 Federal Work-Study jobs (averaging $1470). *Average percent of need met:* 46. *Average financial aid package:* $9054. *Average need-based loan:* $3519. *Average need-based gift aid:* $5027.

APPLYING
Standardized Tests *Required:* math and English exams (for admission). *Recommended:* SAT or ACT (for admission).

Options: electronic application.

Application fee: $40.

Required: essay or personal statement, high school transcript, minimum 2.0 GPA, 2 letters of recommendation, statement of faith, moral/ethical statement. *Recommended:* interview.

Application deadlines: rolling (freshmen), rolling (transfers).

Notification: continuous (freshmen), continuous (transfers).

CONTACT
Mr. Billy Parris, Admissions Recruiter, California Christian College, 5364 E. Belmont Avenue, Fresno, CA 93727. *Phone:* 559-251-4215 Ext. 1002. *Fax:* 559-385-2329. *E-mail:* admissions@calchristiancollege.edu.

California Coast University

Santa Ana, California
http://www.calcoast.edu/

CONTACT
California Coast University, 925 North Spurgeon Street, Santa Ana, CA 92701. *Phone:* 714-547-9625. *Toll-free phone:* 888-CCU-UNIV.

California College of the Arts

San Francisco, California
http://www.cca.edu/

- **Independent** comprehensive, founded 1907
- **Urban** 4-acre campus with easy access to San Francisco, Oakland
- **Endowment** $30.3 million
- **Coed** 1,528 undergraduate students, 94% full-time, 64% women, 36% men

UNDERGRAD STUDENTS
1,442 full-time, 86 part-time. Students come from 49 states and territories; 53 other countries; 32% are from out of state; 6% Black or African American, non-Hispanic/Latino; 12% Hispanic/Latino; 18% Asian, non-Hispanic/Latino; 0.8% Native Hawaiian or other Pacific Islander, non-

Hispanic/Latino; 0.2% American Indian or Alaska Native, non-Hispanic/Latino; 6% Race/ethnicity unknown; 35% international; 9% transferred in; 22% live on campus.

Freshmen:
Admission: 256 enrolled. *Average high school GPA:* 3.3.
Retention: 82% of full-time freshmen returned.

FACULTY
Total: 485, 21% full-time, 56% with terminal degrees.
Student/faculty ratio: 9:1.

ACADEMICS
Calendar: semesters. *Degrees:* bachelor's and master's.

Special study options: academic remediation for entering students, advanced placement credit, double majors, English as a second language, external degree program, independent study, internships, off-campus study, part-time degree program, services for LD students, student-designed majors, study abroad, summer session for credit.

Computers: 400 computers/terminals and 80 ports are available on campus for general student use. Students can access the following: campus intranet, computer help desk, free student e-mail accounts, online (class) grades, online (class) registration, online (class) schedules, online course evaluations, learning management system, media applications, software training, print payments. Campuswide network is available. 100% of college-owned or -operated housing units are wired for high-speed Internet access. Wireless service is available via classrooms, computer centers, computer labs, dorm rooms, learning centers, libraries, student centers.
Library: Meyer Library plus 1 other.

STUDENT LIFE
Housing options: coed, special housing for students with disabilities. Campus housing is university owned and leased by the school. Freshman applicants given priority for college housing.

Activities and organizations: student-run radio station, Student of Color Coalition, International Student Alliance, Chimera Council, Animation Resource Center, MyChina, national fraternities, national sororities.

Campus security: 24-hour emergency response devices and patrols, late-night transport/escort service, controlled dormitory access.

Student services: personal/psychological counseling.

COSTS & FINANCIAL AID
Costs (2018–19) *Tuition:* $48,648 full-time, $2027 per unit part-time. *Required fees:* $490 full-time, $170 per term part-time. *Room only:* $10,136. Room and board charges vary according to housing facility. *Payment plan:* installment. *Waivers:* employees or children of employees.

Financial Aid Of all full-time matriculated undergraduates who enrolled in 2017, 708 applied for aid, 664 were judged to have need, 36 had their need fully met. In 2017, 396 non-need-based awards were made. *Average percent of need met:* 61. *Average financial aid package:* $32,759. *Average need-based loan:* $4665. *Average need-based gift aid:* $27,933. *Average non-need-based aid:* $11,884. *Average indebtedness upon graduation:* $32,017.

APPLYING
Required: essay or personal statement, minimum 2.0 GPA, 1 letter of recommendation, portfolio of creative work. *Required for some:* high school transcript, interview.

CONTACT
Mr. Arnold Icasiano, Director of Admissions, California College of the Arts, 1111 Eighth Street, San Francisco, CA 94107. *Phone:* 415-703-9523 Ext. 9532. *Toll-free phone:* 800-447-1ART. *Fax:* 415-703-9539. *E-mail:* enroll@cca.edu.

California College San Diego

National City, California
http://www.cc-sd.edu/

CONTACT
California College San Diego, 700 Bay Marina Drive, Suite 100, National City, CA 91950. *Toll-free phone:* 800-622-3188.

California College San Diego
San Diego, California
http://www.cc-sd.edu/

CONTACT
Tana Sanderson, Director of Admission, California College San Diego, 6602 Convoy Court, Suite 100, San Diego, CA 92111. *Phone:* 619-295-5785. *Toll-free phone:* 800-622-3188. *E-mail:* tana.sanderson@cc-sd.edu.

California College San Diego
San Marcos, California
http://www.cc-sd.edu/

CONTACT
California College San Diego, 277 Rancheros Drive, Suite 200, San Marcos, CA 92069. *Toll-free phone:* 800-622-3188.

California Institute of Integral Studies
San Francisco, California
http://www.ciis.edu/
- **Independent** upper-level, founded 1968
- **Urban** campus with easy access to San Francisco
- **Endowment** $1.9 million
- **Coed** 50 undergraduate students, 94% full-time, 82% women, 18% men
- **Minimally difficult** entrance level

UNDERGRAD STUDENTS
47 full-time, 3 part-time. Students come from 4 states and territories; 4 other countries; 1% are from out of state; 14% Black or African American, non-Hispanic/Latino; 14% Hispanic/Latino; 2% Asian, non-Hispanic/Latino; 14% Two or more races, non-Hispanic/Latino; 8% international; 62% transferred in.

FACULTY
Total: 199, 32% full-time.
Student/faculty ratio: 11:1.

ACADEMICS
Calendar: semesters. *Degrees:* bachelor's, master's, doctoral, and postbachelor's certificates.

Special study options: accelerated degree program, adult/continuing education programs, distance learning, external degree program, independent study, summer session for credit.

Computers: 25 computers/terminals are available on campus for general student use. Students can access the following: campus intranet, free student e-mail accounts, online (class) grades, online (class) registration, online (class) schedules. Campuswide network is available. Wireless service is available via classrooms, libraries, student centers.
Library: The Laurance S. Rockefeller Library plus 1 other.

STUDENT LIFE
Housing options: college housing not available.

Activities and organizations: drama/theater group, Student Alliance, People of Color, Queer@CIIS, International Students and Friends, AWARE - Awaking to Whiteness and Racism Everywhere.

Student services: personal/psychological counseling.

COSTS & FINANCIAL AID
Costs (2018–19) *Tuition:* $19,792 full-time, $825 per unit part-time. *Required fees:* $430 full-time, $215 per term part-time. *Payment plan:* installment. *Waivers:* employees or children of employees.

Financial Aid Of all full-time matriculated undergraduates who enrolled in 2015, 86 applied for aid, 86 were judged to have need, 4 had their need fully met. 6 Federal Work-Study jobs (averaging $3208). *Average percent of need met:* 22. *Average financial aid package:* $18,625. *Average need-based loan:* $5799. *Average need-based gift aid:* $6193.

APPLYING
Options: electronic application.
Application fee: $65.

CONTACT
Admissions Counselor, California Institute of Integral Studies, 1453 Mission Street, San Francisco, CA 94103. *Phone:* 415-575-6156. *Fax:* 415-575-1268. *E-mail:* admissions@ciis.edu.

California Institute of Technology
Pasadena, California
http://www.caltech.edu/
- **Independent** university, founded 1891
- **Suburban** 124-acre campus with easy access to Los Angeles
- **Endowment** $2.6 billion
- **Coed** 961 undergraduate students, 100% full-time, 45% women, 55% men
- **Most difficult** entrance level, 8% of applicants were admitted

UNDERGRAD STUDENTS
961 full-time. Students come from 47 states and territories; 23 other countries; 66% are from out of state; 1% Black or African American, non-Hispanic/Latino; 12% Hispanic/Latino; 43% Asian, non-Hispanic/Latino; 7% Two or more races, non-Hispanic/Latino; 9% international; 0.3% transferred in; 85% live on campus.

Freshmen:
Admission: 7,339 applied, 568 admitted, 235 enrolled. *Test scores:* ACT scores over 18: 100%; ACT scores over 24: 100%; ACT scores over 30: 100%.
Retention: 98% of full-time freshmen returned.

FACULTY
Total: 374, 89% full-time, 95% with terminal degrees.
Student/faculty ratio: 3:1.

ACADEMICS
Calendar: quarters. *Degrees:* bachelor's, master's, doctoral, and post-master's certificates.

Special study options: cooperative education, double majors, English as a second language, independent study, off-campus study, services for LD students, student-designed majors, study abroad. *ROTC:* Army (c), Air Force (c).

Unusual degree programs: 3-2 engineering with Bowdoin College, Bryn Mawr College, Grinnell College, Haverford College, Mt. Holyoke College, Oberlin College, Occidental College, Ohio Wesleyan University, Pomona College, Reed College, Spelman College, Wesleyan University, Whitman College.

Computers: 75 computers/terminals and 1,250 ports are available on campus for general student use. Students can access the following: campus intranet, computer help desk, free student e-mail accounts, online (class) grades, online (class) registration, online (class) schedules. Campuswide network is available. 100% of college-owned or -operated housing units are wired for high-speed Internet access. Wireless service is available via entire campus.
Library: Sherman Fairchild Library plus 5 others. *Books:* 276,184 (physical), 61,096 (digital/electronic); *Serial titles:* 6,184 (physical), 5,596 (digital/electronic); *Databases:* 197. Weekly public service hours: 168; study areas open 24 hours, 5–7 days a week; students can reserve study rooms.

STUDENT LIFE
Housing options: on-campus residence required for freshman year; coed, special housing for students with disabilities. Campus housing is university owned. Freshman campus housing is guaranteed.

Activities and organizations: drama/theater group, student-run newspaper, choral group, Instrumental music groups, Entrepreneur's Club, Glee Club, Theater Arts, Ultimate Disc Club.

Athletics Member NCAA. All Division III. *Intercollegiate sports:* baseball M, basketball M/W, cross-country running M/W, fencing M/W, soccer M/W, swimming and diving M/W, tennis M/W, track and field M/W, volleyball W, water polo M/W. *Intramural sports:* badminton M(c)/W(c), basketball M/W, soccer M/W, table tennis M/W, ultimate Frisbee M(c)/W(c), volleyball M/W.

Campus security: 24-hour emergency response devices and patrols, late-night transport/escort service, controlled dormitory access.

Student services: health clinic, personal/psychological counseling, women's center.

COSTS & FINANCIAL AID

Costs (2017–18) *One-time required fee:* $500. *Comprehensive fee:* $64,704 includes full-time tuition ($48,111), mandatory fees ($1797), and room and board ($14,796). *College room only:* $8391. Room and board charges vary according to housing facility. *Payment plans:* installment, deferred payment. *Waivers:* employees or children of employees.

Financial Aid Of all full-time matriculated undergrads who enrolled in 2017, 575 applied for aid, 495 were judged to have need, 495 had their need fully met. 251 Federal Work-Study jobs (averaging $3305). 47 state and other part-time jobs (averaging $2563). *Average percent of need met:* 100. *Average financial aid package:* $49,951. *Average need-based loan:* $3622. *Average need-based gift aid:* $45,797. *Average indebtedness upon graduation:* $16,777.

APPLYING

Standardized Tests *Required:* SAT or ACT (for admission), SAT and SAT Subject Tests or ACT (for admission).

Options: electronic application, early admission, early action, deferred entrance.

Application fee: $75.

Required: essay or personal statement, high school transcript, 2 letters of recommendation.

Application deadlines: 1/3 (freshmen), 2/15 (transfers), 11/1 (early action).

Notification: 4/1 (freshmen), 5/1 (transfers), 12/15 (early action).

CONTACT

Mr. Jarrid James Whitney, Executive Director of Admissions, California Institute of Technology, 383 South Hill Avenue, Mail Code 10-90, Pasadena, CA 91125. *Phone:* 626-395-6341. *Fax:* 626-683-3026.

California Institute of the Arts

Valencia, California

http://www.calarts.edu/

CONTACT

Molly Ryan, Director of Admissions, California Institute of the Arts, 24700 McBean Parkway, Valencia, CA 91355-2340. *Phone:* 661-255-1050. *Toll-free phone:* 800-545-2787. *Fax:* 661-253-7710. *E-mail:* admiss@calarts.edu.

California Intercontinental University

Irvine, California

http://caluniversity.edu/

CONTACT

John Ramsay, Director of Admission, California Intercontinental University, 17310 Red Hill Avenue, #200, Irvine, CA 92614. *Phone:* 909-396-6090. *Toll-free phone:* 866-687-2258. *Fax:* 909-804-5151. *E-mail:* admissions@caluniversity.com.

California Lutheran University

Thousand Oaks, California

http://www.callutheran.edu/

- **Independent Lutheran** comprehensive, founded 1959
- **Suburban** 290-acre campus with easy access to Los Angeles
- **Endowment** $95.7 million
- **Coed** 2,963 undergraduate students, 96% full-time, 57% women, 43% men
- **Moderately difficult** entrance level, 73% of applicants were admitted

UNDERGRAD STUDENTS

2,858 full-time, 105 part-time. Students come from 35 states and territories; 27 other countries; 12% are from out of state; 4% Black or African American, non-Hispanic/Latino; 31% Hispanic/Latino; 5% Asian, non-Hispanic/Latino; 0.3% Native Hawaiian or other Pacific Islander, non-Hispanic/Latino; 0.3% American Indian or Alaska Native, non-Hispanic/Latino; 8% Two or more races, non-Hispanic/Latino; 3% Race/ethnicity unknown; 4% international; 9% transferred in; 51% live on campus.

Freshmen:

Admission: 5,251 applied, 3,820 admitted, 585 enrolled. *Average high school GPA:* 3.7. *Test scores:* SAT evidence-based reading and writing scores over 500: 90%; SAT math scores over 500: 87%; ACT scores over 18: 96%; SAT evidence-based reading and writing scores over 600: 37%; SAT math scores over 600: 32%; ACT scores over 24: 55%; SAT evidence-based reading and writing scores over 700: 4%; SAT math scores over 700: 6%; ACT scores over 30: 10%.

Retention: 85% of full-time freshmen returned.

FACULTY

Total: 445, 43% full-time, 60% with terminal degrees.

Student/faculty ratio: 16:1.

ACADEMICS

Calendar: semesters. *Degrees:* certificates, bachelor's, master's, doctoral, post-master's, and postbachelor's certificates.

Special study options: accelerated degree program, adult/continuing education programs, advanced placement credit, cooperative education, double majors, honors programs, independent study, internships, off-campus study, part-time degree program, services for LD students, student-designed majors, study abroad, summer session for credit. *ROTC:* Army (c), Air Force (c).

Unusual degree programs: 3-2 computer science, political public policy and administration.

Computers: 334 computers/terminals are available on campus for general student use. Students can access the following: campus intranet, computer help desk, free student e-mail accounts, online (class) grades, online (class) registration, online (class) schedules. Campuswide network is available. 100% of college-owned or -operated housing units are wired for high-speed Internet access. Wireless service is available via entire campus.

Library: Pearson Library. *Books:* 120,019 (physical), 246,484 (digital/electronic); *Serial titles:* 27 (physical), 34 (digital/electronic); *Databases:* 163. Weekly public service hours: 102; students can reserve study rooms.

STUDENT LIFE

Housing options: on-campus residence required through junior year; coed, special housing for students with disabilities. Campus housing is university owned. Freshman campus housing is guaranteed.

Activities and organizations: drama/theater group, student-run newspaper, radio and television station, choral group, Student Government, recreation, sports fan, or club sports related, service organizations, campus ministry or other religiously affiliated organization, multicultural organizations.

Athletics Member NCAA. All Division III. *Intercollegiate sports:* baseball M, basketball M/W, cheerleading M/W, cross-country running M/W, football M, golf M/W, soccer M/W, softball W, swimming and diving M/W, tennis M/W, track and field M/W, volleyball M/W, water polo M/W. *Intramural sports:* basketball M(c)/W(c), bowling M(c)/W(c), football M(c)/W(c), ice hockey M(c)/W(c), lacrosse M(c)/W(c), rugby M(c)/W(c), soccer M(c)/W(c), softball M(c)/W(c), tennis M(c)/W(c), ultimate Frisbee M(c)/W(c), volleyball M(c)/W(c), water polo M(c)/W(c), wrestling M(c)/W(c).

Campus security: 24-hour emergency response devices and patrols, late-night transport/escort service, controlled dormitory access, escort service, shuttle service.

Student services: health clinic, personal/psychological counseling, women's center.

COSTS & FINANCIAL AID

Costs (2017–18) *Comprehensive fee:* $54,683 includes full-time tuition ($40,880), mandatory fees ($483), and room and board ($13,320). Part-time tuition: $1315 per unit. *College room only:* $7150. Room and board charges vary according to board plan and housing facility. *Payment plan:* installment. *Waivers:* employees or children of employees.

Financial Aid Of all full-time matriculated undergraduates who enrolled in 2017, 2,771 applied for aid, 2,065 were judged to have need, 452 had their need fully met. 260 Federal Work-Study jobs (averaging $2500). In 2017, 688 non-need-based awards were made. *Average percent of need met:* 79. *Average financial aid package:* $36,600. *Average need-based loan:* $4840. *Average need-based gift aid:* $27,600. *Average non-need-based aid:* $18,860. *Average indebtedness upon graduation:* $34,220.

APPLYING

Standardized Tests *Required:* SAT or ACT (for admission).

Options: electronic application, early action, deferred entrance.

Application fee: $25.

Required: essay or personal statement, high school transcript, minimum 2.8 GPA, 1 letter of recommendation. *Recommended:* minimum 3.0 GPA, interview.

Application deadlines: 1/1 (freshmen), 6/1 (transfers), 11/1 (early action).

Notification: 4/1 (freshmen), continuous (transfers), 1/15 (early action).

CONTACT

Dr. Michael Elgarico, Dean of Undergraduate Enrollment, California Lutheran University, Office of Admission, #1350, Thousand Oaks, CA 91360. *Phone:* 805-493-3135. *Toll-free phone:* 877-258-3678. *Fax:* 805-493-3114. *E-mail:* cluadm@clunet.edu.

California Miramar University

San Diego, California

http://www.calmu.edu/

CONTACT

Jean Van Slyke, Director of Admissions, California Miramar University, 3550 Camino Del Rio North, Suite 208, San Diego, CA 92108. *Phone:* 858-653-3000. *Toll-free phone:* 877-570-5678. *Fax:* 858-653-6786. *E-mail:* admissions@calmu.edu.

California Polytechnic State University, San Luis Obispo

San Luis Obispo, California

http://www.calpoly.edu/

- **State-supported** comprehensive, founded 1901, part of California State University System
- **Suburban** 6000-acre campus
- **Coed** 21,297 undergraduate students, 96% full-time, 48% women, 52% men
- **Moderately difficult** entrance level, 35% of applicants were admitted

UNDERGRAD STUDENTS

20,530 full-time, 767 part-time. 14% are from out of state; 0.8% Black or African American, non-Hispanic/Latino; 17% Hispanic/Latino; 13% Asian, non-Hispanic/Latino; 0.2% Native Hawaiian or other Pacific Islander, non-Hispanic/Latino; 0.1% American Indian or Alaska Native, non-Hispanic/Latino; 8% Two or more races, non-Hispanic/Latino; 5% Race/ethnicity unknown; 2% international; 4% transferred in; 36% live on campus.

Freshmen:

Admission: 48,588 applied, 16,817 admitted, 5,253 enrolled. *Average high school GPA:* 4.0. *Test scores:* SAT evidence-based reading and writing scores over 500: 100%; SAT math scores over 500: 100%; ACT scores over 18: 100%; SAT evidence-based reading and writing scores over 600: 80%; SAT math scores over 600: 80%; ACT scores over 24: 91%; SAT evidence-based reading and writing scores over 700: 22%; SAT math scores over 700: 31%; ACT scores over 30: 40%.

Retention: 95% of full-time freshmen returned.

FACULTY

Total: 1,473, 65% full-time, 59% with terminal degrees.

Student/faculty ratio: 19:1.

ACADEMICS

Calendar: quarters. *Degrees:* bachelor's, master's, and postbachelor's certificates.

Special study options: academic remediation for entering students, advanced placement credit, cooperative education, distance learning, double majors, English as a second language, honors programs, internships, off-campus study, part-time degree program, services for LD students, study abroad, summer session for credit. *ROTC:* Army (b).

Computers: Students can access the following: campus intranet, free student e-mail accounts, online (class) grades, online (class) registration, online (class) schedules. Campuswide network is available. Wireless service is available via classrooms, computer centers, computer labs, dorm rooms, learning centers, libraries, student centers.

Library: Robert E. Kennedy Library.

STUDENT LIFE

Housing options: on-campus residence required for freshman year; coed, special housing for students with disabilities. Campus housing is university owned.

Activities and organizations: drama/theater group, student-run newspaper, radio and television station, choral group, marching band, national fraternities, national sororities.

Athletics Member NCAA. All Division I except football (Division I-AA). *Intercollegiate sports:* baseball M(s), basketball M(s)/W(s), cross-country running M(s)/W(s), golf M(s)/W(s), soccer M(s)/W(s), softball W(s), swimming and diving M(s)/W(s), tennis M(s)/W(s), track and field M(s)/W(s), volleyball W(s), wrestling M(s). *Intramural sports:* badminton M/W, basketball M/W, football M, racquetball M/W, soccer M/W, softball M/W, table tennis M/W, tennis M/W, volleyball M/W.

Campus security: 24-hour emergency response devices and patrols, student patrols, late-night transport/escort service.

Student services: health clinic, personal/psychological counseling, women's center, legal services.

COSTS & FINANCIAL AID

Costs (2017–18) *Tuition:* state resident $5742 full-time, $3330 per year part-time; nonresident $17,622 full-time, $8082 per year part-time. Full-time tuition and fees vary according to course load, degree level, and program. Part-time tuition and fees vary according to course load, degree level, and program. *Required fees:* $3690 full-time, $3219 per year part-time. *Room and board:* $13,115; room only: $7792. Room and board charges vary according to housing facility. *Payment plan:* installment. *Waivers:* employees or children of employees.

Financial Aid Of all full-time matriculated undergraduates who enrolled in 2016, 11,669 applied for aid, 7,832 were judged to have need, 670 had their need fully met. In 2016, 2472 non-need-based awards were made. *Average percent of need met:* 58. *Average financial aid package:* $10,456. *Average need-based loan:* $4094. *Average need-based gift aid:* $3563. *Average non-need-based aid:* $2301. *Average indebtedness upon graduation:* $21,852.

APPLYING

Standardized Tests *Required:* SAT or ACT (for admission).

Options: electronic application.

Application fee: $55.

Required: high school transcript.

Application deadlines: 11/30 (freshmen), 11/30 (transfers).

Notification: 4/1 (freshmen), 4/1 (transfers).

CONTACT

Mr. James Maraviglia, Vice Provost for Enrollment Development and Chief Marketing Officer, California Polytechnic State University, San Luis Obispo, Admissions Office, 1 Grand Avenue, San Luis Obispo, CA 93407-0031. *Phone:* 805-756-2913. *Fax:* 805-756-5911. *E-mail:* admissions@calpoly.edu.

California State Polytechnic University, Pomona

Pomona, California

http://www.cpp.edu/

- **State-supported** comprehensive, founded 1938, part of California State University System
- **Urban** 1400-acre campus with easy access to Los Angeles
- **Endowment** $96.1 million
- **Coed** 24,319 undergraduate students, 89% full-time, 46% women, 54% men
- **Moderately difficult** entrance level, 55% of applicants were admitted

UNDERGRAD STUDENTS

21,668 full-time, 2,651 part-time. Students come from 34 states and territories; 107 other countries; 1% are from out of state; 3% Black or African American, non-Hispanic/Latino; 43% Hispanic/Latino; 22% Asian, non-Hispanic/Latino; 0.2% Native Hawaiian or other Pacific Islander, non-Hispanic/Latino; 0.2% American Indian or Alaska Native, non-Hispanic/Latino; 4% Two or more races, non-Hispanic/Latino; 3% Race/ethnicity unknown; 7% international; 13% transferred in; 10% live on campus.

Freshmen:
Admission: 36,574 applied, 20,194 admitted, 3,786 enrolled. *Average high school GPA:* 3.5. *Test scores:* SAT evidence-based reading and writing scores over 500: 79%; SAT math scores over 500: 80%; ACT scores over 18: 89%; SAT evidence-based reading and writing scores over 600: 31%; SAT math scores over 600: 37%; ACT scores over 24: 48%; SAT evidence-based reading and writing scores over 700: 4%; SAT math scores over 700: 9%; ACT scores over 30: 11%.
Retention: 87% of full-time freshmen returned.

FACULTY
Total: 1,244, 49% full-time, 55% with terminal degrees.
Student/faculty ratio: 25:1.

ACADEMICS
Calendar: quarters. *Degrees:* bachelor's, master's, and doctoral.
Special study options: academic remediation for entering students, adult/continuing education programs, advanced placement credit, cooperative education, distance learning, double majors, English as a second language, freshman honors college, honors programs, internships, off-campus study, part-time degree program, services for LD students, study abroad, summer session for credit. *ROTC:* Army (b).
Computers: 2,117 computers/terminals and 3,588 ports are available on campus for general student use. Students can access the following: campus intranet, computer help desk, free student e-mail accounts, online (class) grades, online (class) schedules. Campuswide network is available. 100% of college-owned or -operated housing units are wired for high-speed Internet access. Wireless service is available via entire campus.
Library: University Library. *Books:* 576,734 (physical), 246,874 (digital/electronic); *Serial titles:* 278,011 (physical), 13,335 (digital/electronic); *Databases:* 143. Weekly public service hours: 92; study areas open 24 hours, 5–7 days a week; students can reserve study rooms.

STUDENT LIFE
Housing options: on-campus residence required for freshman year; coed, special housing for students with disabilities. Campus housing is university owned and is provided by a third party. Freshman applicants given priority for college housing.
Activities and organizations: drama/theater group, student-run newspaper, choral group, Rose Float Club, Mexican American Student Association (MASA), Barkada - Filipino American Student Association, American Marketing Association, Cal Poly Society of Accountants, national fraternities, national sororities.
Athletics Member NCAA. All Division II. *Intercollegiate sports:* baseball M(s), basketball M(s)/W(s), cross-country running M(s)/W(s), soccer M(s)/W(s), track and field M(s)/W(s), volleyball W(s). *Intramural sports:* basketball M/W, bowling M/W, football M/W, softball M/W, volleyball M/W.
Campus security: 24-hour emergency response devices and patrols, student patrols, late-night transport/escort service, controlled dormitory access, video camera surveillance.
Student services: health clinic, personal/psychological counseling, women's center.

COSTS & FINANCIAL AID
Costs (2018–19) *Tuition:* state resident $5742 full-time; nonresident $17,622 full-time, $264 per credit hour part-time. Full-time tuition and fees vary according to course load, degree level, and program. Part-time tuition and fees vary according to course load, degree level, and program. *Required fees:* $1555 full-time. *Room and board:* $14,514; room only: $9027. Room and board charges vary according to board plan and housing facility. *Payment plans:* installment, deferred payment. *Waivers:* employees or children of employees.
Financial Aid Of all full-time matriculated undergraduates who enrolled in 2017, 16,917 applied for aid, 14,942 were judged to have need, 385 had their need fully met. 303 Federal Work-Study jobs (averaging $2802). In 2017, 13 non-need-based awards were made. *Average percent of need met:* 54. *Average financial aid package:* $11,067. *Average need-based loan:* $4454. *Average need-based gift aid:* $10,122. *Average non-need-based aid:* $1535. *Average indebtedness upon graduation:* $22,228.

APPLYING
Standardized Tests *Required:* SAT or ACT (for admission).
Options: electronic application.
Application fee: $55.
Required: high school transcript, minimum 2.0 GPA.
Application deadlines: 11/30 (freshmen), 11/30 (transfers).
Notification: continuous (freshmen), 5/1 (transfers).

CONTACT
Ms. Deborah L. Brandon, Executive Director of Admissions & Enrollment Planning, California State Polytechnic University, Pomona, 3801 W Temple Ave, 98-T2, Pomona, CA 91768. *Phone:* 909-869-3427. *Fax:* 909-869-5315. *E-mail:* dlbrandon@cpp.edu.

California State University, Bakersfield
Bakersfield, California
http://www.csub.edu/
- **State-supported** comprehensive, founded 1970, part of California State University System
- **Urban** 575-acre campus
- **Coed**
- 100% of applicants were admitted

FACULTY
Student/faculty ratio: 26:1.

ACADEMICS
Calendar: semesters. *Degrees:* bachelor's, master's, and doctoral.
Library: Walter W. Stiern Library.

STUDENT LIFE
Housing options: coed.
Athletics Member NCAA. All Division II except wrestling (Division I).
Campus security: 24-hour emergency response devices and patrols, late-night transport/escort service.

COSTS & FINANCIAL AID
Costs (2017–18) *Tuition:* state resident $3330 per year part-time; nonresident $8082 per year part-time. Full-time tuition and fees vary according to course load. Part-time tuition and fees vary according to course load. *Required fees:* $1404 per year part-time. *Room and board:* Room and board charges vary according to board plan and housing facility.
Financial Aid Of all full-time matriculated undergraduates who enrolled in 2016, 6,327 applied for aid, 5,647 were judged to have need, 784 had their need fully met. *Average percent of need met:* 55. *Average financial aid package:* $11,346. *Average need-based loan:* $4022. *Average need-based gift aid:* $9762. *Average indebtedness upon graduation:* $17,454.

APPLYING
Standardized Tests *Required for some:* SAT or ACT (for admission).
Options: electronic application, deferred entrance.
Application fee: $55.
Required: high school transcript.

CONTACT
Debra Blowers, Assistant Director, Admissions and Evaluations, California State University, Bakersfield, 9001 Stockdale Highway, Balersfield, CA 93311-1099. *Phone:* 661-664-3036. *Toll-free phone:* 800-788-2782. *E-mail:* admissions@csub.edu.

California State University Channel Islands
Camarillo, California
http://www.csuci.edu/

CONTACT
Ms. Ginger Reyes, California State University Channel Islands, One University Drive, Camarillo, CA 93012. *Phone:* 805-437-8520. *Fax:* 805-437-8519. *E-mail:* prospective.student@csuci.edu.

California State University, Chico

Chico, California

http://www.csuchico.edu/

- **State-supported** comprehensive, founded 1887, part of California State University System
- **Small-town** 119-acre campus
- **Endowment** $54.8 million
- **Coed**
- **Moderately difficult** entrance level

FACULTY

Student/faculty ratio: 24:1.

ACADEMICS

Calendar: semesters. *Degrees:* certificates, bachelor's, master's, post-master's, and postbachelor's certificates.

Library: Meriam Library plus 1 other. *Books:* 923,470 (physical), 180,505 (digital/electronic); *Serial titles:* 660 (physical). Study areas open 24 hours, 5–7 days a week; students can reserve study rooms.

STUDENT LIFE

Housing options: coed, women-only, special housing for students with disabilities. Campus housing is university owned. Freshman applicants given priority for college housing.

Activities and organizations: drama/theater group, student-run newspaper, radio station, choral group, Pre-Medical Association, Health Professionals Association (HPA), Audio Engineering Society, Student Association Of Social Work SASW (Undergraduate), Recreation Hospitality and Parks Society (RHAPS), national fraternities, national sororities.

Athletics Member NCAA. All Division II.

Campus security: 24-hour emergency response devices and patrols, student patrols, late-night transport/escort service, controlled dormitory access, crime prevention workshops, RAD self-defense program, Chico Safe Rides, blue light emergency phones, freshmen safety orientation.

Student services: health clinic, personal/psychological counseling, women's center, legal services.

COSTS & FINANCIAL AID

Costs (2017–18) *Tuition:* state resident $7044 full-time; nonresident $18,204 full-time. Full-time tuition and fees vary according to degree level. Part-time tuition and fees vary according to course load and degree level. *Required fees:* $5472 full-time. *Room and board:* $12,536. Room and board charges vary according to board plan and housing facility. *Payment plans:* installment, deferred payment.

Financial Aid Of all full-time matriculated undergraduates who enrolled in 2015, 12,000 applied for aid, 10,261 were judged to have need, 1,576 had their need fully met. In 2015, 445 non-need-based awards were made. *Average percent of need met:* 76. *Average financial aid package:* $16,081. *Average need-based loan:* $4534. *Average need-based gift aid:* $9941. *Average non-need-based aid:* $1226.

APPLYING

Standardized Tests *Required:* SAT or ACT (for admission).

Options: electronic application, deferred entrance.

Application fee: $55.

Required: high school transcript, GPA from 10th/11th grade college preparatory courses.

CONTACT

Admissions Counselor, California State University, Chico, 400 West First Street, Chico, CA 95929-0722. *Phone:* 530-898-6322. *Toll-free phone:* 800-542-4426. *Fax:* 530-898-6456. *E-mail:* info@csuchico.edu.

California State University, Dominguez Hills

Carson, California

http://www.csudh.edu/

- **State-supported** comprehensive, founded 1960, part of California State University System
- **Urban** 350-acre campus with easy access to Los Angeles
- **Endowment** $11.0 million
- **Coed** 13,116 undergraduate students, 77% full-time, 63% women, 37% men
- **Moderately difficult** entrance level, 77% of applicants were admitted

UNDERGRAD STUDENTS

10,043 full-time, 3,073 part-time. Students come from 15 states and territories; 37 other countries; 12% Black or African American, non-Hispanic/Latino; 62% Hispanic/Latino; 9% Asian, non-Hispanic/Latino; 0.3% Native Hawaiian or other Pacific Islander, non-Hispanic/Latino; 0.1% American Indian or Alaska Native, non-Hispanic/Latino; 3% Two or more races, non-Hispanic/Latino; 3% Race/ethnicity unknown; 5% international; 21% transferred in; 5% live on campus.

Freshmen:

Admission: 12,094 applied, 9,333 admitted, 1,678 enrolled. *Average high school GPA:* 3.1. *Test scores:* SAT evidence-based reading and writing scores over 500: 27%; SAT math scores over 500: 23%; ACT scores over 18: 52%; SAT evidence-based reading and writing scores over 600: 5%; SAT math scores over 600: 7%; ACT scores over 24: 4%.

Retention: 77% of full-time freshmen returned.

FACULTY

Total: 842, 33% full-time, 46% with terminal degrees.

Student/faculty ratio: 21:1.

ACADEMICS

Calendar: semesters. *Degrees:* bachelor's, master's, post-master's, and postbachelor's certificates.

Special study options: academic remediation for entering students, accelerated degree program, advanced placement credit, cooperative education, distance learning, double majors, external degree program, honors programs, independent study, off-campus study, part-time degree program, services for LD students, student-designed majors, study abroad, summer session for credit. *ROTC:* Army (b), Air Force (c).

Computers: 1,100 computers/terminals and 1,100 ports are available on campus for general student use. Students can access the following: campus intranet, computer help desk, free student e-mail accounts, online (class) grades, online (class) registration, online (class) schedules. Campuswide network is available. 100% of college-owned or -operated housing units are wired for high-speed Internet access. Wireless service is available via entire campus.

Library: Leo F. Cain Educational Resource Center. *Books:* 457,885 (physical), 300,523 (digital/electronic); *Serial titles:* 6,542 (physical), 75,366 (digital/electronic); *Databases:* 94. Weekly public service hours: 81; students can reserve study rooms.

STUDENT LIFE

Housing options: men-only, women-only, special housing for students with disabilities. Campus housing is university owned. Freshman applicants given priority for college housing.

Activities and organizations: drama/theater group, student-run newspaper, radio station, choral group, American Marketing Association, Phi Sigma Sigma, Organization of African Studies, Latino Student Business Association, Circle K, national fraternities, national sororities.

Athletics Member NCAA. All Division II. *Intercollegiate sports:* baseball M(s), basketball M(s)/W(s), golf M(s), soccer M(s)/W(s), softball W(s), track and field W(s), volleyball W(s). *Intramural sports:* basketball M/W, football M/W, soccer M/W, softball M/W, swimming and diving M/W, tennis M/W, volleyball M/W, weight lifting M/W.

Campus security: 24-hour emergency response devices and patrols, student patrols, late-night transport/escort service.

Student services: health clinic, personal/psychological counseling, women's center.

COSTS & FINANCIAL AID

Costs (2018–19) *Tuition:* state resident $6937 full-time, $3330 per year part-time; nonresident $16,441 full-time, $396 per unit part-time. Full-time tuition and fees vary according to course load, program, and reciprocity agreements. Part-time tuition and fees vary according to course load, program, and reciprocity agreements. *Required fees:* $1195 full-time, $1195 per year part-time. *Room and board:* $12,540. Room and board charges vary according to housing facility. *Payment plan:* installment. *Waivers:* senior citizens and employees or children of employees.

Financial Aid Of all full-time matriculated undergraduates who enrolled in 2016, 6,789 applied for aid, 6,545 were judged to have need, 112 had their need fully met. 146 Federal Work-Study jobs (averaging $1571). In 2016, 163 non-need-based awards were made. *Average percent of need met:* 34. *Average financial aid package:* $6211. *Average need-based loan:* $2337. *Average need-based gift aid:* $5229. *Average non-need-based aid:* $4604. *Average indebtedness upon graduation:* $15,880. *Financial aid deadline:* 5/15.

APPLYING

Standardized Tests *Required for some:* SAT or ACT (for admission).

Options: electronic application.

Application fee: $55.

Required: high school transcript.

Application deadlines: rolling (freshmen), rolling (transfers).

Notification: continuous (freshmen), continuous (transfers).

CONTACT

Information Center, California State University, Dominguez Hills, 1000 East Victoria Street, Carson, CA 90747-0001. *Phone:* 310-243-3696. *E-mail:* info@csudh.edu.

California State University, East Bay
Hayward, California
http://www.csueastbay.edu/

- **State-supported** comprehensive, founded 1957, part of California State University System
- **Suburban** 343-acre campus with easy access to San Francisco Bay Area
- **Coed** 12,998 undergraduate students, 87% full-time, 62% women, 38% men
- **Minimally difficult** entrance level, 74% of applicants were admitted

UNDERGRAD STUDENTS

11,306 full-time, 1,692 part-time. Students come from 21 states and territories; 54 other countries; 1% are from out of state; 10% Black or African American, non-Hispanic/Latino; 34% Hispanic/Latino; 24% Asian, non-Hispanic/Latino; 0.9% Native Hawaiian or other Pacific Islander, non-Hispanic/Latino; 0.2% American Indian or Alaska Native, non-Hispanic/Latino; 6% Two or more races, non-Hispanic/Latino; 4% Race/ethnicity unknown; 6% international; 18% transferred in.

Freshmen:
Admission: 15,963 applied, 11,824 admitted, 1,420 enrolled. *Average high school GPA:* 3.2. *Test scores:* SAT evidence-based reading and writing scores over 500: 51%; SAT math scores over 500: 49%; ACT scores over 18: 58%; SAT evidence-based reading and writing scores over 600: 10%; SAT math scores over 600: 9%; ACT scores over 24: 9%; SAT evidence-based reading and writing scores over 700: 1%; SAT math scores over 700: 1%; ACT scores over 30: 1%.

Retention: 75% of full-time freshmen returned.

FACULTY
Total: 882, 44% full-time.

Student/faculty ratio: 22:1.

ACADEMICS
Calendar: quarters. *Degrees:* certificates, bachelor's, master's, doctoral, and postbachelor's certificates.

Special study options: academic remediation for entering students, accelerated degree program, adult/continuing education programs, advanced placement credit, cooperative education, distance learning, double majors, English as a second language, honors programs, independent study, internships, off-campus study, part-time degree program, services for LD students, student-designed majors, study abroad, summer session for credit.

Computers: 700 computers/terminals are available on campus for general student use. Students can access the following: campus intranet, computer help desk, free student e-mail accounts, online (class) grades, online (class) registration, online (class) schedules. Campuswide network is available. 100% of college-owned or -operated housing units are wired for high-speed Internet access. Wireless service is available via entire campus.

Library: Hayward Campus Library. *Books:* 630,855 (physical), 233,485 (digital/electronic); *Serial titles:* 10,905 (physical), 107,791 (digital/electronic); *Databases:* 133. Weekly public service hours: 101; students can reserve study rooms.

STUDENT LIFE
Housing options: coed, special housing for students with disabilities. Campus housing is university owned and leased by the school. Freshman applicants given priority for college housing.

Activities and organizations: drama/theater group, student-run newspaper, choral group, marching band, Tau Sigma Hour Society, East Bay Student Nursing Association, Golden Key Honor Society, Black Student Union, Sigma Sigma Sigma Society, national fraternities, national sororities.

Athletics Member NCAA, NAIA. All NCAA Division II. *Intercollegiate sports:* baseball M(s), basketball M(s)/W(s), cross-country running M(s)/W(s), golf M(s)/W(s), soccer M(s)/W(s), softball W(s), swimming and diving W(s), track and field M(s)/W(s), volleyball W(s), water polo W(s). *Intramural sports:* badminton M/W, basketball M/W, golf M/W, gymnastics M, racquetball M/W, soccer M/W, softball M/W, swimming and diving M/W, tennis M/W, volleyball M/W, weight lifting M/W.

Campus security: 24-hour emergency response devices and patrols, student patrols, late-night transport/escort service, controlled dormitory access.

Student services: health clinic, personal/psychological counseling.

COSTS & FINANCIAL AID
Costs (2018–19) *Tuition:* state resident $3330 per term part-time; nonresident $7290 per term part-time. Full-time tuition and fees vary according to course load, program, and reciprocity agreements. Part-time tuition and fees vary according to course load, program, and reciprocity agreements. *Required fees:* $364 per term part-time. *Room and board:* Room and board charges vary according to board plan, housing facility, and student level. *Payment plan:* installment. *Waivers:* senior citizens and employees or children of employees.

Financial Aid Of all full-time matriculated undergraduates who enrolled in 2016, 7,847 applied for aid, 7,676 were judged to have need, 189 had their need fully met. *Average percent of need met:* 55. *Average financial aid package:* $10,778. *Average need-based loan:* $6352. *Average need-based gift aid:* $8545. *Average indebtedness upon graduation:* $19,149.

APPLYING
Standardized Tests *Required for some:* SAT or ACT (for admission).

Options: electronic application.

Application fee: $55.

Required: high school transcript, minimum 2.0 GPA, California State University eligibility index.

Application deadlines: 11/30 (freshmen), 11/30 (transfers).

Notification: continuous (freshmen), continuous (transfers).

CONTACT
Dave Vasques, Associate Director for Admissions, California State University, East Bay, 25800 Carlos Bee Boulevard, Hayward, CA 94542-3000. *Phone:* 510-885-2029. *E-mail:* dave.vasquez@csueastbay.edu.

California State University, Fresno
Fresno, California
http://www.csufresno.edu/

- **State-supported** comprehensive, founded 1911, part of California State University System
- **Urban** 1399-acre campus
- **Coed**
- **Minimally difficult** entrance level

FACULTY
Student/faculty ratio: 21:1.

ACADEMICS
Calendar: semesters. *Degrees:* bachelor's, master's, doctoral, post-master's, and postbachelor's certificates.
Library: Henry Madden Library.

STUDENT LIFE
Housing options: coed, men-only, women-only. Campus housing is university owned.

Activities and organizations: drama/theater group, student-run newspaper, radio station, choral group, marching band, national fraternities, national sororities.

Athletics Member NCAA. All Division I except football (Division I-A).

Campus security: 24-hour emergency response devices and patrols, late-night transport/escort service, controlled dormitory access.

Student services: health clinic, personal/psychological counseling, women's center.

FINANCIAL AID
Financial Aid Of all full-time matriculated undergraduates who enrolled in 2017, 15,772 applied for aid, 14,753 were judged to have need, 2,485 had their need fully met. 183 Federal Work-Study jobs (averaging $5423). In 2017, 470 non-need-based awards were made. *Average percent of need met:* 79. *Average financial aid package:* $13,051. *Average need-based loan:* $4224. *Average need-based gift aid:* $10,486. *Average non-need-based aid:* $2901. *Average indebtedness upon graduation:* $18,308.

APPLYING
Standardized Tests *Required:* SAT or ACT (for admission).
Options: electronic application.
Application fee: $56.
Required: high school transcript, minimum 2.0 GPA.

CONTACT
Mr. Andy Hernandez, Admissions Officer, California State University, Fresno, 5150 North Maple Avenue, M/S JA 57, Fresno, CA 93740-8026. *Phone:* 559-278-6115. *Fax:* 559-278-4812. *E-mail:* andyhe@csufresno.edu.

California State University, Fullerton
Fullerton, California
http://www.fullerton.edu/

- **State-supported** comprehensive, founded 1957, part of California State University System
- **Suburban** 236-acre campus with easy access to Los Angeles
- **Endowment** $52.6 million
- **Coed** 64,304 undergraduate students
- **Moderately difficult** entrance level, 46% of applicants were admitted

UNDERGRAD STUDENTS
Students come from 65 other countries; 1% are from out of state; 2% Black or African American, non-Hispanic/Latino; 43% Hispanic/Latino; 21% Asian, non-Hispanic/Latino; 0.2% Native Hawaiian or other Pacific Islander, non-Hispanic/Latino; 0.1% American Indian or Alaska Native, non-Hispanic/Latino; 4% Two or more races, non-Hispanic/Latino; 4% Race/ethnicity unknown; 6% international; 6% live on campus.

Freshmen:
Admission: 45,808 applied, 20,943 admitted. *Average high school GPA:* 3.6.
Retention: 87% of full-time freshmen returned.

FACULTY
Total: 2,284, 44% full-time, 52% with terminal degrees.
Student/faculty ratio: 30:1.

ACADEMICS
Calendar: semesters. *Degrees:* bachelor's, master's, doctoral, post-master's, and postbachelor's certificates.

Special study options: academic remediation for entering students, adult/continuing education programs, advanced placement credit, cooperative education, distance learning, double majors, honors programs, independent study, internships, off-campus study, part-time degree program, services for LD students, student-designed majors, study abroad, summer session for credit. *ROTC:* Army (b).

Computers: 2,000 computers/terminals are available on campus for general student use. Students can access the following: campus intranet, computer help desk, free student e-mail accounts, online (class) grades, online (class) registration, online (class) schedules. Campuswide network is available. Wireless service is available via entire campus.
Library: Pollak Library.

STUDENT LIFE
Housing options: coed. Campus housing is university owned. Freshman applicants given priority for college housing.

Activities and organizations: drama/theater group, student-run newspaper, radio station, choral group, Pan-Hellenic Council, American Marketing Association, Lacrosse Club, Samaritans (volunteer service club), Human Services Student Association, national fraternities, national sororities.

Athletics Member NCAA. All Division I. *Intercollegiate sports:* archery M(c)/W(c), baseball M(s), basketball M(s)/W(s), bowling M(c)/W(c), cross-country running M(s)/W(s), equestrian sports M(c)/W(c), golf M(s)/W(s), ice hockey M(c)/W(c), lacrosse M(c)/W(c), rugby M(c)/W(c), sailing M(c)/W(c), skiing (downhill) M(c)/W(c), soccer M(s)/W(s), softball W(s), tennis W(s), track and field M(s)/W(s), ultimate Frisbee M(c)/W(c), volleyball M(c)/W(c), water polo M(c)/W(c). *Intramural sports:* badminton M/W, basketball M/W, bowling M/W, football M/W, racquetball M/W, soccer M/W, softball M/W, volleyball M/W.

Campus security: 24-hour emergency response devices and patrols, student patrols, late-night transport/escort service, controlled dormitory access.

Student services: health clinic, personal/psychological counseling, women's center, legal services.

COSTS & FINANCIAL AID
Costs (2017–18) *Tuition:* state resident $5742 full-time, $3330 per year part-time; nonresident $18,734 full-time, $8082 per year part-time. Full-time tuition and fees vary according to course load, degree level, and program. Part-time tuition and fees vary according to course load, degree level, and program. *Required fees:* $1108 full-time, $1108 per year part-time. *Room and board:* $15,642. Room and board charges vary according to board plan and housing facility. *Payment plans:* installment, deferred payment. *Waivers:* senior citizens and employees or children of employees.

Financial Aid Of all full-time matriculated undergraduates who enrolled in 2016, 18,943 applied for aid, 18,127 were judged to have need, 15,425 had their need fully met. In 2016, 1292 non-need-based awards were made. *Average percent of need met:* 76. *Average financial aid package:* $9341. *Average need-based loan:* $1638. *Average need-based gift aid:* $5369. *Average non-need-based aid:* $1683. *Average indebtedness upon graduation:* $14,965.

APPLYING
Options: electronic application.
Application fee: $55.
Required: high school transcript, minimum 2.0 GPA.
Application deadlines: 11/30 (freshmen), 11/30 (transfers).
Notification: continuous (freshmen), continuous (transfers).

CONTACT
Ms. Nancy J. Dority, Assistant Vice President of Enrollment Services, California State University, Fullerton, Office of Admissions and Records, PO Box 34080, Fullerton, CA 92834-9480. *Phone:* 657-278-2370. *Fax:* 657-278-2356. *E-mail:* admissions@fullerton.edu.

California State University, Long Beach

Long Beach, California

http://www.csulb.edu/

- **State-supported** comprehensive, founded 1949, part of California State University System
- **Suburban** 320-acre campus with easy access to Los Angeles
- **Endowment** $57.0 million
- **Coed** 31,351 undergraduate students, 87% full-time, 57% women, 43% men
- **Moderately difficult** entrance level, 29% of applicants were admitted

UNDERGRAD STUDENTS

27,344 full-time, 4,007 part-time. Students come from 40 states and territories; 90 other countries; 0.8% are from out of state; 12% transferred in; 20% live on campus.

Freshmen:

Admission: 61,806 applied, 17,650 admitted, 4,138 enrolled. *Average high school GPA:* 3.5. *Test scores:* SAT evidence-based reading and writing scores over 500: 71%; SAT math scores over 500: 77%; ACT scores over 18: 89%; SAT evidence-based reading and writing scores over 600: 24%; SAT math scores over 600: 42%; ACT scores over 24: 48%; SAT evidence-based reading and writing scores over 700: 4%; SAT math scores over 700: 6%; ACT scores over 30: 8%.

Retention: 86% of full-time freshmen returned.

FACULTY

Total: 2,279, 46% full-time, 59% with terminal degrees.

Student/faculty ratio: 24:1.

ACADEMICS

Calendar: semesters. *Degrees:* bachelor's, master's, doctoral, and postbachelor's certificates.

Special study options: accelerated degree program, adult/continuing education programs, double majors, English as a second language, honors programs, independent study, internships, part-time degree program, student-designed majors, study abroad. *ROTC:* Army (b), Air Force (c).

Computers: 2,000 computers/terminals are available on campus for general student use. Students can access the following: campus intranet, computer help desk, free student e-mail accounts, online (class) grades, online (class) registration, online (class) schedules. Campuswide network is available. Wireless service is available via entire campus.

Library: CSULB University Library. *Books:* 746,820 (physical), 764,807 (digital/electronic); *Serial titles:* 16,579 (physical), 69,287 (digital/electronic); *Databases:* 227. Weekly public service hours: 97.

STUDENT LIFE

Housing options: coed.

Activities and organizations: drama/theater group, student-run newspaper, radio and television station, choral group, national fraternities, national sororities.

Athletics Member NCAA. All Division I. *Intercollegiate sports:* archery M(c)/W(c), baseball M(s), basketball M(s)/W(s), bowling M(c)/W(c), cheerleading M(c)/W(c), crew M(c)/W(c), cross-country running M(s)/W(s), golf M(s)/W(s), rugby M(c)/W(c), sailing M(c)/W(c), sand volleyball W(s), skiing (downhill) M(c)/W(c), soccer M/W(s), softball W(s), tennis W(s), track and field M(s)/W(s), triathlon M(c)/W(c), ultimate Frisbee M(c)/W(c), volleyball M(s)/W(s), water polo M(s)/W(s), weight lifting M(c)/W(c), wrestling M(c)/W(c). *Intramural sports:* basketball M/W, cheerleading M/W, racquetball M/W, sand volleyball W, softball W, tennis W.

Campus security: 24-hour emergency response devices and patrols, student patrols, late-night transport/escort service, controlled dormitory access.

Student services: health clinic, personal/psychological counseling, women's center, legal services.

COSTS & FINANCIAL AID

Costs (2018–19) *Tuition:* state resident $5742 full-time; nonresident $16,038 full-time. Full-time tuition and fees vary according to degree level and program. Part-time tuition and fees vary according to course load, degree level, and program. *Required fees:* $1056 full-time. *Room and board:* $12,750; room only: $8200. Room and board charges vary according to board plan. *Payment plan:* installment. *Waivers:* senior citizens and employees or children of employees.

Financial Aid Of all full-time matriculated undergraduates who enrolled in 2017, 23,709 applied for aid, 21,216 were judged to have need, 9,668 had their need fully met. *Average percent of need met:* 78. *Average financial aid package:* $13,720. *Average need-based loan:* $3949. *Average need-based gift aid:* $6709. *Average indebtedness upon graduation:* $19,062.

APPLYING

Standardized Tests *Required:* SAT or ACT (for admission). *Recommended:* ACT (for admission).

Options: electronic application.

Application fee: $55.

Required: high school transcript. *Required for some:* minimum 3.0 GPA.

Application deadlines: 11/30 (freshmen), 11/30 (transfers).

Notification: continuous (freshmen), continuous (transfers).

CONTACT

Mrs. Janice Miller, Director, Admin Ops and Policy, ES Admissions, California State University, Long Beach, Brotman Hall, 1250 Bellflower Boulevard, Long Beach, CA 90840. *Phone:* 562-985-7827. *E-mail:* janice.miller@csulb.edu.

California State University, Los Angeles

Los Angeles, California

http://www.calstatela.edu/

- **State-supported** comprehensive, founded 1947, part of California State University System
- **Urban** 173-acre campus with easy access to Los Angeles
- **Endowment** $23.6 million
- **Coed** 24,629 undergraduate students, 85% full-time, 57% women, 43% men
- **Moderately difficult** entrance level, 46% of applicants were admitted

UNDERGRAD STUDENTS

20,881 full-time, 3,748 part-time. 4% Black or African American, non-Hispanic/Latino; 66% Hispanic/Latino; 14% Asian, non-Hispanic/Latino; 0.1% Native Hawaiian or other Pacific Islander, non-Hispanic/Latino; 0.1% American Indian or Alaska Native, non-Hispanic/Latino; 2% Two or more races, non-Hispanic/Latino; 2% Race/ethnicity unknown; 7% international; 27% transferred in.

Freshmen:

Admission: 37,396 applied, 17,369 admitted, 3,556 enrolled. *Average high school GPA:* 3.2. *Test scores:* ACT scores over 18: 52%; ACT scores over 24: 8%; ACT scores over 30: 1%.

Retention: 80% of full-time freshmen returned.

FACULTY

Total: 1,718, 41% full-time, 49% with terminal degrees.

Student/faculty ratio: 24:1.

ACADEMICS

Calendar: quarters. *Degrees:* certificates, bachelor's, master's, doctoral, and postbachelor's certificates.

Special study options: academic remediation for entering students, accelerated degree program, adult/continuing education programs, advanced placement credit, cooperative education, distance learning, double majors, English as a second language, freshman honors college, honors programs, independent study, internships, off-campus study, part-time degree program, services for LD students, student-designed majors, study abroad, summer session for credit. *ROTC:* Army (c), Air Force (c).

Unusual degree programs: 3-2 nursing.

Computers: 1,500 computers/terminals are available on campus for general student use. Students can access the following: campus intranet, computer help desk, free student e-mail accounts, online (class) grades, online (class) registration, online (class) schedules. Campuswide network is available. 100% of college-owned or -operated housing units are wired for high-speed Internet access. Wireless service is available via

classrooms, computer centers, computer labs, dorm rooms, learning centers, libraries, student centers.
Library: John F. Kennedy Memorial Library.

STUDENT LIFE
Housing options: special housing for students with disabilities. Campus housing is university owned.

Activities and organizations: drama/theater group, student-run newspaper, radio and television station, choral group, Society of Hispanic Engineering and Science Students, Institute of Electrical and Electronics Engineer, Sigma Delta PI, Asian Unified, Society of Automotive Engineers, national fraternities, national sororities.

Athletics Member NCAA. All Division II. *Intercollegiate sports:* baseball M(s), basketball M(s)/W(s), cross-country running W(s), soccer M(s)/W(s), tennis W(s), track and field M(s)/W(s), volleyball W(s). *Intramural sports:* basketball M/W, bowling M/W, gymnastics M/W, racquetball M/W, skiing (cross-country) M/W, soccer M/W, softball M/W, swimming and diving M/W, tennis M/W, track and field M/W, volleyball M/W, water polo M/W, wrestling M.

Campus security: 24-hour emergency response devices, student patrols, late-night transport/escort service.

Student services: health clinic, personal/psychological counseling, women's center, legal services.

COSTS & FINANCIAL AID
Costs (2017–18) *Tuition:* state resident $6632 full-time; nonresident $16,136 full-time. Full-time tuition and fees vary according to course level and course load. Part-time tuition and fees vary according to course level and course load. *Room and board:* $13,356. Room and board charges vary according to board plan and housing facility. *Payment plan:* installment. *Waivers:* employees or children of employees.

Financial Aid Of all full-time matriculated undergraduates who enrolled in 2016, 18,428 applied for aid, 17,549 were judged to have need, 3,110 had their need fully met. In 2016, 298 non-need-based awards were made. *Average percent of need met:* 65. *Average financial aid package:* $10,811. *Average need-based loan:* $4084. *Average need-based gift aid:* $8293. *Average non-need-based aid:* $2313. *Average indebtedness upon graduation:* $16,362.

APPLYING
Standardized Tests *Required for some:* SAT or ACT (for admission).

Options: electronic application, early admission.

Application fee: $55.

Required: high school transcript.

Application deadlines: 11/30 (freshmen), 11/30 (transfers).

Notification: 8/30 (freshmen), 8/30 (transfers).

CONTACT
Vince Lopez, Director of Outreach and Recruitment, California State University, Los Angeles, 5151 State University Drive, Los Angeles, CA 90032-8530. *Phone:* 323-343-3839. *E-mail:* admission@calstatela.edu.

California State University Maritime Academy
Vallejo, California
http://www.csum.edu/
- **State-supported** comprehensive, founded 1929, part of California State University System
- **Suburban** 64-acre campus with easy access to San Francisco
- **Coed** 1,050 undergraduate students, 96% full-time, 18% women, 82% men
- **Moderately difficult** entrance level, 67% of applicants were admitted

UNDERGRAD STUDENTS
1,007 full-time, 43 part-time. 13% are from out of state; 2% Black or African American, non-Hispanic/Latino; 20% Hispanic/Latino; 9% Asian, non-Hispanic/Latino; 0.6% Native Hawaiian or other Pacific Islander, non-Hispanic/Latino; 0.3% American Indian or Alaska Native, non-Hispanic/Latino; 12% Two or more races, non-Hispanic/Latino; 7%

Race/ethnicity unknown; 0.8% international; 6% transferred in; 66% live on campus.

Freshmen:
Admission: 1,156 applied, 769 admitted, 223 enrolled. *Average high school GPA:* 3.4. *Test scores:* SAT evidence-based reading and writing scores over 500: 90%; SAT math scores over 500: 89%; ACT scores over 18: 93%; SAT evidence-based reading and writing scores over 600: 36%; SAT math scores over 600: 47%; ACT scores over 24: 59%; SAT evidence-based reading and writing scores over 700: 3%; SAT math scores over 700: 5%; ACT scores over 30: 11%.
Retention: 75% of full-time freshmen returned.

FACULTY
Total: 106, 67% full-time.
Student/faculty ratio: 16:1.

ACADEMICS
Calendar: semesters. *Degrees:* bachelor's and master's.

Special study options: academic remediation for entering students, advanced placement credit, internships, study abroad, summer session for credit. *ROTC:* Navy (c), Air Force (c).

Computers: Students can access the following: campus intranet, computer help desk, free student e-mail accounts, online (class) grades, online (class) registration, online (class) schedules. Campuswide network is available. 100% of college-owned or -operated housing units are wired for high-speed Internet access. Wireless service is available via entire campus.

STUDENT LIFE
Housing options: on-campus residence required through senior year; coed. Campus housing is university owned. Freshman campus housing is guaranteed.

Activities and organizations: student-run newspaper, choral group, Sailing Club, Dive Club, drill team.

Athletics Member NAIA. *Intercollegiate sports:* basketball M(s)/W(s), crew M/W, golf M(s)/W, rugby M, sailing M/W, soccer M(s), volleyball W(s), water polo M/W. *Intramural sports:* baseball M, basketball M/W, football M/W, golf M/W, racquetball M/W, rugby M, sailing M/W, softball M/W, tennis M/W, volleyball M/W.

Campus security: 24-hour patrols, student patrols.

Student services: health clinic, personal/psychological counseling.

COSTS & FINANCIAL AID
Costs (2017–18) *Tuition:* state resident $5472 full-time, $1665 per term part-time; nonresident $11,160 full-time, $396 per credit hour part-time. Full-time tuition and fees vary according to course load and reciprocity agreements. Part-time tuition and fees vary according to course load and reciprocity agreements. *Required fees:* $2888 full-time, $3198 per term part-time. *Room and board:* $12,807. Room and board charges vary according to board plan. *Payment plan:* installment. *Waivers:* employees or children of employees.

Financial Aid Of all full-time matriculated undergraduates who enrolled in 2016, 575 applied for aid, 526 were judged to have need, 42 had their need fully met. *Average need-based loan:* $4588. *Average need-based gift aid:* $8575. *Average indebtedness upon graduation:* $24,052.

APPLYING
Standardized Tests *Required:* SAT or ACT (for admission).

Options: electronic application, early action.

Application fee: $55.

Required: high school transcript, minimum 2.0 GPA, health form.

Application deadlines: 11/30 (freshmen), 10/31 (early action).

Notification: continuous (freshmen), continuous (transfers), 12/15 (early action).

CONTACT
California State University Maritime Academy, 200 Maritime Academy Drive, Vallejo, CA 94590. *Phone:* 707-654-1330. *Toll-free phone:* 800-561-1945.

California State University, Monterey Bay

Seaside, California

http://www.csumb.edu/

- **State-supported** comprehensive, founded 1994, part of California State University System
- **Small-town** 1387-acre campus with easy access to San Jose
- **Coed** 6,771 undergraduate students, 90% full-time, 63% women, 37% men
- **Moderately difficult** entrance level, 53% of applicants were admitted

UNDERGRAD STUDENTS

6,111 full-time, 660 part-time. 2% are from out of state; 5% Black or African American, non-Hispanic/Latino; 40% Hispanic/Latino; 6% Asian, non-Hispanic/Latino; 1% Native Hawaiian or other Pacific Islander, non-Hispanic/Latino; 0.8% American Indian or Alaska Native, non-Hispanic/Latino; 8% Two or more races, non-Hispanic/Latino; 4% Race/ethnicity unknown; 5% international; 13% transferred in.

Freshmen:

Admission: 13,112 applied, 6,976 admitted, 926 enrolled. *Average high school GPA:* 3.4. *Test scores:* SAT evidence-based reading and writing scores over 500: 74%; SAT math scores over 500: 68%; ACT scores over 18: 79%; SAT evidence-based reading and writing scores over 600: 23%; SAT math scores over 600: 18%; ACT scores over 24: 28%; SAT evidence-based reading and writing scores over 700: 2%; SAT math scores over 700: 1%; ACT scores over 30: 3%.

Retention: 79% of full-time freshmen returned.

FACULTY

Total: 487, 34% full-time, 50% with terminal degrees.

Student/faculty ratio: 26:1.

ACADEMICS

Calendar: semesters. *Degrees:* bachelor's and master's.

Special study options: academic remediation for entering students, accelerated degree program, advanced placement credit, cooperative education, distance learning, double majors, independent study, internships, off-campus study, part-time degree program, services for LD students, student-designed majors, study abroad, summer session for credit. *ROTC:* Air Force (c).

Computers: Students can access the following: campus intranet, computer help desk, free student e-mail accounts, online (class) grades, online (class) registration, online (class) schedules. Campuswide network is available. 100% of college-owned or -operated housing units are wired for high-speed Internet access. Wireless service is available via entire campus.

Library: The Tanimura & Antle Family Memorial Library.

STUDENT LIFE

Housing options: on-campus residence required through sophomore year; coed, special housing for students with disabilities. Campus housing is university owned. Freshman applicants given priority for college housing.

Activities and organizations: drama/theater group, student-run newspaper, radio station, choral group, national fraternities, national sororities.

Athletics Member NCAA. All Division II. *Intercollegiate sports:* baseball M(s), basketball M(s)/W(s), cross-country running M(s)/W(s), golf M(s)/W(s), sailing M/W, soccer M(s)/W(s), softball W(s), volleyball W(s), water polo W(s). *Intramural sports:* basketball M/W, football M, soccer M/W, softball M/W, ultimate Frisbee M/W, volleyball M/W.

Campus security: 24-hour emergency response devices and patrols, student patrols, late-night transport/escort service, controlled dormitory access.

Student services: health clinic, personal/psychological counseling, women's center.

COSTS & FINANCIAL AID

Costs (2017–18) *Tuition:* state resident $5742 full-time; nonresident $17,622 full-time. *Required fees:* $1301 full-time. *Room and board:* $12,396. Room and board charges vary according to board plan and housing facility.

Financial Aid Of all full-time matriculated undergraduates who enrolled in 2017, 4,808 applied for aid, 4,334 were judged to have need, 499 had their need fully met. In 2017, 113 non-need-based awards were made. *Average percent of need met:* 70. *Average financial aid package:* $11,621. *Average need-based loan:* $4479. *Average need-based gift aid:* $9987. *Average non-need-based aid:* $1679. *Average indebtedness upon graduation:* $19,962. *Financial aid deadline:* 8/30.

APPLYING

Standardized Tests *Required:* SAT or ACT (for admission).

Options: electronic application, deferred entrance.

Application fee: $55.

Required: high school transcript, minimum 2.0 GPA.

Application deadlines: 11/30 (freshmen), 11/30 (transfers).

CONTACT

Assistant Director of Recruitment, California State University, Monterey Bay, 100 Campus Center, Seaside, CA 93955. *Phone:* 831-582-3738. *Fax:* 831-582-3783. *E-mail:* admissions@csumb.edu.

California State University, Northridge

Northridge, California

http://www.csun.edu/

- **State-supported** comprehensive, founded 1958, part of California State University System
- **Urban** 356-acre campus with easy access to Los Angeles
- **Coed** 35,552 undergraduate students, 81% full-time, 54% women, 46% men
- **Moderately difficult** entrance level, 48% of applicants were admitted

UNDERGRAD STUDENTS

28,969 full-time, 6,583 part-time. 5% Black or African American, non-Hispanic/Latino; 46% Hispanic/Latino; 11% Asian, non-Hispanic/Latino; 0.1% Native Hawaiian or other Pacific Islander, non-Hispanic/Latino; 0.1% American Indian or Alaska Native, non-Hispanic/Latino; 3% Two or more races, non-Hispanic/Latino; 4% Race/ethnicity unknown; 9% international.

Freshmen:

Admission: 32,913 applied, 15,876 admitted, 4,499 enrolled. *Average high school GPA:* 3.2.

Retention: 77% of full-time freshmen returned.

FACULTY

Total: 2,125, 42% full-time, 50% with terminal degrees.

Student/faculty ratio: 27:1.

ACADEMICS

Calendar: semesters. *Degrees:* bachelor's, master's, and doctoral.

Special study options: academic remediation for entering students, adult/continuing education programs, advanced placement credit, distance learning, double majors, English as a second language, independent study, internships, off-campus study, part-time degree program, services for LD students, student-designed majors, study abroad, summer session for credit. *ROTC:* Army (c), Air Force (c).

Computers: Students can access the following: online (class) registration. Campuswide network is available.

Library: Oviatt Library plus 1 other. Students can reserve study rooms.

STUDENT LIFE

Activities and organizations: drama/theater group, student-run newspaper, radio station, choral group, national fraternities, national sororities.

Athletics Member NCAA. All Division I except football (Division II). *Intercollegiate sports:* baseball M(s), basketball M(s)/W(s), cross-country running M(s)/W(s), football M(s), golf M(s), soccer M(s), softball W(s), swimming and diving M(s)/W(s), tennis M(s)/W(s), track and field M(s)/W(s), volleyball M(s)/W(s). *Intramural sports:* baseball M, basketball M/W, bowling M(c)/W(c), cross-country running M/W, football M/W, golf M, ice hockey M(c), racquetball M/W, rugby M(c), sailing M(c)/W(c), skiing (downhill) M(c)/W(c), soccer M/W, softball W, swimming and diving M/W, table tennis M(c)/W(c), tennis W, track and field M/W, volleyball M/W.

Campus security: 24-hour emergency response devices, late-night transport/escort service.

Student services: health clinic, personal/psychological counseling, women's center.

COSTS & FINANCIAL AID
Costs (2017–18) *Tuition:* state resident $6870 full-time; nonresident $396 per unit part-time. *Room and board:* $10,402. Room and board charges vary according to board plan and housing facility. *Payment plan:* installment. *Waivers:* senior citizens and employees or children of employees.

Financial Aid Of all full-time matriculated undergraduates who enrolled in 2016, 23,508 applied for aid, 22,712 were judged to have need. In 2016, 4877 non-need-based awards were made. *Average financial aid package:* $18,771. *Average need-based loan:* $5999. *Average need-based gift aid:* $16,656. *Average non-need-based aid:* $1988. *Average indebtedness upon graduation:* $16,876.

APPLYING
Standardized Tests *Required:* SAT or ACT (for admission).

Options: electronic application.

Application fee: $55.

Required: high school transcript.

Notification: continuous (freshmen), continuous (transfers).

CONTACT
Juana Maria Valdivia, Director, Student Outreach and Recruitment, California State University, Northridge, Bayramian Hall 19, 18111 Nordhoff Street, Northridge, CA 91330-8212. *Phone:* 818-677-2967. *E-mail:* outreach.recruitment@csun.edu.

California State University, Sacramento
Sacramento, California
http://www.csus.edu/

- **State-supported** comprehensive, founded 1947, part of California State University System
- **Urban** 300-acre campus
- **Coed** 28,064 undergraduate students, 81% full-time, 56% women, 44% men
- **Moderately difficult** entrance level, 68% of applicants were admitted

UNDERGRAD STUDENTS
22,829 full-time, 5,235 part-time. 1% are from out of state; 6% Black or African American, non-Hispanic/Latino; 31% Hispanic/Latino; 21% Asian, non-Hispanic/Latino; 0.7% Native Hawaiian or other Pacific Islander, non-Hispanic/Latino; 0.3% American Indian or Alaska Native, non-Hispanic/Latino; 6% Two or more races, non-Hispanic/Latino; 6% Race/ethnicity unknown; 3% international; 13% transferred in; 7% live on campus.

Freshmen:
Admission: 24,137 applied, 16,351 admitted, 3,590 enrolled. *Average high school GPA:* 3.4. *Test scores:* SAT evidence-based reading and writing scores over 500: 64%; SAT math scores over 500: 63%; ACT scores over 18: 72%; SAT evidence-based reading and writing scores over 600: 16%; SAT math scores over 600: 16%; ACT scores over 24: 20%; SAT evidence-based reading and writing scores over 700: 1%; SAT math scores over 700: 1%; ACT scores over 30: 3%.
Retention: 83% of full-time freshmen returned.

FACULTY
Total: 1,648, 42% full-time, 55% with terminal degrees.
Student/faculty ratio: 25:1.

ACADEMICS
Calendar: semesters. *Degrees:* bachelor's, master's, and doctoral.
Special study options: accelerated degree program, adult/continuing education programs, advanced placement credit, cooperative education, distance learning, double majors, English as a second language, honors programs, independent study, internships, off-campus study, part-time degree program, services for LD students, student-designed majors, study abroad, summer session for credit. *ROTC:* Army (c), Air Force (b).

Computers: Students can access the following: computer help desk, free student e-mail accounts, online (class) grades, online (class) registration, online (class) schedules, online transcripts. Campuswide network is available. Wireless service is available via entire campus.
Library: California State University, Sacramento Library. Students can reserve study rooms.

STUDENT LIFE
Housing options: coed, special housing for students with disabilities. Campus housing is university owned.

Activities and organizations: drama/theater group, student-run newspaper, radio station, choral group, marching band, national fraternities, national sororities.

Athletics Member NCAA. All Division I except football (Division I-AA). *Intercollegiate sports:* baseball M(s), basketball M(s)/W(s), bowling M(c)/W(c), cheerleading M/W, crew M(s)/W(s), cross-country running M(s)/W(s), golf M(s)/W, gymnastics W(s), ice hockey M(c), lacrosse M(c)/W(c), racquetball M(c)/W(c), rugby M(c), skiing (downhill) M(c)/W(c), soccer M(s)/W(s), softball W(s), tennis M(s)/W(s), track and field M(s)/W(s), volleyball M(c)/W(s). *Intramural sports:* basketball M/W, crew M/W, football M/W, golf M/W, ice hockey M, skiing (downhill) M/W, soccer M/W, softball M/W, table tennis M/W, tennis M/W, volleyball M/W, water polo M/W, weight lifting M/W.

Campus security: 24-hour emergency response devices and patrols, student patrols, late-night transport/escort service, controlled dormitory access.

Student services: health clinic, personal/psychological counseling, women's center, legal services.

COSTS & FINANCIAL AID
Costs (2018–19) *Tuition:* state resident $5742 full-time, $1665 per term part-time; nonresident $396 per credit hour part-time. *Required fees:* $1192 full-time, $731 per term part-time. *Room and board:* $14,396; room only: $9774. Room and board charges vary according to board plan and housing facility. *Payment plan:* installment. *Waivers:* employees or children of employees.

Financial Aid Of all full-time matriculated undergraduates who enrolled in 2016, 19,743 applied for aid, 17,735 were judged to have need, 1,216 had their need fully met. In 2016, 37 non-need-based awards were made. *Average percent of need met:* 60. *Average financial aid package:* $10,572. *Average need-based loan:* $4136. *Average need-based gift aid:* $8712. *Average non-need-based aid:* $1675. *Average indebtedness upon graduation:* $20,052.

APPLYING
Standardized Tests *Required:* SAT or ACT (for admission).

Options: electronic application, early action.

Application fee: $55.

Required: minimum 2.0 GPA. *Required for some:* high school transcript.

Application deadlines: 11/30 (freshmen), 11/30 (transfers).

Notification: continuous until 3/1 (freshmen), 3/1 (transfers), 12/1 (early action).

CONTACT
Brian Henley, Director of Admissions and Outreach, California State University, Sacramento, 6000 J Street, Lassen Hall, Sacramento, CA 95819-6048. *Phone:* 916-278-7766. *Fax:* 916-278-5603. *E-mail:* admissions@csus.edu.

California State University, San Bernardino
San Bernardino, California
http://www.csusb.edu/

- **State-supported** comprehensive, founded 1965, part of California State University System
- **Suburban** 430-acre campus with easy access to Los Angeles
- **Coed** 18,243 undergraduate students, 90% full-time, 60% women, 40% men
- **Moderately difficult** entrance level, 57% of applicants were admitted

UNDERGRAD STUDENTS
16,341 full-time, 1,902 part-time. Students come from 24 states and territories; 76 other countries; 0.3% are from out of state; 5% Black or

African American, non-Hispanic/Latino; 64% Hispanic/Latino; 5% Asian, non-Hispanic/Latino; 0.2% Native Hawaiian or other Pacific Islander, non-Hispanic/Latino; 0.2% American Indian or Alaska Native, non-Hispanic/Latino; 3% Two or more races, non-Hispanic/Latino; 4% Race/ethnicity unknown; 7% international; 13% transferred in; 7% live on campus.

Freshmen:
Admission: 15,637 applied, 8,934 admitted, 2,517 enrolled. *Average high school GPA:* 3.3. *Test scores:* SAT evidence-based reading and writing scores over 500: 53%; SAT math scores over 500: 54%; ACT scores over 18: 58%; SAT evidence-based reading and writing scores over 600: 9%; SAT math scores over 600: 9%; ACT scores over 24: 8%; ACT scores over 30: 1%.
Retention: 85% of full-time freshmen returned.

FACULTY
Total: 1,017, 45% full-time, 47% with terminal degrees.
Student/faculty ratio: 28:1.

ACADEMICS
Calendar: quarters. *Degrees:* certificates, bachelor's, master's, doctoral, and postbachelor's certificates.
Special study options: academic remediation for entering students, accelerated degree program, advanced placement credit, cooperative education, distance learning, double majors, honors programs, independent study, internships, off-campus study, part-time degree program, services for LD students, student-designed majors, study abroad, summer session for credit. *ROTC:* Army (b), Air Force (b).
Computers: Students can access the following: computer help desk, free student e-mail accounts, online (class) grades, online (class) registration, online (class) schedules. Campuswide network is available. Wireless service is available via entire campus.
Library: Pfau Library.

STUDENT LIFE
Housing options: coed, women-only, special housing for students with disabilities. Campus housing is university owned and is provided by a third party. Freshman applicants given priority for college housing.
Activities and organizations: drama/theater group, student-run newspaper, radio and television station, choral group, national fraternities, national sororities.
Athletics Member NCAA. All Division II. *Intercollegiate sports:* baseball M(s), basketball M(s)/W(s), cross-country running W, golf M(s), soccer M(s)/W(s), softball W(s), track and field W, volleyball W(s).
Campus security: 24-hour emergency response devices and patrols, student patrols, late-night transport/escort service, residence staff on call 24 hours.
Student services: health clinic, personal/psychological counseling, women's center, legal services.

COSTS & FINANCIAL AID
Costs (2018–19) *Tuition:* state resident $5472 full-time; nonresident $11,180 full-time, $264 per credit hour part-time. *Required fees:* $1184 full-time. *Room and board:* $12,711. Room and board charges vary according to board plan and housing facility. *Payment plan:* installment. *Waivers:* senior citizens and employees or children of employees.
Financial Aid Of all full-time matriculated undergraduates who enrolled in 2016, 14,696 applied for aid, 13,868 were judged to have need, 1,298 had their need fully met. 326 Federal Work-Study jobs (averaging $4073). In 2016, 35 non-need-based awards were made. *Average percent of need met:* 64. *Average financial aid package:* $9430. *Average need-based loan:* $4165. *Average need-based gift aid:* $9944. *Average non-need-based aid:* $3690. *Average indebtedness upon graduation:* $22,452.

APPLYING
Standardized Tests *Recommended:* SAT or ACT (for admission).
Options: electronic application, early admission, early action.
Application fee: $55.
Required: high school transcript, minimum 2.0 GPA.
Application deadlines: rolling (freshmen), rolling (transfers).
Notification: continuous (freshmen), continuous (transfers).

CONTACT
Julie Rogers, Assistant Director of Admissions and Evaluations, California State University, San Bernardino, 5500 University Parkway, University Hall, Room 115, San Bernardino, CA 92407-2397. *Phone:* 909-537-5211. *Fax:* 909-537-7034. *E-mail:* moreinfo@mail.csusb.edu.

California State University, San Marcos
San Marcos, California
http://www.csusm.edu/
- **State-supported** comprehensive, founded 1990, part of California State University System
- **Suburban** 304-acre campus with easy access to San Diego
- **Coed** 13,316 undergraduate students, 83% full-time, 61% women, 39% men
- **Moderately difficult** entrance level, 77% of applicants were admitted

UNDERGRAD STUDENTS
11,079 full-time, 2,237 part-time. 2% are from out of state; 3% Black or African American, non-Hispanic/Latino; 45% Hispanic/Latino; 9% Asian, non-Hispanic/Latino; 0.3% Native Hawaiian or other Pacific Islander, non-Hispanic/Latino; 0.3% American Indian or Alaska Native, non-Hispanic/Latino; 5% Two or more races, non-Hispanic/Latino; 5% Race/ethnicity unknown; 5% international; 13% transferred in; 80% live on campus.

Freshmen:
Admission: 14,129 applied, 10,864 admitted, 2,499 enrolled. *Average high school GPA:* 3.3. *Test scores:* SAT evidence-based reading and writing scores over 500: 36%; SAT math scores over 500: 43%; ACT scores over 18: 75%; SAT evidence-based reading and writing scores over 600: 6%; SAT math scores over 600: 7%; ACT scores over 24: 19%; ACT scores over 30: 1%.
Retention: 79% of full-time freshmen returned.

FACULTY
Total: 865, 33% full-time.
Student/faculty ratio: 26:1.

ACADEMICS
Calendar: semesters. *Degrees:* bachelor's and master's.
Special study options: academic remediation for entering students, adult/continuing education programs, advanced placement credit, distance learning, double majors, English as a second language, independent study, internships, off-campus study, part-time degree program, services for LD students, student-designed majors, study abroad, summer session for credit. *ROTC:* Army (b), Navy (c), Air Force (c).
Computers: Students can access the following: computer help desk, free student e-mail accounts, online (class) registration. Campuswide network is available.
Library: Kellogg Library. *Books:* 215,402 (physical), 268,189 (digital/electronic); *Serial titles:* 3,130 (physical), 81,643 (digital/electronic); *Databases:* 100. Weekly public service hours: 100; students can reserve study rooms.

STUDENT LIFE
Housing options: special housing for students with disabilities. Campus housing is provided by a third party.
Activities and organizations: drama/theater group, student-run newspaper, choral group, national fraternities, national sororities.
Athletics Member NCAA. All Division I. *Intercollegiate sports:* baseball M, basketball M/W, cross-country running M/W, golf M/W, soccer M/W, softball W, track and field M/W, volleyball W.
Campus security: 24-hour emergency response devices and patrols, student patrols, late-night transport/escort service.
Student services: health clinic, personal/psychological counseling, women's center.

COSTS & FINANCIAL AID
Costs (2018–19) *Tuition:* state resident $5742 full-time; nonresident $14,670 full-time, $396 per unit part-time. Part-time tuition and fees vary according to course load. *Required fees:* $7648 full-time, $2433 per term part-time. *Room and board:* $13,227. Room and board charges vary

according to housing facility. *Waivers:* senior citizens and employees or children of employees.

Financial Aid Of all full-time matriculated undergraduates who enrolled in 2016, 8,394 applied for aid, 7,314 were judged to have need, 202 had their need fully met. In 2016, 9 non-need-based awards were made. *Average percent of need met:* 43. *Average financial aid package:* $10,594. *Average need-based loan:* $4144. *Average need-based gift aid:* $8875. *Average non-need-based aid:* $1515. *Average indebtedness upon graduation:* $23,734.

APPLYING
Standardized Tests *Required:* SAT or ACT (for admission).
Options: electronic application.
Application fee: $65.
Required: high school transcript.
Application deadlines: 11/30 (freshmen), 11/30 (transfers).
Notification: continuous (freshmen), continuous (transfers).

CONTACT
Scott Hagg, Director of Admissions, California State University, San Marcos, 333 South Twin Oaks Valley Road, San Marcos, CA 92096-0001. *Phone:* 760-750-4848. *Fax:* 760-750-3248. *E-mail:* apply@csusm.edu.

California State University, Stanislaus
Turlock, California
http://www.csustan.edu/
- **State-supported** comprehensive, founded 1957, part of California State University System
- **Suburban** 228-acre campus
- **Endowment** $11.6 million
- **Coed** 8,891 undergraduate students, 84% full-time, 65% women, 35% men
- **Moderately difficult** entrance level, 77% of applicants were admitted

UNDERGRAD STUDENTS
7,460 full-time, 1,431 part-time. Students come from 17 states and territories; 18 other countries; 1% are from out of state; 2% Black or African American, non-Hispanic/Latino; 53% Hispanic/Latino; 10% Asian, non-Hispanic/Latino; 0.5% Native Hawaiian or other Pacific Islander, non-Hispanic/Latino; 0.3% American Indian or Alaska Native, non-Hispanic/Latino; 4% Two or more races, non-Hispanic/Latino; 5% Race/ethnicity unknown; 4% international; 11% transferred in; 8% live on campus.

Freshmen:
Admission: 8,069 applied, 6,218 admitted, 1,422 enrolled. *Average high school GPA:* 3.3. *Test scores:* SAT evidence-based reading and writing scores over 500: 57%; SAT math scores over 500: 54%; ACT scores over 18: 62%; SAT evidence-based reading and writing scores over 600: 11%; SAT math scores over 600: 8%; ACT scores over 24: 13%; SAT evidence-based reading and writing scores over 700: 1%; SAT math scores over 700: 1%; ACT scores over 30: 1%.
Retention: 81% of full-time freshmen returned.

FACULTY
Total: 651, 52% full-time, 56% with terminal degrees.
Student/faculty ratio: 23:1.

ACADEMICS
Calendar: semesters. *Degrees:* bachelor's, master's, and doctoral.
Special study options: academic remediation for entering students, advanced placement credit, cooperative education, distance learning, double majors, English as a second language, honors programs, independent study, internships, off-campus study, part-time degree program, services for LD students, student-designed majors, study abroad, summer session for credit.
Computers: 200 computers/terminals are available on campus for general student use. Students can access the following: computer help desk, free student e-mail accounts, online (class) grades, online (class) registration, online (class) schedules. Campuswide network is available. 100% of college-owned or -operated housing units are wired for high-speed Internet access. Wireless service is available via entire campus.

Library: Vasche Library. *Books:* 514,045 (physical), 8,002 (digital/electronic); *Serial titles:* 634 (physical), 60,803 (digital/electronic); *Databases:* 187. Weekly public service hours: 90; students can reserve study rooms.

STUDENT LIFE
Housing options: coed. Campus housing is university owned and leased by the school.
Activities and organizations: drama/theater group, student-run newspaper, radio station, choral group, Alpha Xi Delta, Phi Sigma Sigma, Kappa Sigma, Tau Kappa Epsilon, Theta Chi, national fraternities, national sororities.
Athletics Member NCAA. All Division II. *Intercollegiate sports:* baseball M(s), basketball M(s)/W(s), cross-country running M(s)/W(s), golf M(s), soccer M(s)/W(s), softball W(s), tennis W(s), track and field M(s)/W(s), volleyball W(s). *Intramural sports:* basketball M/W, cheerleading M(c)/W(c), football M/W, soccer M/W, ultimate Frisbee M/W, volleyball M/W.
Campus security: 24-hour emergency response devices and patrols, student patrols, late-night transport/escort service, controlled dormitory access.
Student services: health clinic, personal/psychological counseling, women's center.

COSTS & FINANCIAL AID
Costs (2017–18) *Tuition:* state resident $5742 full-time; nonresident $17,622 full-time. Full-time tuition and fees vary according to reciprocity agreements. Part-time tuition and fees vary according to reciprocity agreements. *Required fees:* $1296 full-time. *Room and board:* $8670; room only: $6507. Room and board charges vary according to board plan and housing facility. *Payment plan:* installment. *Waivers:* employees or children of employees.

Financial Aid Of all full-time matriculated undergraduates who enrolled in 2017, 6,300 applied for aid, 5,830 were judged to have need, 5,763 had their need fully met. 52 Federal Work-Study jobs (averaging $3689). In 2017, 225 non-need-based awards were made. *Average percent of need met:* 92. *Average financial aid package:* $17,143. *Average need-based loan:* $4053. *Average need-based gift aid:* $10,334. *Average non-need-based aid:* $1901. *Average indebtedness upon graduation:* $18,960.

APPLYING
Standardized Tests *Required for some:* SAT or ACT (for admission).
Options: electronic application.
Application fee: $55.
Required for some: high school transcript. *Recommended:* minimum 3.0 GPA.
Application deadlines: 11/30 (freshmen), 11/30 (transfers).
Notification: continuous (freshmen), continuous (transfers).

CONTACT
Student Outreach, California State University, Stanislaus, One University Circle, Turlock, CA 95382. *Phone:* 209-667-3070. *Toll-free phone:* 800-300-7420. *Fax:* 209-667-3394. *E-mail:* outreach_help_desk@csustan.edu.

California University of Management and Sciences
Anaheim, California
http://www.calums.edu/

CONTACT
California University of Management and Sciences, 721 North Euclid Street, Anaheim, CA 92801.

Chamberlain College of Nursing
Rancho Cordova, California
http://www.chamberlain.edu/

CONTACT
Chamberlain College of Nursing, 10971 Sun Center Drive, Rancho Cordova, CA 95670.

Chapman University

Orange, California

http://www.chapman.edu/

- **Independent** comprehensive, founded 1861, affiliated with Christian Church (Disciples of Christ)
- **Suburban** 78-acre campus with easy access to Los Angeles
- **Endowment** $352.6 million
- **Coed** 7,020 undergraduate students, 93% full-time, 60% women, 40% men
- **Very difficult** entrance level, 74% of applicants were admitted

UNDERGRAD STUDENTS

6,515 full-time, 505 part-time. Students come from 50 states and territories; 57 other countries; 31% are from out of state; 2% Black or African American, non-Hispanic/Latino; 15% Hispanic/Latino; 12% Asian, non-Hispanic/Latino; 0.3% Native Hawaiian or other Pacific Islander, non-Hispanic/Latino; 0.1% American Indian or Alaska Native, non-Hispanic/Latino; 7% Two or more races, non-Hispanic/Latino; 6% Race/ethnicity unknown; 4% international; 6% transferred in; 33% live on campus.

Freshmen:
Admission: 10,170 applied, 7,539 admitted, 1,696 enrolled. *Average high school GPA:* 3.7. *Test scores:* SAT evidence-based reading and writing scores over 500: 99%; SAT math scores over 500: 98%; ACT scores over 18: 100%; SAT evidence-based reading and writing scores over 600: 77%; SAT math scores over 600: 70%; ACT scores over 24: 88%; SAT evidence-based reading and writing scores over 700: 17%; SAT math scores over 700: 18%; ACT scores over 30: 26%.
Retention: 91% of full-time freshmen returned.

FACULTY

Total: 1,089, 45% full-time.
Student/faculty ratio: 14:1.

ACADEMICS

Calendar: 4-1-4. *Degrees:* bachelor's, master's, and doctoral.

Special study options: academic remediation for entering students, adult/continuing education programs, advanced placement credit, distance learning, double majors, honors programs, independent study, internships, off-campus study, part-time degree program, services for LD students, student-designed majors, study abroad, summer session for credit. *ROTC:* Army (c), Air Force (c).

Unusual degree programs: 3-2 business administration; engineering with University of California, Irvine.

Computers: Students can access the following: campus intranet, computer help desk, free student e-mail accounts, online (class) grades, online (class) registration, online (class) schedules. Campuswide network is available. 100% of college-owned or -operated housing units are wired for high-speed Internet access. Wireless service is available via entire campus.

Library: Leatherby Libraries plus 1 other. *Books:* 339,051 (physical), 17,371 (digital/electronic); *Serial titles:* 267 (physical), 69,372 (digital/electronic); *Databases:* 287. Weekly public service hours: 127; students can reserve study rooms.

STUDENT LIFE

Housing options: coed, special housing for students with disabilities. Campus housing is university owned. Freshman campus housing is guaranteed.

Activities and organizations: drama/theater group, student-run newspaper, radio station, choral group, national fraternities, national sororities.

Athletics Member NCAA. All Division III. *Intercollegiate sports:* baseball M, basketball M/W, cheerleading W(c), crew M(c)/W(c), cross-country running M/W, equestrian sports W(c), football M, golf M, ice hockey M(c), lacrosse M(c)/W, soccer M/W, softball W, swimming and diving M/W, tennis M/W, track and field M/W, volleyball M(c)/W, water polo M/W. *Intramural sports:* basketball M/W, soccer M/W, ultimate Frisbee M/W, volleyball M/W.

Campus security: 24-hour emergency response devices and patrols, late-night transport/escort service, controlled dormitory access, full safety education program.

Student services: health clinic, personal/psychological counseling.

COSTS & FINANCIAL AID

Costs (2018–19) *Comprehensive fee:* $68,552 includes full-time tuition ($52,340), mandatory fees ($384), and room and board ($15,828). Part-time tuition: $1625 per credit hour. Part-time tuition and fees vary according to course load. *College room only:* $10,900. Room and board charges vary according to board plan and housing facility. *Payment plans:* tuition prepayment, installment, deferred payment. *Waivers:* employees or children of employees.

Financial Aid Of all full-time matriculated undergraduates who enrolled in 2016, 3,944 applied for aid, 3,458 were judged to have need, 411 had their need fully met. 2,046 Federal Work-Study jobs (averaging $2847). In 2016, 385 non-need-based awards were made. *Average percent of need met:* 69. *Average financial aid package:* $32,620. *Average need-based loan:* $4493. *Average need-based gift aid:* $16,989. *Average non-need-based aid:* $16,916. *Average indebtedness upon graduation:* $26,926.

APPLYING

Standardized Tests *Required:* SAT or ACT (for admission). *Recommended:* SAT Subject Tests (for admission).

Options: electronic application, early decision, early action.

Application fee: $70.

Required: essay or personal statement, high school transcript, 1 letter of recommendation. *Required for some:* audition for music, dance, and theatre majors; portfolio for art and film majors; supplemental application for all talent-based majors.

Application deadlines: 1/15 (freshmen), 2/15 (transfers), 11/1 (early action).
Early decision deadline: 11/1.
Notification: 3/15 (freshmen), 4/15 (transfers), 1/10 (early action).

CONTACT

Ms. Marcela Mejia-Martinez, Director of Undergraduate Admission, Chapman University, One University Drive, Orange, CA 92866. *Phone:* 714-997-6711. *Toll-free phone:* 888-CUAPPLY. *Fax:* 714-997-6713. *E-mail:* admit@chapman.edu.

Charles R. Drew University of Medicine and Science

Los Angeles, California

http://www.cdrewu.edu/

- **Independent** comprehensive, founded 1966
- **Urban** 11-acre campus with easy access to Los Angeles
- **Endowment** $90.0 million
- **Coed** 139 undergraduate students, 82% full-time, 58% women, 42% men
- **Moderately difficult** entrance level, 90% of applicants were admitted

UNDERGRAD STUDENTS

114 full-time, 25 part-time. Students come from 3 states and territories; 5 other countries; 2% are from out of state; 25% Black or African American, non-Hispanic/Latino; 45% Hispanic/Latino; 15% Asian, non-Hispanic/Latino; 2% Two or more races, non-Hispanic/Latino; 1% Race/ethnicity unknown; 4% international; 37% transferred in.

Freshmen:
Admission: 61 applied, 55 admitted, 19 enrolled.

FACULTY

Total: 201, 23% full-time, 78% with terminal degrees.
Student/faculty ratio: 10:1.

ACADEMICS

Calendar: semesters. *Degrees:* associate, bachelor's, master's, doctoral, post-master's, and postbachelor's certificates.

Special study options: academic remediation for entering students, adult/continuing education programs, advanced placement credit, independent study, internships, part-time degree program, services for LD students, study abroad, summer session for credit.

Computers: 90 computers/terminals are available on campus for general student use. Students can access the following: computer help desk, free student e-mail accounts, online (class) grades, online (class) registration, online (class) schedules, Campus wide wireless network. Campuswide network is available. Wireless service is available via entire campus.

Library: Health Sciences Library. *Books:* 6,436 (physical), 3,500 (digital/electronic); *Serial titles:* 596 (physical), 11,765 (digital/electronic); *Databases:* 38. Weekly public service hours: 91; students can reserve study rooms.

STUDENT LIFE
Housing options: Campus housing is provided by a third party.

Activities and organizations: Student Government, Critical Exploration of Academic Literature (CEAL), Charles R. Drew University Alumni Association, Pre-Health Society, Pre-Dental Society.

Campus security: 24-hour emergency response devices, late-night transport/escort service.

Student services: personal/psychological counseling.

COSTS & FINANCIAL AID
Costs (2018–19) *One-time required fee:* $100. *Tuition:* $13,872 full-time, $578 per unit part-time. Full-time tuition and fees vary according to course load, degree level, and program. Part-time tuition and fees vary according to course load, degree level, and program. *Payment plan:* installment.

Financial Aid *Financial aid deadline:* 7/31.

APPLYING
Standardized Tests *Required for some:* SAT or ACT (for admission).

Options: electronic application, early admission, early decision, early action, deferred entrance.

Application fee: $35.

Required: essay or personal statement, high school transcript, minimum 2.0 GPA. *Required for some:* pre-admission assessment exams.

Application deadlines: 7/30 (freshmen), 7/30 (transfers).

Notification: continuous (freshmen), continuous (transfers).

CONTACT
Charles R. Drew University of Medicine and Science, 1731 East 120th Street, Los Angeles, CA 90059.

Claremont McKenna College

Claremont, California
http://www.cmc.edu/
- **Independent** comprehensive, founded 1946
- **Suburban** 69-acre campus with easy access to Los Angeles
- **Endowment** $784.4 million
- **Coed** 1,347 undergraduate students
- **Most difficult** entrance level, 9% of applicants were admitted

UNDERGRAD STUDENTS
Students come from 46 states and territories; 38 other countries; 56% are from out of state; 97% live on campus.

Freshmen:
Admission: 6,342 applied, 599 admitted. *Test scores:* ACT scores over 18: 100%; ACT scores over 24: 100%; ACT scores over 30: 81%.
Retention: 93% of full-time freshmen returned.

FACULTY
Total: 171, 84% full-time, 98% with terminal degrees.
Student/faculty ratio: 8:1.

ACADEMICS
Calendar: semesters. *Degrees:* bachelor's and master's.
Special study options: advanced placement credit, double majors, honors programs, independent study, internships, off-campus study, services for LD students, student-designed majors, study abroad. *ROTC:* Army (b), Air Force (c).

Unusual degree programs: 3-2 engineering with Columbia University, Harvey Mudd College.

Computers: 220 computers/terminals are available on campus for general student use. Students can access the following: campus intranet, computer help desk, free student e-mail accounts, online (class) grades, online (class) registration, online (class) schedules. Campuswide network is available. 100% of college-owned or -operated housing units are wired for high-speed Internet access. Wireless service is available via entire campus.

Library: Claremont Colleges Library plus 2 others. *Books:* 995,122 (physical), 881,347 (digital/electronic); *Serial titles:* 7,660 (physical), 132,102 (digital/electronic); *Databases:* 404. Weekly public service hours: 111; students can reserve study rooms.

STUDENT LIFE
Housing options: on-campus residence required for freshman year; coed, special housing for students with disabilities. Campus housing is university owned. Freshman campus housing is guaranteed.

Activities and organizations: drama/theater group, student-run newspaper, radio station, choral group, The Forum - student newspaper, ASCMC - student government, Debate/Forensics Club, SOURCE, Rotaract.

Athletics Member NCAA. All Division III. *Intercollegiate sports:* archery M(c)/W(c), baseball M, basketball M/W, cheerleading M(c)/W(c), cross-country running M/W, equestrian sports M(c)/W(c), fencing M(c)/W(c), field hockey M(c)/W(c), football M, golf M/W, lacrosse M(c)/W, rugby M(c)/W(c), sailing M(c)/W(c), skiing (downhill) M(c)/W(c), soccer M/W, softball W, swimming and diving M/W, tennis M/W, track and field M/W, volleyball M(c)/W, water polo M/W. *Intramural sports:* basketball M/W, bowling M/W, crew M/W, football M, soccer M/W, squash M/W, table tennis M/W, tennis M/W, ultimate Frisbee M/W, volleyball M/W, water polo M/W, weight lifting M/W.

Campus security: 24-hour emergency response devices and patrols, student patrols, late-night transport/escort service, controlled dormitory access.

Student services: health clinic, personal/psychological counseling.

COSTS & FINANCIAL AID
Costs (2017–18) *One-time required fee:* $500. *Comprehensive fee:* $69,045 includes full-time tuition ($52,580), mandatory fees ($245), and room and board ($16,220). Part-time tuition: $8763 per course. Part-time tuition and fees vary according to course load. *College room only:* $8730. Room and board charges vary according to board plan and housing facility. *Payment plan:* installment. *Waivers:* employees or children of employees.

Financial Aid Of all full-time matriculated undergraduates who enrolled in 2016, 643 applied for aid, 531 were judged to have need, 531 had their need fully met. In 2016, 78 non-need-based awards were made. *Average percent of need met:* 100. *Average financial aid package:* $46,129. *Average need-based loan:* $4266. *Average need-based gift aid:* $42,445. *Average non-need-based aid:* $15,744. *Average indebtedness upon graduation:* $23,375. *Financial aid deadline:* 2/1.

APPLYING
Standardized Tests *Required:* SAT or ACT (for admission). *Required for some:* SAT Subject Tests (for admission), TOEFL or IELTS for students for whom English is not their first language and the primary language of instruction in high school was not English.

Options: electronic application, early decision, deferred entrance.

Application fee: $70.

Required: essay or personal statement, high school transcript, 3 letters of recommendation. *Required for some:* interview.

Application deadlines: 1/1 (freshmen), 4/1 (transfers).

Early decision deadline: 11/1 (for plan 1), 1/1 (for plan 2).

Notification: 4/1 (freshmen), 5/15 (transfers), 12/15 (early decision plan 1), 2/15 (early decision plan 2).

CONTACT
Ms. Jennifer Sandoval-Dancs, Director of Admission, Claremont McKenna College, Office of Admission and Financial Aid, 888 Columbia Avenue, Claremont, CA 91711. *Phone:* 909-621-8088. *Fax:* 909-621-8516. *E-mail:* jennifer.sandoval@cmc.edu.

Cogswell Polytechnical College

San Jose, California
http://www.cogswell.edu/
- **Proprietary** comprehensive, founded 1887
- **Suburban** 2-acre campus with easy access to San Francisco, San Jose
- **Coed** 608 undergraduate students, 72% full-time, 29% women, 71% men
- **Moderately difficult** entrance level, 65% of applicants were admitted

UNDERGRAD STUDENTS

436 full-time, 172 part-time. Students come from 13 states and territories; 3 other countries; 7% are from out of state; 5% Black or African American, non-Hispanic/Latino; 20% Hispanic/Latino; 22% Asian, non-Hispanic/Latino; 1% Native Hawaiian or other Pacific Islander, non-Hispanic/Latino; 0.8% American Indian or Alaska Native, non-Hispanic/Latino; 7% Two or more races, non-Hispanic/Latino; 7% Race/ethnicity unknown; 2% international; 8% transferred in.

Freshmen:

Admission: 231 applied, 149 admitted, 72 enrolled. *Average high school GPA:* 3.1. *Test scores:* SAT math scores over 500: 90%; ACT scores over 18: 100%; SAT math scores over 600: 40%; ACT scores over 24: 75%; SAT math scores over 700: 12%; ACT scores over 30: 25%.

Retention: 78% of full-time freshmen returned.

FACULTY

Total: 89, 18% full-time, 22% with terminal degrees.
Student/faculty ratio: 13:1.

ACADEMICS

Calendar: semesters. *Degrees:* bachelor's and master's.

Special study options: academic remediation for entering students, adult/continuing education programs, advanced placement credit, cooperative education, distance learning, double majors, internships, part-time degree program, summer session for credit.

Computers: 224 computers/terminals are available on campus for general student use. Students can access the following: computer help desk, free student e-mail accounts, online (class) grades, online (class) registration, online (class) schedules. Campuswide network is available. Wireless service is available via entire campus.

Library: Cogswell College Library. *Books:* 5,007 (physical); *Serial titles:* 920 (physical); *Databases:* 14.

STUDENT LIFE

Housing options: coed. Campus housing is provided by a third party. Freshman applicants given priority for college housing.

Activities and organizations: choral group, ASB, Game Development club, Audio Production and Engineering club, Comic Club, E-Sports.

Campus security: 24-hour emergency response devices.

Student services: personal/psychological counseling.

COSTS & FINANCIAL AID

Costs (2017–18) *Tuition:* $18,648 full-time, $777 per credit part-time. Full-time tuition and fees vary according to course load. Part-time tuition and fees vary according to course load. *Required fees:* $1000 full-time. *Room only:* $9000. Room and board charges vary according to housing facility. *Payment plan:* deferred payment. *Waivers:* employees or children of employees.

Financial Aid Of all full-time matriculated undergraduates who enrolled in 2015, 17 Federal Work-Study jobs (averaging $2328).

APPLYING

Standardized Tests *Recommended:* SAT or ACT (for admission).

Options: electronic application, deferred entrance.

Required: essay or personal statement, high school transcript, minimum 2.0 GPA. *Required for some:* letters of recommendation, portfolio for Digital Art and Animation, Digital Audio Technology and Game Design Art majors. *Recommended:* minimum 2.7 GPA, interview.

Application deadlines: rolling (freshmen), rolling (out-of-state freshmen), rolling (transfers).

Notification: continuous (freshmen), continuous (out-of-state freshmen), continuous (transfers).

CONTACT

Richard Henson, Director of Admissions, Cogswell Polytechnical College, 191 Baypointe Parkway, San Jose, CA 95134. *Phone:* 408-498-5103 Ext. 103. *Toll-free phone:* 800-264-7955. *Fax:* 408-747-0764. *E-mail:* rhenson@cogswell.edu.

The Colburn School Conservatory of Music

Los Angeles, California

http://www.colburnschool.edu/

CONTACT

Ms. Jessica Cameron, Manager of Admissions, The Colburn School Conservatory of Music, 200 South Grand Avenue, Los Angeles, CA 90012. *Phone:* 213-621-4534. *Fax:* 213-625-0371. *E-mail:* admissions@colburnschool.edu.

Coleman University

San Diego, California

http://www.coleman.edu/

- **Independent** comprehensive, founded 1963
- **Suburban** 3-acre campus
- **Coed** 477 undergraduate students
- **Minimally difficult** entrance level, 100% of applicants were admitted

Freshmen:

Admission: 12 applied, 12 admitted.

ACADEMICS

Calendar: quarters. *Degrees:* associate, bachelor's, and master's.

Special study options: accelerated degree program, distance learning, honors programs, part-time degree program, services for LD students, summer session for credit.

Computers: Campuswide network is available.
Library: Coleman College LaMesa Library.

STUDENT LIFE

Housing options: college housing not available.

Activities and organizations: Veterans Club, Cybersecurity Club, Gaming Club.

Campus security: 24-hour emergency response devices and patrols, late-night transport/escort service.

Student services: personal/psychological counseling.

APPLYING

Options: early admission, deferred entrance.

Application fee: $100.

Required: essay or personal statement, high school transcript, interview.

Application deadlines: 8/1 (freshmen), rolling (transfers).

Notification: continuous (freshmen), continuous (transfers).

CONTACT

Coleman University, 8888 Balboa Avenue, San Diego, CA 92123. *Toll-free phone:* 800-430-2030.

Columbia College Hollywood

Tarzana, California

http://www.columbiacollege.edu/

CONTACT

Carmen Munoz, Admissions Director, Columbia College Hollywood, 18618 Oxnard Street, Tarzana, CA 91356. *Phone:* 818-345-8414 Ext. 203. *Toll-free phone:* 800-785-0585. *Fax:* 818-345-9053. *E-mail:* admissions@columbiacollege.edu.

Concordia University Irvine

Irvine, California

http://www.cui.edu/

- **Independent** comprehensive, founded 1972, affiliated with Lutheran Church–Missouri Synod, part of The Concordia University System
- **Suburban** 70-acre campus with easy access to Los Angeles
- **Endowment** $29.8 million
- **Coed** 1,853 undergraduate students, 89% full-time, 62% women, 38% men
- **Moderately difficult** entrance level, 58% of applicants were admitted

UNDERGRAD STUDENTS

1,645 full-time, 208 part-time. Students come from 31 other countries; 18% are from out of state; 5% Black or African American, non-Hispanic/Latino; 23% Hispanic/Latino; 8% Asian, non-Hispanic/Latino; 0.4% Native Hawaiian or other Pacific Islander, non-Hispanic/Latino; 0.3% American Indian or Alaska Native, non-Hispanic/Latino; 7% Two or more races, non-Hispanic/Latino; 1% Race/ethnicity unknown; 5% international; 7% transferred in; 52% live on campus.

Freshmen:
Admission: 4,979 applied, 2,910 admitted, 328 enrolled. *Average high school GPA:* 3.4. *Test scores:* SAT evidence-based reading and writing scores over 500: 82%; SAT math scores over 500: 78%; ACT scores over 18: 93%; SAT evidence-based reading and writing scores over 600: 34%; SAT math scores over 600: 21%; ACT scores over 24: 46%; SAT evidence-based reading and writing scores over 700: 5%; SAT math scores over 700: 3%; ACT scores over 30: 8%.

Retention: 75% of full-time freshmen returned.

FACULTY

Total: 396, 31% full-time, 37% with terminal degrees.

Student/faculty ratio: 17:1.

ACADEMICS

Calendar: semesters. *Degrees:* associate, bachelor's, master's, and doctoral (associate's degree for international students only).

Special study options: academic remediation for entering students, accelerated degree program, adult/continuing education programs, advanced placement credit, distance learning, double majors, honors programs, independent study, internships, off-campus study, part-time degree program, services for LD students, study abroad, summer session for credit.

Computers: 64 computers/terminals are available on campus for general student use. Students can access the following: computer help desk, free student e-mail accounts, online (class) grades, online (class) registration, online (class) schedules. Campuswide network is available. 100% of college-owned or -operated housing units are wired for high-speed Internet access. Wireless service is available via entire campus.

Library: Concordia University Library. *Books:* 75,355 (physical), 131,618 (digital/electronic); *Serial titles:* 91 (physical), 503,537 (digital/electronic); *Databases:* 34. Weekly public service hours: 85.

STUDENT LIFE

Housing options: coed, women-only, special housing for students with disabilities. Campus housing is university owned. Freshman campus housing is guaranteed.

Activities and organizations: drama/theater group, student-run newspaper, choral group, intramurals, Screaming Eagles, Lacrosse, Abbey West, LEAD Student Activities.

Athletics Member NCAA. All Division II. *Intercollegiate sports:* baseball M(s), basketball M(s)/W(s), cross-country running M(s)/W(s), lacrosse M(s)(c)/W(s)(c), soccer M(s)/W(s), softball W(s), swimming and diving M(s)/W(s), tennis M(s)/W(s), track and field M(s)/W(s), volleyball M(s)/W(s), water polo M(s)/W(s). *Intramural sports:* basketball M/W, bowling M/W, cheerleading M(c)/W(c), football M/W, soccer M/W, softball M/W, track and field M/W, ultimate Frisbee M/W, volleyball M/W.

Campus security: 24-hour emergency response devices and patrols, student patrols, late-night transport/escort service, lighted walkways, 24-hour dispatch.

Student services: health clinic, personal/psychological counseling.

COSTS & FINANCIAL AID

Costs (2018–19) *Comprehensive fee:* $46,700 includes full-time tuition ($34,700), mandatory fees ($700), and room and board ($11,300). Full-time tuition and fees vary according to course load. Part-time tuition and fees vary according to course load. *College room only:* $6510. Room and board charges vary according to board plan and housing facility. *Payment plan:* installment. *Waivers:* employees or children of employees.

Financial Aid Of all full-time matriculated undergraduates who enrolled in 2017, 1,310 applied for aid, 1,152 were judged to have need, 149 had their need fully met. 86 Federal Work-Study jobs (averaging $2238). In 2017, 281 non-need-based awards were made. *Average percent of need met:* 61. *Average financial aid package:* $22,186. *Average need-based loan:* $4515. *Average need-based gift aid:* $19,406. *Average non-need-based aid:* $10,787. *Average indebtedness upon graduation:* $32,754. *Financial aid deadline:* 3/2.

APPLYING

Standardized Tests *Required:* SAT or ACT (for admission).

Options: electronic application, early action, deferred entrance.

Application fee: $50.

Required: high school transcript. *Recommended:* essay or personal statement, minimum 2.8 GPA, 1 letter of recommendation, interview.

Application deadlines: rolling (freshmen), rolling (transfers), 12/1 (early action).

Notification: continuous (freshmen), continuous (transfers), 12/15 (early action).

CONTACT

Mr. Doug Wible, Director of Undergraduate Admissions, Concordia University Irvine, 1530 Concordia West, Irvine, CA 92612-3299. *Phone:* 800-229-1200. *Toll-free phone:* 800-229-1200. *Fax:* 949-214-3520. *E-mail:* admission@cui.edu.

Design Institute of San Diego

San Diego, California
http://www.disd.edu/

- **Proprietary** 4-year, founded 1977
- **Urban** campus with easy access to San Diego
- **Coed** 126 undergraduate students, 63% full-time, 89% women, 11% men

UNDERGRAD STUDENTS

80 full-time, 46 part-time. Students come from 28 states and territories; 5 other countries; 7% Black or African American, non-Hispanic/Latino; 17% Hispanic/Latino; 10% Asian, non-Hispanic/Latino; 0.8% Native Hawaiian or other Pacific Islander, non-Hispanic/Latino; 2% American Indian or Alaska Native, non-Hispanic/Latino; 0.8% Two or more races, non-Hispanic/Latino; 6% international; 10% transferred in.

Freshmen:
Admission: 2 enrolled.

Retention: 75% of full-time freshmen returned.

FACULTY

Total: 26, 19% full-time.

Student/faculty ratio: 9:1.

ACADEMICS

Calendar: semesters. *Degree:* bachelor's.

Special study options: adult/continuing education programs, internships, part-time degree program, services for LD students, student-designed majors, study abroad, summer session for credit.

Computers: 64 computers/terminals are available on campus for general student use. Students can access the following: campus intranet, free student e-mail accounts, computer lab tutors and support from the IT Department. Campuswide network is available. Wireless service is available via classrooms, computer centers, computer labs, libraries.

Library: DISD Library. *Books:* 6,179 (physical); *Serial titles:* 84 (physical). Weekly public service hours: 56.

STUDENT LIFE

Housing options: college housing not available.

Activities and organizations: ASID Student Chapter, IIDA Student Chapter, Student Mentor Program, Student Ambassador.

Campus security: security guard patrols during the semester from 5:30 - 10:30 pm Monday - Thursday. No classes on Friday past 5:00 pm.

COSTS

Costs (2018–19) *Tuition:* $22,500 full-time, $938 per unit part-time. Full-time tuition and fees vary according to class time, course load, and program. Part-time tuition and fees vary according to class time, course load, and program. *Required fees:* $10 full-time, $10 per year part-time. *Payment plans:* installment, deferred payment. *Waivers:* employees or children of employees.

APPLYING

Required: essay or personal statement, high school transcript, 2 letters of recommendation. *Required for some:* official transcripts from all colleges attended. *Recommended:* minimum 2.0 GPA, interview.

CONTACT
Mr. Christopher Pfeil, Admissions, Design Institute of San Diego, 8555 Commerce Avenue, San Diego, CA 92121. *Phone:* 858-566-1200 Ext. 1025. *Toll-free phone:* 800-619-4337. *Fax:* 858-566-2711. *E-mail:* admissions@disd.edu.

DeVry University–Folsom Campus
Folsom, California
http://www.devry.edu/

CONTACT
DeVry University–Folsom Campus, 950 Iron Point Road, Folsom, CA 95630. *Toll-free phone:* 866-338-7934.

DeVry University–Fremont Campus
Fremont, California
http://www.devry.edu/

CONTACT
Admissions Office, DeVry University–Fremont Campus, 6600 Dumbarton Circle, Fremont, CA 94555. *Phone:* 510-574-1200. *Toll-free phone:* 866-338-7934.

DeVry University–Long Beach Campus
Long Beach, California
http://www.devry.edu/

CONTACT
Admissions Office, DeVry University–Long Beach Campus, 3880 Kilroy Airport Way, Long Beach, CA 90806. *Phone:* 562-427-0861. *Toll-free phone:* 866-338-7934.

DeVry University–Pomona Campus
Pomona, California
http://www.devry.edu/

- **Proprietary** comprehensive, founded 1983, part of DeVry University
- **Urban** campus
- **Coed**
- **Minimally difficult** entrance level

FACULTY
Student/faculty ratio: 19:1.

ACADEMICS
Calendar: semesters. *Degrees:* associate, bachelor's, master's, and postbachelor's certificates.

STUDENT LIFE
Housing options: college housing not available.

COSTS
Costs (2017–18) *Tuition:* $14,700 full-time. *Required fees:* $500 full-time.

APPLYING
Options: deferred entrance.
Application fee: $30.
Required: high school transcript, interview.

CONTACT
DeVry University–Pomona Campus, 901 Corporate Center Drive, Pomona, CA 91768. *Phone:* 909-622-8866. *Toll-free phone:* 866-338-7934.

DeVry University–San Diego Campus
San Diego, California
http://www.devry.edu/

CONTACT
Admissions Office, DeVry University–San Diego Campus, 2655 Camino Del Rio North, Suite 350, San Diego, CA 92108-1633. *Phone:* 619-683-2446. *Toll-free phone:* 866-338-7934.

DeVry University–Sherman Oaks Campus
Sherman Oaks, California
http://www.devry.edu/

CONTACT
Admissions Office, DeVry University–Sherman Oaks Campus, 15301 Ventura Boulevard, D-100, Sherman Oaks, CA 91403. *Phone:* 818-713-8111. *Toll-free phone:* 866-338-7934.

Dominican University of California
San Rafael, California
http://www.dominican.edu/

- **Independent** comprehensive, founded 1890, affiliated with Roman Catholic Church
- **Suburban** 85-acre campus with easy access to San Francisco
- **Endowment** $28.3 million
- **Coed** 1,302 undergraduate students, 87% full-time, 74% women, 26% men
- **Moderately difficult** entrance level, 76% of applicants were admitted

UNDERGRAD STUDENTS
1,135 full-time, 167 part-time. Students come from 27 states and territories; 13 other countries; 9% are from out of state; 5% Black or African American, non-Hispanic/Latino; 20% Hispanic/Latino; 26% Asian, non-Hispanic/Latino; 1% Native Hawaiian or other Pacific Islander, non-Hispanic/Latino; 0.7% American Indian or Alaska Native, non-Hispanic/Latino; 7% Two or more races, non-Hispanic/Latino; 7% Race/ethnicity unknown; 1% international; 4% transferred in; 35% live on campus.

Freshmen:
Admission: 1,867 applied, 1,410 admitted, 242 enrolled. *Average high school GPA:* 3.7. *Test scores:* SAT evidence-based reading and writing scores over 500: 88%; SAT math scores over 500: 83%; ACT scores over 18: 92%; SAT evidence-based reading and writing scores over 600: 36%; SAT math scores over 600: 25%; ACT scores over 24: 37%; SAT evidence-based reading and writing scores over 700: 2%; SAT math scores over 700: 1%; ACT scores over 30: 3%.
Retention: 86% of full-time freshmen returned.

FACULTY
Total: 328, 32% full-time, 41% with terminal degrees.
Student/faculty ratio: 9:1.

ACADEMICS
Calendar: semesters. *Degrees:* bachelor's and master's.

Special study options: accelerated degree program, adult/continuing education programs, distance learning, double majors, external degree program, honors programs, independent study, internships, off-campus study, part-time degree program, student-designed majors, study abroad.

Unusual degree programs: 3-2 business administration; nursing; occupational therapy.

Computers: 195 computers/terminals and 700 ports are available on campus for general student use. Students can access the following: computer help desk, free student e-mail accounts, online (class) grades, online (class) registration, online (class) schedules, office software. Campuswide network is available. 100% of college-owned or -operated housing units are wired for high-speed Internet access. Wireless service is available via entire campus.

Library: Archbishop Alemany Library. *Books:* 110,523 (physical); *Databases:* 84.

STUDENT LIFE

Housing options: coed, special housing for students with disabilities. Campus housing is university owned. Freshman applicants given priority for college housing.

Activities and organizations: drama/theater group, student-run newspaper, radio station, choral group, Filipino Cultural Club, BSU, Perceptions, Global Ambassadors, Intramural Club/Programming.

Athletics Member NCAA. All Division II. *Intercollegiate sports:* basketball M(s)/W(s), cross-country running M(s)/W(s), golf M(s)/W(s), lacrosse M(s), soccer M(s)/W(s), softball W(s), tennis W(s), volleyball W(s). *Intramural sports:* badminton M/W, bowling M/W, cheerleading W, sailing M/W, skiing (downhill) M/W, soccer M/W, softball M/W, table tennis M/W, tennis M/W, ultimate Frisbee M/W, volleyball M/W, weight lifting M/W.

Campus security: 24-hour patrols, late-night transport/escort service, controlled dormitory access.

Student services: health clinic, personal/psychological counseling.

COSTS & FINANCIAL AID

Costs (2018–19) *Comprehensive fee:* $59,340 includes full-time tuition ($44,240), mandatory fees ($450), and room and board ($14,650). Full-time tuition and fees vary according to course load. Part-time tuition: $1850 per credit hour. Part-time tuition and fees vary according to course load. *Required fees:* $150 per term part-time. *College room only:* $8280. Room and board charges vary according to board plan. *Payment plan:* installment. *Waivers:* employees or children of employees.

Financial Aid Of all full-time matriculated undergraduates who enrolled in 2016, 1,043 applied for aid, 953 were judged to have need, 135 had their need fully met. 205 Federal Work-Study jobs (averaging $1735). 12 state and other part-time jobs (averaging $13,650). In 2016, 218 non-need-based awards were made. *Average percent of need met:* 67. *Average financial aid package:* $28,594. *Average need-based loan:* $4603. *Average need-based gift aid:* $24,123. *Average non-need-based aid:* $17,006. *Average indebtedness upon graduation:* $37,827.

APPLYING

Standardized Tests *Required:* SAT or ACT (for admission).

Options: electronic application, deferred entrance.

Required: essay or personal statement, high school transcript, minimum 2.0 GPA, 1 letter of recommendation. *Recommended:* interview.

Application deadlines: 2/1 (freshmen), 2/1 (transfers).

Notification: continuous until 10/15 (freshmen), continuous (transfers).

CONTACT

Mr. Rich Toledo, Assistant Vice President, Undergraduate Admissions, Dominican University of California, 50 Acacia Avenue, San Rafael, CA 94901-2298. *Phone:* 415-485-3206. *Toll-free phone:* 888-323-6763. *Fax:* 415-485-3287. *E-mail:* rich.toledo@dominican.edu.

Epic Bible College
Sacramento, California
http://epic.edu/

CONTACT

Ms. Sheila Knoll, Assistant Director of Records, Epic Bible College, 4330 Auburn Boulevard, Sacramento, CA 95841. *Phone:* 916-348-4689. *E-mail:* kclarke@tlbc.edu.

Feather River College
Quincy, California
http://www.frc.edu/

- **District-supported** primarily 2-year, founded 1968, part of California Community College System
- **Rural** 420-acre campus
- **Endowment** $48,167
- **Coed** 2,079 undergraduate students, 26% full-time, 48% women, 51% men
- **Noncompetitive** entrance level

UNDERGRAD STUDENTS

546 full-time, 1,522 part-time. Students come from 30 states and territories; 7 other countries; 8% are from out of state; 11% Black or African American, non-Hispanic/Latino; 30% Hispanic/Latino; 6% Asian, non-Hispanic/Latino; 1% Native Hawaiian or other Pacific Islander, non-Hispanic/Latino; 2% American Indian or Alaska Native, non-Hispanic/Latino; 6% Race/ethnicity unknown; 0.9% international; 19% transferred in.

Freshmen:
Admission: 495 enrolled.

FACULTY

Total: 98, 27% full-time, 12% with terminal degrees.

Student/faculty ratio: 21:1.

ACADEMICS

Calendar: semesters plus summer and winter terms. *Degrees:* certificates, diplomas, associate, and bachelor's.

Special study options: academic remediation for entering students, adult/continuing education programs, advanced placement credit, cooperative education, distance learning, double majors, English as a second language, independent study, part-time degree program, services for LD students, summer session for credit.

Computers: 116 computers/terminals are available on campus for general student use. Students can access the following: computer help desk, free student e-mail accounts, online (class) grades, online (class) registration, online (class) schedules. Campuswide network is available. 100% of college-owned or -operated housing units are wired for high-speed Internet access. Wireless service is available via entire campus.

Library: Feather River College Library. *Books:* 24,291 (physical), 350,000 (digital/electronic); *Serial titles:* 98 (physical), 28,376 (digital/electronic); *Databases:* 35. Weekly public service hours: 61; students can reserve study rooms.

STUDENT LIFE

Housing options: coed. Campus housing is provided by a third party.

Activities and organizations: drama/theater group, choral group, Phi Theta Kappa Honor Society, International and Cultural Club, Horse Show Team, Student Environmental Association, Student Alliance for Equity.

Athletics *Intercollegiate sports:* baseball M, basketball M/W, cross-country running W, equestrian sports M(s)/W(s), football M, sand volleyball W, soccer M/W, softball W, track and field W, volleyball W.

Campus security: student patrols, part-time private security company patrols.

Student services: health clinic, personal/psychological counseling.

COSTS & FINANCIAL AID

Costs (2017–18) *Tuition:* state resident $1380 full-time, $46 per credit part-time; nonresident $8430 full-time, $281 per credit part-time. Full-time tuition and fees vary according to course load. Part-time tuition and fees vary according to course load. *Required fees:* $81 full-time, $2 per credit part-time, $18 per term part-time. *Room only:* $5350. Room and board charges vary according to housing facility. *Payment plan:* installment.

Financial Aid Of all full-time matriculated undergraduates who enrolled in 2016, 22 Federal Work-Study jobs (averaging $750). 103 state and other part-time jobs (averaging $1504).

APPLYING

Standardized Tests *Recommended:* ACCUPLACER.

Options: electronic application.

CONTACT

Mrs. Leslie Mikesell, Director of Admissions and Records, Feather River College, 570 Golden Eagle Avenue, Quincy, CA 95971. *Phone:* 530-283-0202 Ext. 285. *Toll-free phone:* 800-442-9799. *E-mail:* info@frc.edu.

FIDM/Fashion Institute of Design & Merchandising, Los Angeles Campus

Los Angeles, California
http://www.fidm.edu/

- **Proprietary** 4-year, founded 1969, part of FIDM/Fashion Institute of Design & Merchandising
- **Urban** campus with easy access to Los Angeles
- **Coed** 2,367 undergraduate students, 89% full-time, 88% women, 12% men
- **Moderately difficult** entrance level, 39% of applicants were admitted

UNDERGRAD STUDENTS
2,113 full-time, 254 part-time. Students come from 49 states and territories; 51 other countries; 48% are from out of state; 14% transferred in.

Freshmen:
Admission: 1,538 applied, 607 admitted, 372 enrolled. *Average high school GPA:* 2.9.

Retention: 93% of full-time freshmen returned.

FACULTY
Total: 297, 13% full-time.
Student/faculty ratio: 13:1.

ACADEMICS
Calendar: quarters. *Degrees:* associate and bachelor's (also includes Orange County Campus).

Special study options: academic remediation for entering students, accelerated degree program, adult/continuing education programs, advanced placement credit, cooperative education, distance learning, English as a second language, independent study, internships, off-campus study, part-time degree program, services for LD students, study abroad, summer session for credit.

Computers: 433 computers/terminals and 20 ports are available on campus for general student use. Students can access the following: campus intranet, computer help desk, free student e-mail accounts, online (class) grades, online (class) registration, online (class) schedules. Campuswide network is available. Wireless service is available via classrooms, computer centers, computer labs, learning centers, libraries, student centers.

Library: FIDM Los Angeles Campus Library. *Books:* 48,534 (physical), 2,778 (digital/electronic); *Serial titles:* 548 (physical); *Databases:* 39. Students can reserve study rooms.

STUDENT LIFE
Housing options: college housing not available.

Activities and organizations: Cross-Cultural Student Alliance, Fashion Industry Club, Phi Theta Kappa Honor Society, Student Council, FIDM MODE Magazine.

Campus security: 24-hour emergency response devices and patrols, late-night transport/escort service.

Student services: personal/psychological counseling.

COSTS
Costs (2018–19) *Tuition:* $31,760 full-time, $685 per credit hour part-time. Full-time tuition and fees vary according to course load, degree level, and program. Part-time tuition and fees vary according to course load, degree level, and program. *Required fees:* $1185 full-time. *Payment plan:* installment. *Waivers:* employees or children of employees.

APPLYING
Standardized Tests *Recommended:* SAT and SAT Subject Tests or ACT (for admission).

Options: electronic application, deferred entrance.

Application fee: $225.

Required: essay or personal statement, high school transcript, minimum 2.5 GPA, 3 letters of recommendation, interview, major-determined project.

Application deadlines: rolling (freshmen), rolling (transfers).

CONTACT
Ms. Susan Aronson, Executive Director of Admissions, FIDM/Fashion Institute of Design & Merchandising, Los Angeles Campus, 919 South Grand Avenue, Los Angeles, CA 90015. *Phone:* 213-624-1200 Ext. 5400. *Toll-free phone:* 800-624-1200. *E-mail:* saronson@fidm.edu.

FIDM/Fashion Institute of Design & Merchandising, San Francisco Campus

San Francisco, California
http://www.fidm.edu/

- **Proprietary** 4-year, founded 1973, part of FIDM/Fashion Institute of Design & Merchandising
- **Urban** campus with easy access to San Francisco
- **Coed** 279 undergraduate students, 82% full-time, 89% women, 11% men
- **Moderately difficult** entrance level, 37% of applicants were admitted

UNDERGRAD STUDENTS
229 full-time, 50 part-time. Students come from 15 states and territories; 13 other countries; 6% are from out of state; 21% transferred in.

Freshmen:
Admission: 198 applied, 73 admitted, 44 enrolled. *Average high school GPA:* 2.9.

Retention: 96% of full-time freshmen returned.

FACULTY
Total: 40.
Student/faculty ratio: 7:1.

ACADEMICS
Calendar: quarters. *Degrees:* associate and bachelor's.

Special study options: academic remediation for entering students, accelerated degree program, adult/continuing education programs, advanced placement credit, cooperative education, distance learning, English as a second language, honors programs, independent study, internships, off-campus study, part-time degree program, services for LD students, study abroad, summer session for credit.

Computers: 135 computers/terminals are available on campus for general student use. Students can access the following: campus intranet, computer help desk, free student e-mail accounts, online (class) grades, online (class) registration, online (class) schedules. Campuswide network is available. Wireless service is available via classrooms, computer centers, computer labs, libraries, student centers.

Library: FIDM San Francisco Library. Students can reserve study rooms.

STUDENT LIFE
Housing options: college housing not available.

Activities and organizations: Cross-Cultural Student Alliance, Fashion Industry Club, Phi Theta Kappa- National Honor Society, Student Council, FIDM MODE Magazine.

Campus security: 24-hour emergency response devices and patrols, security escorts.

Student services: personal/psychological counseling.

COSTS
Costs (2018–19) *Tuition:* $32,075 full-time, $685 per credit hour part-time. Full-time tuition and fees vary according to degree level and program. Part-time tuition and fees vary according to degree level and program. *Required fees:* $1152 full-time. *Payment plan:* installment. *Waivers:* employees or children of employees.

APPLYING
Standardized Tests *Recommended:* SAT or ACT (for admission).

Options: electronic application, deferred entrance.

Application fee: $225.

Required: essay or personal statement, high school transcript, minimum 2.5 GPA, 3 letters of recommendation, interview, major-determined project.

Application deadlines: rolling (freshmen), rolling (transfers).

CONTACT
Ms. Sheryl Badalamenti, Director of Admissions, FIDM/Fashion Institute of Design & Merchandising, San Francisco Campus, 55 Stockton Street,

San Francisco, CA 94108-5829. *Phone:* 415-433-6691 Ext. 1550. *Toll-free phone:* 800-422-3436. *E-mail:* sbadalamenti@fidm.edu.

Fremont College
Cerritos, California
http://www.fremont.edu/

CONTACT
Natasha Dawson, Director of Admissions, Fremont College, 18000 Studebaker Road, Suite 900A, Cerritos, CA 90703. *Phone:* 562-809-5100. *Toll-free phone:* 800-373-6668. *Fax:* 562-809-5100. *E-mail:* info@fremont.edu.

Fresno Pacific University
Fresno, California
http://www.fresno.edu/

- **Independent** comprehensive, founded 1944, affiliated with Mennonite Brethren Church
- **Suburban** 50-acre campus with easy access to Fresno
- **Coed**
- **Moderately difficult** entrance level

FACULTY
Student/faculty ratio: 13:1.

ACADEMICS
Calendar: semesters. *Degrees:* certificates, associate, bachelor's, master's, and postbachelor's certificates.
Library: Hiebert Library.

STUDENT LIFE
Housing options: on-campus residence required through junior year; men-only, women-only, special housing for students with disabilities. Campus housing is university owned and leased by the school. Freshman campus housing is guaranteed.

Activities and organizations: drama/theater group, student-run newspaper, choral group.

Athletics Member NCAA. All Division II.

Campus security: 24-hour emergency response devices and patrols, student patrols, late-night transport/escort service, controlled dormitory access, 24-hour monitored closed-circuit security cameras.

Student services: health clinic, personal/psychological counseling.

COSTS & FINANCIAL AID
Costs (2017–18) *Comprehensive fee:* $38,848 includes full-time tuition ($29,988), mandatory fees ($460), and room and board ($8400). Full-time tuition and fees vary according to course level, degree level, program, and student level. Part-time tuition: $1071 per credit. Part-time tuition and fees vary according to course level, degree level, program, and student level. *Required fees:* $230 per term part-time. *College room only:* $4160. Room and board charges vary according to board plan and housing facility.

Financial Aid Of all full-time matriculated undergraduates who enrolled in 2016, 1,892 applied for aid, 1,784 were judged to have need, 146 had their need fully met. In 2016, 178 non-need-based awards were made. *Average percent of need met:* 50. *Average financial aid package:* $21,383. *Average need-based loan:* $8159. *Average need-based gift aid:* $8362. *Average non-need-based aid:* $10,883.

APPLYING
Standardized Tests *Required:* SAT or ACT (for admission).

Options: electronic application, early admission, deferred entrance.

Application fee: $40.

Required: essay or personal statement, high school transcript, 1 letter of recommendation. *Required for some:* interview. *Recommended:* minimum 3.1 GPA.

CONTACT
Andy Johnson, Director of Undergraduate Admissions, Fresno Pacific University, 1717 South Chestnut Avenue, Fresno, CA 93727. *Phone:* 559-453-2000. *Toll-free phone:* 800-660-6089. *Fax:* 559-453-2007. *E-mail:* andy.johnson@fresno.edu.

Golden Gate University
San Francisco, California
http://www.ggu.edu/

- **Independent** university, founded 1901
- **Urban** campus with easy access to San Francisco Bay Area
- **Endowment** $29.8 million
- **Coed** 475 undergraduate students, 49% full-time, 43% women, 57% men
- **Moderately difficult** entrance level

UNDERGRAD STUDENTS
231 full-time, 244 part-time. Students come from 14 states and territories; 6% are from out of state; 0.7% Black or African American, non-Hispanic/Latino; 17% Hispanic/Latino; 2% Asian, non-Hispanic/Latino; 27% Native Hawaiian or other Pacific Islander, non-Hispanic/Latino; 13% American Indian or Alaska Native, non-Hispanic/Latino; 4% Two or more races, non-Hispanic/Latino; 25% Race/ethnicity unknown; 2% international; 96% transferred in.

FACULTY
Total: 489, 6% full-time, 31% with terminal degrees.
Student/faculty ratio: 16:1.

ACADEMICS
Calendar: trimesters. *Degrees:* certificates, associate, bachelor's, master's, doctoral, and postbachelor's certificates.

Special study options: academic remediation for entering students, accelerated degree program, adult/continuing education programs, advanced placement credit, distance learning, English as a second language, internships, off-campus study, part-time degree program, summer session for credit.

Computers: 40 computers/terminals and 12 ports are available on campus for general student use. Students can access the following: campus intranet, online (class) registration, online (class) schedules. Campuswide network is available. Wireless service is available via entire campus.
Library: Golden Gate University Library plus 1 other. *Books:* 43,127 (physical), 15,700 (digital/electronic); *Serial titles:* 55,000 (digital/electronic); *Databases:* 116. Weekly public service hours: 90; students can reserve study rooms.

STUDENT LIFE
Housing options: college housing not available.

Activities and organizations: student-run newspaper, American Marketing Association, Korean Student Association, Japanese Student Association, Thai Student Association, Computing Society.

Athletics *Intramural sports:* cross-country running M(c)/W(c), racquetball M(c)/W(c), tennis M(c)/W(c).

Campus security: late-night transport/escort service.

Student services: personal/psychological counseling.

COSTS & FINANCIAL AID
Costs (2017–18) *Tuition:* $15,840 full-time, $8580 per year part-time. Full-time tuition and fees vary according to course load, degree level, and program. Part-time tuition and fees vary according to course load and program. *Required fees:* $255 full-time. *Payment plans:* installment, deferred payment. *Waivers:* children of alumni and employees or children of employees.

Financial Aid Of all full-time matriculated undergraduates who enrolled in 2013, 299 applied for aid, 239 were judged to have need, 49 had their need fully met. 18 Federal Work-Study jobs (averaging $5000). In 2013, 49 non-need-based awards were made. *Average percent of need met:* 20. *Average financial aid package:* $10,350. *Average need-based loan:* $5500. *Average need-based gift aid:* $3750. *Average non-need-based aid:* $3750.

APPLYING
Options: electronic application, deferred entrance.

Application fee: $55.

Required: high school transcript, minimum 2.0 GPA. *Required for some:* minimum 3.2 GPA, interview. *Recommended:* essay or personal statement, minimum 3.0 GPA.

Application deadlines: rolling (freshmen), rolling (transfers).

Notification: continuous (freshmen), continuous (transfers).

CONTACT
Mr. Louis D. Riccardi Jr., Director of Enrollment Services, Golden Gate University, 536 Mission Street, San Francisco, CA 94105-2968. *Phone:* 415-442-7800. *Toll-free phone:* 800-448-3381. *Fax:* 415-442-7807. *E-mail:* info@ggu.edu.

Grace Mission University
Fullerton, California
http://www.gm.edu/

CONTACT
Grace Mission University, 1645 West Valencia Drive, Fullerton, CA 92833.

Gurnick Academy of Medical Arts
San Mateo, California
http://www.gurnick.edu/
- **Proprietary** primarily 2-year
- **Coed**

ACADEMICS
Degrees: certificates, diplomas, associate, and bachelor's.

CONTACT
Gurnick Academy of Medical Arts, 2121 South El Camino Real, Building C 2000, San Mateo, CA 94403.

Harvey Mudd College
Claremont, California
http://www.hmc.edu/
- **Independent** 4-year, founded 1955, part of The Claremont Colleges
- **Suburban** 33-acre campus with easy access to Los Angeles
- **Endowment** $298.9 million
- **Coed** 844 undergraduate students, 100% full-time, 48% women, 52% men
- **Most difficult** entrance level, 15% of applicants were admitted

UNDERGRAD STUDENTS
844 full-time. 57% are from out of state; 4% Black or African American, non-Hispanic/Latino; 18% Hispanic/Latino; 17% Asian, non-Hispanic/Latino; 0.5% Native Hawaiian or other Pacific Islander, non-Hispanic/Latino; 0.5% American Indian or Alaska Native, non-Hispanic/Latino; 11% Two or more races, non-Hispanic/Latino; 5% Race/ethnicity unknown; 10% international; 0.4% transferred in.

Freshmen:
Admission: 4,078 applied, 629 admitted, 225 enrolled. *Test scores:* SAT evidence-based reading and writing scores over 500: 99%; SAT math scores over 500: 100%; ACT scores over 18: 100%; SAT evidence-based reading and writing scores over 600: 98%; SAT math scores over 600: 100%; ACT scores over 24: 100%; SAT evidence-based reading and writing scores over 700: 87%; SAT math scores over 700: 97%; ACT scores over 30: 98%.
Retention: 98% of full-time freshmen returned.

FACULTY
Total: 115, 92% full-time, 99% with terminal degrees.
Student/faculty ratio: 8:1.

ACADEMICS
Calendar: semesters. *Degree:* bachelor's.
Special study options: double majors, internships, off-campus study, services for LD students, student-designed majors, study abroad. *ROTC:* Army (c), Air Force (c).
Unusual degree programs: engineering with Offered to students from Claremont McKenna College and Scripps College.
Computers: Students can access the following: campus intranet, computer help desk, free student e-mail accounts, online (class) grades, online (class) registration, online (class) schedules. Campuswide network is available. 100% of college-owned or -operated housing units are wired for high-speed Internet access. Wireless service is available via entire campus.

Library: Claremont Colleges Library plus 1 other.
STUDENT LIFE
Housing options: on-campus residence required for freshman year; coed. Campus housing is university owned. Freshman campus housing is guaranteed.
Activities and organizations: drama/theater group, student-run newspaper, radio station, choral group, Claremont Colleges Ballroom Dance Company, Science Bus, Society of Women Engineers (SWE), Intervarsity Christian Fellowship, Gonzo Unicycle Madness (Unicycle Club).
Athletics Member NCAA. All Division III. *Intercollegiate sports:* baseball M, basketball M/W, cross-country running M/W, equestrian sports M(c)/W(c), fencing.M(c)/W(c), field hockey M(c)/W(c), football M, golf M/W, lacrosse M(c)/W, rugby M(c)/W(c), soccer M/W, softball W, swimming and diving M/W, tennis M/W, track and field M/W, ultimate Frisbee M(c)/W(c), volleyball M(c)/W, water polo M/W. *Intramural sports:* basketball M/W, bowling M/W, football M/W, soccer M/W(c), table tennis M/W, tennis M(c)/W(c), water polo M/W.
Campus security: 24-hour emergency response devices and patrols, late-night transport/escort service, controlled dormitory access.
Student services: health clinic, personal/psychological counseling, women's center.

COSTS & FINANCIAL AID
Costs (2017–18) *One-time required fee:* $250. *Comprehensive fee:* $72,228 includes full-time tuition ($54,347), mandatory fees ($289), and room and board ($17,592). Part-time tuition: $1698 per unit. Part-time tuition and fees vary according to course load. *College room only:* $9554. Room and board charges vary according to board plan. *Payment plan:* installment. *Waivers:* employees or children of employees.
Financial Aid Of all full-time matriculated undergraduates who enrolled in 2016, 483 applied for aid, 414 were judged to have need, 414 had their need fully met. 121 Federal Work-Study jobs (averaging $839). 25 state and other part-time jobs (averaging $7783). In 2016, 162 non-need-based awards were made. *Average percent of need met:* 100. *Average financial aid package:* $43,248. *Average need-based loan:* $5657. *Average need-based gift aid:* $40,138. *Average non-need-based aid:* $12,696. *Average indebtedness upon graduation:* $25,041. *Financial aid deadline:* 2/1.

APPLYING
Standardized Tests *Required:* SAT or ACT (for admission), SAT Subject Tests (for admission).
Options: electronic application, early admission, early decision, deferred entrance.
Application fee: $70.
Required: essay or personal statement, high school transcript, 3 letters of recommendation. *Recommended:* interview.
Application deadlines: 1/5 (freshmen), 4/1 (transfers).
Early decision deadline: 11/15 (for plan 1), 1/5 (for plan 2).
Notification: 4/1 (freshmen), 5/15 (transfers), 12/15 (early decision plan 1), 2/15 (early decision plan 2).

CONTACT
Harvey Mudd College, 301 Platt Boulevard, Claremont, CA 91711-5994.

Henley-Putnam University
San Jose, California
http://www.henley-putnam.edu/

CONTACT
Henley-Putnam University, 2107 N. First Street, Suite 210, San Jose, CA 95131. *Phone:* 408-453-9900 Ext. 9928. *Toll-free phone:* 888-852-8746.

★ Holy Names University
Oakland, California
http://www.hnu.edu/
- **Independent Roman Catholic** comprehensive, founded 1868
- **Urban** 60-acre campus with easy access to San Francisco
- **Coed** 591 undergraduate students, 92% full-time, 64% women, 36% men
- **Moderately difficult** entrance level, 53% of applicants were admitted

UNDERGRAD STUDENTS
543 full-time, 48 part-time. 7% are from out of state; 18% Black or African American, non-Hispanic/Latino; 43% Hispanic/Latino; 9% Asian, non-Hispanic/Latino; 2% Native Hawaiian or other Pacific Islander, non-Hispanic/Latino; 0.2% American Indian or Alaska Native, non-Hispanic/Latino; 3% Two or more races, non-Hispanic/Latino; 3% Race/ethnicity unknown; 3% international; 51% live on campus.

Freshmen:
Admission: 2,713 applied, 1,426 admitted, 205 enrolled.
Retention: 82% of full-time freshmen returned.

FACULTY
Total: 169, 30% full-time.
Student/faculty ratio: 8:1.

ACADEMICS
Calendar: semesters. *Degrees:* certificates, bachelor's, master's, post-master's, and postbachelor's certificates.

Special study options: academic remediation for entering students, accelerated degree program, adult/continuing education programs, advanced placement credit, distance learning, double majors, English as a second language, honors programs, independent study, internships, part-time degree program, services for LD students, student-designed majors, study abroad, summer session for credit. *ROTC:* Army (c), Air Force (c).

Unusual degree programs: 3-2 business administration.

Computers: 92 computers/terminals are available on campus for general student use. Students can access the following: computer help desk, free student e-mail accounts, online (class) grades, online (class) registration, online (class) schedules. Campuswide network is available. 100% of college-owned or -operated housing units are wired for high-speed Internet access. Wireless service is available via entire campus.
Library: Cushing Library. *Books:* 41,811 (physical), 137,046 (digital/electronic); *Databases:* 49. Students can reserve study rooms.

STUDENT LIFE
Housing options: coed. Campus housing is university owned. Freshman campus housing is guaranteed.

Activities and organizations: drama/theater group, choral group, Drama Club, Latinos Unidos, Black Student Union, Biology Club, Hiking Club.

Athletics Member NCAA. All Division II. *Intercollegiate sports:* baseball M(s), basketball M(s)/W(s), cross-country running M(s)/W(s), golf M(s)/W(s), soccer M(s)/W(s), softball W(s), tennis M(s)/W(s), track and field M(s), volleyball M(c)/W(s).

Campus security: 24-hour emergency response devices, late-night transport/escort service, controlled dormitory access, 24-hour security main gate.

Student services: personal/psychological counseling.

COSTS & FINANCIAL AID
Costs (2018–19) *Comprehensive fee:* $52,506 includes full-time tuition ($38,800), mandatory fees ($516), and room and board ($13,190). Full-time tuition and fees vary according to course level, course load, degree level, program, and reciprocity agreements. Part-time tuition: $1331 per unit. Part-time tuition and fees vary according to course level, course load, degree level, program, and reciprocity agreements. *Required fees:* $258 per term part-time. *College room only:* $6812. Room and board charges vary according to board plan and housing facility. *Payment plan:* installment. *Waivers:* employees or children of employees.

Financial Aid Of all full-time matriculated undergraduates who enrolled in 2006, 373 applied for aid, 247 were judged to have need, 58 had their need fully met. 50 Federal Work-Study jobs (averaging $1699). 53 state and other part-time jobs (averaging $1750). In 2006, 77 non-need-based awards were made. *Average percent of need met:* 43. *Average financial aid package:* $15,554. *Average need-based loan:* $4154. *Average need-based gift aid:* $13,258. *Average non-need-based aid:* $10,557. *Average indebtedness upon graduation:* $10,500. *Financial aid deadline:* 6/30.

APPLYING
Standardized Tests *Required:* SAT or ACT (for admission).

Options: electronic application, deferred entrance.

Application fee: $20.

Required: essay or personal statement, high school transcript, 1 letter of recommendation, minimum 1 recommendation. *Required for some:* interview.

Application deadlines: rolling (freshmen), rolling (transfers).

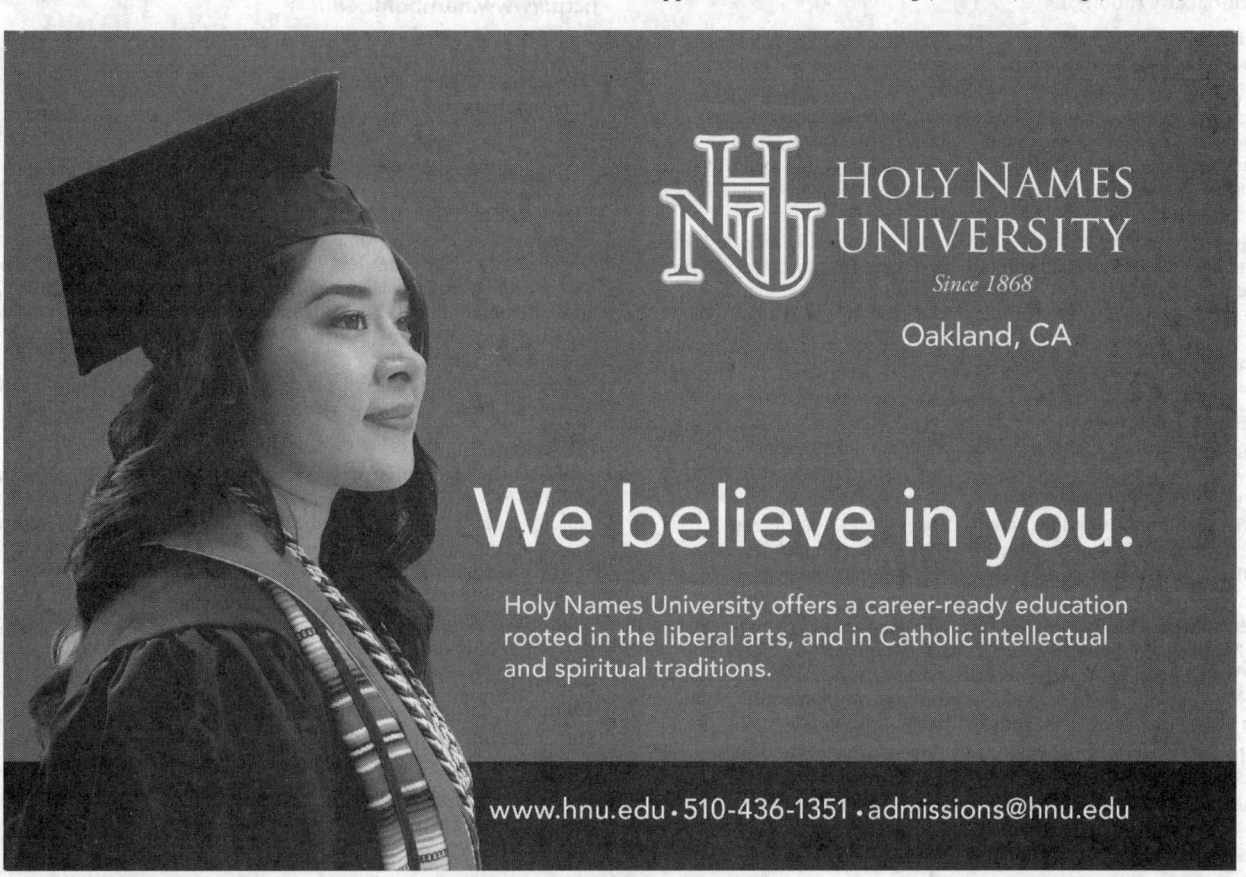

Notification: continuous (freshmen), continuous (transfers).

CONTACT
Holy Names University, 3500 Mountain Boulevard, Oakland, CA 94619. *Phone:* 510-436-1351. *Toll-free phone:* 800-430-1321. *Fax:* 510-436-1325. *E-mail:* admissions@hnu.edu.

See previous page for display ad and page 1312 for the College Close-Up.

Hope International University

Fullerton, California
http://www.hiu.edu/

- **Independent** comprehensive, founded 1928, affiliated with Christian Churches and Churches of Christ
- **Suburban** 16-acre campus with easy access to Los Angeles
- **Coed** 726 undergraduate students, 80% full-time, 56% women, 44% men
- **Moderately difficult** entrance level, 28% of applicants were admitted

UNDERGRAD STUDENTS
582 full-time, 144 part-time. 7% are from out of state; 8% Black or African American, non-Hispanic/Latino; 29% Hispanic/Latino; 4% Asian, non-Hispanic/Latino; 0.6% Native Hawaiian or other Pacific Islander, non-Hispanic/Latino; 1% American Indian or Alaska Native, non-Hispanic/Latino; 13% Two or more races, non-Hispanic/Latino; 5% Race/ethnicity unknown; 2% international; 17% transferred in; 48% live on campus.

Freshmen:
Admission: 786 applied, 223 admitted, 96 enrolled. *Average high school GPA:* 3.2. *Test scores:* SAT evidence-based reading and writing scores over 500: 52%; SAT math scores over 500: 54%; ACT scores over 18: 67%; SAT evidence-based reading and writing scores over 600: 8%; SAT math scores over 600: 10%; ACT scores over 24: 34%; SAT evidence-based reading and writing scores over 700: 3%; SAT math scores over 700: 3%; ACT scores over 30: 10%.
Retention: 72% of full-time freshmen returned.

FACULTY
Total: 234, 17% full-time, 38% with terminal degrees.
Student/faculty ratio: 9:1.

ACADEMICS
Calendar: 4-1-4. *Degrees:* certificates, associate, bachelor's, master's, and postbachelor's certificates.

Special study options: academic remediation for entering students, adult/continuing education programs, advanced placement credit, distance learning, double majors, English as a second language, independent study, internships, off-campus study, part-time degree program, services for LD students, study abroad. *ROTC:* Army (c).

Computers: Students can access the following: computer help desk, free student e-mail accounts, online (class) grades, online (class) registration, online (class) schedules, 30 Internet hotspots on campus. Campuswide network is available. 100% of college-owned and -operated housing units are wired for high-speed Internet access. Wireless service is available via entire campus.
Library: Darling Library.

STUDENT LIFE
Housing options: on-campus residence required through sophomore year; men-only, women-only. Campus housing is university owned. Freshman campus housing is guaranteed.

Activities and organizations: drama/theater group, student-run newspaper, choral group, Campus Ministries, International Student Organization, Musical Theater, Student Government, Student Publications.

Athletics Member NAIA, NCCAA. *Intercollegiate sports:* basketball M(s)/W(s), cheerleading M/W, cross-country running M(s)/W(s), golf M(s)/W(s), soccer M(s)/W(s), softball W(s), tennis M(s)/W(s), track and field M(s)/W(s), volleyball M(s)/W(s). *Intramural sports:* table tennis M/W, ultimate Frisbee M/W, volleyball M/W.

Campus security: 24-hour emergency response devices and patrols, late-night transport/escort service, controlled dormitory access.

Student services: personal/psychological counseling.

COSTS & FINANCIAL AID
Costs (2017–18) *Comprehensive fee:* $41,730 includes full-time tuition ($30,700), mandatory fees ($1100), and room and board ($9930). Full-time tuition and fees vary according to course level, course load, degree level, location, program, and reciprocity agreements. Part-time tuition: $1395 per credit hour. Part-time tuition and fees vary according to course level, course load, degree level, location, program, and reciprocity agreements. *College room only:* $4900. Room and board charges vary according to board plan. *Payment plan:* installment. *Waivers:* employees or children of employees.

Financial Aid Of all full-time matriculated undergraduates who enrolled in 2015, 355 applied for aid, 323 were judged to have need, 7 had their need fully met. 61 Federal Work-Study jobs (averaging $2000). 97 state and other part-time jobs (averaging $2000). In 2015, 14 non-need-based awards were made. *Average percent of need met:* 42. *Average financial aid package:* $20,029. *Average need-based loan:* $4819. *Average need-based gift aid:* $15,971. *Average non-need-based aid:* $9407. *Average indebtedness upon graduation:* $28,438.

APPLYING
Standardized Tests *Required:* SAT or ACT (for admission).
Options: electronic application.
Application fee: $40.
Required: essay or personal statement, high school transcript, minimum 2.5 GPA, 2 letters of recommendation, rank in upper 50% of high school class. *Required for some:* interview.
Application deadlines: rolling (freshmen), rolling (out-of-state freshmen), rolling (transfers).
Notification: continuous (freshmen), continuous (out-of-state freshmen), continuous (transfers).

CONTACT
Hope International University, 2500 East Nutwood Avenue, Fullerton, CA 92831-3138. *Toll-free phone:* 866-722-HOPE.

Humboldt State University

Arcata, California
http://www.humboldt.edu/

- **State-supported** comprehensive, founded 1913, part of California State University System
- **Rural** 161-acre campus
- **Endowment** $30.6 million
- **Coed** 7,774 undergraduate students, 93% full-time, 57% women, 43% men
- **Minimally difficult** entrance level, 58% of applicants were admitted

UNDERGRAD STUDENTS
7,236 full-time, 538 part-time. Students come from 51 states and territories; 20 other countries; 7% are from out of state; 4% Black or African American, non-Hispanic/Latino; 35% Hispanic/Latino; 3% Asian, non-Hispanic/Latino; 0.2% Native Hawaiian or other Pacific Islander, non-Hispanic/Latino; 1% American Indian or Alaska Native, non-Hispanic/Latino; 7% Two or more races, non-Hispanic/Latino; 7% Race/ethnicity unknown; 1% international; 12% transferred in; 26% live on campus.

Freshmen:
Admission: 11,562 applied, 6,720 admitted, 1,210 enrolled. *Average high school GPA:* 3.2. *Test scores:* SAT evidence-based reading and writing scores over 500: 83%; SAT math scores over 500: 82%; ACT scores over 18: 78%; SAT evidence-based reading and writing scores over 600: 52%; SAT math scores over 600: 29%; ACT scores over 24: 31%; SAT evidence-based reading and writing scores over 700: 3%; SAT math scores over 700: 4%; ACT scores over 30: 4%.
Retention: 68% of full-time freshmen returned.

FACULTY
Total: 574, 45% full-time, 58% with terminal degrees.
Student/faculty ratio: 22:1.

ACADEMICS
Calendar: semesters. *Degrees:* bachelor's, master's, post-master's, and postbachelor's certificates.

Special study options: academic remediation for entering students, adult/continuing education programs, advanced placement credit, cooperative education, distance learning, double majors, English as a second language, honors programs, independent study, internships, off-campus study, part-time degree program, services for LD students, student-designed majors, study abroad, summer session for credit.

Computers: 1,098 computers/terminals are available on campus for general student use. Students can access the following: campus intranet, computer help desk, free student e-mail accounts, online (class) grades, online (class) registration, online (class) schedules. Campuswide network is available. 100% of college-owned or -operated housing units are wired for high-speed Internet access. Wireless service is available via entire campus.

Library: Humbolot State University Library. *Books:* 445,765 (physical), 72,209 (digital/electronic); *Serial titles:* 34,235 (physical), 190 (digital/electronic); *Databases:* 98. Weekly public service hours: 100; students can reserve study rooms.

STUDENT LIFE
Housing options: coed. Campus housing is university owned. Freshman campus housing is guaranteed.

Activities and organizations: drama/theater group, student-run newspaper, radio station, choral group, marching band, Bicycle Learning Center, Campus Center for Appropriate Technology (CCAT), Youth Educational Services, HOLA, MECHA, national fraternities, national sororities.

Athletics Member NCAA. All Division II. *Intercollegiate sports:* basketball M(s)/W(s), cheerleading M(c)/W(c), crew M(c)/W, cross-country running M(s)/W(s), football M(s), lacrosse M(c)/W(c), soccer M(s)/W(s), softball W(s), track and field M(s)/W(s), volleyball W(s). *Intramural sports:* archery M(c)/W(c), baseball M(c), basketball M/W, fencing M(c)/W(c), rugby M(c)/W(c), soccer M/W, ultimate Frisbee M(c)/W(c), volleyball M(c), water polo M(c).

Campus security: 24-hour emergency response devices and patrols, late-night transport/escort service, controlled dormitory access.

Student services: health clinic, personal/psychological counseling, women's center.

COSTS & FINANCIAL AID
Costs (2018–19) *Tuition:* state resident $5742 full-time, $3330 per term part-time; nonresident $17,622 full-time, $396 per credit hour part-time. Full-time tuition and fees vary according to degree level. Part-time tuition and fees vary according to course load and degree level. *Required fees:* $1750 full-time, $1314 per term part-time. *Room and board:* $13,056; room only: $6610. Room and board charges vary according to board plan and housing facility. *Payment plan:* installment. *Waivers:* employees or children of employees.

Financial Aid Of all full-time matriculated undergraduates who enrolled in 2016, 6,547 applied for aid, 5,857 were judged to have need, 393 had their need fully met. 309 Federal Work-Study jobs (averaging $2040). In 2016, 289 non-need-based awards were made. *Average percent of need met:* 68. *Average financial aid package:* $13,650. *Average need-based loan:* $7074. *Average need-based gift aid:* $8692. *Average non-need-based aid:* $722. *Average indebtedness upon graduation:* $24,337.

APPLYING
Standardized Tests *Required for some:* SAT or ACT (for admission).
Options: electronic application, deferred entrance.
Application fee: $55.
Required: high school transcript, minimum 2.0 GPA.
Application deadlines: 11/30 (freshmen), 11/30 (transfers).
Notification: continuous (freshmen), continuous (transfers).

CONTACT
Mr. Steven Ladwig, Associate Director of Admissions, Humboldt State University, 1 Harpst Street, Arcata, CA 95521. *Phone:* 707-826-4402. *Toll-free phone:* 866-850-9556. *Fax:* 707-826-6190. *E-mail:* hsuinfo@humboldt.edu.

Humphreys University
Stockton, California
http://www.humphreys.edu/
CONTACT
Humphreys University, 6650 Inglewood Avenue, Stockton, CA 95207-3896. *Phone:* 209-235-2901.

Interior Designers Institute
Newport Beach, California
http://www.idi.edu/
CONTACT
Interior Designers Institute, 1061 Camelback Road, Newport Beach, CA 92660.

John F. Kennedy University
Pleasant Hill, California
http://www.jfku.edu/
CONTACT
Ms. Jen Miller-Hogg, Director of Admissions, John F. Kennedy University, 100 Ellinwood Way, Pleasant Hill, CA 94523-4817. *Phone:* 925-969-3584. *Toll-free phone:* 800-696-JFKU. *E-mail:* jmhogg@jfku.edu.

John Paul the Great Catholic University
Escondido, California
http://www.jpcatholic.edu/
• **Independent** comprehensive, founded 2006, affiliated with Roman Catholic Church
• **Urban** 3-acre campus with easy access to San Diego
• **Coed** 260 undergraduate students, 95% full-time, 48% women, 52% men
• **Moderately difficult** entrance level, 95% of applicants were admitted

UNDERGRAD STUDENTS
247 full-time, 13 part-time. Students come from 39 states and territories; 3 other countries; 52% are from out of state; 0.8% Black or African American, non-Hispanic/Latino; 24% Hispanic/Latino; 3% Asian, non-Hispanic/Latino; 0.4% Native Hawaiian or other Pacific Islander, non-Hispanic/Latino; 3% Two or more races, non-Hispanic/Latino; 16% Race/ethnicity unknown; 2% international; 11% transferred in; 77% live on campus.

Freshmen:
Admission: 201 applied, 191 admitted, 77 enrolled. *Average high school GPA:* 3.5. *Test scores:* SAT evidence-based reading and writing scores over 500: 87%; SAT math scores over 500: 69%; ACT scores over 18: 96%; SAT evidence-based reading and writing scores over 600: 45%; SAT math scores over 600: 16%; ACT scores over 24: 42%; SAT evidence-based reading and writing scores over 700: 11%; ACT scores over 30: 13%.
Retention: 80% of full-time freshmen returned.

FACULTY
Total: 41, 22% full-time, 24% with terminal degrees.
Student/faculty ratio: 15:1.

ACADEMICS
Calendar: quarters. *Degrees:* bachelor's, master's, and postbachelor's certificates.

Special study options: advanced placement credit, distance learning, double majors, independent study, internships, part-time degree program, study abroad, summer session for credit.

Computers: 35 computers/terminals are available on campus for general student use. Students can access the following: computer help desk. Campuswide network is available. 100% of college-owned or -operated housing units are wired for high-speed Internet access. Wireless service is available via entire campus.
Library: John Paul the Great Catholic University Library.

STUDENT LIFE

Housing options: on-campus residence required through senior year; men-only, women-only. Campus housing is leased by the school. Freshman campus housing is guaranteed.

Activities and organizations: drama/theater group, student-run newspaper, choral group, Student government, Knights of Columbus, Flag football, Swing dance club, Gaming club.

Campus security: student patrols, leased campus housing provides their own security.

Student services: personal/psychological counseling.

COSTS & FINANCIAL AID

Costs (2018–19) *Tuition:* $25,200 full-time, $667 per credit part-time. Full-time tuition and fees vary according to degree level. Part-time tuition and fees vary according to degree level. No tuition increase for student's term of enrollment. *Required fees:* $900 full-time. *Room only:* $7650. Room and board charges vary according to housing facility.

Financial Aid Of all full-time matriculated undergraduates who enrolled in 2016, 143 applied for aid, 143 were judged to have need, 11 had their need fully met. In 2016, 42 non-need-based awards were made. *Average percent of need met:* 43. *Average financial aid package:* $16,979. *Average need-based loan:* $3907. *Average need-based gift aid:* $13,798. *Average non-need-based aid:* $8312.

APPLYING

Standardized Tests *Required for some:* SAT or ACT (for admission).

Options: electronic application, deferred entrance.

Application fee: $50.

Required: essay or personal statement, high school transcript, minimum 2.6 GPA. *Recommended:* interview.

Application deadlines: rolling (freshmen), rolling (transfers).

Notification: continuous (freshmen), continuous (transfers).

CONTACT

Mr. Martin Harold, Vice President of Admissions, John Paul the Great Catholic University, 220 W. Grand Avenue, Escondido, CA 92025. *Phone:* 858-653-6740 Ext. 1101. *Fax:* 858-653-3791. *E-mail:* mharold@jpcatholic.com.

Laguna College of Art & Design

Laguna Beach, California
http://www.lcad.edu/

- **Independent** comprehensive, founded 1962
- **Small-town** 9-acre campus with easy access to Los Angeles
- **Endowment** $1.7 million
- **Coed** 567 undergraduate students
- **Very difficult** entrance level, 39% of applicants were admitted

UNDERGRAD STUDENTS

Students come from 32 states and territories; 13 other countries; 42% are from out of state; 2% Black or African American, non-Hispanic/Latino; 19% Hispanic/Latino; 18% Asian, non-Hispanic/Latino; 0.7% Native Hawaiian or other Pacific Islander, non-Hispanic/Latino; 0.5% American Indian or Alaska Native, non-Hispanic/Latino; 3% Two or more races, non-Hispanic/Latino; 4% Race/ethnicity unknown; 2% international; 11% live on campus.

Freshmen:
Admission: 472 applied, 185 admitted. *Average high school GPA:* 3.3. *Test scores:* ACT scores over 18: 100%; ACT scores over 24: 80%; ACT scores over 30: 10%.

Retention: 97% of full-time freshmen returned.

FACULTY

Total: 146, 12% full-time, 42% with terminal degrees.

Student/faculty ratio: 12:1.

ACADEMICS

Calendar: semesters. *Degrees:* certificates, bachelor's, master's, and postbachelor's certificates.

Special study options: double majors, independent study, internships, off-campus study, part-time degree program, services for LD students.

Computers: 85 computers/terminals are available on campus for general student use. Students can access the following: campus intranet, computer help desk, free student e-mail accounts, online (class) grades, online (class) registration, online (class) schedules. Campuswide network is available. 100% of college-owned or -operated housing units are wired for high-speed Internet access. Wireless service is available via entire campus.
Library: Dennis and Leslie Power Library plus 1 other. Weekly public service hours: 54.

STUDENT LIFE

Housing options: coed. Campus housing is leased by the school. Freshman applicants given priority for college housing.

Campus security: 24-hour patrols, late-night transport/escort service.

Student services: personal/psychological counseling.

COSTS & FINANCIAL AID

Costs (2018–19) *Tuition:* $30,700 full-time, $1267 per unit part-time. Full-time tuition and fees vary according to course load and degree level. Part-time tuition and fees vary according to course load and degree level. *Room only:* $10,000. *Payment plan:* installment. *Waivers:* employees or children of employees.

Financial Aid Of all full-time matriculated undergraduates who enrolled in 2016, 28 Federal Work-Study jobs (averaging $1752). *Average indebtedness upon graduation:* $38,000.

APPLYING

Standardized Tests *Recommended:* SAT or ACT (for admission).

Options: early admission, deferred entrance.

Application fee: $45.

Required: essay or personal statement, high school transcript, minimum 2.5 GPA, portfolio. *Required for some:* 2 letters of recommendation, interview.

Application deadlines: rolling (freshmen), rolling (transfers).

Notification: continuous (freshmen), continuous (transfers).

CONTACT

Madison Keyes, Admissions Coordinator, Laguna College of Art & Design, 2222 Laguna Canyon Road, Laguna Beach, CA 92651. *Phone:* 949-376-6000 Ext. 248. *Toll-free phone:* 800-255-0762. *E-mail:* mkeyes@lcad.edu.

La Sierra University

Riverside, California
http://www.lasierra.edu/

- **Independent Seventh-day Adventist** comprehensive, founded 1922, part of Seventh-Day Adventist Education System
- **Suburban** 100-acre campus with easy access to Los Angeles
- **Endowment** $17.2 million
- **Coed** 1,935 undergraduate students, 90% full-time, 60% women, 40% men
- **Minimally difficult** entrance level, 49% of applicants were admitted

UNDERGRAD STUDENTS

1,735 full-time, 200 part-time. Students come from 47 states and territories; 41 other countries; 8% are from out of state; 7% Black or African American, non-Hispanic/Latino; 47% Hispanic/Latino; 15% Asian, non-Hispanic/Latino; 2% Native Hawaiian or other Pacific Islander, non-Hispanic/Latino; 0.4% American Indian or Alaska Native, non-Hispanic/Latino; 4% Two or more races, non-Hispanic/Latino; 0.3% Race/ethnicity unknown; 12% international; 9% transferred in; 31% live on campus.

Freshmen:
Admission: 5,162 applied, 2,552 admitted, 421 enrolled. *Average high school GPA:* 3.3. *Test scores:* ACT scores over 18: 66%; ACT scores over 24: 19%; ACT scores over 30: 4%.

Retention: 63% of full-time freshmen returned.

FACULTY

Total: 115, 82% full-time, 70% with terminal degrees.

Student/faculty ratio: 15:1.

ACADEMICS

Calendar: quarters. *Degrees:* certificates, bachelor's, master's, doctoral, post-master's, and postbachelor's certificates.

Special study options: academic remediation for entering students, accelerated degree program, adult/continuing education programs, advanced placement credit, distance learning, double majors, English as a second language, honors programs, independent study, internships, off-campus study, part-time degree program, services for LD students, student-designed majors, study abroad, summer session for credit.

Unusual degree programs: 3-2 business administration; criminal justice.

Computers: 300 computers/terminals are available on campus for general student use. Students can access the following: computer help desk, free student e-mail accounts, online (class) grades, online (class) registration, online (class) schedules, student portals. Campuswide network is available. Wireless service is available via entire campus.

Library: University Library plus 1 other. *Books:* 254,620 (physical), 380,806 (digital/electronic); *Serial titles:* 386,353 (physical); *Databases:* 79. Weekly public service hours: 76; students can reserve study rooms.

STUDENT LIFE

Housing options: coed, men-only, women-only, cooperative, special housing for students with disabilities. Campus housing is university owned. Freshman campus housing is guaranteed.

Activities and organizations: drama/theater group, student-run newspaper, choral group, Pre Dentistry, Pre Med, Enactus (SIFE), International Club, Black Student Association.

Athletics Member NAIA. *Intercollegiate sports:* basketball M/W, golf M, soccer M, softball W, volleyball W. *Intramural sports:* baseball M, basketball M/W, soccer M, softball W, volleyball W.

Campus security: 24-hour emergency response devices and patrols, student patrols, late-night transport/escort service, controlled dormitory access.

Student services: health clinic, personal/psychological counseling, women's center.

COSTS & FINANCIAL AID

Costs (2018–19) *Comprehensive fee:* $40,380 includes full-time tuition ($31,140), mandatory fees ($990), and room and board ($8250). Full-time tuition and fees vary according to course load, degree level, location, and program. Part-time tuition: $865 per quarter hour. Part-time tuition and fees vary according to course load, degree level, location, and program. *Room and board:* Room and board charges vary according to board plan and housing facility. *Payment plan:* installment. *Waivers:* employees or children of employees.

Financial Aid Of all full-time matriculated undergraduates who enrolled in 2014, 1,617 applied for aid, 1,524 were judged to have need, 114 had their need fully met. In 2014, 330 non-need-based awards were made. *Average percent of need met:* 69. *Average financial aid package:* $22,616. *Average need-based loan:* $5264. *Average need-based gift aid:* $20,429. *Average non-need-based aid:* $8262. *Average indebtedness upon graduation:* $36,251. *Financial aid deadline:* 8/15.

APPLYING

Standardized Tests *Required:* SAT or ACT (for admission).

Options: electronic application, deferred entrance.

Required: high school transcript, minimum 2.0 GPA, Eligibility Index Table (combination of GPA and test scores). *Required for some:* essay or personal statement, 1 letter of recommendation, interview. *Recommended:* minimum 2.0 GPA.

Application deadlines: 2/1 (freshmen), rolling (out-of-state freshmen), 7/1 (transfers).

Notification: continuous (freshmen), continuous (out-of-state freshmen), continuous (transfers).

CONTACT

Ms. Ivy Teheda, Associate Director of Admissions, La Sierra University, 4500 Riverwalk Parkway, Riverside, CA 92505. *Phone:* 951-785-2957. *Toll-free phone:* 800-874-5587. *Fax:* 951-785-2447. *E-mail:* iteheda@lasierra.edu.

Life Pacific College
San Dimas, California
http://www.lifepacific.edu/

CONTACT

Ms. Dorienne Elston, Director of Admissions, Life Pacific College, 1100 Covina Boulevard, San Dimas, CA 91773-3298. *Phone:* 909-599-5433 Ext. 314. *Toll-free phone:* 877-886-5433 Ext. 314. *Fax:* 909-706-3070. *E-mail:* adm@lifepacific.edu.

Lincoln University
Oakland, California
http://www.lincolnuca.edu/

- **Independent** comprehensive, founded 1919
- **Urban** campus
- **Coed** 177 undergraduate students, 52% full-time, 59% women, 41% men
- **Minimally difficult** entrance level, 57% of applicants were admitted

UNDERGRAD STUDENTS

92 full-time, 85 part-time. Students come from 20 other countries; 6% Black or African American, non-Hispanic/Latino; 6% Hispanic/Latino; 18% Asian, non-Hispanic/Latino; 2% Native Hawaiian or other Pacific Islander, non-Hispanic/Latino; 6% Two or more races, non-Hispanic/Latino; 52% international.

Freshmen:
Admission: 111 applied, 63 admitted. *Average high school GPA:* 2.6.

FACULTY
Total: 34, 41% full-time, 79% with terminal degrees.

Student/faculty ratio: 17:1.

ACADEMICS

Calendar: semesters. *Degrees:* bachelor's, master's, and doctoral.

Special study options: double majors, summer session for credit.

Computers: 39 computers/terminals are available on campus for general student use. Students can access the following: computer help desk, free student e-mail accounts, online (class) schedules. Campuswide network is available. Wireless service is available via entire campus.

Library: Lincoln University Library. *Books:* 14,400 (physical), 128,000 (digital/electronic); *Serial titles:* 350 (physical), 5,050 (digital/electronic); *Databases:* 19.

STUDENT LIFE

Housing options: college housing not available.

Campus security: 24-hour emergency response devices.

Student services: personal/psychological counseling.

COSTS

Costs (2017–18) *Tuition:* $10,800 full-time, $435 per unit part-time. Full-time tuition and fees vary according to course level, course load, degree level, and program. Part-time tuition and fees vary according to course level, course load, degree level, and program. *Required fees:* $425 full-time, $425 per year part-time. *Payment plan:* installment.

APPLYING

Options: electronic application, deferred entrance.

Application fee: $75.

Required: essay or personal statement, high school transcript, minimum 2.0 GPA. *Required for some:* letters of recommendation, interview.

Application deadlines: 7/13 (freshmen), 8/8 (transfers).

CONTACT

Mr. Sunny Saggi, Admissions Officer, Lincoln University, 401 15th Street, Oakland, CA 94612. *Phone:* 510-628-8010 Ext. 8011. *Toll-free phone:* 888-810-9998. *Fax:* 510-628-8012. *E-mail:* admissions@lincolnuca.edu.

Loma Linda University

Loma Linda, California
http://www.llu.edu/

CONTACT
Admissions Office, Loma Linda University, 11139 Anderson Street, Loma Linda, CA 92350. *Phone:* 909-558-1000. *Toll-free phone:* 800-422-4558.

Los Angeles Film School

Hollywood, California
http://www.lafilm.edu/

- **Proprietary** 4-year, founded 1999
- **Urban** campus with easy access to Hollywood
- **Coed**
- **Noncompetitive** entrance level

ACADEMICS
Calendar: continuous. *Degrees:* associate and bachelor's.
Library: Main Library plus 1 other.

STUDENT LIFE
Housing options: college housing not available.
Campus security: 24-hour patrols.

APPLYING
Options: electronic application.
Application fee: $75.
Required: essay or personal statement, high school transcript, interview.

CONTACT
Los Angeles Film School, 6363 Sunset Boulevard, Hollywood, CA 90028. *Toll-free phone:* 877-952-3456.

Loyola Marymount University

Los Angeles, California
http://www.lmu.edu/

- **Independent Roman Catholic** comprehensive, founded 1911
- **Suburban** 142-acre campus with easy access to Los Angeles
- **Endowment** $457.5 million
- **Coed** 6,391 undergraduate students, 96% full-time, 56% women, 44% men
- **52% of applicants were admitted**

UNDERGRAD STUDENTS
6,164 full-time, 227 part-time. Students come from 80 other countries; 29% are from out of state; 7% Black or African American, non-Hispanic/Latino; 21% Hispanic/Latino; 10% Asian, non-Hispanic/Latino; 0.2% Native Hawaiian or other Pacific Islander, non-Hispanic/Latino; 0.1% American Indian or Alaska Native, non-Hispanic/Latino; 7% Two or more races, non-Hispanic/Latino; 10% international; 6% transferred in; 53% live on campus.

Freshmen:
Admission: 15,381 applied, 8,072 admitted, 1,446 enrolled. *Average high school GPA:* 3.8. *Test scores:* SAT evidence-based reading and writing scores over 500: 98%; SAT math scores over 500: 98%; ACT scores over 18: 100%; SAT evidence-based reading and writing scores over 600: 77%; SAT math scores over 600: 69%; ACT scores over 24: 94%; SAT evidence-based reading and writing scores over 700: 19%; SAT math scores over 700: 19%; ACT scores over 30: 38%.
Retention: 91% of full-time freshmen returned.

ACADEMICS
Calendar: semesters. *Degrees:* bachelor's, master's, doctoral, post-master's, and postbachelor's certificates.
Special study options: accelerated degree program, advanced placement credit, distance learning, double majors, English as a second language, honors programs, independent study, internships, part-time degree program, student-designed majors, study abroad. *ROTC:* Army (c), Air Force (b).

Unusual degree programs: 3-2 engineering.
Computers: 820 computers/terminals are available on campus for general student use. Students can access the following: campus intranet, computer help desk, free student e-mail accounts, online (class) grades, online (class) registration, online (class) schedules. Campuswide network is available. 100% of college-owned or -operated housing units are wired for high-speed Internet access. Wireless service is available via entire campus.
Library: William H. Hannon Library. Study areas open 24 hours, 5–7 days a week; students can reserve study rooms.

STUDENT LIFE
Housing options: coed, men-only, women-only, special housing for students with disabilities. Campus housing is university owned. Freshman applicants given priority for college housing.
Activities and organizations: drama/theater group, student-run newspaper, radio and television station, choral group, national fraternities, national sororities.
Athletics Member NCAA. All Division I. *Intercollegiate sports:* baseball M(s), basketball M(s)/W(s), cheerleading M/W, crew M/W(s), cross-country running M(s)/W(s), golf M(s), soccer M(s)/W(s), softball W(s), swimming and diving W(s), tennis M(s)/W(s), track and field M/W, volleyball W(s), water polo M(s)/W(s). *Intramural sports:* baseball M(c), basketball M/W(c), football M/W, ice hockey M(c), lacrosse M(c)/W(c), rugby M(c), sand volleyball M/W, skiing (downhill) M(c)/W(c), soccer M(c)/W(c), table tennis M/W, tennis M(c)/W(c), volleyball M(c)/W(c).
Campus security: 24-hour emergency response devices and patrols, late-night transport/escort service, controlled dormitory access.
Student services: health clinic, personal/psychological counseling.

COSTS & FINANCIAL AID
Costs (2017–18) *One-time required fee:* $250. *Comprehensive fee:* $60,826 includes full-time tuition ($45,460), mandatory fees ($676), and room and board ($14,690). Full-time tuition and fees vary according to reciprocity agreements. Part-time tuition: $1897 per credit hour. Part-time tuition and fees vary according to course load. *Required fees:* $8 per unit part-time, $64 per term part-time. *College room only:* $10,290. Room and board charges vary according to board plan and housing facility. *Payment plan:* installment. *Waivers:* employees or children of employees.
Financial Aid Of all full-time matriculated undergraduates who enrolled in 2016, 4,322 applied for aid, 3,226 were judged to have need, 666 had their need fully met. 1,384 Federal Work-Study jobs (averaging $1949). 2,285 state and other part-time jobs (averaging $2053). In 2016, 1617 non-need-based awards were made. *Average percent of need met:* 65. *Average financial aid package:* $29,281. *Average need-based loan:* $5688. *Average need-based gift aid:* $20,916. *Average non-need-based aid:* $11,113. *Average indebtedness upon graduation:* $32,560.

APPLYING
Standardized Tests *Required:* SAT or ACT (for admission).
Options: electronic application, early admission, early decision, early action, deferred entrance.
Application fee: $60.
Required: essay or personal statement, high school transcript, 1 letter of recommendation. *Required for some:* portfolio or audition required for animation, dance, music, and theatre arts programs, portfolio optional for production (film and television) and studio arts programs. *Recommended:* portfolio or audition required for animation, dance, music, and theatre arts programs, portfolio optional for production (film and television) and studio arts programs.
Application deadlines: 1/15 (freshmen), 3/15 (transfers), 11/1 (early action).
Early decision deadline: 11/1.
Notification: continuous (freshmen), continuous (transfers), 12/1 (early decision), 12/20 (early action).

CONTACT
Loyola Marymount University, One LMU Drive, Los Angeles, CA 90045-2659. *Phone:* 310-338-2750. *Toll-free phone:* 800-LMU-INFO.

Marymount California University

Rancho Palos Verdes, California
http://www.marymountcalifornia.edu/

- **Independent Roman Catholic** comprehensive, founded 1932
- **Suburban** 26-acre campus with easy access to Los Angeles
- **Endowment** $10.7 million
- **Coed** 935 undergraduate students, 95% full-time, 50% women, 50% men
- **Minimally difficult** entrance level, 83% of applicants were admitted

UNDERGRAD STUDENTS
892 full-time, 43 part-time. Students come from 26 states and territories; 33 other countries; 9% are from out of state; 8% Black or African American, non-Hispanic/Latino; 41% Hispanic/Latino; 5% Asian, non-Hispanic/Latino; 0.3% Native Hawaiian or other Pacific Islander, non-Hispanic/Latino; 0.4% American Indian or Alaska Native, non-Hispanic/Latino; 2% Two or more races, non-Hispanic/Latino; 7% Race/ethnicity unknown; 17% international; 12% transferred in; 36% live on campus.

Freshmen:
Admission: 1,683 applied, 1,391 admitted, 236 enrolled. *Average high school GPA:* 3.0. *Test scores:* SAT evidence-based reading and writing scores over 500: 46%; SAT math scores over 500: 30%; ACT scores over 18: 69%; SAT evidence-based reading and writing scores over 600: 8%; SAT math scores over 600: 7%; ACT scores over 24: 16%; SAT evidence-based reading and writing scores over 700: 2%; SAT math scores over 700: 2%; ACT scores over 30: 3%.

Retention: 63% of full-time freshmen returned.

FACULTY
Total: 99, 37% full-time, 40% with terminal degrees.
Student/faculty ratio: 16:1.

ACADEMICS
Calendar: semesters. *Degrees:* associate, bachelor's, and master's.

Special study options: academic remediation for entering students, accelerated degree program, adult/continuing education programs, advanced placement credit, cooperative education, distance learning, English as a second language, honors programs, independent study, internships, off-campus study, part-time degree program, services for LD students, study abroad, summer session for credit.

Unusual degree programs: 3-2 business administration.

Computers: 210 computers/terminals are available on campus for general student use. Students can access the following: campus intranet, computer help desk, free student e-mail accounts, online (class) grades, online (class) registration, online (class) schedules. Campuswide network is available. 100% of college-owned or -operated housing units are wired for high-speed Internet access. Wireless service is available via entire campus.
Library: College Library plus 1 other. *Books:* 23,246 (physical), 135,971 (digital/electronic); *Serial titles:* 255 (physical), 30,329 (digital/electronic); *Databases:* 51. Weekly public service hours: 60; students can reserve study rooms.

STUDENT LIFE
Housing options: coed. Campus housing is university owned. Freshman applicants given priority for college housing.

Activities and organizations: drama/theater group, choral group, Latinos Unidos, Student Veterans Organization, Marymount Pride, Black Student Union, Society for Advancement of Management (SAM).

Athletics Member NAIA. *Intercollegiate sports:* baseball M(s), golf M(s)/W(s), lacrosse M(s)/W(s), soccer M(s)/W(s), track and field M(s). *Intramural sports:* basketball M/W, golf M/W, lacrosse M/W, soccer M/W, softball M/W, swimming and diving M/W, track and field M/W, volleyball M/W.

Campus security: 24-hour emergency response devices and patrols, late-night transport/escort service, controlled dormitory access.

Student services: health clinic, personal/psychological counseling.

COSTS & FINANCIAL AID
Costs (2018–19) *One-time required fee:* $300. *Comprehensive fee:* $50,296 includes full-time tuition ($34,134), mandatory fees ($1750), and room and board ($14,412). Part-time tuition: $1475 per credit hour. *Required fees:* $600 per year part-time. *College room only:* $9004. Room and board charges vary according to board plan and housing facility.

Payment plan: installment. *Waivers:* senior citizens and employees or children of employees.

Financial Aid Of all full-time matriculated undergraduates who enrolled in 2017, 631 applied for aid, 626 were judged to have need, 156 had their need fully met. In 2017, 18 non-need-based awards were made. *Average percent of need met:* 81. *Average financial aid package:* $34,826. *Average need-based loan:* $4396. *Average need-based gift aid:* $23,634. *Average non-need-based aid:* $14,142. *Average indebtedness upon graduation:* $31,562. *Financial aid deadline:* 2/15.

APPLYING
Standardized Tests *Recommended:* SAT or ACT (for admission).
Options: electronic application, early admission, deferred entrance.
Application fee: $50.
Required: high school transcript. *Required for some:* essay or personal statement, interview. *Recommended:* minimum 2.0 GPA.
Application deadlines: 8/15 (freshmen), 8/15 (transfers).
Notification: continuous until 9/1 (freshmen), continuous until 9/1 (transfers).

CONTACT
Meshach Puerto, Assistant Director of Admissions, Marymount California University, 30800 Palos Verdes Drive East, Rancho Palos Verdes, CA 90275. *Phone:* 310-377-5501 Ext. 7378. *Fax:* 310-303-7698. *E-mail:* mpuerto@marymountcalifornia.edu.

The Master's University

Santa Clarita, California
http://www.masters.edu/

- **Independent nondenominational** comprehensive, founded 1927
- **Suburban** 110-acre campus with easy access to Los Angeles
- **Endowment** $15.4 million
- **Coed** 1,340 undergraduate students, 73% full-time, 46% women, 54% men
- **Moderately difficult** entrance level, 66% of applicants were admitted

UNDERGRAD STUDENTS
975 full-time, 365 part-time. Students come from 40 states and territories; 25 other countries; 36% are from out of state; 2% Black or African American, non-Hispanic/Latino; 10% Hispanic/Latino; 5% Asian, non-Hispanic/Latino; 0.1% Native Hawaiian or other Pacific Islander, non-Hispanic/Latino; 0.1% American Indian or Alaska Native, non-Hispanic/Latino; 6% Two or more races, non-Hispanic/Latino; 10% Race/ethnicity unknown; 4% international; 7% transferred in; 74% live on campus.

Freshmen:
Admission: 617 applied, 406 admitted, 164 enrolled. *Average high school GPA:* 3.7. *Test scores:* SAT evidence-based reading and writing scores over 500: 87%; SAT math scores over 500: 80%; ACT scores over 18: 97%; SAT evidence-based reading and writing scores over 600: 45%; SAT math scores over 600: 28%; ACT scores over 24: 48%; SAT evidence-based reading and writing scores over 700: 11%; SAT math scores over 700: 7%; ACT scores over 30: 13%.

Retention: 85% of full-time freshmen returned.

FACULTY
Total: 212, 24% full-time, 33% with terminal degrees.
Student/faculty ratio: 12:1.

ACADEMICS
Calendar: semesters. *Degrees:* bachelor's, master's, and doctoral.

Special study options: academic remediation for entering students, accelerated degree program, adult/continuing education programs, advanced placement credit, cooperative education, distance learning, double majors, external degree program, independent study, internships, part-time degree program, services for LD students, study abroad, summer session for credit. *ROTC:* Army (c), Air Force (c).

Computers: 57 computers/terminals are available on campus for general student use. Students can access the following: campus intranet, computer help desk, free student e-mail accounts, online (class) grades, online (class) registration, online (class) schedules. Campuswide network is available. 100% of college-owned or -operated housing units are wired for high-speed Internet access. Wireless service is available via entire campus.

Library: Robert L. Powell Library plus 1 other. *Books:* 98,047 (physical), 210,005 (digital/electronic); *Serial titles:* 657 (physical), 18,615 (digital/electronic); *Databases:* 33. Weekly public service hours: 74.

STUDENT LIFE

Housing options: on-campus residence required through junior year; men-only, women-only. Campus housing is university owned. Freshman campus housing is guaranteed.

Activities and organizations: drama/theater group, choral group, University Singers Choir, Summer Missions, Intramural Sports, Church Ministries, Theatre Arts Group.

Athletics Member NAIA. *Intercollegiate sports:* baseball M(s), basketball M(s)/W(s), cross-country running M(s)/W(s), golf M(s), soccer M(s)/W(s), track and field M(s)/W(s), volleyball W(s). *Intramural sports:* basketball M/W, football M/W, soccer M/W, volleyball M/W.

Campus security: 24-hour patrols.

Student services: health clinic, personal/psychological counseling.

COSTS & FINANCIAL AID

Costs (2018–19) *Comprehensive fee:* $36,590 includes full-time tuition ($24,950), mandatory fees ($440), and room and board ($11,200). Full-time tuition and fees vary according to class time, course load, location, and program. Part-time tuition: $1050 per credit hour. Part-time tuition and fees vary according to class time, course load, location, and program. *Room and board:* Room and board charges vary according to board plan. *Payment plan:* installment. *Waivers:* employees or children of employees.

Financial Aid Of all full-time matriculated undergraduates who enrolled in 2015, 878 applied for aid, 758 were judged to have need, 101 had their need fully met. 60 Federal Work-Study jobs (averaging $2577). 174 state and other part-time jobs (averaging $1904). In 2015, 143 non-need-based awards were made. *Average percent of need met:* 66. *Average financial aid package:* $22,088. *Average need-based loan:* $4249. *Average need-based gift aid:* $18,112. *Average non-need-based aid:* $9865. *Average indebtedness upon graduation:* $29,133.

APPLYING

Standardized Tests *Required:* SAT or ACT (for admission).

Options: electronic application, early admission, early action, deferred entrance.

Application fee: $40.

Required: essay or personal statement, high school transcript, minimum 2.8 GPA, 2 letters of recommendation. *Recommended:* interview.

Application deadlines: 9/1 (freshmen), 9/1 (transfers), 11/15 (early action).

Notification: continuous until 11/1 (freshmen), continuous until 3/2 (transfers), 12/1 (early action).

CONTACT

Mr. Dariu Dumitru, Director of Admissions, The Master's University, 21726 Placerita Canyon Road, Santa Clarita, CA 91321. *Phone:* 661-362-2363. *Toll-free phone:* 800-568-6248. *Fax:* 661-362-2718. *E-mail:* admissions@masters.edu.

Menlo College
Atherton, California
http://www.menlo.edu/

- **Independent** 4-year, founded 1927
- **Small-town** 45-acre campus with easy access to San Francisco
- **Endowment** $25.6 million
- **Coed**
- **Moderately difficult** entrance level

FACULTY
Student/faculty ratio: 14:1.

ACADEMICS
Calendar: semesters. *Degree:* bachelor's.
Library: Bowman Library. *Books:* 47,340 (physical), 17,379 (digital/electronic); *Serial titles:* 76 (physical); *Databases:* 42. Weekly public service hours: 95; students can reserve study rooms.

STUDENT LIFE

Housing options: on-campus residence required through sophomore year; coed, men-only, women-only. Campus housing is university owned.

Activities and organizations: student-run newspaper, International Club, Student Government, SERV, Finance Club, Hawaiian Club.

Athletics Member NAIA.

Campus security: 24-hour emergency response devices and patrols, controlled dormitory access.

Student services: personal/psychological counseling, women's center.

COSTS & FINANCIAL AID

Costs (2017–18) *Comprehensive fee:* $55,030 includes full-time tuition ($40,625), mandatory fees ($725), and room and board ($13,680). Part-time tuition: $1693 per unit. *Required fees:* $181 per term part-time. *Room and board:* Room and board charges vary according to housing facility.

Financial Aid Of all full-time matriculated undergraduates who enrolled in 2014, 522 applied for aid, 478 were judged to have need, 54 had their need fully met. 345 Federal Work-Study jobs (averaging $1024). In 2014, 168 non-need-based awards were made. *Average percent of need met:* 66. *Average financial aid package:* $28,874. *Average need-based loan:* $3741. *Average need-based gift aid:* $25,073. *Average non-need-based aid:* $12,737. *Average indebtedness upon graduation:* $29,943.

APPLYING

Standardized Tests *Required:* SAT or ACT (for admission).

Options: electronic application, early admission, early action, deferred entrance.

Application fee: $40.

Required: essay or personal statement, high school transcript, 1 letter of recommendation. *Recommended:* minimum 2.5 GPA, interview.

CONTACT

Priscila DeSouza, Associate Dean of Enrollment Management, Menlo College, 1000 El Camino Real, Atherton, CA 94027. *Phone:* 650-543-3786. *Toll-free phone:* 800-556-3656. *Fax:* 650-543-4496. *E-mail:* admissions@menlo.edu.

★ Mills College
Oakland, California
http://www.mills.edu/

- **Independent** comprehensive, founded 1852
- **Urban** 135-acre campus with easy access to San Francisco
- **Endowment** $184.9 million
- **Undergraduate: women only; graduate: coed** 768 undergraduate students, 96% full-time, 100% women
- **Moderately difficult** entrance level, 87% of applicants were admitted

UNDERGRAD STUDENTS

739 full-time, 29 part-time. Students come from 37 states and territories; 4 other countries; 19% are from out of state; 9% Black or African American, non-Hispanic/Latino; 28% Hispanic/Latino; 10% Asian, non-Hispanic/Latino; 0.1% Native Hawaiian or other Pacific Islander, non-Hispanic/Latino; 0.4% American Indian or Alaska Native, non-Hispanic/Latino; 9% Two or more races, non-Hispanic/Latino; 0.5% Race/ethnicity unknown; 0.9% international; 11% transferred in; 64% live on campus.

Freshmen:
Admission: 965 applied, 837 admitted, 174 enrolled. *Average high school GPA:* 3.5.
Retention: 77% of full-time freshmen returned.

FACULTY
Total: 174, 47% full-time, 72% with terminal degrees.
Student/faculty ratio: 10:1.

ACADEMICS
Calendar: semesters. *Degrees:* certificates, bachelor's, master's, doctoral, and postbachelor's certificates.

Special study options: accelerated degree program, adult/continuing education programs, advanced placement credit, cooperative education, double majors, independent study, internships, off-campus study, part-time degree program, services for LD students, student-designed majors, study abroad, summer session for credit. *ROTC:* Army (c).

Unusual degree programs: 3-2 engineering with University of Southern California; education, public policy, infant mental health, mathematics.

Computers: 335 computers/terminals and 3,000 ports are available on campus for general student use. Students can access the following: campus intranet, computer help desk, free student e-mail accounts, online (class) grades, online (class) registration, online (class) schedules, online degree audit. Campuswide network is available. 100% of college-owned or -operated housing units are wired for high-speed Internet access. Wireless service is available via entire campus.

Library: F. W. Olin Library. *Books:* 190,417 (physical), 156,636 (digital/electronic); *Serial titles:* 153 (physical), 51,607 (digital/electronic); *Databases:* 39. Weekly public service hours: 89; students can reserve study rooms.

STUDENT LIFE

Housing options: coed, women-only, cooperative, special housing for students with disabilities. Campus housing is university owned. Freshman campus housing is guaranteed.

Activities and organizations: drama/theater group, student-run newspaper, choral group, Associated Students of Mills College, The Campanil, The Mills Choir, Mujeres Unidas, Asian Pacific Islander Student Association.

Athletics Member NCAA. All Division III. *Intercollegiate sports:* crew W, cross-country running W, rowing W, soccer W, swimming and diving W, tennis W, volleyball W. *Intramural sports:* basketball W, cheerleading W(c), soccer W, softball W(c), track and field W(c), volleyball W.

Campus security: 24-hour emergency response devices and patrols, late-night transport/escort service, controlled dormitory access.

Student services: health clinic, personal/psychological counseling, women's center.

COSTS & FINANCIAL AID

Costs (2018–19) *Comprehensive fee:* $43,705 includes full-time tuition ($28,765), mandatory fees ($1492), and room and board ($13,448). Full-time tuition and fees vary according to course load. Part-time tuition: $1199 per semester hour. Part-time tuition and fees vary according to course load. *College room only:* $7064. Room and board charges vary according to board plan and housing facility. *Payment plan:* installment. *Waivers:* employees or children of employees.

Financial Aid Of all full-time matriculated undergraduates who enrolled in 2016, 697 applied for aid, 652 were judged to have need, 95 had their need fully met. 318 Federal Work-Study jobs (averaging $2667). 315 state and other part-time jobs (averaging $3376). In 2016, 33 non-need-based awards were made. *Average percent of need met:* 81. *Average financial aid package:* $42,502. *Average need-based loan:* $7141. *Average need-based gift aid:* $35,497. *Average non-need-based aid:* $20,894. *Average indebtedness upon graduation:* $33,327. *Financial aid deadline:* 2/15.

APPLYING

Options: electronic application, early admission, early action, deferred entrance.

Application fee: $50.

Required: essay or personal statement, high school transcript, 1 letter of recommendation, college transcripts. *Recommended:* interview.

Application deadlines: 1/15 (freshmen), 3/1 (transfers), 11/15 (early action).

Notification: 3/30 (freshmen), 4/1 (transfers), 12/1 (early action).

CONTACT

Mrs. Robynne Royster, Director of Undergraduate Admissions, Mills College, 5000 MacArthur Boulevard, Oakland, CA 94613-1301. *Phone:* 510-430-2135. *Toll-free phone:* 800-87-MILLS. *Fax:* 510-430-3314. *E-mail:* admission@mills.edu.

See below for display ad and page 1344 for the College Close-Up.

Mount Saint Mary's University
Los Angeles, California
http://www.msmu.edu/

- **Independent Roman Catholic** comprehensive, founded 1925
- **Urban** 56-acre campus with easy access to Los Angeles
- **Endowment** $138.5 million
- **Coed, primarily women** 2,601 undergraduate students, 79% full-time, 94% women, 6% men

UNDERGRAD STUDENTS

2,054 full-time, 547 part-time. Students come from 12 states and territories; 16 other countries; 3% are from out of state; 7% Black or African American, non-Hispanic/Latino; 64% Hispanic/Latino; 15% Asian, non-Hispanic/Latino; 0.5% Native Hawaiian or other Pacific Islander, non-Hispanic/Latino; 0.2% American Indian or Alaska Native, non-Hispanic/Latino; 2% Two or more races, non-Hispanic/Latino; 4% Race/ethnicity unknown; 0.1% international; 2% transferred in; 24% live on campus.

Freshmen:

Admission: 496 enrolled. *Average high school GPA:* 3.4. *Test scores:* SAT evidence-based reading and writing scores over 500: 64%; SAT math scores over 500: 55%; ACT scores over 18: 65%; SAT evidence-based reading and writing scores over 600: 14%; SAT math scores over 600: 9%; ACT scores over 24: 14%.

Retention: 76% of full-time freshmen returned.

FACULTY

Total: 453, 23% full-time, 41% with terminal degrees.

Student/faculty ratio: 11:1.

ACADEMICS

Calendar: semesters. *Degrees:* associate, bachelor's, master's, doctoral, and post-master's certificates.

Special study options: academic remediation for entering students, accelerated degree program, advanced placement credit, cooperative education, distance learning, double majors, English as a second language, honors programs, independent study, internships, off-campus study, part-time degree program, services for LD students, student-designed majors, study abroad, summer session for credit.

Computers: 170 computers/terminals are available on campus for general student use. Students can access the following: campus intranet, computer help desk, free student e-mail accounts, online (class) grades, online (class) registration, online (class) schedules. Campuswide network is available. 100% of college-owned or -operated housing units are wired for high-speed Internet access. Wireless service is available via entire campus.

Library: Charles Willard Coe Library plus 1 other. *Books:* 88,758 (physical), 396,855 (digital/electronic); *Serial titles:* 168 (physical), 39,316 (digital/electronic); *Databases:* 215. Weekly public service hours: 91; study areas open 24 hours, 5–7 days a week.

STUDENT LIFE

Housing options: men-only, women-only. Campus housing is university owned. Freshman applicants given priority for college housing.

Activities and organizations: drama/theater group, student-run newspaper, choral group, Sakura Society, Pangkat Pilipino, MSMU Women in Film, Athenian Print, Na Pua O Ka'Aina (NPOKA), national sororities.

Athletics *Intramural sports:* basketball M/W, soccer M/W, softball M/W, swimming and diving M/W, tennis M/W, volleyball M/W.

Campus security: 24-hour emergency response devices and patrols, late-night transport/escort service, controlled dormitory access.

Student services: health clinic, personal/psychological counseling, women's center.

COSTS & FINANCIAL AID

Costs (2018–19) *Comprehensive fee:* $53,405 includes full-time tuition ($40,018), mandatory fees ($1152), and room and board ($12,235). Full-time tuition and fees vary according to course load, degree level, and program. Part-time tuition and fees vary according to course load, degree level, and program. *Room and board:* Room and board charges vary according to board plan and housing facility. *Payment plan:* installment. *Waivers:* employees or children of employees.

Financial Aid Of all full-time matriculated undergraduates who enrolled in 2017, 2,375 applied for aid, 2,310 were judged to have need, 201 had their need fully met. In 2017, 162 non-need-based awards were made. *Average percent of need met:* 41. *Average financial aid package:* $27,877. *Average need-based loan:* $4384. *Average need-based gift aid:* $19,318. *Average non-need-based aid:* $11,774. *Average indebtedness upon graduation:* $35,161.

APPLYING

Standardized Tests *Required for some:* SAT or ACT (for admission).

Required: essay or personal statement, high school transcript, minimum 2.5 GPA, 1 letter of recommendation. *Recommended:* 2 letters of recommendation, interview.

CONTACT

Erika Yamasaki, Director of Admissions, Mount Saint Mary's University, 12001 Chalon Road, Los Angeles, CA 90049-1599. *Phone:* 800-999-9893. *Toll-free phone:* 800-999-9893. *Fax:* 310-954-4259. *E-mail:* admissions@msmu.edu.

★ Mt. Sierra College

Monrovia, California

http://www.mtsierra.edu/

CONTACT

Mt. Sierra College, 800 Royal Oaks Drive, Monrovia, CA 91016. *Phone:* 888-486-9818. *Toll-free phone:* 888-828-8000.

See next page for display ad and page 1354 for the College Close-Up.

Musicians Institute

Hollywood, California

http://www.mi.edu/

CONTACT

Musicians Institute, 1655 North McCadden Place, Hollywood, CA 90028. *Phone:* 323-860-4345. *Toll-free phone:* 800-255-PLAY.

National University

La Jolla, California

http://www.nu.edu/

- **Independent** comprehensive, founded 1971, part of National University System
- **Urban** campus with easy access to San Diego
- **Coed** 7,877 undergraduate students, 37% full-time, 55% women, 45% men
- **Noncompetitive** entrance level

UNDERGRAD STUDENTS

2,899 full-time, 4,978 part-time. Students come from 49 states and territories; 53 other countries; 10% are from out of state; 9% Black or African American, non-Hispanic/Latino; 25% Hispanic/Latino; 9% Asian, non-Hispanic/Latino; 1% Native Hawaiian or other Pacific Islander, non-Hispanic/Latino; 0.5% American Indian or Alaska Native, non-Hispanic/Latino; 5% Two or more races, non-Hispanic/Latino; 12% Race/ethnicity unknown; 2% international; 10% transferred in.

Freshmen:

Admission: 146 enrolled.

FACULTY

Total: 1,325, 22% full-time, 45% with terminal degrees.

Student/faculty ratio: 17:1.

ACADEMICS

Calendar: continuous. *Degrees:* certificates, associate, bachelor's, master's, post-master's, and postbachelor's certificates.

Special study options: academic remediation for entering students, accelerated degree program, adult/continuing education programs, advanced placement credit, cooperative education, distance learning, double majors, English as a second language, independent study, internships, off-campus study, part-time degree program, services for LD students, study abroad, summer session for credit. *ROTC:* Army (c), Air Force (c).

Computers: 2,800 computers/terminals are available on campus for general student use. Students can access the following: computer help desk, free student e-mail accounts, online (class) grades, online (class) registration, online (class) schedules. Campuswide network is available. Wireless service is available via entire campus.

Library: National University Library. *Books:* 212,626 (physical), 319,622 (digital/electronic); *Serial titles:* 3,490 (physical), 92,431 (digital/electronic); *Databases:* 190. Weekly public service hours: 72; students can reserve study rooms.

STUDENT LIFE
Housing options: college housing not available.

Campus security: 24-hour emergency response devices and patrols, late-night transport/escort service.

COSTS & FINANCIAL AID
Costs (2018–19) *One-time required fee:* $60. *Tuition:* $13,032 full-time, $362 per unit part-time. *Payment plan:* deferred payment. *Waivers:* employees or children of employees.

Financial Aid Of all full-time matriculated undergraduates who enrolled in 2015, 4,546 applied for aid, 3,863 were judged to have need, 235 had their need fully met. In 2015, 21 non-need-based awards were made. *Average percent of need met:* 48. *Average financial aid package:* $7768. *Average need-based loan:* $5505. *Average need-based gift aid:* $3240. *Average non-need-based aid:* $2076. *Average indebtedness upon graduation:* $52,986.

APPLYING
Options: electronic application, deferred entrance.

Application fee: $60.

Required: high school transcript, minimum 2.0 GPA, interview. *Required for some:* essay or personal statement.

Application deadlines: rolling (freshmen), rolling (transfers).

Notification: continuous (freshmen), continuous (transfers).

CONTACT
National University, 11255 North Torrey Pines Road, La Jolla, CA 92037-1011. *Toll-free phone:* 800-628-8648.

NewSchool of Architecture and Design
San Diego, California
http://www.newschoolarch.edu/

CONTACT
Kirk Nielson, Director of Enrollment and Field Recruitment, NewSchool of Architecture and Design, 1249 F Street, San Diego, CA 92101. *Phone:* 619-684-8841. *Toll-free phone:* 800-490-7081. *E-mail:* knielson@newschoolarch.edu.

New York Film Academy
Burbank, California
http://www.nyfa.edu/
- **Independent** comprehensive, founded 1992
- **Suburban** campus with easy access to Los Angeles, New York, Miami
- **Coed**

ACADEMICS
Degrees: certificates, associate, bachelor's, and master's.

APPLYING
Standardized Tests *Required:* SAT or ACT (for admission).

Application fee: $50.

Required: essay or personal statement, high school transcript, 2 letters of recommendation, portfolio.

CONTACT
Admissions Office, New York Film Academy, 3300 Riverside Drive, Burbank, CA 91505. *Phone:* 818-333-3558. *Fax:* 818-333 3557. *E-mail:* studios@nyfa.edu.

Northcentral University
San Diego, California
http://www.ncu.edu/
- **Proprietary** upper-level
- **Coed** 89 undergraduate students, 16% full-time, 72% women, 28% men
- **Minimally difficult** entrance level

UNDERGRAD STUDENTS
14 full-time, 75 part-time. Students come from 29 states and territories; 1 other country; 21% Black or African American, non-Hispanic/Latino; 9% Hispanic/Latino; 2% Asian, non-Hispanic/Latino; 1% American Indian or Alaska Native, non-Hispanic/Latino; 3% Two or more races, non-Hispanic/Latino; 35% Race/ethnicity unknown; 15% transferred in.

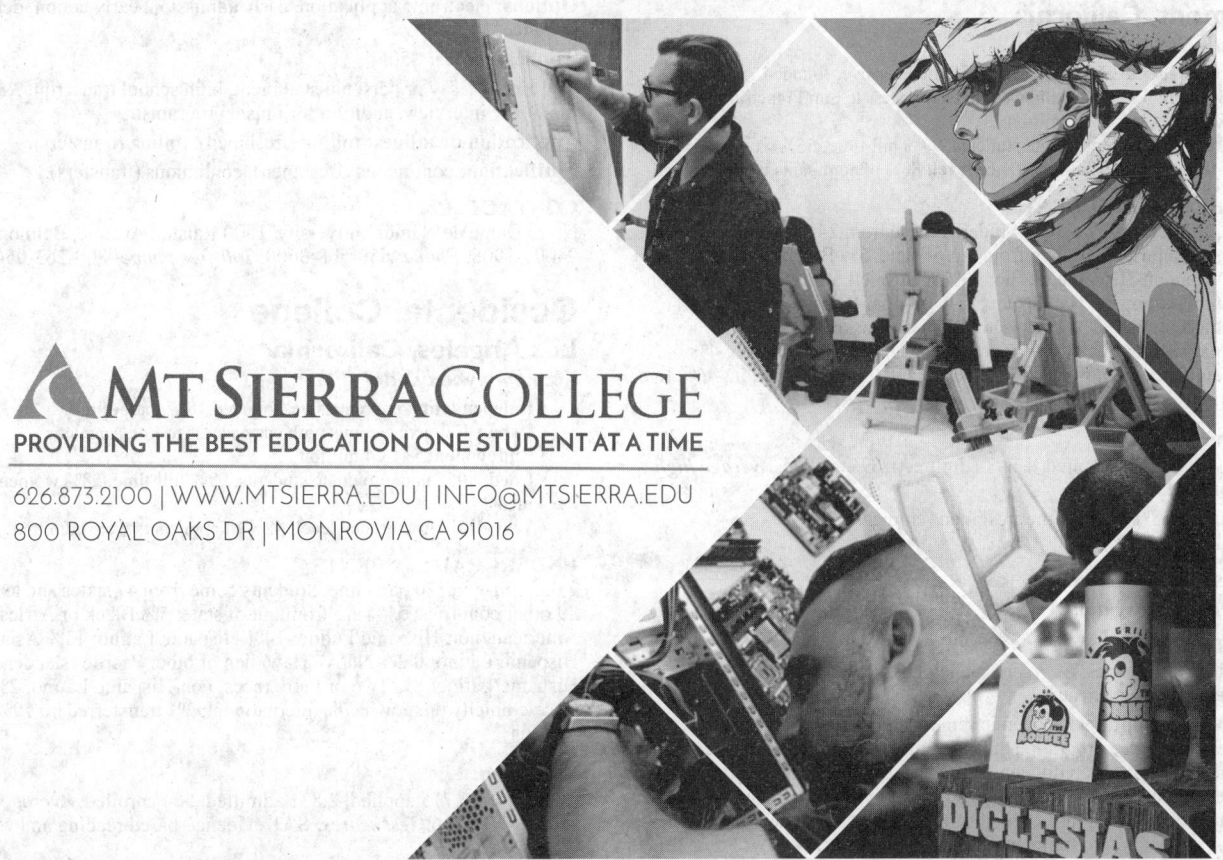
A ★ indicates that the school has detailed information with a Premium Profile on Petersons.com.

www.petersons.com 133

FACULTY

Total: 478, 19% full-time, 100% with terminal degrees.

ACADEMICS

Calendar: continuous. *Degrees:* bachelor's, master's, doctoral, post-master's, and postbachelor's certificates (offers only distance learning programs).

Special study options: accelerated degree program, distance learning, part-time degree program, services for LD students.

Computers: Students can access the following: free student e-mail accounts, online (class) grades, online (class) registration.

Library: Northcentral University Library (Virtual). *Databases:* 123. Weekly public service hours: 79.

COSTS

Costs (2017–18) *One-time required fee:* $450. *Tuition:* $10,680 full-time, $1335 per course part-time. No tuition increase for student's term of enrollment. *Required fees:* $1335 per course part-time. *Payment plans:* tuition prepayment, installment. *Waivers:* employees or children of employees.

APPLYING

Options: electronic application.

Notification: continuous (transfers).

CONTACT

Northcentral University, 2488 Historic Decatur Road, Suite 100, San Diego, CA 92106. *Phone:* 866-776-0331. *Toll-free phone:* 866-776-0331.

Northwestern Polytechnic University

Fremont, California

http://www.npu.edu/

CONTACT

Mr. Michael Tang, Admission Officer, Northwestern Polytechnic University, 47671 Westinghouse Drive, Fremont, CA 94539. *Phone:* 510-592-9688 Ext. 15. *Fax:* 510-657-8975. *E-mail:* admission@npu.edu.

Notre Dame de Namur University

Belmont, California

http://www.ndnu.edu/

- **Independent Roman Catholic** comprehensive, founded 1851
- **Suburban** 50-acre campus with easy access to San Francisco
- **Endowment** $22.5 million
- **Coed** 937 undergraduate students, 77% full-time, 66% women, 34% men
- **Moderately difficult** entrance level, 80% of applicants were admitted

UNDERGRAD STUDENTS

722 full-time, 215 part-time. Students come from 24 states and territories; 27 other countries; 10% are from out of state; 6% Black or African American, non-Hispanic/Latino; 43% Hispanic/Latino; 11% Asian, non-Hispanic/Latino; 2% Native Hawaiian or other Pacific Islander, non-Hispanic/Latino; 0.2% American Indian or Alaska Native, non-Hispanic/Latino; 5% Two or more races, non-Hispanic/Latino; 4% Race/ethnicity unknown; 6% international; 10% transferred in; 46% live on campus.

Freshmen:

Admission: 2,056 applied, 1,647 admitted, 169 enrolled. *Average high school GPA:* 3.1.

Retention: 68% of full-time freshmen returned.

FACULTY

Total: 230, 23% full-time.

Student/faculty ratio: 11:1.

ACADEMICS

Calendar: semesters. *Degrees:* bachelor's, master's, doctoral, and postbachelor's certificates.

Special study options: academic remediation for entering students, accelerated degree program, adult/continuing education programs, advanced placement credit, cooperative education, double majors, English as a second language, independent study, internships, off-campus study, part-time degree program, services for LD students, student-designed majors, study abroad, summer session for credit. *ROTC:* Air Force (c).

Computers: 100 computers/terminals and 100 ports are available on campus for general student use. Students can access the following: campus intranet, computer help desk, free student e-mail accounts, online (class) grades, online (class) registration, online (class) schedules. Campuswide network is available. Wireless service is available via classrooms, computer centers, computer labs, dorm rooms, learning centers, libraries, student centers.

Library: The Carl Gellert and Celia Berta Gellert Library plus 1 other. *Books:* 88,990 (physical), 194,534 (digital/electronic); *Databases:* 50.

STUDENT LIFE

Housing options: on-campus residence required through sophomore year; coed. Campus housing is university owned. Freshman campus housing is guaranteed.

Activities and organizations: drama/theater group, student-run newspaper, choral group.

Athletics Member NCAA. All Division II. *Intercollegiate sports:* basketball M(s)/W(s), cross-country running M(s)/W(s), golf M(s), lacrosse M(s), soccer M(s)/W(s), softball W(s), track and field M(s)/W(s), volleyball W(s).

Campus security: 24-hour emergency response devices and patrols, late-night transport/escort service, controlled dormitory access.

Student services: health clinic, personal/psychological counseling.

COSTS & FINANCIAL AID

Costs (2018–19) *Comprehensive fee:* $49,844 includes full-time tuition ($34,910), mandatory fees ($440), and room and board ($14,494). Part-time tuition: $1126 per credit hour. *College room only:* $9312. *Payment plan:* installment. *Waivers:* employees or children of employees.

Financial Aid Of all full-time matriculated undergraduates who enrolled in 2014, 773 applied for aid, 726 were judged to have need, 42 had their need fully met. In 2014, 40 non-need-based awards were made. *Average percent of need met:* 58. *Average financial aid package:* $24,678. *Average need-based loan:* $4921. *Average need-based gift aid:* $20,114. *Average non-need-based aid:* $10,524. *Average indebtedness upon graduation:* $31,348.

APPLYING

Standardized Tests *Required:* SAT or ACT (for admission).

Options: electronic application, early admission, early action, deferred entrance.

Application fee: $50.

Required: essay or personal statement, high school transcript. *Required for some:* interview, audition for music programs.

Application deadlines: rolling (freshmen), rolling (transfers).

Notification: continuous (freshmen), continuous (transfers).

CONTACT

Notre Dame de Namur University, 1500 Ralston Avenue, Belmont, CA 94002-1908. *Phone:* 650-508-3600. *Toll-free phone:* 800-263-0545.

Occidental College

Los Angeles, California

http://www.oxy.edu/

- **Independent** comprehensive, founded 1887, part of n/a
- **Urban** 120-acre campus with easy access to Los Angeles
- **Endowment** $413.4 million
- **Coed** 2,055 undergraduate students, 99% full-time, 58% women, 42% men
- **Very difficult** entrance level, 42% of applicants were admitted

UNDERGRAD STUDENTS

2,035 full-time, 20 part-time. Students come from 47 states and territories; 29 other countries; 51% are from out of state; 5% Black or African American, non-Hispanic/Latino; 14% Hispanic/Latino; 13% Asian, non-Hispanic/Latino; 0.2% Native Hawaiian or other Pacific Islander, non-Hispanic/Latino; 8% Two or more races, non-Hispanic/Latino; 2% Race/ethnicity unknown; 7% international; 2% transferred in; 79% live on campus.

Freshmen:

Admission: 6,775 applied, 2,831 admitted, 564 enrolled. *Average high school GPA:* 3.6. *Test scores:* SAT evidence-based reading and writing

scores over 500: 100%; SAT math scores over 500: 100%; ACT scores over 18: 100%; SAT evidence-based reading and writing scores over 600: 96%; SAT math scores over 600: 91%; ACT scores over 24: 98%; SAT evidence-based reading and writing scores over 700: 46%; SAT math scores over 700: 40%; ACT scores over 30: 51%.

Retention: 91% of full-time freshmen returned.

FACULTY
Total: 277, 68% full-time.
Student/faculty ratio: 9:1.

ACADEMICS
Calendar: semesters. *Degrees:* diplomas, bachelor's, and master's.

Special study options: advanced placement credit, double majors, honors programs, independent study, internships, off-campus study, services for LD students, student-designed majors, study abroad. *ROTC:* Army (c), Air Force (c).

Unusual degree programs: 3-2 engineering with California Institute of Technology, Columbia University; law with Columbia University, biotechnology with Keck Graduate Institute.

Computers: 200 computers/terminals are available on campus for general student use. Students can access the following: campus intranet, computer help desk, free student e-mail accounts, online (class) grades, online (class) registration, online (class) schedules. Campuswide network is available. 98% of college-owned or -operated housing units are wired for high-speed Internet access. Wireless service is available via entire campus.

Library: Mary Norton Clapp Library and Academic Commons plus 2 others. Study areas open 24 hours, 5–7 days a week; students can reserve study rooms.

STUDENT LIFE
Housing options: on-campus residence required through junior year; coed, women-only. Campus housing is university owned. Freshman campus housing is guaranteed.

Activities and organizations: drama/theater group, student-run newspaper, radio station, choral group, Dance Production, Hiking Club, Ski and Snowboard Club, Black Student Alliance, Asian American Tutorial Project, national fraternities, national sororities.

Athletics Member NCAA. All Division III. *Intercollegiate sports:* baseball M, basketball M/W, cross-country running M/W, football M, golf M/W, lacrosse M(c)/W, rugby M(c)/W(c), soccer M/W, softball W, swimming and diving M/W, tennis M/W, track and field M/W, ultimate Frisbee M(c)/W(c), volleyball W, water polo M/W. *Intramural sports:* basketball M/W, cheerleading W(c), ice hockey M(c), soccer M/W.

Campus security: 24-hour emergency response devices and patrols, late-night transport/escort service, controlled dormitory access, Surveillance cameras; emergency notification system.

Student services: health clinic, personal/psychological counseling, women's center.

COSTS & FINANCIAL AID
Costs (2017–18) *Comprehensive fee:* $67,806 includes full-time tuition ($52,260), mandatory fees ($578), and room and board ($14,968). Part-time tuition: $2177 per unit. Part-time tuition and fees vary according to course load. *Required fees:* $578 per year part-time. *College room only:* $8518. Room and board charges vary according to board plan. *Payment plans:* tuition prepayment, installment. *Waivers:* employees or children of employees.

Financial Aid Of all full-time matriculated undergraduates who enrolled in 2016, 1,320 applied for aid, 1,139 were judged to have need, 1,138 had their need fully met. 776 Federal Work-Study jobs (averaging $2747). 170 state and other part-time jobs (averaging $1364). In 2016, 245 non-need-based awards were made. *Average percent of need met:* 100. *Average financial aid package:* $47,741. *Average need-based loan:* $6074. *Average need-based gift aid:* $40,172. *Average non-need-based aid:* $11,614. *Average indebtedness upon graduation:* $32,008. *Financial aid deadline:* 1/15.

APPLYING
Standardized Tests *Required:* SAT or ACT (for admission). *Recommended:* SAT Subject Tests (for admission).

Options: electronic application, early admission, early decision, deferred entrance.

Application fee: $65.

Required: essay or personal statement, high school transcript, 2 letters of recommendation. *Recommended:* interview.

Application deadlines: 1/15 (freshmen), 4/1 (transfers).

Early decision deadline: 11/15 (for plan 1), 1/1 (for plan 2).

Notification: 3/25 (freshmen), 5/1 (transfers), 12/15 (early decision plan 1), 2/1 (early decision plan 2).

CONTACT
Mr. Vince Cuseo, Vice President of Enrollment and Dean of the College, Occidental College, 1600 Campus Road, Los Angeles, CA 90041. *Phone:* 323-259-2700. *Toll-free phone:* 800-825-5262. *Fax:* 323-341-4875. *E-mail:* admission@oxy.edu.

Otis College of Art and Design
Los Angeles, California
http://www.otis.edu/

CONTACT
Otis College of Art and Design, 9045 Lincoln Boulevard, Los Angeles, CA 90045-9785. *Phone:* 310-665-2577. *Toll-free phone:* 800-527-OTIS.

Pacific College
Costa Mesa, California
http://www.pacific-college.edu/

CONTACT
Pacific College, 3160 Red Hill Avenue, Costa Mesa, CA 92626.

Pacific Oaks College
Pasadena, California
http://www.pacificoaks.edu/

CONTACT
Ms. Augusta Pickens, Office of Admissions, Pacific Oaks College, 5 Westmoreland Place, Pasadena, CA 91103. *Phone:* 626-397-1349. *Toll-free phone:* 877-314-2380. *Fax:* 626-666-1220. *E-mail:* admissions@pacificoaks.edu.

Pacific States University
Los Angeles, California
http://www.psuca.edu/
- **Independent** comprehensive, founded 1928
- **Urban** 1-acre campus
- **Coed**
- **Noncompetitive** entrance level

FACULTY
Student/faculty ratio: 5:1.

ACADEMICS
Calendar: quarters. *Degrees:* certificates, diplomas, bachelor's, master's, doctoral, and postbachelor's certificates.
Library: University Library plus 1 other. Students can reserve study rooms.

STUDENT LIFE
Housing options: coed. Campus housing is university owned.
Campus security: patrols by trained security personnel during campus hours.

APPLYING
Standardized Tests *Required for some:* TOEFL or IELTS. *Recommended:* SAT or ACT (for admission).

Options: electronic application, deferred entrance.

Application fee: $100.

Required: high school transcript, minimum 2.5 GPA. *Recommended:* essay or personal statement.

CONTACT
Mr. Maawiya Ayeva, Director of Admissions, Pacific States University, 3424 Wilshire Boulevard, 12th Floor, Los Angeles, CA 90010. *Phone:*

323-731-2383 Ext. 202. *Toll-free phone:* 888-200-0383. *Fax:* 323-731-7276. *E-mail:* admissions@psuca.edu.

Pacific Union College
Angwin, California
http://www.puc.edu/

CONTACT
Mr. Craig Philpott, Associate Director, Admissions, Pacific Union College, Enrollment Services, One Angwin Avenue, Angwin, CA 94508. *Phone:* 800-862-7080. *Toll-free phone:* 800-862-7080. *Fax:* 707-965-6671. *E-mail:* enroll@puc.edu.

Palo Alto University
Palo Alto, California
http://www.paloaltou.edu/
- **Independent** upper-level
- **Rural** campus with easy access to San Francisco Bay Area/Silicon Valley
- **Endowment** $2.4 million
- **Coed** 121 undergraduate students, 93% full-time, 64% women, 36% men

UNDERGRAD STUDENTS
113 full-time, 8 part-time. Students come from 1 other state; 4 other countries; 0.8% Black or African American, non-Hispanic/Latino; 7% Hispanic/Latino; 9% Native Hawaiian or other Pacific Islander, non-Hispanic/Latino; 0.8% American Indian or Alaska Native, non-Hispanic/Latino; 2% Two or more races, non-Hispanic/Latino; 68% Race/ethnicity unknown; 7% international; 49% transferred in.

FACULTY
Total: 25, 8% full-time, 64% with terminal degrees.
Student/faculty ratio: 12:1.

ACADEMICS
Calendar: quarters. *Degrees:* bachelor's, master's, and doctoral.

Special study options: academic remediation for entering students, distance learning, internships, services for LD students, summer session for credit.

Computers: 14 computers/terminals are available on campus for general student use. Students can access the following: campus intranet, computer help desk, free student e-mail accounts, online (class) grades, online (class) registration, online (class) schedules. Campuswide network is available. Wireless service is available via entire campus.
Library: Omar Seddiqui Research Library. *Books:* 1,771 (physical), 257,269 (digital/electronic); *Serial titles:* 2 (physical), 221,448 (digital/electronic); *Databases:* 53. Weekly public service hours: 71; students can reserve study rooms.

STUDENT LIFE
Housing options: college housing not available.
Student services: personal/psychological counseling.

COSTS
Costs (2018–19) *Tuition:* $17,451 full-time. Full-time tuition and fees vary according to class time. No tuition increase for student's term of enrollment. *Required fees:* $5301 full-time. *Payment plan:* installment. *Waivers:* employees or children of employees.

APPLYING
Options: electronic application, deferred entrance.
Notification: continuous (transfers).

CONTACT
Mr. Lenard Wilson, Assistant Director of Undergraduate Admissions, Palo Alto University, 1791 Arastradero Road, Palo Alto, CA 94304. *Phone:* 650-417-2050. *Toll-free phone:* 800-818-6136. *E-mail:* undergrad@paloaltou.edu.

Patten University
Oakland, California
http://patten.edu/

CONTACT
Ms. Kim Guerra, Director of Admissions, Patten University, 2433 Coolidge Avenue, Oakland, CA 94601-2699. *Phone:* 510-261-8500 Ext. 7763. *Toll-free phone:* 877-4PATTEN. *Fax:* 510-534-4344.

Pepperdine University
Malibu, California
http://www.pepperdine.edu/
- **Independent** university, founded 1937, affiliated with Church of Christ
- **Suburban** 830-acre campus with easy access to Los Angeles
- **Endowment** $861.6 million
- **Coed** 3,604 undergraduate students, 92% full-time, 59% women, 41% men
- **Very difficult** entrance level, 40% of applicants were admitted

UNDERGRAD STUDENTS
3,300 full-time, 304 part-time. Students come from 53 states and territories; 68 other countries; 45% are from out of state; 4% Black or African American, non-Hispanic/Latino; 14% Hispanic/Latino; 10% Asian, non-Hispanic/Latino; 0.3% Native Hawaiian or other Pacific Islander, non-Hispanic/Latino; 0.4% American Indian or Alaska Native, non-Hispanic/Latino; 6% Two or more races, non-Hispanic/Latino; 3% Race/ethnicity unknown; 11% international; 2% transferred in; 52% live on campus.

Freshmen:
Admission: 11,704 applied, 4,664 admitted, 862 enrolled. *Average high school GPA:* 3.6. *Test scores:* ACT scores over 18: 100%; ACT scores over 24: 89%; ACT scores over 30: 35%.
Retention: 90% of full-time freshmen returned.

FACULTY
Total: 678, 58% full-time, 75% with terminal degrees.
Student/faculty ratio: 13:1.

ACADEMICS
Calendar: semesters. *Degrees:* bachelor's, master's, and doctoral.

Special study options: adult/continuing education programs, advanced placement credit, distance learning, double majors, honors programs, independent study, internships, part-time degree program, services for LD students, student-designed majors, study abroad, summer session for credit. *ROTC:* Army (c), Air Force (c).

Unusual degree programs: 3-2 engineering with University of Southern California, Washington University in St. Louis.

Computers: 218 computers/terminals and 139 ports are available on campus for general student use. Students can access the following: campus intranet, computer help desk, free student e-mail accounts, online (class) grades, online (class) registration, online (class) schedules. Campuswide network is available. 100% of college-owned or -operated housing units are wired for high-speed Internet access. Wireless service is available via entire campus.
Library: Payson Library plus 5 others. *Books:* 348,364 (physical), 237,133 (digital/electronic); *Serial titles:* 411 (physical), 61,042 (digital/electronic); *Databases:* 150. Weekly public service hours: 112; students can reserve study rooms.

STUDENT LIFE
Housing options: on-campus residence required through sophomore year; men-only, women-only, special housing for students with disabilities. Campus housing is university owned. Freshman campus housing is guaranteed.

Activities and organizations: drama/theater group, student-run newspaper, radio and television station, choral group, Latino Student Association, Black Student Union, Panhellenic Council, Interfraternity Council, International Justice Mission, national fraternities, national sororities.

Athletics Member NCAA. All Division I. *Intercollegiate sports:* baseball M(s), basketball M(s)/W(s), cross-country running M(s)/W(s), golf M(s)/W(s), soccer M(c)/W(s), swimming and diving W(s), tennis

M(s)/W(s), track and field M(s)/W(s), triathlon W, volleyball M(s)/W(s), water polo M(s). *Intramural sports:* basketball M/W, football M/W, golf M(c)/W(c), lacrosse M(c)/W(c), rugby M(c), soccer M/W, tennis M(c)/W(c), ultimate Frisbee M(c)/W(c), volleyball M/W.

Campus security: 24-hour emergency response devices and patrols, student patrols, late-night transport/escort service, controlled dormitory access, front gate security, 24-hour security in residence halls, controlled access, crime prevention programs.

Student services: health clinic, personal/psychological counseling.

COSTS & FINANCIAL AID

Costs (2018–19) *Comprehensive fee:* $69,252 includes full-time tuition ($53,680), mandatory fees ($252), and room and board ($15,320). Part-time tuition: $1685 per credit hour. *Room and board:* Room and board charges vary according to board plan and housing facility. *Payment plan:* installment. *Waivers:* employees or children of employees.

Financial Aid Of all full-time matriculated undergraduates who enrolled in 2016, 3,176 applied for aid, 1,647 were judged to have need, 305 had their need fully met. 901 Federal Work-Study jobs (averaging $1217). 230 state and other part-time jobs (averaging $1029). In 2016, 815 non-need-based awards were made. *Average percent of need met:* 75. *Average financial aid package:* $39,927. *Average need-based loan:* $5877. *Average need-based gift aid:* $36,283. *Average non-need-based aid:* $18,084. *Average indebtedness upon graduation:* $29,640.

APPLYING

Standardized Tests *Required:* SAT or ACT (for admission).

Options: electronic application.

Application fee: $65.

Required: essay or personal statement, high school transcript, 2 letters of recommendation.

Application deadlines: 1/5 (freshmen), 1/5 (transfers).

Notification: 4/1 (freshmen), 4/1 (transfers).

CONTACT

Mr. Falone Serna, Director of Admission, Enrollment Management, Pepperdine University, 24255 Pacific Coast Highway, Malibu, CA 90263. *Phone:* 310-506-4392. *E-mail:* falone.serna@pepperdine.edu.

See below for display ad and page 1384 for the College Close-Up.

Pima Medical Institute
Chula Vista, California
http://www.pmi.edu/

CONTACT

Admissions Office, Pima Medical Institute, 780 Bay Boulevard, Chula Vista, CA 91910. *Phone:* 619-425-3200. *Toll-free phone:* 800-477-PIMA.

Pitzer College
Claremont, California
http://www.pitzer.edu/

- **Independent** 4-year, founded 1963, part of The Claremont Colleges Consortium
- **Suburban** 35-acre campus with easy access to Los Angeles
- **Endowment** $127.0 million
- **Coed** 1,112 undergraduate students, 97% full-time, 54% women, 46% men
- **Very difficult** entrance level, 16% of applicants were admitted

UNDERGRAD STUDENTS

1,074 full-time, 38 part-time. Students come from 44 states and territories; 31 other countries; 55% are from out of state; 6% Black or African American, non-Hispanic/Latino; 15% Hispanic/Latino; 9% Asian, non-Hispanic/Latino; 0.1% Native Hawaiian or other Pacific Islander, non-Hispanic/Latino; 0.4% American Indian or Alaska Native, non-Hispanic/Latino; 7% Two or more races, non-Hispanic/Latino; 5% Race/ethnicity unknown; 11% international; 2% transferred in; 72% live on campus.

A ★ *indicates that the school has detailed information with a Premium Profile on Petersons.com.*

Freshmen:

Admission: 3,753 applied, 608 admitted, 262 enrolled. *Average high school GPA:* 3.9. *Test scores:* SAT evidence-based reading and writing scores over 500: 100%; SAT math scores over 500: 100%; ACT scores over 18: 100%; SAT evidence-based reading and writing scores over 600: 90%; SAT math scores over 600: 95%; ACT scores over 24: 99%; SAT evidence-based reading and writing scores over 700: 47%; SAT math scores over 700: 58%; ACT scores over 30: 69%.

Retention: 95% of full-time freshmen returned.

FACULTY
Total: 118, 69% full-time, 100% with terminal degrees.
Student/faculty ratio: 11:1.

ACADEMICS
Calendar: semesters. *Degree:* bachelor's.

Special study options: adult/continuing education programs, advanced placement credit, cooperative education, double majors, English as a second language, honors programs, independent study, internships, off-campus study, part-time degree program, services for LD students, student-designed majors, study abroad, summer session for credit. *ROTC:* Army (c), Air Force (c).

Unusual degree programs: 3-2 business administration with Claremont Graduate University; public administration, mathematics, psychology with Claremont Graduate University.

Computers: Students can access the following: campus intranet, computer help desk, free student e-mail accounts, online (class) grades, online (class) registration, online (class) schedules. Campuswide network is available. 100% of college-owned or -operated housing units are wired for high-speed Internet access. Wireless service is available via entire campus.
Library: Honnold Library plus 3 others. Students can reserve study rooms.

STUDENT LIFE
Housing options: on-campus residence required for freshman year; coed, cooperative, special housing for students with disabilities. Campus housing is university owned. Freshman campus housing is guaranteed.

Activities and organizations: drama/theater group, student-run newspaper, radio station, choral group, Student Senate, The Other Side, Without A Box, Residence Hall Association, PAct (Pitzer Activities).

Athletics Member NCAA. All Division III. *Intercollegiate sports:* baseball M, basketball M/W, cross-country running M/W, football M, golf M/W, lacrosse W, soccer M/W, softball W, swimming and diving M/W, tennis M/W, track and field M/W, volleyball W, water polo M/W. *Intramural sports:* badminton M(c)/W(c), basketball M/W, equestrian sports M(c)/W(c), fencing M(c)/W(c), field hockey M(c)/W(c), football M, ice hockey M(c)/W(c), lacrosse M(c), rugby M(c)/W(c), soccer M/W(c), tennis M(c)/W(c), ultimate Frisbee M(c)/W(c), volleyball M(c)/W(c).

Campus security: 24-hour emergency response devices and patrols, late-night transport/escort service, controlled dormitory access, LiveSafe App, CUC and Campus Safety Emergency RSS Feed.

Student services: health clinic, personal/psychological counseling, women's center.

COSTS & FINANCIAL AID
Costs (2017–18) *Comprehensive fee:* $68,500 includes full-time tuition ($51,964), mandatory fees ($272), and room and board ($16,264). Part-time tuition and fees vary according to course load. *Room and board:* Room and board charges vary according to board plan. *Payment plans:* installment, deferred payment. *Waivers:* employees or children of employees.

Financial Aid Of all full-time matriculated undergraduates who enrolled in 2016, 492 applied for aid, 414 were judged to have need, 406 had their need fully met. In 2016, 12 non-need-based awards were made. *Average percent of need met:* 100. *Average financial aid package:* $45,338. *Average need-based loan:* $4101. *Average need-based gift aid:* $40,447. *Average non-need-based aid:* $6187. *Average indebtedness upon graduation:* $21,569. *Financial aid deadline:* 2/1.

APPLYING
Standardized Tests *Required for some:* SAT or ACT (for admission).
Options: electronic application, early decision, deferred entrance.

Application fee: $70.

Required: essay or personal statement, high school transcript, minimum 2.0 GPA, 3 letters of recommendation. *Recommended:* interview.

Application deadlines: 1/1 (freshmen), 4/1 (transfers).

Early decision deadline: 11/15 (for plan 1), 1/1 (for plan 2).

Notification: 4/1 (freshmen), 5/15 (transfers), 12/18 (early decision plan 1), 2/12 (early decision plan 2).

CONTACT
Ms. Yvonne Berumen, Vice President for Admission and Financial Aid, Pitzer College, 1050 North Mills Avenue, Claremont, CA 91711-6101. *Phone:* 909-621-8129. *Toll-free phone:* 800-748-9371. *Fax:* 909-621-8770. *E-mail:* admission@pitzer.edu.

Platt College
Alhambra, California
http://www.plattcollege.edu/

CONTACT
Mr. Detroit Whiteside, Director of Admissions, Platt College, 1000 South Fremont A9W, Alhambra, CA 91803. *Phone:* 323-258-8050. *Toll-free phone:* 888-866-6697 (in-state); 888-80-PLATT (out-of-state).

Platt College
Ontario, California
http://www.plattcollege.edu/

CONTACT
Ms. Jennifer Abandonato, Director of Admissions, Platt College, 3700 Inland Empire Boulevard, Ontario, CA 91764. *Phone:* 909-941-9410. *Toll-free phone:* 888-80-PLATT.

Platt College
Riverside, California
http://www.plattcollege.edu/

CONTACT
Platt College, 6465 Sycamore Canyon Boulevard, Suite 100, Riverside, CA 92507. *Toll-free phone:* 888-807-5288.

★ Platt College San Diego
San Diego, California
http://www.platt.edu/

CONTACT
Mr. Steve Gallup, Director of Admissions, Platt College San Diego, 6250 El Cajon Boulevard, San Diego, CA 92115-3919. *Phone:* 619-265-0107. *Toll-free phone:* 866-752-8826. *Fax:* 619-265-8655. *E-mail:* sgallup@platt.edu.

See next page for display ad and page 1386 for the College Close-Up.

Point Loma Nazarene University
San Diego, California
http://www.pointloma.edu/

- **Independent Nazarene** comprehensive, founded 1902
- **Suburban** 93-acre campus with easy access to San Diego
- **Coed** 3,150 undergraduate students, 83% full-time, 65% women, 35% men
- **Moderately difficult** entrance level, 76% of applicants were admitted

UNDERGRAD STUDENTS
2,621 full-time, 529 part-time. Students come from 43 states and territories; 24 other countries; 17% are from out of state; 2% Black or African American, non-Hispanic/Latino; 26% Hispanic/Latino; 7% Asian, non-Hispanic/Latino; 1% Native Hawaiian or other Pacific Islander, non-Hispanic/Latino; 0.3% American Indian or Alaska Native, non-Hispanic/Latino; 8% Two or more races, non-Hispanic/Latino; 2% Race/ethnicity unknown; 1% international; 11% transferred in; 56% live on campus.

Freshmen:
Admission: 3,007 applied, 2,294 admitted, 618 enrolled. *Average high school GPA:* 3.8. *Test scores:* SAT evidence-based reading and writing scores over 500: 96%; SAT math scores over 500: 95%; ACT scores over 18: 99%; SAT evidence-based reading and writing scores over 600: 58%; SAT math scores over 600: 47%; ACT scores over 24: 73%; SAT evidence-based reading and writing scores over 700: 7%; SAT math scores over 700: 6%; ACT scores over 30: 16%.
Retention: 89% of full-time freshmen returned.

FACULTY
Total: 474, 30% full-time, 46% with terminal degrees.
Student/faculty ratio: 14:1.

ACADEMICS
Calendar: semesters. *Degrees:* certificates, bachelor's, master's, doctoral, and post-master's certificates.
Special study options: academic remediation for entering students, accelerated degree program, adult/continuing education programs, advanced placement credit, distance learning, double majors, external degree program, honors programs, independent study, internships, off-campus study, part-time degree program, services for LD students, study abroad, summer session for credit. *ROTC:* Army (c), Navy (c), Air Force (c).
Computers: 346 computers/terminals and 5,320 ports are available on campus for general student use. Students can access the following: campus intranet, computer help desk, free student e-mail accounts, online (class) grades, online (class) registration, online (class) schedules. Campuswide network is available. 100% of college-owned or -operated housing units are wired for high-speed Internet access. Wireless service is available via entire campus.
Library: Ryan Library.

STUDENT LIFE
Housing options: on-campus residence required through sophomore year; men-only, women-only, special housing for students with disabilities. Campus housing is university owned. Freshman campus housing is guaranteed.

Activities and organizations: drama/theater group, student-run newspaper, radio and television station, choral group.
Athletics Member NCAA. All Division II. *Intercollegiate sports:* baseball M(s), basketball M(s)/W(s), cross-country running W(s), golf W(s), soccer M(s)/W(s), tennis M(s)/W(s), track and field W(s), volleyball W(s). *Intramural sports:* basketball M/W, cheerleading M(c)/W(c), football M/W, rugby M(c)/W(c), soccer M/W, softball M/W, tennis M/W, volleyball M/W.
Campus security: 24-hour patrols, student patrols, late-night transport/escort service.
Student services: health clinic, personal/psychological counseling, women's center.

COSTS & FINANCIAL AID
Costs (2018–19) *Comprehensive fee:* $46,150 includes full-time tuition ($35,100), mandatory fees ($600), and room and board ($10,450). Full-time tuition and fees vary according to course load and program. Part-time tuition: $1465 per credit hour. Part-time tuition and fees vary according to course load and program. *Room and board:* Room and board charges vary according to board plan. *Payment plan:* installment. *Waivers:* senior citizens and employees or children of employees.
Financial Aid Of all full-time matriculated undergraduates who enrolled in 2016, 2,012 applied for aid, 1,694 were judged to have need, 236 had their need fully met. In 2016, 534 non-need-based awards were made. *Average percent of need met:* 62. *Average financial aid package:* $22,975. *Average need-based loan:* $4874. *Average need-based gift aid:* $17,171. *Average non-need-based aid:* $10,421. *Average indebtedness upon graduation:* $35,414.

APPLYING
Standardized Tests *Required:* SAT or ACT (for admission). *Recommended:* SAT (for admission), ACT (for admission).
Options: electronic application, early action.
Application fee: $55.
Required: essay or personal statement, high school transcript, minimum 2.8 GPA, 2 letters of recommendation.
Application deadlines: 2/15 (freshmen), 11/15 (early action).

Notification: 4/1 (freshmen), 12/21 (early action).

CONTACT
Shannon Hutchison, Director of Undergraduate Admissions, Point Loma
Nazarene University, 3900 Lomaland Drive, San Diego, CA 92106.
Phone: 619-849-2541. *Toll-free phone:* 800-733-7770. *Fax:* 619-849-2601.
E-mail: admissions@pointloma.edu.

Pomona College
Claremont, California
http://www.pomona.edu/

- **Independent** 4-year, founded 1887
- **Suburban** 140-acre campus with easy access to Los Angeles
- **Endowment** $2.2 billion
- **Coed** 1,704 undergraduate students, 99% full-time, 50% women, 50% men
- **Most difficult** entrance level, 8% of applicants were admitted

UNDERGRAD STUDENTS
1,683 full-time, 21 part-time. Students come from 53 states and territories;
63 other countries; 70% are from out of state; 9% Black or African
American, non-Hispanic/Latino; 16% Hispanic/Latino; 14% Asian, non-
Hispanic/Latino; 0.3% Native Hawaiian or other Pacific Islander, non-
Hispanic/Latino; 0.5% American Indian or Alaska Native, non-
Hispanic/Latino; 7% Two or more races, non-Hispanic/Latino; 6%
Race/ethnicity unknown; 12% international; 1% transferred in; 98% live
on campus.

Freshmen:
Admission: 9,045 applied, 756 admitted, 412 enrolled. *Test scores:* SAT
evidence-based reading and writing scores over 500: 100%; SAT math
scores over 500: 100%; ACT scores over 18: 100%; SAT evidence-based
reading and writing scores over 600: 99%; SAT math scores over 600:
94%; ACT scores over 24: 100%; SAT evidence-based reading and
writing scores over 700: 72%; SAT math scores over 700: 67%; ACT
scores over 30: 81%.
Retention: 98% of full-time freshmen returned.

FACULTY
Total: 240, 78% full-time, 93% with terminal degrees.
Student/faculty ratio: 8:1.

ACADEMICS
Calendar: semesters. *Degree:* bachelor's.
Special study options: advanced placement credit, double majors,
independent study, internships, off-campus study, services for LD
students, student-designed majors, study abroad. *ROTC:* Army (c), Air
Force (c).
Unusual degree programs: 3-2 engineering with California Institute of
Technology, Washington University in St. Louis, Dartmouth College.
Computers: 180 computers/terminals are available on campus for general
student use. Students can access the following: computer help desk, free
student e-mail accounts, online (class) grades, online (class) registration,
online (class) schedules. Campuswide network is available. 100% of
college-owned or -operated housing units are wired for high-speed
Internet access. Wireless service is available via entire campus.
Library: Honnold/Mudd Library plus 4 others.

STUDENT LIFE
Housing options: on-campus residence required for freshman year; coed.
Campus housing is university owned. Freshman campus housing is
guaranteed.
Activities and organizations: drama/theater group, student-run
newspaper, radio station, choral group, Student Government, music/
choral organizations, service organizations, intramural sports, outdoor
activities club.
Athletics Member NCAA. All Division III. *Intercollegiate sports:*
baseball M, basketball M/W, cross-country running M/W, football M, golf
M/W, lacrosse W, soccer M/W, softball W, swimming and diving M/W,
tennis M/W, track and field M/W, ultimate Frisbee M(c)/W(c), volleyball
M(c)/W, water polo M/W. *Intramural sports:* badminton M(c)/W(c),
basketball M/W, crew W(c), cross-country running M/W, equestrian
sports M(c)/W(c), fencing M/W, field hockey M(c)/W(c), football M, golf
M/W, lacrosse M(c), racquetball M/W, rock climbing M/W, skiing (cross-
country) M(c)/W(c), skiing (downhill) M(c)/W(c), soccer M/W, softball
M/W, squash M/W, swimming and diving M/W, tennis M/W, track and
field M/W, ultimate Frisbee M, volleyball M/W, water polo M/W.
Campus security: 24-hour emergency response devices and patrols, late-
night transport/escort service, controlled dormitory access.
Student services: health clinic, personal/psychological counseling,
women's center.

COSTS & FINANCIAL AID
Costs (2018–19) *Comprehensive fee:* $69,496 includes full-time tuition
($52,412), mandatory fees ($368), and room and board ($16,716). *Room
and board:* Room and board charges vary according to board plan.
Payment plan: installment. *Waivers:* employees or children of employees.
Financial Aid Of all full-time matriculated undergraduates who enrolled
in 2015, 1,148 applied for aid, 917 were judged to have need, 917 had
their need fully met. 153 Federal Work-Study jobs (averaging $1566). 676
state and other part-time jobs (averaging $2300). In 2015, 2 non-need-
based awards were made. *Average percent of need met:* 100. *Average
financial aid package:* $48,034. *Average need-based gift aid:* $46,039.
Average non-need-based aid: $5000. *Average indebtedness upon
graduation:* $18,738. *Financial aid deadline:* 3/1.

APPLYING
Standardized Tests *Required:* SAT or ACT (for admission).
Options: electronic application, early admission, early decision, deferred
entrance.
Application fee: $70.
Required: essay or personal statement, high school transcript, 2 letters of
recommendation. *Recommended:* supplemental forms for visual and
performing arts and science research.
Application deadlines: 1/1 (freshmen), 2/15 (transfers).
Early decision deadline: 11/1 (for plan 1), 1/1 (for plan 2).
Notification: 4/1 (freshmen), 4/1 (transfers), 12/15 (early decision plan 1),
2/15 (early decision plan 2).
CONTACT
Pomona College, 333 North College Way, Claremont, CA 91711.

Providence Christian College
Pasadena, California
http://www.providencecc.edu/

CONTACT
Providence Christian College, 1539 East Howard Street, Pasadena, CA
91124.

SAE Expression College
Emeryville, California
http://www.sae.edu/

CONTACT
SAE Expression College, 6601 Shellmound Street, Emeryville, CA
94608. *Toll-free phone:* 877-833-8800.

Saint Mary's College of California
Moraga, California
http://www.stmarys-ca.edu/

- **Independent Roman Catholic** upper-level, founded 1863
- **Suburban** 420-acre campus with easy access to San Francisco
- **Endowment** $178.6 million
- **Coed** 2,780 undergraduate students, 94% full-time, 59% women, 41% men
- **Moderately difficult** entrance level, 82% of applicants were admitted

UNDERGRAD STUDENTS
2,614 full-time, 166 part-time. Students come from 43 states and
territories; 30 other countries; 12% are from out of state; 4% Black or
African American, non-Hispanic/Latino; 26% Hispanic/Latino; 11%
Asian, non-Hispanic/Latino; 1% Native Hawaiian or other Pacific
Islander, non-Hispanic/Latino; 0.4% American Indian or Alaska Native,
non-Hispanic/Latino; 6% Two or more races, non-Hispanic/Latino; 3%

Race/ethnicity unknown; 3% international; 6% transferred in; 60% live on campus.

Freshmen:
Admission: 4,676 applied, 3,815 admitted.

FACULTY
Total: 500, 45% full-time, 43% with terminal degrees.
Student/faculty ratio: 11:1.

ACADEMICS
Calendar: 4-1-4. *Degrees:* bachelor's, master's, and doctoral.

Special study options: adult/continuing education programs, advanced placement credit, double majors, honors programs, independent study, internships, off-campus study, part-time degree program, services for LD students, student-designed majors, study abroad, summer session for credit. *ROTC:* Army (c).

Unusual degree programs: 3-2 engineering with Washington University in St. Louis, University of Southern California; education.

Computers: 244 computers/terminals and 1,800 ports are available on campus for general student use. Students can access the following: campus intranet, computer help desk, free student e-mail accounts, online (class) grades, online (class) registration, online (class) schedules, student accounts. Campuswide network is available. 100% of college-owned or -operated housing units are wired for high-speed Internet access. Wireless service is available via entire campus.
Library: St. Albert Hall Library. *Books:* 179,912 (physical), 179,777 (digital/electronic); *Serial titles:* 926 (physical), 150,000 (digital/electronic); *Databases:* 219. Weekly public service hours: 102; study areas open 24 hours, 5–7 days a week; students can reserve study rooms.

STUDENT LIFE
Housing options: coed, men-only, special housing for students with disabilities. Campus housing is university owned. Freshman campus housing is guaranteed.

Activities and organizations: drama/theater group, student-run newspaper, radio station, choral group, Gael Force, Campus Activities Board, LASA-Latin American Student Association-Black Student Union, La Hermandad, Asian Pacific American Student Association.

Athletics Member NCAA. All Division I. *Intercollegiate sports:* baseball M(s), basketball M(s)/W(s), cheerleading W, crew M/W(s), cross-country running M(s)/W(s), fencing M(c)/W(c), golf M(s), lacrosse M(c), rugby M(c)/W(c), sand volleyball W(s), soccer M(s)/W(s), softball W(s), tennis M(s)/W(s), track and field M(s)/W(s), volleyball W(s), water polo M(c)/W(c). *Intramural sports:* badminton M/W, baseball M(c), basketball M/W, football M/W, lacrosse W(c), soccer M(c)/W(c), softball M/W, table tennis M/W, tennis M(c)/W(c), ultimate Frisbee M/W, volleyball M(c)/W(c).

Campus security: 24-hour emergency response devices and patrols, late-night transport/escort service.

Student services: health clinic, personal/psychological counseling, women's center.

COSTS & FINANCIAL AID
Costs (2018–19) *Comprehensive fee:* $62,650 includes full-time tuition ($47,130), mandatory fees ($150), and room and board ($15,370). Part-time tuition: $5906 per course. *Required fees:* $75 per term part-time. *Room and board:* Room and board charges vary according to board plan and housing facility. *Payment plan:* installment. *Waivers:* employees or children of employees.
Financial Aid Of all full-time matriculated undergraduates who enrolled in 2015, 2,134 applied for aid, 1,932 were judged to have need, 163 had their need fully met. In 2015, 406 non-need-based awards were made. *Average percent of need met:* 62. *Average financial aid package:* $27,902. *Average need-based loan:* $4702. *Average need-based gift aid:* $23,119. *Average non-need-based aid:* $15,766. *Average indebtedness upon graduation:* $31,203.

APPLYING
Standardized Tests *Required:* SAT or ACT (for admission).
Options: electronic application, early action, deferred entrance.
Application fee: $60.

Application deadlines: 7/1 (transfers), 11/15 (early action).
Notification: continuous (transfers), 1/1 (early action).

CONTACT
Angelica Moore Ed.D., Dean of Admissions, Saint Mary's College of California, 1928 St. Marys Road, P.M.B. 4800, Moraga, CA 94575. *Phone:* 925-631-4553. *Toll-free phone:* 800-800-4SMC. *Fax:* 925-376-7193. *E-mail:* smcadmit@stmarys-ca.edu.

Samuel Merritt University
Oakland, California
http://www.samuelmerritt.edu/
- **Independent** upper-level, founded 1909
- **Urban** 1-acre campus with easy access to San Francisco
- **Endowment** $47.1 million
- **Coed, primarily women** 919 undergraduate students, 61% full-time, 82% women, 18% men

UNDERGRAD STUDENTS
564 full-time, 355 part-time. Students come from 3 states and territories; 0.2% are from out of state; 6% Black or African American, non-Hispanic/Latino; 22% Hispanic/Latino; 23% Asian, non-Hispanic/Latino; 1% Native Hawaiian or other Pacific Islander, non-Hispanic/Latino; 0.1% American Indian or Alaska Native, non-Hispanic/Latino; 6% Two or more races, non-Hispanic/Latino; 8% Race/ethnicity unknown; 24% transferred in.

FACULTY
Total: 392, 42% full-time, 39% with terminal degrees.
Student/faculty ratio: 10:1.

ACADEMICS
Calendar: trimesters. *Degrees:* bachelor's, master's, doctoral, and post-master's certificates (bachelor's degree offered jointly with Saint Mary's College of California).

Special study options: academic remediation for entering students, accelerated degree program, advanced placement credit, cooperative education, distance learning, independent study, internships, off-campus study, part-time degree program, services for LD students.

Computers: 160 computers/terminals are available on campus for general student use. Students can access the following: campus intranet, computer help desk, free student e-mail accounts, online (class) grades, online (class) registration, online (class) schedules. Campuswide network is available. Wireless service is available via entire campus.
Library: John A. Graziano Memorial Library. *Books:* 8,453 (physical), 337 (digital/electronic); *Serial titles:* 714 (physical), 19,832 (digital/electronic); *Databases:* 22. Weekly public service hours: 86; students can reserve study rooms.

STUDENT LIFE
Housing options: college housing not available.

Activities and organizations: Student Body Association, California Podiatric Medical Students'; Association (CPMSA), International Healthcare Club, Community Service Honor Society, Scholars in Service.

Campus security: 24-hour emergency response devices and patrols, late-night transport/escort service, 24-hour controlled access.

Student services: health clinic, personal/psychological counseling.

FINANCIAL AID
Financial Aid Of all full-time matriculated undergraduates who enrolled in 2016, 678 applied for aid, 663 were judged to have need. 138 Federal Work-Study jobs (averaging $1903). *Average percent of need met:* 19. *Average financial aid package:* $11,861. *Average need-based loan:* $6110. *Average need-based gift aid:* $13,002.

APPLYING
Options: electronic application.
Application fee: $45.
Notification: 3/15 (transfers).

CONTACT
Samuel Merritt University, 3100 Telegraph Avenue, Oakland, CA 94609-3108. *Phone:* 510-869-1508. *Toll-free phone:* 800-607-6377.

San Diego Christian College
Santee, California
http://www.sdcc.edu/

CONTACT
Christine Roberts, Admissions Director, San Diego Christian College, 200 Riverview Parkway, Santee, CA 92017. *Phone:* 619-201-8760. *Toll-free phone:* 800-676-2242. *Fax:* 619-201-8749. *E-mail:* christine.roberts@sdcc.edu.

San Diego State University
San Diego, California
http://www.sdsu.edu/

- **State-supported** university, founded 1897, part of California State University System
- **Urban** 288-acre campus with easy access to San Diego
- **Endowment** $268.4 million
- **Coed** 30,165 undergraduate students, 90% full-time, 54% women, 46% men
- **Moderately difficult** entrance level, 35% of applicants were admitted

UNDERGRAD STUDENTS
27,028 full-time, 3,137 part-time. Students come from 52 states and territories; 114 other countries; 10% are from out of state; 4% Black or African American, non-Hispanic/Latino; 31% Hispanic/Latino; 13% Asian, non-Hispanic/Latino; 0.2% Native Hawaiian or other Pacific Islander, non-Hispanic/Latino; 0.4% American Indian or Alaska Native, non-Hispanic/Latino; 7% Two or more races, non-Hispanic/Latino; 4% Race/ethnicity unknown; 7% international; 11% transferred in; 14% live on campus.

Freshmen:
Admission: 60,697 applied, 21,379 admitted, 5,366 enrolled. *Average high school GPA:* 3.7. *Test scores:* SAT evidence-based reading and writing scores over 500: 93%; SAT math scores over 500: 92%; ACT scores over 18: 97%; SAT evidence-based reading and writing scores over 600: 50%; SAT math scores over 600: 48%; ACT scores over 24: 68%; SAT evidence-based reading and writing scores over 700: 5%; SAT math scores over 700: 8%; ACT scores over 30: 15%.
Retention: 89% of full-time freshmen returned.

FACULTY
Total: 1,794, 49% full-time, 62% with terminal degrees.
Student/faculty ratio: 27:1.

ACADEMICS
Calendar: semesters. *Degrees:* bachelor's, master's, doctoral, and postbachelor's certificates.
Special study options: advanced placement credit, distance learning, double majors, English as a second language, external degree program, freshman honors college, honors programs, independent study, internships, off-campus study, part-time degree program, services for LD students, student-designed majors, study abroad, summer session for credit. *ROTC:* Army (b), Navy (b), Air Force (b).
Computers: 2,000 computers/terminals are available on campus for general student use. Students can access the following: computer help desk, free student e-mail accounts, online (class) grades, online (class) registration, online (class) schedules, learning management system. Campuswide network is available. 100% of college-owned or -operated housing units are wired for high-speed Internet access. Wireless service is available via entire campus.
Library: Malcolm A. Love Library. *Books:* 1.3 million (physical), 1.0 million (digital/electronic); *Serial titles:* 45,107 (physical), 92,142 (digital/electronic); *Databases:* 317. Weekly public service hours: 168; study areas open 24 hours, 5–7 days a week; students can reserve study rooms.

STUDENT LIFE
Housing options: on-campus residence required for freshman year; coed, special housing for students with disabilities. Campus housing is university owned. Freshman applicants given priority for college housing.
Activities and organizations: drama/theater group, student-run newspaper, radio and television station, choral group, marching band, AB Samahan, Asian Pacific Student Alliance, Enviro-Business Society,

M.E.Ch.A de SDSU, Social fraternities and sororities, including both general and culturally based organizations, national fraternities, national sororities.
Athletics Member NCAA. All Division I. *Intercollegiate sports:* baseball M(s), basketball M(s)/W(s), cross-country running W(s), football M(s), golf M(s)/W(s), lacrosse W(s), rowing W(s), soccer M(s)/W(s), softball W(s), swimming and diving W(s), tennis M(s)/W(s), track and field W(s), volleyball W(s), water polo W(s). *Intramural sports:* basketball M/W, bowling M/W, football M/W, ice hockey M(c), lacrosse M(c)/W(c), rowing M(c)/W(c), rugby M(c), skiing (downhill) M(c)/W(c), soccer M(c)/W(c), softball M/W, tennis M(c)/W(c), triathlon M(c)/W(c), ultimate Frisbee M(c)/W(c), volleyball M(c)/W(c), water polo M(c)/W(c).
Campus security: 24-hour emergency response devices and patrols, student patrols, late-night transport/escort service.
Student services: health clinic, personal/psychological counseling, women's center.

COSTS & FINANCIAL AID
Costs (2017–18) *Tuition:* state resident $5742 full-time; nonresident $17,622 full-time. Full-time tuition and fees vary according to course load, degree level, and location. Part-time tuition and fees vary according to course load, degree level, and location. *Required fees:* $1718 full-time. *Room and board:* $15,966. Room and board charges vary according to board plan and housing facility. *Payment plan:* installment. *Waivers:* employees or children of employees.
Financial Aid Of all full-time matriculated undergraduates who enrolled in 2017, 18,000 applied for aid, 14,600 were judged to have need, 2,800 had their need fully met. 770 Federal Work-Study jobs (averaging $2200). In 2017, 1500 non-need-based awards were made. *Average percent of need met:* 67. *Average financial aid package:* $9700. *Average need-based loan:* $4100. *Average need-based gift aid:* $9500. *Average non-need-based aid:* $2000. *Average indebtedness upon graduation:* $19,633. *Financial aid deadline:* 3/2.

APPLYING
Standardized Tests *Required:* SAT or ACT (for admission).
Options: electronic application.
Application fee: $55.
Required: high school transcript.
Application deadlines: 11/30 (freshmen), 11/30 (transfers).
Notification: 3/1 (freshmen), 3/1 (transfers).

CONTACT
Office of Admissions, San Diego State University, 5500 Campanile Drive, San Diego, CA 92182-7455. *Phone:* 619-594-6336. *Toll-free phone:* 855-594-6336 (in-state); 855-594-3983 (out-of-state). *E-mail:* admissions@sdsu.edu.

San Diego State University–Imperial Valley Campus
Calexico, California
http://www.ivcampus.sdsu.edu/

CONTACT
Aracely Bororquez, Admissions Department, San Diego State University–Imperial Valley Campus, 720 Heber Avenue, Calexico, CA 92231. *Phone:* 760-768-5506. *Fax:* 760-768-5589. *E-mail:* transfer@mail.sdsu.edu.

San Francisco Art Institute
San Francisco, California
http://www.sfai.edu/

- **Independent** comprehensive, founded 1871
- **Urban** 4-acre campus with easy access to San Francisco
- **Endowment** $10.3 million
- **Coed** 299 undergraduate students, 93% full-time, 63% women, 37% men
- **Moderately difficult** entrance level, 75% of applicants were admitted

UNDERGRAD STUDENTS
279 full-time, 20 part-time. Students come from 37 states and territories; 20 other countries; 64% are from out of state; 2% Black or African American, non-Hispanic/Latino; 15% Hispanic/Latino; 8% Asian, non-Hispanic/Latino; 8% Two or more races, non-Hispanic/Latino;

5% Race/ethnicity unknown; 21% international; 14% transferred in; 36% live on campus.

Freshmen:
Admission: 451 applied, 337 admitted, 53 enrolled. *Average high school GPA:* 3.1. *Test scores:* ACT scores over 18: 100%; ACT scores over 24: 50%.
Retention: 51% of full-time freshmen returned.

FACULTY
Total: 92, 24% full-time, 84% with terminal degrees.
Student/faculty ratio: 9:1.

ACADEMICS
Calendar: semesters. *Degrees:* bachelor's, master's, and postbachelor's certificates.
Special study options: academic remediation for entering students, distance learning, English as a second language, honors programs, independent study, internships, off-campus study, services for LD students, study abroad, summer session for credit.
Computers: 150 computers/terminals are available on campus for general student use. Students can access the following: computer help desk, free student e-mail accounts, online (class) grades, online (class) registration, online (class) schedules. Campuswide network is available. 100% of college-owned or -operated housing units are wired for high-speed Internet access. Wireless service is available via entire campus.
Library: Anne Bremer Memorial Library plus 1 other. *Books:* 32,775 (physical); *Serial titles:* 126 (physical), 791 (digital/electronic); *Databases:* 6. Weekly public service hours: 59.

STUDENT LIFE
Housing options: on-campus residence required for freshman year; coed. Campus housing is leased by the school and is provided by a third party. Freshman applicants given priority for college housing.
Activities and organizations: student-run newspaper, radio station, Student Union, LOGS (Legion of Graduate Students), Film Club, Photo Club, SFAeye.
Campus security: 24-hour patrols, security cameras.
Student services: personal/psychological counseling.

COSTS & FINANCIAL AID
Costs (2018–19) *One-time required fee:* $200. *Comprehensive fee:* $62,243 includes full-time tuition ($45,664), mandatory fees ($870), and room and board ($15,709). Full-time tuition and fees vary according to degree level. Part-time tuition: $2000 per credit. Part-time tuition and fees vary according to degree level. *College room only:* $11,650. Room and board charges vary according to housing facility. *Payment plan:* installment. *Waivers:* employees or children of employees.
Financial Aid Of all full-time matriculated undergraduates who enrolled in 2017, 182 applied for aid, 159 were judged to have need, 17 had their need fully met. In 2017, 111 non-need-based awards were made. *Average percent of need met:* 49. *Average financial aid package:* $16,140. *Average need-based loan:* $2416. *Average need-based gift aid:* $5679. *Average non-need-based aid:* $8361. *Average indebtedness upon graduation:* $27,137.

APPLYING
Standardized Tests *Recommended:* SAT or ACT (for admission).
Options: electronic application, early action, deferred entrance.
Application fee: $75.
Required: essay or personal statement, high school transcript, 1 letter of recommendation, portfolio and artist statement for BFA applicants, critical essay for BA applicants. *Recommended:* minimum 2.5 GPA, interview.
Application deadlines: rolling (freshmen), rolling (transfers), 11/15 (early action).
Notification: continuous (freshmen), continuous (transfers).

CONTACT
Office of Admissions, San Francisco Art Institute, 800 Chestnut Street, San Francisco, CA 94133. *Phone:* 415-749-4500. *Toll-free phone:* 800-345-SFAI. *Fax:* 415-749-4592. *E-mail:* admissions@sfai.edu.

San Francisco Conservatory of Music
San Francisco, California
http://www.sfcm.edu/
- **Independent** comprehensive, founded 1917
- **Urban** 2-acre campus with easy access to San Francisco Bay Area
- **Endowment** $41.3 million
- **Coed** 205 undergraduate students, 100% full-time, 43% women, 57% men

UNDERGRAD STUDENTS
204 full-time, 1 part-time. Students come from 25 states and territories; 15 other countries; 55% are from out of state; 6% Black or African American, non-Hispanic/Latino; 6% Hispanic/Latino; 8% Asian, non-Hispanic/Latino; 1% American Indian or Alaska Native, non-Hispanic/Latino; 9% Two or more races, non-Hispanic/Latino; 5% Race/ethnicity unknown; 30% international; 3% transferred in; 64% live on campus.

Freshmen:
Admission: 61 enrolled.
Retention: 76% of full-time freshmen returned.

FACULTY
Total: 134, 22% full-time, 19% with terminal degrees.
Student/faculty ratio: 7:1.

ACADEMICS
Calendar: semesters. *Degrees:* diplomas, bachelor's, master's, post-master's, and postbachelor's certificates.
Special study options: academic remediation for entering students, advanced placement credit, cooperative education, English as a second language, independent study, internships, services for LD students.
Computers: 12 computers/terminals and 350 ports are available on campus for general student use. Students can access the following: campus intranet, computer help desk, free student e-mail accounts, online (class) grades, online (class) registration, online (class) schedules. Campuswide network is available. 100% of college-owned or -operated housing units are wired for high-speed Internet access. Wireless service is available via entire campus.
Library: San Francisco Conservatory of Music Library. *Books:* 24,129 (physical), 31,094 (digital/electronic); *Serial titles:* 64 (physical), 448 (digital/electronic); *Databases:* 11. Weekly public service hours: 72.

STUDENT LIFE
Housing options: on-campus residence required through sophomore year; coed. Campus housing is leased by the school and is provided by a third party. Freshman campus housing is guaranteed.
Activities and organizations: drama/theater group, choral group, Yoga Group, Student Counsel.
Campus security: 24-hour emergency response devices and patrols, controlled dormitory access, resident assistant on-call for residential hall residents, after hours on-call mental health counceling.
Student services: personal/psychological counseling.

COSTS & FINANCIAL AID
Costs (2017–18) *One-time required fee:* $50. *Comprehensive fee:* $60,970 includes full-time tuition ($43,700), mandatory fees ($1110), and room and board ($16,160). Part-time tuition: $1924 per credit. Part-time tuition and fees vary according to course load. *Required fees:* $1110 per year part-time. *College room only:* $12,460. Room and board charges vary according to board plan and housing facility. *Payment plan:* installment. *Waivers:* employees or children of employees.
Financial Aid Of all full-time matriculated undergraduates who enrolled in 2017, 182 applied for aid, 170 were judged to have need, 16 had their need fully met. 23 Federal Work-Study jobs (averaging $2500). In 2017, 21 non-need-based awards were made. *Average percent of need met:* 75. *Average financial aid package:* $35,000. *Average need-based loan:* $7500. *Average need-based gift aid:* $23,000. *Average non-need-based aid:* $18,300. *Average indebtedness upon graduation:* $42,000. *Financial aid deadline:* 3/1.

APPLYING

Required: essay or personal statement, high school transcript, minimum 2.5 GPA, 2 letters of recommendation, audition, pre-screen recording in select areas. *Required for some:* interview.

CONTACT

Ms. Melissa Cocco-Mitten, Director of Admissions, San Francisco Conservatory of Music, 50 Oak Street, San Francisco, CA 94102. *Phone:* 415-503-6231. *Fax:* 415-503-6299. *E-mail:* admit@sfcm.edu.

San Francisco State University

San Francisco, California

http://www.sfsu.edu/

- **State-supported** university, founded 1899, part of California State University System
- **Urban** 142-acre campus
- **Endowment** $83.7 million
- **Coed** 26,617 undergraduate students, 83% full-time, 56% women, 44% men
- **Moderately difficult** entrance level, 73% of applicants were admitted

UNDERGRAD STUDENTS

22,200 full-time, 4,417 part-time. 1% are from out of state; 5% Black or African American, non-Hispanic/Latino; 33% Hispanic/Latino; 26% Asian, non-Hispanic/Latino; 0.4% Native Hawaiian or other Pacific Islander, non-Hispanic/Latino; 0.2% American Indian or Alaska Native, non-Hispanic/Latino; 6% Two or more races, non-Hispanic/Latino; 4% Race/ethnicity unknown; 7% international; 14% transferred in; 15% live on campus.

Freshmen:

Admission: 23,252 applied, 16,904 admitted, 4,323 enrolled. *Average high school GPA:* 3.2. *Test scores:* SAT evidence-based reading and writing scores over 500: 69%; SAT math scores over 500: 66%; ACT scores over 18: 77%; SAT evidence-based reading and writing scores over 600: 20%; SAT math scores over 600: 16%; ACT scores over 24: 26%; SAT evidence-based reading and writing scores over 700: 2%; SAT math scores over 700: 2%; ACT scores over 30: 4%.

Retention: 79% of full-time freshmen returned.

FACULTY

Total: 1,763, 60% full-time, 47% with terminal degrees.

ACADEMICS

Calendar: semesters. *Degrees:* certificates, bachelor's, master's, doctoral, post-master's, and postbachelor's certificates.

Special study options: academic remediation for entering students, accelerated degree program, adult/continuing education programs, advanced placement credit, cooperative education, distance learning, double majors, English as a second language, honors programs, independent study, internships, off-campus study, part-time degree program, services for LD students, student-designed majors, study abroad, summer session for credit. *ROTC:* Army (c), Air Force (c).

Computers: 2,000 computers/terminals and 800 ports are available on campus for general student use. Students can access the following: campus intranet, computer help desk, free student e-mail accounts, online (class) grades, online (class) registration, online (class) schedules. Campuswide network is available. 100% of college-owned or -operated housing units are wired for high-speed Internet access. Wireless service is available via entire campus.

Library: J. Paul Leonard Library. Study areas open 24 hours, 5–7 days a week; students can reserve study rooms.

STUDENT LIFE

Housing options: coed, women-only, special housing for students with disabilities. Campus housing is university owned. Freshman applicants given priority for college housing.

Activities and organizations: drama/theater group, student-run newspaper, radio and television station, choral group, national fraternities, national sororities.

Athletics Member NCAA. All Division II. *Intercollegiate sports:* baseball M(s), basketball M(s)/W(s), cross-country running M(s)/W(s), soccer M(s)/W(s), softball W(s), track and field W(s), volleyball W(s), wrestling M(s). *Intramural sports:* basketball M/W, cheerleading

M(c)/W(c), ice hockey M(c)/W(c), rugby M(c)/W(c), soccer M/W, tennis M/W, volleyball M/W, water polo M(c)/W(c).

Campus security: 24-hour emergency response devices and patrols, student patrols, late-night transport/escort service, controlled dormitory access.

Student services: health clinic, personal/psychological counseling, women's center, legal services.

COSTS & FINANCIAL AID

Costs (2017–18) *Tuition:* state resident $5742 full-time, $1665 per term part-time; nonresident $17,622 full-time, $4041 per term part-time. Full-time tuition and fees vary according to course load. Part-time tuition and fees vary according to course load. *Required fees:* $1512 full-time, $756 per term part-time. *Room and board:* $13,248; room only: $8752. Room and board charges vary according to board plan and housing facility. *Payment plan:* installment. *Waivers:* senior citizens and employees or children of employees.

Financial Aid Of all full-time matriculated undergraduates who enrolled in 2017, 17,449 applied for aid, 15,910 were judged to have need, 2,710 had their need fully met. In 2017, 312 non-need-based awards were made. *Average percent of need met:* 64. *Average financial aid package:* $15,520. *Average need-based loan:* $4353. *Average need-based gift aid:* $8871. *Average non-need-based aid:* $2535. *Average indebtedness upon graduation:* $19,347.

APPLYING

Standardized Tests *Required:* SAT or ACT (for admission).

Options: electronic application.

Application fee: $55.

Required: high school transcript.

Application deadlines: 11/30 (freshmen), 11/30 (transfers).

Notification: 12/1 (freshmen), 12/1 (transfers).

CONTACT

Admissions Officer, San Francisco State University, 1600 Holloway Avenue, San Francisco, CA 94132-1722. *Phone:* 415-338-1113. *Fax:* 415-338-7196. *E-mail:* ugadmit@sfsu.edu.

San Jose State University

San Jose, California

http://www.sjsu.edu/

CONTACT

Admissions Office, San Jose State University, One Washington Square, San Jose, CA 95192-0001. *Phone:* 408-283-7500. *Fax:* 408-924-2050. *E-mail:* admissions@sjsu.edu.

Santa Barbara Business College

Bakersfield, California

http://www.sbbcollege.edu/

CONTACT

Santa Barbara Business College, 5300 California Avenue, Bakersfield, CA 93309.

Santa Barbara Business College

Santa Maria, California

http://www.sbbcollege.edu/

CONTACT

Santa Barbara Business College, 303 East Plaza Drive, Santa Maria, CA 93454.

Santa Barbara Business College

Ventura, California

http://www.sbbcollege.edu/

CONTACT

Santa Barbara Business College, 4839 Market Street, Ventura, CA 93003.

Santa Clara University

Santa Clara, California
http://www.scu.edu/

- **Independent Roman Catholic (Jesuit)** university, founded 1851
- **Suburban** 106-acre campus with easy access to San Francisco, San Jose
- **Endowment** $905.9 million
- **Coed** 5,499 undergraduate students, 98% full-time, 50% women, 50% men
- **Very difficult** entrance level, 54% of applicants were admitted

UNDERGRAD STUDENTS

5,411 full-time, 88 part-time. Students come from 53 states and territories; 36 other countries; 29% are from out of state; 3% Black or African American, non-Hispanic/Latino; 18% Hispanic/Latino; 16% Asian, non-Hispanic/Latino; 0.2% Native Hawaiian or other Pacific Islander, non-Hispanic/Latino; 0.1% American Indian or Alaska Native, non-Hispanic/Latino; 7% Two or more races, non-Hispanic/Latino; 2% Race/ethnicity unknown; 4% international; 3% transferred in; 56% live on campus.

Freshmen:

Admission: 15,061 applied, 8,067 admitted, 1,404 enrolled. *Average high school GPA:* 3.7. *Test scores:* SAT evidence-based reading and writing scores over 500: 98%; SAT math scores over 500: 100%; ACT scores over 18: 100%; SAT evidence-based reading and writing scores over 600: 89%; SAT math scores over 600: 91%; ACT scores over 24: 98%; SAT evidence-based reading and writing scores over 700: 36%; SAT math scores over 700: 44%; ACT scores over 30: 58%.

Retention: 94% of full-time freshmen returned.

FACULTY

Total: 906, 60% full-time, 82% with terminal degrees.

Student/faculty ratio: 11:1.

ACADEMICS

Calendar: quarters. *Degrees:* bachelor's, master's, doctoral, and postbachelor's certificates.

Special study options: advanced placement credit, cooperative education, double majors, honors programs, independent study, internships, off-campus study, services for LD students, student-designed majors, study abroad, summer session for credit. *ROTC:* Army (b), Air Force (c).

Computers: Students can access the following: campus intranet, computer help desk, free student e-mail accounts, online (class) grades, online (class) registration, online (class) schedules. Campuswide network is available. 100% of college-owned or -operated housing units are wired for high-speed Internet access. Wireless service is available via entire campus.

Library: University Library plus 1 other. *Books:* 606,483 (physical), 658,072 (digital/electronic); *Serial titles:* 14,096 (physical), 84,245 (digital/electronic); *Databases:* 356. Weekly public service hours: 121; students can reserve study rooms.

STUDENT LIFE

Housing options: coed, special housing for students with disabilities. Campus housing is university owned. Freshman applicants given priority for college housing.

Activities and organizations: drama/theater group, student-run newspaper, radio station, choral group, marching band.

Athletics Member NCAA. All Division I. *Intercollegiate sports:* baseball M(s), basketball M(s)/W(s), cross-country running M(s)/W(s), equestrian sports M(c)/W(c), field hockey W(c), golf M(s)/W(s), ice hockey M(c), lacrosse M(c)/W(c), rowing M/W, rugby M(c)/W(c), sailing M(c)/W(c), sand volleyball W, soccer M(s)/W(s), softball W(s), swimming and diving M(c)/W(c), tennis M(s)/W(s), track and field M(s)/W(s), triathlon M(c)/W(c), ultimate Frisbee M(c)/W(c), volleyball M(c)/W(s), water polo M(s)/W(s). *Intramural sports:* badminton M/W, basketball M/W, football M/W, soccer M/W, softball M/W, table tennis M/W, tennis M/W, volleyball M/W.

Campus security: 24-hour emergency response devices and patrols, late-night transport/escort service, controlled dormitory access.

Student services: health clinic, personal/psychological counseling.

COSTS & FINANCIAL AID

Costs (2017–18) *Comprehensive fee:* $64,345 includes full-time tuition ($49,233), mandatory fees ($625), and room and board ($14,487). Part-time tuition: $1368 per unit. Part-time tuition and fees vary according to course load. *Room and board:* Room and board charges vary according to board plan and housing facility. *Payment plan:* installment. *Waivers:* employees or children of employees.

Financial Aid Of all full-time matriculated undergraduates who enrolled in 2017, 3,175 applied for aid, 2,423 were judged to have need, 732 had their need fully met. 325 Federal Work-Study jobs (averaging $3208). In 2017, 1515 non-need-based awards were made. *Average percent of need met:* 77. *Average financial aid package:* $37,051. *Average need-based loan:* $4563. *Average need-based gift aid:* $28,976. *Average non-need-based aid:* $16,185. *Average indebtedness upon graduation:* $28,808.

APPLYING

Standardized Tests *Required:* SAT or ACT (for admission).

Options: electronic application, early admission, early decision, early action, deferred entrance.

Application fee: $60.

Required: essay or personal statement, high school transcript, 1 letter of recommendation.

Application deadlines: 1/7 (freshmen), 4/15 (transfers), 11/1 (early action).

Early decision deadline: 11/1.

Notification: 4/1 (freshmen), continuous (transfers), 12/23 (early decision), 12/23 (early action).

CONTACT

Mrs. Eva Blanco Masias, Dean of Undergraduate Admissions, Santa Clara University, 500 El Camino Real, Santa Clara, CA 95053. *Phone:* 408-554-4700. *Fax:* 408-554-5255. *E-mail:* admission@scu.edu.

Scripps College

Claremont, California
http://www.scrippscollege.edu/

- **Independent** 4-year, founded 1926
- **Suburban** 37-acre campus with easy access to Los Angeles
- **Women only** 1,059 undergraduate students, 100% full-time
- **Very difficult** entrance level, 33% of applicants were admitted

UNDERGRAD STUDENTS

1,056 full-time, 3 part-time. 50% are from out of state; 4% Black or African American, non-Hispanic/Latino; 13% Hispanic/Latino; 16% Asian, non-Hispanic/Latino; 0.2% Native Hawaiian or other Pacific Islander, non-Hispanic/Latino; 5% Two or more races, non-Hispanic/Latino; 4% Race/ethnicity unknown; 6% international; 100% live on campus.

Freshmen:

Admission: 2,841 applied, 948 admitted, 327 enrolled. *Average high school GPA:* 4.1. *Test scores:* SAT evidence-based reading and writing scores over 500: 100%; SAT math scores over 500: 100%; ACT scores over 18: 100%; SAT evidence-based reading and writing scores over 600: 96%; SAT math scores over 600: 92%; ACT scores over 24: 100%; SAT evidence-based reading and writing scores over 700: 60%; SAT math scores over 700: 46%; ACT scores over 30: 73%.

Retention: 92% of full-time freshmen returned.

FACULTY

Total: 125, 75% full-time, 96% with terminal degrees.

Student/faculty ratio: 10:1.

ACADEMICS

Calendar: semesters. *Degrees:* bachelor's and postbachelor's certificates.

Special study options: accelerated degree program, advanced placement credit, cooperative education, double majors, independent study, internships, off-campus study, services for LD students, student-designed majors, study abroad. *ROTC:* Army (c), Air Force (c).

Unusual degree programs: 3-2 business administration with Claremont Graduate University; engineering with Harvey Mudd College, Columbia University; American politics, economics, philosophy, public policy, international studies, religion with Claremont Graduate University.

Computers: Students can access the following: campus intranet, computer help desk, free student e-mail accounts, online (class) grades, online (class) registration, online (class) schedules, 2 ports per dorm room. Campuswide network is available. 100% of college-owned or -operated housing units are wired for high-speed Internet access. Wireless service is available via entire campus.

Library: Honnold Library plus 2 others. Students can reserve study rooms.

STUDENT LIFE

Housing options: on-campus residence required for freshman year; women-only, special housing for students with disabilities. Campus housing is university owned. Freshman campus housing is guaranteed.

Activities and organizations: drama/theater group, student-run newspaper, radio station, choral group, Scripps Associated Students.

Athletics Member NCAA. All Division III. *Intercollegiate sports:* basketball W, cross-country running W, equestrian sports W(c), fencing W(c), golf W, lacrosse W, rugby W(c), skiing (downhill) W(c), soccer W, softball W, swimming and diving W, tennis W, track and field W, ultimate Frisbee W(c), volleyball W, water polo W. *Intramural sports:* basketball W, soccer W, softball W, volleyball W, water polo W.

Campus security: 24-hour emergency response devices and patrols, late-night transport/escort service, controlled dormitory access.

Student services: health clinic, personal/psychological counseling, women's center.

COSTS & FINANCIAL AID

Costs (2017–18) *Comprehensive fee:* $69,260 includes full-time tuition ($52,748), mandatory fees ($218), and room and board ($16,294). Full-time tuition and fees vary according to course load and degree level. Part-time tuition: $6594 per course. Part-time tuition and fees vary according to course load and degree level. *College room only:* $8872. Room and board charges vary according to board plan. *Payment plans:* tuition prepayment, installment. *Waivers:* employees or children of employees.

Financial Aid Of all full-time matriculated undergraduates who enrolled in 2016, 482 applied for aid, 371 were judged to have need, 371 had their need fully met. In 2016, 211 non-need-based awards were made. *Average percent of need met:* 100. *Average financial aid package:* $46,503. *Average need-based loan:* $3625. *Average need-based gift aid:* $37,532. *Average non-need-based aid:* $16,667. *Average indebtedness upon graduation:* $19,639. *Financial aid deadline:* 2/1.

APPLYING

Standardized Tests *Required:* SAT or ACT (for admission).

Options: electronic application, early admission, early decision, deferred entrance.

Application fee: $60.

Required: essay or personal statement, high school transcript, 2 letters of recommendation, school report completed by the student's secondary school counselor. *Recommended:* minimum 3.0 GPA.

Application deadlines: 1/1 (freshmen), 4/1 (transfers).

Early decision deadline: 11/15 (for plan 1), 1/1 (for plan 2).

Notification: 4/1 (freshmen), 4/1 (out-of-state freshmen), 5/15 (transfers), 12/15 (early decision plan 1), 2/15 (early decision plan 2).

CONTACT

Laura Stratton, Director of Admission, Scripps College, 1030 Columbia Avenue, Claremont, CA 91711. *Phone:* 909-621-8149. *Toll-free phone:* 800-770-1333. *Fax:* 909-607-7508. *E-mail:* admission@scrippscollege.edu.

Shasta Bible College
Redding, California
http://www.shasta.edu/

CONTACT

Connie Barton, Registrar, Shasta Bible College, 2951 Goodwater Avenue, Redding, CA 96002. *Phone:* 530-221-4275 Ext. 26. *Toll-free phone:* 800-800-4SBC. *Fax:* 530-221-6929. *E-mail:* registrar@shasta.edu.

Simpson University
Redding, California
http://www.simpsonu.edu/

- **Independent** comprehensive, founded 1921, affiliated with The Christian and Missionary Alliance
- **Suburban** 100-acre campus
- **Endowment** $5.9 million
- **Coed**
- **Moderately difficult** entrance level

FACULTY

Student/faculty ratio: 11:1.

ACADEMICS

Calendar: semesters. *Degrees:* certificates, associate, bachelor's, master's, post-master's, and postbachelor's certificates.

Library: Start-Kilgour Memorial Library. *Books:* 103,721 (physical), 369,714 (digital/electronic); *Serial titles:* 340 (physical), 28,286 (digital/electronic); *Databases:* 54. Weekly public service hours: 93; students can reserve study rooms.

STUDENT LIFE

Housing options: on-campus residence required through junior year; men-only, women-only, special housing for students with disabilities. Campus housing is university owned. Freshman campus housing is guaranteed.

Activities and organizations: drama/theater group, student-run newspaper, choral group, Summer Missions Trips, Biology Club, Boxing Club.

Athletics Member NAIA, NCCAA.

Campus security: 24-hour emergency response devices and patrols, student patrols, late-night transport/escort service, controlled dormitory access, emergency whistle program and monthly campus safety meetings.

Student services: health clinic, personal/psychological counseling.

COSTS & FINANCIAL AID

Costs (2017–18) *Comprehensive fee:* $35,700 includes full-time tuition ($27,250), mandatory fees ($100), and room and board ($8350). Full-time tuition and fees vary according to course load. Part-time tuition: $1150 per credit hour. Part-time tuition and fees vary according to course load. *Room and board:* Room and board charges vary according to board plan and housing facility.

Financial Aid Of all full-time matriculated undergraduates who enrolled in 2016, 702 applied for aid, 628 were judged to have need, 70 had their need fully met. 58 Federal Work-Study jobs (averaging $1229). In 2016, 29 non-need-based awards were made. *Average percent of need met:* 59. *Average financial aid package:* $17,174. *Average need-based loan:* $4556. *Average need-based gift aid:* $11,606. *Average non-need-based aid:* $10,039. *Average indebtedness upon graduation:* $26,938.

APPLYING

Standardized Tests *Required:* SAT or ACT (for admission). *Recommended:* SAT and SAT Subject Tests or ACT (for admission).

Options: electronic application, early action, deferred entrance.

Application fee: $35.

Required: essay or personal statement, high school transcript, minimum 3.0 GPA, 1 letter of recommendation, Christian commitment. *Required for some:* interview.

CONTACT

Mr. Molly McKeever, Director of Undergraduate Admissions, Simpson University, 2211 College View Drive, Redding, CA 96003-8606. *Phone:* 530-226-5600. *Toll-free phone:* 888-9-SIMPSON. *Fax:* 530-226-4861. *E-mail:* admissions@simpsonu.edu.

Soka University of America

Aliso Viejo, California

http://www.soka.edu/

- **Independent** comprehensive, founded 1987
- **Suburban** 103-acre campus with easy access to Los Angeles, San Diego
- **Endowment** $1.2 billion
- **Coed** 412 undergraduate students, 100% full-time, 62% women, 38% men
- **Most difficult** entrance level, 37% of applicants were admitted

UNDERGRAD STUDENTS

411 full-time, 1 part-time. Students come from 30 states and territories; 31 other countries; 46% are from out of state; 4% Black or African American, non-Hispanic/Latino; 10% Hispanic/Latino; 13% Asian, non-Hispanic/Latino; 0.5% Native Hawaiian or other Pacific Islander, non-Hispanic/Latino; 7% Two or more races, non-Hispanic/Latino; 2% Race/ethnicity unknown; 43% international; 99% live on campus.

Freshmen:

Admission: 489 applied, 182 admitted, 107 enrolled. *Average high school GPA:* 4.0. *Test scores:* SAT evidence-based reading and writing scores over 500: 99%; SAT math scores over 500: 100%; ACT scores over 18: 100%; SAT evidence-based reading and writing scores over 600: 65%; SAT math scores over 600: 76%; ACT scores over 24: 95%; SAT evidence-based reading and writing scores over 700: 15%; SAT math scores over 700: 30%; ACT scores over 30: 42%.

Retention: 94% of full-time freshmen returned.

FACULTY

Total: 68, 65% full-time, 84% with terminal degrees.

Student/faculty ratio: 8:1.

ACADEMICS

Calendar: semesters. *Degrees:* bachelor's and master's.

Special study options: cooperative education, independent study, internships, off-campus study, services for LD students, study abroad.

Computers: 100 computers/terminals and 100 ports are available on campus for general student use. Students can access the following: campus intranet, computer help desk, free student e-mail accounts, online (class) grades, online (class) registration, online (class) schedules, course and administrative applications. Campuswide network is available. 100% of college-owned or -operated housing units are wired for high-speed Internet access. Wireless service is available via entire campus. **Library:** Daisaku and Kaneko Ikeda Library. *Books:* 95,080 (physical), 261,022 (digital/electronic); *Serial titles:* 96 (physical), 7,563 (digital/electronic); *Databases:* 170. Study areas open 24 hours, 5–7 days a week; students can reserve study rooms.

STUDENT LIFE

Housing options: on-campus residence required through senior year; coed, men-only, women-only, cooperative, special housing for students with disabilities. Campus housing is university owned. Freshman campus housing is guaranteed.

Activities and organizations: choral group, Josho Daiko (Japanese Drum Club), Rhythmission (Hip Hop Dance Club), Sualseros (Salsa Dance Club), Ka Pilina Ho'olokahi (Hawaiian Dance Club), Soul Wings (Choir).

Athletics Member NAIA. *Intercollegiate sports:* cross-country running M(s)/W(s), golf W, soccer M(s)/W(s), swimming and diving M(s)/W(s), track and field M(s)/W(s). *Intramural sports:* archery M(c)/W(c), baseball M(c), basketball M(c)/W(c), cheerleading M(c)/W(c), tennis M(c)/W(c), volleyball M(c)/W(c).

Campus security: 24-hour emergency response devices and patrols, student patrols, late-night transport/escort service, controlled dormitory access.

Student services: health clinic, personal/psychological counseling.

COSTS & FINANCIAL AID

Costs (2018–19) *Comprehensive fee:* $45,510 includes full-time tuition ($31,310), mandatory fees ($1670), and room and board ($12,530). Full-time tuition and fees vary according to class time, course level, course load, and program. Part-time tuition: $1305 per credit hour. Part-time tuition and fees vary according to class time, course level, course load, and program. *Room and board:* Room and board charges vary according to board plan. *Payment plans:* installment, deferred payment. *Waivers:* employees or children of employees.

Financial Aid Of all full-time matriculated undergraduates who enrolled in 2017, 411 applied for aid, 350 were judged to have need, 249 had their need fully met. 34 Federal Work-Study jobs (averaging $1969). In 2017, 30 non-need-based awards were made. *Average percent of need met:* 88. *Average financial aid package:* $36,220. *Average need-based loan:* $4092. *Average need-based gift aid:* $24,414. *Average non-need-based aid:* $19,131. *Average indebtedness upon graduation:* $29,024. *Financial aid deadline:* 3/2.

APPLYING

Standardized Tests *Required:* SAT or ACT (for admission).

Options: electronic application, early admission, early action, deferred entrance.

Application fee: $45.

Required: essay or personal statement, high school transcript, 2 letters of recommendation, IERF evaluation for course work completed abroad. *Recommended:* interview.

Application deadlines: 1/15 (freshmen), 11/1 (early action).

Notification: 3/1 (freshmen), 3/1 (out-of-state freshmen), 12/1 (early action).

CONTACT

Erica Espejo, Admission Operations Coordinator, Soka University of America, Enrollment Services, 1 University Drive, Aliso Viejo, CA 92656. *Phone:* 949-480-4151 Ext. 4151. *Toll-free phone:* 888-600-SOKA. *Fax:* 949-480-4151. *E-mail:* eespejo@soka.edu.

Sonoma State University

Rohnert Park, California

http://www.sonoma.edu/

- **State-supported** comprehensive, founded 1960, part of California State University System
- **Small-town** 280-acre campus with easy access to San Francisco
- **Endowment** $47.1 million
- **Coed** 8,551 undergraduate students, 92% full-time, 62% women, 38% men
- **Moderately difficult** entrance level, 82% of applicants were admitted

UNDERGRAD STUDENTS

7,857 full-time, 694 part-time. 2% Black or African American, non-Hispanic/Latino; 33% Hispanic/Latino; 5% Asian, non-Hispanic/Latino; 0.3% Native Hawaiian or other Pacific Islander, non-Hispanic/Latino; 0.5% American Indian or Alaska Native, non-Hispanic/Latino; 7% Two or more races, non-Hispanic/Latino; 7% Race/ethnicity unknown; 2% international; 9% transferred in; 22% live on campus.

Freshmen:

Admission: 15,711 applied, 12,888 admitted, 1,784 enrolled. *Average high school GPA:* 3.3. *Test scores:* SAT evidence-based reading and writing scores over 500: 76%; SAT math scores over 500: 70%; ACT scores over 18: 83%; SAT evidence-based reading and writing scores over 600: 22%; SAT math scores over 600: 17%; ACT scores over 24: 28%; SAT evidence-based reading and writing scores over 700: 1%; SAT math scores over 700: 1%; ACT scores over 30: 2%.

Retention: 77% of full-time freshmen returned.

FACULTY

Total: 568, 44% full-time, 63% with terminal degrees.

Student/faculty ratio: 23:1.

ACADEMICS

Calendar: semesters. *Degrees:* bachelor's and master's.

Special study options: academic remediation for entering students, accelerated degree program, adult/continuing education programs, advanced placement credit, cooperative education, distance learning, double majors, English as a second language, honors programs, independent study, internships, off-campus study, part-time degree program, services for LD students, student-designed majors, study abroad, summer session for credit. *ROTC:* Army (c), Air Force (c).

Computers: Students can access the following: computer help desk, free student e-mail accounts, online (class) grades, online (class) registration,

online (class) schedules. Campuswide network is available. 100% of college-owned or -operated housing units are wired for high-speed Internet access. Wireless service is available via entire campus.
Library: Jean and Charles Schultz Information Center plus 1 other. Students can reserve study rooms.

STUDENT LIFE
Housing options: coed, special housing for students with disabilities. Campus housing is university owned. Freshman applicants given priority for college housing.

Activities and organizations: drama/theater group, student-run newspaper, radio station, choral group, national fraternities, national sororities.

Athletics Member NCAA. All Division II. *Intercollegiate sports:* baseball M(s), basketball M(s)/W(s), cross-country running W, golf M/W, soccer M(s)/W(s), softball W(s), tennis M(s)/W(s), track and field W, volleyball W(s), water polo W. *Intramural sports:* archery M(c)/W(c), basketball M/W, cheerleading M/W, crew M/W, cross-country running M, fencing M/W, football M/W, lacrosse M(c)/W(c), rock climbing M/W, rowing M/W, soccer M/W, ultimate Frisbee M(c)/W(c), volleyball M(c)/W(c).

Campus security: 24-hour emergency response devices and patrols, student patrols, late-night transport/escort service, controlled dormitory access.

Student services: health clinic, personal/psychological counseling, women's center, legal services.

COSTS & FINANCIAL AID
Costs (2017–18) *Tuition:* $3330 per year part-time; state resident $5742 full-time; nonresident $17,622 full-time. Full-time tuition and fees vary according to course load and degree level. Part-time tuition and fees vary according to course load and degree level. *Required fees:* $1982 full-time. *Room and board:* $13,554. Room and board charges vary according to board plan and housing facility. *Payment plan:* installment. *Waivers:* employees or children of employees.

Financial Aid Of all full-time matriculated undergraduates who enrolled in 2017, 5,735 applied for aid, 4,708 were judged to have need, 225 had their need fully met. In 2017, 61 non-need-based awards were made. *Average percent of need met:* 51. *Average financial aid package:* $10,616. *Average need-based loan:* $3112. *Average need-based gift aid:* $10,045. *Average non-need-based aid:* $2374. *Average indebtedness upon graduation:* $21,799.

APPLYING
Standardized Tests *Required:* SAT or ACT (for admission).
Options: electronic application, early admission.
Application fee: $55.
Required: high school transcript.
Application deadlines: rolling (freshmen), rolling (transfers).
Notification: continuous (freshmen), continuous (transfers).

CONTACT
Ms. Natalie Kalogiannis, Director of Admissions, Sonoma State University, 1801 East Cotati Avenue, Rohnert Park, CA 94928-3609. *Phone:* 707-664-2874. *E-mail:* natalie.kalogiannis@sonoma.edu.

Southern California Institute of Architecture
Los Angeles, California
http://www.sciarc.edu/

CONTACT
Jamie Black, Admissions Counselor, Southern California Institute of Architecture, 960 East Third Street, Los Angeles, CA 90013. *Phone:* 213-356-5320. *Fax:* 213-613-2260. *E-mail:* admissions@sciarc.edu.

Southern California Institute of Technology
Anaheim, California
http://www.scitech.edu/

CONTACT
Mrs. Sam Rokni, Southern California Institute of Technology, 525 N. Muller Street, Anaheim, CA 92801. *Phone:* 714-300-0300 Ext. 227. *Fax:* 714-300-0311. *E-mail:* admissions@scitech.edu.

Southern California Seminary
El Cajon, California
http://www.socalsem.edu/

CONTACT
Southern California Seminary, 2075 East Madison Avenue, El Cajon, CA 92019. *Phone:* 619-201-8959. *Toll-free phone:* 888-389-7244.

Stanbridge University
Irvine, California
http://www.stanbridge.edu/

CONTACT
Stanbridge University, 2041 Business Center Drive, Irvine, CA 92612.

Stanford University
Stanford, California
http://www.stanford.edu/

- **Independent** university, founded 1891
- **Suburban** 8180-acre campus with easy access to San Francisco, San Jose
- **Coed** 7,034 undergraduate students, 100% full-time, 49% women, 51% men
- **Most difficult** entrance level, 5% of applicants were admitted

UNDERGRAD STUDENTS
7,034 full-time. Students come from 52 states and territories; 76 other countries; 58% are from out of state; 6% Black or African American, non-Hispanic/Latino; 16% Hispanic/Latino; 21% Asian, non-Hispanic/Latino; 0.3% Native Hawaiian or other Pacific Islander, non-Hispanic/Latino; 1% American Indian or Alaska Native, non-Hispanic/Latino; 10% Two or more races, non-Hispanic/Latino; 0.2% Race/ethnicity unknown; 9% international; 0.6% transferred in; 93% live on campus.

Freshmen:
Admission: 43,997 applied, 2,118 admitted, 1,738 enrolled. *Average high school GPA:* 3.9. *Test scores:* ACT scores over 18: 100%; ACT scores over 24: 99%; ACT scores over 30: 87%.
Retention: 98% of full-time freshmen returned.

FACULTY
Total: 1,637, 99% full-time, 99% with terminal degrees.
Student/faculty ratio: 4:1.

ACADEMICS
Calendar: quarters. *Degrees:* bachelor's, master's, doctoral, and postbachelor's certificates.
Special study options: advanced placement credit, distance learning, double majors, English as a second language, honors programs, independent study, internships, off-campus study, services for LD students, student-designed majors, study abroad, summer session for credit. *ROTC:* Army (c), Navy (c), Air Force (c).
Computers: 1,000 computers/terminals are available on campus for general student use. Students can access the following: campus intranet, computer help desk, free student e-mail accounts, online (class) grades, online (class) registration, online (class) schedules. Campuswide network is available. 100% of college-owned or -operated housing units are wired for high-speed Internet access. Wireless service is available via entire campus.
Library: Green Library plus 20 others. *Books:* 9.5 million (physical), 1.5 million (digital/electronic); *Serial titles:* 77,000 (physical). Study areas open 24 hours, 5–7 days a week; students can reserve study rooms.

STUDENT LIFE

Housing options: on-campus residence required for freshman year; coed, women-only, cooperative, special housing for students with disabilities. Campus housing is university owned. Freshman campus housing is guaranteed.

Activities and organizations: drama/theater group, student-run newspaper, radio and television station, choral group, marching band, Ram's Head (theatre club), Axe Committee (athletic support), Business Association of Stanford Entrepreneurial Students, Asian-American Student Association, Stanford Daily, national fraternities, national sororities.

Athletics Member NCAA, NAIA. All NCAA Division I. *Intercollegiate sports:* archery M(c)/W(c), badminton M(c)/W(c), baseball M(s), basketball M(s)/W(s), cheerleading M(c)/W(c), crew M(s)/W(s), cross-country running M(s)/W(s), equestrian sports M(c)/W(c), fencing M(s)/W(s), field hockey W(s), football M(s), golf M(s)/W(s), gymnastics M(s)/W(s), ice hockey M(c), lacrosse M(c)/W(s), racquetball M(c)/W(c), rock climbing M(c)/W(c), rowing M(s)/W(s), rugby M(c)/W(c), sailing M/W, sand volleyball W, skiing (downhill) M(c)/W(c), soccer M(s)/W(s), softball W(s), squash M(c)/W(s), swimming and diving M(s)/W(s), tennis M(s)/W(s), track and field M(s)/W(s), triathlon M(c)/W(c), ultimate Frisbee M(c)/W(c), volleyball M(s)/W(s), water polo M(s)/W(s), wrestling M(s). *Intramural sports:* badminton M/W, baseball M(c), basketball M(c)/W(c), bowling M/W, cross-country running M(c)/W(c), football M/W, golf M(c)/W(c), lacrosse W(c), racquetball M/W, rock climbing M/W, sand volleyball M/W, soccer M(c)/W(c), softball M/W, swimming and diving M(c)/W(c), table tennis M(c)/W(c), tennis M(c)/W(c), track and field M/W, ultimate Frisbee M/W, volleyball M/W, water polo M/W.

Campus security: 24-hour emergency response devices and patrols, late-night transport/escort service, controlled dormitory access.

Student services: health clinic, personal/psychological counseling, women's center, legal services.

COSTS & FINANCIAL AID

Costs (2017–18) *Comprehensive fee:* $64,729 includes full-time tuition ($48,987), mandatory fees ($630), and room and board ($15,112). *Room and board:* Room and board charges vary according to board plan. *Payment plan:* installment. *Waivers:* employees or children of employees.

Financial Aid Of all full-time matriculated undergraduates who enrolled in 2016, 3,714 applied for aid, 3,362 were judged to have need, 3,048 had their need fully met. 549 Federal Work-Study jobs, 1,782 state and other part-time jobs (averaging $2296). In 2016, 24 non-need-based awards were made. *Average percent of need met:* 100. *Average financial aid package:* $51,729. *Average need-based loan:* $3059. *Average need-based gift aid:* $48,039. *Average non-need-based aid:* $10,434. *Average indebtedness upon graduation:* $20,205.

APPLYING

Standardized Tests *Required:* SAT or ACT (for admission). *Recommended:* SAT Subject Tests (for admission).

Options: electronic application, early action, deferred entrance.

Application fee: $90.

Required: essay or personal statement, high school transcript, 2 letters of recommendation.

Application deadlines: 1/3 (freshmen), 3/15 (transfers), 11/1 (early action).

Notification: 4/1 (freshmen), 5/15 (transfers), 12/15 (early action).

CONTACT

Stanford University, 450 Serra Mall, Stanford, CA 94305-2004.

Studio School

Los Angeles, California

http://www.studioschool.org/

CONTACT

Studio School, 1201 West 5th Street, Los Angeles, CA 90017.

SUM Bible College & Theological Seminary

Oakland, California

http://www.sum.edu/

CONTACT

Admissions, SUM Bible College & Theological Seminary, 735 105th Avenue, Oakland, CA 94603. *Phone:* 510-567-6174. *Toll-free phone:* 888-567-6174. *Fax:* 510-568-1024.

Thomas Aquinas College

Santa Paula, California

http://www.thomasaquinas.edu/

- **Independent Roman Catholic** 4-year, founded 1971
- **Rural** 131-acre campus with easy access to Los Angeles
- **Endowment** $22.5 million
- **Coed** 370 undergraduate students, 100% full-time, 52% women, 48% men
- **Very difficult** entrance level, 72% of applicants were admitted

UNDERGRAD STUDENTS

370 full-time. Students come from 43 states and territories; 7 other countries; 60% are from out of state; 0.8% Black or African American, non-Hispanic/Latino; 16% Hispanic/Latino; 2% Asian, non-Hispanic/Latino; 0.3% Native Hawaiian or other Pacific Islander, non-Hispanic/Latino; 0.5% American Indian or Alaska Native, non-Hispanic/Latino; 5% Two or more races, non-Hispanic/Latino; 1% Race/ethnicity unknown; 2% international; 99% live on campus.

Freshmen:

Admission: 192 applied, 138 admitted, 90 enrolled. *Average high school GPA:* 3.8. *Test scores:* SAT evidence-based reading and writing scores over 500: 98%; SAT math scores over 500: 100%; ACT scores over 18: 100%; SAT evidence-based reading and writing scores over 600: 92%; SAT math scores over 600: 63%; ACT scores over 24: 92%; SAT evidence-based reading and writing scores over 700: 43%; SAT math scores over 700: 19%; ACT scores over 30: 36%.

Retention: 90% of full-time freshmen returned.

FACULTY

Total: 39, 79% full-time, 85% with terminal degrees.

Student/faculty ratio: 11:1.

ACADEMICS

Calendar: semesters. *Degree:* bachelor's.

Special study options: cooperative education.

Computers: 20 computers/terminals and 16 ports are available on campus for general student use. Students can access the following: computer help desk, free student e-mail accounts. Campuswide network is available.

Library: St. Bernardine Library. *Books:* 62,852 (physical); *Serial titles:* 78 (physical). Students can reserve study rooms.

STUDENT LIFE

Housing options: on-campus residence required through senior year; men-only, women-only. Campus housing is university owned. Freshman campus housing is guaranteed.

Activities and organizations: drama/theater group, choral group, Musical Groups (Choir, Chamber Orchestra), Theatre Groups, Language Clubs, Pro-Life Ministry, Religious groups.

Athletics *Intramural sports:* basketball M/W, football M, soccer M/W, softball M/W, table tennis M/W, tennis M/W, ultimate Frisbee M/W, volleyball M/W.

Campus security: daily security patrol.

Student services: personal/psychological counseling.

COSTS & FINANCIAL AID

Costs (2017–18) *Comprehensive fee:* $32,450 includes full-time tuition ($24,500) and room and board ($7950). *Payment plan:* installment.

Financial Aid Of all full-time matriculated undergraduates who enrolled in 2017, 262 applied for aid, 258 were judged to have need, 258 had their need fully met. 236 state and other part-time jobs (averaging $4796). *Average percent of need met:* 100. *Average financial aid package:*

$20,095. *Average need-based loan:* $4650. *Average need-based gift aid:* $13,585. *Average indebtedness upon graduation:* $19,269. *Financial aid deadline:* 3/2.

APPLYING
Standardized Tests *Required:* SAT or ACT (for admission).
Options: electronic application.
Required: essay or personal statement, high school transcript, 3 letters of recommendation. *Required for some:* interview. *Recommended:* minimum 3.0 GPA.
Application deadlines: rolling (freshmen), rolling (out-of-state freshmen).
Notification: continuous (freshmen), continuous (out-of-state freshmen).

CONTACT
Mr. Jonathan P. Daly, Director of Admissions, Thomas Aquinas College, 10000 Ojai Road, Santa Paula, CA 93060-9621. *Phone:* 805-525-4417 Ext. 5901. *Toll-free phone:* 800-634-9797. *Fax:* 805-421-5905. *E-mail:* admissions@thomasaquinas.edu.

Touro College Los Angeles
West Hollywood, California
http://www.touro.edu/losangeles/
- **Independent** 4-year, founded 2005
- **Coed**

ACADEMICS
Calendar: semesters. *Degree:* bachelor's.

COSTS
Costs (2017–18) *Tuition:* $16,800 full-time, $700 per credit part-time. No tuition increase for student's term of enrollment. *Required fees:* $150 full-time. *Payment plan:* installment. *Waivers:* employees or children of employees.

CONTACT
Touro College Los Angeles, 1317 North Crescent Heights Boulevard, West Hollywood, CA 90046.

Touro University Worldwide
Los Alamitos, California
http://www.tuw.edu/
- **Independent** comprehensive
- **Coed** 484 undergraduate students, 50% full-time, 70% women, 30% men

UNDERGRAD STUDENTS
244 full-time, 240 part-time. Students come from 39 states and territories; 2 other countries; 21% Black or African American, non-Hispanic/Latino; 9% Hispanic/Latino; 3% Asian, non-Hispanic/Latino; 0.6% Native Hawaiian or other Pacific Islander, non-Hispanic/Latino; 7% Two or more races, non-Hispanic/Latino; 25% Race/ethnicity unknown; 19% transferred in.

Freshmen:
Admission: 24 enrolled.
Retention: 50% of full-time freshmen returned.

FACULTY
Total: 119, 11% full-time, 78% with terminal degrees.
Student/faculty ratio: 22:1.

ACADEMICS
Degrees: associate, bachelor's, master's, and doctoral.
Special study options: distance learning, honors programs, internships, part-time degree program, services for LD students.
Computers: Students can access the following: online (class) grades, online (class) registration, online (class) schedules.

COSTS
Costs (2018–19) *Tuition:* $10,800 full-time, $400 per credit hour part-time. Full-time tuition and fees vary according to program. Part-time tuition and fees vary according to program. No tuition increase for student's term of enrollment. *Payment plans:* tuition prepayment, installment. *Waivers:* employees or children of employees.

APPLYING
Options: electronic application.

CONTACT
Touro University Worldwide, 10601 Calle Lee, Suite 179, Los Alamitos, CA 90720.

Trident University International
Cypress, California
http://www.trident.edu/

CONTACT
Trident University International, 5757 Plaza Drive, Suite 100, Cypress, CA 90630. *Phone:* 800-579-3197.

United States University
San Diego, California
http://www.usuniversity.edu/

CONTACT
Admissions, United States University, 7675 Mission Valley Road, San Diego, CA 92108. *Phone:* 619-477-6310. *Toll-free phone:* 888-422-3381. *Fax:* 619-477-7340.

University of Antelope Valley
Lancaster, California
http://www.uav.edu/

CONTACT
University of Antelope Valley, 44055 North Sierra Highway, Lancaster, CA 93534.

University of California, Berkeley
Berkeley, California
http://www.berkeley.edu/

CONTACT
University of California, Berkeley, Berkeley, CA 94720-1500.

University of California, Davis
Davis, California
http://www.ucdavis.edu/
- **State-supported** university, founded 1908, part of University of California System
- **Suburban** 5300-acre campus with easy access to San Francisco
- **Coed** 30,145 undergraduate students, 97% full-time, 60% women, 40% men
- **Very difficult** entrance level, 44% of applicants were admitted

UNDERGRAD STUDENTS
29,362 full-time, 783 part-time. 5% are from out of state; 2% Black or African American, non-Hispanic/Latino; 21% Hispanic/Latino; 28% Asian, non-Hispanic/Latino; 0.4% Native Hawaiian or other Pacific Islander, non-Hispanic/Latino; 0.2% American Indian or Alaska Native, non-Hispanic/Latino; 5% Two or more races, non-Hispanic/Latino; 2% Race/ethnicity unknown; 16% international; 12% transferred in; 25% live on campus.

Freshmen:
Admission: 70,214 applied, 30,573 admitted, 5,852 enrolled. *Average high school GPA:* 4.0. *Test scores:* SAT evidence-based reading and writing scores over 500: 92%; SAT math scores over 500: 94%; ACT scores over 18: 98%; SAT evidence-based reading and writing scores over 600: 53%; SAT math scores over 600: 65%; ACT scores over 24: 84%; SAT evidence-based reading and writing scores over 700: 10%; SAT math scores over 700: 29%; ACT scores over 30: 37%.
Retention: 93% of full-time freshmen returned.

ACADEMICS
Calendar: quarters. *Degrees:* bachelor's, master's, doctoral, post-master's, and postbachelor's certificates.

Special study options: academic remediation for entering students, adult/continuing education programs, advanced placement credit, double majors, English as a second language, freshman honors college, honors programs, independent study, internships, part-time degree program, services for LD students, student-designed majors, study abroad, summer session for credit. *ROTC:* Army (b), Navy (c), Air Force (c).

Computers: Students can access the following: campus intranet, computer help desk, free student e-mail accounts, online (class) grades, online (class) registration, online (class) schedules, software packages. Campuswide network is available. 100% of college-owned or -operated housing units are wired for high-speed Internet access. Wireless service is available via classrooms, libraries.

Library: Peter J. Shields Library plus 6 others. *Books:* 4.7 million (physical), 865,504 (digital/electronic); *Serial titles:* 121,933 (physical).

STUDENT LIFE
Housing options: coed, women-only, cooperative, special housing for students with disabilities. Campus housing is university owned, leased by the school and is provided by a third party. Freshman campus housing is guaranteed.

Activities and organizations: drama/theater group, student-run newspaper, radio and television station, choral group, marching band, national fraternities, national sororities.

Athletics Member NCAA. All Division I except football (Division I-AA). *Intercollegiate sports:* baseball M(s), basketball M(s)/W(s), cross-country running M(s)/W(s), field hockey W(s), golf M(s)/W(s), gymnastics W(s), lacrosse W(s), soccer M(s)/W(s), softball W(s), swimming and diving W(s), tennis M(s)/W(s), track and field M(s)/W(s), volleyball W(s), water polo M(s)/W(s). *Intramural sports:* archery M(c)/W(c), badminton M(c)/W(c), basketball M/W, crew M(c)/W(c), equestrian sports M(c)/W(c), fencing M(c)/W(c), football M/W, golf M/W, gymnastics M(c), ice hockey M(c)/W, lacrosse M(c)/W(c), racquetball M(c)/W(c), riflery M(c)/W(c), rugby M(c), sailing M(c)/W(c), skiing (cross-country) M(c)/W(c), skiing (downhill) M(c)/W(c), soccer M/W, softball M/W, swimming and diving W(c), table tennis M/W, tennis M/W, volleyball M(c)/W, water polo W(c).

Campus security: 24-hour emergency response devices and patrols, student patrols, late-night transport/escort service, controlled dormitory access, Campus Violence Prevention Program (CVPP).

Student services: health clinic, personal/psychological counseling, women's center, legal services.

COSTS & FINANCIAL AID
Costs (2018–19) *Tuition:* state resident $11,502 full-time; nonresident $40,497 full-time. *Required fees:* $2961 full-time. *Room and board:* $15,765. Room and board charges vary according to board plan.

Financial Aid Of all full-time matriculated undergraduates who enrolled in 2017, 20,459 applied for aid, 17,702 were judged to have need, 3,787 had their need fully met. In 2017, 1060 non-need-based awards were made. *Average percent of need met:* 81. *Average financial aid package:* $21,951. *Average need-based loan:* $6165. *Average need-based gift aid:* $18,761. *Average non-need-based aid:* $6623. *Average indebtedness upon graduation:* $19,124.

APPLYING
Standardized Tests *Required:* SAT or ACT (for admission).

Options: electronic application.

Application fee: $70.

Required: essay or personal statement, high school transcript, high school subject requirements.

Application deadlines: 11/30 (freshmen), 11/30 (transfers).

Notification: 3/15 (freshmen), continuous until 3/15 (transfers).

CONTACT
University of California, Davis, CA. *E-mail:* undergraduateadmissions@ucdavis.edu.

University of California, Irvine
Irvine, California
http://www.uci.edu/
- **State-supported** university, founded 1965, part of University of California System
- **Suburban** 1477-acre campus with easy access to Los Angeles
- **Coed** 29,307 undergraduate students, 98% full-time, 53% women, 47% men
- **Very difficult** entrance level, 37% of applicants were admitted

UNDERGRAD STUDENTS
28,851 full-time, 456 part-time. Students come from 46 states and territories; 76 other countries; 3% are from out of state; 2% Black or African American, non-Hispanic/Latino; 26% Hispanic/Latino; 36% Asian, non-Hispanic/Latino; 0.3% Native Hawaiian or other Pacific Islander, non-Hispanic/Latino; 4% Two or more races, non-Hispanic/Latino; 1% Race/ethnicity unknown; 17% international; 10% transferred in; 39% live on campus.

Freshmen:
Admission: 85,102 applied, 31,063 admitted, 6,545 enrolled. *Average high school GPA:* 4.0. *Test scores:* SAT evidence-based reading and writing scores over 500: 99%; SAT math scores over 500: 97%; SAT evidence-based reading and writing scores over 600: 67%; SAT math scores over 600: 72%; SAT evidence-based reading and writing scores over 700: 20%; SAT math scores over 700: 37%.

Retention: 94% of full-time freshmen returned.

FACULTY
Total: 1,634, 79% full-time, 98% with terminal degrees.

Student/faculty ratio: 18:1.

ACADEMICS
Calendar: quarters. *Degrees:* bachelor's, master's, doctoral, and postbachelor's certificates.

Special study options: accelerated degree program, advanced placement credit, distance learning, double majors, English as a second language, honors programs, independent study, internships, off-campus study, services for LD students, study abroad, summer session for credit. *ROTC:* Army (b), Air Force (c).

Computers: 1,500 computers/terminals are available on campus for general student use. Students can access the following: campus intranet, computer help desk, free student e-mail accounts, online (class) grades, online (class) registration, online (class) schedules. Campuswide network is available. 100% of college-owned or -operated housing units are wired for high-speed Internet access. Wireless service is available via entire campus.

Library: Langson Library plus 4 others. *Books:* 2.3 million (physical), 1.3 million (digital/electronic); *Serial titles:* 4,559 (physical), 146,177 (digital/electronic); *Databases:* 1,486. Study areas open 24 hours, 5–7 days a week; students can reserve study rooms.

STUDENT LIFE
Housing options: coed, men-only, women-only, special housing for students with disabilities. Campus housing is university owned and is provided by a third party. Freshman campus housing is guaranteed.

Activities and organizations: drama/theater group, student-run newspaper, radio station, choral group, marching band, national fraternities, national sororities.

Athletics Member NCAA. All Division I. *Intercollegiate sports:* archery M(c)/W(c), badminton M(c)/W(c), baseball M(s), basketball M(s)/W(s), crew M(c)/W(c), cross-country running M(s)/W(s), fencing M(c)/W(c), golf M(s)/W(s), lacrosse M(c)/W(c), rugby M(c)/W(c), sailing M(c)/W(c), soccer M(s)/W(s), table tennis M(c)/W(c), tennis M(s)/W(s), track and field M(s)/W(s), ultimate Frisbee M(c)/W(c), volleyball M(s)/W(s), water polo M(s)/W(s), wrestling M(c)/W(c). *Intramural sports:* basketball M/W, bowling M/W, football M/W, racquetball M/W, soccer M/W, softball M/W, swimming and diving M/W, table tennis M/W, tennis M/W, track and field M/W, ultimate Frisbee M/W, volleyball M/W, water polo M/W, wrestling M/W.

Campus security: 24-hour emergency response devices and patrols, student patrols, late-night transport/escort service, controlled dormitory access.

Student services: health clinic, personal/psychological counseling.

COSTS & FINANCIAL AID

Costs (2017–18) *Tuition:* state resident $11,502 full-time; nonresident $39,516 full-time. *Required fees:* $4014 full-time. *Room and board:* $14,829. Room and board charges vary according to board plan and housing facility. *Payment plan:* installment. *Waivers:* employees or children of employees.

Financial Aid Of all full-time matriculated undergraduates who enrolled in 2015, 19,466 applied for aid, 17,395 were judged to have need, 3,709 had their need fully met. In 2015, 478 non-need-based awards were made. *Average percent of need met:* 82. *Average financial aid package:* $23,022. *Average need-based loan:* $6753. *Average need-based gift aid:* $19,149. *Average non-need-based aid:* $7814. *Average indebtedness upon graduation:* $20,628. *Financial aid deadline:* 6/26.

APPLYING

Standardized Tests *Required:* SAT or ACT (for admission).

Options: electronic application.

Application fee: $70.

Required: essay or personal statement, high school transcript.

Application deadlines: 11/30 (freshmen), 11/30 (transfers).

Notification: 3/31 (freshmen), 4/30 (transfers).

CONTACT

University of California, Irvine, Office of Admissions and Relations with Schools, 260 Aldrich Hall, Irvine, CA 92697-1075. *Phone:* 949-824-6703. *Fax:* 949-824-2951. *E-mail:* admissions@uci.edu.

University of California, Los Angeles
Los Angeles, California
http://www.ucla.edu/

- **State-supported** university, founded 1919, part of University of California System
- **Urban** 419-acre campus with easy access to Los Angeles
- **Endowment** $3.6 billion
- **Coed** 31,002 undergraduate students, 98% full-time, 57% women, 43% men
- **Very difficult** entrance level, 18% of applicants were admitted

UNDERGRAD STUDENTS

30,458 full-time, 544 part-time. 12% are from out of state; 0.2% Black or African American, non-Hispanic/Latino; 22% Hispanic/Latino; 0.3% Asian, non-Hispanic/Latino; 27% Native Hawaiian or other Pacific Islander, non-Hispanic/Latino; 3% American Indian or Alaska Native, non-Hispanic/Latino; 5% Two or more races, non-Hispanic/Latino; 2% Race/ethnicity unknown; 12% international; 10% transferred in.

Freshmen:

Admission: 97,121 applied, 17,474 admitted, 6,038 enrolled. *Average high school GPA:* 4.4. *Test scores:* ACT scores over 18: 99%; ACT scores over 24: 86%; ACT scores over 30: 57%.

Retention: 97% of full-time freshmen returned.

FACULTY

Total: 2,706, 58% full-time, 92% with terminal degrees.

Student/faculty ratio: 17:1.

ACADEMICS

Calendar: quarters. *Degrees:* bachelor's, master's, and doctoral.

Special study options: accelerated degree program, advanced placement credit, double majors, freshman honors college, independent study, internships, off-campus study, services for LD students, student-designed majors, study abroad, summer session for credit. *ROTC:* Army (b), Navy (b), Air Force (b).

Computers: 4,000 computers/terminals are available on campus for general student use. Students can access the following: campus intranet, computer help desk, free student e-mail accounts, online (class) grades, online (class) registration, online (class) schedules, 24/7 Chat with a Librarian. Campuswide network is available. 100% of college-owned or -operated housing units are wired for high-speed Internet access. Wireless service is available via entire campus.

Library: Charles E. Young Research Library plus 13 others. *Books:* 13.8 million (physical), 2.1 million (digital/electronic); *Serial titles:* 9,543 (physical), 99,598 (digital/electronic); *Databases:* 1,794. Weekly public service hours: 104; study areas open 24 hours, 5–7 days a week; students can reserve study rooms.

STUDENT LIFE

Housing options: coed, cooperative, special housing for students with disabilities. Campus housing is university owned. Freshman campus housing is guaranteed.

Activities and organizations: drama/theater group, student-run newspaper, radio and television station, choral group, marching band, national fraternities, national sororities.

Athletics Member NCAA. All Division I except football (Division I-A). *Intercollegiate sports:* baseball M(s), basketball M(s)/W(s), crew W(s), cross-country running M(s)/W(s), golf M(s)/W(s), gymnastics W(s), soccer M(s)/W(s), softball W(s), swimming and diving W(s), tennis M(s)/W(s), track and field M(s)/W(s), volleyball M(s)/W(s), water polo M(s)/W(s). *Intramural sports:* archery M/W, badminton M/W, basketball M/W, bowling M/W, crew M/W, cross-country running M/W, fencing M/W, field hockey W, football M/W, golf M/W, gymnastics M/W, ice hockey M/W, lacrosse M/W, racquetball M/W, riflery M/W, rugby M/W, sailing M/W, skiing (cross-country) M/W, skiing (downhill) M/W, soccer M/W, softball M/W, squash M/W, swimming and diving M/W, table tennis M/W, tennis M/W, track and field M/W, ultimate Frisbee M/W, volleyball M/W, water polo M/W.

Campus security: 24-hour emergency response devices and patrols, student patrols, late-night transport/escort service, controlled dormitory access.

Student services: health clinic, personal/psychological counseling, women's center, legal services.

COSTS & FINANCIAL AID

Costs (2017–18) *One-time required fee:* $165. *Tuition:* state resident $11,502 full-time; nonresident $39,516 full-time. *Required fees:* $2082 full-time. *Room and board:* $15,143. Room and board charges vary according to board plan and housing facility.

Financial Aid Of all full-time matriculated undergraduates who enrolled in 2017, 17,808 applied for aid, 16,365 were judged to have need, 4,199 had their need fully met. In 2017, 983 non-need-based awards were made. *Average percent of need met:* 83. *Average financial aid package:* $23,980. *Average need-based loan:* $7488. *Average need-based gift aid:* $20,489. *Average non-need-based aid:* $5633. *Average indebtedness upon graduation:* $22,013.

APPLYING

Standardized Tests *Required:* SAT or ACT (for admission).

Options: electronic application.

Application fee: $70.

Required: essay or personal statement, high school transcript.

Application deadlines: 11/30 (freshmen), 11/30 (transfers).

Notification: 3/31 (freshmen), 4/30 (transfers).

CONTACT

University of California, Los Angeles, 405 Hilgard Avenue, Los Angeles, CA 90095. *Phone:* 310-825-3101.

University of California, Merced
Merced, California
http://www.ucmerced.edu/

CONTACT

Mr. Ruben Lubers, Assistant Director, Admissions and Outreach, University of California, Merced, 5200 North Lake Road, Merced, CA 95343. *Phone:* 209-228-4241. *E-mail:* admissions@ucmerced.edu.

University of California, Riverside
Riverside, California
http://www.ucr.edu/

- **State-supported** university, founded 1954, part of University of California System
- **Suburban** 1200-acre campus with easy access to Los Angeles
- **Coed** 20,069 undergraduate students, 98% full-time, 54% women, 46% men
- **Very difficult** entrance level, 57% of applicants were admitted

UNDERGRAD STUDENTS

19,716 full-time, 353 part-time. Students come from 23 states and territories; 95 other countries; 0.6% are from out of state; 3% Black or African American, non-Hispanic/Latino; 41% Hispanic/Latino; 34% Asian, non-Hispanic/Latino; 0.2% Native Hawaiian or other Pacific Islander, non-Hispanic/Latino; 0.1% American Indian or Alaska Native, non-Hispanic/Latino; 6% Two or more races, non-Hispanic/Latino; 1% Race/ethnicity unknown; 3% international; 7% transferred in; 31% live on campus.

Freshmen:

Admission: 43,682 applied, 25,001 admitted, 4,598 enrolled. *Average high school GPA:* 3.7. *Test scores:* SAT evidence-based reading and writing scores over 500: 92%; SAT math scores over 500: 92%; ACT scores over 18: 98%; SAT evidence-based reading and writing scores over 600: 48%; SAT math scores over 600: 49%; ACT scores over 24: 66%; SAT evidence-based reading and writing scores over 700: 7%; SAT math scores over 700: 14%; ACT scores over 30: 19%.

Retention: 89% of full-time freshmen returned.

FACULTY

Total: 1,164, 84% full-time, 98% with terminal degrees.

Student/faculty ratio: 22:1.

ACADEMICS

Calendar: quarters. *Degrees:* bachelor's, master's, and doctoral.

Special study options: accelerated degree program, adult/continuing education programs, advanced placement credit, distance learning, double majors, honors programs, independent study, internships, off-campus study, part-time degree program, services for LD students, study abroad, summer session for credit. *ROTC:* Army (c), Air Force (c).

Unusual degree programs: 3-2 engineering.

Computers: 556 computers/terminals are available on campus for general student use. Students can access the following: campus intranet, computer help desk, free student e-mail accounts, online (class) grades, online (class) registration, online (class) schedules, online viewing of financial information. Campuswide network is available. 100% of college-owned or -operated housing units are wired for high-speed Internet access. Wireless service is available via entire campus.

Library: Tomas Rivera Library plus 4 others. *Books:* 3.0 million (physical), 938,175 (digital/electronic); *Serial titles:* 71,249 (physical); *Databases:* 1,713. Weekly public service hours: 96; study areas open 24 hours, 5–7 days a week; students can reserve study rooms.

STUDENT LIFE

Housing options: coed, special housing for students with disabilities. Campus housing is university owned and is provided by a third party. Freshman campus housing is guaranteed.

Activities and organizations: drama/theater group, student-run newspaper, radio station, choral group, American Red Cross at University of California Riverside, American Medical Student Association, Running Club At UCR, Katipunan Pilipino Student Organization, Circle K International, national fraternities, national sororities.

Athletics Member NCAA. All Division I. *Intercollegiate sports:* baseball M(s), basketball M(s)/W(s), cross-country running M(s)/W(s), golf M(s), soccer M(s)/W(s), softball W(s), tennis M/W, volleyball W(s). *Intramural sports:* badminton M/W, basketball M/W, racquetball M/W, rugby M(c)/W(c), soccer M/W, softball M/W, table tennis M(c)/W(c), tennis M/W, volleyball M/W, wrestling M(c).

Campus security: 24-hour emergency response devices and patrols, student patrols, late-night transport/escort service, controlled dormitory access.

Student services: health clinic, personal/psychological counseling, women's center, legal services.

COSTS & FINANCIAL AID

Costs (2017–18) *Tuition:* state resident $11,502 full-time, $5751 per year part-time; nonresident $39,516 full-time, $19,758 per year part-time. Full-time tuition and fees vary according to course load. Part-time tuition and fees vary according to course load. *Required fees:* $4140 full-time. *Room and board:* $17,000. Room and board charges vary according to board plan and housing facility. *Payment plan:* deferred payment.

Financial Aid Of all full-time matriculated undergraduates who enrolled in 2017, 16,943 applied for aid, 15,572 were judged to have need, 3,922 had their need fully met. 2,972 Federal Work-Study jobs (averaging $1621). In 2017, 822 non-need-based awards were made. *Average percent of need met:* 89. *Average financial aid package:* $23,578. *Average need-based loan:* $5547. *Average need-based gift aid:* $18,125. *Average non-need-based aid:* $8154. *Average indebtedness upon graduation:* $21,104.

APPLYING

Standardized Tests *Required:* SAT or ACT (for admission).

Options: electronic application.

Application fee: $70.

Required: essay or personal statement, high school transcript, minimum 3.0 GPA.

Application deadlines: 11/30 (freshmen), 11/30 (transfers).

Notification: 3/31 (freshmen), continuous until 3/1 (transfers).

CONTACT

Ms. Emily D. Engelschall, Director, Undergraduate Admissions, University of California, Riverside, 3221 Student Services, 900 University Avenue, Riverside, CA 92521. *Phone:* 951-827-3986. *Fax:* 951-827-6346. *E-mail:* discover@ucr.edu.

 # University of California, San Diego

La Jolla, California

http://www.ucsd.edu/

- **State-supported** university, founded 1959, part of University of California System
- **Suburban** 1976-acre campus with easy access to San Diego
- **Coed** 28,587 undergraduate students, 98% full-time, 49% women, 51% men
- **Very difficult** entrance level, 34% of applicants were admitted

UNDERGRAD STUDENTS

28,067 full-time, 425 part-time. Students come from 52 states and territories; 92 other countries; 6% are from out of state; 2% Black or African American, non-Hispanic/Latino; 18% Hispanic/Latino; 38% Asian, non-Hispanic/Latino; 0.2% Native Hawaiian or other Pacific Islander, non-Hispanic/Latino; 0.4% American Indian or Alaska Native, non-Hispanic/Latino; 3% Race/ethnicity unknown; 20% international; 10% transferred in; 39% live on campus.

Freshmen:

Admission: 88,428 applied, 30,212 admitted, 5,694 enrolled. *Average high school GPA:* 4.1. *Test scores:* SAT evidence-based reading and writing scores over 500: 87%; SAT math scores over 500: 94%; ACT scores over 18: 99%; SAT evidence-based reading and writing scores over 600: 54%; SAT math scores over 600: 75%; ACT scores over 24: 87%; SAT evidence-based reading and writing scores over 700: 15%; SAT math scores over 700: 35%; ACT scores over 30: 52%.

Retention: 94% of full-time freshmen returned.

FACULTY

Total: 1,348, 83% full-time, 98% with terminal degrees.

Student/faculty ratio: 19:1.

ACADEMICS

Calendar: quarters. *Degrees:* bachelor's, master's, and doctoral.

Special study options: accelerated degree program, advanced placement credit, cooperative education, double majors, English as a second language, freshman honors college, honors programs, independent study, internships, off-campus study, services for LD students, student-designed majors, study abroad, summer session for credit. *ROTC:* Army (c), Navy (c), Air Force (c).

Computers: Students can access the following: campus intranet, computer help desk, free student e-mail accounts, online (class) grades, online (class) registration, online (class) schedules. Campuswide network is available. 100% of college-owned or -operated housing units are wired for high-speed Internet access. Wireless service is available via entire campus.

Library: Geisel Library plus 1 other. *Books:* 3.5 million (physical), 958,000 (digital/electronic). Study areas open 24 hours, 5–7 days a week; students can reserve study rooms.

STUDENT LIFE

Housing options: coed, special housing for students with disabilities. Campus housing is university owned. Freshman campus housing is guaranteed.

Activities and organizations: drama/theater group, student-run newspaper, radio and television station, choral group, marching band, national fraternities, national sororities.

Athletics Member NCAA. All Division II. *Intercollegiate sports:* baseball M, basketball M/W, crew M/W, cross-country running M/W, fencing M/W, golf M, soccer M/W, softball W, swimming and diving M/W, tennis M/W, track and field M/W, volleyball M/W, water polo M/W. *Intramural sports:* basketball M/W, bowling M/W, equestrian sports M(c)/W(c), football M(c)/W(c), ice hockey M, lacrosse M(c)/W(c), racquetball M/W, sailing M(c)/W(c), skiing (downhill) M(c)/W(c), soccer M/W, softball M/W, table tennis M/W, tennis M/W, ultimate Frisbee M(c)/W(c), volleyball M/W, water polo M/W.

Campus security: 24-hour emergency response devices and patrols, student patrols, late-night transport/escort service, crime prevention programs.

Student services: health clinic, personal/psychological counseling, women's center, legal services.

COSTS & FINANCIAL AID

Costs (2017–18) *One-time required fee:* $174. *Tuition:* state resident $12,630 full-time; nonresident $40,644 full-time. *Required fees:* $1420 full-time. *Room and board:* $13,307. Room and board charges vary according to board plan and housing facility.

Financial Aid Of all full-time matriculated undergraduates who enrolled in 2016, 17,287 applied for aid, 15,003 were judged to have need, 4,952 had their need fully met. In 2016, 548 non-need-based awards were made. *Average percent of need met:* 86. *Average financial aid package:* $22,499. *Average need-based loan:* $5880. *Average need-based gift aid:* $18,412. *Average non-need-based aid:* $11,001. *Average indebtedness upon graduation:* $21,830.

APPLYING

Standardized Tests *Required:* SAT or ACT (for admission), SAT and SAT Subject Tests or ACT (for admission), ACT Assessment with Writing or SAT Reasoning Test, plus two SAT Subject Tests (for admission).

Options: electronic application.

Application fee: $70.

Required: essay or personal statement, high school transcript, minimum 2.8 GPA. *Required for some:* minimum 3.4 GPA.

Notification: 3/31 (freshmen).

CONTACT

Ms. Adele Brumfield, Assistant Vice Chancellor, Enrollment Management, University of California, San Diego, 9500 Gilman Drive, 0021, La Jolla, CA 92093-0021. *Phone:* 858-534-3156. *E-mail:* admissionsreply@ucsd.edu.

See below for display ad and page 1456 for the College Close-Up.

University of California, Santa Barbara

Santa Barbara, California

http://www.ucsb.edu/

- **State-supported** university, founded 1909, part of University of California System
- **Suburban** 989-acre campus
- **Endowment** $155.0 million
- **Coed** 22,186 undergraduate students, 98% full-time, 54% women, 46% men
- **Very difficult** entrance level, 33% of applicants were admitted

UNDERGRAD STUDENTS

21,776 full-time, 410 part-time. Students come from 51 states and territories; 81 other countries; 4% are from out of state; 10% transferred in; 38% live on campus.

Freshmen:
Admission: 80,319 applied, 26,295 admitted, 4,538 enrolled. *Average high school GPA:* 4.1. *Test scores:* SAT evidence-based reading and writing scores over 500: 99%; SAT math scores over 500: 99%; ACT scores over 18: 99%; SAT evidence-based reading and writing scores over 600: 85%; SAT math scores over 600: 81%; ACT scores over 24: 86%; SAT evidence-based reading and writing scores over 700: 36%; SAT math scores over 700: 46%; ACT scores over 30: 51%.
Retention: 92% of full-time freshmen returned.

FACULTY
Total: 1,163, 85% full-time, 100% with terminal degrees.
Student/faculty ratio: 17:1.

ACADEMICS
Calendar: quarters plus 6-week summer term. *Degrees:* bachelor's, master's, doctoral, post-master's, and postbachelor's certificates.
Special study options: accelerated degree program, advanced placement credit, cooperative education, double majors, English as a second language, honors programs, independent study, internships, off-campus study, services for LD students, student-designed majors, study abroad, summer session for credit. *ROTC:* Army (b), Air Force (c).
Computers: Students can access the following: computer help desk, free student e-mail accounts, online (class) grades, online (class) registration, online (class) schedules. Campuswide network is available. 100% of college-owned or -operated housing units are wired for high-speed Internet access. Wireless service is available via classrooms, computer labs, dorm rooms, libraries, student centers.
Library: Davidson Library plus 1 other. Weekly public service hours: 96; study areas open 24 hours, 5–7 days a week; students can reserve study rooms.

STUDENT LIFE
Housing options: coed, cooperative. Campus housing is university owned and is provided by a third party. Freshman applicants given priority for college housing.
Activities and organizations: drama/theater group, student-run newspaper, radio and television station, choral group, national fraternities, national sororities.
Athletics Member NCAA. All Division I. *Intercollegiate sports:* baseball M(s), basketball M(s)/W(s), bowling M(c)/W(c), crew M(c)/W(c), cross-country running M(s)/W(s), equestrian sports M(c)/W(c), fencing M(c)/W(c), field hockey W(c), golf M(s), gymnastics M(s)/W(s), lacrosse M(c)/W(c), rugby M(c), sailing M(c)/W(c), skiing (downhill) M(c)/W(c), soccer M(s)/W(s), softball W(s), swimming and diving M(s)/W(s), tennis M(s)/W(s), track and field M(s)/W(s), ultimate Frisbee M(c)/W(c), volleyball M(s)/W(s), water polo M(s)/W(s). *Intramural sports:* badminton M/W, basketball M/W, bowling M/W, cross-country running M/W, football M/W, golf M/W, gymnastics M/W, racquetball M/W, soccer M/W, softball M/W, squash M/W, tennis M/W, ultimate Frisbee M/W, volleyball M/W, water polo M/W.
Campus security: 24-hour emergency response devices and patrols, student patrols, late-night transport/escort service, controlled dormitory access.
Student services: health clinic, personal/psychological counseling, women's center, legal services.

COSTS & FINANCIAL AID
Costs (2018–19) *Tuition:* state resident $11,502 full-time; nonresident $39,516 full-time. *Required fees:* $2970 full-time. *Room and board:* $15,673. Room and board charges vary according to board plan and housing facility. *Payment plan:* installment.
Financial Aid Of all full-time matriculated undergraduates who enrolled in 2016, 14,954 applied for aid, 12,705 were judged to have need, 2,286 had their need fully met. In 2016, 428 non-need-based awards were made. *Average percent of need met:* 79. *Average financial aid package:* $22,544. *Average need-based loan:* $6477. *Average need-based gift aid:* $18,999. *Average non-need-based aid:* $7952. *Average indebtedness upon graduation:* $21,001.

APPLYING
Standardized Tests *Required:* SAT or ACT (for admission). *Recommended:* SAT Subject Tests (for admission).
Options: electronic application.

Application fee: $70.
Required: essay or personal statement, high school transcript. *Required for some:* interview.
Application deadlines: 11/30 (freshmen), 11/30 (transfers).
Notification: 3/31 (freshmen), 5/1 (transfers).

CONTACT
Office of Admissions, University of California, Santa Barbara, 1210 Cheadle Hall, Santa Barbara, CA 93106-2014. *Phone:* 805-893-2881. *Fax:* 805-893-2676. *E-mail:* admissions@sa.ucsb.edu.

University of California, Santa Cruz
Santa Cruz, California
http://www.ucsc.edu/
- **State-supported** university, founded 1965, part of University of California System
- **Small-town** 2000-acre campus with easy access to San Francisco, San Jose
- **Endowment** $190.1 million
- **Coed** 17,577 undergraduate students, 97% full-time, 50% women, 50% men
- **Very difficult** entrance level, 51% of applicants were admitted

UNDERGRAD STUDENTS
17,082 full-time, 495 part-time. Students come from 47 states and territories; 55 other countries; 4% are from out of state; 2% Black or African American, non-Hispanic/Latino; 28% Hispanic/Latino; 22% Asian, non-Hispanic/Latino; 0.2% Native Hawaiian or other Pacific Islander, non-Hispanic/Latino; 0.1% American Indian or Alaska Native, non-Hispanic/Latino; 8% Two or more races, non-Hispanic/Latino; 2% Race/ethnicity unknown; 6% international; 7% transferred in; 98% live on campus.

Freshmen:
Admission: 52,065 applied, 26,643 admitted, 4,047 enrolled. *Average high school GPA:* 3.5. *Test scores:* SAT evidence-based reading and writing scores over 500: 97%; SAT math scores over 500: 97%; ACT scores over 18: 98%; SAT evidence-based reading and writing scores over 600: 69%; SAT math scores over 600: 68%; ACT scores over 24: 79%; SAT evidence-based reading and writing scores over 700: 18%; SAT math scores over 700: 23%; ACT scores over 30: 29%.
Retention: 90% of full-time freshmen returned.

FACULTY
Student/faculty ratio: 19:1.

ACADEMICS
Calendar: quarters. *Degrees:* bachelor's, master's, doctoral, and postbachelor's certificates.
Special study options: accelerated degree program, advanced placement credit, cooperative education, double majors, freshman honors college, honors programs, independent study, internships, off-campus study, services for LD students, student-designed majors, study abroad, summer session for credit. *ROTC:* Army (c), Navy (c), Air Force (c).
Computers: Students can access the following: campus intranet, computer help desk, free student e-mail accounts, online (class) grades, online (class) registration, online (class) schedules. Campuswide network is available. 100% of college-owned or -operated housing units are wired for high-speed Internet access. Wireless service is available via entire campus.
Library: UCSC Library. *Books:* 1.4 million (physical), 1.2 million (digital/electronic); *Serial titles:* 44,205 (physical), 66,601 (digital/electronic); *Databases:* 436. Weekly public service hours: 102; students can reserve study rooms.

STUDENT LIFE
Housing options: coed, men-only, women-only, cooperative. Campus housing is university owned. Freshman campus housing is guaranteed.
Activities and organizations: drama/theater group, student-run newspaper, radio and television station, choral group, marching band, Bayanihan (formerly Filipino Student Association), Black Student Union, City on a Hill Press, College Panhellenic & Inter-Greek Council, Movimiento Estudiantil Chicano de Aztlan, national fraternities, national sororities.

Athletics Member NCAA. All Division III. *Intercollegiate sports:* badminton M(c)/W(c), basketball M/W, cheerleading M(c)/W(c), cross-country running M/W, equestrian sports M(c)/W(c), fencing M(c)/W(c), golf W, lacrosse M(c)/W(c), racquetball M(c)/W(c), rugby M(c)/W(c), sailing M(c)/W(c), soccer M/W, softball W(c), swimming and diving M/W, tennis M/W, track and field M/W, triathlon M(c)/W(c), ultimate Frisbee M(c)/W(c), volleyball M/W, water polo M(c)/W(c). *Intramural sports:* basketball M/W, soccer M/W, softball M/W, ultimate Frisbee M/W, volleyball M/W, water polo M/W.

Campus security: 24-hour emergency response devices and patrols, late-night transport/escort service, controlled dormitory access, evening main gate security, campus police force and fire station.

Student services: health clinic, personal/psychological counseling, women's center.

COSTS & FINANCIAL AID

Costs (2017–18) *Tuition:* state resident $11,502 full-time; nonresident $39,516 full-time. Part-time tuition and fees vary according to course load. *Required fees:* $2526 full-time. *Room and board:* $16,055. Room and board charges vary according to board plan and housing facility. *Payment plan:* installment.

Financial Aid Of all full-time matriculated undergraduates who enrolled in 2017, 12,285 applied for aid, 10,555 were judged to have need, 2,757 had their need fully met. 1,163 Federal Work-Study jobs (averaging $2549). In 2017, 1403 non-need-based awards were made. *Average percent of need met:* 84. *Average financial aid package:* $25,754. *Average need-based loan:* $6726. *Average need-based gift aid:* $21,030. *Average non-need-based aid:* $5392. *Average indebtedness upon graduation:* $22,804. *Financial aid deadline:* 3/2.

APPLYING

Standardized Tests *Required:* SAT or ACT (for admission).

Options: electronic application.

Application fee: $70.

Required: essay or personal statement, high school transcript, minimum high school GPA of 3.0 for California residents, 3.4 for non-residents.

Application deadlines: 11/30 (freshmen), 11/30 (transfers).

Notification: 3/31 (freshmen), 4/30 (transfers).

CONTACT

Blia Yang, Interim Director, Admissions, University of California, Santa Cruz, 1156 High Street, Santa Cruz, CA 95064. *Phone:* 831-459-4008. *Fax:* 831-459-4452. *E-mail:* admissions@ucsc.edu.

University of La Verne

La Verne, California

http://www.laverne.edu/

- **Independent** university, founded 1891
- **Suburban** 66-acre campus with easy access to Los Angeles
- **Coed** 2,753 undergraduate students, 97% full-time, 58% women, 42% men
- **Moderately difficult** entrance level, 48% of applicants were admitted

UNDERGRAD STUDENTS

2,673 full-time, 80 part-time. Students come from 22 states and territories; 36 other countries; 4% are from out of state; 5% Black or African American, non-Hispanic/Latino; 57% Hispanic/Latino; 6% Asian, non-Hispanic/Latino; 0.7% Native Hawaiian or other Pacific Islander, non-Hispanic/Latino; 0.1% American Indian or Alaska Native, non-Hispanic/Latino; 5% Two or more races, non-Hispanic/Latino; 2% Race/ethnicity unknown; 6% international; 7% transferred in; 30% live on campus.

Freshmen:

Admission: 8,012 applied, 3,879 admitted, 606 enrolled. *Average high school GPA:* 3.5. *Test scores:* SAT evidence-based reading and writing scores over 500: 86%; SAT math scores over 500: 83%; ACT scores over 18: 96%; SAT evidence-based reading and writing scores over 600: 26%; SAT math scores over 600: 25%; ACT scores over 24: 41%; SAT

evidence-based reading and writing scores over 700: 2%; SAT math scores over 700: 4%; ACT scores over 30: 5%.

Retention: 79% of full-time freshmen returned.

FACULTY

Total: 516, 44% full-time.

Student/faculty ratio: 12:1.

ACADEMICS

Calendar: 4-1-4. *Degrees:* certificates, bachelor's, master's, and doctoral (also offers continuing education program with significant enrollment not reflected in profile).

Special study options: academic remediation for entering students, adult/continuing education programs, advanced placement credit, distance learning, double majors, English as a second language, freshman honors college, honors programs, independent study, internships, off-campus study, part-time degree program, services for LD students, student-designed majors, study abroad, summer session for credit. *ROTC:* Army (c).

Computers: Students can access the following: computer help desk, free student e-mail accounts, online (class) grades, online (class) registration, online (class) schedules, MyLaVerne (online). Campuswide network is available. 100% of college-owned or -operated housing units are wired for high-speed Internet access. Wireless service is available via entire campus.

Library: Wilson Library. Students can reserve study rooms.

STUDENT LIFE

Housing options: coed, men-only, women-only. Campus housing is university owned.

Activities and organizations: drama/theater group, student-run newspaper, radio and television station, choral group, Associated Students of La Verne, Latino Student Forum, Black Student Union, Psi Chi, Voices in Action, national fraternities, national sororities.

Athletics Member NCAA. All Division III. *Intercollegiate sports:* baseball M, basketball M/W, cross-country running M/W, football M, golf M, soccer M/W, softball W, swimming and diving M/W, tennis M/W, track and field M/W, volleyball W, water polo M/W.

Campus security: 24-hour emergency response devices and patrols, late-night transport/escort service, controlled dormitory access.

Student services: health clinic, personal/psychological counseling.

COSTS & FINANCIAL AID

Costs (2017–18) *Comprehensive fee:* $54,590 includes full-time tuition ($39,916), mandatory fees ($1534), and room and board ($13,140). Full-time tuition and fees vary according to location. Part-time tuition: $1180 per credit hour. Part-time tuition and fees vary according to location. *College room only:* $7030. Room and board charges vary according to board plan and housing facility. *Payment plans:* installment, deferred payment. *Waivers:* employees or children of employees.

Financial Aid Of all full-time matriculated undergraduates who enrolled in 2017, 2,357 applied for aid, 2,248 were judged to have need, 146 had their need fully met. In 2017, 361 non-need-based awards were made. *Average percent of need met:* 68. *Average financial aid package:* $32,166. *Average need-based loan:* $4646. *Average need-based gift aid:* $20,027. *Average non-need-based aid:* $11,038. *Average indebtedness upon graduation:* $33,384.

APPLYING

Standardized Tests *Required:* SAT or ACT (for admission).

Options: electronic application, deferred entrance.

Application fee: $50.

Required: essay or personal statement, high school transcript, 2 letters of recommendation.

Application deadlines: 2/1 (freshmen), 4/1 (transfers).

Notification: continuous (freshmen), continuous (transfers).

CONTACT

Mr. Erasmo Fuentes, Associate Director of Admission, University of La Verne, 1950 Third Street, La Verne, CA 91750. *Phone:* 800-876-4858. *Toll-free phone:* 800-876-4858. *Fax:* 909-392-2714. *E-mail:* admissions@ulv.edu.

University of Phoenix–Bay Area Campus

San Jose, California
http://www.phoenix.edu/

CONTACT
Marc Booker, Sr. Director, Office of Admissions and Evaluation, University of Phoenix–Bay Area Campus, 4035 South Riverpoint Parkway, Mail Stop CF-L101, Phoenix, AZ 85040-1958. *Phone:* 602-557-4609. *Toll-free phone:* 866-766-0766. *Fax:* 480-643-1156.

University of Phoenix–Central Valley Campus

Fresno, California
http://www.phoenix.edu/

CONTACT
Marc Booker, Sr. Director, Office of Admissions and Evaluation, University of Phoenix–Central Valley Campus, 4035 South Riverpoint Parkway, Mail Stop CF-L101, Phoenix, AZ 85040. *Phone:* 602-557-4609. *Toll-free phone:* 866-766-0766. *Fax:* 480-643-1156.

University of Phoenix–Sacramento Valley Campus

Sacramento, California
http://www.phoenix.edu/

CONTACT
Marc Booker, Sr. Director, Office of Admissions and Evaluation, University of Phoenix–Sacramento Valley Campus, 4035 South Riverpoint Parkway, Mail Stop CF-L101, Phoenix, AZ 85040. *Phone:* 602-557-4609. *Toll-free phone:* 866-766-0766. *Fax:* 480-643-1156.

University of Phoenix–San Diego Campus

San Diego, California
http://www.phoenix.edu/

CONTACT
Marc Booker, Sr. Director, Office of Admissions and Evaluation, University of Phoenix–San Diego Campus, 4035 South Riverpoint Parkway, Mail Stop CF-L101, Phoenix, AZ 85040. *Phone:* 602-557-4609. *Toll-free phone:* 866-766-0766. *Fax:* 480-643-1156.

University of Redlands

Redlands, California
http://www.redlands.edu/

CONTACT
Ms. Belinda Sandoval Zazueta, Director of Undergraduate Admission, University of Redlands, 1200 East Colton Avenue, PO Box 3080, Redlands, CA 92373-0999. *Phone:* 909-748-8074. *Toll-free phone:* 800-455-5064. *Fax:* 909-335-4089. *E-mail:* belinda_sandoval@redlands.edu.

See next page for display ad and page 1478 for the College Close-Up.

University of Saint Katherine

San Marcos, California
http://www.usk.edu/

CONTACT
Dean Marina Karavokiris, Dean of Admissions and Registrar, University of Saint Katherine, 1637 Capalina Road, San Marcos, CA 92069. *Phone:* 760-471-1316 Ext. 307. *Fax:* 760-471-1314. *E-mail:* admissions@stkath.org.

University of San Diego

San Diego, California
http://www.sandiego.edu/

- **Independent Roman Catholic** university, founded 1949
- **Urban** 180-acre campus with easy access to San Diego
- **Endowment** $503.6 million
- **Coed** 5,774 undergraduate students, 97% full-time, 54% women, 46% men
- **Very difficult** entrance level, 50% of applicants were admitted

UNDERGRAD STUDENTS
5,605 full-time, 169 part-time. Students come from 50 states and territories; 75 other countries; 38% are from out of state; 4% Black or African American, non-Hispanic/Latino; 20% Hispanic/Latino; 7% Asian, non-Hispanic/Latino; 0.3% Native Hawaiian or other Pacific Islander, non-Hispanic/Latino; 0.3% American Indian or Alaska Native, non-Hispanic/Latino; 6% Two or more races, non-Hispanic/Latino; 2% Race/ethnicity unknown; 9% international; 6% transferred in; 46% live on campus.

Freshmen:
Admission: 14,739 applied, 7,339 admitted, 1,210 enrolled. *Average high school GPA:* 3.9. *Test scores:* SAT evidence-based reading and writing scores over 500: 99%; SAT math scores over 500: 98%; ACT scores over 18: 100%; SAT evidence-based reading and writing scores over 600: 74%; SAT math scores over 600: 69%; ACT scores over 24: 90%; SAT evidence-based reading and writing scores over 700: 14%; SAT math scores over 700: 15%; ACT scores over 30: 35%.
Retention: 90% of full-time freshmen returned.

FACULTY
Total: 909, 50% full-time, 78% with terminal degrees.
Student/faculty ratio: 14:1.

ACADEMICS
Calendar: 4-1-4. *Degrees:* bachelor's, master's, doctoral, and postbachelor's certificates.

Special study options: advanced placement credit, double majors, English as a second language, honors programs, independent study, internships, part-time degree program, services for LD students, study abroad, summer session for credit. *ROTC:* Army (c), Navy (b), Air Force (c).

Computers: 951 computers/terminals and 4,250 ports are available on campus for general student use. Students can access the following: campus intranet, computer help desk, free student e-mail accounts, online (class) grades, online (class) registration, online (class) schedules. Campuswide network is available. 100% of college-owned or -operated housing units are wired for high-speed Internet access. Wireless service is available via entire campus.

Library: Helen K. and James S. Copley Library plus 1 other. *Books:* 566,393 (physical), 834,947 (digital/electronic); *Serial titles:* 6,403 (physical), 75,037 (digital/electronic); *Databases:* 331. Weekly public service hours: 116; students can reserve study rooms.

STUDENT LIFE
Housing options: on-campus residence required through sophomore year; coed, men-only, women-only, special housing for students with disabilities. Campus housing is university owned. Freshman campus housing is guaranteed.

Activities and organizations: drama/theater group, student-run newspaper, radio and television station, choral group, marching band, Marine Science Club, Entrepreneurship Club, USD Chapter American Marketing Association, International Student Organization, Student International Business Council, national fraternities, national sororities.

Athletics Member NCAA. All Division I except football (Division I-AA). *Intercollegiate sports:* baseball M(s), basketball M(s)/W(s), crew M/W(s), cross-country running M(s)/W(s), equestrian sports M(c)/W(c), golf M(s), lacrosse M(c)/W(c), rock climbing M(c)/W(c), rugby M(c), soccer M(s)/W(s), softball W(s), swimming and diving W(s), tennis M(s)/W(s), track and field W(s), ultimate Frisbee M(c)/W(c), volleyball M(c)/W(s). *Intramural sports:* baseball M(c), basketball M/W, cross-country running M(c)/W(c), football M/W, golf M(c), ice hockey M(c), soccer M(c)/W(c), softball M/W, tennis M(c)/W(c), ultimate Frisbee M/W, volleyball M/W(c), water polo M(c).

University of Redlands

Offering a distinctive residential liberal arts experience in a unique natural setting in historic inland Southern California.

UNIVERSITY OF
Redlands

www.redlands.edu

Campus security: 24-hour emergency response devices and patrols, late-night transport/escort service, controlled dormitory access.

Student services: health clinic, personal/psychological counseling, women's center, legal services.

COSTS & FINANCIAL AID

Costs (2018–19) *Comprehensive fee:* $62,338 includes full-time tuition ($48,750), mandatory fees ($608), and room and board ($12,980). Part-time tuition: $1680 per credit. Part-time tuition and fees vary according to course load. *Required fees:* $376 per year part-time. *Room and board:* Room and board charges vary according to board plan and housing facility. *Payment plan:* installment. *Waivers:* employees or children of employees.

Financial Aid Of all full-time matriculated undergraduates who enrolled in 2016, 3,214 applied for aid, 2,758 were judged to have need, 387 had their need fully met. 508 Federal Work-Study jobs (averaging $2294). In 2016, 1072 non-need-based awards were made. *Average percent of need met:* 71. *Average financial aid package:* $33,737. *Average need-based loan:* $7488. *Average need-based gift aid:* $26,679. *Average non-need-based aid:* $15,419. *Average indebtedness upon graduation:* $30,854.

APPLYING

Standardized Tests *Required:* SAT or ACT (for admission).

Options: electronic application, deferred entrance.

Application fee: $55.

Required: essay or personal statement, high school transcript, 1 letter of recommendation.

Application deadlines: 12/15 (freshmen), 3/1 (transfers).

Notification: 4/1 (freshmen), continuous until 6/30 (transfers).

CONTACT

Ms. Minh-Ha Hoang, Director of Admissions, University of San Diego, 5998 Alcala Park, San Diego, CA 92110. *Phone:* 619-260-4506. *Toll-free phone:* 800-248-4873. *Fax:* 619-260-6836. *E-mail:* admissions@sandiego.edu.

 University of San Francisco
San Francisco, California
http://www.usfca.edu/

- **Independent Roman Catholic (Jesuit)** university, founded 1855
- **Urban** 55-acre campus
- **Endowment** $345.5 million
- **Coed** 6,847 undergraduate students, 96% full-time, 62% women, 38% men
- **Moderately difficult** entrance level, 66% of applicants were admitted

UNDERGRAD STUDENTS

6,586 full-time, 261 part-time. Students come from 57 states and territories; 80 other countries; 18% are from out of state; 4% Black or African American, non-Hispanic/Latino; 22% Hispanic/Latino; 22% Asian, non-Hispanic/Latino; 0.7% Native Hawaiian or other Pacific Islander, non-Hispanic/Latino; 0.3% American Indian or Alaska Native, non-Hispanic/Latino; 7% Two or more races, non-Hispanic/Latino; 2% Race/ethnicity unknown; 17% international; 6% transferred in; 21% live on campus.

Freshmen:
Admission: 16,313 applied, 10,707 admitted, 1,532 enrolled. *Average high school GPA:* 3.4. *Test scores:* SAT evidence-based reading and writing scores over 500: 94%; SAT math scores over 500: 94%; ACT scores over 18: 99%; SAT evidence-based reading and writing scores over 600: 54%; SAT math scores over 600: 47%; ACT scores over 24: 66%; SAT evidence-based reading and writing scores over 700: 8%; SAT math scores over 700: 10%; ACT scores over 30: 14%.
Retention: 85% of full-time freshmen returned.

FACULTY

Total: 1,182, 42% full-time, 63% with terminal degrees.

Student/faculty ratio: 14:1.

ACADEMICS

Calendar: 4-1-4. *Degrees:* certificates, bachelor's, master's, doctoral, post-master's, and postbachelor's certificates.

California

Special study options: accelerated degree program, adult/continuing education programs, advanced placement credit, cooperative education, distance learning, double majors, English as a second language, external degree program, freshman honors college, honors programs, independent study, internships, off-campus study, part-time degree program, services for LD students, student-designed majors, study abroad, summer session for credit. *ROTC:* Army (b), Air Force (c).

Unusual degree programs: 3-2 engineering with University of Southern California.

Computers: 186 computers/terminals are available on campus for general student use. Students can access the following: campus intranet, computer help desk, free student e-mail accounts, online (class) grades, online (class) registration, online (class) schedules. Campuswide network is available. 100% of college-owned or -operated housing units are wired for high-speed Internet access. Wireless service is available via classrooms, computer centers, computer labs, dorm rooms, learning centers, libraries, student centers.

Library: Gleeson Library|Geschke Center plus 1 other. *Books:* 775,128 (physical), 586,739 (digital/electronic); *Serial titles:* 7,960 (physical), 135,406 (digital/electronic); *Databases:* 342. Weekly public service hours: 138; study areas open 24 hours, 5–7 days a week; students can reserve study rooms.

STUDENT LIFE

Housing options: on-campus residence required for freshman year; coed, women-only. Campus housing is university owned and leased by the school. Freshman campus housing is guaranteed.

Activities and organizations: drama/theater group, student-run newspaper, radio and television station, choral group, marching band, national fraternities, national sororities.

Athletics Member NCAA. All Division I. *Intercollegiate sports:* baseball M(s), basketball M(s)/W(s), cross-country running M(s)/W(s), golf M(s)/W(s), soccer M(s)/W(s), softball M(c)/W(c), tennis M(s)/W(s), track and field M/W(s), volleyball M(c)/W(s). *Intramural sports:* basketball M/W, bowling M/W, fencing M(c)/W(c), football M/W, golf M(c)/W(c), lacrosse M(c), racquetball M/W, rugby M(c)/W(c), skiing (cross-country) M(c)/W(c), soccer M/W, softball M/W, swimming and diving M/W, table tennis M/W, tennis M/W, volleyball M/W.

Campus security: 24-hour emergency response devices and patrols, student patrols, late-night transport/escort service, controlled dormitory access.

Student services: health clinic, personal/psychological counseling, women's center.

COSTS & FINANCIAL AID

Costs (2018–19) *Comprehensive fee:* $62,896 includes full-time tuition ($47,550), mandatory fees ($516), and room and board ($14,830). Full-time tuition and fees vary according to course load, degree level, location, program, and reciprocity agreements. Part-time tuition: $1690 per credit hour. Part-time tuition and fees vary according to course load, degree level, location, program, and reciprocity agreements. *Required fees:* $258 per term part-time. *College room only:* $10,010. Room and board charges vary according to board plan and housing facility. *Payment plan:* installment. *Waivers:* employees or children of employees.

Financial Aid Of all full-time matriculated undergraduates who enrolled in 2016, 3,971 applied for aid, 3,540 were judged to have need, 2,140 had their need fully met. 941 Federal Work-Study jobs (averaging $4890). 1,850 state and other part-time jobs (averaging $5361). In 2016, 1018 non-need-based awards were made. *Average percent of need met:* 77. *Average financial aid package:* $35,963. *Average need-based loan:* $4925. *Average need-based gift aid:* $21,451. *Average non-need-based aid:* $13,208. *Average indebtedness upon graduation:* $34,114. *Financial aid deadline:* 2/15.

APPLYING

Standardized Tests *Required:* SAT or ACT (for admission). *Required for some:* TOEFL, IELTS or PTE Academic if English is not the student's native language.

Options: electronic application, early admission, early decision, early action, deferred entrance.

Application fee: $65.

Required: essay or personal statement, high school transcript, 1 letter of recommendation. *Recommended:* minimum 3.0 GPA.

Application deadlines: 1/15 (freshmen), rolling (transfers), 11/1 (early action).

Early decision deadline: 11/1.

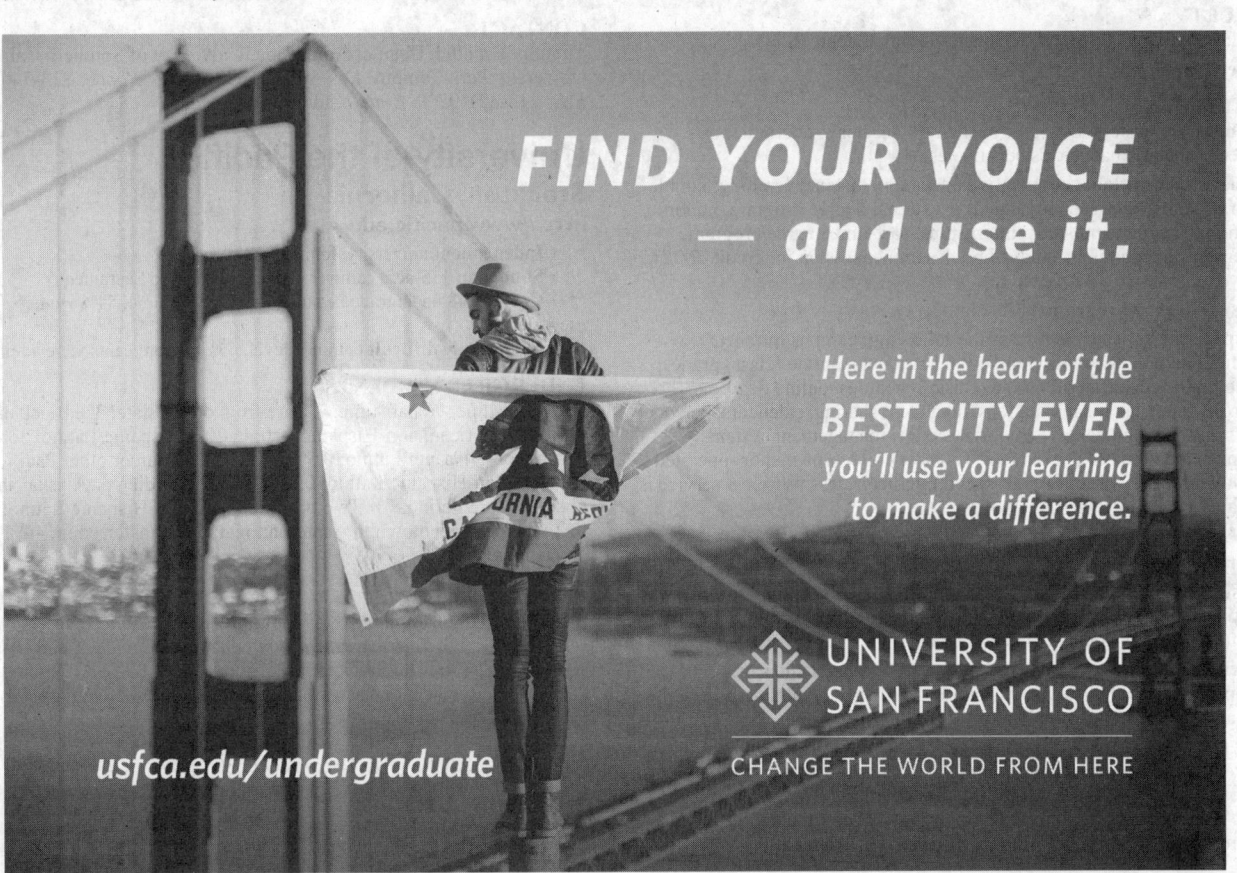

A ★ *indicates that the school has detailed information with a Premium Profile on Petersons.com.* **www.petersons.com 159**

Notification: continuous until 3/15 (freshmen), continuous until 4/1 (transfers), 12/1 (early decision), 12/14 (early action).

CONTACT
April Crabtree, Assistant Vice Provost, Undergraduate Admission, University of San Francisco, 2130 Fulton Street, San Francisco, CA 94117-1080. *Phone:* 415-422-5287. *Toll-free phone:* 800-CALL-USF. *E-mail:* admissions@usfca.edu.

See previous page for display ad and page 1480 for the College Close-Up.

University of Southern California
Los Angeles, California
http://www.usc.edu/

- **Independent** university, founded 1880
- **Urban** 229-acre campus with easy access to Los Angeles
- **Endowment** $4.6 billion
- **Coed** 19,170 undergraduate students, 97% full-time, 52% women, 48% men
- **Most difficult** entrance level, 16% of applicants were admitted

UNDERGRAD STUDENTS
18,631 full-time, 539 part-time. Students come from 8 states and territories; 6 other countries; 35% are from out of state; 5% Black or African American, non-Hispanic/Latino; 14% Hispanic/Latino; 20% Asian, non-Hispanic/Latino; 0.2% Native Hawaiian or other Pacific Islander, non-Hispanic/Latino; 0.1% American Indian or Alaska Native, non-Hispanic/Latino; 6% Two or more races, non-Hispanic/Latino; 2% Race/ethnicity unknown; 14% international; 7% transferred in; 30% live on campus.

Freshmen:
Admission: 56,676 applied, 9,042 admitted, 3,358 enrolled. *Average high school GPA:* 3.8. *Test scores:* SAT evidence-based reading and writing scores over 500: 99%; SAT math scores over 500: 99%; ACT scores over 18: 100%; SAT evidence-based reading and writing scores over 600: 92%; SAT math scores over 600: 88%; ACT scores over 24: 98%; SAT evidence-based reading and writing scores over 700: 46%; SAT math scores over 700: 58%; ACT scores over 30: 79%.

FACULTY
Total: 3,523, 61% full-time, 83% with terminal degrees.
Student/faculty ratio: 8:1.

ACADEMICS
Calendar: semesters. *Degrees:* bachelor's, master's, doctoral, post-master's, and postbachelor's certificates.
Special study options: cooperative education, distance learning, double majors, English as a second language, external degree program, honors programs, independent study, internships, part-time degree program, student-designed majors, study abroad, summer session for credit. *ROTC:* Army (b), Navy (b), Air Force (b).
Unusual degree programs: 3-2 engineering.
Computers: Students can access the following: campus intranet, computer help desk, free student e-mail accounts, online (class) grades, online (class) registration, online (class) schedules, online degree progress, financial aid applications, document sharing, calendars, personal Web space, customizable Web portal, course management systems. Campuswide network is available. 100% of college-owned or -operated housing units are wired for high-speed Internet access. Wireless service is available via entire campus.
Library: Doheny Memorial Library plus 23 others.

STUDENT LIFE
Housing options: coed, special housing for students with disabilities. Campus housing is university owned and is provided by a third party. Freshman campus housing is guaranteed.
Activities and organizations: drama/theater group, student-run newspaper, radio and television station, choral group, marching band, national fraternities, national sororities.
Athletics Member NCAA. All Division I except football (Division I-A). *Intercollegiate sports:* archery M(c)/W(c), badminton M(c)/W(c), baseball M(s), basketball M(s)/W(s), cheerleading M(c)/W(c), crew M(c)/W(s), cross-country running M(c)/W(s), equestrian sports W(c), fencing W(c), field hockey W(c), golf M(s)/W(s), gymnastics W(c), ice

hockey M(c)/W(c), lacrosse M(c)/W(s), racquetball M(c)/W(c), rock climbing M(c)/W(c), rugby M(c)/W(c), sailing W(c), skiing (downhill) M(c)/W(c), soccer M(c)/W(s), softball W(c), squash M(c)/W(c), swimming and diving M(s)/W(s), tennis M(s)/W(s), track and field M(s)/W(s), ultimate Frisbee M(c)/W(c), volleyball M(s)/W(s), water polo M(s)/W(s). *Intramural sports:* badminton M/W, basketball M/W, cross-country running M/W, football M/W, golf M/W, racquetball M/W, soccer M/W, softball M/W, tennis M/W, ultimate Frisbee M/W, volleyball M/W.
Campus security: 24-hour emergency response devices and patrols, student patrols, late-night transport/escort service, controlled dormitory access.
Student services: health clinic, personal/psychological counseling, women's center, legal services.

COSTS & FINANCIAL AID
Costs (2018–19) *One-time required fee:* $350. *Comprehensive fee:* $69,208 includes full-time tuition ($53,448), mandatory fees ($875), and room and board ($14,885). Full-time tuition and fees vary according to program. Part-time tuition: $1800 per credit hour. Part-time tuition and fees vary according to course load and program. *College room only:* $8985. Room and board charges vary according to board plan and housing facility. *Payment plans:* tuition prepayment, installment. *Waivers:* employees or children of employees.
Financial Aid Of all full-time matriculated undergraduates who enrolled in 2016, 8,830 applied for aid, 6,657 were judged to have need, 5,599 had their need fully met. In 2016, 3519 non-need-based awards were made. *Average percent of need met:* 100. *Average financial aid package:* $49,835. *Average need-based loan:* $7043. *Average need-based gift aid:* $36,496. *Average non-need-based aid:* $20,209. *Average indebtedness upon graduation:* $29,080.

APPLYING
Standardized Tests *Required:* SAT or ACT (for admission).
Options: electronic application, deferred entrance.
Application fee: $85.
Required: essay or personal statement, high school transcript.
Application deadlines: 1/15 (freshmen), 2/1 (transfers).
Notification: 4/1 (freshmen), 4/1 (out-of-state freshmen), 6/1 (transfers).

CONTACT
Timothy Brunold, Dean of Admission, University of Southern California, University Park Campus, Los Angeles, CA 90089. *Phone:* 213-740-1111. *Fax:* 213-821-0200. *E-mail:* admitusc@usc.edu.

University of the Pacific
Stockton, California
http://www.pacific.edu/

- **Independent** university, founded 1851
- **Suburban** 175-acre campus with easy access to Sacramento
- **Coed** 3,548 undergraduate students, 97% full-time, 54% women, 46% men
- **Moderately difficult** entrance level, 65% of applicants were admitted

UNDERGRAD STUDENTS
3,452 full-time, 96 part-time. 7% are from out of state; 3% Black or African American, non-Hispanic/Latino; 20% Hispanic/Latino; 36% Asian, non-Hispanic/Latino; 0.5% Native Hawaiian or other Pacific Islander, non-Hispanic/Latino; 0.4% American Indian or Alaska Native, non-Hispanic/Latino; 7% Two or more races, non-Hispanic/Latino; 3% Race/ethnicity unknown; 6% international; 6% transferred in; 44% live on campus.

Freshmen:
Admission: 13,064 applied, 8,475 admitted, 899 enrolled. *Average high school GPA:* 3.5. *Test scores:* SAT evidence-based reading and writing scores over 500: 89%; SAT math scores over 500: 89%; ACT scores over 18: 97%; SAT evidence-based reading and writing scores over 600: 49%; SAT math scores over 600: 49%; ACT scores over 24: 62%; SAT evidence-based reading and writing scores over 700: 13%; SAT math scores over 700: 21%; ACT scores over 30: 27%.
Retention: 85% of full-time freshmen returned.

FACULTY
Total: 823, 54% full-time, 71% with terminal degrees.

Student/faculty ratio: 13:1.

ACADEMICS
Calendar: semesters. *Degrees:* bachelor's, master's, and doctoral.

Special study options: academic remediation for entering students, accelerated degree program, advanced placement credit, cooperative education, double majors, English as a second language, honors programs, independent study, internships, part-time degree program, services for LD students, student-designed majors, summer session for credit. *ROTC:* Air Force (c).

Computers: Students can access the following: campus intranet, computer help desk, free student e-mail accounts, online (class) grades, online (class) registration, online (class) schedules. Campuswide network is available. Wireless service is available via entire campus.
Library: University of the Pacific Library plus 1 other.

STUDENT LIFE
Housing options: on-campus residence required through sophomore year; coed, cooperative. Campus housing is university owned. Freshman campus housing is guaranteed.

Activities and organizations: drama/theater group, student-run newspaper, radio station, choral group, national fraternities, national sororities.

Athletics Member NCAA. All Division I. *Intercollegiate sports:* baseball M(s), basketball M(s)/W(s), cross-country running W(s), field hockey W(s), golf M(s), soccer W(s), softball W(s), swimming and diving M(s)/W(s), tennis M(s)/W(s), volleyball M(s)/W(s), water polo M(s)/W(s). *Intramural sports:* badminton M(c)/W(c), basketball M/W, bowling M/W, football M/W, golf M, lacrosse M(c)/W(c), rugby M(c), soccer M(c)/W(c), tennis M/W, volleyball W.

Campus security: 24-hour emergency response devices and patrols, late-night transport/escort service, controlled dormitory access.
Student services: health clinic, personal/psychological counseling, legal services.

COSTS & FINANCIAL AID
Costs (2017–18) *Comprehensive fee:* $59,702 includes full-time tuition ($45,786), mandatory fees ($560), and room and board ($13,356). Part-time tuition: $1579 per credit hour. Part-time tuition and fees vary according to course load. *Room and board:* Room and board charges vary according to board plan and housing facility. *Payment plan:* deferred payment. *Waivers:* employees or children of employees.

Financial Aid Of all full-time matriculated undergraduates who enrolled in 2017, 2,654 applied for aid, 2,467 were judged to have need, 285 had their need fully met. In 2017, 567 non-need-based awards were made. *Average percent of need met:* 56. *Average financial aid package:* $34,876. *Average need-based loan:* $8596. *Average need-based gift aid:* $28,134. *Average non-need-based aid:* $14,033. *Average indebtedness upon graduation:* $28,759.

APPLYING
Standardized Tests *Required:* SAT or ACT (for admission). *Recommended:* SAT and SAT Subject Tests or ACT (for admission).

Options: electronic application, early action.
Application fee: $35.
Required: essay or personal statement, high school transcript.
Application deadlines: 8/15 (freshmen), 8/15 (transfers), 11/15 (early action).
Notification: continuous (freshmen), continuous (transfers), 1/15 (early action).

CONTACT
Mr. Rich Toledo, Director of Admissions, University of the Pacific, 3601 Pacific Avenue, Stockton, CA 95211-0197. *Phone:* 209-946-2211. *Fax:* 209-946-2413. *E-mail:* admissions@pacific.edu.

University of the People
Pasadena, California
http://www.uopeople.edu/

CONTACT
University of the People, 225 South Lake Avenue, Suite 300, Pasadena, CA 91101.

University of the West
Rosemead, California
http://www.uwest.edu/
- **Independent** comprehensive, founded 1991
- **Suburban** 10-acre campus with easy access to Los Angeles, Pasadena, Long Beach
- **Coed**
- **Minimally difficult** entrance level

FACULTY
Student/faculty ratio: 10:1.

ACADEMICS
Calendar: semesters. *Degrees:* certificates, diplomas, bachelor's, master's, doctoral, post-master's, and postbachelor's certificates.
Library: University of the West Library plus 1 other. Students can reserve study rooms.

STUDENT LIFE
Housing options: coed, special housing for students with disabilities. Campus housing is university owned. Freshman campus housing is guaranteed.

Activities and organizations: Buddhawest Club, Music Club, Explorer Club, Badminton Club, Chaplaincy Club.

Campus security: 24-hour emergency response devices and patrols, controlled dormitory access.

Student services: personal/psychological counseling.

COSTS & FINANCIAL AID
Costs (2017–18) *One-time required fee:* $50. *Comprehensive fee:* $21,584 includes full-time tuition ($13,800), mandatory fees ($900), and room and board ($6884). Full-time tuition and fees vary according to course load, degree level, and program. Part-time tuition: $460 per credit hour. Part-time tuition and fees vary according to course load, degree level, and program. *Required fees:* $640 per year part-time. *Room and board:* Room and board charges vary according to board plan.

Financial Aid Of all full-time matriculated undergraduates who enrolled in 2003, 30 applied for aid, 18 were judged to have need. 20 state and other part-time jobs.

APPLYING
Options: electronic application, deferred entrance.
Application fee: $50.
Required: essay or personal statement, high school transcript, minimum 2.0 GPA, 3 letters of recommendation. *Required for some:* interview.

CONTACT
University of the West, 1409 Walnut Grove Avenue, Rosemead, CA 91770. *Phone:* 626-571-8811 Ext. 311.

Vanguard University of Southern California
Costa Mesa, California
http://www.vanguard.edu/
- **Independent** comprehensive, founded 1920, affiliated with Assemblies of God
- **Suburban** 38-acre campus with easy access to Los Angeles
- **Coed** 1,805 undergraduate students, 84% full-time, 65% women, 35% men
- **Moderately difficult** entrance level, 47% of applicants were admitted

UNDERGRAD STUDENTS
1,511 full-time, 294 part-time. 11% are from out of state; 5% Black or African American, non-Hispanic/Latino; 40% Hispanic/Latino; 3% Asian, non-Hispanic/Latino; 1% Native Hawaiian or other Pacific Islander, non-Hispanic/Latino; 0.1% American Indian or Alaska Native, non-Hispanic/Latino; 4% Two or more races, non-Hispanic/Latino; 6% Race/ethnicity unknown; 0.8% international; 6% transferred in; 50% live on campus.

Freshmen:
Admission: 3,087 applied, 1,441 admitted, 433 enrolled. *Average high school GPA:* 3.3. *Test scores:* SAT evidence-based reading and writing

scores over 500: 64%; SAT math scores over 500: 55%; ACT scores over 18: 77%; SAT evidence-based reading and writing scores over 600: 16%; SAT math scores over 600: 10%; ACT scores over 24: 24%; SAT evidence-based reading and writing scores over 700: 2%; SAT math scores over 700: 1%; ACT scores over 30: 3%.

FACULTY
Total: 247, 28% full-time, 47% with terminal degrees.
Student/faculty ratio: 14:1.

ACADEMICS
Calendar: semesters. *Degrees:* certificates, associate, bachelor's, master's, and postbachelor's certificates.

Special study options: accelerated degree program, adult/continuing education programs, advanced placement credit, distance learning, double majors, independent study, internships, off-campus study, part-time degree program, services for LD students, study abroad, summer session for credit. *ROTC:* Army (c), Air Force (c).

Computers: 100 computers/terminals and 50 ports are available on campus for general student use. Students can access the following: computer help desk, free student e-mail accounts, online (class) grades, online (class) registration, online (class) schedules. Campuswide network is available. 100% of college-owned or -operated housing units are wired for high-speed Internet access. Wireless service is available via entire campus.
Library: O. Cope Budge Library. Students can reserve study rooms.

STUDENT LIFE
Housing options: coed, men-only, women-only. Campus housing is university owned. Freshman campus housing is guaranteed.

Activities and organizations: drama/theater group, student-run newspaper, choral group, local outreach, Global Missions, student organizations/clubs, choral groups.

Athletics Member NAIA. *Intercollegiate sports:* baseball M(s), basketball M(s)/W(s), cross-country running M(s)/W(s), soccer M(s)/W(s), softball W(s), track and field M(s)/W(s), volleyball W(s). *Intramural sports:* basketball M/W, football M/W, soccer M/W, softball M/W, volleyball M/W.

Campus security: 24-hour emergency response devices and patrols, student patrols, late-night transport/escort service, controlled dormitory access.

Student services: health clinic, personal/psychological counseling, women's center.

COSTS & FINANCIAL AID
Costs (2018–19) *Tuition:* $33,200 full-time, $1384 per credit hour part-time. Full-time tuition and fees vary according to class time, course level, course load, degree level, location, and program. Part-time tuition and fees vary according to class time, course level, course load, degree level, and program. *Required fees:* $500 full-time. *Room only:* Room and board charges vary according to board plan, gender, housing facility, and student level. *Payment plan:* installment. *Waivers:* employees or children of employees.

Financial Aid Of all full-time matriculated undergraduates who enrolled in 2017, 1,319 applied for aid, 1,310 were judged to have need, 1,310 had their need fully met. In 2017, 1392 non-need-based awards were made. *Average financial aid package:* $14,614. *Average need-based gift aid:* $7303. *Average non-need-based aid:* $8075. *Average indebtedness upon graduation:* $31,614. *Financial aid deadline:* 3/2.

APPLYING
Standardized Tests *Required:* SAT or ACT (for admission).
Options: electronic application, early admission, early action, deferred entrance.
Application fee: $45.
Required: essay or personal statement, high school transcript, minimum 2.8 GPA, 2 letters of recommendation. *Required for some:* interview.
Application deadlines: 8/1 (freshmen), 12/1 (early action).
Notification: 5/1 (freshmen), continuous (transfers).

CONTACT
Kristi Pruett, Undergraduate Admissions, Vanguard University of Southern California, 55 Fair Drive, Costa Mesa, CA 92626. *Phone:* 800-722-6279 Ext. 4107. *Toll-free phone:* 800-722-6279. *Fax:* 714-966-5471. *E-mail:* admissions@vanguard.edu.

West Coast Ultrasound Institute
Beverly Hills, California
http://wcui.edu/

CONTACT
West Coast Ultrasound Institute, 291 S. La Cienega Boulevard, Suite 500, Beverly Hills, CA 90211.

West Coast University
Anaheim, California
http://westcoastuniversity.edu/

CONTACT
West Coast University, 1477 S. Manchester Avenue, Anaheim, CA 92802.

West Coast University
North Hollywood, California
http://www.westcoastuniversity.edu/

CONTACT
Mr. Roger A. Miller, Dean of Admissions and Registrar, West Coast University, 12215 Victory Boulevard, North Hollywood, CA 91606. *Phone:* 213-427-4400. *Toll-free phone:* 866-508-2684. *E-mail:* info@katz.wcula.edu.

West Coast University
Ontario, California
http://westcoastuniversity.edu/

CONTACT
West Coast University, 2855 E. Guasti Road, Ontario, CA 91761.

Westmont College
Santa Barbara, California
http://www.westmont.edu/

- **Independent nondenominational** 4-year, founded 1937
- **Suburban** 113-acre campus with easy access to Los Angeles
- **Endowment** $75.0 million
- **Coed** 1,303 undergraduate students, 100% full-time, 61% women, 39% men
- **Moderately difficult** entrance level, 85% of applicants were admitted

UNDERGRAD STUDENTS
1,298 full-time, 5 part-time. Students come from 41 states and territories; 20 other countries; 27% are from out of state; 2% Black or African American, non-Hispanic/Latino; 18% Hispanic/Latino; 7% Asian, non-Hispanic/Latino; 0.4% Native Hawaiian or other Pacific Islander, non-Hispanic/Latino; 0.4% American Indian or Alaska Native, non-Hispanic/Latino; 6% Two or more races, non-Hispanic/Latino; 3% Race/ethnicity unknown; 1% international; 4% transferred in; 85% live on campus.

Freshmen:
Admission: 1,818 applied, 1,540 admitted, 353 enrolled. *Average high school GPA:* 3.8. *Test scores:* ACT scores over 18: 99%; ACT scores over 24: 70%; ACT scores over 30: 25%.
Retention: 81% of full-time freshmen returned.

FACULTY
Total: 157, 60% full-time, 67% with terminal degrees.
Student/faculty ratio: 11:1.

ACADEMICS
Calendar: semesters. *Degrees:* bachelor's and postbachelor's certificates.
Special study options: academic remediation for entering students, accelerated degree program, advanced placement credit, double majors, honors programs, internships, off-campus study, services for LD students,

student-designed majors, study abroad, summer session for credit. *ROTC:* Army (c), Air Force (c).

Unusual degree programs: 3-2 engineering with Washington University in St. Louis; Boston University; University of Southern California; University of California, Berkeley, Los Angeles, and Santa Barbara; California Polytechnic State University; Stanford University.

Computers: 100 computers/terminals are available on campus for general student use. Students can access the following: campus intranet, computer help desk, free student e-mail accounts, online (class) grades, online (class) registration, online (class) schedules. Campuswide network is available. 100% of college-owned or -operated housing units are wired for high-speed Internet access. Wireless service is available via entire campus.

Library: Roger John Voskuyl Library. *Books:* 134,000 (physical), 158,000 (digital/electronic); *Databases:* 100. Weekly public service hours: 100; study areas open 24 hours, 5–7 days a week; students can reserve study rooms.

STUDENT LIFE

Housing options: on-campus residence required through senior year; coed, cooperative, special housing for students with disabilities. Campus housing is university owned. Freshman campus housing is guaranteed.

Activities and organizations: drama/theater group, student-run newspaper, choral group, Student Ministries, Student Government, Competitive Athletics, Music, Art and Theater ensembles, Intramural Sports.

Athletics Member NAIA. *Intercollegiate sports:* baseball M(s), basketball M(s)/W(s), cross-country running M(s)/W(s), equestrian sports M(c), rugby M(c), soccer M(s)/W(s), tennis M(s)/W(s), track and field M(s)/W(s), volleyball M(c)/W(s). *Intramural sports:* badminton M/W, basketball M/W, bowling M/W, cross-country running M/W, football M/W, golf M/W, racquetball M/W, soccer M(c)/W, softball M/W, table tennis M/W, tennis M/W, ultimate Frisbee M(c), volleyball M/W, water polo M/W.

Campus security: 24-hour emergency response devices and patrols, late-night transport/escort service, controlled dormitory access.

Student services: health clinic, personal/psychological counseling, women's center.

COSTS & FINANCIAL AID

Costs (2017–18) *One-time required fee:* $300. *Comprehensive fee:* $57,930 includes full-time tuition ($42,890), mandatory fees ($1154), and room and board ($13,886). *College room only:* $8610. Room and board charges vary according to board plan and housing facility. *Payment plan:* installment. *Waivers:* employees or children of employees.

Financial Aid Of all full-time matriculated undergraduates who enrolled in 2017, 1,027 applied for aid, 896 were judged to have need, 202 had their need fully met. 389 Federal Work-Study jobs (averaging $1900). In 2017, 304 non-need-based awards were made. *Average percent of need met:* 80. *Average financial aid package:* $33,174. *Average need-based loan:* $6011. *Average need-based gift aid:* $27,067. *Average non-need-based aid:* $16,606. *Average indebtedness upon graduation:* $33,407.

APPLYING

Standardized Tests *Required:* SAT or ACT (for admission).

Options: electronic application, early action.

Application fee: $50.

Required: essay or personal statement, high school transcript, 1 letter of recommendation. *Required for some:* interview. *Recommended:* interview.

Application deadlines: 2/15 (freshmen), 3/1 (transfers), 11/15 (early action).

Notification: continuous until 3/1 (freshmen), continuous until 3/15 (transfers), 12/15 (early action).

CONTACT

Westmont College, 955 La Paz Road, Santa Barbara, CA 93108-1099. *Toll-free phone:* 800-777-9011.

See below for display ad and page 1498 for the College Close-Up.

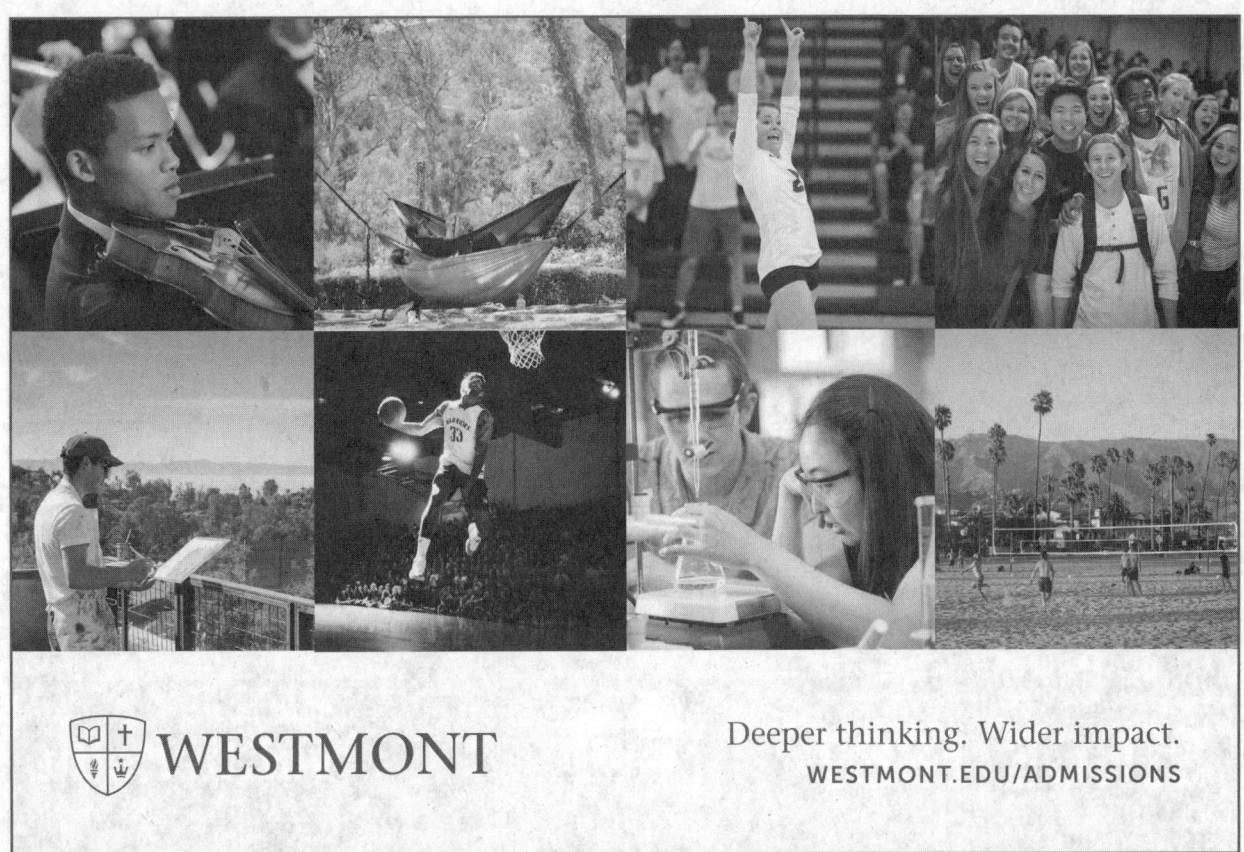

WESTMONT

Deeper thinking. Wider impact.
WESTMONT.EDU/ADMISSIONS

★ Whittier College
Whittier, California
http://www.whittier.edu/

- **Independent** comprehensive, founded 1887
- **Suburban** 95-acre campus with easy access to Los Angeles
- **Endowment** $90.7 million
- **Coed** 1,681 undergraduate students, 98% full-time, 57% women, 43% men
- **Moderately difficult** entrance level, 74% of applicants were admitted

UNDERGRAD STUDENTS

1,640 full-time, 41 part-time. Students come from 32 states and territories; 27 other countries; 23% are from out of state; 5% Black or African American, non-Hispanic/Latino; 50% Hispanic/Latino; 7% Asian, non-Hispanic/Latino; 0.5% Native Hawaiian or other Pacific Islander, non-Hispanic/Latino; 0.4% American Indian or Alaska Native, non-Hispanic/Latino; 7% Two or more races, non-Hispanic/Latino; 0.5% Race/ethnicity unknown; 3% international; 5% transferred in; 50% live on campus.

Freshmen:

Admission: 5,773 applied, 4,277 admitted, 520 enrolled. *Average high school GPA:* 3.5. *Test scores:* SAT evidence-based reading and writing scores over 500: 81%; SAT math scores over 500: 77%; ACT scores over 18: 92%; SAT evidence-based reading and writing scores over 600: 35%; SAT math scores over 600: 27%; ACT scores over 24: 46%; SAT evidence-based reading and writing scores over 700: 4%; SAT math scores over 700: 2%; ACT scores over 30: 7%.

Retention: 78% of full-time freshmen returned.

FACULTY

Total: 165, 72% full-time, 81% with terminal degrees.
Student/faculty ratio: 12:1.

ACADEMICS

Calendar: 4-1-4. *Degrees:* bachelor's, master's, and doctoral.

Special study options: academic remediation for entering students, accelerated degree program, adult/continuing education programs, advanced placement credit, distance learning, double majors, independent study, internships, off-campus study, services for LD students, student-designed majors, study abroad, summer session for credit. *ROTC:* Army (c).

Unusual degree programs: 3-2 engineering with University of Southern California, University of Minnesota.

Computers: 175 computers/terminals and 175 ports are available on campus for general student use. Students can access the following: campus intranet, computer help desk, free student e-mail accounts, online (class) grades, online (class) registration, online (class) schedules. Campuswide network is available. 100% of college-owned or -operated housing units are wired for high-speed Internet access. Wireless service is available via entire campus.

Library: Bonnie Bell Wardman Library plus 1 other. *Books:* 177,410 (physical), 154,491 (digital/electronic); *Serial titles:* 2,730 (physical), 222,633 (digital/electronic); *Databases:* 60. Study areas open 24 hours, 5–7 days a week; students can reserve study rooms.

STUDENT LIFE

Housing options: on-campus residence required through junior year; coed, special housing for students with disabilities. Campus housing is university owned. Freshman campus housing is guaranteed.

Activities and organizations: drama/theater group, student-run newspaper, radio and television station, choral group, Hispanic Students Association, Hawaiian Islander Club, Black Student Union, Asian Students Association, Environment & Sustainability - Raising Awareness for the Environment / Urban Agriculture / Food Recovery Network.

Athletics Member NCAA. All Division III. *Intercollegiate sports:* baseball M, basketball M/W, cross-country running M/W, football M, golf M/W, lacrosse M/W, soccer M/W, softball W, swimming and diving M/W, tennis M/W, track and field M/W, volleyball W, water polo M/W. *Intramural sports:* basketball M/W, softball M/W, volleyball M/W.

Campus security: 24-hour emergency response devices and patrols, late-night transport/escort service, controlled dormitory access.

Student services: health clinic, personal/psychological counseling.

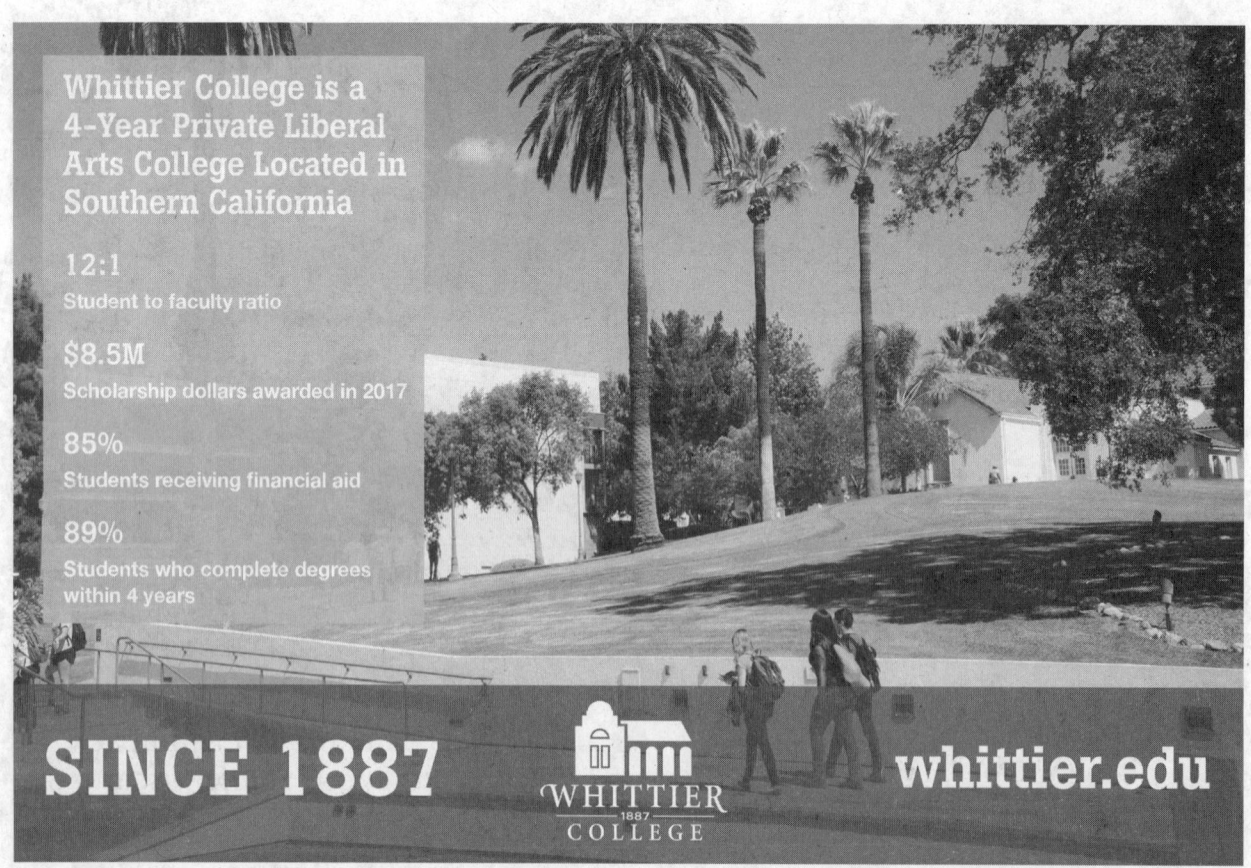

Whittier College is a 4-Year Private Liberal Arts College Located in Southern California

12:1
Student to faculty ratio

$8.5M
Scholarship dollars awarded in 2017

85%
Students receiving financial aid

89%
Students who complete degrees within 4 years

SINCE 1887

WHITTIER
1887
COLLEGE

whittier.edu

COSTS & FINANCIAL AID

Costs (2017–18) *Comprehensive fee:* $59,448 includes full-time tuition ($45,730), mandatory fees ($390), and room and board ($13,328). Full-time tuition and fees vary according to course load. Part-time tuition: $1905 per semester hour. Part-time tuition and fees vary according to course load. *College room only:* $7198. Room and board charges vary according to board plan. *Payment plan:* installment. *Waivers:* employees or children of employees.

Financial Aid Of all full-time matriculated undergraduates who enrolled in 2017, 1,376 applied for aid, 1,284 were judged to have need, 203 had their need fully met. 238 Federal Work-Study jobs (averaging $2270). 580 state and other part-time jobs (averaging $1952). In 2017, 293 non-need-based awards were made. *Average percent of need met:* 79. *Average financial aid package:* $37,931. *Average need-based loan:* $5687. *Average need-based gift aid:* $34,151. *Average non-need-based aid:* $22,612. *Average indebtedness upon graduation:* $32,258. *Financial aid deadline:* 6/30.

APPLYING

Standardized Tests *Required for some:* SAT or ACT (for admission). *Recommended:* SAT Subject Tests (for admission).

Options: electronic application, early action, deferred entrance.

Application fee: $50.

Required: essay or personal statement, high school transcript, minimum 2.0 GPA, 2 letters of recommendation. *Required for some:* minimum 3.0 GPA. *Recommended:* minimum 2.5 GPA, interview.

Application deadlines: rolling (freshmen), rolling (transfers), 11/15 (early action).

Notification: continuous (freshmen), 3/1 (transfers), 12/30 (early action).

CONTACT

Ms. Janine Bissic, Director of Admission, Whittier College, Office of Admission, 13406 East Philadelphia Street, Whittier, CA 90608-0634. *Phone:* 562-907-4238. *Fax:* 562-907-4870. *E-mail:* admission@whittier.edu.

See previous page for display ad and page 1504 for the College Close-Up.

William Jessup University
Rocklin, California
http://www.jessup.edu/

CONTACT
Traditional Undergraduate Admission, William Jessup University, 2121 University Avenue, Rocklin, CA 95765. *Phone:* 916-577-2222. *Fax:* 916-577-2220. *E-mail:* admissions@jessup.edu.

Woodbury University
Burbank, California
http://www.woodbury.edu/
- **Independent** comprehensive, founded 1884
- **Suburban** 22-acre campus with easy access to Los Angeles
- **Coed** 1,024 undergraduate students, 90% full-time, 50% women, 50% men
- **Moderately difficult** entrance level, 62% of applicants were admitted

UNDERGRAD STUDENTS
923 full-time, 101 part-time. 15% are from out of state; 3% Black or African American, non-Hispanic/Latino; 31% Hispanic/Latino; 9% Asian, non-Hispanic/Latino; 0.4% Native Hawaiian or other Pacific Islander, non-Hispanic/Latino; 0.3% American Indian or Alaska Native, non-Hispanic/Latino; 3% Two or more races, non-Hispanic/Latino; 0.6% Race/ethnicity unknown; 21% international; 14% transferred in; 18% live on campus.

Freshmen:
Admission: 1,327 applied, 818 admitted, 116 enrolled. *Average high school GPA:* 3.3. *Test scores:* ACT scores over 18: 81%; ACT scores over 24: 44%; ACT scores over 30: 11%.
Retention: 73% of full-time freshmen returned.

FACULTY
Total: 213, 33% full-time, 49% with terminal degrees.
Student/faculty ratio: 9:1.

ACADEMICS
Calendar: semesters. *Degrees:* bachelor's and master's.

Special study options: academic remediation for entering students, advanced placement credit, double majors, independent study, internships, part-time degree program, services for LD students, student-designed majors, study abroad, summer session for credit.

Computers: Students can access the following: campus intranet, computer help desk, free student e-mail accounts, online (class) grades, online (class) registration, online (class) schedules. Campuswide network is available. 100% of college-owned or -operated housing units are wired for high-speed Internet access. Wireless service is available via classrooms, computer centers, computer labs, learning centers, libraries, student centers.

Library: Los Angeles Times Library. *Books:* 56,582 (physical), 75,462 (digital/electronic); *Serial titles:* 321 (physical), 46,655 (digital/electronic); *Databases:* 40.

STUDENT LIFE
Housing options: coed. Campus housing is university owned and is provided by a third party. Freshman applicants given priority for college housing.

Activities and organizations: national fraternities, national sororities.

Campus security: 24-hour patrols, late-night transport/escort service, controlled dormitory access.

Student services: health clinic, personal/psychological counseling.

COSTS & FINANCIAL AID
Costs (2018–19) *Comprehensive fee:* $51,700 includes full-time tuition ($38,370), mandatory fees ($1410), and room and board ($11,920). Full-time tuition and fees vary according to course load, degree level, and program. Part-time tuition: $1249 per credit hour. Part-time tuition and fees vary according to course load, degree level, and program. *Required fees:* $705 per term part-time. *College room only:* $7150. Room and board charges vary according to board plan, housing facility, and location. *Payment plan:* deferred payment. *Waivers:* employees or children of employees.

Financial Aid Of all full-time matriculated undergraduates who enrolled in 2016, 639 applied for aid, 607 were judged to have need, 11 had their need fully met. In 2016, 102 non-need-based awards were made. *Average percent of need met:* 51. *Average financial aid package:* $23,976. *Average need-based loan:* $4465. *Average need-based gift aid:* $19,919. *Average non-need-based aid:* $11,133. *Average indebtedness upon graduation:* $41,211. *Financial aid deadline:* 2/1.

APPLYING
Standardized Tests *Recommended:* SAT or ACT (for admission).

Options: electronic application, deferred entrance.

Application fee: $75.

Required: high school transcript, minimum 2.3 GPA. *Recommended:* essay or personal statement, 1 letter of recommendation.

Application deadlines: rolling (freshmen), rolling (out-of-state freshmen), rolling (transfers).

Notification: continuous (freshmen), continuous (out-of-state freshmen), continuous (transfers).

CONTACT
Woodbury University, 7500 North Glenoaks Boulevard, Burbank, CA 91504. *Phone:* 818-252-5225. *Toll-free phone:* 800-784-WOOD. *E-mail:* info@woodbury.edu.

World Mission University
Los Angeles, California
http://www.wmu.edu/

CONTACT
World Mission University, 500 Shatto Place, Suite 600, Los Angeles, CA 90020.

Yeshiva Ohr Elchonon Chabad/West Coast Talmudical Seminary

Los Angeles, California
http://www.yoec.edu/

CONTACT
Rabbi Ezra Binyomin Schochet, Dean, Yeshiva Ohr Elchonon Chabad/West Coast Talmudical Seminary, 7215 Waring Avenue, Los Angeles, CA 90046-7660. *Phone:* 323-937-3763. *E-mail:* roshyeshiva@yoec.edu.

Zaytuna College

Berkeley, California
http://www.zaytuna.edu/

CONTACT
Yusuf Samara, Admissions, Zaytuna College, 2401 Le Conte Avenue, Berkeley, CA 94709. *Phone:* 510-900-3156. *E-mail:* admissions@zaytuna.org.

COLORADO

Adams State University

Alamosa, Colorado
http://www.adams.edu/

- **State-supported** comprehensive, founded 1921
- **Small-town** 90-acre campus with easy access to Pueblo
- **Endowment** $64,882
- **Coed** 1,949 undergraduate students, 78% full-time, 47% women, 53% men
- **Moderately difficult** entrance level, 99% of applicants were admitted

UNDERGRAD STUDENTS
1,517 full-time, 432 part-time. 6% Black or African American, non-Hispanic/Latino; 35% Hispanic/Latino; 0.6% Asian, non-Hispanic/Latino; 0.8% Native Hawaiian or other Pacific Islander, non-Hispanic/Latino; 2% American Indian or Alaska Native, non-Hispanic/Latino; 4% Two or more races, non-Hispanic/Latino; 12% Race/ethnicity unknown; 0.7% international; 11% transferred in; 53% live on campus.

Freshmen:
Admission: 1,791 applied, 1,771 admitted, 397 enrolled. *Average high school GPA:* 3.1. *Test scores:* SAT evidence-based reading and writing scores over 500: 44%; SAT math scores over 500: 52%; ACT scores over 18: 80%; SAT evidence-based reading and writing scores over 600: 6%; SAT math scores over 600: 5%; ACT scores over 24: 21%; ACT scores over 30: 2%.

Retention: 61% of full-time freshmen returned.

FACULTY
Total: 254, 44% full-time, 43% with terminal degrees.
Student/faculty ratio: 15:1.

ACADEMICS
Calendar: semesters. *Degrees:* associate, bachelor's, master's, and doctoral.

Special study options: academic remediation for entering students, accelerated degree program, adult/continuing education programs, advanced placement credit, cooperative education, distance learning, double majors, external degree program, independent study, internships, off-campus study, part-time degree program, services for LD students, student-designed majors, study abroad, summer session for credit.

Computers: 322 computers/terminals are available on campus for general student use. Students can access the following: campus intranet, computer help desk, free student e-mail accounts, online (class) grades, online (class) registration, online (class) schedules. Campuswide network is available. 100% of college-owned or -operated housing units are wired for high-speed Internet access. Wireless service is available via entire campus.

Library: Nielsen Library. *Books:* 252 (physical), 891 (digital/electronic); *Serial titles:* 102 (physical), 372 (digital/electronic); *Databases:* 60. Weekly public service hours: 84.

STUDENT LIFE
Housing options: on-campus residence required through sophomore year; coed, men-only, women-only. Campus housing is university owned. Freshman campus housing is guaranteed.

Activities and organizations: drama/theater group, student-run newspaper, radio station, choral group, marching band, Student Programming Board, Student government, Semillas de la Tierra, Newman Club, Fellowship of Christian Athletes.

Athletics Member NCAA. All Division II. *Intercollegiate sports:* baseball M(s), basketball M(s)/W(s), cross-country running M(s)/W(s), football M(s), golf M(s)/W(s), lacrosse M(s)/W(s), soccer M(s)/W(s), softball W(s), swimming and diving M(s)/W(s), track and field M(s)/W(s), volleyball W(s), wrestling M(s). *Intramural sports:* basketball M/W, bowling M/W, cheerleading M(c)/W(c), football M/W, golf M(c)/W(c), racquetball M/W, rock climbing M/W, rugby M(c)/W(c), skiing (cross-country) M/W, skiing (downhill) M/W, soccer M/W, softball M/W, swimming and diving M/W, volleyball M/W, water polo M/W.

Campus security: 24-hour emergency response devices and patrols, student patrols, late-night transport/escort service, controlled dormitory access.

Student services: personal/psychological counseling.

COSTS & FINANCIAL AID
Costs (2017–18) *Tuition:* state resident $5736 full-time, $316 per credit hour part-time; nonresident $16,752 full-time, $698 per credit hour part-time. Full-time tuition and fees vary according to course load. Part-time tuition and fees vary according to course load. No tuition increase for student's term of enrollment. *Required fees:* $3708 full-time, $151 per credit hour part-time. *Room and board:* $7215; room only: $4900. Room and board charges vary according to board plan and housing facility. *Payment plans:* installment, deferred payment. *Waivers:* senior citizens and employees or children of employees.

Financial Aid Of all full-time matriculated undergraduates who enrolled in 2017, 1,506 applied for aid, 1,199 were judged to have need, 76 had their need fully met. *Average percent of need met:* 64. *Average financial aid package:* $13,827. *Average need-based loan:* $4131. *Average need-based gift aid:* $9080. *Average indebtedness upon graduation:* $24,958.

APPLYING
Standardized Tests *Required:* SAT or ACT (for admission).

Options: electronic application, early admission, deferred entrance.

Application fee: $30.

Required: high school transcript, minimum 2.0 GPA. *Required for some:* essay or personal statement, audition for music majors, portfolio for art majors.

Application deadlines: rolling (freshmen), rolling (transfers).

Notification: continuous (freshmen), continuous (transfers).

CONTACT
Adams State University, 208 Edgemont Boulevard, Alamosa, CO 81101. *Toll-free phone:* 800-824-6494.

American Sentinel University

Aurora, Colorado
http://www.americansentinel.edu/

CONTACT
Natalie Nixon, Vice President of Admission, American Sentinel University, 2260 South Xanadu Way, Suite 310, Aurora, CO 80014. *Phone:* 800-729-2427. *Toll-free phone:* 800-729-2427. *Fax:* 866-505-2450. *E-mail:* natalie.nixon@americansentinel.edu.

Argosy University, Denver

Denver, Colorado
http://www.argosy.edu/locations/denver/

CONTACT
Argosy University, Denver, 7600 East Eastman Avenue, Denver, CO 80231. *Phone:* 303-923-4110. *Toll-free phone:* 866-431-5981.

The Art Institute of Colorado
Denver, Colorado
http://www.artinstitutes.edu/denver/

CONTACT
The Art Institute of Colorado, 1200 Lincoln Street, Denver, CO 80203. *Phone:* 303-837-0825. *Toll-free phone:* 800-275-2420.

Aspen University
Denver, Colorado
http://www.aspen.edu/

CONTACT
Aspen University, 720 South Colorado Boulevard, Suite 1150N, Denver, CO 80246-1930. *Phone:* 303-333-4224. *Toll-free phone:* 800-441-4746.

CollegeAmerica–Colorado Springs
Colorado Springs, Colorado
http://www.collegeamerica.edu/

CONTACT
CollegeAmerica–Colorado Springs, 2020 North Academy Boulevard, Colorado Springs, CO 80909. *Phone:* 719-637-0600. *Toll-free phone:* 800-622-2894.

CollegeAmerica–Fort Collins
Fort Collins, Colorado
http://www.collegeamerica.edu/
- **Independent** primarily 2-year, founded 1962
- **Suburban** campus
- **Coed**
- **Minimally difficult** entrance level

ACADEMICS
Calendar: continuous. *Degrees:* associate and bachelor's.

STUDENT LIFE
Housing options: college housing not available.

APPLYING
Required: essay or personal statement, high school transcript, interview. *Recommended:* minimum 2.0 GPA.

CONTACT
CollegeAmerica–Fort Collins, 4601 South Mason Street, Fort Collins, CO 80525. *Phone:* 970-223-6060 Ext. 8002. *Toll-free phone:* 800-622-2894.

Colorado Christian University
Lakewood, Colorado
http://www.ccu.edu/
- **Independent interdenominational** comprehensive, founded 1914
- **Suburban** 26-acre campus with easy access to Denver
- **Coed** 1,343 undergraduate students
- **Moderately difficult** entrance level, 62% of applicants were admitted

UNDERGRAD STUDENTS
Students come from 50 states and territories; 17 other countries; 50% are from out of state; 55% live on campus.

Freshmen:
Admission: 1,925 applied, 1,199 admitted. *Average high school GPA:* 3.7.
Retention: 78% of full-time freshmen returned.

FACULTY
Student/faculty ratio: 15:1.

ACADEMICS
Calendar: semesters. *Degrees:* associate, bachelor's, and master's.

Special study options: academic remediation for entering students, accelerated degree program, adult/continuing education programs, advanced placement credit, cooperative education, distance learning, double majors, honors programs, independent study, internships, off-campus study, part-time degree program, services for LD students, student-designed majors, study abroad, summer session for credit. *ROTC:* Army (c).

Computers: Students can access the following: online (class) registration. Campuswide network is available. 100% of college-owned or -operated housing units are wired for high-speed Internet access. Wireless service is available via classrooms, computer centers, computer labs, dorm rooms, learning centers, libraries, student centers.
Library: Clifton Fowler Library.

STUDENT LIFE
Housing options: on-campus residence required through sophomore year; men-only, women-only, special housing for students with disabilities. Campus housing is university owned and leased by the school. Freshman campus housing is guaranteed.

Activities and organizations: drama/theater group, choral group.

Athletics Member NCAA. All Division II. *Intercollegiate sports:* baseball M(s), basketball M(s)/W(s), cross-country running M(s)/W(s), golf M(s)/W(s), soccer M(s)/W(s), softball W(s), tennis M(s)/W(s), track and field M(s)/W(s), volleyball W(s). *Intramural sports:* cheerleading W(c), ice hockey M(c), sand volleyball M/W, skiing (downhill) M/W, table tennis M/W, ultimate Frisbee M/W.

Campus security: 24-hour emergency response devices and patrols, student patrols.

Student services: health clinic, personal/psychological counseling, women's center.

COSTS & FINANCIAL AID
Costs (2018–19) *Comprehensive fee:* $40,886 includes full-time tuition ($29,870), mandatory fees ($500), and room and board ($10,516). Full-time tuition and fees vary according to course load. Part-time tuition and fees vary according to course load. *College room only:* $2915. Room and board charges vary according to board plan and housing facility.

Financial Aid Of all full-time matriculated undergraduates who enrolled in 2004, 750 applied for aid, 615 were judged to have need, 55 had their need fully met. 16 Federal Work-Study jobs (averaging $2000). In 2004, 252 non-need-based awards were made. *Average percent of need met:* 54. *Average financial aid package:* $8931. *Average need-based loan:* $3946. *Average need-based gift aid:* $6056. *Average non-need-based aid:* $12,655. *Average indebtedness upon graduation:* $18,633.

APPLYING
Standardized Tests *Required:* SAT or ACT (for admission).

Options: electronic application, early admission, deferred entrance.

Application fee: $30.

Required: essay or personal statement, high school transcript, 2 letters of recommendation, interview, Spiritual Recommendation. *Required for some:* minimum 2.8 GPA, 3 letters of recommendation, interview.

Application deadlines: 8/1 (freshmen), 8/1 (transfers).

Notification: continuous (transfers).

CONTACT
Jo Leda Martin, Director of Admissions, Colorado Christian University, 8787 West Alameda Ave, Lakewood, CO 80226. *Phone:* 303-963-3206. *Toll-free phone:* 800-44-FAITH. *Fax:* 303-963-3201. *E-mail:* jomartin@ccu.edu.

The Colorado College
Colorado Springs, Colorado
http://www.coloradocollege.edu/
- **Independent** comprehensive, founded 1874
- **Urban** 90-acre campus with easy access to Denver
- **Endowment** $683.2 million
- **Coed** 2,101 undergraduate students, 99% full-time, 54% women, 46% men
- **Very difficult** entrance level, 16% of applicants were admitted

UNDERGRAD STUDENTS
2,084 full-time, 17 part-time. Students come from 52 states and territories; 55 other countries; 83% are from out of state; 3% Black or African American, non-Hispanic/Latino; 9% Hispanic/Latino; 4% Asian, non-Hispanic/Latino; 0.5% American Indian or Alaska Native, non-Hispanic/Latino; 9% Two or more races, non-Hispanic/Latino; 1%

Race/ethnicity unknown; 8% international; 1% transferred in; 75% live on campus.

Freshmen:
Admission: 7,894 applied, 1,262 admitted, 533 enrolled. *Test scores:* ACT scores over 18: 100%; ACT scores over 24: 98%; ACT scores over 30: 65%.
Retention: 96% of full-time freshmen returned.

FACULTY
Total: 232, 80% full-time, 91% with terminal degrees.
Student/faculty ratio: 10:1.

ACADEMICS
Calendar: 8 blocks of 3 1/2 week courses. *Degrees:* bachelor's, master's, and postbachelor's certificates (master's degree in education only).

Special study options: advanced placement credit, double majors, English as a second language, independent study, internships, off-campus study, services for LD students, student-designed majors, study abroad, summer session for credit. *ROTC:* Army (c).

Unusual degree programs: 3-2 engineering with Rensselaer Polytechnic Institute, Washington University in St. Louis, University of Southern California, Columbia University.

Computers: 396 computers/terminals are available on campus for general student use. Students can access the following: campus intranet, computer help desk, free student e-mail accounts, online (class) grades, online (class) registration, online (class) schedules. Campuswide network is available. 100% of college-owned or -operated housing units are wired for high-speed Internet access. Wireless service is available via entire campus.
Library: Tutt Library plus 1 other. *Books:* 419,811 (physical), 344,607 (digital/electronic); *Serial titles:* 4,322 (physical), 73,232 (digital/electronic); *Databases:* 320. Students can reserve study rooms.

STUDENT LIFE
Housing options: on-campus residence required through junior year; coed, men-only, women-only. Campus housing is university owned. Freshman campus housing is guaranteed.

Activities and organizations: drama/theater group, student-run newspaper, choral group, national fraternities, national sororities.

Athletics Member NCAA. All Division III except ice hockey (Division I), soccer (Division I). *Intercollegiate sports:* baseball M(c), basketball M/W, cross-country running M/W, equestrian sports M(c)/W(c), ice hockey M(s)/W(c), lacrosse M/W, rugby M(c)/W(c), skiing (downhill) M(c)/W(c), soccer M/W(s), softball W(c), swimming and diving M/W, tennis M/W, track and field M/W, ultimate Frisbee M(c)/W(c), volleyball W, water polo W(c). *Intramural sports:* basketball M/W, football M, ice hockey M/W, racquetball M/W, soccer M/W, softball M/W, table tennis M/W, ultimate Frisbee M/W, volleyball M/W.

Campus security: 24-hour emergency response devices and patrols, late-night transport/escort service, controlled dormitory access, whistle program, student escort service, good campus lighting.

Student services: health clinic, personal/psychological counseling.

COSTS & FINANCIAL AID
Costs (2017–18) *One-time required fee:* $150. *Comprehensive fee:* $64,894 includes full-time tuition ($52,380), mandatory fees ($438), and room and board ($12,076). Part-time tuition: $8803 per course. Part-time tuition and fees vary according to course load. *Required fees:* $2201 per credit hour part-time. *College room only:* $7240. Room and board charges vary according to board plan and housing facility. *Payment plan:* installment. *Waivers:* employees or children of employees.

Financial Aid Of all full-time matriculated undergraduates who enrolled in 2017, 801 applied for aid, 665 were judged to have need, 665 had their need fully met. 330 Federal Work-Study jobs (averaging $1855). 188 state and other part-time jobs (averaging $1914). In 2017, 128 non-need-based awards were made. *Average percent of need met:* 100. *Average financial aid package:* $48,900. *Average need-based loan:* $4316. *Average need-based gift aid:* $45,251. *Average non-need-based aid:* $14,736. *Average indebtedness upon graduation:* $20,742. *Financial aid deadline:* 2/15.

APPLYING
Standardized Tests *Required for some:* SAT or ACT (for admission).
Options: electronic application, early decision, early action, deferred entrance.

Application fee: $60.
Required: essay or personal statement, high school transcript, 2 letters of recommendation. *Recommended:* interview.
Application deadlines: 1/15 (freshmen), 3/1 (transfers), 11/10 (early action).
Early decision deadline: 11/10 (for plan 1), 1/15 (for plan 2).
Notification: 4/1 (freshmen), 5/1 (transfers), 12/15 (early decision plan 1), 2/10 (early decision plan 2), 12/20 (early action).

CONTACT
Mr. Carlos Jiminez, Director of Admission, Outreach and Recruitment, The Colorado College, 14 East Cache La Poudre Street, Colorado Springs, CO 80903-3294. *Phone:* 719-389-6344. *Toll-free phone:* 800-542-7214. *Fax:* 719-389-6816. *E-mail:* admission@coloradocollege.edu.

Colorado Mesa University
Grand Junction, Colorado
http://www.coloradomesa.edu/
- **State-supported** comprehensive, founded 1925
- **Suburban** 90-acre campus
- **Endowment** $27.7 million
- **Coed** 9,595 undergraduate students, 76% full-time, 54% women, 46% men
- **Minimally difficult** entrance level, 82% of applicants were admitted

UNDERGRAD STUDENTS
7,277 full-time, 2,318 part-time. Students come from 47 states and territories; 14 other countries; 14% are from out of state; 2% Black or African American, non-Hispanic/Latino; 18% Hispanic/Latino; 2% Asian, non-Hispanic/Latino; 0.5% Native Hawaiian or other Pacific Islander, non-Hispanic/Latino; 0.7% American Indian or Alaska Native, non-Hispanic/Latino; 4% Two or more races, non-Hispanic/Latino; 2% Race/ethnicity unknown; 1% international; 7% transferred in; 23% live on campus.

Freshmen:
Admission: 6,982 applied, 5,702 admitted, 2,023 enrolled. *Average high school GPA:* 3.1. *Test scores:* SAT evidence-based reading and writing scores over 500: 71%; SAT math scores over 500: 68%; ACT scores over 18: 82%; SAT evidence-based reading and writing scores over 600: 26%; SAT math scores over 600: 22%; ACT scores over 24: 29%; SAT evidence-based reading and writing scores over 700: 3%; SAT math scores over 700: 2%; ACT scores over 30: 3%.
Retention: 74% of full-time freshmen returned.

FACULTY
Total: 572, 52% full-time.
Student/faculty ratio: 21:1.

ACADEMICS
Calendar: semesters. *Degrees:* certificates, associate, bachelor's, master's, doctoral, and postbachelor's certificates.

Special study options: academic remediation for entering students, accelerated degree program, advanced placement credit, distance learning, double majors, honors programs, internships, off-campus study, part-time degree program, services for LD students, study abroad, summer session for credit.

Unusual degree programs: 3-2 business administration.

Computers: 525 computers/terminals are available on campus for general student use. Students can access the following: campus intranet, computer help desk, free student e-mail accounts, online (class) grades, online (class) registration, online (class) schedules. Campuswide network is available. 100% of college-owned or -operated housing units are wired for high-speed Internet access. Wireless service is available via entire campus.
Library: John U. Tomlinson Library. *Books:* 202,919 (physical), 162,000 (digital/electronic); *Databases:* 116. Weekly public service hours: 94; study areas open 24 hours, 5–7 days a week; students can reserve study rooms.

STUDENT LIFE
Housing options: on-campus residence required through junior year; coed, special housing for students with disabilities. Campus housing is university owned. Freshman applicants given priority for college housing.

Activities and organizations: drama/theater group, student-run newspaper, radio and television station, choral group, marching band, Environmental Club, Student Body Association, KMSA radio station, Rodeo Club, Campus Residents Association, national fraternities, national sororities.

Athletics Member NCAA. All Division II. *Intercollegiate sports:* baseball M(s), basketball M(s)/W(s), cheerleading M/W, cross-country running M(s)/W(s), football M(s), golf M(s)/W(s), lacrosse M(s)/W(s), rugby M(c)/W(c), sand volleyball W(s), skiing (cross-country) M(c)/W(c), skiing (downhill) M(c)/W(c), soccer M(s)/W(s), softball W(s), swimming and diving M(s)/W(s), tennis M(s)/W(s), track and field M(s)/W(s), volleyball W(s), wrestling M(s). *Intramural sports:* basketball M(c)/W(c), fencing M(c)/W(c), football M/W, ice hockey M(c), lacrosse M(c)/W(c), rugby M(c)/W(c), skiing (downhill) M(c)/W(c), soccer M(c)/W(c), softball M/W, swimming and diving M(c)/W(c), table tennis M(c)/W(c), tennis M(c)/W(c), ultimate Frisbee M(c)/W(c), volleyball M(c)/W(c).

Campus security: 24-hour emergency response devices and patrols, late-night transport/escort service, controlled dormitory access.

Student services: health clinic, personal/psychological counseling, legal services.

COSTS & FINANCIAL AID

Costs (2017–18) *Tuition:* state resident $8100 full-time, $270 per credit hour part-time; nonresident $20,910 full-time, $697 per credit hour part-time. Full-time tuition and fees vary according to course load. Part-time tuition and fees vary according to course load. *Required fees:* $872 full-time, $29 per credit hour part-time. *Room and board:* $10,735; room only: $5930. Room and board charges vary according to board plan and housing facility. *Payment plan:* installment. *Waivers:* employees or children of employees.

Financial Aid Of all full-time matriculated undergraduates who enrolled in 2016, 5,849 applied for aid, 4,679 were judged to have need, 788 had their need fully met. In 2016, 489 non-need-based awards were made. *Average percent of need met:* 61. *Average financial aid package:* $9301. *Average need-based loan:* $3729. *Average need-based gift aid:* $6936. *Average non-need-based aid:* $3685. *Average indebtedness upon graduation:* $28,101.

APPLYING

Standardized Tests *Required:* SAT or ACT (for admission).

Options: electronic application, deferred entrance.

Application fee: $30.

Required: high school transcript. *Recommended:* 2 letters of recommendation.

Application deadlines: rolling (freshmen), rolling (transfers).

Notification: continuous (freshmen), continuous (transfers).

CONTACT
Admissions, Colorado Mesa University, 1100 North Avenue, Grand Junction, CO 81501. *Phone:* 970-248-1875. *Toll-free phone:* 800-982-MESA. *Fax:* 970-248-1973. *E-mail:* admissions@coloradomeas.edu.

Colorado Mountain College
Glenwood Springs, Colorado
http://www.coloradomtn.edu/

CONTACT
Vicky Butler, Admissions Assistant, Colorado Mountain College, 3000 CR 114, Glenwood Springs, CO 81601. *Phone:* 970-947-8276. *Toll-free phone:* 800-621-8559. *E-mail:* vvalentine@coloradomtn.edu.

Colorado Mountain College
Leadville, Colorado
http://www.coloradomtn.edu/

CONTACT
Ms. Mary Laing, Admissions Assistant, Colorado Mountain College, 901South Highway 24, Leadville, CO 80461. *Phone:* 719-486-4292. *Toll-free phone:* 800-621-8559. *E-mail:* joinus@coloradomtn.edu.

Colorado Mountain College
Steamboat Springs, Colorado
http://www.coloradomtn.edu/

CONTACT
Ms. Jackie Brazill, Admissions Assistant, Colorado Mountain College, 1275 Crawford Avenue, Steamboat Springs, CO 80487. *Phone:* 970-870-4417 Ext. 4417. *Toll-free phone:* 800-621-8559. *E-mail:* jbrazill@coloradomtn.edu.

Colorado School of Mines
Golden, Colorado
http://www.mines.edu/

- **State-supported** university, founded 1874
- **Small-town** 499-acre campus with easy access to Denver, Boulder, Colorado Springs
- **Endowment** $234.2 million
- **Coed**
- **Very difficult** entrance level

FACULTY
Student/faculty ratio: 15:1.

ACADEMICS
Calendar: semesters. *Degrees:* bachelor's, master's, doctoral, and post-master's certificates.
Library: Arthur Lakes Library. *Books:* 503,801 (physical), 134,211 (digital/electronic); *Serial titles:* 578 (physical), 104,424 (digital/electronic); *Databases:* 128. Weekly public service hours: 107; students can reserve study rooms.

STUDENT LIFE
Housing options: on-campus residence required for freshman year; coed. Campus housing is university owned and is provided by a third party. Freshman campus housing is guaranteed.

Activities and organizations: drama/theater group, student-run newspaper, radio station, choral group, marching band, Society of Women Engineers, Residence Hall Association, Associated Students of Colorado School of Mines, Student Professional Societies/ and/ Religious Organizations, Multicultural Engineering Program, national fraternities, national sororities.

Athletics Member NCAA. All Division II.

Campus security: 24-hour emergency response devices and patrols, late-night transport/escort service, controlled dormitory access, fully trained police officers.

Student services: health clinic, personal/psychological counseling, women's center.

COSTS & FINANCIAL AID
Costs (2017–18) *Tuition:* state resident $16,170 full-time, $539 per credit hour part-time; nonresident $35,220 full-time, $1174 per credit hour part-time. Full-time tuition and fees vary according to course load. *Required fees:* $2216 full-time. *Room and board:* $11,897. Room and board charges vary according to board plan and housing facility.

Financial Aid Of all full-time matriculated undergraduates who enrolled in 2016, 2,807 applied for aid, 1,968 were judged to have need, 425 had their need fully met. 384 Federal Work-Study jobs (averaging $1749). 2,038 state and other part-time jobs (averaging $2428). In 2016, 1405 non-need-based awards were made. *Average percent of need met:* 58. *Average financial aid package:* $13,912. *Average need-based loan:* $4652. *Average need-based gift aid:* $5869. *Average non-need-based aid:* $8272. *Average indebtedness upon graduation:* $32,221.

APPLYING
Standardized Tests *Required:* SAT or ACT (for admission).
Options: electronic application, deferred entrance.
Application fee: $45.
Required: high school transcript. *Required for some:* essay or personal statement, interview. *Recommended:* minimum 3.8 GPA, rank in upper quartile of high school class.

CONTACT
Mrs. Marisa Garcia, Assistant Director of Enrollment Management, Colorado School of Mines, Admissions Office, Starzer Welcome Center,

1812 Illinois Street, Golden, CO 80401. *Phone:* 303-273-3220. *Toll-free phone:* 800-446-9488 Ext. 3220. *Fax:* 303-273-3509. *E-mail:* admissions@mines.edu.

Colorado State University

Fort Collins, Colorado

http://www.colostate.edu/

- **State-supported** university, founded 1870, part of Colorado State University System
- **Urban** 4773-acre campus with easy access to Denver
- **Endowment** $330.2 million
- **Coed** 25,903 undergraduate students, 85% full-time, 52% women, 48% men
- **Moderately difficult** entrance level, 83% of applicants were admitted

UNDERGRAD STUDENTS

21,969 full-time, 3,934 part-time. Students come from 55 states and territories; 79 other countries; 24% are from out of state; 2% Black or African American, non-Hispanic/Latino; 12% Hispanic/Latino; 2% Asian, non-Hispanic/Latino; 0.2% Native Hawaiian or other Pacific Islander, non-Hispanic/Latino; 0.5% American Indian or Alaska Native, non-Hispanic/Latino; 3% Two or more races, non-Hispanic/Latino; 2% Race/ethnicity unknown; 4% international; 7% transferred in; 26% live on campus.

Freshmen:

Admission: 23,137 applied, 19,116 admitted, 5,038 enrolled. *Average high school GPA:* 3.6. *Test scores:* SAT evidence-based reading and writing scores over 500: 93%; SAT math scores over 500: 92%; ACT scores over 18: 98%; SAT evidence-based reading and writing scores over 600: 57%; SAT math scores over 600: 49%; ACT scores over 24: 64%; SAT evidence-based reading and writing scores over 700: 10%; SAT math scores over 700: 9%; ACT scores over 30: 14%.

Retention: 84% of full-time freshmen returned.

FACULTY

Total: 2,164, 61% full-time.

Student/faculty ratio: 18:1.

ACADEMICS

Calendar: semesters. *Degrees:* bachelor's, master's, doctoral, and postbachelor's certificates.

Special study options: accelerated degree program, adult/continuing education programs, advanced placement credit, cooperative education, distance learning, double majors, English as a second language, honors programs, independent study, internships, off-campus study, part-time degree program, services for LD students, study abroad, summer session for credit. *ROTC:* Army (b), Air Force (b).

Unusual degree programs: 3-2 engineering.

Computers: 1,700 computers/terminals and 3,000 ports are available on campus for general student use. Students can access the following: campus intranet, computer help desk, free student e-mail accounts, online (class) grades, online (class) registration, online (class) schedules, personalized portal services including transcripts and financials (billing, financial aid). Campuswide network is available. 100% of college-owned or -operated housing units are wired for high-speed Internet access. Wireless service is available via classrooms, computer centers, computer labs, dorm rooms, learning centers, libraries, student centers.

Library: William E. Morgan Library plus 1 other. *Books:* 2.0 million (physical), 537,992 (digital/electronic); *Serial titles:* 40,446 (physical), 84,523 (digital/electronic); *Databases:* 322. Weekly public service hours: 108; study areas open 24 hours, 5–7 days a week; students can reserve study rooms.

STUDENT LIFE

Housing options: on-campus residence required for freshman year; coed, special housing for students with disabilities. Campus housing is university owned. Freshman campus housing is guaranteed.

Activities and organizations: drama/theater group, student-run newspaper, radio and television station, choral group, marching band, CSU Photography Club, Biomedical Student Association, Outdoor Club, Criminal Justice Organization, Indian Student Association, national fraternities, national sororities.

Athletics Member NCAA. All Division I except football (Division I-A). *Intercollegiate sports:* baseball M(c), basketball M(s)/W(s), crew M(c)/W(c), cross-country running M(s)/W(s), field hockey M(c)/W(c), golf M(s)/W(s), ice hockey M(c)/W(c), lacrosse M(c)/W(c), riflery M(c)/W(c), rock climbing M(c)/W(c), rowing M(c)/W(c), rugby M(c)/W(c), skiing (downhill) M(c)/W(c), soccer M(c)/W(s), softball W(s), swimming and diving M(c)/W(s), table tennis M(c)/W(c), tennis M(c)/W(s), track and field M(s)/W(s), triathlon M(c)/W(c), ultimate Frisbee M(c)/W(c), volleyball M(c)/W(s), water polo M(c)/W(c), wrestling M(c)/W(c). *Intramural sports:* badminton M/W, basketball M/W, bowling M/W, golf M/W, racquetball M/W, sand volleyball M/W, soccer M/W, softball M/W, table tennis M/W, tennis M/W, track and field M/W, ultimate Frisbee M/W, volleyball M/W, water polo M/W.

Campus security: 24-hour emergency response devices and patrols, student patrols, late-night transport/escort service, controlled dormitory access.

Student services: health clinic, personal/psychological counseling, women's center, legal services.

COSTS & FINANCIAL AID

Costs (2017–18) *Tuition:* state resident $9152 full-time, $416 per credit hour part-time; nonresident $26,660 full-time, $1333 per credit hour part-time. Full-time tuition and fees vary according to course level, course load, program, reciprocity agreements, and student level. Part-time tuition and fees vary according to course level, course load, program, reciprocity agreements, and student level. *Required fees:* $2336 full-time, $58 per credit hour part-time, $290 per term part-time. *Room and board:* $11,514; room only: $5578. Room and board charges vary according to board plan, housing facility, and location. *Waivers:* employees or children of employees.

Financial Aid Of all full-time matriculated undergraduates who enrolled in 2016, 15,747 applied for aid, 11,257 were judged to have need, 2,649 had their need fully met. 613 Federal Work-Study jobs (averaging $2124). 1,150 state and other part-time jobs (averaging $2065). In 2016, 3178 non-need-based awards were made. *Average percent of need met:* 82. *Average financial aid package:* $11,635. *Average need-based loan:* $6583. *Average need-based gift aid:* $8223. *Average non-need-based aid:* $4971. *Average indebtedness upon graduation:* $26,348.

APPLYING

Standardized Tests *Required:* SAT or ACT (for admission).

Options: electronic application, early action, deferred entrance.

Application fee: $50.

Required: essay or personal statement, high school transcript, 1 letter of recommendation.

Application deadlines: 8/1 (freshmen), 6/1 (transfers), 12/1 (early action).

Notification: continuous until 9/15 (freshmen), continuous (transfers), 2/1 (early action).

CONTACT

Kelly Nolin, Associate Director of Admission, Recruitment and Outreach, Colorado State University, Ammons Hall (1062), Fort Collins, CO 80523-1062. *Phone:* 970-491-6909. *Fax:* 970-491-7799. *E-mail:* admissions@colostate.edu.

Colorado State University–Global Campus

Greenwood Village, Colorado

http://csuglobal.edu/

CONTACT

Colorado State University–Global Campus, 8000 E. Maplewood Avenue, Greenwood Village, CO 80111. *Toll-free phone:* 800-920-6723.

Colorado State University–Pueblo
Pueblo, Colorado
http://www.csupueblo.edu/

- **State-supported** comprehensive, founded 1933, part of Colorado State University System
- **Small-town** 275-acre campus with easy access to Colorado Springs
- **Endowment** $18.0 million
- **Coed** 4,621 undergraduate students, 71% full-time, 52% women, 48% men
- **Minimally difficult** entrance level, 95% of applicants were admitted

UNDERGRAD STUDENTS
3,292 full-time, 1,329 part-time. Students come from 41 states and territories; 31 other countries; 14% are from out of state; 6% Black or African American, non-Hispanic/Latino; 31% Hispanic/Latino; 1% Asian, non-Hispanic/Latino; 0.3% Native Hawaiian or other Pacific Islander, non-Hispanic/Latino; 0.7% American Indian or Alaska Native, non-Hispanic/Latino; 5% Two or more races, non-Hispanic/Latino; 6% Race/ethnicity unknown; 2% international; 7% transferred in; 20% live on campus.

Freshmen:
Admission: 5,899 applied, 5,624 admitted, 726 enrolled. *Average high school GPA:* 3.2. *Test scores:* SAT evidence-based reading and writing scores over 500: 59%; SAT math scores over 500: 64%; ACT scores over 18: 82%; SAT evidence-based reading and writing scores over 600: 22%; SAT math scores over 600: 16%; ACT scores over 24: 21%; SAT evidence-based reading and writing scores over 700: 5%; SAT math scores over 700: 2%; ACT scores over 30: 2%.
Retention: 63% of full-time freshmen returned.

FACULTY
Total: 382, 49% full-time.
Student/faculty ratio: 14:1.

ACADEMICS
Calendar: semesters. *Degrees:* bachelor's and master's.
Special study options: academic remediation for entering students, accelerated degree program, advanced placement credit, cooperative education, distance learning, double majors, English as a second language, external degree program, honors programs, independent study, internships, off-campus study, part-time degree program, services for LD students, study abroad, summer session for credit. *ROTC:* Army (b).
Unusual degree programs: 3-2 business administration; biochemistry, biology, and chemistry programs; combined M.B.A. computer information systems, construction management, and management programs.
Computers: 870 computers/terminals are available on campus for general student use. Students can access the following: campus intranet, computer help desk, free student e-mail accounts, online (class) grades, online (class) registration, online (class) schedules. Campuswide network is available. 100% of college-owned or -operated housing units are wired for high-speed Internet access. Wireless service is available via classrooms, computer centers, computer labs, dorm rooms, learning centers, libraries, student centers.
Library: CSU-Pueblo University Library. *Books:* 179,038 (physical), 206,058 (digital/electronic); *Serial titles:* 2,878 (physical), 106,420 (digital/electronic); *Databases:* 192. Weekly public service hours: 93; students can reserve study rooms.

STUDENT LIFE
Housing options: on-campus residence required through sophomore year; coed. Campus housing is university owned. Freshman campus housing is guaranteed.
Activities and organizations: student-run newspaper, radio and television station, choral group, marching band, Fellowship of Christian Athletes, Black Student Union, Latinx Student Union, National Society of Leadership and Success, Southern Colorado Assoc. of Nursing Students (SCANS), national fraternities, national sororities.
Athletics Member NCAA. All Division II. *Intercollegiate sports:* baseball M(s), basketball M(s)/W(s), cheerleading M/W, cross-country running M(s)/W(s), football M(s), golf M(s)/W(s), lacrosse M(s)/W(s), racquetball M/W, soccer M(s)/W(s), softball M/W(s), squash M, swimming and diving W(s), tennis M(s)/W(s), track and field M(s)/W(s), volleyball W(s), wrestling M(s). *Intramural sports:* baseball M(c), basketball M/W, rock climbing M(c)/W(c), rugby M(c), soccer M(c)/W, softball M/W, volleyball M/W(c).

Campus security: 24-hour emergency response devices and patrols, student patrols, late-night transport/escort service, controlled dormitory access, parking and building checks.
Student services: health clinic, personal/psychological counseling.

COSTS & FINANCIAL AID
Costs (2018–19) *Tuition:* state resident $10,394 full-time, $346 per credit hour part-time; nonresident $17,930 full-time, $598 per credit hour part-time. Full-time tuition and fees vary according to degree level, program, and reciprocity agreements. Part-time tuition and fees vary according to degree level, program, and reciprocity agreements. *Required fees:* $2457 full-time, $82 per credit hour part-time, $1228 per term part-time. *Room and board:* $10,068; room only: $6008. Room and board charges vary according to board plan and housing facility. *Payment plan:* installment. *Waivers:* employees or children of employees.

Financial Aid Of all full-time matriculated undergraduates who enrolled in 2015, 2,933 applied for aid, 2,521 were judged to have need, 168 had their need fully met. 686 Federal Work-Study jobs (averaging $3000). 1,109 state and other part-time jobs (averaging $3000). In 2015, 333 non-need-based awards were made. *Average percent of need met:* 51. *Average financial aid package:* $9865. *Average need-based loan:* $3723. *Average need-based gift aid:* $7340. *Average non-need-based aid:* $3361. *Average indebtedness upon graduation:* $28,914.

APPLYING
Standardized Tests *Required:* SAT or ACT (for admission).
Options: electronic application, deferred entrance.
Application fee: $25.
Required: high school transcript, minimum 2.0 GPA. *Required for some:* essay or personal statement.
Application deadlines: 8/1 (freshmen), 8/1 (transfers).
Notification: continuous (freshmen), continuous (transfers).

CONTACT
Tiffany Kingrey, Director of Admissions, Colorado State University–Pueblo, 2200 Bonforte Boulevard, Pueblo, CO 81001-4901. *Phone:* 719-549-2462. *Fax:* 719-549-2419. *E-mail:* info@csupueblo.edu.

Colorado Technical University Aurora
Aurora, Colorado
http://www.coloradotech.edu/

CONTACT
Rosaland Giboney, Associate Director of Admissions, Colorado Technical University Aurora, 3151 South Vaughn Way, Aurora, CO 80014. *Phone:* 888-404-7555. *Toll-free phone:* 888-309-6555. *E-mail:* rgiboney@coloradotech.edu.

Colorado Technical University Colorado Springs
Colorado Springs, Colorado
http://www.coloradotech.edu/

CONTACT
Beth Braaten, Vice President of Admissions, Colorado Technical University Colorado Springs, 4435 North Chestnut Street, Colorado Springs, CO 80907. *Phone:* 888-404-7555. *Toll-free phone:* 866-942-6555. *E-mail:* bbraaten@coloradotech.edu.

Colorado Technical University Online
Colorado Springs, Colorado
http://www.coloradotech.edu/

CONTACT
William Beckley, Chief Admission Officer, Colorado Technical University Online, 4435 North Chestnut Street, Colorado Springs, CO 80907. *Phone:* 888-404-7555. *Toll-free phone:* 866-813-1836.

Denver College of Nursing
Denver, Colorado
http://www.denvercollegeofnursing.edu/

CONTACT
Denver College of Nursing, 1401 19th Street, Denver, CO 80202. *Toll-free phone:* 888-479-5550.

DeVry University–Westminster Campus
Westminster, Colorado
http://www.devry.edu/
- **Proprietary** comprehensive, founded 1945
- **Urban** campus
- **Coed**

FACULTY
Student/faculty ratio: 14:1.

ACADEMICS
Calendar: semesters. *Degrees:* associate, bachelor's, master's, and postbachelor's certificates.

COSTS & FINANCIAL AID
Costs (2017–18) *Tuition:* $14,420 full-time. *Required fees:* $500 full-time.

Financial Aid Of all full-time matriculated undergraduates who enrolled in 2007, 148 applied for aid, 136 were judged to have need, 6 had their need fully met. In 2007, 17 non-need-based awards were made. *Average percent of need met:* 37. *Average financial aid package:* $11,971. *Average need-based loan:* $8024. *Average need-based gift aid:* $6094. *Average non-need-based aid:* $13,350. *Average indebtedness upon graduation:* $11,071.

APPLYING
Options: deferred entrance.
Application fee: $30.

CONTACT
Admissions Office, DeVry University–Westminster Campus, 1870 West 122nd Avenue, Westminster, CO 80234-2010. *Phone:* 303-280-7400. *Toll-free phone:* 866-338-7934.

Ecotech Institute
Aurora, Colorado
http://www.ecotechinstitute.com/

CONTACT
Ecotech Institute, 1400 South Abilene Street, Aurora, CO 80012.

Fort Lewis College
Durango, Colorado
http://www.fortlewis.edu/
- **State-supported** comprehensive, founded 1911
- **Small-town** 350-acre campus
- **Endowment** $8.2 million
- **Coed** 3,299 undergraduate students, 89% full-time, 52% women, 48% men
- **Moderately difficult** entrance level, 83% of applicants were admitted

UNDERGRAD STUDENTS
2,921 full-time, 378 part-time. Students come from 22 other countries; 52% are from out of state; 1% Black or African American, non-Hispanic/Latino; 11% Hispanic/Latino; 0.7% Asian, non-Hispanic/Latino; 0.2% Native Hawaiian or other Pacific Islander, non-Hispanic/Latino; 26% American Indian or Alaska Native, non-Hispanic/Latino; 9% Two or more races, non-Hispanic/Latino; 3% Race/ethnicity unknown; 0.4% international; 9% transferred in; 42% live on campus.

Freshmen:
Admission: 4,473 applied, 3,722 admitted, 706 enrolled. *Average high school GPA:* 3.3. *Test scores:* SAT evidence-based reading and writing scores over 500: 78%; SAT math scores over 500: 81%; ACT scores over 18: 91%; SAT evidence-based reading and writing scores over 600: 29%; SAT math scores over 600: 27%; ACT scores over 24: 36%; SAT evidence-based reading and writing scores over 700: 3%; SAT math scores over 700: 4%; ACT scores over 30: 4%.

Retention: 59% of full-time freshmen returned.

FACULTY
Total: 264, 69% full-time, 71% with terminal degrees.
Student/faculty ratio: 15:1.

ACADEMICS
Calendar: semesters modified trimesters. *Degrees:* certificates, bachelor's, master's, and postbachelor's certificates.

Special study options: academic remediation for entering students, advanced placement credit, double majors, honors programs, independent study, internships, services for LD students, student-designed majors, study abroad, summer session for credit.

Unusual degree programs: 3-2 social work with University of Denver.

Computers: 825 computers/terminals are available on campus for general student use. Students can access the following: campus intranet, computer help desk, free student e-mail accounts, online (class) grades, online (class) registration, online (class) schedules. Campuswide network is available. 100% of college-owned or -operated housing units are wired for high-speed Internet access. Wireless service is available via entire campus.

Library: John F. Reed Library plus 1 other. *Books:* 140,272 (physical), 210,346 (digital/electronic); *Serial titles:* 4 (physical), 170,201 (digital/electronic); *Databases:* 76. Weekly public service hours: 80; study areas open 24 hours, 5–7 days a week; students can reserve study rooms.

STUDENT LIFE
Housing options: on-campus residence required for freshman year; coed, special housing for students with disabilities. Campus housing is university owned. Freshman applicants given priority for college housing.

Activities and organizations: drama/theater group, student-run newspaper, radio station, KDUR - Campus/community radio, Environmental Center, Student Union Productions, Dance Co-Motion, Master Plan Ministries.

Athletics Member NCAA. All Division II. *Intercollegiate sports:* baseball M(c), basketball M(s)/W(s), cheerleading M(c)/W(c), cross-country running M(s)/W(s), fencing M(c)/W(c), football M(s), golf M(s)/W(s), ice hockey M(c), lacrosse M(c)/W(s), rock climbing M(c)/W(c), rugby M(c)/W(c), skiing (cross-country) M(c)/W(c), skiing (downhill) M(c)/W(c), soccer M(s)/W(s), softball W(s), tennis M(c)/W(c), track and field W(s), ultimate Frisbee M(c)/W(c), volleyball W(s), wrestling M(c)/W(c). *Intramural sports:* badminton M/W, basketball M/W, football M/W, golf M/W, racquetball M/W, soccer M/W, softball M/W, ultimate Frisbee M/W, volleyball M/W.

Campus security: 24-hour emergency response devices and patrols, late-night transport/escort service, controlled dormitory access.

Student services: health clinic, personal/psychological counseling, legal services.

COSTS & FINANCIAL AID
Costs (2017–18) *Tuition:* state resident $3720 full-time, $280 per credit hour part-time; nonresident $16,872 full-time, $703 per credit hour part-time. Full-time tuition and fees vary according to course load and reciprocity agreements. Part-time tuition and fees vary according to course load and reciprocity agreements. *Required fees:* $1889 full-time, $63 per credit hour part-time. *Room and board:* $9416; room only: $4708. Room and board charges vary according to board plan and housing facility. *Payment plan:* installment. *Waivers:* minority students, senior citizens, and employees or children of employees.

Financial Aid Of all full-time matriculated undergraduates who enrolled in 2016, 2,110 applied for aid, 1,771 were judged to have need, 289 had their need fully met. 157 Federal Work-Study jobs (averaging $1754). 250 state and other part-time jobs (averaging $1932). In 2016, 477 non-need-based awards were made. *Average percent of need met:* 90. *Average financial aid package:* $16,444. *Average need-based loan:* $3981. *Average need-based gift aid:* $4959. *Average non-need-based aid:* $4588. *Average indebtedness upon graduation:* $20,988.

APPLYING
Standardized Tests *Required:* SAT or ACT (for admission).

Options: electronic application, deferred entrance.

Application fee: $40.

Required: high school transcript. *Required for some:* interview. *Recommended:* essay or personal statement, 2 letters of recommendation.

CONTACT

Fort Lewis College, 1000 Rim Drive, Durango, CO 81301-3999. *Phone:* 970-247-7184. *Toll-free phone:* 877-FLC-COLO.

Johnson & Wales University

Denver, Colorado

http://www.jwu.edu/denver/

CONTACT

Kim Medina, Director of Admissions, Johnson & Wales University, 7150 Montview Boulevard, Denver, CO 80220. *Phone:* 303-256-9300. *Toll-free phone:* 877-598-3368. *Fax:* 303-598-3368. *E-mail:* den@ admissions.jwu.edu.

Metropolitan State University of Denver

Denver, Colorado

http://www.msudenver.edu/

- **State-supported** comprehensive, founded 1963
- **Urban** 175-acre campus with easy access to Denver
- **Endowment** $7.1 million
- **Coed** 19,666 undergraduate students, 65% full-time, 53% women, 47% men
- **Minimally difficult** entrance level, 64% of applicants were admitted

UNDERGRAD STUDENTS

12,759 full-time, 6,907 part-time. 4% are from out of state; 6% Black or African American, non-Hispanic/Latino; 27% Hispanic/Latino; 4% Asian, non-Hispanic/Latino; 0.3% Native Hawaiian or other Pacific Islander, non-Hispanic/Latino; 0.5% American Indian or Alaska Native, non-Hispanic/Latino; 5% Two or more races, non-Hispanic/Latino; 3% Race/ethnicity unknown; 0.6% international; 11% transferred in.

Freshmen:
Admission: 11,435 applied, 7,348 admitted, 2,548 enrolled. *Average high school GPA:* 3.0. *Test scores:* SAT evidence-based reading and writing scores over 500: 60%; SAT math scores over 500: 60%; ACT scores over 18: 72%; SAT evidence-based reading and writing scores over 600: 20%; SAT math scores over 600: 13%; ACT scores over 24: 18%; ACT scores over 30: 2%.

Retention: 62% of full-time freshmen returned.

FACULTY

Total: 1,449, 39% full-time, 36% with terminal degrees.

Student/faculty ratio: 17:1.

ACADEMICS

Calendar: semesters. *Degrees:* certificates, bachelor's, master's, and postbachelor's certificates.

Special study options: accelerated degree program, adult/continuing education programs, advanced placement credit, cooperative education, distance learning, double majors, external degree program, honors programs, independent study, internships, off-campus study, part-time degree program, services for LD students, student-designed majors, study abroad, summer session for credit. *ROTC:* Army (b), Air Force (c).

Computers: 808 computers/terminals are available on campus for general student use. Students can access the following: computer help desk, free student e-mail accounts, online (class) grades, online (class) registration, online (class) schedules. Campuswide network is available. Wireless service is available via entire campus.

Library: Auraria Library.

STUDENT LIFE

Housing options: college housing not available.

Activities and organizations: drama/theater group, student-run newspaper, radio and television station, choral group, national fraternities, national sororities.

Athletics Member NCAA. All Division II. *Intercollegiate sports:* baseball M(s), basketball M(s)/W(s), cross-country running M/W, golf W(s), soccer M(s)/W(s), softball W(s), tennis M(s)/W(s), track and field M/W, volleyball W(s). *Intramural sports:* baseball M(c)/W(c), cheerleading M(c)/W(c), fencing M(c)/W(c), football M(c), ice hockey M(c), lacrosse M(c), rugby M(c), soccer M(c), squash M(c)/W, swimming and diving M(c)/W(c), ultimate Frisbee M(c)/W(c), volleyball M(c)/W(c).

Campus security: 24-hour emergency response devices and patrols, late-night transport/escort service.

Student services: health clinic, personal/psychological counseling, women's center, legal services.

COSTS & FINANCIAL AID

Costs (2017–18) *Tuition:* state resident $6062 full-time; nonresident $18,859 full-time. Full-time tuition and fees vary according to course load and location. Part-time tuition and fees vary according to course load and location. *Required fees:* $1290 full-time. *Payment plans:* installment, deferred payment. *Waivers:* senior citizens.

Financial Aid Of all full-time matriculated undergraduates who enrolled in 2016, 9,539 applied for aid, 8,141 were judged to have need, 459 had their need fully met. 157 Federal Work-Study jobs (averaging $3585). 698 state and other part-time jobs (averaging $3555). In 2016, 626 non-need-based awards were made. *Average percent of need met:* 56. *Average financial aid package:* $9130. *Average need-based loan:* $4089. *Average need-based gift aid:* $6697. *Average non-need-based aid:* $1779. *Average indebtedness upon graduation:* $25,805.

APPLYING

Standardized Tests *Required:* SAT or ACT (for admission). *Required for some:* SAT (for admission), ACT (for admission).

Options: electronic application, deferred entrance.

Application fee: $25.

Required: high school transcript. *Recommended:* minimum 2.0 GPA.

Application deadlines: 7/1 (freshmen), rolling (transfers).

Notification: continuous (freshmen), continuous (transfers).

CONTACT

Associate Director of Admissions, Metropolitan State University of Denver, 890 Auraria Parkway, Denver, CO 80204. *Phone:* 303-556-2615.

Naropa University

Boulder, Colorado

http://www.naropa.edu/

- **Independent** comprehensive, founded 1974
- **Urban** 12-acre campus with easy access to Denver
- **Endowment** $7.6 million
- **Coed** 397 undergraduate students, 92% full-time, 65% women, 35% men
- **Moderately difficult** entrance level, 100% of applicants were admitted

UNDERGRAD STUDENTS

367 full-time, 30 part-time. Students come from 41 states and territories; 12 other countries; 63% are from out of state; 1% Black or African American, non-Hispanic/Latino; 11% Hispanic/Latino; 1% Asian, non-Hispanic/Latino; 0.3% Native Hawaiian or other Pacific Islander, non-Hispanic/Latino; 0.3% American Indian or Alaska Native, non-Hispanic/Latino; 10% Two or more races, non-Hispanic/Latino; 12% Race/ethnicity unknown; 3% international; 22% transferred in; 18% live on campus.

Freshmen:
Admission: 105 applied, 105 admitted, 40 enrolled. *Average high school GPA:* 3.1.

Retention: 58% of full-time freshmen returned.

FACULTY

Total: 153, 33% full-time, 42% with terminal degrees.

Student/faculty ratio: 9:1.

ACADEMICS

Calendar: semesters. *Degrees:* bachelor's and master's.

Special study options: advanced placement credit, cooperative education, double majors, independent study, internships, off-campus study, part-time degree program, services for LD students, student-designed majors, study abroad, summer session for credit.

Computers: 48 computers/terminals are available on campus for general student use. Students can access the following: campus intranet, computer help desk, free student e-mail accounts, online (class) grades, online (class) registration, online (class) schedules. Campuswide network is available. 100% of college-owned or -operated housing units are wired for high-speed Internet access. Wireless service is available via entire campus.
Library: Allen Ginsberg Library plus 2 others. *Books:* 36,333 (physical), 177,800 (digital/electronic); *Serial titles:* 335 (physical), 33,467 (digital/electronic); *Databases:* 47. Weekly public service hours: 69.

STUDENT LIFE
Housing options: on-campus residence required for freshman year; men-only, women-only. Campus housing is university owned. Freshman campus housing is guaranteed.

Activities and organizations: drama/theater group, choral group, Student Union of Naropa, ROOT: Reconnecting on Outdoor Terrain, Team Tapas (yoga club), Community of Color and Allies, Naropa Zazen.

Campus security: late-night transport/escort service, controlled dormitory access, foot and vehicle patrol 4:30 pm to midnight, 24 hour on-call Safety and Security Manager.

Student services: personal/psychological counseling.

FINANCIAL AID
Financial Aid Of all full-time matriculated undergraduates who enrolled in 2015, 272 applied for aid, 251 were judged to have need, 1 had their need fully met. 168 Federal Work-Study jobs (averaging $3077). 11 state and other part-time jobs (averaging $2455). In 2015, 15 non-need-based awards were made. *Average percent of need met:* 90. *Average financial aid package:* $37,077. *Average need-based loan:* $11,519. *Average need-based gift aid:* $24,862. *Average non-need-based aid:* $6858. *Average indebtedness upon graduation:* $38,199.

APPLYING
Options: electronic application, deferred entrance.
Application fee: $50.
Required: high school transcript. *Required for some:* essay or personal statement, 1 letter of recommendation, interview.
Application deadlines: rolling (freshmen), rolling (transfers).
Notification: continuous (freshmen), continuous (transfers).

CONTACT
Ms. Karen Wills, Assistant Dean of Undergraduate Admissions, Naropa University, 2130 Arapahoe Avenue, Boulder, CO 80302. *Phone:* 303-245-4693. *Toll-free phone:* 800-772-6951. *Fax:* 303-546-3536. *E-mail:* kwills@naropa.edu.

National American University
Centennial, Colorado
http://www.national.edu/

CONTACT
National American University, 8242 South University Boulevard, Suite 100, Centennial, CO 80122. *Toll-free phone:* 877-628-5211.

National American University
Colorado Springs, Colorado
http://www.national.edu/

CONTACT
National American University, 1079 Space Center Drive, Suite 140, Colorado Springs, CO 80915. *Toll-free phone:* 855-369-9397.

National American University
Colorado Springs, Colorado
http://www.national.edu/

CONTACT
Director of Admissions, National American University, 1915 Jamboree Drive, Suite 185, Colorado Springs, CO 80920. *Phone:* 719-590-8300. *Toll-free phone:* 855-369-9397. *E-mail:* csadmissions@national.edu.

Pima Medical Institute
Denver, Colorado
http://www.pmi.edu/

CONTACT
Admissions Office, Pima Medical Institute, 7475 Dakin Street, Denver, CO 80221. *Phone:* 303-426-1800. *Toll-free phone:* 800-477-PIMA.

Platt College
Aurora, Colorado
http://www.plattcolorado.edu/

CONTACT
Admissions Office, Platt College, 3100 South Parker Road, Suite 200, Aurora, CO 80014-3141. *Phone:* 303-369-5151.

Pueblo Community College
Pueblo, Colorado
http://www.pueblocc.edu/

- **State-supported** primarily 2-year, founded 1933, part of Colorado Community College System
- **Urban** 35-acre campus
- **Endowment** $1.1 million
- **Coed** 5,993 undergraduate students, 34% full-time, 58% women, 42% men
- **Noncompetitive** entrance level, 100% of applicants were admitted

UNDERGRAD STUDENTS
2,041 full-time, 3,952 part-time. Students come from 23 states and territories; 0.8% are from out of state; 3% Black or African American, non-Hispanic/Latino; 32% Hispanic/Latino; 1% Asian, non-Hispanic/Latino; 0.3% Native Hawaiian or other Pacific Islander, non-Hispanic/Latino; 2% American Indian or Alaska Native, non-Hispanic/Latino; 3% Two or more races, non-Hispanic/Latino; 2% Race/ethnicity unknown; 0.8% international; 8% transferred in.

Freshmen:
Admission: 1,164 applied, 1,164 admitted, 701 enrolled.
Retention: 10% of full-time freshmen returned.

FACULTY
Total: 427, 26% full-time.
Student/faculty ratio: 16:1.

ACADEMICS
Calendar: semesters. *Degrees:* certificates, associate, and bachelor's.
Special study options: academic remediation for entering students, accelerated degree program, advanced placement credit, cooperative education, distance learning, double majors, English as a second language, honors programs, independent study, internships, part-time degree program, services for LD students, summer session for credit.
Computers: 1,180 computers/terminals are available on campus for general student use. Students can access the following: campus intranet, computer help desk, free student e-mail accounts, online (class) grades, online (class) registration, online (class) schedules. Campuswide network is available. Wireless service is available via classrooms, computer centers, computer labs, learning centers, libraries, student centers.
Library: PCC Library. *Books:* 19,162 (physical), 33,004 (digital/electronic); *Serial titles:* 695 (physical), 7,707 (digital/electronic); *Databases:* 12. Weekly public service hours: 60.

STUDENT LIFE
Housing options: college housing not available.

Activities and organizations: drama/theater group, choral group, Phi Theta Kappa, Welding Club, Culinary Arts Club, Performing Arts Club, Art Club.

Campus security: 24-hour emergency response devices and patrols, late-night transport/escort service.

Student services: health clinic, personal/psychological counseling.

COSTS
Costs (2018–19) *Tuition:* state resident $7365 full-time, $180 per credit hour part-time; nonresident $17,858 full-time, $595 per credit hour part-

time. Full-time tuition and fees vary according to course load, degree level, location, program, and reciprocity agreements. Part-time tuition and fees vary according to course load, degree level, location, program, and reciprocity agreements. *Required fees:* $733 full-time, $21 per credit hour part-time, $58 per term part-time. *Payment plans:* installment, deferred payment. *Waivers:* employees or children of employees.

APPLYING
Options: electronic application, early admission, deferred entrance.
Application deadlines: rolling (freshmen), rolling (transfers).
Notification: continuous until 9/1 (freshmen), continuous until 9/1 (transfers).

CONTACT
Mrs. Barbara Benedict, Director of Admissions and Records, Pueblo Community College, 900 West Orman Avenue, Pueblo, CO 81004. *Phone:* 719-549-3039. *Toll-free phone:* 888-642-6017. *Fax:* 719-549-3012. *E-mail:* barbara.benedict@pueblocc.edu.

Regis University
Denver, Colorado
http://www.regis.edu/
- **Independent Roman Catholic (Jesuit)** comprehensive, founded 1877
- **Urban** 90-acre campus with easy access to Denver, Colorado
- **Endowment** $55.8 million
- **Coed** 3,874 undergraduate students, 61% full-time, 61% women, 39% men
- **Moderately difficult** entrance level, 60% of applicants were admitted

UNDERGRAD STUDENTS
2,378 full-time, 1,496 part-time. 38% are from out of state; 4% Black or African American, non-Hispanic/Latino; 21% Hispanic/Latino; 5% Asian, non-Hispanic/Latino; 0.2% Native Hawaiian or other Pacific Islander, non-Hispanic/Latino; 0.5% American Indian or Alaska Native, non-Hispanic/Latino; 4% Two or more races, non-Hispanic/Latino; 7% Race/ethnicity unknown; 1% international; 7% transferred in.

Freshmen:
Admission: 7,388 applied, 4,427 admitted, 540 enrolled. *Average high school GPA:* 3.5. *Test scores:* SAT evidence-based reading and writing scores over 500: 94%; SAT math scores over 500: 83%; ACT scores over 18: 97%; SAT evidence-based reading and writing scores over 600: 47%; SAT math scores over 600: 35%; ACT scores over 24: 54%; SAT evidence-based reading and writing scores over 700: 6%; SAT math scores over 700: 7%; ACT scores over 30: 10%.
Retention: 80% of full-time freshmen returned.

FACULTY
Total: 779, 41% full-time, 33% with terminal degrees.
Student/faculty ratio: 13:1.

ACADEMICS
Calendar: semesters. *Degrees:* certificates, bachelor's, master's, doctoral, post-master's, and postbachelor's certificates.
Special study options: academic remediation for entering students, accelerated degree program, adult/continuing education programs, advanced placement credit, cooperative education, distance learning, double majors, freshman honors college, honors programs, independent study, internships, off-campus study, part-time degree program, services for LD students, student-designed majors, study abroad, summer session for credit. *ROTC:* Army (c), Navy (c), Air Force (c).
Unusual degree programs: 3-2 engineering with Washington University in St. Louis.
Computers: 600 computers/terminals and 24 ports are available on campus for general student use. Students can access the following: campus intranet, computer help desk, free student e-mail accounts, online (class) grades, online (class) registration, online (class) schedules. Campuswide network is available. Wireless service is available via entire campus.
Library: Dayton Memorial Library. *Books:* 393,000 (physical), 118,000 (digital/electronic); *Databases:* 248. Students can reserve study rooms.

STUDENT LIFE
Housing options: on-campus residence required for freshman year; coed, special housing for students with disabilities. Campus housing is university owned. Freshman applicants given priority for college housing.
Activities and organizations: drama/theater group, student-run newspaper, radio station, choral group.
Athletics Member NCAA. All Division II. *Intercollegiate sports:* baseball M(s), basketball M(s)/W(s), cross-country running M(s)/W(s), golf M(s)/W(s), lacrosse W(s), soccer M(s)/W(s), softball W(s), volleyball W(s). *Intramural sports:* badminton M/W, basketball M/W, lacrosse M, rugby M/W, soccer M/W, table tennis M/W, tennis M/W, ultimate Frisbee M/W, volleyball M/W.
Campus security: 24-hour emergency response devices and patrols, student patrols, late-night transport/escort service, controlled dormitory access.
Student services: health clinic, personal/psychological counseling.

COSTS & FINANCIAL AID
Costs (2018–19) *Comprehensive fee:* $48,370 includes full-time tuition ($36,460), mandatory fees ($350), and room and board ($11,560). Full-time tuition and fees vary according to class time, course level, course load, degree level, location, program, reciprocity agreements, and student level. Part-time tuition: $1139 per semester hour. Part-time tuition and fees vary according to class time, course level, course load, degree level, location, program, reciprocity agreements, and student level. *College room only:* $6600. Room and board charges vary according to board plan and housing facility. *Payment plans:* installment, deferred payment. *Waivers:* employees or children of employees.
Financial Aid Of all full-time matriculated undergraduates who enrolled in 2016, 1,789 applied for aid, 1,575 were judged to have need, 237 had their need fully met. 407 Federal Work-Study jobs (averaging $1873). 663 state and other part-time jobs (averaging $2573). In 2016, 532 non-need-based awards were made. *Average percent of need met:* 78. *Average financial aid package:* $28,259. *Average need-based loan:* $4405. *Average need-based gift aid:* $18,816. *Average non-need-based aid:* $14,934. *Average indebtedness upon graduation:* $28,153.

APPLYING
Standardized Tests *Required:* SAT or ACT (for admission).
Options: electronic application, deferred entrance.
Required: essay or personal statement, high school transcript. *Required for some:* 1 letter of recommendation, interview.
Notification: continuous (transfers).

CONTACT
Ms. Sarah Engel, Director of Admissions, Regis University, 3333 Regis Boulevard, Mail Code A-12, Denver, CO 80221. *Phone:* 303-458-4938. *Toll-free phone:* 800-388-2366 Ext. 4900. *Fax:* 303-964-5534. *E-mail:* sengel@regis.edu.

Rocky Mountain College of Art + Design
Lakewood, Colorado
http://www.rmcad.edu/

CONTACT
Mr. Marc Abraham, Director of Admissions, Rocky Mountain College of Art + Design, 1600 Pierce Street, Lakewood, CO 80214. *Phone:* 321-256-9223. *Toll-free phone:* 800-888-ARTS. *E-mail:* mabraham@rmcad.edu.

United States Air Force Academy
Colorado Springs, Colorado
http://www.usafa.edu/
- **Federally supported** 4-year, founded 1954
- **Suburban** 18,000-acre campus with easy access to Colorado Springs, Denver
- **Endowment** $106.7 million
- **Coed**
- **Most difficult** entrance level

FACULTY
Student/faculty ratio: 9:1.

ACADEMICS

Calendar: semesters. *Degree:* bachelor's.

Library: McDermott Library plus 1 other. *Books:* 463,745 (physical), 74,225 (digital/electronic); *Serial titles:* 229 (physical), 325 (digital/electronic); *Databases:* 36. Weekly public service hours: 83.

STUDENT LIFE

Housing options: on-campus residence required through senior year; coed. Campus housing is university owned. Freshman campus housing is guaranteed.

Activities and organizations: drama/theater group, student-run radio station, choral group, marching band, Recreational Ski Club, Men's and Women's Rugby Club, Cycling Club, Aviation Club, Drum and Bugle Corps.

Athletics Member NCAA. All Division I.

Campus security: 24-hour emergency response devices and patrols, late-night transport/escort service, controlled dormitory access, self-defense education, well-lit campus, Charge of Quarters.

Student services: health clinic, personal/psychological counseling, women's center, legal services.

COSTS

Costs (2017–18) *Comprehensive fee:* Tuition, room and board, and medical and dental care are provided by the US government. Each cadet receives a salary from which to pay for uniforms, supplies, and personal expenses.

APPLYING

Standardized Tests *Required:* SAT or ACT (for admission).

Options: electronic application.

Required: essay or personal statement, high school transcript, 1 letter of recommendation, interview, authorized nomination, Candidate Fitness Assessment, medical examination.

CONTACT

Dr. Phillip Prosseda, CHIEF, Selections Division, United States Air Force Academy, HQ USAFA/RRS, 2304 Cadet Drive, Suite 2400, USAF Academy, CO 80840-5025. *Phone:* 800-443-9266. *Toll-free phone:* 800-443-9266. *Fax:* 719-333-3012.

University of Colorado Boulder

Boulder, Colorado

http://www.colorado.edu/

- **State-supported** university, founded 1876, part of University of Colorado System
- **Suburban** 600-acre campus with easy access to Denver
- **Endowment** $596.0 million
- **Coed** 29,091 undergraduate students, 93% full-time, 44% women, 56% men
- **Moderately difficult** entrance level, 80% of applicants were admitted

UNDERGRAD STUDENTS

26,917 full-time, 2,174 part-time. Students come from 52 states and territories; 82 other countries; 42% are from out of state; 2% Black or African American, non-Hispanic/Latino; 12% Hispanic/Latino; 6% Asian, non-Hispanic/Latino; 0.1% Native Hawaiian or other Pacific Islander, non-Hispanic/Latino; 0.2% American Indian or Alaska Native, non-Hispanic/Latino; 5% Two or more races, non-Hispanic/Latino; 0.6% Race/ethnicity unknown; 7% international; 5% transferred in; 28% live on campus.

Freshmen:

Admission: 36,149 applied, 28,861 admitted, 6,570 enrolled. *Average high school GPA:* 3.7. *Test scores:* SAT evidence-based reading and writing scores over 500: 97%; SAT math scores over 500: 96%; ACT scores over 18: 99%; SAT evidence-based reading and writing scores over 600: 66%; SAT math scores over 600: 63%; ACT scores over 24: 83%; SAT evidence-based reading and writing scores over 700: 14%; SAT math scores over 700: 19%; ACT scores over 30: 30%.

Retention: 88% of full-time freshmen returned.

ACADEMICS

Calendar: semesters. *Degrees:* bachelor's, master's, doctoral, and post-master's certificates.

Special study options: accelerated degree program, adult/continuing education programs, advanced placement credit, cooperative education, distance learning, double majors, English as a second language, freshman honors college, honors programs, independent study, internships, off-

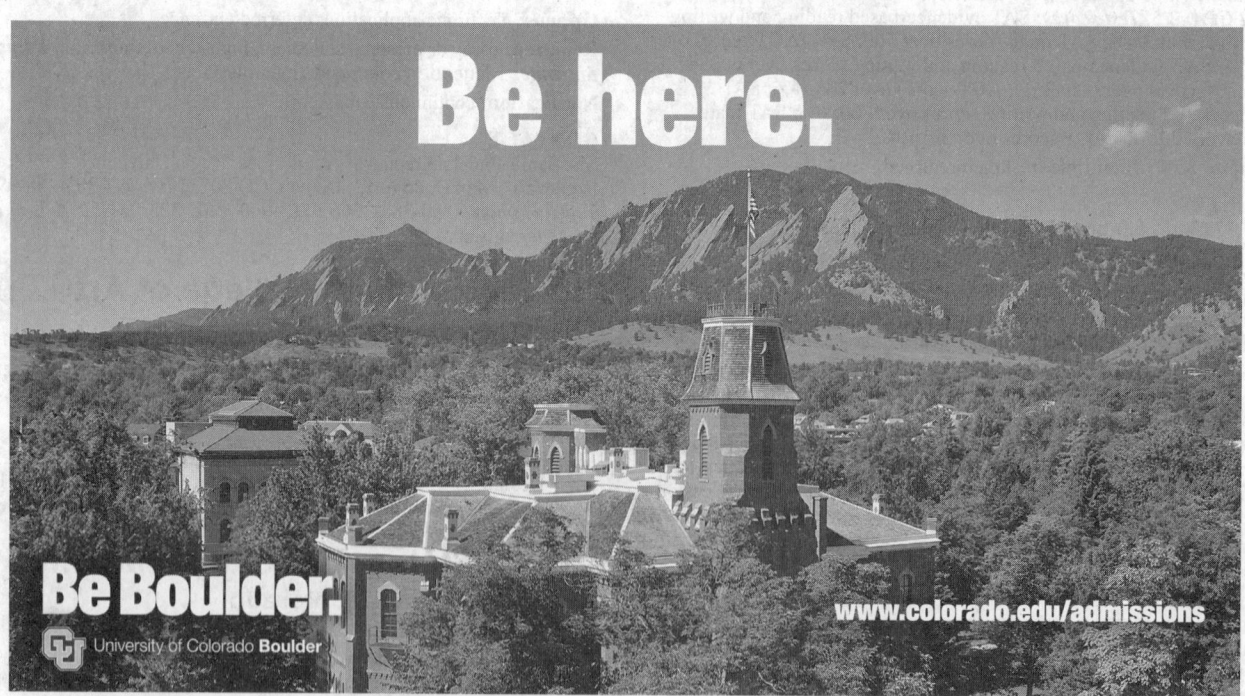

Be here.

Be Boulder.

University of Colorado **Boulder**

www.colorado.edu/admissions

18:1
student to
faculty ratio

3,900+

#1
college town in America
(American Institue for Economic Research, 2017)

300+

campus study, part-time degree program, services for LD students, student-designed majors, study abroad, summer session for credit. *ROTC:* Army (b), Navy (b), Air Force (b).

Computers: 1,689 computers/terminals and 60,000 ports are available on campus for general student use. Students can access the following: campus intranet, computer help desk, free student e-mail accounts, online (class) grades, online (class) registration, online (class) schedules, training, tutorials, workshops, seminars, standard and academic software, student government voting. Campuswide network is available. 100% of college-owned or -operated housing units are wired for high-speed Internet access. Wireless service is available via entire campus.

Library: Norlin Library plus 5 others. *Books:* 664,601 (physical), 984,952 (digital/electronic); *Databases:* 594. Students can reserve study rooms.

STUDENT LIFE

Housing options: on-campus residence required for freshman year; coed, special housing for students with disabilities. Campus housing is university owned and is provided by a third party. Freshman campus housing is guaranteed.

Activities and organizations: drama/theater group, student-run newspaper, radio and television station, choral group, marching band, Student Government, CU Gaming, Boulder Freeride, Neuroscience Club, Association of Holistic Wellness, national fraternities, national sororities.

Athletics Member NCAA. All Division I except football (Division I-A). *Intercollegiate sports:* baseball M(c)/W(c), basketball M(s)/W(s), cheerleading M/W, crew M(c)/W(c), cross-country running M(s)/W(s), equestrian sports M(c)/W(c), fencing M(c)/W(c), field hockey M(c)/W(c), golf M(s)/W(s), ice hockey M(c)/W(c), lacrosse M(c)/W(c), racquetball M(c)/W(c), rugby M(c)/W(c), skiing (cross-country) M(s)/W(s), skiing (downhill) M(s)/W(s), soccer M(c)/W(c), softball W(c), swimming and diving M(c)/W(c), tennis M(c)/W(s), track and field M(s)/W(s), triathlon M(c)/W(c), ultimate Frisbee M(c)/W(c), volleyball M(c)/W(s), water polo M(c)/W(c), wrestling M(c)/W(c). *Intramural sports:* badminton M/W, basketball M/W, ice hockey M/W, soccer M/W, tennis M/W, ultimate Frisbee M/W, volleyball M/W, water polo M/W.

Campus security: 24-hour patrols, student patrols, late-night transport/escort service, controlled dormitory access, University police department, LifeLine Response app connecting to police dispatch center.

Student services: health clinic, personal/psychological counseling, women's center, legal services.

COSTS & FINANCIAL AID

Costs (2017–18) *One-time required fee:* $182. *Tuition:* state resident $10,248 full-time; nonresident $34,382 full-time. Full-time tuition and fees vary according to program. Part-time tuition and fees vary according to course load and program. No tuition increase for student's term of enrollment. *Required fees:* $1838 full-time. *Room and board:* $13,998. Room and board charges vary according to board plan, housing facility, and location. *Payment plan:* installment. *Waivers:* senior citizens and employees or children of employees.

Financial Aid Of all full-time matriculated undergraduates who enrolled in 2017, 13,509 applied for aid, 9,668 were judged to have need, 3,716 had their need fully met. 882 Federal Work-Study jobs (averaging $1729). 869 state and other part-time jobs (averaging $2653). In 2017, 7250 non-need-based awards were made. *Average percent of need met:* 80. *Average financial aid package:* $16,699. *Average need-based loan:* $6578. *Average need-based gift aid:* $11,091. *Average non-need-based aid:* $9134. *Average indebtedness upon graduation:* $27,680.

APPLYING

Standardized Tests *Required:* SAT or ACT (for admission).

Options: electronic application, early action, deferred entrance.

Application fee: $50.

Required: essay or personal statement, high school transcript, 1 letter of recommendation. *Required for some:* audition for music program. *Recommended:* minimum 3.0 GPA.

Application deadlines: 1/15 (freshmen), 3/1 (transfers), 11/15 (early action).

Notification: 4/1 (freshmen), continuous until 3/1 (transfers), 2/1 (early action).

CONTACT
Admissions Office, University of Colorado Boulder, Regent Administrative Center 125, 552 UCB, Boulder, CO 80309. *Phone:* 303-492-6301. *Fax:* 303-735-2501. *E-mail:* apply@colorado.edu.

See previous page for display ad and page 1460 for the College Close-Up.

University of Colorado Colorado Springs
Colorado Springs, Colorado
http://www.uccs.edu/

- **State-supported** university, founded 1965, part of University of Colorado System
- **Urban** 532-acre campus with easy access to Colorado Springs
- **Coed** 10,808 undergraduate students, 76% full-time, 52% women, 48% men
- **Moderately difficult** entrance level, 93% of applicants were admitted

UNDERGRAD STUDENTS
8,171 full-time, 2,637 part-time. Students come from 44 states and territories; 71 other countries; 12% are from out of state; 4% Black or African American, non-Hispanic/Latino; 18% Hispanic/Latino; 3% Asian, non-Hispanic/Latino; 0.3% Native Hawaiian or other Pacific Islander, non-Hispanic/Latino; 0.2% American Indian or Alaska Native, non-Hispanic/Latino; 8% Two or more races, non-Hispanic/Latino; 1% Race/ethnicity unknown; 0.9% international; 12% transferred in; 16% live on campus.

Freshmen:
Admission: 9,909 applied, 9,197 admitted, 2,045 enrolled. *Average high school GPA:* 3.4. *Test scores:* SAT evidence-based reading and writing scores over 500: 85%; SAT math scores over 500: 81%; ACT scores over 18: 94%; SAT evidence-based reading and writing scores over 600: 40%; SAT math scores over 600: 36%; ACT scores over 24: 47%; SAT evidence-based reading and writing scores over 700: 6%; SAT math scores over 700: 5%; ACT scores over 30: 7%.

Retention: 66% of full-time freshmen returned.

FACULTY
Total: 774, 57% full-time, 44% with terminal degrees.

Student/faculty ratio: 19:1.

ACADEMICS
Calendar: semesters. *Degrees:* bachelor's, master's, doctoral, post-master's, and postbachelor's certificates.

Special study options: accelerated degree program, advanced placement credit, cooperative education, distance learning, double majors, English as a second language, honors programs, independent study, internships, off-campus study, part-time degree program, services for LD students, student-designed majors, study abroad, summer session for credit. *ROTC:* Army (b).

Unusual degree programs: 3-2 engineering; chemistry, biochemistry, communication, criminal justice, electrical engineering, math, mechanical engineering, sociology.

Computers: Students can access the following: campus intranet, computer help desk, free student e-mail accounts, online (class) grades, online (class) registration, online (class) schedules, student portal, learning management system. Campuswide network is available. 100% of college-owned or -operated housing units are wired for high-speed Internet access. Wireless service is available via entire campus.

Library: Kraemer Family Library. *Books:* 337,790 (physical), 168,770 (digital/electronic); *Serial titles:* 3,020 (physical); *Databases:* 154. Students can reserve study rooms.

STUDENT LIFE
Housing options: on-campus residence required for freshman year; coed. Campus housing is university owned. Freshman applicants given priority for college housing.

Activities and organizations: drama/theater group, student-run newspaper, radio and television station, choral group, Fans Initiating Growth Honor and Tradition (spirit club), Pi Beta Phi, Sustainability Club, Gamers (computing), El Circulo, national fraternities, national sororities.

Athletics Member NCAA. All Division II. *Intercollegiate sports:* baseball M(s), basketball M(s)/W(s), cross-country running M(s)/W(s), golf M(s)/W(s), lacrosse W(s), soccer M(s)/W(s), softball W(s), track and field M(s)/W(s), volleyball W(s).

Campus security: 24-hour emergency response devices and patrols, late-night transport/escort service, controlled dormitory access, emergency text messaging, state-authorized campus police and public safety department.

Student services: health clinic, personal/psychological counseling.

COSTS & FINANCIAL AID

Costs (2017–18) *One-time required fee:* $140. *Tuition:* state resident $8610 full-time, $287 per credit hour part-time; nonresident $22,590 full-time, $753 per credit hour part-time. Full-time tuition and fees vary according to course load, degree level, location, program, reciprocity agreements, and student level. Part-time tuition and fees vary according to course load, degree level, location, program, reciprocity agreements, and student level. *Required fees:* $1591 full-time. *Room and board:* $10,100. Room and board charges vary according to board plan, housing facility, and student level. *Payment plan:* installment. *Waivers:* employees or children of employees.

Financial Aid Of all full-time matriculated undergraduates who enrolled in 2016, 4,783 applied for aid, 3,709 were judged to have need, 154 had their need fully met. 189 Federal Work-Study jobs (averaging $2848). 246 state and other part-time jobs (averaging $3703). In 2016, 510 non-need-based awards were made. *Average percent of need met:* 43. *Average financial aid package:* $8629. *Average need-based loan:* $4363. *Average need-based gift aid:* $7237. *Average non-need-based aid:* $2823. *Average indebtedness upon graduation:* $25,042.

APPLYING

Standardized Tests *Required:* SAT or ACT (for admission).

Options: electronic application, deferred entrance.

Application fee: $50.

Required: high school transcript.

Application deadlines: rolling (freshmen), rolling (transfers).

Notification: continuous (freshmen), continuous (transfers).

CONTACT

Mr. Chris Beiswanger, Director of Admissions Services, University of Colorado Colorado Springs, 1420 Austin Bluffs Parkway, Colorado Springs, CO 80918. *Phone:* 719-255-3088. *Toll-free phone:* 800-990-8227 Ext. 3383. *E-mail:* cbeiswan@uccs.edu.

University of Colorado Denver

Denver, Colorado

http://www.ucdenver.edu/

- **State-supported** university, founded 1912, part of University of Colorado System
- **Urban** 171-acre campus with easy access to Denver, CO
- **Endowment** $493.1 million
- **Coed** 15,586 undergraduate students, 56% full-time, 55% women, 45% men
- **Moderately difficult** entrance level, 65% of applicants were admitted

UNDERGRAD STUDENTS

8,671 full-time, 6,915 part-time. Students come from 49 states and territories; 68 other countries; 9% are from out of state; 5% Black or African American, non-Hispanic/Latino; 21% Hispanic/Latino; 10% Asian, non-Hispanic/Latino; 0.1% Native Hawaiian or other Pacific Islander, non-Hispanic/Latino; 0.4% American Indian or Alaska Native, non-Hispanic/Latino; 6% Two or more races, non-Hispanic/Latino; 2% Race/ethnicity unknown; 8% international; 10% transferred in.

Freshmen:

Admission: 11,373 applied, 7,418 admitted, 1,513 enrolled. *Average high school GPA:* 3.4. *Test scores:* SAT evidence-based reading and writing scores over 500: 91%; SAT math scores over 500: 87%; ACT scores over 18: 95%; SAT evidence-based reading and writing scores over 600: 46%; SAT math scores over 600: 39%; ACT scores over 24: 50%; SAT evidence-based reading and writing scores over 700: 5%; SAT math scores over 700: 9%; ACT scores over 30: 9%.

Retention: 67% of full-time freshmen returned.

FACULTY

Total: 4,825, 83% full-time, 60% with terminal degrees.

Student/faculty ratio: 15:1.

ACADEMICS

Calendar: semesters. *Degrees:* bachelor's, master's, doctoral, post-master's, and postbachelor's certificates.

Special study options: accelerated degree program, advanced placement credit, cooperative education, distance learning, double majors, English as a second language, honors programs, independent study, internships, off-campus study, part-time degree program, services for LD students, student-designed majors, study abroad, summer session for credit. *ROTC:* Army (c), Air Force (c).

Unusual degree programs: 3-2 criminal justice.

Computers: 750 computers/terminals are available on campus for general student use. Students can access the following: campus intranet, computer help desk, free student e-mail accounts, online (class) grades, online (class) registration, online (class) schedules. Campuswide network is available. 100% of college-owned or -operated housing units are wired for high-speed Internet access. Wireless service is available via entire campus.

Library: Auraria Library plus 1 other. *Books:* 573,818 (physical), 325,936 (digital/electronic); *Serial titles:* 5,780 (physical), 92,591 (digital/electronic); *Databases:* 308. Weekly public service hours: 85; students can reserve study rooms.

STUDENT LIFE

Housing options: college housing not availableCampus housing is provided by a third party.

Activities and organizations: drama/theater group, student-run newspaper, choral group, Veterans Student Organization (Service), Golden Key Honor Society (Academic), Minority Association for Pre-Health Students (Health), Future Doctors of Denver, Intercultural Club Beijing (Cultural and Social).

Athletics *Intramural sports:* basketball M(c)/W(c), cheerleading M(c)/W(c), cross-country running M(c)/W(c), golf M(c)/W(c), ice hockey M(c), lacrosse M(c)/W(c), soccer M(c)/W(c), tennis M(c)/W(c), ultimate Frisbee M(c)/W(c), volleyball W(c).

Campus security: 24-hour emergency response devices and patrols, student patrols, late-night transport/escort service.

Student services: health clinic, personal/psychological counseling, women's center.

COSTS & FINANCIAL AID

Costs (2017–18) *Tuition:* state resident $9720 full-time, $324 per credit hour part-time; nonresident $29,910 full-time, $997 per credit hour part-time. Full-time tuition and fees vary according to course level, course load, degree level, location, program, reciprocity agreements, and student level. Part-time tuition and fees vary according to course level, course load, degree level, location, program, reciprocity agreements, and student level. *Required fees:* $1538 full-time, $918 per year part-time. *Room and board:* $12,190; room only: $8290. Room and board charges vary according to board plan. *Payment plans:* installment, deferred payment. *Waivers:* employees or children of employees.

Financial Aid Of all full-time matriculated undergraduates who enrolled in 2016, 6,088 applied for aid, 5,195 were judged to have need, 54 had their need fully met. 332 Federal Work-Study jobs (averaging $3396). 321 state and other part-time jobs (averaging $3666). In 2016, 530 non-need-based awards were made. *Average percent of need met:* 49. *Average financial aid package:* $9482. *Average need-based loan:* $3815. *Average need-based gift aid:* $7466. *Average non-need-based aid:* $2614. *Average indebtedness upon graduation:* $20,941.

APPLYING

Standardized Tests *Required:* SAT or ACT (for admission).

Options: electronic application, deferred entrance.

Application fee: $50.

Required: minimum 2.5 GPA. *Required for some:* minimum 3.0 GPA, audition, portfolio, entrance exam.

Application deadlines: 8/1 (freshmen), rolling (out-of-state freshmen), 8/1 (transfers).

Notification: continuous (freshmen), continuous (out-of-state freshmen), continuous (transfers).

CONTACT

Catherine Wilson, Office of Admissions, University of Colorado Denver, PO Box 173364, Campus Box 167, Denver, CO 80217. *Phone:* 303-315-2601. *E-mail:* admissions@ucdenver.edu.

University of Denver

Denver, Colorado

http://www.du.edu/

- **Independent** university, founded 1864
- **Urban** 125-acre campus with easy access to Denver
- **Endowment** $711.3 million
- **Coed** 5,765 undergraduate students, 95% full-time, 53% women, 47% men
- **Moderately difficult** entrance level, 58% of applicants were admitted

UNDERGRAD STUDENTS

5,494 full-time, 271 part-time. Students come from 57 states and territories; 52 other countries; 62% are from out of state; 2% Black or African American, non-Hispanic/Latino; 11% Hispanic/Latino; 4% Asian, non-Hispanic/Latino; 0.1% Native Hawaiian or other Pacific Islander, non-Hispanic/Latino; 0.2% American Indian or Alaska Native, non-Hispanic/Latino; 4% Two or more races, non-Hispanic/Latino; 2% Race/ethnicity unknown; 7% international; 3% transferred in; 50% live on campus.

Freshmen:

Admission: 19,904 applied, 11,554 admitted, 1,504 enrolled. *Average high school GPA:* 3.7. *Test scores:* SAT evidence-based reading and writing scores over 500: 97%; SAT math scores over 500: 96%; ACT scores over 18: 99%; SAT evidence-based reading and writing scores over 600: 71%; SAT math scores over 600: 64%; ACT scores over 24: 85%; SAT evidence-based reading and writing scores over 700: 15%; SAT math scores over 700: 13%; ACT scores over 30: 32%.

Retention: 87% of full-time freshmen returned.

FACULTY

Total: 1,290, 57% full-time, 67% with terminal degrees.

Student/faculty ratio: 11:1.

ACADEMICS

Calendar: quarters semesters for law school. *Degrees:* certificates, bachelor's, master's, doctoral, post-master's, and postbachelor's certificates.

Special study options: accelerated degree program, adult/continuing education programs, advanced placement credit, cooperative education, distance learning, double majors, English as a second language, freshman honors college, honors programs, independent study, internships, off-campus study, part-time degree program, services for LD students, student-designed majors, study abroad, summer session for credit. *ROTC:* Army (c), Air Force (c).

Unusual degree programs: 3-2 business administration; engineering; social work; art history, public policy, accounting, international studies, education, environmental science, geography.

Computers: 150 computers/terminals and 36,000 ports are available on campus for general student use. Students can access the following: campus intranet, computer help desk, free student e-mail accounts, online (class) grades, online (class) registration, online (class) schedules. Campuswide network is available. 95% of college-owned or -operated housing units are wired for high-speed Internet access. Wireless service is available via entire campus.

Library: Anderson Academic Commons plus 1 other. *Books:* 1.7 million (physical), 2.3 million (digital/electronic); *Serial titles:* 594,063 (physical), 218,954 (digital/electronic); *Databases:* 1,306. Weekly public service hours: 145; study areas open 24 hours, 5–7 days a week; students can reserve study rooms.

STUDENT LIFE

Housing options: on-campus residence required through sophomore year; coed, cooperative. Campus housing is university owned. Freshman campus housing is guaranteed.

Activities and organizations: drama/theater group, student-run newspaper, radio station, choral group, Club Sports Council, Alpine Club, DU Programs Board, Greek Life Council, Residence Hall Association, national fraternities, national sororities.

Athletics Member NCAA. All Division I. *Intercollegiate sports:* baseball M(c), basketball M(s)/W(s), cross-country running M(c)/W(c), equestrian sports M(c)/W(c), golf M(s)/W(s), gymnastics W(s), ice hockey

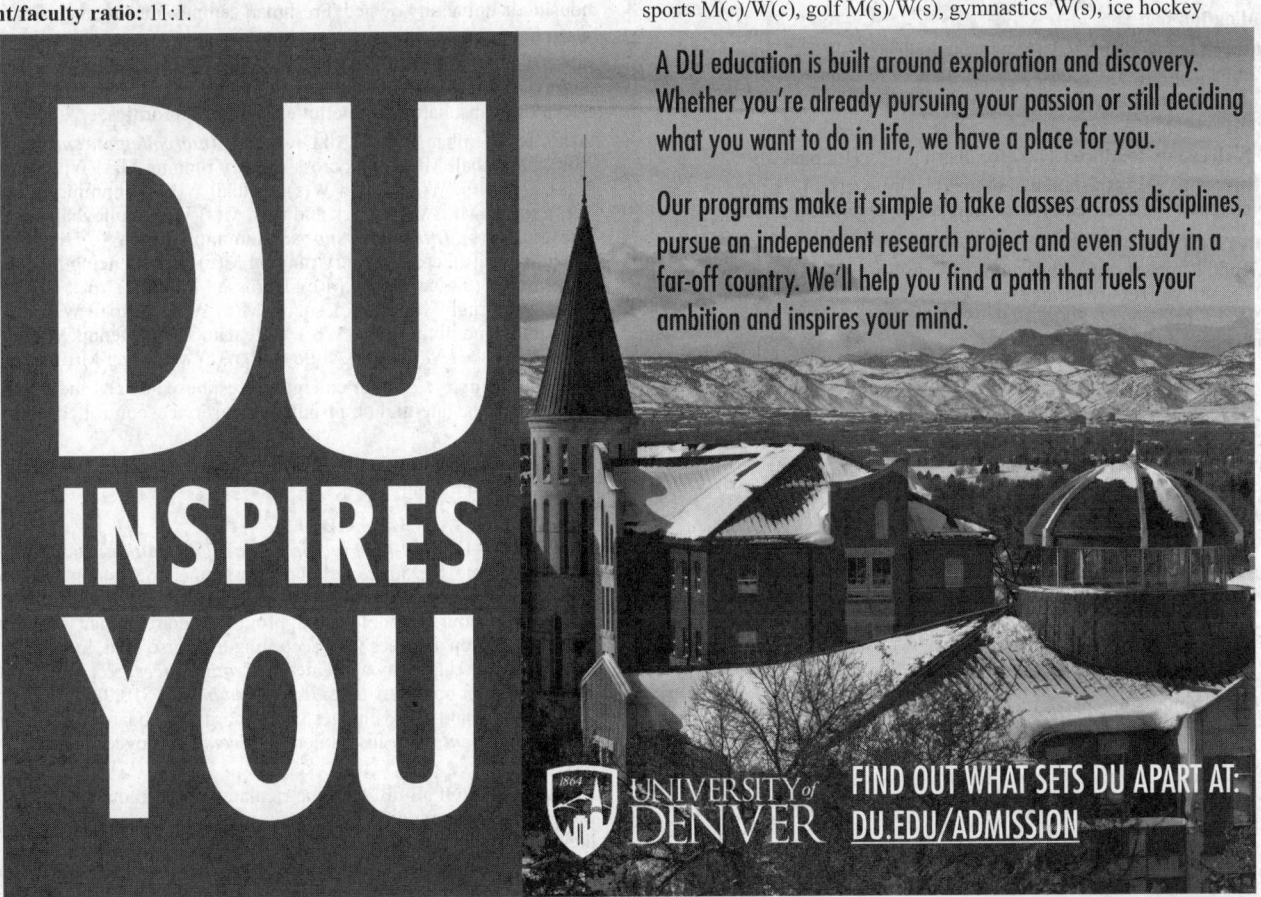

A DU education is built around exploration and discovery. Whether you're already pursuing your passion or still deciding what you want to do in life, we have a place for you.

Our programs make it simple to take classes across disciplines, pursue an independent research project and even study in a far-off country. We'll help you find a path that fuels your ambition and inspires your mind.

UNIVERSITY of DENVER

FIND OUT WHAT SETS DU APART AT: DU.EDU/ADMISSION

M(s)/W(c), lacrosse M(s)/W(s), racquetball M(c)/W(c), skiing (cross-country) M(s)/W(s), skiing (downhill) M(s)/W(s), soccer M(s)/W(s), softball W(c), swimming and diving M(s)/W(s), tennis M(s)/W(s), volleyball W(s), water polo M(c)/W(c). *Intramural sports:* basketball M/W, field hockey M(c)/W(c), football M/W, golf M(c)/W(c), gymnastics W(c), ice hockey M(c)/W(c), lacrosse M(c)/W(c), racquetball M(c)/W(c), rock climbing M(c)/W(c), rowing M(c), rugby M(c)/W(c), skiing (downhill) M(c)/W(c), soccer M(c)/W(c), softball M/W, swimming and diving M(c)/W(c), table tennis M/W, tennis M(c)/W(c), ultimate Frisbee M(c)/W(c), volleyball M(c)/W(c).

Campus security: 24-hour emergency response devices and patrols, late-night transport/escort service, controlled dormitory access, 24-hour locked residence hall entrances.

Student services: health clinic, personal/psychological counseling, women's center.

COSTS & FINANCIAL AID

Costs (2018–19) *Comprehensive fee:* $63,561 includes full-time tuition ($49,392), mandatory fees ($1164), and room and board ($13,005). Full-time tuition and fees vary according to course load and program. Part-time tuition: $1372 per credit hour. Part-time tuition and fees vary according to course load and program. *College room only:* $8100. Room and board charges vary according to board plan and housing facility. *Payment plans:* installment, deferred payment. *Waivers:* senior citizens and employees or children of employees.

Financial Aid Of all full-time matriculated undergraduates who enrolled in 2017, 3,010 applied for aid, 2,333 were judged to have need, 782 had their need fully met. 471 Federal Work-Study jobs (averaging $2825). 195 state and other part-time jobs (averaging $3128). In 2017, 2197 non-need-based awards were made. *Average percent of need met:* 86. *Average financial aid package:* $40,587. *Average need-based loan:* $4291. *Average need-based gift aid:* $34,077. *Average non-need-based aid:* $18,280. *Average indebtedness upon graduation:* $31,526.

APPLYING

Standardized Tests *Required:* SAT or ACT (for admission).

Options: electronic application, early admission, early decision, early action, deferred entrance.

Application fee: $65.

Required: essay or personal statement, high school transcript, 1 letter of recommendation. *Recommended:* 2 letters of recommendation.

Application deadlines: 1/15 (freshmen), rolling (transfers), 11/1 (early action).

Early decision deadline: 11/1 (for plan 1), 1/15 (for plan 2).

Notification: 3/15 (freshmen), continuous (transfers), 12/15 (early decision plan 1), 2/20 (early decision plan 2), 1/15 (early action).

CONTACT

Mr. Todd Rinehart, Vice Chancellor for Enrollment, University of Denver, 2197 South University Boulevard, Denver, CO 80208. *Phone:* 303-871-3125. *Toll-free phone:* 800-525-9495. *Fax:* 303-871-3301. *E-mail:* admission@du.edu.

See previous page for display ad and page 1462 for the College Close-Up.

University of Northern Colorado

Greeley, Colorado

http://www.unco.edu/

- **State-supported** university, founded 1890
- **Suburban** 250-acre campus with easy access to Denver
- **Endowment** $82.8 million
- **Coed** 9,977 undergraduate students, 83% full-time, 65% women, 35% men
- **Moderately difficult** entrance level, 89% of applicants were admitted

UNDERGRAD STUDENTS

8,319 full-time, 1,658 part-time. Students come from 50 states and territories; 35 other countries; 16% are from out of state; 4% Black or African American, non-Hispanic/Latino; 19% Hispanic/Latino; 2% Asian, non-Hispanic/Latino; 0.1% Native Hawaiian or other Pacific Islander, non-Hispanic/Latino; 0.4% American Indian or Alaska Native, non-Hispanic/Latino; 4% Two or more races, non-Hispanic/Latino; 10% Race/ethnicity unknown; 2% international; 8% transferred in; 36% live on campus.

Freshmen:

Admission: 7,481 applied, 6,665 admitted, 2,047 enrolled. *Average high school GPA:* 3.4. *Test scores:* SAT evidence-based reading and writing scores over 500: 80%; SAT math scores over 500: 74%; ACT scores over 18: 89%; SAT evidence-based reading and writing scores over 600: 38%; SAT math scores over 600: 31%; ACT scores over 24: 39%; SAT evidence-based reading and writing scores over 700: 6%; SAT math scores over 700: 5%; ACT scores over 30: 6%.

Retention: 71% of full-time freshmen returned.

FACULTY

Total: 852, 59% full-time, 50% with terminal degrees.

Student/faculty ratio: 18:1.

ACADEMICS

Calendar: semesters. *Degrees:* bachelor's, master's, and doctoral.

Special study options: accelerated degree program, adult/continuing education programs, advanced placement credit, cooperative education, distance learning, double majors, English as a second language, external degree program, honors programs, independent study, internships, off-campus study, part-time degree program, services for LD students, student-designed majors, study abroad, summer session for credit. *ROTC:* Army (b), Air Force (b).

Computers: 1,723 computers/terminals and 825 ports are available on campus for general student use. Students can access the following: computer help desk, free student e-mail accounts, online (class) grades, online (class) registration, online (class) schedules. Campuswide network is available. 100% of college-owned or -operated housing units are wired for high-speed Internet access. Wireless service is available via entire campus.

Library: James A. Michener Library plus 2 others. *Books:* 1.3 million (physical), 433,961 (digital/electronic); *Serial titles:* 19,580 (physical), 85,901 (digital/electronic); *Databases:* 192. Weekly public service hours: 97; students can reserve study rooms.

STUDENT LIFE

Housing options: on-campus residence required for freshman year; coed, women-only, special housing for students with disabilities. Campus housing is university owned. Freshman campus housing is guaranteed.

Activities and organizations: drama/theater group, student-run newspaper, choral group, marching band, Fraternities and Sororities, Club Sports, Campus Religious/Spiritual Organizations, Academic Clubs, Services Clubs, national fraternities, national sororities.

Athletics Member NCAA. All Division I. *Intercollegiate sports:* baseball M(s), basketball M(s)/W(s), cross-country running M(s)/W(s), football M(s), golf M(s)/W(s), soccer W(s), softball W(s), swimming and diving W(s), tennis M(s)/W(s), track and field M(s)/W(s), volleyball W(s), wrestling M(s). *Intramural sports:* badminton M(c)/W(c), baseball M(c), basketball M(c), cross-country running M(c)/W(c), fencing M(c)/W(c), golf M(c)/W(c), ice hockey M(c), lacrosse M(c)/W(c), rock climbing M(c)/W(c), rugby M(c)/W(c), soccer M(c)/W(c), softball M/W, swimming and diving M(c)/W(c), table tennis M/W, tennis M(c)/W(c), ultimate Frisbee M(c)/W(c), volleyball W(c), wrestling M(c)/W(c).

Campus security: 24-hour emergency response devices and patrols, student patrols, late-night transport/escort service, controlled dormitory access.

Student services: health clinic, personal/psychological counseling, women's center, legal services.

COSTS & FINANCIAL AID

Costs (2018–19) *One-time required fee:* $250. *Tuition:* state resident $7374 full-time, $295 per credit hour part-time; nonresident $18,960 full-time, $755 per credit hour part-time. Full-time tuition and fees vary according to course load, location, program, and reciprocity agreements. Part-time tuition and fees vary according to course load, location, program, and reciprocity agreements. *Required fees:* $2171 full-time, $127 per credit hour part-time. *Room and board:* $10,982; room only: $5202. Room and board charges vary according to board plan and housing facility. *Payment plan:* installment. *Waivers:* employees or children of employees.

Financial Aid Of all full-time matriculated undergraduates who enrolled in 2016, 6,847 applied for aid, 5,265 were judged to have need, 1,164 had their need fully met. 191 Federal Work-Study jobs (averaging $2436). 566 state and other part-time jobs (averaging $2331). In 2016, 1297 non-need-based awards were made. *Average percent of need met:* 72. *Average financial aid package:* $13,815. *Average need-based loan:* $4561. *Average need-based gift aid:* $7228. *Average non-need-based aid:* $3141. *Average indebtedness upon graduation:* $24,844.

APPLYING
Standardized Tests *Required:* SAT or ACT (for admission).
Options: electronic application, deferred entrance.
Application fee: $45.
Required: high school transcript. *Required for some:* essay or personal statement.
Application deadlines: 8/1 (freshmen), 8/1 (transfers).
Notification: continuous (freshmen), continuous (transfers).

CONTACT
Sean Broghammer, Director of Admissions, University of Northern Colorado, Campus Box 10, Carter Hall 3006, Greeley, CO 80639. *Phone:* 970-351-2881. *Toll-free phone:* 888-700-4UNC. *Fax:* 970-351-2984. *E-mail:* admissions@unco.edu.

Western State Colorado University
Gunnison, Colorado
http://www.western.edu/
- **State-supported** comprehensive, founded 1901
- **Rural** 381-acre campus
- **Coed** 2,429 undergraduate students, 75% full-time, 43% women, 57% men
- **Moderately difficult** entrance level, 86% of applicants were admitted

UNDERGRAD STUDENTS
1,832 full-time, 597 part-time. 70% are from out of state; 3% Black or African American, non-Hispanic/Latino; 11% Hispanic/Latino; 0.7% Asian, non-Hispanic/Latino; 0.3% Native Hawaiian or other Pacific Islander, non-Hispanic/Latino; 0.7% American Indian or Alaska Native, non-Hispanic/Latino; 5% Two or more races, non-Hispanic/Latino; 8% Race/ethnicity unknown; 0.5% international; 6% transferred in; 37% live on campus.

Freshmen:
Admission: 1,955 applied, 1,681 admitted, 447 enrolled. *Average high school GPA:* 3.1. *Test scores:* SAT evidence-based reading and writing scores over 500: 75%; SAT math scores over 500: 78%; ACT scores over 18: 92%; SAT evidence-based reading and writing scores over 600: 26%; SAT math scores over 600: 29%; ACT scores over 24: 38%; SAT evidence-based reading and writing scores over 700: 4%; SAT math scores over 700: 1%; ACT scores over 30: 5%.
Retention: 64% of full-time freshmen returned.

FACULTY
Total: 169, 72% full-time, 75% with terminal degrees.
Student/faculty ratio: 18:1.

ACADEMICS
Calendar: semesters. *Degrees:* bachelor's, master's, and postbachelor's certificates.
Special study options: academic remediation for entering students, adult/continuing education programs, advanced placement credit, double majors, honors programs, independent study, internships, off-campus study, part-time degree program, services for LD students, study abroad, summer session for credit.
Computers: Students can access the following: computer help desk, free student e-mail accounts, online (class) grades, online (class) registration, online (class) schedules. Campuswide network is available. 100% of college-owned or -operated housing units are wired for high-speed Internet access. Wireless service is available via entire campus.
Library: Leslie J. Savage Library plus 1 other. Weekly public service hours: 101; students can reserve study rooms.

STUDENT LIFE
Housing options: on-campus residence required through sophomore year; coed, special housing for students with disabilities. Campus housing is university owned. Freshman campus housing is guaranteed.

Activities and organizations: drama/theater group, student-run newspaper, radio and television station, choral group, Mountain Search and Rescue Team, Student Government Association, Rodeo Club, wilderness pursuits, Peak Productions.
Athletics Member NCAA. All Division II. *Intercollegiate sports:* baseball M(c), basketball M(s)/W(s), cheerleading M(c)/W(c), cross-country running M(s)/W(s), football M(s), ice hockey M(c), lacrosse M(c)/W(c), rock climbing M(c)/W(c), rugby M(c)/W(c), skiing (cross-country) M(c)/W(c), skiing (downhill) M(c)/W(c), soccer M(c)/W(s), swimming and diving W(s), track and field M(s)/W(s), volleyball M(c)/W(s), wrestling M(s)/W(c). *Intramural sports:* basketball M/W, football M/W, golf M/W, soccer M/W, softball M/W, table tennis M/W, tennis M/W, ultimate Frisbee M/W, volleyball M/W.
Campus security: 24-hour emergency response devices and patrols, student patrols, late-night transport/escort service, controlled dormitory access.
Student services: health clinic, personal/psychological counseling.

COSTS & FINANCIAL AID
Costs (2017–18) *Tuition:* state resident $6624 full-time, $276 per credit hour part-time; nonresident $18,096 full-time, $754 per credit hour part-time. Full-time tuition and fees vary according to course load and reciprocity agreements. Part-time tuition and fees vary according to course load and reciprocity agreements. *Required fees:* $3178 full-time. *Room and board:* $9546; room only: $5030. Room and board charges vary according to board plan and housing facility. *Payment plans:* installment, deferred payment. *Waivers:* senior citizens and employees or children of employees.
Financial Aid Of all full-time matriculated undergraduates who enrolled in 2017, 1,619 applied for aid, 1,038 were judged to have need, 24 had their need fully met. In 2017, 470 non-need-based awards were made. *Average percent of need met:* 33. *Average financial aid package:* $11,207. *Average need-based loan:* $4142. *Average need-based gift aid:* $8821. *Average non-need-based aid:* $2403. *Average indebtedness upon graduation:* $26,950.

APPLYING
Standardized Tests *Required:* SAT or ACT (for admission).
Options: electronic application, deferred entrance.
Application fee: $30.
Required: essay or personal statement, high school transcript, interview. *Recommended:* minimum 2.5 GPA.
Notification: continuous until 11/15 (freshmen), continuous (transfers).

CONTACT
Western State Colorado University, 600 North Adams Street, Gunnison, CO 81231. *Phone:* 970-943-2211. *Toll-free phone:* 800-876-5309. *E-mail:* admissions@western.edu.

CONNECTICUT

Albertus Magnus College
New Haven, Connecticut
http://www.albertus.edu/
- **Independent Roman Catholic** comprehensive, founded 1925
- **Suburban** 50-acre campus
- **Coed**
- **Moderately difficult** entrance level

FACULTY
Student/faculty ratio: 14:1.

ACADEMICS
Calendar: semesters. *Degrees:* certificates, diplomas, associate, bachelor's, master's, post-master's, and postbachelor's certificates.
Library: Rosary Hall. *Books:* 38,339 (physical), 148,500 (digital/electronic); *Databases:* 88.

STUDENT LIFE
Housing options: coed, women-only. Campus housing is university owned. Freshman applicants given priority for college housing.

COLLEGES AT-A-GLANCE

Activities and organizations: drama/theater group, choral group, Student Alumni Association, Student Government Association, M.A.L.E.S Club, Service Club, Honors Club.

Athletics Member NCAA. All Division III.

Campus security: 24-hour emergency response devices and patrols, late-night transport/escort service, controlled dormitory access.

Student services: health clinic, personal/psychological counseling.

COSTS & FINANCIAL AID

Costs (2017–18) *Comprehensive fee:* $45,506 includes full-time tuition ($31,000), mandatory fees ($490), and room and board ($14,016). Full-time tuition and fees vary according to program. Part-time tuition and fees vary according to program. *Room and board:* Room and board charges vary according to board plan.

Financial Aid Of all full-time matriculated undergraduates who enrolled in 2017, 940 applied for aid, 889 were judged to have need, 47 had their need fully met. In 2017, 12 non-need-based awards were made. *Average percent of need met:* 51. *Average financial aid package:* $17,021. *Average need-based loan:* $4370. *Average need-based gift aid:* $12,555. *Average non-need-based aid:* $12,497. *Average indebtedness upon graduation:* $36,908.

APPLYING

Standardized Tests *Required:* SAT or ACT (for admission). *Recommended:* SAT Subject Tests (for admission).

Options: electronic application, deferred entrance.

Application fee: $35.

Required: high school transcript, minimum 2.0 GPA, 1 letter of recommendation. *Required for some:* essay or personal statement, interview.

CONTACT

Anthony Reich, Director of Admission, Albertus Magnus College, 700 Prospect Street, New Haven, CT 06511-1189. *Phone:* 203-773-5032 Ext. 5032. *Toll-free phone:* 800-578-9160. *E-mail:* admissions@albertus.edu.

Bais Binyomin Academy

Stamford, Connecticut

CONTACT

Director of Admissions, Bais Binyomin Academy, 132 Prospect Street, Stamford, CT 06901-1202. *Phone:* 203-325-4351.

Central Connecticut State University

New Britain, Connecticut

http://www.ccsu.edu/

- **State-supported** comprehensive, founded 1849, part of Connecticut State Colleges & Universities (CSCU)
- **Suburban** 314-acre campus
- **Endowment** $71.2 million
- **Coed** 9,554 undergraduate students, 80% full-time, 47% women, 53% men
- **Moderately difficult** entrance level, 67% of applicants were admitted

UNDERGRAD STUDENTS

7,605 full-time, 1,949 part-time. Students come from 30 states and territories; 16 other countries; 3% are from out of state; 13% Black or African American, non-Hispanic/Latino; 14% Hispanic/Latino; 4% Asian, non-Hispanic/Latino; 0.1% Native Hawaiian or other Pacific Islander, non-Hispanic/Latino; 0.1% American Indian or Alaska Native, non-Hispanic/Latino; 3% Two or more races, non-Hispanic/Latino; 3% Race/ethnicity unknown; 2% international; 11% transferred in; 24% live on campus.

Freshmen:

Admission: 7,870 applied, 5,254 admitted, 1,433 enrolled. *Average high school GPA:* 3.1. *Test scores:* SAT evidence-based reading and writing scores over 500: 76%; SAT math scores over 500: 67%; ACT scores over 18: 89%; SAT evidence-based reading and writing scores over 600: 22%; SAT math scores over 600: 17%; ACT scores over 24: 27%; SAT evidence-based reading and writing scores over 700: 1%; SAT math scores over 700: 1%; ACT scores over 30: 7%.

Retention: 76% of full-time freshmen returned.

FACULTY

Total: 932, 48% full-time, 54% with terminal degrees.

Student/faculty ratio: 16:1.

ACADEMICS

Calendar: semesters. *Degrees:* certificates, bachelor's, master's, doctoral, post-master's, and postbachelor's certificates.

Special study options: academic remediation for entering students, adult/continuing education programs, advanced placement credit, cooperative education, distance learning, double majors, English as a second language, honors programs, independent study, internships, off-campus study, part-time degree program, services for LD students, student-designed majors, study abroad, summer session for credit. *ROTC:* Army (c), Air Force (c).

Computers: 750 computers/terminals are available on campus for general student use. Students can access the following: campus intranet, computer help desk, free student e-mail accounts, online (class) grades, online (class) registration, online (class) schedules. Campuswide network is available. 100% of college-owned or -operated housing units are wired for high-speed Internet access. Wireless service is available via entire campus.

Library: Elihu Burritt Library plus 1 other. *Books:* 451,499 (physical), 160,771 (digital/electronic); *Serial titles:* 4,177 (physical), 87,138 (digital/electronic); *Databases:* 147. Weekly public service hours: 84.

STUDENT LIFE

Housing options: coed, women-only, special housing for students with disabilities. Campus housing is university owned.

Activities and organizations: drama/theater group, student-run newspaper, radio and television station, choral group, Inter-Residence Council, student radio station, Program Board (C.A.N.), Student Government Association, A Cappella Society, national fraternities, national sororities.

Athletics Member NCAA. All Division I except football (Division I-AA). *Intercollegiate sports:* baseball M(s), basketball M(s)/W(s), cross-country running M(s)/W(s), golf M(s)/W(s), lacrosse W(s), soccer M(s)/W(s), softball W(s), swimming and diving W(s), track and field M(s)/W(s), volleyball W(s). *Intramural sports:* basketball M/W, fencing M(c)/W(c), field hockey W(c), football M, gymnastics M/W, lacrosse M(c)/W, rugby M(c)/W(c), soccer M/W, softball W, swimming and diving W, volleyball W.

Campus security: 24-hour emergency response devices and patrols, student patrols, late-night transport/escort service, controlled dormitory access.

Student services: health clinic, personal/psychological counseling, women's center.

COSTS & FINANCIAL AID

Costs (2017–18) *Tuition:* state resident $5424 full-time, $226 per credit part-time; nonresident $16,882 full-time, $226 per credit part-time. Full-time tuition and fees vary according to course level, course load, and program. Part-time tuition and fees vary according to course level, course load, and program. *Required fees:* $4801 full-time, $275 per credit part-time, $78 per term part-time. *Room and board:* $11,816; room only: $6820. Room and board charges vary according to board plan and housing facility. *Payment plan:* installment. *Waivers:* senior citizens and employees or children of employees.

Financial Aid Of all full-time matriculated undergraduates who enrolled in 2017, 6,944 applied for aid, 6,039 were judged to have need, 5,119 had their need fully met. 275 Federal Work-Study jobs (averaging $1500). In 2017, 102 non-need-based awards were made. *Average percent of need met:* 63. *Average financial aid package:* $8551. *Average need-based loan:* $3356. *Average need-based gift aid:* $6573. *Average non-need-based aid:* $3149. *Average indebtedness upon graduation:* $5831.

APPLYING

Standardized Tests *Required:* SAT or ACT (for admission).

Options: electronic application.

Application fee: $50.

Required: essay or personal statement, high school transcript, minimum 2.0 GPA, 2 letters of recommendation. *Required for some:* interview, high school class rank.

Application deadlines: 5/1 (freshmen), 5/1 (transfers).

Notification: continuous until 10/15 (freshmen), continuous until 10/15 (transfers).

CONTACT
Central Connecticut State University, 1615 Stanley Street, New Britain, CT 06050. *Phone:* 860-832-2285. *Toll-free phone:* 888-733-2278. *Fax:* 860-832-2522. *E-mail:* admissions@ccsu.edu.

Charter Oak State College

New Britain, Connecticut
http://www.charteroak.edu/
- **State-supported** comprehensive, founded 1973, part of Connecticut State Colleges & Universities (CSCU)
- **Suburban** campus with easy access to Hartford, CT
- **Coed** 1,416 undergraduate students, 20% full-time, 68% women, 32% men
- **Noncompetitive** entrance level

UNDERGRAD STUDENTS
290 full-time, 1,126 part-time. Students come from 43 states and territories; 20% are from out of state; 17% Black or African American, non-Hispanic/Latino; 16% Hispanic/Latino; 2% Asian, non-Hispanic/Latino; 0.4% American Indian or Alaska Native, non-Hispanic/Latino; 3% Two or more races, non-Hispanic/Latino; 5% Race/ethnicity unknown; 0.7% international.

FACULTY
Total: 186, 55% with terminal degrees.
Student/faculty ratio: 12:1.

ACADEMICS
Calendar: semesters. *Degrees:* certificates, associate, bachelor's, and master's (offers only external degree programs).

Special study options: accelerated degree program, adult/continuing education programs, advanced placement credit, distance learning, double majors, external degree program, independent study, off-campus study, part-time degree program, services for LD students, student-designed majors, summer session for credit.

Computers: Students can access the following: computer help desk, free student e-mail accounts, online (class) grades, online (class) registration, online (class) schedules. Campuswide network is available. Wireless service is available via entire campus.

STUDENT LIFE
Housing options: college housing not available.

COSTS & FINANCIAL AID
Costs (2017–18) *Tuition:* state resident $8940 full-time, $298 per credit part-time; nonresident $11,760 full-time, $392 per credit part-time. Full-time tuition and fees vary according to course load. Part-time tuition and fees vary according to course load. *Required fees:* $831 full-time, $277 per term part-time. *Payment plan:* installment.

Financial Aid Of all full-time matriculated undergraduates who enrolled in 2016, 265 applied for aid, 244 were judged to have need, 7 had their need fully met. In 2016, 2 non-need-based awards were made. *Average percent of need met:* 44. *Average financial aid package:* $7129. *Average need-based loan:* $4178. *Average need-based gift aid:* $4303. *Average non-need-based aid:* $1884.

APPLYING
Options: electronic application, deferred entrance.
Application fee: $75.
Required: 9 college-level credits, 16 years of age.
Notification: continuous (transfers).

CONTACT
Charter Oak State College, CT. *Phone:* 860-515-3858.

Connecticut College

New London, Connecticut
http://www.conncoll.edu/
- **Independent** comprehensive, founded 1911
- **Small-town** 750-acre campus with easy access to Providence, RI
- **Endowment** $299.6 million
- **Coed** 1,817 undergraduate students, 97% full-time, 63% women, 37% men
- **Very difficult** entrance level, 38% of applicants were admitted

UNDERGRAD STUDENTS
1,766 full-time, 51 part-time. Students come from 40 states and territories; 41 other countries; 82% are from out of state; 4% Black or African American, non-Hispanic/Latino; 8% Hispanic/Latino; 4% Asian, non-Hispanic/Latino; 0.1% Native Hawaiian or other Pacific Islander, non-Hispanic/Latino; 0.1% American Indian or Alaska Native, non-Hispanic/Latino; 3% Two or more races, non-Hispanic/Latino; 1% Race/ethnicity unknown; 8% international; 1% transferred in; 99% live on campus.

Freshmen:
Admission: 5,434 applied, 2,063 admitted, 444 enrolled. *Test scores:* SAT evidence-based reading and writing scores over 500: 100%; SAT math scores over 500: 98%; ACT scores over 18: 100%; SAT evidence-based reading and writing scores over 600: 91%; SAT math scores over 600: 84%; ACT scores over 24: 99%; SAT evidence-based reading and writing scores over 700: 34%; SAT math scores over 700: 24%; ACT scores over 30: 64%.
Retention: 91% of full-time freshmen returned.

FACULTY
Total: 248, 73% full-time, 85% with terminal degrees.
Student/faculty ratio: 9:1.

ACADEMICS
Calendar: semesters. *Degree:* bachelor's.

Special study options: accelerated degree program, adult/continuing education programs, advanced placement credit, double majors, independent study, internships, off-campus study, part-time degree program, services for LD students, student-designed majors, study abroad.

Unusual degree programs: 3-2 engineering with Washington University in St. Louis.

Computers: Students can access the following: campus intranet, computer help desk, free student e-mail accounts, online (class) grades, online (class) registration, online (class) schedules, learning management system. Campuswide network is available. 100% of college-owned or -operated housing units are wired for high-speed Internet access. Wireless service is available via classrooms, computer centers, computer labs, dorm rooms, learning centers, libraries, student centers.
Library: Charles Shain Library plus 1 other.

STUDENT LIFE
Housing options: on-campus residence required through junior year; coed. Campus housing is university owned. Freshman campus housing is guaranteed.

Activities and organizations: drama/theater group, student-run newspaper, radio station, choral group.

Athletics Member NCAA. All Division III. *Intercollegiate sports:* basketball M/W, cross-country running M/W, field hockey W, ice hockey M/W, lacrosse M/W, rowing M/W, sailing M/W, soccer M/W, squash M/W, swimming and diving M/W, tennis M/W, track and field M/W, volleyball W, water polo M/W. *Intramural sports:* basketball M/W, racquetball M/W, soccer M/W, softball M/W, squash M/W, tennis M/W, volleyball M/W.

Campus security: 24-hour emergency response devices and patrols, late-night transport/escort service, controlled dormitory access.

Student services: health clinic, personal/psychological counseling, women's center.

COSTS & FINANCIAL AID
Costs (2017–18) *Comprehensive fee:* $67,440 includes full-time tuition ($52,530), mandatory fees ($320), and room and board ($14,590). Part-time tuition: $1563 per credit hour. *College room only:* $8420. *Payment plan:* installment. *Waivers:* employees or children of employees.

Financial Aid Of all full-time matriculated undergraduates who enrolled in 2016, 1,125 applied for aid, 1,036 were judged to have need, 1,036 had their need fully met. *Average percent of need met:* 100. *Average financial aid package:* $40,891. *Average need-based loan:* $4497. *Average need-based gift aid:* $37,745. *Average indebtedness upon graduation:* $27,514.

APPLYING

Options: electronic application, early decision, deferred entrance.

Required: essay or personal statement, high school transcript, 2 letters of recommendation. *Recommended:* interview.

Application deadlines: 1/1 (freshmen), 4/1 (transfers).

Early decision deadline: 11/15 (for plan 1), 1/1 (for plan 2).

Notification: 3/31 (freshmen), 5/15 (transfers), 12/15 (early decision plan 1), 2/15 (early decision plan 2).

CONTACT

Andrew Strickler, Dean of Admission and Financial Aid, Connecticut College, 270 Mohegan Avenue, New London, CT 06320. *Phone:* 860-439-2200. *E-mail:* admission@conncoll.edu.

Eastern Connecticut State University

Willimantic, Connecticut

http://www.easternct.edu/

CONTACT

Eastern Connecticut State University, CT. *Phone:* 860-465-4381.

Fairfield University

Fairfield, Connecticut

http://www.fairfield.edu/

- **Independent Roman Catholic (Jesuit)** comprehensive, founded 1942
- **Suburban** 200-acre campus with easy access to New York City
- **Endowment** $349.2 million
- **Coed** 4,113 undergraduate students, 94% full-time, 60% women, 40% men
- **Very difficult** entrance level, 61% of applicants were admitted

UNDERGRAD STUDENTS

3,879 full-time, 234 part-time. Students come from 37 states and territories; 48 other countries; 71% are from out of state; 2% Black or African American, non-Hispanic/Latino; 8% Hispanic/Latino; 2% Asian, non-Hispanic/Latino; 0.0% Native Hawaiian or other Pacific Islander, non-Hispanic/Latino; 0.1% American Indian or Alaska Native, non-Hispanic/Latino; 2% Two or more races, non-Hispanic/Latino; 5% Race/ethnicity unknown; 3% international; 1% transferred in; 71% live on campus.

Freshmen:

Admission: 11,218 applied, 6,794 admitted, 994 enrolled. *Average high school GPA:* 3.5. *Test scores:* SAT evidence-based reading and writing scores over 500: 99%; SAT math scores over 500: 99%; ACT scores over 18: 100%; SAT evidence-based reading and writing scores over 600: 70%; SAT math scores over 600: 70%; ACT scores over 24: 91%; SAT evidence-based reading and writing scores over 700: 10%; SAT math scores over 700: 10%; ACT scores over 30: 19%.

Retention: 90% of full-time freshmen returned.

FACULTY

Total: 589, 46% full-time, 65% with terminal degrees.

Student/faculty ratio: 12:1.

ACADEMICS

Calendar: semesters. *Degrees:* bachelor's, master's, doctoral, post-master's, and postbachelor's certificates.

Special study options: accelerated degree program, adult/continuing education programs, advanced placement credit, distance learning, double majors, honors programs, independent study, internships, off-campus study, part-time degree program, services for LD students, student-designed majors, study abroad, summer session for credit. *ROTC:* Army (c), Air Force (c).

Computers: 131 computers/terminals are available on campus for general student use. Students can access the following: campus intranet, computer help desk, free student e-mail accounts, online (class) grades, online (class) registration, online (class) schedules. Campuswide network is available. 100% of college-owned or -operated housing units are wired for high-speed Internet access. Wireless service is available via entire campus.

Library: DiMenna-Nyselius Library. *Books:* 376,556 (physical), 892,810 (digital/electronic); *Serial titles:* 1,292 (physical), 58,084 (digital/electronic); *Databases:* 183. Weekly public service hours: 104; study areas open 24 hours, 5–7 days a week; students can reserve study rooms.

STUDENT LIFE

Housing options: coed, special housing for students with disabilities. Campus housing is university owned. Freshman campus housing is guaranteed.

Activities and organizations: drama/theater group, student-run newspaper, radio and television station, choral group, Fairfield University Student Association (FUSA), Commuter Student Association, Fairfield United, Intramural/Club Sports, Glee Club.

Athletics Member NCAA. All Division I. *Intercollegiate sports:* baseball M(s), basketball M(s)/W(s), crew M(s)/W(s), cross-country running M(s)/W(s), field hockey W(s), golf M(s)/W(s), lacrosse M(s)/W(s), soccer M(s)/W(s), softball W(s), swimming and diving M(s)/W(s), tennis M(s)/W(s), volleyball W(s). *Intramural sports:* baseball M(c), basketball M(c)/W(c), cheerleading M(c)/W(c), cross-country running M(c)/W(c), equestrian sports M(c)/W(c), field hockey W(c), golf M(c)/W(c), ice hockey M(c), lacrosse M(c)/W(c), rugby M(c)/W(c), sailing M(c)/W(c), skiing (downhill) M(c)/W(c), soccer M(c)/W(c), softball M/W, table tennis M/W, tennis M(c)/W(c), ultimate Frisbee M(c)/W(c), volleyball M(c)/W(c), wrestling M(c).

Campus security: 24-hour emergency response devices and patrols, late-night transport/escort service, controlled dormitory access, EMT public safety officers, bike patrol, closed circuit television system, crime prevention seminars and the LiveSafe mobile safety app.

Student services: health clinic, personal/psychological counseling.

COSTS & FINANCIAL AID

Costs (2017–18) *One-time required fee:* $300. *Comprehensive fee:* $61,445 includes full-time tuition ($46,490), mandatory fees ($675), and room and board ($14,280). Full-time tuition and fees vary according to class time, course level, course load, degree level, and program. Part-time tuition: $725 per credit hour. Part-time tuition and fees vary according to class time, course level, course load, degree level, and program. *Required fees:* $60 per term part-time. *College room only:* $8750. Room and board charges vary according to board plan and housing facility. *Payment plan:* installment. *Waivers:* employees or children of employees.

Financial Aid Of all full-time matriculated undergraduates who enrolled in 2017, 2,484 applied for aid, 1,758 were judged to have need, 594 had their need fully met. 540 Federal Work-Study jobs (averaging $1175). In 2017, 1533 non-need-based awards were made. *Average percent of need met:* 84. *Average financial aid package:* $34,731. *Average need-based loan:* $4863. *Average need-based gift aid:* $27,572. *Average non-need-based aid:* $14,987. *Average indebtedness upon graduation:* $32,186. *Financial aid deadline:* 1/15.

APPLYING

Options: electronic application, early admission, early decision, early action, deferred entrance.

Application fee: $60.

Required: essay or personal statement, high school transcript, 1 letter of recommendation. *Recommended:* interview.

Application deadlines: 1/15 (freshmen), 4/1 (transfers), 11/1 (early action).

Early decision deadline: 11/15 (for plan 1), 1/15 (for plan 2).

Notification: 4/1 (freshmen), 12/15 (early decision plan 1), 2/15 (early decision plan 2), 12/20 (early action).

CONTACT

Alison Hildenbrand, Director of Admission, Fairfield University, 1073 North Benson Road, Fairfield, CT 06824. *Phone:* 203-254-4100. *Fax:* 203-254-4199. *E-mail:* admis@fairfield.edu.

Goodwin College
East Hartford, Connecticut
http://www.goodwin.edu/

CONTACT
Mr. Nicholas Lentino, Assistant Vice President for Admissions, Goodwin College, One Riverside Drive, East Hartford, CT 06118. *Phone:* 860-727-6765. *Toll-free phone:* 800-889-3282. *Fax:* 860-291-9550. *E-mail:* nlentino@goodwin.edu.

Holy Apostles College and Seminary
Cromwell, Connecticut
http://www.holyapostles.edu/

CONTACT
Fr. Peter Samuel Kucer, Academic Dean, Holy Apostles College and Seminary, 33 Prospect Hill Road, Cromwell, CT 06416. *Phone:* 860-632-3063. *Fax:* 860-632-3030. *E-mail:* pkucer@holyapostles.edu.

Lincoln College of New England
Southington, Connecticut
http://www.lincolncollegene.edu/
- **Proprietary** 4-year, founded 1966
- **Small-town** 32-acre campus with easy access to Hartford
- **Coed** 465 undergraduate students, 63% full-time, 81% women, 19% men
- **Minimally difficult** entrance level, 99% of applicants were admitted

UNDERGRAD STUDENTS
295 full-time, 170 part-time. 12% are from out of state; 17% Black or African American, non-Hispanic/Latino; 14% Hispanic/Latino; 3% Asian, non-Hispanic/Latino; 0.6% American Indian or Alaska Native, non-Hispanic/Latino; 6% Two or more races, non-Hispanic/Latino; 9% Race/ethnicity unknown; 15% transferred in.

Freshmen:
Admission: 111 applied, 110 admitted, 67 enrolled.
Retention: 52% of full-time freshmen returned.

FACULTY
Total: 75, 20% full-time, 19% with terminal degrees.
Student/faculty ratio: 14:1.

ACADEMICS
Calendar: semesters. *Degrees:* certificates, associate, and bachelor's.
Special study options: academic remediation for entering students, adult/continuing education programs, advanced placement credit, distance learning, English as a second language, independent study, internships, part-time degree program, services for LD students, summer session for credit.
Computers: 54 computers/terminals are available on campus for general student use. Students can access the following: free student e-mail accounts, online (class) grades, online (class) schedules.
Library: Anthony A. Pupillo Library. *Books:* 11,844 (physical); *Serial titles:* 58 (physical); *Databases:* 92. Weekly public service hours: 61; students can reserve study rooms.

STUDENT LIFE
Housing options: coed, special housing for students with disabilities. Campus housing is university owned. Freshman applicants given priority for college housing.
Activities and organizations: Student Government Association, Student Ambassador Club, Criminal Justice Club, Mortuary Science, Dental.
Campus security: 24-hour patrols, late-night transport/escort service.

COSTS & FINANCIAL AID
Costs (2018–19) *Comprehensive fee:* $26,250 includes full-time tuition ($18,780), mandatory fees ($1270), and room and board ($6200). Part-time tuition: $710 per credit hour. Part-time tuition and fees vary according to course load. *Required fees:* $635 per term part-time. *College room only:* $4500. Room and board charges vary according to board plan. *Payment plan:* installment. *Waivers:* employees or children of employees.

Financial Aid Of all full-time matriculated undergraduates who enrolled in 2016, 92 Federal Work-Study jobs (averaging $2000). 30 state and other part-time jobs.

APPLYING
Options: electronic application.
Application fee: $25.
Required: high school transcript. *Required for some:* interview. *Recommended:* essay or personal statement.
Application deadlines: rolling (freshmen), rolling (out-of-state freshmen), rolling (transfers).
Notification: continuous (freshmen), continuous (out-of-state freshmen), continuous (transfers).

CONTACT
Ms. Tammy Murphy, Director of Admissions, Lincoln College of New England, 2279 Mount Vernon Road, Southington, CT 06489. *Phone:* 860-628-4751 Ext. 41904. *Toll-free phone:* 800-825-0087. *Fax:* 860-628-6444. *E-mail:* tmurphy@lincolncollegene.edu.

Mitchell College
New London, Connecticut
http://www.mitchell.edu/

CONTACT
Mr. Bob Martin, Director of Admissions, Mitchell College, 437 Pequot Avenue, New London, CT 06320. *Phone:* 860-701-5178. *Toll-free phone:* 800-443-2811. *Fax:* 860-444-1209. *E-mail:* admissions@mitchell.edu.

Paier College of Art, Inc.
Hamden, Connecticut
http://www.paiercollegeofart.edu/
- **Proprietary** 4-year, founded 1946
- **Suburban** 3-acre campus with easy access to New York City
- **Coed** 79 undergraduate students, 61% full-time, 70% women, 30% men

UNDERGRAD STUDENTS
48 full-time, 31 part-time. Students come from 2 states and territories; 1 other country; 11% Black or African American, non-Hispanic/Latino; 11% Hispanic/Latino; 5% Asian, non-Hispanic/Latino; 4% Two or more races, non-Hispanic/Latino; 5% Race/ethnicity unknown; 10% transferred in.

Freshmen:
Admission: 6 enrolled. *Average high school GPA:* 3.4.
Retention: 92% of full-time freshmen returned.

FACULTY
Total: 24, 33% full-time, 71% with terminal degrees.
Student/faculty ratio: 3:1.

ACADEMICS
Calendar: semesters plus 1 summer session. *Degree:* certificates, diplomas, and bachelor's.
Special study options: academic remediation for entering students, advanced placement credit, independent study, internships, part-time degree program, services for LD students, study abroad.
Computers: 50 computers/terminals are available on campus for general student use. Students can access the following: online (class) grades, online (class) schedules. Wireless service is available via entire campus.
Library: Adele K. Paier Memorial Library. *Books:* 14,300 (physical), 167 (digital/electronic); *Serial titles:* 80 (physical).

STUDENT LIFE
Housing options: college housing not available.
Activities and organizations: student-run newspaper, Student Council, School Newspaper.

COSTS & FINANCIAL AID
Costs (2018–19) *Tuition:* $16,600 full-time, $550 per credit hour part-time. Part-time tuition and fees vary according to course load. *Required fees:* $470 full-time, $190 per term part-time. *Payment plan:* installment.
Financial Aid Of all full-time matriculated undergraduates who enrolled in 1999, 102 applied for aid, 92 were judged to have need, 1 had their need

fully met. *Average percent of need met:* 62. *Average financial aid package:* $6717. *Average need-based loan:* $3446. *Average need-based gift aid:* $3460. *Average indebtedness upon graduation:* $13,536.

APPLYING
Standardized Tests *Required:* SAT or ACT (for admission).
Required: high school transcript, minimum 2.0 GPA, 2 letters of recommendation, interview, portfolio, interview. *Recommended:* essay or personal statement.

CONTACT
Mrs. Lynn Pascale, Admissions Secretary, Paier College of Art, Inc., 20 Gorham Avenue, Hamden, CT 06514. *Phone:* 203-287-3031. *Fax:* 203-287-3021. *E-mail:* paier.admission@snet.net.

Post University
Waterbury, Connecticut
http://www.post.edu/

- **Independent** comprehensive, founded 1890
- **Suburban** 70-acre campus with easy access to Hartford
- **Coed** 7,844 undergraduate students, 33% full-time, 65% women, 35% men
- **Moderately difficult** entrance level, 63% of applicants were admitted

UNDERGRAD STUDENTS
2,617 full-time, 5,227 part-time. Students come from 29 states and territories; 24 other countries; 71% are from out of state; 25% Black or African American, non-Hispanic/Latino; 7% Hispanic/Latino; 1% Asian, non-Hispanic/Latino; 0.5% Native Hawaiian or other Pacific Islander, non-Hispanic/Latino; 0.8% American Indian or Alaska Native, non-Hispanic/Latino; 5% Two or more races, non-Hispanic/Latino; 19% Race/ethnicity unknown; 1% international; 31% transferred in; 51% live on campus.

Freshmen:
Admission: 4,078 applied, 2,583 admitted, 747 enrolled. *Average high school GPA:* 2.7. *Test scores:* ACT scores over 18: 71%; ACT scores over 24: 41%; ACT scores over 30: 2%.
Retention: 39% of full-time freshmen returned.

FACULTY
Student/faculty ratio: 20:1.

ACADEMICS
Calendar: semesters. *Degrees:* certificates, associate, bachelor's, master's, post-master's, and postbachelor's certificates.
Special study options: accelerated degree program, advanced placement credit, cooperative education, distance learning, double majors, English as a second language, freshman honors college, honors programs, independent study, internships, off-campus study, part-time degree program, services for LD students, summer session for credit.
Computers: 150 computers/terminals and 150 ports are available on campus for general student use. Students can access the following: campus intranet, computer help desk, free student e-mail accounts, online (class) grades, online (class) registration, online (class) schedules, software applications. Campuswide network is available. 100% of college-owned or -operated housing units are wired for high-speed Internet access. Wireless service is available via entire campus.
Library: Trauriq Library and Resource Center. *Books:* 10,320 (physical), 160,000 (digital/electronic); *Serial titles:* 250 (physical), 36,199 (digital/electronic); *Databases:* 43. Weekly public service hours: 75; students can reserve study rooms.

STUDENT LIFE
Housing options: coed, special housing for students with disabilities. Campus housing is university owned.
Activities and organizations: drama/theater group, choral group, Equine Club, Newman Club, GSA, Accounting Club, Choir.
Athletics Member NCAA. All Division II. *Intercollegiate sports:* baseball M(s), basketball M(s)/W(s), cross-country running M(s)/W(s), equestrian sports M(c)/W(c), football M(c), golf M(s)/W(s), ice hockey M(c)/W(c), lacrosse M(s)/W(s), soccer M(s)/W(s), softball W(s), tennis M(s)/W(s), track and field M(s)/W(s), volleyball W(s). *Intramural sports:* basketball M/W, bowling W, cheerleading W(c).

Campus security: 24-hour emergency response devices and patrols, late-night transport/escort service, controlled dormitory access, annual and semi-annual emergency preparedness training for students and staff.
Student services: health clinic, personal/psychological counseling.

COSTS & FINANCIAL AID
Costs (2018–19) *Comprehensive fee:* $40,150 includes full-time tuition ($28,250), mandatory fees ($1300), and room and board ($10,600). Full-time tuition and fees vary according to class time, course level, course load, degree level, location, program, and student level. Part-time tuition: $945 per credit hour. Part-time tuition and fees vary according to class time, course level, course load, degree level, location, program, and student level. *Room and board:* Room and board charges vary according to housing facility. *Payment plans:* tuition prepayment, installment. *Waivers:* senior citizens and employees or children of employees.
Financial Aid Of all full-time matriculated undergraduates who enrolled in 2014, 619 applied for aid, 595 were judged to have need, 87 had their need fully met. In 2014, 12 non-need-based awards were made. *Average percent of need met:* 58. *Average financial aid package:* $19,829. *Average need-based loan:* $4023. *Average need-based gift aid:* $15,866. *Average non-need-based aid:* $9807. *Average indebtedness upon graduation:* $20,246.

APPLYING
Standardized Tests *Required:* SAT or ACT (for admission).
Options: electronic application, deferred entrance.
Required: high school transcript, minimum 2.0 GPA, 1 letter of recommendation. *Recommended:* essay or personal statement, interview.
Application deadlines: rolling (freshmen), rolling (transfers).
Notification: continuous (freshmen), continuous (transfers).

CONTACT
Post University, 800 Country Club Road, Waterbury, CT 06723-2540. *Toll-free phone:* 800-345-2562.

Quinnipiac University
Hamden, Connecticut
http://www.qu.edu/

- **Independent** comprehensive, founded 1929
- **Suburban** 600-acre campus with easy access to New Haven, Hartford
- **Endowment** $481.6 million
- **Coed** 7,305 undergraduate students
- **Moderately difficult** entrance level, 74% of applicants were admitted

UNDERGRAD STUDENTS
Students come from 45 states and territories; 51 other countries; 71% are from out of state; 4% Black or African American, non-Hispanic/Latino; 9% Hispanic/Latino; 3% Asian, non-Hispanic/Latino; 0.1% American Indian or Alaska Native, non-Hispanic/Latino; 3% Two or more races, non-Hispanic/Latino; 2% Race/ethnicity unknown; 2% international; 75% live on campus.

Freshmen:
Admission: 22,071 applied, 16,305 admitted. *Average high school GPA:* 3.5. *Test scores:* SAT evidence-based reading and writing scores over 500: 92%; SAT math scores over 500: 89%; ACT scores over 18: 98%; SAT evidence-based reading and writing scores over 600: 46%; SAT math scores over 600: 40%; ACT scores over 24: 68%; SAT evidence-based reading and writing scores over 700: 4%; SAT math scores over 700: 5%; ACT scores over 30: 11%.
Retention: 86% of full-time freshmen returned.

FACULTY
Total: 1,084, 35% full-time, 55% with terminal degrees.
Student/faculty ratio: 16:1.

ACADEMICS
Calendar: semesters. *Degrees:* bachelor's, master's, doctoral, post-master's, and postbachelor's certificates.
Special study options: accelerated degree program, advanced placement credit, distance learning, double majors, honors programs, independent study, internships, part-time degree program, services for LD students, study abroad, summer session for credit. *ROTC:* Army (c), Air Force (c).

Computers: 600 computers/terminals and 2,500 ports are available on campus for general student use. Students can access the following: campus intranet, computer help desk, free student e-mail accounts, online (class) grades, online (class) registration, online (class) schedules, e-commerce and &Q;; card for local merchants, food service, dorm card access. Campuswide network is available. 100% of college-owned or -operated housing units are wired for high-speed Internet access. Wireless service is available via entire campus.

Library: Arnold Bernhard Library plus 3 others. *Books:* 135,000 (physical), 500,000 (digital/electronic); *Databases:* 190. Weekly public service hours: 93; study areas open 24 hours, 5–7 days a week; students can reserve study rooms.

STUDENT LIFE

Housing options: coed. Campus housing is university owned. Freshman campus housing is guaranteed.

Activities and organizations: drama/theater group, student-run newspaper, radio and television station, choral group, Student Government, Social Programming Board, Drama Club, Chronicle (student newspaper), dance company, national fraternities, national sororities.

Athletics Member NCAA. All Division I. *Intercollegiate sports:* baseball M(s), basketball M(s)/W(s), cross-country running M(s)/W(s), field hockey W(s), golf W(s), gymnastics W(s), ice hockey M(s)/W(s), lacrosse M(s)/W(s), rugby W(s), soccer M(s)/W(s), softball W(s), tennis M(s)/W(s), track and field W(s), volleyball W(s). *Intramural sports:* baseball M, basketball M/W, bowling M/W, field hockey W, soccer M/W, softball W, tennis M/W, volleyball M/W.

Campus security: 24-hour emergency response devices and patrols, late-night transport/escort service, controlled dormitory access, text message emergency notification system.

Student services: health clinic, personal/psychological counseling, women's center.

COSTS & FINANCIAL AID

Costs (2018–19) *One-time required fee:* $1045. *Comprehensive fee:* $62,950 includes full-time tuition ($45,540), mandatory fees ($2420), and room and board ($14,990). Part-time tuition: $1045 per credit hour. Part-time tuition and fees vary according to class time and course load. *Required fees:* $45 per credit hour part-time. *Room and board:* Room and board charges vary according to board plan and housing facility. *Payment plan:* installment. *Waivers:* employees or children of employees.

Financial Aid Of all full-time matriculated undergraduates who enrolled in 2017, 5,136 applied for aid, 4,425 were judged to have need, 701 had their need fully met. 1,745 Federal Work-Study jobs (averaging $2062). In 2017, 1813 non-need-based awards were made. *Average percent of need met:* 65. *Average financial aid package:* $28,707. *Average need-based loan:* $4429. *Average need-based gift aid:* $22,734. *Average non-need-based aid:* $16,877. *Average indebtedness upon graduation:* $48,894.

APPLYING

Standardized Tests *Required for some:* SAT or ACT (for admission).

Options: electronic application, early decision, deferred entrance.

Application fee: $65.

Required: essay or personal statement, high school transcript, 1 letter of recommendation. *Required for some:* minimum 3.0 GPA. *Recommended:* minimum 3.0 GPA, interview.

Application deadlines: 2/1 (freshmen), 4/1 (transfers).

Early decision deadline: 11/1.

Notification: continuous (freshmen), continuous (out-of-state freshmen), continuous (transfers).

CONTACT

Ms. Joan Isaac-Mohr, Vice President for Admissions and Financial Aid, Quinnipiac University, 275 Mount Carmel Avenue, Hamden, CT 06518. *Phone:* 203-582-8600. *Toll-free phone:* 800-462-1944. *Fax:* 203-582-8906. *E-mail:* admissions@qu.edu.

See below for display ad and page 1390 for the College Close-Up.

Sacred Heart University

Fairfield, Connecticut
http://www.sacredheart.edu/

- **Independent Roman Catholic** comprehensive, founded 1963
- **Suburban** 350-acre campus with easy access to New York City
- **Endowment** $157.8 million
- **Coed** 5,603 undergraduate students, 89% full-time, 64% women, 36% men
- **Moderately difficult** entrance level, 60% of applicants were admitted

UNDERGRAD STUDENTS
4,982 full-time, 621 part-time. Students come from 42 states and territories; 26 other countries; 65% are from out of state; 4% Black or African American, non-Hispanic/Latino; 10% Hispanic/Latino; 2% Asian, non-Hispanic/Latino; 0.1% Native Hawaiian or other Pacific Islander, non-Hispanic/Latino; 0.1% American Indian or Alaska Native, non-Hispanic/Latino; 2% Two or more races, non-Hispanic/Latino; 6% Race/ethnicity unknown; 1% international; 2% transferred in; 52% live on campus.

Freshmen:
Admission: 9,992 applied, 6,023 admitted, 1,387 enrolled. **Average high school GPA:** 3.5. **Test scores:** SAT evidence-based reading and writing scores over 500: 94%; SAT math scores over 500: 93%; ACT scores over 18: 100%; SAT evidence-based reading and writing scores over 600: 33%; SAT math scores over 600: 31%; ACT scores over 24: 66%; SAT evidence-based reading and writing scores over 700: 2%; SAT math scores over 700: 2%; ACT scores over 30: 5%.
Retention: 84% of full-time freshmen returned.

FACULTY
Student/faculty ratio: 14:1.

ACADEMICS
Calendar: semesters. **Degrees:** bachelor's, master's, doctoral, and post-master's certificates (also offers part-time program with significant enrollment not reflected in profile).
Special study options: academic remediation for entering students, accelerated degree program, adult/continuing education programs, advanced placement credit, cooperative education, distance learning, double majors, English as a second language, honors programs, independent study, internships, part-time degree program, services for LD students, student-designed majors, study abroad, summer session for credit. **ROTC:** Air Force (c).
Unusual degree programs: 3-2 engineering with Columbia University, Rensselaer Polytechnic Institute; health professions and a law program with Seton Hall University, pre-pharmacy with University of St. Joseph's.
Computers: 499 computers/terminals are available on campus for general student use. Students can access the following: computer help desk, free student e-mail accounts, online (class) grades, online (class) registration. Campuswide network is available. 100% of college-owned or -operated housing units are wired for high-speed Internet access. Wireless service is available via entire campus.
Library: Ryan Matura Library plus 1 other. **Books:** 89,498 (physical), 205,348 (digital/electronic); **Serial titles:** 400 (physical), 52,686 (digital/electronic); **Databases:** 135. Weekly public service hours: 119; students can reserve study rooms.

STUDENT LIFE
Housing options: on-campus residence required through sophomore year; coed, special housing for students with disabilities. Campus housing is university owned and leased by the school. Freshman campus housing is guaranteed.
Activities and organizations: drama/theater group, student-run newspaper, radio and television station, choral group, marching band, Alpha Sigma Lambda Honor Society, Inter Resident Council, Student Nursing Association, Habitat for Humanity, Pre-PT Club, national fraternities, national sororities.
Athletics Member NCAA. All Division I except football (Division I-AA). **Intercollegiate sports:** baseball M(s), basketball M(s)/W(s), bowling W(s), cheerleading W(c), crew W(s), cross-country running M(s)/W(s), equestrian sports W(s), fencing M(s)/W, field hockey W(s), golf M(s)/W(s), ice hockey M(s)/W(s), lacrosse M(s)/W(s), rugby W(s), soccer M(s)/W(s), softball W(s), swimming and diving W(s), tennis M(s)/W(s),

track and field M(s)/W(s), volleyball M(s)/W(s), wrestling M(s).
Intramural sports: baseball M(c), basketball M(c)/W(c), bowling M(c), cross-country running M(c)/W(c), field hockey W(c), golf M(c)/W(c), gymnastics M(c)/W(c), ice hockey M(c), lacrosse M(c)/W(c), rugby M(c), sailing M(c)/W(c), soccer M(c)/W(c), softball W(c), tennis M(c)/W(c), triathlon M(c)/W(c), ultimate Frisbee M(c), volleyball M(c)/W(c), weight lifting M(c)/W(c), wrestling M(c).
Campus security: 24-hour emergency response devices and patrols, late-night transport/escort service, controlled dormitory access, Bystander Intervention, Personal Safety Escort Program, Silent Witness Program, crime prevention announcements, SHU Safe App.
Student services: health clinic, personal/psychological counseling.

COSTS & FINANCIAL AID
Costs (2017–18) Comprehensive fee: $54,590 includes full-time tuition ($39,570), mandatory fees ($250), and room and board ($14,770). Part-time tuition: $600 per credit hour. Part-time tuition and fees vary according to course load. **Required fees:** $115 per term part-time. **College room only:** $10,100. Room and board charges vary according to board plan and housing facility. **Payment plan:** installment. **Waivers:** employees or children of employees.
Financial Aid Of all full-time matriculated undergraduates who enrolled in 2017, 3,959 applied for aid, 3,343 were judged to have need, 540 had their need fully met. 1,037 Federal Work-Study jobs (averaging $1679). 650 state and other part-time jobs (averaging $1281). In 2017, 4789 non-need-based awards were made. **Average percent of need met:** 57. **Average financial aid package:** $20,729. **Average need-based loan:** $4952. **Average need-based gift aid:** $16,376. **Average non-need-based aid:** $12,447. **Average indebtedness upon graduation:** $42,033.

APPLYING
Options: electronic application, early admission, early decision, early action, deferred entrance.
Application fee: $50.
Required: high school transcript, 1 letter of recommendation. **Required for some:** interview, interview for Early Decision candidates. **Recommended:** essay or personal statement.
Application deadlines: rolling (freshmen), 12/15 (early action).
Early decision deadline: 12/1.
Notification: continuous (freshmen), continuous (transfers), 12/15 (early decision), 1/31 (early action).

CONTACT
Mr. Kevin O'Sullivan, Executive Director of Undergraduate Admissions, Sacred Heart University, 5151 Park Avenue, Fairfield, CT 06825. *Phone:* 203-371-7880. *Fax:* 203-365-7607. *E-mail:* swartzk2@sacredheart.edu.

St. Vincent's College

Bridgeport, Connecticut
http://www.stvincentscollege.edu/

- **Independent** primarily 2-year, founded 1991, affiliated with Roman Catholic Church
- **Urban** campus with easy access to New York City
- **Endowment** $4.1 million
- **Coed**

FACULTY
Student/faculty ratio: 14:1.

ACADEMICS
Calendar: semesters. **Degrees:** certificates, associate, and bachelor's.
Library: Daniel T. Banks Health Science Library. **Books:** 1,500 (physical), 84,000 (digital/electronic); **Serial titles:** 81 (physical); **Databases:** 5. Weekly public service hours: 40; students can reserve study rooms.

STUDENT LIFE
Housing options: college housing not available.
Activities and organizations: Radiography Club, Student Nurses Association, SALUTE (veterans national honor society), Phi Theta Kappa (honor society).
Campus security: 24-hour emergency response devices and patrols, late-night transport/escort service.

COSTS & FINANCIAL AID

Costs (2017–18) *Tuition:* $14,520 full-time, $605 per credit hour part-time. Full-time tuition and fees vary according to course load. Part-time tuition and fees vary according to course load. *Required fees:* $1043 full-time, $1043 per year part-time.

Financial Aid Of all full-time matriculated undergraduates who enrolled in 2015, 45 applied for aid, 45 were judged to have need. *Average percent of need met:* 34. *Average financial aid package:* $8755. *Average need-based loan:* $4070. *Average need-based gift aid:* $5754. *Average indebtedness upon graduation:* $35,263.

APPLYING

Standardized Tests *Recommended:* SAT or ACT (for admission).

Required: high school transcript. *Recommended:* minimum 2.0 GPA.

CONTACT

St. Vincent's College, 2800 Main Street, Bridgeport, CT 06606-4292. *Toll-free phone:* 800-873-1013.

Southern Connecticut State University

New Haven, Connecticut

http://www.southernct.edu/

- **State-supported** comprehensive, founded 1893, part of Connecticut State Colleges & Universities (CSCU)
- **Suburban** 168-acre campus with easy access to New York City
- **Coed**
- **Moderately difficult** entrance level

FACULTY

Student/faculty ratio: 14:1.

ACADEMICS

Calendar: semesters. *Degrees:* bachelor's, master's, doctoral, post-master's, and postbachelor's certificates.
Library: Hilton C. Buley Library. *Books:* 478,191 (physical), 135,134 (digital/electronic); *Serial titles:* 14,528 (physical), 158 (digital/electronic); *Databases:* 203. Students can reserve study rooms.

STUDENT LIFE

Housing options: coed, special housing for students with disabilities. Campus housing is university owned. Freshman campus housing is guaranteed.

Activities and organizations: drama/theater group, student-run newspaper, radio and television station, choral group, marching band, Student Government Association, Psychology Club, Habitat for Humanity, Crescent Players, Black Student Union, national fraternities, national sororities.

Athletics Member NCAA. All Division II.

Campus security: 24-hour emergency response devices and patrols, late-night transport/escort service, controlled dormitory access.

Student services: health clinic, personal/psychological counseling, women's center.

COSTS & FINANCIAL AID

Costs (2017–18) *Tuition:* state resident $5424 full-time, $569 per credit hour part-time; nonresident $16,882 full-time, $569 per credit hour part-time. Full-time tuition and fees vary according to course load and reciprocity agreements. Part-time tuition and fees vary according to course load. *Required fees:* $5114 full-time, $55 per term part-time. *Room and board:* $12,432; room only: $6842. Room and board charges vary according to board plan and housing facility. *Payment plans:* installment, deferred payment.

Financial Aid Of all full-time matriculated undergraduates who enrolled in 2016, 5,412 applied for aid, 4,582 were judged to have need, 1,145 had their need fully met. 96 Federal Work-Study jobs (averaging $4196). In 2016, 210 non-need-based awards were made. *Average percent of need met:* 68. *Average financial aid package:* $14,501. *Average need-based loan:* $4359. *Average need-based gift aid:* $6639. *Average non-need-based aid:* $4636. *Average indebtedness upon graduation:* $28,370. *Financial aid deadline:* 3/9.

APPLYING

Standardized Tests *Required:* SAT or ACT (for admission).

Options: electronic application, deferred entrance.

Application fee: $50.

Required: essay or personal statement, high school transcript.

CONTACT

Mrs. Alexis S. Haakonsen, Director of Admissions, Southern Connecticut State University, Admissions House, 131 Farnham Avenue, New Haven, CT 06515-1202. *Phone:* 203-392-5652. *Fax:* 203-392-5727. *E-mail:* haakonsena1@southernct.edu.

Trinity College

Hartford, Connecticut

http://www.trincoll.edu/

CONTACT

Trinity College, 300 Summit Street, Hartford, CT 06106-3100. *Phone:* 860-297-2180.

United States Coast Guard Academy

New London, Connecticut

http://www.uscga.edu/

- **Federally supported** 4-year, founded 1876
- **Suburban** 103-acre campus with easy access to Providence, Hartford
- **Coed** 1,045 undergraduate students, 100% full-time, 35% women, 65% men
- **Very difficult** entrance level, 15% of applicants were admitted

UNDERGRAD STUDENTS

1,045 full-time. Students come from 52 states and territories; 12 other countries; 95% are from out of state; 6% Black or African American, non-Hispanic/Latino; 9% Hispanic/Latino; 7% Asian, non-Hispanic/Latino; 0.2% Native Hawaiian or other Pacific Islander, non-Hispanic/Latino; 0.3% American Indian or Alaska Native, non-Hispanic/Latino; 9% Two or more races, non-Hispanic/Latino; 0.9% Race/ethnicity unknown; 3% international; 100% live on campus.

Freshmen:
Admission: 2,021 applied, 304 admitted, 290 enrolled. *Average high school GPA:* 3.8. *Test scores:* SAT evidence-based reading and writing scores over 500: 98%; SAT math scores over 500: 100%; ACT scores over 18: 99%; SAT evidence-based reading and writing scores over 600: 73%; SAT math scores over 600: 82%; ACT scores over 24: 90%; SAT evidence-based reading and writing scores over 700: 19%; SAT math scores over 700: 18%; ACT scores over 30: 39%.

Retention: 95% of full-time freshmen returned.

FACULTY

Total: 161, 86% full-time, 51% with terminal degrees.
Student/faculty ratio: 7:1.

ACADEMICS

Calendar: semesters. *Degree:* bachelor's.

Special study options: academic remediation for entering students, advanced placement credit, double majors, honors programs, independent study, internships, off-campus study, summer session for credit.

Computers: 280 computers/terminals are available on campus for general student use. Students can access the following: campus intranet, computer help desk, free student e-mail accounts, online (class) grades, online (class) schedules. Campuswide network is available. 100% of college-owned or -operated housing units are wired for high-speed Internet access. Wireless service is available via classrooms, dorm rooms, libraries, student centers.
Library: USCG Academy Library. Students can reserve study rooms.

STUDENT LIFE

Housing options: on-campus residence required through senior year; coed. Campus housing is university owned. Freshman campus housing is guaranteed.

Activities and organizations: drama/theater group, choral group, marching band, Club Sports, Musical activities, Multicultural Club, Officers Christian Fellowship, International Dance Club.

Athletics Member NCAA. All Division III. *Intercollegiate sports:* baseball M, basketball M/W, cheerleading W(c), crew M/W, cross-country running M/W, football M, ice hockey M(c)/W(c), lacrosse M(c)/W(c), riflery M/W, rugby M(c)/W(c), sailing M/W, soccer M/W, softball W, swimming and diving M/W, tennis M, track and field M/W, volleyball W, water polo M(c)/W(c), wrestling M. *Intramural sports:* basketball M/W, bowling M/W, equestrian sports M(c)/W(c), fencing M(c)/W(c), football M, golf M/W, racquetball M/W, sailing M/W, skiing (downhill) M/W, soccer M/W, softball M/W, table tennis M/W, track and field M/W, ultimate Frisbee M/W, volleyball M/W, water polo M/W, weight lifting M/W, wrestling M.

Campus security: 24-hour patrols, late-night transport/escort service, controlled dormitory access, cadets staff a 24-hour Watch Office.

Student services: health clinic, personal/psychological counseling, legal services.

APPLYING
Standardized Tests *Required:* SAT or ACT (for admission).

Options: electronic application, early action, deferred entrance.

Required: essay or personal statement, high school transcript, 3 letters of recommendation, medical examination, physical fitness examination. *Recommended:* interview.

Application deadlines: 2/1 (freshmen), rolling (out-of-state freshmen), 2/1 (transfers), 11/15 (early action).

Notification: continuous until 4/15 (freshmen), continuous until 4/15 (out-of-state freshmen), continuous until 4/15 (transfers), 2/1 (early action).

CONTACT
Mr. Daniel V. Pinch, Associate Director of Admissions for Outreach, United States Coast Guard Academy, 31 Mohegan Avenue, New London, CT 06320-4195. *Phone:* 860-701-6327. *Toll-free phone:* 800-883-8724. *Fax:* 860-701-6700. *E-mail:* daniel.v.pinch@uscga.edu.

University of Bridgeport
Bridgeport, Connecticut
http://www.bridgeport.edu/

- **Independent** comprehensive, founded 1927
- **Urban** 86-acre campus with easy access to New York City
- **Endowment** $38.0 million
- **Coed** 3,129 undergraduate students, 74% full-time, 64% women, 36% men
- **Moderately difficult** entrance level, 54% of applicants were admitted

UNDERGRAD STUDENTS
2,300 full-time, 829 part-time. Students come from 40 states and territories; 48 other countries; 32% are from out of state; 34% Black or African American, non-Hispanic/Latino; 22% Hispanic/Latino; 4% Asian, non-Hispanic/Latino; 0.2% Native Hawaiian or other Pacific Islander, non-Hispanic/Latino; 0.8% American Indian or Alaska Native, non-Hispanic/Latino; 1% Two or more races, non-Hispanic/Latino; 13% international; 10% transferred in; 37% live on campus.

Freshmen:
Admission: 7,947 applied, 4,283 admitted, 550 enrolled. *Average high school GPA:* 3.0. *Test scores:* SAT evidence-based reading and writing scores over 500: 52%; SAT math scores over 500: 37%; ACT scores over 18: 85%; SAT evidence-based reading and writing scores over 600: 6%; SAT math scores over 600: 7%; ACT scores over 24: 26%; SAT evidence-based reading and writing scores over 700: 1%; SAT math scores over 700: 1%; ACT scores over 30: 2%.

Retention: 71% of full-time freshmen returned.

FACULTY
Total: 559, 26% full-time.

Student/faculty ratio: 16:1.

ACADEMICS
Calendar: semesters. *Degrees:* certificates, associate, bachelor's, master's, doctoral, post-master's, and postbachelor's certificates.

Special study options: academic remediation for entering students, accelerated degree program, adult/continuing education programs, advanced placement credit, cooperative education, distance learning, double majors, English as a second language, honors programs, independent study, internships, off-campus study, part-time degree program, services for LD students, student-designed majors, study abroad, summer session for credit.

Computers: 300 computers/terminals and 300 ports are available on campus for general student use. Students can access the following: computer help desk, free student e-mail accounts, online (class) grades, online (class) registration, online (class) schedules. Campuswide network is available. 100% of college-owned or -operated housing units are wired for high-speed Internet access. Wireless service is available via classrooms, computer centers, computer labs, dorm rooms, learning centers, libraries, student centers.

Library: Wahlstrom Library. *Books:* 144,829 (physical), 210,775 (digital/electronic); *Serial titles:* 957 (physical), 68,477 (digital/electronic); *Databases:* 81. Weekly public service hours: 90.

STUDENT LIFE
Housing options: on-campus residence required through sophomore year; coed. Campus housing is university owned. Freshman campus housing is guaranteed.

Activities and organizations: student-run newspaper, choral group, Student Congress, International Relations Club, Black Students Alliance, Latin America Club, Martial Arts Club, national fraternities, national sororities.

Athletics Member NCAA. All Division II. *Intercollegiate sports:* baseball M(s), basketball M(s)/W(s), cross-country running M(s)/W(s), gymnastics W(s), lacrosse W(s), soccer M(s)/W(s), softball W(s), swimming and diving M(s)/W(s), volleyball W(s). *Intramural sports:* basketball M/W, football M/W, golf M/W, racquetball M/W, soccer M/W, softball M/W, tennis M/W.

Campus security: 24-hour emergency response devices and patrols, student patrols, late-night transport/escort service, controlled dormitory access.

Student services: health clinic, personal/psychological counseling.

COSTS & FINANCIAL AID
Costs (2017–18) *Comprehensive fee:* $45,840 includes full-time tuition ($30,150), mandatory fees ($2100), and room and board ($13,590). Full-time tuition and fees vary according to course load and program. Part-time tuition: $1005 per credit hour. Part-time tuition and fees vary according to course load and program. *Required fees:* $215 per term part-time. *Room and board:* Room and board charges vary according to board plan and housing facility. *Payment plans:* installment, deferred payment. *Waivers:* senior citizens and employees or children of employees.

Financial Aid Of all full-time matriculated undergraduates who enrolled in 2016, 2,185 applied for aid, 1,886 were judged to have need, 219 had their need fully met. In 2016, 299 non-need-based awards were made. *Average percent of need met:* 60. *Average financial aid package:* $28,677. *Average need-based loan:* $7000. *Average need-based gift aid:* $14,193. *Average non-need-based aid:* $14,220. *Average indebtedness upon graduation:* $21,200.

APPLYING
Standardized Tests *Required:* SAT or ACT (for admission).

Options: electronic application, early admission, deferred entrance.

Application fee: $25.

Required: essay or personal statement, high school transcript, minimum 2.0 GPA. *Required for some:* 2 letters of recommendation, interview, portfolio, audition. *Recommended:* 1 letter of recommendation, interview.

Application deadlines: rolling (freshmen), rolling (transfers).

Notification: continuous (freshmen), continuous (transfers).

CONTACT
Ms. Jessica N. Crowley Goddu, Director of Undergraduate Admissions, University of Bridgeport, 126 Park Avenue, Bridgeport, CT 06604. *Phone:* 203-576-4812. *Toll-free phone:* 800-EXCEL-UB. *Fax:* 203-576-4941. *E-mail:* admit@bridgeport.edu.

University of Connecticut
Storrs, Connecticut
http://www.uconn.edu/

CONTACT
Nathan Fuerst, Director of Undergraduate Admissions, University of Connecticut, 2131 Hillside Road, U-88, Storrs, CT 06269. *Phone:* 860-486-3137. *Fax:* 860-486-1476. *E-mail:* beahusky@uconn.edu.

 # University of Hartford
West Hartford, Connecticut
http://www.hartford.edu/

- **Independent** comprehensive, founded 1877
- **Suburban** 320-acre campus with easy access to Hartford
- **Endowment** $164.5 million
- **Coed** 5,069 undergraduate students, 88% full-time, 51% women, 49% men
- **Moderately difficult** entrance level, 81% of applicants were admitted

UNDERGRAD STUDENTS
4,460 full-time, 609 part-time. Students come from 47 states and territories; 45 other countries; 45% are from out of state; 15% Black or African American, non-Hispanic/Latino; 13% Hispanic/Latino; 4% Asian, non-Hispanic/Latino; 0.1% Native Hawaiian or other Pacific Islander, non-Hispanic/Latino; 0.3% American Indian or Alaska Native, non-Hispanic/Latino; 4% Two or more races, non-Hispanic/Latino; 3% Race/ethnicity unknown; 6% international; 5% transferred in; 61% live on campus.

Freshmen:
Admission: 14,043 applied, 11,360 admitted, 1,334 enrolled. *Average high school GPA:* 3.1. *Test scores:* SAT evidence-based reading and writing scores over 500: 87%; SAT math scores over 500: 80%; ACT scores over 18: 98%; SAT evidence-based reading and writing scores over 600: 33%; SAT math scores over 600: 29%; ACT scores over 24: 47%; SAT evidence-based reading and writing scores over 700: 5%; SAT math scores over 700: 5%; ACT scores over 30: 10%.
Retention: 73% of full-time freshmen returned.

FACULTY
Total: 875, 41% full-time.
Student/faculty ratio: 9:1.

ACADEMICS
Calendar: semesters. *Degrees:* certificates, diplomas, associate, bachelor's, master's, doctoral, post-master's, and postbachelor's certificates.
Special study options: academic remediation for entering students, adult/continuing education programs, advanced placement credit, cooperative education, distance learning, double majors, English as a second language, honors programs, independent study, internships, off-campus study, part-time degree program, services for LD students, student-designed majors, study abroad, summer session for credit. *ROTC:* Army (c), Air Force (c).
Computers: 400 computers/terminals are available on campus for general student use. Students can access the following: campus intranet, computer help desk, free student e-mail accounts, online (class) grades, online (class) registration, online (class) schedules, student Web pages. Campuswide network is available. 100% of college-owned or -operated housing units are wired for high-speed Internet access. Wireless service is available via entire campus.
Library: Mortensen Library plus 1 other. *Books:* 287,556 (physical), 2,540 (digital/electronic); *Serial titles:* 1,479 (physical), 56,360 (digital/electronic); *Databases:* 229. Weekly public service hours: 104.

STUDENT LIFE
Housing options: coed, women-only, special housing for students with disabilities. Campus housing is university owned and leased by the school. Freshman campus housing is guaranteed.
Activities and organizations: drama/theater group, student-run newspaper, radio and television station, choral group, Program Council, Brothers and Sisters United, Hillel, Student Government Association, Residence Hall Association, national fraternities, national sororities.

Athletics Member NCAA. All Division I. *Intercollegiate sports:* badminton M(c)/W(c), baseball M(s), basketball M(s)/W(s), cross-country running M(s)/W(s), golf M(s)/W(s), lacrosse M(s), racquetball M(c)/W(c), rugby M(c)/W(c), soccer M(s)/W(s), softball W(s), track and field M/W, volleyball M(c)/W(s). *Intramural sports:* badminton M/W, basketball M/W, football M/W, racquetball M/W, soccer M/W, softball M/W, tennis M/W, ultimate Frisbee M/W, volleyball M/W.

Campus security: 24-hour emergency response devices and patrols, late-night transport/escort service, controlled dormitory access, bicycle patrols.

Student services: health clinic, personal/psychological counseling, women's center, legal services.

COSTS & FINANCIAL AID
Costs (2018–19) *Comprehensive fee:* $53,170 includes full-time tuition ($37,802), mandatory fees ($2892), and room and board ($12,476). Full-time tuition and fees vary according to program. Part-time tuition and fees vary according to course load and program. *College room only:* $8008. Room and board charges vary according to board plan and housing facility. *Payment plans:* tuition prepayment, installment. *Waivers:* senior citizens and employees or children of employees.

Financial Aid Of all full-time matriculated undergraduates who enrolled in 2017, 3,590 applied for aid, 3,273 were judged to have need, 424 had their need fully met. 516 Federal Work-Study jobs (averaging $1916). In 2017, 868 non-need-based awards were made. *Average percent of need met:* 68. *Average financial aid package:* $27,599. *Average need-based loan:* $4621. *Average need-based gift aid:* $22,152. *Average non-need-based aid:* $16,666.

APPLYING
Standardized Tests *Required:* SAT or ACT (for admission).
Options: electronic application, early admission, early action, deferred entrance.
Application fee: $35.
Required: high school transcript. *Recommended:* essay or personal statement, 2 letters of recommendation, interview.
Application deadlines: rolling (freshmen), rolling (transfers).
Notification: continuous (freshmen), continuous (transfers).

CONTACT
Mr. Richard Zeiser, Dean of Admissions, University of Hartford, 200 Bloomfield Avenue, West Hartford, CT 06117. *Phone:* 860-768-4296. *Toll-free phone:* 800-947-4303. *Fax:* 860-768-4961. *E-mail:* admissions@hartford.edu.

 # University of New Haven
West Haven, Connecticut
http://www.newhaven.edu/

- **Independent** comprehensive, founded 1920
- **Suburban** 82-acre campus with easy access to New Haven
- **Coed** 5,216 undergraduate students, 93% full-time, 53% women, 47% men
- **Moderately difficult** entrance level, 88% of applicants were admitted

UNDERGRAD STUDENTS
4,831 full-time, 385 part-time. Students come from 42 states and territories; 36 other countries; 56% are from out of state; 12% Black or African American, non-Hispanic/Latino; 12% Hispanic/Latino; 3% Asian, non-Hispanic/Latino; 0.1% Native Hawaiian or other Pacific Islander, non-Hispanic/Latino; 0.3% American Indian or Alaska Native, non-Hispanic/Latino; 1% Two or more races, non-Hispanic/Latino; 6% Race/ethnicity unknown; 6% international; 5% transferred in; 52% live on campus.

Freshmen:
Admission: 9,953 applied, 8,735 admitted, 1,449 enrolled. *Average high school GPA:* 3.4. *Test scores:* SAT evidence-based reading and writing scores over 500: 83%; SAT math scores over 500: 77%; ACT scores over 18: 94%; SAT evidence-based reading and writing scores over 600: 33%; SAT math scores over 600: 26%; ACT scores over 24: 50%; SAT evidence-based reading and writing scores over 700: 3%; SAT math scores over 700: 3%; ACT scores over 30: 8%.
Retention: 79% of full-time freshmen returned.

FACULTY
Total: 647, 41% full-time, 60% with terminal degrees.
Student/faculty ratio: 16:1.

ACADEMICS
Calendar: 4-1-4. *Degrees:* certificates, associate, bachelor's, master's, doctoral, post-master's, and postbachelor's certificates.

Special study options: academic remediation for entering students, accelerated degree program, adult/continuing education programs, advanced placement credit, cooperative education, distance learning, double majors, English as a second language, honors programs, independent study, internships, off-campus study, part-time degree program, services for LD students, study abroad, summer session for credit. *ROTC:* Army (b), Air Force (c).

Computers: Students can access the following: campus intranet, computer help desk, free student e-mail accounts, online (class) grades, online (class) registration, online (class) schedules, computer repair services. Campuswide network is available. Wireless service is available via entire campus.

Library: Marvin K. Peterson Library.

STUDENT LIFE
Housing options: coed, special housing for students with disabilities. Campus housing is university owned and leased by the school. Freshman campus housing is guaranteed.

Activities and organizations: drama/theater group, student-run newspaper, radio station, marching band, national fraternities, national sororities.

Athletics Member NCAA. All Division II. *Intercollegiate sports:* baseball M(s), basketball M(s)/W(s), cross-country running M(s)/W(s), field hockey W(s), football M(s), ice hockey M(c), lacrosse M(c)/W(s), rugby M(c), soccer M(s)/W(s), softball W(s), tennis W(s), track and field M(s)/W(s), ultimate Frisbee M(c)/W(c), volleyball M(c)/W(s), wrestling M(c). *Intramural sports:* basketball M/W, cheerleading M/W, racquetball M/W, soccer M/W, softball M/W, tennis M/W, volleyball M/W.

Campus security: 24-hour emergency response devices and patrols, student patrols, late-night transport/escort service, controlled dormitory access, vehicle, bicycle and foot patrols, crime prevention programs.

Student services: health clinic, personal/psychological counseling.

COSTS & FINANCIAL AID
Costs (2017–18) *Comprehensive fee:* $53,780 includes full-time tuition ($36,770), mandatory fees ($1400), and room and board ($15,610). Full-time tuition and fees vary according to course load, location, and program. Part-time tuition: $1225 per credit hour. Part-time tuition and fees vary according to class time, course load, location, and program. *Required fees:* $65 per term part-time. *College room only:* $9860. Room and board charges vary according to board plan, housing facility, and location. *Payment plan:* installment. *Waivers:* senior citizens and employees or children of employees.

Financial Aid Of all full-time matriculated undergraduates who enrolled in 2017, 4,032 applied for aid, 3,714 were judged to have need, 546 had their need fully met. In 2017, 696 non-need-based awards were made. *Average percent of need met:* 59. *Average financial aid package:* $23,082. *Average need-based loan:* $4267. *Average need-based gift aid:* $19,708. *Average non-need-based aid:* $16,299. *Average indebtedness upon graduation:* $49,941.

APPLYING
Standardized Tests *Required:* SAT or ACT (for admission).

Options: electronic application, early decision, early action.

Application fee: $50.

Required: essay or personal statement, high school transcript, 1 letter of recommendation. *Recommended:* interview.

Application deadlines: rolling (freshmen), rolling (out-of-state freshmen), rolling (transfers), 12/15 (early action).

Early decision deadline: 12/1.

Notification: continuous (freshmen), continuous (out-of-state freshmen), continuous (transfers), 12/15 (early decision), 1/15 (early action).

CONTACT
Mr. Jason Riendeau, Director of Undergraduate Admissions, University of New Haven, Bayer Hall, 300 Boston Post Road, West Haven, CT 06516. *Phone:* 203-932-2920. *Toll-free phone:* 800-342-5864. *E-mail:* jriendeau@newhaven.edu.

See below for display ad and page 1472 for the College Close-Up.

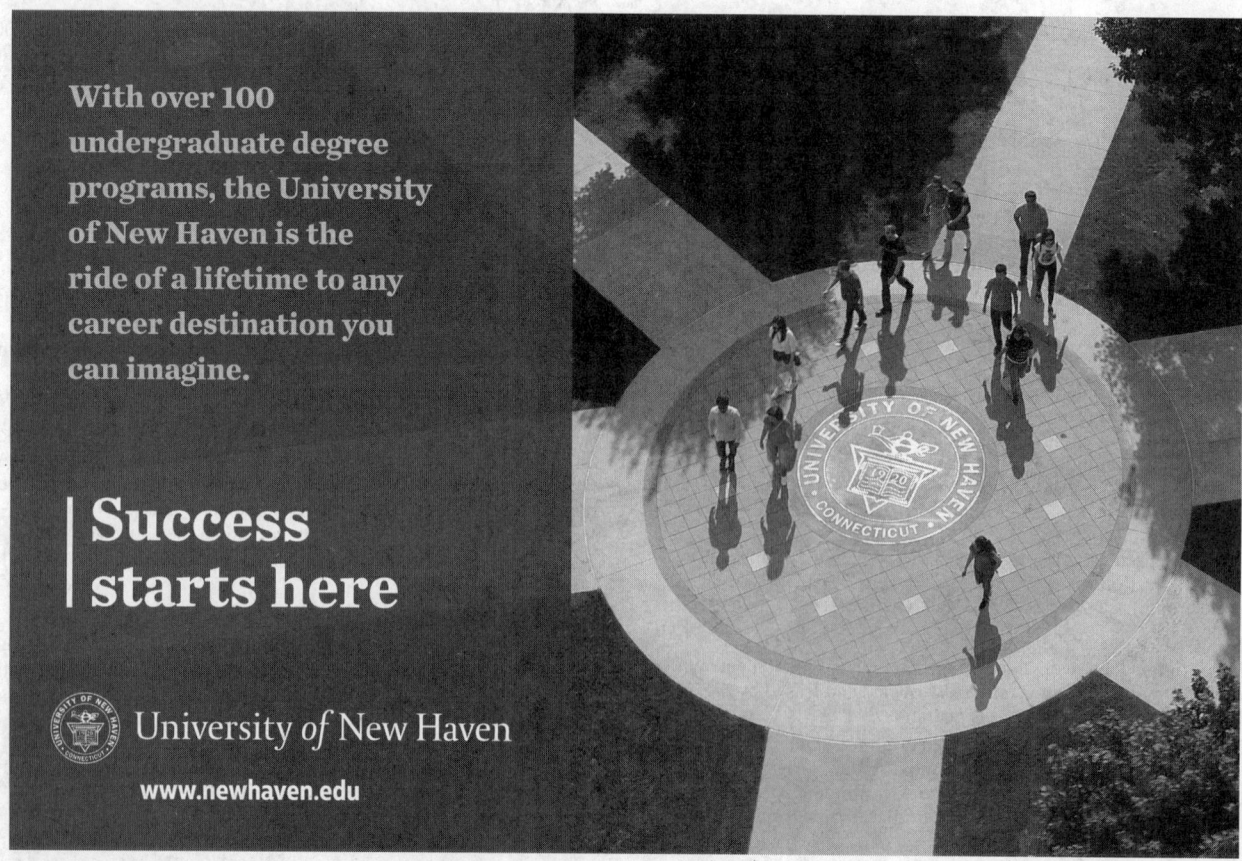

University of Saint Joseph
West Hartford, Connecticut
http://www.usj.edu/
- **Independent Roman Catholic** comprehensive, founded 1932
- **Suburban** 90-acre campus with easy access to Hartford
- **Coed, primarily women** 810 undergraduate students, 81% full-time, 98% women, 2% men
- **Moderately difficult** entrance level, 90% of applicants were admitted

UNDERGRAD STUDENTS
654 full-time, 156 part-time. Students come from 15 states and territories; 5% are from out of state; 14% Black or African American, non-Hispanic/Latino; 15% Hispanic/Latino; 5% Asian, non-Hispanic/Latino; 0.2% American Indian or Alaska Native, non-Hispanic/Latino; 1% Two or more races, non-Hispanic/Latino; 11% Race/ethnicity unknown; 0.9% international; 7% transferred in; 51% live on campus.

Freshmen:
Admission: 649 applied, 586 admitted, 134 enrolled. *Average high school GPA:* 3.4. *Test scores:* SAT evidence-based reading and writing scores over 500: 82%; SAT math scores over 500: 60%; ACT scores over 18: 100%; SAT evidence-based reading and writing scores over 600: 21%; SAT math scores over 600: 13%; ACT scores over 24: 14%; SAT evidence-based reading and writing scores over 700: 3%.
Retention: 75% of full-time freshmen returned.

FACULTY
Total: 301, 45% full-time.
Student/faculty ratio: 9:1.

ACADEMICS
Calendar: semesters. *Degrees:* certificates, bachelor's, master's, doctoral, post-master's, and postbachelor's certificates.

Special study options: accelerated degree program, adult/continuing education programs, advanced placement credit, distance learning, double majors, honors programs, independent study, internships, off-campus study, part-time degree program, services for LD students, student-designed majors, study abroad, summer session for credit.

Computers: 72 computers/terminals are available on campus for general student use. Students can access the following: campus intranet, computer help desk, free student e-mail accounts, online (class) grades, online (class) registration, online (class) schedules. Campuswide network is available. 100% of college-owned or -operated housing units are wired for high-speed Internet access. Wireless service is available via classrooms, computer centers, computer labs, dorm rooms, libraries, student centers.
Library: Pope Pius XII Library.

STUDENT LIFE
Housing options: coed, women-only, special housing for students with disabilities. Campus housing is university owned.

Activities and organizations: drama/theater group, choral group.

Athletics Member NCAA. All Division III. *Intercollegiate sports:* basketball W, cross-country running W, lacrosse W, soccer W, softball W, swimming and diving W, tennis W, volleyball W. *Intramural sports:* badminton M/W, basketball M/W, cross-country running M(c)/W(c), field hockey W(c).

Campus security: 24-hour emergency response devices and patrols, late-night transport/escort service, controlled dormitory access.

Student services: health clinic, personal/psychological counseling.

COSTS & FINANCIAL AID
Costs (2018–19) *Comprehensive fee:* $50,600 includes full-time tuition ($37,360), mandatory fees ($1812), and room and board ($11,428). Full-time tuition and fees vary according to course load, degree level, location, program, and student level. Part-time tuition: $818 per credit hour. Part-time tuition and fees vary according to course load, degree level, location, program, and student level. *Required fees:* $58 per credit hour part-time. *College room only:* $6438. Room and board charges vary according to board plan and housing facility. *Payment plan:* installment. *Waivers:* employees or children of employees.

Financial Aid Of all full-time matriculated undergraduates who enrolled in 2017, 598 applied for aid, 572 were judged to have need, 81 had their need fully met. 166 Federal Work-Study jobs (averaging $1711). 121 state and other part-time jobs (averaging $1792). In 2017, 45 non-need-based awards were made. *Average percent of need met:* 73. *Average financial aid package:* $27,986. *Average need-based loan:* $5814. *Average need-based gift aid:* $22,970. *Average non-need-based aid:* $15,954. *Average indebtedness upon graduation:* $38,916.

APPLYING
Standardized Tests *Required for some:* SAT or ACT (for admission).
Options: electronic application, deferred entrance.
Application fee: $50.
Required: high school transcript, 1 letter of recommendation. *Recommended:* essay or personal statement, interview.
Application deadlines: rolling (freshmen), rolling (transfers).
Notification: continuous (freshmen), continuous (transfers).

CONTACT
University of Saint Joseph, 1678 Asylum Avenue, West Hartford, CT 06117-2700. *Toll-free phone:* 866-442-8752.

Wesleyan University
Middletown, Connecticut
http://www.wesleyan.edu/
- **Independent** university, founded 1831
- **Suburban** 316-acre campus with easy access to Hartford, CT; New Haven, CT; Springfield, MA
- **Endowment** $967.2 million
- **Coed** 2,976 undergraduate students, 97% full-time, 54% women, 46% men
- **Most difficult** entrance level, 16% of applicants were admitted

UNDERGRAD STUDENTS
2,896 full-time, 80 part-time. Students come from 54 states and territories; 53 other countries; 92% are from out of state; 6% Black or African American, non-Hispanic/Latino; 11% Hispanic/Latino; 8% Asian, non-Hispanic/Latino; 0.1% Native Hawaiian or other Pacific Islander, non-Hispanic/Latino; 0.1% American Indian or Alaska Native, non-Hispanic/Latino; 5% Two or more races, non-Hispanic/Latino; 3% Race/ethnicity unknown; 12% international; 2% transferred in; 100% live on campus.

Freshmen:
Admission: 12,360 applied, 2,013 admitted, 761 enrolled. *Test scores:* SAT evidence-based reading and writing scores over 500: 100%; SAT math scores over 500: 100%; ACT scores over 18: 100%; SAT evidence-based reading and writing scores over 600: 92%; SAT math scores over 600: 89%; ACT scores over 24: 96%; SAT evidence-based reading and writing scores over 700: 57%; SAT math scores over 700: 53%; ACT scores over 30: 72%.
Retention: 95% of full-time freshmen returned.

FACULTY
Total: 441, 84% full-time, 87% with terminal degrees.
Student/faculty ratio: 8:1.

ACADEMICS
Calendar: semesters. *Degrees:* bachelor's, master's, doctoral, and post-master's certificates.

Special study options: accelerated degree program, advanced placement credit, double majors, honors programs, independent study, internships, off-campus study, services for LD students, student-designed majors, study abroad, summer session for credit. *ROTC:* Air Force (c).

Unusual degree programs: 3-2 engineering with Columbia University, California Institute of Technology, Dartmouth College.

Computers: 118 computers/terminals and 7,200 ports are available on campus for general student use. Students can access the following: campus intranet, computer help desk, free student e-mail accounts, online (class) registration, online (class) schedules, electronic portfolio, course drop/add, learning management system, software training. Campuswide network is available. 100% of college-owned or -operated housing units are wired for high-speed Internet access. Wireless service is available via entire campus.
Library: Olin Memorial Library plus 1 other. *Books:* 1.2 million (physical), 502,915 (digital/electronic); *Serial titles:* 7,507 (physical), 86,968 (digital/electronic); *Databases:* 332. Weekly public service hours: 113.

STUDENT LIFE

Housing options: on-campus residence required through senior year; coed, men-only, women-only, special housing for students with disabilities. Campus housing is university owned. Freshman campus housing is guaranteed.

Activities and organizations: drama/theater group, student-run newspaper, radio station, choral group, Mock Trial, Athletic Clubs, Spectrum, Burlesque, Espwesso, national fraternities, national sororities.

Athletics Member NCAA. All Division III. *Intercollegiate sports:* badminton M(c)/W(c), baseball M, basketball M/W, crew M/W, cross-country running M/W, equestrian sports M(c)/W(c), fencing M(c)/W(c), field hockey W, football M, golf M, ice hockey M/W, lacrosse M/W, rugby M(c)/W(c), sailing M(c)/W(c), soccer M/W, softball W, squash M/W, swimming and diving M/W, tennis M/W, track and field M/W, ultimate Frisbee M(c)/W(c), volleyball W, water polo M(c)/W(c), wrestling M. *Intramural sports:* basketball M/W, ice hockey M/W, soccer M/W, softball M/W, squash M/W, ultimate Frisbee M/W, water polo M/W.

Campus security: 24-hour emergency response devices and patrols, late-night transport/escort service, controlled dormitory access, Self-defense classes offered by certified instructors.

Student services: health clinic, personal/psychological counseling.

COSTS & FINANCIAL AID

Costs (2017–18) *Comprehensive fee:* $66,940 includes full-time tuition ($52,174), mandatory fees ($300), and room and board ($14,466). *Room and board:* Room and board charges vary according to board plan and student level. *Payment plan:* installment.

Financial Aid Of all full-time matriculated undergraduates who enrolled in 2017, 1,316 applied for aid, 1,282 were judged to have need, 1,282 had their need fully met. 994 Federal Work-Study jobs (averaging $2502). 166 state and other part-time jobs (averaging $2564). In 2017, 18 non-need-based awards were made. *Average percent of need met:* 100. *Average financial aid package:* $51,397. *Average need-based loan:* $4306. *Average need-based gift aid:* $47,206. *Average non-need-based aid:* $43,431. *Average indebtedness upon graduation:* $22,930. *Financial aid deadline:* 2/15.

APPLYING

Standardized Tests *Required for some:* SAT and SAT Subject Tests or ACT (for admission).

Options: electronic application, early admission, early decision, deferred entrance.

Application fee: $55.

Required: essay or personal statement, high school transcript, 2 letters of recommendation. *Required for some:* interview. *Recommended:* interview.

Application deadlines: 1/1 (freshmen), 3/15 (transfers).

Early decision deadline: 11/15 (for plan 1), 1/1 (for plan 2).

Notification: 4/1 (freshmen), 5/15 (transfers), 12/15 (early decision plan 1), 2/15 (early decision plan 2).

CONTACT

Ms. Nancy Hargrave Meislahn, Dean of Admission and Financial Aid, Wesleyan University, Stewart M. Reid House, Admission Office, 70 Wyllys Avenue, Middletown, CT 06459. *Phone:* 860-685-3000. *Fax:* 860-685-3001. *E-mail:* admission@wesleyan.edu.

Western Connecticut State University

Danbury, Connecticut

http://www.wcsu.edu/

- **State-supported** comprehensive, founded 1903, part of Connecticut State Colleges & Universities (CSCU)
- **Urban** 340-acre campus with easy access to New York City
- **Endowment** $18.9 million
- **Coed** 5,082 undergraduate students, 80% full-time, 52% women, 48% men
- **Moderately difficult** entrance level, 71% of applicants were admitted

UNDERGRAD STUDENTS

4,089 full-time, 993 part-time. Students come from 13 states and territories; 7 other countries; 9% are from out of state; 11% Black or African American, non-Hispanic/Latino; 18% Hispanic/Latino; 4% Asian, non-Hispanic/Latino; 0.1% Native Hawaiian or other Pacific Islander, non-Hispanic/Latino; 0.2% American Indian or Alaska Native, non-Hispanic/Latino; 3% Two or more races, non-Hispanic/Latino; 3% Race/ethnicity unknown; 0.2% international; 11% transferred in; 29% live on campus.

Freshmen:

Admission: 5,671 applied, 4,017 admitted, 827 enrolled. *Test scores:* SAT evidence-based reading and writing scores over 500: 79%; SAT math scores over 500: 72%; SAT evidence-based reading and writing scores over 600: 23%; SAT math scores over 600: 14%; SAT evidence-based reading and writing scores over 700: 2%; SAT math scores over 700: 1%. *Retention:* 73% of full-time freshmen returned.

FACULTY

Total: 620, 35% full-time, 32% with terminal degrees.

Student/faculty ratio: 13:1.

ACADEMICS

Calendar: semesters. *Degrees:* associate, bachelor's, master's, doctoral, and post-master's certificates.

Special study options: advanced placement credit, cooperative education, distance learning, honors programs, independent study, internships, part-time degree program, services for LD students, student-designed majors, study abroad, summer session for credit. *ROTC:* Army (c), Air Force (c).

Computers: 666 computers/terminals and 1,065 ports are available on campus for general student use. Students can access the following: computer help desk, free student e-mail accounts, online (class) grades, online (class) registration, online (class) schedules, online payment. Campuswide network is available. 100% of college-owned or -operated housing units are wired for high-speed Internet access. Wireless service is available via entire campus.

Library: Ruth Haas Library plus 2 others. *Books:* 204,701 (physical), 240,140 (digital/electronic); *Serial titles:* 302 (physical), 67,162 (digital/electronic); *Databases:* 188. Weekly public service hours: 144; students can reserve study rooms.

STUDENT LIFE

Housing options: coed. Campus housing is university owned.

Activities and organizations: drama/theater group, student-run newspaper, radio station, choral group, National Society of Collegiate Scholars, Criminology Club, Jazz Club, American Marketing Club, Meteorology, national fraternities, national sororities.

Athletics Member NCAA. All Division III. *Intercollegiate sports:* baseball M, basketball M/W, cheerleading W(c), field hockey W, football M, lacrosse M/W, soccer M/W, softball W, swimming and diving W, tennis M/W, volleyball W. *Intramural sports:* basketball M/W, football M, ice hockey M(c), rock climbing M(c)/W(c), soccer M/W, softball W.

Campus security: 24-hour emergency response devices and patrols, student patrols, late-night transport/escort service, controlled dormitory access.

Student services: health clinic, personal/psychological counseling, women's center.

COSTS & FINANCIAL AID

Costs (2017–18) *Tuition:* state resident $10,458 full-time, $226 per credit hour part-time; nonresident $23,147 full-time, $226 per credit hour part-time. Full-time tuition and fees vary according to course load, program, and reciprocity agreements. *Required fees:* $269 per credit hour part-time, $60 per term part-time. *Room and board:* $12,416; room only: $7108. Room and board charges vary according to board plan and housing facility. *Payment plan:* installment. *Waivers:* senior citizens and employees or children of employees.

Financial Aid Of all full-time matriculated undergraduates who enrolled in 2016, 3,416 applied for aid, 2,850 were judged to have need, 372 had their need fully met. 61 Federal Work-Study jobs (averaging $1810). In 2016, 63 non-need-based awards were made. *Average percent of need met:* 42. *Average financial aid package:* $8593. *Average need-based loan:* $4368. *Average need-based gift aid:* $5302. *Average non-need-based aid:* $9223. *Average indebtedness upon graduation:* $35,177. *Financial aid deadline:* 3/15.

WESTERN CONNECTICUT STATE UNIVERSITY

UNDERGRADUATE & GRADUATE DEGREE PROGRAMS IN ARTS & SCIENCES, BUSINESS, PROFESSIONAL STUDIES AND VISUAL & PERFORMING ARTS

ACCOUNTING Financial, Managerial
AMERICAN STUDIES
ANTHROPOLOGY/SOCIOLOGY
APPLIED COMPUTING*
ART Graphic Design, Illustration, Photography, Studio Art
BIOLOGY
BIOLOGY Bioscience, Ecological
BUSINESS ADMINISTRATION/UNDECLARED
CHEMISTRY
CHEMISTRY/BIOCHEMISTRY
COMMUNICATION Communication Studies, Relational
COMPUTER SCIENCE
DIGITAL & INTERACTIVE MEDIA*
EARTH & PLANETARY SCIENCES
ECONOMICS
EDUCATION (ELEMENTARY 1–6) Interdisciplinary
EDUCATION (SECONDARY 7–12) Biology, Chemistry, Earth Science, English, History w/ Social Studies minor, Mathematics, Spanish
ENGLISH
FINANCE Financial Management, Financial Investments & Markets
HEALTH EDUCATION (PK-12)
HEALTH PROMOTION STUDIES Allied Health; Community Health; Holistic & Integrative; Wellness Management
HISTORY
JUSTICE & LAW ADMINISTRATION Corrections, Law Enforcement, Legal Studies, Paralegal Studies, Criminology

LIBERAL ARTS (2-year Associate or 4-year B.A.*)
MANAGEMENT Human Resources, Small Business & Entrepreneurial, Supervisory
MANAGEMENT INFORMATION SYSTEMS
MANAGEMENT INFORMATION SYSTEMS: INFORMATION SECURITY
MARKETING
MARKETING: DIGITAL & INTERACTIVE
MATHEMATICS
MATHEMATICS: COMPUTER SCIENCE
MEDIA ARTS Media Studies, Production
METEOROLOGY
MUSIC
MUSIC: AUDIO & MUSIC PRODUCTION
MUSIC: JAZZ STUDIES
MUSIC: PERFORMANCE
MUSIC EDUCATION (K–12)
MUSICAL THEATRE
NURSING
NURSING: RN TO BSN
POLITICAL SCIENCE
PROFESSIONAL WRITING Business, Creative, General, Journalism/Freelance, Public Relations
PSYCHOLOGY
SOCIAL SCIENCES
SOCIAL SCIENCES Anthropology/Sociology, Family, Global, Multicultural
SOCIAL WORK
SPANISH
THEATRE ARTS Design/Technology, Drama Studies, Management, Performance
UNDECLARED

* PENDING BOARD OF REGENTS APPROVAL

181 WHITE STREET, DANBURY, CONN.
WWW.WCSU.EDU

WESTERN CONNECTICUT STATE UNIVERSITY

APPLYING

Standardized Tests *Recommended:* SAT or ACT (for admission).

Options: electronic application, deferred entrance.

Application fee: $50.

Required: high school transcript. *Required for some:* essay or personal statement, interview.

Application deadlines: rolling (freshmen), rolling (transfers).

Notification: continuous (freshmen), continuous (transfers).

CONTACT
Office of University Admissions, Western Connecticut State University, 181 White Street, Danbury, CT 06810. *Phone:* 203-837-9000. *Toll-free phone:* 877-837-WCSU. *Fax:* 203-837-8338. *E-mail:* admissions@wcsu.edu.

See this page for display ad and page 1496 for the College Close-Up.

Yale University
New Haven, Connecticut
http://www.yale.edu/

- **Independent** university, founded 1701
- **Urban** 342-acre campus with easy access to New York City
- **Endowment** $25.6 billion
- **Coed**
- **Most difficult** entrance level

FACULTY
Student/faculty ratio: 6:1.

ACADEMICS
Calendar: semesters. *Degrees:* bachelor's, master's, doctoral, and post-master's certificates.
Library: Sterling Memorial Library plus 15 others. *Books:* 13.8 million (physical), 1.8 million (digital/electronic). Weekly public service hours: 93; students can reserve study rooms.

STUDENT LIFE
Housing options: on-campus residence required through sophomore year; coed, special housing for students with disabilities. Campus housing is university owned. Freshman campus housing is guaranteed.

Activities and organizations: drama/theater group, student-run newspaper, radio and television station, choral group, marching band, national fraternities, national sororities.

Athletics Member NCAA. All Division I except football (Division I-AA).

Campus security: 24-hour emergency response devices and patrols, late-night transport/escort service, controlled dormitory access.

Student services: health clinic, personal/psychological counseling, women's center.

COSTS & FINANCIAL AID
Costs (2017–18) *Comprehensive fee:* $66,900 includes full-time tuition ($51,400) and room and board ($15,500). *College room only:* $8700. Room and board charges vary according to board plan.

Financial Aid Of all full-time matriculated undergraduates who enrolled in 2016, 2,891 applied for aid, 2,733 were judged to have need, 2,733 had their need fully met. *Average percent of need met:* 100. *Average financial aid package:* $52,894. *Average need-based loan:* $2725. *Average need-based gift aid:* $50,565. *Average indebtedness upon graduation:* $13,625. *Financial aid deadline:* 3/1.

APPLYING
Standardized Tests *Required:* SAT or ACT (for admission). *Recommended:* SAT Subject Tests (for admission).

Options: electronic application, early action, deferred entrance.

Application fee: $80.

Required: essay or personal statement, high school transcript, 3 letters of recommendation. *Recommended:* interview.

CONTACT
Undergraduate Admissions, Yale University, Yale University, PO Box 208234, New Haven, CT 06520. *Phone:* 203-432-9300. *E-mail:* student.questions@yale.edu.

DELAWARE

Delaware State University
Dover, Delaware
http://www.desu.edu/

- **State-supported** university, founded 1891, part of Delaware Higher Education Commission
- **Small-town** 400-acre campus
- **Coed** 4,051 undergraduate students, 88% full-time, 65% women, 35% men
- **Moderately difficult** entrance level, 45% of applicants were admitted

UNDERGRAD STUDENTS
3,571 full-time, 480 part-time. 51% are from out of state; 75% Black or African American, non-Hispanic/Latino; 7% Hispanic/Latino; 0.6% Asian, non-Hispanic/Latino; 0.1% Native Hawaiian or other Pacific Islander, non-Hispanic/Latino; 0.3% American Indian or Alaska Native, non-Hispanic/Latino; 5% Two or more races, non-Hispanic/Latino; 0.4% Race/ethnicity unknown; 2% international; 5% transferred in; 58% live on campus.

Freshmen:
Admission: 7,636 applied, 3,450 admitted, 951 enrolled. *Average high school GPA:* 3.1. *Test scores:* SAT evidence-based reading and writing scores over 500: 31%; SAT math scores over 500: 25%; ACT scores over 18: 63%; SAT evidence-based reading and writing scores over 600: 2%; SAT math scores over 600: 5%; ACT scores over 24: 7%; SAT math scores over 700: 1%; ACT scores over 30: 2%.

Retention: 71% of full-time freshmen returned.

ACADEMICS
Calendar: semesters. *Degrees:* certificates, bachelor's, master's, and doctoral.

Special study options: academic remediation for entering students, accelerated degree program, adult/continuing education programs, advanced placement credit, cooperative education, distance learning, double majors, English as a second language, honors programs, independent study, internships, off-campus study, part-time degree program, services for LD students, study abroad, summer session for credit. *ROTC:* Army (b), Air Force (b).

Computers: Students can access the following: campus intranet, computer help desk, free student e-mail accounts, online (class) grades, online (class) registration, online (class) schedules. Campuswide network is available. Wireless service is available via classrooms, computer centers, computer labs, learning centers, libraries, student centers.
Library: William C. Jason Library.

STUDENT LIFE
Housing options: coed, men-only, women-only. Campus housing is university owned. Freshman applicants given priority for college housing.

Activities and organizations: drama/theater group, student-run newspaper, radio and television station, choral group, marching band, SGA, NPHC, Women's Senate, RHA, Men's Council, national fraternities, national sororities.

Athletics Member NCAA. All Division I except football (Division I-AA). *Intercollegiate sports:* baseball M(s), basketball M(s)/W(s), bowling W(s), cheerleading M(s)/W(s), cross-country running M(s)/W(s), equestrian sports W(s), soccer W(s), softball W(s), tennis W(s), track and field M(s)/W(s), volleyball W(s). *Intramural sports:* basketball M/W, football M(c)/W(c), soccer M/W, softball M/W, swimming and diving M/W, table tennis M/W, tennis M/W, track and field M/W, volleyball W.

Campus security: 24-hour emergency response devices and patrols, student patrols, late-night transport/escort service, controlled dormitory access.

Student services: health clinic, personal/psychological counseling, women's center.

COSTS & FINANCIAL AID
Costs (2017–18) *Tuition:* state resident $7868 full-time, $280 per credit hour part-time; nonresident $16,904 full-time, $638 per credit hour part-time. Full-time tuition and fees vary according to course load, reciprocity agreements, and student level. Part-time tuition and fees vary according to course load, reciprocity agreements, and student level. *Required fees:* $300 per term part-time. *Room and board:* $11,054; room only: $6976. Room and board charges vary according to board plan and housing facility. *Payment plans:* installment, deferred payment. *Waivers:* senior citizens and employees or children of employees.

Financial Aid Of all full-time matriculated undergraduates who enrolled in 2015, 3,301 applied for aid, 2,971 were judged to have need, 276 had their need fully met. In 2015, 91 non-need-based awards were made. *Average percent of need met:* 47. *Average financial aid package:* $10,617. *Average need-based loan:* $3883. *Average need-based gift aid:* $5250. *Average non-need-based aid:* $4530. *Average indebtedness upon graduation:* $36,812.

APPLYING
Options: electronic application, early admission.

Application fee: $35.

Required: high school transcript, minimum 2.0 GPA.

CONTACT
Mrs. Erin Hill, Executive Director for Admissions, Delaware State University, 1200 North DuPont Highway, Dover, DE 19901-2277. *Phone:* 302-857-6351. *Toll-free phone:* 800-845-2544. *Fax:* 302-857-6352. *E-mail:* ehill@desu.edu.

Goldey-Beacom College
Wilmington, Delaware
http://www.gbc.edu/

CONTACT
Mr. Larry Eby, Director of Admissions, Goldey-Beacom College, 4701 Limestone Road, Wilmington, DE 19808. *Phone:* 302-225-6289. *Toll-free phone:* 800-833-4877. *Fax:* 302-996-5408. *E-mail:* admissions@gbc.edu.

Strayer University–Christiana Campus
Newark, Delaware
http://www.strayer.edu/delaware/christiana/

CONTACT
Strayer University–Christiana Campus, 240 Continental Drive, Suite 108, Newark, DE 19713. *Toll-free phone:* 888-311-0355.

University of Delaware
Newark, Delaware
http://www.udel.edu/

- **State-related** university, founded 1743
- **Small-town** 1000-acre campus with easy access to Philadelphia, Baltimore
- **Coed**
- **Moderately difficult** entrance level

FACULTY
Student/faculty ratio: 13:1.

ACADEMICS
Calendar: 4-1-4. *Degrees:* associate, bachelor's, master's, and doctoral.
Library: Hugh Morris Library.

STUDENT LIFE
Housing options: on-campus residence required for freshman year; coed, women-only, special housing for students with disabilities. Campus housing is university owned. Freshman campus housing is guaranteed.

Activities and organizations: drama/theater group, student-run newspaper, radio station, choral group, marching band, national fraternities, national sororities.

Athletics Member NCAA. All Division I except football (Division I-AA).

Campus security: 24-hour emergency response devices and patrols, student patrols, late-night transport/escort service, controlled dormitory access.

Student services: health clinic, personal/psychological counseling, women's center.

COSTS & FINANCIAL AID

Costs (2017–18) *Tuition:* state resident $11,870 full-time, $495 per credit hour part-time; nonresident $31,860 full-time, $1328 per credit hour part-time. *Required fees:* $1290 full-time. *Room and board:* $12,332; room only: $7462. Room and board charges vary according to board plan and housing facility.

Financial Aid Of all full-time matriculated undergraduates who enrolled in 2016, 11,568 applied for aid, 8,260 were judged to have need, 830 had their need fully met. In 2016, 3407 non-need-based awards were made. *Average percent of need met:* 55. *Average financial aid package:* $13,017. *Average need-based loan:* $4483. *Average need-based gift aid:* $9506. *Average non-need-based aid:* $7523. *Average indebtedness upon graduation:* $34,144. *Financial aid deadline:* 3/15.

APPLYING

Standardized Tests *Required:* SAT or ACT (for admission). *Required for some:* SAT Subject Tests (for admission). *Recommended:* SAT Subject Tests (for admission).

Options: electronic application, early admission, deferred entrance.

Application fee: $75.

Required: essay or personal statement, high school transcript, 1 letter of recommendation.

CONTACT

Dr. Douglas Zander, Director of Admissions, University of Delaware, 122 University Visitors Center, Newark, DE 19716. *Phone:* 302-831-8123. *Fax:* 302-831-6905. *E-mail:* admissions@udel.edu.

Wesley College
Dover, Delaware
http://www.wesley.edu/

CONTACT

Mr. Christopher Jester, Assistant Director of Undergraduate Admissions, Wesley College, 120 North State Street, Dover, DE 19901-3875. *Phone:* 302-736-2468. *Toll-free phone:* 800-937-5398. *E-mail:* christopher.jester@wesley.edu.

Wilmington University
New Castle, Delaware
http://www.wilmu.edu/
- **Independent** university, founded 1967
- **Suburban** 17-acre campus with easy access to Philadelphia
- **Endowment** $73.9 million
- **Coed** 8,440 undergraduate students, 36% full-time, 65% women, 35% men
- **Noncompetitive** entrance level, 99% of applicants were admitted

UNDERGRAD STUDENTS

3,037 full-time, 5,403 part-time. Students come from 45 states and territories; 74 other countries; 33% are from out of state; 21% Black or African American, non-Hispanic/Latino; 2% Hispanic/Latino; 2% Asian, non-Hispanic/Latino; 0.2% Native Hawaiian or other Pacific Islander, non-Hispanic/Latino; 1% American Indian or Alaska Native, non-Hispanic/Latino; 6% Two or more races, non-Hispanic/Latino; 23% Race/ethnicity unknown; 2% international; 12% transferred in.

Freshmen:
Admission: 1,662 applied, 1,648 admitted, 746 enrolled.
Retention: 64% of full-time freshmen returned.

FACULTY
Total: 2,466, 5% full-time.
Student/faculty ratio: 17:1.

ACADEMICS
Calendar: semesters. *Degrees:* certificates, associate, bachelor's, master's, doctoral, post-master's, and postbachelor's certificates.

Special study options: academic remediation for entering students, accelerated degree program, adult/continuing education programs, cooperative education, distance learning, double majors, English as a second language, external degree program, independent study, internships, part-time degree program, study abroad, summer session for credit. *ROTC:* Army (c), Air Force (c).

Computers: 600 computers/terminals are available on campus for general student use. Students can access the following: free student e-mail accounts, online (class) grades, online (class) registration, online (class) schedules. Campuswide network is available. Wireless service is available via entire campus.

Library: Robert C. and Dorothy M. Peoples Library plus 1 other. *Books:* 104,530 (physical), 179,000 (digital/electronic); *Serial titles:* 50 (physical), 98,000 (digital/electronic).

STUDENT LIFE

Housing options: college housing not available.

Activities and organizations: Student Government Association, Green Team, Photography Club, WU Student United Way, Wildcat Cheerleaders.

Athletics Member NCAA. All Division II. *Intercollegiate sports:* baseball M(s), basketball M(s)/W(s), bowling W(s), cross-country running M(s)/W(s), softball W(s), volleyball W(s).

Campus security: 24-hour emergency response devices and patrols, late-night transport/escort service.

COSTS & FINANCIAL AID

Costs (2017–18) *Tuition:* $8712 full-time, $363 per credit part-time. Full-time tuition and fees vary according to location. Part-time tuition and fees vary according to location. *Required fees:* $50 full-time, $25 per term part-time. *Payment plan:* installment. *Waivers:* employees or children of employees.

Financial Aid Of all full-time matriculated undergraduates who enrolled in 2004, 1,217 applied for aid, 900 were judged to have need. 25 Federal Work-Study jobs (averaging $2000). In 2004, 74 non-need-based awards were made. *Average percent of need met:* 48. *Average financial aid package:* $5770. *Average need-based loan:* $3889. *Average need-based gift aid:* $2464. *Average non-need-based aid:* $1100. *Average indebtedness upon graduation:* $17,486.

APPLYING

Options: electronic application, early admission, deferred entrance.

Application fee: $25.

Required: high school transcript. *Recommended:* interview.

Application deadlines: rolling (freshmen), rolling (transfers).

Notification: continuous (freshmen), continuous (transfers).

CONTACT

Ms. Laura Morris, Director of Admissions, Wilmington University, 320 North DuPont Highway, New Castle, DE 19720-6491. *Phone:* 302-295-1179. *Toll-free phone:* 877-967-5464. *E-mail:* undergradadmissions@wilmu.edu.

DISTRICT OF COLUMBIA

American University
Washington, District of Columbia
http://www.american.edu/
- **Independent Methodist** university, founded 1893
- **Suburban** 84-acre campus with easy access to Washington, DC
- **Endowment** $622.0 million
- **Coed** 8,123 undergraduate students, 96% full-time, 62% women, 38% men
- **Very difficult** entrance level, 29% of applicants were admitted

UNDERGRAD STUDENTS

7,764 full-time, 359 part-time. Students come from 54 states and territories; 97 other countries; 82% are from out of state; 7% Black or African American, non-Hispanic/Latino; 14% Hispanic/Latino; 7% Asian, non-Hispanic/Latino; 0.1% American Indian or Alaska Native, non-Hispanic/Latino; 4% Two or more races, non-Hispanic/Latino; 3% Race/ethnicity unknown; 8% international; 2% transferred in.

Freshmen:
Admission: 18,699 applied, 5,498 admitted, 1,785 enrolled. *Average high school GPA:* 3.6. *Test scores:* SAT evidence-based reading and writing

scores over 500: 99%; SAT math scores over 500: 97%; ACT scores over 18: 100%; SAT evidence-based reading and writing scores over 600: 82%; SAT math scores over 600: 60%; ACT scores over 24: 91%; SAT evidence-based reading and writing scores over 700: 22%; SAT math scores over 700: 11%; ACT scores over 30: 34%.

Retention: 90% of full-time freshmen returned.

FACULTY

Total: 1,466, 54% full-time, 51% with terminal degrees.
Student/faculty ratio: 11:1.

ACADEMICS

Calendar: semesters. *Degrees:* certificates, associate, bachelor's, master's, doctoral, and postbachelor's certificates.

Special study options: accelerated degree program, advanced placement credit, cooperative education, distance learning, double majors, English as a second language, honors programs, independent study, internships, off-campus study, part-time degree program, services for LD students, student-designed majors, study abroad, summer session for credit. *ROTC:* Army (c), Air Force (c).

Unusual degree programs: 3-2 engineering with University of Maryland, College Park.

Computers: 700 computers/terminals and 7,000 ports are available on campus for general student use. Students can access the following: campus intranet, computer help desk, free student e-mail accounts, online (class) grades, online (class) registration, online (class) schedules, online e-support through learning management system. Campuswide network is available. 100% of college-owned or -operated housing units are wired for high-speed Internet access. Wireless service is available via entire campus.

Library: Bender Library plus 1 other. *Books:* 700,000 (physical), 800,000 (digital/electronic); *Serial titles:* 650 (physical), 145,000 (digital/electronic); *Databases:* 500. Study areas open 24 hours, 5–7 days a week; students can reserve study rooms.

STUDENT LIFE

Housing options: coed, special housing for students with disabilities. Campus housing is university owned and leased by the school. Freshman campus housing is guaranteed.

Activities and organizations: drama/theater group, student-run newspaper, radio and television station, choral group, Kennedy Political Union, Habitat for Humanity, Student government, Amnesty International, Multiple Ethnic and religious organizations, national fraternities, national sororities.

Athletics Member NCAA. All Division I. *Intercollegiate sports:* basketball M(s)/W(s), cross-country running M(s)/W(s), field hockey W(s), lacrosse W(s), soccer M(s)/W(s), swimming and diving M/W, track and field M(s)/W(s), volleyball W(s), wrestling M(s). *Intramural sports:* baseball M(c)/W(c), basketball M/W, crew M(c)/W(c), equestrian sports M(c)/W(c), field hockey M(c)/W(c), football M/W, golf M(c)/W(c), gymnastics M(c)/W(c), ice hockey M(c)/W(c), lacrosse M(c)/W(c), rugby M(c)/W(c), sailing M(c)/W(c), soccer M/W, table tennis M/W, tennis M/W, track and field M/W, ultimate Frisbee M(c)/W(c), volleyball M/W, water polo M/W, weight lifting M.

Campus security: 24-hour emergency response devices and patrols, late-night transport/escort service, controlled dormitory access, e-mail and text emergency notification system, special events security, safe ride home program, self defense training.

Student services: health clinic, personal/psychological counseling, women's center.

COSTS & FINANCIAL AID

Costs (2018–19) *Comprehensive fee:* $63,339 includes full-time tuition ($47,640), mandatory fees ($819), and room and board ($14,880). Full-time tuition and fees vary according to course load. Part-time tuition: $1587 per credit hour. Part-time tuition and fees vary according to course load. *Required fees:* $170 per term part-time. *College room only:* $9996. Room and board charges vary according to board plan, housing facility, and location. *Payment plans:* tuition prepayment, installment. *Waivers:* employees or children of employees.

Financial Aid Of all full-time matriculated undergraduates who enrolled in 2017, 4,583 applied for aid, 3,868 were judged to have need, 716 had their need fully met. 1,700 Federal Work-Study jobs (averaging $1530). In 2017, 604 non-need-based awards were made. *Average percent of need*

met: 72. *Average financial aid package:* $33,279. *Average need-based loan:* $4506. *Average need-based gift aid:* $26,625. *Average non-need-based aid:* $14,165. *Financial aid deadline:* 1/15.

APPLYING

Options: electronic application, early admission, early decision, deferred entrance.

Application fee: $70.

Required: essay or personal statement, high school transcript. *Recommended:* 2 letters of recommendation.

Application deadlines: 1/15 (freshmen), 3/1 (transfers).

Early decision deadline: 11/15 (for plan 1), 1/15 (for plan 2).

Notification: 4/1 (freshmen), continuous (transfers), 12/31 (early decision plan 1), 2/15 (early decision plan 2).

CONTACT

Dr. Andrea Felder, Asst Vice Provost, Undergraduate Admissions, American University, 4400 Massachusetts Avenue, NW, Washington, DC 20016-8001. *Phone:* 202-885-6000. *E-mail:* admissions@american.edu.

The Catholic University of America
Washington, District of Columbia
http://www.catholic.edu/

- **Independent** university, founded 1887, affiliated with Roman Catholic Church
- **Urban** 176-acre campus with easy access to Washington DC
- **Coed** 3,313 undergraduate students, 96% full-time, 54% women, 46% men

UNDERGRAD STUDENTS

3,194 full-time, 119 part-time. Students come from 49 states and territories; 28 other countries; 99% are from out of state; 5% Black or African American, non-Hispanic/Latino; 13% Hispanic/Latino; 4% Asian, non-Hispanic/Latino; 0.2% American Indian or Alaska Native, non-Hispanic/Latino; 5% Two or more races, non-Hispanic/Latino; 3% Race/ethnicity unknown; 6% international; 3% transferred in; 58% live on campus.

Freshmen:
Admission: 831 enrolled. *Average high school GPA:* 3.4. *Test scores:* SAT evidence-based reading and writing scores over 500: 95%; SAT math scores over 500: 94%; ACT scores over 18: 100%; SAT evidence-based reading and writing scores over 600: 61%; SAT math scores over 600: 49%; ACT scores over 24: 74%; SAT evidence-based reading and writing scores over 700: 17%; SAT math scores over 700: 11%; ACT scores over 30: 23%.

Retention: 86% of full-time freshmen returned.

FACULTY

Total: 755, 53% full-time, 50% with terminal degrees.
Student/faculty ratio: 7:1.

ACADEMICS

Calendar: semesters. *Degrees:* certificates, bachelor's, master's, doctoral, post-master's, and postbachelor's certificates.

Special study options: accelerated degree program, adult/continuing education programs, advanced placement credit, cooperative education, distance learning, double majors, English as a second language, external degree program, honors programs, independent study, internships, off-campus study, part-time degree program, services for LD students, study abroad, summer session for credit. *ROTC:* Army (c), Navy (c), Air Force (c).

Unusual degree programs: 3-2 business administration; engineering; nursing; social work; architecture, accounting, education, psychology.

Computers: 542 computers/terminals and 13,403 ports are available on campus for general student use. Students can access the following: campus intranet, computer help desk, free student e-mail accounts, online (class) grades, online (class) registration, online (class) schedules. Campuswide network is available. 100% of college-owned or -operated housing units are wired for high-speed Internet access. Wireless service is available via entire campus.

Library: Mullen Library plus 1 other. *Books:* 734,247 (physical), 390,119 (digital/electronic); *Serial titles:* 342,482 (physical), 135,001 (digital/electronic); *Databases:* 482. Weekly public service hours: 102.

STUDENT LIFE

Housing options: on-campus residence required through sophomore year; men-only, women-only. Campus housing is university owned. Freshman campus housing is guaranteed.

Activities and organizations: drama/theater group, student-run newspaper, radio station, choral group, College Republicans, Habitat for Humanity, Student Nurse's Association, Cardinals for Life, College Democrats, national fraternities, national sororities.

Athletics Member NCAA. All Division III. *Intercollegiate sports:* baseball M, basketball M/W, cross-country running M/W, field hockey W, football M, lacrosse M/W, soccer M/W, softball W, swimming and diving M/W, tennis M/W, track and field M/W, volleyball W. *Intramural sports:* badminton M/W, basketball M/W, cheerleading M(c)/W(c), crew M(c)/W(c), football M, ice hockey M(c)/W(c), lacrosse M(c), racquetball M/W, rowing M(c)/W(c), rugby M(c)/W(c), sailing M(c)/W(c), soccer M/W, softball M/W, tennis M/W, track and field M/W, ultimate Frisbee M(c)/W(c), volleyball M/W.

Campus security: 24-hour emergency response devices and patrols, late-night transport/escort service, controlled dormitory access, controlled access of academic buildings.

Student services: health clinic, personal/psychological counseling, legal services.

COSTS & FINANCIAL AID

Costs (2017–18) *One-time required fee:* $440. *Comprehensive fee:* $58,376 includes full-time tuition ($43,300), mandatory fees ($760), and room and board ($14,316). Full-time tuition and fees vary according to program. Part-time tuition: $1715 per credit hour. Part-time tuition and fees vary according to course load and program. *Required fees:* $430 per year part-time. *Room and board:* Room and board charges vary according to board plan and housing facility. *Payment plan:* installment. *Waivers:* children of alumni and employees or children of employees.

Financial Aid Of all full-time matriculated undergraduates who enrolled in 2017, 2,141 applied for aid, 1,843 were judged to have need, 793 had their need fully met. 221 Federal Work-Study jobs (averaging $1824). In 2017, 1022 non-need-based awards were made. *Average percent of need met:* 81. *Average financial aid package:* $30,182. *Average need-based loan:* $4923. *Average need-based gift aid:* $26,356. *Average non-need-based aid:* $19,597. *Average indebtedness upon graduation:* $36,542. *Financial aid deadline:* 4/10.

APPLYING

Required: essay or personal statement, high school transcript, 1 letter of recommendation. *Recommended:* minimum 3.0 GPA, interview.

CONTACT

James Dewey-Rosenfeld, Dean of Undergraduate Admission, The Catholic University of America, 102 Father O'Connell Hall, 620 Michigan Avenue, NE, Washington, DC 20064. *Phone:* 202-319-5305. *Toll-free phone:* 800-673-2772. *Fax:* 202-319-6533. *E-mail:* cua-admissions@cua.edu.

See below for display ad and page 1258 for the College Close-Up.

Gallaudet University

Washington, District of Columbia

http://www.gallaudet.edu/

- **Independent** university, founded 1864
- **Urban** 99-acre campus
- **Coed**
- **Moderately difficult** entrance level

FACULTY

Student/faculty ratio: 7:1.

ACADEMICS

Calendar: semesters. *Degrees:* bachelor's, master's, doctoral, post-master's, and postbachelor's certificates (Undergraduate programs are open primarily to the students with hearing-impairments).

Library: Merrill Learning Center. *Books:* 121,359 (physical), 547,506 (digital/electronic); *Serial titles:* 4,142 (physical), 71,930 (digital/electronic); *Databases:* 79. Weekly public service hours: 90; students can reserve study rooms.

STUDENT LIFE

Housing options: coed, special housing for students with disabilities. Campus housing is university owned.

Activities and organizations: drama/theater group, student-run newspaper, television station, Student Body Government, The Buff and Blue, Rainbow Society, Green Grow, national fraternities, national sororities.

Athletics Member NCAA. All Division III.

Campus security: 24-hour emergency response devices and patrols, late-night transport/escort service, controlled dormitory access.

Student services: health clinic, personal/psychological counseling.

COSTS & FINANCIAL AID

Costs (2017–18) *Comprehensive fee:* $30,088 includes full-time tuition ($16,032), mandatory fees ($526), and room and board ($13,530). Full-time tuition and fees vary according to course load. Part-time tuition: $668 per credit hour. Part-time tuition and fees vary according to course load. *College room only:* $7400. Room and board charges vary according to board plan and housing facility. *Payment plans:* installment, deferred payment.

Financial Aid Of all full-time matriculated undergraduates who enrolled in 2016, 985 applied for aid, 918 were judged to have need, 174 had their need fully met. In 2016, 40 non-need-based awards were made. *Average percent of need met:* 75. *Average financial aid package:* $21,472. *Average need-based loan:* $4115. *Average need-based gift aid:* $20,580. *Average non-need-based aid:* $5812. *Average indebtedness upon graduation:* $15,767.

APPLYING

Standardized Tests *Required:* SAT or ACT (for admission). *Recommended:* ACT (for admission).

Options: electronic application, deferred entrance.

Application fee: $50.

Required: essay or personal statement, high school transcript, 2 letters of recommendation, audiogram. *Required for some:* interview.

CONTACT

Gallaudet University, 800 Florida Avenue, NE, Washington, DC 20002-3625. *Phone:* 202-651-5750. *Toll-free phone:* 800-995-0550.

Georgetown University
Washington, District of Columbia
http://www.georgetown.edu/

- **Independent Roman Catholic (Jesuit)** university, founded 1789
- **Urban** 104-acre campus with easy access to Washington, DC
- **Coed** 7,463 undergraduate students, 94% full-time, 56% women, 44% men
- **Most difficult** entrance level, 16% of applicants were admitted

UNDERGRAD STUDENTS

6,987 full-time, 476 part-time. Students come from 52 states and territories; 105 other countries; 98% are from out of state; 6% Black or African American, non-Hispanic/Latino; 10% Hispanic/Latino; 9% Asian, non-Hispanic/Latino; 0.1% Native Hawaiian or other Pacific Islander, non-Hispanic/Latino; 4% Two or more races, non-Hispanic/Latino; 4% Race/ethnicity unknown; 14% international; 3% transferred in; 78% live on campus.

Freshmen:

Admission: 21,462 applied, 3,365 admitted, 1,597 enrolled. *Test scores:* SAT evidence-based reading and writing scores over 500: 100%; SAT math scores over 500: 100%; ACT scores over 18: 100%; SAT evidence-based reading and writing scores over 600: 95%; SAT math scores over 600: 91%; ACT scores over 24: 97%; SAT evidence-based reading and writing scores over 700: 67%; SAT math scores over 700: 63%; ACT scores over 30: 80%.

Retention: 96% of full-time freshmen returned.

FACULTY

Total: 2,166, 48% full-time, 51% with terminal degrees.

Student/faculty ratio: 11:1.

ACADEMICS

Calendar: semesters. *Degrees:* certificates, bachelor's, master's, doctoral, post-master's, and postbachelor's certificates.

Special study options: academic remediation for entering students, adult/continuing education programs, advanced placement credit, distance learning, double majors, English as a second language, honors programs, independent study, internships, off-campus study, part-time degree program, services for LD students, student-designed majors, study abroad, summer session for credit. *ROTC:* Army (b), Navy (c), Air Force (c).

Unusual degree programs: 3-2 foreign service.

Computers: 430 computers/terminals and 1,000 ports are available on campus for general student use. Students can access the following: computer help desk, free student e-mail accounts, online (class) grades, online (class) registration, online (class) schedules. Campuswide network is available. 100% of college-owned or -operated housing units are wired for high-speed Internet access. Wireless service is available via entire campus.

Library: Joseph Mark Lauinger Memorial Library plus 6 others. *Books:* 2.4 million (physical), 1.9 million (digital/electronic); *Serial titles:* 52,479 (physical), 275,836 (digital/electronic); *Databases:* 1,556. Weekly public service hours: 100; study areas open 24 hours, 5–7 days a week; students can reserve study rooms.

STUDENT LIFE

Housing options: on-campus residence required through sophomore year; coed, special housing for students with disabilities. Campus housing is university owned. Freshman campus housing is guaranteed.

Activities and organizations: drama/theater group, student-run newspaper, radio and television station, choral group, Georgetown University Student Association (Student Government), International Relations Club, College Democrats, Georgetown University Grilling Society, Black Student Alliance.

Athletics Member NCAA. All Division I except football (Division I-AA). *Intercollegiate sports:* baseball M(s), basketball M(s)/W(s), crew M(s)/W(s), cross-country running M(s)/W(s), field hockey W(s), golf M(s)/W(s), ice hockey M(c), lacrosse M(s)/W(s), rugby M(c)/W(c), sailing M/W, soccer M(s)/W(s), softball W(s), swimming and diving M/W(s), tennis M/W(s), track and field M(s)/W(s), ultimate Frisbee M(c)/W(c), volleyball M(c)/W(s), water polo M(c). *Intramural sports:* basketball M/W, cross-country running M/W, football M/W, golf M/W, racquetball M/W, soccer M/W, softball M/W, squash M/W, table tennis M/W, tennis M/W, track and field M/W, ultimate Frisbee M, volleyball M/W.

Campus security: 24-hour emergency response devices and patrols, late-night transport/escort service, controlled dormitory access, student guards at residence halls and academic facilities.

Student services: health clinic, personal/psychological counseling, women's center.

COSTS & FINANCIAL AID

Costs (2017–18) *Comprehensive fee:* $68,970 includes full-time tuition ($51,720), mandatory fees ($580), and room and board ($16,670). Full-time tuition and fees vary according to course load and program. Part-time tuition: $2155 per credit hour. Part-time tuition and fees vary according to course load and program. *College room only:* $11,000. Room and board charges vary according to board plan and housing facility. *Payment plan:* installment.

Financial Aid Of all full-time matriculated undergraduates who enrolled in 2017, 3,564 applied for aid, 2,659 were judged to have need, 2,659 had their need fully met. 2,620 Federal Work-Study jobs (averaging $2890). *Average percent of need met:* 100. *Average financial aid package:* $46,571. *Average need-based loan:* $4115. *Average need-based gift aid:* $72,258. *Average indebtedness upon graduation:* $23,387. *Financial aid deadline:* 2/1.

APPLYING

Standardized Tests *Required:* SAT or ACT (for admission). *Recommended:* SAT Subject Tests (for admission).

Options: electronic application, early action, deferred entrance.

Application fee: $75.

Required: essay or personal statement, high school transcript, 2 letters of recommendation, interview.

Application deadlines: 1/10 (freshmen), 3/1 (transfers), 11/1 (early action).

Notification: 4/1 (freshmen), 6/1 (transfers), 12/15 (early action).

CONTACT
Dean Charles A. Deacon, Dean of Undergraduate Admissions, Georgetown University, 37th and O Street, NW, Washington, DC 20057. *Phone:* 202-687-3600. *Fax:* 202-687-5084.

The George Washington University
Washington, District of Columbia
http://www.gwu.edu/
- **Independent** university, founded 1821
- **Urban** 36-acre campus
- **Coed** 11,999 undergraduate students, 91% full-time, 60% women, 40% men
- **Most difficult** entrance level, 41% of applicants were admitted

UNDERGRAD STUDENTS
10,893 full-time, 1,106 part-time. Students come from 57 states and territories; 97 other countries; 97% are from out of state; 7% Black or African American, non-Hispanic/Latino; 10% Hispanic/Latino; 10% Asian, non-Hispanic/Latino; 0.1% Native Hawaiian or other Pacific Islander, non-Hispanic/Latino; 0.1% American Indian or Alaska Native, non-Hispanic/Latino; 4% Two or more races, non-Hispanic/Latino; 6% Race/ethnicity unknown; 11% international; 6% transferred in; 61% live on campus.

Freshmen:
Admission: 26,987 applied, 11,059 admitted, 2,610 enrolled. *Test scores:* SAT evidence-based reading and writing scores over 500: 100%; SAT math scores over 500: 100%; ACT scores over 18: 100%; SAT evidence-based reading and writing scores over 600: 91%; SAT math scores over 600: 89%; ACT scores over 24: 98%; SAT evidence-based reading and writing scores over 700: 41%; SAT math scores over 700: 41%; ACT scores over 30: 63%.
Retention: 91% of full-time freshmen returned.

ACADEMICS
Calendar: semesters. *Degrees:* certificates, associate, bachelor's, master's, doctoral, post-master's, and postbachelor's certificates.
Special study options: accelerated degree program, adult/continuing education programs, advanced placement credit, cooperative education, distance learning, double majors, honors programs, independent study, internships, off-campus study, part-time degree program, services for LD students, student-designed majors, study abroad, summer session for credit. *ROTC:* Army (c), Navy (b), Air Force (c).
Unusual degree programs: 3-2 business administration; engineering; chemical toxicology, art therapy, economics, engineering economics, operations research.
Computers: Campuswide network is available.
Library: Gelman Library.

STUDENT LIFE
Housing options: on-campus residence required through sophomore year; coed, women-only. Campus housing is university owned. Freshman campus housing is guaranteed.
Activities and organizations: drama/theater group, student-run newspaper, radio and television station, choral group, marching band, Program Board, Student Association, Residence Hall Association, College Democrats, College Republicans, national fraternities, national sororities.
Athletics Member NCAA. All Division I. *Intercollegiate sports:* baseball M(s), basketball M(s)/W(s), crew M(s)/W(s), cross-country running M(s)/W(s), golf M(s), gymnastics W(s), soccer M(s)/W(s), swimming and diving M(s)/W(s), tennis M(s)/W(s), volleyball W(s), water polo M(s). *Intramural sports:* badminton M(c)/W(c), basketball M/W, bowling M(c)/W(c), equestrian sports M(c)/W(c), fencing M(c)/W(c), football M/W, lacrosse M(c), racquetball M/W, rugby M(c), sailing M(c)/W(c), soccer M/W, softball M/W, squash M(c)/W, swimming and diving M/W, tennis M/W, volleyball M(c)/W, water polo M/W.
Campus security: 24-hour emergency response devices and patrols, late-night transport/escort service, controlled dormitory access.

Student services: health clinic, personal/psychological counseling, legal services.

COSTS & FINANCIAL AID
Costs (2017–18) *Comprehensive fee:* $66,518 includes full-time tuition ($53,435), mandatory fees ($83), and room and board ($13,000). Full-time tuition and fees vary according to student level. Part-time tuition: $1520 per credit hour. Part-time tuition and fees vary according to course load. No tuition increase for student's term of enrollment. *Required fees:* $3 per credit hour part-time. *College room only:* $8900. Room and board charges vary according to housing facility. *Payment plan:* installment. *Waivers:* employees or children of employees.
Financial Aid Of all full-time matriculated undergraduates who enrolled in 2015, 5,607 applied for aid, 4,611 were judged to have need, 2,171 had their need fully met. In 2015, 2718 non-need-based awards were made. *Average percent of need met:* 87. *Average financial aid package:* $43,674. *Average need-based loan:* $5809. *Average need-based gift aid:* $29,433. *Average non-need-based aid:* $19,541. *Average indebtedness upon graduation:* $33,305. *Financial aid deadline:* 2/1.

APPLYING
Standardized Tests *Required for some:* SAT or ACT (for admission), SAT and SAT Subject Tests or ACT (for admission).
Options: electronic application, early admission, early decision, deferred entrance.
Application fee: $75.
Required: essay or personal statement, high school transcript, 2 letters of recommendation.
Early decision deadline: 11/1.
Notification: 4/1 (freshmen), continuous (transfers), 4/1 (early decision).

CONTACT
The George Washington University, 2121 I Street, NW, Washington, DC 20052. *Phone:* 202-994-6040.

Howard University
Washington, District of Columbia
http://www.howard.edu/
CONTACT
Tammy McCants, Associate Director of Admissions, Howard University, 2400 Sixth Street N.W., Suite 111, Washington, DC 20059. *Phone:* 202-806-2763. *Toll-free phone:* 800-822-6363. *Fax:* 202-806-4465. *E-mail:* admission@howard.edu.

National Intelligence University
Washington, District of Columbia
http://www.ni-u.edu/
CONTACT
National Intelligence University, Washington, DC 20340-5100.

Strayer University–Takoma Park Campus
Washington, District of Columbia
http://www.strayer.edu/district-columbia/takoma-park/
CONTACT
Strayer University–Takoma Park Campus, 6830 Laurel Street, NW, Washington, DC 20012. *Toll-free phone:* 888-311-0355.

Strayer University–Washington Campus
Washington, District of Columbia
http://www.strayer.edu/district-columbia/washington/
CONTACT
Strayer University–Washington Campus, 1133 15th Street, NW, Washington, DC 20025. *Toll-free phone:* 888-311-0355.

Trinity Washington University
Washington, District of Columbia
http://www.trinitydc.edu/

CONTACT
Director of Admissions, Trinity Washington University, 125 Michigan Avenue, NE, Washington, DC 20017-1094. *Phone:* 800-492-6882. *Toll-free phone:* 800-IWANTTC. *E-mail:* admissions@trinitydc.edu.

University of the District of Columbia
Washington, District of Columbia
http://www.udc.edu/

CONTACT
Ms. Nicole L. Daniels, Director of Undergraduate Recruitment and Admissions, University of the District of Columbia, 4200 Connecticut Avenue NW, Washington, DC 20008. *Phone:* 202-274-6430. *Fax:* 202-274-5553. *E-mail:* nicole.daniels@udc.edu.

University of the Potomac
Washington, District of Columbia
http://www.potomac.edu/

- **Proprietary** comprehensive, founded 1991
- **Urban** campus with easy access to Washington DC; Tysons, VA
- **Coed** 109 undergraduate students, 100% full-time, 37% women, 63% men
- **Noncompetitive** entrance level, 96% of applicants were admitted

UNDERGRAD STUDENTS
109 full-time. Students come from 12 states and territories; 10 other countries; 60% are from out of state; 43% Black or African American, non-Hispanic/Latino; 3% Hispanic/Latino; 0.9% American Indian or Alaska Native, non-Hispanic/Latino; 0.9% Two or more races, non-Hispanic/Latino; 2% Race/ethnicity unknown; 35% international; 11% transferred in.

Freshmen:
Admission: 114 applied, 109 admitted, 23 enrolled.
Retention: 67% of full-time freshmen returned.

FACULTY
Total: 52, 6% full-time, 35% with terminal degrees.
Student/faculty ratio: 5:1.

ACADEMICS
Calendar: 6 8-week terms. *Degrees:* certificates, associate, bachelor's, and master's.

Special study options: adult/continuing education programs, distance learning, external degree program, honors programs, part-time degree program, services for LD students.

Computers: 28 computers/terminals are available on campus for general student use. Students can access the following: campus intranet, free student e-mail accounts, online (class) grades, online (class) schedules, student portal, access to learning management system. Campuswide network is available. Wireless service is available via entire campus.

Library: Learning Resource Center - Washington Campus plus 1 other. *Books:* 4,500 (physical); *Serial titles:* 20 (physical), 5 (digital/electronic); *Databases:* 5. Weekly public service hours: 35.

STUDENT LIFE
Housing options: college housing not available.
Campus security: late-night transport/escort service.

COSTS
Costs (2017–18) *One-time required fee:* $125. *Tuition:* $12,984 full-time, $541 per credit hour part-time. No tuition increase for student's term of enrollment. *Required fees:* $900 full-time, $450 per term part-time. *Payment plans:* tuition prepayment, installment.

APPLYING
Options: electronic application.
Required: interview.

Application deadlines: rolling (freshmen), rolling (transfers).
Notification: continuous (freshmen), continuous (transfers).

CONTACT
Gina Rice-Holland, Director of Admissions, University of the Potomac, 1401 H Street NW, Suite 100, Washington, DC 20005. *Phone:* 202-274-2338. *Toll-free phone:* 888-686-0876. *E-mail:* gina.riceholland@potomac.edu.

FLORIDA

Adventist University of Health Sciences
Orlando, Florida
http://www.adu.edu/

- **Independent** comprehensive, founded 1992
- **Urban** 9-acre campus with easy access to Orlando
- **Endowment** $7.8 million
- **Coed** 1,491 undergraduate students, 39% full-time, 80% women, 20% men
- **Minimally difficult** entrance level, 97% of applicants were admitted

UNDERGRAD STUDENTS
575 full-time, 916 part-time. Students come from 44 states and territories; 13 other countries; 23% are from out of state; 16% Black or African American, non-Hispanic/Latino; 30% Hispanic/Latino; 6% Asian, non-Hispanic/Latino; 0.4% Native Hawaiian or other Pacific Islander, non-Hispanic/Latino; 0.2% American Indian or Alaska Native, non-Hispanic/Latino; 3% Two or more races, non-Hispanic/Latino; 4% Race/ethnicity unknown; 0.9% international; 12% transferred in; 10% live on campus.

Freshmen:
Admission: 317 applied, 307 admitted, 107 enrolled. *Test scores:* SAT evidence-based reading and writing scores over 500: 53%; SAT math scores over 500: 37%; ACT scores over 18: 62%; SAT evidence-based reading and writing scores over 600: 10%; SAT math scores over 600: 4%; ACT scores over 24: 10%; SAT evidence-based reading and writing scores over 700: 2%; SAT math scores over 700: 1%.
Retention: 79% of full-time freshmen returned.

FACULTY
Total: 242, 37% full-time, 31% with terminal degrees.
Student/faculty ratio: 8:1.

ACADEMICS
Calendar: trimesters. *Degrees:* certificates, associate, bachelor's, master's, doctoral, and postbachelor's certificates.

Special study options: academic remediation for entering students, distance learning, double majors, freshman honors college, independent study, internships, services for LD students, summer session for credit.

Computers: 47 computers/terminals are available on campus for general student use. Students can access the following: campus intranet, computer help desk, free student e-mail accounts, online (class) grades, online (class) registration, online (class) schedules, Online Registration. Campuswide network is available. Wireless service is available via entire campus.

Library: R. A. Williams Library. *Books:* 11,997 (physical), 19,145 (digital/electronic); *Serial titles:* 27 (physical), 27,744 (digital/electronic); *Databases:* 119. Weekly public service hours: 65; students can reserve study rooms.

STUDENT LIFE
Housing options: coed. Campus housing is leased by the school.

Activities and organizations: drama/theater group, choral group, Student Nursing Association, Student Occupational Therapy Association, Pre Physician Assistant, Pre Medical School, Campus Ministries.

Campus security: 24-hour emergency response devices and patrols, late-night transport/escort service, controlled dormitory access.

Student services: personal/psychological counseling.

COSTS & FINANCIAL AID

Costs (2018–19) *Tuition:* $14,550 full-time, $485 per credit hour part-time. *Required fees:* $600 full-time, $300 per term part-time. *Room only:* $4200. *Payment plans:* installment, deferred payment. *Waivers:* employees or children of employees.

Financial Aid *Financial aid deadline:* 7/22.

APPLYING

Standardized Tests *Required for some:* SAT or ACT (for admission), TOEFL for non-native English Speakers.

Options: electronic application, early admission, early action, deferred entrance.

Application fee: $20.

Required: high school transcript, minimum 2.5 GPA.

Application deadlines: 7/1 (freshmen), 7/1 (transfers), 5/1 (early action).

Notification: continuous until 7/15 (freshmen), continuous until 7/15 (transfers).

CONTACT

Adventist University of Health Sciences, 671 Winyah Drive, Orlando, FL 32803. *Phone:* 407-303-7742. *Toll-free phone:* 800-500-7747.

Altierus Career College

Tampa, Florida
http://www.altierus.edu/

CONTACT

Altierus Career College, 3319 West Hillsborough Avenue, Tampa, FL 33614. *Phone:* 813-879-6000 Ext. 129.

American College for Medical Careers

Orlando, Florida
http://www.acmc.edu/

CONTACT

American College for Medical Careers, 5959 Lake Ellenor Drive, Orlando, FL 32809. *Toll-free phone:* 888-599-7887.

Argosy University, Sarasota

Sarasota, Florida
http://www.argosy.edu/locations/sarasota/

CONTACT

Argosy University, Sarasota, 5250 17th Street, Sarasota, FL 34235. *Phone:* 941-379-0404. *Toll-free phone:* 800-331-5995.

Argosy University, Tampa

Tampa, Florida
http://www.argosy.edu/locations/tampa/

CONTACT

Argosy University, Tampa, 1403 North Howard Avenue, Tampa, FL 33607. *Phone:* 813-393-5290. *Toll-free phone:* 800-850-6488.

The Art Institute of Fort Lauderdale

Fort Lauderdale, Florida
http://www.artinstitutes.edu/fortlauderdale/

CONTACT

The Art Institute of Fort Lauderdale, 1799 Southeast 17th Street, Fort Lauderdale, FL 33316. *Phone:* 954-463-3000. *Toll-free phone:* 800-275-7603.

The Art Institute of Tampa, a branch of Miami International University of Art & Design

Tampa, Florida
http://www.artinstitutes.edu/tampa/

CONTACT

The Art Institute of Tampa, a branch of Miami International University of Art & Design, Parkside at Tampa Bay Park, 4401 North Himes Avenue, Suite 150, Tampa, FL 33614. *Phone:* 813-873-2112. *Toll-free phone:* 866-703-3277.

Atlantis University

Miami, Florida
http://www.atlantisuniversity.edu/

CONTACT

Atlantis University, 1442 Biscayne Boulevard, Miami, FL 33132.

Ave Maria University

Ave Maria, Florida
http://www.avemaria.edu/

CONTACT

Ave Maria University, 5050 Ave Maria Boulevard, Ave Maria, FL 34142. *Phone:* 239-280-2487. *Toll-free phone:* 877-283-8648. *Fax:* 239-280-2559.

★ The Baptist College of Florida

Graceville, Florida
http://www.baptistcollege.edu/

- **Independent Southern Baptist** comprehensive, founded 1943
- **Small-town** 250-acre campus
- **Endowment** $7.8 million
- **Coed** 427 undergraduate students, 66% full-time, 42% women, 58% men
- **Noncompetitive** entrance level, 62% of applicants were admitted

UNDERGRAD STUDENTS

280 full-time, 147 part-time. Students come from 16 states and territories; 1 other country; 25% are from out of state; 7% Black or African American, non-Hispanic/Latino; 4% Hispanic/Latino; 0.2% Asian, non-Hispanic/Latino; 0.7% Native Hawaiian or other Pacific Islander, non-Hispanic/Latino; 0.5% American Indian or Alaska Native, non-Hispanic/Latino; 2% Two or more races, non-Hispanic/Latino; 10% Race/ethnicity unknown; 0.2% international; 9% transferred in; 39% live on campus.

Freshmen:

Admission: 113 applied, 70 admitted, 39 enrolled.

Retention: 74% of full-time freshmen returned.

FACULTY

Total: 67, 39% full-time, 48% with terminal degrees.

Student/faculty ratio: 9:1.

ACADEMICS

Calendar: semesters. *Degrees:* associate, bachelor's, and master's.

Special study options: academic remediation for entering students, advanced placement credit, distance learning, double majors, independent study, internships, part-time degree program, services for LD students, summer session for credit.

Computers: 25 computers/terminals are available on campus for general student use. Students can access the following: free student e-mail accounts, online (class) grades, online (class) registration, online (class) schedules. Campuswide network is available. Wireless service is available via entire campus.

Library: Ida J. MacMillan Library plus 1 other. *Books:* 90,006 (physical), 88,931 (digital/electronic); *Serial titles:* 5,602 (physical), 5,602 (digital/electronic); *Databases:* 16. Weekly public service hours: 66.

STUDENT LIFE

Housing options: on-campus residence required through sophomore year; men-only, women-only, special housing for students with disabilities. Campus housing is university owned. Freshman campus housing is guaranteed.

Activities and organizations: drama/theater group, choral group, Baptist Collegiate Ministry, College Choir, AACC.

Athletics *Intramural sports:* basketball M/W, fencing M/W, football M/W, soccer M/W, softball M/W, ultimate Frisbee M/W, volleyball M/W.

Campus security: student patrols, patrols by police officers 11 pm to 7 am.

Student services: personal/psychological counseling.

COSTS & FINANCIAL AID

Costs (2017–18) *Comprehensive fee:* $15,238 includes full-time tuition ($10,200), mandatory fees ($900), and room and board ($4138). Full-time tuition and fees vary according to location and program. Part-time tuition: $340 per credit hour. Part-time tuition and fees vary according to location and program. *Required fees:* $30 per credit part-time. *Room and board:* Room and board charges vary according to board plan and housing facility. *Waivers:* employees or children of employees.

Financial Aid Of all full-time matriculated undergraduates who enrolled in 2016, 336 applied for aid, 295 were judged to have need, 9 had their need fully met. 24 Federal Work-Study jobs (averaging $2163). In 2016, 20 non-need-based awards were made. *Average percent of need met:* 41. *Average financial aid package:* $8517. *Average need-based loan:* $3520. *Average need-based gift aid:* $5993. *Average non-need-based aid:* $1872. *Average indebtedness upon graduation:* $24,444. *Financial aid deadline:* 4/15.

APPLYING

Standardized Tests *Required:* SAT or ACT (for admission).

Options: electronic application, deferred entrance.

Application fee: $25.

Required: essay or personal statement, high school transcript, minimum 2.5 GPA, 2 letters of recommendation, Christian/church member for 1 year minimum. *Recommended:* interview.

Application deadlines: 8/11 (freshmen), 8/11 (transfers).
Notification: continuous (freshmen), continuous (transfers).

CONTACT

The Baptist College of Florida, 5400 College Drive, Graceville, FL 32440. *Phone:* 850-263-3261 Ext. 460. *Toll-free phone:* 800-328-2660 Ext. 460.

Barry University
Miami Shores, Florida
http://www.barry.edu/

- **Independent Roman Catholic** university, founded 1940
- **Suburban** 122-acre campus with easy access to Miami
- **Coed** 3,505 undergraduate students, 85% full-time, 60% women, 40% men
- **Moderately difficult** entrance level, 85% of applicants were admitted

UNDERGRAD STUDENTS

2,991 full-time, 514 part-time. 20% are from out of state; 34% Black or African American, non-Hispanic/Latino; 34% Hispanic/Latino; 1% Asian, non-Hispanic/Latino; 0.2% Native Hawaiian or other Pacific Islander, non-Hispanic/Latino; 0.5% American Indian or Alaska Native, non-Hispanic/Latino; 1% Two or more races, non-Hispanic/Latino; 1% Race/ethnicity unknown; 8% international; 16% transferred in; 30% live on campus.

Freshmen:

Admission: 5,110 applied, 4,350 admitted, 604 enrolled. *Test scores:* SAT evidence-based reading and writing scores over 500: 43%; SAT math scores over 500: 28%; ACT scores over 18: 71%; SAT evidence-based reading and writing scores over 600: 4%; SAT math scores over 600: 2%; ACT scores over 24: 8%; SAT evidence-based reading and writing scores over 700: 1%; ACT scores over 30: 1%.

Retention: 61% of full-time freshmen returned.

FACULTY

Total: 735, 44% full-time.

Student/faculty ratio: 13:1.

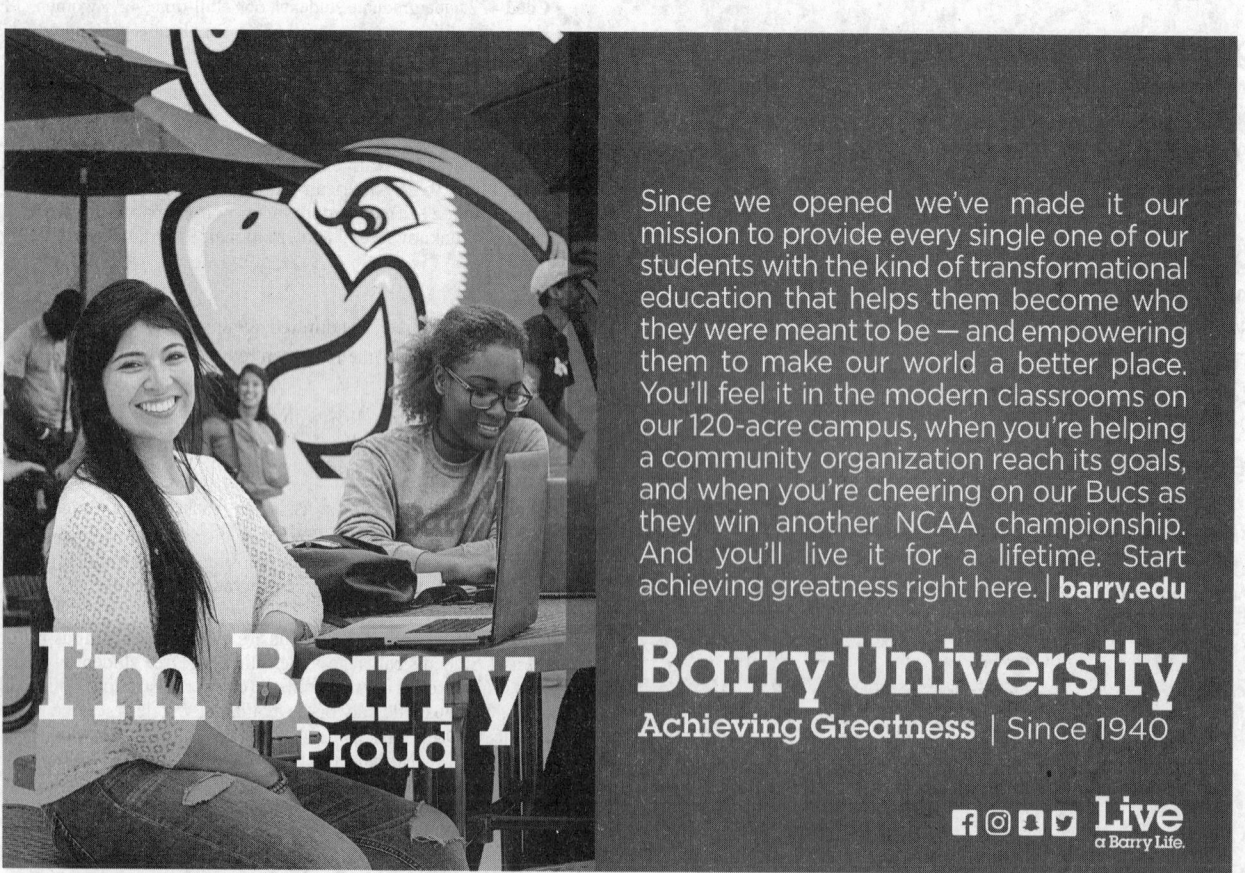

ACADEMICS

Calendar: semesters. *Degrees:* certificates, bachelor's, master's, doctoral, post-master's, and postbachelor's certificates.

Special study options: academic remediation for entering students, accelerated degree program, adult/continuing education programs, advanced placement credit, distance learning, double majors, English as a second language, honors programs, independent study, internships, off-campus study, part-time degree program, services for LD students, study abroad, summer session for credit. *ROTC:* Army (c), Air Force (c).

Unusual degree programs: 3-2 engineering with University of Miami.

Computers: 368 computers/terminals are available on campus for general student use. Students can access the following: campus intranet, computer help desk, free student e-mail accounts, online (class) grades, online (class) registration, online (class) schedules, learning management system. Campuswide network is available. Wireless service is available via computer centers, computer labs, learning centers, student centers.

Library: Monsignor William Barry Memorial Library plus 1 other.

STUDENT LIFE

Housing options: on-campus residence required for freshman year; coed, men-only, women-only, special housing for students with disabilities. Campus housing is university owned.

Activities and organizations: drama/theater group, student-run newspaper, radio and television station, choral group, Student Government Association, Campus Activities Board, SCUBA Society, Caribbean Students Association, Jamaican Association, national fraternities, national sororities.

Athletics Member NCAA. All Division II. *Intercollegiate sports:* baseball M(s), basketball M(s)/W(s), crew W(s), golf M(s)/W(s), soccer M(s)/W(s), softball W(s), tennis M(s)/W(s), volleyball W(s). *Intramural sports:* basketball M/W, football M/W, golf M/W, soccer M/W, softball M/W, volleyball M/W.

Campus security: 24-hour emergency response devices and patrols, late-night transport/escort service.

Student services: health clinic, personal/psychological counseling.

COSTS & FINANCIAL AID

Costs (2018–19) *Comprehensive fee:* $40,800 includes full-time tuition ($29,700) and room and board ($11,100). Part-time tuition: $925 per credit hour. Part-time tuition and fees vary according to course load. *Room and board:* Room and board charges vary according to housing facility. *Payment plans:* installment, deferred payment. *Waivers:* employees or children of employees.

Financial Aid Of all full-time matriculated undergraduates who enrolled in 2017, 2,325 applied for aid, 2,256 were judged to have need, 86 had their need fully met. In 2017, 259 non-need-based awards were made. *Average percent of need met:* 55. *Average financial aid package:* $22,133. *Average need-based loan:* $4290. *Average need-based gift aid:* $9369. *Average non-need-based aid:* $10,068. *Average indebtedness upon graduation:* $38,176.

APPLYING

Standardized Tests *Required:* SAT or ACT (for admission).

Options: electronic application, early admission, deferred entrance.

Application fee: $30.

Required: high school transcript, minimum 2.0 GPA. *Required for some:* essay or personal statement. *Recommended:* interview.

Application deadlines: rolling (freshmen), rolling (transfers).

Notification: continuous (freshmen), continuous (transfers).

CONTACT

Barry University, 11300 Northeast Second Avenue, Miami Shores, FL 33161-6695. *Phone:* 305-899-3394. *Toll-free phone:* 800-695-2279.

See previous page for display ad and page 1242 for the College Close-Up.

Beacon College

Leesburg, Florida

http://www.beaconcollege.edu/

- **Independent** 4-year, founded 1989
- **Small-town** 19-acre campus with easy access to Orlando
- **Endowment** $83,990
- **Coed** 348 undergraduate students, 99% full-time, 41% women, 59% men
- **Moderately difficult** entrance level, 53% of applicants were admitted

UNDERGRAD STUDENTS

344 full-time, 4 part-time. Students come from 37 states and territories; 3 other countries; 71% are from out of state; 15% Black or African American, non-Hispanic/Latino; 6% Hispanic/Latino; 3% Asian, non-Hispanic/Latino; 0.3% Native Hawaiian or other Pacific Islander, non-Hispanic/Latino; 0.6% American Indian or Alaska Native, non-Hispanic/Latino; 5% Two or more races, non-Hispanic/Latino; 1% international; 10% transferred in; 85% live on campus.

Freshmen:

Admission: 261 applied, 138 admitted, 82 enrolled. *Average high school GPA:* 2.9.

Retention: 68% of full-time freshmen returned.

FACULTY

Total: 37, 76% full-time, 54% with terminal degrees.

Student/faculty ratio: 11:1.

ACADEMICS

Calendar: semesters. *Degree:* bachelor's.

Special study options: academic remediation for entering students, adult/continuing education programs, advanced placement credit, cooperative education, double majors, honors programs, independent study, internships, services for LD students, study abroad, summer session for credit.

Computers: 150 computers/terminals and 450 ports are available on campus for general student use. Students can access the following: campus intranet, computer help desk, free student e-mail accounts, online (class) grades, online (class) schedules. Campuswide network is available. 100% of college-owned or -operated housing units are wired for high-speed Internet access. Wireless service is available via entire campus.

Library: Beacon College Library. *Books:* 11,113 (physical), 346,154 (digital/electronic); *Serial titles:* 40 (physical); *Databases:* 15. Weekly public service hours: 76; students can reserve study rooms.

STUDENT LIFE

Housing options: coed. Campus housing is university owned and leased by the school. Freshman campus housing is guaranteed.

Activities and organizations: drama/theater group, student-run radio station, Gamma Beta Phi, Performance Club, Psychology & Human Services Club, Nerd Culture Club, Equine Club, national fraternities, national sororities.

Campus security: 24-hour emergency response devices and patrols, student patrols, late-night transport/escort service.

Student services: health clinic, personal/psychological counseling.

COSTS & FINANCIAL AID

Costs (2017–18) *Comprehensive fee:* $48,878 includes full-time tuition ($37,788) and room and board ($11,090). Full-time tuition and fees vary according to course load. Part-time tuition: $1260 per credit hour. Part-time tuition and fees vary according to course load. *College room only:* $7048. Room and board charges vary according to housing facility. *Payment plan:* installment. *Waivers:* employees or children of employees.

Financial Aid Of all full-time matriculated undergraduates who enrolled in 2015, 137 applied for aid, 118 were judged to have need. In 2015, 67 non-need-based awards were made. *Average financial aid package:* $12,366. *Average need-based loan:* $3438. *Average need-based gift aid:* $18,625. *Average non-need-based aid:* $4470. *Average indebtedness upon graduation:* $27,000.

APPLYING

Options: electronic application, early admission, deferred entrance.

Application fee: $50.

Florida

COLLEGES AT-A-GLANCE

Required: high school transcript, 3 letters of recommendation, psycho-educational evaluation showing diagnosed learning disability or ADHD. *Recommended:* minimum 2.0 GPA, interview.

Application deadlines: rolling (freshmen), rolling (transfers).

Notification: 8/1 (freshmen), 8/1 (transfers).

CONTACT
Ms. Dale Herold, Vice President of Admissions and Enrollment Management, Beacon College, 105 East Main Street, Leesburg, FL 34748. *Phone:* 352-638-9778. *Fax:* 352-787-0796. *E-mail:* dherold@beaconcollege.edu.

Belhaven University
Orlando, Florida
http://orlando.belhaven.edu/

CONTACT
Jeremy Couch, Director of Admission, Belhaven University, 5200 Vineland Road, Suite 100, Orlando, FL 32811. *Phone:* 407-804-1424. *Toll-free phone:* 877-804-1424. *Fax:* 407-661-1732. *E-mail:* orlando@belhaven.edu.

Bethune-Cookman University
Daytona Beach, Florida
http://www.cookman.edu/

- **Independent Methodist** comprehensive, founded 1904
- **Urban** 60-acre campus with easy access to Orlando
- **Endowment** $47.9 million
- **Coed** 3,992 undergraduate students, 94% full-time, 62% women, 38% men
- **Minimally difficult** entrance level, 54% of applicants were admitted

UNDERGRAD STUDENTS
3,755 full-time, 237 part-time. Students come from 40 states and territories; 20 other countries; 27% are from out of state; 78% Black or African American, non-Hispanic/Latino; 3% Hispanic/Latino; 0.1% Asian, non-Hispanic/Latino; 0.1% American Indian or Alaska Native, non-Hispanic/Latino; 2% Two or more races, non-Hispanic/Latino; 14% Race/ethnicity unknown; 2% international; 3% transferred in; 66% live on campus.

Freshmen:
Admission: 11,652 applied, 6,326 admitted, 1,180 enrolled. *Average high school GPA:* 2.9. *Test scores:* ACT scores over 18: 32%; ACT scores over 24: 2%.

Retention: 67% of full-time freshmen returned.

FACULTY
Total: 278, 70% full-time.

Student/faculty ratio: 16:1.

ACADEMICS
Calendar: semesters. *Degrees:* bachelor's and master's.

Special study options: academic remediation for entering students, accelerated degree program, adult/continuing education programs, advanced placement credit, cooperative education, distance learning, double majors, honors programs, independent study, internships, part-time degree program, study abroad, summer session for credit. *ROTC:* Army (c), Air Force (c).

Unusual degree programs: engineering with Tuskegee University, University of Florida, Florida Atlantic University, Florida Agricultural and Mechanical University, University of Central Florida.

Computers: 846 computers/terminals and 1,471 ports are available on campus for general student use. Students can access the following: campus intranet, computer help desk, free student e-mail accounts, online (class) grades, online (class) registration, online (class) schedules. Campuswide network is available. 100% of college-owned or -operated housing units are wired for high-speed Internet access. Wireless service is available via entire campus.

Library: Carl S. Swisher Library plus 1 other. *Books:* 83,794 (physical), 269,009 (digital/electronic); *Serial titles:* 20 (physical), 36,000 (digital/electronic); *Databases:* 34. Weekly public service hours: 92; study areas open 24 hours, 5–7 days a week; students can reserve study rooms.

STUDENT LIFE
Housing options: on-campus residence required through sophomore year; coed, men-only, women-only. Campus housing is university owned. Freshman campus housing is guaranteed.

Activities and organizations: drama/theater group, student-run newspaper, radio station, choral group, marching band, National Council of Negro Women, Gamma Sigma Sigma Sorority, Phenomenal Woman Think Tank, What's Next Dance Company, NAACP, national fraternities, national sororities.

Athletics Member NCAA, NAIA. All NCAA Division I except football (Division I-AA). *Intercollegiate sports:* baseball M(s), basketball M(s)/W(s), bowling W(s), cheerleading W, cross-country running M(s)/W(s), golf M(s)/W(s), softball W(s), tennis M(s)/W(s), track and field M(s)/W(s), volleyball W(s). *Intramural sports:* basketball M/W, bowling M/W, football M, racquetball W, soccer M/W, table tennis W.

Campus security: 24-hour emergency response devices and patrols, student patrols, late-night transport/escort service.

Student services: health clinic, personal/psychological counseling.

COSTS & FINANCIAL AID
Costs (2018–19) *Comprehensive fee:* $23,322 includes full-time tuition ($13,440), mandatory fees ($970), and room and board ($8912). Part-time tuition: $560 per credit hour. Part-time tuition and fees vary according to course load. *Required fees:* $50 per credit hour part-time. *Room and board:* Room and board charges vary according to housing facility. *Payment plan:* installment. *Waivers:* employees or children of employees.

Financial Aid Of all full-time matriculated undergraduates who enrolled in 2017, 3,565 applied for aid, 3,443 were judged to have need, 161 had their need fully met. 200 Federal Work-Study jobs (averaging $2500). 100 state and other part-time jobs (averaging $2000). In 2017, 92 non-need-based awards were made. *Average percent of need met:* 53. *Average financial aid package:* $14,838. *Average need-based loan:* $4031. *Average need-based gift aid:* $11,272. *Average non-need-based aid:* $8557. *Average indebtedness upon graduation:* $40,601.

APPLYING
Standardized Tests *Required:* SAT or ACT (for admission).

Options: electronic application, early admission, deferred entrance.

Application fee: $25.

Required: high school transcript, minimum 2.3 GPA, 1 letter of recommendation, medical history. *Required for some:* interview. *Recommended:* essay or personal statement.

Application deadlines: 6/30 (freshmen), 6/30 (transfers).

Notification: continuous (freshmen), continuous (transfers).

CONTACT
Treran Porter, Director of Recruitment, Bethune-Cookman University, FL. *Phone:* 386-481-2603. *Toll-free phone:* 800-448-0228. *E-mail:* portert@cookman.edu.

Broward College
Fort Lauderdale, Florida
http://www.broward.edu/

CONTACT
Mr. Willie J. Alexander, Associate Vice President for Student Affairs/College Registrar, Broward College, 225 East Las Olas Boulevard, Fort Lauderdale, FL 33301. *Phone:* 954-201-7471. *Fax:* 954-201-7466. *E-mail:* walexand@broward.edu.

Carlos Albizu University, Miami Campus
Miami, Florida
http://www.albizu.edu/

CONTACT
Ms. Maria Elena Torres, Admissions Officer, Carlos Albizu University, Miami Campus, 2173 NW 99 Avenue, Miami, FL 33172. *Phone:* 305-593-1223 Ext. 3134. *Toll-free phone:* 888-GO-TO-CAU (in-state); 800-GO-TO-CAU (out-of-state). *Fax:* 305-593-1854. *E-mail:* matorres@albizu.edu.

Chamberlain College of Nursing

Jacksonville, Florida
http://www.chamberlain.edu/
- Proprietary 4-year
- Coed

FACULTY
Student/faculty ratio: 11:1.

ACADEMICS
Calendar: semesters. *Degree:* bachelor's.

STUDENT LIFE
Housing options: college housing not available.

COSTS
Costs (2017–18) *Tuition:* $18,900 full-time. *Required fees:* $600 full-time.

APPLYING
Standardized Tests *Required:* SAT or ACT (for admission).
Options: deferred entrance.
Application fee: $95.

CONTACT
Admissions, Chamberlain College of Nursing, 5200 Belfort Road, Jacksonville, FL 32256. *Phone:* 904-251-8100. *Toll-free phone:* 877-751-5783.

Chamberlain College of Nursing

Miramar, Florida
http://www.chamberlain.edu/
- Proprietary 4-year
- Coed
- Moderately difficult entrance level

FACULTY
Student/faculty ratio: 9:1.

ACADEMICS
Degree: bachelor's.

STUDENT LIFE
Housing options: college housing not available.

COSTS
Costs (2017–18) *Tuition:* $18,900 full-time. *Required fees:* $600 full-time.

APPLYING
Standardized Tests *Required:* SAT or ACT (for admission).
Options: deferred entrance.
Application fee: $95.

CONTACT
Director of Recruitment, Chamberlain College of Nursing, 2300 SW 145th Avenue, Miramar, FL 33027. *Phone:* 954-885-3510. *Toll-free phone:* 877-751-5783.

Chipola College

Marianna, Florida
http://www.chipola.edu/
- State-supported primarily 2-year, founded 1947
- Rural 105-acre campus
- Coed 2,104 undergraduate students, 41% full-time, 61% women, 39% men
- Noncompetitive entrance level

UNDERGRAD STUDENTS
859 full-time, 1,245 part-time. Students come from 7 states and territories; 6 other countries; 8% are from out of state; 15% Black or African American, non-Hispanic/Latino; 5% Hispanic/Latino; 0.7% Asian, non-Hispanic/Latino; 0.1% Native Hawaiian or other Pacific Islander, non-Hispanic/Latino; 1% American Indian or Alaska Native, non-Hispanic/Latino; 3% Two or more races, non-Hispanic/Latino; 1% Race/ethnicity unknown; 0.5% international; 7% transferred in.

Freshmen:
Admission: 264 enrolled. *Average high school GPA:* 2.5. *Test scores:* ACT scores over 18: 81%; ACT scores over 24: 25%; ACT scores over 30: 3%.

FACULTY
Total: 127, 31% full-time, 13% with terminal degrees.
Student/faculty ratio: 24:1.

ACADEMICS
Calendar: semesters. *Degrees:* certificates, associate, and bachelor's.

Special study options: academic remediation for entering students, adult/continuing education programs, advanced placement credit, distance learning, honors programs, independent study, part-time degree program, services for LD students, summer session for credit.

Computers: 80 computers/terminals are available on campus for general student use. Students can access the following: campus intranet, computer help desk, free student e-mail accounts, online (class) grades, online (class) registration, online (class) schedules. Campuswide network is available. 80% of college-owned or -operated housing units are wired for high-speed Internet access. Wireless service is available via classrooms, computer centers, computer labs, dorm rooms, learning centers, libraries, student centers.
Library: Chipola Library. *Books:* 30,000 (physical), 67,000 (digital/electronic); *Serial titles:* 150 (physical); *Databases:* 100. Weekly public service hours: 60; students can reserve study rooms.

STUDENT LIFE
Housing options: college housing not available.

Activities and organizations: drama/theater group, student-run newspaper, choral group.

Athletics Member NJCAA. *Intercollegiate sports:* baseball M(s), basketball M(s)/W(s), softball W(s).

Campus security: night security personnel.

COSTS
Costs (2018–19) *Tuition:* state resident $104 per credit hour part-time; nonresident $298 per credit hour part-time. Full-time tuition and fees vary according to degree level. Part-time tuition and fees vary according to degree level. *Waivers:* senior citizens.

APPLYING
Options: early admission.
Required: high school transcript.
Application deadlines: rolling (freshmen), rolling (transfers).
Notification: continuous (freshmen), continuous (transfers).

CONTACT
Mrs. Kathy L. Rehberg, Registrar, Chipola College, 3094 Indian Circle, Marianna, FL 32446-3065. *Phone:* 850-718-2233. *Fax:* 850-718-2287. *E-mail:* rehbergk@chipola.edu.

City College

Altamonte Springs, Florida
http://www.citycollege.edu/

CONTACT
Ms. Kimberly Bowden, Director of Admissions, City College, 177 Montgomery Road, Altamonte Springs, FL 32714. *Phone:* 352-335-4000. *Fax:* 352-335-4303. *E-mail:* kbowden@citycollege.edu.

City College

Fort Lauderdale, Florida
http://www.citycollege.edu/

CONTACT
City College, 2000 West Commercial Boulevard, Suite 200, Fort Lauderdale, FL 33309. *Phone:* 954-492-5353. *Toll-free phone:* 866-314-5681.

City College
Gainesville, Florida
http://www.citycollege.edu/

CONTACT
Admissions Office, City College, 7001 Northwest 4th Boulevard, Gainesville, FL 32607. *Phone:* 352-335-4000.

City College
Hollywood, Florida
http://www.citycollege.edu/

CONTACT
City College, 6565 Taft Street, Hollywood, FL 33024. *Toll-free phone:* 866-314-5681.

City College
Miami, Florida
http://www.citycollege.edu/

CONTACT
Admissions Office, City College, 9300 South Dadeland Boulevard, Suite PH, Miami, FL 33156. *Phone:* 305-666-9242. *Fax:* 305-666-9243.

College of Business and Technology–Main Campus
Miami, Florida
http://www.cbt.edu/

- **Proprietary** primarily 2-year, founded 1988
- **Urban** campus
- **Coed** 10 undergraduate students, 100% full-time, 80% women, 20% men
- **Minimally difficult** entrance level

UNDERGRAD STUDENTS
10 full-time. Students come from 1 other state; 100% Hispanic/Latino.

Freshmen:
Admission: 10 enrolled.

FACULTY
Total: 1, 100% full-time.
Student/faculty ratio: 10:1.

ACADEMICS
Calendar: semesters. *Degrees:* certificates, diplomas, associate, and bachelor's.
Special study options: academic remediation for entering students, adult/continuing education programs, cooperative education, English as a second language, independent study.
Computers: 15 computers/terminals are available on campus for general student use. Students can access the following: campus intranet, computer help desk, free student e-mail accounts, online (class) grades, online (class) schedules. Campuswide network is available. Wireless service is available via entire campus.
Library: CBT College-Miami Branch Library (Use Flagler). *Books:* 590 (physical); *Serial titles:* 8 (physical); *Databases:* 50.

STUDENT LIFE
Housing options: college housing not available.
Campus security: security guard posted at main entrance, local police department.

COSTS
Costs (2018–19) *Tuition:* $11,952 full-time. *Required fees:* $1500 full-time. *Payment plan:* installment.

APPLYING
Application fee: $25.
Required: high school transcript, interview.

CONTACT
College of Business and Technology–Main Campus, 8700 West Flagler Street, Suite 420, Miami, FL 33174. *Phone:* 305-273-4499 Ext. 1100.

College of Business and Technology–Miami Gardens
Miami Gardens, Florida
http://www.cbt.edu/

- **Proprietary** primarily 2-year, founded 2012
- **Urban** campus with easy access to Miami
- **Coed** 108 undergraduate students, 84% full-time, 28% women, 56% men
- **Minimally difficult** entrance level

UNDERGRAD STUDENTS
91 full-time. Students come from 1 other state; 18% Black or African American, non-Hispanic/Latino; 81% Hispanic/Latino.

Freshmen:
Admission: 16 enrolled.

FACULTY
Total: 15, 20% full-time, 13% with terminal degrees.
Student/faculty ratio: 15:1.

ACADEMICS
Calendar: semesters. *Degrees:* certificates, diplomas, associate, and bachelor's.
Special study options: academic remediation for entering students, adult/continuing education programs, cooperative education, independent study, services for LD students.
Computers: 50 computers/terminals are available on campus for general student use. Students can access the following: campus intranet, computer help desk, free student e-mail accounts, online (class) grades, online (class) schedules. Campuswide network is available. Wireless service is available via entire campus.
Library: CBT College–Miami Gardens Library. *Books:* 1,085 (physical); *Serial titles:* 18 (physical); *Databases:* 50.

STUDENT LIFE
Housing options: college housing not available.
Campus security: local police department.

COSTS
Costs (2018–19) *Tuition:* $11,952 full-time. *Required fees:* $1500 full-time. *Payment plan:* installment.

APPLYING
Application fee: $25.
Required: high school transcript, interview.

CONTACT
College of Business and Technology–Miami Gardens, 5190 NW 167 Street, Miami Gardens, FL 33014. *Phone:* 305-273-4499 Ext. 1100.

College of Central Florida
Ocala, Florida
http://www.cf.edu/

- **State and locally supported** primarily 2-year, founded 1957, part of Florida Community College System
- **Small-town** 139-acre campus
- **Endowment** $65.4 million
- **Coed** 7,931 undergraduate students, 38% full-time, 63% women, 37% men
- **Noncompetitive** entrance level, 55% of applicants were admitted

UNDERGRAD STUDENTS
3,036 full-time, 4,895 part-time. 16% are from out of state.

Freshmen:
Admission: 4,416 applied, 2,430 admitted, 1,503 enrolled.

FACULTY
Total: 374, 37% full-time, 10% with terminal degrees.

ACADEMICS
Calendar: semesters. *Degrees:* certificates, diplomas, associate, and bachelor's.
Special study options: academic remediation for entering students, adult/continuing education programs, advanced placement credit,

cooperative education, distance learning, English as a second language, freshman honors college, honors programs, independent study, internships, part-time degree program, services for LD students, summer session for credit.

Computers: 2,500 computers/terminals are available on campus for general student use. Students can access the following: campus intranet, computer help desk, online (class) grades, online (class) registration, online (class) schedules. Campuswide network is available. Wireless service is available via classrooms, computer centers, computer labs, learning centers, libraries, student centers.

Library: Clifford B. Stearns Learning Resources Center. *Books:* 75,935 (physical), 43,910 (digital/electronic); *Databases:* 152. Students can reserve study rooms.

STUDENT LIFE
Housing options: college housing not available.

Activities and organizations: drama/theater group, student-run newspaper, choral group, Inspirational Choir, Model United Nations, Performing Arts, Phi Theta Kappa (PTK), Student Nurses Association.

Athletics Member NJCAA. *Intercollegiate sports:* baseball M(s), basketball M(s)/W(s), softball W(s), volleyball W(s). *Intramural sports:* bowling M/W.

Campus security: 24-hour emergency response devices and patrols, student patrols, late-night transport/escort service.

Student services: personal/psychological counseling.

COSTS & FINANCIAL AID
Costs (2017–18) *Tuition:* state resident $5044 full-time, $107 per credit hour part-time; nonresident $20,252 full-time, $422 per credit hour part-time. Full-time tuition and fees vary according to course level, degree level, program, and student level. Part-time tuition and fees vary according to course level, degree level, program, and student level. *Waivers:* employees or children of employees.

Financial Aid *Average indebtedness upon graduation:* $2164.

APPLYING
Options: electronic application, early admission.
Application fee: $30.
Required: high school transcript.
Application deadlines: rolling (freshmen), rolling (transfers).
Notification: continuous (freshmen), continuous (transfers).

CONTACT
Ms. Devona Sewell, Registrar, Admission and Records, College of Central Florida, 3001 SW College Road, Ocala, FL 34474. *Phone:* 352-237-2111 Ext. 1398. *Fax:* 352-873-5882. *E-mail:* sewelld@cf.edu.

Daytona State College

Daytona Beach, Florida
http://www.daytonastate.edu/

- **State-supported** primarily 2-year, founded 1958, part of Florida College System
- **Suburban** 115-acre campus with easy access to Orlando
- **Endowment** $12.9 million
- **Coed** 13,141 undergraduate students, 39% full-time, 60% women, 40% men
- **Noncompetitive** entrance level

UNDERGRAD STUDENTS
5,185 full-time, 7,956 part-time. Students come from 38 states and territories; 27 other countries; 1% are from out of state; 12% Black or African American, non-Hispanic/Latino; 17% Hispanic/Latino; 2% Asian, non-Hispanic/Latino; 0.2% Native Hawaiian or other Pacific Islander, non-Hispanic/Latino; 0.2% American Indian or Alaska Native, non-Hispanic/Latino; 3% Two or more races, non-Hispanic/Latino; 1% Race/ethnicity unknown; 0.4% international; 4% transferred in.

Freshmen:
Admission: 1,346 enrolled.

FACULTY
Total: 916, 31% full-time, 16% with terminal degrees.

Student/faculty ratio: 16:1.

ACADEMICS
Calendar: semesters. *Degrees:* certificates, diplomas, associate, and bachelor's.

Special study options: academic remediation for entering students, adult/continuing education programs, advanced placement credit, cooperative education, distance learning, English as a second language, external degree program, freshman honors college, honors programs, independent study, internships, off-campus study, part-time degree program, services for LD students, study abroad, summer session for credit. *ROTC:* Army (c), Air Force (c).

Computers: 3,200 computers/terminals are available on campus for general student use. Students can access the following: campus intranet, computer help desk, free student e-mail accounts, online (class) grades, online (class) registration, online (class) schedules. Campuswide network is available. Wireless service is available via entire campus.

Library: Mary Karl Memorial Learning Resources Center plus 1 other. *Books:* 40,415 (physical), 185,001 (digital/electronic); *Serial titles:* 221 (physical), 46,685 (digital/electronic); *Databases:* 100. Weekly public service hours: 68; students can reserve study rooms.

STUDENT LIFE
Housing options: college housing not available.

Activities and organizations: drama/theater group, student-run newspaper, choral group, Phi Theta Kappa International Honors Society, Student Government Association, Student Occupational Therapy Club, Business Club, Student Paralegal Club, national fraternities, national sororities.

Athletics Member NJCAA. *Intercollegiate sports:* baseball M(s), basketball M(s)/W(s), golf W(s), soccer M(s)/W(s), softball W(s), volleyball W(s). *Intramural sports:* basketball M/W, football M/W, soccer M/W, table tennis M/W, volleyball M/W.

Campus security: 24-hour emergency response devices and patrols, late-night transport/escort service, emergency alert system capable of delivering text messages, voice calls, and email messages to college email accounts.

Student services: personal/psychological counseling, women's center.

COSTS & FINANCIAL AID
Costs (2018–19) *Tuition:* state resident $3071 full-time, $102 per credit hour part-time; nonresident $11,960 full-time, $399 per credit hour part-time. Full-time tuition and fees vary according to course level and course load. Part-time tuition and fees vary according to course level and course load. *Required fees:* $38 full-time, $1 per credit hour part-time. *Payment plan:* installment. *Waivers:* employees or children of employees.

Financial Aid Of all full-time matriculated undergraduates who enrolled in 2016, 131 Federal Work-Study jobs (averaging $1978). *Average need-based gift aid:* $1870.

APPLYING
Options: electronic application, early admission, deferred entrance.
Required: high school transcript.
Application deadlines: rolling (freshmen), rolling (transfers).
Notification: continuous (freshmen), continuous (transfers).

CONTACT
Dr. Karen Sanders, Director of Admissions and Recruitment, Daytona State College, 1200 International Speedway Boulevard, Daytona Beach, FL 32114. *Phone:* 386-506-3050. *E-mail:* karen.sanders@daytonastate.edu.

DeVry University–Jacksonville Campus

Jacksonville, Florida
http://www.devry.edu/

CONTACT
Admissions Office, DeVry University–Jacksonville Campus, 5200 Belfort Road, Suite 175, Jacksonville, FL 32256-6040. *Phone:* 904-367-4942. *Toll-free phone:* 866-338-7934.

DeVry University–Miramar Campus

Miramar, Florida

http://www.devry.edu/

- **Proprietary** comprehensive, founded 2002, part of DeVry University
- **Coed**
- **Minimally difficult** entrance level

FACULTY
Student/faculty ratio: 18:1.

ACADEMICS
Calendar: semesters. *Degrees:* associate, bachelor's, master's, and postbachelor's certificates.

STUDENT LIFE
Housing options: college housing not available.

COSTS & FINANCIAL AID
Costs (2017–18) *Tuition:* $14,728 full-time. *Required fees:* $500 full-time.

Financial Aid Of all full-time matriculated undergraduates who enrolled in 2007, 204 applied for aid, 197 were judged to have need, 2 had their need fully met. In 2007, 35 non-need-based awards were made. *Average percent of need met:* 38. *Average financial aid package:* $12,172. *Average need-based loan:* $7414. *Average need-based gift aid:* $7044. *Average non-need-based aid:* $12,256. *Average indebtedness upon graduation:* $51,131.

APPLYING
Options: deferred entrance.

Application fee: $30.

Required: high school transcript, interview.

CONTACT
DeVry University–Miramar Campus, 2300 Southwest 145th Avenue, Miramar, FL 33027. *Phone:* 954-499-9775. *Toll-free phone:* 866-338-7934.

DeVry University–Orlando Campus

Orlando, Florida

http://www.devry.edu/

- **Proprietary** comprehensive, founded 2000, part of DeVry University
- **Urban** campus
- **Coed**
- **Minimally difficult** entrance level

FACULTY
Student/faculty ratio: 31:1.

ACADEMICS
Calendar: semesters. *Degrees:* associate, bachelor's, master's, and postbachelor's certificates.
Library: Learning Resource Center.

STUDENT LIFE
Housing options: college housing not available.

COSTS & FINANCIAL AID
Costs (2017–18) *Tuition:* $14,728 full-time. *Required fees:* $500 full-time.

Financial Aid Of all full-time matriculated undergraduates who enrolled in 2007, 314 applied for aid, 294 were judged to have need, 2 had their need fully met. In 2007, 35 non-need-based awards were made. *Average percent of need met:* 33. *Average financial aid package:* $10,774. *Average need-based loan:* $7062. *Average need-based gift aid:* $5608. *Average non-need-based aid:* $18,240. *Average indebtedness upon graduation:* $23,511.

APPLYING
Options: deferred entrance.

Application fee: $30.

Required: high school transcript, interview.

CONTACT
DeVry University–Orlando Campus, 7352 Greenbriar Parkway, Orlando, FL 32819. *Phone:* 407-345-2800. *Toll-free phone:* 866-338-7934.

Eastern Florida State College

Cocoa, Florida

http://www.easternflorida.edu/

CONTACT
Ms. Stephanie Burnette, Registrar, Eastern Florida State College, 1519 Clearlake Road, Cocoa, FL 32922-6597. *Phone:* 321-433-7271. *Fax:* 321-433-7172. *E-mail:* cocoaadmissions@brevardcc.edu.

Eckerd College

St. Petersburg, Florida

http://www.eckerd.edu/

- **Independent Presbyterian** 4-year, founded 1958
- **Suburban** 188-acre campus with easy access to Tampa
- **Endowment** $55.9 million
- **Coed** 1,957 undergraduate students, 98% full-time, 66% women, 34% men
- **Moderately difficult** entrance level, 73% of applicants were admitted

UNDERGRAD STUDENTS
1,909 full-time, 48 part-time. Students come from 46 states and territories; 42 other countries; 78% are from out of state; 3% Black or African American, non-Hispanic/Latino; 9% Hispanic/Latino; 2% Asian, non-Hispanic/Latino; 0.2% Native Hawaiian or other Pacific Islander, non-Hispanic/Latino; 0.3% American Indian or Alaska Native, non-Hispanic/Latino; 3% Two or more races, non-Hispanic/Latino; 0.7% Race/ethnicity unknown; 4% international; 2% transferred in; 87% live on campus.

Freshmen:
Admission: 4,525 applied, 3,291 admitted, 561 enrolled. *Average high school GPA:* 3.4. *Test scores:* SAT evidence-based reading and writing scores over 500: 94%; SAT math scores over 500: 85%; ACT scores over 18: 99%; SAT evidence-based reading and writing scores over 600: 47%; SAT math scores over 600: 31%; ACT scores over 24: 68%; SAT evidence-based reading and writing scores over 700: 7%; SAT math scores over 700: 5%; ACT scores over 30: 18%.
Retention: 81% of full-time freshmen returned.

FACULTY
Total: 184, 80% full-time, 77% with terminal degrees.
Student/faculty ratio: 12:1.

ACADEMICS
Calendar: 4-1-4. *Degree:* bachelor's.

Special study options: accelerated degree program, adult/continuing education programs, advanced placement credit, double majors, external degree program, honors programs, independent study, internships, off-campus study, part-time degree program, services for LD students, student-designed majors, study abroad, summer session for credit. *ROTC:* Army (c), Air Force (c).

Unusual degree programs: 3-2 engineering with Columbia University.

Computers: 300 computers/terminals and 2,000 ports are available on campus for general student use. Students can access the following: campus intranet, computer help desk, free student e-mail accounts, online (class) grades, online (class) registration, online (class) schedules, free computer repair shop. Campuswide network is available. 100% of college-owned or -operated housing units are wired for high-speed Internet access. Wireless service is available via entire campus.
Library: Peter Armacost Library. *Books:* 155,959 (physical), 167,858 (digital/electronic); *Serial titles:* 972 (physical), 101,999 (digital/electronic); *Databases:* 199.

STUDENT LIFE
Housing options: on-campus residence required for freshman year; coed, women-only. Campus housing is university owned. Freshman campus housing is guaranteed.

Activities and organizations: drama/theater group, student-run newspaper, radio and television station, choral group, Marine Science Club, Water Search and Rescue Team, The Current (student newspaper), A cappella Vocal Group, Organization of Students.

Athletics Member NCAA. All Division II. *Intercollegiate sports:* baseball M(s), basketball M(s)/W(s), golf M(s)/W(s), sailing M/W, soccer

M(s)/W(s), softball W(s), tennis M(s)/W(s), volleyball W(s). *Intramural sports:* baseball M, basketball M/W, bowling M/W, cheerleading M(c)/W(c), equestrian sports M(c)/W(c), field hockey M(c)/W(c), football M(c)/W(c), golf M(c)/W(c), lacrosse M(c)/W(c), rugby M(c)/W(c), sailing M/W, soccer M(c)/W(c), softball M/W, swimming and diving M(c)/W(c), table tennis M/W, tennis M(c)/W(c), ultimate Frisbee M(c)/W(c), volleyball M/W.

Campus security: 24-hour emergency response devices and patrols, student patrols, late-night transport/escort service, controlled dormitory access.

Student services: health clinic, personal/psychological counseling, women's center.

COSTS & FINANCIAL AID
Costs (2018–19) *Comprehensive fee:* $55,206 includes full-time tuition ($42,428), mandatory fees ($616), and room and board ($12,162). *College room only:* $6362. Room and board charges vary according to board plan and housing facility. *Payment plan:* installment. *Waivers:* employees or children of employees.

Financial Aid Of all full-time matriculated undergraduates who enrolled in 2017, 1,316 applied for aid, 1,158 were judged to have need, 550 had their need fully met. 917 Federal Work-Study jobs (averaging $2000). In 2017, 607 non-need-based awards were made. *Average percent of need met:* 88. *Average financial aid package:* $36,810. *Average need-based loan:* $4476. *Average need-based gift aid:* $25,494. *Average non-need-based aid:* $17,555. *Average indebtedness upon graduation:* $33,484.

APPLYING
Standardized Tests *Required:* SAT or ACT (for admission). *Recommended:* SAT Subject Tests (for admission).

Options: electronic application, early action, deferred entrance.

Application fee: $40.

Required: essay or personal statement, high school transcript. *Recommended:* interview.

Application deadlines: rolling (freshmen), rolling (transfers), 11/15 (early action).

Notification: continuous (freshmen), continuous (transfers), 12/15 (early action).

CONTACT
Ms. Lucille Lopez, Campus Visit Coordinator, Eckerd College, 4200 54th Avenue South, St. Petersburg, FL 33711. *Phone:* 727-864-8331. *Toll-free phone:* 800-456-9009. *Fax:* 727-866-2304. *E-mail:* admissions@eckerd.edu.

Edward Waters College
Jacksonville, Florida
http://www.ewc.edu/

CONTACT
Edward Waters College, 1658 Kings Road, Jacksonville, FL 32209-6199. *Phone:* 904-470-8202. *Toll-free phone:* 888-898-3191.

★ Embry-Riddle Aeronautical University–Daytona
Daytona Beach, Florida
http://www.daytonabeach.erau.edu/
- **Independent** university, founded 1926
- **Suburban** 289-acre campus with easy access to Orlando
- **Coed** 5,729 undergraduate students, 94% full-time, 22% women, 78% men
- **Moderately difficult** entrance level, 71% of applicants were admitted

UNDERGRAD STUDENTS
5,378 full-time, 351 part-time. Students come from 54 states and territories; 64% are from out of state; 5% Black or African American, non-Hispanic/Latino; 7% Hispanic/Latino; 5% Asian, non-Hispanic/Latino; 0.3% Native Hawaiian or other Pacific Islander, non-Hispanic/Latino; 0.2% American Indian or Alaska Native, non-Hispanic/Latino; 7% Two or more races, non-Hispanic/Latino; 7% Race/ethnicity unknown; 12% international; 5% transferred in; 40% live on campus.

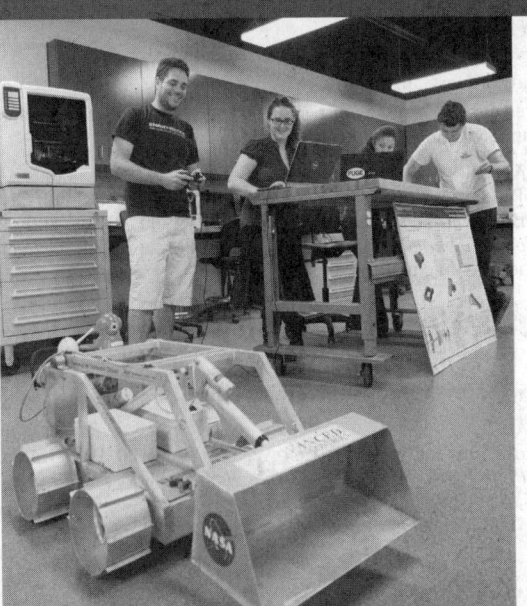
A ★ indicates that the school has detailed information with a Premium Profile on Petersons.com.

Freshmen:

Admission: 4,564 applied, 3,239 admitted, 1,357 enrolled. *Average high school GPA:* 3.7. *Test scores:* SAT evidence-based reading and writing scores over 500: 92%; SAT math scores over 500: 92%; ACT scores over 18: 97%; SAT evidence-based reading and writing scores over 600: 52%; SAT math scores over 600: 54%; ACT scores over 24: 65%; SAT evidence-based reading and writing scores over 700: 9%; SAT math scores over 700: 14%; ACT scores over 30: 17%.
Retention: 80% of full-time freshmen returned.

FACULTY
Total: 432, 75% full-time, 63% with terminal degrees.

ACADEMICS
Calendar: semesters. *Degrees:* associate, bachelor's, master's, and doctoral.

Special study options: academic remediation for entering students, accelerated degree program, advanced placement credit, cooperative education, double majors, English as a second language, honors programs, internships, part-time degree program, services for LD students, study abroad, summer session for credit. *ROTC:* Army (b), Navy (b), Air Force (b).

Computers: Students can access the following: campus intranet, computer help desk, free student e-mail accounts, online (class) grades, online (class) registration, online (class) schedules. Campuswide network is available. 100% of college-owned or -operated housing units are wired for high-speed Internet access. Wireless service is available via entire campus.

Library: Jack R. Hunt Memorial Library. *Books:* 53,612 (physical), 92,114 (digital/electronic); *Serial titles:* 459 (physical), 69,595 (digital/electronic); *Databases:* 98. Students can reserve study rooms.

STUDENT LIFE
Housing options: on-campus residence required for freshman year; coed. Campus housing is university owned. Freshman campus housing is guaranteed.

Activities and organizations: drama/theater group, student-run newspaper, radio station, choral group, Eagle Wing, Future Professional Pilots Association, African Student Association, Caribbean Student Association, Sigma Gamma Tau, national fraternities, national sororities.

Athletics Member NCAA, NAIA. All NCAA Division II except golf (Division I). *Intercollegiate sports:* baseball M(s), basketball M(s)/W(s), cheerleading M/W, cross-country running M(s)/W(s), golf M(s)/W(s), lacrosse M(s)/W(s), rowing M(s)/W(s), soccer M(s)/W(s), softball W(s), tennis M(s)/W(s), track and field M(s)/W(s), volleyball W(s). *Intramural sports:* archery M(c)/W(c), basketball M(c)/W(c), equestrian sports M(c)/W(c), football M/W, golf M/W, ice hockey M(c), lacrosse M(c), racquetball M(c)/W(c), rowing M(c)/W(c), rugby M(c), soccer M/W, softball M/W, swimming and diving M(c)/W(c), table tennis M/W, tennis M/W, ultimate Frisbee M(c)/W(c), volleyball M/W.

Campus security: 24-hour emergency response devices and patrols, student patrols, late-night transport/escort service, controlled dormitory access.

Student services: health clinic, personal/psychological counseling, women's center.

COSTS & FINANCIAL AID
Costs (2018–19) *Comprehensive fee:* $47,152 includes full-time tuition ($34,292), mandatory fees ($1422), and room and board ($11,438). Part-time tuition: $1433 per credit hour. *Required fees:* $711 per term part-time. *College room only:* $6900. Room and board charges vary according to board plan, housing facility, and location. *Payment plan:* installment. *Waivers:* employees or children of employees.

Financial Aid Of all full-time matriculated undergraduates who enrolled in 2017, 3,742 applied for aid, 3,037 were judged to have need. 187 Federal Work-Study jobs (averaging $1909). 1,206 state and other part-time jobs (averaging $2816). *Average financial aid package:* $16,996. *Average need-based loan:* $4487. *Average need-based gift aid:* $14,976.

APPLYING
Standardized Tests *Recommended:* SAT or ACT (for admission).

Options: electronic application, deferred entrance.
Application fee: $50.
Required: high school transcript, minimum 2.0 GPA, 2 letters of recommendation. *Required for some:* medical examination for flight students. *Recommended:* essay or personal statement, minimum 3.0 GPA, 3 letters of recommendation.
Application deadlines: rolling (freshmen), rolling (out-of-state freshmen), rolling (transfers).
Notification: continuous (freshmen), continuous (out-of-state freshmen), continuous (transfers).

CONTACT
Embry-Riddle Aeronautical University–Daytona, 600 South Clyde Morris Boulevard, Daytona Beach, FL 32114-3900. *Phone:* 386-226-6100. *Toll-free phone:* 800-862-2416. *Fax:* 386-226-7070. *E-mail:* dbadmit@erau.edu.

See previous page for display ad and page 1282 for the College Close-Up.

Embry-Riddle Aeronautical University–Worldwide
Daytona Beach, Florida
http://www.worldwide.erau.edu/

- **Independent** comprehensive, founded 1970
- **Endowment** $111.3 million
- **Coed**
- **Minimally difficult** entrance level

ACADEMICS
Calendar: 5 9-week terms with monthly starts. *Degrees:* certificates, associate, bachelor's, master's, doctoral, and postbachelor's certificates (programs offered at 100 military bases worldwide).
Library: Jack R. Hunt Memorial Library located in Daytona Beach. *Books:* 54,106 (physical), 76,328 (digital/electronic); *Serial titles:* 1,521 (physical), 48,948 (digital/electronic); *Databases:* 106.

STUDENT LIFE
Campus security: ERAU Worldwide does not have a physical campus; courses are offered online and at military bases worldwide.

COSTS & FINANCIAL AID
Costs (2017–18) *Tuition:* $9000 full-time, $375 per credit hour part-time. Full-time tuition and fees vary according to program. Part-time tuition and fees vary according to program. *Required fees:* $76 full-time. *Room only:* Room and board charges vary according to location.

Financial Aid Of all full-time matriculated undergraduates who enrolled in 2017, 1,166 applied for aid, 1,116 were judged to have need. *Average financial aid package:* $5326. *Average need-based loan:* $4402. *Average need-based gift aid:* $4534.

APPLYING
Options: electronic application, deferred entrance.
Application fee: $50.
Required for some: essay or personal statement, high school transcript, minimum 2.0 GPA, 2 letters of recommendation.

CONTACT
Embry-Riddle Aeronautical University–Worldwide, 600 South Clyde Morris Boulevard, Daytona Beach, FL 32114-3900. *Phone:* 800-522-6787. *Toll-free phone:* 800-522-6787. *Fax:* 386-226-6984. *E-mail:* worldwide@erau.edu.

Everglades University
Boca Raton, Florida
http://www.evergladesuniversity.edu/

CONTACT
Everglades University, 5002 T-Rex Avenue, Suite 100, Boca Raton, FL 33431. *Phone:* 561-912-1211. *Toll-free phone:* 888-772-6077.

Everglades University

Maitland, Florida
http://www.evergladesuniversity.edu/

CONTACT
Everglades University, 850 Trafalgar Court, Suite 100, Maitland, FL 32751. *Phone:* 407-277-0311. *Toll-free phone:* 866-289-1078.

Everglades University

Sarasota, Florida
http://www.evergladesuniversity.edu/

CONTACT
Everglades University, 6001 Lake Osprey Drive #110, Sarasota, FL 34240. *Phone:* 866-289-1078. *Toll-free phone:* 888-854-8308.

Flagler College

St. Augustine, Florida
http://www.flagler.edu/

- **Independent** comprehensive, founded 1968
- **Small-town** 49-acre campus with easy access to Jacksonville
- **Endowment** $49.0 million
- **Coed** 2,676 undergraduate students, 52% full-time, 65% women, 35% men
- **57%** of applicants were admitted

UNDERGRAD STUDENTS
1,392 full-time, 1,284 part-time. Students come from 46 states and territories; 51 other countries; 43% are from out of state; 4% Black or African American, non-Hispanic/Latino; 6% Hispanic/Latino; 0.9% Asian, non-Hispanic/Latino; 0.1% Native Hawaiian or other Pacific Islander, non-Hispanic/Latino; 0.3% American Indian or Alaska Native, non-Hispanic/Latino; 3% Two or more races, non-Hispanic/Latino; 5% Race/ethnicity unknown; 4% international; 7% transferred in; 44% live on campus.

Freshmen:
Admission: 4,921 applied, 2,785 admitted, 1,935 enrolled. *Average high school GPA:* 3.5. *Test scores:* SAT evidence-based reading and writing scores over 500: 86%; SAT math scores over 500: 45%; ACT scores over 18: 97%; SAT evidence-based reading and writing scores over 600: 32%; SAT math scores over 600: 5%; ACT scores over 24: 47%; SAT evidence-based reading and writing scores over 700: 3%; ACT scores over 30: 6%.

Retention: 72% of full-time freshmen returned.

FACULTY
Total: 249, 49% full-time, 51% with terminal degrees.
Student/faculty ratio: 16:1.

ACADEMICS
Calendar: semesters. *Degrees:* bachelor's and master's.

Special study options: academic remediation for entering students, adult/continuing education programs, advanced placement credit, cooperative education, distance learning, double majors, honors programs, independent study, internships, part-time degree program, services for LD students, study abroad, summer session for credit.

Computers: 343 computers/terminals are available on campus for general student use. Students can access the following: campus intranet, computer help desk, free student e-mail accounts, online (class) grades, online (class) registration, online (class) schedules, local and remote printing to campus printers, remote access to intranet files. Campuswide network is available. 100% of college-owned or -operated housing units are wired for high-speed Internet access. Wireless service is available via entire campus.

Library: Proctor Library. *Books:* 102,047 (physical), 212,689 (digital/electronic); *Serial titles:* 630 (physical), 44,000 (digital/electronic); *Databases:* 60. Weekly public service hours: 100; students can reserve study rooms.

STUDENT LIFE
Housing options: men-only, women-only. Campus housing is university owned. Freshman campus housing is guaranteed.

Activities and organizations: drama/theater group, student-run newspaper, radio station, choral group, Student Government Association, Inter-Varsity, International Student Club, Flagler College Volunteers, Phi Alpha Omega (women's service club).

Athletics Member NCAA. All Division II. *Intercollegiate sports:* baseball M(s), basketball M(s)/W(s), cheerleading W, cross-country running M(s)/W(s), golf M(s)/W(s), soccer M(s)/W(s), softball M/W(s), tennis M(s)/W(s), track and field M(s)/W(s), volleyball W(s). *Intramural sports:* badminton M/W, basketball M/W, bowling M/W, football M/W, golf M/W, lacrosse M(c), soccer M/W, softball W, swimming and diving M/W, table tennis M/W, tennis M/W, volleyball M/W, weight lifting M/W.

Campus security: 24-hour emergency response devices and patrols, student patrols, late-night transport/escort service, controlled dormitory access, transport/escort service is provided from 6:00 pm until 6:00 am daily.

Student services: health clinic, personal/psychological counseling.

COSTS & FINANCIAL AID
Costs (2018–19) *Comprehensive fee:* $30,290 includes full-time tuition ($18,850), mandatory fees ($100), and room and board ($11,340). Full-time tuition and fees vary according to location. Part-time tuition: $645 per credit hour. Part-time tuition and fees vary according to location. *College room only:* $5800. Room and board charges vary according to board plan and housing facility. *Payment plan:* installment. *Waivers:* employees or children of employees.

Financial Aid Of all full-time matriculated undergraduates who enrolled in 2016, 1,941 applied for aid, 1,553 were judged to have need, 216 had their need fully met. 261 Federal Work-Study jobs (averaging $1400). 57 state and other part-time jobs (averaging $1400). In 2016, 452 non-need-based awards were made. *Average percent of need met:* 57. *Average financial aid package:* $12,151. *Average need-based loan:* $4047. *Average need-based gift aid:* $8522. *Average non-need-based aid:* $2573. *Average indebtedness upon graduation:* $29,267.

APPLYING
Standardized Tests *Required:* SAT or ACT (for admission).

Options: electronic application, early admission, early decision, deferred entrance.

Application fee: $50.

Required: essay or personal statement, high school transcript, letters of recommendation. *Required for some:* interview, interview for early admission.

Application deadlines: 3/1 (freshmen), rolling (transfers).

Early decision deadline: 11/1.

Notification: 3/31 (freshmen), continuous (transfers), 12/15 (early decision).

CONTACT
Ms. Rachel Branch, Director of Admissions, Flagler College, 74 King Street, St. Augustine, FL 32085. *Phone:* 904-819-6294. *Toll-free phone:* 800-304-4208. *Fax:* 904-819-6466. *E-mail:* rbranch@flagler.edu.

Flagler College–Tallahassee

Tallahassee, Florida
http://www.flagler.edu/

CONTACT
Flagler College–Tallahassee, 444 Appleyard Drive, Tallahassee, FL 32304.

Florida Agricultural and Mechanical University

Tallahassee, Florida
http://www.famu.edu/

- **State-supported** university, founded 1887, part of State University System of Florida
- **Urban** 419-acre campus with easy access to Jacksonville
- **Endowment** $122.0 million
- **Coed** 8,024 undergraduate students, 86% full-time, 65% women, 35% men
- **Moderately difficult** entrance level, 46% of applicants were admitted

UNDERGRAD STUDENTS

6,875 full-time, 1,149 part-time. Students come from 43 states and territories; 38 other countries; 13% are from out of state; 89% Black or African American, non-Hispanic/Latino; 3% Hispanic/Latino; 0.4% Asian, non-Hispanic/Latino; 0.1% American Indian or Alaska Native, non-Hispanic/Latino; 3% Two or more races, non-Hispanic/Latino; 0.8% international; 6% transferred in; 32% live on campus.

Freshmen:

Admission: 7,533 applied, 3,437 admitted, 1,684 enrolled. *Average high school GPA:* 3.3. *Test scores:* SAT evidence-based reading and writing scores over 500: 81%; SAT math scores over 500: 81%; ACT scores over 18: 85%; SAT evidence-based reading and writing scores over 600: 16%; SAT math scores over 600: 12%; ACT scores over 24: 14%; SAT evidence-based reading and writing scores over 700: 1%; SAT math scores over 700: 1%; ACT scores over 30: 2%.

Retention: 83% of full-time freshmen returned.

FACULTY

Total: 675, 80% full-time, 59% with terminal degrees.

Student/faculty ratio: 16:1.

ACADEMICS

Calendar: semesters. *Degrees:* associate, bachelor's, master's, doctoral, and post-master's certificates.

Special study options: academic remediation for entering students, accelerated degree program, adult/continuing education programs, advanced placement credit, cooperative education, distance learning, double majors, honors programs, independent study, internships, off-campus study, part-time degree program, services for LD students, study abroad, summer session for credit. *ROTC:* Army (b), Navy (b), Air Force (c).

Unusual degree programs: 3-2 business administration; occupational therapy, architecture.

Computers: 4,000 computers/terminals and 8,000 ports are available on campus for general student use. Students can access the following: campus intranet, computer help desk, free student e-mail accounts, online (class) grades, online (class) registration, online (class) schedules. Campuswide network is available. 100% of college-owned or -operated housing units are wired for high-speed Internet access. Wireless service is available via classrooms, computer centers, computer labs, dorm rooms, learning centers, libraries, student centers.

Library: Samuel H. Coleman Memorial Library plus 4 others. *Books:* 109,342 (physical), 450,711 (digital/electronic); *Serial titles:* 16,025 (physical), 396,052 (digital/electronic); *Databases:* 320. Weekly public service hours: 135; study areas open 24 hours, 5–7 days a week; students can reserve study rooms.

STUDENT LIFE

Housing options: on-campus residence required for freshman year; coed, men-only, women-only, special housing for students with disabilities. Campus housing is university owned. Freshman applicants given priority for college housing.

Activities and organizations: drama/theater group, student-run newspaper, radio and television station, choral group, marching band, National Council of Negro Women, FAMU Chapter, American Society of Mechanical Engineers, Psi Chi International Honor Society, Caribbean Student Association, Academy of Student Pharmacists/Student National Pharmaceutical Association, national fraternities, national sororities.

Athletics Member NCAA. All Division I except football (Division I-AA). *Intercollegiate sports:* baseball M(s), basketball M(s)/W(s), bowling W(s), cheerleading M/W, cross-country running M(s)/W(s), golf M(s)/W(s), softball W(s), swimming and diving M(s)/W(s), tennis M(s)/W(s), track and field M(s)/W(s), volleyball W(s). *Intramural sports:* badminton M/W, basketball M/W, bowling M/W, cheerleading W, football M, golf M/W, gymnastics M/W, racquetball M/W, skiing (downhill) M/W, soccer M/W, softball M/W, swimming and diving M/W, table tennis M/W, tennis M/W, track and field M/W, ultimate Frisbee M/W, volleyball M/W, weight lifting M/W, wrestling M/W.

Campus security: 24-hour emergency response devices and patrols, late-night transport/escort service, controlled dormitory access.

Student services: health clinic, personal/psychological counseling.

COSTS & FINANCIAL AID

Costs (2018–19) *Tuition:* state resident $5645 full-time, $188 per credit hour part-time; nonresident $17,585 full-time, $188 per credit hour part-time. *Required fees:* $140 full-time. *Room and board:* $10,594; room only: $6012. Room and board charges vary according to board plan and housing facility. *Payment plan:* tuition prepayment. *Waivers:* senior citizens and employees or children of employees.

Financial Aid Of all full-time matriculated undergraduates who enrolled in 2016, 6,306 applied for aid, 5,593 were judged to have need, 613 had their need fully met. 240 Federal Work-Study jobs (averaging $1913). In 2016, 163 non-need-based awards were made. *Average percent of need met:* 62. *Average financial aid package:* $13,408. *Average need-based loan:* $4036. *Average need-based gift aid:* $5899. *Average non-need-based aid:* $10,014. *Average indebtedness upon graduation:* $7454.

APPLYING

Standardized Tests *Required:* SAT or ACT (for admission).

Options: electronic application, early admission.

Application fee: $30.

Required: essay or personal statement, high school transcript, minimum 2.5 GPA, 3 letters of recommendation. *Required for some:* interview, audition for music major applicants. *Recommended:* minimum 3.0 GPA.

Application deadlines: 5/15 (freshmen), 5/15 (transfers).

Notification: continuous (freshmen), continuous (out-of-state freshmen), continuous (transfers).

CONTACT

Ms. Barbara R. Cox, Director, Admissions, Florida Agricultural and Mechanical University, Office of Admissions, Florida A & M University, Tallahassee, FL 32307. *Phone:* 850-599-3796. *Toll-free phone:* 866-642-1198. *Fax:* 850-599-3069. *E-mail:* ugrdadmissions@famu.edu.

Florida Atlantic University
Boca Raton, Florida
http://www.fau.edu/

- **State-supported** university, founded 1961, part of State University System of Florida
- **Suburban** 850-acre campus with easy access to Miami, Fort Lauderdale, West Palm Beach
- **Endowment** $282.2 million
- **Coed** 25,025 undergraduate students, 65% full-time, 56% women, 44% men
- **Moderately difficult** entrance level, 60% of applicants were admitted

UNDERGRAD STUDENTS

16,325 full-time, 8,700 part-time. Students come from 48 states and territories; 125 other countries; 5% are from out of state; 20% Black or African American, non-Hispanic/Latino; 27% Hispanic/Latino; 4% Asian, non-Hispanic/Latino; 0.1% Native Hawaiian or other Pacific Islander, non-Hispanic/Latino; 0.2% American Indian or Alaska Native, non-Hispanic/Latino; 4% Two or more races, non-Hispanic/Latino; 0.8% Race/ethnicity unknown; 3% international; 10% transferred in; 17% live on campus.

Freshmen:

Admission: 15,176 applied, 9,107 admitted, 2,768 enrolled. *Average high school GPA:* 4.0. *Test scores:* ACT scores over 18: 98%; ACT scores over 24: 39%; ACT scores over 30: 5%.

Retention: 80% of full-time freshmen returned.

FACULTY

Total: 1,321, 63% full-time, 65% with terminal degrees.

Student/faculty ratio: 24:1.

ACADEMICS

Calendar: semesters. *Degrees:* certificates, associate, bachelor's, master's, doctoral, and post-master's certificates.

Special study options: accelerated degree program, adult/continuing education programs, advanced placement credit, cooperative education, distance learning, double majors, English as a second language, freshman honors college, honors programs, independent study, internships, off-campus study, part-time degree program, services for LD students, study abroad, summer session for credit. *ROTC:* Army (b), Air Force (c).

Unusual degree programs: 3-2 business administration; engineering; nursing; architecture, mathematics.

Computers: 1,350 computers/terminals are available on campus for general student use. Students can access the following: campus intranet, computer help desk, free student e-mail accounts, online (class) grades, online (class) registration, online (class) schedules. Campuswide network is available. 100% of college-owned or -operated housing units are wired for high-speed Internet access. Wireless service is available via entire campus.

Library: S. E. Wimberly Library plus 2 others. *Books:* 1.4 million (physical), 1.2 million (digital/electronic); *Serial titles:* 29,249 (physical), 105,472 (digital/electronic); *Databases:* 581. Study areas open 24 hours, 5–7 days a week.

STUDENT LIFE

Housing options: on-campus residence required for freshman year; coed, women-only. Campus housing is university owned. Freshman campus housing is guaranteed.

Activities and organizations: drama/theater group, student-run newspaper, radio and television station, choral group, marching band, American Society of Civil Engineers, Dive Club, Pre-Law Society, Submarine Club, American Criminal Justice Society, national fraternities, national sororities.

Athletics Member NCAA. All Division I. *Intercollegiate sports:* baseball M(s), basketball M(s)/W(s), cheerleading M/W, cross-country running M/W, football M(s), golf M(s)/W(s), soccer M/W, softball W(s), swimming and diving M/W, tennis M/W, track and field W, volleyball W(s). *Intramural sports:* baseball M/W, bowling M/W, football M, ice hockey M(c)/W(c), lacrosse M(c), rock climbing M(c)/W(c), rugby M(c)/W(c), sailing M(c)/W(c), soccer M/W, softball W, table tennis M/W, ultimate Frisbee M/W, volleyball M/W, weight lifting M(c), wrestling M(c).

Campus security: 24-hour emergency response devices and patrols, student patrols, late-night transport/escort service, controlled dormitory access.

Student services: health clinic, personal/psychological counseling, women's center.

COSTS & FINANCIAL AID

Costs (2018–19) *Tuition:* state resident $6039 full-time, $105 per credit hour part-time; nonresident $21,595 full-time, $599 per credit hour part-time. Full-time tuition and fees vary according to course load. Part-time tuition and fees vary according to course load. *Required fees:* $96 per credit hour part-time. *Room and board:* $10,388; room only: $6730. Room and board charges vary according to board plan and housing facility. *Payment plans:* installment, deferred payment. *Waivers:* senior citizens and employees or children of employees.

Financial Aid Of all full-time matriculated undergraduates who enrolled in 2017, 11,529 applied for aid, 9,778 were judged to have need, 1,251 had their need fully met. 250 Federal Work-Study jobs (averaging $2103). 5 state and other part-time jobs (averaging $3331). In 2017, 181 non-need-based awards were made. *Average percent of need met:* 64. *Average financial aid package:* $13,750. *Average need-based loan:* $7070. *Average need-based gift aid:* $7347. *Average non-need-based aid:* $4220. *Average indebtedness upon graduation:* $22,818.

APPLYING

Standardized Tests *Required:* SAT or ACT (for admission).

Options: electronic application, early admission, deferred entrance.

Application fee: $30.

Required: high school transcript.

Application deadlines: 5/1 (freshmen), 5/1 (transfers).

Notification: continuous (freshmen), continuous (transfers).

CONTACT

Ms. Mary Edmunds, Associate Director, Florida Atlantic University, 777 Glades Road, PO Box 3091, Boca Raton, FL 33431-0991. *Phone:* 561-297-3040. *Fax:* 561-297-2758. *E-mail:* recruitment@fau.edu.

Florida College
Temple Terrace, Florida
http://www.floridacollege.edu/

- **Independent** 4-year, founded 1944
- **Suburban** 95-acre campus with easy access to Tampa
- **Endowment** $16.5 million
- **Coed** 508 undergraduate students, 96% full-time, 52% women, 48% men
- **Moderately difficult** entrance level, 74% of applicants were admitted

UNDERGRAD STUDENTS

490 full-time, 18 part-time. Students come from 34 states and territories; 11 other countries; 51% are from out of state; 6% Black or African American, non-Hispanic/Latino; 9% Hispanic/Latino; 0.2% Asian, non-Hispanic/Latino; 0.4% Native Hawaiian or other Pacific Islander, non-Hispanic/Latino; 1% American Indian or Alaska Native, non-Hispanic/Latino; 4% Two or more races, non-Hispanic/Latino; 2% Race/ethnicity unknown; 3% international; 81% live on campus.

Freshmen:

Admission: 263 applied, 194 admitted, 127 enrolled. *Test scores:* SAT evidence-based reading and writing scores over 500: 57%; SAT math scores over 500: 57%; ACT scores over 18: 83%; SAT evidence-based reading and writing scores over 600: 33%; SAT math scores over 600: 19%; ACT scores over 24: 48%; SAT evidence-based reading and writing scores over 700: 14%; SAT math scores over 700: 5%; ACT scores over 30: 10%.

FACULTY

Total: 52, 65% full-time.

Student/faculty ratio: 13:1.

ACADEMICS

Calendar: semesters. *Degrees:* associate and bachelor's.

Special study options: academic remediation for entering students, advanced placement credit, independent study, summer session for credit. *ROTC:* Army (c), Air Force (c).

Computers: 85 computers/terminals are available on campus for general student use. Students can access the following: campus intranet, computer help desk, free student e-mail accounts, online (class) grades, online (class) schedules. Campuswide network is available. 100% of college-owned or -operated housing units are wired for high-speed Internet access. Wireless service is available via classrooms, computer centers, computer labs, dorm rooms, libraries, student centers.

Library: Chatlos Library.

STUDENT LIFE

Housing options: on-campus residence required through sophomore year; men-only, women-only. Campus housing is university owned. Freshman campus housing is guaranteed.

Activities and organizations: drama/theater group, choral group, Co-ed Societies, ROTARACT CLUB, NAFME, SBGA, Footlighters.

Athletics Member NAIA, USCAA. *Intercollegiate sports:* basketball M(s)/W, cheerleading W, cross-country running M/W, soccer M(s)/W(s), volleyball W(s). *Intramural sports:* basketball M/W, football M/W, soccer M/W, softball M/W, ultimate Frisbee M/W, volleyball M/W.

Campus security: controlled dormitory access, evening patrols by trained security personnel.

Student services: health clinic, personal/psychological counseling.

COSTS & FINANCIAL AID

Costs (2017–18) *Comprehensive fee:* $25,562 includes full-time tuition ($16,142), mandatory fees ($1000), and room and board ($8420). Part-time tuition: $637 per credit hour. Part-time tuition and fees vary according to course load. *College room only:* $4270. Room and board charges vary according to board plan and housing facility. *Payment plan:* installment. *Waivers:* employees or children of employees.

Financial Aid Of all full-time matriculated undergraduates who enrolled in 2015, 434 applied for aid, 372 were judged to have need, 41 had their need fully met. 35 Federal Work-Study jobs (averaging $665). In 2015, 75 non-need-based awards were made. *Average percent of need met:* 56. *Average financial aid package:* $10,644. *Average need-based loan:* $4113. *Average need-based gift aid:* $7068. *Average non-need-based aid:* $4048.

APPLYING

Standardized Tests *Required:* SAT or ACT (for admission).

Options: electronic application.

Application fee: $40.

Required: high school transcript, minimum 2.0 GPA, 2 letters of recommendation. *Required for some:* essay for international students.

Application deadlines: 8/1 (freshmen), 8/1 (transfers).

Notification: continuous (freshmen), continuous (transfers).

CONTACT

Mrs. Colleen Engel, Assistant Director of Admissions, Florida College, 119 North Glen Arven Avenue, Temple Terrace, FL 33617. *Phone:* 813-988-5131 Ext. 152. *Fax:* 813-899-6772. *E-mail:* admissions@ floridacollege.edu.

Florida Gateway College

Lake City, Florida

http://www.fgc.edu/

CONTACT

Admissions, Florida Gateway College, 149 SE College Place, Lake City, FL 32025-8703. *Phone:* 386-755-4236. *E-mail:* admissions@fgc.edu.

Florida Gulf Coast University

Fort Myers, Florida

http://www.fgcu.edu/

- **State-supported** comprehensive, founded 1991, part of State University System of Florida
- **Suburban** 760-acre campus
- **Endowment** $72.9 million
- **Coed** 13,820 undergraduate students, 79% full-time, 56% women, 44% men
- **Moderately difficult** entrance level, 64% of applicants were admitted

UNDERGRAD STUDENTS

10,947 full-time, 2,873 part-time. Students come from 45 states and territories; 84 other countries; 7% are from out of state; 7% Black or African American, non-Hispanic/Latino; 21% Hispanic/Latino; 2% Asian, non-Hispanic/Latino; 0.2% Native Hawaiian or other Pacific Islander, non-Hispanic/Latino; 0.2% American Indian or Alaska Native, non-Hispanic/Latino; 3% Two or more races, non-Hispanic/Latino; 1% Race/ethnicity unknown; 2% international; 7% transferred in; 22% live on campus.

Freshmen:
Admission: 13,832 applied, 8,889 admitted, 2,632 enrolled. *Average high school GPA:* 3.9. *Test scores:* SAT evidence-based reading and writing scores over 500: 98%; SAT math scores over 500: 94%; ACT scores over 18: 98%; SAT evidence-based reading and writing scores over 600: 35%; SAT math scores over 600: 25%; ACT scores over 24: 41%; SAT evidence-based reading and writing scores over 700: 3%; SAT math scores over 700: 2%; ACT scores over 30: 4%.
Retention: 80% of full-time freshmen returned.

FACULTY

Total: 760, 61% full-time, 45% with terminal degrees.

Student/faculty ratio: 22:1.

ACADEMICS

Calendar: semesters. *Degrees:* certificates, associate, bachelor's, master's, doctoral, and post-master's certificates.

Special study options: academic remediation for entering students, accelerated degree program, advanced placement credit, cooperative education, distance learning, double majors, honors programs, independent study, internships, off-campus study, part-time degree program, services for LD students, study abroad, summer session for credit.

Computers: 1,029 computers/terminals are available on campus for general student use. Students can access the following: computer help desk, free student e-mail accounts, online (class) registration, online (class) schedules, online admissions and advising. Campuswide network is available. 100% of college-owned or -operated housing units are wired for high-speed Internet access. Wireless service is available via entire campus.

Library: Library Services plus 1 other. *Books:* 242,131 (physical), 73,000 (digital/electronic); *Serial titles:* 128,865 (digital/electronic); *Databases:* 389. Students can reserve study rooms.

STUDENT LIFE

Housing options: coed. Campus housing is university owned.

Activities and organizations: drama/theater group, student-run newspaper, Student Government, Ignite (Religious Organization), International Club, Martial Arts Club, Physical Therapy Association, national fraternities, national sororities.

Athletics Member NCAA. All Division I. *Intercollegiate sports:* baseball M(s), basketball M(s)/W(s), cheerleading W, cross-country running M(s)/W(s), golf M(s)/W(s), soccer M(s)/W(s), softball W(s), swimming and diving W(s), tennis M(s)/W(s), volleyball W(s). *Intramural sports:* basketball M/W, cross-country running M(c)/W(c), fencing M(c)/W(c), football M/W, ice hockey M(c), lacrosse M(c)/W(c), sailing M(c)/W(c), skiing (downhill) M(c)/W(c), soccer M/W, softball M/W, swimming and diving M(c)/W(c), table tennis M/W, tennis M(c)/W(c), ultimate Frisbee M/W, volleyball M/W, water polo M/W, weight lifting M(c)/W(c), wrestling M(c)/W(c).

Campus security: 24-hour emergency response devices and patrols, late-night transport/escort service.

Student services: health clinic, personal/psychological counseling.

COSTS & FINANCIAL AID

Costs (2018–19) *Tuition:* state resident $4191 full-time; nonresident $22,328 full-time. Full-time tuition and fees vary according to course load. Part-time tuition and fees vary according to course load. *Required fees:* $1927 full-time. *Room and board:* $8620; room only: $4820. Room and board charges vary according to board plan.

Financial Aid Of all full-time matriculated undergraduates who enrolled in 2016, 7,440 applied for aid, 5,102 were judged to have need, 476 had their need fully met. 258 Federal Work-Study jobs (averaging $419,774). 9 state and other part-time jobs (averaging $18,531). In 2016, 304 non-need-based awards were made. *Average percent of need met:* 57. *Average financial aid package:* $9892. *Average need-based loan:* $7335. *Average need-based gift aid:* $5443. *Average non-need-based aid:* $3297. *Average indebtedness upon graduation:* $24,879. *Financial aid deadline:* 6/30.

APPLYING

Standardized Tests *Required:* SAT or ACT (for admission).

Options: electronic application, deferred entrance.

Application fee: $30.

Required: high school transcript, minimum 2.5 GPA.

Application deadlines: 5/1 (freshmen), 7/1 (transfers).

Notification: continuous (freshmen), continuous (transfers).

CONTACT

Florida Gulf Coast University, 10501 FGCU Boulevard South, Fort Myers, FL 33965-6565. *Phone:* 239-590-7878. *Toll-free phone:* 888-889-1095.

Florida Institute of Technology

Melbourne, Florida

http://www.fit.edu/

- **Independent** university, founded 1958
- **Suburban** 130-acre campus with easy access to Orlando
- **Coed** 3,635 undergraduate students, 90% full-time, 29% women, 71% men
- **Moderately difficult** entrance level, 63% of applicants were admitted

UNDERGRAD STUDENTS

3,269 full-time, 366 part-time. Students come from 52 states and territories; 110 other countries; 50% are from out of state; 6% Black or African American, non-Hispanic/Latino; 9% Hispanic/Latino; 3% Asian, non-Hispanic/Latino; 0.4% Native Hawaiian or other Pacific Islander, non-Hispanic/Latino; 0.2% American Indian or Alaska Native, non-Hispanic/Latino; 2% Two or more races, non-Hispanic/Latino; 2% Race/ethnicity unknown; 32% international; 6% transferred in; 45% live on campus.

Freshmen:
Admission: 8,898 applied, 5,647 admitted, 721 enrolled. *Average high school GPA:* 3.7. *Test scores:* SAT evidence-based reading and writing scores over 500: 93%; ACT scores over 18: 99%; SAT evidence-based reading and writing scores over 600: 53%; ACT scores over 24: 82%; SAT evidence-based reading and writing scores over 700: 8%; ACT scores over 30: 24%.
Retention: 80% of full-time freshmen returned.

FACULTY
Total: 526, 58% full-time, 79% with terminal degrees.
Student/faculty ratio: 15:1.

ACADEMICS
Calendar: semesters. *Degrees:* bachelor's, master's, doctoral, and post-master's certificates.

Special study options: academic remediation for entering students, accelerated degree program, adult/continuing education programs, advanced placement credit, cooperative education, distance learning, double majors, English as a second language, independent study, internships, part-time degree program, services for LD students, student-designed majors, study abroad, summer session for credit. *ROTC:* Army (b).

Computers: 254 computers/terminals and 100 ports are available on campus for general student use. Students can access the following: campus intranet, computer help desk, free student e-mail accounts, online (class) grades, online (class) registration, online (class) schedules. Campuswide network is available. 100% of college-owned or -operated housing units are wired for high-speed Internet access. Wireless service is available via classrooms, computer centers, computer labs, dorm rooms, learning centers, libraries, student centers.
Library: Evans Library. *Books:* 131,564 (physical), 728,454 (digital/electronic); *Serial titles:* 1,605 (physical), 56,994 (digital/electronic); *Databases:* 161. Weekly public service hours: 96; students can reserve study rooms.

STUDENT LIFE
Housing options: on-campus residence required through sophomore year; coed. Campus housing is university owned. Freshman campus housing is guaranteed.
Activities and organizations: drama/theater group, student-run newspaper, radio and television station, choral group, Florida Institute of Technology Society for Science Fiction and Fantasy (FITSSFF), International Student Services Organization (ISSO), Student Government Association (SGA), Surf Club, Campus Activities Board, national fraternities, national sororities.
Athletics Member NCAA. All Division II. *Intercollegiate sports:* baseball M(s), basketball M(s)/W(s), crew M(s)/W(s), cross-country running M(s)/W(s), football M(s), golf M(s)/W(s), lacrosse M(s)/W(s), soccer M(s)/W(s), softball W(s), swimming and diving M(s)/W(s), tennis M(s)/W(s), track and field M(s)/W(s), volleyball W(s). *Intramural sports:* archery M(c)/W(c), badminton M/W, baseball M(c)/W(c), bowling M(c)/W(c), fencing M(c)/W(c), ice hockey M(c)/W(c), rugby M(c)/W(c), sailing M(c)/W(c), soccer M/W, tennis M/W, triathlon M(c)/W(c), ultimate Frisbee M/W, volleyball M/W.
Campus security: 24-hour emergency response devices and patrols, late-night transport/escort service, controlled dormitory access.
Student services: health clinic, personal/psychological counseling, women's center.

COSTS & FINANCIAL AID
Costs (2018–19) *Comprehensive fee:* $54,730 includes full-time tuition ($41,100), mandatory fees ($750), and room and board ($12,880). Full-time tuition and fees vary according to course load and program. Part-time tuition: $1170 per credit hour. *College room only:* $7000. Room and board charges vary according to board plan and housing facility. *Payment plan:* installment. *Waivers:* senior citizens and employees or children of employees.
Financial Aid Of all full-time matriculated undergraduates who enrolled in 2017, 1,871 applied for aid, 1,682 were judged to have need, 570 had their need fully met. 363 Federal Work-Study jobs (averaging $2500). 455 state and other part-time jobs (averaging $6342). In 2017, 999 non-need-based awards were made. *Average percent of need met:* 84. *Average financial aid package:* $37,796. *Average need-based loan:* $5288.

Average need-based gift aid: $26,815. *Average non-need-based aid:* $15,373. *Average indebtedness upon graduation:* $33,135.

APPLYING
Standardized Tests *Required:* SAT or ACT (for admission).
Options: electronic application, deferred entrance.
Required: essay or personal statement, high school transcript, minimum 2.6 GPA, 1 letter of recommendation. *Recommended:* minimum 3.3 GPA, interview.
Application deadlines: rolling (freshmen), rolling (transfers).
Notification: continuous (freshmen), continuous (transfers).

CONTACT
Florida Institute of Technology, 150 West University Boulevard, Melbourne, FL 32901-6975. *Toll-free phone:* 800-888-4348.

Florida International University
Miami, Florida
http://www.fiu.edu/
- **State-supported** university, founded 1965, part of State University System of Florida
- **Urban** 576-acre campus with easy access to Miami
- **Endowment** $196.3 million
- **Coed** 47,586 undergraduate students, 56% full-time, 57% women, 43% men
- **Moderately difficult** entrance level, 51% of applicants were admitted

UNDERGRAD STUDENTS
26,697 full-time, 20,889 part-time. Students come from 47 states and territories; 140 other countries; 4% are from out of state; 13% Black or African American, non-Hispanic/Latino; 67% Hispanic/Latino; 2% Asian, non-Hispanic/Latino; 0.1% Native Hawaiian or other Pacific Islander, non-Hispanic/Latino; 0.1% American Indian or Alaska Native, non-Hispanic/Latino; 3% Two or more races, non-Hispanic/Latino; 0.6% Race/ethnicity unknown; 6% international; 11% transferred in; 7% live on campus.

Freshmen:
Admission: 14,861 applied, 7,596 admitted, 4,298 enrolled. *Average high school GPA:* 4.0. *Test scores:* SAT evidence-based reading and writing scores over 500: 99%; SAT math scores over 500: 97%; ACT scores over 18: 99%; SAT evidence-based reading and writing scores over 600: 55%; SAT math scores over 600: 37%; ACT scores over 24: 55%; SAT evidence-based reading and writing scores over 700: 6%; SAT math scores over 700: 3%; ACT scores over 30: 6%.
Retention: 89% of full-time freshmen returned.

FACULTY
Total: 2,440, 52% full-time, 67% with terminal degrees.
Student/faculty ratio: 25:1.

ACADEMICS
Calendar: semesters. *Degrees:* bachelor's, master's, doctoral, and postbachelor's certificates.

Special study options: accelerated degree program, adult/continuing education programs, advanced placement credit, cooperative education, distance learning, double majors, freshman honors college, honors programs, independent study, internships, off-campus study, part-time degree program, services for LD students, study abroad, summer session for credit. *ROTC:* Army (b), Air Force (b).

Computers: Students can access the following: computer help desk, free student e-mail accounts, online (class) grades, online (class) registration, online (class) schedules, online financial and cashier's information; financial, campus maps information available on cell phones. Campuswide network is available. 100% of college-owned or -operated housing units are wired for high-speed Internet access. Wireless service is available via entire campus.
Library: Steven and Dorothea Green Library plus 4 others. *Books:* 1.5 million (physical), 443,863 (digital/electronic); *Serial titles:* 63,945 (physical), 111,662 (digital/electronic); *Databases:* 808. Weekly public service hours: 112; students can reserve study rooms.

STUDENT LIFE
Housing options: coed. Campus housing is university owned.

Activities and organizations: drama/theater group, student-run newspaper, radio station, choral group, marching band, Students for Community Service, Black Student Leadership Council, Hospitality Management Student Club, Hispanic Students Association, Haitian Students Organization, national fraternities, national sororities.

Athletics Member NCAA. All Division I. *Intercollegiate sports:* baseball M(s), basketball M(s)/W(s), cross-country running M(s)/W(s), football M(s), golf W(s), soccer M(s)/W(s), softball W(s), swimming and diving W(s), tennis W(s), track and field M(s)/W(s), volleyball W(s). *Intramural sports:* badminton M(c)/W(c), baseball M(c), basketball M/W, crew M(c)/W(c), cross-country running M(c)/W(c), equestrian sports M(c)/W(c), football M/W, golf W, lacrosse M(c)/W(c), racquetball M/W, rugby M(c)/W(c), sailing M/W, soccer M/W, softball M/W, swimming and diving M(c)/W(c), table tennis M/W, tennis M(c)/W(c), ultimate Frisbee M/W, volleyball M/W, weight lifting M/W, wrestling M(c)/W(c).

Campus security: 24-hour emergency response devices and patrols, late-night transport/escort service, controlled dormitory access.

Student services: health clinic, personal/psychological counseling, women's center.

COSTS & FINANCIAL AID

Costs (2017–18) *Tuition:* state resident $6168 full-time, $206 per credit hour part-time; nonresident $18,566 full-time, $619 per credit hour part-time. *Required fees:* $390 full-time. *Room and board:* $10,882; room only: $6984. Room and board charges vary according to board plan and housing facility. *Payment plan:* installment. *Waivers:* employees or children of employees.

Financial Aid Of all full-time matriculated undergraduates who enrolled in 2015, 18,636 applied for aid, 18,395 were judged to have need, 1,362 had their need fully met. In 2015, 1009 non-need-based awards were made. *Average percent of need met:* 23. *Average financial aid package:* $8370. *Average need-based loan:* $4666. *Average need-based gift aid:* $5654. *Average non-need-based aid:* $2234. *Average indebtedness upon graduation:* $19,915. *Financial aid deadline:* 5/15.

APPLYING

Standardized Tests *Required:* SAT or ACT (for admission). *Required for some:* TOEFL for applicants whose native language is not English.

Options: electronic application.

Application fee: $30.

Required: high school transcript. *Required for some:* portfolio or audition.

Application deadlines: 11/1 (freshmen), rolling (out-of-state freshmen), rolling (transfers).

Notification: continuous (freshmen), continuous (out-of-state freshmen), continuous (transfers).

CONTACT
Ms. Jody Glassman, Director of Admissions, Florida International University, 11200 SW Eighth Street, PC 140, Miami, FL 33199. *Phone:* 305-348-3662. *E-mail:* admiss@fiu.edu.

Florida Keys Community College

Key West, Florida

http://www.fkcc.edu/

- **State-supported** primarily 2-year, founded 1965, part of Florida College System
- **Small-town** 20-acre campus
- **Coed** 1,030 undergraduate students, 35% full-time, 58% women, 42% men
- **Noncompetitive** entrance level

UNDERGRAD STUDENTS
363 full-time, 667 part-time. 9% Black or African American, non-Hispanic/Latino; 27% Hispanic/Latino; 2% Asian, non-Hispanic/Latino; 0.4% Native Hawaiian or other Pacific Islander, non-Hispanic/Latino; 0.3% American Indian or Alaska Native, non-Hispanic/Latino; 3% Two or more races, non-Hispanic/Latino; 4% Race/ethnicity unknown; 0.9% international; 10% transferred in.

Freshmen:
Admission: 198 enrolled.

FACULTY
Total: 28.
Student/faculty ratio: 12:1.

ACADEMICS
Calendar: semesters. *Degrees:* certificates, associate, and bachelor's.

Special study options: academic remediation for entering students, adult/continuing education programs, advanced placement credit, cooperative education, distance learning, double majors, English as a second language, independent study, internships, part-time degree program, services for LD students, student-designed majors, summer session for credit.

Computers: Students can access the following: campus intranet, computer help desk, free student e-mail accounts, online (class) grades, online (class) registration, online (class) schedules. Campuswide network is available. 100% of college-owned or -operated housing units are wired for high-speed Internet access. Wireless service is available via entire campus.

Library: Florida Keys Community College Library. Students can reserve study rooms.

STUDENT LIFE
Housing options: coed. Campus housing is university owned.

Activities and organizations: choral group.

Campus security: 24-hour patrols.

Student services: personal/psychological counseling.

COSTS & FINANCIAL AID
Costs (2018–19) *Tuition:* state resident $109 per credit hour part-time; nonresident $439 per credit hour part-time. Full-time tuition and fees vary according to degree level. Part-time tuition and fees vary according to degree level. *Room only:* $10,508. Room and board charges vary according to board plan. *Payment plan:* installment. *Waivers:* employees or children of employees.

Financial Aid Of all full-time matriculated undergraduates who enrolled in 2016, 30 Federal Work-Study jobs (averaging $2000).

APPLYING
Options: electronic application, early admission, deferred entrance.

Application fee: $30.

Required for some: essay or personal statement, high school transcript, letters of recommendation.

Application deadlines: rolling (freshmen), rolling (transfers).

Notification: continuous (freshmen), continuous (transfers).

CONTACT
Florida Keys Community College, 5901 College Road, Key West, FL 33040-4397. *Phone:* 305-296-9081 Ext. 237.

Florida Memorial University

Miami-Dade, Florida

http://www.fmuniv.edu/

CONTACT
Mrs. Peggy Murray Martin, Director of Admissions and International Student Advisor, Florida Memorial University, 15800 NW 42nd Avenue, Miami-Dade, FL 33054. *Phone:* 305-626-3147. *Toll-free phone:* 800-822-1362.

Florida National University

Hialeah, Florida

http://www.fnu.edu/

- **Proprietary** comprehensive, founded 1982
- **Urban** 4-acre campus with easy access to Miami
- **Coed** 4,023 undergraduate students, 72% full-time, 71% women, 29% men
- **Moderately difficult** entrance level, 95% of applicants were admitted

UNDERGRAD STUDENTS
2,899 full-time, 1,124 part-time. Students come from 22 states and territories; 31 other countries; 1% are from out of state; 3% Black or African American, non-Hispanic/Latino; 82% Hispanic/Latino; 0.3% Asian, non-Hispanic/Latino; 0.1% Native Hawaiian or other Pacific

Islander, non-Hispanic/Latino; 0.1% American Indian or Alaska Native, non-Hispanic/Latino; 0.6% Two or more races, non-Hispanic/Latino; 0.1% Race/ethnicity unknown; 13% international; 7% transferred in.

Freshmen:
Admission: 1,785 applied, 1,687 admitted, 866 enrolled.
Retention: 98% of full-time freshmen returned.

FACULTY
Total: 150, 53% full-time, 15% with terminal degrees.
Student/faculty ratio: 31:1.

ACADEMICS
Calendar: semesters. *Degrees:* certificates, diplomas, associate, bachelor's, master's, post-master's, and postbachelor's certificates.
Special study options: academic remediation for entering students, accelerated degree program, adult/continuing education programs, advanced placement credit, cooperative education, distance learning, English as a second language, independent study, internships, part-time degree program, services for LD students, summer session for credit.
Computers: 300 computers/terminals are available on campus for general student use. Students can access the following: computer help desk, free student e-mail accounts, online (class) grades, online (class) registration, online (class) schedules. Campuswide network is available. Wireless service is available via entire campus.
Library: Hialeah Campus Library plus 1 other. *Books:* 21,521 (physical), 144,218 (digital/electronic); *Serial titles:* 55 (physical), 196,357 (digital/electronic); *Databases:* 32. Weekly public service hours: 69; students can reserve study rooms.

STUDENT LIFE
Housing options: college housing not available.
Activities and organizations: student-run newspaper, Student Government Association, Bible Club, Salsa Club, W.I.C.S (Women Community Service), Criminal Justice Society, national fraternities.
Athletics Member USCAA. *Intercollegiate sports:* baseball M(s), basketball M(s), soccer M(s)/W(s), volleyball W(s).
Campus security: 24-hour emergency response devices.

COSTS & FINANCIAL AID
Costs (2018–19) *Tuition:* $13,200 full-time, $550 per credit hour part-time. Full-time tuition and fees vary according to course level. Part-time tuition and fees vary according to course level. No tuition increase for student's term of enrollment. *Required fees:* $650 full-time. *Payment plans:* tuition prepayment, installment. *Waivers:* employees or children of employees.
Financial Aid Of all full-time matriculated undergraduates who enrolled in 2016, 1,920 applied for aid, 1,824 were judged to have need. 19 Federal Work-Study jobs (averaging $4500). *Average indebtedness upon graduation:* $10,982.

APPLYING
Standardized Tests *Required:* SAT or ACT (for admission).
Options: electronic application, deferred entrance.
Required: high school transcript, interview.
Application deadlines: rolling (freshmen), rolling (transfers).
Notification: continuous (freshmen), continuous (transfers).

CONTACT
Mr. Robert Lopez, Director of Admissions, Florida National University, 4425 W. Jose Regueiro (20th) Avenue, Hialeah, FL 33012. *Phone:* 305-821-3333. *Fax:* 305-362-0595. *E-mail:* rlopez@fnu.edu.

★ Florida Southern College
Lakeland, Florida
http://www.flsouthern.edu/
- **Independent** comprehensive, founded 1885, affiliated with United Methodist Church
- **Suburban** 113-acre campus with easy access to Tampa, Orlando
- **Coed** 2,633 undergraduate students, 90% full-time, 65% women, 35% men
- **Moderately difficult** entrance level, 51% of applicants were admitted

UNDERGRAD STUDENTS
2,364 full-time, 269 part-time. Students come from 49 states and territories; 52 other countries; 38% are from out of state; 5% Black or African American, non-Hispanic/Latino; 10% Hispanic/Latino; 3% Asian, non-Hispanic/Latino; 0.1% Native Hawaiian or other Pacific Islander, non-Hispanic/Latino; 1% American Indian or Alaska Native, non-Hispanic/Latino; 0.6% Two or more races, non-Hispanic/Latino; 2% Race/ethnicity unknown; 4% international; 4% transferred in; 92% live on campus.

Freshmen:
Admission: 5,983 applied, 3,062 admitted, 722 enrolled. *Average high school GPA:* 3.7. *Test scores:* SAT evidence-based reading and writing scores over 500: 91%; SAT math scores over 500: 89%; ACT scores over 18: 100%; SAT evidence-based reading and writing scores over 600: 43%; SAT math scores over 600: 32%; ACT scores over 24: 67%; SAT evidence-based reading and writing scores over 700: 7%; SAT math scores over 700: 3%; ACT scores over 30: 10%.
Retention: 80% of full-time freshmen returned.

FACULTY
Total: 287, 48% full-time, 63% with terminal degrees.
Student/faculty ratio: 15:1.

ACADEMICS
Calendar: semesters. *Degrees:* bachelor's, master's, and doctoral.
Special study options: accelerated degree program, adult/continuing education programs, advanced placement credit, distance learning, double majors, external degree program, honors programs, independent study, internships, off-campus study, part-time degree program, student-designed majors, study abroad, summer session for credit. *ROTC:* Army (b), Air Force (c).
Unusual degree programs: 3-2 business administration; engineering with Washington University in St. Louis; environmental science with Duke University, accounting/accountancy with Florida Southern College, medicine with Lake Erie College of Osteopathic Medicine.
Computers: 490 computers/terminals and 65 ports are available on campus for general student use. Students can access the following: campus intranet, computer help desk, free student e-mail accounts, online (class) grades, online (class) registration, online (class) schedules, campus portal. Campuswide network is available. 100% of college-owned or -operated housing units are wired for high-speed Internet access. Wireless service is available via entire campus.
Library: Roux Library plus 1 other. *Books:* 160,667 (physical), 167,731 (digital/electronic); *Serial titles:* 22 (physical), 97,772 (digital/electronic); *Databases:* 118. Weekly public service hours: 104; students can reserve study rooms.

STUDENT LIFE
Housing options: on-campus residence required through senior year; coed, men-only, women-only, special housing for students with disabilities. Campus housing is university owned. Freshman campus housing is guaranteed.
Activities and organizations: drama/theater group, student-run newspaper, television station, choral group, National Society for Leadership and Success, Association of Campus Entertainment, Association of Honors Students, Beyond (Campus Ministry), Multicultural Student Council, national fraternities, national sororities.
Athletics Member NCAA. All Division II. *Intercollegiate sports:* baseball M(s), basketball M(s)/W(s), cheerleading W(c), cross-country running M(s)/W(s), equestrian sports W(c), golf M(s)/W(s), lacrosse M(s)/W(s), soccer M(s)/W(s), softball W(s), swimming and diving M(s)/W(s), tennis M(s)/W(s), track and field M/W, volleyball W(s). *Intramural sports:* basketball M/W, bowling M/W, football M/W, soccer M/W, softball M/W, swimming and diving M/W, tennis M/W, ultimate Frisbee M/W, volleyball M/W, water polo M/W.
Campus security: 24-hour emergency response devices and patrols, student patrols, late-night transport/escort service, controlled dormitory access.
Student services: health clinic, personal/psychological counseling.

COSTS & FINANCIAL AID
Costs (2017–18) *Comprehensive fee:* $45,978 includes full-time tuition ($34,074), mandatory fees ($700), and room and board ($11,204). Part-time tuition: $970 per credit hour. Part-time tuition and fees vary

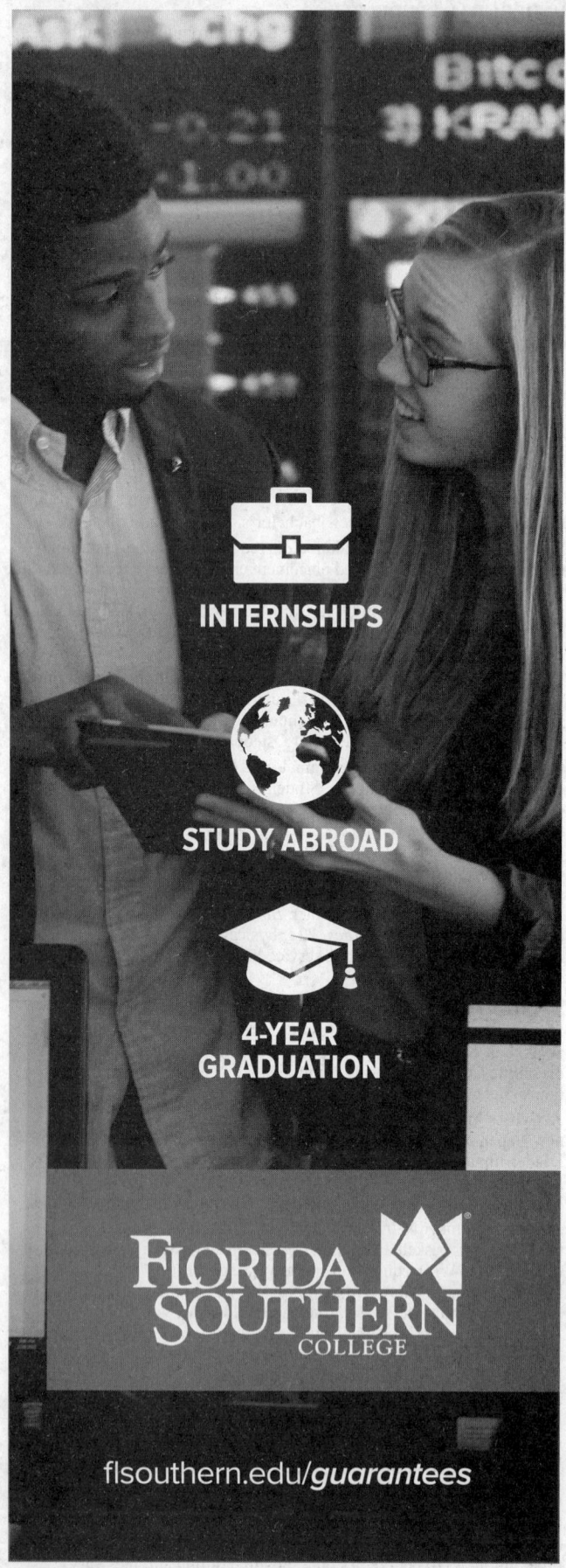

according to class time and course load. *College room only:* $6700. Room and board charges vary according to board plan and housing facility. *Payment plan:* installment. *Waivers:* children of alumni and employees or children of employees.

Financial Aid Of all full-time matriculated undergraduates who enrolled in 2017, 1,863 applied for aid, 1,583 were judged to have need, 447 had their need fully met. 118 Federal Work-Study jobs (averaging $2586). In 2017, 751 non-need-based awards were made. *Average percent of need met:* 75. *Average financial aid package:* $28,756. *Average need-based loan:* $5466. *Average need-based gift aid:* $22,505. *Average non-need-based aid:* $21,720. *Average indebtedness upon graduation:* $25,493. *Financial aid deadline:* 7/1.

APPLYING
Standardized Tests *Required:* SAT or ACT (for admission).

Options: electronic application, early admission, early decision, deferred entrance.

Required: high school transcript, minimum 2.0 GPA, 1 letter of recommendation. *Recommended:* essay or personal statement, interview.

Application deadlines: 3/1 (freshmen), rolling (transfers).

Early decision deadline: 12/1.

Notification: continuous (freshmen), continuous (transfers), 12/15 (early decision).

CONTACT
Florida Southern College, 111 Lake Hollingsworth Drive, Lakeland, FL 33801-5698. *Phone:* 863-680-4131. *Toll-free phone:* 800-274-4131.

See this page for display ad and page 1294 for the College Close-Up.

Florida SouthWestern State College
Fort Myers, Florida
http://www.fsw.edu/

- **State and locally supported** primarily 2-year, founded 1962, part of Florida College System
- **Urban** 413-acre campus
- **Endowment** $731,365
- **Coed**
- **Noncompetitive** entrance level

FACULTY
Student/faculty ratio: 31:1.

ACADEMICS
Calendar: semesters. *Degrees:* certificates, associate, and bachelor's.
Library: Richard H. Rush Library. *Books:* 45,355 (physical), 28,410 (digital/electronic); *Databases:* 128. Weekly public service hours: 79.

STUDENT LIFE
Housing options: coed. Campus housing is university owned.

Activities and organizations: drama/theater group, choral group.

Athletics Member NJCAA.

Campus security: 24-hour emergency response devices and patrols, late-night transport/escort service, controlled dormitory access, Rave Guardian app for students, faculty, and staff.

FINANCIAL AID
Financial Aid Of all full-time matriculated undergraduates who enrolled in 2014, 3,887 applied for aid, 3,311 were judged to have need, 68 had their need fully met. In 2014, 166 non-need-based awards were made. *Average percent of need met:* 47. *Average financial aid package:* $6172. *Average need-based loan:* $3461. *Average need-based gift aid:* $5119. *Average non-need-based aid:* $2588.

APPLYING
Options: electronic application, early admission, deferred entrance.

Application fee: $30.

Required: high school transcript.

CONTACT
FSW Admissions, Florida SouthWestern State College, 8099 College Parkway, Fort Myers, FL 33919. *Phone:* 239-489-9054. *Fax:* 239-489-9094. *E-mail:* admissions@fsw.edu.

Florida State College at Jacksonville
Jacksonville, Florida
http://www.fscj.edu/

CONTACT
Dr. Peter Biegel, Registrar, Florida State College at Jacksonville, 501 West State Street, Jacksonville, FL 32202. *Phone:* 904-632-5112. *Toll-free phone:* 888-873-1145. *E-mail:* pbiegel@fscj.edu.

Florida State University
Tallahassee, Florida
http://www.fsu.edu/

- **State-supported** university, founded 1851, part of State University System of Florida
- **Suburban** 477-acre campus
- **Endowment** $639.4 million
- **Coed** 33,093 undergraduate students, 89% full-time, 56% women, 44% men
- **Very difficult** entrance level, 49% of applicants were admitted

UNDERGRAD STUDENTS
29,370 full-time, 3,723 part-time. Students come from 51 states and territories; 102 other countries; 11% are from out of state; 8% Black or African American, non-Hispanic/Latino; 20% Hispanic/Latino; 2% Asian, non-Hispanic/Latino; 0.1% Native Hawaiian or other Pacific Islander, non-Hispanic/Latino; 0.2% American Indian or Alaska Native, non-Hispanic/Latino; 4% Two or more races, non-Hispanic/Latino; 2% Race/ethnicity unknown; 2% international; 6% transferred in; 20% live on campus.

Freshmen:
Admission: 35,334 applied, 17,381 admitted, 6,494 enrolled. *Average high school GPA:* 4.0. *Test scores:* SAT evidence-based reading and writing scores over 500: 99%; SAT math scores over 500: 99%; ACT scores over 18: 100%; SAT evidence-based reading and writing scores over 600: 79%; SAT math scores over 600: 69%; ACT scores over 24: 95%; SAT evidence-based reading and writing scores over 700: 13%; SAT math scores over 700: 10%; ACT scores over 30: 26%.
Retention: 94% of full-time freshmen returned.

FACULTY
Total: 1,774, 82% full-time, 87% with terminal degrees.
Student/faculty ratio: 22:1.

ACADEMICS
Calendar: semesters. *Degrees:* certificates, associate, bachelor's, master's, doctoral, post-master's, and postbachelor's certificates.
Special study options: accelerated degree program, advanced placement credit, cooperative education, distance learning, double majors, English as a second language, honors programs, independent study, internships, off-campus study, part-time degree program, services for LD students, study abroad, summer session for credit. *ROTC:* Army (b), Navy (c), Air Force (b).
Unusual degree programs: 3-2 engineering; education, criminology, mathematics, computer science, statistics, law.
Computers: 1,100 computers/terminals are available on campus for general student use. Students can access the following: computer help desk, free student e-mail accounts, online (class) grades, online (class) registration, online (class) schedules, course home pages, course search, online fee payment. Campuswide network is available. 100% of college-owned or -operated housing units are wired for high-speed Internet access. Wireless service is available via entire campus.
Library: Robert Manning Strozier Library plus 8 others. *Books:* 2.3 million (physical), 1.6 million (digital/electronic); *Serial titles:* 125,007 (digital/electronic); *Databases:* 1,144. Weekly public service hours: 134; study areas open 24 hours, 5–7 days a week; students can reserve study rooms.

STUDENT LIFE
Housing options: coed, special housing for students with disabilities. Campus housing is university owned. Freshman applicants given priority for college housing.

Activities and organizations: drama/theater group, student-run newspaper, radio and television station, choral group, marching band, Student Government, Honors Program, Golden Key Honor Society, Marching Chiefs, Intramural Sports, national fraternities, national sororities.
Athletics Member NCAA. All Division I except football (Division I-A). *Intercollegiate sports:* baseball M(s), basketball M(s)/W(s), bowling M(c)/W(c), cheerleading M/W, cross-country running M(s)/W(s), golf M(s)/W(s), rugby M(c)/W(c), sand volleyball W(s), soccer M(c)/W(s), softball W(s), swimming and diving M(s)/W(s), table tennis M(c)/W(c), tennis M(s)/W(s), track and field M(s)/W(s), volleyball M(c)/W(s). *Intramural sports:* badminton M(c)/W(c), baseball M(c), basketball M/W, bowling M/W, cheerleading W(c), crew M(c)/W(c), equestrian sports M(c)/W(c), fencing M(c)/W(c), field hockey M(c)/W(c), football M/W, golf M/W, gymnastics M(c)/W(c), ice hockey M(c)/W(c), lacrosse M(c)/W(c), racquetball M/W, sailing M(c)/W(c), sand volleyball M/W, soccer M/W, softball M/W(c), swimming and diving M(c)/W(c), table tennis M/W, tennis M/W, track and field M/W, ultimate Frisbee M(c)/W(c), volleyball M(c)/W(c), water polo M(c)/W(c), weight lifting M/W, wrestling M/W.
Campus security: 24-hour emergency response devices and patrols, late-night transport/escort service, controlled dormitory access.
Student services: health clinic, personal/psychological counseling, women's center, legal services.

COSTS & FINANCIAL AID
Costs (2018–19) *Tuition:* state resident $4640 full-time, $216 per credit hour part-time; nonresident $19,806 full-time, $721 per credit hour part-time. Full-time tuition and fees vary according to course load, degree level, and location. Part-time tuition and fees vary according to course load, degree level, and location. *Required fees:* $1867 full-time. *Room and board:* $10,458; room only: $6380. Room and board charges vary according to board plan and housing facility. *Payment plans:* tuition prepayment, installment. *Waivers:* senior citizens and employees or children of employees.
Financial Aid Of all full-time matriculated undergraduates who enrolled in 2016, 20,291 applied for aid, 14,299 were judged to have need, 1,545 had their need fully met. 855 Federal Work-Study jobs (averaging $2400). 21 state and other part-time jobs (averaging $2400). In 2016, 4466 non-need-based awards were made. *Average percent of need met:* 65. *Average financial aid package:* $13,013. *Average need-based loan:* $4450. *Average need-based gift aid:* $10,859. *Average non-need-based aid:* $4987. *Average indebtedness upon graduation:* $23,679.

APPLYING
Standardized Tests *Required:* SAT or ACT (for admission).
Options: electronic application, early admission, deferred entrance.
Application fee: $30.
Required: high school transcript. *Recommended:* essay or personal statement.
Application deadlines: 2/7 (freshmen), 6/1 (transfers).
Notification: 3/28 (freshmen), continuous (transfers).

CONTACT
Florida State University, 600 West College Avenue, Tallahassee, FL 32306. *Phone:* 850-644-1389.

Fortis College
Cutler Bay, Florida
http://www.fortis.edu/

CONTACT
Fortis College, 19600 South Dixie Highway, Suite B, Cutler Bay, FL 33157. *Toll-free phone:* 855-4-FORTIS.

Full Sail University
Winter Park, Florida
http://www.fullsail.edu/

CONTACT
Ms. Mary Beth Plank, Director of Admissions, Full Sail University, 3300 University Boulevard, Winter Park, FL 32792-7437. *Phone:* 407-679-6333. *Toll-free phone:* 800-226-7625. *E-mail:* admissions@fullsail.com.

Gulf Coast State College

Panama City, Florida

http://www.gulfcoast.edu/

- **State-supported** primarily 2-year, founded 1957, part of Florida College System
- **Urban** 80-acre campus
- **Endowment** $30.5 million
- **Coed**
- **Noncompetitive** entrance level

FACULTY
Student/faculty ratio: 19:1.

ACADEMICS
Calendar: semesters. *Degrees:* certificates, associate, and bachelor's.
Library: Gulf Coast State College Library. *Books:* 44,254 (physical), 58,468 (digital/electronic); *Databases:* 152.

STUDENT LIFE
Housing options: college housing not available.
Activities and organizations: drama/theater group, student-run newspaper, radio and television station, choral group.
Athletics Member NJCAA.
Campus security: 24-hour patrols, late-night transport/escort service, patrols by trained security personnel during campus hours.
Student services: personal/psychological counseling.

COSTS & FINANCIAL AID
Costs (2017–18) *Tuition:* state resident $2370 full-time, $99 per credit hour part-time; nonresident $8633 full-time, $360 per credit hour part-time. Full-time tuition and fees vary according to degree level. Part-time tuition and fees vary according to degree level. *Required fees:* $620 full-time, $26 per credit hour part-time.
Financial Aid Of all full-time matriculated undergraduates who enrolled in 2016, 145 Federal Work-Study jobs (averaging $3200). 60 state and other part-time jobs (averaging $2600).

APPLYING
Options: electronic application, early admission, deferred entrance.
Application fee: $20.
Required: high school transcript.

CONTACT
Mrs. Sam Wagner, Application Process Specialist, Gulf Coast State College, 5230 West U.S. Highway 98, Panama City, FL 32401. *Phone:* 850-769-1551 Ext. 2936. *Fax:* 850-913-3308. *E-mail:* swagner1@gulfcoast.edu.

Herzing University

Winter Park, Florida

http://www.herzing.edu/orlando

CONTACT
Herzing University, 1865 SR 436, Winter Park, FL 32792. *Toll-free phone:* 800-596-0724.

Hobe Sound Bible College

Hobe Sound, Florida

http://www.hsbc.edu/

- **Independent nondenominational** 4-year, founded 1960
- **Small-town** 84-acre campus
- **Endowment** $755,758
- **Coed**
- **Noncompetitive** entrance level, 100% of applicants were admitted

Freshmen:
Admission: 29 applied, 29 admitted.

FACULTY
Total: 22, 36% full-time, 27% with terminal degrees.
Student/faculty ratio: 13:1.

ACADEMICS
Calendar: semesters. *Degrees:* certificates, associate, and bachelor's.
Special study options: academic remediation for entering students, advanced placement credit, distance learning, double majors, English as a second language, external degree program, independent study, internships, summer session for credit.
Computers: 13 computers/terminals are available on campus for general student use. Students can access the following: campus intranet, free student e-mail accounts, online (class) grades. Campuswide network is available. Wireless service is available via classrooms, computer labs, dorm rooms, learning centers, libraries.
Library: College Library.

STUDENT LIFE
Housing options: on-campus residence required through senior year; men-only, women-only.
Activities and organizations: choral group.
Campus security: student patrols, late-night transport/escort service, controlled dormitory access.

COSTS & FINANCIAL AID
Costs (2018–19) *Comprehensive fee:* $12,710 includes full-time tuition ($5600), mandatory fees ($940), and room and board ($6170). Part-time tuition: $325 per credit hour. Part-time tuition and fees vary according to course load. *Required fees:* $940 per year part-time. *College room only:* $2370. *Payment plans:* installment, deferred payment. *Waivers:* employees or children of employees.
Financial Aid *Average financial aid package:* $3550. *Average indebtedness upon graduation:* $7000.

APPLYING
Standardized Tests *Required:* SAT or ACT (for admission).
Options: early admission.
Application fee: $25.
Required: essay or personal statement, high school transcript, 3 letters of recommendation, photograph, medical report.
Application deadlines: rolling (freshmen), rolling (transfers).
Notification: continuous until 8/30 (freshmen), continuous until 8/30 (transfers).

CONTACT
Mrs. Elizabeth McMillan, Director of Admissions, Hobe Sound Bible College, PO Box 1065, Hobe Sound, FL 33475-1065. *Phone:* 772-545-1400 Ext. 1019. *E-mail:* elizabethmcmillan@hsbc.edu.

Hodges University

Naples, Florida

http://www.hodges.edu/

CONTACT
Hodges University, 2655 Northbrooke Drive, Naples, FL 34119. *Phone:* 239-513-1122 Ext. 6104. *Toll-free phone:* 800-466-8017.

Indian River State College

Fort Pierce, Florida

http://www.irsc.edu/

CONTACT
Mr. Eileen Storck, Dean of Educational Services, Indian River State College, 3209 Virginia Avenue, Fort Pierce, FL 34981-5596. *Phone:* 772-462-7361. *Toll-free phone:* 866-792-4772. *E-mail:* estrock@irsc.edu.

Jacksonville University

Jacksonville, Florida

http://www.ju.edu/

- **Independent** comprehensive, founded 1934
- **Suburban** 260-acre campus with easy access to Jacksonville, Saint Augustine
- **Coed** 2,877 undergraduate students, 76% full-time, 61% women, 39% men
- **Moderately difficult** entrance level, 87% of applicants were admitted

UNDERGRAD STUDENTS

2,180 full-time, 697 part-time. Students come from 48 states and territories; 47 other countries; 33% are from out of state; 19% Black or African American, non-Hispanic/Latino; 11% Hispanic/Latino; 2% Asian, non-Hispanic/Latino; 0.4% Native Hawaiian or other Pacific Islander, non-Hispanic/Latino; 0.5% American Indian or Alaska Native, non-Hispanic/Latino; 4% Two or more races, non-Hispanic/Latino; 1% Race/ethnicity unknown; 7% international; 3% transferred in; 41% live on campus.

Freshmen:

Admission: 2,978 applied, 2,582 admitted, 576 enrolled. *Average high school GPA:* 3.3. *Test scores:* SAT evidence-based reading and writing scores over 500: 67%; SAT math scores over 500: 54%; ACT scores over 18: 92%; SAT evidence-based reading and writing scores over 600: 16%; SAT math scores over 600: 18%; ACT scores over 24: 52%; ACT scores over 30: 7%.

Retention: 71% of full-time freshmen returned.

FACULTY

Total: 412, 55% full-time, 52% with terminal degrees.

Student/faculty ratio: 11:1.

ACADEMICS

Calendar: semesters. *Degrees:* bachelor's, master's, doctoral, post-master's, and postbachelor's certificates.

Special study options: academic remediation for entering students, accelerated degree program, adult/continuing education programs, advanced placement credit, cooperative education, distance learning, double majors, English as a second language, freshman honors college, honors programs, independent study, internships, off-campus study, part-time degree program, services for LD students, student-designed majors, study abroad, summer session for credit. *ROTC:* Army (b), Navy (b).

Unusual degree programs: 3-2 business administration; engineering; nursing; mathematics.

Computers: 400 computers/terminals and 1,205 ports are available on campus for general student use. Students can access the following: campus intranet, computer help desk, free student e-mail accounts, online (class) grades, online (class) registration, online (class) schedules, learning management systems. Campuswide network is available. 100% of college-owned or -operated housing units are wired for high-speed Internet access. Wireless service is available via entire campus.

Library: Carl S. Swisher Library. *Books:* 213,571 (physical), 251,492 (digital/electronic); *Serial titles:* 5,833 (physical); *Databases:* 67. Weekly public service hours: 88; students can reserve study rooms.

STUDENT LIFE

Housing options: on-campus residence required through junior year; coed, men-only, women-only, special housing for students with disabilities. Campus housing is university owned. Freshman campus housing is guaranteed.

Activities and organizations: drama/theater group, student-run newspaper, radio and television station, choral group, marching band, Student Veterans of America - Special Interest, Pi Kappa Alpha - Fraternity, Honor Student Association - Academic, Dolphin Divers - Special Interest, Alpha Delta Pi - Sorority, national fraternities, national sororities.

Athletics Member NCAA. All Division I except football (Division I-AA). *Intercollegiate sports:* baseball M(s), basketball M(s)/W(s), crew M(s)/W(s), cross-country running M/W(s), golf M(s)/W(s), lacrosse M(s)/W(s), sand volleyball W, soccer M(s)/W(s), softball W(s), track and field W(s), volleyball W(s). *Intramural sports:* basketball M/W, cheerleading M(c)/W(c), football M/W, riflery M(c)/W(c), sailing M(c)/W(c), sand volleyball M/W, soccer M/W, softball M/W, ultimate Frisbee M/W, volleyball M/W.

Campus security: 24-hour emergency response devices and patrols, student patrols, late-night transport/escort service, controlled dormitory access, trained security patrols during evening hours.

Student services: health clinic, personal/psychological counseling.

COSTS & FINANCIAL AID

Costs (2017–18) *Comprehensive fee:* $49,210 includes full-time tuition ($35,260) and room and board ($13,950). Full-time tuition and fees vary according to course level, course load, degree level, and program. Part-time tuition: $1175 per credit hour. Part-time tuition and fees vary according to course level, course load, degree level, and program. *Required fees:* $580 per credit hour part-time. *College room only:* $9150. Room and board charges vary according to board plan and housing facility. *Payment plan:* deferred payment. *Waivers:* employees or children of employees.

Financial Aid Of all full-time matriculated undergraduates who enrolled in 2017, 2,098 applied for aid, 1,578 were judged to have need, 444 had their need fully met. 252 Federal Work-Study jobs (averaging $894). 70 state and other part-time jobs (averaging $491). In 2017, 306 non-need-based awards were made. *Average percent of need met:* 75. *Average financial aid package:* $26,452. *Average need-based loan:* $3369. *Average need-based gift aid:* $19,345. *Average non-need-based aid:* $15,448.

APPLYING

Options: electronic application, early admission, deferred entrance.

Application fee: $30.

Required: high school transcript, minimum 2.0 GPA. *Required for some:* essay or personal statement, 2 letters of recommendation, audition for music, dance, and theater majors; portfolio for art, computer art, and design majors; interview for the Honors Program. *Recommended:* interview.

Application deadlines: rolling (freshmen), rolling (transfers).

Notification: continuous (freshmen), continuous (transfers).

CONTACT

Mrs. Allana Forte, Director of Admissions and Recruitment, Jacksonville University, 2800 University Boulevard North, Office of Admissions, Jacksonville, FL 32211. *Phone:* 904-256-7000. *Toll-free phone:* 800-225-2027. *Fax:* 904-256-7012. *E-mail:* admissions@ju.edu.

Johnson & Wales University

North Miami, Florida

http://www.jwu.edu/northmiami/

CONTACT

Jeff Greenip, Director of Admissions, Johnson & Wales University, 1701 Northeast 127th Street, North Miami, FL 33181. *Phone:* 305-892-7600. *Toll-free phone:* 866-598-3567. *Fax:* 305-892-7020. *E-mail:* mia@admissions.jwu.edu.

Johnson University Florida

Kissimmee, Florida

http://www.johnsonu.edu/

- **Independent** comprehensive, founded 1976, affiliated with Christian Churches and Churches of Christ
- **Small-town** 40-acre campus with easy access to Orlando
- **Coed** 180 undergraduate students, 92% full-time, 40% women, 60% men
- **Minimally difficult** entrance level, 93% of applicants were admitted

UNDERGRAD STUDENTS

166 full-time, 14 part-time. 15% are from out of state; 11% Black or African American, non-Hispanic/Latino; 17% Hispanic/Latino; 0.6% Asian, non-Hispanic/Latino; 0.6% Native Hawaiian or other Pacific Islander, non-Hispanic/Latino; 2% Two or more races, non-Hispanic/Latino; 6% Race/ethnicity unknown; 2% international; 11% transferred in; 75% live on campus.

Freshmen:

Admission: 97 applied, 90 admitted, 56 enrolled. *Average high school GPA:* 3.1. *Test scores:* SAT evidence-based reading and writing scores over 500: 30%; SAT math scores over 500: 35%; ACT scores over 18: 30%; SAT math scores over 600: 3%.

Retention: 67% of full-time freshmen returned.

FACULTY

Total: 30, 33% full-time, 60% with terminal degrees.

Student/faculty ratio: 10:1.

ACADEMICS

Calendar: semesters. *Degrees:* certificates, associate, bachelor's, and master's.

Special study options: adult/continuing education programs, advanced placement credit, distance learning, double majors, independent study, internships, part-time degree program, study abroad, summer session for credit.

Computers: Students can access the following: computer help desk, free student e-mail accounts, online (class) grades, online (class) registration, online (class) schedules. Campuswide network is available. 100% of college-owned or -operated housing units are wired for high-speed Internet access. Wireless service is available via entire campus.

Library: Library.

STUDENT LIFE

Housing options: Campus housing is university owned.

Activities and organizations: choral group, Student Government Association, Harvesters (Missions), SunRunners club, Timothy club (preachers), Indoor Soccer.

Athletics Member NCCAA. *Intercollegiate sports:* basketball M, soccer M, volleyball W. *Intramural sports:* field hockey M(c), ultimate Frisbee M(c).

Campus security: controlled dormitory access, late night trained security patrol.

Student services: personal/psychological counseling.

COSTS & FINANCIAL AID

Costs (2018–19) *Comprehensive fee:* $22,760 includes full-time tuition ($14,880), mandatory fees ($1180), and room and board ($6700). Full-time tuition and fees vary according to course load and degree level. Part-time tuition: $470 per credit hour. Part-time tuition and fees vary according to degree level. *College room only:* $3000. *Payment plan:* installment. *Waivers:* employees or children of employees.

Financial Aid Of all full-time matriculated undergraduates who enrolled in 2005, 186 applied for aid, 186 were judged to have need, 5 had their need fully met. 38 Federal Work-Study jobs (averaging $1103). In 2005, 10 non-need-based awards were made. *Average percent of need met:* 46. *Average financial aid package:* $5947. *Average need-based loan:* $3418. *Average need-based gift aid:* $2788. *Average non-need-based aid:* $2000. *Average indebtedness upon graduation:* $15,353. *Financial aid deadline:* 7/15.

APPLYING

Standardized Tests *Required:* SAT or ACT (for admission).

Options: electronic application, early admission, deferred entrance.

Application fee: $35.

Required: essay or personal statement, high school transcript, minimum 2.5 GPA, 3 letters of recommendation. *Required for some:* interview.

Application deadlines: 7/15 (freshmen), 7/15 (transfers).

Early decision deadline: 7/15 (for plan 1), 7/15 (for plan 2).

Notification: continuous until 8/15 (freshmen), continuous until 8/15 (transfers), 8/15 (early decision plan 1), 8/15 (early decision plan 2).

CONTACT

Kirsys Asenjo, Director of Admissions, Johnson University Florida, 1011 Bill Beck Boulevard, Kissimmee, FL 34744. *Phone:* 407-569-1380. *Toll-free phone:* 888-468-6322. *Fax:* 321-206-2007. *E-mail:* kasenjo@johnsonu.edu.

Jose Maria Vargas University

Pembroke Pines, Florida

http://www.jmvu.edu/

CONTACT

Jose Maria Vargas University, 10131 Pines Boulevard, Pembroke Pines, FL 33026.

Keiser University

Fort Lauderdale, Florida

http://www.keiseruniversity.edu/

- **Independent** university, founded 1977
- **Urban** campus
- **Coed** 16,039 undergraduate students, 75% full-time, 68% women, 32% men

UNDERGRAD STUDENTS

12,007 full-time, 4,032 part-time. Students come from 54 states and territories; 11% are from out of state; 20% Black or African American, non-Hispanic/Latino; 31% Hispanic/Latino; 2% Asian, non-Hispanic/Latino; 0.3% American Indian or Alaska Native, non-Hispanic/Latino; 4% Two or more races, non-Hispanic/Latino; 3% Race/ethnicity unknown; 0.3% international; 4% transferred in.

Freshmen:

Admission: 2,289 enrolled.

Retention: 90% of full-time freshmen returned.

FACULTY

Total: 1,440, 71% full-time.

Student/faculty ratio: 12:1.

ACADEMICS

Calendar: 3 semesters per year. *Degrees:* associate, bachelor's, master's, doctoral, and post-master's certificates (profile includes data from campuses located in Daytona Beach, Fort Lauderdale, Fort Myers, Jacksonville, Lakeland, Melbourne, Miami, Orlando, Pembroke Pines, Port St. Lucie, Sarasota, Tallahassee, Tampa, and West Palm Beach; not all programs offered at all locations, but many classes offered 100% online).

Special study options: advanced placement credit, distance learning, English as a second language, internships, part-time degree program, summer session for credit.

Computers: Students can access the following: free student e-mail accounts, online (class) grades, online (class) registration, online (class) schedules. Campuswide network is available. Wireless service is available via entire campus.

Library: Keiser University Library. *Books:* 150,394 (physical), 145,000 (digital/electronic); *Serial titles:* 188 (physical), 29 (digital/electronic); *Databases:* 257.

STUDENT LIFE

Housing options: college housing not available.

Activities and organizations: Student Government Association, Phi Theta Kappa, Sigma Beta Delta International Honor Society, Alpha Phi Sigma National Honor Society, Student Nurses Association.

Athletics Member NAIA. *Intercollegiate sports:* baseball M, basketball M/W, cross-country running M/W, golf M/W, lacrosse M/W, soccer M/W, softball W, swimming and diving M/W, tennis M/W, track and field M/W, volleyball W.

Campus security: 24-hour patrols, late-night transport/escort service, AlertNow Rapid Communications Service, Campus Response Teams.

FINANCIAL AID

Financial Aid Of all full-time matriculated undergraduates who enrolled in 2015, 17,735 applied for aid, 17,735 were judged to have need, 17,735 had their need fully met. 47 Federal Work-Study jobs (averaging $2890). *Average financial aid package:* $5512. *Average need-based loan:* $10,068. *Average need-based gift aid:* $5512.

APPLYING

Standardized Tests *Required:* SAT or ACT or Wonderlic aptitude test (for admission).

Options: electronic application.

Application fee: $55.

Required: high school transcript.

Application deadlines: rolling (freshmen), rolling (transfers).

Notification: continuous (freshmen), continuous (transfers).

CONTACT

Keiser University, 1500 NW 49th Street, Fort Lauderdale, FL 33309. *Phone:* 954-439-2720. *Toll-free phone:* 888-534-7379.

Lynn University
Boca Raton, Florida
http://www.lynn.edu/
- **Independent** comprehensive, founded 1962
- **Suburban** 123-acre campus with easy access to Fort Lauderdale
- **Coed** 2,204 undergraduate students, 83% full-time, 48% women, 52% men
- **Moderately difficult** entrance level, 85% of applicants were admitted

UNDERGRAD STUDENTS
1,826 full-time, 378 part-time. Students come from 44 states and territories; 81 other countries; 41% are from out of state; 11% Black or African American, non-Hispanic/Latino; 15% Hispanic/Latino; 1% Asian, non-Hispanic/Latino; 0.3% American Indian or Alaska Native, non-Hispanic/Latino; 1% Two or more races, non-Hispanic/Latino; 11% Race/ethnicity unknown; 17% international; 18% transferred in; 46% live on campus.

Freshmen:
Admission: 3,003 applied, 2,541 admitted, 482 enrolled. *Average high school GPA:* 3.0. *Test scores:* SAT math scores over 500: 70%; ACT scores over 18: 87%; SAT math scores over 600: 11%; ACT scores over 24: 29%; ACT scores over 30: 1%.
Retention: 69% of full-time freshmen returned.

FACULTY
Total: 183, 69% full-time, 54% with terminal degrees.
Student/faculty ratio: 17:1.

ACADEMICS
Calendar: semesters plus 3 summer sessions. *Degrees:* associate, bachelor's, master's, doctoral, post-master's, and postbachelor's certificates.
Special study options: academic remediation for entering students, accelerated degree program, advanced placement credit, cooperative education, distance learning, double majors, English as a second language, independent study, internships, part-time degree program, services for LD students, student-designed majors, study abroad, summer session for credit. *ROTC:* Air Force (c).
Computers: 150 computers/terminals are available on campus for general student use. Students can access the following: campus intranet, computer help desk, free student e-mail accounts, online (class) grades, online (class) schedules, online registration with advisor approval for juniors, seniors and MBA students. Campuswide network is available. 100% of college-owned or -operated housing units are wired for high-speed Internet access. Wireless service is available via entire campus.
Library: Eugene M. and Christine E. Lynn Library. *Books:* 58,952 (physical), 239,257 (digital/electronic); *Serial titles:* 401 (physical), 43,029 (digital/electronic); *Databases:* 118. Weekly public service hours: 96.

STUDENT LIFE
Housing options: on-campus residence required through sophomore year; coed, special housing for students with disabilities. Campus housing is university owned. Freshman campus housing is guaranteed.
Activities and organizations: drama/theater group, student-run newspaper, radio and television station, Knights of the Round Table, intramural groups, student newspaper, Student Activities Board, Greek Life, national fraternities, national sororities.
Athletics Member NCAA. All Division II. *Intercollegiate sports:* baseball M(s), basketball M(s)/W(s), cross-country running M(s)/W(s), golf M(s)/W(s), lacrosse M(s), soccer M(s)/W(s), softball W(s), swimming and diving W(s), tennis M(s)/W(s), track and field W(s), volleyball W(s). *Intramural sports:* basketball M/W, soccer M/W, tennis M/W, ultimate Frisbee M/W, volleyball M/W.
Campus security: 24-hour emergency response devices and patrols, late-night transport/escort service, controlled dormitory access, video monitor at residence entrances.
Student services: health clinic, personal/psychological counseling, women's center.

COSTS & FINANCIAL AID
Costs (2018–19) *One-time required fee:* $1000. *Comprehensive fee:* $50,380 includes full-time tuition ($35,960), mandatory fees ($2250), and room and board ($12,170). Full-time tuition and fees vary according to degree level and program. Part-time tuition: $1040 per credit hour. Part-time tuition and fees vary according to course load and program. *Room and board:* Room and board charges vary according to board plan and housing facility. *Payment plans:* installment, deferred payment. *Waivers:* employees or children of employees.
Financial Aid Of all full-time matriculated undergraduates who enrolled in 2017, 1,550 applied for aid, 756 were judged to have need, 752 had their need fully met. 224 Federal Work-Study jobs (averaging $2055). 35 state and other part-time jobs (averaging $8516). In 2017, 523 non-need-based awards were made. *Average percent of need met:* 52. *Average financial aid package:* $22,741. *Average need-based loan:* $4751. *Average need-based gift aid:* $10,401. *Average non-need-based aid:* $10,810. *Average indebtedness upon graduation:* $32,533.

APPLYING
Standardized Tests *Recommended:* SAT or ACT (for admission).
Options: electronic application, early admission, early action, deferred entrance.
Application fee: $45.
Required: essay or personal statement, high school transcript. *Required for some:* audition for Conservatory of Music. *Recommended:* interview.
Application deadlines: 3/1 (freshmen), rolling (transfers), 11/15 (early action).
Notification: continuous until 12/15 (freshmen), continuous (transfers), 12/15 (early action).
CONTACT
Stefano Papaleo, Director of Undergraduate Admission, Lynn University, Admission, 3601 North Military Trail, Boca Raton, FL 33431. *Phone:* 561-237-7831. *Toll-free phone:* 800-888-5966. *Fax:* 561-237-7100. *E-mail:* spapaleo@lynn.edu.

Marconi International University
Pembroke Pines, Florida
http://www.marconiinternationaluniversity.edu/
CONTACT
Admissions, Marconi International University, 1806 Flamingo Road, Suite 120, Pembroke Pines, FL 33028. *Phone:* 954-374-4701. *E-mail:* info@marconiinternational.org.

Miami Dade College
Miami, Florida
http://www.mdc.edu/
- **State and locally supported** primarily 2-year, founded 1960, part of Florida College System
- **Urban** campus
- **Endowment** $137.1 million
- **Coed** 56,001 undergraduate students, 42% full-time, 57% women, 43% men
- **Noncompetitive** entrance level, 100% of applicants were admitted

UNDERGRAD STUDENTS
23,589 full-time, 32,412 part-time. Students come from 37 states and territories; 165 other countries; 0.4% are from out of state; 14% Black or African American, non-Hispanic/Latino; 70% Hispanic/Latino; 1% Asian, non-Hispanic/Latino; 0.1% Native Hawaiian or other Pacific Islander, non-Hispanic/Latino; 0.1% American Indian or Alaska Native, non-Hispanic/Latino; 0.6% Two or more races, non-Hispanic/Latino; 2% Race/ethnicity unknown; 6% international; 0.1% transferred in.

Freshmen:
Admission: 44,910 applied, 44,910 admitted, 12,173 enrolled.
FACULTY
Total: 2,355, 30% full-time, 25% with terminal degrees.
Student/faculty ratio: 26:1.

ACADEMICS
Calendar: 16-16-6-6. *Degrees:* certificates, associate, bachelor's, and postbachelor's certificates.

Special study options: academic remediation for entering students, accelerated degree program, adult/continuing education programs, advanced placement credit, cooperative education, distance learning, English as a second language, freshman honors college, honors programs, independent study, internships, off-campus study, part-time degree program, services for LD students, study abroad, summer session for credit. *ROTC:* Army (b), Air Force (c).

Computers: 9,655 computers/terminals and 1,500 ports are available on campus for general student use. Students can access the following: campus intranet, computer help desk, free student e-mail accounts, online (class) grades, online (class) registration, online (class) schedules, admissions, student feedback of faculty, financial aid. Campuswide network is available. Wireless service is available via entire campus.

Library: Miami Dade College Learning Resources plus 9 others. *Books:* 185,820 (physical), 60,221 (digital/electronic); *Serial titles:* 708 (physical), 46,482 (digital/electronic); *Databases:* 126. Weekly public service hours: 69; students can reserve study rooms.

STUDENT LIFE

Housing options: college housing not available.

Activities and organizations: drama/theater group, student-run newspaper, radio and television station, choral group, Student Government Association, Phi Theta Kappa, Phi Beta Lambda (business), Future Educators of America Professional, Kappa Delta Pi Honor Society (education).

Athletics Member NCAA, NJCAA. All NCAA Division I. *Intercollegiate sports:* baseball M(s), basketball M(s)/W(s), softball W(s), volleyball W(s).

Campus security: 24-hour emergency response devices and patrols, student patrols, late-night transport/escort service, Emergency Mass Notification System (EMNS), campus public address systems, LiveSafe mobile safety App for students/employees.

Student services: health clinic, personal/psychological counseling.

COSTS & FINANCIAL AID

Costs (2017–18) *One-time required fee:* $30. *Tuition:* state resident $1987 full-time, $83 per credit hour part-time; nonresident $7947 full-time, $331 per credit hour part-time. Full-time tuition and fees vary according to course load, degree level, and program. Part-time tuition and fees vary according to course load, degree level, and program. *Required fees:* $851 full-time, $35 per credit hour part-time. *Waivers:* employees or children of employees.

Financial Aid Of all full-time matriculated undergraduates who enrolled in 2016, 800 Federal Work-Study jobs (averaging $5000). 125 state and other part-time jobs (averaging $5000).

APPLYING

Options: electronic application, early admission.

Application fee: $30.

Required: high school transcript.

Application deadlines: rolling (freshmen), rolling (transfers).

Notification: continuous (freshmen), continuous (transfers).

CONTACT

Ms. Elisabet Vizoso, Interim College Registrar, Miami Dade College, 11011 SW 104th Street, Miami, FL 33176. *Phone:* 305-237-2206. *Fax:* 305-237-2532. *E-mail:* evizoso@mdc.edu.

Miami International University of Art & Design

Miami, Florida

http://www.artinstitutes.edu/miami/

CONTACT

Miami International University of Art & Design, 1501 Biscayne Boulevard, Suite 100, Miami, FL 33132-1418. *Phone:* 305-428-5700. *Toll-free phone:* 800-225-9023.

Miami Regional University

Miami Springs, Florida

http://www.mru.edu/

CONTACT

Miami Regional University, 700 South Royal Poinciana Boulevard, Miami Springs, FL 33166.

Millennia Atlantic University

Doral, Florida

http://www.maufl.edu/

CONTACT

Millennia Atlantic University, 3801 NW 97th Avenue, Doral, FL 33178.

New College of Florida

Sarasota, Florida

http://www.ncf.edu/

- **State-supported** comprehensive, founded 1960, part of State University System of Florida
- **Suburban** 119-acre campus with easy access to Tampa-St. Petersburg
- **Endowment** $40.4 million
- **Coed** 835 undergraduate students, 100% full-time, 63% women, 37% men
- **Very difficult** entrance level, 69% of applicants were admitted

UNDERGRAD STUDENTS

835 full-time. Students come from 38 states and territories; 19 other countries; 18% are from out of state; 3% Black or African American, non-Hispanic/Latino; 18% Hispanic/Latino; 3% Asian, non-Hispanic/Latino; 3% Two or more races, non-Hispanic/Latino; 2% Race/ethnicity unknown; 2% international; 4% transferred in; 79% live on campus.

Freshmen:

Admission: 1,353 applied, 933 admitted, 199 enrolled. *Average high school GPA:* 4.0. *Test scores:* SAT evidence-based reading and writing scores over 500: 100%; SAT math scores over 500: 99%; ACT scores over 18: 100%; SAT evidence-based reading and writing scores over 600: 86%; SAT math scores over 600: 58%; ACT scores over 24: 88%; SAT evidence-based reading and writing scores over 700: 31%; SAT math scores over 700: 19%; ACT scores over 30: 35%.

Retention: 79% of full-time freshmen returned.

FACULTY

Total: 108, 73% full-time, 91% with terminal degrees.

Student/faculty ratio: 10:1.

ACADEMICS

Calendar: 4-1-4. *Degrees:* bachelor's and master's.

Special study options: accelerated degree program, double majors, freshman honors college, honors programs, independent study, internships, off-campus study, services for LD students, student-designed majors, study abroad, summer session for credit.

Computers: 105 computers/terminals and 1,356 ports are available on campus for general student use. Students can access the following: campus intranet, computer help desk, free student e-mail accounts, online (class) grades, online (class) registration, online (class) schedules. Campuswide network is available. 100% of college-owned or -operated housing units are wired for high-speed Internet access. Wireless service is available via classrooms, computer labs, dorm rooms, learning centers, libraries, student centers.

Library: Jane Bancroft Cook Library. *Books:* 223,507 (physical), 28,571 (digital/electronic); *Serial titles:* 1,701 (physical), 1,899 (digital/electronic); *Databases:* 210. Weekly public service hours: 96.

STUDENT LIFE

Housing options: on-campus residence required through senior year; coed, special housing for students with disabilities. Campus housing is university owned. Freshman campus housing is guaranteed.

Activities and organizations: drama/theater group, student-run newspaper, radio station, choral group, Dance Collective, Queery, New College Student Alliance, Generation Action, NCF Democrats.

Athletics *Intercollegiate sports:* sailing M/W. *Intramural sports:* basketball M/W, golf M/W, racquetball M/W, sailing M(c)/W(c), sand volleyball M/W, soccer M(c)/W(c), softball M(c)/W(c), swimming and diving M(c)/W(c), table tennis M(c)/W(c), tennis M(c)/W(c), triathlon M(c)/W(c), ultimate Frisbee M(c)/W(c), weight lifting M/W, wrestling M/W.

Campus security: 24-hour emergency response devices and patrols, student patrols, late-night transport/escort service, controlled dormitory access, campus police are state certified police officers and available 24/7.

Student services: health clinic, personal/psychological counseling.

COSTS & FINANCIAL AID
Costs (2017–18) *Tuition:* state resident $6916 full-time; nonresident $29,944 full-time. *Room and board:* $9264; room only: $6603. Room and board charges vary according to board plan and housing facility. *Payment plan:* installment.

Financial Aid Of all full-time matriculated undergraduates who enrolled in 2017, 673 applied for aid, 479 were judged to have need, 148 had their need fully met. 30 Federal Work-Study jobs (averaging $1156). In 2017, 285 non-need-based awards were made. *Average percent of need met:* 86. *Average financial aid package:* $14,822. *Average need-based loan:* $3600. *Average need-based gift aid:* $9932. *Average non-need-based aid:* $2514. *Average indebtedness upon graduation:* $16,297.

APPLYING
Standardized Tests *Required:* SAT or ACT (for admission).

Options: electronic application, early admission, early decision, deferred entrance.

Application fee: $30.

Required: essay or personal statement, high school transcript, 1 letter of recommendation. *Recommended:* minimum 3.0 GPA.

Application deadlines: 4/15 (freshmen), 7/1 (transfers).

Notification: 4/25 (freshmen), 7/31 (transfers).

CONTACT
Office of Admissions, New College of Florida, 5800 Bay Shore Road, Sarasota, FL 34243-2109. *Phone:* 941-487-5000. *Fax:* 941-487-5010. *E-mail:* admissions@ncf.edu.

See below for display ad and page 1362 for the College Close-Up.

New World School of the Arts
Miami, Florida
http://www.mdc.edu/nwsa/

- **State-supported** 4-year, founded 1984
- **Urban** 5-acre campus with easy access to Miami-Dade, Broward, Palm Beach Counties
- **Endowment** $8.3 million
- **Coed** 335 undergraduate students, 100% full-time, 57% women, 43% men
- **Noncompetitive** entrance level, 52% of applicants were admitted

UNDERGRAD STUDENTS
335 full-time. Students come from 12 states and territories; 9 other countries; 4% are from out of state; 13% Black or African American, non-Hispanic/Latino; 62% Hispanic/Latino; 4% Asian, non-Hispanic/Latino; 6% Two or more races, non-Hispanic/Latino; 6% transferred in.

Freshmen:
Admission: 384 applied, 200 admitted, 123 enrolled. *Average high school GPA:* 3.0.
Retention: 70% of full-time freshmen returned.

FACULTY
Total: 77, 29% full-time.
Student/faculty ratio: 5:1.

ACADEMICS
Calendar: semesters. *Degrees:* associate and bachelor's.

Special study options: academic remediation for entering students, advanced placement credit, cooperative education, distance learning, English as a second language, freshman honors college, independent

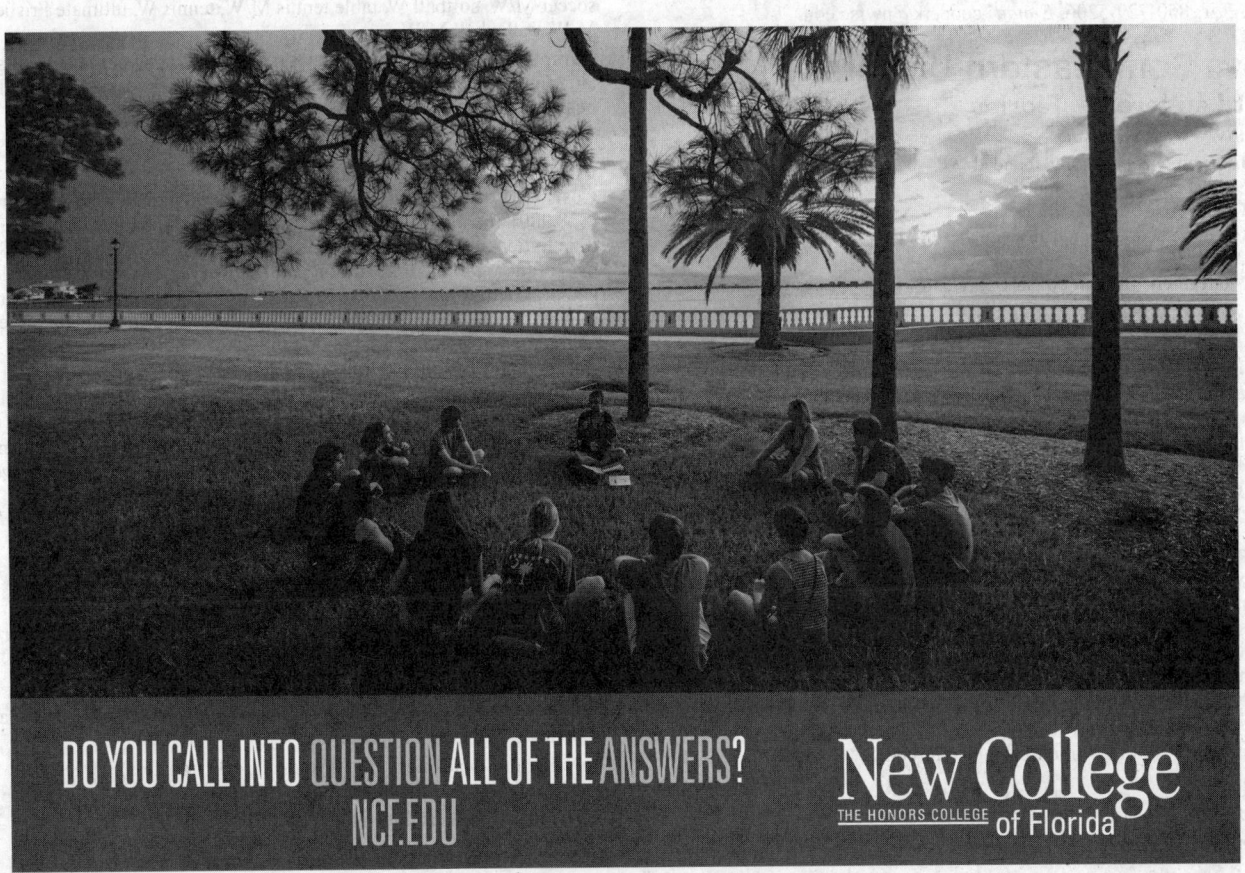

---

study, internships, services for LD students, study abroad, summer session for credit.

Computers: 100 computers/terminals are available on campus for general student use. Students can access the following: campus intranet, computer help desk, free student e-mail accounts, online (class) grades, online (class) registration. Campuswide network is available. Wireless service is available via entire campus.

Library: Miami Dade Community College library (Wolfson Campus) plus 1 other. Students can reserve study rooms.

STUDENT LIFE

Housing options: college housing not available.

Activities and organizations: Student Government.

Campus security: 24-hour emergency response devices and patrols.

Student services: personal/psychological counseling.

APPLYING

Standardized Tests *Recommended:* SAT or ACT (for admission).

Options: electronic application, early decision.

Required: essay or personal statement, high school transcript, 2 letters of recommendation, interview, audition or portfolio submission.

Application deadlines: rolling (freshmen), rolling (out-of-state freshmen), rolling (transfers).

Notification: continuous (freshmen), continuous (transfers), rolling (early decision).

CONTACT

Eloisa Ferrer, Recruitment and Admissions Coordinator, New World School of the Arts, 300 NE 2nd Avenue, Miami, FL 33132. *Phone:* 305-237-7408. *Fax:* 305-237-3794. *E-mail:* eferrer2@mdc.edu.

Northwest Florida State College

Niceville, Florida

http://www.nwfsc.edu/

CONTACT

Ms. Karen Cooper, Director of Admissions, Northwest Florida State College, 100 College Boulevard, Niceville, FL 32578. *Phone:* 850-729-4901. *Fax:* 850-729-5206. *E-mail:* cooperk@nwfsc.edu.

Nova Southeastern University

Fort Lauderdale, Florida

http://www.nova.edu/

- **Independent** university, founded 1964
- **Suburban** 314-acre campus
- **Endowment** $117.8 million
- **Coed** 4,497 undergraduate students, 70% full-time, 71% women, 29% men
- **Moderately difficult** entrance level, 58% of applicants were admitted

UNDERGRAD STUDENTS

3,154 full-time, 1,343 part-time. Students come from 47 states and territories; 66 other countries; 22% are from out of state; 15% Black or African American, non-Hispanic/Latino; 27% Hispanic/Latino; 10% Asian, non-Hispanic/Latino; 0.1% Native Hawaiian or other Pacific Islander, non-Hispanic/Latino; 0.2% American Indian or Alaska Native, non-Hispanic/Latino; 3% Two or more races, non-Hispanic/Latino; 4% Race/ethnicity unknown; 6% international; 13% transferred in; 25% live on campus.

Freshmen:

Admission: 7,779 applied, 4,525 admitted, 984 enrolled. *Average high school GPA:* 4.0. *Test scores:* SAT evidence-based reading and writing scores over 500: 96%; SAT math scores over 500: 90%; ACT scores over 18: 98%; SAT evidence-based reading and writing scores over 600: 51%; SAT math scores over 600: 43%; ACT scores over 24: 68%; SAT evidence-based reading and writing scores over 700: 6%; SAT math scores over 700: 7%; ACT scores over 30: 17%.

Retention: 79% of full-time freshmen returned.

FACULTY

Total: 1,602, 50% full-time, 76% with terminal degrees.

Student/faculty ratio: 17:1.

ACADEMICS

Calendar: trimesters. *Degrees:* certificates, associate, bachelor's, master's, doctoral, post-master's, and postbachelor's certificates.

Special study options: academic remediation for entering students, adult/continuing education programs, advanced placement credit, distance learning, double majors, freshman honors college, honors programs, independent study, internships, off-campus study, part-time degree program, services for LD students, study abroad, summer session for credit.

Unusual degree programs: 3-2 business administration; computer science, criminal justice, humanities and social sciences.

Computers: 3,000 computers/terminals and 6,000 ports are available on campus for general student use. Students can access the following: campus intranet, computer help desk, free student e-mail accounts, online (class) grades, online (class) registration, online (class) schedules. Campuswide network is available. 100% of college-owned or -operated housing units are wired for high-speed Internet access. Wireless service is available via entire campus.

Library: Alvin Sherman Library, Research, and Information Technology Center plus 4 others. *Books:* 498,823 (physical), 379,928 (digital/electronic); *Serial titles:* 6,035 (physical), 20,738 (digital/electronic); *Databases:* 577. Study areas open 24 hours, 5–7 days a week; students can reserve study rooms.

STUDENT LIFE

Housing options: on-campus residence required through sophomore year; coed, special housing for students with disabilities. Campus housing is university owned. Freshman campus housing is guaranteed.

Activities and organizations: drama/theater group, student-run newspaper, radio and television station, choral group, HOSA: Future Health Professionals, Make-a Meal Service Organization, Student Government Association, Delta Epsilon Iota, Pre-Med, national fraternities, national sororities.

Athletics Member NCAA. All Division II. *Intercollegiate sports:* baseball M(s), basketball M(s)/W(s), cheerleading W, crew W(s), cross-country running M(s)/W(s), golf M(s)/W(s), soccer M(s)/W(s), softball W(s), swimming and diving M(s)/W(s), tennis W(s), track and field M(s)/W(s), volleyball W(s). *Intramural sports:* badminton M/W, basketball M/W, equestrian sports M/W, racquetball M/W, rowing W, soccer M/W, softball W, table tennis M/W, tennis W, ultimate Frisbee M/W, volleyball M/W.

Campus security: 24-hour emergency response devices and patrols, late-night transport/escort service, controlled dormitory access, shuttle bus service.

Student services: health clinic, personal/psychological counseling.

COSTS & FINANCIAL AID

Costs (2017–18) *Comprehensive fee:* $42,490 includes full-time tuition ($28,980), mandatory fees ($960), and room and board ($12,550). Full-time tuition and fees vary according to program. Part-time tuition: $966 per credit hour. Part-time tuition and fees vary according to course load and program. *Room and board:* Room and board charges vary according to board plan and housing facility. *Payment plans:* installment, deferred payment. *Waivers:* employees or children of employees.

Financial Aid Of all full-time matriculated undergraduates who enrolled in 2017, 2,559 applied for aid, 2,251 were judged to have need, 301 had their need fully met. 1,144 Federal Work-Study jobs (averaging $6106). 458 state and other part-time jobs (averaging $1061). In 2017, 736 non-need-based awards were made. *Average percent of need met:* 73. *Average financial aid package:* $30,300. *Average need-based loan:* $3305. *Average need-based gift aid:* $17,639. *Average non-need-based aid:* $12,165. *Average indebtedness upon graduation:* $32,127.

APPLYING

Standardized Tests *Required:* SAT or ACT (for admission).

Options: electronic application, early admission, early decision, early action, deferred entrance.

Application fee: $50.

Required: minimum 3.0 GPA. *Required for some:* essay or personal statement, high school transcript, .

Application deadlines: 2/1 (freshmen), 4/1 (transfers), 11/1 (early action).

Early decision deadline: 11/1.

Notification: continuous (freshmen), 10/16 (early decision), rolling (early action).

CONTACT
Nova Southeastern University, 3301 College Avenue, Fort Lauderdale, FL 33314-7796. *Phone:* 954-262-8000. *Toll-free phone:* 800-541-NOVA.

Palm Beach Atlantic University
West Palm Beach, Florida
http://www.pba.edu/
- **Independent nondenominational** comprehensive, founded 1968
- **Urban** 100-acre campus with easy access to Miami-Dade County
- **Endowment** $81.2 million
- **Coed** 3,003 undergraduate students, 78% full-time, 63% women, 37% men
- **Moderately difficult** entrance level, 97% of applicants were admitted

UNDERGRAD STUDENTS
2,350 full-time, 653 part-time. Students come from 48 states and territories; 28 other countries; 34% are from out of state; 10% Black or African American, non-Hispanic/Latino; 15% Hispanic/Latino; 2% Asian, non-Hispanic/Latino; 0.3% Native Hawaiian or other Pacific Islander, non-Hispanic/Latino; 0.3% American Indian or Alaska Native, non-Hispanic/Latino; 3% Two or more races, non-Hispanic/Latino; 2% Race/ethnicity unknown; 3% international; 9% transferred in; 49% live on campus.

Freshmen:
Admission: 1,380 applied, 1,344 admitted, 533 enrolled. *Average high school GPA:* 3.6. *Test scores:* SAT evidence-based reading and writing scores over 500: 77%; SAT math scores over 500: 68%; ACT scores over 18: 92%; SAT evidence-based reading and writing scores over 600: 34%; SAT math scores over 600: 23%; ACT scores over 24: 44%; SAT evidence-based reading and writing scores over 700: 3%; SAT math scores over 700: 2%; ACT scores over 30: 9%.
Retention: 76% of full-time freshmen returned.

FACULTY
Total: 373, 46% full-time, 62% with terminal degrees.
Student/faculty ratio: 12:1.

ACADEMICS
Calendar: semesters. *Degrees:* bachelor's, master's, and doctoral.
Special study options: academic remediation for entering students, accelerated degree program, adult/continuing education programs, advanced placement credit, distance learning, double majors, honors programs, independent study, internships, off-campus study, part-time degree program, services for LD students, student-designed majors, study abroad, summer session for credit. *ROTC:* Army (c).
Unusual degree programs: 3-2 divinity.
Computers: 350 computers/terminals are available on campus for general student use. Students can access the following: campus intranet, computer help desk, free student e-mail accounts, online (class) grades, online (class) registration, online (class) schedules. Campuswide network is available. 100% of college-owned or -operated housing units are wired for high-speed Internet access. Wireless service is available via entire campus.
Library: Warren Library plus 1 other. *Books:* 143,334 (physical), 126,921 (digital/electronic); *Serial titles:* 114 (physical), 121,795 (digital/electronic); *Databases:* 143. Weekly public service hours: 100; students can reserve study rooms.

STUDENT LIFE
Housing options: on-campus residence required through sophomore year; coed, men-only, women-only. Campus housing is university owned and leased by the school. Freshman campus housing is guaranteed.
Activities and organizations: drama/theater group, student-run newspaper, choral group, Impact Leadership Team, Nursing Student Association, Nurses Christian Fellowship, Student Government, Sigma Alpha Omega.
Athletics Member NCAA. All Division II. *Intercollegiate sports:* baseball M(s), basketball M(s)/W(s), cheerleading M(c)/W(c), crew M(c)/W(c), cross-country running M(s)/W(s), golf M(s)/W(s), lacrosse M(s)/W(s), soccer M(s)/W(s), softball W(s), tennis M(s)/W(s), track and field M(s)/W(s), volleyball W(s). *Intramural sports:* basketball M/W,

sand volleyball M/W, soccer M(c)/W, softball M/W, ultimate Frisbee M/W, volleyball M/W.
Campus security: 24-hour emergency response devices and patrols, late-night transport/escort service, controlled dormitory access, lighted pathways/sidewalks, self-defense education, closed-circuit television system.
Student services: health clinic, personal/psychological counseling.

COSTS & FINANCIAL AID
Costs (2018–19) *Comprehensive fee:* $41,580 includes full-time tuition ($30,990), mandatory fees ($460), and room and board ($10,130). Full-time tuition and fees vary according to course load, location, and program. Part-time tuition: $745 per credit hour. Part-time tuition and fees vary according to course load, location, and program. *Required fees:* $145 per term part-time. *College room only:* $5370. Room and board charges vary according to board plan and housing facility. *Payment plan:* installment. *Waivers:* children of alumni and employees or children of employees.
Financial Aid Of all full-time matriculated undergraduates who enrolled in 2017, 1,945 applied for aid, 1,696 were judged to have need, 278 had their need fully met. 205 Federal Work-Study jobs (averaging $3186). 12 state and other part-time jobs (averaging $3010). In 2017, 586 non-need-based awards were made. *Average percent of need met:* 63. *Average financial aid package:* $21,938. *Average need-based loan:* $3868. *Average need-based gift aid:* $19,029. *Average non-need-based aid:* $12,397. *Average indebtedness upon graduation:* $26,907.

APPLYING
Standardized Tests *Required:* SAT or ACT (for admission).
Options: electronic application, early admission, early action, deferred entrance.
Application fee: $50.
Required: essay or personal statement, high school transcript. *Required for some:* interview.
Application deadlines: rolling (freshmen), rolling (transfers), 5/1 (early action).
Notification: continuous (freshmen), continuous (transfers), 6/1 (early action).

CONTACT
Mr. Joseph Bryan, Assistant Vice President for Admissions, Palm Beach Atlantic University, 901 South Flagler Drive, PO Box 24708, West Palm Beach, FL 33416-4708. *Phone:* 561-803-2102. *Toll-free phone:* 888-GO-TO-PBA. *Fax:* 561-803-2115. *E-mail:* joseph_bryan@pba.edu.

Palm Beach State College
Lake Worth, Florida
http://www.palmbeachstate.edu/
- **State-supported** 4-year, founded 1933, part of Florida College System
- **Urban** 114-acre campus with easy access to West Palm Beach
- **Endowment** $18.3 million
- **Coed** 30,052 undergraduate students, 28% full-time, 57% women, 43% men
- **Noncompetitive** entrance level, 100% of applicants were admitted

UNDERGRAD STUDENTS
8,303 full-time, 21,749 part-time. Students come from 23 states and territories; 26% Black or African American, non-Hispanic/Latino; 31% Hispanic/Latino; 3% Asian, non-Hispanic/Latino; 0.2% Native Hawaiian or other Pacific Islander, non-Hispanic/Latino; 0.2% American Indian or Alaska Native, non-Hispanic/Latino; 2% Two or more races, non-Hispanic/Latino; 4% Race/ethnicity unknown; 2% international; 4% transferred in.

Freshmen:
Admission: 5,653 applied, 5,653 admitted, 5,653 enrolled.

FACULTY
Total: 1,170, 28% full-time.
Student/faculty ratio: 23:1.

ACADEMICS
Calendar: semesters. *Degrees:* certificates, diplomas, associate, and bachelor's.

Special study options: academic remediation for entering students, adult/continuing education programs, advanced placement credit, cooperative education, distance learning, double majors, English as a second language, freshman honors college, honors programs, independent study, internships, off-campus study, part-time degree program, services for LD students, student-designed majors, study abroad, summer session for credit.

Computers: Students can access the following: computer help desk, free student e-mail accounts, online (class) registration. Campuswide network is available. Wireless service is available via entire campus.

Library: Harold C. Manor Library plus 5 others. Weekly public service hours: 72; students can reserve study rooms.

STUDENT LIFE
Housing options: college housing not available.

Activities and organizations: drama/theater group, student-run newspaper, choral group, Student Government, Phi Theta Kappa, Students for International Understanding, Black Student Union, Drama Club, national fraternities.

Athletics Member NJCAA. *Intercollegiate sports:* baseball M(s), basketball M(s)/W(s), softball W(s), volleyball W(s).

Campus security: 24-hour emergency response devices and patrols.

Student services: health clinic, personal/psychological counseling, women's center.

COSTS
Costs (2018–19) *One-time required fee:* $40. *Tuition:* state resident $3050 full-time, $101 per credit hour part-time; nonresident $11,740 full-time, $363 per credit hour part-time. Full-time tuition and fees vary according to degree level. Part-time tuition and fees vary according to degree level. *Required fees:* $20 full-time.

APPLYING
Standardized Tests *Recommended:* SAT and SAT Subject Tests or ACT (for admission).

Options: electronic application, early admission, deferred entrance.

Application fee: $40.

Required: high school transcript.

Application deadlines: 8/20 (freshmen), 8/20 (transfers).

Notification: continuous until 8/20 (freshmen), continuous until 8/20 (transfers).

CONTACT
Palm Beach State College, 4200 Congress Avenue, Lake Worth, FL 33461-4796.

Pasco-Hernando State College

New Port Richey, Florida
http://www.phsc.edu/

CONTACT
Ms. Estela Carrion, Director of Admissions and Student Records, Pasco-Hernando State College, 10230 Ridge Road, New Port Richey, FL 34654-5199. *Phone:* 727-816-3261. *Toll-free phone:* 877-TRY-PHSC. *Fax:* 727-816-3389. *E-mail:* carrioe@phsc.edu.

Pensacola Christian College

Pensacola, Florida
http://www.pcci.edu/

CONTACT
Pensacola Christian College, 250 Brent Lane, Pensacola, FL 32503-2267. *Toll-free phone:* 800-722-4636.

Pensacola State College

Pensacola, Florida
http://www.pensacolastate.edu/
- **State-supported** primarily 2-year, founded 1948, part of Florida College System
- **Urban** 130-acre campus with easy access to Mobile, Alabama
- **Endowment** $11.3 million
- **Coed** 9,655 undergraduate students, 37% full-time, 61% women, 39% men
- **Noncompetitive** entrance level, 100% of applicants were admitted

UNDERGRAD STUDENTS
3,583 full-time, 6,072 part-time. Students come from 37 states and territories; 5% are from out of state; 15% Black or African American, non-Hispanic/Latino; 7% Hispanic/Latino; 3% Asian, non-Hispanic/Latino; 0.4% Native Hawaiian or other Pacific Islander, non-Hispanic/Latino; 0.8% American Indian or Alaska Native, non-Hispanic/Latino; 6% Two or more races, non-Hispanic/Latino; 2% Race/ethnicity unknown; 0.4% international; 7% transferred in.

Freshmen:
Admission: 2,892 applied, 2,892 admitted, 1,049 enrolled. *Average high school GPA:* 3.0.
Retention: 72% of full-time freshmen returned.

FACULTY
Total: 599, 30% full-time, 6% with terminal degrees.
Student/faculty ratio: 19:1.

ACADEMICS
Calendar: semesters. *Degrees:* certificates, diplomas, associate, and bachelor's.

Special study options: academic remediation for entering students, adult/continuing education programs, advanced placement credit, cooperative education, distance learning, double majors, English as a second language, external degree program, honors programs, independent study, internships, part-time degree program, services for LD students, summer session for credit. *ROTC:* Army (b).

Computers: 1,700 computers/terminals are available on campus for general student use. Students can access the following: campus intranet, computer help desk, free student e-mail accounts, online (class) grades, online (class) registration, online (class) schedules. Campuswide network is available. Wireless service is available via entire campus.

Library: Edward M. Chadbourne Library plus 3 others. Students can reserve study rooms.

STUDENT LIFE
Housing options: college housing not available.

Activities and organizations: drama/theater group, student-run newspaper, choral group, Student Government Association, Health Occupations Students of America (HOSA), SkillsUSA, African-American Student Association, Forestry Club.

Athletics Member NJCAA. *Intercollegiate sports:* baseball M(s), basketball M(s)/W(s), softball W(s), volleyball W(s). *Intramural sports:* archery M/W, badminton M/W, basketball M/W, bowling M/W, racquetball M/W, soccer M/W, softball W, tennis M/W, volleyball M/W.

Campus security: 24-hour emergency response devices and patrols, late-night transport/escort service.

Student services: personal/psychological counseling.

COSTS & FINANCIAL AID
Costs (2018–19) *One-time required fee:* $30. *Tuition:* state resident $3137 full-time, $105 per credit hour part-time; nonresident $12,593 full-time, $420 per credit hour part-time. Full-time tuition and fees vary according to course level and degree level. Part-time tuition and fees vary according to course level and degree level. *Payment plan:* deferred payment. *Waivers:* senior citizens and employees or children of employees.

Financial Aid Of all full-time matriculated undergraduates who enrolled in 2016, 120 Federal Work-Study jobs (averaging $3000).

APPLYING
Options: electronic application, early admission.

Application fee: $30.

Required: high school transcript.

Application deadlines: 8/30 (freshmen), 8/30 (transfers).

Notification: continuous until 8/30 (freshmen), continuous until 8/30 (transfers).

CONTACT
Ms. Kathy Dutremble, Registrar, Pensacola State College, 1000 College Boulevard, Pensacola, FL 32504. *Phone:* 850-484-2076. *Fax:* 850-484-1020. *E-mail:* kdutremble@pensacolastate.edu.

Polk State College
Winter Haven, Florida
http://www.polk.edu/

- **State-supported** 4-year, founded 1964, part of Florida College System
- **Suburban** 98-acre campus with easy access to Orlando, Tampa
- **Coed** 10,659 undergraduate students, 34% full-time, 63% women, 37% men
- **Noncompetitive** entrance level

UNDERGRAD STUDENTS
3,627 full-time, 7,032 part-time. Students come from 6 states and territories; 5 other countries; 1% are from out of state; 16% Black or African American, non-Hispanic/Latino; 22% Hispanic/Latino; 2% Asian, non-Hispanic/Latino; 0.1% Native Hawaiian or other Pacific Islander, non-Hispanic/Latino; 0.2% American Indian or Alaska Native, non-Hispanic/Latino; 3% Two or more races, non-Hispanic/Latino; 3% Race/ethnicity unknown; 0.9% international; 5% transferred in.

Freshmen:
Admission: 1,088 enrolled.

FACULTY
Total: 392, 41% full-time, 22% with terminal degrees.
Student/faculty ratio: 25:1.

ACADEMICS
Calendar: semesters 16-16-6-6. *Degrees:* certificates, diplomas, associate, and bachelor's.

Special study options: academic remediation for entering students, accelerated degree program, adult/continuing education programs, advanced placement credit, cooperative education, distance learning, double majors, English as a second language, honors programs, independent study, internships, off-campus study, part-time degree program, services for LD students, study abroad, summer session for credit. *ROTC:* Army (c), Air Force (c).

Computers: 800 computers/terminals are available on campus for general student use. Students can access the following: computer help desk, free student e-mail accounts, online (class) grades, online (class) registration, online (class) schedules. Campuswide network is available. Wireless service is available via entire campus.
Library: Polk State College Libraries plus 1 other. *Books:* 82,640 (physical), 110,114 (digital/electronic).

STUDENT LIFE
Housing options: college housing not available.
Activities and organizations: drama/theater group, choral group, Florida Student Nursing Association, Honors Program Student Council, Phi Theta Kappa (PTK), Student Government Association, SALO (Student Activities and Leadership Office).
Athletics Member NJCAA. *Intercollegiate sports:* baseball M(s), basketball M(s), sand volleyball W(s), soccer W(s), softball W(s), volleyball W(s). *Intramural sports:* basketball M/W, bowling M/W, cheerleading M/W, football M/W, sand volleyball W, table tennis M/W, volleyball W.
Campus security: 24-hour emergency response devices and patrols.
Student services: personal/psychological counseling, legal services.

COSTS
Costs (2018–19) *Tuition:* state resident $112 per credit hour part-time; nonresident $409 per credit hour part-time. Full-time tuition and fees vary according to course level, course load, and degree level. Part-time tuition and fees vary according to course level, course load, and degree level. *Waivers:* employees or children of employees.

APPLYING
Options: electronic application, early admission, deferred entrance.

Required: high school transcript.

Application deadlines: rolling (freshmen), rolling (transfers).

Notification: continuous (freshmen), continuous (transfers).

CONTACT
Polk State College, 999 Avenue H, NE, Winter Haven, FL 33881-4299. *Phone:* 863-297-1021.

Polytechnic University of Puerto Rico, Miami Campus
Miami, Florida
http://www.pupr.edu/miami/

- **Independent** comprehensive
- **Urban** campus with easy access to Miami-Dade
- **Coed**

Freshmen:
Average high school GPA: 2.0.

FACULTY
Student/faculty ratio: 10:1.

ACADEMICS
Degrees: bachelor's and master's.

STUDENT LIFE
Housing options: college housing not available.

COSTS
Costs (2017–18) *Tuition:* $11,340 full-time, $315 per credit part-time. Full-time tuition and fees vary according to course load and degree level. Part-time tuition and fees vary according to course load and degree level. No tuition increase for student's term of enrollment. *Required fees:* $750 full-time, $250 per term part-time. *Payment plans:* installment, deferred payment. *Waivers:* employees or children of employees.

APPLYING
Options: electronic application.
Application fee: $30.

CONTACT
Polytechnic University of Puerto Rico, Miami Campus, 8180 Northwest 36th Street, Suite 401, Miami, FL 33166. *Phone:* 305-418-8000. *Toll-free phone:* 888-729-7659.

Polytechnic University of Puerto Rico, Orlando Campus
Orlando, Florida
http://www.pupr.edu/orlando/

CONTACT
Teresa Cardona, Director of Recruitment and Admission, Polytechnic University of Puerto Rico, Orlando Campus, 550 North Econlockhatchee Trail, Orlando, FL 32825. *Phone:* 407-677-7000. *Toll-free phone:* 888-577-POLY. *Fax:* 407-677-5082.

Rasmussen College Fort Myers
Fort Myers, Florida
http://www.rasmussen.edu/

- **Proprietary** 4-year, part of Rasmussen College System
- **Suburban** campus
- **Coed**
- **Minimally difficult** entrance level

FACULTY
Student/faculty ratio: 22:1.

ACADEMICS
Calendar: quarters. *Degrees:* certificates, diplomas, associate, and bachelor's.
Library: Rasmussen College Library - Fort Myers.

STUDENT LIFE
Housing options: college housing not available.

COSTS

Costs (2017–18) *Tuition:* $11,055 full-time, $290 per credit hour part-time. Full-time tuition and fees vary according to course level, course load, degree level, location, and program. Part-time tuition and fees vary according to course level, course load, degree level, location, and program. No tuition increase for student's term of enrollment. *Required fees:* $1695 full-time, $44 per credit hour part-time. *Payment plans:* installment, deferred payment.

APPLYING

Standardized Tests *Required:* institutional exam (for admission).

Options: electronic application, early admission, deferred entrance.

Required: high school transcript, minimum 2.0 GPA. *Required for some:* interview.

CONTACT

Ms. Susan Hammerstrom, Director of Admissions, Rasmussen College Fort Myers, 9160 Forum Corporate Parkway, Suite 100, Fort Myers, FL 33905. *Phone:* 239-477-2100. *Toll-free phone:* 888-549-6755. *E-mail:* susan.hammerstrom@rasmussen.edu.

Rasmussen College Land O' Lakes

Land O' Lakes, Florida

http://www.rasmussen.edu/

- **Proprietary** 4-year, part of Rasmussen College System
- **Suburban** campus
- **Coed**
- **Minimally difficult** entrance level

FACULTY

Student/faculty ratio: 22:1.

ACADEMICS

Calendar: quarters. *Degrees:* certificates, diplomas, associate, and bachelor's.

Library: Rasmussen College Library - Land O' Lakes.

STUDENT LIFE

Housing options: college housing not available.

COSTS

Costs (2017–18) *Tuition:* $11,055 full-time, $290 per credit hour part-time. Full-time tuition and fees vary according to course level, course load, degree level, location, and program. Part-time tuition and fees vary according to course level, course load, degree level, location, and program. No tuition increase for student's term of enrollment. *Required fees:* $1695 full-time, $44 per credit hour part-time. *Payment plans:* installment, deferred payment.

APPLYING

Standardized Tests *Required:* institutional exam (for admission).

Options: electronic application, early admission, deferred entrance.

Required: high school transcript, minimum 2.0 GPA. *Required for some:* interview.

CONTACT

Ms. Susan Hammerstrom, Director of Admissions, Rasmussen College Land O' Lakes, 18600 Fernview Street, Land O' Lakes, FL 34638. *Phone:* 813-435-3601. *Toll-free phone:* 888-549-6755. *E-mail:* susan.hammerstrom@rasmussen.edu.

Rasmussen College New Port Richey

New Port Richey, Florida

http://www.rasmussen.edu/

- **Proprietary** 4-year, part of Rasmussen College System
- **Suburban** campus
- **Coed** 680 undergraduate students, 84% full-time, 84% women, 16% men
- **Minimally difficult** entrance level, 93% of applicants were admitted

UNDERGRAD STUDENTS

573 full-time, 107 part-time.

Freshmen:

Admission: 29 applied, 27 admitted, 27 enrolled.

FACULTY

Total: 36, 47% full-time.

Student/faculty ratio: 22:1.

ACADEMICS

Calendar: quarters. *Degrees:* certificates, diplomas, associate, bachelor's, master's, and postbachelor's certificates.

Special study options: academic remediation for entering students, accelerated degree program, adult/continuing education programs, distance learning, double majors, internships, part-time degree program, summer session for credit.

Computers: 118 computers/terminals are available on campus for general student use. Students can access the following: computer help desk, free student e-mail accounts, online (class) grades, online (class) schedules. Campuswide network is available. Wireless service is available via entire campus.

Library: Rasmussen College Library - New Port Richey.

STUDENT LIFE

Housing options: college housing not available.

COSTS & FINANCIAL AID

Costs (2017–18) *Tuition:* $11,055 full-time, $290 per credit hour part-time. Full-time tuition and fees vary according to course level, course load, degree level, location, and program. Part-time tuition and fees vary according to course level, course load, degree level, location, and program. No tuition increase for student's term of enrollment. *Required fees:* $1695 full-time, $44 per credit hour part-time. *Payment plans:* installment, deferred payment. *Waivers:* employees or children of employees.

Financial Aid Of all full-time matriculated undergraduates who enrolled in 2016, 6 Federal Work-Study jobs.

APPLYING

Standardized Tests *Required:* institutional exam (for admission).

Options: electronic application, early admission, deferred entrance.

Required: high school transcript, minimum 2.0 GPA. *Required for some:* interview.

Application deadlines: rolling (freshmen), rolling (transfers).

CONTACT

Dwayne Bertotto, Vice President of Admissions and Student Experience, Rasmussen College New Port Richey, 8300 Norman Center Drive, Suite 300, Bloomington, MN 55437. *Phone:* 952-806-3958. *Toll-free phone:* 888-549-6755. *E-mail:* dwayne.bertotto@rasmussen.edu.

Rasmussen College Ocala

Ocala, Florida

http://www.rasmussen.edu/

- **Proprietary** 4-year, founded 1984, part of Rasmussen College System
- **Suburban** campus with easy access to Orlando
- **Coed** 1,447 undergraduate students, 82% full-time, 85% women, 15% men
- **Minimally difficult** entrance level, 92% of applicants were admitted

UNDERGRAD STUDENTS

1,182 full-time, 265 part-time.

Freshmen:

Admission: 92 applied, 85 admitted, 85 enrolled.

FACULTY

Total: 44, 23% full-time.

Student/faculty ratio: 22:1.

ACADEMICS

Calendar: quarters. *Degrees:* certificates, diplomas, associate, and bachelor's.

Special study options: academic remediation for entering students, accelerated degree program, adult/continuing education programs, distance learning, double majors, internships, part-time degree program, summer session for credit.

Computers: 124 computers/terminals are available on campus for general student use. Students can access the following: computer help desk, free student e-mail accounts, online (class) grades, online (class) schedules.

Campuswide network is available. Wireless service is available via entire campus.
Library: Rasmussen College Library - Ocala.

STUDENT LIFE
Housing options: college housing not available.

COSTS
Costs (2017–18) *Tuition:* $11,055 full-time, $290 per credit hour part-time. Full-time tuition and fees vary according to course level, course load, degree level, location, and program. Part-time tuition and fees vary according to course level, course load, degree level, location, and program. No tuition increase for student's term of enrollment. *Required fees:* $1695 full-time, $44 per credit hour part-time. *Payment plans:* installment, deferred payment. *Waivers:* employees or children of employees.

APPLYING
Standardized Tests *Required:* institutional exam (for admission).
Options: electronic application, early admission, deferred entrance.
Required: high school transcript, minimum 2.0 GPA. *Required for some:* interview.
Application deadlines: rolling (freshmen), rolling (transfers).

CONTACT
Dwayne Bertotto, Vice President of Admissions and Student Experience, Rasmussen College Ocala, 8300 Norman Center Drive, Suite 300, Bloomington, MN 55437. *Phone:* 952-806-3958. *Toll-free phone:* 888-549-6755. *E-mail:* dwayne.bertotto@rasmussen.edu.

Rasmussen College Ocala School of Nursing
Ocala, Florida
http://www.rasmussen.edu/
- **Proprietary** 4-year, part of Rasmussen College System
- **Suburban** campus
- **Coed**
- **Minimally difficult** entrance level

FACULTY
Student/faculty ratio: 22:1.

ACADEMICS
Calendar: quarters. *Degrees:* associate and bachelor's.
Library: Rasmussen College Library - Ocala.

STUDENT LIFE
Housing options: college housing not available.

COSTS
Costs (2017–18) *Tuition:* $11,055 full-time, $395 per credit hour part-time. Full-time tuition and fees vary according to course level, course load, degree level, location, and program. Part-time tuition and fees vary according to course level, course load, degree level, location, and program. No tuition increase for student's term of enrollment. *Required fees:* $1695 full-time, $44 per credit hour part-time. *Payment plans:* installment, deferred payment.

APPLYING
Standardized Tests *Required:* institutional exam (for admission).
Options: electronic application, early admission, deferred entrance.
Required: high school transcript, minimum 2.0 GPA. *Required for some:* interview.

CONTACT
Ms. Susan Hammerstrom, Director of Admissions, Rasmussen College Ocala School of Nursing, 2100 SW 22nd Place, Ocala, FL 34471. *Phone:* 352-291-8560. *Toll-free phone:* 888-549-6755. *E-mail:* susan.hammerstrom@rasmussen.edu.

Rasmussen College Tampa/Brandon
Tampa, Florida
http://www.rasmussen.edu/
- **Proprietary** 4-year, part of Rasmussen College System
- **Suburban** campus
- **Coed**
- **Minimally difficult** entrance level

FACULTY
Student/faculty ratio: 22:1.

ACADEMICS
Calendar: quarters. *Degrees:* certificates, diplomas, associate, and bachelor's.
Library: Rasmussen College Library - Tampa.

STUDENT LIFE
Housing options: college housing not available.

COSTS
Costs (2017–18) *Tuition:* $11,055 full-time, $290 per credit hour part-time. Full-time tuition and fees vary according to course level, course load, degree level, location, and program. Part-time tuition and fees vary according to course level, course load, degree level, location, and program. No tuition increase for student's term of enrollment. *Required fees:* $1695 full-time, $44 per credit hour part-time. *Payment plans:* installment, deferred payment.

APPLYING
Standardized Tests *Required:* institutional exam (for admission).
Options: electronic application, early admission, deferred entrance.
Required: high school transcript, minimum 2.0 GPA. *Required for some:* interview.

CONTACT
Ms. Susan Hammerstrom, Director of Admissions, Rasmussen College Tampa/Brandon, 4042 Park Oaks Boulevard, Suite 100, Tampa, FL 33610. *Phone:* 813-246-7600. *Toll-free phone:* 888-549-6755. *E-mail:* susan.hammerstrom@rasmussen.edu.

Ringling College of Art and Design
Sarasota, Florida
http://www.ringling.edu/
- **Independent** 4-year, founded 1931
- **Urban** 49-acre campus with easy access to Tampa-St. Petersburg
- **Endowment** $47.5 million
- **Coed** 1,456 undergraduate students, 96% full-time, 68% women, 32% men
- **Moderately difficult** entrance level, 64% of applicants were admitted

UNDERGRAD STUDENTS
1,395 full-time, 61 part-time. Students come from 48 states and territories; 56 other countries; 54% are from out of state; 4% Black or African American, non-Hispanic/Latino; 17% Hispanic/Latino; 9% Asian, non-Hispanic/Latino; 0.1% Native Hawaiian or other Pacific Islander, non-Hispanic/Latino; 0.3% American Indian or Alaska Native, non-Hispanic/Latino; 4% Two or more races, non-Hispanic/Latino; 2% Race/ethnicity unknown; 16% international; 6% transferred in; 71% live on campus.

Freshmen:
Admission: 1,995 applied, 1,275 admitted, 367 enrolled. *Average high school GPA:* 3.3.
Retention: 84% of full-time freshmen returned.

FACULTY
Total: 173, 65% full-time, 53% with terminal degrees.
Student/faculty ratio: 11:1.

ACADEMICS
Calendar: semesters. *Degree:* bachelor's.
Special study options: academic remediation for entering students, advanced placement credit, English as a second language, independent study, internships, off-campus study, part-time degree program, services for LD students, study abroad, summer session for credit.

Computers: 1,000 computers/terminals are available on campus for general student use. Students can access the following: campus intranet, computer help desk, free student e-mail accounts, online (class) grades, online (class) registration, online (class) schedules, central file storage, high performance computing labs. Campuswide network is available. 100% of college-owned or -operated housing units are wired for high-speed Internet access. Wireless service is available via entire campus.
Library: Alfred R. Goldstein Library. *Books:* 51,891 (physical), 133,879 (digital/electronic); *Serial titles:* 12,169 (physical); *Databases:* 28. Weekly public service hours: 84; study areas open 24 hours, 5–7 days a week; students can reserve study rooms.

STUDENT LIFE

Housing options: coed, men-only, women-only. Campus housing is university owned. Freshman applicants given priority for college housing.

Activities and organizations: drama/theater group, student-run television station, choral group, Student Government Association, Digital Painting Sketch Club, Resident Student Association, MOSAIC, Quidditch Team.

Athletics *Intramural sports:* football M(c)/W(c).

Campus security: 24-hour emergency response devices and patrols, late-night transport/escort service, controlled dormitory access, lighted campus.

Student services: health clinic, personal/psychological counseling, legal services.

COSTS & FINANCIAL AID

Costs (2018–19) *Comprehensive fee:* $61,090 includes full-time tuition ($42,330), mandatory fees ($4090), and room and board ($14,670). Full-time tuition and fees vary according to course load, program, and student level. Part-time tuition: $1972 per credit hour. Part-time tuition and fees vary according to program and student level. *Room and board:* Room and board charges vary according to board plan and housing facility. *Payment plan:* installment. *Waivers:* employees or children of employees.

Financial Aid Of all full-time matriculated undergraduates who enrolled in 2016, 935 applied for aid, 863 were judged to have need, 44 had their need fully met. In 2016, 314 non-need-based awards were made. *Average percent of need met:* 48. *Average financial aid package:* $24,503. *Average need-based loan:* $7807. *Average need-based gift aid:* $15,839. *Average non-need-based aid:* $11,663. *Average indebtedness upon graduation:* $44,384.

APPLYING

Options: electronic application, early action, deferred entrance.

Application fee: $70.

Required: essay or personal statement, high school transcript, minimum 2.0 GPA, 2 letters of recommendation, portfolio, resume. *Recommended:* interview.

Application deadlines: rolling (freshmen), rolling (transfers), 11/1 (early action).

Notification: continuous (freshmen), continuous (transfers), 12/15 (early action).

CONTACT

Ringling College of Art and Design, 2700 North Tamiami Trail, Sarasota, FL 34234-5895. *Phone:* 941-359-7523. *Toll-free phone:* 800-255-7695. *E-mail:* admissions@ringling.edu.

Rollins College

Winter Park, Florida

http://www.rollins.edu/

- **Independent** comprehensive, founded 1885
- **Suburban** 80-acre campus with easy access to Orlando
- **Endowment** $368.8 million
- **Coed** 1,984 undergraduate students, 100% full-time, 61% women, 39% men
- **Moderately difficult** entrance level, 64% of applicants were admitted

UNDERGRAD STUDENTS

1,977 full-time, 7 part-time. Students come from 41 states and territories; 57 other countries; 42% are from out of state; 4% Black or African American, non-Hispanic/Latino; 16% Hispanic/Latino; 3% Asian, non-Hispanic/Latino; 0.2% American Indian or Alaska Native, non-Hispanic/Latino; 4% Two or more races, non-Hispanic/Latino; 3% Race/ethnicity unknown; 10% international; 3% transferred in; 60% live on campus.

Freshmen:
Admission: 5,297 applied, 3,384 admitted, 530 enrolled. *Average high school GPA:* 3.3. *Test scores:* SAT evidence-based reading and writing scores over 500: 100%; SAT math scores over 500: 100%; ACT scores over 18: 100%; SAT evidence-based reading and writing scores over 600: 82%; SAT math scores over 600: 70%; ACT scores over 24: 94%; SAT evidence-based reading and writing scores over 700: 18%; SAT math scores over 700: 14%; ACT scores over 30: 26%.

Retention: 83% of full-time freshmen returned.

FACULTY

Total: 232, 100% full-time, 90% with terminal degrees.

Student/faculty ratio: 10:1.

ACADEMICS

Calendar: semesters. *Degrees:* bachelor's, master's, and doctoral.

Special study options: academic remediation for entering students, accelerated degree program, adult/continuing education programs, advanced placement credit, double majors, honors programs, independent study, internships, off-campus study, part-time degree program, services for LD students, student-designed majors, study abroad, summer session for credit.

Unusual degree programs: 3-2 business administration with Rollins College; engineering with Columbia University, Washington University in St. Louis, Auburn University; Environmental management with Duke University.

Computers: 254 computers/terminals are available on campus for general student use. Students can access the following: campus intranet, computer help desk, free student e-mail accounts, online (class) grades, online (class) registration, online (class) schedules. Campuswide network is available. 100% of college-owned or -operated housing units are wired for high-speed Internet access. Wireless service is available via entire campus.
Library: Olin Library. *Books:* 259,302 (physical), 200,491 (digital/electronic); *Serial titles:* 2,358 (physical), 134,353 (digital/electronic); *Databases:* 80. Study areas open 24 hours, 5–7 days a week; students can reserve study rooms.

STUDENT LIFE

Housing options: on-campus residence required through sophomore year; coed, men-only, women-only, special housing for students with disabilities. Campus housing is university owned. Freshman campus housing is guaranteed.

Activities and organizations: drama/theater group, student-run newspaper, radio and television station, choral group, Black Student Union, Student Government Association, Eco-Rollins, Spectrum, WPRK 91.5, national fraternities, national sororities.

Athletics Member NCAA. All Division II. *Intercollegiate sports:* baseball M(s), basketball M(s)/W(s), crew M/W, cross-country running M/W, golf M(s)/W(s), lacrosse M/W, sailing M/W, skiing (downhill) M/W, soccer M(s)/W(s), softball W(s), swimming and diving M/W, tennis M(s)/W(s), volleyball W(s). *Intramural sports:* baseball M, basketball M/W, bowling M/W, equestrian sports W(c), ice hockey M(c), soccer M/W, softball M/W, table tennis M/W, tennis M/W, ultimate Frisbee M/W, volleyball M/W.

Campus security: 24-hour emergency response devices and patrols, late-night transport/escort service, controlled dormitory access.

Student services: health clinic, personal/psychological counseling, women's center.

COSTS & FINANCIAL AID

Costs (2018–19) *Comprehensive fee:* $64,500 includes full-time tuition ($49,760) and room and board ($14,740). *College room only:* $8720. Room and board charges vary according to housing facility. *Payment plan:* installment. *Waivers:* employees or children of employees.

Financial Aid Of all full-time matriculated undergraduates who enrolled in 2017, 1,167 applied for aid, 1,039 were judged to have need, 285 had their need fully met. 232 Federal Work-Study jobs (averaging $2172). 1 state and other part-time job (averaging $6250). In 2017, 637 non-need-based awards were made. *Average percent of need met:* 80. *Average financial aid package:* $39,094. *Average need-based loan:* $4252.

Average need-based gift aid: $33,915. *Average non-need-based aid:* $25,295. *Average indebtedness upon graduation:* $32,700.

APPLYING
Standardized Tests *Required:* Selection of Test Score Waived Option (TSWO) or official SAT/ACT scores (for admission).

Options: electronic application, early admission, early decision, deferred entrance.

Application fee: $50.

Required: essay or personal statement, high school transcript, 1 letter of recommendation. *Recommended:* minimum 2.0 GPA, interview.

Application deadlines: 2/1 (freshmen), 4/15 (transfers).

Early decision deadline: 11/15 (for plan 1), 12/15 (for plan 2).

Notification: 4/1 (freshmen), continuous (transfers), 1/15 (early decision plan 1), 1/15 (early decision plan 2).

CONTACT
Dr. Faye Tydlaska, Vice President of Enrollment Management and Marketing, Rollins College, 1000 Holt Avenue, Campus Box 2720, Winter Park, FL 32789. *Phone:* 407-646-2000 Ext. 2161. *E-mail:* admissions@rollins.edu.

St. John Vianney College Seminary
Miami, Florida
http://www.sjvcs.edu/

CONTACT
Br. Edward Van Merrienboer, Academic Dean, St. John Vianney College Seminary, 2900 Southwest 87th Avenue, Miami, FL 33165-3244. *Phone:* 305-223-4561 Ext. 13.

Saint Leo University
Saint Leo, Florida
http://www.saintleo.edu/
- **Independent Roman Catholic** comprehensive, founded 1889
- **Rural** 280-acre campus with easy access to Tampa, Orlando
- **Endowment** $58.1 million
- **Coed** 2,264 undergraduate students, 97% full-time, 57% women, 43% men
- **Moderately difficult** entrance level, 70% of applicants were admitted

UNDERGRAD STUDENTS
2,192 full-time, 72 part-time. Students come from 47 states and territories; 63 other countries; 30% are from out of state; 14% Black or African American, non-Hispanic/Latino; 19% Hispanic/Latino; 2% Asian, non-Hispanic/Latino; 0.3% American Indian or Alaska Native, non-Hispanic/Latino; 2% Two or more races, non-Hispanic/Latino; 7% Race/ethnicity unknown; 12% international; 6% transferred in; 67% live on campus.

Freshmen:
Admission: 4,501 applied, 3,139 admitted, 610 enrolled. *Average high school GPA:* 3.5. *Test scores:* ACT scores over 18: 97%; ACT scores over 24: 38%; ACT scores over 30: 7%.
Retention: 72% of full-time freshmen returned.

FACULTY
Total: 211, 61% full-time, 64% with terminal degrees.
Student/faculty ratio: 14:1.

ACADEMICS
Calendar: semesters. *Degrees:* certificates, associate, bachelor's, master's, doctoral, and postbachelor's certificates.

Special study options: academic remediation for entering students, accelerated degree program, adult/continuing education programs, advanced placement credit, distance learning, double majors, English as a second language, honors programs, independent study, internships, part-time degree program, services for LD students, study abroad, summer session for credit. *ROTC:* Army (b), Air Force (b).

Computers: 150 computers/terminals are available on campus for general student use. Students can access the following: campus intranet, computer help desk, free student e-mail accounts, online (class) grades, online (class) registration, online (class) schedules. Campuswide network is available. 100% of college-owned or -operated housing units are wired for high-speed Internet access. Wireless service is available via classrooms, computer centers, computer labs, dorm rooms, learning centers, libraries, student centers.

Library: Cannon Memorial Library plus 1 other. *Books:* 97,155 (physical), 403,383 (digital/electronic); *Serial titles:* 265 (physical), 170,845 (digital/electronic); *Databases:* 72. Weekly public service hours: 119.

STUDENT LIFE
Housing options: on-campus residence required through junior year; coed, men-only, women-only, special housing for students with disabilities. Campus housing is university owned. Freshman applicants given priority for college housing.

Activities and organizations: drama/theater group, student-run newspaper, choral group, Caribbean Student Association, Alpha Phi Omega, Intercultural Student Association, Opus Fides, Pacioli Accounting Club, national fraternities, national sororities.

Athletics Member NCAA. All Division II. *Intercollegiate sports:* baseball M(s), basketball M(s)/W(s), cross-country running M(s)/W(s), golf M(s)/W(s), lacrosse M(s)/W(s), soccer M(s)/W(s), softball W(s), swimming and diving M(s)/W(s), tennis M(s)/W(s), track and field M(s)/W(s), volleyball W(s). *Intramural sports:* basketball M/W, bowling M/W, field hockey M/W, football M/W, sand volleyball M/W, soccer M/W, ultimate Frisbee M/W.

Campus security: 24-hour emergency response devices and patrols, late-night transport/escort service, controlled dormitory access, surveillance cameras in parking lots.

Student services: health clinic, personal/psychological counseling.

COSTS & FINANCIAL AID
Costs (2017–18) *Comprehensive fee:* $32,540 includes full-time tuition ($21,600), mandatory fees ($370), and room and board ($10,570). *College room only:* $5620. Room and board charges vary according to board plan and housing facility. *Payment plans:* installment, deferred payment. *Waivers:* employees or children of employees.

Financial Aid Of all full-time matriculated undergraduates who enrolled in 2017, 1,690 applied for aid, 1,496 were judged to have need, 265 had their need fully met. 425 Federal Work-Study jobs (averaging $4254). 5 state and other part-time jobs (averaging $4460). In 2017, 516 non-need-based awards were made. *Average percent of need met:* 73. *Average financial aid package:* $22,237. *Average need-based loan:* $4111. *Average need-based gift aid:* $16,931. *Average non-need-based aid:* $7317. *Average indebtedness upon graduation:* $40,359.

APPLYING
Standardized Tests *Recommended:* SAT or ACT (for admission).

Options: electronic application, early admission, deferred entrance.

Application fee: $40.

Required: high school transcript, 1 letter of recommendation. *Recommended:* interview.

Application deadlines: rolling (freshmen), rolling (transfers).

Notification: continuous (freshmen), continuous (transfers).

CONTACT
Saint Leo University, MC 2008, PO Box 6665, Saint Leo, FL 33574-6665. *Phone:* 352-588-8283. *Toll-free phone:* 800-334-5532. *Fax:* 352-588-8257. *E-mail:* admissions@saintleo.edu.

St. Petersburg College
St. Petersburg, Florida
http://www.spcollege.edu/
- **State and locally supported** 4-year, founded 1927
- **Suburban** 410-acre campus with easy access to Tampa
- **Coed**
- **Noncompetitive** entrance level

ACADEMICS
Calendar: semesters. *Degrees:* certificates, diplomas, associate, and bachelor's.
Library: M. M. Bennett Library.

STUDENT LIFE
Housing options: college housing not available.

Activities and organizations: drama/theater group, student-run newspaper, choral group.

Athletics Member NJCAA.

Campus security: late-night transport/escort service.

Student services: women's center.

COSTS

Costs (2017–18) *Tuition:* state resident $2428 full-time, $113 per credit hour part-time; nonresident $9717 full-time, $389 per credit hour part-time. *Required fees:* $957 full-time.

APPLYING

Options: electronic application, early admission.

Application fee: $30.

Required: high school transcript.

CONTACT

Ms. Eva Christensen, Director of Admissions and Records, St. Petersburg College, PO Box 13489, St. Petersburg, FL 33733-3489. *Phone:* 727-341-3166. *E-mail:* information@spcollege.edu.

St. Thomas University
Miami Gardens, Florida
http://www.stu.edu/

- **Independent Roman Catholic** university, founded 1961
- **Suburban** 140-acre campus with easy access to Miami, FL
- **Endowment** $25.6 million
- **Coed** 2,912 undergraduate students, 32% full-time, 58% women, 42% men

UNDERGRAD STUDENTS

932 full-time, 1,980 part-time. Students come from 28 states and territories; 23 other countries; 11% are from out of state; 26% Black or African American, non-Hispanic/Latino; 44% Hispanic/Latino; 0.3% Asian, non-Hispanic/Latino; 2% Two or more races, non-Hispanic/Latino; 5% Race/ethnicity unknown; 15% international; 10% transferred in; 40% live on campus.

Freshmen:

Admission: 229 enrolled. *Average high school GPA:* 3.2. *Test scores:* SAT evidence-based reading and writing scores over 500: 48%; SAT math scores over 500: 55%; ACT scores over 18: 75%; SAT evidence-based reading and writing scores over 600: 10%; SAT math scores over 600: 16%; ACT scores over 24: 16%; SAT evidence-based reading and writing scores over 700: 1%; SAT math scores over 700: 1%; ACT scores over 30: 1%.

Retention: 68% of full-time freshmen returned.

FACULTY

Total: 497, 19% full-time.

Student/faculty ratio: 11:1.

ACADEMICS

Calendar: semesters. *Degrees:* certificates, bachelor's, master's, doctoral, post-master's, and postbachelor's certificates.

Special study options: academic remediation for entering students, accelerated degree program, adult/continuing education programs, advanced placement credit, distance learning, double majors, English as a second language, external degree program, honors programs, independent study, internships, part-time degree program, services for LD students, study abroad, summer session for credit. *ROTC:* Air Force (c).

Computers: 100 computers/terminals and 20 ports are available on campus for general student use. Students can access the following: campus intranet, computer help desk, free student e-mail accounts, online (class) grades, online (class) registration, online (class) schedules. Campuswide network is available. 100% of college-owned or -operated housing units are wired for high-speed Internet access. Wireless service is available via entire campus.

Library: St. Thomas University Library plus 1 other. *Books:* 555,242 (physical), 479,232 (digital/electronic); *Serial titles:* 146,423 (physical),

146,423 (digital/electronic); *Databases:* 410. Weekly public service hours: 101; students can reserve study rooms.

STUDENT LIFE

Housing options: coed. Campus housing is university owned.

Activities and organizations: choral group, marching band, Psychology Club, Nursing Students Association, Criminal Justice, Caribbean Students Association, Future Teachers of America.

Athletics Member NAIA. *Intercollegiate sports:* baseball M(s), basketball M(s)/W(s), cheerleading W(s), cross-country running M(s)/W(s), golf M(s)/W, sand volleyball W(s), soccer M(s)/W(s), softball W(s), tennis M(s)/W(s), track and field M(s)/W(s), volleyball W(s). *Intramural sports:* badminton M/W, baseball M, basketball M/W, cross-country running M/W, football M/W, golf M/W, racquetball M/W, sand volleyball M/W, soccer M/W, softball M/W, table tennis M/W, tennis M/W, volleyball M/W.

Campus security: 24-hour emergency response devices and patrols, late-night transport/escort service, controlled dormitory access.

Student services: health clinic, personal/psychological counseling.

COSTS & FINANCIAL AID

Costs (2018–19) *Comprehensive fee:* $42,780 includes full-time tuition ($30,900), mandatory fees ($180), and room and board ($11,700). Full-time tuition and fees vary according to course load and program. Part-time tuition: $618 per credit hour. Part-time tuition and fees vary according to course load and program. *Required fees:* $75 per course part-time, $120 per course part-time. *College room only:* $7200. Room and board charges vary according to board plan and housing facility. *Payment plans:* installment, deferred payment. *Waivers:* employees or children of employees.

Financial Aid Of all full-time matriculated undergraduates who enrolled in 2015, 806 applied for aid, 790 were judged to have need.

APPLYING

Standardized Tests *Recommended:* SAT or ACT (for admission).

Required: high school transcript, minimum 2.5 GPA. *Required for some:* interview. *Recommended:* essay or personal statement, 1 letter of recommendation.

CONTACT

Mr. Anthony Noriega, Associate Director of Admissions, St. Thomas University, 16401 Northwest 37th Avenue, Miami Gardens, FL 33054-6459. *Phone:* 305-628-6617. *Toll-free phone:* 800-367-9010. *E-mail:* ajnoriega@stu.edu.

San Ignacio University
Doral, Florida
http://www.sanignaciouniversity.edu/

CONTACT
San Ignacio University, 10395 NW 41st Street, Suite 125, Doral, FL 33178.

Santa Fe College
Gainesville, Florida
http://www.sfcollege.edu/

CONTACT
Santa Fe College, 3000 Northwest 83rd Street, Gainesville, FL 32606. *Phone:* 352-395-4177.

Schiller International University
Largo, Florida
http://www.schiller.edu/

CONTACT
Admissions Officer, Schiller International University, Largo, FL 33770. *Toll-free phone:* 800-261-9571 (in-state); 800-261-9751 (out-of-state). *Fax:* 727-738-6376. *E-mail:* admissions@schiller.edu.

Seminole State College of Florida

Sanford, Florida

http://www.seminolestate.edu/

- **State and locally supported** primarily 2-year, founded 1966, part of Florida College System
- **Small-town** 200-acre campus with easy access to Orlando
- **Endowment** $24.6 million
- **Coed** 17,706 undergraduate students, 35% full-time, 55% women, 45% men
- **Noncompetitive** entrance level, 64% of applicants were admitted

UNDERGRAD STUDENTS

6,137 full-time, 11,569 part-time. Students come from 21 states and territories; 68 other countries; 3% are from out of state; 16% Black or African American, non-Hispanic/Latino; 24% Hispanic/Latino; 3% Asian, non-Hispanic/Latino; 0.3% Native Hawaiian or other Pacific Islander, non-Hispanic/Latino; 0.3% American Indian or Alaska Native, non-Hispanic/Latino; 3% Two or more races, non-Hispanic/Latino; 3% Race/ethnicity unknown; 2% international; 7% transferred in.

Freshmen:
Admission: 4,587 applied, 2,941 admitted, 2,670 enrolled.
Retention: 52% of full-time freshmen returned.

FACULTY

Total: 798, 26% full-time, 22% with terminal degrees.
Student/faculty ratio: 26:1.

ACADEMICS

Calendar: semesters. *Degrees:* certificates, diplomas, associate, bachelor's, and postbachelor's certificates.

Special study options: academic remediation for entering students, accelerated degree program, adult/continuing education programs, advanced placement credit, cooperative education, distance learning, double majors, English as a second language, external degree program, honors programs, independent study, internships, part-time degree program, services for LD students, study abroad, summer session for credit. *ROTC:* Army (b).

Computers: 300 computers/terminals are available on campus for general student use. Students can access the following: campus intranet, computer help desk, free student e-mail accounts, online (class) grades, online (class) registration, online (class) schedules, online syllabi. Campuswide network is available. Wireless service is available via entire campus.
Library: Seminole State Library at Sanford Lake Mary plus 3 others. *Books:* 67,023 (physical), 145,374 (digital/electronic); *Serial titles:* 520 (physical), 18,003 (digital/electronic); *Databases:* 130. Weekly public service hours: 60; students can reserve study rooms.

STUDENT LIFE

Housing options: college housing not available.

Activities and organizations: drama/theater group, student-run newspaper, choral group, Phi Beta Lambda, Phi Theta Kappa, Student Government Association, Sigma Phi Gamma, Hispanic Student Association.

Athletics Member NJCAA. *Intercollegiate sports:* baseball M(s), golf W(s), softball W(s).

Campus security: 24-hour emergency response devices and patrols, late-night transport/escort service.

Student services: personal/psychological counseling.

COSTS

Costs (2018–19) *Tuition:* state resident $3131 full-time, $104 per credit hour part-time; nonresident $12,739 full-time, $382 per credit hour part-time. Full-time tuition and fees vary according to degree level. Part-time tuition and fees vary according to degree level. *Payment plan:* deferred payment. *Waivers:* senior citizens and employees or children of employees.

APPLYING

Options: electronic application, early admission, deferred entrance.
Required: high school transcript, minimum 2.0 GPA.
Application deadlines: rolling (freshmen), rolling (transfers).
Notification: continuous (freshmen), continuous (transfers).

CONTACT

Seminole State College of Florida, 100 Weldon Boulevard, Sanford, FL 32773-6199.

Southeastern University

Lakeland, Florida

http://www.seu.edu/

- **Independent** comprehensive, founded 1935, affiliated with Assemblies of God
- **Suburban** 87-acre campus with easy access to Tampa, Orlando
- **Endowment** $9.3 million
- **Coed** 6,240 undergraduate students, 69% full-time, 56% women, 44% men
- **Minimally difficult** entrance level, 98% of applicants were admitted

UNDERGRAD STUDENTS

4,288 full-time, 1,952 part-time. Students come from 52 states and territories; 33 other countries; 47% are from out of state; 13% Black or African American, non-Hispanic/Latino; 19% Hispanic/Latino; 2% Asian, non-Hispanic/Latino; 0.5% Native Hawaiian or other Pacific Islander, non-Hispanic/Latino; 0.5% American Indian or Alaska Native, non-Hispanic/Latino; 5% Race/ethnicity unknown; 1% international; 20% transferred in; 32% live on campus.

Freshmen:
Admission: 1,258 applied, 1,228 admitted, 1,225 enrolled. *Average high school GPA:* 3.4. *Test scores:* SAT evidence-based reading and writing scores over 500: 62%; SAT math scores over 500: 75%; ACT scores over 18: 79%; SAT evidence-based reading and writing scores over 600: 16%; SAT math scores over 600: 28%; ACT scores over 24: 28%; SAT evidence-based reading and writing scores over 700: 1%; SAT math scores over 700: 3%; ACT scores over 30: 3%.

Retention: 68% of full-time freshmen returned.

FACULTY

Total: 467, 34% full-time, 33% with terminal degrees.
Student/faculty ratio: 20:1.

ACADEMICS

Calendar: semesters. *Degrees:* certificates, associate, bachelor's, master's, doctoral, post-master's, and postbachelor's certificates.

Special study options: academic remediation for entering students, adult/continuing education programs, advanced placement credit, cooperative education, distance learning, double majors, honors programs, independent study, internships, off-campus study, part-time degree program, services for LD students, study abroad, summer session for credit. *ROTC:* Army (c).

Computers: 220 computers/terminals are available on campus for general student use. Students can access the following: campus intranet, computer help desk, free student e-mail accounts, online (class) grades, online (class) registration, online (class) schedules, network programs. Campuswide network is available. 100% of college-owned or -operated housing units are wired for high-speed Internet access. Wireless service is available via entire campus.
Library: Steelman Library. *Books:* 79,844 (physical), 215,769 (digital/electronic).

STUDENT LIFE

Housing options: on-campus residence required through sophomore year; men-only, women-only. Campus housing is university owned. Freshman campus housing is guaranteed.

Activities and organizations: drama/theater group, student-run newspaper, radio and television station, choral group.

Athletics Member NAIA. *Intercollegiate sports:* baseball M(s), basketball M(s)/W(s), cheerleading M/W, cross-country running M(s)/W(s), football M(s), golf M(s)/W(s), soccer M(s)/W(s), softball W(s), tennis M(s)/W(s), volleyball W(s), wrestling M(s). *Intramural sports:* basketball M/W, football M/W, soccer M/W, softball M/W, ultimate Frisbee M/W, volleyball M/W.

Campus security: 24-hour emergency response devices and patrols, late-night transport/escort service, controlled dormitory access.

Student services: health clinic, personal/psychological counseling.

COSTS & FINANCIAL AID

Costs (2018–19) *Comprehensive fee:* $34,910 includes full-time tuition ($24,360), mandatory fees ($1000), and room and board ($9550). Full-time tuition and fees vary according to class time, degree level, location, and reciprocity agreements. Part-time tuition: $1015 per credit hour. Part-time tuition and fees vary according to class time, course load, degree level, location, and reciprocity agreements. *Required fees:* $200 per term part-time. *Room and board:* Room and board charges vary according to board plan and housing facility. *Payment plan:* installment. *Waivers:* employees or children of employees.

Financial Aid Of all full-time matriculated undergraduates who enrolled in 2017, 3,734 applied for aid, 3,307 were judged to have need, 419 had their need fully met. 86 Federal Work-Study jobs (averaging $2029). In 2017, 822 non-need-based awards were made. *Average percent of need met:* 61. *Average financial aid package:* $15,554. *Average need-based loan:* $4107. *Average need-based gift aid:* $6252. *Average non-need-based aid:* $9024. *Average indebtedness upon graduation:* $29,810.

APPLYING

Standardized Tests *Required:* SAT or ACT (for admission).

Options: electronic application, early admission, deferred entrance.

Application fee: $40.

Required: essay or personal statement, high school transcript, 1 letter of recommendation. *Required for some:* interview.

Application deadlines: 5/1 (freshmen), 7/1 (transfers).

Notification: 6/1 (freshmen), continuous (transfers).

CONTACT

Ms. Sarah Clark, Executive Director of Admission, Southeastern University, 1000 Longfellow Boulevard, Lakeland, FL 33801. *Phone:* 863-667-5018. *Toll-free phone:* 800-500-8760. *E-mail:* admission@seu.edu.

Southern Technical College

Fort Myers, Florida

http://www.southerntech.edu/locations/ft-myers/

CONTACT

Ms. Tiffany Quinlan, Director of Admissions, Southern Technical College, 1685 Medical Lane, Fort Myers, FL 33907. *Phone:* 239-939-4766. *Toll-free phone:* 877-347-5492. *Fax:* 239-936-4040. *E-mail:* tquinlan@southerntech.edu.

Southern Technical College

Tampa, Florida

http://www.southerntech.edu/locations/tampa/

CONTACT

Admissions, Southern Technical College, 3910 Riga Boulevard, Tampa, FL 33619. *Phone:* 813-630-4401. *Toll-free phone:* 877-347-5492.

South Florida Bible College and Theological Seminary

Deerfield Beach, Florida

http://www.sfbc.edu/

CONTACT

South Florida Bible College and Theological Seminary, 2200 SW 10th Street, Deerfield Beach, FL 33442.

South Florida State College

Avon Park, Florida

http://www.southflorida.edu/

- **State-supported** primarily 2-year, founded 1965, part of Florida State College System
- **Rural** 228-acre campus with easy access to Tampa, St. Petersburg, Orlando
- **Endowment** $6.2 million
- **Coed** 2,885 undergraduate students, 34% full-time, 64% women, 36% men
- **Noncompetitive** entrance level

UNDERGRAD STUDENTS

975 full-time, 1,910 part-time. 3% are from out of state; 11% Black or African American, non-Hispanic/Latino; 37% Hispanic/Latino; 2% Asian, non-Hispanic/Latino; 0.3% Native Hawaiian or other Pacific Islander, non-Hispanic/Latino; 0.2% American Indian or Alaska Native, non-Hispanic/Latino; 2% Two or more races, non-Hispanic/Latino; 2% Race/ethnicity unknown; 1% international; 4% transferred in.

Freshmen:
Admission: 663 applied, 413 enrolled. *Average high school GPA:* 3.1.

FACULTY
Total: 156, 38% full-time, 16% with terminal degrees.

Student/faculty ratio: 16:1.

ACADEMICS

Calendar: semesters. *Degrees:* certificates, diplomas, associate, and bachelor's.

Special study options: academic remediation for entering students, adult/continuing education programs, advanced placement credit, cooperative education, distance learning, English as a second language, independent study, internships, part-time degree program, services for LD students, summer session for credit.

Computers: 85 computers/terminals are available on campus for general student use. Students can access the following: campus intranet, computer help desk, free student e-mail accounts, online (class) grades, online (class) registration, online (class) schedules. Campuswide network is available. 100% of college-owned or -operated housing units are wired for high-speed Internet access. Wireless service is available via classrooms, computer centers, computer labs, learning centers, libraries, student centers.

Library: Library Services.

STUDENT LIFE

Housing options: Campus housing is provided by a third party.

Activities and organizations: Phi Theta Kappa, Phi Beta Lambda, Art Club, Anime and Gaming Club, Basketball Club.

Athletics Member NJCAA. *Intercollegiate sports:* baseball M(s), cross-country running W(s), softball W(s), volleyball W(s). *Intramural sports:* basketball M(c)/W(c), soccer M(c)/W(c).

Campus security: 24-hour emergency response devices and patrols, late-night transport/escort service.

Student services: personal/psychological counseling.

COSTS & FINANCIAL AID

Costs (2018–19) *One-time required fee:* $15. *Tuition:* state resident $2593 full-time, $105 per credit hour part-time; nonresident $9722 full-time, $394 per credit hour part-time. Full-time tuition and fees vary according to course level, course load, degree level, and program. Part-time tuition and fees vary according to course level, course load, degree level, and program. *Room and board:* $6040; room only: $2040. *Payment plan:* installment. *Waivers:* employees or children of employees.

Financial Aid *Average need-based gift aid:* $4666. *Average indebtedness upon graduation:* $3083.

APPLYING

Options: electronic application, early admission, deferred entrance.

Application fee: $15.

Required: high school transcript.

Notification: continuous (freshmen).

CONTACT
Ms. Brenda Desantiago, Admissions, South Florida State College, 600 West College Drive, Avon Park, FL 33825. *Phone:* 863-784-7416.

South University
Royal Palm Beach, Florida
http://www.southuniversity.edu/west-palm-beach/

CONTACT
South University, University Centre, 9801 Belvedere Road, Royal Palm Beach, FL 33411. *Phone:* 561-273-6500. *Toll-free phone:* 866-629-2902.

South University
Tampa, Florida
http://www.southuniversity.edu/tampa/

CONTACT
South University, 4401 North Himes Avenue, Suite 175, Tampa, FL 33614. *Phone:* 813-393-3800. *Toll-free phone:* 800-846-1472.

State College of Florida Manatee-Sarasota
Bradenton, Florida
http://www.scf.edu/
- **State-supported** 4-year, founded 1957, part of Florida Community College System
- **Suburban** 100-acre campus with easy access to Tampa-St. Petersburg
- **Coed**
- **Noncompetitive** entrance level

ACADEMICS
Calendar: semesters. *Degrees:* certificates, associate, and bachelor's.
Library: Sara Harlee Library. *Books:* 129,690 (physical), 731,905 (digital/electronic); *Databases:* 140.

STUDENT LIFE
Housing options: college housing not available.
Activities and organizations: drama/theater group, student-run newspaper, choral group, Student Government Association, Phi Theta Kappa, American Chemical Society Student Affiliate, Campus Ministry, Medical Community Club.
Athletics Member NJCAA.
Campus security: 24-hour emergency response devices and patrols, late-night transport/escort service.

FINANCIAL AID
Financial Aid Of all full-time matriculated undergraduates who enrolled in 2016, 82 Federal Work-Study jobs (averaging $2800). *Financial aid deadline:* 8/15.

APPLYING
Options: electronic application, early admission.
Required: high school transcript.

CONTACT
Ms. MariLynn Lewy, Assistant Vice President of Student Services, State College of Florida Manatee-Sarasota, Bradenton, FL 34206. *Phone:* 941-752-5384. *Fax:* 941-727-6380. *E-mail:* lewym@scf.edu.

Stetson University
DeLand, Florida
http://www.stetson.edu/
- **Independent** comprehensive, founded 1883
- **Small-town** 159-acre campus with easy access to Orlando
- **Endowment** $228.7 million
- **Coed** 3,081 undergraduate students, 99% full-time, 57% women, 43% men
- **Moderately difficult** entrance level, 68% of applicants were admitted

UNDERGRAD STUDENTS
3,044 full-time, 37 part-time. Students come from 49 states and territories; 64 other countries; 27% are from out of state; 8% Black or African American, non-Hispanic/Latino; 16% Hispanic/Latino; 2% Asian, non-Hispanic/Latino; 0.1% Native Hawaiian or other Pacific Islander, non-Hispanic/Latino; 0.4% American Indian or Alaska Native, non-Hispanic/Latino; 4% Two or more races, non-Hispanic/Latino; 2% Race/ethnicity unknown; 6% international; 3% transferred in; 66% live on campus.

Freshmen:
Admission: 11,732 applied, 7,958 admitted, 864 enrolled. *Average high school GPA:* 3.8. *Test scores:* SAT evidence-based reading and writing scores over 500: 96%; SAT math scores over 500: 93%; ACT scores over 18: 99%; SAT evidence-based reading and writing scores over 600: 61%; SAT math scores over 600: 44%; ACT scores over 24: 72%; SAT evidence-based reading and writing scores over 700: 11%; SAT math scores over 700: 8%; ACT scores over 30: 18%.
Retention: 78% of full-time freshmen returned.

FACULTY
Total: 430, 62% full-time, 81% with terminal degrees.
Student/faculty ratio: 13:1.

ACADEMICS
Calendar: semesters. *Degrees:* bachelor's, master's, doctoral, and post-master's certificates.
Special study options: accelerated degree program, advanced placement credit, distance learning, double majors, honors programs, independent study, internships, off-campus study, part-time degree program, services for LD students, student-designed majors, study abroad, summer session for credit. *ROTC:* Army (c).
Unusual degree programs: 3-2 engineering; forestry with Duke University; environmental management with Duke University, public administration with American University.
Computers: 500 computers/terminals are available on campus for general student use. Students can access the following: campus intranet, computer help desk, free student e-mail accounts, online (class) grades, online (class) registration, online (class) schedules. Campuswide network is available. 100% of college-owned or -operated housing units are wired for high-speed Internet access. Wireless service is available via entire campus.
Library: duPont-Ball Library plus 1 other. *Books:* 205,846 (physical), 188,390 (digital/electronic); *Serial titles:* 295 (physical), 115,751 (digital/electronic); *Databases:* 145. Weekly public service hours: 99; students can reserve study rooms.

STUDENT LIFE
Housing options: on-campus residence required through junior year; coed, men-only, women-only. Campus housing is university owned and leased by the school. Freshman campus housing is guaranteed.
Activities and organizations: drama/theater group, student-run newspaper, radio station, choral group, Caribbean Student Association, Fellowship of Christian Athletes, Kaleidoscope (promotes inclusivity), Enactus (social action), Model United Nations, national fraternities, national sororities.
Athletics Member NCAA. All Division I. *Intercollegiate sports:* baseball M(s), basketball M(s)/W(s), crew M(s)/W(s), cross-country running M(s)/W(s), football M, golf M(s)/W(s), lacrosse W(s), soccer M(s)/W(s), softball W(s), tennis M(s)/W(s), volleyball W(s). *Intramural sports:* baseball M(c), basketball M/W(c), equestrian sports M(c)/W(c), golf M(c)/W(c), ice hockey M(c)/W(c), lacrosse M(c)/W(c), riflery M(c)/W(c), sand volleyball M/W, soccer M(c)/W(c), softball M/W(c), tennis M/W, ultimate Frisbee M(c)/W(c), volleyball M/W(c).
Campus security: 24-hour emergency response devices and patrols, student patrols, late-night transport/escort service, controlled dormitory access.
Student services: health clinic, personal/psychological counseling.

COSTS & FINANCIAL AID
Costs (2018–19) *Comprehensive fee:* $59,082 includes full-time tuition ($45,670), mandatory fees ($360), and room and board ($13,052). Part-time tuition: $1150 per credit hour. *College room only:* $7512. Room and board charges vary according to board plan. *Payment plan:* installment. *Waivers:* employees or children of employees.
Financial Aid Of all full-time matriculated undergraduates who enrolled in 2017, 2,299 applied for aid, 2,056 were judged to have need, 429 had

their need fully met. 68 state and other part-time jobs (averaging $3832). In 2017, 788 non-need-based awards were made. *Average percent of need met:* 76. *Average financial aid package:* $36,776. *Average need-based loan:* $5110. *Average need-based gift aid:* $29,996. *Average non-need-based aid:* $24,126. *Average indebtedness upon graduation:* $31,457.

APPLYING
Standardized Tests *Required for some:* SAT or ACT (for admission).
Options: electronic application, deferred entrance.
Application fee: $50.
Required: essay or personal statement, high school transcript, 1 letter of recommendation. *Recommended:* interview.
Application deadlines: rolling (freshmen), rolling (transfers).
Notification: continuous (freshmen), continuous (transfers).

CONTACT
Mr. Rick Ellis, Director of Admissions, Stetson University, 421 N. Woodland Boulevard, Unit 8378, DeLand, FL 32723. *Phone:* 386-822-7100. *Toll-free phone:* 800-688-0101. *Fax:* 386-822-7112. *E-mail:* admissions@stetson.edu.

Strayer University–Baymeadows Campus
Jacksonville, Florida
http://www.strayer.edu/florida/baymeadows/

CONTACT
Strayer University–Baymeadows Campus, 8375 Dix Ellis Trail, Suite 200, Jacksonville, FL 32256. *Toll-free phone:* 888-311-0355.

Strayer University–Fort Lauderdale Campus
Fort Lauderdale, Florida
http://www.strayer.edu/florida/fort-lauderdale/

CONTACT
Strayer University–Fort Lauderdale Campus, 2307 West Broward Boulevard, Suite 100, Fort Lauderdale, FL 33312. *Toll-free phone:* 888-311-0355.

Strayer University–Maitland Campus
Maitland, Florida
http://www.strayer.edu/florida/maitland/

CONTACT
Strayer University–Maitland Campus, 901 North Lake Destiny Road, Suite 370, Maitland, FL 32751. *Toll-free phone:* 888-311-0355.

Strayer University–Miramar Campus
Hollywood, Florida
http://www.strayer.edu/florida/miramar/

CONTACT
Strayer University–Miramar Campus, 15620 Southwest 29th Street, Hollywood, FL 33027. *Toll-free phone:* 888-311-0355.

Strayer University–Orlando East Campus
Orlando, Florida
http://www.strayer.edu/florida/orlando-east/

CONTACT
Strayer University–Orlando East Campus, 2200 North Alafaya Trail, Suite 500, Orlando, FL 32826. *Toll-free phone:* 888-311-0355.

Strayer University–Palm Beach Gardens Campus
West Palm Beach, Florida
http://www.strayer.edu/florida/palm-beach-gardens/

CONTACT
Strayer University–Palm Beach Gardens Campus, 11025 RCA Center Drive, Suite 200, West Palm Beach, FL 33410. *Toll-free phone:* 888-311-0355.

Strayer University–Sand Lake Campus
Orlando, Florida
http://www.strayer.edu/florida/sand-lake/

CONTACT
Strayer University–Sand Lake Campus, 8541 South Park Circle, Building 900, Orlando, FL 32819. *Toll-free phone:* 888-311-0355.

Strayer University–Tampa East Campus
Tampa, Florida
http://www.strayer.edu/florida/tampa-east/

CONTACT
Strayer University–Tampa East Campus, 5650 Breckenridge Park Drive, Suite 300, Tampa, FL 33610. *Toll-free phone:* 888-311-0355.

Strayer University–Tampa Westshore Campus
Tampa, Florida
http://www.strayer.edu/florida/tampa-westshore/

CONTACT
Strayer University–Tampa Westshore Campus, 4902 Eisenhower Boulevard, Suite 100, Tampa, FL 33634. *Toll-free phone:* 888-311-0355.

Tallahassee Community College
Tallahassee, Florida
http://www.tcc.fl.edu/

- **State and locally supported** primarily 2-year, founded 1966, part of Florida College System
- **Suburban** 214-acre campus
- **Endowment** $9.3 million
- **Coed** 11,782 undergraduate students, 49% full-time, 54% women, 46% men
- **Noncompetitive** entrance level

UNDERGRAD STUDENTS
5,830 full-time, 5,952 part-time. Students come from 15 states and territories; 78 other countries; 6% are from out of state; 30% Black or African American, non-Hispanic/Latino; 13% Hispanic/Latino; 2% Asian, non-Hispanic/Latino; 0.1% Native Hawaiian or other Pacific Islander, non-Hispanic/Latino; 0.3% American Indian or Alaska Native, non-Hispanic/Latino; 3% Two or more races, non-Hispanic/Latino; 3% Race/ethnicity unknown; 1% international; 6% transferred in.

Freshmen:
Admission: 2,562 admitted, 2,510 enrolled.
Retention: 56% of full-time freshmen returned.

FACULTY
Total: 724, 24% full-time, 69% with terminal degrees.
Student/faculty ratio: 22:1.

ACADEMICS
Calendar: semesters. *Degrees:* certificates, associate, and bachelor's.
Special study options: academic remediation for entering students, accelerated degree program, adult/continuing education programs,

advanced placement credit, distance learning, English as a second language, external degree program, honors programs, independent study, off-campus study, part-time degree program, services for LD students, study abroad, summer session for credit. *ROTC:* Army (c), Navy (c), Air Force (c).

Computers: 1,733 computers/terminals are available on campus for general student use. Students can access the following: campus intranet, computer help desk, free student e-mail accounts, online (class) grades, online (class) registration, online (class) schedules. Campuswide network is available. Wireless service is available via entire campus.
Library: Tallahassee Community College Library. *Books:* 82,774 (physical), 53,129 (digital/electronic); *Serial titles:* 59 (physical), 42,687 (digital/electronic); *Databases:* 105. Weekly public service hours: 68; students can reserve study rooms.

STUDENT LIFE
Housing options: college housing not available.

Activities and organizations: drama/theater group, student-run newspaper, choral group, Student Government Association, International Student Organization, Phi Theta Kappa, Model United Nations, Honors Council.

Athletics Member NJCAA. *Intercollegiate sports:* baseball M(s), basketball M(s)/W(s), softball W(s). *Intramural sports:* basketball M/W, football M/W, soccer M/W, softball M/W, volleyball M/W.

Campus security: 24-hour emergency response devices and patrols, late-night transport/escort service.

Student services: personal/psychological counseling.

COSTS & FINANCIAL AID
Costs (2018–19) *Tuition:* state resident $2002 full-time, $101 per credit hour part-time; nonresident $7982 full-time, $387 per credit hour part-time. Full-time tuition and fees vary according to course load. Part-time tuition and fees vary according to course load. *Required fees:* $24 full-time, $24 per year part-time. *Payment plans:* installment, deferred payment. *Waivers:* employees or children of employees.

Financial Aid Of all full-time matriculated undergraduates who enrolled in 2016, 3,920 applied for aid, 2,778 were judged to have need. 110 Federal Work-Study jobs (averaging $2217). *Average financial aid package:* $3840. *Average need-based gift aid:* $3656.

APPLYING
Options: electronic application, early admission, deferred entrance.
Required: high school transcript.
Application deadlines: 8/1 (freshmen), 8/1 (transfers).

CONTACT
Student Success Center, Tallahassee Community College, 444 Appleyard Drive, Tallahassee, FL 32304-2895. *Phone:* 850-201-8555. *E-mail:* admissions@tcc.fl.edu.

Talmudic University
Miami Beach, Florida
http://www.talmudicu.edu/

CONTACT
Rabbi Yeshaya Greenberg, Dean of Students, Talmudic University, 4000 Alton Road, Miami Beach, FL 33140. *Phone:* 305-534-7050. *Fax:* 305-534-8444. *E-mail:* yandtg@gmail.com.

Trinity Baptist College
Jacksonville, Florida
http://www.tbc.edu/
- **Independent Baptist** comprehensive, founded 1974
- **Urban** 148-acre campus with easy access to Jacksonville
- **Coed**
- **Moderately difficult** entrance level

ACADEMICS
Calendar: semesters. *Degrees:* associate, bachelor's, and master's.

STUDENT LIFE
Housing options: on-campus residence required through junior year; men-only, women-only. Campus housing is university owned. Freshman campus housing is guaranteed.

Activities and organizations: drama/theater group, student-run newspaper, choral group.

Athletics Member NCCAA.

Campus security: 24-hour emergency response devices and patrols, controlled dormitory access.

Student services: health clinic, personal/psychological counseling.

COSTS & FINANCIAL AID
Costs (2017–18) *Comprehensive fee:* $18,040 includes full-time tuition ($10,490), mandatory fees ($1150), and room and board ($6400). Full-time tuition and fees vary according to course load and program. Part-time tuition: $438 per credit hour. Part-time tuition and fees vary according to course load and program. *Required fees:* $438 per credit hour part-time, $575 per term part-time. *College room only:* $3163.
Financial Aid *Financial aid deadline:* 4/15.

APPLYING
Standardized Tests *Required for some:* SAT or ACT (for admission).
Options: electronic application, early admission.
Application fee: $35.
Required: essay or personal statement, high school transcript, 2 letters of recommendation. *Required for some:* interview.

CONTACT
Melissa Gibson, Trinity Baptist College, 800 Hammond Boulevard, Jacksonville, FL 32219. *Phone:* 904-596-2307. *Toll-free phone:* 800-786-2206. *E-mail:* mgibson@tbc.edu.

Trinity College of Florida
Trinity, Florida
http://www.trinitycollege.edu/
- **Independent nondenominational** 4-year, founded 1932
- **Small-town** 40-acre campus with easy access to Tampa
- **Endowment** $726,911
- **Coed** 189 undergraduate students, 86% full-time, 46% women, 54% men
- **Noncompetitive** entrance level, 92% of applicants were admitted

UNDERGRAD STUDENTS
163 full-time, 26 part-time. Students come from 15 states and territories; 3 other countries; 10% are from out of state; 26% Black or African American, non-Hispanic/Latino; 18% Hispanic/Latino; 2% Asian, non-Hispanic/Latino; 1% American Indian or Alaska Native, non-Hispanic/Latino; 12% Race/ethnicity unknown; 2% international; 25% transferred in; 49% live on campus.

Freshmen:
Admission: 61 applied, 56 admitted, 38 enrolled. *Average high school GPA:* 3.1. *Test scores:* SAT evidence-based reading and writing scores over 500: 26%; SAT math scores over 500: 32%; ACT scores over 18: 57%; ACT scores over 24: 5%; ACT scores over 30: 1%.
Retention: 54% of full-time freshmen returned.

FACULTY
Total: 22, 36% full-time, 32% with terminal degrees.
Student/faculty ratio: 9:1.

ACADEMICS
Calendar: semesters. *Degrees:* certificates, associate, and bachelor's.

Special study options: academic remediation for entering students, accelerated degree program, adult/continuing education programs, advanced placement credit, cooperative education, distance learning, double majors, honors programs, independent study, off-campus study, part-time degree program, services for LD students, summer session for credit.

Computers: 17 computers/terminals and 144 ports are available on campus for general student use. Students can access the following: campus intranet, computer help desk, free student e-mail accounts, online (class) grades, online (class) registration, online (class) schedules. Campuswide network is available. 100% of college-owned or -operated

housing units are wired for high-speed Internet access. Wireless service is available via entire campus.

Library: Raymond H. Center, M.D. Library. *Books:* 33,116 (physical), 165,300 (digital/electronic); *Serial titles:* 38 (physical); *Databases:* 9. Weekly public service hours: 60.

STUDENT LIFE

Housing options: men-only, women-only, special housing for students with disabilities. Campus housing is university owned and leased by the school. Freshman campus housing is guaranteed.

Activities and organizations: choral group, Student Government Association, Great Commission Missionary Fellowship, Prayer Group, Trinity Against Trafficking.

Athletics Member NCCAA. *Intercollegiate sports:* basketball M/W, soccer M, volleyball W.

Campus security: student patrols, security cameras.

Student services: personal/psychological counseling.

COSTS & FINANCIAL AID

Costs (2018–19) *Comprehensive fee:* $23,315 includes full-time tuition ($15,300), mandatory fees ($1040), and room and board ($6975). Full-time tuition and fees vary according to course load and program. Part-time tuition: $510 per credit hour. Part-time tuition and fees vary according to course load and program. *Required fees:* $520 per term part-time. *Payment plan:* installment. *Waivers:* senior citizens and employees or children of employees.

Financial Aid Of all full-time matriculated undergraduates who enrolled in 2017, 140 applied for aid, 130 were judged to have need, 14 had their need fully met. 14 Federal Work-Study jobs (averaging $2501). 1 state and other part-time job (averaging $4860). In 2017, 15 non-need-based awards were made. *Average percent of need met:* 60. *Average financial aid package:* $11,276. *Average need-based loan:* $3878. *Average need-based gift aid:* $8024. *Average non-need-based aid:* $3987. *Average indebtedness upon graduation:* $31,757.

APPLYING

Standardized Tests *Required:* SAT or ACT (for admission).

Options: electronic application, deferred entrance.

Application fee: $35.

Required: essay or personal statement, high school transcript, 2 letters of recommendation. *Required for some:* interview. *Recommended:* minimum 2.2 GPA.

Application deadlines: 7/31 (freshmen), 7/31 (transfers).

Notification: continuous (freshmen), continuous (out-of-state freshmen), continuous (transfers).

CONTACT

Mr. Alton Shady, Admissions Representative, Trinity College of Florida, 2430 Welbilt Boulevard, Trinity, FL 34655. *Phone:* 727-376-6911 Ext. 309. *Toll-free phone:* 800-388-0869. *Fax:* 727-569-1410. *E-mail:* ashady@trinitycollege.edu.

Unilatina International College

Miramar, Florida

http://www.unilatina.edu/

CONTACT

Unilatina International College, 3130 Commerce Parkway, Miramar, FL 33025.

University of Central Florida

Orlando, Florida

http://www.ucf.edu/

- **State-supported** university, founded 1963, part of State University System of Florida
- **Suburban** 1415-acre campus with easy access to Orlando.
- **Endowment** $155.2 million
- **Coed** 56,972 undergraduate students, 70% full-time, 54% women, 46% men
- **Moderately difficult** entrance level, 50% of applicants were admitted

UNDERGRAD STUDENTS

39,962 full-time, 17,010 part-time. Students come from 50 states and territories; 140 other countries; 6% are from out of state; 11% Black or African American, non-Hispanic/Latino; 26% Hispanic/Latino; 6% Asian, non-Hispanic/Latino; 0.2% Native Hawaiian or other Pacific Islander, non-Hispanic/Latino; 0.2% American Indian or Alaska Native, non-Hispanic/Latino; 4% Two or more races, non-Hispanic/Latino; 0.8% Race/ethnicity unknown; 2% international; 12% transferred in; 18% live on campus.

Freshmen:
Admission: 37,693 applied, 18,810 admitted, 6,860 enrolled. *Average high school GPA:* 3.9. *Test scores:* SAT evidence-based reading and writing scores over 500: 99%; SAT math scores over 500: 99%; ACT scores over 18: 100%; SAT evidence-based reading and writing scores over 600: 67%; SAT math scores over 600: 59%; ACT scores over 24: 78%; SAT evidence-based reading and writing scores over 700: 11%; SAT math scores over 700: 11%; ACT scores over 30: 19%.

Retention: 90% of full-time freshmen returned.

FACULTY

Total: 2,051, 77% full-time, 74% with terminal degrees.

Student/faculty ratio: 30:1.

ACADEMICS

Calendar: semesters. *Degrees:* certificates, associate, bachelor's, master's, doctoral, post-master's, and postbachelor's certificates.

Special study options: accelerated degree program, adult/continuing education programs, advanced placement credit, cooperative education, distance learning, double majors, English as a second language, freshman honors college, honors programs, independent study, internships, off-campus study, part-time degree program, services for LD students, study abroad, summer session for credit. *ROTC:* Army (b), Air Force (b).

Unusual degree programs: 3-2 engineering; nursing; history, communicative sciences and disorders, computer science, law.

Computers: 4,113 computers/terminals and 500 ports are available on campus for general student use. Students can access the following: campus intranet, computer help desk, free student e-mail accounts, online (class) grades, online (class) registration, online (class) schedules. Campuswide network is available. 100% of college-owned or -operated housing units are wired for high-speed Internet access. Wireless service is available via entire campus.

Library: University Library plus 1 other. *Books:* 1.6 million (physical), 157,535 (digital/electronic); *Serial titles:* 737 (physical), 68,194 (digital/electronic); *Databases:* 481. Weekly public service hours: 106; students can reserve study rooms.

STUDENT LIFE

Housing options: coed, special housing for students with disabilities. Campus housing is university owned and is provided by a third party. Freshman applicants given priority for college housing.

Activities and organizations: drama/theater group, student-run radio and television station, choral group, marching band, Volunteer UCF, RWC Intramural Sports, Fraternity and Sorority Life, Multicultural Student Center and Organizations, Knight-thon Dance Marathon, national fraternities, national sororities.

Athletics Member NCAA. All Division I except football (Division I-A). *Intercollegiate sports:* baseball M(s), basketball M(s)/W(s), cheerleading W(s), crew W(s), cross-country running W(s), golf M(s)/W(s), soccer M(s)/W(s), softball W(s), tennis M(s)/W(s), track and field W(s), volleyball W(s). *Intramural sports:* badminton M/W, baseball M, basketball M/W, bowling M(c)/W(c), crew M(c)/W, equestrian sports M(c)/W(c), fencing M(c), golf M/W, ice hockey M(c), lacrosse M(c)/W(c), racquetball M/W, rock climbing M(c)/W(c), rugby M(c)/W(c), soccer M/W, softball W(c), swimming and diving M(c)/W(c), table tennis M(c)/W(c), tennis M/W, triathlon M(c)/W(c), ultimate Frisbee M(c)/W(c), volleyball M/W, water polo M(c)/W(c), wrestling M(c)/W(c).

Campus security: 24-hour emergency response devices and patrols, late-night transport/escort service, controlled dormitory access.

Student services: health clinic, personal/psychological counseling, women's center, legal services.

COSTS & FINANCIAL AID

Costs (2017–18) *Tuition:* state resident $6368 full-time, $212 per credit hour part-time; nonresident $22,467 full-time, $749 per credit hour part-

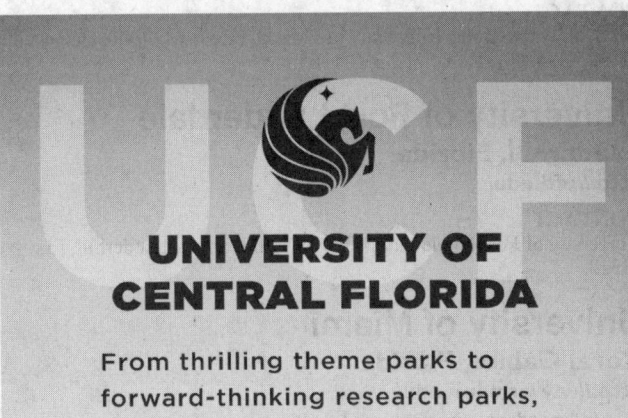

UNIVERSITY OF CENTRAL FLORIDA

From thrilling theme parks to forward-thinking research parks, Orlando has made its mark on the world's stage. Home to the nation's second-largest university, this dynamic area has the ability to attract, develop and unleash creative talent.

To learn more about the UCF Knights, visit **ucf.edu**.

time. Full-time tuition and fees vary according to course load. Part-time tuition and fees vary according to course load. *Room and board:* $10,011; room only: $5400. Room and board charges vary according to board plan and housing facility. *Payment plans:* tuition prepayment, deferred payment. *Waivers:* senior citizens and employees or children of employees.

Financial Aid Of all full-time matriculated undergraduates who enrolled in 2016, 30,552 applied for aid, 23,929 were judged to have need, 1,630 had their need fully met. 997 Federal Work-Study jobs (averaging $3335). In 2016, 1689 non-need-based awards were made. *Average percent of need met:* 55. *Average financial aid package:* $8655. *Average need-based loan:* $4645. *Average need-based gift aid:* $5796. *Average non-need-based aid:* $4041. *Average indebtedness upon graduation:* $21,818. *Financial aid deadline:* 6/30.

APPLYING
Standardized Tests *Required:* SAT or ACT (for admission).

Options: electronic application, early admission.

Application fee: $30.

Required: minimum 2.5 GPA. *Required for some:* high school transcript. *Recommended:* essay or personal statement.

Application deadlines: 5/1 (freshmen), 7/1 (transfers).

Notification: continuous (freshmen), continuous (transfers).

CONTACT
Dr. Gordon Chavis Jr., Associate Vice President, Undergraduate Admissions, Student Financial Assistance and Outreach Programs, University of Central Florida, PO Box 160111, Orlando, FL 32816-0111. *Phone:* 407-823-3000. *Fax:* 407-823-5625. *E-mail:* admission@ucf.edu.

See this page for display ad and page 1458 for the College Close-Up.

University of Florida
Gainesville, Florida
http://www.ufl.edu/
- **State-supported** university, founded 1853, part of Board of Trustees
- **Suburban** 2000-acre campus with easy access to Jacksonville
- **Endowment** $1.6 billion
- **Coed** 35,246 undergraduate students, 89% full-time, 56% women, 44% men
- **Very difficult** entrance level, 42% of applicants were admitted

UNDERGRAD STUDENTS
31,383 full-time, 3,863 part-time. Students come from 51 states and territories; 130 other countries; 6% are from out of state; 6% Black or African American, non-Hispanic/Latino; 21% Hispanic/Latino; 8% Asian, non-Hispanic/Latino; 0.6% Native Hawaiian or other Pacific Islander, non-Hispanic/Latino; 0.2% American Indian or Alaska Native, non-Hispanic/Latino; 3% Two or more races, non-Hispanic/Latino; 3% Race/ethnicity unknown; 3% international; 5% transferred in; 22% live on campus.

Freshmen:
Admission: 32,747 applied, 13,758 admitted, 6,423 enrolled. *Average high school GPA:* 4.4. *Test scores:* SAT evidence-based reading and writing scores over 500: 99%; SAT math scores over 500: 99%; ACT scores over 18: 100%; SAT evidence-based reading and writing scores over 600: 85%; SAT math scores over 600: 83%; ACT scores over 24: 96%; SAT evidence-based reading and writing scores over 700: 25%; SAT math scores over 700: 30%; ACT scores over 30: 54%.

ACADEMICS
Calendar: semesters. *Degrees:* certificates, associate, bachelor's, master's, doctoral, post-master's, and postbachelor's certificates.

Special study options: accelerated degree program, adult/continuing education programs, advanced placement credit, cooperative education, distance learning, double majors, English as a second language, external degree program, honors programs, independent study, internships, off-campus study, part-time degree program, services for LD students, student-designed majors, study abroad, summer session for credit. *ROTC:* Army (b), Navy (b), Air Force (b).

Unusual degree programs: 3-2 business administration; engineering with The University of the Virgin Islands; forestry.

Computers: 1,327 computers/terminals and 245 ports are available on campus for general student use. Students can access the following: campus intranet, free student e-mail accounts, online (class) grades, online (class) registration, online (class) schedules, course management system; virtual labs/applications. Campuswide network is available. 100% of college-owned or -operated housing units are wired for high-speed Internet access. Wireless service is available via entire campus.

Library: George A. Smathers Libraries plus 7 others. *Books:* 4.5 million (physical), 1.5 million (digital/electronic); *Serial titles:* 1,978 (physical), 145,196 (digital/electronic); *Databases:* 1,574. Weekly public service hours: 152; study areas open 24 hours, 5–7 days a week; students can reserve study rooms.

STUDENT LIFE

Housing options: coed, special housing for students with disabilities. Campus housing is university owned and is provided by a third party.

Activities and organizations: drama/theater group, student-run newspaper, radio and television station, choral group, marching band, VISA - Volunteers for International Student Affairs, Fellowship of Christian Athletes, Black Student Union, Hispanic Student Association, Asian American Student Union, national fraternities, national sororities.

Athletics Member NCAA. All Division I. *Intercollegiate sports:* baseball M(s), basketball M(s)/W(s), bowling M(c)/W(c), cheerleading M(s)/W(s), cross-country running M(s)/W(s), football M(s), golf M(s)/W(s), gymnastics W(s), lacrosse W(s), racquetball M(c)/W(c), soccer M/W(s), softball W(s), swimming and diving M(s)/W(s), table tennis M(c)/W(c), tennis M(s)/W(s), track and field M(s)/W(s), ultimate Frisbee M(c)/W(c), volleyball M/W(s). *Intramural sports:* archery M(c)/W(c), badminton M(c)/W(c), baseball M(c), basketball M/W, bowling M/W, cheerleading W(c), crew M(c)/W(c), cross-country running M(c)/W(c), equestrian sports M(c)/W(c), fencing M(c)/W(c), field hockey M(c)/W(c), football M/W, golf M(c)/W(c), gymnastics W(c), ice hockey M(c), lacrosse M(c)/W(c), racquetball M/W, rock climbing M(c)/W(c), rugby M(c)/W(c), sailing M(c)/W(c), sand volleyball M/W, soccer M/W, softball M/W, swimming and diving M/W, table tennis M/W, tennis M/W, track and field M/W, ultimate Frisbee M/W, volleyball M/W, water polo M(c)/W(c), weight lifting M(c)/W(c), wrestling M(c)/W(c).

Campus security: 24-hour emergency response devices and patrols, student patrols, late-night transport/escort service, controlled dormitory access, crime and rape prevention programs.

Student services: health clinic, personal/psychological counseling, women's center, legal services.

COSTS & FINANCIAL AID

Costs (2017–18) *Tuition:* state resident $4477 full-time, $149 per credit hour part-time; nonresident $25,694 full-time, $856 per credit hour part-time. Full-time tuition and fees vary according to course level, course load, location, program, and reciprocity agreements. Part-time tuition and fees vary according to course level, course load, location, program, and reciprocity agreements. *Required fees:* $1904 full-time. *Room and board:* $9910; room only: $5440. Room and board charges vary according to board plan and housing facility. *Waivers:* senior citizens and employees or children of employees.

Financial Aid Of all full-time matriculated undergraduates who enrolled in 2016, 21,465 applied for aid, 16,044 were judged to have need, 3,541 had their need fully met. 1,048 Federal Work-Study jobs (averaging $1970). 5,059 state and other part-time jobs (averaging $1856). In 2016, 1940 non-need-based awards were made. *Average percent of need met:* 97. *Average financial aid package:* $12,982. *Average need-based loan:* $4472. *Average need-based gift aid:* $7612. *Average non-need-based aid:* $2717. *Average indebtedness upon graduation:* $22,192.

APPLYING

Standardized Tests *Required:* SAT or ACT (for admission). *Required for some:* SAT Subject Tests (for admission).

Options: electronic application.

Application fee: $30.

Required: essay or personal statement. *Required for some:* high school transcript.

Application deadlines: 3/1 (freshmen), rolling (transfers).

Notification: 2/9 (freshmen), continuous (transfers).

CONTACT

Office of Admissions, University of Florida, PO Box 114000, Gainesville, FL 32611-4000. *Phone:* 352-392-1365.

University of Fort Lauderdale
Lauderhill, Florida
http://uftl.edu/

CONTACT
University of Fort Lauderdale, 4093 NW 16th Street, Lauderhill, FL 33313.

University of Miami
Coral Gables, Florida
http://www.miami.edu/

- **Independent** university, founded 1925
- **Suburban** 239-acre campus with easy access to Miami
- **Endowment** $948.6 million
- **Coed** 10,832 undergraduate students, 94% full-time, 52% women, 48% men
- **Very difficult** entrance level, 36% of applicants were admitted

UNDERGRAD STUDENTS

10,216 full-time, 616 part-time. Students come from 53 states and territories; 102 other countries; 55% are from out of state; 8% Black or African American, non-Hispanic/Latino; 23% Hispanic/Latino; 5% Asian, non-Hispanic/Latino; 0.1% American Indian or Alaska Native, non-Hispanic/Latino; 3% Two or more races, non-Hispanic/Latino; 4% Race/ethnicity unknown; 15% international; 6% transferred in; 39% live on campus.

Freshmen:

Admission: 30,634 applied, 10,936 admitted, 2,211 enrolled. *Average high school GPA:* 3.5. *Test scores:* SAT evidence-based reading and writing scores over 500: 98%; SAT math scores over 500: 99%; ACT scores over 18: 99%; SAT evidence-based reading and writing scores over 600: 81%; SAT math scores over 600: 82%; ACT scores over 24: 94%; SAT evidence-based reading and writing scores over 700: 24%; SAT math scores over 700: 38%; ACT scores over 30: 56%.

Retention: 91% of full-time freshmen returned.

FACULTY
Total: 1,614, 69% full-time, 79% with terminal degrees.
Student/faculty ratio: 12:1.

ACADEMICS

Calendar: semesters. *Degrees:* certificates, bachelor's, master's, doctoral, post-master's, and postbachelor's certificates.

Special study options: academic remediation for entering students, accelerated degree program, advanced placement credit, cooperative education, distance learning, double majors, English as a second language, honors programs, independent study, internships, off-campus study, part-time degree program, services for LD students, student-designed majors, study abroad, summer session for credit. *ROTC:* Army (b), Air Force (b).

Unusual degree programs: 3-2 engineering; nursing; Law.

Computers: 400 computers/terminals and 600 ports are available on campus for general student use. Students can access the following: campus intranet, computer help desk, free student e-mail accounts, online (class) grades, online (class) registration, online (class) schedules, online bill payment, online housing registration. Campuswide network is available. 100% of college-owned or -operated housing units are wired for high-speed Internet access. Wireless service is available via entire campus.

Library: Otto G. Richter Library plus 6 others. *Books:* 2.8 million (physical), 1.0 million (digital/electronic); *Serial titles:* 1,216 (physical), 113,585 (digital/electronic); *Databases:* 677. Weekly public service hours: 118; students can reserve study rooms.

STUDENT LIFE

Housing options: on-campus residence required for freshman year; coed, special housing for students with disabilities. Campus housing is university owned. Freshman campus housing is guaranteed.

Activities and organizations: drama/theater group, student-run newspaper, radio and television station, choral group, marching band,

Hurricane Productions, Federation of Club Sports, Association of Greek Letter Organizations, Panhellenic Council, Scuba Club, national fraternities, national sororities.

Athletics Member NCAA. All Division I except football (Division I-A). *Intercollegiate sports:* baseball M(s), basketball M(s)/W(s), cheerleading M/W, crew W(s), cross-country running M(s)/W(s), golf W(s), soccer W(s), swimming and diving M(s)/W(s), tennis M(s)/W(s), track and field M(s)/W(s), volleyball W(s). *Intramural sports:* badminton M(c)/W(c), baseball M(c), basketball M/W, cross-country running M(c)/W(c), equestrian sports M(c)/W(c), fencing M(c)/W(c), field hockey W(c), football M/W, golf M(c)/W(c), ice hockey M(c), lacrosse M(c)/W(c), racquetball M(c)/W(c), rock climbing M(c)/W(c), rugby M(c)/W(c), sailing M(c)/W(c), soccer M(c)/W(c), softball M/W, squash M(c)/W(c), swimming and diving M(c)/W(c), table tennis M(c)/W(c), tennis M(c)/W(c), ultimate Frisbee M(c)/W(c), volleyball M(c)/W(c), water polo M(c)/W(c), weight lifting M/W, wrestling M(c)/W(c).

Campus security: 24-hour emergency response devices and patrols, student patrols, late-night transport/escort service, controlled dormitory access, programs, seminars, activities, classes and publications are available to students, faculty, staff, parents and friends.

Student services: health clinic, personal/psychological counseling.

COSTS & FINANCIAL AID

Costs (2017–18) *Comprehensive fee:* $62,150 includes full-time tuition ($47,040), mandatory fees ($1444), and room and board ($13,666). Full-time tuition and fees vary according to course load. Part-time tuition: $1960 per credit hour. Part-time tuition and fees vary according to course load and program. *College room only:* $7880. Room and board charges vary according to board plan and housing facility. *Payment plan:* installment. *Waivers:* employees or children of employees.

Financial Aid Of all full-time matriculated undergraduates who enrolled in 2016, 5,292 applied for aid, 4,252 were judged to have need, 3,495 had their need fully met. 2,539 Federal Work-Study jobs (averaging $3086). 209 state and other part-time jobs (averaging $3269). In 2016, 2908 non-need-based awards were made. *Average percent of need met:* 86. *Average financial aid package:* $45,111. *Average need-based loan:* $2325. *Average need-based gift aid:* $29,853. *Average non-need-based aid:* $18,825. *Average indebtedness upon graduation:* $25,000. *Financial aid deadline:* 4/15.

APPLYING

Standardized Tests *Required:* SAT or ACT (for admission). *Required for some:* SAT and SAT Subject Tests or ACT (for admission).

Options: electronic application, early admission, early decision, early action, deferred entrance.

Application fee: $70.

Required: essay or personal statement, high school transcript, 1 letter of recommendation. *Required for some:* college transcript(s) and statement of good standing from prior institution(s), auditions for selected academic programs.

Application deadlines: 1/1 (freshmen), 11/1 (early action).

Early decision deadline: 11/1 (for plan 1), 1/1 (for plan 2).

Notification: 4/1 (freshmen), 1/1 (early decision plan 1), 3/1 (early decision plan 2), 2/1 (early action).

CONTACT

Mr. Mark Reid, Executive Director of Admission, University of Miami, PO Box 248025, Coral Gables, FL 33124. *Phone:* 305-284-4323. *Fax:* 305-284-6605. *E-mail:* mreid@miami.edu.

University of North Florida
Jacksonville, Florida
http://www.unf.edu/

- **State-supported** comprehensive, founded 1965, part of State University System of Florida
- **Urban** 1300-acre campus with easy access to Jacksonville, FL
- **Endowment** $97.4 million
- **Coed** 14,255 undergraduate students, 72% full-time, 56% women, 44% men
- **Moderately difficult** entrance level, 59% of applicants were admitted

UNDERGRAD STUDENTS

10,223 full-time, 4,032 part-time. Students come from 47 states and territories; 54 other countries; 4% are from out of state; 9% Black or African American, non-Hispanic/Latino; 12% Hispanic/Latino; 5% Asian, non-Hispanic/Latino; 0.1% Native Hawaiian or other Pacific Islander, non-Hispanic/Latino; 0.2% American Indian or Alaska Native, non-Hispanic/Latino; 5% Two or more races, non-Hispanic/Latino; 0.4% Race/ethnicity unknown; 2% international; 11% transferred in; 24% live on campus.

Freshmen:

Admission: 14,305 applied, 8,399 admitted, 2,291 enrolled. *Average high school GPA:* 3.9. *Test scores:* SAT evidence-based reading and writing scores over 500: 96%; SAT math scores over 500: 95%; ACT scores over 18: 100%; SAT evidence-based reading and writing scores over 600: 54%; SAT math scores over 600: 48%; ACT scores over 24: 49%; SAT evidence-based reading and writing scores over 700: 7%; SAT math scores over 700: 6%; ACT scores over 30: 5%.

Retention: 81% of full-time freshmen returned.

FACULTY

Total: 967, 59% full-time, 62% with terminal degrees.

Student/faculty ratio: 18:1.

ACADEMICS

Calendar: semesters. *Degrees:* associate, bachelor's, master's, doctoral, post-master's, and postbachelor's certificates (doctoral degree in education only).

Special study options: accelerated degree program, adult/continuing education programs, advanced placement credit, cooperative education, distance learning, double majors, English as a second language, honors programs, independent study, internships, off-campus study, part-time degree program, services for LD students, study abroad, summer session for credit. *ROTC:* Army (b), Navy (c).

Unusual degree programs: 3-2 computer science.

Computers: 700 computers/terminals are available on campus for general student use. Students can access the following: campus intranet, computer help desk, free student e-mail accounts, online (class) grades, online (class) registration, online (class) schedules, reduced prices for students on certain business and design software. Campuswide network is available. 100% of college-owned or -operated housing units are wired for high-speed Internet access. Wireless service is available via entire campus.

Library: Thomas G. Carpenter Library. *Books:* 579,242 (physical), 296,992 (digital/electronic); *Serial titles:* 16,185 (physical), 44,772 (digital/electronic); *Databases:* 269. Students can reserve study rooms.

STUDENT LIFE

Housing options: coed, special housing for students with disabilities. Campus housing is university owned. Freshman campus housing is guaranteed.

Activities and organizations: drama/theater group, student-run newspaper, radio and television station, choral group, Student Government Association, African American Student Association, International Student Association, Filipino Student Association, National Education Association, national fraternities, national sororities.

Athletics Member NCAA. All Division I. *Intercollegiate sports:* baseball M(s), basketball M(s)/W(s), cross-country running M(s)/W(s), golf M(s)/W, soccer M(s)/W(s), softball W(s), swimming and diving W(s), tennis M(s)/W(s), track and field M(s)/W(s), volleyball W(s). *Intramural sports:* badminton M/W, basketball M/W, bowling M/W, fencing M(c)/W(c), football M/W, golf M/W, lacrosse M(c)/W(c), racquetball M(c)/W(c), rugby M(c), sailing M(c)/W(c), soccer M/W, swimming and diving M/W, table tennis M/W, track and field M/W, ultimate Frisbee M(c)/W(c), volleyball M(c)/W(c).

Campus security: 24-hour emergency response devices and patrols, late-night transport/escort service, controlled dormitory access, electronic parking lot security.

Student services: health clinic, personal/psychological counseling, women's center.

COSTS & FINANCIAL AID

Costs (2017–18) *Tuition:* state resident $4281 full-time, $143 per credit hour part-time; nonresident $17,999 full-time, $600 per credit hour part-time. Full-time tuition and fees vary according to course load. Part-time tuition and fees vary according to course load. *Required fees:* $2113 full-time, $70 per credit hour part-time. *Room and board:* $9772; room only: $5772. Room and board charges vary according to board plan and housing facility. *Payment plan:* installment. *Waivers:* senior citizens and employees or children of employees.

Financial Aid Of all full-time matriculated undergraduates who enrolled in 2017, 7,083 applied for aid, 4,268 were judged to have need, 305 had their need fully met. 143 Federal Work-Study jobs (averaging $3244). In 2017, 1408 non-need-based awards were made. *Average percent of need met:* 89. *Average financial aid package:* $8820. *Average need-based loan:* $4140. *Average need-based gift aid:* $6444. *Average non-need-based aid:* $3092. *Average indebtedness upon graduation:* $18,787.

APPLYING
Standardized Tests *Required:* SAT or ACT (for admission).
Options: electronic application, deferred entrance.
Application fee: $30.
Required: high school transcript, minimum 2.5 GPA. *Required for some:* essay or personal statement. *Recommended:* minimum 3.0 GPA.
Application deadlines: rolling (freshmen), 5/10 (transfers).
Notification: continuous (freshmen), continuous (transfers).

CONTACT
Ms. Karen Lucas, Director of Admissions, University of North Florida, 1 UNF Drive, Jacksonville, FL 32224. *Phone:* 904-620-5252. *Fax:* 904-620-2014. *E-mail:* admissions@unf.edu.

University of South Florida

Tampa, Florida
http://www.usf.edu/

- **State-supported** university, founded 1956, part of State University System of Florida
- **Urban** 1562-acre campus
- **Endowment** $417.4 million
- **Coed**
- **Moderately difficult** entrance level

FACULTY
Student/faculty ratio: 24:1.

ACADEMICS
Calendar: semesters. *Degrees:* associate, bachelor's, master's, and doctoral.
Library: Tampa Campus Library plus 5 others. *Books:* 1.8 million (physical), 652,513 (digital/electronic); *Serial titles:* 537 (physical), 58,975 (digital/electronic); *Databases:* 930. Weekly public service hours: 116; study areas open 24 hours, 5–7 days a week; students can reserve study rooms.

STUDENT LIFE
Housing options: on-campus residence required for freshman year; special housing for students with disabilities. Campus housing is university owned. Freshman campus housing is guaranteed.
Activities and organizations: drama/theater group, student-run newspaper, radio and television station, choral group, marching band, Student Government, Campus Activities Board, USF Ambassadors, Student Admissions Representatives, national fraternities, national sororities.
Athletics Member NCAA. All Division I except football (Division I-A).
Campus security: 24-hour emergency response devices and patrols, student patrols, late-night transport/escort service, controlled dormitory access, residence hall lobby personnel 8 pm to 6 am.
Student services: health clinic, personal/psychological counseling, women's center, legal services.

COSTS & FINANCIAL AID
Costs (2017–18) *Tuition:* state resident $6336 full-time, $211 per credit hour part-time; nonresident $17,250 full-time, $575 per credit hour part-time. Full-time tuition and fees vary according to location. Part-time tuition and fees vary according to location. *Required fees:* $74 full-time, $74 per year part-time. *Room and board:* $10,325; room only: $6588.

Room and board charges vary according to board plan, housing facility, and location.

Financial Aid Of all full-time matriculated undergraduates who enrolled in 2016, 20,584 applied for aid, 17,329 were judged to have need, 1,674 had their need fully met. 761 Federal Work-Study jobs (averaging $3219). 258 state and other part-time jobs (averaging $1615). In 2016, 2546 non-need-based awards were made. *Average percent of need met:* 58. *Average financial aid package:* $11,260. *Average need-based loan:* $6609. *Average need-based gift aid:* $7417. *Average non-need-based aid:* $2844. *Average indebtedness upon graduation:* $21,799.

APPLYING
Standardized Tests *Required:* SAT or ACT (for admission).
Options: electronic application, early admission, deferred entrance.
Application fee: $30.
Required: minimum 2.0 GPA. *Required for some:* high school transcript, 1 letter of recommendation.

CONTACT
University of South Florida, Office of Undergraduate Admissions, 4202 East Fowler Avenue, Tampa, FL 33620-9951. *Phone:* 813-974-3350. *Fax:* 813-974-9689. *E-mail:* admissions@usf.edu.

University of South Florida, St. Petersburg

St. Petersburg, Florida
http://www.usfsp.edu/

- **State-supported** comprehensive, founded 1965, part of University of South Florida System
- **Urban** 48-acre campus with easy access to Tampa
- **Endowment** $19.1 million
- **Coed** 4,334 undergraduate students, 65% full-time, 63% women, 37% men

UNDERGRAD STUDENTS
2,837 full-time, 1,497 part-time. 4% are from out of state; 8% Black or African American, non-Hispanic/Latino; 17% Hispanic/Latino; 3% Asian, non-Hispanic/Latino; 0.1% Native Hawaiian or other Pacific Islander, non-Hispanic/Latino; 0.3% American Indian or Alaska Native, non-Hispanic/Latino; 4% Two or more races, non-Hispanic/Latino; 3% Race/ethnicity unknown; 0.7% international; 13% transferred in; 17% live on campus.

Freshmen:
Admission: 645 enrolled. *Average high school GPA:* 3.7. *Test scores:* SAT evidence-based reading and writing scores over 500: 99%; SAT math scores over 500: 96%; ACT scores over 18: 98%; SAT evidence-based reading and writing scores over 600: 48%; SAT math scores over 600: 27%; ACT scores over 24: 48%; SAT evidence-based reading and writing scores over 700: 4%; SAT math scores over 700: 2%; ACT scores over 30: 4%.

FACULTY
Total: 301, 52% full-time, 58% with terminal degrees.
Student/faculty ratio: 16:1.

ACADEMICS
Calendar: semesters. *Degrees:* certificates, bachelor's, and master's.
Special study options: distance learning, double majors, freshman honors college, honors programs, independent study, internships, services for LD students, study abroad, summer session for credit. *ROTC:* Army (b).
Computers: 125 computers/terminals and 350 ports are available on campus for general student use. Students can access the following: computer help desk, free student e-mail accounts, online (class) grades, online (class) registration, online (class) schedules. Campuswide network is available. 100% of college-owned or -operated housing units are wired for high-speed Internet access. Wireless service is available via entire campus.
Library: Nelson Poynter Memorial Library. *Books:* 212,904 (physical), 693,313 (digital/electronic); *Serial titles:* 7,817 (physical), 64,928 (digital/electronic); *Databases:* 939. Weekly public service hours: 79; students can reserve study rooms.

STUDENT LIFE

Housing options: on-campus residence required for freshman year; coed. Campus housing is university owned and is provided by a third party. Freshman applicants given priority for college housing.

Activities and organizations: drama/theater group, student-run newspaper, radio station, Student Government, Harborside Activities Board, Delta Sigma Pi, Multicultural Activities Council, HERD Step Team.

Athletics *Intercollegiate sports:* baseball M(c), sailing W(c). *Intramural sports:* basketball M/W, football M/W, sailing M/W, soccer M/W, volleyball M/W.

Campus security: 24-hour emergency response devices and patrols, late-night transport/escort service, controlled dormitory access.

Student services: health clinic, personal/psychological counseling.

COSTS

Costs (2017–18) *Tuition:* state resident $4206 full-time, $140 per credit hour part-time; nonresident $15,120 full-time, $504 per credit hour part-time. *Required fees:* $1615 full-time, $54 per credit hour part-time. *Room and board:* $10,808. Room and board charges vary according to board plan and housing facility. *Payment plan:* installment. *Waivers:* employees or children of employees.

APPLYING

Standardized Tests *Required:* SAT or ACT (for admission).

Required: high school transcript, minimum 2.5 GPA.

CONTACT

University of South Florida, St. Petersburg, 140 Seventh Avenue South, St. Petersburg, FL 33701. *Phone:* 727-873-4142. *Fax:* 727-873-4525. *E-mail:* admissions@usfsp.edu.

University of South Florida Sarasota-Manatee

Sarasota, Florida

http://www.usfsm.edu/

- **State-supported** comprehensive, founded 1956, part of University of South Florida System
- **Urban** 31-acre campus with easy access to Tampa
- **Endowment** $10.2 million
- **Coed** 1,935 undergraduate students, 54% full-time, 61% women, 39% men

UNDERGRAD STUDENTS

1,048 full-time, 887 part-time. Students come from 27 states and territories; 22 other countries; 3% are from out of state; 5% Black or African American, non-Hispanic/Latino; 16% Hispanic/Latino; 2% Asian, non-Hispanic/Latino; 0.4% American Indian or Alaska Native, non-Hispanic/Latino; 3% Two or more races, non-Hispanic/Latino; 2% Race/ethnicity unknown; 2% international; 17% transferred in.

Freshmen:
Admission: 135 enrolled. *Average high school GPA:* 3.8. *Test scores:* SAT evidence-based reading and writing scores over 500: 97%; SAT math scores over 500: 100%; ACT scores over 18: 101%; SAT evidence-based reading and writing scores over 600: 42%; SAT math scores over 600: 33%; ACT scores over 24: 63%; SAT evidence-based reading and writing scores over 700: 3%; SAT math scores over 700: 4%; ACT scores over 30: 8%.

Retention: 83% of full-time freshmen returned.

FACULTY

Total: 151, 56% full-time, 62% with terminal degrees.
Student/faculty ratio: 14:1.

ACADEMICS

Calendar: semesters. *Degrees:* certificates, associate, bachelor's, master's, and post-master's certificates.

Special study options: advanced placement credit, distance learning, double majors, honors programs, independent study, internships, part-time degree program, services for LD students, study abroad, summer session for credit. *ROTC:* Army (c), Navy (c), Air Force (c).

Computers: 56 computers/terminals and 450 ports are available on campus for general student use. Students can access the following: campus intranet, computer help desk, free student e-mail accounts, online (class) grades, online (class) registration, online (class) schedules. Campuswide network is available. Wireless service is available via entire campus.

Library: USF Libraries. *Books:* 1,231 (physical), 676,353 (digital/electronic); *Serial titles:* 61,782 (digital/electronic); *Databases:* 959. Weekly public service hours: 96; students can reserve study rooms.

STUDENT LIFE

Housing options: college housing not available.

Activities and organizations: Box Office Bulls, The Adventure Club, Gamers'; Club, Student Veteran Society, The Criminology Club.

Campus security: 24-hour emergency response devices and patrols, late-night transport/escort service.

Student services: health clinic, personal/psychological counseling.

COSTS

Costs (2017–18) *Tuition:* state resident $151 per credit hour part-time; nonresident $487 per credit hour part-time. Full-time tuition and fees vary according to course load and program. Part-time tuition and fees vary according to course load and program. *Required fees:* $1381 full-time, $46 per credit hour part-time, $74 per credit hour part-time. *Waivers:* employees or children of employees.

APPLYING

Standardized Tests *Required:* SAT or ACT (for admission). *Recommended:* SAT Subject Tests (for admission).

Required: high school transcript, minimum 3.3 GPA. *Required for some:* minimum 3.3 GPA, interview. *Recommended:* essay or personal statement, minimum 3.3 GPA, 2 letters of recommendation.

CONTACT

Mr. Andy Telatovich, Director, Admissions, University of South Florida Sarasota-Manatee, 8350 N. Tamiami Trail, C107, Sarasota, FL 34232. *Phone:* 941-359-4330. *Fax:* 941-359-4236. *E-mail:* atelatovich@sar.usf.edu.

The University of Tampa

Tampa, Florida

http://www.ut.edu/

- **Independent** comprehensive, founded 1931
- **Urban** 110-acre campus with easy access to Tampa-St. Petersburg, Clearwater
- **Coed** 7,974 undergraduate students, 97% full-time, 58% women, 42% men
- **Moderately difficult** entrance level, 53% of applicants were admitted

UNDERGRAD STUDENTS

7,728 full-time, 246 part-time. Students come from 50 states and territories; 140 other countries; 70% are from out of state; 5% Black or African American, non-Hispanic/Latino; 13% Hispanic/Latino; 2% Asian, non-Hispanic/Latino; 0.1% Native Hawaiian or other Pacific Islander, non-Hispanic/Latino; 0.1% American Indian or Alaska Native, non-Hispanic/Latino; 3% Two or more races, non-Hispanic/Latino; 6% Race/ethnicity unknown; 10% international; 7% transferred in; 53% live on campus.

Freshmen:
Admission: 20,495 applied, 10,915 admitted, 2,141 enrolled. *Average high school GPA:* 3.4. *Test scores:* SAT evidence-based reading and writing scores over 500: 93%; SAT math scores over 500: 92%; ACT scores over 18: 100%; SAT evidence-based reading and writing scores over 600: 38%; SAT math scores over 600: 34%; ACT scores over 24: 56%; SAT evidence-based reading and writing scores over 700: 3%; SAT math scores over 700: 2%; ACT scores over 30: 8%.

Retention: 78% of full-time freshmen returned.

FACULTY

Total: 742, 46% full-time, 58% with terminal degrees.
Student/faculty ratio: 17:1.

ACADEMICS

Calendar: semesters. *Degrees:* certificates, bachelor's, master's, and post-master's certificates.

Special study options: academic remediation for entering students, adult/continuing education programs, advanced placement credit, cooperative education, double majors, English as a second language, honors programs, independent study, internships, part-time degree program, services for LD students, study abroad, summer session for credit. *ROTC:* Army (b), Navy (c), Air Force (c).

Unusual degree programs: 3-2 chemistry/business administration.

Computers: 802 computers/terminals and 8,000 ports are available on campus for general student use. Students can access the following: campus intranet, computer help desk, free student e-mail accounts, online (class) grades, online (class) registration, online (class) schedules. Campuswide network is available. 100% of college-owned or -operated housing units are wired for high-speed Internet access. Wireless service is available via entire campus.

Library: Macdonald Kelce Library. *Books:* 195,067 (physical), 145,016 (digital/electronic); *Serial titles:* 1,214 (physical), 190,560 (digital/electronic); *Databases:* 214. Weekly public service hours: 100; students can reserve study rooms.

STUDENT LIFE

Housing options: coed, special housing for students with disabilities. Campus housing is university owned and leased by the school. Freshman applicants given priority for college housing.

Activities and organizations: drama/theater group, student-run newspaper, radio and television station, choral group, Greek Life, student government, PEACE (volunteer organization), Student Productions, Minaret, national fraternities, national sororities.

Athletics Member NCAA. All Division II except lacrosse (Division I), track and field (Division I). *Intercollegiate sports:* baseball M(s), basketball M(s)/W(s), crew W(s), cross-country running M(s)/W(s), golf M(s)/W(s), lacrosse M(s)/W(s), soccer M(s)/W(s), softball W(s), swimming and diving M(s)/W(s), tennis W(s), track and field M(s)/W(s), volleyball W(s). *Intramural sports:* basketball M/W, cheerleading W(c), crew M(c), equestrian sports W(c), field hockey M(c)/W(c), football M/W, golf M/W, ice hockey M(c), soccer M/W, softball M/W, swimming and diving M/W, tennis M(c)/W(c), ultimate Frisbee M/W, volleyball M/W.

Campus security: 24-hour emergency response devices and patrols, student patrols, late-night transport/escort service, controlled dormitory access.

Student services: health clinic, personal/psychological counseling, women's center.

COSTS & FINANCIAL AID

Costs (2017–18) *One-time required fee:* $85. *Comprehensive fee:* $38,928 includes full-time tuition ($26,504), mandatory fees ($1922), and room and board ($10,502). Full-time tuition and fees vary according to class time, course load, and program. Part-time tuition: $564 per credit hour. Part-time tuition and fees vary according to class time, course load, and program. *Required fees:* $40 per term part-time. *College room only:* $5546. Room and board charges vary according to board plan and housing facility. *Payment plan:* installment. *Waivers:* employees or children of employees.

Financial Aid Of all full-time matriculated undergraduates who enrolled in 2017, 5,605 applied for aid, 4,611 were judged to have need, 368 had their need fully met. 404 Federal Work-Study jobs (averaging $2000). 248 state and other part-time jobs (averaging $2000). In 2017, 2271 non-need-based awards were made. *Average percent of need met:* 60. *Average financial aid package:* $17,438. *Average need-based loan:* $4279. *Average need-based gift aid:* $13,686. *Average non-need-based aid:* $7997. *Average indebtedness upon graduation:* $32,048.

APPLYING

Standardized Tests *Required:* SAT or ACT (for admission).

Options: electronic application, early admission, early action, deferred entrance.

Application fee: $40.

Required: essay or personal statement, high school transcript, minimum 2.0 GPA. *Required for some:* 1 letter of recommendation. *Recommended:* interview.

Application deadlines: rolling (freshmen), rolling (transfers), 11/15 (early action).

Notification: continuous until 10/1 (freshmen), continuous (transfers), 12/15 (early action).

CONTACT

Mr. Dennis Nostrand, Vice President for Enrollment, The University of Tampa, 401 West Kennedy Boulevard, Tampa, FL 33606-1480. *Phone:* 813-257-1808. *Toll-free phone:* 888-646-2738 (in-state); 888-MINARET (out-of-state). *Fax:* 813-258-7398. *E-mail:* admissions@ut.edu.

University of West Florida
Pensacola, Florida
http://www.uwf.edu/

CONTACT

Katie Condon, Director of Admissions, University of West Florida, Admissions, 11000 University Parkway, Pensacola, FL 32514. *Phone:* 850-474-2230. *Toll-free phone:* 800-263-1074. *Fax:* 850-474-3460. *E-mail:* admissions@uwf.edu.

Valencia College
Orlando, Florida
http://valenciacollege.edu/

- **State-supported** 4-year, founded 1967, part of Florida College System
- **Urban** 654-acre campus with easy access to Orlando
- **Endowment** $70.3 million
- **Coed** 44,833 undergraduate students, 36% full-time, 57% women, 43% men
- **98%** of applicants were admitted

UNDERGRAD STUDENTS

16,165 full-time, 28,668 part-time. Students come from 20 states and territories; 182 other countries; 4% are from out of state; 16% Black or African American, non-Hispanic/Latino; 35% Hispanic/Latino; 4% Asian, non-Hispanic/Latino; 0.3% Native Hawaiian or other Pacific Islander, non-Hispanic/Latino; 0.3% American Indian or Alaska Native, non-Hispanic/Latino; 3% Two or more races, non-Hispanic/Latino; 12% Race/ethnicity unknown; 4% international; 7% transferred in.

Freshmen:
Admission: 11,352 applied, 11,148 admitted, 8,959 enrolled.

FACULTY

Total: 1,956, 30% full-time, 22% with terminal degrees.

Student/faculty ratio: 23:1.

ACADEMICS

Calendar: semesters. *Degrees:* certificates, diplomas, associate, and bachelor's.

Special study options: academic remediation for entering students, accelerated degree program, adult/continuing education programs, advanced placement credit, cooperative education, distance learning, double majors, English as a second language, external degree program, freshman honors college, honors programs, independent study, internships, part-time degree program, services for LD students, study abroad, summer session for credit. *ROTC:* Army (c), Navy (c).

Computers: Students can access the following: campus intranet, computer help desk, free student e-mail accounts, online (class) grades, online (class) registration, online (class) schedules, education plans, Â?what if analysisÂ? degree audit, degree plan, view and print unofficial transcripts, order official transcripts, career exploration. Campuswide network is available. Wireless service is available via entire campus.

Library: Library plus 4 others. *Books:* 153,869 (physical), 180,848 (digital/electronic); *Serial titles:* 261 (physical), 52,262 (digital/electronic); *Databases:* 188. Weekly public service hours: 87; students can reserve study rooms.

STUDENT LIFE

Housing options: college housing not available.

Activities and organizations: drama/theater group, student-run newspaper, choral group, National Society for Leadership and Success, PTK, Honors, Gay-Straight Alliance, Valencia Hospitality.

Athletics *Intramural sports:* basketball M/W, soccer M/W, volleyball M/W.

Campus security: 24-hour emergency response devices and patrols, late-night transport/escort service, video monitoring for certain areas.

Student services: personal/psychological counseling.

COSTS & FINANCIAL AID

Costs (2018–19) *Tuition:* state resident $2473 full-time; nonresident $9383 full-time. Full-time tuition and fees vary according to degree level. Part-time tuition and fees vary according to degree level. *Payment plan:* installment. *Waivers:* senior citizens and employees or children of employees.

Financial Aid Of all full-time matriculated undergraduates who enrolled in 2010, 21,366 applied for aid, 17,532 were judged to have need, 485 had their need fully met. 242 Federal Work-Study jobs (averaging $2608). 27 state and other part-time jobs (averaging $2738). In 2010, 93 non-need-based awards were made. *Average percent of need met:* 46. *Average financial aid package:* $7383. *Average need-based loan:* $3242. *Average need-based gift aid:* $3430. *Average non-need-based aid:* $642.

APPLYING

Options: electronic application, early admission, deferred entrance.

Application fee: $35.

Required for some: high school transcript, professional license for some allied health bachelors programs. *Recommended:* high school transcript.

Application deadlines: rolling (freshmen), rolling (out-of-state freshmen), rolling (transfers).

CONTACT

Dr. Linda K. Herlocker, Assistant Vice President of Admissions and Records, Valencia College, West Campus, MC 4-8, 1800 S. Kirkman Road, SSB 104-D, Orlando, FL 32811-2302. *Phone:* 407-582-1511. *Fax:* 407-582-1866. *E-mail:* lherlocker@valenciacollege.edu.

Warner University
Lake Wales, Florida
http://www.warner.edu/

CONTACT

Mr. Jason Roe, Director of Admissions, Warner University, Warner Southern Center, 13895 Highway 27, Lake Wales, FL 33859. *Phone:* 863-638-7212 Ext. 7213. *Toll-free phone:* 800-309-9563. *Fax:* 863-638-1472. *E-mail:* admissions@warner.edu.

 # Webber International University
Babson Park, Florida
http://www.webber.edu/

• **Independent** comprehensive, founded 1927
• **Small-town** 110-acre campus with easy access to Orlando
• **Coed** 627 undergraduate students, 93% full-time, 29% women, 71% men
• **Moderately difficult** entrance level, 49% of applicants were admitted

UNDERGRAD STUDENTS

585 full-time, 42 part-time. Students come from 24 states and territories; 20 other countries; 20% are from out of state; 33% Black or African American, non-Hispanic/Latino; 12% Hispanic/Latino; 0.5% Asian, non-Hispanic/Latino; 1% Native Hawaiian or other Pacific Islander, non-Hispanic/Latino; 0.2% American Indian or Alaska Native, non-Hispanic/Latino; 1% Two or more races, non-Hispanic/Latino; 19% international; 12% transferred in; 53% live on campus.

Freshmen:

Admission: 912 applied, 447 admitted, 173 enrolled. *Average high school GPA:* 2.9. *Test scores:* ACT scores over 18: 73%; ACT scores over 24: 7%. *Retention:* 52% of full-time freshmen returned.

FACULTY

Total: 41, 51% full-time, 46% with terminal degrees.

Student/faculty ratio: 21:1.

ACADEMICS

Calendar: semesters. *Degrees:* associate, bachelor's, and master's.

Special study options: academic remediation for entering students, accelerated degree program, adult/continuing education programs, advanced placement credit, cooperative education, distance learning, double majors, freshman honors college, honors programs, internships, part-time degree program, services for LD students, study abroad, summer session for credit.

Computers: 92 computers/terminals are available on campus for general student use. Students can access the following: campus intranet, computer help desk, free student e-mail accounts, online (class) grades, online (class) registration, online (class) schedules. Campuswide network is available. 100% of college-owned or -operated housing units are wired for high-speed Internet access. Wireless service is available via entire campus.

Library: Grace and Roger Babson Library. *Books:* 1,041 (physical); *Databases:* 127. Weekly public service hours: 70; students can reserve study rooms.

STUDENT LIFE

Housing options: on-campus residence required through sophomore year; men-only, women-only. Campus housing is university owned. Freshman campus housing is guaranteed.

Activities and organizations: student-run newspaper, Student Leadership Association, Phi Beta Lambda, Society of International Students, Fellowship of Christian Athletes, Rotaract.

Athletics Member NAIA. *Intercollegiate sports:* baseball M(s), basketball M(s)/W(s), bowling M(s)/W(s), cross-country running M(s)/W(s), football M(s), golf M(s)/W(s), sand volleyball M(s)/W(s), soccer M(s)/W(s), softball W(s), tennis M(s)/W(s), track and field M(s)/W(s), triathlon M(s)/W(s), volleyball M(s)/W(s).

Campus security: 24-hour emergency response devices and patrols, late-night transport/escort service.

Student services: health clinic, personal/psychological counseling.

COSTS & FINANCIAL AID

Costs (2018–19) *Comprehensive fee:* $35,410 includes full-time tuition ($23,380), mandatory fees ($2736), and room and board ($9294). Full-time tuition and fees vary according to class time, course load, and program. Part-time tuition: $366 per credit hour. Part-time tuition and fees vary according to class time, course load, and program. *Room and board:* Room and board charges vary according to board plan, gender, and housing facility. *Payment plan:* installment. *Waivers:* children of alumni, adult students, senior citizens, and employees or children of employees.

Financial Aid Of all full-time matriculated undergraduates who enrolled in 2017, 453 applied for aid, 428 were judged to have need, 32 had their need fully met. 49 Federal Work-Study jobs (averaging $1008). 44 state and other part-time jobs (averaging $1218). In 2017, 121 non-need-based awards were made. *Average percent of need met:* 62. *Average financial aid package:* $20,525. *Average need-based loan:* $4028. *Average need-based gift aid:* $17,076. *Average non-need-based aid:* $9199. *Average indebtedness upon graduation:* $26,682. *Financial aid deadline:* 8/1.

APPLYING

Standardized Tests *Required for some:* SAT or ACT (for admission).

Options: electronic application.

Application fee: $35.

Required: high school transcript, minimum 2.0 GPA. *Required for some:* letters of recommendation, interview. *Recommended:* essay or personal statement.

Application deadlines: 8/1 (freshmen), 8/1 (transfers).

Notification: continuous (freshmen), continuous (transfers).

CONTACT

Office of Admissions, Webber International University, PO Box 96, Babson Park, FL 33827. *Phone:* 863-638-2910. *Toll-free phone:* 800-741-1844. *Fax:* 863-638-1591. *E-mail:* admissions@webber.edu.

West Coast University
Doral, Florida
http://westcoastuniversity.edu/

CONTACT

West Coast University, 9250 NW 36th Street, Doral, FL 33178.

Yeshiva Gedolah Rabbinical College
Miami Beach, Florida

CONTACT
Yeshiva Gedolah Rabbinical College, 1140 Alton Road, Miami Beach, FL 33139.

GEORGIA

Abraham Baldwin Agricultural College
Tifton, Georgia
http://www.abac.edu/

CONTACT
Mrs. Donna Webb, Director of Enrollment Services, Abraham Baldwin Agricultural College, Box 4, 2802 Moore Highway, Tifton, GA 31793-2601. *Phone:* 229-391-5004. *Toll-free phone:* 800-733-3653. *Fax:* 229-391-5002. *E-mail:* dwebb@abac.edu.

Agnes Scott College
Decatur, Georgia
http://www.agnesscott.edu/

- **Independent** 4-year, founded 1889, affiliated with Presbyterian Church (U.S.A.)
- **Urban** 100-acre campus with easy access to Atlanta
- **Endowment** $229.9 million
- **Women only** 921 undergraduate students, 99% full-time
- **Moderately difficult** entrance level, 66% of applicants were admitted

UNDERGRAD STUDENTS
913 full-time, 8 part-time. Students come from 46 states and territories; 27 other countries; 46% are from out of state; 29% Black or African American, non-Hispanic/Latino; 12% Hispanic/Latino; 7% Asian, non-Hispanic/Latino; 0.2% Native Hawaiian or other Pacific Islander, non-Hispanic/Latino; 0.2% American Indian or Alaska Native, non-Hispanic/Latino; 7% Two or more races, non-Hispanic/Latino; 2% Race/ethnicity unknown; 8% international; 1% transferred in; 84% live on campus.

Freshmen:
Admission: 1,534 applied, 1,006 admitted, 251 enrolled. *Average high school GPA:* 3.8. *Test scores:* SAT evidence-based reading and writing scores over 500: 97%; SAT math scores over 500: 93%; ACT scores over 18: 99%; SAT evidence-based reading and writing scores over 600: 63%; SAT math scores over 600: 30%; ACT scores over 24: 77%; SAT evidence-based reading and writing scores over 700: 23%; SAT math scores over 700: 4%; ACT scores over 30: 27%.
Retention: 87% of full-time freshmen returned.

FACULTY
Total: 120, 67% full-time, 81% with terminal degrees.
Student/faculty ratio: 10:1.

ACADEMICS
Calendar: semesters. *Degree:* bachelor's.

Special study options: accelerated degree program, adult/continuing education programs, advanced placement credit, distance learning, double majors, independent study, internships, off-campus study, part-time degree program, services for LD students, student-designed majors, study abroad, summer session for credit. *ROTC:* Army (c), Air Force (c).

Unusual degree programs: 3-2 engineering with Georgia Institute of Technology; nursing with Emory University; computer science with Emory University.

Computers: 450 computers/terminals are available on campus for general student use. Students can access the following: campus intranet, computer help desk, free student e-mail accounts, online (class) grades, online (class) registration, online (class) schedules. Campuswide network is available. 100% of college-owned or -operated housing units are wired for high-speed Internet access. Wireless service is available via entire campus.
Library: McCain Library. *Books:* 239,851 (physical), 57,182 (digital/electronic); *Databases:* 373. Weekly public service hours: 104; study areas open 24 hours, 5–7 days a week.

STUDENT LIFE
Housing options: on-campus residence required through senior year; women-only. Campus housing is university owned. Freshman campus housing is guaranteed.
Activities and organizations: drama/theater group, student-run newspaper, radio station, choral group, marching band.
Athletics Member NCAA. All Division III. *Intercollegiate sports:* basketball W, cross-country running W, soccer W, softball W, tennis W, volleyball W. *Intramural sports:* archery W, badminton W, cheerleading W(c), lacrosse W(c), swimming and diving W(c), tennis W.
Campus security: 24-hour emergency response devices and patrols, late-night transport/escort service, controlled dormitory access, security systems in apartments, public safety facility, surveillance equipment, key required for residence hall entry.
Student services: health clinic, personal/psychological counseling.

COSTS & FINANCIAL AID
Costs (2018–19) *One-time required fee:* $200. *Comprehensive fee:* $53,490 includes full-time tuition ($40,920), mandatory fees ($240), and room and board ($12,330). Part-time tuition: $1705 per credit hour. Part-time tuition and fees vary according to course load. *Room and board:* Room and board charges vary according to board plan and housing facility. *Payment plan:* installment. *Waivers:* employees or children of employees.

Financial Aid Of all full-time matriculated undergraduates who enrolled in 2017, 743 applied for aid, 677 were judged to have need, 150 had their need fully met. In 2017, 207 non-need-based awards were made. *Average percent of need met:* 85. *Average financial aid package:* $36,231. *Average need-based loan:* $4344. *Average need-based gift aid:* $30,022. *Average non-need-based aid:* $27,576. *Average indebtedness upon graduation:* $32,276. *Financial aid deadline:* 5/1.

APPLYING
Standardized Tests *Required for some:* SAT or ACT (for admission), SAT and SAT Subject Tests or ACT (for admission).
Options: electronic application, early admission, early decision, early action, deferred entrance.
Required: essay or personal statement, high school transcript. *Recommended:* interview.
Application deadlines: 5/1 (freshmen), 6/1 (transfers), 11/15 (early action).
Early decision deadline: 11/1.
Notification: 4/15 (freshmen), continuous (transfers), 12/1 (early decision), 1/15 (early action).

CONTACT
Agnes Scott College, 141 East College Avenue, Decatur, GA 30030-3797. *Phone:* 404-471-6285. *Toll-free phone:* 800-868-8602.

Albany State University
Albany, Georgia
http://www.asurams.edu/

- **State-supported** comprehensive, founded 1903, part of University System of Georgia
- **Urban** 232-acre campus
- **Endowment** $1.8 million
- **Coed**
- **Minimally difficult** entrance level

FACULTY
Student/faculty ratio: 19:1.

ACADEMICS
Calendar: semesters. *Degrees:* bachelor's, master's, and post-master's certificates.
Library: James Pendergrast Memorial Library.

STUDENT LIFE

Housing options: on-campus residence required for freshman year; men-only, women-only. Campus housing is university owned. Freshman applicants given priority for college housing.

Activities and organizations: drama/theater group, student-run newspaper, radio and television station, choral group, marching band, ASU Anointed Gospel Choir, ASU Pan-Hellenic Council (Greeks), Peer Educators, SIFE (Students In Free Enterprise), Student Government Association, national fraternities, national sororities.

Athletics Member NCAA. All Division II.

Campus security: 24-hour emergency response devices and patrols, late-night transport/escort service, controlled dormitory access, ConnectED Emergency E-mail, Emergency sirens, Active Shooter Team, Certified Police Officers.

Student services: health clinic, personal/psychological counseling.

COSTS & FINANCIAL AID

Costs (2017–18) *Tuition:* state resident $3965 full-time, $165 per credit hour part-time; nonresident $14,426 full-time, $601 per credit hour part-time. Full-time tuition and fees vary according to course load and degree level. Part-time tuition and fees vary according to course load and degree level. *Required fees:* $1710 full-time. *Room and board:* $8874; room only: $5266. Room and board charges vary according to board plan and housing facility.

Financial Aid Of all full-time matriculated undergraduates who enrolled in 2014, 2,729 applied for aid, 2,616 were judged to have need, 234 had their need fully met. In 2014, 1 non-need-based awards were made. *Average percent of need met:* 71. *Average financial aid package:* $5164. *Average need-based loan:* $2402. *Average need-based gift aid:* $2595. *Average non-need-based aid:* $1500. *Average indebtedness upon graduation:* $39,014. *Financial aid deadline:* 6/30.

APPLYING

Standardized Tests *Required:* SAT or ACT (for admission). *Required for some:* SAT and SAT Subject Tests or ACT (for admission).

Options: electronic application, early admission, deferred entrance.

Application fee: $25.

Required: high school transcript, minimum 2.2 GPA.

CONTACT

Interim Director, Enrollment Services, Albany State University, 504 College Drive, Albany, GA 31705-2717. *Phone:* 229-430-4646. *Toll-free phone:* 800-822-7267. *Fax:* 229-430-4105. *E-mail:* enrollmentservices@asurams.edu.

American InterContinental University Atlanta

Atlanta, Georgia
http://www.aiuniv.edu/

CONTACT

American InterContinental University Atlanta, 6600 Peachtree-Dunwoody Road, 500 Embassy Row, Atlanta, GA 30328. *Phone:* 877-564-6248. *Toll-free phone:* 800-353-1744. *Fax:* 877-564-6248.

Argosy University, Atlanta

Atlanta, Georgia
http://www.argosy.edu/locations/atlanta/

CONTACT

Argosy University, Atlanta, 980 Hammond Drive, Suite 100, Atlanta, GA 30328. *Phone:* 770-671-1200. *Toll-free phone:* 888-671-4777.

The Art Institute of Atlanta

Atlanta, Georgia
http://www.artinstitutes.edu/atlanta/

CONTACT

The Art Institute of Atlanta, 6600 Peachtree Dunwoody Road, NE, 100 Embassy Row, Atlanta, GA 30328. *Phone:* 770-394-8300. *Toll-free phone:* 800-275-4242.

Ashworth College

Norcross, Georgia
http://www.ashworthcollege.edu/

CONTACT

Mr. Eric Ryall, Registrar, Ashworth College, 6625 The Corners Parkway, Suite 500, Norcross, GA 30092. *Phone:* 770-729-8400 Ext. 5297. *Toll-free phone:* 800-957-5412.

Augusta University

Augusta, Georgia
http://www.augusta.edu/

- **State-supported** university, founded 1828, part of University System of Georgia
- **Urban** 670-acre campus
- **Endowment** $9.4 million
- **Coed**
- 59% of applicants were admitted

ACADEMICS

Calendar: semesters. *Degrees:* associate, bachelor's, master's, doctoral, post-master's, and postbachelor's certificates.

Library: Main Library plus 2 others.

STUDENT LIFE

Housing options: coed. Campus housing is university owned.

Activities and organizations: drama/theater group, student-run newspaper, choral group, national fraternities, national sororities.

Athletics Member NCAA. All Division II except men's and women's golf (Division I).

Campus security: 24-hour emergency response devices and patrols, late-night transport/escort service.

Student services: health clinic, personal/psychological counseling.

COSTS & FINANCIAL AID

Costs (2017–18) *Tuition:* state resident $6592 full-time, $220 per credit hour part-time; nonresident $21,300 full-time, $710 per credit hour part-time. Full-time tuition and fees vary according to course load, location, and program. Part-time tuition and fees vary according to course load, location, and program. *Required fees:* $1690 full-time. *Room and board:* $13,200. Room and board charges vary according to board plan and housing facility.

Financial Aid Of all full-time matriculated undergraduates who enrolled in 2016, 3,070 applied for aid, 2,452 were judged to have need, 167 had their need fully met. 169 Federal Work-Study jobs (averaging $2931). In 2016, 42 non-need-based awards were made. *Average financial aid package:* $2390. *Average need-based loan:* $2159. *Average need-based gift aid:* $2216. *Average non-need-based aid:* $1421. *Financial aid deadline:* 3/1.

APPLYING

Standardized Tests *Required:* SAT or ACT (for admission).

Options: electronic application, early action.

Application fee: $50.

Required: Freshman Index (FI). *Required for some:* high school transcript.

CONTACT

Augusta University, 1120 15th Street, Augusta, GA 30912. *Phone:* 706-737-1632. *Toll-free phone:* 800-519-3388.

Berry College

Mount Berry, Georgia
http://www.berry.edu/

- **Independent interdenominational** comprehensive, founded 1902
- **Suburban** 27,000-acre campus with easy access to Atlanta
- **Endowment** $968.5 million
- **Coed** 1,978 undergraduate students, 98% full-time, 61% women, 39% men
- **Moderately difficult** entrance level, 62% of applicants were admitted

UNDERGRAD STUDENTS

1,945 full-time, 33 part-time. Students come from 37 states and territories; 9 other countries; 32% are from out of state; 5% Black or African American, non-Hispanic/Latino; 7% Hispanic/Latino; 2% Asian, non-Hispanic/Latino; 0.1% Native Hawaiian or other Pacific Islander, non-Hispanic/Latino; 0.3% American Indian or Alaska Native, non-Hispanic/Latino; 3% Two or more races, non-Hispanic/Latino; 2% Race/ethnicity unknown; 0.6% international; 2% transferred in; 89% live on campus.

Freshmen:

Admission: 3,883 applied, 2,392 admitted, 553 enrolled. *Average high school GPA:* 3.7. *Test scores:* SAT evidence-based reading and writing scores over 500: 96%; SAT math scores over 500: 95%; ACT scores over 18: 100%; SAT evidence-based reading and writing scores over 600: 62%; SAT math scores over 600: 45%; ACT scores over 24: 77%; SAT evidence-based reading and writing scores over 700: 16%; SAT math scores over 700: 5%; ACT scores over 30: 17%.

Retention: 78% of full-time freshmen returned.

FACULTY

Total: 230, 72% full-time, 80% with terminal degrees.

Student/faculty ratio: 11:1.

ACADEMICS

Calendar: semesters. *Degrees:* bachelor's and master's.

Special study options: adult/continuing education programs, advanced placement credit, double majors, honors programs, independent study, internships, part-time degree program, services for LD students, student-designed majors, study abroad, summer session for credit.

Unusual degree programs: 3-2 engineering with Georgia Institute of Technology, Kennesaw State University; nursing with Emory University.

Computers: 200 computers/terminals and 80 ports are available on campus for general student use. Students can access the following: campus intranet, computer help desk, free student e-mail accounts, online (class) grades, online (class) registration, online (class) schedules. Campuswide network is available. 100% of college-owned or -operated housing units are wired for high-speed Internet access. Wireless service is available via classrooms, computer centers, computer labs, dorm rooms, learning centers, libraries, student centers.

Library: Memorial Library plus 1 other. *Books:* 246,222 (physical), 664,520 (digital/electronic); *Serial titles:* 7,978 (physical), 44,764 (digital/electronic); *Databases:* 224. Weekly public service hours: 106; students can reserve study rooms.

STUDENT LIFE

Housing options: on-campus residence required through senior year; coed, men-only, women-only. Campus housing is university owned. Freshman campus housing is guaranteed.

Activities and organizations: drama/theater group, student-run newspaper, choral group, Student Government Association, Campus Outreach, Block-n-Bridle, Allied Health, Athletes Bettering the Community.

Athletics Member NCAA. All Division III. *Intercollegiate sports:* baseball M, basketball M/W, cross-country running M/W, equestrian sports W, football M, golf M/W, lacrosse M/W, soccer M/W, softball W, swimming and diving M/W, tennis M/W, track and field M/W, volleyball W. *Intramural sports:* basketball M/W, cheerleading M(c)/W(c), crew M(c)/W(c), football M/W, golf M/W, racquetball M/W, rowing M(c)/W(c), sand volleyball M/W, soccer M/W, softball M/W, swimming and diving M/W, tennis M/W, ultimate Frisbee M/W, volleyball M/W.

Campus security: 24-hour emergency response devices and patrols, controlled dormitory access, lighted pathways, gated campus, mobile police patrols, identification of valuables, limited access to campus, on-campus police officers.

Student services: health clinic, personal/psychological counseling.

COSTS & FINANCIAL AID

Costs (2017–18) *Comprehensive fee:* $47,436 includes full-time tuition ($34,950), mandatory fees ($226), and room and board ($12,260). Part-time tuition: $1165 per credit hour. *College room only:* $6930. Room and board charges vary according to board plan and housing facility. *Payment plan:* installment. *Waivers:* senior citizens and employees or children of employees.

Financial Aid Of all full-time matriculated undergraduates who enrolled in 2017, 1,681 applied for aid, 1,381 were judged to have need, 348 had their need fully met. 201 Federal Work-Study jobs (averaging $3626). 179 state and other part-time jobs (averaging $4679). In 2017, 556 non-need-based awards were made. *Average percent of need met:* 85. *Average financial aid package:* $29,832. *Average need-based loan:* $5110. *Average need-based gift aid:* $24,949. *Average non-need-based aid:* $15,182. *Average indebtedness upon graduation:* $27,378.

APPLYING

Standardized Tests *Required:* SAT or ACT (for admission).

Options: electronic application, early admission, early decision, early action.

Required: essay or personal statement, high school transcript, 1 letter of recommendation. *Required for some:* 2 letters of recommendation. *Recommended:* interview.

Application deadlines: 7/20 (freshmen), 7/20 (transfers).

Notification: continuous (freshmen), continuous (transfers).

CONTACT

Mr. Timothy Tarpley, Director of Operations, Enrollment Management, Berry College, PO Box 490159, 2277 Martha Berry Highway, NW, Mount Berry, GA 30149-0159. *Phone:* 706-236-2215. *Toll-free phone:* 800-237-7942. *E-mail:* admissions@berry.edu.

Beulah Heights University

Atlanta, Georgia

http://www.beulah.edu/

- **Independent Pentecostal** comprehensive, founded 1918
- **Urban** 10-acre campus with easy access to Atlanta
- **Coed** 349 undergraduate students, 52% full-time, 49% women, 51% men
- **Noncompetitive** entrance level, 100% of applicants were admitted

UNDERGRAD STUDENTS

181 full-time, 168 part-time. Students come from 22 states and territories; 12 other countries; 30% are from out of state; 73% Black or African American, non-Hispanic/Latino; 4% Hispanic/Latino; 7% Asian, non-Hispanic/Latino; 11% Race/ethnicity unknown; 0.5% international; 15% transferred in; 14% live on campus.

Freshmen:

Admission: 16 applied, 16 admitted, 16 enrolled. *Average high school GPA:* 3.0.

Retention: 57% of full-time freshmen returned.

FACULTY

Total: 97, 12% full-time, 45% with terminal degrees.

Student/faculty ratio: 5:1.

ACADEMICS

Calendar: semesters. *Degrees:* associate, bachelor's, master's, and doctoral.

Special study options: academic remediation for entering students, accelerated degree program, adult/continuing education programs, advanced placement credit, cooperative education, distance learning, double majors, English as a second language, independent study, internships, off-campus study, part-time degree program, services for LD students, summer session for credit.

Unusual degree programs: 3-2 religious studies or leadership studies/divinity, leadership, religious studies.

Computers: 28 computers/terminals are available on campus for general student use. Students can access the following: campus intranet, computer help desk, free student e-mail accounts, online (class) registration, online (class) schedules. Campuswide network is available. 100% of college-owned or -operated housing units are wired for high-speed Internet access. Wireless service is available via entire campus.

Library: Barth Memorial Library. *Books:* 51,672 (physical). Weekly public service hours: 57.

STUDENT LIFE

Housing options: men-only, women-only. Campus housing is university owned.

Activities and organizations: student-run newspaper, choral group, Chapel Choir, Student Government Association, Club Give.

Campus security: 24-hour emergency response devices and patrols.
Student services: personal/psychological counseling.

COSTS & FINANCIAL AID
Costs (2017–18) *Tuition:* $9270 full-time, $309 per credit hour part-time. Full-time tuition and fees vary according to course load. *Required fees:* $610 full-time. *Room only:* $6000. Room and board charges vary according to housing facility. *Payment plans:* installment, deferred payment. *Waivers:* employees or children of employees.

Financial Aid Of all full-time matriculated undergraduates who enrolled in 2009, 113 applied for aid, 113 were judged to have need. 13 Federal Work-Study jobs (averaging $4335). *Average percent of need met:* 75. *Average financial aid package:* $5619. *Average need-based loan:* $2250. *Average need-based gift aid:* $3500. *Average indebtedness upon graduation:* $40,000.

APPLYING
Standardized Tests *Required for some:* TOEFL for international students. *Recommended:* SAT or ACT (for admission).
Options: electronic application, early admission.
Application fee: $50.
Required: essay or personal statement, high school transcript, minimum 2.0 GPA, 2 letters of recommendation, Statement of Faith.
Recommended: interview.
Application deadlines: rolling (freshmen), rolling (transfers).
Notification: continuous (freshmen), continuous (transfers).

CONTACT
Mrs. Bianca Phillips, Admissions Coordinator, Beulah Heights University, 892 Berne Street, SE, Atlanta, GA 30316. *Phone:* 404-627-2681 Ext. 117. *Toll-free phone:* 888-777-BHBC. *E-mail:* bianca.phillips@beulah.edu.

Brenau University

Gainesville, Georgia
http://www.brenau.edu/
- **Independent** comprehensive, founded 1878
- **Small-town** 57-acre campus with easy access to Atlanta
- **Endowment** $45.3 million
- **Coed, primarily women** 1,736 undergraduate students, 62% full-time, 91% women, 9% men
- **Moderately difficult** entrance level, 42% of applicants were admitted

UNDERGRAD STUDENTS
1,080 full-time, 656 part-time. Students come from 40 states and territories; 23 other countries; 7% are from out of state; 32% Black or African American, non-Hispanic/Latino; 8% Hispanic/Latino; 2% Asian, non-Hispanic/Latino; 0.2% American Indian or Alaska Native, non-Hispanic/Latino; 3% Two or more races, non-Hispanic/Latino; 4% Race/ethnicity unknown; 4% international; 25% transferred in; 27% live on campus.

Freshmen:
Admission: 2,140 applied, 897 admitted, 310 enrolled.
Retention: 65% of full-time freshmen returned.

FACULTY
Total: 284, 45% full-time, 65% with terminal degrees.
Student/faculty ratio: 11:1.

ACADEMICS
Calendar: semesters. *Degrees:* certificates, associate, bachelor's, master's, doctoral, post-master's, and postbachelor's certificates (also offers coed evening and weekend programs with significant enrollment not reflected in profile).
Special study options: academic remediation for entering students, accelerated degree program, advanced placement credit, distance learning, double majors, honors programs, independent study, internships, part-time degree program, services for LD students, study abroad, summer session for credit.
Computers: 157 computers/terminals and 190 ports are available on campus for general student use. Students can access the following: campus intranet, computer help desk, free student e-mail accounts, online

(class) grades, online (class) registration, online (class) schedules. Campuswide network is available. 100% of college-owned or -operated housing units are wired for high-speed Internet access. Wireless service is available via entire campus.
Library: Brenau Trustee Library. *Books:* 78,624 (physical), 343,819 (digital/electronic); *Serial titles:* 194 (physical), 42,250 (digital/electronic); *Databases:* 114. Weekly public service hours: 84; students can reserve study rooms.

STUDENT LIFE
Housing options: on-campus residence required through junior year; men-only, women-only, special housing for students with disabilities. Campus housing is university owned. Freshman campus housing is guaranteed.
Activities and organizations: drama/theater group, student-run newspaper, radio station, choral group, Student Government Association/Student Activities Board, International Club, national sororities.
Athletics Member NAIA. *Intercollegiate sports:* basketball W(s), cheerleading W(s), crew W(c), cross-country running W(s), golf W(s), soccer W(s), softball W(s), swimming and diving W(s), tennis W(s), track and field W(s), volleyball W(s).
Campus security: 24-hour emergency response devices and patrols, late-night transport/escort service.
Student services: health clinic, personal/psychological counseling, women's center.

COSTS & FINANCIAL AID
Costs (2018–19) *Comprehensive fee:* $41,468 includes full-time tuition ($28,650), mandatory fees ($400), and room and board ($12,418). Full-time tuition and fees vary according to class time, degree level, location, and program. Part-time tuition: $955 per semester hour. Part-time tuition and fees vary according to program. *Required fees:* $200 per term part-time. *Payment plans:* installment, deferred payment. *Waivers:* employees or children of employees.

Financial Aid Of all full-time matriculated undergraduates who enrolled in 2016, 922 applied for aid, 851 were judged to have need, 91 had their need fully met. 134 Federal Work-Study jobs (averaging $1852). In 2016, 116 non-need-based awards were made. *Average percent of need met:* 73. *Average financial aid package:* $21,389. *Average need-based loan:* $8830. *Average need-based gift aid:* $13,418. *Average non-need-based aid:* $11,759. *Average indebtedness upon graduation:* $33,375.

APPLYING
Options: electronic application, deferred entrance.
Required for some: essay or personal statement, high school transcript, interview.
Application deadlines: rolling (freshmen), rolling (out-of-state freshmen), rolling (transfers).
Notification: continuous (freshmen), continuous (out-of-state freshmen), continuous (transfers).

CONTACT
Ray Lian, Brenau University, Admissions, 500 Washington Street, SE, Gainesville, GA 30501. *Phone:* 770-534-6171. *Toll-free phone:* 800-252-5119. *Fax:* 770-538-4701. *E-mail:* rlian@brenau.edu.

Brewton-Parker College

Mt. Vernon, Georgia
http://www.bpc.edu/
- **Independent Southern Baptist** 4-year, founded 1904
- **Rural** 280-acre campus
- **Coed** 783 undergraduate students, 56% full-time, 42% women, 58% men
- **Minimally difficult** entrance level, 54% of applicants were admitted

UNDERGRAD STUDENTS
438 full-time, 345 part-time. Students come from 18 states and territories; 6 other countries; 11% are from out of state; 18% Black or African American, non-Hispanic/Latino; 4% Hispanic/Latino; 0.4% Asian, non-Hispanic/Latino; 0.5% Native Hawaiian or other Pacific Islander, non-Hispanic/Latino; 0.1% American Indian or Alaska Native, non-Hispanic/Latino; 2% Two or more races, non-Hispanic/Latino; 48% Race/ethnicity unknown; 0.6% international; 7% transferred in; 67% live on campus.

Freshmen:
Admission: 589 applied, 319 admitted, 167 enrolled. *Average high school GPA:* 3.0. *Test scores:* ACT scores over 18: 54%; ACT scores over 24: 7%; ACT scores over 30: 4%.
Retention: 49% of full-time freshmen returned.

FACULTY
Total: 75, 39% full-time, 43% with terminal degrees.
Student/faculty ratio: 13:1.

ACADEMICS
Calendar: semesters. *Degrees:* associate, bachelor's, and postbachelor's certificates.
Special study options: academic remediation for entering students, accelerated degree program, advanced placement credit, cooperative education, distance learning, double majors, honors programs, independent study, internships, part-time degree program, services for LD students, summer session for credit.
Computers: 99 computers/terminals are available on campus for general student use. Students can access the following: campus intranet, computer help desk, free student e-mail accounts, online (class) grades, online (class) registration, online (class) schedules, Printers. Campuswide network is available. 100% of college-owned or -operated housing units are wired for high-speed Internet access. Wireless service is available via entire campus.
Library: Fountain-New Library. *Books:* 88,734 (physical); *Serial titles:* 6,729 (physical); *Databases:* 290. Weekly public service hours: 78; students can reserve study rooms.

STUDENT LIFE
Housing options: on-campus residence required through junior year; men-only, women-only. Campus housing is university owned. Freshman campus housing is guaranteed.
Activities and organizations: drama/theater group, student-run newspaper, choral group, Council of Intramural Activities, Student Activities Council, Student Government Association, Circle K, Baptist Student Union.
Athletics Member NAIA. *Intercollegiate sports:* baseball M(s), basketball M(s)/W(s), cross-country running M(s)/W(s), golf M(s), soccer M(s)/W(s), softball W(s), tennis M(s)/W(s), track and field M(s)/W(s), volleyball M(s)/W(s), wrestling M(s)/W(s). *Intramural sports:* basketball M/W, football M/W, softball M/W, table tennis M/W, tennis M/W, ultimate Frisbee M/W, volleyball M/W.
Campus security: 24-hour emergency response devices, controlled dormitory access, campus security is provided from 6 pm to 6 am.
Student services: personal/psychological counseling.

COSTS & FINANCIAL AID
Costs (2018–19) *One-time required fee:* $200. *Comprehensive fee:* $26,620 includes full-time tuition ($16,940), mandatory fees ($1300), and room and board ($8380). Full-time tuition and fees vary according to course load, location, and program. Part-time tuition: $500 per credit hour. Part-time tuition and fees vary according to course load, location, and program. *Required fees:* $700 per year part-time. *College room only:* $3300. Room and board charges vary according to board plan and housing facility. *Payment plan:* installment. *Waivers:* senior citizens and employees or children of employees.
Financial Aid Of all full-time matriculated undergraduates who enrolled in 2009, 819 applied for aid, 736 were judged to have need, 118 had their need fully met. 170 Federal Work-Study jobs (averaging $676). 114 state and other part-time jobs (averaging $466). In 2009, 96 non-need-based awards were made. *Average percent of need met:* 71. *Average financial aid package:* $11,736. *Average need-based loan:* $3436. *Average need-based gift aid:* $9011. *Average non-need-based aid:* $3915. *Average indebtedness upon graduation:* $28,231. *Financial aid deadline:* 5/1.

APPLYING
Standardized Tests *Required:* SAT or ACT (for admission).
Options: electronic application.
Application fee: $35.
Required: high school transcript, minimum 2.0 GPA.

Application deadlines: 8/1 (freshmen), rolling (transfers).
Notification: continuous (freshmen), continuous (transfers).

CONTACT
Ms. Tiffany Quarterman, Admissions Office Manager, Brewton-Parker College, PO Box 197, Mount Vernon, GA 30445. *Phone:* 912-583-3250. *Toll-free phone:* 800-342-1087. *Fax:* 912-583-3598. *E-mail:* admissions@bpc.edu.

Carver College
Atlanta, Georgia
http://www.carver.edu/
- **Independent nondenominational** 4-year, founded 1943
- **Urban** 16-acre campus with easy access to Atlanta
- **Coed**
- **Noncompetitive** entrance level

FACULTY
Student/faculty ratio: 6:1.

ACADEMICS
Calendar: semesters. *Degrees:* certificates, associate, and bachelor's.
Library: Carver Bible College Library plus 1 other. Study areas open 24 hours, 5–7 days a week; students can reserve study rooms.

STUDENT LIFE
Housing options: men-only, women-only. Campus housing is leased by the school.
Activities and organizations: drama/theater group, choral group, Student Government Association, Student Missions Organization, Carver Praise Team, Thespian Club.
Athletics Member NCCAA.
Campus security: 24-hour patrols, late-night transport/escort service.
Student services: personal/psychological counseling.

APPLYING
Application fee: $35.
Required: essay or personal statement, high school transcript, minimum 2.0 GPA, 2 letters of recommendation. *Required for some:* interview. *Recommended:* interview.

CONTACT
Bertha Mack, Admissions Officer, Carver College, 3870 Cascade Road SW, Atlanta, GA 30331. *Phone:* 404-527-4520 Ext. 209. *Fax:* 404-527-4524. *E-mail:* info@carver.edu.

Chamberlain College of Nursing
Atlanta, Georgia
http://www.chamberlain.edu/
- **Proprietary** 4-year
- **Coed**

FACULTY
Student/faculty ratio: 8:1.

ACADEMICS
Degree: bachelor's.

STUDENT LIFE
Housing options: college housing not available.

COSTS
Costs (2017–18) *Tuition:* $18,900 full-time. *Required fees:* $600 full-time.

APPLYING
Standardized Tests *Required:* SAT or ACT (for admission).
Options: deferred entrance.
Application fee: $95.

CONTACT
Chamberlain College of Nursing, 5775 Peachtree Dunwoody Road NE, Suite A-100, Atlanta, GA 30342. *Toll-free phone:* 877-751-5783.

Clark Atlanta University
Atlanta, Georgia
http://www.cau.edu/
- **Independent United Methodist** university, founded 1865
- **Urban** 126-acre campus
- **Endowment** $68.5 million
- **Coed** 3,302 undergraduate students, 97% full-time, 72% women, 28% men
- **Moderately difficult** entrance level, 58% of applicants were admitted

UNDERGRAD STUDENTS
3,187 full-time, 115 part-time. Students come from 43 states and territories; 10 other countries; 64% are from out of state; 85% Black or African American, non-Hispanic/Latino; 0.1% Hispanic/Latino; 0.1% Asian, non-Hispanic/Latino; 0.1% American Indian or Alaska Native, non-Hispanic/Latino; 9% Race/ethnicity unknown; 6% international; 6% transferred in; 64% live on campus.

Freshmen:
Admission: 13,940 applied, 8,075 admitted, 914 enrolled. *Average high school GPA:* 3.2. *Test scores:* SAT evidence-based reading and writing scores over 500: 58%; SAT math scores over 500: 49%; ACT scores over 18: 76%; SAT evidence-based reading and writing scores over 600: 7%; SAT math scores over 600: 3%; ACT scores over 24: 15%.
Retention: 70% of full-time freshmen returned.

FACULTY
Total: 281, 64% full-time, 55% with terminal degrees.
Student/faculty ratio: 20:1.

ACADEMICS
Calendar: semesters. *Degrees:* bachelor's, master's, doctoral, post-master's, and postbachelor's certificates.

Special study options: academic remediation for entering students, accelerated degree program, adult/continuing education programs, advanced placement credit, cooperative education, double majors, honors programs, independent study, internships, off-campus study, part-time degree program, services for LD students, study abroad, summer session for credit. *ROTC:* Army (c), Navy (c).

Unusual degree programs: 3-2 engineering with Georgia Institute of Technology, Boston University, North Carolina Agricultural and Technical State University.

Computers: 741 computers/terminals and 2,000 ports are available on campus for general student use. Students can access the following: computer help desk, free student e-mail accounts, online (class) grades, online (class) registration, online (class) schedules. Campuswide network is available. 100% of college-owned or -operated housing units are wired for high-speed Internet access. Wireless service is available via entire campus.
Library: Robert W. Woodruff Library.

STUDENT LIFE
Housing options: on-campus residence required through sophomore year; coed, men-only, women-only. Campus housing is university owned and is provided by a third party. Freshman applicants given priority for college housing.

Activities and organizations: drama/theater group, student-run newspaper, radio and television station, choral group, marching band, Spirit Boosters, Pre-Alumni Council, Campus Activities Board, Orientation Guides, National Association for the Advancement of Colored People, national fraternities, national sororities.

Athletics Member NCAA. All Division II. *Intercollegiate sports:* baseball M(s), basketball M(s)/W(s), cross-country running M(s)/W(s), football M(s), softball W(s), tennis W(s), track and field M(s)/W(s), volleyball W(s). *Intramural sports:* basketball M/W, football M, softball W, tennis W, track and field M/W, volleyball M/W.

Campus security: 24-hour emergency response devices and patrols, late-night transport/escort service, controlled dormitory access.

Student services: health clinic, personal/psychological counseling.

COSTS & FINANCIAL AID
Costs (2017–18) *Comprehensive fee:* $33,960 includes full-time tuition ($20,476), mandatory fees ($2606), and room and board ($10,878). Part-time tuition: $853 per credit hour. *Required fees:* $1207 per term part-time. *Room and board:* Room and board charges vary according to board plan and housing facility. *Payment plan:* installment. *Waivers:* employees or children of employees.

Financial Aid Of all full-time matriculated undergraduates who enrolled in 2016, 2,780 applied for aid, 2,638 were judged to have need, 1,261 had their need fully met. 201 Federal Work-Study jobs (averaging $1740). *Average percent of need met:* 45. *Average financial aid package:* $7324. *Average need-based loan:* $2453. *Average need-based gift aid:* $5425. *Average indebtedness upon graduation:* $40,393.

APPLYING
Standardized Tests *Required:* SAT or ACT (for admission).
Options: electronic application, early admission, deferred entrance.
Application fee: $35.
Required: essay or personal statement, high school transcript, minimum 2.5 GPA, 2 letters of recommendation. *Required for some:* interview.
Application deadlines: 6/1 (freshmen), 6/1 (transfers).
Notification: continuous (freshmen), continuous (out-of-state freshmen), continuous (transfers).

CONTACT
Ms. Lorri Rice, Director of Recruitment and Admissions, Clark Atlanta University, 223 James P. Brawley Drive, SW, Atlanta, GA 30314. *Phone:* 404-880-8043. *Toll-free phone:* 800-688-3228. *Fax:* 404-880-6174. *E-mail:* cauadmissions@cau.edu.

Clayton State University
Morrow, Georgia
http://www.clayton.edu/
- **State-supported** comprehensive, founded 1969, part of University System of Georgia
- **Suburban** 163-acre campus with easy access to Atlanta
- **Coed** 6,555 undergraduate students, 57% full-time, 69% women, 31% men
- **Minimally difficult** entrance level, 48% of applicants were admitted

UNDERGRAD STUDENTS
3,742 full-time, 2,813 part-time. 4% are from out of state; 61% Black or African American, non-Hispanic/Latino; 6% Hispanic/Latino; 6% Asian, non-Hispanic/Latino; 0.1% Native Hawaiian or other Pacific Islander, non-Hispanic/Latino; 0.2% American Indian or Alaska Native, non-Hispanic/Latino; 3% Two or more races, non-Hispanic/Latino; 3% Race/ethnicity unknown; 1% international; 12% transferred in; 18% live on campus.

Freshmen:
Admission: 2,117 applied, 1,010 admitted, 643 enrolled. *Average high school GPA:* 3.0. *Test scores:* SAT evidence-based reading and writing scores over 500: 43%; SAT math scores over 500: 30%; ACT scores over 18: 85%; SAT evidence-based reading and writing scores over 600: 6%; SAT math scores over 600: 5%; ACT scores over 24: 16%; ACT scores over 30: 1%.
Retention: 68% of full-time freshmen returned.

FACULTY
Total: 346, 67% full-time, 67% with terminal degrees.
Student/faculty ratio: 17:1.

ACADEMICS
Calendar: semesters. *Degrees:* certificates, associate, bachelor's, and master's.

Special study options: academic remediation for entering students, adult/continuing education programs, advanced placement credit, cooperative education, distance learning, double majors, English as a second language, freshman honors college, honors programs, independent study, internships, off-campus study, part-time degree program, services for LD students, student-designed majors, study abroad, summer session for credit. *ROTC:* Army (c), Navy (c), Air Force (c).

Computers: 3,500 computers/terminals are available on campus for general student use. Students can access the following: computer help desk, free student e-mail accounts, online (class) grades, online (class) registration, online (class) schedules. Campuswide network is available.

100% of college-owned or -operated housing units are wired for high-speed Internet access. Wireless service is available via entire campus. **Library:** Clayton State University Library.

STUDENT LIFE

Housing options: on-campus residence required for freshman year; coed. Campus housing is university owned. Freshman applicants given priority for college housing.

Activities and organizations: drama/theater group, student-run newspaper, radio station, choral group, national fraternities, national sororities.

Athletics Member NCAA. All Division II. *Intercollegiate sports:* basketball M(s)/W(s), cheerleading W(s)(c), cross-country running M(s)/W(s), golf M(s), soccer M(s)/W(s), tennis W(s), track and field M(s)/W(s). *Intramural sports:* bowling M/W, softball M/W, table tennis M/W, volleyball M/W.

Campus security: 24-hour emergency response devices and patrols, late-night transport/escort service, controlled dormitory access, lighted pathways.

Student services: health clinic, personal/psychological counseling.

COSTS & FINANCIAL AID

Costs (2017–18) *Tuition:* state resident $4956 full-time, $165 per credit hour part-time; nonresident $18,032 full-time, $601 per credit hour part-time. Full-time tuition and fees vary according to course load. Part-time tuition and fees vary according to course load. *Required fees:* $1454 full-time, $727 per term part-time. *Room and board:* $10,490. Room and board charges vary according to board plan and housing facility. *Waivers:* senior citizens and employees or children of employees.

Financial Aid Of all full-time matriculated undergraduates who enrolled in 2017, 3,251 applied for aid, 3,029 were judged to have need, 86 had their need fully met. 67 Federal Work-Study jobs (averaging $4556). In 2017, 25 non-need-based awards were made. *Average percent of need met:* 47. *Average financial aid package:* $10,024. *Average need-based loan:* $4067. *Average need-based gift aid:* $7108. *Average non-need-based aid:* $2045. *Average indebtedness upon graduation:* $30,423.

APPLYING

Standardized Tests *Required:* SAT or ACT (for admission).

Options: electronic application, early admission, deferred entrance.

Application fee: $40.

Required: high school transcript, proof of immunization.

Notification: continuous (freshmen), continuous (transfers).

CONTACT

Admissions, Clayton State University, 2000 Clayton State Boulevard, Morrow, GA 30260-0285. *Phone:* 678-466-4115. *Fax:* 678-466-4149. *E-mail:* csc-info@clayton.edu.

College of Coastal Georgia

Brunswick, Georgia

http://www.ccga.edu/

- **State-supported** 4-year, founded 1961, part of University System of Georgia
- **Small-town** 193-acre campus with easy access to Jacksonville
- **Endowment** $7.9 million
- **Coed** 3,663 undergraduate students, 61% full-time, 67% women, 33% men
- **Minimally difficult** entrance level, 95% of applicants were admitted

UNDERGRAD STUDENTS

2,217 full-time, 1,446 part-time. Students come from 42 states and territories; 43 other countries; 8% are from out of state; 18% Black or African American, non-Hispanic/Latino; 6% Hispanic/Latino; 2% Asian, non-Hispanic/Latino; 0.2% Native Hawaiian or other Pacific Islander, non-Hispanic/Latino; 0.3% American Indian or Alaska Native, non-Hispanic/Latino; 4% Two or more races, non-Hispanic/Latino; 2% Race/ethnicity unknown; 1% international; 8% transferred in; 18% live on campus.

Freshmen:

Admission: 1,562 applied, 1,479 admitted, 809 enrolled. *Average high school GPA:* 3.0. *Test scores:* SAT evidence-based reading and writing scores over 500: 43%; SAT math scores over 500: 27%; ACT scores over 18: 63%; SAT evidence-based reading and writing scores over 600: 5%; SAT math scores over 600: 4%; ACT scores over 24: 13%; ACT scores over 30: 1%.

Retention: 58% of full-time freshmen returned.

FACULTY

Total: 214, 47% full-time, 55% with terminal degrees.

Student/faculty ratio: 19:1.

ACADEMICS

Calendar: semesters. *Degrees:* associate and bachelor's.

Special study options: academic remediation for entering students, advanced placement credit, distance learning, double majors, honors programs, internships, part-time degree program, services for LD students, study abroad, summer session for credit.

Computers: 395 computers/terminals and 300 ports are available on campus for general student use. Students can access the following: computer help desk, free student e-mail accounts, online (class) grades, online (class) registration, online (class) schedules. Campuswide network is available. 100% of college-owned or -operated housing units are wired for high-speed Internet access. Wireless service is available via entire campus. **Library:** Clara Wood Gould Memorial Library. *Books:* 54,662 (physical), 150,476 (digital/electronic); *Serial titles:* 109 (physical), 168,333 (digital/electronic); *Databases:* 338. Weekly public service hours: 77; students can reserve study rooms.

STUDENT LIFE

Housing options: on-campus residence required for freshman year; coed. Campus housing is university owned, leased by the school and is provided by a third party. Freshman campus housing is guaranteed.

Activities and organizations: student-run newspaper, International Association, Coastal Georgia Association of Nursing Students, Urban Gaming Club, Association of Coastal Educators, CCGA Biology Club.

Athletics Member NAIA. *Intercollegiate sports:* basketball M(s)/W(s), golf M(s)/W(s), softball W(s), tennis M(s)/W(s), volleyball W(s). *Intramural sports:* baseball M(c), basketball M/W, bowling M, cheerleading W(c), football M/W, golf M/W, lacrosse W(c), sailing M(c)/W(c), soccer M/W, softball M/W, ultimate Frisbee M/W.

Campus security: 24-hour emergency response devices and patrols, late-night transport/escort service, controlled dormitory access.

Student services: health clinic, personal/psychological counseling.

COSTS & FINANCIAL AID

Costs (2018–19) *One-time required fee:* $25. *Tuition:* state resident $2451 full-time, $104 per credit hour part-time; nonresident $9058 full-time, $385 per credit hour part-time. Full-time tuition and fees vary according to course load. Part-time tuition and fees vary according to course load. *Required fees:* $1520 full-time, $455 per term part-time. *Room and board:* $9520; room only: $6300. Room and board charges vary according to board plan, housing facility, and location. *Payment plan:* installment. *Waivers:* senior citizens and employees or children of employees.

Financial Aid Of all full-time matriculated undergraduates who enrolled in 2016, 2,359 applied for aid, 1,941 were judged to have need. 27 Federal Work-Study jobs (averaging $3203). *Average financial aid package:* $6705. *Average need-based loan:* $3500. *Average need-based gift aid:* $3457. *Average indebtedness upon graduation:* $25,455. *Financial aid deadline:* 6/1.

APPLYING

Standardized Tests *Required:* SAT or ACT (for admission).

Options: electronic application, early admission, deferred entrance.

Application fee: $25.

Required: high school transcript, minimum 2.0 GPA, immunization records, proof of residency.

Application deadlines: 8/24 (freshmen), 8/24 (transfers).

Notification: continuous (freshmen), continuous (transfers).

CONTACT

Ms. Aerial Dickerson, Associate Director of Admissions, College of Coastal Georgia, One College Drive, Brunswick, GA 31520. *Phone:* 912-279-5730. *Toll-free phone:* 800-675-7235. *Fax:* 912-262-3072. *E-mail:* admiss@ccga.edu.

Columbus State University
Columbus, Georgia
http://www.columbusstate.edu/
- **State-supported** comprehensive, founded 1958, part of University System of Georgia
- **Suburban** 132-acre campus with easy access to Atlanta
- **Coed** 6,798 undergraduate students, 69% full-time, 59% women, 41% men
- **Minimally difficult** entrance level, 53% of applicants were admitted

UNDERGRAD STUDENTS
4,693 full-time, 2,105 part-time. Students come from 31 states and territories; 35 other countries; 15% are from out of state; 38% Black or African American, non-Hispanic/Latino; 6% Hispanic/Latino; 2% Asian, non-Hispanic/Latino; 0.1% Native Hawaiian or other Pacific Islander, non-Hispanic/Latino; 0.4% American Indian or Alaska Native, non-Hispanic/Latino; 2% Two or more races, non-Hispanic/Latino; 1% international; 10% transferred in; 20% live on campus.

Freshmen:
Admission: 3,483 applied, 1,860 admitted, 958 enrolled. *Average high school GPA:* 3.1. *Test scores:* SAT evidence-based reading and writing scores over 500: 55%; SAT math scores over 500: 40%; ACT scores over 18: 83%; SAT evidence-based reading and writing scores over 600: 8%; SAT math scores over 600: 9%; ACT scores over 24: 24%; SAT evidence-based reading and writing scores over 700: 2%; ACT scores over 30: 2%.
Retention: 76% of full-time freshmen returned.

FACULTY
Total: 564, 52% full-time, 49% with terminal degrees.
Student/faculty ratio: 17:1.

ACADEMICS
Calendar: semesters. *Degrees:* certificates, associate, bachelor's, master's, doctoral, post-master's, and postbachelor's certificates.
Special study options: academic remediation for entering students, accelerated degree program, adult/continuing education programs, advanced placement credit, cooperative education, distance learning, double majors, English as a second language, freshman honors college, honors programs, independent study, internships, off-campus study, part-time degree program, services for LD students, study abroad, summer session for credit. *ROTC:* Army (b).
Unusual degree programs: 3-2 engineering with Georgia Institute of Technology.
Computers: 3,053 computers/terminals and 1,765 ports are available on campus for general student use. Students can access the following: campus intranet, computer help desk, free student e-mail accounts, online (class) grades, online (class) registration, online (class) schedules. Campuswide network is available. 100% of college-owned or -operated housing units are wired for high-speed Internet access. Wireless service is available via entire campus.
Library: Simon Schwob Memorial Library plus 1 other. *Books:* 379,660 (physical); *Serial titles:* 1,103 (physical).

STUDENT LIFE
Housing options: on-campus residence required for freshman year; coed, men-only, women-only, special housing for students with disabilities. Campus housing is university owned. Freshman applicants given priority for college housing.
Activities and organizations: drama/theater group, student-run newspaper, choral group, Student Government Association, Student Activities Council, Campus Ministry Association, African Students Association, SABER Student Newspaper, national fraternities, national sororities.
Athletics Member NCAA. All Division II. *Intercollegiate sports:* baseball M(s), basketball M(s)/W(s), cross-country running M(s)/W(s), golf M(s)/W(s), soccer W(s), softball W(s), tennis M(s)/W(s), track and field M(s)/W(s), volleyball W(s). *Intramural sports:* baseball M, basketball M/W, cross-country running M/W, football M, lacrosse M(c), racquetball M/W, riflery M(c)/W(c), skiing (downhill) M/W, soccer M/W, softball W, ultimate Frisbee M/W, volleyball M/W, wrestling M(c).
Campus security: 24-hour emergency response devices and patrols, late-night transport/escort service, controlled dormitory access.
Student services: health clinic, personal/psychological counseling.

COSTS & FINANCIAL AID
Costs (2017–18) *Tuition:* state resident $5330 full-time, $178 per credit hour part-time; nonresident $18,812 full-time, $627 per credit hour part-time. Full-time tuition and fees vary according to course load, degree level, and program. Part-time tuition and fees vary according to course load, degree level, and program. *Required fees:* $1870 full-time, $935 per term part-time. *Room and board:* $10,550; room only: $6580. Room and board charges vary according to board plan and housing facility. *Waivers:* senior citizens.
Financial Aid Of all full-time matriculated undergraduates who enrolled in 2016, 4,110 applied for aid, 3,416 were judged to have need, 533 had their need fully met. In 2016, 185 non-need-based awards were made. *Average percent of need met:* 69. *Average financial aid package:* $9309. *Average need-based loan:* $4314. *Average need-based gift aid:* $4915. *Average non-need-based aid:* $1695. *Average indebtedness upon graduation:* $31,676.

APPLYING
Standardized Tests *Required:* SAT or ACT (for admission).
Options: electronic application, early admission, deferred entrance.
Application fee: $40.
Required: high school transcript, minimum 2.5 GPA, proof of immunization.
Application deadlines: 6/30 (freshmen), 6/30 (transfers).
Notification: continuous (freshmen), continuous (transfers).

CONTACT
Columbus State University, 4225 University Avenue, Columbus, GA 31907-5645. *Phone:* 706-507-8827. *Toll-free phone:* 866-264-2035.

Covenant College
Lookout Mountain, Georgia
http://www.covenant.edu/
- **Independent** comprehensive, founded 1955, affiliated with Presbyterian Church in America
- **Suburban** 350-acre campus
- **Coed** 1,030 undergraduate students, 95% full-time, 53% women, 47% men
- **Moderately difficult** entrance level, 95% of applicants were admitted

UNDERGRAD STUDENTS
983 full-time, 47 part-time. 70% are from out of state; 3% Black or African American, non-Hispanic/Latino; 3% Hispanic/Latino; 0.9% Asian, non-Hispanic/Latino; 4% Two or more races, non-Hispanic/Latino; 0.2% Race/ethnicity unknown; 3% international; 3% transferred in; 85% live on campus.

Freshmen:
Admission: 692 applied, 659 admitted, 263 enrolled. *Average high school GPA:* 3.6. *Test scores:* SAT evidence-based reading and writing scores over 500: 97%; SAT math scores over 500: 91%; ACT scores over 18: 99%; SAT evidence-based reading and writing scores over 600: 66%; SAT math scores over 600: 53%; ACT scores over 24: 76%; SAT evidence-based reading and writing scores over 700: 21%; SAT math scores over 700: 10%; ACT scores over 30: 29%.
Retention: 87% of full-time freshmen returned.

FACULTY
Total: 103, 62% full-time, 73% with terminal degrees.
Student/faculty ratio: 13:1.

ACADEMICS
Calendar: semesters. *Degrees:* bachelor's and master's (master's degree in education only).
Special study options: academic remediation for entering students, adult/continuing education programs, advanced placement credit, double majors, English as a second language, independent study, internships, off-campus study, part-time degree program, services for LD students, student-designed majors, study abroad, summer session for credit. *ROTC:* Army (c).
Computers: Students can access the following: computer help desk, free student e-mail accounts, online (class) registration, online student information

system. Campuswide network is available. 100% of college-owned or -operated housing units are wired for high-speed Internet access. Wireless service is available via classrooms, computer labs, dorm rooms, libraries. **Library:** Kresge Memorial Library.

STUDENT LIFE

Housing options: on-campus residence required through junior year; coed. Campus housing is university owned. Freshman campus housing is guaranteed.

Activities and organizations: drama/theater group, student-run newspaper, radio station, choral group.

Athletics Member NCAA, NAIA, NCCAA. All NCAA Division III. *Intercollegiate sports:* baseball M, basketball M/W, cross-country running M/W, golf M/W, soccer M/W, softball W, tennis M/W, volleyball W. *Intramural sports:* badminton M/W, basketball M/W, football M, soccer M/W, volleyball M/W.

Campus security: controlled dormitory access, night security guards.

Student services: health clinic, personal/psychological counseling, women's center.

COSTS & FINANCIAL AID

Costs (2018–19) *Comprehensive fee:* $44,590 includes full-time tuition ($33,360), mandatory fees ($970), and room and board ($10,260). Part-time tuition: $1430 per credit hour.

Financial Aid Of all full-time matriculated undergraduates who enrolled in 2015, 776 applied for aid, 664 were judged to have need, 207 had their need fully met. In 2015, 314 non-need-based awards were made. *Average percent of need met:* 79. *Average financial aid package:* $25,772. *Average need-based loan:* $6841. *Average need-based gift aid:* $19,425. *Average non-need-based aid:* $13,013. *Average indebtedness upon graduation:* $24,484.

APPLYING

Standardized Tests *Required:* SAT or ACT (for admission).

Options: electronic application, early admission, early action, deferred entrance.

Application fee: $35.

Required: essay or personal statement, high school transcript, minimum 2.5 GPA, 2 letters of recommendation, interview.

CONTACT

Mr. Philip Howlett, Assistant Director of Admissions, Covenant College, 14049 Scenic Highway, Lookout Mountain, GA 30750. *Phone:* 706-419-1145. *Toll-free phone:* 888-451-2683. *Fax:* 706-820-0893. *E-mail:* admissions@covenant.edu.

Dalton State College

Dalton, Georgia

http://www.daltonstate.edu/

- **State-supported** 4-year, founded 1963, part of University System of Georgia
- **Small-town** 144-acre campus
- **Endowment** $33.6 million
- **Coed**
- **Noncompetitive** entrance level

FACULTY

Student/faculty ratio: 19:1.

ACADEMICS

Calendar: semesters. *Degrees:* certificates, associate, and bachelor's.
Library: Derrell C. Roberts Library. *Books:* 143,415 (physical), 99,973 (digital/electronic); *Databases:* 72. Students can reserve study rooms.

STUDENT LIFE

Housing options: coed, special housing for students with disabilities. Campus housing is university owned.

Activities and organizations: Lambda Alpha Eplison (Criminal Justice), Rotaract, College Republicans, Beta Chi Nu (Biology), LASO (Latin American Student Organization), national fraternities, national sororities.

Athletics Member NAIA.

Campus security: 24-hour emergency response devices and patrols.

COSTS & FINANCIAL AID

Costs (2017–18) *One-time required fee:* $200. *Tuition:* state resident $3064 full-time, $102 per credit hour part-time; nonresident $11,322 full-time, $377 per credit hour part-time. Full-time tuition and fees vary according to course load and program. Part-time tuition and fees vary according to course load and program. *Required fees:* $1052 full-time, $365 per year part-time, $365 per term part-time. *Room and board:* $7970; room only: $4972. Room and board charges vary according to board plan.

Financial Aid Of all full-time matriculated undergraduates who enrolled in 2014, 2,154 applied for aid, 1,874 were judged to have need, 978 had their need fully met. In 2014, 813 non-need-based awards were made. *Average percent of need met:* 84. *Average financial aid package:* $2850. *Average need-based loan:* $4750. *Average need-based gift aid:* $3500. *Average non-need-based aid:* $895. *Average indebtedness upon graduation:* $3000. *Financial aid deadline:* 7/1.

APPLYING

Standardized Tests *Required:* SAT or ACT (for admission).

Options: electronic application, deferred entrance.

Application fee: $30.

Required: high school transcript.

CONTACT

Katherine Logan, Director of Admissions, Dalton State College, 650 College Drive, Dalton, GA 30720-3797. *Phone:* 706-272-4524. *Toll-free phone:* 800-829-4436. *Fax:* 706-272-2530. *E-mail:* klogan@daltonstate.edu.

DeVry University–Alpharetta Campus

Alpharetta, Georgia

http://www.devry.edu/

CONTACT

Admissions Office, DeVry University–Alpharetta Campus, 2555 Northwinds Parkway, Alpharetta, GA 30009. *Phone:* 770-619-3600. *Toll-free phone:* 866-338-7934.

DeVry University–Decatur Campus

Decatur, Georgia

http://www.devry.edu/

- **Proprietary** comprehensive, founded 1969, part of DeVry University
- **Suburban** campus
- **Coed**
- **Minimally difficult** entrance level

FACULTY

Student/faculty ratio: 21:1.

ACADEMICS

Calendar: semesters. *Degrees:* associate, bachelor's, master's, and postbachelor's certificates.
Library: Learning Resource Center.

STUDENT LIFE

Housing options: college housing not available.

COSTS

Costs (2017–18) *Tuition:* $14,644 full-time. *Required fees:* $500 full-time.

APPLYING

Options: deferred entrance.

Application fee: $30.

Required: high school transcript, interview.

CONTACT

DeVry University–Decatur Campus, 1 West Court Square, Suite 100, Decatur, GA 30030. *Phone:* 404-270-2700. *Toll-free phone:* 866-338-7934.

East Georgia State College

Swainsboro, Georgia

http://www.ega.edu/

- **State-supported** primarily 2-year, founded 1973, part of University System of Georgia
- **Rural** 207-acre campus
- **Coed**
- **Minimally difficult** entrance level

FACULTY
Student/faculty ratio: 26:1.

ACADEMICS
Calendar: semesters. *Degrees:* certificates, associate, and bachelor's.
Library: East Georgia College Library. Students can reserve study rooms.

STUDENT LIFE
Housing options: coed. Campus housing is provided by a third party.
Activities and organizations: drama/theater group, student-run newspaper, choral group.
Athletics Member NJCAA.
Campus security: 24-hour patrols, late-night transport/escort service, controlled dormitory access.
Student services: health clinic, personal/psychological counseling.

COSTS & FINANCIAL AID
Costs (2017–18) *One-time required fee:* $35. *Tuition:* state resident $2726 full-time, $91 per credit hour part-time; nonresident $10,320 full-time, $344 per credit hour part-time. Full-time tuition and fees vary according to class time, course load, location, and student level. Part-time tuition and fees vary according to class time, course load, location, and student level. *Required fees:* $886 full-time, $443 per term part-time. *Room and board:* $8504; room only: $5960. Room and board charges vary according to location.
Financial Aid Of all full-time matriculated undergraduates who enrolled in 2016, 43 Federal Work-Study jobs (averaging $1560).

APPLYING
Options: early admission, deferred entrance.
Application fee: $20.
Required: high school transcript.

CONTACT
East Georgia State College, 131 College Circle, Swainsboro, GA 30401-2699. *Phone:* 478-289-2112.

Emmanuel College

Franklin Springs, Georgia

http://www.ec.edu/

- **Independent** 4-year, founded 1919, affiliated with Pentecostal Holiness Church
- **Rural** 90-acre campus with easy access to Atlanta, GA
- **Endowment** $5.1 million
- **Coed** 952 undergraduate students, 86% full-time, 48% women, 52% men
- **Minimally difficult** entrance level, 43% of applicants were admitted

UNDERGRAD STUDENTS
822 full-time, 130 part-time. Students come from 30 states and territories; 20 other countries; 25% are from out of state; 13% Black or African American, non-Hispanic/Latino; 7% Hispanic/Latino; 0.9% Asian, non-Hispanic/Latino; 0.5% Native Hawaiian or other Pacific Islander, non-Hispanic/Latino; 0.1% American Indian or Alaska Native, non-Hispanic/Latino; 3% Two or more races, non-Hispanic/Latino; 7% international; 5% transferred in; 59% live on campus.

Freshmen:
Admission: 1,119 applied, 482 admitted, 263 enrolled. *Average high school GPA:* 3.2.
Retention: 61% of full-time freshmen returned.

FACULTY
Total: 79, 63% full-time, 52% with terminal degrees.
Student/faculty ratio: 15:1.

ACADEMICS
Calendar: semesters. *Degrees:* associate and bachelor's.
Special study options: advanced placement credit, distance learning, honors programs, independent study, internships, part-time degree program, services for LD students, study abroad, summer session for credit.
Unusual degree programs: 3-2 psychology with Richmont University.
Computers: 80 computers/terminals are available on campus for general student use. Students can access the following: campus intranet, computer help desk, free student e-mail accounts, online (class) grades, online (class) registration, online (class) schedules. Campuswide network is available. 100% of college-owned or -operated housing units are wired for high-speed Internet access. Wireless service is available via entire campus.
Library: Shaw-Leslie Library plus 1 other. *Books:* 41,206 (physical), 50,364 (digital/electronic); *Serial titles:* 99 (physical); *Databases:* 124. Weekly public service hours: 84; students can reserve study rooms.

STUDENT LIFE
Housing options: on-campus residence required through sophomore year; men-only, women-only. Campus housing is university owned. Freshman campus housing is guaranteed.
Activities and organizations: drama/theater group, choral group, Students in Free Enterprise (SIFE), Fellowship of Christian Athletes, SOS, BSU, International Students Club.
Athletics Member NCAA, NCCAA. All NCAA Division II. *Intercollegiate sports:* archery M(s)/W(s), baseball M(s), basketball M(s)/W(s), bowling M(s)/W(s), cross-country running M(s)/W(s), golf M(s)/W(s), lacrosse M(s)/W(s), riflery M(s)/W(s), soccer M(s)/W(s), softball W(s), swimming and diving M(s)/W(s), tennis M(s)/W(s), track and field M(s)/W(s), volleyball M(s)/W(s), wrestling M(s)/W(s). *Intramural sports:* basketball M/W, football M/W, golf M/W, soccer M/W, tennis M/W, track and field M/W, volleyball M/W, weight lifting M/W.
Campus security: 24-hour patrols.
Student services: personal/psychological counseling.

COSTS & FINANCIAL AID
Costs (2017–18) *Comprehensive fee:* $27,598 includes full-time tuition ($19,370), mandatory fees ($340), and room and board ($7888). Part-time tuition: $815 per credit hour. *Room and board:* Room and board charges vary according to housing facility. *Payment plan:* installment. *Waivers:* senior citizens and employees or children of employees.
Financial Aid Of all full-time matriculated undergraduates who enrolled in 2017, 672 applied for aid, 593 were judged to have need, 118 had their need fully met. 71 Federal Work-Study jobs (averaging $849). 142 state and other part-time jobs (averaging $962). In 2017, 87 non-need-based awards were made. *Average percent of need met:* 69. *Average financial aid package:* $16,046. *Average need-based loan:* $3615. *Average need-based gift aid:* $12,524. *Average non-need-based aid:* $4232. *Average indebtedness upon graduation:* $24,840. *Financial aid deadline:* 6/15.

APPLYING
Standardized Tests *Required:* SAT or ACT (for admission).
Options: electronic application, early admission, deferred entrance.
Application fee: $25.
Required: essay or personal statement, high school transcript. *Required for some:* interview.
Application deadlines: 8/1 (freshmen), 8/1 (transfers).
Notification: continuous until 8/1 (freshmen), continuous until 8/1 (transfers).

CONTACT
Ms. Kelley Garrett, Director of Admissions, Emmanuel College, PO Box 129, 181 Spring Street, Franklin Springs, GA 30639-0129. *Phone:* 706-245-7226 Ext. 2814. *Toll-free phone:* 800-860-8800. *E-mail:* admissions@ec.edu.

Emory University

Atlanta, Georgia

http://www.emory.edu/

- **Independent Methodist** university, founded 1836
- **Suburban** 631-acre campus with easy access to Atlanta
- **Endowment** $6.9 billion
- **Coed** 6,937 undergraduate students, 98% full-time, 60% women, 40% men
- **Most difficult** entrance level, 22% of applicants were admitted

UNDERGRAD STUDENTS

6,794 full-time, 143 part-time. Students come from 55 states and territories; 84 other countries; 78% are from out of state; 8% Black or African American, non-Hispanic/Latino; 9% Hispanic/Latino; 20% Asian, non-Hispanic/Latino; 0.1% American Indian or Alaska Native, non-Hispanic/Latino; 4% Two or more races, non-Hispanic/Latino; 2% Race/ethnicity unknown; 16% international; 1% transferred in; 65% live on campus.

Freshmen:
Admission: 23,747 applied, 5,234 admitted, 1,388 enrolled. *Average high school GPA:* 3.8. *Test scores:* SAT evidence-based reading and writing scores over 500: 100%; SAT math scores over 500: 100%; ACT scores over 18: 100%; SAT evidence-based reading and writing scores over 600: 97%; SAT math scores over 600: 96%; ACT scores over 24: 100%; SAT evidence-based reading and writing scores over 700: 59%; SAT math scores over 700: 67%; ACT scores over 30: 83%.
Retention: 93% of full-time freshmen returned.

FACULTY

Total: 1,222, 87% full-time, 93% with terminal degrees.
Student/faculty ratio: 9:1.

ACADEMICS

Calendar: semesters. *Degrees:* bachelor's, master's, doctoral, post-master's, and postbachelor's certificates (enrollment figures include Emory University, Oxford College; application data for main campus only).

Special study options: advanced placement credit, cooperative education, double majors, English as a second language, honors programs, independent study, internships, off-campus study, services for LD students, study abroad, summer session for credit. *ROTC:* Army (c), Navy (c), Air Force (c).

Unusual degree programs: 3-2 business administration; engineering with Georgia Institute of Technology; nursing.

Computers: Students can access the following: campus intranet, computer help desk, free student e-mail accounts, online (class) grades, online (class) registration, online (class) schedules, computer repair system. Campuswide network is available. 100% of college-owned or -operated housing units are wired for high-speed Internet access. Wireless service is available via entire campus.
Library: Robert W. Woodruff Library plus 8 others. *Books:* 2.3 million (physical), 943,697 (digital/electronic); *Serial titles:* 78,038 (physical), 156,766 (digital/electronic); *Databases:* 892.

STUDENT LIFE

Housing options: on-campus residence required through sophomore year; coed. Campus housing is university owned. Freshman campus housing is guaranteed.

Activities and organizations: drama/theater group, student-run newspaper, radio and television station, choral group, Volunteer Emory, music/theater, Student Government, Outdoor Emory, Hillel, national fraternities, national sororities.

Athletics Member NCAA. All Division III. *Intercollegiate sports:* badminton M(c)/W(c), baseball M, basketball M/W, crew M(c)/W(c), cross-country running M/W, equestrian sports M(c)/W(c), fencing M(c)/W(c), field hockey M(c)/W(c), golf M(c)/W(c), gymnastics W(c), lacrosse M(c)/W(c), rock climbing M(c)/W(c), rugby M(c), sailing M(c)/W(c), soccer M/W, softball W, squash M(c)/W(c), swimming and diving M/W, tennis M/W, track and field M/W, ultimate Frisbee M(c)/W(c), volleyball M/W, water polo M(c)/W(c), weight lifting M(c)/W(c). *Intramural sports:* basketball M/W, football M/W, golf M, soccer M/W, softball W, swimming and diving M/W, table tennis M/W, tennis M/W, volleyball W.

Campus security: 24-hour emergency response devices and patrols, student patrols, late-night transport/escort service, controlled dormitory access.

Student services: health clinic, personal/psychological counseling, women's center, legal services.

COSTS & FINANCIAL AID

Costs (2018–19) *Comprehensive fee:* $65,762 includes full-time tuition ($50,590), mandatory fees ($716), and room and board ($14,456). Part-time tuition: $2108 per credit hour. *College room only:* $8306. Room and board charges vary according to board plan and housing facility. *Payment plan:* installment. *Waivers:* employees or children of employees.
Financial Aid Of all full-time matriculated undergraduates who enrolled in 2017, 3,409 applied for aid, 2,992 were judged to have need, 2,869 had their need fully met. In 2017, 332 non-need-based awards were made. *Average percent of need met:* 99. *Average financial aid package:* $43,777. *Average need-based loan:* $6154. *Average need-based gift aid:* $39,571. *Average non-need-based aid:* $26,925. *Average indebtedness upon graduation:* $28,262. *Financial aid deadline:* 3/1.

APPLYING

Standardized Tests *Required:* SAT or ACT (for admission).
Options: electronic application, early admission, early decision, deferred entrance.
Application fee: $75.
Required: essay or personal statement, high school transcript, 2 letters of recommendation.
Application deadlines: 1/1 (freshmen), 3/15 (transfers).
Early decision deadline: 11/1 (for plan 1), 1/1 (for plan 2).
Notification: 4/1 (freshmen), 4/30 (transfers), 12/15 (early decision plan 1), 2/15 (early decision plan 2).

CONTACT

Dr. John Latting, Dean of Admission, Emory University, 1390 Oxford Road NE, 3rd Floor, Atlanta, GA 30322-1100. *Phone:* 404-727-6036. *Toll-free phone:* 800-727-6036. *Fax:* 404-727-4303. *E-mail:* admiss@emory.edu.

Fort Valley State University

Fort Valley, Georgia

http://www.fvsu.edu/

CONTACT

Mr. Donald Moore, Director of Admissions and Recruitment, Fort Valley State University, 1005 State University Drive, Fort Valley, GA 31030. *Phone:* 478-825-6307. *Toll-free phone:* 877-462-3878. *Fax:* 478-825-6169. *E-mail:* admissap@fvsu.edu.

Georgia College & State University

Milledgeville, Georgia

http://www.gcsu.edu/

- **State-supported** comprehensive, founded 1889, part of University System of Georgia
- **Small-town** 680-acre campus
- **Endowment** $40.6 million
- **Coed** 5,987 undergraduate students, 91% full-time, 62% women, 38% men
- **Moderately difficult** entrance level, 79% of applicants were admitted

UNDERGRAD STUDENTS

5,442 full-time, 545 part-time. Students come from 24 states and territories; 34 other countries; 1% are from out of state; 5% Black or African American, non-Hispanic/Latino; 5% Hispanic/Latino; 1% Asian, non-Hispanic/Latino; 0.1% Native Hawaiian or other Pacific Islander, non-Hispanic/Latino; 0.2% American Indian or Alaska Native, non-Hispanic/Latino; 3% Two or more races, non-Hispanic/Latino; 0.3% Race/ethnicity unknown; 0.5% international; 5% transferred in; 33% live on campus.

Freshmen:
Admission: 4,089 applied, 3,230 admitted, 1,443 enrolled. *Average high school GPA:* 3.5. *Test scores:* SAT evidence-based reading and writing scores over 500: 98%; SAT math scores over 500: 92%; ACT scores over

18: 100%; SAT evidence-based reading and writing scores over 600: 54%; SAT math scores over 600: 38%; ACT scores over 24: 65%; SAT evidence-based reading and writing scores over 700: 7%; SAT math scores over 700: 4%; ACT scores over 30: 7%.

Retention: 84% of full-time freshmen returned.

FACULTY
Total: 406, 81% full-time, 71% with terminal degrees.
Student/faculty ratio: 17:1.

ACADEMICS
Calendar: semesters. *Degrees:* certificates, bachelor's, master's, doctoral, and post-master's certificates.

Special study options: accelerated degree program, advanced placement credit, distance learning, double majors, English as a second language, external degree program, freshman honors college, honors programs, independent study, internships, part-time degree program, services for LD students, student-designed majors, study abroad, summer session for credit. *ROTC:* Army (c).

Unusual degree programs: 3-2 engineering with Georgia Institute of Technology.

Computers: 900 computers/terminals and 6,295 ports are available on campus for general student use. Students can access the following: campus intranet, computer help desk, free student e-mail accounts, online (class) grades, online (class) registration, online (class) schedules. Campuswide network is available. 100% of college-owned or -operated housing units are wired for high-speed Internet access. Wireless service is available via entire campus.

Library: Ina Dillard Russell Library plus 1 other. *Books:* 175,159 (physical), 576,315 (digital/electronic); *Serial titles:* 4,951 (physical), 232,257 (digital/electronic); *Databases:* 379. Weekly public service hours: 102; students can reserve study rooms.

STUDENT LIFE
Housing options: on-campus residence required for freshman year; coed, special housing for students with disabilities. Campus housing is university owned and leased by the school. Freshman campus housing is guaranteed.

Activities and organizations: drama/theater group, student-run newspaper, radio station, choral group, Resident Student Association, Alpha Lambda Delta, Circle K, Georgia College Miracle, Wesley Foundation of Campus Ministries, national fraternities, national sororities.

Athletics Member NCAA. All Division II. *Intercollegiate sports:* baseball M(s), basketball M(s)/W(s), cheerleading M/W, cross-country running M(s)/W(s), golf M(s), soccer W(s), softball W(s), tennis M(s)/W(s), volleyball W(s). *Intramural sports:* baseball M(c), basketball M/W, equestrian sports W(c), football M/W, golf M(c), ice hockey M(c), lacrosse M(c)/W(c), rugby M(c)/W(c), soccer M(c)/W(c), softball M(c)/W(c), swimming and diving W(c), tennis M(c)/W(c), ultimate Frisbee M(c)/W(c), volleyball M/W(c), water polo M(c)/W(c).

Campus security: 24-hour emergency response devices and patrols, student patrols, late-night transport/escort service, controlled dormitory access.

Student services: health clinic, personal/psychological counseling, women's center.

COSTS & FINANCIAL AID
Costs (2017–18) *Tuition:* state resident $7324 full-time; nonresident $26,038 full-time. Full-time tuition and fees vary according to course load, location, and program. Part-time tuition and fees vary according to course load, location, and program. *Required fees:* $2022 full-time. *Room and board:* $12,538; room only: $6938. Room and board charges vary according to board plan and housing facility. *Payment plan:* installment. *Waivers:* senior citizens and employees or children of employees.

Financial Aid Of all full-time matriculated undergraduates who enrolled in 2017, 4,202 applied for aid, 2,818 were judged to have need, 404 had their need fully met. In 2017, 197 non-need-based awards were made. *Average percent of need met:* 58. *Average financial aid package:* $10,745. *Average need-based loan:* $4520. *Average need-based gift aid:* $4577. *Average non-need-based aid:* $2258. *Average indebtedness upon graduation:* $30,407.

APPLYING
Standardized Tests *Required:* SAT or ACT (for admission). *Required for some:* SAT Subject Tests (for admission).

Options: electronic application, early admission, early action, deferred entrance.

Application fee: $40.

Required: proof of immunization. *Required for some:* essay or personal statement, high school transcript, .

Application deadlines: 4/1 (freshmen), rolling (out-of-state freshmen), 7/1 (transfers), 11/1 (early action).

Notification: continuous (freshmen), continuous (out-of-state freshmen), continuous (transfers).

CONTACT
Mr. Ramon Blakley, Director of Admissions, Undergraduate, Georgia College & State University, CPO Box 023, Milledgeville, GA 31061. *Phone:* 478-445-1283. *Toll-free phone:* 800-342-0471. *Fax:* 478-445-3653. *E-mail:* admissions@gcsu.edu.

Georgia Gwinnett College
Lawrenceville, Georgia
http://www.ggc.edu/
- **State-supported** 4-year, part of University System of Georgia
- **Suburban** 260-acre campus with easy access to Atlanta
- **Coed** 12,287 undergraduate students, 67% full-time, 56% women, 44% men
- **Noncompetitive** entrance level, 88% of applicants were admitted

UNDERGRAD STUDENTS
8,289 full-time, 3,998 part-time. Students come from 36 states and territories; 122 other countries; 1% are from out of state; 32% Black or African American, non-Hispanic/Latino; 19% Hispanic/Latino; 11% Asian, non-Hispanic/Latino; 0.2% Native Hawaiian or other Pacific Islander, non-Hispanic/Latino; 0.1% American Indian or Alaska Native, non-Hispanic/Latino; 3% Two or more races, non-Hispanic/Latino; 0.8% Race/ethnicity unknown; 2% international; 6% transferred in; 5% live on campus.

Freshmen:
Admission: 4,073 applied, 3,573 admitted, 2,444 enrolled. *Average high school GPA:* 2.9. *Test scores:* SAT evidence-based reading and writing scores over 500: 57%; SAT math scores over 500: 55%; ACT scores over 18: 65%; SAT evidence-based reading and writing scores over 600: 13%; SAT math scores over 600: 10%; ACT scores over 24: 15%; SAT evidence-based reading and writing scores over 700: 1%; SAT math scores over 700: 1%; ACT scores over 30: 1%.

Retention: 67% of full-time freshmen returned.

FACULTY
Total: 674, 67% full-time, 64% with terminal degrees.
Student/faculty ratio: 18:1.

ACADEMICS
Calendar: semesters. *Degrees:* associate and bachelor's.

Special study options: academic remediation for entering students, advanced placement credit, double majors, English as a second language, honors programs, internships, part-time degree program, services for LD students, study abroad, summer session for credit. *ROTC:* Army (b).

Computers: 243 computers/terminals are available on campus for general student use. Students can access the following: campus intranet, computer help desk, free student e-mail accounts, online (class) grades, online (class) registration, online (class) schedules. Campuswide network is available. 100% of college-owned or -operated housing units are wired for high-speed Internet access. Wireless service is available via entire campus.

Library: Daniel J. Kaufman Library and Learning Center. *Books:* 76,355 (physical), 118,119 (digital/electronic); *Serial titles:* 141 (physical), 5,119 (digital/electronic); *Databases:* 112. Weekly public service hours: 79; students can reserve study rooms.

STUDENT LIFE
Housing options: coed. Campus housing is university owned. Freshman campus housing is guaranteed.

Athletics Member NAIA. *Intercollegiate sports:* baseball M, soccer M/W, softball W, tennis M/W.

Campus security: 24-hour emergency response devices and patrols, student patrols, late-night transport/escort service, controlled dormitory access.

Student services: health clinic, personal/psychological counseling.

COSTS

Costs (2018–19) *Tuition:* state resident $3920 full-time, $131 per credit hour part-time; nonresident $14,634 full-time, $488 per credit hour part-time. Full-time tuition and fees vary according to course load. Part-time tuition and fees vary according to course load. *Required fees:* $1714 full-time, $480 per term part-time. *Room and board:* $12,874; room only: $9744. Room and board charges vary according to board plan and housing facility. *Payment plans:* installment, deferred payment. *Waivers:* senior citizens and employees or children of employees.

APPLYING

Standardized Tests *Required:* SAT or ACT (for admission).

Options: electronic application, deferred entrance.

Application fee: $20.

Required: high school transcript, minimum 2.0 GPA.

Application deadlines: 6/1 (freshmen), rolling (transfers).

CONTACT

Admissions Office, Georgia Gwinnett College, 1000 University Center Lane, Lawrenceville, GA 30043. *Phone:* 678-407-5313. *Toll-free phone:* 877-704-4422. *E-mail:* ggcadmissions@ggc.edu.

Georgia Highlands College

Rome, Georgia

http://www.highlands.edu/

- **State-supported** primarily 2-year, founded 1970, part of University System of Georgia
- **Suburban** 226-acre campus with easy access to Atlanta
- **Endowment** $39,054
- **Coed** 6,003 undergraduate students, 47% full-time, 62% women, 38% men
- **Noncompetitive** entrance level

UNDERGRAD STUDENTS

2,828 full-time, 3,175 part-time. Students come from 23 states and territories; 1% are from out of state; 16% Black or African American, non-Hispanic/Latino; 14% Hispanic/Latino; 2% Asian, non-Hispanic/Latino; 0.1% Native Hawaiian or other Pacific Islander, non-Hispanic/Latino; 0.2% American Indian or Alaska Native, non-Hispanic/Latino; 3% Two or more races, non-Hispanic/Latino; 0.1% Race/ethnicity unknown; 6% transferred in.

Freshmen:
Admission: 1,374 enrolled. *Average high school GPA:* 3.0.
Retention: 67% of full-time freshmen returned.

FACULTY

Total: 277, 47% full-time, 25% with terminal degrees.

Student/faculty ratio: 21:1.

ACADEMICS

Calendar: semesters. *Degrees:* associate and bachelor's.

Special study options: academic remediation for entering students, advanced placement credit, cooperative education, distance learning, double majors, honors programs, independent study, part-time degree program, services for LD students, study abroad, summer session for credit.

Computers: 867 computers/terminals are available on campus for general student use. Students can access the following: campus intranet, free student e-mail accounts, online (class) grades, online (class) registration, online (class) schedules. Campuswide network is available. Wireless service is available via entire campus.

Library: Georgia Highlands College Library–Floyd Campus plus 4 others. *Books:* 79,592 (physical), 178,561 (digital/electronic); *Serial titles:* 48 (physical), 4,380 (digital/electronic); *Databases:* 382. Weekly public service hours: 58; students can reserve study rooms.

STUDENT LIFE

Housing options: college housing not available.

Activities and organizations: student-run newspaper, Association of Nursing Students, Green Highlands, Brother 2 Brother, Student Government Association, Phi Theta Kappa.

Athletics Member NJCAA. *Intercollegiate sports:* baseball M(s), basketball M(s)/W(s), softball W(s). *Intramural sports:* basketball M/W, cheerleading M/W, football M/W, golf M/W, skiing (downhill) M/W, table tennis M/W, tennis M/W, ultimate Frisbee M/W, volleyball M/W, weight lifting M/W.

Campus security: 24-hour emergency response devices and patrols, emergency phone/email alert system.

Student services: personal/psychological counseling.

COSTS & FINANCIAL AID

Costs (2018–19) *Tuition:* state resident $2780 full-time, $93 per credit hour part-time; nonresident $10,526 full-time, $351 per credit hour part-time. Full-time tuition and fees vary according to course load and location. Part-time tuition and fees vary according to course load and location. *Required fees:* $1064 full-time, $412 per term part-time. *Payment plan:* installment. *Waivers:* senior citizens.

Financial Aid Of all full-time matriculated undergraduates who enrolled in 2016, 50 Federal Work-Study jobs (averaging $3500).

APPLYING

Options: electronic application, deferred entrance.

Application fee: $30.

Required: high school transcript, minimum 2.0 GPA.

Application deadlines: 7/15 (freshmen), 7/15 (transfers).

Notification: continuous (freshmen), continuous (transfers).

CONTACT

Charlene Graham, Assistant Director of Admissions, Georgia Highlands College, 3175 Cedartown Highway, Rome, GA 30161. *Phone:* 706-295-6339. *Toll-free phone:* 800-332-2406. *Fax:* 706-295-6341. *E-mail:* cgraham@highlands.edu.

Georgia Institute of Technology

Atlanta, Georgia

http://www.gatech.edu/

- **State-supported** university, founded 1885, part of University System of Georgia
- **Urban** 400-acre campus
- **Endowment** $2.0 billion
- **Coed** 15,572 undergraduate students, 96% full-time, 38% women, 62% men
- 23% of applicants were admitted

UNDERGRAD STUDENTS

14,898 full-time, 674 part-time. Students come from 54 states and territories; 127 other countries; 35% are from out of state; 7% Black or African American, non-Hispanic/Latino; 7% Hispanic/Latino; 21% Asian, non-Hispanic/Latino; 4% Two or more races, non-Hispanic/Latino; 4% Race/ethnicity unknown; 9% international; 4% transferred in; 43% live on campus.

Freshmen:
Admission: 31,497 applied, 7,369 admitted, 2,860 enrolled. *Average high school GPA:* 4.0. *Test scores:* SAT evidence-based reading and writing scores over 500: 52%; SAT math scores over 500: 100%; ACT scores over 18: 100%; SAT evidence-based reading and writing scores over 600: 51%; SAT math scores over 600: 98%; ACT scores over 24: 98%; SAT evidence-based reading and writing scores over 700: 38%; SAT math scores over 700: 84%; ACT scores over 30: 83%.
Retention: 97% of full-time freshmen returned.

FACULTY

Total: 1,285, 87% full-time, 4% with terminal degrees.

Student/faculty ratio: 22:1.

ACADEMICS

Calendar: semesters. *Degrees:* bachelor's, master's, and doctoral.

Special study options: academic remediation for entering students, accelerated degree program, advanced placement credit, cooperative education, distance learning, English as a second language, honors programs, independent study, internships, off-campus study, part-time degree program, services for LD students, student-designed majors, study abroad, summer session for credit. *ROTC:* Army (b), Navy (b), Air Force (b).

Unusual degree programs: 3-2 engineering with Georgia Institute of Technology.

Computers: 2,500 computers/terminals and 22,981 ports are available on campus for general student use. Students can access the following: campus intranet, computer help desk, free student e-mail accounts, online (class) grades, online (class) registration, online (class) schedules, access to a virtual lab environment from a personal device or GT computer. Campuswide network is available. 100% of college-owned or -operated housing units are wired for high-speed Internet access. Wireless service is available via entire campus.

Library: Georgia Institute of Technology Library plus 1 other. *Books:* 909,730 (physical), 1.0 million (digital/electronic); *Serial titles:* 12,999 (physical), 29,621 (digital/electronic); *Databases:* 336. Weekly public service hours: 168; study areas open 24 hours, 5–7 days a week; students can reserve study rooms.

STUDENT LIFE

Housing options: coed, men-only, women-only, special housing for students with disabilities. Campus housing is university owned. Freshman campus housing is guaranteed.

Activities and organizations: drama/theater group, student-run newspaper, radio and television station, choral group, marching band, national fraternities, national sororities.

Athletics Member NCAA. All Division I. *Intercollegiate sports:* baseball M(s), basketball M(s)/W(s), cheerleading M(s)/W(s), cross-country running M(s)/W(s), football M(s), golf M(s), softball W(s), swimming and diving M(s)/W(s), tennis M(s)/W(s), track and field M(s)/W(s), volleyball W(s). *Intramural sports:* archery M(c)/W(c), badminton M(c)/W(c), baseball M(c)/W(c), basketball M/W, bowling M/W, crew M(c)/W(c), equestrian sports M(c)/W(c), fencing M(c)/W(c), field hockey M(c)/W(c), golf M(c)/W(c), gymnastics M(c)/W(c), ice hockey M(c)/W(c), lacrosse M(c)/W(c), racquetball M/W, rowing M(c)/W(c), rugby M(c)/W(c), sailing M(c)/W(c), soccer M/W, softball M, squash M(c)/W(c), swimming and diving M(c)/W(c), tennis M(c)/W(c), triathlon M(c)/W(c), ultimate Frisbee M(c)/W(c), volleyball M/W, water polo M(c)/W(c), weight lifting M(c), wrestling M(c).

Campus security: 24-hour emergency response devices and patrols, late-night transport/escort service, controlled dormitory access, lighted pathways/sidewalks, emergency notification system, self-defense education, emergency telephones, shuttle buses, video cameras.

Student services: health clinic, personal/psychological counseling, women's center, legal services.

COSTS & FINANCIAL AID

Costs (2017–18) *Tuition:* state resident $10,008 full-time, $2974 per term part-time; nonresident $30,604 full-time, $9081 per term part-time. Part-time tuition and fees vary according to course load. *Required fees:* $2410 full-time, $1205 per term part-time. *Room and board:* $14,126; room only: $9286. Room and board charges vary according to board plan, housing facility, and student level. *Payment plan:* deferred payment. *Waivers:* senior citizens and employees or children of employees.

Financial Aid Of all full-time matriculated undergraduates who enrolled in 2016, 9,499 applied for aid, 6,104 were judged to have need, 2,301 had their need fully met. 399 Federal Work-Study jobs (averaging $1686). In 2016, 1127 non-need-based awards were made. *Average percent of need met:* 54. *Average financial aid package:* $13,016. *Average need-based loan:* $4046. *Average need-based gift aid:* $7194. *Average non-need-based aid:* $5690. *Average indebtedness upon graduation:* $32,398. *Financial aid deadline:* 1/31.

APPLYING

Standardized Tests *Required:* SAT or ACT (for admission).

Options: electronic application, early admission, early action, deferred entrance.

Application fee: $75.

Required: essay or personal statement, high school transcript.

Application deadlines: 1/1 (freshmen), 3/1 (transfers), 10/15 (early action).

Notification: 3/15 (freshmen), 6/15 (transfers), 1/13 (early action).

CONTACT

Mr. Rick A. Clark Jr., Director of Undergraduate Admissions, Georgia Institute of Technology, Office of Undergraduate Admission, Atlanta, GA 30332-0320. *Phone:* 404-894-4154. *Fax:* 404-894-9511. *E-mail:* admission@gatech.edu.

Georgia Military College
Milledgeville, Georgia
http://www.gmc.edu/

- **Public** primarily 2-year, founded 1879
- **Small-town** campus
- **Endowment** $1.5 million
- **Coed** 8,595 undergraduate students, 50% full-time, 61% women, 39% men
- **Noncompetitive** entrance level, 78% of applicants were admitted

UNDERGRAD STUDENTS

4,270 full-time, 4,325 part-time. Students come from 36 states and territories; 12 other countries; 4% are from out of state; 42% Black or African American, non-Hispanic/Latino; 7% Hispanic/Latino; 2% Asian, non-Hispanic/Latino; 0.4% Native Hawaiian or other Pacific Islander, non-Hispanic/Latino; 3% American Indian or Alaska Native, non-Hispanic/Latino; 0.2% Two or more races, non-Hispanic/Latino; 2% Race/ethnicity unknown; 0.2% international; 29% transferred in; 3% live on campus.

Freshmen:
Admission: 3,475 applied, 2,717 admitted, 1,492 enrolled.
Retention: 46% of full-time freshmen returned.

FACULTY
Total: 890, 14% full-time.
Student/faculty ratio: 15:1.

ACADEMICS
Calendar: quarters. *Degrees:* associate and bachelor's.

Special study options: academic remediation for entering students, advanced placement credit, cooperative education, distance learning, double majors, independent study, off-campus study, part-time degree program, services for LD students, student-designed majors, study abroad, summer session for credit. *ROTC:* Army (b).

Computers: 835 computers/terminals are available on campus for general student use. Students can access the following: campus intranet, computer help desk, free student e-mail accounts, online (class) grades, online (class) registration, online (class) schedules. Campuswide network is available. 100% of college-owned or -operated housing units are wired for high-speed Internet access. Wireless service is available via entire campus.

Library: Sibley Cone Library plus 1 other. *Books:* 38,125 (physical), 57,769 (digital/electronic); *Serial titles:* 52 (physical); *Databases:* 331. Weekly public service hours: 68.

STUDENT LIFE

Housing options: on-campus residence required through sophomore year; coed. Campus housing is university owned. Freshman campus housing is guaranteed.

Activities and organizations: drama/theater group, student-run newspaper, choral group, Student Government Association, Alpha Phi Omega National Service Fraternity, Phi Theta Kappa, Drama Club, Biology Club.

Athletics Member NJCAA. *Intercollegiate sports:* cross-country running M/W, football M(s), golf M/W, riflery M/W, soccer M(s)/W(s), softball W(s). *Intramural sports:* badminton M/W, basketball M/W, golf M/W, softball M/W, tennis M/W, volleyball M/W.

Campus security: 24-hour emergency response devices and patrols, controlled dormitory access.

Student services: health clinic.

COSTS & FINANCIAL AID

Costs (2018–19) *Tuition:* state resident $5445 full-time, $121 per credit hour part-time; nonresident $5445 full-time, $121 per credit hour part-time. Full-time tuition and fees vary according to location. Part-time tuition and fees vary according to location. *Required fees:* $679 full-time, $15 per credit hour part-time. *Room and board:* $7500; room only:

$3150. Room and board charges vary according to location. *Waivers:* senior citizens and employees or children of employees.

Financial Aid Of all full-time matriculated undergraduates who enrolled in 2012, 6,554 applied for aid, 6,132 were judged to have need, 282 had their need fully met. 121 Federal Work-Study jobs (averaging $1614). In 2012, 61 non-need-based awards were made. *Average percent of need met:* 47. *Average financial aid package:* $9567. *Average need-based loan:* $3189. *Average need-based gift aid:* $4626. *Average non-need-based aid:* $2226.

APPLYING

Options: electronic application, early admission, deferred entrance.

Application fee: $35.

Required for some: high school transcript, interview.

Application deadlines: rolling (freshmen), rolling (transfers).

CONTACT

Georgia Military College, 201 East Greene Street, Old Capitol Building, Milledgeville, GA 31061-3398. *Phone:* 478-387-4890. *Toll-free phone:* 800-342-0413.

Georgia Southern University

Statesboro, Georgia

http://www.georgiasouthern.edu/

- **State-supported** university, founded 1906, part of University System of Georgia
- **Small-town** 900-acre campus
- **Endowment** $47.7 million
- **Coed** 17,759 undergraduate students, 89% full-time, 50% women, 50% men
- **Moderately difficult** entrance level, 68% of applicants were admitted

UNDERGRAD STUDENTS

15,755 full-time, 2,004 part-time. Students come from 49 states and territories; 73 other countries; 5% are from out of state; 24% Black or African American, non-Hispanic/Latino; 5% Hispanic/Latino; 2% Asian, non-Hispanic/Latino; 0.1% Native Hawaiian or other Pacific Islander, non-Hispanic/Latino; 0.5% American Indian or Alaska Native, non-Hispanic/Latino; 2% Two or more races, non-Hispanic/Latino; 1% Race/ethnicity unknown; 2% international; 6% transferred in; 28% live on campus.

Freshmen:

Admission: 9,202 applied, 6,284 admitted, 3,508 enrolled. *Average high school GPA:* 3.3. *Test scores:* SAT evidence-based reading and writing scores over 500: 99%; SAT math scores over 500: 97%; ACT scores over 18: 99%; SAT evidence-based reading and writing scores over 600: 48%; SAT math scores over 600: 30%; ACT scores over 24: 46%; SAT evidence-based reading and writing scores over 700: 4%; SAT math scores over 700: 3%; ACT scores over 30: 6%.

Retention: 80% of full-time freshmen returned.

FACULTY

Total: 866, 90% full-time, 81% with terminal degrees.

Student/faculty ratio: 22:1.

ACADEMICS

Calendar: semesters. *Degrees:* certificates, bachelor's, master's, doctoral, post-master's, and postbachelor's certificates.

Special study options: academic remediation for entering students, accelerated degree program, adult/continuing education programs, advanced placement credit, cooperative education, distance learning, double majors, English as a second language, honors programs, independent study, internships, off-campus study, part-time degree program, services for LD students, student-designed majors, study abroad, summer session for credit. *ROTC:* Army (b).

Unusual degree programs: 3-2 engineering with Georgia Institute of Technology; nursing.

Computers: 3,743 computers/terminals and 5,200 ports are available on campus for general student use. Students can access the following: campus intranet, computer help desk, free student e-mail accounts, online (class) grades, online (class) registration, online (class) schedules, online degree audit, online career services, and online healthcare. Campuswide network is available. 100% of college-owned or -operated housing units are wired for high-speed Internet access. Wireless service is available via entire campus.

Library: Henderson Library. *Books:* 1.0 million (physical), 374,473 (digital/electronic); *Serial titles:* 14,993 (physical), 94,948 (digital/electronic); *Databases:* 332. Weekly public service hours: 143; study areas open 24 hours, 5–7 days a week; students can reserve study rooms.

STUDENT LIFE

Housing options: on-campus residence required for freshman year; coed, special housing for students with disabilities. Campus housing is university owned. Freshman applicants given priority for college housing.

Activities and organizations: drama/theater group, student-run newspaper, radio station, choral group, marching band, Residence Hall Association, Campus Religious Ministries, Student Government Association, Club Sports and Recreation, Greek Life, national fraternities, national sororities.

Athletics Member NCAA. All Division I. *Intercollegiate sports:* baseball M(s), basketball M(s)/W(s), cheerleading M/W, cross-country running W(s), football M(s), golf M(s)/W(s), riflery W(s), soccer M(s)/W(s), softball W(s), swimming and diving W(s), tennis M(s)/W(s), track and field W(s), volleyball W(s). *Intramural sports:* archery M/W, baseball M(c), basketball M/W, bowling M/W, cheerleading M(c)/W(c), cross-country running M(c)/W(c), equestrian sports M(c)/W(c), fencing M(c)/W(c), football M/W, golf M/W, lacrosse M(c)/W(c), riflery M(c)/W(c), rugby M(c)/W(c), soccer M/W, softball M/W, swimming and diving M(c)/W(c), tennis M/W, track and field M(c)/W(c), ultimate Frisbee M/W, volleyball M/W, water polo M(c)/W(c), wrestling M(c).

Campus security: 24-hour emergency response devices and patrols, student patrols, late-night transport/escort service, controlled dormitory access, bike police and services.

Student services: health clinic, personal/psychological counseling, women's center, legal services.

COSTS & FINANCIAL AID

Costs (2017–18) *Tuition:* state resident $4798 full-time, $178 per credit hour part-time; nonresident $16,930 full-time, $627 per credit hour part-time. Full-time tuition and fees vary according to course load, degree level, location, and program. Part-time tuition and fees vary according to course load, degree level, location, and program. *Required fees:* $2092 full-time, $1046 per term part-time. *Room and board:* $9650; room only: $5900. Room and board charges vary according to board plan and housing facility. *Payment plan:* installment. *Waivers:* senior citizens and employees or children of employees.

Financial Aid Of all full-time matriculated undergraduates who enrolled in 2016, 14,429 applied for aid, 10,324 were judged to have need, 1,098 had their need fully met. 265 Federal Work-Study jobs (averaging $1671). In 2016, 389 non-need-based awards were made. *Average percent of need met:* 55. *Average financial aid package:* $10,410. *Average need-based loan:* $5594. *Average need-based gift aid:* $6837. *Average non-need-based aid:* $1734. *Average indebtedness upon graduation:* $29,724.

APPLYING

Standardized Tests *Required:* SAT or ACT (for admission).

Options: electronic application, early admission, deferred entrance.

Application fee: $30.

Required: minimum 2.5 GPA. *Required for some:* high school transcript.

Application deadlines: 5/1 (freshmen), 8/1 (transfers).

Notification: continuous (freshmen), continuous (transfers).

CONTACT

Miss Amy Smith, Director, Georgia Southern University, PO Box 8024, Statesboro, GA 30460. *Phone:* 912-478-5391. *Fax:* 912-478-7240. *E-mail:* admissions@georgiasouthern.edu.

Georgia Southern University–Armstrong Campus
Savannah, Georgia
http://www.georgiasouthern.edu/
- **State-supported** comprehensive, founded 1935, part of University System of Georgia
- **Suburban** 267-acre campus
- **Endowment** $12.2 million
- **Coed** 6,281 undergraduate students, 72% full-time, 66% women, 34% men

UNDERGRAD STUDENTS
4,513 full-time, 1,768 part-time. Students come from 43 states and territories; 67 other countries; 13% are from out of state; 26% Black or African American, non-Hispanic/Latino; 8% Hispanic/Latino; 3% Asian, non-Hispanic/Latino; 0.3% Native Hawaiian or other Pacific Islander, non-Hispanic/Latino; 0.4% American Indian or Alaska Native, non-Hispanic/Latino; 5% Two or more races, non-Hispanic/Latino; 0.2% Race/ethnicity unknown; 2% international; 9% transferred in; 19% live on campus.

Freshmen:
Admission: 840 enrolled. *Average high school GPA:* 3.2. *Test scores:* SAT evidence-based reading and writing scores over 500: 76%; SAT math scores over 500: 79%; ACT scores over 18: 86%; SAT evidence-based reading and writing scores over 600: 20%; SAT math scores over 600: 20%; ACT scores over 24: 22%; SAT evidence-based reading and writing scores over 700: 2%; SAT math scores over 700: 1%; ACT scores over 30: 3%.
Retention: 65% of full-time freshmen returned.

FACULTY
Total: 478, 61% full-time.
Student/faculty ratio: 16:1.

ACADEMICS
Calendar: semesters. *Degrees:* certificates, associate, bachelor's, master's, doctoral, post-master's, and postbachelor's certificates.

Special study options: academic remediation for entering students, adult/continuing education programs, advanced placement credit, cooperative education, distance learning, double majors, honors programs, independent study, internships, off-campus study, part-time degree program, services for LD students, study abroad, summer session for credit. *ROTC:* Army (b), Navy (c).

Computers: 300 computers/terminals are available on campus for general student use. Students can access the following: campus intranet, computer help desk, free student e-mail accounts, online (class) grades, online (class) registration, online (class) schedules. Campuswide network is available. 100% of college-owned or -operated housing units are wired for high-speed Internet access. Wireless service is available via entire campus.
Library: Lane Library plus 1 other. *Books:* 207,421 (physical), 215,400 (digital/electronic); *Serial titles:* 500 (physical), 2,000 (digital/electronic); *Databases:* 300. Weekly public service hours: 108; students can reserve study rooms.

STUDENT LIFE
Housing options: on-campus residence required for freshman year; coed. Campus housing is leased by the school and is provided by a third party. Freshman applicants given priority for college housing.

Activities and organizations: drama/theater group, student-run newspaper, choral group, Hispanic Outreach and Leadership at Armstrong (HOLA), Student Government Association, Campus Union Board, Gay Straight Alliance, Collegiate 100, national fraternities, national sororities.

Athletics *Intramural sports:* archery M(c)/W(c), baseball M(c), basketball M(c)/W(c), rugby M(c), soccer M(c)/W(c), table tennis M/W, tennis M(c)/W(c), ultimate Frisbee M(c)/W(c), volleyball M/W.

Campus security: 24-hour emergency response devices and patrols, student patrols, late-night transport/escort service, controlled dormitory access, personal safety app.

Student services: health clinic, personal/psychological counseling.

COSTS & FINANCIAL AID
Costs (2017–18) *Tuition:* state resident $4956 full-time, $165 per credit hour part-time; nonresident $18,032 full-time, $601 per credit hour part-time. Full-time tuition and fees vary according to course load, location, and program. Part-time tuition and fees vary according to course load, location, and program. *Required fees:* $1474 full-time, $612 per term part-time. *Room and board:* $10,856; room only: $6658. Room and board charges vary according to board plan and housing facility. *Payment plan:* installment. *Waivers:* senior citizens and employees or children of employees.

Financial Aid Of all full-time matriculated undergraduates who enrolled in 2015, 4,018 applied for aid, 3,981 were judged to have need. In 2015, 129 non-need-based awards were made. *Average need-based loan:* $3500. *Average need-based gift aid:* $1500. *Average non-need-based aid:* $1515. *Financial aid deadline:* 4/20.

APPLYING
Standardized Tests *Required:* SAT or ACT (for admission). *Required for some:* SAT Subject Tests (for admission).
Required: high school transcript, minimum 2.5 GPA.

CONTACT
Amy Smither, Director of Admissions, Georgia Southern University–Armstrong Campus, 11935 Abercorn St, Savannah, GA 31419. *Phone:* 912-478-5391. *Toll-free phone:* 800-633-2349. *Fax:* 912-344-3417. *E-mail:* amysmith@georgiasouthern.com.

Georgia Southwestern State University
Americus, Georgia
http://www.gsw.edu/
- **State-supported** comprehensive, founded 1906, part of University System of Georgia
- **Small-town** 250-acre campus
- **Endowment** $35.6 million
- **Coed** 2,606 undergraduate students, 68% full-time, 63% women, 37% men
- **Moderately difficult** entrance level, 67% of applicants were admitted

UNDERGRAD STUDENTS
1,779 full-time, 827 part-time. Students come from 25 states and territories; 33 other countries; 4% are from out of state; 26% Black or African American, non-Hispanic/Latino; 6% Hispanic/Latino; 1% Asian, non-Hispanic/Latino; 0.2% Native Hawaiian or other Pacific Islander, non-Hispanic/Latino; 0.2% American Indian or Alaska Native, non-Hispanic/Latino; 2% Two or more races, non-Hispanic/Latino; 0.3% Race/ethnicity unknown; 2% international; 10% transferred in; 32% live on campus.

Freshmen:
Admission: 1,279 applied, 863 admitted, 452 enrolled. *Average high school GPA:* 3.3. *Test scores:* SAT evidence-based reading and writing scores over 500: 68%; SAT math scores over 500: 57%; ACT scores over 18: 88%; SAT evidence-based reading and writing scores over 600: 16%; SAT math scores over 600: 9%; ACT scores over 24: 22%.
Retention: 65% of full-time freshmen returned.

FACULTY
Total: 166, 72% full-time, 58% with terminal degrees.
Student/faculty ratio: 18:1.

ACADEMICS
Calendar: semesters. *Degrees:* bachelor's, master's, post-master's, and postbachelor's certificates.

Special study options: academic remediation for entering students, accelerated degree program, advanced placement credit, distance learning, double majors, English as a second language, honors programs, internships, part-time degree program, services for LD students, study abroad, summer session for credit.

Unusual degree programs: engineering with Georgia Institute of Technology.

Computers: 260 computers/terminals are available on campus for general student use. Students can access the following: free student e-mail accounts, online (class) grades, online (class) registration, online (class) schedules. Campuswide network is available. 100% of college-owned or -operated housing units are wired for high-speed Internet access. Wireless service is available via dorm rooms, learning centers, libraries, student centers.

Library: James Earl Carter Library. *Books:* 207,635 (physical), 68,397 (digital/electronic); *Serial titles:* 76 (physical), 81 (digital/electronic); *Databases:* 277. Weekly public service hours: 72; students can reserve study rooms.

STUDENT LIFE

Housing options: on-campus residence required through sophomore year; coed. Campus housing is university owned. Freshman applicants given priority for college housing.

Activities and organizations: drama/theater group, student-run newspaper, choral group, National sororities and fraternities, African Student Association, Enactus, Outdoor Club, International Student Association, national fraternities, national sororities.

Athletics Member NCAA. All Division II. *Intercollegiate sports:* baseball M(s), basketball M(s)/W(s), cross-country running W(s), golf M(s), soccer M(s)/W(s), softball W(s), tennis M(s)/W(s). *Intramural sports:* basketball M/W, racquetball M/W, ultimate Frisbee M/W, volleyball M/W.

Campus security: 24-hour emergency response devices and patrols, late-night transport/escort service, controlled dormitory access.

Student services: health clinic, personal/psychological counseling.

COSTS & FINANCIAL AID

Costs (2017–18) *Tuition:* state resident $4956 full-time, $165 per credit hour part-time; nonresident $18,032 full-time, $601 per credit hour part-time. Full-time tuition and fees vary according to course load, location, and program. Part-time tuition and fees vary according to course load, location, and program. *Required fees:* $1376 full-time. *Room and board:* $7910; room only: $3970. Room and board charges vary according to board plan and housing facility. *Waivers:* senior citizens.

Financial Aid Of all full-time matriculated undergraduates who enrolled in 2016, 1,577 applied for aid, 1,288 were judged to have need, 164 had their need fully met. 56 Federal Work-Study jobs (averaging $2207). In 2016, 124 non-need-based awards were made. *Average percent of need met:* 60. *Average financial aid package:* $9480. *Average need-based loan:* $3984. *Average need-based gift aid:* $4902. *Average non-need-based aid:* $1977. *Average indebtedness upon graduation:* $28,469. *Financial aid deadline:* 6/15.

APPLYING

Standardized Tests *Required:* SAT or ACT (for admission).

Options: electronic application, early admission, deferred entrance.

Application fee: $25.

Required: high school transcript, minimum 2.0 GPA, college preparatory curriculum. *Recommended:* interview.

Application deadlines: 7/21 (freshmen), 7/21 (transfers).

Notification: continuous (freshmen), continuous (transfers).

CONTACT

Mr. David Jenkins, Assistant Director of Admissions, Georgia Southwestern State University, Americus, GA 31709. *Phone:* 229-928-1273. *Toll-free phone:* 800-338-0082. *Fax:* 229-931-2983. *E-mail:* admissions@gsw.edu.

Georgia State University

Atlanta, Georgia

http://www.gsu.edu/

- **State-supported** university, founded 1913, part of University System of Georgia
- **Urban** 109-acre campus with easy access to Atlanta
- **Endowment** $155.3 million
- **Coed** 25,790 undergraduate students, 77% full-time, 59% women, 41% men
- **Moderately difficult** entrance level, 52% of applicants were admitted

UNDERGRAD STUDENTS

19,909 full-time, 5,881 part-time. Students come from 53 states and territories; 124 other countries; 4% are from out of state; 42% Black or African American, non-Hispanic/Latino; 11% Hispanic/Latino; 14% Asian, non-Hispanic/Latino; 0.1% Native Hawaiian or other Pacific Islander, non-Hispanic/Latino; 0.1% American Indian or Alaska Native, non-Hispanic/Latino; 6% Two or more races, non-Hispanic/Latino; 1% Race/ethnicity unknown; 2% international; 6% transferred in; 22% live on campus.

Freshmen:

Admission: 18,971 applied, 9,898 admitted, 4,270 enrolled. *Average high school GPA:* 3.4. *Test scores:* SAT evidence-based reading and writing scores over 500: 76%; SAT math scores over 500: 66%; ACT scores over 18: 95%; SAT evidence-based reading and writing scores over 600: 18%; SAT math scores over 600: 22%; ACT scores over 24: 44%; SAT evidence-based reading and writing scores over 700: 3%; SAT math scores over 700: 3%; ACT scores over 30: 8%.

Retention: 77% of full-time freshmen returned.

FACULTY

Total: 1,547, 75% full-time, 84% with terminal degrees.

Student/faculty ratio: 23:1.

ACADEMICS

Calendar: semesters. *Degrees:* certificates, associate, bachelor's, master's, doctoral, post-master's, and postbachelor's certificates.

Special study options: advanced placement credit, cooperative education, distance learning, double majors, English as a second language, honors programs, independent study, internships, part-time degree program, services for LD students, study abroad, summer session for credit. *ROTC:* Army (b), Navy (c), Air Force (c).

Computers: 2,040 computers/terminals and 28,716 ports are available on campus for general student use. Students can access the following: computer help desk, free student e-mail accounts, online (class) grades, online (class) registration, online (class) schedules. Campuswide network is available. 100% of college-owned or -operated housing units are wired for high-speed Internet access. Wireless service is available via entire campus.

Library: University Library plus 6 others. *Books:* 2.0 million (physical), 645,924 (digital/electronic); *Serial titles:* 11,156 (digital/electronic). Students can reserve study rooms.

STUDENT LIFE

Housing options: coed, special housing for students with disabilities. Campus housing is university owned and leased by the school. Freshman applicants given priority for college housing.

Activities and organizations: drama/theater group, student-run newspaper, radio and television station, choral group, marching band, Spotlight Programs Board, Fraternities/Sororities, Service Organizations, Academic Organizations, Sports Clubs, national fraternities, national sororities.

Athletics Member NCAA. All Division I. *Intercollegiate sports:* baseball M(s), basketball M(s)/W(s), cross-country running W(s), football M(s), golf M(s)/W(s), rugby M(c), soccer M(s)/W(s), softball W(s), squash M(c)/W(c), swimming and diving M(c)/W(c), table tennis M(c)/W(c), tennis M(s)/W(s), track and field W(s), ultimate Frisbee M(c)/W(c), volleyball W(s). *Intramural sports:* badminton M(c)/W(c), basketball M/W, bowling M/W, crew M(c)/W(c), equestrian sports M(c)/W(c), football M/W, golf M/W, lacrosse M(c)/W(c), racquetball M/W, rock climbing M(c)/W(c), soccer M/W, table tennis M/W, ultimate Frisbee M/W, volleyball M/W, wrestling M(c)/W(c).

Campus security: 24-hour emergency response devices and patrols, late-night transport/escort service, controlled dormitory access, Emergency Notification System.

Student services: health clinic, personal/psychological counseling.

COSTS & FINANCIAL AID

Costs (2017–18) *Tuition:* state resident $8730 full-time, $291 per credit hour part-time; nonresident $27,304 full-time, $910 per credit hour part-time. Part-time tuition and fees vary according to course load. *Required fees:* $2128 full-time, $1064 per term part-time. *Room and board:* $14,392; room only: $10,560. Room and board charges vary according to board plan and housing facility. *Waivers:* senior citizens and employees or children of employees.

Financial Aid Of all full-time matriculated undergraduates who enrolled in 2016, 22,320 applied for aid, 19,350 were judged to have need, 1,104 had their need fully met. *Average percent of need met:* 53. *Average financial aid package:* $10,626. *Average need-based gift aid:* $5109.

Average indebtedness upon graduation: $30,167. *Financial aid deadline:* 4/1.

APPLYING
Standardized Tests *Required:* SAT or ACT (for admission).

Options: electronic application, early admission, early action, deferred entrance.

Application fee: $60.

Required: essay or personal statement, high school transcript, minimum 2.8 GPA, 1 letter of recommendation, college preparatory curriculum as specified by the University System of Georgia Board of Regents, combined SAT of 830, minimum Freshman Index of 2500.

Application deadlines: 3/1 (freshmen), 8/1 (transfers), 11/15 (early action).

Notification: 5/1 (freshmen), continuous (transfers), 12/15 (early action).

CONTACT
Scott Burke, Director of Admissions, Georgia State University, PO Box 4009, Atlanta, GA 30302-4009. *Phone:* 404-413-2500. *Fax:* 404-413-2002. *E-mail:* onestopshop@gsu.edu.

Gordon State College
Barnesville, Georgia
http://www.gordonstate.edu/
- **State-supported** primarily 2-year, founded 1852, part of University System of Georgia
- **Small-town** 235-acre campus with easy access to Atlanta
- **Coed** 3,986 undergraduate students
- **83% of applicants were admitted**

UNDERGRAD STUDENTS
0.8% are from out of state; 38% Black or African American, non-Hispanic/Latino; 4% Hispanic/Latino; 1% Asian, non-Hispanic/Latino; 0.1% American Indian or Alaska Native, non-Hispanic/Latino; 4% Two or more races, non-Hispanic/Latino; 0.5% Race/ethnicity unknown.

Freshmen:
Admission: 2,973 applied, 2,470 admitted.

FACULTY
Total: 197, 62% full-time.
Student/faculty ratio: 21:1.

ACADEMICS
Calendar: semesters. *Degrees:* associate and bachelor's.

Special study options: academic remediation for entering students, accelerated degree program, adult/continuing education programs, advanced placement credit, cooperative education, distance learning, double majors, honors programs, internships, off-campus study, part-time degree program, services for LD students, study abroad, summer session for credit.

Computers: 466 computers/terminals and 1,000 ports are available on campus for general student use. Students can access the following: campus intranet, computer help desk, free student e-mail accounts, online (class) grades, online (class) registration, online (class) schedules. Campuswide network is available. 100% of college-owned or -operated housing units are wired for high-speed Internet access. Wireless service is available via entire campus.
Library: Dorothy W. Hightower Collaborative Learning Center and Library. *Books:* 103,423 (physical), 35,999 (digital/electronic); *Serial titles:* 401 (physical), 87,985 (digital/electronic); *Databases:* 325. Weekly public service hours: 73.

STUDENT LIFE
Housing options: on-campus residence required for freshman year; coed. Campus housing is university owned. Freshman applicants given priority for college housing.

Activities and organizations: drama/theater group, student-run newspaper, choral group, Campus Activity Board, Student Government Association, Earth Wind Fire (science club), Student African American Brotherhood (SAAB), Swazi Step Team.

Athletics Member NJCAA. *Intercollegiate sports:* baseball M, basketball M, soccer M/W, softball W.

Campus security: 24-hour emergency response devices and patrols, student patrols, controlled dormitory access, Resident Assistants and Resident Directors in housing, parking patrol.
Student services: health clinic, personal/psychological counseling.

COSTS & FINANCIAL AID
Costs (2018–19) *Tuition:* state resident $3828 full-time, $103 per credit hour part-time; nonresident $10,010 full-time, $378 per credit hour part-time. *Required fees:* $1100 full-time, $550 per term part-time. *Room and board:* $8408. Room and board charges vary according to board plan and housing facility. *Payment plan:* installment.

Financial Aid Of all full-time matriculated undergraduates who enrolled in 2016, 75 Federal Work-Study jobs (averaging $1850).

APPLYING
Standardized Tests *Required:* SAT or ACT (for admission).
Options: electronic application, early admission.
Application fee: $30.
Required: high school transcript.
Application deadlines: rolling (freshmen), rolling (transfers).

CONTACT
Gordon State College, 419 College Drive, Barnesville, GA 30204-1762. *Phone:* 678-359-5021. *Toll-free phone:* 800-282-6504.

Herzing University
Atlanta, Georgia
http://www.herzing.edu/atlanta/
CONTACT
Herzing University, 3393 Peachtree Road, NE, Suite 1003, Atlanta, GA 30326. *Toll-free phone:* 800-596-0724.

Kennesaw State University
Kennesaw, Georgia
http://www.kennesaw.edu/
- **State-supported** comprehensive, founded 1963, part of University System of Georgia
- **Suburban** 602-acre campus with easy access to Atlanta
- **Endowment** $37.8 million
- **Coed** 32,945 undergraduate students, 75% full-time, 48% women, 52% men
- **Moderately difficult** entrance level, 61% of applicants were admitted

UNDERGRAD STUDENTS
24,869 full-time, 8,076 part-time. Students come from 53 states and territories; 135 other countries; 12% are from out of state; 21% Black or African American, non-Hispanic/Latino; 10% Hispanic/Latino; 5% Asian, non-Hispanic/Latino; 0.1% Native Hawaiian or other Pacific Islander, non-Hispanic/Latino; 0.2% American Indian or Alaska Native, non-Hispanic/Latino; 5% Two or more races, non-Hispanic/Latino; 2% Race/ethnicity unknown; 2% international; 8% transferred in; 15% live on campus.

Freshmen:
Admission: 13,998 applied, 8,487 admitted, 5,238 enrolled. *Average high school GPA:* 3.3. *Test scores:* SAT evidence-based reading and writing scores over 500: 97%; SAT math scores over 500: 96%; ACT scores over 18: 98%; SAT evidence-based reading and writing scores over 600: 43%; SAT math scores over 600: 33%; ACT scores over 24: 45%; SAT evidence-based reading and writing scores over 700: 4%; SAT math scores over 700: 4%; ACT scores over 30: 7%.
Retention: 78% of full-time freshmen returned.

FACULTY
Total: 1,994, 58% full-time, 61% with terminal degrees.
Student/faculty ratio: 20:1.

ACADEMICS
Calendar: semesters. *Degrees:* certificates, bachelor's, master's, doctoral, post-master's, and postbachelor's certificates.
Special study options: adult/continuing education programs, advanced placement credit, cooperative education, distance learning, double majors,

English as a second language, freshman honors college, honors programs, internships, off-campus study, part-time degree program, services for LD students, study abroad, summer session for credit. *ROTC:* Army (c), Air Force (c).

Computers: 4,500 computers/terminals and 38,000 ports are available on campus for general student use. Students can access the following: campus intranet, computer help desk, free student e-mail accounts, online (class) grades, online (class) registration, online (class) schedules. Campuswide network is available. 100% of college-owned or -operated housing units are wired for high-speed Internet access. Wireless service is available via classrooms, computer centers, computer labs, dorm rooms, learning centers, libraries, student centers.

Library: KSU Library System plus 1 other. *Books:* 439,577 (physical), 667,799 (digital/electronic); *Serial titles:* 1,281 (physical), 114,983 (digital/electronic); *Databases:* 408. Weekly public service hours: 95; students can reserve study rooms.

STUDENT LIFE

Housing options: coed, special housing for students with disabilities. Campus housing is provided by a third party. Freshman applicants given priority for college housing.

Activities and organizations: drama/theater group, student-run newspaper, radio station, choral group, marching band, Kennesaw Activities Board, African American Student Alliance, Phi Eta Sigma Honor Society, International Student Association, KSU eSports Organization, national fraternities, national sororities.

Athletics Member NCAA. All Division I except football (Division I-AA). *Intercollegiate sports:* baseball M(s), basketball M(s)/W(s), cross-country running M(s)/W(s), golf M(s)/W(s), lacrosse W(s), soccer W(s), softball W(s), tennis M(s)/W(s), track and field M(s)/W(s), volleyball W(s). *Intramural sports:* archery M(c)/W(c), baseball M(c), basketball M/W, bowling M/W, cross-country running M(c)/W(c), equestrian sports W(c), fencing M(c)/W(c), football M/W, golf M/W, gymnastics M(c)/W(c), ice hockey M(c), lacrosse M(c)/W(c), racquetball M/W, rugby M(c)/W(c), sand volleyball M/W, soccer M/W, softball M/W, swimming and diving M(c)/W(c), table tennis M(c), tennis M/W, ultimate Frisbee M(c)/W(c), volleyball M(c)/W(c), weight lifting M(c)/W(c).

Campus security: 24-hour emergency response devices and patrols, student patrols, late-night transport/escort service, controlled dormitory access, campus advisory Web page; early notification system; sirens; rapid email, text, and phone messages to all staff and students.

Student services: health clinic, personal/psychological counseling.

COSTS & FINANCIAL AID

Costs (2017–18) *Tuition:* state resident $5426 full-time, $181 per credit hour part-time; nonresident $19,152 full-time, $638 per credit hour part-time. Full-time tuition and fees vary according to course load, degree level, location, program, and student level. Part-time tuition and fees vary according to course load, degree level, location, program, and student level. *Required fees:* $2006 full-time, $1003 per term part-time. *Room and board:* $11,467. Room and board charges vary according to board plan, housing facility, and student level. *Payment plans:* installment, deferred payment. *Waivers:* senior citizens and employees or children of employees.

Financial Aid Of all full-time matriculated undergraduates who enrolled in 2016, 21,674 applied for aid, 17,780 were judged to have need, 698 had their need fully met. In 2016, 189 non-need-based awards were made. *Average percent of need met:* 38. *Average financial aid package:* $8426. *Average need-based loan:* $3475. *Average need-based gift aid:* $4654. *Average non-need-based aid:* $1229. *Average indebtedness upon graduation:* $25,613.

APPLYING

Standardized Tests *Required:* SAT or ACT (for admission), (for admission).

Options: electronic application, early admission.

Application fee: $40.

Required: high school transcript, minimum 2.5 GPA.

Application deadlines: 4/1 (freshmen), 6/15 (transfers).

Notification: continuous (freshmen), continuous (transfers).

CONTACT

Admissions Office, Kennesaw State University, 3391 Town Point Drive, Suite 1000, Mail Drop #9111, Kennesaw, GA 30144. *Phone:* 770-423-6300. *Fax:* 470-578-9169. *E-mail:* ksuadmit@kennesaw.edu.

LaGrange College

LaGrange, Georgia

http://www.lagrange.edu/

- **Independent United Methodist** comprehensive, founded 1831
- **Small-town** 120-acre campus with easy access to Atlanta
- **Endowment** $56.2 million
- **Coed** 937 undergraduate students, 95% full-time, 51% women, 49% men
- **Moderately difficult** entrance level, 57% of applicants were admitted

UNDERGRAD STUDENTS

888 full-time, 49 part-time. Students come from 18 states and territories; 7 other countries; 15% are from out of state; 22% Black or African American, non-Hispanic/Latino; 1% Hispanic/Latino; 0.9% Asian, non-Hispanic/Latino; 0.2% American Indian or Alaska Native, non-Hispanic/Latino; 3% Two or more races, non-Hispanic/Latino; 0.1% Race/ethnicity unknown; 0.8% international; 9% transferred in; 59% live on campus.

Freshmen:

Admission: 1,548 applied, 879 admitted, 274 enrolled. *Average high school GPA:* 3.5. *Test scores:* SAT evidence-based reading and writing scores over 500: 86%; SAT math scores over 500: 76%; ACT scores over 18: 99%; SAT evidence-based reading and writing scores over 600: 26%; SAT math scores over 600: 18%; ACT scores over 24: 29%; SAT evidence-based reading and writing scores over 700: 3%; SAT math scores over 700: 2%; ACT scores over 30: 4%.

Retention: 65% of full-time freshmen returned.

FACULTY

Total: 120, 63% full-time, 61% with terminal degrees.

Student/faculty ratio: 11:1.

ACADEMICS

Calendar: 4-1-4. *Degrees:* bachelor's and master's.

Special study options: accelerated degree program, adult/continuing education programs, advanced placement credit, distance learning, double majors, independent study, internships, part-time degree program, services for LD students, student-designed majors, study abroad, summer session for credit.

Unusual degree programs: 3-2 engineering with Georgia Institute of Technology, Auburn University.

Computers: 116 computers/terminals and 960 ports are available on campus for general student use. Students can access the following: campus intranet, free student e-mail accounts, online (class) grades, online (class) registration, online (class) schedules. Campuswide network is available. 100% of college-owned or -operated housing units are wired for high-speed Internet access. Wireless service is available via entire campus.

Library: Frank and Laura Lewis Library. *Books:* 99,049 (physical), 245,721 (digital/electronic); *Serial titles:* 75 (physical), 41 (digital/electronic); *Databases:* 366. Weekly public service hours: 84; study areas open 24 hours, 5–7 days a week; students can reserve study rooms.

STUDENT LIFE

Housing options: on-campus residence required through senior year; coed, men-only, women-only, special housing for students with disabilities. Campus housing is university owned. Freshman campus housing is guaranteed.

Activities and organizations: drama/theater group, student-run newspaper, choral group, marching band, Greek Life, Campus Circle, Sports Management Club, WILD, Black Male Initiative, national fraternities, national sororities.

Athletics Member NCAA. All Division III. *Intercollegiate sports:* baseball M, basketball M/W, cheerleading W, cross-country running M/W, football M, golf M, lacrosse W, soccer M/W, softball W, swimming and diving M/W, tennis M/W, volleyball W. *Intramural sports:* basketball M/W, softball M/W, table tennis M/W, water polo M/W.

Campus security: 24-hour patrols, controlled dormitory access, mass notification system (e2Campus) to send emergency messages to students and employees.

Student services: health clinic, personal/psychological counseling.

COSTS & FINANCIAL AID
Costs (2017–18) *One-time required fee:* $150. *Comprehensive fee:* $41,110 includes full-time tuition ($29,150), mandatory fees ($330), and room and board ($11,630). Full-time tuition and fees vary according to class time, course load, degree level, and program. Part-time tuition: $1200 per semester hour. Part-time tuition and fees vary according to class time, course load, degree level, and program. *College room only:* $6430. Room and board charges vary according to board plan and housing facility. *Payment plan:* installment. *Waivers:* senior citizens and employees or children of employees.

Financial Aid Of all full-time matriculated undergraduates who enrolled in 2016, 802 applied for aid, 742 were judged to have need, 121 had their need fully met. In 2016, 57 non-need-based awards were made. *Average percent of need met:* 90. *Average financial aid package:* $25,146. *Average need-based loan:* $4046. *Average need-based gift aid:* $6763. *Average non-need-based aid:* $14,715. *Average indebtedness upon graduation:* $35,580.

APPLYING
Standardized Tests *Required:* SAT or ACT (for admission). *Required for some:* SAT (for admission), ACT (for admission).

Options: electronic application, deferred entrance.

Required: essay or personal statement, high school transcript. *Required for some:* minimum 2.5 GPA, 3 letters of recommendation, interview.

Application deadlines: rolling (freshmen), rolling (transfers).

Notification: continuous (freshmen), continuous (transfers).

CONTACT
Ms. Holly Phillips, Administrative Coordinator, LaGrange College, 601 Broad Street, LaGrange, GA 30240-2999. *Phone:* 706-880-8005. *Toll-free phone:* 800-593-2885. *Fax:* 706-880-8010. *E-mail:* hphillips@lagrange.edu.

Life University
Marietta, Georgia
http://www.life.edu/
- **Independent** comprehensive, founded 1974
- **Suburban** 96-acre campus with easy access to Atlanta Metro
- **Coed** 755 undergraduate students, 83% full-time, 54% women, 46% men
- **Minimally difficult** entrance level, 92% of applicants were admitted

UNDERGRAD STUDENTS
624 full-time, 131 part-time. Students come from 53 states and territories; 42 other countries; 62% are from out of state; 26% Black or African American, non-Hispanic/Latino; 13% Hispanic/Latino; 2% Asian, non-Hispanic/Latino; 2% American Indian or Alaska Native, non-Hispanic/Latino; 3% Race/ethnicity unknown; 7% international; 12% transferred in; 10% live on campus.

Freshmen:
Admission: 280 applied, 258 admitted, 115 enrolled. *Average high school GPA:* 3.1. *Test scores:* ACT scores over 18: 78%; ACT scores over 24: 11%.

Retention: 59% of full-time freshmen returned.

FACULTY
Total: 183, 70% full-time, 80% with terminal degrees.

Student/faculty ratio: 12:1.

ACADEMICS
Calendar: quarters. *Degrees:* certificates, associate, bachelor's, master's, and doctoral.

Special study options: academic remediation for entering students, accelerated degree program, advanced placement credit, cooperative education, distance learning, double majors, English as a second language, independent study, internships, off-campus study, part-time degree program, services for LD students, student-designed majors, study abroad, summer session for credit.

Computers: Students can access the following: campus intranet, computer help desk, free student e-mail accounts, online (class) grades, online (class) registration. Campuswide network is available. 100% of college-owned or -operated housing units are wired for high-speed Internet access. Wireless service is available via entire campus.

Library: Library & Learning Services. *Books:* 35,643 (physical), 363,658 (digital/electronic); *Serial titles:* 61 (physical), 31,104 (digital/electronic); *Databases:* 25. Weekly public service hours: 98; students can reserve study rooms.

STUDENT LIFE
Housing options: coed. Campus housing is university owned.

Activities and organizations: student-run newspaper, Student Ambassadors, Jewish Life, Student Nutrition and Dietetics Association, Gay Straight Alliance, Hispanic Club.

Athletics Member NAIA. *Intercollegiate sports:* basketball M(s)/W(s), cross-country running W(s), ice hockey M(s), rugby M(s)/W(s), soccer M(s)/W(s), swimming and diving W(s), track and field W(s), volleyball W(s), wrestling M(s)/W(s). *Intramural sports:* basketball M/W, cross-country running M/W, rugby M/W, soccer M, softball M/W, table tennis M, tennis M/W, volleyball M/W, weight lifting M/W.

Campus security: 24-hour emergency response devices and patrols, controlled dormitory access.

Student services: health clinic, personal/psychological counseling.

COSTS & FINANCIAL AID
Costs (2017–18) *Comprehensive fee:* $26,115 includes full-time tuition ($10,665), mandatory fees ($1050), and room and board ($14,400). Full-time tuition and fees vary according to course load. Part-time tuition: $237 per credit hour. *College room only:* $5100. Room and board charges vary according to housing facility. *Payment plan:* installment. *Waivers:* employees or children of employees.

Financial Aid Of all full-time matriculated undergraduates who enrolled in 2016, 475 applied for aid, 436 were judged to have need, 3 had their need fully met. *Average percent of need met:* 27. *Average financial aid package:* $10,000. *Average need-based loan:* $4600. *Average need-based gift aid:* $5400. *Average indebtedness upon graduation:* $38,800.

APPLYING
Standardized Tests *Recommended:* SAT or ACT (for admission).

Options: electronic application.

Application fee: $50.

Required: high school transcript, minimum 2.0 GPA.

Notification: continuous (freshmen), continuous (transfers).

CONTACT
Miss Robyn Stanley, Executive Director Enrollment Management, Life University, 1269 Barclay Circle, Marietta, GA 30060. *Phone:* 770-426-2877. *Toll-free phone:* 800-543-3202. *Fax:* 770-426-2895. *E-mail:* robyn.stanley@life.edu.

Luther Rice College & Seminary
Lithonia, Georgia
http://www.lutherrice.edu/
- **Independent Baptist** comprehensive, founded 1962
- **Suburban** 5-acre campus with easy access to Atlanta
- **Endowment** $556,351
- **Coed** 351 undergraduate students, 17% full-time, 30% women, 70% men
- **Noncompetitive** entrance level

UNDERGRAD STUDENTS
58 full-time, 293 part-time. Students come from 29 states and territories; 2 other countries; 42% are from out of state; 43% Black or African American, non-Hispanic/Latino; 1% Hispanic/Latino; 0.6% Asian, non-Hispanic/Latino; 0.3% American Indian or Alaska Native, non-Hispanic/Latino; 0.6% Race/ethnicity unknown; 48% transferred in.

Freshmen:
Admission: 31 applied, 17 enrolled. *Average high school GPA:* 2.6.

Retention: 50% of full-time freshmen returned.

FACULTY
Total: 35, 43% full-time, 74% with terminal degrees.

Student/faculty ratio: 24:1.

ACADEMICS

Calendar: semesters. *Degrees:* bachelor's, master's, and doctoral.

Special study options: adult/continuing education programs, cooperative education, distance learning, independent study, part-time degree program, summer session for credit.

Computers: 13 computers/terminals are available on campus for general student use. Students can access the following: free student e-mail accounts, online (class) grades, online (class) registration, online (class) schedules, Online tutoring. Campuswide network is available. Wireless service is available via entire campus.

Library: Smith Library. Weekly public service hours: 41.

STUDENT LIFE

Housing options: college housing not available.

Activities and organizations: SGA - Student Government Association.

Campus security: 24-hour emergency response devices.

Student services: personal/psychological counseling.

COSTS

Costs (2017–18) *One-time required fee:* $175. *Tuition:* $8100 full-time, $270 per credit hour part-time. Full-time tuition and fees vary according to degree level and location. *Required fees:* $950 full-time, $95 per course part-time. *Room only:* Room and board charges vary according to location. *Payment plan:* installment. *Waivers:* employees or children of employees.

APPLYING

Options: electronic application.

Application fee: $50.

Required: essay or personal statement, high school transcript, letters of recommendation, Bible exam.

Application deadlines: rolling (freshmen), rolling (transfers).

CONTACT

Laura Powell, Admissions Associate, Luther Rice College & Seminary, 3038 Evans Mill Road, Lithonia, GA 30038. *Phone:* 770-484-1204 Ext. 5278. *Toll-free phone:* 800-442-1577. *Fax:* 770-484-1155. *E-mail:* admissions@lutherrice.edu.

Mercer University

Macon, Georgia

http://www.mercer.edu/

- **Independent Baptist** university, founded 1833
- **Urban** 150-acre campus
- **Endowment** $319.1 million
- **Coed** 3,224 undergraduate students, 98% full-time, 53% women, 47% men
- **Moderately difficult** entrance level, 73% of applicants were admitted

UNDERGRAD STUDENTS

3,172 full-time, 52 part-time. Students come from 38 states and territories; 38 other countries; 17% are from out of state; 19% Black or African American, non-Hispanic/Latino; 6% Hispanic/Latino; 9% Asian, non-Hispanic/Latino; 0.1% Native Hawaiian or other Pacific Islander, non-Hispanic/Latino; 0.2% American Indian or Alaska Native, non-Hispanic/Latino; 4% Two or more races, non-Hispanic/Latino; 3% Race/ethnicity unknown; 3% international; 3% transferred in; 78% live on campus.

Freshmen:

Admission: 4,749 applied, 3,479 admitted, 890 enrolled. *Average high school GPA:* 3.9. *Test scores:* SAT evidence-based reading and writing scores over 500: 100%; SAT math scores over 500: 99%; ACT scores over 18: 100%; SAT evidence-based reading and writing scores over 600: 72%; SAT math scores over 600: 64%; ACT scores over 24: 88%; SAT evidence-based reading and writing scores over 700: 13%; SAT math scores over 700: 14%; ACT scores over 30: 28%.

Retention: 86% of full-time freshmen returned.

FACULTY

Total: 743, 52% full-time, 76% with terminal degrees.

Student/faculty ratio: 13:1.

ACADEMICS

Calendar: semesters. *Degrees:* certificates, bachelor's, master's, doctoral, and post-master's certificates.

Special study options: accelerated degree program, adult/continuing education programs, advanced placement credit, cooperative education, distance learning, double majors, English as a second language, honors programs, independent study, internships, off-campus study, part-time degree program, services for LD students, student-designed majors, study abroad, summer session for credit. *ROTC:* Army (b).

Unusual degree programs: 3-2 engineering; nursing; pharmacy, physical therapy, physicians assistant.

Computers: Students can access the following: campus intranet, computer help desk, free student e-mail accounts, online (class) grades, online (class) registration, online (class) schedules. Campuswide network is available. 100% of college-owned or -operated housing units are wired for high-speed Internet access. Wireless service is available via entire campus.

Library: Jack Tarver Library plus 3 others. *Books:* 551,308 (physical), 775,934 (digital/electronic); *Serial titles:* 4,242 (physical), 172,037 (digital/electronic); *Databases:* 226. Study areas open 24 hours, 5–7 days a week; students can reserve study rooms.

STUDENT LIFE

Housing options: on-campus residence required through junior year; coed, men-only, women-only, special housing for students with disabilities. Campus housing is university owned and is provided by a third party. Freshman campus housing is guaranteed.

Activities and organizations: drama/theater group, student-run newspaper, radio station, choral group, marching band, national fraternities, national sororities.

Athletics Member NCAA. All Division I. *Intercollegiate sports:* baseball M(s), basketball M(s)/W(s), cross-country running M(s)/W(s), football M(s), golf M(s)/W(s), lacrosse M(s)/W(s), sand volleyball M(s), soccer M(s)/W(s), softball W(s), tennis M(s)/W(s), track and field W(s), volleyball W(s). *Intramural sports:* basketball M/W, cheerleading M/W, equestrian sports M/W, fencing M(c)/W(c), golf M/W, lacrosse M(c), soccer M(c)/W(c), swimming and diving M(c)/W(c), table tennis M/W, tennis M/W, volleyball M/W, wrestling M(c).

Campus security: 24-hour emergency response devices and patrols, student patrols, late-night transport/escort service, controlled dormitory access, patrols by police officers.

Student services: health clinic, personal/psychological counseling.

COSTS & FINANCIAL AID

Costs (2017–18) *Comprehensive fee:* $48,153 includes full-time tuition ($35,700), mandatory fees ($300), and room and board ($12,153). Full-time tuition and fees vary according to location. Part-time tuition: $1190 per credit hour. Part-time tuition and fees vary according to course load and location. *Required fees:* $10 per credit hour part-time. *College room only:* $6174. Room and board charges vary according to board plan, housing facility, location, and student level. *Payment plan:* installment. *Waivers:* employees or children of employees.

Financial Aid Of all full-time matriculated undergraduates who enrolled in 2017, 3,166 applied for aid, 2,223 were judged to have need, 877 had their need fully met. 789 Federal Work-Study jobs (averaging $2032). In 2017, 862 non-need-based awards were made. *Average percent of need met:* 85. *Average financial aid package:* $35,680. *Average need-based loan:* $10,276. *Average need-based gift aid:* $25,059. *Average non-need-based aid:* $20,044. *Average indebtedness upon graduation:* $26,429.

APPLYING

Standardized Tests *Required:* SAT or ACT (for admission).

Options: electronic application, early action, deferred entrance.

Application fee: $50.

Required: essay or personal statement, high school transcript, minimum 3.3 GPA, 1 letter of recommendation. *Required for some:* interview. *Recommended:* interview.

Application deadlines: 7/1 (freshmen), rolling (transfers), 3/1 (early action).

Notification: continuous (freshmen), continuous (transfers), rolling (early action).

CONTACT

Ms. Kelly L. Holloway, Director of Freshman Admissions, Mercer University, 1501 Mercer University Drive, Macon, GA 31207-0003. *Phone:* 478-301-5125. *Toll-free phone:* 800-MERCER-U. *Fax:* 478-301-2828. *E-mail:* holloway_kl@mercer.edu.

Middle Georgia State University
Macon, Georgia
http://www.mga.edu/

- **State-supported** comprehensive, founded 2015, part of University System of Georgia
- **Urban** 419-acre campus with easy access to Atlanta
- **Endowment** $874,853
- **Coed** 7,221 undergraduate students, 62% full-time, 58% women, 42% men
- **Minimally difficult** entrance level, 94% of applicants were admitted

UNDERGRAD STUDENTS

4,507 full-time, 2,714 part-time. Students come from 32 states and territories; 6 other countries; 2% are from out of state; 33% Black or African American, non-Hispanic/Latino; 5% Hispanic/Latino; 3% Asian, non-Hispanic/Latino; 0.1% Native Hawaiian or other Pacific Islander, non-Hispanic/Latino; 0.1% American Indian or Alaska Native, non-Hispanic/Latino; 3% Two or more races, non-Hispanic/Latino; 0.4% Race/ethnicity unknown; 0.2% international; 9% transferred in; 19% live on campus.

Freshmen:
Admission: 4,841 applied, 4,549 admitted, 2,209 enrolled. *Average high school GPA:* 3.0. *Test scores:* SAT evidence-based reading and writing scores over 500: 44%; SAT math scores over 500: 32%; ACT scores over 18: 64%; SAT evidence-based reading and writing scores over 600: 6%; SAT math scores over 600: 6%; ACT scores over 24: 12%; SAT evidence-based reading and writing scores over 700: 1%; ACT scores over 30: 1%.

Retention: 65% of full-time freshmen returned.

FACULTY

Total: 387, 66% full-time, 48% with terminal degrees.

Student/faculty ratio: 19:1.

ACADEMICS

Calendar: semesters. *Degrees:* certificates, associate, bachelor's, master's, and postbachelor's certificates.

Special study options: academic remediation for entering students, advanced placement credit, cooperative education, distance learning, double majors, honors programs, independent study, internships, part-time degree program, services for LD students, study abroad, summer session for credit.

Computers: 500 computers/terminals are available on campus for general student use. Students can access the following: campus intranet, computer help desk, free student e-mail accounts, online (class) grades, online (class) registration, online (class) schedules. Campuswide network is available. 100% of college-owned or -operated housing units are wired for high-speed Internet access. Wireless service is available via entire campus.

Library: Macon State University Library. *Books:* 125,996 (physical), 246,646 (digital/electronic); *Serial titles:* 85 (physical), 51,575 (digital/electronic); *Databases:* 138. Weekly public service hours: 23; students can reserve study rooms.

STUDENT LIFE

Housing options: on-campus residence required for freshman year; coed. Campus housing is university owned.

Activities and organizations: drama/theater group, student-run newspaper, television station, choral group, marching band, Brothers of Leadership and Distinction (BOLD), Middle Georgia State Association of Nursing Students (MGSANS), Black Student Unification (BSU), Student Government Association (SGA), International Students and Studies Association (ISSA), national fraternities, national sororities.

Athletics Member NAIA. *Intercollegiate sports:* baseball M(s), basketball M(s)/W(s), cross-country running W(s), soccer M/W(s), softball W(s), tennis M(s)/W(s), volleyball W(s). *Intramural sports:* basketball M/W, cheerleading M(c)/W(c), equestrian sports M(c)/W(c), football M(c), soccer M/W, softball M/W.

Campus security: 24-hour emergency response devices and patrols, late-night transport/escort service.

Student services: health clinic, personal/psychological counseling.

COSTS & FINANCIAL AID

Costs (2018–19) *Tuition:* state resident $3326 full-time, $111 per credit hour part-time; nonresident $8960 full-time, $410 per credit hour part-time. Full-time tuition and fees vary according to program. Part-time tuition and fees vary according to program. *Required fees:* $1282 full-time. *Room and board:* $7614; room only: $5390. Room and board charges vary according to board plan, housing facility, and location. *Payment plan:* installment. *Waivers:* senior citizens and employees or children of employees.

Financial Aid Of all full-time matriculated undergraduates who enrolled in 2015, 7,540 applied for aid, 7,540 were judged to have need. 87 Federal Work-Study jobs (averaging $2385). *Average financial aid package:* $4309. *Average need-based loan:* $3520. *Average need-based gift aid:* $4091. *Average non-need-based aid:* $1000.

APPLYING

Standardized Tests *Required:* SAT or ACT (for admission).

Options: electronic application, early admission.

Application fee: $30.

Required: high school transcript, minimum 2.0 GPA.

Application deadlines: rolling (freshmen), rolling (transfers).

Notification: continuous (freshmen), continuous (transfers).

CONTACT

Middle Georgia State University, 100 University Parkway, Macon, GA 31206. *Toll-free phone:* 877-238-8664.

Morehouse College
Atlanta, Georgia
http://www.morehouse.edu/

- **Independent** 4-year, founded 1867
- **Urban** 66-acre campus with easy access to Atlanta, Georgia
- **Men only** 2,202 undergraduate students, 95% full-time
- **Moderately difficult** entrance level, 74% of applicants were admitted

UNDERGRAD STUDENTS

2,090 full-time, 112 part-time. Students come from 41 states and territories; 13 other countries; 73% are from out of state; 94% Black or African American, non-Hispanic/Latino; 0.6% Hispanic/Latino; 0.1% Asian, non-Hispanic/Latino; 0.2% American Indian or Alaska Native, non-Hispanic/Latino; 2% Two or more races, non-Hispanic/Latino; 1% Race/ethnicity unknown; 1% international; 3% transferred in; 61% live on campus.

Freshmen:
Admission: 2,349 applied, 1,748 admitted, 617 enrolled. *Average high school GPA:* 3.2. *Test scores:* SAT evidence-based reading and writing scores over 500: 69%; SAT math scores over 500: 65%; ACT scores over 18: 77%; SAT evidence-based reading and writing scores over 600: 23%; SAT math scores over 600: 16%; ACT scores over 24: 20%; SAT evidence-based reading and writing scores over 700: 2%; SAT math scores over 700: 1%; ACT scores over 30: 3%.

Retention: 80% of full-time freshmen returned.

FACULTY

Total: 234, 76% full-time.

Student/faculty ratio: 11:1.

ACADEMICS

Calendar: semesters. *Degree:* bachelor's.

Special study options: academic remediation for entering students, advanced placement credit, cooperative education, double majors, honors programs, independent study, internships, off-campus study, part-time degree program, services for LD students, study abroad, summer session for credit. *ROTC:* Army (b), Navy (b), Air Force (c).

Unusual degree programs: 3-2 engineering with Auburn University, Clarkson University, Columbia University, Dartmouth College, Georgia Institute of Technology, Indiana University–Purdue University Indianapolis, Notre Dame University, North Carolina Agricultural and Technical State University.

Computers: 1,158 computers/terminals are available on campus for general student use. Students can access the following: campus intranet, computer help desk, free student e-mail accounts, online (class) grades, online (class) registration, online (class) schedules, on-campus computer repair service, computer helpline. Campuswide network is available. 100% of college-owned or -operated housing units are wired for high-speed Internet access. Wireless service is available via entire campus.

Library: Atlanta University Center Robert R. Woodruff Library. Students can reserve study rooms.

STUDENT LIFE

Housing options: on-campus residence required through junior year; men-only. Campus housing is university owned. Freshman campus housing is guaranteed.

Activities and organizations: drama/theater group, student-run newspaper, choral group, marching band, Morehouse College Glee Club, Morehouse Business Association, SGA, Morehouse Public Health Association, Pre-Law Society, national fraternities.

Athletics Member NCAA. All Division II. *Intercollegiate sports:* baseball M(s), basketball M(s), cross-country running M(s), football M(s), golf M, tennis M(s), track and field M(s). *Intramural sports:* basketball M, football M, golf M, lacrosse M(c), soccer M, swimming and diving M, table tennis M(c), tennis M, volleyball M, wrestling M(c).

Campus security: 24-hour patrols, late-night transport/escort service, controlled dormitory access, emergency call boxes, safety tips and awareness training.

Student services: health clinic, personal/psychological counseling.

COSTS & FINANCIAL AID

Costs (2018–19) *Comprehensive fee:* $41,012 includes full-time tuition ($25,368), mandatory fees ($2206), and room and board ($13,438). Full-time tuition and fees vary according to course load. Part-time tuition and fees vary according to course load. *College room only:* $7510. Room and board charges vary according to board plan and housing facility. *Payment plan:* installment. *Waivers:* employees or children of employees.

Financial Aid Of all full-time matriculated undergraduates who enrolled in 2017, 1,956 applied for aid, 1,712 were judged to have need. In 2017, 24 non-need-based awards were made. *Average financial aid package:* $23,565. *Average need-based loan:* $4349. *Average need-based gift aid:* $20,851. *Average non-need-based aid:* $38,487. *Average indebtedness upon graduation:* $31,833. *Financial aid deadline:* 4/1.

APPLYING

Standardized Tests *Required:* SAT or ACT (for admission). *Recommended:* SAT and SAT Subject Tests or ACT (for admission).

Options: electronic application, early admission, early decision, early action, deferred entrance.

Application fee: $50.

Required: essay or personal statement, high school transcript, interview. *Recommended:* minimum 3.0 GPA.

Application deadlines: 2/1 (freshmen), 2/1 (transfers), 11/1 (early action).

Notification: 3/15 (freshmen), 3/15 (transfers), 12/15 (early action).

CONTACT

Morehouse College, 830 Westview Drive, SW, Atlanta, GA 30314. *Phone:* 470-639-0391. *Toll-free phone:* 800-851-1254.

Oglethorpe University

Atlanta, Georgia

http://www.oglethorpe.edu/

- **Independent** 4-year, founded 1835
- **Suburban** 102-acre campus with easy access to Atlanta
- **Endowment** $31.7 million
- **Coed** 1,250 undergraduate students, 93% full-time, 59% women, 41% men
- **Very difficult** entrance level, 78% of applicants were admitted

UNDERGRAD STUDENTS

1,166 full-time, 84 part-time. Students come from 33 states and territories; 38 other countries; 24% are from out of state; 24% Black or African American, non-Hispanic/Latino; 11% Hispanic/Latino; 4% Asian, non-Hispanic/Latino; 0.2% Native Hawaiian or other Pacific Islander, non-Hispanic/Latino; 0.8% American Indian or Alaska Native, non-Hispanic/Latino; 2% Two or more races, non-Hispanic/Latino; 13% Race/ethnicity unknown; 8% international; 3% transferred in; 57% live on campus.

Freshmen:
Admission: 2,768 applied, 2,172 admitted, 334 enrolled. *Average high school GPA:* 3.6.
Retention: 77% of full-time freshmen returned.

ACADEMICS

Calendar: semesters. *Degree:* bachelor's.

Special study options: accelerated degree program, adult/continuing education programs, advanced placement credit, cooperative education, double majors, honors programs, independent study, internships, off-campus study, part-time degree program, services for LD students, student-designed majors, study abroad, summer session for credit. *ROTC:* Army (c), Navy (c), Air Force (c).

Computers: 45 computers/terminals and 575 ports are available on campus for general student use. Students can access the following: campus intranet, computer help desk, free student e-mail accounts, online (class) grades, online (class) registration, online (class) schedules. Campuswide network is available. 688% of college-owned or -operated housing units are wired for high-speed Internet access. Wireless service is available via entire campus.

Library: Philip Weltner Library. *Books:* 160,614 (physical), 871,647 (digital/electronic); *Serial titles:* 782 (physical), 26,900 (digital/electronic); *Databases:* 310. Weekly public service hours: 82; study areas open 24 hours, 5–7 days a week.

STUDENT LIFE

Housing options: on-campus residence required through sophomore year; coed. Campus housing is university owned. Freshman campus housing is guaranteed.

Activities and organizations: drama/theater group, student-run newspaper, choral group, national fraternities, national sororities.

Athletics Member NCAA. All Division III. *Intercollegiate sports:* baseball M, basketball M/W, cross-country running M/W, golf M/W, lacrosse M/W, soccer M/W, tennis M/W, track and field M/W, volleyball W. *Intramural sports:* badminton M/W, basketball M/W, football M/W, softball M/W, table tennis M/W, ultimate Frisbee M/W, volleyball M/W.

Campus security: 24-hour emergency response devices and patrols, late-night transport/escort service, controlled dormitory access.

Student services: health clinic, personal/psychological counseling.

COSTS & FINANCIAL AID

Costs (2017–18) *Comprehensive fee:* $49,785 includes full-time tuition ($36,400), mandatory fees ($425), and room and board ($12,960). Full-time tuition and fees vary according to degree level. Part-time tuition: $1525 per credit hour. Part-time tuition and fees vary according to class time, course load, and degree level. *College room only:* $4210. Room and board charges vary according to housing facility and location. *Payment plans:* tuition prepayment, installment. *Waivers:* employees or children of employees.

Financial Aid Of all full-time matriculated undergraduates who enrolled in 2017, 944 applied for aid, 875 were judged to have need, 147 had their need fully met. 101 Federal Work-Study jobs (averaging $1713). In 2017, 294 non-need-based awards were made. *Average percent of need met:* 75. *Average financial aid package:* $31,801. *Average need-based loan:* $4199. *Average need-based gift aid:* $27,055. *Average non-need-based aid:* $21,483. *Average indebtedness upon graduation:* $28,495.

APPLYING

Standardized Tests *Required:* SAT or ACT (for admission).

Options: electronic application, early admission, early action, deferred entrance.

Application fee: $50.

Required: essay or personal statement, high school transcript, 1 letter of recommendation. *Required for some:* interview. *Recommended:* minimum 2.5 GPA, interview.

Application deadlines: rolling (freshmen), rolling (transfers), 12/5 (early action).

Notification: continuous (freshmen), continuous (transfers), 12/20 (early action).

CONTACT
Oglethorpe University, 4484 Peachtree Road, NE, Atlanta, GA 30319-2797. *Toll-free phone:* 800-428-4484.

Paine College
Augusta, Georgia
http://www.paine.edu/

- **Independent Methodist** 4-year, founded 1882
- **Urban** 65-acre campus with easy access to Columbia, SC
- **Endowment** $8.4 million
- **Coed**
- **Minimally difficult** entrance level

FACULTY
Student/faculty ratio: 10:1.

ACADEMICS
Calendar: semesters. *Degree:* bachelor's.
Library: Collins-Callaway Library. *Books:* 70,791 (physical), 137,762 (digital/electronic); *Serial titles:* 205 (physical). Weekly public service hours: 83; students can reserve study rooms.

STUDENT LIFE
Housing options: men-only, women-only. Campus housing is university owned. Freshman applicants given priority for college housing.

Activities and organizations: drama/theater group, student-run newspaper, choral group, Wesley Fellowship, Alpha Kappa Mu National Honor Society, International Student Association, National Association for the Advancement of Colored People, Creme de la Creme Models, national fraternities, national sororities.

Athletics Member NCAA. All Division II.

Campus security: 24-hour emergency response devices and patrols, late-night transport/escort service.

Student services: personal/psychological counseling.

COSTS & FINANCIAL AID
Costs (2017–18) *Comprehensive fee:* $20,888 includes full-time tuition ($12,706), mandatory fees ($1520), and room and board ($6662). Full-time tuition and fees vary according to class time and course load. Part-time tuition: $529 per credit hour. Part-time tuition and fees vary according to class time and course load. *College room only:* $3136. Room and board charges vary according to housing facility. *Payment plans:* installment, deferred payment.

Financial Aid *Average indebtedness upon graduation:* $2304.

APPLYING
Standardized Tests *Required:* SAT or ACT (for admission).

Options: electronic application, early admission, deferred entrance.

Application fee: $25.

Required: high school transcript, minimum 2.0 GPA, 2 letters of recommendation. *Required for some:* score of 500 on each Georgia high school exit exam.

CONTACT
Mr. R. Wayne Woodson, Dean of Students, Paine College, 1235 15th Street, Augusta, GA 30901-3182. *Phone:* 706-821-8320. *Toll-free phone:* 800-476-7703. *Fax:* 706-821-8691. *E-mail:* rwoodson@paine.edu.

Piedmont College
Demorest, Georgia
http://www.piedmont.edu/

- **Independent** comprehensive, founded 1897, affiliated with United Church of Christ
- **Rural** 186-acre campus with easy access to Atlanta
- **Endowment** $51.9 million
- **Coed** 1,281 undergraduate students, 91% full-time, 66% women, 34% men
- **Moderately difficult** entrance level, 60% of applicants were admitted

UNDERGRAD STUDENTS
1,160 full-time, 121 part-time. Students come from 22 states and territories; 4 other countries; 8% are from out of state; 10% Black or African American, non-Hispanic/Latino; 8% Hispanic/Latino; 1% Asian, non-Hispanic/Latino; 0.4% American Indian or Alaska Native, non-Hispanic/Latino; 14% Race/ethnicity unknown; 10% transferred in; 68% live on campus.

Freshmen:
Admission: 1,287 applied, 766 admitted, 291 enrolled. *Average high school GPA:* 3.4. *Test scores:* SAT evidence-based reading and writing scores over 500: 71%; SAT math scores over 500: 61%; ACT scores over 18: 87%; SAT evidence-based reading and writing scores over 600: 21%; SAT math scores over 600: 12%; ACT scores over 24: 28%; ACT scores over 30: 3%.
Retention: 66% of full-time freshmen returned.

FACULTY
Total: 291, 44% full-time, 74% with terminal degrees.
Student/faculty ratio: 10:1.

ACADEMICS
Calendar: semesters. *Degrees:* certificates, bachelor's, master's, doctoral, and post-master's certificates.

Special study options: accelerated degree program, adult/continuing education programs, advanced placement credit, cooperative education, distance learning, double majors, honors programs, independent study, internships, off-campus study, part-time degree program, services for LD students, student-designed majors, study abroad, summer session for credit.

Unusual degree programs: 3-2 engineering with Georgia Institute of Technology.

Computers: 150 computers/terminals are available on campus for general student use. Students can access the following: campus intranet, computer help desk, free student e-mail accounts, online (class) grades, online (class) registration, online (class) schedules. Campuswide network is available. Wireless service is available via classrooms, computer centers, computer labs, dorm rooms, learning centers, libraries, student centers.
Library: Arrendale Library plus 2 others. *Books:* 99,693 (physical), 416,680 (digital/electronic); *Serial titles:* 24,272 (digital/electronic). Students can reserve study rooms.

STUDENT LIFE
Housing options: on-campus residence required through sophomore year; coed, men-only, women-only, special housing for students with disabilities. Campus housing is university owned. Freshman campus housing is guaranteed.

Activities and organizations: drama/theater group, student-run newspaper, radio and television station, choral group, Campus Activity Board, Student Government Association, Team Piedmont, National Society of Leadership and Success, American Marketing Association-Piedmont Chapter.

Athletics Member NCAA. All Division III. *Intercollegiate sports:* baseball M, basketball M/W, cross-country running M/W, golf M/W, lacrosse M/W, soccer M/W, softball W, tennis M/W, track and field M/W, volleyball W. *Intramural sports:* cheerleading W.

Campus security: 24-hour emergency response devices and patrols, late-night transport/escort service.

Student services: personal/psychological counseling.

COSTS & FINANCIAL AID
Costs (2017–18) *Comprehensive fee:* $34,334 includes full-time tuition ($24,264), mandatory fees ($200), and room and board ($9870). Full-time tuition and fees vary according to course load, degree level, location, and program. Part-time tuition: $1011 per credit hour. Part-time tuition and fees vary according to course load, degree level, location, and program. *Required fees:* $100 per term part-time. *College room only:* $5502. Room and board charges vary according to board plan. *Payment plan:* installment. *Waivers:* employees or children of employees.

Financial Aid Of all full-time matriculated undergraduates who enrolled in 2017, 1,061 applied for aid, 948 were judged to have need, 159 had their need fully met. 81 Federal Work-Study jobs (averaging $2189). 267 state and other part-time jobs (averaging $2534). In 2017, 167 non-need-based awards were made. *Average percent of need met:* 69. *Average financial aid package:* $20,522. *Average need-based loan:* $4375. *Average need-based gift aid:* $16,583. *Average non-need-based aid:* $10,583. *Average indebtedness upon graduation:* $29,160.

APPLYING

Standardized Tests *Required:* SAT or ACT (for admission).

Options: electronic application, early admission, deferred entrance.

Required: high school transcript. *Required for some:* interview. *Recommended:* essay or personal statement.

Application deadlines: 7/1 (freshmen), 7/1 (transfers).

CONTACT

Ms. Brenda Boonstra, Director of Undergraduate Admissions, Piedmont College, PO Box 10, 165 Central Avenue, Demorest, GA 30535. *Phone:* 706-776-0103 Ext. 1188. *Toll-free phone:* 800-277-7020. *Fax:* 706-776-6635. *E-mail:* bboonstra@piedmont.edu.

Point University

West Point, Georgia

http://point.edu/

- **Independent Christian** comprehensive, founded 1937
- **Small-town** campus with easy access to Atlanta, GA and Montgomery, AL
- **Coed** 1,926 undergraduate students, 58% full-time, 54% women, 46% men
- **Moderately difficult** entrance level, 35% of applicants were admitted

UNDERGRAD STUDENTS

1,119 full-time, 807 part-time. Students come from 30 states and territories; 18 other countries; 18% are from out of state; 32% Black or African American, non-Hispanic/Latino; 6% Hispanic/Latino; 1% Asian, non-Hispanic/Latino; 0.2% Native Hawaiian or other Pacific Islander, non-Hispanic/Latino; 0.3% American Indian or Alaska Native, non-Hispanic/Latino; 6% Two or more races, non-Hispanic/Latino; 6% Race/ethnicity unknown; 2% international; 8% transferred in; 39% live on campus.

Freshmen:

Admission: 1,406 applied, 493 admitted, 278 enrolled. *Average high school GPA:* 3.1. *Test scores:* SAT evidence-based reading and writing scores over 500: 45%; SAT math scores over 500: 43%; ACT scores over 18: 64%; SAT evidence-based reading and writing scores over 600: 9%; SAT math scores over 600: 7%; ACT scores over 24: 11%; ACT scores over 30: 1%.

Retention: 52% of full-time freshmen returned.

FACULTY

Total: 192, 23% full-time, 38% with terminal degrees.

Student/faculty ratio: 15:1.

ACADEMICS

Calendar: semesters. *Degrees:* certificates, associate, bachelor's, and master's.

Special study options: accelerated degree program, adult/continuing education programs, advanced placement credit, distance learning, double majors, independent study, part-time degree program, services for LD students, summer session for credit.

Computers: 115 computers/terminals and 50 ports are available on campus for general student use. Students can access the following: campus intranet, computer help desk, free student e-mail accounts, online (class) grades, online (class) registration, online (class) schedules. Campuswide network is available. 100% of college-owned or -operated housing units are wired for high-speed Internet access. Wireless service is available via entire campus.

Library: Point University Library plus 1 other.

STUDENT LIFE

Housing options: on-campus residence required through sophomore year; men-only, women-only. Campus housing is leased by the school. Freshman campus housing is guaranteed.

Activities and organizations: choral group, marching band, Student Government Association, Community Concert Band, Campus Life Ministers, Campus Activities Board, Fellowship of Christian Athletes (FCA).

Athletics Member NAIA, NCCAA. *Intercollegiate sports:* baseball M(s), basketball M(s)/W(s), cheerleading M(s)/W(s), cross-country running M(s)/W(s), football M(s), golf M(s)/W(s), lacrosse M(s)/W(s), soccer M(s)/W(s), softball W(s), swimming and diving M(s)/W(s), tennis

M(s)/W(s), volleyball W(s). *Intramural sports:* basketball M/W, football M/W, sand volleyball M/W, softball M/W, table tennis M/W, ultimate Frisbee M/W, volleyball M/W.

Campus security: 24-hour patrols.

Student services: personal/psychological counseling.

COSTS

Costs (2017–18) *Comprehensive fee:* $28,500 includes full-time tuition ($19,500), mandatory fees ($1100), and room and board ($7900). Full-time tuition and fees vary according to course load. Part-time tuition and fees vary according to course load. *College room only:* $4500. *Payment plan:* installment. *Waivers:* employees or children of employees.

APPLYING

Options: electronic application, deferred entrance.

Required: high school transcript, minimum 2.0 GPA, 1 letter of recommendation. *Required for some:* essay or personal statement, college transcript if applicable.

Application deadlines: 8/1 (freshmen), rolling (out-of-state freshmen), 8/1 (transfers).

Notification: continuous (freshmen), continuous (out-of-state freshmen), continuous (transfers).

CONTACT

Mr. Rusty Hassell, Exective Director of Enrollment, Point University, 507 West 10th Street, West Point, GA 31833. *Phone:* 706-385-1000. *Toll-free phone:* 855-37-POINT. *Fax:* 706-645-9473. *E-mail:* admissions@point.edu.

Reinhardt University

Waleska, Georgia

http://www.reinhardt.edu/

CONTACT

Ms. Julie Fleming, Director of Admissions, Reinhardt University, 7300 Reinhardt College Circle, Waleska, GA 30183-0128. *Phone:* 770-720-5526. *Fax:* 770-720-5602. *E-mail:* admissions@mail.reinhardt.edu.

Savannah College of Art and Design

Savannah, Georgia

http://www.scad.edu/

- **Independent** comprehensive, founded 1978
- **Urban** campus
- **Coed** 11,324 undergraduate students, 84% full-time, 67% women, 33% men
- **Moderately difficult** entrance level, 71% of applicants were admitted

UNDERGRAD STUDENTS

9,474 full-time, 1,850 part-time. Students come from 54 states and territories; 107 other countries; 80% are from out of state; 10% Black or African American, non-Hispanic/Latino; 8% Hispanic/Latino; 5% Asian, non-Hispanic/Latino; 0.5% Native Hawaiian or other Pacific Islander, non-Hispanic/Latino; 0.5% American Indian or Alaska Native, non-Hispanic/Latino; 3% Race/ethnicity unknown; 21% international; 6% transferred in; 43% live on campus.

Freshmen:

Admission: 11,723 applied, 8,329 admitted, 2,534 enrolled. *Average high school GPA:* 3.5. *Test scores:* SAT evidence-based reading and writing scores over 500: 90%; SAT math scores over 500: 79%; ACT scores over 18: 93%; SAT evidence-based reading and writing scores over 600: 44%; SAT math scores over 600: 28%; ACT scores over 24: 53%; SAT evidence-based reading and writing scores over 700: 6%; SAT math scores over 700: 4%; ACT scores over 30: 11%.

Retention: 84% of full-time freshmen returned.

FACULTY

Total: 694, 78% full-time, 82% with terminal degrees.

Student/faculty ratio: 20:1.

ACADEMICS

Calendar: quarters. *Degrees:* certificates, bachelor's, and master's.

Special study options: accelerated degree program, advanced placement credit, cooperative education, distance learning, double majors, English as a second language, independent study, internships, off-campus study, part-time degree program, services for LD students, study abroad, summer session for credit.

Computers: 3,464 computers/terminals are available on campus for general student use. Students can access the following: campus intranet, computer help desk, free student e-mail accounts, online (class) grades, online (class) registration, online (class) schedules. Campuswide network is available. 100% of college-owned or -operated housing units are wired for high-speed Internet access. Wireless service is available via entire campus.

Library: Jen Library plus 4 others. *Books:* 260,879 (physical), 199,797 (digital/electronic); *Serial titles:* 949 (physical), 48,391 (digital/electronic); *Databases:* 89. Weekly public service hours: 105; students can reserve study rooms.

STUDENT LIFE
Housing options: coed, special housing for students with disabilities. Campus housing is university owned and leased by the school. Freshman applicants given priority for college housing.

Activities and organizations: drama/theater group, student-run newspaper, radio station, choral group.

Athletics Member NAIA. *Intercollegiate sports:* bowling M(s)/W(s), cross-country running M(s)/W(s), equestrian sports M(s)/W(s), golf M(s)/W(s), lacrosse M(s)/W(s), soccer M(s)/W(s), swimming and diving M(s)/W(s), tennis M(s)/W(s), track and field M/W. *Intramural sports:* badminton M/W, basketball M/W, fencing M(c)/W(c), sand volleyball M/W, soccer M/W, table tennis M/W, volleyball M/W.

Campus security: 24-hour emergency response devices and patrols, late-night transport/escort service, controlled dormitory access, video camera surveillance.

Student services: health clinic, personal/psychological counseling.

COSTS & FINANCIAL AID
Costs (2018–19) *One-time required fee:* $500. *Comprehensive fee:* $51,180 includes full-time tuition ($36,630) and room and board ($14,550). Full-time tuition and fees vary according to course load and degree level. Part-time tuition: $4070 per course. Part-time tuition and fees vary according to course load and degree level. *College room only:* $9591. Room and board charges vary according to board plan, housing facility, and location. *Payment plan:* installment. *Waivers:* employees or children of employees.

Financial Aid Of all full-time matriculated undergraduates who enrolled in 2016, 5,114 applied for aid, 4,405 were judged to have need, 359 had their need fully met. 384 Federal Work-Study jobs (averaging $1495). 810 state and other part-time jobs (averaging $1617). In 2016, 3785 non-need-based awards were made. *Average percent of need met:* 43. *Average financial aid package:* $18,094. *Average need-based loan:* $4284. *Average need-based gift aid:* $14,225. *Average non-need-based aid:* $10,720. *Average indebtedness upon graduation:* $39,022.

APPLYING
Standardized Tests *Required:* SAT or ACT (for admission), TOEFL scores are required for International students (for admission).

Options: electronic application, early admission, deferred entrance.

Application fee: $70.

Required for some: essay or personal statement, high school transcript, interview, portfolio/audition for performing arts, riding, writing, or visual arts. *Recommended:* essay or personal statement, interview.

Application deadlines: rolling (freshmen), rolling (transfers).

Notification: continuous (freshmen), continuous (transfers).

CONTACT
Ms. Rina Gaitonde Le Blanc, Executive Director of Admissions Operations, Savannah College of Art and Design, 342 Bull Street, PO Box 3146, Savannah, GA 31402-3146. *Phone:* 912-525-5100. *Toll-free phone:* 800-869-7223. *E-mail:* admission@scad.edu.

Savannah State University
Savannah, Georgia
http://www.savannahstate.edu/

CONTACT
Mr. Descatur Potier, Assistant Vice President of Academic Affairs for Enrollment Services/Director of Admission, Savannah State University, PO Box 20209, 3219 College Street, Savannah, GA 31404. *Phone:* 912-358-4014. *Toll-free phone:* 800-788-0478. *Fax:* 912-650-8009. *E-mail:* potierd@savannahstate.edu.

Shorter University
Rome, Georgia
http://www.shorter.edu/

- **Independent Baptist** comprehensive, founded 1873
- **Small-town** 155-acre campus with easy access to Atlanta
- **Endowment** $14.8 million
- **Coed**
- **Moderately difficult** entrance level, 61% of applicants were admitted

UNDERGRAD STUDENTS
54% live on campus.

Freshmen:
Admission: 1,820 applied, 1,113 admitted. *Average high school GPA:* 3.3. *Test scores:* ACT scores over 18: 81%; ACT scores over 24: 26%; ACT scores over 30: 2%.

Retention: 53% of full-time freshmen returned.

ACADEMICS
Calendar: semesters. *Degrees:* associate, bachelor's, and master's.

Special study options: academic remediation for entering students, adult/continuing education programs, advanced placement credit, double majors, honors programs, independent study, internships, off-campus study, part-time degree program, services for LD students, student-designed majors, study abroad, summer session for credit.

Computers: 100 computers/terminals are available on campus for general student use. Students can access the following: campus intranet, computer help desk, free student e-mail accounts, online (class) grades, online (class) registration, online (class) schedules. Campuswide network is available. 100% of college-owned or -operated housing units are wired for high-speed Internet access. Wireless service is available via entire campus.

Library: Livingston Library. *Books:* 118,322 (physical), 575,620 (digital/electronic); *Serial titles:* 1,183 (physical), 117,578 (digital/electronic); *Databases:* 233. Students can reserve study rooms.

STUDENT LIFE
Housing options: men-only, women-only. Campus housing is university owned. Freshman applicants given priority for college housing.

Activities and organizations: drama/theater group, student-run newspaper, radio and television station, choral group, marching band, Baptist Collegiate Ministries, Student Government Association, Fellowship of Christian Athletes, Habitat for Humanity, SAVE (Students Advocating Volunteer Efforts), national fraternities, national sororities.

Athletics Member NCAA. All Division II. *Intercollegiate sports:* baseball M(s), basketball M(s)/W(s), cheerleading M(s)/W(s), cross-country running M(s)/W(s), football M(s), golf M(s)/W(s), soccer M(s)/W(s), softball W(s), tennis M(s)/W(s), track and field M(s)/W(s), volleyball W(s). *Intramural sports:* basketball M/W, bowling M/W, soccer M/W, table tennis M/W, tennis M/W, ultimate Frisbee M/W, volleyball W.

Campus security: 24-hour emergency response devices and patrols.

Student services: health clinic, personal/psychological counseling.

COSTS & FINANCIAL AID
Costs (2017–18) *Comprehensive fee:* $31,070 includes full-time tuition ($21,300), mandatory fees ($370), and room and board ($9400). Full-time tuition and fees vary according to course load, location, and program. Part-time tuition: $550 per credit hour. Part-time tuition and fees vary according to location and program. *Required fees:* $8 per credit hour part-time. *College room only:* $5000. Room and board charges vary according to board plan and housing facility. *Payment plan:* installment. *Waivers:* senior citizens and employees or children of employees.

Financial Aid Of all full-time matriculated undergraduates who enrolled in 2012, 1,198 applied for aid, 1,078 were judged to have need, 197 had their need fully met. In 2012, 124 non-need-based awards were made. *Average percent of need met:* 61. *Average financial aid package:* $16,335. *Average need-based loan:* $4164. *Average need-based gift aid:* $12,863. *Average non-need-based aid:* $5371.

APPLYING
Standardized Tests *Required:* SAT or ACT (for admission).
Options: electronic application, early admission, deferred entrance.
Application fee: $25.
Required: essay or personal statement, high school transcript. *Required for some:* interview, audition for music and theater programs. *Recommended:* minimum 2.0 GPA, 1 letter of recommendation, interview.
Application deadlines: 8/25 (freshmen), 8/25 (transfers).
Notification: continuous (freshmen), continuous (transfers).

CONTACT
Shorter University, 315 Shorter Avenue, Rome, GA 30165. *Phone:* 706-233-7342. *Toll-free phone:* 800-868-6980.

South Georgia State College
Douglas, Georgia
http://www.sgc.edu/

CONTACT
South Georgia State College, 100 West College Park Drive, Douglas, GA 31533-5098. *Phone:* 912-260-4409. *Toll-free phone:* 800-342-6364.

South University
Savannah, Georgia
http://www.southuniversity.edu/savannah/

CONTACT
South University, 709 Mall Boulevard, Savannah, GA 31406. *Phone:* 912-201-8000. *Toll-free phone:* 866-629-2901.

Spelman College
Atlanta, Georgia
http://www.spelman.edu/

- **Independent** 4-year, founded 1881
- **Urban** 39-acre campus with easy access to Atlanta
- **Endowment** $367.9 million
- **Women only** 2,137 undergraduate students, 98% full-time
- **Very difficult** entrance level, 40% of applicants were admitted

UNDERGRAD STUDENTS
2,086 full-time, 51 part-time. Students come from 42 states and territories; 10 other countries; 72% are from out of state; 97% Black or African American, non-Hispanic/Latino; 0.1% Hispanic/Latino; 2% American Indian or Alaska Native, non-Hispanic/Latino; 0.5% Two or more races, non-Hispanic/Latino; 0.8% international; 2% transferred in; 67% live on campus.

Freshmen:
Admission: 8,344 applied, 3,342 admitted, 548 enrolled. *Average high school GPA:* 3.7. *Test scores:* SAT evidence-based reading and writing scores over 500: 97%; SAT math scores over 500: 89%; ACT scores over 18: 98%; SAT evidence-based reading and writing scores over 600: 43%; SAT math scores over 600: 22%; ACT scores over 24: 47%; SAT evidence-based reading and writing scores over 700: 5%; SAT math scores over 700: 3%; ACT scores over 30: 3%.
Retention: 89% of full-time freshmen returned.

FACULTY
Total: 241, 72% full-time, 83% with terminal degrees.
Student/faculty ratio: 11:1.

ACADEMICS
Calendar: semesters. *Degree:* bachelor's.

Special study options: adult/continuing education programs, advanced placement credit, cooperative education, double majors, honors programs, independent study, internships, off-campus study, part-time degree program, services for LD students, student-designed majors, study abroad. *ROTC:* Army (c), Navy (c), Air Force (c).
Unusual degree programs: 3-2 engineering with North Carolina Agricultural and Technical State University, Rensselaer Polytechnic Institute, Georgia Institute of Technology, Boston University, The University of Alabama in Huntsville, Auburn University.
Computers: 700 computers/terminals and 1,500 ports are available on campus for general student use. Students can access the following: computer help desk, free student e-mail accounts, online (class) grades, online (class) registration, online (class) schedules. Campuswide network is available. 100% of college-owned or -operated housing units are wired for high-speed Internet access. Wireless service is available via entire campus.
Library: Robert Woodruff Library plus 1 other. *Books:* 489,081 (physical), 139,636 (digital/electronic); *Serial titles:* 987 (physical), 122,146 (digital/electronic); *Databases:* 317. Weekly public service hours: 95; students can reserve study rooms.

STUDENT LIFE
Housing options: on-campus residence required through sophomore year; women-only. Campus housing is university owned and leased by the school. Freshman applicants given priority for college housing.
Activities and organizations: drama/theater group, student-run newspaper, choral group, Glee Club, Theater Program, Student Government, Honors Program, Religious Groups, national sororities.
Campus security: 24-hour emergency response devices and patrols, late-night transport/escort service, controlled dormitory access, lighted pathways/sidewalks.
Student services: health clinic, personal/psychological counseling, women's center.

COSTS & FINANCIAL AID
Costs (2017–18) *One-time required fee:* $250. *Comprehensive fee:* $41,642 includes full-time tuition ($24,382), mandatory fees ($3799), and room and board ($13,461). Full-time tuition and fees vary according to course load. Part-time tuition: $1010 per credit hour. Part-time tuition and fees vary according to course load. *Required fees:* $1010 per credit hour part-time, $1900 per term part-time. *Room and board:* Room and board charges vary according to board plan and housing facility. *Payment plans:* installment, deferred payment. *Waivers:* employees or children of employees.
Financial Aid Of all full-time matriculated undergraduates who enrolled in 2016, 1,853 applied for aid, 1,700 were judged to have need, 14 had their need fully met. In 2016, 15 non-need-based awards were made. *Average percent of need met:* 33. *Average financial aid package:* $16,900. *Average need-based loan:* $5013. *Average need-based gift aid:* $12,410. *Average non-need-based aid:* $35,697. *Average indebtedness upon graduation:* $38,430.

APPLYING
Standardized Tests *Required:* SAT or ACT (for admission). *Required for some:* SAT and SAT Subject Tests or ACT (for admission), SAT Subject Tests (for admission).
Options: electronic application, early admission, early decision, early action, deferred entrance.
Application fee: $35.
Required: essay or personal statement, high school transcript, minimum 2.0 GPA, 2 letters of recommendation. *Required for some:* interview.
Application deadlines: 2/1 (freshmen), 4/1 (transfers), 11/15 (early action).
Early decision deadline: 11/1.
Notification: 4/1 (freshmen), 5/1 (transfers), 12/15 (early decision), 12/31 (early action).

CONTACT
Ms. Tiffany Nelson, Director of Admissions, Spelman College, 350 Spelman Lane, SW, Atlanta, GA 30314-4399. *Phone:* 800-982-2411. *Toll-free phone:* 800-982-2411. *Fax:* 404-270-5201. *E-mail:* admiss@spelman.edu.

Strayer University–Augusta Campus
Augusta, Georgia
http://www.strayer.edu/georgia/augusta/

CONTACT
Strayer University–Augusta Campus, 1330 Augusta West Parkway, Augusta, GA 30909. *Toll-free phone:* 888-311-0355.

Strayer University–Chamblee Campus
Atlanta, Georgia
http://www.strayer.edu/georgia/chamblee/

CONTACT
Strayer University–Chamblee Campus, 3355 Northeast Expressway, Suite 100, Atlanta, GA 30341. *Toll-free phone:* 888-311-0355.

Strayer University–Cobb County Campus
Atlanta, Georgia
http://www.strayer.edu/georgia/cobb-county/

CONTACT
Strayer University–Cobb County Campus, 3101 Towercreek Parkway, SE, Suite 700, Atlanta, GA 30339. *Toll-free phone:* 888-311-0355.

Strayer University–Columbus Campus
Columbus, Georgia
http://www.strayer.edu/georgia/columbus/

CONTACT
Strayer University–Columbus Campus, 6003 Veterans Parkway, Suite 100, Columbus, GA 31909. *Toll-free phone:* 888-311-0355.

Strayer University–Douglasville Campus
Douglasville, Georgia
http://www.strayer.edu/georgia/douglasville/

CONTACT
Strayer University–Douglasville Campus, 4655 Timber Ridge Drive, Douglasville, GA 30135. *Toll-free phone:* 888-311-0355.

Strayer University–Lithonia Campus
Lithonia, Georgia
http://www.strayer.edu/georgia/lithonia/

CONTACT
Strayer University–Lithonia Campus, 3120 Stonecrest Boulevard, Suite 200, Lithonia, GA 30038. *Toll-free phone:* 888-311-0355.

Strayer University–Morrow Campus
Morrow, Georgia
http://www.strayer.edu/georgia/morrow/

CONTACT
Strayer University–Morrow Campus, 3000 Corporate Center Drive, Suite 100, Morrow, GA 30260. *Toll-free phone:* 888-311-0355.

Strayer University–Roswell Campus
Roswell, Georgia
http://www.strayer.edu/georgia/roswell/

CONTACT
Strayer University–Roswell Campus, 100 Mansell Court East, Suite 100, Roswell, GA 30076. *Toll-free phone:* 888-311-0355.

Strayer University–Savannah Campus
Savannah, Georgia
http://www.strayer.edu/georgia/savannah/

CONTACT
Strayer University–Savannah Campus, 20 Martin Court, Savannah, GA 31419. *Toll-free phone:* 888-311-0355.

Thomas University
Thomasville, Georgia
http://www.thomasu.edu/

- **Independent** comprehensive, founded 1950
- **Small-town** 24-acre campus
- **Endowment** $4.2 million
- **Coed** 1,114 undergraduate students, 39% full-time, 64% women, 36% men
- **Minimally difficult** entrance level, 23% of applicants were admitted

UNDERGRAD STUDENTS
438 full-time, 676 part-time. Students come from 14 states and territories; 11 other countries; 35% are from out of state; 34% transferred in; 9% live on campus.

Freshmen:
Admission: 359 applied, 81 admitted, 79 enrolled.

FACULTY
Total: 53, 96% full-time, 70% with terminal degrees.
Student/faculty ratio: 6:1.

ACADEMICS
Calendar: semesters. *Degrees:* associate, bachelor's, master's, post-master's, and postbachelor's certificates.

Special study options: academic remediation for entering students, accelerated degree program, adult/continuing education programs, advanced placement credit, cooperative education, distance learning, double majors, independent study, internships, part-time degree program, services for LD students, study abroad, summer session for credit.

Computers: 80 computers/terminals are available on campus for general student use. Students can access the following: campus intranet, computer help desk, free student e-mail accounts, online (class) grades, online (class) registration, online (class) schedules. Campuswide network is available. 100% of college-owned or -operated housing units are wired for high-speed Internet access. Wireless service is available via entire campus.
Library: Thomas University Library plus 1 other. Weekly public service hours: 60.

STUDENT LIFE
Housing options: on-campus residence required through sophomore year; coed. Campus housing is university owned. Freshman applicants given priority for college housing.

Activities and organizations: drama/theater group, student-run newspaper, choral group, Student Government Association, Professional Management Association, National Society for Leadership and Success.

Athletics Member NAIA. *Intercollegiate sports:* baseball M(s), golf M(s)/W, soccer M(s)/W(s), softball W(s). *Intramural sports:* football M/W, table tennis M/W, tennis M/W, volleyball M/W.

Campus security: late-night transport/escort service, controlled dormitory access, evening security guards.
Student services: personal/psychological counseling.

COSTS & FINANCIAL AID
Costs (2018–19) *Comprehensive fee:* $23,980 includes full-time tuition ($15,940), mandatory fees ($1000), and room and board ($7040). Part-time tuition: $630 per credit hour. *Required fees:* $550 per year part-time. *College room only:* $6000. Room and board charges vary according to housing facility. *Payment plan:* installment.

Financial Aid Of all full-time matriculated undergraduates who enrolled in 2016, 101 applied for aid. 41 Federal Work-Study jobs (averaging $1584).

APPLYING
Options: electronic application, early admission, deferred entrance.

Application fee: $25.

Required: high school transcript.

Application deadlines: rolling (freshmen), rolling (transfers).

Notification: continuous (freshmen), continuous (transfers).

CONTACT
Mrs. Rita Gagliano, Office of Admission, Thomas University, 1501 Millpond Road, Thomasville, GA 31792. *Phone:* 229-227-6942. *Toll-free phone:* 800-538-9784. *Fax:* 229-227-6919. *E-mail:* rgagliano@thomasu.edu.

Toccoa Falls College
Toccoa Falls, Georgia
http://www.tfc.edu/

- **Independent interdenominational** 4-year, founded 1907
- **Small-town** 1100-acre campus with easy access to Atlanta, GA metro area
- **Endowment** $2.8 million
- **Coed** 1,411 undergraduate students, 62% full-time, 59% women, 41% men
- **Moderately difficult** entrance level, 59% of applicants were admitted

UNDERGRAD STUDENTS
872 full-time, 539 part-time. Students come from 30 states and territories; 8 other countries; 35% are from out of state; 8% Black or African American, non-Hispanic/Latino; 5% Hispanic/Latino; 6% Asian, non-Hispanic/Latino; 0.2% Native Hawaiian or other Pacific Islander, non-Hispanic/Latino; 0.1% American Indian or Alaska Native, non-Hispanic/Latino; 2% Two or more races, non-Hispanic/Latino; 1% Race/ethnicity unknown; 2% international; 4% transferred in; 28% live on campus.

Freshmen:
Admission: 843 applied, 495 admitted, 217 enrolled. *Average high school GPA:* 3.4. *Test scores:* SAT evidence-based reading and writing scores over 500: 65%; SAT math scores over 500: 54%; ACT scores over 18: 79%; SAT evidence-based reading and writing scores over 600: 26%; SAT math scores over 600: 11%; ACT scores over 24: 24%; SAT evidence-based reading and writing scores over 700: 4%; SAT math scores over 700: 2%; ACT scores over 30: 1%.

Retention: 65% of full-time freshmen returned.

FACULTY
Total: 125, 35% full-time, 36% with terminal degrees.

Student/faculty ratio: 15:1.

ACADEMICS
Calendar: 4-1-4. *Degrees:* certificates, associate, and bachelor's.

Special study options: advanced placement credit, distance learning, double majors, independent study, internships, part-time degree program, services for LD students, study abroad, summer session for credit.

Computers: 40 computers/terminals are available on campus for general student use. Students can access the following: campus intranet, free student e-mail accounts, online (class) grades, online (class) registration, online (class) schedules. Campuswide network is available. 95% of college-owned or -operated housing units are wired for high-speed Internet access. Wireless service is available via entire campus.

Library: Seby Jones Library plus 1 other. *Books:* 55,113 (physical), 630,445 (digital/electronic); *Serial titles:* 79 (physical), 73,000 (digital/electronic); *Databases:* 282. Weekly public service hours: 82; students can reserve study rooms.

STUDENT LIFE
Housing options: on-campus residence required through junior year; men-only, women-only. Campus housing is university owned. Freshman campus housing is guaranteed.

Activities and organizations: drama/theater group, student-run newspaper, radio station, choral group, Outdoor Club, Hmong Student Fellowship, The Justice Campaign, Toccoa Falls for Life, Theatrical Society.

Athletics Member NCCAA. *Intercollegiate sports:* baseball M, basketball M/W, soccer M/W, volleyball W. *Intramural sports:* basketball M/W, cross-country running M(c)/W(c), football M/W, soccer M/W, softball M/W, ultimate Frisbee M/W, volleyball M/W.

Campus security: student patrols.

Student services: health clinic, personal/psychological counseling.

COSTS & FINANCIAL AID
Costs (2018–19) *Comprehensive fee:* $31,074 includes full-time tuition ($21,974), mandatory fees ($770), and room and board ($8330). Full-time tuition and fees vary according to location. Part-time tuition: $916 per credit hour. Part-time tuition and fees vary according to location. *Required fees:* $770 per year part-time. *Room and board:* Room and board charges vary according to board plan. *Payment plan:* installment. *Waivers:* employees or children of employees.

Financial Aid Of all full-time matriculated undergraduates who enrolled in 2016, 688 applied for aid, 632 were judged to have need, 84 had their need fully met. In 2016, 60 non-need-based awards were made. *Average percent of need met:* 66. *Average financial aid package:* $16,791. *Average need-based loan:* $3670. *Average need-based gift aid:* $13,571. *Average non-need-based aid:* $10,284. *Average indebtedness upon graduation:* $26,653.

APPLYING
Standardized Tests *Required:* SAT or ACT (for admission).

Options: electronic application, early admission, deferred entrance.

Application fee: $30.

Required: essay or personal statement, high school transcript, minimum 2.0 GPA, 1 letter of recommendation. *Required for some:* interview.

Application deadlines: rolling (freshmen), rolling (out-of-state freshmen), rolling (transfers).

Notification: continuous (freshmen), continuous (out-of-state freshmen), continuous (transfers).

CONTACT
Mr. Ronnie Stewart, Toccoa Falls College, 107 Kincaid Drive, MSC 899, Toccoa Falls, GA 30598. *Phone:* 706-886-6831 Ext. 5378. *Toll-free phone:* 888-785-5624. *Fax:* 706-282-6012. *E-mail:* rstewart@tfc.edu.

Truett McConnell University
Cleveland, Georgia
http://www.truett.edu/

- **Independent Baptist** comprehensive, founded 1946
- **Rural** 200-acre campus with easy access to Atlanta
- **Coed** 2,152 undergraduate students, 34% full-time, 56% women, 44% men
- **Minimally difficult** entrance level, 91% of applicants were admitted

UNDERGRAD STUDENTS
740 full-time, 1,412 part-time. Students come from 17 states and territories; 15 other countries; 9% are from out of state; 8% Black or African American, non-Hispanic/Latino; 6% Hispanic/Latino; 0.4% Asian, non-Hispanic/Latino; 0.1% American Indian or Alaska Native, non-Hispanic/Latino; 2% Race/ethnicity unknown; 2% international; 2% transferred in.

Freshmen:
Admission: 543 applied, 492 admitted, 222 enrolled. *Average high school GPA:* 3.4. *Test scores:* ACT scores over 18: 66%; ACT scores over 24: 13%; ACT scores over 30: 1%.

Retention: 63% of full-time freshmen returned.

FACULTY
Total: 52.

Student/faculty ratio: 15:1.

ACADEMICS
Calendar: semesters. *Degrees:* bachelor's and master's.

Special study options: academic remediation for entering students, accelerated degree program, advanced placement credit, distance learning, double majors, services for LD students, summer session for credit.

Computers: 40 computers/terminals are available on campus for general student use. Students can access the following: computer help desk, free student e-mail accounts, online (class) grades, online (class) registration, online (class) schedules. Campuswide network is available. 100% of college-owned or -operated housing units are wired for high-speed Internet access. Wireless service is available via entire campus.

Library: Cofer Library.

STUDENT LIFE

Housing options: on-campus residence required through senior year; men-only, women-only. Campus housing is university owned.

Activities and organizations: choral group.

Athletics Member NAIA. *Intercollegiate sports:* baseball M(s), basketball M(s)/W(s), cross-country running M(s)/W(s), golf M(s)/W(s), lacrosse W(s), soccer M(s)/W(s), softball W(s), volleyball W(s), wrestling M(s). *Intramural sports:* football M/W.

Campus security: 24-hour weekday patrols, 10-hour weekend patrols by trained security personnel.

COSTS & FINANCIAL AID

Costs (2017–18) *Comprehensive fee:* $26,880 includes full-time tuition ($18,570), mandatory fees ($910), and room and board ($7400). Full-time tuition and fees vary according to course load, degree level, location, and program. Part-time tuition: $774 per credit hour. Part-time tuition and fees vary according to course load, degree level, location, and program. *Required fees:* $455 per term part-time. *Room and board:* Room and board charges vary according to housing facility. *Payment plan:* installment. *Waivers:* employees or children of employees.

Financial Aid Of all full-time matriculated undergraduates who enrolled in 2017, 661 applied for aid, 581 were judged to have need, 110 had their need fully met. 24 Federal Work-Study jobs (averaging $1834). In 2017, 107 non-need-based awards were made. *Average percent of need met:* 70. *Average financial aid package:* $15,836. *Average need-based loan:* $4826. *Average need-based gift aid:* $12,437. *Average non-need-based aid:* $6850. *Average indebtedness upon graduation:* $29,757.

APPLYING

Standardized Tests *Required:* SAT or ACT (for admission).

Options: electronic application, early admission, deferred entrance.

Required: high school transcript, minimum 2.0 GPA. *Required for some:* essay or personal statement, 1 letter of recommendation, interview.

Application deadlines: 8/1 (freshmen), 8/1 (transfers).

Notification: continuous (freshmen), continuous (transfers).

CONTACT

Truett McConnell University, 100 Alumni Drive, Cleveland, GA 30528. *Phone:* 706-865-2134 Ext. 4301. *Toll-free phone:* 800-226-8621.

University of Georgia
Athens, Georgia
http://www.uga.edu/

- **State-supported** university, founded 1785, part of University System of Georgia
- **Suburban** 767-acre campus with easy access to Atlanta
- **Endowment** $1.2 billion
- **Coed** 28,848 undergraduate students, 94% full-time, 57% women, 43% men
- **Moderately difficult** entrance level, 54% of applicants were admitted

UNDERGRAD STUDENTS

27,142 full-time, 1,706 part-time. Students come from 54 states and territories; 123 other countries; 11% are from out of state; 8% Black or African American, non-Hispanic/Latino; 6% Hispanic/Latino; 10% Asian, non-Hispanic/Latino; 0.1% Native Hawaiian or other Pacific Islander, non-Hispanic/Latino; 0.1% American Indian or Alaska Native, non-Hispanic/Latino; 4% Two or more races, non-Hispanic/Latino; 0.9% Race/ethnicity unknown; 2% international; 5% transferred in; 33% live on campus.

Freshmen:

Admission: 24,165 applied, 13,052 admitted, 5,826 enrolled. *Average high school GPA:* 4.0. *Test scores:* SAT evidence-based reading and writing scores over 500: 99%; SAT math scores over 500: 98%; ACT scores over 18: 100%; SAT evidence-based reading and writing scores over 600: 84%; SAT math scores over 600: 72%; ACT scores over 24: 92%; SAT evidence-based reading and writing scores over 700: 23%; SAT math scores over 700: 21%; ACT scores over 30: 45%.

Retention: 96% of full-time freshmen returned.

FACULTY

Total: 2,307, 88% full-time, 91% with terminal degrees.

Student/faculty ratio: 17:1.

ACADEMICS

Calendar: semesters. *Degrees:* certificates, bachelor's, master's, doctoral, post-master's, and postbachelor's certificates.

Special study options: academic remediation for entering students, accelerated degree program, adult/continuing education programs, advanced placement credit, cooperative education, distance learning, double majors, external degree program, honors programs, independent study, internships, off-campus study, part-time degree program, services for LD students, student-designed majors, study abroad, summer session for credit. *ROTC:* Army (b), Air Force (b).

Computers: Students can access the following: campus intranet, computer help desk, free student e-mail accounts, online (class) grades, online (class) registration, online (class) schedules. Campuswide network is available. 100% of college-owned or -operated housing units are wired for high-speed Internet access. Wireless service is available via entire campus.

Library: Ilah Dunlap Little Memorial Library plus 4 others. *Books:* 5.2 million (digital/electronic). Students can reserve study rooms.

STUDENT LIFE

Housing options: on-campus residence required for freshman year; coed, women-only, special housing for students with disabilities. Campus housing is university owned. Freshman campus housing is guaranteed.

Activities and organizations: drama/theater group, student-run newspaper, radio station, choral group, marching band, Intramural Sports, Recreational sports program, Communiversity, University Union, Red Coat Band, national fraternities, national sororities.

Athletics Member NCAA. All Division I except football (Division I-A). *Intercollegiate sports:* badminton M(c)/W(c), baseball M(s), basketball M(s)/W(s), cheerleading M(c)/W(c), crew M(c)/W(c), cross-country running M(s)/W(s), equestrian sports M(c)/W(s), fencing M(c)/W(c), golf M(s)/W(s), gymnastics M(c)/W(s), ice hockey M(c), lacrosse M(c)/W(c), racquetball M(c)/W(c), rugby M(c)/W(c), sailing M(c)/W(c), soccer M(c)/W(s), softball W(s), swimming and diving M(s)/W(s), tennis M(s)/W(s), track and field M(s)/W(s), ultimate Frisbee M(c)/W(c), volleyball M(c)/W(c), water polo M(c)/W(c), wrestling M(c). *Intramural sports:* badminton M/W, basketball M/W, football M/W, golf M/W, racquetball M/W, soccer M/W, softball M/W, tennis M/W, ultimate Frisbee M/W, volleyball M/W, water polo M/W.

Campus security: 24-hour emergency response devices and patrols, late-night transport/escort service, controlled dormitory access.

Student services: health clinic, personal/psychological counseling, women's center, legal services.

COSTS & FINANCIAL AID

Costs (2017–18) *Tuition:* state resident $9552 full-time; nonresident $28,126 full-time. Full-time tuition and fees vary according to course load, location, and program. Part-time tuition and fees vary according to course load, location, and program. *Required fees:* $2266 full-time. *Room and board:* $10,060; room only: $6104. Room and board charges vary according to board plan and housing facility. *Waivers:* senior citizens.

Financial Aid Of all full-time matriculated undergraduates who enrolled in 2017, 19,275 applied for aid, 11,988 were judged to have need, 2,649 had their need fully met. 388 Federal Work-Study jobs (averaging $2414). In 2017, 1119 non-need-based awards were made. *Average percent of need met:* 72. *Average financial aid package:* $12,182. *Average need-based loan:* $4191. *Average need-based gift aid:* $9317. *Average non-need-based aid:* $2640. *Average indebtedness upon graduation:* $23,403.

APPLYING

Standardized Tests *Required:* SAT or ACT (for admission).

Options: electronic application, early admission, early action, deferred entrance.

Application fee: $60.

Required: high school transcript, counselor evaluation. *Recommended:* essay or personal statement, minimum 2.0 GPA.

Application deadlines: 1/8 (freshmen), 4/1 (transfers), 10/15 (early action).

Notification: 4/1 (freshmen), continuous (transfers), 12/1 (early action).

CONTACT
Mr. Charles Carabello, Associate Director for Enrollment Management, University of Georgia, Terrell Hall, Athens, GA 30602. *Phone:* 706-542-8776. *Fax:* 706-542-1466. *E-mail:* admproc@uga.edu.

University of North Georgia
Dahlonega, Georgia
http://www.ung.edu/

- **State-supported** comprehensive, founded 1873, part of University System of Georgia
- **Small-town** 1077-acre campus with easy access to Atlanta
- **Endowment** $58.4 million
- **Coed** 18,173 undergraduate students, 70% full-time, 56% women, 44% men
- **Moderately difficult** entrance level

UNDERGRAD STUDENTS
12,712 full-time, 5,461 part-time. Students come from 46 states and territories; 96 other countries; 4% are from out of state; 4% Black or African American, non-Hispanic/Latino; 12% Hispanic/Latino; 3% Asian, non-Hispanic/Latino; 0.2% Native Hawaiian or other Pacific Islander, non-Hispanic/Latino; 0.2% American Indian or Alaska Native, non-Hispanic/Latino; 3% Two or more races, non-Hispanic/Latino; 0.9% Race/ethnicity unknown; 2% international; 3% transferred in; 22% live on campus.

Freshmen:
Admission: 4,392 applied, 3,964 enrolled. *Average high school GPA:* 3.6. *Test scores:* SAT evidence-based reading and writing scores over 500: 89%; SAT math scores over 500: 81%; ACT scores over 18: 100%; SAT evidence-based reading and writing scores over 600: 21%; SAT math scores over 600: 24%; ACT scores over 24: 67%; SAT evidence-based reading and writing scores over 700: 3%; SAT math scores over 700: 1%; ACT scores over 30: 8%.
Retention: 81% of full-time freshmen returned.

FACULTY
Total: 984, 69% full-time, 56% with terminal degrees.
Student/faculty ratio: 19:1.

ACADEMICS
Calendar: semesters. *Degrees:* certificates, associate, bachelor's, master's, doctoral, post-master's, and postbachelor's certificates.
Special study options: academic remediation for entering students, accelerated degree program, advanced placement credit, cooperative education, distance learning, double majors, English as a second language, freshman honors college, honors programs, independent study, internships, part-time degree program, services for LD students, study abroad, summer session for credit. *ROTC:* Army (b).
Unusual degree programs: 3-2 engineering with Georgia Institute of Technology, Clemson University.
Computers: 3,500 computers/terminals and 6,300 ports are available on campus for general student use. Students can access the following: campus intranet, computer help desk, free student e-mail accounts, online (class) grades, online (class) registration, online (class) schedules. Campuswide network is available. 100% of college-owned or -operated housing units are wired for high-speed Internet access. Wireless service is available via entire campus.
Library: Library Technology Center plus 4 others. *Books:* 195,525 (physical), 433,929 (digital/electronic); *Serial titles:* 168 (physical); *Databases:* 298. Weekly public service hours: 94; students can reserve study rooms.

STUDENT LIFE
Housing options: on-campus residence required through sophomore year; coed, men-only, women-only, special housing for students with disabilities. Campus housing is university owned. Freshman applicants given priority for college housing.
Activities and organizations: drama/theater group, student-run newspaper, radio station, choral group, marching band, Student Government Association, Commuter Council, Graduate Student Senate, Student Activities Board, Greek organizations, national fraternities, national sororities.

Athletics Member NCAA. All Division II. *Intercollegiate sports:* baseball M(s), basketball M(s)/W(s), cheerleading M/W, cross-country running M(c)/W(s), equestrian sports W(c), golf M(s)/W(s), lacrosse M(c)/W(c), riflery M(s)/W(s), soccer M(s)/W(s), softball W(s), tennis M(s)/W(s), wrestling M(c). *Intramural sports:* basketball M/W, football M/W, golf M(c)/W(c), rugby M/W, soccer M/W, softball M/W, table tennis M/W, ultimate Frisbee M/W, volleyball M/W, water polo M/W.
Campus security: 24-hour emergency response devices and patrols, late-night transport/escort service, controlled dormitory access.
Student services: health clinic, personal/psychological counseling.

COSTS & FINANCIAL AID
Costs (2018–19) *Tuition:* state resident $5569 full-time, $182 per credit hour part-time; nonresident $19,657 full-time, $642 per credit hour part-time. Full-time tuition and fees vary according to course load, degree level, and location. Part-time tuition and fees vary according to course load, degree level, and location. *Required fees:* $1826 full-time. *Room and board:* $10,800; room only: $5520. Room and board charges vary according to board plan and housing facility. *Payment plan:* installment. *Waivers:* senior citizens and employees or children of employees.
Financial Aid Of all full-time matriculated undergraduates who enrolled in 2017, 9,951 applied for aid, 8,147 were judged to have need, 4,523 had their need fully met. 178 Federal Work-Study jobs (averaging $1195). In 2017, 1275 non-need-based awards were made. *Average percent of need met:* 79. *Average financial aid package:* $4910. *Average need-based loan:* $3519. *Average need-based gift aid:* $4375. *Average non-need-based aid:* $3808. *Average indebtedness upon graduation:* $19,129.

APPLYING
Standardized Tests *Required:* SAT or ACT (for admission).
Options: electronic application, early admission.
Application fee: $30.
Required: high school transcript, minimum 2.0 GPA, proof of immunization.
Application deadlines: 7/1 (freshmen), rolling (transfers).
Notification: continuous (freshmen), continuous (transfers).

CONTACT
Molly Potts, Director of Admissions, University of North Georgia, Admissions Center, 3820 Mundy Mill Road, Oakwood, GA 30566. *Phone:* 678-717-3849. *Toll-free phone:* 800-498-9581. *E-mail:* molly.potts@ung.edu.

University of West Georgia
Carrollton, Georgia
http://www.westga.edu/

- **State-supported** comprehensive, founded 1933, part of University System of Georgia
- **Rural** 645-acre campus with easy access to Atlanta
- **Endowment** $29.2 million
- **Coed** 11,252 undergraduate students, 79% full-time, 63% women, 37% men
- **Moderately difficult** entrance level, 59% of applicants were admitted

UNDERGRAD STUDENTS
8,938 full-time, 2,314 part-time. Students come from 25 states and territories; 65 other countries; 6% are from out of state; 38% Black or African American, non-Hispanic/Latino; 6% Hispanic/Latino; 1% Asian, non-Hispanic/Latino; 0.1% Native Hawaiian or other Pacific Islander, non-Hispanic/Latino; 0.1% American Indian or Alaska Native, non-Hispanic/Latino; 4% Two or more races, non-Hispanic/Latino; 2% Race/ethnicity unknown; 1% international; 7% transferred in; 27% live on campus.

Freshmen:
Admission: 7,909 applied, 4,636 admitted, 2,264 enrolled. *Average high school GPA:* 3.2. *Test scores:* SAT math scores over 500: 33%; ACT scores over 18: 87%; SAT math scores over 600: 4%; ACT scores over 24: 16%; ACT scores over 30: 1%.
Retention: 72% of full-time freshmen returned.

FACULTY
Total: 705, 64% full-time, 65% with terminal degrees.

Student/faculty ratio: 20:1.

ACADEMICS
Calendar: semesters. *Degrees:* bachelor's, master's, doctoral, post-master's, and postbachelor's certificates.

Special study options: accelerated degree program, advanced placement credit, cooperative education, distance learning, double majors, external degree program, freshman honors college, honors programs, independent study, internships, off-campus study, part-time degree program, services for LD students, study abroad, summer session for credit. *ROTC:* Air Force (c).

Unusual degree programs: 3-2 engineering with Auburn University, Mercer University.

Computers: 1,200 computers/terminals are available on campus for general student use. Students can access the following: campus intranet, computer help desk, free student e-mail accounts, online (class) grades, online (class) registration, online (class) schedules. Campuswide n etwork is available. 100% of college-owned or -operated housing units are wired for high-speed Internet access. Wireless service is available via entire campus.

Library: Irvine Sullivan Ingram Library plus 1 other. Weekly public service hours: 137; study areas open 24 hours, 5–7 days a week; students can reserve study rooms.

STUDENT LIFE
Housing options: on-campus residence required for freshman year; coed, women-only, special housing for students with disabilities. Campus housing is university owned and leased by the school. Freshman campus housing is guaranteed.

Activities and organizations: drama/theater group, student-run newspaper, radio and television station, choral group, marching band, Black Student Alliance, Student Activities Council, Baptist Collegiate Ministries, Campus Outreach, United Voices Gospel Choir, national fraternities, national sororities.

Athletics Member NCAA. All Division II. *Intercollegiate sports:* baseball M(s), basketball M(s)/W(s), cheerleading W(s), cross-country running M(s)/W(s), football M(s), golf M(s)/W(s), soccer W(s), softball W(s), tennis W(s), track and field W(s), volleyball W(s). *Intramural sports:* baseball M(c), basketball M(c)/W(c), equestrian sports W(c), golf M/W, lacrosse M(c), rock climbing M(c)/W(c), soccer M(c), ultimate Frisbee M/W, weight lifting M/W, wrestling M(c).

Campus security: 24-hour emergency response devices and patrols, student patrols, late-night transport/escort service, controlled dormitory access.

Student services: health clinic, personal/psychological counseling.

COSTS & FINANCIAL AID
Costs (2018–19) *Tuition:* state resident $5330 full-time, $178 per semester hour part-time; nonresident $18,812 full-time, $627 per semester hour part-time. Full-time tuition and fees vary according to course load, degree level, location, and program. Part-time tuition and fees vary according to course load, degree level, location, and program. *Required fees:* $1962 full-time. *Room and board:* $10,218; room only: $5450. Room and board charges vary according to board plan and housing facility. *Payment plan:* installment. *Waivers:* senior citizens and employees or children of employees.

Financial Aid Of all full-time matriculated undergraduates who enrolled in 2017, 8,113 applied for aid, 6,617 were judged to have need, 4,131 had their need fully met. In 2017, 509 non-need-based awards were made. *Average percent of need met:* 53. *Average financial aid package:* $8828. *Average need-based loan:* $3964. *Average need-based gift aid:* $5013. *Average non-need-based aid:* $2299. *Average indebtedness upon graduation:* $29,000. *Financial aid deadline:* 7/1.

APPLYING
Standardized Tests *Required:* SAT or ACT (for admission).

Options: electronic application, early admission, deferred entrance.

Application fee: $40.

Required: minimum 2.6 GPA, proof of immunization. *Required for some:* high school transcript.

Application deadlines: rolling (freshmen), rolling (transfers).

Notification: continuous (freshmen), continuous (transfers).

CONTACT
University of West Georgia, 1601 Maple Street, Carrollton, GA 30118. *Phone:* 678-839-5600.

Valdosta State University
Valdosta, Georgia
http://www.valdosta.edu/
- **State-supported** university, founded 1906, part of University System of Georgia
- **Small-town** 180-acre campus
- **Endowment** $7.5 million
- **Coed** 8,778 undergraduate students, 82% full-time, 62% women, 38% men
- **Moderately difficult** entrance level, 74% of applicants were admitted

UNDERGRAD STUDENTS
7,166 full-time, 1,612 part-time. Students come from 46 states and territories; 54 other countries; 14% are from out of state; 38% Black or African American, non-Hispanic/Latino; 6% Hispanic/Latino; 1% Asian, non-Hispanic/Latino; 0.1% Native Hawaiian or other Pacific Islander, non-Hispanic/Latino; 0.2% American Indian or Alaska Native, non-Hispanic/Latino; 4% Two or more races, non-Hispanic/Latino; 0.6% Race/ethnicity unknown; 2% international; 8% transferred in; 28% live on campus.

Freshmen:
Admission: 5,303 applied, 3,933 admitted, 1,628 enrolled. *Average high school GPA:* 3.1. *Test scores:* SAT evidence-based reading and writing scores over 500: 82%; SAT math scores over 500: 67%; ACT scores over 18: 90%; SAT evidence-based reading and writing scores over 600: 20%; SAT math scores over 600: 10%; ACT scores over 24: 21%; SAT evidence-based reading and writing scores over 700: 1%; ACT scores over 30: 1%.

Retention: 69% of full-time freshmen returned.

FACULTY
Total: 559, 75% full-time, 68% with terminal degrees.

Student/faculty ratio: 20:1.

ACADEMICS
Calendar: semesters. *Degrees:* certificates, associate, bachelor's, master's, doctoral, post-master's, and postbachelor's certificates.

Special study options: accelerated degree program, adult/continuing education programs, advanced placement credit, cooperative education, distance learning, double majors, English as a second language, external degree program, honors programs, independent study, internships, off-campus study, part-time degree program, services for LD students, study abroad, summer session for credit. *ROTC:* Air Force (b).

Unusual degree programs: 3-2 engineering with Georgia Institute of Technology.

Computers: 1,691 computers/terminals are available on campus for general student use. Students can access the following: campus intranet, computer help desk, free student e-mail accounts, online (class) grades, online (class) registration, online (class) schedules. Campuswide network is available. 100% of college-owned or -operated housing units are wired for high-speed Internet access. Wireless service is available via entire campus.

Library: Odum Library. *Books:* 579,774 (physical), 408,139 (digital/electronic); *Serial titles:* 10,877 (physical), 39,852 (digital/electronic); *Databases:* 237. Students can reserve study rooms.

STUDENT LIFE
Housing options: on-campus residence required for freshman year; coed, special housing for students with disabilities. Campus housing is university owned. Freshman applicants given priority for college housing.

Activities and organizations: drama/theater group, student-run newspaper, radio and television station, choral group, marching band, Black Student League, Enactus, Psychology Club, Collegiate women of VSU, College Republican Society, national fraternities, national sororities.

Athletics Member NCAA. All Division II. *Intercollegiate sports:* baseball M(s), basketball M(s)/W(s), cheerleading M/W, cross-country running M(s)/W(s), football M(s), golf M(s), soccer W(s), softball W(s), tennis M(s)/W(s), volleyball W(s). *Intramural sports:* basketball M/W, bowling M/W, football M/W, golf M/W, lacrosse M(c), rugby M(c), soccer M/W, softball M/W, table tennis M/W, tennis M/W, ultimate Frisbee M/W, volleyball M/W.

Campus security: 24-hour emergency response devices and patrols, late-night transport/escort service, controlled dormitory access, bicycle patrols, security cameras, mobile security app.

Student services: health clinic, personal/psychological counseling.

COSTS & FINANCIAL AID

Costs (2018–19) *Tuition:* state resident $4264 full-time, $178 per credit hour part-time; nonresident $15,050 full-time, $627 per credit hour part-time. Full-time tuition and fees vary according to course load, location, program, and reciprocity agreements. Part-time tuition and fees vary according to course load, location, program, and reciprocity agreements. *Required fees:* $2146 full-time. *Room and board:* $7900; room only: $4060. Room and board charges vary according to board plan and housing facility. *Payment plan:* installment. *Waivers:* employees or children of employees.

Financial Aid Of all full-time matriculated undergraduates who enrolled in 2015, 6,194 applied for aid, 5,323 were judged to have need, 781 had their need fully met. In 2015, 77 non-need-based awards were made. *Average percent of need met:* 78. *Average financial aid package:* $15,919. *Average need-based loan:* $3464. *Average need-based gift aid:* $6361. *Average non-need-based aid:* $2478. *Average indebtedness upon graduation:* $29,607.

APPLYING

Standardized Tests *Required:* SAT or ACT (for admission).

Options: electronic application, deferred entrance.

Application fee: $40.

Required: high school transcript.

Application deadlines: 6/15 (freshmen), rolling (out-of-state freshmen), 6/15 (transfers).

Notification: continuous until 9/1 (freshmen), continuous until 8/1 (out-of-state freshmen), continuous until 8/1 (transfers).

CONTACT

Mr. Ryan M. Hogan, Director of Admissions, Valdosta State University, Office of Admissions, 1500 North Patterson Street, Valdosta, GA 31698. *Phone:* 229-333-5791. *Toll-free phone:* 800-618-1878. *Fax:* 229-333-5482. *E-mail:* admissions@valdosta.edu.

Wesleyan College
Macon, Georgia
http://www.wesleyancollege.edu/

- **Independent United Methodist** comprehensive, founded 1836
- **Suburban** 200-acre campus with easy access to Atlanta
- **Endowment** $58.6 million
- **Undergraduate:** women only; graduate: coed
- **Moderately difficult** entrance level

FACULTY
Student/faculty ratio: 15:1.

ACADEMICS
Calendar: semesters. *Degrees:* bachelor's and master's.
Library: Willet Memorial Library. Study areas open 24 hours, 5–7 days a week; students can reserve study rooms.

STUDENT LIFE
Housing options: women-only, special housing for students with disabilities. Campus housing is university owned. Freshman campus housing is guaranteed.

Activities and organizations: drama/theater group, student-run newspaper, choral group, Student Government Association (SGA), Black Student Alliance (BSA), A.X.I.S. (Association of eXemplary International Students), GLBAL (Gay, Lesbian, Bi-sexual Alliance), Campus Activities Board (CAB).

Athletics Member NCAA. All Division III.

Campus security: 24-hour emergency response devices and patrols, late-night transport/escort service.

Student services: health clinic, personal/psychological counseling, women's center.

COSTS & FINANCIAL AID

Costs (2017–18) *One-time required fee:* $250. *Comprehensive fee:* $31,940 includes full-time tuition ($21,370), mandatory fees ($1000), and room and board ($9570). Full-time tuition and fees vary according to class time, course load, and program. Part-time tuition: $510 per semester hour. Part-time tuition and fees vary according to class time and course load. *Required fees:* $40 per semester hour part-time. *Room and board:* Room and board charges vary according to housing facility.

Financial Aid Of all full-time matriculated undergraduates who enrolled in 2016, 345 applied for aid, 320 were judged to have need, 61 had their need fully met. In 2016, 85 non-need-based awards were made. *Average percent of need met:* 74. *Average financial aid package:* $20,567. *Average need-based loan:* $5880. *Average need-based gift aid:* $15,880. *Average non-need-based aid:* $10,742. *Average indebtedness upon graduation:* $35,392. *Financial aid deadline:* 6/1.

APPLYING

Standardized Tests *Required:* SAT or ACT (for admission).

Options: electronic application, early admission, early decision, early action, deferred entrance.

Application fee: $30.

Required: high school transcript, minimum 2.0 GPA, 1 letter of recommendation. *Required for some:* interview. *Recommended:* essay or personal statement, 2 letters of recommendation.

CONTACT

Ms. Danielle Lodge, Executive Director of Enrollment, Wesleyan College, 4760 Forsyth Road, Macon, GA 31210-4462. *Phone:* 478-757-5206. *Toll-free phone:* 800-447-6610. *Fax:* 478-757-4030. *E-mail:* admissions@wesleyancollege.edu.

Young Harris College
Young Harris, Georgia
http://www.yhc.edu/

CONTACT
Mr. Clinton G. Hobbs, Vice President for Enrollment Management, Young Harris College, PO Box 116, Young Harris, GA 30582-0098. *Phone:* 706-379-3111. *Toll-free phone:* 800-241-3754. *Fax:* 706-379-3108. *E-mail:* admissions@yhc.edu.

HAWAII

Argosy University, Hawai`i
Honolulu, Hawaii
http://www.argosy.edu/locations/hawaii/

CONTACT
Argosy University, Hawai`i, 1001 Bishop Street, Suite 400, Honolulu, HI 96813. *Phone:* 808-536-5555. *Toll-free phone:* 888-323-2777.

Brigham Young University–Hawaii
Laie, Hawaii
http://www.byuh.edu/

CONTACT
Mr. Arapata P. Meha, Brigham Young University–Hawaii, 55-220 Kulanui Street, Laie, HI 96762-1294. *Phone:* 808-675-3731. *Fax:* 808-675-3741. *E-mail:* admissions@byuh.edu.

Chaminade University of Honolulu
Honolulu, Hawaii
http://www.chaminade.edu/

- **Independent Roman Catholic** comprehensive, founded 1955
- **Urban** 62-acre campus with easy access to Honolulu
- **Endowment** $19.1 million
- **Coed** 1,157 undergraduate students, 97% full-time, 71% women, 29% men
- **Moderately difficult** entrance level, 91% of applicants were admitted

UNDERGRAD STUDENTS

1,125 full-time, 32 part-time. Students come from 39 states and territories; 11 other countries; 29% are from out of state; 3% Black or African American, non-Hispanic/Latino; 4% Hispanic/Latino; 37% Asian, non-Hispanic/Latino; 26% Native Hawaiian or other Pacific Islander, non-Hispanic/Latino; 0.4% American Indian or Alaska Native, non-Hispanic/Latino; 10% Two or more races, non-Hispanic/Latino; 4% Race/ethnicity unknown; 1% international; 10% transferred in; 23% live on campus.

Freshmen:

Admission: 742 applied, 674 admitted, 212 enrolled. *Average high school GPA:* 3.4. *Test scores:* ACT scores over 18: 88%; ACT scores over 24: 20%.

Retention: 77% of full-time freshmen returned.

FACULTY

Total: 138, 66% full-time.

Student/faculty ratio: 11:1.

ACADEMICS

Calendar: semesters. *Degrees:* associate, bachelor's, master's, post-master's, and postbachelor's certificates.

Special study options: academic remediation for entering students, accelerated degree program, adult/continuing education programs, advanced placement credit, distance learning, double majors, independent study, internships, off-campus study, part-time degree program, study abroad, summer session for credit. *ROTC:* Army (c), Air Force (c).

Computers: 200 computers/terminals are available on campus for general student use. Students can access the following: computer help desk, free student e-mail accounts, online (class) grades, online (class) registration, online (class) schedules. Campuswide network is available. 100% of college-owned or -operated housing units are wired for high-speed Internet access. Wireless service is available via entire campus.

Library: Sullivan Library. *Books:* 47,508 (physical), 133,757 (digital/electronic); *Serial titles:* 142 (physical), 36,441 (digital/electronic); *Databases:* 99.

STUDENT LIFE

Housing options: coed, women-only, special housing for students with disabilities. Campus housing is university owned and leased by the school.

Activities and organizations: drama/theater group, student-run newspaper, radio station, choral group, Lumana O Samoa (Samoan Club), Kaimi Lalakea (Hawaiian Club), Rotaract, Residence Hall Association, Chaminade Student Government Association.

Athletics Member NCAA. All Division II. *Intercollegiate sports:* basketball M(s)/W(s), cross-country running M(s)/W(s), golf M(s), soccer M(s)/W(s), softball W(s), tennis W(s), volleyball W(s). *Intramural sports:* basketball M/W.

Campus security: 24-hour emergency response devices and patrols, late-night transport/escort service, controlled dormitory access.

Student services: personal/psychological counseling.

COSTS & FINANCIAL AID

Costs (2018–19) *One-time required fee:* $180. *Comprehensive fee:* $39,004 includes full-time tuition ($25,260), mandatory fees ($114), and room and board ($13,630). Full-time tuition and fees vary according to course load, location, and program. Part-time tuition: $842 per credit. Part-time tuition and fees vary according to course load, location, and program. *Room and board:* Room and board charges vary according to board plan and housing facility. *Payment plan:* installment. *Waivers:* employees or children of employees.

Financial Aid Of all full-time matriculated undergraduates who enrolled in 2016, 937 applied for aid, 823 were judged to have need, 90 had their need fully met. In 2016, 298 non-need-based awards were made. *Average percent of need met:* 61. *Average financial aid package:* $17,701. *Average need-based loan:* $4187. *Average need-based gift aid:* $4608. *Average non-need-based aid:* $8967. *Average indebtedness upon graduation:* $26,191.

APPLYING

Standardized Tests *Required:* SAT or ACT (for admission), TOEFL for international students (for admission).

Options: electronic application, deferred entrance.

Application fee: $50.

Required: essay or personal statement, high school transcript, minimum 2.5 GPA. *Required for some:* minimum 2.8 GPA, 2 letters of recommendation, interview. *Recommended:* minimum 3.0 GPA.

Application deadlines: rolling (freshmen), rolling (transfers).

Notification: continuous (freshmen), continuous (transfers).

CONTACT

Office of Admissions, Chaminade University of Honolulu, 3140 Waialae Avenue, Honolulu, HI 96816-1578. *Phone:* 808-735-8340. *Toll-free phone:* 800-735-3733. *Fax:* 808-739-4647. *E-mail:* admissions@chaminade.edu.

Hawai`i Pacific University

Honolulu, Hawaii

http://www.hpu.edu/

- **Independent** comprehensive, founded 1965
- **Urban** 140-acre campus
- **Endowment** $44.4 million
- **Coed** 3,560 undergraduate students, 68% full-time, 60% women, 40% men
- **Moderately difficult** entrance level, 75% of applicants were admitted

UNDERGRAD STUDENTS

2,411 full-time, 1,149 part-time. Students come from 54 states and territories; 55 other countries; 42% are from out of state; 5% Black or African American, non-Hispanic/Latino; 14% Hispanic/Latino; 15% Asian, non-Hispanic/Latino; 2% Native Hawaiian or other Pacific Islander, non-Hispanic/Latino; 0.6% American Indian or Alaska Native, non-Hispanic/Latino; 15% Two or more races, non-Hispanic/Latino; 13% Race/ethnicity unknown; 10% international; 9% transferred in; 14% live on campus.

Freshmen:

Admission: 6,551 applied, 4,892 admitted, 500 enrolled. *Average high school GPA:* 3.5. *Test scores:* SAT evidence-based reading and writing scores over 500: 81%; SAT math scores over 500: 73%; ACT scores over 18: 90%; SAT evidence-based reading and writing scores over 600: 29%; SAT math scores over 600: 23%; ACT scores over 24: 41%; SAT evidence-based reading and writing scores over 700: 3%; SAT math scores over 700: 2%; ACT scores over 30: 2%.

Retention: 65% of full-time freshmen returned.

FACULTY

Total: 359, 42% full-time.

Student/faculty ratio: 12:1.

ACADEMICS

Calendar: semesters. *Degrees:* certificates, associate, bachelor's, master's, doctoral, post-master's, and postbachelor's certificates.

Special study options: academic remediation for entering students, accelerated degree program, adult/continuing education programs, advanced placement credit, cooperative education, distance learning, double majors, English as a second language, freshman honors college, honors programs, independent study, internships, off-campus study, part-time degree program, services for LD students, student-designed majors, study abroad, summer session for credit. *ROTC:* Army (c), Air Force (c).

Unusual degree programs: 3-2 engineering with Washington University in St. Louis, University of Southern California.

Computers: 200 computers/terminals are available on campus for general student use. Students can access the following: campus intranet, computer help desk, free student e-mail accounts, online (class) grades, online (class) registration, online (class) schedules. Campuswide network is available. Wireless service is available via entire campus.

Library: Meader Library plus 2 others. *Books:* 103,021 (physical), 191,075 (digital/electronic); *Serial titles:* 64 (physical), 4,520 (digital/electronic); *Databases:* 101. Students can reserve study rooms.

STUDENT LIFE

Housing options: coed. Campus housing is university owned. Freshman applicants given priority for college housing.

Activities and organizations: drama/theater group, student-run newspaper, choral group, Student Government Association, Campus

Activities Board, Student Nurses Association, Travel Industry Management Student Organization, Christian Student Organization.

Athletics Member NCAA. All Division II. *Intercollegiate sports:* baseball M(s), basketball M(s)/W(s), cross-country running M(s)/W(s), golf M(s)/W(s), gymnastics W(s), soccer M(s)/W(s), softball W(s), tennis M(s)/W(s), volleyball W(s). *Intramural sports:* basketball M/W, soccer M/W, tennis M/W, volleyball M/W.

Campus security: 24-hour emergency response devices and patrols, late-night transport/escort service, controlled dormitory access, emergency notification, patrol system and emergency exit alarms in residence halls.

Student services: health clinic, personal/psychological counseling.

COSTS & FINANCIAL AID

Costs (2018–19) *Comprehensive fee:* $40,780 includes full-time tuition ($25,630), mandatory fees ($350), and room and board ($14,800). Full-time tuition and fees vary according to course level, course load, degree level, location, program, and student level. Part-time tuition: $855 per credit. Part-time tuition and fees vary according to course level, course load, degree level, location, program, and student level. *Required fees:* $25 per term part-time. *Room and board:* Room and board charges vary according to board plan, housing facility, and location. *Payment plan:* installment. *Waivers:* employees or children of employees.

Financial Aid Of all full-time matriculated undergraduates who enrolled in 2016, 1,602 applied for aid, 1,408 were judged to have need, 230 had their need fully met. 455 Federal Work-Study jobs (averaging $2834). In 2016, 619 non-need-based awards were made. *Average percent of need met:* 48. *Average financial aid package:* $15,142. *Average need-based loan:* $4345. *Average need-based gift aid:* $4549. *Average non-need-based aid:* $9260. *Average indebtedness upon graduation:* $28,893.

APPLYING

Standardized Tests *Required:* SAT or ACT (for admission). *Required for some:* TOEFL or IELTS.

Options: electronic application, early action, deferred entrance.

Application fee: $50.

Required: high school transcript, minimum 2.5 GPA. *Required for some:* interview. *Recommended:* essay or personal statement, 2 letters of recommendation.

Application deadlines: rolling (freshmen), rolling (transfers).

Notification: continuous (transfers).

CONTACT
Marissa Bratton, Director of Admissions, Hawai`i Pacific University, 1 Aloha Tower Drive, Honolulu, HI 96813. *Phone:* 808-544-0238. *Toll-free phone:* 866-225-5478. *Fax:* 808-544-1136. *E-mail:* admissions@hpu.edu.

Pacific Rim Christian University
Honolulu, Hawaii
http://www.pacrim.edu/

CONTACT
Pacific Rim Christian University, 2223 Ho'one'e Place, Honolulu, HI 96819.

Remington College–Honolulu Campus
Honolulu, Hawaii
http://www.remingtoncollege.edu/

CONTACT
Louis LaMair, Director of Recruitment, Remington College–Honolulu Campus, 1111 Bishop Street, Suite 400, Honolulu, HI 96813. *Phone:* 808-942-1000. *Toll-free phone:* 800-323-8122. *Fax:* 808-533-3064. *E-mail:* louis.lamair@remingtoncollege.edu.

University of Hawaii at Hilo
Hilo, Hawaii
http://hilo.hawaii.edu/

CONTACT
University of Hawaii at Hilo, Admissions, 200 W. Kawili Street, Hilo, HI 96720. *Phone:* 808-932-7446. *Toll-free phone:* 800-897-4456. *Fax:* 808-932-7459. *E-mail:* uhhadm@hawaii.edu.

University of Hawaii at Manoa
Honolulu, Hawaii
http://manoa.hawaii.edu/

- **State-supported** university, founded 1907, part of University of Hawaii System
- **Urban** 320-acre campus with easy access to Honolulu
- **Coed** 12,881 undergraduate students, 83% full-time, 56% women, 44% men
- **Moderately difficult** entrance level, 83% of applicants were admitted

UNDERGRAD STUDENTS
10,702 full-time, 2,179 part-time. Students come from 50 states and territories; 67 other countries; 27% are from out of state; 2% Black or African American, non-Hispanic/Latino; 2% Hispanic/Latino; 40% Asian, non-Hispanic/Latino; 17% Native Hawaiian or other Pacific Islander, non-Hispanic/Latino; 0.4% American Indian or Alaska Native, non-Hispanic/Latino; 16% Two or more races, non-Hispanic/Latino; 0.2% Race/ethnicity unknown; 3% international; 12% transferred in; 25% live on campus.

Freshmen:
Admission: 8,523 applied, 7,069 admitted, 1,959 enrolled. *Average high school GPA:* 3.5. *Test scores:* ACT scores over 18: 96%; ACT scores over 24: 48%; ACT scores over 30: 8%.

Retention: 79% of full-time freshmen returned.

FACULTY
Total: 1,404, 82% full-time, 90% with terminal degrees.
Student/faculty ratio: 10:1.

ACADEMICS
Calendar: semesters. *Degrees:* bachelor's, master's, doctoral, and postbachelor's certificates.

Special study options: advanced placement credit, cooperative education, distance learning, double majors, English as a second language, honors programs, independent study, internships, off-campus study, part-time degree program, services for LD students, student-designed majors, study abroad, summer session for credit. *ROTC:* Army (b), Air Force (b).

Computers: 117 computers/terminals and 6 ports are available on campus for general student use. Students can access the following: campus intranet, computer help desk, free student e-mail accounts, online (class) grades, online (class) registration, online (class) schedules. Campuswide network is available. 100% of college-owned or -operated housing units are wired for high-speed Internet access. Wireless service is available via entire campus.

Library: Hamilton Library plus 6 others. *Books:* 3.3 million (physical), 229,160 (digital/electronic); *Serial titles:* 21,504 (physical), 55,502 (digital/electronic); *Databases:* 304. Weekly public service hours: 93; study areas open 24 hours, 5–7 days a week; students can reserve study rooms.

STUDENT LIFE
Housing options: coed, special housing for students with disabilities. Campus housing is university owned. Freshman applicants given priority for college housing.

Activities and organizations: drama/theater group, student-run newspaper, radio station, choral group, marching band, Biology Club, Pre-Medical Association, International Student Association, Katipunan, Timpuyog, national fraternities, national sororities.

Athletics Member NCAA. All Division I except football (Division I-A). *Intercollegiate sports:* archery M, baseball M(s), basketball M(s)/W(s), cheerleading M(s)/W(s), cross-country running W(s), golf M(s)/W(s), sailing M/W, soccer W(s), softball W(s), swimming and diving M(s)/W(s), tennis M(s)/W(s), track and field W(s), volleyball M(s)/W(s),

Idaho

COLLEGES AT-A-GLANCE

water polo W(s). *Intramural sports:* badminton M/W, basketball M/W, crew M/W, cross-country running M/W, golf M/W, rugby M, sailing M/W, soccer M, softball M, swimming and diving M/W, table tennis M/W, tennis M/W, track and field M/W, ultimate Frisbee M/W, volleyball M/W, weight lifting M/W, wrestling M/W.

Campus security: 24-hour emergency response devices and patrols, student patrols, late-night transport/escort service, controlled dormitory access.

Student services: health clinic, personal/psychological counseling, women's center.

COSTS & FINANCIAL AID

Costs (2018–19) *Tuition:* state resident $11,088 full-time, $462 per credit hour part-time; nonresident $33,120 full-time, $1380 per credit hour part-time. Full-time tuition and fees vary according to class time, course level, course load, degree level, program, reciprocity agreements, and student level. Part-time tuition and fees vary according to class time, course level, course load, degree level, program, reciprocity agreements, and student level. *Required fees:* $882 full-time, $462 per term part-time. *Room and board:* $13,689; room only: $9663. Room and board charges vary according to board plan and housing facility. *Payment plan:* installment. *Waivers:* minority students, adult students, senior citizens, and employees or children of employees.

Financial Aid Of all full-time matriculated undergraduates who enrolled in 2017, 432 Federal Work-Study jobs (averaging $2849). *Average indebtedness upon graduation:* $24,233.

APPLYING

Standardized Tests *Required:* SAT or ACT (for admission). *Recommended:* SAT (for admission), ACT (for admission).

Options: electronic application.

Application fee: $70.

Required: high school transcript, minimum 2.8 GPA.

Application deadlines: 3/1 (freshmen), 3/1 (transfers).

Notification: continuous (freshmen), continuous (transfers).

CONTACT

Ms. Lisa Buto, Student Services Specialist, University of Hawaii at Manoa, 2600 Campus Road, Room 001, Honolulu, HI 96822. *Phone:* 808-956-8975. *Toll-free phone:* 800-823-9771. *Fax:* 808-956-4148. *E-mail:* uhmanoa.admissions@hawaii.edu.

University of Hawaii Maui College

Kahului, Hawaii

http://maui.hawaii.edu/

CONTACT

Mr. Stephen Kameda, Director of Admissions and Records, University of Hawaii Maui College, 310 Kaahumanu Avenue, Kahului, HI 96732. *Phone:* 808-984-3267. *Toll-free phone:* 800-479-6692. *Fax:* 808-984-3872. *E-mail:* skameda@hawaii.edu.

University of Hawaii–West Oahu

Kapolei, Hawaii

http://www.uhwo.hawaii.edu/

CONTACT

Mr. Craig Morimoto, University of Hawaii–West Oahu, HI. *Phone:* 808-689-2916. *Toll-free phone:* 866-299-8656. *E-mail:* uhwoadm@hawaii.edu.

University of Phoenix–Hawaii Campus

Honolulu, Hawaii

http://www.phoenix.edu/

CONTACT

Marc Booker, Sr. Director, Office of Admissions and Evaluation, University of Phoenix–Hawaii Campus, 4035 South Riverpoint Parkway, Mail Stop CF-L101, Phoenix, AZ 85040. *Phone:* 602-557-4609. *Toll-free phone:* 866-766-0766. *Fax:* 480-643-1156.

IDAHO

Boise Bible College

Boise, Idaho

http://www.boisebible.edu/

CONTACT

Russell Grove, Director of Admissions, Boise Bible College, 8695 West Marigold Street, Boise, ID 83714-1220. *Phone:* 208-376-7731. *Toll-free phone:* 800-893-7755. *Fax:* 208-376-7743. *E-mail:* rgrove@boisebible.edu.

Boise State University

Boise, Idaho

http://www.boisestate.edu/

- **State-supported** university, founded 1932, part of Idaho System of Higher Education
- **Urban** 287-acre campus
- **Coed** 20,767 undergraduate students, 60% full-time, 56% women, 44% men
- **Moderately difficult** entrance level, 82% of applicants were admitted

UNDERGRAD STUDENTS

12,477 full-time, 8,290 part-time. Students come from 50 states and territories; 58 other countries; 2% Black or African American, non-Hispanic/Latino; 13% Hispanic/Latino; 2% Asian, non-Hispanic/Latino; 0.4% Native Hawaiian or other Pacific Islander, non-Hispanic/Latino; 0.4% American Indian or Alaska Native, non-Hispanic/Latino; 4% Two or more races, non-Hispanic/Latino; 2% Race/ethnicity unknown; 2% international; 7% transferred in; 31% live on campus.

Freshmen:
Admission: 8,330 applied, 6,808 admitted, 2,788 enrolled. *Average high school GPA:* 3.5. *Test scores:* ACT scores over 18: 92%; ACT scores over 24: 43%; ACT scores over 30: 6%.

Retention: 80% of full-time freshmen returned.

FACULTY

Total: 1,526, 50% full-time, 40% with terminal degrees.

ACADEMICS

Calendar: semesters. *Degrees:* associate, bachelor's, master's, doctoral, and postbachelor's certificates.

Special study options: academic remediation for entering students, adult/continuing education programs, advanced placement credit, cooperative education, distance learning, double majors, English as a second language, freshman honors college, honors programs, independent study, internships, off-campus study, part-time degree program, services for LD students, student-designed majors, study abroad, summer session for credit. *ROTC:* Army (b).

Computers: 900 computers/terminals are available on campus for general student use. Students can access the following: campus intranet, computer help desk, free student e-mail accounts, online (class) grades, online (class) registration, online (class) schedules. Campuswide network is available. 100% of college-owned or -operated housing units are wired for high-speed Internet access. Wireless service is available via classrooms, computer centers, computer labs, dorm rooms, learning centers, libraries, student centers.

Library: Albertson's Library plus 1 other. *Books:* 644,899 (physical), 60,977 (digital/electronic); *Serial titles:* 112,213 (digital/electronic); *Databases:* 303. Weekly public service hours: 115; study areas open 24 hours, 5–7 days a week; students can reserve study rooms.

STUDENT LIFE

Housing options: coed, men-only, women-only. Campus housing is university owned. Freshman applicants given priority for college housing.

Activities and organizations: drama/theater group, student-run newspaper, radio station, choral group, marching band, national fraternities, national sororities.

Athletics Member NCAA. All Division I except football (Division I-A). *Intercollegiate sports:* basketball M(s)/W(s), cross-country running M(s)/W(s), golf M(s)/W(s), gymnastics W(s), soccer W(s), softball W(s), swimming and diving W(s), tennis M(s)/W(s), track and field M(s)/W(s), volleyball W(s). *Intramural sports:* baseball M, basketball M/W, golf

A ★ *indicates that the school has detailed information with a Premium Profile on Petersons.com.*

www.petersons.com 285

M/W, lacrosse M(c)/W(c), rugby M(c)/W(c), soccer M(c)/W(c), softball W(c), swimming and diving M/W, track and field M/W, triathlon M/W, ultimate Frisbee M(c)/W(c), volleyball M(c)/W(c), water polo M/W.

Campus security: 24-hour emergency response devices and patrols, late-night transport/escort service, controlled dormitory access.

Student services: health clinic, personal/psychological counseling, women's center, legal services.

COSTS & FINANCIAL AID

Costs (2017–18) *Tuition:* state resident $5043 full-time, $205 per credit hour part-time; nonresident $20,359 full-time, $500 per credit hour part-time. Full-time tuition and fees vary according to course load, program, and reciprocity agreements. Part-time tuition and fees vary according to course load and program. *Required fees:* $2283 full-time, $100 per term part-time. *Room and board:* $7750; room only: $3850. Room and board charges vary according to board plan and housing facility. *Payment plan:* installment. *Waivers:* senior citizens and employees or children of employees.

Financial Aid Of all full-time matriculated undergraduates who enrolled in 2016, 7,424 applied for aid, 7,332 were judged to have need, 990 had their need fully met. 192 Federal Work-Study jobs (averaging $2260). 216 state and other part-time jobs (averaging $2090). In 2016, 311 non-need-based awards were made. *Average percent of need met:* 58. *Average financial aid package:* $10,136. *Average need-based loan:* $4386. *Average need-based gift aid:* $5750. *Average non-need-based aid:* $2111. *Average indebtedness upon graduation:* $27,974. *Financial aid deadline:* 6/30.

APPLYING

Standardized Tests *Required for some:* SAT or ACT (for admission).

Options: electronic application.

Application fee: $50.

Required for some: high school transcript.

Application deadlines: rolling (freshmen), rolling (transfers).

Notification: continuous (freshmen), continuous (transfers).

CONTACT

Ms. Kelly Talbert, Director/Admissions, Boise State University, 1910 University Drive, Boise, ID 83725. *Phone:* 208-426-3844. *Toll-free phone:* 800-824-7017. *E-mail:* bsuinfo@boisestate.edu.

Brigham Young University–Idaho

Rexburg, Idaho

http://www.byui.edu/

- **Independent** 4-year, founded 1888, affiliated with The Church of Jesus Christ of Latter-day Saints
- **Small-town** 255-acre campus
- **Coed** 32,458 undergraduate students, 51% full-time, 58% women, 42% men
- **Moderately difficult** entrance level, 96% of applicants were admitted

UNDERGRAD STUDENTS

16,538 full-time, 15,920 part-time. Students come from 53 states and territories; 116 other countries; 78% are from out of state; 0.6% Black or African American, non-Hispanic/Latino; 3% Hispanic/Latino; 1% Asian, non-Hispanic/Latino; 0.7% Native Hawaiian or other Pacific Islander, non-Hispanic/Latino; 0.3% American Indian or Alaska Native, non-Hispanic/Latino; 6% Two or more races, non-Hispanic/Latino; 2% Race/ethnicity unknown; 9% international; 8% transferred in.

Freshmen:

Admission: 8,034 applied, 7,699 admitted, 4,188 enrolled. *Test scores:* ACT scores over 18: 91%; ACT scores over 24: 39%; ACT scores over 30: 3%.

Retention: 71% of full-time freshmen returned.

FACULTY

Total: 792, 61% full-time.

Student/faculty ratio: 25:1.

ACADEMICS

Calendar: semesters. *Degrees:* associate and bachelor's.

Special study options: academic remediation for entering students, accelerated degree program, adult/continuing education programs,

advanced placement credit, honors programs, internships, part-time degree program, services for LD students, summer session for credit. *ROTC:* Army (b).

Computers: Students can access the following: online (class) registration. Campuswide network is available. Wireless service is available via entire campus.

Library: David O. McKay Library. Students can reserve study rooms.

STUDENT LIFE

Housing options: men-only, women-only. Campus housing is university owned.

Activities and organizations: drama/theater group, student-run newspaper, radio station, choral group, national fraternities, national sororities.

Campus security: 24-hour emergency response devices and patrols, late-night transport/escort service.

Student services: health clinic, personal/psychological counseling, legal services.

COSTS & FINANCIAL AID

Costs (2017–18) *Comprehensive fee:* $4319 includes full-time tuition ($2009), mandatory fees ($14), and room and board ($2296). Part-time tuition: $167 per credit hour. *Room and board:* Room and board charges vary according to housing facility and location. *Waivers:* employees or children of employees.

Financial Aid Of all full-time matriculated undergraduates who enrolled in 2016, 2,400 state and other part-time jobs.

APPLYING

Standardized Tests *Required:* SAT or ACT (for admission).

Options: electronic application.

Application fee: $35.

Required: essay or personal statement, high school transcript, interview.

Application deadlines: 2/15 (freshmen), 3/15 (transfers).

Notification: 4/1 (freshmen), 3/15 (transfers).

CONTACT

Brigham Young University–Idaho, 525 South Center Street, Rexburg, ID 83460. *Phone:* 208-496-1310.

The College of Idaho

Caldwell, Idaho

http://www.collegeofidaho.edu/

- **Independent** comprehensive, founded 1891
- **Suburban** 50-acre campus
- **Coed** 943 undergraduate students, 95% full-time, 50% women, 50% men
- **Moderately difficult** entrance level, 76% of applicants were admitted

UNDERGRAD STUDENTS

896 full-time, 47 part-time. 66% are from out of state; 4% Black or African American, non-Hispanic/Latino; 14% Hispanic/Latino; 2% Asian, non-Hispanic/Latino; 1% Native Hawaiian or other Pacific Islander, non-Hispanic/Latino; 0.5% American Indian or Alaska Native, non-Hispanic/Latino; 4% Two or more races, non-Hispanic/Latino; 4% Race/ethnicity unknown; 6% international; 5% transferred in; 68% live on campus.

Freshmen:

Admission: 1,665 applied, 1,263 admitted, 268 enrolled. *Test scores:* SAT evidence-based reading and writing scores over 500: 86%; SAT math scores over 500: 76%; ACT scores over 18: 94%; SAT evidence-based reading and writing scores over 600: 39%; SAT math scores over 600: 24%; ACT scores over 24: 49%; SAT evidence-based reading and writing scores over 700: 9%; SAT math scores over 700: 7%; ACT scores over 30: 8%.

Retention: 77% of full-time freshmen returned.

FACULTY

Total: 142, 61% full-time, 57% with terminal degrees.

Student/faculty ratio: 9:1.

ACADEMICS

Calendar: 12-6-12 week calendar. *Degrees:* bachelor's and master's.

Special study options: academic remediation for entering students, advanced placement credit, cooperative education, double majors, English as a second language, honors programs, independent study, internships, off-campus study, part-time degree program, services for LD students, study abroad, summer session for credit. *ROTC:* Army (c).

Unusual degree programs: 3-2 engineering with Washington University in St. Louis, Columbia University; nursing with Idaho State University.

Computers: Students can access the following: campus intranet, computer help desk, free student e-mail accounts, online (class) grades, online (class) registration, online (class) schedules, online course syllabi, course assignments, course discussion. Campuswide network is available. 100% of college-owned or -operated housing units are wired for high-speed Internet access. Wireless service is available via entire campus.

Library: Terteling Library.

STUDENT LIFE

Housing options: on-campus residence required through junior year; coed, special housing for students with disabilities. Campus housing is university owned. Freshman campus housing is guaranteed.

Activities and organizations: drama/theater group, student-run newspaper, choral group, marching band, national fraternities, national sororities.

Athletics Member NAIA. *Intercollegiate sports:* baseball M(s), basketball M(s)/W(s), cross-country running M(s)/W(s), golf M(s)/W(s), lacrosse M(c)/W(c), skiing (cross-country) M/W, skiing (downhill) M(s)/W(s), soccer M(s)/W(s), softball W(s), swimming and diving M(s)/W(s), tennis W(s), track and field M(s)/W(s), volleyball W(s). *Intramural sports:* badminton M/W, basketball M/W, football M/W, soccer M/W, softball M/W, ultimate Frisbee M/W, volleyball M/W.

Campus security: 24-hour emergency response devices and patrols, student patrols, late-night transport/escort service, controlled dormitory access.

Student services: health clinic, personal/psychological counseling, women's center.

COSTS & FINANCIAL AID

Costs (2018–19) *Comprehensive fee:* $39,852 includes full-time tuition ($29,400), mandatory fees ($755), and room and board ($9697). Part-time tuition: $1225 per credit. *Room and board:* Room and board charges vary according to board plan and housing facility. *Payment plan:* installment. *Waivers:* employees or children of employees.

Financial Aid Of all full-time matriculated undergraduates who enrolled in 2017, 755 applied for aid, 586 were judged to have need, 147 had their need fully met. In 2017, 296 non-need-based awards were made. *Average percent of need met:* 50. *Average financial aid package:* $27,221. *Average need-based loan:* $4397. *Average need-based gift aid:* $4208. *Average non-need-based aid:* $19,426. *Average indebtedness upon graduation:* $7202.

APPLYING

Options: electronic application, early admission, early action, deferred entrance.

Required: essay or personal statement, high school transcript, 1 letter of recommendation. *Recommended:* interview, class rank, extracurricular resumé.

Application deadlines: 2/16 (freshmen), 8/1 (transfers), 11/16 (early action).

Notification: continuous (freshmen), continuous (transfers), 12/21 (early action).

CONTACT

Vice President of Enrollment Management, The College of Idaho, 2112 Cleveland Boulevard, Caldwell, ID 83605-4432. *Phone:* 208-459-5319. *Toll-free phone:* 800-244-3246. *Fax:* 208-459-. *E-mail:* admission@collegeofidaho.edu.

Idaho State University

Pocatello, Idaho

http://www.isu.edu/

- **State-supported** university, founded 1901
- **Urban** 1100-acre campus
- **Coed** 10,688 undergraduate students, 59% full-time, 56% women, 43% men
- **Minimally difficult** entrance level, 100% of applicants were admitted

UNDERGRAD STUDENTS

6,278 full-time, 4,405 part-time. 9% are from out of state; 1% Black or African American, non-Hispanic/Latino; 13% Hispanic/Latino; 1% Asian, non-Hispanic/Latino; 0.3% Native Hawaiian or other Pacific Islander, non-Hispanic/Latino; 2% American Indian or Alaska Native, non-Hispanic/Latino; 3% Two or more races, non-Hispanic/Latino; 2% Race/ethnicity unknown; 7% international; 4% transferred in; 15% live on campus.

Freshmen:
Admission: 3,284 applied, 3,279 admitted, 1,364 enrolled. *Average high school GPA:* 3.2. *Test scores:* SAT evidence-based reading and writing scores over 500: 60%; SAT math scores over 500: 56%; ACT scores over 18: 80%; SAT evidence-based reading and writing scores over 600: 19%; SAT math scores over 600: 17%; ACT scores over 24: 32%; SAT evidence-based reading and writing scores over 700: 3%; SAT math scores over 700: 3%; ACT scores over 30: 7%.
Retention: 65% of full-time freshmen returned.

FACULTY

Total: 771, 77% full-time.
Student/faculty ratio: 14:1.

ACADEMICS

Calendar: semesters. *Degrees:* certificates, bachelor's, master's, doctoral, post-master's, and postbachelor's certificates.

Special study options: academic remediation for entering students, accelerated degree program, adult/continuing education programs, advanced placement credit, cooperative education, distance learning, double majors, English as a second language, honors programs, independent study, internships, off-campus study, part-time degree program, services for LD students, student-designed majors, study abroad, summer session for credit. *ROTC:* Army (b).

Computers: Students can access the following: computer help desk, free student e-mail accounts, online (class) grades, online (class) registration, online (class) schedules. Campuswide network is available. 100% of college-owned or -operated housing units are wired for high-speed Internet access. Wireless service is available via entire campus.

Library: Eli M. Oboler Library. Weekly public service hours: 103; students can reserve study rooms.

STUDENT LIFE

Housing options: coed, men-only, women-only, special housing for students with disabilities. Campus housing is university owned.

Activities and organizations: drama/theater group, student-run newspaper, radio and television station, choral group, marching band, national fraternities, national sororities.

Athletics Member NCAA. All Division I except football (Division I-AA). *Intercollegiate sports:* basketball M(s)/W(s), cross-country running M(s)/W(s), golf W(s), soccer W(s), softball W(s), tennis M(s)/W(s), track and field M(s)/W(s), volleyball W(s). *Intramural sports:* basketball M/W, cross-country running M/W, football M, golf W, rock climbing M(c)/W(c), soccer M/W, softball M/W, tennis M/W, track and field M/W, volleyball M/W.

Campus security: 24-hour emergency response devices and patrols, late-night transport/escort service, controlled dormitory access.

Student services: health clinic, personal/psychological counseling, women's center.

COSTS & FINANCIAL AID

Costs (2017–18) *Tuition:* state resident $5425 full-time, $359 per credit hour part-time; nonresident $20,201 full-time, $599 per credit hour part-time. Full-time tuition and fees vary according to course load, program, and reciprocity agreements. Part-time tuition and fees vary according to course load. No tuition increase for student's term of enrollment.

A ★ indicates that the school has detailed information with a Premium Profile on Petersons.com.

Required fees: $1741 full-time. *Room and board:* $7024; room only: $2790. Room and board charges vary according to board plan, housing facility, and location. *Payment plan:* installment. *Waivers:* senior citizens and employees or children of employees.

Financial Aid Of all full-time matriculated undergraduates who enrolled in 2015, 4,967 applied for aid, 4,333 were judged to have need, 199 had their need fully met. In 2015, 518 non-need-based awards were made. *Average percent of need met:* 46. *Average financial aid package:* $8494. *Average need-based loan:* $3834. *Average need-based gift aid:* $4686. *Average non-need-based aid:* $2251. *Average indebtedness upon graduation:* $30,617.

APPLYING
Standardized Tests *Required:* SAT or ACT (for admission). *Recommended:* ACT (for admission).

Options: electronic application, early admission, deferred entrance.

Application fee: $50.

Required: high school transcript, minimum 2.0 GPA.

Application deadlines: rolling (freshmen), rolling (transfers).

Notification: continuous (freshmen), continuous (transfers).

CONTACT
Admissions Office, Idaho State University, 921 South 8th, Stop 8270, Pocatello, ID 83209-8270. *Phone:* 208-282-2475. *Fax:* 208-282-4511. *E-mail:* admiss@isu.edu.

Lewis-Clark State College

Lewiston, Idaho
http://www.lcsc.edu/

CONTACT
Soo Lee Bruce-Smith, Coordinator of New Student Recruitment, Lewis-Clark State College, 500 Eighth Avenue, Lewiston, ID 83501-2698. *Phone:* 208-792-2210. *Toll-free phone:* 800-933-5272. *Fax:* 208-792-2876. *E-mail:* admissions@lcsc.edu.

New Saint Andrews College

Moscow, Idaho
http://www.nsa.edu/

- **Independent Christian** comprehensive, founded 1993
- **Small-town** campus
- **Coed** 140 undergraduate students, 91% full-time, 58% women, 42% men
- **Moderately difficult** entrance level, 93% of applicants were admitted

UNDERGRAD STUDENTS
128 full-time, 12 part-time. Students come from 28 states and territories; 5 other countries; 93% are from out of state; 4% Hispanic/Latino; 2% Asian, non-Hispanic/Latino; 0.8% American Indian or Alaska Native, non-Hispanic/Latino; 0.8% Two or more races, non-Hispanic/Latino; 8% Race/ethnicity unknown; 7% international.

Freshmen:
Admission: 68 applied, 63 admitted, 31 enrolled. *Test scores:* ACT scores over 18: 99%; ACT scores over 24: 81%; ACT scores over 30: 36%.

Retention: 76% of full-time freshmen returned.

FACULTY
Total: 18, 33% full-time, 50% with terminal degrees.
Student/faculty ratio: 12:1.

ACADEMICS
Calendar: 4 8-week terms. *Degrees:* associate, bachelor's, master's, and postbachelor's certificates.

Special study options: advanced placement credit, independent study, part-time degree program, summer session for credit.

Computers: 4 computers/terminals are available on campus for general student use. Students can access the following: campus intranet, free student e-mail accounts, online (class) grades, online (class) registration, online (class) schedules. Campuswide network is available. Wireless service is available via entire campus.

Library: Tyndale Library plus 1 other. Students can reserve study rooms.

STUDENT LIFE
Housing options: college housing not available.

Activities and organizations: drama/theater group, choral group, Students for the Relief of the Oppressed, Nursing Home Visits and Elderly Assistance (snow and leaf removal, firewood distribution), Blood Drives, Fall Carnival, St. Andrews Day Food Bank Drive.

Athletics *Intramural sports:* rugby M(c), soccer M(c), volleyball W(c).

Campus security: 24-hour emergency response devices.

Student services: personal/psychological counseling.

COSTS
Costs (2018–19) *Tuition:* $475 per credit hour part-time. Full-time tuition and fees vary according to course load and program. Part-time tuition and fees vary according to program. *Payment plan:* installment. *Waivers:* children of alumni and employees or children of employees.

APPLYING
Standardized Tests *Required:* SAT or ACT (for admission).

Options: electronic application, deferred entrance.

Application fee: $40.

Required: essay or personal statement, high school transcript, 2 letters of recommendation. *Required for some:* interview.

Application deadlines: 2/15 (freshmen), 2/15 (transfers).

Notification: 3/15 (freshmen), 3/15 (transfers).

CONTACT
Mr. John Sawyer, Director of Student Recruitment, New Saint Andrews College, PO Box 9025, Moscow, ID 83843. *Phone:* 208-882-1566 Ext. 100. *Fax:* 208-882-4293. *E-mail:* info@nsa.edu.

★ Northwest Nazarene University

Nampa, Idaho
http://www.nnu.edu/

- **Independent** comprehensive, founded 1913, affiliated with Church of the Nazarene
- **Small-town** 85-acre campus with easy access to Boise
- **Coed** 1,530 undergraduate students, 75% full-time, 58% women, 42% men
- **Moderately difficult** entrance level, 96% of applicants were admitted

UNDERGRAD STUDENTS
1,154 full-time, 376 part-time. 42% are from out of state; 2% Black or African American, non-Hispanic/Latino; 7% Hispanic/Latino; 2% Asian, non-Hispanic/Latino; 0.1% Native Hawaiian or other Pacific Islander, non-Hispanic/Latino; 0.5% American Indian or Alaska Native, non-Hispanic/Latino; 4% Two or more races, non-Hispanic/Latino; 5% Race/ethnicity unknown; 4% international; 5% transferred in; 71% live on campus.

Freshmen:
Admission: 818 applied, 783 admitted, 289 enrolled. *Average high school GPA:* 3.6. *Test scores:* SAT evidence-based reading and writing scores over 500: 88%; SAT math scores over 500: 76%; ACT scores over 18: 94%; SAT evidence-based reading and writing scores over 600: 45%; SAT math scores over 600: 28%; ACT scores over 24: 52%; SAT evidence-based reading and writing scores over 700: 5%; SAT math scores over 700: 4%; ACT scores over 30: 7%.

Retention: 76% of full-time freshmen returned.

FACULTY
Total: 119, 99% full-time, 67% with terminal degrees.
Student/faculty ratio: 16:1.

ACADEMICS
Calendar: semesters. *Degrees:* associate, bachelor's, master's, doctoral, post-master's, and postbachelor's certificates.

Special study options: academic remediation for entering students, accelerated degree program, adult/continuing education programs, advanced placement credit, cooperative education, distance learning, double majors, English as a second language, freshman honors college, honors programs, independent study, internships, off-campus study, part-time degree program, services for LD students, student-designed majors, study abroad, summer session for credit. *ROTC:* Army (b).

Computers: Students can access the following: campus intranet, computer help desk, free student e-mail accounts, online (class) grades, online (class) registration, online (class) schedules. Campuswide network is available. 99% of college-owned or -operated housing units are wired for high-speed Internet access. Wireless service is available via entire campus.
Library: John E. Riley Library.

STUDENT LIFE
Housing options: on-campus residence required through sophomore year; men-only, women-only, special housing for students with disabilities. Campus housing is university owned. Freshman campus housing is guaranteed.

Activities and organizations: drama/theater group, student-run newspaper, choral group, Students in Free Enterprise (SIFE), Student Government Association, Fellowship of Christian Athletes, The Crusader newspaper, The Oasis yearbook.

Athletics Member NCAA. All Division II. *Intercollegiate sports:* baseball M(s), basketball M(s)/W(s), cheerleading W(c), cross-country running M(s)/W(s), golf M(s)/W(s), soccer M/W(s), softball W(s), track and field M(s)/W(s), volleyball W(s). *Intramural sports:* basketball M/W, cross-country running M/W, football M/W, lacrosse W, softball M/W, table tennis M/W, tennis M/W, ultimate Frisbee M/W, volleyball M/W.

Campus security: 24-hour emergency response devices and patrols, student patrols, late-night transport/escort service, controlled dormitory access, residence hall check-in system, on-campus police hub.

Student services: health clinic, personal/psychological counseling.

COSTS & FINANCIAL AID
Costs (2018–19) *Comprehensive fee:* $36,700 includes full-time tuition ($29,300) and room and board ($7400). Full-time tuition and fees vary according to class time, course load, degree level, location, program, and reciprocity agreements. Part-time tuition: $1200 per credit hour. Part-time tuition and fees vary according to class time, location, and program. *College room only:* $3550. Room and board charges vary according to board plan. *Payment plan:* installment. *Waivers:* senior citizens and employees or children of employees.

Financial Aid Of all full-time matriculated undergraduates who enrolled in 2016, 985 applied for aid, 901 were judged to have need, 187 had their need fully met. 95 Federal Work-Study jobs (averaging $731). In 2016, 187 non-need-based awards were made. *Average percent of need met:* 73. *Average financial aid package:* $21,877. *Average need-based loan:* $8199. *Average need-based gift aid:* $5014. *Average non-need-based aid:* $10,815. *Average indebtedness upon graduation:* $31,318.

APPLYING
Standardized Tests *Required:* SAT or ACT (for admission).
Options: electronic application, early action, deferred entrance.
Required: essay or personal statement, high school transcript, minimum 2.5 GPA, 2 letters of recommendation. *Required for some:* interview.
Application deadlines: 8/15 (freshmen), 8/15 (transfers), 12/15 (early action).
Notification: continuous (freshmen), continuous (transfers), 1/15 (early action).

CONTACT
Northwest Nazarene University, 623 S. University Boulevard, Nampa, ID 83686-5897. *Phone:* 208-467-8950. *Toll-free phone:* 877-668-4968.

Stevens-Henager College
Boise, Idaho
http://www.stevenshenager.edu/
CONTACT
David Breck, Director of Admission, Stevens-Henager College, 1444 South Entertainment Avenue, Boise, ID 83709. *Phone:* 208-383-4540. *Toll-free phone:* 800-622-2640. *Fax:* 208-345-6999.

Stevens-Henager College
Idaho Falls, Idaho
http://www.stevenshenager.edu/
CONTACT
Stevens-Henager College, 901 Pier View Drive, Suite 105, Idaho Falls, ID 83402. *Toll-free phone:* 800-622-2640.

University of Idaho
Moscow, Idaho
http://www.uidaho.edu/
- **State-supported** university, founded 1889
- **Small-town** 810-acre campus
- **Endowment** $263.8 million
- **Coed** 9,885 undergraduate students, 72% full-time, 50% women, 50% men
- **Moderately difficult** entrance level, 73% of applicants were admitted

UNDERGRAD STUDENTS
7,166 full-time, 2,719 part-time. Students come from 51 states and territories; 57 other countries; 21% are from out of state; 1% Black or African American, non-Hispanic/Latino; 11% Hispanic/Latino; 2% Asian, non-Hispanic/Latino; 0.3% Native Hawaiian or other Pacific Islander, non-Hispanic/Latino; 0.6% American Indian or Alaska Native, non-Hispanic/Latino; 4% Two or more races, non-Hispanic/Latino; 7% Race/ethnicity unknown; 4% international; 6% transferred in; 36% live on campus.

Freshmen:
Admission: 7,087 applied, 5,180 admitted, 1,538 enrolled. *Average high school GPA:* 3.4. *Test scores:* SAT evidence-based reading and writing scores over 500: 82%; SAT math scores over 500: 76%; ACT scores over 18: 90%; SAT evidence-based reading and writing scores over 600: 38%; SAT math scores over 600: 30%; ACT scores over 24: 48%; SAT evidence-based reading and writing scores over 700: 7%; SAT math scores over 700: 5%; ACT scores over 30: 9%.
Retention: 82% of full-time freshmen returned.

FACULTY
Total: 798, 85% full-time, 82% with terminal degrees.
Student/faculty ratio: 14:1.

ACADEMICS
Calendar: semesters. *Degrees:* certificates, bachelor's, master's, doctoral, post-master's, and postbachelor's certificates.

Special study options: academic remediation for entering students, accelerated degree program, adult/continuing education programs, advanced placement credit, cooperative education, distance learning, double majors, English as a second language, honors programs, independent study, internships, off-campus study, part-time degree program, services for LD students, study abroad, summer session for credit. *ROTC:* Army (b), Navy (b), Air Force (c).

Unusual degree programs: architecture.

Computers: 510 computers/terminals are available on campus for general student use. Students can access the following: campus intranet, computer help desk, free student e-mail accounts, online (class) grades, online (class) registration, online (class) schedules. Campuswide network is available. 100% of college-owned or -operated housing units are wired for high-speed Internet access. Wireless service is available via entire campus.
Library: University of Idaho Library plus 1 other. *Books:* 1.5 million (physical), 876,025 (digital/electronic); *Serial titles:* 143,154 (physical), 189,954 (digital/electronic).

STUDENT LIFE
Housing options: on-campus residence required for freshman year; coed, men-only, women-only, cooperative, special housing for students with disabilities. Campus housing is university owned. Freshman campus housing is guaranteed.

Activities and organizations: drama/theater group, student-run newspaper, radio and television station, choral group, marching band, Student Alumni Relations Board (SARB), Associate Students University of Idaho (ASUI), Vandal Volunteers Club, Earth Club, Gender and Sexuality Alliance, national fraternities, national sororities.

Athletics Member NCAA. All Division I except football (Division I-A). *Intercollegiate sports:* basketball M(s)/W(s), cross-country running M(s)/W(s), golf M(s)/W(s), soccer W(s), swimming and diving W(s), tennis M(s)/W(s), track and field M(s)/W(s), volleyball W(s). *Intramural sports:* badminton M/W, baseball M, basketball M/W, cheerleading M, equestrian sports M(c)/W(c), football M, golf M/W, ice hockey M(c)/W(c), lacrosse M(c)/W(c), racquetball M/W, rock climbing M(c)/W(c), rugby M(c)/W(c), sand volleyball M/W, skiing (cross-country) M/W, skiing (downhill) M(c)/W(c), soccer M/W, softball M/W, swimming and diving M/W, table tennis M/W, tennis M/W, track and field M/W, ultimate Frisbee M/W, volleyball M/W, water polo M(c)/W(c), weight lifting M/W, wrestling M.

Campus security: 24-hour emergency response devices and patrols, late-night transport/escort service, controlled dormitory access, contracted services with the city of Moscow police department.

Student services: health clinic, personal/psychological counseling, women's center.

COSTS & FINANCIAL AID

Costs (2017–18) *Tuition:* state resident $5346 full-time, $312 per credit hour part-time; nonresident $21,670 full-time, $1129 per credit hour part-time. Full-time tuition and fees vary according to course load, program, and reciprocity agreements. Part-time tuition and fees vary according to program and reciprocity agreements. *Required fees:* $2142 full-time, $62 per credit hour part-time. *Room and board:* $8670. Room and board charges vary according to board plan and housing facility. *Payment plan:* installment. *Waivers:* employees or children of employees.

Financial Aid Of all full-time matriculated undergraduates who enrolled in 2016, 6,228 applied for aid, 5,050 were judged to have need, 1,573 had their need fully met. 464 Federal Work-Study jobs (averaging $1335). 146 state and other part-time jobs (averaging $1486). In 2016, 1675 non-need-based awards were made. *Average percent of need met:* 78. *Average financial aid package:* $13,785. *Average need-based loan:* $6671. *Average need-based gift aid:* $4596. *Average non-need-based aid:* $5239. *Average indebtedness upon graduation:* $25,145.

APPLYING

Standardized Tests *Required:* SAT or ACT (for admission).

Options: electronic application, deferred entrance.

Application fee: $60.

Required: high school transcript, minimum 2.2 GPA. *Required for some:* essay or personal statement.

Application deadlines: 8/1 (freshmen), rolling (transfers).

Notification: continuous (freshmen), continuous (transfers).

CONTACT

Ms. Melissa Goodwin, Associate Director, Admissions, University of Idaho, 875 Perimeter Drive, MS 4264, Moscow, ID 83844-4264. *Phone:* 208-885-6326. *Toll-free phone:* 888-884-3246. *Fax:* 208-885-9119. *E-mail:* admissions@uidaho.edu.

ILLINOIS

Ambria College of Nursing

Hoffman Estates, Illinois

http://www.ambria.edu/

CONTACT

Ambria College of Nursing, 5210 Trillium Boulevard, Hoffman Estates, IL 60192.

American Academy of Art

Chicago, Illinois

http://www.aaart.edu/

- **Independent** 4-year, founded 1923
- **Urban** campus with easy access to Chicago
- **Coed** 260 undergraduate students, 74% full-time, 62% women, 38% men
- **Moderately difficult** entrance level

UNDERGRAD STUDENTS

193 full-time, 67 part-time. Students come from 7 states and territories; 18% are from out of state; 10% Black or African American, non-Hispanic/Latino; 36% Hispanic/Latino; 4% Asian, non-Hispanic/Latino; 0.8% Native Hawaiian or other Pacific Islander, non-Hispanic/Latino; 0.4% American Indian or Alaska Native, non-Hispanic/Latino; 5% Two or more races, non-Hispanic/Latino; 2% transferred in.

Freshmen:
Admission: 56 enrolled.
Retention: 75% of full-time freshmen returned.

FACULTY

Total: 26, 100% full-time, 4% with terminal degrees.

Student/faculty ratio: 14:1.

ACADEMICS

Calendar: semesters. *Degree:* bachelor's.

Special study options: academic remediation for entering students, accelerated degree program, adult/continuing education programs, independent study, internships, part-time degree program, study abroad, summer session for credit.

Library: Irving Shapiro Library.

STUDENT LIFE

Housing options: Campus housing is leased by the school.

Campus security: 24-hour emergency response devices.

COSTS & FINANCIAL AID

Costs (2017–18) *Tuition:* $1025 per credit hour part-time. Full-time tuition and fees vary according to course load. Part-time tuition and fees vary according to course load. *Payment plan:* installment. *Waivers:* employees or children of employees.

Financial Aid *Average percent of need met:* 70.

APPLYING

Options: electronic application.

Application fee: $25.

Required: high school transcript, interview.

Application deadlines: rolling (freshmen), rolling (transfers).

CONTACT

Mr. Stuart Rosenbloom, Director of Admissions, American Academy of Art, 332 South Michigan Avenue, Suite 300, Chicago, IL 60604-4302. *Phone:* 312-461-0600 Ext. 129. *Toll-free phone:* 888-461-0600. *E-mail:* srosenbloom@aaart.edu.

American InterContinental University Online

Schaumburg, Illinois

http://www.aiuniv.edu/

CONTACT

Jennifer Ziegenmier, Senior Vice President of Admissions and Marketing, American InterContinental University Online, 231 N. Martingale Road, 6th Floor, Schaumburg, IL 60173. *Phone:* 877-564-6248. *Toll-free phone:* 877-701-3800. *E-mail:* jziegenmier@aiuonline.edu.

Argosy University, Chicago

Chicago, Illinois

http://www.argosy.edu/chicago-illinois/default.aspx

CONTACT

Argosy University, Chicago, 225 North Michigan Avenue, Suite 1300, Chicago, IL 60601. *Phone:* 312-777-7600. *Toll-free phone:* 800-626-4123.

Argosy University, Schaumburg

Schaumburg, Illinois

http://www.argosy.edu/locations/chicago-schaumburg/

CONTACT
Argosy University, Schaumburg, 999 North Plaza Drive, Suite 111, Schaumburg, IL 60173-5403. *Phone:* 847-969-4900. *Toll-free phone:* 866-290-2777.

Augustana College

Rock Island, Illinois

http://www.augustana.edu/

- **Independent** 4-year, founded 1860, affiliated with Evangelical Lutheran Church in America
- **Suburban** 115-acre campus
- **Endowment** $168.8 million
- **Coed** 2,647 undergraduate students, 100% full-time, 58% women, 42% men
- **Moderately difficult** entrance level, 59% of applicants were admitted

UNDERGRAD STUDENTS
2,637 full-time, 10 part-time. Students come from 32 states and territories; 42 other countries; 15% are from out of state; 4% Black or African American, non-Hispanic/Latino; 10% Hispanic/Latino; 2% Asian, non-Hispanic/Latino; 0.2% Native Hawaiian or other Pacific Islander, non-Hispanic/Latino; 3% Two or more races, non-Hispanic/Latino; 0.9% Race/ethnicity unknown; 7% international; 2% transferred in; 71% live on campus.

Freshmen:
Admission: 6,739 applied, 3,976 admitted, 735 enrolled. *Average high school GPA:* 3.3.
Retention: 87% of full-time freshmen returned.

FACULTY
Total: 264, 74% full-time.
Student/faculty ratio: 12:1.

ACADEMICS
Calendar: quarters. *Degree:* bachelor's.
Special study options: advanced placement credit, double majors, English as a second language, honors programs, independent study, internships, off-campus study, part-time degree program, services for LD students, student-designed majors, study abroad, summer session for credit.
Unusual degree programs: 3-2 engineering with Washington University in St. Louis, Northern Illinois University; forestry with Duke University; nursing with Trinity College; accounting with Wake Forest University, occupational therapy and/or physical therapy with Washington University in St. Louis, landscape architecture and veterinary medicine with University of Illinois, optometry with Illinois College of Optometry, pre-Law with Capital University.
Computers: 600 computers/terminals and 1,800 ports are available on campus for general student use. Students can access the following: campus intranet, computer help desk, free student e-mail accounts, online (class) grades, online (class) registration, online (class) schedules. Campuswide network is available. 100% of college-owned or -operated housing units are wired for high-speed Internet access. Wireless service is available via entire campus.
Library: Thomas Tredway Library plus 1 other. *Books:* 128,238 (physical), 4,470 (digital/electronic); *Serial titles:* 233 (physical), 120,219 (digital/electronic); *Databases:* 106. Weekly public service hours: 100.

STUDENT LIFE
Housing options: on-campus residence required through junior year; coed. Campus housing is university owned. Freshman campus housing is guaranteed.
Activities and organizations: drama/theater group, student-run newspaper, radio station, choral group, College Union Board of Managers, Student Government Association, student newspaper, student radio station, service organizations (APO, Dance Marathon committee).
Athletics Member NCAA. All Division III. *Intercollegiate sports:* baseball M, basketball M/W, cheerleading W(c), crew M(c)/W(c), cross-country running M/W, equestrian sports M(c)/W(c), fencing M(c)/W(c), football M, golf M/W, ice hockey M(c), lacrosse M/W, soccer M/W, softball W, swimming and diving M/W, tennis M/W, track and field M/W, ultimate Frisbee M(c)/W(c), volleyball M(c)/W, water polo M(c)/W(c), wrestling M. *Intramural sports:* badminton M/W, basketball M/W, bowling M/W, cross-country running M/W, football M/W, golf M/W, racquetball M/W, rugby M, skiing (cross-country) M/W, skiing (downhill) M/W, soccer M/W, softball M/W, swimming and diving M/W, table tennis M/W, tennis M/W, track and field M/W, ultimate Frisbee M/W, volleyball M/W, wrestling M.

Campus security: 24-hour emergency response devices and patrols, late-night transport/escort service, controlled dormitory access.
Student services: personal/psychological counseling.

COSTS & FINANCIAL AID
Costs (2018–19) *Comprehensive fee:* $52,707 includes full-time tuition ($42,135) and room and board ($10,572). Part-time tuition: $1808 per credit. Part-time tuition and fees vary according to course load. *College room only:* $5079. Room and board charges vary according to board plan and housing facility. *Payment plans:* tuition prepayment, installment. *Waivers:* employees or children of employees.
Financial Aid Of all full-time matriculated undergraduates who enrolled in 2016, 2,265 applied for aid, 1,928 were judged to have need, 426 had their need fully met. 1,313 Federal Work-Study jobs (averaging $2339). In 2016, 570 non-need-based awards were made. *Average percent of need met:* 86. *Average financial aid package:* $30,840. *Average need-based loan:* $4825. *Average need-based gift aid:* $24,787. *Average non-need-based aid:* $21,096. *Average indebtedness upon graduation:* $34,964.

APPLYING
Options: electronic application, early admission, early decision, early action, deferred entrance.
Required: high school transcript. *Required for some:* essay or personal statement, interview. *Recommended:* essay or personal statement, 1 letter of recommendation, interview.
Application deadlines: rolling (freshmen), rolling (out-of-state freshmen), rolling (transfers), 11/1 (early action).
Early decision deadline: 11/1.
Notification: continuous (freshmen), continuous (out-of-state freshmen), continuous (transfers), 11/15 (early decision), 12/1 (early action).

CONTACT
W. Kent Barnds, Vice President of Enrollment Management, Augustana College, 639 38th Street, Rock Island, IL 61201. *Phone:* 309-794-7662. *Toll-free phone:* 800-798-8100. *Fax:* 309-794-8797. *E-mail:* admissions@augustana.edu.

Aurora University

Aurora, Illinois

http://www.aurora.edu/

- **Independent** comprehensive, founded 1893
- **Suburban** 70-acre campus with easy access to Chicago
- **Endowment** $43.1 million
- **Coed** 3,933 undergraduate students, 88% full-time, 65% women, 35% men
- **Moderately difficult** entrance level, 87% of applicants were admitted

UNDERGRAD STUDENTS
3,461 full-time, 472 part-time. Students come from 39 states and territories; 4 other countries; 12% are from out of state; 8% Black or African American, non-Hispanic/Latino; 30% Hispanic/Latino; 2% Asian, non-Hispanic/Latino; 0.2% Native Hawaiian or other Pacific Islander, non-Hispanic/Latino; 0.4% American Indian or Alaska Native, non-Hispanic/Latino; 3% Two or more races, non-Hispanic/Latino; 6% Race/ethnicity unknown; 0.3% international; 14% transferred in; 18% live on campus.

Freshmen:
Admission: 3,061 applied, 2,673 admitted, 801 enrolled. *Average high school GPA:* 3.3. *Test scores:* SAT evidence-based reading and writing scores over 500: 62%; SAT math scores over 500: 60%; ACT scores over 18: 93%; SAT evidence-based reading and writing scores over 600: 13%; SAT math scores over 600: 15%; ACT scores over 24: 25%; SAT evidence-based reading and writing scores over 700: 1%; ACT scores over 30: 1%.

Retention: 74% of full-time freshmen returned.

FACULTY
Total: 451, 31% full-time.
Student/faculty ratio: 18:1.

ACADEMICS
Calendar: semesters. *Degrees:* bachelor's, master's, doctoral, and post-master's certificates.

Special study options: academic remediation for entering students, accelerated degree program, adult/continuing education programs, advanced placement credit, distance learning, double majors, independent study, internships, off-campus study, part-time degree program, services for LD students, student-designed majors, study abroad, summer session for credit. *ROTC:* Army (c).

Computers: 254 computers/terminals are available on campus for general student use. Students can access the following: campus intranet, computer help desk, free student e-mail accounts, online (class) grades, online (class) registration, online (class) schedules, learning management system. Campuswide network is available. 100% of college-owned or -operated housing units are wired for high-speed Internet access. Wireless service is available via classrooms, computer labs, dorm rooms, learning centers, libraries, student centers.

Library: Charles B. Phillips Library plus 1 other. *Books:* 14,969 (physical), 160,012 (digital/electronic); *Serial titles:* 46,444 (digital/electronic); *Databases:* 61. Weekly public service hours: 96; students can reserve study rooms.

STUDENT LIFE
Housing options: coed. Campus housing is university owned. Freshman applicants given priority for college housing.

Activities and organizations: drama/theater group, student-run newspaper, radio and television station, choral group, Latin American Student Organization, American Marketing Association, Student Nursing Association, Phi Eta Sigma, Spartan Athletic Training Student Organization, national fraternities, national sororities.

Athletics Member NCAA. All Division III. *Intercollegiate sports:* baseball M, basketball M/W, bowling W, cross-country running M/W, football M, golf M/W, ice hockey M/W, lacrosse M/W, soccer M/W, softball W, tennis M/W, track and field M/W, volleyball W. *Intramural sports:* badminton M/W, basketball M/W, cheerleading W(c), football M/W, ice hockey M(c), racquetball M/W, soccer M/W, softball M/W, table tennis M/W, ultimate Frisbee M/W, volleyball M/W.

Campus security: 24-hour emergency response devices and patrols, late-night transport/escort service, controlled dormitory access.

Student services: health clinic, personal/psychological counseling.

COSTS & FINANCIAL AID
Costs (2018–19) **Comprehensive fee:** $35,960 includes full-time tuition ($24,000), mandatory fees ($260), and room and board ($11,700). Full-time tuition and fees vary according to course load, location, and program. Part-time tuition: $690 per semester hour. Part-time tuition and fees vary according to course load, location, and program. *Room and board:* Room and board charges vary according to board plan, housing facility, and location. *Payment plans:* installment, deferred payment. *Waivers:* children of alumni and employees or children of employees.

Financial Aid Of all full-time matriculated undergraduates who enrolled in 2017, 2,989 applied for aid, 2,790 were judged to have need, 262 had their need fully met. 2,030 Federal Work-Study jobs (averaging $1906). 33 state and other part-time jobs (averaging $9644). In 2017, 587 non-need-based awards were made. *Average percent of need met:* 78. *Average financial aid package:* $20,674. *Average need-based loan:* $3521. *Average need-based gift aid:* $14,929. *Average non-need-based aid:* $10,241. *Average indebtedness upon graduation:* $27,117.

APPLYING
Standardized Tests *Required:* SAT or ACT (for admission).

Options: electronic application, deferred entrance.

Required: high school transcript, minimum 2.0 GPA. *Required for some:* essay or personal statement, 2 letters of recommendation, interview.

Application deadlines: rolling (freshmen), rolling (transfers).

Notification: continuous (freshmen), continuous (transfers).

CONTACT
Mr. James Lancaster, Vice President for Enrollment, Aurora University, 347 South Gladstone Avenue, Aurora, IL 60506-4892. *Phone:* 630-844-5533. *Toll-free phone:* 800-742-5281. *Fax:* 630-844-5535. *E-mail:* admission@aurora.edu.

Benedictine University
Lisle, Illinois
http://www.ben.edu/

- **Independent Roman Catholic** comprehensive, founded 1887
- **Suburban** 108-acre campus with easy access to Chicago
- **Endowment** $33.8 million
- **Coed** 2,885 undergraduate students, 86% full-time, 48% women, 52% men
- **Moderately difficult** entrance level, 62% of applicants were admitted

UNDERGRAD STUDENTS
2,473 full-time, 412 part-time. Students come from 49 states and territories; 16 other countries; 7% are from out of state; 8% Black or African American, non-Hispanic/Latino; 17% Hispanic/Latino; 15% Asian, non-Hispanic/Latino; 0.3% Native Hawaiian or other Pacific Islander, non-Hispanic/Latino; 0.6% American Indian or Alaska Native, non-Hispanic/Latino; 14% Race/ethnicity unknown; 0.8% international; 13% transferred in; 22% live on campus.

Freshmen:
Admission: 5,334 applied, 3,318 admitted, 423 enrolled. *Average high school GPA:* 3.3. *Test scores:* ACT scores over 18: 90%; ACT scores over 24: 36%; ACT scores over 30: 6%.

Retention: 73% of full-time freshmen returned.

FACULTY
Total: 585, 27% full-time, 51% with terminal degrees.
Student/faculty ratio: 12:1.

ACADEMICS
Calendar: semesters. *Degrees:* certificates, diplomas, bachelor's, master's, doctoral, and postbachelor's certificates.

Special study options: academic remediation for entering students, accelerated degree program, adult/continuing education programs, advanced placement credit, distance learning, double majors, English as a second language, honors programs, independent study, internships, off-campus study, part-time degree program, services for LD students, study abroad, summer session for credit. *ROTC:* Army (c).

Unusual degree programs: 3-2 engineering with University of Illinois at Urbana–Champaign, Illinois Institute of Technology, Purdue University; nursing with Rush University.

Computers: 275 computers/terminals and 275 ports are available on campus for general student use. Students can access the following: computer help desk, free student e-mail accounts, online (class) grades, online (class) registration, online (class) schedules. Campuswide network is available. 100% of college-owned or -operated housing units are wired for high-speed Internet access. Wireless service is available via entire campus.

Library: Benedictine Library. *Books:* 110,801 (physical), 119,224 (digital/electronic); *Serial titles:* 1,498 (physical), 127,691 (digital/electronic); *Databases:* 86. Weekly public service hours: 83; students can reserve study rooms.

STUDENT LIFE
Housing options: coed, men-only, women-only, special housing for students with disabilities. Campus housing is university owned. Freshman campus housing is guaranteed.

Activities and organizations: student-run newspaper, radio and television station, choral group, Student Senate, MSA-Muslim Student Association, AMSA-American Medical Student Association, The Candor-Student Newspaper, Programming Board.

Athletics Member NCAA. All Division III. *Intercollegiate sports:* baseball M, basketball M/W, cross-country running M/W, golf M/W, lacrosse M/W, soccer M/W, softball W, track and field M/W, volleyball W. *Intramural sports:* basketball M/W, bowling M/W, cheerleading W(c), football M, lacrosse M(c), softball M/W, table tennis M/W, volleyball M/W.

Campus security: 24-hour emergency response devices and patrols, late-night transport/escort service, controlled dormitory access.

Student services: health clinic, personal/psychological counseling.

COSTS & FINANCIAL AID

Costs (2018–19) *Comprehensive fee:* $43,770 includes full-time tuition ($32,700), mandatory fees ($1590), and room and board ($9480). Full-time tuition and fees vary according to course load, degree level, and location. Part-time tuition: $1090 per credit hour. Part-time tuition and fees vary according to course load, degree level, and location. *Required fees:* $60 per credit hour part-time. *College room only:* $7800. Room and board charges vary according to board plan, housing facility, and location. *Payment plan:* installment. *Waivers:* employees or children of employees.

Financial Aid Of all full-time matriculated undergraduates who enrolled in 2017, 2,074 applied for aid, 1,973 were judged to have need. In 2017, 370 non-need-based awards were made. *Average financial aid package:* $23,183. *Average need-based loan:* $4594. *Average need-based gift aid:* $8392. *Average non-need-based aid:* $12,349. *Average indebtedness upon graduation:* $23,959.

APPLYING

Standardized Tests *Required:* SAT or ACT (for admission).

Options: electronic application, deferred entrance.

Application fee: $40.

Required: essay or personal statement, high school transcript. *Required for some:* interview. *Recommended:* rank in upper 50% of high school class.

Application deadlines: rolling (freshmen), rolling (out-of-state freshmen), rolling (transfers), rolling (early action).

Early decision deadline: rolling (for plan 1), rolling (for plan 2).

Notification: continuous (freshmen), continuous (transfers), rolling (early decision plan 1), rolling (early decision plan 2), rolling (early action).

CONTACT

Mr. Edward Robinson, Vice President for Enrollment Management, Benedictine University, 5700 College Road, Lisle, IL 60532-0900. *Toll-free phone:* 888-829-6363. *E-mail:* admissions@ben.edu.

Blackburn College

Carlinville, Illinois

http://www.blackburn.edu/

- **Independent Presbyterian** 4-year, founded 1837
- **Small-town** 80-acre campus with easy access to St. Louis
- **Endowment** $18.8 million
- **Coed** 596 undergraduate students, 96% full-time, 54% women, 46% men
- **Moderately difficult** entrance level, 52% of applicants were admitted

UNDERGRAD STUDENTS

572 full-time, 24 part-time. Students come from 22 states and territories; 4 other countries; 11% are from out of state; 12% Black or African American, non-Hispanic/Latino; 3% Hispanic/Latino; 0.9% Asian, non-Hispanic/Latino; 0.2% Native Hawaiian or other Pacific Islander, non-Hispanic/Latino; 0.2% American Indian or Alaska Native, non-Hispanic/Latino; 4% Two or more races, non-Hispanic/Latino; 2% Race/ethnicity unknown; 1% international; 7% transferred in; 69% live on campus.

Freshmen:

Admission: 1,001 applied, 517 admitted, 170 enrolled. *Average high school GPA:* 3.3. *Test scores:* ACT scores over 18: 78%; ACT scores over 24: 21%; ACT scores over 30: 2%.

Retention: 65% of full-time freshmen returned.

FACULTY

Total: 68, 47% full-time, 47% with terminal degrees.

Student/faculty ratio: 13:1.

ACADEMICS

Calendar: semesters. *Degree:* bachelor's.

Special study options: advanced placement credit, cooperative education, double majors, honors programs, independent study, internships, off-campus study, services for LD students, student-designed majors, study abroad, summer session for credit.

Unusual degree programs: 3-2 engineering with Washington University in St. Louis, University of Missouri–Kansas City; nursing with St. John's College (Springfield).

Computers: 202 computers/terminals are available on campus for general student use. Students can access the following: computer help desk, free student e-mail accounts, online (class) grades, online (class) registration, online (class) schedules. Campuswide network is available. 100% of college-owned or -operated housing units are wired for high-speed Internet access. Wireless service is available via entire campus.

Library: Lumpkin Learning Commons. *Books:* 62,000 (physical); *Serial titles:* 40 (physical); *Databases:* 21. Weekly public service hours: 80; students can reserve study rooms.

STUDENT LIFE

Housing options: on-campus residence required through junior year; coed, women-only. Campus housing is university owned. Freshman campus housing is guaranteed.

Activities and organizations: drama/theater group, student-run newspaper, radio station, choral group, Habitat for Humanity, Pre-Health Professions, Running Club, Trading Card Games, Spectrum.

Athletics Member NCAA. All Division III. *Intercollegiate sports:* baseball M, basketball M/W, cross-country running M/W, golf M, soccer M/W, softball W, tennis W, volleyball W. *Intramural sports:* badminton M/W, basketball M/W, football M/W, golf M/W, racquetball M/W, soccer M/W, softball M/W, table tennis M/W, tennis M/W, ultimate Frisbee M/W, volleyball M/W.

Campus security: student patrols, late-night transport/escort service.

Student services: personal/psychological counseling.

COSTS & FINANCIAL AID

Costs (2017–18) *Comprehensive fee:* $29,652 includes full-time tuition ($21,582), mandatory fees ($410), and room and board ($7660). Full-time tuition and fees vary according to student level. Part-time tuition: $720 per credit hour. Part-time tuition and fees vary according to student level. *Required fees:* $190 per year part-time. *College room only:* $4448. Room and board charges vary according to board plan. *Payment plan:* installment. *Waivers:* employees or children of employees.

Financial Aid Of all full-time matriculated undergraduates who enrolled in 2009, 581 applied for aid, 502 were judged to have need, 194 had their need fully met. 388 Federal Work-Study jobs (averaging $2653). 113 state and other part-time jobs (averaging $2337). In 2009, 62 non-need-based awards were made. *Average percent of need met:* 80. *Average financial aid package:* $13,873. *Average need-based loan:* $4107. *Average need-based gift aid:* $11,209. *Average non-need-based aid:* $5163. *Average indebtedness upon graduation:* $20,077.

APPLYING

Standardized Tests *Required:* SAT or ACT (for admission).

Options: electronic application, deferred entrance.

Required: high school transcript, minimum 2.0 GPA. *Required for some:* essay or personal statement, 3 letters of recommendation, interview. *Recommended:* minimum 2.5 GPA.

Application deadlines: rolling (freshmen), rolling (transfers).

Notification: continuous (freshmen), continuous (transfers).

CONTACT

Mrs. Alisha Kapp, Director of Admission, Blackburn College, 700 College Avenue, Carlinville, IL 62626. *Phone:* 217-854-5110. *Toll-free phone:* 800-233-3550. *E-mail:* alisha.kapp@blackburn.edu.

Blessing-Rieman College of Nursing & Health Sciences

Quincy, Illinois

http://www.brcn.edu/

CONTACT

Ms. Heather Mutter, Admissions Counselor, Blessing-Rieman College of Nursing & Health Sciences, Broadway at 11th Street, POB 7005, Quincy, IL 62305-7005. *Phone:* 217-228-5520 Ext. 6979. *Toll-free phone:* 800-877-9140. *Fax:* 217-223-4661. *E-mail:* admissions@brcn.edu.

★ Bradley University

Peoria, Illinois
http://www.bradley.edu/

- **Independent** comprehensive, founded 1897
- **Suburban** 85-acre campus
- **Endowment** $299.8 million
- **Coed** 4,649 undergraduate students, 97% full-time, 51% women, 49% men
- **Moderately difficult** entrance level, 71% of applicants were admitted

UNDERGRAD STUDENTS

4,512 full-time, 137 part-time. Students come from 37 states and territories; 38 other countries; 18% are from out of state; 7% Black or African American, non-Hispanic/Latino; 10% Hispanic/Latino; 4% Asian, non-Hispanic/Latino; 0.1% American Indian or Alaska Native, non-Hispanic/Latino; 2% Two or more races, non-Hispanic/Latino; 2% Race/ethnicity unknown; 2% international; 5% transferred in; 62% live on campus.

Freshmen:

Admission: 10,232 applied, 7,303 admitted, 1,265 enrolled. *Average high school GPA:* 3.6. *Test scores:* SAT evidence-based reading and writing scores over 500: 91%; SAT math scores over 500: 88%; ACT scores over 18: 100%; SAT evidence-based reading and writing scores over 600: 53%; SAT math scores over 600: 43%; ACT scores over 24: 63%; SAT evidence-based reading and writing scores over 700: 7%; SAT math scores over 700: 10%; ACT scores over 30: 13%.

Retention: 87% of full-time freshmen returned.

FACULTY

Total: 603, 59% full-time, 47% with terminal degrees.
Student/faculty ratio: 12:1.

ACADEMICS

Calendar: semesters. *Degrees:* bachelor's, master's, doctoral, post-master's, and postbachelor's certificates.

Special study options: accelerated degree program, advanced placement credit, cooperative education, distance learning, double majors, honors programs, independent study, internships, off-campus study, part-time degree program, services for LD students, student-designed majors, study abroad, summer session for credit. *ROTC:* Army (b).

Computers: 80 computers/terminals and 3,123 ports are available on campus for general student use. Students can access the following: campus intranet, computer help desk, free student e-mail accounts, online (class) grades, online (class) registration, online (class) schedules, Online directory, catalog, library materials and other resources. Campuswide network is available. 100% of college-owned or -operated housing units are wired for high-speed Internet access. Wireless service is available via entire campus.

Library: Cullom-Davis Library. *Books:* 377,381 (physical), 33,819 (digital/electronic); *Serial titles:* 228 (physical), 55,411 (digital/electronic); *Databases:* 54. Weekly public service hours: 108; students can reserve study rooms.

STUDENT LIFE

Housing options: on-campus residence required through sophomore year; coed. Campus housing is university owned, leased by the school and is provided by a third party. Freshman campus housing is guaranteed.

Activities and organizations: drama/theater group, student-run newspaper, radio and television station, choral group, Activities Council of Bradley University, CRU (Campus Christian group), Fraternity/Sorority Life, Service on Saturday, Alpha Phi Omega (Coed Service), national fraternities, national sororities.

Athletics Member NCAA. All Division I. *Intercollegiate sports:* baseball M(s), basketball M(s)/W(s), cheerleading M/W, cross-country running M(s)/W(s), golf M(s)/W(s), soccer M(s), softball W(s), table tennis M(c), tennis W(s), track and field M(s)/W(s), volleyball M(c)/W(s), wrestling M(c). *Intramural sports:* badminton M/W, baseball M(c), basketball M/W, bowling M/W, fencing M(c)/W(c), football M/W, golf M/W, ice hockey M(c), lacrosse M(c)/W(c), racquetball M/W, rock climbing M(c)/W(c), soccer M(c)/W(c), softball M/W(c), swimming and diving M/W, table tennis M/W, tennis M/W, triathlon M(c)/W(c), ultimate Frisbee M(c)/W(c), volleyball M/W, water polo M(c)/W(c), wrestling M/W.

Campus security: 24-hour emergency response devices and patrols, student patrols, late-night transport/escort service, controlled dormitory access, emergency text messaging, mass notification/emergency communication system in 20 academic buildings.

Student services: health clinic, personal/psychological counseling.

COSTS & FINANCIAL AID

Costs (2017–18) *One-time required fee:* $200. *Comprehensive fee:* $43,240 includes full-time tuition ($32,540), mandatory fees ($390), and room and board ($10,310). Full-time tuition and fees vary according to course load and program. Part-time tuition: $870 per credit hour. Part-time tuition and fees vary according to course load and program. *Required fees:* $390 per year part-time. *College room only:* $5960. Room and board charges vary according to board plan and housing facility. *Payment plans:* installment, deferred payment. *Waivers:* senior citizens and employees or children of employees.

Financial Aid Of all full-time matriculated undergraduates who enrolled in 2017, 3,784 applied for aid, 3,239 were judged to have need, 499 had their need fully met. 388 Federal Work-Study jobs (averaging $1961). In 2017, 1218 non-need-based awards were made. *Average percent of need met:* 72. *Average financial aid package:* $23,839. *Average need-based loan:* $6388. *Average need-based gift aid:* $18,905. *Average non-need-based aid:* $11,754. *Average indebtedness upon graduation:* $28,432.

APPLYING

Standardized Tests *Required:* SAT or ACT (for admission).

Options: electronic application, deferred entrance.

Application fee: $35.

Required: essay or personal statement, high school transcript. *Required for some:* audition required of music majors and recommended for theatre majors, portfolio recommended for art majors. *Recommended:* minimum 2.8 GPA, 1 letter of recommendation, interview.

Application deadlines: rolling (freshmen), rolling (transfers).

Notification: continuous (freshmen), continuous (transfers).

CONTACT

Dr. Justin Ball, Vice President for Enrollment Management, Bradley University, 1501 W. Bradley Avenue, Peoria, IL 61625. *Phone:* 309-677-1000. *Toll-free phone:* 800-447-6460. *Fax:* 309-677-2797. *E-mail:* admissions@bradley.edu.

Chamberlain College of Nursing

Addison, Illinois
http://www.chamberlain.edu/

- **Proprietary** comprehensive
- **Coed**

FACULTY
Student/faculty ratio: 24:1.

ACADEMICS
Calendar: semesters. *Degrees:* bachelor's, master's, doctoral, and post-master's certificates.

STUDENT LIFE
Housing options: college housing not available.

COSTS
Costs (2017–18) *Tuition:* $18,900 full-time. *Required fees:* $600 full-time.

APPLYING
Standardized Tests *Required:* SAT or ACT (for admission).

Options: deferred entrance.

Application fee: $95.

CONTACT
Admissions, Chamberlain College of Nursing, 1221 North Swift Road, Addison, IL 60101. *Phone:* 630-953-3680. *Toll-free phone:* 877-751-5783.

Chamberlain College of Nursing

Chicago, Illinois
http://www.chamberlain.edu/
- **Proprietary** 4-year
- **Coed**

FACULTY
Student/faculty ratio: 11:1.

ACADEMICS
Calendar: semesters. *Degree:* bachelor's.

STUDENT LIFE
Housing options: college housing not available.

COSTS
Costs (2017–18) *Tuition:* $18,900 full-time. *Required fees:* $600 full-time.

APPLYING
Standardized Tests *Required:* SAT or ACT (for admission).
Options: deferred entrance.
Application fee: $95.

CONTACT
Admissions, Chamberlain College of Nursing, 3300 North Campbell Avenue, Chicago, IL 60618. *Phone:* 773-961-3000. *Toll-free phone:* 877-751-5783.

Chamberlain College of Nursing

Tinley Park, Illinois
http://www.chamberlain.edu/
- **Proprietary** 4-year
- **Coed**

FACULTY
Student/faculty ratio: 11:1.

ACADEMICS
Degree: bachelor's.

STUDENT LIFE
Housing options: college housing not available.

COSTS
Costs (2017–18) *Tuition:* $18,900 full-time. *Required fees:* $600 full-time.

APPLYING
Standardized Tests *Required:* SAT or ACT (for admission).
Options: deferred entrance.
Application fee: $95.

CONTACT
Chamberlain College of Nursing, 18624 West Creek Drive, Tinley Park, IL 60477. *Toll-free phone:* 877-751-5783.

Chicago State University

Chicago, Illinois
http://www.csu.edu/

CONTACT
Mr. John Martinez, Associate Director of Admissions, Chicago State University, 95th Street at King Drive, ADM 200, Chicago, IL 60628. *Phone:* 773-995-3578. *Fax:* 773-995-3820. *E-mail:* jmarti21@csu.edu.

Columbia College Chicago

Chicago, Illinois
http://www.colum.edu/
- **Independent** comprehensive, founded 1890
- **Urban** campus with easy access to Chicago
- **Coed** 7,027 undergraduate students, 92% full-time, 54% women, 46% men
- **Minimally difficult** entrance level, 92% of applicants were admitted

UNDERGRAD STUDENTS
6,436 full-time, 591 part-time. Students come from 56 states and territories; 51 other countries; 46% are from out of state; 13% Black or African American, non-Hispanic/Latino; 15% Hispanic/Latino; 4% Asian, non-Hispanic/Latino; 0.1% Native Hawaiian or other Pacific Islander, non-Hispanic/Latino; 0.2% American Indian or Alaska Native, non-Hispanic/Latino; 4% Two or more races, non-Hispanic/Latino; 5% Race/ethnicity unknown; 4% international; 10% transferred in; 32% live on campus.

Freshmen:
Admission: 8,117 applied, 7,438 admitted, 1,443 enrolled. *Average high school GPA:* 3.3. *Test scores:* ACT scores over 18: 89%; ACT scores over 24: 44%; ACT scores over 30: 7%.
Retention: 66% of full-time freshmen returned.

FACULTY
Total: 979, 28% full-time.
Student/faculty ratio: 14:1.

ACADEMICS
Calendar: semesters. *Degrees:* bachelor's, master's, and postbachelor's certificates.

Special study options: academic remediation for entering students, adult/continuing education programs, advanced placement credit, cooperative education, distance learning, double majors, English as a second language, honors programs, independent study, internships, off-campus study, part-time degree program, services for LD students, study abroad, summer session for credit.

Computers: Students can access the following: campus intranet, computer help desk, free student e-mail accounts, online (class) grades, online (class) registration, online (class) schedules. Campuswide network is available. 100% of college-owned or -operated housing units are wired for high-speed Internet access. Wireless service is available via entire campus.
Library: Columbia College Chicago Library. *Books:* 295,362 (physical), 61,291 (digital/electronic); *Serial titles:* 553 (physical); *Databases:* 180. Weekly public service hours: 87; students can reserve study rooms.

STUDENT LIFE
Housing options: coed. Campus housing is university owned and leased by the school. Freshman applicants given priority for college housing.

Activities and organizations: drama/theater group, student-run newspaper, radio and television station, choral group.

Athletics *Intramural sports:* basketball M/W.

Campus security: 24-hour emergency response devices and patrols, late-night transport/escort service, controlled dormitory access.

Student services: health clinic, personal/psychological counseling.

COSTS & FINANCIAL AID
Costs (2018–19) *Comprehensive fee:* $41,321 includes full-time tuition ($26,090), mandatory fees ($1219), and room and board ($14,012). Full-time tuition and fees vary according to course load and degree level. Part-time tuition: $901 per credit hour. Part-time tuition and fees vary according to course load and degree level. *Room and board:* Room and board charges vary according to housing facility. *Payment plan:* installment. *Waivers:* employees or children of employees.

Financial Aid Of all full-time matriculated undergraduates who enrolled in 2016, 5,923 applied for aid, 4,798 were judged to have need, 936 had their need fully met. In 2016, 36 non-need-based awards were made. *Average percent of need met:* 55. *Average financial aid package:* $9862. *Average need-based gift aid:* $10,531. *Average non-need-based aid:* $19,659. *Average indebtedness upon graduation:* $33,208.

APPLYING
Options: electronic application, deferred entrance.
Application fee: $35.
Required: essay or personal statement, high school transcript. *Required for some:* digital portfolio/video audition. *Recommended:* minimum 2.0 GPA, 1 letter of recommendation, interview.

CONTACT
Columbia College Chicago, 600 South Michigan Avenue, Room 301-B, Chicago, IL 60605-1996. *Phone:* 312-369-7130. *E-mail:* admissions@colum.edu.

Concordia University Chicago

River Forest, Illinois

http://www.cuchicago.edu/

- **Independent** comprehensive, founded 1864, affiliated with Lutheran Church–Missouri Synod, part of Concordia University System
- **Suburban** 40-acre campus with easy access to Chicago
- **Coed** 1,413 undergraduate students, 92% full-time, 59% women, 41% men
- **Moderately difficult** entrance level, 75% of applicants were admitted

UNDERGRAD STUDENTS

1,301 full-time, 112 part-time. Students come from 39 states and territories; 9 other countries; 25% are from out of state; 14% Black or African American, non-Hispanic/Latino; 30% Hispanic/Latino; 3% Asian, non-Hispanic/Latino; 0.3% Native Hawaiian or other Pacific Islander, non-Hispanic/Latino; 0.3% American Indian or Alaska Native, non-Hispanic/Latino; 3% Two or more races, non-Hispanic/Latino; 2% Race/ethnicity unknown; 2% international; 8% transferred in; 36% live on campus.

Freshmen:

Admission: 4,755 applied, 3,553 admitted, 327 enrolled. *Average high school GPA:* 3.1. *Test scores:* SAT evidence-based reading and writing scores over 500: 71%; SAT math scores over 500: 78%; ACT scores over 18: 95%; SAT evidence-based reading and writing scores over 600: 28%; SAT math scores over 600: 11%; ACT scores over 24: 30%; SAT evidence-based reading and writing scores over 700: 3%; SAT math scores over 700: 2%; ACT scores over 30: 7%.

Retention: 67% of full-time freshmen returned.

FACULTY

Total: 502, 50% full-time, 59% with terminal degrees.

Student/faculty ratio: 10:1.

ACADEMICS

Calendar: semesters. *Degrees:* certificates, associate, bachelor's, master's, doctoral, and post-master's certificates.

Special study options: accelerated degree program, adult/continuing education programs, distance learning, double majors, honors programs, independent study, internships, part-time degree program, student-designed majors, study abroad.

Computers: Students can access the following: campus intranet, computer help desk, free student e-mail accounts, online (class) grades, online (class) registration, online (class) schedules. Campuswide network is available. 100% of college-owned or -operated housing units are wired for high-speed Internet access. Wireless service is available via entire campus.

Library: Klinck Memorial Library. *Books:* 160,000 (physical); *Databases:* 80. Weekly public service hours: 89; students can reserve study rooms.

STUDENT LIFE

Housing options: coed. Campus housing is university owned. Freshman campus housing is guaranteed.

Activities and organizations: drama/theater group, student-run newspaper, radio and television station, choral group, Campus Ministry, College Life, Student Government Association, Campus Activities Board, Art Club.

Athletics Member NCAA. All Division III. *Intercollegiate sports:* basketball M/W, cheerleading W, cross-country running M/W, football M, lacrosse M/W, soccer M/W, tennis M/W, track and field M/W, volleyball W. *Intramural sports:* baseball M(c), basketball M(c)/W(c), soccer M(c)/W(c), softball W(c), ultimate Frisbee M(c)/W(c), volleyball M(c)/W(c).

Campus security: 24-hour emergency response devices and patrols, student patrols, late-night transport/escort service, controlled dormitory access, emergency call boxes.

Student services: health clinic, personal/psychological counseling.

COSTS & FINANCIAL AID

Costs (2018–19) *Comprehensive fee:* $41,826 includes full-time tuition ($31,146), mandatory fees ($932), and room and board ($9748). Full-time tuition and fees vary according to course load, degree level, and reciprocity agreements. Part-time tuition: $937 per credit hour. Part-time tuition and fees vary according to course load, degree level, and reciprocity agreements. *College room only:* $6126. Room and board charges vary according to board plan and housing facility. *Payment plan:* installment. *Waivers:* children of alumni, senior citizens, and employees or children of employees.

Financial Aid Of all full-time matriculated undergraduates who enrolled in 2015, 1,265 applied for aid, 1,167 were judged to have need, 175 had their need fully met. In 2015, 141 non-need-based awards were made. *Average percent of need met:* 75. *Average financial aid package:* $20,605. *Average need-based loan:* $4264. *Average need-based gift aid:* $16,518. *Average non-need-based aid:* $13,473. *Average indebtedness upon graduation:* $32,549. *Financial aid deadline:* 6/1.

APPLYING

Standardized Tests *Required:* SAT or ACT (for admission).

Options: electronic application, early admission, deferred entrance.

Required: high school transcript, minimum 2.0 GPA, 1 letter of recommendation, general college preparatory program for degree seeking students. *Required for some:* essay or personal statement, interview.

Application deadlines: rolling (freshmen), rolling (out-of-state freshmen), rolling (transfers).

CONTACT

Ms. Gwen Kanelos, Director of Admission, Concordia University Chicago, 7400 Augusta Street, River Forest, IL 60305. *Phone:* 708-209-3101. *Toll-free phone:* 800-285-2668. *Fax:* 708-209-3473. *E-mail:* gwen.kanelos@cuchicago.edu.

DePaul University

Chicago, Illinois

http://www.depaul.edu/

- **Independent Roman Catholic** university, founded 1898
- **Urban** 38-acre campus with easy access to Chicago
- **Endowment** $492.4 million
- **Coed** 14,816 undergraduate students, 87% full-time, 52% women, 48% men
- **Moderately difficult** entrance level, 72% of applicants were admitted

UNDERGRAD STUDENTS

12,886 full-time, 1,930 part-time. Students come from 51 states and territories; 97 other countries; 24% are from out of state; 8% Black or African American, non-Hispanic/Latino; 19% Hispanic/Latino; 9% Asian, non-Hispanic/Latino; 0.2% Native Hawaiian or other Pacific Islander, non-Hispanic/Latino; 0.1% American Indian or Alaska Native, non-Hispanic/Latino; 4% Two or more races, non-Hispanic/Latino; 3% Race/ethnicity unknown; 3% international; 8% transferred in; 18% live on campus.

Freshmen:

Admission: 21,613 applied, 15,506 admitted, 2,542 enrolled. *Average high school GPA:* 3.6. *Test scores:* SAT evidence-based reading and writing scores over 500: 93%; SAT math scores over 500: 91%; ACT scores over 18: 97%; SAT evidence-based reading and writing scores over 600: 56%; SAT math scores over 600: 45%; ACT scores over 24: 66%; SAT evidence-based reading and writing scores over 700: 13%; SAT math scores over 700: 7%; ACT scores over 30: 17%.

Retention: 84% of full-time freshmen returned.

FACULTY

Total: 1,855, 49% full-time, 60% with terminal degrees.

Student/faculty ratio: 16:1.

ACADEMICS

Calendar: quarters College of Law on semester system. *Degrees:* certificates, bachelor's, master's, doctoral, post-master's, and postbachelor's certificates.

Special study options: academic remediation for entering students, accelerated degree program, adult/continuing education programs, advanced placement credit, distance learning, double majors, English as a second language, freshman honors college, honors programs, independent study, internships, off-campus study, part-time degree program, services for LD students, study abroad, summer session for credit. *ROTC:* Army (b).

Unusual degree programs: 3-2 engineering with Illinois Institute of Technology; accountancy, animation, anthropology, biological science, chemistry, communications and media, communications studies, computer game development, computer science, digital cinema, economics, English, environmental science, environmental studies, geography, health science, history, journalism, math.

Computers: Students can access the following: campus intranet, computer help desk, free student e-mail accounts, online (class) grades, online (class) registration, online (class) schedules, tuition payments, degree progress, financial aid, and transcript requests, housing services, student employment information. Campuswide network is available. 100% of college-owned or -operated housing units are wired for high-speed Internet access. Wireless service is available via entire campus.
Library: John T. Richardson Library plus 2 others. *Books:* 1.1 million (physical), 335,025 (digital/electronic); *Serial titles:* 12,015 (physical), 80,609 (digital/electronic). Students can reserve study rooms.

STUDENT LIFE
Housing options: coed, special housing for students with disabilities. Campus housing is university owned, leased by the school and is provided by a third party. Freshman applicants given priority for college housing.

Activities and organizations: drama/theater group, student-run newspaper, radio station, choral group, DePaul Fundamental Research in Academic Gaming, DePaul Community Service Association (DCSA), Black Student Union, DemonTHON, DePaul's Voices for the Animals, national fraternities, national sororities.

Athletics Member NCAA. All Division I. *Intercollegiate sports:* basketball M(s)/W(s), cross-country running M(s)/W(s), golf M(s), soccer M(s)/W(s), softball W(s), tennis M(s)/W(s), track and field M(s)/W(s), volleyball W(s). *Intramural sports:* badminton M(c)/W(c), baseball M(c)/W(c), basketball M/W(c), crew M(c)/W(c), fencing M(c)/W(c), football M/W, golf M(c)/W(c), ice hockey M(c)/W(c), lacrosse M(c)/W(c), racquetball M/W, rock climbing M(c)/W(c), rowing M(c)/W(c), rugby M(c)/W(c), sailing M(c)/W(c), skiing (downhill) M(c)/W(c), soccer M(c)/W(c), softball M/W, swimming and diving M(c)/W(c), table tennis M(c)/W(c), tennis M(c)/W(c), ultimate Frisbee M(c)/W(c), volleyball M(c)/W(c), water polo M(c)/W(c).

Campus security: 24-hour emergency response devices and patrols, late-night transport/escort service, controlled dormitory access, security lighting, prevention/awareness programs, on-campus police officers, video cameras, smoke detectors in residence halls.

Student services: health clinic, personal/psychological counseling, women's center, legal services.

COSTS & FINANCIAL AID
Costs (2017–18) *Tuition:* $38,410 full-time, $615 per credit hour part-time. Full-time tuition and fees vary according to course load and program. Part-time tuition and fees vary according to course load and program. *Room only:* Room and board charges vary according to board plan, housing facility, and location. *Payment plans:* installment, deferred payment. *Waivers:* employees or children of employees.

Financial Aid Of all full-time matriculated undergraduates who enrolled in 2016, 10,144 applied for aid, 9,005 were judged to have need, 896 had their need fully met. 734 Federal Work-Study jobs (averaging $3659). 2,313 state and other part-time jobs (averaging $3005). In 2016, 2532 non-need-based awards were made. *Average percent of need met:* 62. *Average financial aid package:* $23,589. *Average need-based loan:* $4269. *Average need-based gift aid:* $12,156. *Average non-need-based aid:* $15,348. *Average indebtedness upon graduation:* $30,115.

APPLYING
Standardized Tests *Recommended:* SAT or ACT (for admission).
Options: electronic application, early action, deferred entrance.
Required: high school transcript, minimum 2.3 GPA, letters of recommendation. *Required for some:* minimum 3.0 GPA, interview, audition/interview for School of Music and Theatre. *Recommended:* essay or personal statement, minimum 2.8 GPA.
Application deadlines: 2/1 (freshmen), rolling (transfers), 11/15 (early action).
Notification: 3/15 (freshmen), continuous (transfers), 1/15 (early action).

CONTACT
Carlene Klaas-Kennelly, Dean of Undergraduate Admission, DePaul University, 1 East Jackson Boulevard, Suite 900, Chicago, IL 60604.

Phone: 312-362-8300. *Toll-free phone:* 800-4DE-PAUL. *E-mail:* admission@depaul.edu.

DeVry University–Addison Campus
Addison, Illinois
http://www.devry.edu/

CONTACT
Admissions Office, DeVry University–Addison Campus, 1221 North Swift Road, Addison, IL 60101-6106. *Phone:* 630-953-1300. *Toll-free phone:* 866-338-7934.

DeVry University–Chicago Campus
Chicago, Illinois
http://www.devry.edu/
- **Proprietary** comprehensive, founded 1931, part of DeVry University
- **Urban** campus
- **Coed**
- **Minimally difficult** entrance level

FACULTY
Student/faculty ratio: 16:1.

ACADEMICS
Calendar: semesters. *Degrees:* associate, bachelor's, master's, and postbachelor's certificates.
Library: Learning Resource Center.

STUDENT LIFE
Housing options: college housing not available.

COSTS & FINANCIAL AID
Costs (2017–18) *Tuition:* $14,364 full-time. *Required fees:* $500 full-time.

Financial Aid Of all full-time matriculated undergraduates who enrolled in 2007, 479 applied for aid, 467 were judged to have need, 5 had their need fully met. In 2007, 14 non-need-based awards were made. *Average percent of need met:* 48. *Average financial aid package:* $16,145. *Average need-based loan:* $8033. *Average need-based gift aid:* $8371. *Average non-need-based aid:* $11,220. *Average indebtedness upon graduation:* $49,157.

APPLYING
Application fee: $30.
Required: high school transcript, interview.

CONTACT
DeVry University–Chicago Campus, 3300 North Campbell Avenue, Chicago, IL 60618. *Phone:* 773-929-8500. *Toll-free phone:* 866-338-7934.

DeVry University Online
Addison, Illinois
http://www.devry.edu/
- **Proprietary** comprehensive, founded 2000
- **Coed**

FACULTY
Student/faculty ratio: 14:1.

ACADEMICS
Calendar: semesters. *Degrees:* associate, bachelor's, master's, and postbachelor's certificates.

STUDENT LIFE
Housing options: college housing not available.

COSTS & FINANCIAL AID
Costs (2017–18) *Tuition:* $14,364 full-time. *Required fees:* $500 full-time.

Financial Aid Of all full-time matriculated undergraduates who enrolled in 2006, 810 applied for aid, 785 were judged to have need, 9 had their need fully met. In 2006, 146 non-need-based awards were made. *Average percent of need met:* 36. *Average financial aid package:* $10,560. *Average need-based loan:* $6201. *Average need-based gift aid:* $7114.

Average non-need-based aid: $10,591. *Average indebtedness upon graduation:* $35,423.

APPLYING
Options: deferred entrance.
Application fee: $30.
Required: high school transcript, interview.

CONTACT
DeVry University Online, 1221 North Swift Road, Addison, IL 60101. *Phone:* 877-496-9050. *Toll-free phone:* 866-338-7934.

DeVry University–Tinley Park Campus
Tinley Park, Illinois
http://www.devry.edu/

CONTACT
Admissions Office, DeVry University–Tinley Park Campus, 18624 West Creek Drive, Tinley Park, IL 60477 . *Phone:* 708-342-3300. *Toll-free phone:* 866-338-7934.

Dominican University
River Forest, Illinois
http://www.dom.edu/
- **Independent Roman Catholic** comprehensive, founded 1901
- **Suburban** 30-acre campus with easy access to Chicago
- **Endowment** $33.0 million
- **Coed** 2,171 undergraduate students, 93% full-time, 67% women, 33% men
- **Moderately difficult** entrance level, 65% of applicants were admitted

UNDERGRAD STUDENTS
2,014 full-time, 157 part-time. Students come from 30 states and territories; 9 other countries; 6% are from out of state; 7% Black or African American, non-Hispanic/Latino; 51% Hispanic/Latino; 3% Asian, non-Hispanic/Latino; 0.2% Native Hawaiian or other Pacific Islander, non-Hispanic/Latino; 0.1% American Indian or Alaska Native, non-Hispanic/Latino; 0.8% Two or more races, non-Hispanic/Latino; 2% Race/ethnicity unknown; 2% international; 7% transferred in; 26% live on campus.

Freshmen:
Admission: 4,697 applied, 3,052 admitted, 441 enrolled. *Average high school GPA:* 3.7. *Test scores:* SAT evidence-based reading and writing scores over 500: 81%; SAT math scores over 500: 75%; ACT scores over 18: 94%; SAT evidence-based reading and writing scores over 600: 34%; SAT math scores over 600: 16%; ACT scores over 24: 35%; ACT scores over 30: 5%.
Retention: 81% of full-time freshmen returned.

FACULTY
Total: 418, 38% full-time, 63% with terminal degrees.
Student/faculty ratio: 11:1.

ACADEMICS
Calendar: semesters. *Degrees:* bachelor's, master's, doctoral, post-master's, and postbachelor's certificates.

Special study options: academic remediation for entering students, accelerated degree program, adult/continuing education programs, advanced placement credit, distance learning, double majors, English as a second language, honors programs, independent study, internships, off-campus study, part-time degree program, services for LD students, student-designed majors, study abroad, summer session for credit.

Unusual degree programs: 3-2 business administration; engineering with Illinois Institute of Technology; nursing; social work; library science, pharmacy with Midwestern University.

Computers: 550 computers/terminals and 4,000 ports are available on campus for general student use. Students can access the following: campus intranet, computer help desk, free student e-mail accounts, online (class) grades, online (class) registration, online (class) schedules. Campuswide network is available. 100% of college-owned or -operated housing units are wired for high-speed Internet access. Wireless service is available via entire campus.

Library: Rebecca Crown Library. *Books:* 247,967 (physical), 9,389 (digital/electronic); *Serial titles:* 280 (physical), 53,047 (digital/electronic); *Databases:* 114. Weekly public service hours: 100; students can reserve study rooms.

STUDENT LIFE
Housing options: coed, women-only, special housing for students with disabilities. Campus housing is university owned and leased by the school. Freshman applicants given priority for college housing.

Activities and organizations: drama/theater group, student-run newspaper, choral group, Polish Club, Commuter Student Association, Nutrition Club, Organization of Latin American Students, Fashion Club.

Athletics Member NCAA. All Division III. *Intercollegiate sports:* baseball M, basketball M/W, cross-country running M/W, golf M, soccer M/W, softball W, tennis M/W, volleyball M/W. *Intramural sports:* basketball M/W, bowling M/W, football M/W, racquetball M/W, soccer M/W, ultimate Frisbee M/W, volleyball M/W.

Campus security: 24-hour emergency response devices and patrols, student patrols, late-night transport/escort service, controlled dormitory access, door alarms.

Student services: health clinic, personal/psychological counseling.

COSTS & FINANCIAL AID
Costs (2018–19) *One-time required fee:* $150. *Comprehensive fee:* $43,675 includes full-time tuition ($32,964), mandatory fees ($470), and room and board ($10,241). Full-time tuition and fees vary according to course load, program, and reciprocity agreements. Part-time tuition: $1100 per credit hour. Part-time tuition and fees vary according to course load, program, and reciprocity agreements. *Required fees:* $90 per term part-time. *Room and board:* Room and board charges vary according to board plan and housing facility. *Payment plan:* deferred payment. *Waivers:* employees or children of employees.

Financial Aid Of all full-time matriculated undergraduates who enrolled in 2017, 1,864 applied for aid, 1,758 were judged to have need, 175 had their need fully met. In 2017, 221 non-need-based awards were made. *Average percent of need met:* 71. *Average financial aid package:* $23,125. *Average need-based loan:* $4266. *Average need-based gift aid:* $19,644. *Average non-need-based aid:* $15,808. *Average indebtedness upon graduation:* $28,659.

APPLYING
Standardized Tests *Required:* SAT or ACT (for admission).
Options: electronic application, deferred entrance.
Application fee: $25.
Required: high school transcript. *Required for some:* interview. *Recommended:* essay or personal statement, minimum 2.5 GPA.
Application deadlines: rolling (freshmen), rolling (transfers).
Notification: continuous (freshmen), continuous (transfers).

CONTACT
Mr. Glenn Hamilton, Assistant Vice President, Enrollment Management, Dominican University, 7900 West Division Street, River Forest, IL 60305. *Phone:* 708-524-6800. *Toll-free phone:* 800-828-8475. *Fax:* 708-524-6864. *E-mail:* domadmis@dom.edu.

Eastern Illinois University
Charleston, Illinois
http://www.eiu.edu/
- **State-supported** comprehensive, founded 1895
- **Small-town** 320-acre campus
- **Endowment** $76.9 million
- **Coed**
- **Moderately difficult** entrance level

FACULTY
Student/faculty ratio: 14:1.

ACADEMICS
Calendar: semesters. *Degrees:* bachelor's, master's, post-master's, and postbachelor's certificates.
Library: Booth Library. *Books:* 1.0 million (physical), 1.3 million (digital/electronic); *Serial titles:* 161 (physical), 45,276 (digital/electronic); *Databases:* 244. Weekly public service hours: 98.

STUDENT LIFE

Housing options: on-campus residence required for freshman year; coed, men-only, women-only. Campus housing is university owned. Freshman campus housing is guaranteed.

Activities and organizations: drama/theater group, student-run newspaper, radio and television station, choral group, marching band, Greek Organizations, Black Student Union, Intramural Sports, University Board, Religious Student Organizations, national fraternities, national sororities.

Athletics Member NCAA. All Division I except football (Division I-AA).

Campus security: 24-hour emergency response devices and patrols, student patrols, controlled dormitory access, AlertEIU and warning sirens, self-defense education, shuttle buses, lighted pathways and sidewalks.

Student services: health clinic, personal/psychological counseling, women's center, legal services.

COSTS & FINANCIAL AID

Costs (2017–18) *Tuition:* state resident $8760 full-time, $292 per credit hour part-time; nonresident $10,950 full-time, $365 per credit hour part-time. Full-time tuition and fees vary according to course load and student level. Part-time tuition and fees vary according to course load and student level. No tuition increase for student's term of enrollment. *Required fees:* $2918 full-time, $111 per credit hour part-time. *Room and board:* $9736. Room and board charges vary according to board plan and housing facility.

Financial Aid Of all full-time matriculated undergraduates who enrolled in 2017, 3,693 applied for aid, 3,017 were judged to have need, 294 had their need fully met. In 2017, 521 non-need-based awards were made. *Average percent of need met:* 57. *Average financial aid package:* $13,067. *Average need-based loan:* $4424. *Average need-based gift aid:* $8459. *Average non-need-based aid:* $3671. *Average indebtedness upon graduation:* $30,695.

APPLYING

Standardized Tests *Required:* SAT or ACT (for admission).

Options: electronic application, deferred entrance.

Application fee: $30.

Required: high school transcript, minimum 2.3 GPA. *Required for some:* essay or personal statement, 1 letter of recommendation, audition for music program.

CONTACT

Denise Lee, Assistant Director of Admissions, Eastern Illinois University, 600 Lincoln Avenue, Charleston, IL 61920. *Phone:* 217-581-7975. *Toll-free phone:* 877-581-2348. *Fax:* 217-581-7060. *E-mail:* dalee@eiu.edu.

East-West University

Chicago, Illinois

http://www.eastwest.edu/

CONTACT

Bryan Lambert, Director of Enrollment, East-West University, 816 South Michigan Avenue, Chicago, IL 60605-2103. *Phone:* 312-939-0112 Ext. 1701.

★ Elmhurst College

Elmhurst, Illinois

http://www.elmhurst.edu/

- **Independent** comprehensive, founded 1871, affiliated with United Church of Christ
- **Suburban** 38-acre campus with easy access to Chicago
- **Endowment** $94.8 million
- **Coed** 2,875 undergraduate students, 95% full-time, 61% women, 39% men
- **Moderately difficult** entrance level, 71% of applicants were admitted

UNDERGRAD STUDENTS

2,732 full-time, 143 part-time. Students come from 33 states and territories; 25 other countries; 9% are from out of state; 5% Black or African American, non-Hispanic/Latino; 21% Hispanic/Latino; 5% Asian, non-Hispanic/Latino; 0.1% Native Hawaiian or other Pacific Islander, non-Hispanic/Latino; 0.1% American Indian or Alaska Native, non-Hispanic/Latino; 4% Two or more races, non-Hispanic/Latino; 3% Race/ethnicity unknown; 13% transferred in; 32% live on campus.

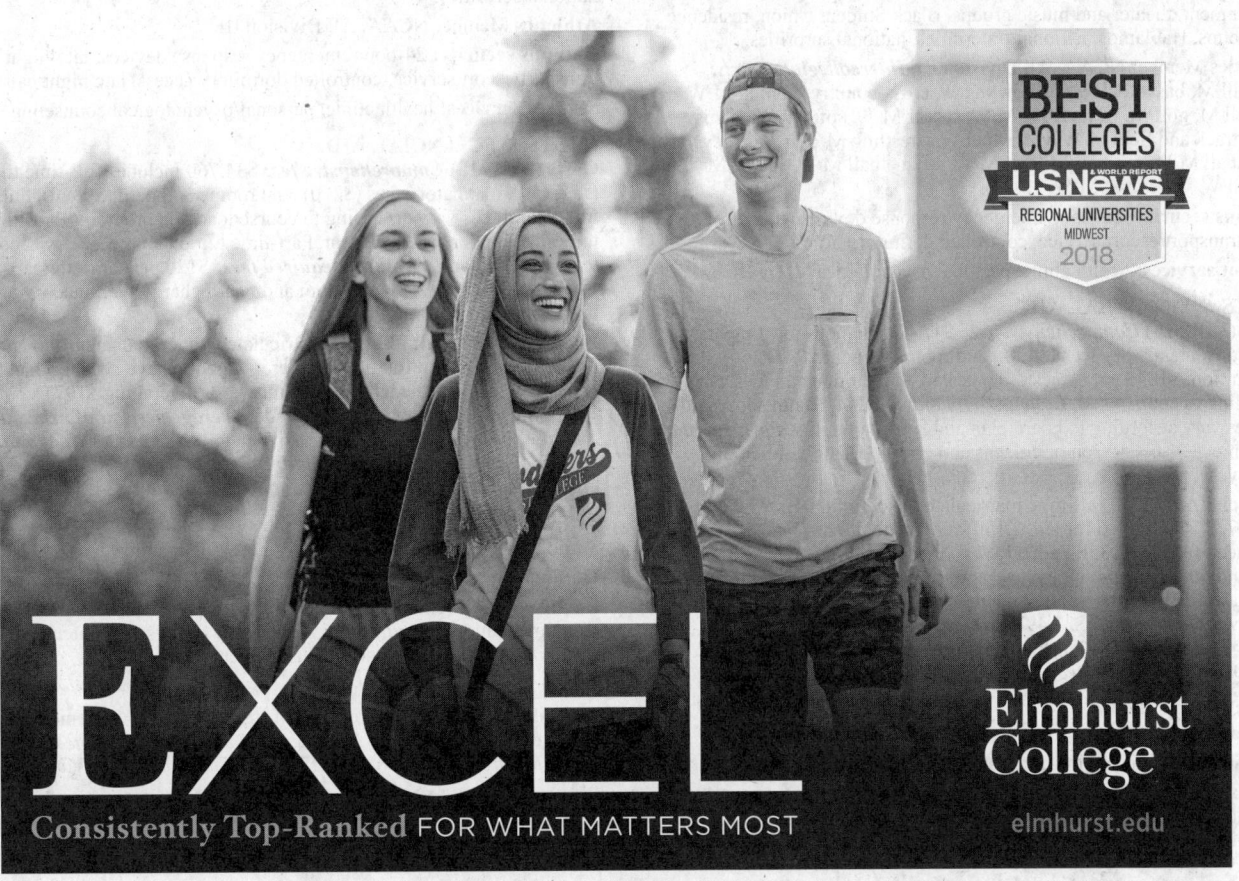

Freshmen:

Admission: 3,645 applied, 2,571 admitted, 497 enrolled. *Average high school GPA:* 3.5. *Test scores:* SAT evidence-based reading and writing scores over 500: 78%; SAT math scores over 500: 73%; ACT scores over 18: 92%; SAT evidence-based reading and writing scores over 600: 24%; SAT math scores over 600: 29%; ACT scores over 24: 43%; SAT evidence-based reading and writing scores over 700: 2%; SAT math scores over 700: 5%; ACT scores over 30: 6%.

Retention: 75% of full-time freshmen returned.

FACULTY
Total: 381, 40% full-time, 45% with terminal degrees.
Student/faculty ratio: 14:1.

ACADEMICS
Calendar: 4-1-4. *Degrees:* bachelor's and master's.

Special study options: academic remediation for entering students, accelerated degree program, adult/continuing education programs, advanced placement credit, cooperative education, double majors, honors programs, independent study, internships, off-campus study, part-time degree program, services for LD students, study abroad, summer session for credit. *ROTC:* Army (c), Air Force (c).

Unusual degree programs: 3-2 engineering with University of Illinois at Urbana–Champaign, University of Southern California.

Computers: 800 computers/terminals are available on campus for general student use. Students can access the following: campus intranet, computer help desk, free student e-mail accounts, online (class) grades, online (class) registration, online (class) schedules. Campuswide network is available. 100% of college-owned or -operated housing units are wired for high-speed Internet access. Wireless service is available via classrooms, computer labs, dorm rooms, libraries, student centers.
Library: Buehler Library.

STUDENT LIFE
Housing options: coed. Campus housing is university owned, leased by the school and is provided by a third party. Freshman applicants given priority for college housing.

Activities and organizations: drama/theater group, student-run newspaper, radio station, choral group, Programming Board and Student Government, theater and music groups, Black Student Union, residence life groups, Hablamos, national fraternities, national sororities.

Athletics Member NCAA. All Division III. *Intercollegiate sports:* baseball M, basketball M/W, bowling W, cross-country running M/W, football M, golf M/W, lacrosse M/W, soccer M/W, softball W, tennis M/W, track and field M/W, volleyball W, wrestling M. *Intramural sports:* basketball M/W, football M, golf M/W, racquetball M/W, soccer M/W, softball W, volleyball M/W.

Campus security: 24-hour emergency response devices and patrols, late-night transport/escort service, controlled dormitory access.

Student services: health clinic, personal/psychological counseling.

COSTS & FINANCIAL AID
Costs (2018–19) *Comprehensive fee:* $47,421 includes full-time tuition ($36,755), mandatory fees ($300), and room and board ($10,366). Part-time tuition: $1045 per semester hour. Part-time tuition and fees vary according to course load. *College room only:* $6244. Room and board charges vary according to board plan and housing facility. *Payment plan:* installment. *Waivers:* senior citizens and employees or children of employees.

Financial Aid Of all full-time matriculated undergraduates who enrolled in 2017, 2,306 applied for aid, 2,130 were judged to have need, 391 had their need fully met. 356 Federal Work-Study jobs (averaging $611). 328 state and other part-time jobs (averaging $1365). In 2017, 174 non-need-based awards were made. *Average percent of need met:* 73. *Average financial aid package:* $27,497. *Average need-based loan:* $4417. *Average need-based gift aid:* $22,917. *Average non-need-based aid:* $15,901. *Average indebtedness upon graduation:* $29,925.

APPLYING
Standardized Tests *Required:* SAT or ACT (for admission).
Options: electronic application, early action, deferred entrance.
Required: high school transcript. *Required for some:* essay or personal statement, interview. *Recommended:* essay or personal statement, interview.

Application deadlines: rolling (freshmen), rolling (transfers).
Notification: continuous (freshmen), continuous (transfers).

CONTACT
Mrs. Stephanie Levenson, Executive Director of Admission, Elmhurst College, Elmhurst College, Admission Office, 190 South Prospect Avenue, Elmhurst, IL 60126-3296. *Phone:* 630-617-3400. *Toll-free phone:* 800-697-1871. *Fax:* 630-617-5501. *E-mail:* admit@elmhurst.edu.

See previous page for display ad and page 1280 for the College Close-Up.

Eureka College
Eureka, Illinois
http://www.eureka.edu/

- **Independent** 4-year, founded 1855, affiliated with Christian Church (Disciples of Christ)
- **Small-town** 64-acre campus
- **Endowment** $25.3 million
- **Coed**
- **Minimally difficult** entrance level

FACULTY
Student/faculty ratio: 13:1.

ACADEMICS
Calendar: semesters 4 8-week terms. *Degree:* bachelor's.
Library: Melick Library. *Books:* 81,371 (physical), 7,171 (digital/electronic); *Serial titles:* 532 (physical), 919 (digital/electronic); *Databases:* 11. Weekly public service hours: 70; students can reserve study rooms.

STUDENT LIFE
Housing options: on-campus residence required through senior year; coed, men-only, women-only. Campus housing is university owned. Freshman campus housing is guaranteed.

Activities and organizations: drama/theater group, student-run newspaper, choral group, Student Senate, Campus Activities Board (CAB), Alpha Phi Omega, Student Alliance for Greener Environments (SAGE), Multicultural Student Union (MCSU), national fraternities, national sororities.

Athletics Member NCAA. All Division III.

Campus security: 24-hour emergency response devices, late-night transport/escort service, controlled dormitory access, late night patrols.

Student services: health clinic, personal/psychological counseling.

COSTS & FINANCIAL AID
Costs (2017–18) *Comprehensive fee:* $34,760 includes full-time tuition ($25,150), mandatory fees ($240), and room and board ($9370). Full-time tuition and fees vary according to course load and program. Part-time tuition: $700 per semester hour. Part-time tuition and fees vary according to course load and program. *Required fees:* $120 per semester part-time. *College room only:* $4490. Room and board charges vary according to board plan and housing facility.

Financial Aid Of all full-time matriculated undergraduates who enrolled in 2017, 512 applied for aid, 449 were judged to have need, 35 had their need fully met. 119 Federal Work-Study jobs (averaging $1971). In 2017, 130 non-need-based awards were made. *Average percent of need met:* 59. *Average financial aid package:* $16,506. *Average need-based loan:* $3267. *Average need-based gift aid:* $13,239. *Average non-need-based aid:* $8278. *Average indebtedness upon graduation:* $34,180.

APPLYING
Standardized Tests *Required:* SAT or ACT (for admission).
Options: electronic application.
Required: high school transcript, minimum 2.3 GPA, 1 letter of recommendation. *Required for some:* essay or personal statement. *Recommended:* essay or personal statement, interview.

CONTACT
Mr. Mike Murtagh, Vice President of Institutional Advancement, Eureka College, 300 East College Avenue, Eureka, IL 61530. *Phone:* 309-467-6315. *Toll-free phone:* 888-4-EUREKA. *E-mail:* mmurtagh@eureka.edu.

Governors State University

University Park, Illinois

http://www.govst.edu/

- **State-supported** university, founded 1969
- **Suburban** 742-acre campus with easy access to Chicago
- **Endowment** $2.1 million
- **Coed** 3,326 undergraduate students, 56% full-time, 63% women, 37% men
- **Moderately difficult** entrance level, 43% of applicants were admitted

UNDERGRAD STUDENTS

1,879 full-time, 1,447 part-time. Students come from 16 states and territories; 35 other countries; 2% are from out of state; 40% Black or African American, non-Hispanic/Latino; 13% Hispanic/Latino; 2% Asian, non-Hispanic/Latino; 0.1% Native Hawaiian or other Pacific Islander, non-Hispanic/Latino; 0.1% American Indian or Alaska Native, non-Hispanic/Latino; 3% Two or more races, non-Hispanic/Latino; 9% Race/ethnicity unknown; 1% international; 23% transferred in; 7% live on campus.

Freshmen:

Admission: 1,305 applied, 561 admitted, 199 enrolled. *Average high school GPA:* 2.8. *Test scores:* ACT scores over 18: 63%; ACT scores over 24: 9%.

Retention: 54% of full-time freshmen returned.

FACULTY

Total: 470, 49% full-time, 36% with terminal degrees.

ACADEMICS

Calendar: semesters. *Degrees:* certificates, bachelor's, master's, doctoral, post-master's, and postbachelor's certificates.

Special study options: adult/continuing education programs, advanced placement credit, distance learning, double majors, English as a second language, external degree program, honors programs, independent study, internships, off-campus study, part-time degree program, services for LD students, student-designed majors, study abroad, summer session for credit. *ROTC:* Air Force (c).

Computers: Students can access the following: campus intranet, computer help desk, free student e-mail accounts, online (class) grades, online (class) registration, online (class) schedules, student portal. Campuswide network is available. 100% of college-owned or -operated housing units are wired for high-speed Internet access. Wireless service is available via entire campus.
Library: University Library. *Books:* 284,377 (physical), 339,176 (digital/electronic); *Serial titles:* 2,438 (physical), 11,484 (digital/electronic); *Databases:* 176. Weekly public service hours: 75; students can reserve study rooms.

STUDENT LIFE

Housing options: coed. Campus housing is university owned.

Activities and organizations: student-run newspaper, choral group.

Athletics Member NAIA. *Intercollegiate sports:* basketball M(s)/W(s), cross-country running M(s)/W(s), golf M(s)/W(s), volleyball M(s)/W(s). *Intramural sports:* basketball M/W, table tennis M/W.

Campus security: 24-hour emergency response devices and patrols, late-night transport/escort service, controlled dormitory access.

Student services: health clinic, personal/psychological counseling.

COSTS & FINANCIAL AID

Costs (2018–19) *Tuition:* state resident $9390 full-time, $313 per credit hour part-time; nonresident $18,780 full-time, $626 per credit hour part-time. Full-time tuition and fees vary according to course load, degree level, and reciprocity agreements. Part-time tuition and fees vary according to course load, degree level, and reciprocity agreements. No tuition increase for student's term of enrollment. *Required fees:* $2356 full-time, $76 per credit hour part-time, $38 per term part-time. *Room and board:* $10,104; room only: $8104. Room and board charges vary according to board plan and housing facility. *Payment plan:* installment. *Waivers:* senior citizens and employees or children of employees.

Financial Aid Of all full-time matriculated undergraduates who enrolled in 2016, 1,818 were judged to have need, 86 had their need fully met. 141 Federal Work-Study jobs (averaging $2248). In 2016, 272 non-need-based

awards were made. *Average percent of need met:* 58. *Average financial aid package:* $11,536. *Average need-based loan:* $8959. *Average need-based gift aid:* $9223. *Average non-need-based aid:* $2526. *Financial aid deadline:* 10/1.

APPLYING

Standardized Tests *Required:* SAT and SAT Subject Tests or ACT (for admission).

Options: electronic application, early admission, early decision, deferred entrance.

Application fee: $25.

Required: high school transcript, minimum 2.8 GPA. *Required for some:* essay or personal statement, interview.

Early decision deadline: 11/15.

Notification: continuous (transfers), 12/15 (early decision).

CONTACT

Mr. Paul McGuinness, Director, Admissions, Governors State University, One University Parkway, University Park, IL 60484. *Phone:* 708-235-7308 Ext. 7308. *Toll-free phone:* 800-478-8478. *E-mail:* pmcguinness@govst.edu.

Greenville University

Greenville, Illinois

http://www.greenville.edu/

- **Independent Free Methodist** comprehensive, founded 1892
- **Small-town** 50-acre campus with easy access to St. Louis
- **Endowment** $16.3 million
- **Coed** 985 undergraduate students, 90% full-time, 49% women, 51% men
- **Moderately difficult** entrance level, 66% of applicants were admitted

UNDERGRAD STUDENTS

887 full-time, 98 part-time. Students come from 39 states and territories; 14 other countries; 31% are from out of state; 13% Black or African American, non-Hispanic/Latino; 6% Hispanic/Latino; 1% Asian, non-Hispanic/Latino; 69% Native Hawaiian or other Pacific Islander, non-Hispanic/Latino; 0.4% American Indian or Alaska Native, non-Hispanic/Latino; 2% Two or more races, non-Hispanic/Latino; 4% Race/ethnicity unknown; 4% international; 10% transferred in; 73% live on campus.

Freshmen:

Admission: 1,287 applied, 852 admitted, 220 enrolled. *Average high school GPA:* 3.3. *Test scores:* ACT scores over 18: 84%; ACT scores over 24: 32%; ACT scores over 30: 6%.

Retention: 73% of full-time freshmen returned.

FACULTY

Total: 168, 35% full-time, 38% with terminal degrees.

Student/faculty ratio: 13:1.

ACADEMICS

Calendar: 4-1-4. *Degrees:* bachelor's and master's.

Special study options: academic remediation for entering students, accelerated degree program, adult/continuing education programs, advanced placement credit, cooperative education, distance learning, double majors, external degree program, honors programs, independent study, internships, off-campus study, part-time degree program, student-designed majors, study abroad, summer session for credit.

Unusual degree programs: 3-2 engineering with University of Illinois at Urbana–Champaign, Washington University in St. Louis; nursing with St. John's College, Southern Illinois University Edwardsville, Mennonite College of Nursing; chiropractic with Logan College of Chiropractic.

Computers: 50 computers/terminals are available on campus for general student use. Students can access the following: campus intranet, computer help desk, free student e-mail accounts, online (class) grades, online (class) registration, online (class) schedules. Campuswide network is available. 100% of college-owned or -operated housing units are wired for high-speed Internet access. Wireless service is available via entire campus.
Library: Ruby E. Dare Library. *Books:* 131,047 (physical), 7,408 (digital/electronic). Students can reserve study rooms.

STUDENT LIFE

Housing options: on-campus residence required through senior year; men-only, women-only. Campus housing is university owned. Freshman campus housing is guaranteed.

Activities and organizations: drama/theater group, student-run newspaper, radio station, choral group, marching band, Campus Activity Board, Panther Corps Marching Band, Greenville College Student Association, Habitat for Humanity, Music and Entertainment Industry Student Association.

Athletics Member NCAA, NCCAA. All NCAA Division III. *Intercollegiate sports:* baseball M, basketball M/W, cross-country running M/W, football M, golf M/W, soccer M/W, softball W, tennis M/W, track and field M/W, volleyball M/W. *Intramural sports:* basketball M/W, cheerleading W, football M/W, softball M/W, ultimate Frisbee M/W, volleyball M/W.

Campus security: 24-hour emergency response devices and patrols, late-night transport/escort service, controlled dormitory access.

Student services: personal/psychological counseling.

COSTS & FINANCIAL AID

Costs (2018–19) *Comprehensive fee:* $36,556 includes full-time tuition ($26,778), mandatory fees ($330), and room and board ($9448). Full-time tuition and fees vary according to degree level and program. Part-time tuition: $434 per credit hour. Part-time tuition and fees vary according to course load, degree level, and program. *College room only:* $4798. Room and board charges vary according to housing facility. *Payment plan:* installment. *Waivers:* senior citizens and employees or children of employees.

Financial Aid Of all full-time matriculated undergraduates who enrolled in 2016, 816 applied for aid, 751 were judged to have need, 90 had their need fully met. 143 Federal Work-Study jobs (averaging $1354). In 2016, 143 non-need-based awards were made. *Average percent of need met:* 73. *Average financial aid package:* $20,558. *Average need-based loan:* $4163. *Average need-based gift aid:* $17,065. *Average non-need-based aid:* $10,918. *Average indebtedness upon graduation:* $28,724.

APPLYING

Standardized Tests *Required:* SAT or ACT (for admission).

Options: electronic application, early admission, deferred entrance.

Required: essay or personal statement, high school transcript, minimum 2.3 GPA, agreement to lifestyle statement. *Required for some:* interview.

Application deadlines: rolling (freshmen), rolling (transfers).

Notification: continuous (freshmen), continuous (transfers).

CONTACT

Mr. Karl Hatton, Dean of Admissions, Greenville University, 315 East College Avenue, Greenville, IL 62246. *Phone:* 618-664-7100. *Toll-free phone:* 800-345-4440. *Fax:* 618-664-9841. *E-mail:* admissions@greenville.edu.

Hebrew Theological College

Skokie, Illinois
http://www.htc.edu/

CONTACT
Rabbi Berish Cardash, Hebrew Theological College, 7135 North Carpenter Road, Skokie, IL 60077-3263. *Phone:* 847-982-2500.

Illinois College

Jacksonville, Illinois
http://www.ic.edu/

- **Independent interdenominational** comprehensive, founded 1829
- **Small-town** 62-acre campus with easy access to St. Louis
- **Coed** 959 undergraduate students, 99% full-time, 51% women, 49% men
- **Moderately difficult** entrance level, 55% of applicants were admitted

UNDERGRAD STUDENTS

950 full-time, 9 part-time. 14% are from out of state; 11% Black or African American, non-Hispanic/Latino; 9% Hispanic/Latino; 1% Asian, non-Hispanic/Latino; 0.1% Native Hawaiian or other Pacific Islander, non-Hispanic/Latino; 0.2% American Indian or Alaska Native, non-

Hispanic/Latino; 3% Two or more races, non-Hispanic/Latino; 5% international; 4% transferred in; 85% live on campus.

Freshmen:
Admission: 4,121 applied, 2,261 admitted, 258 enrolled. *Average high school GPA:* 3.5. *Test scores:* SAT evidence-based reading and writing scores over 500: 67%; SAT math scores over 500: 87%; ACT scores over 18: 89%; SAT evidence-based reading and writing scores over 600: 33%; SAT math scores over 600: 27%; ACT scores over 24: 35%; SAT math scores over 700: 7%; ACT scores over 30: 4%.

Retention: 77% of full-time freshmen returned.

FACULTY
Total: 91, 82% full-time, 73% with terminal degrees.
Student/faculty ratio: 12:1.

ACADEMICS
Calendar: semesters. *Degrees:* bachelor's and master's.
Computers: Students can access the following: computer help desk, free student e-mail accounts, online (class) grades, online (class) registration, online (class) schedules. Campuswide network is available. Wireless service is available via entire campus.
Library: Schewe Library.

STUDENT LIFE
Housing options: on-campus residence required through sophomore year; coed, men-only, women-only. Campus housing is university owned. Freshman campus housing is guaranteed.

Athletics Member NCAA. All Division III. *Intercollegiate sports:* baseball M, cheerleading W, cross-country running M/W, football M, golf M/W, soccer M/W, softball W, swimming and diving M/W, tennis M/W, track and field M/W, volleyball W. *Intramural sports:* badminton M/W, basketball M/W, fencing M/W, football M, racquetball M/W, softball M/W, swimming and diving M/W, volleyball M/W, water polo M/W, weight lifting M/W.

Campus security: 24-hour emergency response devices and patrols, late-night transport/escort service, controlled dormitory access.

COSTS & FINANCIAL AID
Costs (2018–19) *Comprehensive fee:* $42,370 includes full-time tuition ($32,540), mandatory fees ($550), and room and board ($9280). Part-time tuition: $990 per credit hour. Part-time tuition and fees vary according to course load. *Room and board:* Room and board charges vary according to board plan and housing facility. *Payment plan:* installment. *Waivers:* employees or children of employees.

Financial Aid Of all full-time matriculated undergraduates who enrolled in 2016, 866 applied for aid, 798 were judged to have need, 188 had their need fully met. In 2016, 150 non-need-based awards were made. *Average percent of need met:* 87. *Average financial aid package:* $27,933. *Average need-based loan:* $4566. *Average need-based gift aid:* $23,190. *Average non-need-based aid:* $17,694. *Average indebtedness upon graduation:* $32,740.

APPLYING
Options: electronic application, early admission, early action, deferred entrance.

Required: high school transcript, 1 letter of recommendation. *Required for some:* essay or personal statement. *Recommended:* essay or personal statement, minimum 2.5 GPA, interview.

Notification: continuous until 9/15 (freshmen).

CONTACT
Mr. Rick Bystry, Associate Director of Admission, Illinois College, 1101 West College, Jacksonville, IL 62650. *Phone:* 217-245-3030. *Toll-free phone:* 866-464-5265. *Fax:* 217-245-3034. *E-mail:* admissions@ic.edu.

The Illinois Institute of Art–Chicago

Chicago, Illinois
http://www.artinstitutes.edu/chicago/

CONTACT
The Illinois Institute of Art–Chicago, 350 North Orleans Street, Chicago, IL 60654. *Phone:* 312-280-3500. *Toll-free phone:* 800-351-3450.

The Illinois Institute of Art–Schaumburg

Schaumburg, Illinois

http://www.artinstitutes.edu/schaumburg/

CONTACT

The Illinois Institute of Art–Schaumburg, 1000 North Plaza Drive, Suite 100, Schaumburg, IL 60173. *Phone:* 847-619-3450. *Toll-free phone:* 800-314-3450.

Illinois Institute of Technology

Chicago, Illinois

http://www.iit.edu/

CONTACT

Ms. Toni Riley, Director, Undergraduate Admissions Office, Illinois Institute of Technology, Office of Undergraduate Admission, Perlstein 101, 10 West 33rd Street, Chicago, IL 60616. *Phone:* 312-567-5239. *Toll-free phone:* 800-448-2329. *E-mail:* admission@iit.edu.

Illinois State University

Normal, Illinois

http://www.illinoisstate.edu/

- **State-supported** university, founded 1857
- **Suburban** 1111-acre campus
- **Endowment** $112.7 million
- **Coed** 18,330 undergraduate students, 94% full-time, 55% women, 45% men
- **Minimally difficult** entrance level, 89% of applicants were admitted

UNDERGRAD STUDENTS

17,165 full-time, 1,165 part-time. Students come from 47 states and territories; 69 other countries; 2% are from out of state; 9% Black or African American, non-Hispanic/Latino; 10% Hispanic/Latino; 2% Asian, non-Hispanic/Latino; 0.1% Native Hawaiian or other Pacific Islander, non-Hispanic/Latino; 0.2% American Indian or Alaska Native, non-Hispanic/Latino; 3% Two or more races, non-Hispanic/Latino; 0.3% Race/ethnicity unknown; 0.5% international; 10% transferred in; 31% live on campus.

Freshmen:

Admission: 12,078 applied, 10,735 admitted, 3,352 enrolled. *Average high school GPA:* 3.4. *Test scores:* ACT scores over 18: 99%; ACT scores over 24: 45%; ACT scores over 30: 11%.
Retention: 81% of full-time freshmen returned.

FACULTY

Total: 1,290, 68% full-time, 66% with terminal degrees.
Student/faculty ratio: 17:1.

ACADEMICS

Calendar: semesters. *Degrees:* certificates, bachelor's, master's, doctoral, post-master's, and postbachelor's certificates.

Special study options: academic remediation for entering students, accelerated degree program, adult/continuing education programs, advanced placement credit, cooperative education, distance learning, double majors, English as a second language, honors programs, independent study, internships, off-campus study, part-time degree program, services for LD students, student-designed majors, study abroad, summer session for credit. *ROTC:* Army (b).

Unusual degree programs: 3-2 engineering with University of Illinois, Bradley University.

Computers: 2,500 computers/terminals and 2,500 ports are available on campus for general student use. Students can access the following: computer help desk, free student e-mail accounts, online (class) grades, online (class) registration, online (class) schedules. Campuswide network is available. 100% of college-owned or -operated housing units are wired for high-speed Internet access. Wireless service is available via entire campus.

Library: Milner Library. *Books:* 1.4 million (physical), 190,817 (digital/electronic); *Serial titles:* 97,570 (digital/electronic); *Databases:* 251. Students can reserve study rooms.

STUDENT LIFE

Housing options: on-campus residence required through sophomore year; coed, women-only, special housing for students with disabilities. Campus housing is university owned. Freshman campus housing is guaranteed.

Activities and organizations: drama/theater group, student-run newspaper, radio and television station, choral group, marching band, national fraternities, national sororities.

Athletics Member NCAA. All Division I except football (Division I-AA). *Intercollegiate sports:* baseball M(s), basketball M(s)/W(s), cross-country running M(s)/W(s), golf M(s)/W(s), gymnastics W(s), soccer W(s), softball W(s), swimming and diving W(s), tennis M(s)/W(s), track and field M(s)/W(s), volleyball W(s). *Intramural sports:* badminton M(c)/W(c), baseball M(c), basketball M/W(c), cheerleading W(c), cross-country running M(c)/W(c), equestrian sports M(c)/W(c), fencing M(c)/W(c), golf M(c)/W(c), ice hockey M(c), lacrosse M(c)/W(c), rugby M(c)/W(c), soccer M(c)/W(c), softball M(c)/W(c), table tennis M(c)/W(c), tennis M(c)/W(c), triathlon M(c)/W(c), ultimate Frisbee M(c)/W(c), volleyball M(c)/W(c), water polo M(c)/W(c), wrestling M(c)/W(c).

Campus security: 24-hour emergency response devices and patrols, student patrols, late-night transport/escort service, controlled dormitory access.

Student services: health clinic, personal/psychological counseling, women's center, legal services.

COSTS & FINANCIAL AID

Costs (2018–19) *Tuition:* state resident $11,108 full-time, $370 per credit hour part-time; nonresident $22,215 full-time, $741 per credit hour part-time. Full-time tuition and fees vary according to degree level. Part-time tuition and fees vary according to degree level. No tuition increase for student's term of enrollment. *Required fees:* $2953 full-time, $82 per credit hour part-time. *Room and board:* $9850; room only: $5334. Room and board charges vary according to board plan and housing facility. *Payment plan:* installment. *Waivers:* minority students, senior citizens, and employees or children of employees.

Financial Aid Of all full-time matriculated undergraduates who enrolled in 2015, 13,206 applied for aid, 11,081 were judged to have need, 3,224 had their need fully met. 307 Federal Work-Study jobs (averaging $2034). 51 state and other part-time jobs (averaging $2462). In 2015, 949 non-need-based awards were made. *Average percent of need met:* 72. *Average financial aid package:* $10,444. *Average need-based loan:* $4345. *Average need-based gift aid:* $9736. *Average non-need-based aid:* $2697. *Average indebtedness upon graduation:* $29,006.

APPLYING

Standardized Tests *Required:* SAT or ACT (for admission).

Options: electronic application.

Application fee: $50.

Required for some: interview. *Recommended:* essay or personal statement, high school transcript.

Application deadlines: 4/1 (freshmen), rolling (transfers).

Notification: continuous (freshmen), continuous (out-of-state freshmen), continuous (transfers).

CONTACT

Mr. Jeff Mavros, Director of Admissions, Illinois State University, Campus Box 2200, Normal, IL 61790-2200. *Phone:* 309-438-2181. *Toll-free phone:* 800-366-2478. *Fax:* 309-438-3932. *E-mail:* admissions@ilstu.edu.

Illinois Wesleyan University

Bloomington, Illinois

http://www.iwu.edu/

- **Independent** 4-year, founded 1850
- **Suburban** 85-acre campus
- **Endowment** $206.7 million
- **Coed** 1,649 undergraduate students, 100% full-time, 55% women, 45% men
- **Very difficult** entrance level, 61% of applicants were admitted

UNDERGRAD STUDENTS

1,646 full-time, 3 part-time. Students come from 31 states and territories; 23 other countries; 14% are from out of state; 5% Black or African

American, non-Hispanic/Latino; 8% Hispanic/Latino; 6% Asian, non-Hispanic/Latino; 0.1% Native Hawaiian or other Pacific Islander, non-Hispanic/Latino; 2% Two or more races, non-Hispanic/Latino; 1% Race/ethnicity unknown; 8% international; 2% transferred in; 79% live on campus.

Freshmen:
Admission: 3,697 applied, 2,250 admitted, 378 enrolled. *Average high school GPA:* 3.7. *Test scores:* ACT scores over 18: 100%; ACT scores over 24: 79%; ACT scores over 30: 20%.

Retention: 89% of full-time freshmen returned.

FACULTY
Total: 193, 74% full-time, 84% with terminal degrees.
Student/faculty ratio: 10:1.

ACADEMICS
Calendar: 4-4-1. *Degree:* bachelor's.

Special study options: advanced placement credit, distance learning, double majors, English as a second language, honors programs, independent study, internships, off-campus study, services for LD students, student-designed majors, study abroad. *ROTC:* Army (c).

Unusual degree programs: 3-2 engineering with Case Western Reserve University, Northwestern University, Washington University in St. Louis, Dartmouth College, University of Illinois; forestry with Duke University; occupational therapy.

Computers: 400 computers/terminals are available on campus for general student use. Students can access the following: campus intranet, computer help desk, free student e-mail accounts, online (class) grades, online (class) registration, online (class) schedules. Campuswide network is available. 100% of college-owned or -operated housing units are wired for high-speed Internet access. Wireless service is available via entire campus.

Library: The Ames Library. *Books:* 193,789 (physical), 35,089 (digital/electronic); *Serial titles:* 2,056 (physical), 80,933 (digital/electronic); *Databases:* 181. Students can reserve study rooms.

STUDENT LIFE
Housing options: on-campus residence required through junior year; coed, special housing for students with disabilities. Campus housing is university owned. Freshman campus housing is guaranteed.

Activities and organizations: drama/theater group, student-run newspaper, radio and television station, choral group, national fraternities, national sororities.

Athletics Member NCAA. All Division III. *Intercollegiate sports:* baseball M, basketball M/W, cheerleading M(c)/W(c), cross-country running M/W, football M, golf M/W, lacrosse M/W, soccer M/W, softball W, swimming and diving M/W, tennis M/W, track and field M/W, ultimate Frisbee M(c)/W(c), volleyball M(c)/W, water polo M(c). *Intramural sports:* badminton M/W, basketball M/W, football M/W, golf M/W, racquetball M/W, soccer M/W, softball M/W, tennis M/W, volleyball M/W.

Campus security: 24-hour emergency response devices and patrols, late-night transport/escort service, controlled dormitory access, emergency response team.

Student services: health clinic, personal/psychological counseling.

COSTS & FINANCIAL AID
Costs (2018–19) *Comprehensive fee:* $58,620 includes full-time tuition ($47,434), mandatory fees ($202), and room and board ($10,984). Part-time tuition: $1482 per credit hour. *College room only:* $6878. Room and board charges vary according to housing facility. *Payment plan:* installment. *Waivers:* employees or children of employees.

Financial Aid Of all full-time matriculated undergraduates who enrolled in 2017, 1,264 applied for aid, 1,065 were judged to have need, 188 had their need fully met. In 2017, 550 non-need-based awards were made. *Average percent of need met:* 85. *Average financial aid package:* $34,735. *Average need-based loan:* $5853. *Average need-based gift aid:* $27,990. *Average non-need-based aid:* $19,202. *Average indebtedness upon graduation:* $36,036.

APPLYING
Standardized Tests *Required:* SAT or ACT (for admission).
Options: electronic application, early admission, early action, deferred entrance.

Required: essay or personal statement, high school transcript, minimum 2.0 GPA, 1 letter of recommendation. *Recommended:* minimum 3.0 GPA, 2 letters of recommendation, interview.

Notification: 12/15 (early action).

CONTACT
Mr. Greg King, Associate Vice President for Enrollment Management, Illinois Wesleyan University, PO Box 2900, Bloomington, IL 61702-2900. *Phone:* 309-556-3031. *Toll-free phone:* 800-332-2498. *Fax:* 309-556-3820. *E-mail:* iwuadmit@iwu.edu.

Judson University

Elgin, Illinois

http://www.judsonu.edu/

- **Independent Baptist** comprehensive, founded 1963
- **Suburban** 90-acre campus with easy access to Chicago
- **Endowment** $11.2 million
- **Coed** 1,081 undergraduate students, 70% full-time, 55% women, 45% men
- **Moderately difficult** entrance level, 71% of applicants were admitted

UNDERGRAD STUDENTS
761 full-time, 320 part-time. Students come from 29 states and territories; 26 other countries; 18% are from out of state; 9% Black or African American, non-Hispanic/Latino; 22% Hispanic/Latino; 2% Asian, non-Hispanic/Latino; 0.3% Native Hawaiian or other Pacific Islander, non-Hispanic/Latino; 0.3% American Indian or Alaska Native, non-Hispanic/Latino; 2% Two or more races, non-Hispanic/Latino; 12% Race/ethnicity unknown; 4% international; 15% transferred in; 65% live on campus.

Freshmen:
Admission: 757 applied, 539 admitted, 181 enrolled. *Average high school GPA:* 3.3. *Test scores:* SAT evidence-based reading and writing scores over 500: 53%; SAT math scores over 500: 55%; ACT scores over 18: 84%; SAT evidence-based reading and writing scores over 600: 25%; SAT math scores over 600: 19%; ACT scores over 24: 36%; SAT evidence-based reading and writing scores over 700: 2%; SAT math scores over 700: 2%; ACT scores over 30: 3%.

Retention: 71% of full-time freshmen returned.

FACULTY
Total: 194, 30% full-time, 29% with terminal degrees.
Student/faculty ratio: 10:1.

ACADEMICS
Calendar: semesters. *Degrees:* certificates, associate, bachelor's, master's, and doctoral.

Special study options: academic remediation for entering students, accelerated degree program, adult/continuing education programs, advanced placement credit, distance learning, double majors, honors programs, independent study, internships, off-campus study, part-time degree program, services for LD students, student-designed majors, study abroad, summer session for credit. *ROTC:* Army (c).

Computers: 140 computers/terminals are available on campus for general student use. Students can access the following: campus intranet, computer help desk, free student e-mail accounts, online (class) grades, online (class) registration, online (class) schedules. Campuswide network is available. 100% of college-owned or -operated housing units are wired for high-speed Internet access. Wireless service is available via entire campus.

Library: Benjamin P. Browne Library. *Books:* 141,240 (physical), 2,243 (digital/electronic); *Serial titles:* 158 (physical), 48,401 (digital/electronic); *Databases:* 53. Weekly public service hours: 83; students can reserve study rooms.

STUDENT LIFE
Housing options: on-campus residence required through senior year; coed, men-only, women-only, special housing for students with disabilities. Campus housing is university owned. Freshman campus housing is guaranteed.

Activities and organizations: drama/theater group, choral group, Judson Student Organization, University Ministries, Judson Choir, Fellowship of Christian Athletes, Judson Business Society.

Athletics Member NAIA, NCCAA. *Intercollegiate sports:* baseball M(s), basketball M(s)/W(s), bowling M(s)/W(s), cheerleading M(s)/W(s), cross-country running M(s)/W(s), golf M(s)/W(s), soccer M(s)/W(s), softball W(s), tennis M(s)/W(s), track and field M(s)/W(s), volleyball M(s)/W(s). *Intramural sports:* basketball M/W, soccer M/W, volleyball M/W.

Campus security: 24-hour emergency response devices and patrols, controlled dormitory access.

Student services: health clinic, personal/psychological counseling.

COSTS & FINANCIAL AID
Costs (2018–19) *One-time required fee:* $100. *Comprehensive fee:* $39,848 includes full-time tuition ($28,834), mandatory fees ($1026), and room and board ($9988). Full-time tuition and fees vary according to class time, course load, degree level, and program. Part-time tuition: $1185 per credit hour. Part-time tuition and fees vary according to class time, course load, degree level, and program. *College room only:* $7764. Room and board charges vary according to board plan. *Payment plan:* deferred payment. *Waivers:* adult students, senior citizens, and employees or children of employees.

Financial Aid Of all full-time matriculated undergraduates who enrolled in 2015, 729 applied for aid, 678 were judged to have need, 538 had their need fully met. 271 Federal Work-Study jobs (averaging $1610). In 2015, 99 non-need-based awards were made. *Average percent of need met:* 62. *Average financial aid package:* $18,502. *Average need-based loan:* $4719. *Average need-based gift aid:* $9762. *Average non-need-based aid:* $7582. *Financial aid deadline:* 8/1.

APPLYING
Standardized Tests *Required:* SAT or ACT (for admission).
Options: electronic application.
Application fee: $50.
Required: high school transcript, minimum 2.5 GPA, minimum ACT score of 21, lifestyle statement. *Required for some:* essay or personal statement, . *Recommended:* essay or personal statement.
Application deadlines: rolling (freshmen), rolling (transfers).
Notification: continuous (freshmen), continuous (transfers).

CONTACT
Mrs. Nancy Binger, Executive Director of Enrollment Services, Judson University, 1151 North State Street, Elgin, IL 60123. *Phone:* 847-628-2512. *Toll-free phone:* 800-879-5376. *Fax:* 847-628-2526. *E-mail:* nbinger@judsonu.edu.

Kendall College
Chicago, Illinois
http://www.kendall.edu/
- **Proprietary** 4-year, founded 1934, part of Laureate International Universities
- **Urban** campus with easy access to Chicago
- **Coed**
- **Minimally difficult** entrance level

FACULTY
Student/faculty ratio: 8:1.

ACADEMICS
Calendar: quarters. *Degrees:* associate and bachelor's.
Library: Iva Freeman Library. *Books:* 11,484 (physical); *Serial titles:* 56 (physical); *Databases:* 23. Weekly public service hours: 61.

STUDENT LIFE
Housing options: coed. Campus housing is leased by the school.
Activities and organizations: International Club, SEED Club, Soccer Club, Meditation Club, Kendall Cares Community Service.
Campus security: 24-hour emergency response devices and patrols, controlled dormitory access, 24-hour security at dorms.
Student services: personal/psychological counseling.

FINANCIAL AID
Financial Aid Of all full-time matriculated undergraduates who enrolled in 2016, 527 applied for aid, 490 were judged to have need, 47 had their need fully met. In 2016, 14 non-need-based awards were made. *Average percent of need met:* 58. *Average financial aid package:* $16,522.

Average need-based loan: $3773. *Average need-based gift aid:* $6560. *Average non-need-based aid:* $6649.

APPLYING
Standardized Tests *Required for some:* SAT or ACT (for admission).
Options: electronic application, deferred entrance.
Application fee: $25.
Required: essay or personal statement, high school transcript, interview. *Recommended:* minimum 2.0 GPA.

CONTACT
Ms. Angela Batchelor, Manager of Enrollment, Kendall College, 900 North Branch Street, Chicago, IL 60642. *Toll-free phone:* 888-90-KENDALL. *E-mail:* info@kendall.edu.

Knox College
Galesburg, Illinois
http://www.knox.edu/
- **Independent** 4-year, founded 1837
- **Small-town** 82-acre campus with easy access to Peoria, Quad Cities
- **Endowment** $143.2 million
- **Coed** 1,356 undergraduate students, 98% full-time, 57% women, 43% men
- **Very difficult** entrance level, 72% of applicants were admitted

UNDERGRAD STUDENTS
1,334 full-time, 22 part-time. Students come from 46 states and territories; 46 other countries; 55% are from out of state; 8% Black or African American, non-Hispanic/Latino; 15% Hispanic/Latino; 5% Asian, non-Hispanic/Latino; 0.1% Native Hawaiian or other Pacific Islander, non-Hispanic/Latino; 6% Two or more races, non-Hispanic/Latino; 2% Race/ethnicity unknown; 17% international; 2% transferred in; 89% live on campus.

Freshmen:
Admission: 3,222 applied, 2,305 admitted, 358 enrolled. *Average high school GPA:* 3.4. *Test scores:* SAT evidence-based reading and writing scores over 500: 96%; SAT math scores over 500: 95%; ACT scores over 18: 99%; SAT evidence-based reading and writing scores over 600: 65%; SAT math scores over 600: 60%; ACT scores over 24: 74%; SAT evidence-based reading and writing scores over 700: 13%; SAT math scores over 700: 23%; ACT scores over 30: 26%.
Retention: 87% of full-time freshmen returned.

FACULTY
Total: 140, 79% full-time, 84% with terminal degrees.
Student/faculty ratio: 11:1.

ACADEMICS
Calendar: trimesters. *Degree:* bachelor's.
Special study options: advanced placement credit, double majors, English as a second language, honors programs, independent study, internships, off-campus study, part-time degree program, services for LD students, student-designed majors, study abroad.
Unusual degree programs: 3-2 engineering with University of Illinois at Urbana–Champaign, Washington University in St. Louis, Columbia University, Rensselaer Polytechnic Institute; forestry with Duke University; nursing with Rush University.
Computers: 275 computers/terminals are available on campus for general student use. Students can access the following: campus intranet, computer help desk, free student e-mail accounts, online (class) grades, online (class) registration, online (class) schedules, transcripts, learning management system. Campuswide network is available. 100% of college-owned or -operated housing units are wired for high-speed Internet access. Wireless service is available via entire campus.
Library: Henry M. Seymour Library plus 1 other. *Books:* 338,862 (physical), 10,401 (digital/electronic); *Serial titles:* 157 (physical), 35,779 (digital/electronic); *Databases:* 79. Weekly public service hours: 106; students can reserve study rooms.

STUDENT LIFE
Housing options: on-campus residence required through junior year; coed, men-only, women-only, special housing for students with

disabilities. Campus housing is university owned. Freshman campus housing is guaranteed.

Activities and organizations: drama/theater group, student-run newspaper, radio station, choral group, Student-Run Radio Station (WVKC), Best Buddies (Assistance and Friendship for Individuals with Intellectual Disabilities), Student Newspaper (The Knox Student), Common Ground, Terpsichore (Dance Collective), national fraternities, national sororities.

Athletics Member NCAA. All Division III. *Intercollegiate sports:* baseball M, basketball M/W, cross-country running M/W, football M, golf M/W, soccer M/W, softball W, swimming and diving M/W, tennis M/W, track and field M/W, volleyball W. *Intramural sports:* basketball M/W, equestrian sports M(c)/W(c), soccer M/W, ultimate Frisbee M(c)/W(c), volleyball M/W, water polo M(c)/W(c).

Campus security: 24-hour emergency response devices and patrols, late-night transport/escort service.

Student services: health clinic, personal/psychological counseling.

COSTS & FINANCIAL AID

Costs (2018–19) *Comprehensive fee:* $56,424 includes full-time tuition ($45,783), mandatory fees ($771), and room and board ($9870). Full-time tuition and fees vary according to course load. Part-time tuition: $5087 per credit. Part-time tuition and fees vary according to course load. *College room only:* $4941. Room and board charges vary according to housing facility. *Payment plan:* installment. *Waivers:* employees or children of employees.

Financial Aid Of all full-time matriculated undergraduates who enrolled in 2017, 1,215 applied for aid, 1,130 were judged to have need, 388 had their need fully met. 681 Federal Work-Study jobs (averaging $2200). In 2017, 175 non-need-based awards were made. *Average percent of need met:* 86. *Average financial aid package:* $35,746. *Average need-based loan:* $4280. *Average need-based gift aid:* $28,374. *Average non-need-based aid:* $21,835. *Average indebtedness upon graduation:* $31,235.

APPLYING

Options: electronic application, early admission, early decision, early action, deferred entrance.

Application fee: $50.

Required: essay or personal statement, high school transcript, 2 letters of recommendation. *Recommended:* interview.

Application deadlines: 4/1 (transfers), 12/1 (early action).

Early decision deadline: 11/1.

Notification: 3/15 (freshmen), 5/1 (transfers), 11/15 (early decision), 1/15 (early action).

CONTACT

Mr. Paul Steenis, Dean of Admission, Knox College, 2 East South Street, Campus Box148, Galesburg, IL 61401. *Phone:* 309-341-7100. *Toll-free phone:* 800-678-KNOX. *Fax:* 309-341-7070. *E-mail:* admission@knox.edu.

Lake Forest College
Lake Forest, Illinois
http://www.lakeforest.edu/

- **Independent** comprehensive, founded 1857
- **Suburban** 107-acre campus with easy access to Chicago
- **Endowment** $83.9 million
- **Coed**
- **Moderately difficult** entrance level

FACULTY
Student/faculty ratio: 12:1.

ACADEMICS
Calendar: semesters. *Degrees:* bachelor's, master's, and postbachelor's certificates.
Library: Donnelley and Lee Library. *Books:* 294,734 (physical), 169,997 (digital/electronic); *Serial titles:* 49,666 (physical), 68,879 (digital/electronic); *Databases:* 72. Weekly public service hours: 91; study areas open 24 hours, 5–7 days a week; students can reserve study rooms.

STUDENT LIFE
Housing options: on-campus residence required through junior year; coed. Campus housing is university owned. Freshman applicants given priority for college housing.

Activities and organizations: drama/theater group, student-run newspaper, radio station, choral group, Student Government, Athletic Council, United Black Association, Alpha Phi, PRIDE, national fraternities, national sororities.

Athletics Member NCAA. All Division III.

Campus security: 24-hour emergency response devices and patrols, student patrols, late-night transport/escort service, controlled dormitory access.

Student services: health clinic, personal/psychological counseling.

COSTS & FINANCIAL AID

Costs (2017–18) *Comprehensive fee:* $55,600 includes full-time tuition ($44,824), mandatory fees ($724), and room and board ($10,052). Full-time tuition and fees vary according to course load and degree level. Part-time tuition: $5603 per course. Part-time tuition and fees vary according to course load and degree level. *Required fees:* $724 per year part-time. *College room only:* $4800. Room and board charges vary according to board plan and housing facility.

Financial Aid *Financial aid deadline:* 5/1.

APPLYING

Standardized Tests *Recommended:* SAT or ACT (for admission).

Options: electronic application, early decision, early action, deferred entrance.

Required: essay or personal statement, high school transcript, 1 letter of recommendation. *Recommended:* interview.

CONTACT

Christopher Ellertson, Vice President for Enrollment, Lake Forest College, 555 North Sheridan Road, Lake Forest, IL 60045-2338. *Phone:* 847-735-5000. *Toll-free phone:* 800-828-4751. *Fax:* 847-735-6271. *E-mail:* admissions@lakeforest.edu.

Lakeview College of Nursing
Danville, Illinois
http://www.lakeviewcol.edu/

- **Independent** upper-level, founded 1987
- **Small-town** 1-acre campus
- **Coed, primarily women**
- **Moderately difficult** entrance level

FACULTY
Student/faculty ratio: 12:1.

ACADEMICS
Calendar: semesters. *Degree:* bachelor's.
Library: Lakeview College of Nursing Library plus 1 other.

STUDENT LIFE
Housing options: college housing not available.

Campus security: 24-hour emergency response devices and patrols.

COSTS & FINANCIAL AID

Costs (2017–18) *Tuition:* $13,200 full-time, $440 per credit hour part-time. Full-time tuition and fees vary according to course level, course load, and location. Part-time tuition and fees vary according to course level, course load, and location. *Required fees:* $2410 full-time, $65 per credit hour part-time.

Financial Aid Of all full-time matriculated undergraduates who enrolled in 2017, 384 applied for aid, 371 were judged to have need. *Average percent of need met:* 82. *Average financial aid package:* $22,950. *Average need-based loan:* $5500. *Average need-based gift aid:* $5750. *Financial aid deadline:* 10/1.

APPLYING

Standardized Tests *Required:* Nursing Admission Test (for admission).

Options: early admission.

Application fee: $100.

CONTACT
Admissions Office, Lakeview College of Nursing, 903 North Logan Avenue, Danville, IL 61832. *Phone:* 217-709-0920. *Fax:* 217-709-0953. *E-mail:* admission@lakeviewcol.edu.

Lewis University
Romeoville, Illinois
http://www.lewisu.edu/
- **Independent** comprehensive, founded 1932, affiliated with Roman Catholic Church
- **Suburban** 410-acre campus with easy access to Chicago
- **Coed** 4,506 undergraduate students, 82% full-time, 53% women, 47% men
- **Moderately difficult** entrance level, 54% of applicants were admitted

UNDERGRAD STUDENTS
3,687 full-time, 819 part-time. Students come from 33 states and territories; 26 other countries; 9% are from out of state; 5% Black or African American, non-Hispanic/Latino; 20% Hispanic/Latino; 4% Asian, non-Hispanic/Latino; 0.1% Native Hawaiian or other Pacific Islander, non-Hispanic/Latino; 0.2% American Indian or Alaska Native, non-Hispanic/Latino; 3% Two or more races, non-Hispanic/Latino; 8% Race/ethnicity unknown; 2% international; 12% transferred in; 22% live on campus.

Freshmen:
Admission: 5,447 applied, 2,932 admitted, 609 enrolled. *Average high school GPA:* 3.5. *Test scores:* SAT evidence-based reading and writing scores over 500: 62%; SAT math scores over 500: 67%; ACT scores over 18: 97%; SAT evidence-based reading and writing scores over 600: 29%; SAT math scores over 600: 34%; ACT scores over 24: 44%; SAT evidence-based reading and writing scores over 700: 7%; SAT math scores over 700: 4%; ACT scores over 30: 6%.
Retention: 80% of full-time freshmen returned.

FACULTY
Total: 675, 33% full-time, 28% with terminal degrees.
Student/faculty ratio: 13:1.

ACADEMICS
Calendar: semesters. *Degrees:* certificates, associate, bachelor's, master's, doctoral, post-master's, and postbachelor's certificates.
Special study options: academic remediation for entering students, accelerated degree program, adult/continuing education programs, advanced placement credit, distance learning, double majors, English as a second language, honors programs, independent study, internships, off-campus study, part-time degree program, services for LD students, student-designed majors, study abroad, summer session for credit. *ROTC:* Army (c), Air Force (c).
Computers: 350 computers/terminals are available on campus for general student use. Students can access the following: campus intranet, computer help desk, free student e-mail accounts, online (class) grades, online (class) registration, online (class) schedules, online help desk, online billing, online financial aid, online payments, online admission application, online housing application, online application for graduation, online Blackboard course management system, online tutoring. Campuswide network is available. 100% of college-owned or -operated housing units are wired for high-speed Internet access. Wireless service is available via entire campus.
Library: Lewis University Library. *Books:* 120,468 (physical), 527,534 (digital/electronic); *Serial titles:* 1,622 (physical), 151,185 (digital/electronic); *Databases:* 115. Weekly public service hours: 102; students can reserve study rooms.

STUDENT LIFE
Housing options: coed. Campus housing is university owned. Freshman campus housing is guaranteed.
Activities and organizations: drama/theater group, student-run newspaper, radio and television station, choral group, Student Governing Board, Student Nurses Association, Latin American Student Organization, Theta Kappa Pi Sorority, Delta Sigma Pi (business fraternity), national fraternities, national sororities.
Athletics Member NCAA. All Division II except volleyball (Division I).
Intercollegiate sports: badminton M(c)/W(c), baseball M(s), basketball M(s)/W(s), bowling W(s); cheerleading W(s)(c), cross-country running M(s)/W(s), golf M(s)/W(s), ice hockey M(c), lacrosse W(s), soccer M(s)/W(s), softball W(s), swimming and diving M(s)/W(s), tennis M(s)/W(s), track and field M(s)/W(s), volleyball M(s)/W(s), water polo M(c)/W(c). *Intramural sports:* archery M(c)/W(c), badminton M/W, baseball M(c), basketball M(c)/W(c), bowling M/W, football M/W, lacrosse M(c)/W(c), rugby M(c)/W(c), sand volleyball M/W, soccer M(c)/W(c), softball M/W, table tennis M/W, ultimate Frisbee M(c)/W(c), volleyball M(c)/W(c), water polo M/W, weight lifting M(c)/W(c).
Campus security: 24-hour emergency response devices and patrols, late-night transport/escort service, controlled dormitory access, Emergency notification system.
Student services: health clinic, personal/psychological counseling.

COSTS & FINANCIAL AID
Costs (2018–19) *Comprehensive fee:* $43,028 includes full-time tuition ($32,300), mandatory fees ($150), and room and board ($10,578). Full-time tuition and fees vary according to course load, location, and program. Part-time tuition: $948 per credit hour. Part-time tuition and fees vary according to course load, location, and program. *Required fees:* $75 per term part-time. *Room and board:* Room and board charges vary according to board plan and housing facility. *Payment plan:* installment. *Waivers:* children of alumni and employees or children of employees.
Financial Aid Of all full-time matriculated undergraduates who enrolled in 2017, 3,134 applied for aid, 2,805 were judged to have need, 556 had their need fully met. In 2017, 605 non-need-based awards were made. *Average percent of need met:* 86. *Average financial aid package:* $25,119. *Average need-based loan:* $4425. *Average need-based gift aid:* $15,882. *Average non-need-based aid:* $11,661. *Average indebtedness upon graduation:* $34,006. *Financial aid deadline:* 5/1.

APPLYING
Standardized Tests *Required:* SAT or ACT (for admission).
Options: electronic application, deferred entrance.
Application fee: $40.
Required: high school transcript, minimum 2.0 GPA. *Required for some:* interview.
Application deadlines: 8/1 (freshmen), rolling (transfers).
Notification: continuous (freshmen), continuous (transfers).

CONTACT
Mr. Ryan Cockerill, Director of Admission, Lewis University, Unit #297, One University Parkway, Romeoville, IL 60446. *Phone:* 815-836-5237. *Toll-free phone:* 800-897-9000. *Fax:* 815-836-5002. *E-mail:* cockerry@lewisu.edu.

Lincoln Christian University
Lincoln, Illinois
http://www.lincolnchristian.edu/
- **Independent** comprehensive, founded 1944, affiliated with Christian Churches and Churches of Christ
- **Small-town** 100-acre campus
- **Endowment** $5.2 million
- **Coed** 464 undergraduate students, 75% full-time, 51% women, 49% men
- **Moderately difficult** entrance level, 62% of applicants were admitted

UNDERGRAD STUDENTS
347 full-time, 117 part-time. Students come from 31 states and territories; 3 other countries; 30% are from out of state; 7% Black or African American, non-Hispanic/Latino; 2% Hispanic/Latino; 0.6% Asian, non-Hispanic/Latino; 0.4% American Indian or Alaska Native, non-Hispanic/Latino; 2% Two or more races, non-Hispanic/Latino; 2% Race/ethnicity unknown; 3% international; 7% transferred in; 22% live on campus.

Freshmen:
Admission: 301 applied, 187 admitted, 82 enrolled. *Average high school GPA:* 3.2.
Retention: 85% of full-time freshmen returned.

FACULTY
Total: 69, 48% full-time, 62% with terminal degrees.
Student/faculty ratio: 12:1.

ACADEMICS

Calendar: semesters. *Degrees:* associate, bachelor's, master's, and doctoral.

Special study options: academic remediation for entering students, adult/continuing education programs, advanced placement credit, cooperative education, distance learning, double majors, external degree program, honors programs, independent study, internships, off-campus study, part-time degree program, services for LD students, study abroad, summer session for credit.

Computers: 51 computers/terminals are available on campus for general student use. Students can access the following: campus intranet, computer help desk, free student e-mail accounts, online (class) grades, online (class) registration, online (class) schedules. Campuswide network is available. 100% of college-owned or -operated housing units are wired for high-speed Internet access. Wireless service is available via entire campus.

Library: Jessie Eury Library. *Books:* 92,813 (physical), 55,082 (digital/electronic); *Serial titles:* 719 (physical), 15,442 (digital/electronic); *Databases:* 52. Weekly public service hours: 82; students can reserve study rooms.

STUDENT LIFE

Housing options: on-campus residence required through senior year; men-only, women-only. Campus housing is university owned. Freshman campus housing is guaranteed.

Activities and organizations: drama/theater group, choral group, Chorale, Student Cabinet, American Association of Christian Counselors (AACC) - Student Chapter, Cheerleading.

Athletics Member NAIA, NCCAA. *Intercollegiate sports:* baseball M(s), basketball M(s)/W(s), soccer M(s)/W(s), volleyball W(s). *Intramural sports:* badminton M/W, basketball M/W, soccer M/W, ultimate Frisbee M/W, volleyball M/W.

Campus security: 24-hour emergency response devices, student patrols, controlled dormitory access, 24-hour emergency alert hotline.

Student services: personal/psychological counseling.

COSTS & FINANCIAL AID

Costs (2018–19) *Comprehensive fee:* $20,764 includes full-time tuition ($13,200) and room and board ($7564). Part-time tuition: $440 per credit hour. *College room only:* $3600. *Payment plan:* installment. *Waivers:* senior citizens and employees or children of employees.

Financial Aid Of all full-time matriculated undergraduates who enrolled in 2015, 392 applied for aid, 349 were judged to have need, 22 had their need fully met. 60 Federal Work-Study jobs (averaging $1945). 120 state and other part-time jobs (averaging $1910). In 2015, 64 non-need-based awards were made. *Average percent of need met:* 52. *Average financial aid package:* $10,199. *Average need-based loan:* $3805. *Average need-based gift aid:* $7018. *Average non-need-based aid:* $2866. *Average indebtedness upon graduation:* $32,138.

APPLYING

Standardized Tests *Required:* SAT or ACT (for admission).

Options: electronic application, deferred entrance.

Required: essay or personal statement, 3 letters of recommendation. *Required for some:* high school transcript, interview.

Application deadlines: rolling (freshmen), rolling (out-of-state freshmen), rolling (transfers).

Notification: continuous (freshmen), continuous (out-of-state freshmen), continuous (transfers).

CONTACT

Mrs. Mary K. Davis, Admissions Office Manager, Lincoln Christian University, 100 Campus View Drive, Lincoln, IL 62656. *Phone:* 217-732-3168 Ext. 2251. *Toll-free phone:* 888-522-5228. *Fax:* 217-732-4199. *E-mail:* enroll@lincolnchristian.edu.

Lincoln College

Lincoln, Illinois

http://www.lincolncollege.edu/

- **Independent** 4-year, founded 1865
- **Small-town** 42-acre campus
- **Endowment** $20.5 million
- **Coed** 1,120 undergraduate students, 67% full-time, 55% women, 45% men
- **Minimally difficult** entrance level, 68% of applicants were admitted

UNDERGRAD STUDENTS

754 full-time, 366 part-time. Students come from 18 states and territories; 8 other countries; 7% are from out of state; 44% Black or African American, non-Hispanic/Latino; 7% Hispanic/Latino; 0.4% Asian, non-Hispanic/Latino; 0.1% American Indian or Alaska Native, non-Hispanic/Latino; 5% Two or more races, non-Hispanic/Latino; 2% Race/ethnicity unknown; 1% international; 7% transferred in.

Freshmen:

Admission: 1,537 applied, 1,045 admitted, 297 enrolled. *Average high school GPA:* 2.6.

Retention: 65% of full-time freshmen returned.

FACULTY

Total: 114, 31% full-time.

Student/faculty ratio: 14:1.

ACADEMICS

Calendar: semesters. *Degrees:* associate and bachelor's.

Special study options: academic remediation for entering students, accelerated degree program, freshman honors college, honors programs, independent study, internships, part-time degree program, services for LD students, summer session for credit.

Computers: Students can access the following: campus intranet, computer help desk, free student e-mail accounts, online (class) grades, online (class) schedules. Campuswide network is available. Wireless service is available via entire campus.

Library: McKinstry Library. *Books:* 23,449 (physical), 182,420 (digital/electronic); *Serial titles:* 3 (physical); *Databases:* 38. Students can reserve study rooms.

STUDENT LIFE

Housing options: on-campus residence required through sophomore year; men-only, women-only. Campus housing is university owned. Freshman campus housing is guaranteed.

Activities and organizations: drama/theater group, student-run radio and television station, choral group, Black Student Union, Phi Theta Kappa, Purple Pulse, Student Activities Board, Woment of Worth.

Athletics Member NJCAA. *Intercollegiate sports:* baseball M(s), basketball M(s)/W(s), cheerleading M(s)(c)/W(s)(c), cross-country running M(s)/W(s), golf M(s)/W(s), soccer M(s)/W(s), softball W(s), swimming and diving M(s)/W(s), track and field M(s)/W(s), volleyball M(s)(c)/W(s), wrestling M(s). *Intramural sports:* basketball M/W, football M/W, sand volleyball M/W, softball M/W, table tennis M/W.

Campus security: 24-hour emergency response devices and patrols, controlled dormitory access.

Student services: health clinic, personal/psychological counseling.

COSTS & FINANCIAL AID

Costs (2018–19) *One-time required fee:* $50. *Comprehensive fee:* $26,300 includes full-time tuition ($17,500), mandatory fees ($1100), and room and board ($7700). Part-time tuition: $310 per credit hour. No tuition increase for student's term of enrollment. *College room only:* $3000. Room and board charges vary according to housing facility. *Payment plans:* tuition prepayment, installment. *Waivers:* employees or children of employees.

Financial Aid Of all full-time matriculated undergraduates who enrolled in 2016, 200 Federal Work-Study jobs (averaging $900).

APPLYING

Standardized Tests *Required:* SAT or ACT (for admission).

Options: electronic application, early admission, deferred entrance.

Required: high school transcript, minimum 2.0 GPA. *Required for some:* essay or personal statement, 2 letters of recommendation, interview.

Application deadlines: rolling (freshmen), rolling (out-of-state freshmen), rolling (transfers).

CONTACT
Lincoln College, 300 Keokuk Street, Lincoln, IL 62656-1699. *Phone:* 217-735-7251 Ext. 7251. *Toll-free phone:* 800-569-0558.

Loyola University Chicago
Chicago, Illinois
http://www.luc.edu/
- **Independent Roman Catholic (Jesuit)** university, founded 1870
- **Urban** 105-acre campus
- **Endowment** $593.5 million
- **Coed** 11,420 undergraduate students, 94% full-time, 66% women, 34% men
- **Moderately difficult** entrance level, 71% of applicants were admitted

UNDERGRAD STUDENTS
10,681 full-time, 739 part-time. Students come from 52 states and territories; 103 other countries; 35% are from out of state; 6% Black or African American, non-Hispanic/Latino; 16% Hispanic/Latino; 12% Asian, non-Hispanic/Latino; 0.3% Native Hawaiian or other Pacific Islander, non-Hispanic/Latino; 0.1% American Indian or Alaska Native, non-Hispanic/Latino; 4% Two or more races, non-Hispanic/Latino; 1% Race/ethnicity unknown; 5% international; 5% transferred in; 40% live on campus.

Freshmen:
Admission: 23,571 applied, 16,639 admitted, 2,654 enrolled. *Average high school GPA:* 3.7. *Test scores:* SAT evidence-based reading and writing scores over 500: 99%; SAT math scores over 500: 94%; ACT scores over 18: 100%; SAT evidence-based reading and writing scores over 600: 63%; SAT math scores over 600: 49%; ACT scores over 24: 81%; SAT evidence-based reading and writing scores over 700: 12%; SAT math scores over 700: 10%; ACT scores over 30: 23%.
Retention: 83% of full-time freshmen returned.

FACULTY
Total: 1,566, 53% full-time.
Student/faculty ratio: 14:1.

ACADEMICS
Calendar: semesters. *Degrees:* certificates, associate, bachelor's, master's, doctoral, post-master's, and postbachelor's certificates (also offers adult part-time program with significant enrollment not reflected in profile).
Special study options: accelerated degree program, adult/continuing education programs, advanced placement credit, cooperative education, distance learning, double majors, English as a second language, freshman honors college, honors programs, independent study, internships, off-campus study, part-time degree program, services for LD students, study abroad, summer session for credit. *ROTC:* Army (b), Navy (c), Air Force (c).
Unusual degree programs: 3-2 business administration; engineering; social work; political science, sociology, psychology/applied social psychology, computers, biology, accounting, information technology, criminal justice and criminology.
Computers: 1,300 computers/terminals are available on campus for general student use. Students can access the following: campus intranet, computer help desk, free student e-mail accounts, online (class) grades, online (class) registration, online (class) schedules. Campuswide network is available. 100% of college-owned or -operated housing units are wired for high-speed Internet access. Wireless service is available via entire campus.
Library: Cudahy Library plus 7 others. *Books:* 1.9 million (physical), 568,720 (digital/electronic); *Serial titles:* 2,245 (physical), 58,389 (digital/electronic); *Databases:* 545. Weekly public service hours: 144; study areas open 24 hours, 5–7 days a week; students can reserve study rooms.

STUDENT LIFE
Housing options: on-campus residence required through sophomore year; coed, special housing for students with disabilities. Campus housing is university owned. Freshman campus housing is guaranteed.

Activities and organizations: drama/theater group, student-run newspaper, radio station, choral group, Panhellenic Council, National Society of Collegiate Scholars, Vegetarian and Vegan Society, Interfraternity Council, American Medical Student Association, national fraternities, national sororities.
Athletics Member NCAA. All Division I. *Intercollegiate sports:* basketball M(s)/W(s), cross-country running M(s)/W(s), golf M(s)/W(s), soccer M(s)/W(s), softball W(s), track and field M(s)/W(s), volleyball M(s)/W(s). *Intramural sports:* badminton M/W, baseball M(c), basketball M/W, cross-country running M(c)/W(c), field hockey W(c), football M(c)/W(c), golf M(c)/W(c), ice hockey M(c)/W(c), lacrosse M(c)/W(c), racquetball M/W, rugby M(c)/W(c), soccer M(c)/W(c), softball W(c), swimming and diving M(c)/W(c), table tennis M/W, tennis M(c)/W(c), ultimate Frisbee M(c)/W(c), volleyball M(c)/W(c), water polo M(c)/W(c).
Campus security: 24-hour emergency response devices, late-night transport/escort service, controlled dormitory access, Loyola Alert (special service to provide personalized, time-sensitive alerts to students, faculty, staff and other personnel).
Student services: health clinic, personal/psychological counseling, women's center.

COSTS & FINANCIAL AID
Costs (2018–19) *Tuition:* $42,720 full-time, $788 per credit hour part-time. Full-time tuition and fees vary according to degree level, location, program, and student level. Part-time tuition and fees vary according to course load. *Required fees:* $1088 full-time, $350 per year part-time. *Room only:* Room and board charges vary according to board plan, housing facility, and location. *Payment plans:* installment, deferred payment. *Waivers:* senior citizens and employees or children of employees.
Financial Aid Of all full-time matriculated undergraduates who enrolled in 2017, 7,797 applied for aid, 6,846 were judged to have need, 945 had their need fully met. 5,021 Federal Work-Study jobs (averaging $2790). In 2017, 3097 non-need-based awards were made. *Average percent of need met:* 81. *Average financial aid package:* $34,844. *Average need-based loan:* $4617. *Average need-based gift aid:* $21,420. *Average non-need-based aid:* $16,444. *Average indebtedness upon graduation:* $34,973.

APPLYING
Standardized Tests *Required:* SAT or ACT (for admission).
Options: electronic application.
Required: essay or personal statement, high school transcript, minimum 2.0 GPA. *Recommended:* letters of recommendation, interview.
Notification: continuous (freshmen), continuous (transfers).

CONTACT
Ms. Erin Moriarty, Director of Undergraduate Admissions, Loyola University Chicago, 1032 West Sheridan Road, Chicago, IL 60660. *Phone:* 773-508-3079. *Toll-free phone:* 800-262-2373. *E-mail:* admission@luc.edu.

MacMurray College
Jacksonville, Illinois
http://www.mac.edu/
- **Independent United Methodist** 4-year, founded 1846
- **Small-town** 60-acre campus
- **Endowment** $13.5 million
- **Coed**
- **Moderately difficult** entrance level

ACADEMICS
Calendar: semesters. *Degrees:* associate and bachelor's.
Library: Henry Pfeiffer Library. *Books:* 87,300 (physical), 4,591 (digital/electronic); *Serial titles:* 893 (physical), 13,638 (digital/electronic); *Databases:* 42. Weekly public service hours: 85.

STUDENT LIFE
Housing options: on-campus residence required through junior year; coed. Campus housing is university owned. Freshman campus housing is guaranteed.

Activities and organizations: drama/theater group, choral group, Campus Activity Board, MacMurray Student Association, Helping Hands, Belles Lettres, Phi Nu.
Athletics Member NCAA. All Division III.

Campus security: 24-hour emergency response devices and patrols, student patrols, late-night transport/escort service, controlled dormitory access.

Student services: health clinic, personal/psychological counseling.

COSTS & FINANCIAL AID

Costs (2017–18) *Comprehensive fee:* $35,020 includes full-time tuition ($25,340), mandatory fees ($760), and room and board ($8920). Full-time tuition and fees vary according to course load and location. Part-time tuition: $780 per credit hour. Part-time tuition and fees vary according to course load and location. *Required fees:* $40 per credit hour part-time, $10 per term part-time. *Room and board:* Room and board charges vary according to housing facility. *Payment plans:* installment, deferred payment.

Financial Aid Of all full-time matriculated undergraduates who enrolled in 2016, 512 applied for aid, 481 were judged to have need, 98 had their need fully met. 313 Federal Work-Study jobs (averaging $1510). In 2016, 43 non-need-based awards were made. *Average percent of need met:* 80. *Average financial aid package:* $21,509. *Average need-based loan:* $5134. *Average need-based gift aid:* $16,287. *Average non-need-based aid:* $11,288. *Average indebtedness upon graduation:* $36,877.

APPLYING

Standardized Tests *Required:* SAT or ACT (for admission).

Options: electronic application, early admission.

Required: high school transcript, minimum 2.5 GPA. *Required for some:* essay or personal statement.

CONTACT

Kristen Chenoweth, Associate Director of Admissions, MacMurray College, 447 East College Avenue, Jacksonville, IL 62650. *Phone:* 217-479-7063. *Toll-free phone:* 800-252-7485. *Fax:* 217-291-0702. *E-mail:* kristen.chenoweth@mac.edu.

McKendree University

Lebanon, Illinois

http://www.mckendree.edu/

- **Independent** university, founded 1828, affiliated with United Methodist Church
- **Suburban** 235-acre campus with easy access to St. Louis, MO; Belleville, IL
- **Coed** 2,104 undergraduate students, 80% full-time, 54% women, 46% men
- **Moderately difficult** entrance level, 62% of applicants were admitted

UNDERGRAD STUDENTS

1,692 full-time, 412 part-time. Students come from 40 states and territories; 38 other countries; 27% are from out of state; 13% Black or African American, non-Hispanic/Latino; 4% Hispanic/Latino; 0.6% Asian, non-Hispanic/Latino; 0.1% Native Hawaiian or other Pacific Islander, non-Hispanic/Latino; 0.3% American Indian or Alaska Native, non-Hispanic/Latino; 3% Two or more races, non-Hispanic/Latino; 10% Race/ethnicity unknown; 3% international; 5% transferred in; 77% live on campus.

Freshmen:

Admission: 2,206 applied, 1,361 admitted, 364 enrolled. *Average high school GPA:* 3.5. *Test scores:* SAT evidence-based reading and writing scores over 500: 71%; SAT math scores over 500: 70%; ACT scores over 18: 95%; SAT evidence-based reading and writing scores over 600: 23%; SAT math scores over 600: 11%; ACT scores over 24: 37%; ACT scores over 30: 5%.

Retention: 75% of full-time freshmen returned.

FACULTY

Total: 278, 35% full-time, 46% with terminal degrees.

Student/faculty ratio: 14:1.

ACADEMICS

Calendar: semesters. *Degrees:* associate, bachelor's, master's, doctoral, and post-master's certificates.

Special study options: academic remediation for entering students, accelerated degree program, adult/continuing education programs, advanced placement credit, cooperative education, distance learning, double majors, freshman honors college, honors programs, independent study, internships, off-campus study, part-time degree program, services for LD students, student-designed majors, study abroad, summer session for credit. *ROTC:* Army (c), Air Force (c).

Unusual degree programs: 3-2 Occupational Therapy with Washington University in St. Louis.

Computers: 380 computers/terminals are available on campus for general student use. Students can access the following: campus intranet, computer help desk, free student e-mail accounts, online (class) grades, online (class) registration, online (class) schedules. Campuswide network is available. 100% of college-owned or -operated housing units are wired for high-speed Internet access. Wireless service is available via entire campus.

Library: Holman Library. *Books:* 76,806 (physical), 11,853 (digital/electronic); *Serial titles:* 5,099 (physical), 7,229 (digital/electronic); *Databases:* 59. Students can reserve study rooms.

STUDENT LIFE

Housing options: on-campus residence required through junior year; coed, special housing for students with disabilities. Campus housing is university owned and leased by the school. Freshman campus housing is guaranteed.

Activities and organizations: drama/theater group, student-run newspaper, radio station, choral group, marching band, Center for Public Service, Wonders of Wellness, Campus Ministries, APO, Debate, national fraternities, national sororities.

Athletics Member NCAA. All Division II except volleyball (Division I). *Intercollegiate sports:* baseball M(s), basketball M(s)/W(s), bowling M(c)/W(s), cheerleading M(s)(c)/W(s)(c), cross-country running M(s)/W(s), fencing M(c)/W(c), football M(s), golf M(s)/W(s), ice hockey M(c)/W(c), lacrosse W(s), soccer M(s)/W(s), softball W(s), swimming and diving M(s)/W(s), tennis M(s)/W(s), track and field M(s)/W(s), volleyball M(s)/W(s), water polo M(s)/W(s), weight lifting M(c)/W(c), wrestling M(s)/W(s)(c). *Intramural sports:* basketball M/W, football M/W, softball M/W, ultimate Frisbee M/W, volleyball M/W.

Campus security: 24-hour emergency response devices and patrols, student patrols, late-night transport/escort service, controlled dormitory access.

Student services: health clinic, personal/psychological counseling.

COSTS & FINANCIAL AID

Costs (2018–19) *Comprehensive fee:* $40,440 includes full-time tuition ($29,420), mandatory fees ($1100), and room and board ($9920). Full-time tuition and fees vary according to course load, degree level, and location. Part-time tuition: $960 per credit hour. Part-time tuition and fees vary according to course load, degree level, and location. *College room only:* $5120. Room and board charges vary according to board plan and housing facility. *Payment plans:* installment, deferred payment. *Waivers:* children of alumni and employees or children of employees.

Financial Aid Of all full-time matriculated undergraduates who enrolled in 2016, 1,580 applied for aid, 1,440 were judged to have need, 268 had their need fully met. 881 Federal Work-Study jobs (averaging $1785). 67 state and other part-time jobs (averaging $1138). In 2016, 314 non-need-based awards were made. *Average percent of need met:* 71. *Average financial aid package:* $21,099. *Average need-based loan:* $4321. *Average need-based gift aid:* $18,025. *Average non-need-based aid:* $11,530. *Average indebtedness upon graduation:* $28,375.

APPLYING

Standardized Tests *Required:* SAT or ACT (for admission).

Options: electronic application, deferred entrance.

Required: essay or personal statement, high school transcript, minimum 2.5 GPA, 1 letter of recommendation, rank in upper 50% of high school class, minimum ACT score of 20. *Required for some:* interview.

Application deadlines: rolling (freshmen), rolling (transfers).

Notification: continuous (freshmen), continuous (transfers).

CONTACT

Mrs. Josie Blasdel, Director of Undergraduate Admission, McKendree University, 701 College Road, Lebanon, IL 62254. *Phone:* 618-537-6836. *Toll-free phone:* 800-232-7228. *E-mail:* jlblasdel@mckendree.edu.

Methodist College

Peoria, Illinois

http://www.methodistcol.edu/

CONTACT
Methodist College, 415 St. Mark Court, Peoria, IL 61603.

Midstate College

Peoria, Illinois

http://www.midstate.edu/

CONTACT
Ms. Jessica Hancock, Director of Admissions, Midstate College, 411 West Northmoor Road, Peoria, IL 61614. *Phone:* 309-692-4092. *Toll-free phone:* 800-251-4299. *Fax:* 309-692-3893. *E-mail:* jhancock2@midstate.edu.

Millikin University

Decatur, Illinois

http://www.millikin.edu/

- **Independent** comprehensive, founded 1901, affiliated with Presbyterian Church (U.S.A.)
- **Suburban** 75-acre campus
- **Endowment** $110.5 million
- **Coed** 1,950 undergraduate students, 94% full-time, 57% women, 43% men
- **Moderately difficult** entrance level, 65% of applicants were admitted

UNDERGRAD STUDENTS

1,840 full-time, 110 part-time. Students come from 37 states and territories; 24 other countries; 17% are from out of state; 15% Black or African American, non-Hispanic/Latino; 7% Hispanic/Latino; 1% Asian, non-Hispanic/Latino; 0.1% Native Hawaiian or other Pacific Islander, non-Hispanic/Latino; 0.1% American Indian or Alaska Native, non-Hispanic/Latino; 4% Two or more races, non-Hispanic/Latino; 1% Race/ethnicity unknown; 2% international; 6% transferred in; 58% live on campus.

Freshmen:
Admission: 3,431 applied, 2,216 admitted, 474 enrolled. *Average high school GPA:* 3.4. *Test scores:* SAT evidence-based reading and writing scores over 500: 90%; SAT math scores over 500: 90%; ACT scores over 18: 88%; SAT evidence-based reading and writing scores over 600: 47%; SAT math scores over 600: 34%; ACT scores over 24: 39%; SAT evidence-based reading and writing scores over 700: 5%; SAT math scores over 700: 5%; ACT scores over 30: 7%.
Retention: 76% of full-time freshmen returned.

FACULTY

Total: 272, 55% full-time, 51% with terminal degrees.
Student/faculty ratio: 10:1.

ACADEMICS

Calendar: semesters. *Degrees:* certificates, bachelor's, master's, doctoral, and postbachelor's certificates.

Special study options: academic remediation for entering students, accelerated degree program, adult/continuing education programs, advanced placement credit, distance learning, double majors, English as a second language, honors programs, independent study, internships, off-campus study, part-time degree program, services for LD students, student-designed majors, study abroad, summer session for credit.

Unusual degree programs: 3-2 engineering with Washington University in St. Louis, University of Missouri–Kansas City; occupational therapy with Washington University, pharmacy with Midwestern University.

Computers: 255 computers/terminals and 300 ports are available on campus for general student use. Students can access the following: computer help desk, free student e-mail accounts, online (class) grades, online (class) registration, online (class) schedules, online degree audit, online financials (view and pay bills, financial aid). Campuswide network is available. 100% of college-owned or -operated housing units are wired for high-speed Internet access. Wireless service is available via classrooms, computer centers, computer labs, dorm rooms, learning centers, libraries, student centers.

Library: Staley Library. *Books:* 189,000 (physical), 82,000 (digital/electronic); *Serial titles:* 1,000 (physical), 53,000 (digital/electronic); *Databases:* 80. Weekly public service hours: 113; students can reserve study rooms.

STUDENT LIFE

Housing options: on-campus residence required through junior year; coed, special housing for students with disabilities. Campus housing is university owned, leased by the school and is provided by a third party. Freshman campus housing is guaranteed.

Activities and organizations: drama/theater group, student-run newspaper, radio station, choral group, University Center Board, Multicultural Student Council, Student Housing Council, Panhellenic Council, Interfraternity Council, national fraternities, national sororities.

Athletics Member NCAA. All Division III. *Intercollegiate sports:* baseball M, basketball M/W, cross-country running M/W, football M, golf M/W, soccer M/W, softball W, swimming and diving M/W, tennis M/W, track and field M/W, triathlon W, volleyball W, wrestling M. *Intramural sports:* basketball M/W, cheerleading M(c)/W(c), football M/W, soccer M/W, softball M/W, ultimate Frisbee M/W, volleyball M/W.

Campus security: 24-hour emergency response devices and patrols, late-night transport/escort service, controlled dormitory access, emergency notification program.

Student services: health clinic, personal/psychological counseling, women's center.

COSTS & FINANCIAL AID

Costs (2017–18) *Comprehensive fee:* $44,148 includes full-time tuition ($32,274), mandatory fees ($792), and room and board ($11,082). Part-time tuition: $465 per credit hour. *Required fees:* $22 per credit hour part-time. *College room only:* $8356. Room and board charges vary according to board plan, housing facility, and student level. *Payment plan:* installment. *Waivers:* employees or children of employees.

Financial Aid Of all full-time matriculated undergraduates who enrolled in 2016, 1,636 applied for aid, 1,487 were judged to have need, 554 had their need fully met. 439 Federal Work-Study jobs (averaging $1013). 440 state and other part-time jobs (averaging $658). In 2016, 144 non-need-based awards were made. *Average percent of need met:* 85. *Average financial aid package:* $24,841. *Average need-based loan:* $4644. *Average need-based gift aid:* $8596. *Average non-need-based aid:* $16,300. *Average indebtedness upon graduation:* $33,146.

APPLYING

Standardized Tests *Required:* SAT or ACT (for admission).

Options: electronic application, deferred entrance.

Required: high school transcript, minimum 2.0 GPA, 2 letters of recommendation. *Required for some:* audition for music/theatre, art portfolio review. *Recommended:* interview.

Application deadlines: rolling (freshmen), rolling (transfers).

Notification: continuous (freshmen), continuous (transfers).

CONTACT

Mr. Kevin McIntyre, Dean of Admission, Millikin University, 1184 West Main Street, Decatur, IL 62522-2084. *Phone:* 217-424-6210. *Toll-free phone:* 800-373-7733. *Fax:* 217-425-4669. *E-mail:* admis@millikin.edu.

Monmouth College

Monmouth, Illinois

http://www.monmouthcollege.edu/

- **Independent** 4-year, founded 1853, affiliated with Presbyterian Church
- **Small-town** 112-acre campus
- **Endowment** $113.8 million
- **Coed** 1,033 undergraduate students
- **Moderately difficult** entrance level, 67% of applicants were admitted

UNDERGRAD STUDENTS

Students come from 32 states and territories; 33 other countries; 11% are from out of state; 11% Black or African American, non-Hispanic/Latino; 10% Hispanic/Latino; 1% Asian, non-Hispanic/Latino; 0.2% American Indian or Alaska Native, non-Hispanic/Latino; 3% Two or more races, non-Hispanic/Latino; 5% Race/ethnicity unknown; 7% international; 91% live on campus.

Freshmen:

Admission: 2,428 applied, 1,628 admitted. *Average high school GPA:* 3.3. *Test scores:* SAT evidence-based reading and writing scores over 500: 62%; SAT math scores over 500: 62%; ACT scores over 18: 92%; SAT evidence-based reading and writing scores over 600: 14%; SAT math scores over 600: 5%; ACT scores over 24: 40%; ACT scores over 30: 6%.

Retention: 71% of full-time freshmen returned.

FACULTY

Total: 125, 73% full-time, 71% with terminal degrees.

Student/faculty ratio: 11:1.

ACADEMICS

Calendar: semesters. *Degree:* bachelor's.

Special study options: academic remediation for entering students, advanced placement credit, double majors, English as a second language, honors programs, independent study, internships, off-campus study, part-time degree program, services for LD students, student-designed majors, study abroad. *ROTC:* Army (c).

Unusual degree programs: 3-2 engineering with Case Western Reserve University, University of Southern California, Illinois Institute of Technology; nursing with Rush University; architecture with Washington University in St. Louis, occupational therapy, medical technology with Rush University.

Computers: 140 computers/terminals are available on campus for general student use. Students can access the following: campus intranet, computer help desk, free student e-mail accounts, online (class) grades, online (class) registration, online (class) schedules. Campuswide network is available. 100% of college-owned or -operated housing units are wired for high-speed Internet access. Wireless service is available via entire campus.

Library: Hewes Library. *Books:* 206,954 (physical), 33,996 (digital/electronic); *Serial titles:* 3,400 (physical), 28,190 (digital/electronic); *Databases:* 115. Weekly public service hours: 96; students can reserve study rooms.

STUDENT LIFE

Housing options: on-campus residence required through senior year; coed, men-only, women-only, special housing for students with disabilities. Campus housing is university owned. Freshman campus housing is guaranteed.

Activities and organizations: drama/theater group, student-run newspaper, radio and television station, choral group, marching band, Fighting Scots Marching Band and Jazz Band, Associated Students of Monmouth College, Crimson Masque (theatre), Alternative Spring Break, Coalition for Ethnic Awareness, national fraternities, national sororities.

Athletics Member NCAA. All Division III. *Intercollegiate sports:* baseball M, basketball M/W, cross-country running M/W, football M, golf M/W, lacrosse M/W, soccer M/W, softball W, swimming and diving M/W, tennis M/W, track and field M/W, volleyball W, water polo M/W. *Intramural sports:* archery M/W, badminton M/W, baseball M, cheerleading W(c), soccer M/W, swimming and diving M/W, table tennis M/W, tennis M/W, ultimate Frisbee M/W, volleyball M/W, water polo M(c)/W(c), wrestling M.

Campus security: 24-hour emergency response devices and patrols, late-night transport/escort service, controlled dormitory access, full-time Director of Campus Security.

Student services: personal/psychological counseling.

COSTS & FINANCIAL AID

Costs (2018–19) *Comprehensive fee:* $46,640 includes full-time tuition ($37,674) and room and board ($8966). Part-time tuition: $4709 per course. *College room only:* $5054. Room and board charges vary according to housing facility. *Payment plan:* installment. *Waivers:* employees or children of employees.

Financial Aid Of all full-time matriculated undergraduates who enrolled in 2017, 903 applied for aid, 851 were judged to have need, 207 had their need fully met. 456 Federal Work-Study jobs (averaging $1341). In 2017, 149 non-need-based awards were made. *Average percent of need met:* 89. *Average financial aid package:* $34,091. *Average need-based loan:*

$4832. *Average need-based gift aid:* $28,485. *Average non-need-based aid:* $21,863. *Average indebtedness upon graduation:* $33,333.

APPLYING

Standardized Tests *Required:* SAT or ACT (for admission).

Options: electronic application, deferred entrance.

Required: high school transcript. *Required for some:* interview. *Recommended:* essay or personal statement, minimum 2.7 GPA, letters of recommendation, interview.

Application deadlines: rolling (freshmen), rolling (transfers).

Notification: continuous (freshmen), continuous (transfers).

CONTACT

Mr. Trent Gilbert, Vice President for Enrollment Management, Monmouth College, 700 East Broadway, Monmouth, IL 61462-1988. *Phone:* 309-457-2131. *Toll-free phone:* 800-747-2687. *Fax:* 309-457-2141. *E-mail:* admissions@monmouthcollege.edu.

Moody Bible Institute

Chicago, Illinois
http://www.moody.edu/

CONTACT

Ms. Jacqueline Holman, Admissions Office, Moody Bible Institute, 820 North LaSalle Boulevard, Chicago, IL 60610. *Phone:* 312-329-4307. *Toll-free phone:* 800-967-4MBI. *Fax:* 312-329-8987. *E-mail:* admissions@moody.edu.

Morthland College

West Frankfort, Illinois
http://www.morthland.edu/

CONTACT

Morthland College, 202 East Oak Street, West Frankfort, IL 62896.

National Louis University

Chicago, Illinois
http://www.nl.edu/

- **Independent** university, founded 1886
- **Urban** 12-acre campus
- **Coed** 1,885 undergraduate students, 66% full-time, 73% women, 27% men
- **Moderately difficult** entrance level, 86% of applicants were admitted

UNDERGRAD STUDENTS

1,250 full-time, 635 part-time. Students come from 20 states and territories; 3% are from out of state; 29% Black or African American, non-Hispanic/Latino; 47% Hispanic/Latino; 2% Asian, non-Hispanic/Latino; 0.2% Native Hawaiian or other Pacific Islander, non-Hispanic/Latino; 0.2% American Indian or Alaska Native, non-Hispanic/Latino; 1% Two or more races, non-Hispanic/Latino; 3% Race/ethnicity unknown; 0.6% international; 15% transferred in.

Freshmen:

Admission: 2,713 applied, 2,322 admitted, 502 enrolled. *Average high school GPA:* 2.7.

Retention: 68% of full-time freshmen returned.

FACULTY

Total: 290, 47% full-time.

Student/faculty ratio: 17:1.

ACADEMICS

Calendar: quarters. *Degrees:* bachelor's, master's, doctoral, post-master's, and postbachelor's certificates.

Special study options: academic remediation for entering students, accelerated degree program, adult/continuing education programs, advanced placement credit, distance learning, English as a second language, independent study, internships, part-time degree program, services for LD students, summer session for credit.

Computers: Students can access the following: campus intranet, computer help desk, free student e-mail accounts, online (class) grades,

online (class) registration, online (class) schedules. Campuswide network is available. Wireless service is available via entire campus.
Library: NLU Library.

STUDENT LIFE
Housing options: college housing not available.

Campus security: 24-hour emergency response devices and patrols.

Student services: personal/psychological counseling.

COSTS & FINANCIAL AID
Costs (2017–18) *Tuition:* $12,456 full-time, $470 per credit hour part-time. Full-time tuition and fees vary according to course load and degree level. Part-time tuition and fees vary according to course load and degree level. *Required fees:* $390 full-time.

Financial Aid Of all full-time matriculated undergraduates who enrolled in 2011, 772 applied for aid, 736 were judged to have need, 10 had their need fully met. 66 Federal Work-Study jobs (averaging $3890). In 2011, 52 non-need-based awards were made. *Average percent of need met:* 43. *Average financial aid package:* $12,225. *Average need-based loan:* $4426. *Average need-based gift aid:* $8302. *Average non-need-based aid:* $5605. *Average indebtedness upon graduation:* $29,900.

APPLYING
Standardized Tests *Recommended:* SAT or ACT (for admission).

Options: electronic application, deferred entrance.

Required: high school transcript, minimum 2.0 GPA. *Recommended:* interview.

Application deadlines: rolling (freshmen), rolling (transfers).

Notification: continuous (freshmen), continuous (transfers).

CONTACT
National Louis University, 1000 Capitol Drive, Wheeling, IL 60090. *Phone:* 888-NLU-TODAY. *Toll-free phone:* 888-658-8632.

North Central College
Naperville, Illinois
http://www.northcentralcollege.edu/
- **Independent United Methodist** comprehensive, founded 1861
- **Suburban** 68-acre campus with easy access to Chicago
- **Endowment** $110.0 million
- **Coed** 2,769 undergraduate students, 95% full-time, 54% women, 46% men
- **Moderately difficult** entrance level, 54% of applicants were admitted

UNDERGRAD STUDENTS
2,634 full-time, 135 part-time. Students come from 27 states and territories; 45 other countries; 7% are from out of state; 4% Black or African American, non-Hispanic/Latino; 15% Hispanic/Latino; 3% Asian, non-Hispanic/Latino; 0.1% Native Hawaiian or other Pacific Islander, non-Hispanic/Latino; 0.1% American Indian or Alaska Native, non-Hispanic/Latino; 4% Two or more races, non-Hispanic/Latino; 7% Race/ethnicity unknown; 3% international; 9% transferred in; 49% live on campus.

Freshmen:
Admission: 7,220 applied, 3,928 admitted, 603 enrolled. *Average high school GPA:* 3.7. *Test scores:* ACT scores over 18: 99%; ACT scores over 24: 59%; ACT scores over 30: 11%.

Retention: 79% of full-time freshmen returned.

FACULTY
Total: 283, 53% full-time, 63% with terminal degrees.

Student/faculty ratio: 14:1.

ACADEMICS
Calendar: quarters. *Degrees:* bachelor's, master's, and postbachelor's certificates.

Special study options: academic remediation for entering students, accelerated degree program, advanced placement credit, distance learning, double majors, English as a second language, honors programs, independent study, internships, off-campus study, part-time degree program, services for LD students, student-designed majors, study abroad, summer session for credit. *ROTC:* Army (c), Air Force (c).

Unusual degree programs: 3-2 engineering with Washington University in St. Louis; University of Illinois at Urbana–Champaign; Marquette University; University of Minnesota, Twin Cities Campus.

Computers: 450 computers/terminals are available on campus for general student use. Students can access the following: campus intranet, computer help desk, free student e-mail accounts, online (class) grades, online (class) registration, online (class) schedules, software packages. Campuswide network is available. 100% of college-owned or -operated housing units are wired for high-speed Internet access. Wireless service is available via classrooms, computer centers, computer labs, dorm rooms, learning centers, libraries, student centers.

Library: Oesterle Library. *Books:* 135,388 (physical), 74,330 (digital/electronic); *Databases:* 137.

STUDENT LIFE
Housing options: on-campus residence required through sophomore year; coed, men-only, women-only, special housing for students with disabilities. Campus housing is university owned. Freshman applicants given priority for college housing.

Activities and organizations: drama/theater group, student-run newspaper, radio station, choral group, marching band, College Union Activities Board, WONC (student radio station), Cardinals in Action (service group), ENACTUS (Students in Free Enterprise SIFE), Residence Hall Association.

Athletics Member NCAA. All Division III. *Intercollegiate sports:* baseball M, basketball M/W, bowling W, cheerleading W, cross-country running M/W, football M, golf M/W, lacrosse M/W, soccer M/W, softball W, swimming and diving M/W, tennis M/W, track and field M/W, triathlon W, volleyball M/W, wrestling M. *Intramural sports:* badminton M/W, basketball M/W, football M/W, golf M/W, racquetball M/W, soccer M/W, softball M/W, ultimate Frisbee M/W, volleyball M/W.

Campus security: 24-hour emergency response devices and patrols, late-night transport/escort service, controlled dormitory access.

Student services: health clinic, personal/psychological counseling.

COSTS & FINANCIAL AID
Costs (2017–18) *Comprehensive fee:* $48,399 includes full-time tuition ($37,569), mandatory fees ($180), and room and board ($10,650). Part-time tuition: $1044 per credit hour. Part-time tuition and fees vary according to course load. *Required fees:* $20 per term part-time. *College room only:* $7317. Room and board charges vary according to housing facility. *Payment plan:* installment. *Waivers:* senior citizens and employees or children of employees.

Financial Aid Of all full-time matriculated undergraduates who enrolled in 2017, 2,266 applied for aid, 2,042 were judged to have need, 383 had their need fully met. 1,527 Federal Work-Study jobs (averaging $233). In 2017, 566 non-need-based awards were made. *Average percent of need met:* 79. *Average financial aid package:* $27,601. *Average need-based loan:* $4564. *Average need-based gift aid:* $22,447. *Average non-need-based aid:* $18,225. *Average indebtedness upon graduation:* $38,267.

APPLYING
Standardized Tests *Required:* SAT or ACT (for admission). *Recommended:* ACT (for admission).

Options: electronic application, deferred entrance.

Application fee: $25.

Required: high school transcript, minimum 2.5 GPA. *Required for some:* interview. *Recommended:* essay or personal statement, 1 letter of recommendation.

Application deadlines: rolling (freshmen), rolling (transfers).

Notification: continuous (freshmen), continuous (transfers).

CONTACT
Ms. Martha Stolze, Dean of Admission, North Central College, 30 North Brainard Street, PO Box 3063, Naperville, IL 60566-7063. *Phone:* 630-637-5800. *Toll-free phone:* 800-411-1861. *Fax:* 630-637-5819. *E-mail:* admissions@noctrl.edu.

Northeastern Illinois University

Chicago, Illinois

http://www.neiu.edu/

- **State-supported** comprehensive, founded 1961
- **Urban** 67-acre campus with easy access to Chicago
- **Endowment** $768,031
- **Coed**
- **Minimally difficult** entrance level

FACULTY

Student/faculty ratio: 14:1.

ACADEMICS

Calendar: semesters. *Degrees:* certificates, bachelor's, and master's.

Library: Ronald Williams Library plus 3 others. *Books:* 688,147 (physical), 156,705 (digital/electronic); *Serial titles:* 742 (physical), 86,898 (digital/electronic); *Databases:* 188. Weekly public service hours: 92.

STUDENT LIFE

Housing options: coed. Campus housing is provided by a third party.

Activities and organizations: drama/theater group, student-run newspaper, radio station, choral group, Student Government Association, United Greek Council, ASSW - Association of Student Social Workers, Accounting Associates, Computer Science Society, national fraternities, national sororities.

Campus security: 24-hour emergency response devices and patrols, late-night transport/escort service, controlled dormitory access.

Student services: health clinic, personal/psychological counseling, women's center.

COSTS & FINANCIAL AID

Costs (2017–18) *Tuition:* state resident $11,320 full-time, $377 per credit hour part-time; nonresident $22,639 full-time, $755 per credit hour part-time. Full-time tuition and fees vary according to course load, degree level, and program. Part-time tuition and fees vary according to course load, degree level, and program. No tuition increase for student's term of enrollment. *Required fees:* $2100 full-time, $70 per credit hour part-time, $3 per term part-time. *Room and board:* $11,424; room only: $8424. Room and board charges vary according to housing facility. *Payment plans:* installment, deferred payment.

Financial Aid Of all full-time matriculated undergraduates who enrolled in 2016, 3,473 applied for aid, 2,897 were judged to have need, 117 had their need fully met. In 2016, 80 non-need-based awards were made. *Average percent of need met:* 17. *Average financial aid package:* $8549. *Average need-based loan:* $4277. *Average need-based gift aid:* $6882. *Average non-need-based aid:* $1936. *Average indebtedness upon graduation:* $16,247.

APPLYING

Standardized Tests *Required:* SAT or ACT (for admission).

Options: electronic application, deferred entrance.

Application fee: $30.

Required: high school transcript.

CONTACT

Ms. Zarrin Kerwell, Admissions Counselor, Northeastern Illinois University, 5500 North St. Louis Avenue, Chicago, IL 60625. *Phone:* 773-442-4026. *Fax:* 773-794-6243. *E-mail:* admrec@neiu.edu.

Northern Illinois University

De Kalb, Illinois

http://www.niu.edu/

- **State-supported** university, founded 1895
- **Small-town** 650-acre campus with easy access to Chicago
- **Endowment** $3.1 million
- **Coed** 13,454 undergraduate students, 88% full-time, 50% women, 50% men
- **Moderately difficult** entrance level, 53% of applicants were admitted

UNDERGRAD STUDENTS

11,788 full-time, 1,666 part-time. Students come from 42 states and territories; 48 other countries; 3% are from out of state; 16% Black or African American, non-Hispanic/Latino; 18% Hispanic/Latino; 5% Asian, non-Hispanic/Latino; 0.1% Native Hawaiian or other Pacific Islander, non-Hispanic/Latino; 0.1% American Indian or Alaska Native, non-Hispanic/Latino; 4% Two or more races, non-Hispanic/Latino; 0.4% Race/ethnicity unknown; 2% international; 13% transferred in; 27% live on campus.

Freshmen:

Admission: 14,641 applied, 7,806 admitted, 1,852 enrolled. *Average high school GPA:* 3.3. *Test scores:* ACT scores over 18: 86%; ACT scores over 24: 32%; ACT scores over 30: 5%.

Retention: 73% of full-time freshmen returned.

FACULTY

Total: 1,067, 76% full-time, 74% with terminal degrees.

Student/faculty ratio: 14:1.

ACADEMICS

Calendar: semesters. *Degrees:* bachelor's, master's, and doctoral.

Special study options: accelerated degree program, adult/continuing education programs, advanced placement credit, cooperative education, double majors, honors programs, independent study, internships, off-campus study, part-time degree program, services for LD students, student-designed majors, study abroad, summer session for credit. *ROTC:* Army (b), Air Force (c).

Computers: 1,500 computers/terminals are available on campus for general student use. Students can access the following: computer help desk, free student e-mail accounts, online (class) grades, online (class) registration, online (class) schedules. Campuswide network is available. 100% of college-owned or -operated housing units are wired for high-speed Internet access. Wireless service is available via entire campus.

Library: Founders Memorial Library plus 4 others. *Books:* 1.8 million (physical), 589,600 (digital/electronic); *Serial titles:* 1,600 (physical), 81,832 (digital/electronic); *Databases:* 309. Weekly public service hours: 100; students can reserve study rooms.

STUDENT LIFE

Housing options: on-campus residence required through senior year; coed. Campus housing is university owned. Freshman applicants given priority for college housing.

Activities and organizations: drama/theater group, student-run newspaper, radio station, choral group, marching band, American Marketing Association, Delta Sigma Pi, Pi Sigma Epsilon, Black Choir, Student Volunteer Choir, national fraternities, national sororities.

Athletics Member NCAA. All Division I except football (Division I-A). *Intercollegiate sports:* baseball M(s), basketball M(s)/W(s), cross-country running W, golf M(s)/W(s), gymnastics W(s), soccer M(s)/W(s), softball W(s), swimming and diving M(s)/W(s), tennis M(s)/W(s), volleyball W(s), wrestling M(s). *Intramural sports:* archery M(c)/W(c), badminton M/W, basketball M/W, bowling M(c)/W(c), cross-country running W, football M/W, golf M/W, ice hockey M(c)/W(c), lacrosse M(c)/W(c), racquetball M/W, rugby M(c)/W(c), skiing (downhill) M(c)/W(c), soccer M/W, softball M/W, table tennis M/W, tennis M/W, track and field M(c)/W(c), volleyball M/W, water polo M(c)/W(c), weight lifting M(c)/W(c).

Campus security: 24-hour emergency response devices and patrols, student patrols, late-night transport/escort service, controlled dormitory access.

Student services: health clinic, personal/psychological counseling, women's center, legal services.

COSTS & FINANCIAL AID

Costs (2017–18) *Tuition:* state resident $9466 full-time, $440 per credit hour part-time; nonresident $18,931 full-time, $793 per credit hour part-time. Part-time tuition and fees vary according to course load and location. *Required fees:* $2796 full-time, $94 per credit hour part-time, $125 per term part-time. *Room and board:* $10,880. Room and board charges vary according to student level. *Payment plan:* installment. *Waivers:* senior citizens and employees or children of employees.

Financial Aid Of all full-time matriculated undergraduates who enrolled in 2016, 10,723 applied for aid, 9,309 were judged to have need, 667 had their need fully met. 5,830 Federal Work-Study jobs (averaging $2641). In 2016, 1154 non-need-based awards were made. *Average percent of need met:* 61. *Average financial aid package:* $12,759. *Average need-based loan:* $4662. *Average need-based gift aid:* $8232. *Average non-need-based aid:* $4194. *Average indebtedness upon graduation:* $34,708.

APPLYING

Standardized Tests *Required:* SAT or ACT (for admission).

Options: electronic application.

Application fee: $40.

Required: high school transcript, high school class rank.

Application deadlines: 8/1 (freshmen), 8/1 (transfers).

Notification: continuous (freshmen), continuous (transfers).

CONTACT

Katy Saalfeld, Acting Director of Admissions, Northern Illinois University, Student Affairs & Enrollment Management, DeKalb, IL 60115-2857. *Phone:* 815-753-0446. *Toll-free phone:* 800-892-3050. *E-mail:* admissions@niu.edu.

North Park University

Chicago, Illinois

http://www.northpark.edu/

CONTACT

Office of Admissions, North Park University, 3225 West Foster Avenue, Chicago, IL 60625-4895. *Phone:* 773-244-5500. *Toll-free phone:* 800-888-NPC8. *Fax:* 773-583-0858. *E-mail:* afao@northpark.edu.

Northwestern University

Evanston, Illinois

http://www.northwestern.edu/

- **Independent** university, founded 1851
- **Suburban** 250-acre campus with easy access to Chicago
- **Coed** 8,278 undergraduate students, 98% full-time, 50% women, 50% men
- **Most difficult** entrance level, 9% of applicants were admitted

UNDERGRAD STUDENTS

8,117 full-time, 161 part-time. Students come from 75 other countries; 68% are from out of state; 6% Black or African American, non-Hispanic/Latino; 13% Hispanic/Latino; 17% Asian, non-Hispanic/Latino; 0.1% American Indian or Alaska Native, non-Hispanic/Latino; 5% Two or more races, non-Hispanic/Latino; 3% Race/ethnicity unknown; 9% international; 2% transferred in; 52% live on campus.

Freshmen:

Admission: 37,259 applied, 3,442 admitted, 1,903 enrolled. *Test scores:* SAT evidence-based reading and writing scores over 500: 99%; SAT math scores over 500: 99%; ACT scores over 18: 100%; SAT evidence-based reading and writing scores over 600: 96%; SAT math scores over 600: 98%; ACT scores over 24: 99%; SAT evidence-based reading and writing scores over 700: 72%; SAT math scores over 700: 79%; ACT scores over 30: 89%.

Retention: 98% of full-time freshmen returned.

FACULTY

Total: 1,731, 85% full-time, 100% with terminal degrees.

Student/faculty ratio: 7:1.

ACADEMICS

Calendar: quarters. *Degrees:* certificates, bachelor's, master's, doctoral, and post-master's certificates.

Special study options: accelerated degree program, adult/continuing education programs, advanced placement credit, cooperative education, double majors, honors programs, independent study, internships, part-time degree program, services for LD students, student-designed majors, study abroad, summer session for credit. *ROTC:* Army (c), Navy (b), Air Force (c).

Computers: Students can access the following: campus intranet, computer help desk, free student e-mail accounts, online (class) grades, online (class) registration, online (class) schedules. Campuswide network is available. 100% of college-owned or -operated housing units are wired for high-speed Internet access. Wireless service is available via entire campus.

Library: University Library plus 6 others.

STUDENT LIFE

Housing options: coed, men-only, women-only. Campus housing is university owned. Freshman campus housing is guaranteed.

Activities and organizations: drama/theater group, student-run newspaper, radio and television station, choral group, marching band, national fraternities, national sororities.

Athletics Member NCAA. All Division I.

Campus security: 24-hour emergency response devices and patrols, late-night transport/escort service, controlled dormitory access.

Student services: health clinic, personal/psychological counseling, women's center.

COSTS & FINANCIAL AID

Costs (2017–18) *Comprehensive fee:* $68,725 includes full-time tuition ($52,239), mandatory fees ($439), and room and board ($16,047). *Room and board:* Room and board charges vary according to board plan and housing facility. *Payment plan:* installment.

Financial Aid Of all full-time matriculated undergraduates who enrolled in 2017, 4,174 applied for aid, 3,723 were judged to have need, 3,723 had their need fully met. In 2017, 326 non-need-based awards were made. *Average percent of need met:* 100. *Average financial aid package:* $49,030. *Average need-based loan:* $4339. *Average need-based gift aid:* $46,720. *Average non-need-based aid:* $4923. *Average indebtedness upon graduation:* $19,718. *Financial aid deadline:* 3/5.

APPLYING

Standardized Tests *Required:* SAT or ACT (for admission). *Required for some:* SAT Subject Tests (for admission).

Options: electronic application, early admission, early decision, deferred entrance.

Application fee: $75.

Required: essay or personal statement, high school transcript, 1 letter of recommendation. *Required for some:* audition for music program.

Application deadlines: 1/1 (freshmen), 3/15 (transfers).

Early decision deadline: 11/1.

Notification: 4/1 (freshmen), continuous (transfers), 12/15 (early decision).

CONTACT

Mr. Christopher Watson, Assistant Vice President for Student Outreach and Dean of Undergraduate Admission, Northwestern University, 1801 Hinman Ave, PO Box 3060, Evanston, IL 60208. *Phone:* 847-491-7271. *E-mail:* ug-admission@northwestern.edu.

Olivet Nazarene University

Bourbonnais, Illinois

http://www.olivet.edu/

- **Independent** comprehensive, founded 1907, affiliated with Church of the Nazarene
- **Small-town** 275-acre campus with easy access to Chicago
- **Endowment** $33.2 million
- **Coed** 3,371 undergraduate students, 92% full-time, 59% women, 41% men
- **Moderately difficult** entrance level, 66% of applicants were admitted

UNDERGRAD STUDENTS

3,113 full-time, 258 part-time. Students come from 46 states and territories; 19 other countries; 36% are from out of state; 8% Black or African American, non-Hispanic/Latino; 8% Hispanic/Latino; 3% Asian, non-Hispanic/Latino; 0.1% Native Hawaiian or other Pacific Islander, non-Hispanic/Latino; 0.2% American Indian or Alaska Native, non-Hispanic/Latino; 3% Two or more races, non-Hispanic/Latino; 0.3% Race/ethnicity unknown; 1% international; 9% transferred in; 77% live on campus.

Freshmen:

Admission: 3,964 applied, 2,623 admitted, 752 enrolled. *Average high school GPA:* 3.5.

Retention: 78% of full-time freshmen returned.

FACULTY

Total: 453, 28% full-time.

Student/faculty ratio: 19:1.

ACADEMICS

Calendar: semesters. *Degrees:* bachelor's, master's, and doctoral.

Special study options: academic remediation for entering students, adult/continuing education programs, advanced placement credit, cooperative education, distance learning, double majors, honors programs, independent study, internships, off-campus study, part-time degree program, services for LD students, student-designed majors, study abroad, summer session for credit. *ROTC:* Army (b).

Computers: Students can access the following: campus intranet, computer help desk, free student e-mail accounts, online (class) grades, online (class) registration, online (class) schedules. Campuswide network is available. 100% of college-owned or -operated housing units are wired for high-speed Internet access. Wireless service is available via entire campus.

Library: Benner Library. *Books:* 127,535 (physical), 215,890 (digital/electronic); *Serial titles:* 627 (physical), 65,313 (digital/electronic); *Databases:* 263. Students can reserve study rooms.

STUDENT LIFE

Housing options: on-campus residence required through senior year; men-only, women-only. Campus housing is university owned. Freshman campus housing is guaranteed.

Activities and organizations: drama/theater group, student-run newspaper, radio station, choral group, marching band, Fellowship of Christian Athletes, C.A.U.S.E. (College and University Serving and Enabling), Diakonia, Student Education Association, Women's Residence Association.

Athletics Member NAIA, NCCAA. *Intercollegiate sports:* baseball M(s), basketball M(s)/W(s), cheerleading M(s)/W(s), cross-country running M(s)/W(s), football M(s), golf M(s), soccer M(s)/W(s), softball W(s), tennis M(s)/W(s), track and field M(s)/W(s), volleyball W(s). *Intramural sports:* baseball M, basketball M/W, football M/W, golf M/W, racquetball M/W, soccer M/W, softball M/W, table tennis M/W, tennis M/W, track and field M/W, volleyball M/W.

Campus security: 24-hour patrols, late-night transport/escort service.

Student services: health clinic, personal/psychological counseling.

COSTS & FINANCIAL AID

Costs (2017–18) *Comprehensive fee:* $42,840 includes full-time tuition ($33,950), mandatory fees ($990), and room and board ($7900). Full-time tuition and fees vary according to course load. Part-time tuition: $1415 per semester hour. Part-time tuition and fees vary according to course load. *Room and board:* Room and board charges vary according to board plan. *Payment plan:* installment. *Waivers:* employees or children of employees.

Financial Aid Of all full-time matriculated undergraduates who enrolled in 2017, 2,597 applied for aid, 2,378 were judged to have need, 663 had their need fully met. In 2017, 527 non-need-based awards were made. *Average percent of need met:* 85. *Average financial aid package:* $29,045. *Average need-based loan:* $4363. *Average need-based gift aid:* $23,977. *Average non-need-based aid:* $15,977. *Average indebtedness upon graduation:* $33,847.

APPLYING

Standardized Tests *Required:* SAT or ACT (for admission).

Options: electronic application, deferred entrance.

Application fee: $25.

Required: high school transcript, minimum 2.0 GPA. *Required for some:* 2 letters of recommendation. *Recommended:* essay or personal statement, interview.

Application deadlines: rolling (freshmen), rolling (transfers).

Notification: continuous (freshmen), continuous (transfers).

CONTACT

Mr. Jordan Gerstenberger, Director of Recruitment, Olivet Nazarene University, One University Avenue, Bourbonnais, IL 60914. *Phone:* 815-928-5595. *Toll-free phone:* 800-648-1463.

See below for display ad and page 1378 for the College Close-Up.

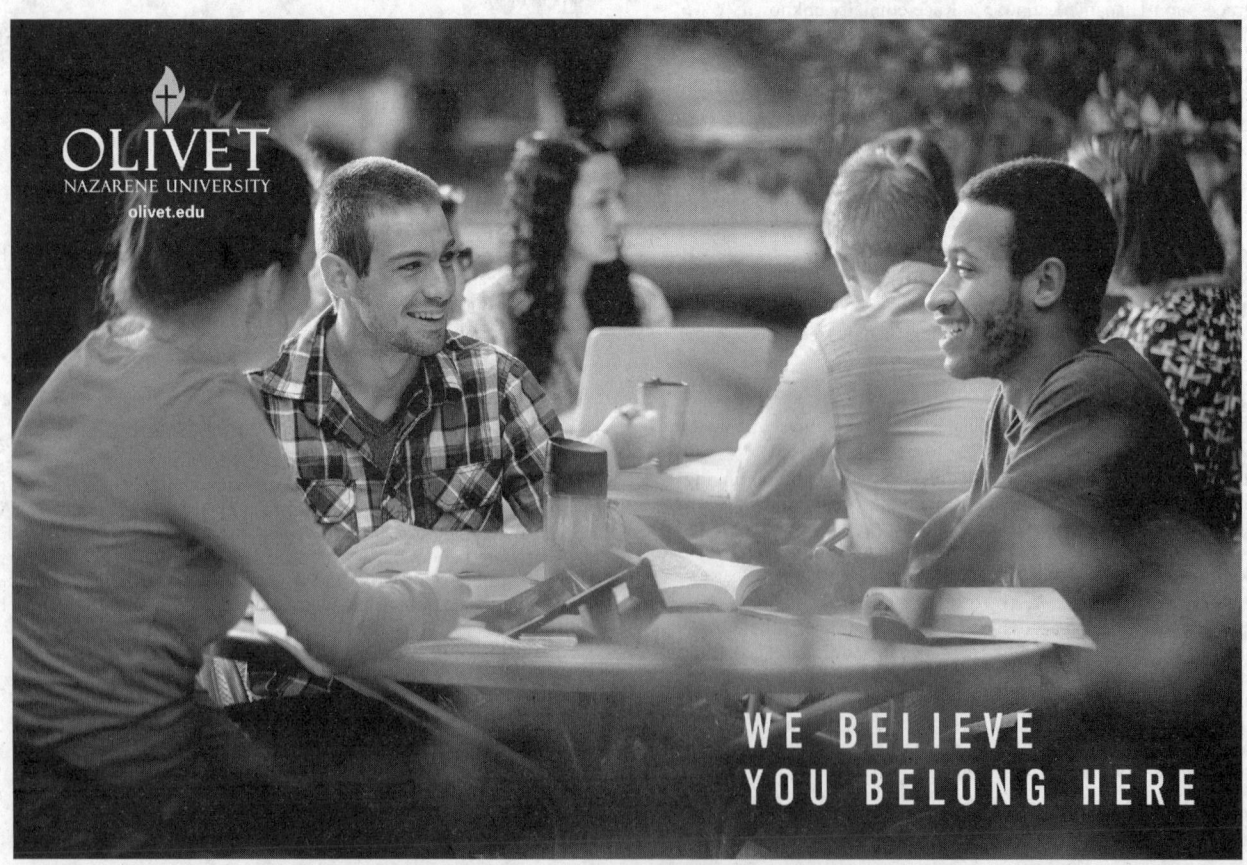

Principia College

Elsah, Illinois

http://www.principiacollege.edu/

- **Independent Christian Science** 4-year, founded 1910
- **Rural** 2600-acre campus with easy access to St. Louis
- **Endowment** $377.5 million
- **Coed** 455 undergraduate students, 97% full-time, 49% women, 51% men
- **Moderately difficult** entrance level, 91% of applicants were admitted

UNDERGRAD STUDENTS

441 full-time, 14 part-time. Students come from 37 states and territories; 30 other countries; 88% are from out of state; 2% Black or African American, non-Hispanic/Latino; 2% Hispanic/Latino; 2% Asian, non-Hispanic/Latino; 0.4% Native Hawaiian or other Pacific Islander, non-Hispanic/Latino; 0.2% American Indian or Alaska Native, non-Hispanic/Latino; 0.9% Two or more races, non-Hispanic/Latino; 2% Race/ethnicity unknown; 18% international; 2% transferred in; 97% live on campus.

Freshmen:

Admission: 134 applied, 122 admitted, 85 enrolled. *Average high school GPA:* 3.3. *Test scores:* SAT evidence-based reading and writing scores over 500: 81%; SAT math scores over 500: 81%; ACT scores over 18: 78%; SAT evidence-based reading and writing scores over 600: 45%; SAT math scores over 600: 36%; ACT scores over 24: 48%; SAT evidence-based reading and writing scores over 700: 9%; SAT math scores over 700: 4%; ACT scores over 30: 8%.

Retention: 87% of full-time freshmen returned.

FACULTY

Total: 78, 87% full-time, 62% with terminal degrees.

Student/faculty ratio: 6:1.

ACADEMICS

Calendar: semesters. *Degree:* bachelor's.

Special study options: advanced placement credit, double majors, independent study, internships, off-campus study, part-time degree program, student-designed majors, study abroad, summer session for credit.

Unusual degree programs: 3-2 engineering with University of Minnesota, Southern Illinois University Edwardsville; education with University of Missouri, St. Louis.

Computers: 100 computers/terminals are available on campus for general student use. Students can access the following: campus intranet, computer help desk, free student e-mail accounts, online (class) grades, online (class) registration, online (class) schedules. Campuswide network is available. 100% of college-owned or -operated housing units are wired for high-speed Internet access. Wireless service is available via classrooms, computer centers, computer labs, dorm rooms, learning centers, libraries, student centers.

Library: Marshall Brooks Library plus 1 other. *Books:* 168,085 (physical), 338,122 (digital/electronic); *Serial titles:* 237 (physical), 99,238 (digital/electronic); *Databases:* 96. Weekly public service hours: 90; students can reserve study rooms.

STUDENT LIFE

Housing options: on-campus residence required through senior year; coed, men-only, women-only. Campus housing is university owned. Freshman campus housing is guaranteed.

Activities and organizations: drama/theater group, student-run newspaper, radio and television station, choral group, Christian Science Organization, Community Service Team, Solidarity (Multi-club group), Rugby Club, Student Government.

Athletics Member NCAA. All Division III. *Intercollegiate sports:* baseball M, basketball M/W, cross-country running M/W, lacrosse W(c), rugby M(c), soccer M/W, softball W, swimming and diving M/W, tennis M/W, track and field M/W, volleyball W. *Intramural sports:* basketball M/W, soccer M/W, softball M/W.

Campus security: 24-hour emergency response devices and patrols, controlled dormitory access.

Student services: health clinic.

COSTS & FINANCIAL AID

Costs (2018–19) *Comprehensive fee:* $41,080 includes full-time tuition ($28,770), mandatory fees ($700), and room and board ($11,610). Full-time tuition and fees vary according to course load. Part-time tuition: $944 per credit hour. Part-time tuition and fees vary according to course load. *College room only:* $5510. Room and board charges vary according to board plan. *Payment plan:* installment. *Waivers:* employees or children of employees.

Financial Aid Of all full-time matriculated undergraduates who enrolled in 2017, 325 applied for aid, 318 were judged to have need, 173 had their need fully met. In 2017, 96 non-need-based awards were made. *Average percent of need met:* 93. *Average financial aid package:* $31,771. *Average need-based loan:* $5558. *Average need-based gift aid:* $28,101. *Average non-need-based aid:* $22,714. *Average indebtedness upon graduation:* $18,335.

APPLYING

Standardized Tests *Required:* SAT or ACT (for admission).

Options: electronic application, deferred entrance.

Required: essay or personal statement, high school transcript, minimum 2.4 GPA, 3 letters of recommendation, Christian Science commitment. *Required for some:* interview. *Recommended:* interview.

Application deadlines: rolling (freshmen), rolling (transfers).

Notification: continuous (freshmen), continuous (transfers).

CONTACT

Ms. Tami Gavaletz, Director of Admissions and Financial Aid, Principia College, 1 Maybeck Place, Elsah, IL 62028. *Phone:* 618-374-5187. *Toll-free phone:* 800-277-4648 Ext. 2804.

Quincy University

Quincy, Illinois

http://www.quincy.edu/

CONTACT

Ms. Abby Wayman, Associate Director, Admissions, Quincy University, Admissions Office, 1800 College Avenue, Quincy, IL 62301-2699. *Phone:* 217-228-5432 Ext. 3414. *Toll-free phone:* 800-688-4295. *E-mail:* admissions@quincy.edu.

Rasmussen College Aurora

Aurora, Illinois

http://www.rasmussen.edu/

- **Proprietary** 4-year, part of Rasmussen College System
- **Suburban** campus
- **Coed**
- **Minimally difficult** entrance level

FACULTY

Student/faculty ratio: 22:1.

ACADEMICS

Calendar: quarters. *Degrees:* certificates, diplomas, associate, and bachelor's.

Library: Rasmussen College Library - Aurora.

STUDENT LIFE

Housing options: college housing not available.

COSTS

Costs (2017–18) *Tuition:* $11,055 full-time, $290 per credit hour part-time. Full-time tuition and fees vary according to course level, course load, degree level, location, and program. Part-time tuition and fees vary according to course level, course load, degree level, location, and program. No tuition increase for student's term of enrollment. *Required fees:* $1695 full-time, $44 per credit hour part-time. *Payment plans:* installment, deferred payment.

APPLYING

Standardized Tests *Required:* institutional exam (for admission).

Options: electronic application, early admission, deferred entrance.

Required: high school transcript, minimum 2.0 GPA. *Required for some:* interview.

CONTACT

Ms. Susan Hammerstrom, Director of Admissions, Rasmussen College Aurora, 2363 Sequoia Drive, Aurora, IL 60506. *Phone:* 630-888-3500. *Toll-free phone:* 888-549-6755. *E-mail:* susan.hammerstrom@ rasmussen.edu.

Rasmussen College Mokena/ Tinley Park

Mokena, Illinois

http://www.rasmussen.edu/

- **Proprietary** 4-year, part of Rasmussen College System
- **Suburban** campus
- **Coed**
- **Minimally difficult** entrance level

FACULTY

Student/faculty ratio: 22:1.

ACADEMICS

Calendar: quarters. *Degrees:* certificates, diplomas, associate, and bachelor's.
Library: Rasmussen College Library - Mokena.

STUDENT LIFE

Housing options: college housing not available.

COSTS

Costs (2017–18) *Tuition:* $11,055 full-time, $290 per credit hour part-time. Full-time tuition and fees vary according to course level, course load, degree level, location, and program. Part-time tuition and fees vary according to course level, course load, degree level, location, and program. No tuition increase for student's term of enrollment. *Required fees:* $1695 full-time, $44 per credit hour part-time. *Payment plans:* installment, deferred payment.

APPLYING

Standardized Tests *Required:* institutional exam (for admission).

Options: electronic application, early admission, deferred entrance.

Required: high school transcript, minimum 2.0 GPA. *Required for some:* interview.

CONTACT

Ms. Susan Hammerstrom, Director of Admissions, Rasmussen College Mokena/Tinley Park, 8650 West Spring Lake Road, Mokena, IL 60448. *Phone:* 815-534-3300. *Toll-free phone:* 888-549-6755.

Rasmussen College Rockford

Rockford, Illinois

http://www.rasmussen.edu/

- **Proprietary** 4-year, part of Rasmussen College System
- **Suburban** campus
- **Coed** 630 undergraduate students, 83% full-time, 86% women, 14% men
- **Minimally difficult** entrance level, 94% of applicants were admitted

UNDERGRAD STUDENTS

525 full-time, 105 part-time.

Freshmen:

Admission: 33 applied, 31 admitted, 31 enrolled.

FACULTY

Total: 54, 22% full-time.
Student/faculty ratio: 22:1.

ACADEMICS

Calendar: quarters. *Degrees:* certificates, diplomas, associate, and bachelor's.

Special study options: academic remediation for entering students, accelerated degree program, adult/continuing education programs, distance learning, double majors, internships, part-time degree program, summer session for credit.

Computers: 103 computers/terminals are available on campus for general student use. Students can access the following: computer help desk, free student e-mail accounts, online (class) grades, online (class) schedules. Campuswide network is available. Wireless service is available via entire campus.
Library: Rasmussen College Library - Rockford.

STUDENT LIFE

Housing options: college housing not available.

COSTS

Costs (2017–18) *Tuition:* $11,055 full-time, $290 per credit hour part-time. Full-time tuition and fees vary according to course level, course load, degree level, location, and program. Part-time tuition and fees vary according to course level, course load, degree level, location, and program. No tuition increase for student's term of enrollment. *Required fees:* $1695 full-time, $44 per credit hour part-time. *Payment plans:* installment, deferred payment. *Waivers:* employees or children of employees.

APPLYING

Standardized Tests *Required:* institutional exam (for admission).

Options: electronic application, early admission, deferred entrance.

Required: high school transcript, minimum 2.0 GPA. *Required for some:* interview.

Application deadlines: rolling (freshmen), rolling (transfers).

CONTACT

Dwayne Bertotto, Vice President of Admissions and Student Experience, Rasmussen College Rockford, 8300 Norman Center Drive, Suite 300, Bloomington, MN 55437. *Phone:* 952-806-3958. *Toll-free phone:* 888-549-6755. *E-mail:* dwayne.bertotto@rasmussen.edu.

Rasmussen College Romeoville/Joliet

Romeoville, Illinois

http://www.rasmussen.edu/

- **Proprietary** 4-year, part of Rasmussen College System
- **Suburban** campus
- **Coed**
- **Minimally difficult** entrance level

FACULTY

Student/faculty ratio: 22:1.

ACADEMICS

Calendar: quarters. *Degrees:* certificates, diplomas, associate, and bachelor's.
Library: Rasmussen College Library - Romeoville.

STUDENT LIFE

Housing options: college housing not available.

COSTS

Costs (2017–18) *Tuition:* $11,055 full-time, $290 per credit hour part-time. Full-time tuition and fees vary according to course level, course load, degree level, location, and program. Part-time tuition and fees vary according to course level, course load, degree level, location, and program. No tuition increase for student's term of enrollment. *Required fees:* $1695 full-time, $44 per credit hour part-time. *Payment plans:* installment, deferred payment.

APPLYING

Standardized Tests *Required:* institutional exam (for admission).

Options: electronic application, early admission, deferred entrance.

Required: high school transcript, minimum 2.0 GPA. *Required for some:* interview.

CONTACT

Ms. Susan Hammerstrom, Director of Admissions, Rasmussen College Romeoville/Joliet, 1400 West Normantown Road, Romeoville, IL 60446. *Phone:* 815-306-2600. *Toll-free phone:* 888-549-6755. *E-mail:* susan.hammerstrom@rasmussen.edu.

Resurrection University

Chicago, Illinois

http://www.resu.edu/

- **Independent** upper-level, founded 1982
- **Urban** 10-acre campus with easy access to Chicago
- **Endowment** $1.5 million
- **Coed** 602 undergraduate students, 83% full-time, 81% women, 19% men
- **Moderately difficult** entrance level

UNDERGRAD STUDENTS
499 full-time, 103 part-time. Students come from 6 states and territories; 1% are from out of state; 16% Black or African American, non-Hispanic/Latino; 25% Hispanic/Latino; 13% Asian, non-Hispanic/Latino; 0.3% Native Hawaiian or other Pacific Islander, non-Hispanic/Latino; 0.6% American Indian or Alaska Native, non-Hispanic/Latino; 5% Two or more races, non-Hispanic/Latino; 6% Race/ethnicity unknown; 40% transferred in.

FACULTY
Total: 59, 44% full-time, 10% with terminal degrees.
Student/faculty ratio: 7:1.

ACADEMICS
Calendar: semesters. *Degrees:* certificates, bachelor's, master's, doctoral, and postbachelor's certificates.

Special study options: academic remediation for entering students, accelerated degree program, advanced placement credit, independent study, part-time degree program, summer session for credit.

Computers: 36 computers/terminals are available on campus for general student use. Students can access the following: campus intranet, computer help desk, free student e-mail accounts, online (class) grades, online (class) registration, online (class) schedules. Campuswide network is available. Wireless service is available via entire campus.
Library: Resurrection University Library.

STUDENT LIFE
Housing options: college housing not available.

Campus security: 24-hour emergency response devices and patrols, late-night transport/escort service.

Student services: personal/psychological counseling.

COSTS & FINANCIAL AID
Costs (2018–19) *One-time required fee:* $150. *Tuition:* $37,578 full-time. Full-time tuition and fees vary according to course load, degree level, and program. Part-time tuition and fees vary according to course load, degree level, and program. *Required fees:* $870 full-time. *Payment plan:* installment.

Financial Aid Of all full-time matriculated undergraduates who enrolled in 2016, 434 applied for aid, 434 were judged to have need, 98 had their need fully met. In 2016, 6 non-need-based awards were made. *Average percent of need met:* 80. *Average financial aid package:* $18,775. *Average need-based loan:* $5500. *Average need-based gift aid:* $5000. *Average non-need-based aid:* $2000.

APPLYING
Standardized Tests *Required for some:* TEAS.

Options: electronic application, deferred entrance.

Application fee: $50.

Notification: 5/15 (transfers).

CONTACT
Resurrection University, 1431 N. Claremont Avenue, Chicago, IL 60622. *Phone:* 773-252-5307.

Robert Morris University Illinois

Chicago, Illinois

http://www.robertmorris.edu/

- **Independent** comprehensive, founded 1913
- **Urban** campus with easy access to Chicago
- **Endowment** $17.9 million
- **Coed** 2,003 undergraduate students, 95% full-time, 44% women, 56% men
- **Minimally difficult** entrance level, 16% of applicants were admitted

UNDERGRAD STUDENTS
1,895 full-time, 108 part-time. Students come from 39 states and territories; 10 other countries; 13% are from out of state; 25% Black or African American, non-Hispanic/Latino; 31% Hispanic/Latino; 3% Asian, non-Hispanic/Latino; 0.2% Native Hawaiian or other Pacific Islander, non-Hispanic/Latino; 0.1% American Indian or Alaska Native, non-Hispanic/Latino; 2% Two or more races, non-Hispanic/Latino; 3% Race/ethnicity unknown; 0.9% international; 15% transferred in; 11% live on campus.

Freshmen:
Admission: 2,705 applied, 427 admitted, 427 enrolled. *Average high school GPA:* 2.7. *Test scores:* ACT scores over 18: 58%; ACT scores over 24: 15%; ACT scores over 30: 1%.
Retention: 49% of full-time freshmen returned.

FACULTY
Total: 184, 28% full-time, 24% with terminal degrees.
Student/faculty ratio: 21:1.

ACADEMICS
Calendar: 5 10-week academic sessions per year. *Degrees:* associate, bachelor's, and master's.

Special study options: accelerated degree program, adult/continuing education programs, advanced placement credit, double majors, honors programs, internships, part-time degree program, services for LD students, study abroad, summer session for credit. *ROTC:* Army (c).

Computers: 1,307 computers/terminals are available on campus for general student use. Students can access the following: computer help desk, free student e-mail accounts, online (class) grades, online (class) registration, online (class) schedules, online credentials, online payments, online student accounts, online degree audit. Campuswide network is available. 100% of college-owned or -operated housing units are wired for high-speed Internet access. Wireless service is available via entire campus.
Library: Information Technology Library. *Books:* 165,268 (physical), 58,182 (digital/electronic); *Databases:* 37. Weekly public service hours: 74; students can reserve study rooms.

STUDENT LIFE
Housing options: coed. Campus housing is leased by the school. Freshman applicants given priority for college housing.

Activities and organizations: drama/theater group, student-run newspaper, choral group, marching band, UNA-USA, Eagles United for a Cause, Eagles Soaring for a Change, Cooks for a Cause, Eagle Newspaper.

Athletics Member NAIA, USCAA. *Intercollegiate sports:* baseball M(s), basketball M(s)/W(s), bowling M(s)/W(s), cheerleading M(s)/W(s), cross-country running M(s)/W(s), football M(s), golf M(s)/W(s), ice hockey M/W, lacrosse M(s)/W(s), soccer M(s)/W(s), softball W(s), track and field M(s)/W(s), volleyball M(s)/W(s).

Campus security: late-night transport/escort service, controlled dormitory access, Urban campus has multiple security officers at all times who are off-duty Chicago police officers.

Student services: personal/psychological counseling.

COSTS & FINANCIAL AID
Costs (2018–19) *Tuition:* $28,050 full-time, $775 per quarter hour part-time. Part-time tuition and fees vary according to course load. *Required fees:* $480 full-time. *Payment plan:* installment. *Waivers:* employees or children of employees.

Financial Aid Of all full-time matriculated undergraduates who enrolled in 2016, 2,653 applied for aid, 2,586 were judged to have need, 119 had their need fully met. 146 Federal Work-Study jobs (averaging $2239). In 2016, 93 non-need-based awards were made. *Average percent of need met:* 56. *Average financial aid package:* $17,114. *Average need-based loan:* $4198. *Average need-based gift aid:* $13,866. *Average non-need-based aid:* $18,623. *Average indebtedness upon graduation:* $34,382.

APPLYING
Standardized Tests *Required for some:* SAT or ACT (for admission), ACT for nursing and surgical technology programs.

Options: electronic application, deferred entrance.

Application fee: $20.

Required for some: high school transcript. *Recommended:* interview.

Application deadlines: rolling (freshmen), rolling (out-of-state freshmen), rolling (transfers).

Notification: continuous (freshmen), continuous (out-of-state freshmen), continuous (transfers).

CONTACT

Admissions Office, Robert Morris University Illinois, 401 South State Street, Chicago, IL 60605. *Phone:* 800-762-5960. *Toll-free phone:* 800-762-5960. *Fax:* 312-935-4440. *E-mail:* enroll@robertmorris.edu.

Rockford University

Rockford, Illinois

http://www.rockford.edu/

- **Independent** comprehensive, founded 1847
- **Suburban** 150-acre campus with easy access to Chicago
- **Coed** 1,061 undergraduate students, 86% full-time, 55% women, 45% men

UNDERGRAD STUDENTS

917 full-time, 144 part-time. 33% are from out of state; 10% Black or African American, non-Hispanic/Latino; 15% Hispanic/Latino; 2% Asian, non-Hispanic/Latino; 0.2% American Indian or Alaska Native, non-Hispanic/Latino; 3% Two or more races, non-Hispanic/Latino; 3% Race/ethnicity unknown; 4% international; 13% transferred in; 32% live on campus.

Freshmen:

Admission: 152 enrolled. *Average high school GPA:* 3.2. *Test scores:* SAT evidence-based reading and writing scores over 500: 50%; SAT math scores over 500: 50%; ACT scores over 18: 93%; SAT math scores over 600: 13%; ACT scores over 24: 24%; ACT scores over 30: 3%.

Retention: 66% of full-time freshmen returned.

FACULTY

Student/faculty ratio: 10:1.

ACADEMICS

Calendar: semesters. *Degrees:* bachelor's, master's, and postbachelor's certificates.

Special study options: academic remediation for entering students, accelerated degree program, adult/continuing education programs, advanced placement credit, distance learning, double majors, English as a second language, honors programs, independent study, internships, off-campus study, part-time degree program, services for LD students, study abroad, summer session for credit.

Computers: 94 computers/terminals and 4 ports are available on campus for general student use. Students can access the following: campus intranet, computer help desk, free student e-mail accounts, online (class) grades, online (class) registration, online (class) schedules, online bill payment. Campuswide network is available. 100% of college-owned or -operated housing units are wired for high-speed Internet access. Wireless service is available via entire campus.

Library: Howard Colman Library. *Books:* 134,831 (physical), 140,140 (digital/electronic); *Serial titles:* 157 (physical), 23,000 (digital/electronic); *Databases:* 27. Weekly public service hours: 85; students can reserve study rooms.

STUDENT LIFE

Housing options: coed, special housing for students with disabilities. Campus housing is university owned.

Activities and organizations: drama/theater group, student-run newspaper, radio station, choral group, Campus Activities Board, Multicultural Club, Student Government Association, Nursing Student Organization, Alpha Helix.

Athletics Member NCAA. All Division III. *Intercollegiate sports:* baseball M, basketball M/W, cross-country running M/W, football M, soccer M/W, softball W, track and field M/W, volleyball W. *Intramural sports:* basketball M/W, football M/W, volleyball W.

Campus security: 24-hour emergency response devices and patrols, student patrols, late-night transport/escort service, controlled dormitory access.

Student services: health clinic, personal/psychological counseling.

COSTS & FINANCIAL AID

Costs (2018–19) *Comprehensive fee:* $39,590 includes full-time tuition ($30,800), mandatory fees ($130), and room and board ($8660). Full-time tuition and fees vary according to course load. Part-time tuition: $795 per credit hour. Part-time tuition and fees vary according to course load. *College room only:* $4700. Room and board charges vary according to board plan and housing facility. *Payment plan:* installment. *Waivers:* employees or children of employees.

Financial Aid Of all full-time matriculated undergraduates who enrolled in 2016, 837 applied for aid, 789 were judged to have need, 80 had their need fully met. 142 Federal Work-Study jobs (averaging $630). 149 state and other part-time jobs (averaging $2083). In 2016, 89 non-need-based awards were made. *Average percent of need met:* 65. *Average financial aid package:* $20,212. *Average need-based loan:* $4937. *Average need-based gift aid:* $15,734. *Average non-need-based aid:* $11,202. *Average indebtedness upon graduation:* $38,951.

APPLYING

Standardized Tests *Required:* SAT or ACT (for admission).

Required: high school transcript. *Required for some:* essay or personal statement, minimum 2.7 GPA, 2 letters of recommendation. *Recommended:* minimum 2.7 GPA.

CONTACT

Ms. Jennifer Nordstrom, Associate Vice President for Undergraduate Admission, Rockford University, 5050 East State Street, Rockford, IL 61108-2393. *Phone:* 815-226-4050. *Toll-free phone:* 800-892-2984. *Fax:* 815-226-2822. *E-mail:* admissions@rockford.edu.

Roosevelt University

Chicago, Illinois

http://www.roosevelt.edu/

- **Independent** comprehensive, founded 1945
- **Urban** campus with easy access to Chicago
- **Endowment** $109.6 million
- **Coed** 2,514 undergraduate students, 84% full-time, 63% women, 37% men
- **Moderately difficult** entrance level, 70% of applicants were admitted

UNDERGRAD STUDENTS

2,115 full-time, 399 part-time. Students come from 39 states and territories; 44 other countries; 17% are from out of state; 17% Black or African American, non-Hispanic/Latino; 25% Hispanic/Latino; 6% Asian, non-Hispanic/Latino; 0.2% Native Hawaiian or other Pacific Islander, non-Hispanic/Latino; 0.4% American Indian or Alaska Native, non-Hispanic/Latino; 3% Two or more races, non-Hispanic/Latino; 1% Race/ethnicity unknown; 4% international; 16% transferred in; 20% live on campus.

Freshmen:

Admission: 4,018 applied, 2,793 admitted, 360 enrolled. *Average high school GPA:* 3.4. *Test scores:* SAT evidence-based reading and writing scores over 500: 50%; SAT math scores over 500: 45%; ACT scores over 18: 98%; ACT scores over 24: 37%; ACT scores over 30: 4%.

Retention: 64% of full-time freshmen returned.

FACULTY

Total: 622, 38% full-time, 89% with terminal degrees.

Student/faculty ratio: 10:1.

ACADEMICS

Calendar: semesters. *Degrees:* bachelor's, master's, doctoral, and postbachelor's certificates.

Special study options: academic remediation for entering students, accelerated degree program, adult/continuing education programs, advanced placement credit, cooperative education, distance learning, double majors, English as a second language, honors programs, independent study, internships, off-campus study, part-time degree program, services for LD students, student-designed majors, study abroad, summer session for credit.

Computers: 646 computers/terminals are available on campus for general student use. Students can access the following: campus intranet, computer help desk, free student e-mail accounts, online (class) grades, online (class) registration, online (class) schedules. Campuswide network is available. 100% of college-owned or -operated housing units are wired for high-speed Internet access. Wireless service is available via entire campus.

Library: Murray-Green Library plus 4 others. *Books:* 152,557 (physical), 43,963 (digital/electronic); *Serial titles:* 174 (physical), 41,406 (digital/electronic); *Databases:* 198.

STUDENT LIFE

Housing options: on-campus residence required through sophomore year; coed. Campus housing is university owned, leased by the school and is provided by a third party. Freshman campus housing is guaranteed.

Activities and organizations: student-run newspaper, radio station, SPEED Programming Board, Student Government Association, Roosevelt Black Student Union, Alpha Phi Omega Co-ed Service Fraternity, Alpha Gamma Delta Sorority Inc., national fraternities, national sororities.

Athletics Member NAIA. *Intercollegiate sports:* baseball M, basketball M/W, cross-country running M/W, golf M, soccer M/W, softball W, tennis M/W, track and field M/W, volleyball W. *Intramural sports:* basketball M/W, cheerleading W(c).

Campus security: 24-hour emergency response devices and patrols, late-night transport/escort service, controlled dormitory access.

Student services: personal/psychological counseling.

COSTS & FINANCIAL AID

Costs (2018–19) *Comprehensive fee:* $43,055 includes full-time tuition ($29,832) and room and board ($13,223). Full-time tuition and fees vary according to program. Part-time tuition: $797 per credit hour. Part-time tuition and fees vary according to program. *Required fees:* $288 per term part-time. *Room and board:* Room and board charges vary according to board plan and housing facility. *Payment plan:* installment. *Waivers:* employees or children of employees.

Financial Aid Of all full-time matriculated undergraduates who enrolled in 2014, 2,812 applied for aid, 2,397 were judged to have need, 169 had their need fully met. In 2014, 500 non-need-based awards were made. *Average percent of need met:* 75. *Average financial aid package:* $22,318. *Average need-based loan:* $8800. *Average need-based gift aid:* $9000. *Average non-need-based aid:* $7000.

APPLYING

Standardized Tests *Required:* SAT or ACT (for admission).

Options: electronic application, deferred entrance.

Application fee: $25.

Required: high school transcript, minimum 2.5 GPA, audition for music and theater programs. *Required for some:* essay or personal statement, interview. *Recommended:* essay or personal statement.

Notification: continuous (freshmen), continuous (transfers).

CONTACT

Mr. Al Nunez, Director of Admission, Roosevelt University, 430 S Michigan Ave, Chicago, IL 60605. *Phone:* 312-341-2187. *Toll-free phone:* 877-APPLYRU. *E-mail:* anunez13@roosevelt.edu.

Rush University

Chicago, Illinois

http://www.rushu.rush.edu/

CONTACT

Rush University, 600 South Paulina, Chicago, IL 60612-3832. *Phone:* 312-942-7100.

Saint Anthony College of Nursing

Rockford, Illinois

http://www.sacn.edu/

- **Independent Roman Catholic** upper-level, founded 1915
- **Suburban** 7-acre campus with easy access to Chicago
- **Coed, primarily women**
- **Moderately difficult** entrance level

FACULTY

Student/faculty ratio: 7:1.

ACADEMICS

Calendar: semesters. *Degrees:* bachelor's, master's, doctoral, and post-master's certificates.

Library: Sister Mary Linus Learning Resource Center. Students can reserve study rooms.

STUDENT LIFE

Housing options: college housing not available.

Activities and organizations: Student Organization.

Campus security: 24-hour patrols.

Student services: health clinic, personal/psychological counseling, legal services.

COSTS & FINANCIAL AID

Costs (2017–18) *Tuition:* $24,226 full-time, $758 per credit hour part-time. Full-time tuition and fees vary according to course load, program, and student level. Part-time tuition and fees vary according to course load, program, and student level. *Required fees:* $1116 full-time. *Payment plans:* installment, deferred payment.

Financial Aid Of all full-time matriculated undergraduates who enrolled in 2015, 154 applied for aid, 145 were judged to have need, 3 had their need fully met. In 2015, 1 non-need-based awards were made. *Average percent of need met:* 38. *Average financial aid package:* $9203. *Average need-based loan:* $4268. *Average need-based gift aid:* $7100. *Average non-need-based aid:* $4000.

APPLYING

Options: electronic application.

Application fee: $75.

CONTACT

Ms. April Lipnitzky, Enrollment Management Coordinator, Saint Anthony College of Nursing, 5658 East State Street, Rockford, IL 61108-2468. *Phone:* 815-227-2141. *Fax:* 815-227-2730. *E-mail:* admissions@sacn.edu.

St. Augustine College

Chicago, Illinois

http://www.staugustine.edu/

CONTACT

Ms. Gloria Quiroz, Director of Admissions, St. Augustine College, 1333-1345 West Argyle, Chicago, IL 60640-3501. *Phone:* 773-878-3256. *Fax:* 773-878-0937. *E-mail:* info@staugustine.edu.

Saint Francis Medical Center College of Nursing

Peoria, Illinois

http://www.sfmccon.edu/

- **Independent Roman Catholic** upper-level, founded 1986
- **Urban** campus
- **Coed, primarily women** 402 undergraduate students, 77% full-time, 88% women, 12% men
- **84%** of applicants were admitted

UNDERGRAD STUDENTS

311 full-time, 91 part-time. Students come from 3 states and territories; 4 other countries; 1% are from out of state; 5% Black or African American, non-Hispanic/Latino; 5% Hispanic/Latino; 2% Asian, non-Hispanic/Latino; 2% Two or more races, non-Hispanic/Latino; 0.5% Race/ethnicity unknown; 1% international; 30% transferred in; 20% live on campus.

Freshmen:
Admission: 90 applied, 76 admitted.

FACULTY

Total: 54, 69% full-time, 20% with terminal degrees.

Student/faculty ratio: 10:1.

ACADEMICS

Calendar: semesters. *Degrees:* bachelor's, master's, doctoral, and post-master's certificates.

Special study options: academic remediation for entering students, accelerated degree program, adult/continuing education programs, advanced placement credit, distance learning, independent study, part-time degree program, summer session for credit.

Computers: 62 computers/terminals and 53 ports are available on campus for general student use. Students can access the following: computer help desk, online (class) grades, online (class) registration, online (class) schedules. Campuswide network is available. 100% of college-owned or -operated housing units are wired for high-speed Internet access. Wireless service is available via entire campus.

Library: Sister Mary Ludgera Pieperbeck Learning and Resource Center plus 1 other. *Books:* 4,054 (physical), 298 (digital/electronic); *Serial titles:* 126 (physical); *Databases:* 57. Students can reserve study rooms.

STUDENT LIFE

Housing options: coed. Campus housing is university owned.

Activities and organizations: Student Senate, SNAI, Minority Student Association, Tau Omicron.

Campus security: 24-hour emergency response devices and patrols, late-night transport/escort service, controlled dormitory access.

Student services: health clinic, personal/psychological counseling.

COSTS & FINANCIAL AID

Costs (2018–19) *Tuition:* $20,020 full-time, $616 per semester hour part-time. Full-time tuition and fees vary according to course load, degree level, program, and student level. Part-time tuition and fees vary according to course load, degree level, program, and student level. *Required fees:* $1037 full-time, $215 per term part-time. *Room only:* $1850. *Payment plan:* installment. *Waivers:* employees or children of employees.

Financial Aid Of all full-time matriculated undergraduates who enrolled in 2017, 265 applied for aid, 210 were judged to have need, 9 had their need fully met. In 2017, 25 non-need-based awards were made. *Average percent of need met:* 41. *Average financial aid package:* $10,953. *Average need-based loan:* $5721. *Average need-based gift aid:* $7143. *Average non-need-based aid:* $2522.

APPLYING

Options: deferred entrance.

Application fee: $50.

Notification: 10/15 (transfers).

CONTACT

Saint Francis Medical Center College of Nursing, 511 Northeast Greenleaf Street, Peoria, IL 61603-3783. *Phone:* 309-624-8980.

St. John's College
Springfield, Illinois
http://www.sjcs.edu/

CONTACT

St. John's College, 729 East Carpenter Street, Springfield, IL 62702. *Phone:* 217-525-5628.

Saint Xavier University
Chicago, Illinois
http://www.sxu.edu/

CONTACT

Dr. Kathleen Carlson, Vice President, Saint Xavier University, 3700 West 103rd Street, Chicago, IL 60655-3105. *Phone:* 773-298-3305. *Toll-free phone:* 800-462-9288. *E-mail:* carlson@sxu.edu.

School of the Art Institute of Chicago
Chicago, Illinois
http://www.saic.edu/

- **Independent** comprehensive, founded 1866
- **Urban** 1-acre campus with easy access to Chicago
- **Coed**
- **Very difficult** entrance level

FACULTY
Student/faculty ratio: 11:1.

ACADEMICS

Calendar: semesters. *Degrees:* bachelor's, master's, and postbachelor's certificates.

Library: The John M. Flaxman Library plus 1 other. *Books:* 110,287 (physical), 203,725 (digital/electronic); *Serial titles:* 19,541 (physical), 204,634 (digital/electronic); *Databases:* 177.

STUDENT LIFE

Housing options: coed, special housing for students with disabilities. Campus housing is university owned.

Activities and organizations: drama/theater group, student-run newspaper, radio and television station, Student Association/Student Union Galleries, Korean Student Association, InterVarsity, Curatorial Community, Good 'Ol Futbol.

Campus security: 24-hour emergency response devices and patrols, late-night transport/escort service, controlled dormitory access.

Student services: health clinic, personal/psychological counseling.

COSTS

Costs (2017–18) *Comprehensive fee:* $62,910 includes full-time tuition ($46,560), mandatory fees ($860), and room and board ($15,490). Full-time tuition and fees vary according to course load, degree level, and program. Part-time tuition: $1552 per credit hour. Part-time tuition and fees vary according to course load, degree level, and program. *Required fees:* $295 per term part-time. *College room only:* $11,900. Room and board charges vary according to board plan and housing facility.

APPLYING

Standardized Tests *Required:* SAT or ACT (for admission).

Options: electronic application, early action, deferred entrance.

Application fee: $65.

Required: essay or personal statement, high school transcript. *Recommended:* interview.

CONTACT

Ms. Asia Mitchell, Director, Undergraduate Admissions, School of the Art Institute of Chicago, 36 South Wabash, Chicago, IL 60603. *Phone:* 312-629-6100. *Toll-free phone:* 800-232-SAIC. *Fax:* 312-629-6101. *E-mail:* ugadmiss@saic.edu.

Southern Illinois University Carbondale
Carbondale, Illinois
http://www.siu.edu/

- **State-supported** university, founded 1869, part of Southern Illinois University
- **Rural** 1136-acre campus with easy access to St. Louis
- **Coed** 10,987 undergraduate students, 86% full-time, 46% women, 54% men
- **Moderately difficult** entrance level, 76% of applicants were admitted

UNDERGRAD STUDENTS

9,455 full-time, 1,532 part-time. Students come from 46 states and territories; 47 other countries; 17% are from out of state; 16% Black or African American, non-Hispanic/Latino; 9% Hispanic/Latino; 2% Asian, non-Hispanic/Latino; 0.1% Native Hawaiian or other Pacific Islander, non-Hispanic/Latino; 0.3% American Indian or Alaska Native, non-Hispanic/Latino; 4% Two or more races, non-Hispanic/Latino; 0.1% Race/ethnicity unknown; 4% international; 14% transferred in; 22% live on campus.

Freshmen:

Admission: 7,941 applied, 6,049 admitted, 1,319 enrolled. *Average high school GPA:* 3.1. *Test scores:* ACT scores over 18: 93%; ACT scores over 24: 40%; ACT scores over 30: 7%.

Retention: 68% of full-time freshmen returned.

FACULTY

Total: 998, 83% full-time, 69% with terminal degrees.

Student/faculty ratio: 14:1.

ACADEMICS

Calendar: semesters plus 8-week summer session. *Degrees:* certificates, associate, bachelor's, master's, doctoral, and postbachelor's certificates.

Special study options: academic remediation for entering students, accelerated degree program, adult/continuing education programs, advanced placement credit, cooperative education, distance learning, double majors, English as a second language, honors programs, independent study, internships, off-campus study, part-time degree program, services for LD students, student-designed majors, study abroad, summer session for credit. *ROTC:* Army (b), Air Force (b).

Computers: 1,900 computers/terminals are available on campus for general student use. Students can access the following: computer help desk, free student e-mail accounts, online (class) grades, online (class) registration, online (class) schedules. Campuswide network is available. 100% of college-owned or -operated housing units are wired for high-speed Internet access. Wireless service is available via classrooms, computer centers, computer labs, dorm rooms, learning centers, libraries, student centers.

Library: Morris Library plus 1 other. *Books:* 2.6 million (physical), 389,774 (digital/electronic); *Serial titles:* 303 (physical), 58,572 (digital/electronic); *Databases:* 165. Weekly public service hours: 100; students can reserve study rooms.

STUDENT LIFE

Housing options: on-campus residence required for freshman year; coed, men-only, women-only, cooperative, special housing for students with disabilities. Campus housing is university owned. Freshman campus housing is guaranteed.

Activities and organizations: drama/theater group, student-run newspaper, radio and television station, choral group, marching band, Inter-Greek Council, Undergraduate Student Government, Black Affairs Council, Residence Hall Association, Equestrian Club, national fraternities, national sororities.

Athletics Member NCAA. All Division I except football (Division I-AA). *Intercollegiate sports:* baseball M(s), basketball M(s)/W(s), cheerleading M/W, cross-country running M(s)/W(s), golf M(s)/W(s), softball W(s), swimming and diving M(s)/W(s), track and field M(s)/W(s), volleyball W(s). *Intramural sports:* archery M(c)/W(c), badminton M(c)/W(c), baseball M(c), basketball M/W, bowling M(c)/W(c), equestrian sports M(c)/W(c), fencing M(c)/W(c), gymnastics M(c)/W(c), lacrosse M(c), racquetball M/W, rock climbing M(c)/W(c), rugby M(c)/W(c), sailing M(c)/W(c), soccer M(c)/W(c), softball W(c), swimming and diving W, table tennis M(c)/W(c), tennis M(c)/W(c), triathlon M(c)/W(c), ultimate Frisbee M(c)/W(c), volleyball M(c)/W(c), water polo M(c)/W(c), weight lifting M(c)/W(c), wrestling M(c)/W(c).

Campus security: 24-hour emergency response devices and patrols, student patrols, late-night transport/escort service, controlled dormitory access, well-lit pathways, night safety vans, student transit system.

Student services: health clinic, personal/psychological counseling, women's center, legal services.

COSTS & FINANCIAL AID

Costs (2017–18) *Tuition:* state resident $9450 full-time, $315 per credit hour part-time; nonresident $23,625 full-time, $788 per credit hour part-time. Full-time tuition and fees vary according to course load, location, program, reciprocity agreements, and student level. Part-time tuition and fees vary according to course load, location, program, reciprocity agreements, and student level. No tuition increase for student's term of enrollment. *Required fees:* $4486 full-time, $1001 per credit hour part-time. *Room and board:* $10,622. Room and board charges vary according to board plan and housing facility. *Payment plan:* installment. *Waivers:* children of alumni, senior citizens, and employees or children of employees.

Financial Aid Of all full-time matriculated undergraduates who enrolled in 2016, 7,562 applied for aid, 6,661 were judged to have need, 666 had their need fully met. 1,382 Federal Work-Study jobs (averaging $1291). In 2016, 416 non-need-based awards were made. *Average percent of need met:* 61. *Average financial aid package:* $15,046. *Average need-based loan:* $4693. *Average need-based gift aid:* $7904. *Average non-need-based aid:* $6693. *Average indebtedness upon graduation:* $29,637.

APPLYING

Standardized Tests *Required:* SAT or ACT (for admission).

Options: electronic application, deferred entrance.

Application fee: $40.

Required: high school transcript.

Application deadlines: rolling (freshmen), rolling (out-of-state freshmen), rolling (transfers).

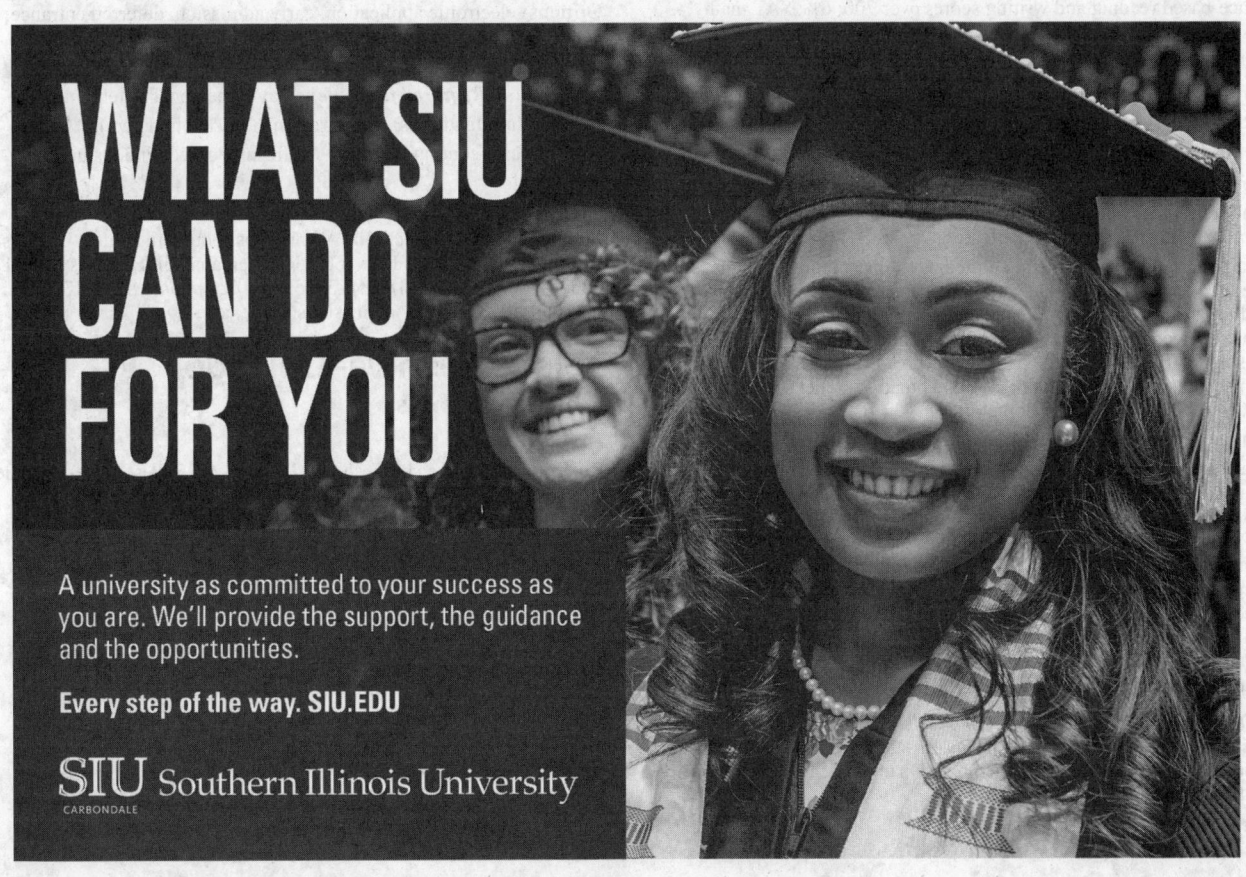

Notification: continuous (freshmen), continuous (out-of-state freshmen), continuous (transfers).

CONTACT

Tamora Workman, Director of the Registrar's Office, Southern Illinois University Carbondale, Office of Registrar, 1263 Lincoln Drive, MC 4701, Carbondale, IL 62901. *Phone:* 618-453-2963. *Fax:* 618-453-2915. *E-mail:* regstrar@siu.edu.

See previous page for display ad and page 1428 for the College Close-Up.

Southern Illinois University Edwardsville

Edwardsville, Illinois

http://www.siue.edu/

- **State-supported** university, founded 1957, part of Southern Illinois University
- **Suburban** 2660-acre campus with easy access to St. Louis
- **Endowment** $22.4 million
- **Coed** 11,402 undergraduate students, 84% full-time, 53% women, 47% men
- **Moderately difficult** entrance level, 90% of applicants were admitted

UNDERGRAD STUDENTS

9,550 full-time, 1,852 part-time. Students come from 39 states and territories; 42 other countries; 12% are from out of state; 14% Black or African American, non-Hispanic/Latino; 5% Hispanic/Latino; 2% Asian, non-Hispanic/Latino; 0.1% Native Hawaiian or other Pacific Islander, non-Hispanic/Latino; 0.3% American Indian or Alaska Native, non-Hispanic/Latino; 3% Two or more races, non-Hispanic/Latino; 1% Race/ethnicity unknown; 1% international; 12% transferred in; 28% live on campus.

Freshmen:

Admission: 6,273 applied, 5,615 admitted, 1,797 enrolled. *Average high school GPA:* 3.5. *Test scores:* SAT evidence-based reading and writing scores over 500: 72%; SAT math scores over 500: 75%; ACT scores over 18: 95%; SAT evidence-based reading and writing scores over 600: 27%; SAT math scores over 600: 28%; ACT scores over 24: 45%; SAT evidence-based reading and writing scores over 700: 6%; SAT math scores over 700: 9%; ACT scores over 30: 8%.

Retention: 73% of full-time freshmen returned.

FACULTY

Total: 852, 70% full-time, 67% with terminal degrees.
Student/faculty ratio: 19:1.

ACADEMICS

Calendar: semesters. *Degrees:* bachelor's, master's, doctoral, post-master's, and postbachelor's certificates.

Special study options: academic remediation for entering students, accelerated degree program, advanced placement credit, cooperative education, distance learning, double majors, English as a second language, external degree program, honors programs, independent study, internships, off-campus study, part-time degree program, services for LD students, student-designed majors, study abroad, summer session for credit. *ROTC:* Army (b), Air Force (c).

Unusual degree programs: 3-2 engineering.

Computers: 315 computers/terminals are available on campus for general student use. Students can access the following: campus intranet, computer help desk, free student e-mail accounts, online (class) grades, online (class) registration, online (class) schedules, online job finder. Campuswide network is available. 100% of college-owned or -operated housing units are wired for high-speed Internet access. Wireless service is available via entire campus.

Library: Lovejoy Library. *Books:* 735,648 (physical), 89,572 (digital/electronic); *Serial titles:* 145 (physical), 34,715 (digital/electronic). Students can reserve study rooms.

STUDENT LIFE

Housing options: coed, special housing for students with disabilities. Campus housing is university owned. Freshman applicants given priority for college housing.

Activities and organizations: drama/theater group, student-run newspaper, radio station, choral group, Fraternity and Sorority Life, Campus Activities Board, Sports Clubs/Intramurals, Dance Marathon, Student Government, national fraternities, national sororities.

Athletics Member NCAA. All Division I. *Intercollegiate sports:* baseball M(s), basketball M(s)/W(s), cross-country running M(s)/W(s), golf M(s), soccer M(s)/W(s), softball W(s), tennis W(s), track and field M(s)/W(s), volleyball W(s), wrestling M(s). *Intramural sports:* archery M(c)/W(c), badminton M/W, baseball M(c), basketball M/W, bowling M/W, cheerleading M/W, cross-country running M/W, fencing M/W, football M(c), golf M(c)/W(c), ice hockey M(c), lacrosse M(c)/W(c), racquetball M/W, rock climbing M/W, skiing (downhill) M(c)/W(c), soccer M/W, softball M/W, swimming and diving M(c)/W(c), table tennis M/W, tennis M/W, ultimate Frisbee M(c)/W(c), volleyball M(c)/W(c), water polo M(c)/W(c), weight lifting M(c)/W(c), wrestling M(c).

Campus security: 24-hour emergency response devices and patrols, late-night transport/escort service, controlled dormitory access.

Student services: health clinic, personal/psychological counseling.

COSTS & FINANCIAL AID

Costs (2018–19) *Tuition:* state resident $9123 full-time; nonresident $9123 full-time. Full-time tuition and fees vary according to course load, degree level, location, and program. Part-time tuition and fees vary according to course load, degree level, location, and program. No tuition increase for student's term of enrollment. *Required fees:* $3009 full-time. *Room and board:* $9730; room only: $6170. Room and board charges vary according to board plan, housing facility, and student level. *Payment plan:* installment. *Waivers:* children of alumni and employees or children of employees.

Financial Aid Of all full-time matriculated undergraduates who enrolled in 2015, 8,167 applied for aid, 6,499 were judged to have need, 2,442 had their need fully met. In 2015, 521 non-need-based awards were made. *Average percent of need met:* 60. *Average financial aid package:* $11,223. *Average need-based loan:* $4496. *Average need-based gift aid:* $7760. *Average non-need-based aid:* $5113. *Average indebtedness upon graduation:* $22,277.

APPLYING

Standardized Tests *Required:* SAT or ACT (for admission).

Options: electronic application, early admission, deferred entrance.

Application fee: $40.

Required: high school transcript, minimum 2.0 GPA, college transcript(s). *Required for some:* essay or personal statement.

Application deadlines: 7/19 (freshmen), 7/19 (transfers).

Notification: continuous until 9/1 (freshmen), continuous until 9/1 (transfers).

CONTACT

Mr. Todd Burrell, Director of Admissions, Southern Illinois University Edwardsville, Campus Box 1600, Rendleman Hall, Edwardsville, IL 62026-1600. *Phone:* 618-650-3705. *Toll-free phone:* 800-447-SIUE. *Fax:* 618-650-5013. *E-mail:* admissions@siue.edu.

Telshe Yeshiva–Chicago

Chicago, Illinois

CONTACT

Rosh Hayeshiva, Telshe Yeshiva–Chicago, 3535 West Foster Avenue, Chicago, IL 60625-5598. *Phone:* 773-463-7738.

Trinity Christian College

Palos Heights, Illinois

http://www.trnty.edu/

- **Independent Christian Reformed** comprehensive, founded 1959
- **Suburban** 53-acre campus with easy access to Chicago
- **Endowment** $10.8 million
- **Coed** 1,107 undergraduate students, 82% full-time, 67% women, 33% men
- **Moderately difficult** entrance level

UNDERGRAD STUDENTS

907 full-time, 200 part-time. Students come from 29 states and territories; 10 other countries; 31% are from out of state; 8% Black or African American, non-Hispanic/Latino; 12% Hispanic/Latino; 1% Asian, non-Hispanic/Latino; 0.1% Native Hawaiian or other Pacific Islander, non-Hispanic/Latino; 0.2% American Indian or Alaska Native, non-Hispanic/Latino; 1% Two or more races, non-Hispanic/Latino; 3% Race/ethnicity unknown; 9% international; 6% transferred in; 42% live on campus.

Freshmen:

Admission: 889 applied, 192 enrolled. *Average high school GPA:* 3.5. *Test scores:* SAT evidence-based reading and writing scores over 500: 100%; SAT math scores over 500: 80%; ACT scores over 18: 90%; SAT evidence-based reading and writing scores over 600: 33%; SAT math scores over 600: 25%; ACT scores over 24: 42%; SAT math scores over 700: 5%; ACT scores over 30: 5%.

Retention: 83% of full-time freshmen returned.

FACULTY

Total: 151, 46% full-time, 42% with terminal degrees.

Student/faculty ratio: 10:1.

ACADEMICS

Calendar: semesters plus 2 week interim term. *Degrees:* bachelor's and master's.

Special study options: academic remediation for entering students, accelerated degree program, adult/continuing education programs, advanced placement credit, cooperative education, distance learning, double majors, English as a second language, honors programs, independent study, internships, off-campus study, part-time degree program, services for LD students, study abroad, summer session for credit.

Computers: 170 computers/terminals are available on campus for general student use. Students can access the following: campus intranet, computer help desk, free student e-mail accounts, online (class) grades, online (class) registration, online (class) schedules. Campuswide network is available. 100% of college-owned or -operated housing units are wired for high-speed Internet access. Wireless service is available via entire campus.

Library: Jennie Huizenga Memorial Library plus 1 other. *Books:* 60,951 (physical), 6,449 (digital/electronic); *Serial titles:* 20 (physical), 45,797 (digital/electronic); *Databases:* 61. Weekly public service hours: 84; students can reserve study rooms.

STUDENT LIFE

Housing options: coed. Campus housing is university owned. Freshman campus housing is guaranteed.

Activities and organizations: drama/theater group, student-run newspaper, choral group, Student Association, Student ministries, Campus newspaper, Pro-Life Task Force, PACE (prison tutoring program).

Athletics Member NAIA, NCCAA. *Intercollegiate sports:* baseball M(s), basketball M(s)/W(s), cross-country running M(s)/W(s), golf M(s)/W, soccer M(s)/W(s), softball W(s), track and field M(s)/W(s), volleyball M/W(s). *Intramural sports:* basketball M/W, soccer M/W, volleyball M/W.

Campus security: 24-hour emergency response devices and patrols, student patrols, late-night transport/escort service, controlled dormitory access, security cameras, Code Blue Emergency Phones.

Student services: personal/psychological counseling.

COSTS & FINANCIAL AID

Costs (2018–19) *One-time required fee:* $225. *Comprehensive fee:* $39,740 includes full-time tuition ($29,700), mandatory fees ($250), and room and board ($9790). Full-time tuition and fees vary according to course load and degree level. Part-time tuition: $942 per credit hour. Part-time tuition and fees vary according to course load and degree level. *Room and board:* Room and board charges vary according to board plan and housing facility. *Payment plan:* installment. *Waivers:* employees or children of employees.

Financial Aid Of all full-time matriculated undergraduates who enrolled in 2017, 770 applied for aid, 697 were judged to have need, 115 had their need fully met. In 2017, 99 non-need-based awards were made. *Average percent of need met:* 73. *Average financial aid package:* $20,865. *Average need-based loan:* $4589. *Average need-based gift aid:* $16,760.

Average non-need-based aid: $10,560. *Average indebtedness upon graduation:* $29,978.

APPLYING

Standardized Tests *Required:* SAT or ACT (for admission).

Options: electronic application, deferred entrance.

Application fee: $30.

Required: essay or personal statement, high school transcript, minimum 2.5 GPA, interview. *Required for some:* 1 letter of recommendation, ACT Composite score of 19 or combined SAT score of 980.

Application deadlines: rolling (freshmen), rolling (transfers).

Notification: continuous (freshmen), continuous (transfers).

CONTACT

Jeremy Klyn, Director of Admissions, Trinity Christian College, 6601 West College Drive, Palos Heights, IL 60463. *Phone:* 708-293-4712. *Toll-free phone:* 866-TRIN-4-ME. *Fax:* 708-239-4826. *E-mail:* admissions@trnty.edu.

Trinity College of Nursing and Health Sciences
Rock Island, Illinois
http://www.trinitycollegeqc.edu/

CONTACT

Ms. Lori Perez, Admissions Representative, Trinity College of Nursing and Health Sciences, 2122 25th Avenue, Rock Island, IL 61201. *Phone:* 309-779-7700. *Fax:* 309-779-7748. *E-mail:* perezlj@ihs.org.

Trinity International University
Deerfield, Illinois
http://www.tiu.edu/

CONTACT

Mr. Aaron Mahl, Director of Undergraduate Admissions, Trinity International University, 2065 Half Day Road, Deerfield, IL 60015-1284. *Phone:* 847-317-7000. *Toll-free phone:* 800-822-3225. *Fax:* 847-317-8097. *E-mail:* tcadmissions@tiu.edu.

University of Chicago
Chicago, Illinois
http://www.uchicago.edu/

- **Independent** university, founded 1890
- **Urban** 217-acre campus with easy access to Chicago
- **Endowment** $7.8 billion
- **Coed** 6,264 undergraduate students, 100% full-time, 49% women, 51% men
- **Most difficult** entrance level, 9% of applicants were admitted

UNDERGRAD STUDENTS

6,242 full-time, 22 part-time. Students come from 50 states and territories; 77 other countries; 82% are from out of state; 5% Black or African American, non-Hispanic/Latino; 13% Hispanic/Latino; 18% Asian, non-Hispanic/Latino; 0.1% American Indian or Alaska Native, non-Hispanic/Latino; 6% Two or more races, non-Hispanic/Latino; 2% Race/ethnicity unknown; 13% international; 0.6% transferred in; 54% live on campus.

Freshmen:

Admission: 27,694 applied, 2,419 admitted, 1,736 enrolled. *Average high school GPA:* 4.5. *Test scores:* SAT evidence-based reading and writing scores over 500: 100%; SAT math scores over 500: 100%; ACT scores over 18: 100%; SAT evidence-based reading and writing scores over 600: 100%; SAT math scores over 600: 100%; ACT scores over 24: 100%; SAT evidence-based reading and writing scores over 700: 92%; SAT math scores over 700: 92%; ACT scores over 30: 95%.

Retention: 99% of full-time freshmen returned.

FACULTY

Total: 1,671, 84% full-time, 99% with terminal degrees.

Student/faculty ratio: 5:1.

ACADEMICS

Calendar: quarters. *Degrees:* bachelor's, master's, and doctoral.

Special study options: accelerated degree program, advanced placement credit, double majors, English as a second language, independent study, internships, off-campus study, services for LD students, student-designed majors, study abroad, summer session for credit. *ROTC:* Army (c), Air Force (c).

Unusual degree programs: 3-2 social work; public policy, social sciences, international relations.

Computers: Students can access the following: campus intranet, computer help desk, free student e-mail accounts, online (class) grades, online (class) registration, online (class) schedules. Campuswide network is available. Wireless service is available via entire campus.

Library: Joseph Regenstein Library plus 5 others. Students can reserve study rooms.

STUDENT LIFE

Housing options: on-campus residence required for freshman year; coed, special housing for students with disabilities. Campus housing is university owned. Freshman campus housing is guaranteed.

Activities and organizations: drama/theater group, student-run newspaper, radio station, choral group, University Theatre, Model United Nations, Council on University Programming, South Asian Students Association, Splash, national fraternities, national sororities.

Athletics Member NCAA. All Division III. *Intercollegiate sports:* baseball M, basketball M/W, cross-country running M/W, football M, soccer M/W, softball W, swimming and diving M/W, tennis M/W, track and field M/W, volleyball W, wrestling M. *Intramural sports:* badminton M/W, basketball M/W, bowling M/W, racquetball M/W, sailing W(c), soccer M/W, softball M/W, swimming and diving M/W, table tennis M/W, tennis M/W, track and field M/W, ultimate Frisbee M/W, volleyball M/W.

Campus security: 24-hour emergency response devices and patrols, student patrols, late-night transport/escort service, controlled dormitory access.

Student services: health clinic, personal/psychological counseling, women's center.

COSTS & FINANCIAL AID

Costs (2017–18) *One-time required fee:* $1209. *Comprehensive fee:* $70,551 includes full-time tuition ($53,292), mandatory fees ($1533), and room and board ($15,726). Full-time tuition and fees vary according to course load. Part-time tuition and fees vary according to course load. *Room and board:* Room and board charges vary according to board plan and housing facility. *Payment plan:* installment. *Waivers:* employees or children of employees.

Financial Aid Of all full-time matriculated undergraduates who enrolled in 2017, 3,289 applied for aid, 2,661 were judged to have need, 2,661 had their need fully met. *Average percent of need met:* 100. *Average financial aid package:* $52,643. *Average need-based loan:* $3777. *Average need-based gift aid:* $46,460. *Average indebtedness upon graduation:* $23,401.

APPLYING

Standardized Tests *Required:* SAT or ACT (for admission).

Options: electronic application, early admission, early decision, early action, deferred entrance.

Application fee: $75.

Required: essay or personal statement, high school transcript, 2 letters of recommendation.

Application deadlines: 1/1 (freshmen), 3/1 (transfers), 11/1 (early action).

Notification: 4/1 (freshmen), 5/9 (transfers), 12/17 (early action).

CONTACT

Mr. James G. Nondorf, Vice President for Enrollment and Student Advancement and Dean of Admissions and Financial Aid, University of Chicago, Rosenwald Hall, 1101 East 58th Street, Suite 105, Chicago, IL 60637. *Phone:* 773-702-8650. *Fax:* 773-702-4199. *E-mail:* collegeadmissions@uchicago.edu.

University of Illinois at Chicago
Chicago, Illinois
http://www.uic.edu/

- **State-supported** university, founded 1946, part of University of Illinois System
- **Urban** 240-acre campus with easy access to Chicago
- **Endowment** $321.6 million
- **Coed** 19,447 undergraduate students, 92% full-time, 50% women, 50% men
- **Moderately difficult** entrance level, 77% of applicants were admitted

UNDERGRAD STUDENTS

17,961 full-time, 1,486 part-time. Students come from 65 other countries; 3% are from out of state; 8% Black or African American, non-Hispanic/Latino; 33% Hispanic/Latino; 21% Asian, non-Hispanic/Latino; 0.1% Native Hawaiian or other Pacific Islander, non-Hispanic/Latino; 0.1% American Indian or Alaska Native, non-Hispanic/Latino; 3% Two or more races, non-Hispanic/Latino; 0.7% Race/ethnicity unknown; 5% international; 11% transferred in; 15% live on campus.

Freshmen:

Admission: 18,768 applied, 14,467 admitted, 4,050 enrolled. *Average high school GPA:* 3.3. *Test scores:* SAT evidence-based reading and writing scores over 500: 86%; SAT math scores over 500: 90%; ACT scores over 18: 96%; SAT evidence-based reading and writing scores over 600: 49%; SAT math scores over 600: 59%; ACT scores over 24: 46%; SAT evidence-based reading and writing scores over 700: 9%; SAT math scores over 700: 19%; ACT scores over 30: 8%.

Retention: 80% of full-time freshmen returned.

FACULTY

Total: 1,613, 74% full-time, 82% with terminal degrees.

Student/faculty ratio: 17:1.

ACADEMICS

Calendar: semesters. *Degrees:* bachelor's, master's, doctoral, post-master's, and postbachelor's certificates.

Special study options: academic remediation for entering students, accelerated degree program, advanced placement credit, cooperative education, distance learning, double majors, freshman honors college, honors programs, independent study, internships, off-campus study, part-time degree program, services for LD students, student-designed majors, study abroad, summer session for credit. *ROTC:* Army (b), Navy (c), Air Force (c).

Computers: 1,052 computers/terminals are available on campus for general student use. Students can access the following: campus intranet, computer help desk, free student e-mail accounts, online (class) grades, online (class) registration, online (class) schedules. Campuswide network is available. 100% of college-owned or -operated housing units are wired for high-speed Internet access. Wireless service is available via entire campus.

Library: Richard J. Daley Library plus 2 others. *Books:* 1.6 million (physical), 617,614 (digital/electronic); *Serial titles:* 61,000 (digital/electronic); *Databases:* 100. Weekly public service hours: 140; study areas open 24 hours, 5–7 days a week; students can reserve study rooms.

STUDENT LIFE

Housing options: coed. Campus housing is university owned.

Activities and organizations: drama/theater group, student-run newspaper, radio station, choral group, Muslim Student Association, Alternative Spring Break, Filipinos in Alliance, Society of Future Physicians, Ski and Snowboard Club, national fraternities, national sororities.

Athletics Member NCAA. All Division I. *Intercollegiate sports:* baseball M(s), basketball M(s)/W(s), cross-country running M(s)/W(s), gymnastics M(s)/W(s), soccer M(s), softball W(s), swimming and diving M(s)/W(s), tennis M(s)/W(s), track and field M(s)/W(s), volleyball W(s). *Intramural sports:* badminton M/W, basketball M/W, bowling M/W, fencing M(c)/W(c), field hockey W, football M/W, golf M/W, racquetball M/W, rugby M(c)/W(c), soccer M/W, softball M/W, squash M/W, table tennis M/W, tennis M/W, volleyball M(c)/W, water polo M(c)/W(c), wrestling M.

Campus security: 24-hour emergency response devices and patrols, student patrols, late-night transport/escort service, controlled dormitory access, housing ID stickers, guest escort policy, 24-hour closed circuit videos for exits and entrances, security screen for first floor.

Student services: health clinic, personal/psychological counseling, women's center, legal services.

COSTS & FINANCIAL AID
Costs (2018–19) *Tuition:* state resident $10,584 full-time, $394 per credit hour part-time; nonresident $23,440 full-time, $803 per credit hour part-time. Full-time tuition and fees vary according to degree level and program. Part-time tuition and fees vary according to course load, degree level, and program. No tuition increase for student's term of enrollment. *Required fees:* $3030 full-time. *Room and board:* $10,960; room only: $7930. Room and board charges vary according to board plan and housing facility. *Payment plan:* installment. *Waivers:* senior citizens and employees or children of employees.

Financial Aid Of all full-time matriculated undergraduates who enrolled in 2016, 13,775 applied for aid, 12,474 were judged to have need, 1,120 had their need fully met. 856 Federal Work-Study jobs (averaging $3000). 3,162 state and other part-time jobs (averaging $2500). In 2016, 578 non-need-based awards were made. *Average percent of need met:* 61. *Average financial aid package:* $14,729. *Average need-based loan:* $4349. *Average need-based gift aid:* $12,993. *Average non-need-based aid:* $5663. *Average indebtedness upon graduation:* $23,076.

APPLYING
Standardized Tests *Required:* SAT or ACT (for admission).

Options: electronic application, early admission, early action.

Application fee: $50.

Required: essay or personal statement, high school transcript. *Required for some:* audition for music and theater majors, portfolio for art majors.

Application deadlines: 1/15 (freshmen), 3/31 (transfers).

Notification: continuous until 11/30 (freshmen), continuous (transfers).

CONTACT
Ms. Maureen Woods, Associate Director, Admissions Undergraduate, University of Illinois at Chicago, Chicago. *Phone:* 312-996-4111. *Fax:* 312-413-7628. *E-mail:* uic.admit@uic.edu.

University of Illinois at Springfield
Springfield, Illinois
http://www.uis.edu/
- **State-supported** comprehensive, founded 1969, part of University of Illinois System
- **Suburban** 746-acre campus
- **Endowment** $17.8 million
- **Coed** 2,932 undergraduate students, 65% full-time, 49% women, 51% men
- **Moderately difficult** entrance level, 52% of applicants were admitted

UNDERGRAD STUDENTS
1,903 full-time, 1,029 part-time. Students come from 44 states and territories; 27 other countries; 14% are from out of state; 13% Black or African American, non-Hispanic/Latino; 9% Hispanic/Latino; 3% Asian, non-Hispanic/Latino; 0.1% Native Hawaiian or other Pacific Islander, non-Hispanic/Latino; 0.3% American Indian or Alaska Native, non-Hispanic/Latino; 3% Two or more races, non-Hispanic/Latino; 1% Race/ethnicity unknown; 4% international; 18% transferred in; 30% live on campus.

Freshmen:
Admission: 1,746 applied, 915 admitted, 278 enrolled. *Average high school GPA:* 3.6. *Test scores:* ACT scores over 18: 93%; ACT scores over 24: 48%; ACT scores over 30: 10%.
Retention: 78% of full-time freshmen returned.

FACULTY
Total: 375, 57% full-time, 63% with terminal degrees.
Student/faculty ratio: 13:1.

ACADEMICS
Calendar: semesters. *Degrees:* bachelor's, master's, doctoral, post-master's, and postbachelor's certificates.

Special study options: academic remediation for entering students, advanced placement credit, cooperative education, distance learning, English as a second language, honors programs, independent study, internships, off-campus study, part-time degree program, services for LD students, study abroad, summer session for credit.

Computers: 560 computers/terminals and 63 ports are available on campus for general student use. Students can access the following: campus intranet, computer help desk, free student e-mail accounts, online (class) grades, online (class) registration, online (class) schedules. Campuswide network is available. 100% of college-owned or -operated housing units are wired for high-speed Internet access. Wireless service is available via entire campus.

Library: Norris L Brookens Library plus 1 other. *Books:* 460,486 (physical), 213,074 (digital/electronic); *Serial titles:* 9,843 (physical), 14,828 (digital/electronic); *Databases:* 172. Weekly public service hours: 90; students can reserve study rooms.

STUDENT LIFE
Housing options: on-campus residence required for freshman year; coed, special housing for students with disabilities. Campus housing is university owned. Freshman campus housing is guaranteed.

Activities and organizations: drama/theater group, student-run newspaper, radio station, choral group, Student Activities Committee, Black Student Union, Christian Student Fellowship, Dance Marathon, Club Dodgeball, national fraternities, national sororities.

Athletics Member NCAA. All Division II. *Intercollegiate sports:* baseball M(s), basketball M(s)/W(s), cheerleading M(s)/W(s), cross-country running M(s)/W(s), golf M(s)/W(s), soccer M(s)/W(s), softball W(s), tennis M(s)/W(s), track and field M(s)/W(s), volleyball W(s). *Intramural sports:* badminton M(c)/W(c), basketball M/W, football M/W, racquetball M/W, sand volleyball M/W, soccer M(c)/W, softball M/W, squash M(c)/W(c), table tennis M/W, tennis M/W, ultimate Frisbee M/W, volleyball M(c)/W(c).

Campus security: 24-hour emergency response devices and patrols, late-night transport/escort service, controlled dormitory access.

Student services: health clinic, personal/psychological counseling, women's center.

COSTS & FINANCIAL AID
Costs (2017–18) *Tuition:* state resident $9405 full-time, $314 per credit hour part-time; nonresident $18,930 full-time, $631 per credit hour part-time. Full-time tuition and fees vary according to course load. Part-time tuition and fees vary according to course load. No tuition increase for student's term of enrollment. *Required fees:* $3040 full-time, $18 per credit hour part-time, $1111 per term part-time. *Room and board:* $11,660; room only: $7460. Room and board charges vary according to board plan and housing facility. *Payment plan:* installment. *Waivers:* senior citizens and employees or children of employees.

Financial Aid Of all full-time matriculated undergraduates who enrolled in 2016, 1,559 applied for aid, 1,274 were judged to have need, 165 had their need fully met. In 2016, 280 non-need-based awards were made. *Average percent of need met:* 69. *Average financial aid package:* $13,348. *Average need-based loan:* $4159. *Average need-based gift aid:* $10,770. *Average non-need-based aid:* $8323. *Average indebtedness upon graduation:* $25,313. *Financial aid deadline:* 11/15.

APPLYING
Standardized Tests *Required:* SAT or ACT (for admission). *Recommended:* SAT and SAT Subject Tests or ACT (for admission).

Options: electronic application, deferred entrance.

Application fee: $50.

Required: high school transcript.

Application deadlines: rolling (freshmen), rolling (transfers).

Notification: continuous (transfers).

CONTACT
Fernando Planas, Director of Admissions, University of Illinois at Springfield, One University Plaza, MS UHB 1080, Springfield, IL 62703-5407. *Phone:* 217-206-4847. *Toll-free phone:* 888-977-4847. *E-mail:* admissions@uis.edu.

University of Illinois at Urbana–Champaign

Champaign, Illinois
http://www.illinois.edu/

CONTACT
Stacey Kostell, Director of Admissions, University of Illinois at Urbana–Champaign, 901 West Illinois, Urbana, IL 61801. *Phone:* 217-333-0302. *Fax:* 217-244-4614. *E-mail:* ugradadmissions@uiuc.edu.

University of St. Francis

Joliet, Illinois
http://www.stfrancis.edu/

- **Independent Roman Catholic** comprehensive, founded 1920
- **Suburban** 18-acre campus with easy access to Chicago
- **Endowment** $16.5 million
- **Coed** 1,371 undergraduate students, 93% full-time, 63% women, 37% men
- **Moderately difficult** entrance level, 52% of applicants were admitted

UNDERGRAD STUDENTS
1,273 full-time, 98 part-time. Students come from 20 states and territories; 7 other countries; 5% are from out of state; 8% Black or African American, non-Hispanic/Latino; 22% Hispanic/Latino; 2% Asian, non-Hispanic/Latino; 0.2% Native Hawaiian or other Pacific Islander, non-Hispanic/Latino; 0.3% American Indian or Alaska Native, non-Hispanic/Latino; 4% Two or more races, non-Hispanic/Latino; 0.4% Race/ethnicity unknown; 4% international; 13% transferred in; 25% live on campus.

Freshmen:
Admission: 1,560 applied, 806 admitted, 229 enrolled. *Average high school GPA:* 3.5. *Test scores:* SAT evidence-based reading and writing scores over 500: 71%; SAT math scores over 500: 93%; ACT scores over 18: 97%; SAT evidence-based reading and writing scores over 600: 50%; SAT math scores over 600: 36%; ACT scores over 24: 36%; SAT math scores over 700: 7%; ACT scores over 30: 4%.

Retention: 80% of full-time freshmen returned.

FACULTY
Total: 266, 36% full-time, 50% with terminal degrees.

Student/faculty ratio: 12:1.

ACADEMICS
Calendar: semesters. *Degrees:* certificates, bachelor's, master's, doctoral, post-master's, and postbachelor's certificates.

Special study options: academic remediation for entering students, accelerated degree program, adult/continuing education programs, advanced placement credit, distance learning, double majors, English as a second language, honors programs, independent study, internships, off-campus study, part-time degree program, services for LD students, student-designed majors, study abroad, summer session for credit. *ROTC:* Army (c).

Computers: 560 computers/terminals and 2,300 ports are available on campus for general student use. Students can access the following: campus intranet, computer help desk, free student e-mail accounts, online (class) grades, online (class) registration, online (class) schedules, billing/payment. Campuswide network is available. 100% of college-owned or -operated housing units are wired for high-speed Internet access. Wireless service is available via entire campus.

Library: Brown Library. *Books:* 113,077 (physical), 4,118 (digital/electronic); *Serial titles:* 605 (physical), 113 (digital/electronic); *Databases:* 76. Weekly public service hours: 74; students can reserve study rooms.

STUDENT LIFE
Housing options: coed, special housing for students with disabilities. Campus housing is university owned. Freshman campus housing is guaranteed.

Activities and organizations: drama/theater group, student-run newspaper, radio and television station, choral group, Student Nurses Association, Student Business Association, Justice League, Student Athletic Advisory Committee, Unidos Vamos a Alcanzar (UVA), national sororities.

Athletics Member NAIA. *Intercollegiate sports:* baseball M(s), basketball M(s)/W(s), bowling M(s)/W(s), cheerleading M(s)/W(s), cross-country running M(s)/W(s), football M(s), golf M(s)/W(s), soccer M(s)/W(s), softball W(s), tennis M(s)/W(s), track and field M(s)/W(s), volleyball W(s). *Intramural sports:* basketball M/W, bowling M/W, table tennis M/W, volleyball M/W.

Campus security: 24-hour emergency response devices and patrols, student patrols, late-night transport/escort service, controlled dormitory access, First Response trained security personnel.

Student services: health clinic, personal/psychological counseling.

COSTS & FINANCIAL AID
Costs (2018–19) *Tuition:* $32,000 full-time, $825 per credit hour part-time. Full-time tuition and fees vary according to degree level, location, and program. Part-time tuition and fees vary according to degree level and program. *Required fees:* $320 full-time, $75 per term part-time. *Room only:* Room and board charges vary according to housing facility. *Payment plans:* installment, deferred payment. *Waivers:* children of alumni and employees or children of employees.

Financial Aid Of all full-time matriculated undergraduates who enrolled in 2017, 1,153 applied for aid, 1,055 were judged to have need, 214 had their need fully met. 126 Federal Work-Study jobs (averaging $2477). 300 state and other part-time jobs (averaging $2500). In 2017, 175 non-need-based awards were made. *Average percent of need met:* 80. *Average financial aid package:* $24,259. *Average need-based loan:* $4662. *Average need-based gift aid:* $20,129. *Average non-need-based aid:* $10,691. *Average indebtedness upon graduation:* $32,838.

APPLYING
Standardized Tests *Required:* SAT or ACT (for admission).

Options: electronic application, deferred entrance.

Required: high school transcript, minimum 2.5 GPA. *Required for some:* essay or personal statement, 2 letters of recommendation, interview.

Notification: continuous (freshmen), continuous (transfers).

CONTACT
Mr. Eric Ruiz, Director of Freshman Admissions, University of St. Francis, 500 North Wilcox Street, Joliet, IL 60435-6188. *Phone:* 800-735-7500. *Toll-free phone:* 800-735-7500. *Fax:* 815-740-5070. *E-mail:* eruiz@stfrancis.edu.

VanderCook College of Music

Chicago, Illinois
http://www.vandercook.edu/

- **Independent** comprehensive, founded 1909
- **Urban** 1-acre campus with easy access to Chicago
- **Endowment** $514,572
- **Coed** 122 undergraduate students, 72% full-time, 44% women, 56% men

UNDERGRAD STUDENTS
88 full-time, 34 part-time. Students come from 12 states and territories; 2 other countries; 20% are from out of state; 2% Black or African American, non-Hispanic/Latino; 18% Hispanic/Latino; 0.8% Native Hawaiian or other Pacific Islander, non-Hispanic/Latino; 2% Two or more races, non-Hispanic/Latino; 5% Race/ethnicity unknown; 2% international; 2% transferred in; 18% live on campus.

Freshmen:
Admission: 15 enrolled. *Average high school GPA:* 3.0. *Test scores:* SAT evidence-based reading and writing scores over 500: 100%; SAT math scores over 500: 100%; ACT scores over 18: 100%; ACT scores over 24: 43%; ACT scores over 30: 14%.

Retention: 73% of full-time freshmen returned.

FACULTY
Total: 37, 35% full-time, 27% with terminal degrees.

Student/faculty ratio: 3:1.

ACADEMICS
Calendar: semesters. *Degrees:* bachelor's and master's.

Special study options: academic remediation for entering students, advanced placement credit, independent study.

Computers: 21 computers/terminals are available on campus for general student use. Students can access the following: free student e-mail accounts. Campuswide network is available. 100% of college-owned or -operated housing units are wired for high-speed Internet access. Wireless service is available via entire campus.

Library: Harry Ruppel Memorial Library plus 1 other. *Books:* 16,985 (physical), 6,827 (digital/electronic); *Serial titles:* 200 (physical), 100 (digital/electronic); *Databases:* 28. Weekly public service hours: 54; students can reserve study rooms.

STUDENT LIFE
Housing options: college housing not available; coed, special housing for students with disabilities. Campus housing is provided by a third party.

Activities and organizations: student-run radio station, choral group, NAfME (National Association for Music Education), ACDA (American Choral Directors Association), NBA (National Band Association), ASTA (American String Teachers Association), national fraternities, national sororities.

Campus security: 24-hour emergency response devices and patrols, late-night transport/escort service, controlled dormitory access.

Student services: health clinic, personal/psychological counseling.

COSTS & FINANCIAL AID
Costs (2018–19) *Tuition:* $26,548 full-time, $1115 per semester hour part-time. Full-time tuition and fees vary according to course level, course load, and program. Part-time tuition and fees vary according to course level, course load, and program. *Required fees:* $1886 full-time, $1510 per year part-time. *Payment plan:* installment. *Waivers:* employees or children of employees.

Financial Aid Of all full-time matriculated undergraduates who enrolled in 2016, 98 applied for aid, 84 were judged to have need. 27 Federal Work-Study jobs (averaging $748). 7 state and other part-time jobs (averaging $611). In 2016, 18 non-need-based awards were made. *Average financial aid package:* $15,524. *Average need-based loan:* $4523. *Average need-based gift aid:* $10,190. *Average non-need-based aid:* $8927. *Average indebtedness upon graduation:* $42,886.

APPLYING
Standardized Tests *Required:* SAT or ACT (for admission).

Required: essay or personal statement, high school transcript, 3 letters of recommendation, interview, audition on the applicant's primary instrument or voice. *Required for some:* minimum 3.0 GPA. *Recommended:* minimum 3.0 GPA.

CONTACT
Mrs. LeeAnn L. Meyer, Director of Admissions and Retention, VanderCook College of Music, 3140 South Federal Street, Chicago, IL 60616. *Phone:* 312-788-1120 Ext. 230. *Fax:* 312-225-5211. *E-mail:* admissions@vandercook.edu.

Western Illinois University
Macomb, Illinois
http://www.wiu.edu/

- **State-supported** comprehensive, founded 1899
- **Small-town** 1050-acre campus with easy access to Quad Cities; Peoria, IL; Springfield, IL
- **Endowment** $49.3 million
- **Coed** 7,599 undergraduate students, 88% full-time, 51% women, 49% men
- **Moderately difficult** entrance level, 60% of applicants were admitted

UNDERGRAD STUDENTS
6,668 full-time, 931 part-time. Students come from 39 states and territories; 61 other countries; 10% are from out of state; 22% Black or African American, non-Hispanic/Latino; 12% Hispanic/Latino; 0.9% Asian, non-Hispanic/Latino; 0.1% American Indian or Alaska Native, non-Hispanic/Latino; 3% Two or more races, non-Hispanic/Latino; 2% Race/ethnicity unknown; 1% international; 11% transferred in; 44% live on campus.

Freshmen:
Admission: 9,767 applied, 5,857 admitted, 1,206 enrolled. *Average high school GPA:* 3.2. *Test scores:* ACT scores over 18: 79%; ACT scores over 24: 20%; ACT scores over 30: 4%.

Retention: 68% of full-time freshmen returned.

FACULTY
Total: 608, 91% full-time, 69% with terminal degrees.
Student/faculty ratio: 14:1.

ACADEMICS
Calendar: semesters. *Degrees:* bachelor's, master's, doctoral, post-master's, and postbachelor's certificates.

Special study options: academic remediation for entering students, adult/continuing education programs, advanced placement credit, distance learning, double majors, English as a second language, external degree program, freshman honors college, honors programs, independent study, internships, off-campus study, part-time degree program, services for LD students, student-designed majors, study abroad, summer session for credit. *ROTC:* Army (b).

Unusual degree programs: 3-2 engineering with University of Iowa, University of Illinois; arts and sciences/clinical laboratory science; general studies/chiropractic with Palmer College of Chiropractic.

Computers: 632 computers/terminals and 1,012 ports are available on campus for general student use. Students can access the following: computer help desk, free student e-mail accounts, online (class) grades, online (class) registration, online (class) schedules. Campuswide network is available. 100% of college-owned or -operated housing units are wired for high-speed Internet access. Wireless service is available via entire campus.

Library: Leslie Malpass Library plus 4 others. *Books:* 765,743 (physical), 149,893 (digital/electronic); *Serial titles:* 153,468 (physical), 79,966 (digital/electronic); *Databases:* 126.

STUDENT LIFE
Housing options: on-campus residence required through sophomore year; coed, men-only, women-only, special housing for students with disabilities. Campus housing is university owned. Freshman campus housing is guaranteed.

Activities and organizations: drama/theater group, student-run newspaper, radio and television station, choral group, marching band, Student Government Association, Black Student Association, University Union Board, Western's All Volunteer Effort (WAVE), Inter Hall Council, national fraternities, national sororities.

Athletics Member NCAA. All Division I except football (Division I-AA). *Intercollegiate sports:* baseball M(s), basketball M(s)/W(s), cross-country running M(s)/W(s), golf M(s)/W, soccer M(s)/W(s), softball W(s), swimming and diving M(s)/W(s), tennis W(s), track and field M(s)/W(s), volleyball W(s). *Intramural sports:* badminton M(c)/W(c), baseball M(c), basketball M/W, bowling M(c), cheerleading M/W, cross-country running M/W, equestrian sports M(c)/W(c), fencing M(c)/W(c), football M/W, golf M/W, ice hockey M(c), lacrosse M(c), racquetball M/W, rugby M/W, sand volleyball M/W, soccer M/W, softball M/W, swimming and diving M/W, table tennis M/W, tennis M/W, ultimate Frisbee M(c)/W(c), volleyball M/W, water polo M/W, wrestling M.

Campus security: 24-hour emergency response devices and patrols, student patrols, late-night transport/escort service, controlled dormitory access.

Student services: health clinic, personal/psychological counseling, women's center, legal services.

COSTS & FINANCIAL AID
Costs (2017–18) *One-time required fee:* $200. *Tuition:* state resident $8541 full-time, $285 per credit hour part-time; nonresident $8541 full-time, $285 per credit hour part-time. Full-time tuition and fees vary according to course load, location, and student level. Part-time tuition and fees vary according to course load, location, and student level. No tuition increase for student's term of enrollment. *Required fees:* $2726 full-time, $90 per credit hour part-time. *Room and board:* $9630; room only: $5880. Room and board charges vary according to board plan, housing facility, and student level. *Payment plan:* installment. *Waivers:* senior citizens and employees or children of employees.

Financial Aid Of all full-time matriculated undergraduates who enrolled in 2017, 5,747 applied for aid, 5,138 were judged to have need, 1,296 had their need fully met. 175 Federal Work-Study jobs (averaging $2754). 1,437 state and other part-time jobs (averaging $1654). In 2017, 358 non-need-based awards were made. *Average percent of need met:* 62. *Average financial aid package:* $12,356. *Average need-based loan:* $4286.

Average need-based gift aid: $9653. *Average non-need-based aid:* $3401. *Average indebtedness upon graduation:* $29,422.

APPLYING

Standardized Tests *Required:* SAT or ACT (for admission).

Options: electronic application, deferred entrance.

Application fee: $30.

Required: high school transcript, minimum 2.5 GPA.

Application deadlines: 5/15 (freshmen), rolling (transfers).

Notification: continuous (freshmen), continuous (transfers).

CONTACT

Western Illinois University, 1 University Circle, Macomb, IL 61455-1390. *Phone:* 309-298-3157. *Toll-free phone:* 877-742-5948.

Wheaton College

Wheaton, Illinois

http://www.wheaton.edu/

- **Independent nondenominational** comprehensive, founded 1860
- **Suburban** 80-acre campus with easy access to Chicago
- **Endowment** $446.4 million
- **Coed** 2,391 undergraduate students, 97% full-time, 54% women, 46% men
- **Very difficult** entrance level, 85% of applicants were admitted

UNDERGRAD STUDENTS

2,310 full-time, 81 part-time. Students come from 50 states and territories; 40 other countries; 72% are from out of state; 3% Black or African American, non-Hispanic/Latino; 6% Hispanic/Latino; 9% Asian, non-Hispanic/Latino; 0.2% American Indian or Alaska Native, non-Hispanic/Latino; 4% Two or more races, non-Hispanic/Latino; 0.3% Race/ethnicity unknown; 3% international; 2% transferred in; 89% live on campus.

Freshmen:

Admission: 1,693 applied, 1,439 admitted, 580 enrolled. *Average high school GPA:* 3.7. *Test scores:* SAT evidence-based reading and writing scores over 500: 99%; SAT math scores over 500: 97%; ACT scores over 18: 100%; SAT evidence-based reading and writing scores over 600: 90%; SAT math scores over 600: 77%; ACT scores over 24: 93%; SAT evidence-based reading and writing scores over 700: 42%; SAT math scores over 700: 25%; ACT scores over 30: 48%.

Retention: 93% of full-time freshmen returned.

FACULTY

Total: 321, 69% full-time, 79% with terminal degrees.

Student/faculty ratio: 11:1.

ACADEMICS

Calendar: semesters. *Degrees:* bachelor's, master's, doctoral, and postbachelor's certificates.

Special study options: advanced placement credit, double majors, independent study, internships, off-campus study, services for LD students, student-designed majors, study abroad, summer session for credit. *ROTC:* Army (b), Air Force (c).

Unusual degree programs: 3-2 engineering with Illinois Institute of Technology; nursing with Emory University, Indiana Wesleyan University.

Computers: 325 computers/terminals and 3,500 ports are available on campus for general student use. Students can access the following: campus intranet, computer help desk, free student e-mail accounts, online (class) grades, online (class) registration, online (class) schedules, financial information, degree requirements evaluation. Campuswide network is available. 100% of college-owned or -operated housing units are wired for high-speed Internet access. Wireless service is available via entire campus.

Library: Buswell Memorial Library. *Books:* 518,164 (physical), 226,974 (digital/electronic); *Serial titles:* 389 (physical), 6,182 (digital/electronic); *Databases:* 249. Weekly public service hours: 94; students can reserve study rooms.

STUDENT LIFE

Housing options: on-campus residence required through senior year; coed, men-only, women-only, cooperative, special housing for students with disabilities. Campus housing is university owned. Freshman campus housing is guaranteed.

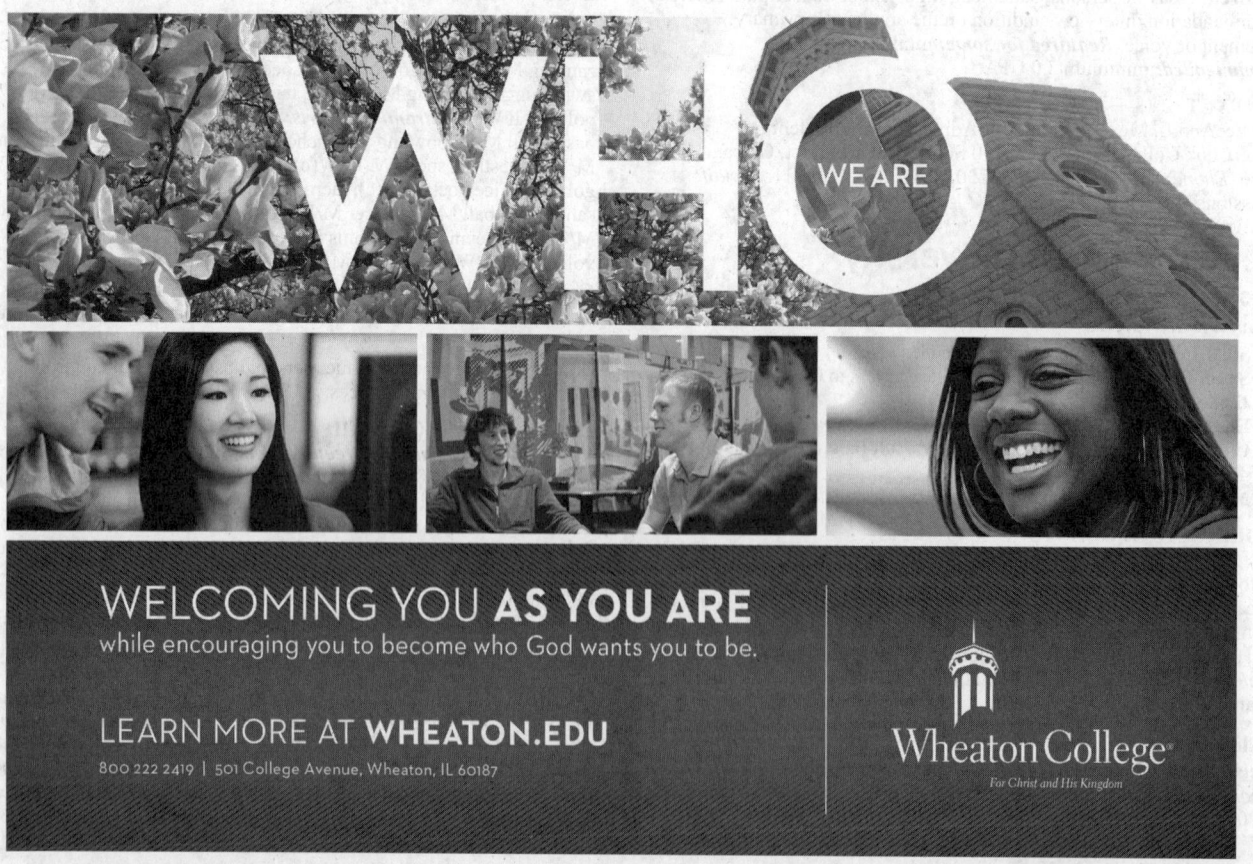

WHO WE ARE

WELCOMING YOU **AS YOU ARE**
while encouraging you to become who God wants you to be.

LEARN MORE AT **WHEATON.EDU**

800 222 2419 | 501 College Avenue, Wheaton, IL 60187

Wheaton College
For Christ and His Kingdom

Activities and organizations: drama/theater group, student-run newspaper, choral group, Discipleship small groups, intramurals, Club Sports, Christian Service Council, New Student Orientation.

Athletics Member NCAA. All Division III. *Intercollegiate sports:* baseball M, basketball M/W, cheerleading W(c), crew M(c)/W(c), cross-country running M/W, football M, golf M/W, ice hockey M(c), lacrosse M(c)/W(c), rowing M(c)/W, soccer M/W, softball W, swimming and diving M/W, tennis M/W, track and field M/W, volleyball W, wrestling M. *Intramural sports:* badminton M/W, basketball M/W, golf M/W, soccer M/W, softball M, ultimate Frisbee M/W, volleyball M/W.

Campus security: 24-hour emergency response devices and patrols, student patrols, late-night transport/escort service, controlled dormitory access.

Student services: health clinic, personal/psychological counseling.

COSTS & FINANCIAL AID
Costs (2018–19) *Comprehensive fee:* $46,600 includes full-time tuition ($36,420) and room and board ($10,180). Full-time tuition and fees vary according to program. Part-time tuition: $1518 per credit hour. Part-time tuition and fees vary according to course load and program. *College room only:* $6000. Room and board charges vary according to board plan and housing facility. *Payment plans:* installment, deferred payment.

Financial Aid Of all full-time matriculated undergraduates who enrolled in 2017, 1,468 applied for aid, 1,294 were judged to have need, 282 had their need fully met. 143 Federal Work-Study jobs (averaging $1374). In 2017, 532 non-need-based awards were made. *Average percent of need met:* 84. *Average financial aid package:* $25,883. *Average need-based loan:* $5422. *Average need-based gift aid:* $21,171. *Average non-need-based aid:* $7358. *Average indebtedness upon graduation:* $27,543.

APPLYING
Standardized Tests *Required:* SAT or ACT (for admission).

Options: electronic application, early action, deferred entrance.

Application fee: $50.

Required: essay or personal statement, high school transcript, 2 letters of recommendation. *Recommended:* interview.

Application deadlines: 1/10 (freshmen), 3/1 (transfers), 11/1 (early action).

Notification: 4/1 (freshmen), 4/1 (transfers), 12/31 (early action).

CONTACT
Jason Kircher, Interim Director of Admissions, Wheaton College, 501 College Avenue, Wheaton, IL 60187-5593. *Phone:* 630-752-5011. *Toll-free phone:* 800-222-2419. *Fax:* 630-752-5285. *E-mail:* admissions@wheaton.edu.

See previous page for display ad and page 1502 for the College Close-Up.

INDIANA

Anderson University

Anderson, Indiana
http://www.anderson.edu/
- **Independent** comprehensive, founded 1917, affiliated with Church of God
- **Suburban** 163-acre campus with easy access to Indianapolis
- **Endowment** $33.7 million
- **Coed** 1,566 undergraduate students, 91% full-time, 59% women, 41% men
- **Moderately difficult** entrance level, 65% of applicants were admitted

UNDERGRAD STUDENTS
1,431 full-time, 135 part-time. Students come from 39 states and territories; 18 other countries; 24% are from out of state; 9% Black or African American, non-Hispanic/Latino; 2% Hispanic/Latino; 1% Asian, non-Hispanic/Latino; 0.3% Native Hawaiian or other Pacific Islander, non-Hispanic/Latino; 1% American Indian or Alaska Native, non-Hispanic/Latino; 0.4% Two or more races, non-Hispanic/Latino; 2% Race/ethnicity unknown; 2% international; 4% transferred in; 65% live on campus.

Freshmen:
Admission: 2,236 applied, 1,459 admitted, 347 enrolled. *Average high school GPA:* 3.4. *Test scores:* SAT evidence-based reading and writing scores over 500: 52%; SAT math scores over 500: 57%; ACT scores over 18: 83%; SAT evidence-based reading and writing scores over 600: 15%; SAT math scores over 600: 13%; ACT scores over 24: 41%; SAT evidence-based reading and writing scores over 700: 2%; SAT math scores over 700: 1%; ACT scores over 30: 3%.

Retention: 73% of full-time freshmen returned.

FACULTY
Total: 252, 42% full-time, 35% with terminal degrees.
Student/faculty ratio: 10:1.

ACADEMICS
Calendar: semesters. *Degrees:* associate, bachelor's, master's, and doctoral.

Special study options: academic remediation for entering students, accelerated degree program, adult/continuing education programs, advanced placement credit, distance learning, double majors, honors programs, independent study, internships, off-campus study, part-time degree program, services for LD students, student-designed majors, study abroad, summer session for credit.

Unusual degree programs: 3-2 engineering with Purdue University.

Computers: 300 computers/terminals are available on campus for general student use. Students can access the following: campus intranet, computer help desk, free student e-mail accounts, online (class) grades, online (class) registration, online (class) schedules, microcomputer software. Campuswide network is available. 100% of college-owned or -operated housing units are wired for high-speed Internet access. Wireless service is available via entire campus.

Library: Robert A. Nicholson Library. *Books:* 318,141 (physical), 261,900 (digital/electronic); *Serial titles:* 7,348 (physical), 53,279 (digital/electronic); *Databases:* 136. Weekly public service hours: 95; study areas open 24 hours, 5–7 days a week; students can reserve study rooms.

STUDENT LIFE
Housing options: on-campus residence required through junior year; men-only, women-only. Campus housing is university owned. Freshman campus housing is guaranteed.

Activities and organizations: drama/theater group, student-run newspaper, radio station, choral group, Adult and Continuing Education Students Association, Multicultural Student Union, Campus Ministries.

Athletics Member NCAA. All Division III. *Intercollegiate sports:* baseball M, basketball M/W, cross-country running M/W, football M, golf M/W, soccer M/W, softball W, swimming and diving M/W, tennis M/W, track and field M/W, volleyball W. *Intramural sports:* badminton M/W, basketball M/W, bowling M/W, cheerleading M(c)/W(c), rugby M(c), soccer M/W, softball M/W, tennis M/W, volleyball M/W.

Campus security: 24-hour emergency response devices and patrols, student patrols, late-night transport/escort service, controlled dormitory access, 24-hour crime line.

Student services: health clinic, personal/psychological counseling.

COSTS & FINANCIAL AID
Costs (2017–18) *Comprehensive fee:* $39,450 includes full-time tuition ($29,210), mandatory fees ($500), and room and board ($9740). Part-time tuition: $1218 per semester hour. Part-time tuition and fees vary according to course load. *College room only:* $6120. Room and board charges vary according to board plan and housing facility. *Payment plan:* installment. *Waivers:* employees or children of employees.

Financial Aid Of all full-time matriculated undergraduates who enrolled in 2014, 1,549 applied for aid, 1,410 were judged to have need, 604 had their need fully met. In 2014, 307 non-need-based awards were made. *Average percent of need met:* 88. *Average financial aid package:* $23,905. *Average need-based loan:* $10,011. *Average need-based gift aid:* $15,932. *Average non-need-based aid:* $14,313.

APPLYING
Standardized Tests *Required:* SAT or ACT (for admission).
Options: electronic application, deferred entrance.
Application fee: $25.

Required: high school transcript, minimum 2.0 GPA, 2 letters of recommendation, lifestyle statement. *Required for some:* interview. *Recommended:* essay or personal statement.

Application deadlines: 7/1 (freshmen), rolling (transfers).

Notification: 9/1 (freshmen), continuous until 9/1 (transfers).

CONTACT
Ms. Kynan Simison, Director of Admissions, Anderson University, 1100 East 5th Street, Anderson, IN 46012-3495. *Phone:* 765-641-4076. *Toll-free phone:* 800-428-6414. *Fax:* 765-641-3851. *E-mail:* info@anderson.edu.

The Art Institute of Indianapolis
Indianapolis, Indiana
http://www.artinstitutes.edu/indianapolis/

CONTACT
The Art Institute of Indianapolis, 3500 Depauw Boulevard, Suite 1010, Indianapolis, IN 46268. *Phone:* 317-613-4800. *Toll-free phone:* 866-441-9031.

Ball State University
Muncie, Indiana
http://www.bsu.edu/

- **State-supported** university, founded 1918
- **Suburban** 1140-acre campus with easy access to Indianapolis
- **Endowment** $201.8 million
- **Coed** 17,004 undergraduate students, 89% full-time, 60% women, 40% men

UNDERGRAD STUDENTS
15,203 full-time, 1,801 part-time. Students come from 44 states and territories; 33 other countries; 15% are from out of state; 8% Black or African American, non-Hispanic/Latino; 5% Hispanic/Latino; 1% Asian, non-Hispanic/Latino; 0.1% Native Hawaiian or other Pacific Islander, non-Hispanic/Latino; 3% Two or more races, non-Hispanic/Latino; 1% Race/ethnicity unknown; 1% international; 5% transferred in; 44% live on campus.

Freshmen:
Admission: 3,985 enrolled. *Average high school GPA:* 3.5. *Test scores:* SAT evidence-based reading and writing scores over 500: 93%; SAT math scores over 500: 87%; ACT scores over 18: 98%; SAT evidence-based reading and writing scores over 600: 35%; SAT math scores over 600: 25%; ACT scores over 24: 42%; SAT evidence-based reading and writing scores over 700: 4%; SAT math scores over 700: 2%; ACT scores over 30: 6%.

Retention: 79% of full-time freshmen returned.

FACULTY
Total: 1,291, 79% full-time, 72% with terminal degrees.

Student/faculty ratio: 17:1.

ACADEMICS
Calendar: semesters. *Degrees:* certificates, bachelor's, master's, doctoral, post-master's, and postbachelor's certificates.

Special study options: accelerated degree program, adult/continuing education programs, advanced placement credit, cooperative education, distance learning, double majors, English as a second language, external degree program, freshman honors college, honors programs, independent study, internships, part-time degree program, services for LD students, student-designed majors, study abroad, summer session for credit. *ROTC:* Army (b).

Computers: 578 computers/terminals and 9,337 ports are available on campus for general student use. Students can access the following: campus intranet, computer help desk, free student e-mail accounts, online (class) grades, online (class) registration, online (class) schedules, room reservations, testing and test results, manage and pay tuition, order/buy textbooks, request room repairs, order transcripts, manage meal plan, manage and prepay long distance service, undergraduate degree progress report. Campuswide network is available. 100% of college-owned or -operated housing units are wired for high-speed Internet access. Wireless service is available via entire campus.

Library: Bracken Library plus 2 others. *Books:* 822,983 (physical), 15,244 (digital/electronic); *Serial titles:* 13,599 (physical), 103,640 (digital/electronic); *Databases:* 296. Weekly public service hours: 123; students can reserve study rooms.

STUDENT LIFE
Housing options: on-campus residence required for freshman year; coed, men-only, women-only, special housing for students with disabilities. Campus housing is university owned. Freshman campus housing is guaranteed.

Activities and organizations: drama/theater group, student-run newspaper, radio and television station, choral group, marching band, Student Voluntary Services, National Society of Collegiate Scholars, Dance Marathon, Cardinal Catholic, National Society of Leadership and Success, national fraternities, national sororities.

Athletics Member NCAA. All Division I except football (Division I-A). *Intercollegiate sports:* baseball M(s)/W(c), basketball M(s)/W(s), bowling M(c)/W(c), cheerleading M/W, cross-country running W(s), equestrian sports M(c)/W(c), fencing M(c)/W(c), field hockey W(s), golf M(s)/W(s), gymnastics W(s), lacrosse M(c)/W(c), racquetball M(c)/W(c), rock climbing M(c)/W(c), rugby M(c)/W(c), soccer M(c)/W(s), softball W(s), swimming and diving M(s)/W(s), tennis M(s)/W(s), track and field W(s), triathlon M(c)/W(c), ultimate Frisbee M(c)/W(c), volleyball M(s)/W(s), water polo M(c)/W(c), wrestling M(c). *Intramural sports:* archery M(c)/W(c), badminton M/W, basketball M/W, bowling M/W, golf M/W, gymnastics W(c), ice hockey M(c), racquetball M/W, soccer M/W, softball M/W, swimming and diving M/W, table tennis M/W, tennis M/W, track and field M/W, ultimate Frisbee M/W, volleyball M/W.

Campus security: 24-hour emergency response devices and patrols, late-night transport/escort service, controlled dormitory access.

Student services: health clinic, personal/psychological counseling, women's center, legal services.

COSTS & FINANCIAL AID
Costs (2017–18) *Tuition:* state resident $9112 full-time, $300 per credit hour part-time; nonresident $25,280 full-time, $1001 per credit hour part-time. Full-time tuition and fees vary according to program and reciprocity agreements. Part-time tuition and fees vary according to course load, program, and reciprocity agreements. *Required fees:* $662 full-time. *Room and board:* $10,034. Room and board charges vary according to board plan and housing facility. *Payment plan:* installment. *Waivers:* senior citizens and employees or children of employees.

Financial Aid Of all full-time matriculated undergraduates who enrolled in 2017, 13,152 applied for aid, 10,516 were judged to have need, 4,139 had their need fully met. In 2017, 1912 non-need-based awards were made. *Average percent of need met:* 71. *Average financial aid package:* $13,416. *Average need-based loan:* $4394. *Average need-based gift aid:* $6216. *Average non-need-based aid:* $8198. *Average indebtedness upon graduation:* $28,295.

APPLYING
Standardized Tests *Required for some:* SAT or ACT (for admission).

Required: high school transcript. *Required for some:* essay or personal statement.

CONTACT
Ball State University, 2000 West University Avenue, Muncie, IN 47306. *Phone:* 765-285-8300. *Toll-free phone:* 800-482-4BSU.

Bethel College
Mishawaka, Indiana
http://www.bethelcollege.edu/

- **Independent** comprehensive, founded 1947, affiliated with Missionary Church
- **Suburban** 80-acre campus
- **Endowment** $9.3 million
- **Coed** 1,294 undergraduate students, 80% full-time, 64% women, 36% men
- **Minimally difficult** entrance level, 90% of applicants were admitted

UNDERGRAD STUDENTS
1,033 full-time, 261 part-time. Students come from 29 states and territories; 15 other countries; 27% are from out of state; 10% Black or African American, non-Hispanic/Latino; 8% Hispanic/Latino; 2% Asian,

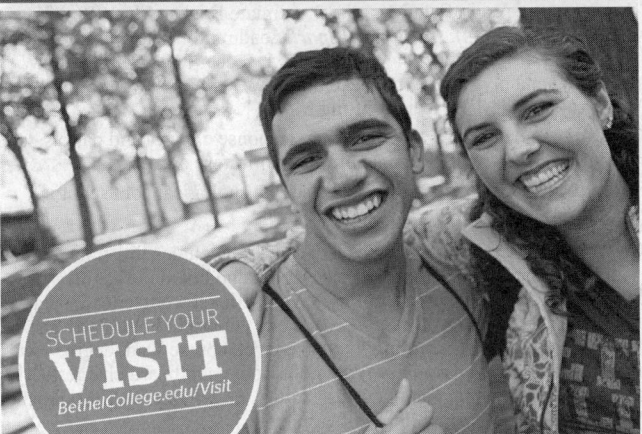

BETHEL COLLEGE AT A GLANCE

SPIRITED COMMUNITY

Going to college is about much more than earning a degree. On our diverse campus, you'll connect with students from across the United States and every corner of the globe.

ENGAGED IN MIND AND HEART

Our professors love to watch as the concepts they teach come alive in your heart, in your mind and in your life. With more than 50 areas of study, you are able to study what you love and put it to use in the real world.

REAL WORLD, REAL SERVICE

Your learning is not limited to the four walls of the classroom. Bethel offers community-focused ministries and internships as well as study abroad programs in places like Australia, China, Oxford, Spain or Uganda to prepare you as a servant-leader.

NATIONALLY RECOGNIZED

1001 BETHEL CIRCLE, MISHAWAKA, IN 46545
800.422.4101 • BethelCollege.edu

non-Hispanic/Latino; 0.1% American Indian or Alaska Native, non-Hispanic/Latino; 5% Two or more races, non-Hispanic/Latino; 0.8% Race/ethnicity unknown; 2% international; 10% transferred in; 52% live on campus.

Freshmen:
Admission: 1,065 applied, 956 admitted, 233 enrolled. *Average high school GPA:* 3.4. *Test scores:* SAT evidence-based reading and writing scores over 500: 69%; SAT math scores over 500: 65%; ACT scores over 18: 83%; SAT evidence-based reading and writing scores over 600: 25%; SAT math scores over 600: 19%; ACT scores over 24: 40%; SAT evidence-based reading and writing scores over 700: 4%; SAT math scores over 700: 4%; ACT scores over 30: 4%.
Retention: 78% of full-time freshmen returned.

FACULTY
Total: 183, 37% full-time, 33% with terminal degrees.
Student/faculty ratio: 12:1.

ACADEMICS
Calendar: semesters. *Degrees:* associate, bachelor's, and master's.
Special study options: academic remediation for entering students, accelerated degree program, adult/continuing education programs, advanced placement credit, distance learning, double majors, external degree program, honors programs, independent study, internships, off-campus study, part-time degree program, services for LD students, student-designed majors, study abroad, summer session for credit. *ROTC:* Army (c), Air Force (c).
Unusual degree programs: 3-2 engineering with University of Notre Dame, Trine University.
Computers: 160 computers/terminals and 440 ports are available on campus for general student use. Students can access the following: campus intranet, computer help desk, free student e-mail accounts, online (class) grades, online (class) schedules. Campuswide network is available. 100% of college-owned or -operated housing units are wired for high-speed Internet access. Wireless service is available via entire campus.
Library: Otis and Elizabeth Bowen Library. *Books:* 80,904 (physical), 174,107 (digital/electronic); *Serial titles:* 473 (physical), 58,644 (digital/electronic); *Databases:* 89. Weekly public service hours: 79.

STUDENT LIFE
Housing options: on-campus residence required through sophomore year; men-only, women-only. Campus housing is university owned.
Activities and organizations: drama/theater group, student-run newspaper, radio station, choral group, Student Government, Psychology Club, America Sign Language Club.
Athletics Member NAIA, NCCAA. *Intercollegiate sports:* baseball M(s), basketball M(s)/W(s), cheerleading M(s)/W(s), cross-country running M(s)/W(s), golf M(s)/W(s), lacrosse W(s), rugby M(s), soccer M(s)/W(s), softball W(s), tennis M(s)/W(s), track and field M(s)/W(s), volleyball W(s). *Intramural sports:* basketball M/W, volleyball M/W.
Campus security: 24-hour emergency response devices and patrols, late-night transport/escort service, controlled dormitory access.
Student services: health clinic, personal/psychological counseling.

COSTS & FINANCIAL AID
Costs (2018–19) *Comprehensive fee:* $37,590 includes full-time tuition ($28,140), mandatory fees ($450), and room and board ($9000). Full-time tuition and fees vary according to program. Part-time tuition: $895 per credit hour. Part-time tuition and fees vary according to course load and program. *Required fees:* $250 per year part-time. *College room only:* $4280. Room and board charges vary according to board plan and housing facility. *Payment plan:* installment. *Waivers:* employees or children of employees.
Financial Aid Of all full-time matriculated undergraduates who enrolled in 2017, 69 Federal Work-Study jobs (averaging $1512). In 2017, 121 non-need-based awards were made. *Average non-need-based aid:* $12,724. *Average indebtedness upon graduation:* $33,565. *Financial aid deadline:* 4/15.

APPLYING
Standardized Tests *Required:* SAT or ACT (for admission).
Options: electronic application, early admission, deferred entrance.

Required: high school transcript, minimum 2.0 GPA. *Recommended:* essay or personal statement, minimum 2.5 GPA, interview.

Application deadlines: 8/15 (freshmen), 8/15 (transfers).

Notification: continuous (freshmen), continuous (transfers).

CONTACT

Stephanie Hochstetler, Director of Admission, Bethel College, 1001 Bethel Circle, Mishawaka, IN 46545. *Phone:* 574-807-7600. *Toll-free phone:* 800-422-4101. *Fax:* 574-807-7650. *E-mail:* admissions@bethelcollege.edu.

See previous page for display ad and page 1246 for the College Close-Up.

Butler University

Indianapolis, Indiana

http://www.butler.edu/

- **Independent** comprehensive, founded 1855
- **Suburban** 295-acre campus with easy access to Indianapolis
- **Endowment** $207.1 million
- **Coed** 4,229 undergraduate students, 99% full-time, 60% women, 40% men
- **Moderately difficult** entrance level, 65% of applicants were admitted

UNDERGRAD STUDENTS

4,179 full-time, 50 part-time. Students come from 48 states and territories; 39 other countries; 53% are from out of state; 4% Black or African American, non-Hispanic/Latino; 4% Hispanic/Latino; 3% Asian, non-Hispanic/Latino; 0.2% American Indian or Alaska Native, non-Hispanic/Latino; 3% Two or more races, non-Hispanic/Latino; 2% Race/ethnicity unknown; 1% international; 2% transferred in; 67% live on campus.

Freshmen:

Admission: 14,635 applied, 9,532 admitted, 1,054 enrolled. *Average high school GPA:* 3.8. *Test scores:* SAT evidence-based reading and writing scores over 500: 99%; SAT math scores over 500: 97%; ACT scores over 18: 100%; SAT evidence-based reading and writing scores over 600: 63%; SAT math scores over 600: 60%; ACT scores over 24: 84%; SAT evidence-based reading and writing scores over 700: 13%; SAT math scores over 700: 12%; ACT scores over 30: 30%.

Retention: 89% of full-time freshmen returned.

FACULTY

Total: 568, 64% full-time.

Student/faculty ratio: 11:1.

ACADEMICS

Calendar: semesters. *Degrees:* bachelor's, master's, doctoral, and postbachelor's certificates.

Special study options: accelerated degree program, advanced placement credit, cooperative education, distance learning, double majors, honors programs, independent study, internships, off-campus study, services for LD students, student-designed majors, study abroad, summer session for credit. *ROTC:* Army (c), Air Force (c).

Unusual degree programs: 3-2 engineering with Indiana University–Purdue University Indianapolis.

Computers: 490 computers/terminals are available on campus for general student use. Students can access the following: campus intranet, computer help desk, free student e-mail accounts, online (class) grades, online (class) registration, online (class) schedules. Campuswide network is available. 100% of college-owned or -operated housing units are wired for high-speed Internet access. Wireless service is available via entire campus. **Library:** Irwin Library plus 2 others. *Books:* 197,610 (physical), 307,297 (digital/electronic); *Serial titles:* 2,327 (physical), 59,443 (digital/electronic); *Databases:* 265. Weekly public service hours: 106; students can reserve study rooms.

STUDENT LIFE

Housing options: on-campus residence required through junior year; coed, women-only. Campus housing is university owned. Freshman campus housing is guaranteed.

Activities and organizations: drama/theater group, student-run newspaper, radio and television station, choral group, marching band, Pre-Pharmacy Club, American Chemical Society Students Affiliate, Answers for Autism (Butler University Chapter), Delta Delta Delta, Kappa Psi Pharmaceutical Fraternity, national fraternities, national sororities.

Athletics Member NCAA. All Division I except football (Division I-AA). *Intercollegiate sports:* baseball M(s), basketball M(s)/W(s), crew M(c)/W(c), cross-country running M(s)/W(s), equestrian sports W(c), golf M(s)/W(s), ice hockey M(c), lacrosse M(c)/W(s), rugby M(c), soccer M(s)/W(s), softball W(s), swimming and diving M(c)/W, tennis M(s)/W(s), track and field M(s)/W(s), ultimate Frisbee M(c)/W(c), volleyball M(c)/W(s). *Intramural sports:* badminton M/W, baseball M, basketball M/W, bowling M/W, football M, soccer M/W, softball M/W, swimming and diving M/W, table tennis M/W, tennis M/W, track and field M/W, volleyball M/W, weight lifting M/W.

Campus security: 24-hour emergency response devices and patrols, late-night transport/escort service, controlled dormitory access.

Student services: health clinic, personal/psychological counseling.

COSTS & FINANCIAL AID

Costs (2018–19) *Comprehensive fee:* $55,810 includes full-time tuition ($40,160), mandatory fees ($960), and room and board ($14,690). Full-time tuition and fees vary according to course level, course load, degree level, and program. Part-time tuition: $1670 per credit hour. Part-time tuition and fees vary according to course level, course load, degree level, and program. *College room only:* $7660. Room and board charges vary according to board plan and housing facility. *Payment plan:* installment. *Waivers:* employees or children of employees.

Financial Aid Of all full-time matriculated undergraduates who enrolled in 2017, 4,205 applied for aid, 2,611 were judged to have need, 298 had their need fully met. 326 Federal Work-Study jobs (averaging $974). In 2017, 1567 non-need-based awards were made. *Average percent of need met:* 65. *Average financial aid package:* $25,357. *Average need-based loan:* $5043. *Average need-based gift aid:* $20,935. *Average non-need-based aid:* $14,312. *Average indebtedness upon graduation:* $40,393.

APPLYING

Standardized Tests *Required:* SAT or ACT (for admission).

Options: electronic application, early action, deferred entrance.

Required: essay or personal statement, high school transcript. *Required for some:* audition, interview, portfolio; 4 years of math and science strongly recommended for COPHS majors and natural sciences.

Application deadlines: 2/1 (freshmen), 8/15 (transfers), 11/1 (early action).

Notification: continuous (freshmen), continuous (transfers), 12/20 (early action).

CONTACT

Mr. Delorean Menifee, Director of Admission, Butler University, 4600 Sunset Avenue, Indianapolis, IN 46208-3485. *Phone:* 317-940-8100. *Toll-free phone:* 888-940-8100. *Fax:* 317-940-8150. *E-mail:* admission@butler.edu.

Calumet College of Saint Joseph

Whiting, Indiana

http://www.ccsj.edu/

- **Independent Roman Catholic** comprehensive, founded 1951
- **Urban** 25-acre campus with easy access to Chicago
- **Endowment** $4.1 million
- **Coed** 624 undergraduate students, 68% full-time, 45% women, 55% men
- **Noncompetitive** entrance level, 33% of applicants were admitted

UNDERGRAD STUDENTS

427 full-time, 197 part-time. Students come from 22 states and territories; 15 other countries; 49% are from out of state; 22% Black or African American, non-Hispanic/Latino; 30% Hispanic/Latino; 1% Asian, non-Hispanic/Latino; 0.2% Native Hawaiian or other Pacific Islander, non-Hispanic/Latino; 0.3% American Indian or Alaska Native, non-Hispanic/Latino; 2% Two or more races, non-Hispanic/Latino; 3% Race/ethnicity unknown; 0.2% international; 12% transferred in.

Freshmen:

Admission: 436 applied, 143 admitted, 98 enrolled. *Average high school GPA:* 2.7. *Test scores:* ACT scores over 18: 58%; ACT scores over 24: 10%.

Retention: 52% of full-time freshmen returned.

FACULTY
Total: 92, 33% full-time, 50% with terminal degrees.
Student/faculty ratio: 10:1.

ACADEMICS
Calendar: semesters. *Degrees:* certificates, associate, bachelor's, and master's.

Special study options: academic remediation for entering students, accelerated degree program, adult/continuing education programs, advanced placement credit, cooperative education, distance learning, double majors, external degree program, honors programs, independent study, internships, part-time degree program, services for LD students, summer session for credit.

Computers: 241 computers/terminals are available on campus for general student use. Students can access the following: computer help desk, free student e-mail accounts, online (class) grades, online (class) schedules. Campuswide network is available. Wireless service is available via entire campus.
Library: Mary Gorman Specker Memorial Library. *Books:* 10,000 (physical), 7,128 (digital/electronic); *Serial titles:* 2 (physical); *Databases:* 62. Weekly public service hours: 63.

STUDENT LIFE
Housing options: college housing not available.

Activities and organizations: drama/theater group, student-run newspaper, Student Government, Los Amigos Hispanic Club, Criminal Justice Club, Drama Club, GIVE.

Athletics Member NAIA. *Intercollegiate sports:* baseball M(s), basketball M(s)/W(s), bowling M(s)/W(s), cross-country running M(s)/W(s), golf M(s)/W(s), soccer M(s)/W(s), softball W(s), tennis M(s)/W(s), track and field M(s)/W(s), volleyball M(s)/W(s), wrestling M(s).

Campus security: day and night security, emergency alert system.

Student services: personal/psychological counseling.

COSTS & FINANCIAL AID
Costs (2018–19) *Tuition:* $18,900 full-time. Full-time tuition and fees vary according to course load and program. Part-time tuition and fees vary according to course load and program. No tuition increase for student's term of enrollment. *Required fees:* $970 full-time. *Payment plan:* deferred payment. *Waivers:* children of alumni, senior citizens, and employees or children of employees.

Financial Aid Of all full-time matriculated undergraduates who enrolled in 2017, 384 applied for aid, 349 were judged to have need, 43 had their need fully met. 22 Federal Work-Study jobs (averaging $809). In 2017, 14 non-need-based awards were made. *Average percent of need met:* 48. *Average financial aid package:* $16,372. *Average need-based loan:* $3820. *Average need-based gift aid:* $9634. *Average non-need-based aid:* $2427. *Average indebtedness upon graduation:* $24,431.

APPLYING
Standardized Tests *Required:* ACCUPLACER (for admission). *Recommended:* SAT or ACT (for admission).

Options: electronic application, deferred entrance.

Required: high school transcript. *Required for some:* essay or personal statement, 1 letter of recommendation. *Recommended:* minimum 2.0 GPA, interview.

Application deadlines: rolling (freshmen), rolling (out-of-state freshmen), rolling (transfers).

Notification: continuous (freshmen), continuous (transfers).

CONTACT
Mr. Andy Marks, Director of Enrollment, Calumet College of Saint Joseph, 2400 New York Avenue, Whiting, IN 46394. *Phone:* 219-473-4295. *Toll-free phone:* 877-700-9100. *Fax:* 219-473-4336. *E-mail:* admissions@ccsj.edu.

Chamberlain College of Nursing
Indianapolis, Indiana
http://www.chamberlain.edu/
- Proprietary 4-year
- Coed

FACULTY
Student/faculty ratio: 10:1.

ACADEMICS
Degree: bachelor's.

COSTS
Costs (2017–18) *Tuition:* $18,900 full-time. *Required fees:* $600 full-time.

APPLYING
Standardized Tests *Required:* SAT or ACT (for admission).

Options: deferred entrance.

Application fee: $95.

CONTACT
Chamberlain College of Nursing, 9100 Keystone Crossing, Indianapolis, IN 46240. *Toll-free phone:* 877-751-5783.

Crossroads Bible College
Indianapolis, Indiana
http://www.crossroads.edu/

CONTACT
Michael Garrison, Admissions Counselor, Crossroads Bible College, 601 North Shortridge Road, Indianapolis, IN 46219. *Phone:* 317-789-8266. *Toll-free phone:* 800-822-3119. *E-mail:* admissions@crossroads.edu.

DePauw University
Greencastle, Indiana
http://www.depauw.edu/
- **Independent** 4-year, founded 1837, affiliated with United Methodist Church
- **Small-town** 655-acre campus with easy access to Indianapolis
- **Endowment** $614.6 million
- **Coed** 2,158 undergraduate students, 99% full-time, 52% women, 48% men
- **Moderately difficult** entrance level, 67% of applicants were admitted

UNDERGRAD STUDENTS
2,140 full-time, 18 part-time. 5% Black or African American, non-Hispanic/Latino; 7% Hispanic/Latino; 4% Asian, non-Hispanic/Latino; 0.4% American Indian or Alaska Native, non-Hispanic/Latino; 5% Two or more races, non-Hispanic/Latino; 2% Race/ethnicity unknown; 10% international; 0.7% transferred in; 96% live on campus.

Freshmen:
Admission: 5,173 applied, 3,479 admitted, 595 enrolled. *Average high school GPA:* 3.8. *Test scores:* SAT evidence-based reading and writing scores over 500: 96%; SAT math scores over 500: 93%; ACT scores over 18: 98%; SAT evidence-based reading and writing scores over 600: 56%; SAT math scores over 600: 52%; ACT scores over 24: 75%; SAT evidence-based reading and writing scores over 700: 10%; SAT math scores over 700: 20%; ACT scores over 30: 21%.

Retention: 89% of full-time freshmen returned.

FACULTY
Total: 264, 86% full-time, 93% with terminal degrees.
Student/faculty ratio: 9:1.

ACADEMICS
Calendar: 4-1-4. *Degree:* bachelor's.

Special study options: advanced placement credit, cooperative education, double majors, English as a second language, honors programs, independent study, internships, off-campus study, part-time degree program, services for LD students, student-designed majors, study abroad. *ROTC:* Army (c), Air Force (c).

Unusual degree programs: 3-2 engineering with Columbia University, Washington University in St. Louis.

Computers: Students can access the following: campus intranet, computer help desk, free student e-mail accounts, online (class) grades, online (class) registration, online (class) schedules. Campuswide network is available. 100% of college-owned or -operated housing units

are wired for high-speed Internet access. Wireless service is available via entire campus.

Library: Roy O. West Library plus 2 others. Study areas open 24 hours, 5–7 days a week; students can reserve study rooms.

STUDENT LIFE

Housing options: on-campus residence required through senior year; coed, special housing for students with disabilities. Campus housing is university owned. Freshman campus housing is guaranteed.

Activities and organizations: drama/theater group, student-run newspaper, radio and television station, choral group, national fraternities, national sororities.

Athletics Member NCAA. All Division III. *Intercollegiate sports:* baseball M, basketball M/W, cheerleading M(c)/W(c), crew M(c)/W(c), cross-country running M/W, field hockey W, football M, golf M/W, lacrosse M/W, rugby M(c), soccer M/W, softball W, swimming and diving M/W, tennis M/W, track and field M/W, volleyball W. *Intramural sports:* badminton M/W, basketball M/W, bowling M/W, football M/W, golf M, racquetball M/W, soccer M/W, softball M/W, table tennis M/W, tennis M/W, ultimate Frisbee M/W, volleyball M/W.

Campus security: 24-hour emergency response devices and patrols, student patrols, late-night transport/escort service, controlled dormitory access.

Student services: health clinic, personal/psychological counseling, women's center.

COSTS & FINANCIAL AID

Costs (2017–18) *Comprehensive fee:* $60,367 includes full-time tuition ($47,026), mandatory fees ($812), and room and board ($12,529). Part-time tuition: $1470 per credit hour. *Room and board:* Room and board charges vary according to board plan. *Payment plan:* installment. *Waivers:* employees or children of employees.

Financial Aid Of all full-time matriculated undergraduates who enrolled in 2016, 1,487 applied for aid, 1,305 were judged to have need, 349 had their need fully met. In 2016, 840 non-need-based awards were made. *Average percent of need met:* 89. *Average financial aid package:* $39,790. *Average need-based loan:* $4920. *Average need-based gift aid:* $34,859. *Average non-need-based aid:* $17,350. *Average indebtedness upon graduation:* $22,770. *Financial aid deadline:* 2/1.

APPLYING

Standardized Tests *Required:* SAT or ACT (for admission).

Options: electronic application, early admission, early decision, early action, deferred entrance.

Required: essay or personal statement, high school transcript, 1 letter of recommendation. *Recommended:* interview.

Application deadlines: 2/1 (freshmen), 3/1 (transfers), 12/1 (early action).

Early decision deadline: 11/1.

Notification: continuous until 12/15 (freshmen), continuous (out-of-state freshmen), 4/1 (transfers), 12/1 (early decision), 1/15 (early action).

CONTACT

Ms. Rachel Schmidtke, Director of Recruitment, DePauw University, 204 East Seminary Street, Greencastle, IN 46135. *Phone:* 765-658-4104. *Toll-free phone:* 800-447-2495. *Fax:* 765-658-4007. *E-mail:* rachelschmidtke@depauw.edu.

★ Earlham College
Richmond, Indiana
http://www.earlham.edu/

- **Independent** comprehensive, founded 1847, affiliated with Society of Friends
- **Small-town** 800-acre campus with easy access to Cincinnati, Indianapolis, Dayton
- **Endowment** $425.4 million
- **Coed** 1,067 undergraduate students, 99% full-time, 56% women, 44% men
- **Very difficult** entrance level, 52% of applicants were admitted

UNDERGRAD STUDENTS

1,051 full-time, 16 part-time. Students come from 47 states and territories; 54 other countries; 82% are from out of state; 11% Black or African American, non-Hispanic/Latino; 7% Hispanic/Latino; 6% Asian, non-

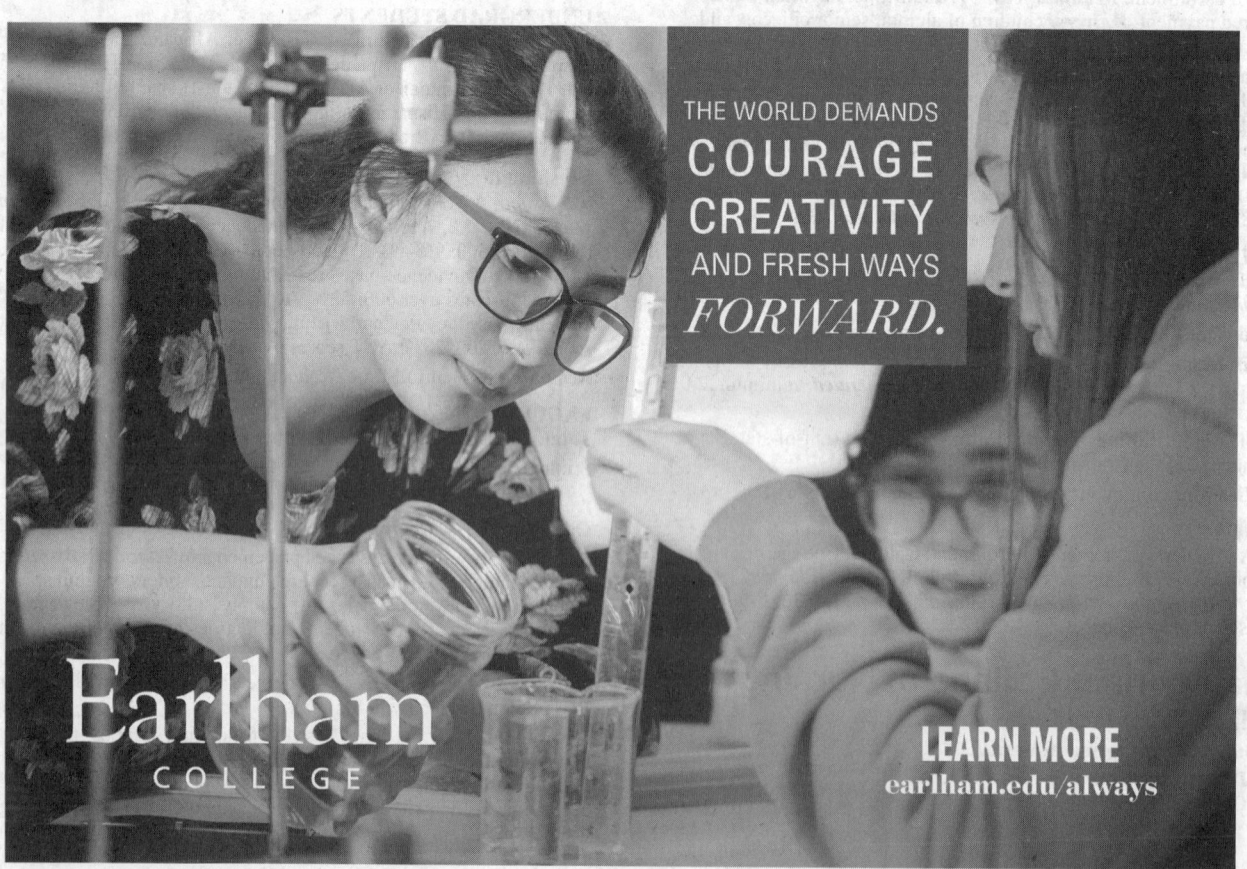

Hispanic/Latino; 0.1% Native Hawaiian or other Pacific Islander, non-Hispanic/Latino; 0.8% American Indian or Alaska Native, non-Hispanic/Latino; 0.2% Two or more races, non-Hispanic/Latino; 4% Race/ethnicity unknown; 21% international; 0.9% transferred in; 98% live on campus.

Freshmen:
Admission: 2,799 applied, 1,452 admitted, 287 enrolled. *Average high school GPA:* 3.7. *Test scores:* SAT evidence-based reading and writing scores over 500: 97%; SAT math scores over 500: 98%; ACT scores over 18: 100%; SAT evidence-based reading and writing scores over 600: 78%; SAT math scores over 600: 71%; ACT scores over 24: 83%; SAT evidence-based reading and writing scores over 700: 26%; SAT math scores over 700: 26%; ACT scores over 30: 26%.
Retention: 86% of full-time freshmen returned.

FACULTY
Total: 110, 96% full-time, 94% with terminal degrees.
Student/faculty ratio: 10:1.

ACADEMICS
Calendar: semesters. *Degrees:* bachelor's, master's, and postbachelor's certificates.
Special study options: cooperative education, double majors, English as a second language, honors programs, independent study, internships, off-campus study, services for LD students, student-designed majors, study abroad.
Unusual degree programs: 3-2 engineering with Columbia University, University of Minnesota, Rensselaer Polytechnic Institute.
Computers: 266 computers/terminals are available on campus for general student use. Students can access the following: campus intranet, computer help desk, free student e-mail accounts, online (class) grades, online (class) registration, online (class) schedules. Campuswide network is available. 100% of college-owned or -operated housing units are wired for high-speed Internet access. Wireless service is available via entire campus.
Library: Lilly Library plus 1 other. Students can reserve study rooms.

STUDENT LIFE
Housing options: on-campus residence required through senior year; coed, men-only, women-only, special housing for students with disabilities. Campus housing is university owned. Freshman campus housing is guaranteed.
Activities and organizations: drama/theater group, student-run newspaper, radio station, choral group, Gospel Revelations Chorus, Dance Alloy, club sports, Student Government, Black Student Union.
Athletics Member NCAA. All Division III. *Intercollegiate sports:* baseball M, basketball M/W, cheerleading M(c)/W(c), cross-country running M/W, equestrian sports M(c)/W(c), field hockey W, football M, golf M/W, lacrosse M(c)/W(c), rugby M(c)/W(c), soccer M/W, tennis M/W, track and field M/W, ultimate Frisbee M(c)/W(c), volleyball M(c)/W. *Intramural sports:* basketball M/W, bowling M/W, football M, racquetball M/W, rock climbing M/W, soccer M/W, ultimate Frisbee M/W.
Campus security: 24-hour emergency response devices and patrols, student patrols, late-night transport/escort service, controlled dormitory access.
Student services: health clinic, personal/psychological counseling, women's center.

COSTS & FINANCIAL AID
Costs (2018–19) *Comprehensive fee:* $56,850 includes full-time tuition ($45,500), mandatory fees ($950), and room and board ($10,400). Full-time tuition and fees vary according to course load and program. Part-time tuition: $1517 per credit hour. Part-time tuition and fees vary according to course load and program. *College room only:* $5500. Room and board charges vary according to board plan. *Payment plans:* installment, deferred payment. *Waivers:* employees or children of employees.
Financial Aid Of all full-time matriculated undergraduates who enrolled in 2017, 934 applied for aid, 894 were judged to have need, 449 had their need fully met. 650 Federal Work-Study jobs (averaging $2200). In 2017, 118 non-need-based awards were made. *Average percent of need met:* 94. *Average financial aid package:* $42,386. *Average need-based loan:* $4974. *Average need-based gift aid:* $37,896. *Average non-need-based*

aid: $22,981. *Average indebtedness upon graduation:* $27,830. *Financial aid deadline:* 3/1.

APPLYING
Standardized Tests *Required for some:* SAT or ACT (for admission).
Options: electronic application, early admission, early decision, early action, deferred entrance.
Required: essay or personal statement, high school transcript, minimum 3.0 GPA, 2 letters of recommendation. *Recommended:* interview.
Application deadlines: 2/15 (freshmen), 4/1 (transfers), 12/1 (early action).
Early decision deadline: 11/15.
Notification: 4/1 (freshmen), continuous until 5/1 (transfers), 12/15 (early decision), 1/15 (early action).

CONTACT
Josh Stevens, Director of Admissions, Earlham College, 801 National Road West, Richmond, IN 47374. *Phone:* 765-983-1600. *Toll-free phone:* 800-327-5426. *Fax:* 765-983-1560. *E-mail:* admission@earlham.edu.

See previous page for display ad and page 1276 for the College Close-Up.

Franklin College
Franklin, Indiana
http://www.franklincollege.edu/
- **Independent** comprehensive, founded 1834, affiliated with American Baptist Churches in the U.S.A.
- **Suburban** 207-acre campus with easy access to Indianapolis
- **Endowment** $84.6 million
- **Coed** 1,016 undergraduate students, 95% full-time, 52% women, 48% men
- **Moderately difficult** entrance level, 62% of applicants were admitted

UNDERGRAD STUDENTS
962 full-time, 54 part-time. Students come from 17 states and territories; 3 other countries; 8% are from out of state; 4% Black or African American, non-Hispanic/Latino; 3% Hispanic/Latino; 0.8% Asian, non-Hispanic/Latino; 0.3% American Indian or Alaska Native, non-Hispanic/Latino; 3% Two or more races, non-Hispanic/Latino; 2% Race/ethnicity unknown; 0.3% international; 3% transferred in; 69% live on campus.

Freshmen:
Admission: 2,301 applied, 1,418 admitted, 267 enrolled. *Average high school GPA:* 3.5. *Test scores:* SAT evidence-based reading and writing scores over 500: 79%; SAT math scores over 500: 80%; ACT scores over 18: 89%; SAT evidence-based reading and writing scores over 600: 29%; SAT math scores over 600: 22%; ACT scores over 24: 39%; SAT evidence-based reading and writing scores over 700: 3%; SAT math scores over 700: 3%; ACT scores over 30: 6%.
Retention: 75% of full-time freshmen returned.

FACULTY
Total: 123, 61% full-time, 65% with terminal degrees.
Student/faculty ratio: 11:1.

ACADEMICS
Calendar: 4-1-4. *Degrees:* bachelor's and master's.
Special study options: academic remediation for entering students, advanced placement credit, cooperative education, double majors, English as a second language, independent study, internships, off-campus study, part-time degree program, services for LD students, student-designed majors, study abroad, summer session for credit. *ROTC:* Army (c).
Unusual degree programs: 3-2 engineering with Indiana University–Purdue University Indianapolis; athletic training with Franklin College, public health with Indiana University-Purdue University Indianapolis.
Computers: 150 computers/terminals are available on campus for general student use. Students can access the following: campus intranet, computer help desk, free student e-mail accounts, online (class) grades, online (class) registration, online (class) schedules. Campuswide network is available. 100% of college-owned or -operated housing units are wired for high-speed Internet access. Wireless service is available via classrooms, computer centers, computer labs, dorm rooms, learning centers, libraries, student centers.

Library: Hamilton Library. *Books:* 104,767 (physical), 1.5 million (digital/electronic); *Serial titles:* 33,498 (physical), 136,773 (digital/electronic); *Databases:* 78. Weekly public service hours: 83; students can reserve study rooms.

STUDENT LIFE

Housing options: on-campus residence required through junior year; coed, men-only, women-only, special housing for students with disabilities. Campus housing is university owned. Freshman campus housing is guaranteed.

Activities and organizations: drama/theater group, student-run newspaper, radio station, choral group, Student Entertainment Board, Student Congress, FC Volunteers, national fraternities, national sororities.

Athletics Member NCAA. All Division III. *Intercollegiate sports:* baseball M, basketball M/W, cheerleading W(c), cross-country running M/W, football M, golf M/W, lacrosse W, soccer M/W, softball W, swimming and diving M/W, tennis M/W, track and field M/W, volleyball W. *Intramural sports:* basketball M/W.

Campus security: 24-hour emergency response devices and patrols, student patrols, late-night transport/escort service, controlled dormitory access.

Student services: health clinic, personal/psychological counseling.

COSTS & FINANCIAL AID

Costs (2017–18) *Comprehensive fee:* $40,135 includes full-time tuition ($30,735), mandatory fees ($185), and room and board ($9215). Full-time tuition and fees vary according to course load and degree level. Part-time tuition: $445 per credit hour. Part-time tuition and fees vary according to course load and degree level. *Required fees:* $6 per credit hour part-time. *College room only:* $5490. Room and board charges vary according to board plan. *Payment plan:* installment. *Waivers:* senior citizens and employees or children of employees.

Financial Aid Of all full-time matriculated undergraduates who enrolled in 2016, 906 applied for aid, 816 were judged to have need, 122 had their need fully met. In 2016, 143 non-need-based awards were made. *Average percent of need met:* 72. *Average financial aid package:* $22,129. *Average need-based loan:* $4294. *Average need-based gift aid:* $18,625. *Average non-need-based aid:* $13,321. *Average indebtedness upon graduation:* $36,145.

APPLYING

Standardized Tests *Required:* SAT or ACT (for admission).

Options: electronic application, deferred entrance.

Application fee: $40.

Required: high school transcript. *Required for some:* interview. *Recommended:* essay or personal statement.

Application deadlines: rolling (freshmen), rolling (out-of-state freshmen), rolling (transfers).

Notification: continuous (freshmen), continuous (out-of-state freshmen), continuous (transfers).

CONTACT

Ms. Tara Evans, Director of Admissions, Franklin College, 101 Branigin Boulevard, Franklin, IN 46131-2623. *Phone:* 317-738-8075. *Toll-free phone:* 800-852-0232. *Fax:* 317-738-8075. *E-mail:* admissions@franklincollege.edu.

Goshen College

Goshen, Indiana

http://www.goshen.edu/

- **Independent Mennonite** comprehensive, founded 1894
- **Small-town** 135-acre campus
- **Endowment** $107.4 million
- **Coed** 883 undergraduate students, 92% full-time, 64% women, 36% men
- **Moderately difficult** entrance level, 65% of applicants were admitted

UNDERGRAD STUDENTS

816 full-time, 67 part-time. Students come from 35 states and territories; 22 other countries; 58% are from out of state; 4% Black or African American, non-Hispanic/Latino; 20% Hispanic/Latino; 2% Asian, non-Hispanic/Latino; 0.1% Native Hawaiian or other Pacific Islander, non-Hispanic/Latino; 0.2% American Indian or Alaska Native, non-Hispanic/Latino; 2% Two or more races, non-Hispanic/Latino; 0.8%

Race/ethnicity unknown; 7% international; 6% transferred in; 53% live on campus.

Freshmen:

Admission: 1,185 applied, 772 admitted, 215 enrolled. *Average high school GPA:* 3.5. *Test scores:* SAT evidence-based reading and writing scores over 500: 75%; SAT math scores over 500: 72%; ACT scores over 18: 87%; SAT evidence-based reading and writing scores over 600: 34%; SAT math scores over 600: 34%; ACT scores over 24: 51%; SAT evidence-based reading and writing scores over 700: 6%; SAT math scores over 700: 4%; ACT scores over 30: 11%.

Retention: 78% of full-time freshmen returned.

FACULTY

Total: 101, 65% full-time, 51% with terminal degrees.

Student/faculty ratio: 11:1.

ACADEMICS

Calendar: semesters. *Degrees:* bachelor's and master's.

Special study options: academic remediation for entering students, accelerated degree program, adult/continuing education programs, advanced placement credit, distance learning, double majors, independent study, internships, off-campus study, part-time degree program, services for LD students, student-designed majors, study abroad, summer session for credit.

Unusual degree programs: 3-2 engineering with Case Western Reserve University, University of Illinois at Urbana–Champaign, University of Notre Dame, Washington University in St. Louis.

Computers: 160 computers/terminals and 2,000 ports are available on campus for general student use. Students can access the following: campus intranet, computer help desk, free student e-mail accounts, online (class) grades, online (class) registration, online (class) schedules. Campuswide network is available. 100% of college-owned or -operated housing units are wired for high-speed Internet access. Wireless service is available via entire campus.

Library: The Harold and Wilma Good Library plus 1 other. *Books:* 106,274 (physical), 157,167 (digital/electronic); *Serial titles:* 2,769 (physical), 30,977 (digital/electronic); *Databases:* 69. Weekly public service hours: 81; students can reserve study rooms.

STUDENT LIFE

Housing options: on-campus residence required through junior year; coed, men-only, women-only, special housing for students with disabilities. Campus housing is university owned. Freshman campus housing is guaranteed.

Activities and organizations: drama/theater group, student-run newspaper, radio and television station, choral group, International Student Club, Latino Student Union, PAX - Peace Club, Goshen Student Women's Organization, Business Club.

Athletics Member NAIA. *Intercollegiate sports:* baseball M(s), basketball M(s)/W(s), cross-country running M(s)/W(s), golf M(s), soccer M(s)/W(s), softball W(s), tennis M(s)/W(s), track and field M(s)/W(s), volleyball M(s)/W(s). *Intramural sports:* badminton M/W, baseball M, basketball M/W, racquetball M/W, soccer M/W, softball W, table tennis M/W, tennis M/W, ultimate Frisbee M/W, volleyball M/W.

Campus security: 24-hour emergency response devices and patrols, late-night transport/escort service, controlled dormitory access.

Student services: health clinic, personal/psychological counseling.

COSTS & FINANCIAL AID

Costs (2018–19) *Comprehensive fee:* $44,350 includes full-time tuition ($33,700) and room and board ($10,650). Full-time tuition and fees vary according to degree level and program. Part-time tuition: $1380 per credit hour. Part-time tuition and fees vary according to course load, degree level, and program. *College room only:* $5670. Room and board charges vary according to board plan and housing facility. *Payment plan:* installment. *Waivers:* employees or children of employees.

Financial Aid Of all full-time matriculated undergraduates who enrolled in 2017, 662 applied for aid, 616 were judged to have need, 110 had their need fully met. 341 Federal Work-Study jobs (averaging $1066). 55 state and other part-time jobs (averaging $1815). In 2017, 180 non-need-based awards were made. *Average percent of need met:* 83. *Average financial aid package:* $27,982. *Average need-based loan:* $5251. *Average need-*

based gift aid: $23,549. *Average non-need-based aid:* $14,275. *Average indebtedness upon graduation:* $27,062.

APPLYING
Standardized Tests *Required:* SAT or ACT (for admission).
Options: electronic application, deferred entrance.
Application fee: $25.
Required: minimum 2.0 GPA. *Required for some:* essay or personal statement, high school transcript. *Recommended:* minimum 2.8 GPA, 1 letter of recommendation, interview, rank in upper 50% of high school class.
Application deadlines: 8/15 (freshmen), 8/15 (transfers).
Notification: continuous (freshmen), continuous (transfers).

CONTACT
Goshen College, 1700 South Main Street, Goshen, IN 46526-4794. *Toll-free phone:* 800-348-7422.

Grace College
Winona Lake, Indiana
http://www.grace.edu/
- **Independent** comprehensive, founded 1948, affiliated with Fellowship of Grace Brethren Churches
- **Small-town** 160-acre campus
- **Endowment** $12.3 million
- **Coed**
- **Moderately difficult** entrance level

FACULTY
Student/faculty ratio: 22:1.

ACADEMICS
Calendar: semesters. *Degrees:* certificates, diplomas, associate, bachelor's, master's, and doctoral.
Library: Morgan Library.

STUDENT LIFE
Housing options: on-campus residence required through senior year; men-only, women-only. Campus housing is university owned. Freshman campus housing is guaranteed.
Activities and organizations: drama/theater group, student-run newspaper, choral group, Grace Ministries in Action, Student Activities Board, Funfest, women's ministries, Breakout.
Athletics Member NAIA, NCCAA.
Campus security: 24-hour emergency response devices and patrols, student patrols, late-night transport/escort service, controlled dormitory access.
Student services: health clinic, personal/psychological counseling.

COSTS & FINANCIAL AID
Costs (2017–18) *Comprehensive fee:* $31,524 includes full-time tuition ($23,120) and room and board ($8404). Full-time tuition and fees vary according to degree level, location, and student level. Part-time tuition: $824 per credit hour. Part-time tuition and fees vary according to degree level and location. *College room only:* $4378. Room and board charges vary according to board plan and housing facility.
Financial Aid Of all full-time matriculated undergraduates who enrolled in 2009, 1,276 applied for aid, 1,273 were judged to have need. *Average financial aid package:* $11,338.

APPLYING
Standardized Tests *Required:* SAT or ACT (for admission).
Options: electronic application, early admission, early action, deferred entrance.
Application fee: $30.
Required: essay or personal statement, high school transcript, minimum 2.3 GPA, 2 letters of recommendation, personal statement of faith. *Required for some:* interview.

CONTACT
Mrs. Nikki Sproul, Admissions Office, Grace College, 200 Seminary Drive, Winona Lake, IN 46590. *Phone:* 574-372-5100 Ext. 6008. *Toll-free phone:* 800-54-GRACE. *Fax:* 574-372-5120. *E-mail:* enroll@grace.edu.

Hanover College
Hanover, Indiana
http://www.hanover.edu/
- **Independent Presbyterian** 4-year, founded 1827
- **Rural** 630-acre campus with easy access to Louisville
- **Endowment** $136.2 million
- **Coed**
- **Moderately difficult** entrance level

FACULTY
Student/faculty ratio: 12:1.

ACADEMICS
Calendar: 4-4-1. *Degree:* bachelor's.
Library: Duggan Library. Students can reserve study rooms.

STUDENT LIFE
Housing options: on-campus residence required through senior year; coed, men-only, women-only. Campus housing is university owned and leased by the school. Freshman campus housing is guaranteed.
Activities and organizations: drama/theater group, student-run newspaper, radio and television station, choral group, marching band, Delight Ministries, Alpha Lambda Delta, Love Out Loud, Art Club, International Club, national fraternities, national sororities.
Athletics Member NCAA. All Division III.
Campus security: 24-hour emergency response devices and patrols, late-night transport/escort service, controlled dormitory access.
Student services: health clinic, personal/psychological counseling.

COSTS & FINANCIAL AID
Costs (2017–18) *One-time required fee:* $350. *Comprehensive fee:* $47,750 includes full-time tuition ($35,750), mandatory fees ($770), and room and board ($11,230). Full-time tuition and fees vary according to reciprocity agreements. Part-time tuition: $3972 per unit. Part-time tuition and fees vary according to course load and reciprocity agreements. *College room only:* $5600. Room and board charges vary according to housing facility.
Financial Aid Of all full-time matriculated undergraduates who enrolled in 2016, 929 applied for aid, 840 were judged to have need, 229 had their need fully met. 347 Federal Work-Study jobs (averaging $1513). In 2016, 233 non-need-based awards were made. *Average percent of need met:* 82. *Average financial aid package:* $29,314. *Average need-based loan:* $4212. *Average need-based gift aid:* $25,419. *Average non-need-based aid:* $20,679. *Average indebtedness upon graduation:* $30,835.

APPLYING
Standardized Tests *Required:* SAT or ACT (for admission).
Options: electronic application, early admission, early action, deferred entrance.
Required: essay or personal statement, high school transcript, 1 letter of recommendation. *Recommended:* interview.

CONTACT
Ms. Victoria Hidalgo, Director of Admission, Hanover College, 517 Ball Drive, Hanover, IN 47243. *Phone:* 812-866-7031. *Toll-free phone:* 800-213-2178. *Fax:* 812-866-7098. *E-mail:* admission@hanover.edu.

Harrison College
Indianapolis, Indiana
http://www.harrison.edu/

CONTACT
Mr. Jason Howanec, Vice President of Enrollment, Harrison College, 500 N. Meridian Street, Indianapolis, IN 46204. *Phone:* 888-544-4422. *Toll-free phone:* 888-544-4422. *E-mail:* admissions@harrison.edu.

Holy Cross College
Notre Dame, Indiana
http://www.hcc-nd.edu/
- **Independent Roman Catholic** 4-year, founded 1966
- **Suburban** 150-acre campus with easy access to Chicago, Indianapolis
- **Coed**
- **Moderately difficult** entrance level

FACULTY
Student/faculty ratio: 14:1.

ACADEMICS
Calendar: semesters. *Degrees:* associate and bachelor's.
Library: McKenna Library. *Books:* 21,257 (physical), 10,401 (digital/electronic); *Serial titles:* 74 (physical); *Databases:* 55. Weekly public service hours: 86.

STUDENT LIFE
Housing options: on-campus residence required through sophomore year; men-only, women-only. Campus housing is university owned and leased by the school. Freshman campus housing is guaranteed.

Activities and organizations: drama/theater group, choral group, marching band, Student Government Association, Campus Ministry, Intramural athletics, Commuter Student Organization, SAGE.

Athletics Member NAIA.

Campus security: 24-hour emergency response devices, late-night transport/escort service, controlled dormitory access.

Student services: health clinic, personal/psychological counseling.

APPLYING
Standardized Tests *Required:* SAT or ACT (for admission).

Options: electronic application, deferred entrance.

Required: high school transcript. *Required for some:* essay or personal statement. *Recommended:* essay or personal statement, 2 letters of recommendation, interview.

CONTACT
Holy Cross College, 54515 SR 933 N., PO Box 308, Notre Dame, IN 46556. *Phone:* 574-239-8338. *E-mail:* admissions@hcc-nd.edu.

Horizon University

Indianapolis, Indiana
http://www.horizonuniversity.edu/
- **Independent** 4-year, founded 1993
- **Suburban** 100-acre campus with easy access to Indianapolis, IN
- **Coed**
- **Noncompetitive** entrance level

FACULTY
Student/faculty ratio: 2:1.

ACADEMICS
Calendar: semesters. *Degrees:* certificates, associate, and bachelor's.

Special study options: adult/continuing education programs, advanced placement credit, distance learning, part-time degree program, summer session for credit.

Computers: Students can access the following: online (class) grades, online (class) registration, online (class) schedules. Wireless service is available via entire campus.

STUDENT LIFE
Housing options: college housing not available.

COSTS
Costs (2018–19) *Tuition:* $9000 full-time, $250 per semester hour part-time. *Required fees:* $300 full-time, $100 per term part-time. *Payment plan:* installment. *Waivers:* employees or children of employees.

APPLYING
Options: electronic application.

Required: essay or personal statement, high school transcript, minimum 2.0 GPA, 2 letters of recommendation, interview.

CONTACT
Horizon University, 7700 Indian Lake Road, Indianapolis, IN 46236. *Toll-free phone:* 800-553-HORIZON.

Huntington University

Huntington, Indiana
http://www.huntington.edu/
- **Independent** comprehensive, founded 1897, affiliated with Church of the United Brethren in Christ
- **Small-town** 170-acre campus with easy access to Fort Wayne
- **Endowment** $25.2 million
- **Coed**
- **Moderately difficult** entrance level

FACULTY
Student/faculty ratio: 13:1.

ACADEMICS
Calendar: 4-1-4. *Degrees:* associate, bachelor's, master's, and doctoral.
Library: RichLyn Library.

STUDENT LIFE
Housing options: on-campus residence required through junior year; men-only, women-only, special housing for students with disabilities. Campus housing is university owned. Freshman campus housing is guaranteed.

Activities and organizations: drama/theater group, student-run newspaper, radio and television station, choral group, Friesen Center for Volunteer Service, Student Government Association, Multicultural Activities Council, Student Activities Board, Intramural Sports.

Athletics Member NAIA, NCCAA.

Campus security: 24-hour emergency response devices, late-night transport/escort service, campus police on duty from 6 pm to 6 am.

COSTS & FINANCIAL AID
Costs (2017–18) *Comprehensive fee:* $33,996 includes full-time tuition ($24,694), mandatory fees ($846), and room and board ($8456). Full-time tuition and fees vary according to course load, degree level, and program. Part-time tuition and fees vary according to course load, degree level, and program. *Required fees:* $420 per credit hour part-time. *College room only:* $3980. Room and board charges vary according to board plan.

Financial Aid Of all full-time matriculated undergraduates who enrolled in 2017, 598 applied for aid, 537 were judged to have need, 38 had their need fully met. In 2017, 268 non-need-based awards were made. *Average percent of need met:* 87. *Average financial aid package:* $19,060. *Average need-based loan:* $4562. *Average need-based gift aid:* $14,851. *Average non-need-based aid:* $9626. *Average indebtedness upon graduation:* $32,515.

APPLYING
Standardized Tests *Required:* SAT or ACT (for admission).

Options: electronic application, deferred entrance.

Application fee: $20.

Required: essay or personal statement, high school transcript, minimum 2.3 GPA. *Recommended:* interview.

CONTACT
Huntington University, 2303 College Avenue, Huntington, IN 46750-1299. *Phone:* 260-356-6000. *Toll-free phone:* 800-642-6493.

Indiana State University

Terre Haute, Indiana
http://www.indstate.edu/
- **State-supported** university, founded 1865
- **Small-town** 435-acre campus with easy access to Indianapolis
- **Endowment** $47.4 million
- **Coed** 11,591 undergraduate students, 81% full-time, 55% women, 45% men
- **Moderately difficult** entrance level, 85% of applicants were admitted

UNDERGRAD STUDENTS
9,369 full-time, 2,222 part-time. Students come from 53 states and territories; 71 other countries; 20% are from out of state; 18% Black or African American, non-Hispanic/Latino; 4% Hispanic/Latino; 1% Asian, non-Hispanic/Latino; 0.3% American Indian or Alaska Native, non-Hispanic/Latino; 4% Two or more races, non-Hispanic/Latino; 3% Race/ethnicity unknown; 4% international; 8% transferred in; 29% live on campus.

Freshmen:
Admission: 11,720 applied, 9,904 admitted, 2,688 enrolled. *Average high school GPA:* 3.1. *Test scores:* SAT evidence-based reading and writing scores over 500: 55%; SAT math scores over 500: 51%; ACT scores over 18: 66%; SAT evidence-based reading and writing scores over 600: 13%; SAT math scores over 600: 11%; ACT scores over 24: 22%; SAT evidence-based reading and writing scores over 700: 1%; SAT math scores over 700: 1%; ACT scores over 30: 2%.
Retention: 68% of full-time freshmen returned.

FACULTY
Total: 684, 67% full-time, 62% with terminal degrees.
Student/faculty ratio: 21:1.

ACADEMICS
Calendar: semesters. *Degrees:* certificates, bachelor's, master's, doctoral, post-master's, and postbachelor's certificates.

Special study options: academic remediation for entering students, accelerated degree program, adult/continuing education programs, advanced placement credit, cooperative education, distance learning, double majors, English as a second language, freshman honors college, honors programs, independent study, internships, off-campus study, part-time degree program, services for LD students, study abroad, summer session for credit. *ROTC:* Army (b), Air Force (b).

Computers: 988 computers/terminals are available on campus for general student use. Students can access the following: campus intranet, computer help desk, free student e-mail accounts, online (class) grades, online (class) registration, online (class) schedules. Campuswide network is available. 100% of college-owned or -operated housing units are wired for high-speed Internet access. Wireless service is available via entire campus.

Library: Cunningham Memorial Library plus 1 other. *Books:* 1.0 million (physical), 920,661 (digital/electronic); *Serial titles:* 80,200 (digital/electronic); *Databases:* 313. Weekly public service hours: 132; study areas open 24 hours, 5–7 days a week; students can reserve study rooms.

STUDENT LIFE
Housing options: on-campus residence required for freshman year; coed, men-only, women-only, special housing for students with disabilities. Campus housing is university owned. Freshman campus housing is guaranteed.

Activities and organizations: drama/theater group, student-run newspaper, radio station, choral group, marching band, Union Board, Student Government Association, Panhellenic Council (sororities), Interfraternity Council (fraternities), Residence Hall Association, national fraternities, national sororities.

Athletics Member NCAA. All Division I except football (Division I-AA). *Intercollegiate sports:* baseball M(s), basketball M(s)/W(s), cross-country running M(s)/W(s), golf W(s), soccer W(s), softball W(s), swimming and diving W(s), track and field M(s)/W(s), volleyball W(s). *Intramural sports:* badminton M/W, basketball M/W, bowling M(c)/W(c), rugby M(c)/W(c), sand volleyball M/W, soccer M(c)/W(c), softball M/W, swimming and diving M/W, tennis M(c)/W(c), track and field M/W, ultimate Frisbee M(c)/W(c), volleyball M(c)/W(c), wrestling M(c).

Campus security: 24-hour emergency response devices and patrols, student patrols, late-night transport/escort service.

Student services: health clinic, personal/psychological counseling, women's center.

COSTS & FINANCIAL AID
Costs (2017–18) *Tuition:* state resident $8716 full-time, $316 per credit hour part-time; nonresident $19,252 full-time, $682 per credit hour part-time. Full-time tuition and fees vary according to reciprocity agreements. Part-time tuition and fees vary according to course load and reciprocity agreements. *Required fees:* $200 full-time, $100 per term part-time. *Room and board:* $9883. Room and board charges vary according to board plan, housing facility, and student level. *Payment plans:* installment, deferred payment. *Waivers:* senior citizens and employees or children of employees.

Financial Aid Of all full-time matriculated undergraduates who enrolled in 2015, 8,312 applied for aid, 7,121 were judged to have need, 1,023 had their need fully met. In 2015, 890 non-need-based awards were made. *Average percent of need met:* 82. *Average financial aid package:* $10,813. *Average need-based loan:* $3898. *Average need-based gift aid:* $5792. *Average non-need-based aid:* $4153. *Average indebtedness upon graduation:* $27,705. *Financial aid deadline:* 7/1.

APPLYING
Standardized Tests *Required:* SAT or ACT (for admission).
Options: electronic application, deferred entrance.
Application fee: $25.
Required: high school transcript. *Required for some:* interview. *Recommended:* minimum 2.5 GPA.
Notification: continuous (freshmen), continuous (transfers).

CONTACT
Mr. Richard Toomey, Assistant Vice President of Enrollment Management, Indiana State University, 318 North Sixth Street, John W. Moore Welcome Center, Terre Haute, IN 47809-9989. *Phone:* 812-237-2121. *Toll-free phone:* 800-468-6478. *Fax:* 812-237-8023. *E-mail:* admissions@indstate.edu.

Indiana Tech
Fort Wayne, Indiana
http://www.indianatech.edu/
- **Independent** comprehensive, founded 1930
- **Urban** 42-acre campus
- **Endowment** $123.2 million
- **Coed** 7,170 undergraduate students, 59% full-time, 61% women, 39% men
- **Moderately difficult** entrance level, 70% of applicants were admitted

UNDERGRAD STUDENTS
4,247 full-time, 2,923 part-time. Students come from 49 states and territories; 57 other countries; 48% are from out of state; 35% Black or African American, non-Hispanic/Latino; 4% Hispanic/Latino; 0.5% Asian, non-Hispanic/Latino; 0.1% Native Hawaiian or other Pacific Islander, non-Hispanic/Latino; 0.4% American Indian or Alaska Native, non-Hispanic/Latino; 3% Two or more races, non-Hispanic/Latino; 15% Race/ethnicity unknown; 5% international; 7% transferred in; 55% live on campus.

Freshmen:
Admission: 3,059 applied, 2,138 admitted, 1,320 enrolled. *Average high school GPA:* 3.0. *Test scores:* SAT evidence-based reading and writing scores over 500: 62%; SAT math scores over 500: 63%; ACT scores over 18: 73%; SAT evidence-based reading and writing scores over 600: 19%; SAT math scores over 600: 18%; ACT scores over 24: 27%; SAT evidence-based reading and writing scores over 700: 2%; SAT math scores over 700: 2%; ACT scores over 30: 3%.
Retention: 60% of full-time freshmen returned.

FACULTY
Total: 530, 11% full-time, 5% with terminal degrees.
Student/faculty ratio: 20:1.

ACADEMICS
Calendar: semesters. *Degrees:* associate, bachelor's, master's, and doctoral.

Special study options: academic remediation for entering students, accelerated degree program, adult/continuing education programs, advanced placement credit, cooperative education, distance learning, double majors, English as a second language, external degree program, freshman honors college, honors programs, independent study, internships, part-time degree program, services for LD students, student-designed majors, study abroad, summer session for credit. *ROTC:* Army (c).

Computers: 460 computers/terminals and 460 ports are available on campus for general student use. Students can access the following: computer help desk, free student e-mail accounts, online (class) grades, online (class) registration, online (class) schedules. Campuswide network is available. 100% of college-owned or -operated housing units are wired for high-speed Internet access. Wireless service is available via entire campus.

Library: McMillen Library. *Books:* 15,633 (physical), 60,903 (digital/electronic); *Serial titles:* 182 (physical), 500,000 (digital/electronic); *Databases:* 10. Weekly public service hours: 72; students can reserve study rooms.

STUDENT LIFE

Housing options: on-campus residence required through sophomore year; coed. Campus housing is university owned.

Activities and organizations: Multicultural Club, NSBE, Indiana Tech Gaming Society, Tech LOL, Cyber Defense Club of Indiana Tech, national fraternities.

Athletics Member NAIA. *Intercollegiate sports:* baseball M(s), basketball M(s)/W(s), bowling M(s)/W(s), cheerleading M(s)/W(s), cross-country running M(s)/W(s), golf M(s)/W(s), ice hockey M(s), lacrosse M(s)/W(s), soccer M(s)/W(s), softball W(s), tennis M(s)/W(s), track and field M(s)/W(s), volleyball W(s), wrestling M(s). *Intramural sports:* basketball M/W, bowling M/W, football M, soccer M/W, table tennis M/W, ultimate Frisbee M/W, volleyball M/W.

Campus security: 24-hour emergency response devices and patrols, student patrols, late-night transport/escort service, controlled dormitory access.

Student services: personal/psychological counseling.

COSTS & FINANCIAL AID

Costs (2018–19) *Tuition:* $520 per credit hour part-time. Full-time tuition and fees vary according to course load and program. Part-time tuition and fees vary according to course load and program. No tuition increase for student's term of enrollment. *Required fees:* $165 per term part-time. *Room only:* Room and board charges vary according to board plan and housing facility. *Payment plan:* installment. *Waivers:* minority students, children of alumni, adult students, senior citizens, and employees or children of employees.

Financial Aid Of all full-time matriculated undergraduates who enrolled in 2016, 3,701 applied for aid, 3,515 were judged to have need, 1,148 had their need fully met. 88 Federal Work-Study jobs (averaging $1401). In 2016, 59 non-need-based awards were made. *Average percent of need met:* 39. *Average financial aid package:* $17,004. *Average need-based loan:* $3129. *Average need-based gift aid:* $9535. *Average non-need-based aid:* $9494. *Average indebtedness upon graduation:* $41,844.

APPLYING

Standardized Tests *Required:* SAT or ACT (for admission). *Recommended:* AP Exam Results.

Options: electronic application.

Required: high school transcript, minimum 2.0 GPA. *Required for some:* essay or personal statement, minimum 3.0 GPA, 2 letters of recommendation, interview, interview.

Application deadlines: 8/15 (freshmen), 8/15 (transfers).

Notification: continuous until 8/15 (freshmen), continuous until 8/15 (transfers).

CONTACT

Mr. Robert Confer, Director of Admissions, Indiana Tech, 1600 East Washington Boulevard, Fort Wayne, IN 46803. *Phone:* 260-422-5561 Ext. 2424. *Toll-free phone:* 800-937-2448. *Fax:* 260-422-7696. *E-mail:* admissions@indianatech.edu.

Indiana University Bloomington

Bloomington, Indiana

http://www.iub.edu/

- **State-supported** university, founded 1820, part of Indiana University System
- **Small-town** 1939-acre campus with easy access to Indianapolis
- **Endowment** $1.2 billion
- **Coed** 33,429 undergraduate students, 96% full-time, 49% women, 51% men
- **Moderately difficult** entrance level, 76% of applicants were admitted

UNDERGRAD STUDENTS

32,212 full-time, 1,217 part-time. Students come from 52 states and territories; 120 other countries; 34% are from out of state; 4% Black or African American, non-Hispanic/Latino; 6% Hispanic/Latino; 5% Asian, non-Hispanic/Latino; 0.1% American Indian or Alaska Native, non-Hispanic/Latino; 4% Two or more races, non-Hispanic/Latino; 0.3% Race/ethnicity unknown; 11% international; 2% transferred in; 36% live on campus.

Freshmen:

Admission: 41,939 applied, 31,878 admitted, 8,001 enrolled. *Average high school GPA:* 3.7. *Test scores:* SAT evidence-based reading and writing scores over 500: 96%; SAT math scores over 500: 96%; ACT scores over 18: 99%; SAT evidence-based reading and writing scores over 600: 64%; SAT math scores over 600: 63%; ACT scores over 24: 83%; SAT evidence-based reading and writing scores over 700: 14%; SAT math scores over 700: 20%; ACT scores over 30: 36%.

Retention: 91% of full-time freshmen returned.

FACULTY

Total: 2,456, 86% full-time, 77% with terminal degrees.

Student/faculty ratio: 17:1.

ACADEMICS

Calendar: semesters plus summer sessions. *Degrees:* certificates, associate, bachelor's, master's, doctoral, and postbachelor's certificates.

Special study options: academic remediation for entering students, accelerated degree program, adult/continuing education programs, advanced placement credit, cooperative education, distance learning, double majors, English as a second language, external degree program, freshman honors college, honors programs, independent study, internships, off-campus study, part-time degree program, services for LD students, student-designed majors, study abroad, summer session for credit. *ROTC:* Army (b), Air Force (b).

Unusual degree programs: 3-2 business administration.

Computers: 2,150 computers/terminals are available on campus for general student use. Students can access the following: campus intranet, computer help desk, free student e-mail accounts, online (class) grades, online (class) registration, online (class) schedules. Campuswide network is available. 95% of college-owned or -operated housing units are wired for high-speed Internet access. Wireless service is available via entire campus.

Library: Indiana University Library plus 18 others. *Books:* 5.3 million (physical), 1.3 million (digital/electronic); *Serial titles:* 165,443 (physical), 79,521 (digital/electronic); *Databases:* 1,965. Study areas open 24 hours, 5–7 days a week; students can reserve study rooms.

STUDENT LIFE

Housing options: on-campus residence required for freshman year; coed, men-only, women-only, cooperative, special housing for students with disabilities. Campus housing is university owned. Freshman applicants given priority for college housing.

Activities and organizations: drama/theater group, student-run newspaper, radio and television station, choral group, marching band, Union Board, Student Association, Student Foundation, Habitat for Humanity, Student Athletic Board, national fraternities, national sororities.

Athletics Member NCAA. All Division I. *Intercollegiate sports:* baseball M(s), basketball M(s)/W(s), cross-country running M(s)/W(s), field hockey W, football M(s), golf M(s)/W(s), rowing W(s), soccer M(s)/W(s), softball W(s), swimming and diving M(s)/W(s), tennis M(s)/W(s), track and field M(s)/W(s), volleyball W(s), water polo W(s), wrestling M(s). *Intramural sports:* badminton M(c)/W(c), baseball M(c)/W(c), basketball M(c)/W(c), crew M(c)/W(c), cross-country running M(c)/W(c), equestrian sports M(c)/W(c), fencing M(c)/W(c), field hockey W(c), golf M(c)/W(c), gymnastics M(c)/W(c), ice hockey M(c)/W(c), lacrosse M(c)/W(c), racquetball M/W, rowing M(c)/W(c), rugby M(c)/W(c), sailing M(c)/W(c), skiing (downhill) M(c)/W(c), soccer M(c)/W(c), softball M/W, swimming and diving M(c)/W(c), table tennis M/W, tennis M(c)/W(c), track and field M/W, ultimate Frisbee M(c)/W(c), volleyball M(c)/W(c), water polo M(c)/W(c).

Campus security: 24-hour emergency response devices and patrols, late-night transport/escort service, safety seminars, lighted pathways, escort service, shuttle bus service.

Student services: health clinic, personal/psychological counseling, women's center, legal services.

COSTS & FINANCIAL AID

Costs (2018–19) *Tuition:* state resident $9342 full-time, $292 per credit hour part-time; nonresident $34,117 full-time, $1066 per credit hour part-time. Full-time tuition and fees vary according to location and program. Part-time tuition and fees vary according to course load, location, and program. *Required fees:* $1339 full-time. *Room and* *board:* Room and board charges vary according to board plan and housing facility. *Payment plans:* installment, deferred payment. *Waivers:* employees or children of employees.

Financial Aid Of all full-time matriculated undergraduates who enrolled in 2016, 18,747 applied for aid, 13,183 were judged to have need, 3,359 had their need fully met. 555 Federal Work-Study jobs (averaging $1967). In 2016, 10179 non-need-based awards were made. *Average percent of need met:* 69. *Average financial aid package:* $13,500. *Average need-based loan:* $4454. *Average need-based gift aid:* $11,445. *Average non-need-based aid:* $5626. *Average indebtedness upon graduation:* $28,792.

APPLYING
Standardized Tests *Required:* SAT or ACT (for admission). *Recommended:* SAT Subject Tests (for admission).

Options: electronic application, early action, deferred entrance.

Application fee: $65.

Required: high school transcript. *Recommended:* interview.

Application deadlines: rolling (freshmen), rolling (transfers).

Notification: continuous until 1/15 (freshmen), continuous (transfers).

CONTACT
Ms. Sacha Thieme, Executive Director of Admissions, Indiana University Bloomington, 300 North Jordan Avenue, Bloomington, IN 47405-1106. *Phone:* 812-855-0661. *Fax:* 812-855-5102. *E-mail:* iuadmit@indiana.edu.

Indiana University East
Richmond, Indiana
http://www.iue.edu/

- **State-supported** comprehensive, founded 1971, part of Indiana University System
- **Small-town** 182-acre campus with easy access to Indianapolis
- **Endowment** $5.0 million
- **Coed** 3,292 undergraduate students, 57% full-time, 64% women, 36% men
- **Moderately difficult** entrance level, 70% of applicants were admitted

UNDERGRAD STUDENTS
1,887 full-time, 1,405 part-time. Students come from 41 states and territories; 40 other countries; 24% are from out of state; 5% Black or African American, non-Hispanic/Latino; 4% Hispanic/Latino; 1% Asian, non-Hispanic/Latino; 0.4% American Indian or Alaska Native, non-Hispanic/Latino; 3% Two or more races, non-Hispanic/Latino; 1% Race/ethnicity unknown; 1% international; 11% transferred in.

Freshmen:
Admission: 1,279 applied, 891 admitted, 396 enrolled. *Average high school GPA:* 3.2. *Test scores:* SAT evidence-based reading and writing scores over 500: 61%; SAT math scores over 500: 60%; ACT scores over 18: 82%; SAT evidence-based reading and writing scores over 600: 15%; SAT math scores over 600: 11%; ACT scores over 24: 23%; SAT evidence-based reading and writing scores over 700: 1%; SAT math scores over 700: 1%; ACT scores over 30: 2%.

Retention: 66% of full-time freshmen returned.

FACULTY
Total: 287, 41% full-time, 45% with terminal degrees.

Student/faculty ratio: 14:1.

ACADEMICS
Calendar: semesters. *Degrees:* certificates, bachelor's, master's, and postbachelor's certificates.

Special study options: academic remediation for entering students, accelerated degree program, adult/continuing education programs, advanced placement credit, cooperative education, distance learning, double majors, external degree program, honors programs, independent study, internships, off-campus study, part-time degree program, services for LD students, study abroad, summer session for credit.

Computers: 196 computers/terminals are available on campus for general student use. Students can access the following: campus intranet, computer help desk, free student e-mail accounts, online (class) grades, online (class) registration, online (class) schedules. Campuswide network is available. Wireless service is available via entire campus.

Library: IU East Campus Library. *Books:* 21,975 (physical), 171,759 (digital/electronic); *Serial titles:* 2 (physical), 93,538 (digital/electronic); *Databases:* 512. Students can reserve study rooms.

STUDENT LIFE
Housing options: college housing not available.

Activities and organizations: drama/theater group, student-run newspaper, television station, choral group, Student Government Association.

Athletics Member NAIA. *Intercollegiate sports:* basketball M/W, cross-country running M/W, golf M/W, soccer M/W, tennis M/W, track and field M/W, volleyball W.

Campus security: 24-hour emergency response devices, late-night transport/escort service, safety awareness, lighted pathways, 14-hour foot and vehicle patrol.

Student services: personal/psychological counseling.

COSTS & FINANCIAL AID
Costs (2018–19) *Tuition:* state resident $6727 full-time, $224 per credit hour part-time; nonresident $18,783 full-time, $626 per credit hour part-time. Full-time tuition and fees vary according to course load, location, program, and reciprocity agreements. Part-time tuition and fees vary according to course load, location, program, and reciprocity agreements. *Required fees:* $617 full-time. *Payment plans:* installment, deferred payment. *Waivers:* employees or children of employees.

Financial Aid Of all full-time matriculated undergraduates who enrolled in 2016, 1,669 applied for aid, 1,421 were judged to have need, 241 had their need fully met. 50 Federal Work-Study jobs (averaging $2355). In 2016, 124 non-need-based awards were made. *Average percent of need met:* 68. *Average financial aid package:* $8822. *Average need-based loan:* $3867. *Average need-based gift aid:* $7046. *Average non-need-based aid:* $2009. *Average indebtedness upon graduation:* $22,392.

APPLYING
Standardized Tests *Required:* SAT or ACT (for admission).

Options: electronic application, early admission, deferred entrance.

Application fee: $35.

Required: high school transcript, Core 40 high school curriculum for recent Indiana graduates, minimum of 28 semester hours of college preparatory courses for nonresidents. *Recommended:* minimum 2.0 GPA.

Application deadlines: rolling (freshmen), rolling (transfers).

Notification: continuous (freshmen), continuous (transfers).

CONTACT
Ms. Molly Vanderpool, Executive Director, Recruitment and Transitions, Admissions, Indiana University East, 2325 Chester Boulevard, Whitewater Hall 151, Richmond, IN 47374-1289. *Phone:* 765-973-8208. *Toll-free phone:* 800-959-EAST. *Fax:* 765-973-8209. *E-mail:* applynow@iue.edu.

Indiana University Kokomo
Kokomo, Indiana
http://www.iuk.edu/

- **State-supported** comprehensive, founded 1945, part of Indiana University System
- **Small-town** 52-acre campus with easy access to Indianapolis
- **Endowment** $6.0 million
- **Coed** 2,876 undergraduate students, 77% full-time, 64% women, 36% men
- **Minimally difficult** entrance level, 70% of applicants were admitted

UNDERGRAD STUDENTS
2,215 full-time, 661 part-time. Students come from 12 states and territories; 28 other countries; 2% are from out of state; 4% Black or African American, non-Hispanic/Latino; 5% Hispanic/Latino; 0.9% Asian, non-Hispanic/Latino; 0.1% Native Hawaiian or other Pacific Islander, non-Hispanic/Latino; 0.3% American Indian or Alaska Native, non-Hispanic/Latino; 3% Two or more races, non-Hispanic/Latino; 3% Race/ethnicity unknown; 1% international; 9% transferred in.

Freshmen:
Admission: 1,770 applied, 1,244 admitted, 605 enrolled. *Average high school GPA:* 3.2. *Test scores:* SAT evidence-based reading and writing scores over 500: 68%; SAT math scores over 500: 63%; ACT scores over 18: 72%; SAT evidence-based reading and writing scores over 600: 14%; SAT math scores over 600: 11%; ACT scores over 24: 17%; SAT evidence-based reading and writing scores over 700: 1%; SAT math scores over 700: 1%; ACT scores over 30: 1%.
Retention: 60% of full-time freshmen returned.

FACULTY

Total: 241, 51% full-time, 40% with terminal degrees.
Student/faculty ratio: 16:1.

ACADEMICS

Calendar: semesters. *Degrees:* certificates, associate, bachelor's, master's, and postbachelor's certificates.

Special study options: academic remediation for entering students, accelerated degree program, adult/continuing education programs, advanced placement credit, distance learning, double majors, English as a second language, external degree program, freshman honors college, honors programs, independent study, internships, part-time degree program, services for LD students, study abroad, summer session for credit. *ROTC:* Army (b).

Computers: 325 computers/terminals are available on campus for general student use. Students can access the following: campus intranet, computer help desk, free student e-mail accounts, online (class) grades, online (class) registration, online (class) schedules. Campuswide network is available. Wireless service is available via entire campus.
Library: IU Kokomo Library. *Books:* 93,410 (physical), 884,363 (digital/electronic); *Serial titles:* 1,512 (physical), 101,301 (digital/electronic); *Databases:* 367. Students can reserve study rooms.

STUDENT LIFE

Housing options: college housing not available.

Activities and organizations: drama/theater group, student-run newspaper, choral group, national sororities.

Athletics Member NAIA. *Intercollegiate sports:* baseball M, basketball M/W, cross-country running M/W, golf M/W, soccer W, tennis W, track and field M/W, volleyball W. *Intramural sports:* basketball M/W, cheerleading W(c), soccer M/W.

Campus security: 24-hour patrols, late-night transport/escort service, campus police, lighted pathways.

Student services: personal/psychological counseling.

COSTS & FINANCIAL AID

Costs (2018–19) *Tuition:* state resident $6727 full-time, $224 per credit hour part-time; nonresident $18,783 full-time, $626 per credit hour part-time. Full-time tuition and fees vary according to course load, location, and program. Part-time tuition and fees vary according to course load, location, and program. *Required fees:* $617 full-time.
Payment plans: installment, deferred payment. *Waivers:* employees or children of employees.

Financial Aid Of all full-time matriculated undergraduates who enrolled in 2016, 1,842 applied for aid, 1,475 were judged to have need, 227 had their need fully met. 99 Federal Work-Study jobs (averaging $1877). In 2016, 141 non-need-based awards were made. *Average percent of need met:* 67. *Average financial aid package:* $8575. *Average need-based loan:* $3552. *Average need-based gift aid:* $7246. *Average non-need-based aid:* $1414. *Average indebtedness upon graduation:* $23,664. *Financial aid deadline:* 6/30.

APPLYING

Standardized Tests *Required:* SAT or ACT (for admission).
Options: electronic application, deferred entrance.
Application fee: $35.
Required: high school transcript.
Notification: continuous (freshmen), continuous (transfers).

CONTACT

Ms. Angie Siders, Director of Admissions, Indiana University Kokomo, Kelley Student Center, Room 230, 2300 South Washington Street, Kokomo, IN 46904-9003. *Phone:* 765-455-9217. *Toll-free phone:* 888-875-4485. *Fax:* 765-455-9537. *E-mail:* iuadmis@iuk.edu.

Indiana University Northwest
Gary, Indiana
http://www.iun.edu/

- **State-supported** comprehensive, founded 1959, part of Indiana University System
- **Urban** 43-acre campus with easy access to Chicago
- **Endowment** $9.8 million
- **Coed** 3,700 undergraduate students, 70% full-time, 70% women, 30% men
- **Minimally difficult** entrance level, 74% of applicants were admitted

UNDERGRAD STUDENTS

2,608 full-time, 1,092 part-time. Students come from 9 states and territories; 36 other countries; 3% are from out of state; 18% Black or African American, non-Hispanic/Latino; 22% Hispanic/Latino; 3% Asian, non-Hispanic/Latino; 0.2% American Indian or Alaska Native, non-Hispanic/Latino; 3% Two or more races, non-Hispanic/Latino; 1% Race/ethnicity unknown; 0.5% international; 7% transferred in.

Freshmen:
Admission: 1,749 applied, 1,302 admitted, 606 enrolled. *Average high school GPA:* 3.0. *Test scores:* SAT evidence-based reading and writing scores over 500: 52%; SAT math scores over 500: 47%; ACT scores over 18: 74%; SAT evidence-based reading and writing scores over 600: 11%; SAT math scores over 600: 9%; ACT scores over 24: 18%; SAT evidence-based reading and writing scores over 700: 1%; SAT math scores over 700: 1%; ACT scores over 30: 3%.
Retention: 69% of full-time freshmen returned.

FACULTY

Total: 364, 45% full-time, 47% with terminal degrees.
Student/faculty ratio: 14:1.

ACADEMICS

Calendar: semesters. *Degrees:* certificates, associate, bachelor's, master's, and postbachelor's certificates.

Special study options: academic remediation for entering students, accelerated degree program, adult/continuing education programs, advanced placement credit, cooperative education, distance learning, double majors, external degree program, honors programs, independent study, internships, off-campus study, part-time degree program, services for LD students, student-designed majors, study abroad, summer session for credit. *ROTC:* Army (b).

Computers: 605 computers/terminals are available on campus for general student use. Students can access the following: campus intranet, computer help desk, free student e-mail accounts, online (class) grades, online (class) registration, online (class) schedules. Campuswide network is available. Wireless service is available via entire campus.
Library: IUN Library. *Books:* 500,000 (physical), 605,000 (digital/electronic); *Databases:* 325. Students can reserve study rooms.

STUDENT LIFE

Housing options: college housing not available.

Activities and organizations: drama/theater group, student-run newspaper, radio station, Student Government Association, Student Ambassadors, Art Club, Modern Languages Club, national fraternities, national sororities.

Athletics Member NAIA. *Intercollegiate sports:* basketball M(s)/W(s), cross-country running M(s)/W(s), golf M(s)/W(s), volleyball W(s).
Intramural sports: basketball M/W, cheerleading M(c)/W(c), cross-country running M(c)/W(c), football M(c)/W(c), ice hockey M(c)/W(c), soccer M(c)/W(c), softball M(c)/W(c), volleyball M/W.

Campus security: 24-hour emergency response devices and patrols, late-night transport/escort service, lighted pathways.

Student services: health clinic, personal/psychological counseling.

COSTS & FINANCIAL AID

Costs (2018–19) *Tuition:* state resident $6727 full-time, $224 per credit hour part-time; nonresident $18,783 full-time, $626 per credit hour part-time. Full-time tuition and fees vary according to course load, location, and program. Part-time tuition and fees vary according to course load, location, and program. *Required fees:* $617 full-time.
Payment plans: installment, deferred payment. *Waivers:* employees or children of employees.

Financial Aid Of all full-time matriculated undergraduates who enrolled in 2016, 2,342 applied for aid, 1,874 were judged to have need, 242 had their need fully met. 76 Federal Work-Study jobs (averaging $1769). In 2016, 218 non-need-based awards were made. *Average percent of need met:* 65. *Average financial aid package:* $8390. *Average need-based loan:* $3611. *Average need-based gift aid:* $7259. *Average non-need-based aid:* $3379. *Average indebtedness upon graduation:* $28,241.

APPLYING
Standardized Tests *Required:* SAT or ACT (for admission).
Options: electronic application, deferred entrance.
Application fee: $35.
Required: high school transcript, minimum 2.0 GPA.
Application deadlines: rolling (freshmen), rolling (transfers).
Notification: continuous (freshmen), continuous (transfers).

CONTACT
Office of Admissions, Indiana University Northwest, Hawthorn Hall 100, 3400 Broadway, Gary, IN 46408-1197. *Phone:* 219-980-6991. *Toll-free phone:* 800-968-7486. *Fax:* 219-981-4219. *E-mail:* admit@iun.edu.

Indiana University–Purdue University Fort Wayne

Fort Wayne, Indiana
http://www.ipfw.edu/

CONTACT
Angela Morren, Undergraduate Applications Coordinator, Indiana University–Purdue University Fort Wayne, 2101 East Coliseum Boulevard, Fort Wayne, IN 46805-1499. *Phone:* 260-481-6142. *Toll-free phone:* 800-324-4739. *Fax:* 260-481-6880. *E-mail:* morrena@ipfw.edu.

Indiana University–Purdue University Indianapolis

Indianapolis, Indiana
http://www.iupui.edu/

- **State-supported** university, founded 1969, part of Indiana University System
- **Urban** 534-acre campus with easy access to Indianapolis
- **Endowment** $928.6 million
- **Coed** 21,610 undergraduate students, 81% full-time, 56% women, 44% men
- **Moderately difficult** entrance level, 80% of applicants were admitted

UNDERGRAD STUDENTS
17,521 full-time, 4,089 part-time. Students come from 40 states and territories; 131 other countries; 4% are from out of state; 10% Black or African American, non-Hispanic/Latino; 7% Hispanic/Latino; 4% Asian, non-Hispanic/Latino; 0.1% Native Hawaiian or other Pacific Islander, non-Hispanic/Latino; 0.1% American Indian or Alaska Native, non-Hispanic/Latino; 4% Two or more races, non-Hispanic/Latino; 0.6% Race/ethnicity unknown; 4% international; 7% transferred in; 11% live on campus.

Freshmen:
Admission: 11,091 applied, 8,834 admitted, 4,093 enrolled. *Average high school GPA:* 3.5. *Test scores:* SAT evidence-based reading and writing scores over 500: 78%; SAT math scores over 500: 75%; ACT scores over 18: 87%; SAT evidence-based reading and writing scores over 600: 29%; SAT math scores over 600: 24%; ACT scores over 24: 44%; SAT evidence-based reading and writing scores over 700: 3%; SAT math scores over 700: 4%; ACT scores over 30: 7%.
Retention: 75% of full-time freshmen returned.

FACULTY
Total: 3,528, 68% full-time, 69% with terminal degrees.
Student/faculty ratio: 17:1.

ACADEMICS
Calendar: semesters. *Degrees:* certificates, associate, bachelor's, master's, doctoral, post-master's, and postbachelor's certificates.

Special study options: academic remediation for entering students, accelerated degree program, adult/continuing education programs, advanced placement credit, cooperative education, distance learning, double majors, English as a second language, external degree program, freshman honors college, honors programs, independent study, internships, off-campus study, part-time degree program, services for LD students, student-designed majors, study abroad, summer session for credit. *ROTC:* Army (b), Air Force (c).

Computers: 1,158 computers/terminals are available on campus for general student use. Students can access the following: campus intranet, computer help desk, free student e-mail accounts, online (class) grades, online (class) registration, online (class) schedules. Campuswide network is available. 100% of college-owned or -operated housing units are wired for high-speed Internet access. Wireless service is available via entire campus.
Library: University Library plus 4 others. *Books:* 1.2 million (physical), 918,183 (digital/electronic); *Serial titles:* 55,126 (physical), 64,180 (digital/electronic); *Databases:* 909. Study areas open 24 hours, 5–7 days a week; students can reserve study rooms.

STUDENT LIFE
Housing options: coed. Campus housing is university owned.
Activities and organizations: drama/theater group, student-run newspaper, choral group, national fraternities, national sororities.
Athletics Member NCAA. All Division I. *Intercollegiate sports:* basketball M(s)/W(s), cheerleading M/W, cross-country running M(s)/W(s), golf M(s)/W(s), soccer M(s)/W(s), softball W(s), swimming and diving M(s)/W(s), tennis M(s)/W(s), track and field M(s)/W(s), volleyball W(s). *Intramural sports:* baseball M(c)/W(c), basketball M/W, crew M(c)/W(c), cross-country running M/W, equestrian sports M(c)/W(c), fencing M(c)/W(c), football M/W, golf M/W, ice hockey M(c)/W(c), rowing M(c)/W(c), rugby M(c)/W(c), soccer M/W, softball M/W, swimming and diving M(c)/W(c), table tennis M(c)/W(c), tennis M(c)/W(c), ultimate Frisbee M/W, volleyball M/W.
Campus security: 24-hour emergency response devices and patrols, late-night transport/escort service, controlled dormitory access, lighted pathways, self-defense education.
Student services: health clinic, personal/psychological counseling, women's center.

COSTS & FINANCIAL AID
Costs (2018–19) *Tuition:* state resident $8371 full-time, $279 per credit hour part-time; nonresident $28,727 full-time, $958 per credit hour part-time. Full-time tuition and fees vary according to course load, location, and program. Part-time tuition and fees vary according to course load, location, and program. *Required fees:* $1094 full-time. *Room and board:* Room and board charges vary according to board plan and housing facility. *Payment plan:* deferred payment. *Waivers:* employees or children of employees.
Financial Aid Of all full-time matriculated undergraduates who enrolled in 2016, 14,280 applied for aid, 11,520 were judged to have need, 2,188 had their need fully met. 455 Federal Work-Study jobs (averaging $2408). In 2016, 1997 non-need-based awards were made. *Average percent of need met:* 67. *Average financial aid package:* $11,003. *Average need-based loan:* $4030. *Average need-based gift aid:* $9382. *Average non-need-based aid:* $5269. *Average indebtedness upon graduation:* $29,065.

APPLYING
Standardized Tests *Required:* SAT or ACT (for admission).
Options: electronic application.
Application fee: $65.
Required: high school transcript. *Required for some:* interview. *Recommended:* portfolio for art program.
Application deadlines: 5/1 (freshmen), rolling (transfers).
Notification: continuous (freshmen), continuous (transfers).

CONTACT
Indiana University–Purdue University Indianapolis, 420 University Boulevard, Campus Center 255, Indianapolis, IN 46202-5143. *Phone:* 317-274-4591. *Fax:* 317-278-1862. *E-mail:* apply@iupui.edu.

Indiana University South Bend
South Bend, Indiana
http://www.iusb.edu/

- **State-supported** comprehensive, founded 1922, part of Indiana University System
- **Suburban** 104-acre campus with easy access to Chicago
- **Endowment** $17.0 million
- **Coed** 4,876 undergraduate students, 77% full-time, 62% women, 38% men
- **Moderately difficult** entrance level, 78% of applicants were admitted

UNDERGRAD STUDENTS
3,767 full-time, 1,109 part-time. Students come from 20 states and territories; 43 other countries; 5% are from out of state; 8% Black or African American, non-Hispanic/Latino; 11% Hispanic/Latino; 2% Asian, non-Hispanic/Latino; 0.1% Native Hawaiian or other Pacific Islander, non-Hispanic/Latino; 0.3% American Indian or Alaska Native, non-Hispanic/Latino; 4% Two or more races, non-Hispanic/Latino; 0.7% Race/ethnicity unknown; 3% international; 7% transferred in; 8% live on campus.

Freshmen:
Admission: 2,580 applied, 2,005 admitted, 982 enrolled. *Average high school GPA:* 3.1. *Test scores:* SAT evidence-based reading and writing scores over 500: 62%; SAT math scores over 500: 56%; ACT scores over 18: 80%; SAT evidence-based reading and writing scores over 600: 17%; SAT math scores over 600: 11%; ACT scores over 24: 27%; SAT evidence-based reading and writing scores over 700: 2%; SAT math scores over 700: 1%; ACT scores over 30: 3%.
Retention: 66% of full-time freshmen returned.

FACULTY
Total: 453, 57% full-time, 55% with terminal degrees.
Student/faculty ratio: 13:1.

ACADEMICS
Calendar: semesters. *Degrees:* certificates, diplomas, associate, bachelor's, master's, and postbachelor's certificates.

Special study options: accelerated degree program, adult/continuing education programs, advanced placement credit, distance learning, double majors, English as a second language, external degree program, freshman honors college, honors programs, independent study, internships, off-campus study, part-time degree program, services for LD students, study abroad, summer session for credit. *ROTC:* Army (c), Navy (c), Air Force (c).

Computers: 780 computers/terminals are available on campus for general student use. Students can access the following: campus intranet, computer help desk, free student e-mail accounts, online (class) grades, online (class) registration, online (class) schedules. Campuswide network is available. 100% of college-owned or -operated housing units are wired for high-speed Internet access. Wireless service is available via entire campus.
Library: Franklin D. Schurz Library. *Books:* 354,095 (physical), 399,246 (digital/electronic); *Serial titles:* 7,369 (physical), 103,806 (digital/electronic); *Databases:* 307. Students can reserve study rooms.

STUDENT LIFE
Housing options: coed. Campus housing is university owned.

Activities and organizations: drama/theater group, student-run newspaper, choral group, national fraternities, national sororities.

Athletics Member NAIA. *Intercollegiate sports:* baseball M(s), basketball M(s)/W(s), cross-country running M(s)/W(s), golf M(s)/W(s), softball W(s), tennis M(s)/W(s), volleyball W(s). *Intramural sports:* archery M(c)/W(c), badminton M/W, basketball M/W, cheerleading M(c)/W(c), cross-country running M(c)/W(c), equestrian sports M(c)/W(c), football M/W, golf M(c)/W(c), racquetball M/W, soccer M(c)/W(c), softball M/W, table tennis M/W, volleyball M/W(c).

Campus security: 24-hour emergency response devices and patrols, late-night transport/escort service, safety seminars, lighted pathways.

Student services: health clinic, personal/psychological counseling, women's center.

COSTS & FINANCIAL AID
Costs (2018–19) *Tuition:* state resident $6727 full-time, $224 per credit hour part-time; nonresident $18,783 full-time, $626 per credit hour part-time. Full-time tuition and fees vary according to course load, location, and program. Part-time tuition and fees vary according to course load, location, and program. *Required fees:* $617 full-time. *Room and board:* Room and board charges vary according to housing facility. *Payment plans:* installment, deferred payment. *Waivers:* employees or children of employees.

Financial Aid Of all full-time matriculated undergraduates who enrolled in 2016, 3,235 applied for aid, 2,714 were judged to have need, 403 had their need fully met. 229 Federal Work-Study jobs (averaging $1973). In 2016, 295 non-need-based awards were made. *Average percent of need met:* 67. *Average financial aid package:* $8881. *Average need-based loan:* $3649. *Average need-based gift aid:* $7297. *Average non-need-based aid:* $2203. *Average indebtedness upon graduation:* $25,780.

APPLYING
Standardized Tests *Required:* SAT or ACT (for admission).
Options: electronic application, deferred entrance.
Application fee: $35.
Required: high school transcript, minimum 2.0 GPA. *Required for some:* interview.
Application deadlines: rolling (freshmen), rolling (transfers).
Notification: continuous (freshmen), continuous (transfers).

CONTACT
Ms. Constance Peterson-Miller, Director of Admissions, Indiana University South Bend, 1700 Mishawaka Avenue, PO Box 7111, South Bend, IN 46634-7111. *Phone:* 574-520-4839. *Toll-free phone:* 877-GO-2-IUSB. *Fax:* 574-520-4834. *E-mail:* admissions@iusb.edu.

 # Indiana University Southeast
New Albany, Indiana
http://www.ius.edu/

- **State-supported** comprehensive, founded 1941, part of Indiana University System
- **Suburban** 180-acre campus with easy access to Louisville
- **Endowment** $14.1 million
- **Coed** 4,823 undergraduate students, 67% full-time, 60% women, 40% men
- **Minimally difficult** entrance level, 83% of applicants were admitted

UNDERGRAD STUDENTS
3,218 full-time, 1,605 part-time. Students come from 20 states and territories; 43 other countries; 31% are from out of state; 7% Black or African American, non-Hispanic/Latino; 4% Hispanic/Latino; 1% Asian, non-Hispanic/Latino; 0.1% Native Hawaiian or other Pacific Islander, non-Hispanic/Latino; 0.1% American Indian or Alaska Native, non-Hispanic/Latino; 3% Two or more races, non-Hispanic/Latino; 0.6% Race/ethnicity unknown; 0.6% international; 8% transferred in; 8% live on campus.

Freshmen:
Admission: 2,273 applied, 1,881 admitted, 927 enrolled. *Average high school GPA:* 3.2. *Test scores:* SAT evidence-based reading and writing scores over 500: 69%; SAT math scores over 500: 64%; ACT scores over 18: 71%; SAT evidence-based reading and writing scores over 600: 17%; SAT math scores over 600: 10%; ACT scores over 24: 19%; SAT evidence-based reading and writing scores over 700: 2%; SAT math scores over 700: 1%; ACT scores over 30: 2%.
Retention: 59% of full-time freshmen returned.

FACULTY
Total: 438, 49% full-time, 54% with terminal degrees.
Student/faculty ratio: 14:1.

ACADEMICS
Calendar: semesters. *Degrees:* certificates, associate, bachelor's, master's, and postbachelor's certificates.

Special study options: academic remediation for entering students, accelerated degree program, adult/continuing education programs, advanced placement credit, distance learning, double majors, English as a second language, external degree program, honors programs, independent study, internships, off-campus study, part-time degree program, services for LD students, student-designed majors, study abroad, summer session for credit. *ROTC:* Army (c), Air Force (c).

Computers: 924 computers/terminals are available on campus for general student use. Students can access the following: campus intranet, computer help desk, free student e-mail accounts, online (class) grades, online (class) registration, online (class) schedules. Campuswide network is available. 100% of college-owned or -operated housing units are wired for high-speed Internet access. Wireless service is available via entire campus.

Library: IU Southeast Library. *Books:* 367,848 (physical), 904,000 (digital/electronic); *Serial titles:* 342 (physical), 183,000 (digital/electronic); *Databases:* 340. Students can reserve study rooms.

STUDENT LIFE
Housing options: coed. Campus housing is university owned.

Activities and organizations: drama/theater group, student-run newspaper, choral group, national fraternities, national sororities.

Athletics Member NAIA. *Intercollegiate sports:* baseball M(s), basketball M(s)/W(s), softball W(s), tennis M(s)/W(s), volleyball W(s). *Intramural sports:* basketball M/W, football M/W, golf M/W, soccer M/W, softball M/W, ultimate Frisbee M/W, volleyball M/W, weight lifting M.

Campus security: 24-hour emergency response devices and patrols, self-defense education, lighted pathways, police department on campus.

Student services: personal/psychological counseling.

COSTS & FINANCIAL AID
Costs (2018–19) *Tuition:* state resident $6727 full-time, $224 per credit hour part-time; nonresident $18,783 full-time, $626 per credit hour part-time. Full-time tuition and fees vary according to course load, location, program, and reciprocity agreements. Part-time tuition and fees vary according to course load, location, program, and reciprocity agreements. *Required fees:* $617 full-time. *Room and board:* Room and board charges vary according to board plan and housing facility. *Payment plans:* installment, deferred payment. *Waivers:* employees or children of employees.

Financial Aid Of all full-time matriculated undergraduates who enrolled in 2016, 2,780 applied for aid, 2,205 were judged to have need, 254 had their need fully met. 134 Federal Work-Study jobs (averaging $1494). In 2016, 234 non-need-based awards were made. *Average percent of need met:* 63. *Average financial aid package:* $8245. *Average need-based loan:* $3750. *Average need-based gift aid:* $6727. *Average non-need-based aid:* $1706. *Average indebtedness upon graduation:* $23,845.

APPLYING
Standardized Tests *Required:* SAT or ACT (for admission).
Options: electronic application, early admission, deferred entrance.
Application fee: $35.
Required: high school transcript. *Required for some:* interview.
Application deadlines: rolling (freshmen), rolling (transfers).
Notification: continuous (freshmen), continuous (transfers).

CONTACT
Ms. Christopher Crews, Director of Recruitment and Admission, Indiana University Southeast, University Center South Room 102, 4201 Grant Line Road, New Albany, IN 47150. *Phone:* 812-941-2212. *Toll-free phone:* 800-852-8835. *Fax:* 812-941-2595. *E-mail:* admissions@ius.edu.

Indiana Wesleyan University
Marion, Indiana
http://www.indwes.edu/
- **Independent Wesleyan** comprehensive, founded 1920
- **Small-town** 300-acre campus with easy access to Indianapolis
- **Coed** 2,799 undergraduate students, 94% full-time, 65% women, 35% men
- **Moderately difficult** entrance level, 72% of applicants were admitted

UNDERGRAD STUDENTS
2,634 full-time, 165 part-time. 4% Black or African American, non-Hispanic/Latino; 4% Hispanic/Latino; 2% Asian, non-Hispanic/Latino; 0.2% American Indian or Alaska Native, non-Hispanic/Latino; 4% Two or more races, non-Hispanic/Latino; 2% Race/ethnicity unknown; 1% international; 4% transferred in; 82% live on campus.

Freshmen:
Admission: 3,796 applied, 2,734 admitted, 787 enrolled. *Average high school GPA:* 3.6. *Test scores:* ACT scores over 18: 94%; ACT scores over 24: 51%; ACT scores over 30: 10%.
Retention: 82% of full-time freshmen returned.

FACULTY
Total: 267, 60% full-time, 54% with terminal degrees.
Student/faculty ratio: 13:1.

ACADEMICS
Calendar: semesters. *Degrees:* associate, bachelor's, master's, doctoral, post-master's, and postbachelor's certificates (also offers adult program with significant enrollment not reflected in profile).

Special study options: academic remediation for entering students, advanced placement credit, distance learning, double majors, freshman honors college, honors programs, independent study, internships, off-campus study, part-time degree program, services for LD students, study abroad, summer session for credit. *ROTC:* Army (b).

Computers: Students can access the following: campus intranet, computer help desk, free student e-mail accounts, online (class) grades, online (class) registration, online (class) schedules. Campuswide network is available. Wireless service is available via entire campus.
Library: Lewis A. Jackson Library. Students can reserve study rooms.

STUDENT LIFE
Housing options: on-campus residence required through junior year; men-only, women-only. Campus housing is university owned. Freshman campus housing is guaranteed.

Activities and organizations: drama/theater group, student-run newspaper, radio and television station, choral group, Student Government Organization, Student Activities Council, University Players, World Christian Fellowship, Sixth Man Club.

Athletics Member NAIA, NCCAA. *Intercollegiate sports:* baseball M(s), basketball M(s)/W(s), cheerleading M(s)/W(s), cross-country running M(s)/W(s), golf M(s)/W(s), soccer M(s)/W(s), softball W(s), swimming and diving W, tennis M(s)/W(s), track and field M(s)/W(s), volleyball W(s). *Intramural sports:* badminton M/W, basketball M/W, bowling M/W, football M, golf M/W, racquetball M/W, soccer M/W, softball M/W, swimming and diving M/W, table tennis M/W, tennis M/W, ultimate Frisbee M/W, volleyball M/W, weight lifting M/W.

Campus security: 24-hour emergency response devices and patrols, late-night transport/escort service, controlled dormitory access.

Student services: health clinic, personal/psychological counseling.

COSTS & FINANCIAL AID
Costs (2018–19) *Comprehensive fee:* $34,292 includes full-time tuition ($25,980) and room and board ($8312). Full-time tuition and fees vary according to course load and degree level. Part-time tuition: $555 per credit hour. Part-time tuition and fees vary according to course load and degree level. *College room only:* $4154. Room and board charges vary according to board plan. *Payment plans:* installment, deferred payment. *Waivers:* employees or children of employees.

Financial Aid Of all full-time matriculated undergraduates who enrolled in 2017, 2,323 applied for aid, 2,051 were judged to have need, 1,198 had their need fully met. In 2017, 271 non-need-based awards were made. *Average percent of need met:* 92. *Average financial aid package:* $29,681. *Average need-based loan:* $4009. *Average need-based gift aid:* $3548. *Average non-need-based aid:* $9802. *Average indebtedness upon graduation:* $30,355.

APPLYING
Standardized Tests *Required:* SAT or ACT (for admission). *Required for some:* TOEFL for non-English speaking and some non-resident alien students.
Options: electronic application, deferred entrance.
Required: essay or personal statement, high school transcript, minimum 2.5 GPA, 2 letters of recommendation.

CONTACT
Mr. Adam Farmer, Director of Admissions, Indiana Wesleyan University, 4201 South Washington Street, Marion, IN 46953. *Phone:* 866-468-6498

Ext. 2138. *Toll-free phone:* 866-468-6498. *E-mail:* admissions@ indwes.edu.

International Business College

Fort Wayne, Indiana
http://www.ibcfortwayne.edu/

CONTACT
Admissions Office, International Business College, 5699 Coventry Lane, Fort Wayne, IN 46804. *Phone:* 260-459-4500. *Toll-free phone:* 800-589-6363.

Manchester University

North Manchester, Indiana
http://www.manchester.edu/

- **Independent** comprehensive, founded 1889, affiliated with Church of the Brethren
- **Small-town** 125-acre campus
- **Endowment** $60.2 million
- **Coed** 1,262 undergraduate students, 99% full-time, 52% women, 48% men
- **Moderately difficult** entrance level, 62% of applicants were admitted

UNDERGRAD STUDENTS
1,244 full-time, 18 part-time. Students come from 20 states and territories; 19 other countries; 14% are from out of state; 7% Black or African American, non-Hispanic/Latino; 7% Hispanic/Latino; 1% Asian, non-Hispanic/Latino; 0.2% American Indian or Alaska Native, non-Hispanic/Latino; 4% Two or more races, non-Hispanic/Latino; 3% Race/ethnicity unknown; 4% international; 2% transferred in; 73% live on campus.

Freshmen:
Admission: 4,115 applied, 2,541 admitted, 397 enrolled. *Average high school GPA:* 3.4. *Test scores:* ACT scores over 18: 80%; ACT scores over 24: 32%; ACT scores over 30: 3%.
Retention: 63% of full-time freshmen returned.

FACULTY
Total: 112, 68% full-time, 68% with terminal degrees.
Student/faculty ratio: 14:1.

ACADEMICS
Calendar: 4-1-4. *Degrees:* associate, bachelor's, master's, and doctoral.
Special study options: accelerated degree program, advanced placement credit, distance learning, double majors, honors programs, independent study, internships, off-campus study, part-time degree program, services for LD students, student-designed majors, study abroad, summer session for credit.
Unusual degree programs: 3-2 engineering with Washington University in St. Louis, Purdue University, Ohio State University, Columbia University.
Computers: 226 computers/terminals are available on campus for general student use. Students can access the following: campus intranet, computer help desk, free student e-mail accounts, online (class) grades, online (class) registration, online (class) schedules. Campuswide network is available. 100% of college-owned or -operated housing units are wired for high-speed Internet access. Wireless service is available via classrooms, computer centers, computer labs, dorm rooms, learning centers, libraries, student centers.
Library: Funderburg Library. Study areas open 24 hours, 5–7 days a week.

STUDENT LIFE
Housing options: on-campus residence required through junior year; coed, special housing for students with disabilities. Campus housing is university owned. Freshman campus housing is guaranteed.
Activities and organizations: drama/theater group, student-run newspaper, radio station, choral group, College of Business Club, Manchester University Athletic Training Club, Fellowship of Christian Athletes, Student Education Association, Pre-Professionals of Science Club.
Athletics Member NCAA. All Division III. *Intercollegiate sports:* baseball M, basketball M/W, cheerleading W, cross-country running M/W,

football M, golf M/W, soccer M/W, softball W, swimming and diving M/W, tennis M/W, track and field M/W, volleyball W, wrestling M. *Intramural sports:* basketball M/W, football M/W, soccer M/W, softball M/W, volleyball M/W.
Campus security: 24-hour patrols, student patrols, late-night transport/escort service, alarm system, locked residence hall entrances.
Student services: health clinic, personal/psychological counseling.

COSTS & FINANCIAL AID
Costs (2018–19) *One-time required fee:* $250. *Comprehensive fee:* $42,338 includes full-time tuition ($31,500), mandatory fees ($1258), and room and board ($9580). Part-time tuition: $725 per credit hour. Part-time tuition and fees vary according to course load. *Required fees:* $35 per credit hour part-time. *College room only:* $5250. Room and board charges vary according to board plan and housing facility. *Payment plan:* installment. *Waivers:* employees or children of employees.
Financial Aid Of all full-time matriculated undergraduates who enrolled in 2017, 1,132 applied for aid, 1,043 were judged to have need, 127 had their need fully met. In 2017, 67 non-need-based awards were made. *Average percent of need met:* 86. *Average financial aid package:* $30,161. *Average need-based loan:* $3907. *Average need-based gift aid:* $24,312. *Average non-need-based aid:* $17,676. *Average indebtedness upon graduation:* $32,920.

APPLYING
Options: electronic application, deferred entrance.
Application fee: $25.
Required: high school transcript, 1 letter of recommendation, rank in upper 50% of high school class. *Required for some:* minimum 3.0 GPA. *Recommended:* minimum 2.3 GPA.
Application deadlines: rolling (freshmen), rolling (transfers).
Notification: continuous (freshmen), continuous (transfers).

CONTACT
Ms. Brandi Chauncey, Director of Admissions, Manchester University, 604 East College Ave., North Manchester, IN 46962. *Phone:* 260-982-5232. *Toll-free phone:* 800-852-3648. *E-mail:* bcchauncey@ manchester.edu.

Marian University

Indianapolis, Indiana
http://www.marian.edu/

- **Independent Roman Catholic** comprehensive, founded 1851
- **Suburban** 114-acre campus with easy access to Indianapolis
- **Endowment** $47.1 million
- **Coed** 2,303 undergraduate students, 85% full-time, 62% women, 38% men
- **Moderately difficult** entrance level, 59% of applicants were admitted

UNDERGRAD STUDENTS
1,961 full-time, 342 part-time. Students come from 36 states and territories; 18 other countries; 23% are from out of state; 11% Black or African American, non-Hispanic/Latino; 5% Hispanic/Latino; 2% Asian, non-Hispanic/Latino; 0.2% Native Hawaiian or other Pacific Islander, non-Hispanic/Latino; 0.2% American Indian or Alaska Native, non-Hispanic/Latino; 3% Two or more races, non-Hispanic/Latino; 3% Race/ethnicity unknown; 1% international; 7% transferred in; 40% live on campus.

Freshmen:
Admission: 2,246 applied, 1,320 admitted, 338 enrolled. *Average high school GPA:* 3.5. *Test scores:* SAT evidence-based reading and writing scores over 500: 77%; SAT math scores over 500: 76%; ACT scores over 18: 91%; SAT evidence-based reading and writing scores over 600: 27%; SAT math scores over 600: 27%; ACT scores over 24: 39%; SAT evidence-based reading and writing scores over 700: 2%; SAT math scores over 700: 3%; ACT scores over 30: 5%.
Retention: 78% of full-time freshmen returned.

FACULTY
Total: 270, 56% full-time, 50% with terminal degrees.
Student/faculty ratio: 14:1.

ACADEMICS

Calendar: semesters. *Degrees:* associate, bachelor's, master's, and doctoral.

Special study options: academic remediation for entering students, accelerated degree program, adult/continuing education programs, advanced placement credit, cooperative education, distance learning, double majors, honors programs, independent study, internships, off-campus study, part-time degree program, services for LD students, study abroad, summer session for credit. *ROTC:* Army (c).

Computers: 118 computers/terminals are available on campus for general student use. Students can access the following: computer help desk, free student e-mail accounts, online (class) grades, online (class) registration, online (class) schedules. Campuswide network is available. 100% of college-owned or -operated housing units are wired for high-speed Internet access. Wireless service is available via entire campus.

Library: Mother Theresa Hackelmeier Memorial Library. *Books:* 80,118 (physical); *Serial titles:* 150 (physical), 44,749 (digital/electronic). Weekly public service hours: 95.

STUDENT LIFE

Housing options: on-campus residence required through junior year; coed. Campus housing is university owned. Freshman campus housing is guaranteed.

Activities and organizations: drama/theater group, student-run newspaper, choral group, marching band, Student Government Association, College Mentors for Kids, Best Buddies, Knight Nation, Sophia Club.

Athletics Member NAIA. *Intercollegiate sports:* baseball M(s), basketball M(s)/W(s), bowling M(s)/W(s), cheerleading M(s)(c)/W(s)(c), cross-country running M(s)/W(s), football M(s), golf M(s)/W(s), lacrosse W(s), soccer M(s)/W(s), softball W(s), tennis M(s)/W(s), track and field M(s)/W(s), volleyball W(s), wrestling M(s). *Intramural sports:* basketball M/W, cheerleading M/W, football M/W, ultimate Frisbee M/W, volleyball M/W.

Campus security: 24-hour emergency response devices and patrols, student patrols, late-night transport/escort service, controlled dormitory access.

Student services: health clinic, personal/psychological counseling.

COSTS & FINANCIAL AID

Costs (2018–19) *Comprehensive fee:* $44,640 includes full-time tuition ($34,000) and room and board ($10,640). Part-time tuition: $1500 per credit hour. *College room only:* $5200. Room and board charges vary according to housing facility. *Payment plan:* installment. *Waivers:* children of alumni and employees or children of employees.

Financial Aid Of all full-time matriculated undergraduates who enrolled in 2008, 1,192 applied for aid, 1,068 were judged to have need, 231 had their need fully met. 200 Federal Work-Study jobs (averaging $1500). In 2008, 185 non-need-based awards were made. *Average percent of need met:* 75. *Average financial aid package:* $19,509. *Average need-based loan:* $4478. *Average need-based gift aid:* $11,188. *Average non-need-based aid:* $12,191. *Average indebtedness upon graduation:* $23,467.

APPLYING

Standardized Tests *Required:* SAT or ACT (for admission).

Options: electronic application, deferred entrance.

Application fee: $35.

Required: high school transcript, college transcripts for transfer students. *Required for some:* essay or personal statement, 1 letter of recommendation, interview.

Application deadlines: 8/1 (freshmen), 8/1 (transfers).

Notification: continuous (freshmen), continuous (out-of-state freshmen), continuous (transfers).

CONTACT

Ms. Luann Brames, Director of Freshmen Admission, Marian University, 3200 Cold Spring Road, Indianapolis, IN 46222-1997. *Phone:* 317-955-6300. *Toll-free phone:* 800-772-7264. *Fax:* 317-955-6401. *E-mail:* admissions@marian.edu.

Martin University
Indianapolis, Indiana
http://www.martin.edu/

CONTACT
Ms. Brenda Shaheed, Director of Enrollment Management, Martin University, 2171 Avondale Place, PO Box 18567, Indianapolis, IN 46218-3867. *Phone:* 317-543-3237. *Fax:* 317-543-4790.

Mid-America College of Funeral Service
Jeffersonville, Indiana
http://www.mid-america.edu/

CONTACT
Mr. Richard Nelson, Dean of Students, Mid-America College of Funeral Service, 3111 Hamburg Pike, Jeffersonville, IN 47130-9630. *Phone:* 812-288-8878. *Toll-free phone:* 800-221-6158. *Fax:* 812-288-5942. *E-mail:* macfs@mindspring.com.

National American University
Indianapolis, Indiana
http://www.national.edu/

CONTACT
Dr. Rhonda Parker, Campus Director, National American University, 3600 Woodview Trace, Suite 200, Indianapolis, IN 46268. *Phone:* 317-578-7353. *Toll-free phone:* 800-609-1430.

Oakland City University
Oakland City, Indiana
http://www.oak.edu/
- **Independent General Baptist** comprehensive, founded 1885
- **Rural** 20-acre campus
- **Endowment** $5.0 million
- **Coed** 1,113 undergraduate students, 51% full-time, 56% women, 44% men
- **Minimally difficult** entrance level, 67% of applicants were admitted

UNDERGRAD STUDENTS
572 full-time, 541 part-time. Students come from 18 states and territories; 11 other countries; 19% are from out of state; 6% Black or African American, non-Hispanic/Latino; 2% Hispanic/Latino; 0.2% Asian, non-Hispanic/Latino; 0.4% American Indian or Alaska Native, non-Hispanic/Latino; 1% Two or more races, non-Hispanic/Latino; 10% Race/ethnicity unknown; 3% international; 4% transferred in; 36% live on campus.

Freshmen:
Admission: 595 applied, 399 admitted, 99 enrolled. *Average high school GPA:* 3.3. *Test scores:* SAT evidence-based reading and writing scores over 500: 66%; SAT math scores over 500: 69%; ACT scores over 18: 79%; SAT evidence-based reading and writing scores over 600: 18%; SAT math scores over 600: 15%; ACT scores over 24: 25%.
Retention: 76% of full-time freshmen returned.

FACULTY
Total: 187, 19% full-time.
Student/faculty ratio: 12:1.

ACADEMICS
Calendar: semesters. *Degrees:* certificates, associate, bachelor's, master's, and doctoral.

Special study options: academic remediation for entering students, accelerated degree program, adult/continuing education programs, advanced placement credit, distance learning, external degree program, part-time degree program, services for LD students, summer session for credit.

Computers: 200 computers/terminals are available on campus for general student use. Students can access the following: campus intranet, computer help desk, free student e-mail accounts, online (class) grades, online

COLLEGES AT-A-GLANCE

(class) registration, online (class) schedules. Campuswide network is available. Wireless service is available via entire campus.
Library: Barger-Richardson Library. *Books:* 84,412 (physical), 17,690 (digital/electronic); *Serial titles:* 79 (physical), 50,255 (digital/electronic); *Databases:* 52.

STUDENT LIFE
Housing options: men-only, women-only. Campus housing is university owned. Freshman campus housing is guaranteed.

Activities and organizations: drama/theater group, student-run newspaper, choral group, Student Government Association, Good News Players, Art Guild, FOCUS, intramural sports.

Athletics Member NCAA, NCCAA. All NCAA Division II. *Intercollegiate sports:* baseball M(s), basketball M(s)/W(s), cheerleading W(s), cross-country running M(s)/W(s), golf M(s)/W(s), soccer M(s)/W(s), softball W(s), tennis M(s)/W(s), volleyball W(s). *Intramural sports:* basketball M/W, bowling M/W, football M/W, softball M/W, table tennis M/W, tennis M/W, volleyball M/W.

Campus security: 24-hour patrols, student patrols.

Student services: personal/psychological counseling.

COSTS & FINANCIAL AID
Costs (2018–19) *Comprehensive fee:* $33,900 includes full-time tuition ($24,000) and room and board ($9900). Full-time tuition and fees vary according to degree level. Part-time tuition: $800 per credit hour. *Room and board:* Room and board charges vary according to board plan and housing facility. *Payment plan:* deferred payment. *Waivers:* employees or children of employees.

Financial Aid Of all full-time matriculated undergraduates who enrolled in 2016, 435 applied for aid, 435 were judged to have need. *Average percent of need met:* 34. *Average financial aid package:* $21,053. *Average need-based gift aid:* $11,567.

APPLYING
Standardized Tests *Required for some:* SAT or ACT (for admission).

Options: electronic application, early admission, deferred entrance.

Application fee: $35.

Required: high school transcript, minimum 2.0 GPA. *Recommended:* essay or personal statement, interview.

CONTACT
Miss Jennifer Cates, Assistant Director of Admissions, Oakland City University, 138 North Lucretia Street, Oakland City, IN 47660. *Phone:* 812-749-1220. *Toll-free phone:* 800-737-5125. *E-mail:* jcates@oak.edu.

Purdue University
West Lafayette, Indiana
http://www.purdue.edu/

- **State-supported** university, founded 1869, part of Purdue University System
- **Suburban** 2660-acre campus with easy access to Indianapolis
- **Endowment** $2.4 billion
- **Coed** 31,006 undergraduate students, 96% full-time, 43% women, 57% men
- **Moderately difficult** entrance level, 57% of applicants were admitted

UNDERGRAD STUDENTS
29,629 full-time, 1,377 part-time. Students come from 44 states and territories; 104 other countries; 36% are from out of state; 3% Black or African American, non-Hispanic/Latino; 5% Hispanic/Latino; 8% Asian, non-Hispanic/Latino; 0.1% Native Hawaiian or other Pacific Islander, non-Hispanic/Latino; 0.1% American Indian or Alaska Native, non-Hispanic/Latino; 3% Two or more races, non-Hispanic/Latino; 2% Race/ethnicity unknown; 16% international; 3% transferred in; 40% live on campus.

Freshmen:
Admission: 48,912 applied, 28,092 admitted, 7,566 enrolled. *Average high school GPA:* 3.8. *Test scores:* SAT evidence-based reading and writing scores over 500: 97%; SAT math scores over 500: 97%; ACT scores over 18: 99%; SAT evidence-based reading and writing scores over 600: 65%; SAT math scores over 600: 69%; ACT scores over 24: 85%; SAT evidence-based reading and writing scores over 700: 16%; SAT math scores over 700: 31%; ACT scores over 30: 40%.

Retention: 92% of full-time freshmen returned.

FACULTY
Total: 2,642, 87% full-time, 96% with terminal degrees.
Student/faculty ratio: 13:1.

ACADEMICS
Calendar: semesters. *Degrees:* certificates, associate, bachelor's, master's, doctoral, post-master's, and postbachelor's certificates.

Special study options: accelerated degree program, adult/continuing education programs, cooperative education, distance learning, double majors, English as a second language, honors programs, independent study, part-time degree program, services for LD students, study abroad, summer session for credit. *ROTC:* Army (b), Navy (b), Air Force (b).

Unusual degree programs: 3-2 business administration; engineering; forestry; nursing; social work; pharmacy.

Computers: 5,237 computers/terminals and 77,239 ports are available on campus for general student use. Students can access the following: campus intranet, free student e-mail accounts, online (class) grades, online (class) schedules. Campuswide network is available. 100% of college-owned or -operated housing units are wired for high-speed Internet access. Wireless service is available via entire campus.
Library: Purdue University Libraries plus 9 others. *Books:* 968,500 (physical), 2.2 million (digital/electronic); *Serial titles:* 34,790 (physical), 123,000 (digital/electronic); *Databases:* 575. Weekly public service hours: 168; study areas open 24 hours, 5–7 days a week; students can reserve study rooms.

STUDENT LIFE
Housing options: coed, men-only, women-only, cooperative, special housing for students with disabilities. Campus housing is university owned. Freshman applicants given priority for college housing.

Activities and organizations: drama/theater group, student-run newspaper, radio station, choral group, marching band, Purdue Student Government, FSCL Councils, RHA, Society of Women Engineers, AG Council, national fraternities, national sororities.

Athletics Member NCAA. All Division I except football (Division I-A). *Intercollegiate sports:* baseball M(s), basketball M(s)/W(s), cross-country running M(s)/W(s), golf M(s)/W(s), soccer W(s), softball W(s), swimming and diving M(s)/W(s), tennis M(s)/W(s), track and field M(s)/W(s), volleyball W(s), wrestling M(s). *Intramural sports:* archery M(c)/W(c), badminton M(c)/W(c), baseball M(c), basketball M(c)/W(c), bowling M(c)/W(c), crew M(c)/W(c), cross-country running M(c)/W(c), equestrian sports M(c)/W(c), fencing M(c)/W(c), gymnastics M(c)/W(c), ice hockey M(c), lacrosse M(c)/W(c), racquetball M(c)/W(c), riflery M(c)/W(c), rock climbing M(c)/W(c), rugby M(c)/W(c), sailing M(c)/W(c), soccer M(c)/W(c), squash M(c)/W(c), swimming and diving M(c)/W(c), table tennis M(c)/W(c), tennis M(c)/W(c), track and field M(c)/W(c), ultimate Frisbee M(c)/W(c), volleyball M(c)/W(c), water polo M(c)/W(c).

Campus security: 24-hour emergency response devices and patrols, student patrols, late-night transport/escort service, controlled dormitory access.

Student services: health clinic, personal/psychological counseling, women's center, legal services.

COSTS & FINANCIAL AID
Costs (2018–19) *Tuition:* state resident $9208 full-time, $330 per credit hour part-time; nonresident $28,010 full-time, $930 per credit hour part-time. Full-time tuition and fees vary according to course load and program. Part-time tuition and fees vary according to course load. *Required fees:* $784 full-time, $18 per credit hour part-time. *Room and board:* $10,030; room only: $4860. Room and board charges vary according to board plan and housing facility. *Payment plan:* installment. *Waivers:* senior citizens and employees or children of employees.

Financial Aid Of all full-time matriculated undergraduates who enrolled in 2016, 16,737 applied for aid, 11,986 were judged to have need, 5,636 had their need fully met. 1,772 Federal Work-Study jobs (averaging $2229). In 2016, 3772 non-need-based awards were made. *Average percent of need met:* 85. *Average financial aid package:* $13,849. *Average need-based loan:* $5117. *Average need-based gift aid:* $13,404. *Average non-need-based aid:* $5959. *Average indebtedness upon graduation:* $27,530.

Indiana

COLLEGES AT-A-GLANCE

APPLYING

Standardized Tests *Required:* SAT or ACT (for admission).

Options: electronic application, early admission, early action, deferred entrance.

Application fee: $60.

Required: essay or personal statement, high school transcript.

Application deadlines: rolling (freshmen), rolling (transfers), 11/1 (early action).

Notification: 12/12 (freshmen), 12/12 (early action).

CONTACT

Ms. Kristina M Wong Davis, Vice Provost for Enrollment Management, Purdue University, 475 Stadium Mall Drive, Schleman Hall, West Lafayette, IN 47907-2050. *Phone:* 765-494-9116. *Fax:* 765-494-0544. *E-mail:* admissions@purdue.edu.

Purdue University Northwest

Hammond, Indiana

http://www.pnw.edu/

- **State-supported** comprehensive, founded 2016, part of Purdue University System
- **Urban** 454-acre campus with easy access to Chicago
- **Coed** 11,134 undergraduate students, 55% full-time, 57% women, 43% men
- **Moderately difficult** entrance level, 92% of applicants were admitted

UNDERGRAD STUDENTS

6,172 full-time, 4,962 part-time. Students come from 32 states and territories; 44 other countries; 9% are from out of state; 10% Black or African American, non-Hispanic/Latino; 18% Hispanic/Latino; 2% Asian, non-Hispanic/Latino; 0.1% Native Hawaiian or other Pacific Islander, non-Hispanic/Latino; 0.2% American Indian or Alaska Native, non-Hispanic/Latino; 3% Two or more races, non-Hispanic/Latino; 1% Race/ethnicity unknown; 4% international; 9% transferred in; 6% live on campus.

Freshmen:

Admission: 1,984 applied, 1,823 admitted, 1,125 enrolled. *Average high school GPA:* 3.4. *Test scores:* SAT evidence-based reading and writing scores over 500: 74%; SAT math scores over 500: 69%; ACT scores over 18: 85%; SAT evidence-based reading and writing scores over 600: 21%; SAT math scores over 600: 16%; ACT scores over 24: 31%; SAT evidence-based reading and writing scores over 700: 1%; SAT math scores over 700: 1%; ACT scores over 30: 3%.

Retention: 68% of full-time freshmen returned.

FACULTY

Total: 706, 54% full-time, 44% with terminal degrees.

Student/faculty ratio: 16:1.

ACADEMICS

Calendar: semesters. *Degrees:* certificates, associate, bachelor's, master's, doctoral, post-master's, and postbachelor's certificates.

Special study options: academic remediation for entering students, accelerated degree program, adult/continuing education programs, advanced placement credit, cooperative education, distance learning, double majors, English as a second language, freshman honors college, honors programs, independent study, internships, part-time degree program, services for LD students, study abroad, summer session for credit. *ROTC:* Army (b).

Computers: 1,700 computers/terminals and 1,700 ports are available on campus for general student use. Students can access the following: campus intranet, computer help desk, free student e-mail accounts, online (class) grades, online (class) registration, online (class) schedules. Campuswide network is available. 100% of college-owned or -operated housing units are wired for high-speed Internet access. Wireless service is available via entire campus.

Library: Purdue University Northwest Libraries plus 2 others. *Books:* 261,544 (physical), 55,227 (digital/electronic); *Serial titles:* 4,010 (physical), 80,047 (digital/electronic); *Databases:* 174. Weekly public service hours: 138.

STUDENT LIFE

Housing options: coed. Campus housing is university owned.

Activities and organizations: drama/theater group, student-run newspaper, choral group, Black Student Union, Women in Business, National Society of Black Engineers, American Sign Language Club, Student Athlete Advisory Committee, national fraternities, national sororities.

Athletics Member NCAA, NAIA. All NCAA Division II. *Intercollegiate sports:* baseball M(s), basketball M(s)/W(s), cross-country running M(s)/W(s), golf M(s)/W(s), soccer M(s)/W(s), softball W(s), tennis M(s)/W(s), volleyball W(s). *Intramural sports:* badminton M/W, basketball M/W, bowling M/W, football M/W, golf M/W, racquetball M/W, soccer M/W, softball M/W, table tennis M/W, ultimate Frisbee M/W, volleyball M/W, weight lifting M/W, wrestling M/W.

Campus security: 24-hour emergency response devices and patrols, student patrols, late-night transport/escort service, controlled dormitory access.

Student services: health clinic, personal/psychological counseling.

COSTS & FINANCIAL AID

Costs (2017–18) *Tuition:* state resident $6839 full-time, $228 per credit hour part-time; nonresident $16,386 full-time, $546 per credit hour part-time. Full-time tuition and fees vary according to course level and program. Part-time tuition and fees vary according to program. *Required fees:* $743 full-time, $25 per credit hour part-time. *Room and board:* $7597; room only: $5595. Room and board charges vary according to housing facility. *Payment plans:* installment, deferred payment. *Waivers:* senior citizens and employees or children of employees.

Financial Aid Of all full-time matriculated undergraduates who enrolled in 2014, 4,236 applied for aid, 3,567 were judged to have need, 172 had their need fully met. 105 Federal Work-Study jobs (averaging $2322). In 2014, 215 non-need-based awards were made. *Average percent of need met:* 11. *Average financial aid package:* $7768. *Average need-based loan:* $3388. *Average need-based gift aid:* $5782. *Average non-need-based aid:* $3124. *Average indebtedness upon graduation:* $27,902.

APPLYING

Standardized Tests *Required:* SAT or ACT (for admission).

Options: electronic application.

Application fee: $25.

Required: high school transcript, minimum 2.0 GPA.

Application deadlines: 8/1 (freshmen), 8/1 (transfers).

Notification: continuous (freshmen), continuous (out-of-state freshmen), continuous (transfers).

CONTACT

Purdue University Northwest, 2200 169th Street, Hammond, IN 46323-2094. *Phone:* 219-989-2768. *Toll-free phone:* 800-447-8738.

Rose-Hulman Institute of Technology

Terre Haute, Indiana

http://www.rose-hulman.edu/

- **Independent** comprehensive, founded 1874
- **Suburban** 200-acre campus with easy access to Indianapolis
- **Endowment** $206.2 million
- **Coed, primarily men** 2,168 undergraduate students, 99% full-time, 25% women, 75% men
- **Very difficult** entrance level, 61% of applicants were admitted

UNDERGRAD STUDENTS

2,147 full-time, 21 part-time. Students come from 49 states and territories; 11 other countries; 64% are from out of state; 3% Black or African American, non-Hispanic/Latino; 5% Hispanic/Latino; 5% Asian, non-Hispanic/Latino; 0.1% Native Hawaiian or other Pacific Islander, non-Hispanic/Latino; 0.1% American Indian or Alaska Native, non-Hispanic/Latino; 5% Two or more races, non-Hispanic/Latino; 0.6% Race/ethnicity unknown; 15% international; 0.9% transferred in; 58% live on campus.

Freshmen:

Admission: 4,473 applied, 2,726 admitted, 557 enrolled. *Average high school GPA:* 4.0. *Test scores:* SAT evidence-based reading and writing scores over 500: 99%; SAT math scores over 500: 100%; ACT scores over 18: 100%; SAT evidence-based reading and writing scores over 600: 77%; SAT math scores over 600: 94%; ACT scores over 24: 97%; SAT

A ★ *indicates that the school has detailed information with a Premium Profile on Petersons.com.*   **www.petersons.com 351**

COLLEGES AT-A-GLANCE

evidence-based reading and writing scores over 700: 23%; SAT math scores over 700: 52%; ACT scores over 30: 53%.

Retention: 91% of full-time freshmen returned.

FACULTY

Total: 202, 94% full-time, 99% with terminal degrees.

Student/faculty ratio: 11:1.

ACADEMICS

Calendar: quarters. *Degrees:* bachelor's and master's.

Special study options: accelerated degree program, adult/continuing education programs, advanced placement credit, cooperative education, double majors, English as a second language, independent study, off-campus study, services for LD students, study abroad, summer session for credit. *ROTC:* Army (b), Air Force (b).

Computers: 48 computers/terminals and 8,000 ports are available on campus for general student use. Students can access the following: campus intranet, computer help desk, free student e-mail accounts, online (class) grades, online (class) registration, online (class) schedules. Campuswide network is available. 100% of college-owned or -operated housing units are wired for high-speed Internet access. Wireless service is available via classrooms, computer centers, computer labs, dorm rooms, learning centers, libraries, student centers.

Library: John A. Logan Library. *Books:* 29,406 (physical), 301,291 (digital/electronic); *Serial titles:* 42 (physical), 41,278 (digital/electronic); *Databases:* 33. Weekly public service hours: 101; students can reserve study rooms.

STUDENT LIFE

Housing options: on-campus residence required for freshman year; coed, men-only. Campus housing is university owned. Freshman applicants given priority for college housing.

Activities and organizations: drama/theater group, student-run newspaper, radio station, choral group, Residence Hall Association, Student Activities Board, Branam Innovation Center competition teams, Drama Club, Diversity organizations, national fraternities, national sororities.

Athletics Member NCAA. All Division III. *Intercollegiate sports:* baseball M, basketball M/W, cross-country running M/W, football M, golf M/W, soccer M/W, softball W, swimming and diving M/W, tennis M/W, track and field M/W, volleyball W. *Intramural sports:* badminton M/W, basketball M/W, bowling M/W, cross-country running M/W, golf M/W, lacrosse M(c)/W(c), racquetball M/W, skiing (downhill) M(c)/W(c), soccer M/W, softball M/W, swimming and diving M/W, table tennis M/W, tennis M/W, track and field M/W, ultimate Frisbee M/W, volleyball M/W.

Campus security: 24-hour emergency response devices and patrols, late-night transport/escort service, controlled dormitory access.

Student services: health clinic, personal/psychological counseling.

COSTS & FINANCIAL AID

Costs (2017–18) *One-time required fee:* $2250. *Comprehensive fee:* $59,823 includes full-time tuition ($44,847), mandatory fees ($915), and room and board ($14,061). Full-time tuition and fees vary according to course load. Part-time tuition: $1309 per credit hour. Part-time tuition and fees vary according to course load. *College room only:* $8559. Room and board charges vary according to board plan. *Payment plans:* tuition prepayment, installment. *Waivers:* employees or children of employees.

Financial Aid Of all full-time matriculated undergraduates who enrolled in 2017, 1,431 applied for aid, 1,241 were judged to have need, 988 had their need fully met. 742 Federal Work-Study jobs (averaging $1272). In 2017, 871 non-need-based awards were made. *Average percent of need met:* 69. *Average financial aid package:* $30,070. *Average need-based loan:* $5716. *Average need-based gift aid:* $26,898. *Average non-need-based aid:* $12,343. *Average indebtedness upon graduation:* $45,345.

APPLYING

Standardized Tests *Required:* SAT or ACT (for admission).

Options: electronic application, early action, deferred entrance.

Application fee: $50.

Required: essay or personal statement, high school transcript, 1 letter of recommendation, curricular prerequisites.

Application deadlines: 2/1 (freshmen), 11/1 (early action).

Notification: 3/15 (freshmen), continuous (transfers), 12/16 (early action).

CONTACT

Mrs. Lisa Norton, Dean of Admissions, Rose-Hulman Institute of Technology, 5500 Wabash Avenue, CM 1, Terre Haute, IN 47803-3920. *Phone:* 812-877-8213. *Toll-free phone:* 800-248-7448. *Fax:* 812-877-8941. *E-mail:* admissions@rose-hulman.edu.

Saint Mary-of-the-Woods College
Saint Mary of the Woods, Indiana
http://www.smwc.edu/

- **Independent Roman Catholic** comprehensive, founded 1840
- **Rural** 67-acre campus with easy access to Indianapolis
- **Coed, primarily women** 756 undergraduate students, 53% full-time, 90% women, 10% men
- **Minimally difficult** entrance level, 75% of applicants were admitted

UNDERGRAD STUDENTS

397 full-time, 359 part-time. 28% are from out of state; 4% Black or African American, non-Hispanic/Latino; 2% Hispanic/Latino; 1% Asian, non-Hispanic/Latino; 0.3% Native Hawaiian or other Pacific Islander, non-Hispanic/Latino; 0.6% American Indian or Alaska Native, non-Hispanic/Latino; 2% Two or more races, non-Hispanic/Latino; 9% Race/ethnicity unknown; 0.8% international; 12% transferred in; 42% live on campus.

Freshmen:

Admission: 578 applied, 434 admitted, 135 enrolled. *Average high school GPA:* 3.3. *Test scores:* SAT evidence-based reading and writing scores over 500: 52%; SAT math scores over 500: 47%; ACT scores over 18: 76%; SAT evidence-based reading and writing scores over 600: 11%; SAT math scores over 600: 11%; ACT scores over 24: 24%; ACT scores over 30: 2%.

Retention: 66% of full-time freshmen returned.

FACULTY

Total: 142, 35% full-time.

Student/faculty ratio: 7:1.

ACADEMICS

Calendar: semesters. *Degrees:* certificates, associate, bachelor's, master's, and postbachelor's certificates (also offers external degree program with significant enrollment not reflected in profile).

Special study options: academic remediation for entering students, accelerated degree program, adult/continuing education programs, advanced placement credit, distance learning, double majors, external degree program, honors programs, independent study, internships, off-campus study, part-time degree program, services for LD students, student-designed majors, study abroad, summer session for credit. *ROTC:* Army (c), Navy (c), Air Force (c).

Unusual degree programs: 3-2 business administration.

Computers: Students can access the following: campus intranet, computer help desk, free student e-mail accounts, online (class) grades, online (class) schedules. Campuswide network is available. 100% of college-owned or -operated housing units are wired for high-speed Internet access. Wireless service is available via entire campus.

Library: Rooney Library.

STUDENT LIFE

Housing options: on-campus residence required through senior year; coed, special housing for students with disabilities. Campus housing is university owned. Freshman campus housing is guaranteed.

Activities and organizations: drama/theater group, student-run newspaper, choral group.

Athletics Member USCAA. *Intercollegiate sports:* basketball W(s), cross-country running W(s), equestrian sports W(s), golf W(s), soccer W(s), softball W(s).

Campus security: 24-hour emergency response devices and patrols, late-night transport/escort service, Resident Assistants (RAs) patrol the residence hall 3-4 times per night.

Student services: health clinic, personal/psychological counseling.

COSTS & FINANCIAL AID

Costs (2018–19) *Comprehensive fee:* $40,424 includes full-time tuition ($29,510) and room and board ($10,914). Full-time tuition and fees vary according to location, program, and student level. Part-time tuition: $496 per credit hour. Part-time tuition and fees vary according to course load, location, program, and student level. No tuition increase for student's term of enrollment. *College room only:* $6614. Room and board charges vary according to housing facility. *Payment plan:* installment. *Waivers:* employees or children of employees.

Financial Aid Of all full-time matriculated undergraduates who enrolled in 2016, 398 applied for aid, 398 were judged to have need. *Average financial aid package:* $21,973. *Average need-based loan:* $3987. *Average need-based gift aid:* $18,000. *Financial aid deadline:* 3/10.

APPLYING
Standardized Tests *Required:* SAT or ACT (for admission).

Options: electronic application, early admission, deferred entrance.

Required: high school transcript, minimum 2.0 GPA. *Required for some:* essay or personal statement, minimum 1.0 GPA, official transcripts from all previous institutions for transfers; proof of RN license, valid driver's license, and background check for RN-to-BSN program; background check and Praxis II scores for teacher licensure. *Recommended:* essay or personal statement.

CONTACT
Ryan McDonald, Director of Campus Admissions, Saint Mary-of-the-Woods College, Rooney Library, 1 St. Mary of the Woods College, St Mary of the Woods, IN 47876. *Phone:* 812-535-5106. *Toll-free phone:* 800-926-SMWC. *Fax:* 812-535-5010. *E-mail:* rmcdonald@smwc.edu.

Saint Mary's College
Notre Dame, Indiana
http://www.saintmarys.edu/
- **Independent Roman Catholic** comprehensive, founded 1844
- **Suburban** 100-acre campus
- **Endowment** $164.9 million
- **Women only**
- **Moderately difficult** entrance level

FACULTY
Student/faculty ratio: 10:1.

ACADEMICS
Calendar: semesters. *Degrees:* bachelor's, master's, and doctoral.
Library: Cushwa-Leighton Library. *Books:* 260,077 (physical), 140,170 (digital/electronic); *Serial titles:* 4,136 (physical), 205,506 (digital/electronic); *Databases:* 74. Weekly public service hours: 54; study areas open 24 hours, 5–7 days a week; students can reserve study rooms.

STUDENT LIFE
Housing options: on-campus residence required through junior year; women-only, special housing for students with disabilities. Campus housing is university owned. Freshman campus housing is guaranteed.

Activities and organizations: drama/theater group, student-run newspaper, radio and television station, choral group, marching band, Student Government Association, Dance Marathon, Class Boards, Residence Hall Association, Student Diversity Board.

Athletics Member NCAA. All Division III.

Campus security: 24-hour emergency response devices and patrols, late-night transport/escort service, controlled dormitory access.

Student services: health clinic, personal/psychological counseling, women's center.

COSTS & FINANCIAL AID
Costs (2017–18) *One-time required fee:* $150. *Comprehensive fee:* $52,900 includes full-time tuition ($39,980), mandatory fees ($820), and room and board ($12,100). Full-time tuition and fees vary according to course load. Part-time tuition: $1500 per credit hour. Part-time tuition and fees vary according to course load. *College room only:* $7500. Room and board charges vary according to board plan and housing facility.

Financial Aid Of all full-time matriculated undergraduates who enrolled in 2017, 1,475 applied for aid, 1,060 were judged to have need, 201 had their need fully met. 275 Federal Work-Study jobs (averaging $1606). 3 state and other part-time jobs (averaging $2000). In 2017, 393 non-need-based awards were made. *Average percent of need met:* 86. *Average financial aid package:* $35,934. *Average need-based loan:* $6737. *Average need-based gift aid:* $29,333. *Average non-need-based aid:*

$15,305. *Average indebtedness upon graduation:* $33,698. *Financial aid deadline:* 3/1.

APPLYING
Standardized Tests *Required:* SAT or ACT (for admission).

Options: electronic application, early admission, early decision, deferred entrance.

Required: essay or personal statement, high school transcript, 1 letter of recommendation, 16 high school academic units, at least two years of study of the same foreign language. *Recommended:* interview.

CONTACT
Sarah Dvorak, Director of Admission, Saint Mary's College, Notre Dame, IN 46556. *Phone:* 574-284-4587. *Toll-free phone:* 800-551-7621. *Fax:* 574-284-4841. *E-mail:* sdvorak@saintmarys.edu.

See next page for display ad and page 1414 for the College Close-Up.

Taylor University
Upland, Indiana
http://www.taylor.edu/
- **Independent interdenominational** comprehensive, founded 1846
- **Rural** 950-acre campus with easy access to Indianapolis
- **Endowment** $89.6 million
- **Coed** 2,110 undergraduate students, 87% full-time, 56% women, 44% men
- **Moderately difficult** entrance level, 87% of applicants were admitted

UNDERGRAD STUDENTS
1,840 full-time, 270 part-time. Students come from 45 states and territories; 36 other countries; 58% are from out of state; 4% Black or African American, non-Hispanic/Latino; 4% Hispanic/Latino; 3% Asian, non-Hispanic/Latino; 0.3% Native Hawaiian or other Pacific Islander, non-Hispanic/Latino; 0.8% American Indian or Alaska Native, non-Hispanic/Latino; 0.1% Two or more races, non-Hispanic/Latino; 5% international; 3% transferred in; 89% live on campus.

Freshmen:
Admission: 1,673 applied, 1,452 admitted, 448 enrolled. *Average high school GPA:* 3.8. *Test scores:* SAT evidence-based reading and writing scores over 500: 89%; SAT math scores over 500: 86%; ACT scores over 18: 95%; SAT evidence-based reading and writing scores over 600: 54%; SAT math scores over 600: 41%; ACT scores over 24: 67%; SAT evidence-based reading and writing scores over 700: 12%; SAT math scores over 700: 11%; ACT scores over 30: 20%.

Retention: 90% of full-time freshmen returned.

FACULTY
Total: 193, 69% full-time, 72% with terminal degrees.
Student/faculty ratio: 13:1.

ACADEMICS
Calendar: 4-1-4. *Degrees:* diplomas, bachelor's, and master's.

Special study options: academic remediation for entering students, advanced placement credit, cooperative education, distance learning, double majors, English as a second language, honors programs, independent study, internships, off-campus study, part-time degree program, services for LD students, student-designed majors, study abroad, summer session for credit.

Computers: 375 computers/terminals are available on campus for general student use. Students can access the following: campus intranet, computer help desk, free student e-mail accounts, online (class) grades, online (class) registration, online (class) schedules. Campuswide network is available. 100% of college-owned or -operated housing units are wired for high-speed Internet access. Wireless service is available via entire campus.
Library: Zondervan Library. *Books:* 170,640 (physical), 277,813 (digital/electronic); *Serial titles:* 279 (physical); *Databases:* 118. Weekly public service hours: 96; study areas open 24 hours, 5–7 days a week.

STUDENT LIFE
Housing options: on-campus residence required through junior year; men-only, women-only. Campus housing is university owned and is provided by a third party. Freshman campus housing is guaranteed.

Activities and organizations: drama/theater group, student-run newspaper, radio and television station, choral group, Spring Break Missions, Lighthouse, Alpha Pi Lota, Encounter, Kappa Delta Pi.

Athletics Member NAIA. *Intercollegiate sports:* baseball M(s), basketball M(s)/W(s), cross-country running M(s)/W(s), football M(s), golf M(s)/W(s), lacrosse M, soccer M(s)/W(s), softball W(s), tennis M(s)/W(s), track and field M(s)/W(s), volleyball W(s). *Intramural sports:* badminton M/W, basketball M/W, equestrian sports W(c), lacrosse M(c)/W(c), racquetball M/W, soccer M/W, softball M/W, tennis M/W, ultimate Frisbee M/W, volleyball M/W.

Campus security: 24-hour patrols, student patrols, late-night transport/escort service, controlled dormitory access.

Student services: health clinic, personal/psychological counseling.

COSTS & FINANCIAL AID

Costs (2017–18) *Comprehensive fee:* $42,130 includes full-time tuition ($32,640), mandatory fees ($245), and room and board ($9245). Full-time tuition and fees vary according to course load. Part-time tuition: $1150 per credit hour. Part-time tuition and fees vary according to course load. *Required fees:* $40 per term part-time. *College room only:* $4860. Room and board charges vary according to board plan and housing facility. *Payment plan:* installment. *Waivers:* senior citizens and employees or children of employees.

Financial Aid Of all full-time matriculated undergraduates who enrolled in 2017, 1,344 applied for aid, 1,137 were judged to have need, 318 had their need fully met. 882 Federal Work-Study jobs (averaging $639). In 2017, 540 non-need-based awards were made. *Average percent of need met:* 76. *Average financial aid package:* $23,875. *Average need-based loan:* $4600. *Average need-based gift aid:* $19,706. *Average non-need-based aid:* $12,528. *Average indebtedness upon graduation:* $28,094. *Financial aid deadline:* 4/15.

APPLYING

Standardized Tests *Required:* SAT or ACT (for admission).

Options: electronic application, early action, deferred entrance.

Application fee: $25.

Required: essay or personal statement, high school transcript, 2 letters of recommendation, interview. *Recommended:* minimum 2.8 GPA.

Application deadlines: rolling (freshmen), rolling (transfers).

Notification: continuous (freshmen), continuous (transfers).

CONTACT

Morgan Riessen, Visit Coordinator, Taylor University, 236 West Reade Avenue, Upland, IN 46989-1001. *Phone:* 765-998-5560. *Toll-free phone:* 800-882-3456. *Fax:* 765-998-4925. *E-mail:* admissions@taylor.edu.

★ Trine University
Angola, Indiana
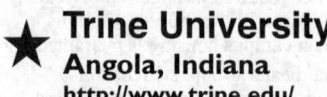
http://www.trine.edu/

- **Independent** comprehensive, founded 1884
- **Small-town** 400-acre campus
- **Endowment** $32.0 million
- **Coed** 4,104 undergraduate students, 47% full-time, 45% women, 55% men
- **Moderately difficult** entrance level, 66% of applicants were admitted

UNDERGRAD STUDENTS

1,920 full-time, 2,184 part-time. Students come from 37 states and territories; 26 other countries; 20% are from out of state; 6% Black or African American, non-Hispanic/Latino; 8% Hispanic/Latino; 2% Asian, non-Hispanic/Latino; 0.2% Native Hawaiian or other Pacific Islander, non-Hispanic/Latino; 0.3% American Indian or Alaska Native, non-Hispanic/Latino; 4% Two or more races, non-Hispanic/Latino; 2% Race/ethnicity unknown; 5% international; 2% transferred in; 71% live on campus.

Freshmen:

Admission: 3,597 applied, 2,360 admitted, 602 enrolled. *Average high school GPA:* 3.5. *Test scores:* SAT evidence-based reading and writing scores over 500: 68%; SAT math scores over 500: 70%; ACT scores over 18: 96%; SAT evidence-based reading and writing scores over 600: 14%; SAT math scores over 600: 23%; ACT scores over 24: 57%; SAT

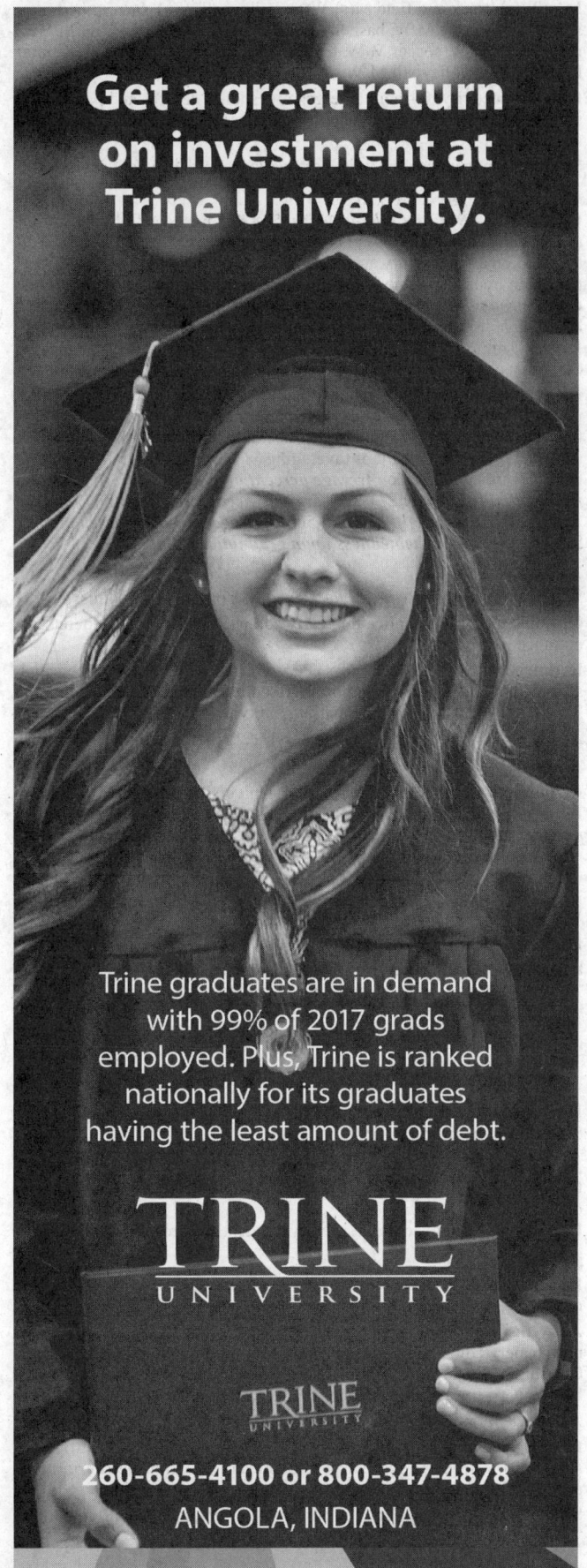

evidence-based reading and writing scores over 700: 2%; SAT math scores over 700: 2%; ACT scores over 30: 13%.
Retention: 80% of full-time freshmen returned.

FACULTY
Total: 165, 68% full-time.
Student/faculty ratio: 16:1.

ACADEMICS
Calendar: semesters. *Degrees:* associate, bachelor's, master's, and doctoral.

Special study options: academic remediation for entering students, adult/continuing education programs, advanced placement credit, cooperative education, distance learning, double majors, English as a second language, honors programs, independent study, internships, part-time degree program, services for LD students, student-designed majors, study abroad, summer session for credit. *ROTC:* Air Force (c).

Unusual degree programs: 3-2 engineering.

Computers: 400 computers/terminals and 1,100 ports are available on campus for general student use. Students can access the following: computer help desk, free student e-mail accounts, online (class) grades, online (class) registration, online (class) schedules, online campus billing accounts, course management system. Campuswide network is available. 100% of college-owned or -operated housing units are wired for high-speed Internet access. Wireless service is available via entire campus.
Library: Sponsel Library plus 1 other. *Books:* 23,523 (physical), 225,584 (digital/electronic); *Serial titles:* 19 (physical), 21,141 (digital/electronic); *Databases:* 87.

STUDENT LIFE
Housing options: on-campus residence required through senior year; coed, men-only, women-only, special housing for students with disabilities. Campus housing is university owned and is provided by a third party. Freshman campus housing is guaranteed.

Activities and organizations: drama/theater group, student-run radio station, choral group, marching band, Campus Christian House, Society of Women Engineers, Multicultural Student Organization, SPEAK, Trine Disc Golf Collective, national fraternities, national sororities.

Athletics Member NCAA. All Division III. *Intercollegiate sports:* baseball M, basketball M/W, bowling M(c)/W(c), cross-country running M/W, field hockey W, football M, golf M/W, ice hockey M/W, lacrosse M/W, soccer M/W, softball W, tennis M/W, track and field M/W, triathlon W, volleyball M/W, wrestling M. *Intramural sports:* basketball M/W, football M, golf M/W, sand volleyball M/W, skiing (downhill) M(c)/W(c), table tennis M(c)/W(c), ultimate Frisbee M(c)/W(c), volleyball M/W.

Campus security: 24-hour emergency response devices and patrols, late-night transport/escort service, controlled dormitory access.

Student services: health clinic, personal/psychological counseling.

COSTS & FINANCIAL AID
Costs (2017–18) *Comprehensive fee:* $42,110 includes full-time tuition ($31,080), mandatory fees ($460), and room and board ($10,570). Full-time tuition and fees vary according to degree level, location, and program. Part-time tuition: $970 per credit hour. Part-time tuition and fees vary according to degree level, location, and program. *Room and board:* Room and board charges vary according to board plan and housing facility. *Payment plan:* installment. *Waivers:* senior citizens and employees or children of employees.

Financial Aid Of all full-time matriculated undergraduates who enrolled in 2017, 1,761 applied for aid, 1,581 were judged to have need, 334 had their need fully met. In 2017, 240 non-need-based awards were made. *Average percent of need met:* 81. *Average financial aid package:* $27,853. *Average need-based loan:* $5053. *Average need-based gift aid:* $21,962. *Average non-need-based aid:* $14,882. *Average indebtedness upon graduation:* $38,161.

APPLYING
Standardized Tests *Required:* SAT or ACT (for admission).
Options: electronic application, deferred entrance.
Required: high school transcript, minimum 2.5 GPA. *Recommended:* essay or personal statement, 2 letters of recommendation, interview.
Application deadlines: 8/1 (freshmen), 8/1 (transfers).
Notification: 8/15 (freshmen), continuous until 8/15 (transfers).

CONTACT
Ms. Theresa Knight, Admission Coordinator, Trine University, 1 University Avenue, Angola, IN 46703. *Phone:* 260-665-4132. *Toll-free phone:* 800-347-4878. *E-mail:* admit@trine.edu.

See previous page for display ad and page 1448 for the College Close-Up.

University of Evansville
Evansville, Indiana
http://www.evansville.edu/

- **Independent** comprehensive, founded 1854, affiliated with United Methodist Church
- **Urban** 75-acre campus
- **Endowment** $127.8 million
- **Coed** 2,342 undergraduate students, 86% full-time, 56% women, 44% men
- **Moderately difficult** entrance level, 70% of applicants were admitted

UNDERGRAD STUDENTS
2,024 full-time, 318 part-time. Students come from 44 states and territories; 55 other countries; 35% are from out of state; 3% Black or African American, non-Hispanic/Latino; 3% Hispanic/Latino; 2% Asian, non-Hispanic/Latino; 0.1% American Indian or Alaska Native, non-Hispanic/Latino; 2% Two or more races, non-Hispanic/Latino; 11% Race/ethnicity unknown; 14% international; 3% transferred in; 51% live on campus.

Freshmen:
Admission: 3,825 applied, 2,676 admitted, 442 enrolled. *Average high school GPA:* 3.7. *Test scores:* SAT evidence-based reading and writing scores over 500: 91%; SAT math scores over 500: 94%; ACT scores over 18: 97%; SAT evidence-based reading and writing scores over 600: 50%; SAT math scores over 600: 52%; ACT scores over 24: 65%; SAT evidence-based reading and writing scores over 700: 13%; SAT math scores over 700: 13%; ACT scores over 30: 22%.
Retention: 84% of full-time freshmen returned.

FACULTY
Total: 262, 66% full-time, 68% with terminal degrees.
Student/faculty ratio: 11:1.

ACADEMICS
Calendar: semesters. *Degrees:* associate, bachelor's, master's, and doctoral.
Special study options: accelerated degree program, adult/continuing education programs, advanced placement credit, cooperative education, distance learning, double majors, English as a second language, honors programs, independent study, internships, part-time degree program, services for LD students, student-designed majors, study abroad, summer session for credit. *ROTC:* Army (c).
Computers: 219 computers/terminals and 3,273 ports are available on campus for general student use. Students can access the following: campus intranet, computer help desk, free student e-mail accounts, online (class) grades, online (class) registration, online (class) schedules. Campuswide network is available. 100% of college-owned or -operated housing units are wired for high-speed Internet access. Wireless service is available via entire campus.
Library: University of Evansville Libraries. *Books:* 235,259 (physical), 222,903 (digital/electronic); *Serial titles:* 56,159 (digital/electronic); *Databases:* 128. Weekly public service hours: 97; students can reserve study rooms.

STUDENT LIFE
Housing options: on-campus residence required through sophomore year; coed, men-only, women-only, special housing for students with disabilities. Campus housing is university owned. Freshman campus housing is guaranteed.
Activities and organizations: drama/theater group, student-run newspaper, radio station, choral group, Resident Students Association, International Club, PT Club, Newman Club, Venturing, national fraternities, national sororities.
Athletics Member NCAA. All Division I. *Intercollegiate sports:* baseball M(s), basketball M(s)/W(s), cross-country running M(s)/W(s), golf M(s)/W(s), soccer M(s)/W(s), softball W(s), swimming and diving M(s)/W(s), track and field M(s)/W(s), volleyball W(s). *Intramural sports:* badminton M/W, basketball M/W, cross-country running M/W, racquetball M/W, soccer M/W, tennis M/W, track and field M/W, ultimate Frisbee M/W, volleyball M/W.
Campus security: 24-hour emergency response devices and patrols, student patrols, late-night transport/escort service, controlled dormitory access.
Student services: health clinic, personal/psychological counseling.

COSTS & FINANCIAL AID
Costs (2018–19) *Comprehensive fee:* $48,876 includes full-time tuition ($35,300), mandatory fees ($1116), and room and board ($12,460). Full-time tuition and fees vary according to location. Part-time tuition: $990 per credit hour. Part-time tuition and fees vary according to course load. *College room only:* $6540. Room and board charges vary according to board plan, housing facility, and location. *Payment plan:* installment. *Waivers:* minority students, children of alumni, adult students, senior citizens, and employees or children of employees.
Financial Aid Of all full-time matriculated undergraduates who enrolled in 2017, 1,460 applied for aid, 1,295 were judged to have need, 631 had their need fully met. 385 Federal Work-Study jobs (averaging $1656). 98 state and other part-time jobs (averaging $1745). In 2017, 538 non-need-based awards were made. *Average percent of need met:* 87. *Average financial aid package:* $31,270. *Average need-based loan:* $4795. *Average need-based gift aid:* $23,566. *Average non-need-based aid:* $20,251. *Average indebtedness upon graduation:* $30,533.

APPLYING
Standardized Tests *Required for some:* SAT or ACT (for admission).
Options: electronic application, early admission, early action, deferred entrance.
Required: high school transcript. *Required for some:* essay or personal statement, interview, SAT and/or ACT scores. *Recommended:* minimum 3.0 GPA, 1 letter of recommendation, interview.
Application deadlines: 8/15 (transfers), 12/1 (early action).

CONTACT
Kenton Hargis, Director of Admission, University of Evansville, 1800 Lincoln Avenue, Evansville, IN 47722. *Phone:* 812-488-2142. *Toll-free phone:* 800-423-8633 Ext. 2468. *E-mail:* kh88@evansville.edu.

See next page for display ad and page 1466 for the College Close-Up.

University of Indianapolis
Indianapolis, Indiana
http://www.uindy.edu/

- **Independent** comprehensive, founded 1902, affiliated with United Methodist Church
- **Urban** 65-acre campus with easy access to Indianapolis
- **Coed**
- **Moderately difficult** entrance level

FACULTY
Student/faculty ratio: 12:1.

ACADEMICS
Calendar: semesters. *Degrees:* associate, bachelor's, master's, and doctoral.
Library: Krannert Memorial Library. Students can reserve study rooms.

STUDENT LIFE
Housing options: coed, women-only. Campus housing is university owned.
Activities and organizations: drama/theater group, student-run newspaper, radio and television station, choral group, Fellowship of Christian Athletes, Intercultural Association, Circle K, Indianapolis Student Government, Residence Hall Association.
Athletics Member NCAA. All Division II.
Campus security: 24-hour emergency response devices and patrols, student patrols, late-night transport/escort service, controlled dormitory access, emergency call boxes.
Student services: health clinic, personal/psychological counseling.

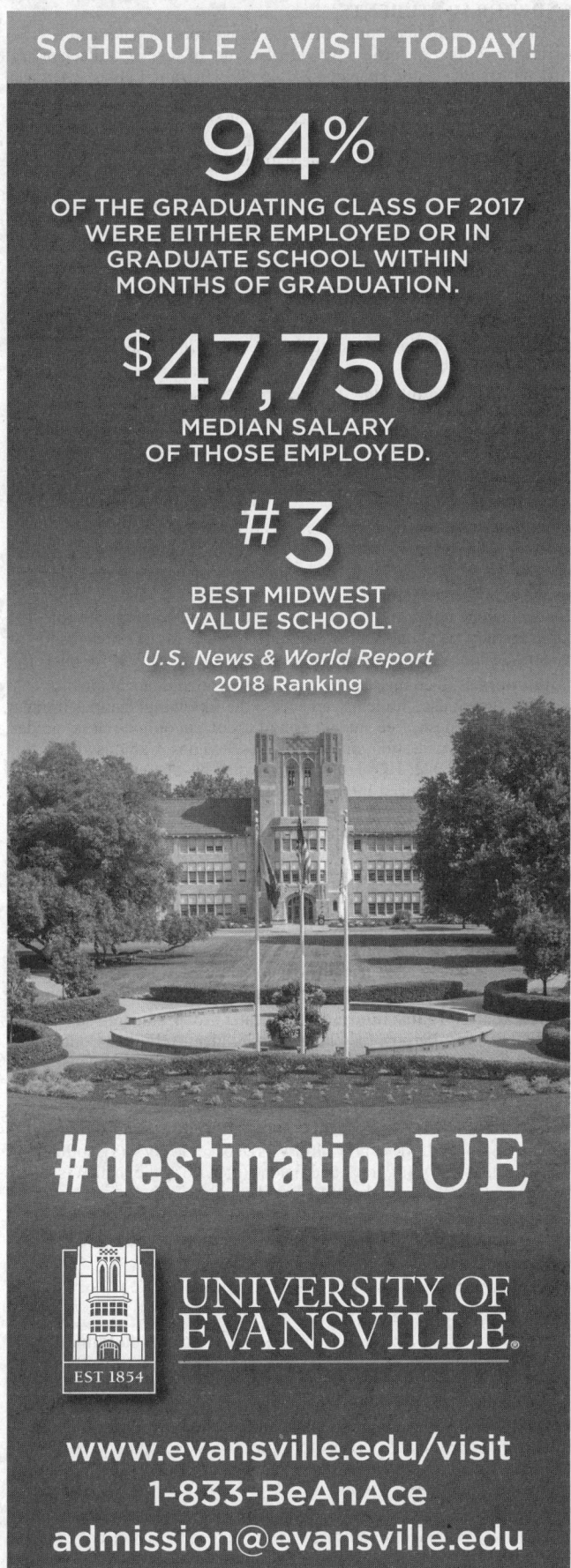

COSTS & FINANCIAL AID

Costs (2017–18) *Comprehensive fee:* $38,378 includes full-time tuition ($27,860), mandatory fees ($530), and room and board ($9988). Full-time tuition and fees vary according to class time. Part-time tuition: $1152 per credit hour. Part-time tuition and fees vary according to class time and course load. *Required fees:* $50 per term part-time. *College room only:* $5126. Room and board charges vary according to board plan and housing facility. *Payment plans:* installment, deferred payment.

Financial Aid Of all full-time matriculated undergraduates who enrolled in 2015, 3,253 applied for aid, 2,856 were judged to have need, 312 had their need fully met. 332 Federal Work-Study jobs (averaging $881). 165 state and other part-time jobs (averaging $7212). In 2015, 579 non-need-based awards were made. *Average percent of need met:* 64. *Average financial aid package:* $18,471. *Average need-based loan:* $4565. *Average need-based gift aid:* $8390. *Average non-need-based aid:* $10,214. *Average indebtedness upon graduation:* $36,304.

APPLYING

Standardized Tests *Required:* SAT or ACT (for admission).

Options: electronic application, deferred entrance.

Application fee: $25.

Required: high school transcript, minimum 2.0 GPA. *Required for some:* interview.

CONTACT

Mr. Ronald Wilks, Associate Vice President of Admissions, University of Indianapolis, 1400 East Hanna Avenue, Indianapolis, IN 46227-3697. *Phone:* 317-788-3216. *Toll-free phone:* 800-232-8634 Ext. 3216. *Fax:* 317-788-3300. *E-mail:* admissions@uindy.edu.

University of Notre Dame

Notre Dame, Indiana

http://www.nd.edu/

- **Independent Roman Catholic** university, founded 1842
- **Suburban** 1250-acre campus
- **Endowment** $12.0 billion
- **Coed** 8,576 undergraduate students, 100% full-time, 47% women, 53% men
- **Most difficult** entrance level, 19% of applicants were admitted

UNDERGRAD STUDENTS

8,557 full-time, 19 part-time. Students come from 52 states and territories; 68 other countries; 92% are from out of state; 4% Black or African American, non-Hispanic/Latino; 10% Hispanic/Latino; 5% Asian, non-Hispanic/Latino; 0.1% Native Hawaiian or other Pacific Islander, non-Hispanic/Latino; 0.2% American Indian or Alaska Native, non-Hispanic/Latino; 5% Two or more races, non-Hispanic/Latino; 0.6% Race/ethnicity unknown; 6% international; 2% transferred in; 79% live on campus.

Freshmen:
Admission: 19,567 applied, 3,702 admitted, 2,051 enrolled. *Test scores:* SAT evidence-based reading and writing scores over 500: 99%; SAT math scores over 500: 99%; ACT scores over 18: 100%; SAT evidence-based reading and writing scores over 600: 96%; SAT math scores over 600: 96%; ACT scores over 24: 99%; SAT evidence-based reading and writing scores over 700: 65%; SAT math scores over 700: 70%; ACT scores over 30: 89%.

Retention: 98% of full-time freshmen returned.

FACULTY

Total: 1,348, 88% full-time, 87% with terminal degrees.

Student/faculty ratio: 10:1.

ACADEMICS

Calendar: semesters. *Degrees:* bachelor's, master's, and doctoral.

Special study options: advanced placement credit, distance learning, double majors, honors programs, independent study, internships, off-campus study, services for LD students, student-designed majors, study abroad, summer session for credit. *ROTC:* Army (b), Navy (b), Air Force (b).

Computers: 232 computers/terminals are available on campus for general student use. Students can access the following: computer help desk, free student e-mail accounts, online (class) grades, online (class) registration,

online (class) schedules. Campuswide network is available. Wireless service is available via entire campus.

Library: Hesburgh Library plus 10 others.

STUDENT LIFE

Housing options: on-campus residence required for freshman year; men-only, women-only. Campus housing is university owned. Freshman campus housing is guaranteed.

Activities and organizations: drama/theater group, student-run newspaper, radio station, choral group, marching band, marching band, Circle K, Finance Club, Notre Dame/St. Mary's Right to Life.

Athletics Member NCAA. All Division I except football (Division I-A). *Intercollegiate sports:* baseball M(s), basketball M(s)/W(s), crew W(s), cross-country running M(s)/W(s), fencing M(s)/W(s), golf M(s)/W(s), ice hockey M(s), lacrosse M(s)/W(s), soccer M(s)/W(s), softball W(s), swimming and diving M(s)/W(s), tennis M(s)/W(s), track and field M(s)/W(s), volleyball W(s). *Intramural sports:* badminton M/W, baseball M, basketball M/W, bowling M(c)/W(c), crew M(c), equestrian sports M(c)/W(c), field hockey W(c), football M/W, golf M/W, gymnastics M(c)/W(c), ice hockey M/W(c), lacrosse M/W, racquetball M/W, rugby M(c)/W(c), sailing M(c)/W(c), skiing (cross-country) M(c)/W(c), skiing (downhill) M(c)/W(c), soccer M/W, softball M/W, squash M(c)/W(c), table tennis M/W, tennis M/W, ultimate Frisbee M/W, volleyball M(c)/W(c), water polo M(c)/W(c), wrestling M(c).

Campus security: 24-hour emergency response devices and patrols, student patrols, late-night transport/escort service, controlled dormitory access, crime prevention and personal safety workshops, full-time trained police investigators, fire sprinklers in all residence halls.

Student services: health clinic, personal/psychological counseling, women's center.

COSTS & FINANCIAL AID

Costs (2018–19) *Comprehensive fee:* $68,801 includes full-time tuition ($52,884), mandatory fees ($507), and room and board ($15,410). Part-time tuition: $2201 per credit hour. *Payment plan:* installment. *Waivers:* employees or children of employees.

Financial Aid Of all full-time matriculated undergraduates who enrolled in 2017, 4,937 applied for aid, 4,135 were judged to have need, 4,089 had their need fully met. 1,319 Federal Work-Study jobs (averaging $2631). 3,231 state and other part-time jobs (averaging $3402). In 2017, 388 non-need-based awards were made. *Average percent of need met:* 100. *Average financial aid package:* $49,410. *Average need-based loan:* $493. *Average need-based gift aid:* $38,921. *Average non-need-based aid:* $13,517. *Average indebtedness upon graduation:* $29,254.

APPLYING

Standardized Tests *Required:* SAT or ACT (for admission). *Required for some:* SAT Subject Tests (for admission).

Options: electronic application, early action, deferred entrance.

Application fee: $75.

Required: essay or personal statement, high school transcript, 1 letter of recommendation.

Application deadlines: 1/1 (freshmen), 3/15 (transfers), 11/1 (early action).

Notification: 4/10 (freshmen), 12/21 (early action).

CONTACT

Office of Undergraduate Admissions, University of Notre Dame, 220 Main Building, Notre Dame, IN 46556-5612. *Phone:* 574-631-7505. *Fax:* 574-631-8865. *E-mail:* admissions@nd.edu.

University of Saint Francis

Fort Wayne, Indiana

http://www.sf.edu/

- **Independent Roman Catholic** comprehensive, founded 1890
- **Urban** 100-acre campus
- **Endowment** $22.8 million
- **Coed** 1,906 undergraduate students, 80% full-time, 71% women, 29% men
- **Noncompetitive** entrance level, 99% of applicants were admitted

UNDERGRAD STUDENTS

1,523 full-time, 383 part-time. Students come from 16 states and territories; 7 other countries; 10% are from out of state; 7% Black or African American, non-Hispanic/Latino; 7% Hispanic/Latino; 2% Asian, non-Hispanic/Latino; 0.2% Native Hawaiian or other Pacific Islander, non-Hispanic/Latino; 0.1% American Indian or Alaska Native, non-Hispanic/Latino; 3% Two or more races, non-Hispanic/Latino; 2% Race/ethnicity unknown; 0.7% international; 10% transferred in; 22% live on campus.

Freshmen:

Admission: 1,249 applied, 1,233 admitted, 454 enrolled. *Average high school GPA:* 3.4. *Test scores:* SAT evidence-based reading and writing scores over 500: 69%; SAT math scores over 500: 69%; ACT scores over 18: 85%; SAT evidence-based reading and writing scores over 600: 21%; SAT math scores over 600: 16%; ACT scores over 24: 30%; SAT evidence-based reading and writing scores over 700: 2%; ACT scores over 30: 4%.

Retention: 72% of full-time freshmen returned.

FACULTY

Total: 299, 45% full-time, 28% with terminal degrees.

Student/faculty ratio: 10:1.

ACADEMICS

Calendar: semesters. *Degrees:* certificates, associate, bachelor's, master's, doctoral, post-master's, and postbachelor's certificates.

Special study options: academic remediation for entering students, advanced placement credit, cooperative education, distance learning, double majors, honors programs, independent study, internships, off-campus study, part-time degree program, services for LD students, student-designed majors, summer session for credit. *ROTC:* Army (c).

Computers: 120 computers/terminals are available on campus for general student use. Students can access the following: campus intranet, computer help desk, free student e-mail accounts, online (class) grades, online (class) registration, online (class) schedules. Campuswide network is available. 100% of college-owned or -operated housing units are wired for high-speed Internet access. Wireless service is available via entire campus.

Library: Lee and Jim Vann Library. *Books:* 67,110 (physical), 182,832 (digital/electronic); *Serial titles:* 798 (physical), 39,156 (digital/electronic); *Databases:* 110. Weekly public service hours: 86; study areas open 24 hours, 5–7 days a week; students can reserve study rooms.

STUDENT LIFE

Housing options: on-campus residence required through sophomore year; coed, special housing for students with disabilities. Campus housing is university owned. Freshman applicants given priority for college housing.

Activities and organizations: drama/theater group, student-run newspaper, choral group, marching band, Student Activities Council, Student Government Association, Intramural Sports, Residence Hall Association, Artists in Action.

Athletics Member NAIA. *Intercollegiate sports:* baseball M(s), basketball M(s)/W(s), cheerleading M(s)/W(s), cross-country running M(s)/W(s), football M(s), golf M(s)/W(s), soccer M(s)/W(s), softball W(s), tennis M(s)/W(s), track and field M(s)/W(s), volleyball W(s). *Intramural sports:* basketball M/W, volleyball M/W.

Campus security: 24-hour emergency response devices and patrols, late-night transport/escort service, controlled dormitory access, video surveillance system.

Student services: personal/psychological counseling.

COSTS & FINANCIAL AID

Costs (2018–19) *Comprehensive fee:* $40,270 includes full-time tuition ($29,360), mandatory fees ($1070), and room and board ($9840). Full-time tuition and fees vary according to course load. Part-time tuition: $935 per credit hour. Part-time tuition and fees vary according to course load. *Required fees:* $30 per credit hour part-time, $150 per term part-time. *Room and board:* Room and board charges vary according to board plan and housing facility. *Payment plan:* installment. *Waivers:* employees or children of employees.

Financial Aid Of all full-time matriculated undergraduates who enrolled in 2009, 1,477 applied for aid, 1,316 were judged to have need, 258 had their need fully met. 629 Federal Work-Study jobs (averaging $1411). In 2009, 146 non-need-based awards were made. *Average percent of need* *met:* 72. *Average financial aid package:* $16,158. *Average need-based loan:* $4028. *Average need-based gift aid:* $12,247. *Average non-need-based aid:* $5446. *Average indebtedness upon graduation:* $28,428. *Financial aid deadline:* 6/30.

APPLYING

Standardized Tests *Required:* SAT or ACT (for admission).

Options: electronic application, deferred entrance.

Required: high school transcript, minimum 2.3 GPA. *Required for some:* essay or personal statement, interview. *Recommended:* essay or personal statement.

Application deadlines: rolling (freshmen), rolling (transfers).

Notification: continuous until 8/1 (freshmen), continuous until 8/1 (transfers).

CONTACT

Mr. Joel Wincowski, Interim Vice President for Enrollment Management, University of Saint Francis, 2701 Spring Street, Fort Wayne, IN 46808. *Phone:* 260-399-7700 Ext. 6314. *Toll-free phone:* 800-729-4732. *E-mail:* admis@sf.edu.

 University of Southern Indiana
Evansville, Indiana
http://www.usi.edu/
- **State-supported** comprehensive, founded 1965, part of Indiana Commission for Higher Education
- **Suburban** 1400-acre campus
- **Coed** 7,706 undergraduate students, 85% full-time, 62% women, 38% men
- **Moderately difficult** entrance level, 94% of applicants were admitted

UNDERGRAD STUDENTS

6,538 full-time, 1,168 part-time. Students come from 31 states and territories; 44 other countries; 13% are from out of state; 4% Black or African American, non-Hispanic/Latino; 3% Hispanic/Latino; 1% Asian, non-Hispanic/Latino; 0.1% Native Hawaiian or other Pacific Islander, non-Hispanic/Latino; 0.2% American Indian or Alaska Native, non-Hispanic/Latino; 2% Two or more races, non-Hispanic/Latino; 0.1% Race/ethnicity unknown; 2% international; 6% transferred in; 32% live on campus.

Freshmen:

Admission: 4,569 applied, 4,277 admitted, 1,722 enrolled. *Average high school GPA:* 3.4. *Test scores:* SAT evidence-based reading and writing scores over 500: 72%; SAT math scores over 500: 71%; ACT scores over 18: 88%; SAT evidence-based reading and writing scores over 600: 22%; SAT math scores over 600: 17%; ACT scores over 24: 36%; SAT evidence-based reading and writing scores over 700: 2%; SAT math scores over 700: 2%; ACT scores over 30: 4%.

Retention: 71% of full-time freshmen returned.

FACULTY

Total: 686, 51% full-time, 46% with terminal degrees.

Student/faculty ratio: 17:1.

ACADEMICS

Calendar: semesters. *Degrees:* certificates, associate, bachelor's, master's, doctoral, post-master's, and postbachelor's certificates.

Special study options: academic remediation for entering students, accelerated degree program, adult/continuing education programs, advanced placement credit, cooperative education, distance learning, double majors, English as a second language, honors programs, independent study, internships, part-time degree program, services for LD students, study abroad, summer session for credit. *ROTC:* Army (b).

Computers: 1,165 computers/terminals are available on campus for general student use. Students can access the following: campus intranet, computer help desk, free student e-mail accounts, online (class) grades, online (class) registration, online (class) schedules. Campuswide network is available. 100% of college-owned or -operated housing units are wired for high-speed Internet access. Wireless service is available via entire campus.

Library: David L. Rice Library. *Books:* 241,710 (physical), 230,844 (digital/electronic); *Serial titles:* 1,075 (physical), 141,229 (digital/electronic); *Databases:* 168. Weekly public service hours: 114; students can reserve study rooms.

STUDENT LIFE

Housing options: coed, special housing for students with disabilities. Campus housing is university owned.

Activities and organizations: drama/theater group, student-run newspaper, radio and television station, choral group, Sororities, Fraternities, Riley Dance Marathon, Activities Programming Board, Student Government Association, national fraternities, national sororities.

Athletics Member NCAA. All Division II. *Intercollegiate sports:* baseball M(s), basketball M(s)/W(s), cheerleading M(c)/W(c), cross-country running M(s)/W(s), golf M(s)/W(s), soccer M(s)/W(s), softball W(s), tennis M(s)/W(s), track and field M(s)/W(s), volleyball W(s). *Intramural sports:* badminton M/W, basketball M/W, bowling M/W, football M/W, golf M/W, rugby M(c)/W(c), sand volleyball M/W, soccer M/W, softball M/W, table tennis M/W, tennis M/W, ultimate Frisbee M(c)/W(c), volleyball M/W, wrestling M(c).

Campus security: 24-hour emergency response devices and patrols, student patrols, late-night transport/escort service, controlled dormitory access.

Student services: health clinic, personal/psychological counseling.

COSTS & FINANCIAL AID

Costs (2017–18) *One-time required fee:* $450. *Tuition:* state resident $7460 full-time, $249 per credit hour part-time; nonresident $18,116 full-time, $604 per credit hour part-time. Full-time tuition and fees vary according to course level, course load, program, and reciprocity agreements. Part-time tuition and fees vary according to course level, course load, program, and reciprocity agreements. *Required fees:* $510 full-time, $23 per term part-time. *Room and board:* $8838; room only: $4668. Room and board charges vary according to board plan and housing facility. *Payment plan:* installment. *Waivers:* employees or children of employees.

Financial Aid Of all full-time matriculated undergraduates who enrolled in 2017, 5,450 applied for aid, 4,191 were judged to have need, 1,261 had their need fully met. 98 Federal Work-Study jobs (averaging $1995). In 2017, 1113 non-need-based awards were made. *Average percent of need met:* 80. *Average financial aid package:* $9456. *Average need-based loan:* $3273. *Average need-based gift aid:* $8140. *Average non-need-based aid:* $3931. *Average indebtedness upon graduation:* $24,568.

APPLYING

Standardized Tests *Required:* SAT or ACT (for admission).

Options: electronic application.

Application fee: $40.

Required: high school transcript. *Required for some:* interview. *Recommended:* minimum 2.5 GPA.

Notification: continuous (freshmen).

CONTACT

Mr. Rashad Smith, Director of Undergraduate Admissions, University of Southern Indiana, 8600 University Boulevard, Evansville, IN 47712-3590. *Phone:* 812-464-1765. *Toll-free phone:* 800-467-1965. *Fax:* 812-465-7154. *E-mail:* enroll@usi.edu.

Valparaiso University
Valparaiso, Indiana
http://www.valpo.edu/
- **Independent** comprehensive, founded 1859, affiliated with Lutheran Church
- **Small-town** 350-acre campus with easy access to Chicago
- **Endowment** $235.2 million
- **Coed** 3,251 undergraduate students, 98% full-time, 55% women, 45% men
- **Moderately difficult** entrance level, 84% of applicants were admitted

UNDERGRAD STUDENTS

3,180 full-time, 71 part-time. Students come from 43 states and territories; 27 other countries; 57% are from out of state; 6% Black or African American, non-Hispanic/Latino; 9% Hispanic/Latino; 2% Asian, non-Hispanic/Latino; 0.2% American Indian or Alaska Native, non-Hispanic/Latino; 3% Two or more races, non-Hispanic/Latino; 3%

Race/ethnicity unknown; 5% international; 7% transferred in; 64% live on campus.

Freshmen:
Admission: 7,954 applied, 6,704 admitted, 807 enrolled. *Average high school GPA:* 3.7. *Test scores:* SAT evidence-based reading and writing scores over 500: 93%; SAT math scores over 500: 91%; ACT scores over 18: 99%; SAT evidence-based reading and writing scores over 600: 43%; SAT math scores over 600: 43%; ACT scores over 24: 71%; SAT evidence-based reading and writing scores over 700: 6%; SAT math scores over 700: 7%; ACT scores over 30: 21%.
Retention: 83% of full-time freshmen returned.

FACULTY
Total: 417, 74% full-time, 75% with terminal degrees.
Student/faculty ratio: 11:1.

ACADEMICS
Calendar: semesters. *Degrees:* certificates, associate, bachelor's, master's, doctoral, post-master's, and postbachelor's certificates.

Special study options: accelerated degree program, adult/continuing education programs, advanced placement credit, cooperative education, distance learning, double majors, English as a second language, freshman honors college, honors programs, independent study, internships, off-campus study, part-time degree program, services for LD students, student-designed majors, study abroad, summer session for credit. *ROTC:* Army (c), Air Force (c).

Unusual degree programs: 3-2 physician assistant.

Computers: 500 computers/terminals are available on campus for general student use. Students can access the following: campus intranet, computer help desk, free student e-mail accounts, online (class) grades, online (class) registration, online (class) schedules, Web academic information, degree audit, online course evaluations. Campuswide network is available. 100% of college-owned or -operated housing units are wired for high-speed Internet access. Wireless service is available via classrooms, computer centers, computer labs, dorm rooms, learning centers, libraries, student centers.
Library: Christopher Center for Library and Information Resources plus 1 other. *Books:* 545,491 (physical); *Serial titles:* 2,588 (physical), 79,749 (digital/electronic). Weekly public service hours: 112.

STUDENT LIFE
Housing options: on-campus residence required through junior year; coed, women-only. Campus housing is university owned and leased by the school. Freshman campus housing is guaranteed.

Activities and organizations: drama/theater group, student-run newspaper, radio station, choral group, Student Government, Student volunteer organization, Chapel programs, Union Board, national fraternities, national sororities.

Athletics Member NCAA. All Division I except football (Division I-AA). *Intercollegiate sports:* baseball M(s), basketball M(s)/W(s), bowling W(s), cross-country running M(s)/W(s), golf M(s)/W(s), soccer M(s)/W(s), softball W(s), swimming and diving M(s)/W(s), tennis M(s)/W(s), track and field M(s)/W(s), volleyball W(s). *Intramural sports:* badminton M/W, basketball M/W, bowling M/W, cheerleading M/W, football M/W, golf M/W, racquetball M/W, soccer M(c)/W(c), softball M/W, table tennis M/W, tennis M(c)/W(c), triathlon M/W, ultimate Frisbee M(c)/W(c), volleyball M/W.

Campus security: 24-hour emergency response devices and patrols, late-night transport/escort service, controlled dormitory access.
Student services: health clinic, personal/psychological counseling, legal services.

COSTS & FINANCIAL AID
Costs (2018–19) *Comprehensive fee:* $52,120 includes full-time tuition ($39,000), mandatory fees ($1260), and room and board ($11,860). Full-time tuition and fees vary according to course load and program. Part-time tuition: $1715 per credit hour. Part-time tuition and fees vary according to course load and program. *College room only:* $7280. Room and board charges vary according to housing facility and student level. *Payment plans:* tuition prepayment, installment. *Waivers:* employees or children of employees.

Financial Aid Of all full-time matriculated undergraduates who enrolled in 2016, 2,707 applied for aid, 2,443 were judged to have need, 974 had

their need fully met. 556 Federal Work-Study jobs (averaging $1375). 940 state and other part-time jobs (averaging $2065). In 2016, 626 non-need-based awards were made. *Average percent of need met:* 93. *Average financial aid package:* $30,984. *Average need-based loan:* $4948. *Average need-based gift aid:* $28,710. *Average non-need-based aid:* $17,064. *Average indebtedness upon graduation:* $37,978.

APPLYING
Standardized Tests *Required:* SAT or ACT (for admission).
Options: electronic application, deferred entrance.
Required: essay or personal statement, high school transcript. *Required for some:* interview. *Recommended:* 2 letters of recommendation, interview.
Application deadlines: rolling (freshmen), rolling (transfers).
Notification: continuous (freshmen), continuous (transfers).

CONTACT
Mr. Bart Harvey, Director of Freshman Admission and Operations, Valparaiso University, Kretzmann Hall, 1700 Chapel Drive, Valparaiso, IN 46383-6493. *Phone:* 219-464-5011. *Toll-free phone:* 888-GO-VALPO. *Fax:* 219-464-6898. *E-mail:* undergrad.admission@valpo.edu.

Vincennes University

Vincennes, Indiana
http://www.vinu.edu/
- **State-supported** primarily 2-year, founded 1801
- **Small-town** 160-acre campus
- **Coed** 18,904 undergraduate students, 28% full-time, 45% women, 55% men
- **Noncompetitive** entrance level, 79% of applicants were admitted

UNDERGRAD STUDENTS
5,359 full-time, 13,545 part-time. Students come from 40 states and territories; 15 other countries; 18% are from out of state; 10% Black or African American, non-Hispanic/Latino; 10% Hispanic/Latino; 0.6% Asian, non-Hispanic/Latino; 0.2% Native Hawaiian or other Pacific Islander, non-Hispanic/Latino; 0.3% American Indian or Alaska Native, non-Hispanic/Latino; 2% Two or more races, non-Hispanic/Latino; 5% Race/ethnicity unknown; 0.7% international; 1% transferred in; 40% live on campus.

Freshmen:
Admission: 5,486 applied, 4,346 admitted, 2,332 enrolled.
Retention: 52% of full-time freshmen returned.

FACULTY
Total: 1,351, 15% full-time.
Student/faculty ratio: 16:1.

ACADEMICS
Calendar: semesters. *Degrees:* certificates, associate, and bachelor's.
Special study options: academic remediation for entering students, accelerated degree program, adult/continuing education programs, advanced placement credit, distance learning, double majors, English as a second language, external degree program, freshman honors college, honors programs, independent study, internships, off-campus study, part-time degree program, services for LD students, student-designed majors, summer session for credit. *ROTC:* Army (b).

Computers: 1,500 computers/terminals are available on campus for general student use. Campuswide network is available.
Library: Shake Learning Resource Center.

STUDENT LIFE
Housing options: on-campus residence required for freshman year; coed, men-only, women-only. Campus housing is university owned. Freshman campus housing is guaranteed.

Activities and organizations: drama/theater group, student-run newspaper, radio and television station, choral group, national fraternities, national sororities.

Athletics Member NJCAA. *Intercollegiate sports:* baseball M, basketball M/W, bowling M, cross-country running M/W, golf M, track and field M/W, volleyball W.

Campus security: 24-hour emergency response devices and patrols, student patrols, late-night transport/escort service, controlled dormitory access, surveillance cameras.

Student services: health clinic, personal/psychological counseling.

COSTS

Costs (2017–18) *Tuition:* state resident $5270 full-time; nonresident $13,100 full-time. Full-time tuition and fees vary according to course level, course load, location, program, reciprocity agreements, and student level. Part-time tuition and fees vary according to course level, course load, location, program, reciprocity agreements, and student level. *Required fees:* $467 full-time. *Room and board:* $9702. Room and board charges vary according to board plan, gender, and housing facility. *Payment plan:* installment. *Waivers:* senior citizens and employees or children of employees.

APPLYING

Options: electronic application, deferred entrance.

Application fee: $20.

Required: high school transcript. *Required for some:* interview.

Application deadlines: rolling (freshmen), rolling (transfers).

Notification: continuous until 8/1 (freshmen), continuous (transfers).

CONTACT

Vincennes University, 1002 North First Street, Vincennes, IN 47591. *Phone:* 812-888-4313. *Toll-free phone:* 800-742-9198.

Wabash College
Crawfordsville, Indiana
http://www.wabash.edu/

- **Independent** 4-year, founded 1832
- **Small-town** 60-acre campus with easy access to Indianapolis
- **Endowment** $340.2 million
- **Men only** 864 undergraduate students, 100% full-time
- **Moderately difficult** entrance level, 63% of applicants were admitted

UNDERGRAD STUDENTS

864 full-time. Students come from 28 states and territories; 18 other countries; 26% are from out of state; 6% Black or African American, non-Hispanic/Latino; 8% Hispanic/Latino; 1% Asian, non-Hispanic/Latino; 0.1% American Indian or Alaska Native, non-Hispanic/Latino; 3% Two or more races, non-Hispanic/Latino; 2% Race/ethnicity unknown; 7% international; 2% transferred in; 96% live on campus.

Freshmen:
Admission: 1,304 applied, 821 admitted, 232 enrolled. *Average high school GPA:* 3.7. *Test scores:* SAT math scores over 500: 93%; ACT scores over 18: 93%; SAT math scores over 600: 48%; ACT scores over 24: 60%; SAT math scores over 700: 13%; ACT scores over 30: 15%.
Retention: 87% of full-time freshmen returned.

FACULTY

Total: 105, 78% full-time, 93% with terminal degrees.

Student/faculty ratio: 10:1.

ACADEMICS

Calendar: semesters. *Degree:* bachelor's.

Special study options: advanced placement credit, double majors, independent study, internships, off-campus study, services for LD students, student-designed majors, study abroad.

Unusual degree programs: 3-2 engineering with Purdue University, Columbia University, Washington University in St. Louis.

Computers: 380 computers/terminals and 2,600 ports are available on campus for general student use. Students can access the following: campus intranet, computer help desk, free student e-mail accounts, online (class) grades, online (class) registration, online (class) schedules, online course management, degree audit, expenses. Campuswide network is available. 100% of college-owned or -operated housing units are wired for high-speed Internet access. Wireless service is available via entire campus.

Library: Lilly Library. *Books:* 199,060 (physical), 262,577 (digital/electronic); *Serial titles:* 2,047 (physical), 35,603 (digital/electronic); *Databases:* 82. Weekly public service hours: 112.

STUDENT LIFE

Housing options: on-campus residence required through junior year; men-only. Campus housing is university owned. Freshman campus housing is guaranteed.

Activities and organizations: drama/theater group, student-run newspaper, radio station, choral group, Inter-Fraternity Council, Malcolm X Institute for Black Studies, Sphinx Club, Student Government, College Mentors for Kids, national fraternities.

Athletics Member NCAA. All Division III. *Intercollegiate sports:* baseball M, basketball M, cross-country running M, football M, golf M, lacrosse M, rugby M(c), soccer M, swimming and diving M, tennis M, track and field M, ultimate Frisbee M(c), wrestling M. *Intramural sports:* basketball M, bowling M, football M, racquetball M, soccer M, softball M.

Campus security: 24-hour emergency response devices and patrols.

Student services: health clinic, personal/psychological counseling.

COSTS & FINANCIAL AID

Costs (2018–19) *Comprehensive fee:* $53,500 includes full-time tuition ($42,800), mandatory fees ($850), and room and board ($9850). Part-time tuition: $1783 per semester hour. Part-time tuition and fees vary according to course load. *Required fees:* $50 per term part-time. *College room only:* $5250. Room and board charges vary according to board plan and housing facility. *Payment plans:* tuition prepayment, installment. *Waivers:* employees or children of employees.

Financial Aid Of all full-time matriculated undergraduates who enrolled in 2017, 798 applied for aid, 653 were judged to have need, 526 had their need fully met. 207 Federal Work-Study jobs (averaging $2912). 312 state and other part-time jobs (averaging $2876). In 2017, 206 non-need-based awards were made. *Average percent of need met:* 94. *Average financial aid package:* $37,666. *Average need-based loan:* $4348. *Average need-based gift aid:* $30,123. *Average non-need-based aid:* $22,589. *Average indebtedness upon graduation:* $35,726.

APPLYING

Standardized Tests *Required:* SAT or ACT (for admission).

Options: electronic application, early admission, early decision, early action, deferred entrance.

Application fee: $50.

Required: high school transcript, 1 letter of recommendation, high school report. *Required for some:* interview. *Recommended:* interview.

Application deadlines: 1/15 (freshmen), rolling (transfers), 11/1 (early action).

Early decision deadline: 10/15.

Notification: continuous (freshmen), continuous (transfers), 11/16 (early decision), 12/11 (early action).

CONTACT

Mr. Charles Timmons, Associate Dean for Enrollment, Wabash College, PO Box 362, Crawfordsville, IN 47933-0352. *Phone:* 765-361-6225. *Toll-free phone:* 800-345-5385. *Fax:* 765-361-6437. *E-mail:* admissions@wabash.edu.

IOWA

Allen College
Waterloo, Iowa
http://www.allencollege.edu/

- **Independent** comprehensive, founded 1989
- **Suburban** 20-acre campus
- **Endowment** $6.9 million
- **Coed, primarily women** 329 undergraduate students, 80% full-time, 91% women, 9% men
- **Moderately difficult** entrance level

UNDERGRAD STUDENTS

262 full-time, 67 part-time. Students come from 9 states and territories; 2 other countries; 7% are from out of state; 0.6% Black or African American, non-Hispanic/Latino; 1% Hispanic/Latino; 0.6% Asian, non-Hispanic/Latino; 0.3% Native Hawaiian or other Pacific Islander, non-

Hispanic/Latino; 0.3% American Indian or Alaska Native, non-Hispanic/Latino; 2% Two or more races, non-Hispanic/Latino; 5% Race/ethnicity unknown; 0.6% international; 38% transferred in.

FACULTY
Total: 54, 78% full-time, 31% with terminal degrees.
Student/faculty ratio: 17:1.

ACADEMICS
Calendar: semesters. *Degrees:* certificates, associate, bachelor's, master's, doctoral, and post-master's certificates (liberal arts and general education courses offered at either University of North Iowa or Wartburg College).
Special study options: accelerated degree program, advanced placement credit, cooperative education, distance learning, honors programs, independent study, internships, off-campus study, part-time degree program. *ROTC:* Army (c).
Unusual degree programs: 3-2 nursing with Wartburg College, Loras College, Central College, Simpson College.
Computers: 32 computers/terminals are available on campus for general student use. Students can access the following: campus intranet, computer help desk, free student e-mail accounts, online (class) grades, online (class) schedules, online proctoring exams. Campuswide network is available. 100% of college-owned or -operated housing units are wired for high-speed Internet access. Wireless service is available via entire campus.
Library: Barrett Library plus 1 other. *Books:* 13,226 (physical), 5,000 (digital/electronic); *Serial titles:* 211 (physical), 3,000 (digital/electronic); *Databases:* 45. Weekly public service hours: 50; study areas open 24 hours, 5–7 days a week; students can reserve study rooms.

STUDENT LIFE
Housing options: college housing not availableCampus housing is provided by a third party.
Activities and organizations: choral group, Allen Student Nurses's Association, Nurses'; Christian Fellowship.
Campus security: 24-hour patrols, late-night transport/escort service, controlled dormitory access.
Student services: health clinic, personal/psychological counseling.

COSTS & FINANCIAL AID
Costs (2017–18) *Comprehensive fee:* $25,507 includes full-time tuition ($16,884), mandatory fees ($1342), and room and board ($7281). Full-time tuition and fees vary according to course load, degree level, and program. Part-time tuition: $603 per credit hour. Part-time tuition and fees vary according to course load, degree level, and program. *Required fees:* $81 per credit hour part-time. *College room only:* $3641. *Payment plan:* deferred payment.
Financial Aid Of all full-time matriculated undergraduates who enrolled in 2015, 249 applied for aid, 203 were judged to have need, 10 had their need fully met. 12 Federal Work-Study jobs (averaging $5000). In 2015, 23 non-need-based awards were made. *Average percent of need met:* 51. *Average financial aid package:* $11,217. *Average need-based loan:* $5101. *Average need-based gift aid:* $8419. *Average non-need-based aid:* $1250.

APPLYING
Standardized Tests *Required for some:* SAT or ACT (for admission), ATI, TEAS for undergraduate pre-licensure students.
Options: electronic application.
Application fee: $50.
Required for some: essay or personal statement, high school transcript, 1 letter of recommendation, interview.
Application deadlines: 2/1 (freshmen), 2/1 (transfers).
Notification: continuous until 3/1 (freshmen), continuous until 3/1 (transfers).

CONTACT
Jamie Jordan, Administrative Assistant, Student Services, Allen College, Barrett Forum, 1825 Logan Avenue, Waterloo, IA 50703. *Phone:* 319-226-2014. *Fax:* 319-226-2010. *E-mail:* admissions@allencollege.edu.

Briar Cliff University
Sioux City, Iowa
http://www.briarcliff.edu/
- **Independent Roman Catholic** comprehensive, founded 1930
- **Suburban** 75-acre campus
- **Coed**
- **Moderately difficult** entrance level

FACULTY
Student/faculty ratio: 14:1.

ACADEMICS
Calendar: 3 10-week terms plus two 5-week summer sessions. *Degrees:* associate, bachelor's, master's, doctoral, post-master's, and postbachelor's certificates.
Library: Bishop Mueller Library.

STUDENT LIFE
Housing options: on-campus residence required through junior year; coed. Campus housing is university owned. Freshman campus housing is guaranteed.
Activities and organizations: drama/theater group, student-run newspaper, radio station, choral group, Residence Hall Association, Briar Cliff Student Government, Choices, Blue Crew, Catholic Daughters of America.
Athletics Member NAIA.
Campus security: 24-hour emergency response devices and patrols, student patrols, late-night transport/escort service, controlled dormitory access.
Student services: health clinic, personal/psychological counseling.

COSTS & FINANCIAL AID
Costs (2017–18) *Comprehensive fee:* $38,872 includes full-time tuition ($28,650), mandatory fees ($1136), and room and board ($9086). Full-time tuition and fees vary according to class time, course load, degree level, location, and program. Part-time tuition: $956 per credit hour. Part-time tuition and fees vary according to class time, course load, degree level, location, and program. *College room only:* $4300. Room and board charges vary according to board plan, housing facility, and location. *Payment plans:* installment, deferred payment.
Financial Aid Of all full-time matriculated undergraduates who enrolled in 2015, 778 applied for aid, 656 were judged to have need, 156 had their need fully met. In 2015, 133 non-need-based awards were made. *Average percent of need met:* 26. *Average financial aid package:* $30,582. *Average need-based loan:* $4837. *Average need-based gift aid:* $14,647. *Average non-need-based aid:* $2524. *Average indebtedness upon graduation:* $29,484. *Financial aid deadline:* 3/15.

APPLYING
Standardized Tests *Required:* SAT or ACT (for admission).
Options: electronic application, early admission, deferred entrance.
Application fee: $20.
Required: high school transcript, minimum 2.0 GPA. *Required for some:* essay or personal statement, 3 letters of recommendation, interview.

CONTACT
Mr. Brian Eben, Assistant Vice President for Enrollment Management, Briar Cliff University, 3303 Rebecca Street, Sioux City, IA 51104. *Phone:* 712-279-5200. *Toll-free phone:* 800-662-3303. *Fax:* 712-279-1632. *E-mail:* admissions@briarcliff.edu.

Buena Vista University
Storm Lake, Iowa
http://www.bvu.edu/
- **Independent** comprehensive, founded 1891, affiliated with Presbyterian Church (U.S.A.)
- **Small-town** 60-acre campus
- **Endowment** $135.0 million
- **Coed** 786 undergraduate students, 97% full-time, 49% women, 51% men
- **Moderately difficult** entrance level, 64% of applicants were admitted

UNDERGRAD STUDENTS

766 full-time, 20 part-time. Students come from 27 states and territories; 15 other countries; 26% are from out of state; 5% Black or African American, non-Hispanic/Latino; 7% Hispanic/Latino; 1% Asian, non-Hispanic/Latino; 0.1% Native Hawaiian or other Pacific Islander, non-Hispanic/Latino; 0.3% American Indian or Alaska Native, non-Hispanic/Latino; 5% Two or more races, non-Hispanic/Latino; 5% Race/ethnicity unknown; 3% international; 6% transferred in; 90% live on campus.

Freshmen:
Admission: 1,477 applied, 943 admitted, 203 enrolled. *Average high school GPA:* 3.3. *Test scores:* ACT scores over 18: 87%; ACT scores over 24: 32%; ACT scores over 30: 6%.
Retention: 77% of full-time freshmen returned.

FACULTY

Total: 116, 70% full-time, 59% with terminal degrees.
Student/faculty ratio: 9:1.

ACADEMICS

Calendar: 4-1-4. *Degrees:* bachelor's and master's.
Special study options: academic remediation for entering students, adult/continuing education programs, advanced placement credit, distance learning, double majors, English as a second language, external degree program, honors programs, independent study, internships, off-campus study, part-time degree program, services for LD students, student-designed majors, study abroad, summer session for credit. *ROTC:* Army (b).
Unusual degree programs: 3-2 engineering with Washington University in St. Louis.
Computers: Students can access the following: campus intranet, computer help desk, free student e-mail accounts, online (class) grades, online (class) registration, online (class) schedules. Campuswide network is available. 100% of college-owned or -operated housing units are wired for high-speed Internet access. Wireless service is available via entire campus.
Library: BVU Library. *Books:* 108,603 (physical), 146,418 (digital/electronic); *Serial titles:* 1,157 (physical), 39,974 (digital/electronic); *Databases:* 66. Weekly public service hours: 94; students can reserve study rooms.

STUDENT LIFE

Housing options: on-campus residence required through senior year; coed, special housing for students with disabilities. Campus housing is university owned. Freshman campus housing is guaranteed.
Activities and organizations: drama/theater group, student-run newspaper, radio and television station, choral group, Student Activities Board, Orientation Team, Esprit De Corps, Student Senate, Student Mobilizing Outreach and Volunteer Efforts.
Athletics Member NCAA. All Division III. *Intercollegiate sports:* baseball M, basketball M/W, cross-country running M/W, football M, golf M/W, soccer M/W, softball W, tennis M/W, track and field M/W, volleyball W, wrestling M. *Intramural sports:* basketball M/W, racquetball M/W, softball M/W, table tennis M/W, tennis M/W, volleyball M/W.
Campus security: 24-hour emergency response devices, late-night transport/escort service, controlled dormitory access, night security patrols.
Student services: health clinic, personal/psychological counseling.

COSTS & FINANCIAL AID

Costs (2017–18) *Comprehensive fee:* $42,344 includes full-time tuition ($32,854) and room and board ($9490). Full-time tuition and fees vary according to location. Part-time tuition: $1105 per credit hour. Part-time tuition and fees vary according to location. *College room only:* $4774. Room and board charges vary according to board plan and housing facility. *Payment plan:* installment. *Waivers:* employees or children of employees.
Financial Aid Of all full-time matriculated undergraduates who enrolled in 2017, 688 applied for aid, 634 were judged to have need, 132 had their need fully met. In 2017, 120 non-need-based awards were made. *Average percent of need met:* 83. *Average financial aid package:* $29,026. *Average need-based loan:* $5359. *Average need-based gift aid:* $23,634.

Average non-need-based aid: $18,429. *Average indebtedness upon graduation:* $36,299.

APPLYING

Standardized Tests *Required:* SAT or ACT (for admission). *Recommended:* ACT (for admission).
Options: electronic application, deferred entrance.
Required: high school transcript. *Required for some:* essay or personal statement, interview. *Recommended:* minimum 3.0 GPA.
Notification: continuous (freshmen), continuous (transfers).

CONTACT

Michael Fox, Director of Admissions, Buena Vista University, 610 West Fourth Street, Storm Lake, IA 50588. *Phone:* 712-749-2078. *Toll-free phone:* 800-383-9600. *E-mail:* admissions@bvu.edu.

Central College
Pella, Iowa
http://www.central.edu/

CONTACT

Chevy Freiburger, Director of Admission, Central College, 812 University, Pella, IA 50112. *Phone:* 641-628-7637. *Toll-free phone:* 877-462-3687. *Fax:* 641-628-5983. *E-mail:* freiburgerc@central.edu.

Clarke University
Dubuque, Iowa
http://www.clarke.edu/

- **Independent Roman Catholic** comprehensive, founded 1843
- **Urban** 55-acre campus
- **Endowment** $31.3 million
- **Coed** 774 undergraduate students, 91% full-time, 64% women, 36% men
- **Moderately difficult** entrance level, 63% of applicants were admitted

UNDERGRAD STUDENTS

708 full-time, 66 part-time. Students come from 32 states and territories; 8 other countries; 50% are from out of state; 6% Black or African American, non-Hispanic/Latino; 7% Hispanic/Latino; 1% Asian, non-Hispanic/Latino; 0.7% Native Hawaiian or other Pacific Islander, non-Hispanic/Latino; 0.5% American Indian or Alaska Native, non-Hispanic/Latino; 2% Two or more races, non-Hispanic/Latino; 0.8% Race/ethnicity unknown; 1% international; 8% transferred in; 55% live on campus.

Freshmen:
Admission: 1,149 applied, 726 admitted, 162 enrolled. *Average high school GPA:* 3.4. *Test scores:* ACT scores over 18: 92%; ACT scores over 24: 39%; ACT scores over 30: 5%.
Retention: 75% of full-time freshmen returned.

FACULTY

Total: 90, 98% full-time, 90% with terminal degrees.
Student/faculty ratio: 8:1.

ACADEMICS

Calendar: semesters. *Degrees:* associate, bachelor's, master's, and doctoral.
Special study options: accelerated degree program, adult/continuing education programs, advanced placement credit, cooperative education, distance learning, double majors, honors programs, independent study, internships, off-campus study, part-time degree program, services for LD students, student-designed majors, study abroad, summer session for credit. *ROTC:* Army (c).
Computers: 237 computers/terminals are available on campus for general student use. Students can access the following: campus intranet, computer help desk, free student e-mail accounts, online (class) grades, online (class) registration, online (class) schedules. Campuswide network is available. 100% of college-owned or -operated housing units are wired for high-speed Internet access. Wireless service is available via entire campus.
Library: Nicholas J. Schrupp Library. *Books:* 76,525 (physical), 136,800 (digital/electronic); *Serial titles:* 150 (physical), 53,000 (digital/electronic); *Databases:* 60. Weekly public service hours: 90.

STUDENT LIFE

Housing options: on-campus residence required through sophomore year; coed, men-only, women-only. Campus housing is university owned. Freshman campus housing is guaranteed.

Activities and organizations: drama/theater group, choral group, Admissions Student Team, Student Multicultural Organization, Concert Choir, Campus Ministry, Student Government.

Athletics Member NAIA. *Intercollegiate sports:* baseball M(s), basketball M(s)/W(s), bowling M(s)/W(s), cheerleading W, cross-country running M(s)/W(s), football M(s), golf M(s)/W(s), lacrosse M(s)/W(s), soccer M(s)/W(s), softball W(s), track and field M(s)/W(s), volleyball M(s)/W(s). *Intramural sports:* badminton M/W, basketball M/W, bowling M/W, football M/W, golf M/W, skiing (cross-country) M/W, skiing (downhill) M/W, softball M/W, table tennis M/W, tennis M/W, track and field M/W, volleyball M/W, weight lifting M/W.

Campus security: 24-hour emergency response devices and patrols, late-night transport/escort service, controlled dormitory access.

Student services: health clinic, personal/psychological counseling.

COSTS & FINANCIAL AID

Costs (2018–19) *Comprehensive fee:* $42,950 includes full-time tuition ($32,300), mandatory fees ($1050), and room and board ($9600). Part-time tuition: $720 per credit hour. *College room only:* $4600. Room and board charges vary according to board plan. *Payment plans:* installment, deferred payment. *Waivers:* employees or children of employees.

Financial Aid Of all full-time matriculated undergraduates who enrolled in 2017, 636 applied for aid, 590 were judged to have need, 147 had their need fully met. 417 Federal Work-Study jobs (averaging $2000). In 2017, 89 non-need-based awards were made. *Average percent of need met:* 74. *Average financial aid package:* $27,131. *Average need-based loan:* $4489. *Average need-based gift aid:* $21,991. *Average non-need-based aid:* $22,042. *Average indebtedness upon graduation:* $39,907.

APPLYING

Standardized Tests *Required:* SAT or ACT (for admission).

Options: electronic application, deferred entrance.

Application fee: $25.

Required: high school transcript, minimum 2.0 GPA.

Application deadlines: rolling (freshmen), rolling (transfers).

Notification: 7/15 (freshmen), continuous until 8/15 (transfers).

CONTACT

Mrs. Alicia Schmitt, Associate Director of Admissions, Clarke University, 1550 Clarke Drive, Dubuque, IA 52001-3198. *Phone:* 563-588-6373. *Toll-free phone:* 800-383-2345. *E-mail:* admissions@clarke.edu.

Coe College

Cedar Rapids, Iowa

http://www.coe.edu/

- **Independent** 4-year, founded 1851, affiliated with Presbyterian Church
- **Urban** 53-acre campus
- **Endowment** $85.6 million
- **Coed** 1,394 undergraduate students, 98% full-time, 56% women, 44% men
- **Moderately difficult** entrance level, 56% of applicants were admitted

UNDERGRAD STUDENTS

1,369 full-time, 25 part-time. Students come from 37 states and territories; 20 other countries; 58% are from out of state; 8% Black or African American, non-Hispanic/Latino; 10% Hispanic/Latino; 4% Asian, non-Hispanic/Latino; 0.1% Native Hawaiian or other Pacific Islander, non-Hispanic/Latino; 0.4% American Indian or Alaska Native, non-Hispanic/Latino; 3% Two or more races, non-Hispanic/Latino; 3% Race/ethnicity unknown; 2% international; 3% transferred in; 86% live on campus.

Freshmen:

Admission: 7,002 applied, 3,937 admitted, 400 enrolled. *Average high school GPA:* 3.6. *Test scores:* SAT evidence-based reading and writing scores over 500: 88%; SAT math scores over 500: 98%; ACT scores over 18: 100%; SAT evidence-based reading and writing scores over 600: 43%; SAT math scores over 600: 45%; ACT scores over 24: 86%; SAT

evidence-based reading and writing scores over 700: 18%; SAT math scores over 700: 18%; ACT scores over 30: 42%.

Retention: 81% of full-time freshmen returned.

FACULTY

Total: 177, 57% full-time, 63% with terminal degrees.

Student/faculty ratio: 11:1.

ACADEMICS

Calendar: 4-4-1. *Degree:* bachelor's.

Special study options: advanced placement credit, double majors, English as a second language, honors programs, independent study, internships, off-campus study, part-time degree program, services for LD students, student-designed majors, study abroad, summer session for credit. *ROTC:* Army (b), Air Force (c).

Unusual degree programs: 3-2 engineering; public health with University of Iowa; law with University of Iowa.

Computers: 450 computers/terminals and 2,000 ports are available on campus for general student use. Students can access the following: campus intranet, computer help desk, free student e-mail accounts, online (class) grades, online (class) registration, online (class) schedules. Campuswide network is available. 100% of college-owned or -operated housing units are wired for high-speed Internet access. Wireless service is available via entire campus.

Library: Stewart Memorial Library plus 1 other. *Books:* 238,645 (physical), 289,126 (digital/electronic); *Serial titles:* 751 (physical), 3,630 (digital/electronic); *Databases:* 140. Weekly public service hours: 106.

STUDENT LIFE

Housing options: on-campus residence required through senior year; coed, men-only, women-only, special housing for students with disabilities. Campus housing is university owned. Freshman campus housing is guaranteed.

Activities and organizations: drama/theater group, student-run newspaper, radio station, choral group, Multicultural Fusion, Coe Alliance, Student Senate, Habitat for Humanity, International Club, national fraternities, national sororities.

Athletics Member NCAA. All Division III. *Intercollegiate sports:* baseball M, basketball M/W, cross-country running M/W, football M, golf M/W, soccer M/W, softball W, swimming and diving M/W, tennis M/W, track and field M/W, volleyball W, wrestling M. *Intramural sports:* lacrosse M/W, rock climbing M/W, soccer M/W, ultimate Frisbee M(c)/W(c), volleyball W.

Campus security: 24-hour emergency response devices and patrols, late-night transport/escort service, controlled dormitory access.

Student services: health clinic, personal/psychological counseling.

COSTS & FINANCIAL AID

Costs (2018–19) *Comprehensive fee:* $54,480 includes full-time tuition ($44,700), mandatory fees ($300), and room and board ($9480). Part-time tuition: $5587 per course. Part-time tuition and fees vary according to course load. *Room and board:* Room and board charges vary according to board plan and housing facility. *Payment plan:* installment. *Waivers:* adult students, senior citizens, and employees or children of employees.

Financial Aid Of all full-time matriculated undergraduates who enrolled in 2017, 1,197 applied for aid, 1,116 were judged to have need, 229 had their need fully met. 617 Federal Work-Study jobs (averaging $1706). 226 state and other part-time jobs (averaging $1550). In 2017, 223 non-need-based awards were made. *Average percent of need met:* 84. *Average financial aid package:* $35,630. *Average need-based loan:* $5144. *Average need-based gift aid:* $30,679. *Average non-need-based aid:* $25,052. *Average indebtedness upon graduation:* $36,022.

APPLYING

Standardized Tests *Required:* SAT or ACT (for admission).

Options: electronic application, early admission, early action, deferred entrance.

Application fee: $30.

Required: essay or personal statement, high school transcript, 1 letter of recommendation. *Recommended:* minimum 3.0 GPA, interview.

Application deadlines: 3/1 (freshmen), rolling (transfers), 12/10 (early action).

Notification: 3/15 (freshmen), continuous (transfers).

CONTACT
Julie Staker, Vice President for Admission and Marketing, Coe College, 1220 1st Avenue NE, Cedar Rapids, IA 52402-5070. *Phone:* 319-399-8500. *Toll-free phone:* 877-225-5263. *Fax:* 319-399-8816. *E-mail:* admission@coe.edu.

Cornell College
Mount Vernon, Iowa
http://www.cornellcollege.edu/
- **Independent Methodist** 4-year, founded 1853
- **Small-town** 129-acre campus
- **Endowment** $67.0 million
- **Coed** 1,009 undergraduate students, 99% full-time, 49% women, 51% men
- **Moderately difficult** entrance level, 71% of applicants were admitted

UNDERGRAD STUDENTS
1,003 full-time, 6 part-time. Students come from 46 states and territories; 21 other countries; 81% are from out of state; 6% Black or African American, non-Hispanic/Latino; 9% Hispanic/Latino; 3% Asian, non-Hispanic/Latino; 1% American Indian or Alaska Native, non-Hispanic/Latino; 2% Two or more races, non-Hispanic/Latino; 4% Race/ethnicity unknown; 5% international; 3% transferred in; 88% live on campus.

Freshmen:
Admission: 1,965 applied, 1,394 admitted, 300 enrolled. *Average high school GPA:* 3.5. *Test scores:* SAT evidence-based reading and writing scores over 500: 93%; SAT math scores over 500: 93%; ACT scores over 18: 98%; SAT evidence-based reading and writing scores over 600: 63%; SAT math scores over 600: 54%; ACT scores over 24: 68%; SAT evidence-based reading and writing scores over 700: 20%; SAT math scores over 700: 25%; ACT scores over 30: 21%.
Retention: 81% of full-time freshmen returned.

FACULTY
Total: 112, 70% full-time, 78% with terminal degrees.
Student/faculty ratio: 11:1.

ACADEMICS
Calendar: 8 3.5 week terms. *Degree:* bachelor's.
Special study options: advanced placement credit, double majors, English as a second language, independent study, internships, off-campus study, services for LD students, student-designed majors, study abroad.
Unusual degree programs: 3-2 engineering with University of Minnesota; forestry with Duke University; architecture with Washington University in St. Louis.
Computers: 259 computers/terminals and 1,200 ports are available on campus for general student use. Students can access the following: campus intranet, computer help desk, free student e-mail accounts, online (class) grades, online (class) registration, online (class) schedules. Campuswide network is available. 100% of college-owned or -operated housing units are wired for high-speed Internet access. Wireless service is available via entire campus.
Library: Cole Library plus 1 other. *Books:* 232,914 (physical); *Serial titles:* 491 (digital/electronic). Weekly public service hours: 70; students can reserve study rooms.

STUDENT LIFE
Housing options: on-campus residence required through senior year; coed, women-only. Campus housing is university owned and leased by the school. Freshman campus housing is guaranteed.
Activities and organizations: drama/theater group, student-run newspaper, radio station, choral group, Student-initiated Living-Learning Community, Chess and Games, Environmental Club, Performing Arts and Activities Council, Alliance.
Athletics Member NCAA. All Division III. *Intercollegiate sports:* baseball M, basketball M/W, cross-country running M/W, football M, lacrosse M/W, soccer M/W, softball W, tennis M/W, track and field M/W, ultimate Frisbee M(c)/W(c), volleyball M(c)/W, wrestling M. *Intramural sports:* badminton M/W, basketball M/W, bowling M/W, cheerleading M/W, fencing M(c)/W(c), football M/W, golf M/W, ice hockey M/W, lacrosse M(c)/W(c), racquetball M/W, soccer M/W, softball M/W, table tennis M/W, tennis M/W, track and field M/W, ultimate Frisbee M/W, volleyball M/W, weight lifting M/W, wrestling M/W.
Campus security: 24-hour emergency response devices and patrols, late-night transport/escort service, controlled dormitory access.
Student services: health clinic, personal/psychological counseling.

COSTS & FINANCIAL AID
Costs (2018–19) *Comprehensive fee:* $51,683 includes full-time tuition ($41,874), mandatory fees ($425), and room and board ($9384). Part-time tuition: $5232 per course. Part-time tuition and fees vary according to course load. *College room only:* $4326. Room and board charges vary according to board plan and housing facility. *Payment plan:* installment. *Waivers:* employees or children of employees.
Financial Aid Of all full-time matriculated undergraduates who enrolled in 2017, 799 applied for aid, 708 were judged to have need, 149 had their need fully met. 350 Federal Work-Study jobs (averaging $1655). 117 state and other part-time jobs (averaging $950). In 2017, 276 non-need-based awards were made. *Average percent of need met:* 80. *Average financial aid package:* $30,999. *Average need-based loan:* $4505. *Average need-based gift aid:* $26,977. *Average non-need-based aid:* $21,726. *Average indebtedness upon graduation:* $34,130.

APPLYING
Standardized Tests *Recommended:* SAT or ACT (for admission).
Options: electronic application, early admission, early decision, early action, deferred entrance.
Application fee: $30.
Required: essay or personal statement, high school transcript, 1 letter of recommendation.
Application deadlines: 2/1 (freshmen), 3/1 (transfers), 12/1 (early action).
Early decision deadline: 11/1 (for plan 1), 2/1 (for plan 2).
Notification: 3/20 (freshmen), continuous (transfers), 12/15 (early decision plan 1), 3/15 (early decision plan 2), 2/1 (early action).

CONTACT
Ms. Marie Schofer, Director of Admissions, Cornell College, 600 First Street SW, Mount Vernon, IA 52314-1098. *Phone:* 319-895-4159. *Toll-free phone:* 800-747-1112. *Fax:* 319-895-4451. *E-mail:* admission@cornellcollege.edu.

Divine Word College
Epworth, Iowa
http://www.dwci.edu/
CONTACT
Divine Word College, 102 Jacoby Drive SW, Epworth, IA 52045-0380. *Phone:* 563-876-3353. *Toll-free phone:* 800-553-3321.

Dordt College
Sioux Center, Iowa
http://www.dordt.edu/
CONTACT
Mr. Howard Wislon, Vice President for Enrollment, Dordt College, 498 4th Avenue, NE, Sioux Center, IA 51250-1697. *Phone:* 712-722-6080. *Toll-free phone:* 800-343-6738. *Fax:* 712-722-6035. *E-mail:* admissions@dordt.edu.

Drake University
Des Moines, Iowa
http://www.drake.edu/
- **Independent** university, founded 1881
- **Urban** 120-acre campus
- **Endowment** $210.6 million
- **Coed** 3,098 undergraduate students, 95% full-time, 57% women, 43% men
- **Moderately difficult** entrance level, 69% of applicants were admitted

UNDERGRAD STUDENTS
2,955 full-time, 143 part-time. Students come from 45 states and territories; 37 other countries; 69% are from out of state; 5% Black or

African American, non-Hispanic/Latino; 5% Hispanic/Latino; 3% Asian, non-Hispanic/Latino; 0.1% American Indian or Alaska Native, non-Hispanic/Latino; 3% Two or more races, non-Hispanic/Latino; 0.8% Race/ethnicity unknown; 6% international; 4% transferred in; 70% live on campus.

Freshmen:
Admission: 5,574 applied, 3,835 admitted, 758 enrolled. *Average high school GPA:* 3.7. *Test scores:* SAT evidence-based reading and writing scores over 500: 93%; SAT math scores over 500: 93%; ACT scores over 18: 99%; SAT evidence-based reading and writing scores over 600: 65%; SAT math scores over 600: 60%; ACT scores over 24: 82%; SAT evidence-based reading and writing scores over 700: 13%; SAT math scores over 700: 27%; ACT scores over 30: 32%.
Retention: 87% of full-time freshmen returned.

FACULTY
Total: 478, 65% full-time, 67% with terminal degrees.

ACADEMICS
Calendar: semesters. *Degrees:* bachelor's, master's, doctoral, post-master's, and postbachelor's certificates.

Special study options: accelerated degree program, advanced placement credit, cooperative education, distance learning, double majors, English as a second language, honors programs, independent study, internships, off-campus study, part-time degree program, services for LD students, student-designed majors, study abroad, summer session for credit. *ROTC:* Army (c), Air Force (c).

Unusual degree programs: 3-2 journalism and law, arts and sciences and law, accounting.

Computers: Students can access the following: campus intranet, computer help desk, free student e-mail accounts, online (class) grades, online (class) registration, online (class) schedules. Campuswide network is available. 100% of college-owned or -operated housing units are wired for high-speed Internet access. Wireless service is available via classrooms, computer centers, computer labs, dorm rooms, libraries, student centers.

Library: Cowles Library plus 1 other. Study areas open 24 hours, 5–7 days a week; students can reserve study rooms.

STUDENT LIFE
Housing options: on-campus residence required through sophomore year; coed. Campus housing is university owned and is provided by a third party. Freshman campus housing is guaranteed.

Activities and organizations: drama/theater group, student-run newspaper, radio and television station, choral group, marching band, Student Activities Board, Drake Magazine, Dog Pound Pep Squad, Alpha Phi Omega, Residence Hall Association, national fraternities, national sororities.

Athletics Member NCAA. All Division I except football (Division I-AA). *Intercollegiate sports:* basketball M(s)/W(s), cheerleading M(s)/W(s), crew W, cross-country running M(s)/W(s), golf M(s)/W, soccer M(s)/W(s), softball W(s), tennis M(s)/W(s), track and field M(s)/W(s), volleyball W(s). *Intramural sports:* badminton M/W, basketball M/W, football M/W, golf M/W, racquetball M/W, soccer M(c)/W, softball M/W, swimming and diving M/W, tennis M/W, volleyball M/W(c).

Campus security: 24-hour emergency response devices and patrols, late-night transport/escort service, controlled dormitory access, 24-hour desk attendants in residence halls.

Student services: health clinic, personal/psychological counseling, legal services.

COSTS & FINANCIAL AID
Costs (2018–19) *Comprehensive fee:* $51,554 includes full-time tuition ($41,250), mandatory fees ($146), and room and board ($10,158). Full-time tuition and fees vary according to course load, degree level, program, and student level. Part-time tuition: $775 per credit hour. Part-time tuition and fees vary according to class time, degree level, and program. No tuition increase for student's term of enrollment. *College room only:* $5486. Room and board charges vary according to board plan and housing facility. *Payment plan:* installment. *Waivers:* children of alumni, senior citizens, and employees or children of employees.

Financial Aid Of all full-time matriculated undergraduates who enrolled in 2017, 2,119 applied for aid, 1,796 were judged to have need, 494 had their need fully met. 1,458 Federal Work-Study jobs (averaging $1914). In

2017, 937 non-need-based awards were made. *Average percent of need met:* 77. *Average financial aid package:* $28,868. *Average need-based loan:* $5573. *Average need-based gift aid:* $20,625. *Average non-need-based aid:* $15,950. *Average indebtedness upon graduation:* $34,600.

APPLYING
Standardized Tests *Required for some:* SAT or ACT (for admission).
Options: electronic application, early admission, deferred entrance.
Required: essay or personal statement, high school transcript. *Recommended:* interview.
Application deadlines: 3/1 (freshmen), rolling (transfers).
Notification: continuous (freshmen), continuous (transfers).

CONTACT
Drake University, 2507 University Avenue, Des Moines, IA 50311. *Phone:* 515-271-3182. *Toll-free phone:* 800-44-DRAKE Ext. 3181. *E-mail:* admission@drake.edu.

Emmaus Bible College
Dubuque, Iowa
http://www.emmaus.edu/
- **Independent nondenominational** 4-year, founded 1941
- **Small-town** 22-acre campus
- **Coed** 269 undergraduate students, 92% full-time, 56% women, 44% men
- **Noncompetitive** entrance level, 58% of applicants were admitted

UNDERGRAD STUDENTS
248 full-time, 21 part-time. 57% are from out of state; 4% Black or African American, non-Hispanic/Latino; 6% Hispanic/Latino; 5% Asian, non-Hispanic/Latino; 2% American Indian or Alaska Native, non-Hispanic/Latino; 4% Two or more races, non-Hispanic/Latino; 6% Race/ethnicity unknown; 8% transferred in; 90% live on campus.

Freshmen:
Admission: 193 applied, 111 admitted, 61 enrolled. *Average high school GPA:* 3.5. *Test scores:* SAT evidence-based reading and writing scores over 500: 89%; SAT math scores over 500: 72%; ACT scores over 18: 83%; SAT evidence-based reading and writing scores over 600: 45%; SAT math scores over 600: 17%; ACT scores over 24: 47%; SAT evidence-based reading and writing scores over 700: 6%; SAT math scores over 700: 6%; ACT scores over 30: 13%.
Retention: 70% of full-time freshmen returned.

FACULTY
Total: 39, 51% full-time, 18% with terminal degrees.
Student/faculty ratio: 10:1.

ACADEMICS
Calendar: semesters. *Degrees:* certificates, associate, and bachelor's.

Special study options: advanced placement credit, distance learning, double majors, independent study, internships, off-campus study, part-time degree program, services for LD students, summer session for credit.

Computers: Students can access the following: campus intranet, computer help desk, free student e-mail accounts, online (class) grades, online (class) registration, online (class) schedules. Campuswide network is available. 226% of college-owned or -operated housing units are wired for high-speed Internet access. Wireless service is available via entire campus.

Library: The Emmaus Bible College Library plus 1 other. Weekly public service hours: 130.

STUDENT LIFE
Housing options: on-campus residence required through senior year; men-only, women-only. Campus housing is university owned. Freshman campus housing is guaranteed.

Activities and organizations: choral group.

Athletics Member NCCAA. *Intercollegiate sports:* basketball M/W, soccer M, volleyball W. *Intramural sports:* badminton M/W, basketball M/W, golf M/W, racquetball M/W, soccer M/W, softball M/W, table tennis M/W, tennis M/W, ultimate Frisbee M/W, volleyball M/W.

Campus security: 24-hour emergency response devices, student patrols, controlled dormitory access.

Student services: personal/psychological counseling.

COSTS

Costs (2018–19) *Comprehensive fee:* $26,900 includes full-time tuition ($18,400) and room and board ($8500). Full-time tuition and fees vary according to course load. Part-time tuition: $765 per credit hour. *Payment plan:* installment. *Waivers:* employees or children of employees.

APPLYING

Standardized Tests *Required:* SAT or ACT (for admission).

Options: electronic application, deferred entrance.

Required: essay or personal statement, high school transcript, minimum 2.0 GPA, 1 letter of recommendation.

Application deadlines: 8/1 (freshmen), 8/1 (transfers).

Notification: continuous (freshmen), continuous (transfers).

CONTACT

Emmaus Bible College, 2570 Asbury Road, Dubuque, IA 52001-3097. *Toll-free phone:* 800-397-2425.

Faith Baptist Bible College and Theological Seminary

Ankeny, Iowa

http://www.faith.edu/

- **Independent** comprehensive, founded 1921, affiliated with General Association of Regular Baptist Churches
- **Suburban** 52-acre campus
- **Endowment** $4.0 million
- **Coed**
- **Minimally difficult** entrance level

FACULTY

Student/faculty ratio: 11:1.

ACADEMICS

Calendar: semesters. *Degrees:* certificates, associate, bachelor's, and master's.
Library: John L. Patten Library.

STUDENT LIFE

Housing options: on-campus residence required through senior year; men-only, women-only, special housing for students with disabilities. Campus housing is university owned. Freshman campus housing is guaranteed.

Activities and organizations: drama/theater group, choral group, Student Association, Student Missionary Fellowship, Intramural Sports, Photo Club, Chapel Orchestra.

Athletics Member NCCAA.

Campus security: 24-hour emergency response devices and patrols, late-night transport/escort service.

Student services: personal/psychological counseling.

COSTS & FINANCIAL AID

Costs (2017–18) *Comprehensive fee:* $23,566 includes full-time tuition ($16,274), mandatory fees ($492), and room and board ($6800). Full-time tuition and fees vary according to course load. Part-time tuition: $595 per credit hour. *Required fees:* $246 per term part-time. *College room only:* $3230.

Financial Aid Of all full-time matriculated undergraduates who enrolled in 2004, 311 applied for aid, 290 were judged to have need, 5 had their need fully met. In 2004, 21 non-need-based awards were made. *Average percent of need met:* 48. *Average financial aid package:* $7124. *Average need-based loan:* $3142. *Average need-based gift aid:* $6299. *Average non-need-based aid:* $2465. *Average indebtedness upon graduation:* $15,006.

APPLYING

Standardized Tests *Required:* SAT or ACT (for admission).

Options: electronic application, deferred entrance.

Application fee: $45.

Required: essay or personal statement, high school transcript, 2 letters of recommendation. *Required for some:* interview. *Recommended:* minimum 2.0 GPA.

CONTACT

Miss Mary Tubbs, Admissions Coordinator, Faith Baptist Bible College and Theological Seminary, 1900 NW 4th Street, Ankeny, IA 50023. *Phone:* 515-964-0601. *Toll-free phone:* 888-FAITH 4U. *Fax:* 515-964-1638. *E-mail:* admissions@faith.edu.

Graceland University

Lamoni, Iowa

http://www.graceland.edu/

- **Independent Community of Christ** comprehensive, founded 1895
- **Small-town** 170-acre campus with easy access to Des Moines
- **Endowment** $50.9 million
- **Coed** 1,404 undergraduate students, 76% full-time, 56% women, 44% men
- **Moderately difficult** entrance level, 56% of applicants were admitted

UNDERGRAD STUDENTS

1,061 full-time, 343 part-time. Students come from 42 states and territories; 26 other countries; 77% are from out of state; 10% Black or African American, non-Hispanic/Latino; 9% Hispanic/Latino; 1% Asian, non-Hispanic/Latino; 1% Native Hawaiian or other Pacific Islander, non-Hispanic/Latino; 0.4% American Indian or Alaska Native, non-Hispanic/Latino; 4% Two or more races, non-Hispanic/Latino; 17% Race/ethnicity unknown; 3% international; 9% transferred in; 71% live on campus.

Freshmen:
Admission: 2,800 applied, 1,572 admitted, 255 enrolled. *Average high school GPA:* 3.2. *Test scores:* SAT evidence-based reading and writing scores over 500: 41%; SAT math scores over 500: 58%; ACT scores over 18: 82%; SAT evidence-based reading and writing scores over 600: 7%; SAT math scores over 600: 8%; ACT scores over 24: 18%; ACT scores over 30: 2%.
Retention: 62% of full-time freshmen returned.

FACULTY

Total: 83, 76% full-time, 61% with terminal degrees.

Student/faculty ratio: 17:1.

ACADEMICS

Calendar: 4-1-4. *Degrees:* certificates, bachelor's, master's, doctoral, post-master's, and postbachelor's certificates.

Special study options: academic remediation for entering students, accelerated degree program, adult/continuing education programs, advanced placement credit, cooperative education, distance learning, double majors, freshman honors college, honors programs, independent study, internships, part-time degree program, services for LD students, student-designed majors, study abroad, summer session for credit.

Computers: 179 computers/terminals are available on campus for general student use. Students can access the following: campus intranet, computer help desk, free student e-mail accounts, online (class) grades, online (class) registration, online (class) schedules. Campuswide network is available. 100% of college-owned or -operated housing units are wired for high-speed Internet access. Wireless service is available via classrooms, computer centers, computer labs, dorm rooms, learning centers, libraries, student centers.

Library: F. M. Smith Library. *Books:* 80,000 (physical), 350,000 (digital/electronic); *Serial titles:* 153 (physical), 60 (digital/electronic); *Databases:* 50. Weekly public service hours: 80; students can reserve study rooms.

STUDENT LIFE

Housing options: on-campus residence required through senior year; men-only, women-only, special housing for students with disabilities. Campus housing is university owned. Freshman campus housing is guaranteed.

Activities and organizations: drama/theater group, student-run newspaper, radio station, choral group, marching band, Black Student Union, Latin Club, Enactus, Social Equality Alliance, Communication Club.

Athletics Member NAIA. *Intercollegiate sports:* baseball M(s), basketball M(s)/W(s), cheerleading M(s)/W(s), cross-country running M(s)/W(s), football M(s), golf M(s)/W(s), soccer M(s)/W(s), softball W(s), track and field M(s)/W(s), volleyball M(s)/W(s), wrestling M(s).

Intramural sports: basketball M/W, football M/W, soccer M/W, softball M/W, table tennis M/W, ultimate Frisbee M/W, volleyball M/W.

Campus security: 24-hour emergency response devices, late-night transport/escort service, controlled dormitory access.

Student services: health clinic, personal/psychological counseling.

COSTS & FINANCIAL AID

Costs (2018–19) *Comprehensive fee:* $38,000 includes full-time tuition ($28,600), mandatory fees ($640), and room and board ($8760). Full-time tuition and fees vary according to course load, degree level, location, and program. Part-time tuition: $800 per semester hour. Part-time tuition and fees vary according to course load, degree level, location, and program. *Required fees:* $320 per semester part-time. *College room only:* $3370. Room and board charges vary according to board plan, housing facility, and location. *Payment plan:* installment. *Waivers:* senior citizens and employees or children of employees.

Financial Aid Of all full-time matriculated undergraduates who enrolled in 2017, 993 applied for aid, 920 were judged to have need, 124 had their need fully met. 276 Federal Work-Study jobs (averaging $905). 505 state and other part-time jobs (averaging $1148). In 2017, 151 non-need-based awards were made. *Average percent of need met:* 74. *Average financial aid package:* $24,479. *Average need-based loan:* $4562. *Average need-based gift aid:* $20,085. *Average non-need-based aid:* $14,231. *Average indebtedness upon graduation:* $32,120.

APPLYING

Standardized Tests *Required:* SAT or ACT (for admission), TOEFL or IELTS for all students whose first language is not English (for admission).

Options: electronic application.

Required: high school transcript, 2 of the following: minimum high school GPA of 2.5 or rank in top half of class or minimum of 21 on ACT or 960 on the SAT. *Required for some:* essay or personal statement, 2 letters of recommendation, interview.

Application deadlines: rolling (freshmen), rolling (transfers).

Notification: continuous (freshmen), continuous (transfers).

CONTACT

Mr. Kevin Brown, Director of Admissions, Graceland University, 1 University Place, Lamoni, IA 50140. *Phone:* 641-784-5149. *Toll-free phone:* 866-GRACELAND. *Fax:* 641-784-5480. *E-mail:* admissions@graceland.edu.

★ Grand View University
Des Moines, Iowa
http://www.grandview.edu/

- **Independent** comprehensive, founded 1896, affiliated with Evangelical Lutheran Church in America
- **Urban** 25-acre campus
- **Endowment** $22.6 million
- **Coed** 1,788 undergraduate students, 88% full-time, 56% women, 44% men
- **Minimally difficult** entrance level, 93% of applicants were admitted

UNDERGRAD STUDENTS

1,574 full-time, 214 part-time. Students come from 38 states and territories; 38 other countries; 7% are from out of state; 7% Black or African American, non-Hispanic/Latino; 5% Hispanic/Latino; 3% Asian, non-Hispanic/Latino; 0.2% Native Hawaiian or other Pacific Islander, non-Hispanic/Latino; 0.4% American Indian or Alaska Native, non-Hispanic/Latino; 6% Two or more races, non-Hispanic/Latino; 9% Race/ethnicity unknown; 3% international; 14% transferred in; 55% live on campus.

Freshmen:
Admission: 820 applied, 760 admitted, 331 enrolled. *Average high school GPA:* 3.3. *Test scores:* SAT evidence-based reading and writing scores over 500: 45%; SAT math scores over 500: 55%; ACT scores over 18: 87%; SAT evidence-based reading and writing scores over 600: 9%; SAT math scores over 600: 20%; ACT scores over 24: 23%; SAT math scores over 700: 8%; ACT scores over 30: 1%.
Retention: 67% of full-time freshmen returned.

FACULTY

Total: 222, 40% full-time, 43% with terminal degrees.

Student/faculty ratio: 13:1.

ACADEMICS

Calendar: semesters. *Degrees:* certificates, bachelor's, master's, and postbachelor's certificates.

Special study options: academic remediation for entering students, accelerated degree program, adult/continuing education programs, advanced placement credit, cooperative education, distance learning, double majors, English as a second language, freshman honors college, honors programs, independent study, internships, off-campus study, part-time degree program, services for LD students, student-designed majors, study abroad, summer session for credit. *ROTC:* Army (c), Air Force (c).

Unusual degree programs: 3-2 engineering with Iowa State University.

Computers: 336 computers/terminals are available on campus for general student use. Students can access the following: campus intranet, computer help desk, free student e-mail accounts, online (class) grades, online (class) registration, online (class) schedules. Campuswide network is available. 100% of college-owned or -operated housing units are wired for high-speed Internet access. Wireless service is available via classrooms, computer labs, libraries, student centers.

Library: Grand View University Library plus 1 other. *Books:* 88,382 (physical), 45,490 (digital/electronic); *Serial titles:* 514 (physical), 75,889 (digital/electronic); *Databases:* 29. Weekly public service hours: 86.

STUDENT LIFE

Housing options: on-campus residence required through junior year; coed. Campus housing is university owned. Freshman applicants given priority for college housing.

Activities and organizations: drama/theater group, student-run newspaper, radio station, choral group, Nursing Student Association, Art Club, Science Club, Education Club, Business Club.

Athletics Member NAIA. *Intercollegiate sports:* baseball M(s), basketball M(s)/W(s), bowling M(s)/W(s), cheerleading M(s)/W(s), cross-country running M(s)/W(s), football M(s), golf M(s)/W(s), riflery M(s)/W(s), soccer M(s)/W(s), softball W(s), tennis M(s)/W(s), track and field M(s)/W(s), volleyball M(s)/W(s), wrestling M(s). *Intramural sports:* basketball M/W, football M/W, soccer M/W, table tennis M/W, ultimate Frisbee M/W, volleyball M/W.

Campus security: 24-hour emergency response devices and patrols, late-night transport/escort service, controlled dormitory access, night security patrols.

Student services: health clinic, personal/psychological counseling.

COSTS & FINANCIAL AID

Costs (2018–19) *Comprehensive fee:* $36,696 includes full-time tuition ($26,922), mandatory fees ($596), and room and board ($9178). Full-time tuition and fees vary according to class time and course load. Part-time tuition: $669 per credit hour. Part-time tuition and fees vary according to class time and course load. *Room and board:* Room and board charges vary according to board plan and housing facility. *Payment plan:* installment. *Waivers:* children of alumni, senior citizens, and employees or children of employees.

Financial Aid Of all full-time matriculated undergraduates who enrolled in 2016, 1,499 applied for aid, 1,348 were judged to have need, 361 had their need fully met. 336 Federal Work-Study jobs (averaging $1354). In 2016, 261 non-need-based awards were made. *Average percent of need met:* 78. *Average financial aid package:* $19,738. *Average need-based loan:* $4535. *Average need-based gift aid:* $17,665. *Average non-need-based aid:* $9015. *Average indebtedness upon graduation:* $37,158.

APPLYING

Standardized Tests *Required:* SAT or ACT (for admission).

Options: electronic application.

Required: high school transcript. *Recommended:* minimum 2.0 GPA.

Application deadlines: 8/15 (freshmen), 8/15 (transfers).

Notification: 9/15 (freshmen), continuous until 9/15 (transfers).

CONTACT

Mr. Ryan Thompson, Director of Admissions, Grand View University, 1200 Grandview Avenue, Des Moines, IA 50316-1599. *Phone:* 515-263-2810. *Toll-free phone:* 800-444-6083. *Fax:* 515-263-2974. *E-mail:* admissions@grandview.edu.

See previous page for display ad and page 1300 for the College Close-Up.

Grinnell College
Grinnell, Iowa
http://www.grinnell.edu/

- **Independent** 4-year, founded 1846
- **Small-town** 120-acre campus
- **Endowment** $1.9 billion
- **Coed** 1,712 undergraduate students, 97% full-time, 53% women, 47% men
- **Very difficult** entrance level, 29% of applicants were admitted

UNDERGRAD STUDENTS

1,662 full-time, 50 part-time. Students come from 52 states and territories; 51 other countries; 92% are from out of state; 6% Black or African American, non-Hispanic/Latino; 7% Hispanic/Latino; 8% Asian, non-Hispanic/Latino; 4% Two or more races, non-Hispanic/Latino; 5% Race/ethnicity unknown; 19% international; 0.2% transferred in; 88% live on campus.

Freshmen:
Admission: 5,850 applied, 1,689 admitted, 447 enrolled. *Test scores:* SAT evidence-based reading and writing scores over 500: 100%; SAT math scores over 500: 100%; ACT scores over 18: 100%; SAT evidence-based reading and writing scores over 600: 94%; SAT math scores over 600: 94%; ACT scores over 24: 100%; SAT evidence-based reading and writing scores over 700: 50%; SAT math scores over 700: 64%; ACT scores over 30: 84%.
Retention: 96% of full-time freshmen returned.

FACULTY

Total: 209, 85% full-time, 91% with terminal degrees.
Student/faculty ratio: 9:1.

ACADEMICS

Calendar: semesters. *Degree:* bachelor's.

Special study options: accelerated degree program, advanced placement credit, double majors, independent study, internships, off-campus study, services for LD students, student-designed majors, study abroad.

Unusual degree programs: 3-2 engineering with Columbia University, California Institute of Technology, Rensselaer Polytechnic Institute, Washington University in St. Louis; architecture with Washington University in St. Louis, law at Columbia University.

Computers: 200 computers/terminals are available on campus for general student use. Students can access the following: campus intranet, computer help desk, free student e-mail accounts, online (class) grades, online (class) registration, online (class) schedules. Campuswide network is available. 100% of college-owned or -operated housing units are wired for high-speed Internet access. Wireless service is available via entire campus.

Library: Burling Library plus 2 others. *Books:* 488,334 (physical), 474,326 (digital/electronic); *Serial titles:* 6,491 (physical), 11,577 (digital/electronic); *Databases:* 346. Weekly public service hours: 109.

STUDENT LIFE

Housing options: on-campus residence required through sophomore year; coed, cooperative, special housing for students with disabilities. Campus housing is university owned. Freshman campus housing is guaranteed.

Activities and organizations: drama/theater group, student-run newspaper, radio station, choral group, Concerned Black Students, International Student Organization, Student Organization of Latinas/Latinos, Campus Democrats, Ultimate Frisbee.

Athletics Member NCAA. All Division III. *Intercollegiate sports:* baseball M, basketball M/W, cross-country running M/W, football M, golf M/W, soccer M/W, softball W, swimming and diving M/W, tennis M/W, track and field M/W, volleyball W. *Intramural sports:* archery M(c)/W(c), badminton M/W, baseball M(c)/W(c), basketball M/W, equestrian sports M(c)/W(c), fencing M(c)/W(c), rugby M(c)/W(c), sailing M(c)/W(c), soccer M/W, softball M/W, tennis M/W, ultimate Frisbee M(c)/W, volleyball M/W, water polo M/W.

Campus security: 24-hour emergency response devices and patrols, student patrols, late-night transport/escort service, controlled dormitory access.

Student services: health clinic, personal/psychological counseling.

COSTS & FINANCIAL AID

Costs (2018–19) *Comprehensive fee:* $65,202 includes full-time tuition ($51,924), mandatory fees ($468), and room and board ($12,810). Part-time tuition: $1571 per credit hour. *College room only:* $6050. Room and board charges vary according to board plan and housing facility. *Payment plan:* installment. *Waivers:* employees or children of employees.

Financial Aid Of all full-time matriculated undergraduates who enrolled in 2017, 1,198 applied for aid, 1,078 were judged to have need, 1,078 had their need fully met. 562 Federal Work-Study jobs (averaging $1928). 581 state and other part-time jobs (averaging $2078). In 2017, 339 non-need-based awards were made. *Average percent of need met:* 100. *Average financial aid package:* $47,561. *Average need-based loan:* $4129. *Average need-based gift aid:* $41,344. *Average non-need-based aid:* $18,444. *Average indebtedness upon graduation:* $19,392. *Financial aid deadline:* 1/15.

APPLYING

Standardized Tests *Required:* SAT or ACT (for admission).

Options: electronic application, early admission, early decision, deferred entrance.

Required: essay or personal statement, high school transcript, 3 letters of recommendation. *Recommended:* interview.

Application deadlines: 1/15 (freshmen), 4/1 (transfers).

Early decision deadline: 11/15 (for plan 1), 1/1 (for plan 2).

Notification: 4/1 (freshmen), 5/20 (transfers), 12/15 (early decision plan 1), 2/1 (early decision plan 2).

CONTACT

Ms. Sarah Fischer, Director of Admission, Grinnell College, 1103 Park Street, Grinnell, IA 50112. *Phone:* 641-269-3600. *Toll-free phone:* 800-247-0113. *Fax:* 641-269-4800. *E-mail:* askgrin@grinnell.edu.

Hamilton Technical College

Davenport, Iowa

http://www.hamiltontechcollege.edu/

CONTACT

Hamilton Technical College, 1011 East 53rd Street, Davenport, IA 52807-2653. *Phone:* 563-386-3570. *Toll-free phone:* 866-966-4825.

INSTE Bible College

Ankeny, Iowa

http://www.inste.edu/

CONTACT

Admissions, INSTE Bible College, 2302 SW 3rd Street, Ankeny, IA 50023. *Phone:* 515-289-9200. *Fax:* 515-289-9201. *E-mail:* inste@inste.edu.

Iowa State University of Science and Technology

Ames, Iowa

http://www.iastate.edu/

- **State-supported** university, founded 1858
- **Suburban** 1795-acre campus with easy access to Des Moines
- **Endowment** $838.9 million
- **Coed** 30,406 undergraduate students, 94% full-time, 42% women, 58% men
- **Moderately difficult** entrance level, 89% of applicants were admitted

UNDERGRAD STUDENTS

28,590 full-time, 1,816 part-time. Students come from 53 states and territories; 124 other countries; 35% are from out of state; 3% Black or African American, non-Hispanic/Latino; 5% Hispanic/Latino; 3% Asian, non-Hispanic/Latino; 0.1% Native Hawaiian or other Pacific Islander, non-Hispanic/Latino; 0.2% American Indian or Alaska Native, non-Hispanic/Latino; 2% Two or more races, non-Hispanic/Latino; 5% Race/ethnicity unknown; 7% international; 6% transferred in; 41% live on campus.

Freshmen:

Admission: 19,262 applied, 17,208 admitted, 5,944 enrolled. *Average high school GPA:* 3.5. *Test scores:* SAT evidence-based reading and writing scores over 500: 83%; SAT math scores over 500: 90%; ACT scores over 18: 97%; SAT evidence-based reading and writing scores over 600: 46%; SAT math scores over 600: 60%; ACT scores over 24: 63%; SAT evidence-based reading and writing scores over 700: 11%; SAT math scores over 700: 18%; ACT scores over 30: 17%.

Retention: 88% of full-time freshmen returned.

FACULTY

Total: 1,874, 83% full-time, 88% with terminal degrees.

Student/faculty ratio: 19:1.

ACADEMICS

Calendar: semesters. *Degrees:* bachelor's, master's, doctoral, post-master's, and postbachelor's certificates.

Special study options: academic remediation for entering students, accelerated degree program, adult/continuing education programs, advanced placement credit, cooperative education, distance learning, double majors, English as a second language, external degree program, freshman honors college, honors programs, independent study, internships, off-campus study, part-time degree program, services for LD students, student-designed majors, study abroad, summer session for credit. *ROTC:* Army (b), Navy (b), Air Force (b).

Unusual degree programs: 3-2 engineering with William Penn College.

Computers: 2,527 computers/terminals are available on campus for general student use. Students can access the following: campus intranet, computer help desk, free student e-mail accounts, online (class) grades, online (class) registration, online (class) schedules, network services. Campuswide network is available. 100% of college-owned or -operated housing units are wired for high-speed Internet access. Wireless service is available via entire campus.

Library: Parks Library (University Library) plus 1 other. *Books:* 2.9 million (physical), 447,689 (digital/electronic); *Serial titles:* 25,754 (physical), 95,371 (digital/electronic); *Databases:* 303. Weekly public service hours: 113; students can reserve study rooms.

STUDENT LIFE

Housing options: coed, men-only, women-only, special housing for students with disabilities. Campus housing is university owned.

Activities and organizations: drama/theater group, student-run newspaper, radio and television station, choral group, marching band, Greek Life, Intramural Sports Activities, Club Sports, national fraternities, national sororities.

Athletics Member NCAA. All Division I except football (Division I-A). *Intercollegiate sports:* basketball M(s)/W(s), cross-country running M(s)/W(s), golf M(s)/W(s), gymnastics W(s), soccer W(s), softball W(s), swimming and diving M(s)/W(s), tennis W(s), track and field M(s)/W(s), volleyball W(s), wrestling M(s). *Intramural sports:* archery M(c)/W(c), badminton M(c)/W(c), baseball M(c)/W(c), basketball M/W, bowling M(c)/W(c), crew M(c)/W(c), cross-country running M/W, equestrian sports M(c)/W(c), fencing M(c)/W(c), football M/W, golf M/W, gymnastics W, ice hockey M/W, lacrosse M(c)/W(c), racquetball M(c)/W(c), riflery M(c)/W(c), rugby M(c)/W(c), sailing M(c)/W(c), sand volleyball M/W, skiing (cross-country) M(c)/W(c), skiing (downhill) M(c)/W(c), soccer M(c)/W(c), softball M/W, swimming and diving M/W, table tennis M/W, tennis M/W, track and field M/W, ultimate Frisbee M/W, volleyball M/W, water polo M(c)/W(c), weight lifting M(c)/W(c), wrestling M/W.

Campus security: 24-hour emergency response devices and patrols, late-night transport/escort service, controlled dormitory access, crime prevention programs, threat assessment team, motor vehicle help van.

Student services: health clinic, personal/psychological counseling, women's center, legal services.

COSTS & FINANCIAL AID

Costs (2017–18) *Tuition:* state resident $7456 full-time, $311 per credit hour part-time; nonresident $21,292 full-time, $888 per credit hour part-time. Full-time tuition and fees vary according to class time, degree level, program, and student level. Part-time tuition and fees vary according to class time, course load, degree level, program, and student level. *Required fees:* $1180 full-time. *Room and board:* $8546; room only: $4562. Room and board charges vary according to board plan and housing facility. *Payment plans:* installment, deferred payment.

Financial Aid Of all full-time matriculated undergraduates who enrolled in 2016, 21,603 applied for aid, 14,163 were judged to have need, 2,966 had their need fully met. 1,336 Federal Work-Study jobs (averaging $1079). 11,355 state and other part-time jobs (averaging $2068). In 2016, 10064 non-need-based awards were made. *Average percent of need met:* 79. *Average financial aid package:* $12,456. *Average need-based loan:* $4408. *Average need-based gift aid:* $7606. *Average non-need-based aid:* $3463. *Average indebtedness upon graduation:* $27,643.

APPLYING
Standardized Tests *Required:* SAT or ACT (for admission).
Options: electronic application, early admission, deferred entrance.
Application fee: $40.
Required: high school transcript, minimum Regent Admission Index (RAI) of 245, high school course requirements.
Application deadlines: rolling (freshmen), rolling (transfers).
Notification: continuous (freshmen), continuous (transfers).

CONTACT
Phillip B. Caffrey, Associate Director for Admissions, Iowa State University of Science and Technology, 100 Enrollment Services, 2433 Union Dr., Ames, IA 50011-2042. *Phone:* 515-294-5836. *Toll-free phone:* 800-262-3810. *Fax:* 515-294-2592. *E-mail:* pbcaffr@iastate.edu.

Iowa Wesleyan University
Mount Pleasant, Iowa
http://www.iw.edu/

- **Independent United Methodist** 4-year, founded 1842
- **Small-town** 60-acre campus
- **Endowment** $9.7 million
- **Coed**
- **Moderately difficult** entrance level

FACULTY
Student/faculty ratio: 10:1.

ACADEMICS
Calendar: semesters. *Degree:* bachelor's.
Library: Chadwick Library plus 1 other. *Books:* 93,754 (physical), 3,338 (digital/electronic); *Serial titles:* 2,169 (physical), 4,827 (digital/electronic); *Databases:* 32. Weekly public service hours: 80; students can reserve study rooms.

STUDENT LIFE
Housing options: on-campus residence required through senior year; coed, men-only, women-only. Campus housing is university owned. Freshman campus housing is guaranteed.
Activities and organizations: choral group, Student Union Board, Student Government Association, Behavioral Science Club, Student Nurses Association, Homecoming Committee.
Athletics Member NCAA. All Division III.
Campus security: late-night transport/escort service, controlled dormitory access, evening patrols by trained security personnel.
Student services: personal/psychological counseling.

COSTS & FINANCIAL AID
Costs (2017–18) *Comprehensive fee:* $41,000 includes full-time tuition ($29,500), mandatory fees ($1000), and room and board ($10,500). Part-time tuition: $745 per credit hour. Part-time tuition and fees vary according to class time, course load, and location. *College room only:* $4000. Room and board charges vary according to housing facility. *Payment plans:* installment, deferred payment.

Financial Aid Of all full-time matriculated undergraduates who enrolled in 2016, 448 applied for aid, 448 were judged to have need, 51 had their need fully met. 84 Federal Work-Study jobs (averaging $800). In 2016, 14 non-need-based awards were made. *Average percent of need met:* 68. *Average financial aid package:* $21,546. *Average need-based loan:* $2382. *Average need-based gift aid:* $13,646. *Average non-need-based aid:* $15,437. *Average indebtedness upon graduation:* $33,152.

APPLYING
Standardized Tests *Required:* SAT or ACT (for admission).

Options: electronic application, early admission, deferred entrance.
Application fee: $20.
Required: high school transcript, minimum 2.5 GPA, minimum ACT score of 19 or SAT of 890. *Required for some:* essay or personal statement, 1 letter of recommendation, interview.

CONTACT
Julie Duplessis, Director of Enrollment, Iowa Wesleyan University, 601 N. Main Street, Mount Pleasant, IA 52641. *Phone:* 319-385-6208. *Toll-free phone:* 800-582-2383. *Fax:* 319-385-6240. *E-mail:* julie.duplessis@iw.edu.

Kaplan University, Cedar Falls
Cedar Falls, Iowa
http://www.kaplanuniversity.edu/

CONTACT
Kaplan University, Cedar Falls, 7009 Nordic Drive, Cedar Falls, IA 50613. *Phone:* 319-277-0220. *Toll-free phone:* 800-987-7734.

Kaplan University, Cedar Rapids
Cedar Rapids, Iowa
http://www.kaplanuniversity.edu/

CONTACT
Kaplan University, Cedar Rapids, 3165 Edgewood Parkway, SW, Cedar Rapids, IA 52404. *Phone:* 319-363-0481. *Toll-free phone:* 800-987-7734.

Kaplan University, Davenport
Davenport, Iowa
http://www.kaplanuniversity.edu/

CONTACT
Kaplan University, Davenport, 1801 East Kimberly Road, Suite 1, Davenport, IA 52807. *Phone:* 563-355-3500. *Toll-free phone:* 800-987-7734.

Kaplan University, Des Moines
Urbandale, Iowa
http://www.kaplanuniversity.edu/

CONTACT
Kaplan University, Des Moines, 4655 121st Street, Urbandale, IA 50323. *Phone:* 515-727-2100. *Toll-free phone:* 800-987-7734.

Kaplan University, Mason City
Mason City, Iowa
http://www.kaplanuniversity.edu/

CONTACT
Kaplan University, Mason City, 2570 4th Street, SW, Mason City, IA 50401. *Phone:* 641-423-2530. *Toll-free phone:* 800-987-7734.

Loras College
Dubuque, Iowa
http://www.loras.edu/

- **Independent Roman Catholic** comprehensive, founded 1839
- **Suburban** 64-acre campus
- **Endowment** $36.8 million
- **Coed** 1,397 undergraduate students, 96% full-time, 48% women, 52% men
- **Moderately difficult** entrance level, 95% of applicants were admitted

UNDERGRAD STUDENTS
1,335 full-time, 62 part-time. Students come from 25 states and territories; 9 other countries; 58% are from out of state; 2% Black or African American, non-Hispanic/Latino; 8% Hispanic/Latino; 0.8% Asian, non-Hispanic/Latino; 0.1% Native Hawaiian or other Pacific Islander, non-Hispanic/Latino; 0.1% American Indian or Alaska Native, non-Hispanic/Latino; 2% Two or more races, non-Hispanic/Latino; 5%

Race/ethnicity unknown; 2% international; 4% transferred in; 65% live on campus.

Freshmen:
Admission: 1,159 applied, 1,102 admitted, 337 enrolled. *Average high school GPA:* 3.4. *Test scores:* SAT evidence-based reading and writing scores over 500: 89%; SAT math scores over 500: 100%; ACT scores over 18: 97%; SAT evidence-based reading and writing scores over 600: 11%; SAT math scores over 600: 44%; ACT scores over 24: 44%; ACT scores over 30: 4%.
Retention: 76% of full-time freshmen returned.

FACULTY
Total: 143, 71% full-time, 73% with terminal degrees.
Student/faculty ratio: 12:1.

ACADEMICS
Calendar: semesters plus January term. *Degrees:* bachelor's, master's, and postbachelor's certificates.

Special study options: academic remediation for entering students, advanced placement credit, cooperative education, distance learning, double majors, honors programs, independent study, internships, off-campus study, part-time degree program, services for LD students, student-designed majors, study abroad, summer session for credit. *ROTC:* Army (c).

Unusual degree programs: 3-2 business administration; nursing with Allen College; athletic training.

Computers: 5 computers/terminals and 991 ports are available on campus for general student use. Students can access the following: campus intranet, computer help desk, free student e-mail accounts, online (class) grades, online (class) registration, online (class) schedules. Campuswide network is available. 100% of college-owned or -operated housing units are wired for high-speed Internet access. Wireless service is available via entire campus.

Library: Loras College Library. *Books:* 215,732 (physical), 141,947 (digital/electronic); *Serial titles:* 146 (physical), 52,920 (digital/electronic); *Databases:* 64. Weekly public service hours: 91; students can reserve study rooms.

STUDENT LIFE
Housing options: on-campus residence required through junior year; coed, men-only, women-only. Campus housing is university owned. Freshman campus housing is guaranteed.

Activities and organizations: drama/theater group, student-run newspaper, radio and television station, choral group, Dance Marathon, Campus Activities Board, DuBuddies, Social Work Club, American Chemical Society, national fraternities, national sororities.

Athletics Member NCAA. All Division III. *Intercollegiate sports:* baseball M, basketball M/W, cheerleading M(c)/W(c), cross-country running M/W, football M, golf M/W, ice hockey M(c)/W(c), lacrosse W, rugby M(c)/W(c), soccer M/W, softball W, swimming and diving M/W, tennis M/W, track and field M/W, ultimate Frisbee M(c)/W(c), volleyball M/W, wrestling M. *Intramural sports:* basketball M/W, racquetball M/W, soccer M/W, softball M/W, volleyball M/W.

Campus security: 24-hour emergency response devices and patrols, late-night transport/escort service, controlled dormitory access, online anonymous reporting system.

Student services: health clinic, personal/psychological counseling.

COSTS & FINANCIAL AID
Costs (2018–19) *Comprehensive fee:* $42,459 includes full-time tuition ($32,524), mandatory fees ($1660), and room and board ($8275). Full-time tuition and fees vary according to course load and degree level. Part-time tuition: $725 per credit hour. *Required fees:* $42 per credit hour part-time. *College room only:* $4000. Room and board charges vary according to board plan and housing facility. *Payment plan:* installment. *Waivers:* employees or children of employees.

Financial Aid Of all full-time matriculated undergraduates who enrolled in 2017, 1,157 applied for aid, 1,005 were judged to have need, 335 had their need fully met. 563 Federal Work-Study jobs (averaging $2339). 10 state and other part-time jobs (averaging $1250). In 2017, 327 non-need-based awards were made. *Average percent of need met:* 89. *Average financial aid package:* $27,733. *Average need-based loan:* $4968.

Average need-based gift aid: $21,256. *Average non-need-based aid:* $18,242. *Average indebtedness upon graduation:* $34,156.

APPLYING
Standardized Tests *Required:* SAT or ACT (for admission).
Options: electronic application, deferred entrance.
Required: high school transcript, minimum 2.5 GPA. *Required for some:* essay or personal statement, 1 letter of recommendation, interview. *Recommended:* essay or personal statement, 1 letter of recommendation.
Application deadlines: rolling (freshmen), rolling (out-of-state freshmen), rolling (transfers).
Notification: continuous (freshmen), continuous (out-of-state freshmen), continuous (transfers).

CONTACT
Loras College, 1450 Alta Vista Street, Dubuque, IA 52001. *Phone:* 800-245-6727. *Toll-free phone:* 800-245-6727. *Fax:* 563-588-7119. *E-mail:* admissions@loras.edu.

Luther College
Decorah, Iowa
http://www.luther.edu/

- **Independent** 4-year, founded 1861, affiliated with Evangelical Lutheran Church in America
- **Small-town** 200-acre campus
- **Endowment** $161.8 million
- **Coed** 2,053 undergraduate students, 98% full-time, 55% women, 45% men
- **Moderately difficult** entrance level, 65% of applicants were admitted

UNDERGRAD STUDENTS
2,014 full-time, 39 part-time. Students come from 39 states and territories; 74 other countries; 71% are from out of state; 2% Black or African American, non-Hispanic/Latino; 5% Hispanic/Latino; 1% Asian, non-Hispanic/Latino; 0.1% Native Hawaiian or other Pacific Islander, non-Hispanic/Latino; 0.4% American Indian or Alaska Native, non-Hispanic/Latino; 2% Two or more races, non-Hispanic/Latino; 0.2% Race/ethnicity unknown; 8% international; 1% transferred in; 93% live on campus.

Freshmen:
Admission: 4,288 applied, 2,791 admitted, 517 enrolled. *Average high school GPA:* 3.7. *Test scores:* SAT evidence-based reading and writing scores over 500: 76%; SAT math scores over 500: 83%; ACT scores over 18: 98%; SAT evidence-based reading and writing scores over 600: 45%; SAT math scores over 600: 48%; ACT scores over 24: 68%; SAT evidence-based reading and writing scores over 700: 14%; SAT math scores over 700: 17%; ACT scores over 30: 20%.
Retention: 83% of full-time freshmen returned.

FACULTY
Total: 208, 81% full-time, 85% with terminal degrees.
Student/faculty ratio: 11:1.

ACADEMICS
Calendar: 4-1-4. *Degree:* bachelor's.

Special study options: academic remediation for entering students, advanced placement credit, double majors, honors programs, independent study, internships, off-campus study, part-time degree program, services for LD students, student-designed majors, study abroad, summer session for credit.

Unusual degree programs: 3-2 engineering with Washington University in St. Louis; University of Minnesota, Twin Cities Campus.

Computers: 592 computers/terminals are available on campus for general student use. Students can access the following: campus intranet, computer help desk, free student e-mail accounts, online (class) grades, online (class) registration, online (class) schedules. Campuswide network is available. 100% of college-owned or -operated housing units are wired for high-speed Internet access. Wireless service is available via entire campus.

Library: Preus Library. *Books:* 202,938 (physical), 292,640 (digital/electronic); *Serial titles:* 17,086 (physical), 17,086 (digital/electronic); *Databases:* 99. Weekly public service hours: 104; students can reserve study rooms.

STUDENT LIFE

Housing options: on-campus residence required through senior year; coed, special housing for students with disabilities. Campus housing is university owned. Freshman campus housing is guaranteed.

Activities and organizations: drama/theater group, student-run newspaper, radio station, choral group, Alpha Phi Omega, college ministries, recreational sports, Student Activities Council, Diversity groups.

Athletics Member NCAA. All Division III. *Intercollegiate sports:* baseball M, basketball M/W, cross-country running M/W, football M, golf M/W, soccer M/W, softball W, swimming and diving M/W, tennis M/W, track and field M/W, ultimate Frisbee M(c)/W(c), volleyball W, wrestling M. *Intramural sports:* archery M/W, badminton M/W, basketball M/W, bowling M/W, football M/W, golf M/W, lacrosse W(c), racquetball M/W, rugby M(c)/W(c), soccer M/W, softball M/W, table tennis M/W, tennis M/W, track and field M/W, ultimate Frisbee M(c)/W(c), volleyball M/W.

Campus security: 24-hour emergency response devices and patrols, late-night transport/escort service, controlled dormitory access.

Student services: health clinic, personal/psychological counseling, women's center.

COSTS & FINANCIAL AID

Costs (2018–19) *Comprehensive fee:* $51,750 includes full-time tuition ($41,950), mandatory fees ($340), and room and board ($9460). Full-time tuition and fees vary according to course load. Part-time tuition: $1498 per credit hour. Part-time tuition and fees vary according to course load. *College room only:* $4420. Room and board charges vary according to board plan and housing facility. *Payment plan:* installment. *Waivers:* employees or children of employees.

Financial Aid Of all full-time matriculated undergraduates who enrolled in 2017, 1,749 applied for aid, 1,565 were judged to have need, 593 had their need fully met. 770 Federal Work-Study jobs (averaging $2055). 897 state and other part-time jobs (averaging $1769). In 2017, 443 non-need-based awards were made. *Average percent of need met:* 89. *Average financial aid package:* $35,397. *Average need-based loan:* $7319. *Average need-based gift aid:* $27,778. *Average non-need-based aid:* $21,053. *Average indebtedness upon graduation:* $36,685.

APPLYING

Standardized Tests *Required:* SAT or ACT (for admission).

Options: electronic application, deferred entrance.

Required: essay or personal statement, high school transcript, 1 letter of recommendation. *Recommended:* interview.

Notification: continuous (freshmen), continuous (transfers).

CONTACT

Mr. Derek Hartl, Associate Vice President and Director of Admissions, Luther College, 700 College Drive, Decorah, IA 52101. *Phone:* 563-387-1433. *Toll-free phone:* 800-458-8437. *Fax:* 563-387-2159. *E-mail:* hartde01@luther.edu.

See below for display ad and page 1332 for the College Close-Up.

Maharishi University of Management

Fairfield, Iowa

http://www.mum.edu/

- **Independent** university, founded 1971
- **Small-town** 242-acre campus
- **Coed** 326 undergraduate students, 81% full-time, 58% women, 42% men
- **Moderately difficult** entrance level, 89% of applicants were admitted

UNDERGRAD STUDENTS

263 full-time, 63 part-time. 82% are from out of state; 9% Black or African American, non-Hispanic/Latino; 8% Hispanic/Latino; 3% Asian, non-Hispanic/Latino; 0.3% Native Hawaiian or other Pacific Islander, non-Hispanic/Latino; 0.9% American Indian or Alaska Native, non-Hispanic/Latino; 3% Two or more races, non-Hispanic/Latino; 41% Race/ethnicity unknown; 5% international; 13% transferred in; 82% live on campus.

Freshmen:

Admission: 83 applied, 74 admitted, 19 enrolled. *Average high school GPA:* 3.0.

Retention: 71% of full-time freshmen returned.

FACULTY

Total: 128, 63% full-time, 20% with terminal degrees.

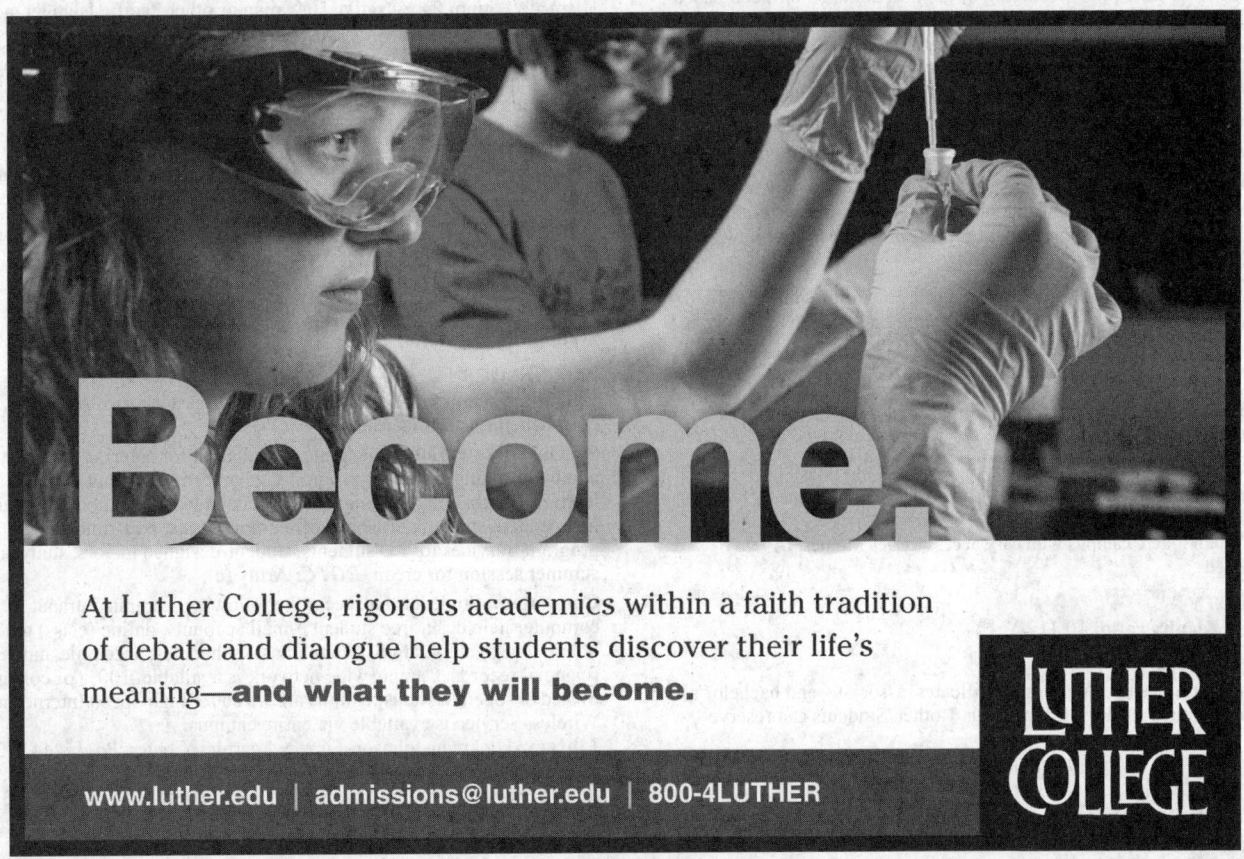

At Luther College, rigorous academics within a faith tradition of debate and dialogue help students discover their life's meaning—**and what they will become.**

www.luther.edu | admissions@luther.edu | 800-4LUTHER

LUTHER COLLEGE

Student/faculty ratio: 9:1.

ACADEMICS

Calendar: semesters. *Degrees:* certificates, bachelor's, master's, doctoral, and postbachelor's certificates.

Special study options: adult/continuing education programs, double majors, English as a second language, independent study, off-campus study, student-designed majors.

Computers: Students can access the following: campus intranet, computer help desk, free student e-mail accounts, online (class) grades, online (class) schedules. Campuswide network is available. 100% of college-owned or -operated housing units are wired for high-speed Internet access. Wireless service is available via entire campus.
Library: Maharishi University of Management Library. Weekly public service hours: 55.

STUDENT LIFE

Housing options: on-campus residence required through senior year; men-only, women-only. Campus housing is university owned. Freshman campus housing is guaranteed.

Athletics *Intercollegiate sports:* soccer M(c)/W(c), ultimate Frisbee M(c)/W(c), volleyball M(c)/W(c). *Intramural sports:* archery M/W, badminton M/W, basketball M/W, football M/W, gymnastics M/W, rock climbing M/W, sailing M/W, soccer M/W, table tennis M/W, tennis M/W, ultimate Frisbee M/W, volleyball M/W.

Campus security: 24-hour emergency response devices and patrols, late-night transport/escort service, controlled dormitory access.

Student services: health clinic, personal/psychological counseling.

COSTS & FINANCIAL AID

Costs (2017–18) *Comprehensive fee:* $34,930 includes full-time tuition ($27,000), mandatory fees ($530), and room and board ($7400). Part-time tuition: $450 per unit. Part-time tuition and fees vary according to course load. *Room and board:* Room and board charges vary according to housing facility. *Payment plan:* installment. *Waivers:* employees or children of employees.

Financial Aid Of all full-time matriculated undergraduates who enrolled in 2006, 150 applied for aid, 148 were judged to have need, 32 had their need fully met. 120 Federal Work-Study jobs (averaging $1422). 7 state and other part-time jobs (averaging $2729). In 2006, 5 non-need-based awards were made. *Average percent of need met:* 89. *Average financial aid package:* $23,963. *Average need-based loan:* $8281. *Average need-based gift aid:* $14,082. *Average non-need-based aid:* $9300. *Average indebtedness upon graduation:* $22,691.

APPLYING

Options: electronic application, early admission, deferred entrance.
Application fee: $20.

Required: essay or personal statement, high school transcript, minimum 2.5 GPA, 2 letters of recommendation. *Recommended:* interview.

CONTACT

Maharishi University of Management, Office of Admissions, Fairfield, IA 52557. *Phone:* 641-472-1110. *Toll-free phone:* 800-369-6480. *Fax:* 641-472-1179. *E-mail:* admissions@mum.edu.

Mercy College of Health Sciences

Des Moines, Iowa

http://www.mchs.edu/
- **Independent** 4-year, founded 1995, affiliated with Roman Catholic Church
- **Urban** 5-acre campus with easy access to Des Moines, IA
- **Coed**

FACULTY
Student/faculty ratio: 10:1.

ACADEMICS
Calendar: semesters. *Degrees:* certificates, associate, and bachelor's.
Library: Mercy College Library plus 1 other. Students can reserve study rooms.

STUDENT LIFE
Housing options: college housing not available.

Activities and organizations: student senate, Campus Ministry, Science Club, Mercy College Association of Nursing Students, Zeta Chi—At Large Chapter.

Campus security: 24-hour emergency response devices and patrols, late-night transport/escort service.

Student services: personal/psychological counseling.

COSTS
Costs (2017–18) *Tuition:* $17,600 full-time, $610 per credit hour part-time. Full-time tuition and fees vary according to program. Part-time tuition and fees vary according to course load.

APPLYING
Standardized Tests *Recommended:* ACT (for admission).
Required: high school transcript, minimum 2.3 GPA.

CONTACT
Heather Gaumer, Director of Admissions, Mercy College of Health Sciences, 921 Sixth Avenue, Des Moines, IA 50309-1200. *Phone:* 515-643-6604. *Toll-free phone:* 800-637-2994. *Fax:* 515-643-6698. *E-mail:* hgaumer@mercydesmoines.org.

Morningside College

Sioux City, Iowa

http://www.morningside.edu/
- **Independent** comprehensive, founded 1894, affiliated with United Methodist Church
- **Suburban** 69-acre campus with easy access to Omaha, NE
- **Endowment** $44.9 million
- **Coed** 1,322 undergraduate students, 95% full-time, 53% women, 47% men
- **Moderately difficult** entrance level, 55% of applicants were admitted

UNDERGRAD STUDENTS
1,252 full-time, 70 part-time. Students come from 30 states and territories; 19 other countries; 46% are from out of state; 2% Black or African American, non-Hispanic/Latino; 8% Hispanic/Latino; 0.9% Asian, non-Hispanic/Latino; 0.4% Native Hawaiian or other Pacific Islander, non-Hispanic/Latino; 0.6% American Indian or Alaska Native, non-Hispanic/Latino; 3% Two or more races, non-Hispanic/Latino; 4% Race/ethnicity unknown; 5% international; 4% transferred in; 60% live on campus.

Freshmen:
Admission: 4,603 applied, 2,540 admitted, 354 enrolled. *Average high school GPA:* 3.4. *Test scores:* ACT scores over 18: 93%; ACT scores over 24: 35%; ACT scores over 30: 5%.
Retention: 70% of full-time freshmen returned.

FACULTY
Total: 233, 33% full-time, 53% with terminal degrees.
Student/faculty ratio: 14:1.

ACADEMICS
Calendar: semesters. *Degrees:* bachelor's, master's, post-master's, and postbachelor's certificates.

Special study options: academic remediation for entering students, adult/continuing education programs, advanced placement credit, distance learning, double majors, English as a second language, honors programs, independent study, internships, off-campus study, part-time degree program, services for LD students, student-designed majors, study abroad, summer session for credit. *ROTC:* Army (c).

Computers: Students can access the following: campus intranet, computer help desk, free student e-mail accounts, online (class) grades, online (class) registration, online (class) schedules, academic and financial records. Campuswide network is available. 100% of college-owned or -operated housing units are wired for high-speed Internet access. Wireless service is available via entire campus.
Library: Hickman-Johnson-Furrow Learning Center. *Books:* 44,113 (physical), 179,888 (digital/electronic); *Serial titles:* 110 (physical), 73 (digital/electronic); *Databases:* 43. Weekly public service hours: 93.

STUDENT LIFE

Housing options: on-campus residence required through junior year; coed. Campus housing is university owned. Freshman campus housing is guaranteed.

Activities and organizations: drama/theater group, student-run newspaper, radio and television station, choral group, marching band, Student Government/Activities Council, Student Ambassadors, Homecoming Committee, national fraternities, national sororities.

Athletics Member NCAA, NAIA. All NCAA Division II. *Intercollegiate sports:* baseball M(s), basketball M(s)/W(s), bowling M/W, cross-country running M(s)/W(s), football M(s), golf M(s)/W(s), soccer M(s)/W(s), softball W(s), swimming and diving M(s)/W(s), tennis M(s)/W(s), track and field M(s)/W(s), volleyball W(s), wrestling M(s). *Intramural sports:* basketball M/W, bowling M/W, ultimate Frisbee M/W, volleyball M/W.

Campus security: 24-hour emergency response devices and patrols, student patrols, late-night transport/escort service, controlled dormitory access.

Student services: health clinic, personal/psychological counseling, women's center.

COSTS & FINANCIAL AID

Costs (2017–18) *Comprehensive fee:* $39,780 includes full-time tuition ($28,890), mandatory fees ($1500), and room and board ($9390). Full-time tuition and fees vary according to program. Part-time tuition: $910 per credit hour. Part-time tuition and fees vary according to course load and program. *College room only:* $5090. Room and board charges vary according to housing facility. *Payment plan:* installment. *Waivers:* children of alumni, senior citizens, and employees or children of employees.

Financial Aid Of all full-time matriculated undergraduates who enrolled in 2017, 1,107 applied for aid, 994 were judged to have need, 238 had their need fully met. 542 Federal Work-Study jobs (averaging $1346). 265 state and other part-time jobs (averaging $2000). In 2017, 257 non-need-based awards were made. *Average percent of need met:* 74. *Average financial aid package:* $24,135. *Average need-based loan:* $4635. *Average need-based gift aid:* $6366. *Average non-need-based aid:* $15,529. *Average indebtedness upon graduation:* $36,449.

APPLYING

Standardized Tests *Required:* SAT or ACT (for admission).

Options: electronic application, deferred entrance.

Required: high school transcript, minimum 2.5 GPA, minimum ACT score of 20 or SAT of 1410 and either rank in top half of class or 2.5 GPA. *Recommended:* interview.

Application deadlines: rolling (freshmen), rolling (transfers).

Notification: continuous (freshmen), continuous (transfers).

CONTACT

Mrs. Stephanie Peters, Director of Admissions, Morningside College, 1501 Morningside Avenue, Sioux City, IA 51106. *Phone:* 712-274-5111. *Toll-free phone:* 800-831-0806 Ext. 5111. *Fax:* 712-274-5101. *E-mail:* mscadm@morningside.edu.

Mount Mercy University
Cedar Rapids, Iowa
http://www.mtmercy.edu/

- **Independent Roman Catholic** comprehensive, founded 1928
- **Suburban** 40-acre campus with easy access to Iowa City
- **Endowment** $26.4 million
- **Coed** 1,518 undergraduate students, 71% full-time, 68% women, 32% men
- **Moderately difficult** entrance level, 57% of applicants were admitted

UNDERGRAD STUDENTS

1,083 full-time, 434 part-time. Students come from 28 states and territories; 33 other countries; 10% are from out of state; 7% Black or African American, non-Hispanic/Latino; 1% Hispanic/Latino; 2% Asian, non-Hispanic/Latino; 0.5% Native Hawaiian or other Pacific Islander, non-Hispanic/Latino; 2% American Indian or Alaska Native, non-Hispanic/Latino; 2% Two or more races, non-Hispanic/Latino; 4% Race/ethnicity unknown; 4% international; 15% transferred in; 40% live on campus.

Freshmen:

Admission: 1,457 applied, 834 admitted, 239 enrolled. *Average high school GPA:* 3.4. *Test scores:* ACT scores over 18: 88%; ACT scores over 24: 33%; ACT scores over 30: 5%.

Retention: 73% of full-time freshmen returned.

FACULTY

Total: 160, 52% full-time, 48% with terminal degrees.

Student/faculty ratio: 15:1.

ACADEMICS

Calendar: 4-1-4. *Degrees:* bachelor's, master's, and doctoral.

Special study options: academic remediation for entering students, accelerated degree program, adult/continuing education programs, advanced placement credit, double majors, external degree program, honors programs, independent study, internships, off-campus study, part-time degree program, services for LD students, study abroad, summer session for credit.

Computers: 120 computers/terminals and 200 ports are available on campus for general student use. Students can access the following: campus intranet, computer help desk, free student e-mail accounts, online (class) grades, online (class) registration, online (class) schedules. Campuswide network is available. 100% of college-owned or -operated housing units are wired for high-speed Internet access. Wireless service is available via entire campus.

Library: Busse Library. *Books:* 124,017 (physical), 191,793 (digital/electronic); *Serial titles:* 3,972 (physical). Students can reserve study rooms.

STUDENT LIFE

Housing options: on-campus residence required through sophomore year; coed, men-only, women-only. Campus housing is university owned. Freshman campus housing is guaranteed.

Activities and organizations: drama/theater group, student-run newspaper, choral group, Student Ambassadors, Mount Mercy University Association of Nursing Students, Cheerleaders, Black Student Union, Student Government Association.

Athletics Member NCAA, NAIA. All NCAA Division III. *Intercollegiate sports:* baseball M(s), basketball M(s)/W(s), bowling M(s)/W(s), cheerleading M(s)/W(s), cross-country running M(s)/W(s), golf M(s)/W(s), soccer M(s)/W(s), softball W(s), track and field M(s)/W(s), volleyball M(s)/W(s). *Intramural sports:* baseball M, basketball M/W, bowling M/W, cheerleading W, football M/W, racquetball M/W, tennis M/W, volleyball M/W, weight lifting M/W.

Campus security: 24-hour emergency response devices and patrols, student patrols, late-night transport/escort service, controlled dormitory access, Department of Public Safety operational 24-hours a day, 7 days a week.

Student services: health clinic, personal/psychological counseling.

COSTS & FINANCIAL AID

Costs (2018–19) *Comprehensive fee:* $41,532 includes full-time tuition ($31,598), mandatory fees ($400), and room and board ($9534). Full-time tuition and fees vary according to course load. Part-time tuition: $958 per credit hour. Part-time tuition and fees vary according to course load. *Required fees:* $200 per year part-time. *Room and board:* Room and board charges vary according to board plan and housing facility. *Payment plan:* installment. *Waivers:* employees or children of employees.

Financial Aid Of all full-time matriculated undergraduates who enrolled in 2016, 999 applied for aid, 921 were judged to have need, 170 had their need fully met. In 2016, 176 non-need-based awards were made. *Average percent of need met:* 75. *Average financial aid package:* $24,022. *Average need-based loan:* $3857. *Average need-based gift aid:* $20,438. *Average non-need-based aid:* $13,346. *Average indebtedness upon graduation:* $25,739.

APPLYING

Standardized Tests *Required:* SAT or ACT (for admission).

Options: electronic application, deferred entrance.

Required: high school transcript, minimum 2.5 GPA. *Required for some:* 1 letter of recommendation.

Application deadlines: 8/15 (freshmen), 8/15 (transfers).

Notification: continuous (freshmen), continuous (transfers).

CONTACT
Dr. Teresa Crumley, Dean of Admission, Mount Mercy University, 1330 Elmhurst Drive, NE, Cedar Rapids, IA 52402. *Phone:* 319-368-6460. *Toll-free phone:* 800-248-4504. *Fax:* 319-363-5270. *E-mail:* tcrumley@ mtmercy.edu.

Northwestern College

Orange City, Iowa
http://www.nwciowa.edu/

- **Independent** comprehensive, founded 1882, affiliated with Reformed Church in America
- **Small-town** 100-acre campus
- **Endowment** $49.4 million
- **Coed** 1,049 undergraduate students, 95% full-time, 56% women, 44% men
- **Moderately difficult** entrance level, 68% of applicants were admitted

UNDERGRAD STUDENTS
997 full-time, 52 part-time. Students come from 31 states and territories; 20 other countries; 42% are from out of state; 1% Black or African American, non-Hispanic/Latino; 4% Hispanic/Latino; 1% Asian, non-Hispanic/Latino; 0.2% American Indian or Alaska Native, non-Hispanic/Latino; 2% Two or more races, non-Hispanic/Latino; 5% Race/ethnicity unknown; 3% international; 1% transferred in; 92% live on campus.

Freshmen:
Admission: 1,959 applied, 1,334 admitted, 281 enrolled. *Average high school GPA:* 3.6. *Test scores:* SAT evidence-based reading and writing scores over 500: 74%; SAT math scores over 500: 77%; ACT scores over 18: 97%; SAT evidence-based reading and writing scores over 600: 24%; SAT math scores over 600: 31%; ACT scores over 24: 55%; SAT math scores over 700: 8%; ACT scores over 30: 15%.
Retention: 77% of full-time freshmen returned.

FACULTY
Total: 141, 58% full-time.
Student/faculty ratio: 11:1.

ACADEMICS
Calendar: semesters. *Degrees:* bachelor's, master's, and postbachelor's certificates.
Special study options: academic remediation for entering students, advanced placement credit, cooperative education, distance learning, double majors, English as a second language, honors programs, independent study, internships, off-campus study, services for LD students, student-designed majors, study abroad, summer session for credit.
Unusual degree programs: 3-2 engineering with Washington University in St. Louis.
Computers: 250 computers/terminals and 1,200 ports are available on campus for general student use. Students can access the following: campus intranet, computer help desk, free student e-mail accounts, online (class) grades, online (class) registration, online (class) schedules, online degree audits. Campuswide network is available. 100% of college-owned or -operated housing units are wired for high-speed Internet access. Wireless service is available via entire campus.
Library: DeWitt Learning Commons plus 1 other. *Books:* 80,887 (physical), 151,137 (digital/electronic); *Serial titles:* 2,286 (physical), 80,593 (digital/electronic); *Databases:* 65. Weekly public service hours: 98; students can reserve study rooms.

STUDENT LIFE
Housing options: on-campus residence required through senior year; men-only, women-only, special housing for students with disabilities. Campus housing is university owned. Freshman campus housing is guaranteed.
Activities and organizations: drama/theater group, student-run newspaper, choral group, Drama Ministries Ensemble, A cappella Choir, Discipleship Groups, Fellowship of Christian Athletes, International Club.
Athletics Member NAIA. *Intercollegiate sports:* baseball M(s), basketball M(s)/W(s), cheerleading M(s)/W(s), cross-country running M(s)/W(s), football M(s), golf M(s)/W(s), rugby W(c), soccer M(s)/W(s), softball W(s), tennis M(s)/W(s), track and field M(s)/W(s), volleyball W(s), wrestling M(s). *Intramural sports:* badminton M/W, basketball M/W, bowling M/W, football M/W, golf M/W, racquetball M/W, soccer M/W, softball M/W, table tennis M/W, tennis M/W, ultimate Frisbee M/W, volleyball M/W.
Campus security: 24-hour emergency response devices, controlled dormitory access.
Student services: health clinic, personal/psychological counseling.

COSTS & FINANCIAL AID
Costs (2018–19) *Comprehensive fee:* $40,300 includes full-time tuition ($30,900), mandatory fees ($200), and room and board ($9200). Part-time tuition: $650 per credit hour. Part-time tuition and fees vary according to course load. *Required fees:* $75 per term part-time. *Room and board:* Room and board charges vary according to board plan and housing facility. *Payment plans:* tuition prepayment, installment. *Waivers:* employees or children of employees.
Financial Aid Of all full-time matriculated undergraduates who enrolled in 2017, 845 applied for aid, 734 were judged to have need, 444 had their need fully met. 144 Federal Work-Study jobs (averaging $1550). 666 state and other part-time jobs (averaging $1089). In 2017, 253 non-need-based awards were made. *Average percent of need met:* 93. *Average financial aid package:* $25,672. *Average need-based loan:* $4947. *Average need-based gift aid:* $7244. *Average non-need-based aid:* $12,162. *Average indebtedness upon graduation:* $32,164.

APPLYING
Standardized Tests *Required:* SAT or ACT (for admission).
Options: electronic application, early admission, deferred entrance.
Required: essay or personal statement, high school transcript, minimum 2.0 GPA. *Recommended:* minimum 2.5 GPA, 1 letter of recommendation, interview.
Application deadlines: rolling (freshmen), rolling (transfers).
Notification: continuous (freshmen), continuous (transfers).

CONTACT
Mrs. Jackie Davis, Director of Admissions, Northwestern College, 101 7th Street SW, Orange City, IA 51041. *Phone:* 712-737-7114. *Toll-free phone:* 800-747-4757. *Fax:* 712-707-7164. *E-mail:* admissions@ nwciowa.edu.

Palmer College of Chiropractic

Davenport, Iowa
http://www.palmer.edu/

CONTACT
Ms. Lisa Gisel, Undergraduate Admissions Representative, Palmer College of Chiropractic, 1000 Brady Street, Davenport, IA 52803-5287. *Phone:* 563-884-5743. *Toll-free phone:* 800-722-3648. *Fax:* 563-884-5226. *E-mail:* lisa.gisel@palmer.edu.

St. Ambrose University

Davenport, Iowa
http://www.sau.edu/

- **Independent Roman Catholic** comprehensive, founded 1882
- **Urban** 118-acre campus
- **Endowment** $139.8 million
- **Coed** 2,370 undergraduate students, 93% full-time, 56% women, 44% men
- **Moderately difficult** entrance level, 61% of applicants were admitted

UNDERGRAD STUDENTS
2,215 full-time, 155 part-time. Students come from 28 states and territories; 24 other countries; 62% are from out of state; 5% Black or African American, non-Hispanic/Latino; 8% Hispanic/Latino; 1% Asian, non-Hispanic/Latino; 0.2% Native Hawaiian or other Pacific Islander, non-Hispanic/Latino; 0.1% American Indian or Alaska Native, non-Hispanic/Latino; 3% Two or more races, non-Hispanic/Latino; 4% Race/ethnicity unknown; 5% international; 9% transferred in; 66% live on campus.

Freshmen:
Admission: 5,351 applied, 3,244 admitted, 550 enrolled. *Average high school GPA:* 3.3. *Test scores:* ACT scores over 18: 98%; ACT scores over 24: 39%; ACT scores over 30: 5%.
Retention: 78% of full-time freshmen returned.

FACULTY
Total: 346, 59% full-time, 57% with terminal degrees.
Student/faculty ratio: 12:1.

ACADEMICS
Calendar: semesters. *Degrees:* bachelor's, master's, doctoral, and post-master's certificates.

Special study options: academic remediation for entering students, accelerated degree program, adult/continuing education programs, advanced placement credit, cooperative education, distance learning, double majors, English as a second language, honors programs, independent study, internships, off-campus study, part-time degree program, services for LD students, student-designed majors, study abroad, summer session for credit.

Unusual degree programs: 3-2 social work; physical therapy, criminal justice.

Computers: 507 computers/terminals and 517 ports are available on campus for general student use. Students can access the following: campus intranet, computer help desk, free student e-mail accounts, online (class) registration, online (class) schedules, online course syllabi, online payments. Campuswide network is available. 100% of college-owned or -operated housing units are wired for high-speed Internet access. Wireless service is available via entire campus.
Library: SAU Library plus 1 other. *Books:* 172,923 (physical), 13,678 (digital/electronic); *Serial titles:* 502 (physical); *Databases:* 85. Weekly public service hours: 95; students can reserve study rooms.

STUDENT LIFE
Housing options: on-campus residence required through sophomore year; coed, men-only, women-only, special housing for students with disabilities. Campus housing is university owned. Freshman campus housing is guaranteed.

Activities and organizations: drama/theater group, student-run newspaper, radio and television station, choral group, marching band, Dance Marathon, Habitat for Humanity, Biology Club, Ambrosians for Peace and Justice, SPTO - Student Physical Therapy Organization.

Athletics Member NAIA. *Intercollegiate sports:* baseball M(s), basketball M(s)/W(s), bowling M(s)/W(s), cheerleading M(s)/W(s), cross-country running M(s)/W(s), football M(s), golf M(s)/W(s), lacrosse M(s), soccer M(s)/W(s), softball W(s), swimming and diving M(s)/W(s), tennis M(s)/W(s), track and field M(s)/W(s), volleyball M(s)/W(s). *Intramural sports:* basketball M/W, bowling M/W, cross-country running M(c)/W(c), football M/W, racquetball M(c)/W(c), rugby M(c)/W(c), sand volleyball M/W, soccer M/W, softball M/W, table tennis M/W, volleyball M/W.

Campus security: 24-hour emergency response devices and patrols, student patrols, late-night transport/escort service, controlled dormitory access, off-duty officer available three nights/week for 4.5 hours per night, twelve cameras record various public areas on campus.

Student services: health clinic, personal/psychological counseling.

COSTS & FINANCIAL AID
Costs (2018–19) *Comprehensive fee:* $41,364 includes full-time tuition ($30,614), mandatory fees ($280), and room and board ($10,470). Full-time tuition and fees vary according to course load and location. Part-time tuition: $942 per credit hour. Part-time tuition and fees vary according to course load and location. *Required fees:* $280 per term part-time. *College room only:* $6384. Room and board charges vary according to board plan and housing facility. *Payment plans:* installment, deferred payment.
Waivers: employees or children of employees.

Financial Aid Of all full-time matriculated undergraduates who enrolled in 2016, 1,870 applied for aid, 1,669 were judged to have need, 389 had their need fully met. In 2016, 419 non-need-based awards were made. *Average percent of need met:* 77. *Average financial aid package:* $22,886. *Average need-based loan:* $4423. *Average need-based gift aid:* $17,899. *Average non-need-based aid:* $13,462.

APPLYING
Standardized Tests *Required:* SAT or ACT (for admission).

Options: electronic application, deferred entrance.
Required: high school transcript, minimum 2.5 GPA. *Required for some:* interview. *Recommended:* interview.
Application deadlines: rolling (freshmen), rolling (transfers).
Notification: 10/1 (freshmen), continuous (transfers).

CONTACT
Ms. Allison Conklin, Associate Director of First Year Admissions, St. Ambrose University, 518 W Locust Street, Davenport, IA 52803. *Phone:* 563-333-6300. *Toll-free phone:* 800-383-2627. *Fax:* 563-333-6297. *E-mail:* conklinallisonj@sau.edu.

St. Luke's College
Sioux City, Iowa
http://stlukescollege.edu/
- **Independent** primarily 2-year, founded 1967
- **Rural** 3-acre campus with easy access to Omaha
- **Endowment** $1.1 million
- **Coed** 274 undergraduate students, 43% full-time, 89% women, 11% men
- **Minimally difficult** entrance level, 27% of applicants were admitted

UNDERGRAD STUDENTS
118 full-time, 156 part-time. Students come from 14 states and territories; 1 other country; 36% are from out of state; 2% Black or African American, non-Hispanic/Latino; 9% Hispanic/Latino; 2% Asian, non-Hispanic/Latino; 0.4% Native Hawaiian or other Pacific Islander, non-Hispanic/Latino; 1% American Indian or Alaska Native, non-Hispanic/Latino; 2% Two or more races, non-Hispanic/Latino; 3% Race/ethnicity unknown; 8% transferred in.

Freshmen:
Admission: 15 applied, 4 admitted, 4 enrolled. *Average high school GPA:* 3.6. *Test scores:* ACT scores over 18: 75%; ACT scores over 24: 25%.
Retention: 100% of full-time freshmen returned.

FACULTY
Total: 42, 62% full-time, 12% with terminal degrees.
Student/faculty ratio: 6:1.

ACADEMICS
Calendar: semesters. *Degrees:* certificates, associate, and bachelor's.
Special study options: advanced placement credit, distance learning, internships, services for LD students, summer session for credit.
Computers: 9 computers/terminals are available on campus for general student use. Students can access the following: campus intranet, computer help desk, free student e-mail accounts, online (class) grades, online (class) registration, online (class) schedules. Campuswide network is available. Wireless service is available via entire campus.
Library:*Books:* 2,531 (physical); *Serial titles:* 63 (physical); *Databases:* 7. Weekly public service hours: 65.

STUDENT LIFE
Housing options: college housing not available.
Campus security: 24-hour emergency response devices and patrols, late-night transport/escort service.
Student services: health clinic, personal/psychological counseling.

COSTS & FINANCIAL AID
Costs (2018–19) *Tuition:* $18,900 full-time. Full-time tuition and fees vary according to course load, degree level, and program. Part-time tuition and fees vary according to course load, degree level, and program. *Required fees:* $1560 full-time. *Payment plans:* installment, deferred payment. *Waivers:* employees or children of employees.
Financial Aid Of all full-time matriculated undergraduates who enrolled in 2016, 93 applied for aid, 93 were judged to have need. 7 Federal Work-Study jobs (averaging $1671). *Average percent of need met:* 80. *Average financial aid package:* $12,430. *Average need-based loan:* $6512. *Average need-based gift aid:* $4756. *Average indebtedness upon graduation:* $14,158.

APPLYING
Standardized Tests *Required:* SAT or ACT (for admission).
Options: electronic application.

Iowa

Required: essay or personal statement, high school transcript, minimum 2.5 GPA, interview.
Notification: continuous (transfers).

CONTACT
Ms. Sherry McCarthy, Admissions Coordinator, St. Luke's College, 2720 Stone Park Boulevard, Sioux City, IA 51104. *Phone:* 712-279-3149. *Toll-free phone:* 800-352-4660 Ext. 3149. *Fax:* 712-233-8017. *E-mail:* sherry.mccarthy@stlukescollege.edu.

Shiloh University

Kalona, Iowa

http://www.shilohuniversity.edu/

- **Independent** comprehensive, founded 2007
- **Small-town** 200-acre campus
- **Coed** 23 undergraduate students, 4% full-time, 43% women, 57% men
- **Noncompetitive** entrance level

UNDERGRAD STUDENTS
1 full-time, 22 part-time. Students come from 4 states and territories; 1 other country; 61% are from out of state; 7% Native Hawaiian or other Pacific Islander, non-Hispanic/Latino; 7% international; 343% transferred in.

FACULTY
Total: 37, 14% full-time, 43% with terminal degrees.
Student/faculty ratio: 1:1.

ACADEMICS
Degrees: certificates, associate, bachelor's, master's, doctoral, and postbachelor's certificates.
Special study options: distance learning, off-campus study, part-time degree program, services for LD students, summer session for credit.
Library: University e-Library. *Databases:* 2.

COSTS
Costs (2017–18) *Tuition:* $3600 full-time, $150 per credit hour part-time. Full-time tuition and fees vary according to course load. Part-time tuition and fees vary according to course load. *Required fees:* $10 full-time, $10 per year part-time. *Payment plan:* installment.

APPLYING
Options: electronic application, early admission, deferred entrance.
Required: essay or personal statement, high school transcript, minimum 2.0 GPA.
Application deadlines: 7/5 (freshmen), 7/5 (transfers).
Notification: 7/19 (freshmen), 7/19 (transfers).

CONTACT
Mr. Andrew R. Thompson, Admissions Coordinator, Shiloh University, 100 Shiloh Drive, Kalona, IA 52247. *Phone:* 319-656-2447. *Fax:* 319-656-2448. *E-mail:* admissions@shilohuniversity.edu.

Simpson College

Indianola, Iowa

http://www.simpson.edu/

- **Independent United Methodist** comprehensive, founded 1860
- **Suburban** 85-acre campus with easy access to Des Moines
- **Endowment** $84.6 million
- **Coed** 1,432 undergraduate students, 89% full-time, 54% women, 46% men
- **Moderately difficult** entrance level, 83% of applicants were admitted

UNDERGRAD STUDENTS
1,280 full-time, 152 part-time. Students come from 29 states and territories; 6 other countries; 19% are from out of state; 2% Black or African American, non-Hispanic/Latino; 4% Hispanic/Latino; 2% Asian, non-Hispanic/Latino; 0.2% Native Hawaiian or other Pacific Islander, non-Hispanic/Latino; 0.1% American Indian or Alaska Native, non-Hispanic/Latino; 2% Two or more races, non-Hispanic/Latino; 6% Race/ethnicity unknown; 1% international; 5% transferred in; 77% live on campus.

Freshmen:
Admission: 1,265 applied, 1,044 admitted, 298 enrolled. *Test scores:* ACT scores over 18: 96%; ACT scores over 24: 57%; ACT scores over 30: 11%.
Retention: 80% of full-time freshmen returned.

FACULTY
Total: 194, 54% full-time, 57% with terminal degrees.
Student/faculty ratio: 10:1.

ACADEMICS
Calendar: 4-4-1. *Degrees:* bachelor's, master's, and postbachelor's certificates.
Special study options: accelerated degree program, adult/continuing education programs, advanced placement credit, cooperative education, distance learning, double majors, honors programs, independent study, internships, off-campus study, part-time degree program, services for LD students, student-designed majors, study abroad, summer session for credit.
Unusual degree programs: 3-2 engineering with Washington University in St. Louis, Iowa State University, University of Minnesota; nursing with Allen College.
Computers: 425 computers/terminals are available on campus for general student use. Students can access the following: campus intranet, computer help desk, free student e-mail accounts, online (class) grades, online (class) registration, online (class) schedules. Campuswide network is available. 100% of college-owned or -operated housing units are wired for high-speed Internet access. Wireless service is available via entire campus.
Library: Dunn Library. *Books:* 116,870 (physical), 168,359 (digital/electronic); *Serial titles:* 234 (physical), 278,513 (digital/electronic); *Databases:* 38. Weekly public service hours: 95.

STUDENT LIFE
Housing options: on-campus residence required through junior year; coed, men-only, women-only. Campus housing is university owned. Freshman campus housing is guaranteed.
Activities and organizations: drama/theater group, student-run newspaper, radio station, choral group, Religious Life Community, Campus Activities Board, Student Government Association, Residence Hall Association, intramurals, national fraternities, national sororities.
Athletics Member NCAA. All Division III. *Intercollegiate sports:* baseball M, basketball M/W, cheerleading M/W, cross-country running M/W, football M, golf M/W, soccer M/W, softball W, swimming and diving M/W, tennis M/W, track and field M/W, volleyball W, wrestling M. *Intramural sports:* badminton M/W, basketball M/W, bowling M/W, football M/W, golf M/W, racquetball M/W, rugby M(c)/W(c), soccer M/W, softball M/W, swimming and diving M/W, table tennis M/W, tennis M/W, ultimate Frisbee M/W, volleyball M/W.
Campus security: 24-hour emergency response devices and patrols, student patrols, late-night transport/escort service, controlled dormitory access, SAFE (Simpson Alert for Emergencies) provides phone calls in case of campus security/weather emergencies.
Student services: health clinic, personal/psychological counseling, women's center.

COSTS & FINANCIAL AID
Costs (2018–19) *One-time required fee:* $200. *Comprehensive fee:* $47,524 includes full-time tuition ($38,412), mandatory fees ($732), and room and board ($8380). Full-time tuition and fees vary according to class time, course load, degree level, and program. Part-time tuition: $375 per credit hour. Part-time tuition and fees vary according to class time, course load, degree level, and program. *Required fees:* $6 per credit hour part-time. *College room only:* $4062. Room and board charges vary according to board plan and housing facility. *Payment plan:* installment. *Waivers:* children of alumni, senior citizens, and employees or children of employees.
Financial Aid Of all full-time matriculated undergraduates who enrolled in 2017, 1,272 applied for aid, 1,055 were judged to have need, 230 had their need fully met. 295 Federal Work-Study jobs (averaging $1377). 490 state and other part-time jobs (averaging $1473). In 2017, 195 non-need-based awards were made. *Average percent of need met:* 80. *Average financial aid package:* $29,443. *Average need-based loan:* $4950.

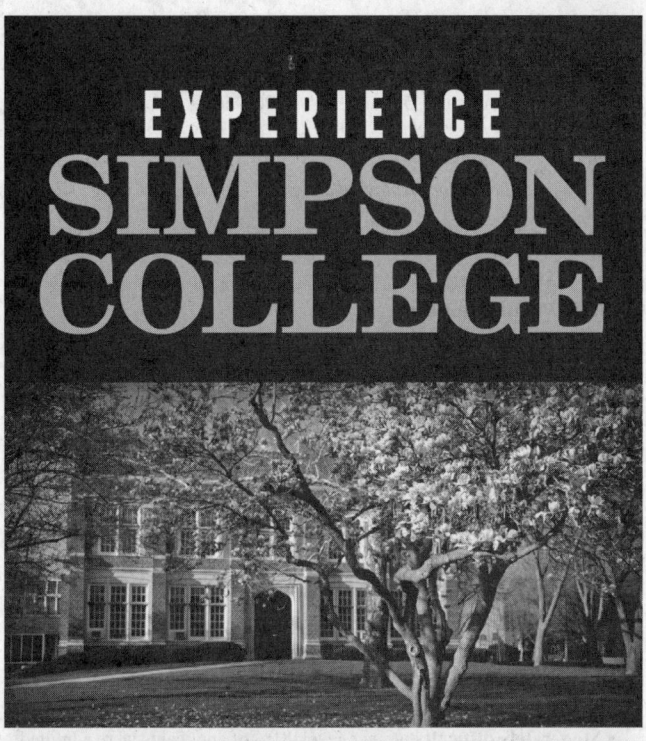

- **1,300** undergraduate students

- Minutes from **DES MOINES**—#1 Best City for Young Professionals *(Forbes)*

- Excellent **INTERNSHIP OPPORTUNITIES**

- Personalized education with **4-4-1 CALENDAR**

- Unique **STUDY ABROAD PROGRAMS**

- Home to **NATIONALLY ACCLAIMED** fine arts programs, championship DIII athletic teams and the 2018 National Debate Champions

- **BEST VALUE**—100% of full-time students receive grants or scholarships

INDIANOLA, IOWA
SIMPSON.EDU

Average need-based gift aid: $23,867. *Average non-need-based aid:* $21,045. *Average indebtedness upon graduation:* $38,155.

APPLYING
Standardized Tests *Required:* SAT or ACT (for admission).
Options: electronic application, deferred entrance.
Required: high school transcript, guidance counselor recommendation form. *Recommended:* minimum 3.0 GPA, interview.
Application deadlines: 8/15 (freshmen), 8/15 (transfers).
Notification: continuous (freshmen), continuous (transfers).

CONTACT
Simpson College, 701 North C Street, Indianola, IA 50125-1297. *Toll-free phone:* 800-362-2454.

See this page for display ad and page 1424 for the College Close-Up.

 University of Dubuque
Dubuque, Iowa
http://www.dbq.edu/
- **Independent Presbyterian** comprehensive, founded 1852
- **Suburban** 77-acre campus
- **Endowment** $132.6 million
- **Coed** 1,965 undergraduate students, 87% full-time, 42% women, 58% men
- **Moderately difficult** entrance level, 74% of applicants were admitted

UNDERGRAD STUDENTS
1,710 full-time, 255 part-time. Students come from 42 states and territories; 28 other countries; 54% are from out of state; 15% Black or African American, non-Hispanic/Latino; 9% Hispanic/Latino; 2% Asian, non-Hispanic/Latino; 0.4% Native Hawaiian or other Pacific Islander, non-Hispanic/Latino; 0.2% American Indian or Alaska Native, non-Hispanic/Latino; 3% Two or more races, non-Hispanic/Latino; 4% Race/ethnicity unknown; 6% international; 8% transferred in; 45% live on campus.

Freshmen:
Admission: 1,761 applied, 1,306 admitted, 518 enrolled. *Average high school GPA:* 2.9. *Test scores:* SAT evidence-based reading and writing scores over 500: 55%; SAT math scores over 500: 57%; ACT scores over 18: 63%; SAT evidence-based reading and writing scores over 600: 10%; SAT math scores over 600: 12%; ACT scores over 24: 15%; ACT scores over 30: 1%.
Retention: 58% of full-time freshmen returned.

FACULTY
Total: 385, 27% full-time, 23% with terminal degrees.
Student/faculty ratio: 13:1.

ACADEMICS
Calendar: 4-1-4. *Degrees:* associate, bachelor's, master's, and doctoral.
Special study options: academic remediation for entering students, accelerated degree program, adult/continuing education programs, advanced placement credit, distance learning, double majors, honors programs, independent study, internships, off-campus study, part-time degree program, services for LD students, student-designed majors, study abroad, summer session for credit. *ROTC:* Army (b).
Unusual degree programs: 3-2 business administration; communications, theology.
Computers: 244 computers/terminals are available on campus for general student use. Students can access the following: campus intranet, computer help desk, free student e-mail accounts, online (class) grades, online (class) registration, online (class) schedules. Campuswide network is available. 100% of college-owned or -operated housing units are wired for high-speed Internet access. Wireless service is available via entire campus.
Library: Charles C. Myers Library. *Books:* 134,278 (physical), 178,036 (digital/electronic); *Serial titles:* 180 (physical), 30,070 (digital/electronic); *Databases:* 58. Weekly public service hours: 109.

STUDENT LIFE
Housing options: on-campus residence required through junior year; coed, special housing for students with disabilities. Campus housing is university owned. Freshman campus housing is guaranteed.

Activities and organizations: drama/theater group, student-run newspaper, choral group, Greek Council, Saudi Student Organization, Student Nurses Association, Accounting Club, ROTC.

Athletics Member NCAA. All Division III. *Intercollegiate sports:* baseball M, basketball M/W, cross-country running M/W, football M, golf M/W, soccer M/W, softball W, tennis M/W, track and field M/W, volleyball W, wrestling M. *Intramural sports:* badminton M/W, basketball M/W, bowling M/W, cheerleading M(c)/W(c), football M/W, golf M/W, soccer M/W, softball M/W, table tennis M/W, tennis M/W, ultimate Frisbee M/W, volleyball M/W.

Campus security: 24-hour patrols, late-night transport/escort service, controlled dormitory access.

Student services: health clinic, personal/psychological counseling.

COSTS & FINANCIAL AID
Costs (2017–18) *One-time required fee:* $100. *Comprehensive fee:* $39,160 includes full-time tuition ($28,360), mandatory fees ($1350), and room and board ($9450). Part-time tuition: $850 per credit hour. *Room and board:* Room and board charges vary according to board plan and housing facility. *Payment plan:* installment. *Waivers:* employees or children of employees.

Financial Aid Of all full-time matriculated undergraduates who enrolled in 2017, 1,583 applied for aid, 1,493 were judged to have need, 220 had their need fully met. 193 Federal Work-Study jobs (averaging $2000). 180 state and other part-time jobs (averaging $2000). In 2017, 186 non-need-based awards were made. *Average percent of need met:* 61. *Average financial aid package:* $25,561. *Average need-based loan:* $6673. *Average need-based gift aid:* $19,452. *Average non-need-based aid:* $11,896. *Average indebtedness upon graduation:* $30,353.

APPLYING
Standardized Tests *Required:* SAT or ACT (for admission).
Options: electronic application, deferred entrance.
Application fee: $25.
Required: essay or personal statement, high school transcript, 2 letters of recommendation. *Recommended:* interview.
Application deadlines: rolling (freshmen), rolling (transfers).

Notification: continuous (freshmen), continuous (transfers).

CONTACT
Mr. Bob Broshous, Director of Admissions, University of Dubuque, 2000 University Avenue, Dubuque, IA 52001-5099. *Phone:* 563-589-3199. *Toll-free phone:* 800-722-5583. *Fax:* 563-589-3690. *E-mail:* admissns@dbq.edu.

See below for display ad and page 1464 for the College Close-Up.

The University of Iowa

Iowa City, Iowa
http://www.uiowa.edu/

CONTACT
Debra Miller, Sr. Associate Director, Undergraduate Evaluation, The University of Iowa, 108 Calvin Hall, Iowa City, IA 52242. *Phone:* 319-335-3847. *Toll-free phone:* 800-553-4692. *Fax:* 319-335-1535. *E-mail:* admissions@uiowa.edu.

University of Northern Iowa

Cedar Falls, Iowa
http://www.uni.edu/

- **State-supported** comprehensive, founded 1876, part of Board of Regents, State of Iowa
- **Suburban** 908-acre campus
- **Endowment** $126.6 million
- **Coed** 10,005 undergraduate students, 91% full-time, 57% women, 43% men
- **Moderately difficult** entrance level, 81% of applicants were admitted

UNDERGRAD STUDENTS
9,100 full-time, 905 part-time. Students come from 32 states and territories; 65 other countries; 6% are from out of state; 3% Black or African American, non-Hispanic/Latino; 4% Hispanic/Latino; 1% Asian, non-Hispanic/Latino; 0.1% Native Hawaiian or other Pacific Islander, non-Hispanic/Latino; 0.3% American Indian or Alaska Native, non-Hispanic/Latino; 2% Two or more races, non-Hispanic/Latino; 4%

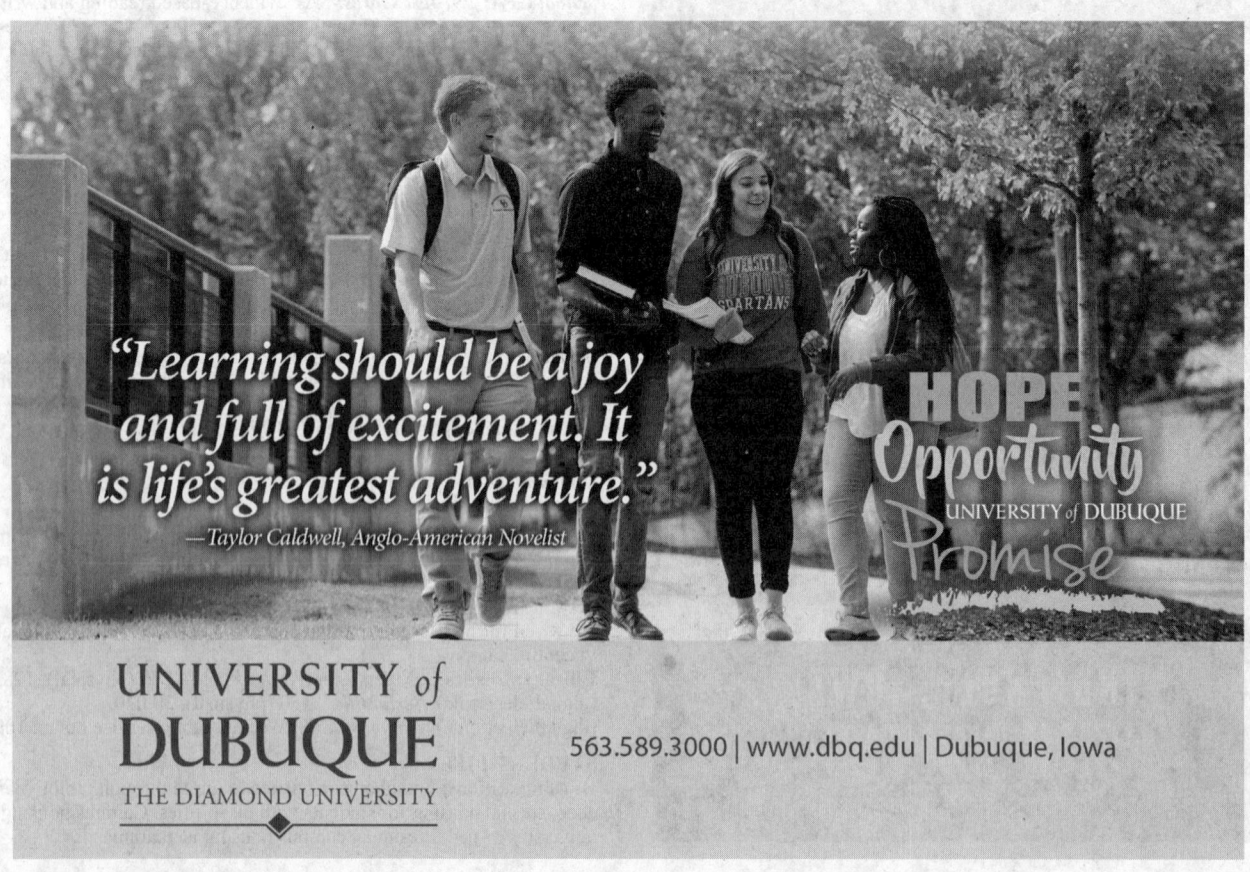

Race/ethnicity unknown; 4% international; 9% transferred in; 38% live on campus.

Freshmen:
Admission: 5,494 applied, 4,441 admitted, 1,834 enrolled. *Average high school GPA:* 3.5. *Test scores:* ACT scores over 18: 95%; ACT scores over 24: 41%; ACT scores over 30: 6%.
Retention: 81% of full-time freshmen returned.

FACULTY
Total: 703, 72% full-time, 67% with terminal degrees.
Student/faculty ratio: 18:1.

ACADEMICS
Calendar: semesters. *Degrees:* bachelor's, master's, and doctoral.
Special study options: academic remediation for entering students, accelerated degree program, adult/continuing education programs, advanced placement credit, cooperative education, distance learning, double majors, English as a second language, external degree program, honors programs, independent study, internships, off-campus study, part-time degree program, services for LD students, student-designed majors, study abroad, summer session for credit. *ROTC:* Army (b).
Unusual degree programs: 3-2 nursing with Allen College, University of Iowa; medical technology with University of Iowa Medical School, cytotechnology with Mayo School of Health-Related Sciences and Mercy College of Health Sciences, chiropractic with Logan College of Chiropractic and Palmer College of Chiropractic.
Computers: 1,900 computers/terminals are available on campus for general student use. Students can access the following: campus intranet, computer help desk, free student e-mail accounts, online (class) grades, online (class) registration, online (class) schedules, student account, degree audit, program of study. Campuswide network is available. 100% of college-owned or -operated housing units are wired for high-speed Internet access. Wireless service is available via entire campus.
Library: Rod Library plus 1 other. *Books:* 776,654 (physical), 464,215 (digital/electronic); *Serial titles:* 22,329 (physical), 105,088 (digital/electronic); *Databases:* 210. Weekly public service hours: 97; students can reserve study rooms.

STUDENT LIFE
Housing options: coed, special housing for students with disabilities. Campus housing is university owned. Freshman campus housing is guaranteed.
Activities and organizations: drama/theater group, student-run newspaper, radio station, choral group, marching band, Dance Marathon, Colleges Against Cancer/Relay for Life, Accounting Club, Phi Eta Sigma, Students Today Alumni Tomorrow, national fraternities, national sororities.
Athletics Member NCAA. All Division I except football (Division I-AA). *Intercollegiate sports:* basketball M(s)/W(s), cross-country running M(s)/W(s), golf M(s)/W(s), soccer W(s), softball W(s), swimming and diving W(s), tennis W(s), track and field M(s)/W(s), volleyball W(s), wrestling M(s). *Intramural sports:* badminton M/W, baseball M(c), basketball M/W, bowling M(c)/W(c), cheerleading M/W, crew M(c)/W(c), cross-country running M(c)/W(c), football M(c), golf M(c)/W(c), ice hockey M(c), racquetball M(c)/W(c), rugby M(c)/W(c), skiing (downhill) M(c)/W(c), soccer M(c)/W(c), softball M(c)/W(c), swimming and diving M(c)/W(c), table tennis M/W, tennis M(c)/W(c), track and field M(c)/W(c), ultimate Frisbee M(c)/W(c), volleyball M/W(c).
Campus security: 24-hour emergency response devices and patrols, student patrols, late-night transport/escort service, controlled dormitory access, automatic external defibrillators, silent witness online, vehicle assistance.
Student services: health clinic, personal/psychological counseling.

COSTS & FINANCIAL AID
Costs (2017–18) *Tuition:* state resident $7456 full-time, $311 per credit hour part-time; nonresident $17,998 full-time, $750 per credit hour part-time. Full-time tuition and fees vary according to course load and program. Part-time tuition and fees vary according to course load and program. *Required fees:* $1243 full-time. *Room and board:* $8781; room only: $4473. Room and board charges vary according to board plan and housing facility. *Payment plan:* installment.

Financial Aid Of all full-time matriculated undergraduates who enrolled in 2015, 6,973 applied for aid, 5,431 were judged to have need, 805 had their need fully met. 452 Federal Work-Study jobs (averaging $1507). In 2015, 972 non-need-based awards were made. *Average percent of need met:* 65. *Average financial aid package:* $8363. *Average need-based loan:* $4343. *Average need-based gift aid:* $4714. *Average non-need-based aid:* $3304. *Average indebtedness upon graduation:* $24,325.

APPLYING
Standardized Tests *Required:* SAT or ACT (for admission). *Recommended:* SAT (for admission), ACT (for admission).
Options: electronic application, deferred entrance.
Application fee: $40.
Required: high school transcript, 4 years of English; 3 years each of math, science and social studies; 2 or more years of electives, which may include foreign language and fine arts. *Required for some:* interview.
Application deadlines: 8/15 (freshmen), 8/15 (transfers).
Notification: 7/1 (freshmen), 8/1 (transfers).

CONTACT
Amy S. Schipper, Associate Director, Recruitment/Communications, University of Northern Iowa, 002 Gilchrist, Cedar Falls, IA 50614. *Phone:* 319-273-2281. *Toll-free phone:* 800-772-2037. *Fax:* 319-273-2885. *E-mail:* admissions@uni.edu.

Upper Iowa University
Fayette, Iowa
http://www.uiu.edu/
- **Independent** comprehensive, founded 1857
- **Rural** 100-acre campus with easy access to Minneapolis-St. Paul, Chicago
- **Endowment** $17.1 million
- **Coed** 4,275 undergraduate students, 49% full-time, 62% women, 38% men
- **Moderately difficult** entrance level, 56% of applicants were admitted

UNDERGRAD STUDENTS
2,110 full-time, 2,165 part-time. Students come from 50 states and territories; 46 other countries; 55% are from out of state; 18% Black or African American, non-Hispanic/Latino; 5% Hispanic/Latino; 2% Asian, non-Hispanic/Latino; 0.2% Native Hawaiian or other Pacific Islander, non-Hispanic/Latino; 0.4% American Indian or Alaska Native, non-Hispanic/Latino; 2% Two or more races, non-Hispanic/Latino; 3% Race/ethnicity unknown; 12% international; 12% transferred in; 56% live on campus.

Freshmen:
Admission: 1,901 applied, 1,056 admitted, 221 enrolled. *Average high school GPA:* 3.1.
Retention: 60% of full-time freshmen returned.

FACULTY
Total: 518, 14% full-time, 37% with terminal degrees.
Student/faculty ratio: 17:1.

ACADEMICS
Calendar: 6 8-week terms. *Degrees:* certificates, associate, bachelor's, and master's (enrollment figures include extended learning centers and online and distance education programs).
Special study options: academic remediation for entering students, accelerated degree program, adult/continuing education programs, advanced placement credit, cooperative education, distance learning, double majors, English as a second language, external degree program, freshman honors college, honors programs, independent study, internships, off-campus study, part-time degree program, services for LD students, student-designed majors, study abroad, summer session for credit.
Computers: 360 computers/terminals and 360 ports are available on campus for general student use. Students can access the following: campus intranet, computer help desk, free student e-mail accounts, online (class) grades, online (class) registration, online (class) schedules. Campuswide network is available. 100% of college-owned or -operated housing units are wired for high-speed Internet access. Wireless service is

available via classrooms, computer centers, computer labs, dorm rooms, learning centers, libraries, student centers.

Library: Henderson Wilder Library. *Books:* 68,870 (physical), 7,450 (digital/electronic); *Serial titles:* 211 (physical), 83,993 (digital/electronic); *Databases:* 40. Weekly public service hours: 85.

STUDENT LIFE

Housing options: on-campus residence required through junior year; coed, men-only, women-only. Campus housing is university owned. Freshman campus housing is guaranteed.

Activities and organizations: drama/theater group, student-run newspaper, choral group, Student Athlete Advisory Committee, Peacock Alumni for Student Traditions, UIU Science and Environment Club, Student Government Association, Peacocks for Progress.

Athletics Member NCAA. All Division II. *Intercollegiate sports:* baseball M(s), basketball M(s)/W(s), cross-country running W(s), football M(s), golf M(s)/W(s), soccer M(s)/W(s), softball W(s), tennis W(s), track and field W(s), volleyball W(s), wrestling M(s). *Intramural sports:* badminton M/W, basketball M/W, bowling M/W, cheerleading M(c)/W(c), football M, golf M/W, soccer M/W, softball M/W, table tennis M/W, ultimate Frisbee M/W, volleyball M/W.

Campus security: late-night transport/escort service, controlled dormitory access.

Student services: personal/psychological counseling.

COSTS & FINANCIAL AID

Costs (2018–19) *Comprehensive fee:* $38,910 includes full-time tuition ($29,700), mandatory fees ($750), and room and board ($8460). Full-time tuition and fees vary according to degree level, location, and program. *College room only:* $3900. Room and board charges vary according to board plan, housing facility, and location. *Payment plan:* installment. *Waivers:* employees or children of employees.

Financial Aid Of all full-time matriculated undergraduates who enrolled in 2016, 1,838 applied for aid, 1,634 were judged to have need, 163 had their need fully met. 371 Federal Work-Study jobs (averaging $1877). In 2016, 4 non-need-based awards were made. *Average percent of need met:* 58. *Average financial aid package:* $14,614. *Average need-based loan:* $4740. *Average need-based gift aid:* $4907. *Average non-need-based aid:* $938. *Average indebtedness upon graduation:* $26,488.

APPLYING

Standardized Tests *Required:* SAT or ACT (for admission).

Options: electronic application.

Required: high school transcript, minimum 2.0 GPA.

Application deadlines: rolling (freshmen), rolling (transfers).

CONTACT

Ms. Kathy Franken, Vice President of Enrollment Management, Upper Iowa University, 605 Washington Street, Parker Fox Hall, Fayette, IA 52142. *Phone:* 563-425-5868. *Toll-free phone:* 800-553-4150. *Fax:* 563-4255323. *E-mail:* frankenk@uiu.edu.

Vatterott College

Des Moines, Iowa

http://www.vatterott.edu/

CONTACT

Mr. Dana Smith, Co-Director, Vatterott College, 7000 Fleur Drive, Suite 290, Des Moines, IA 50321. *Phone:* 515-309-9000. *Toll-free phone:* 888-553-6627. *Fax:* 515-309-0366.

Waldorf University

Forest City, Iowa

http://www.waldorf.edu/

- **Independent Lutheran** comprehensive, founded 1903, part of Columbia Southern Education Group
- **Rural** 51-acre campus
- **Coed** 2,126 undergraduate students, 71% full-time, 37% women, 63% men
- **Moderately difficult** entrance level, 72% of applicants were admitted

UNDERGRAD STUDENTS

1,517 full-time, 609 part-time. Students come from 50 states and territories; 24 other countries; 83% are from out of state; 12% Black or African American, non-Hispanic/Latino; 9% Hispanic/Latino; 2% Asian, non-Hispanic/Latino; 0.2% Native Hawaiian or other Pacific Islander, non-Hispanic/Latino; 0.8% American Indian or Alaska Native, non-Hispanic/Latino; 0.9% Two or more races, non-Hispanic/Latino; 15% Race/ethnicity unknown; 1% international; 4% transferred in; 70% live on campus.

Freshmen:

Admission: 771 applied, 554 admitted, 131 enrolled. *Average high school GPA:* 3.1. *Test scores:* SAT evidence-based reading and writing scores over 500: 58%; SAT math scores over 500: 61%; ACT scores over 18: 82%; SAT evidence-based reading and writing scores over 600: 8%; SAT math scores over 600: 13%; ACT scores over 24: 18%; SAT evidence-based reading and writing scores over 700: 3%.

Retention: 46% of full-time freshmen returned.

FACULTY

Total: 171, 27% full-time, 47% with terminal degrees.

Student/faculty ratio: 19:1.

ACADEMICS

Calendar: semesters. *Degrees:* certificates, associate, bachelor's, and master's.

Special study options: academic remediation for entering students, adult/continuing education programs, advanced placement credit, cooperative education, distance learning, double majors, freshman honors college, honors programs, independent study, internships, part-time degree program, services for LD students, summer session for credit.

Computers: 621 computers/terminals are available on campus for general student use. Students can access the following: campus intranet, computer help desk, free student e-mail accounts, online (class) grades, online (class) schedules. Campuswide network is available. 100% of college-owned or -operated housing units are wired for high-speed Internet access. Wireless service is available via entire campus.

Library: Luise V. Hanson Library. *Books:* 55,884 (physical), 152,040 (digital/electronic); *Serial titles:* 394 (physical); *Databases:* 87. Weekly public service hours: 97; students can reserve study rooms.

STUDENT LIFE

Housing options: on-campus residence required through junior year; coed, men-only, women-only, cooperative, special housing for students with disabilities. Campus housing is university owned and leased by the school. Freshman campus housing is guaranteed.

Activities and organizations: drama/theater group, student-run newspaper, radio and television station, choral group, Student Activities Team, Education Club, Campus Ministry groups, intramurals, Radio/TV/ Newspaper.

Athletics Member NAIA. *Intercollegiate sports:* baseball M(s), basketball M(s)/W(s), bowling M(s)/W(s), cheerleading M(s)/W(s), cross-country running M(s)/W(s), football M(s), golf M(s)/W(s), ice hockey M, soccer M(s)/W(s), softball W(s), track and field M(s)/W(s), volleyball W(s), wrestling M(s)/W(s). *Intramural sports:* basketball M/W, bowling M/W, football M, racquetball M/W, soccer M/W, softball M/W, table tennis M/W, tennis M/W, ultimate Frisbee M/W, volleyball M/W.

Campus security: 24-hour emergency response devices, student patrols, late-night transport/escort service, controlled dormitory access, evening and night patrols by trained security personnel, camera surveillance system.

Student services: health clinic, personal/psychological counseling.

COSTS & FINANCIAL AID

Costs (2018–19) *Comprehensive fee:* $29,600 includes full-time tuition ($20,934), mandatory fees ($1142), and room and board ($7524). Full-time tuition and fees vary according to class time, course load, and program. Part-time tuition: $295 per credit hour. *Room and board:* Room and board charges vary according to board plan and housing facility. *Payment plans:* installment, deferred payment. *Waivers:* employees or children of employees.

Financial Aid Of all full-time matriculated undergraduates who enrolled in 2015, 1,030 applied for aid, 959 were judged to have need, 98 had their need fully met. In 2015, 111 non-need-based awards were made. *Average percent of need met:* 62. *Average financial aid package:* $13,783.

Average need-based loan: $4414. *Average need-based gift aid:* $10,658. *Average non-need-based aid:* $7090. *Average indebtedness upon graduation:* $33,494.

APPLYING

Standardized Tests *Required:* SAT or ACT (for admission).

Options: electronic application.

Required: high school transcript. *Required for some:* 1 letter of recommendation, interview. *Recommended:* minimum 2.0 GPA.

Application deadlines: rolling (freshmen), rolling (transfers).

Notification: continuous (freshmen), continuous (transfers).

CONTACT

Waldorf University, 106 South 6th Street, Forest City, IA 50436. *Toll-free phone:* 800-292-1903.

Wartburg College

Waverly, Iowa

http://www.wartburg.edu/

- **Independent Lutheran** 4-year, founded 1852
- **Small-town** 170-acre campus
- **Endowment** $73.9 million
- **Coed** 1,527 undergraduate students, 96% full-time, 53% women, 47% men
- **Moderately difficult** entrance level, 77% of applicants were admitted

UNDERGRAD STUDENTS

1,470 full-time, 57 part-time. Students come from 30 states and territories; 55 other countries; 33% are from out of state; 5% Black or African American, non-Hispanic/Latino; 5% Hispanic/Latino; 1% Asian, non-Hispanic/Latino; 0.1% Native Hawaiian or other Pacific Islander, non-Hispanic/Latino; 3% Two or more races, non-Hispanic/Latino; 3% Race/ethnicity unknown; 8% international; 2% transferred in; 86% live on campus.

Freshmen:

Admission: 4,342 applied, 3,339 admitted, 451 enrolled. *Average high school GPA:* 3.6. *Test scores:* SAT evidence-based reading and writing scores over 500: 68%; SAT math scores over 500: 68%; ACT scores over 18: 94%; SAT evidence-based reading and writing scores over 600: 21%; SAT math scores over 600: 26%; ACT scores over 24: 47%; SAT evidence-based reading and writing scores over 700: 3%; SAT math scores over 700: 3%; ACT scores over 30: 10%.

Retention: 79% of full-time freshmen returned.

FACULTY

Total: 160, 59% full-time, 55% with terminal degrees.
Student/faculty ratio: 11:1.

ACADEMICS

Calendar: 4-4-1. *Degree:* bachelor's.

Special study options: academic remediation for entering students, accelerated degree program, advanced placement credit, double majors, honors programs, independent study, internships, off-campus study, part-time degree program, services for LD students, student-designed majors, study abroad, summer session for credit.

Unusual degree programs: 3-2 engineering with Iowa State University; nursing with Allen College; pre-seminary with Wartburg Seminary, clinical laboratory science with Mercy College of Health Sciences, pre-Law with The University of Iowa, museum studies with Western Illinois University.

Computers: 349 computers/terminals are available on campus for general student use. Students can access the following: campus intranet, computer help desk, free student e-mail accounts, online (class) grades, online (class) registration, online (class) schedules, billing, satellite. Campuswide network is available. 100% of college-owned or -operated housing units are wired for high-speed Internet access. Wireless service is available via entire campus.

Library: Vogel Library. *Books:* 127,680 (physical), 156,930 (digital/electronic); *Serial titles:* 1,615 (physical), 54,863 (digital/electronic); *Databases:* 93. Weekly public service hours: 91.

STUDENT LIFE

Housing options: on-campus residence required through senior year; coed, men-only, women-only, special housing for students with disabilities. Campus housing is university owned. Freshman campus housing is guaranteed.

Activities and organizations: drama/theater group, student-run newspaper, radio and television station, choral group, Entertainment To Knight, Student Senate, Campus Ministry, Symphonic Band, Wartburg Choir.

Athletics Member NCAA. All Division III. *Intercollegiate sports:* baseball M, basketball M/W, bowling M/W, cross-country running M/W, football M, golf M/W, lacrosse W, soccer M/W, softball W, tennis M/W, track and field M/W, volleyball W, wrestling M. *Intramural sports:* basketball M/W, bowling M/W, cheerleading W(c), golf M/W, sand volleyball M/W, soccer M/W, softball M/W.

Campus security: 24-hour emergency response devices and patrols, late-night transport/escort service, controlled dormitory access.

Student services: health clinic, personal/psychological counseling.

COSTS & FINANCIAL AID

Costs (2018–19) *Comprehensive fee:* $51,275 includes full-time tuition ($40,220), mandatory fees ($1060), and room and board ($9995). Part-time tuition: $2100 per course. Part-time tuition and fees vary according to course load. *Required fees:* $120 per year part-time. *College room only:* $5075. Room and board charges vary according to board plan and housing facility. *Payment plan:* installment. *Waivers:* employees or children of employees.

Financial Aid Of all full-time matriculated undergraduates who enrolled in 2016, 1,214 applied for aid, 1,043 were judged to have need, 209 had their need fully met. 523 Federal Work-Study jobs (averaging $885). 462 state and other part-time jobs (averaging $1962). In 2016, 362 non-need-based awards were made. *Average percent of need met:* 82. *Average financial aid package:* $30,082. *Average need-based loan:* $5502. *Average need-based gift aid:* $25,286. *Average non-need-based aid:* $22,209. *Average indebtedness upon graduation:* $37,551.

APPLYING

Standardized Tests *Required:* SAT or ACT (for admission).

Options: electronic application, early action, deferred entrance.

Required: high school transcript, minimum 2.5 GPA. *Recommended:* letters of recommendation, secondary school report.

Application deadlines: rolling (freshmen), rolling (transfers), 12/1 (early action).

Notification: continuous (freshmen), continuous (transfers).

CONTACT

Tara Winter, Director of Student Recruitment, Wartburg College, 100 Wartburg Boulevard, PO Box 1003, Waverly, IA 50677-0903. *Phone:* 319-352-8475. *Toll-free phone:* 800-772-2085. *Fax:* 319-352-8579. *E-mail:* admissions@wartburg.edu.

William Penn University

Oskaloosa, Iowa

http://www.wmpenn.edu/

- **Independent** comprehensive, founded 1873, affiliated with Society of Friends
- **Rural** 60-acre campus with easy access to Des Moines
- **Endowment** $4.7 million
- **Coed** 1,315 undergraduate students
- **Moderately difficult** entrance level, 56% of applicants were admitted

UNDERGRAD STUDENTS

Students come from 46 states and territories; 22 other countries; 47% are from out of state; 22% Black or African American, non-Hispanic/Latino; 10% Hispanic/Latino; 1% Asian, non-Hispanic/Latino; 0.3% Native Hawaiian or other Pacific Islander, non-Hispanic/Latino; 0.9% American Indian or Alaska Native, non-Hispanic/Latino; 2% Two or more races, non-Hispanic/Latino; 4% Race/ethnicity unknown; 5% international; 55% live on campus.

Freshmen:

Admission: 1,219 applied, 688 admitted. *Average high school GPA:* 2.9. *Test scores:* ACT scores over 18: 59%; ACT scores over 24: 7%.

Retention: 51% of full-time freshmen returned.

FACULTY
Total: 134, 34% full-time, 24% with terminal degrees.
Student/faculty ratio: 18:1.

ACADEMICS
Calendar: semesters. *Degrees:* bachelor's and master's.

Special study options: academic remediation for entering students, adult/continuing education programs, advanced placement credit, cooperative education, distance learning, double majors, honors programs, independent study, internships, part-time degree program, services for LD students, study abroad, summer session for credit.

Unusual degree programs: 3-2 engineering with Iowa State University.

Computers: 200 computers/terminals and 665 ports are available on campus for general student use. Students can access the following: computer help desk, free student e-mail accounts, online (class) grades, online (class) schedules. Campuswide network is available. 100% of college-owned or -operated housing units are wired for high-speed Internet access. Wireless service is available via entire campus.
Library: Wilcox Library plus 1 other. *Books:* 61,804 (physical), 162,694 (digital/electronic); *Serial titles:* 54 (physical), 48,768 (digital/electronic); *Databases:* 38. Weekly public service hours: 92; students can reserve study rooms.

STUDENT LIFE
Housing options: on-campus residence required through sophomore year; coed, men-only, women-only. Campus housing is university owned. Freshman campus housing is guaranteed.

Activities and organizations: drama/theater group, student-run newspaper, radio and television station, choral group, marching band, Greek Council, Biology Club, Education Club, Student Government Association, Computer Club.

Athletics Member NAIA. *Intercollegiate sports:* baseball M(s), basketball M(s)/W(s), bowling M(s)/W(s), cheerleading M(s)/W(s), cross-country running M(s)/W(s), football M(s), golf M(s)/W(s), soccer M(s)/W(s), softball W(s), track and field M(s)/W(s), volleyball W(s), wrestling M(s). *Intramural sports:* badminton M/W, basketball M/W, golf M/W, rugby M/W, sand volleyball M/W, soccer M/W, ultimate Frisbee M/W, volleyball M/W, weight lifting M/W.

Campus security: 24-hour emergency response devices and patrols, late-night transport/escort service, controlled dormitory access.

Student services: health clinic, personal/psychological counseling.

COSTS & FINANCIAL AID
Costs (2018–19) *Comprehensive fee:* $32,552 includes full-time tuition ($24,870), mandatory fees ($730), and room and board ($6952). Full-time tuition and fees vary according to class time, course load, degree level, location, and program. Part-time tuition and fees vary according to class time, course load, degree level, location, and program. *College room only:* $3102. Room and board charges vary according to housing facility. *Payment plan:* installment. *Waivers:* senior citizens and employees or children of employees.

Financial Aid Of all full-time matriculated undergraduates who enrolled in 2005, 808 applied for aid, 768 were judged to have need, 238 had their need fully met. 511 Federal Work-Study jobs (averaging $1287). 1 state and other part-time job (averaging $1103). In 2005, 2 non-need-based awards were made. *Average percent of need met:* 82. *Average financial aid package:* $17,782. *Average need-based loan:* $4600. *Average need-based gift aid:* $11,300. *Average non-need-based aid:* $4500. *Average indebtedness upon graduation:* $22,169.

APPLYING
Standardized Tests *Required:* SAT or ACT (for admission).
Options: electronic application, deferred entrance.
Required: high school transcript, minimum 2.0 GPA. *Required for some:* essay or personal statement, letters of recommendation, interview.
Application deadlines: rolling (freshmen), rolling (transfers).
Notification: continuous (freshmen), continuous (transfers).

CONTACT
Ms. Kerra Strong, Vice President for Enrollment Management, William Penn University, 201 Trueblood Avenue, Oskaloosa, IA 52577-1799.

Phone: 641-673-1012. *Fax:* 641-673-2113. *E-mail:* admissions@wmpenn.edu.

KANSAS

Baker University
Baldwin City, Kansas
http://www.bakeru.edu/

- **Independent United Methodist** comprehensive, founded 1858
- **Small-town** 26-acre campus with easy access to Kansas City
- **Endowment** $38.5 million
- **Coed** 1,159 undergraduate students, 73% full-time, 52% women, 48% men
- **Moderately difficult** entrance level, 86% of applicants were admitted

UNDERGRAD STUDENTS
849 full-time, 310 part-time. Students come from 30 states and territories; 20 other countries; 32% are from out of state; 10% Black or African American, non-Hispanic/Latino; 8% Hispanic/Latino; 0.5% Asian, non-Hispanic/Latino; 0.5% Native Hawaiian or other Pacific Islander, non-Hispanic/Latino; 1% American Indian or Alaska Native, non-Hispanic/Latino; 5% Two or more races, non-Hispanic/Latino; 2% Race/ethnicity unknown; 3% international; 4% transferred in; 83% live on campus.

Freshmen:
Admission: 803 applied, 688 admitted, 256 enrolled. *Average high school GPA:* 3.5. *Test scores:* ACT scores over 18: 96%; ACT scores over 24: 48%; ACT scores over 30: 4%.
Retention: 68% of full-time freshmen returned.

FACULTY
Total: 100, 56% full-time, 58% with terminal degrees.
Student/faculty ratio: 13:1.

ACADEMICS
Calendar: 4-1-4 semesters for nursing program. *Degrees:* bachelor's, master's, and doctoral (profile includes information primarily for undergraduate residential campus in Baldwin City, KS).

Special study options: advanced placement credit, double majors, honors programs, independent study, internships, services for LD students, student-designed majors, study abroad, summer session for credit. *ROTC:* Army (c), Air Force (c).

Unusual degree programs: 3-2 engineering with Washington University in St. Louis, University of Kansas, Kansas State University, University of Missouri–Kansas City.

Computers: 140 computers/terminals are available on campus for general student use. Students can access the following: computer help desk, free student e-mail accounts, online (class) grades, online (class) registration, online (class) schedules. Campuswide network is available. 100% of college-owned or -operated housing units are wired for high-speed Internet access. Wireless service is available via entire campus.
Library: Baker University Library. *Books:* 69,073 (physical), 170,620 (digital/electronic); *Serial titles:* 1,285 (physical), 276 (digital/electronic); *Databases:* 48. Weekly public service hours: 73; study areas open 24 hours, 5–7 days a week; students can reserve study rooms.

STUDENT LIFE
Housing options: on-campus residence required through senior year; coed, men-only, women-only, special housing for students with disabilities. Campus housing is university owned. Freshman campus housing is guaranteed.

Activities and organizations: drama/theater group, student-run newspaper, radio and television station, choral group, Exercise Science Student Alliance, Baker University Speech Choir, Mungano, Student Senate, Student Activities Council, national fraternities, national sororities.

Athletics Member NAIA. *Intercollegiate sports:* baseball M(s), basketball M(s)/W(s), bowling W(s), cheerleading M(s)/W(s), cross-country running M(s)/W(s), football M(s), golf M(s)/W(s), soccer M(s)/W(s), softball W(s), tennis M(s)/W(s), track and field M(s)/W(s), volleyball W(s), wrestling M(s). *Intramural sports:* basketball M/W, football M/W, softball M/W, table tennis M/W, volleyball M/W.

Campus security: 24-hour emergency response devices and patrols, controlled dormitory access.

Student services: health clinic, personal/psychological counseling.

COSTS & FINANCIAL AID

Costs (2017–18) *One-time required fee:* $80. *Comprehensive fee:* $37,190 includes full-time tuition ($28,430), mandatory fees ($450), and room and board ($8310). Full-time tuition and fees vary according to course load, degree level, location, and program. Part-time tuition: $890 per credit hour. Part-time tuition and fees vary according to course load, degree level, location, and program. *Required fees:* $200 per year part-time. *College room only:* $3910. Room and board charges vary according to board plan and housing facility. *Payment plan:* installment. *Waivers:* senior citizens and employees or children of employees.

Financial Aid Of all full-time matriculated undergraduates who enrolled in 2016, 749 applied for aid, 650 were judged to have need. In 2016, 89 non-need-based awards were made. *Average financial aid package:* $25,766. *Average need-based loan:* $3972. *Average need-based gift aid:* $6142. *Average non-need-based aid:* $10,496. *Average indebtedness upon graduation:* $31,937.

APPLYING

Standardized Tests *Required:* SAT or ACT (for admission).

Options: electronic application, deferred entrance.

Required: high school transcript. *Required for some:* essay or personal statement, 1 letter of recommendation, interview.

Application deadlines: rolling (freshmen), rolling (transfers).

CONTACT

Mrs. Cheryl McCrary, Director of Enrollment Management, Baker University, PO Box 65, Baldwin City, KS 66006-0065. *Phone:* 785-594-8327. *Toll-free phone:* 800-873-4282. *Fax:* 785-594-8353. *E-mail:* admissions@bakeru.edu.

Barclay College

Haviland, Kansas

http://www.barclaycollege.edu/

- **Independent** comprehensive, founded 1917, affiliated with Society of Friends
- **Rural** 17-acre campus
- **Endowment** $1.5 million
- **Coed** 229 undergraduate students, 78% full-time, 50% women, 50% men
- **Minimally difficult** entrance level, 67% of applicants were admitted

UNDERGRAD STUDENTS

178 full-time, 51 part-time. Students come from 34 states and territories; 7 other countries; 56% are from out of state; 16% Black or African American, non-Hispanic/Latino; 6% Hispanic/Latino; 0.9% Asian, non-Hispanic/Latino; 2% American Indian or Alaska Native, non-Hispanic/Latino; 2% Two or more races, non-Hispanic/Latino; 3% Race/ethnicity unknown; 2% international; 11% transferred in; 78% live on campus.

Freshmen:

Admission: 109 applied, 73 admitted, 39 enrolled. *Test scores:* SAT evidence-based reading and writing scores over 500: 60%; SAT math scores over 500: 20%; ACT scores over 18: 71%; ACT scores over 24: 10%; ACT scores over 30: 3%.

Retention: 65% of full-time freshmen returned.

FACULTY

Total: 42, 60% full-time, 33% with terminal degrees.

Student/faculty ratio: 10:1.

ACADEMICS

Calendar: semesters. *Degrees:* certificates, associate, bachelor's, and master's.

Special study options: academic remediation for entering students, adult/continuing education programs, advanced placement credit, distance learning, double majors, external degree program, independent study, internships, off-campus study, part-time degree program.

Unusual degree programs: 3-2 nursing with Pratt Community College, Hutchinson Community College.

Computers: 28 computers/terminals are available on campus for general student use. Students can access the following: campus intranet, computer help desk, free student e-mail accounts, online (class) grades, online (class) registration, online (class) schedules. Campuswide network is available. 100% of college-owned or -operated housing units are wired for high-speed Internet access. Wireless service is available via entire campus.

Library: Worden Memorial Library. *Books:* 44,420 (physical), 23 (digital/electronic); *Serial titles:* 410 (physical), 4 (digital/electronic); *Databases:* 48. Weekly public service hours: 95.

STUDENT LIFE

Housing options: on-campus residence required through senior year; men-only, women-only. Campus housing is university owned. Freshman campus housing is guaranteed.

Activities and organizations: drama/theater group, choral group.

Athletics Member NCCAA. *Intercollegiate sports:* basketball M/W, cheerleading M/W, soccer M, tennis M/W, volleyball W. *Intramural sports:* basketball M/W, volleyball M/W.

Campus security: student patrols.

Student services: personal/psychological counseling.

COSTS & FINANCIAL AID

Costs (2017–18) *Comprehensive fee:* $28,990 includes full-time tuition ($15,000), mandatory fees ($4640), and room and board ($9350). Part-time tuition: $295 per credit hour. Part-time tuition and fees vary according to course load. *Room and board:* Room and board charges vary according to board plan and housing facility. *Payment plan:* installment. *Waivers:* employees or children of employees.

Financial Aid Of all full-time matriculated undergraduates who enrolled in 2017, 146 applied for aid, 146 were judged to have need. 53 Federal Work-Study jobs (averaging $1545). 53 state and other part-time jobs (averaging $1545). In 2017, 11 non-need-based awards were made. *Average percent of need met:* 45. *Average financial aid package:* $19,529. *Average need-based loan:* $7685. *Average need-based gift aid:* $11,843. *Average non-need-based aid:* $13,869. *Average indebtedness upon graduation:* $19,926.

APPLYING

Standardized Tests *Required:* SAT or ACT (for admission).

Options: electronic application, early admission, deferred entrance.

Application fee: $15.

Required: essay or personal statement, high school transcript, minimum 2.3 GPA, 2 letters of recommendation, interview.

Application deadlines: 9/1 (freshmen), 9/1 (transfers).

Notification: continuous (freshmen), continuous (transfers).

CONTACT

Mr. Justin Kendall, Admissions Recruiter, Barclay College, 607 North Kingman, Haviland, KS 67059. *Phone:* 620-862-5252 Ext. 21. *Toll-free phone:* 800-862-0226. *Fax:* 620-862-5242. *E-mail:* jkendall@barclaycollege.edu.

Benedictine College

Atchison, Kansas

http://www.benedictine.edu/

- **Independent Roman Catholic** comprehensive, founded 1859
- **Small-town** 225-acre campus with easy access to Kansas City
- **Endowment** $24.3 million
- **Coed** 2,071 undergraduate students, 87% full-time, 55% women, 45% men
- **Minimally difficult** entrance level, 97% of applicants were admitted

UNDERGRAD STUDENTS

1,806 full-time, 265 part-time. Students come from 49 states and territories; 16 other countries; 76% are from out of state; 3% Black or African American, non-Hispanic/Latino; 7% Hispanic/Latino; 0.8% Asian, non-Hispanic/Latino; 0.3% Native Hawaiian or other Pacific Islander, non-Hispanic/Latino; 0.6% American Indian or Alaska Native, non-Hispanic/Latino; 0.3% Two or more races, non-Hispanic/Latino; 7%

Race/ethnicity unknown; 2% international; 4% transferred in; 82% live on campus.

Freshmen:
Admission: 2,367 applied, 2,307 admitted, 438 enrolled. *Average high school GPA:* 3.5. *Test scores:* ACT scores over 18: 95%; ACT scores over 24: 63%; ACT scores over 30: 18%.
Retention: 79% of full-time freshmen returned.

FACULTY
Total: 200, 58% full-time, 45% with terminal degrees.
Student/faculty ratio: 13:1.

ACADEMICS
Calendar: semesters. *Degrees:* certificates, diplomas, associate, bachelor's, master's, and postbachelor's certificates.

Special study options: academic remediation for entering students, advanced placement credit, cooperative education, distance learning, double majors, English as a second language, honors programs, independent study, internships, off-campus study, part-time degree program, services for LD students, student-designed majors, study abroad, summer session for credit. *ROTC:* Army (c).

Computers: 100 computers/terminals and 1,800 ports are available on campus for general student use. Students can access the following: computer help desk, free student e-mail accounts, online (class) grades, online (class) registration, online (class) schedules. Campuswide network is available. 100% of college-owned or -operated housing units are wired for high-speed Internet access. Wireless service is available via entire campus.
Library: Benedictine College Library. *Books:* 198,277 (physical), 139,987 (digital/electronic); *Serial titles:* 45,794 (physical), 400 (digital/electronic); *Databases:* 88. Weekly public service hours: 85.

STUDENT LIFE
Housing options: on-campus residence required through senior year; men-only, women-only. Campus housing is university owned. Freshman campus housing is guaranteed.

Activities and organizations: drama/theater group, student-run newspaper, choral group, marching band, Student Government, ENACTUS, Knights of Columbus, Concert Chorale/Chamber Singers, Ravens Respect Life.

Athletics Member NAIA. *Intercollegiate sports:* baseball M(s), basketball M(s)/W(s), cheerleading W(s), cross-country running M(s)/W(s), football M(s), lacrosse M/W, soccer M(s)/W(s), softball W(s), track and field M(s)/W(s), volleyball W(s), wrestling M(s). *Intramural sports:* basketball M/W, football M/W, golf M/W, lacrosse M/W, racquetball M/W, rugby M/W, soccer M/W, softball M/W, table tennis M/W, ultimate Frisbee M/W, volleyball M/W.

Campus security: 24-hour emergency response devices and patrols, late-night transport/escort service, controlled dormitory access.

Student services: health clinic, personal/psychological counseling.

COSTS & FINANCIAL AID
Costs (2017–18) *Comprehensive fee:* $38,380 includes full-time tuition ($27,730), mandatory fees ($750), and room and board ($9900). Full-time tuition and fees vary according to course load and degree level. Part-time tuition: $800 per credit hour. Part-time tuition and fees vary according to course load and degree level. *Required fees:* $50 per credit hour part-time. *College room only:* $5400. Room and board charges vary according to board plan and housing facility. *Payment plan:* installment. *Waivers:* senior citizens and employees or children of employees.

Financial Aid Of all full-time matriculated undergraduates who enrolled in 2017, 1,441 applied for aid, 1,228 were judged to have need, 295 had their need fully met. 291 Federal Work-Study jobs (averaging $620). In 2017, 571 non-need-based awards were made. *Average percent of need met:* 80. *Average financial aid package:* $23,698. *Average need-based loan:* $4984. *Average need-based gift aid:* $15,796. *Average non-need-based aid:* $12,748. *Average indebtedness upon graduation:* $29,196.

APPLYING
Standardized Tests *Required:* SAT or ACT (for admission).
Options: electronic application, deferred entrance.
Application fee: $50.

Required: high school transcript, minimum 2.0 GPA, 1 letter of recommendation. *Required for some:* interview.
Application deadlines: rolling (freshmen), rolling (transfers).
Notification: continuous (freshmen), continuous (transfers).

CONTACT
Mr. Pete Helgesen, Dean of Enrollment Management, Benedictine College, 1020 North 2nd Street, Atchison, KS 66002-1499. *Phone:* 913-367-5340 Ext. 2476. *Toll-free phone:* 800-467-5340. *E-mail:* phelgesen@benedictine.edu.

Bethany College
Lindsborg, Kansas
http://www.bethanylb.edu/

CONTACT
Katie Laier, Dean of Admissions and Financial Aid, Bethany College, 335 East Swensson Avenue, Lindsborg, KS 67456-1895. *Phone:* 785-227-3311 Ext. 8344. *Toll-free phone:* 800-826-2281. *Fax:* 785-227-8993. *E-mail:* admissions@bethanylb.edu.

Bethel College
North Newton, Kansas
http://www.bethelks.edu/

- **Independent** 4-year, founded 1887, affiliated with Mennonite Church USA
- **Small-town** 90-acre campus with easy access to Wichita
- **Endowment** $17.2 million
- **Coed** 503 undergraduate students, 97% full-time, 53% women, 47% men
- **Moderately difficult** entrance level, 56% of applicants were admitted

UNDERGRAD STUDENTS
489 full-time, 14 part-time. Students come from 29 states and territories; 5 other countries; 35% are from out of state; 16% Black or African American, non-Hispanic/Latino; 9% Hispanic/Latino; 2% Asian, non-Hispanic/Latino; 0.2% Native Hawaiian or other Pacific Islander, non-Hispanic/Latino; 0.4% American Indian or Alaska Native, non-Hispanic/Latino; 4% Two or more races, non-Hispanic/Latino; 0.2% Race/ethnicity unknown; 1% international; 18% transferred in; 68% live on campus.

Freshmen:
Admission: 770 applied, 431 admitted, 124 enrolled. *Average high school GPA:* 3.4. *Test scores:* ACT scores over 18: 97%; ACT scores over 24: 36%; ACT scores over 30: 6%.
Retention: 60% of full-time freshmen returned.

FACULTY
Total: 81, 52% full-time, 37% with terminal degrees.
Student/faculty ratio: 10:1.

ACADEMICS
Calendar: 4-1-4. *Degree:* bachelor's.

Special study options: adult/continuing education programs, advanced placement credit, cooperative education, double majors, honors programs, independent study, internships, part-time degree program, services for LD students, student-designed majors, study abroad, summer session for credit.

Computers: 62 computers/terminals and 500 ports are available on campus for general student use. Students can access the following: campus intranet, computer help desk, free student e-mail accounts, online (class) grades, online (class) registration, online (class) schedules. Campuswide network is available. 100% of college-owned or -operated housing units are wired for high-speed Internet access. Wireless service is available via entire campus.
Library: Mantz Library plus 1 other. *Books:* 119,391 (physical), 149,966 (digital/electronic); *Serial titles:* 3,157 (physical), 107,370 (digital/electronic); *Databases:* 80. Weekly public service hours: 88; students can reserve study rooms.

STUDENT LIFE
Housing options: on-campus residence required through senior year; coed, special housing for students with disabilities. Campus housing is university owned. Freshman campus housing is guaranteed.

Activities and organizations: drama/theater group, student-run newspaper, radio and television station, choral group, Student Activities Committee, Student Alumni Association, Students for Social Change, Intramurals, KBCU FM 88.1.

Athletics Member NAIA. *Intercollegiate sports:* basketball M(s)/W(s), cross-country running M(s)/W(s), football M(s), golf M(s)/W(s), soccer M(s)/W(s), tennis M(s)/W(s), track and field M(s)/W(s), volleyball W(s). *Intramural sports:* badminton M/W, basketball M/W, cheerleading M/W, cross-country running M/W, golf M/W, soccer M/W, softball W, tennis M/W, track and field M/W, ultimate Frisbee M/W, volleyball M/W.

Campus security: 24-hour emergency response devices and patrols, controlled dormitory access, SMS Alert System.

Student services: health clinic, personal/psychological counseling.

COSTS & FINANCIAL AID
Costs (2018–19) *Comprehensive fee:* $37,390 includes full-time tuition ($28,300), mandatory fees ($240), and room and board ($8850). Part-time tuition: $773 per credit hour. Part-time tuition and fees vary according to course load. *College room only:* $4340. Room and board charges vary according to board plan, housing facility, and student level. *Payment plans:* installment, deferred payment. *Waivers:* minority students, children of alumni, senior citizens, and employees or children of employees.

Financial Aid Of all full-time matriculated undergraduates who enrolled in 2016, 414 applied for aid, 401 were judged to have need, 90 had their need fully met. In 2016, 56 non-need-based awards were made. *Average percent of need met:* 82. *Average financial aid package:* $24,986. *Average need-based loan:* $8204. *Average need-based gift aid:* $5398. *Average non-need-based aid:* $12,020. *Average indebtedness upon graduation:* $5633.

APPLYING
Standardized Tests *Recommended:* SAT (for admission), ACT (for admission), SAT or ACT (for admission), SAT Subject Tests (for admission).

Options: electronic application, deferred entrance.

Required: high school transcript, minimum 2.5 GPA. *Required for some:* essay or personal statement, 2 letters of recommendation. *Recommended:* interview.

Application deadlines: rolling (freshmen), rolling (transfers), rolling (early action).

Early decision deadline: rolling (for plan 1), rolling (for plan 2).

Notification: continuous (freshmen), continuous (transfers), rolling (early decision plan 1), rolling (early decision plan 2), rolling (early action).

CONTACT
Mr. Andy Johnson, Vice President for Admissions, Bethel College, 300 East 27th Street, North Newton, KS 67117-0531. *Phone:* 316-284-5230. *Toll-free phone:* 800-522-1887 Ext. 230. *Fax:* 316-284-5870. *E-mail:* admissions@bethelks.edu.

Central Christian College of Kansas
McPherson, Kansas
http://www.centralchristian.edu/

CONTACT
Central Christian College of Kansas, 1200 South Main, PO Box 1403, McPherson, KS 67460-5799. *Phone:* 620-241-0723 Ext. 380. *Toll-free phone:* 800-835-0078.

Cleveland University–Kansas City
Overland Park, Kansas
http://www.cleveland.edu/

CONTACT
Ms. Melissa Denton, Director of Admissions, Cleveland University–Kansas City, 10850 Lowell Avenue, Overland Park, KS 66210. *Phone:*

913-234-0750. *Toll-free phone:* 800-467-2252. *Fax:* 913-234-0906. *E-mail:* kc.admissions@cleveland.edu.

Donnelly College
Kansas City, Kansas
http://www.donnelly.edu/
- **Independent Roman Catholic** primarily 2-year, founded 1949
- **Urban** 4-acre campus
- **Coed** 294 undergraduate students, 61% full-time, 74% women, 26% men
- **Noncompetitive** entrance level, 100% of applicants were admitted

UNDERGRAD STUDENTS
179 full-time, 115 part-time. Students come from 2 states and territories; 24 other countries; 31% are from out of state; 33% Black or African American, non-Hispanic/Latino; 39% Hispanic/Latino; 6% Asian, non-Hispanic/Latino; 0.7% Native Hawaiian or other Pacific Islander, non-Hispanic/Latino; 2% American Indian or Alaska Native, non-Hispanic/Latino; 4% Two or more races, non-Hispanic/Latino; 1% international; 16% transferred in.

Freshmen:
Admission: 349 applied, 349 admitted, 55 enrolled.
Retention: 55% of full-time freshmen returned.

FACULTY
Student/faculty ratio: 11:1.

ACADEMICS
Calendar: semesters. *Degrees:* certificates, associate, and bachelor's.

Special study options: academic remediation for entering students, advanced placement credit, distance learning, English as a second language, external degree program, honors programs, independent study, part-time degree program, services for LD students, summer session for credit.

Computers: Students can access the following: campus intranet, computer help desk, free student e-mail accounts, online (class) grades, online (class) registration, online (class) schedules. Campuswide network is available. Wireless service is available via entire campus.
Library: Trant Memorial Library plus 1 other.

STUDENT LIFE
Housing options: college housing not available; men-only, women-only. Campus housing is university owned.

Activities and organizations: Organization of Student Leadership, Student Ambassadors, Healthy Student Task Force, Men's Soccer Club, Women's Soccer Club.

Athletics *Intramural sports:* basketball M/W, soccer M/W, volleyball M/W.

Campus security: 24-hour emergency response devices.

Student services: personal/psychological counseling.

COSTS
Costs (2017–18) *Tuition:* $6960 full-time, $290 per credit hour part-time. Full-time tuition and fees vary according to degree level, location, and program. Part-time tuition and fees vary according to degree level and location. *Required fees:* $180 full-time, $5 per credit hour part-time, $30 per term part-time. *Payment plan:* installment. *Waivers:* senior citizens and employees or children of employees.

APPLYING
Options: electronic application, early admission, deferred entrance.
Recommended: high school transcript.
Application deadlines: rolling (freshmen), rolling (transfers).

CONTACT
Ms. Kimkisha Stevenson, Director of Admissions, Donnelly College, 608 North 18th Street, Kansas City, KS 66102. *Phone:* 913-621-8762. *Fax:* 913-621-8719. *E-mail:* admissions@donnelly.edu.

Emporia State University

Emporia, Kansas
http://www.emporia.edu/

- **State-supported** comprehensive, founded 1863, part of Kansas State Board of Regents
- **Small-town** 207-acre campus with easy access to Wichita
- **Endowment** $74.4 million
- **Coed** 3,605 undergraduate students, 93% full-time, 62% women, 38% men
- **Noncompetitive** entrance level, 83% of applicants were admitted

UNDERGRAD STUDENTS
3,340 full-time, 265 part-time. Students come from 20 states and territories; 50 other countries; 10% are from out of state; 5% Black or African American, non-Hispanic/Latino; 7% Hispanic/Latino; 0.9% Asian, non-Hispanic/Latino; 0.1% Native Hawaiian or other Pacific Islander, non-Hispanic/Latino; 0.4% American Indian or Alaska Native, non-Hispanic/Latino; 8% Two or more races, non-Hispanic/Latino; 2% Race/ethnicity unknown; 7% international; 10% transferred in; 17% live on campus.

Freshmen:
Admission: 1,693 applied, 1,401 admitted, 606 enrolled. *Average high school GPA:* 3.4. *Test scores:* ACT scores over 18: 88%; ACT scores over 24: 34%; ACT scores over 30: 4%.

Retention: 73% of full-time freshmen returned.

FACULTY
Total: 278, 89% full-time, 77% with terminal degrees.
Student/faculty ratio: 17:1.

ACADEMICS
Calendar: semesters. *Degrees:* bachelor's, master's, doctoral, post-master's, and postbachelor's certificates.

Special study options: academic remediation for entering students, accelerated degree program, adult/continuing education programs, advanced placement credit, cooperative education, distance learning, double majors, English as a second language, freshman honors college, honors programs, independent study, internships, off-campus study, part-time degree program, services for LD students, study abroad, summer session for credit.

Unusual degree programs: 3-2 engineering with Kansas State University, University of Kansas, Wichita State University.

Computers: 410 computers/terminals are available on campus for general student use. Students can access the following: campus intranet, computer help desk, free student e-mail accounts, online (class) grades, online (class) registration, online (class) schedules. Campuswide network is available. 100% of college-owned or -operated housing units are wired for high-speed Internet access. Wireless service is available via entire campus.

Library: William Allen White Library plus 1 other. *Books:* 389,595 (physical), 153,016 (digital/electronic); *Serial titles:* 35,153 (physical), 278 (digital/electronic); *Databases:* 97. Weekly public service hours: 79; study areas open 24 hours, 5–7 days a week; students can reserve study rooms.

STUDENT LIFE
Housing options: on-campus residence required for freshman year; coed, men-only, women-only, special housing for students with disabilities. Campus housing is university owned. Freshman campus housing is guaranteed.

Activities and organizations: drama/theater group, student-run newspaper, radio station, choral group, marching band, Phi Eta Sigma, Student Chapter of the American Library Association of ESU, TradPlus Student Organization, Arabic Culture Student Organization, Emporia Kansas Association of Nursing Students, national fraternities, national sororities.

Athletics Member NCAA. All Division II. *Intercollegiate sports:* baseball M(s), basketball M(s)/W(s), cheerleading M(s)/W(s), cross-country running M(s)/W(s), football M(s), soccer W(s), softball W(s), tennis M(s)/W(s), track and field M(s)/W(s), volleyball W(s). *Intramural sports:* badminton M/W, basketball M/W, fencing M(c)/W(c), football M/W, rugby M(c), soccer M(c)/W(c), softball M/W, table tennis M/W, tennis M/W, volleyball M/W.

Campus security: 24-hour emergency response devices and patrols, student patrols, late-night transport/escort service, controlled dormitory access, 24-hour residence hall monitoring, safety and self-awareness programs.

Student services: health clinic, personal/psychological counseling, women's center, legal services.

COSTS & FINANCIAL AID
Costs (2017–18) *Tuition:* state resident $5027 full-time, $168 per credit hour part-time; nonresident $18,600 full-time, $620 per credit hour part-time. Full-time tuition and fees vary according to course load, degree level, and location. Part-time tuition and fees vary according to course load, degree level, and location. *Required fees:* $1318 full-time, $81 per credit hour part-time. *Room and board:* $8684; room only: $5130. Room and board charges vary according to board plan, housing facility, and location. *Payment plans:* installment, deferred payment. *Waivers:* senior citizens and employees or children of employees.

Financial Aid Of all full-time matriculated undergraduates who enrolled in 2017, 2,561 applied for aid, 2,180 were judged to have need, 288 had their need fully met. 184 Federal Work-Study jobs (averaging $2185). 18 state and other part-time jobs (averaging $2683). In 2017, 598 non-need-based awards were made. *Average percent of need met:* 60. *Average financial aid package:* $9540. *Average need-based loan:* $6670. *Average need-based gift aid:* $5716. *Average non-need-based aid:* $2982. *Average indebtedness upon graduation:* $22,816.

APPLYING
Standardized Tests *Required:* SAT or ACT (for admission).

Options: electronic application, early admission, deferred entrance.

Application fee: $30.

Required: high school transcript, minimum ACT score of 21, or rank in the top 1/3 and completed QA core classes with cum 2.0 GPA, 22 Math subscore, or completed 4th year of math. *Recommended:* minimum 2.0 GPA.

Application deadlines: rolling (freshmen), rolling (transfers).

Notification: continuous (freshmen), continuous (transfers).

CONTACT
Ms. Roxie Pearson, Associate Director of Data Management, Emporia State University, 1 Kellogg Circle, Campus Box 4034, Emporia, KS 66801-5087. *Phone:* 620-341-5465. *Toll-free phone:* 877-GOTOESU (in-state); 877-468-6378 (out-of-state). *Fax:* 620-341-5599. *E-mail:* go2esu@emporia.edu.

Fort Hays State University

Hays, Kansas
http://www.fhsu.edu/

CONTACT
Tricia Cline, Director, Admissions, Fort Hays State University, 600 Park Street, Hays, KS 67601-4099. *Phone:* 785-628-4091. *Toll-free phone:* 800-628-FHSU. *E-mail:* tcline@fhsu.edu.

Friends University

Wichita, Kansas
http://www.friends.edu/

- **Independent** comprehensive, founded 1898, affiliated with Christian non-denominational
- **Urban** 55-acre campus
- **Endowment** $49.1 million
- **Coed** 1,146 undergraduate students, 79% full-time, 56% women, 44% men
- **Moderately difficult** entrance level, 48% of applicants were admitted

UNDERGRAD STUDENTS
906 full-time, 240 part-time. Students come from 38 states and territories; 15 other countries; 20% are from out of state; 9% Black or African American, non-Hispanic/Latino; 11% Hispanic/Latino; 0.9% Asian, non-Hispanic/Latino; 0.2% Native Hawaiian or other Pacific Islander, non-Hispanic/Latino; 2% American Indian or Alaska Native, non-Hispanic/Latino; 1% Two or more races, non-Hispanic/Latino; 11% Race/ethnicity unknown; 16% transferred in; 25% live on campus.

Freshmen:
Admission: 881 applied, 423 admitted, 176 enrolled. *Average high school GPA:* 3.5. *Test scores:* SAT evidence-based reading and writing scores over 500: 67%; SAT math scores over 500: 72%; ACT scores over 18: 89%; SAT evidence-based reading and writing scores over 600: 11%; SAT math scores over 600: 39%; ACT scores over 24: 36%; SAT math scores over 700: 6%; ACT scores over 30: 4%.

Retention: 74% of full-time freshmen returned.

FACULTY
Total: 282, 22% full-time, 29% with terminal degrees.
Student/faculty ratio: 10:1.

ACADEMICS
Calendar: semesters. *Degrees:* bachelor's and master's.

Special study options: academic remediation for entering students, accelerated degree program, adult/continuing education programs, advanced placement credit, cooperative education, distance learning, double majors, honors programs, independent study, internships, off-campus study, part-time degree program, services for LD students, student-designed majors, study abroad, summer session for credit.

Computers: 360 computers/terminals are available on campus for general student use. Students can access the following: campus intranet, computer help desk, free student e-mail accounts, online (class) grades, online (class) registration, online (class) schedules. Campuswide network is available. 90% of college-owned or -operated housing units are wired for high-speed Internet access. Wireless service is available via entire campus.
Library: Edmund Stanley Library plus 1 other. *Books:* 88,223 (physical), 141,741 (digital/electronic); *Serial titles:* 202 (physical); *Databases:* 102.

STUDENT LIFE
Housing options: on-campus residence required for freshman year; coed. Campus housing is university owned.

Activities and organizations: drama/theater group, choral group, Concert Choir, Singing Quakers, Zoo Science Club, Psychology Club, Spanish Club.

Athletics Member NAIA. *Intercollegiate sports:* baseball M(s), basketball M(s)/W(s), cheerleading M(s)/W(s), cross-country running M(s)/W(s), football M(s), golf W(s), soccer M(s)/W(s), softball W(s), tennis M(s)/W(s), track and field M(s)/W(s), volleyball W(s). *Intramural sports:* basketball M/W, football M/W, racquetball M/W, sand volleyball M/W, soccer M/W, table tennis M/W, tennis M/W, ultimate Frisbee M/W, volleyball M/W.

Campus security: 24-hour emergency response devices and patrols, late-night transport/escort service, controlled dormitory access.

Student services: health clinic, personal/psychological counseling.

COSTS & FINANCIAL AID
Costs (2018–19) Comprehensive fee: $36,387 includes full-time tuition ($27,965), mandatory fees ($450), and room and board ($7972). Full-time tuition and fees vary according to class time, course load, degree level, and location. Part-time tuition: $932 per credit hour. Part-time tuition and fees vary according to class time, course load, degree level, and location. *College room only:* $3800. Room and board charges vary according to board plan and housing facility. *Payment plan:* installment. *Waivers:* senior citizens and employees or children of employees.

Financial Aid Of all full-time matriculated undergraduates who enrolled in 2015, 905 applied for aid, 805 were judged to have need, 283 had their need fully met. 204 Federal Work-Study jobs (averaging $1091). 252 state and other part-time jobs (averaging $1306). In 2015, 100 non-need-based awards were made. *Average percent of need met:* 82. *Average financial aid package:* $16,394. *Average need-based loan:* $4158. *Average need-based gift aid:* $8359. *Average non-need-based aid:* $8975. *Average indebtedness upon graduation:* $28,175.

APPLYING
Standardized Tests *Required for some:* SAT or ACT (for admission). *Recommended:* ACT (for admission), SAT and SAT Subject Tests or ACT (for admission).

Options: electronic application.

Required for some: high school transcript, minimum 2.0 GPA, interview, audition for music, dance and theater programs; portfolio for art program.

Application deadlines: rolling (freshmen), rolling (transfers).

Notification: continuous (freshmen), continuous (transfers).

CONTACT
Mrs. Miya Williams, Director of Admissions, Friends University, 2100 West University Avenue, Wichita, KS 67213. *Phone:* 316-295-5100. *Toll-free phone:* 800-794-6945. *Fax:* 316-295-5101. *E-mail:* learn@friends.edu.

Grantham University
Lenexa, Kansas
http://www.grantham.edu/

CONTACT
Mr. Les Hyde, Vice President Admissions, Grantham University, 7200 NW 86th Street, Kansas City, MO 64153. *Phone:* 800-955-2527. *Toll-free phone:* 800-955-2527. *Fax:* 816-595-5757. *E-mail:* admissions@grantham.edu.

Haskell Indian Nations University
Lawrence, Kansas
http://www.haskell.edu/

CONTACT
Ms. Patty Grant, Recruitment Officer, Haskell Indian Nations University, 155 Indian Avenue, #5031, Lawrence, KS 66046-4800. *Phone:* 785-749-8437 Ext. 437.

Hesston College
Hesston, Kansas
http://www.hesston.edu/
- **Independent Mennonite** primarily 2-year, founded 1909
- **Small-town** 50-acre campus with easy access to Wichita
- **Endowment** $12.9 million
- **Coed** 442 undergraduate students, 91% full-time, 60% women, 40% men
- **Noncompetitive** entrance level, 56% of applicants were admitted

UNDERGRAD STUDENTS
403 full-time, 39 part-time. Students come from 29 states and territories; 15 other countries; 43% are from out of state; 5% Black or African American, non-Hispanic/Latino; 12% Hispanic/Latino; 2% Asian, non-Hispanic/Latino; 0.2% American Indian or Alaska Native, non-Hispanic/Latino; 3% Two or more races, non-Hispanic/Latino; 0.7% Race/ethnicity unknown; 13% international; 8% transferred in; 69% live on campus.

Freshmen:
Admission: 562 applied, 312 admitted, 166 enrolled. *Average high school GPA:* 3.3. *Test scores:* SAT evidence-based reading and writing scores over 500: 54%; SAT math scores over 500: 63%; ACT scores over 18: 86%; SAT evidence-based reading and writing scores over 600: 30%; SAT math scores over 600: 30%; ACT scores over 24: 23%; SAT evidence-based reading and writing scores over 700: 3%; SAT math scores over 700: 3%; ACT scores over 30: 1%.

Retention: 77% of full-time freshmen returned.

FACULTY
Total: 53, 72% full-time, 25% with terminal degrees.
Student/faculty ratio: 8:1.

ACADEMICS
Calendar: semesters. *Degrees:* associate and bachelor's.

Special study options: academic remediation for entering students, adult/continuing education programs, advanced placement credit, cooperative education, double majors, English as a second language, independent study, internships, part-time degree program, services for LD students, summer session for credit.

Computers: 115 computers/terminals are available on campus for general student use. Students can access the following: computer help desk, free student e-mail accounts, online (class) grades, online (class) registration, online (class) schedules. Campuswide network is available. 100% of college-owned or -operated housing units are wired for high-speed Internet access. Wireless service is available via classrooms, computer centers, computer labs, dorm rooms, learning centers, libraries, student centers.

Library: Mary Miller Library. Students can reserve study rooms.

STUDENT LIFE

Housing options: on-campus residence required through sophomore year; men-only, women-only. Campus housing is university owned. Freshman campus housing is guaranteed.

Activities and organizations: drama/theater group, student-run newspaper, choral group, Peace and Service Club, Intramural Sports, Ministry Assistants.

Athletics Member NJCAA. *Intercollegiate sports:* baseball M(s), basketball M(s)/W(s), cross-country running M(s)/W(s), golf M(s), soccer M(s)/W(s), softball W(s), tennis M(s)/W(s), track and field M(s)/W(s), volleyball W(s). *Intramural sports:* basketball M/W, golf M(c)/W(c), sand volleyball M/W, soccer M/W, ultimate Frisbee M/W, volleyball M/W.

Campus security: 24-hour emergency response devices, controlled dormitory access.

Student services: personal/psychological counseling.

COSTS & FINANCIAL AID

Costs (2018–19) *Comprehensive fee:* $35,700 includes full-time tuition ($26,460), mandatory fees ($440), and room and board ($8800). Full-time tuition and fees vary according to course load and program. Part-time tuition: $1102 per credit hour. Part-time tuition and fees vary according to course load. *Required fees:* $110 per term part-time. *Payment plans:* installment, deferred payment. *Waivers:* employees or children of employees.

Financial Aid Of all full-time matriculated undergraduates who enrolled in 2016, 120 Federal Work-Study jobs (averaging $800).

APPLYING

Standardized Tests *Required:* SAT or ACT (for admission).

Options: electronic application, early admission, deferred entrance.

Required: high school transcript. *Required for some:* 2 letters of recommendation, interview.

Application deadlines: rolling (freshmen), rolling (out-of-state freshmen), rolling (transfers).

CONTACT

Rachel Swartzendruber-Miller, Vice President of Admissions, Hesston College, Hesston, KS 67062. *Phone:* 620-327-8206. *Toll-free phone:* 800-995-2757. *Fax:* 620-327-8300. *E-mail:* admissions@hesston.edu.

Kansas State University
Manhattan, Kansas
http://www.k-state.edu/

- **State-supported** university, founded 1863, part of Kansas Board of Regents
- **Suburban** 668-acre campus
- **Endowment** $506.4 million
- **Coed** 18,488 undergraduate students, 91% full-time, 47% women, 53% men
- **Minimally difficult** entrance level, 95% of applicants were admitted

UNDERGRAD STUDENTS

16,770 full-time, 1,718 part-time. Students come from 52 states and territories; 81 other countries; 18% are from out of state; 3% Black or African American, non-Hispanic/Latino; 7% Hispanic/Latino; 1% Asian, non-Hispanic/Latino; 0.1% Native Hawaiian or other Pacific Islander, non-Hispanic/Latino; 0.5% American Indian or Alaska Native, non-Hispanic/Latino; 4% Two or more races, non-Hispanic/Latino; 0.9% Race/ethnicity unknown; 5% international; 7% transferred in; 24% live on campus.

Freshmen:

Admission: 8,310 applied, 7,864 admitted, 3,350 enrolled. *Average high school GPA:* 3.5. *Test scores:* ACT scores over 18: 97%; ACT scores over 24: 59%; ACT scores over 30: 16%.

Retention: 84% of full-time freshmen returned.

FACULTY

Total: 1,281, 86% full-time, 80% with terminal degrees.

Student/faculty ratio: 18:1.

ACADEMICS

Calendar: semesters. *Degrees:* certificates, associate, bachelor's, master's, doctoral, and postbachelor's certificates.

Special study options: academic remediation for entering students, accelerated degree program, adult/continuing education programs, advanced placement credit, cooperative education, distance learning, double majors, English as a second language, freshman honors college, honors programs, independent study, internships, off-campus study, part-time degree program, services for LD students, study abroad, summer session for credit. *ROTC:* Army (b), Air Force (b).

Unusual degree programs: 3-2 engineering; biology, kinesiology, horticulture, master of public health, biochemistry, mathematics, human nutrition, hospitality management, agricultural economics, political science/master of public administration, accounting/MBA, architectural engineering, industrial engineering, bio/ag engineering.

Computers: Students can access the following: computer help desk, free student e-mail accounts, online (class) grades, online (class) registration, online (class) schedules. Campuswide network is available. Wireless service is available via entire campus.

Library: Hale Library plus 3 others. *Books:* 1.3 million (physical), 1.5 million (digital/electronic); *Serial titles:* 51,881 (physical), 114,285 (digital/electronic); *Databases:* 278. Weekly public service hours: 80; study areas open 24 hours, 5–7 days a week; students can reserve study rooms.

STUDENT LIFE

Housing options: coed, men-only, women-only, cooperative. Campus housing is university owned.

Activities and organizations: drama/theater group, student-run newspaper, radio and television station, choral group, marching band, athletic department groups, marching band, Union Governing Board, theater productions, debate team, national fraternities, national sororities.

Athletics Member NCAA. All Division I except football (Division I-A). *Intercollegiate sports:* baseball M(s), basketball M(s)/W(s), crew W(s), cross-country running M(s)/W(s), golf M(s)/W(s), soccer W, tennis W(s), track and field M(s)/W(s), volleyball W(s). *Intramural sports:* badminton M/W, basketball M/W, bowling M/W, crew M/W, cross-country running M/W, football M/W, golf M/W, ice hockey M, lacrosse M, racquetball M/W, soccer M/W, softball M/W, table tennis M/W, tennis M/W, track and field M/W, volleyball M/W, water polo M/W, weight lifting M/W, wrestling M.

Campus security: 24-hour emergency response devices and patrols, late-night transport/escort service, controlled dormitory access.

Student services: health clinic, personal/psychological counseling, women's center, legal services.

COSTS & FINANCIAL AID

Costs (2017–18) *Tuition:* state resident $9273 full-time; nonresident $24,630 full-time. Full-time tuition and fees vary according to course level, course load, degree level, location, program, and reciprocity agreements. Part-time tuition and fees vary according to course level, course load, degree level, location, program, and reciprocity agreements. *Required fees:* $862 full-time. *Room and board:* $9430. Room and board charges vary according to board plan, housing facility, and location. *Payment plans:* installment, deferred payment. *Waivers:* employees or children of employees.

Financial Aid Of all full-time matriculated undergraduates who enrolled in 2015, 12,011 applied for aid, 8,925 were judged to have need, 1,676 had their need fully met. In 2015, 1596 non-need-based awards were made. *Average percent of need met:* 78. *Average financial aid package:* $12,646. *Average need-based loan:* $4501. *Average need-based gift aid:* $4329. *Average non-need-based aid:* $4250. *Average indebtedness upon graduation:* $27,198.

APPLYING

Standardized Tests *Required for some:* SAT or ACT (for admission). *Recommended:* SAT or ACT (for admission).

Options: electronic application, early admission.

Application fee: $40.

Required: high school transcript, minimum 2.0 GPA, minimum ACT composite of 21 or top third of high school graduating class.

Application deadlines: rolling (freshmen), rolling (transfers).

Notification: continuous (freshmen), continuous (transfers).

CONTACT

Ms. Molly McGaughey, Associate Director of Admissions, Kansas State University, 119 Anderson Hall, Manhattan, KS 66506. *Phone:* 785-532-6250. *Toll-free phone:* 800-432-8270. *Fax:* 785-532-6393. *E-mail:* k-state@k-state.edu.

Kansas State University Polytechnic Campus

Salina, Kansas

http://www.polytechnic.k-state.edu/

CONTACT

Kansas State University Polytechnic Campus, 2310 Centennial Road, Salina, KS 67401.

Kansas Wesleyan University

Salina, Kansas

http://www.kwu.edu/

- **Independent United Methodist** comprehensive, founded 1886
- **Small-town** 28-acre campus
- **Endowment** $27.2 million
- **Coed** 693 undergraduate students, 91% full-time, 41% women, 59% men
- **Moderately difficult** entrance level, 54% of applicants were admitted

UNDERGRAD STUDENTS

631 full-time, 62 part-time. Students come from 34 states and territories; 8 other countries; 55% are from out of state; 14% Black or African American, non-Hispanic/Latino; 16% Hispanic/Latino; 0.4% Asian, non-Hispanic/Latino; 0.4% Native Hawaiian or other Pacific Islander, non-Hispanic/Latino; 0.3% American Indian or Alaska Native, non-Hispanic/Latino; 4% Two or more races, non-Hispanic/Latino; 0.9% Race/ethnicity unknown; 2% international; 13% transferred in; 66% live on campus.

Freshmen:

Admission: 809 applied, 434 admitted, 184 enrolled. *Average high school GPA:* 3.3.

Retention: 54% of full-time freshmen returned.

FACULTY

Total: 78, 58% full-time, 50% with terminal degrees.
Student/faculty ratio: 13:1.

ACADEMICS

Calendar: semesters plus summer term. *Degrees:* associate, bachelor's, and master's.

Special study options: academic remediation for entering students, advanced placement credit, distance learning, double majors, honors programs, independent study, internships, off-campus study, part-time degree program, services for LD students, student-designed majors, study abroad, summer session for credit.

Unusual degree programs: 3-2 engineering with Washington University in St. Louis; ecospheric Studies with Western Colorado State University.

Computers: 195 computers/terminals are available on campus for general student use. Students can access the following: computer help desk, free student e-mail accounts, online (class) grades, online (class) registration, online (class) schedules. Campuswide network is available. 100% of college-owned or -operated housing units are wired for high-speed Internet access. Wireless service is available via entire campus.
Library: Memorial Library. *Books:* 71,409 (physical), 6,730 (digital/electronic); *Serial titles:* 402 (physical); *Databases:* 57. Weekly public service hours: 83; students can reserve study rooms.

STUDENT LIFE

Housing options: on-campus residence required through sophomore year; coed, men-only, women-only. Campus housing is university owned. Freshman campus housing is guaranteed.

Activities and organizations: drama/theater group, student-run newspaper, radio and television station, choral group, Fellowship of Christian Athletes, Student Government, Wesleyan Chorale, Coyote Gaming Club, Coyote Activities Board.

Athletics Member NAIA. *Intercollegiate sports:* baseball M(s), basketball M(s)/W(s), bowling M(s)/W(s), cheerleading M(s)/W(s), cross-country running M(s)/W(s), football M(s), golf M(s)/W(s), soccer M(s)/W(s), softball W(s), tennis M(s)/W(s), track and field M(s)/W(s), volleyball W(s), wrestling M(s). *Intramural sports:* basketball M/W, bowling M/W, football M/W, softball M/W, table tennis M/W, volleyball M/W.

Campus security: 24-hour emergency response devices, student patrols, late-night transport/escort service, controlled dormitory access, evening patrols by security.

Student services: personal/psychological counseling.

COSTS & FINANCIAL AID

Costs (2018–19) *One-time required fee:* $300. *Comprehensive fee:* $39,000 includes full-time tuition ($29,500) and room and board ($9500). Part-time tuition: $3000 per term. Part-time tuition and fees vary according to course load. *Room and board:* Room and board charges vary according to housing facility. *Payment plan:* installment. *Waivers:* children of alumni, senior citizens, and employees or children of employees.

Financial Aid Of all full-time matriculated undergraduates who enrolled in 2016, 657 applied for aid, 559 were judged to have need, 105 had their need fully met. 98 Federal Work-Study jobs (averaging $1488). 31 state and other part-time jobs (averaging $828). In 2016, 82 non-need-based awards were made. *Average percent of need met:* 68. *Average financial aid package:* $21,316. *Average need-based loan:* $4294. *Average need-based gift aid:* $7695. *Average non-need-based aid:* $11,252. *Average indebtedness upon graduation:* $34,526.

APPLYING

Standardized Tests *Required:* SAT or ACT (for admission).

Options: electronic application, deferred entrance.

Application fee: $20.

Required: high school transcript, minimum 2.5 GPA. *Required for some:* essay or personal statement, interview.

Application deadlines: rolling (freshmen), rolling (transfers).

Notification: continuous (freshmen), continuous (transfers).

CONTACT

Mr. Esteban Paredes, Director of Admissions, Kansas Wesleyan University, 100 East Claflin Avenue, Box 20, Salina, KS 67401. *Phone:* 785-833-4307. *Toll-free phone:* 800-874-1154 Ext. 1285. *Fax:* 785-404-1485. *E-mail:* esteban.paredes@kwu.edu.

Manhattan Christian College

Manhattan, Kansas

http://www.mccks.edu/

CONTACT

Ms. Connie Hill, Admissions Office Manager, Manhattan Christian College, 1415 Anderson Avenue, Manhattan, KS 66502. *Phone:* 877-246-4622 Ext. 212. *Toll-free phone:* 877-246-4622. *E-mail:* teka.wilson@mccks.edu.

McPherson College

McPherson, Kansas

http://www.mcpherson.edu/

- **Independent** comprehensive, founded 1887, affiliated with Church of the Brethren
- **Small-town** 26-acre campus
- **Endowment** $39.1 million
- **Coed** 725 undergraduate students, 93% full-time, 36% women, 64% men
- **Moderately difficult** entrance level, 27% of applicants were admitted

UNDERGRAD STUDENTS

673 full-time, 52 part-time. Students come from 34 states and territories; 16 other countries; 53% are from out of state; 13% Black or African American, non-Hispanic/Latino; 14% Hispanic/Latino; 1% Asian, non-Hispanic/Latino; 0.1% Native Hawaiian or other Pacific Islander, non-Hispanic/Latino; 2% American Indian or Alaska Native, non-Hispanic/Latino; 0.6% Two or more races, non-Hispanic/Latino; 4% Race/ethnicity unknown; 1% international; 12% transferred in; 66% live on campus.

Freshmen:

Admission: 759 applied, 202 admitted, 202 enrolled. *Average high school GPA:* 3.2. *Test scores:* SAT evidence-based reading and writing scores over 500: 100%; SAT math scores over 500: 72%; ACT scores over 18: 99%; SAT evidence-based reading and writing scores over 600: 38%; SAT math scores over 600: 8%; ACT scores over 24: 23%; ACT scores over 30: 1%.

Retention: 63% of full-time freshmen returned.

FACULTY

Total: 47, 91% full-time, 72% with terminal degrees.

Student/faculty ratio: 13:1.

ACADEMICS

Calendar: 4-1-4. *Degrees:* bachelor's and master's.

Special study options: academic remediation for entering students, double majors, English as a second language, independent study, internships, off-campus study, part-time degree program, services for LD students, student-designed majors, study abroad, summer session for credit.

Computers: 190 computers/terminals and 190 ports are available on campus for general student use. Students can access the following: campus intranet, computer help desk, free student e-mail accounts, online (class) grades, online (class) registration, online (class) schedules. Campuswide network is available. Wireless service is available via entire campus.

Library: Miller Library. *Books:* 42,629 (physical), 164,814 (digital/electronic); *Serial titles:* 681 (physical), 92,937 (digital/electronic); *Databases:* 65. Weekly public service hours: 86; students can reserve study rooms.

STUDENT LIFE

Housing options: coed, men-only, women-only, special housing for students with disabilities. Campus housing is university owned and leased by the school. Freshman campus housing is guaranteed.

Activities and organizations: drama/theater group, student-run newspaper, choral group, Student Activities Board, Student Government Association, CARS Club, Business Club, Multicultural Student Association.

Athletics Member NAIA. *Intercollegiate sports:* baseball M, basketball M/W, cheerleading M/W, cross-country running M/W, football M, soccer M/W, softball W, tennis M/W, track and field M/W, volleyball W. *Intramural sports:* basketball M/W, football M/W, soccer M/W, softball M/W, table tennis M/W, ultimate Frisbee M/W, volleyball M/W.

Campus security: student patrols, controlled dormitory access, Security cameras.

Student services: health clinic, personal/psychological counseling.

COSTS & FINANCIAL AID

Costs (2018–19) *Comprehensive fee:* $37,362 includes full-time tuition ($28,161), mandatory fees ($790), and room and board ($8411). Full-time tuition and fees vary according to course load. Part-time tuition: $430 per credit hour. Part-time tuition and fees vary according to course load.

Required fees: $50 per term part-time. *Payment plan:* installment. *Waivers:* senior citizens and employees or children of employees.

Financial Aid Of all full-time matriculated undergraduates who enrolled in 2016, 558 applied for aid, 558 were judged to have need, 129 had their need fully met. In 2016, 54 non-need-based awards were made. *Average percent of need met:* 82. *Average financial aid package:* $24,898. *Average need-based loan:* $8592. *Average need-based gift aid:* $5722. *Average non-need-based aid:* $14,626. *Average indebtedness upon graduation:* $28,615.

APPLYING

Standardized Tests *Required:* SAT or ACT (for admission).

Options: electronic application, deferred entrance.

Required: high school transcript, minimum 2.0 GPA.

Application deadlines: 8/12 (freshmen), rolling (out-of-state freshmen), rolling (transfers).

Notification: continuous (freshmen), continuous (transfers).

CONTACT

Ms. Sara Brubaker, Director of Admissions Operations and Financial Aid, McPherson College, 1600 East Euclid, McPherson, KS 67460. *Phone:*

800-365-7402. *Toll-free phone:* 800-365-7402. *E-mail:* admiss@ mcpherson.edu.

MidAmerica Nazarene University
Olathe, Kansas
http://www.mnu.edu/

- **Independent** comprehensive, founded 1966, affiliated with Church of the Nazarene
- **Suburban** 105-acre campus with easy access to Kansas City
- **Endowment** $10.6 million
- **Coed** 1,308 undergraduate students, 76% full-time, 59% women, 41% men
- **Minimally difficult** entrance level, 66% of applicants were admitted

UNDERGRAD STUDENTS

998 full-time, 310 part-time. Students come from 43 states and territories; 17 other countries; 40% are from out of state; 12% Black or African American, non-Hispanic/Latino; 8% Hispanic/Latino; 2% Asian, non-Hispanic/Latino; 0.8% Native Hawaiian or other Pacific Islander, non-Hispanic/Latino; 1% American Indian or Alaska Native, non-Hispanic/Latino; 3% Two or more races, non-Hispanic/Latino; 15% Race/ethnicity unknown; 7% transferred in; 56% live on campus.

Freshmen:

Admission: 957 applied, 628 admitted, 223 enrolled. *Average high school GPA:* 3.3. *Test scores:* SAT evidence-based reading and writing scores over 500: 58%; SAT math scores over 500: 65%; ACT scores over 18: 81%; SAT evidence-based reading and writing scores over 600: 24%; SAT math scores over 600: 24%; ACT scores over 24: 32%; SAT evidence-based reading and writing scores over 700: 3%; SAT math scores over 700: 3%; ACT scores over 30: 6%.

Retention: 63% of full-time freshmen returned.

FACULTY

Total: 270, 33% full-time, 32% with terminal degrees.

Student/faculty ratio: 7:1.

ACADEMICS

Calendar: semesters. *Degrees:* associate, bachelor's, master's, post-master's, and postbachelor's certificates.

Special study options: academic remediation for entering students, accelerated degree program, adult/continuing education programs, advanced placement credit, cooperative education, distance learning, double majors, English as a second language, freshman honors college, honors programs, independent study, internships, off-campus study, part-time degree program, services for LD students, student-designed majors, study abroad, summer session for credit. *ROTC:* Army (c), Air Force (c).

Unusual degree programs: 3-2 nursing.

Computers: 85 computers/terminals and 100 ports are available on campus for general student use. Students can access the following: campus intranet, computer help desk, free student e-mail accounts, online (class) grades, online (class) registration, online (class) schedules. Campuswide network is available. 100% of college-owned or -operated housing units are wired for high-speed Internet access. Wireless service is available via entire campus.

Library: Mabee Library. *Books:* 88,000 (physical), 249,000 (digital/electronic); *Serial titles:* 397 (physical), 25 (digital/electronic); *Databases:* 35. Weekly public service hours: 81; study areas open 24 hours, 5–7 days a week; students can reserve study rooms.

STUDENT LIFE

Housing options: on-campus residence required through senior year; men-only, women-only, special housing for students with disabilities. Campus housing is university owned. Freshman campus housing is guaranteed.

Activities and organizations: drama/theater group, student-run newspaper, radio and television station, choral group, LOL - Loving on Littles, S.M.I.L.E. - Students Ministering in the Lives of Elderly, Center for Grace, Freedom Fire, Students for Social Justice.

Athletics Member NAIA. *Intercollegiate sports:* baseball M(s), basketball M(s)/W(s), cheerleading M(s)/W(s), cross-country running M(s)/W(s), football M(s), soccer M(s)/W(s), softball W(s), track and field M(s)/W(s), volleyball W(s). *Intramural sports:* basketball M/W, football

M/W, soccer M/W, softball M/W, tennis M/W, volleyball M/W, weight lifting M.

Campus security: 24-hour emergency response devices and patrols, student patrols, late-night transport/escort service, controlled dormitory access.

Student services: personal/psychological counseling.

COSTS & FINANCIAL AID

Costs (2018–19) *Comprehensive fee:* $39,444 includes full-time tuition ($29,986), mandatory fees ($750), and room and board ($8708). Full-time tuition and fees vary according to course load, degree level, program, and reciprocity agreements. Part-time tuition: $1119 per credit hour. Part-time tuition and fees vary according to course load, degree level, program, and reciprocity agreements. *College room only:* $4834. Room and board charges vary according to board plan and housing facility. *Payment plan:* installment. *Waivers:* senior citizens and employees or children of employees.

Financial Aid Of all full-time matriculated undergraduates who enrolled in 2016, 839 applied for aid, 793 were judged to have need, 242 had their need fully met. 100 Federal Work-Study jobs (averaging $1370). In 2016, 146 non-need-based awards were made. *Average percent of need met:* 75. *Average financial aid package:* $25,027. *Average need-based loan:* $7772. *Average need-based gift aid:* $17,239. *Average non-need-based aid:* $17,631. *Average indebtedness upon graduation:* $33,018.

APPLYING

Standardized Tests *Required for some:* SAT or ACT (for admission). *Recommended:* TOEFL for international applicants.

Options: electronic application, deferred entrance.

Required: high school transcript, minimum 2.0 GPA.

Application deadlines: 8/1 (freshmen), 8/1 (transfers).

Notification: continuous (freshmen), continuous (transfers).

CONTACT

Meghan Luoma, MidAmerica Nazarene University, 2030 College Avenue, Olathe, IN 66062. *Phone:* 913-971-3783. *Toll-free phone:* 800-800-8887. *E-mail:* mvluoma@mnu.edu.

National American University

Overland Park, Kansas

http://www.national.edu/

CONTACT

Admissions Office, National American University, 10310 Mastin Street, Overland Park, KS 66212. *Toll-free phone:* 866-628-1288.

National American University

Wichita, Kansas

http://www.national.edu/

CONTACT

National American University, 7309 East 21st Street, Suite G40, Wichita, KS 67206. *Toll-free phone:* 877-628-9424.

National American University

Wichita, Kansas

http://www.national.edu/

CONTACT

National American University, 8428 West 13th Street North, Suite 120, Wichita, KS 67212. *Toll-free phone:* 877-628-9424.

Nazarene Bible College

Lenexa, Kansas

http://www.nbc.edu/

- **Independent** 4-year, founded 1967, affiliated with Church of the Nazarene
- **Urban** 64-acre campus with easy access to Colorado Springs
- **Coed**
- **Noncompetitive** entrance level

FACULTY

Student/faculty ratio: 6:1.

ACADEMICS

Calendar: trimesters. *Degrees:* certificates, diplomas, associate, and bachelor's.

Library: Trimble Library. *Books:* 47,287 (physical), 1,502 (digital/electronic); *Serial titles:* 285 (physical), 3,145 (digital/electronic); *Databases:* 14. Weekly public service hours: 51.

STUDENT LIFE

Housing options: college housing not available.

Campus security: 24-hour security personnel on campus.

Student services: personal/psychological counseling.

COSTS & FINANCIAL AID

Costs (2017–18) *Tuition:* $10,800 full-time, $450 per credit hour part-time. Full-time tuition and fees vary according to program and reciprocity agreements. Part-time tuition and fees vary according to program and reciprocity agreements. *Required fees:* $960 full-time, $40 per credit hour part-time.

Financial Aid Of all full-time matriculated undergraduates who enrolled in 2014, 122 applied for aid, 89 were judged to have need, 84 had their need fully met. *Average percent of need met:* 96. *Average financial aid package:* $7695. *Average need-based loan:* $3337. *Average need-based gift aid:* $4527. *Average indebtedness upon graduation:* $33,289.

APPLYING

Options: electronic application, deferred entrance.

Required: official transcripts from all prior colleges. *Required for some:* high school transcript.

CONTACT

Scott McConnaughey, Director of Admissions/Admissions Counselor, Nazarene Bible College, 1111 Academy Park Loop, Colorado Springs, CO 80910-3704. *Phone:* 719-884-5062. *Toll-free phone:* 800-873-3873. *Fax:* 719-884-5039. *E-mail:* semcconnaughey@nbc.edu.

Newman University

Wichita, Kansas

http://www.newmanu.edu/

- **Independent Roman Catholic** comprehensive, founded 1933
- **Urban** 61-acre campus with easy access to Sedgwick County
- **Coed** 1,198 undergraduate students, 85% full-time, 66% women, 34% men
- **Minimally difficult** entrance level, 64% of applicants were admitted

UNDERGRAD STUDENTS

1,013 full-time, 185 part-time. 17% are from out of state; 6% Black or African American, non-Hispanic/Latino; 15% Hispanic/Latino; 5% Asian, non-Hispanic/Latino; 1% American Indian or Alaska Native, non-Hispanic/Latino; 2% Two or more races, non-Hispanic/Latino; 1% Race/ethnicity unknown; 8% international; 12% transferred in; 23% live on campus.

Freshmen:

Admission: 1,084 applied, 692 admitted, 212 enrolled. *Average high school GPA:* 3.6. *Test scores:* SAT evidence-based reading and writing scores over 500: 91%; SAT math scores over 500: 73%; ACT scores over 18: 93%; SAT evidence-based reading and writing scores over 600: 45%; SAT math scores over 600: 64%; ACT scores over 24: 35%; ACT scores over 30: 7%.

Retention: 80% of full-time freshmen returned.

FACULTY

Total: 202, 41% full-time, 33% with terminal degrees.

Student/faculty ratio: 11:1.

ACADEMICS

Calendar: semesters. *Degrees:* associate, bachelor's, and master's.

Special study options: academic remediation for entering students, accelerated degree program, adult/continuing education programs, advanced placement credit, cooperative education, distance learning, double majors, honors programs, independent study, internships, off-campus study, part-time degree program, services for LD students, student-designed majors, study abroad, summer session for credit.

Unusual degree programs: 3-2 occupational therapy with Washington University in St. Louis.

Computers: Students can access the following: computer help desk, free student e-mail accounts, online (class) grades, online (class) registration, online (class) schedules. Campuswide network is available. 100% of college-owned or -operated housing units are wired for high-speed Internet access. Wireless service is available via entire campus.

Library: Dugan Library. Students can reserve study rooms.

STUDENT LIFE

Housing options: on-campus residence required for freshman year; coed. Campus housing is university owned. Freshman campus housing is guaranteed.

Activities and organizations: drama/theater group, student-run newspaper, choral group, Newman University Medical Professionals Club (NUMPC), National Society of Leadership and Success, Student Athlete Advisory Committee, Swing Dance Club, Hispanic American Leadership Organization (HALO).

Athletics Member NCAA. All Division II. *Intercollegiate sports:* baseball M(s), basketball M(s)/W(s), bowling M(s)(c)/W(s)(c), cross-country running M(s)/W(s), golf M(s)/W(s), soccer M(s)/W(s), softball W(s), tennis M(s)/W(s), volleyball W(s), wrestling M(s). *Intramural sports:* baseball M, basketball M/W, bowling M/W, football M/W, golf M/W, soccer M/W, softball M/W, table tennis M/W, triathlon M/W, ultimate Frisbee M/W, volleyball M/W, weight lifting M/W.

Campus security: 24-hour emergency response devices and patrols, student patrols, late-night transport/escort service, controlled dormitory access.

Student services: personal/psychological counseling.

COSTS & FINANCIAL AID

Costs (2018–19) *Comprehensive fee:* $38,970 includes full-time tuition ($29,260), mandatory fees ($1304), and room and board ($8406). Part-time tuition: $976 per credit hour. Part-time tuition and fees vary according to course load. *College room only:* $4484. Room and board charges vary according to board plan and housing facility. *Payment plan:* installment. *Waivers:* employees or children of employees.

Financial Aid Of all full-time matriculated undergraduates who enrolled in 2015, 825 applied for aid, 662 were judged to have need, 129 had their need fully met. In 2015, 826 non-need-based awards were made. *Average percent of need met:* 37. *Average financial aid package:* $11,476. *Average need-based loan:* $2255. *Average need-based gift aid:* $3198. *Average non-need-based aid:* $5499. *Average indebtedness upon graduation:* $3809.

APPLYING

Standardized Tests *Required for some:* SAT or ACT (for admission).

Options: electronic application, early admission, deferred entrance.

Required: high school transcript, minimum 2.0 GPA. *Recommended:* interview.

Application deadlines: rolling (freshmen), rolling (transfers).

Notification: continuous (freshmen), continuous (transfers).

CONTACT

Kristen English, Director of Undergraduate Admissions, Newman University, 3100 McCormick Avenue, Wichita, KS 67213. *Phone:* 316-942-4291 Ext. 2146. *Toll-free phone:* 877-NEWMANU. *Fax:* 316-942-4483. *E-mail:* englishk@newmanu.edu.

Ottawa University

Ottawa, Kansas

http://www.ottawa.edu/

- **Independent American Baptist Churches in the USA** comprehensive, founded 1865
- **Small-town** 64-acre campus with easy access to Kansas City
- **Endowment** $17.6 million
- **Coed** 1,755 undergraduate students, 38% full-time, 60% women, 40% men
- **Moderately difficult** entrance level, 98% of applicants were admitted

UNDERGRAD STUDENTS

674 full-time, 1,081 part-time. Students come from 44 states and territories; 3 other countries; 33% are from out of state; 12% Black or African American, non-Hispanic/Latino; 12% Hispanic/Latino; 2% Asian, non-Hispanic/Latino; 0.3% Native Hawaiian or other Pacific Islander, non-Hispanic/Latino; 3% American Indian or Alaska Native, non-Hispanic/Latino; 4% Two or more races, non-Hispanic/Latino; 6% Race/ethnicity unknown; 80% transferred in; 63% live on campus.

Freshmen:

Admission: 1,732 applied, 1,689 admitted, 253 enrolled. *Average high school GPA:* 3.1. *Test scores:* ACT scores over 18: 84%; ACT scores over 24: 23%.

Retention: 57% of full-time freshmen returned.

FACULTY

Total: 36, 69% full-time, 50% with terminal degrees.

Student/faculty ratio: 18:1.

ACADEMICS

Calendar: semesters. *Degrees:* certificates, bachelor's, and master's (also offers master's, adult, international and on-line education programs with significant enrollment not reflected in profile).

Special study options: advanced placement credit, distance learning, double majors, independent study, internships, part-time degree program, student-designed majors, study abroad, summer session for credit.

Computers: 40 computers/terminals are available on campus for general student use. Students can access the following: campus intranet, computer help desk, free student e-mail accounts, online (class) grades, online (class) registration, online (class) schedules. Campuswide network is available. Wireless service is available via entire campus.

Library: Myers Library. Students can reserve study rooms.

STUDENT LIFE

Housing options: on-campus residence required through junior year; coed, women-only. Campus housing is university owned. Freshman campus housing is guaranteed.

Activities and organizations: drama/theater group, student-run newspaper, radio station, choral group, Christian Faith In Action, Student Activities Force, Education Club, Whole Earth Club, Fellowship of Christian Athletes.

Athletics Member NAIA. *Intercollegiate sports:* baseball M(s), basketball M(s)/W(s), bowling M(s)/W(s), cheerleading M(s)/W(s), cross-country running M(s)/W(s), football M(s), golf M(s)/W(s), lacrosse M(s)/W(s), soccer M(s)/W(s), softball W(s), tennis M(s)/W(s), track and field M(s)/W(s), volleyball W(s), wrestling M(s)/W(s). *Intramural sports:* basketball M/W, volleyball M/W, weight lifting M/W.

Campus security: 24-hour emergency response devices and patrols, controlled dormitory access, locked residence hall entrances.

Student services: health clinic, personal/psychological counseling.

COSTS

Costs (2018–19) *Comprehensive fee:* $35,690 includes full-time tuition ($28,410), mandatory fees ($1280), and room and board ($6000). Full-time tuition and fees vary according to course load and program. Part-time tuition: $1185 per credit hour. Part-time tuition and fees vary according to course load and program. *Required fees:* $531 per year part-time. *College room only:* $5000. Room and board charges vary according to board plan and housing facility. *Payment plan:* installment. *Waivers:* employees or children of employees.

APPLYING

Standardized Tests *Required:* SAT or ACT (for admission).

Options: electronic application.

Application fee: $25.

Required: high school transcript, minimum 2.5 GPA, rank in upper 50% of high school class. *Required for some:* essay or personal statement. *Recommended:* 2 letters of recommendation, interview.

Application deadlines: rolling (freshmen), rolling (transfers).

Notification: continuous (freshmen), continuous (transfers).

CONTACT

Ottawa University, 1001 South Cedar, Ottawa, KS 66067-3399. *Toll-free phone:* 800-755-5200.

Pittsburg State University

Pittsburg, Kansas
http://www.pittstate.edu/

- **State-supported** comprehensive, founded 1903, part of Kansas State Board of Regents
- **Small-town** 630-acre campus
- **Coed** 5,706 undergraduate students, 90% full-time, 48% women, 52% men
- **Minimally difficult** entrance level, 87% of applicants were admitted

UNDERGRAD STUDENTS
5,109 full-time, 597 part-time. 31% are from out of state; 4% Black or African American, non-Hispanic/Latino; 6% Hispanic/Latino; 0.9% Asian, non-Hispanic/Latino; 0.2% Native Hawaiian or other Pacific Islander, non-Hispanic/Latino; 1% American Indian or Alaska Native, non-Hispanic/Latino; 6% Two or more races, non-Hispanic/Latino; 0.2% Race/ethnicity unknown; 3% international; 9% transferred in.

Freshmen:
Admission: 2,486 applied, 2,168 admitted, 979 enrolled. *Average high school GPA:* 3.3. *Test scores:* ACT scores over 18: 90%; ACT scores over 24: 35%; ACT scores over 30: 5%.
Retention: 74% of full-time freshmen returned.

FACULTY
Total: 382, 76% full-time, 65% with terminal degrees.
Student/faculty ratio: 18:1.

ACADEMICS
Calendar: semesters. *Degrees:* certificates, associate, bachelor's, master's, doctoral, post-master's, and postbachelor's certificates.
Special study options: accelerated degree program, adult/continuing education programs, distance learning, double majors, freshman honors college, honors programs, independent study, internships, off-campus study, part-time degree program, services for LD students, student-designed majors, study abroad, summer session for credit.
ROTC: Army (b).
Computers: Students can access the following: campus intranet, computer help desk, free student e-mail accounts, online (class) grades, online (class) registration, online (class) schedules. Campuswide network is available. 100% of college-owned or -operated housing units are wired for high-speed Internet access. Wireless service is available via entire campus.
Library: Leonard H. Axe Library plus 2 others.

STUDENT LIFE
Housing options: on-campus residence required for freshman year; coed, special housing for students with disabilities. Campus housing is university owned. Freshman applicants given priority for college housing.
Activities and organizations: drama/theater group, student-run newspaper, radio and television station, choral group, marching band, Student Government Association, student yearbook, student newspaper, Student Activities Council, Students in Free Enterprise (SIFE), national fraternities, national sororities.
Athletics Member NCAA. All Division II. *Intercollegiate sports:* baseball M(s), basketball M(s)/W(s), cheerleading M(s)/W(s), cross-country running M(s)/W(s), football M(s), golf M(s), softball W(s), track and field M(s)/W(s), volleyball W(s). *Intramural sports:* badminton M/W, basketball M/W, football M/W, lacrosse M(c), racquetball M/W, rugby M(c), soccer M(c)/W(c), softball M/W, table tennis M/W, tennis M/W, ultimate Frisbee M/W, volleyball M/W.
Campus security: 24-hour emergency response devices and patrols, late-night transport/escort service, controlled dormitory access.
Student services: health clinic, personal/psychological counseling, legal services.

COSTS & FINANCIAL AID
Costs (2017–18) *Tuition:* state resident $5548 full-time, $185 per credit hour part-time; nonresident $16,600 full-time, $554 per credit hour part-time. *Required fees:* $1552 full-time, $66 per credit hour part-time. *Room and board:* $7700. Room and board charges vary according to board plan. *Payment plan:* installment. *Waivers:* employees or children of employees.
Financial Aid In 2016, 1994 non-need-based awards were made. *Average financial aid package:* $7092. *Average need-based loan:* $3990. *Average*

need-based gift aid: $4542. *Average non-need-based aid:* $2521. *Average indebtedness upon graduation:* $24,389.

APPLYING
Standardized Tests *Required:* ACT (for admission).
Options: electronic application, deferred entrance.
Application fee: $30.
Required: high school transcript. *Required for some:* minimum 2.0 GPA.
Application deadlines: rolling (freshmen), rolling (transfers).

CONTACT
Director of Admission, Pittsburg State University, 1701 South Broadway, Pittsburg, KS 66762. *Phone:* 620-235-4251. *Toll-free phone:* 800-854-7488. *Fax:* 620-235-6003. *E-mail:* psuadmit@pittstate.edu.

Rasmussen College Kansas City/Overland Park

Overland Park, Kansas
http://www.rasmussen.edu/

- **Proprietary** 4-year, founded 2013, part of Rasmussen College System
- **Suburban** campus
- **Coed**
- **Minimally difficult** entrance level

FACULTY
Student/faculty ratio: 22:1.

ACADEMICS
Calendar: quarters. *Degrees:* certificates, diplomas, associate, bachelor's, and postbachelor's certificates.
Library: Rasmussen College Library - Kansas City/Overland Park.

STUDENT LIFE
Housing options: college housing not available.

COSTS
Costs (2017–18) *Tuition:* $11,055 full-time, $290 per credit hour part-time. Full-time tuition and fees vary according to course level, course load, degree level, location, and program. Part-time tuition and fees vary according to course level, course load, degree level, location, and program. No tuition increase for student's term of enrollment. *Required fees:* $1695 full-time, $44 per credit hour part-time. *Payment plans:* installment, deferred payment.

APPLYING
Standardized Tests *Required:* institutional exam (for admission).
Options: electronic application, early admission, deferred entrance.
Required: high school transcript, minimum 2.0 GPA. *Required for some:* interview.

CONTACT
Ms. Susan Hammerstrom, Director of Admissions, Rasmussen College Kansas City/Overland Park, 11600 College Boulevard, Overland Park, KS 66210. *Phone:* 913-491-7870. *Toll-free phone:* 888-549-6755. *E-mail:* susan.hammerstrom@rasmussen.edu.

Rasmussen College Topeka

Topeka, Kansas
http://www.rasmussen.edu/

- **Proprietary** 4-year, founded 2013, part of Rasmussen College System
- **Suburban** campus
- **Coed**
- **Minimally difficult** entrance level

FACULTY
Student/faculty ratio: 22:1.

ACADEMICS
Calendar: quarters. *Degrees:* certificates, diplomas, associate, bachelor's, and postbachelor's certificates.
Library: Rasmussen College Library - Topeka.

STUDENT LIFE
Housing options: college housing not available.

COSTS

Costs (2017–18) *Tuition:* $11,055 full-time, $290 per credit hour part-time. Full-time tuition and fees vary according to course level, course load, degree level, location, and program. Part-time tuition and fees vary according to course level, course load, degree level, location, and program. No tuition increase for student's term of enrollment. *Required fees:* $1695 full-time, $44 per credit hour part-time. *Payment plans:* installment, deferred payment.

APPLYING

Standardized Tests *Required:* institutional exam (for admission).

Options: electronic application, early admission, deferred entrance.

Required: high school transcript, minimum 2.0 GPA. *Required for some:* interview.

CONTACT

Ms. Susan Hammerstrom, Director of Admissions, Rasmussen College Topeka, 620 SW Governor View, Topeka, KS 66606. *Phone:* 785-228-7320. *Toll-free phone:* 888-549-6755. *E-mail:* susan.hammerstrom@rasmussen.edu.

Southwestern College

Winfield, Kansas

http://www.sckans.edu/

- **Independent United Methodist** comprehensive, founded 1885
- **Small-town** 70-acre campus with easy access to Wichita
- **Endowment** $26.5 million
- **Coed** 1,147 undergraduate students, 50% full-time, 37% women, 63% men
- **Minimally difficult** entrance level, 97% of applicants were admitted

UNDERGRAD STUDENTS

577 full-time, 570 part-time. Students come from 43 states and territories; 18 other countries; 61% are from out of state; 11% Black or African American, non-Hispanic/Latino; 9% Hispanic/Latino; 1% Asian, non-Hispanic/Latino; 0.3% Native Hawaiian or other Pacific Islander, non-Hispanic/Latino; 1% American Indian or Alaska Native, non-Hispanic/Latino; 4% Two or more races, non-Hispanic/Latino; 26% Race/ethnicity unknown; 5% international; 15% transferred in; 37% live on campus.

Freshmen:
Admission: 512 applied, 496 admitted, 189 enrolled. *Average high school GPA:* 3.2. *Test scores:* SAT evidence-based reading and writing scores over 500: 43%; SAT math scores over 500: 38%; ACT scores over 18: 88%; SAT evidence-based reading and writing scores over 600: 4%; SAT math scores over 600: 6%; ACT scores over 24: 19%; ACT scores over 30: 3%.
Retention: 62% of full-time freshmen returned.

FACULTY

Total: 167, 26% full-time, 34% with terminal degrees.
Student/faculty ratio: 10:1.

ACADEMICS

Calendar: semesters. *Degrees:* certificates, bachelor's, master's, doctoral, and postbachelor's certificates.

Special study options: academic remediation for entering students, accelerated degree program, adult/continuing education programs, advanced placement credit, distance learning, double majors, English as a second language, honors programs, independent study, internships, off-campus study, part-time degree program, services for LD students, student-designed majors, study abroad, summer session for credit.

Computers: 45 computers/terminals and 30 ports are available on campus for general student use. Students can access the following: campus intranet, computer help desk, free student e-mail accounts, online (class) grades, online (class) registration, online (class) schedules, everything in Self-Service and BlackBoard. Campuswide network is available. 100% of college-owned or -operated housing units are wired for high-speed Internet access. Wireless service is available via entire campus.
Library: Harold and Mary Ellen Deets Library. *Books:* 49,349 (physical), 479,970 (digital/electronic); *Serial titles:* 10 (physical), 21,560 (digital/electronic); *Databases:* 84. Weekly public service hours: 91; students can reserve study rooms.

STUDENT LIFE

Housing options: on-campus residence required through sophomore year; coed, men-only, women-only. Campus housing is university owned. Freshman campus housing is guaranteed.

Activities and organizations: drama/theater group, student-run newspaper, radio and television station, choral group, Discipleship SC, Leadership SC, Student Foundation, Student Government Association, Gaming Club.

Athletics Member NAIA. *Intercollegiate sports:* baseball M(s), basketball M(s)/W(s), cross-country running M(s)/W(s), football M(s), golf M(s)/W(s), soccer M(s)/W(s), softball W(s), tennis M(s)/W(s), track and field M(s)/W(s), volleyball W(s), wrestling W(s). *Intramural sports:* basketball M/W, cheerleading M(c)/W(c), swimming and diving M(c)/W(c), ultimate Frisbee M(c)/W(c).

Campus security: 24-hour emergency response devices and patrols, late-night transport/escort service, controlled dormitory access.

Student services: personal/psychological counseling.

COSTS & FINANCIAL AID

Costs (2018–19) *Comprehensive fee:* $37,910 includes full-time tuition ($30,000), mandatory fees ($150), and room and board ($7760). Full-time tuition and fees vary according to course load, degree level, location, and program. Part-time tuition: $1250 per credit hour. Part-time tuition and fees vary according to course load, degree level, location, and program. *College room only:* $3620. Room and board charges vary according to board plan and housing facility. *Payment plan:* installment. *Waivers:* senior citizens and employees or children of employees.

Financial Aid Of all full-time matriculated undergraduates who enrolled in 2016, 433 applied for aid, 398 were judged to have need, 62 had their need fully met. 145 Federal Work-Study jobs (averaging $1583). 74 state and other part-time jobs (averaging $1435). In 2016, 79 non-need-based awards were made. *Average percent of need met:* 77. *Average financial aid package:* $23,291. *Average need-based loan:* $5825. *Average need-based gift aid:* $17,112. *Average non-need-based aid:* $9839. *Average indebtedness upon graduation:* $39,231.

APPLYING

Standardized Tests *Required:* SAT or ACT (for admission).

Options: electronic application.

Application fee: $25.

Required: high school transcript, minimum 2.6 GPA. *Required for some:* essay or personal statement, 2 letters of recommendation.

Application deadlines: 8/25 (freshmen), 8/25 (transfers).

Notification: continuous (freshmen), continuous (out-of-state freshmen), continuous (transfers).

CONTACT

Southwestern College, 100 College Street, Winfield, KS 67156-2499. *Phone:* 620-229-6241. *Toll-free phone:* 800-846-1543.

Sterling College

Sterling, Kansas

http://www.sterling.edu/

- **Independent Presbyterian** 4-year, founded 1887
- **Rural** 46-acre campus
- **Endowment** $16.0 million
- **Coed**
- **Minimally difficult** entrance level

ACADEMICS

Calendar: 4-1-4. *Degree:* bachelor's.
Library: Mabee Library. *Books:* 50,908 (physical), 80,159 (digital/electronic); *Serial titles:* 74 (physical); *Databases:* 28. Weekly public service hours: 75; students can reserve study rooms.

STUDENT LIFE

Housing options: on-campus residence required through senior year; men-only, women-only. Campus housing is university owned. Freshman campus housing is guaranteed.

Activities and organizations: drama/theater group, student-run newspaper, radio and television station, choral group, Fellowship of Christian Athletes, Student Activities Council, Bible study groups, theatre, Mission teams.

Athletics Member NAIA.

Campus security: controlled dormitory access, late night security patrol.

Student services: health clinic, personal/psychological counseling.

COSTS & FINANCIAL AID
Costs (2017–18) *One-time required fee:* $100. *Comprehensive fee:* $33,065 includes full-time tuition ($23,985), mandatory fees ($500), and room and board ($8580). Full-time tuition and fees vary according to course load. Part-time tuition: $448 per credit hour. Part-time tuition and fees vary according to course load. *Room and board:* Room and board charges vary according to board plan and housing facility.

Financial Aid Of all full-time matriculated undergraduates who enrolled in 2016, 546 applied for aid, 469 were judged to have need, 113 had their need fully met. In 2016, 72 non-need-based awards were made. *Average percent of need met:* 82. *Average financial aid package:* $22,213. *Average need-based loan:* $5696. *Average need-based gift aid:* $11,049. *Average non-need-based aid:* $10,084. *Average indebtedness upon graduation:* $28,221.

APPLYING
Standardized Tests *Required:* SAT or ACT (for admission).

Options: electronic application, deferred entrance.

Application fee: $25.

Required: high school transcript, minimum 2.2 GPA. *Required for some:* 2 letters of recommendation. *Recommended:* essay or personal statement, interview.

CONTACT
Marge Jones, Admissions Office Manager, Sterling College, 125 West Cooper, Sterling, KS 67579. *Phone:* 620-278-4275. *Toll-free phone:* 800-346-1017. *Fax:* 620-278-4416. *E-mail:* admissions@sterling.edu.

Tabor College
Hillsboro, Kansas
http://www.tabor.edu/

- **Independent Mennonite Brethren** comprehensive, founded 1908
- **Small-town** 87-acre campus with easy access to Wichita
- **Endowment** $9.4 million
- **Coed** 711 undergraduate students, 78% full-time, 46% women, 54% men
- **Moderately difficult** entrance level, 52% of applicants were admitted

UNDERGRAD STUDENTS
554 full-time, 157 part-time. Students come from 35 states and territories; 15 other countries; 49% are from out of state; 11% Black or African American, non-Hispanic/Latino; 15% Hispanic/Latino; 0.4% Asian, non-Hispanic/Latino; 0.7% Native Hawaiian or other Pacific Islander, non-Hispanic/Latino; 0.8% American Indian or Alaska Native, non-Hispanic/Latino; 4% Two or more races, non-Hispanic/Latino; 2% Race/ethnicity unknown; 3% international; 12% transferred in; 92% live on campus.

Freshmen:
Admission: 1,017 applied, 526 admitted, 149 enrolled. *Average high school GPA:* 3.3. *Test scores:* SAT evidence-based reading and writing scores over 500: 46%; SAT math scores over 500: 30%; ACT scores over 18: 86%; SAT evidence-based reading and writing scores over 600: 6%; ACT scores over 24: 29%; ACT scores over 30: 4%.

Retention: 60% of full-time freshmen returned.

FACULTY
Total: 118, 32% full-time, 45% with terminal degrees.

Student/faculty ratio: 10:1.

ACADEMICS
Calendar: 4-1-4 (adult and graduate studies programs run by cohort groups). *Degrees:* associate, bachelor's, and master's.

Special study options: academic remediation for entering students, accelerated degree program, adult/continuing education programs, advanced placement credit, cooperative education, distance learning, double majors, honors programs, independent study, internships, off-campus study, part-time degree program, services for LD students, student-designed majors, study abroad.

Computers: 35 computers/terminals are available on campus for general student use. Students can access the following: computer help desk, free student e-mail accounts, online (class) grades, online (class) schedules, online registration for Hillsboro undergraduate students. Campuswide network is available. 100% of college-owned or -operated housing units are wired for high-speed Internet access. Wireless service is available via entire campus.

Library: Tabor College Library. *Books:* 61,550 (physical), 225,000 (digital/electronic); *Serial titles:* 148 (physical), 5,000 (digital/electronic); *Databases:* 41. Weekly public service hours: 85; students can reserve study rooms.

STUDENT LIFE
Housing options: on-campus residence required through senior year; men-only, women-only, special housing for students with disabilities. Campus housing is university owned.

Activities and organizations: drama/theater group, student-run newspaper, choral group, Student Activities Board, CHUMS (Challenging, Helping and Understanding through Mentorship), Intramurals, WUMP (Wichita Urban Ministries Plunge), Multi-Cultural Student Union.

Athletics Member NAIA. *Intercollegiate sports:* baseball M(s), basketball M(s)/W(s), cheerleading M(s)/W(s), cross-country running M(s)/W(s), football M(s), golf M/W, soccer M(s)/W(s), softball W(s), swimming and diving M(s)/W(s), tennis M(s)/W(s), track and field M(s)/W(s), volleyball W(s). *Intramural sports:* basketball M/W, soccer M/W, softball M/W, volleyball M/W.

Campus security: Emergency Alert System.

Student services: personal/psychological counseling.

COSTS & FINANCIAL AID
Costs (2018–19) *Comprehensive fee:* $36,797 includes full-time tuition ($26,300), mandatory fees ($920), and room and board ($9577). Full-time tuition and fees vary according to course load and degree level. Part-time tuition: $510 per credit hour. Part-time tuition and fees vary according to course load and degree level. *Room and board:* Room and board charges vary according to board plan and housing facility. *Payment plan:* installment. *Waivers:* employees or children of employees.

Financial Aid Of all full-time matriculated undergraduates who enrolled in 2014, 542 applied for aid, 448 were judged to have need, 60 had their need fully met. In 2014, 93 non-need-based awards were made. *Average percent of need met:* 73. *Average financial aid package:* $22,141. *Average need-based loan:* $5417. *Average need-based gift aid:* $5487. *Average non-need-based aid:* $11,390. *Average indebtedness upon graduation:* $47,172. *Financial aid deadline:* 8/15.

APPLYING
Standardized Tests *Required:* SAT or ACT (for admission).

Options: electronic application, deferred entrance.

Application fee: $50.

Required: essay or personal statement, high school transcript, minimum 2.0 GPA, validation of high school graduation date for transfers. *Recommended:* interview.

Application deadlines: rolling (freshmen), rolling (transfers).

Notification: continuous (freshmen), continuous (transfers).

CONTACT
Ms. Kelly Dugger, Assistant Director of Admissions, Tabor College, 400 South Jefferson, Hillsboro, KS 67063. *Phone:* 620-947-3121 Ext. 1724. *Toll-free phone:* 800-822-6799. *Fax:* 620-947-3789. *E-mail:* kellydugger@tabor.edu.

The University of Kansas
Lawrence, Kansas
http://www.ku.edu/

- **State-supported** university, founded 1866, part of Kansas Board of Regents
- **Suburban** 1000-acre campus with easy access to Kansas City
- **Endowment** $1.6 billion
- **Coed** 19,338 undergraduate students, 89% full-time, 51% women, 49% men
- **Moderately difficult** entrance level, 93% of applicants were admitted

UNDERGRAD STUDENTS

17,151 full-time, 2,187 part-time. Students come from 53 states and territories; 76 other countries; 28% are from out of state; 4% Black or African American, non-Hispanic/Latino; 8% Hispanic/Latino; 5% Asian, non-Hispanic/Latino; 0.1% Native Hawaiian or other Pacific Islander, non-Hispanic/Latino; 0.3% American Indian or Alaska Native, non-Hispanic/Latino; 5% Two or more races, non-Hispanic/Latino; 0.6% Race/ethnicity unknown; 6% international; 6% transferred in; 26% live on campus.

Freshmen:
Admission: 14,538 applied, 13,576 admitted, 4,153 enrolled. *Average high school GPA:* 3.6. *Test scores:* ACT scores over 18: 99%; ACT scores over 24: 69%; ACT scores over 30: 18%.
Retention: 83% of full-time freshmen returned.

FACULTY

Total: 1,625, 84% full-time, 83% with terminal degrees.
Student/faculty ratio: 17:1.

ACADEMICS

Calendar: semesters. *Degrees:* certificates, bachelor's, master's, doctoral, post-master's, and postbachelor's certificates (University of Kansas is a single institution with academic programs and facilities at two primary locations: Lawrence and Kansas City).

Special study options: academic remediation for entering students, accelerated degree program, adult/continuing education programs, advanced placement credit, cooperative education, distance learning, double majors, English as a second language, freshman honors college, honors programs, independent study, internships, part-time degree program, services for LD students, study abroad, summer session for credit. *ROTC:* Army (b), Navy (b), Air Force (b).

Computers: 1,500 computers/terminals are available on campus for general student use. Students can access the following: campus intranet, computer help desk, free student e-mail accounts, online (class) grades, online (class) registration, online (class) schedules, online payments. Campuswide network is available. 100% of college-owned or -operated housing units are wired for high-speed Internet access. Wireless service is available via entire campus.

Library: Watson Library plus 11 others. *Books:* 4.7 million (physical), 1.0 million (digital/electronic). Weekly public service hours: 168; study areas open 24 hours, 5–7 days a week; students can reserve study rooms.

STUDENT LIFE

Housing options: coed, men-only, women-only, cooperative. Campus housing is university owned.

Activities and organizations: drama/theater group, student-run newspaper, radio and television station, choral group, marching band, KU Adventure Club, Panhellenic Association, Center for Community Outreach, Pre-Nursing Club, American Red Cross Club, national fraternities, national sororities.

Athletics Member NCAA. All Division I except football (Division I-A). *Intercollegiate sports:* baseball M(s), basketball M(s)/W(s), crew W(s), cross-country running M(s)/W(s), golf M(s)/W(s), rugby M(c), soccer W(s), softball W(s), swimming and diving W(s), tennis W(s), track and field M(s)/W(s), volleyball W(s). *Intramural sports:* badminton M(c)/W(c), baseball M(c), basketball M/W, crew M(c)/W(c), football M/W, golf M(c)/W(c), gymnastics M(c)/W(c), ice hockey M(c), lacrosse M(c)/W(c), racquetball M/W, rock climbing M(c)/W(c), rugby M(c)/W(c), sailing M(c)/W(c), sand volleyball M/W, soccer M(c)/W(c), softball W(c), swimming and diving M(c)/W(c), table tennis M/W, tennis M/W, ultimate Frisbee M(c)/W(c), volleyball M(c)/W(c), water polo M(c)/W(c), weight lifting M(c)/W(c).

Campus security: 24-hour emergency response devices and patrols, late-night transport/escort service, controlled dormitory access, University police department.

Student services: health clinic, personal/psychological counseling, women's center, legal services.

COSTS & FINANCIAL AID

Costs (2017–18) *Tuition:* state resident $9818 full-time, $327 per credit hour part-time; nonresident $25,586 full-time, $853 per credit hour part-time. Full-time tuition and fees vary according to reciprocity agreements. Part-time tuition and fees vary according to reciprocity agreements. *Required fees:* $1006 full-time, $79 per credit hour part-time. *Room and*

board: $10,060; room only: $5910. Room and board charges vary according to board plan and housing facility. *Payment plan:* installment. *Waivers:* employees or children of employees.

Financial Aid Of all full-time matriculated undergraduates who enrolled in 2016, 11,064 applied for aid, 8,121 were judged to have need, 3,060 had their need fully met. 693 Federal Work-Study jobs (averaging $2097). 58 state and other part-time jobs (averaging $4425). In 2016, 3367 non-need-based awards were made. *Average percent of need met:* 76. *Average financial aid package:* $15,412. *Average need-based loan:* $4494. *Average need-based gift aid:* $7340. *Average non-need-based aid:* $5896. *Average indebtedness upon graduation:* $28,462.

APPLYING

Standardized Tests *Required:* SAT or ACT (for admission).
Options: electronic application.
Application fee: $40.
Required: high school transcript, minimum 3.0 GPA, Kansas Qualified Admissions Curriculum with minimum 2.0 GPA for state residents and 2.5 for nonresidents and minimum 3.0 overall GPA and ACT score of 24/SAT of 1160 or minimum 3.25 overall GPA and ACT score of 21/SAT of 1060.
Application deadlines: 8/13 (freshmen), 8/7 (transfers).
Notification: continuous (freshmen), continuous (transfers).

CONTACT

Ms. Lisa Pinamonti Kress, Director of Admissions, The University of Kansas, KU Visitor Center, 1502 Iowa Street, Lawrence, KS 66045-7576. *Phone:* 785-864-3911. *Toll-free phone:* 888-686-7323. *Fax:* 785-864-5017. *E-mail:* adm@ku.edu.

University of Saint Mary

Leavenworth, Kansas

http://www.stmary.edu/

- **Independent Roman Catholic** comprehensive, founded 1923
- **Small-town** 240-acre campus with easy access to Kansas City
- **Endowment** $19.8 million
- **Coed** 748 undergraduate students, 86% full-time, 48% women, 52% men
- **Moderately difficult** entrance level, 49% of applicants were admitted

UNDERGRAD STUDENTS

641 full-time, 107 part-time. Students come from 40 states and territories; 2 other countries; 50% are from out of state; 12% Black or African American, non-Hispanic/Latino; 14% Hispanic/Latino; 2% Asian, non-Hispanic/Latino; 0.5% Native Hawaiian or other Pacific Islander, non-Hispanic/Latino; 0.8% American Indian or Alaska Native, non-Hispanic/Latino; 0.7% Two or more races, non-Hispanic/Latino; 14% Race/ethnicity unknown; 0.9% international; 14% transferred in; 37% live on campus.

Freshmen:
Admission: 1,001 applied, 492 admitted, 145 enrolled. *Average high school GPA:* 3.2. *Test scores:* SAT evidence-based reading and writing scores over 500: 69%; SAT math scores over 500: 67%; ACT scores over 18: 94%; SAT evidence-based reading and writing scores over 600: 18%; SAT math scores over 600: 13%; ACT scores over 24: 30%; SAT evidence-based reading and writing scores over 700: 5%; SAT math scores over 700: 5%; ACT scores over 30: 4%.
Retention: 66% of full-time freshmen returned.

FACULTY

Total: 183, 35% full-time, 45% with terminal degrees.
Student/faculty ratio: 9:1.

ACADEMICS

Calendar: semesters. *Degrees:* associate, bachelor's, master's, and doctoral.

Special study options: academic remediation for entering students, adult/continuing education programs, advanced placement credit, cooperative education, distance learning, double majors, honors programs, independent study, internships, off-campus study, part-time degree program, services for LD students, student-designed majors, study abroad, summer session for credit. *ROTC:* Army (c), Air Force (c).

Computers: 30 computers/terminals are available on campus for general student use. Students can access the following: campus intranet, computer help desk, free student e-mail accounts, online (class) grades, online (class) registration, online (class) schedules. Campuswide network is available. 100% of college-owned or -operated housing units are wired for high-speed Internet access. Wireless service is available via entire campus.

Library: De Paul Library plus 1 other. *Books:* 75,000 (physical), 10,500 (digital/electronic); *Serial titles:* 15 (physical), 38,459 (digital/electronic); *Databases:* 63. Weekly public service hours: 68; students can reserve study rooms.

STUDENT LIFE
Housing options: on-campus residence required through sophomore year; coed. Campus housing is university owned. Freshman campus housing is guaranteed.

Activities and organizations: drama/theater group, choral group, Student Government Association, BACCHUS, Theatrical Union, campus ministry, Amnesty International.

Athletics Member NAIA. *Intercollegiate sports:* baseball M(s), basketball M(s)/W(s), cheerleading M(s)/W(s), cross-country running M(s)/W(s), football M(s), lacrosse M(s)/W(s), soccer M(s)/W(s), softball W(s), track and field M(s)/W(s), volleyball W(s), wrestling M(s)/W(s). *Intramural sports:* basketball M/W, table tennis M/W, ultimate Frisbee M/W.

Campus security: 24-hour patrols, late-night transport/escort service, controlled dormitory access.

Student services: personal/psychological counseling.

COSTS & FINANCIAL AID
Costs (2018–19) *Comprehensive fee:* $36,830 includes full-time tuition ($27,880), mandatory fees ($810), and room and board ($8140). Full-time tuition and fees vary according to class time, course load, degree level, location, program, and reciprocity agreements. Part-time tuition: $645 per credit hour. Part-time tuition and fees vary according to class time, course load, degree level, location, program, and reciprocity agreements. *Room and board:* Room and board charges vary according to board plan and housing facility. *Payment plan:* installment. *Waivers:* senior citizens and employees or children of employees.

Financial Aid *Average percent of need met:* 82.

APPLYING
Standardized Tests *Required:* SAT or ACT (for admission).

Options: electronic application.

Application fee: $25.

Required: high school transcript, minimum 2.5 GPA.

Application deadlines: rolling (freshmen), rolling (transfers).

Notification: continuous (freshmen), continuous (transfers).

CONTACT
Mr. John Shultz, Vice President of Admissions and Marketing, University of Saint Mary, 4100 South 4th Street, Leavenworth, KS 66048. *Phone:* 913-758-6329. *Toll-free phone:* 800-752-7043. *E-mail:* admiss@ stmary.edu.

Washburn University
Topeka, Kansas
http://www.washburn.edu/
- **City-supported** comprehensive, founded 1865
- **Urban** 160-acre campus with easy access to Kansas City
- **Endowment** $172.4 million
- **Coed**
- **Noncompetitive** entrance level

FACULTY
Student/faculty ratio: 12:1.

ACADEMICS
Calendar: semesters. *Degrees:* certificates, associate, bachelor's, master's, doctoral, post-master's, and postbachelor's certificates.
Library: Mabee Library plus 1 other. *Books:* 441,448 (physical), 292,840 (digital/electronic); *Serial titles:* 93,914 (physical); *Databases:* 182. Weekly public service hours: 104; students can reserve study rooms.

STUDENT LIFE
Housing options: coed. Campus housing is university owned.

Activities and organizations: drama/theater group, student-run newspaper, television station, choral group, marching band, national fraternities, national sororities.

Athletics Member NCAA. All Division II.

Campus security: 24-hour emergency response devices and patrols, student patrols, late-night transport/escort service.

Student services: health clinic, personal/psychological counseling, legal services.

COSTS & FINANCIAL AID
Costs (2017–18) *Tuition:* state resident $8190 full-time, $273 per credit hour part-time; nonresident $18,510 full-time, $617 per credit hour part-time. Full-time tuition and fees vary according to program. Part-time tuition and fees vary according to program. *Required fees:* $110 full-time. *Room and board:* $7527; room only: $4287. Room and board charges vary according to board plan and housing facility.

Financial Aid Of all full-time matriculated undergraduates who enrolled in 2016, 3,366 applied for aid, 2,314 were judged to have need, 286 had their need fully met. In 2016, 521 non-need-based awards were made. *Average percent of need met:* 37. *Average financial aid package:* $9580. *Average need-based loan:* $4128. *Average need-based gift aid:* $5140. *Average non-need-based aid:* $3331. *Average indebtedness upon graduation:* $23,552.

APPLYING
Standardized Tests *Required:* ACT (for admission).

Options: electronic application.

Application fee: $20.

Required: high school transcript.

CONTACT
Ms. Kris Klima, Director of Admissions, Washburn University, 1700 SW College, MO 114, Topeka, KS 66621. *Phone:* 785-670-1030. *Toll-free phone:* 800-332-0291. *Fax:* 785-670-1113. *E-mail:* admissions@ washburn.edu.

Wichita State University
Wichita, Kansas
http://www.wichita.edu/
- **State-supported** university, founded 1895, part of Kansas Board of Regents
- **Urban** 335-acre campus
- **Endowment** $302.0 million
- **Coed** 12,398 undergraduate students, 71% full-time, 54% women, 46% men
- **Minimally difficult** entrance level, 97% of applicants were admitted

UNDERGRAD STUDENTS
8,749 full-time, 3,649 part-time. Students come from 48 states and territories; 96 other countries; 9% are from out of state; 6% Black or African American, non-Hispanic/Latino; 12% Hispanic/Latino; 7% Asian, non-Hispanic/Latino; 0.1% Native Hawaiian or other Pacific Islander, non-Hispanic/Latino; 0.6% American Indian or Alaska Native, non-Hispanic/Latino; 5% Two or more races, non-Hispanic/Latino; 3% Race/ethnicity unknown; 8% international; 10% transferred in; 11% live on campus.

Freshmen:
Admission: 5,469 applied, 5,309 admitted, 1,510 enrolled. *Average high school GPA:* 3.4. *Test scores:* SAT evidence-based reading and writing scores over 500: 79%; SAT math scores over 500: 80%; ACT scores over 18: 92%; SAT evidence-based reading and writing scores over 600: 33%; SAT math scores over 600: 38%; ACT scores over 24: 46%; SAT evidence-based reading and writing scores over 700: 8%; SAT math scores over 700: 10%; ACT scores over 30: 10%.

Retention: 73% of full-time freshmen returned.

FACULTY
Total: 771, 65% full-time, 55% with terminal degrees.
Student/faculty ratio: 20:1.

ACADEMICS

Calendar: semesters. *Degrees:* certificates, associate, bachelor's, master's, doctoral, post-master's, and postbachelor's certificates.

Special study options: academic remediation for entering students, accelerated degree program, adult/continuing education programs, advanced placement credit, cooperative education, distance learning, double majors, English as a second language, freshman honors college, honors programs, independent study, internships, off-campus study, part-time degree program, services for LD students, study abroad, summer session for credit.

Computers: 1,500 computers/terminals are available on campus for general student use. Students can access the following: computer help desk, free student e-mail accounts, online (class) grades, online (class) registration, online (class) schedules, learning management system. Campuswide network is available. 100% of college-owned or -operated housing units are wired for high-speed Internet access. Wireless service is available via entire campus.

Library: Ablah Library plus 2 others. *Books:* 1.9 million (physical), 475,186 (digital/electronic); *Serial titles:* 460 (physical), 94,566 (digital/electronic); *Databases:* 269. Study areas open 24 hours, 5–7 days a week; students can reserve study rooms.

STUDENT LIFE

Housing options: on-campus residence required for freshman year; coed, special housing for students with disabilities. Campus housing is university owned. Freshman campus housing is guaranteed.

Activities and organizations: drama/theater group, student-run newspaper, radio station, choral group, national fraternities, national sororities.

Athletics Member NCAA. All Division I. *Intercollegiate sports:* baseball M(s), basketball M(s)/W(s), bowling M(s)/W(s), cheerleading M(s)/W(s), cross-country running M(s)/W(s), golf M(s)/W(s), softball W(s), tennis M(s)/W(s), track and field M(s)/W(s), volleyball W(s). *Intramural sports:* basketball M/W, bowling M/W, crew M/W, golf M/W, rowing M/W, softball W, swimming and diving M/W, tennis M/W, track and field M/W, volleyball W.

Campus security: 24-hour emergency response devices and patrols, student patrols, late-night transport/escort service, controlled dormitory access, bicycle patrols by campus security.

Student services: health clinic, personal/psychological counseling, women's center.

COSTS & FINANCIAL AID

Costs (2017–18) *Tuition:* state resident $6545 full-time, $218 per credit hour part-time; nonresident $15,503 full-time, $517 per credit hour part-time. Full-time tuition and fees vary according to course level, course load, degree level, and program. Part-time tuition and fees vary according to course level, course load, degree level, and program. *Required fees:* $1780 full-time, $8 per credit hour part-time. *Room and board:* $6782. Room and board charges vary according to board plan and housing facility. *Payment plan:* installment. *Waivers:* senior citizens and employees or children of employees.

Financial Aid Of all full-time matriculated undergraduates who enrolled in 2016, 6,289 applied for aid, 4,839 were judged to have need, 800 had their need fully met. 106 Federal Work-Study jobs (averaging $2623). 87 state and other part-time jobs (averaging $908). In 2016, 1355 non-need-based awards were made. *Average percent of need met:* 63. *Average financial aid package:* $7927. *Average need-based loan:* $2134. *Average need-based gift aid:* $4838. *Average non-need-based aid:* $1235. *Average indebtedness upon graduation:* $25,380.

APPLYING

Standardized Tests *Required for some:* SAT or ACT (for admission). *Recommended:* SAT or ACT (for admission).

Options: electronic application, deferred entrance.

Application fee: $30.

Required: high school transcript. *Required for some:* minimum 2.5 GPA, rank in upper one-third of high school class or complete the pre-college curriculum with a minimum 2.0 GPA (2.5 GPA for nonresidents).

Application deadlines: rolling (freshmen), rolling (out-of-state freshmen), rolling (transfers).

Notification: continuous (freshmen), continuous (out-of-state freshmen), continuous (transfers).

CONTACT

Wichita State University, 1845 North Fairmount, Wichita, KS 67260. *Phone:* 316-978-3085. *Toll-free phone:* 800-362-2594.

KENTUCKY

Alice Lloyd College

Pippa Passes, Kentucky

http://www.alc.edu/

- **Independent** 4-year, founded 1923
- **Rural** 175-acre campus
- **Endowment** $40.8 million
- **Coed** 598 undergraduate students, 97% full-time, 53% women, 47% men

UNDERGRAD STUDENTS

578 full-time, 20 part-time. Students come from 7 states and territories; 4 other countries; 16% are from out of state; 2% Black or African American, non-Hispanic/Latino; 1% Hispanic/Latino; 0.2% Asian, non-Hispanic/Latino; 0.3% Native Hawaiian or other Pacific Islander, non-Hispanic/Latino; 0.3% Two or more races, non-Hispanic/Latino; 1% Race/ethnicity unknown; 0.7% international; 4% transferred in; 70% live on campus.

Freshmen:
Admission: 220 enrolled. *Average high school GPA:* 3.6. *Test scores:* SAT evidence-based reading and writing scores over 500: 50%; SAT math scores over 500: 38%; ACT scores over 18: 83%; SAT evidence-based reading and writing scores over 600: 12%; ACT scores over 24: 18%; ACT scores over 30: 3%.

Retention: 60% of full-time freshmen returned.

FACULTY

Total: 47, 62% full-time, 51% with terminal degrees.

Student/faculty ratio: 17:1.

ACADEMICS

Calendar: semesters. *Degree:* bachelor's.

Special study options: academic remediation for entering students, advanced placement credit, double majors, independent study, internships, part-time degree program, study abroad.

Unusual degree programs: 3-2 nursing with University of Kentucky, Eastern Kentucky University.

Computers: 146 computers/terminals and 557 ports are available on campus for general student use. Students can access the following: campus intranet, computer help desk, free student e-mail accounts. Campuswide network is available. 100% of college-owned or -operated housing units are wired for high-speed Internet access. Wireless service is available via entire campus.

Library: McGaw Library and Learning Center. *Books:* 63,050 (physical), 170,956 (digital/electronic); *Serial titles:* 57 (physical), 23,210 (digital/electronic); *Databases:* 105. Weekly public service hours: 74; students can reserve study rooms.

STUDENT LIFE

Housing options: men-only, women-only. Campus housing is university owned.

Activities and organizations: drama/theater group, student-run newspaper, radio and television station, choral group, Voices of Appalachia, Intramurals, Baptist Collegiate Ministries, Allied Health Sciences Club, Alpha Chi National Honor Society.

Athletics Member NAIA, NCCAA. *Intercollegiate sports:* baseball M(s), basketball M(s)/W(s), cheerleading W, cross-country running M/W, golf M, softball W, tennis M/W, volleyball W. *Intramural sports:* basketball M/W, softball M, volleyball M/W, weight lifting M.

Campus security: 24-hour emergency response devices and patrols, late-night transport/escort service, controlled dormitory access, video cameras.

Student services: health clinic, personal/psychological counseling.

COSTS & FINANCIAL AID

Costs (2018–19) *Comprehensive fee:* includes mandatory fees ($2150) and room and board ($6880). Part-time tuition: $225 per credit hour. The cost of tuition is covered by a combination of scholarships and other financial aid. *College room only:* $3300. *Payment plan:* installment.

Financial Aid Of all full-time matriculated undergraduates who enrolled in 2016, 584 applied for aid, 533 were judged to have need, 68 had their need fully met. 418 Federal Work-Study jobs (averaging $2320). 168 state and other part-time jobs (averaging $2320). In 2016, 57 non-need-based awards were made. *Average percent of need met:* 71. *Average financial aid package:* $13,681. *Average need-based loan:* $2197. *Average need-based gift aid:* $9872. *Average non-need-based aid:* $5919. *Average indebtedness upon graduation:* $10,141.

APPLYING
Standardized Tests *Required:* SAT or ACT (for admission).
Required: high school transcript, minimum 2.3 GPA, interview. *Required for some:* essay or personal statement, 2 letters of recommendation.

CONTACT
Mr. JD Cornett, Director of Admissions, Alice Lloyd College, 100 Purpose Road, Pippa Passes, KY 41844. *Phone:* 606-368-6134. *Toll-free phone:* 888-280-4252. *Fax:* 606-368-6038. *E-mail:* jdcornett@alc.edu.

American National University
Lexington, Kentucky
http://www.an.edu/

CONTACT
Kim Thomasson, Campus Director, American National University, 2376 Sir Barton Way, Lexington, KY 40509. *Phone:* 859-253-0621. *Toll-free phone:* 888-9-JOBREADY.

American National University
Louisville, Kentucky
http://www.an.edu/

CONTACT
Vincent C. Tinebra, Campus Director, American National University, 4205 Dixie Highway, Louisville, KY 40216. *Phone:* 502-447-7634. *Toll-free phone:* 888-9-JOBREADY.

Asbury University
Wilmore, Kentucky
http://www.asbury.edu/
- **Independent nondenominational** comprehensive, founded 1890
- **Small-town** 400-acre campus with easy access to Lexington, KY
- **Endowment** $47.8 million
- **Coed** 1,717 undergraduate students, 77% full-time, 60% women, 40% men
- **Moderately difficult** entrance level, 70% of applicants were admitted

UNDERGRAD STUDENTS
1,323 full-time, 394 part-time. Students come from 41 states and territories; 35 other countries; 47% are from out of state; 4% Black or African American, non-Hispanic/Latino; 6% Hispanic/Latino; 2% Asian, non-Hispanic/Latino; 0.2% Native Hawaiian or other Pacific Islander, non-Hispanic/Latino; 0.6% American Indian or Alaska Native, non-Hispanic/Latino; 3% Two or more races, non-Hispanic/Latino; 3% Race/ethnicity unknown; 4% international; 3% transferred in; 85% live on campus.

Freshmen:
Admission: 1,105 applied, 777 admitted, 318 enrolled. *Average high school GPA:* 3.7. *Test scores:* SAT evidence-based reading and writing scores over 500: 82%; SAT math scores over 500: 71%; ACT scores over 18: 94%; SAT evidence-based reading and writing scores over 600: 49%; SAT math scores over 600: 35%; ACT scores over 24: 51%; SAT evidence-based reading and writing scores over 700: 13%; SAT math scores over 700: 7%; ACT scores over 30: 15%.
Retention: 85% of full-time freshmen returned.

FACULTY
Total: 204, 46% full-time, 51% with terminal degrees.

Student/faculty ratio: 13:1.

ACADEMICS
Calendar: semesters. *Degrees:* associate, bachelor's, and master's.
Special study options: adult/continuing education programs, advanced placement credit, distance learning, double majors, internships, off-campus study, services for LD students, study abroad, summer session for credit. *ROTC:* Army (c), Air Force (c).
Unusual degree programs: 3-2 engineering with University of Kentucky; nursing with University of Kentucky.
Computers: 250 computers/terminals and 950 ports are available on campus for general student use. Students can access the following: campus intranet, computer help desk, free student e-mail accounts, online (class) grades, online (class) registration, online (class) schedules. Campuswide network is available. 100% of college-owned or -operated housing units are wired for high-speed Internet access. Wireless service is available via classrooms, computer centers, computer labs, dorm rooms, learning centers, libraries, student centers.
Library: Kinlaw Library. *Books:* 157,131 (physical), 168,625 (digital/electronic); *Serial titles:* 442 (physical), 37,780 (digital/electronic); *Databases:* 60. Weekly public service hours: 88; students can reserve study rooms.

STUDENT LIFE
Housing options: on-campus residence required through senior year; men-only, women-only. Campus housing is university owned. Freshman campus housing is guaranteed.
Activities and organizations: drama/theater group, student-run newspaper, radio and television station, choral group, Asbury Student Congress, Spiritual Life Board, Summer Ministry Teams, Asbury Outdoors, WGM Global Cafe.
Athletics Member NAIA, NCCAA. *Intercollegiate sports:* baseball M(s), basketball M(s)/W(s), cheerleading M/W, cross-country running M(s)/W(s), golf M(s)/W(s), lacrosse M(s)/W(s), soccer M(s)/W(s), softball W(s), swimming and diving M(s)/W(s), tennis M(s)/W(s), track and field M(s)/W(s), volleyball W(s). *Intramural sports:* basketball M/W, football M/W, racquetball M/W, soccer M/W, softball M/W, ultimate Frisbee M/W, volleyball M/W.
Campus security: 24-hour emergency response devices, late-night transport/escort service, controlled dormitory access, late night security personnel.
Student services: health clinic, personal/psychological counseling.

COSTS & FINANCIAL AID
Costs (2017–18) *Comprehensive fee:* $36,450 includes full-time tuition ($29,302), mandatory fees ($198), and room and board ($6950). Full-time tuition and fees vary according to course load and program. Part-time tuition: $1127 per credit hour. Part-time tuition and fees vary according to course load and program. *Room and board:* Room and board charges vary according to board plan and housing facility. *Payment plan:* installment. *Waivers:* senior citizens and employees or children of employees.
Financial Aid Of all full-time matriculated undergraduates who enrolled in 2015, 1,127 applied for aid, 1,017 were judged to have need. 326 Federal Work-Study jobs (averaging $1711). *Average indebtedness upon graduation:* $30,123.

APPLYING
Standardized Tests *Required:* SAT or ACT (for admission).
Options: electronic application, early admission, deferred entrance.
Required: essay or personal statement, high school transcript, minimum 2.5 GPA, 1 letter of recommendation.
Application deadlines: rolling (freshmen), rolling (out-of-state freshmen), rolling (transfers).
Notification: continuous (freshmen), continuous (out-of-state freshmen), continuous (transfers).

CONTACT
Mr. Brandon Combs, Director of Undergraduate Admissions, Asbury University, One Macklem Drive, Wilmore, KY 40390. *Phone:* 800-888-1818. *Toll-free phone:* 800-888-1818. *E-mail:* admissions@asbury.edu.

Beckfield College

Florence, Kentucky

http://www.beckfield.edu/

CONTACT

Mrs. Leah Boerger, Director of Admissions, Beckfield College, 16 Spiral Drive, Florence, KY 41042. *Phone:* 859-371-9393. *E-mail:* lboerger@beckfield.edu.

Bellarmine University

Louisville, Kentucky

http://www.bellarmine.edu/

- **Independent Roman Catholic** comprehensive, founded 1950
- **Suburban** 175-acre campus with easy access to Louisville
- **Endowment** $50.5 million
- **Coed** 2,544 undergraduate students, 95% full-time, 64% women, 36% men
- **Moderately difficult** entrance level, 89% of applicants were admitted

UNDERGRAD STUDENTS

2,410 full-time, 134 part-time. Students come from 47 states and territories; 26 other countries; 30% are from out of state; 5% Black or African American, non-Hispanic/Latino; 4% Hispanic/Latino; 2% Asian, non-Hispanic/Latino; 0.1% Native Hawaiian or other Pacific Islander, non-Hispanic/Latino; 0.2% American Indian or Alaska Native, non-Hispanic/Latino; 3% Two or more races, non-Hispanic/Latino; 3% Race/ethnicity unknown; 1% international; 2% transferred in; 38% live on campus.

Freshmen:

Admission: 5,692 applied, 5,080 admitted, 681 enrolled. *Average high school GPA:* 3.5. *Test scores:* SAT evidence-based reading and writing scores over 500: 79%; SAT math scores over 500: 78%; ACT scores over 18: 100%; SAT evidence-based reading and writing scores over 600: 28%; SAT math scores over 600: 23%; ACT scores over 24: 62%; SAT evidence-based reading and writing scores over 700: 5%; SAT math scores over 700: 2%; ACT scores over 30: 11%.

Retention: 72% of full-time freshmen returned.

FACULTY

Total: 445, 40% full-time, 57% with terminal degrees.

Student/faculty ratio: 12:1.

ACADEMICS

Calendar: semesters. *Degrees:* certificates, bachelor's, master's, doctoral, and postbachelor's certificates.

Special study options: accelerated degree program, adult/continuing education programs, advanced placement credit, cooperative education, distance learning, double majors, freshman honors college, honors programs, independent study, internships, part-time degree program, services for LD students, student-designed majors, study abroad, summer session for credit. *ROTC:* Army (c), Air Force (c).

Unusual degree programs: 3-2 business administration.

Computers: 440 computers/terminals and 440 ports are available on campus for general student use. Students can access the following: campus intranet, computer help desk, free student e-mail accounts, online (class) grades, online (class) registration, online (class) schedules, mobile app. Campuswide network is available. 100% of college-owned or -operated housing units are wired for high-speed Internet access. Wireless service is available via entire campus.

Library: W. L. Lyons Brown Library. *Books:* 121,125 (physical), 233,857 (digital/electronic); *Serial titles:* 207 (physical), 88,144 (digital/electronic); *Databases:* 145. Weekly public service hours: 140; study areas open 24 hours, 5–7 days a week.

STUDENT LIFE

Housing options: on-campus residence required through junior year; coed, men-only, women-only, special housing for students with disabilities. Campus housing is university owned. Freshman campus housing is guaranteed.

Activities and organizations: drama/theater group, student-run newspaper, radio station, choral group, Student Government, Bellarmine Activities Council, Knights Nation, Fellowship of Christian Athletes, Delta Sigma Pi, national fraternities, national sororities.

Athletics Member NCAA. All Division II except lacrosse (Division I). *Intercollegiate sports:* baseball M(s), basketball M(s)/W(s), cheerleading M(s)/W(s), cross-country running M(s)/W(s), field hockey W(s), golf M(s)/W(s), lacrosse M(s), soccer M(s)/W(s), softball W(s), swimming and diving M(s)/W(s), tennis M(s)/W(s), track and field M(s)/W(s), volleyball W(s), wrestling M(s). *Intramural sports:* basketball M/W, bowling M(c)/W(c), football M/W, golf M/W, soccer M/W, softball M/W, swimming and diving M/W, table tennis M/W, tennis M/W, ultimate Frisbee M/W, volleyball M/W.

Campus security: 24-hour emergency response devices and patrols, student patrols, late-night transport/escort service, controlled dormitory access, 24-hour locked residence hall entrances, security cameras.

Student services: health clinic, personal/psychological counseling.

COSTS & FINANCIAL AID

Costs (2018–19) *One-time required fee:* $400. *Comprehensive fee:* $54,050 includes full-time tuition ($40,250), mandatory fees ($1550), and room and board ($12,250). Full-time tuition and fees vary according to course load, degree level, location, and program. Part-time tuition: $935 per credit hour. Part-time tuition and fees vary according to course load, degree level, location, and program. *College room only:* $7630. Room and board charges vary according to board plan and housing facility. *Payment plan:* installment. *Waivers:* employees or children of employees.

Financial Aid Of all full-time matriculated undergraduates who enrolled in 2016, 2,192 applied for aid, 1,935 were judged to have need, 408 had their need fully met. In 2016, 483 non-need-based awards were made. *Average percent of need met:* 74. *Average financial aid package:* $30,651. *Average need-based loan:* $4475. *Average need-based gift aid:* $23,040. *Average non-need-based aid:* $21,948. *Average indebtedness upon graduation:* $30,759.

APPLYING

Standardized Tests *Required:* SAT or ACT (for admission).

Options: electronic application, early admission, early action, deferred entrance.

Application fee: $25.

Required: high school transcript, minimum 2.5 GPA, 1 letter of recommendation. *Required for some:* essay or personal statement. *Recommended:* interview.

Application deadlines: 8/15 (freshmen), rolling (transfers), 11/1 (early action).

Notification: continuous until 9/1 (freshmen), continuous (transfers), 11/15 (early action).

CONTACT

Mr. Timothy A. Sturgeon, Dean of Admission, Bellarmine University, 2001 Newburg Road, Louisville, KY 40205-0671. *Phone:* 502-272-8131. *Toll-free phone:* 800-274-4723 Ext. 8131. *E-mail:* admissions@bellarmine.edu.

Berea College

Berea, Kentucky

http://www.berea.edu/

- **Independent** 4-year, founded 1855
- **Small-town** 140-acre campus
- **Endowment** $1.2 billion
- **Coed** 1,670 undergraduate students, 97% full-time, 58% women, 42% men
- **Moderately difficult** entrance level, 35% of applicants were admitted

UNDERGRAD STUDENTS

1,615 full-time, 55 part-time. Students come from 42 states and territories; 76 other countries; 52% are from out of state; 15% Black or African American, non-Hispanic/Latino; 11% Hispanic/Latino; 2% Asian, non-Hispanic/Latino; 0.1% Native Hawaiian or other Pacific Islander, non-Hispanic/Latino; 0.2% American Indian or Alaska Native, non-Hispanic/Latino; 7% Two or more races, non-Hispanic/Latino; 0.7% Race/ethnicity unknown; 8% international; 3% transferred in; 89% live on campus.

Freshmen:
Admission: 1,712 applied, 600 admitted, 432 enrolled. *Average high school GPA:* 3.5. *Test scores:* SAT evidence-based reading and writing scores over 500: 73%; SAT math scores over 500: 70%; ACT scores over 18: 100%; SAT evidence-based reading and writing scores over 600: 23%; SAT math scores over 600: 27%; ACT scores over 24: 53%; SAT evidence-based reading and writing scores over 700: 5%; SAT math scores over 700: 5%; ACT scores over 30: 6%.
Retention: 80% of full-time freshmen returned.

FACULTY
Total: 184, 74% full-time, 80% with terminal degrees.
Student/faculty ratio: 10:1.

ACADEMICS
Calendar: semesters. *Degree:* bachelor's.

Special study options: academic remediation for entering students, advanced placement credit, double majors, English as a second language, honors programs, independent study, internships, off-campus study, services for LD students, student-designed majors, study abroad, summer session for credit.

Unusual degree programs: 3-2 engineering with University of Kentucky.

Computers: 7,000 ports are available on campus for general student use. Students can access the following: campus intranet, computer help desk, free student e-mail accounts, online (class) grades, online (class) registration, online (class) schedules. Campuswide network is available. 100% of college-owned or -operated housing units are wired for high-speed Internet access. Wireless service is available via entire campus.
Library: Hutchins Library plus 1 other. *Books:* 350,474 (physical), 238,135 (digital/electronic); *Serial titles:* 261 (physical), 28,567 (digital/electronic). Weekly public service hours: 94; students can reserve study rooms.

STUDENT LIFE
Housing options: on-campus residence required through senior year; men-only, women-only. Campus housing is university owned. Freshman campus housing is guaranteed.

Activities and organizations: drama/theater group, student-run newspaper, choral group, Campus Activities Board, Cosmopolitan Club, CELTS (Center for Excellence in Learning through Service), Black Cultural Center, African Student Association.

Athletics Member NCAA. All Division III. *Intercollegiate sports:* baseball M, basketball M/W, cross-country running M/W, golf M, soccer M/W, softball W, tennis M/W, track and field M/W, volleyball W. *Intramural sports:* basketball M/W, football M/W, racquetball M/W, soccer M/W, softball M/W, ultimate Frisbee M/W, volleyball M/W.

Campus security: 24-hour emergency response devices and patrols, late-night transport/escort service, controlled dormitory access, crime prevention programs.

Student services: health clinic, personal/psychological counseling, women's center.

COSTS & FINANCIAL AID
Costs (2017–18) *Comprehensive fee:* includes mandatory fees ($560) and room and board ($6534). Financial aid is provided to all students for tuition costs.

Financial Aid Of all full-time matriculated undergraduates who enrolled in 2016, 1,612 applied for aid, 1,612 were judged to have need. *Average percent of need met:* 95. *Average financial aid package:* $34,714. *Average need-based loan:* $1781. *Average need-based gift aid:* $32,288. *Average indebtedness upon graduation:* $7468. *Financial aid deadline:* 5/1.

APPLYING
Standardized Tests *Required:* SAT or ACT (for admission).
Options: electronic application.
Required: essay or personal statement, high school transcript, interview. *Recommended:* 2 letters of recommendation.
Application deadlines: 4/30 (freshmen), 3/31 (transfers).
Notification: continuous (freshmen), continuous until 4/15 (transfers).

CONTACT
Mr. Luke Hodson, Director of Admissions, Berea College, CPO 2220, Berea, KY 40404. *Phone:* 859-985-3500. *Toll-free phone:* 800-326-5948. *Fax:* 859-985-3512. *E-mail:* admissions@berea.edu.

Brescia University
Owensboro, Kentucky
http://www.brescia.edu/
- **Independent Roman Catholic** comprehensive, founded 1950
- **Urban** 9-acre campus
- **Endowment** $12.4 million
- **Coed** 1,272 undergraduate students, 56% full-time, 65% women, 35% men
- **Moderately difficult** entrance level, 42% of applicants were admitted

UNDERGRAD STUDENTS
709 full-time, 563 part-time. Students come from 48 states and territories; 7 other countries; 56% are from out of state; 15% Black or African American, non-Hispanic/Latino; 7% Hispanic/Latino; 1% Asian, non-Hispanic/Latino; 0.2% Native Hawaiian or other Pacific Islander, non-Hispanic/Latino; 0.3% American Indian or Alaska Native, non-Hispanic/Latino; 0.3% Two or more races, non-Hispanic/Latino; 14% Race/ethnicity unknown; 1% international; 9% transferred in; 41% live on campus.

Freshmen:
Admission: 4,158 applied, 1,763 admitted, 121 enrolled. *Average high school GPA:* 3.0. *Test scores:* ACT scores over 18: 87%; ACT scores over 24: 29%; ACT scores over 30: 2%.
Retention: 64% of full-time freshmen returned.

FACULTY
Total: 124, 39% full-time.
Student/faculty ratio: 12:1.

ACADEMICS
Calendar: semesters. *Degrees:* certificates, associate, bachelor's, master's, and postbachelor's certificates.

Special study options: academic remediation for entering students, adult/continuing education programs, advanced placement credit, distance learning, double majors, honors programs, independent study, internships, off-campus study, part-time degree program, services for LD students, student-designed majors, study abroad, summer session for credit.

Computers: 90 computers/terminals and 90 ports are available on campus for general student use. Students can access the following: computer help desk, free student e-mail accounts, online (class) grades, online (class) schedules. Campuswide network is available. 100% of college-owned or -operated housing units are wired for high-speed Internet access. Wireless service is available via entire campus.
Library: Fr. Leonard Alvey Library. *Books:* 72,970 (physical), 1,245 (digital/electronic); *Databases:* 75. Students can reserve study rooms.

STUDENT LIFE
Housing options: on-campus residence required through junior year; coed, men-only, women-only. Campus housing is university owned. Freshman applicants given priority for college housing.

Activities and organizations: drama/theater group, student-run newspaper, choral group, Student Government, Alpha Chi, Kentucky Education Association, National Society for Speech Language and Hearing Association, ZEST.

Athletics Member NAIA. *Intercollegiate sports:* baseball M(s), basketball M(s)/W(s), cross-country running M(s)/W(s), golf M(s)/W(s), soccer M(s)/W(s), softball W(s), track and field M/W(s), volleyball W(s). *Intramural sports:* basketball M/W, soccer M/W, table tennis M/W, volleyball M/W.

Campus security: 24-hour emergency response devices, late-night transport/escort service, controlled dormitory access.

Student services: personal/psychological counseling.

COSTS & FINANCIAL AID
Costs (2018–19) *One-time required fee:* $200. *Comprehensive fee:* $31,450 includes full-time tuition ($21,500), mandatory fees ($600), and room and board ($9350). Full-time tuition and fees vary according to course load, degree level, and location. Part-time tuition: $590 per credit

hour. Part-time tuition and fees vary according to course load, degree level, and location. *Room and board:* Room and board charges vary according to board plan and housing facility. *Payment plan:* installment. *Waivers:* senior citizens and employees or children of employees.

Financial Aid Of all full-time matriculated undergraduates who enrolled in 2015, 925 applied for aid, 899 were judged to have need. 50 Federal Work-Study jobs (averaging $909). 48 state and other part-time jobs (averaging $849). In 2015, 57 non-need-based awards were made. *Average financial aid package:* $25,489. *Average need-based loan:* $3414. *Average need-based gift aid:* $7811. *Average non-need-based aid:* $16,191. *Average indebtedness upon graduation:* $19,060.

APPLYING
Standardized Tests *Required:* SAT or ACT (for admission).
Options: electronic application, deferred entrance.
Application fee: $25.
Required: high school transcript. *Required for some:* essay or personal statement, 1 letter of recommendation, interview.
Application deadlines: rolling (freshmen), rolling (transfers).
Notification: continuous (freshmen), continuous (transfers).

CONTACT
Brescia University, 717 Frederica Street, Owensboro, KY 42301-3023. *Phone:* 270-686-4241 Ext. 241. *Toll-free phone:* 877-273-7242.

Campbellsville University

Campbellsville, Kentucky
http://www.campbellsville.edu/

- **Independent** comprehensive, founded 1906, affiliated with Kentucky Baptist Convention
- **Small-town** 90-acre campus
- **Endowment** $14.0 million
- **Coed** 4,099 undergraduate students, 52% full-time, 59% women, 41% men
- **Moderately difficult** entrance level, 69% of applicants were admitted

UNDERGRAD STUDENTS
2,120 full-time, 1,979 part-time. Students come from 44 states and territories; 39 other countries; 16% are from out of state; 9% Black or African American, non-Hispanic/Latino; 3% Hispanic/Latino; 1% Asian, non-Hispanic/Latino; 0.1% Native Hawaiian or other Pacific Islander, non-Hispanic/Latino; 0.3% American Indian or Alaska Native, non-Hispanic/Latino; 2% Two or more races, non-Hispanic/Latino; 4% Race/ethnicity unknown; 4% international; 5% transferred in; 36% live on campus.

Freshmen:
Admission: 2,770 applied, 1,900 admitted, 540 enrolled. *Average high school GPA:* 3.3. *Test scores:* SAT evidence-based reading and writing scores over 500: 56%; SAT math scores over 500: 61%; ACT scores over 18: 80%; SAT evidence-based reading and writing scores over 600: 15%; SAT math scores over 600: 10%; ACT scores over 24: 27%; ACT scores over 30: 3%.
Retention: 65% of full-time freshmen returned.

FACULTY
Total: 285, 59% full-time, 37% with terminal degrees.
Student/faculty ratio: 23:1.

ACADEMICS
Calendar: semesters. *Degrees:* certificates, associate, bachelor's, master's, doctoral, post-master's, and postbachelor's certificates.
Special study options: academic remediation for entering students, accelerated degree program, adult/continuing education programs, advanced placement credit, cooperative education, distance learning, double majors, English as a second language, honors programs, independent study, internships, off-campus study, part-time degree program, services for LD students, study abroad, summer session for credit. *ROTC:* Army (c).
Computers: 220 computers/terminals are available on campus for general student use. Students can access the following: campus intranet, computer help desk, free student e-mail accounts, online (class) grades, online (class)

registration, online (class) schedules. Campuswide network is available. 100% of college-owned or -operated housing units are wired for high-speed Internet access. Wireless service is available via entire campus.
Library: Montgomery Library. *Books:* 173,113 (physical), 239,581 (digital/electronic); *Serial titles:* 67 (physical); *Databases:* 77. Weekly public service hours: 77; students can reserve study rooms.

STUDENT LIFE
Housing options: on-campus residence required through sophomore year; men-only, women-only. Campus housing is university owned. Freshman campus housing is guaranteed.

Activities and organizations: drama/theater group, student-run newspaper, radio and television station, choral group, marching band, Baptist Campus Ministries, Student Government Association, International Student Association, Green Minds, KANS (Nursing Society).

Athletics Member NAIA, NCCAA. *Intercollegiate sports:* archery M(s)/W(s), baseball M(s), basketball M(s)/W(s), bowling M(s)/W(s), cheerleading M(s)/W(s), cross-country running M(s)/W(s), football M(s), golf M(s)/W(s), soccer M(s)/W(s), softball W(s), swimming and diving M(s)/W(s), tennis M(s)/W(s), track and field M(s)/W(s), volleyball M(s)/W(s), wrestling M(s)/W(s). *Intramural sports:* basketball M/W, bowling M/W, football M/W, racquetball M/W, sand volleyball M/W, soccer M/W, softball M/W, swimming and diving M/W, table tennis M/W, tennis M/W, ultimate Frisbee M/W, volleyball M/W, weight lifting M/W.

Campus security: 24-hour emergency response devices and patrols, student patrols, late-night transport/escort service, controlled dormitory access.

Student services: health clinic, personal/psychological counseling.

COSTS & FINANCIAL AID
Costs (2017–18) *Comprehensive fee:* $33,400 includes full-time tuition ($24,900), mandatory fees ($500), and room and board ($8000). Full-time tuition and fees vary according to course load, location, and program. Part-time tuition: $1038 per credit hour. Part-time tuition and fees vary according to class time, course load, location, and program. *Required fees:* $250 per year part-time. *Room and board:* Room and board charges vary according to housing facility. *Payment plan:* installment. *Waivers:* adult students, senior citizens, and employees or children of employees.

Financial Aid Of all full-time matriculated undergraduates who enrolled in 2016, 1,646 applied for aid, 1,531 were judged to have need, 266 had their need fully met. In 2016, 138 non-need-based awards were made. *Average percent of need met:* 76. *Average financial aid package:* $19,583. *Average need-based loan:* $3503. *Average need-based gift aid:* $17,119. *Average non-need-based aid:* $11,711. *Average indebtedness upon graduation:* $21,756.

APPLYING
Standardized Tests *Required:* SAT or ACT (for admission).
Options: electronic application, deferred entrance.
Application fee: $20.
Required: high school transcript, minimum 2.0 GPA. *Recommended:* essay or personal statement, minimum 3.0 GPA, interview.
Application deadlines: rolling (freshmen), rolling (transfers).
Notification: continuous (freshmen), continuous (transfers).

CONTACT
Mrs. Paula S. Caldwell, Director of Admissions, Campbellsville University, 1 University Drive, UPO 782, Campbellsville, KY 42718-2799. *Phone:* 270-789-5220 Ext. 5007. *Toll-free phone:* 800-264-6014. *Fax:* 270-789-5071. *E-mail:* admissions@campbellsville.edu.

Centre College

Danville, Kentucky
http://www.centre.edu/

- **Independent** 4-year, founded 1819, affiliated with Presbyterian Church (U.S.A.)
- **Small-town** 160-acre campus
- **Endowment** $269.4 million
- **Coed** 1,450 undergraduate students, 100% full-time, 51% women, 49% men
- **Very difficult** entrance level, 76% of applicants were admitted

UNDERGRAD STUDENTS
1,449 full-time, 1 part-time. Students come from 46 states and territories; 17 other countries; 44% are from out of state; 5% Black or African American, non-Hispanic/Latino; 5% Hispanic/Latino; 5% Asian, non-Hispanic/Latino; 0.1% Native Hawaiian or other Pacific Islander, non-Hispanic/Latino; 0.2% American Indian or Alaska Native, non-Hispanic/Latino; 3% Two or more races, non-Hispanic/Latino; 1% Race/ethnicity unknown; 7% international; 0.4% transferred in; 98% live on campus.

Freshmen:
Admission: 2,454 applied, 1,873 admitted, 401 enrolled. *Average high school GPA:* 3.6. *Test scores:* SAT evidence-based reading and writing scores over 500: 99%; SAT math scores over 500: 100%; ACT scores over 18: 100%; SAT evidence-based reading and writing scores over 600: 74%; SAT math scores over 600: 67%; ACT scores over 24: 92%; SAT evidence-based reading and writing scores over 700: 20%; SAT math scores over 700: 36%; ACT scores over 30: 45%.
Retention: 91% of full-time freshmen returned.

FACULTY
Total: 137, 94% full-time, 94% with terminal degrees.
Student/faculty ratio: 10:1.

ACADEMICS
Calendar: 4-1-4. *Degree:* bachelor's.
Special study options: advanced placement credit, cooperative education, double majors, honors programs, independent study, internships, off-campus study, services for LD students, student-designed majors, study abroad. *ROTC:* Army (c), Air Force (c).
Unusual degree programs: 3-2 engineering with Washington University in St. Louis, Vanderbilt University, University of Kentucky.
Computers: 425 computers/terminals and 1,500 ports are available on campus for general student use. Students can access the following: campus intranet, computer help desk, free student e-mail accounts, online (class) grades, online (class) registration, online (class) schedules. Campuswide network is available. 100% of college-owned or -operated housing units are wired for high-speed Internet access. Wireless service is available via entire campus.
Library: Doherty Library. *Books:* 231,820 (physical), 33,042 (digital/electronic); *Serial titles:* 536 (physical), 27,570 (digital/electronic); *Databases:* 530. Weekly public service hours: 113; study areas open 24 hours, 5–7 days a week; students can reserve study rooms.

STUDENT LIFE
Housing options: on-campus residence required through senior year; coed, men-only, women-only, special housing for students with disabilities. Campus housing is university owned. Freshman campus housing is guaranteed.
Activities and organizations: drama/theater group, student-run newspaper, radio station, choral group, Student Government Association, Centre Action Reaches Everyone, Student Activities Council, Christian fellowship group, Diversity Student Union, national fraternities, national sororities.
Athletics Member NCAA. All Division III. *Intercollegiate sports:* baseball M, basketball M/W, cheerleading W, cross-country running M/W, field hockey W, football M, golf M/W, lacrosse M/W, soccer M/W, softball W, swimming and diving M/W, tennis M/W, track and field M/W, volleyball W. *Intramural sports:* basketball M/W, football M/W, golf M/W, soccer M/W, softball M/W, tennis M/W, volleyball M/W.
Campus security: 24-hour emergency response devices and patrols, late-night transport/escort service, controlled dormitory access.
Student services: health clinic, personal/psychological counseling.

COSTS & FINANCIAL AID
Costs (2018–19) *Comprehensive fee:* $52,180 includes full-time tuition ($41,700) and room and board ($10,480). Part-time tuition: $1446 per credit hour. *College room only:* $5240. Room and board charges vary according to housing facility. *Payment plan:* installment. *Waivers:* employees or children of employees.
Financial Aid Of all full-time matriculated undergraduates who enrolled in 2016, 1,021 applied for aid, 789 were judged to have need, 255 had their need fully met. 334 Federal Work-Study jobs (averaging $1665). In 2016, 582 non-need-based awards were made. *Average percent of need met:* 86. *Average financial aid package:* $32,001. *Average need-based loan:* $4512. *Average need-based gift aid:* $28,880. *Average non-need-based aid:* $20,689. *Average indebtedness upon graduation:* $26,740. *Financial aid deadline:* 1/31.

APPLYING
Standardized Tests *Required:* SAT or ACT (for admission).
Options: electronic application, early admission, early decision, early action, deferred entrance.
Required: essay or personal statement, high school transcript, 1 letter of recommendation. *Recommended:* interview.
Application deadlines: 1/15 (freshmen), rolling (transfers), 12/1 (early action).
Early decision deadline: 11/15.
Notification: 3/31 (freshmen), 12/15 (early decision), 1/15 (early action).

CONTACT
Mr. Bob Nesmith, Dean of Admission and Student Financial Aid, Centre College, 600 West Walnut Street, Danville, KY 40422-1394. *Phone:* 859-238-5350. *Toll-free phone:* 800-423-6236. *Fax:* 859-238-5373. *E-mail:* admission@centre.edu.

Clear Creek Baptist Bible College
Pineville, Kentucky
http://www.ccbbc.edu/

CONTACT
Mr. Billy Howell, Director of Admissions, Clear Creek Baptist Bible College, 300 Clear Creek Road, Pineville, KY 40977. *Phone:* 606-337-3196 Ext. 103. *Fax:* 606-337-1631. *E-mail:* bhowell@ccbbc.edu.

Eastern Kentucky University
Richmond, Kentucky
http://www.eku.edu/

CONTACT
Ms. Stephanie Leigh Whaley, Director of Admissions, Eastern Kentucky University, SSB CPO 54, 521 Lancaster Avenue, Richmond, KY 40475-3102. *Phone:* 859-622-2106. *Toll-free phone:* 800-465-9191. *Fax:* 859-622-8024. *E-mail:* admissions@eku.edu.

Galen College of Nursing
Louisville, Kentucky
http://www.galencollege.edu/

CONTACT
Galen College of Nursing, 1031 Zorn Avenue, Suite 400, Louisville, KY 40207. *Toll-free phone:* 877-223-7040.

Georgetown College
Georgetown, Kentucky
http://www.georgetowncollege.edu/
- **Independent** comprehensive, founded 1829, affiliated with Baptist Church
- **Suburban** 104-acre campus with easy access to Cincinnati, OH; Louisville, KY
- **Endowment** $30.9 million
- **Coed** 1,060 undergraduate students, 92% full-time, 54% women, 46% men
- **Moderately difficult** entrance level, 67% of applicants were admitted

UNDERGRAD STUDENTS
975 full-time, 85 part-time. Students come from 32 states and territories; 11 other countries; 74% are from out of state; 9% Black or African American, non-Hispanic/Latino; 0.1% Hispanic/Latino; 0.8% Asian, non-Hispanic/Latino; 0.5% American Indian or Alaska Native, non-Hispanic/Latino; 5% Two or more races, non-Hispanic/Latino; 6% Race/ethnicity unknown; 0.6% international; 4% transferred in; 90% live on campus.

Kentucky

Freshmen:
Admission: 2,498 applied, 1,682 admitted, 305 enrolled. *Average high school GPA:* 3.4. *Test scores:* ACT scores over 18: 96%; ACT scores over 24: 49%; ACT scores over 30: 6%.

FACULTY
Total: 166, 52% full-time, 66% with terminal degrees.
Student/faculty ratio: 11:1.

ACADEMICS
Calendar: semesters. *Degrees:* certificates, diplomas, bachelor's, master's, and postbachelor's certificates.

Special study options: advanced placement credit, cooperative education, distance learning, double majors, English as a second language, honors programs, independent study, internships, off-campus study, part-time degree program, services for LD students, student-designed majors, study abroad, summer session for credit. *ROTC:* Army (c), Air Force (c).

Unusual degree programs: 3-2 engineering with University of Kentucky; nursing with University of Kentucky; diplomacy and international commerce with University of Kentucky.

Computers: 135 computers/terminals and 2,000 ports are available on campus for general student use. Students can access the following: campus intranet, computer help desk, free student e-mail accounts, online (class) grades, online (class) registration, online (class) schedules, library apps for smartphones. Campuswide network is available. 100% of college-owned or -operated housing units are wired for high-speed Internet access. Wireless service is available via entire campus.
Library: Anna Ashcraft Ensor Learning Resource Center. *Books:* 121,081 (physical), 327,868 (digital/electronic); *Serial titles:* 1,108 (physical), 43,132 (digital/electronic); *Databases:* 107. Weekly public service hours: 91.

STUDENT LIFE
Housing options: on-campus residence required through senior year; men-only, women-only. Campus housing is university owned and leased by the school. Freshman campus housing is guaranteed.

Activities and organizations: drama/theater group, student-run newspaper, radio station, choral group, national fraternities, national sororities.

Athletics Member NAIA. *Intercollegiate sports:* baseball M(s), basketball M(s)/W(s), cheerleading W(s), cross-country running M(s)/W(s), football M(s), golf M(s)/W(s), lacrosse W(s), soccer M(s)/W(s), softball W(s), tennis M(s)/W(s), track and field M(s)/W(s), volleyball W(s). *Intramural sports:* basketball M/W, football M/W, golf M/W, racquetball M/W, soccer M/W, softball M/W, table tennis M/W, tennis M/W, ultimate Frisbee M/W, volleyball M/W.

Campus security: 24-hour patrols, late-night transport/escort service, controlled dormitory access.

Student services: health clinic, personal/psychological counseling.

COSTS & FINANCIAL AID
Costs (2018–19) *Comprehensive fee:* $48,430 includes full-time tuition ($38,650) and room and board ($9780). Full-time tuition and fees vary according to course load and degree level. Part-time tuition and fees vary according to course load and degree level. *College room only:* $4720. Room and board charges vary according to board plan and housing facility. *Payment plan:* installment. *Waivers:* employees or children of employees.

Financial Aid Of all full-time matriculated undergraduates who enrolled in 2014, 884 applied for aid, 805 were judged to have need, 56 had their need fully met. 545 Federal Work-Study jobs (averaging $916). In 2014, 71 non-need-based awards were made. *Average percent of need met:* 86. *Average financial aid package:* $29,023. *Average need-based loan:* $3018. *Average need-based gift aid:* $14,998. *Average non-need-based aid:* $13,372. *Average indebtedness upon graduation:* $31,267.

APPLYING
Standardized Tests *Required:* SAT or ACT (for admission).
Options: electronic application, deferred entrance.
Required: high school transcript, minimum 2.0 GPA. *Required for some:* essay or personal statement, interview.
Application deadlines: rolling (freshmen), rolling (transfers).
Notification: continuous (freshmen), continuous (transfers).

CONTACT
Mr. Jeremiah Tudor, Senior Associate Director of Admissions, Georgetown College, 400 East College Street, Georgetown, KY 40324. *Phone:* 502-863-8727. *Toll-free phone:* 800-788-9985. *Fax:* 502-868-7733. *E-mail:* admissions@georgetowncollege.edu.

Kentucky Christian University
Grayson, Kentucky
http://www.kcu.edu/

CONTACT
Ms. Heather Stacy, Director of Admissions, Kentucky Christian University, 100 Academic Parkway, Grayson, KY 41143. *Phone:* 606-474-3284. *Toll-free phone:* 800-522-3181. *Fax:* 606-474-3155. *E-mail:* sgreer@kcu.edu.

Kentucky Mountain Bible College
Jackson, Kentucky
http://www.kmbc.edu/
- **Independent interdenominational** 4-year, founded 1931
- **Rural** 500-acre campus with easy access to Lexington
- **Coed** 83 undergraduate students, 81% full-time, 35% women, 65% men
- **Minimally difficult** entrance level, 50% of applicants were admitted

UNDERGRAD STUDENTS
67 full-time, 16 part-time. Students come from 16 states and territories; 3 other countries; 70% are from out of state; 11% transferred in; 92% live on campus.

Freshmen:
Admission: 72 applied, 36 admitted, 16 enrolled. *Average high school GPA:* 3.4. *Test scores:* ACT scores over 18: 91%; ACT scores over 24: 37%.
Retention: 66% of full-time freshmen returned.

FACULTY
Total: 14, 7% full-time, 7% with terminal degrees.
Student/faculty ratio: 13:1.

ACADEMICS
Calendar: semesters. *Degrees:* associate and bachelor's.

Special study options: academic remediation for entering students, cooperative education, distance learning, independent study, internships, part-time degree program.

Computers: 4 computers/terminals are available on campus for general student use. Students can access the following: campus intranet, free student e-mail accounts, online (class) grades, online (class) registration, online (class) schedules. Campuswide network is available. 100% of college-owned or -operated housing units are wired for high-speed Internet access. Wireless service is available via entire campus.
Library: Gibson Library plus 1 other. *Books:* 34,770 (physical), 52 (digital/electronic); *Serial titles:* 111 (physical). Weekly public service hours: 70.

STUDENT LIFE
Housing options: on-campus residence required through senior year; men-only, women-only. Campus housing is university owned. Freshman campus housing is guaranteed.

Activities and organizations: drama/theater group, student-run newspaper, choral group, Missionary Involvement, Class Organizations.
Athletics *Intramural sports:* basketball M, volleyball W.
Campus security: student patrols.
Student services: personal/psychological counseling.

COSTS & FINANCIAL AID
Costs (2018–19) *One-time required fee:* $640. *Comprehensive fee:* $13,180 includes full-time tuition ($7520), mandatory fees ($710), and room and board ($4950). Full-time tuition and fees vary according to program. Part-time tuition: $235 per credit hour. Part-time tuition and fees vary according to program. *Required fees:* $250 per term part-time. *College room only:* $1800. Room and board charges vary according to housing facility. *Payment plan:* installment. *Waivers:* employees or children of employees.

Financial Aid Of all full-time matriculated undergraduates who enrolled in 2015, 54 applied for aid, 53 were judged to have need, 5 had their need fully met. In 2015, 7 non-need-based awards were made. *Average percent of need met:* 66. *Average financial aid package:* $9336. *Average need-based loan:* $3707. *Average need-based gift aid:* $5889. *Average non-need-based aid:* $2808. *Average indebtedness upon graduation:* $7370.

APPLYING
Standardized Tests *Required:* ACT (for admission).

Application fee: $25.

Required: essay or personal statement, high school transcript, minimum 2.0 GPA, testimony of Christian belief and practice. *Recommended:* minimum 2.0 GPA, interview.

Application deadlines: rolling (freshmen), rolling (transfers).

Notification: continuous (freshmen), continuous (transfers).

CONTACT
Mr. David Lorimer, Director of Recruiting, Kentucky Mountain Bible College, PO Box 10, Vancleve, KY 41385. *Phone:* 606-693-5000 Ext. 138. *Toll-free phone:* 800-879-KMBC. *Fax:* 606-693-4884. *E-mail:* dlorimer@kmbc.edu.

Kentucky State University
Frankfort, Kentucky
http://www.kysu.edu/
- **State-related** comprehensive, founded 1886
- **Small-town** 916-acre campus with easy access to Louisville
- **Endowment** $16.6 million
- **Coed** 1,757 undergraduate students, 64% full-time, 60% women, 40% men

UNDERGRAD STUDENTS
1,122 full-time, 635 part-time. Students come from 39 states and territories; 14 other countries; 31% are from out of state; 53% Black or African American, non-Hispanic/Latino; 16% Hispanic/Latino; 0.9% Asian, non-Hispanic/Latino; 1% Native Hawaiian or other Pacific Islander, non-Hispanic/Latino; 0.5% American Indian or Alaska Native, non-Hispanic/Latino; 4% Two or more races, non-Hispanic/Latino; 4% Race/ethnicity unknown; 1% international; 9% transferred in; 36% live on campus.

Freshmen:
Admission: 318 enrolled. *Average high school GPA:* 2.8. *Test scores:* ACT scores over 18: 56%; ACT scores over 24: 9%.

Retention: 68% of full-time freshmen returned.

FACULTY
Total: 130, 82% full-time, 59% with terminal degrees.
Student/faculty ratio: 11:1.

ACADEMICS
Calendar: semesters. *Degrees:* certificates, associate, bachelor's, master's, and doctoral.

Special study options: academic remediation for entering students, adult/continuing education programs, advanced placement credit, cooperative education, distance learning, double majors, external degree program, freshman honors college, honors programs, independent study, internships, part-time degree program, services for LD students, student-designed majors, study abroad, summer session for credit. *ROTC:* Army (c), Air Force (c).

Unusual degree programs: 3-2 engineering with University of Kentucky.

Computers: 142 computers/terminals and 92 ports are available on campus for general student use. Students can access the following: campus intranet, computer help desk, free student e-mail accounts, online (class) grades, online (class) registration, online (class) schedules, student bill-pay, address verification, ability to accept financial aid awards. Campuswide network is available. 100% of college-owned or -operated housing units are wired for high-speed Internet access. Wireless service is available via entire campus.

Library: Paul G. Blazer Library. *Books:* 170,726 (physical), 23,417 (digital/electronic); *Serial titles:* 1,894 (physical), 38,647 (digital/electronic); *Databases:* 56. Weekly public service hours: 101; study areas open 24 hours, 5–7 days a week.

STUDENT LIFE
Housing options: on-campus residence required through sophomore year; coed, men-only, women-only, special housing for students with disabilities. Campus housing is university owned. Freshman campus housing is guaranteed.

Activities and organizations: drama/theater group, student-run newspaper, choral group, marching band, Collegiate100, Alpha Phi Omega, Drive Our Peer's Education DOPE, Student Ambassador's, Alpha Phi Alpha, national fraternities, national sororities.

Athletics Member NCAA. All Division II. *Intercollegiate sports:* baseball M(s), basketball M(s)/W(s), cross-country running M(s)/W(s), football M(s), golf M(s), softball W(s), track and field M(s)/W(s), volleyball W(s). *Intramural sports:* badminton M/W, basketball M/W, cheerleading W(c), gymnastics M/W, racquetball M/W, volleyball W.

Campus security: 24-hour emergency response devices and patrols, student patrols, late-night transport/escort service, controlled dormitory access.

Student services: health clinic, personal/psychological counseling.

COSTS & FINANCIAL AID
Costs (2018–19) *Tuition:* state resident $7406 full-time, $325 per credit hour part-time; nonresident $18,314 full-time, $802 per credit hour part-time. Full-time tuition and fees vary according to course load. Part-time tuition and fees vary according to course load. *Required fees:* $390 full-time. *Room and board:* $6690; room only: $3340. Room and board charges vary according to board plan and housing facility. *Payment plan:* installment. *Waivers:* senior citizens and employees or children of employees.

Financial Aid Of all full-time matriculated undergraduates who enrolled in 2017, 1,066 applied for aid, 972 were judged to have need, 149 had their need fully met. 129 Federal Work-Study jobs (averaging $3658). 41 state and other part-time jobs (averaging $2639). In 2017, 85 non-need-based awards were made. *Average percent of need met:* 80. *Average financial aid package:* $12,829. *Average need-based loan:* $4085. *Average need-based gift aid:* $9162. *Average non-need-based aid:* $4570. *Average indebtedness upon graduation:* $29,553.

APPLYING
Standardized Tests *Required:* SAT or ACT (for admission).

Required: high school transcript, minimum 2.5 GPA, minimum ACT score of 18.

CONTACT
Kentucky State University, 320 Hill Student Center, 400 East Main Street, Frankfort, KY 40601. *Phone:* 502-597-6813. *Toll-free phone:* 877-367-5978. *Fax:* 502-597-5814. *E-mail:* admissions@kysu.edu.

Kentucky Wesleyan College
Owensboro, Kentucky
http://www.kwc.edu/
- **Independent Methodist** 4-year, founded 1858
- **Suburban** 52-acre campus
- **Endowment** $34.3 million
- **Coed**
- **Moderately difficult** entrance level

FACULTY
Student/faculty ratio: 11:1.

ACADEMICS
Calendar: semesters. *Degree:* bachelor's.
Library: Library Learning Center. Students can reserve study rooms.

STUDENT LIFE
Housing options: on-campus residence required through senior year; coed, men-only, women-only, special housing for students with disabilities. Campus housing is university owned. Freshman campus housing is guaranteed.

Activities and organizations: drama/theater group, student-run newspaper, radio station, choral group, Student Government Association, Student Activities Programming Board, Campus Ministries, Pre Professional, St Jude Up 'Til Dawn Executive Board, national fraternities, national sororities.

Athletics Member NCAA. All Division II.

Campus security: 24-hour emergency response devices, late-night transport/escort service, 12-hour patrols by trained security personnel.

Student services: health clinic, personal/psychological counseling, women's center.

COSTS & FINANCIAL AID

Costs (2017–18) *Comprehensive fee:* $34,666 includes full-time tuition ($24,290), mandatory fees ($780), and room and board ($9596). Full-time tuition and fees vary according to course load. Part-time tuition: $700 per credit hour. Part-time tuition and fees vary according to course load. *Required fees:* $700 per term part-time. *Room and board:* Room and board charges vary according to board plan and housing facility. *Payment plans:* installment, deferred payment.

Financial Aid *Average indebtedness upon graduation:* $24,150. *Financial aid deadline:* 3/15.

APPLYING

Standardized Tests *Required:* SAT or ACT (for admission).

Options: electronic application, early admission, deferred entrance.

Required: high school transcript.

CONTACT

Kentucky Wesleyan College, 3000 Frederica Street, Owensboro, KY 42301. *Phone:* 270-852-3120. *Toll-free phone:* 800-999-0592 (in-state); 800-990-0592 (out-of-state).

Lindsey Wilson College

Columbia, Kentucky

http://www.lindsey.edu/

- **Independent United Methodist** comprehensive, founded 1903
- **Rural** 225-acre campus
- **Endowment** $24.3 million
- **Coed** 2,068 undergraduate students, 93% full-time, 61% women, 39% men
- **Minimally difficult** entrance level, 92% of applicants were admitted

UNDERGRAD STUDENTS

1,919 full-time, 149 part-time. Students come from 30 states and territories; 35 other countries; 20% are from out of state; 8% Black or African American, non-Hispanic/Latino; 0.8% Hispanic/Latino; 0.4% Asian, non-Hispanic/Latino; 0.1% Native Hawaiian or other Pacific Islander, non-Hispanic/Latino; 0.3% American Indian or Alaska Native, non-Hispanic/Latino; 2% Two or more races, non-Hispanic/Latino; 26% Race/ethnicity unknown; 12% transferred in; 52% live on campus.

Freshmen:

Admission: 2,090 applied, 1,915 admitted, 547 enrolled. *Average high school GPA:* 3.3. *Test scores:* ACT scores over 18: 86%; ACT scores over 24: 27%; ACT scores over 30: 3%.

Retention: 57% of full-time freshmen returned.

FACULTY

Total: 239, 45% full-time, 36% with terminal degrees.

Student/faculty ratio: 13:1.

ACADEMICS

Calendar: semesters. *Degrees:* associate, bachelor's, master's, and doctoral.

Special study options: academic remediation for entering students, accelerated degree program, adult/continuing education programs, advanced placement credit, cooperative education, double majors, English as a second language, independent study, internships, off-campus study, part-time degree program, services for LD students, student-designed majors, study abroad, summer session for credit.

Computers: 120 computers/terminals are available on campus for general student use. Students can access the following: campus intranet, computer help desk, free student e-mail accounts, online (class) grades, online (class) registration, online (class) schedules. Campuswide network is available. 100% of college-owned or -operated housing units are wired for high-speed Internet access. Wireless service is available via entire campus.

Library: Katie Murrell Library.

STUDENT LIFE

Housing options: on-campus residence required through senior year; men-only, women-only. Campus housing is university owned. Freshman campus housing is guaranteed.

Activities and organizations: drama/theater group, student-run newspaper, choral group, marching band.

Athletics Member NAIA. *Intercollegiate sports:* baseball M(s), basketball M(s)/W(s), bowling M(s)/W(s), cheerleading M(s)/W(s), cross-country running M(s)/W(s), football M(s)/W(s), golf M(s)/W(s), soccer M(s)/W(s), softball W(s), swimming and diving M(s)/W(s), tennis M(s)/W(s), track and field M(s)/W(s), volleyball W(s), wrestling M(s). *Intramural sports:* basketball M/W, football M/W, softball M/W, table tennis M/W, tennis M/W, volleyball M/W, weight lifting M/W.

Campus security: 24-hour emergency response devices and patrols.

Student services: health clinic, personal/psychological counseling, women's center.

COSTS & FINANCIAL AID

Costs (2018–19) *Comprehensive fee:* $34,235 includes full-time tuition ($24,600), mandatory fees ($250), and room and board ($9385). Full-time tuition and fees vary according to class time, degree level, and location. Part-time tuition: $1025 per credit hour. Part-time tuition and fees vary according to class time, degree level, and location. *Required fees:* $50 per term part-time. *College room only:* $3400. *Payment plan:* installment. *Waivers:* senior citizens and employees or children of employees.

Financial Aid Of all full-time matriculated undergraduates who enrolled in 2017, 1,893 applied for aid, 1,789 were judged to have need, 413 had their need fully met. 225 Federal Work-Study jobs (averaging $2178). 23 state and other part-time jobs (averaging $2479). *Average need-based loan:* $4183. *Average need-based gift aid:* $19,576. *Average indebtedness upon graduation:* $28,870.

APPLYING

Standardized Tests *Required for some:* SAT or ACT (for admission).

Options: electronic application.

Required: high school transcript. *Recommended:* interview.

Application deadlines: rolling (freshmen), rolling (transfers).

Notification: continuous (freshmen), continuous (transfers).

CONTACT

Mrs. Charity Ferguson, Assistant Director of Admissions, Lindsey Wilson College, 210 Lindsey Wilson Street, Columbia, KY 42728-1298. *Phone:* 270-384-8100. *Toll-free phone:* 800-264-0138. *Fax:* 270-384-8591.

Midway University

Midway, Kentucky

http://www.midway.edu/

CONTACT

Midway University, 512 East Stephens Street, Midway, KY 40347-1120. *Phone:* 859-846-5799. *Toll-free phone:* 800-755-0031.

Morehead State University

Morehead, Kentucky

http://www.moreheadstate.edu/

- **State-supported** comprehensive, founded 1922
- **Small-town** 1187-acre campus
- **Endowment** $43.0 million
- **Coed** 9,665 undergraduate students, 60% full-time, 60% women, 40% men
- **Minimally difficult** entrance level, 80% of applicants were admitted

UNDERGRAD STUDENTS

5,835 full-time, 3,830 part-time. Students come from 44 states and territories; 24 other countries; 13% are from out of state; 3% Black or African American, non-Hispanic/Latino; 2% Hispanic/Latino; 0.6% Asian, non-Hispanic/Latino; 0.1% Native Hawaiian or other Pacific Islander, non-Hispanic/Latino; 0.2% American Indian or Alaska Native, non-Hispanic/Latino; 2% Two or more races, non-Hispanic/Latino; 0.9% Race/ethnicity unknown; 2% international; 5% transferred in; 42% live on campus.

Freshmen:
Admission: 5,392 applied, 4,293 admitted, 1,271 enrolled. *Average high school GPA:* 3.5. *Test scores:* SAT evidence-based reading and writing scores over 500: 11%; SAT math scores over 500: 33%; ACT scores over 18: 95%; SAT evidence-based reading and writing scores over 600: 11%; SAT math scores over 600: 11%; ACT scores over 24: 43%; ACT scores over 30: 5%.
Retention: 72% of full-time freshmen returned.

FACULTY
Total: 411, 77% full-time.
Student/faculty ratio: 15:1.

ACADEMICS
Calendar: semesters. *Degrees:* certificates, associate, bachelor's, master's, doctoral, post-master's, and postbachelor's certificates.

Special study options: academic remediation for entering students, accelerated degree program, adult/continuing education programs, advanced placement credit, cooperative education, distance learning, double majors, English as a second language, honors programs, independent study, internships, off-campus study, part-time degree program, services for LD students, student-designed majors, study abroad, summer session for credit. *ROTC:* Army (b).

Unusual degree programs: 3-2 engineering with University of Kentucky.

Computers: 950 computers/terminals and 25 ports are available on campus for general student use. Students can access the following: campus intranet, computer help desk, free student e-mail accounts, online (class) grades, online (class) registration, online (class) schedules. Campuswide network is available. 100% of college-owned or -operated housing units are wired for high-speed Internet access. Wireless service is available via entire campus.

Library: Camden Carroll Library. *Books:* 339,640 (physical), 121,456 (digital/electronic); *Serial titles:* 29,191 (physical), 72,511 (digital/electronic); *Databases:* 152. Weekly public service hours: 95; students can reserve study rooms.

STUDENT LIFE
Housing options: on-campus residence required through sophomore year; coed, special housing for students with disabilities. Campus housing is university owned. Freshman applicants given priority for college housing.

Activities and organizations: drama/theater group, student-run newspaper, radio and television station, choral group, marching band, Delta Tau Delta Fraternity, Delta Gamma, Phi Sigma Pi (Honors), Baptist Campus Ministries (BCM), Collegiate Future Farmers of America (FFA), national fraternities, national sororities.

Athletics Member NCAA. All Division I except football (Division I-AA). *Intercollegiate sports:* baseball M(s), basketball M(s)/W(s), bowling M(c)/W(c), cheerleading M(s)/W(s), cross-country running M(s)/W(s), equestrian sports M(c)/W(c), golf M(s)/W(s), riflery M(s)/W(s), soccer W(s), softball W(s), track and field M(s)/W(s), volleyball W(s). *Intramural sports:* badminton M/W, basketball M/W, bowling M/W, football M/W, golf M/W, racquetball M/W, soccer M(c), softball M/W, table tennis M/W, tennis M/W, ultimate Frisbee M/W, volleyball M/W.

Campus security: 24-hour emergency response devices and patrols, student patrols, late-night transport/escort service, controlled dormitory access, LiveSafe app—a two-way communication safety app between students and University Police.

Student services: health clinic, personal/psychological counseling.

COSTS & FINANCIAL AID
Costs (2017–18) *Tuition:* state resident $8950 full-time, $374 per credit hour part-time; nonresident $13,426 full-time, $561 per credit hour part-time. Full-time tuition and fees vary according to course load, degree level, location, reciprocity agreements, and student level. Part-time tuition and fees vary according to course load, degree level, location, reciprocity agreements, and student level. *Room and board:* $9436; room only: $5270. Room and board charges vary according to board plan and housing facility. *Payment plans:* installment, deferred payment. *Waivers:* minority students, children of alumni, senior citizens, and employees or children of employees.

Financial Aid Of all full-time matriculated undergraduates who enrolled in 2017, 4,858 applied for aid, 4,257 were judged to have need, 713 had their need fully met. 341 Federal Work-Study jobs (averaging $2327). 765 state and other part-time jobs (averaging $2659). In 2017, 833 non-need-based awards were made. *Average percent of need met:* 61. *Average financial aid package:* $11,532. *Average need-based loan:* $3769. *Average need-based gift aid:* $5783. *Average non-need-based aid:* $7684. *Average indebtedness upon graduation:* $26,623.

APPLYING
Standardized Tests *Required:* SAT or ACT (for admission).

Options: electronic application, early admission, deferred entrance.

Application fee: $30.

Required: high school transcript. *Required for some:* essay or personal statement, 1 letter of recommendation, interview.

Application deadlines: rolling (freshmen), rolling (out-of-state freshmen), rolling (transfers).

Notification: continuous (freshmen), continuous (out-of-state freshmen), continuous (transfers).

CONTACT
Mr. Tim Rhodes, Assistant Vice President for Enrollment Services, Morehead State University, 407 Enrollment Services Center, Morehead, KY 40351. *Phone:* 606-783-2000. *Toll-free phone:* 800-585-6781. *Fax:* 606-783-5038. *E-mail:* admissions@moreheadstate.edu.

Murray State University
Murray, Kentucky
http://www.murraystate.edu/
- **State-supported** university, founded 1922
- **Small-town** 261-acre campus
- **Endowment** $19.2 million
- **Coed** 8,886 undergraduate students, 79% full-time, 58% women, 42% men
- **Moderately difficult** entrance level, 85% of applicants were admitted

UNDERGRAD STUDENTS
6,980 full-time, 1,906 part-time. Students come from 44 states and territories; 42 other countries; 32% are from out of state; 6% Black or African American, non-Hispanic/Latino; 2% Hispanic/Latino; 1% Asian, non-Hispanic/Latino; 0.1% Native Hawaiian or other Pacific Islander, non-Hispanic/Latino; 0.2% American Indian or Alaska Native, non-Hispanic/Latino; 2% Two or more races, non-Hispanic/Latino; 3% Race/ethnicity unknown; 4% international; 7% transferred in; 33% live on campus.

Freshmen:
Admission: 6,479 applied, 5,530 admitted, 1,502 enrolled. *Average high school GPA:* 3.5. *Test scores:* ACT scores over 18: 99%; ACT scores over 24: 52%; ACT scores over 30: 9%.
Retention: 74% of full-time freshmen returned.

FACULTY
Total: 686, 65% full-time, 62% with terminal degrees.
Student/faculty ratio: 15:1.

ACADEMICS
Calendar: semesters. *Degrees:* certificates, bachelor's, master's, doctoral, and postbachelor's certificates.

Special study options: academic remediation for entering students, adult/continuing education programs, advanced placement credit, cooperative education, distance learning, double majors, English as a second language, external degree program, freshman honors college, honors programs, independent study, internships, off-campus study, part-time degree program, services for LD students, student-designed majors, study abroad, summer session for credit. *ROTC:* Army (b).

Computers: Students can access the following: campus intranet, computer help desk, free student e-mail accounts, online (class) grades, online (class) registration, online (class) schedules, billing accounts, course evaluation forms, receive instant campus alerts, secure on-campus housing, pre-order of food or take-out. Campuswide network is available. 100% of college-owned or -operated housing units are wired for high-speed Internet access. Wireless service is available via entire campus.
Library: Waterfield Library plus 4 others. *Books:* 363,292 (physical), 193,453 (digital/electronic); *Serial titles:* 317 (physical), 639 (digital/electronic); *Databases:* 128. Weekly public service hours: 107; students can reserve study rooms.

STUDENT LIFE

Housing options: on-campus residence required through sophomore year; coed, women-only, special housing for students with disabilities. Campus housing is university owned. Freshman applicants given priority for college housing.

Activities and organizations: drama/theater group, student-run newspaper, television station, choral group, marching band, Racer Band, Student Government Association, National Panhellenic Council, International Student Organization, MSU Student Ambassadors, national fraternities, national sororities.

Athletics Member NCAA. All Division I except football (Division I-AA). *Intercollegiate sports:* baseball M(s), basketball M(s)/W(s), cheerleading M(c)/W(c), crew M(c)/W(c), cross-country running M/W(s), equestrian sports M(c)/W(c), golf M(s)/W(s), riflery M(s)/W(s), rowing M(c)/W(c), soccer W(s), softball W(s), tennis W(s), track and field W(s), volleyball W(s). *Intramural sports:* archery M(c)/W(c), basketball M/W, bowling M/W, fencing M(c)/W(c), football M/W, golf M/W, racquetball M(c)/W(c), rugby M(c), soccer M/W, softball M/W, swimming and diving M/W, table tennis M/W, tennis M/W, ultimate Frisbee M/W, volleyball M/W, water polo M/W.

Campus security: 24-hour emergency response devices and patrols, student patrols, late-night transport/escort service, controlled dormitory access, LiveSafe, a mobile safety app.

Student services: health clinic, personal/psychological counseling, women's center.

COSTS & FINANCIAL AID

Costs (2017–18) *Tuition:* state resident $8340 full-time, $368 per credit hour part-time; nonresident $22,728 full-time, $993 per credit hour part-time. Full-time tuition and fees vary according to course load and reciprocity agreements. Part-time tuition and fees vary according to reciprocity agreements. *Room and board:* $8906; room only: $5246. Room and board charges vary according to board plan and housing facility. *Payment plan:* installment. *Waivers:* senior citizens and employees or children of employees.

Financial Aid Of all full-time matriculated undergraduates who enrolled in 2017, 6,040 applied for aid, 4,601 were judged to have need, 1,147 had their need fully met. 442 Federal Work-Study jobs (averaging $1375). 2,686 state and other part-time jobs (averaging $2088). In 2017, 768 non-need-based awards were made. *Average percent of need met:* 34. *Average financial aid package:* $12,274. *Average need-based loan:* $6428. *Average need-based gift aid:* $6258. *Average non-need-based aid:* $5487. *Average indebtedness upon graduation:* $27,564.

APPLYING

Standardized Tests *Required:* SAT or ACT (for admission). *Recommended:* ACT (for admission).

Options: electronic application, early admission.

Application fee: $40.

Required: high school transcript, minimum 3.0 GPA, minimum ACT composite score of 18 or SAT score of 870, rank in the top half of high school class or minimum 3.0 GPA; high school curriculum criteria.

Application deadlines: rolling (freshmen), rolling (out-of-state freshmen), rolling (transfers).

Notification: continuous (freshmen), continuous (out-of-state freshmen), continuous (transfers).

CONTACT

Ms. Stacy Bell, Assistant Director of Undergraduate Admissions, Murray State University, 102 Curris Center, Murray, KY 42701-0009. *Phone:* 270-809-3741. *Toll-free phone:* 800-272-4678. *Fax:* 270-809-3780. *E-mail:* msu.admissions@murraystate.edu.

Northern Kentucky University
Highland Heights, Kentucky
http://www.nku.edu/

- **State-supported** comprehensive, founded 1968
- **Suburban** 426-acre campus with easy access to Cincinnati
- **Endowment** $89.9 million
- **Coed** 12,347 undergraduate students, 73% full-time, 56% women, 44% men
- **90% of applicants were admitted**

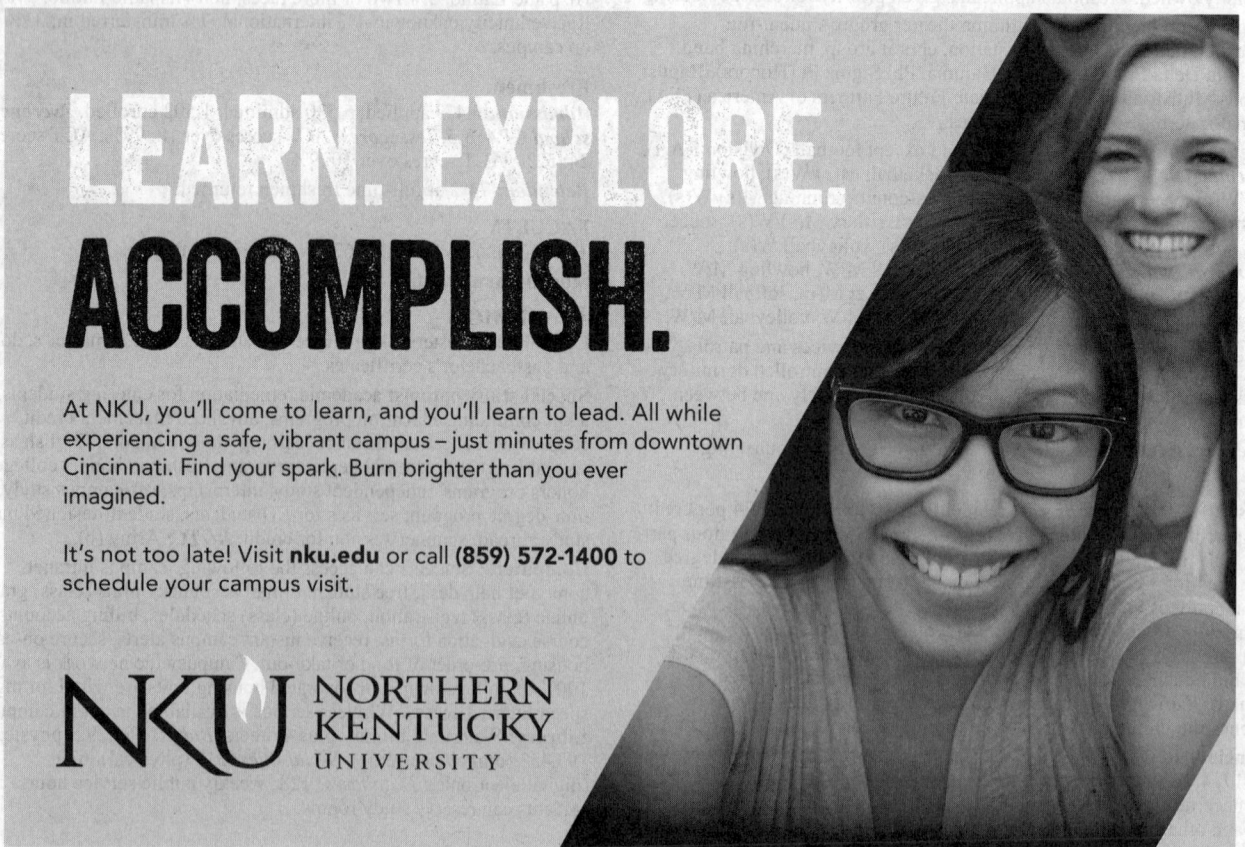

UNDERGRAD STUDENTS

8,980 full-time, 3,367 part-time. Students come from 42 states and territories; 58 other countries; 32% are from out of state; 7% Black or African American, non-Hispanic/Latino; 3% Hispanic/Latino; 1% Asian, non-Hispanic/Latino; 0.1% Native Hawaiian or other Pacific Islander, non-Hispanic/Latino; 0.2% American Indian or Alaska Native, non-Hispanic/Latino; 3% Two or more races, non-Hispanic/Latino; 0.7% Race/ethnicity unknown; 3% international; 6% transferred in; 15% live on campus.

Freshmen:

Admission: 5,852 applied, 5,289 admitted, 2,145 enrolled. *Average high school GPA:* 3.4. *Test scores:* ACT scores over 18: 95%; ACT scores over 24: 45%; ACT scores over 30: 7%.

Retention: 71% of full-time freshmen returned.

FACULTY

Total: 1,032, 55% full-time, 52% with terminal degrees.

ACADEMICS

Calendar: semesters. *Degrees:* certificates, bachelor's, master's, doctoral, post-master's, and postbachelor's certificates.

Special study options: academic remediation for entering students, accelerated degree program, adult/continuing education programs, advanced placement credit, cooperative education, distance learning, double majors, English as a second language, honors programs, independent study, internships, off-campus study, part-time degree program, services for LD students, student-designed majors, study abroad, summer session for credit. *ROTC:* Army (c), Air Force (c).

Unusual degree programs: 3-2 engineering with University of Louisville, University of Kentucky; law with Mount St. Joseph University.

Computers: 200 computers/terminals and 1,500 ports are available on campus for general student use. Students can access the following: campus intranet, computer help desk, free student e-mail accounts, online (class) grades, online (class) registration, online (class) schedules. Campuswide network is available. 100% of college-owned or -operated housing units are wired for high-speed Internet access. Wireless service is available via entire campus.

Library: W. Frank Steely Library plus 1 other. *Books:* 327,172 (physical), 39,448 (digital/electronic); *Serial titles:* 56,176 (digital/electronic); *Databases:* 110. Weekly public service hours: 104; students can reserve study rooms.

STUDENT LIFE

Housing options: on-campus residence required for freshman year; coed, special housing for students with disabilities. Campus housing is university owned. Freshman applicants given priority for college housing.

Activities and organizations: drama/theater group, student-run newspaper, radio and television station, choral group, Sororities, Fraternities, Freshmen Service Leadership Committee, Student Alumni Association, Activities Programming Board, national fraternities, national sororities.

Athletics Member NCAA. All Division I. *Intercollegiate sports:* baseball M(s), basketball M(s)/W(s), cheerleading M(s)/W(s), cross-country running M(s)/W(s), golf M(s)/W(s), soccer M(s)/W(s), softball W(s), tennis M(s)/W(s), track and field M(s)/W(s), volleyball W(s). *Intramural sports:* badminton M(c)/W(c), basketball M/W, bowling M(c)/W(c), cross-country running M(c)/W(c), equestrian sports M(c)/W(c), lacrosse M(c)/W(c), rock climbing M(c)/W(c), skiing (downhill) W(c), soccer M(c)/W(c), tennis M/W, ultimate Frisbee M/W, volleyball M/W, water polo M/W, weight lifting M/W.

Campus security: 24-hour emergency response devices and patrols, late-night transport/escort service, controlled dormitory access.

Student services: health clinic, personal/psychological counseling, women's center, legal services.

COSTS & FINANCIAL AID

Costs (2017–18) *Tuition:* state resident $9360 full-time, $390 per credit hour part-time; nonresident $18,720 full-time, $780 per credit hour part-time. Full-time tuition and fees vary according to course load, program, and reciprocity agreements. Part-time tuition and fees vary according to course load, program, and reciprocity agreements. *Required fees:* $384 full-time, $16 per credit hour part-time. *Room and board:* $9732. Room and board charges vary according to board plan and housing facility.

Payment plan: installment. *Waivers:* children of alumni, senior citizens, and employees or children of employees.

Financial Aid Of all full-time matriculated undergraduates who enrolled in 2016, 7,260 applied for aid, 5,907 were judged to have need, 1,226 had their need fully met. In 2016, 1239 non-need-based awards were made. *Average percent of need met:* 64. *Average financial aid package:* $10,941. *Average need-based loan:* $4506. *Average need-based gift aid:* $5623. *Average non-need-based aid:* $7085. *Average indebtedness upon graduation:* $27,612.

APPLYING

Standardized Tests *Required:* SAT or ACT (for admission).

Options: electronic application.

Application fee: $40.

Required: high school transcript, minimum 2.0 GPA.

Application deadlines: 8/20 (freshmen), 8/1 (transfers).

Notification: continuous (freshmen), continuous (transfers).

CONTACT

Mrs. Melissa Gorbandt, Office of Admissions, Northern Kentucky University, Lucas Administrative Center, 400 Nunn Drive, Highland Heights, KY 41099. *Phone:* 859-572-5220. *Toll-free phone:* 800-637-9948. *Fax:* 859-572-6665. *E-mail:* beanorse@nku.edu.

See previous page for display ad and page 1370 for the College Close-Up.

Simmons College of Kentucky
Louisville, Kentucky
http://www.simmonscollegeky.edu/

CONTACT
Simmons College of Kentucky, 1018 South 7th Street, Louisville, KY 40203.

The Southern Baptist Theological Seminary
Louisville, Kentucky
http://www.sbts.edu/

CONTACT
Dr. Daniel DeWitt, The Southern Baptist Theological Seminary, 2825 Lexington Road, Louisville, KY 40280-0004. *Phone:* 502-897-4011 Ext. 4617.

Spalding University
Louisville, Kentucky
http://www.spalding.edu/

- **Independent** comprehensive, founded 1814, affiliated with Roman Catholic Church
- **Urban** 24-acre campus with easy access to Louisville
- **Endowment** $16.6 million
- **Coed**
- **Moderately difficult** entrance level

FACULTY
Student/faculty ratio: 12:1.

ACADEMICS
Calendar: other. *Degrees:* associate, bachelor's, master's, doctoral, post-master's, and postbachelor's certificates.

Library: Spalding Library. *Books:* 70,000 (physical), 425,638 (digital/electronic); *Serial titles:* 102 (physical), 100,000 (digital/electronic); *Databases:* 70. Students can reserve study rooms.

STUDENT LIFE
Housing options: coed, special housing for students with disabilities. Campus housing is university owned.

Activities and organizations: student-run radio station, choral group, Egan Service Learning Program, Student Occupational Therapy Association, Spalding University Nursing Students, Campus Activities Board, Best Buddies.

Athletics Member NCAA. All Division III.

Campus security: 24-hour emergency response devices and patrols, late-night transport/escort service, controlled dormitory access.

Student services: personal/psychological counseling.

COSTS & FINANCIAL AID

Costs (2017–18) *Comprehensive fee:* $31,900 includes full-time tuition ($24,000) and room and board ($7900). Full-time tuition and fees vary according to course load, degree level, and program. Part-time tuition: $800 per credit hour. Part-time tuition and fees vary according to course load, degree level, and program. *College room only:* $4800. Room and board charges vary according to board plan.

Financial Aid *Average percent of need met:* 75. *Average financial aid package:* $11,500.

APPLYING

Standardized Tests *Required:* SAT or ACT (for admission).

Options: electronic application, early admission, deferred entrance.

Application fee: $20.

Required: high school transcript, minimum 2.5 GPA. *Required for some:* essay or personal statement. *Recommended:* interview.

CONTACT

Mr. Matt Elder, Director, Undergraduate Admissions, Spalding University, 845 South Third Street, Louisville, KY 40203. *Phone:* 502-873-4177. *Toll-free phone:* 800-896-8941. *Fax:* 502-992-2418. *E-mail:* melder@spalding.edu.

Spencerian College

Louisville, Kentucky

http://www.spencerian.edu/

- **Proprietary** primarily 2-year, founded 1892
- **Urban** 4-acre campus
- **Coed** 405 undergraduate students, 56% full-time, 84% women, 16% men
- **Minimally difficult** entrance level

UNDERGRAD STUDENTS

226 full-time, 179 part-time. Students come from 5 states and territories; 17% are from out of state; 18% Black or African American, non-Hispanic/Latino; 2% Hispanic/Latino; 1% Asian, non-Hispanic/Latino; 0.3% Native Hawaiian or other Pacific Islander, non-Hispanic/Latino; 0.3% American Indian or Alaska Native, non-Hispanic/Latino; 12% Two or more races, non-Hispanic/Latino; 10% Race/ethnicity unknown; 14% transferred in; 1% live on campus.

Freshmen:

Admission: 103 enrolled.

FACULTY

Student/faculty ratio: 6:1.

ACADEMICS

Calendar: quarters. *Degrees:* certificates, diplomas, associate, and bachelor's.

Special study options: distance learning, internships, summer session for credit.

Computers: Students can access the following: free student e-mail accounts, online (class) grades, online (class) schedules. Campuswide network is available.

Library: Spencerian College Learning Resource Center.

STUDENT LIFE

Housing options: coed. Campus housing is university owned.

Campus security: security on campus during school hours.

COSTS

Costs (2017–18) *Comprehensive fee:* $31,080 includes full-time tuition ($19,800), mandatory fees ($1725), and room and board ($9555). Full-time tuition and fees vary according to class time, degree level, and program. Part-time tuition: $395 per credit hour. Part-time tuition and fees vary according to class time, degree level, and program. *Required fees:* $60 per course part-time. *College room only:* $6435. Room and board charges vary according to housing facility. *Waivers:* children of alumni and employees or children of employees.

APPLYING

Application fee: $50.

Required: high school transcript. *Required for some:* essay or personal statement, interview, specific selective admission criteria for some medical programs.

Notification: continuous (freshmen), continuous (transfers).

CONTACT

Spencerian College, 4000 Dupont Circle, Louisville, KY 40207. *Phone:* 502-447-1000 Ext. 7808. *Toll-free phone:* 800-264-1799.

Sullivan College of Technology and Design

Louisville, Kentucky

http://www.sctd.edu/

CONTACT

Ms. Heather Wilson, Director of Admissions, Sullivan College of Technology and Design, 3901 Atkinson Square Drive, Louisville, KY 40218. *Phone:* 502-456-6509 Ext. 8220. *Toll-free phone:* 800-884-6528. *Fax:* 502-456-2341. *E-mail:* hwilson@sctd.edu.

Sullivan University

Louisville, Kentucky

http://www.sullivan.edu/

- **Proprietary** comprehensive, founded 1962, part of The Sullivan University System, Inc.
- **Suburban** 15-acre campus
- **Coed** 2,600 undergraduate students, 51% full-time, 61% women, 39% men
- **Minimally difficult** entrance level, 80% of applicants were admitted

UNDERGRAD STUDENTS

1,324 full-time, 1,276 part-time. Students come from 35 states and territories; 27 other countries; 21% are from out of state; 17% Black or African American, non-Hispanic/Latino; 0.1% Hispanic/Latino; 2% Asian, non-Hispanic/Latino; 0.2% Native Hawaiian or other Pacific Islander, non-Hispanic/Latino; 0.5% American Indian or Alaska Native, non-Hispanic/Latino; 9% Two or more races, non-Hispanic/Latino; 20% Race/ethnicity unknown; 0.3% international; 9% live on campus.

Freshmen:

Admission: 1,232 applied, 990 admitted, 467 enrolled. *Test scores:* SAT evidence-based reading and writing scores over 500: 78%; SAT math scores over 500: 100%; ACT scores over 18: 63%; SAT evidence-based reading and writing scores over 600: 22%; ACT scores over 24: 16%.

FACULTY

Total: 266, 45% full-time.

Student/faculty ratio: 19:1.

ACADEMICS

Calendar: quarters. *Degrees:* certificates, diplomas, associate, bachelor's, master's, doctoral, and postbachelor's certificates.

Special study options: academic remediation for entering students, accelerated degree program, adult/continuing education programs, cooperative education, distance learning, double majors, independent study, internships, part-time degree program, services for LD students, student-designed majors.

Computers: 93 computers/terminals are available on campus for general student use. Students can access the following: campus intranet, computer help desk, free student e-mail accounts, online (class) grades, online (class) registration, online (class) schedules. Campuswide network is available. 100% of college-owned or -operated housing units are wired for high-speed Internet access. Wireless service is available via entire campus.

Library: Sullivan University Library and Learning Resource Center. *Books:* 30,229 (physical), 67,284 (digital/electronic); *Serial titles:* 29 (physical), 133,343 (digital/electronic); *Databases:* 170. Weekly public service hours: 86.

STUDENT LIFE

Housing options: coed, men-only, women-only, special housing for students with disabilities. Campus housing is university owned. Freshman campus housing is guaranteed.

Activities and organizations: Student Activities Committee, Student Veterans Association, Sullivan Christian Fellowship, Chess Club, Phi Beta Lambda.

Athletics *Intramural sports:* basketball M/W, bowling M/W, sand volleyball M/W, soccer M/W, softball M/W, ultimate Frisbee M/W, volleyball M/W, weight lifting M/W.

Campus security: 24-hour patrols, late-night transport/escort service, controlled dormitory access.

Student services: personal/psychological counseling.

FINANCIAL AID

Financial Aid Of all full-time matriculated undergraduates who enrolled in 2002, 6,028 applied for aid, 5,247 were judged to have need. 31 Federal Work-Study jobs (averaging $2065). In 2002, 374 non-need-based awards were made. *Average non-need-based aid:* $2000. *Average indebtedness upon graduation:* $15,000.

APPLYING

Standardized Tests *Recommended:* SAT or ACT (for admission).

Options: electronic application, deferred entrance.

Application fee: $30.

Required: high school transcript, interview. *Required for some:* essay or personal statement, criminal background check and no felony convictions.

Application deadlines: rolling (freshmen), rolling (transfers).

Notification: continuous (freshmen), continuous (transfers).

CONTACT

Ms. Heather Cunningham, Senior Director of Admissions, Sullivan University, 3101 Bardstown Road, Louisville, KY 40205. *Phone:* 502-456-6505. *Toll-free phone:* 800-844-1354. *Fax:* 502-456-0040. *E-mail:* admissions@sullivan.edu.

Thomas More College
Crestview Hills, Kentucky
http://www.thomasmore.edu/

- **Independent Roman Catholic** comprehensive, founded 1921
- **Suburban** 100-acre campus with easy access to Cincinnati
- **Endowment** $20.7 million
- **Coed**
- **Moderately difficult** entrance level

FACULTY

Student/faculty ratio: 16:1.

ACADEMICS

Calendar: semesters. *Degrees:* certificates, associate, bachelor's, and master's.

Library: Thomas More College Library plus 1 other. *Books:* 87,667 (physical), 3,056 (digital/electronic); *Serial titles:* 329 (physical); *Databases:* 65. Weekly public service hours: 76.

STUDENT LIFE

Housing options: on-campus residence required through sophomore year; men-only, women-only, special housing for students with disabilities. Campus housing is university owned. Freshman campus housing is guaranteed.

Activities and organizations: drama/theater group, choral group, marching band, Student Government Association, Student Activities Board, More Ministry, Outdoors Adventure Club, Education Club, national fraternities, national sororities.

Athletics Member NCAA. All Division III.

Campus security: 24-hour emergency response devices and patrols, late-night transport/escort service, controlled dormitory access.

Student services: health clinic, personal/psychological counseling.

COSTS & FINANCIAL AID

Costs (2017–18) *One-time required fee:* $125. *Comprehensive fee:* $37,862 includes full-time tuition ($28,850), mandatory fees ($1420), and room and board ($7592). Part-time tuition: $635 per credit hour. *Required fees:* $71 per credit hour part-time. *College room only:* $4200. Room and board charges vary according to board plan and housing facility.

Financial Aid Of all full-time matriculated undergraduates who enrolled in 2017, 1,175 applied for aid, 1,066 were judged to have need, 244 had

their need fully met. 134 Federal Work-Study jobs (averaging $1016). 241 state and other part-time jobs (averaging $1150). In 2017, 220 non-need-based awards were made. *Average percent of need met:* 68. *Average financial aid package:* $20,806. *Average need-based loan:* $3672. *Average need-based gift aid:* $16,765. *Average non-need-based aid:* $14,643. *Average indebtedness upon graduation:* $32,908.

APPLYING

Standardized Tests *Required:* SAT or ACT (for admission).

Options: electronic application, deferred entrance.

Application fee: $25.

Required: high school transcript, minimum 2.5 GPA.

CONTACT

Justin Vogel, Director of Admissions, Thomas More College, 333 Thomas More Parkway, Crestview Hills, KY 41017-3495. *Phone:* 859-344-3307. *Toll-free phone:* 800-825-4557. *Fax:* 859-344-3444. *E-mail:* admissions@thomasmore.edu.

Transylvania University
Lexington, Kentucky
http://www.transy.edu/

- **Independent** 4-year, founded 1780, affiliated with Christian Church (Disciples of Christ)
- **Urban** 40-acre campus with easy access to Cincinnati, Louisville
- **Endowment** $179.2 million
- **Coed** 963 undergraduate students, 100% full-time, 60% women, 40% men
- **Very difficult** entrance level, 95% of applicants were admitted

UNDERGRAD STUDENTS

959 full-time, 4 part-time. Students come from 30 states and territories; 7 other countries; 22% are from out of state; 4% Black or African American, non-Hispanic/Latino; 5% Hispanic/Latino; 1% Asian, non-Hispanic/Latino; 0.1% American Indian or Alaska Native, non-Hispanic/Latino; 4% Two or more races, non-Hispanic/Latino; 4% Race/ethnicity unknown; 3% international; 1% transferred in; 74% live on campus.

Freshmen:

Admission: 1,567 applied, 1,496 admitted, 281 enrolled. *Average high school GPA:* 3.7. *Test scores:* SAT evidence-based reading and writing scores over 500: 97%; SAT math scores over 500: 96%; ACT scores over 18: 100%; SAT evidence-based reading and writing scores over 600: 82%; SAT math scores over 600: 63%; ACT scores over 24: 87%; SAT evidence-based reading and writing scores over 700: 26%; SAT math scores over 700: 19%; ACT scores over 30: 32%.

Retention: 82% of full-time freshmen returned.

FACULTY

Total: 103, 80% full-time, 86% with terminal degrees.

Student/faculty ratio: 11:1.

ACADEMICS

Calendar: 4-4-1. *Degree:* bachelor's.

Special study options: advanced placement credit, double majors, independent study, internships, off-campus study, part-time degree program, services for LD students, student-designed majors, study abroad, summer session for credit. *ROTC:* Army (c), Air Force (c).

Unusual degree programs: 3-2 engineering with University of Kentucky, Vanderbilt University.

Computers: 90 computers/terminals are available on campus for general student use. Students can access the following: campus intranet, computer help desk, free student e-mail accounts, online (class) grades, online (class) registration, online (class) schedules. Campuswide network is available. 100% of college-owned or -operated housing units are wired for high-speed Internet access. Wireless service is available via entire campus.

Library: J. Douglas Gay Jr./Frances Carrick Thomas Library. *Books:* 124,199 (physical), 170,342 (digital/electronic); *Serial titles:* 530 (physical), 23,600 (digital/electronic); *Databases:* 70. Weekly public service hours: 102; students can reserve study rooms.

STUDENT LIFE

Housing options: on-campus residence required through junior year; coed, men-only, women-only, special housing for students with disabilities. Campus housing is university owned. Freshman campus housing is guaranteed.

Activities and organizations: drama/theater group, student-run newspaper, radio station, choral group, Student Government Association, Delta Sigma Phi, Phi Mu, Delta Delta Delta, Chi Omega, national fraternities, national sororities.

Athletics Member NCAA. All Division III. *Intercollegiate sports:* baseball M, basketball M/W, cheerleading M/W, cross-country running M/W, equestrian sports M/W, field hockey W, golf M/W, lacrosse M/W, soccer M/W, softball W, swimming and diving M/W, tennis M/W, track and field M/W, volleyball W. *Intramural sports:* badminton M/W, basketball M/W, soccer M/W, softball M/W, table tennis M/W, ultimate Frisbee M/W, volleyball M/W.

Campus security: 24-hour emergency response devices and patrols, late-night transport/escort service, controlled dormitory access.

Student services: health clinic, personal/psychological counseling.

COSTS & FINANCIAL AID

Costs (2018–19) *Comprehensive fee:* $49,210 includes full-time tuition ($37,170), mandatory fees ($1580), and room and board ($10,460). Part-time tuition: $4130 per course. Part-time tuition and fees vary according to course load. *College room only:* $5920. Room and board charges vary according to board plan and housing facility. *Payment plan:* installment. *Waivers:* employees or children of employees.

Financial Aid Of all full-time matriculated undergraduates who enrolled in 2016, 731 applied for aid, 628 were judged to have need, 145 had their need fully met. 310 Federal Work-Study jobs (averaging $1656). 40 state and other part-time jobs (averaging $5641). In 2016, 315 non-need-based awards were made. *Average percent of need met:* 81. *Average financial aid package:* $28,085. *Average need-based loan:* $4284. *Average need-based gift aid:* $24,196. *Average non-need-based aid:* $17,513. *Average indebtedness upon graduation:* $30,514.

APPLYING

Options: electronic application, early admission, early action, deferred entrance.

Required: essay or personal statement, high school transcript, minimum 2.8 GPA, 2 letters of recommendation. *Required for some:* interview. *Recommended:* interview.

Application deadlines: 11/15 (freshmen), rolling (transfers), 11/1 (early action).

Notification: 12/1 (freshmen), 12/1 (early action).

CONTACT

Dr. Holly Sheilley, Vice President for Enrollment and Student Life, Transylvania University, 300 North Broadway, Lexington, KY 40508-1797. *Phone:* 859-233-8242. *Toll-free phone:* 800-872-6798. *Fax:* 859-281-3649. *E-mail:* admissions@transy.edu.

Union College

Barbourville, Kentucky

http://www.unionky.edu/

- **Independent United Methodist** comprehensive, founded 1879
- **Small-town** 100-acre campus
- **Coed**
- **Moderately difficult** entrance level

FACULTY

Student/faculty ratio: 12:1.

ACADEMICS

Calendar: semesters. *Degrees:* bachelor's, master's, post-master's, and postbachelor's certificates.

Library: Weeks-Townsend Memorial Library plus 1 other.

STUDENT LIFE

Housing options: on-campus residence required through sophomore year; men-only, women-only. Campus housing is university owned. Freshman campus housing is guaranteed.

Activities and organizations: drama/theater group, choral group.

Athletics Member NAIA.

Campus security: 24-hour emergency response devices and patrols, late-night transport/escort service, controlled dormitory access.

Student services: health clinic, personal/psychological counseling.

COSTS & FINANCIAL AID

Costs (2017–18) *Comprehensive fee:* $33,480 includes full-time tuition ($24,590), mandatory fees ($1490), and room and board ($7400). Full-time tuition and fees vary according to location and program. Part-time tuition: $345 per credit hour. Part-time tuition and fees vary according to location and program. *College room only:* $3300. Room and board charges vary according to housing facility.

Financial Aid Of all full-time matriculated undergraduates who enrolled in 2015, 625 applied for aid, 586 were judged to have need, 91 had their need fully met. In 2015, 79 non-need-based awards were made. *Average percent of need met:* 69. *Average financial aid package:* $22,057. *Average need-based loan:* $4203. *Average need-based gift aid:* $18,268. *Average non-need-based aid:* $15,481. *Average indebtedness upon graduation:* $32,691.

APPLYING

Standardized Tests *Required:* SAT or ACT (for admission).

Options: electronic application, deferred entrance.

Application fee: $10.

Required: high school transcript, minimum 2.0 GPA. *Required for some:* interview.

CONTACT

Mr. Craig Grooms, Director: Undergraduate Enrollment, Union College, 310 College Street, Barbourville, KY 40906. *Phone:* 606-546-4151 Ext. 1709. *Toll-free phone:* 800-489-8646. *Fax:* 606-546-1667. *E-mail:* cgrooms@unionky.edu.

University of Kentucky

Lexington, Kentucky

http://www.uky.edu/

- **State-supported** university, founded 1865
- **Urban** 813-acre campus with easy access to Cincinnati, Louisville
- **Coed** 22,425 undergraduate students, 92% full-time, 55% women, 45% men
- **Moderately difficult** entrance level, 96% of applicants were admitted

UNDERGRAD STUDENTS

20,657 full-time, 1,768 part-time. Students come from 54 states and territories; 77 other countries; 31% are from out of state; 8% Black or African American, non-Hispanic/Latino; 5% Hispanic/Latino; 3% Asian, non-Hispanic/Latino; 0.1% Native Hawaiian or other Pacific Islander, non-Hispanic/Latino; 0.2% American Indian or Alaska Native, non-Hispanic/Latino; 4% Two or more races, non-Hispanic/Latino; 3% Race/ethnicity unknown; 2% international; 4% transferred in; 33% live on campus.

Freshmen:

Admission: 18,925 applied, 18,125 admitted, 4,855 enrolled. *Average high school GPA:* 3.7. *Test scores:* SAT evidence-based reading and writing scores over 500: 78%; SAT math scores over 500: 74%; ACT scores over 18: 98%; SAT evidence-based reading and writing scores over 600: 28%; SAT math scores over 600: 36%; ACT scores over 24: 65%; SAT evidence-based reading and writing scores over 700: 11%; SAT math scores over 700: 17%; ACT scores over 30: 20%.

Retention: 83% of full-time freshmen returned.

ACADEMICS

Calendar: semesters. *Degrees:* certificates, bachelor's, master's, doctoral, post-master's, and postbachelor's certificates.

Special study options: academic remediation for entering students, accelerated degree program, adult/continuing education programs, advanced placement credit, cooperative education, distance learning, double majors, English as a second language, honors programs, independent study, internships, off-campus study, part-time degree program, services for LD students, student-designed majors, study abroad, summer session for credit. *ROTC:* Army (b), Air Force (b).

Unusual degree programs: 3-2 business administration.

Computers: 730 computers/terminals are available on campus for general student use. Students can access the following: campus intranet, computer help desk, free student e-mail accounts, online (class) registration, online (class) schedules. Campuswide network is available. 100% of college-owned or -operated housing units are wired for high-speed Internet access. Wireless service is available via entire campus.

Library: William T. Young Library plus 10 others. Study areas open 24 hours, 5–7 days a week; students can reserve study rooms.

STUDENT LIFE

Housing options: coed, men-only. Campus housing is university owned, leased by the school and is provided by a third party. Freshman applicants given priority for college housing.

Activities and organizations: drama/theater group, student-run newspaper, radio and television station, choral group, marching band, Student Activities Board, Student Government Association, Campus Progressive Coalition, Ski and Snowboard Club, Society of Women Engineers, national fraternities, national sororities.

Athletics Member NCAA. All Division I except football (Division I-A). *Intercollegiate sports:* baseball M(s), basketball M(s)/W(s), cross-country running M(s)/W(s), golf M(s)/W(s), gymnastics W(s), riflery M(s)/W(s), soccer M(s)/W(s), softball W(s), swimming and diving M(s)/W(s), tennis M(s)/W(s), track and field M(s)/W(s), volleyball W(s). *Intramural sports:* archery M/W, badminton M/W, basketball M/W, fencing M/W, football M/W, golf M/W, ice hockey M, lacrosse M, rugby M, soccer M/W, softball M/W, swimming and diving M/W, table tennis M/W, tennis M/W, track and field M/W, volleyball M/W.

Campus security: 24-hour emergency response devices and patrols, late-night transport/escort service, controlled dormitory access.

Student services: health clinic, personal/psychological counseling, women's center, legal services.

COSTS & FINANCIAL AID

Costs (2017–18) *Tuition:* state resident $11,772 full-time, $477 per credit hour part-time; nonresident $27,856 full-time, $1145 per credit hour part-time. Full-time tuition and fees vary according to location, program, reciprocity agreements, and student level. Part-time tuition and fees vary according to course load, location, program, reciprocity agreements, and student level. *Required fees:* $1362 full-time, $43 per credit hour part-time. *Room and board:* $12,184. Room and board charges vary according to board plan and housing facility. *Payment plan:* installment. *Waivers:* employees or children of employees.

Financial Aid Of all full-time matriculated undergraduates who enrolled in 2016, 13,213 applied for aid, 10,489 were judged to have need, 1,876 had their need fully met. In 2016, 5318 non-need-based awards were made. *Average percent of need met:* 54. *Average financial aid package:* $12,392. *Average need-based loan:* $4502. *Average need-based gift aid:* $5664. *Average non-need-based aid:* $9475. *Average indebtedness upon graduation:* $42,090.

APPLYING

Standardized Tests *Required:* SAT or ACT (for admission).

Options: electronic application, early admission, early action, deferred entrance.

Application fee: $50.

Required: essay or personal statement, high school transcript, minimum 2.0 GPA, 1 letter of recommendation.

Application deadlines: 2/15 (freshmen), rolling (transfers), 12/1 (early action).

Notification: continuous until 5/1 (freshmen), continuous until 5/1 (out-of-state freshmen), continuous (transfers), rolling (early action).

CONTACT

Scott McDonald, University of Kentucky, 100 W.D. Funkhouser Building, Lexington, KY 40506-0054. *Phone:* 859-257-2000. *Toll-free phone:* 866-900-GO-UK. *Fax:* 859-257-3823. *E-mail:* admission@uky.edu.

University of Louisville

Louisville, Kentucky

http://www.louisville.edu/

- **State-supported** university, founded 1798
- **Urban** 640-acre campus with easy access to Louisville
- **Endowment** $719.0 million
- **Coed** 15,547 undergraduate students, 77% full-time, 51% women, 49% men
- **Moderately difficult** entrance level, 73% of applicants were admitted

UNDERGRAD STUDENTS

12,025 full-time, 3,522 part-time. Students come from 53 states and territories; 94 other countries; 17% are from out of state; 11% Black or African American, non-Hispanic/Latino; 5% Hispanic/Latino; 4% Asian, non-Hispanic/Latino; 0.1% American Indian or Alaska Native, non-Hispanic/Latino; 5% Two or more races, non-Hispanic/Latino; 0.1% Race/ethnicity unknown; 1% international; 6% transferred in; 34% live on campus.

Freshmen:

Admission: 10,165 applied, 7,377 admitted, 2,796 enrolled. *Average high school GPA:* 3.6. *Test scores:* SAT evidence-based reading and writing scores over 500: 60%; SAT math scores over 500: 73%; ACT scores over 18: 99%; SAT evidence-based reading and writing scores over 600: 28%; SAT math scores over 600: 27%; ACT scores over 24: 61%; SAT evidence-based reading and writing scores over 700: 13%; SAT math scores over 700: 6%; ACT scores over 30: 19%.

Retention: 81% of full-time freshmen returned.

FACULTY

Total: 1,336, 70% full-time, 72% with terminal degrees.

Student/faculty ratio: 15:1.

ACADEMICS

Calendar: semesters. *Degrees:* certificates, associate, bachelor's, master's, doctoral, post-master's, and postbachelor's certificates.

Special study options: academic remediation for entering students, accelerated degree program, adult/continuing education programs, advanced placement credit, cooperative education, distance learning, double majors, English as a second language, honors programs, independent study, internships, off-campus study, part-time degree program, services for LD students, study abroad, summer session for credit. *ROTC:* Army (b), Air Force (b).

Unusual degree programs: 3-2 engineering.

Computers: 400 computers/terminals are available on campus for general student use. Students can access the following: computer help desk, free student e-mail accounts, online (class) grades, online (class) registration, online (class) schedules. Campuswide network is available. 100% of college-owned or -operated housing units are wired for high-speed Internet access. Wireless service is available via entire campus.

Library: William F. Ekstrom Library plus 6 others. *Books:* 1.6 million (physical), 367,856 (digital/electronic); *Serial titles:* 2,158 (physical), 90,689 (digital/electronic); *Databases:* 345. Weekly public service hours: 97; study areas open 24 hours, 5–7 days a week; students can reserve study rooms.

STUDENT LIFE

Housing options: on-campus residence required for freshman year; coed, men-only, women-only, special housing for students with disabilities. Campus housing is university owned and leased by the school. Freshman campus housing is guaranteed.

Activities and organizations: drama/theater group, student-run newspaper, choral group, marching band, Baptist Campus Ministry, Society of Porter Scholars, Association of Black Students, Common Ground, Raise Red Dance Marathon, national fraternities, national sororities.

Athletics Member NCAA. All Division I except football (Division I-A). *Intercollegiate sports:* baseball M(s), basketball M(s)/W(s), cheerleading M(s)/W(s), cross-country running M(s)/W(s), field hockey W(s), golf M(s)/W(s), lacrosse W(s), rowing W(s), soccer M(s)/W(s), softball W(s), swimming and diving M(s)/W(s), tennis M(s)/W(s), track and field M(s)/W(s), volleyball W(s). *Intramural sports:* badminton M/W, basketball M/W, bowling M/W, cross-country running M/W, equestrian sports W(c), fencing M/W, football M/W, golf M/W, ice hockey M, lacrosse M(c)/W(c), racquetball M/W, rugby M(c), soccer M/W, softball

W, swimming and diving M/W, table tennis M/W, tennis M/W, track and field M/W, ultimate Frisbee M/W, volleyball M/W.

Campus security: 24-hour emergency response devices and patrols, late-night transport/escort service, controlled dormitory access, alert notification system.

Student services: health clinic, personal/psychological counseling, women's center.

COSTS & FINANCIAL AID
Costs (2017–18) *Tuition:* state resident $11,068 full-time, $462 per credit hour part-time; nonresident $26,090 full-time, $1088 per credit hour part-time. Full-time tuition and fees vary according to reciprocity agreements. Part-time tuition and fees vary according to course load and reciprocity agreements. *Required fees:* $196 full-time. *Room and board:* $8700; room only: $5970. Room and board charges vary according to board plan and housing facility. *Payment plan:* installment. *Waivers:* senior citizens and employees or children of employees.

Financial Aid Of all full-time matriculated undergraduates who enrolled in 2017, 9,001 applied for aid, 7,418 were judged to have need, 1,385 had their need fully met. 355 Federal Work-Study jobs (averaging $3682). In 2017, 2264 non-need-based awards were made. *Average percent of need met:* 60. *Average financial aid package:* $12,382. *Average need-based loan:* $4206. *Average need-based gift aid:* $9548. *Average non-need-based aid:* $6750. *Average indebtedness upon graduation:* $23,556.

APPLYING
Standardized Tests *Required for some:* SAT or ACT (for admission), TOEFL for students whose primary language is not English.

Options: electronic application, deferred entrance.

Application fee: $50.

Required: high school transcript, minimum 2.5 GPA.

Application deadlines: rolling (freshmen), rolling (transfers).

Notification: continuous (transfers).

CONTACT
Ms. Jenny L. Sawyer, Executive Director of Admissions, University of Louisville, 2301 South Third Street, Houchens Room 150, Louisville, KY 40292-0001. *Phone:* 502-852-6531. *Toll-free phone:* 800-334-8635. *Fax:* 502-852-4776. *E-mail:* admitme@louisville.edu.

University of Pikeville
Pikeville, Kentucky
http://www.upike.edu/
- **Independent** comprehensive, founded 1889, affiliated with Presbyterian Church (U.S.A.)
- **Small-town** 25-acre campus
- **Endowment** $15.4 million
- **Coed** 1,599 undergraduate students, 66% full-time, 53% women, 44% men
- **Noncompetitive** entrance level, 100% of applicants were admitted

UNDERGRAD STUDENTS
1,049 full-time, 510 part-time. Students come from 29 states and territories; 13 other countries; 20% are from out of state; 6% Black or African American, non-Hispanic/Latino; 0.8% Hispanic/Latino; 0.8% Asian, non-Hispanic/Latino; 0.1% Native Hawaiian or other Pacific Islander, non-Hispanic/Latino; 0.8% American Indian or Alaska Native, non-Hispanic/Latino; 2% international; 7% transferred in; 50% live on campus.

Freshmen:
Admission: 2,299 applied, 2,299 admitted, 279 enrolled. *Average high school GPA:* 3.2. *Test scores:* SAT evidence-based reading and writing scores over 500: 40%; SAT math scores over 500: 44%; ACT scores over 18: 78%; SAT evidence-based reading and writing scores over 600: 4%; SAT math scores over 600: 4%; ACT scores over 24: 24%; ACT scores over 30: 2%.

Retention: 57% of full-time freshmen returned.

FACULTY
Total: 105, 62% full-time, 47% with terminal degrees.
Student/faculty ratio: 14:1.

ACADEMICS
Calendar: semesters. *Degrees:* associate, bachelor's, master's, and doctoral.

Special study options: academic remediation for entering students, advanced placement credit, distance learning, double majors, English as a second language, internships, part-time degree program, services for LD students, student-designed majors, study abroad, summer session for credit. *ROTC:* Army (b).

Computers: 308 computers/terminals are available on campus for general student use. Students can access the following: computer help desk, free student e-mail accounts, online (class) grades, online (class) schedules. Campuswide network is available. 100% of college-owned or -operated housing units are wired for high-speed Internet access. Wireless service is available via entire campus.

Library: Allara Library plus 2 others. *Books:* 73,924 (physical), 214,499 (digital/electronic); *Serial titles:* 1,437 (physical), 88,386 (digital/electronic); *Databases:* 73. Weekly public service hours: 105; students can reserve study rooms.

STUDENT LIFE
Housing options: coed, men-only, women-only. Campus housing is university owned.

Activities and organizations: drama/theater group, student-run newspaper, television station, choral group, Student Government, Phi Beta Lambda, Lambda Sigma, Concert Choir, Student Nurses at UPIKE.

Athletics Member NAIA. *Intercollegiate sports:* archery M(s)/W(s), baseball M(s), basketball M(s)/W(s), bowling M(s)/W(s), cheerleading M(s)/W(s), cross-country running M(s)/W(s), football M(s), golf M(s)/W(s), soccer M(s)/W(s), softball W(s), tennis M(s)/W(s), track and field M(s)/W(s), volleyball W(s). *Intramural sports:* basketball M/W, football M.

Campus security: 24-hour patrols, controlled dormitory access.
Student services: health clinic.

COSTS & FINANCIAL AID
Costs (2018–19) *Comprehensive fee:* $28,750 includes full-time tuition ($20,800), mandatory fees ($150), and room and board ($7800). Full-time tuition and fees vary according to course load. Part-time tuition: $867 per semester hour. Part-time tuition and fees vary according to course load. *Room and board:* Room and board charges vary according to housing facility. *Payment plan:* installment. *Waivers:* senior citizens and employees or children of employees.

Financial Aid Of all full-time matriculated undergraduates who enrolled in 2017, 1,043 applied for aid, 1,035 were judged to have need, 612 had their need fully met. 255 Federal Work-Study jobs (averaging $1852). *Average percent of need met:* 90. *Average financial aid package:* $20,102. *Average need-based loan:* $4255. *Average need-based gift aid:* $17,433. *Average indebtedness upon graduation:* $23,876.

APPLYING
Standardized Tests *Required:* SAT or ACT (for admission).
Options: electronic application, deferred entrance.
Required: high school transcript.
Application deadlines: 8/15 (freshmen), 8/15 (transfers).
Notification: continuous (freshmen), continuous (transfers).

CONTACT
Mr. John Yancey, Director of Admissions, University of Pikeville, 147 Sycamore Street, Pikeville, KY 41501. *Phone:* 606-218-5251. *Toll-free phone:* 866-232-7700. *Fax:* 606-218-5255. *E-mail:* wewantyou@pc.edu.

University of the Cumberlands
Williamsburg, Kentucky
http://www.ucumberlands.edu/
- **Independent Kentucky Baptist** university, founded 1889
- **Rural** 150-acre campus with easy access to Knoxville
- **Coed**
- **Moderately difficult** entrance level

FACULTY
Student/faculty ratio: 15:1.

ACADEMICS

Calendar: semesters. *Degrees:* associate, bachelor's, master's, doctoral, post-master's, and postbachelor's certificates.

Library: Norma Perkins Hagan Memorial Library plus 1 other. *Books:* 127,545 (physical), 325,906 (digital/electronic); *Serial titles:* 428 (physical), 63,756 (digital/electronic); *Databases:* 83. Weekly public service hours: 79.

STUDENT LIFE

Housing options: on-campus residence required through senior year; men-only, women-only. Campus housing is university owned. Freshman campus housing is guaranteed.

Activities and organizations: drama/theater group, student-run newspaper, radio and television station, choral group, marching band, Campus Activity Board, Baptist Campus Ministries, Mountain Outreach, Appalachian Ministries, Student Government Association.

Athletics Member NAIA.

Campus security: 24-hour emergency response devices and patrols, student patrols, late-night transport/escort service.

Student services: health clinic, personal/psychological counseling.

COSTS & FINANCIAL AID

Costs (2017–18) *Comprehensive fee:* $32,000 includes full-time tuition ($22,640), mandatory fees ($360), and room and board ($9000). Part-time tuition: $720 per credit hour. Part-time tuition and fees vary according to course load. *Required fees:* $90 per term part-time.

Financial Aid Of all full-time matriculated undergraduates who enrolled in 2015, 1,529 applied for aid, 1,447 were judged to have need, 253 had their need fully met. 830 Federal Work-Study jobs (averaging $1939). 11 state and other part-time jobs (averaging $2095). In 2015, 179 non-need-based awards were made. *Average percent of need met:* 76. *Average financial aid package:* $19,977. *Average need-based loan:* $3737. *Average need-based gift aid:* $16,231. *Average non-need-based aid:* $10,469. *Average indebtedness upon graduation:* $25,198.

APPLYING

Standardized Tests *Required:* SAT or ACT (for admission).

Options: electronic application, deferred entrance.

Required: high school transcript, minimum 2.0 GPA.

CONTACT

Mrs. Erica Harris, Director of Admissions, University of the Cumberlands, 6178 College Station Drive, Williamsburg, KY 40769. *Phone:* 606-539-4241. *Toll-free phone:* 800-343-1609. *Fax:* 606-539-4303. *E-mail:* admiss@ucumberlands.edu.

Western Kentucky University

Bowling Green, Kentucky

http://www.wku.edu/

- **State-supported** comprehensive, founded 1906
- **Suburban** 235-acre campus with easy access to Nashville
- **Endowment** $152.5 million
- **Coed** 17,656 undergraduate students, 73% full-time, 59% women, 41% men
- **Minimally difficult** entrance level, 95% of applicants were admitted

UNDERGRAD STUDENTS

12,919 full-time, 4,737 part-time. Students come from 41 states and territories; 59 other countries; 21% are from out of state; 8% Black or African American, non-Hispanic/Latino; 3% Hispanic/Latino; 2% Asian, non-Hispanic/Latino; 0.1% Native Hawaiian or other Pacific Islander, non-Hispanic/Latino; 0.3% American Indian or Alaska Native, non-Hispanic/Latino; 3% Two or more races, non-Hispanic/Latino; 1% Race/ethnicity unknown; 4% international; 6% transferred in; 33% live on campus.

Freshmen:

Admission: 9,804 applied, 9,358 admitted, 3,116 enrolled. *Average high school GPA:* 3.3. *Test scores:* SAT evidence-based reading and writing scores over 500: 75%; SAT math scores over 500: 69%; ACT scores over 18: 85%; SAT evidence-based reading and writing scores over 600: 27%; SAT math scores over 600: 18%; ACT scores over 24: 43%; SAT evidence-based reading and writing scores over 700: 2%; SAT math scores over 700: 2%; ACT scores over 30: 10%.

Retention: 70% of full-time freshmen returned.

FACULTY

Total: 1,192, 63% full-time, 59% with terminal degrees.

Student/faculty ratio: 18:1.

ACADEMICS

Calendar: semesters. *Degrees:* certificates, associate, bachelor's, master's, doctoral, post-master's, and postbachelor's certificates.

Special study options: academic remediation for entering students, accelerated degree program, adult/continuing education programs, advanced placement credit, cooperative education, distance learning, double majors, English as a second language, freshman honors college, honors programs, independent study, internships, off-campus study, part-time degree program, services for LD students, student-designed majors, study abroad, summer session for credit. *ROTC:* Army (b), Air Force (c).

Unusual degree programs: 3-2 physics, applied sciences, engineering.

Computers: 350 computers/terminals are available on campus for general student use. Students can access the following: campus intranet, computer help desk, free student e-mail accounts, online (class) grades, online (class) registration, online (class) schedules. Campuswide network is available. 100% of college-owned or -operated housing units are wired for high-speed Internet access. Wireless service is available via entire campus.

Library: Helm-Cravens Library plus 2 others. *Books:* 801,946 (physical), 89,239 (digital/electronic); *Serial titles:* 540 (physical), 2,460 (digital/electronic); *Databases:* 246. Weekly public service hours: 107; students can reserve study rooms.

STUDENT LIFE

Housing options: on-campus residence required through sophomore year; coed, men-only, women-only. Campus housing is university owned. Freshman applicants given priority for college housing.

Activities and organizations: drama/theater group, student-run newspaper, radio and television station, choral group, marching band, Student Government Association, Campus Activities Board, Campus Crusade for Christ, Campus Ministries, Residence Hall Association, national fraternities, national sororities.

Athletics Member NCAA. All Division I except football (Division I-A). *Intercollegiate sports:* baseball M(s), basketball M(s)/W(s), cross-country running M(s)/W(s), golf M(s)/W(s), soccer W, softball W(s), tennis W(s), track and field M(s)/W(s), volleyball W(s). *Intramural sports:* badminton M(c)/W(c), basketball M/W, fencing M(c)/W(c), football M/W, golf M/W, lacrosse M(c)/W(c), racquetball M/W, rugby M(c)/W(c), soccer M/W, softball M/W, tennis M/W, triathlon M(c)/W(c), ultimate Frisbee M/W, volleyball M/W.

Campus security: 24-hour emergency response devices and patrols, student patrols, late-night transport/escort service, controlled dormitory access.

Student services: health clinic, personal/psychological counseling, women's center, legal services.

COSTS & FINANCIAL AID

Costs (2017–18) *Tuition:* state resident $10,202 full-time, $425 per credit hour part-time; nonresident $25,512 full-time, $1063 per credit hour part-time. Full-time tuition and fees vary according to reciprocity agreements. Part-time tuition and fees vary according to reciprocity agreements. *Room and board:* $8350; room only: $4600. Room and board charges vary according to board plan and housing facility. *Payment plan:* installment. *Waivers:* senior citizens and employees or children of employees.

Financial Aid Of all full-time matriculated undergraduates who enrolled in 2016, 10,216 applied for aid, 8,114 were judged to have need, 1,864 had their need fully met. 795 Federal Work-Study jobs (averaging $1754). 1,911 state and other part-time jobs (averaging $2502). In 2016, 1726 non-need-based awards were made. *Average percent of need met:* 23. *Average financial aid package:* $14,550. *Average need-based loan:* $3864. *Average need-based gift aid:* $5169. *Average non-need-based aid:* $6561. *Average indebtedness upon graduation:* $27,654.

APPLYING

Standardized Tests *Required:* SAT or ACT (for admission).

Options: electronic application, deferred entrance.

Application fee: $45.

Required: high school transcript, minimum ACT composite score of 20 or greater, SAT combined score of 1020 or greater (940 or greater for tests taken prior to March 2016), unweighted high school GPA of 2.50 or higher, or minimum on Composite Admission Index score.

Application deadlines: 8/1 (freshmen), 8/1 (transfers).

Notification: continuous (freshmen), continuous (transfers).

CONTACT
Western Kentucky University, 1906 College Heights Boulevard, Bowling Green, KY 42101. *Phone:* 270-7452551. *Toll-free phone:* 800-495-8463.

LOUISIANA

 ## Centenary College of Louisiana
Shreveport, Louisiana
http://www.centenary.edu/

- **Independent United Methodist** comprehensive, founded 1825
- **Urban** 65-acre campus with easy access to Shreveport
- **Coed** 533 undergraduate students, 98% full-time, 56% women, 44% men
- **Moderately difficult** entrance level, 62% of applicants were admitted

UNDERGRAD STUDENTS
524 full-time, 9 part-time. 40% are from out of state; 16% Black or African American, non-Hispanic/Latino; 10% Hispanic/Latino; 3% Asian, non-Hispanic/Latino; 0.2% Native Hawaiian or other Pacific Islander, non-Hispanic/Latino; 0.9% American Indian or Alaska Native, non-Hispanic/Latino; 5% Two or more races, non-Hispanic/Latino; 2% international; 4% transferred in.

Freshmen:
Admission: 848 applied, 524 admitted, 173 enrolled. *Average high school GPA:* 3.6. *Test scores:* SAT evidence-based reading and writing scores over 500: 86%; SAT math scores over 500: 91%; ACT scores over 18: 100%; SAT evidence-based reading and writing scores over 600: 33%; SAT math scores over 600: 29%; ACT scores over 24: 58%; SAT evidence-based reading and writing scores over 700: 4%; SAT math scores over 700: 2%; ACT scores over 30: 15%.

Retention: 78% of full-time freshmen returned.

FACULTY
Total: 80, 69% full-time, 76% with terminal degrees.
Student/faculty ratio: 9:1.

ACADEMICS
Calendar: 4-4-1. *Degrees:* bachelor's and master's.

Special study options: advanced placement credit, double majors, honors programs, independent study, internships, off-campus study, part-time degree program, services for LD students, student-designed majors, study abroad, summer session for credit.

Unusual degree programs: 3-2 engineering; speech pathology.

Computers: Students can access the following: free student e-mail accounts, online (class) grades, online (class) registration, online (class) schedules. Campuswide network is available. Wireless service is available via classrooms, computer labs, dorm rooms, libraries, student centers.
Library: Magale Library plus 1 other. *Books:* 151,971 (physical), 155,940 (digital/electronic); *Serial titles:* 9,794 (physical), 255,780 (digital/electronic); *Databases:* 323. Weekly public service hours: 82; students can reserve study rooms.

STUDENT LIFE
Housing options: on-campus residence required through senior year; coed. Campus housing is university owned. Freshman campus housing is guaranteed.

Activities and organizations: drama/theater group, student-run newspaper, radio station, choral group, Intramural sports, Residence Life (Centenary Activities Board), Fellowship of Christian Athletes, Christian Leadership Center, Media Group, national fraternities, national sororities.

Athletics Member NCAA. All Division III. *Intercollegiate sports:* baseball M, basketball M/W, golf M/W, gymnastics W, lacrosse M(c), soccer M/W, softball W, swimming and diving M/W, tennis M/W,

triathlon W, volleyball W. *Intramural sports:* basketball M/W, football M/W, soccer M/W, softball M/W, volleyball M/W.

Campus security: 24-hour emergency response devices and patrols, late-night transport/escort service, controlled dormitory access.

Student services: health clinic, personal/psychological counseling.

COSTS & FINANCIAL AID
Costs (2018–19) *One-time required fee:* $250. *Comprehensive fee:* $49,980 includes full-time tuition ($36,580) and room and board ($13,400). Full-time tuition and fees vary according to course load and degree level. Part-time tuition: $1524 per credit hour. Part-time tuition and fees vary according to course load and degree level. *Room and board:* Room and board charges vary according to board plan, housing facility, and student level. *Payment plan:* installment. *Waivers:* employees or children of employees.

Financial Aid Of all full-time matriculated undergraduates who enrolled in 2017, 463 applied for aid, 407 were judged to have need, 92 had their need fully met. 167 Federal Work-Study jobs (averaging $2285). 53 state and other part-time jobs (averaging $1582). In 2017, 109 non-need-based awards were made. *Average percent of need met:* 75. *Average financial aid package:* $30,528. *Average need-based loan:* $4501. *Average need-based gift aid:* $26,816. *Average non-need-based aid:* $22,400. *Average indebtedness upon graduation:* $32,900.

APPLYING
Standardized Tests *Required:* SAT or ACT (for admission).

Options: electronic application, early admission, early action, deferred entrance.

Required: essay or personal statement, high school transcript. *Required for some:* interview. *Recommended:* letters of recommendation, interview.

Application deadlines: rolling (freshmen), rolling (transfers), 12/15 (early action).

Notification: continuous (freshmen), continuous (transfers).

CONTACT
Ms. Lauren Carlton Hawkins, Associate Director of Admission, Recruitment, Centenary College of Louisiana, Office of Admission, 2911 Centenary Boulevard, Shreveport, LA 71104. *Phone:* 318-869-5131. *Toll-free phone:* 800-234-4448. *Fax:* 318-869-5005. *E-mail:* lcarlton@centenary.edu.

Dillard University
New Orleans, Louisiana
http://www.dillard.edu/

CONTACT
Ms. Monica White, Director for Recruitment, Admissions and Programming, Dillard University, 2601 Gentilly Boulevard, New Orleans, LA 70122-3097. *Phone:* 504-816-4374. *Toll-free phone:* 800-216-8094. *Fax:* 504-816-4895. *E-mail:* acyprian@dillard.edu.

Franciscan Missionaries of Our Lady University
Baton Rouge, Louisiana
http://www.franu.edu/

- **Independent Roman Catholic** comprehensive, founded 1990
- **Urban** 5-acre campus with easy access to New Orleans
- **Coed** 1,185 undergraduate students, 48% full-time, 86% women, 14% men
- **Minimally difficult** entrance level, 48% of applicants were admitted

UNDERGRAD STUDENTS
566 full-time, 619 part-time. 10% are from out of state; 18% Black or African American, non-Hispanic/Latino; 9% Hispanic/Latino; 3% Asian, non-Hispanic/Latino; 0.4% Native Hawaiian or other Pacific Islander, non-Hispanic/Latino; 0.8% American Indian or Alaska Native, non-Hispanic/Latino; 6% Race/ethnicity unknown.

Freshmen:
Admission: 291 applied, 140 admitted, 95 enrolled.
Retention: 75% of full-time freshmen returned.

ACADEMICS

Calendar: semesters. *Degrees:* certificates, associate, bachelor's, master's, doctoral, and postbachelor's certificates.

Special study options: advanced placement credit, distance learning, off-campus study, part-time degree program, services for LD students, summer session for credit. *ROTC:* Army (c), Air Force (c).

Unusual degree programs: 3-2 biology/physician's assistant.

Computers: 150 computers/terminals are available on campus for general student use. Students can access the following: campus intranet, computer help desk, free student e-mail accounts, online (class) grades, online (class) registration, online (class) schedules. Campuswide network is available. Wireless service is available via entire campus.
Library: Students can reserve study rooms.

STUDENT LIFE

Housing options: college housing not available.

Activities and organizations: Student Government Association, Cultural Arts Association, Christian Fellowship Association, Mathematics/Science Association.

Campus security: 24-hour patrols.

Student services: health clinic, personal/psychological counseling.

COSTS & FINANCIAL AID

Costs (2018–19) *Tuition:* $12,161 full-time, $507 per credit hour part-time. Full-time tuition and fees vary according to course load, degree level, and program. Part-time tuition and fees vary according to course load, degree level, and program. *Required fees:* $1126 full-time. *Payment plan:* installment.

Financial Aid Of all full-time matriculated undergraduates who enrolled in 2008, 684 applied for aid, 546 were judged to have need, 10 had their need fully met. *Average financial aid package:* $5175. *Average need-based loan:* $3664. *Average need-based gift aid:* $2486. *Average indebtedness upon graduation:* $12,019.

APPLYING

Standardized Tests *Required:* SAT or ACT (for admission).

Options: electronic application, early admission, deferred entrance.

Application fee: $35.

Required: high school transcript, minimum 2.5 GPA.

Application deadlines: 8/1 (freshmen), rolling (transfers).

Notification: continuous (freshmen).

CONTACT

Franciscan Missionaries of Our Lady University, LA. *Phone:* 225-768-1718. *E-mail:* admissions@franu.edu.

Grambling State University
Grambling, Louisiana
http://www.gram.edu/

- **State-supported** university, founded 1901, part of University of Louisiana System
- **Small-town** 590-acre campus with easy access to Shreveport
- **Endowment** $6.8 million
- **Coed** 4,089 undergraduate students, 91% full-time, 58% women, 42% men
- **Noncompetitive** entrance level, 45% of applicants were admitted

UNDERGRAD STUDENTS

3,732 full-time, 357 part-time. Students come from 42 states and territories; 25 other countries; 33% are from out of state; 89% Black or African American, non-Hispanic/Latino; 1% Hispanic/Latino; 0.1% Asian, non-Hispanic/Latino; 0.0% Native Hawaiian or other Pacific Islander, non-Hispanic/Latino; 0.2% American Indian or Alaska Native, non-Hispanic/Latino; 2% Two or more races, non-Hispanic/Latino; 0.6% Race/ethnicity unknown; 5% international; 6% transferred in.

Freshmen:

Admission: 6,340 applied, 2,862 admitted, 922 enrolled. *Average high school GPA:* 2.8. *Test scores:* SAT evidence-based reading and writing scores over 500: 33%; SAT math scores over 500: 20%; ACT scores over 18: 59%; SAT math scores over 600: 1%; ACT scores over 24: 5%.

Retention: 68% of full-time freshmen returned.

FACULTY

Total: 176, 91% full-time, 64% with terminal degrees.

Student/faculty ratio: 26:1.

ACADEMICS

Calendar: semesters. *Degrees:* bachelor's, master's, doctoral, and post-master's certificates.

Special study options: academic remediation for entering students, adult/continuing education programs, advanced placement credit, cooperative education, distance learning, double majors, honors programs, internships, off-campus study, part-time degree program, services for LD students, summer session for credit. *ROTC:* Army (b), Air Force (c).

Computers: 500 computers/terminals and 500 ports are available on campus for general student use. Students can access the following: campus intranet, computer help desk, free student e-mail accounts, online (class) grades, online (class) registration, online (class) schedules. Campuswide network is available. 100% of college-owned or -operated housing units are wired for high-speed Internet access. Wireless service is available via entire campus.

Library: A. C. Lewis Memorial Library. *Books:* 127,508 (physical), 205,483 (digital/electronic); *Serial titles:* 835 (physical), 51,728 (digital/electronic); *Databases:* 101. Weekly public service hours: 49; students can reserve study rooms.

STUDENT LIFE

Housing options: on-campus residence required through sophomore year; coed, men-only, women-only, special housing for students with disabilities. Campus housing is university owned and leased by the school. Freshman applicants given priority for college housing.

Activities and organizations: drama/theater group, student-run newspaper, radio and television station, choral group, marching band, Tiger Marching Band, Black Dynasty Modeling Troupe, Academic and Professional Clubs, sororities, fraternities, national fraternities, national sororities.

Athletics Member NCAA. All Division I except football (Division I-AA). *Intercollegiate sports:* baseball M(s), basketball M(s)/W(s), bowling W(s), cross-country running M/W, soccer W, softball W(s), tennis W(s), track and field M(s)/W(s), volleyball W(s). *Intramural sports:* badminton M(c)/W(c), basketball M/W, bowling M(c)/W(c), racquetball M(c)/W(c), soccer M(c)/W(c), softball W, table tennis M/W, tennis M(c)/W(c), volleyball M(c)/W(c), weight lifting M/W.

Campus security: 24-hour emergency response devices and patrols, student patrols, late-night transport/escort service, controlled dormitory access.

Student services: health clinic, personal/psychological counseling.

COSTS & FINANCIAL AID

Costs (2018–19) *Tuition:* state resident $5140 full-time; nonresident $14,163 full-time. Full-time tuition and fees vary according to course load, degree level, and student level. Part-time tuition and fees vary according to course load, degree level, and student level. *Required fees:* $2295 full-time. *Room and board:* $10,054; room only: $6500. Room and board charges vary according to housing facility. *Payment plans:* installment, deferred payment. *Waivers:* children of alumni, senior citizens, and employees or children of employees.

Financial Aid Of all full-time matriculated undergraduates who enrolled in 2017, 3,460 applied for aid, 3,013 were judged to have need. In 2017, 39 non-need-based awards were made. *Average financial aid package:* $4045. *Average need-based loan:* $4068. *Average need-based gift aid:* $4579. *Average non-need-based aid:* $2477. *Average indebtedness upon graduation:* $47,162. *Financial aid deadline:* 6/1.

APPLYING

Standardized Tests *Required:* SAT or ACT (for admission).

Options: electronic application, early admission.

Application fee: $20.

Required: high school transcript, minimum 2.0 GPA, 19 units from Required Core 4 Curriculum including no more than one developmental course.

Application deadlines: 8/15 (freshmen), 7/15 (transfers).

Notification: 4/1 (freshmen), continuous until 6/15 (transfers).

CONTACT
DeVaria Hudson, Director of Admissions and Recruitment, Grambling State University, GSU Box 4200, Grambling, LA 71245. *Phone:* 318-274-6100. *Toll-free phone:* 800-569-4714. *Fax:* 318-274-3292. *E-mail:* hudsond@gram.edu.

Herzing University
Kenner, Louisiana
http://www.herzing.edu/new-orleans

CONTACT
Herzing University, 2500 Williams Boulevard, Kenner, LA 70062. *Toll-free phone:* 800-596-0724.

Louisiana College
Pineville, Louisiana
http://www.lacollege.edu/

- **Independent Southern Baptist** comprehensive, founded 1906
- **Small-town** 81-acre campus
- **Coed** 989 undergraduate students, 88% full-time, 46% women, 54% men
- **Moderately difficult** entrance level, 67% of applicants were admitted

UNDERGRAD STUDENTS
872 full-time, 117 part-time. Students come from 21 states and territories; 19 other countries; 10% are from out of state; 25% Black or African American, non-Hispanic/Latino; 3% Hispanic/Latino; 1% Asian, non-Hispanic/Latino; 0.1% Native Hawaiian or other Pacific Islander, non-Hispanic/Latino; 1% American Indian or Alaska Native, non-Hispanic/Latino; 2% Two or more races, non-Hispanic/Latino; 0.5% Race/ethnicity unknown; 3% international; 9% transferred in; 55% live on campus.

Freshmen:
Admission: 530 applied, 357 admitted, 306 enrolled. *Average high school GPA:* 3.2. *Test scores:* SAT evidence-based reading and writing scores over 500: 83%; SAT math scores over 500: 67%; ACT scores over 18: 92%; SAT evidence-based reading and writing scores over 600: 33%; SAT math scores over 600: 33%; ACT scores over 24: 25%; ACT scores over 30: 2%.
Retention: 55% of full-time freshmen returned.

FACULTY
Total: 104, 69% full-time, 61% with terminal degrees.
Student/faculty ratio: 12:1.

ACADEMICS
Calendar: semesters. *Degrees:* certificates, associate, bachelor's, and master's.
Special study options: academic remediation for entering students, accelerated degree program, adult/continuing education programs, advanced placement credit, distance learning, double majors, English as a second language, honors programs, independent study, internships, off-campus study, part-time degree program, services for LD students, student-designed majors, summer session for credit.
Unusual degree programs: 3-2 engineering with Louisiana Tech University.
Computers: 323 computers/terminals are available on campus for general student use. Students can access the following: campus intranet, computer help desk, free student e-mail accounts, online (class) grades, online (class) registration, online (class) schedules. Campuswide network is available. 100% of college-owned or -operated housing units are wired for high-speed Internet access. Wireless service is available via entire campus.
Library: Richard W. Norton Memorial Library. *Books:* 124,328 (physical), 281,138 (digital/electronic); *Serial titles:* 369 (physical), 28,876 (digital/electronic); *Databases:* 112. Weekly public service hours: 70; students can reserve study rooms.

STUDENT LIFE
Housing options: on-campus residence required through sophomore year; coed, men-only, women-only. Campus housing is university owned. Freshman campus housing is guaranteed.

Activities and organizations: drama/theater group, student-run radio and television station, choral group, marching band, Baptist Collegiate Ministry, Delta Xi Omega, Student Government Association, Union Board, Lambda Chi Beta.

Athletics Member NCAA. All Division III. *Intercollegiate sports:* baseball M, basketball M/W, cross-country running M/W, football M, golf M/W, soccer M/W, softball W, tennis M/W, track and field M/W, volleyball W. *Intramural sports:* badminton M/W, basketball M/W, cheerleading M/W, football M/W, soccer M/W, softball M/W, table tennis M/W, ultimate Frisbee M/W, volleyball M/W.

Campus security: 24-hour emergency response devices and patrols, student patrols, late-night transport/escort service, controlled dormitory access.

Student services: health clinic, personal/psychological counseling.

COSTS & FINANCIAL AID
Costs (2018–19) *Comprehensive fee:* $21,274 includes full-time tuition ($16,000) and room and board ($5274). Full-time tuition and fees vary according to program. Part-time tuition: $500 per credit hour. Part-time tuition and fees vary according to course load and program. *College room only:* $2132. Room and board charges vary according to board plan and housing facility. *Payment plan:* installment. *Waivers:* senior citizens and employees or children of employees.
Financial Aid *Average indebtedness upon graduation:* $22,969.

APPLYING
Standardized Tests *Required:* SAT or ACT (for admission). *Recommended:* ACT (for admission).
Options: electronic application.
Application fee: $25.
Required: high school transcript, minimum 2.0 GPA. *Required for some:* essay or personal statement.
Application deadlines: rolling (freshmen), rolling (out-of-state freshmen), rolling (transfers).
Notification: continuous (freshmen), continuous (out-of-state freshmen), continuous (transfers).

CONTACT
Ms. Renee Melder, Assistant Director of Admissions, Louisiana College, LC Box 566, Pineville, LA 71359. *Phone:* 318-487-7439. *Toll-free phone:* 800-487-1906. *E-mail:* admissions@lacollege.edu.

Louisiana Culinary Institute
Baton Rouge, Louisiana
http://www.lci.edu/

CONTACT
Louisiana Culinary Institute, 10550 Airline Highway, Baton Rouge, LA 70816. *Toll-free phone:* 877-533-3198.

Louisiana State University and Agricultural & Mechanical College
Baton Rouge, Louisiana
http://www.lsu.edu/

- **State-supported** university, founded 1860, part of Louisiana State University System
- **Urban** 2000-acre campus with easy access to New Orleans
- **Endowment** $436.8 million
- **Coed** 25,444 undergraduate students, 87% full-time, 52% women, 48% men
- **Moderately difficult** entrance level, 74% of applicants were admitted

UNDERGRAD STUDENTS
22,060 full-time, 3,384 part-time. 17% are from out of state; 12% Black or African American, non-Hispanic/Latino; 6% Hispanic/Latino; 4% Asian, non-Hispanic/Latino; 0.1% Native Hawaiian or other Pacific Islander, non-Hispanic/Latino; 0.4% American Indian or Alaska Native, non-Hispanic/Latino; 2% Two or more races, non-Hispanic/Latino; 0.9% Race/ethnicity unknown; 2% international; 3% transferred in; 23% live on campus.

Freshmen:

Admission: 17,907 applied, 13,236 admitted, 4,917 enrolled. *Average high school GPA:* 3.4. *Test scores:* SAT evidence-based reading and writing scores over 500: 92%; SAT math scores over 500: 96%; ACT scores over 18: 100%; SAT evidence-based reading and writing scores over 600: 42%; SAT math scores over 600: 46%; ACT scores over 24: 68%; SAT evidence-based reading and writing scores over 700: 8%; SAT math scores over 700: 12%; ACT scores over 30: 19%.

Retention: 83% of full-time freshmen returned.

FACULTY

Total: 1,489, 89% full-time, 83% with terminal degrees.

Student/faculty ratio: 20:1.

ACADEMICS

Calendar: semesters. *Degrees:* certificates, bachelor's, master's, doctoral, post-master's, and postbachelor's certificates.

Special study options: accelerated degree program, adult/continuing education programs, advanced placement credit, cooperative education, distance learning, double majors, English as a second language, freshman honors college, honors programs, independent study, internships, off-campus study, part-time degree program, services for LD students, student-designed majors, study abroad, summer session for credit. *ROTC:* Army (b), Navy (c), Air Force (b).

Computers: 1,180 computers/terminals and 8,300 ports are available on campus for general student use. Students can access the following: computer help desk, free student e-mail accounts, online (class) grades, online (class) registration, online (class) schedules, free software for download, storage, discounts on hardware, virtual computer lab. Campuswide network is available. 100% of college-owned or -operated housing units are wired for high-speed Internet access. Wireless service is available via entire campus.

Library: Troy H. Middleton Library plus 4 others. *Books:* 3.0 million (physical), 583,654 (digital/electronic); *Serial titles:* 633,678 (physical), 332,761 (digital/electronic); *Databases:* 367. Study areas open 24 hours, 5–7 days a week; students can reserve study rooms.

STUDENT LIFE

Housing options: on-campus residence required for freshman year; coed, men-only, women-only, special housing for students with disabilities. Campus housing is university owned. Freshman campus housing is guaranteed.

Activities and organizations: drama/theater group, student-run newspaper, radio and television station, choral group, marching band, intramural athletics, student political organizations, student professional organizations, religious organizations, cultural organizations, national fraternities, national sororities.

Athletics Member NCAA. All Division I except football (Division I-A). *Intercollegiate sports:* baseball M(s), basketball M(s)/W(s), cheerleading M/W, cross-country running M(s)/W(s), golf M(s)/W(s), gymnastics W(s), soccer W(s), softball W(s), swimming and diving M(s)/W(s), tennis M(s)/W(s), track and field M(s)/W(s), volleyball W(s). *Intramural sports:* badminton M/W, baseball M(c), basketball M(c)/W, cross-country running M(c)/W(c), equestrian sports W(c), football M/W, golf M/W, ice hockey M(c)/W(c), lacrosse M(c)/W(c), racquetball M/W, rock climbing M/W, rowing M(c)/W(c), rugby M(c)/W(c), sand volleyball M/W, soccer M(c)/W(c), softball M/W, table tennis M(c)/W(c), tennis M(c)/W(c), triathlon M(c)/W(c), ultimate Frisbee M(c)/W(c), volleyball M(c)/W(c), water polo M(c)/W(c), weight lifting M(c)/W(c).

Campus security: 24-hour emergency response devices and patrols, late-night transport/escort service, controlled dormitory access, self-defense education, crime prevention programs.

Student services: health clinic, personal/psychological counseling, women's center, legal services.

COSTS & FINANCIAL AID

Costs (2017–18) *Tuition:* state resident $8038 full-time; nonresident $24,715 full-time. Full-time tuition and fees vary according to course load. Part-time tuition and fees vary according to course load. *Required fees:* $3336 full-time. *Room and board:* $11,750; room only: $7740. Room and board charges vary according to board plan and housing facility. *Payment plan:* deferred payment. *Waivers:* employees or children of employees.

Financial Aid Of all full-time matriculated undergraduates who enrolled in 2016, 15,768 applied for aid, 11,734 were judged to have need, 2,144 had their need fully met. 1,035 Federal Work-Study jobs (averaging $2000). 3,995 state and other part-time jobs (averaging $2300). In 2016, 4245 non-need-based awards were made. *Average percent of need met:* 63. *Average financial aid package:* $15,278. *Average need-based loan:* $6845. *Average need-based gift aid:* $10,104. *Average non-need-based aid:* $4063. *Average indebtedness upon graduation:* $24,933.

APPLYING

Standardized Tests *Required:* SAT or ACT (for admission).

Options: electronic application, early admission, deferred entrance.

Application fee: $50.

Required: high school transcript, minimum 3.0 GPA. *Required for some:* essay or personal statement, letters of recommendation.

Application deadlines: 4/15 (freshmen), 4/15 (transfers).

Notification: continuous (freshmen), continuous (transfers).

CONTACT

Mr. Emmett Brown, Interim Associate Director, Undergraduate Admissions, Louisiana State University and Agricultural & Mechanical College, 1146 Pleasant Hall, Baton Rouge, LA 70803. *Phone:* 225-578-1175. *Fax:* 225-578-4433. *E-mail:* cbrow63@lsu.edu.

Louisiana State University at Alexandria

Alexandria, Louisiana

http://www.lsua.edu/

- **State-supported** 4-year, founded 1960, part of Louisiana State University System
- **Rural** 3114-acre campus
- **Endowment** $15.3 million
- **Coed**
- **Moderately difficult** entrance level

FACULTY

Student/faculty ratio: 18:1.

ACADEMICS

Calendar: semesters. *Degrees:* certificates, associate, and bachelor's.

Library: James C. Bolton Library. *Books:* 123,993 (physical), 224,774 (digital/electronic); *Serial titles:* 505 (physical), 501,390 (digital/electronic); *Databases:* 85. Students can reserve study rooms.

STUDENT LIFE

Housing options: on-campus residence required for freshman year; coed, special housing for students with disabilities. Campus housing is university owned. Freshman applicants given priority for college housing.

Activities and organizations: drama/theater group, student-run newspaper, choral group, Student Government Association.

Athletics Member NAIA.

Campus security: 24-hour emergency response devices and patrols.

Student services: health clinic, personal/psychological counseling.

COSTS & FINANCIAL AID

Costs (2017–18) *Tuition:* state resident $6158 full-time, $204 per credit hour part-time; nonresident $13,150 full-time, $303 per credit hour part-time. *Required fees:* $4927 full-time, $47 per credit hour part-time, $15 per term part-time. *Room and board:* $7770; room only: $4320. Room and board charges vary according to board plan and housing facility.

Financial Aid Of all full-time matriculated undergraduates who enrolled in 2016, 53 Federal Work-Study jobs (averaging $1226). 76 state and other part-time jobs (averaging $1261).

APPLYING

Standardized Tests *Required:* SAT or ACT (for admission).

Options: electronic application, early admission.

Application fee: $20.

Required: high school transcript. *Required for some:* minimum 2.0 GPA.

CONTACT

Ms. Shelly Kieffer, Director of Enrollment Management, Louisiana State University at Alexandria, 8100 Highway 71 South, Alexandria, LA

71302-9121. *Phone:* 318-473-6424. *Toll-free phone:* 888-473-6417. *Fax:* 318-473-6418. *E-mail:* admissions@lsua.edu.

Louisiana State University Health Sciences Center

New Orleans, Louisiana
http://www.lsuhsc.edu/

- **State-supported** university, founded 1931, part of Louisiana State University System
- **Urban** 80-acre campus with easy access to New Orleans
- **Endowment** $120.1 million
- **Coed** 921 undergraduate students, 76% full-time, 87% women, 13% men

UNDERGRAD STUDENTS
696 full-time, 225 part-time. Students come from 19 states and territories; 10 other countries; 6% are from out of state; 10% Black or African American, non-Hispanic/Latino; 6% Hispanic/Latino; 5% Asian, non-Hispanic/Latino; 0.4% American Indian or Alaska Native, non-Hispanic/Latino; 2% Two or more races, non-Hispanic/Latino; 1% Race/ethnicity unknown; 0.1% international; 25% transferred in; 10% live on campus.

FACULTY
Total: 897, 76% full-time, 86% with terminal degrees.
Student/faculty ratio: 4:1.

ACADEMICS
Calendar: varies by academic program. *Degrees:* associate, bachelor's, master's, and doctoral.

Special study options: academic remediation for entering students, accelerated degree program, adult/continuing education programs, advanced placement credit, cooperative education, distance learning, double majors, independent study, internships, services for LD students, summer session for credit. *ROTC:* Army (c), Navy (c), Air Force (c).

Computers: 120 computers/terminals and 3,800 ports are available on campus for general student use. Students can access the following: campus intranet, computer help desk, free student e-mail accounts, online (class) grades, online (class) registration, online (class) schedules. Campuswide network is available. 100% of college-owned or -operated housing units are wired for high-speed Internet access. Wireless service is available via entire campus.
Library: John P. Ische Library plus 2 others. *Books:* 61,199 (physical); *Serial titles:* 4,968 (physical), 3,068 (digital/electronic); *Databases:* 204. Weekly public service hours: 97; study areas open 24 hours, 5–7 days a week.

STUDENT LIFE
Housing options: coed, special housing for students with disabilities. Campus housing is university owned.

Campus security: 24-hour emergency response devices and patrols, late-night transport/escort service, controlled dormitory access.

Student services: health clinic, personal/psychological counseling.

COSTS
Costs (2018–19) *Tuition:* state resident $5612 full-time, $357 per semester hour part-time; nonresident $12,394 full-time, $424 per semester hour part-time. Full-time tuition and fees vary according to degree level, program, and reciprocity agreements. Part-time tuition and fees vary according to course load, degree level, program, and reciprocity agreements. *Required fees:* $2696 full-time, $158 per semester hour part-time. *Room only:* $5598. Room and board charges vary according to housing facility.

APPLYING
Options: electronic application.
Application fee: $50.
Notification: 8/1 (transfers).

CONTACT
Louisiana State University Health Sciences Center, 433 Bolivar Street, New Orleans, LA 70112-2223.

Louisiana State University in Shreveport

Shreveport, Louisiana
http://www.lsus.edu/

CONTACT
Louisiana State University in Shreveport, 1 University Place, Shreveport, LA 71115-2399. *Phone:* 318-797-5063. *Toll-free phone:* 800-229-5957.

Louisiana Tech University

Ruston, Louisiana
http://www.latech.edu/

- **State-supported** university, founded 1894, part of University of Louisiana System
- **Small-town** 247-acre campus
- **Coed**
- **Moderately difficult** entrance level

FACULTY
Student/faculty ratio: 26:1.

ACADEMICS
Calendar: quarters. *Degrees:* associate, bachelor's, master's, doctoral, post-master's, and postbachelor's certificates.
Library: Prescott Memorial Library.

STUDENT LIFE
Housing options: on-campus residence required through sophomore year; men-only, women-only, special housing for students with disabilities. Campus housing is university owned and is provided by a third party.

Activities and organizations: drama/theater group, student-run newspaper, radio and television station, choral group, marching band, Student Government Association, Association of Women's Studies, Union Board, national fraternities, national sororities.

Athletics Member NCAA. All Division I except football (Division I-A).

Campus security: 24-hour emergency response devices and patrols, student patrols, late-night transport/escort service, controlled dormitory access.

Student services: health clinic, personal/psychological counseling, legal services.

COSTS & FINANCIAL AID
Costs (2017–18) *Tuition:* state resident $6400 full-time, $402 per credit hour part-time; nonresident $15,313 full-time, $773 per credit hour part-time. Full-time tuition and fees vary according to course load, location, and program. Part-time tuition and fees vary according to course load, location, and program. *Required fees:* $3245 full-time. *Room and board:* $6360; room only: $2910. Room and board charges vary according to board plan and housing facility. *Payment plans:* installment, deferred payment.

Financial Aid Of all full-time matriculated undergraduates who enrolled in 2016, 6,346 applied for aid, 4,443 were judged to have need, 851 had their need fully met. 327 Federal Work-Study jobs (averaging $1969). 1,251 state and other part-time jobs (averaging $2083). In 2016, 1726 non-need-based awards were made. *Average percent of need met:* 80. *Average financial aid package:* $11,358. *Average need-based loan:* $3668. *Average need-based gift aid:* $9484. *Average non-need-based aid:* $4502. *Average indebtedness upon graduation:* $22,262.

APPLYING
Standardized Tests *Required:* SAT or ACT (for admission). *Recommended:* ACT (for admission).

Options: early admission.

Application fee: $20.

Required: high school transcript, minimum 2.2 GPA.

CONTACT
Mrs. Jan B. Albritton, Director of Admissions, Louisiana Tech University, PO Box 3168, Ruston, LA 71272. *Phone:* 318-257-3036. *Toll-free phone:* 800-528-3241. *Fax:* 318-257-2499. *E-mail:* bulldog@latech.edu.

Loyola University New Orleans

New Orleans, Louisiana

http://www.loyno.edu/

- **Independent Roman Catholic (Jesuit)** comprehensive, founded 1912
- **Suburban** 22-acre campus with easy access to New Orleans
- **Endowment** $234.0 million
- **Coed** 2,602 undergraduate students, 94% full-time, 62% women, 38% men
- **Moderately difficult** entrance level, 69% of applicants were admitted

UNDERGRAD STUDENTS

2,446 full-time, 156 part-time. Students come from 48 states and territories; 42 other countries; 57% are from out of state; 14% Black or African American, non-Hispanic/Latino; 16% Hispanic/Latino; 3% Asian, non-Hispanic/Latino; 0.1% Native Hawaiian or other Pacific Islander, non-Hispanic/Latino; 0.3% American Indian or Alaska Native, non-Hispanic/Latino; 5% Two or more races, non-Hispanic/Latino; 7% Race/ethnicity unknown; 3% international; 3% transferred in; 54% live on campus.

Freshmen:

Admission: 5,112 applied, 3,533 admitted, 803 enrolled. *Average high school GPA:* 3.6. *Test scores:* SAT evidence-based reading and writing scores over 500: 97%; SAT math scores over 500: 83%; ACT scores over 18: 100%; SAT evidence-based reading and writing scores over 600: 55%; SAT math scores over 600: 36%; ACT scores over 24: 65%; SAT evidence-based reading and writing scores over 700: 10%; SAT math scores over 700: 6%; ACT scores over 30: 14%.

Retention: 80% of full-time freshmen returned.

FACULTY

Total: 437, 55% full-time, 70% with terminal degrees.

Student/faculty ratio: 11:1.

ACADEMICS

Calendar: semesters. *Degrees:* bachelor's, master's, doctoral, post-master's, and postbachelor's certificates.

Special study options: accelerated degree program, adult/continuing education programs, advanced placement credit, cooperative education, distance learning, double majors, English as a second language, external degree program, honors programs, independent study, internships, off-campus study, part-time degree program, services for LD students, student-designed majors, study abroad, summer session for credit. *ROTC:* Army (c), Navy (c), Air Force (c).

Unusual degree programs: 3-2 engineering with University of New Orleans, The Catholic University of America.

Computers: 300 computers/terminals and 2,500 ports are available on campus for general student use. Students can access the following: campus intranet, computer help desk, free student e-mail accounts, online (class) grades, online (class) registration, online (class) schedules. Campuswide network is available. 100% of college-owned or -operated housing units are wired for high-speed Internet access. Wireless service is available via entire campus.

Library: Monroe Library plus 1 other. *Books:* 387,652 (physical), 42,637 (digital/electronic); *Serial titles:* 221,718 (physical). Weekly public service hours: 114; students can reserve study rooms.

STUDENT LIFE

Housing options: on-campus residence required through sophomore year; coed, special housing for students with disabilities. Campus housing is university owned. Freshman campus housing is guaranteed.

Activities and organizations: drama/theater group, student-run newspaper, radio station, choral group, Panhellenic Council, Black Student Union, Loyola University Community Action Plan, Quidditch, Interfraternity Council, national fraternities, national sororities.

Athletics Member NAIA. *Intercollegiate sports:* baseball M, basketball M(s)/W(s), cheerleading M(s)/W(s), cross-country running M(s)/W(s), golf M(s)/W(s), swimming and diving M(s)/W(s), table tennis M/W, tennis M(s)/W(s), track and field M(s)/W(s), volleyball W(s). *Intramural sports:* basketball M/W, football M/W, racquetball M/W, soccer M/W, softball M/W, volleyball M/W, weight lifting M/W.

Campus security: 24-hour emergency response devices and patrols, student patrols, late-night transport/escort service, controlled dormitory access, self-defense education, bicycle patrols, closed circuit TV monitors, door alarms, crime prevention programs, card access control.

Student services: health clinic, personal/psychological counseling, women's center.

COSTS & FINANCIAL AID

Costs (2018–19) *One-time required fee:* $250. *Comprehensive fee:* $53,072 includes full-time tuition ($38,126), mandatory fees ($1566), and room and board ($13,380). Full-time tuition and fees vary according to class time, course load, and degree level. Part-time tuition: $1073 per credit hour. Part-time tuition and fees vary according to class time and degree level. *Required fees:* $402 per term part-time. *College room only:* $7430. Room and board charges vary according to board plan and housing facility. *Payment plan:* installment. *Waivers:* senior citizens and employees or children of employees.

Financial Aid Of all full-time matriculated undergraduates who enrolled in 2017, 2,052 applied for aid, 1,819 were judged to have need, 315 had their need fully met. 767 Federal Work-Study jobs (averaging $1600). In 2017, 522 non-need-based awards were made. *Average percent of need met:* 79. *Average financial aid package:* $33,676. *Average need-based loan:* $4402. *Average need-based gift aid:* $29,558. *Average non-need-based aid:* $16,800.

APPLYING

Standardized Tests *Required:* SAT or ACT (for admission).

Options: electronic application, early admission.

Required: essay or personal statement, high school transcript, 1 letter of recommendation. *Required for some:* interview. *Recommended:* interview.

Application deadlines: rolling (freshmen), rolling (transfers).

Notification: continuous (freshmen).

CONTACT

John Head, Vice President for Enrollment Management, Loyola University New Orleans, 6363 St. Charles Avenue, Campus Box 18, New Orleans, LA 70118. *Phone:* 504-865-3240. *Toll-free phone:* 800-4-LOYOLA. *Fax:* 504-865-3383. *E-mail:* johnhead@loyno.edu.

McNeese State University

Lake Charles, Louisiana

http://www.mcneese.edu/

- **State-supported** comprehensive, founded 1939, part of University of Louisiana System
- **Suburban** 766-acre campus
- **Coed** 6,965 undergraduate students, 80% full-time, 60% women, 40% men
- **Moderately difficult** entrance level, 62% of applicants were admitted

UNDERGRAD STUDENTS

5,567 full-time, 1,398 part-time. Students come from 38 states and territories; 68 other countries; 7% are from out of state; 16% Black or African American, non-Hispanic/Latino; 3% Hispanic/Latino; 2% Asian, non-Hispanic/Latino; 0.1% Native Hawaiian or other Pacific Islander, non-Hispanic/Latino; 0.5% American Indian or Alaska Native, non-Hispanic/Latino; 4% Two or more races, non-Hispanic/Latino; 6% international; 5% transferred in.

Freshmen:

Admission: 3,300 applied, 2,054 admitted, 1,322 enrolled. *Average high school GPA:* 3.5.

Retention: 68% of full-time freshmen returned.

FACULTY

Total: 451, 55% full-time, 48% with terminal degrees.

Student/faculty ratio: 21:1.

ACADEMICS

Calendar: semesters. *Degrees:* associate, bachelor's, master's, post-master's, and postbachelor's certificates.

Special study options: academic remediation for entering students, accelerated degree program, advanced placement credit, cooperative education, distance learning, double majors, English as a second language, freshman honors college, honors programs, independent study, internships, off-campus study, part-time degree program, services for LD students, study abroad, summer session for credit.

Computers: Students can access the following: computer help desk, free student e-mail accounts, online (class) grades, online (class) registration, online (class) schedules. Campuswide network is available. 100% of college-owned or -operated housing units are wired for high-speed Internet access. Wireless service is available via entire campus.
Library: Frazar Memorial Library plus 1 other.

STUDENT LIFE
Housing options: coed. Campus housing is university owned and leased by the school.

Activities and organizations: drama/theater group, student-run newspaper, choral group, marching band, Student Government Association, International Students Association, Resident Student Association, national fraternities, national sororities.

Athletics Member NCAA. All Division I except football (Division I-AA). *Intercollegiate sports:* baseball M(s), basketball M(s)/W(s), cross-country running M(s)/W(s), golf M(s)/W(s), soccer W(s), softball W(s), tennis W(s), track and field M(s)/W(s), volleyball W(s). *Intramural sports:* badminton M/W, baseball M, basketball M/W, football M/W, golf M/W, racquetball M/W, soccer M/W, softball W, swimming and diving M/W, table tennis M/W, tennis M/W, ultimate Frisbee M/W, volleyball M/W, water polo M/W, weight lifting M/W.

Campus security: 24-hour emergency response devices and patrols, late-night transport/escort service, controlled dormitory access.

Student services: health clinic, personal/psychological counseling, women's center.

COSTS & FINANCIAL AID
Costs (2017–18) *Tuition:* state resident $6574 full-time; nonresident $11,574 full-time. Full-time tuition and fees vary according to course load. Part-time tuition and fees vary according to course load. *Required fees:* $2427 full-time. *Room and board:* $7314; room only: $4100. Room and board charges vary according to board plan and housing facility. *Payment plan:* installment. *Waivers:* senior citizens and employees or children of employees.

Financial Aid Of all full-time matriculated undergraduates who enrolled in 2014, 4,704 applied for aid, 3,627 were judged to have need, 408 had their need fully met. *Average percent of need met:* 61. *Average financial aid package:* $9508. *Average need-based loan:* $3711. *Average need-based gift aid:* $4838.

APPLYING
Standardized Tests *Required:* SAT or ACT (for admission).
Options: electronic application, early admission, deferred entrance.
Application fee: $20.
Required: high school transcript, minimum 2.0 GPA, Louisiana Board of Regents high school Core 4 curriculum, no more than one developmental course.
Application deadlines: rolling (freshmen), rolling (transfers).
Notification: continuous (freshmen), continuous (transfers).

CONTACT
Ms. Kourtney Istre, Director of Admissions and Recruiting, McNeese State University, Box 91740, Lake Charles, LA 70609. *Phone:* 337-475-5505. *Toll-free phone:* 800-622-3352. *Fax:* 337-475-5978. *E-mail:* kistre@mcneese.edu.

New Orleans Baptist Theological Seminary
New Orleans, Louisiana
http://www.nobts.edu/

CONTACT
Dr. Paul E. Gregoire Jr., Registrar/Director of Admissions, New Orleans Baptist Theological Seminary, 3939 Gentilly Boulevard, New Orleans, LA 70126-4858. *Phone:* 504-282-4455 Ext. 3337. *Toll-free phone:* 800-662-8701.

Nicholls State University
Thibodaux, Louisiana
http://www.nicholls.edu/

CONTACT
Mrs. Becky L. Durocher, Director of Admissions, Nicholls State University, PO Box 2004-NSU, Thibodaux, LA 70310. *Phone:* 985-448-4507. *Toll-free phone:* 877-NICHOLLS. *Fax:* 985-448-4929. *E-mail:* nicholls@nicholls.edu.

Northwestern State University of Louisiana
Natchitoches, Louisiana
http://www.nsula.edu/

- **State-supported** comprehensive, founded 1884, part of University of Louisiana System
- **Small-town** 916-acre campus
- **Endowment** $15.4 million
- **Coed** 9,452 undergraduate students, 58% full-time, 69% women, 31% men
- **Moderately difficult** entrance level, 62% of applicants were admitted

UNDERGRAD STUDENTS
5,471 full-time, 3,981 part-time. Students come from 56 states and territories; 27 other countries; 8% are from out of state; 28% Black or African American, non-Hispanic/Latino; 6% Hispanic/Latino; 0.8% Asian, non-Hispanic/Latino; 0.2% Native Hawaiian or other Pacific Islander, non-Hispanic/Latino; 2% American Indian or Alaska Native, non-Hispanic/Latino; 4% Two or more races, non-Hispanic/Latino; 2% Race/ethnicity unknown; 1% international; 8% transferred in.

Freshmen:
Admission: 5,494 applied, 3,431 admitted, 1,542 enrolled. *Average high school GPA:* 3.3. *Test scores:* SAT evidence-based reading and writing scores over 500: 52%; SAT math scores over 500: 52%; ACT scores over 18: 90%; SAT evidence-based reading and writing scores over 600: 14%; SAT math scores over 600: 17%; ACT scores over 24: 28%; ACT scores over 30: 4%.
Retention: 75% of full-time freshmen returned.

FACULTY
Total: 469, 65% full-time, 48% with terminal degrees.
Student/faculty ratio: 19:1.

ACADEMICS
Calendar: semesters. *Degrees:* associate, bachelor's, master's, doctoral, post-master's, and postbachelor's certificates.

Special study options: adult/continuing education programs, advanced placement credit, cooperative education, distance learning, double majors, freshman honors college, honors programs, independent study, internships, part-time degree program, services for LD students, study abroad, summer session for credit. *ROTC:* Army (b), Air Force (c).

Computers: 1,500 computers/terminals and 1,500 ports are available on campus for general student use. Students can access the following: computer help desk, free student e-mail accounts, online (class) grades, online (class) registration, online (class) schedules. Campuswide network is available. 100% of college-owned or -operated housing units are wired for high-speed Internet access. Wireless service is available via classrooms, computer centers, computer labs, dorm rooms, learning centers, libraries, student centers.
Library: Eugene P. Watson Memorial Library plus 1 other. *Books:* 310,849 (physical), 38,166 (digital/electronic); *Serial titles:* 329 (physical), 230 (digital/electronic); *Databases:* 111. Weekly public service hours: 87; students can reserve study rooms.

STUDENT LIFE
Housing options: coed, special housing for students with disabilities. Campus housing is university owned and is provided by a third party. Freshman applicants given priority for college housing.

Activities and organizations: drama/theater group, student-run newspaper, radio and television station, choral group, marching band, Student Activities Board, Student Government Associate, College Panhellenic Council, national fraternities, national sororities.

Athletics Member NCAA. All Division I except football (Division I-AA). *Intercollegiate sports:* baseball M(s), basketball M(s)/W(s), cheerleading M(s)/W(s), cross-country running M(s)/W(s), soccer W(s), softball W(s), tennis W(s), track and field M(s)/W(s), volleyball W(s). *Intramural sports:* archery M(c)/W(c), badminton M/W, basketball M/W, bowling M/W, crew M(c)/W(c), fencing M(c)/W(c), football M/W, racquetball M/W, softball M/W, swimming and diving M/W, table tennis M/W, tennis M/W, volleyball M/W.

Campus security: 24-hour emergency response devices and patrols, student patrols, late-night transport/escort service, controlled dormitory access.

Student services: health clinic, personal/psychological counseling.

COSTS & FINANCIAL AID
Costs (2017–18) *Tuition:* state resident $5180 full-time; nonresident $15,968 full-time. Full-time tuition and fees vary according to course load and location. Part-time tuition and fees vary according to course load and location. *Required fees:* $3408 full-time. *Room and board:* $9086; room only: $5490. Room and board charges vary according to board plan, housing facility, and location. *Payment plan:* installment. *Waivers:* senior citizens and employees or children of employees.

Financial Aid Of all full-time matriculated undergraduates who enrolled in 2015, 4,388 applied for aid, 3,653 were judged to have need, 391 had their need fully met. In 2015, 337 non-need-based awards were made. *Average percent of need met:* 21. *Average financial aid package:* $13,863. *Average need-based loan:* $6915. *Average need-based gift aid:* $7342. *Average non-need-based aid:* $3962. *Average indebtedness upon graduation:* $41,500.

APPLYING
Standardized Tests *Required:* SAT or ACT (for admission).

Options: electronic application, deferred entrance.

Application fee: $20.

Required: high school transcript, minimum 2.4 GPA, college preparatory curriculum.

Application deadlines: 7/6 (freshmen), 7/6 (transfers).

Notification: continuous (freshmen), continuous (out-of-state freshmen), continuous (transfers).

CONTACT
Ms. Jana Lucky, Director of University Recruiting, Northwestern State University of Louisiana, 175 Sam Sibley Drive, Recruiting Office, Student Services Center, 1st Floor, Natchitoches, LA 71497. *Phone:* 318-357-4503. *Toll-free phone:* 800-327-1903. *Fax:* 318-357-5567. *E-mail:* recruiting@nsula.edu.

Saint Joseph Seminary College
Saint Benedict, Louisiana
http://www.sjasc.edu/

CONTACT
Saint Joseph Seminary College, 75376 River Road, St. Benedict, LA 70457. *Phone:* 985-867-2273. *Fax:* 985-327-1085. *E-mail:* registrar@sjasc.edu.

Southeastern Louisiana University
Hammond, Louisiana
http://www.southeastern.edu/

- **State-supported** comprehensive, founded 1925, part of University of Louisiana System
- **Small-town** 375-acre campus with easy access to New Orleans
- **Endowment** $49.8 million
- **Coed** 13,340 undergraduate students, 67% full-time, 62% women, 38% men
- **Moderately difficult** entrance level, 88% of applicants were admitted

UNDERGRAD STUDENTS
8,998 full-time, 4,342 part-time. Students come from 42 states and territories; 55 other countries; 5% are from out of state; 19% Black or African American, non-Hispanic/Latino; 7% Hispanic/Latino; 1% Asian, non-Hispanic/Latino; 0.1% Native Hawaiian or other Pacific Islander, non-Hispanic/Latino; 0.3% American Indian or Alaska Native, non-Hispanic/Latino; 4% Two or more races, non-Hispanic/Latino; 5% Race/ethnicity unknown; 2% international; 5% transferred in; 21% live on campus.

Freshmen:
Admission: 4,402 applied, 3,892 admitted, 2,736 enrolled. *Average high school GPA:* 3.3. *Test scores:* ACT scores over 18: 97%; ACT scores over 24: 35%; ACT scores over 30: 3%.
Retention: 66% of full-time freshmen returned.

FACULTY
Total: 593, 83% full-time, 61% with terminal degrees.
Student/faculty ratio: 19:1.

ACADEMICS
Calendar: semesters. *Degrees:* associate, bachelor's, master's, doctoral, post-master's, and postbachelor's certificates.

Special study options: academic remediation for entering students, accelerated degree program, adult/continuing education programs, advanced placement credit, distance learning, double majors, English as a second language, honors programs, independent study, internships, off-campus study, part-time degree program, services for LD students, study abroad, summer session for credit. *ROTC:* Army (b).

Computers: 1,031 computers/terminals and 600 ports are available on campus for general student use. Students can access the following: campus intranet, computer help desk, free student e-mail accounts, online (class) grades, online (class) registration, online (class) schedules, campus Webmail, student newspaper, transcripts, bookstore. Campuswide network is available. 100% of college-owned or -operated housing units are wired for high-speed Internet access. Wireless service is available via classrooms, computer centers, computer labs, dorm rooms, learning centers, libraries, student centers.

Library: Linus A. Sims Memorial Library plus 1 other. *Books:* 1.5 million (physical), 368,573 (digital/electronic); *Serial titles:* 768 (physical), 344 (digital/electronic). Students can reserve study rooms.

STUDENT LIFE
Housing options: coed, women-only, special housing for students with disabilities. Campus housing is university owned.

Activities and organizations: drama/theater group, student-run newspaper, radio and television station, choral group, marching band, Student Government Association, Gamma Beta Phi, Black Student Union, NAACP, All Greek Organization, national fraternities, national sororities.

Athletics Member NCAA. All Division I except football (Division I-AA). *Intercollegiate sports:* baseball M(s), basketball M(s)/W(s), cross-country running M(s)/W(s), golf M(s), soccer W(s), softball W(s), tennis W(s), track and field M(s)/W(s), volleyball W(s). *Intramural sports:* baseball M/W, basketball M/W, football M/W, racquetball M/W, rugby M(c), soccer M/W, softball M/W, tennis M/W, volleyball M/W, weight lifting M/W.

Campus security: 24-hour emergency response devices and patrols, student patrols, late-night transport/escort service, controlled dormitory access, video cameras, motorist assistance.

Student services: health clinic, personal/psychological counseling.

COSTS & FINANCIAL AID
Costs (2017–18) *Tuition:* state resident $5777 full-time, $340 per credit hour part-time; nonresident $18,255 full-time, $340 per credit hour part-time. Full-time tuition and fees vary according to course load. Part-time tuition and fees vary according to course load. No tuition increase for student's term of enrollment. *Required fees:* $2376 full-time. *Room and board:* $8340; room only: $4940. Room and board charges vary according to board plan and housing facility. *Payment plan:* installment. *Waivers:* employees or children of employees.

Financial Aid Of all full-time matriculated undergraduates who enrolled in 2016, 7,264 applied for aid, 5,636 were judged to have need, 531 had their need fully met. 168 Federal Work-Study jobs (averaging $1992). 854 state and other part-time jobs (averaging $1907). In 2016, 850 non-need-based awards were made. *Average financial aid package:* $9450. *Average need-based loan:* $3779. *Average need-based gift aid:* $5198. *Average non-need-based aid:* $1561. *Average indebtedness upon graduation:* $20,164.

APPLYING
Standardized Tests *Required:* SAT or ACT (for admission).

Options: electronic application, early admission, deferred entrance.

Application fee: $20.

Required: high school transcript, minimum 2.4 GPA, proof of immunization; college transcripts and statement of good standing required for some.

Application deadlines: 8/1 (freshmen), 8/1 (transfers).

Notification: continuous until 10/15 (freshmen), continuous until 10/15 (transfers).

CONTACT
Southeastern Louisiana University, 548 Ned McGehee Drive, Hammond, LA 70402. *Phone:* 985-549-5629. *Toll-free phone:* 800-222-7358.

Southern University and Agricultural and Mechanical College
Baton Rouge, Louisiana
http://www.subr.edu/

CONTACT
Ms. Velva Thomas, Director of Admissions, Southern University and Agricultural and Mechanical College, PO Box 9901, Baton Rouge, LA 70813. *Phone:* 225-771-2430. *Fax:* 225-771-2500. *E-mail:* velva_thomas@subr.edu.

Southern University at New Orleans
New Orleans, Louisiana
http://www.suno.edu/

CONTACT
Southern University at New Orleans, 6400 Press Drive, New Orleans, LA 70126-1009. *Phone:* 504-286-5033.

Southwest University
Kenner, Louisiana
http://www.southwest.edu/

CONTACT
Admissions Office, Southwest University, 2200 Veterans Memorial Boulevard, Kenner, LA 70062. *Phone:* 504-468-2900. *Toll-free phone:* 800-433-5923. *Fax:* 504-468-3213. *E-mail:* admissions@southwest.edu.

Tulane University
New Orleans, Louisiana
http://www.tulane.edu/

- **Independent** university, founded 1834
- **Urban** 110-acre campus
- **Endowment** $1.6 billion
- **Coed** 6,571 undergraduate students, 100% full-time, 59% women, 41% men
- **Very difficult** entrance level, 21% of applicants were admitted

UNDERGRAD STUDENTS
6,540 full-time, 31 part-time. Students come from 53 states and territories; 55 other countries; 77% are from out of state; 4% Black or African American, non-Hispanic/Latino; 7% Hispanic/Latino; 5% Asian, non-Hispanic/Latino; 0.2% Native Hawaiian or other Pacific Islander, non-Hispanic/Latino; 0.2% American Indian or Alaska Native, non-Hispanic/Latino; 4% Two or more races, non-Hispanic/Latino; 1% Race/ethnicity unknown; 4% international; 1% transferred in; 48% live on campus.

Freshmen:
Admission: 35,622 applied, 7,657 admitted, 1,905 enrolled. *Average high school GPA:* 3.6. *Test scores:* SAT evidence-based reading and writing scores over 500: 98%; SAT math scores over 500: 99%; ACT scores over 18: 100%; SAT evidence-based reading and writing scores over 600: 93%; SAT math scores over 600: 96%; ACT scores over 24: 98%; SAT evidence-based reading and writing scores over 700: 61%; SAT math scores over 700: 59%; ACT scores over 30: 79%.

Retention: 93% of full-time freshmen returned.

FACULTY
Total: 1,188, 65% full-time, 79% with terminal degrees.
Student/faculty ratio: 8:1.

ACADEMICS
Calendar: semesters plus 3 summer sessions. *Degrees:* certificates, bachelor's, master's, doctoral, and postbachelor's certificates.

Special study options: accelerated degree program, adult/continuing education programs, advanced placement credit, cooperative education, distance learning, double majors, English as a second language, freshman honors college, honors programs, independent study, internships, off-campus study, part-time degree program, services for LD students, student-designed majors, study abroad, summer session for credit. *ROTC:* Army (b), Navy (b), Air Force (b).

Unusual degree programs: 3-2 business administration; public health tropical medicine, science and engineering.

Computers: 556 computers/terminals are available on campus for general student use. Students can access the following: campus intranet, computer help desk, free student e-mail accounts, online (class) grades, online (class) registration, online (class) schedules. Campuswide network is available. 100% of college-owned or -operated housing units are wired for high-speed Internet access. Wireless service is available via entire campus.
Library: Howard Tilton Memorial Library plus 8 others. *Books:* 4.6 million (physical); *Serial titles:* 72,300 (physical). Study areas open 24 hours, 5–7 days a week.

STUDENT LIFE
Housing options: on-campus residence required through sophomore year; coed, women-only, special housing for students with disabilities. Campus housing is university owned. Freshman campus housing is guaranteed.

Activities and organizations: drama/theater group, student-run newspaper, radio and television station, choral group, marching band, Community Action Council of Tulane Students (CACTUS), Associated Student Body, Tulane University Campus Programming (TUCP), Association of Club Sports (ACS), National Pan-Hellenic Council, national fraternities, national sororities.

Athletics Member NCAA. All Division I except football (Division I-A). *Intercollegiate sports:* baseball M(s), basketball M(s)/W(s), crew M(c)/W(c), cross-country running M(s)/W(s), golf W(s), gymnastics M(c)/W(c), ice hockey M(c)/W(c), lacrosse M(c)/W(c), rugby M(c), sailing M(c)/W(c), soccer M(c)/W(s), swimming and diving M(c)/W(s), tennis M(s)/W(s), track and field M(c)/W(s), volleyball M(c)/W(s), water polo M(c)/W(c). *Intramural sports:* baseball M(c), cheerleading M(c)/W(c), crew M(c)/W(c), cross-country running M(c), fencing M(c)/W(c), field hockey M(c)/W(c), gymnastics M(c)/W(c), ice hockey M(c), lacrosse M(c)/W(c), racquetball M(c)/W(c), rock climbing M(c)/W(c), rugby M(c), sailing M(c)/W(c), soccer M(c)/W(c), swimming and diving M(c)/W(c), tennis M(c)/W(c), track and field M(c)/W, ultimate Frisbee M(c)/W(c), volleyball M(c)/W(c), water polo M(c)/W(c).

Campus security: 24-hour emergency response devices and patrols, student patrols, late-night transport/escort service, controlled dormitory access, on and off-campus shuttle service, crime prevention programs, lighted pathways.

Student services: health clinic, personal/psychological counseling, women's center, legal services.

COSTS & FINANCIAL AID
Costs (2017–18) *Comprehensive fee:* $67,496 includes full-time tuition ($48,920), mandatory fees ($4040), and room and board ($14,536). *College room only:* $8342. Room and board charges vary according to board plan, housing facility, and student level. *Payment plans:* tuition prepayment, installment. *Waivers:* employees or children of employees.

Financial Aid Of all full-time matriculated undergraduates who enrolled in 2017, 2,894 applied for aid, 2,105 were judged to have need, 1,461 had their need fully met. 1,020 Federal Work-Study jobs (averaging $3772). 130 state and other part-time jobs (averaging $8598). In 2017, 2520 non-need-based awards were made. *Average percent of need met:* 96. *Average financial aid package:* $47,540. *Average need-based loan:* $7766. *Average need-based gift aid:* $34,996. *Average non-need-based aid:* $26,091. *Average indebtedness upon graduation:* $33,717.

APPLYING
Standardized Tests *Required:* SAT or ACT (for admission).

Options: electronic application, early decision, early action, deferred entrance.

Required: essay or personal statement, high school transcript, 1 letter of recommendation.

Application deadlines: 11/15 (freshmen), 11/15 (early action).

Early decision deadline: 11/1 (for plan 1), 1/5 (for plan 2).

Notification: 4/1 (freshmen), 12/15 (early decision plan 1), 1/19 (early decision plan 2), 11/15 (early action).

CONTACT
Satyajit Dattagupta, Vice President for Enrollment Management and Dean of Admissions, Tulane University, Office of Admissions, 210 Gibson Hall, New Orleans, LA 70118. *Phone:* 504-865-5731. *Toll-free phone:* 800-873-9283. *Fax:* 504-862-8715. *E-mail:* undergrad.admission@tulane.edu.

University of Holy Cross

New Orleans, Louisiana
http://www.uhcno.edu/

CONTACT
Donna Kennedy, Director of Admissions and Financial Aid, University of Holy Cross, 4123 Woodland Drive, New Orleans, LA 70131-7399. *Phone:* 504-398-2175. *Toll-free phone:* 800-259-7744. *E-mail:* dkennedy@olhcc.edu.

University of Louisiana at Lafayette

Lafayette, Louisiana
http://www.louisiana.edu/

CONTACT
Mr. Andy Benoit Jr., Assistant Vice President for Enrollment Management and Director of Enrollment Services and Recruitment, University of Louisiana at Lafayette, PO Drawer 41210, Lafayette, LA 70504. *Phone:* 337-482-6473. *Toll-free phone:* 800-752-6553. *Fax:* 337-482-1317. *E-mail:* admissions@louisiana.edu.

University of Louisiana at Monroe

Monroe, Louisiana
http://www.ulm.edu/

- **State-supported** university, founded 1931, part of University of Louisiana System
- **Urban** 238-acre campus
- **Endowment** $50.6 million
- **Coed** 7,948 undergraduate students, 66% full-time, 63% women, 37% men
- **Moderately difficult** entrance level, 72% of applicants were admitted

UNDERGRAD STUDENTS
5,212 full-time, 2,736 part-time. Students come from 45 states and territories; 48 other countries; 9% are from out of state; 23% Black or African American, non-Hispanic/Latino; 2% Hispanic/Latino; 2% Asian, non-Hispanic/Latino; 0.1% Native Hawaiian or other Pacific Islander, non-Hispanic/Latino; 0.4% American Indian or Alaska Native, non-Hispanic/Latino; 3% Two or more races, non-Hispanic/Latino; 2% Race/ethnicity unknown; 3% international; 6% transferred in; 30% live on campus.

Freshmen:
Admission: 3,969 applied, 2,840 admitted, 1,364 enrolled. *Average high school GPA:* 3.4. *Test scores:* SAT evidence-based reading and writing scores over 500: 11%; SAT math scores over 500: 11%; ACT scores over 18: 95%; SAT evidence-based reading and writing scores over 600: 11%; SAT math scores over 600: 11%; ACT scores over 24: 35%; ACT scores over 30: 7%.

FACULTY
Total: 480, 68% full-time.
Student/faculty ratio: 19:1.

ACADEMICS
Calendar: semesters. *Degrees:* associate, bachelor's, master's, doctoral, post-master's, and postbachelor's certificates.

Special study options: academic remediation for entering students, accelerated degree program, adult/continuing education programs, advanced placement credit, cooperative education, distance learning, double majors, English as a second language, external degree program, honors programs, independent study, internships, off-campus study, part-time degree program, services for LD students, study abroad, summer session for credit. *ROTC:* Army (c).

Computers: Students can access the following: campus intranet, computer help desk, free student e-mail accounts, online (class) grades, online (class) registration, online (class) schedules. Campuswide network is available. 100% of college-owned or -operated housing units are wired for high-speed Internet access. Wireless service is available via entire campus.

Library: University Library. *Books:* 150,255 (physical), 293,246 (digital/electronic); *Serial titles:* 245 (physical), 93,407 (digital/electronic); *Databases:* 101. Students can reserve study rooms.

STUDENT LIFE
Housing options: coed, men-only, women-only. Campus housing is university owned and leased by the school. Freshman applicants given priority for college housing.

Activities and organizations: drama/theater group, student-run newspaper, radio and television station, choral group, marching band, Maroon Platoon, Alpha Lambda Delta, Louisiana Pharmacist Alliance, Association for Students in Kinesiology, Pre-Pharmacy Organization/Sound of Today, national fraternities, national sororities.

Athletics Member NCAA. All Division I except football (Division I-A). *Intercollegiate sports:* baseball M(s), basketball M(s)/W(s), cross-country running M(s)/W(s), golf M(s)/W(s), sand volleyball W(s), soccer W(s), softball W(s), tennis W(s), track and field M(s)/W(s), volleyball W(s).

Campus security: 24-hour emergency response devices and patrols, student patrols, late-night transport/escort service, controlled dormitory access.

Student services: health clinic, personal/psychological counseling.

COSTS & FINANCIAL AID
Costs (2017–18) *Tuition:* state resident $5788 full-time, $364 per credit hour part-time; nonresident $17,888 full-time, $364 per credit hour part-time. Full-time tuition and fees vary according to course load, degree level, and program. Part-time tuition and fees vary according to course load, degree level, and program. *Required fees:* $2682 full-time, $320 per credit hour part-time. *Room and board:* $7454; room only: $4282. Room and board charges vary according to board plan and housing facility. *Payment plan:* installment. *Waivers:* senior citizens and employees or children of employees.

Financial Aid Of all full-time matriculated undergraduates who enrolled in 2017, 4,317 applied for aid, 3,408 were judged to have need, 610 had their need fully met. 404 Federal Work-Study jobs (averaging $1159). In 2017, 1503 non-need-based awards were made. *Average percent of need met:* 56. *Average financial aid package:* $7821. *Average need-based loan:* $1987. *Average need-based gift aid:* $2658. *Average non-need-based aid:* $3854.

APPLYING
Standardized Tests *Required:* SAT or ACT (for admission).

Options: electronic application, early admission.

Application fee: $20.

Required: high school transcript, minimum 2.4 GPA.

Application deadlines: rolling (freshmen), rolling (transfers).

Notification: continuous (freshmen), continuous (transfers).

CONTACT
Ms. Mary Peterson, Coordinator of Enrollment Services, University of Louisiana at Monroe, Office of Recruitment and Admissions, University Library, 202, Monroe, LA 71209. *Phone:* 318-342-5397. *Toll-free phone:* 800-372-5127. *Fax:* 318-342-1915. *E-mail:* peterson@ulm.edu.

Louisiana

University of New Orleans

New Orleans, Louisiana
http://www.uno.edu/

- **State-supported** university, founded 1958, part of University of Louisiana System
- **Urban** 345-acre campus
- **Coed** 6,472 undergraduate students, 73% full-time, 50% women, 50% men
- 57% of applicants were admitted

UNDERGRAD STUDENTS

4,737 full-time, 1,735 part-time. 15% Black or African American, non-Hispanic/Latino; 13% Hispanic/Latino; 9% Asian, non-Hispanic/Latino; 0.1% Native Hawaiian or other Pacific Islander, non-Hispanic/Latino; 0.3% American Indian or Alaska Native, non-Hispanic/Latino; 4% Two or more races, non-Hispanic/Latino; 3% Race/ethnicity unknown; 4% international; 10% transferred in.

Freshmen:
Admission: 3,739 applied, 2,115 admitted, 960 enrolled. *Average high school GPA:* 3.2. *Test scores:* SAT evidence-based reading and writing scores over 500: 80%; SAT math scores over 500: 84%; ACT scores over 18: 95%; SAT evidence-based reading and writing scores over 600: 51%; SAT math scores over 600: 33%; ACT scores over 24: 38%; SAT evidence-based reading and writing scores over 700: 8%; SAT math scores over 700: 8%; ACT scores over 30: 7%.
Retention: 62% of full-time freshmen returned.

FACULTY
Total: 387, 63% full-time, 68% with terminal degrees.
Student/faculty ratio: 22:1.

ACADEMICS
Calendar: semesters. *Degrees:* bachelor's, master's, doctoral, and postbachelor's certificates.

Special study options: advanced placement credit, cooperative education, distance learning, double majors, English as a second language, honors programs, independent study, internships, part-time degree program, services for LD students, study abroad, summer session for credit. *ROTC:* Army (c), Navy (c), Air Force (c).

Computers: 1,050 computers/terminals are available on campus for general student use. Students can access the following: campus intranet, computer help desk, free student e-mail accounts, online (class) grades, online (class) registration, online (class) schedules, learning management system. Campuswide network is available. 100% of college-owned or - operated housing units are wired for high-speed Internet access. Wireless service is available via entire campus.

Library: Earl K. Long Library. *Books:* 1.0 million (physical), 220,863 (digital/electronic); *Serial titles:* 25,831 (physical), 55,551 (digital/electronic); *Databases:* 154. Students can reserve study rooms.

STUDENT LIFE
Housing options: coed. Campus housing is university owned and is provided by a third party. Freshman applicants given priority for college housing.

Activities and organizations: drama/theater group, student-run newspaper, choral group, Student Activities Council, Student Government, International Student Organization, Vietnamese American Student Association, Greek Life, national fraternities, national sororities.

Athletics Member NCAA. All Division I. *Intercollegiate sports:* baseball M(s), basketball M(s)/W(s), cross-country running M(s)/W(s), golf M(s), tennis M(s)/W(s), track and field M(s)/W(s), volleyball W(s). *Intramural sports:* basketball M/W, sailing M(c)/W(c), soccer M/W, softball M/W, table tennis M(c)/W(c), volleyball M/W, weight lifting M(c)/W(c), wrestling M(c)/W(c).

Campus security: 24-hour emergency response devices and patrols, late-night transport/escort service, controlled dormitory access.

Student services: health clinic, personal/psychological counseling, women's center, legal services.

COSTS & FINANCIAL AID
Costs (2017–18) *Tuition:* state resident $6090 full-time; nonresident $10,926 full-time. Full-time tuition and fees vary according to course load. Part-time tuition and fees vary according to course load. *Required*

fees: $2604 full-time. *Room and board:* $10,575. Room and board charges vary according to board plan and housing facility. *Payment plans:* installment, deferred payment. *Waivers:* senior citizens and employees or children of employees.

Financial Aid Of all full-time matriculated undergraduates who enrolled in 2016, 3,680 applied for aid, 3,094 were judged to have need, 386 had their need fully met. In 2016, 325 non-need-based awards were made. *Average percent of need met:* 64. *Average financial aid package:* $9587. *Average need-based loan:* $3813. *Average need-based gift aid:* $5126. *Average non-need-based aid:* $2605. *Average indebtedness upon graduation:* $20,723. *Financial aid deadline:* 6/30.

APPLYING
Standardized Tests *Required:* SAT or ACT (for admission).
Options: electronic application, deferred entrance.
Application fee: $25.
Required: high school transcript.

CONTACT
Mr. Brett Hornsby, Director, Enrollment Operations, University of New Orleans, Privateer Enrollment Center, University of New Orleans, 105 Earl K. Long Library, New Orleans, LA 70148. *Phone:* 504-280-7394. *Toll-free phone:* 888-514-4275. *Fax:* 504-280-3973. *E-mail:* bjhornsb@uno.edu.

Xavier University of Louisiana

New Orleans, Louisiana
http://www.xula.edu/

- **Independent Roman Catholic** comprehensive, founded 1925
- **Urban** 23-acre campus
- **Coed** 2,293 undergraduate students, 94% full-time, 73% women, 27% men
- **Moderately difficult** entrance level, 64% of applicants were admitted

UNDERGRAD STUDENTS

2,155 full-time, 138 part-time. 46% are from out of state; 78% Black or African American, non-Hispanic/Latino; 3% Hispanic/Latino; 7% Asian, non-Hispanic/Latino; 0.1% Native Hawaiian or other Pacific Islander, non-Hispanic/Latino; 0.1% American Indian or Alaska Native, non-Hispanic/Latino; 4% Two or more races, non-Hispanic/Latino; 4% Race/ethnicity unknown; 2% international; 4% transferred in; 48% live on campus.

Freshmen:
Admission: 7,164 applied, 4,589 admitted, 716 enrolled. *Average high school GPA:* 3.4. *Test scores:* SAT evidence-based reading and writing scores over 500: 75%; SAT math scores over 500: 66%; ACT scores over 18: 93%; SAT evidence-based reading and writing scores over 600: 25%; SAT math scores over 600: 19%; ACT scores over 24: 37%; SAT evidence-based reading and writing scores over 700: 4%; SAT math scores over 700: 3%; ACT scores over 30: 4%.
Retention: 70% of full-time freshmen returned.

FACULTY
Total: 243, 90% full-time, 88% with terminal degrees.
Student/faculty ratio: 14:1.

ACADEMICS
Calendar: semesters. *Degrees:* bachelor's, master's, and doctoral.

Special study options: academic remediation for entering students, accelerated degree program, adult/continuing education programs, advanced placement credit, cooperative education, distance learning, double majors, freshman honors college, honors programs, independent study, internships, off-campus study, part-time degree program, services for LD students, study abroad, summer session for credit. *ROTC:* Army (c), Navy (c), Air Force (c).

Unusual degree programs: 3-2 business administration with Tulane University; engineering with Tulane University, University of Maryland, University of New Orleans, Georgia Institute of Technology, University of Wisconsin–Madison, Morgan State University, Southern University and Agricultural and Mechanical College; biostatistics with Louisiana State University Medical Center.

Computers: Students can access the following: computer help desk, free student e-mail accounts, online (class) grades, online (class) registration,

online (class) schedules. Campuswide network is available. 100% of college-owned or -operated housing units are wired for high-speed Internet access. Wireless service is available via entire campus.
Library: Xavier Library.

STUDENT LIFE

Housing options: coed, men-only, women-only, special housing for students with disabilities. Campus housing is university owned. Freshman applicants given priority for college housing.

Activities and organizations: drama/theater group, student-run newspaper, television station, choral group, national fraternities, national sororities.

Athletics Member NAIA. *Intercollegiate sports:* basketball M(s)/W(s), cross-country running M/W, tennis M(s)/W(s). *Intramural sports:* badminton M/W, basketball M/W, football M/W, golf M/W, softball M/W, swimming and diving M/W, table tennis M/W, tennis M/W, track and field M/W, volleyball M/W.

Campus security: 24-hour emergency response devices and patrols, student patrols, bicycle patrols.

Student services: health clinic, personal/psychological counseling.

COSTS & FINANCIAL AID

Costs (2017–18) *Comprehensive fee:* $33,280 includes full-time tuition ($21,212), mandatory fees ($2534), and room and board ($9534). Part-time tuition: $884 per credit hour. Part-time tuition and fees vary according to course load. *Required fees:* $250 per term part-time. *Room and board:* Room and board charges vary according to housing facility. *Payment plan:* installment. *Waivers:* employees or children of employees.

Financial Aid Of all full-time matriculated undergraduates who enrolled in 2015, 2,078 applied for aid, 1,862 were judged to have need, 8 had their need fully met. In 2015, 103 non-need-based awards were made. *Average financial aid package:* $22,248. *Average need-based loan:* $5932. *Average need-based gift aid:* $5834. *Average non-need-based aid:* $13,048. *Average indebtedness upon graduation:* $22,142.

APPLYING

Standardized Tests *Required:* SAT or ACT (for admission).

Options: electronic application, deferred entrance.

Required: high school transcript, minimum 2.0 GPA, 1 letter of recommendation. *Required for some:* interview.

Notification: continuous (freshmen).

CONTACT

Mr. Winston Brown, Dean of Admissions, Xavier University of Louisiana, 7325 Palmetto Street, New Orleans, LA 70125. *Phone:* 504-520-7388. *Toll-free phone:* 877-XAVIERU. *Fax:* 504-520-7941. *E-mail:* apply@xula.edu.

MAINE

Bates College

Lewiston, Maine
http://www.bates.edu/

- **Independent** 4-year, founded 1855
- **Small-town** 133-acre campus
- **Endowment** $293.8 million
- **Coed** 1,787 undergraduate students, 100% full-time, 51% women, 49% men
- **Very difficult** entrance level, 22% of applicants were admitted

UNDERGRAD STUDENTS

1,787 full-time. Students come from 43 states and territories; 59 other countries; 90% are from out of state; 5% Black or African American, non-Hispanic/Latino; 9% Hispanic/Latino; 4% Asian, non-Hispanic/Latino; 0.1% Native Hawaiian or other Pacific Islander, non-Hispanic/Latino; 0.1% American Indian or Alaska Native, non-Hispanic/Latino; 5% Two or more races, non-Hispanic/Latino; 0.3% Race/ethnicity unknown; 7% international; 0.2% transferred in; 92% live on campus.

Freshmen:

Admission: 5,316 applied, 1,166 admitted, 510 enrolled. *Test scores:* SAT evidence-based reading and writing scores over 500: 98%; SAT math scores over 500: 99%; ACT scores over 18: 100%; SAT evidence-based reading and writing scores over 600: 90%; SAT math scores over 600: 86%; ACT scores over 24: 95%; SAT evidence-based reading and writing scores over 700: 48%; SAT math scores over 700: 38%; ACT scores over 30: 70%.

Retention: 95% of full-time freshmen returned.

FACULTY
Total: 195, 92% full-time, 94% with terminal degrees.
Student/faculty ratio: 10:1.

ACADEMICS
Calendar: 4-4-1. *Degree:* bachelor's.

Special study options: accelerated degree program, advanced placement credit, cooperative education, double majors, honors programs, independent study, internships, off-campus study, services for LD students, student-designed majors, study abroad.

Unusual degree programs: 3-2 engineering with Columbia University, Rensselaer Polytechnic Institute, Case Western Reserve University, Washington University in St. Louis, Dartmouth College.

Computers: 400 computers/terminals and 2,075 ports are available on campus for general student use. Students can access the following: computer help desk, free student e-mail accounts, online (class) grades, online (class) registration, online (class) schedules, course Web pages; course management system; software applications for learning, teaching and research; online course evaluation, transcripts, major declaration, degree audit, financial records. Campuswide network is available. 100% of college-owned or -operated housing units are wired for high-speed Internet access. Wireless service is available via classrooms, computer labs, dorm rooms, learning centers, libraries, student centers.
Library: Ladd Library plus 1 other. *Books:* 602,011 (physical), 725,335 (digital/electronic); *Databases:* 371.

STUDENT LIFE

Housing options: on-campus residence required through senior year; coed, men-only, women-only. Campus housing is university owned. Freshman campus housing is guaranteed.

Activities and organizations: drama/theater group, student-run newspaper, radio station, choral group, Outing Club (outdoor recreation), International Club, Chase Hall Committee (student activities planning), Representative Assembly, WRBC (student radio station).

Athletics Member NCAA. All Division III. *Intercollegiate sports:* baseball M, basketball M/W, crew M/W, cross-country running M/W, equestrian sports M(c)/W(c), fencing M(c)/W(c), field hockey W, football M, golf M/W, ice hockey M(c)/W(c), lacrosse M/W, rugby M(c)/W(c), sailing M(c)/W(c), skiing (cross-country) M/W, skiing (downhill) M/W, soccer M/W, softball W, squash M/W, swimming and diving M/W, tennis M/W, track and field M/W, ultimate Frisbee M(c)/W(c), volleyball M(c)/W, water polo M(c)/W(c). *Intramural sports:* basketball M/W, bowling M/W, ice hockey M/W, racquetball M/W, soccer M/W, softball M/W, squash M/W, tennis M/W, volleyball M/W.

Campus security: 24-hour emergency response devices and patrols, student patrols, late-night transport/escort service, controlled dormitory access, emergency contact/notification system.

Student services: health clinic, personal/psychological counseling, women's center.

COSTS & FINANCIAL AID

Costs (2017–18) *Comprehensive fee:* $66,720 includes full-time tuition ($52,042) and room and board ($14,678). *Payment plans:* tuition prepayment, installment. *Waivers:* employees or children of employees.

Financial Aid Of all full-time matriculated undergraduates who enrolled in 2016, 849 applied for aid, 774 were judged to have need, 774 had their need fully met. 446 Federal Work-Study jobs (averaging $1750). 309 state and other part-time jobs (averaging $1757). *Average percent of need met:* 100. *Average financial aid package:* $45,494. *Average need-based loan:* $3064. *Average need-based gift aid:* $41,478. *Average indebtedness upon graduation:* $22,845. *Financial aid deadline:* 2/1.

APPLYING

Options: electronic application, early admission, early decision, deferred entrance.

Application fee: $60.

Required: essay or personal statement, high school transcript, 3 letters of recommendation. *Recommended:* interview.

Application deadlines: 1/1 (freshmen), 3/1 (transfers).

Early decision deadline: 11/15 (for plan 1), 1/1 (for plan 2).

Notification: 4/1 (freshmen), 4/30 (transfers), 12/20 (early decision plan 1), 2/15 (early decision plan 2).

CONTACT

Leigh Weisenburger, Dean of Admission and Financial Aid, Bates College, 23 Campus Avenue, Lindholm House, Lewiston, ME 04240-6028. *Phone:* 855-228-3755. *Toll-free phone:* 855-228-3755. *Fax:* 207-786-6025. *E-mail:* admission@bates.edu.

Bowdoin College

Brunswick, Maine

http://www.bowdoin.edu/

- **Independent** 4-year, founded 1794
- **Small-town** 207-acre campus with easy access to Portland
- **Endowment** $1.5 billion
- **Coed** 1,816 undergraduate students, 100% full-time, 50% women, 50% men
- **Most difficult** entrance level, 14% of applicants were admitted

UNDERGRAD STUDENTS

1,813 full-time, 3 part-time. Students come from 46 states and territories; 35 other countries; 89% are from out of state; 6% Black or African American, non-Hispanic/Latino; 11% Hispanic/Latino; 7% Asian, non-Hispanic/Latino; 0.1% Native Hawaiian or other Pacific Islander, non-Hispanic/Latino; 0.3% American Indian or Alaska Native, non-Hispanic/Latino; 7% Two or more races, non-Hispanic/Latino; 1% Race/ethnicity unknown; 5% international; 0.2% transferred in; 90% live on campus.

Freshmen:

Admission: 7,251 applied, 988 admitted, 501 enrolled.

Retention: 96% of full-time freshmen returned.

FACULTY

Total: 228, 85% full-time, 97% with terminal degrees.

Student/faculty ratio: 9:1.

ACADEMICS

Calendar: semesters. *Degree:* bachelor's.

Special study options: accelerated degree program, advanced placement credit, double majors, independent study, off-campus study, services for LD students, student-designed majors, study abroad.

Unusual degree programs: 3-2 engineering with California Institute of Technology, Columbia University, Dartmouth College, University of Maine Orono; law with Columbia University.

Computers: 500 computers/terminals and 600 ports are available on campus for general student use. Students can access the following: campus intranet, computer help desk, free student e-mail accounts, online (class) grades, online (class) registration, online (class) schedules, computer repair; training classes; 24/7 software support; free equipment loaner pool: laptops, video and digital cameras, sound and lighting systems, iPads; movie streaming service; free office software; digital media lab. Campuswide network is available. 100% of college-owned or -operated housing units are wired for high-speed Internet access. Wireless service is available via entire campus.

Library: Hawthorne-Longfellow Library plus 3 others. *Books:* 1.2 million (physical), 1.1 million (digital/electronic); *Serial titles:* 7,146 (physical), 80,997 (digital/electronic); *Databases:* 515. Weekly public service hours: 112; students can reserve study rooms.

STUDENT LIFE

Housing options: on-campus residence required through sophomore year; coed, special housing for students with disabilities. Campus housing is university owned. Freshman campus housing is guaranteed.

Activities and organizations: drama/theater group, student-run newspaper, radio station, choral group, Outing Club, Intramural sports, Community Service Volunteer Programs, WBOR 91.1 FM Radio, Bowdoin Orient Student Newspaper.

Athletics Member NCAA. All Division III except men's and women's sailing (Division I), men's and women's skiing (cross-country) (Division I), men's and women's squash (Division I). *Intercollegiate sports:* baseball M, basketball M/W, crew M(c)/W(c), cross-country running M/W, equestrian sports M(c)/W(c), fencing M(c)/W(c), field hockey W, football M, golf M/W, ice hockey M/W, lacrosse M/W, rugby M(c)/W, sailing M/W, skiing (cross-country) M/W, soccer M/W, softball W, squash M/W, swimming and diving M/W, tennis M/W, track and field M/W, ultimate Frisbee M(c)/W(c), volleyball M(c)/W, water polo M(c)/W(c). *Intramural sports:* badminton M/W, basketball M/W, cheerleading M(c)/W(c), field hockey M/W, ice hockey M/W, lacrosse M(c), skiing (downhill) M(c)/W(c), soccer M/W, softball M/W, tennis M(c)/W(c).

Campus security: 24-hour emergency response devices and patrols, late-night transport/escort service, controlled dormitory access, self-defense education, safe ride service, emergency notification system.

Student services: health clinic, personal/psychological counseling, women's center.

COSTS & FINANCIAL AID

Costs (2017–18) *Comprehensive fee:* $65,980 includes full-time tuition ($51,344), mandatory fees ($504), and room and board ($14,132). Part-time tuition: $1003 per credit hour. *College room only:* $6604. Room and board charges vary according to board plan. *Payment plans:* installment, deferred payment. *Waivers:* employees or children of employees.

Financial Aid Of all full-time matriculated undergraduates who enrolled in 2017, 925 applied for aid, 832 were judged to have need, 832 had their need fully met. 530 Federal Work-Study jobs (averaging $1850). 252 state and other part-time jobs (averaging $1848). In 2017, 32 non-need-based awards were made. *Average percent of need met:* 100. *Average financial aid package:* $46,562. *Average need-based gift aid:* $44,824. *Average non-need-based aid:* $1000. *Average indebtedness upon graduation:* $23,174. *Financial aid deadline:* 2/15.

APPLYING

Options: electronic application, early admission, early decision, deferred entrance.

Application fee: $65.

Required: essay or personal statement, high school transcript, 3 letters of recommendation. *Recommended:* interview.

Application deadlines: 1/1 (freshmen), 3/1 (transfers).

Early decision deadline: 11/15 (for plan 1), 1/1 (for plan 2).

Notification: 3/20 (freshmen), 5/1 (transfers), 12/15 (early decision plan 1), 2/15 (early decision plan 2).

CONTACT

Claudia Marroquin, Director of Admissions, Bowdoin College, 255 Maine Street, Brunswick, ME 04011. *Phone:* 207-725-3100. *Fax:* 207-725-3101. *E-mail:* admissions@bowdoin.edu.

Colby College

Waterville, Maine

http://www.colby.edu/

- **Independent** 4-year, founded 1813
- **Small-town** 714-acre campus with easy access to Portland, ME
- **Endowment** $775.1 million
- **Coed** 1,917 undergraduate students, 100% full-time, 52% women, 48% men
- **Most difficult** entrance level, 16% of applicants were admitted

UNDERGRAD STUDENTS

1,917 full-time. Students come from 47 states and territories; 52 other countries; 89% are from out of state; 4% Black or African American, non-Hispanic/Latino; 7% Hispanic/Latino; 7% Asian, non-Hispanic/Latino; 0.2% Native Hawaiian or other Pacific Islander, non-Hispanic/Latino; 0.4% American Indian or Alaska Native, non-Hispanic/Latino; 5% Two or more races, non-Hispanic/Latino; 2% Race/ethnicity unknown; 10% international; 0.3% transferred in; 95% live on campus.

Freshmen:
Admission: 11,190 applied, 1,767 admitted, 552 enrolled. *Test scores:* SAT evidence-based reading and writing scores over 500: 100%; SAT math scores over 500: 100%; ACT scores over 18: 100%; SAT evidence-based reading and writing scores over 600: 95%; SAT math scores over 600: 93%; ACT scores over 24: 100%; SAT evidence-based reading and writing scores over 700: 61%; SAT math scores over 700: 60%; ACT scores over 30: 84%.
Retention: 94% of full-time freshmen returned.

ACADEMICS
Calendar: 4-1-4. *Degree:* bachelor's.
Special study options: advanced placement credit, double majors, honors programs, independent study, internships, off-campus study, services for LD students, student-designed majors, study abroad. *ROTC:* Army (c).
Unusual degree programs: 3-2 engineering with Dartmouth College, Columbia University.
Computers: 158 computers/terminals and 3,000 ports are available on campus for general student use. Students can access the following: campus intranet, computer help desk, free student e-mail accounts, online (class) grades, online (class) registration, online (class) schedules, software license for every student computer, unlimited technology training, video editing lab, high performance natural science research computing, GIS lab. Campuswide network is available. 100% of college-owned or -operated housing units are wired for high-speed Internet access. Wireless service is available via entire campus.
Library: Miller Library plus 3 others. *Books:* 545,763 (physical), 595,720 (digital/electronic); *Serial titles:* 22,931 (physical), 100,911 (digital/electronic); *Databases:* 701. Weekly public service hours: 119; study areas open 24 hours, 5–7 days a week.

STUDENT LIFE
Housing options: on-campus residence required through senior year; coed, cooperative, special housing for students with disabilities. Campus housing is university owned. Freshman campus housing is guaranteed.
Activities and organizations: drama/theater group, student-run newspaper, radio station, choral group, Outing Club, volunteer center, WMHB-FM (College Radio Station), Student Government, Powder and Wig (theater).
Athletics Member NCAA. All Division III except men's and women's skiing (cross-country) (Division I), men's and women's skiing (downhill) (Division I). *Intercollegiate sports:* baseball M, basketball M/W, crew M/W, cross-country running M/W, fencing M(c)/W(c), field hockey W, football M, golf M/W, ice hockey M/W, lacrosse M/W, rugby M(c)/W(c), sailing M(c)/W(c), skiing (cross-country) M/W, skiing (downhill) M/W, soccer M/W, softball W, squash M/W, swimming and diving M/W, tennis M/W, track and field M/W, ultimate Frisbee M(c)/W(c), volleyball M(c)/W, water polo M(c)/W(c). *Intramural sports:* basketball M/W, field hockey M/W, football M/W, soccer M/W, softball M/W, tennis M/W.
Campus security: 24-hour emergency response devices and patrols, student patrols, late-night transport/escort service, controlled dormitory access, campus lighting, student emergency response team, self-defense class, property ID program, party monitors.
Student services: health clinic, personal/psychological counseling, women's center.

COSTS & FINANCIAL AID
Costs (2017–18) *Comprehensive fee:* $66,780 includes full-time tuition ($50,890), mandatory fees ($2230), and room and board ($13,660). Part-time tuition: $1960 per credit hour. Part-time tuition and fees vary according to course load. *Payment plan:* installment. *Waivers:* employees or children of employees.
Financial Aid Of all full-time matriculated undergraduates who enrolled in 2017, 935 applied for aid, 813 were judged to have need, 796 had their need fully met. In 2017, 6 non-need-based awards were made. *Average percent of need met:* 100. *Average financial aid package:* $48,467. *Average need-based gift aid:* $46,775. *Average non-need-based aid:* $433. *Average indebtedness upon graduation:* $34,745. *Financial aid deadline:* 2/1.

APPLYING
Standardized Tests *Required for some:* SAT or ACT (for admission), SAT and SAT Subject Tests or ACT (for admission).

Options: electronic application, early admission, early decision, deferred entrance.
Required: essay or personal statement, high school transcript, 2 letters of recommendation. *Recommended:* interview.
Application deadlines: 1/1 (freshmen), 3/1 (transfers).
Early decision deadline: 11/15 (for plan 1), 1/1 (for plan 2).
Notification: 4/1 (freshmen), 4/1 (out-of-state freshmen), 5/15 (transfers), 12/15 (early decision plan 1), 2/15 (early decision plan 2).

CONTACT
Denise Walden, Associate Director of Admissions, Colby College, 4000 Mayflower Hill, Waterville, ME 04901-8840. *Phone:* 207-859-4800. *Toll-free phone:* 800-723-3032. *Fax:* 207-859-4828. *E-mail:* admissions@colby.edu.

College of the Atlantic
Bar Harbor, Maine
http://www.coa.edu/
- **Independent** comprehensive, founded 1969
- **Small-town** 35-acre campus
- **Endowment** $53.0 million
- **Coed** 349 undergraduate students, 95% full-time, 75% women, 25% men
- **Very difficult** entrance level, 68% of applicants were admitted

UNDERGRAD STUDENTS
330 full-time, 19 part-time. Students come from 33 states and territories; 41 other countries; 78% are from out of state; 1% Black or African American, non-Hispanic/Latino; 3% Hispanic/Latino; 3% Asian, non-Hispanic/Latino; 0.3% American Indian or Alaska Native, non-Hispanic/Latino; 2% Two or more races, non-Hispanic/Latino; 5% Race/ethnicity unknown; 21% international; 6% transferred in; 46% live on campus.

Freshmen:
Admission: 474 applied, 322 admitted, 91 enrolled. *Average high school GPA:* 3.7. *Test scores:* SAT evidence-based reading and writing scores over 500: 97%; SAT math scores over 500: 94%; ACT scores over 18: 100%; SAT evidence-based reading and writing scores over 600: 91%; SAT math scores over 600: 50%; ACT scores over 24: 95%; SAT evidence-based reading and writing scores over 700: 32%; SAT math scores over 700: 18%; ACT scores over 30: 33%.
Retention: 76% of full-time freshmen returned.

FACULTY
Total: 53, 49% full-time, 68% with terminal degrees.
Student/faculty ratio: 10:1.

ACADEMICS
Calendar: trimesters. *Degrees:* bachelor's and master's.
Special study options: academic remediation for entering students, accelerated degree program, advanced placement credit, cooperative education, independent study, internships, off-campus study, part-time degree program, services for LD students, student-designed majors, study abroad, summer session for credit.
Computers: 45 computers/terminals and 85 ports are available on campus for general student use. Students can access the following: computer help desk, free student e-mail accounts, online (class) grades, online (class) registration, online (class) schedules, online billing, transcript, financial aid, course management system. Campuswide network is available. 100% of college-owned or -operated housing units are wired for high-speed Internet access. Wireless service is available via entire campus.
Library: Thorndike Library. *Books:* 45,700 (physical), 15,500 (digital/electronic); *Serial titles:* 400 (physical), 62,600 (digital/electronic); *Databases:* 76. Weekly public service hours: 101; students can reserve study rooms.

STUDENT LIFE
Housing options: on-campus residence required for freshman year; coed. Campus housing is university owned. Freshman campus housing is guaranteed.
Activities and organizations: drama/theater group, student-run newspaper, choral group, Earth in Brackets [earth], Outing Club, Campus Committee for Sustainability, Spectrum (LGBTQ+), Futbol (soccer) Club.

Athletics *Intramural sports:* badminton M/W, basketball M/W, bowling M/W, cross-country running M/W, fencing M/W, ice hockey M/W, rock climbing M/W, sailing M/W, skiing (cross-country) M/W, soccer M/W, softball M/W, table tennis M/W, ultimate Frisbee M/W, volleyball M/W, water polo M/W.

Campus security: 24-hour emergency response devices and patrols, late-night transport/escort service.

Student services: health clinic, personal/psychological counseling.

COSTS & FINANCIAL AID

Costs (2018–19) *Comprehensive fee:* $53,289 includes full-time tuition ($42,993), mandatory fees ($549), and room and board ($9747). Full-time tuition and fees vary according to course load and degree level. Part-time tuition: $4777 per credit. Part-time tuition and fees vary according to course load and degree level. *Required fees:* $183 per term part-time. *College room only:* $6210. Room and board charges vary according to board plan. *Payment plan:* installment. *Waivers:* employees or children of employees.

Financial Aid Of all full-time matriculated undergraduates who enrolled in 2017, 298 applied for aid, 273 were judged to have need, 23 had their need fully met. 178 Federal Work-Study jobs (averaging $2862). 85 state and other part-time jobs (averaging $2906). In 2017, 43 non-need-based awards were made. *Average percent of need met:* 96. *Average financial aid package:* $42,122. *Average need-based loan:* $4831. *Average need-based gift aid:* $36,071. *Average non-need-based aid:* $14,515. *Average indebtedness upon graduation:* $24,228. *Financial aid deadline:* 2/1.

APPLYING

Options: electronic application, early admission, early decision, deferred entrance.

Application fee: $50.

Required: essay or personal statement, high school transcript, 3 letters of recommendation. *Recommended:* minimum 3.0 GPA, interview.

Application deadlines: 2/1 (freshmen), 3/15 (transfers).

Early decision deadline: 12/1 (for plan 1), 1/15 (for plan 2).

Notification: 4/1 (freshmen), 4/15 (transfers), 12/15 (early decision plan 1), 1/30 (early decision plan 2).

CONTACT

Ms. Heather Albert-Knopp, Dean of Admission, College of the Atlantic, 105 Eden Street, Bar Harbor, ME 04609-1198. *Phone:* 207-288-5015. *Toll-free phone:* 800-528-0025. *Fax:* 207-288-4126. *E-mail:* inquiry@coa.edu.

Husson University

Bangor, Maine

http://www.husson.edu/

- **Independent** comprehensive, founded 1898
- **Suburban** 208-acre campus
- **Endowment** $17.3 million
- **Coed** 2,763 undergraduate students, 83% full-time, 56% women, 44% men
- **Moderately difficult** entrance level, 80% of applicants were admitted

UNDERGRAD STUDENTS

2,298 full-time, 465 part-time. Students come from 29 states and territories; 28 other countries; 28% are from out of state; 4% Black or African American, non-Hispanic/Latino; 2% Hispanic/Latino; 1% Asian, non-Hispanic/Latino; 0.2% Native Hawaiian or other Pacific Islander, non-Hispanic/Latino; 0.3% American Indian or Alaska Native, non-Hispanic/Latino; 2% Two or more races, non-Hispanic/Latino; 2% Race/ethnicity unknown; 3% international; 5% transferred in; 39% live on campus.

Freshmen:

Admission: 2,460 applied, 1,974 admitted, 577 enrolled. *Average high school GPA:* 3.3. *Test scores:* ACT scores over 18: 68%; ACT scores over 24: 13%.

Retention: 76% of full-time freshmen returned.

FACULTY

Total: 341, 41% full-time, 48% with terminal degrees.

Student/faculty ratio: 15:1.

ACADEMICS

Calendar: semesters. *Degrees:* certificates, associate, bachelor's, master's, doctoral, post-master's, and postbachelor's certificates.

Special study options: academic remediation for entering students, adult/continuing education programs, advanced placement credit, cooperative education, distance learning, double majors, English as a second language, independent study, internships, off-campus study, part-time degree program, services for LD students, student-designed majors, study abroad, summer session for credit. *ROTC:* Army (b), Navy (c).

Unusual degree programs: 3-2 business administration; nursing; occupational therapy, criminal justice administration.

Computers: 131 computers/terminals and 131 ports are available on campus for general student use. Students can access the following: campus intranet, computer help desk, free student e-mail accounts, online (class) grades, online (class) registration, online (class) schedules. Campuswide network is available. 100% of college-owned or -operated housing units are wired for high-speed Internet access. Wireless service is available via entire campus.

Library: Sawyer Library. *Books:* 41,659 (physical), 5,539 (digital/electronic); *Serial titles:* 74 (physical), 151 (digital/electronic); *Databases:* 91. Weekly public service hours: 98; study areas open 24 hours, 5–7 days a week; students can reserve study rooms.

STUDENT LIFE

Housing options: on-campus residence required through sophomore year; coed. Campus housing is university owned. Freshman campus housing is guaranteed.

Activities and organizations: drama/theater group, student-run radio station, choral group, Organization of Student Nurses, Organization of Physical Therapy Students, Outdoors Club, International Student Association, Habitat for Humanity, national fraternities, national sororities.

Athletics Member NCAA. All Division III. *Intercollegiate sports:* baseball M, basketball M/W, cross-country running M/W, field hockey W, football M, golf M/W, lacrosse M/W, soccer M/W, softball W, swimming and diving M/W, tennis W, track and field M/W, volleyball W. *Intramural sports:* basketball M/W, cheerleading M(c)/W(c), football M/W, ice hockey M(c), soccer M/W, softball M/W, volleyball M/W, wrestling M(c).

Campus security: 24-hour emergency response devices and patrols, late-night transport/escort service, controlled dormitory access.

Student services: health clinic, personal/psychological counseling.

COSTS & FINANCIAL AID

Costs (2018–19) *One-time required fee:* $150. *Comprehensive fee:* $27,430 includes full-time tuition ($17,100), mandatory fees ($500), and room and board ($9830). Full-time tuition and fees vary according to class time and location. Part-time tuition: $570 per credit. Part-time tuition and fees vary according to class time, course load, and location. *Required fees:* $120 per year part-time. *College room only:* $4950. Room and board charges vary according to board plan and housing facility. *Payment plans:* tuition prepayment, installment. *Waivers:* senior citizens and employees or children of employees.

Financial Aid Of all full-time matriculated undergraduates who enrolled in 2017, 2,111 applied for aid, 1,901 were judged to have need, 177 had their need fully met. 413 Federal Work-Study jobs (averaging $1600). In 2017, 333 non-need-based awards were made. *Average percent of need met:* 67. *Average financial aid package:* $15,074. *Average need-based loan:* $4287. *Average need-based gift aid:* $8919. *Average non-need-based aid:* $3793. *Average indebtedness upon graduation:* $33,412. *Financial aid deadline:* 4/15.

APPLYING

Standardized Tests *Required:* SAT or ACT (for admission).

Options: electronic application, deferred entrance.

Application fee: $40.

Required: essay or personal statement, high school transcript, 1 letter of recommendation. *Recommended:* minimum 3.0 GPA, interview.

Application deadlines: 8/15 (freshmen), 8/15 (transfers).

Notification: continuous (freshmen), continuous (transfers).

CONTACT

Mr. Adam Smith, Director of Undergraduate Admissions, Husson University, 1 College Circle, Bangor, ME 04401-2999. *Phone:* 207-404-

5643. *Toll-free phone:* 800-4-HUSSON. *Fax:* 207-941-7935. *E-mail:* smithad@husson.edu.

Kaplan University, Augusta
Augusta, Maine
http://www.kaplanuniversity.edu/

CONTACT
Kaplan University, Augusta, 14 Marketplace Drive, Augusta, ME 04330. *Toll-free phone:* 888-561-4343.

Maine College of Art
Portland, Maine
http://www.meca.edu/

CONTACT
Maine College of Art, 522 Congress Street, Portland, ME 04101. *Phone:* 207-699-5023. *Toll-free phone:* 800-699-1509.

Maine College of Health Professions
Lewiston, Maine
http://www.mchp.edu/

- **Independent** primarily 2-year, founded 1891
- **Urban** campus
- **Coed** 188 undergraduate students, 23% full-time, 88% women, 12% men
- **Moderately difficult** entrance level, 46% of applicants were admitted

UNDERGRAD STUDENTS
44 full-time, 144 part-time. Students come from 1 other state; 2% Black or African American, non-Hispanic/Latino; 1% Hispanic/Latino; 2% Asian, non-Hispanic/Latino; 0.5% American Indian or Alaska Native, non-Hispanic/Latino; 2% Two or more races, non-Hispanic/Latino; 10% Race/ethnicity unknown; 50% transferred in; 4% live on campus.

Freshmen:
Admission: 13 applied, 6 admitted, 9 enrolled. *Average high school GPA:* 3.6.

FACULTY
Total: 19, 89% full-time, 16% with terminal degrees.
Student/faculty ratio: 5:1.

ACADEMICS
Calendar: semesters. *Degrees:* certificates, associate, and bachelor's.
Special study options: advanced placement credit, off-campus study, services for LD students, summer session for credit.
Computers: 30 computers/terminals are available on campus for general student use. Students can access the following: campus intranet, computer help desk, free student e-mail accounts, online (class) grades, online (class) schedules. Wireless service is available via entire campus.
Library: Gerrish True Health Sciences Library plus 1 other. *Books:* 2,816 (physical), 172 (digital/electronic); *Databases:* 17. Study areas open 24 hours, 5–7 days a week.

STUDENT LIFE
Housing options: coed. Campus housing is university owned.
Activities and organizations: Student Government.
Campus security: 24-hour emergency response devices and patrols, late-night transport/escort service, controlled dormitory access.
Student services: health clinic, personal/psychological counseling.

COSTS & FINANCIAL AID
Costs (2018–19) *Tuition:* $10,720 full-time, $5360 per year part-time. Full-time tuition and fees vary according to program. Part-time tuition and fees vary according to program. *Required fees:* $1525 full-time, $1525 per term part-time. *Room only:* $2350. *Payment plan:* installment. *Waivers:* employees or children of employees.
Financial Aid Of all full-time matriculated undergraduates who enrolled in 2017, 72 applied for aid.

APPLYING
Standardized Tests *Required for some:* SAT or ACT (for admission), HESI Entrance Exam for nursing, ACCUPLACER.

Options: electronic application.
Application fee: $50.
Required: essay or personal statement, high school transcript, high school or college-level algebra, second math, biology, chemistry.
Notification: 5/1 (freshmen).

CONTACT
Ms. Erica Watson, Admissions Director, Maine College of Health Professions, 70 Middle Street, Lewiston, ME 04240. *Phone:* 207-795-2843. *Fax:* 207-795-2849. *E-mail:* watsoner@mchp.edu.

Maine Maritime Academy
Castine, Maine
http://www.mainemaritime.edu/

CONTACT
Maine Maritime Academy, 1 Pleasant Street, Castine, ME 04420. *Phone:* 207-326-2215. *Toll-free phone:* 800-464-6565 (in-state); 800-227-8465 (out-of-state).

Saint Joseph's College of Maine
Standish, Maine
http://www.sjcme.edu/

CONTACT
Kathleen Davis, Vice President for Enrollment Management, Saint Joseph's College of Maine, 278 Whites Bridge Road, Standish, ME 04084-5263. *Phone:* 207-893-7746. *Toll-free phone:* 800-338-7057. *Fax:* 207-893-7862. *E-mail:* admission@sjcme.edu.

Thomas College
Waterville, Maine
http://www.thomas.edu/

CONTACT
Ms. Angela Stinchfield, Director of Admissions, Thomas College, 180 West River Road, Waterville, ME 04901. *Phone:* 207-859-1101. *Toll-free phone:* 800-339-7001. *Fax:* 207-859-1114. *E-mail:* admiss@thomas.edu.

★ Unity College
Unity, Maine
http://www.unity.edu/

- **Independent** comprehensive, founded 1965
- **Rural** 300-acre campus
- **Endowment** $14.0 million
- **Coed** 704 undergraduate students, 99% full-time, 51% women, 49% men
- **Moderately difficult** entrance level, 89% of applicants were admitted

UNDERGRAD STUDENTS
694 full-time, 10 part-time. Students come from 32 states and territories; 1 other country; 74% are from out of state; 0.7% Black or African American, non-Hispanic/Latino; 1% Hispanic/Latino; 0.9% Asian, non-Hispanic/Latino; 2% American Indian or Alaska Native, non-Hispanic/Latino; 3% Two or more races, non-Hispanic/Latino; 6% Race/ethnicity unknown; 8% transferred in; 70% live on campus.

Freshmen:
Admission: 915 applied, 812 admitted, 175 enrolled. *Average high school GPA:* 3.3.
Retention: 64% of full-time freshmen returned.

FACULTY
Student/faculty ratio: 14:1.

ACADEMICS
Calendar: semesters. *Degrees:* bachelor's, master's, and postbachelor's certificates.
Special study options: academic remediation for entering students, accelerated degree program, advanced placement credit, cooperative education, double majors, honors programs, independent study, internships, off-campus study, part-time degree program, services for LD students, study abroad, summer session for credit.

Computers: 140 computers/terminals and 150 ports are available on campus for general student use. Students can access the following: campus intranet, computer help desk, free student e-mail accounts, online (class) grades, online (class) registration, online (class) schedules. Campuswide network is available. 100% of college-owned or -operated housing units are wired for high-speed Internet access. Wireless service is available via entire campus.

Library: Dorothy Webb Quimby Library. *Books:* 52,723 (physical), 15,329 (digital/electronic); *Databases:* 72. Weekly public service hours: 40.

STUDENT LIFE

Housing options: on-campus residence required through sophomore year; coed, men-only, women-only, cooperative, special housing for students with disabilities. Campus housing is university owned. Freshman campus housing is guaranteed.

Activities and organizations: drama/theater group, choral group, Woodsmen Team, Ultimate Frisbee, Outing Club.

Athletics Member USCAA. *Intercollegiate sports:* basketball M/W, cross-country running M/W, soccer M/W, volleyball W. *Intramural sports:* baseball M, basketball M/W, cross-country running M/W, golf M/W, ice hockey M/W, soccer W, softball M/W, table tennis M/W, tennis M/W, ultimate Frisbee M/W, volleyball M/W, weight lifting M/W.

Campus security: 24-hour emergency response devices and patrols, security cameras in certain areas.

Student services: health clinic, personal/psychological counseling.

COSTS & FINANCIAL AID

Costs (2017–18) *Comprehensive fee:* $38,750 includes full-time tuition ($27,150), mandatory fees ($1200), and room and board ($10,400). Part-time tuition: $980 per credit. *Room and board:* Room and board charges vary according to board plan and housing facility. *Payment plan:* installment. *Waivers:* employees or children of employees.

Financial Aid Of all full-time matriculated undergraduates who enrolled in 2017, 641 applied for aid, 584 were judged to have need, 63 had their need fully met. 429 Federal Work-Study jobs (averaging $1429). 16 state and other part-time jobs (averaging $1597). In 2017, 106 non-need-based awards were made. *Average percent of need met:* 72. *Average financial aid package:* $20,848. *Average need-based loan:* $7120. *Average need-based gift aid:* $13,718. *Average non-need-based aid:* $9602.

APPLYING

Standardized Tests *Recommended:* SAT or ACT (for admission).

Options: electronic application, early action, deferred entrance.

Required: essay or personal statement, high school transcript. *Required for some:* interview. *Recommended:* minimum 2.5 GPA, interview.

Application deadlines: rolling (freshmen), rolling (out-of-state freshmen), rolling (transfers), 12/15 (early action).

Notification: continuous (freshmen), continuous (out-of-state freshmen), continuous (transfers), 12/31 (early action).

CONTACT

Mr. Joe Saltalamachia, Director of Admissions, Unity College, 90 Quaker Hill Road, Unity, ME 04988. *Phone:* 207-509-7205. *E-mail:* jsalty@unity.edu.

 # University of Maine
Orono, Maine
http://www.umaine.edu/

- **State-supported** university, founded 1865, part of University of Maine System
- **Small-town** 660-acre campus
- **Coed** 9,279 undergraduate students, 88% full-time, 47% women, 53% men
- **Moderately difficult** entrance level, 92% of applicants were admitted

UNDERGRAD STUDENTS

8,204 full-time, 1,075 part-time. Students come from 49 states and territories; 29 other countries; 35% are from out of state; 2% Black or African American, non-Hispanic/Latino; 4% Hispanic/Latino; 2% Asian, non-Hispanic/Latino; 1% American Indian or Alaska Native, non-Hispanic/Latino; 3% Two or more races, non-Hispanic/Latino; 2% Race/ethnicity unknown; 2% international; 4% transferred in; 40% live on campus.

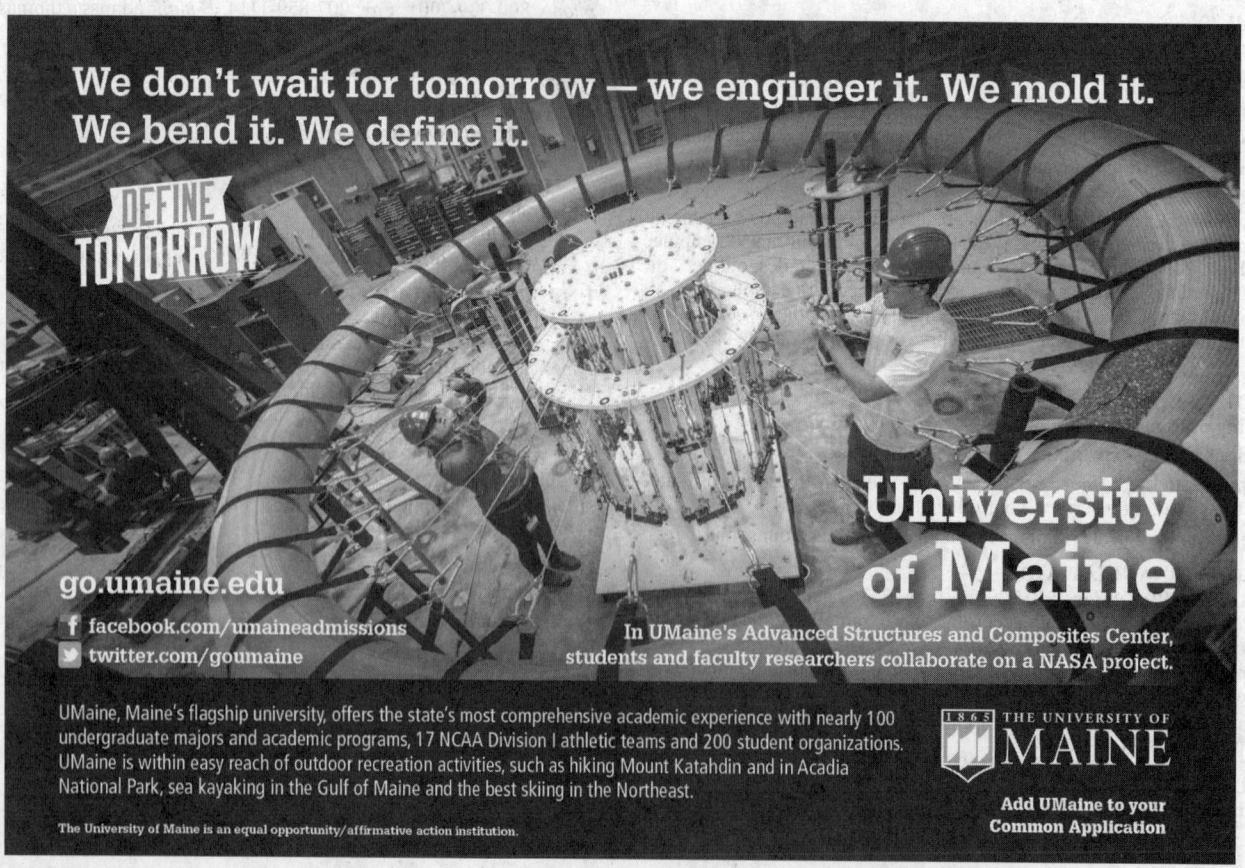

We don't wait for tomorrow — we engineer it. We mold it. We bend it. We define it.

DEFINE TOMORROW

go.umaine.edu

facebook.com/umaineadmissions
twitter.com/goumaine

University of Maine

In UMaine's Advanced Structures and Composites Center, students and faculty researchers collaborate on a NASA project.

UMaine, Maine's flagship university, offers the state's most comprehensive academic experience with nearly 100 undergraduate majors and academic programs, 17 NCAA Division I athletic teams and 200 student organizations. UMaine is within easy reach of outdoor recreation activities, such as hiking Mount Katahdin and in Acadia National Park, sea kayaking in the Gulf of Maine and the best skiing in the Northeast.

1865 THE UNIVERSITY OF MAINE

Add UMaine to your Common Application

The University of Maine is an equal opportunity/affirmative action institution.

Freshmen:
Admission: 13,231 applied, 12,207 admitted, 2,299 enrolled. *Average high school GPA:* 3.3. *Test scores:* SAT evidence-based reading and writing scores over 500: 89%; SAT math scores over 500: 85%; ACT scores over 18: 96%; SAT evidence-based reading and writing scores over 600: 41%; SAT math scores over 600: 34%; ACT scores over 24: 58%; SAT evidence-based reading and writing scores over 700: 6%; SAT math scores over 700: 6%; ACT scores over 30: 11%.
Retention: 75% of full-time freshmen returned.

FACULTY
Total: 838, 61% full-time, 61% with terminal degrees.
Student/faculty ratio: 16:1.

ACADEMICS
Calendar: semesters. *Degrees:* bachelor's, master's, doctoral, post-master's, and postbachelor's certificates.

Special study options: accelerated degree program, advanced placement credit, distance learning, double majors, English as a second language, freshman honors college, honors programs, independent study, internships, off-campus study, part-time degree program, services for LD students, student-designed majors, study abroad, summer session for credit. *ROTC:* Army (b), Navy (b).

Computers: 600 computers/terminals are available on campus for general student use. Students can access the following: campus intranet, computer help desk, free student e-mail accounts, online (class) grades, online (class) registration, online (class) schedules, online housing and financial aid information. Campuswide network is available. 100% of college-owned or -operated housing units are wired for high-speed Internet access. Wireless service is available via entire campus.
Library: Fogler Library. *Books:* 1.2 million (physical), 893,818 (digital/electronic); *Serial titles:* 65,908 (physical), 130,590 (digital/electronic); *Databases:* 367. Weekly public service hours: 103; students can reserve study rooms.

STUDENT LIFE
Housing options: on-campus residence required for freshman year; coed, special housing for students with disabilities. Campus housing is university owned. Freshman campus housing is guaranteed.

Activities and organizations: drama/theater group, student-run newspaper, radio station, choral group, marching band, Fraternity and Sorority Life, Alternative Breaks, UMaine Student Government, Campus Activities Board, Wilde Stein, national fraternities, national sororities.

Athletics Member NCAA. All Division I except football (Division I-AA). *Intercollegiate sports:* baseball M(s), basketball M(s)/W(s), cheerleading M(c)/W(c), cross-country running M(s)/W(s), field hockey W(s), ice hockey M(s)/W(s), soccer M(c)/W(s), softball W(s), swimming and diving M/W(s), tennis M(c)/W(c), track and field M(s)/W(s). *Intramural sports:* badminton M/W, baseball M(c), basketball M/W, crew M(c)/W(c), equestrian sports M(c)/W(c), fencing M(c)/W(c), field hockey M(c)/W(c), football M(c), golf M(c)/W(c), ice hockey M(c)/W(c), lacrosse M(c)/W(c), racquetball M/W, rock climbing M(c)/W(c), rugby M(c)/W(c), skiing (cross-country) M/W, skiing (downhill) M(c)/W(c), soccer M/W, softball M/W, swimming and diving M/W, table tennis M/W, tennis M/W, track and field M/W, ultimate Frisbee M(c)/W(c), volleyball M(c)/W(c), water polo M/W, wrestling M(c).

Campus security: 24-hour emergency response devices and patrols, late-night transport/escort service, controlled dormitory access, area emergency text and email message system.

Student services: health clinic, personal/psychological counseling, women's center, legal services.

COSTS & FINANCIAL AID
Costs (2017–18) *Tuition:* state resident $8580 full-time, $286 per credit hour part-time; nonresident $27,960 full-time, $932 per credit hour part-time. Full-time tuition and fees vary according to course load. Part-time tuition and fees vary according to course load. *Required fees:* $2322 full-time. *Room and board:* $10,136; room only: $5272. Room and board charges vary according to board plan and housing facility. *Payment plan:* installment. *Waivers:* senior citizens and employees or children of employees.

Financial Aid Of all full-time matriculated undergraduates who enrolled in 2017, 6,857 applied for aid, 5,599 were judged to have need, 958 had their need fully met. 727 Federal Work-Study jobs (averaging $2383). In 2017, 1738 non-need-based awards were made. *Average percent of need met:* 67. *Average financial aid package:* $13,589. *Average need-based loan:* $4510. *Average need-based gift aid:* $8803. *Average non-need-based aid:* $6280. *Average indebtedness upon graduation:* $34,741.

APPLYING
Standardized Tests *Required:* SAT or ACT (for admission).
Options: electronic application, early admission, early action, deferred entrance.
Application fee: $40.
Required: essay or personal statement, high school transcript, letters of recommendation. *Required for some:* audition for music majors.
Application deadlines: 2/1 (freshmen), rolling (transfers), 12/1 (early action).
Notification: continuous (freshmen), continuous (transfers), 1/15 (early action).

CONTACT
Lateef O'Connor, Senior Associate Director of Admissions, University of Maine, 5713 Chadbourne Hall, Orono, ME 04469-5713. *Phone:* 207-581-1561. *Toll-free phone:* 877-486-2364. *Fax:* 207-581-1213. *E-mail:* um-admit@maine.edu.

See previous page for display ad and page 1468 for the College Close-Up.

University of Maine at Augusta
Augusta, Maine
http://www.uma.edu/

CONTACT
Pamela Proulx-Curry, Interim Dean of Enrollment Services, University of Maine at Augusta, 46 University Drive, Robinson Hall, Augusta, ME 04330. *Phone:* 207-621-3465. *Toll-free phone:* 877-862-1234 Ext. 3185 (in-state); 877-862-1234 (out-of-state). *Fax:* 207-621-3333. *E-mail:* umaadm@maine.edu.

University of Maine at Farmington
Farmington, Maine
http://www.umf.maine.edu/
- **State-supported** comprehensive, founded 1863, part of University of Maine System
- **Small-town** 55-acre campus
- **Endowment** $13.1 million
- **Coed** 1,811 undergraduate students, 92% full-time, 66% women, 34% men

UNDERGRAD STUDENTS
1,673 full-time, 138 part-time. Students come from 28 states and territories; 8 other countries; 16% are from out of state; 2% Black or African American, non-Hispanic/Latino; 2% Hispanic/Latino; 0.6% Asian, non-Hispanic/Latino; 0.1% Native Hawaiian or other Pacific Islander, non-Hispanic/Latino; 0.4% American Indian or Alaska Native, non-Hispanic/Latino; 2% Two or more races, non-Hispanic/Latino; 5% Race/ethnicity unknown; 0.9% international; 6% transferred in; 53% live on campus.

Freshmen:
Admission: 426 enrolled. *Average high school GPA:* 3.1. *Test scores:* SAT evidence-based reading and writing scores over 500: 77%; SAT math scores over 500: 66%; ACT scores over 18: 95%; SAT evidence-based reading and writing scores over 600: 28%; SAT math scores over 600: 15%; ACT scores over 24: 60%; SAT evidence-based reading and writing scores over 700: 2%; SAT math scores over 700: 1%.
Retention: 72% of full-time freshmen returned.

FACULTY
Total: 202, 56% full-time, 62% with terminal degrees.
Student/faculty ratio: 13:1.

ACADEMICS
Calendar: semesters 3 summer sessions: one of 5 weeks and two of 4 weeks each. *Degrees:* certificates, bachelor's, master's, and postbachelor's certificates.

Special study options: academic remediation for entering students, accelerated degree program, advanced placement credit, distance learning, double majors, honors programs, independent study, internships, off-campus study, part-time degree program, services for LD students, student-designed majors, study abroad, summer session for credit.

Unusual degree programs: 3-2 social work with University of Southern Maine; Logan University.

Computers: 220 computers/terminals and 3,000 ports are available on campus for general student use. Students can access the following: campus intranet, computer help desk, free student e-mail accounts, online (class) grades, online (class) registration, online (class) schedules. Campuswide network is available. 100% of college-owned or -operated housing units are wired for high-speed Internet access. Wireless service is available via entire campus.

Library: Mantor Library plus 1 other. Weekly public service hours: 88; students can reserve study rooms.

STUDENT LIFE
Housing options: on-campus residence required for freshman year; coed, women-only, cooperative, special housing for students with disabilities. Campus housing is university owned. Freshman campus housing is guaranteed.

Activities and organizations: drama/theater group, student-run newspaper, radio station, choral group, Bust-A-Move Beavers, Commuter Council, Intervarsity Christian Fellowship, Student Senate, Campus Residence Council.

Athletics Member NCAA. All Division III. *Intercollegiate sports:* baseball M, basketball M/W, cross-country running M/W, field hockey W, golf M, lacrosse W, skiing (cross-country) M/W, skiing (downhill) M/W, soccer M/W, softball W, tennis M(c)/W(c), track and field M/W. *Intramural sports:* basketball M/W, cheerleading M(c)/W(c), equestrian sports M(c)/W(c), football M/W, ice hockey M(c)/W(c), rugby M(c)/W(c), skiing (cross-country) M(c)/W(c), skiing (downhill) M(c)/W(c), soccer M/W, softball M/W, swimming and diving M/W, tennis M/W, ultimate Frisbee M(c)/W(c), volleyball M/W.

Campus security: 24-hour emergency response devices and patrols, student patrols, late-night transport/escort service, controlled dormitory access, safety whistles, security cameras.

Student services: health clinic, personal/psychological counseling.

COSTS & FINANCIAL AID
Costs (2017–18) *Tuition:* state resident $8576 full-time, $268 per credit hour part-time; nonresident $18,144 full-time, $567 per credit hour part-time. Full-time tuition and fees vary according to course load and reciprocity agreements. Part-time tuition and fees vary according to course load and reciprocity agreements. *Required fees:* $882 full-time. *Room and board:* $9334; room only: $5038. Room and board charges vary according to board plan and housing facility. *Payment plan:* installment. *Waivers:* minority students, children of alumni, senior citizens, and employees or children of employees.

Financial Aid Of all full-time matriculated undergraduates who enrolled in 2014, 1,535 applied for aid, 1,332 were judged to have need, 610 had their need fully met. In 2014, 58 non-need-based awards were made. *Average percent of need met:* 83. *Average financial aid package:* $13,876. *Average need-based loan:* $6910. *Average need-based gift aid:* $7079. *Average non-need-based aid:* $2789. *Average indebtedness upon graduation:* $31,529.

APPLYING
Required: high school transcript, 1 letter of recommendation. *Required for some:* essay or personal statement, Minimum 2.75 GPA for College of Education transfers, 2.5 for Health and Rehabilitation, 2.0 for all others. *Recommended:* essay or personal statement, interview.

CONTACT
Lisa Ellrich, Associate Director of Admissions, University of Maine at Farmington, 246 Main Street, Farmington, ME 04938-1994. *Phone:* 207-778-7050. *E-mail:* ellrich@maine.edu.

University of Maine at Fort Kent
Fort Kent, Maine
http://www.umfk.maine.edu/
- **State-supported** 4-year, founded 1878, part of University of Maine System
- **Rural** 52-acre campus
- **Endowment** $3.1 million
- **Coed** 1,760 undergraduate students, 33% full-time, 71% women, 29% men
- **Minimally difficult** entrance level, 97% of applicants were admitted

UNDERGRAD STUDENTS
582 full-time, 1,178 part-time. Students come from 26 states and territories; 26 other countries; 14% are from out of state; 2% Black or African American, non-Hispanic/Latino; 2% Hispanic/Latino; 0.5% Asian, non-Hispanic/Latino; 0.1% Native Hawaiian or other Pacific Islander, non-Hispanic/Latino; 0.7% American Indian or Alaska Native, non-Hispanic/Latino; 2% Two or more races, non-Hispanic/Latino; 36% Race/ethnicity unknown; 4% international; 13% transferred in; 29% live on campus.

Freshmen:
Admission: 572 applied, 556 admitted, 135 enrolled. *Average high school GPA:* 3.4. *Test scores:* SAT evidence-based reading and writing scores over 500: 54%; SAT math scores over 500: 52%; ACT scores over 18: 83%; SAT evidence-based reading and writing scores over 600: 7%; SAT math scores over 600: 5%; ACT scores over 24: 17%.
Retention: 61% of full-time freshmen returned.

FACULTY
Total: 93, 37% full-time, 23% with terminal degrees.
Student/faculty ratio: 14:1.

ACADEMICS
Calendar: semesters. *Degrees:* associate and bachelor's.

Special study options: academic remediation for entering students, accelerated degree program, advanced placement credit, cooperative education, distance learning, double majors, English as a second language, external degree program, honors programs, independent study, internships, part-time degree program, services for LD students, student-designed majors, summer session for credit.

Computers: 100 computers/terminals are available on campus for general student use. Students can access the following: campus intranet, computer help desk, free student e-mail accounts, online (class) grades, online (class) registration, online (class) schedules. Campuswide network is available. 100% of college-owned or -operated housing units are wired for high-speed Internet access. Wireless service is available via entire campus.

Library: Waneta Blake Library. *Books:* 44,058 (physical), 9,361 (digital/electronic); *Serial titles:* 92 (physical), 61,183 (digital/electronic); *Databases:* 106. Weekly public service hours: 88; students can reserve study rooms.

STUDENT LIFE
Housing options: on-campus residence required for freshman year; coed. Campus housing is university owned. Freshman applicants given priority for college housing.

Activities and organizations: drama/theater group, Student Nurses Organization, Student Teachers Educational Professional Society, Student Senate, Student Activities Board, Dorm Council, national fraternities, national sororities.

Athletics Member USCAA. *Intercollegiate sports:* basketball M/W, soccer M/W, volleyball W. *Intramural sports:* basketball M/W, softball M/W, volleyball M/W.

Campus security: controlled dormitory access, night patrols by security personnel 11pm-7am.

Student services: health clinic, personal/psychological counseling.

COSTS & FINANCIAL AID
Costs (2018–19) *Tuition:* state resident $6990 full-time, $233 per credit hour part-time; nonresident $11,190 full-time, $373 per credit hour part-time. *Required fees:* $1125 full-time, $75 per credit hour part-time. *Room and board:* $7910; room only: $4250. Room and board charges vary

according to board plan and housing facility. *Payment plan:* installment. *Waivers:* senior citizens and employees or children of employees.

Financial Aid Of all full-time matriculated undergraduates who enrolled in 2016, 478 applied for aid, 389 were judged to have need, 194 had their need fully met. 98 Federal Work-Study jobs (averaging $1143). In 2016, 28 non-need-based awards were made. *Average percent of need met:* 79. *Average financial aid package:* $11,258. *Average need-based loan:* $6502. *Average need-based gift aid:* $6324. *Average non-need-based aid:* $2813. *Average indebtedness upon graduation:* $24,096.

APPLYING
Standardized Tests *Required for some:* SAT or ACT (for admission).
Options: electronic application, deferred entrance.
Application fee: $40.
Required: essay or personal statement, high school transcript. *Required for some:* interview.
Application deadlines: rolling (freshmen), rolling (out-of-state freshmen), rolling (transfers).
Notification: continuous (freshmen), continuous (out-of-state freshmen), continuous (transfers).

CONTACT
University of Maine at Fort Kent, 23 University Drive, Fort Kent, ME 04743-1292. *Phone:* 207-834-7600. *Toll-free phone:* 888-TRY-UMFK.

University of Maine at Machias
Machias, Maine
http://www.machias.edu/

- **State-supported** 4-year, founded 1909, part of University of Maine System
- **Rural** 42-acre campus
- **Coed** 701 undergraduate students, 52% full-time, 69% women, 31% men
- **Moderately difficult** entrance level, 91% of applicants were admitted

UNDERGRAD STUDENTS
367 full-time, 334 part-time. 11% are from out of state; 2% Black or African American, non-Hispanic/Latino; 6% Hispanic/Latino; 0.4% Asian, non-Hispanic/Latino; 0.2% Native Hawaiian or other Pacific Islander, non-Hispanic/Latino; 4% American Indian or Alaska Native, non-Hispanic/Latino; 2% Two or more races, non-Hispanic/Latino; 3% Race/ethnicity unknown; 0.4% international; 5% transferred in; 56% live on campus.

Freshmen:
Admission: 514 applied, 470 admitted, 99 enrolled.
Retention: 63% of full-time freshmen returned.

FACULTY
Total: 68, 41% full-time, 60% with terminal degrees.
Student/faculty ratio: 12:1.

ACADEMICS
Calendar: semesters. *Degrees:* certificates, associate, and bachelor's.
Special study options: academic remediation for entering students, advanced placement credit, cooperative education, distance learning, double majors, independent study, internships, off-campus study, part-time degree program, services for LD students, student-designed majors, study abroad, summer session for credit.
Library: Merrill Library.

STUDENT LIFE
Housing options: on-campus residence required through sophomore year; coed, special housing for students with disabilities. Campus housing is university owned.
Athletics Member NAIA. *Intercollegiate sports:* basketball M/W, cross-country running M/W, lacrosse M(c)/W(c), soccer M/W, volleyball W. *Intramural sports:* basketball M/W, cheerleading W, fencing M/W, football M/W, soccer M/W, softball W, water polo M/W.

COSTS & FINANCIAL AID
Costs (2017–18) *Tuition:* state resident $6840 full-time, $228 per semester hour part-time; nonresident $18,480 full-time, $616 per semester hour part-time. Full-time tuition and fees vary according to course load and reciprocity agreements. Part-time tuition and fees vary according to

course load and reciprocity agreements. *Required fees:* $886 full-time. *Room and board:* $8490; room only: $4330. Room and board charges vary according to housing facility. *Payment plan:* installment. *Waivers:* senior citizens and employees or children of employees.

Financial Aid Of all full-time matriculated undergraduates who enrolled in 2016, 394 applied for aid, 354 were judged to have need, 217 had their need fully met. In 2016, 2 non-need-based awards were made. *Average percent of need met:* 83. *Average financial aid package:* $14,175. *Average need-based loan:* $6053. *Average need-based gift aid:* $8858. *Average non-need-based aid:* $750. *Average indebtedness upon graduation:* $25,702.

APPLYING
Options: electronic application, early admission, early action, deferred entrance.
Application fee: $40.
Required: essay or personal statement, high school transcript, 1 letter of recommendation. *Required for some:* minimum 2.0 GPA, interview. *Recommended:* minimum 2.5 GPA, 2 letters of recommendation, interview.

CONTACT
Director of Admissions, University of Maine at Machias, 9 O'Brien Avenue, Machias, ME 04654. *Phone:* 207-255-1318. *Toll-free phone:* 888-GOTOUMM (in-state); 888-468-6866 (out-of-state). *Fax:* 207-255-1363. *E-mail:* ummadmissions@maine.edu.

University of Maine at Presque Isle
Presque Isle, Maine
http://www.umpi.edu/

- **State-supported** 4-year, founded 1903, part of University of Maine System
- **Small-town** 150-acre campus
- **Endowment** $1.3 million
- **Coed** 1,408 undergraduate students, 50% full-time, 62% women, 38% men
- **Minimally difficult** entrance level, 95% of applicants were admitted

UNDERGRAD STUDENTS
710 full-time, 698 part-time. Students come from 28 states and territories; 9 other countries; 16% are from out of state; 2% Black or African American, non-Hispanic/Latino; 2% Hispanic/Latino; 0.7% Asian, non-Hispanic/Latino; 1% American Indian or Alaska Native, non-Hispanic/Latino; 3% Two or more races, non-Hispanic/Latino; 11% Race/ethnicity unknown; 3% international; 9% transferred in; 33% live on campus.

Freshmen:
Admission: 1,424 applied, 1,359 admitted, 171 enrolled. *Average high school GPA:* 2.9. *Test scores:* SAT evidence-based reading and writing scores over 500: 61%; SAT math scores over 500: 51%; ACT scores over 18: 90%; SAT evidence-based reading and writing scores over 600: 18%; SAT math scores over 600: 13%; ACT scores over 24: 20%; SAT evidence-based reading and writing scores over 700: 1%; SAT math scores over 700: 1%.
Retention: 57% of full-time freshmen returned.

FACULTY
Total: 102, 41% full-time, 40% with terminal degrees.
Student/faculty ratio: 13:1.

ACADEMICS
Calendar: semesters. *Degrees:* certificates, associate, and bachelor's.
Special study options: academic remediation for entering students, accelerated degree program, adult/continuing education programs, advanced placement credit, cooperative education, distance learning, double majors, honors programs, independent study, internships, off-campus study, part-time degree program, services for LD students, student-designed majors, study abroad, summer session for credit.
Computers: Students can access the following: campus intranet, computer help desk, free student e-mail accounts, online (class) grades, online (class) registration, online (class) schedules. Campuswide network is available. 100% of college-owned or -operated housing units

are wired for high-speed Internet access. Wireless service is available via entire campus.

Library: Center for Innovative Learning plus 1 other. Weekly public service hours: 72.

STUDENT LIFE

Housing options: coed, special housing for students with disabilities. Campus housing is university owned. Freshman applicants given priority for college housing.

Activities and organizations: student-run newspaper, radio station, national fraternities, national sororities.

Athletics Member NCAA, USCAA. All Division III except men's and women's skiing (cross-country) (Division I). *Intercollegiate sports:* baseball M, basketball M/W, cross-country running M/W, golf M, skiing (cross-country) M/W, soccer M/W, softball W, volleyball W. *Intramural sports:* basketball M/W, cross-country running M/W, ice hockey M(c)/W(c), skiing (cross-country) M/W, skiing (downhill) M/W, soccer M/W, softball M/W, tennis M, track and field W, volleyball M/W.

Campus security: student patrols, late-night transport/escort service, controlled dormitory access.

Student services: health clinic, personal/psychological counseling.

COSTS & FINANCIAL AID

Costs (2018–19) *Tuition:* state resident $6990 full-time; nonresident $11,190 full-time. Full-time tuition and fees vary according to course load. Part-time tuition and fees vary according to course load. *Required fees:* $1044 full-time. *Room and board:* $8406; room only: $4850. Room and board charges vary according to board plan. *Payment plan:* installment. *Waivers:* senior citizens and employees or children of employees.

Financial Aid Of all full-time matriculated undergraduates who enrolled in 2017, 559 applied for aid, 503 were judged to have need, 298 had their need fully met. In 2017, 20 non-need-based awards were made. *Average percent of need met:* 82. *Average financial aid package:* $11,451. *Average need-based loan:* $5063. *Average need-based gift aid:* $6592. *Average non-need-based aid:* $3047. *Average indebtedness upon graduation:* $23,574.

APPLYING

Options: electronic application, early admission, deferred entrance.

Required: essay or personal statement, high school transcript, 1 letter of recommendation. *Required for some:* interview. *Recommended:* minimum 2.0 GPA.

Application deadlines: rolling (freshmen), rolling (out-of-state freshmen), rolling (transfers).

CONTACT

Patricia Armstrong, Director of Admission, University of Maine at Presque Isle, 181 Main Street, Presque Isle, ME 04769. *Phone:* 207-768-9533. *E-mail:* patricia.armstrong@umpi.edu.

University of New England
Biddeford, Maine
http://www.une.edu/

- **Independent** comprehensive, founded 1831
- **Small-town** 540-acre campus
- **Endowment** $35.5 million
- **Coed** 4,423 undergraduate students, 53% full-time, 75% women, 25% men
- **Moderately difficult** entrance level, 81% of applicants were admitted

UNDERGRAD STUDENTS

2,361 full-time, 2,062 part-time. Students come from 39 states and territories; 6 other countries; 70% are from out of state; 2% Black or African American, non-Hispanic/Latino; 0.1% Hispanic/Latino; 5% Asian, non-Hispanic/Latino; 0.1% Native Hawaiian or other Pacific Islander, non-Hispanic/Latino; 0.5% American Indian or Alaska Native, non-Hispanic/Latino; 0.9% Two or more races, non-Hispanic/Latino; 23% Race/ethnicity unknown; 0.3% international; 2% transferred in; 65% live on campus.

Freshmen:
Admission: 5,087 applied, 4,107 admitted, 651 enrolled. *Average high school GPA:* 3.4. *Test scores:* SAT evidence-based reading and writing scores over 500: 87%; SAT math scores over 500: 80%; ACT scores over 18: 97%; SAT evidence-based reading and writing scores over 600: 34%; SAT math scores over 600: 26%; ACT scores over 24: 52%; SAT evidence-based reading and writing scores over 700: 3%; SAT math scores over 700: 2%; ACT scores over 30: 9%.

Retention: 78% of full-time freshmen returned.

FACULTY

Total: 599, 48% full-time, 56% with terminal degrees.

Student/faculty ratio: 13:1.

ACADEMICS

Calendar: semesters. *Degrees:* bachelor's, master's, doctoral, post-master's, and postbachelor's certificates.

Special study options: academic remediation for entering students, accelerated degree program, adult/continuing education programs, advanced placement credit, cooperative education, distance learning, double majors, honors programs, independent study, internships, off-campus study, part-time degree program, services for LD students, study abroad, summer session for credit. *ROTC:* Army (c).

Unusual degree programs: 3-2 physician assistant.

Computers: 91 computers/terminals are available on campus for general student use. Students can access the following: campus intranet, computer help desk, free student e-mail accounts, online (class) grades, online (class) registration, online (class) schedules. Campuswide network is available. 100% of college-owned or -operated housing units are wired for high-speed Internet access. Wireless service is available via entire campus.

Library: Jack S. Ketchum Library plus 1 other. *Books:* 135,000 (physical), 1.2 million (digital/electronic); *Serial titles:* 140,000 (digital/electronic); *Databases:* 200. Weekly public service hours: 146; study areas open 24 hours, 5–7 days a week; students can reserve study rooms.

STUDENT LIFE

Housing options: on-campus residence required through junior year; coed, women-only, special housing for students with disabilities. Campus housing is university owned. Freshman campus housing is guaranteed.

Activities and organizations: drama/theater group, student-run newspaper, choral group, Student Government, Outing Club, Campus Programming Board, Earth's Eco, Dance Team.

Athletics Member NCAA. All Division III. *Intercollegiate sports:* basketball M/W, cross-country running M/W, field hockey W, football M, golf M, ice hockey M/W, lacrosse M/W, rugby W, soccer M/W, softball W, swimming and diving W, volleyball W. *Intramural sports:* baseball M(c), basketball M/W, cheerleading M(c)/W(c), equestrian sports M(c)/W(c), gymnastics M(c)/W(c), ice hockey M(c)/W(c), racquetball M/W, rugby M(c)/W(c), sailing M(c)/W(c), soccer M/W, softball M/W, swimming and diving M(c), table tennis M/W, tennis M(c)/W(c), track and field M(c)/W(c), ultimate Frisbee M/W, volleyball M(c)/W(c), water polo W(c).

Campus security: 24-hour emergency response devices and patrols, late-night transport/escort service, controlled dormitory access.

Student services: health clinic, personal/psychological counseling.

COSTS

Costs (2017–18) *Comprehensive fee:* $50,110 includes full-time tuition ($35,240), mandatory fees ($1290), and room and board ($13,580). Full-time tuition and fees vary according to course load and program. Part-time tuition: $1240 per credit hour. Part-time tuition and fees vary according to course load and program. *Required fees:* $1290 per term part-time. *Room and board:* Room and board charges vary according to board plan and housing facility. *Payment plan:* installment. *Waivers:* children of alumni and employees or children of employees.

APPLYING

Standardized Tests *Required:* SAT or ACT (for admission).

Options: electronic application, early admission, early action, deferred entrance.

Application fee: $40.

Required: essay or personal statement, high school transcript. *Recommended:* 1 letter of recommendation.

Application deadlines: 2/15 (freshmen), rolling (transfers), 12/1 (early action).

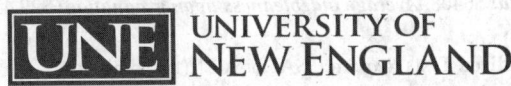
Notification: continuous (freshmen), continuous (transfers), rolling (early action).

CONTACT
Peter Heeley, Senior Associate Director of Undergraduate Admission, University of New England, 11 Hills Beach Road, Biddeford, ME 04005-9526. *Phone:* 800-477-4863. *Toll-free phone:* 800-477-4863. *Fax:* 207-602-5900. *E-mail:* admissions@une.edu.

See this page for display ad and page 1470 for the College Close-Up.

University of Southern Maine
Portland, Maine
http://www.usm.maine.edu/

- **State-supported** comprehensive, founded 1878, part of University of Maine System
- **Urban** 144-acre campus
- **Endowment** $38.5 million
- **Coed** 6,189 undergraduate students, 61% full-time, 58% women, 42% men
- **Moderately difficult** entrance level, 80% of applicants were admitted

UNDERGRAD STUDENTS
3,750 full-time, 2,439 part-time. Students come from 38 states and territories; 16 other countries; 12% are from out of state; 4% Black or African American, non-Hispanic/Latino; 2% Hispanic/Latino; 2% Asian, non-Hispanic/Latino; 0.7% American Indian or Alaska Native, non-Hispanic/Latino; 3% Two or more races, non-Hispanic/Latino; 14% Race/ethnicity unknown; 1% international; 11% transferred in; 24% live on campus.

Freshmen:
Admission: 4,111 applied, 3,299 admitted, 805 enrolled. *Average high school GPA:* 3.2. *Test scores:* ACT scores over 18: 84%; ACT scores over 24: 39%; ACT scores over 30: 2%.
Retention: 63% of full-time freshmen returned.

FACULTY
Total: 662, 40% full-time, 46% with terminal degrees.
Student/faculty ratio: 14:1.

ACADEMICS
Calendar: semesters. *Degrees:* certificates, bachelor's, master's, doctoral, post-master's, and postbachelor's certificates.

Special study options: academic remediation for entering students, accelerated degree program, adult/continuing education programs, advanced placement credit, cooperative education, distance learning, double majors, English as a second language, honors programs, independent study, internships, off-campus study, part-time degree program, services for LD students, student-designed majors, study abroad, summer session for credit. *ROTC:* Army (c), Air Force (c).

Unusual degree programs: 3-2 business administration.

Computers: 219 computers/terminals are available on campus for general student use. Students can access the following: campus intranet, computer help desk, free student e-mail accounts, online (class) grades, online (class) registration, online (class) schedules. Campuswide network is available. 100% of college-owned or -operated housing units are wired for high-speed Internet access. Wireless service is available via entire campus.
Library: Glickman Library plus 3 others.

STUDENT LIFE
Housing options: coed, special housing for students with disabilities. Campus housing is university owned. Freshman applicants given priority for college housing.

Activities and organizations: drama/theater group, student-run newspaper, radio station, choral group, Outing and Ski Clubs, Gorham Events Board, Commuter Student Group, Circle K, national fraternities, national sororities.

Athletics Member NCAA. All Division III. *Intercollegiate sports:* baseball M, basketball M/W, cross-country running M/W, fencing M/W(c), field hockey W, golf M/W, ice hockey M/W, lacrosse M/W, sailing M/W, soccer M/W, softball W, tennis M/W, track and field M/W, volleyball W, wrestling M. *Intramural sports:* baseball M, basketball M/W, cheerleading M(c)/W(c), football M/W, ice hockey M/W, lacrosse

M(c)/W(c), racquetball M/W, rugby M(c)/W(c), skiing (downhill) M(c)/W(c), soccer M/W, softball M/W, squash M/W, table tennis M/W, tennis M/W, ultimate Frisbee M/W, volleyball M/W, weight lifting M/W.

Campus security: 24-hour emergency response devices and patrols, late-night transport/escort service, controlled dormitory access, security lighting, preventive programs within residence halls.

Student services: health clinic, personal/psychological counseling, women's center, legal services.

COSTS & FINANCIAL AID

Costs (2017–18) *Tuition:* state resident $7860 full-time, $262 per credit hour part-time; nonresident $20,670 full-time, $689 per credit hour part-time. Full-time tuition and fees vary according to course load, degree level, and reciprocity agreements. Part-time tuition and fees vary according to course load, degree level, and reciprocity agreements. *Required fees:* $1360 full-time, $1360 per year part-time. *Room and board:* $9200; room only: $5000. Room and board charges vary according to board plan and housing facility. *Payment plan:* installment. *Waivers:* employees or children of employees.

Financial Aid Of all full-time matriculated undergraduates who enrolled in 2015, 3,267 applied for aid, 2,788 were judged to have need, 1,646 had their need fully met. In 2015, 152 non-need-based awards were made. *Average percent of need met:* 79. *Average financial aid package:* $13,894. *Average need-based loan:* $6939. *Average need-based gift aid:* $7911. *Average non-need-based aid:* $3741.

APPLYING

Standardized Tests *Required:* SAT (for admission).

Options: electronic application, early admission, deferred entrance.

Application fee: $40.

Required: essay or personal statement, high school transcript. *Required for some:* interview, audition for music majors. *Recommended:* 1 letter of recommendation, interview.

Notification: continuous (freshmen), continuous (out-of-state freshmen), continuous (transfers).

CONTACT

Admissions, University of Southern Maine, Portland, ME 04104-9300. *Phone:* 207-780-5670. *Toll-free phone:* 800-800-4USM Ext. 5670. *E-mail:* admitusm@maine.edu.

MARYLAND

Bais HaMedrash and Mesivta of Baltimore
Baltimore, Maryland

CONTACT
Bais HaMedrash and Mesivta of Baltimore, 6823 Old Pimlico Road, Baltimore, MD 21209.

Bowie State University
Bowie, Maryland
http://www.bowiestate.edu/

- **State-supported** comprehensive, founded 1865, part of University System of Maryland
- **Small-town** 295-acre campus with easy access to Baltimore and Washington, DC
- **Coed** 4,711 undergraduate students, 84% full-time, 62% women, 38% men
- **Minimally difficult** entrance level, 41% of applicants were admitted

UNDERGRAD STUDENTS
3,939 full-time, 772 part-time. Students come from 31 states and territories; 9% are from out of state; 86% Black or African American, non-Hispanic/Latino; 3% Hispanic/Latino; 1% Asian, non-Hispanic/Latino; 0.1% Native Hawaiian or other Pacific Islander, non-Hispanic/Latino; 0.1% American Indian or Alaska Native, non-Hispanic/Latino; 4% Two or more races, non-Hispanic/Latino; 2% Race/ethnicity unknown; 1% international; 35% live on campus.

Freshmen:
Admission: 6,720 applied, 2,775 admitted, 967 enrolled. *Average high school GPA:* 2.5.
Retention: 70% of full-time freshmen returned.

FACULTY
Total: 414, 52% full-time, 88% with terminal degrees.
Student/faculty ratio: 16:1.

ACADEMICS
Calendar: semesters. *Degrees:* certificates, bachelor's, master's, doctoral, and postbachelor's certificates.

Special study options: academic remediation for entering students, adult/continuing education programs, advanced placement credit, cooperative education, distance learning, double majors, external degree program, honors programs, independent study, internships, off-campus study, part-time degree program, services for LD students, study abroad, summer session for credit. *ROTC:* Army (b).

Unusual degree programs: 3-2 engineering with George Washington University, University of Maryland College Park, Howard University.

Computers: 3,950 computers/terminals are available on campus for general student use. Students can access the following: computer help desk, free student e-mail accounts, online (class) grades, online (class) registration. Campuswide network is available. Wireless service is available via entire campus.

Library: Thurgood Marshall Library. Students can reserve study rooms.

STUDENT LIFE
Housing options: coed, men-only, women-only. Campus housing is university owned and is provided by a third party. Freshman applicants given priority for college housing.

Activities and organizations: drama/theater group, student-run newspaper, radio and television station, choral group, marching band, Honda Campus All-Star Challenge, national fraternities, national sororities.

Athletics Member NCAA. All Division II. *Intercollegiate sports:* basketball M(s)/W(s), bowling W, cross-country running M(s)/W(s), football M(s), softball W(s), tennis W(s), track and field M(s)/W(s), volleyball W(s).

Campus security: 24-hour emergency response devices and patrols, student patrols, late-night transport/escort service, controlled dormitory access.

Student services: health clinic, personal/psychological counseling.

COSTS & FINANCIAL AID
Costs (2017–18) *Tuition:* state resident $5426 full-time, $239 per credit hour part-time; nonresident $16,016 full-time, $673 per credit hour part-time. Part-time tuition and fees vary according to course load. *Required fees:* $2637 full-time, $119 per credit hour part-time. *Room and board:* $11,340; room only: $7180. Room and board charges vary according to board plan and housing facility. *Payment plans:* installment, deferred payment. *Waivers:* senior citizens and employees or children of employees.

Financial Aid Of all full-time matriculated undergraduates who enrolled in 2017, 3,177 applied for aid, 3,164 were judged to have need, 485 had their need fully met. 85 Federal Work-Study jobs (averaging $2875). In 2017, 49 non-need-based awards were made. *Average percent of need met:* 43. *Average financial aid package:* $8736. *Average need-based loan:* $4017. *Average need-based gift aid:* $7113. *Average non-need-based aid:* $6408. *Average indebtedness upon graduation:* $29,433.

APPLYING
Standardized Tests *Required:* SAT or ACT (for admission).

Options: electronic application.

Application fee: $40.

Required: high school transcript, minimum 2.5 GPA.

Application deadlines: 4/1 (freshmen), 4/1 (transfers).

Notification: continuous (freshmen), continuous (transfers).

CONTACT
Mrs. Shirley Holt, Assistant Director of Admissions, Bowie State University, Administration Building, 1st Floor. *Phone:* 301-860-3415. *Toll-free phone:* 877-772-6943. *Fax:* 301-860-3438. *E-mail:* sholt@bowiestate.edu.

Capitol Technology University
Laurel, Maryland
http://www.captechu.edu/

CONTACT
Capitol Technology University, 11301 Springfield Road, Laurel, MD 20708-9759. *Phone:* 301-953-3200 Ext. 3033. *Toll-free phone:* 800-950-1992.

Cecil College
North East, Maryland
http://www.cecil.edu/
- **County-supported** primarily 2-year, founded 1968
- **Small-town** 159-acre campus with easy access to Baltimore
- **Coed** 2,468 undergraduate students, 35% full-time, 64% women, 36% men
- **Noncompetitive** entrance level

UNDERGRAD STUDENTS
867 full-time, 1,601 part-time. Students come from 9 states and territories; 21 other countries; 16% are from out of state; 10% Black or African American, non-Hispanic/Latino; 6% Hispanic/Latino; 1% Asian, non-Hispanic/Latino; 0.1% Native Hawaiian or other Pacific Islander, non-Hispanic/Latino; 0.3% American Indian or Alaska Native, non-Hispanic/Latino; 5% Two or more races, non-Hispanic/Latino; 1% Race/ethnicity unknown; 0.6% international; 4% transferred in.

Freshmen:
Admission: 409 enrolled.
Retention: 56% of full-time freshmen returned.

FACULTY
Total: 295, 17% full-time, 5% with terminal degrees.
Student/faculty ratio: 11:1.

ACADEMICS
Calendar: semesters. *Degrees:* certificates, associate, and bachelor's.
Special study options: academic remediation for entering students, accelerated degree program, adult/continuing education programs, advanced placement credit, cooperative education, distance learning, double majors, English as a second language, independent study, internships, off-campus study, part-time degree program, services for LD students, summer session for credit.
Computers: 105 computers/terminals are available on campus for general student use. Students can access the following: computer help desk, free student e-mail accounts, online (class) grades, online (class) registration, online (class) schedules. Campuswide network is available. Wireless service is available via entire campus.
Library: Cecil County Veterans Memorial Library.

STUDENT LIFE
Activities and organizations: drama/theater group, Student Government, Non-Traditional Student Organization, Student Nurses Association, national fraternities.
Athletics Member NJCAA. *Intercollegiate sports:* baseball M(s), basketball M(s)/W(s), golf M, lacrosse M(c), soccer M(s)/W(s), softball W(s), tennis W(s), volleyball W(s).
Campus security: 24-hour emergency response devices, late-night transport/escort service, armed patrols from 6:30 am until 7:00 pm.
Student services: personal/psychological counseling, women's center.

COSTS
Costs (2018–19) *Tuition:* area resident $3270 full-time, $109 per credit hour part-time; state resident $6090 full-time, $203 per credit hour part-time; nonresident $7530 full-time, $251 per credit hour part-time.
Required fees: $735 full-time. *Payment plan:* deferred payment.
Waivers: senior citizens and employees or children of employees.

APPLYING
Options: electronic application, early admission, deferred entrance.
Required: high school transcript.
Application deadlines: rolling (freshmen), rolling (transfers).
Notification: continuous (freshmen), continuous (transfers).

CONTACT
Dr. Christy Dryer, Cecil College, One Seahawk Drive, North East, MD 21901-1999. *Phone:* 410-287-6060. *Fax:* 410-287-1001. *E-mail:* cdryer@cecil.edu.

Coppin State University
Baltimore, Maryland
http://www.coppin.edu/

CONTACT
Ms. Michelle Gross, Director of Admissions, Coppin State University, 2500 West North Avenue, Baltimore, MD 21216-3698. *Phone:* 410-951-3600. *Toll-free phone:* 800-635-3674. *Fax:* 410-523-7351. *E-mail:* mgross@coppin.edu.

Faith Theological Seminary
Baltimore, Maryland
http://www.fts.edu/

CONTACT
Faith Theological Seminary, 529 Walker Avenue, Baltimore, MD 21212. *Phone:* 410-323-6211.

Frostburg State University
Frostburg, Maryland
http://www.frostburg.edu/
- **State-supported** comprehensive, founded 1898, part of University System of Maryland
- **Small-town** 260-acre campus with easy access to Baltimore and Washington, DC
- **Endowment** $25.1 million
- **Coed** 4,725 undergraduate students, 81% full-time, 52% women, 48% men
- **Moderately difficult** entrance level, 72% of applicants were admitted

UNDERGRAD STUDENTS
3,849 full-time, 876 part-time. Students come from 31 states and territories; 41 other countries; 7% are from out of state; 31% Black or African American, non-Hispanic/Latino; 6% Hispanic/Latino; 2% Asian, non-Hispanic/Latino; 0.1% American Indian or Alaska Native, non-Hispanic/Latino; 4% Two or more races, non-Hispanic/Latino; 1% Race/ethnicity unknown; 4% international; 10% transferred in; 28% live on campus.

Freshmen:
Admission: 3,436 applied, 2,484 admitted, 774 enrolled. *Average high school GPA:* 3.2. *Test scores:* SAT evidence-based reading and writing scores over 500: 60%; SAT math scores over 500: 54%; ACT scores over 18: 67%; SAT evidence-based reading and writing scores over 600: 13%; SAT math scores over 600: 13%; ACT scores over 24: 21%; SAT evidence-based reading and writing scores over 700: 1%; SAT math scores over 700: 1%; ACT scores over 30: 1%.
Retention: 74% of full-time freshmen returned.

FACULTY
Total: 390, 64% full-time, 58% with terminal degrees.
Student/faculty ratio: 15:1.

ACADEMICS
Calendar: semesters. *Degrees:* bachelor's, master's, and doctoral.
Special study options: adult/continuing education programs, advanced placement credit, cooperative education, distance learning, double majors, freshman honors college, honors programs, independent study, internships, off-campus study, part-time degree program, services for LD students, study abroad, summer session for credit.
Unusual degree programs: 3-2 business administration; engineering with University of Maryland, College Park.
Computers: 577 computers/terminals are available on campus for general student use. Students can access the following: campus intranet, computer help desk, free student e-mail accounts, online (class) grades, online (class) registration, online (class) schedules. Campuswide network is available. 100% of college-owned or -operated housing units

are wired for high-speed Internet access. Wireless service is available via entire campus.

Library: Lewis J. Ort Library.

STUDENT LIFE

Housing options: coed, men-only, women-only. Campus housing is university owned and is provided by a third party.

Activities and organizations: drama/theater group, student-run newspaper, radio and television station, choral group, marching band, Student Government Association, Black Student Association, Campus Activities Board, Residence Hall Association, University Programming Council, national fraternities, national sororities.

Athletics Member NCAA. All Division III. *Intercollegiate sports:* baseball M, basketball M/W, cross-country running M/W, field hockey W, football M, lacrosse M/W, soccer M/W, softball W, swimming and diving M/W, tennis M/W, track and field M/W, volleyball W. *Intramural sports:* basketball M/W, football M/W, lacrosse M(c), racquetball M/W, rugby M(c), soccer M/W, softball M/W, tennis M/W, volleyball M(c)/W, wrestling M.

Campus security: 24-hour emergency response devices and patrols, student patrols, late-night transport/escort service, controlled dormitory access, bicycle patrols.

Student services: health clinic, personal/psychological counseling, women's center.

COSTS & FINANCIAL AID

Costs (2018–19) *Tuition:* state resident $6468 full-time, $267 per credit hour part-time; nonresident $19,816 full-time, $556 per credit hour part-time. Full-time tuition and fees vary according to location. Part-time tuition and fees vary according to course load and location. *Required fees:* $2446 full-time, $115 per credit hour part-time, $26 per term part-time. *Room and board:* $9210; room only: $4520. Room and board charges vary according to board plan and housing facility. *Payment plans:* installment, deferred payment. *Waivers:* senior citizens and employees or children of employees.

Financial Aid Of all full-time matriculated undergraduates who enrolled in 2017, 3,480 applied for aid, 2,669 were judged to have need, 386 had their need fully met. 130 Federal Work-Study jobs (averaging $674). In 2017, 853 non-need-based awards were made. *Average percent of need met:* 59. *Average financial aid package:* $9993. *Average need-based loan:* $3932. *Average need-based gift aid:* $7651. *Average non-need-based aid:* $3427. *Average indebtedness upon graduation:* $29,802.

APPLYING

Standardized Tests *Required:* SAT or ACT (for admission).

Options: electronic application, early admission.

Application fee: $30.

Required: high school transcript, minimum 2.0 GPA. *Required for some:* essay or personal statement. *Recommended:* interview.

Application deadlines: 2/15 (freshmen), 2/30 (out-of-state freshmen), 6/1 (transfers).

CONTACT

Frostburg State University, 101 Braddock Road, Frostburg, MD 21532-1099. *Phone:* 301-687-4201.

Goucher College

Baltimore, Maryland

http://www.goucher.edu/

- **Independent** comprehensive, founded 1885
- **Suburban** 287-acre campus with easy access to Baltimore and Washington, DC
- **Endowment** $201.5 million
- **Coed**
- **Moderately difficult** entrance level

FACULTY

Student/faculty ratio: 10:1.

ACADEMICS

Calendar: semesters. *Degrees:* bachelor's, master's, and postbachelor's certificates.

Library: Goucher College Library plus 1 other. *Books:* 250,000 (physical), 300,000 (digital/electronic); *Serial titles:* 96,000

(digital/electronic); *Databases:* 120. Weekly public service hours: 168; study areas open 24 hours, 5–7 days a week.

STUDENT LIFE

Housing options: on-campus residence required through senior year; coed, men-only, women-only, special housing for students with disabilities. Campus housing is university owned. Freshman applicants given priority for college housing.

Activities and organizations: drama/theater group, student-run newspaper, radio station, choral group, Ultimate Frisbee, Yoga Club, Hip Hop Team, Umoja: The Black Student Union, Model Senate.

Athletics Member NCAA. All Division III.

Campus security: 24-hour emergency response devices and patrols, late-night transport/escort service, controlled dormitory access, E2 campus alerts.

Student services: health clinic, personal/psychological counseling.

COSTS & FINANCIAL AID

Costs (2017–18) *Comprehensive fee:* $56,110 includes full-time tuition ($42,600), mandatory fees ($840), and room and board ($12,670). Part-time tuition: $1420 per credit hour. *Room and board:* Room and board charges vary according to board plan and housing facility. *Payment plans:* tuition prepayment, installment.

Financial Aid Of all full-time matriculated undergraduates who enrolled in 2017, 1,072 applied for aid, 959 were judged to have need, 217 had their need fully met. 397 Federal Work-Study jobs (averaging $1863). In 2017, 432 non-need-based awards were made. *Average percent of need met:* 82. *Average financial aid package:* $36,918. *Average need-based loan:* $4071. *Average need-based gift uid:* $32,630. *Average non-need-based aid:* $19,119. *Average indebtedness upon graduation:* $33,702.

APPLYING

Options: electronic application, early admission, early decision, early action, deferred entrance.

Application fee: $55.

Required: essay or personal statement, a short video, digital application, signed statement of academic integrity, two works from high school career (one of which must be a graded writing assignment) for Goucher Video Application. *Required for some:* high school transcript. *Recommended:* 3 letters of recommendation, interview.

CONTACT

Mr. Carlton E. Surbeck, Director of Admissions, Goucher College, 1021 Dulaney Valley Road, Baltimore, MD 21204. *Phone:* 410-337-6100. *Toll-free phone:* 800-468-2437. *Fax:* 410-337-6354. *E-mail:* admissions@goucher.edu.

Hood College

Frederick, Maryland

http://www.hood.edu/

- **Independent** comprehensive, founded 1893
- **Suburban** 50-acre campus with easy access to Baltimore and Washington, DC
- **Endowment** $91.3 million
- **Coed** 1,128 undergraduate students, 93% full-time, 62% women, 38% men
- **Moderately difficult** entrance level, 81% of applicants were admitted

UNDERGRAD STUDENTS

1,048 full-time, 80 part-time. Students come from 29 states and territories; 11 other countries; 24% are from out of state; 17% Black or African American, non-Hispanic/Latino; 11% Hispanic/Latino; 3% Asian, non-Hispanic/Latino; 0.1% Native Hawaiian or other Pacific Islander, non-Hispanic/Latino; 0.1% American Indian or Alaska Native, non-Hispanic/Latino; 6% Two or more races, non-Hispanic/Latino; 4% Race/ethnicity unknown; 2% international; 8% transferred in; 52% live on campus.

Freshmen:

Admission: 1,431 applied, 1,161 admitted, 256 enrolled. *Average high school GPA:* 3.4.

Retention: 78% of full-time freshmen returned.

FACULTY

Total: 248, 42% full-time, 60% with terminal degrees.

Student/faculty ratio: 10:1.

ACADEMICS

Calendar: semesters. *Degrees:* certificates, bachelor's, master's, doctoral, and postbachelor's certificates (also offers adult program with significant enrollment not reflected in profile).

Special study options: academic remediation for entering students, advanced placement credit, double majors, honors programs, independent study, internships, off-campus study, part-time degree program, services for LD students, student-designed majors, study abroad, summer session for credit. *ROTC:* Army (b).

Unusual degree programs: 3-2 business administration; nursing; social work; communication arts, integrated marketing communications, education.

Computers: 470 computers/terminals are available on campus for general student use. Students can access the following: campus intranet, computer help desk, free student e-mail accounts, online (class) grades, online (class) registration, online (class) schedules, Virtual Computer Lab (VCL). Campuswide network is available. 100% of college-owned or -operated housing units are wired for high-speed Internet access. Wireless service is available via entire campus.

Library: Beneficial-Hodson Library and Information Technology Center plus 1 other. *Books:* 172,311 (physical), 295,531 (digital/electronic); *Serial titles:* 235 (physical), 42,000 (digital/electronic); *Databases:* 96. Students can reserve study rooms.

STUDENT LIFE

Housing options: on-campus residence required through junior year; coed. Campus housing is university owned. Freshman campus housing is guaranteed.

Activities and organizations: drama/theater group, student-run newspaper, radio station, choral group, Black Student Union (BSU), Campus Activities Board (CAB), International Club, Queer Student Union (QSU), Enactus.

Athletics Member NCAA. All Division III. *Intercollegiate sports:* baseball M, basketball M/W, cross-country running M/W, equestrian sports M(c)/W(c), field hockey W, golf M/W, lacrosse M/W, soccer M/W, softball W, swimming and diving M/W, tennis M/W, track and field M/W, volleyball W. *Intramural sports:* cheerleading W(c).

Campus security: 24-hour emergency response devices and patrols, late-night transport/escort service, controlled dormitory access.

Student services: health clinic, personal/psychological counseling.

COSTS & FINANCIAL AID

Costs (2018–19) *Comprehensive fee:* $52,192 includes full-time tuition ($38,910), mandatory fees ($582), and room and board ($12,700). Part-time tuition: $1134 per credit hour. *Required fees:* $188 per term part-time. *College room only:* $6600. Room and board charges vary according to board plan. *Payment plan:* installment. *Waivers:* senior citizens and employees or children of employees.

Financial Aid Of all full-time matriculated undergraduates who enrolled in 2017, 936 applied for aid, 867 were judged to have need, 156 had their need fully met. In 2017, 158 non-need-based awards were made. *Average percent of need met:* 73. *Average financial aid package:* $30,919. *Average need-based loan:* $4568. *Average need-based gift aid:* $26,886. *Average non-need-based aid:* $17,472. *Average indebtedness upon graduation:* $35,823.

APPLYING

Options: electronic application.

Required: essay or personal statement, high school transcript, minimum 2.0 GPA, 2 letters of recommendation. *Recommended:* interview.

Application deadlines: rolling (freshmen), rolling (out-of-state freshmen), rolling (transfers).

Notification: continuous (freshmen), continuous (out-of-state freshmen), continuous (transfers).

CONTACT

William Brown, Vice President for Enrollment Management, Hood College, 401 Rosemont Avenue, Frederick, MD 21701. *Phone:* 301-696-3400. *Toll-free phone:* 800-922-1599. *Fax:* 301-696-3819. *E-mail:* admission@hood.edu.

Johns Hopkins University
Baltimore, Maryland
http://www.jhu.edu/

- **Independent** university, founded 1876
- **Urban** 140-acre campus with easy access to Baltimore and Washington, DC
- **Endowment** $3.8 billion
- **Coed** 5,465 undergraduate students, 99% full-time, 51% women, 49% men
- 12% of applicants were admitted

UNDERGRAD STUDENTS

5,432 full-time, 32 part-time. Students come from 52 states and territories; 77 other countries; 89% are from out of state; 6% Black or African American, non-Hispanic/Latino; 14% Hispanic/Latino; 26% Asian, non-Hispanic/Latino; 0.2% Native Hawaiian or other Pacific Islander, non-Hispanic/Latino; 0.1% American Indian or Alaska Native, non-Hispanic/Latino; 5% Two or more races, non-Hispanic/Latino; 5% Race/ethnicity unknown; 9% international; 1% transferred in; 51% live on campus.

Freshmen:

Admission: 26,578 applied, 3,115 admitted, 1,345 enrolled. *Average high school GPA:* 3.9. *Test scores:* SAT evidence-based reading and writing scores over 500: 100%; SAT math scores over 500: 100%; ACT scores over 18: 100%; SAT evidence-based reading and writing scores over 600: 99%; SAT math scores over 600: 99%; ACT scores over 24: 100%; SAT evidence-based reading and writing scores over 700: 87%; SAT math scores over 700: 87%; ACT scores over 30: 97%.

Retention: 97% of full-time freshmen returned.

FACULTY

Total: 655, 97% full-time, 94% with terminal degrees.

Student/faculty ratio: 8:1.

ACADEMICS

Calendar: 4-1-4. *Degrees:* certificates, diplomas, bachelor's, master's, doctoral, and postbachelor's certificates.

Special study options: advanced placement credit, double majors, independent study, internships, off-campus study, services for LD students, student-designed majors, study abroad, summer session for credit. *ROTC:* Army (b), Air Force (c).

Unusual degree programs: 3-2 engineering; international studies with Johns Hopkins University, biology, classics, German, history, neuroscience, public policy, mathematics, education.

Computers: 175 computers/terminals and 4,000 ports are available on campus for general student use. Students can access the following: campus intranet, computer help desk, free student e-mail accounts, online (class) grades, online (class) registration, online (class) schedules. Campuswide network is available. 100% of college-owned or -operated housing units are wired for high-speed Internet access. Wireless service is available via entire campus.

Library: The Sheridan Libraries plus 2 others. *Books:* 4.1 million (physical); *Serial titles:* 52,351 (physical), 132,176 (digital/electronic); *Databases:* 648. Study areas open 24 hours, 5–7 days a week; students can reserve study rooms.

STUDENT LIFE

Housing options: on-campus residence required through sophomore year; coed, special housing for students with disabilities. Campus housing is university owned and leased by the school. Freshman campus housing is guaranteed.

Activities and organizations: drama/theater group, student-run newspaper, radio station, choral group, national fraternities, national sororities.

Athletics Member NCAA. All Division III except men's and women's lacrosse (Division I). *Intercollegiate sports:* baseball M, basketball M/W, cross-country running M/W, fencing M/W, field hockey W, football M, lacrosse M(s)/W(s), soccer M/W, swimming and diving M/W, tennis M/W, track and field M/W, volleyball W, water polo M, wrestling M. *Intramural sports:* badminton M(c)/W(c), baseball M(c), basketball M/W, cheerleading W(c), equestrian sports M(c)/W(c), field hockey W(c), football M/W, golf M(c)/W(c), ice hockey M(c), lacrosse M(c)/W(c),

IF IT CAN
BE IMAGINED,
IT CAN BE
ACHIEVED AT
JOHNS HOPKINS.

JOHNS HOPKINS
UNIVERSITY

APPLY.JHU.EDU

racquetball M(c)/W(c), riflery M(c)/W(c), rock climbing M/W, rugby M(c)/W(c), soccer M/W, softball W(c), squash M(c)/W(c), swimming and diving M(c)/W(c), table tennis M(c)/W(c), tennis M(c)/W(c), track and field M(c)/W(c), triathlon M(c)/W(c), ultimate Frisbee M(c)/W(c), volleyball M(c)/W(c), water polo M(c)/W(c), wrestling M(c).

Campus security: 24-hour emergency response devices and patrols, student patrols, late-night transport/escort service, controlled dormitory access, CCTV monitoring of public areas.

Student services: health clinic, personal/psychological counseling, women's center.

COSTS & FINANCIAL AID

Costs (2017–18) *One-time required fee:* $500. *Comprehensive fee:* $67,580 includes full-time tuition ($52,170) and room and board ($15,410). Part-time tuition: $1740 per credit hour. *College room only:* $8912. Room and board charges vary according to board plan and housing facility. *Payment plan:* installment. *Waivers:* employees or children of employees.

Financial Aid Of all full-time matriculated undergraduates who enrolled in 2015, 3,043 applied for aid, 2,554 were judged to have need, 2,552 had their need fully met. 1,696 Federal Work-Study jobs (averaging $2428). In 2015, 87 non-need-based awards were made. *Average percent of need met:* 100. *Average financial aid package:* $39,344. *Average need-based loan:* $4384. *Average need-based gift aid:* $36,687. *Average non-need-based aid:* $27,941. *Average indebtedness upon graduation:* $24,702. *Financial aid deadline:* 3/1.

APPLYING

Standardized Tests *Required:* SAT or ACT (for admission). *Recommended:* SAT and SAT Subject Tests or ACT (for admission).

Options: electronic application, early decision, deferred entrance.

Application fee: $70.

Required: essay or personal statement, high school transcript, 2 letters of recommendation.

Application deadlines: 1/1 (freshmen), 1/1 (transfers).

Early decision deadline: 11/1.

Notification: 4/1 (freshmen), 4/1 (transfers), 12/15 (early decision).

CONTACT

Johns Hopkins University, 3400 North Charles Street, Baltimore, MD 21218.

See this page for display ad and page 1316 for the College Close-Up.

Kaplan University, Hagerstown

Hagerstown, Maryland
http://www.kaplanuniversity.edu/

CONTACT

Kaplan University, Hagerstown, 18618 Crestwood Drive, Hagerstown, MD 21742. *Phone:* 301-739-2680 Ext. 217. *Toll-free phone:* 800-987-7734.

Loyola University Maryland

Baltimore, Maryland
http://www.loyola.edu/

- **Independent Roman Catholic (Jesuit)** university, founded 1852
- **Urban** 89-acre campus with easy access to Washington, DC
- **Endowment** $193.8 million
- **Coed**
- **Moderately difficult** entrance level

FACULTY

Student/faculty ratio: 12:1.

ACADEMICS

Calendar: semesters. *Degrees:* bachelor's, master's, doctoral, post-master's, and postbachelor's certificates.
Library: Loyola/Notre Dame Library plus 1 other.

STUDENT LIFE

Housing options: coed, cooperative. Freshman campus housing is guaranteed.

Activities and organizations: drama/theater group, student-run newspaper, radio and television station, choral group, Student

Government Association, Resident Affairs Council (RAC), Relay for Life, Resident Assistants (RA), The Evergreens.

Athletics Member NCAA. All Division I.

Campus security: 24-hour emergency response devices and patrols, late-night transport/escort service, controlled dormitory access.

Student services: health clinic, personal/psychological counseling, women's center.

COSTS & FINANCIAL AID
Costs (2017–18) *One-time required fee:* $1240. *Comprehensive fee:* $61,875 includes full-time tuition ($46,160), mandatory fees ($1565), and room and board ($14,150). Full-time tuition and fees vary according to course load. Part-time tuition: $745 per credit. Part-time tuition and fees vary according to course load. *Room and board:* Room and board charges vary according to board plan and housing facility.

Financial Aid Of all full-time matriculated undergraduates who enrolled in 2015, 2,614 applied for aid, 2,232 were judged to have need, 2,075 had their need fully met. In 2015, 611 non-need-based awards were made. *Average percent of need met:* 91. *Average financial aid package:* $32,100. *Average need-based loan:* $6750. *Average need-based gift aid:* $24,200. *Average non-need-based aid:* $14,960. *Average indebtedness upon graduation:* $36,208. *Financial aid deadline:* 1/15.

APPLYING
Options: electronic application, early admission, early decision, early action, deferred entrance.

Application fee: $60.

Required: essay or personal statement, high school transcript.

CONTACT
Loyola University Maryland, 4501 North Charles Street, Baltimore, MD 21210-2699. *Phone:* 410-617-2000. *Toll-free phone:* 800-221-9107.

See below for display ad and page 1330 for the College Close-Up.

Maple Springs Baptist Bible College and Seminary
Capitol Heights, Maryland
http://www.msbbcs.edu/

CONTACT
Ms. Jeannie Bowman, Assistant Director of Admissions and Records, Maple Springs Baptist Bible College and Seminary, 4130 Belt Road, Capitol Heights, MD 20743. *Phone:* 301-736-3631. *Fax:* 301-735-6507.

Maryland Institute College of Art
Baltimore, Maryland
http://www.mica.edu/

- **Independent** comprehensive, founded 1826
- **Urban** 16-acre campus with easy access to Washington, DC
- **Endowment** $86.1 million
- **Coed** 1,694 undergraduate students, 99% full-time, 75% women, 25% men
- **Very difficult** entrance level, 62% of applicants were admitted

UNDERGRAD STUDENTS
1,674 full-time, 20 part-time. Students come from 43 states and territories; 46 other countries; 74% are from out of state; 7% Black or African American, non-Hispanic/Latino; 3% Hispanic/Latino; 11% Asian, non-Hispanic/Latino; 0.2% Native Hawaiian or other Pacific Islander, non-Hispanic/Latino; 0.1% American Indian or Alaska Native, non-Hispanic/Latino; 12% Two or more races, non-Hispanic/Latino; 2% Race/ethnicity unknown; 24% international; 4% transferred in; 88% live on campus.

Freshmen:
Admission: 3,636 applied, 2,240 admitted, 423 enrolled. *Average high school GPA:* 3.5.
Retention: 86% of full-time freshmen returned.

FACULTY
Total: 433, 39% full-time, 76% with terminal degrees.

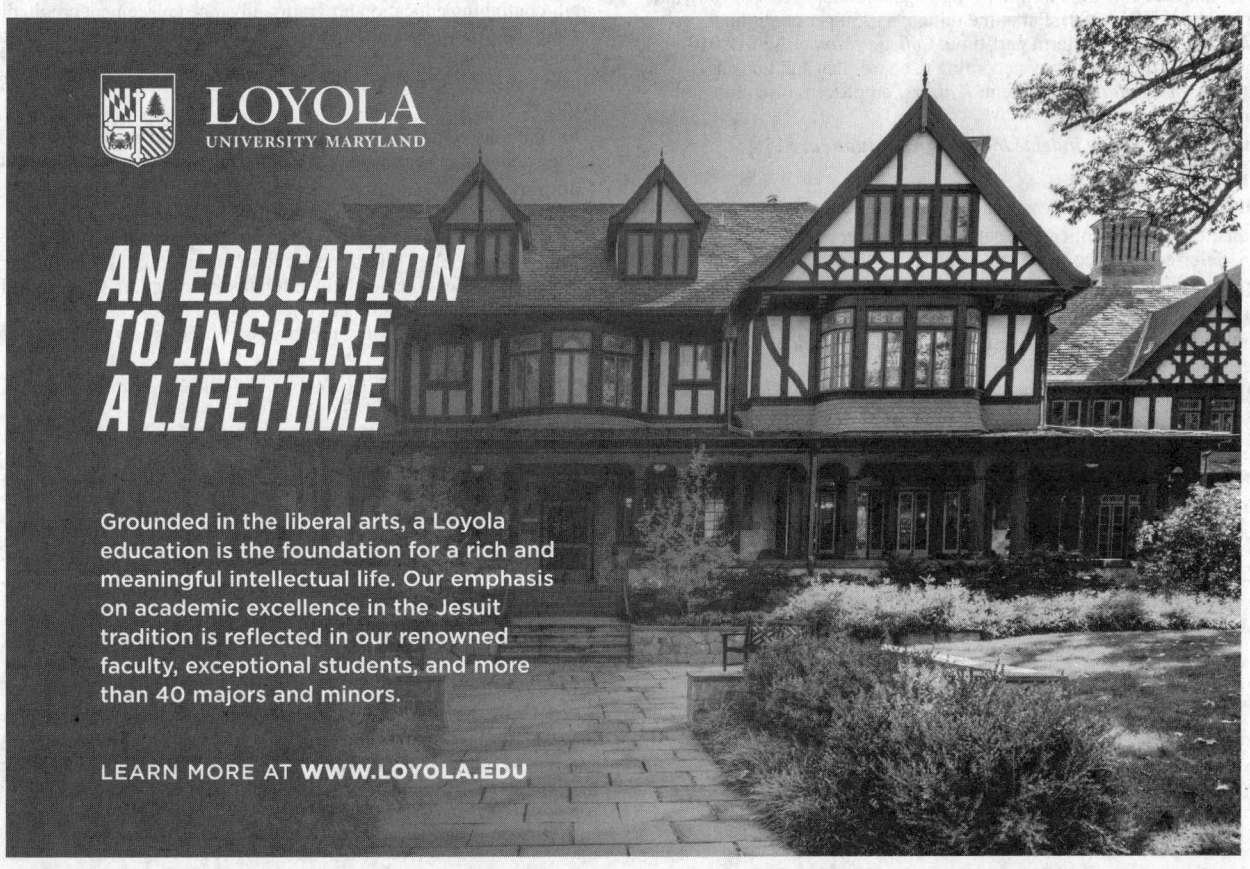

Student/faculty ratio: 8:1.

ACADEMICS

Calendar: semesters. *Degrees:* bachelor's, master's, and postbachelor's certificates.

Special study options: accelerated degree program, adult/continuing education programs, advanced placement credit, distance learning, double majors, English as a second language, independent study, internships, off-campus study, services for LD students, student-designed majors, study abroad, summer session for credit. *ROTC:* Army (c).

Computers: 750 computers/terminals and 3,000 ports are available on campus for general student use. Students can access the following: campus intranet, computer help desk, free student e-mail accounts, online (class) grades, online (class) registration, online (class) schedules, Campus Portal, online gallery space, Behance image portfolio system, Google Apps, Lynda.com web-based training, network storage space, personal websites, online software training tutorials, Canvas learning management system, printing services. Campuswide network is available. 100% of college-owned or -operated housing units are wired for high-speed Internet access. Wireless service is available via entire campus.

Library: Decker Library. *Books:* 75,897 (physical), 172,505 (digital/electronic); *Serial titles:* 391 (physical); *Databases:* 35. Weekly public service hours: 70; students can reserve study rooms.

STUDENT LIFE

Housing options: on-campus residence required through sophomore year; coed, special housing for students with disabilities. Campus housing is university owned. Freshman campus housing is guaranteed.

Activities and organizations: drama/theater group, student-run radio station, choral group, Haunted House, Urban Gaming Club, Oy , Korean International Student Association, MICA Design League.

Campus security: 24-hour emergency response devices and patrols, student patrols, late-night transport/escort service, controlled dormitory access, self-defense education, 24-hour building security, safety awareness programs, campus patrols by city police.

Student services: health clinic, personal/psychological counseling.

COSTS & FINANCIAL AID

Costs (2018–19) *One-time required fee:* $190. *Comprehensive fee:* $61,910 includes full-time tuition ($46,870), mandatory fees ($1760), and room and board ($13,280). Part-time tuition: $1950 per credit hour. *Required fees:* $880 per term part-time. *College room only:* $10,010. Room and board charges vary according to board plan and housing facility. *Payment plan:* installment. *Waivers:* employees or children of employees.

Financial Aid *Average indebtedness upon graduation:* $17,472.

APPLYING

Standardized Tests *Required:* SAT or ACT (for admission).

Options: electronic application, early admission, early decision, early action, deferred entrance.

Application fee: $70.

Required: essay or personal statement, high school transcript, 3 letters of recommendation, art portfolio, test scores, and a list of activities and interests. *Recommended:* interview.

Application deadlines: 2/1 (freshmen), 4/1 (transfers), 12/1 (early action).

Early decision deadline: 11/1.

Notification: 2/26 (freshmen), 4/25 (transfers), 12/1 (early decision), 1/15 (early action).

CONTACT

Maryland Institute College of Art, 1300 Mount Royal Avenue, Baltimore, MD 21217.

McDaniel College

Westminster, Maryland

http://www.mcdaniel.edu/

- **Independent** comprehensive, founded 1867
- **Suburban** 160-acre campus with easy access to Baltimore and Washington, DC
- **Endowment** $109.3 million
- **Coed** 1,577 undergraduate students, 97% full-time, 51% women, 49% men
- **Moderately difficult** entrance level, 85% of applicants were admitted

UNDERGRAD STUDENTS

1,536 full-time, 41 part-time. Students come from 39 states and territories; 35 other countries; 34% are from out of state; 14% Black or African American, non-Hispanic/Latino; 6% Hispanic/Latino; 3% Asian, non-Hispanic/Latino; 0.1% Native Hawaiian or other Pacific Islander, non-Hispanic/Latino; 0.3% American Indian or Alaska Native, non-Hispanic/Latino; 4% Two or more races, non-Hispanic/Latino; 4% Race/ethnicity unknown; 4% international; 4% transferred in; 82% live on campus.

Freshmen:
Admission: 2,814 applied, 2,392 admitted, 450 enrolled. *Average high school GPA:* 3.5. *Test scores:* SAT evidence-based reading and writing scores over 500: 91%; SAT math scores over 500: 84%; ACT scores over 18: 100%; SAT evidence-based reading and writing scores over 600: 40%; SAT math scores over 600: 32%; ACT scores over 24: 52%; SAT evidence-based reading and writing scores over 700: 7%; SAT math scores over 700: 5%; ACT scores over 30: 17%.

Retention: 81% of full-time freshmen returned.

FACULTY

Total: 564, 24% full-time, 45% with terminal degrees.

Student/faculty ratio: 11:1.

ACADEMICS

Calendar: 4-1-4. *Degrees:* bachelor's, master's, and postbachelor's certificates.

Special study options: academic remediation for entering students, adult/continuing education programs, advanced placement credit, distance learning, double majors, honors programs, independent study, internships, off-campus study, part-time degree program, services for LD students, student-designed majors, study abroad, summer session for credit. *ROTC:* Army (b).

Unusual degree programs: 3-2 gerontology, human services management, music education, secondary education, special education.

Computers: 138 computers/terminals and 1,500 ports are available on campus for general student use. Students can access the following: campus intranet, computer help desk, free student e-mail accounts, online (class) grades, online (class) registration, online (class) schedules, online billing summaries, financial aid letter, tax information. Campuswide network is available. 100% of college-owned or -operated housing units are wired for high-speed Internet access. Wireless service is available via entire campus.

Library: Hoover Library. *Books:* 182,835 (physical), 177,580 (digital/electronic); *Serial titles:* 1,420 (physical), 65,808 (digital/electronic); *Databases:* 81. Study areas open 24 hours, 5–7 days a week; students can reserve study rooms.

STUDENT LIFE

Housing options: on-campus residence required through junior year; coed, special housing for students with disabilities. Campus housing is university owned. Freshman campus housing is guaranteed.

Activities and organizations: drama/theater group, student-run newspaper, radio and television station, choral group, Student Government Association, Black Student Union, International Club, Maryland State Legislature, McDaniel Allies, national fraternities, national sororities.

Athletics Member NCAA. All Division III. *Intercollegiate sports:* baseball M, basketball M/W, cross-country running M/W, field hockey W, football M, golf M/W, lacrosse M/W, soccer M/W, softball W, swimming and diving M/W, tennis M/W, track and field M/W, volleyball W, wrestling M. *Intramural sports:* basketball M/W, cheerleading

M(c)/W(c), football M/W, golf M/W, soccer M/W, softball M/W, ultimate Frisbee M/W, volleyball M/W.

Campus security: 24-hour emergency response devices and patrols, late-night transport/escort service, patrol force containing campus police, all certified to US DOT First Responder standards.

Student services: health clinic, personal/psychological counseling.

COSTS & FINANCIAL AID

Costs (2017–18) *Comprehensive fee:* $52,910 includes full-time tuition ($41,800) and room and board ($11,110). Full-time tuition and fees vary according to course load. Part-time tuition: $1306 per credit hour. Part-time tuition and fees vary according to course load and reciprocity agreements. *College room only:* $5100. Room and board charges vary according to board plan and housing facility. *Payment plan:* installment. *Waivers:* employees or children of employees.

Financial Aid Of all full-time matriculated undergraduates who enrolled in 2017, 1,317 applied for aid, 1,230 were judged to have need, 268 had their need fully met. In 2017, 288 non-need-based awards were made. *Average percent of need met:* 85. *Average financial aid package:* $36,984. *Average need-based loan:* $3306. *Average need-based gift aid:* $32,586. *Average non-need-based aid:* $18,680. *Average indebtedness upon graduation:* $34,099. *Financial aid deadline:* 4/1.

APPLYING

Standardized Tests *Required:* SAT or ACT (for admission).

Options: electronic application, early admission, early decision, early action, deferred entrance.

Application fee: $50.

Required: essay or personal statement, high school transcript, minimum 2.5 GPA, 2 letters of recommendation. *Required for some:* interview. *Recommended:* interview.

Application deadlines: 2/1 (freshmen), 6/1 (transfers), 11/15 (early action).

Early decision deadline: 11/1 (for plan 1), 1/15 (for plan 2).

Notification: 3/1 (freshmen), 6/15 (transfers), 12/1 (early decision plan 1), 2/1 (early decision plan 2), 12/15 (early action).

CONTACT

Ms. Florence Hines, Vice President for Enrollment Management and Dean of Admissions, McDaniel College, 2 College Hill, Westminster, MD 21157-4390. *Phone:* 410-857-2230. *Toll-free phone:* 800-638-5005. *Fax:* 410-857-2757. *E-mail:* admissions@mcdaniel.edu.

Morgan State University
Baltimore, Maryland
http://www.morgan.edu/

CONTACT
Ms. Shonda Gray, Acting Director of Admissions and Recruitment, Morgan State University, 1700 East Cold Spring Lane, Baltimore, MD 21251. *Phone:* 443-885-3000. *Toll-free phone:* 800-332-6674. *E-mail:* shantell.saunders@morgan.edu.

Mount St. Mary's University
Emmitsburg, Maryland
http://www.msmary.edu/

- **Independent Roman Catholic** comprehensive, founded 1808
- **Rural** 1500-acre campus with easy access to Baltimore and Washington, DC
- **Endowment** $50.3 million
- **Coed** 1,817 undergraduate students, 93% full-time, 52% women, 48% men
- **Moderately difficult** entrance level, 64% of applicants were admitted

UNDERGRAD STUDENTS
1,696 full-time, 121 part-time. Students come from 43 states and territories; 10 other countries; 43% are from out of state; 17% Black or African American, non-Hispanic/Latino; 11% Hispanic/Latino; 3% Asian, non-Hispanic/Latino; 0.2% Native Hawaiian or other Pacific Islander, non-Hispanic/Latino; 0.5% American Indian or Alaska Native, non-Hispanic/Latino; 4% Two or more races, non-Hispanic/Latino; 1%

Race/ethnicity unknown; 0.7% international; 3% transferred in; 80% live on campus.

Freshmen:
Admission: 6,130 applied, 3,937 admitted, 524 enrolled. *Average high school GPA:* 3.3. *Test scores:* SAT evidence-based reading and writing scores over 500: 79%; SAT math scores over 500: 68%; ACT scores over 18: 81%; SAT evidence-based reading and writing scores over 600: 27%; SAT math scores over 600: 22%; ACT scores over 24: 34%; SAT evidence-based reading and writing scores over 700: 3%; SAT math scores over 700: 3%; ACT scores over 30: 3%.
Retention: 76% of full-time freshmen returned.

FACULTY
Total: 208, 62% full-time, 65% with terminal degrees.
Student/faculty ratio: 13:1.

ACADEMICS
Calendar: semesters. *Degrees:* bachelor's, master's, post-master's, and postbachelor's certificates.

Special study options: academic remediation for entering students, accelerated degree program, adult/continuing education programs, advanced placement credit, double majors, honors programs, independent study, internships, off-campus study, part-time degree program, services for LD students, student-designed majors, study abroad, summer session for credit. *ROTC:* Army (c).

Unusual degree programs: 3-2 nursing with University of Maryland, Shenandoah University.

Computers: 80 computers/terminals are available on campus for general student use. Students can access the following: campus intranet, computer help desk, free student e-mail accounts, online (class) grades, online (class) registration, online (class) schedules, tuition payment, course management system. Campuswide network is available. 100% of college-owned or -operated housing units are wired for high-speed Internet access. Wireless service is available via entire campus.
Library: Phillips Library. *Books:* 149,657 (physical), 280,598 (digital/electronic); *Serial titles:* 1,207 (physical), 26,497 (digital/electronic); *Databases:* 157.

STUDENT LIFE
Housing options: on-campus residence required for freshman year; coed, special housing for students with disabilities. Campus housing is university owned. Freshman campus housing is guaranteed.

Activities and organizations: drama/theater group, student-run newspaper, radio station, choral group, Mount Students for Life, CRUX - Outdoor Adventures, Campus Ministry Student Organization, FOCUS, Mount Chorale.

Athletics Member NCAA. All Division I. *Intercollegiate sports:* baseball M(s), basketball M(s)/W(s), bowling W(s), cheerleading M/W, cross-country running M(s)/W(s), equestrian sports M(c)/W(c), field hockey W(c), golf M(s)/W(s), gymnastics M(s)/W(s), ice hockey M(c), lacrosse M(s)/W(s), rugby M(c)/W(c), soccer M(s)/W(s), softball W(s), swimming and diving M(s)/W(s), tennis M(s)/W(s), track and field M(s)/W(s), ultimate Frisbee M(c)/W(c), volleyball W(c). *Intramural sports:* baseball M(c), basketball M/W, field hockey W, racquetball M/W, sand volleyball M/W, soccer M(c), softball W(c), tennis M/W.

Campus security: 24-hour emergency response devices and patrols, late-night transport/escort service, controlled dormitory access.

Student services: health clinic, personal/psychological counseling.

COSTS & FINANCIAL AID
Costs (2017–18) *Comprehensive fee:* $53,380 includes full-time tuition ($39,200), mandatory fees ($1350), and room and board ($12,830). Full-time tuition and fees vary according to location and program. Part-time tuition: $1275 per credit hour. Part-time tuition and fees vary according to location and program. *College room only:* $6500. Room and board charges vary according to housing facility. *Payment plan:* installment. *Waivers:* employees or children of employees.

Financial Aid Of all full-time matriculated undergraduates who enrolled in 2017, 1,378 applied for aid, 1,239 were judged to have need, 279 had their need fully met. 107 Federal Work-Study jobs (averaging $1970). 522 state and other part-time jobs (averaging $1473). In 2017, 398 non-need-based awards were made. *Average percent of need met:* 74. *Average financial aid package:* $29,515. *Average need-based loan:* $4723.

Average need-based gift aid: $24,811. *Average non-need-based aid:* $18,997. *Average indebtedness upon graduation:* $36,112. *Financial aid deadline:* 3/1.

APPLYING

Standardized Tests *Required:* SAT or ACT (for admission).

Options: electronic application, early action, deferred entrance.

Application fee: $45.

Required: high school transcript, minimum 2.0 GPA, 1 letter of recommendation. *Recommended:* essay or personal statement, minimum 3.0 GPA, interview.

Application deadlines: 3/1 (freshmen), 6/1 (transfers), 12/1 (early action).

Notification: continuous (freshmen), continuous (transfers), 12/25 (early action).

CONTACT

Mr. Eric M. Danielson, Director of Admissions, Mount St. Mary's University, 16300 Old Emmitsburg Road, Emmitsburg, MD 21727. *Phone:* 301-447-5505. *Toll-free phone:* 800-448-4347. *Fax:* 301-447-5818. *E-mail:* admissions@msmary.edu.

Ner Israel Rabbinical College

Baltimore, Maryland

CONTACT

Ner Israel Rabbinical College, 400 Mount Wilson Lane, Baltimore, MD 21208. *Phone:* 410-484-7200.

Notre Dame of Maryland University

Baltimore, Maryland

http://www.ndm.edu/

CONTACT

Angela Baumler, Director of Admissions (Women's College), Notre Dame of Maryland University, 4701 North Charles Street, Baltimore, MD 21210. *Phone:* 410-532-5330. *Toll-free phone:* 800-435-0200. *E-mail:* abaumler@ndm.edu.

Peabody Conservatory of The Johns Hopkins University

Baltimore, Maryland

http://www.peabody.jhu.edu/

CONTACT

Mr. David Lane, Director of Admissions, Peabody Conservatory of The Johns Hopkins University, Peabody Conservatory Admissions Office, One East Mount Vernon Place, Baltimore, MD 21202-2397. *Phone:* 410-234-4848. *Toll-free phone:* 800-368-2521.

St. John's College

Annapolis, Maryland

http://www.sjc.edu/

- **Independent** comprehensive, founded 1696
- **Small-town** 36-acre campus with easy access to Washington, D.C. and Baltimore, MD
- **Endowment** $168.5 million
- **Coed** 458 undergraduate students, 100% full-time, 47% women, 53% men
- **Moderately difficult** entrance level, 55% of applicants were admitted

UNDERGRAD STUDENTS

458 full-time. Students come from 42 states and territories; 35 other countries; 62% are from out of state; 2% Black or African American, non-Hispanic/Latino; 6% Hispanic/Latino; 4% Asian, non-Hispanic/Latino; 3% Two or more races, non-Hispanic/Latino; 22% international; 3% transferred in; 70% live on campus.

Freshmen:

Admission: 753 applied, 411 admitted, 122 enrolled. *Average high school GPA:* 3.5. *Test scores:* SAT evidence-based reading and writing scores over 500: 98%; SAT math scores over 500: 96%; ACT scores over 18: 100%; SAT evidence-based reading and writing scores over 600: 87%; SAT math scores over 600: 70%; ACT scores over 24: 93%; SAT evidence-based reading and writing scores over 700: 53%; SAT math scores over 700: 28%; ACT scores over 30: 64%.

Retention: 87% of full-time freshmen returned.

FACULTY

Total: 72, 90% full-time, 86% with terminal degrees.

Student/faculty ratio: 7:1.

ACADEMICS

Calendar: semesters. *Degrees:* bachelor's and master's.

Special study options: internships, off-campus study, services for LD students, study abroad.

Computers: 26 computers/terminals and 500 ports are available on campus for general student use. Students can access the following: campus intranet, computer help desk, free student e-mail accounts, free wi-fi access throughout the campus; support for bring-your-own mobile devices. Campuswide network is available. 100% of college-owned or -operated housing units are wired for high-speed Internet access. Wireless service is available via entire campus.

Library: Greenfield Library plus 1 other. *Books:* 108,811 (physical), 486 (digital/electronic); *Serial titles:* 127 (physical), 1,439 (digital/electronic); *Databases:* 14. Weekly public service hours: 94; students can reserve study rooms.

STUDENT LIFE

Housing options: on-campus residence required for freshman year; coed, special housing for students with disabilities. Campus housing is university owned. Freshman campus housing is guaranteed.

Activities and organizations: drama/theater group, student-run newspaper, choral group, King William's Players (drama), Reality (social), Delegate Council (student government), Waltz (social), Student Committee on Instruction (advisory).

Athletics Member USCAA. *Intercollegiate sports:* crew M(c)/W(c), fencing M(c)/W(c), sailing M(c)/W(c). *Intramural sports:* basketball M/W, crew M/W, fencing M/W, sailing M/W, soccer M/W, swimming and diving M/W, ultimate Frisbee M/W, volleyball M/W, weight lifting M/W.

Campus security: 24-hour emergency response devices and patrols, late-night transport/escort service, controlled dormitory access, Personal Whistle Safety Program, Operation ID (identification of valuables), LiveSafe App.

Student services: health clinic, personal/psychological counseling.

COSTS & FINANCIAL AID

Costs (2017–18) *One-time required fee:* $125. *Comprehensive fee:* $63,904 includes full-time tuition ($51,200), mandatory fees ($470), and room and board ($12,234). *College room only:* $5984. Room and board charges vary according to board plan and housing facility. *Payment plans:* tuition prepayment, installment. *Waivers:* employees or children of employees.

Financial Aid Of all full-time matriculated undergraduates who enrolled in 2017, 360 applied for aid, 318 were judged to have need, 80 had their need fully met. 55 Federal Work-Study jobs (averaging $2700). 125 state and other part-time jobs (averaging $2700). In 2017, 103 non-need-based awards were made. *Average percent of need met:* 87. *Average financial aid package:* $41,116. *Average need-based loan:* $4734. *Average need-based gift aid:* $36,575. *Average non-need-based aid:* $19,170. *Average indebtedness upon graduation:* $16,705.

APPLYING

Standardized Tests *Required for some:* SAT or ACT (for admission), SAT/ACT, TOEFL/IELTS or interview for international applicants; SAT/ACT/CLT for homeschooled students and applicants who have not and will not graduate high school. *Recommended:* SAT/ACT, TOEFL/IELTS or interview for international applicants; SAT/ACT/CLT for homeschooled students and applicants who have not and will not graduate high school.

Options: electronic application, early admission, early action, deferred entrance.

Required: essay or personal statement, high school transcript, 2 letters of recommendation. *Required for some:* outline of curriculum for home-schooled applicants. *Recommended:* interview.

Application deadlines: rolling (freshmen), 11/15 (early action). **Notification:** continuous (freshmen), 12/15 (early action).

CONTACT
Mr. Benjamin Baum, Director of Admissions, St. John's College, 60 College Avenue, Annapolis, MD 21401. *Phone:* 410-626-2522. *Toll-free phone:* 800-727-9238. *Fax:* 410-269-7916. *E-mail:* annapolis.admissions@sjc.edu.

St. Mary's College of Maryland
St. Mary's City, Maryland
http://www.smcm.edu/

- **State-supported** comprehensive, founded 1840
- **Rural** 361-acre campus
- **Endowment** $34.2 million
- **Coed** 1,570 undergraduate students, 97% full-time, 58% women, 42% men
- **Moderately difficult** entrance level, 82% of applicants were admitted

UNDERGRAD STUDENTS
1,516 full-time, 54 part-time. Students come from 26 states and territories; 11 other countries; 7% are from out of state; 9% Black or African American, non-Hispanic/Latino; 8% Hispanic/Latino; 4% Asian, non-Hispanic/Latino; 0.1% Native Hawaiian or other Pacific Islander, non-Hispanic/Latino; 0.3% American Indian or Alaska Native, non-Hispanic/Latino; 5% Two or more races, non-Hispanic/Latino; 2% Race/ethnicity unknown; 1% international; 6% transferred in; 82% live on campus.

Freshmen:
Admission: 1,655 applied, 1,364 admitted, 342 enrolled. *Average high school GPA:* 3.3. *Test scores:* SAT evidence-based reading and writing scores over 500: 89%; SAT math scores over 500: 88%; ACT scores over 18: 94%; SAT evidence-based reading and writing scores over 600: 55%; SAT math scores over 600: 38%; ACT scores over 24: 59%; SAT evidence-based reading and writing scores over 700: 12%; SAT math scores over 700: 6%; ACT scores over 30: 20%.
Retention: 87% of full-time freshmen returned.

FACULTY
Total: 199, 70% full-time, 75% with terminal degrees.
Student/faculty ratio: 10:1.

ACADEMICS
Calendar: semesters. *Degrees:* bachelor's and master's.
Special study options: advanced placement credit, cooperative education, double majors, freshman honors college, independent study, internships, part-time degree program, services for LD students, student-designed majors, study abroad, summer session for credit.
Computers: 395 computers/terminals and 500 ports are available on campus for general student use. Students can access the following: campus intranet, computer help desk, free student e-mail accounts, online (class) grades, online (class) registration, online (class) schedules, learning management system. Campuswide network is available. 100% of college-owned or -operated housing units are wired for high-speed Internet access. Wireless service is available via entire campus.
Library: Library, Archives, and Media Center. *Books:* 149,367 (physical), 112,402 (digital/electronic); *Serial titles:* 487 (physical); *Databases:* 109. Weekly public service hours: 106; study areas open 24 hours, 5–7 days a week; students can reserve study rooms.

STUDENT LIFE
Housing options: coed, men-only, women-only, special housing for students with disabilities. Campus housing is university owned. Freshman campus housing is guaranteed.
Activities and organizations: drama/theater group, student-run newspaper, radio station, choral group, Dance Club, Humans vs. Zombies, InterVarsity Christian Fellowship, Habitat for Humanity, History Club.
Athletics Member NCAA. All Division III. *Intercollegiate sports:* baseball M, basketball M/W, crew M(c)/W(c), cross-country running M/W, equestrian sports M(c)/W(c), fencing M(c)/W(c), field hockey W, lacrosse M/W, rock climbing M(c)/W(c), rowing M/W, rugby M(c)/W(c), sailing M/W, soccer M/W, softball W(c), swimming and diving M/W, tennis M/W, ultimate Frisbee M(c)/W(c), volleyball W. *Intramural sports:* badminton M/W, basketball M/W, soccer M/W, volleyball M/W.
Campus security: 24-hour emergency response devices and patrols, late-night transport/escort service, controlled dormitory access.
Student services: health clinic, personal/psychological counseling.

COSTS & FINANCIAL AID
Costs (2018–19) *Tuition:* state resident $11,646 full-time, $200 per credit hour part-time; nonresident $27,097 full-time, $200 per credit hour part-time. Full-time tuition and fees vary according to course load. Part-time tuition and fees vary according to course load. *Required fees:* $2850 full-time. *Room and board:* $12,816; room only: $7400. Room and board charges vary according to board plan and housing facility. *Payment plan:* installment. *Waivers:* senior citizens and employees or children of employees.
Financial Aid Of all full-time matriculated undergraduates who enrolled in 2016, 1,126 applied for aid, 817 were judged to have need, 34 had their need fully met. 177 Federal Work-Study jobs (averaging $960). In 2016, 407 non-need-based awards were made. *Average percent of need met:* 68. *Average financial aid package:* $12,454. *Average need-based loan:* $4272. *Average need-based gift aid:* $10,240. *Average non-need-based aid:* $4084. *Average indebtedness upon graduation:* $21,911.

APPLYING
Standardized Tests *Required:* SAT or ACT (for admission).
Options: electronic application, early action, deferred entrance.
Application fee: $50.
Required: essay or personal statement, high school transcript, 2 letters of recommendation, Common Application. *Recommended:* interview.
Application deadlines: 2/15 (freshmen), 4/1 (transfers), 11/15 (early action).
Notification: continuous until 4/1 (freshmen), continuous until 5/1 (transfers), 12/20 (early action).

CONTACT
Mr. David Hautanen Jr., Vice President for Enrollment Management, St. Mary's College of Maryland, 47645 College Drive, St. Mary's City, MD 20686-3001. *Phone:* 240-895-5000. *Toll-free phone:* 800-492-7181. *Fax:* 240-895-5001. *E-mail:* admissions@smcm.edu.

Salisbury University
Salisbury, Maryland
http://www.salisbury.edu/

- **State-supported** comprehensive, founded 1925, part of University System of Maryland
- **Small-town** 185-acre campus
- **Endowment** $67.7 million
- **Coed** 7,782 undergraduate students, 92% full-time, 56% women, 44% men
- **Moderately difficult** entrance level, 65% of applicants were admitted

UNDERGRAD STUDENTS
7,191 full-time, 591 part-time. Students come from 29 states and territories; 33 other countries; 13% are from out of state; 14% Black or African American, non-Hispanic/Latino; 4% Hispanic/Latino; 4% Asian, non-Hispanic/Latino; 0.2% Native Hawaiian or other Pacific Islander, non-Hispanic/Latino; 0.7% American Indian or Alaska Native, non-Hispanic/Latino; 3% Two or more races, non-Hispanic/Latino; 3% Race/ethnicity unknown; 1% international; 11% transferred in; 31% live on campus.

Freshmen:
Admission: 8,171 applied, 5,313 admitted, 1,328 enrolled. *Average high school GPA:* 3.6. *Test scores:* SAT evidence-based reading and writing scores over 500: 95%; SAT math scores over 500: 94%; ACT scores over 18: 89%; SAT evidence-based reading and writing scores over 600: 52%; SAT math scores over 600: 43%; ACT scores over 24: 31%; SAT evidence-based reading and writing scores over 700: 4%; SAT math scores over 700: 3%; ACT scores over 30: 1%.
Retention: 83% of full-time freshmen returned.

FACULTY
Total: 666, 65% full-time, 62% with terminal degrees.

Student/faculty ratio: 16:1.

ACADEMICS

Calendar: 4-1-4. *Degrees:* bachelor's, master's, doctoral, post-master's, and postbachelor's certificates.

Special study options: accelerated degree program, advanced placement credit, cooperative education, distance learning, double majors, English as a second language, freshman honors college, honors programs, independent study, internships, off-campus study, part-time degree program, services for LD students, student-designed majors, study abroad, summer session for credit. *ROTC:* Army (b), Air Force (c).

Unusual degree programs: 3-2 engineering with University of Maryland, College Park; Old Dominion University; Widener University; social work with University of Maryland Eastern Shore; biology and environmental marine science with University of Maryland Eastern Shore.

Computers: 1,000 computers/terminals and 3,552 ports are available on campus for general student use. Students can access the following: campus intranet, computer help desk, free student e-mail accounts, online (class) grades, online (class) registration, online (class) schedules, university accounts, student web hosting. Campuswide network is available. 100% of college-owned or -operated housing units are wired for high-speed Internet access. Wireless service is available via entire campus.

Library: SU Libraries plus 2 others. *Books:* 264,146 (physical), 269 (digital/electronic); *Serial titles:* 692 (physical), 150 (digital/electronic); *Databases:* 106. Weekly public service hours: 111; study areas open 24 hours, 5–7 days a week; students can reserve study rooms.

STUDENT LIFE

Housing options: on-campus residence required through sophomore year; coed, special housing for students with disabilities. Campus housing is university owned. Freshman applicants given priority for college housing.

Activities and organizations: drama/theater group, student-run newspaper, radio and television station, choral group, Student Government Association, Radio (WXSU) / SU TV / The Flyer Newspaper, Student Organization for Activity Planning (SOAP), Campus Crusade for Christ, Union of African American Students, national fraternities, national sororities.

Athletics Member NCAA. All Division III. *Intercollegiate sports:* baseball M, basketball M/W, cross-country running M/W, field hockey W, football M, lacrosse M/W, soccer M/W, softball W, swimming and diving M/W, tennis M/W, track and field M/W, volleyball W. *Intramural sports:* basketball M/W, cheerleading M(c)/W(c), equestrian sports M(c)/W(c), field hockey M(c)/W(c), golf M/W, gymnastics M(c)/W(c), ice hockey M(c), lacrosse M(c)/W(c), rock climbing M/W, rugby M(c)/W(c), sailing M(c)/W(c), sand volleyball M/W, soccer M/W, softball M/W, ultimate Frisbee M(c)/W(c), volleyball M/W, weight lifting M(c)/W(c).

Campus security: 24-hour emergency response devices and patrols, student patrols, late-night transport/escort service, controlled dormitory access, video surveillance system, shuttle buses, emergency notification system, self-defense education.

Student services: health clinic, personal/psychological counseling.

COSTS & FINANCIAL AID

Costs (2017–18) *Tuition:* state resident $6982 full-time, $287 per credit hour part-time; nonresident $16,022 full-time, $662 per credit hour part-time. *Required fees:* $2600 full-time, $92 per credit hour part-time. *Room and board:* $11,550; room only: $6750. Room and board charges vary according to board plan and housing facility. *Payment plan:* installment. *Waivers:* senior citizens and employees or children of employees.

Financial Aid Of all full-time matriculated undergraduates who enrolled in 2016, 5,373 applied for aid, 3,972 were judged to have need, 464 had their need fully met. 76 Federal Work-Study jobs (averaging $1817). In 2016, 563 non-need-based awards were made. *Average percent of need met:* 53. *Average financial aid package:* $8186. *Average need-based loan:* $4017. *Average need-based gift aid:* $6190. *Average non-need-based aid:* $2612. *Average indebtedness upon graduation:* $26,940.

APPLYING

Standardized Tests *Required for some:* SAT (for admission), ACT (for admission), SAT or ACT (for admission).

Options: electronic application, early admission, early decision, early action, deferred entrance.

Application fee: $50.

Required: essay or personal statement, minimum 2.0 GPA. *Required for some:* high school transcript.

Application deadlines: 1/15 (freshmen), rolling (transfers), 12/1 (early action).

Early decision deadline: 11/15.

Notification: 3/15 (freshmen), continuous (transfers), 12/15 (early decision), 1/15 (early action).

CONTACT

Ms. Elizabeth Skoglund, Director of Admissions, Salisbury University, Admissions House, 1101 Camden Avenue, Salisbury, MD 21801. *Phone:* 410-543-6161. *Toll-free phone:* 888-543-0148. *Fax:* 410-546-6016. *E-mail:* admissions@salisbury.edu.

Stevenson University
Stevenson, Maryland
http://www.stevenson.edu/

- **Independent** comprehensive, founded 1952
- **Suburban** 163-acre campus with easy access to Baltimore
- **Endowment** $82.7 million
- **Coed** 3,397 undergraduate students, 86% full-time, 66% women, 34% men
- **Moderately difficult** entrance level, 61% of applicants were admitted

UNDERGRAD STUDENTS

2,926 full-time, 471 part-time. Students come from 32 states and territories; 5 other countries; 23% are from out of state; 28% Black or African American, non-Hispanic/Latino; 6% Hispanic/Latino; 4% Asian, non-Hispanic/Latino; 0.1% Native Hawaiian or other Pacific Islander, non-Hispanic/Latino; 0.1% American Indian or Alaska Native, non-Hispanic/Latino; 5% Two or more races, non-Hispanic/Latino; 3% Race/ethnicity unknown; 0.4% international; 5% transferred in; 52% live on campus.

Freshmen:
Admission: 5,533 applied, 3,368 admitted, 688 enrolled. *Average high school GPA:* 3.1. *Test scores:* SAT evidence-based reading and writing scores over 500: 83%; SAT math scores over 500: 78%; ACT scores over 18: 87%; SAT evidence-based reading and writing scores over 600: 29%; SAT math scores over 600: 24%; ACT scores over 24: 30%; SAT evidence-based reading and writing scores over 700: 3%; SAT math scores over 700: 3%; ACT scores over 30: 4%.

Retention: 81% of full-time freshmen returned.

FACULTY
Total: 462, 29% full-time, 53% with terminal degrees.
Student/faculty ratio: 16:1.

ACADEMICS
Calendar: semesters. *Degrees:* bachelor's, master's, and postbachelor's certificates.

Special study options: academic remediation for entering students, accelerated degree program, adult/continuing education programs, advanced placement credit, cooperative education, distance learning, double majors, honors programs, independent study, internships, off-campus study, part-time degree program, services for LD students, student-designed majors, study abroad, summer session for credit. *ROTC:* Army (c), Air Force (c).

Computers: 515 computers/terminals and 3,000 ports are available on campus for general student use. Students can access the following: campus intranet, computer help desk, free student e-mail accounts, online (class) grades, online (class) registration, online (class) schedules. Campuswide network is available. 100% of college-owned or -operated housing units are wired for high-speed Internet access. Wireless service is available via entire campus.

Library: Stevenson University Learning Resource Center-Greenspring Campus plus 2 others. *Books:* 67,987 (physical), 342,648 (digital/electronic); *Serial titles:* 476 (physical), 72,885 (digital/electronic); *Databases:* 88. Weekly public service hours: 136; students can reserve study rooms.

STUDENT LIFE
Housing options: coed. Campus housing is university owned. Freshman applicants given priority for college housing.

Activities and organizations: drama/theater group, student-run newspaper, radio station, choral group, marching band, Relay for Life, Mustang Activities Programming, Black Student Union, American Chemical Society, Phi Sigma Sigma, national fraternities, national sororities.

Athletics Member NCAA. All Division III. *Intercollegiate sports:* baseball M, basketball M/W, cheerleading M/W, cross-country running M/W, field hockey W, football M, golf M/W, ice hockey M/W, lacrosse M/W, soccer M/W, softball M, tennis M/W, track and field M/W, volleyball M/W. *Intramural sports:* badminton M, baseball M, basketball M/W, field hockey W, football M/W, ice hockey M, soccer M/W, softball W, tennis M/W, volleyball M/W.

Campus security: 24-hour emergency response devices and patrols, late-night transport/escort service, controlled dormitory access, patrols by trained security personnel during campus hours.

Student services: health clinic, personal/psychological counseling.

COSTS & FINANCIAL AID

Costs (2018–19) *Comprehensive fee:* $49,312 includes full-time tuition ($33,690), mandatory fees ($2492), and room and board ($13,130). Full-time tuition and fees vary according to course load and degree level. Part-time tuition: $835 per credit hour. Part-time tuition and fees vary according to degree level. *Required fees:* $75 per term part-time. *College room only:* $8492. Room and board charges vary according to board plan and housing facility. *Payment plan:* installment. *Waivers:* employees or children of employees.

Financial Aid Of all full-time matriculated undergraduates who enrolled in 2017, 2,544 applied for aid, 2,347 were judged to have need, 253 had their need fully met. 156 Federal Work-Study jobs (averaging $2043). In 2017, 500 non-need-based awards were made. *Average percent of need met:* 66. *Average financial aid package:* $23,636. *Average need-based loan:* $4294. *Average need-based gift aid:* $20,387. *Average non-need-based aid:* $14,939. *Average indebtedness upon graduation:* $37,000.

APPLYING

Standardized Tests *Required:* SAT or ACT (for admission).

Options: electronic application, deferred entrance.

Application fee: $40.

Required: essay or personal statement, high school transcript, 1 letter of recommendation. *Required for some:* interview.

Application deadlines: rolling (freshmen), rolling (transfers).

Notification: continuous (freshmen), continuous (transfers).

CONTACT
Mr. Mark Hergan, Vice President, Enrollment Management, Stevenson University, 1525 Greenspring Valley Road, Stevenson, MD 21153. *Phone:* 410-486-7001. *Toll-free phone:* 877-468-6852 (in-state); 877-468-3852 (out-of-state). *Fax:* 410-352-4440. *E-mail:* admissions@stevenson.edu.

Stratford University

Baltimore, Maryland
http://www.stratford.edu/

- **Proprietary** comprehensive, founded 1972
- **Urban** 6-acre campus with easy access to Baltimore and Washington, DC
- **Coed**
- **Minimally difficult** entrance level

ACADEMICS
Calendar: quarters. *Degrees:* associate, bachelor's, and master's.
Library: Learning Resource Center.

COSTS
Costs (2017–18) *One-time required fee:* $100. *Tuition:* $24,975 full-time, $1665 per course part-time. Full-time tuition and fees vary according to course level, course load, degree level, and program. Part-time tuition and fees vary according to course level, course load, degree level, and program.

APPLYING
Options: electronic application.
Application fee: $50.
Required: high school transcript, interview. *Required for some:* 1 letter of recommendation. *Recommended:* essay or personal statement.

CONTACT
Admissions, Stratford University, 210 South Central Avenue, Baltimore, MD 21202. *Phone:* 410-752-4710. *Toll-free phone:* 800-624-9926 (in-state); 800-624-9926 Ext. 120 (out-of-state). *E-mail:* baadmissions@stratford.edu.

Strayer University–Anne Arundel Campus

Millersville, Maryland
http://www.strayer.edu/maryland/anne-arundel/

CONTACT
Strayer University–Anne Arundel Campus, 1520 Jabez Run, Suite 100, Millersville, MD 21108. *Toll-free phone:* 888-311-0355.

Strayer University–Owings Mills Campus

Owings Mills, Maryland
http://www.strayer.edu/maryland/owings-mills/

CONTACT
Strayer University–Owings Mills Campus, 500 Redland Court, Suite 100, Owings Mills, MD 21117. *Toll-free phone:* 888-311-0355.

Strayer University–Prince George's Campus

Suitland, Maryland
http://www.strayer.edu/maryland/prince-georges/

CONTACT
Strayer University–Prince George's Campus, 5110 Auth Way, Suitland, MD 20746. *Toll-free phone:* 888-311-0355.

Strayer University–Rockville Campus

Rockville, Maryland
http://www.strayer.edu/maryland/rockville/

CONTACT
Strayer University–Rockville Campus, 1803 Research Boulevard, Suite 110, Rockville, MD 20850. *Toll-free phone:* 888-311-0355.

Strayer University–White Marsh Campus

Baltimore, Maryland
http://www.strayer.edu/maryland/white-marsh/

CONTACT
Strayer University–White Marsh Campus, 9920 Franklin Square Drive, Suite 200, Baltimore, MD 21236. *Toll-free phone:* 888-311-0355.

Towson University

Towson, Maryland
http://www.towson.edu/

- **State-supported** university, founded 1866, part of University System of Maryland
- **Suburban** 329-acre campus with easy access to Baltimore and Washington, DC
- **Endowment** $76.0 million
- **Coed** 19,596 undergraduate students, 87% full-time, 60% women, 40% men
- **Moderately difficult** entrance level, 77% of applicants were admitted

UNDERGRAD STUDENTS
17,106 full-time, 2,490 part-time. Students come from 45 states and territories; 74 other countries; 13% are from out of state; 21% Black or African American, non-Hispanic/Latino; 8% Hispanic/Latino; 6% Asian, non-Hispanic/Latino; 0.1% Native Hawaiian or other Pacific Islander, non-Hispanic/Latino; 0.2% American Indian or Alaska Native, non-

Boston

Hispanic/Latino; 5% Two or more races, non-Hispanic/Latino; 2% Race/ethnicity unknown; 1% international; 12% transferred in; 26% live on campus.

Freshmen:

Admission: 12,747 applied, 9,854 admitted, 2,741 enrolled. **Average high school GPA:** 3.6. **Test scores:** SAT evidence-based reading and writing scores over 500: 93%; SAT math scores over 500: 88%; ACT scores over 18: 97%; SAT evidence-based reading and writing scores over 600: 34%; SAT math scores over 600: 26%; ACT scores over 24: 41%; SAT evidence-based reading and writing scores over 700: 2%; SAT math scores over 700: 2%; ACT scores over 30: 4%.

Retention: 85% of full-time freshmen returned.

FACULTY
Total: 1,711, 52% full-time, 54% with terminal degrees.
Student/faculty ratio: 17:1.

ACADEMICS
Calendar: semesters. *Degrees:* bachelor's, master's, doctoral, post-master's, and postbachelor's certificates.

Special study options: academic remediation for entering students, adult/continuing education programs, advanced placement credit, cooperative education, distance learning, double majors, English as a second language, freshman honors college, honors programs, independent study, internships, off-campus study, part-time degree program, services for LD students, student-designed majors, study abroad, summer session for credit. **ROTC:** Army (c), Air Force (c).

Unusual degree programs: 3-2 engineering with University of Maryland, College Park; law with University of Baltimore School of Law.

Computers: 2,500 computers/terminals and 8,445 ports are available on campus for general student use. Students can access the following: computer help desk, free student e-mail accounts, online (class) grades, online (class) registration, online (class) schedules. Campuswide network is available. 100% of college-owned or -operated housing units are wired for high-speed Internet access. Wireless service is available via entire campus.

Library: Cook Library. *Books:* 402,034 (physical), 245,801 (digital/electronic); *Serial titles:* 326 (physical), 29,155 (digital/electronic); *Databases:* 196. Weekly public service hours: 109; study areas open 24 hours, 5–7 days a week; students can reserve study rooms.

STUDENT LIFE
Housing options: coed, special housing for students with disabilities. Campus housing is university owned and is provided by a third party. Freshman campus housing is guaranteed.

Activities and organizations: drama/theater group, student-run newspaper, radio and television station, choral group, marching band, University Residence Government, Latin American Student Organization, Black Student Union, Hillel, African Diaspora Club, national fraternities, national sororities.

Athletics Member NCAA. All Division I except football (Division I-A). *Intercollegiate sports:* baseball M(s), basketball M(s)/W(s), cross-country running W(s), field hockey W(s), golf M(s)/W(s), gymnastics W(s), lacrosse M(s)/W(s), soccer W(s), softball W(s), swimming and diving M(s)/W(s), tennis W(s), track and field W(s), ultimate Frisbee M/W, volleyball M/W(s). *Intramural sports:* badminton M/W, basketball M/W, cheerleading M(c)/W(c), cross-country running M(c)/W(c), equestrian sports M(c)/W(c), field hockey M(c)/W(c), golf M(c)/W(c), gymnastics M(c)/W(c), ice hockey M(c)/W(c), lacrosse M(c)/W(c), riflery M(c)/W(c), rugby M(c)/W(c), soccer M/W, softball M/W, swimming and diving M(c)/W(c), table tennis M/W, tennis M(c)/W(c), track and field M(c)/W(c), ultimate Frisbee M(c)/W(c), volleyball M/W, water polo M(c)/W(c), wrestling M(c)/W(c).

Campus security: 24-hour emergency response devices and patrols, late-night transport/escort service, controlled dormitory access.

Student services: health clinic, personal/psychological counseling, women's center.

COSTS & FINANCIAL AID
Costs (2017–18) *Tuition:* state resident $6692 full-time, $288 per credit hour part-time; nonresident $19,138 full-time, $806 per credit hour part-time. Full-time tuition and fees vary according to course load and location. Part-time tuition and fees vary according to course load and location. **Required fees:** $3002 full-time, $130 per credit hour part-time. **Room and board:** $12,544; room only: $6984. Room and board charges vary according to board plan and housing facility. **Payment plan:** installment. **Waivers:** senior citizens and employees or children of employees.

Financial Aid Of all full-time matriculated undergraduates who enrolled in 2017, 12,624 applied for aid, 9,840 were judged to have need, 951 had their need fully met. 708 Federal Work-Study jobs (averaging $1763). In 2017, 1014 non-need-based awards were made. **Average percent of need met:** 57. **Average financial aid package:** $10,468. **Average need-based loan:** $4055. **Average need-based gift aid:** $9180. **Average non-need-based aid:** $5099. **Average indebtedness upon graduation:** $26,460.

APPLYING
Standardized Tests *Required:* SAT or ACT (for admission).
Options: electronic application, early admission, early action, deferred entrance.
Application fee: $45.
Required: essay or personal statement, high school transcript. **Required for some:** interview. **Recommended:** minimum 3.0 GPA, 2 letters of recommendation, resume or activity list.
Application deadlines: 1/17 (freshmen), 1/17 (transfers).
Notification: continuous (freshmen), continuous (transfers).

CONTACT
Mr. David Fedorchak, Director of University Admissions, Towson University, 8000 York Road, Towson, MD 21252. *Phone:* 410-704-2113. *Fax:* 410-704-3030. *E-mail:* admissions@towson.edu.

United States Naval Academy
Annapolis, Maryland
http://www.usna.edu/

CONTACT
Capt. Ann Kubera, Director of Admissions, United States Naval Academy, 52 King George Street, Annapolis, MD 21402. *Phone:* 410-293-4361. *Toll-free phone:* 888-249-7707. *Fax:* 410-293-4348. *E-mail:* webmail@usna.edu.

University of Baltimore
Baltimore, Maryland
http://www.ubalt.edu/

CONTACT
David Waggoner, Associate Vice President of Admission, University of Baltimore, 1420 North Charles Street, Baltimore, MD 21201. *Phone:* 410-837-4777. *Fax:* 410-837-4793. *E-mail:* admission@ubalt.edu.

University of Maryland, Baltimore County
Baltimore, Maryland
http://www.umbc.edu/

- **State-supported** university, founded 1963, part of University System of Maryland
- **Suburban** 530-acre campus with easy access to Washington, DC
- **Endowment** $92.0 million
- **Coed** 11,234 undergraduate students, 85% full-time, 45% women, 55% men
- **Moderately difficult** entrance level, 60% of applicants were admitted

UNDERGRAD STUDENTS
9,543 full-time, 1,691 part-time. Students come from 44 states and territories; 81 other countries; 5% are from out of state; 18% Black or African American, non-Hispanic/Latino; 7% Hispanic/Latino; 22% Asian, non-Hispanic/Latino; 0.1% Native Hawaiian or other Pacific Islander, non-Hispanic/Latino; 0.2% American Indian or Alaska Native, non-Hispanic/Latino; 4% Two or more races, non-Hispanic/Latino; 3% Race/ethnicity unknown; 4% international; 10% transferred in; 35% live on campus.

Maryland

COLLEGES AT-A-GLANCE

Freshmen:
Admission: 11,201 applied, 6,744 admitted, 1,772 enrolled. *Average high school GPA:* 3.8. *Test scores:* SAT evidence-based reading and writing scores over 500: 98%; SAT math scores over 500: 99%; ACT scores over 18: 98%; SAT evidence-based reading and writing scores over 600: 68%; SAT math scores over 600: 66%; ACT scores over 24: 80%; SAT evidence-based reading and writing scores over 700: 12%; SAT math scores over 700: 15%; ACT scores over 30: 22%.
Retention: 88% of full-time freshmen returned.

FACULTY
Total: 838, 65% full-time, 68% with terminal degrees.
Student/faculty ratio: 18:1.

ACADEMICS
Calendar: 4-1-4. *Degrees:* bachelor's, master's, doctoral, and postbachelor's certificates.

Special study options: academic remediation for entering students, adult/continuing education programs, advanced placement credit, cooperative education, distance learning, double majors, English as a second language, external degree program, freshman honors college, honors programs, independent study, internships, off-campus study, part-time degree program, services for LD students, student-designed majors, study abroad, summer session for credit. *ROTC:* Army (c), Navy (b), Air Force (c).

Computers: 1,065 computers/terminals and 4,000 ports are available on campus for general student use. Students can access the following: campus intranet, computer help desk, free student e-mail accounts, online (class) grades, online (class) registration, online (class) schedules, billing, housing, parking, degree audit and advising. Campuswide network is available. 100% of college-owned or -operated housing units are wired for high-speed Internet access. Wireless service is available via entire campus.
Library: Albin O. Kuhn Library and Gallery. *Books:* 703,486 (physical), 175,156 (digital/electronic); *Serial titles:* 27,505 (physical), 142,969 (digital/electronic); *Databases:* 388. Weekly public service hours: 94; study areas open 24 hours, 5–7 days a week; students can reserve study rooms.

STUDENT LIFE
Housing options: coed, special housing for students with disabilities. Campus housing is university owned and is provided by a third party. Freshman campus housing is guaranteed.

Activities and organizations: drama/theater group, student-run newspaper, radio station, choral group, Student Government Association, Student Events Board, Retriever Weekly, Resident Student Association, WMBC, Campus Radio, national fraternities, national sororities.

Athletics Member NCAA. All Division I except field hockey (Division II). *Intercollegiate sports:* baseball M(s), basketball M(s)/W(s), crew M(c)/W(c), cross-country running M(s)/W(s), equestrian sports M/W, fencing M(c)/W(c), field hockey W, ice hockey M(c), lacrosse M(s)/W(s), rugby M(c)/W(c), sailing M(c)/W(c), sand volleyball M/W, soccer M(s)/W(s), softball W(s), swimming and diving M(s)/W(s), track and field M(s)/W(s), ultimate Frisbee M(c)/W(c), volleyball M(c)/W(s), wrestling M(c). *Intramural sports:* basketball M/W, football M/W, lacrosse M(c)/W(c), soccer M(c)/W(c), softball M/W, tennis M(c)/W(c), volleyball M/W(c).

Campus security: 24-hour emergency response devices and patrols, late-night transport/escort service.
Student services: health clinic, personal/psychological counseling, women's center.

COSTS & FINANCIAL AID
Costs (2017–18) *One-time required fee:* $125. *Tuition:* state resident $8368 full-time, $347 per credit hour part-time; nonresident $22,504 full-time, $934 per credit hour part-time. Full-time tuition and fees vary according to location and program. Part-time tuition and fees vary according to location and program. *Required fees:* $3150 full-time, $136 per credit hour part-time. *Room and board:* $11,486; room only: $6966. Room and board charges vary according to board plan and housing facility. *Payment plan:* installment. *Waivers:* senior citizens and employees or children of employees.
Financial Aid Of all full-time matriculated undergraduates who enrolled in 2017, 6,424 applied for aid, 5,240 were judged to have need, 548 had

their need fully met. 163 Federal Work-Study jobs (averaging $1559). 118 state and other part-time jobs (averaging $10,410). In 2017, 1617 non-need-based awards were made. *Average percent of need met:* 55. *Average financial aid package:* $11,033. *Average need-based loan:* $4310. *Average need-based gift aid:* $9312. *Average non-need-based aid:* $8128. *Average indebtedness upon graduation:* $27,221.

APPLYING
Standardized Tests *Required:* SAT (for admission), ACT (for admission), SAT or ACT (for admission).
Options: electronic application, early admission, early action, deferred entrance.
Application fee: $50.
Required: essay or personal statement, high school transcript. *Recommended:* minimum 3.0 GPA, 2 letters of recommendation.
Application deadlines: 2/1 (freshmen), 12/15 (transfers), 11/1 (early action).
Notification: continuous (freshmen), continuous (transfers), 12/15 (early action).

CONTACT
Mr. Dale Bittinger, Director of Admissions, University of Maryland, Baltimore County, 1000 Hilltop Circle, Baltimore, MD 21250. *Phone:* 410-455-2291. *Toll-free phone:* 800-UMBC-4U2 (in-state); 800-862-2402 (out-of-state). *Fax:* 410-455-1094. *E-mail:* admissions@umbc.edu.

University of Maryland, College Park
College Park, Maryland
http://www.maryland.edu/
- **State-supported** university, founded 1856, part of University System of Maryland
- **Suburban** 1335-acre campus with easy access to Baltimore and Washington, DC
- **Endowment** $483.2 million
- **Coed** 29,868 undergraduate students, 93% full-time, 47% women, 53% men
- **Moderately difficult** entrance level, 44% of applicants were admitted

UNDERGRAD STUDENTS
27,708 full-time, 2,160 part-time. Students come from 51 states and territories; 63 other countries; 22% are from out of state; 12% Black or African American, non-Hispanic/Latino; 10% Hispanic/Latino; 17% Asian, non-Hispanic/Latino; 0.1% Native Hawaiian or other Pacific Islander, non-Hispanic/Latino; 0.1% American Indian or Alaska Native, non-Hispanic/Latino; 4% Two or more races, non-Hispanic/Latino; 1% Race/ethnicity unknown; 5% international; 7% transferred in; 40% live on campus.

Freshmen:
Admission: 33,907 applied, 15,081 admitted, 4,141 enrolled. *Average high school GPA:* 4.3. *Test scores:* SAT evidence-based reading and writing scores over 500: 99%; SAT math scores over 500: 99%; ACT scores over 18: 100%; SAT evidence-based reading and writing scores over 600: 87%; SAT math scores over 600: 88%; ACT scores over 24: 96%; SAT evidence-based reading and writing scores over 700: 39%; SAT math scores over 700: 52%; ACT scores over 30: 68%.
Retention: 96% of full-time freshmen returned.

FACULTY
Total: 2,633, 70% full-time, 81% with terminal degrees.
Student/faculty ratio: 18:1.

ACADEMICS
Calendar: semesters. *Degrees:* certificates, bachelor's, master's, doctoral, post-master's, and postbachelor's certificates.

Special study options: academic remediation for entering students, accelerated degree program, adult/continuing education programs, advanced placement credit, cooperative education, distance learning, double majors, English as a second language, external degree program, honors programs, independent study, internships, off-campus study, part-time degree program, services for LD students, student-designed majors, study abroad, summer session for credit. *ROTC:* Army (b), Navy (c), Air Force (b).

Computers: Students can access the following: campus intranet, computer help desk, free student e-mail accounts, online (class) grades, online (class) registration, online (class) schedules, student account information, financial aid summary. Campuswide network is available. 100% of college-owned or -operated housing units are wired for high-speed Internet access. Wireless service is available via entire campus.

Library: McKeldin Library plus 6 others. *Books:* 2.2 million (physical), 2.2 million (digital/electronic); *Serial titles:* 17,485 (physical), 110,240 (digital/electronic); *Databases:* 935. Weekly public service hours: 140; study areas open 24 hours, 5–7 days a week; students can reserve study rooms.

STUDENT LIFE

Housing options: coed, women-only, cooperative, special housing for students with disabilities. Campus housing is university owned and is provided by a third party. Freshman campus housing is guaranteed.

Activities and organizations: drama/theater group, student-run newspaper, radio and television station, choral group, marching band, Student Government Association, Residence Hall Association, Black Student Union, Asian-American Student Union/Jewish Student Union, Commuter Students Association, national fraternities, national sororities.

Athletics Member NCAA. All Division I. *Intercollegiate sports:* baseball M(s), basketball M(s)/W(s), cross-country running W(s), field hockey W(s), football M(s), golf M(s)/W(s), gymnastics W(s), lacrosse M(s)/W(s), soccer M(s)/W(s), softball W(s), swimming and diving M/W, tennis W(s), track and field M/W(s), volleyball W(s), wrestling M(s). *Intramural sports:* badminton M(c)/W(c), baseball M(c), basketball M(c)/W(c), crew M(c)/W(c), cross-country running M(c)/W(c), equestrian sports M(c)/W(c), fencing M(c)/W(c), field hockey W(c), football M/W, golf M(c)/W(c), ice hockey M(c)/W(c), lacrosse M(c)/W(c), racquetball M(c)/W(c), rock climbing M(c)/W(c), rugby M(c)/W(c), sailing M(c)/W(c), soccer M(c)/W(c), softball W(c), squash M(c)/W(c), swimming and diving M(c)/W(c), table tennis M(c)/W(c), tennis M(c)/W(c), ultimate Frisbee M/W, volleyball M(c)/W(c), water polo M(c)/W(c), wrestling M(c).

Campus security: 24-hour emergency response devices and patrols, student patrols, late-night transport/escort service, controlled dormitory access, campus police, video camera surveillance.

Student services: health clinic, personal/psychological counseling, women's center, legal services.

COSTS & FINANCIAL AID

Costs (2017–18) *Tuition:* state resident $8481 full-time, $353 per credit hour part-time; nonresident $31,688 full-time, $1321 per credit hour part-time. Full-time tuition and fees vary according to location, program, and student level. Part-time tuition and fees vary according to course load, location, program, and student level. *Required fees:* $1918 full-time, $447 per term part-time. *Room and board:* $12,082; room only: $7190. Room and board charges vary according to board plan and housing facility. *Payment plans:* installment, deferred payment. *Waivers:* employees or children of employees.

Financial Aid Of all full-time matriculated undergraduates who enrolled in 2016, 15,508 applied for aid, 10,883 were judged to have need, 1,697 had their need fully met. In 2016, 3543 non-need-based awards were made. *Average percent of need met:* 66. *Average financial aid package:* $12,410. *Average need-based loan:* $4775. *Average need-based gift aid:* $9978. *Average non-need-based aid:* $6919. *Average indebtedness upon graduation:* $28,122.

APPLYING

Standardized Tests *Required:* SAT or ACT (for admission).

Options: electronic application, early admission, early action, deferred entrance.

Application fee: $65.

Required: essay or personal statement, high school transcript. *Required for some:* Resume of activities, audition for music applicants, drawing requirement for architecture applicants. *Recommended:* 2 letters of recommendation.

Application deadlines: 1/20 (freshmen), 6/1 (transfers), 11/1 (early action).

Notification: 4/1 (freshmen), continuous (transfers), 1/31 (early action).

CONTACT

Ms. Barbara Gill, Associate Vice President, Enrollment Management, University of Maryland, College Park, College Park, MD 20742. *Phone:* 301-314-8385. *Toll-free phone:* 800-422-5867. *Fax:* 301-314-9693.

University of Maryland Eastern Shore
Princess Anne, Maryland
http://www.umes.edu/

- **State-supported** university, founded 1886, part of University System of Maryland
- **Rural** 745-acre campus
- **Endowment** $27.9 million
- **Coed** 2,862 undergraduate students, 90% full-time, 55% women, 45% men
- **Moderately difficult** entrance level, 39% of applicants were admitted

UNDERGRAD STUDENTS

2,573 full-time, 289 part-time. Students come from 30 states and territories; 33 other countries; 17% are from out of state; 75% Black or African American, non-Hispanic/Latino; 4% Hispanic/Latino; 1% Asian, non-Hispanic/Latino; 0.1% Native Hawaiian or other Pacific Islander, non-Hispanic/Latino; 0.2% American Indian or Alaska Native, non-Hispanic/Latino; 5% Two or more races, non-Hispanic/Latino; 0.3% Race/ethnicity unknown; 3% international; 5% transferred in; 60% live on campus.

Freshmen:
Admission: 7,827 applied, 3,053 admitted, 565 enrolled. *Average high school GPA:* 3.0. *Test scores:* ACT scores over 18: 40%; ACT scores over 24: 5%.

Retention: 64% of full-time freshmen returned.

FACULTY

Total: 307, 68% full-time, 66% with terminal degrees.
Student/faculty ratio: 13:1.

ACADEMICS

Calendar: semesters. *Degrees:* certificates, bachelor's, master's, and doctoral.

Special study options: part-time degree program. *ROTC:* Army (c).

Computers: Students can access the following: computer help desk, free student e-mail accounts, online (class) grades, online (class) registration, online (class) schedules. Campuswide network is available. Wireless service is available via entire campus.

Library: Frederick Douglass Library. *Books:* 137,271 (physical), 27,434 (digital/electronic); *Serial titles:* 459 (physical), 1,019 (digital/electronic); *Databases:* 134. Study areas open 24 hours, 5–7 days a week; students can reserve study rooms.

STUDENT LIFE

Housing options: coed, men-only, women-only. Campus housing is university owned and leased by the school.

Athletics Member NCAA. All Division I. *Intercollegiate sports:* baseball M(s), basketball M(s)/W(s), cheerleading M/W, cross-country running M/W, softball W, tennis M(s)/W, track and field M/W, volleyball W, wrestling M. *Intramural sports:* basketball M/W, bowling W, cheerleading M/W, cross-country running M/W, soccer M/W, softball W, swimming and diving M/W, table tennis M/W, tennis M/W, track and field M/W, volleyball M/W, wrestling M.

Campus security: 24-hour emergency response devices and patrols, student patrols, late-night transport/escort service, controlled dormitory access.

FINANCIAL AID

Financial Aid Of all full-time matriculated undergraduates who enrolled in 2015, 3,133 applied for aid, 2,697 were judged to have need, 21 had their need fully met. 88 Federal Work-Study jobs (averaging $2955). In 2015, 92 non-need-based awards were made. *Average percent of need met:* 34. *Average financial aid package:* $4416. *Average need-based loan:* $3996. *Average need-based gift aid:* $3337. *Average non-need-based aid:* $4545. *Average indebtedness upon graduation:* $9861.

APPLYING

Standardized Tests *Required:* SAT or ACT (for admission).

Options: electronic application, deferred entrance.

Application fee: $25.

Required: essay or personal statement, high school transcript, minimum 2.5 GPA, 3 letters of recommendation. *Required for some:* interview.

Application deadlines: 7/15 (freshmen), 5/1 (transfers).

CONTACT
University of Maryland Eastern Shore, 11868 Academic Oval, Princess Anne, MD 21853. *Phone:* 410-651-6410.

University of Maryland University College

Adelphi, Maryland
http://www.umuc.edu/

- **State-supported** comprehensive, founded 1947, part of University System of Maryland
- **Suburban** campus with easy access to Washington, DC
- **Coed** 45,604 undergraduate students, 21% full-time, 44% women, 56% men
- **Noncompetitive** entrance level, 100% of applicants were admitted

UNDERGRAD STUDENTS
9,714 full-time, 35,890 part-time. Students come from 52 states and territories; 34 other countries; 59% are from out of state; 26% Black or African American, non-Hispanic/Latino; 13% Hispanic/Latino; 5% Asian, non-Hispanic/Latino; 0.9% Native Hawaiian or other Pacific Islander, non-Hispanic/Latino; 0.5% American Indian or Alaska Native, non-Hispanic/Latino; 5% Two or more races, non-Hispanic/Latino; 8% Race/ethnicity unknown; 2% international; 22% transferred in.

Freshmen:
Admission: 2,496 applied, 2,496 admitted, 676 enrolled.

FACULTY
Total: 3,691, 5% full-time, 56% with terminal degrees.
Student/faculty ratio: 19:1.

ACADEMICS
Calendar: semesters. *Degrees:* certificates, associate, bachelor's, master's, doctoral, and postbachelor's certificates (offers primarily part-time evening and weekend degree programs at more than 30 off-campus locations in Maryland and the Washington, DC area, and more than 180 military communities in Europe and Asia with military enrollment not reflected in this profile; associate of arts program available to military students only).

Special study options: academic remediation for entering students, accelerated degree program, advanced placement credit, cooperative education, distance learning, double majors, external degree program, independent study, internships, off-campus study, part-time degree program, services for LD students, summer session for credit.

Computers: 484 computers/terminals are available on campus for general student use. Students can access the following: campus intranet, computer help desk, free student e-mail accounts, online (class) grades, online (class) registration, online (class) schedules. Campuswide network is available. Wireless service is available via entire campus.
Library: Information and Library Services plus 1 other. *Books:* 1,234 (physical), 110,587 (digital/electronic); *Serial titles:* 149,268 (physical); *Databases:* 102. Weekly public service hours: 95.

STUDENT LIFE
Housing options: college housing not available.

Campus security: 24-hour emergency response devices and patrols, late-night transport/escort service.

COSTS & FINANCIAL AID
Costs (2018–19) *Tuition:* state resident $6936 full-time, $289 per credit hour part-time; nonresident $11,976 full-time, $499 per credit hour part-time. *Required fees:* $360 full-time. *Payment plan:* installment. *Waivers:* senior citizens and employees or children of employees.

Financial Aid Of all full-time matriculated undergraduates who enrolled in 2016, 5,932 applied for aid, 5,660 were judged to have need, 46 had their need fully met. *Average percent of need met:* 27. *Average financial aid package:* $6959. *Average need-based loan:* $4244. *Average need-based gift aid:* $4776.

APPLYING
Options: electronic application, early decision, deferred entrance.
Application fee: $50.
Required: high school transcript.
Application deadlines: rolling (freshmen), rolling (transfers).
Notification: continuous (freshmen), continuous (transfers).

CONTACT
University of Maryland University College, 3501 University Boulevard East, Adelphi, MD 20783. *Phone:* 800-888-UMUC (8682). *Toll-free phone:* 800-888-8682. *E-mail:* enroll@umuc.edu.

Washington Adventist University

Takoma Park, Maryland
http://www.wau.edu/

CONTACT
Elaine Oliver, Associate Vice President, Enrollment Services, Washington Adventist University, 7600 Flower Avenue, Takoma Park, MD 20912. *Phone:* 301-891-4502. *Toll-free phone:* 800-835-4212. *Fax:* 301-971-4230. *E-mail:* enroll@cuc.edu.

Washington College

Chestertown, Maryland
http://www.washcoll.edu/

- **Independent** 4-year, founded 1782
- **Small-town** 140-acre campus with easy access to Baltimore and Washington, DC
- **Endowment** $220.0 million
- **Coed** 1,484 undergraduate students, 98% full-time, 58% women, 42% men
- **Moderately difficult** entrance level, 48% of applicants were admitted

UNDERGRAD STUDENTS
1,456 full-time, 28 part-time. Students come from 38 states and territories; 26 other countries; 54% are from out of state; 8% Black or African American, non-Hispanic/Latino; 6% Hispanic/Latino; 3% Asian, non-Hispanic/Latino; 0.1% Native Hawaiian or other Pacific Islander, non-Hispanic/Latino; 0.7% American Indian or Alaska Native, non-Hispanic/Latino; 0.5% Two or more races, non-Hispanic/Latino; 4% Race/ethnicity unknown; 10% international; 2% transferred in; 85% live on campus.

Freshmen:
Admission: 5,515 applied, 2,626 admitted, 368 enrolled. *Average high school GPA:* 3.7. *Test scores:* SAT evidence-based reading and writing scores over 500: 93%; SAT math scores over 500: 88%; ACT scores over 18: 97%; SAT evidence-based reading and writing scores over 600: 56%; SAT math scores over 600: 42%; ACT scores over 24: 70%; SAT evidence-based reading and writing scores over 700: 16%; SAT math scores over 700: 7%; ACT scores over 30: 20%.

Retention: 85% of full-time freshmen returned.

FACULTY
Total: 175, 66% full-time, 82% with terminal degrees.
Student/faculty ratio: 11:1.

ACADEMICS
Calendar: semesters. *Degree:* bachelor's.

Special study options: accelerated degree program, double majors, English as a second language, honors programs, independent study, internships, off-campus study, part-time degree program, services for LD students, student-designed majors, study abroad, summer session for credit.

Unusual degree programs: 3-2 engineering with Columbia University; nursing with University of Maryland; pharmacy with University of Maryland.

Computers: 100 computers/terminals and 1,450 ports are available on campus for general student use. Students can access the following: campus intranet, computer help desk, free student e-mail accounts, online (class) grades, online (class) registration, online (class) schedules. Campuswide network is available. 100% of college-owned or -operated

housing units are wired for high-speed Internet access. Wireless service is available via entire campus.
Library: Clifton M. Miller Library.

STUDENT LIFE

Housing options: on-campus residence required through sophomore year; coed, men-only, women-only, special housing for students with disabilities. Campus housing is university owned. Freshman campus housing is guaranteed.

Activities and organizations: drama/theater group, student-run newspaper, radio station, choral group, Presidential Fellows, Dance Club, Habitat for Humanity, Peer Mentor, Animal Impact Club, national fraternities, national sororities.

Athletics Member NCAA. All Division III. *Intercollegiate sports:* baseball M, basketball M/W, cheerleading W(c), crew M/W, equestrian sports M(c)/W(c), field hockey W, ice hockey M(c), lacrosse M/W, rugby M(c)/W(c), sailing M/W, soccer M/W, softball W, swimming and diving M/W, tennis M/W, volleyball W, water polo M(c)/W(c). *Intramural sports:* badminton M/W, basketball M/W, football M/W, lacrosse M(c), racquetball M/W, rugby M/W, sailing M/W, soccer M/W, squash M/W, table tennis M/W, tennis M/W, ultimate Frisbee M/W, volleyball M/W.

Campus security: 24-hour emergency response devices and patrols, student patrols, late-night transport/escort service, controlled dormitory access, LiveSafe mobile app.

Student services: health clinic, personal/psychological counseling.

COSTS & FINANCIAL AID

Costs (2018–19) *Comprehensive fee:* $59,196 includes full-time tuition ($45,888), mandatory fees ($1118), and room and board ($12,190). Part-time tuition: $1912 per credit hour. Part-time tuition and fees vary according to course load. No tuition increase for student's term of enrollment. *College room only:* $5776. Room and board charges vary according to board plan, housing facility, and location. *Payment plans:* tuition prepayment, installment. *Waivers:* employees or children of employees.

Financial Aid Of all full-time matriculated undergraduates who enrolled in 2017, 1,077 applied for aid, 961 were judged to have need, 162 had their need fully met. 163 Federal Work-Study jobs (averaging $1484). In 2017, 368 non-need-based awards were made. *Average percent of need met:* 76. *Average financial aid package:* $32,393. *Average need-based loan:* $4293. *Average need-based gift aid:* $29,254. *Average non-need-based aid:* $18,106. *Average indebtedness upon graduation:* $30,462.

APPLYING

Standardized Tests *Required:* SAT or ACT (for admission).

Options: electronic application, early admission, early decision, early action, deferred entrance.

Required: essay or personal statement, high school transcript, 1 letter of recommendation. *Required for some:* interview. *Recommended:* interview.

Application deadlines: 2/15 (freshmen), rolling (transfers), 12/1 (early action).

Early decision deadline: 11/15 (for plan 1), 12/15 (for plan 2).

Notification: continuous (freshmen), continuous (transfers), 12/15 (early decision plan 1), 1/15 (early decision plan 2), 1/15 (early action).

CONTACT

Washington College, 300 Washington Avenue, Chestertown, MD 21620. *Phone:* 410-778-7700. *Toll-free phone:* 800-422-1782. *Fax:* 410-778-7287. *E-mail:* wc_admissions@washcoll.edu.

Yeshiva College of the Nation's Capital

Silver Spring, Maryland
http://www.yeshiva.edu/

CONTACT
Yeshiva College of the Nation's Capital, 1216 Arcola Avenue, Silver Spring, MD 20902.

MASSACHUSETTS

American International College

Springfield, Massachusetts
http://www.aic.edu/

- **Independent** comprehensive, founded 1885
- **Urban** 58-acre campus
- **Endowment** $15.0 million
- **Coed** 1,372 undergraduate students, 91% full-time, 59% women, 41% men
- **Minimally difficult** entrance level, 72% of applicants were admitted

UNDERGRAD STUDENTS

1,254 full-time, 118 part-time. Students come from 30 states and territories; 20 other countries; 62% are from out of state; 24% Black or African American, non-Hispanic/Latino; 19% Hispanic/Latino; 1% Asian, non-Hispanic/Latino; 0.4% Native Hawaiian or other Pacific Islander, non-Hispanic/Latino; 0.5% American Indian or Alaska Native, non-Hispanic/Latino; 3% Two or more races, non-Hispanic/Latino; 10% Race/ethnicity unknown; 3% international; 10% transferred in; 49% live on campus.

Freshmen:

Admission: 1,988 applied, 1,428 admitted, 373 enrolled. *Average high school GPA:* 2.9. *Test scores:* SAT evidence-based reading and writing scores over 500: 57%; SAT math scores over 500: 52%; ACT scores over 18: 66%; SAT evidence-based reading and writing scores over 600: 7%; SAT math scores over 600: 8%; ACT scores over 24: 13%.

Retention: 62% of full-time freshmen returned.

FACULTY

Total: 320, 23% full-time, 44% with terminal degrees.

Student/faculty ratio: 18:1.

ACADEMICS

Calendar: semesters. *Degrees:* associate, bachelor's, master's, doctoral, post-master's, and postbachelor's certificates.

Special study options: academic remediation for entering students, accelerated degree program, adult/continuing education programs, advanced placement credit, distance learning, double majors, honors programs, independent study, internships, off-campus study, part-time degree program, services for LD students, study abroad, summer session for credit. *ROTC:* Army (c), Air Force (c).

Unusual degree programs: 3-2 business administration; occupational therapy; education.

Computers: 230 computers/terminals and 100 ports are available on campus for general student use. Students can access the following: campus intranet, computer help desk, free student e-mail accounts, online (class) grades, online (class) registration, online (class) schedules. Campuswide network is available. 100% of college-owned or -operated housing units are wired for high-speed Internet access. Wireless service is available via entire campus.
Library: James J. Shea Sr. Library. *Books:* 56,511 (physical), 179,160 (digital/electronic); *Serial titles:* 183 (physical), 962 (digital/electronic); *Databases:* 64. Weekly public service hours: 100; students can reserve study rooms.

STUDENT LIFE

Housing options: on-campus residence required through sophomore year; coed, women-only. Campus housing is university owned. Freshman campus housing is guaranteed.

Activities and organizations: drama/theater group, student-run newspaper, choral group, Student Activities Committee, Model Congress, PRIDE (Persons Ready in Defense of Ebony), Student Government, School newspaper.

Athletics Member NCAA. All Division II except ice hockey (Division I), rugby (Division I). *Intercollegiate sports:* baseball M(s), basketball M(s)/W(s), cross-country running M(s)/W(s), field hockey W(s), football M(s), golf M(s)/W(s), ice hockey M(s), lacrosse M(s)/W(s), rugby M(s)(c)/W(s), soccer M(s)/W(s), softball W(s), tennis W(s), track and field M(s)/W(s), volleyball W(s), wrestling M(s). *Intramural sports:* basketball M/W, cheerleading M(c)/W(c), softball M/W, volleyball M/W.

Campus security: 24-hour emergency response devices and patrols, late-night transport/escort service, controlled dormitory access.

Student services: health clinic, personal/psychological counseling.

COSTS & FINANCIAL AID
Costs (2018–19) *Comprehensive fee:* $49,980 includes full-time tuition ($35,680) and room and board ($14,300). Full-time tuition and fees vary according to course load and program. Part-time tuition: $735 per credit hour. Part-time tuition and fees vary according to course load. *Required fees:* $30 per term part-time. *College room only:* $7140. Room and board charges vary according to board plan and housing facility. *Payment plan:* installment. *Waivers:* employees or children of employees.

Financial Aid Of all full-time matriculated undergraduates who enrolled in 2013, 1,394 applied for aid, 1,333 were judged to have need, 159 had their need fully met. 466 Federal Work-Study jobs (averaging $640). 161 state and other part-time jobs (averaging $1190). *Average percent of need met:* 70. *Average financial aid package:* $23,969. *Average need-based loan:* $4133. *Average need-based gift aid:* $19,916. *Average indebtedness upon graduation:* $35,587.

APPLYING
Options: electronic application, deferred entrance.

Required: high school transcript. *Recommended:* essay or personal statement, 1 letter of recommendation.

Application deadlines: 9/7 (freshmen), 9/7 (transfers).

Notification: continuous (freshmen), continuous (transfers).

CONTACT
Mr. Jonathan Scully, Director of Undergraduate Admissions, American International College, 1000 State Street, Springfield, MA 01109-3189. *Phone:* 413-205-3270. *Toll-free phone:* 800-242-3142. *Fax:* 413-205-3051. *E-mail:* jonathan.scully@aic.edu.

Amherst College
Amherst, Massachusetts
http://www.amherst.edu/
- **Independent** 4-year, founded 1821
- **Small-town** 1020-acre campus
- **Coed** 1,836 undergraduate students, 100% full-time, 49% women, 51% men
- **Most difficult** entrance level, 13% of applicants were admitted

UNDERGRAD STUDENTS
1,836 full-time. Students come from 48 states and territories; 58 other countries; 86% are from out of state; 11% Black or African American, non-Hispanic/Latino; 13% Hispanic/Latino; 14% Asian, non-Hispanic/Latino; 0.1% Native Hawaiian or other Pacific Islander, non-Hispanic/Latino; 0.6% American Indian or Alaska Native, non-Hispanic/Latino; 5% Two or more races, non-Hispanic/Latino; 3% Race/ethnicity unknown; 9% international; 0.9% transferred in; 97% live on campus.

Freshmen:
Admission: 9,285 applied, 1,198 admitted, 471 enrolled. *Test scores:* SAT evidence-based reading and writing scores over 500: 100%; SAT math scores over 500: 100%; ACT scores over 18: 100%; SAT evidence-based reading and writing scores over 600: 99%; SAT math scores over 600: 99%; ACT scores over 24: 100%; SAT evidence-based reading and writing scores over 700: 83%; SAT math scores over 700: 85%; ACT scores over 30: 94%.
Retention: 96% of full-time freshmen returned.

FACULTY
Total: 291, 77% full-time, 89% with terminal degrees.
Student/faculty ratio: 8:1.

ACADEMICS
Calendar: semesters. *Degree:* bachelor's.
Special study options: double majors, independent study, internships, off-campus study, services for LD students, student-designed majors, study abroad. *ROTC:* Army (c), Air Force (c).
Unusual degree programs: 3-2 engineering with Dartmouth College.

Computers: Students can access the following: campus intranet, computer help desk, free student e-mail accounts, online (class) grades, online (class) registration, online (class) schedules. Campuswide network is available. 100% of college-owned or -operated housing units are wired for high-speed Internet access. Wireless service is available via entire campus.
Library: Robert Frost Library plus 3 others.

STUDENT LIFE
Housing options: on-campus residence required for freshman year; coed, women-only, cooperative, special housing for students with disabilities. Campus housing is university owned. Freshman campus housing is guaranteed.

Activities and organizations: drama/theater group, student-run newspaper, radio station, choral group, Association of Amherst Students, Black Students Union, Student Publications (e.g., Amherst Student, Indicator), A Capella Groups (e.g., Zumbye's, Bluestockings), Amherst Dance.

Athletics Member NCAA. All Division III. *Intercollegiate sports:* baseball M, basketball M/W, cheerleading W(c), crew M(c)/W(c), cross-country running M/W, equestrian sports M(c)/W(c), fencing M(c)/W(c), field hockey W, football M, golf M/W, ice hockey M/W, lacrosse M/W, rugby M(c)/W(c), sailing M(c)/W(c), skiing (downhill) M(c)/W(c), soccer M/W, softball W, squash M/W, swimming and diving M/W, tennis M/W, track and field M/W, ultimate Frisbee M(c)/W(c), volleyball M(c)/W, water polo M(c)/W(c), wrestling M(c)/W(c). *Intramural sports:* badminton M/W, basketball M/W, golf M/W, ice hockey M/W, rock climbing M/W, soccer M/W, softball M/W, squash M/W, tennis M/W, track and field M/W, volleyball M/W.

Campus security: 24-hour emergency response devices and patrols, late-night transport/escort service, controlled dormitory access.

Student services: health clinic, personal/psychological counseling, women's center.

COSTS & FINANCIAL AID
Costs (2017–18) *Comprehensive fee:* $68,500 includes full-time tuition ($53,430), mandatory fees ($880), and room and board ($14,190). *College room only:* $7690. *Payment plan:* installment.

Financial Aid Of all full-time matriculated undergraduates who enrolled in 2017, 1,229 applied for aid, 1,102 were judged to have need, 1,102 had their need fully met. 715 Federal Work-Study jobs (averaging $1901). 171 state and other part-time jobs (averaging $1965). *Average percent of need met:* 100. *Average financial aid package:* $53,052. *Average need-based loan:* $505. *Average need-based gift aid:* $51,841. *Average indebtedness upon graduation:* $19,075.

APPLYING
Standardized Tests *Required:* SAT or ACT (for admission).

Options: electronic application, early admission, early decision, deferred entrance.

Application fee: $65.

Required: essay or personal statement, high school transcript, 3 letters of recommendation, Amherst College Supplement.

Application deadlines: 1/1 (freshmen), 3/1 (transfers).

Early decision deadline: 11/1.

Notification: 4/1 (freshmen), 5/15 (transfers), 12/15 (early decision).

CONTACT
Katharine L. Fretwell, Dean of Admission and Financial Aid, Amherst College, PO Box 5000, Amherst, MA 01002-5000. *Phone:* 413-542-2328. *Fax:* 413-542-2040. *E-mail:* admission@amherst.edu.

Anna Maria College
Paxton, Massachusetts
http://www.annamaria.edu/

CONTACT
Mr. Peter Miller, Dean of Admissions and Financial Aid, Anna Maria College, 50 Sunset Lane, Paxton, MA 01612. *Phone:* 508-849-3586. *Fax:* 508-849-3362. *E-mail:* admissions@annamaria.edu.

Assumption College
Worcester, Massachusetts
http://www.assumption.edu/

- **Independent Roman Catholic** comprehensive, founded 1904
- **Suburban** 180-acre campus with easy access to Boston
- **Endowment** $102.5 million
- **Coed** 1,940 undergraduate students, 99% full-time, 58% women, 42% men
- **Moderately difficult** entrance level, 79% of applicants were admitted

UNDERGRAD STUDENTS

1,925 full-time, 15 part-time. Students come from 29 states and territories; 21 other countries; 35% are from out of state; 5% Black or African American, non-Hispanic/Latino; 7% Hispanic/Latino; 3% Asian, non-Hispanic/Latino; 0.2% Native Hawaiian or other Pacific Islander, non-Hispanic/Latino; 0.1% American Indian or Alaska Native, non-Hispanic/Latino; 2% Two or more races, non-Hispanic/Latino; 4% Race/ethnicity unknown; 2% international; 1% transferred in; 85% live on campus.

Freshmen:
Admission: 4,508 applied, 3,561 admitted, 492 enrolled. *Average high school GPA:* 3.3. *Test scores:* SAT evidence-based reading and writing scores over 500: 93%; SAT math scores over 500: 92%; ACT scores over 18: 100%; SAT evidence-based reading and writing scores over 600: 43%; SAT math scores over 600: 37%; ACT scores over 24: 69%; SAT evidence-based reading and writing scores over 700: 6%; SAT math scores over 700: 4%; ACT scores over 30: 18%.

Retention: 82% of full-time freshmen returned.

FACULTY
Total: 231, 62% full-time, 77% with terminal degrees.
Student/faculty ratio: 11:1.

ACADEMICS
Calendar: semesters. *Degrees:* bachelor's, master's, post-master's, and postbachelor's certificates.

Special study options: advanced placement credit, double majors, honors programs, independent study, internships, off-campus study, part-time degree program, services for LD students, student-designed majors, study abroad, summer session for credit. *ROTC:* Army (c), Air Force (c).

Unusual degree programs: 3-2 business administration; engineering with University of Notre Dame; Washington University at St. Louis; forestry with Duke University; special education, rehabilitation counseling, school counseling; law (JD) with Duquesne U School of Law, Western NE College School of Law, Vermont Law School; optometry with New England College of Optometry; osteopathic medicine with Des Moines U; environmental science with Duke U.

Computers: 361 computers/terminals and 2,476 ports are available on campus for general student use. Students can access the following: campus intranet, computer help desk, free student e-mail accounts, online (class) grades, online (class) registration, online (class) schedules. Campuswide network is available. 100% of college-owned or -operated housing units are wired for high-speed Internet access. Wireless service is available via entire campus.
Library: Emmanuel d'Alzon Library. *Books:* 131,961 (physical), 159,279 (digital/electronic); *Serial titles:* 2,163 (physical), 45,363 (digital/electronic); *Databases:* 78. Weekly public service hours: 102; students can reserve study rooms.

STUDENT LIFE
Housing options: coed, women-only, special housing for students with disabilities. Campus housing is university owned. Freshman campus housing is guaranteed.

Activities and organizations: drama/theater group, student-run newspaper, television station, choral group, Volunteer center, Campus Activities Board, Student Government, Campus Ministry, intramural sports.

Athletics Member NCAA. All Division II. *Intercollegiate sports:* baseball M, basketball M(s)/W(s), cheerleading M(c)/W(c), cross-country running M/W, equestrian sports M(c)/W(c), field hockey W, football M, golf M, ice hockey M, lacrosse M/W, rowing W, soccer M/W, softball W, swimming and diving W, tennis M/W, track and field M/W, ultimate Frisbee M(c)/W(c), volleyball M(c)/W. *Intramural sports:* basketball

M/W, football M/W, golf M/W, ice hockey M/W, racquetball M/W, soccer M/W, softball M/W, swimming and diving M/W, table tennis M/W, tennis M/W, volleyball M/W.

Campus security: 24-hour emergency response devices and patrols, student patrols, late-night transport/escort service, controlled dormitory access, front gate security, well-lit pathways.

Student services: health clinic, personal/psychological counseling.

COSTS & FINANCIAL AID
Costs (2018–19) *Comprehensive fee:* $53,642 includes full-time tuition ($40,208), mandatory fees ($750), and room and board ($12,684). Full-time tuition and fees vary according to course load, reciprocity agreements, and student level. Part-time tuition: $1184 per credit hour. Part-time tuition and fees vary according to course load. *Room and board:* Room and board charges vary according to housing facility. *Waivers:* employees or children of employees.

Financial Aid Of all full-time matriculated undergraduates who enrolled in 2017, 1,606 applied for aid, 1,442 were judged to have need, 399 had their need fully met. 456 Federal Work-Study jobs (averaging $1652). In 2017, 415 non-need-based awards were made. *Average percent of need met:* 76. *Average financial aid package:* $27,681. *Average need-based loan:* $4561. *Average need-based gift aid:* $22,325. *Average non-need-based aid:* $15,806. *Financial aid deadline:* 2/15.

APPLYING
Options: electronic application, early decision, early action, deferred entrance.

Application fee: $50.

Required: essay or personal statement, high school transcript, 1 letter of recommendation. *Recommended:* interview.

Application deadlines: 2/15 (freshmen), 7/1 (transfers), 11/1 (early action).

Early decision deadline: 11/1.

Notification: continuous (freshmen), continuous (transfers), 12/8 (early decision), 12/15 (early action).

CONTACT
Assumption College, 500 Salisbury Street, Worcester, MA 01609-1296. *Phone:* 508-767-7286. *Toll-free phone:* 866-477-7776.

See next page for display ad and page 1234 for the College Close-Up.

Babson College
Wellesley, Massachusetts
http://www.babson.edu/

- **Independent** comprehensive, founded 1919
- **Suburban** 370-acre campus with easy access to Boston
- **Endowment** $348.6 million
- **Coed** 2,342 undergraduate students, 100% full-time, 48% women, 52% men
- **Very difficult** entrance level, 24% of applicants were admitted

UNDERGRAD STUDENTS

2,342 full-time. Students come from 49 states and territories; 80 other countries; 73% are from out of state; 5% Black or African American, non-Hispanic/Latino; 11% Hispanic/Latino; 12% Asian, non-Hispanic/Latino; 0.1% Native Hawaiian or other Pacific Islander, non-Hispanic/Latino; 0.1% American Indian or Alaska Native, non-Hispanic/Latino; 2% Two or more races, non-Hispanic/Latino; 5% Race/ethnicity unknown; 28% international; 2% transferred in; 79% live on campus.

Freshmen:
Admission: 7,122 applied, 1,722 admitted, 550 enrolled. *Test scores:* SAT evidence-based reading and writing scores over 500: 100%; SAT math scores over 500: 100%; ACT scores over 18: 100%; SAT evidence-based reading and writing scores over 600: 87%; SAT math scores over 600: 85%; ACT scores over 24: 97%; SAT evidence-based reading and writing scores over 700: 16%; SAT math scores over 700: 36%; ACT scores over 30: 50%.

Retention: 96% of full-time freshmen returned.

FACULTY
Total: 266, 69% full-time, 76% with terminal degrees.
Student/faculty ratio: 11:1.

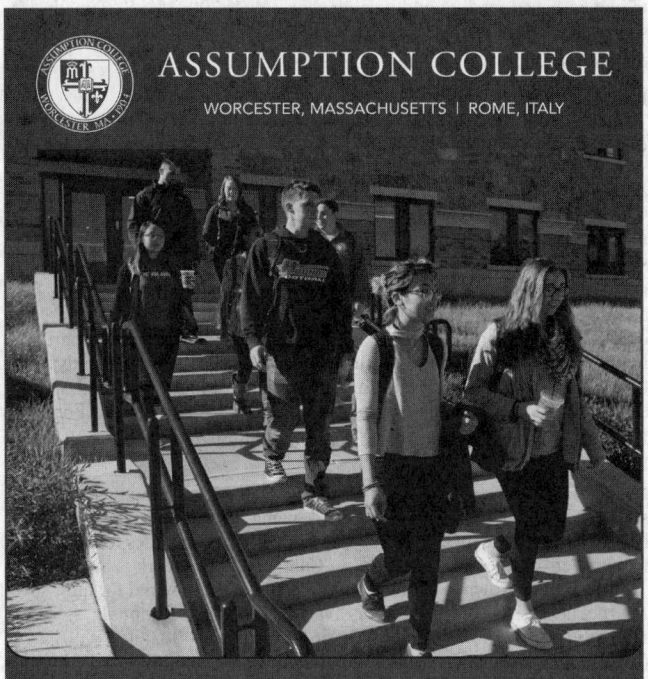

Find yourself *here*.

:: Choose among **30** majors and **47** minors in the liberal arts, sciences, business and professional studies

:: **2,000** undergraduates from **29** states and **21** countries

:: **90%** of the undergraduates live on campus for all **4** years

:: Located in the **2nd-largest** city in New England, with **35,000** college students overall

:: **Ranked as one of the best colleges** in the nation by *Princeton Review* and a **"Best Value"** by *U.S. News & World Report*

Visit the 4th-oldest Catholic college in New England

www.assumption.edu

Light the way.

ACADEMICS

Calendar: semesters. *Degrees:* bachelor's, master's, and postbachelor's certificates.

Special study options: advanced placement credit, freshman honors college, honors programs, independent study, internships, off-campus study, services for LD students, student-designed majors, study abroad, summer session for credit. *ROTC:* Army (c).

Computers: Students can access the following: campus intranet, computer help desk, free student e-mail accounts, online (class) grades, online (class) registration, online (class) schedules. Campuswide network is available. Wireless service is available via entire campus.

Library: Horn Library plus 1 other.

STUDENT LIFE

Housing options: on-campus residence required for freshman year; coed, men-only, special housing for students with disabilities. Campus housing is university owned. Freshman campus housing is guaranteed.

Activities and organizations: drama/theater group, student-run newspaper, radio station, choral group, national fraternities, national sororities.

Athletics Member NCAA. All Division III. *Intercollegiate sports:* baseball M, basketball M/W, cheerleading W(c), cross-country running M/W, field hockey W, golf M, ice hockey M/W(c), lacrosse M/W, rugby M(c)/W(c), skiing (downhill) M/W, soccer M/W, softball W, swimming and diving M/W, tennis M/W, track and field M/W, volleyball W. *Intramural sports:* basketball M/W, football M, ice hockey M/W, racquetball M/W, soccer M/W, softball M/W, squash M/W, tennis M/W, ultimate Frisbee M/W, volleyball M/W, wrestling M(c).

Campus security: 24-hour emergency response devices and patrols, late-night transport/escort service, controlled dormitory access.

Student services: health clinic, personal/psychological counseling, women's center.

COSTS & FINANCIAL AID

Costs (2018–19) *Comprehensive fee:* $67,416 includes full-time tuition ($51,104) and room and board ($16,312). *Room and board:* Room and board charges vary according to board plan and housing facility. *Payment plan:* installment. *Waivers:* employees or children of employees.

Financial Aid Of all full-time matriculated undergraduates who enrolled in 2017, 1,077 applied for aid, 946 were judged to have need, 616 had their need fully met. In 2017, 142 non-need-based awards were made. *Average percent of need met:* 98. *Average financial aid package:* $42,671. *Average need-based loan:* $4915. *Average need-based gift aid:* $39,436. *Average non-need-based aid:* $18,631. *Average indebtedness upon graduation:* $35,013. *Financial aid deadline:* 2/1.

APPLYING

Standardized Tests *Required:* SAT or ACT (for admission). *Recommended:* TOEFL or IELTS for non-native English speakers.

Options: electronic application, early decision, early action, deferred entrance.

Application fee: $75.

Required: essay or personal statement, high school transcript, 2 letters of recommendation. *Recommended:* interview.

Application deadlines: 1/3 (freshmen), 3/15 (transfers), 11/1 (early action).

Early decision deadline: 11/1.

Notification: 4/1 (freshmen), 5/15 (transfers), 12/15 (early decision), 1/1 (early action).

CONTACT

Mrs. Adrienne Ramsey, Associate Director of Undergraduate Admission, Babson College, Lunder Undergraduate Admission Center, Babson Park, MA 02457-0310. *Phone:* 781-239-5522. *Toll-free phone:* 800-488-3696. *Fax:* 781-239-4135. *E-mail:* ugradadmission@babson.edu.

See next page for display ad and page 1236 for the College Close-Up.

Bard College at Simon's Rock

Great Barrington, Massachusetts
http://www.simons-rock.edu/

CONTACT
Chandra Joos deKoven, Director of Admissions, Bard College at Simon's Rock, 84 Alford Road, Great Barrington, MA 01230-9702. *Phone:* 800-235-7186. *Toll-free phone:* 800-235-7186. *Fax:* 413-541-0081. *E-mail:* admit@simons-rock.edu.

Bay Path University

Longmeadow, Massachusetts
http://www.baypath.edu/

- **Independent** comprehensive, founded 1897
- **Suburban** 48-acre campus with easy access to Hartford, CT and Boston, MA
- **Endowment** $41.5 million
- **Undergraduate: women only; graduate: coed** 1,947 undergraduate students, 70% full-time, 100% women
- **Moderately difficult** entrance level, 63% of applicants were admitted

UNDERGRAD STUDENTS
1,367 full-time, 580 part-time. Students come from 8 states and territories; 5 other countries; 42% are from out of state; 13% Black or African American, non-Hispanic/Latino; 19% Hispanic/Latino; 2% Asian, non-Hispanic/Latino; 0.1% Native Hawaiian or other Pacific Islander, non-Hispanic/Latino; 0.3% American Indian or Alaska Native, non-Hispanic/Latino; 3% Two or more races, non-Hispanic/Latino; 5% Race/ethnicity unknown; 0.6% international; 4% transferred in; 45% live on campus.

Freshmen:
Admission: 1,470 applied, 924 admitted, 144 enrolled. *Average high school GPA:* 3.4. *Test scores:* SAT evidence-based reading and writing scores over 500: 75%; SAT math scores over 500: 65%; ACT scores over 18: 93%; SAT evidence-based reading and writing scores over 600: 32%; SAT math scores over 600: 17%; ACT scores over 24: 36%; SAT

evidence-based reading and writing scores over 700: 1%; SAT math scores over 700: 3%; ACT scores over 30: 7%.
Retention: 70% of full-time freshmen returned.

FACULTY
Total: 478, 15% full-time, 36% with terminal degrees.
Student/faculty ratio: 13:1.

ACADEMICS
Calendar: semesters. *Degrees:* certificates, associate, bachelor's, master's, doctoral, post-master's, and postbachelor's certificates.

Special study options: academic remediation for entering students, accelerated degree program, adult/continuing education programs, advanced placement credit, cooperative education, distance learning, double majors, English as a second language, external degree program, honors programs, independent study, internships, off-campus study, part-time degree program, services for LD students, student-designed majors, study abroad, summer session for credit. *ROTC:* Army (c), Air Force (c).

Unusual degree programs: 3-2 business administration; occupational therapy.

Computers: 235 computers/terminals are available on campus for general student use. Students can access the following: campus intranet, computer help desk, free student e-mail accounts, online (class) grades, online (class) registration, online (class) schedules. Campuswide network is available. 100% of college-owned or -operated housing units are wired for high-speed Internet access. Wireless service is available via entire campus.
Library: Hatch Library. *Books:* 52,565 (physical), 408,000 (digital/electronic); *Serial titles:* 80 (physical), 55,000 (digital/electronic); *Databases:* 110. Weekly public service hours: 86; students can reserve study rooms.

STUDENT LIFE
Housing options: women-only. Campus housing is university owned. Freshman campus housing is guaranteed.

Activities and organizations: drama/theater group, choral group, Habitat for Humanity, Tactical Team, Wellness Wildcats, Women of Culture, Alliance Club.

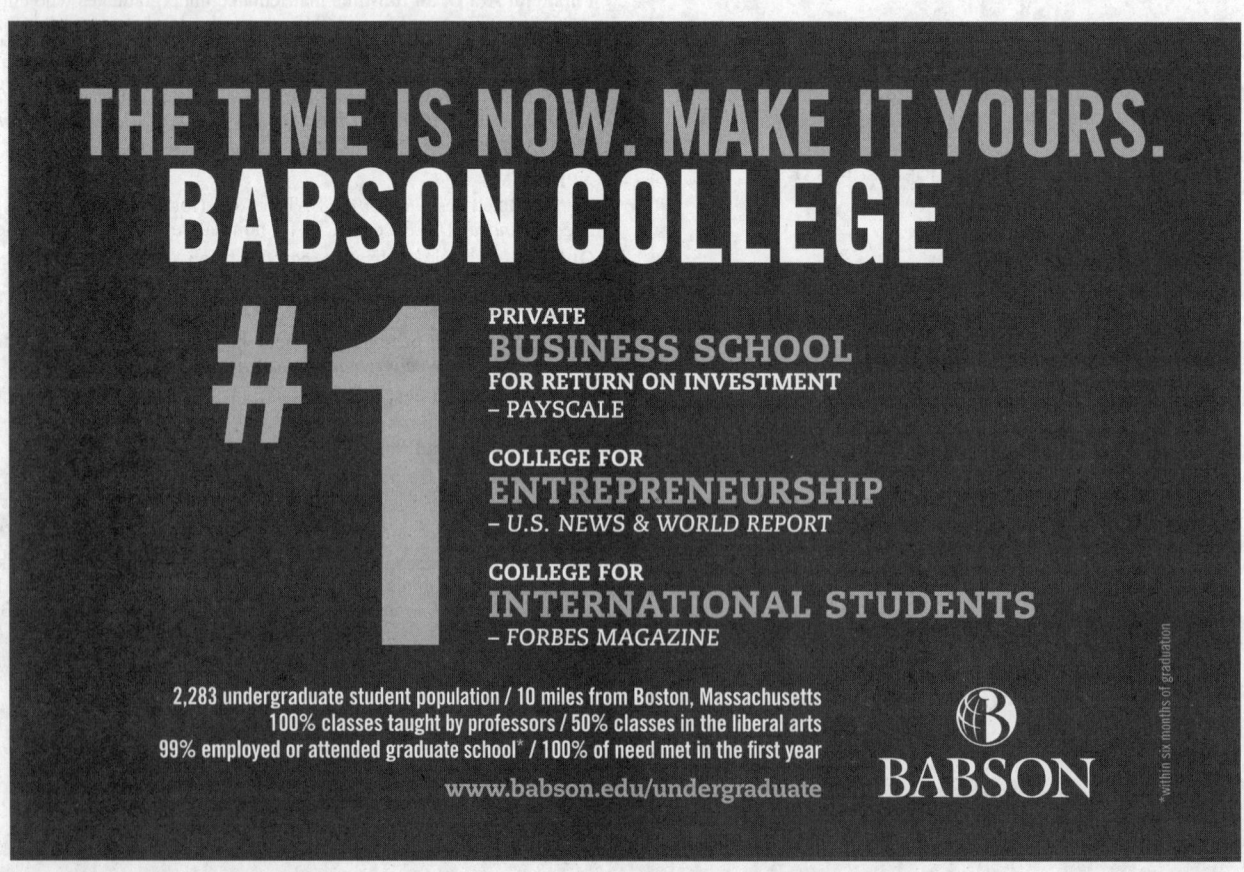

Athletics Member NCAA. All Division III. *Intercollegiate sports:* basketball W, cross-country running W, field hockey W, lacrosse W, soccer W, softball W, volleyball W. *Intramural sports:* swimming and diving W(c), track and field W(c).

Campus security: 24-hour emergency response devices and patrols, late-night transport/escort service, controlled dormitory access.

Student services: health clinic, personal/psychological counseling.

COSTS & FINANCIAL AID

Costs (2017–18) *Comprehensive fee:* $46,356 includes full-time tuition ($33,557) and room and board ($12,799). Part-time tuition: $510 per credit hour. Part-time tuition and fees vary according to course load. *Room and board:* Room and board charges vary according to board plan. *Payment plan:* installment. *Waivers:* employees or children of employees.

Financial Aid Of all full-time matriculated undergraduates who enrolled in 2016, 624 applied for aid, 589 were judged to have need, 46 had their need fully met. 113 Federal Work-Study jobs (averaging $2500). 72 state and other part-time jobs (averaging $2500). In 2016, 63 non-need-based awards were made. *Average percent of need met:* 72. *Average financial aid package:* $26,392. *Average need-based loan:* $4886. *Average need-based gift aid:* $21,203. *Average non-need-based aid:* $14,176. *Average indebtedness upon graduation:* $29,954.

APPLYING

Options: electronic application, early action, deferred entrance.

Required for some: essay or personal statement, high school transcript, interview. *Recommended:* minimum 2.0 GPA, interview.

Application deadlines: 8/1 (freshmen), rolling (transfers).

Notification: continuous (transfers).

CONTACT

Dawn Bryden, Dean of Traditional Undergraduate Enrollment and Admissions, Bay Path University, 588 Longmeadow Street, Longmeadow, MA 01106-2292. *Phone:* 413-565-1235. *Toll-free phone:* 800-782-7284 Ext. 1331. *E-mail:* dbryden@baypath.edu.

★ Bay State College
Boston, Massachusetts
http://www.baystate.edu/

CONTACT

Kimberly Odusami, Director of Admissions, Bay State College, 122 Commonwealth Avenue, Boston, MA 02116. *Phone:* 617-217-9186. *Toll-free phone:* 800-81-LEARN. *E-mail:* admissions@baystate.edu.

Becker College
Worcester, Massachusetts
http://www.becker.edu/

- **Independent** comprehensive, founded 1784
- **Urban** 100-acre campus with easy access to Boston, MA; Providence, RI; Hartford, CT
- **Coed** 1,882 undergraduate students, 81% full-time, 58% women, 42% men
- **Moderately difficult** entrance level, 69% of applicants were admitted

UNDERGRAD STUDENTS

1,530 full-time, 352 part-time. Students come from 37 states and territories; 29 other countries; 38% are from out of state; 7% Black or African American, non-Hispanic/Latino; 8% Hispanic/Latino; 2% Asian, non-Hispanic/Latino; 0.1% Native Hawaiian or other Pacific Islander, non-Hispanic/Latino; 0.7% American Indian or Alaska Native, non-Hispanic/Latino; 3% Two or more races, non-Hispanic/Latino; 6% Race/ethnicity unknown; 0.8% international; 7% transferred in; 55% live on campus.

Freshmen:

Admission: 4,972 applied, 3,451 admitted, 381 enrolled. *Average high school GPA:* 3.1. *Test scores:* SAT evidence-based reading and writing scores over 500: 73%; SAT math scores over 500: 67%; ACT scores over 18: 87%; SAT evidence-based reading and writing scores over 600: 23%; SAT math scores over 600: 17%; ACT scores over 24: 53%; SAT evidence-based reading and writing scores over 700: 2%; SAT math scores over 700: 2%; ACT scores over 30: 8%.

Retention: 73% of full-time freshmen returned.

FACULTY

Total: 267, 18% full-time, 18% with terminal degrees.

Student/faculty ratio: 14:1.

ACADEMICS

Calendar: semesters. *Degrees:* certificates, associate, bachelor's, and master's (also includes Leicester, MA small town campus).

Special study options: academic remediation for entering students, accelerated degree program, adult/continuing education programs, advanced placement credit, cooperative education, distance learning, double majors, independent study, internships, off-campus study, part-time degree program, services for LD students, study abroad, summer session for credit. *ROTC:* Army (c), Navy (c), Air Force (c).

Unusual degree programs: 3-2 business administration; nursing; mental health counseling.

Computers: 404 computers/terminals and 370 ports are available on campus for general student use. Students can access the following: campus intranet, computer help desk, free student e-mail accounts, online (class) grades, online (class) registration, online (class) schedules, Portal, 24X7 Library Chat, 24X7 online Tutoring. Campuswide network is available. 100% of college-owned or -operated housing units are wired for high-speed Internet access. Wireless service is available via entire campus.

Library: Ruska Library plus 1 other. *Books:* 14,869 (physical), 46,845 (digital/electronic); *Serial titles:* 15 (physical), 74 (digital/electronic); *Databases:* 68. Weekly public service hours: 168; study areas open 24 hours, 5–7 days a week; students can reserve study rooms.

STUDENT LIFE

Housing options: coed. Campus housing is university owned and leased by the school.

Activities and organizations: drama/theater group, student-run newspaper, choral group, Campus Activities Board (CAB), Animal Health Club/Pre-Veterinary Club, International Game Developers Association (IGDA), Dance Club, Marine Wildlife Conversation Club.

Athletics *Intercollegiate sports:* baseball M, basketball M/W, cheerleading M(c)/W(c), equestrian sports M/W, field hockey W, football M, golf M, ice hockey M/W, lacrosse M/W, soccer M/W, softball W, tennis M/W, ultimate Frisbee M(c)/W(c), volleyball W.

Campus security: 24-hour emergency response devices and patrols, late-night transport/escort service, controlled dormitory access.

Student services: health clinic, personal/psychological counseling.

COSTS & FINANCIAL AID

Costs (2018–19) *One-time required fee:* $200. *Comprehensive fee:* $53,000 includes full-time tuition ($35,600), mandatory fees ($3600), and room and board ($13,800). Full-time tuition and fees vary according to class time, course load, and program. Part-time tuition: $1483 per credit. Part-time tuition and fees vary according to class time, course load, and program. *Room and board:* Room and board charges vary according to housing facility. *Payment plan:* installment. *Waivers:* employees or children of employees.

Financial Aid Of all full-time matriculated undergraduates who enrolled in 2016, 1,427 applied for aid, 1,362 were judged to have need, 3 had their need fully met. In 2016, 179 non-need-based awards were made. *Average percent of need met:* 56. *Average financial aid package:* $21,224. *Average need-based loan:* $4124. *Average need-based gift aid:* $17,978. *Average non-need-based aid:* $12,586.

APPLYING

Standardized Tests *Required:* SAT or ACT (for admission).

Options: electronic application, early admission, early decision, early action.

Required: high school transcript, minimum 2.0 GPA. *Recommended:* essay or personal statement, letters of recommendation, interview.

Application deadlines: rolling (freshmen), rolling (transfers), 11/15 (early action).

Early decision deadline: 11/15.

Notification: continuous (freshmen), continuous (transfers), 12/15 (early decision), 12/15 (early action).

CONTACT

Mr. Michael Perron, Dean of Admissions, Becker College, 61 Sever Street, Worcester, MA 01609. *Phone:* 508-373-9400. *Toll-free phone:* 877-5BECKER. *Fax:* 508-890-1500. *E-mail:* admissions@becker.edu.

Benjamin Franklin Institute of Technology

Boston, Massachusetts
http://www.bfit.edu/

CONTACT

Ms. Brittainy Johnson, Associate Director of Admissions, Benjamin Franklin Institute of Technology, Boston, MA 02116. *Phone:* 617-423-4630 Ext. 122. *Toll-free phone:* 877-400-BFIT. *Fax:* 617-482-3706. *E-mail:* bjohnson@bfit.edu.

Bentley University

Waltham, Massachusetts
http://www.bentley.edu/

- **Independent** comprehensive, founded 1917
- **Suburban** 163-acre campus with easy access to Boston
- **Endowment** $271.8 million
- **Coed** 4,272 undergraduate students, 98% full-time, 41% women, 59% men
- **Very difficult** entrance level, 44% of applicants were admitted

UNDERGRAD STUDENTS

4,171 full-time, 101 part-time. Students come from 44 states and territories; 75 other countries; 58% are from out of state; 3% Black or African American, non-Hispanic/Latino; 7% Hispanic/Latino; 8% Asian, non-Hispanic/Latino; 0.1% Native Hawaiian or other Pacific Islander, non-Hispanic/Latino; 2% Two or more races, non-Hispanic/Latino; 4% Race/ethnicity unknown; 14% international; 2% transferred in; 78% live on campus.

Freshmen:

Admission: 8,867 applied, 3,915 admitted, 1,018 enrolled. *Test scores:* SAT evidence-based reading and writing scores over 500: 99%; SAT math scores over 500: 99%; ACT scores over 18: 100%; SAT evidence-based reading and writing scores over 600: 74%; SAT math scores over 600: 85%; ACT scores over 24: 97%; SAT evidence-based reading and writing scores over 700: 12%; SAT math scores over 700: 32%; ACT scores over 30: 37%.

Retention: 92% of full-time freshmen returned.

FACULTY

Total: 450, 65% full-time, 61% with terminal degrees.
Student/faculty ratio: 11:1.

ACADEMICS

Calendar: semesters. *Degrees:* bachelor's, master's, doctoral, post-master's, and postbachelor's certificates.

Special study options: advanced placement credit, double majors, English as a second language, honors programs, independent study, internships, off-campus study, part-time degree program, services for LD students, study abroad, summer session for credit. *ROTC:* Army (c), Air Force (c).

Computers: 4,620 computers/terminals and 10,752 ports are available on campus for general student use. Students can access the following: campus intranet, computer help desk, free student e-mail accounts, online (class) grades, online (class) registration, online (class) schedules, grade checking; online admission; blackboard; resume review; student employment; interlibary loan; free software. Campuswide network is available. 100% of college-owned or -operated housing units are wired for high-speed Internet access. Wireless service is available via entire campus.

Library: Bentley Library. *Books:* 187,590 (physical), 206,692 (digital/electronic); *Serial titles:* 2,550 (physical), 101,266 (digital/electronic); *Databases:* 106. Weekly public service hours: 110; students can reserve study rooms.

STUDENT LIFE

Housing options: coed, special housing for students with disabilities. Campus housing is university owned. Freshman campus housing is guaranteed.

Activities and organizations: drama/theater group, student-run newspaper, radio station, choral group, South Asian Student Association, Campus Activities Board, Delta Sigma Pi, Bentley Investment Group, National Association of Black Accountants, national fraternities, national sororities.

Athletics Member NCAA. All Division II except ice hockey (Division I). *Intercollegiate sports:* baseball M, basketball M(s)/W(s), cross-country running M/W, field hockey W, football M, golf M, ice hockey M(s), lacrosse M/W, soccer M/W, softball W, swimming and diving M/W, tennis M/W, track and field M/W, volleyball W. *Intramural sports:* basketball M/W, cheerleading W(c), equestrian sports W(c), football M, golf M(c)/W(c), ice hockey M(c), rugby M(c)/W(c), sailing M(c)/W(c), soccer M/W, softball M/W, triathlon M(c)/W(c), ultimate Frisbee M/W, volleyball M/W.

Campus security: 24-hour emergency response devices and patrols, late-night transport/escort service, controlled dormitory access, security cameras, Community Policing Team, self-defense classes, CPR and first-aid training, anonymous crime reporting, fire drills.

Student services: health clinic, personal/psychological counseling, women's center.

COSTS & FINANCIAL AID

Costs (2018–19) *Comprehensive fee:* $66,200 includes full-time tuition ($48,180), mandatory fees ($1700), and room and board ($16,320). Part-time tuition and fees vary according to course load. *College room only:* $9900. Room and board charges vary according to board plan and housing facility. *Payment plan:* installment. *Waivers:* employees or children of employees.

Financial Aid Of all full-time matriculated undergraduates who enrolled in 2016, 2,396 applied for aid, 1,764 were judged to have need, 689 had their need fully met. 876 Federal Work-Study jobs (averaging $1817). 816 state and other part-time jobs (averaging $1161). In 2016, 905 non-need-based awards were made. *Average percent of need met:* 93. *Average financial aid package:* $36,161. *Average need-based loan:* $5062. *Average need-based gift aid:* $31,187. *Average non-need-based aid:* $19,746. *Average indebtedness upon graduation:* $31,889. *Financial aid deadline:* 1/7.

APPLYING

Standardized Tests *Required:* SAT or ACT (for admission), TOEFL or IELTS is required for non-native English speakers (for admission).

Options: electronic application, early admission, early decision, deferred entrance.

Application fee: $75.

Required: essay or personal statement, high school transcript, 2 letters of recommendation. *Recommended:* interview.

Application deadlines: 1/7 (freshmen), 4/1 (transfers).

Early decision deadline: 11/15.

Notification: 3/31 (freshmen), continuous (transfers), 12/20 (early decision).

CONTACT

Office of Undergraduate Admissions, Bentley University, 175 Forest Street, Waltham, MA 02452. *Phone:* 781-891-2244. *Toll-free phone:* 800-523-2354. *Fax:* 781-891-3414. *E-mail:* ugadmission@bentley.edu.

See next page for display ad and page 1244 for the College Close-Up.

Berklee College of Music

Boston, Massachusetts
http://www.berklee.edu/

CONTACT

Mr. Damien Bracken, Director of Admissions, Berklee College of Music, 1140 Boylston Street, Boston, MA 02215-3693. *Phone:* 617-747-2222. *Toll-free phone:* 800-BERKLEE. *Fax:* 617-747-2047. *E-mail:* admissions@berklee.edu.

BUSINESS IS EVERYWHERE. PREPARE HERE.

A Bentley education is based in business and integrated with the best of the arts and sciences. Here, just minutes from Boston, you'll make a better, more complete you: confident, capable, and ready to take on the complex challenges that will come your way.

bentley.edu/ undergraduate

Bloomberg BusinessWeek Ranks Bentley among the top 20 undergraduate programs in the nation.

BENTLEY
UNIVERSITY

PDF12/17UG.255.17

Boston Architectural College

Boston, Massachusetts
http://www.the-bac.edu/

- **Independent** comprehensive, founded 1889
- **Urban** 1-acre campus with easy access to Boston
- **Endowment** $10.1 million
- **Coed** 472 undergraduate students, 75% full-time, 42% women, 58% men
- **Noncompetitive** entrance level, 15% of applicants were admitted

UNDERGRAD STUDENTS
354 full-time, 118 part-time. 6% Black or African American, non-Hispanic/Latino; 17% Hispanic/Latino; 9% Asian, non-Hispanic/Latino; 0.3% Native Hawaiian or other Pacific Islander, non-Hispanic/Latino; 0.3% American Indian or Alaska Native, non-Hispanic/Latino; 4% Two or more races, non-Hispanic/Latino; 8% Race/ethnicity unknown; 5% international.

Freshmen:
Admission: 178 applied, 26 admitted, 24 enrolled.
Retention: 75% of full-time freshmen returned.

FACULTY
Total: 264, 10% full-time, 100% with terminal degrees.
Student/faculty ratio: 4:1.

ACADEMICS
Calendar: semesters. *Degrees:* certificates, bachelor's, and master's.
Special study options: adult/continuing education programs, advanced placement credit, distance learning, independent study, internships, off-campus study, services for LD students, summer session for credit.
Computers: 84 computers/terminals are available on campus for general student use. Students can access the following: campus intranet, computer help desk, free student e-mail accounts, online (class) grades, online (class) registration, online (class) schedules. Campuswide network is available. Wireless service is available via entire campus.
Library: Shaw and Stone Library. *Books:* 42,224 (physical), 117,108 (digital/electronic); *Serial titles:* 613 (physical), 313,728 (digital/electronic); *Databases:* 73. Weekly public service hours: 71.

STUDENT LIFE
Housing options: college housing not available.
Activities and organizations: Student Government Association, Student American Society of Landscape Architects, BAC Interior Design Society (IIDA and ASID), National Organization of Minority Architecture Students (NOMAS), American Institute of Architectural Students.
Campus security: 24-hour emergency response devices and patrols, late-night transport/escort service, electronically operated building access, closed-circuit TV systems.
Student services: personal/psychological counseling, legal services.

COSTS & FINANCIAL AID
Costs (2017–18) *Tuition:* $20,424 full-time, $1702 per credit hour part-time. Full-time tuition and fees vary according to course load and program. Part-time tuition and fees vary according to course load and program. *Required fees:* $750 full-time, $225 per term part-time. *Payment plan:* installment. *Waivers:* employees or children of employees.
Financial Aid Of all full-time matriculated undergraduates who enrolled in 2016, 98 applied for aid, 93 were judged to have need, 1 had their need fully met. 18 Federal Work-Study jobs (averaging $2915). In 2016, 9 non-need-based awards were made. *Average percent of need met:* 33. *Average financial aid package:* $11,472. *Average need-based loan:* $5643. *Average need-based gift aid:* $6941. *Average non-need-based aid:* $2740.

APPLYING
Options: electronic application.
Required: essay or personal statement, high school transcript, resumé and creative exercise. *Recommended:* interview.

CONTACT
Ms. Meredith Spinnato, Director of Admission Office, Boston Architectural College, 320 Newbury Street, Boston, MA 02115-2795. *Phone:* 617-585-0123. *Fax:* 617-585-0121. *E-mail:* admissions@the-bac.edu.

Boston Baptist College

Boston, Massachusetts

http://www.boston.edu/

CONTACT

Mrs. Kim Melton, Director of Admissions, Boston Baptist College, 950 Metropolitan Avenue, Boston, MA 02136. *Phone:* 617-364-3510 Ext. 233. *Toll-free phone:* 888-235-2014. *Fax:* 617-399-8220. *E-mail:* kmelton@boston.edu.

Boston College

Chestnut Hill, Massachusetts

http://www.bc.edu/

- **Independent Roman Catholic (Jesuit)** university, founded 1863
- **Suburban** 338-acre campus with easy access to Boston
- **Endowment** $2.4 billion
- **Coed** 9,358 undergraduate students, 100% full-time, 53% women, 47% men
- **Very difficult** entrance level, 32% of applicants were admitted

UNDERGRAD STUDENTS

9,358 full-time. Students come from 54 states and territories; 65 other countries; 74% are from out of state; 4% Black or African American, non-Hispanic/Latino; 11% Hispanic/Latino; 10% Asian, non-Hispanic/Latino; 3% Two or more races, non-Hispanic/Latino; 4% Race/ethnicity unknown; 7% international; 0.8% transferred in; 84% live on campus.

Freshmen:

Admission: 28,454 applied, 9,223 admitted, 2,412 enrolled. *Test scores:* SAT evidence-based reading and writing scores over 500: 99%; SAT math scores over 500: 99%; ACT scores over 18: 100%; SAT evidence-based reading and writing scores over 600: 93%; SAT math scores over 600: 91%; ACT scores over 24: 98%; SAT evidence-based reading and writing scores over 700: 51%; SAT math scores over 700: 55%; ACT scores over 30: 84%.

Retention: 95% of full-time freshmen returned.

FACULTY

Total: 1,641, 50% full-time, 92% with terminal degrees.

Student/faculty ratio: 12:1.

ACADEMICS

Calendar: semesters. *Degrees:* certificates, bachelor's, master's, doctoral, and post-master's certificates (also offers continuing education program with significant enrollment not reflected in profile).

Special study options: accelerated degree program, advanced placement credit, double majors, honors programs, independent study, internships, off-campus study, part-time degree program, services for LD students, student-designed majors, study abroad, summer session for credit. *ROTC:* Army (c), Navy (c), Air Force (c).

Computers: 1,000 computers/terminals are available on campus for general student use. Students can access the following: campus intranet, computer help desk, free student e-mail accounts, online (class) grades, online (class) registration, online (class) schedules. Campuswide network is available. 100% of college-owned or -operated housing units are wired for high-speed Internet access. Wireless service is available via entire campus.

Library: O'Neill Library plus 8 others. *Books:* 3.3 million (physical), 844,953 (digital/electronic); *Serial titles:* 3,725 (physical), 43,552 (digital/electronic). Study areas open 24 hours, 5–7 days a week; students can reserve study rooms.

STUDENT LIFE

Housing options: coed, women-only. Campus housing is university owned. Freshman campus housing is guaranteed.

Activities and organizations: drama/theater group, student-run newspaper, radio and television station, choral group, marching band, UGBC and individual School Senates, Asian Caucus, Appalachia Volunteers, Dance Marathon, 4Boston.

Athletics Member NCAA. All Division I except football (Division I-A). *Intercollegiate sports:* baseball M(s), basketball M(s)/W(s), cheerleading M(c)/W(c), crew W(s), cross-country running M(s)/W(s), fencing M/W, field hockey W(s), golf M(s)/W(s), ice hockey M(s)/W(s), lacrosse W(s),

sailing M/W, skiing (downhill) M/W, soccer M(s)/W(s), softball W(s), swimming and diving M(s)/W(s), tennis M(s)/W(s), track and field M(s)/W(s), volleyball W(s). *Intramural sports:* badminton M/W, basketball M(c)/W(c), crew M(c), cross-country running M(c)/W(c), equestrian sports M(c)/W(c), field hockey W(c), golf M(c)/W(c), ice hockey M/W, lacrosse M(c)/W(c), racquetball M/W, rugby M(c)/W(c), soccer M(c)/W(c), softball M/W, squash M/W, tennis M/W, track and field M(c)/W(c), ultimate Frisbee M(c)/W(c), volleyball M(c)/W, water polo M(c)/W(c).

Campus security: 24-hour emergency response devices and patrols, late-night transport/escort service, controlled dormitory access, emergency text alerts, self defense training, student EMT program.

Student services: health clinic, personal/psychological counseling, women's center.

COSTS & FINANCIAL AID

Costs (2017–18) *One-time required fee:* $555. *Comprehensive fee:* $67,488 includes full-time tuition ($52,500), mandatory fees ($846), and room and board ($14,142). *College room only:* $8830. Room and board charges vary according to housing facility. *Payment plan:* installment. *Waivers:* employees or children of employees.

Financial Aid Of all full-time matriculated undergraduates who enrolled in 2016, 4,189 applied for aid, 3,705 were judged to have need, 3,705 had their need fully met. In 2016, 212 non-need-based awards were made. *Average percent of need met:* 100. *Average financial aid package:* $41,056. *Average need-based loan:* $4329. *Average need-based gift aid:* $37,716. *Average non-need-based aid:* $21,634. *Average indebtedness upon graduation:* $20,481.

APPLYING

Standardized Tests *Required:* SAT or ACT (for admission).

Options: electronic application, early admission, early action, deferred entrance.

Application fee: $80.

Required: essay or personal statement, high school transcript, 2 letters of recommendation.

Application deadlines: 1/1 (freshmen), 3/15 (transfers), 11/1 (early action).

Notification: 4/15 (freshmen), 6/1 (transfers), 12/25 (early action).

CONTACT

Office of Undergraduate Admissions, Boston College, 140 Commonwealth Avenue, Devlin 208, Chestnut Hill, MA 02467-3809. *Phone:* 617-552-3100. *Toll-free phone:* 800-360-2522. *Fax:* 617-552-0798.

See page 1248 for the College Close-Up.

Boston University

Boston, Massachusetts

http://www.bu.edu/

- **Independent** university, founded 1839
- **Urban** 134-acre campus with easy access to Boston
- **Endowment** $2.0 billion
- **Coed** 18,080 undergraduate students, 93% full-time, 60% women, 40% men
- **Very difficult** entrance level, 25% of applicants were admitted

UNDERGRAD STUDENTS

16,839 full-time, 1,241 part-time. Students come from 52 states and territories; 118 other countries; 80% are from out of state; 4% Black or African American, non-Hispanic/Latino; 11% Hispanic/Latino; 14% Asian, non-Hispanic/Latino; 0.1% Native Hawaiian or other Pacific Islander, non-Hispanic/Latino; 0.0% American Indian or Alaska Native, non-Hispanic/Latino; 4% Two or more races, non-Hispanic/Latino; 7% Race/ethnicity unknown; 21% international; 4% transferred in; 75% live on campus.

Freshmen:

Admission: 60,825 applied, 15,273 admitted, 3,498 enrolled. *Average high school GPA:* 3.7. *Test scores:* SAT evidence-based reading and writing scores over 500: 100%; SAT math scores over 500: 100%; ACT scores over 18: 100%; SAT evidence-based reading and writing scores over 600: 92%; SAT math scores over 600: 93%; ACT scores over 24:

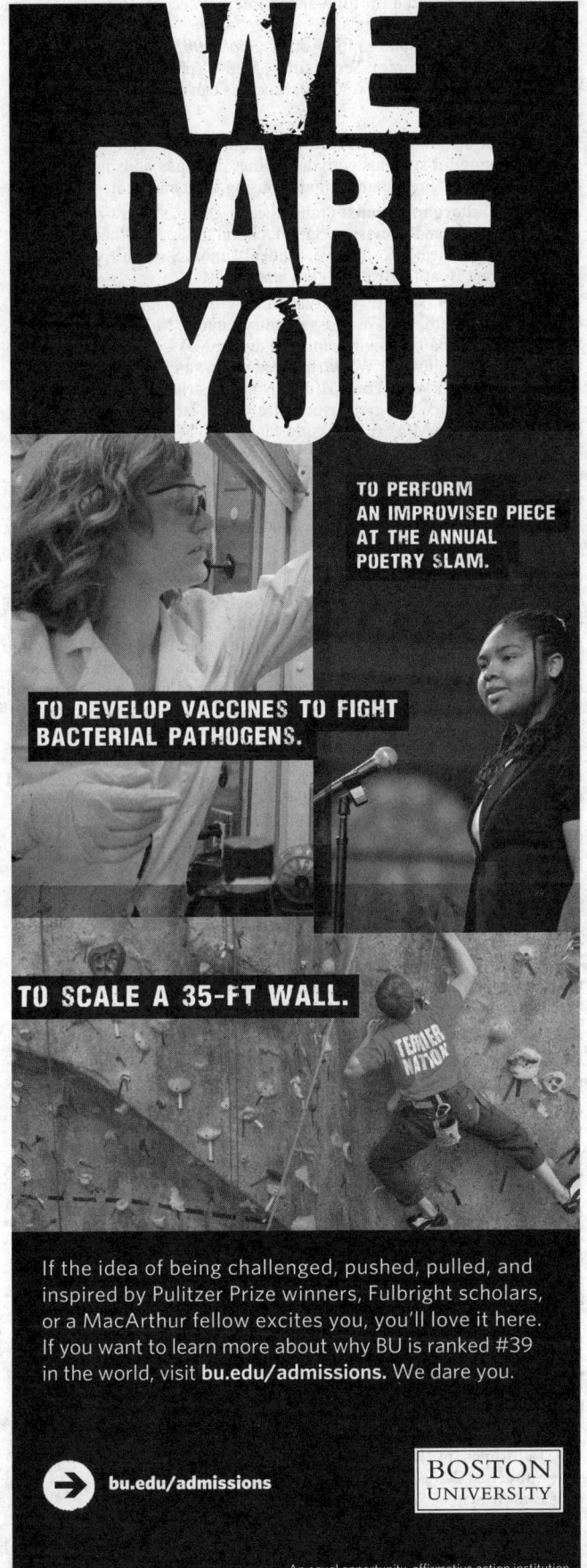

99%; SAT evidence-based reading and writing scores over 700: 38%; SAT math scores over 700: 55%; ACT scores over 30: 64%.
Retention: 93% of full-time freshmen returned.

FACULTY
Total: 2,673, 69% full-time, 61% with terminal degrees.
Student/faculty ratio: 10:1.

ACADEMICS
Calendar: semesters. *Degrees:* certificates, bachelor's, master's, doctoral, post-master's, and postbachelor's certificates.
Special study options: accelerated degree program, adult/continuing education programs, advanced placement credit, cooperative education, distance learning, double majors, English as a second language, freshman honors college, honors programs, independent study, internships, off-campus study, part-time degree program, services for LD students, student-designed majors, study abroad, summer session for credit. *ROTC:* Army (b), Navy (b), Air Force (b).
Computers: 250 computers/terminals and 1,650 ports are available on campus for general student use. Students can access the following: campus intranet, computer help desk, free student e-mail accounts, online (class) registration, online (class) schedules, research and educational networks. Campuswide network is available. 100% of college-owned or -operated housing units are wired for high-speed Internet access. Wireless service is available via classrooms, computer labs, dorm rooms, libraries, student centers.
Library: Mugar Memorial Library plus 20 others. *Books:* 1.2 million (physical), 1.7 million (digital/electronic); *Serial titles:* 227,677 (physical), 103,216 (digital/electronic); *Databases:* 591. Weekly public service hours: 123; students can reserve study rooms.

STUDENT LIFE
Housing options: on-campus residence required for freshman year; coed, women-only, cooperative, special housing for students with disabilities. Campus housing is university owned. Freshman campus housing is guaranteed.
Activities and organizations: drama/theater group, student-run newspaper, radio and television station, choral group, marching band, performing and Acappella groups, cultural organizations, service organizations, Student Government, residence hall associations, national fraternities, national sororities.
Athletics Member NCAA. All Division I. *Intercollegiate sports:* badminton M(c)/W(c), baseball M(c), basketball M(s)/W(s), cheerleading M(c)/W(c), crew M(s)/W(s), cross-country running M(s)/W(s), equestrian sports M(c)/W(c), fencing M(c)/W(c), field hockey W(s), golf M(c)/W(s), gymnastics M(c)/W(c), ice hockey M(s)/W(s), lacrosse M(s)/W(s), rowing M(s)/W(s), rugby M(c)/W(c), sailing M(c)/W(c), skiing (downhill) M(c)/W(c), soccer M(s)/W(s), softball W(s), squash M(c)/W(c), swimming and diving M(s)/W(s), table tennis M(c)/W(c), tennis M/W(s), track and field M(s)/W(s), triathlon M(c)/W(c), ultimate Frisbee M(c)/W(c), volleyball M(c)/W(c), water polo M(c)/W(c). *Intramural sports:* basketball M/W, football M/W, ice hockey M(c)/W(c), rowing M(c)/W(c), soccer M(c)/W(c), softball M/W, volleyball M/W.
Campus security: 24-hour emergency response devices and patrols, late-night transport/escort service, controlled dormitory access, security personnel at residence hall entrances, self-defense education, well-lit sidewalks, Emergency Alert System, Blue Light System.
Student services: health clinic, personal/psychological counseling, women's center.

COSTS & FINANCIAL AID
Costs (2017–18) *Comprehensive fee:* $67,352 includes full-time tuition ($50,980), mandatory fees ($1102), and room and board ($15,270). Full-time tuition and fees vary according to class time and course load. Part-time tuition: $1593 per credit hour. Part-time tuition and fees vary according to class time, course level, and course load. *Required fees:* $60 per term part-time. *College room only:* $10,080. Room and board charges vary according to board plan, housing facility, and location. *Payment plans:* tuition prepayment, installment. *Waivers:* employees or children of employees.
Financial Aid Of all full-time matriculated undergraduates who enrolled in 2017, 7,333 applied for aid, 6,439 were judged to have need, 1,453 had their need fully met. 3,001 Federal Work-Study jobs (averaging $2283). In 2017, 1085 non-need-based awards were made. *Average percent of need*

met: 84. *Average financial aid package:* $42,180. *Average need-based loan:* $4185. *Average need-based gift aid:* $36,055. *Average non-need-based aid:* $20,755. *Average indebtedness upon graduation:* $40,089. *Financial aid deadline:* 2/1.

APPLYING
Standardized Tests *Required for some:* SAT or ACT (for admission), SAT Subject Tests (for admission).

Options: electronic application, early admission, early decision, deferred entrance.

Application fee: $80.

Required: essay or personal statement, high school transcript, 2 letters of recommendation. *Required for some:* interview, audition, portfolio.

Application deadlines: 1/2 (freshmen), 3/1 (transfers).

Early decision deadline: 11/1 (for plan 1), 1/2 (for plan 2).

Notification: 4/1 (freshmen), continuous until 6/1 (transfers), 12/15 (early decision plan 1), 2/15 (early decision plan 2).

CONTACT
Ms. Kelly A. Walter, Associate Vice President for Enrollment and Dean of Admissions, Boston University, 233 Bay State Road, Boston, MA 02215. *Phone:* 617-353-2300. *Fax:* 617-353-9695. *E-mail:* admissions@bu.edu.

See previous page for display ad and page 1250 for the College Close-Up.

Brandeis University
Waltham, Massachusetts
http://www.brandeis.edu/
- **Independent** university, founded 1948
- **Suburban** 235-acre campus with easy access to Boston
- **Endowment** $976.9 million
- **Coed** 3,635 undergraduate students, 100% full-time, 59% women, 41% men
- **Most difficult** entrance level, 34% of applicants were admitted

UNDERGRAD STUDENTS
3,620 full-time, 15 part-time. Students come from 49 states and territories; 54 other countries; 71% are from out of state; 5% Black or African American, non-Hispanic/Latino; 7% Hispanic/Latino; 13% Asian, non-Hispanic/Latino; 0.2% Native Hawaiian or other Pacific Islander, non-Hispanic/Latino; 0.1% American Indian or Alaska Native, non-Hispanic/Latino; 3% Two or more races, non-Hispanic/Latino; 3% Race/ethnicity unknown; 21% international; 1% transferred in; 75% live on campus.

Freshmen:
Admission: 11,721 applied, 4,011 admitted, 858 enrolled. *Average high school GPA:* 3.9. *Test scores:* SAT evidence-based reading and writing scores over 500: 98%; SAT math scores over 500: 99%; ACT scores over 18: 100%; SAT evidence-based reading and writing scores over 600: 88%; SAT math scores over 600: 88%; ACT scores over 24: 98%; SAT evidence-based reading and writing scores over 700: 36%; SAT math scores over 700: 50%; ACT scores over 30: 71%.
Retention: 94% of full-time freshmen returned.

FACULTY
Total: 554, 65% full-time, 80% with terminal degrees.
Student/faculty ratio: 10:1.

ACADEMICS
Calendar: semesters. *Degrees:* bachelor's, master's, doctoral, and post-master's certificates.

Special study options: advanced placement credit, double majors, independent study, internships, off-campus study, services for LD students, student-designed majors, study abroad, summer session for credit. *ROTC:* Army (c), Air Force (c).

Unusual degree programs: 3-2 engineering with Columbia University.

Computers: 130 computers/terminals are available on campus for general student use. Students can access the following: computer help desk, free student e-mail accounts, online (class) grades, online (class) registration, online (class) schedules, educational software. Campuswide network is available. 100% of college-owned or -operated

housing units are wired for high-speed Internet access. Wireless service is available via entire campus.
Library: Goldfarb Library plus 1 other. *Books:* 993,533 (physical), 1.1 million (digital/electronic); *Serial titles:* 10,606 (physical), 38,001 (digital/electronic); *Databases:* 310. Students can reserve study rooms.

STUDENT LIFE
Housing options: on-campus residence required for freshman year; coed, special housing for students with disabilities. Campus housing is university owned. Freshman campus housing is guaranteed.

Activities and organizations: drama/theater group, student-run newspaper, radio and television station, choral group, Waltham Group, Undergraduate Theater Collective, Student Union, Student Events (Programming Board), BEMCo - student EMTs.

Athletics Member NCAA. All Division III. *Intercollegiate sports:* baseball M, basketball M/W, cross-country running M/W, fencing M/W, soccer M/W, softball W, swimming and diving M/W, tennis M/W, track and field M/W, volleyball W. *Intramural sports:* archery M(c)/W(c), cheerleading M(c)/W(c), crew M(c)/W(c), equestrian sports M(c)/W(c), field hockey M(c)/W(c), gymnastics M(c)/W(c), lacrosse W(c), rugby M(c)/W(c), sailing M(c)/W(c), skiing (downhill) M(c)/W(c), squash M/W, table tennis M/W, ultimate Frisbee M(c)/W(c), volleyball M.

Campus security: 24-hour emergency response devices and patrols, late-night transport/escort service, controlled dormitory access.

Student services: health clinic, personal/psychological counseling, women's center.

COSTS & FINANCIAL AID
Costs (2017–18) *Comprehensive fee:* $68,443 includes full-time tuition ($51,460), mandatory fees ($2077), and room and board ($14,906). Part-time tuition: $1608 per credit. Part-time tuition and fees vary according to course load. *Required fees:* $2077 per year part-time. *College room only:* $8364. Room and board charges vary according to board plan and housing facility. *Payment plan:* installment. *Waivers:* employees or children of employees.

Financial Aid Of all full-time matriculated undergraduates who enrolled in 2016, 1,991 applied for aid, 1,716 were judged to have need, 1,225 had their need fully met. 361 Federal Work-Study jobs (averaging $2599). 30 state and other part-time jobs (averaging $2636). In 2016, 381 non-need-based awards were made. *Average percent of need met:* 96. *Average financial aid package:* $43,353. *Average need-based loan:* $4314. *Average need-based gift aid:* $39,606. *Average non-need-based aid:* $14,333. *Average indebtedness upon graduation:* $33,522.

APPLYING
Standardized Tests *Required:* SAT or ACT (for admission).

Options: electronic application, early admission, early decision, deferred entrance.

Application fee: $80.

Required: essay or personal statement, high school transcript, 1 letter of recommendation. *Recommended:* interview.

Application deadlines: 1/1 (freshmen), 4/1 (transfers).

Early decision deadline: 11/1 (for plan 1), 1/1 (for plan 2).

Notification: 4/1 (freshmen), 5/25 (transfers), 12/15 (early decision plan 1), 2/1 (early decision plan 2).

CONTACT
Jennifer Walker, Dean of Admissions, Brandeis University, 415 South Street, PO Box 549110, Waltham, MA 02454-9110. *Phone:* 781-736-3500. *Toll-free phone:* 800-622-0622. *Fax:* 781-736-3536. *E-mail:* admissions@brandeis.edu.

Bridgewater State University
Bridgewater, Massachusetts
http://www.bridgew.edu/
- **State-supported** comprehensive, founded 1840, part of Massachusetts Department of Higher Education
- **Suburban** 278-acre campus with easy access to Boston
- **Endowment** $37.1 million
- **Coed** 9,558 undergraduate students, 82% full-time, 59% women, 41% men
- **Moderately difficult** entrance level, 80% of applicants were admitted

UNDERGRAD STUDENTS

7,858 full-time, 1,700 part-time. Students come from 29 states and territories; 32 other countries; 4% are from out of state; 11% Black or African American, non-Hispanic/Latino; 7% Hispanic/Latino; 2% Asian, non-Hispanic/Latino; 0.1% Native Hawaiian or other Pacific Islander, non-Hispanic/Latino; 0.2% American Indian or Alaska Native, non-Hispanic/Latino; 4% Two or more races, non-Hispanic/Latino; 1% Race/ethnicity unknown; 0.4% international; 12% transferred in; 42% live on campus.

Freshmen:
Admission: 6,343 applied, 5,097 admitted, 1,506 enrolled. *Average high school GPA:* 3.1. *Test scores:* SAT evidence-based reading and writing scores over 500: 73%; SAT math scores over 500: 71%; ACT scores over 18: 85%; SAT evidence-based reading and writing scores over 600: 21%; SAT math scores over 600: 14%; ACT scores over 24: 30%; SAT evidence-based reading and writing scores over 700: 1%; SAT math scores over 700: 1%; ACT scores over 30: 3%.
Retention: 76% of full-time freshmen returned.

FACULTY

Total: 771, 46% full-time, 64% with terminal degrees.
Student/faculty ratio: 19:1.

ACADEMICS

Calendar: semesters. *Degrees:* bachelor's, master's, post-master's, and postbachelor's certificates.

Special study options: academic remediation for entering students, accelerated degree program, adult/continuing education programs, advanced placement credit, distance learning, double majors, English as a second language, honors programs, independent study, internships, off-campus study, part-time degree program, services for LD students, study abroad, summer session for credit. *ROTC:* Army (c), Air Force (c).

Computers: 780 computers/terminals and 20 ports are available on campus for general student use. Students can access the following: campus intranet, computer help desk, free student e-mail accounts, online (class) grades, online (class) registration, online (class) schedules, student account information, application software. Campuswide network is available. 100% of college-owned or -operated housing units are wired for high-speed Internet access. Wireless service is available via entire campus.
Library: Clement C. Maxwell Library. *Books:* 293,576 (physical), 61,041 (digital/electronic); *Serial titles:* 46,165 (digital/electronic); *Databases:* 193. Weekly public service hours: 93.

STUDENT LIFE

Housing options: coed, special housing for students with disabilities. Campus housing is university owned. Freshman applicants given priority for college housing.

Activities and organizations: drama/theater group, student-run newspaper, radio station, choral group, Dance Company, African American Society (Afro-Am), Program Committee, Panhellenic Association, Inter-Fraternity Council, national fraternities, national sororities.

Athletics Member NCAA. All Division III. *Intercollegiate sports:* baseball M, basketball M/W, cross-country running M/W, field hockey W, football M, lacrosse W, soccer M/W, softball W, swimming and diving M/W, tennis M/W, track and field M/W, volleyball W, wrestling M. *Intramural sports:* badminton M/W, basketball M/W, cheerleading W(c), equestrian sports W(c), football M/W, ice hockey M(c), lacrosse M(c), rugby W(c), soccer M/W, softball M/W, ultimate Frisbee M(c)/W(c), volleyball M/W.

Campus security: 24-hour emergency response devices and patrols, late-night transport/escort service, controlled dormitory access.

Student services: health clinic, personal/psychological counseling.

COSTS & FINANCIAL AID

Costs (2018–19) *Tuition:* state resident $910 full-time, $38 per credit hour part-time; nonresident $7050 full-time, $294 per credit hour part-time. Full-time tuition and fees vary according to course load. *Required fees:* $9402 full-time, $365 per credit hour part-time. *Room and board:* $13,000; room only: $8600. Room and board charges vary according to board plan and housing facility. *Payment plan:* installment. *Waivers:* senior citizens and employees or children of employees.

Financial Aid Of all full-time matriculated undergraduates who enrolled in 2016, 7,044 applied for aid, 5,468 were judged to have need, 765 had their need fully met. 395 Federal Work-Study jobs (averaging $1580). In 2016, 17 non-need-based awards were made. *Average financial aid package:* $8148. *Average need-based loan:* $3709. *Average need-based gift aid:* $5669. *Average non-need-based aid:* $8266. *Average indebtedness upon graduation:* $34,146.

APPLYING

Standardized Tests *Recommended:* SAT (for admission).
Options: electronic application, early action, deferred entrance.
Application fee: $50.
Required: high school transcript, minimum 2.0 GPA. *Recommended:* essay or personal statement, letters of recommendation.
Application deadlines: 2/15 (freshmen), 2/15 (transfers), 11/15 (early action).
Notification: continuous until 4/15 (freshmen), continuous until 4/15 (transfers), 12/15 (early action).

CONTACT

Mr. Gregg Meyer, Dean of University Admissions, Bridgewater State University, Gates House, 40 Cedar Street, Bridgewater, MA 02325. *Phone:* 508-531-1237. *Fax:* 508-531-1746. *E-mail:* admission@bridgew.edu.

Cambridge College
Boston, Massachusetts
http://www.cambridgecollege.edu/

CONTACT

Denise Haile, Director of Admissions, Cambridge College, 1000 Massachusetts Avenue, Cambridge, MA 02138-5304. *Phone:* 800-877-4725. *Toll-free phone:* 800-877-4723. *Fax:* 617-349-3561. *E-mail:* denise.haile@cambridgecollege.edu.

Clark University
Worcester, Massachusetts
http://www.clarku.edu/

- **Independent** university, founded 1887
- **Urban** 50-acre campus with easy access to Boston
- **Endowment** $413.7 million
- **Coed** 2,240 undergraduate students, 98% full-time, 61% women, 39% men
- **Moderately difficult** entrance level, 55% of applicants were admitted

UNDERGRAD STUDENTS

2,199 full-time, 41 part-time. Students come from 48 states and territories; 85 other countries; 58% are from out of state; 4% Black or African American, non-Hispanic/Latino; 8% Hispanic/Latino; 8% Asian, non-Hispanic/Latino; 0.2% American Indian or Alaska Native, non-Hispanic/Latino; 2% Two or more races, non-Hispanic/Latino; 7% Race/ethnicity unknown; 14% international; 2% transferred in; 67% live on campus.

Freshmen:
Admission: 7,914 applied, 4,331 admitted, 615 enrolled. *Average high school GPA:* 3.6. *Test scores:* ACT scores over 18: 100%; ACT scores over 24: 92%; ACT scores over 30: 44%.
Retention: 86% of full-time freshmen returned.

FACULTY

Total: 303, 68% full-time, 93% with terminal degrees.
Student/faculty ratio: 9:1.

ACADEMICS

Calendar: semesters. *Degrees:* bachelor's, master's, doctoral, and post-master's certificates.

Special study options: accelerated degree program, adult/continuing education programs, advanced placement credit, distance learning, double majors, English as a second language, honors programs, independent study, internships, off-campus study, part-time degree program, services for LD students, student-designed majors, study abroad, summer session for credit. *ROTC:* Army (c), Air Force (c).

Unusual degree programs: 3-2 business administration; engineering with Columbia University, Washington University in St. Louis, Worcester

Polytechnic Institute; environmental studies, international development, community planning, biology, biochemistry, chemistry, physics, economics, history, communications, public administration, geographic information systems.

Computers: Students can access the following: campus intranet, computer help desk, free student e-mail accounts, online (class) grades, online (class) registration, online (class) schedules, online course support. Campuswide network is available. 100% of college-owned or -operated housing units are wired for high-speed Internet access. Wireless service is available via entire campus.

Library: Robert Hutchings Goddard Library plus 8 others. Students can reserve study rooms.

STUDENT LIFE

Housing options: on-campus residence required through sophomore year; coed, women-only, special housing for students with disabilities. Campus housing is university owned. Freshman campus housing is guaranteed.

Activities and organizations: drama/theater group, student-run newspaper, radio and television station, choral group, marching band, International Students Association, Science Fiction People of Clark, Outing Club, Hillel, Clark Musical Theater.

Athletics Member NCAA, NAIA. All NCAA Division III. *Intercollegiate sports:* baseball M, basketball M/W, crew M/W, cross-country running M/W, field hockey W, lacrosse M, soccer M/W, softball W, swimming and diving M/W, tennis M/W, volleyball W. *Intramural sports:* basketball M/W, equestrian sports W(c), ice hockey M(c), lacrosse W(c), racquetball M/W, soccer M(c)/W, softball M/W, tennis M(c)/W(c), ultimate Frisbee M(c)/W(c), volleyball M(c)/W(c), water polo M/W.

Campus security: 24-hour emergency response devices and patrols, student patrols, late-night transport/escort service, controlled dormitory access.

Student services: health clinic, personal/psychological counseling, women's center.

COSTS & FINANCIAL AID

Costs (2018–19) *Comprehensive fee:* $54,900 includes full-time tuition ($45,380), mandatory fees ($350), and room and board ($9170). Part-time tuition: $1376 per credit. *Room and board:* Room and board charges vary according to board plan and housing facility. *Payment plans:* tuition prepayment, installment. *Waivers:* employees or children of employees.

Financial Aid Of all full-time matriculated undergraduates who enrolled in 2017, 1,549 applied for aid, 1,199 were judged to have need, 223 had their need fully met. In 2017, 743 non-need-based awards were made. *Average percent of need met:* 90. *Average financial aid package:* $33,996. *Average need-based loan:* $4754. *Average need-based gift aid:* $17,663. *Average non-need-based aid:* $19,010. *Average indebtedness upon graduation:* $34,305. *Financial aid deadline:* 1/15.

APPLYING

Options: electronic application, early admission, early decision, early action, deferred entrance.

Application fee: $60.

Required: essay or personal statement, high school transcript, 2 letters of recommendation. *Recommended:* interview.

Application deadlines: 1/15 (freshmen), 5/1 (transfers), 11/1 (early action).

Early decision deadline: 11/1.

Notification: 4/1 (freshmen), 6/1 (transfers), 12/15 (early decision), 12/15 (early action).

CONTACT

Mr. Donald Honeman, Dean of Admissions, Clark University, Admissions House, 950 Main Street, Worcester, MA 01610. *Phone:* 508-793-7431. *Toll-free phone:* 800-GO-CLARK. *Fax:* 508-793-8821. *E-mail:* admissions@clarku.edu.

College of the Holy Cross
Worcester, Massachusetts
http://www.holycross.edu/

- **Independent Roman Catholic (Jesuit)** 4-year, founded 1843
- **Suburban** 174-acre campus with easy access to Boston
- **Endowment** $748.9 million
- **Coed** 3,051 undergraduate students, 99% full-time, 52% women, 48% men
- **Very difficult** entrance level, 40% of applicants were admitted

UNDERGRAD STUDENTS

3,020 full-time, 31 part-time. Students come from 52 states and territories; 24 other countries; 59% are from out of state; 4% Black or African American, non-Hispanic/Latino; 10% Hispanic/Latino; 5% Asian, non-Hispanic/Latino; 0.1% Native Hawaiian or other Pacific Islander, non-Hispanic/Latino; 0.1% American Indian or Alaska Native, non-Hispanic/Latino; 3% Two or more races, non-Hispanic/Latino; 3% Race/ethnicity unknown; 3% international; 0.5% transferred in; 91% live on campus.

Freshmen:
Admission: 6,622 applied, 2,622 admitted, 818 enrolled. *Test scores:* SAT evidence-based reading and writing scores over 500: 100%; SAT math scores over 500: 100%; ACT scores over 18: 100%; SAT evidence-based reading and writing scores over 600: 91%; SAT math scores over 600: 88%; ACT scores over 24: 99%; SAT evidence-based reading and writing scores over 700: 34%; SAT math scores over 700: 30%; ACT scores over 30: 56%.

Retention: 95% of full-time freshmen returned.

FACULTY
Total: 318, 87% full-time, 92% with terminal degrees.
Student/faculty ratio: 10:1.

ACADEMICS
Calendar: semesters. *Degree:* bachelor's.

Special study options: accelerated degree program, advanced placement credit, double majors, honors programs, independent study, internships, off-campus study, services for LD students, student-designed majors, study abroad, summer session for credit. *ROTC:* Army (c), Navy (b), Air Force (c).

Unusual degree programs: 3-2 engineering with Columbia University.

Computers: 485 computers/terminals are available on campus for general student use. Students can access the following: computer help desk, free student e-mail accounts, online (class) grades, online (class) registration. Campuswide network is available. 100% of college-owned or -operated housing units are wired for high-speed Internet access. Wireless service is available via entire campus.

Library: Dinand Library plus 4 others. *Books:* 649,119 (physical), 317,604 (digital/electronic); *Serial titles:* 510 (physical), 15,127 (digital/electronic); *Databases:* 309. Study areas open 24 hours, 5–7 days a week; students can reserve study rooms.

STUDENT LIFE

Housing options: on-campus residence required through sophomore year; coed, special housing for students with disabilities. Campus housing is university owned. Freshman campus housing is guaranteed.

Activities and organizations: drama/theater group, student-run newspaper, radio station, choral group, marching band, SPUD (community service organization), choral and music groups, Campus Activities Board, Student Government Association, Purple Key Society.

Athletics Member NCAA. All Division I except football (Division I-AA). *Intercollegiate sports:* baseball M, basketball M(s)/W(s), crew M/W(s), cross-country running M/W(s), field hockey W(s), golf M/W, ice hockey M(s)/W, lacrosse M(s)/W(s), soccer M(s)/W(s), softball W(s), swimming and diving M/W(s), tennis M/W, track and field M/W(s), volleyball W(s). *Intramural sports:* baseball M(c), basketball M(c)/W(c), equestrian sports M(c)/W(c), field hockey W(c), football M/W, golf M(c)/W(c), ice hockey M(c), lacrosse M(c)/W(c), rugby M(c)/W(c), sailing M(c)/W(c), skiing (downhill) M(c)/W(c), soccer M(c)/W(c), softball M/W, swimming and diving M(c)/W(c), tennis M(c)/W(c), ultimate Frisbee M(c)/W(c), water polo M/W.

Campus security: 24-hour emergency response devices and patrols, late-night transport/escort service, controlled dormitory access.

Student services: health clinic, personal/psychological counseling.

COSTS & FINANCIAL AID
Costs (2017–18) *Comprehensive fee:* $64,320 includes full-time tuition ($49,980), mandatory fees ($650), and room and board ($13,690). *College room only:* $7390. Room and board charges vary according to board plan and housing facility. *Payment plan:* installment. *Waivers:* employees or children of employees.

Financial Aid Of all full-time matriculated undergraduates who enrolled in 2017, 1,945 applied for aid, 1,593 were judged to have need, 1,593 had their need fully met. In 2017, 42 non-need-based awards were made. *Average percent of need met:* 100. *Average financial aid package:* $40,304. *Average need-based loan:* $5413. *Average need-based gift aid:* $36,836. *Average non-need-based aid:* $33,023. *Average indebtedness upon graduation:* $26,258. *Financial aid deadline:* 1/15.

APPLYING
Options: electronic application, early admission, early decision, deferred entrance.
Application fee: $60.
Required: high school transcript, 2 letters of recommendation. *Recommended:* interview.
Application deadlines: 1/15 (freshmen), 4/1 (transfers).
Early decision deadline: 12/15.
Notification: 4/1 (freshmen), continuous (transfers), 1/15 (early decision).

CONTACT
College of the Holy Cross, 1 College Street, Worcester, MA 01610-2395. *Phone:* 508-793-2443. *Toll-free phone:* 800-442-2421.

Curry College
Milton, Massachusetts
http://www.curry.edu/
- **Independent** comprehensive, founded 1879
- **Suburban** 131-acre campus with easy access to Boston
- **Endowment** $104.5 million
- **Coed** 2,565 undergraduate students, 80% full-time, 60% women, 40% men
- **Moderately difficult** entrance level, 90% of applicants were admitted

UNDERGRAD STUDENTS
2,059 full-time, 506 part-time. Students come from 29 states and territories; 21 other countries; 26% are from out of state; 11% Black or African American, non-Hispanic/Latino; 7% Hispanic/Latino; 3% Asian, non-Hispanic/Latino; 0.2% Native Hawaiian or other Pacific Islander, non-Hispanic/Latino; 0.3% American Indian or Alaska Native, non-Hispanic/Latino; 2% Two or more races, non-Hispanic/Latino; 8% Race/ethnicity unknown; 2% international; 2% transferred in; 84% live on campus.

Freshmen:
Admission: 6,031 applied, 5,431 admitted, 603 enrolled. *Average high school GPA:* 2.9. *Test scores:* SAT evidence-based reading and writing scores over 500: 65%; SAT math scores over 500: 58%; ACT scores over 18: 81%; SAT evidence-based reading and writing scores over 600: 10%; SAT math scores over 600: 7%; ACT scores over 24: 20%.
Retention: 68% of full-time freshmen returned.

FACULTY
Total: 324, 40% full-time, 48% with terminal degrees.
Student/faculty ratio: 13:1.

ACADEMICS
Calendar: semesters. *Degrees:* bachelor's, master's, and post-master's certificates.
Special study options: academic remediation for entering students, accelerated degree program, adult/continuing education programs, advanced placement credit, double majors, English as a second language, honors programs, independent study, internships, off-campus study, part-time degree program, services for LD students, student-designed majors, study abroad, summer session for credit. *ROTC:* Army (c).

Unusual degree programs: 3-2 business administration; education.
Computers: 245 computers/terminals and 2,500 ports are available on campus for general student use. Students can access the following: campus intranet, computer help desk, free student e-mail accounts, online (class) grades, online (class) registration, online (class) schedules. Campuswide network is available. 100% of college-owned or -operated housing units are wired for high-speed Internet access. Wireless service is available via entire campus.
Library: Levin Library plus 1 other. *Books:* 71,564 (physical), 141,518 (digital/electronic); *Serial titles:* 66 (physical), 109,694 (digital/electronic); *Databases:* 101. Weekly public service hours: 98; students can reserve study rooms.

STUDENT LIFE
Housing options: coed, men-only, women-only. Campus housing is university owned.
Activities and organizations: drama/theater group, student-run newspaper, radio and television station, choral group, Student radio station, Student government, Student Program Board, Curry Cares: Community Service, Theatre.
Athletics Member NCAA. All Division III. *Intercollegiate sports:* baseball M, basketball M/W, cross-country running W, equestrian sports M(c)/W(c), football M, ice hockey M/W(c), lacrosse M/W, rugby M(c), soccer M/W, softball W, tennis M/W, volleyball W. *Intramural sports:* badminton M/W, basketball M/W, bowling M/W, cheerleading M(c)/W(c), field hockey W, skiing (downhill) M/W, soccer M/W, softball M/W, tennis M/W, ultimate Frisbee M/W, volleyball M/W.
Campus security: 24-hour emergency response devices and patrols, late-night transport/escort service, controlled dormitory access, campus safety office.
Student services: health clinic, personal/psychological counseling.

COSTS & FINANCIAL AID
Costs (2018–19) *One-time required fee:* $350. *Comprehensive fee:* $55,605 includes full-time tuition ($37,850), mandatory fees ($1870), and room and board ($15,885). Full-time tuition and fees vary according to class time, course load, location, and program. Part-time tuition: $1262 per credit. Part-time tuition and fees vary according to class time, course load, location, and program. *Required fees:* $420 per year part-time. *College room only:* $8535. Room and board charges vary according to board plan and housing facility. *Payment plan:* installment. *Waivers:* children of alumni and employees or children of employees.

Financial Aid Of all full-time matriculated undergraduates who enrolled in 2017, 1,632 applied for aid, 1,586 were judged to have need, 185 had their need fully met. 923 Federal Work-Study jobs (averaging $2338). In 2017, 379 non-need-based awards were made. *Average percent of need met:* 69. *Average financial aid package:* $28,668. *Average need-based loan:* $4394. *Average need-based gift aid:* $24,285. *Average non-need-based aid:* $16,232. *Average indebtedness upon graduation:* $45,947.

APPLYING
Standardized Tests *Required for some:* SAT or ACT (for admission), TOEFL for international applicants whose native language is not English.
Options: electronic application, early admission, early action, deferred entrance.
Application fee: $50.
Required: essay or personal statement, high school transcript, minimum 2.0 GPA, 1 letter of recommendation, Common Application Supplement and Program for Advancement of Learning (PAL), Cognitive and Achievement Testing for PAL. *Required for some:* interview.
Application deadlines: 4/1 (freshmen), 7/1 (transfers), 12/1 (early action).
Notification: continuous (freshmen), continuous (transfers), 12/15 (early action).

CONTACT
Ms. Jane P. Fidler, Vice President of Admission and Dean of Undergraduate Admission, Curry College, 1071 Blue Hill Avenue, Milton, MA 02186. *Phone:* 617-333-2210. *Toll-free phone:* 800-669-0686. *Fax:* 617-333-2114. *E-mail:* curryadm@curry.edu.

Dean College
Franklin, Massachusetts
http://www.dean.edu/

- **Independent** 4-year, founded 1865
- **Suburban** 100-acre campus with easy access to Boston, MA and Providence, RI
- **Endowment** $42.2 million
- **Coed** 1,301 undergraduate students, 85% full-time, 54% women, 46% men
- **Moderately difficult** entrance level, 86% of applicants were admitted

UNDERGRAD STUDENTS

1,101 full-time, 200 part-time. Students come from 35 states and territories; 17 other countries; 48% are from out of state; 14% Black or African American, non-Hispanic/Latino; 8% Hispanic/Latino; 2% Asian, non-Hispanic/Latino; 0.2% Native Hawaiian or other Pacific Islander, non-Hispanic/Latino; 0.6% American Indian or Alaska Native, non-Hispanic/Latino; 4% Two or more races, non-Hispanic/Latino; 12% Race/ethnicity unknown; 5% international; 4% transferred in; 90% live on campus.

Freshmen:
Admission: 4,515 applied, 3,886 admitted, 497 enrolled. *Average high school GPA:* 2.6. *Test scores:* SAT evidence-based reading and writing scores over 500: 51%; SAT math scores over 500: 43%; ACT scores over 18: 58%; SAT evidence-based reading and writing scores over 600: 13%; SAT math scores over 600: 9%; ACT scores over 24: 13%; SAT evidence-based reading and writing scores over 700: 1%; SAT math scores over 700: 2%; ACT scores over 30: 5%.

Retention: 70% of full-time freshmen returned.

FACULTY
Total: 140, 22% full-time, 31% with terminal degrees.

Student/faculty ratio: 17:1.

ACADEMICS
Calendar: semesters. *Degrees:* certificates, associate, and bachelor's.

Special study options: accelerated degree program, adult/continuing education programs, advanced placement credit, distance learning, double majors, English as a second language, honors programs, independent study, internships, off-campus study, part-time degree program, services for LD students, student-designed majors, study abroad, summer session for credit.

Computers: 36 computers/terminals are available on campus for general student use. Students can access the following: campus intranet, computer help desk, free student e-mail accounts, online (class) grades, online (class) registration, online (class) schedules. Campuswide network is available. Wireless service is available via entire campus.

Library: E. Ross Anderson Library. *Books:* 37,000 (physical), 36,000 (digital/electronic); *Serial titles:* 32 (physical), 100,000 (digital/electronic); *Databases:* 58. Weekly public service hours: 76.

STUDENT LIFE
Housing options: on-campus residence required through senior year; coed, men-only, women-only. Campus housing is university owned. Freshman campus housing is guaranteed.

Activities and organizations: drama/theater group, student-run radio and television station, choral group, National Society of Leadership and Success, Student Activities Committee, Residence Hall Association, International Student Association, Dean Community Outreach.

Athletics Member NCAA, USCAA. All Division III. *Intercollegiate sports:* baseball M, basketball M/W, cross-country running M/W, field hockey W, football M, golf M, lacrosse M/W, soccer M/W, softball W, volleyball M/W.

Campus security: 24-hour emergency response devices and patrols, student patrols, late-night transport/escort service, controlled dormitory access.

Student services: health clinic, personal/psychological counseling.

COSTS & FINANCIAL AID
Costs (2018–19) *One-time required fee:* $300. *Comprehensive fee:* $56,270 includes full-time tuition ($39,234), mandatory fees ($200), and room and board ($16,836). Full-time tuition and fees vary according to class time and course load. Part-time tuition: $350 per credit hour. Part-time tuition and fees vary according to class time and course load.

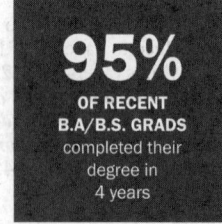

95% OF RECENT B.A/B.S. GRADS completed their degree in 4 years

40 ACADEMIC COACHES available for student support

BACHELOR'S and ASSOCIATE DEGREES

DISCOVER THE DEAN DIFFERENCE

DEAN COLLEGE

877-TRY-DEAN • dean.edu

Required fees: $25 per term part-time. *College room only:* $10,634. Room and board charges vary according to housing facility. *Payment plan:* installment. *Waivers:* employees or children of employees.

Financial Aid Of all full-time matriculated undergraduates who enrolled in 2017, 947 applied for aid, 876 were judged to have need, 99 had their need fully met. In 2017, 265 non-need-based awards were made. *Average percent of need met:* 61. *Average financial aid package:* $27,345. *Average need-based loan:* $3926. *Average need-based gift aid:* $20,456. *Average non-need-based aid:* $14,464. *Average indebtedness upon graduation:* $48,717.

APPLYING

Options: electronic application, early admission, early action, deferred entrance.

Required: high school transcript. *Required for some:* audition for performing arts majors. *Recommended:* essay or personal statement, minimum 2.0 GPA, 1 letter of recommendation, interview.

Application deadlines: rolling (freshmen), rolling (out-of-state freshmen), rolling (transfers), 12/1 (early action).

Notification: continuous (freshmen), 1/15 (early action).

CONTACT

Iris P. Godes, Associate Vice President of Enrollment Services/Dean of Admissions, Dean College, 99 Main Street, Franklin, MA 02038. *Phone:* 508-541-1508. *Toll-free phone:* 877-TRY-DEAN. *Fax:* 508-541-8726. *E-mail:* igodes@dean.edu.

See previous page for display ad and page 1272 for the College Close-Up.

Eastern Nazarene College

Quincy, Massachusetts
http://www.enc.edu/

- **Independent** comprehensive, founded 1900, affiliated with Church of the Nazarene
- **Urban** 17-acre campus with easy access to Boston
- **Coed** 694 undergraduate students, 82% full-time, 57% women, 43% men
- **Moderately difficult** entrance level, 68% of applicants were admitted

UNDERGRAD STUDENTS

571 full-time, 123 part-time. Students come from 37 states and territories; 15 other countries; 40% are from out of state; 21% Black or African American, non-Hispanic/Latino; 13% Hispanic/Latino; 2% Asian, non-Hispanic/Latino; 0.4% Native Hawaiian or other Pacific Islander, non-Hispanic/Latino; 0.1% American Indian or Alaska Native, non-Hispanic/Latino; 4% Two or more races, non-Hispanic/Latino; 1% Race/ethnicity unknown; 4% international; 5% transferred in; 50% live on campus.

Freshmen:

Admission: 1,157 applied, 784 admitted, 153 enrolled.
Retention: 67% of full-time freshmen returned.

ACADEMICS

Calendar: semesters. *Degrees:* associate, bachelor's, and master's.

Special study options: academic remediation for entering students, accelerated degree program, adult/continuing education programs, advanced placement credit, cooperative education, double majors, honors programs, independent study, internships, off-campus study, part-time degree program, services for LD students, study abroad, summer session for credit.

Unusual degree programs: engineering with Boston University; nursing with Boston College; Massachusetts College of Pharmacy.

Computers: 140 computers/terminals are available on campus for general student use. Students can access the following: computer help desk, free student e-mail accounts, online (class) grades, online (class) registration, online (class) schedules. Campuswide network is available. 100% of college-owned or -operated housing units are wired for high-speed Internet access. Wireless service is available via entire campus.

Library: Nease Library. *Books:* 113,825 (physical), 314,187 (digital/electronic); *Serial titles:* 748 (physical), 295,387 (digital/electronic); *Databases:* 90. Weekly public service hours: 95; study areas open 24 hours, 5–7 days a week; students can reserve study rooms.

STUDENT LIFE

Housing options: on-campus residence required through senior year; men-only, women-only, special housing for students with disabilities. Campus housing is university owned. Freshman campus housing is guaranteed.

Activities and organizations: drama/theater group, student-run newspaper, choral group, Gospel Choir, A cappella Choir, Germantown Tutoring, ALANA, Spirit Team.

Athletics Member NCAA. All Division III. *Intercollegiate sports:* baseball M, basketball M/W, cross-country running M/W, golf M, soccer M/W, softball W, tennis M/W, track and field M/W, volleyball M/W. *Intramural sports:* basketball M/W, soccer M/W, swimming and diving M(c)/W(c), ultimate Frisbee M.

Campus security: 24-hour emergency response devices and patrols, student patrols, late-night transport/escort service, controlled dormitory access.

Student services: health clinic, personal/psychological counseling.

COSTS & FINANCIAL AID

Costs (2018–19) *Comprehensive fee:* $35,222 includes full-time tuition ($24,698), mandatory fees ($900), and room and board ($9624). Full-time tuition and fees vary according to class time, course load, degree level, location, program, and reciprocity agreements. Part-time tuition: $1338 per credit hour. Part-time tuition and fees vary according to class time, degree level, location, program, and reciprocity agreements. *Room and board:* Room and board charges vary according to board plan and housing facility. *Payment plan:* installment. *Waivers:* employees or children of employees.

Financial Aid Of all full-time matriculated undergraduates who enrolled in 2014, 761 applied for aid, 395 were judged to have need, 128 had their need fully met. 40 Federal Work-Study jobs (averaging $2500). In 2014, 67 non-need-based awards were made. *Average percent of need met:* 80. *Average financial aid package:* $29,431. *Average need-based loan:* $8837. *Average need-based gift aid:* $17,673. *Average non-need-based aid:* $13,644. *Average indebtedness upon graduation:* $25,251.

APPLYING

Standardized Tests *Required:* SAT or ACT (for admission).

Options: electronic application, early admission, deferred entrance.

Required: high school transcript, minimum 2.0 GPA, 1 letter of recommendation. *Recommended:* essay or personal statement, minimum 3.0 GPA, 2 letters of recommendation, interview.

Application deadlines: rolling (freshmen), rolling (out-of-state freshmen), rolling (transfers).

Notification: continuous (freshmen), continuous (out-of-state freshmen), continuous (transfers).

CONTACT

Ms. Ashley Rudeen, Assistant Director of Admission/International DSO, Eastern Nazarene College, 23 East Elm Avenue, Quincy, MA 02170. *Phone:* 617-745-3861. *Toll-free phone:* 800-88-ENC88. *Fax:* 617-745-3992. *E-mail:* ashley.rudeen@enc.edu.

Elms College

Chicopee, Massachusetts
http://www.elms.edu/

- **Independent Roman Catholic** comprehensive, founded 1928
- **Suburban** 32-acre campus
- **Coed** 1,174 undergraduate students, 83% full-time, 74% women, 26% men
- **Moderately difficult** entrance level, 79% of applicants were admitted

UNDERGRAD STUDENTS

973 full-time, 201 part-time. Students come from 28 states and territories; 21 other countries; 23% are from out of state; 9% Black or African American, non-Hispanic/Latino; 14% Hispanic/Latino; 2% Asian, non-Hispanic/Latino; 0.3% American Indian or Alaska Native, non-Hispanic/Latino; 18% Race/ethnicity unknown; 0.5% international; 4% transferred in; 33% live on campus.

Freshmen:

Admission: 868 applied, 690 admitted, 173 enrolled. *Average high school GPA:* 3.3. *Test scores:* SAT evidence-based reading and writing scores over 500: 63%; SAT math scores over 500: 66%; ACT scores over 18: 66%; SAT evidence-based reading and writing scores over 600: 12%; SAT math scores over 600: 11%; ACT scores over 24: 26%; ACT scores over 30: 13%.

Retention: 84% of full-time freshmen returned.

FACULTY
Total: 187, 35% full-time, 45% with terminal degrees.
Student/faculty ratio: 12:1.

ACADEMICS
Calendar: semesters. *Degrees:* associate, bachelor's, master's, doctoral, post-master's, and postbachelor's certificates.

Special study options: accelerated degree program, adult/continuing education programs, advanced placement credit, cooperative education, distance learning, double majors, English as a second language, independent study, internships, off-campus study, part-time degree program, services for LD students, study abroad, summer session for credit. *ROTC:* Army (c), Air Force (c).

Computers: 175 computers/terminals are available on campus for general student use. Students can access the following: computer help desk, free student e-mail accounts, online (class) grades, online (class) registration, online (class) schedules. Campuswide network is available. Wireless service is available via entire campus.
Library: Alumnae Library.

STUDENT LIFE
Housing options: coed, women-only. Campus housing is university owned. Freshman campus housing is guaranteed.

Activities and organizations: choral group.

Athletics Member NCAA. All Division III. *Intercollegiate sports:* baseball M, basketball M/W, cross-country running M/W, field hockey W, golf M, lacrosse W, soccer M/W, softball W, swimming and diving M/W, track and field M/W, volleyball M/W. *Intramural sports:* basketball M/W, cross-country running M/W, field hockey W, lacrosse M/W, soccer M/W, softball M/W, swimming and diving M/W, volleyball M/W, weight lifting M/W.

Campus security: 24-hour emergency response devices and patrols, controlled dormitory access.

Student services: health clinic, personal/psychological counseling.

COSTS & FINANCIAL AID
Costs (2018–19) *Comprehensive fee:* $48,894 includes full-time tuition ($34,114), mandatory fees ($1674), and room and board ($13,106). Part-time tuition: $691 per credit hour. Part-time tuition and fees vary according to location and program. *Room and board:* Room and board charges vary according to board plan. *Payment plan:* installment. *Waivers:* senior citizens and employees or children of employees.

Financial Aid Of all full-time matriculated undergraduates who enrolled in 2017, 911 applied for aid, 876 were judged to have need, 63 had their need fully met. 96 Federal Work-Study jobs (averaging $1206). In 2017, 71 non-need-based awards were made. *Average percent of need met:* 61. *Average financial aid package:* $22,746. *Average need-based loan:* $4691. *Average need-based gift aid:* $18,925. *Average non-need-based aid:* $14,622. *Average indebtedness upon graduation:* $38,539.

APPLYING
Standardized Tests *Required:* SAT or ACT (for admission).

Options: early admission, deferred entrance.

Required: essay or personal statement, high school transcript, 2 letters of recommendation. *Recommended:* interview.

Application deadlines: rolling (freshmen), rolling (out-of-state freshmen), rolling (transfers).

Notification: continuous (freshmen), continuous (out-of-state freshmen), continuous (transfers).

CONTACT
Mr. Joseph Wagner, Director of Admissions, Elms College, Chicopee, MA 01013-2839. *Phone:* 413-592-3189. *Toll-free phone:* 800-255-ELMS. *Fax:* 413-594-2781. *E-mail:* admissions@elms.edu.

Emerson College
Boston, Massachusetts
http://www.emerson.edu/

- **Independent** comprehensive, founded 1880
- **Urban** campus with easy access to Boston, MA
- **Endowment** $161.1 million
- **Coed** 3,813 undergraduate students, 98% full-time, 59% women, 41% men
- **Very difficult** entrance level, 46% of applicants were admitted

UNDERGRAD STUDENTS
3,748 full-time, 65 part-time. Students come from 53 states and territories; 47 other countries; 79% are from out of state; 3% Black or African American, non-Hispanic/Latino; 12% Hispanic/Latino; 5% Asian, non-Hispanic/Latino; 0.1% Native Hawaiian or other Pacific Islander, non-Hispanic/Latino; 0.2% American Indian or Alaska Native, non-Hispanic/Latino; 4% Two or more races, non-Hispanic/Latino; 2% Race/ethnicity unknown; 9% international; 4% transferred in; 52% live on campus.

Freshmen:
Admission: 10,360 applied, 4,772 admitted, 932 enrolled. *Average high school GPA:* 3.7. *Test scores:* SAT evidence-based reading and writing scores over 500: 100%; SAT math scores over 500: 98%; ACT scores over 18: 100%; SAT evidence-based reading and writing scores over 600: 86%; SAT math scores over 600: 63%; ACT scores over 24: 89%; SAT evidence-based reading and writing scores over 700: 26%; SAT math scores over 700: 14%; ACT scores over 30: 33%.

Retention: 88% of full-time freshmen returned.

FACULTY
Total: 454, 44% full-time, 59% with terminal degrees.
Student/faculty ratio: 13:1.

ACADEMICS
Calendar: semesters. *Degrees:* certificates, bachelor's, master's, and doctoral.

Special study options: adult/continuing education programs, advanced placement credit, double majors, honors programs, independent study, internships, off-campus study, part-time degree program, services for LD students, student-designed majors, study abroad, summer session for credit.

Computers: 480 computers/terminals and 1,900 ports are available on campus for general student use. Students can access the following: computer help desk, free student e-mail accounts, online (class) grades, online (class) registration, online (class) schedules. Campuswide network is available. 100% of college-owned or -operated housing units are wired for high-speed Internet access. Wireless service is available via entire campus.
Library: Iwasaki Library plus 1 other. *Books:* 336,669 (physical), 2,484 (digital/electronic); *Serial titles:* 67,760 (digital/electronic); *Databases:* 125. Weekly public service hours: 93; students can reserve study rooms.

STUDENT LIFE
Housing options: on-campus residence required through junior year; coed. Campus housing is university owned. Freshman campus housing is guaranteed.

Activities and organizations: drama/theater group, student-run newspaper, radio and television station, choral group, EIV (Emerson Independent Video), National Broadcasting Society (student chapter), SPEC (Screenwriting), Entertainment Monthly (entertainment news), Emerson International (international student group), national fraternities, national sororities.

Athletics Member NCAA. All Division III. *Intercollegiate sports:* baseball M, basketball M/W, cross-country running M/W, golf M(c)/W(c), lacrosse M/W, soccer M/W, softball W, tennis M/W, track and field W, volleyball M/W. *Intramural sports:* basketball M/W, soccer M/W, volleyball M/W.

Campus security: 24-hour emergency response devices and patrols, late-night transport/escort service, controlled dormitory access.

Student services: health clinic, personal/psychological counseling.

COSTS & FINANCIAL AID

Costs (2018–19) *Tuition:* $46,016 full-time, $1438 per credit hour part-time. *Required fees:* $836 full-time. *Room only:* Room and board charges vary according to board plan and location. *Payment plan:* installment. *Waivers:* employees or children of employees.

Financial Aid Of all full-time matriculated undergraduates who enrolled in 2016, 2,410 applied for aid, 2,038 were judged to have need, 137 had their need fully met. 383 Federal Work-Study jobs (averaging $1980). 85 state and other part-time jobs (averaging $12,943). In 2016, 361 non-need-based awards were made. *Average percent of need met:* 52. *Average financial aid package:* $21,848. *Average need-based loan:* $4788. *Average need-based gift aid:* $18,820. *Average non-need-based aid:* $15,402. *Average indebtedness upon graduation:* $23,225.

APPLYING

Options: electronic application, early admission, early action, deferred entrance.

Application fee: $65.

Required: essay or personal statement, high school transcript, 1 letter of recommendation. *Required for some:* interview.

Application deadlines: 1/15 (freshmen), 3/15 (transfers), 11/1 (early action).

Notification: continuous until 4/1 (freshmen), continuous until 4/1 (out-of-state freshmen), 5/1 (transfers), 12/15 (early action).

CONTACT

Emerson College, 120 Boylston Street, Boston, MA 02116-4624. *Phone:* 617-824-8600.

See this page for display ad and page 1286 for the College Close-Up.

Emmanuel College
Boston, Massachusetts
http://www.emmanuel.edu/

- **Independent Roman Catholic** comprehensive, founded 1919
- **Urban** 17-acre campus
- **Endowment** $136.6 million
- **Coed** 1,947 undergraduate students, 93% full-time, 73% women, 27% men
- 73% of applicants were admitted

UNDERGRAD STUDENTS

1,804 full-time, 143 part-time. Students come from 32 states and territories; 51 other countries; 42% are from out of state; 5% Black or African American, non-Hispanic/Latino; 10% Hispanic/Latino; 4% Asian, non-Hispanic/Latino; 0.1% Native Hawaiian or other Pacific Islander, non-Hispanic/Latino; 0.2% American Indian or Alaska Native, non-Hispanic/Latino; 3% Two or more races, non-Hispanic/Latino; 8% Race/ethnicity unknown; 1% international; 3% transferred in; 68% live on campus.

Freshmen:
Admission: 5,965 applied, 4,354 admitted, 474 enrolled. *Average high school GPA:* 3.7. *Test scores:* SAT evidence-based reading and writing scores over 500: 97%; SAT math scores over 500: 93%; ACT scores over 18: 100%; SAT evidence-based reading and writing scores over 600: 54%; SAT math scores over 600: 37%; ACT scores over 24: 83%; SAT evidence-based reading and writing scores over 700: 4%; SAT math scores over 700: 3%; ACT scores over 30: 17%.

Retention: 78% of full-time freshmen returned.

FACULTY

Total: 191, 47% full-time, 73% with terminal degrees.

Student/faculty ratio: 13:1.

ACADEMICS

Calendar: semesters. *Degrees:* bachelor's, master's, post-master's, and postbachelor's certificates.

Special study options: advanced placement credit, distance learning, double majors, honors programs, independent study, internships, off-campus study, part-time degree program, services for LD students, student-designed majors, study abroad, summer session for credit. *ROTC:* Army (c).

Computers: 284 computers/terminals are available on campus for general student use. Students can access the following: campus intranet, computer help desk, free student e-mail accounts, online (class) grades, online (class) registration, online (class) schedules. Campuswide network is available. 100% of college-owned or -operated housing units are wired for high-speed Internet access. Wireless service is available via entire campus.

Library: Cardinal Cushing Library. *Books:* 64,408 (physical), 186,664 (digital/electronic); *Serial titles:* 119 (physical), 3,967 (digital/electronic); *Databases:* 60. Weekly public service hours: 112; students can reserve study rooms.

STUDENT LIFE
Housing options: coed. Campus housing is university owned and leased by the school. Freshman campus housing is guaranteed.

Activities and organizations: drama/theater group, student-run newspaper, radio station, choral group, Student Government Association, Biology Club, Emmanuel College Programming Team, Black Student Union, Sister for Sister.

Athletics Member NCAA. All Division III. *Intercollegiate sports:* basketball M/W, cross-country running M/W, golf M, lacrosse M/W, soccer M/W, softball W, track and field M/W, volleyball M/W. *Intramural sports:* baseball M(c), field hockey W(c), ultimate Frisbee M(c)/W(c).

Campus security: 24-hour emergency response devices and patrols, late-night transport/escort service, controlled dormitory access.

Student services: health clinic, personal/psychological counseling.

COSTS & FINANCIAL AID
Costs (2018–19) *One-time required fee:* $350. *Comprehensive fee:* $54,798 includes full-time tuition ($39,544), mandatory fees ($260), and room and board ($14,994). Part-time tuition: $1236 per credit hour. *Room and board:* Room and board charges vary according to board plan and housing facility. *Payment plan:* installment. *Waivers:* employees or children of employees.

Financial Aid Of all full-time matriculated undergraduates who enrolled in 2017, 1,579 applied for aid, 1,444 were judged to have need, 462 had their need fully met. 822 Federal Work-Study jobs (averaging $2034). In 2017, 266 non-need-based awards were made. *Average percent of need met:* 71. *Average financial aid package:* $29,174. *Average need-based loan:* $4529. *Average need-based gift aid:* $24,150. *Average non-need-based aid:* $16,575.

APPLYING
Options: electronic application, early admission, early action, deferred entrance.

Application fee: $60.

Required: essay or personal statement, high school transcript, 2 letters of recommendation. *Recommended:* interview.

Application deadlines: 2/15 (freshmen), 4/1 (transfers), 11/1 (early action).

Notification: continuous until 1/15 (freshmen), 5/1 (transfers), 12/15 (early action).

CONTACT
Ms. Sandra Robbins, Dean for Enrollment, Emmanuel College, Admission Office, 400 The Fenway, Boston, MA 02115. *Phone:* 617-735-9715. *Fax:* 617-735-9801. *E-mail:* enroll@emmanuel.edu.

Endicott College
Beverly, Massachusetts
http://www.endicott.edu/

- **Independent** comprehensive, founded 1939
- **Suburban** 235-acre campus with easy access to Boston
- **Endowment** $78.6 million
- **Coed** 3,482 undergraduate students, 88% full-time, 61% women, 39% men
- **Moderately difficult** entrance level, 81% of applicants were admitted

UNDERGRAD STUDENTS
3,075 full-time, 407 part-time. Students come from 34 states and territories; 33 other countries; 51% are from out of state; 2% Black or African American, non-Hispanic/Latino; 4% Hispanic/Latino; 1% Asian, non-Hispanic/Latino; 0.1% Native Hawaiian or other Pacific Islander, non-Hispanic/Latino; 0.3% American Indian or Alaska Native, non-Hispanic/Latino; 1% Two or more races, non-Hispanic/Latino; 9% Race/ethnicity unknown; 2% international; 4% transferred in; 91% live on campus.

Freshmen:
Admission: 3,623 applied, 2,949 admitted, 780 enrolled. *Average high school GPA:* 3.3. *Test scores:* SAT evidence-based reading and writing scores over 500: 92%; SAT math scores over 500: 87%; ACT scores over 18: 98%; SAT evidence-based reading and writing scores over 600: 32%; SAT math scores over 600: 30%; ACT scores over 24: 50%; SAT evidence-based reading and writing scores over 700: 2%; SAT math scores over 700: 2%; ACT scores over 30: 2%.

Retention: 84% of full-time freshmen returned.

FACULTY
Total: 526, 20% full-time, 41% with terminal degrees.
Student/faculty ratio: 14:1.

ACADEMICS
Calendar: semesters. *Degrees:* certificates, associate, bachelor's, master's, doctoral, post-master's, and postbachelor's certificates.

Special study options: accelerated degree program, adult/continuing education programs, advanced placement credit, cooperative education, distance learning, double majors, English as a second language, honors programs, independent study, internships, off-campus study, part-time degree program, services for LD students, student-designed majors, study abroad, summer session for credit. *ROTC:* Army (c).

Computers: 285 computers/terminals are available on campus for general student use. Students can access the following: campus intranet, computer help desk, free student e-mail accounts, online (class) grades, online (class) registration, online (class) schedules. Campuswide network is available. 100% of college-owned or -operated housing units are wired for high-speed Internet access. Wireless service is available via entire campus.

Library: Diane M. Halle Library. *Books:* 104,213 (physical), 172,731 (digital/electronic); *Serial titles:* 47 (physical), 154,538 (digital/electronic); *Databases:* 175. Weekly public service hours: 97; students can reserve study rooms.

STUDENT LIFE
Housing options: coed, women-only, special housing for students with disabilities. Campus housing is university owned. Freshman campus housing is guaranteed.

Activities and organizations: drama/theater group, student-run newspaper, radio and television station, choral group.

Athletics Member NCAA. All Division III. *Intercollegiate sports:* baseball M, basketball M/W, cheerleading W(c), crew M(c)/W(c), cross-country running M/W, equestrian sports M/W, field hockey W, football M, golf M, ice hockey M/W, lacrosse M/W, rowing M(c)/W(c), rugby M(c)/W(c), soccer M/W, softball W, tennis M/W, track and field W, volleyball M/W. *Intramural sports:* basketball M/W, football M/W, ice hockey M/W, soccer M/W, softball M/W, ultimate Frisbee M/W, volleyball M/W.

Campus security: 24-hour emergency response devices and patrols, student patrols, late-night transport/escort service, controlled dormitory access, crime prevention programs, rape awareness defense, property identification, security cameras, front gate.

Student services: health clinic, personal/psychological counseling.

COSTS & FINANCIAL AID
Costs (2018–19) *Comprehensive fee:* $48,326 includes full-time tuition ($32,350), mandatory fees ($700), and room and board ($15,276). Full-time tuition and fees vary according to location and program. Part-time tuition: $994 per credit hour. Part-time tuition and fees vary according to location and program. *College room only:* $10,530. Room and board charges vary according to housing facility. *Payment plans:* tuition prepayment, installment. *Waivers:* employees or children of employees.

Financial Aid Of all full-time matriculated undergraduates who enrolled in 2017, 2,302 applied for aid, 1,934 were judged to have need, 201 had their need fully met. 787 Federal Work-Study jobs (averaging $2000). In 2017, 668 non-need-based awards were made. *Average percent of need met:* 64. *Average financial aid package:* $20,881. *Average need-based loan:* $4698. *Average need-based gift aid:* $15,942. *Average non-need-based aid:* $9693. *Average indebtedness upon graduation:* $44,159.

APPLYING
Standardized Tests *Required for some:* SAT or ACT (for admission).
Options: electronic application.

Application fee: $50.

Required: essay or personal statement, high school transcript, minimum 2.5 GPA, 1 letter of recommendation. *Required for some:* interview. *Recommended:* interview.

Application deadlines: 2/15 (freshmen), 3/15 (transfers).

Notification: continuous (freshmen), continuous (transfers).

CONTACT
Mr. Thomas J. Redman, Vice President of Admission and Financial Aid, Endicott College, 376 Hale Street, Beverly, MA 01915. *Phone:* 978-921-1000. *Toll-free phone:* 800-325-1114. *Fax:* 978-232-2520. *E-mail:* admissio@endicott.edu.

Fisher College
Boston, Massachusetts
http://www.fisher.edu/
- **Independent** comprehensive, founded 1903
- **Urban** 1-acre campus with easy access to Boston
- **Endowment** $34.0 million
- **Coed** 1,882 undergraduate students, 40% full-time, 73% women, 27% men

UNDERGRAD STUDENTS
748 full-time, 1,134 part-time. Students come from 38 states and territories; 40 other countries; 21% are from out of state; 11% Black or African American, non-Hispanic/Latino; 10% Hispanic/Latino; 0.9% Asian, non-Hispanic/Latino; 0.1% Native Hawaiian or other Pacific Islander, non-Hispanic/Latino; 0.1% American Indian or Alaska Native, non-Hispanic/Latino; 2% Two or more races, non-Hispanic/Latino; 38% Race/ethnicity unknown; 9% international; 3% transferred in; 22% live on campus.

Freshmen:
Admission: 263 enrolled. *Average high school GPA:* 2.5. *Test scores:* SAT evidence-based reading and writing scores over 500: 36%; SAT math scores over 500: 32%; ACT scores over 18: 50%; SAT evidence-based reading and writing scores over 600: 8%; SAT math scores over 600: 8%; ACT scores over 24: 17%.

Retention: 60% of full-time freshmen returned.

FACULTY
Total: 188, 19% full-time, 12% with terminal degrees.
Student/faculty ratio: 16:1.

ACADEMICS
Calendar: semesters. *Degrees:* certificates, associate, bachelor's, and master's.

Special study options: academic remediation for entering students, accelerated degree program, adult/continuing education programs, advanced placement credit, distance learning, English as a second language, honors programs, independent study, internships, off-campus study, part-time degree program, services for LD students, study abroad, summer session for credit. *ROTC:* Army (c).

Computers: 208 computers/terminals are available on campus for general student use. Students can access the following: campus intranet, computer help desk, free student e-mail accounts, online (class) grades, online (class) registration, online (class) schedules. Campuswide network is available. 100% of college-owned or -operated housing units are wired for high-speed Internet access. Wireless service is available via entire campus.
Library: Fisher College Library. *Books:* 23,902 (physical), 105,119 (digital/electronic); *Serial titles:* 40 (physical); *Databases:* 104. Weekly public service hours: 72; study areas open 24 hours, 5–7 days a week; students can reserve study rooms.

STUDENT LIFE
Housing options: coed, women-only. Campus housing is university owned and leased by the school.

Activities and organizations: drama/theater group, choral group, National Society of Leadership and Success (NSLS), Psychology Club, Criminal Justice Club, Fashion Club, Multi-Cultural Club.

Athletics Member NAIA. *Intercollegiate sports:* baseball M, basketball M/W, soccer M/W, softball W.

Campus security: 24-hour emergency response devices and patrols, student patrols, controlled dormitory access.

Student services: health clinic, personal/psychological counseling, women's center.

COSTS & FINANCIAL AID
Costs (2018–19) *Comprehensive fee:* $47,310 includes full-time tuition ($30,389), mandatory fees ($995), and room and board ($15,926). Part-time tuition: $1143 per course. Part-time tuition and fees vary according to course load. *Required fees:* $95 per course part-time. *Room and board:* Room and board charges vary according to housing facility. *Payment plan:* installment. *Waivers:* employees or children of employees.

Financial Aid Of all full-time matriculated undergraduates who enrolled in 2016, 701 applied for aid, 689 were judged to have need. 57 Federal Work-Study jobs (averaging $1141). In 2016, 56 non-need-based awards were made. *Average financial aid package:* $21,050. *Average need-based loan:* $4125. *Average need-based gift aid:* $12,480. *Average non-need-based aid:* $6534. *Average indebtedness upon graduation:* $12,724. *Financial aid deadline:* 3/15.

APPLYING
Standardized Tests *Required for some:* SAT or ACT (for admission).
Required: high school transcript. *Required for some:* essay or personal statement, interview. *Recommended:* minimum 2.0 GPA.

CONTACT
Mr. Robert Melaragni, Vice President of Enrollment Management, Fisher College, Boston, MA 02116. *Phone:* 617-236-8818. *Fax:* 617-236-5473. *E-mail:* admissions@fisher.edu.

Fitchburg State University
Fitchburg, Massachusetts
http://www.fitchburgstate.edu/
- **State-supported** comprehensive, founded 1894, part of Massachusetts Public Higher Education System
- **Suburban** 78-acre campus with easy access to Boston
- **Endowment** $15.6 million
- **Coed** 4,117 undergraduate students, 82% full-time, 53% women, 47% men
- **Moderately difficult** entrance level, 80% of applicants were admitted

UNDERGRAD STUDENTS
3,386 full-time, 731 part-time. Students come from 26 states and territories; 5 other countries; 8% are from out of state; 10% Black or African American, non-Hispanic/Latino; 12% Hispanic/Latino; 3% Asian, non-Hispanic/Latino; 0.1% American Indian or Alaska Native, non-Hispanic/Latino; 3% Two or more races, non-Hispanic/Latino; 2% Race/ethnicity unknown; 0.4% international; 9% transferred in; 57% live on campus.

Freshmen:
Admission: 3,608 applied, 2,888 admitted, 756 enrolled. *Average high school GPA:* 3.0.
Retention: 78% of full-time freshmen returned.

FACULTY
Total: 318, 66% full-time.
Student/faculty ratio: 13:1.

ACADEMICS
Calendar: semesters. *Degrees:* certificates, bachelor's, master's, post-master's, and postbachelor's certificates.

Special study options: academic remediation for entering students, accelerated degree program, adult/continuing education programs, advanced placement credit, distance learning, double majors, honors programs, independent study, internships, off-campus study, part-time degree program, services for LD students, student-designed majors, study abroad, summer session for credit. *ROTC:* Army (b).

Computers: 500 computers/terminals are available on campus for general student use. Students can access the following: computer help desk, free student e-mail accounts, online (class) grades, online (class) registration, online (class) schedules. Campuswide network is available. 100% of college-owned or -operated housing units are wired for high-speed Internet access. Wireless service is available via entire campus.
Library: Amelia V. Galucci-Cirio Library. *Books:* 222,517 (physical); *Databases:* 150. Weekly public service hours: 77.

STUDENT LIFE

Housing options: coed, special housing for students with disabilities. Campus housing is university owned. Freshman applicants given priority for college housing.

Activities and organizations: drama/theater group, student-run newspaper, radio station, choral group, Student Government Association, Dance Club, Activities Board, Greek Council, MASSPIRG, national fraternities, national sororities.

Athletics Member NCAA. All Division III. *Intercollegiate sports:* baseball M, basketball M/W, cross-country running M/W, field hockey W, football M, ice hockey M, lacrosse W, soccer M/W, softball W, track and field M/W. *Intramural sports:* basketball M/W, football M/W, racquetball M/W, soccer M/W, softball M/W, swimming and diving M/W, table tennis M/W, ultimate Frisbee M/W, volleyball M/W, water polo M/W.

Campus security: 24-hour emergency response devices and patrols, student patrols, late-night transport/escort service, controlled dormitory access.

Student services: health clinic, personal/psychological counseling.

COSTS & FINANCIAL AID

Costs (2017–18) *Tuition:* state resident $970 full-time, $40 per credit hour part-time; nonresident $7050 full-time, $294 per credit hour part-time. Full-time tuition and fees vary according to class time and reciprocity agreements. Part-time tuition and fees vary according to class time and reciprocity agreements. *Required fees:* $9185 full-time, $383 per credit hour part-time. *Room and board:* $10,676. Room and board charges vary according to board plan and housing facility. *Payment plan:* installment. *Waivers:* senior citizens and employees or children of employees.

Financial Aid Of all full-time matriculated undergraduates who enrolled in 2016, 3,002 applied for aid, 2,281 were judged to have need. 218 Federal Work-Study jobs (averaging $1525). In 2016, 171 non-need-based awards were made. *Average percent of need met:* 76. *Average financial aid package:* $10,255. *Average need-based loan:* $4489. *Average need-based gift aid:* $6611. *Average non-need-based aid:* $1249. *Average indebtedness upon graduation:* $26,316.

APPLYING

Standardized Tests *Required:* SAT or ACT (for admission).

Options: electronic application, deferred entrance.

Application fee: $50.

Required: essay or personal statement, high school transcript, minimum 2.0 GPA, 16 core courses.

Application deadlines: rolling (freshmen), rolling (transfers).

Notification: continuous (freshmen), continuous (transfers).

CONTACT

Jinawa McNeil, Director of Admissions, Fitchburg State University, 160 Pearl Street, Fitchburg, MA 01420-2697. *Phone:* 978-665-3140. *Toll-free phone:* 800-705-9692. *Fax:* 978-665-4540. *E-mail:* admissions@ fitchburgstate.edu.

Framingham State University

Framingham, Massachusetts

http://www.framingham.edu/

- **State-supported** comprehensive, founded 1839, part of Massachusetts Public Higher Education System
- **Suburban** 77-acre campus with easy access to Boston
- **Endowment** $37.9 million
- **Coed** 4,126 undergraduate students, 86% full-time, 59% women, 41% men
- **Moderately difficult** entrance level, 68% of applicants were admitted

UNDERGRAD STUDENTS

3,558 full-time, 568 part-time. Students come from 15 other countries; 6% are from out of state; 11% Black or African American, non-Hispanic/Latino; 14% Hispanic/Latino; 3% Asian, non-Hispanic/Latino; 0.1% American Indian or Alaska Native, non-Hispanic/Latino; 4% Two or more races, non-Hispanic/Latino; 3% Race/ethnicity unknown; 0.5% international; 10% transferred in; 46% live on campus.

Freshmen:

Admission: 6,039 applied, 4,113 admitted, 764 enrolled. *Average high school GPA:* 3.0. *Test scores:* SAT evidence-based reading and writing scores over 500: 66%; SAT math scores over 500: 63%; ACT scores over 18: 91%; SAT evidence-based reading and writing scores over 600: 15%;

SAT math scores over 600: 11%; ACT scores over 24: 20%; SAT evidence-based reading and writing scores over 700: 1%; ACT scores over 30: 3%.

Retention: 76% of full-time freshmen returned.

FACULTY

Total: 330, 60% full-time.

Student/faculty ratio: 14:1.

ACADEMICS

Calendar: semesters. *Degrees:* bachelor's, master's, and postbachelor's certificates.

Special study options: advanced placement credit, cooperative education, distance learning, double majors, English as a second language, honors programs, independent study, internships, off-campus study, part-time degree program, services for LD students, student-designed majors, study abroad, summer session for credit.

Computers: 216 computers/terminals and 3,500 ports are available on campus for general student use. Students can access the following: free student e-mail accounts, online (class) grades, online (class) registration, online (class) schedules. Campuswide network is available. 100% of college-owned or -operated housing units are wired for high-speed Internet access. Wireless service is available via entire campus.

Library: Henry Whittemore Library. *Books:* 155,690 (physical), 28,774 (digital/electronic); *Serial titles:* 120 (physical); *Databases:* 65. Weekly public service hours: 100.

STUDENT LIFE

Housing options: coed, women-only, special housing for students with disabilities. Campus housing is university owned. Freshman applicants given priority for college housing.

Activities and organizations: drama/theater group, student-run newspaper, radio station, choral group, Dance Club, Student Union Activities Board, Gatepost (student newspaper), Student Government Association, Hilltop Players (theater group).

Athletics Member NCAA. All Division III. *Intercollegiate sports:* baseball M, basketball M/W, cross-country running M/W, field hockey W, football M, ice hockey M, lacrosse W, soccer M/W, softball W, volleyball W. *Intramural sports:* basketball M/W, cheerleading W(c), football M/W, golf M/W, lacrosse M(c), rugby M(c)/W(c), soccer M/W, volleyball M/W, weight lifting M/W.

Campus security: 24-hour emergency response devices and patrols, student patrols, late-night transport/escort service, controlled dormitory access.

Student services: health clinic, personal/psychological counseling, legal services.

COSTS & FINANCIAL AID

Costs (2018–19) *Tuition:* state resident $970 full-time, $162 per course part-time; nonresident $7050 full-time, $1175 per course part-time. Full-time tuition and fees vary according to class time and degree level. Part-time tuition and fees vary according to class time, course load, and degree level. *Required fees:* $8950 full-time, $1556 per course part-time. *Room and board:* $11,820; room only: $7690. Room and board charges vary according to board plan and housing facility. *Payment plans:* tuition prepayment, installment. *Waivers:* senior citizens and employees or children of employees.

Financial Aid Of all full-time matriculated undergraduates who enrolled in 2016, 2,498 applied for aid, 1,971 were judged to have need, 682 had their need fully met. In 2016, 218 non-need-based awards were made. *Average percent of need met:* 60. *Average financial aid package:* $9800. *Average need-based loan:* $5150. *Average need-based gift aid:* $4600. *Average non-need-based aid:* $2100. *Average indebtedness upon graduation:* $30,781.

APPLYING

Standardized Tests *Required:* SAT or ACT (for admission).

Options: electronic application, early action, deferred entrance.

Application fee: $50.

Required: high school transcript, minimum 2.0 GPA, minimum of 16 college preparatory courses in specified areas. *Recommended:* minimum 3.0 GPA.

Application deadlines: 2/15 (freshmen), 11/15 (early action).

Notification: continuous (freshmen), continuous (transfers), 12/15 (early action).

CONTACT
Ms. Shayna Eddy, Associate Dean of Admissions, Framingham State University, 100 State Street, PO Box 9101, Framingham, MA 01701-9101. *Phone:* 508-626-4500. *Fax:* 508-626-4017. *E-mail:* admissions@framingham.edu.

Franklin W. Olin College of Engineering

Needham, Massachusetts
http://www.olin.edu/

- **Independent** 4-year, founded 1997
- **Suburban** 75-acre campus with easy access to Boston
- **Endowment** $376.5 million
- **Coed** 380 undergraduate students, 92% full-time, 48% women, 52% men
- **Most difficult** entrance level, 13% of applicants were admitted

UNDERGRAD STUDENTS
351 full-time, 29 part-time. Students come from 45 states and territories; 11 other countries; 88% are from out of state; 2% Black or African American, non-Hispanic/Latino; 8% Hispanic/Latino; 11% Asian, non-Hispanic/Latino; 7% Two or more races, non-Hispanic/Latino; 13% Race/ethnicity unknown; 10% international; 100% live on campus.

Freshmen:
Admission: 1,062 applied, 142 admitted, 90 enrolled. *Average high school GPA:* 3.8. *Test scores:* SAT evidence-based reading and writing scores over 500: 100%; SAT math scores over 500: 100%; ACT scores over 18: 100%; SAT evidence-based reading and writing scores over 600: 98%; SAT math scores over 600: 100%; ACT scores over 24: 100%; SAT evidence-based reading and writing scores over 700: 79%; SAT math scores over 700: 91%; ACT scores over 30: 98%.

Retention: 99% of full-time freshmen returned.

FACULTY
Total: 59, 69% full-time, 81% with terminal degrees.
Student/faculty ratio: 8:1.

ACADEMICS
Calendar: semesters. *Degree:* bachelor's.

Special study options: independent study, internships, off-campus study, services for LD students, student-designed majors, study abroad.

Computers: 2,364 ports are available on campus for general student use. Students can access the following: campus intranet, computer help desk, free student e-mail accounts, online (class) grades, online (class) registration, online (class) schedules. Campuswide network is available. 100% of college-owned or -operated housing units are wired for high-speed Internet access. Wireless service is available via entire campus.
Library: Franklin W. Olin Library. *Books:* 24,000 (physical), 426,889 (digital/electronic); *Serial titles:* 56 (physical), 179,581 (digital/electronic); *Databases:* 132. Study areas open 24 hours, 5–7 days a week; students can reserve study rooms.

STUDENT LIFE
Housing options: on-campus residence required through senior year; coed, special housing for students with disabilities. Campus housing is university owned. Freshman campus housing is guaranteed.

Activities and organizations: drama/theater group, student-run newspaper, choral group, Council of Olin Representatives, Stay Late and Create, Support, Encourage and Recognize Volunteerism (SERV), Mini Baja, Olin Fire Arts Club.

Athletics *Intercollegiate sports:* soccer M(c)/W(c), ultimate Frisbee M(c)/W(c). *Intramural sports:* basketball M/W, softball M/W, volleyball M/W.

Campus security: 24-hour emergency response devices and patrols, controlled dormitory access.

Student services: health clinic, personal/psychological counseling.

COSTS & FINANCIAL AID
Costs (2018–19) *One-time required fee:* $2656. *Comprehensive fee:* $67,380 includes full-time tuition ($50,400), mandatory fees ($680), and room and board ($16,300). Part-time tuition: $1575 per credit hour. *Payment plan:* installment.

Financial Aid Of all full-time matriculated undergraduates who enrolled in 2017, 187 applied for aid, 162 were judged to have need, 161 had their need fully met. In 2017, 186 non-need-based awards were made. *Average percent of need met:* 99. *Average financial aid package:* $47,140. *Average need-based loan:* $3122. *Average need-based gift aid:* $45,637. *Average non-need-based aid:* $24,333. *Average indebtedness upon graduation:* $23,098. *Financial aid deadline:* 2/15.

APPLYING
Standardized Tests *Required:* SAT or ACT (for admission).

Options: electronic application, deferred entrance.

Application fee: $85.

Required: essay or personal statement, high school transcript, 3 letters of recommendation, interview.

Notification: 3/24 (freshmen).

CONTACT
Franklin W. Olin College of Engineering, 1000 Olin Way, Needham, MA 02492-1200. *Phone:* 781-292-2222. *Fax:* 781-292-2210. *E-mail:* apply@olin.edu.

Gordon College

Wenham, Massachusetts
http://www.gordon.edu/

- **Independent nondenominational** comprehensive, founded 1889
- **Suburban** 485-acre campus with easy access to Boston
- **Endowment** $49.9 million
- **Coed** 1,591 undergraduate students, 96% full-time, 63% women, 37% men
- **Moderately difficult** entrance level, 89% of applicants were admitted

UNDERGRAD STUDENTS
1,528 full-time, 63 part-time. Students come from 44 states and territories; 52 other countries; 65% are from out of state; 6% Black or African American, non-Hispanic/Latino; 8% Hispanic/Latino; 5% Asian, non-Hispanic/Latino; 0.2% Native Hawaiian or other Pacific Islander, non-Hispanic/Latino; 0.1% American Indian or Alaska Native, non-Hispanic/Latino; 3% Two or more races, non-Hispanic/Latino; 9% international; 3% transferred in; 88% live on campus.

Freshmen:
Admission: 2,924 applied, 2,599 admitted, 417 enrolled. *Average high school GPA:* 3.6. *Test scores:* SAT evidence-based reading and writing scores over 500: 89%; SAT math scores over 500: 81%; ACT scores over 18: 94%; SAT evidence-based reading and writing scores over 600: 50%; SAT math scores over 600: 37%; ACT scores over 24: 64%; SAT evidence-based reading and writing scores over 700: 12%; SAT math scores over 700: 10%; ACT scores over 30: 21%.

Retention: 83% of full-time freshmen returned.

FACULTY
Total: 231, 41% full-time, 35% with terminal degrees.
Student/faculty ratio: 11:1.

ACADEMICS
Calendar: semesters. *Degrees:* bachelor's and master's.

Special study options: advanced placement credit, cooperative education, double majors, honors programs, independent study, internships, off-campus study, part-time degree program, services for LD students, student-designed majors, study abroad, summer session for credit. *ROTC:* Army (c).

Unusual degree programs: 3-2 engineering with University of Southern California.

Computers: 100 computers/terminals and 10 ports are available on campus for general student use. Students can access the following: campus intranet, computer help desk, free student e-mail accounts, online (class) grades, online (class) registration, online (class) schedules. Campuswide network is available. 100% of college-owned or -operated housing units are wired for high-speed Internet access. Wireless service is available via entire campus.
Library: Jenks Learning Resource Center. *Books:* 130,608 (physical), 178,400 (digital/electronic); *Serial titles:* 1,603 (physical). Weekly public service hours: 103; students can reserve study rooms.

STUDENT LIFE

Housing options: coed, men-only, women-only, special housing for students with disabilities. Campus housing is university owned. Freshman campus housing is guaranteed.

Activities and organizations: drama/theater group, student-run newspaper, radio station, choral group, Student Government Association, Student ministries and volunteer programs, Diverse music ensembles, Intramural sports, Short-term missions.

Athletics Member NCAA. All Division III. *Intercollegiate sports:* baseball M, basketball M/W, cross-country running M/W, field hockey W, lacrosse M/W, soccer M/W, softball W, swimming and diving M/W, tennis M/W, track and field M/W, volleyball W. *Intramural sports:* badminton M/W, basketball M/W, football M/W, racquetball M/W, rowing M(c)/W(c), soccer M/W, triathlon M/W, volleyball M/W, water polo M/W.

Campus security: 24-hour emergency response devices and patrols, late-night transport/escort service, controlled dormitory access, gated entrance; active treat training; Video Surveillance.

Student services: health clinic, personal/psychological counseling.

COSTS & FINANCIAL AID

Costs (2018–19) *Comprehensive fee:* $48,470 includes full-time tuition ($35,800), mandatory fees ($1600), and room and board ($11,070). Full-time tuition and fees vary according to course load and program. Part-time tuition: $895 per credit. Part-time tuition and fees vary according to course load and program. *College room only:* $7000. Room and board charges vary according to board plan and housing facility. *Payment plan:* installment. *Waivers:* employees or children of employees.

Financial Aid Of all full-time matriculated undergraduates who enrolled in 2017, 1,211 applied for aid, 1,048 were judged to have need, 194 had their need fully met. 395 Federal Work-Study jobs (averaging $639). In 2017, 489 non-need-based awards were made. *Average percent of need met:* 72. *Average financial aid package:* $26,133. *Average need-based loan:* $4777. *Average need-based gift aid:* $21,281. *Average non-need-based aid:* $15,571. *Average indebtedness upon graduation:* $37,780.

APPLYING

Standardized Tests *Required:* SAT or ACT (for admission).

Options: electronic application, early admission, early action, deferred entrance.

Application fee: $50.

Required: essay or personal statement, high school transcript, 1 letter of recommendation, interview, pastoral recommendation and statement of Christian faith. *Recommended:* minimum 3.0 GPA.

Application deadlines: 8/1 (freshmen), rolling (out-of-state freshmen), rolling (transfers), 12/1 (early action).

Notification: continuous until 8/15 (freshmen), continuous until 8/15 (out-of-state freshmen), continuous (transfers), 12/15 (early action).

CONTACT

Miss June Bodoni, Associate Vice President for Enrollment, Gordon College, 255 Grapevine Road, Wenham, MA 01984. *Phone:* 978-867-4218. *Toll-free phone:* 866-464-6736. *Fax:* 978-867-4682. *E-mail:* admissions@gordon.edu.

Hampshire College

Amherst, Massachusetts

http://www.hampshire.edu/

- **Independent** 4-year, founded 1965
- **Small-town** 800-acre campus
- **Endowment** $48.5 million
- **Coed** 1,268 undergraduate students, 100% full-time, 63% women, 37% men
- **Moderately difficult** entrance level, 63% of applicants were admitted

UNDERGRAD STUDENTS

1,268 full-time. 78% are from out of state; 7% Black or African American, non-Hispanic/Latino; 12% Hispanic/Latino; 2% Asian, non-Hispanic/Latino; 0.1% American Indian or Alaska Native, non-Hispanic/Latino; 6% Two or more races, non-Hispanic/Latino; 4% Race/ethnicity unknown; 5% international; 4% transferred in; 84% live on campus.

Freshmen:

Admission: 2,305 applied, 1,448 admitted, 325 enrolled.

Retention: 77% of full-time freshmen returned.

FACULTY

Total: 162, 70% full-time.

Student/faculty ratio: 10:1.

ACADEMICS

Calendar: semesters. *Degree:* bachelor's.

Special study options: advanced placement credit, independent study, internships, off-campus study, services for LD students, student-designed majors, study abroad. *ROTC:* Army (c).

Computers: 205 computers/terminals are available on campus for general student use. Students can access the following: campus intranet, computer help desk, free student e-mail accounts, online (class) grades, online (class) registration, online (class) schedules. Campuswide network is available. 100% of college-owned or -operated housing units are wired for high-speed Internet access. Wireless service is available via entire campus.

Library: Harold F. Johnson Library. *Books:* 125,971 (physical), 194,919 (digital/electronic); *Serial titles:* 753 (physical), 37,716 (digital/electronic); *Databases:* 133. Weekly public service hours: 102; study areas open 24 hours, 5–7 days a week; students can reserve study rooms.

STUDENT LIFE

Housing options: on-campus residence required through senior year; coed, men-only, women-only, special housing for students with disabilities. Campus housing is university owned. Freshman campus housing is guaranteed.

Activities and organizations: drama/theater group, student-run newspaper, radio station, choral group, Red Scare Frisbee, Queer Community Alliance, Excalibur (fantasy/role playing), Sports Coop, Circus Folks Unite.

Athletics Member USCAA. *Intercollegiate sports:* basketball M(c)/W(c), cross-country running M/W, equestrian sports M(c)/W(c), fencing M/W, soccer M/W, ultimate Frisbee M/W. *Intramural sports:* basketball M/W, equestrian sports M(c)/W(c), rock climbing M(c)/W(c), soccer M/W, table tennis M(c)/W(c), ultimate Frisbee M/W.

Campus security: 24-hour emergency response devices and patrols.

Student services: health clinic, personal/psychological counseling, women's center.

COSTS & FINANCIAL AID

Costs (2018–19) *Comprehensive fee:* $63,636 includes full-time tuition ($50,030) and room and board ($13,606). *College room only:* $8520. Room and board charges vary according to board plan. *Payment plan:* installment. *Waivers:* employees or children of employees.

Financial Aid Of all full-time matriculated undergraduates who enrolled in 2016, 997 applied for aid, 860 were judged to have need, 110 had their need fully met. 575 Federal Work-Study jobs (averaging $2900). 253 state and other part-time jobs (averaging $2900). In 2016, 350 non-need-based awards were made. *Average percent of need met:* 93. *Average financial aid package:* $42,326. *Average need-based loan:* $4354. *Average need-based gift aid:* $35,237. *Average non-need-based aid:* $12,652. *Average indebtedness upon graduation:* $21,758.

APPLYING

Options: electronic application, early admission, early decision, early action, deferred entrance.

Required: essay or personal statement, high school transcript, 1 letter of recommendation. *Recommended:* interview.

Application deadlines: 1/15 (freshmen), 3/15 (transfers), 12/1 (early action).

Early decision deadline: 11/15 (for plan 1), 1/1 (for plan 2).

Notification: 4/1 (freshmen), 4/15 (transfers), 12/15 (early decision plan 1), 2/1 (early decision plan 2), 2/1 (early action).

CONTACT

Hampshire College, 893 West Street, Amherst, MA 01002. *Phone:* 413-559-5752. *Toll-free phone:* 877-937-4267. *E-mail:* admissions@hampshire.edu.

Harvard University
Cambridge, Massachusetts
http://www.harvard.edu/

- **Independent** university, founded 1636
- **Urban** 380-acre campus with easy access to Boston
- **Endowment** $37.1 billion
- **Coed** 6,766 undergraduate students, 100% full-time, 48% women, 52% men
- **Most difficult** entrance level, 5% of applicants were admitted

UNDERGRAD STUDENTS
6,764 full-time, 2 part-time. Students come from 55 states and territories; 109 other countries; 84% are from out of state; 8% Black or African American, non-Hispanic/Latino; 11% Hispanic/Latino; 21% Asian, non-Hispanic/Latino; 0.1% Native Hawaiian or other Pacific Islander, non-Hispanic/Latino; 0.2% American Indian or Alaska Native, non-Hispanic/Latino; 7% Two or more races, non-Hispanic/Latino; 2% Race/ethnicity unknown; 11% international; 0.2% transferred in; 98% live on campus.

Freshmen:
Admission: 39,506 applied, 2,037 admitted, 1,685 enrolled. *Average high school GPA:* 4.2. *Test scores:* SAT evidence-based reading and writing scores over 500: 100%; SAT math scores over 500: 100%; ACT scores over 18: 100%; SAT evidence-based reading and writing scores over 600: 99%; SAT math scores over 600: 99%; ACT scores over 24: 100%; SAT evidence-based reading and writing scores over 700: 87%; SAT math scores over 700: 88%; ACT scores over 30: 93%.

Retention: 97% of full-time freshmen returned.

FACULTY
Total: 1,170, 83% full-time, 85% with terminal degrees.
Student/faculty ratio: 6:1.

ACADEMICS
Calendar: semesters. *Degrees:* bachelor's, master's, and doctoral.
Special study options: accelerated degree program, advanced placement credit, double majors, honors programs, independent study, internships, off-campus study, services for LD students, student-designed majors, study abroad, summer session for credit. *ROTC:* Army (b), Navy (b), Air Force (b).
Computers: 605 computers/terminals are available on campus for general student use. Students can access the following: computer help desk, free student e-mail accounts, online (class) grades, online (class) registration, online (class) schedules. Campuswide network is available. 100% of college-owned or -operated housing units are wired for high-speed Internet access. Wireless service is available via entire campus.
Library: Widener Library.

STUDENT LIFE
Housing options: on-campus residence required for freshman year; coed, cooperative, special housing for students with disabilities. Campus housing is university owned. Freshman campus housing is guaranteed.
Activities and organizations: drama/theater group, student-run newspaper, radio and television station, choral group, marching band, Phillips Brooks House Association, Asian-American Association, International Relations Council, Harvard Crimson (newspaper), Harvard/Radcliffe Chorus.
Athletics Member NCAA. All Division I except football (Division I-AA). *Intercollegiate sports:* baseball M, basketball M/W, crew M/W, cross-country running M/W, fencing M/W, field hockey W, golf M/W, ice hockey M/W, lacrosse M/W, rugby W, sailing M/W, skiing (cross-country) M/W, skiing (downhill) M/W, soccer M/W, softball W, squash M/W, swimming and diving M/W, tennis M/W, track and field M/W, volleyball M/W, water polo M/W, wrestling M. *Intramural sports:* archery M(c)/W(c), badminton M(c)/W(c), baseball M(c), basketball M/W, bowling M(c)/W(c), cheerleading M(c)/W(c), cross-country running M/W, fencing M/W, field hockey W(c), golf M(c)/W(c), gymnastics M(c)/W(c), ice hockey M/W, lacrosse M(c)/W(c), rugby M(c), skiing (cross-country) M(c)/W(c), skiing (downhill) M(c)/W(c), soccer M/W, squash M/W, swimming and diving M/W, table tennis M/W, tennis M/W, ultimate Frisbee M/W, volleyball M/W, water polo M(c)/W(c), weight lifting M(c)/W(c), wrestling M(c)/W(c).
Campus security: 24-hour emergency response devices and patrols, late-night transport/escort service, controlled dormitory access, required and optional safety courses.

Student services: health clinic, personal/psychological counseling, women's center.

COSTS & FINANCIAL AID
Costs (2017–18) *Comprehensive fee:* $65,609 includes full-time tuition ($44,990), mandatory fees ($3959), and room and board ($16,660). *College room only:* $10,300. *Payment plans:* tuition prepayment, installment.
Financial Aid Of all full-time matriculated undergraduates who enrolled in 2016, 3,987 applied for aid, 3,675 were judged to have need, 3,675 had their need fully met. 880 Federal Work-Study jobs (averaging $2803). 2,146 state and other part-time jobs (averaging $2872). In 2016, 12 non-need-based awards were made. *Average percent of need met:* 100. *Average financial aid package:* $53,730. *Average need-based loan:* $4270. *Average need-based gift aid:* $50,699. *Average non-need-based aid:* $20,064. *Average indebtedness upon graduation:* $15,114.

APPLYING
Standardized Tests *Required:* SAT or ACT (for admission), SAT Subject Tests (for admission).
Options: electronic application, early admission, early action, deferred entrance.
Application fee: $75.
Required: essay or personal statement, high school transcript. *Recommended:* 2 letters of recommendation, interview.
Application deadlines: 1/1 (freshmen), 3/1 (transfers).
Notification: 4/1 (freshmen), 6/15 (transfers).

CONTACT
Harvard University, Cambridge, MA 02138. *Phone:* 617-495-1551.

Hellenic College
Brookline, Massachusetts
http://www.hchc.edu/

CONTACT
Mr. Gregory Floor, Director of Admissions, Hellenic College, 50 Goddard Avenue, Brookline, MA 02445-7496. *Phone:* 617-850-1285. *Toll-free phone:* 866-424-2338. *Fax:* 617-850-1460. *E-mail:* admissions@ hchc.edu.

Hult International Business School
Cambridge, Massachusetts
http://www.hult.edu/

CONTACT
Hult International Business School, 1 Education Street, Cambridge, MA 02141.

Lasell College
Newton, Massachusetts
http://www.lasell.edu/

- **Independent** comprehensive, founded 1851
- **Suburban** 53-acre campus with easy access to Boston
- **Endowment** $38.0 million
- **Coed** 1,731 undergraduate students, 96% full-time, 64% women, 36% men
- **Moderately difficult** entrance level, 81% of applicants were admitted

UNDERGRAD STUDENTS
1,669 full-time, 62 part-time. Students come from 29 states and territories; 22 other countries; 42% are from out of state; 7% Black or African American, non-Hispanic/Latino; 9% Hispanic/Latino; 2% Asian, non-Hispanic/Latino; 0.1% Native Hawaiian or other Pacific Islander, non-Hispanic/Latino; 0.1% American Indian or Alaska Native, non-Hispanic/Latino; 2% Two or more races, non-Hispanic/Latino; 4% Race/ethnicity unknown; 7% international; 4% transferred in; 74% liveon campus.

Freshmen:
Admission: 3,466 applied, 2,824 admitted, 411 enrolled. *Average high school GPA:* 2.9. *Test scores:* SAT evidence-based reading and writing scores over 500: 77%; SAT math scores over 500: 73%; ACT scores over 18: 78%; SAT evidence-based reading and writing scores over 600: 23%;

SAT math scores over 600: 18%; ACT scores over 24: 23%; SAT evidence-based reading and writing scores over 700: 3%; SAT math scores over 700: 1%; ACT scores over 30: 6%.

Retention: 73% of full-time freshmen returned.

FACULTY
Total: 265, 35% full-time.

Student/faculty ratio: 13:1.

ACADEMICS
Calendar: semesters. *Degrees:* bachelor's and master's.

Special study options: accelerated degree program, advanced placement credit, cooperative education, distance learning, double majors, English as a second language, honors programs, independent study, internships, off-campus study, part-time degree program, services for LD students, student-designed majors, study abroad, summer session for credit.

Unusual degree programs: 3-2 business administration with Lasell College; communication, sport management.

Computers: 219 computers/terminals are available on campus for general student use. Students can access the following: campus intranet, computer help desk, free student e-mail accounts, online (class) grades, online (class) registration, online (class) schedules, online tutoring. Campuswide network is available. 100% of college-owned or -operated housing units are wired for high-speed Internet access. Wireless service is available via entire campus.

Library: Brennan Library. *Books:* 41,761 (physical), 117,808 (digital/electronic); *Serial titles:* 67 (physical), 45,258 (digital/electronic); *Databases:* 86. Weekly public service hours: 83; students can reserve study rooms.

STUDENT LIFE
Housing options: coed, women-only, special housing for students with disabilities. Campus housing is university owned. Freshman campus housing is guaranteed.

Activities and organizations: drama/theater group, student-run newspaper, radio station, choral group, 19851 Chronicle, Campus Activities Board, Hope for Humanity, Lasell College Drama Club, Lasell College Radio (Marathon Monday).

Athletics Member NCAA. All Division III. *Intercollegiate sports:* baseball M, basketball M/W, cross-country running M/W, field hockey W, lacrosse M/W, soccer M/W, softball W, track and field M/W, volleyball M/W. *Intramural sports:* basketball M/W, cheerleading M(c)/W(c), crew M(c)/W(c), rugby M(c)/W(c), skiing (downhill) M(c)/W(c), tennis M(c)/W(c), ultimate Frisbee M(c).

Campus security: 24-hour emergency response devices and patrols, late-night transport/escort service, controlled dormitory access.

Student services: health clinic, personal/psychological counseling.

COSTS & FINANCIAL AID
Costs (2018–19) *Comprehensive fee:* $51,400 includes full-time tuition ($34,700), mandatory fees ($1300), and room and board ($15,400). Part-time tuition: $1155 per credit hour. Part-time tuition and fees vary according to course load. *Required fees:* $325 per term part-time. *Room and board:* Room and board charges vary according to housing facility. *Payment plan:* installment. *Waivers:* children of alumni and employees or children of employees.

Financial Aid Of all full-time matriculated undergraduates who enrolled in 2017, 1,395 applied for aid, 1,303 were judged to have need, 185 had their need fully met. 880 Federal Work-Study jobs (averaging $1860). In 2017, 237 non-need-based awards were made. *Average percent of need met:* 73. *Average financial aid package:* $28,275. *Average need-based loan:* $4240. *Average need-based gift aid:* $23,648. *Average non-need-based aid:* $11,954. *Average indebtedness upon graduation:* $41,455.

APPLYING
Standardized Tests *Required for some:* SAT or ACT (for admission).

Options: electronic application, early action, deferred entrance.

Application fee: $40.

Required: essay or personal statement, high school transcript, 2 letters of recommendation, college preparatory program. *Recommended:* interview.

Application deadlines: 9/1 (freshmen), rolling (transfers), 11/15 (early action).

Notification: continuous until 12/15 (freshmen), continuous (transfers), 12/1 (early action).

CONTACT
Dean James Tweed, Dean of Undergraduate Admission, Lasell College, 1844 Commonwealth Avenue, Newton, MA 02466. *Phone:* 617-243-2225. *Toll-free phone:* 888-LASELL-4. *Fax:* 617-243-2380. *E-mail:* info@lasell.edu.

Lesley University
Cambridge, Massachusetts
http://www.lesley.edu/

- **Independent** comprehensive, founded 1909
- **Urban** campus with easy access to Boston
- **Coed, primarily women** 2,096 undergraduate students, 79% full-time, 77% women, 23% men
- 73% of applicants were admitted

UNDERGRAD STUDENTS
1,653 full-time, 443 part-time. 33% are from out of state; 8% Black or African American, non-Hispanic/Latino; 13% Hispanic/Latino; 5% Asian, non-Hispanic/Latino; 0.1% American Indian or Alaska Native, non-Hispanic/Latino; 4% Two or more races, non-Hispanic/Latino; 5% Race/ethnicity unknown; 3% international; 43% live on campus.

Freshmen:
Admission: 3,165 applied, 2,298 admitted, 383 enrolled. *Average high school GPA:* 3.3. *Test scores:* SAT evidence-based reading and writing scores over 500: 85%; SAT math scores over 500: 74%; ACT scores over 18: 94%; SAT evidence-based reading and writing scores over 600: 40%; SAT math scores over 600: 20%; ACT scores over 24: 55%; SAT evidence-based reading and writing scores over 700: 4%; SAT math scores over 700: 1%; ACT scores over 30: 6%.

Retention: 80% of full-time freshmen returned.

FACULTY
Total: 603, 24% full-time, 39% with terminal degrees.

Student/faculty ratio: 12:1.

ACADEMICS
Calendar: semesters. *Degrees:* certificates, associate, bachelor's, master's, doctoral, post-master's, and postbachelor's certificates.

Special study options: academic remediation for entering students, accelerated degree program, adult/continuing education programs, advanced placement credit, distance learning, double majors, freshman honors college, honors programs, independent study, internships, off-campus study, part-time degree program, services for LD students, student-designed majors, study abroad, summer session for credit.

Computers: Students can access the following: free student e-mail accounts, online (class) registration. Campuswide network is available. Wireless service is available via classrooms, student centers.

Library: Sherrill Library.

STUDENT LIFE
Housing options: coed, women-only. Campus housing is university owned and leased by the school. Freshman applicants given priority for college housing.

Activities and organizations: drama/theater group, student-run newspaper, choral group.

Athletics Member NCAA. All Division III except baseball (Division II). *Intercollegiate sports:* baseball M, basketball M/W, cross-country running M/W, soccer M/W, softball W, volleyball M/W. *Intramural sports:* swimming and diving M/W, tennis M.

Campus security: 24-hour emergency response devices and patrols, late-night transport/escort service, controlled dormitory access.

Student services: health clinic, personal/psychological counseling.

COSTS & FINANCIAL AID
Costs (2018–19) *Comprehensive fee:* $43,830 includes full-time tuition ($27,600) and room and board ($16,230). Full-time tuition and fees vary according to class time, course level, course load, degree level, location, program, and reciprocity agreements. Part-time tuition: $920 per credit hour. *College room only:* $9830. Room and board charges vary according to board plan. *Payment plan:* installment. *Waivers:* employees or children of employees.

Financial Aid Of all full-time matriculated undergraduates who enrolled in 2017, 1,319 applied for aid, 1,145 were judged to have need, 74 had

their need fully met. In 2017, 421 non-need-based awards were made. *Average percent of need met:* 70. *Average financial aid package:* $17,580. *Average need-based loan:* $4685. *Average need-based gift aid:* $12,324. *Average non-need-based aid:* $10,209. *Average indebtedness upon graduation:* $23,000.

APPLYING
Standardized Tests *Required:* SAT or ACT (for admission).

Options: electronic application, early action, deferred entrance.

Required: essay or personal statement, high school transcript. *Recommended:* interview.

Application deadlines: 7/15 (freshmen), rolling (transfers), 12/1 (early action).

Notification: continuous until 1/15 (freshmen), continuous (transfers), 12/23 (early action).

CONTACT
Lesley University, 29 Everett Street, Cambridge, MA 02138-2790. *Phone:* 617-349-8800. *Toll-free phone:* 800-999-1959 Ext. 8800.

Massachusetts College of Art and Design
Boston, Massachusetts
http://www.massart.edu/
- **State-supported** comprehensive, founded 1873, part of Massachusetts Public Higher Education System
- **Urban** 5-acre campus
- **Endowment** $16.0 million
- **Coed** 1,931 undergraduate students, 86% full-time, 70% women, 30% men
- **Moderately difficult** entrance level, 71% of applicants were admitted

UNDERGRAD STUDENTS
1,662 full-time, 269 part-time. Students come from 32 states and territories; 45 other countries; 32% are from out of state; 5% Black or African American, non-Hispanic/Latino; 11% Hispanic/Latino; 8% Asian, non-Hispanic/Latino; 0.1% Native Hawaiian or other Pacific Islander, non-Hispanic/Latino; 0.2% American Indian or Alaska Native, non-Hispanic/Latino; 2% Two or more races, non-Hispanic/Latino; 8% Race/ethnicity unknown; 4% international; 6% transferred in; 41% live on campus.

Freshmen:
Admission: 2,386 applied, 1,686 admitted, 424 enrolled. *Average high school GPA:* 3.5.

Retention: 87% of full-time freshmen returned.

FACULTY
Total: 290, 40% full-time.
Student/faculty ratio: 9:1.

ACADEMICS
Calendar: semesters. *Degrees:* certificates, bachelor's, master's, and postbachelor's certificates.

Special study options: double majors, independent study, internships, off-campus study, part-time degree program, student-designed majors, study abroad, summer session for credit.

Computers: 370 computers/terminals are available on campus for general student use. Students can access the following: campus intranet, computer help desk, free student e-mail accounts, online (class) grades, online (class) registration, online (class) schedules. Campuswide network is available. 100% of college-owned or -operated housing units are wired for high-speed Internet access. Wireless service is available via entire campus.

Library: Morton R. Godine Library. *Books:* 106,885 (physical), 173,498 (digital/electronic); *Databases:* 75.

STUDENT LIFE
Housing options: coed. Campus housing is university owned. Freshman campus housing is guaranteed.

Activities and organizations: drama/theater group, student-run newspaper, radio and television station, choral group, International Students' Club, Design Research Unit, Spectrum, film society, Event Works.

Athletics *Intramural sports:* basketball M/W, cross-country running M/W, field hockey M/W, ice hockey M/W, soccer M/W, softball M/W, table tennis M/W, tennis M/W, volleyball M/W.

Campus security: 24-hour emergency response devices and patrols, late-night transport/escort service, controlled dormitory access, security lighting, self-defense workshops.

Student services: health clinic, personal/psychological counseling, women's center.

COSTS & FINANCIAL AID
Costs (2018–19) *Tuition:* state resident $13,200 full-time; nonresident $36,400 full-time. *Room and board:* $13,500. Room and board charges vary according to board plan and housing facility.

Financial Aid Of all full-time matriculated undergraduates who enrolled in 2017, 1,603 applied for aid, 1,509 were judged to have need. In 2017, 479 non-need-based awards were made. *Average financial aid package:* $10,436. *Average need-based loan:* $4189. *Average need-based gift aid:* $7298. *Average non-need-based aid:* $4245. *Average indebtedness upon graduation:* $26,792.

APPLYING
Options: electronic application, early action, deferred entrance.

Application fee: $70.

Required: essay or personal statement, high school transcript, 2 letters of recommendation, portfolio of 15-20 pieces of artwork completed in the last 2 years. *Recommended:* minimum 3.0 GPA.

Application deadlines: 2/1 (freshmen), 2/1 (transfers), 12/1 (early action).

Notification: 1/5 (early action).

CONTACT
Lauren Wilshusen, Massachusetts College of Art and Design, 621 Huntington Avenue, Boston, MA 02115. *Phone:* 617-879-7222. *Fax:* 617-879-7250. *E-mail:* admissions@massart.edu.

Massachusetts College of Liberal Arts
North Adams, Massachusetts
http://www.mcla.edu/
- **State-supported** comprehensive, founded 1894, part of Massachusetts State University System
- **Small-town** 105-acre campus with easy access to Albany-Schenectady-Troy New York Metro Area
- **Coed** 1,407 undergraduate students, 85% full-time, 62% women, 38% men
- **Moderately difficult** entrance level, 77% of applicants were admitted

UNDERGRAD STUDENTS
1,201 full-time, 206 part-time. Students come from 23 states and territories; 2 other countries; 24% are from out of state; 9% Black or African American, non-Hispanic/Latino; 8% Hispanic/Latino; 2% Asian, non-Hispanic/Latino; 0.1% Native Hawaiian or other Pacific Islander, non-Hispanic/Latino; 0.4% American Indian or Alaska Native, non-Hispanic/Latino; 3% Two or more races, non-Hispanic/Latino; 4% Race/ethnicity unknown; 0.6% international; 10% transferred in; 58% live on campus.

Freshmen:
Admission: 1,947 applied, 1,492 admitted, 289 enrolled. *Average high school GPA:* 3.2. *Test scores:* SAT evidence-based reading and writing scores over 500: 70%; SAT math scores over 500: 75%; ACT scores over 18: 84%; SAT evidence-based reading and writing scores over 600: 21%; SAT math scores over 600: 31%; ACT scores over 24: 36%; SAT evidence-based reading and writing scores over 700: 4%; SAT math scores over 700: 5%; ACT scores over 30: 12%.

Retention: 73% of full-time freshmen returned.

FACULTY
Total: 166, 52% full-time.
Student/faculty ratio: 12:1.

ACADEMICS
Calendar: semesters. *Degrees:* certificates, bachelor's, master's, post-master's, and postbachelor's certificates.

Special study options: academic remediation for entering students, accelerated degree program, adult/continuing education programs, advanced placement credit, cooperative education, distance learning, double majors, honors programs, independent study, internships, off-campus study, part-time degree program, services for LD students, student-designed majors, study abroad, summer session for credit.

Unusual degree programs: 3-2 engineering with University of Massachusetts Amherst; podiatric medicine with the New York School of Podiatric Medicine.

Computers: 140 computers/terminals are available on campus for general student use. Students can access the following: campus intranet, computer help desk, free student e-mail accounts, online (class) grades, online (class) registration, online (class) schedules. Campuswide network is available. 100% of college-owned or -operated housing units are wired for high-speed Internet access. Wireless service is available via entire campus.

Library: Eugene L. Freel Library. *Books:* 130,000 (physical), 205,000 (digital/electronic); *Serial titles:* 1,000 (physical), 43,000 (digital/electronic); *Databases:* 80.

STUDENT LIFE
Housing options: on-campus residence required through junior year; coed, special housing for students with disabilities. Campus housing is university owned. Freshman campus housing is guaranteed.

Activities and organizations: drama/theater group, student-run newspaper, radio and television station, choral group, Student Activities Council, Student Government Association, The Beacon (Student Newspaper), Harlequin-Musical Theatre Company, Dance Company.

Athletics Member NCAA. All Division III. *Intercollegiate sports:* baseball M, basketball M/W, cross-country running M/W, golf M, lacrosse W, soccer M/W, softball W, tennis M/W, volleyball W. *Intramural sports:* basketball M/W, cheerleading W(c), equestrian sports M/W, football M/W, golf M/W, lacrosse M(c), racquetball M/W, rugby M(c)/W(c), skiing (cross-country) M/W, skiing (downhill) M/W, soccer M/W, softball M/W, squash M/W, tennis M/W, ultimate Frisbee M/W, volleyball M/W.

Campus security: 24-hour emergency response devices and patrols, late-night transport/escort service, controlled dormitory access.

Student services: health clinic, personal/psychological counseling, women's center.

COSTS & FINANCIAL AID
Costs (2017–18) *Tuition:* state resident $1030 full-time, $43 per credit part-time; nonresident $9975 full-time, $416 per credit part-time. Full-time tuition and fees vary according to reciprocity agreements. Part-time tuition and fees vary according to course load and reciprocity agreements. *Required fees:* $9105 full-time, $309 per credit part-time. *Room and board:* $10,724. Room and board charges vary according to board plan and housing facility. *Payment plan:* installment. *Waivers:* senior citizens and employees or children of employees.

Financial Aid Of all full-time matriculated undergraduates who enrolled in 2017, 1,115 applied for aid, 953 were judged to have need, 746 had their need fully met. In 2017, 85 non-need-based awards were made. *Average percent of need met:* 76. *Average financial aid package:* $15,345. *Average need-based loan:* $4006. *Average need-based gift aid:* $6475. *Average non-need-based aid:* $3362. *Average indebtedness upon graduation:* $27,883.

APPLYING
Standardized Tests *Required:* SAT or ACT (for admission).

Options: electronic application, early admission, early action, deferred entrance.

Required: essay or personal statement, high school transcript, minimum 3.0 GPA, 1 letter of recommendation. *Required for some:* interview, sliding scale applies (GPA and SAT) if below 3.0.

Application deadlines: rolling (freshmen), rolling (transfers), 12/1 (early action).

Notification: continuous (freshmen), continuous (transfers), 12/15 (early action).

CONTACT
Massachusetts College of Liberal Arts, 375 Church Street, North Adams, MA 01247-4100. *Phone:* 413-662-5410. *Toll-free phone:* 800-989-MCLA.

Massachusetts Institute of Technology
Cambridge, Massachusetts
http://www.mit.edu/

- **Independent** university, founded 1861
- **Urban** 166-acre campus with easy access to Boston
- **Endowment** $14.8 billion
- **Coed** 4,547 undergraduate students, 99% full-time, 46% women, 54% men
- **Most difficult** entrance level, 7% of applicants were admitted

UNDERGRAD STUDENTS
4,510 full-time, 37 part-time. Students come from 55 states and territories; 107 other countries; 90% are from out of state; 6% Black or African American, non-Hispanic/Latino; 14% Hispanic/Latino; 27% Asian, non-Hispanic/Latino; 0.1% American Indian or Alaska Native, non-Hispanic/Latino; 7% Two or more races, non-Hispanic/Latino; 1% Race/ethnicity unknown; 10% international; 0.5% transferred in; 94% live on campus.

Freshmen:
Admission: 20,247 applied, 1,452 admitted, 1,097 enrolled. *Test scores:* SAT evidence-based reading and writing scores over 500: 100%; SAT math scores over 500: 100%; ACT scores over 18: 100%; SAT evidence-based reading and writing scores over 600: 100%; SAT math scores over 600: 100%; ACT scores over 24: 100%; SAT evidence-based reading and writing scores over 700: 88%; SAT math scores over 700: 99%; ACT scores over 30: 99%.
Retention: 99% of full-time freshmen returned.

FACULTY
Total: 1,576, 81% full-time, 88% with terminal degrees.
Student/faculty ratio: 3:1.

ACADEMICS
Calendar: 4-1-4. *Degrees:* bachelor's, master's, and doctoral.
Special study options: advanced placement credit, cooperative education, double majors, English as a second language, independent study, internships, off-campus study, services for LD students, study abroad. *ROTC:* Army (b), Navy (b), Air Force (b).
Computers: 1,050 computers/terminals and 50,000 ports are available on campus for general student use. Students can access the following: campus intranet, computer help desk, free student e-mail accounts, online (class) grades, online (class) registration, online (class) schedules. Campuswide network is available. 100% of college-owned or -operated housing units are wired for high-speed Internet access. Wireless service is available via entire campus.
Library: MIT Libraries plus 5 others. *Books:* 1.7 million (physical), 698,043 (digital/electronic); *Serial titles:* 51,946 (physical), 55,502 (digital/electronic); *Databases:* 351. Weekly public service hours: 95; study areas open 24 hours, 5–7 days a week; students can reserve study rooms.

STUDENT LIFE
Housing options: on-campus residence required for freshman year; coed, women-only, cooperative, special housing for students with disabilities. Campus housing is university owned. Freshman campus housing is guaranteed.

Activities and organizations: drama/theater group, student-run newspaper, radio and television station, choral group, marching band, Educational Studies Program, Dance Troupe, Science Fiction Society, The Tech (student newspaper), Anime Club, national fraternities, national sororities.

Athletics Member NCAA. All Division III except men's and women's crew (Division I), men's and women's rowing (Division I). *Intercollegiate sports:* baseball M, basketball M/W, crew M/W, cross-country running M/W, fencing M/W, field hockey W, football M, lacrosse M/W, riflery M/W, rowing M/W, sailing M/W, soccer M/W, softball W, squash M, swimming and diving M/W, tennis M/W, track and field M/W, volleyball M/W, water polo M. *Intramural sports:* archery M(c)/W(c), badminton M/W, basketball M/W, cheerleading M(c)/W(c), crew M(c)/W(c), golf M(c)/W(c), gymnastics M(c)/W(c), ice hockey M/W, rowing M(c)/W(c), rugby M(c)/W(c), soccer M/W, softball M/W, table tennis M/W, tennis M/W, triathlon M(c)/W(c), ultimate Frisbee M/W, volleyball M/W, water polo M/W, wrestling M(c).

Campus security: 24-hour emergency response devices and patrols, late-night transport/escort service, controlled dormitory access.

Student services: health clinic, personal/psychological counseling.

COSTS & FINANCIAL AID
Costs (2018–19) *Comprehensive fee:* $67,342 includes full-time tuition ($51,520), mandatory fees ($312), and room and board ($15,510). Part-time tuition and fees vary according to course load. *College room only:* $9890. Room and board charges vary according to board plan and housing facility. *Payment plan:* installment. *Waivers:* employees or children of employees.

Financial Aid Of all full-time matriculated undergraduates who enrolled in 2016, 2,912 applied for aid, 2,591 were judged to have need, 2,591 had their need fully met. 567 Federal Work-Study jobs (averaging $2365). 1,331 state and other part-time jobs (averaging $2696). *Average percent of need met:* 100. *Average financial aid package:* $47,451. *Average need-based loan:* $3591. *Average need-based gift aid:* $45,570. *Average indebtedness upon graduation:* $20,048. *Financial aid deadline:* 2/15.

APPLYING
Standardized Tests *Required:* SAT or ACT (for admission), SAT Subject Tests (for admission).

Options: electronic application, early admission, early action, deferred entrance.

Application fee: $75.

Required: essay or personal statement, high school transcript, 2 letters of recommendation. *Recommended:* interview.

Application deadlines: 1/1 (freshmen), 2/15 (transfers), 11/1 (early action).

Notification: 3/20 (freshmen), 5/1 (transfers), 12/20 (early action).

CONTACT
Admissions Counselors, Massachusetts Institute of Technology, 77 Massachusetts Avenue, Building 3-108, Cambridge, MA 02139-4307. *Phone:* 617-253-3400. *Fax:* 617-258-8304. *E-mail:* admissions@mit.edu.

Massachusetts Maritime Academy
Buzzards Bay, Massachusetts
http://www.maritime.edu/

- **State-supported** comprehensive, founded 1891, part of Massachusetts State University System
- **Small-town** 54-acre campus with easy access to Boston, Providence
- **Coed** 1,688 undergraduate students, 95% full-time, 13% women, 87% men
- **Moderately difficult** entrance level, 83% of applicants were admitted

UNDERGRAD STUDENTS
1,607 full-time, 81 part-time. Students come from 32 states and territories; 3 other countries; 20% are from out of state; 1% Black or African American, non-Hispanic/Latino; 3% Hispanic/Latino; 1% Asian, non-Hispanic/Latino; 0.1% American Indian or Alaska Native, non-Hispanic/Latino; 3% Two or more races, non-Hispanic/Latino; 3% Race/ethnicity unknown; 0.9% international; 2% transferred in; 97% live on campus.

Freshmen:
Admission: 838 applied, 697 admitted, 392 enrolled. *Average high school GPA:* 3.2. *Test scores:* SAT evidence-based reading and writing scores over 500: 86%; SAT math scores over 500: 90%; ACT scores over 18: 97%; SAT evidence-based reading and writing scores over 600: 28%; SAT math scores over 600: 28%; ACT scores over 24: 47%; SAT evidence-based reading and writing scores over 700: 2%; SAT math scores over 700: 4%; ACT scores over 30: 7%.

Retention: 88% of full-time freshmen returned.

FACULTY
Total: 143, 61% full-time, 43% with terminal degrees.
Student/faculty ratio: 16:1.

ACADEMICS
Calendar: 4-1-4 plus sea term. *Degrees:* bachelor's and master's.

Special study options: advanced placement credit, cooperative education, distance learning, double majors, independent study, internships, off-campus study, part-time degree program, services for LD students, study abroad, summer session for credit. *ROTC:* Army (c).

Computers: 130 computers/terminals and 1,800 ports are available on campus for general student use. Students can access the following: computer help desk, free student e-mail accounts, online (class) grades, online (class) registration, online (class) schedules, course-supported e-learning. Campuswide network is available. 100% of college-owned or -operated housing units are wired for high-speed Internet access. Wireless service is available via entire campus.
Library: American Bureau of Shipping Information Commons plus 1 other.

STUDENT LIFE
Housing options: on-campus residence required through senior year; coed. Campus housing is university owned and leased by the school. Freshman campus housing is guaranteed.

Activities and organizations: drama/theater group, marching band, Student Government, Intramurals, Regimental Leadership, Band/Honor Guard, NCAA Division 3 Athletics.

Athletics Member NCAA. All Division III. *Intercollegiate sports:* baseball M, crew M/W, cross-country running M/W, football M, lacrosse M/W, sailing M/W, soccer M/W, softball W, track and field M/W, volleyball W. *Intramural sports:* baseball M(c)/W(c), basketball M/W, football M/W, golf M(c)/W(c), ice hockey M(c)/W(c), lacrosse M(c)/W(c), rock climbing M(c)/W(c), rugby M(c)/W(c), soccer M/W, softball M/W, swimming and diving M(c)/W(c), weight lifting M(c)/W(c).

Campus security: 24-hour emergency response devices and patrols, late-night transport/escort service, controlled dormitory access.

Student services: health clinic, personal/psychological counseling, women's center.

COSTS & FINANCIAL AID
Costs (2017–18) *Tuition:* state resident $1714 full-time, $71 per credit part-time; nonresident $19,140 full-time, $798 per credit part-time. Full-time tuition and fees vary according to program and reciprocity agreements. Part-time tuition and fees vary according to program and reciprocity agreements. *Required fees:* $6684 full-time, $267 per credit part-time. *Room and board:* $12,306; room only: $7340. *Payment plan:* installment. *Waivers:* employees or children of employees.

Financial Aid Of all full-time matriculated undergraduates who enrolled in 2016, 1,350 applied for aid, 946 were judged to have need, 321 had their need fully met. 244 Federal Work-Study jobs (averaging $1490). In 2016, 103 non-need-based awards were made. *Average percent of need met:* 77. *Average financial aid package:* $15,186. *Average need-based loan:* $4165. *Average need-based gift aid:* $9929. *Average non-need-based aid:* $3160. *Average indebtedness upon graduation:* $37,414.

APPLYING
Standardized Tests *Required:* SAT or ACT (for admission).

Options: electronic application, early action, deferred entrance.

Application fee: $50.

Required: essay or personal statement, high school transcript, minimum 2.0 GPA, 2 letters of recommendation, minimum college GPA 2.5 if transferring 12-23 credits, minimum college GPA 2.0 for more than 24 transferable credits. *Recommended:* interview.

Application deadlines: rolling (freshmen), rolling (out-of-state freshmen), rolling (transfers), 11/1 (early action).

Notification: continuous (freshmen), continuous (out-of-state freshmen), continuous (transfers), 12/31 (early action).

CONTACT
Mr. Joshua Tefft, Director of Admissions, Massachusetts Maritime Academy, 101 Academy Drive, Flanagan Hall, Buzzards Bay, MA 02532. *Phone:* 508-830-6687. *Toll-free phone:* 800-544-3411. *E-mail:* jtefft@maritime.edu.

MCPHS University
Boston, Massachusetts
http://www.mcphs.edu/

- **Independent** university, founded 1823
- **Urban** 3-acre campus
- **Endowment** $847.8 million
- **Coed** 3,882 undergraduate students, 93% full-time, 71% women, 29% men
- 84% of applicants were admitted

UNDERGRAD STUDENTS

3,624 full-time, 258 part-time. Students come from 42 states and territories; 52 other countries; 40% are from out of state; 7% Black or African American, non-Hispanic/Latino; 7% Hispanic/Latino; 22% Asian, non-Hispanic/Latino; 0.1% Native Hawaiian or other Pacific Islander, non-Hispanic/Latino; 0.2% American Indian or Alaska Native, non-Hispanic/Latino; 2% Two or more races, non-Hispanic/Latino; 7% Race/ethnicity unknown; 15% international; 7% transferred in.

Freshmen:
Admission: 5,526 applied, 4,634 admitted, 769 enrolled. *Average high school GPA:* 3.5.
Retention: 82% of full-time freshmen returned.

FACULTY
Total: 738, 42% full-time.

ACADEMICS
Calendar: semesters. *Degrees:* certificates, bachelor's, master's, doctoral, post-master's, and postbachelor's certificates.

Special study options: accelerated degree program, adult/continuing education programs, advanced placement credit, cooperative education, distance learning, double majors, independent study, internships, off-campus study, part-time degree program, services for LD students, study abroad, summer session for credit.

Computers: 507 computers/terminals are available on campus for general student use. Students can access the following: computer help desk, free student e-mail accounts, online (class) grades, online (class) registration, online (class) schedules. Campuswide network is available. 100% of college-owned or -operated housing units are wired for high-speed Internet access. Wireless service is available via entire campus.
Library: Henrietta DeBenedictis Library plus 2 others.

STUDENT LIFE
Housing options: coed, special housing for students with disabilities. Campus housing is university owned, leased by the school and is provided by a third party. Freshman campus housing is guaranteed.

Activities and organizations: drama/theater group, student-run newspaper, choral group, Residence Hall Council, Vietnamese Student Association, Student Government Association, Campus Activities Board, Student Indian Organization, national fraternities.

Athletics *Intramural sports:* basketball M/W, bowling M/W, cross-country running M/W, field hockey M/W, football M/W, racquetball M/W, soccer M/W, softball M/W, tennis M/W, ultimate Frisbee M/W, volleyball M/W.

Campus security: 24-hour emergency response devices and patrols, late-night transport/escort service, controlled dormitory access, electronically operated academic area entrances, security guards at entrance.

Student services: health clinic, personal/psychological counseling.

COSTS & FINANCIAL AID
Costs (2018–19) *Comprehensive fee:* $49,105 includes full-time tuition ($31,600), mandatory fees ($1105), and room and board ($16,400). Full-time tuition and fees vary according to course load, degree level, location, program, and student level. *College room only:* $13,126. Room and board charges vary according to board plan, housing facility, and location. *Payment plan:* installment. *Waivers:* employees or children of employees.

Financial Aid Of all full-time matriculated undergraduates who enrolled in 2017, 2,640 applied for aid, 2,467 were judged to have need, 834 had their need fully met. In 2017, 885 non-need-based awards were made. *Average percent of need met:* 21. *Average financial aid package:* $8116. *Average need-based loan:* $2941. *Average need-based gift aid:* $5748. *Average non-need-based aid:* $6122. *Average indebtedness upon graduation:* $58,012.

APPLYING
Standardized Tests *Required:* SAT or ACT (for admission).

Options: electronic application, early action, deferred entrance.

Required: essay or personal statement, 1 letter of recommendation. *Required for some:* high school transcript, interview.

Application deadlines: rolling (freshmen), 2/1 (transfers), 11/1 (early action).

Notification: continuous until 2/15 (freshmen), continuous (transfers), 12/1 (early action).

CONTACT
Giselle Colon, Visit Concierge, MCPHS University, 179 Longwood Avenue, Boston, MA 02115. *Phone:* 617-732-2744. *Fax:* 617-732-2118. *E-mail:* admissions@mcphs.edu.

Merrimack College
North Andover, Massachusetts
http://www.merrimack.edu/
- **Independent Roman Catholic** comprehensive, founded 1947
- **Suburban** 220-acre campus with easy access to Boston
- **Endowment** $54.4 million
- **Coed** 3,515 undergraduate students, 95% full-time, 51% women, 49% men
- **Moderately difficult** entrance level, 82% of applicants were admitted

UNDERGRAD STUDENTS
3,346 full-time, 169 part-time. Students come from 34 states and territories; 27 other countries; 29% are from out of state; 3% Black or African American, non-Hispanic/Latino; 7% Hispanic/Latino; 1% Asian, non-Hispanic/Latino; 0.1% Native Hawaiian or other Pacific Islander, non-Hispanic/Latino; 0.1% American Indian or Alaska Native, non-Hispanic/Latino; 1% Two or more races, non-Hispanic/Latino; 8% Race/ethnicity unknown; 2% international; 3% transferred in; 70% live on campus.

Freshmen:
Admission: 8,656 applied, 7,058 admitted, 855 enrolled. *Average high school GPA:* 3.1.
Retention: 80% of full-time freshmen returned.

FACULTY
Total: 429, 43% full-time.
Student/faculty ratio: 14:1.

ACADEMICS
Calendar: semesters. *Degrees:* bachelor's, master's, and post-master's certificates.

Special study options: academic remediation for entering students, accelerated degree program, adult/continuing education programs, advanced placement credit, cooperative education, double majors, honors programs, independent study, internships, off-campus study, part-time degree program, services for LD students, student-designed majors, study abroad, summer session for credit. *ROTC:* Air Force (c).

Computers: Students can access the following: campus intranet, computer help desk, free student e-mail accounts, online (class) grades, online (class) registration, online (class) schedules. Campuswide network is available. 100% of college-owned or -operated housing units are wired for high-speed Internet access. Wireless service is available via entire campus.
Library: McQuade Library.

STUDENT LIFE
Housing options: coed, special housing for students with disabilities. Campus housing is university owned and leased by the school. Freshman campus housing is guaranteed.

Activities and organizations: drama/theater group, student-run newspaper, radio and television station, choral group, national fraternities, national sororities.

Athletics Member NCAA. All Division II except men's and women's ice hockey (Division I). *Intercollegiate sports:* baseball M(s), basketball M(s)/W(s), crew W(s), cross-country running M(s)/W(s), field hockey W(s), football M(s), golf W(s), ice hockey M(s)/W(s), lacrosse M(s)/W(s), soccer M(s)/W(s), softball W(s), swimming and diving W(s), tennis M(s)/W(s), track and field M(s)/W(s), volleyball W(s). *Intramural sports:* badminton M/W, baseball M(c), basketball M/W, cheerleading W(c), cross-country running M(c)/W(c), golf M(c), gymnastics W(c), ice hockey M(c)/W(c), lacrosse M(c)/W(c), rugby M(c)/W(c), soccer M(c)/W, softball M/W(c), ultimate Frisbee M(c)/W(c), volleyball M/W.

Campus security: 24-hour emergency response devices and patrols, late-night transport/escort service, controlled dormitory access, staffed dorm entrances.

Student services: health clinic, personal/psychological counseling.

COSTS & FINANCIAL AID
Costs (2017–18) *Comprehensive fee:* $55,415 includes full-time tuition ($37,910), mandatory fees ($2280), and room and board ($15,225). Full-

time tuition and fees vary according to degree level. Part-time tuition: $1360 per credit. Part-time tuition and fees vary according to class time, course load, and degree level. *Room and board:* Room and board charges vary according to board plan and housing facility. *Payment plan:* installment. *Waivers:* senior citizens and employees or children of employees.

Financial Aid Of all full-time matriculated undergraduates who enrolled in 2017, 2,656 applied for aid, 2,379 were judged to have need, 259 had their need fully met. In 2017, 765 non-need-based awards were made. *Average percent of need met:* 63. *Average financial aid package:* $23,808. *Average need-based loan:* $4436. *Average need-based gift aid:* $20,182. *Average non-need-based aid:* $13,184.

APPLYING

Options: electronic application, early admission, early decision, early action, deferred entrance.

Required: essay or personal statement, high school transcript, 1 letter of recommendation, first quarter senior grades. *Required for some:* interview. *Recommended:* interview.

Application deadlines: 2/15 (freshmen), 8/25 (transfers), 1/15 (early action).

Early decision deadline: 11/15.

Notification: continuous until 3/15 (freshmen), continuous (transfers), 12/15 (early decision), 2/15 (early action).

CONTACT

Admissions Office, Merrimack College, 510 Turnpike St, North Andover, MA 01845. *Phone:* 978-837-5100. *Fax:* 978-837-5133. *E-mail:* admission@merrimack.edu.

Montserrat College of Art

Beverly, Massachusetts

http://www.montserrat.edu/

CONTACT

Mr. Jeffrey Newell, Director of Admissions, Montserrat College of Art, 23 Essex Street, Beverly, MA 01915. *Phone:* 978-921-4242 Ext. 1152. *Toll-free phone:* 800-836-0487. *Fax:* 978-921-4241. *E-mail:* jeffrey.newell@montserrat.edu.

Mount Holyoke College

South Hadley, Massachusetts

http://www.mtholyoke.edu/

- **Independent** comprehensive, founded 1837
- **Small-town** 800-acre campus with easy access to Springfield
- **Endowment** $729.4 million
- **Women only** 2,210 undergraduate students, 98% full-time
- **Very difficult** entrance level, 51% of applicants were admitted

UNDERGRAD STUDENTS

2,161 full-time, 49 part-time. Students come from 46 states and territories; 57 other countries; 53% are from out of state; 5% Black or African American, non-Hispanic/Latino; 7% Hispanic/Latino; 10% Asian, non-Hispanic/Latino; 0.2% American Indian or Alaska Native, non-Hispanic/Latino; 4% Two or more races, non-Hispanic/Latino; 1% Race/ethnicity unknown; 27% international; 2% transferred in; 95% live on campus.

Freshmen:

Admission: 3,446 applied, 1,752 admitted, 529 enrolled. *Average high school GPA:* 3.8.

Retention: 91% of full-time freshmen returned.

FACULTY

Total: 264, 81% full-time, 91% with terminal degrees.

Student/faculty ratio: 9:1.

ACADEMICS

Calendar: semesters. *Degrees:* bachelor's, master's, and postbachelor's certificates.

Special study options: adult/continuing education programs, advanced placement credit, distance learning, double majors, independent study, internships, off-campus study, part-time degree program, services for LD students, student-designed majors, study abroad, summer session for credit. *ROTC:* Army (c), Air Force (c).

Unusual degree programs: 3-2 engineering with Dartmouth College, University of Massachusetts, California Institute of Technology.

Computers: 392 computers/terminals and 3,000 ports are available on campus for general student use. Students can access the following: campus intranet, computer help desk, free student e-mail accounts, online (class) grades, online (class) registration, online (class) schedules, personal Web pages. Campuswide network is available. 100% of college-owned or -operated housing units are wired for high-speed Internet access. Wireless service is available via classrooms, computer centers, computer labs, dorm rooms, learning centers, libraries, student centers.

Library: Williston Memorial Library plus 2 others. *Books:* 662,010 (physical), 853,290 (digital/electronic); *Serial titles:* 603 (physical), 8,098 (digital/electronic); *Databases:* 227. Weekly public service hours: 115; students can reserve study rooms.

STUDENT LIFE

Housing options: on-campus residence required through senior year; women-only, special housing for students with disabilities. Campus housing is university owned. Freshman campus housing is guaranteed.

Activities and organizations: drama/theater group, student-run newspaper, radio station, choral group, Student Government Association, C.A.U.S.E. (Creating Awareness and Unity for Social Equality), MHC Outing Club, Mount Holyoke Symphony Orchestra, Mount Holyoke News.

Athletics Member NCAA. All Division III. *Intercollegiate sports:* basketball W, crew W, cross-country running W, equestrian sports W, field hockey W, golf W, lacrosse W, soccer W, squash W, swimming and diving W, tennis W, track and field W, volleyball W. *Intramural sports:* equestrian sports W(c), fencing W(c), ice hockey W(c), rugby W(c), ultimate Frisbee W(c).

Campus security: 24-hour emergency response devices and patrols, student patrols, late-night transport/escort service, controlled dormitory access, police officers on-campus.

Student services: health clinic, personal/psychological counseling.

COSTS & FINANCIAL AID

Costs (2018–19) *Comprehensive fee:* $64,658 includes full-time tuition ($49,780), mandatory fees ($218), and room and board ($14,660). *College room only:* $7160. *Payment plan:* installment. *Waivers:* employees or children of employees.

Financial Aid Of all full-time matriculated undergraduates who enrolled in 2017, 1,551 applied for aid, 1,420 were judged to have need, 1,420 had their need fully met. 826 Federal Work-Study jobs (averaging $2123). 325 state and other part-time jobs (averaging $2135). In 2017, 282 non-need-based awards were made. *Average percent of need met:* 100. *Average financial aid package:* $40,769. *Average need-based loan:* $4595. *Average need-based gift aid:* $35,067. *Average non-need-based aid:* $21,064. *Average indebtedness upon graduation:* $23,872. *Financial aid deadline:* 3/1.

APPLYING

Options: electronic application, early admission, early decision, deferred entrance.

Application fee: $60.

Required: essay or personal statement, high school transcript, 2 letters of recommendation. *Recommended:* interview.

Application deadlines: 1/15 (freshmen), 3/1 (transfers).

Early decision deadline: 11/15 (for plan 1), 1/1 (for plan 2).

Notification: 4/1 (freshmen), continuous until 4/15 (transfers), 1/1 (early decision plan 1), 2/1 (early decision plan 2).

CONTACT

Ms. Gail Berson, Vice President of Enrollment and Dean of Admission, Mount Holyoke College, Office of Admission, Mount Holyoke College, South Hadley, MA 01075. *Phone:* 413-538-2023. *Fax:* 413-538-2409. *E-mail:* admission@mtholyoke.edu.

Newbury College

Brookline, Massachusetts

http://www.newbury.edu/

CONTACT

Mr. Salvadore Liberto, Vice President of Enrollment Management, Newbury College, 129 Fisher Avenue, Brookline, MA 02445-5796.

Phone: 617-730-7066. *Toll-free phone:* 800-NEWBURY. *Fax:* 617-731-9618. *E-mail:* salvadore.liberto@newbury.edu.

New England College of Business and Finance

Boston, Massachusetts
http://necb.edu/

CONTACT
New England College of Business and Finance, 10 High Street, Suite 204, Boston, MA 02111-2645. *Phone:* 617-951-2350 Ext. 6912. *Toll-free phone:* 800-997-1673.

New England Conservatory of Music

Boston, Massachusetts
http://necmusic.edu/

CONTACT
New England Conservatory of Music, 290 Huntington Avenue, Boston, MA 02115-5000. *Phone:* 617-585-1103.

Nichols College

Dudley, Massachusetts
http://www.nichols.edu/
- **Independent** comprehensive, founded 1815
- **Small-town** 250-acre campus with easy access to Boston
- **Endowment** $13.7 million
- **Coed** 1,301 undergraduate students, 93% full-time, 37% women, 63% men

UNDERGRAD STUDENTS
1,211 full-time, 90 part-time. Students come from 25 states and territories; 11 other countries; 37% are from out of state; 7% Black or African American, non-Hispanic/Latino; 8% Hispanic/Latino; 1% Asian, non-Hispanic/Latino; 4% Two or more races, non-Hispanic/Latino; 2% international; 3% transferred in; 77% live on campus.

Freshmen:
Admission: 373 enrolled. *Average high school GPA:* 2.9. *Test scores:* ACT scores over 18: 76%; ACT scores over 24: 19%.

Retention: 76% of full-time freshmen returned.

FACULTY
Total: 108, 50% full-time, 40% with terminal degrees.
Student/faculty ratio: 17:1.

ACADEMICS
Calendar: semesters. *Degrees:* bachelor's and master's.

Special study options: accelerated degree program, adult/continuing education programs, advanced placement credit, cooperative education, distance learning, double majors, honors programs, independent study, internships, off-campus study, part-time degree program, services for LD students, study abroad, summer session for credit.

Unusual degree programs: 3-2 business administration.

Computers: 154 computers/terminals are available on campus for general student use. Students can access the following: campus intranet, computer help desk, free student e-mail accounts, online (class) grades, online (class) registration, online (class) schedules. Campuswide network is available. 100% of college-owned or -operated housing units are wired for high-speed Internet access. Wireless service is available via entire campus.
Library: Conant Library. *Books:* 28,154 (physical), 144,048 (digital/electronic); *Databases:* 35. Weekly public service hours: 102; study areas open 24 hours, 5–7 days a week; students can reserve study rooms.

STUDENT LIFE
Housing options: coed, men-only, women-only, special housing for students with disabilities. Campus housing is university owned. Freshman campus housing is guaranteed.

Activities and organizations: student-run radio station, Campus Activities Board, Institute for Women's Leadership, Student Government Association, Student Athletic Advisory Council, Student Alumni Association.

Athletics Member NCAA. All Division III. *Intercollegiate sports:* baseball M, basketball M/W, cheerleading M(c)/W(c), cross-country running M/W, field hockey W, football M, golf M, ice hockey M/W, lacrosse M/W, racquetball M(c)/W(c), rugby M(c)/W(c), soccer M/W, softball W, tennis M/W, track and field M/W, volleyball M/W. *Intramural sports:* basketball M/W, bowling M/W, cheerleading M/W, football M/W, ice hockey M(c)/W(c), racquetball M(c)/W(c), rock climbing M/W, sand volleyball M/W, skiing (downhill) M/W, soccer M/W, volleyball M/W.

Campus security: 24-hour emergency response devices and patrols, student patrols, late-night transport/escort service, controlled dormitory access.

Student services: health clinic, personal/psychological counseling, women's center.

COSTS & FINANCIAL AID
Costs (2018–19) *Comprehensive fee:* $47,800 includes full-time tuition ($33,600), mandatory fees ($400), and room and board ($13,800). Part-time tuition: $1120 per credit. Part-time tuition and fees vary according to class time, course load, and location. *Required fees:* $200 per term part-time. *Room and board:* Room and board charges vary according to housing facility. *Payment plan:* installment. *Waivers:* employees or children of employees.

Financial Aid Of all full-time matriculated undergraduates who enrolled in 2017, 1,044 applied for aid, 909 were judged to have need, 233 had their need fully met. 683 Federal Work-Study jobs (averaging $2336). In 2017, 302 non-need-based awards were made. *Average percent of need met:* 81. *Average financial aid package:* $30,653. *Average need-based loan:* $4346. *Average need-based gift aid:* $19,407. *Average non-need-based aid:* $17,915. *Average indebtedness upon graduation:* $34,873.

APPLYING
Standardized Tests *Required for some:* SAT or ACT (for admission).

Required: essay or personal statement, high school transcript, 1 letter of recommendation. *Required for some:* interview. *Recommended:* 2 letters of recommendation.

CONTACT
Mr. Paul Brower, Assistant Dean for Enrollment, Nichols College, 129 Center Road, Dudley, MA 01571. *Phone:* 508-213-2371. *Toll-free phone:* 800-470-3379. *E-mail:* paul.brower@nichols.edu.

Northeastern University

Boston, Massachusetts
http://www.northeastern.edu/
- **Independent** university, founded 1898
- **Urban** 73-acre campus
- **Coed** 18,269 undergraduate students, 100% full-time, 51% women, 49% men
- **Very difficult** entrance level, 27% of applicants were admitted

UNDERGRAD STUDENTS
18,230 full-time, 39 part-time. Students come from 124 other countries; 73% are from out of state; 4% Black or African American, non-Hispanic/Latino; 8% Hispanic/Latino; 13% Asian, non-Hispanic/Latino; 0.0% American Indian or Alaska Native, non-Hispanic/Latino; 4% Two or more races, non-Hispanic/Latino; 6% Race/ethnicity unknown; 18% international; 2% transferred in; 49% live on campus.

Freshmen:
Admission: 54,209 applied, 14,876 admitted, 3,108 enrolled. *Test scores:* SAT evidence-based reading and writing scores over 500: 98%; SAT math scores over 500: 100%; ACT scores over 18: 100%; SAT evidence-based reading and writing scores over 600: 92%; SAT math scores over 600: 94%; ACT scores over 24: 99%; SAT evidence-based reading and writing scores over 700: 65%; SAT math scores over 700: 72%; ACT scores over 30: 94%.

Retention: 97% of full-time freshmen returned.

FACULTY
Total: 1,743, 75% full-time, 84% with terminal degrees.
Student/faculty ratio: 14:1.

ACADEMICS
Calendar: semesters. *Degrees:* bachelor's, master's, doctoral, and post-master's certificates.

Special study options: accelerated degree program, cooperative education, double majors, honors programs, independent study, internships, off-campus study, services for LD students, student-designed majors, study abroad, summer session for credit. *ROTC:* Army (b), Navy (c), Air Force (c).

Computers: Students can access the following: campus intranet, computer help desk, free student e-mail accounts, online (class) grades, online (class) registration, online (class) schedules. Campuswide network is available. 100% of college-owned or -operated housing units are wired for high-speed Internet access. Wireless service is available via entire campus.

Library: Snell Library plus 3 others. *Books:* 530,566 (physical), 589,334 (digital/electronic). Study areas open 24 hours, 5–7 days a week; students can reserve study rooms.

STUDENT LIFE

Housing options: on-campus residence required through sophomore year; coed. Campus housing is university owned and leased by the school. Freshman campus housing is guaranteed.

Activities and organizations: drama/theater group, student-run newspaper, radio and television station, choral group, Student Government Association, Council for University Programs, Resident Student Association, Downhillers Ski and Snowboard Club, Northeastern University Huskiers and Outing Club, national fraternities, national sororities.

Athletics Member NCAA. All Division I. *Intercollegiate sports:* baseball M, basketball M/W, cross-country running M/W, field hockey W, ice hockey M/W, rowing M/W, soccer M/W, swimming and diving W, track and field M/W, volleyball W. *Intramural sports:* basketball M(c)/W(c), ice hockey M(c)/W(c), sand volleyball M(c)/W(c), soccer M(c)/W(c), volleyball M(c)/W(c).

Campus security: 24-hour emergency response devices and patrols, student patrols, late-night transport/escort service, controlled dormitory access, public safety website.

Student services: health clinic, personal/psychological counseling.

COSTS & FINANCIAL AID

Costs (2017–18) *Comprehensive fee:* $65,737 includes full-time tuition ($48,560), mandatory fees ($937), and room and board ($16,240). *College room only:* $8680. Room and board charges vary according to board plan and housing facility. *Payment plan:* installment. *Waivers:* employees or children of employees.

Financial Aid Of all full-time matriculated undergraduates who enrolled in 2016, 8,632 applied for aid, 6,721 were judged to have need, 2,516 had their need fully met. In 2016, 4248 non-need-based awards were made. *Average percent of need met:* 86. *Average financial aid package:* $31,140. *Average need-based loan:* $4958. *Average need-based gift aid:* $27,534. *Average non-need-based aid:* $15,579.

APPLYING

Standardized Tests *Required:* SAT or ACT (for admission).

Options: electronic application, early admission, early decision, early action, deferred entrance.

Application fee: $75.

Application deadlines: 1/1 (freshmen), 4/1 (transfers), 11/1 (early action).

Early decision deadline: 11/1 (for plan 1), 1/1 (for plan 2).

Notification: continuous until 4/1 (freshmen), continuous (transfers), 12/15 (early decision plan 1), 2/15 (early decision plan 2), 12/31 (early action).

CONTACT

Northeastern University, 360 Huntington Avenue, Boston, MA 02115. *Phone:* 617-373-2200. *E-mail:* admissions@northeastern.edu.

See below for display ad and page 1366 for the College Close-Up.

Northpoint Bible College
Haverhill, Massachusetts
http://northpoint.edu/

CONTACT
Helen Brouillette, Admissions Director, Northpoint Bible College, 320 South Main Street, Haverhill, MA 01835. *Phone:* 800-356-4014. *Toll-free phone:* 800-356-4014. *E-mail:* admissions@zbc.edu.

URBAN SPACES

Northeastern University

BOSTON, MASSACHUSETTS

GREEN OASIS

Pine Manor College

Chestnut Hill, Massachusetts

http://www.pmc.edu/

- **Independent** comprehensive, founded 1911
- **Suburban** 50-acre campus
- **Endowment** $11.0 million
- **Coed** 419 undergraduate students, 100% full-time, 48% women, 52% men
- **Moderately difficult** entrance level, 51% of applicants were admitted

UNDERGRAD STUDENTS

417 full-time, 2 part-time. Students come from 25 states and territories; 16 other countries; 52% are from out of state; 24% Black or African American, non-Hispanic/Latino; 15% Hispanic/Latino; 2% Asian, non-Hispanic/Latino; 1% American Indian or Alaska Native, non-Hispanic/Latino; 5% Two or more races, non-Hispanic/Latino; 7% Race/ethnicity unknown; 40% international; 5% transferred in.

Freshmen:
Admission: 588 applied, 301 admitted, 76 enrolled. *Average high school GPA:* 2.6.
Retention: 59% of full-time freshmen returned.

FACULTY

Total: 56, 36% full-time, 36% with terminal degrees.
Student/faculty ratio: 8:1.

ACADEMICS

Calendar: semesters. *Degrees:* associate, bachelor's, and master's.
Special study options: academic remediation for entering students, adult/continuing education programs, advanced placement credit, double majors, English as a second language, external degree program, honors programs, independent study, internships, off-campus study, part-time degree program, services for LD students, student-designed majors, study abroad, summer session for credit.
Computers: 85 computers/terminals are available on campus for general student use. Students can access the following: campus intranet, computer help desk, free student e-mail accounts, online (class) grades, online (class) schedules. Campuswide network is available. 100% of college-owned or -operated housing units are wired for high-speed Internet access. Wireless service is available via entire campus.
Library: Annenberg Library plus 1 other. *Books:* 63,939 (physical), 46,446 (digital/electronic); *Serial titles:* 38 (physical), 8 (digital/electronic); *Databases:* 43. Weekly public service hours: 73; students can reserve study rooms.

STUDENT LIFE

Housing options: coed. Campus housing is university owned.
Activities and organizations: drama/theater group, student-run newspaper, radio station, choral group, African American, Latina, Asian, Native American and All (ALANA), Community Service Committee, International Student Club, The Model UN, Student Government Association (SGA).
Athletics Member NCAA. All Division III. *Intercollegiate sports:* baseball M, basketball M/W, cross-country running M/W, soccer M/W, softball W, volleyball M/W.
Campus security: 24-hour emergency response devices and patrols, student patrols, late-night transport/escort service, controlled dormitory access.
Student services: health clinic, personal/psychological counseling, women's center.

COSTS & FINANCIAL AID

Costs (2017–18) *Comprehensive fee:* $44,290 includes full-time tuition ($29,860), mandatory fees ($1000), and room and board ($13,430). Full-time tuition and fees vary according to course load. Part-time tuition: $930 per credit hour. Part-time tuition and fees vary according to course load. *Required fees:* $1000 per year part-time.
Room and board: Room and board charges vary according to housing facility. *Payment plan:* installment. *Waivers:* children of alumni and employees or children of employees.
Financial Aid Of all full-time matriculated undergraduates who enrolled in 2016, 264 applied for aid, 264 were judged to have need, 11 had their

need fully met. 258 Federal Work-Study jobs (averaging $825). In 2016, 27 non-need-based awards were made. *Average percent of need met:* 69. *Average financial aid package:* $25,335. *Average need-based loan:* $3654. *Average need-based gift aid:* $20,700. *Average non-need-based aid:* $14,485. *Average indebtedness upon graduation:* $34,970.

APPLYING

Options: electronic application, deferred entrance.
Application fee: $25.
Required: essay or personal statement, high school transcript, letters of recommendation. *Recommended:* minimum 2.0 GPA, interview.
Application deadlines: rolling (freshmen), rolling (transfers).
Notification: continuous (freshmen), continuous (transfers).

CONTACT

Pine Manor College, 400 Heath Street, Chestnut Hill, MA 02467. *Phone:* 617-731-7107. *Toll-free phone:* 800-762-1357.

Regis College

Weston, Massachusetts

http://www.regiscollege.edu/

- **Independent Roman Catholic** comprehensive, founded 1927
- **Small-town** 131-acre campus with easy access to Boston
- **Endowment** $33.7 million
- **Coed**
- **Moderately difficult** entrance level

FACULTY

Student/faculty ratio: 11:1.

ACADEMICS

Calendar: semesters. *Degrees:* associate, bachelor's, master's, doctoral, and post-master's certificates.
Library: Regis College Library. *Books:* 108,313 (physical), 421,975 (digital/electronic); *Serial titles:* 126 (physical), 153 (digital/electronic); *Databases:* 58. Weekly public service hours: 108.

STUDENT LIFE

Housing options: coed, women-only. Campus housing is university owned. Freshman campus housing is guaranteed.
Activities and organizations: drama/theater group, student-run newspaper, radio station, choral group, Campus Ministry, SGA-Student Government Association, Asian American Student Organization, Dynasty Step Squad, Black Student Organization.
Athletics Member NCAA. All Division III.
Campus security: 24-hour emergency response devices and patrols, late-night transport/escort service, controlled dormitory access.
Student services: health clinic, personal/psychological counseling.

COSTS & FINANCIAL AID

Costs (2017–18) *Comprehensive fee:* $54,560 includes full-time tuition ($39,820) and room and board ($14,740).
Financial Aid *Average indebtedness upon graduation:* $24,178.

APPLYING

Standardized Tests *Required for some:* SAT or ACT (for admission).
Options: electronic application, early admission, early action, deferred entrance.
Application fee: $50.
Required: essay or personal statement, high school transcript, minimum 2.0 GPA, 2 letters of recommendation. *Required for some:* interview. *Recommended:* minimum 3.0 GPA, interview, rank in upper 50% of high school class.

CONTACT

Dr. Laura Bertonazzi, Dean of Undergraduate Enrollment and Retention, Regis College, 235 Wellesley Street, Weston, MA 02493. *Phone:* 781-768-7060. *Toll-free phone:* 866-438-7344. *Fax:* 781-768-7060. *E-mail:* admission@regiscollege.edu.

See next page for display ad and page 1394 for the College Close-Up.

Salem State University

Salem, Massachusetts
http://www.salemstate.edu/

CONTACT
Dr. Mary Dunn, Assistant Dean for Undergraduate Admissions, Salem State University, 352 Lafayette Street, Salem, MA 01970. *Phone:* 978-542-6202. *Fax:* 978-542-6893. *E-mail:* admissions@salemstate.edu.

Simmons College

Boston, Massachusetts
http://www.simmons.edu/

- **Independent** university, founded 1899
- **Urban** 12-acre campus with easy access to Boston
- **Endowment** $188.2 million
- **Undergraduate: women only; graduate: coed** 1,763 undergraduate students, 88% full-time, 99% women, 1% men
- **Moderately difficult** entrance level, 60% of applicants were admitted

UNDERGRAD STUDENTS
1,553 full-time, 210 part-time. Students come from 33 states and territories; 51 other countries; 40% are from out of state; 6% Black or African American, non-Hispanic/Latino; 6% Hispanic/Latino; 10% Asian, non-Hispanic/Latino; 0.2% Native Hawaiian or other Pacific Islander, non-Hispanic/Latino; 0.1% American Indian or Alaska Native, non-Hispanic/Latino; 5% Two or more races, non-Hispanic/Latino; 3% Race/ethnicity unknown; 5% international; 3% transferred in; 63% live on campus.

Freshmen:
Admission: 3,483 applied, 2,105 admitted, 405 enrolled. *Average high school GPA:* 3.4. *Test scores:* ACT scores over 18: 100%; ACT scores over 24: 75%; ACT scores over 30: 19%.
Retention: 84% of full-time freshmen returned.

FACULTY
Total: 1,071, 23% full-time, 19% with terminal degrees.
Student/faculty ratio: 12:1.

ACADEMICS
Calendar: semesters. *Degrees:* bachelor's, master's, doctoral, and post-master's certificates.
Special study options: accelerated degree program, adult/continuing education programs, advanced placement credit, distance learning, double majors, external degree program, honors programs, independent study, internships, off-campus study, part-time degree program, services for LD students, student-designed majors, study abroad, summer session for credit. *ROTC:* Army (c).
Unusual degree programs: 3-2 business administration; nursing; social work.
Computers: 570 computers/terminals are available on campus for general student use. Students can access the following: campus intranet, computer help desk, free student e-mail accounts, online (class) grades, online (class) registration, online (class) schedules. Campuswide network is available. 100% of college-owned or -operated housing units are wired for high-speed Internet access. Wireless service is available via entire campus.
Library: Beatley Library. *Books:* 154,852 (physical), 37,362 (digital/electronic); *Serial titles:* 13 (physical), 278,000 (digital/electronic); *Databases:* 137. Weekly public service hours: 105; students can reserve study rooms.

STUDENT LIFE
Housing options: on-campus residence required for freshman year; coed, women-only. Campus housing is university owned. Freshman applicants given priority for college housing.
Activities and organizations: drama/theater group, student-run newspaper, radio station, choral group, Simmons College Dance Company, Student Government Association, Simmons Student Nursing Association, Sexuality Women and Gender (SWAG), Class Councils (2018, 2019, 2020, 2021).
Athletics Member NCAA. All Division III. *Intercollegiate sports:* basketball W, crew W, cross-country running W, field hockey W, lacrosse W, soccer W, softball W, swimming and diving W, tennis W, volleyball W. *Intramural sports:* basketball M/W, rugby W(c), soccer M/W, softball M/W, tennis M/W, volleyball M/W.

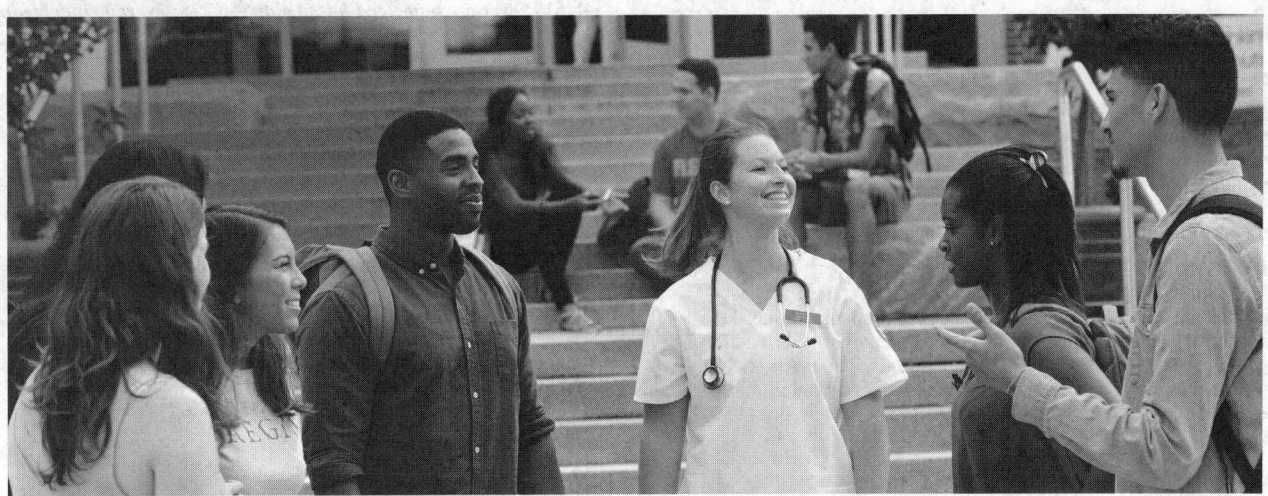

BOLDLY EMPOWERING THE NEXT GENERATION OF LEADERS TO CHANGE LIVES.

See why you belong here. Schedule a campus visit or explore our online tour at **regiscollege.edu/ugvisit**

REGIS

Office of Undergraduate Admission | 235 Wellesley Street, Weston MA | admission@regiscollege.edu

Campus security: 24-hour emergency response devices and patrols, late-night transport/escort service, controlled dormitory access.

Student services: health clinic, personal/psychological counseling, women's center.

COSTS & FINANCIAL AID

Costs (2018–19) *Comprehensive fee:* $56,000 includes full-time tuition ($39,660), mandatory fees ($1140), and room and board ($15,200). Full-time tuition and fees vary according to course load and program. Part-time tuition: $1360 per credit hour. Part-time tuition and fees vary according to course load and program. *Required fees:* $260 per term part-time. *Room and board:* Room and board charges vary according to board plan and location. *Payment plan:* installment. *Waivers:* employees or children of employees.

Financial Aid Of all full-time matriculated undergraduates who enrolled in 2017, 1,277 applied for aid, 1,186 were judged to have need, 142 had their need fully met. 829 Federal Work-Study jobs (averaging $2373). In 2017, 317 non-need-based awards were made. *Average percent of need met:* 76. *Average financial aid package:* $31,887. *Average need-based loan:* $4032. *Average need-based gift aid:* $28,339. *Average non-need-based aid:* $19,131.

APPLYING

Standardized Tests *Required:* SAT or ACT (for admission).

Options: electronic application, early action, deferred entrance.

Application fee: $55.

Required: essay or personal statement, high school transcript, 2 letters of recommendation. *Recommended:* minimum 3.0 GPA, interview.

Application deadlines: 2/1 (freshmen), 4/1 (transfers), 12/1 (early action).

Notification: continuous until 3/15 (freshmen), 3/15 (out-of-state freshmen), 1/15 (early action).

CONTACT

Danielle Navarro, Senior Associate Director of Admission, Simmons College, 300 The Fenway, Boston, MA 02115. *Phone:* 617-521-2512. *Toll-free phone:* 800-345-8468. *Fax:* 617-521-3190. *E-mail:* danielle.navarro@simmons.edu.

Smith College

Northampton, Massachusetts

http://www.smith.edu/

- **Independent** comprehensive, founded 1871
- **Small-town** 147-acre campus with easy access to Hartford
- **Undergraduate: women only; graduate: coed** 2,521 undergraduate students, 99% full-time, 100% women, 0% men
- **Very difficult** entrance level, 32% of applicants were admitted

UNDERGRAD STUDENTS

2,505 full-time, 16 part-time. 79% are from out of state; 7% Black or African American, non-Hispanic/Latino; 10% Hispanic/Latino; 11% Asian, non-Hispanic/Latino; 0.1% Native Hawaiian or other Pacific Islander, non-Hispanic/Latino; 0.1% American Indian or Alaska Native, non-Hispanic/Latino; 4% Two or more races, non-Hispanic/Latino; 6% Race/ethnicity unknown; 14% international; 2% transferred in; 95% live on campus.

Freshmen:
Admission: 5,432 applied, 1,731 admitted, 638 enrolled. *Average high school GPA:* 3.8. *Test scores:* SAT evidence-based reading and writing scores over 500: 100%; SAT math scores over 500: 99%; ACT scores over 18: 100%; SAT evidence-based reading and writing scores over 600: 93%; SAT math scores over 600: 89%; ACT scores over 24: 97%; SAT evidence-based reading and writing scores over 700: 49%; SAT math scores over 700: 45%; ACT scores over 30: 77%.

Retention: 93% of full-time freshmen returned.

ACADEMICS

Calendar: semesters. *Degrees:* bachelor's, master's, doctoral, post-master's, and postbachelor's certificates.

Special study options: accelerated degree program, adult/continuing education programs, double majors, honors programs, independent study,

internships, part-time degree program, student-designed majors, study abroad. *ROTC:* Army (c), Air Force (c).

Computers: Students can access the following: campus intranet, computer help desk, free student e-mail accounts, online (class) grades, online (class) registration, online (class) schedules. Campuswide network is available. 100% of college-owned or -operated housing units are wired for high-speed Internet access. Wireless service is available via classrooms, computer centers, computer labs, dorm rooms, learning centers, libraries, student centers.

Library: Neilson Library.

STUDENT LIFE

Housing options: on-campus residence required through senior year; women-only, cooperative. Campus housing is university owned. Freshman campus housing is guaranteed.

Activities and organizations: drama/theater group, student-run newspaper, radio and television station, choral group.

Athletics Member NCAA. All Division III. *Intercollegiate sports:* basketball W, crew W, cross-country running W, equestrian sports W, field hockey W, lacrosse W, soccer W, softball W, squash W, swimming and diving W, tennis W, track and field W, volleyball W. *Intramural sports:* badminton W(c), cheerleading W(c), crew W(c), equestrian sports W(c), fencing W(c), golf W(c), ice hockey W(c), rock climbing W, rugby W(c), soccer W, squash W, ultimate Frisbee W(c).

Campus security: 24-hour emergency response devices and patrols, late-night transport/escort service, self-defense workshops, emergency telephones, programs in crime and sexual assault prevention.

COSTS & FINANCIAL AID

Costs (2017–18) *Comprehensive fee:* $66,774 includes full-time tuition ($49,760), mandatory fees ($284), and room and board ($16,730). Part-time tuition: $1560 per credit hour. *Payment plans:* tuition prepayment, installment. *Waivers:* employees or children of employees.

Financial Aid Of all full-time matriculated undergraduates who enrolled in 2017, 1,802 applied for aid, 1,550 were judged to have need, 1,550 had their need fully met. In 2017, 188 non-need-based awards were made. *Average percent of need met:* 100. *Average financial aid package:* $51,046. *Average need-based loan:* $4350. *Average need-based gift aid:* $45,819. *Average non-need-based aid:* $16,278. *Average indebtedness upon graduation:* $24,501. *Financial aid deadline:* 1/25.

APPLYING

Standardized Tests *Required for some:* SAT or ACT (for admission).

Options: electronic application, early admission, early decision, deferred entrance.

Required: essay or personal statement, high school transcript, 3 letters of recommendation. *Recommended:* interview.

CONTACT

Ms. Debra Shaver, Dean of Admissions, Smith College, 7 College Lane, Northampton, MA 01063. *Phone:* 413-585-2500. *Toll-free phone:* 800-383-3232. *Fax:* 413-585-2527. *E-mail:* admission@smith.edu.

 # Springfield College

Springfield, Massachusetts

http://www.springfield.edu/

CONTACT

Richard K. Veres, Director of Undergraduate Admissions, Springfield College, 263 Alden Street, Springfield, MA 01109. *Phone:* 413-748-3136. *Toll-free phone:* 800-343-1257. *Fax:* 413-748-3694. *E-mail:* admissions@spfldcol.edu.

See next page for display ad and page 1434 for the College Close-Up.

Stonehill College

Easton, Massachusetts

http://www.stonehill.edu/

- **Independent Roman Catholic** comprehensive, founded 1948
- **Suburban** 384-acre campus with easy access to Boston
- **Endowment** $194.1 million
- **Coed** 2,498 undergraduate students, 99% full-time, 59% women, 41% men
- **Very difficult** entrance level, 72% of applicants were admitted

UNDERGRAD STUDENTS

2,482 full-time, 16 part-time. Students come from 34 states and territories; 11 other countries; 38% are from out of state; 4% Black or African American, non-Hispanic/Latino; 4% Hispanic/Latino; 2% Asian, non-Hispanic/Latino; 2% Two or more races, non-Hispanic/Latino; 2% Race/ethnicity unknown; 0.6% international; 2% transferred in; 89% live on campus.

Freshmen:
Admission: 6,260 applied, 4,515 admitted, 667 enrolled. *Average high school GPA:* 3.3. *Test scores:* SAT evidence-based reading and writing scores over 500: 94%; SAT math scores over 500: 91%; ACT scores over 18: 97%; SAT evidence-based reading and writing scores over 600: 46%; SAT math scores over 600: 45%; ACT scores over 24: 69%; SAT evidence-based reading and writing scores over 700: 6%; SAT math scores over 700: 6%; ACT scores over 30: 18%.
Retention: 85% of full-time freshmen returned.

FACULTY

Total: 284, 60% full-time, 71% with terminal degrees.
Student/faculty ratio: 12:1.

ACADEMICS

Calendar: semesters. *Degrees:* bachelor's and master's.

Special study options: advanced placement credit, double majors, honors programs, independent study, internships, off-campus study, part-time degree program, services for LD students, student-designed majors, study abroad, summer session for credit. *ROTC:* Army (b).

Unusual degree programs: 3-2 engineering with University of Notre Dame.

Computers: 407 computers/terminals and 300 ports are available on campus for general student use. Students can access the following: campus intranet, computer help desk, free student e-mail accounts, online (class) grades, online (class) registration, online (class) schedules, Learning Management System, online degree evaluation/planning, add funds to ID, use at off campus locations, housing contracts and room lottery, financial aid awards, time sheets and payments for campus jobs, ebill. Campuswide network is available. 100% of college-owned or -operated housing units are wired for high-speed Internet access. Wireless service is available via entire campus.

Library: MacPhaidin Library plus 2 others. *Books:* 166,092 (physical), 281,782 (digital/electronic); *Serial titles:* 3,788 (physical), 80,308 (digital/electronic); *Databases:* 71. Weekly public service hours: 110; students can reserve study rooms.

STUDENT LIFE

Housing options: coed, women-only, special housing for students with disabilities. Campus housing is university owned.

Activities and organizations: drama/theater group, student-run newspaper, radio station, choral group, Into the Streets, Recreation/Intramural Sports Teams, Dance Club, Student Government Association, Education Society.

Athletics Member NCAA. All Division II. *Intercollegiate sports:* baseball M(s), basketball M(s)/W(s), bowling M(c)/W(c), cheerleading M(c)/W(c), cross-country running M(s)/W(s), equestrian sports W, field hockey W(s), football M(s), golf M(c)/W(s), ice hockey M, lacrosse M(c)/W(s), rugby M(c)/W(c), soccer M(s)/W(s), softball W(s), tennis M(s)/W(s), track and field M(s)/W(s), ultimate Frisbee M(c)/W(c), volleyball M(c)/W(s). *Intramural sports:* basketball M/W, field hockey M/W, ice hockey M(c)/W(c), soccer M/W, softball M/W, table tennis M/W, tennis M/W, ultimate Frisbee M/W, volleyball M/W(c).

Campus security: 24-hour emergency response devices and patrols, late-night transport/escort service, controlled dormitory access, restricted access on weekends.

Student services: health clinic, personal/psychological counseling.

COSTS & FINANCIAL AID

Costs (2017–18) *Comprehensive fee:* $57,060 includes full-time tuition ($41,300) and room and board ($15,760). Part-time tuition: $1377 per credit hour. Part-time tuition and fees vary according to course load. *College room only:* $9657. Room and board charges vary according to board plan. *Payment plans:* tuition prepayment, installment. *Waivers:* employees or children of employees.

Financial Aid Of all full-time matriculated undergraduates who enrolled in 2016, 1,891 applied for aid, 1,610 were judged to have need, 732 had their need fully met. In 2016, 680 non-need-based awards were made. *Average percent of need met:* 91. *Average financial aid package:* $30,606. *Average need-based loan:* $4660. *Average need-based gift aid:*

$25,017. *Average non-need-based aid:* $17,418. *Average indebtedness upon graduation:* $35,462.

APPLYING
Options: electronic application, early decision, early action, deferred entrance.

Application fee: $60.

Required: essay or personal statement, high school transcript, 2 letters of recommendation. *Recommended:* interview.

Application deadlines: 1/15 (freshmen), 4/1 (transfers), 11/1 (early action).

Early decision deadline: 12/1.

Notification: 3/15 (freshmen), continuous until 5/31 (transfers), 12/31 (early decision), 12/31 (early action).

CONTACT
Stonehill College, 320 Washington Street, Easton, MA 02357-5610. *Phone:* 508-565-1373. *Fax:* 508-565-1545. *E-mail:* admission@ stonehill.edu.

Suffolk University
Boston, Massachusetts
http://www.suffolk.edu/

- **Independent** comprehensive, founded 1906
- **Urban** 2-acre campus with easy access to Boston, MA
- **Endowment** $231.7 million
- **Coed** 5,117 undergraduate students, 95% full-time, 54% women, 46% men
- **Moderately difficult** entrance level, 83% of applicants were admitted

UNDERGRAD STUDENTS
4,849 full-time, 268 part-time. Students come from 45 states and territories; 115 other countries; 32% are from out of state; 5% Black or African American, non-Hispanic/Latino; 12% Hispanic/Latino; 8% Asian, non-Hispanic/Latino; 0.1% Native Hawaiian or other Pacific Islander, non-Hispanic/Latino; 0.1% American Indian or Alaska Native, non-Hispanic/Latino; 2% Two or more races, non-Hispanic/Latino; 4% Race/ethnicity unknown; 22% international; 6% transferred in; 25% live on campus.

Freshmen:
Admission: 8,237 applied, 6,867 admitted, 1,087 enrolled. *Average high school GPA:* 3.2. *Test scores:* SAT evidence-based reading and writing scores over 500: 78%; SAT math scores over 500: 76%; ACT scores over 18: 94%; SAT evidence-based reading and writing scores over 600: 27%; SAT math scores over 600: 19%; ACT scores over 24: 52%; SAT evidence-based reading and writing scores over 700: 2%; SAT math scores over 700: 1%; ACT scores over 30: 5%.

Retention: 77% of full-time freshmen returned.

FACULTY
Total: 685, 51% full-time, 65% with terminal degrees.
Student/faculty ratio: 13:1.

ACADEMICS
Calendar: semesters. *Degrees:* certificates, diplomas, associate, bachelor's, master's, doctoral, post-master's, and postbachelor's certificates (doctoral degree in law).

Special study options: academic remediation for entering students, accelerated degree program, adult/continuing education programs, advanced placement credit, cooperative education, distance learning, double majors, English as a second language, honors programs, independent study, internships, off-campus study, part-time degree program, services for LD students, study abroad, summer session for credit. *ROTC:* Army (c).

Computers: 675 computers/terminals and 8,000 ports are available on campus for general student use. Students can access the following: campus intranet, computer help desk, free student e-mail accounts, online (class) grades, online (class) registration, online (class) schedules. Campuswide network is available. 100% of college-owned or -operated housing units are wired for high-speed Internet access. Wireless service is available via entire campus.

Library: Mildred Sawyer Library plus 3 others. *Books:* 128,945 (physical), 249,567 (digital/electronic); *Serial titles:* 307 (physical), 65,782 (digital/electronic); *Databases:* 174. Weekly public service hours: 103; students can reserve study rooms.

STUDENT LIFE
Housing options: coed. Campus housing is university owned. Freshman applicants given priority for college housing.

Activities and organizations: drama/theater group, student-run newspaper, radio and television station, choral group, Student Government Association, Program Committee, Suffolk Free Radio, Black Student Union, Journey Leadership Program, national fraternities, national sororities.

Athletics Member NCAA. All Division III. *Intercollegiate sports:* baseball M, basketball M/W, cross-country running M/W, golf M/W, ice hockey M/W, soccer M/W, softball W, tennis M/W, track and field M/W, volleyball W. *Intramural sports:* basketball M/W, soccer M/W, softball M/W, volleyball M/W.

Campus security: 24-hour emergency response devices, late-night transport/escort service, controlled dormitory access.

Student services: health clinic, personal/psychological counseling, women's center.

COSTS & FINANCIAL AID
Costs (2018–19) *Tuition:* $38,420 full-time, $1130 per credit hour part-time. Full-time tuition and fees vary according to course level and reciprocity agreements. Part-time tuition and fees vary according to course level, course load, and reciprocity agreements. *Required fees:* $146 full-time, $19 per credit hour part-time. *Room only:* Room and board charges vary according to board plan and housing facility. *Payment plans:* installment, deferred payment. *Waivers:* children of alumni, senior citizens, and employees or children of employees.

Financial Aid Of all full-time matriculated undergraduates who enrolled in 2017, 3,006 applied for aid, 3,006 were judged to have need, 872 had their need fully met. 814 Federal Work-Study jobs (averaging $2356). 433 state and other part-time jobs (averaging $4056). In 2017, 1301 non-need-based awards were made. *Average percent of need met:* 78. *Average financial aid package:* $31,688. *Average need-based loan:* $4446. *Average need-based gift aid:* $8150. *Average non-need-based aid:* $13,994. *Average indebtedness upon graduation:* $28,859. *Financial aid deadline:* 6/30.

APPLYING
Options: electronic application, early action, deferred entrance.

Application fee: $50.

Required: essay or personal statement, high school transcript, 2 letters of recommendation. *Required for some:* interview.

Application deadlines: 2/15 (freshmen), 6/30 (transfers), 11/15 (early action).

Notification: continuous until 3/20 (freshmen), continuous (transfers), 12/15 (early action).

CONTACT
Ms. Donna Grand Pre, Assistant Vice President/Director Undergraduate Admissions, Suffolk University, 8 Ashburton Place, Boston, MA 02108. *Phone:* 617-573-8460. *Toll-free phone:* 800-6-SUFFOLK. *Fax:* 617-742-4291. *E-mail:* admission@suffolk.edu.

Tufts University
Medford, Massachusetts
http://www.tufts.edu/

- **Independent** university, founded 1852
- **Suburban** 150-acre campus with easy access to Boston
- **Coed** 5,541 undergraduate students, 99% full-time, 51% women, 49% men
- **Most difficult** entrance level, 15% of applicants were admitted

UNDERGRAD STUDENTS
5,483 full-time, 58 part-time. Students come from 51 states and territories; 74 other countries; 75% are from out of state; 4% Black or African American, non-Hispanic/Latino; 7% Hispanic/Latino; 12% Asian, non-Hispanic/Latino; 5% Two or more races, non-Hispanic/Latino; 6% Race/ethnicity unknown; 10% international; 0.8% transferred in; 63% live on campus.

Freshmen:
Admission: 21,101 applied, 3,127 admitted, 1,410 enrolled. *Test scores:* SAT evidence-based reading and writing scores over 500: 100%; SAT

math scores over 500: 100%; ACT scores over 18: 97%; SAT evidence-based reading and writing scores over 600: 98%; SAT math scores over 600: 97%; ACT scores over 24: 97%; SAT evidence-based reading and writing scores over 700: 77%; SAT math scores over 700: 79%; ACT scores over 30: 88%.

Retention: 97% of full-time freshmen returned.

FACULTY
Total: 1,077, 63% full-time, 83% with terminal degrees.
Student/faculty ratio: 9:1.

ACADEMICS
Calendar: semesters. *Degrees:* certificates, bachelor's, master's, doctoral, post-master's, and postbachelor's certificates.

Special study options: academic remediation for entering students, adult/continuing education programs, advanced placement credit, cooperative education, double majors, independent study, internships, off-campus study, services for LD students, student-designed majors, study abroad, summer session for credit. *ROTC:* Army (c), Navy (c), Air Force (c).

Unusual degree programs: 3-2 New England Conservatory of Music.

Computers: 1,039 computers/terminals are available on campus for general student use. Students can access the following: campus intranet, computer help desk, free student e-mail accounts, online (class) grades, online (class) registration, online (class) schedules, Cloud storage for all students, staff, and faculty. Campuswide network is available. 100% of college-owned or -operated housing units are wired for high-speed Internet access. Wireless service is available via entire campus.
Library: Tisch Library plus 3 others. *Books:* 1.3 million (physical), 432,877 (digital/electronic); *Serial titles:* 1,012 (physical); *Databases:* 83,216. Weekly public service hours: 110; students can reserve study rooms.

STUDENT LIFE
Housing options: on-campus residence required through sophomore year; coed, women-only, special housing for students with disabilities. Campus housing is university owned. Freshman campus housing is guaranteed.

Activities and organizations: drama/theater group, student-run newspaper, radio and television station, choral group, Leonard Carmichael Society (community service), Tufts Dance Collective, intramural sports, Tufts Daily (newspaper), Tufts Mountain Club, national fraternities, national sororities.

Athletics Member NCAA. All Division III. *Intercollegiate sports:* baseball M, basketball M/W, crew M/W, cross-country running M/W, equestrian sports M(c)/W(c), fencing W, field hockey W, football M, golf M, ice hockey M, lacrosse M/W, rugby M(c)/W(c), sailing M/W, soccer M/W, softball W, squash M/W, swimming and diving M/W, tennis M/W, track and field M/W, ultimate Frisbee M(c)/W(c), volleyball M(c)/W, water polo M(c)/W(c). *Intramural sports:* badminton M/W, baseball M(c), basketball M/W, cheerleading W, fencing M(c), field hockey W(c), football M(c)/W(c), ice hockey M(c), lacrosse M(c)/W(c), racquetball M/W, rock climbing M(c)/W(c), skiing (downhill) M/W, soccer M/W, softball M/W(c), table tennis M(c)/W(c), tennis M/W, volleyball M/W.

Campus security: 24-hour emergency response devices and patrols, late-night transport/escort service, controlled dormitory access, security lighting, call boxes to campus police.

Student services: health clinic, personal/psychological counseling, women's center, legal services.

COSTS & FINANCIAL AID
Costs (2017–18) *Comprehensive fee:* $68,372 includes full-time tuition ($53,152), mandatory fees ($1166), and room and board ($14,054). *College room only:* $7658. Room and board charges vary according to board plan. *Payment plans:* tuition prepayment, installment. *Waivers:* employees or children of employees.
Financial Aid Of all full-time matriculated undergraduates who enrolled in 2017, 2,361 applied for aid, 2,069 were judged to have need, 1,992 had their need fully met. 1,463 Federal Work-Study jobs (averaging $1924). 166 state and other part-time jobs (averaging $1914). In 2017, 139 non-need-based awards were made. *Average percent of need met:* 98. *Average financial aid package:* $45,107. *Average need-based loan:* $3112. *Average need-based gift aid:* $42,763. *Average non-need-based aid:* $4000. *Average indebtedness upon graduation:* $27,367. *Financial aid deadline:* 2/1.

APPLYING
Standardized Tests *Required:* SAT or ACT (for admission). *Required for some:* art portfolio in lieu of Subject Tests for applicants to the School of Museum of Fine Arts.

Options: electronic application, early admission, early decision, deferred entrance.

Application fee: $75.

Required: essay or personal statement, high school transcript, 2 letters of recommendation, Common Application or Coalition Application or QuestBridge Application, the Tufts Supplement. *Recommended:* interview.

Application deadlines: 1/1 (freshmen), 3/15 (transfers).

Early decision deadline: 11/1 (for plan 1), 1/1 (for plan 2).

Notification: 4/1 (freshmen), continuous until 5/15 (transfers), 12/15 (early decision plan 1), 2/15 (early decision plan 2).

CONTACT
Office of Undergraduate Admissions, Tufts University, Bendetson Hall, Medford, MA 02155. *Phone:* 617-627-3170. *Fax:* 617-627-3860. *E-mail:* undergraduate.admissions@tufts.edu.

University of Massachusetts Amherst
Amherst, Massachusetts
http://www.umass.edu/
- **State-supported** university, founded 1863, part of University of Massachusetts
- **Small-town** 1463-acre campus with easy access to Springfield, MA and Hartford, CT
- **Endowment** $323.6 million
- **Coed** 23,388 undergraduate students, 92% full-time, 50% women, 50% men
- **Moderately difficult** entrance level, 57% of applicants were admitted

UNDERGRAD STUDENTS
21,577 full-time, 1,811 part-time. Students come from 51 states and territories; 78 other countries; 18% are from out of state; 4% Black or African American, non-Hispanic/Latino; 6% Hispanic/Latino; 10% Asian, non-Hispanic/Latino; 0.1% Native Hawaiian or other Pacific Islander, non-Hispanic/Latino; 0.1% American Indian or Alaska Native, non-Hispanic/Latino; 3% Two or more races, non-Hispanic/Latino; 6% Race/ethnicity unknown; 6% international; 5% transferred in; 61% live on campus.

Freshmen:
Admission: 41,922 applied, 24,102 admitted, 4,761 enrolled. *Average high school GPA:* 3.9. *Test scores:* SAT evidence-based reading and writing scores over 500: 98%; SAT math scores over 500: 99%; SAT evidence-based reading and writing scores over 600: 71%; SAT math scores over 600: 72%; SAT evidence-based reading and writing scores over 700: 16%; SAT math scores over 700: 22%.

Retention: 91% of full-time freshmen returned.

FACULTY
Total: 1,495, 90% full-time, 92% with terminal degrees.
Student/faculty ratio: 17:1.

ACADEMICS
Calendar: semesters. *Degrees:* certificates, associate, bachelor's, master's, doctoral, and postbachelor's certificates.

Special study options: accelerated degree program, adult/continuing education programs, advanced placement credit, cooperative education, distance learning, double majors, English as a second language, freshman honors college, honors programs, independent study, internships, off-campus study, part-time degree program, services for LD students, student-designed majors, study abroad, summer session for credit. *ROTC:* Army (b), Air Force (b).

Computers: 507 computers/terminals and 430 ports are available on campus for general student use. Students can access the following: computer help desk, free student e-mail accounts, online (class) grades, online (class) registration, online (class) schedules, online housing assignments, bill payment, Learning Management System, file storage, Web hosting, blogs. Campuswide network is available. 100% of college-owned or -operated housing units are wired for high-speed Internet access. Wireless service is available via entire campus.

Library: W. E. B. Du Bois Library plus 1 other. *Books:* 2.7 million (physical), 1.7 million (digital/electronic); *Serial titles:* 115,786 (physical), 115,786 (digital/electronic); *Databases:* 287. Weekly public service hours: 142; study areas open 24 hours, 5–7 days a week; students can reserve study rooms.

STUDENT LIFE

Housing options: on-campus residence required for freshman year; coed, men-only, women-only, special housing for students with disabilities. Campus housing is university owned. Freshman campus housing is guaranteed.

Activities and organizations: drama/theater group, student-run newspaper, radio and television station, choral group, marching band, Minutemen Marching Band, Ski Club, Outing Club, University Programming Council, Student Government Association, national fraternities, national sororities.

Athletics Member NCAA. All Division I except football (Division I-A). *Intercollegiate sports:* baseball M(s), basketball M(s)/W(s), crew W(s), cross-country running M(s)/W(s), field hockey W(s), ice hockey M(s), lacrosse M(s)/W(s), soccer M(s)/W(s), softball W(s), swimming and diving M(s)/W(s), tennis W(s), track and field M(s)/W(s). *Intramural sports:* badminton M/W, baseball M(c), basketball M/W, cheerleading M/W, crew M(c), equestrian sports M(c)/W(c), fencing M(c)/W(c), field hockey W(c), football M/W, golf M(c)/W(c), gymnastics W(c), ice hockey M(c)/W(c), lacrosse M(c)/W(c), racquetball M(c)/W(c), rugby M(c)/W(c), sailing M(c)/W(c), sand volleyball M/W, skiing (downhill) M(c)/W(c), soccer M(c)/W(c), softball W(c), swimming and diving M(c)/W(c), table tennis M(c)/W, tennis M(c)/W(c), triathlon M(c)/W(c), ultimate Frisbee M(c)/W(c), volleyball M(c)/W(c), water polo M(c)/W(c), wrestling M(c)/W(c).

Campus security: 24-hour emergency response devices and patrols, student patrols, late-night transport/escort service, controlled dormitory access.

Student services: health clinic, personal/psychological counseling, women's center, legal services.

COSTS & FINANCIAL AID

Costs (2017–18) *One-time required fee:* $185. *Tuition:* state resident $15,030 full-time, $5264 per term part-time; nonresident $33,096 full-time, $11,685 per term part-time. Full-time tuition and fees vary according to class time, location, program, reciprocity agreements, and student level. Part-time tuition and fees vary according to class time, course load, location, program, reciprocity agreements, and student level. *Required fees:* $381 full-time, $191 per term part-time. *Room and board:* $12,258; room only: $6862. Room and board charges vary according to board plan and housing facility. *Payment plan:* installment. *Waivers:* senior citizens and employees or children of employees.

Financial Aid Of all full-time matriculated undergraduates who enrolled in 2016, 16,906 applied for aid, 11,965 were judged to have need, 1,634 had their need fully met. 2,100 Federal Work-Study jobs (averaging $1454). In 2016, 4929 non-need-based awards were made. *Average percent of need met:* 86. *Average financial aid package:* $17,687. *Average need-based loan:* $4856. *Average need-based gift aid:* $10,708. *Average non-need-based aid:* $4707. *Average indebtedness upon graduation:* $31,860.

APPLYING

Standardized Tests *Required:* SAT or ACT (for admission).

Options: electronic application, early action, deferred entrance.

Application fee: $80.

Required: essay or personal statement, high school transcript, 1 letter of recommendation.

Application deadlines: 1/15 (freshmen), 4/15 (transfers), 11/1 (early action).

Notification: continuous (freshmen), continuous (transfers), 12/15 (early action).

CONTACT

Dr. James Roche, Vice Provost of Enrollment Management, University of Massachusetts Amherst, 255 Whitmore, Amherst, MA 01003. *Phone:* 413-545-0222. *Fax:* 413-545-4312. *E-mail:* mail@admissions.umass.edu.

University of Massachusetts Boston
Boston, Massachusetts
http://www.umb.edu/

- **State-supported** university, founded 1964, part of University of Massachusetts
- **Urban** 120-acre campus
- **Endowment** $74.4 million
- **Coed** 12,660 undergraduate students, 76% full-time, 53% women, 47% men
- **Moderately difficult** entrance level, 75% of applicants were admitted

UNDERGRAD STUDENTS

9,574 full-time, 3,086 part-time. Students come from 38 states and territories; 143 other countries; 5% are from out of state; 16% Black or African American, non-Hispanic/Latino; 15% Hispanic/Latino; 13% Asian, non-Hispanic/Latino; 0.2% American Indian or Alaska Native, non-Hispanic/Latino; 3% Two or more races, non-Hispanic/Latino; 7% Race/ethnicity unknown; 12% international; 12% transferred in.

Freshmen:
Admission: 10,507 applied, 7,896 admitted, 1,881 enrolled. *Average high school GPA:* 3.3. *Test scores:* SAT evidence-based reading and writing scores over 500: 85%; SAT math scores over 500: 89%; ACT scores over 18: 97%; SAT evidence-based reading and writing scores over 600: 32%; SAT math scores over 600: 32%; ACT scores over 24: 49%; SAT evidence-based reading and writing scores over 700: 4%; SAT math scores over 700: 4%; ACT scores over 30: 5%.

Retention: 77% of full-time freshmen returned.

FACULTY

Total: 1,146, 61% full-time, 73% with terminal degrees.

Student/faculty ratio: 17:1.

ACADEMICS

Calendar: semesters. *Degrees:* certificates, bachelor's, master's, doctoral, post-master's, and postbachelor's certificates.

Special study options: academic remediation for entering students, accelerated degree program, adult/continuing education programs, advanced placement credit, cooperative education, distance learning, double majors, English as a second language, freshman honors college, honors programs, independent study, internships, off-campus study, part-time degree program, services for LD students, student-designed majors, study abroad, summer session for credit. *ROTC:* Army (c), Navy (c), Air Force (c).

Computers: 350 computers/terminals are available on campus for general student use. Students can access the following: computer help desk, free student e-mail accounts, online (class) grades, online (class) registration, online (class) schedules. Campuswide network is available. Wireless service is available via entire campus.

Library: Joseph P. Healey Library. *Books:* 459,163 (physical), 547,086 (digital/electronic); *Databases:* 124.

STUDENT LIFE

Housing options: college housing not available.

Activities and organizations: drama/theater group, student-run newspaper, radio station, choral group, Student Arts and Events Council, Haitian Student Association, Golden Key Honor Society, Campus Kitchens, Mass Media.

Athletics Member NCAA. All Division III. *Intercollegiate sports:* baseball M, basketball M/W, cross-country running M/W, ice hockey M/W, lacrosse M, soccer M/W, softball W, tennis M/W, track and field M/W, volleyball W. *Intramural sports:* basketball M/W, bowling M/W, football M, golf M/W, racquetball M/W, soccer M/W, softball M/W, volleyball M/W.

Campus security: 24-hour emergency response devices and patrols, late-night transport/escort service, crime prevention program, bicycle patrols.

Student services: health clinic, personal/psychological counseling, women's center.

COSTS & FINANCIAL AID

Costs (2017–18) *Tuition:* state resident $13,503 full-time, $562 per credit hour part-time; nonresident $32,660 full-time, $1361 per credit hour part-time. Full-time tuition and fees vary according to program. Part-time tuition and fees vary according to program. *Required fees:* $325 full-time, $14 per credit hour part-time.

Financial Aid Of all full-time matriculated undergraduates who enrolled in 2016, 6,820 applied for aid, 6,030 were judged to have need, 2,433 had their need fully met. In 2016, 557 non-need-based awards were made. *Average percent of need met:* 88. *Average financial aid package:* $15,935. *Average need-based loan:* $4198. *Average need-based gift aid:* $9773. *Average non-need-based aid:* $7959. *Average indebtedness upon graduation:* $27,109.

APPLYING
Standardized Tests *Required for some:* SAT or ACT (for admission).

Options: electronic application, early admission, early action, deferred entrance.

Application fee: $60.

Required: high school transcript, minimum 2.5 GPA, 1 letter of recommendation. *Required for some:* essay or personal statement, minimum 2.8 GPA. *Recommended:* essay or personal statement.

Application deadlines: 3/1 (freshmen), 11/1 (early action).

Notification: continuous until 4/30 (freshmen).

CONTACT
Mr. Corey Ford, Director of Undergraduate Admissions, University of Massachusetts Boston, 100 Morrissey Boulevard, Boston, MA 02125-3393. *Phone:* 617-287-6100. *Fax:* 617-287-5999. *E-mail:* enrollment.info@umb.edu.

University of Massachusetts Dartmouth

North Dartmouth, Massachusetts
http://www.umassd.edu/
- **State-supported** university, founded 1895, part of University of Massachusetts
- **Suburban** 710-acre campus with easy access to Boston, Providence
- **Endowment** $54.6 million
- **Coed** 6,763 undergraduate students, 86% full-time, 49% women, 51% men
- **Moderately difficult** entrance level, 84% of applicants were admitted

UNDERGRAD STUDENTS
5,790 full-time, 973 part-time. Students come from 39 states and territories; 41 other countries; 7% are from out of state; 15% Black or African American, non-Hispanic/Latino; 10% Hispanic/Latino; 4% Asian, non-Hispanic/Latino; 0.2% American Indian or Alaska Native, non-Hispanic/Latino; 4% Two or more races, non-Hispanic/Latino; 5% Race/ethnicity unknown; 3% international; 9% transferred in; 52% live on campus.

Freshmen:
Admission: 7,959 applied, 6,707 admitted, 1,333 enrolled. *Average high school GPA:* 3.2. *Test scores:* SAT evidence-based reading and writing scores over 500: 77%; SAT math scores over 500: 75%; ACT scores over 18: 90%; SAT evidence-based reading and writing scores over 600: 26%; SAT math scores over 600: 24%; ACT scores over 24: 42%; SAT evidence-based reading and writing scores over 700: 2%; SAT math scores over 700: 3%; ACT scores over 30: 10%.

Retention: 74% of full-time freshmen returned.

FACULTY
Total: 595, 67% full-time, 65% with terminal degrees.
Student/faculty ratio: 16:1.

ACADEMICS
Calendar: semesters. *Degrees:* certificates, bachelor's, master's, doctoral, post-master's, and postbachelor's certificates.

Special study options: academic remediation for entering students, accelerated degree program, advanced placement credit, cooperative education, distance learning, double majors, English as a second language, honors programs, independent study, internships, off-campus study, part-time degree program, services for LD students, student-designed majors, study abroad, summer session for credit. *ROTC:* Army (c).

Unusual degree programs: 3-2 engineering; nursing; biology, chemistry, crime and justice Studies, English, political science, psychology, computer science, data science.

Computers: 368 computers/terminals and 5,000 ports are available on campus for general student use. Students can access the following: campus intranet, computer help desk, free student e-mail accounts, online (class) grades, online (class) registration, online (class) schedules. Campuswide network is available. 100% of college-owned or -operated housing units are wired for high-speed Internet access. Wireless service is available via classrooms, computer centers, computer labs, learning centers, libraries, student centers.

Library: Claire T. Carney Library plus 1 other. *Books:* 241,507 (physical), 75,709 (digital/electronic); *Serial titles:* 1,407 (physical), 85,115 (digital/electronic); *Databases:* 142. Students can reserve study rooms.

STUDENT LIFE
Housing options: coed, special housing for students with disabilities. Campus housing is university owned.

Activities and organizations: drama/theater group, student-run newspaper, choral group, Outdoor Club, Ski and Snowboard Club, 20 Cent Fiction, Relay for Life, American Red Cross, national fraternities, national sororities.

Athletics Member NCAA. All Division III. *Intercollegiate sports:* baseball M, basketball M/W, cross-country running M/W, equestrian sports W, field hockey W, football M, golf M, ice hockey M, lacrosse M/W, sailing W, soccer M/W, softball W, swimming and diving M/W, tennis M/W, track and field M/W, volleyball W. *Intramural sports:* badminton M/W, basketball M/W, rugby M(c)/W(c), sand volleyball M/W, skiing (downhill) M(c)/W(c), soccer M/W, triathlon M/W, ultimate Frisbee M/W, water polo M/W, weight lifting M/W.

Campus security: 24-hour emergency response devices and patrols, student patrols, late-night transport/escort service, controlled dormitory access.

Student services: health clinic, personal/psychological counseling, women's center.

COSTS & FINANCIAL AID
Costs (2017–18) *One-time required fee:* $100. *Tuition:* state resident $13,166 full-time, $549 per credit part-time; nonresident $27,880 full-time, $1162 per credit part-time. Full-time tuition and fees vary according to class time, program, and reciprocity agreements. Part-time tuition and fees vary according to class time, course load, program, and reciprocity agreements. *Required fees:* $405 full-time, $26 per credit part-time. *Room and board:* $12,936; room only: $4475. Room and board charges vary according to board plan and housing facility. *Payment plan:* installment. *Waivers:* senior citizens and employees or children of employees.

Financial Aid Of all full-time matriculated undergraduates who enrolled in 2017, 4,884 applied for aid, 4,193 were judged to have need, 1,458 had their need fully met. 1,128 Federal Work-Study jobs (averaging $1272). In 2017, 560 non-need-based awards were made. *Average percent of need met:* 83. *Average financial aid package:* $17,361. *Average need-based loan:* $8707. *Average need-based gift aid:* $10,333. *Average non-need-based aid:* $4476. *Average indebtedness upon graduation:* $31,992. *Financial aid deadline:* 6/30.

APPLYING
Standardized Tests *Required:* SAT or ACT (for admission).

Options: electronic application, early admission, early action, deferred entrance.

Application fee: $60.

Required: high school transcript, minimum 2.0 GPA. *Recommended:* essay or personal statement, 1 letter of recommendation.

Application deadlines: rolling (freshmen), rolling (transfers), 11/18 (early action).

Notification: continuous (freshmen), continuous (transfers), 12/15 (early action).

CONTACT
University of Massachusetts Dartmouth, 285 Old Westport Road, North Dartmouth, MA 02747-2300. *Phone:* 508-999-8605. *Fax:* 508-999-8755. *E-mail:* admissions@umassd.edu.

University of Massachusetts Lowell

Lowell, Massachusetts
http://www.uml.edu/

- **State-supported** university, founded 1894, part of University of Massachusetts
- **Urban** 100-acre campus with easy access to Boston
- **Endowment** $84.8 million
- **Coed** 14,013 undergraduate students, 75% full-time, 38% women, 62% men
- **Moderately difficult** entrance level, 69% of applicants were admitted

UNDERGRAD STUDENTS
10,495 full-time, 3,518 part-time. Students come from 50 states and territories; 66 other countries; 9% are from out of state; 6% Black or African American, non-Hispanic/Latino; 11% Hispanic/Latino; 10% Asian, non-Hispanic/Latino; 0.0% Native Hawaiian or other Pacific Islander, non-Hispanic/Latino; 0.1% American Indian or Alaska Native, non-Hispanic/Latino; 3% Two or more races, non-Hispanic/Latino; 5% Race/ethnicity unknown; 4% international; 8% transferred in; 32% live on campus.

Freshmen:
Admission: 11,113 applied, 7,636 admitted, 2,004 enrolled. *Average high school GPA:* 3.6. *Test scores:* SAT evidence-based reading and writing scores over 500: 99%; SAT math scores over 500: 99%; ACT scores over 18: 99%; SAT evidence-based reading and writing scores over 600: 57%; SAT math scores over 600: 61%; ACT scores over 24: 77%; SAT evidence-based reading and writing scores over 700: 8%; SAT math scores over 700: 12%; ACT scores over 30: 22%.
Retention: 86% of full-time freshmen returned.

FACULTY
Total: 1,119, 55% full-time, 70% with terminal degrees.
Student/faculty ratio: 17:1.

ACADEMICS
Calendar: semesters. *Degrees:* certificates, associate, bachelor's, master's, doctoral, post-master's, and postbachelor's certificates.
Special study options: accelerated degree program, adult/continuing education programs, advanced placement credit, cooperative education, distance learning, double majors, honors programs, independent study, internships, off-campus study, part-time degree program, services for LD students, study abroad, summer session for credit. *ROTC:* Army (b), Air Force (b).
Computers: 2,145 computers/terminals and 4,100 ports are available on campus for general student use. Students can access the following: campus intranet, computer help desk, free student e-mail accounts, online (class) grades, online (class) registration, online (class) schedules. Campuswide network is available. 100% of college-owned or -operated housing units are wired for high-speed Internet access. Wireless service is available via entire campus.
Library: O'Leary Library and Learning Commons plus 2 others. *Books:* 224,000 (physical), 192,600 (digital/electronic); *Serial titles:* 5,383 (physical), 125,540 (digital/electronic); *Databases:* 135. Weekly public service hours: 118; students can reserve study rooms.

STUDENT LIFE
Housing options: coed. Campus housing is university owned and leased by the school.
Activities and organizations: drama/theater group, student-run newspaper, radio station, choral group, marching band, Student Government Association, Recreational Sports Clubs, Association of Students of African Origin, WUML (radio station), Campus Activities Programming Association, national fraternities, national sororities.
Athletics Member NCAA. All Division I. *Intercollegiate sports:* baseball M(s), basketball M(s)/W(s), cross-country running M(s)/W(s), field hockey W(s), ice hockey M(s), lacrosse M(s)/W(s), soccer M(s)/W(s), softball W(s), track and field M(s)/W(s), volleyball W(s). *Intramural sports:* badminton M/W, baseball M(c), basketball M/W, cheerleading M(c)/W(c), cross-country running M/W, field hockey W(c), football M/W, golf M(c)/W(c), ice hockey M/W, lacrosse M(c)/W(c), racquetball M/W, rowing M(c)/W(c), rugby M(c)/W(c),

skiing (cross-country) M(c)/W(c), skiing (downhill) M(c)/W(c), soccer M/W, softball M/W, squash M/W, swimming and diving M(c)/W(c), table tennis M/W, tennis M/W, track and field M(c)/W(c), triathlon M/W, ultimate Frisbee M/W, volleyball M/W.
Campus security: 24-hour emergency response devices and patrols, controlled dormitory access, police and security patrols.
Student services: health clinic, personal/psychological counseling.

COSTS & FINANCIAL AID
Costs (2017–18) *Tuition:* state resident $14,350 full-time, $598 per credit hour part-time; nonresident $31,415 full-time, $1309 per credit hour part-time. Part-time tuition and fees vary according to course load. *Required fees:* $450 full-time, $19 per credit hour part-time. *Room and board:* $12,496; room only: $8254. Room and board charges vary according to board plan and housing facility. *Payment plan:* installment. *Waivers:* senior citizens and employees or children of employees.
Financial Aid Of all full-time matriculated undergraduates who enrolled in 2015, 7,331 applied for aid, 5,808 were judged to have need, 2,954 had their need fully met. In 2015, 835 non-need-based awards were made. *Average percent of need met:* 90. *Average financial aid package:* $15,393. *Average need-based loan:* $4410. *Average need-based gift aid:* $8631. *Average non-need-based aid:* $4648. *Average indebtedness upon graduation:* $31,432.

APPLYING
Standardized Tests *Required:* SAT or ACT (for admission). *Required for some:* short answer questions for No Test option.
Options: electronic application, early action, deferred entrance.
Application fee: $60.
Required: essay or personal statement, high school transcript, minimum 3.0 GPA, 1 letter of recommendation. *Required for some:* audition for music students, art portfolio for art majors, three additional short answer questions for No Test option.
Application deadlines: 2/1 (freshmen), 8/15 (transfers), 11/1 (early action).
Notification: 3/10 (freshmen), continuous (transfers), 12/10 (early action).

CONTACT
Admissions Office, University of Massachusetts Lowell, University Crossing, Suite 420, 220 Pawtucket Street, Lowell, MA 01854-2874. *Phone:* 978-934-3931. *Fax:* 978-934-3086. *E-mail:* admissions@uml.edu.

Wellesley College

Wellesley, Massachusetts
http://www.wellesley.edu/

- **Independent** 4-year, founded 1870
- **Suburban** 500-acre campus with easy access to Boston
- **Endowment** $1.9 billion
- **Women only** 2,508 undergraduate students, 95% full-time
- **Most difficult** entrance level, 22% of applicants were admitted

UNDERGRAD STUDENTS
2,374 full-time, 134 part-time. Students come from 50 states and territories; 84 other countries; 87% are from out of state; 6% Black or African American, non-Hispanic/Latino; 12% Hispanic/Latino; 23% Asian, non-Hispanic/Latino; 0.2% American Indian or Alaska Native, non-Hispanic/Latino; 6% Two or more races, non-Hispanic/Latino; 0.1% Race/ethnicity unknown; 13% international; 1% transferred in; 98% live on campus.

Freshmen:
Admission: 5,666 applied, 1,251 admitted, 603 enrolled. *Test scores:* SAT evidence-based reading and writing scores over 500: 100%; SAT math scores over 500: 100%; ACT scores over 18: 100%; SAT evidence-based reading and writing scores over 600: 97%; SAT math scores over 600: 97%; ACT scores over 24: 100%; SAT evidence-based reading and writing scores over 700: 71%; SAT math scores over 700: 60%; ACT scores over 30: 80%.
Retention: 95% of full-time freshmen returned.

FACULTY
Total: 359, 86% full-time, 89% with terminal degrees.

Student/faculty ratio: 7:1.

ACADEMICS

Calendar: semesters. *Degrees:* bachelor's (double bachelor's degree with Massachusetts Institute of Technology).

Special study options: adult/continuing education programs, advanced placement credit, cooperative education, double majors, honors programs, independent study, internships, off-campus study, part-time degree program, services for LD students, student-designed majors, study abroad, summer session for credit. *ROTC:* Army (c), Air Force (c).

Unusual degree programs: 3-2 engineering with Massachusetts Institute of Technology, Dartmouth College, Columbia University; architecture, aeronautics and astronautics, urban studies and planning with Massachusetts Institute of Technology, international economics and finance with Brandeis University.

Computers: 468 computers/terminals and 468 ports are available on campus for general student use. Students can access the following: campus intranet, computer help desk, free student e-mail accounts, online (class) grades, online (class) registration, online (class) schedules. Campuswide network is available. 100% of college-owned or -operated housing units are wired for high-speed Internet access. Wireless service is available via entire campus.

Library: Margaret Clapp Library plus 5 others. *Books:* 717,924 (physical), 770,553 (digital/electronic); *Serial titles:* 319,932 (physical), 94,450 (digital/electronic). Students can reserve study rooms.

STUDENT LIFE

Housing options: women-only, cooperative. Campus housing is university owned. Freshman campus housing is guaranteed.

Activities and organizations: drama/theater group, student-run newspaper, radio and television station, choral group, Student Government, community service organizations, cultural clubs, societies, theater groups.

Athletics Member NCAA. All Division III. *Intercollegiate sports:* basketball W, crew W, cross-country running W, fencing W, field hockey W, golf W, lacrosse W, rugby W(c), sailing W(c), skiing (downhill) W(c), soccer W, softball W, squash W, swimming and diving W, tennis W, track and field W, ultimate Frisbee W(c), volleyball W. *Intramural sports:* archery W, badminton W(c), basketball W, cheerleading W(c), crew W, equestrian sports W(c), ice hockey W(c), racquetball W(c), rock climbing W(c), sailing W(c), skiing (cross-country) W, skiing (downhill) W, soccer W, softball W, squash W(c), swimming and diving W, table tennis W(c), tennis W, volleyball W, water polo W.

Campus security: 24-hour emergency response devices and patrols, late-night transport/escort service, controlled dormitory access.

Student services: health clinic, personal/psychological counseling, women's center.

COSTS & FINANCIAL AID

Costs (2017–18) *Comprehensive fee:* $66,984 includes full-time tuition ($50,840), mandatory fees ($308), and room and board ($15,836). Part-time tuition: $6355 per course. Part-time tuition and fees vary according to course load. *Required fees:* $39 per course part-time. *College room only:* $8040. *Payment plans:* tuition prepayment, installment. *Waivers:* employees or children of employees.

Financial Aid Of all full-time matriculated undergraduates who enrolled in 2016, 1,560 applied for aid, 1,403 were judged to have need, 1,403 had their need fully met. *Average percent of need met:* 100. *Average financial aid package:* $47,527. *Average need-based loan:* $3728. *Average need-based gift aid:* $45,178. *Average indebtedness upon graduation:* $13,415.

APPLYING

Standardized Tests *Required:* SAT or ACT (for admission).

Options: electronic application, early admission, early decision, deferred entrance.

Required: essay or personal statement, high school transcript, 3 letters of recommendation, first senior marking period grades and mid-year report. *Required for some:* interview. *Recommended:* interview.

Application deadlines: 1/15 (freshmen), 3/1 (transfers).

Early decision deadline: 11/1 (for plan 1), 1/1 (for plan 2).

Notification: 4/1 (freshmen), 5/15 (transfers), 12/15 (early decision plan 1), 2/28 (early decision plan 2).

CONTACT
Ms. Grace Cheng, Director of Admission, Wellesley College, 106 Central Street, Wellesley, MA 02481. *Phone:* 781-283-2270. *Fax:* 781-283-3678. *E-mail:* admission@wellesley.edu.

★ Wentworth Institute of Technology
Boston, Massachusetts
http://www.wit.edu/

- **Independent** comprehensive, founded 1904
- **Urban** 31-acre campus with easy access to Boston, MA
- **Endowment** $94.1 million
- **Coed** 4,262 undergraduate students, 92% full-time, 21% women, 79% men
- **Moderately difficult** entrance level, 92% of applicants were admitted

UNDERGRAD STUDENTS

3,904 full-time, 358 part-time. Students come from 29 states and territories; 60 other countries; 34% are from out of state; 4% Black or African American, non-Hispanic/Latino; 10% Hispanic/Latino; 7% Asian, non-Hispanic/Latino; 0.1% American Indian or Alaska Native, non-Hispanic/Latino; 2% Two or more races, non-Hispanic/Latino; 7% Race/ethnicity unknown; 8% international; 4% transferred in; 49% live on campus.

Freshmen:
Admission: 6,172 applied, 5,670 admitted, 967 enrolled. *Average high school GPA:* 3.1. *Test scores:* SAT evidence-based reading and writing scores over 500: 88%; SAT math scores over 500: 95%; ACT scores over 18: 96%; SAT evidence-based reading and writing scores over 600: 39%; SAT math scores over 600: 50%; ACT scores over 24: 58%; SAT evidence-based reading and writing scores over 700: 5%; SAT math scores over 700: 8%; ACT scores over 30: 15%.

Retention: 84% of full-time freshmen returned.

FACULTY

Total: 354, 45% full-time, 25% with terminal degrees.

Student/faculty ratio: 17:1.

ACADEMICS

Calendar: semesters for freshmen and sophomores, trimesters for juniors and seniors. *Degrees:* certificates, associate, bachelor's, and master's.

Special study options: academic remediation for entering students, advanced placement credit, cooperative education, distance learning, internships, off-campus study, part-time degree program, services for LD students, study abroad, summer session for credit. *ROTC:* Army (c), Air Force (c).

Computers: 320 computers/terminals and 200 ports are available on campus for general student use. Students can access the following: campus intranet, computer help desk, free student e-mail accounts, online (class) grades, online (class) registration, online (class) schedules. Campuswide network is available. 100% of college-owned or -operated housing units are wired for high-speed Internet access. Wireless service is available via entire campus.

Library: Douglas D. Schumann Library & Learning Commons plus 1 other. *Books:* 51,754 (physical), 244,116 (digital/electronic); *Serial titles:* 210 (physical), 77,225 (digital/electronic); *Databases:* 75. Weekly public service hours: 100.

STUDENT LIFE

Housing options: on-campus residence required through sophomore year; coed. Campus housing is university owned. Freshman campus housing is guaranteed.

Activities and organizations: student-run radio station, Intramural Sports, Wentworth Events Board, Multicultural Student Association, Phi Sigma Pi, Major Particular Professional Student Associations.

Athletics Member NCAA. All Division III. *Intercollegiate sports:* baseball M, basketball M/W, crew M, cross-country running M, golf M, ice hockey M, lacrosse M/W, rugby M(c)/W(c), soccer M/W, softball W, tennis M/W, ultimate Frisbee M(c)/W(c), volleyball M/W.

Campus security: 24-hour emergency response devices and patrols, student patrols, late-night transport/escort service, controlled dormitory access.

Student services: health clinic, personal/psychological counseling, women's center.

COSTS & FINANCIAL AID

Costs (2017–18) *Comprehensive fee:* $48,821 includes full-time tuition ($32,954), mandatory fees ($2023), and room and board ($13,844). Full-time tuition and fees vary according to class time, course load, and program. Part-time tuition: $1030 per credit hour. Part-time tuition and fees vary according to class time, course load, and program. *Room and board:* Room and board charges vary according to board plan and housing facility. *Payment plan:* installment. *Waivers:* employees or children of employees.

Financial Aid Of all full-time matriculated undergraduates who enrolled in 2017, 3,711 applied for aid, 2,773 were judged to have need, 202 had their need fully met. In 2017, 843 non-need-based awards were made. *Average percent of need met:* 52. *Average financial aid package:* $20,181. *Average need-based loan:* $4585. *Average need-based gift aid:* $14,111. *Average non-need-based aid:* $10,487. *Average indebtedness upon graduation:* $59,419.

APPLYING

Standardized Tests *Required:* SAT or ACT (for admission).

Options: electronic application, deferred entrance.

Application fee: $50.

Required: essay or personal statement, high school transcript, 1 letter of recommendation. *Recommended:* minimum 2.0 GPA, interview.

Application deadlines: 2/15 (freshmen), rolling (out-of-state freshmen), 5/1 (transfers).

Notification: continuous (freshmen), continuous (transfers).

CONTACT

Ms. Amy Dufour, Senior Associate Director of Admissions, Wentworth Institute of Technology, 550 Huntington Avenue, Boston, MA 02115. *Phone:* 617-989-4116. *Toll-free phone:* 800-556-0610. *Fax:* 617-989-4010. *E-mail:* dufoura@wit.edu.

See below for display ad and page 1494 for the College Close-Up.

Western New England University

Springfield, Massachusetts

http://www.wne.edu/

- **Independent** comprehensive, founded 1919
- **Suburban** 215-acre campus
- **Endowment** $73.0 million
- **Coed** 2,736 undergraduate students, 96% full-time, 37% women, 63% men
- **Moderately difficult** entrance level, 81% of applicants were admitted

UNDERGRAD STUDENTS

2,613 full-time, 123 part-time. Students come from 26 states and territories; 22 other countries; 49% are from out of state; 6% Black or African American, non-Hispanic/Latino; 9% Hispanic/Latino; 3% Asian, non-Hispanic/Latino; 0.3% Native Hawaiian or other Pacific Islander, non-Hispanic/Latino; 0.3% American Indian or Alaska Native, non-Hispanic/Latino; 2% Two or more races, non-Hispanic/Latino; 3% Race/ethnicity unknown; 3% international; 4% transferred in; 61% live on campus.

Freshmen:

Admission: 6,645 applied, 5,363 admitted, 770 enrolled. *Average high school GPA:* 3.4. *Test scores:* SAT evidence-based reading and writing scores over 500: 71%; SAT math scores over 500: 78%; ACT scores over 18: 99%; SAT evidence-based reading and writing scores over 600: 11%; SAT math scores over 600: 29%; ACT scores over 24: 60%; SAT evidence-based reading and writing scores over 700: 1%; SAT math scores over 700: 2%; ACT scores over 30: 9%.

Retention: 75% of full-time freshmen returned.

FACULTY

Total: 367, 66% full-time.

Student/faculty ratio: 12:1.

ACADEMICS

Calendar: semesters. *Degrees:* certificates, associate, bachelor's, master's, doctoral, and postbachelor's certificates.

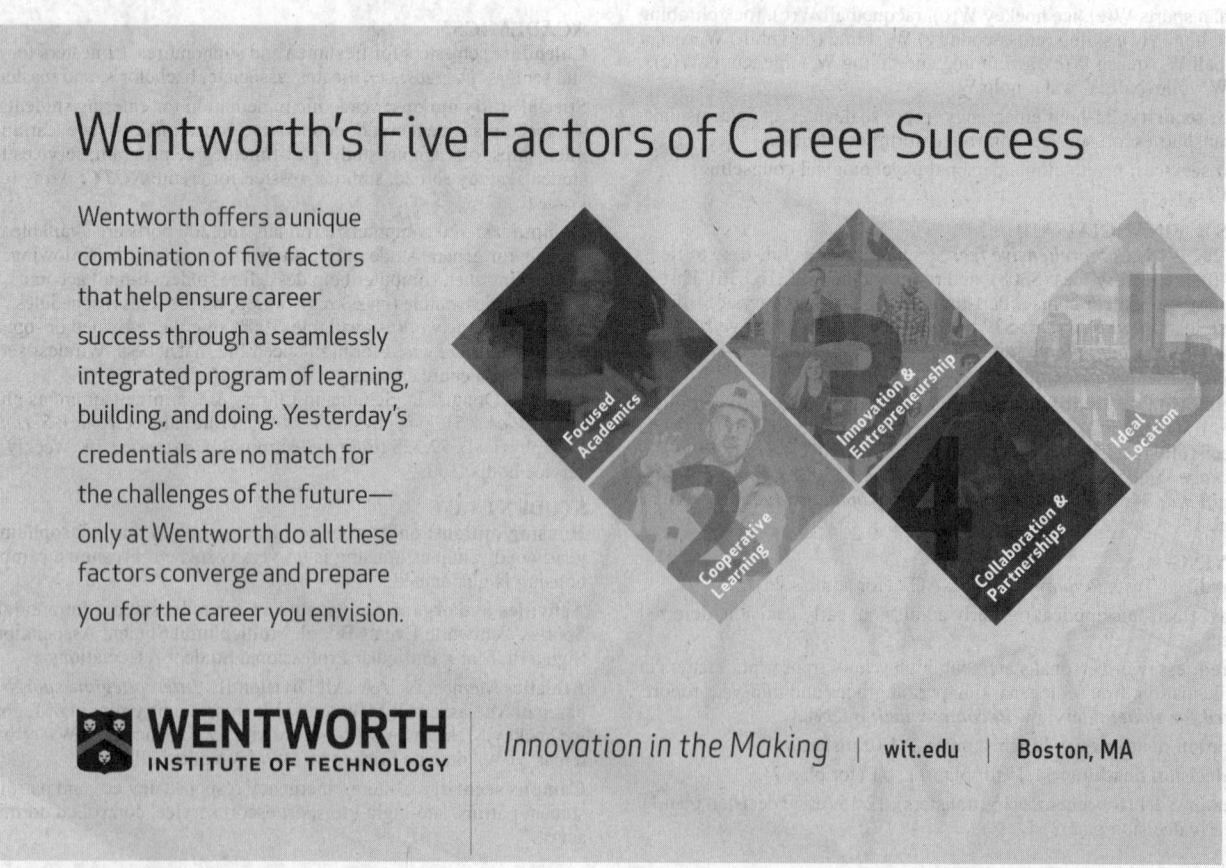

Special study options: accelerated degree program, adult/continuing education programs, advanced placement credit, distance learning, double majors, honors programs, independent study, internships, off-campus study, part-time degree program, services for LD students, study abroad, summer session for credit. *ROTC:* Army (b), Air Force (c).

Unusual degree programs: 3-2 business administration; engineering.

Computers: 530 computers/terminals are available on campus for general student use. Students can access the following: campus intranet, computer help desk, free student e-mail accounts, online (class) grades, online (class) registration, online (class) schedules. Campuswide network is available. 100% of college-owned or -operated housing units are wired for high-speed Internet access. Wireless service is available via entire campus.

Library: D'Amour Library plus 1 other. *Books:* 106,500 (physical), 31,912 (digital/electronic); *Serial titles:* 46 (physical), 109,440 (digital/electronic); *Databases:* 128. Weekly public service hours: 97; study areas open 24 hours, 5–7 days a week.

STUDENT LIFE

Housing options: coed, special housing for students with disabilities. Campus housing is university owned. Freshman campus housing is guaranteed.

Activities and organizations: drama/theater group, student-run newspaper, radio and television station, choral group, Student Senate, Residence Hall Association, Campus Activities Board, student radio station, The Westerner (student newspaper).

Athletics Member NCAA. All Division III. *Intercollegiate sports:* baseball M, basketball M/W, cross-country running M/W, field hockey W, football M, golf M, ice hockey M, lacrosse M/W, soccer M/W, softball W, swimming and diving W, tennis M/W, volleyball W, wrestling M. *Intramural sports:* basketball M/W, bowling M/W, football M/W, racquetball M/W, rugby M(c), soccer M/W, softball M/W, table tennis M/W, volleyball M/W, water polo M/W.

Campus security: 24-hour emergency response devices and patrols, student patrols, late-night transport/escort service, controlled dormitory access, security cameras.

Student services: health clinic, personal/psychological counseling.

COSTS & FINANCIAL AID

Costs (2017–18) *Comprehensive fee:* $49,182 includes full-time tuition ($33,338), mandatory fees ($2402), and room and board ($13,442). Full-time tuition and fees vary according to course load and program. Part-time tuition: $628 per credit. Part-time tuition and fees vary according to course load and program. *Room and board:* Room and board charges vary according to board plan and housing facility. *Payment plans:* tuition prepayment, installment. *Waivers:* employees or children of employees.

Financial Aid Of all full-time matriculated undergraduates who enrolled in 2017, 2,514 applied for aid, 2,056 were judged to have need, 286 had their need fully met. 959 Federal Work-Study jobs (averaging $1935). In 2017, 423 non-need-based awards were made. *Average percent of need met:* 73. *Average financial aid package:* $26,004. *Average need-based loan:* $4373. *Average need-based gift aid:* $20,940. *Average non-need-based aid:* $14,123. *Average indebtedness upon graduation:* $36,517.

APPLYING

Standardized Tests *Required for some:* SAT or ACT (for admission).

Options: electronic application, early admission, deferred entrance.

Application fee: $40.

Required: high school transcript, 1 letter of recommendation.

Recommended: essay or personal statement, interview.

Application deadlines: rolling (freshmen), rolling (transfers).

Notification: continuous (freshmen), continuous (transfers).

CONTACT

Mr. Bryan Gross, Vice President for Enrollment Management, Western New England University, 1215 Wilbraham Road, Springfield, MA 01119. *Phone:* 413-782-1321. *Toll-free phone:* 800-325-1122 Ext. 1321. *Fax:* 413-782-1777. *E-mail:* learn@wne.edu.

Westfield State University
Westfield, Massachusetts
http://www.westfield.ma.edu/

- **State-supported** comprehensive, founded 1839, part of Massachusetts Public Higher Education System
- **Suburban** 256-acre campus
- **Endowment** $5.5 million
- **Coed** 5,552 undergraduate students, 86% full-time, 53% women, 47% men
- **Moderately difficult** entrance level, 85% of applicants were admitted

UNDERGRAD STUDENTS

4,791 full-time, 761 part-time. Students come from 21 states and territories; 18 other countries; 7% are from out of state; 5% Black or African American, non-Hispanic/Latino; 10% Hispanic/Latino; 2% Asian, non-Hispanic/Latino; 0.1% Native Hawaiian or other Pacific Islander, non-Hispanic/Latino; 0.3% American Indian or Alaska Native, non-Hispanic/Latino; 5% Two or more races, non-Hispanic/Latino; 4% Race/ethnicity unknown; 0.4% international; 8% transferred in; 51% live on campus.

Freshmen:
Admission: 4,381 applied, 3,735 admitted, 1,011 enrolled. *Average high school GPA:* 3.1. *Test scores:* SAT evidence-based reading and writing scores over 500: 75%; SAT math scores over 500: 70%; ACT scores over 18: 94%; SAT evidence-based reading and writing scores over 600: 19%; SAT math scores over 600: 14%; ACT scores over 24: 34%; SAT evidence-based reading and writing scores over 700: 1%; SAT math scores over 700: 1%; ACT scores over 30: 6%.
Retention: 79% of full-time freshmen returned.

FACULTY
Total: 524, 44% full-time, 54% with terminal degrees.
Student/faculty ratio: 16:1.

ACADEMICS
Calendar: semesters. *Degrees:* bachelor's, master's, and postbachelor's certificates.

Special study options: adult/continuing education programs, advanced placement credit, distance learning, double majors, honors programs, independent study, internships, off-campus study, part-time degree program, services for LD students, student-designed majors, study abroad, summer session for credit. *ROTC:* Army (c), Air Force (c).

Computers: 814 computers/terminals are available on campus for general student use. Students can access the following: computer help desk, free student e-mail accounts, online (class) grades, online (class) registration, online (class) schedules, online transcripts and billing information, Web portal. Campuswide network is available. 100% of college-owned or -operated housing units are wired for high-speed Internet access. Wireless service is available via entire campus.

Library: Governor Joseph B. Ely Library. *Books:* 129,289 (physical), 160,388 (digital/electronic); *Serial titles:* 5,137 (physical), 25,808 (digital/electronic); *Databases:* 138. Weekly public service hours: 92; students can reserve study rooms.

STUDENT LIFE
Housing options: coed, special housing for students with disabilities. Campus housing is university owned. Freshman applicants given priority for college housing.

Activities and organizations: drama/theater group, student-run newspaper, radio and television station, choral group, Student National Education Association, Student Government Association, Campus Activities Board, The Dance Company, Multicultural Student Association.

Athletics Member NCAA. All Division III. *Intercollegiate sports:* baseball M, basketball M/W, cross-country running M/W, field hockey W, football M, golf M/W, ice hockey M, lacrosse W, soccer M/W, softball W, swimming and diving W, track and field M/W, volleyball W. *Intramural sports:* basketball M, equestrian sports M(c)/W(c), football M, ice hockey M(c)/W(c), lacrosse M(c), rock climbing M(c)/W(c), rugby M(c)/W(c), skiing (downhill) M(c)/W(c), soccer M/W, softball M, ultimate Frisbee M(c)/W(c), volleyball M/W, weight lifting M(c)/W(c).

Campus security: 24-hour emergency response devices and patrols, student patrols, late-night transport/escort service, controlled dormitory access.

Student services: health clinic, personal/psychological counseling, legal services.

COSTS & FINANCIAL AID

Costs (2017–18) *Tuition:* state resident $970 full-time, $306 per credit hour part-time; nonresident $7050 full-time, $306 per credit hour part-time. Full-time tuition and fees vary according to program and reciprocity agreements. Part-time tuition and fees vary according to course load. *Required fees:* $8745 full-time, $75 per term part-time. *Room and board:* $10,689. Room and board charges vary according to board plan and housing facility. *Payment plan:* installment. *Waivers:* senior citizens and employees or children of employees.

Financial Aid Of all full-time matriculated undergraduates who enrolled in 2016, 4,339 applied for aid, 3,123 were judged to have need, 332 had their need fully met. 299 Federal Work-Study jobs (averaging $1454). In 2016, 100 non-need-based awards were made. *Average percent of need met:* 62. *Average financial aid package:* $8746. *Average need-based loan:* $4133. *Average need-based gift aid:* $5798. *Average non-need-based aid:* $3408. *Average indebtedness upon graduation:* $29,050.

APPLYING

Standardized Tests *Required:* SAT or ACT (for admission).

Options: electronic application, deferred entrance.

Application fee: $50.

Required: high school transcript, minimum 3.0 GPA. *Required for some:* interview, audition for music majors, portfolio for art majors, essay and interview for nursing majors, sliding scale minimum high school GPA using SAT/ACT scores for GPAs between 2.0 and 3.0.

Application deadlines: 3/1 (freshmen), 3/1 (transfers).

Notification: continuous until 3/15 (freshmen), continuous until 3/15 (transfers).

CONTACT

Dr. Kelly Hart, Director of Admissions, Westfield State University, 333 Western Avenue, Westfield, MA 01002. *Phone:* 413-572-5218. *Fax:* 413-572-0520. *E-mail:* admission@westfield.ma.edu.

Wheaton College

Norton, Massachusetts

http://www.wheatoncollege.edu/

- **Independent** 4-year, founded 1834
- **Suburban** 478-acre campus with easy access to Boston, MA
- **Endowment** $205.0 million
- **Coed** 1,688 undergraduate students, 99% full-time, 61% women, 39% men
- **Very difficult** entrance level, 48% of applicants were admitted

UNDERGRAD STUDENTS

1,675 full-time, 13 part-time. Students come from 40 states and territories; 71 other countries; 63% are from out of state; 6% Black or African American, non-Hispanic/Latino; 8% Hispanic/Latino; 5% Asian, non-Hispanic/Latino; 0.1% Native Hawaiian or other Pacific Islander, non-Hispanic/Latino; 0.1% American Indian or Alaska Native, non-Hispanic/Latino; 3% Two or more races, non-Hispanic/Latino; 1% Race/ethnicity unknown; 10% international; 0.4% transferred in; 96% live on campus.

Freshmen:

Admission: 6,089 applied, 2,916 admitted, 502 enrolled. *Average high school GPA:* 3.4. *Test scores:* SAT evidence-based reading and writing scores over 500: 96%; SAT math scores over 500: 96%; ACT scores over 18: 100%; SAT evidence-based reading and writing scores over 600: 75%; SAT math scores over 600: 60%; ACT scores over 24: 90%; SAT evidence-based reading and writing scores over 700: 18%; SAT math scores over 700: 16%; ACT scores over 30: 37%.

Retention: 88% of full-time freshmen returned.

FACULTY

Total: 189, 72% full-time, 80% with terminal degrees.

Student/faculty ratio: 10:1.

ACADEMICS

Calendar: semesters. *Degree:* bachelor's.

Special study options: accelerated degree program, advanced placement credit, cooperative education, double majors, honors programs, independent study, internships, off-campus study, services for LD students, student-designed majors, study abroad, summer session for credit. *ROTC:* Army (c).

Unusual degree programs: engineering with Dartmouth College; theology with Andover Newton Theological School, optometry with New England School of Optometry, integrated marketing communication studies with Emerson College, Clark University.

Computers: 196 computers/terminals are available on campus for general student use. Students can access the following: campus intranet, computer help desk, free student e-mail accounts, online (class) grades, online (class) registration, online (class) schedules, assistive technology, online software training, media equipment loan program. Campuswide network is available. 100% of college-owned or -operated housing units are wired for high-speed Internet access. Wireless service is available via entire campus.

Library: Madeleine Clark Wallace Library. *Books:* 342,617 (physical), 159,639 (digital/electronic); *Serial titles:* 131 (physical), 38,862 (digital/electronic); *Databases:* 76. Weekly public service hours: 114; students can reserve study rooms.

STUDENT LIFE

Housing options: coed, women-only, special housing for students with disabilities. Campus housing is university owned. Freshman campus housing is guaranteed.

Activities and organizations: drama/theater group, student-run newspaper, radio station, choral group, Student Government Association, Performance Groups (a capella, dance and improv), Black Student Association (BSA), Programming Activities Council, Feminist Association of Wheaton (FAW).

Athletics Member NCAA. All Division III. *Intercollegiate sports:* baseball M, basketball M/W, cross-country running M/W, field hockey W, lacrosse M/W, soccer M/W, softball W, swimming and diving M/W, tennis M/W, track and field M/W, volleyball W. *Intramural sports:* archery M(c)/W(c), badminton M/W, basketball M/W, cheerleading M(c)/W(c), equestrian sports M(c)/W(c), fencing M(c)/W(c), football M/W, golf M/W, ice hockey M(c)/W(c), rugby M(c)/W(c), soccer M/W, tennis M(c)/W(c), triathlon M(c)/W(c), ultimate Frisbee M(c)/W(c).

Campus security: 24-hour emergency response devices and patrols, student patrols, late-night transport/escort service, controlled dormitory access.

Student services: health clinic, personal/psychological counseling.

COSTS & FINANCIAL AID

Costs (2018–19) *One-time required fee:* $50. *Comprehensive fee:* $66,050 includes full-time tuition ($52,288), mandatory fees ($338), and room and board ($13,424). Part-time tuition: $6536 per course. *College room only:* $7160. *Payment plan:* installment. *Waivers:* employees or children of employees.

Financial Aid Of all full-time matriculated undergraduates who enrolled in 2017, 1,268 applied for aid, 1,158 were judged to have need, 595 had their need fully met. 640 Federal Work-Study jobs (averaging $1900). 358 state and other part-time jobs (averaging $1770). In 2017, 490 non-need-based awards were made. *Average percent of need met:* 94. *Average financial aid package:* $41,564. *Average need-based loan:* $4983. *Average need-based gift aid:* $34,058. *Average non-need-based aid:* $19,953. *Average indebtedness upon graduation:* $35,058. *Financial aid deadline:* 2/1.

APPLYING

Options: electronic application, early admission, early decision, early action, deferred entrance.

Application fee: $60.

Required: essay or personal statement, high school transcript, 2 letters of recommendation. *Recommended:* interview.

Application deadlines: 1/1 (freshmen), 5/1 (transfers), 11/1 (early action).

Early decision deadline: 11/1 (for plan 1), 1/1 (for plan 2).

Notification: 4/1 (freshmen), 5/15 (transfers), 12/15 (early decision plan 1), 2/1 (early decision plan 2), 1/15 (early action).

CONTACT
Grant M. Gosselin, Vice President for Enrollment and Dean of Admission and Student Aid, Wheaton College, 26 East Main Street, Norton, MA 02766. *Phone:* 508-286-8251. *Toll-free phone:* 800-394-6003. *Fax:* 508-286-8271. *E-mail:* admission@wheatoncollege.edu.

Williams College
Williamstown, Massachusetts
http://www.williams.edu/
- **Independent** comprehensive, founded 1793
- **Small-town** 450-acre campus with easy access to Albany NY
- **Endowment** $2.6 billion
- **Coed** 2,061 undergraduate students, 98% full-time, 47% women, 53% men
- **Most difficult** entrance level, 15% of applicants were admitted

UNDERGRAD STUDENTS
2,018 full-time, 43 part-time. Students come from 47 states and territories; 57 other countries; 86% are from out of state; 8% Black or African American, non-Hispanic/Latino; 13% Hispanic/Latino; 13% Asian, non-Hispanic/Latino; 0.1% American Indian or Alaska Native, non-Hispanic/Latino; 6% Two or more races, non-Hispanic/Latino; 1% Race/ethnicity unknown; 8% international; 0.3% transferred in; 93% live on campus.

Freshmen:
Admission: 8,593 applied, 1,253 admitted, 548 enrolled. *Test scores:* SAT evidence-based reading and writing scores over 500: 100%; SAT math scores over 500: 101%; ACT scores over 18: 100%; SAT evidence-based reading and writing scores over 600: 99%; SAT math scores over 600: 97%; ACT scores over 24: 100%; SAT evidence-based reading and writing scores over 700: 78%; SAT math scores over 700: 73%; ACT scores over 30: 87%.
Retention: 98% of full-time freshmen returned.

FACULTY
Total: 364, 80% full-time, 92% with terminal degrees.
Student/faculty ratio: 7:1.

ACADEMICS
Calendar: 4-1-4. *Degrees:* bachelor's and master's.
Special study options: double majors, independent study, internships, off-campus study, services for LD students, student-designed majors, study abroad. *ROTC:* Air Force (c).
Unusual degree programs: 3-2 engineering with Columbia University, Dartmouth College.
Computers: 1,000 computers/terminals are available on campus for general student use. Students can access the following: computer help desk, free student e-mail accounts, online (class) grades, online (class) registration, online (class) schedules. Campuswide network is available. 100% of college-owned or -operated housing units are wired for high-speed Internet access. Wireless service is available via entire campus.
Library: Sawyer Library plus 2 others. *Books:* 998,634 (physical); *Serial titles:* 738 (physical), 93,053 (digital/electronic). Weekly public service hours: 118; study areas open 24 hours, 5–7 days a week; students can reserve study rooms.

STUDENT LIFE
Housing options: on-campus residence required for freshman year; coed, cooperative, special housing for students with disabilities. Campus housing is university owned. Freshman campus housing is guaranteed.
Activities and organizations: drama/theater group, student-run newspaper, radio station, choral group, marching band.
Athletics Member NCAA. All Division III except men's and women's skiing (cross-country) (Division I), men's and women's skiing (downhill) (Division I). *Intercollegiate sports:* badminton M(c)/W(c), baseball M, basketball M/W, crew M/W, cross-country running M/W, equestrian sports M(c)/W(c), fencing M(c)/W(c), field hockey W, football M, golf M/W, ice hockey M/W, lacrosse M/W, rugby M(c)/W(c), sailing M(c)/W(c), skiing (cross-country) M/W, skiing (downhill) M/W, soccer M/W, softball W, squash M/W, swimming and diving M/W, tennis M/W, track and field M/W, ultimate Frisbee M(c)/W(c), volleyball M(c)/W, water polo M(c)/W(c), wrestling M. *Intramural sports:* basketball M/W, bowling M(c)/W(c), gymnastics M/W, ice hockey M/W, skiing (cross-country) M/W, skiing (downhill) M/W, soccer M/W, softball M/W, tennis M(c)/W(c), ultimate Frisbee M(c)/W(c), volleyball M/W, water polo M/W.
Campus security: 24-hour emergency response devices and patrols, student patrols, late-night transport/escort service, controlled dormitory access.
Student services: health clinic, personal/psychological counseling.

COSTS & FINANCIAL AID
Costs (2017–18) *Comprehensive fee:* $67,700 includes full-time tuition ($53,240), mandatory fees ($310), and room and board ($14,150). *College room only:* $7170. Room and board charges vary according to board plan. *Payment plan:* installment.
Financial Aid Of all full-time matriculated undergraduates who enrolled in 2017, 1,175 applied for aid, 1,026 were judged to have need, 1,026 had their need fully met. *Average percent of need met:* 100. *Average financial aid package:* $54,932. *Average need-based loan:* $3012. *Average need-based gift aid:* $51,773. *Average indebtedness upon graduation:* $16,230. *Financial aid deadline:* 1/15.

APPLYING
Standardized Tests *Required:* SAT or ACT (for admission).
Options: electronic application, early admission, early decision, deferred entrance.
Application fee: $65.
Required: essay or personal statement, high school transcript, 2 letters of recommendation.
Application deadlines: 1/1 (freshmen), 4/1 (transfers).
Early decision deadline: 11/15.
Notification: 4/7 (freshmen), 5/15 (transfers), 12/15 (early decision).

CONTACT
Mr. Richard L. Nesbitt, Director of Admission, Williams College, 995 Main Street, Williamstown, MA 01267. *Phone:* 413-597-2211. *Fax:* 413-597-4052. *E-mail:* admission@williams.edu.

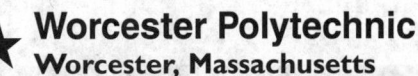

★ Worcester Polytechnic Institute
Worcester, Massachusetts
http://www.wpi.edu/
- **Independent** university, founded 1865
- **Suburban** 95-acre campus with easy access to Boston
- **Endowment** $502.5 million
- **Coed** 4,435 undergraduate students, 97% full-time, 36% women, 64% men
- **Very difficult** entrance level, 48% of applicants were admitted

UNDERGRAD STUDENTS
4,301 full-time, 134 part-time. Students come from 46 states and territories; 69 other countries; 57% are from out of state; 3% Black or African American, non-Hispanic/Latino; 9% Hispanic/Latino; 3% Asian, non-Hispanic/Latino; 0.4% American Indian or Alaska Native, non-Hispanic/Latino; 2% Two or more races, non-Hispanic/Latino; 8% Race/ethnicity unknown; 11% international; 0.9% transferred in; 59% live on campus.

Freshmen:
Admission: 10,331 applied, 5,009 admitted, 1,124 enrolled. *Average high school GPA:* 3.9. *Test scores:* SAT evidence-based reading and writing scores over 500: 99%; SAT math scores over 500: 100%; ACT scores over 18: 100%; SAT evidence-based reading and writing scores over 600: 86%; SAT math scores over 600: 94%; ACT scores over 24: 98%; SAT evidence-based reading and writing scores over 700: 31%; SAT math scores over 700: 49%; ACT scores over 30: 61%.
Retention: 95% of full-time freshmen returned.

FACULTY
Total: 516, 75% full-time, 80% with terminal degrees.
Student/faculty ratio: 13:1.

ACADEMICS
Calendar: 4 7-week terms. *Degrees:* bachelor's, master's, doctoral, and post-master's certificates.

Special study options: accelerated degree program, advanced placement credit, cooperative education, distance learning, double majors, English as a second language, independent study, internships, off-campus study, part-time degree program, services for LD students, student-designed majors, study abroad, summer session for credit. *ROTC:* Army (b), Navy (c), Air Force (b).

Computers: 860 computers/terminals and 800 ports are available on campus for general student use. Students can access the following: campus intranet, computer help desk, free student e-mail accounts, online (class) grades, online (class) registration, online (class) schedules, online course content. Campuswide network is available. 100% of college-owned or -operated housing units are wired for high-speed Internet access. Wireless service is available via entire campus.

Library: George C. Gordon Library plus 1 other. *Books:* 198,648 (physical), 1.4 million (digital/electronic); *Serial titles:* 5,116 (physical), 227,285 (digital/electronic); *Databases:* 490. Weekly public service hours: 107; students can reserve study rooms.

STUDENT LIFE

Housing options: coed, special housing for students with disabilities. Campus housing is university owned. Freshman campus housing is guaranteed.

Activities and organizations: drama/theater group, student-run newspaper, radio station, choral group, Student Government Association, Panhellenic, Interfraternity Council, Intramural and Club Sports, Music Association, national fraternities, national sororities.

Athletics Member NCAA. All Division III. *Intercollegiate sports:* baseball M, basketball M/W, crew M/W, cross-country running M/W, field hockey W, football M, soccer M/W, softball W, swimming and diving M/W, track and field M/W, volleyball W, wrestling M. *Intramural sports:* badminton M(c)/W(c), basketball M/W, cheerleading M(c)/W(c), fencing M(c)/W(c), football M, golf M(c)/W(c), ice hockey M(c), lacrosse M(c)/W(c), racquetball M(c)/W(c), rugby M(c)/W(c), sailing M(c)/W(c), skiing (downhill) M(c)/W(c), soccer M/W, squash M(c)/W(c), table tennis M(c)/W(c), tennis M(c)/W(c), ultimate Frisbee M(c)/W(c), volleyball M/W, water polo M(c)/W(c), wrestling M(c).

Campus security: 24-hour emergency response devices and patrols, student patrols, late-night transport/escort service, controlled dormitory access.

Student services: health clinic, personal/psychological counseling.

COSTS & FINANCIAL AID

Costs (2017–18) *One-time required fee:* $200. *Comprehensive fee:* $62,846 includes full-time tuition ($47,988), mandatory fees ($640), and room and board ($14,218). Part-time tuition: $1333 per credit hour. Part-time tuition and fees vary according to course load. *College room only:* $8122. Room and board charges vary according to board plan and housing facility. *Payment plans:* tuition prepayment, installment, deferred payment. *Waivers:* employees or children of employees.

Financial Aid Of all full-time matriculated undergraduates who enrolled in 2016, 3,136 applied for aid, 2,678 were judged to have need, 1,256 had their need fully met. 466 Federal Work-Study jobs (averaging $1503). In 2016, 1487 non-need-based awards were made. *Average percent of need met:* 81. *Average financial aid package:* $35,614. *Average need-based loan:* $2267. *Average need-based gift aid:* $22,942. *Average non-need-based aid:* $15,800. *Financial aid deadline:* 2/1.

APPLYING

Standardized Tests *Required for some:* IELTS or TOEFL.

Options: electronic application, early admission, early action, deferred entrance.

Application fee: $65.

Required: essay or personal statement, high school transcript, 2 letters of recommendation. *Required for some:* interview.

Application deadlines: 2/1 (freshmen), 4/15 (transfers), 11/1 (early action).

Notification: 4/1 (freshmen), continuous (transfers), 12/20 (early action).

CONTACT

Jennifer Cluett, Director of Undergraduate Admissions, Worcester Polytechnic Institute, 100 Institute Road, Worcester, MA 01609-2280. *Phone:* 508-831-5286. *Fax:* 508-831-5875. *E-mail:* admissions@wpi.edu.

See below for display ad and page 1508 for the College Close-Up.

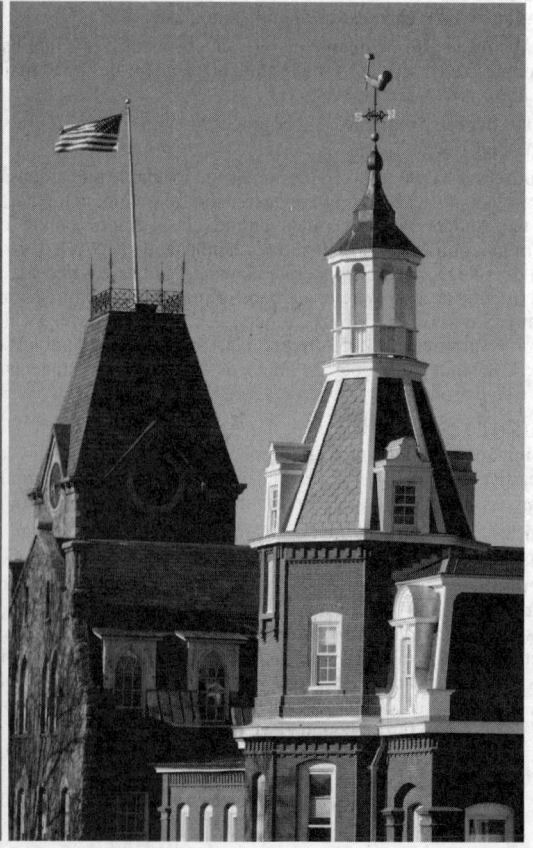

Worcester State University

Worcester, Massachusetts

http://www.worcester.edu/

- **State-supported** comprehensive, founded 1874, part of Massachusetts Public Higher Education System
- **Urban** 58-acre campus with easy access to Boston
- **Endowment** $14.1 million
- **Coed** 5,495 undergraduate students, 76% full-time, 59% women, 41% men
- **Moderately difficult** entrance level, 76% of applicants were admitted

UNDERGRAD STUDENTS

4,153 full-time, 1,342 part-time. Students come from 26 states and territories; 18 other countries; 4% are from out of state; 9% Black or African American, non-Hispanic/Latino; 12% Hispanic/Latino; 5% Asian, non-Hispanic/Latino; 0.3% American Indian or Alaska Native, non-Hispanic/Latino; 3% Two or more races, non-Hispanic/Latino; 4% Race/ethnicity unknown; 0.9% international; 10% transferred in; 30% live on campus.

Freshmen:
Admission: 3,747 applied, 2,860 admitted, 909 enrolled. *Average high school GPA:* 3.3. *Test scores:* SAT evidence-based reading and writing scores over 500: 75%; SAT math scores over 500: 74%; ACT scores over 18: 90%; SAT evidence-based reading and writing scores over 600: 21%; SAT math scores over 600: 17%; ACT scores over 24: 42%; SAT evidence-based reading and writing scores over 700: 1%; SAT math scores over 700: 1%.

Retention: 80% of full-time freshmen returned.

FACULTY

Total: 441, 48% full-time, 50% with terminal degrees.
Student/faculty ratio: 17:1.

ACADEMICS

Calendar: semesters. *Degrees:* bachelor's, master's, post-master's, and postbachelor's certificates.

Special study options: academic remediation for entering students, accelerated degree program, adult/continuing education programs, advanced placement credit, distance learning, double majors, English as a second language, honors programs, independent study, internships, off-campus study, part-time degree program, services for LD students, student-designed majors, study abroad, summer session for credit. *ROTC:* Army (c), Navy (c), Air Force (c).

Computers: Students can access the following: campus intranet, computer help desk, free student e-mail accounts, online (class) grades, online (class) registration, online (class) schedules. Campuswide network is available. 100% of college-owned or -operated housing units are wired for high-speed Internet access. Wireless service is available via entire campus.

Library: Worcester State University Library. *Books:* 143,442 (physical), 152,949 (digital/electronic); *Serial titles:* 76 (physical), 137,540 (digital/electronic); *Databases:* 252. Weekly public service hours: 100.

STUDENT LIFE

Housing options: coed, men-only, women-only, special housing for students with disabilities. Campus housing is university owned.

Activities and organizations: drama/theater group, student-run radio and television station, choral group, Senate, SEC (Student Events Committee), TWA (Third World Alliance), WSCW (radio station), Dance Company/Club.

Athletics Member NCAA. All Division III. *Intercollegiate sports:* baseball M, basketball M/W, cross-country running M/W, field hockey W, football M, golf M/W, ice hockey M, lacrosse W, soccer M/W, softball W, tennis W, track and field M/W, volleyball W. *Intramural sports:* basketball M/W, cheerleading M/W, equestrian sports M/W, lacrosse M/W.

Campus security: 24-hour emergency response devices and patrols, late-night transport/escort service, controlled dormitory access, well-lit campus, limited access to campus at night.

Student services: health clinic, personal/psychological counseling.

COSTS & FINANCIAL AID

Costs (2017–18) *Tuition:* state resident $970 full-time, $40 per credit hour part-time; nonresident $7050 full-time, $294 per credit hour part-time. Full-time tuition and fees vary according to class time, course load, degree level, and reciprocity agreements. Part-time tuition and fees vary according to class time, course load, degree level, and reciprocity agreements. *Required fees:* $8562 full-time, $357 per credit hour part-time. *Room and board:* $12,006; room only: $8256. Room and board charges vary according to board plan and housing facility. *Payment plan:* installment. *Waivers:* senior citizens and employees or children of employees.

Financial Aid Of all full-time matriculated undergraduates who enrolled in 2016, 3,433 applied for aid, 2,474 were judged to have need, 959 had their need fully met. In 2016, 139 non-need-based awards were made. *Average percent of need met:* 80. *Average financial aid package:* $14,842. *Average need-based loan:* $3082. *Average need-based gift aid:* $5116. *Average non-need-based aid:* $2659. *Average indebtedness upon graduation:* $29,137. *Financial aid deadline:* 5/1.

APPLYING

Standardized Tests *Required for some:* SAT or ACT (for admission).

Options: electronic application, early action, deferred entrance.

Application fee: $50.

Required: high school transcript, minimum 2.0 GPA. *Required for some:* essay or personal statement.

Application deadlines: 5/1 (freshmen), rolling (transfers), 11/15 (early action).

Notification: 1/2 (freshmen), continuous (transfers), 12/15 (early action).

CONTACT

Worcester State University, 486 Chandler Street, Administration Building, Worcester, MA 01602-2597. *Phone:* 508-929-8040. *Fax:* 508-929-8183. *E-mail:* admissions@worcester.edu.

MICHIGAN

Adrian College

Adrian, Michigan

http://www.adrian.edu/

CONTACT

Mr. Frank Hribar, Vice President for Enrollment, Adrian College, 110 S. Madison Street, Adrian, MI 49221. *Phone:* 800-877-2246. *Toll-free phone:* 800-877-2246. *Fax:* 517-264-3331. *E-mail:* admissions@adrian.edu.

Albion College

Albion, Michigan

http://www.albion.edu/

- **Independent Methodist** 4-year, founded 1835
- **Small-town** 574-acre campus with easy access to Detroit
- **Endowment** $176.9 million
- **Coed** 1,568 undergraduate students, 99% full-time, 53% women, 47% men
- **Moderately difficult** entrance level, 71% of applicants were admitted

UNDERGRAD STUDENTS

1,554 full-time, 14 part-time. Students come from 28 states and territories; 18 other countries; 23% are from out of state; 13% Black or African American, non-Hispanic/Latino; 9% Hispanic/Latino; 3% Asian, non-Hispanic/Latino; 0.1% Native Hawaiian or other Pacific Islander, non-Hispanic/Latino; 0.2% American Indian or Alaska Native, non-Hispanic/Latino; 3% Two or more races, non-Hispanic/Latino; 5% Race/ethnicity unknown; 2% international; 3% transferred in; 94% live on campus.

Freshmen:
Admission: 3,884 applied, 2,742 admitted, 515 enrolled. *Average high school GPA:* 3.4. *Test scores:* SAT evidence-based reading and writing scores over 500: 80%; SAT math scores over 500: 76%; ACT scores over 18: 96%; SAT evidence-based reading and writing scores over 600: 30%;

SAT math scores over 600: 23%; ACT scores over 24: 44%; SAT evidence-based reading and writing scores over 700: 3%; SAT math scores over 700: 4%; ACT scores over 30: 7%.

Retention: 79% of full-time freshmen returned.

FACULTY

Total: 174, 63% full-time, 74% with terminal degrees.

Student/faculty ratio: 12:1.

ACADEMICS

Calendar: semesters. *Degree:* bachelor's.

Special study options: advanced placement credit, distance learning, double majors, honors programs, independent study, internships, off-campus study, part-time degree program, services for LD students, student-designed majors, study abroad, summer session for credit.

Unusual degree programs: 3-2 engineering with Columbia University, University of Michigan, Case Western Reserve University, Michigan Technological University; forestry with Duke University; nursing with Oakland University.

Computers: 185 computers/terminals and 2,000 ports are available on campus for general student use. Students can access the following: computer help desk, free student e-mail accounts, online (class) grades, online (class) registration, online (class) schedules, online student account and financial aid. Campuswide network is available. 100% of college-owned or -operated housing units are wired for high-speed Internet access. Wireless service is available via classrooms, computer centers, computer labs, dorm rooms, learning centers, libraries, student centers.

Library: Stockwell Mudd Libraries. *Books:* 346,622 (physical), 291,052 (digital/electronic); *Serial titles:* 779 (physical), 76,739 (digital/electronic); *Databases:* 205. Weekly public service hours: 110.

STUDENT LIFE

Housing options: on-campus residence required through senior year; coed, men-only, women-only, cooperative, special housing for students with disabilities. Campus housing is university owned. Freshman campus housing is guaranteed.

Activities and organizations: drama/theater group, student-run newspaper, radio station, choral group, marching band, Greek Life (Fraternities and Sororities), Student Senate (Student Government), Umbrella (Diversity Groups), Union Board (Programming Board), Spiritual Life (Religious Centered groups), national fraternities, national sororities.

Athletics Member NCAA. All Division III. *Intercollegiate sports:* baseball M, basketball M/W, cross-country running M/W, equestrian sports M/W, football M, golf M/W, lacrosse M/W, soccer M/W, softball W, swimming and diving M/W, tennis M/W, track and field M/W, volleyball W. *Intramural sports:* basketball M/W, cheerleading M(c)/W(c), ice hockey M(c)/W(c), racquetball M/W, rugby M/W, sailing M(c)/W(c), soccer M/W, softball M/W, swimming and diving M/W, tennis M/W, ultimate Frisbee M/W, volleyball M/W, water polo M(c)/W(c).

Campus security: 24-hour emergency response devices and patrols, late-night transport/escort service, controlled dormitory access.

Student services: health clinic, personal/psychological counseling, women's center.

COSTS & FINANCIAL AID

Costs (2018–19) *One-time required fee:* $185. *Comprehensive fee:* $57,970 includes full-time tuition ($45,070), mandatory fees ($520), and room and board ($12,380). Full-time tuition and fees vary according to course load. Part-time tuition: $1890 per semester hour. Part-time tuition and fees vary according to course load. *College room only:* $6080. Room and board charges vary according to board plan and housing facility. *Payment plans:* installment, deferred payment. *Waivers:* employees or children of employees.

Financial Aid Of all full-time matriculated undergraduates who enrolled in 2017, 1,295 applied for aid, 1,228 were judged to have need, 209 had their need fully met. 355 Federal Work-Study jobs (averaging $1320). 168 state and other part-time jobs (averaging $1770). In 2017, 324 non-need-based awards were made. *Average percent of need met:* 87. *Average financial aid package:* $40,402. *Average need-based loan:* $4295. *Average need-based gift aid:* $35,978. *Average non-need-based aid:* $23,988. *Average indebtedness upon graduation:* $44,140.

APPLYING

Standardized Tests *Required:* SAT or ACT (for admission).

Options: electronic application, early admission, early action, deferred entrance.

Required: high school transcript, 1 letter of recommendation. *Recommended:* essay or personal statement, interview.

Application deadlines: rolling (freshmen), rolling (out-of-state freshmen), 8/15 (transfers), 12/1 (early action).

Notification: continuous until 10/15 (freshmen), continuous until 10/15 (out-of-state freshmen), continuous until 8/15 (transfers), rolling (early action).

CONTACT

Shar Sanders, Admissions Assistant, Albion College, 611 E. Porter Street, Albion, MI 49224. *Phone:* 517-629-0466. *Toll-free phone:* 800-858-6770. *Fax:* 517-629-0569. *E-mail:* ssanders@albion.edu.

Alma College

Alma, Michigan

http://www.alma.edu/

- **Independent Presbyterian** 4-year, founded 1886
- **Small-town** 128-acre campus with easy access to Lansing
- **Endowment** $120.2 million
- **Coed** 1,426 undergraduate students, 96% full-time, 57% women, 43% men
- **Moderately difficult** entrance level, 64% of applicants were admitted

UNDERGRAD STUDENTS

1,376 full-time, 50 part-time. Students come from 29 states and territories; 10 other countries; 9% are from out of state; 3% Black or African American, non-Hispanic/Latino; 5% Hispanic/Latino; 1% Asian, non-Hispanic/Latino; 0.1% Native Hawaiian or other Pacific Islander, non-Hispanic/Latino; 0.4% American Indian or Alaska Native, non-Hispanic/Latino; 3% Two or more races, non-Hispanic/Latino; 8% Race/ethnicity unknown; 2% international; 3% transferred in; 95% live on campus.

Freshmen:
Admission: 4,728 applied, 3,026 admitted, 408 enrolled. *Average high school GPA:* 3.5. *Test scores:* SAT evidence-based reading and writing scores over 500: 86%; SAT math scores over 500: 83%; ACT scores over 18: 98%; SAT evidence-based reading and writing scores over 600: 39%; SAT math scores over 600: 28%; ACT scores over 24: 44%; SAT evidence-based reading and writing scores over 700: 6%; SAT math scores over 700: 2%; ACT scores over 30: 7%.

Retention: 77% of full-time freshmen returned.

FACULTY

Total: 158, 63% full-time, 65% with terminal degrees.

Student/faculty ratio: 12:1.

ACADEMICS

Calendar: 4-4-1. *Degree:* bachelor's.

Special study options: cooperative education, double majors, honors programs, independent study, internships, off-campus study, services for LD students, student-designed majors, study abroad. *ROTC:* Army (c).

Unusual degree programs: 3-2 engineering with University of Michigan, Kettering University.

Computers: 410 computers/terminals are available on campus for general student use. Students can access the following: campus intranet, computer help desk, free student e-mail accounts, online (class) grades, online (class) registration, online (class) schedules. Campuswide network is available. 100% of college-owned or -operated housing units are wired for high-speed Internet access. Wireless service is available via entire campus.

Library: Kerhl Building-Monteith Library. *Books:* 245,135 (physical), 150,135 (digital/electronic); *Serial titles:* 1,000 (physical). Weekly public service hours: 100; students can reserve study rooms.

STUDENT LIFE

Housing options: on-campus residence required through senior year; coed, special housing for students with disabilities. Campus housing is university owned. Freshman campus housing is guaranteed.

Activities and organizations: drama/theater group, student-run newspaper, choral group, marching band, Alma Ambassadors, Alma

College Union Board, Alma College Otaku Gamers (ACOG), Student Congress, Alpha Phi Omega, national fraternities, national sororities.

Athletics Member NCAA. All Division III. *Intercollegiate sports:* baseball M, basketball M/W, bowling W, cheerleading M/W, cross-country running M/W, football M, golf M/W, lacrosse M/W, soccer M/W, softball W, swimming and diving M/W, tennis M/W, track and field M/W, volleyball W, wrestling M. *Intramural sports:* basketball M/W, sand volleyball M/W, soccer M/W, softball M/W, table tennis M/W, ultimate Frisbee M/W, volleyball M/W.

Campus security: 24-hour emergency response devices, late-night transport/escort service, controlled dormitory access.

Student services: health clinic, personal/psychological counseling.

COSTS & FINANCIAL AID
Costs (2017–18) *Comprehensive fee:* $49,410 includes full-time tuition ($38,348), mandatory fees ($420), and room and board ($10,642). Part-time tuition: $1150 per credit hour. Part-time tuition and fees vary according to course load. *Room and board:* Room and board charges vary according to board plan and housing facility. *Payment plans:* installment, deferred payment. *Waivers:* employees or children of employees.

Financial Aid Of all full-time matriculated undergraduates who enrolled in 2017, 1,264 applied for aid, 1,162 were judged to have need, 129 had their need fully met. 690 Federal Work-Study jobs (averaging $1824). In 2017, 212 non-need-based awards were made. *Average percent of need met:* 70. *Average financial aid package:* $28,542. *Average need-based loan:* $4396. *Average need-based gift aid:* $27,547. *Average non-need-based aid:* $21,776. *Average indebtedness upon graduation:* $39,264.

APPLYING
Standardized Tests *Required:* SAT or ACT (for admission).

Options: electronic application.

Application fee: $25.

Required: essay or personal statement, high school transcript. *Required for some:* interview.

Application deadlines: rolling (freshmen), rolling (out-of-state freshmen), rolling (transfers).

Notification: continuous (freshmen), continuous (out-of-state freshmen), continuous (transfers).

CONTACT
Craig Aimar, Director of Admissions, Alma College, 614 W. Superior Street, Alma, MI 48801-1599. *Phone:* 800-321-2562. *Toll-free phone:* 800-321-ALMA. *E-mail:* admissions@alma.edu.

Andrews University
Berrien Springs, Michigan
http://www.andrews.edu/
- **Independent Seventh-day Adventist** university, founded 1874
- **Small-town** 1650-acre campus
- **Endowment** $53.1 million
- **Coed** 1,704 undergraduate students, 79% full-time, 55% women, 45% men
- **Moderately difficult** entrance level, 58% of applicants were admitted

UNDERGRAD STUDENTS
1,344 full-time, 360 part-time. Students come from 51 states and territories; 67 other countries; 64% are from out of state; 19% Black or African American, non-Hispanic/Latino; 14% Hispanic/Latino; 14% Asian, non-Hispanic/Latino; 0.4% Native Hawaiian or other Pacific Islander, non-Hispanic/Latino; 0.3% American Indian or Alaska Native, non-Hispanic/Latino; 4% Two or more races, non-Hispanic/Latino; 3% Race/ethnicity unknown; 18% international; 7% transferred in; 57% live on campus.

Freshmen:
Admission: 1,554 applied, 896 admitted, 281 enrolled. *Average high school GPA:* 3.6. *Test scores:* SAT evidence-based reading and writing scores over 500: 90%; SAT math scores over 500: 80%; ACT scores over 18: 93%; SAT evidence-based reading and writing scores over 600: 51%; SAT math scores over 600: 42%; ACT scores over 24: 58%; SAT evidence-based reading and writing scores over 700: 12%; SAT math scores over 700: 14%; ACT scores over 30: 22%.

Retention: 87% of full-time freshmen returned.

FACULTY
Total: 276, 79% full-time, 63% with terminal degrees.

Student/faculty ratio: 10:1.

ACADEMICS
Calendar: semesters. *Degrees:* certificates, associate, bachelor's, master's, doctoral, post-master's, and postbachelor's certificates.

Special study options: academic remediation for entering students, accelerated degree program, adult/continuing education programs, advanced placement credit, cooperative education, distance learning, double majors, English as a second language, freshman honors college, honors programs, internships, off-campus study, part-time degree program, student-designed majors, study abroad, summer session for credit.

Unusual degree programs: 3-2 physical therapy and architecture.

Computers: 100 computers/terminals are available on campus for general student use. Students can access the following: campus intranet, computer help desk, free student e-mail accounts, online (class) grades, online (class) registration, online (class) schedules, degree audit. Campuswide network is available. 99% of college-owned or -operated housing units are wired for high-speed Internet access. Wireless service is available via entire campus.

Library: James White Library plus 2 others. *Books:* 950,014 (physical), 394,023 (digital/electronic); *Serial titles:* 1,229 (physical), 198,545 (digital/electronic); *Databases:* 187.

STUDENT LIFE
Housing options: on-campus residence required through senior year; men-only, women-only. Campus housing is university owned. Freshman campus housing is guaranteed.

Activities and organizations: drama/theater group, student-run newspaper, radio station, choral group.

Athletics *Intramural sports:* basketball M/W, football M/W, golf M/W, gymnastics M/W, racquetball M/W, soccer M/W, softball M/W, volleyball M/W, water polo M/W.

Campus security: 24-hour emergency response devices and patrols, controlled dormitory access.

Student services: health clinic, personal/psychological counseling.

COSTS & FINANCIAL AID
Costs (2017–18) *Comprehensive fee:* $37,514 includes full-time tuition ($27,456), mandatory fees ($980), and room and board ($9078). Full-time tuition and fees vary according to course load. Part-time tuition: $1144 per credit hour. Part-time tuition and fees vary according to course load. *Required fees:* $124 per term part-time. *College room only:* $4778. Room and board charges vary according to board plan. *Payment plan:* installment. *Waivers:* senior citizens and employees or children of employees.

Financial Aid Of all full-time matriculated undergraduates who enrolled in 2017, 869 applied for aid, 801 were judged to have need, 129 had their need fully met. 564 Federal Work-Study jobs (averaging $959). In 2017, 521 non-need-based awards were made. *Average percent of need met:* 87. *Average financial aid package:* $31,058. *Average need-based loan:* $4336. *Average need-based gift aid:* $7052. *Average non-need-based aid:* $12,937. *Average indebtedness upon graduation:* $31,845.

APPLYING
Standardized Tests *Required:* SAT or ACT (for admission).

Options: electronic application, deferred entrance.

Application fee: $30.

Required: high school transcript, minimum 2.3 GPA, 2 letters of recommendation.

Application deadlines: rolling (freshmen), rolling (transfers).

Notification: continuous (freshmen), continuous (transfers).

CONTACT
Elivette Diaz, Undergraduate Admissions Coordinator, Andrews University, Berrien Springs, MI 49104. *Phone:* 800-253-2874. *Toll-free phone:* 800-253-2874. *Fax:* 269-471-3228. *E-mail:* enroll@andrews.edu.

★ Aquinas College

Grand Rapids, Michigan

http://www.aquinas.edu/

- **Independent Roman Catholic** comprehensive, founded 1886
- **Suburban** 117-acre campus with easy access to Grand Rapids
- **Endowment** $40.8 million
- **Coed** 1,551 undergraduate students, 85% full-time, 61% women, 39% men
- **Moderately difficult** entrance level, 75% of applicants were admitted

UNDERGRAD STUDENTS

1,317 full-time, 234 part-time. Students come from 25 states and territories; 22 other countries; 5% are from out of state; 3% Black or African American, non-Hispanic/Latino; 6% Hispanic/Latino; 1% Asian, non-Hispanic/Latino; 0.4% American Indian or Alaska Native, non-Hispanic/Latino; 2% Two or more races, non-Hispanic/Latino; 8% Race/ethnicity unknown; 2% international; 4% transferred in; 46% live on campus.

Freshmen:

Admission: 1,875 applied, 1,397 admitted, 314 enrolled. *Average high school GPA:* 3.5. *Test scores:* SAT evidence-based reading and writing scores over 500: 84%; SAT math scores over 500: 75%; ACT scores over 18: 98%; SAT evidence-based reading and writing scores over 600: 31%; SAT math scores over 600: 24%; ACT scores over 24: 53%; SAT evidence-based reading and writing scores over 700: 5%; SAT math scores over 700: 1%; ACT scores over 30: 7%.

Retention: 74% of full-time freshmen returned.

FACULTY

Total: 210, 40% full-time, 44% with terminal degrees.

Student/faculty ratio: 12:1.

ACADEMICS

Calendar: semesters. *Degrees:* associate, bachelor's, and master's.

Special study options: academic remediation for entering students, adult/continuing education programs, advanced placement credit, cooperative education, distance learning, double majors, English as a second language, honors programs, independent study, internships, off-campus study, part-time degree program, services for LD students, student-designed majors, study abroad, summer session for credit.

Computers: 210 computers/terminals are available on campus for general student use. Students can access the following: campus intranet, computer help desk, free student e-mail accounts, online (class) grades, online (class) registration, online (class) schedules. Campuswide network is available. 100% of college-owned or -operated housing units are wired for high-speed Internet access. Wireless service is available via entire campus.

Library: Grace Hauenstein Library plus 1 other. *Books:* 85,348 (physical), 196,003 (digital/electronic); *Serial titles:* 231 (physical); *Databases:* 85. Weekly public service hours: 90; students can reserve study rooms.

STUDENT LIFE

Housing options: on-campus residence required through junior year; coed. Campus housing is university owned. Freshman campus housing is guaranteed.

Activities and organizations: drama/theater group, student-run newspaper, radio station, choral group, Community Senate Programming Board, The Saint (newspaper), Insignis Honors Group, Community Action Volunteers of Aquinas (CAVA), Residence Hall Association.

Athletics Member NAIA. *Intercollegiate sports:* baseball M(s), basketball M(s)/W(s), bowling M(s)/W(s), cheerleading M(s)/W(s), cross-country running M(s)/W(s), golf M(s)/W(s), ice hockey M/W, lacrosse M(s)/W(s), soccer M(s)/W(s), softball W(s), tennis M(s)/W(s), track and field M(s)/W(s), volleyball W(s). *Intramural sports:* basketball M/W, football M/W, golf M, skiing (cross-country) M/W, skiing (downhill) M/W, soccer M/W, softball M/W, tennis M/W, volleyball M/W.

Campus security: 24-hour emergency response devices and patrols, student patrols, late-night transport/escort service, controlled dormitory access.

Student services: health clinic, personal/psychological counseling, women's center.

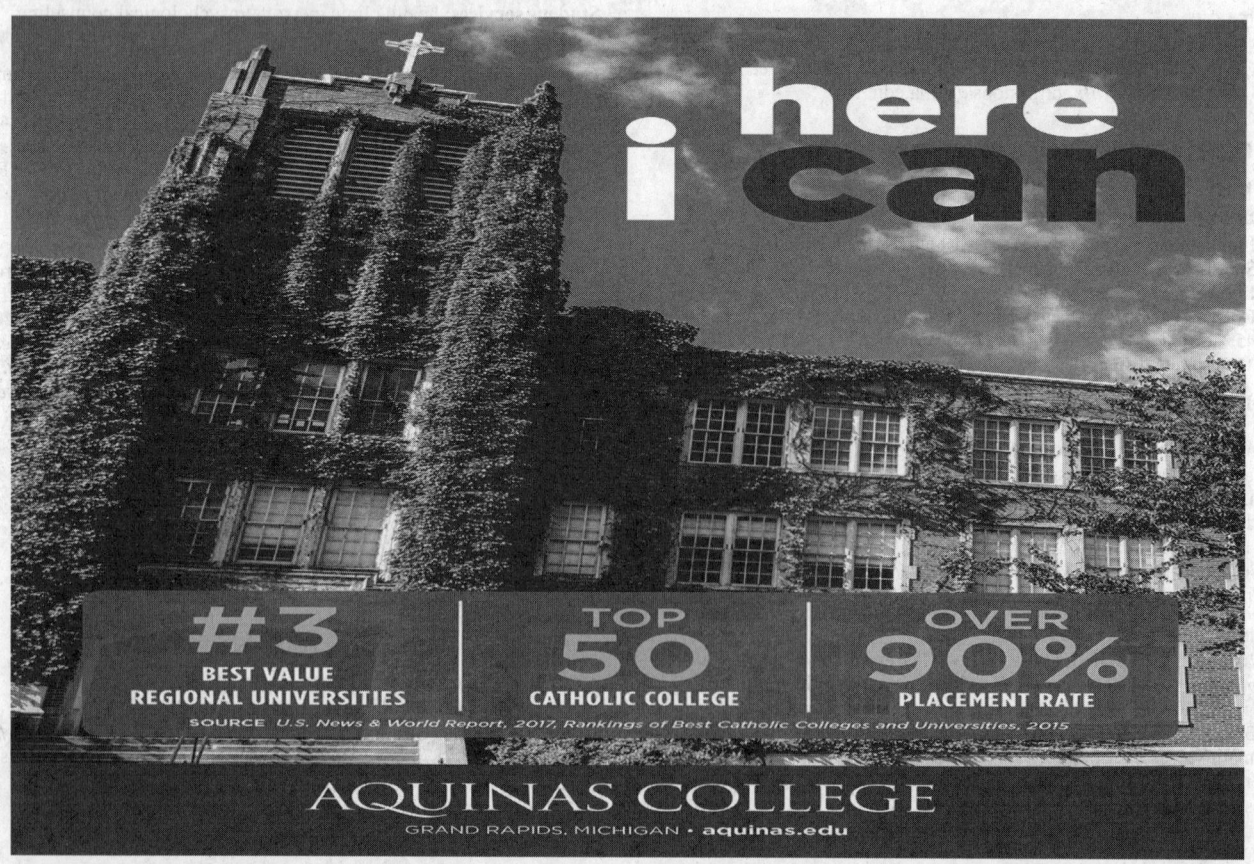

COSTS & FINANCIAL AID

Costs (2018–19) *Comprehensive fee:* $41,906 includes full-time tuition ($31,976), mandatory fees ($598), and room and board ($9332). Full-time tuition and fees vary according to course load. Part-time tuition: $498 per credit hour. Part-time tuition and fees vary according to course load. *Required fees:* $60 per term part-time. *College room only:* $4376. Room and board charges vary according to board plan and housing facility. *Payment plans:* installment, deferred payment. *Waivers:* employees or children of employees.

Financial Aid Of all full-time matriculated undergraduates who enrolled in 2017, 1,111 applied for aid, 1,010 were judged to have need, 205 had their need fully met. 131 Federal Work-Study jobs (averaging $1026). In 2017, 301 non-need-based awards were made. *Average percent of need met:* 83. *Average financial aid package:* $24,384. *Average need-based loan:* $2740. *Average need-based gift aid:* $21,644. *Average non-need-based aid:* $16,822. *Average indebtedness upon graduation:* $29,755.

APPLYING

Standardized Tests *Required:* SAT or ACT (for admission).

Options: electronic application, deferred entrance.

Required: high school transcript, minimum 2.5 GPA. *Required for some:* essay or personal statement, interview.

Application deadlines: rolling (freshmen), rolling (out-of-state freshmen), rolling (transfers).

CONTACT

Ms. Rebecca Roberts, Admissions Office Applications Specialist, Aquinas College, 1700 Fulton Street E., Grand Rapids, MI 49506-1801. *Phone:* 616-632-2900. *Toll-free phone:* 800-678-9593. *Fax:* 616-732-4469. *E-mail:* admissions@aquinas.edu.

See previous page for display ad and page 1232 for the College Close-Up.

The Art Institute of Michigan
Novi, Michigan
http://www.artinstitutes.edu/detroit/

CONTACT
The Art Institute of Michigan, 28125 Cabot Drive, Suite 120, Novi, MI 48377. *Phone:* 248-675-3800. *Toll-free phone:* 800-479-0087.

Baker College
Flint, Michigan
http://www.baker.edu/

CONTACT
Mr. Mark Heaton, System Marketing/Admission, Baker College, 1050 West Bristol Road, Flint, MI 48507-5508. *Phone:* 810-766-4280. *Toll-free phone:* 800-964-4299. *Fax:* 810-766-4279. *E-mail:* mark.heaton@baker.edu.

Calvin College
Grand Rapids, Michigan
http://www.calvin.edu/

- **Independent Christian Reformed** comprehensive, founded 1876
- **Suburban** 400-acre campus with easy access to Grand Rapids
- **Coed** 4,282 undergraduate students, 94% full-time, 59% women, 41% men
- **Moderately difficult** entrance level, 83% of applicants were admitted

UNDERGRAD STUDENTS
4,035 full-time, 247 part-time. Students come from 46 states and territories; 62 other countries; 42% are from out of state; 3% Black or African American, non-Hispanic/Latino; 5% Hispanic/Latino; 5% Asian, non-Hispanic/Latino; 0.1% American Indian or Alaska Native, non-Hispanic/Latino; 3% Two or more races, non-Hispanic/Latino; 2% Race/ethnicity unknown; 12% international; 2% transferred in; 58% live on campus.

Freshmen:
Admission: 3,221 applied, 2,689 admitted, 909 enrolled. *Average high school GPA:* 3.8. *Test scores:* ACT scores over 18: 99%; ACT scores over 24: 74%; ACT scores over 30: 25%.

Retention: 87% of full-time freshmen returned.

FACULTY
Total: 350, 70% full-time, 71% with terminal degrees.
Student/faculty ratio: 13:1.

ACADEMICS
Calendar: 4-1-4. *Degrees:* bachelor's and master's.

Special study options: academic remediation for entering students, accelerated degree program, advanced placement credit, distance learning, double majors, honors programs, independent study, internships, off-campus study, part-time degree program, services for LD students, student-designed majors, study abroad, summer session for credit. *ROTC:* Army (c).

Unusual degree programs: 3-2 occupational therapy with Washington University in St. Louis.

Computers: 1,025 computers/terminals and 2,656 ports are available on campus for general student use. Students can access the following: campus intranet, computer help desk, free student e-mail accounts, online (class) grades, online (class) registration, online (class) schedules. Campuswide network is available. 100% of college-owned or -operated housing units are wired for high-speed Internet access. Wireless service is available via classrooms, computer centers, computer labs, dorm rooms, learning centers, libraries, student centers.

Library: Hekman Library. *Books:* 729,447 (physical), 381,459 (digital/electronic); *Serial titles:* 5,893 (physical), 34,583 (digital/electronic); *Databases:* 137. Weekly public service hours: 90; students can reserve study rooms.

STUDENT LIFE
Housing options: on-campus residence required through sophomore year; men-only, women-only. Campus housing is university owned. Freshman campus housing is guaranteed.

Activities and organizations: drama/theater group, student-run newspaper, choral group, Dance Guild, Pre-Health Professionals, Calvin Outdoor Recreation, National Student Speech, Language, and Hearing Association, African Students Association.

Athletics Member NCAA. All Division III. *Intercollegiate sports:* baseball M, basketball M/W, cross-country running M/W, equestrian sports M(c)/W(c), golf M/W, ice hockey M(c), lacrosse M/W, rugby M(c)/W(c), soccer M/W, softball W, swimming and diving M/W, tennis M/W, track and field M/W, ultimate Frisbee M(c)/W(c), volleyball M(c)/W. *Intramural sports:* badminton M/W, basketball M/W, cross-country running M/W, football M/W, golf M/W, racquetball M/W, rock climbing M/W, sand volleyball M/W, soccer M/W, softball M/W, swimming and diving M/W, table tennis M/W, tennis M/W, track and field M/W, volleyball M/W, water polo M/W.

Campus security: 24-hour emergency response devices and patrols, student patrols, late-night transport/escort service, controlled dormitory access, crime prevention programs, crime alert bulletins.

Student services: health clinic, personal/psychological counseling.

COSTS & FINANCIAL AID
Costs (2017–18) *Comprehensive fee:* $43,090 includes full-time tuition ($33,100) and room and board ($9990). Full-time tuition and fees vary according to degree level, program, and student level. Part-time tuition: $790 per credit hour. Part-time tuition and fees vary according to course load, degree level, and student level. *Room and board:* Room and board charges vary according to board plan and housing facility. *Payment plan:* installment. *Waivers:* employees or children of employees.

Financial Aid Of all full-time matriculated undergraduates who enrolled in 2017, 2,809 applied for aid, 2,095 were judged to have need, 368 had their need fully met. 1,217 Federal Work-Study jobs (averaging $1079). In 2017, 1228 non-need-based awards were made. *Average percent of need met:* 73. *Average financial aid package:* $23,940. *Average need-based loan:* $6077. *Average need-based gift aid:* $18,198. *Average non-need-based aid:* $11,693. *Average indebtedness upon graduation:* $31,478.

APPLYING
Standardized Tests *Required:* SAT or ACT (for admission), or CLT (for admission).

Options: electronic application, deferred entrance.

Application fee: $35.

Required: essay or personal statement, high school transcript, minimum 2.5 GPA, 1 letter of recommendation. *Recommended:* interview.

Application deadlines: 8/15 (freshmen), rolling (transfers).

Notification: continuous (freshmen).

CONTACT

Dr. Ben Arendt, Director of Admissions, Calvin College, 3201 Burton Street, SE, Grand Rapids, MI 49546. *Phone:* 616-526-6106. *Toll-free phone:* 800-688-0122. *Fax:* 616-526-6777. *E-mail:* admissions@calvin.edu.

Central Michigan University

Mount Pleasant, Michigan

http://www.cmich.edu/

- **State-supported** university, founded 1892
- **Small-town** 854-acre campus
- **Endowment** $130.7 million
- **Coed** 17,845 undergraduate students, 87% full-time, 57% women, 43% men
- **Moderately difficult** entrance level, 68% of applicants were admitted

UNDERGRAD STUDENTS

15,590 full-time, 2,255 part-time. Students come from 52 states and territories; 35 other countries; 8% are from out of state; 9% Black or African American, non-Hispanic/Latino; 5% Hispanic/Latino; 1% Asian, non-Hispanic/Latino; 0.1% Native Hawaiian or other Pacific Islander, non-Hispanic/Latino; 0.8% American Indian or Alaska Native, non-Hispanic/Latino; 4% Two or more races, non-Hispanic/Latino; 1% Race/ethnicity unknown; 3% international; 6% transferred in; 37% live on campus.

Freshmen:

Admission: 19,021 applied, 12,887 admitted, 3,076 enrolled. *Average high school GPA:* 3.4. *Test scores:* SAT evidence-based reading and writing scores over 500: 79%; SAT math scores over 500: 76%; ACT scores over 18: 92%; SAT evidence-based reading and writing scores over 600: 31%; SAT math scores over 600: 23%; ACT scores over 24: 46%; SAT evidence-based reading and writing scores over 700: 4%; SAT math scores over 700: 4%; ACT scores over 30: 9%.

Retention: 77% of full-time freshmen returned.

FACULTY

Total: 1,291, 62% full-time, 58% with terminal degrees.

Student/faculty ratio: 20:1.

ACADEMICS

Calendar: semesters. *Degrees:* bachelor's, master's, doctoral, post-master's, and postbachelor's certificates.

Special study options: academic remediation for entering students, accelerated degree program, advanced placement credit, distance learning, double majors, English as a second language, honors programs, independent study, internships, off-campus study, part-time degree program, services for LD students, student-designed majors, study abroad, summer session for credit. *ROTC:* Army (b), Air Force (c).

Unusual degree programs: 3-2 business administration; engineering; apparel product development and merchandising technology, computer science, economics, experimental psychology, higher education administration, history, geographic information science, administration, Spanish, mathematics, political science, human development and family studies.

Computers: 490 computers/terminals and 26,902 ports are available on campus for general student use. Students can access the following: campus intranet, computer help desk, free student e-mail accounts, online (class) grades, online (class) registration, online (class) schedules, learning management system. Campuswide network is available. 100% of college-owned or -operated housing units are wired for high-speed Internet access. Wireless service is available via entire campus.

Library: Charles V. Park Library plus 1 other. *Books:* 734,063 (physical), 423,429 (digital/electronic); *Serial titles:* 6,091 (physical), 72,302 (digital/electronic); *Databases:* 287. Weekly public service hours: 125; students can reserve study rooms.

STUDENT LIFE

Housing options: on-campus residence required through sophomore year; coed, special housing for students with disabilities. Campus housing is university owned. Freshman campus housing is guaranteed.

Activities and organizations: drama/theater group, student-run newspaper, radio and television station, choral group, marching band, national fraternities, national sororities.

Athletics Member NCAA. All Division I except football (Division I-A). *Intercollegiate sports:* baseball M(s), basketball M(s)/W(s), cross-country running M(s)/W(s), field hockey W(s), golf W(s), gymnastics W(s), lacrosse W(s), soccer W(s), softball W(s), track and field M(s)/W(s), volleyball W(s), wrestling M(s). *Intramural sports:* baseball M(c), basketball M/W, bowling M/W, cross-country running M(c)/W(c), equestrian sports M(c)/W(c), football M/W, golf M(c)/W(c), gymnastics M(c)/W(c), ice hockey M(c)/W(c), lacrosse M(c)/W(c), racquetball M/W, rugby M(c)/W(c), sand volleyball M/W, skiing (downhill) M(c)/W(c), soccer M/W, softball M/W, swimming and diving M(c)/W(c), table tennis M/W, tennis M/W, track and field M(c)/W(c), triathlon M(c)/W(c), ultimate Frisbee M(c)/W(c), volleyball M/W, water polo M(c)/W(c), weight lifting M(c)/W(c), wrestling M/W.

Campus security: 24-hour emergency response devices and patrols, late-night transport/escort service.

Student services: health clinic, personal/psychological counseling, women's center.

COSTS & FINANCIAL AID

Costs (2017–18) *Tuition:* state resident $12,510 full-time, $417 per credit hour part-time; nonresident $23,670 full-time, $789 per credit hour part-time. Full-time tuition and fees vary according to location. Part-time tuition and fees vary according to location. *Room and board:* $9736; room only: $4868. Room and board charges vary according to board plan and housing facility. *Payment plan:* installment. *Waivers:* children of alumni, senior citizens, and employees or children of employees.

Financial Aid Of all full-time matriculated undergraduates who enrolled in 2016, 13,224 applied for aid, 10,420 were judged to have need, 3,803 had their need fully met. In 2016, 2283 non-need-based awards were made. *Average percent of need met:* 80. *Average financial aid package:* $13,337. *Average need-based loan:* $7077. *Average need-based gift aid:* $6765. *Average non-need-based aid:* $5471. *Average indebtedness upon graduation:* $33,635.

APPLYING

Standardized Tests *Required:* SAT or ACT (for admission).

Options: electronic application, early admission, early action, deferred entrance.

Application fee: $35.

Required: high school transcript. *Required for some:* essay or personal statement, interview.

Application deadlines: 7/1 (freshmen), rolling (transfers).

Notification: continuous (freshmen), continuous (transfers).

CONTACT

Central Michigan University, Warriner Hall 102, Mt Pleasant, MI 48859. *Phone:* 989-774-3076. *Toll-free phone:* 888-292-5366. *Fax:* 989-774-7267. *E-mail:* cmuadmit@cmich.edu.

Chamberlain College of Nursing

Troy, Michigan

http://www.chamberlain.edu/

- **Proprietary** 4-year
- **Coed**

FACULTY

Student/faculty ratio: 11:1.

ACADEMICS

Degree: bachelor's.

STUDENT LIFE

Housing options: college housing not available.

COSTS

Costs (2017–18) *Tuition:* $18,900 full-time. *Required fees:* $600 full-time.

APPLYING

Standardized Tests *Required:* SAT or ACT (for admission).

Options: deferred entrance.

Application fee: $95.

CONTACT

Chamberlain College of Nursing, 200 Kirts Boulevard, Troy, MI 48084. *Toll-free phone:* 877-751-5783.

Cleary University

Howell, Michigan

http://www.cleary.edu/

CONTACT

Eric Brown, Director of Admissions, Cleary University, 3750 Cleary Drive, Howell, MI 48843. *Phone:* 800-686-1883. *Toll-free phone:* 800-686-1883. *Fax:* 517-338-5075. *E-mail:* admissions@cleary.edu.

 ## College for Creative Studies

Detroit, Michigan

http://www.collegeforcreativestudies.edu/

CONTACT

Office of Admissions, College for Creative Studies, 201 East Kirby, Detroit, MI 48202-4034. *Phone:* 800-952-2787. *Toll-free phone:* 800-952-ARTS. *Fax:* 313-872-2739. *E-mail:* admissions@collegeforcreativestudies.edu.

See below for display ad and page 1262 for the College Close-Up.

Compass College of Cinematic Arts

Grand Rapids, Michigan

http://www.compass.edu/

- **Independent** 4-year
- **Urban** campus
- **Coed** 130 undergraduate students
- **Minimally difficult** entrance level

ACADEMICS

Degrees: associate and bachelor's.

Special study options: academic remediation for entering students, accelerated degree program, advanced placement credit, internships.

Computers: Wireless service is available via entire campus.

APPLYING

Standardized Tests *Recommended:* SAT or ACT (for admission).

Required: essay or personal statement, high school transcript, minimum 2.0 GPA, 2 letters of recommendation, interview, Portfolio of 2 film pieces and 2 non-film pieces.

Application deadlines: rolling (freshmen), rolling (out-of-state freshmen), rolling (transfers).

Notification: continuous (freshmen), continuous (out-of-state freshmen), continuous (transfers).

CONTACT

Compass College of Cinematic Arts, 41 Sheldon Boulevard SE, Grand Rapids, MI 49503.

Concordia University Ann Arbor

Ann Arbor, Michigan

http://www.cuaa.edu/

CONTACT

Mr. Ben Limback, Director of Admissions, Concordia University Ann Arbor, 4090 Geddes Road, Ann Arbor, MI 48105-2797. *Phone:* 734-995-7311. *Toll-free phone:* 877-995-7520 (in-state); 877-955-7520 (out-of-state). *Fax:* 734-995-4610. *E-mail:* admissions@cuaa.edu.

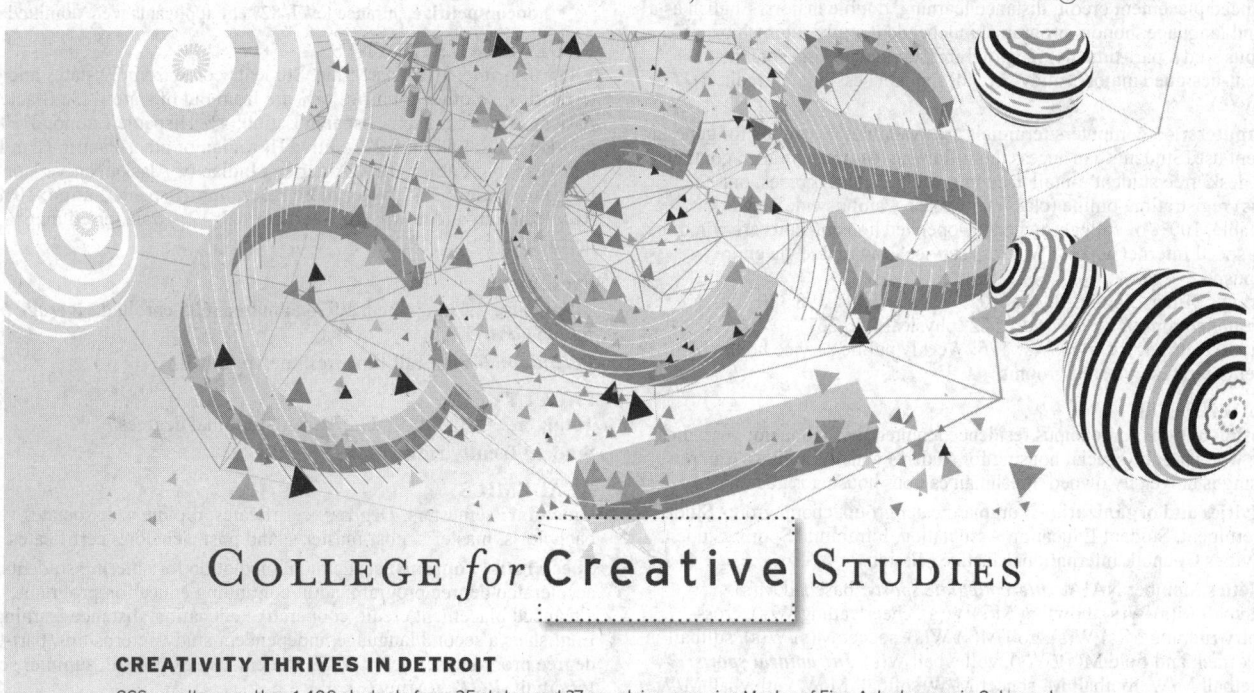

COLLEGE *for* Creative STUDIES

CREATIVITY THRIVES IN DETROIT

CCS enrolls more than 1,400 students from 35 states and 37 countries, pursuing Master of Fine Arts degrees in Color and Materials Design, Integrated Design, Interaction Design and Transportation Design and Bachelor of Fine Arts degrees in Advertising: Copywriting, Advertising: Design, Art Education, Communication Design, Crafts, Entertainment Arts, Fashion Accessories Design, Fine Arts, Illustration, Interior Design, Photography, Product Design and Transportation Design.

VISIT COLLEGEFORCREATIVESTUDIES.EDU

Cornerstone University

Grand Rapids, Michigan

http://www.cornerstone.edu/

- **Independent nondenominational** comprehensive, founded 1941
- **Suburban** 132-acre campus with easy access to Grand Rapids
- **Endowment** $9.2 million
- **Coed** 1,755 undergraduate students, 72% full-time, 62% women, 38% men
- **Minimally difficult** entrance level, 67% of applicants were admitted

UNDERGRAD STUDENTS

1,260 full-time, 495 part-time. Students come from 26 states and territories; 30 other countries; 20% are from out of state; 12% Black or African American, non-Hispanic/Latino; 5% Hispanic/Latino; 2% Asian, non-Hispanic/Latino; 0.1% Native Hawaiian or other Pacific Islander, non-Hispanic/Latino; 0.3% American Indian or Alaska Native, non-Hispanic/Latino; 0.6% Two or more races, non-Hispanic/Latino; 4% international; 6% transferred in; 63% live on campus.

Freshmen:

Admission: 2,737 applied, 1,844 admitted, 287 enrolled. *Average high school GPA:* 3.6. *Test scores:* SAT evidence-based reading and writing scores over 500: 85%; SAT math scores over 500: 85%; ACT scores over 18: 92%; SAT evidence-based reading and writing scores over 600: 40%; SAT math scores over 600: 26%; ACT scores over 24: 48%; SAT evidence-based reading and writing scores over 700: 5%; SAT math scores over 700: 1%; ACT scores over 30: 7%.

Retention: 77% of full-time freshmen returned.

FACULTY

Total: 374, 17% full-time, 36% with terminal degrees.

Student/faculty ratio: 15:1.

ACADEMICS

Calendar: semesters. *Degrees:* diplomas, associate, bachelor's, master's, and doctoral.

Special study options: academic remediation for entering students, accelerated degree program, adult/continuing education programs, advanced placement credit, distance learning, double majors, English as a second language, honors programs, independent study, internships, off-campus study, part-time degree program, services for LD students, student-designed majors, study abroad, summer session for credit. *ROTC:* Army (c).

Computers: 43 computers/terminals are available on campus for general student use. Students can access the following: campus intranet, computer help desk, free student e-mail accounts, online (class) grades, online (class) registration, online (class) schedules. Campuswide network is available. 100% of college-owned or -operated housing units are wired for high-speed Internet access. Wireless service is available via entire campus.

Library: Miller Library. *Books:* 102,008 (physical), 198,380 (digital/electronic); *Serial titles:* 522 (physical), 46,267 (digital/electronic); *Databases:* 176. Weekly public service hours: 85; students can reserve study rooms.

STUDENT LIFE

Housing options: on-campus residence required through junior year; men-only, women-only, special housing for students with disabilities. Campus housing is university owned. Freshman campus housing is guaranteed.

Activities and organizations: drama/theater group, choral group, Student Government, Student Education Association, Intramural Sports, Student Activities Council, International Justice Mission.

Athletics Member NAIA. *Intercollegiate sports:* baseball M(s), basketball M(s)/W(s), bowling M(s)/W(s), cheerleading W(s), cross-country running M(s)/W(s), golf M(s)/W(s), soccer M(s)/W(s), softball W(s), track and field M(s)/W(s), volleyball W(s). *Intramural sports:* basketball M/W, football M, soccer M/W, softball M/W, volleyball M/W.

Campus security: 24-hour emergency response devices and patrols, student patrols, late-night transport/escort service, controlled dormitory access.

Student services: health clinic, personal/psychological counseling.

COSTS & FINANCIAL AID

Costs (2018–19) *Comprehensive fee:* $33,800 includes full-time tuition ($24,500) and room and board ($9300). Full-time tuition and fees vary according to course load and reciprocity agreements. Part-time tuition and fees vary according to course load. *Room and board:* Room and board charges vary according to board plan and housing facility. *Payment plan:* installment. *Waivers:* employees or children of employees.

Financial Aid Of all full-time matriculated undergraduates who enrolled in 2017, 904 applied for aid, 841 were judged to have need, 110 had their need fully met. 183 Federal Work-Study jobs (averaging $941). In 2017, 209 non-need-based awards were made. *Average percent of need met:* 70. *Average financial aid package:* $21,975. *Average need-based loan:* $4154. *Average need-based gift aid:* $17,455. *Average non-need-based aid:* $10,381. *Average indebtedness upon graduation:* $33,729.

APPLYING

Standardized Tests *Required:* SAT or ACT (for admission).

Options: electronic application.

Required: essay or personal statement, high school transcript, minimum 2.5 GPA, 1 letter of recommendation, pastoral letter.

Application deadlines: rolling (freshmen), rolling (transfers).

Notification: continuous (freshmen), continuous (transfers).

CONTACT

Mrs. Lisa Link, Office of Admissions, Cornerstone University, 1001 East Beltline Avenue, NE, Grand Rapids, MI 49525. *Phone:* 616-222-1426. *Toll-free phone:* 800-787-9778. *Fax:* 616-222-1418. *E-mail:* admissions@cornerstone.edu.

Davenport University

Grand Rapids, Michigan

http://www.davenport.edu/

- **Independent** comprehensive, founded 1866
- **Suburban** 77-acre campus with easy access to Grand Rapids
- **Endowment** $20.6 million
- **Coed** 5,642 undergraduate students, 44% full-time, 56% women, 44% men
- **Noncompetitive** entrance level, 82% of applicants were admitted

UNDERGRAD STUDENTS

2,488 full-time, 3,154 part-time. Students come from 39 states and territories; 26 other countries; 6% are from out of state; 11% Black or African American, non-Hispanic/Latino; 4% Hispanic/Latino; 3% Asian, non-Hispanic/Latino; 0.2% Native Hawaiian or other Pacific Islander, non-Hispanic/Latino; 0.5% American Indian or Alaska Native, non-Hispanic/Latino; 3% Two or more races, non-Hispanic/Latino; 10% Race/ethnicity unknown; 3% international; 12% transferred in; 6% live on campus.

Freshmen:

Admission: 2,412 applied, 1,976 admitted, 605 enrolled. *Average high school GPA:* 3.2.

Retention: 74% of full-time freshmen returned.

FACULTY

Total: 832, 16% full-time, 27% with terminal degrees.

Student/faculty ratio: 12:1.

ACADEMICS

Calendar: semesters. *Degrees:* certificates, diplomas, associate, bachelor's, master's, post-master's, and postbachelor's certificates.

Special study options: academic remediation for entering students, accelerated degree program, adult/continuing education programs, advanced placement credit, cooperative education, distance learning, English as a second language, independent study, internships, part-time degree program, services for LD students, study abroad, summer session for credit. *ROTC:* Army (c).

Computers: 3,098 computers/terminals and 315 ports are available on campus for general student use. Students can access the following: campus intranet, computer help desk, free student e-mail accounts, online (class) grades, online (class) registration, online (class) schedules. Campuswide network is available. 100% of college-owned or -operated housing units are wired for high-speed Internet access. Wireless service is available via entire campus.

Library: Margaret D. Sneden Library Information Commons plus 3 others. Students can reserve study rooms.

STUDENT LIFE
Housing options: coed. Campus housing is university owned. Freshman applicants given priority for college housing.

Activities and organizations: marching band, Business Professionals of America, Delta Epsilon Chi, Student Government, Health Occupations Students of America, Connect.

Athletics Member NAIA. *Intercollegiate sports:* baseball M(s), basketball M(s)/W(s), bowling M(s)/W(s), cheerleading W(s), cross-country running M(s)/W(s), football M(s), golf M(s)/W(s), ice hockey M(s)/W(s), lacrosse M(s)/W(s), rugby M(s)/W(s), soccer M(s)/W(s), softball W(s), tennis M(s)/W(s), track and field M(s)/W(s), volleyball W(s).

Campus security: 24-hour emergency response devices and patrols, late-night transport/escort service, controlled dormitory access.

Student services: personal/psychological counseling.

COSTS
Costs (2017–18) *Comprehensive fee:* $27,460 includes full-time tuition ($16,728), mandatory fees ($830), and room and board ($9902). Full-time tuition and fees vary according to location and program. Part-time tuition: $697 per credit hour. Part-time tuition and fees vary according to location and program. *Required fees:* $415 per term part-time. *College room only:* $6324. Room and board charges vary according to board plan and housing facility. *Payment plan:* installment. *Waivers:* employees or children of employees.

APPLYING
Standardized Tests *Recommended:* SAT (for admission), ACT (for admission).

Options: electronic application, deferred entrance.

Application fee: $25.

Required: high school transcript. *Recommended:* interview.

Application deadlines: rolling (freshmen), rolling (transfers).

Notification: continuous (freshmen), continuous (transfers).

CONTACT
Ms. David Lawrence, Executive Director of Admissions, Davenport University, 6191 Kraft Avenue SE, Grand Rapids, MI 49512. *Phone:* 616-451-3511. *Toll-free phone:* 800-686-1600 (in-state); 866-686-1600 (out-of-state). *Fax:* 616-732-1145. *E-mail:* david.lawrence@davenport.edu.

Eastern Michigan University
Ypsilanti, Michigan
http://www.emich.edu/

- **State-supported** comprehensive, founded 1849
- **Suburban** 460-acre campus with easy access to Detroit
- **Endowment** $67.2 million
- **Coed** 16,997 undergraduate students, 73% full-time, 59% women, 41% men
- **Moderately difficult** entrance level, 73% of applicants were admitted

UNDERGRAD STUDENTS
12,395 full-time, 4,602 part-time. 10% are from out of state; 18% Black or African American, non-Hispanic/Latino; 5% Hispanic/Latino; 3% Asian, non-Hispanic/Latino; 0.1% Native Hawaiian or other Pacific Islander, non-Hispanic/Latino; 0.3% American Indian or Alaska Native, non-Hispanic/Latino; 4% Two or more races, non-Hispanic/Latino; 4% Race/ethnicity unknown; 2% international; 9% transferred in; 22% live on campus.

Freshmen:
Admission: 16,012 applied, 11,675 admitted, 2,815 enrolled. *Average high school GPA:* 3.3. *Test scores:* SAT evidence-based reading and writing scores over 500: 75%; SAT math scores over 500: 75%; ACT scores over 18: 87%; SAT evidence-based reading and writing scores over 600: 25%; SAT math scores over 600: 19%; ACT scores over 24: 38%; ACT scores over 30: 6%.

Retention: 72% of full-time freshmen returned.

FACULTY
Total: 1,319, 58% full-time, 57% with terminal degrees.
Student/faculty ratio: 17:1.

ACADEMICS
Calendar: semesters. *Degrees:* bachelor's, master's, doctoral, post-master's, and postbachelor's certificates.

Special study options: academic remediation for entering students, accelerated degree program, advanced placement credit, cooperative education, distance learning, double majors, English as a second language, external degree program, honors programs, independent study, internships, part-time degree program, services for LD students, student-designed majors, study abroad, summer session for credit. *ROTC:* Army (b), Navy (c), Air Force (c).

Unusual degree programs: 3-2 accounting, occupational therapy.

Computers: 1,600 computers/terminals and 200 ports are available on campus for general student use. Students can access the following: campus intranet, computer help desk, free student e-mail accounts, online (class) grades, online (class) registration, online (class) schedules. Campuswide network is available. 100% of college-owned or -operated housing units are wired for high-speed Internet access. Wireless service is available via entire campus.
Library: Bruce T. Halle Library.

STUDENT LIFE
Housing options: on-campus residence required through sophomore year; coed, special housing for students with disabilities. Campus housing is university owned.

Activities and organizations: drama/theater group, student-run newspaper, radio and television station, choral group, marching band, International Student Association, Golden Key International Honor Society, Psychology Club, Indian Student Association, GREEN (Gathering Resources to Educate about our Environment and Nature), national fraternities, national sororities.

Athletics Member NCAA. All Division I except football (Division I-A). *Intercollegiate sports:* baseball M(s), basketball M(s)/W(s), crew W(s), cross-country running M(s)/W(s), golf M(s)/W(s), gymnastics W(s), soccer W(s), softball W(s), swimming and diving M(s)/W(s), tennis W(s), track and field M(s)/W(s), volleyball W(s), wrestling M(s). *Intramural sports:* badminton M/W, basketball M/W, bowling M/W, cross-country running M/W, golf M/W, racquetball M/W, rock climbing M/W, soccer M/W, softball M/W, swimming and diving M/W, table tennis M/W, track and field M/W, ultimate Frisbee M/W, volleyball M/W, weight lifting M/W.

Campus security: 24-hour emergency response devices and patrols, student patrols, late-night transport/escort service, controlled dormitory access, bicycle patrols, local police in dormitories, self-defense education, lighted pathways, bike lock lease program.

Student services: health clinic, personal/psychological counseling, women's center, legal services.

COSTS & FINANCIAL AID
Costs (2017–18) *One-time required fee:* $323. *Tuition:* state resident $12,120 full-time, $323 per credit hour part-time; nonresident $27,711 full-time, $873 per credit hour part-time. Full-time tuition and fees vary according to course level and reciprocity agreements. Part-time tuition and fees vary according to course level and reciprocity agreements. *Required fees:* $1529 full-time, $47 per credit hour part-time, $50 per credit hour part-time. *Room and board:* $9672. Room and board charges vary according to board plan, housing facility, and location. *Payment plan:* installment. *Waivers:* employees or children of employees.

Financial Aid Of all full-time matriculated undergraduates who enrolled in 2016, 10,503 applied for aid, 8,657 were judged to have need, 358 had their need fully met. 595 Federal Work-Study jobs (averaging $2302). In 2016, 2479 non-need-based awards were made. *Average percent of need met:* 47. *Average financial aid package:* $10,030. *Average need-based loan:* $4080. *Average need-based gift aid:* $5707. *Average non-need-based aid:* $5413. *Average indebtedness upon graduation:* $30,205.

APPLYING
Standardized Tests *Required:* SAT or ACT (for admission).

Options: electronic application, deferred entrance.

Application fee: $35.

Required: high school transcript, minimum 2.0 GPA. *Required for some:* 1 letter of recommendation, interview.

Application deadlines: rolling (freshmen), rolling (transfers).

Notification: continuous (freshmen), continuous (transfers).

Michigan

CONTACT
Eastern Michigan University, Ypsilanti, MI 48197. *Phone:* 734-487-3060. *Toll-free phone:* 800-GO TO EMU.

Ferris State University

Big Rapids, Michigan
http://www.ferris.edu/

- **State-supported** comprehensive, founded 1884
- **Small-town** 941-acre campus with easy access to Grand Rapids
- **Endowment** $73.8 million
- **Coed** 12,504 undergraduate students, 68% full-time, 53% women, 47% men
- **Minimally difficult** entrance level, 74% of applicants were admitted

UNDERGRAD STUDENTS
8,469 full-time, 4,035 part-time. Students come from 46 states and territories; 49 other countries; 6% are from out of state; 8% Black or African American, non-Hispanic/Latino; 5% Hispanic/Latino; 2% Asian, non-Hispanic/Latino; 0.1% Native Hawaiian or other Pacific Islander, non-Hispanic/Latino; 0.5% American Indian or Alaska Native, non-Hispanic/Latino; 4% Two or more races, non-Hispanic/Latino; 1% Race/ethnicity unknown; 0.7% international; 10% transferred in; 21% live on campus.

Freshmen:
Admission: 9,926 applied, 7,361 admitted, 1,817 enrolled. *Average high school GPA:* 3.4. *Test scores:* SAT evidence-based reading and writing scores over 500: 67%; SAT math scores over 500: 64%; ACT scores over 18: 85%; SAT evidence-based reading and writing scores over 600: 24%; SAT math scores over 600: 18%; ACT scores over 24: 37%; SAT evidence-based reading and writing scores over 700: 3%; SAT math scores over 700: 3%; ACT scores over 30: 8%.
Retention: 79% of full-time freshmen returned.

FACULTY
Total: 916, 60% full-time, 34% with terminal degrees.
Student/faculty ratio: 16:1.

ACADEMICS
Calendar: semesters. *Degrees:* certificates, associate, bachelor's, master's, doctoral, and postbachelor's certificates.

Special study options: academic remediation for entering students, accelerated degree program, adult/continuing education programs, advanced placement credit, cooperative education, distance learning, double majors, English as a second language, external degree program, freshman honors college, honors programs, independent study, internships, off-campus study, part-time degree program, services for LD students, student-designed majors, study abroad, summer session for credit. *ROTC:* Army (c).

Computers: 1,723 computers/terminals are available on campus for general student use. Students can access the following: computer help desk, free student e-mail accounts, online (class) grades, online (class) registration, online (class) schedules. Campuswide network is available. 100% of college-owned or -operated housing units are wired for high-speed Internet access. Wireless service is available via entire campus.
Library: Ferris Library for Information, Technology and Education. *Books:* 267,897 (physical), 214,655 (digital/electronic); *Serial titles:* 161 (physical), 160,936 (digital/electronic); *Databases:* 183. Weekly public service hours: 93; study areas open 24 hours, 5–7 days a week; students can reserve study rooms.

STUDENT LIFE
Housing options: on-campus residence required for freshman year; coed, special housing for students with disabilities. Campus housing is university owned. Freshman campus housing is guaranteed.

Activities and organizations: drama/theater group, student-run newspaper, radio and television station, choral group, Student American Dental Hygiene Association, Pre-Pharm D, American Pharmacist Association, Student Nurses Association, American Marketing Association, national fraternities, national sororities.

Athletics Member NCAA. All Division II. *Intercollegiate sports:* basketball M(s)/W(s), cross-country running M(s)/W(s), football M(s), golf M(s)/W(s), ice hockey M(s), soccer W(s), softball W(s), tennis M(s)/W(s), track and field M(s)/W(s), volleyball W(s). *Intramural sports:* badminton

M/W, baseball M(c), basketball M/W, bowling M/W, cheerleading M(c)/W(c), equestrian sports W(c), football M/W, golf M(c)/W(c), ice hockey M, lacrosse M(c)/W(c), rugby M(c)/W(c), soccer M/W, softball M/W, table tennis M(c)/W(c), tennis M(c)/W(c), ultimate Frisbee M(c)/W(c), volleyball M/W, weight lifting M(c)/W(c), wrestling M(c).

Campus security: 24-hour emergency response devices, student patrols, late-night transport/escort service, controlled dormitory access.
Student services: health clinic, personal/psychological counseling.

COSTS & FINANCIAL AID
Costs (2017–18) *Tuition:* state resident $12,180 full-time, $406 per credit hour part-time; nonresident $18,270 full-time, $609 per credit hour part-time. Full-time tuition and fees vary according to location, program, and student level. Part-time tuition and fees vary according to location and student level. *Room and board:* $9894. Room and board charges vary according to board plan and housing facility. *Payment plan:* installment. *Waivers:* employees or children of employees.

Financial Aid Of all full-time matriculated undergraduates who enrolled in 2017, 8,149 applied for aid, 6,335 were judged to have need, 984 had their need fully met. 454 Federal Work-Study jobs (averaging $2372). 190 state and other part-time jobs (averaging $1935). In 2017, 1270 non-need-based awards were made. *Average percent of need met:* 66. *Average financial aid package:* $11,610. *Average need-based loan:* $4560. *Average need-based gift aid:* $5130. *Average non-need-based aid:* $4350. *Average indebtedness upon graduation:* $35,600.

APPLYING
Standardized Tests *Required for some:* SAT or ACT (for admission).
Options: electronic application.
Required: high school transcript, minimum 2.5 GPA. *Required for some:* essay or personal statement, interview.
Application deadlines: 8/1 (freshmen), 7/1 (transfers).
Notification: continuous (freshmen), continuous (transfers).

CONTACT
Mr. Jason Daday, Associate Director of Admissions, Ferris State University, 1201 South State Street, CSS 201, Big Rapids, MI 49307-2742. *Phone:* 231-591-3106. *Toll-free phone:* 800-433-7747. *Fax:* 231-591-2242. *E-mail:* dadayja@ferris.edu.

Finlandia University

Hancock, Michigan
http://www.finlandia.edu/

CONTACT
Martin Kinard, Finlandia University, 601 Quincy Street, Hancock, MI 49930. *Phone:* 906-487-7352. *Toll-free phone:* 877-202-5491. *Fax:* 906-487-7383. *E-mail:* admissions@finlandia.edu.

Grace Bible College

Grand Rapids, Michigan
http://www.gbcol.edu/

CONTACT
Mr. Kevin Gilliam, Director of Enrollment, Grace Bible College, 1101 Aldon Street, SW, PO Box 910, Grand Rapids, MI 49509. *Phone:* 616-538-2330 Ext. 239. *Toll-free phone:* 800-968-1887. *Fax:* 616-538-0599. *E-mail:* gbc@gbcol.edu.

Grand Valley State University

Allendale, Michigan
http://www.gvsu.edu/

- **State-supported** comprehensive, founded 1960
- **Small-town** 1391-acre campus with easy access to Grand Rapids
- **Endowment** $102.4 million
- **Coed** 21,937 undergraduate students, 88% full-time, 59% women, 41% men
- **Moderately difficult** entrance level, 81% of applicants were admitted

UNDERGRAD STUDENTS
19,373 full-time, 2,564 part-time. Students come from 42 states and territories; 70 other countries; 7% are from out of state; 5% Black or

African American, non-Hispanic/Latino; 5% Hispanic/Latino; 2% Asian, non-Hispanic/Latino; 0.1% Native Hawaiian or other Pacific Islander, non-Hispanic/Latino; 0.3% American Indian or Alaska Native, non-Hispanic/Latino; 4% Two or more races, non-Hispanic/Latino; 0.4% Race/ethnicity unknown; 1% international; 7% transferred in; 27% live on campus.

Freshmen:
Admission: 17,509 applied, 14,168 admitted, 4,117 enrolled. *Average high school GPA:* 3.6. *Test scores:* SAT evidence-based reading and writing scores over 500: 89%; SAT math scores over 500: 89%; ACT scores over 18: 97%; SAT evidence-based reading and writing scores over 600: 38%; SAT math scores over 600: 32%; ACT scores over 24: 52%; SAT evidence-based reading and writing scores over 700: 4%; SAT math scores over 700: 4%; ACT scores over 30: 9%.

Retention: 83% of full-time freshmen returned.

FACULTY
Total: 1,768, 67% full-time, 58% with terminal degrees.
Student/faculty ratio: 17:1.

ACADEMICS
Calendar: semesters. *Degrees:* certificates, bachelor's, master's, doctoral, post-master's, and postbachelor's certificates.

Special study options: academic remediation for entering students, accelerated degree program, adult/continuing education programs, advanced placement credit, cooperative education, distance learning, double majors, English as a second language, freshman honors college, honors programs, independent study, internships, part-time degree program, services for LD students, study abroad, summer session for credit.

Computers: 2,600 computers/terminals are available on campus for general student use. Students can access the following: campus intranet, computer help desk, free student e-mail accounts, online (class) grades, online (class) registration, online (class) schedules, transcript, degree audit, credit card payments. Campuswide network is available. 100% of college-owned or -operated housing units are wired for high-speed Internet access. Wireless service is available via entire campus.
Library: Mary Idema Pew Library Learning and Information Commons plus 5 others. *Books:* 567,197 (physical), 1.0 million (digital/electronic). Students can reserve study rooms.

STUDENT LIFE
Housing options: coed. Campus housing is university owned. Freshman campus housing is guaranteed.

Activities and organizations: drama/theater group, student-run newspaper, radio and television station, choral group, marching band, Habitat for Humanity, Alternative Breaks, Hospitality and tourism Management Club, Dance Troupe, Colleges Against Cancer, national fraternities, national sororities.

Athletics Member NCAA. All Division II. *Intercollegiate sports:* baseball M(s), basketball M(s)/W(s), cheerleading M(c)/W(c), crew M(c)/W(c), cross-country running M(s)/W(s), football M(s), golf M(s)/W(s), ice hockey M/W, lacrosse M(c)/W, rowing M/W, rugby M(c)/W(c), sailing M(c)/W(c), skiing (downhill) M(c)/W(c), soccer M(c)/W(s), softball W(s), swimming and diving M(s)/W(s), tennis M(s)/W(s), track and field M(s)/W(s), volleyball M(c)/W(s), water polo M(c)/W(c), wrestling M(c). *Intramural sports:* archery M/W, basketball M/W, bowling M/W, cheerleading M/W, crew M/W, cross-country running M/W, fencing M/W, field hockey M/W, football M, golf M/W, gymnastics M/W, lacrosse M/W, racquetball M/W, skiing (cross-country) M/W, skiing (downhill) M/W, soccer M/W, softball M/W, squash M/W, swimming and diving M/W, tennis M/W, volleyball M/W, water polo M/W, weight lifting M/W, wrestling M.

Campus security: 24-hour emergency response devices and patrols, student patrols, late-night transport/escort service, controlled dormitory access.

Student services: health clinic, personal/psychological counseling, women's center.

COSTS & FINANCIAL AID
Costs (2017–18) *Tuition:* state resident $11,994 full-time, $525 per credit hour part-time; nonresident $17,064 full-time, $736 per credit hour part-time. Full-time tuition and fees vary according to course level, course load, program, and student level. Part-time tuition and fees vary according

to course level, course load, program, and student level. *Room and board:* $9000. Room and board charges vary according to board plan and housing facility. *Payment plans:* installment, deferred payment. *Waivers:* employees or children of employees.

Financial Aid Of all full-time matriculated undergraduates who enrolled in 2017, 15,729 applied for aid, 11,550 were judged to have need, 2,043 had their need fully met. 1,376 Federal Work-Study jobs (averaging $2880). In 2017, 3216 non-need-based awards were made. *Average percent of need met:* 67. *Average financial aid package:* $10,093. *Average need-based loan:* $4296. *Average need-based gift aid:* $5409. *Average non-need-based aid:* $3440. *Average indebtedness upon graduation:* $29,675.

APPLYING
Standardized Tests *Required:* SAT or ACT (for admission).
Options: electronic application.
Application fee: $30.
Required: high school transcript. *Required for some:* essay or personal statement, interview.
Application deadlines: 5/1 (freshmen), 7/24 (transfers).
Notification: 5/1 (freshmen), continuous (transfers).

CONTACT
Ms. Jodi Chycinski, Director of Admissions, Grand Valley State University, 1 Campus Drive, Allendale, MI 49401. *Phone:* 616-331-2025. *Toll-free phone:* 800-748-0246. *Fax:* 616-331-2000. *E-mail:* go2gvsu@gvsu.edu.

Great Lakes Christian College
Lansing, Michigan
http://www.glcc.edu/

CONTACT
Mrs. Judy Carter, Admissions Office Manager, Great Lakes Christian College, 6211 West Willow Highway, Lansing, MI 48917-1299. *Phone:* 517-321-0242 Ext. 221. *Toll-free phone:* 800-YES-GLCC. *Fax:* 517-321-5902. *E-mail:* jcarter@glcc.edu.

★ Hillsdale College
Hillsdale, Michigan
http://www.hillsdale.edu/

- **Independent** comprehensive, founded 1844
- **Small-town** 400-acre campus
- **Endowment** $528.4 million
- **Coed** 1,512 undergraduate students, 97% full-time, 49% women, 51% men
- **Very difficult** entrance level, 41% of applicants were admitted

UNDERGRAD STUDENTS
1,463 full-time, 49 part-time. Students come from 50 states and territories; 14 other countries; 65% are from out of state; 1% transferred in; 69% live on campus.

Freshmen:
Admission: 2,080 applied, 863 admitted, 369 enrolled. *Average high school GPA:* 3.9. *Test scores:* SAT evidence-based reading and writing scores over 500: 100%; SAT math scores over 500: 100%; ACT scores over 18: 100%; SAT evidence-based reading and writing scores over 600: 93%; SAT math scores over 600: 83%; ACT scores over 24: 99%; SAT evidence-based reading and writing scores over 700: 49%; SAT math scores over 700: 32%; ACT scores over 30: 66%.

Retention: 92% of full-time freshmen returned.

FACULTY
Total: 199, 69% full-time.
Student/faculty ratio: 10:1.

ACADEMICS
Calendar: semesters. *Degrees:* bachelor's, master's, and doctoral.
Special study options: advanced placement credit, double majors, honors programs, independent study, internships, off-campus study, part-time degree program, student-designed majors, study abroad, summer session for credit.

Unusual degree programs: 3-2 engineering.

Computers: 312 computers/terminals are available on campus for general student use. Students can access the following: campus intranet, computer help desk, free student e-mail accounts, online (class) grades, online (class) registration, online (class) schedules. Campuswide network is available. 95% of college-owned or -operated housing units are wired for high-speed Internet access. Wireless service is available via entire campus.

Library: Michael Alex Mossey Library. *Books:* 252,517 (physical), 2.0 million (digital/electronic); *Serial titles:* 570 (physical), 30,000 (digital/electronic); *Databases:* 235.

STUDENT LIFE

Housing options: on-campus residence required through sophomore year; men-only, women-only, cooperative. Campus housing is university owned. Freshman campus housing is guaranteed.

Activities and organizations: drama/theater group, student-run newspaper, radio station, choral group, College Republicans, InterVarsity, Students for Life, American Chemical Society, PRAXIS - Political Economy Club, national fraternities, national sororities.

Athletics Member NCAA. All Division II. *Intercollegiate sports:* archery M(c)/W(c), baseball M(s), basketball M(s)/W(s), cheerleading W(c), crew M(c)/W(c), cross-country running M(s)/W(s), equestrian sports M(c)/W(c), football M(s), golf M(s), rugby M(c), soccer M(c)/W(c), softball W(s), swimming and diving M(c)/W(s), tennis M(s)/W(s), track and field M(s)/W(s), volleyball M(c)/W(s). *Intramural sports:* basketball M/W, football M/W, golf M, racquetball M/W, rugby M(c), soccer M/W, swimming and diving M(c), table tennis M/W, volleyball M/W, water polo M/W.

Campus security: 24-hour emergency response devices and patrols, student patrols, late-night transport/escort service, controlled dormitory access.

Student services: health clinic, personal/psychological counseling.

COSTS & FINANCIAL AID

Costs (2017–18) *One-time required fee:* $325. *Comprehensive fee:* $37,352 includes full-time tuition ($25,540), mandatory fees ($1202), and room and board ($10,610). Full-time tuition and fees vary according to degree level. Part-time tuition: $1020 per credit hour. Part-time tuition and fees vary according to degree level. *Required fees:* $85 per credit hour part-time, $1202 per year part-time. *College room only:* $5240. Room and board charges vary according to board plan. *Payment plan:* installment. *Waivers:* children of alumni and employees or children of employees.

Financial Aid Of all full-time matriculated undergraduates who enrolled in 2017, 809 applied for aid, 777 were judged to have need, 325 had their need fully met. In 2017, 649 non-need-based awards were made. *Average percent of need met:* 68. *Average financial aid package:* $19,939. *Average need-based loan:* $5996. *Average need-based gift aid:* $8471. *Average non-need-based aid:* $14,430. *Average indebtedness upon graduation:* $28,171.

APPLYING

Standardized Tests *Required:* SAT or ACT (for admission). *Recommended:* SAT Subject Tests (for admission).

Options: electronic application, early admission, early decision.

Application fee: $35.

Required: essay or personal statement, high school transcript, 2 letters of recommendation. *Recommended:* minimum 3.5 GPA, interview, campus visit, college prep courses.

Application deadlines: 4/1 (freshmen), 4/1 (transfers).

Early decision deadline: 11/1.

Notification: continuous (freshmen), continuous (transfers), 12/1 (early decision).

CONTACT

Mr. Douglas Banbury, Vice President Admissions, Hillsdale College, 33 East College Street, Hillsdale, MI 49242-1298. *Phone:* 517-607-2327. *Fax:* 517-607-2223. *E-mail:* admissions@hillsdale.edu.

See below for display ad and page 1308 for the College Close-Up.

Hope College
Holland, Michigan
http://www.hope.edu/

- **Independent** 4-year, founded 1866, affiliated with Reformed Church in America
- **Suburban** 91-acre campus with easy access to Grand Rapids
- **Endowment** $208.0 million
- **Coed** 3,150 undergraduate students, 96% full-time, 61% women, 39% men
- **Moderately difficult** entrance level, 84% of applicants were admitted

UNDERGRAD STUDENTS
3,018 full-time, 132 part-time. Students come from 36 states and territories; 35 other countries; 28% are from out of state; 3% Black or African American, non-Hispanic/Latino; 8% Hispanic/Latino; 2% Asian, non-Hispanic/Latino; 2% Two or more races, non-Hispanic/Latino; 0.7% Race/ethnicity unknown; 3% international; 2% transferred in; 88% live on campus.

Freshmen:
Admission: 3,899 applied, 3,291 admitted, 779 enrolled. *Average high school GPA:* 3.9. *Test scores:* SAT evidence-based reading and writing scores over 500: 94%; SAT math scores over 500: 92%; ACT scores over 18: 100%; SAT evidence-based reading and writing scores over 600: 55%; SAT math scores over 600: 51%; ACT scores over 24: 76%; SAT evidence-based reading and writing scores over 700: 11%; SAT math scores over 700: 10%; ACT scores over 30: 22%.

Retention: 91% of full-time freshmen returned.

FACULTY
Total: 348, 68% full-time.
Student/faculty ratio: 11:1.

ACADEMICS
Calendar: semesters. *Degree:* bachelor's.
Special study options: advanced placement credit, double majors, English as a second language, external degree program, independent study, internships, off-campus study, part-time degree program, services for LD students, student-designed majors, study abroad, summer session for credit. *ROTC:* Army (c).
Computers: 300 computers/terminals and 5,000 ports are available on campus for general student use. Students can access the following: campus intranet, computer help desk, free student e-mail accounts, online (class) grades, online (class) registration, online (class) schedules. Campuswide network is available. 100% of college-owned or -operated housing units are wired for high-speed Internet access. Wireless service is available via entire campus.
Library: Van Wylen Library plus 2 others. *Books:* 247,002 (physical), 242,414 (digital/electronic); *Serial titles:* 2,530 (physical), 41,509 (digital/electronic); *Databases:* 166. Weekly public service hours: 96.

STUDENT LIFE
Housing options: on-campus residence required through junior year; coed, men-only, women-only, special housing for students with disabilities. Campus housing is university owned and leased by the school. Freshman campus housing is guaranteed.
Activities and organizations: drama/theater group, student-run newspaper, radio station, choral group, Social Activities Committee, Greek Life, Dance Marathon, Hockey Club, Relay for Life, national fraternities, national sororities.
Athletics Member NCAA. All Division III. *Intercollegiate sports:* baseball M, basketball M/W, cheerleading M/W, cross-country running M/W, football M, golf M/W, ice hockey M(c), lacrosse M/W, sailing M(c)/W(c), soccer M/W, softball W, swimming and diving M/W, tennis M/W, track and field M/W, volleyball W. *Intramural sports:* badminton M/W, basketball M/W, football M/W, ice hockey M(c), rugby M(c), sailing M(c)/W(c), soccer M/W, softball M/W, tennis M/W, ultimate Frisbee M/W, volleyball M/W, water polo M/W.
Campus security: 24-hour emergency response devices and patrols, late-night transport/escort service, controlled dormitory access.
Student services: health clinic, personal/psychological counseling.

COSTS & FINANCIAL AID
Costs (2018–19) *Comprehensive fee:* $44,320 includes full-time tuition ($33,700), mandatory fees ($310), and room and board ($10,310). Part-time tuition and fees vary according to course load and program. *College room only:* $4730. Room and board charges vary according to board plan. *Payment plan:* installment. *Waivers:* employees or children of employees.
Financial Aid Of all full-time matriculated undergraduates who enrolled in 2017, 2,059 applied for aid, 1,728 were judged to have need, 435 had their need fully met. 136 Federal Work-Study jobs (averaging $2370). 588 state and other part-time jobs (averaging $1103). In 2017, 827 non-need-based awards were made. *Average percent of need met:* 81. *Average financial aid package:* $26,952. *Average need-based loan:* $5287. *Average need-based gift aid:* $20,276. *Average non-need-based aid:* $8812. *Average indebtedness upon graduation:* $33,033.

APPLYING
Standardized Tests *Required:* SAT or ACT (for admission).
Options: electronic application, early admission, deferred entrance.
Application fee: $35.
Required: essay or personal statement, high school transcript. *Required for some:* 1 letter of recommendation. *Recommended:* interview.
Application deadlines: rolling (freshmen), rolling (transfers).
Notification: continuous (freshmen), continuous (transfers).

CONTACT
Admissions Office, Hope College, 69 East 10th Street, PO Box 9000, Holland, MI 49422-9000. *Phone:* 616-395-7850. *Toll-free phone:* 800-968-7850. *E-mail:* admissions@hope.edu.

Kalamazoo College
Kalamazoo, Michigan
http://www.kzoo.edu/

- **Independent** 4-year, founded 1833, affiliated with American Baptist Churches in the U.S.A.
- **Urban** 60-acre campus with easy access to Grand Rapids
- **Endowment** $227.0 million
- **Coed** 1,436 undergraduate students, 99% full-time, 57% women, 43% men
- **Very difficult** entrance level, 73% of applicants were admitted

UNDERGRAD STUDENTS
1,427 full-time, 9 part-time. Students come from 43 states and territories; 28 other countries; 33% are from out of state; 8% Black or African American, non-Hispanic/Latino; 13% Hispanic/Latino; 8% Asian, non-Hispanic/Latino; 0.1% Native Hawaiian or other Pacific Islander, non-Hispanic/Latino; 4% Two or more races, non-Hispanic/Latino; 3% Race/ethnicity unknown; 6% international; 0.8% transferred in; 53% live on campus.

Freshmen:
Admission: 3,434 applied, 2,520 admitted, 448 enrolled. *Average high school GPA:* 3.8. *Test scores:* SAT evidence-based reading and writing scores over 500: 97%; SAT math scores over 500: 95%; ACT scores over 18: 99%; SAT evidence-based reading and writing scores over 600: 75%; SAT math scores over 600: 70%; ACT scores over 24: 87%; SAT evidence-based reading and writing scores over 700: 21%; SAT math scores over 700: 22%; ACT scores over 30: 32%.

Retention: 90% of full-time freshmen returned.

FACULTY
Total: 135, 74% full-time, 90% with terminal degrees.
Student/faculty ratio: 13:1.

ACADEMICS
Calendar: quarters. *Degree:* bachelor's.
Special study options: advanced placement credit, double majors, independent study, internships, off-campus study, services for LD students, student-designed majors, study abroad. *ROTC:* Army (c).
Unusual degree programs: 3-2 engineering with University of Michigan, Washington University in St. Louis.
Computers: 250 computers/terminals are available on campus for general student use. Students can access the following: campus intranet, computer help desk, free student e-mail accounts, online (class) grades, online

(class) registration, online (class) schedules, residential computer consultant. Campuswide network is available. 100% of college-owned or - operated housing units are wired for high-speed Internet access. Wireless service is available via entire campus.

Library: Upjohn Library Commons. *Books:* 272,425 (physical), 162,857 (digital/electronic); *Serial titles:* 2,660 (physical), 176,641 (digital/electronic); *Databases:* 517. Weekly public service hours: 114.

STUDENT LIFE

Housing options: on-campus residence required through junior year; coed, special housing for students with disabilities. Campus housing is university owned. Freshman campus housing is guaranteed.

Activities and organizations: drama/theater group, student-run newspaper, radio station, choral group, Cirque du K, A cappella groups, Food Recovery Network, Women of Color, Swing Club.

Athletics Member NCAA. All Division III. *Intercollegiate sports:* baseball M, basketball M/W, cross-country running M/W, football M, golf M/W, lacrosse M/W, soccer M/W, softball W, swimming and diving M/W, tennis M/W, volleyball W. *Intramural sports:* badminton M/W, basketball M/W, cheerleading M(c)/W(c), lacrosse M(c)/W(c), racquetball M/W, soccer M/W, softball M/W, table tennis M/W, tennis M/W, ultimate Frisbee M(c)/W(c), volleyball M/W.

Campus security: 24-hour emergency response devices and patrols, late-night transport/escort service, controlled dormitory access.

Student services: health clinic, personal/psychological counseling.

COSTS & FINANCIAL AID

Costs (2018–19) *Comprehensive fee:* $58,272 includes full-time tuition ($48,162), mandatory fees ($354), and room and board ($9756). Full-time tuition and fees vary according to course load. Part-time tuition and fees vary according to course load. *College room only:* $4746. Room and board charges vary according to board plan and housing facility. *Payment plan:* installment. *Waivers:* employees or children of employees.

Financial Aid Of all full-time matriculated undergraduates who enrolled in 2016, 1,083 applied for aid, 970 were judged to have need, 394 had their need fully met. In 2016, 399 non-need-based awards were made. *Average percent of need met:* 92. *Average financial aid package:*

$37,979. *Average need-based loan:* $6214. *Average need-based gift aid:* $29,998. *Average non-need-based aid:* $19,558. *Average indebtedness upon graduation:* $27,653.

APPLYING

Options: electronic application, early decision, early action, deferred entrance.

Required: essay or personal statement, high school transcript, 2 letters of recommendation. *Recommended:* minimum 3.0 GPA, interview.

Application deadlines: 1/15 (freshmen), 5/1 (transfers), 11/1 (early action).

Early decision deadline: 11/1 (for plan 1), 2/1 (for plan 2).

Notification: 4/1 (freshmen), 5/15 (transfers), 12/1 (early decision plan 1), 2/15 (early decision plan 2), 12/20 (early action).

CONTACT

Kalamazoo College, 1200 Academy Street, Kalamazoo, MI 49006-3295. *Toll-free phone:* 800-253-3602.

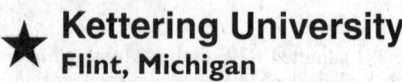

★ Kettering University
Flint, Michigan
http://www.kettering.edu/

- **Independent** comprehensive, founded 1919
- **Urban** 85-acre campus with easy access to Detroit
- **Endowment** $81.3 million
- **Coed** 1,889 undergraduate students, 96% full-time, 19% women, 81% men
- **Very difficult** entrance level, 70% of applicants were admitted

UNDERGRAD STUDENTS

1,807 full-time, 82 part-time. 15% are from out of state; 3% Black or African American, non-Hispanic/Latino; 5% Hispanic/Latino; 4% Asian, non-Hispanic/Latino; 0.3% American Indian or Alaska Native, non-Hispanic/Latino; 3% Two or more races, non-Hispanic/Latino; 5% Race/ethnicity unknown; 4% international; 2% transferred in; 9% live on campus.

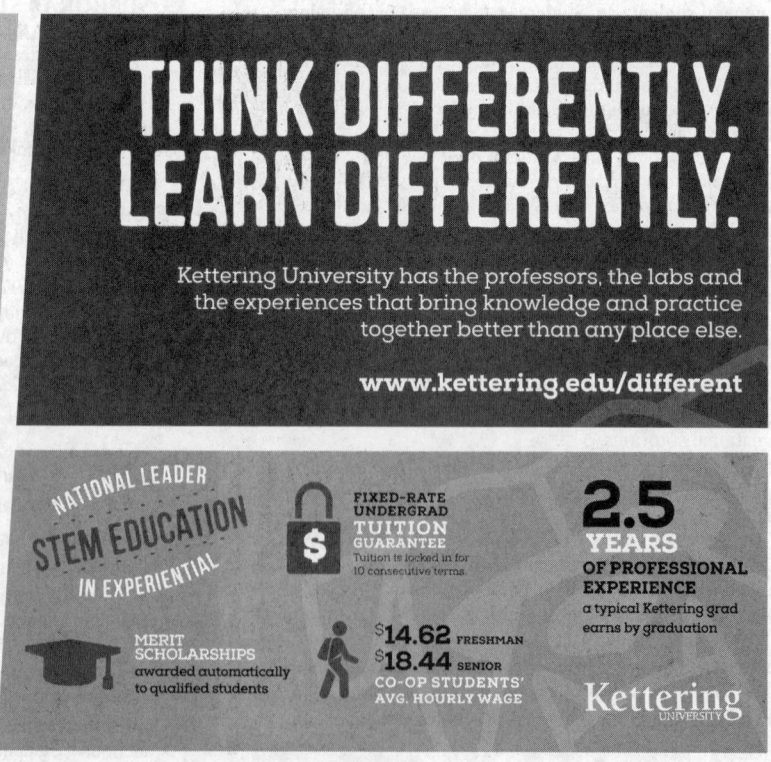

Freshmen:
Admission: 1,931 applied, 1,358 admitted, 371 enrolled. *Average high school GPA:* 3.7. *Test scores:* SAT evidence-based reading and writing scores over 500: 99%; SAT math scores over 500: 99%; ACT scores over 18: 100%; SAT evidence-based reading and writing scores over 600: 62%; SAT math scores over 600: 82%; ACT scores over 24: 85%; SAT evidence-based reading and writing scores over 700: 11%; SAT math scores over 700: 22%; ACT scores over 30: 25%.
Retention: 93% of full-time freshmen returned.

FACULTY
Total: 146, 78% full-time, 68% with terminal degrees.
Student/faculty ratio: 15:1.

ACADEMICS
Calendar: semesters (11 weeks of full-time study plus 12 weeks of paid co-op experience per semester). *Degrees:* bachelor's and master's.
Special study options: advanced placement credit, cooperative education, distance learning, double majors, external degree program, independent study, internships, services for LD students, study abroad, summer session for credit.
Computers: Students can access the following: campus intranet, computer help desk, free student e-mail accounts, online (class) grades, online (class) registration, online (class) schedules. Campuswide network is available. 100% of college-owned or -operated housing units are wired for high-speed Internet access. Wireless service is available via entire campus.
Library: Kettering University Library.

STUDENT LIFE
Housing options: on-campus residence required for freshman year; coed, men-only, women-only, special housing for students with disabilities. Campus housing is university owned and is provided by a third party. Freshman campus housing is guaranteed.
Activities and organizations: student-run newspaper, radio station, choral group, Student Government, Dance Club, Firebirds, Outdoors Club, International Club, national fraternities, national sororities.
Athletics *Intramural sports:* baseball M(c)/W(c), basketball M/W, bowling M/W, football M/W, golf M(c)/W(c), ice hockey M(c)/W(c), lacrosse M(c)/W(c), racquetball M/W, riflery M(c)/W(c), soccer M/W, softball M/W, squash M/W, table tennis M(c)/W(c), tennis M/W, ultimate Frisbee M(c)/W(c), volleyball M/W, water polo M/W.
Campus security: 24-hour emergency response devices and patrols, late-night transport/escort service, controlled dormitory access, security card access to all campus buildings 24/7 except the campus center main entrance which is secure 11pm-7am.
Student services: health clinic, personal/psychological counseling, women's center.

FINANCIAL AID
Financial Aid Of all full-time matriculated undergraduates who enrolled in 2015, 1,747 applied for aid, 1,306 were judged to have need, 129 had their need fully met. In 2015, 446 non-need-based awards were made. *Average percent of need met:* 63. *Average financial aid package:* $21,047. *Average need-based loan:* $4336. *Average need-based gift aid:* $16,951. *Average non-need-based aid:* $13,804.

APPLYING
Standardized Tests *Required:* SAT or ACT (for admission).
Options: electronic application, early action, deferred entrance.
Required: high school transcript. *Required for some:* essay or personal statement. *Recommended:* minimum 3.0 GPA, interview.
Application deadlines: rolling (freshmen), rolling (out-of-state freshmen), rolling (transfers).
Notification: continuous (freshmen), continuous (out-of-state freshmen), continuous (transfers).

CONTACT
Mr. Kip Darcy, Vice President of Marketing, Communications and Enrollment, Kettering University, 1700 University Avenue, Flint, MI 48504-6214. *Phone:* 810-762-9511. *Toll-free phone:* 800-955-4464 Ext. 7865 (in-state); 800-955-4464 (out-of-state). *Fax:* 810-762-9837. *E-mail:* kdarcy@kettering.edu.

See previous page for display ad and page 1318 for the College Close-Up.

Kuyper College
Grand Rapids, Michigan
http://www.kuyper.edu/
• **Independent Christian** 4-year, founded 1939
• **Suburban** 34-acre campus with easy access to Grand Rapids
• **Endowment** $7.4 million
• **Coed**
• **Moderately difficult** entrance level

FACULTY
Student/faculty ratio: 12:1.

ACADEMICS
Calendar: semesters. *Degrees:* certificates, associate, bachelor's, and postbachelor's certificates.
Library: Zondervan Library plus 1 other. *Books:* 78,702 (physical), 14,199 (digital/electronic); *Databases:* 101. Weekly public service hours: 72; students can reserve study rooms.

STUDENT LIFE
Housing options: on-campus residence required through sophomore year; coed. Campus housing is university owned. Freshman campus housing is guaranteed.
Activities and organizations: drama/theater group, choral group, intramurals, Student Activities Club, Helping and Nurturing During Service, Yearbook, Roots.
Campus security: 24-hour emergency response devices, student patrols, late-night transport/escort service, controlled dormitory access.
Student services: health clinic, personal/psychological counseling.

COSTS & FINANCIAL AID
Costs (2017–18) *One-time required fee:* $544. *Comprehensive fee:* $28,344 includes full-time tuition ($20,506), mandatory fees ($584), and room and board ($7254). Full-time tuition and fees vary according to course load and reciprocity agreements. Part-time tuition: $950 per credit hour. Part-time tuition and fees vary according to course load and reciprocity agreements. *Required fees:* $295 per year part-time.
Room and board: Room and board charges vary according to board plan, housing facility, and student level. *Payment plans:* installment, deferred payment.
Financial Aid Of all full-time matriculated undergraduates who enrolled in 2017, 137 applied for aid, 125 were judged to have need, 5 had their need fully met. In 2017, 14 non-need-based awards were made. *Average percent of need met:* 77. *Average financial aid package:* $18,369. *Average need-based loan:* $7496. *Average need-based gift aid:* $12,426. *Average non-need-based aid:* $4644. *Average indebtedness upon graduation:* $36,147.

APPLYING
Standardized Tests *Required:* SAT or ACT (for admission).
Options: electronic application, deferred entrance.
Required: essay or personal statement, high school transcript, minimum 2.5 GPA. *Recommended:* interview.

CONTACT
Admissions Office, Kuyper College, 3333 East Beltline Avenue, NE, Grand Rapids, MI 49525. *Phone:* 616-222-3000 Ext. 632. *Fax:* 616-222-3045. *E-mail:* admissions@kuyper.edu.

Lake Superior State University
Sault Sainte Marie, Michigan
http://www.lssu.edu/

CONTACT
Lake Superior State University, 650 West Easterday Avenue, Sault Sainte Marie, MI 49783. *Phone:* 906-635-2231. *Toll-free phone:* 888-800-LSSU Ext. 2231.

Lawrence Technological University
Southfield, Michigan
http://www.ltu.edu/

- **Independent** university, founded 1932
- **Suburban** 107-acre campus with easy access to Detroit
- **Endowment** $73.7 million
- **Coed** 2,191 undergraduate students, 76% full-time, 26% women, 74% men
- **Moderately difficult** entrance level, 60% of applicants were admitted

UNDERGRAD STUDENTS
1,672 full-time, 519 part-time. Students come from 38 states and territories; 36 other countries; 8% are from out of state; 6% Black or African American, non-Hispanic/Latino; 3% Hispanic/Latino; 3% Asian, non-Hispanic/Latino; 0.3% American Indian or Alaska Native, non-Hispanic/Latino; 2% Two or more races, non-Hispanic/Latino; 0.7% Race/ethnicity unknown; 14% international; 7% transferred in; 36% live on campus.

Freshmen:
Admission: 2,173 applied, 1,296 admitted, 373 enrolled. *Average high school GPA:* 3.5. *Test scores:* SAT evidence-based reading and writing scores over 500: 84%; SAT math scores over 500: 88%; ACT scores over 18: 95%; SAT evidence-based reading and writing scores over 600: 40%; SAT math scores over 600: 45%; ACT scores over 24: 68%; SAT evidence-based reading and writing scores over 700: 4%; SAT math scores over 700: 8%; ACT scores over 30: 19%.
Retention: 82% of full-time freshmen returned.

FACULTY
Total: 341, 37% full-time, 45% with terminal degrees.
Student/faculty ratio: 11:1.

ACADEMICS
Calendar: semesters. *Degrees:* certificates, associate, bachelor's, master's, doctoral, and postbachelor's certificates.

Special study options: academic remediation for entering students, accelerated degree program, adult/continuing education programs, advanced placement credit, cooperative education, distance learning, double majors, English as a second language, honors programs, independent study, internships, off-campus study, part-time degree program, services for LD students, study abroad, summer session for credit. *ROTC:* Air Force (c).

Computers: 2,203 computers/terminals and 3,618 ports are available on campus for general student use. Students can access the following: campus intranet, computer help desk, free student e-mail accounts, online (class) grades, online (class) registration, online (class) schedules, degree audit, Canvas/Blackboard, Banner (student information), personal websites, document collection, Handshake, Placement, Mapworks advising. Campuswide network is available. 100% of college-owned or -operated housing units are wired for high-speed Internet access. Wireless service is available via entire campus.
Library: Lawrence Technological University Library plus 1 other. *Books:* 43,864 (physical), 298,126 (digital/electronic); *Serial titles:* 941 (physical), 44,608 (digital/electronic); *Databases:* 171. Weekly public service hours: 73; students can reserve study rooms.

STUDENT LIFE
Housing options: coed, special housing for students with disabilities. Campus housing is university owned and is provided by a third party. Freshman applicants given priority for college housing.

Activities and organizations: drama/theater group, student-run newspaper, American Institute of Architecture Students, American Society of Mechanical Engineers, Sigma Phi Epsilon, American Society of Civil Engineers, Student Government, national fraternities, national sororities.

Athletics Member NAIA. *Intercollegiate sports:* baseball M(s), basketball M(s)/W(s), bowling M(s)/W(s), cross-country running M(s)/W(s), football M(s), golf M(s)/W(s), ice hockey M, lacrosse M(s)/W(s), soccer M(s)/W(s), softball W(s), tennis M(s)/W(s), volleyball M(s)/W(s). *Intramural sports:* badminton M/W, basketball M/W, golf M/W, ice hockey M(c), racquetball M/W, skiing (downhill) M/W, soccer M/W, softball M/W, table tennis M/W, tennis M/W, track and field M(c)/W(c), ultimate Frisbee M(c)/W(c), volleyball M/W.

Campus security: 24-hour emergency response devices and patrols, late-night transport/escort service, controlled dormitory access.

Student services: personal/psychological counseling.

COSTS & FINANCIAL AID
Costs (2017–18) *Comprehensive fee:* $41,630 includes full-time tuition ($31,410), mandatory fees ($720), and room and board ($9500). Full-time tuition and fees vary according to course level, degree level, location, program, and student level. Part-time tuition: $1047 per credit hour. Part-time tuition and fees vary according to course level, degree level, location, program, and student level. *Required fees:* $360 per term part-time. *College room only:* $6700. Room and board charges vary according to board plan and housing facility. *Payment plan:* installment. *Waivers:* employees or children of employees.

Financial Aid Of all full-time matriculated undergraduates who enrolled in 2016, 1,408 applied for aid, 1,014 were judged to have need, 165 had their need fully met. 80 Federal Work-Study jobs (averaging $1378). In 2016, 348 non-need-based awards were made. *Average percent of need met:* 69. *Average financial aid package:* $24,840. *Average need-based loan:* $7009. *Average need-based gift aid:* $15,970. *Average non-need-based aid:* $15,440. *Average indebtedness upon graduation:* $32,572.

APPLYING
Standardized Tests *Required:* SAT or ACT (for admission).
Options: electronic application, deferred entrance.
Application fee: $30.
Required: high school transcript, minimum 2.5 GPA. *Required for some:* essay or personal statement, minimum 2.8 GPA, 1 letter of recommendation, interview.
Application deadlines: 8/15 (freshmen), 8/15 (transfers).
Notification: continuous until 8/26 (freshmen), continuous until 8/26 (transfers).

CONTACT
Jane Rohrback, Director of Admissions, Lawrence Technological University, 21000 West Ten Mile Road, Southfield, MI 48075. *Phone:* 248-204-3160. *Toll-free phone:* 800-225-5588. *Fax:* 248-204-2228. *E-mail:* admissions@ltu.edu.

Madonna University
Livonia, Michigan
http://www.madonna.edu/

- **Independent Roman Catholic** comprehensive, founded 1947
- **Suburban** 85-acre campus with easy access to Detroit
- **Endowment** $38.9 million
- **Coed** 2,458 undergraduate students, 55% full-time, 65% women, 35% men
- **Moderately difficult** entrance level, 74% of applicants were admitted

UNDERGRAD STUDENTS
1,358 full-time, 1,100 part-time. Students come from 15 states and territories; 7 other countries; 2% are from out of state; 12% Black or African American, non-Hispanic/Latino; 4% Hispanic/Latino; 1% Asian, non-Hispanic/Latino; 0.2% Native Hawaiian or other Pacific Islander, non-Hispanic/Latino; 0.1% American Indian or Alaska Native, non-Hispanic/Latino; 3% Two or more races, non-Hispanic/Latino; 5% Race/ethnicity unknown; 13% international; 16% transferred in; 46% live on campus.

Freshmen:
Admission: 1,009 applied, 750 admitted, 278 enrolled. *Average high school GPA:* 3.2. *Test scores:* SAT evidence-based reading and writing scores over 500: 34%; SAT math scores over 500: 45%; ACT scores over 18: 87%; SAT evidence-based reading and writing scores over 600: 10%; SAT math scores over 600: 8%; ACT scores over 24: 31%; SAT evidence-based reading and writing scores over 700: 3%; ACT scores over 30: 3%.
Retention: 73% of full-time freshmen returned.

FACULTY
Total: 282, 34% full-time, 41% with terminal degrees.
Student/faculty ratio: 13:1.

ACADEMICS

Calendar: semesters. *Degrees:* certificates, diplomas, associate, bachelor's, master's, doctoral, post-master's, and postbachelor's certificates.

Special study options: accelerated degree program, adult/continuing education programs, advanced placement credit, cooperative education, distance learning, double majors, English as a second language, independent study, internships, off-campus study, part-time degree program, services for LD students, student-designed majors, study abroad, summer session for credit. *ROTC:* Army (c).

Computers: 227 computers/terminals and 227 ports are available on campus for general student use. Students can access the following: campus intranet, computer help desk, free student e-mail accounts, online (class) grades, online (class) registration, online (class) schedules, online payments, online statements, online unofficial transcripts. Campuswide network is available. 100% of college-owned or -operated housing units are wired for high-speed Internet access. Wireless service is available via classrooms, computer labs, dorm rooms, learning centers, libraries, student centers.

Library: Madonna University Library. *Books:* 78,541 (physical), 166,468 (digital/electronic); *Serial titles:* 219 (physical), 60,485 (digital/electronic); *Databases:* 135. Weekly public service hours: 97; students can reserve study rooms.

STUDENT LIFE

Housing options: men-only, women-only. Campus housing is university owned. Freshman campus housing is guaranteed.

Activities and organizations: drama/theater group, student-run newspaper, radio and television station, choral group, Campus Ministry, Madonna University Nursing Student Association, Broadcast and Film Club, Society of Future Teachers, Michigan Blood Club.

Athletics Member NAIA. *Intercollegiate sports:* baseball M(s), basketball M(s)/W(s), bowling M(s)/W(s), cross-country running M(s)/W(s), golf M(s)/W(s), lacrosse M(s)/W(s), soccer M(s)/W(s), softball W(s), track and field M(s)/W(s), volleyball W(s). *Intramural sports:* basketball M/W.

Campus security: 24-hour emergency response devices and patrols, late-night transport/escort service, controlled dormitory access.

Student services: personal/psychological counseling.

COSTS & FINANCIAL AID

Costs (2017–18) *Comprehensive fee:* $30,450 includes full-time tuition ($20,700) and room and board ($9750). Full-time tuition and fees vary according to course load and program. Part-time tuition: $690 per credit hour. Part-time tuition and fees vary according to course load and program. *College room only:* $4800. Room and board charges vary according to board plan. *Payment plan:* deferred payment. *Waivers:* senior citizens and employees or children of employees.

Financial Aid Of all full-time matriculated undergraduates who enrolled in 2007, 862 applied for aid, 698 were judged to have need, 122 had their need fully met. In 2007, 172 non-need-based awards were made. *Average percent of need met:* 56. *Average financial aid package:* $7396. *Average need-based loan:* $3862. *Average need-based gift aid:* $4508. *Average non-need-based aid:* $2427.

APPLYING

Standardized Tests *Required:* SAT or ACT (for admission).

Options: electronic application, early decision, deferred entrance.

Application fee: $25.

Required: high school transcript. *Required for some:* essay or personal statement.

Application deadlines: rolling (freshmen), rolling (transfers).

Early decision deadline: 12/1.

Notification: continuous (freshmen), continuous (transfers), 1/15 (early decision).

CONTACT

Mr. Mark A. Schroeder, Director of Undergraduate Admissions, Madonna University, 36600 Schoolcraft Road, Livonia, MI 48150-1173. *Phone:* 734-432-5339. *Toll-free phone:* 800-852-4951. *Fax:* 734-432-5424. *E-mail:* mschroeder@madonna.edu.

Michigan State University
East Lansing, Michigan
http://www.msu.edu/

- **State-supported** university, founded 1855
- **Suburban** 5192-acre campus with easy access to Detroit
- **Endowment** $3.1 billion
- **Coed** 38,996 undergraduate students, 91% full-time, 51% women, 49% men
- **Moderately difficult** entrance level, 72% of applicants were admitted

UNDERGRAD STUDENTS

35,404 full-time, 3,592 part-time. Students come from 109 other countries; 13% are from out of state; 7% Black or African American, non-Hispanic/Latino; 4% Hispanic/Latino; 5% Asian, non-Hispanic/Latino; 0.1% Native Hawaiian or other Pacific Islander, non-Hispanic/Latino; 0.2% American Indian or Alaska Native, non-Hispanic/Latino; 3% Two or more races, non-Hispanic/Latino; 0.7% Race/ethnicity unknown; 12% international; 4% transferred in; 40% live on campus.

Freshmen:
Admission: 36,143 applied, 25,860 admitted, 8,366 enrolled. *Average high school GPA:* 3.7. *Test scores:* SAT evidence-based reading and writing scores over 500: 93%; SAT math scores over 500: 94%; ACT scores over 18: 98%; SAT evidence-based reading and writing scores over 600: 52%; SAT math scores over 600: 53%; ACT scores over 24: 74%; SAT evidence-based reading and writing scores over 700: 9%; SAT math scores over 700: 13%; ACT scores over 30: 18%.

Retention: 91% of full-time freshmen returned.

FACULTY
Total: 2,946, 86% full-time, 85% with terminal degrees.
Student/faculty ratio: 16:1.

ACADEMICS

Calendar: semesters. *Degrees:* certificates, bachelor's, master's, doctoral, and post-master's certificates.

Special study options: academic remediation for entering students, accelerated degree program, adult/continuing education programs, advanced placement credit, cooperative education, distance learning, double majors, English as a second language, freshman honors college, honors programs, independent study, internships, off-campus study, part-time degree program, services for LD students, student-designed majors, study abroad, summer session for credit. *ROTC:* Army (b), Air Force (b).

Unusual degree programs: 3-2 engineering.

Computers: Students can access the following: campus intranet, computer help desk, free student e-mail accounts, online (class) grades, online (class) registration, online (class) schedules. Campuswide network is available. 100% of college-owned or -operated housing units are wired for high-speed Internet access. Wireless service is available via classrooms, computer centers, computer labs, dorm rooms, learning centers, libraries, student centers.

Library: Main Library plus 4 others.

STUDENT LIFE

Housing options: on-campus residence required for freshman year; coed, women-only, cooperative, special housing for students with disabilities. Campus housing is university owned. Freshman campus housing is guaranteed.

Activities and organizations: drama/theater group, student-run newspaper, radio and television station, choral group, marching band, national fraternities, national sororities.

Athletics Member NCAA. All Division I except football (Division I-A). *Intercollegiate sports:* baseball M(s), basketball M(s)/W(s), cheerleading M/W, crew M(c)/W(s), cross-country running M(s)/W(s), equestrian sports M(c)/W(c), fencing M(c)/W(c), field hockey W(s), golf M(s)/W(s), gymnastics W(s), ice hockey M(s)/W(c), lacrosse M(c)/W(c), rowing M(c)/W(s), rugby M(c)/W(c), sailing M(c)/W(c), soccer M(s)/W(s), softball W(s), swimming and diving M(s)/W(s), table tennis M(c)/W(c), tennis M(s)/W(s), track and field M(s)/W(s), volleyball M(c)/W(s), water polo M(c)/W(c), wrestling M(s). *Intramural sports:* baseball M(c), basketball M/W, cheerleading W(c), crew M(c)/W(c), football M/W, ice hockey M/W, racquetball M/W, riflery M/W, rowing M(c)/W(c), rugby M(c)/W(c), sand volleyball M/W, soccer M(c)/W(c), softball M/W, squash

M/W, table tennis M/W, tennis M/W, ultimate Frisbee M(c)/W(c), volleyball M/W, water polo M/W.

Campus security: 24-hour emergency response devices and patrols, late-night transport/escort service, controlled dormitory access, self-defense workshops.

Student services: health clinic, personal/psychological counseling, women's center, legal services.

COSTS & FINANCIAL AID

Costs (2017–18) *Tuition:* state resident $14,460 full-time, $482 per credit hour part-time; nonresident $39,405 full-time, $1314 per credit hour part-time. Full-time tuition and fees vary according to course load, program, and student level. Part-time tuition and fees vary according to course load, program, and student level. *Room and board:* $9976; room only: $4120. Room and board charges vary according to board plan and housing facility. *Payment plan:* deferred payment. *Waivers:* employees or children of employees.

Financial Aid Of all full-time matriculated undergraduates who enrolled in 2017, 21,893 applied for aid, 16,984 were judged to have need, 2,333 had their need fully met. 1,620 Federal Work-Study jobs (averaging $2174). In 2017, 3180 non-need-based awards were made. *Average percent of need met:* 59. *Average financial aid package:* $13,466. *Average need-based loan:* $4020. *Average need-based gift aid:* $10,593. *Average non-need-based aid:* $10,493. *Average indebtedness upon graduation:* $32,310.

APPLYING

Standardized Tests *Required:* SAT or ACT (for admission).

Options: electronic application, deferred entrance.

Application fee: $65.

Required: essay or personal statement, high school transcript.

Application deadlines: rolling (freshmen), rolling (transfers).

Notification: continuous (freshmen), continuous (transfers).

CONTACT

James Cotter, Director of Admissions, Michigan State University, 250 Administration Building, East Lansing, MI 48824. *Phone:* 517-355-8332. *Fax:* 517-353-1647. *E-mail:* admis@msu.edu.

Michigan Technological University

Houghton, Michigan

http://www.mtu.edu/

- **State-supported** university, founded 1885
- **Small-town** 925-acre campus
- **Endowment** $106.4 million
- **Coed** 5,917 undergraduate students, 93% full-time, 27% women, 73% men
- **Moderately difficult** entrance level, 74% of applicants were admitted

UNDERGRAD STUDENTS

5,517 full-time, 400 part-time. Students come from 45 states and territories; 35 other countries; 22% are from out of state; 0.9% Black or African American, non-Hispanic/Latino; 2% Hispanic/Latino; 1% Asian, non-Hispanic/Latino; 0.1% Native Hawaiian or other Pacific Islander, non-Hispanic/Latino; 0.3% American Indian or Alaska Native, non-Hispanic/Latino; 3% Two or more races, non-Hispanic/Latino; 2% Race/ethnicity unknown; 3% international; 3% transferred in; 45% live on campus.

Freshmen:

Admission: 5,469 applied, 4,074 admitted, 1,323 enrolled. *Average high school GPA:* 3.7. *Test scores:* SAT evidence-based reading and writing scores over 500: 96%; SAT math scores over 500: 99%; ACT scores over 18: 100%; SAT evidence-based reading and writing scores over 600: 61%; SAT math scores over 600: 68%; ACT scores over 24: 83%; SAT evidence-based reading and writing scores over 700: 10%; SAT math scores over 700: 17%; ACT scores over 30: 29%.

Retention: 83% of full-time freshmen returned.

FACULTY

Total: 450, 92% full-time, 86% with terminal degrees.

Student/faculty ratio: 12:1.

ACADEMICS

Calendar: semesters. *Degrees:* certificates, associate, bachelor's, master's, doctoral, and postbachelor's certificates.

Special study options: accelerated degree program, advanced placement credit, cooperative education, distance learning, double majors, English as a second language, honors programs, independent study, internships, off-campus study, part-time degree program, services for LD students, study abroad, summer session for credit. *ROTC:* Army (b), Air Force (b).

Unusual degree programs: engineering with Adrian College, Albion College, Augsburg College, Northland College, Olivet College, University of Wisconsin–Superior; forestry with Northland College, University of Wisconsin–Superior.

Computers: 1,079 computers/terminals and 6,082 ports are available on campus for general student use. Students can access the following: campus intranet, computer help desk, free student e-mail accounts, online (class) grades, online (class) registration, online (class) schedules. Campuswide network is available. 100% of college-owned or -operated housing units are wired for high-speed Internet access. Wireless service is available via entire campus.

Library: J. R. Van Pelt and John and Ruanne Opie Library. *Books:* 362,342 (physical), 142,603 (digital/electronic); *Serial titles:* 14,050 (physical), 124,764 (digital/electronic); *Databases:* 347. Weekly public service hours: 105; study areas open 24 hours, 5–7 days a week; students can reserve study rooms.

STUDENT LIFE

Housing options: on-campus residence required for freshman year; coed, special housing for students with disabilities. Campus housing is university owned. Freshman campus housing is guaranteed.

Activities and organizations: drama/theater group, student-run newspaper, radio station, choral group, Indian Students Associate, Society of Women Engineers, Huskies Pep Band, Fishing Club, WMTU, national fraternities, national sororities.

Athletics Member NCAA. All Division II except ice hockey (Division I). *Intercollegiate sports:* archery M(c)/W(c), badminton M(c)/W(c), baseball M(c), basketball M(s)/W(s), cheerleading M(c)/W(c), crew M(c)/W(c), cross-country running M(s)/W(s), fencing M(c)/W(c), football M(s), golf M(c)/W(c), gymnastics M(c)/W(c), ice hockey M(s)/W(c), lacrosse M(c)/W(c), racquetball M(c)/W(c), riflery M(c)/W(c), rugby M(c)/W(c), sailing M(c)/W(c), skiing (cross-country) M(s)/W(s), skiing (downhill) M(c)/W(c), soccer M(c)/W(s), softball W(c), tennis M(s)/W(s), track and field M(s)/W(s), ultimate Frisbee M(c)/W(c), volleyball M(c)/W(s), water polo M(c)/W(c). *Intramural sports:* badminton M/W, basketball M/W, bowling M/W, golf M/W, ice hockey M/W, racquetball M/W, riflery M/W, sand volleyball M/W, soccer M/W, softball M/W, swimming and diving M/W, table tennis M/W, tennis M/W, ultimate Frisbee M/W, volleyball M/W, water polo M/W, weight lifting M(c)/W(c).

Campus security: 24-hour emergency response devices and patrols, late-night transport/escort service, controlled dormitory access.

Student services: health clinic, personal/psychological counseling, women's center.

COSTS & FINANCIAL AID

Costs (2017–18) *Tuition:* state resident $14,774 full-time, $558 per credit hour part-time; nonresident $32,018 full-time, $1186 per credit hour part-time. Full-time tuition and fees vary according to program and student level. Part-time tuition and fees vary according to course load, program, and student level. *Required fees:* $300 full-time, $150 per term part-time. *Room and board:* $10,477; room only: $5827. Room and board charges vary according to board plan and housing facility. *Payment plans:* installment, deferred payment. *Waivers:* children of alumni, senior citizens, and employees or children of employees.

Financial Aid Of all full-time matriculated undergraduates who enrolled in 2017, 4,472 applied for aid, 3,620 were judged to have need, 556 had their need fully met. 196 Federal Work-Study jobs (averaging $1589). In 2017, 1371 non-need-based awards were made. *Average percent of need met:* 71. *Average financial aid package:* $15,463. *Average need-based loan:* $4739. *Average need-based gift aid:* $7481. *Average non-need-based aid:* $5679. *Average indebtedness upon graduation:* $35,834.

APPLYING

Standardized Tests *Required:* SAT or ACT (for admission).

Options: electronic application, deferred entrance.

Required: high school transcript. *Required for some:* essay or personal statement, examples of creative work for some majors in Visual and Performing Arts Department. *Recommended:* minimum 2.8 GPA.

Application deadlines: rolling (freshmen), rolling (transfers).

Notification: continuous (freshmen), continuous (transfers).

CONTACT
Ms. Allison Carter, Director of Admissions, Michigan Technological University, 1400 Townsend Drive, Houghton, MI 49931-1295. *Phone:* 906-487-2335. *Toll-free phone:* 888-MTU-1885. *Fax:* 906-487-2125. *E-mail:* mtu4u@mtu.edu.

Northern Michigan University
Marquette, Michigan
http://www.nmu.edu/

- **State-supported** comprehensive, founded 1899
- **Small-town** 360-acre campus
- **Coed** 7,018 undergraduate students, 88% full-time, 54% women, 46% men
- **74%** of applicants were admitted

UNDERGRAD STUDENTS
6,207 full-time, 811 part-time. 19% are from out of state; 2% Black or African American, non-Hispanic/Latino; 3% Hispanic/Latino; 0.5% Asian, non-Hispanic/Latino; 1% American Indian or Alaska Native, non-Hispanic/Latino; 5% Two or more races, non-Hispanic/Latino; 1% Race/ethnicity unknown; 1% international; 6% transferred in; 42% live on campus.

Freshmen:
Admission: 6,173 applied, 4,591 admitted, 1,501 enrolled. *Average high school GPA:* 3.2. *Test scores:* SAT evidence-based reading and writing scores over 500: 31%; SAT math scores over 500: 38%; ACT scores over 18: 89%; SAT evidence-based reading and writing scores over 600: 5%; SAT math scores over 600: 5%; ACT scores over 24: 42%; ACT scores over 30: 7%.

Retention: 78% of full-time freshmen returned.

FACULTY
Total: 419, 69% full-time, 48% with terminal degrees.

Student/faculty ratio: 20:1.

ACADEMICS
Calendar: semesters. *Degrees:* certificates, associate, bachelor's, master's, doctoral, post-master's, and postbachelor's certificates.

Special study options: accelerated degree program, adult/continuing education programs, cooperative education, distance learning, double majors, English as a second language, honors programs, independent study, internships, part-time degree program, services for LD students, student-designed majors, study abroad, summer session for credit. *ROTC:* Army (b).

Computers: Students can access the following: campus intranet, computer help desk, free student e-mail accounts, online (class) grades, online (class) registration, online (class) schedules. Campuswide network is available. 100% of college-owned or -operated housing units are wired for high-speed Internet access. Wireless service is available via entire campus.

Library: Lydia M. Olson Library.

STUDENT LIFE
Housing options: on-campus residence required through sophomore year; coed, men-only, women-only, special housing for students with disabilities. Campus housing is university owned. Freshman campus housing is guaranteed.

Activities and organizations: drama/theater group, student-run newspaper, radio and television station, choral group, marching band, national fraternities, national sororities.

Athletics Member NCAA. All Division II.

Campus security: 24-hour emergency response devices and patrols, student patrols, late-night transport/escort service, controlled dormitory access.

Student services: health clinic, personal/psychological counseling.

COSTS & FINANCIAL AID
Costs (2018–19) *Tuition:* state resident $9528 full-time, $397 per credit hour part-time; nonresident $15,024 full-time, $626 per credit hour part-time. *Required fees:* $962 full-time. *Room and board:* $10,328; room only: $5498. Room and board charges vary according to board plan, housing facility, and student level. *Payment plans:* installment, deferred payment. *Waivers:* employees or children of employees.

Financial Aid Of all full-time matriculated undergraduates who enrolled in 2016, 5,037 applied for aid, 4,121 were judged to have need, 611 had their need fully met. 518 Federal Work-Study jobs (averaging $1860). In 2016, 604 non-need-based awards were made. *Average percent of need met:* 64. *Average financial aid package:* $9747. *Average need-based loan:* $4225. *Average need-based gift aid:* $4774. *Average non-need-based aid:* $2809. *Average indebtedness upon graduation:* $31,075.

APPLYING
Standardized Tests *Required:* SAT or ACT (for admission).

Options: electronic application, deferred entrance.

Application fee: $35.

Required: high school transcript.

Application deadlines: rolling (freshmen), rolling (transfers).

Notification: continuous (freshmen), continuous (transfers).

CONTACT
Ms. Gerri Daniels, Director of Admissions, Northern Michigan University, 1401 Presque Isle Avenue, Marquette, MI 49855. *Phone:* 906-227-2650. *Toll-free phone:* 800-682-9797. *Fax:* 906-227-1747. *E-mail:* admissions@nmu.edu.

Northwestern Michigan College
Traverse City, Michigan
http://www.nmc.edu/

CONTACT
Catheryn Claerhout, Director of Admissions, Northwestern Michigan College, 1701 E. Front Street, Traverse City, MI 49686. *Phone:* 231-995-1034. *Toll-free phone:* 800-748-0566. *E-mail:* c.claerhout@nmc.edu.

Northwood University, Michigan Campus
Midland, Michigan
http://www.northwood.edu/

- **Independent** comprehensive, founded 1959
- **Small-town** 434-acre campus
- **Endowment** $31.1 million
- **Coed**
- **Moderately difficult** entrance level

FACULTY
Student/faculty ratio: 20:1.

ACADEMICS
Calendar: semesters. *Degrees:* associate, bachelor's, and master's.

Library: Strosacker Library. *Books:* 29,908 (physical); *Databases:* 50. Weekly public service hours: 89; students can reserve study rooms.

STUDENT LIFE
Housing options: on-campus residence required for freshman year; coed, men-only, women-only, special housing for students with disabilities. Campus housing is university owned. Freshman campus housing is guaranteed.

Activities and organizations: drama/theater group, student-run newspaper, Student Senate, intramural sports/club sports, campus art, Northwood University International Auto Show (NUTAS), national fraternities, national sororities.

Athletics Member NCAA. All Division II.

Campus security: 24-hour emergency response devices and patrols, late-night transport/escort service, controlled dormitory access.

Student services: health clinic, personal/psychological counseling.

COSTS & FINANCIAL AID

Costs (2017–18) *Comprehensive fee:* $36,250 includes full-time tuition ($24,770), mandatory fees ($1310), and room and board ($10,170). Full-time tuition and fees vary according to course load and location. Part-time tuition: $953 per semester hour. Part-time tuition and fees vary according to course load and location. *College room only:* $5300. Room and board charges vary according to board plan.

Financial Aid Of all full-time matriculated undergraduates who enrolled in 2017, 950 applied for aid, 831 were judged to have need, 178 had their need fully met. 136 Federal Work-Study jobs (averaging $1531). In 2017, 241 non-need-based awards were made. *Average percent of need met:* 63. *Average financial aid package:* $18,932. *Average need-based loan:* $4422. *Average need-based gift aid:* $6001. *Average non-need-based aid:* $7541. *Average indebtedness upon graduation:* $31,992.

APPLYING

Standardized Tests *Required:* SAT or ACT (for admission).

Options: electronic application, early admission, deferred entrance.

Application fee: $30.

Required: essay or personal statement, high school transcript, minimum 2.0 GPA. *Recommended:* 1 letter of recommendation, interview.

CONTACT

Miss Heidi Schall, Director of Admission, Northwood University, Michigan Campus, 4000 Whiting Drive, Midland, MI 48640. *Phone:* 989-837-4342. *Toll-free phone:* 800-457-7878. *Fax:* 989-837-4490. *E-mail:* miadmit@northwood.edu.

Oakland University

Rochester, Michigan

http://www.oakland.edu/

- **State-supported** university, founded 1957
- **Suburban** 1444-acre campus with easy access to Detroit
- **Endowment** $87.1 million
- **Coed** 15,901 undergraduate students, 79% full-time, 56% women, 44% men
- **Moderately difficult** entrance level, 84% of applicants were admitted

UNDERGRAD STUDENTS

12,549 full-time, 3,352 part-time. Students come from 38 states and territories; 46 other countries; 1% are from out of state; 7% Black or African American, non-Hispanic/Latino; 4% Hispanic/Latino; 5% Asian, non-Hispanic/Latino; 0.1% Native Hawaiian or other Pacific Islander, non-Hispanic/Latino; 0.3% American Indian or Alaska Native, non-Hispanic/Latino; 3% Two or more races, non-Hispanic/Latino; 4% Race/ethnicity unknown; 2% international; 9% transferred in; 16% live on campus.

Freshmen:
Admission: 10,296 applied, 8,691 admitted, 2,456 enrolled. *Average high school GPA:* 3.5. *Test scores:* SAT evidence-based reading and writing scores over 500: 79%; SAT math scores over 500: 78%; ACT scores over 18: 94%; SAT evidence-based reading and writing scores over 600: 33%; SAT math scores over 600: 29%; ACT scores over 24: 55%; SAT evidence-based reading and writing scores over 700: 6%; SAT math scores over 700: 6%; ACT scores over 30: 15%.

Retention: 77% of full-time freshmen returned.

FACULTY

Total: 589.

Student/faculty ratio: 21:1.

ACADEMICS

Calendar: semesters. *Degrees:* bachelor's, master's, doctoral, post-master's, and postbachelor's certificates.

Special study options: academic remediation for entering students, accelerated degree program, advanced placement credit, cooperative education, distance learning, double majors, English as a second language, freshman honors college, honors programs, independent study, internships, off-campus study, part-time degree program, services for LD students, student-designed majors, study abroad, summer session for credit. *ROTC:* Air Force (c).

Computers: Students can access the following: computer help desk, free student e-mail accounts, online (class) grades, online (class) registration, online (class) schedules. Campuswide network is available. 100% of college-owned or -operated housing units are wired for high-speed Internet access. Wireless service is available via entire campus.

Library: Kresge Library plus 1 other. *Books:* 499,352 (physical), 648,059 (digital/electronic); *Serial titles:* 3,674 (physical), 59,485 (digital/electronic); *Databases:* 234. Weekly public service hours: 168; study areas open 24 hours, 5–7 days a week; students can reserve study rooms.

STUDENT LIFE

Housing options: coed, cooperative, special housing for students with disabilities. Campus housing is university owned. Freshman applicants given priority for college housing.

Activities and organizations: drama/theater group, student-run newspaper, radio and television station, choral group, Alternative Break, Beta Alpha Psi, Grizz Gang, Meadow Brook Ball Committee, Student Program Board, national fraternities, national sororities.

Athletics Member NCAA. All Division I. *Intercollegiate sports:* baseball M(s), basketball M(s)/W(s), cheerleading M(c)/W(c), cross-country running M(s)/W(s), football M(c), golf M(s)/W(s), ice hockey M(c), soccer M(s)/W(s), softball W(s), swimming and diving M(s)/W(s), tennis W(s), track and field M(s)/W(s), volleyball W(s). *Intramural sports:* badminton M/W, baseball M(c), basketball M/W(c), bowling M(c)/W(c), cross-country running M(c)/W(c), equestrian sports M(c)/W(c), fencing M(c)/W(c), football M(c), golf M(c)/W(c), ice hockey M(c), lacrosse M(c)/W(c), racquetball M/W, rugby M(c)/W(c), sand volleyball M/W, skiing (downhill) M(c)/W(c), soccer M(c)/W(c), softball M(c)/W(c), swimming and diving M(c)/W(c), table tennis M/W, tennis M(c)/W(c), ultimate Frisbee M(c)/W(c), volleyball M/W/W(c), water polo M(c)/W(c).

Campus security: 24-hour emergency response devices and patrols, student patrols, late-night transport/escort service, controlled dormitory access, state certified police officers, security lighting, extensive camera system, self-defense/alcohol abuse classes.

Student services: health clinic, personal/psychological counseling.

COSTS & FINANCIAL AID

Costs (2017–18) *Tuition:* state resident $12,420 full-time, $414 per credit hour part-time; nonresident $23,873 full-time, $796 per credit hour part-time. Full-time tuition and fees vary according to program and student level. Part-time tuition and fees vary according to program and student level. *Room and board:* $9910. Room and board charges vary according to housing facility. *Payment plans:* installment, deferred payment. *Waivers:* senior citizens and employees or children of employees.

Financial Aid Of all full-time matriculated undergraduates who enrolled in 2015, 9,774 applied for aid, 8,072 were judged to have need, 660 had their need fully met. In 2015, 2311 non-need-based awards were made. *Average percent of need met:* 72. *Average financial aid package:* $13,766. *Average need-based loan:* $4069. *Average need-based gift aid:* $5996. *Average non-need-based aid:* $3885. *Average indebtedness upon graduation:* $27,669.

APPLYING

Standardized Tests *Required:* SAT or ACT (for admission).

Options: electronic application, deferred entrance.

Required: high school transcript, minimum 2.5 GPA. *Required for some:* interview, audition for music, theatre, and dance.

Application deadlines: rolling (freshmen), rolling (transfers).

Notification: continuous until 9/1 (freshmen), continuous (transfers).

CONTACT

Oakland University, 201 Meadow Brook Road, Rochester, MI 48309-4401. *Toll-free phone:* 800-OAK-UNIV.

Olivet College

Olivet, Michigan

http://www.olivetcollege.edu/

- **Independent** comprehensive, founded 1844, affiliated with Congregational Christian Church
- **Small-town** 92-acre campus with easy access to Lansing, Battle Creek
- **Endowment** $16.8 million
- **Coed**
- **Minimally difficult** entrance level

FACULTY
Student/faculty ratio: 16:1.

ACADEMICS
Calendar: 4-4-1. *Degrees:* bachelor's and master's.
Library: Burrage Library plus 1 other. *Books:* 61,268 (physical); *Serial titles:* 211 (physical), 68,401 (digital/electronic); *Databases:* 14. Students can reserve study rooms.

STUDENT LIFE
Housing options: on-campus residence required through junior year; coed, men-only, women-only. Campus housing is university owned. Freshman campus housing is guaranteed.

Activities and organizations: student-run newspaper, radio station, choral group, marching band, Minority Association of Premedical Students, Gay-Straight Alliance, Mathletes, OC Association Computing Machinery, Black Student Union.

Athletics Member NCAA. All Division III.

Campus security: 24-hour patrols, late-night transport/escort service, security cameras in all dorms and campus surveillance.

Student services: women's center.

FINANCIAL AID
Financial Aid Of all full-time matriculated undergraduates who enrolled in 2016, 1,014 applied for aid, 895 were judged to have need, 160 had their need fully met. 196 Federal Work-Study jobs (averaging $908). In 2016, 95 non-need-based awards were made. *Average percent of need met:* 80. *Average financial aid package:* $18,615. *Average need-based loan:* $5155. *Average need-based gift aid:* $14,100. *Average non-need-based aid:* $13,315. *Average indebtedness upon graduation:* $26,872.

APPLYING
Standardized Tests *Required:* SAT or ACT (for admission).

Options: electronic application, deferred entrance.

Application fee: $25.

Required: high school transcript. *Required for some:* essay or personal statement, interview. *Recommended:* minimum 2.6 GPA.

CONTACT
Admissions, Olivet College, 320 S. Main Street, Olivet, MI 49076. *Phone:* 800-456-7189. *Toll-free phone:* 800-456-7189. *E-mail:* admissions@olivetcollege.edu.

Rochester College
Rochester Hills, Michigan
http://www.rc.edu/

CONTACT
Mr. Larry Norman, Dean of Admissions, Rochester College, 800 West Avon Road, Rochester Hills, MI 48307-2764. *Phone:* 248-218-2190. *Toll-free phone:* 800-521-6010. *Fax:* 248-218-2035. *E-mail:* admissions@rc.edu.

Sacred Heart Major Seminary
Detroit, Michigan
http://www.shms.edu/

CONTACT
Fr. Michael Byrnes, Vice Rector, Sacred Heart Major Seminary, 2701 Chicago Boulevard, Detroit, MI 48206. *Phone:* 313-883-8552. *Fax:* 313-868-6400.

Saginaw Valley State University
University Center, Michigan
http://www.svsu.edu/

- **State-supported** comprehensive, founded 1963
- **Small-town** 782-acre campus
- **Endowment** $72.4 million
- **Coed** 7,893 undergraduate students, 84% full-time, 59% women, 41% men
- **Moderately difficult** entrance level, 74% of applicants were admitted

UNDERGRAD STUDENTS
6,601 full-time, 1,292 part-time. Students come from 21 states and territories; 43 other countries; 2% are from out of state; 8% Black or African American, non-Hispanic/Latino; 4% Hispanic/Latino; 0.8% Asian, non-Hispanic/Latino; 0.3% American Indian or Alaska Native, non-Hispanic/Latino; 3% Two or more races, non-Hispanic/Latino; 5% Race/ethnicity unknown; 7% international; 7% transferred in; 30% live on campus.

Freshmen:
Admission: 6,457 applied, 4,768 admitted, 1,230 enrolled. *Average high school GPA:* 3.4. *Test scores:* SAT evidence-based reading and writing scores over 500: 77%; SAT math scores over 500: 73%; ACT scores over 18: 92%; SAT evidence-based reading and writing scores over 600: 29%; SAT math scores over 600: 21%; ACT scores over 24: 42%; SAT evidence-based reading and writing scores over 700: 2%; SAT math scores over 700: 2%; ACT scores over 30: 7%.
Retention: 74% of full-time freshmen returned.

FACULTY
Total: 742, 39% full-time.
Student/faculty ratio: 17:1.

ACADEMICS
Calendar: semesters plus summer session. *Degrees:* bachelor's, master's, doctoral, and post-master's certificates.

Special study options: academic remediation for entering students, accelerated degree program, adult/continuing education programs, advanced placement credit, cooperative education, distance learning, double majors, English as a second language, honors programs, independent study, internships, part-time degree program, services for LD students, student-designed majors, study abroad, summer session for credit.

Computers: 424 computers/terminals are available on campus for general student use. Students can access the following: computer help desk, free student e-mail accounts, online (class) grades, online (class) registration, online (class) schedules. Campuswide network is available. 100% of college-owned or -operated housing units are wired for high-speed Internet access. Wireless service is available via entire campus.
Library: Zahnow Library. *Books:* 217,900 (physical), 107,479 (digital/electronic); *Serial titles:* 127 (physical), 50,164 (digital/electronic); *Databases:* 63. Weekly public service hours: 93.

STUDENT LIFE
Housing options: coed, special housing for students with disabilities. Campus housing is university owned. Freshman applicants given priority for college housing.

Activities and organizations: drama/theater group, student-run newspaper, radio station, choral group, marching band, His House Christian Fellowship, Criminal Justice Society, Delta Sigma Pi, Alpha Phi Omega, International Students Club, national fraternities, national sororities.

Athletics Member NCAA. All Division II. *Intercollegiate sports:* baseball M(s), basketball M(s)/W(s), bowling M(c)/W(c), cheerleading M(c)/W(c), cross-country running M(s)/W(s), equestrian sports M(c)/W(c), football M(s), golf M(s), gymnastics M(c)/W(c), ice hockey M(c)/W(c), lacrosse M(c)/W(c), rugby M(c)/W(c), soccer M(s)/W(s), softball W(s), swimming and diving M(s)/W(s), tennis M(c)/W(s), track and field M(s)/W(s), volleyball W(s), wrestling M(c). *Intramural sports:* badminton M/W, basketball M/W, football M/W, golf M/W, ice hockey M/W, racquetball M/W, soccer M/W, softball M/W, table tennis M/W, tennis M/W, volleyball M/W, water polo M/W.

Campus security: 24-hour emergency response devices and patrols, student patrols, late-night transport/escort service, controlled dormitory access, Sexual Assault Prevention Program.

Student services: health clinic, personal/psychological counseling.

COSTS & FINANCIAL AID
Costs (2017–18) *Tuition:* state resident $9381 full-time, $313 per credit hour part-time; nonresident $22,625 full-time, $754 per credit hour part-time. Full-time tuition and fees vary according to course level, degree level, location, and program. Part-time tuition and fees vary according to course level, degree level, location, and program. *Required fees:* $438 full-time, $15 per credit hour part-time. *Room and board:* $9465; room only: $4592. Room and board charges vary according to board plan and

housing facility. *Payment plan:* installment. *Waivers:* employees or children of employees.

Financial Aid Of all full-time matriculated undergraduates who enrolled in 2017, 4,973 applied for aid, 4,292 were judged to have need. In 2017, 884 non-need-based awards were made. *Average need-based gift aid:* $6421. *Average non-need-based aid:* $6272. *Average indebtedness upon graduation:* $31,695.

APPLYING

Standardized Tests *Required:* SAT or ACT (for admission).

Options: electronic application, deferred entrance.

Application fee: $30.

Required: high school transcript, minimum 2.5 GPA.

Application deadlines: rolling (freshmen), rolling (transfers).

Notification: continuous (freshmen), continuous (transfers).

CONTACT

Jennifer Pahl, Director of Admissions, Saginaw Valley State University, 7400 Bay Road, University Center, MI 48710-0001. *Phone:* 989-964-4200. *Toll-free phone:* 800-968-9500. *Fax:* 989-790-0180. *E-mail:* admissions@svsu.edu.

Schoolcraft College

Livonia, Michigan

http://www.schoolcraft.edu/

- **District-supported** primarily 2-year, founded 1961, part of Michigan Department of Education
- **Suburban** campus with easy access to Detroit
- **Coed** 10,558 undergraduate students, 28% full-time, 53% women, 47% men
- **Noncompetitive** entrance level

UNDERGRAD STUDENTS

2,955 full-time, 7,603 part-time. 14% Black or African American, non-Hispanic/Latino; 5% Hispanic/Latino; 4% Asian, non-Hispanic/Latino; 0.1% Native Hawaiian or other Pacific Islander, non-Hispanic/Latino; 0.6% American Indian or Alaska Native, non-Hispanic/Latino; 3% Two or more races, non-Hispanic/Latino; 7% Race/ethnicity unknown; 2% international; 23% transferred in.

Freshmen:

Admission: 1,906 enrolled. *Average high school GPA:* 2.8.

Retention: 62% of full-time freshmen returned.

FACULTY

Total: 515, 20% full-time.

Student/faculty ratio: 23:1.

ACADEMICS

Calendar: semesters. *Degrees:* certificates, associate, and bachelor's.

Special study options: academic remediation for entering students, advanced placement credit, distance learning, English as a second language, honors programs, independent study, internships, part-time degree program, services for LD students, study abroad, summer session for credit.

Computers: Students can access the following: campus intranet, computer help desk, free student e-mail accounts, online (class) grades, online (class) registration, online (class) schedules. Campuswide network is available. Wireless service is available via entire campus.

Library: Bradner Library plus 1 other. *Books:* 67,778 (physical), 74,201 (digital/electronic); *Databases:* 147. Students can reserve study rooms.

STUDENT LIFE

Housing options: college housing not available.

Activities and organizations: drama/theater group, student-run newspaper, choral group, Phi Theta Kappa, The Schoolcraft Connection Newspaper, Student Activities Board, Project Playhem Gaming Club, Otaku Anime Japanese Animation Club.

Athletics Member NJCAA. *Intercollegiate sports:* baseball M, basketball M(s)/W(s), bowling M/W, cross-country running M/W, golf M, soccer M(s)/W(s), softball W, volleyball W(s).

Campus security: 24-hour emergency response devices and patrols, late-night transport/escort service.

Student services: health clinic, personal/psychological counseling, women's center.

COSTS & FINANCIAL AID

Costs (2017–18) *Tuition:* area resident $3240 full-time, $108 per credit hour part-time; state resident $4710 full-time, $157 per credit hour part-time; nonresident $6930 full-time, $231 per credit hour part-time. *Required fees:* $952 full-time, $23 per credit hour part-time, $43 per term part-time. *Payment plans:* installment, deferred payment. *Waivers:* senior citizens and employees or children of employees.

Financial Aid Of all full-time matriculated undergraduates who enrolled in 2017, 124 Federal Work-Study jobs (averaging $4000).

APPLYING

Options: electronic application, early admission, deferred entrance.

Required for some: high school transcript. *Recommended:* high school transcript.

Application deadlines: rolling (freshmen), rolling (transfers).

CONTACT

Ms. Lisa Bushaw, Director of Admissions, Schoolcraft College, 18600 Haggerty Road, Livonia, MI 48152-2696. *Phone:* 734-462-4683. *E-mail:* admissions@schoolcraft.edu.

Siena Heights University

Adrian, Michigan

http://www.sienaheights.edu/

CONTACT

Ms. Trudy Mohre, Director of Admissions, Siena Heights University, 1247 East Siena Heights Drive, Adrian, MI 49221. *Phone:* 517-264-7185. *Toll-free phone:* 800-521-0009. *E-mail:* tmohre@sienaheights.edu.

South University

Novi, Michigan

http://www.southuniversity.edu/novi.aspx

CONTACT

South University, 41555 Twelve Mile Road, Novi, MI 48377. *Phone:* 248-675-0200. *Toll-free phone:* 877-693-2085.

Spring Arbor University

Spring Arbor, Michigan

http://www.arbor.edu/

CONTACT

Office of Admissions, Spring Arbor University, 106 East Main Street, Spring Arbor, MI 49283-9799. *Phone:* 517-750-1200 Ext. 1468. *Toll-free phone:* 800-968-0011. *Fax:* 517-750-6620. *E-mail:* admissions@arbor.edu.

University of Detroit Mercy

Detroit, Michigan

http://www.udmercy.edu/

- **Independent Roman Catholic (Jesuit)** university, founded 1877
- **Urban** 70-acre campus with easy access to Detroit, MI
- **Endowment** $43.9 million
- **Coed**
- **Moderately difficult** entrance level

FACULTY

Student/faculty ratio: 10:1.

ACADEMICS

Calendar: semesters. *Degrees:* certificates, diplomas, bachelor's, master's, doctoral, post-master's, and postbachelor's certificates.

Library: McNichols Campus Library. *Books:* 468,257 (physical), 175,312 (digital/electronic); *Serial titles:* 107,735 (digital/electronic); *Databases:* 84. Weekly public service hours: 80.

STUDENT LIFE

Housing options: coed. Campus housing is university owned. Freshman campus housing is guaranteed.

Activities and organizations: drama/theater group, student-run newspaper, radio station, choral group, Alpha Phi Omega, Biology Club, Chemistry Club, Pre-Dentistry Club, Greek Organizations - NPC, NIC, and NPHC, national fraternities, national sororities.

Athletics Member NCAA. All Division I.

Campus security: 24-hour emergency response devices and patrols, student patrols, late-night transport/escort service.

Student services: health clinic, personal/psychological counseling.

COSTS & FINANCIAL AID

Costs (2017–18) *Comprehensive fee:* $50,610 includes full-time tuition ($41,158) and room and board ($9452). Full-time tuition and fees vary according to program. Part-time tuition: $1049 per credit hour. Part-time tuition and fees vary according to location and program. *Room and board:* Room and board charges vary according to board plan and housing facility. *Payment plans:* installment, deferred payment.

Financial Aid Of all full-time matriculated undergraduates who enrolled in 2017, 1,905 applied for aid, 1,614 were judged to have need, 75 had their need fully met. In 2017, 612 non-need-based awards were made. *Average percent of need met:* 73. *Average financial aid package:* $34,929. *Average need-based loan:* $5073. *Average need-based gift aid:* $27,922. *Average non-need-based aid:* $21,556. *Average indebtedness upon graduation:* $36,968.

APPLYING

Standardized Tests *Required:* SAT or ACT (for admission).

Options: electronic application, early decision, deferred entrance.

Required: essay or personal statement, high school transcript, minimum 2.5 GPA. *Required for some:* interview. *Recommended:* 1 letter of recommendation, interview.

CONTACT

Office of Admissions, University of Detroit Mercy, 4001 West McNichols Road, Detroit, MI 48221-3038. *Phone:* 313-993-1245. *Toll-free phone:* 800-635-5020. *Fax:* 313-993-3326. *E-mail:* admissions@udmercy.edu.

University of Michigan

Ann Arbor, Michigan

http://www.umich.edu/

- **State-supported** university, founded 1817
- **Urban** 3207-acre campus with easy access to Detroit
- **Endowment** $9.6 billion
- **Coed** 28,983 undergraduate students, 97% full-time, 50% women, 50% men
- **Very difficult** entrance level, 29% of applicants were admitted

UNDERGRAD STUDENTS

27,969 full-time, 1,014 part-time. Students come from 56 states and territories; 87 other countries; 40% are from out of state; 4% Black or African American, non-Hispanic/Latino; 5% Hispanic/Latino; 14% Asian, non-Hispanic/Latino; 0.2% American Indian or Alaska Native, non-Hispanic/Latino; 4% Two or more races, non-Hispanic/Latino; 5% Race/ethnicity unknown; 7% international; 4% transferred in; 32% live on campus.

Freshmen:

Admission: 55,504 applied, 15,871 admitted, 6,689 enrolled. *Average high school GPA:* 3.8. *Test scores:* ACT scores over 18: 99%; ACT scores over 24: 97%; ACT scores over 30: 74%.

Retention: 97% of full-time freshmen returned.

FACULTY

Total: 3,434, 81% full-time, 85% with terminal degrees.

Student/faculty ratio: 15:1.

ACADEMICS

Calendar: trimesters. *Degrees:* bachelor's, master's, doctoral, post-master's, and postbachelor's certificates.

Special study options: accelerated degree program, adult/continuing education programs, advanced placement credit, cooperative education, distance learning, double majors, English as a second language, external degree program, honors programs, independent study, internships, off-campus study, part-time degree program, services for LD students,

student-designed majors, study abroad, summer session for credit. *ROTC:* Army (b), Navy (b), Air Force (b).

Unusual degree programs: 3-2 business administration; engineering.

Computers: 3,940 computers/terminals are available on campus for general student use. Students can access the following: campus intranet, computer help desk, free student e-mail accounts, online (class) grades, online (class) registration, online (class) schedules, file storage, personal Web pages, printing. Campuswide network is available. 100% of college-owned or -operated housing units are wired for high-speed Internet access. Wireless service is available via entire campus.

Library: Shapiro Undergraduate Library plus 9 others. *Books:* 9.0 million (physical), 3.3 million (digital/electronic); *Serial titles:* 464,460 (physical), 163,830 (digital/electronic); *Databases:* 10,078. Weekly public service hours: 168; study areas open 24 hours, 5–7 days a week; students can reserve study rooms.

STUDENT LIFE

Housing options: coed, women-only, cooperative. Campus housing is university owned. Freshman campus housing is guaranteed.

Activities and organizations: drama/theater group, student-run newspaper, radio and television station, choral group, marching band, Hillel Society, K-Grams (Kids'; Program), M-Powered Entrepreneurial Club, Dance Marathon, Alternative Spring Break, national fraternities, national sororities.

Athletics Member NCAA. All Division I except football (Division I-AA). *Intercollegiate sports:* baseball M(s), basketball M(s)/W(s), cheerleading M(s)(c)/W(s)(c), crew M(c)/W(s), cross-country running M(s)/W(s), fencing M(c)/W(c), field hockey W(s), golf M(s)/W(s), gymnastics M(s)/W(s), ice hockey M(s), lacrosse M(s)/W(s), riflery M(c)/W(c), rowing M(c), rugby M(c)/W(c), sailing M(c)/W(c), soccer M(s)/W(s), softball W(s), swimming and diving M(s)/W(s), table tennis M(c)/W(c), tennis M(s)/W(s), track and field M(s)/W(s), triathlon M(c), ultimate Frisbee M(c)/W(c), volleyball M(c)/W(s), water polo M(c)/W(s), wrestling M(s). *Intramural sports:* badminton M/W, baseball M(c), basketball M/W, cross-country running M(c)/W(c), field hockey M/W, gymnastics W(c), ice hockey M(c)/W(c), lacrosse W(c), racquetball M/W, soccer M(c)/W(c), softball W(c), squash M/W, swimming and diving M/W(c), table tennis M/W, tennis M(c)/W(c), track and field M/W, ultimate Frisbee M/W, volleyball M/W(c), water polo W(c), wrestling M(c).

Campus security: 24-hour emergency response devices and patrols, student patrols, late-night transport/escort service, controlled dormitory access, Safewalk (no-cost night-time escorts), SafeRide (no-cost night-time ride service).

Student services: health clinic, personal/psychological counseling, women's center, legal services.

COSTS & FINANCIAL AID

Costs (2017–18) *Tuition:* state resident $14,498 full-time, $573 per credit hour part-time; nonresident $47,148 full-time, $1934 per credit hour part-time. Full-time tuition and fees vary according to course load, degree level, program, and student level. Part-time tuition and fees vary according to course load, degree level, program, and student level. *Required fees:* $328 full-time, $164 per term part-time. *Room and board:* $11,198. Room and board charges vary according to board plan and housing facility. *Payment plan:* installment.

Financial Aid Of all full-time matriculated undergraduates who enrolled in 2016, 14,512 applied for aid, 10,685 were judged to have need, 8,344 had their need fully met. 5,120 Federal Work-Study jobs (averaging $2745). In 2016, 3611 non-need-based awards were made. *Average percent of need met:* 93. *Average financial aid package:* $26,477. *Average need-based loan:* $5314. *Average need-based gift aid:* $19,648. *Average non-need-based aid:* $5568. *Average indebtedness upon graduation:* $25,712. *Financial aid deadline:* 4/30.

APPLYING

Standardized Tests *Required:* SAT or ACT (for admission). *Required for some:* SAT Subject Tests (for admission).

Options: electronic application, early action, deferred entrance.

Application fee: $75.

Required: essay or personal statement, high school transcript, 1 letter of recommendation. *Required for some:* interview, audition for School of Music, Theatre and Dance; portfolio for School of Art and Design.

Application deadlines: 2/1 (freshmen), 2/1 (transfers), 11/1 (early action).

Notification: continuous (freshmen), continuous (transfers), 12/24 (early action).

CONTACT
University of Michigan, Ann Arbor, MI 48109. *Phone:* 734-764-7433.

University of Michigan–Dearborn
Dearborn, Michigan
http://www.umdearborn.edu/

- **State-supported** comprehensive, founded 1959, part of University of Michigan System
- **Suburban** 202-acre campus with easy access to Detroit
- **Endowment** $52.1 million
- **Coed** 7,141 undergraduate students, 72% full-time, 47% women, 53% men
- **Moderately difficult** entrance level, 64% of applicants were admitted

UNDERGRAD STUDENTS
5,137 full-time, 2,004 part-time. Students come from 19 states and territories; 30 other countries; 4% are from out of state; 9% Black or African American, non-Hispanic/Latino; 5% Hispanic/Latino; 8% Asian, non-Hispanic/Latino; 0.2% Native Hawaiian or other Pacific Islander, non-Hispanic/Latino; 0.3% American Indian or Alaska Native, non-Hispanic/Latino; 3% Two or more races, non-Hispanic/Latino; 3% Race/ethnicity unknown; 2% international; 11% transferred in.

Freshmen:
Admission: 5,731 applied, 3,684 admitted, 1,106 enrolled. *Average high school GPA:* 3.6. *Test scores:* SAT evidence-based reading and writing scores over 500: 89%; SAT math scores over 500: 87%; ACT scores over 18: 98%; SAT evidence-based reading and writing scores over 600: 44%; SAT math scores over 600: 44%; ACT scores over 24: 67%; SAT evidence-based reading and writing scores over 700: 6%; SAT math scores over 700: 9%; ACT scores over 30: 17%.
Retention: 81% of full-time freshmen returned.

FACULTY
Total: 567, 58% full-time, 67% with terminal degrees.
Student/faculty ratio: 17:1.

ACADEMICS
Calendar: semesters. *Degrees:* certificates, bachelor's, master's, doctoral, and postbachelor's certificates.

Special study options: academic remediation for entering students, adult/continuing education programs, advanced placement credit, cooperative education, distance learning, double majors, English as a second language, honors programs, independent study, internships, off-campus study, part-time degree program, services for LD students, student-designed majors, study abroad, summer session for credit. *ROTC:* Army (c).

Computers: 1,060 computers/terminals are available on campus for general student use. Students can access the following: campus intranet, computer help desk, free student e-mail accounts, online (class) grades, online (class) registration, online (class) schedules, tuition and application payments accepted online. Campuswide network is available. Wireless service is available via entire campus.
Library: Mardigian Library. *Books:* 277,320 (physical), 617,638 (digital/electronic); *Serial titles:* 390 (physical), 95,980 (digital/electronic); *Databases:* 1,135. Weekly public service hours: 95; students can reserve study rooms.

STUDENT LIFE
Housing options: college housing not available.

Activities and organizations: student-run newspaper, radio and television station, national fraternities, national sororities.

Athletics Member NAIA. *Intercollegiate sports:* baseball M, basketball M(s)/W(s), cheerleading M(c)/W(c), cross-country running M(s)/W(s), ice hockey M(c), lacrosse M(s), soccer M(s)/W, softball W(s), tennis M(c)/W(c), volleyball W(s), wrestling M(c)/W(c). *Intramural sports:* basketball M/W, soccer M/W, volleyball M/W.

Campus security: 24-hour emergency response devices and patrols, late-night transport/escort service, AEDs available around campus.

Student services: personal/psychological counseling, women's center.

COSTS & FINANCIAL AID
Costs (2017–18) *Tuition:* state resident $11,718 full-time, $463 per credit hour part-time; nonresident $23,952 full-time, $953 per credit hour part-time. Full-time tuition and fees vary according to course level, course load, degree level, program, and student level. Part-time tuition and fees vary according to course level, course load, degree level, program, and student level. *Required fees:* $754 full-time, $377 per term part-time. *Payment plan:* installment. *Waivers:* senior citizens and employees or children of employees.

Financial Aid Of all full-time matriculated undergraduates who enrolled in 2016, 3,825 applied for aid, 3,353 were judged to have need, 249 had their need fully met. 221 Federal Work-Study jobs (averaging $1193). 732 state and other part-time jobs (averaging $3974). In 2016, 708 non-need-based awards were made. *Average percent of need met:* 56. *Average financial aid package:* $10,215. *Average need-based loan:* $4383. *Average need-based gift aid:* $6028. *Average non-need-based aid:* $5760. *Average indebtedness upon graduation:* $25,759.

APPLYING
Standardized Tests *Required:* SAT or ACT (for admission).

Options: electronic application, deferred entrance.

Required: high school transcript. *Recommended:* minimum 2.5 GPA.

Application deadlines: rolling (freshmen), rolling (transfers).

Notification: continuous (freshmen), continuous (transfers).

CONTACT
Ms. Deb Peffer, Director of Admissions and Orientation, University of Michigan–Dearborn, 4901 Evergreen Road, Room 1145 UC, Dearborn, MI 48128-1491. *Phone:* 313-593-5100. *Fax:* 313-436-9167. *E-mail:* admissions@umd.umich.edu.

University of Michigan–Flint
Flint, Michigan
http://www.umflint.edu/

- **State-supported** comprehensive, founded 1956, part of University of Michigan System
- **Urban** 76-acre campus with easy access to Detroit, Lansing
- **Endowment** $106.3 million
- **Coed** 6,434 undergraduate students, 59% full-time, 61% women, 39% men
- **Moderately difficult** entrance level, 65% of applicants were admitted

UNDERGRAD STUDENTS
3,809 full-time, 2,625 part-time. Students come from 21 states and territories; 27 other countries; 2% are from out of state; 13% Black or African American, non-Hispanic/Latino; 4% Hispanic/Latino; 2% Asian, non-Hispanic/Latino; 0.1% Native Hawaiian or other Pacific Islander, non-Hispanic/Latino; 0.7% American Indian or Alaska Native, non-Hispanic/Latino; 3% Two or more races, non-Hispanic/Latino; 2% Race/ethnicity unknown; 4% international; 11% transferred in; 6% live on campus.

Freshmen:
Admission: 4,558 applied, 2,968 admitted, 688 enrolled. *Average high school GPA:* 3.4. *Test scores:* SAT evidence-based reading and writing scores over 500: 74%; SAT math scores over 500: 68%; ACT scores over 18: 89%; SAT evidence-based reading and writing scores over 600: 34%; SAT math scores over 600: 23%; ACT scores over 24: 45%; SAT evidence-based reading and writing scores over 700: 5%; SAT math scores over 700: 3%; ACT scores over 30: 9%.
Retention: 77% of full-time freshmen returned.

FACULTY
Total: 573, 57% full-time, 57% with terminal degrees.
Student/faculty ratio: 13:1.

ACADEMICS
Calendar: semesters. *Degrees:* bachelor's, master's, doctoral, post-master's, and postbachelor's certificates.

Special study options: academic remediation for entering students, accelerated degree program, adult/continuing education programs, advanced placement credit, cooperative education, distance learning, double majors, English as a second language, honors programs, independent study, internships, off-campus study, part-time degree program, services for LD students, student-designed majors, study abroad, summer session for credit. *ROTC:* Army (c), Navy (c), Air Force (c).

Unusual degree programs: 3-2 engineering with University of Michigan (Ann Arbor).

Computers: 512 computers/terminals are available on campus for general student use. Students can access the following: campus intranet, computer help desk, free student e-mail accounts, online (class) grades, online (class) registration, online (class) schedules. Campuswide network is available. 100% of college-owned or -operated housing units are wired for high-speed Internet access. Wireless service is available via entire campus.

Library: Frances Willson Thompson Library plus 1 other. *Books:* 251,483 (physical), 981,065 (digital/electronic); *Serial titles:* 1,862 (physical), 163,338 (digital/electronic); *Databases:* 1,387. Weekly public service hours: 96; students can reserve study rooms.

STUDENT LIFE

Housing options: coed. Campus housing is university owned.

Activities and organizations: drama/theater group, student-run newspaper, choral group, Fraternity and Sorority Life, National Society for Leadership and Success, Psychology Club, Baccalaureate Student Nurses Organization, Student Nurse Practitioner Association, national fraternities, national sororities.

Athletics *Intramural sports:* basketball M/W, football M(c), ice hockey M(c)/W(c), lacrosse M(c), soccer M/W, volleyball M/W.

Campus security: 24-hour emergency response devices and patrols, student patrols, late-night transport/escort service, controlled dormitory access.

Student services: personal/psychological counseling, women's center.

COSTS & FINANCIAL AID

Costs (2017–18) *Tuition:* state resident $10,902 full-time, $431 per credit hour part-time; nonresident $21,222 full-time, $858 per credit hour part-time. Full-time tuition and fees vary according to course level, course load, degree level, program, and student level. Part-time tuition and fees vary according to course level, course load, degree level, program, and student level. *Required fees:* $432 full-time, $167 per term part-time. *Room and board:* $8437; room only: $5437. Room and board charges vary according to housing facility. *Payment plan:* installment. *Waivers:* senior citizens.

Financial Aid Of all full-time matriculated undergraduates who enrolled in 2016, 3,132 applied for aid, 2,798 were judged to have need, 70 had their need fully met. 124 Federal Work-Study jobs (averaging $2029). In 2016, 118 non-need-based awards were made. *Average percent of need met:* 68. *Average financial aid package:* $12,813. *Average need-based loan:* $4632. *Average need-based gift aid:* $6312. *Average non-need-based aid:* $4168. *Average indebtedness upon graduation:* $33,258.

APPLYING

Standardized Tests *Required:* SAT or ACT (for admission).

Options: electronic application, deferred entrance.

Application fee: $30.

Required: high school transcript, minimum 2.7 GPA.

Application deadlines: 8/18 (freshmen), 8/18 (transfers).

Notification: continuous (freshmen), continuous (transfers).

CONTACT

Ms. Karen Cuzydlo, Admissions Senior Associate Director, University of Michigan–Flint, 303 East Kearsley Street, 245 University Pavilion, Flint, MI 48502. *Phone:* 810-762-3300. *Toll-free phone:* 800-942-5636. *Fax:* 810-762-3272. *E-mail:* admissions@umflint.edu.

Walsh College of Accountancy and Business Administration
Troy, Michigan
http://www.walshcollege.edu/

- **Independent** upper-level, founded 1922
- **Suburban** 29-acre campus with easy access to Detroit
- **Endowment** $8.4 million
- **Coed** 893 undergraduate students, 9% full-time, 48% women, 52% men
- **Noncompetitive** entrance level

UNDERGRAD STUDENTS

78 full-time, 815 part-time. Students come from 8 states and territories; 35 other countries; 5% Black or African American, non-Hispanic/Latino; 2% Hispanic/Latino; 5% Asian, non-Hispanic/Latino; 0.1% Native Hawaiian or other Pacific Islander, non-Hispanic/Latino; 2% Two or more races, non-Hispanic/Latino; 2% Race/ethnicity unknown; 2% international; 99% transferred in.

FACULTY

Total: 113, 20% full-time, 35% with terminal degrees.

Student/faculty ratio: 15:1.

ACADEMICS

Calendar: 4 11-week semesters. *Degrees:* bachelor's, master's, and postbachelor's certificates.

Special study options: academic remediation for entering students, adult/continuing education programs, advanced placement credit, distance learning, double majors, independent study, internships, off-campus study, part-time degree program, services for LD students, summer session for credit.

Computers: 400 computers/terminals are available on campus for general student use. Students can access the following: campus intranet, computer help desk, free student e-mail accounts, online (class) grades, online (class) registration, online (class) schedules, Campus Wifi. Campuswide network is available. Wireless service is available via entire campus.

Library: Vollbrecht Library plus 1 other. *Books:* 27,985 (physical), 18,425 (digital/electronic); *Serial titles:* 2,262 (physical), 71,676 (digital/electronic); *Databases:* 79. Weekly public service hours: 113.

STUDENT LIFE

Housing options: college housing not available.

Activities and organizations: Delta Mu Delta, Accounting and Taxation Student Organization, International Student Organization, MBA Association, Walsh College Marketing Association.

Campus security: 24-hour emergency response devices.

COSTS

Costs (2017–18) *Tuition:* $16,560 full-time, $8280 per year part-time. Full-time tuition and fees vary according to course level and degree level. Part-time tuition and fees vary according to course level and degree level. *Required fees:* $375 full-time, $375 per year part-time. *Payment plan:* deferred payment. *Waivers:* employees or children of employees.

APPLYING

Options: electronic application, deferred entrance.

Application fee: $35.

Notification: continuous (transfers).

CONTACT

Walsh College of Accountancy and Business Administration, 3838 Livernois Road, Troy, MI 48083. *Phone:* 248-823-1610. *Toll-free phone:* 800-925-7401.

★ Wayne State University
Detroit, Michigan
http://www.wayne.edu/

- **State-supported** university, founded 1868
- **Urban** 195-acre campus with easy access to Detroit
- **Endowment** $366.7 million
- **Coed** 17,322 undergraduate students, 72% full-time, 56% women, 44% men
- **Moderately difficult** entrance level, 67% of applicants were admitted

UNDERGRAD STUDENTS

12,409 full-time, 4,913 part-time. Students come from 39 states and territories; 40 other countries; 2% are from out of state; 17% Black or African American, non-Hispanic/Latino; 5% Hispanic/Latino; 10% Asian, non-Hispanic/Latino; 0.1% Native Hawaiian or other Pacific Islander, non-Hispanic/Latino; 0.2% American Indian or Alaska Native, non-Hispanic/Latino; 4% Two or more races, non-Hispanic/Latino; 3% Race/ethnicity unknown; 2% international; 11% transferred in; 13% live on campus.

Freshmen:

Admission: 15,331 applied, 10,334 admitted, 2,653 enrolled. *Average high school GPA:* 3.4. *Test scores:* SAT evidence-based reading and writing scores over 500: 79%; SAT math scores over 500: 77%; ACT scores over 18: 96%; SAT evidence-based reading and writing scores over 600: 34%; SAT math scores over 600: 26%; ACT scores over 24: 58%; SAT evidence-based reading and writing scores over 700: 3%; SAT math scores over 700: 4%; ACT scores over 30: 16%.

Retention: 81% of full-time freshmen returned.

FACULTY

Total: 1,740, 59% full-time.
Student/faculty ratio: 16:1.

ACADEMICS

Calendar: semesters. *Degrees:* certificates, bachelor's, master's, doctoral, post-master's, and postbachelor's certificates.

Special study options: academic remediation for entering students, accelerated degree program, advanced placement credit, cooperative education, distance learning, double majors, English as a second language, freshman honors college, honors programs, independent study, internships, off-campus study, part-time degree program, services for LD students, study abroad, summer session for credit. *ROTC:* Army (b), Air Force (c).

Unusual degree programs: 3-2 business administration with Northwest University of Politics and Law (NWUPL); engineering.

Computers: Students can access the following: computer help desk, free student e-mail accounts, online (class) grades, online (class) registration, online (class) schedules. Campuswide network is available. 100% of college-owned or -operated housing units are wired for high-speed Internet access. Wireless service is available via entire campus.
Library: David Adamany Undergraduate Library plus 5 others. *Books:* 1.7 million (physical), 1.1 million (digital/electronic); *Serial titles:* 60,832 (physical), 112,521 (digital/electronic); *Databases:* 700. Weekly public service hours: 138; study areas open 24 hours, 5–7 days a week.

STUDENT LIFE

Housing options: coed, special housing for students with disabilities. Campus housing is university owned. Freshman applicants given priority for college housing.

Activities and organizations: drama/theater group, student-run newspaper, radio station, choral group, marching band, national fraternities, national sororities.

Athletics Member NCAA. All Division II. *Intercollegiate sports:* baseball M(s), basketball M(s)/W(s), cross-country running M(s)/W(s), fencing M(s)/W(s), football M(s), golf M(s)/W(s), lacrosse M(c), soccer M(c)/W(c), softball W(s), swimming and diving M(s)/W(s), tennis M(s)/W(s), track and field W(s), volleyball M(c)/W(s). *Intramural sports:* badminton M/W, basketball M/W(c), football M/W, rock climbing M/W, soccer M/W, softball M/W, table tennis M/W, tennis M/W, ultimate Frisbee M/W, volleyball M/W(c).

Campus security: 24-hour emergency response devices and patrols, late-night transport/escort service, controlled dormitory access, VIN etching, bike patrol, safety and defense classes, K-9 unit, victim assistance, confidential tip line.

Student services: health clinic, personal/psychological counseling, legal services.

COSTS & FINANCIAL AID

Costs (2017–18) *One-time required fee:* $250. *Tuition:* state resident $12,264 full-time, $409 per credit hour part-time; nonresident $28,151 full-time, $938 per credit hour part-time. Full-time tuition and fees vary according to course load, program, and student level. Part-time tuition and fees vary according to course load, program, and student level. *Required fees:* $1512 full-time, $36 per credit hour part-time, $221 per term part-time. *Room and board:* $10,106; room only: $6308. Room and board

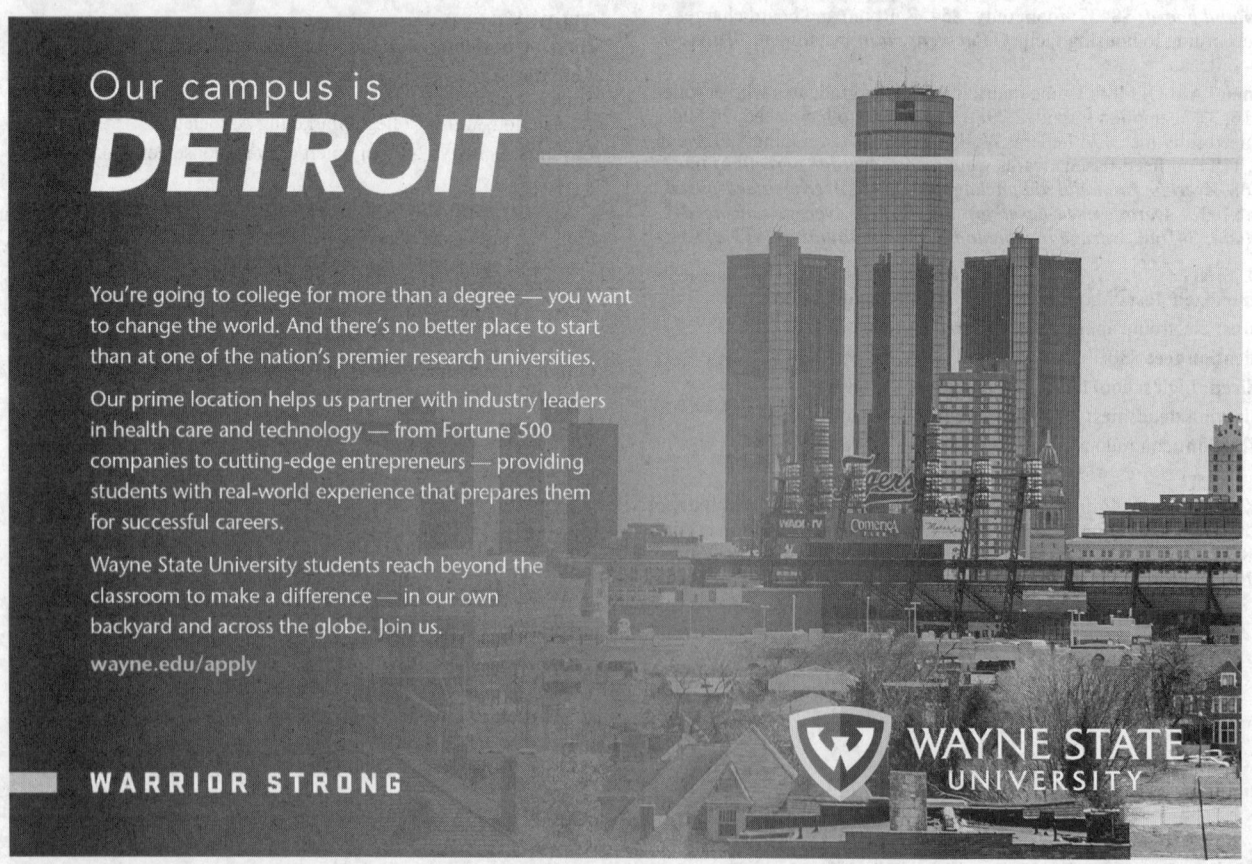

charges vary according to board plan and housing facility. *Payment plan:* installment. *Waivers:* senior citizens and employees or children of employees.

Financial Aid Of all full-time matriculated undergraduates who enrolled in 2016, 9,644 applied for aid, 8,693 were judged to have need, 371 had their need fully met. In 2016, 2022 non-need-based awards were made. *Average percent of need met:* 49. *Average financial aid package:* $10,934. *Average need-based loan:* $4406. *Average need-based gift aid:* $6798. *Average non-need-based aid:* $5383. *Average indebtedness upon graduation:* $27,960. *Financial aid deadline:* 6/30.

APPLYING
Standardized Tests *Required:* SAT or ACT (for admission).

Options: electronic application, deferred entrance.

Application fee: $25.

Required: high school transcript.

Application deadlines: 8/1 (freshmen), 8/15 (transfers).

CONTACT
Ms. Ericka M. Jackson, Director of Undergraduate Admissions, Wayne State University, 42 West Warren, Office of Undergraduate Admissions, Detroit 48202. *Phone:* 313-577-2100. *Toll-free phone:* 877-WSU-INFO. *E-mail:* admissions@wayne.edu.

See previous page for display ad and page 1490 for the College Close-Up.

Western Michigan University
Kalamazoo, Michigan
http://www.wmich.edu/
- **State-supported** university, founded 1903
- **Urban** 1289-acre campus
- **Endowment** $386.6 million
- **Coed** 17,936 undergraduate students, 84% full-time, 50% women, 50% men
- **Moderately difficult** entrance level, 82% of applicants were admitted

UNDERGRAD STUDENTS
15,063 full-time, 2,873 part-time. Students come from 43 states and territories; 57 other countries; 10% are from out of state; 12% Black or African American, non-Hispanic/Latino; 6% Hispanic/Latino; 2% Asian, non-Hispanic/Latino; 0.1% Native Hawaiian or other Pacific Islander, non-Hispanic/Latino; 0.4% American Indian or Alaska Native, non-Hispanic/Latino; 4% Two or more races, non-Hispanic/Latino; 0.7% Race/ethnicity unknown; 4% international; 9% transferred in; 28% live on campus.

Freshmen:
Admission: 14,263 applied, 11,741 admitted, 3,178 enrolled. *Average high school GPA:* 3.4. *Test scores:* SAT evidence-based reading and writing scores over 500: 74%; SAT math scores over 500: 68%; ACT scores over 18: 90%; SAT evidence-based reading and writing scores over 600: 27%; SAT math scores over 600: 21%; ACT scores over 24: 42%; SAT evidence-based reading and writing scores over 700: 3%; SAT math scores over 700: 3%; ACT scores over 30: 6%.

Retention: 78% of full-time freshmen returned.

FACULTY
Total: 1,451, 64% full-time, 49% with terminal degrees.

Student/faculty ratio: 17:1.

ACADEMICS
Calendar: semesters. *Degrees:* certificates, bachelor's, master's, doctoral, post-master's, and postbachelor's certificates.

Special study options: academic remediation for entering students, accelerated degree program, adult/continuing education programs, advanced placement credit, cooperative education, distance learning, double majors, English as a second language, freshman honors college, honors programs, independent study, internships, off-campus study, part-time degree program, services for LD students, student-designed majors, study abroad, summer session for credit. *ROTC:* Army (b).

Computers: 2,250 computers/terminals and 100 ports are available on campus for general student use. Students can access the following: computer help desk, free student e-mail accounts, online (class) grades, online (class) registration, online (class) schedules. Campuswide network is available. 100% of college-owned or -operated housing units are wired for high-speed Internet access. Wireless service is available via entire campus.

Library: Waldo Library plus 4 others. *Books:* 1.8 million (physical), 661,724 (digital/electronic); *Serial titles:* 936 (physical), 80,141 (digital/electronic); *Databases:* 638. Weekly public service hours: 106; students can reserve study rooms.

STUDENT LIFE
Housing options: coed, men-only, women-only, special housing for students with disabilities. Campus housing is university owned. Freshman campus housing is guaranteed.

Activities and organizations: drama/theater group, student-run newspaper, radio station, choral group, marching band, Campus Activities Board, Western Student Association, Young Black Male Support Network, Drive Safe Kalamazoo, Alternative Spring Break, national fraternities, national sororities.

Athletics Member NCAA. All Division I except football (Division I-A). *Intercollegiate sports:* baseball M(s), basketball M(s)/W(s), cross-country running W(s), equestrian sports W(c), golf M(c)/W(s), gymnastics W(s), ice hockey M(s), lacrosse M(c)/W(c), racquetball M/W, rock climbing M(c)/W(c), rugby M(c)/W(c), sailing M(c)/W(c), skiing (downhill) M(c)/W(c), soccer M(s)/W(s), softball W(s), swimming and diving M(c)/W(c), tennis M(s)/W(s), track and field W(s), ultimate Frisbee M(c), volleyball M(c)/W(s), water polo M(c)/W(c). *Intramural sports:* badminton M/W, basketball M/W, golf M/W, ice hockey M/W, racquetball M/W, rock climbing M/W, sand volleyball M/W, soccer M/W, softball M/W, table tennis M/W, tennis M/W, ultimate Frisbee M/W, volleyball M/W.

Campus security: 24-hour emergency response devices and patrols, student patrols, late-night transport/escort service, controlled dormitory access, residence hall security system, engravers for identification of items, free bicycle registration.

Student services: health clinic, personal/psychological counseling, women's center.

COSTS & FINANCIAL AID
Costs (2017–18) *One-time required fee:* $300. *Tuition:* state resident $11,020 full-time, $423 per credit hour part-time; nonresident $13,776 full-time, $529 per credit hour part-time. Full-time tuition and fees vary according to course load, location, program, reciprocity agreements, and student level. Part-time tuition and fees vary according to course load, location, program, reciprocity agreements, and student level. *Required fees:* $923 full-time, $259 per term part-time. *Room and board:* $9848; room only: $5079. Room and board charges vary according to board plan and housing facility. *Payment plan:* installment. *Waivers:* senior citizens and employees or children of employees.

Financial Aid Of all full-time matriculated undergraduates who enrolled in 2016, 11,273 applied for aid, 6,681 were judged to have need, 1,312 had their need fully met. In 2016, 1402 non-need-based awards were made. *Average percent of need met:* 73. *Average financial aid package:* $13,679. *Average need-based loan:* $4002. *Average need-based gift aid:* $5382. *Average non-need-based aid:* $6692. *Average indebtedness upon graduation:* $35,602.

APPLYING
Standardized Tests *Required:* SAT or ACT (for admission).

Options: electronic application.

Application fee: $40.

Required: high school transcript, minimum 2.5 GPA.

Application deadlines: rolling (freshmen), rolling (transfers).

Notification: continuous (freshmen), continuous (transfers).

CONTACT
Western Michigan University, 1903 West Michigan Avenue, Kalamazoo, MI 49008. *Phone:* 269-387-2000. *E-mail:* ask-wmu@wmich.edu.

Yeshiva Beth Yehuda–Yeshiva Gedolah of Greater Detroit
Oak Park, Michigan

CONTACT
Rabbi P. Rushnawitz, Director, Yeshiva Beth Yehuda–Yeshiva Gedolah of Greater Detroit, 24600 Greenfield, Oak Park, MI 48237-1544.

MINNESOTA

Academy College
Bloomington, Minnesota
http://www.academycollege.edu/
- **Proprietary** 4-year, founded 1936
- **Urban** campus
- **Coed** 65 undergraduate students, 69% full-time, 22% women, 78% men
- **Noncompetitive** entrance level

UNDERGRAD STUDENTS
45 full-time, 20 part-time. Students come from 4 states and territories; 5% are from out of state; 8% Black or African American, non-Hispanic/Latino; 2% Hispanic/Latino; 12% Asian, non-Hispanic/Latino; 12% Race/ethnicity unknown.

FACULTY
Student/faculty ratio: 8:1.

ACADEMICS
Calendar: quarters. *Degrees:* diplomas, associate, and bachelor's.

Special study options: academic remediation for entering students, accelerated degree program, adult/continuing education programs, advanced placement credit, cooperative education, distance learning, internships, part-time degree program, summer session for credit.

Computers: 25 computers/terminals are available on campus for general student use. Students can access the following: online (class) registration. Campuswide network is available. Wireless service is available via entire campus.

Library: Learning Resource Center plus 1 other.

STUDENT LIFE
Housing options: college housing not available.

COSTS & FINANCIAL AID
Costs (2017–18) *One-time required fee:* $280. *Tuition:* $17,261 full-time, $455 per credit hour part-time. Full-time tuition and fees vary according to course load and program. Part-time tuition and fees vary according to course load and program. *Required fees:* $120 full-time, $40 per term part-time. *Payment plan:* installment.

Financial Aid Of all full-time matriculated undergraduates who enrolled in 2015, 25 applied for aid, 25 were judged to have need. *Average indebtedness upon graduation:* $14,476.

APPLYING
Options: electronic application, early admission, deferred entrance.
Application fee: $40.
Required: high school transcript, interview.
Notification: continuous (freshmen), continuous (transfers).

CONTACT
Mr. Andrew Scoblionko, Director of Admissions, Academy College, 1600 W 82nd Street, Suite 100, Bloomington, MN 55431. *Phone:* 952-851-0066. *Toll-free phone:* 800-292-9149. *Fax:* 952-851-0094. *E-mail:* admissions@academycollege.edu.

Argosy University, Twin Cities
Eagan, Minnesota
http://www.argosy.edu/locations/twin-cities/

CONTACT
Argosy University, Twin Cities, 1515 Central Parkway, Eagan, MN 55121. *Phone:* 651-846-2882. *Toll-free phone:* 888-844-2004.

Augsburg University
Minneapolis, Minnesota
http://www.augsburg.edu/
- **Independent Lutheran** comprehensive, founded 1869
- **Urban** 23-acre campus with easy access to Minneapolis-St. Paul
- **Coed** 2,427 undergraduate students, 84% full-time, 54% women, 46% men
- **Moderately difficult** entrance level, 45% of applicants were admitted

UNDERGRAD STUDENTS
2,033 full-time, 394 part-time. 11% are from out of state; 13% Black or African American, non-Hispanic/Latino; 8% Hispanic/Latino; 9% Asian, non-Hispanic/Latino; 0.1% Native Hawaiian or other Pacific Islander, non-Hispanic/Latino; 1% American Indian or Alaska Native, non-Hispanic/Latino; 4% Two or more races, non-Hispanic/Latino; 12% Race/ethnicity unknown; 3% international; 11% transferred in; 36% live on campus.

Freshmen:
Admission: 3,163 applied, 1,423 admitted, 436 enrolled. *Average high school GPA:* 3.2. *Test scores:* ACT scores over 18: 88%; ACT scores over 24: 29%; ACT scores over 30: 5%.
Retention: 77% of full-time freshmen returned.

FACULTY
Total: 369, 47% full-time, 64% with terminal degrees.
Student/faculty ratio: 13:1.

ACADEMICS
Calendar: semesters for undergraduate programs; trimesters for graduate programs and weekend college. *Degrees:* certificates, bachelor's, master's, doctoral, and postbachelor's certificates.

Special study options: academic remediation for entering students, adult/continuing education programs, advanced placement credit, cooperative education, double majors, English as a second language, freshman honors college, honors programs, independent study, internships, off-campus study, part-time degree program, services for LD students, student-designed majors, study abroad, summer session for credit. *ROTC:* Army (c), Navy (c), Air Force (c).

Unusual degree programs: 3-2 engineering with Michigan Technological University.

Computers: Students can access the following: campus intranet, computer help desk, free student e-mail accounts, online (class) grades, online (class) registration, online (class) schedules. Campuswide network is available. 100% of college-owned or -operated housing units are wired for high-speed Internet access. Wireless service is available via entire campus.

Library: James G. Lindell Library. Students can reserve study rooms.

STUDENT LIFE
Housing options: coed, special housing for students with disabilities. Campus housing is university owned. Freshman applicants given priority for college housing.

Activities and organizations: drama/theater group, student-run newspaper, radio station, choral group, Pan-Afrikan Student Union, Augsburg Business Organization, Queer Pride Alliance, Students for Racial Justice, Augsburg Asian Student Association.

Athletics Member NCAA. All Division III. *Intercollegiate sports:* baseball M, basketball M/W, cross-country running M/W, football M, golf M/W, ice hockey M/W, lacrosse W, soccer M/W, softball W, swimming and diving W, track and field M/W, volleyball W, wrestling M. *Intramural sports:* basketball M/W, football M, skiing (cross-country) M(c)/W(c), skiing (downhill) M(c)/W(c), softball M/W, volleyball M/W, wrestling M.

Campus security: 24-hour emergency response devices and patrols, student patrols, late-night transport/escort service, controlled dormitory access.

Student services: health clinic, personal/psychological counseling, women's center.

COSTS & FINANCIAL AID
Costs (2018–19) *Comprehensive fee:* $49,080 includes full-time tuition ($38,150), mandatory fees ($650), and room and board ($10,280). Full-time tuition and fees vary according to class time and location. Part-time

tuition: $1192 per credit hour. Part-time tuition and fees vary according to class time and location. *College room only:* $5350. Room and board charges vary according to board plan and housing facility. *Payment plan:* installment. *Waivers:* employees or children of employees.

Financial Aid Of all full-time matriculated undergraduates who enrolled in 2015, 1,790 applied for aid, 1,656 were judged to have need, 176 had their need fully met. In 2015, 328 non-need-based awards were made. *Average percent of need met:* 72. *Average financial aid package:* $28,485. *Average need-based loan:* $4824. *Average need-based gift aid:* $22,652. *Average non-need-based aid:* $14,342. *Average indebtedness upon graduation:* $40,816. *Financial aid deadline:* 8/1.

APPLYING
Standardized Tests *Required:* SAT or ACT (for admission).

Options: electronic application, deferred entrance.

Required: essay or personal statement, high school transcript, 1 letter of recommendation, letter of recommendation from an academic teacher. *Recommended:* minimum 2.8 GPA, interview.

Application deadlines: 8/1 (freshmen), 8/1 (transfers).

Notification: continuous (freshmen), continuous (transfers).

CONTACT
Ms. Keri VanOverschelde, Admissions Operations Program Director, Augsburg University, 2211 Riverside Avenue, Minneapolis, MN 55454-1351. *Phone:* 612-330-1001. *Toll-free phone:* 800-788-5678. *E-mail:* vanovers@augsburg.edu.

Bemidji State University
Bemidji, Minnesota
http://www.bemidjistate.edu/
- **State-supported** comprehensive, founded 1919, part of Minnesota State Colleges and Universities System
- **Small-town** 89-acre campus
- **Coed** 4,833 undergraduate students, 69% full-time, 58% women, 42% men
- **Moderately difficult** entrance level, 66% of applicants were admitted

UNDERGRAD STUDENTS
3,351 full-time, 1,482 part-time. 12% are from out of state; 2% Black or African American, non-Hispanic/Latino; 2% Hispanic/Latino; 1% Asian, non-Hispanic/Latino; 0.1% Native Hawaiian or other Pacific Islander, non-Hispanic/Latino; 3% American Indian or Alaska Native, non-Hispanic/Latino; 3% Two or more races, non-Hispanic/Latino; 7% Race/ethnicity unknown; 2% international; 9% transferred in; 28% live on campus.

Freshmen:
Admission: 4,033 applied, 2,670 admitted, 764 enrolled. *Average high school GPA:* 3.2. *Test scores:* ACT scores over 18: 94%; ACT scores over 24: 31%; ACT scores over 30: 3%.

FACULTY
Total: 241, 66% full-time, 54% with terminal degrees.
Student/faculty ratio: 21:1.

ACADEMICS
Calendar: semesters. *Degrees:* certificates, associate, bachelor's, master's, and postbachelor's certificates.

Special study options: adult/continuing education programs, external degree program, part-time degree program.

Computers: Students can access the following: computer help desk, free student e-mail accounts, online (class) grades, online (class) registration, online (class) schedules. Wireless service is available via entire campus.
Library: A. C. Clark Library.

STUDENT LIFE
Housing options: coed, special housing for students with disabilities. Campus housing is university owned. Freshman applicants given priority for college housing.

Athletics Member NCAA. All Division II except men's and women's ice hockey (Division I). *Intercollegiate sports:* baseball M(s), basketball M(s)/W(s), cross-country running W(s), football M(s), golf M(s)/W(s), ice hockey M(s)/W(s), soccer W(s), softball W(s), tennis W(s), track and field W(s), volleyball W(s). *Intramural sports:* basketball M/W, football M, ice hockey M/W, soccer M/W, softball M/W, volleyball M/W.

Campus security: 24-hour emergency response devices and patrols, late-night transport/escort service, controlled dormitory access.

FINANCIAL AID
Financial Aid Of all full-time matriculated undergraduates who enrolled in 2016, 2,792 applied for aid, 2,072 were judged to have need, 314 had their need fully met. 299 Federal Work-Study jobs (averaging $1284). 194 state and other part-time jobs (averaging $2124). In 2016, 669 non-need-based awards were made. *Average percent of need met:* 61. *Average financial aid package:* $9299. *Average need-based loan:* $4225. *Average need-based gift aid:* $5878. *Average non-need-based aid:* $11,023. *Average indebtedness upon graduation:* $27,171.

APPLYING
Standardized Tests *Required:* SAT or ACT (for admission).
Options: electronic application, early action, deferred entrance.
Application fee: $20.
Required: high school transcript. *Required for some:* essay or personal statement, interview.

CONTACT
Bemidji State University, 1500 Birchmont Drive, NE, Bemidji, MN 56601-2699. *Phone:* 218-755-2040. *Toll-free phone:* 800-475-2001.

Bethany Global University
Bloomington, Minnesota
http://www.bethanygu.edu/

CONTACT
Bethany Global University, 6820 Auto Club Road, Suite C, Bloomington, MN 55438. *Toll-free phone:* 800-323-3417.

Bethany Lutheran College
Mankato, Minnesota
http://www.blc.edu/
- **Independent Lutheran** 4-year, founded 1927
- **Small-town** 50-acre campus with easy access to Minneapolis-St. Paul
- **Endowment** $43.3 million
- **Coed** 651 undergraduate students, 80% full-time, 53% women, 47% men
- **Moderately difficult** entrance level, 79% of applicants were admitted

UNDERGRAD STUDENTS
522 full-time, 129 part-time. Students come from 26 states and territories; 16 other countries; 24% are from out of state; 3% Black or African American, non-Hispanic/Latino; 4% Hispanic/Latino; 0.6% Asian, non-Hispanic/Latino; 0.2% American Indian or Alaska Native, non-Hispanic/Latino; 2% Two or more races, non-Hispanic/Latino; 2% Race/ethnicity unknown; 5% international; 4% transferred in; 64% live on campus.

Freshmen:
Admission: 388 applied, 307 admitted, 129 enrolled. *Average high school GPA:* 3.4. *Test scores:* ACT scores over 18: 94%; ACT scores over 24: 40%; ACT scores over 30: 8%.
Retention: 83% of full-time freshmen returned.

FACULTY
Total: 63, 70% full-time, 35% with terminal degrees.
Student/faculty ratio: 9:1.

ACADEMICS
Calendar: semesters. *Degrees:* certificates, bachelor's, and postbachelor's certificates.

Special study options: academic remediation for entering students, adult/continuing education programs, advanced placement credit, cooperative education, distance learning, double majors, English as a second language, independent study, internships, services for LD students, student-designed majors, study abroad, summer session for credit. *ROTC:* Army (c).

Unusual degree programs: engineering with University of Minnesota, Twin Cities Campus.

Computers: 100 computers/terminals and 400 ports are available on campus for general student use. Students can access the following: campus intranet, computer help desk, free student e-mail accounts, online (class) grades, online (class) registration, online (class) schedules. Campuswide network is available. 100% of college-owned or -operated housing units are wired for high-speed Internet access. Wireless service is available via entire campus.

Library: Memorial Library plus 1 other. *Books:* 65,225 (physical), 20,722 (digital/electronic); *Serial titles:* 451 (physical), 224 (digital/electronic); *Databases:* 88. Weekly public service hours: 88.

STUDENT LIFE

Housing options: on-campus residence required through sophomore year; men-only, women-only. Campus housing is university owned. Freshman campus housing is guaranteed.

Activities and organizations: drama/theater group, student-run newspaper, choral group, Bethany Activities Committee, Student Senate, Scholastic Leadership Society, PAMA (Promoting Awareness, spurring Motivation, and encouraging Action), Bethany Society of Royal Scientists.

Athletics Member NCAA. All Division III. *Intercollegiate sports:* baseball M, basketball M/W, cross-country running M/W, golf M/W, soccer M/W, softball W, tennis M/W, track and field M/W, volleyball W. *Intramural sports:* basketball M/W, football M/W, racquetball M/W, volleyball M/W.

Campus security: 24-hour emergency response devices and patrols, late-night transport/escort service, controlled dormitory access.

Student services: health clinic, personal/psychological counseling.

COSTS & FINANCIAL AID

Costs (2018–19) *One-time required fee:* $130. *Comprehensive fee:* $35,820 includes full-time tuition ($27,100), mandatory fees ($680), and room and board ($8040). Part-time tuition: $1140 per credit hour. Part-time tuition and fees vary according to course load. *Required fees:* $340 per term part-time. *Room and board:* Room and board charges vary according to board plan, housing facility, and student level. *Payment plan:* installment. *Waivers:* senior citizens and employees or children of employees.

Financial Aid Of all full-time matriculated undergraduates who enrolled in 2016, 443 applied for aid, 405 were judged to have need, 71 had their need fully met. 21 Federal Work-Study jobs (averaging $1753). 298 state and other part-time jobs (averaging $1091). In 2016, 67 non-need-based awards were made. *Average percent of need met:* 85. *Average financial aid package:* $21,147. *Average need-based loan:* $4829. *Average need-based gift aid:* $16,844. *Average non-need-based aid:* $9435. *Average indebtedness upon graduation:* $31,654.

APPLYING

Standardized Tests *Required:* SAT or ACT (for admission).

Options: electronic application.

Required: essay or personal statement, high school transcript, minimum 2.4 GPA. *Required for some:* interview. *Recommended:* minimum 3.2 GPA, interview.

Notification: continuous (transfers).

CONTACT

Mr. Daniel Tomhave, Vice President of Admissions and Enrollment Management, Bethany Lutheran College, 700 Luther Drive, Mankato, MN 56001. *Phone:* 507-344-7000 Ext. 451. *Toll-free phone:* 800-944-3066. *Fax:* 507-344-7376. *E-mail:* dtomhave@blc.edu.

★ Bethel University

St. Paul, Minnesota
http://www.bethel.edu/

- **Independent** comprehensive, founded 1871, affiliated with Baptist General Conference
- **Suburban** 289-acre campus with easy access to Minneapolis-St. Paul
- **Endowment** $48.7 million
- **Coed** 2,904 undergraduate students, 83% full-time, 62% women, 38% men
- **Moderately difficult** entrance level, 83% of applicants were admitted

UNDERGRAD STUDENTS

2,407 full-time, 497 part-time. Students come from 24 states and territories; 19% are from out of state; 4% Black or African American, non-Hispanic/Latino; 5% Hispanic/Latino; 3% Asian, non-Hispanic/Latino; 0.2% Native Hawaiian or other Pacific Islander, non-Hispanic/Latino; 0.4% American Indian or Alaska Native, non-Hispanic/Latino; 4% Two or more races, non-Hispanic/Latino; 7% Race/ethnicity unknown; 0.2% international; 4% transferred in; 63% live on campus.

Freshmen:
Admission: 1,812 applied, 1,513 admitted, 598 enrolled. *Average high school GPA:* 3.5. *Test scores:* ACT scores over 18: 96%; ACT scores over 24: 55%; ACT scores over 30: 11%.
Retention: 85% of full-time freshmen returned.

FACULTY

Total: 297, 61% full-time, 67% with terminal degrees.
Student/faculty ratio: 11:1.

ACADEMICS

Calendar: 4-1-4. *Degrees:* associate, bachelor's, master's, doctoral, post-master's, and postbachelor's certificates.

Special study options: academic remediation for entering students, adult/continuing education programs, advanced placement credit, distance learning, double majors, honors programs, independent study, internships, off-campus study, part-time degree program, services for LD students, student-designed majors, study abroad, summer session for credit. *ROTC:* Army (c), Air Force (c).

Unusual degree programs: 3-2 engineering with University of Minnesota.

Computers: 203 computers/terminals are available on campus for general student use. Students can access the following: campus intranet, computer help desk, free student e-mail accounts, online (class) grades, online (class) registration, online (class) schedules. Campuswide network is available. 100% of college-owned or -operated housing units are wired for high-speed Internet access. Wireless service is available via classrooms, computer centers, computer labs, dorm rooms, learning centers, libraries, student centers.

Library: Bethel University Library plus 1 other. *Books:* 141,904 (physical), 153,597 (digital/electronic); *Serial titles:* 890 (physical), 31,538 (digital/electronic); *Databases:* 93. Weekly public service hours: 96; students can reserve study rooms.

STUDENT LIFE

Housing options: on-campus residence required through sophomore year; special housing for students with disabilities. Campus housing is university owned. Freshman campus housing is guaranteed.

Activities and organizations: drama/theater group, student-run newspaper, radio station, choral group, Bethel Student Government, Bethel Business and Economics Association, Bethel Rec Sports, Welcome Week.

Athletics Member NCAA. All Division III. *Intercollegiate sports:* baseball M, basketball M/W, cross-country running M/W, football M, golf M/W, ice hockey M/W, soccer M/W, softball W, tennis M/W, track and field M/W, volleyball M(c)/W. *Intramural sports:* basketball M/W, football M, lacrosse M(c)/W(c), rugby M(c), volleyball M(c)/W.

Campus security: 24-hour emergency response devices and patrols, student patrols, late-night transport/escort service, controlled dormitory access, video surveillance for residence halls, academic buildings, and parking lots.

Student services: health clinic, personal/psychological counseling.

COSTS & FINANCIAL AID

Costs (2018–19) *Comprehensive fee:* $47,820 includes full-time tuition ($37,140), mandatory fees ($160), and room and board ($10,520). Part-time tuition: $1550 per credit. Part-time tuition and fees vary according to course load. *College room only:* $5830. Room and board charges vary according to board plan. *Payment plans:* tuition prepayment, installment. *Waivers:* employees or children of employees.

Financial Aid Of all full-time matriculated undergraduates who enrolled in 2017, 1,994 applied for aid, 1,732 were judged to have need, 352 had their need fully met. In 2017, 538 non-need-based awards were made. *Average percent of need met:* 81. *Average financial aid package:*

$28,736. *Average need-based loan:* $3867. *Average need-based gift aid:* $22,874. *Average non-need-based aid:* $13,577. *Average indebtedness upon graduation:* $36,990.

APPLYING

Standardized Tests *Required:* SAT or ACT (for admission).

Options: electronic application, early admission.

Required: essay or personal statement, high school transcript, rank in upper 50% of high school class. *Required for some:* 2 letters of recommendation. *Recommended:* minimum 2.5 GPA, interview.

Application deadlines: rolling (freshmen), rolling (transfers).

Notification: continuous (freshmen), continuous (transfers).

CONTACT

Office of Admissions, Bethel University, 3900 Bethel Drive, St. Paul, MN 55112. *Phone:* 651-638-6242. *Toll-free phone:* 800-255-8706 Ext. 6242. *Fax:* 651-635-1490. *E-mail:* undergrad-admissions@bethel.edu.

Bethlehem College & Seminary
Minneapolis, Minnesota
http://www.bcsmn.edu/

CONTACT

Bethlehem College & Seminary, 720 13th Avenue South, Minneapolis, MN 55415.

Capella University
Minneapolis, Minnesota
http://www.capella.edu/

CONTACT

Enrollment Services, Capella University, 225 South Sixth Street, Capella Tower, 9th Floor, Minneapolis, MN 55402. *Phone:* 866-2837921. *Toll-free phone:* 866-283-7921. *Fax:* 612-977-5060. *E-mail:* info@capella.edu.

Carleton College
Northfield, Minnesota
http://www.carleton.edu/

- **Independent** 4-year, founded 1866
- **Small-town** 955-acre campus with easy access to Minneapolis-St. Paul
- **Endowment** $828.2 million
- **Coed** 2,078 undergraduate students, 99% full-time, 51% women, 49% men
- **Very difficult** entrance level, 21% of applicants were admitted

UNDERGRAD STUDENTS

2,055 full-time, 23 part-time. Students come from 50 states and territories; 42 other countries; 85% are from out of state; 5% Black or African American, non-Hispanic/Latino; 8% Hispanic/Latino; 8% Asian, non-Hispanic/Latino; 0.0% American Indian or Alaska Native, non-Hispanic/Latino; 6% Two or more races, non-Hispanic/Latino; 2% Race/ethnicity unknown; 10% international; 0.5% transferred in; 100% live on campus.

Freshmen:

Admission: 6,499 applied, 1,378 admitted, 522 enrolled. *Test scores:* SAT evidence-based reading and writing scores over 500: 100%; SAT math scores over 500: 100%; ACT scores over 18: 100%; SAT evidence-based reading and writing scores over 600: 96%; SAT math scores over 600: 94%; ACT scores over 24: 97%; SAT evidence-based reading and writing scores over 700: 70%; SAT math scores over 700: 69%; ACT scores over 30: 81%.

Retention: 96% of full-time freshmen returned.

FACULTY

Total: 261, 81% full-time, 92% with terminal degrees.

Student/faculty ratio: 9:1.

ACADEMICS

Calendar: 3 courses for each of three terms. *Degree:* bachelor's.

Special study options: accelerated degree program, advanced placement credit, double majors, independent study, internships, off-campus study, services for LD students, student-designed majors, study abroad.

Unusual degree programs: 3-2 engineering with Columbia University.

Computers: 250 computers/terminals and 220 ports are available on campus for general student use. Students can access the following: campus intranet, computer help desk, free student e-mail accounts, online (class) grades, online (class) registration, online (class) schedules. Campuswide network is available. 100% of college-owned or -operated housing units are wired for high-speed Internet access. Wireless service is available via entire campus.

Library: Laurence McKinley Gould Library plus 1 other. *Books:* 499,801 (physical), 640,539 (digital/electronic); *Serial titles:* 82,879 (digital/electronic); *Databases:* 31,508. Weekly public service hours: 118.

STUDENT LIFE

Housing options: on-campus residence required through senior year; coed, special housing for students with disabilities. Campus housing is university owned. Freshman campus housing is guaranteed.

Activities and organizations: drama/theater group, student-run newspaper, radio station, choral group, CANOE (Carleton Association of Nature and Outdoor Enthusiasts), Farm Club, Ebony II, WHIMS (Women in Math and Science), Amnesty International.

Athletics Member NCAA. All Division III. *Intercollegiate sports:* badminton M(c)/W(c), baseball M, basketball M/W, cross-country running M/W, equestrian sports M(c)/W(c), fencing M(c)/W(c), field hockey W(c), football M, golf M/W, ice hockey M(c)/W(c), lacrosse M(c)/W(c), rugby M(c)/W(c), sailing M(c)/W(c), skiing (cross-country) M(c)/W(c), skiing (downhill) M(c)/W(c), soccer M/W, softball W, swimming and diving M/W, table tennis M(c)/W(c), tennis M/W, track and field M/W, ultimate Frisbee M(c)/W(c), volleyball M(c)/W, water polo M(c)/W(c). *Intramural sports:* badminton M/W, basketball M/W, soccer M/W, softball M/W, table tennis M/W, tennis M/W, ultimate Frisbee M/W, volleyball M/W.

Campus security: 24-hour emergency response devices and patrols, student patrols, late-night transport/escort service, controlled dormitory access, Emergency Notification Service (cell phone text and email alerts).

Student services: health clinic, personal/psychological counseling, women's center.

COSTS & FINANCIAL AID

Costs (2017–18) *Comprehensive fee:* $66,414 includes full-time tuition ($52,476), mandatory fees ($306), and room and board ($13,632). *College room only:* $7140. Room and board charges vary according to board plan. *Payment plan:* installment. *Waivers:* employees or children of employees.

Financial Aid Of all full-time matriculated undergraduates who enrolled in 2016, 1,758 applied for aid, 1,121 were judged to have need, 1,121 had their need fully met. 359 Federal Work-Study jobs (averaging $2596). 1,341 state and other part-time jobs (averaging $2665). In 2016, 102 non-need-based awards were made. *Average percent of need met:* 100. *Average financial aid package:* $48,110. *Average need-based loan:* $5192. *Average need-based gift aid:* $40,675. *Average non-need-based aid:* $4562. *Average indebtedness upon graduation:* $21,035. *Financial aid deadline:* 1/15.

APPLYING

Standardized Tests *Required:* SAT or ACT (for admission). *Recommended:* SAT Subject Tests (for admission).

Options: electronic application, early admission, early decision, deferred entrance.

Application fee: $30.

Required: essay or personal statement, high school transcript, 2 letters of recommendation, Common Application Supplement. *Recommended:* interview.

Application deadlines: 1/15 (freshmen), 3/31 (transfers).

Early decision deadline: 11/15 (for plan 1), 1/15 (for plan 2).

Notification: 3/31 (freshmen), 5/15 (transfers), 12/15 (early decision plan 1), 2/15 (early decision plan 2).

CONTACT

Carleton College, One North College Street, Northfield, MN 55057-4001. *Phone:* 507-222-4190. *Toll-free phone:* 800-995-2275.

Minnesota

College of Saint Benedict
Saint Joseph, Minnesota
http://www.csbsju.edu/

- **Independent Roman Catholic** 4-year, founded 1913
- **Small-town** 300-acre campus with easy access to Minneapolis-St. Paul
- **Endowment** $72.1 million
- **Women only** 1,937 undergraduate students, 99% full-time
- **Moderately difficult** entrance level, 91% of applicants were admitted

UNDERGRAD STUDENTS
1,916 full-time, 21 part-time. Students come from 32 states and territories; 13 other countries; 16% are from out of state; 3% Black or African American, non-Hispanic/Latino; 7% Hispanic/Latino; 6% Asian, non-Hispanic/Latino; 0.2% Native Hawaiian or other Pacific Islander, non-Hispanic/Latino; 0.9% American Indian or Alaska Native, non-Hispanic/Latino; 0.1% Two or more races, non-Hispanic/Latino; 4% international; 0.8% transferred in; 91% live on campus.

Freshmen:
Admission: 1,775 applied, 1,615 admitted, 519 enrolled. *Average high school GPA:* 3.7. *Test scores:* ACT scores over 18: 98%; ACT scores over 24: 63%; ACT scores over 30: 16%.
Retention: 87% of full-time freshmen returned.

FACULTY
Total: 169, 83% full-time, 83% with terminal degrees.
Student/faculty ratio: 12:1.

ACADEMICS
Calendar: semesters. *Degrees:* bachelor's (coordinate with Saint John's University for men).
Special study options: advanced placement credit, double majors, English as a second language, honors programs, independent study, internships, off-campus study, services for LD students, student-designed majors, study abroad. *ROTC:* Army (c).
Computers: 275 computers/terminals and 4,600 ports are available on campus for general student use. Students can access the following: campus intranet, computer help desk, free student e-mail accounts, online (class) grades, online (class) registration, online (class) schedules, online student accounts. 100% of college-owned or -operated housing units are wired for high-speed Internet access. Wireless service is available via entire campus.
Library: Clemens Library plus 2 others. *Books:* 680,763 (physical), 641,295 (digital/electronic); *Serial titles:* 326 (physical), 44,640 (digital/electronic); *Databases:* 226. Weekly public service hours: 104; students can reserve study rooms.

STUDENT LIFE
Housing options: on-campus residence required through senior year; women-only, special housing for students with disabilities. Campus housing is university owned. Freshman campus housing is guaranteed.
Activities and organizations: drama/theater group, student-run newspaper, radio and television station, choral group, Joint Events Council, Hmong Americans Involving Students, Magis Ministries, Enactus, Archipelago Association.
Athletics Member NCAA. All Division III. *Intercollegiate sports:* basketball W, crew W(c), cross-country running W, golf W, ice hockey W, lacrosse W(c), rugby W(c), skiing (cross-country) W(c), soccer W, softball W, swimming and diving W, tennis W, track and field W, ultimate Frisbee W(c), volleyball W. *Intramural sports:* badminton W, basketball W, football W, racquetball W, soccer W, softball W, tennis W, volleyball W.
Campus security: 24-hour emergency response devices and patrols, student patrols, late-night transport/escort service, controlled dormitory access, well-lit pathways.
Student services: health clinic, personal/psychological counseling, women's center.

COSTS & FINANCIAL AID
Costs (2017–18) *Comprehensive fee:* $54,480 includes full-time tuition ($42,690), mandatory fees ($1048), and room and board ($10,742). Part-time tuition: $1779 per credit hour. Part-time tuition and fees vary according to course load. *College room only:* $5250. Room and board charges vary according to board plan and housing facility. *Payment plan:* installment. *Waivers:* employees or children of employees.
Financial Aid Of all full-time matriculated undergraduates who enrolled in 2017, 1,608 applied for aid, 1,434 were judged to have need, 448 had their need fully met. 423 Federal Work-Study jobs (averaging $2581). 1,005 state and other part-time jobs (averaging $2964). In 2017, 483 non-need-based awards were made. *Average percent of need met:* 89. *Average financial aid package:* $36,390. *Average need-based loan:* $5083. *Average need-based gift aid:* $30,353. *Average non-need-based aid:* $19,980. *Average indebtedness upon graduation:* $42,833.

APPLYING
Standardized Tests *Required:* SAT or ACT (for admission).
Options: electronic application, early action, deferred entrance.
Required: high school transcript, college preparatory program. *Recommended:* minimum 3.0 GPA.
Application deadlines: rolling (transfers), 11/15 (early action).
Notification: continuous until 10/1 (freshmen), continuous until 10/1 (out-of-state freshmen), continuous (transfers), 12/15 (early action).

CONTACT
Ms. Karen Backes, Dean of Admissions, College of Saint Benedict, 37 South College Avenue, St. Joseph, MN 56374. *Phone:* 320-363-5055. *Toll-free phone:* 800-544-1489. *Fax:* 320-363-5650. *E-mail:* admissions@csbsju.edu.

The College of St. Scholastica
Duluth, Minnesota
http://www.css.edu/

- **Independent** comprehensive, founded 1912, affiliated with Roman Catholic Church
- **Suburban** 186-acre campus
- **Endowment** $69.4 million
- **Coed** 2,719 undergraduate students, 80% full-time, 71% women, 29% men
- **Moderately difficult** entrance level, 64% of applicants were admitted

UNDERGRAD STUDENTS
2,179 full-time, 540 part-time. Students come from 50 states and territories; 32 other countries; 14% are from out of state; 3% Black or African American, non-Hispanic/Latino; 4% Hispanic/Latino; 2% Asian, non-Hispanic/Latino; 0.1% Native Hawaiian or other Pacific Islander, non-Hispanic/Latino; 1% American Indian or Alaska Native, non-Hispanic/Latino; 3% Two or more races, non-Hispanic/Latino; 0.3% Race/ethnicity unknown; 2% international; 14% transferred in; 51% live on campus.

Freshmen:
Admission: 3,232 applied, 2,059 admitted, 482 enrolled. *Average high school GPA:* 3.5. *Test scores:* SAT evidence-based reading and writing scores over 500: 53%; SAT math scores over 500: 42%; ACT scores over 18: 95%; SAT evidence-based reading and writing scores over 600: 11%; SAT math scores over 600: 11%; ACT scores over 24: 47%; ACT scores over 30: 7%.
Retention: 80% of full-time freshmen returned.

FACULTY
Total: 419, 53% full-time.
Student/faculty ratio: 14:1.

ACADEMICS
Calendar: semesters. *Degrees:* certificates, bachelor's, master's, doctoral, post-master's, and postbachelor's certificates.
Special study options: accelerated degree program, adult/continuing education programs, advanced placement credit, distance learning, double majors, honors programs, independent study, internships, off-campus study, part-time degree program, services for LD students, student-designed majors, study abroad, summer session for credit. *ROTC:* Air Force (c).
Unusual degree programs: 3-2 occupational therapy.
Computers: 614 computers/terminals are available on campus for general student use. Students can access the following: campus intranet, computer help desk, free student e-mail accounts, online (class) grades, online

(class) registration, online (class) schedules, student account information, transcripts. Campuswide network is available. 100% of college-owned or -operated housing units are wired for high-speed Internet access. Wireless service is available via classrooms, computer centers, computer labs, dorm rooms, learning centers, libraries, student centers.
Library: College of St. Scholastica Library. *Books:* 110,444 (physical), 9,561 (digital/electronic); *Databases:* 124.

STUDENT LIFE
Housing options: on-campus residence required through sophomore year; coed, special housing for students with disabilities. Campus housing is university owned. Freshman applicants given priority for college housing.

Activities and organizations: drama/theater group, student-run newspaper, television station, choral group, Campus Activity Board, Inter-Varsity, Habitat for Humanity, SHIMA, Volunteers Involved Through Action.

Athletics Member NCAA. All Division III. *Intercollegiate sports:* baseball M, basketball M/W, cross-country running M/W, football M, golf M/W, ice hockey M/W, skiing (cross-country) M/W, soccer M/W, softball W, tennis M/W, track and field M/W, volleyball W. *Intramural sports:* basketball M/W, football M/W, soccer M/W, tennis M/W, volleyball M/W.

Campus security: 24-hour emergency response devices and patrols, late-night transport/escort service, controlled dormitory access, student door monitor at night.

Student services: health clinic, personal/psychological counseling.

COSTS & FINANCIAL AID
Costs (2018–19) *Comprehensive fee:* $46,922 includes full-time tuition ($36,614), mandatory fees ($598), and room and board ($9710). Full-time tuition and fees vary according to class time, degree level, and program. Part-time tuition: $1148 per credit hour. Part-time tuition and fees vary according to class time, course load, degree level, and program. *College room only:* $5334. Room and board charges vary according to board plan and housing facility. *Payment plan:* installment. *Waivers:* senior citizens and employees or children of employees.

Financial Aid Of all full-time matriculated undergraduates who enrolled in 2017, 1,900 applied for aid, 1,746 were judged to have need, 372 had their need fully met. In 2017, 131 non-need-based awards were made. *Average percent of need met:* 73. *Average financial aid package:* $26,120. *Average need-based loan:* $4783. *Average need-based gift aid:* $7595. *Average non-need-based aid:* $18,068. *Average indebtedness upon graduation:* $41,133.

APPLYING
Standardized Tests *Required:* SAT or ACT (for admission).

Options: electronic application, deferred entrance.

Required: high school transcript. *Required for some:* interview. *Recommended:* interview.

Application deadlines: rolling (freshmen), rolling (transfers).

Notification: continuous (freshmen), continuous (transfers).

CONTACT
The College of St. Scholastica, 1200 Kenwood Avenue, Duluth, MN 55811-4199. *Toll-free phone:* 800-249-6412.

Concordia College
Moorhead, Minnesota
http://www.concordiacollege.edu/
- **Independent** comprehensive, founded 1891, affiliated with Evangelical Lutheran Church in America
- **Suburban** 113-acre campus
- **Endowment** $111.3 million
- **Coed**
- **Moderately difficult** entrance level

FACULTY
Student/faculty ratio: 11:1.

ACADEMICS
Calendar: semesters. *Degrees:* bachelor's and master's.
Library: Carl B. Ylvisaker Library. *Books:* 347,087 (physical), 134,773 (digital/electronic); *Databases:* 148. Weekly public service hours: 93; students can reserve study rooms.

STUDENT LIFE
Housing options: on-campus residence required through sophomore year; coed. Campus housing is university owned. Freshman campus housing is guaranteed.

Activities and organizations: drama/theater group, student-run newspaper, radio and television station, choral group, Campus Entertainment Commission, Habitat for Humanity, Dance Marathon, Student Government Association, Campus Ministry Commission.

Athletics Member NCAA. All Division III.

Campus security: 24-hour emergency response devices and patrols, controlled dormitory access, well-lighted campus; outdoor campus emergency phones.

Student services: health clinic, personal/psychological counseling, women's center.

COSTS & FINANCIAL AID
Costs (2017–18) *Comprehensive fee:* $46,418 includes full-time tuition ($38,150), mandatory fees ($228), and room and board ($8040). Full-time tuition and fees vary according to course load and degree level. Part-time tuition: $1435 per credit. Part-time tuition and fees vary according to course load and degree level. *Required fees:* $114 per term part-time. *College room only:* $3460. Room and board charges vary according to board plan and housing facility.

Financial Aid Of all full-time matriculated undergraduates who enrolled in 2016, 1,726 applied for aid, 1,483 were judged to have need, 320 had their need fully met. In 2016, 534 non-need-based awards were made. *Average percent of need met:* 91. *Average financial aid package:* $29,701. *Average need-based loan:* $5505. *Average need-based gift aid:* $22,228. *Average non-need-based aid:* $15,926.

APPLYING
Standardized Tests *Required:* SAT or ACT (for admission).

Options: electronic application, early admission, deferred entrance.

Application fee: $20.

Required: high school transcript, 2 letters of recommendation.

CONTACT
Ms. Carola Thorson, Executive Director of Admissions and Scholarships, Concordia College, 901 8th Street South, Moorhead, MN 56562. *Phone:* 218-299-3004. *Toll-free phone:* 800-699-9897. *Fax:* 218-299-4720. *E-mail:* cthorson@cord.edu.

Concordia University, St. Paul
St. Paul, Minnesota
http://www.csp.edu/
- **Independent** comprehensive, founded 1893, affiliated with Lutheran Church–Missouri Synod
- **Urban** 37-acre campus with easy access to Minneapolis-St. Paul
- **Endowment** $48.3 million
- **Coed** 2,851 undergraduate students, 51% full-time, 59% women, 41% men
- **Minimally difficult** entrance level, 55% of applicants were admitted

UNDERGRAD STUDENTS
1,444 full-time, 1,407 part-time. Students come from 50 states and territories; 10 other countries; 26% are from out of state; 12% Black or African American, non-Hispanic/Latino; 4% Hispanic/Latino; 8% Asian, non-Hispanic/Latino; 0.3% Native Hawaiian or other Pacific Islander, non-Hispanic/Latino; 0.4% American Indian or Alaska Native, non-Hispanic/Latino; 4% Two or more races, non-Hispanic/Latino; 6% Race/ethnicity unknown; 4% international; 24% transferred in; 26% live on campus.

Freshmen:
Admission: 1,500 applied, 823 admitted, 246 enrolled. *Average high school GPA:* 3.2. *Test scores:* ACT scores over 18: 82%; ACT scores over 24: 28%; ACT scores over 30: 5%.
Retention: 65% of full-time freshmen returned.

FACULTY
Total: 441, 22% full-time, 32% with terminal degrees.
Student/faculty ratio: 18:1.

ACADEMICS

Calendar: semesters. *Degrees:* certificates, associate, bachelor's, master's, doctoral, post-master's, and postbachelor's certificates.

Special study options: academic remediation for entering students, accelerated degree program, adult/continuing education programs, advanced placement credit, distance learning, double majors, independent study, internships, off-campus study, part-time degree program, services for LD students, student-designed majors, study abroad, summer session for credit. *ROTC:* Army (c), Air Force (c).

Computers: 10 computers/terminals and 150 ports are available on campus for general student use. Students can access the following: campus intranet, computer help desk, free student e-mail accounts, online (class) grades, online (class) registration, online (class) schedules. Campuswide network is available. 100% of college-owned or -operated housing units are wired for high-speed Internet access. Wireless service is available via entire campus.

Library: Library Technology Center. *Books:* 108,345 (physical), 226,902 (digital/electronic); *Serial titles:* 917 (physical), 98,931 (digital/electronic); *Databases:* 178. Weekly public service hours: 74; students can reserve study rooms.

STUDENT LIFE

Housing options: on-campus residence required for freshman year; coed, men-only, women-only, special housing for students with disabilities. Campus housing is university owned. Freshman campus housing is guaranteed.

Activities and organizations: drama/theater group, student-run newspaper, choral group, Southeast Asian Student Organization, United Minds of Joint Action.

Athletics Member NCAA. All Division II. *Intercollegiate sports:* baseball M(s), basketball M(s)/W(s), cross-country running M(s)/W(s), football M(s), golf M(s)/W(s), lacrosse W(s), soccer W(s), softball W(s), track and field M(s)/W(s), volleyball W(s). *Intramural sports:* basketball M/W, football M/W, soccer M/W, volleyball M/W.

Campus security: 24-hour emergency response devices and patrols, student patrols, late-night transport/escort service, controlled dormitory access.

Student services: personal/psychological counseling.

COSTS & FINANCIAL AID

Costs (2018–19) *Comprehensive fee:* $31,775 includes full-time tuition ($22,775) and room and board ($9000). Full-time tuition and fees vary according to degree level and program. Part-time tuition: $600 per credit. Part-time tuition and fees vary according to course load, degree level, and program. *Room and board:* Room and board charges vary according to board plan and housing facility. *Payment plan:* installment. *Waivers:* employees or children of employees.

Financial Aid Of all full-time matriculated undergraduates who enrolled in 2017, 1,201 applied for aid, 1,045 were judged to have need, 113 had their need fully met. 98 Federal Work-Study jobs (averaging $2253). 290 state and other part-time jobs (averaging $2547). In 2017, 120 non-need-based awards were made. *Average percent of need met:* 58. *Average financial aid package:* $14,920. *Average need-based loan:* $4486. *Average need-based gift aid:* $10,647. *Average non-need-based aid:* $5614. *Average indebtedness upon graduation:* $34,686.

APPLYING

Standardized Tests *Required:* SAT or ACT (for admission).

Options: electronic application, early admission, deferred entrance.

Required: high school transcript, 2 letters of recommendation. *Required for some:* essay or personal statement. *Recommended:* minimum 2.0 GPA.

Application deadlines: 8/1 (freshmen), 8/1 (transfers).

Notification: continuous (freshmen), continuous (transfers).

CONTACT

Ms. Leah Martin, Director of Traditional Admission, Concordia University, St. Paul, 1282 Concordia Avenue, St. Paul, MN 55104-5494. *Phone:* 651-641-8230. *Toll-free phone:* 800-333-4705. *Fax:* 651-603-6320. *E-mail:* admission@csp.edu.

Crown College
St. Bonifacius, Minnesota
http://www.crown.edu/

CONTACT
Mr. Bret Hyder, Assistant Director of Admissions, Crown College, 8700 College View Drive, St. Bonifacius, MN 55375-9001. *Phone:* 952-446-4142. *Toll-free phone:* 800-68-CROWN. *Fax:* 952-446-4149. *E-mail:* admissions@crown.edu.

Dunwoody College of Technology
Minneapolis, Minnesota
http://www.dunwoody.edu/

- **Independent** primarily 2-year, founded 1914
- **Urban** 12-acre campus with easy access to Minneapolis-St. Paul
- **Endowment** $22.3 million
- **Coed, primarily men** 1,302 undergraduate students, 82% full-time, 17% women, 83% men
- **Minimally difficult** entrance level, 78% of applicants were admitted

UNDERGRAD STUDENTS
1,073 full-time, 229 part-time. Students come from 3 other countries; 2% are from out of state; 4% Black or African American, non-Hispanic/Latino; 3% Hispanic/Latino; 7% Asian, non-Hispanic/Latino; 0.5% Native Hawaiian or other Pacific Islander, non-Hispanic/Latino; 0.5% American Indian or Alaska Native, non-Hispanic/Latino; 5% Two or more races, non-Hispanic/Latino; 6% Race/ethnicity unknown; 0.2% international; 21% transferred in.

Freshmen:
Admission: 976 applied, 765 admitted, 184 enrolled. *Average high school GPA:* 2.7.

Retention: 89% of full-time freshmen returned.

FACULTY
Total: 165, 52% full-time, 15% with terminal degrees.

Student/faculty ratio: 10:1.

ACADEMICS
Calendar: semesters. *Degrees:* certificates, associate, and bachelor's.

Special study options: academic remediation for entering students, adult/continuing education programs, cooperative education, distance learning, independent study, internships, study abroad, summer session for credit.

Computers: 300 computers/terminals and 1,000 ports are available on campus for general student use. Students can access the following: campus intranet, computer help desk, free student e-mail accounts, online (class) grades, online (class) registration, online (class) schedules. Campuswide network is available. Wireless service is available via entire campus.

Library: Learning Resource Center plus 1 other. *Books:* 5,500 (physical), 179,443 (digital/electronic); *Serial titles:* 133 (physical); *Databases:* 26. Weekly public service hours: 55.

STUDENT LIFE
Housing options: college housing not available.

Activities and organizations: Phi Theta Kappa, Historic Green, Dunwoody Motorsports Club, Architectural Institute of America Student Chapter, Professional Association for Design.

Campus security: 24-hour emergency response devices, late-night transport/escort service.

Student services: women's center.

COSTS & FINANCIAL AID
Costs (2017–18) *Tuition:* $18,826 full-time, $654 per credit part-time. Full-time tuition and fees vary according to course load, degree level, and program. Part-time tuition and fees vary according to course load, degree level, and program. *Required fees:* $1652 full-time, $1458 per term part-time. *Payment plan:* installment. *Waivers:* employees or children of employees.

Financial Aid Of all full-time matriculated undergraduates who enrolled in 2016, 937 applied for aid, 829 were judged to have need, 32 had their need fully met. 24 Federal Work-Study jobs (averaging $3486). 29 state and other part-time jobs (averaging $3052). In 2016, 38 non-need-based awards were made. *Average percent of need met:* 36. *Average financial aid package:* $8856. *Average need-based loan:* $3461. *Average need-based gift aid:* $6950. *Average non-need-based aid:* $3219. *Average indebtedness upon graduation:* $19,167.

APPLYING
Standardized Tests *Required for some:* ACT (for admission).

Options: electronic application.

Application fee: $50.

Required: essay or personal statement, high school transcript. *Required for some:* minimum 3.0 GPA, letters of recommendation, resume, ACT scores. *Recommended:* minimum 2.5 GPA, interview.

Application deadlines: rolling (freshmen), rolling (out-of-state freshmen), rolling (transfers).

Notification: continuous (freshmen), continuous (out-of-state freshmen), continuous (transfers).

CONTACT
Kelly OBrien, Director of Admissions, Dunwoody College of Technology, 818 Dunwoody Boulevard, Minneapolis, MN 55403. *Phone:* 612-381-3302. *Toll-free phone:* 800-292-4625. *Fax:* 612-677-3131. *E-mail:* kobrien@dunwoody.edu.

Gustavus Adolphus College
St. Peter, Minnesota
http://www.gustavus.edu/

- **Independent** 4-year, founded 1862, affiliated with Evangelical Lutheran Church in America
- **Small-town** 340-acre campus with easy access to Minneapolis-St. Paul
- **Endowment** $166.8 million
- **Coed** 2,201 undergraduate students, 99% full-time, 56% women, 44% men
- **Very difficult** entrance level, 68% of applicants were admitted

UNDERGRAD STUDENTS
2,170 full-time, 31 part-time. Students come from 45 states and territories; 26 other countries; 17% are from out of state; 3% Black or African American, non-Hispanic/Latino; 5% Hispanic/Latino; 5% Asian, non-Hispanic/Latino; 0.1% Native Hawaiian or other Pacific Islander, non-Hispanic/Latino; 4% Two or more races, non-Hispanic/Latino; 0.7% Race/ethnicity unknown; 5% international; 0.9% transferred in; 97% live on campus.

Freshmen:
Admission: 4,834 applied, 3,279 admitted, 589 enrolled. *Average high school GPA:* 3.6. *Test scores:* ACT scores over 18: 99%; ACT scores over 24: 78%; ACT scores over 30: 28%.

Retention: 88% of full-time freshmen returned.

FACULTY
Total: 224, 82% full-time, 80% with terminal degrees.

Student/faculty ratio: 11:1.

ACADEMICS
Calendar: 4-1-4. *Degree:* bachelor's.

Special study options: accelerated degree program, advanced placement credit, cooperative education, double majors, honors programs, independent study, internships, off-campus study, services for LD students, student-designed majors, study abroad. *ROTC:* Army (c).

Unusual degree programs: engineering with Minnesota State University, Mankato; University of Minnesota; social work; occupational therapy with Washington University in St. Louis.

Computers: 400 computers/terminals are available on campus for general student use. Students can access the following: computer help desk, free student e-mail accounts, online (class) grades, online (class) registration, online (class) schedules. Campuswide network is available. 100% of college-owned or -operated housing units are wired for high-speed Internet access. Wireless service is available via entire campus.

Library: Folke Bernadotte Memorial Library. *Books:* 326,681 (physical), 53,368 (digital/electronic); *Serial titles:* 1,126 (physical); *Databases:* 108. Students can reserve study rooms.

STUDENT LIFE
Housing options: on-campus residence required through senior year; coed, special housing for students with disabilities. Campus housing is university owned. Freshman campus housing is guaranteed.

Activities and organizations: drama/theater group, student-run newspaper, radio and television station, choral group, Proclaim, Big Partner/Little Partner, Study Buddies, I am...We are, Pound Pals, national fraternities, national sororities.

Athletics Member NCAA. All Division III. *Intercollegiate sports:* baseball M, basketball M/W, cross-country running M/W, football M, golf M/W, gymnastics W, ice hockey M/W, lacrosse M(c), rugby M(c)/W(c), skiing (cross-country) M/W, soccer M/W, softball W, swimming and diving M/W, tennis M/W, track and field M/W, ultimate Frisbee M(c)/W(c), volleyball M(c)/W. *Intramural sports:* badminton M/W, basketball M/W, golf M/W, ice hockey M/W, racquetball M/W, rugby M/W, skiing (cross-country) M/W, skiing (downhill) M/W, soccer M/W, softball M/W, swimming and diving M/W, tennis M/W, track and field M/W, ultimate Frisbee M/W, volleyball M/W, water polo M/W, weight lifting M/W.

Campus security: 24-hour emergency response devices and patrols, late-night transport/escort service, controlled dormitory access.

Student services: health clinic, personal/psychological counseling, women's center.

COSTS & FINANCIAL AID
Costs (2018–19) *One-time required fee:* $490. *Comprehensive fee:* $55,010 includes full-time tuition ($44,900), mandatory fees ($200), and room and board ($9910). Part-time tuition: $7680 per course. *College room only:* $6300. Room and board charges vary according to board plan and housing facility. *Payment plans:* tuition prepayment, installment. *Waivers:* employees or children of employees.

Financial Aid Of all full-time matriculated undergraduates who enrolled in 2017, 1,675 applied for aid, 1,541 were judged to have need, 447 had their need fully met. In 2017, 616 non-need-based awards were made. *Average percent of need met:* 92. *Average financial aid package:* $37,892. *Average need-based loan:* $3480. *Average need-based gift aid:* $32,482. *Average non-need-based aid:* $22,283. *Financial aid deadline:* 4/15.

APPLYING
Options: electronic application, early admission, early action, deferred entrance.

Required: essay or personal statement, high school transcript, 1 letter of recommendation. *Recommended:* interview.

Application deadlines: 4/1 (freshmen), rolling (transfers), rolling (early action).

Notification: continuous (freshmen), continuous (transfers), rolling (early action).

CONTACT
Mr. Richard Aune, Vice President for Enrollment Management, Gustavus Adolphus College, 800 West College Avenue, St. Peter, MN 56082-1498. *Phone:* 507-933-7676. *Toll-free phone:* 800-GUSTAVU(S). *Fax:* 507-933-7474. *E-mail:* admission@gac.edu.

Hamline University
St. Paul, Minnesota
http://www.hamline.edu/

- **Independent** comprehensive, founded 1854, affiliated with United Methodist Church
- **Urban** 60-acre campus with easy access to Minneapolis-St. Paul
- **Coed** 2,168 undergraduate students, 96% full-time, 61% women, 39% men
- **Moderately difficult** entrance level, 70% of applicants were admitted

UNDERGRAD STUDENTS
2,082 full-time, 86 part-time. Students come from 35 states and territories; 39 other countries; 19% are from out of state; 9% Black or African American, non-Hispanic/Latino; 9% Hispanic/Latino; 7% Asian, non-Hispanic/Latino; 0.3% American Indian or Alaska Native, non-Hispanic/Latino; 6% Two or more races, non-Hispanic/Latino; 3% Race/ethnicity unknown; 1% international; 5% transferred in; 38% live on campus.

Freshmen:
Admission: 4,252 applied, 2,989 admitted, 535 enrolled. *Average high school GPA:* 3.4. *Test scores:* SAT evidence-based reading and writing scores over 500: 82%; SAT math scores over 500: 33%; ACT scores over 18: 93%; SAT evidence-based reading and writing scores over 600: 32%; ACT scores over 24: 43%; SAT evidence-based reading and writing scores over 700: 18%; ACT scores over 30: 10%.

Retention: 84% of full-time freshmen returned.

FACULTY
Total: 297, 49% full-time, 56% with terminal degrees.
Student/faculty ratio: 13:1.

ACADEMICS
Calendar: 4-1-4. *Degrees:* certificates, bachelor's, master's, doctoral, post-master's, and postbachelor's certificates.

Special study options: advanced placement credit, distance learning, double majors, English as a second language, honors programs, independent study, internships, off-campus study, part-time degree program, services for LD students, student-designed majors, study abroad, summer session for credit. *ROTC:* Army (c), Air Force (c).

Unusual degree programs: 3-2 engineering.

Computers: 300 computers/terminals are available on campus for general student use. Students can access the following: campus intranet, computer help desk, free student e-mail accounts, online (class) grades, online (class) registration, online (class) schedules. Campuswide network is available. 99% of college-owned or -operated housing units are wired for high-speed Internet access. Wireless service is available via entire campus.

Library: Bush Library. *Books:* 126,680 (physical), 345,792 (digital/electronic); *Serial titles:* 1,455 (physical), 61,526 (digital/electronic); *Databases:* 110. Students can reserve study rooms.

STUDENT LIFE
Housing options: coed, special housing for students with disabilities. Campus housing is university owned. Freshman campus housing is guaranteed.

Activities and organizations: drama/theater group, student-run newspaper, radio and television station, choral group, Anthro Society, Asian Pacific American Coalition, Hamline Student Athlete Advisory Committee, Hand in Hand, Pride BSA, national fraternities, national sororities.

Athletics Member NCAA. All Division III. *Intercollegiate sports:* baseball M, basketball M/W, cheerleading W(c), cross-country running M/W, football M, gymnastics W, ice hockey M/W, lacrosse W, soccer M/W, softball W, swimming and diving M/W, tennis M/W, track and field M/W, volleyball W. *Intramural sports:* basketball M(c)/W(c), football M(c)/W(c), golf M(c)/W(c), lacrosse M(c)/W(c), rock climbing M(c)/W(c), soccer M(c)/W(c), ultimate Frisbee M(c)/W(c), volleyball M(c)/W(c).

Campus security: 24-hour emergency response devices and patrols, student patrols, late-night transport/escort service, controlled dormitory access, security cameras on campus and in residence halls, jump starts offered to those in escort range.

Student services: health clinic, personal/psychological counseling, women's center.

COSTS & FINANCIAL AID
Costs (2018–19) *Comprehensive fee:* $51,656 includes full-time tuition ($40,284), mandatory fees ($1014), and room and board ($10,358). Part-time tuition: $1259 per credit hour. Part-time tuition and fees vary according to course load. *Required fees:* $788 per year part-time. *College room only:* $5100. Room and board charges vary according to board plan and housing facility. *Payment plan:* installment. *Waivers:* employees or children of employees.

Financial Aid Of all full-time matriculated undergraduates who enrolled in 2016, 1,861 applied for aid, 1,728 were judged to have need, 297 had their need fully met. In 2016, 309 non-need-based awards were made. *Average percent of need met:* 79. *Average financial aid package:* $29,877. *Average need-based loan:* $4748. *Average need-based gift aid:* $23,426. *Average non-need-based aid:* $16,630. *Average indebtedness upon graduation:* $34,935.

APPLYING
Standardized Tests *Required:* SAT or ACT (for admission).

Options: electronic application, early admission, early decision, early action, deferred entrance.

Required: high school transcript. *Recommended:* essay or personal statement, 1 letter of recommendation, interview.

Application deadlines: rolling (freshmen), rolling (transfers), 12/1 (early action).

Early decision deadline: 11/1.

Notification: continuous (freshmen), continuous (transfers), 11/15 (early decision).

CONTACT
Admissions Office, Hamline University, 1536 Hewitt Avenue, St. Paul, MN 55104-1284. *Phone:* 651-523-2207. *Toll-free phone:* 800-753-9753. *E-mail:* admission@hamline.edu.

Herzing University
Minneapolis, Minnesota
http://www.herzing.edu/minneapolis

CONTACT
Ms. Shelly Larson, Director of Admissions, Herzing University, 5700 West Broadway, Minneapolis, MN 55428. *Phone:* 763-231-3155. *Toll-free phone:* 800-596-0724. *Fax:* 763-535-9205. *E-mail:* info@mpls.herzing.edu.

Macalester College
St. Paul, Minnesota
http://www.macalester.edu/

- **Independent** 4-year, founded 1874
- **Urban** 53-acre campus
- **Endowment** $747.7 million
- **Coed** 2,136 undergraduate students
- **Very difficult** entrance level, 41% of applicants were admitted

UNDERGRAD STUDENTS
Students come from 53 states and territories; 90 other countries; 83% are from out of state; 3% Black or African American, non-Hispanic/Latino; 7% Hispanic/Latino; 7% Asian, non-Hispanic/Latino; 0.1% Native Hawaiian or other Pacific Islander, non-Hispanic/Latino; 0.1% American Indian or Alaska Native, non-Hispanic/Latino; 6% Two or more races, non-Hispanic/Latino; 0.2% Race/ethnicity unknown; 16% international; 72% live on campus.

Freshmen:
Admission: 5,900 applied, 2,394 admitted. *Test scores:* SAT evidence-based reading and writing scores over 500: 100%; SAT math scores over 500: 99%; ACT scores over 18: 100%; SAT evidence-based reading and writing scores over 600: 95%; SAT math scores over 600: 88%; ACT scores over 24: 99%; SAT evidence-based reading and writing scores over 700: 55%; SAT math scores over 700: 47%; ACT scores over 30: 68%.

Retention: 93% of full-time freshmen returned.

FACULTY
Total: 238, 77% full-time, 82% with terminal degrees.
Student/faculty ratio: 10:1.

ACADEMICS
Calendar: semesters. *Degree:* bachelor's.

Special study options: advanced placement credit, double majors, honors programs, independent study, internships, off-campus study, part-time degree program, services for LD students, student-designed majors, study abroad, summer session for credit. *ROTC:* Army (c), Navy (c), Air Force (c).

Unusual degree programs: 3-2 architecture with Washington University in St. Louis.

Computers: 580 computers/terminals and 2,600 ports are available on campus for general student use. Students can access the following: campus intranet, computer help desk, free student e-mail accounts, online (class) grades, online (class) registration, online (class) schedules, wireless networking, free printing, specialized tools. Campuswide network is available. 100% of college-owned or -operated housing units are wired for high-speed Internet access. Wireless service is available via entire campus.

Library: DeWitt Wallace Library. *Books:* 326,620 (physical), 179,946 (digital/electronic); *Serial titles:* 2,412 (physical), 76,659 (digital/electronic); *Databases:* 202. Weekly public service hours: 109; study areas open 24 hours, 5–7 days a week; students can reserve study rooms.

STUDENT LIFE

Housing options: on-campus residence required through sophomore year; coed, men-only, women-only, cooperative. Campus housing is university owned. Freshman campus housing is guaranteed.

Activities and organizations: drama/theater group, student-run newspaper, radio station, choral group, Program Board, WMCN - Macalester College Radio, The Mac Weekly, Adelante , Outing Club.

Athletics Member NCAA. All Division III. *Intercollegiate sports:* baseball M, basketball M/W, crew M(c)/W(c), cross-country running M/W, football M, golf M/W, ice hockey M(c)/W(c), lacrosse W(c), rugby M(c)/W(c), skiing (cross-country) M(c)/W(c), soccer M/W, softball W, swimming and diving M/W, tennis M/W, track and field M/W, ultimate Frisbee M(c)/W(c), volleyball M(c)/W, water polo M(c)/W. *Intramural sports:* badminton M/W, basketball M/W, racquetball M/W, soccer M/W, softball M/W, table tennis M/W, tennis M(c)/W(c), ultimate Frisbee M/W.

Campus security: 24-hour emergency response devices and patrols, late-night transport/escort service, controlled dormitory access, Rave Alert Notification System (texting/email).

Student services: health clinic, personal/psychological counseling.

COSTS & FINANCIAL AID

Costs (2018–19) *Comprehensive fee:* $66,500 includes full-time tuition ($54,114), mandatory fees ($230), and room and board ($12,156). Full-time tuition and fees vary according to course load. Part-time tuition: $1691 per credit. Part-time tuition and fees vary according to course load. *College room only:* $6526. Room and board charges vary according to board plan and housing facility. *Payment plan:* installment. *Waivers:* employees or children of employees.

Financial Aid Of all full-time matriculated undergraduates who enrolled in 2017, 1,597 applied for aid, 1,448 were judged to have need, 1,448 had their need fully met. In 2017, 256 non-need-based awards were made. *Average percent of need met:* 100. *Average financial aid package:* $45,680. *Average need-based loan:* $5040. *Average need-based gift aid:* $39,177. *Average non-need-based aid:* $15,258. *Average indebtedness upon graduation:* $24,381.

APPLYING

Standardized Tests *Required:* SAT or ACT (for admission).

Options: electronic application, early admission, early decision, deferred entrance.

Application fee: $40.

Required: essay or personal statement, high school transcript, 2 letters of recommendation. *Recommended:* interview.

Application deadlines: 1/15 (freshmen), 4/15 (transfers).

Early decision deadline: 11/15 (for plan 1), 1/1 (for plan 2).

Notification: 3/30 (freshmen), 5/15 (transfers), 12/15 (early decision plan 1), 2/7 (early decision plan 2).

CONTACT
Mr. Jeff Allen, Vice President of Admissions and Financial Aid, Macalester College, 1600 Grand Avenue, St. Paul, MN 55105-1899. *Phone:* 651-696-6357. *Toll-free phone:* 800-231-7974. *Fax:* 651-696-6724. *E-mail:* admissions@macalester.edu.

Martin Luther College
New Ulm, Minnesota
http://www.mlc-wels.edu/

- **Independent** comprehensive, founded 1995, affiliated with Wisconsin Evangelical Lutheran Synod
- **Small-town** 50-acre campus
- **Coed** 859 undergraduate students, 84% full-time, 52% women, 48% men
- **Moderately difficult** entrance level, 83% of applicants were admitted

UNDERGRAD STUDENTS
718 full-time, 141 part-time. 80% are from out of state; 2% Black or African American, non-Hispanic/Latino; 1% Hispanic/Latino; 0.9% Asian, non-Hispanic/Latino; 0.1% American Indian or Alaska Native, non-Hispanic/Latino; 0.5% Two or more races, non-Hispanic/Latino; 2% international; 1% transferred in; 87% live on campus.

Freshmen:
Admission: 293 applied, 244 admitted, 196 enrolled. *Average high school GPA:* 3.5. *Test scores:* ACT scores over 18: 98%; ACT scores over 24: 61%; ACT scores over 30: 13%.
Retention: 87% of full-time freshmen returned.

FACULTY
Total: 75, 69% full-time, 37% with terminal degrees.
Student/faculty ratio: 12:1.

ACADEMICS
Calendar: semesters. *Degrees:* certificates, diplomas, bachelor's, and master's.

Special study options: advanced placement credit, distance learning, double majors, summer session for credit.

Computers: Campuswide network is available.
Library: Martin Luther College Library.

STUDENT LIFE
Housing options: on-campus residence required for freshman year; men-only, women-only, special housing for students with disabilities. Campus housing is university owned. Freshman campus housing is guaranteed.

Activities and organizations: drama/theater group, choral group.

Athletics Member NCAA, NAIA. All NCAA Division III. *Intercollegiate sports:* baseball M, basketball M/W, cross-country running M/W, football M, golf M/W, soccer M/W, softball W, tennis M/W, track and field M/W, volleyball W. *Intramural sports:* badminton M/W, basketball M/W, bowling M/W, football M, soccer M/W, softball M/W, tennis M/W, volleyball M/W.

Student services: health clinic, personal/psychological counseling.

COSTS & FINANCIAL AID
Costs (2017–18) *Comprehensive fee:* $20,470 includes full-time tuition ($14,680) and room and board ($5790). Part-time tuition: $310 per credit. *Payment plan:* installment.

Financial Aid Of all full-time matriculated undergraduates who enrolled in 2016, 602 applied for aid, 525 were judged to have need, 89 had their need fully met. In 2016, 108 non-need-based awards were made. *Average percent of need met:* 73. *Average financial aid package:* $12,279. *Average need-based loan:* $4390. *Average need-based gift aid:* $8218. *Average non-need-based aid:* $2707. *Average indebtedness upon graduation:* $23,239. *Financial aid deadline:* 4/17.

APPLYING
Standardized Tests *Required:* SAT or ACT (for admission).
Options: deferred entrance.
Required: high school transcript, minimum 2.0 GPA.

CONTACT
Martin Luther College, 1995 Luther Court, New Ulm, MN 56073. *Toll-free phone:* 877-MLC-1995.

Metropolitan State University
St. Paul, Minnesota
http://www.metrostate.edu/

CONTACT
Mr. Daryl Johnson, Director, Metropolitan State University, 700 East 7th Street, St. Paul, MN 55106. *Phone:* 651-793-1227. *Fax:* 651-793-1546. *E-mail:* daryl.johnson@metrostate.edu.

Minneapolis College of Art and Design

Minneapolis, Minnesota
http://www.mcad.edu/

- **Independent** comprehensive, founded 1886
- **Urban** 3-acre campus
- **Endowment** $47.9 million
- **Coed** 675 undergraduate students, 98% full-time, 68% women, 32% men
- **Moderately difficult** entrance level, 59% of applicants were admitted

UNDERGRAD STUDENTS

664 full-time, 11 part-time. Students come from 13 other countries; 47% are from out of state; 6% Black or African American, non-Hispanic/Latino; 7% Hispanic/Latino; 8% Asian, non-Hispanic/Latino; 0.1% Native Hawaiian or other Pacific Islander, non-Hispanic/Latino; 2% American Indian or Alaska Native, non-Hispanic/Latino; 2% Two or more races, non-Hispanic/Latino; 7% Race/ethnicity unknown; 2% international; 9% transferred in.

Freshmen:
Admission: 692 applied, 405 admitted, 133 enrolled. *Average high school GPA:* 3.3. *Test scores:* ACT scores over 18: 94%; ACT scores over 24: 46%; ACT scores over 30: 9%.
Retention: 83% of full-time freshmen returned.

FACULTY
Total: 139, 30% full-time, 54% with terminal degrees.
Student/faculty ratio: 10:1.

ACADEMICS
Calendar: semesters. *Degrees:* bachelor's and master's.

Special study options: adult/continuing education programs, advanced placement credit, cooperative education, distance learning, independent study, internships, off-campus study, part-time degree program, services for LD students, study abroad, summer session for credit.

Computers: Students can access the following: campus intranet, computer help desk, free student e-mail accounts, online (class) grades, online (class) registration, online (class) schedules. Campuswide network is available. 100% of college-owned or -operated housing units are wired for high-speed Internet access. Wireless service is available via entire campus.

Library: MCAD Library. *Books:* 50,000 (physical), 145,000 (digital/electronic); *Serial titles:* 329 (physical); *Databases:* 8.

STUDENT LIFE
Housing options: coed. Campus housing is university owned. Freshman applicants given priority for college housing.

Activities and organizations: Peoples Library, Black Artist Student Union, Animation Study Group, Comic Club, Kinda Midnight Movies Club.

Athletics *Intramural sports:* soccer M(c)/W(c), softball M(c)/W(c).

Campus security: 24-hour emergency response devices and patrols, late-night transport/escort service, controlled dormitory access.

Student services: personal/psychological counseling.

COSTS & FINANCIAL AID
Costs (2018–19) *Tuition:* $38,670 full-time, $1612 per credit hour part-time. Part-time tuition and fees vary according to course load. *Required fees:* $450 full-time, $225 per term part-time. *Room only:* $5610. Room and board charges vary according to housing facility. *Payment plan:* installment. *Waivers:* children of alumni and employees or children of employees.

Financial Aid Of all full-time matriculated undergraduates who enrolled in 2014, 546 applied for aid, 490 were judged to have need, 54 had their need fully met. In 2014, 112 non-need-based awards were made. *Average percent of need met:* 68. *Average financial aid package:* $22,825. *Average need-based loan:* $4747. *Average need-based gift aid:* $17,718. *Average non-need-based aid:* $11,165. *Average indebtedness upon graduation:* $33,400. *Financial aid deadline:* 4/1.

APPLYING
Standardized Tests *Required for some:* SAT or ACT (for admission).

Options: electronic application, early action.
Application fee: $50.
Required: essay or personal statement, high school transcript. *Recommended:* interview.
Application deadlines: 5/1 (freshmen), 5/1 (transfers), 12/1 (early action).
Notification: continuous (freshmen), continuous (out-of-state freshmen), continuous (transfers), 12/15 (early action).

CONTACT
Minneapolis College of Art and Design, 2501 Stevens Avenue, Minneapolis, MN 55404-4347. *Phone:* 612-874-3764. *Toll-free phone:* 800-874-6223.

Minnesota State University Mankato

Mankato, Minnesota
http://www.mnsu.edu/

- **State-supported** university, founded 1868, part of Minnesota State Colleges and Universities System
- **Small-town** 303-acre campus with easy access to Minneapolis-St. Paul
- **Coed**

FACULTY
Student/faculty ratio: 20:1.

ACADEMICS
Calendar: semesters. *Degrees:* certificates, associate, bachelor's, master's, doctoral, and post-master's certificates.
Library: Memorial Library.

STUDENT LIFE
Housing options: coed. Campus housing is university owned and leased by the school. Freshman applicants given priority for college housing.

Activities and organizations: drama/theater group, student-run newspaper, radio station, choral group, marching band, national fraternities, national sororities.

Athletics Member NCAA. All Division II except men's and women's ice hockey (Division I).

Campus security: 24-hour emergency response devices and patrols, student patrols, late-night transport/escort service, controlled dormitory access, Night Owl security program in residence halls, closed circuit cameras in parking lots.

Student services: health clinic, personal/psychological counseling, women's center, legal services.

COSTS & FINANCIAL AID
Costs (2017–18) *Tuition:* state resident $7678 full-time, $281 per credit hour part-time; nonresident $15,230 full-time, $604 per credit hour part-time. Full-time tuition and fees vary according to course load, location, program, and reciprocity agreements. Part-time tuition and fees vary according to course load, location, program, and reciprocity agreements. *Required fees:* $985 full-time, $41 per credit hour part-time. *Room and board:* $8475; room only: $5524. Room and board charges vary according to board plan and housing facility.

Financial Aid Of all full-time matriculated undergraduates who enrolled in 2017, 8,082 applied for aid, 5,761 were judged to have need, 1,015 had their need fully met. 328 Federal Work-Study jobs (averaging $4336). 338 state and other part-time jobs (averaging $4087). In 2017, 1051 non-need-based awards were made. *Average percent of need met:* 70. *Average financial aid package:* $9505. *Average need-based loan:* $4350. *Average need-based gift aid:* $5975. *Average non-need-based aid:* $5664. *Average indebtedness upon graduation:* $31,483.

APPLYING
Standardized Tests *Required:* SAT or ACT (for admission).

Required: high school transcript. *Required for some:* essay or personal statement, 1 letter of recommendation, personal statement, letter and senior grades.

CONTACT
Office of Admissions, Minnesota State University Mankato, 122 Taylor Center, Mankato, MN 56001. *Phone:* 507-389-1822. *Toll-free phone:* 800-722-0544. *Fax:* 507-389-1511. *E-mail:* admissions@mnsu.edu.

Minnesota State University Moorhead

Moorhead, Minnesota
http://www.mnstate.edu/

- **State-supported** comprehensive, founded 1885, part of Minnesota State Colleges and Universities System
- **Urban** 119-acre campus
- **Endowment** $22.3 million
- **Coed** 5,147 undergraduate students, 81% full-time, 61% women, 39% men
- **Moderately difficult** entrance level, 60% of applicants were admitted

UNDERGRAD STUDENTS
4,165 full-time, 982 part-time. Students come from 38 states and territories; 51 other countries; 32% are from out of state; 3% Black or African American, non-Hispanic/Latino; 3% Hispanic/Latino; 1% Asian, non-Hispanic/Latino; 0.1% Native Hawaiian or other Pacific Islander, non-Hispanic/Latino; 0.6% American Indian or Alaska Native, non-Hispanic/Latino; 4% Two or more races, non-Hispanic/Latino; 2% Race/ethnicity unknown; 7% international; 9% transferred in; 32% live on campus.

Freshmen:
Admission: 4,400 applied, 2,657 admitted, 844 enrolled. *Average high school GPA:* 3.4. *Test scores:* ACT scores over 18: 94%; ACT scores over 24: 37%; ACT scores over 30: 5%.
Retention: 75% of full-time freshmen returned.

FACULTY
Total: 348, 60% full-time, 65% with terminal degrees.
Student/faculty ratio: 19:1.

ACADEMICS
Calendar: semesters. *Degrees:* certificates, bachelor's, master's, doctoral, post-master's, and postbachelor's certificates.
Special study options: academic remediation for entering students, adult/continuing education programs, advanced placement credit, distance learning, double majors, English as a second language, honors programs, independent study, internships, off-campus study, part-time degree program, services for LD students, student-designed majors, study abroad, summer session for credit. *ROTC:* Army (c), Air Force (c).
Computers: 1,500 computers/terminals are available on campus for general student use. Students can access the following: computer help desk, free student e-mail accounts, online (class) grades, online (class) registration, online (class) schedules. Campuswide network is available. 100% of college-owned or -operated housing units are wired for high-speed Internet access. Wireless service is available via entire campus.
Library: Livingston Lord Library plus 1 other. *Books:* 326,187 (physical), 20,401 (digital/electronic); *Serial titles:* 1,634 (physical), 18,041 (digital/electronic); *Databases:* 84. Weekly public service hours: 79.

STUDENT LIFE
Housing options: coed, special housing for students with disabilities. Campus housing is university owned. Freshman campus housing is guaranteed.
Activities and organizations: drama/theater group, student-run newspaper, radio and television station, choral group, Education Minnesota Student Program, Cinethusiasts, SPECTRUM, NSSLHA / Collegiate SERTOMA, National Society of Leadership and Success, national fraternities, national sororities.
Athletics Member NCAA. All Division II. *Intercollegiate sports:* basketball M(s)/W(s), cheerleading M/W, cross-country running M(s)/W(s), football M(s), golf W(s), soccer W(s), softball W(s), swimming and diving W(s), tennis W(s), track and field M(s)/W(s), volleyball W(s), wrestling M(s). *Intramural sports:* badminton M/W, basketball M/W, football M/W, golf W, ice hockey M/W, soccer M(c)/W(c), softball M/W, tennis M/W, ultimate Frisbee M/W, volleyball M/W.
Campus security: 24-hour emergency response devices and patrols, student patrols, late-night transport/escort service, controlled dormitory access.

Student services: health clinic, personal/psychological counseling, women's center.

COSTS & FINANCIAL AID
Costs (2018–19) *Tuition:* state resident $7410 full-time, $239 per credit hour part-time; nonresident $14,820 full-time, $478 per credit hour part-time. Full-time tuition and fees vary according to course load and reciprocity agreements. Part-time tuition and fees vary according to reciprocity agreements. *Required fees:* $1086 full-time, $45 per credit hour part-time, $543 per term part-time. *Room and board:* $9280; room only: $5950. Room and board charges vary according to board plan and housing facility. *Payment plan:* installment. *Waivers:* senior citizens and employees or children of employees.
Financial Aid Of all full-time matriculated undergraduates who enrolled in 2017, 3,307 applied for aid, 2,553 were judged to have need. 238 Federal Work-Study jobs (averaging $2555). 163 state and other part-time jobs (averaging $2385). *Average financial aid package:* $3211. *Average need-based loan:* $3940. *Average need-based gift aid:* $2716. *Average indebtedness upon graduation:* $32,713.

APPLYING
Standardized Tests *Required:* SAT or ACT (for admission). *Recommended:* ACT (for admission).
Options: electronic application, deferred entrance.
Application fee: $20.
Required: high school transcript.
Application deadlines: rolling (freshmen), rolling (out-of-state freshmen), rolling (transfers).
Notification: continuous (freshmen), continuous (out-of-state freshmen), continuous (transfers).

CONTACT
Minnesota State University Moorhead, 1104 7th Avenue South, Moorhead, MN 56563. *Toll-free phone:* 800-593-7246.

National American University
Bloomington, Minnesota
http://www.national.edu/
CONTACT
Ms. Jennifer Michaelson, Admissions Assistant, National American University, 321 Kansas City Street, Rapid City, SD 57201. *Phone:* 605-394-4827. *Toll-free phone:* 866-628-6387. *E-mail:* jmichaelson@national.edu.

National American University
Brooklyn Center, Minnesota
http://www.national.edu/
CONTACT
Admissions Office, National American University, 6200 Shingle Creek Parkway, Suite 130, Brooklyn Center, MN 55430. *Toll-free phone:* 866-628-6387.

National American University
Burnsville, Minnesota
http://www.national.edu/
CONTACT
National American University, 513 West Travelers Trail, Burnsville, MN 55337. *Toll-free phone:* 866-628-6387.

National American University
Roseville, Minnesota
http://www.national.edu/
CONTACT
Mr. Steve Grunlan, Director of Admissions, National American University, 1550 West Highway 36, Roseville, MN 55113. *Phone:* 651-644-1265. *Toll-free phone:* 866-628-6387.

Minnesota

North Central University

Minneapolis, Minnesota
http://www.northcentral.edu/

CONTACT
Ms. Sigi Shawa, Assistant Director, North Central University, 910 Elliot Avenue, Minneapolis, MN 55404-1322. *Phone:* 612-343-4460. *Toll-free phone:* 800-289-6222. *Fax:* 612-343-4146. *E-mail:* admissions@northcentral.edu.

Oak Hills Christian College

Bemidji, Minnesota
http://www.oakhills.edu/

CONTACT
Shelly Fast, Assistant Director of Admissions, Oak Hills Christian College, 1600 Oak Hills Road SW, Bemidji, MN 56601. *Phone:* 218-751-8670 Ext. 1285. *Toll-free phone:* 888-751-8670 Ext. 1285. *Fax:* 218-751-8825. *E-mail:* admissions@oakhills.edu.

Rasmussen College Blaine

Blaine, Minnesota
http://www.rasmussen.edu/
- **Proprietary** 4-year, part of Rasmussen College System
- **Suburban** campus with easy access to Minneapolis-St. Paul
- **Coed**
- **Minimally difficult** entrance level

FACULTY
Student/faculty ratio: 22:1.

ACADEMICS
Calendar: quarters. *Degrees:* certificates, diplomas, associate, and bachelor's.
Library: Rasmussen College Library - Blaine.

STUDENT LIFE
Housing options: college housing not available.

COSTS
Costs (2017–18) *Tuition:* $11,055 full-time, $290 per credit hour part-time. Full-time tuition and fees vary according to course level, course load, degree level, location, and program. Part-time tuition and fees vary according to course level, course load, degree level, location, and program. No tuition increase for student's term of enrollment. *Required fees:* $1695 full-time, $44 per credit hour part-time. *Payment plans:* installment, deferred payment.

APPLYING
Standardized Tests *Required:* institutional exam (for admission).
Options: electronic application, early admission, deferred entrance.
Required: high school transcript, minimum 2.0 GPA. *Required for some:* interview.

CONTACT
Ms. Susan Hammerstrom, Director of Admissions, Rasmussen College Blaine, 3629 95th Avenue NE, Blaine, MN 55014. *Phone:* 763-795-4720. *Toll-free phone:* 888-549-6755. *E-mail:* susan.hammerstrom@rasmussen.edu.

Rasmussen College Bloomington

Bloomington, Minnesota
http://www.rasmussen.edu/
- **Proprietary** 4-year, founded 1904, part of Rasmussen College System
- **Suburban** campus with easy access to Minneapolis-St. Paul
- **Coed** 997 undergraduate students, 93% full-time, 81% women, 19% men
- **Minimally difficult** entrance level, 92% of applicants were admitted

UNDERGRAD STUDENTS
923 full-time, 74 part-time.

Freshmen:
Admission: 26 applied, 24 admitted, 24 enrolled.

FACULTY
Student/faculty ratio: 22:1.

ACADEMICS
Calendar: quarters. *Degrees:* certificates, diplomas, associate, bachelor's, master's, and postbachelor's certificates.

Special study options: academic remediation for entering students, accelerated degree program, adult/continuing education programs, distance learning, double majors, internships, part-time degree program, summer session for credit.

Computers: 68 computers/terminals are available on campus for general student use. Students can access the following: computer help desk, free student e-mail accounts, online (class) grades, online (class) schedules. Campuswide network is available. Wireless service is available via entire campus.
Library: Rasmussen College Library - Bloomington.

STUDENT LIFE
Housing options: college housing not available.

COSTS & FINANCIAL AID
Costs (2017–18) *Tuition:* $11,055 full-time, $290 per credit hour part-time. Full-time tuition and fees vary according to course level, course load, degree level, location, and program. Part-time tuition and fees vary according to course level, course load, degree level, location, and program. No tuition increase for student's term of enrollment. *Required fees:* $1695 full-time, $44 per credit hour part-time. *Payment plans:* installment, deferred payment. *Waivers:* employees or children of employees.

Financial Aid Of all full-time matriculated undergraduates who enrolled in 2016, 3 state and other part-time jobs (averaging $4338).

APPLYING
Standardized Tests *Required:* institutional exam (for admission).
Options: electronic application, early admission, deferred entrance.
Required: high school transcript, minimum 2.0 GPA. *Required for some:* interview.

Application deadlines: rolling (freshmen), rolling (transfers).

CONTACT
Dwayne Bertotto, Vice President of Admissions and Student Experience, Rasmussen College Bloomington, 8300 Norman Center Drive, Suite 300, Bloomington, MN 55437. *Phone:* 952-806-3958. *Toll-free phone:* 888-549-6755. *E-mail:* dwayne.bertotto@rasmussen.edu.

Rasmussen College Brooklyn Park

Brooklyn Park, Minnesota
http://www.rasmussen.edu/
- **Proprietary** 4-year, part of Rasmussen College System
- **Suburban** campus with easy access to Minneapolis-St. Paul
- **Coed** 568 undergraduate students, 81% full-time, 79% women, 21% men
- **Minimally difficult** entrance level, 79% of applicants were admitted

UNDERGRAD STUDENTS
458 full-time, 110 part-time.

Freshmen:
Admission: 47 applied, 37 admitted, 37 enrolled.

FACULTY
Total: 53, 23% full-time.
Student/faculty ratio: 22:1.

ACADEMICS
Calendar: quarters. *Degrees:* certificates, diplomas, associate, and bachelor's.

Special study options: academic remediation for entering students, accelerated degree program, adult/continuing education programs, distance learning, double majors, internships, part-time degree program, summer session for credit.

Computers: 80 computers/terminals are available on campus for general student use. Students can access the following: computer help desk, free student e-mail accounts, online (class) grades, online (class) schedules. Campuswide network is available. Wireless service is available via entire campus.

Library: Rasmussen College Library - Brooklyn Park.

STUDENT LIFE
Housing options: college housing not available.

COSTS
Costs (2017–18) *Tuition:* $11,055 full-time, $290 per credit hour part-time. Full-time tuition and fees vary according to course level, course load, degree level, location, and program. Part-time tuition and fees vary according to course level, course load, degree level, location, and program. No tuition increase for student's term of enrollment. *Required fees:* $1695 full-time, $44 per credit hour part-time. *Payment plans:* installment, deferred payment. *Waivers:* employees or children of employees.

APPLYING
Standardized Tests *Required:* institutional exam (for admission).
Options: electronic application, early admission, deferred entrance.
Required: high school transcript, minimum 2.0 GPA. *Required for some:* interview.
Application deadlines: rolling (freshmen), rolling (transfers).

CONTACT
Dwayne Bertotto, Vice President of Admissions and Student Experience, Rasmussen College Brooklyn Park, 8300 Norman Center Drive, Suite 300, Bloomington, MN 55437. *Phone:* 952-806-3958. *Toll-free phone:* 888-549-6755. *E-mail:* dwayne.bertotto@rasmussen.edu.

Rasmussen College Eagan

Eagan, Minnesota

http://www.rasmussen.edu/
- **Proprietary** 4-year, founded 1904, part of Rasmussen College System
- **Suburban** campus with easy access to Minneapolis-St. Paul
- **Coed** 506 undergraduate students, 77% full-time, 72% women, 28% men
- **Minimally difficult** entrance level, 93% of applicants were admitted

UNDERGRAD STUDENTS
389 full-time, 117 part-time.

Freshmen:
Admission: 27 applied, 25 admitted, 25 enrolled.

FACULTY
Total: 83, 13% full-time.
Student/faculty ratio: 22:1.

ACADEMICS
Calendar: quarters. *Degrees:* certificates, diplomas, associate, bachelor's, and postbachelor's certificates.
Special study options: academic remediation for entering students, accelerated degree program, adult/continuing education programs, distance learning, double majors, internships, part-time degree program, summer session for credit.
Computers: 93 computers/terminals are available on campus for general student use. Students can access the following: computer help desk, free student e-mail accounts, online (class) grades, online (class) schedules. Campuswide network is available. Wireless service is available via entire campus.
Library: Rasmussen College Library - Eagan.

STUDENT LIFE
Housing options: college housing not available.

COSTS
Costs (2017–18) *Tuition:* $11,055 full-time, $290 per credit hour part-time. Full-time tuition and fees vary according to course level, course load, degree level, location, and program. Part-time tuition and fees vary according to course level, course load, degree level, location, and program. No tuition increase for student's term of enrollment. *Required fees:* $1695 full-time, $44 per credit hour part-time. *Payment plans:* installment, deferred payment. *Waivers:* employees or children of employees.

APPLYING
Standardized Tests *Required:* institutional exam (for admission).
Options: electronic application, early admission, deferred entrance.

Required: high school transcript, minimum 2.0 GPA. *Required for some:* interview.
Application deadlines: rolling (freshmen), rolling (transfers).

CONTACT
Mr. Dwayne Bertotto, Vice President of Admissions and Student Experience, Rasmussen College Eagan, 8300 Norman Center Drive, Suite 300, Bloomington, MN 55437. *Phone:* 952-806-3958. *Toll-free phone:* 888-549-6755. *E-mail:* dwayne.bertotto@rasmussen.edu.

Rasmussen College Lake Elmo/Woodbury

Lake Elmo, Minnesota

http://www.rasmussen.edu/
- **Proprietary** 4-year, part of Rasmussen College System
- **Suburban** campus with easy access to Minneapolis-St. Paul
- **Coed**
- **Minimally difficult** entrance level

FACULTY
Student/faculty ratio: 22:1.

ACADEMICS
Calendar: quarters. *Degrees:* certificates, diplomas, associate, and bachelor's.
Library: Rasmussen College Library - Lake Elmo.

STUDENT LIFE
Housing options: college housing not available.

COSTS
Costs (2017–18) *Tuition:* $11,055 full-time, $290 per credit hour part-time. Full-time tuition and fees vary according to course level, course load, degree level, location, and program. Part-time tuition and fees vary according to course level, course load, degree level, location, and program. No tuition increase for student's term of enrollment. *Required fees:* $1695 full-time, $44 per credit hour part-time. *Payment plans:* installment, deferred payment.

APPLYING
Standardized Tests *Required:* institutional exam (for admission).
Options: electronic application, early admission, deferred entrance.
Required: high school transcript, minimum 2.0 GPA. *Required for some:* interview.

CONTACT
Ms. Susan Hammerstrom, Director of Admissions, Rasmussen College Lake Elmo/Woodbury, 8565 Eagle Point Circle, Lake Elmo, MN 55042. *Phone:* 651-259-6600. *Toll-free phone:* 888-549-6755. *E-mail:* susan.hammerstrom@rasmussen.edu.

Rasmussen College Mankato

Mankato, Minnesota

http://www.rasmussen.edu/
- **Proprietary** 4-year, founded 1904, part of Rasmussen College System
- **Suburban** campus with easy access to Minneapolis-St. Paul
- **Coed** 682 undergraduate students, 88% full-time, 82% women, 18% men
- **Minimally difficult** entrance level, 86% of applicants were admitted

UNDERGRAD STUDENTS
597 full-time, 85 part-time.

Freshmen:
Admission: 37 applied, 32 admitted, 32 enrolled.

FACULTY
Total: 62, 29% full-time.
Student/faculty ratio: 22:1.

ACADEMICS
Calendar: quarters. *Degrees:* certificates, diplomas, associate, bachelor's, master's, and postbachelor's certificates.
Special study options: academic remediation for entering students, accelerated degree program, adult/continuing education programs,

distance learning, double majors, internships, part-time degree program, summer session for credit.

Computers: 116 computers/terminals are available on campus for general student use. Students can access the following: computer help desk, free student e-mail accounts, online (class) grades, online (class) schedules. Campuswide network is available. Wireless service is available via entire campus.
Library: Rasmussen College Library - Mankato.

STUDENT LIFE
Housing options: college housing not available.

COSTS & FINANCIAL AID
Costs (2017–18) *Tuition:* $11,055 full-time, $290 per credit hour part-time. Full-time tuition and fees vary according to course level, course load, degree level, location, and program. Part-time tuition and fees vary according to course level, course load, degree level, location, and program. No tuition increase for student's term of enrollment. *Required fees:* $1695 full-time, $44 per credit hour part-time. *Payment plans:* installment, deferred payment. *Waivers:* employees or children of employees.

Financial Aid Of all full-time matriculated undergraduates who enrolled in 2016, 15 Federal Work-Study jobs (averaging $4000). 13 state and other part-time jobs (averaging $4000).

APPLYING
Standardized Tests *Required:* institutional exam (for admission).
Options: electronic application, early admission, deferred entrance.
Required: high school transcript, minimum 2.0 GPA. *Required for some:* interview.
Application deadlines: rolling (freshmen), rolling (transfers).

CONTACT
Mr. Dwayne Bertotto, Vice President of Admissions and Student Experience, Rasmussen College Mankato, 1400 Madison Avenue, Mankato, MN 56001. *Phone:* 952-806-3958. *Toll-free phone:* 888-549-6755. *E-mail:* dwayne.bertto@rasmussen.edu.

Rasmussen College Moorhead

Moorhead, Minnesota
http://www.rasmussen.edu/

- **Proprietary** 4-year, part of Rasmussen College System
- **Suburban** campus
- **Coed**
- **Minimally difficult** entrance level

FACULTY
Student/faculty ratio: 22:1.

ACADEMICS
Calendar: quarters. *Degrees:* certificates, diplomas, associate, and bachelor's.
Library: Rasmussen College Library - Moorhead.

STUDENT LIFE
Housing options: college housing not available.

COSTS
Costs (2017–18) *Tuition:* $11,055 full-time, $290 per credit hour part-time. Full-time tuition and fees vary according to course level, course load, degree level, location, and program. Part-time tuition and fees vary according to course level, course load, degree level, location, and program. No tuition increase for student's term of enrollment. *Required fees:* $1695 full-time, $44 per credit hour part-time. *Payment plans:* installment, deferred payment.

APPLYING
Standardized Tests *Required:* institutional exam (for admission).
Options: electronic application, early admission, deferred entrance.
Required: high school transcript, minimum 2.0 GPA. *Required for some:* interview.

CONTACT
Ms. Susan Hammerstrom, Director of Admissions, Rasmussen College Moorhead, 1250 29th Avenue South, Moorhead, MN 56560. *Phone:* 218-

304-6200. *Toll-free phone:* 888-549-6755. *E-mail:* susan.hammerstrom@rasmussen.edu.

Rasmussen College St. Cloud

St. Cloud, Minnesota
http://www.rasmussen.edu/

- **Proprietary** 4-year, founded 1904, part of Rasmussen College System
- **Suburban** campus
- **Coed** 765 undergraduate students, 87% full-time, 85% women, 15% men
- **Minimally difficult** entrance level, 92% of applicants were admitted

UNDERGRAD STUDENTS
665 full-time, 100 part-time.

Freshmen:
Admission: 37 applied, 34 admitted, 34 enrolled.

FACULTY
Total: 62, 26% full-time.
Student/faculty ratio: 22:1.

ACADEMICS
Calendar: quarters. *Degrees:* certificates, diplomas, associate, bachelor's, master's, and postbachelor's certificates.

Special study options: academic remediation for entering students, accelerated degree program, adult/continuing education programs, distance learning, double majors, internships, part-time degree program, summer session for credit.

Computers: 91 computers/terminals are available on campus for general student use. Students can access the following: computer help desk, free student e-mail accounts, online (class) grades, online (class) schedules. Campuswide network is available. Wireless service is available via entire campus.
Library: Rasmussen College Library - St. Cloud.

STUDENT LIFE
Housing options: college housing not available.

COSTS & FINANCIAL AID
Costs (2017–18) *Tuition:* $11,055 full-time, $290 per credit hour part-time. Full-time tuition and fees vary according to course level, course load, degree level, location, and program. Part-time tuition and fees vary according to course level, course load, degree level, location, and program. No tuition increase for student's term of enrollment. *Required fees:* $1695 full-time, $44 per credit hour part-time. *Payment plans:* installment, deferred payment. *Waivers:* employees or children of employees.

Financial Aid Of all full-time matriculated undergraduates who enrolled in 2016, 34 Federal Work-Study jobs (averaging $866). 51 state and other part-time jobs (averaging $700).

APPLYING
Standardized Tests *Required:* institutional exam (for admission).
Options: electronic application, early admission, deferred entrance.
Required: high school transcript, minimum 2.0 GPA. *Required for some:* interview.

Application deadlines: rolling (freshmen), rolling (transfers).

CONTACT
Dwayne Bertotto, Vice President of Admissions and Student Experience, Rasmussen College St. Cloud, 8300 Norman Center Drive, Suite 300, Bloomington, MN 55437. *Phone:* 952-806-3958. *Toll-free phone:* 888-549-6755. *E-mail:* dwayne.bertotto@rasmussen.edu.

Rochester Community and Technical College

Rochester, Minnesota
http://www.rctc.edu/

CONTACT
Mr. Troy Tynsky, Director of Admissions, Rochester Community and Technical College, 851 30th Avenue, SE, Rochester, MN 55904-4999. *Phone:* 507-280-3509.

St. Catherine University

St. Paul, Minnesota

http://www.stkate.edu/

- **Independent Roman Catholic** comprehensive, founded 1905
- **Urban** 110-acre campus with easy access to Minneapolis-St. Paul
- **Undergraduate: women only; graduate: coed** 5,258 undergraduate students, 40% full-time, 98% women, 2% men
- **Moderately difficult** entrance level, 70% of applicants were admitted

UNDERGRAD STUDENTS

2,124 full-time, 3,134 part-time. 12% are from out of state; 10% Black or African American, non-Hispanic/Latino; 9% Hispanic/Latino; 11% Asian, non-Hispanic/Latino; 0.2% Native Hawaiian or other Pacific Islander, non-Hispanic/Latino; 0.4% American Indian or Alaska Native, non-Hispanic/Latino; 4% Two or more races, non-Hispanic/Latino; 3% Race/ethnicity unknown; 0.7% international; 11% transferred in; 38% live on campus.

Freshmen:

Admission: 2,682 applied, 1,881 admitted, 399 enrolled. *Average high school GPA:* 3.6. *Test scores:* SAT evidence-based reading and writing scores over 500: 100%; SAT math scores over 500: 88%; ACT scores over 18: 95%; SAT evidence-based reading and writing scores over 600: 59%; SAT math scores over 600: 41%; ACT scores over 24: 47%; SAT evidence-based reading and writing scores over 700: 12%; SAT math scores over 700: 12%; ACT scores over 30: 8%.

Retention: 81% of full-time freshmen returned.

FACULTY

Total: 536, 54% full-time, 43% with terminal degrees.

Student/faculty ratio: 10:1.

ACADEMICS

Calendar: 4-1-4. *Degrees:* certificates, associate, bachelor's, master's, doctoral, and postbachelor's certificates.

Special study options: adult/continuing education programs, distance learning, double majors, honors programs, independent study, internships, part-time degree program, student-designed majors, study abroad. *ROTC:* Army (c), Air Force (c).

Computers: Students can access the following: campus intranet, computer help desk, free student e-mail accounts, online (class) grades, online (class) registration, online (class) schedules, transcript. Campuswide network is available. Wireless service is available via entire campus.

Library: St. Catherine Library.

STUDENT LIFE

Housing options: women-only. Campus housing is university owned. Freshman campus housing is guaranteed.

Activities and organizations: drama/theater group, student-run newspaper, radio station, choral group.

Athletics Member NCAA. All Division III. *Intercollegiate sports:* basketball W, cross-country running W, ice hockey W, soccer W, softball W, swimming and diving W, tennis W, track and field W, volleyball W. *Intramural sports:* basketball W, cheerleading W, cross-country running W, football W, golf W, lacrosse W, racquetball W, soccer W, softball W, swimming and diving W, tennis W, track and field W, volleyball W.

Campus security: 24-hour emergency response devices and patrols, student patrols, late-night transport/escort service, controlled dormitory access.

COSTS & FINANCIAL AID

Costs (2017–18) *Comprehensive fee:* $47,545 includes full-time tuition ($37,590), mandatory fees ($759), and room and board ($9196). Full-time tuition and fees vary according to degree level. Part-time tuition: $1253 per credit hour. Part-time tuition and fees vary according to degree level. *Required fees:* $322 per term part-time. *College room only:* $5400. Room and board charges vary according to board plan and housing facility. *Payment plan:* installment. *Waivers:* senior citizens and employees or children of employees.

Financial Aid Of all full-time matriculated undergraduates who enrolled in 2017, 1,740 applied for aid, 1,500 were judged to have need, 580 had their need fully met. In 2017, 238 non-need-based awards were made. *Average percent of need met:* 90. *Average financial aid package:*

$36,000. *Average need-based loan:* $5200. *Average need-based gift aid:* $9600. *Average non-need-based aid:* $19,000. *Average indebtedness upon graduation:* $38,199.

APPLYING

Standardized Tests *Required:* SAT or ACT (for admission).

Options: deferred entrance.

Required: high school transcript, 1 letter of recommendation. *Required for some:* essay or personal statement, interview. *Recommended:* interview.

CONTACT

Associate Director of Admission and Financial Aid, St. Catherine University, 2004 Randolph Avenue, St. Paul, MN 55105. *Phone:* 651-690-6047. *Toll-free phone:* 800-945-4599. *E-mail:* stkate@stkate.edu.

St. Cloud State University

St. Cloud, Minnesota

http://www.stcloudstate.edu/

- **State-supported** comprehensive, founded 1869, part of Minnesota State Colleges and Universities System
- **Suburban** 100-acre campus with easy access to Minneapolis-St. Paul
- **Endowment** $24.7 million
- **Coed**
- **Moderately difficult** entrance level

FACULTY

Student/faculty ratio: 20:1.

ACADEMICS

Calendar: semesters. *Degrees:* certificates, diplomas, associate, bachelor's, master's, doctoral, post-master's, and postbachelor's certificates.

Library: James W. Miller Learning Resources Center.

STUDENT LIFE

Housing options: coed, men-only, women-only, special housing for students with disabilities. Campus housing is university owned and leased by the school. Freshman applicants given priority for college housing.

Activities and organizations: drama/theater group, student-run newspaper, radio and television station, choral group, Nepalese Student Association, Residence Hall Association, International Student Association, College Panhellenic Council, KVSC - Campus Radio Station, national fraternities, national sororities.

Athletics Member NCAA. All Division II except men's and women's ice hockey (Division I).

Campus security: 24-hour emergency response devices and patrols, student patrols, late-night transport/escort service.

Student services: health clinic, personal/psychological counseling, women's center, legal services.

COSTS & FINANCIAL AID

Costs (2017–18) *Tuition:* state resident $8228 full-time, $241 per credit hour part-time; nonresident $16,462 full-time, $521 per credit hour part-time. Full-time tuition and fees vary according to course load, location, and reciprocity agreements. Part-time tuition and fees vary according to course load, location, and reciprocity agreements. *Required fees:* $39 per credit hour part-time, $65 per term part-time. *Room and board:* $8558. Room and board charges vary according to board plan and housing facility.

Financial Aid Of all full-time matriculated undergraduates who enrolled in 2015, 6,811 applied for aid, 5,313 were judged to have need, 675 had their need fully met. In 2015, 1496 non-need-based awards were made. *Average percent of need met:* 62. *Average financial aid package:* $9708. *Average need-based loan:* $4094. *Average need-based gift aid:* $5639. *Average non-need-based aid:* $9998. *Average indebtedness upon graduation:* $31,305.

APPLYING

Standardized Tests *Required:* SAT or ACT (for admission).

Options: electronic application, deferred entrance.

Application fee: $20.

Required: high school transcript.

CONTACT
Ms. Amber Schultz, Assistant Vice President for Admissions, Marketing, and Recruitment, St. Cloud State University, 720 4th Avenue South, AS 115, St. Cloud, MN 56301-4498. *Phone:* 320-308-3870. *Toll-free phone:* 877-654-7278. *Fax:* 320-308-2243. *E-mail:* scsu4u@stcloudstate.edu.

Saint John's University

Collegeville, Minnesota

http://www.csbsju.edu/

- **Independent Roman Catholic** comprehensive, founded 1857
- **Rural** 2500-acre campus with easy access to Minneapolis-St. Paul
- **Endowment** $179.7 million
- **Undergraduate: men only; graduate: coed** 1,720 undergraduate students, 99% full-time, 100% men
- **Moderately difficult** entrance level, 90% of applicants were admitted

UNDERGRAD STUDENTS

1,703 full-time, 17 part-time. Students come from 36 states and territories; 13 other countries; 20% are from out of state; 5% Black or African American, non-Hispanic/Latino; 8% Hispanic/Latino; 3% Asian, non-Hispanic/Latino; 0.5% Native Hawaiian or other Pacific Islander, non-Hispanic/Latino; 0.7% American Indian or Alaska Native, non-Hispanic/Latino; 0.1% Two or more races, non-Hispanic/Latino; 5% international; 1% transferred in; 91% live on campus.

Freshmen:
Admission: 1,461 applied, 1,315 admitted, 465 enrolled. *Average high school GPA:* 3.5. *Test scores:* ACT scores over 18: 100%; ACT scores over 24: 62%; ACT scores over 30: 16%.

Retention: 88% of full-time freshmen returned.

FACULTY
Total: 157, 83% full-time, 76% with terminal degrees.
Student/faculty ratio: 12:1.

ACADEMICS
Calendar: semesters. *Degrees:* bachelor's and master's (coordinate with College of Saint Benedict for women).

Special study options: advanced placement credit, double majors, English as a second language, honors programs, independent study, internships, off-campus study, services for LD students, student-designed majors, study abroad. *ROTC:* Army (b).

Computers: 275 computers/terminals and 4,600 ports are available on campus for general student use. Students can access the following: campus intranet, computer help desk, free student e-mail accounts, online (class) grades, online (class) registration, online (class) schedules, online student accounts. Campuswide network is available. 100% of college-owned or -operated housing units are wired for high-speed Internet access. Wireless service is available via entire campus.

Library: Alcuin Library plus 2 others. *Books:* 680,763 (physical), 641,295 (digital/electronic); *Serial titles:* 326 (physical), 44,640 (digital/electronic); *Databases:* 226. Weekly public service hours: 104; students can reserve study rooms.

STUDENT LIFE
Housing options: on-campus residence required through senior year; men-only, special housing for students with disabilities. Campus housing is university owned. Freshman campus housing is guaranteed.

Activities and organizations: drama/theater group, student-run newspaper, radio and television station, choral group, Joint Events Council, Hmong Americans Involving Students, Magis Ministries, Enactus, Archipelago Association.

Athletics Member NCAA. All Division III. *Intercollegiate sports:* baseball M, basketball M, crew M(c), cross-country running M, football M, golf M, ice hockey M, lacrosse M(c), riflery M(c), rugby M(c), skiing (cross-country) M(c), soccer M, swimming and diving M, tennis M, track and field M, ultimate Frisbee M(c), volleyball M(c), water polo M(c), wrestling M. *Intramural sports:* basketball M, football M, racquetball M, soccer M, softball M, ultimate Frisbee M, volleyball M.

Campus security: 24-hour emergency response devices and patrols, student patrols, late-night transport/escort service, controlled dormitory access, well-lit pathways, 911 center on campus.

Student services: health clinic, personal/psychological counseling.

COSTS & FINANCIAL AID
Costs (2017–18) *Comprehensive fee:* $53,472 includes full-time tuition ($42,574), mandatory fees ($782), and room and board ($10,116). Part-time tuition: $1774 per credit hour. Part-time tuition and fees vary according to course load. *College room only:* $5070. Room and board charges vary according to board plan and housing facility. *Payment plan:* installment. *Waivers:* employees or children of employees.

Financial Aid Of all full-time matriculated undergraduates who enrolled in 2017, 1,340 applied for aid, 1,178 were judged to have need, 384 had their need fully met. 171 Federal Work-Study jobs (averaging $3400). 875 state and other part-time jobs (averaging $3400). In 2017, 430 non-need-based awards were made. *Average percent of need met:* 90. *Average financial aid package:* $33,379. *Average need-based loan:* $3296. *Average need-based gift aid:* $29,686. *Average non-need-based aid:* $17,270. *Average indebtedness upon graduation:* $41,698.

APPLYING
Standardized Tests *Required:* SAT or ACT (for admission).

Options: electronic application, early action, deferred entrance.

Required: high school transcript, college preparatory program. *Recommended:* minimum 3.0 GPA.

Application deadlines: rolling (transfers), 11/15 (early action).

Notification: continuous (transfers), 12/15 (early action).

CONTACT
Mr. Matt Beirne, Director of Admission, Saint John's University, 2850 Abbey Plaza, Collegeville, MN 56321-7155. *Phone:* 320-363-5060. *Toll-free phone:* 800-544-1489. *Fax:* 320-363-3206. *E-mail:* admissions@csbsju.edu.

Saint Mary's University of Minnesota

Winona, Minnesota

http://www.smumn.edu/

- **Independent Roman Catholic** comprehensive, founded 1912
- **Small-town** 350-acre campus
- **Coed** 1,503 undergraduate students, 75% full-time, 53% women, 47% men
- **Moderately difficult** entrance level, 64% of applicants were admitted

UNDERGRAD STUDENTS

1,129 full-time, 374 part-time. Students come from 31 states and territories; 15 other countries; 45% are from out of state; 8% Black or African American, non-Hispanic/Latino; 8% Hispanic/Latino; 3% Asian, non-Hispanic/Latino; 0.1% Native Hawaiian or other Pacific Islander, non-Hispanic/Latino; 0.5% American Indian or Alaska Native, non-Hispanic/Latino; 0.7% Two or more races, non-Hispanic/Latino; 11% Race/ethnicity unknown; 3% international; 8% transferred in; 93% live on campus.

Freshmen:
Admission: 2,417 applied, 1,556 admitted, 300 enrolled. *Average high school GPA:* 3.4. *Test scores:* SAT evidence-based reading and writing scores over 500: 76%; SAT math scores over 500: 68%; ACT scores over 18: 90%; SAT evidence-based reading and writing scores over 600: 28%; SAT math scores over 600: 28%; ACT scores over 24: 43%; ACT scores over 30: 8%.

Retention: 77% of full-time freshmen returned.

FACULTY
Total: 471, 21% full-time, 49% with terminal degrees.
Student/faculty ratio: 18:1.

ACADEMICS
Calendar: semesters. *Degrees:* certificates, diplomas, bachelor's, master's, doctoral, post-master's, and postbachelor's certificates.

Special study options: academic remediation for entering students, accelerated degree program, adult/continuing education programs, advanced placement credit, cooperative education, distance learning, double majors, English as a second language, honors programs, independent study, internships, off-campus study, part-time degree program, services for LD students, student-designed majors, study abroad, summer session for credit. *ROTC:* Army (c).

Computers: 200 computers/terminals and 50 ports are available on campus for general student use. Students can access the following:

campus intranet, computer help desk, free student e-mail accounts, online (class) grades, online (class) registration, online (class) schedules. Campuswide network is available. 100% of college-owned or -operated housing units are wired for high-speed Internet access. Wireless service is available via computer centers, computer labs, dorm rooms, libraries, student centers.

Library: Fitzgerald Library plus 1 other. *Books:* 210,639 (physical), 10,144 (digital/electronic); *Serial titles:* 169 (physical), 82,154 (digital/electronic); *Databases:* 77. Weekly public service hours: 97; students can reserve study rooms.

STUDENT LIFE

Housing options: on-campus residence required through sophomore year; coed, men-only, women-only, special housing for students with disabilities. Campus housing is university owned. Freshman campus housing is guaranteed.

Activities and organizations: drama/theater group, student-run newspaper, radio station, choral group, Student Activity Committee, PR Business Club, Serving Others United in Love (Soul) - Mission Trips, Colleges Against Cancer, Club Hockey, national fraternities, national sororities.

Athletics Member NCAA. All Division III. *Intercollegiate sports:* baseball M, basketball M/W, cross-country running M/W, golf M/W, ice hockey M/W, soccer M/W, softball W, swimming and diving M/W, tennis M/W, track and field M/W, volleyball W. *Intramural sports:* basketball M/W, cheerleading W(c), fencing M(c)/W(c), field hockey M/W, football M/W, ice hockey M, lacrosse M(c)/W(c), rugby M(c), skiing (downhill) M(c)/W(c), soccer M/W, softball M/W, tennis M/W, ultimate Frisbee M/W, volleyball M/W, water polo M(c)/W(c).

Campus security: 24-hour emergency response devices and patrols, late-night transport/escort service, controlled dormitory access.

Student services: health clinic, personal/psychological counseling.

COSTS & FINANCIAL AID

Costs (2018–19) *Comprehensive fee:* $44,220 includes full-time tuition ($34,500), mandatory fees ($640), and room and board ($9080). Full-time tuition and fees vary according to course load and location. Part-time tuition: $1150 per credit. Part-time tuition and fees vary according to course load and location. *College room only:* $5080. Room and board charges vary according to board plan and housing facility. *Payment plan:* installment. *Waivers:* employees or children of employees.

Financial Aid Of all full-time matriculated undergraduates who enrolled in 2017, 835 applied for aid, 825 were judged to have need, 143 had their need fully met. In 2017, 84 non-need-based awards were made. *Average percent of need met:* 74. *Average financial aid package:* $27,927. *Average need-based loan:* $4311. *Average need-based gift aid:* $18,713. *Average non-need-based aid:* $20,405. *Average indebtedness upon graduation:* $39,917.

APPLYING

Standardized Tests *Required:* SAT or ACT (for admission).

Options: electronic application, early admission, deferred entrance.

Application fee: $25.

Required: essay or personal statement, high school transcript, minimum 2.5 GPA. *Required for some:* interview. *Recommended:* 2 letters of recommendation.

Application deadlines: 5/1 (freshmen), rolling (transfers).

Notification: continuous (freshmen), continuous (transfers).

CONTACT

Mr. Dan Meyer, Vice President for Enrollment, Saint Mary's University of Minnesota, 700 Terrace Heights, Winona, MN 55987. *Phone:* 507-457-1700. *Toll-free phone:* 800-635-5987. *Fax:* 507-457-1722. *E-mail:* dmeyer@smumn.edu.

St. Olaf College
Northfield, Minnesota
http://www.stolaf.edu/

- **Independent Lutheran** 4-year, founded 1874
- **Small-town** 300-acre campus with easy access to Minneapolis-St. Paul
- **Endowment** $498.7 million
- **Coed** 3,035 undergraduate students, 99% full-time, 58% women, 42% men
- **Very difficult** entrance level, 43% of applicants were admitted

UNDERGRAD STUDENTS

3,003 full-time, 32 part-time. Students come from 49 states and territories; 79 other countries; 53% are from out of state; 3% Black or African American, non-Hispanic/Latino; 6% Hispanic/Latino; 7% Asian, non-Hispanic/Latino; 0.1% Native Hawaiian or other Pacific Islander, non-Hispanic/Latino; 3% Two or more races, non-Hispanic/Latino; 0.8% Race/ethnicity unknown; 10% international; 0.8% transferred in; 95% live on campus.

Freshmen:
Admission: 5,949 applied, 2,571 admitted, 786 enrolled. *Average high school GPA:* 3.6. *Test scores:* SAT evidence-based reading and writing scores over 500: 94%; SAT math scores over 500: 93%; ACT scores over 18: 100%; SAT evidence-based reading and writing scores over 600: 70%; SAT math scores over 600: 64%; ACT scores over 24: 87%; SAT evidence-based reading and writing scores over 700: 24%; SAT math scores over 700: 31%; ACT scores over 30: 44%.

Retention: 92% of full-time freshmen returned.

FACULTY
Total: 320, 65% full-time, 83% with terminal degrees.

Student/faculty ratio: 12:1.

ACADEMICS
Calendar: 4-1-4. *Degree:* bachelor's.

Special study options: advanced placement credit, double majors, English as a second language, independent study, internships, off-campus study, part-time degree program, services for LD students, student-designed majors, study abroad, summer session for credit.

Unusual degree programs: 3-2 engineering with Washington University in St. Louis.

Computers: 840 computers/terminals and 3,300 ports are available on campus for general student use. Students can access the following: campus intranet, computer help desk, free student e-mail accounts, online (class) grades, online (class) registration, online (class) schedules. Campuswide network is available. 100% of college-owned or -operated housing units are wired for high-speed Internet access. Wireless service is available via entire campus.

Library: Rolvaag Memorial Library plus 1 other. *Books:* 610,051 (physical), 606,055 (digital/electronic); *Serial titles:* 3,347 (physical), 119,677 (digital/electronic); *Databases:* 349. Weekly public service hours: 112.

STUDENT LIFE

Housing options: on-campus residence required through senior year; coed, special housing for students with disabilities. Campus housing is university owned. Freshman campus housing is guaranteed.

Activities and organizations: drama/theater group, student-run newspaper, radio station, choral group, Student Government Association, Ultimate Frisbee Teams, Ole Spring Relief, Alpha Phi Omega, SARN: Sexual Assault Resource Network.

Athletics Member NCAA. All Division III. *Intercollegiate sports:* baseball M, basketball M/W, cross-country running M/W, football M, golf M/W, ice hockey M/W, skiing (cross-country) M/W, skiing (downhill) M/W, soccer M/W, softball W, swimming and diving M/W, tennis M/W, track and field M/W, volleyball W, wrestling M. *Intramural sports:* badminton M(c)/W(c), basketball M/W, bowling M/W, equestrian sports M(c)/W(c), football M/W, ice hockey M(c), lacrosse M(c)/W(c), rowing M(c)/W(c), rugby M(c)/W(c), sand volleyball M/W, soccer M/W, softball M/W, table tennis M/W, tennis M/W, triathlon M/W, ultimate Frisbee M/W, volleyball M(c)/W, water polo M/W.

Campus security: 24-hour emergency response devices and patrols, late-night transport/escort service, controlled dormitory access, lighted pathways and sidewalks, first-year only dorms.

Student services: health clinic, personal/psychological counseling.

COSTS & FINANCIAL AID

Costs (2018–19) *Comprehensive fee:* $53,040 includes full-time tuition ($47,840) and room and board ($5200). Part-time tuition: $5980 per course. Part-time tuition and fees vary according to course load. *College room only:* $5650. Room and board charges vary according to board plan. *Payment plan:* installment. *Waivers:* senior citizens and employees or children of employees.

Financial Aid Of all full-time matriculated undergraduates who enrolled in 2017, 2,330 applied for aid, 2,203 were judged to have need, 1,622 had their need fully met. 374 Federal Work-Study jobs (averaging $2170). 1,949 state and other part-time jobs (averaging $2133). In 2017, 589 non-need-based awards were made. *Average percent of need met:* 96. *Average financial aid package:* $40,769. *Average need-based loan:* $3167. *Average need-based gift aid:* $33,553. *Average non-need-based aid:* $16,237. *Average indebtedness upon graduation:* $27,002. *Financial aid deadline:* 3/1.

APPLYING

Standardized Tests *Required:* SAT or ACT (for admission).

Options: electronic application, early decision, deferred entrance.

Required: essay or personal statement, high school transcript, 1 letter of recommendation. *Recommended:* 2 letters of recommendation, interview.

Application deadlines: 1/15 (freshmen), 4/1 (transfers).

Early decision deadline: 11/15 (for plan 1), 1/8 (for plan 2).

Notification: 3/20 (freshmen), 5/1 (transfers), 12/15 (early decision plan 1), 2/1 (early decision plan 2).

CONTACT

Dave Wagner, Director of Admissions, St. Olaf College, 1520 St. Olaf Avenue, Northfield, MN 55057. *Phone:* 507-786-3025. *Toll-free phone:* 800-800-3025. *Fax:* 507-786-3832. *E-mail:* admissions@stolaf.edu.

Southwest Minnesota State University

Marshall, Minnesota

http://www.smsu.edu/

CONTACT

Mr. Andrew Hlubeck, Director of Admissions, Southwest Minnesota State University, 1501 State Street, Marshall, MN 56258. *Phone:* 507-537-6286. *Toll-free phone:* 800-642-0684. *Fax:* 507-537-7145. *E-mail:* andrew.hlubek@smsu.edu.

University of Minnesota, Crookston

Crookston, Minnesota

http://www.umcrookston.edu/

- **State-supported** 4-year, founded 1966, part of University of Minnesota System
- **Rural** 237-acre campus
- **Endowment** $15.2 million
- **Coed** 2,823 undergraduate students, 45% full-time, 53% women, 47% men
- **Minimally difficult** entrance level, 78% of applicants were admitted

UNDERGRAD STUDENTS

1,281 full-time, 1,542 part-time. Students come from 45 states and territories; 17 other countries; 30% are from out of state; 7% Black or African American, non-Hispanic/Latino; 4% Hispanic/Latino; 2% Asian, non-Hispanic/Latino; 0.2% Native Hawaiian or other Pacific Islander, non-Hispanic/Latino; 0.4% American Indian or Alaska Native, non-Hispanic/Latino; 2% Two or more races, non-Hispanic/Latino; 2% Race/ethnicity unknown; 5% international; 9% transferred in.

Freshmen:

Admission: 1,073 applied, 839 admitted, 239 enrolled. *Average high school GPA:* 3.2. *Test scores:* ACT scores over 18: 90%; ACT scores over 24: 32%; ACT scores over 30: 4%.

Retention: 65% of full-time freshmen returned.

FACULTY

Total: 116, 61% full-time, 34% with terminal degrees.

Student/faculty ratio: 16:1.

ACADEMICS

Calendar: semesters. *Degree:* bachelor's.

Special study options: academic remediation for entering students, advanced placement credit, cooperative education, distance learning, double majors, English as a second language, honors programs, independent study, internships, off-campus study, part-time degree program, services for LD students, student-designed majors, study abroad, summer session for credit. *ROTC:* Air Force (c).

Computers: 25 computers/terminals are available on campus for general student use. Students can access the following: campus intranet, computer help desk, free student e-mail accounts, online (class) grades, online (class) registration, online (class) schedules, personal Web pages. Campuswide network is available. 100% of college-owned or -operated housing units are wired for high-speed Internet access. Wireless service is available via entire campus.

Library: UMC Library. *Books:* 47,423 (physical), 336,375 (digital/electronic); *Serial titles:* 412 (physical), 8,500 (digital/electronic); *Databases:* 152. Weekly public service hours: 76.

STUDENT LIFE

Housing options: coed, special housing for students with disabilities. Campus housing is university owned. Freshman applicants given priority for college housing.

Activities and organizations: drama/theater group, choral group, National Society for Leadership and Success, Archery Club, Crookston Futbol Club, Choir, Student Athletic Advisory Council, national fraternities.

Athletics Member NCAA. All Division II. *Intercollegiate sports:* baseball M(s), basketball M(s)/W(s), equestrian sports W(s), football M(s), golf M(s)/W(s), soccer W(s), softball W(s), tennis W(s), volleyball W(s). *Intramural sports:* basketball M/W, football M/W, golf M/W, ice hockey M(c), racquetball M/W, soccer M(c)/W, softball M/W, table tennis M/W, tennis M/W, volleyball M/W.

Campus security: 24-hour emergency response devices, student patrols, controlled dormitory access.

Student services: health clinic, personal/psychological counseling, women's center.

COSTS & FINANCIAL AID

Costs (2017–18) *Tuition:* state resident $10,282 full-time, $395 per credit part-time; nonresident $10,282 full-time, $395 per credit part-time. *Required fees:* $1920 full-time, $960 per term part-time. *Room and board:* $7658; room only: $3470. Room and board charges vary according to board plan and housing facility. *Payment plan:* installment. *Waivers:* senior citizens.

Financial Aid Of all full-time matriculated undergraduates who enrolled in 2017, 902 applied for aid, 764 were judged to have need, 212 had their need fully met. In 2017, 72 non-need-based awards were made. *Average percent of need met:* 81. *Average financial aid package:* $13,339. *Average need-based loan:* $4000. *Average need-based gift aid:* $9708. *Average non-need-based aid:* $2466. *Average indebtedness upon graduation:* $26,696.

APPLYING

Standardized Tests *Required:* SAT or ACT (for admission). *Recommended:* ACT (for admission).

Options: electronic application, deferred entrance.

Application fee: $30.

Required: high school transcript, minimum 2.0 GPA, minimum ACT composite score of 21 or SAT of 980.

Application deadlines: rolling (freshmen), rolling (out-of-state freshmen), rolling (transfers).

Notification: continuous (freshmen), continuous (out-of-state freshmen), continuous (transfers).

CONTACT

Michelle Christopherson, Director of Admissions, University of Minnesota, Crookston, 2900 University Avenue, Crookston, MN 56716-5001. *Phone:* 218-281-8679. *Toll-free phone:* 800-862-6466. *E-mail:* mchristo@crk.umn.edu.

University of Minnesota, Duluth

Duluth, Minnesota

http://www.d.umn.edu/

- **State-supported** comprehensive, founded 1947, part of University of Minnesota System
- **Suburban** 250-acre campus
- **Endowment** $161.9 million
- **Coed** 10,135 undergraduate students, 88% full-time, 48% women, 52% men
- **Moderately difficult** entrance level, 77% of applicants were admitted

UNDERGRAD STUDENTS

8,906 full-time, 1,229 part-time. Students come from 40 states and territories; 38 other countries; 12% are from out of state; 2% Black or African American, non-Hispanic/Latino; 3% Hispanic/Latino; 4% Asian, non-Hispanic/Latino; 0.1% Native Hawaiian or other Pacific Islander, non-Hispanic/Latino; 0.4% American Indian or Alaska Native, non-Hispanic/Latino; 3% Two or more races, non-Hispanic/Latino; 0.7% Race/ethnicity unknown; 2% international; 4% transferred in; 32% live on campus.

Freshmen:

Admission: 8,689 applied, 6,660 admitted, 2,275 enrolled. *Average high school GPA:* 3.5. *Test scores:* ACT scores over 18: 98%; ACT scores over 24: 54%; ACT scores over 30: 7%.

Retention: 77% of full-time freshmen returned.

FACULTY

Total: 596, 82% full-time, 66% with terminal degrees.

Student/faculty ratio: 18:1.

ACADEMICS

Calendar: semesters. *Degrees:* certificates, bachelor's, master's, doctoral, and postbachelor's certificates.

Special study options: academic remediation for entering students, adult/continuing education programs, advanced placement credit, distance learning, double majors, English as a second language, honors programs, independent study, internships, off-campus study, part-time degree program, services for LD students, student-designed majors, study abroad, summer session for credit. *ROTC:* Air Force (b).

Computers: 406 computers/terminals are available on campus for general student use. Students can access the following: campus intranet, computer help desk, free student e-mail accounts, online (class) grades, online (class) registration, online (class) schedules. Campuswide network is available. 100% of college-owned or -operated housing units are wired for high-speed Internet access. Wireless service is available via entire campus.

Library: Kathryn A. Martin Library. *Books:* 306,518 (physical), 485,781 (digital/electronic); *Serial titles:* 4,042 (physical), 109,924 (digital/electronic); *Databases:* 150. Weekly public service hours: 94; students can reserve study rooms.

STUDENT LIFE

Housing options: coed, men-only, women-only, special housing for students with disabilities. Campus housing is university owned. Freshman applicants given priority for college housing.

Activities and organizations: drama/theater group, student-run newspaper, radio station, choral group, marching band, UMD Student Association, Newman Catholic Campus Ministries, Panhellenic Council, Coloring Club, Rod and Gun Club at UMD, national fraternities, national sororities.

Athletics Member NCAA. All Division II except men's and women's ice hockey (Division I). *Intercollegiate sports:* badminton M(c)/W(c), baseball M(s), basketball M(s)/W(s), cheerleading W(c), cross-country running M(s)/W(s), football M(s), ice hockey M(s)/W(s), lacrosse M(s)(c)/W(s)(c), rugby M(c)/W(c), skiing (downhill) M(c)/W(c), soccer M(c)/W(c), softball W(s), tennis W(s), track and field M/W, volleyball M(c)/W(s), water polo W. *Intramural sports:* badminton M/W, basketball M/W, bowling M/W, football M/W, golf M/W, ice hockey M/W, rock climbing M(c)/W(c), rowing M(c)/W(c), soccer M/W, softball M/W, swimming and diving M(c)/W(c), table tennis M(c)/W(c), tennis W, ultimate Frisbee M(c)/W(c), volleyball M/W, water polo M(c)/W(c), wrestling M(c).

Campus security: 24-hour emergency response devices and patrols, late-night transport/escort service.

Student services: health clinic, personal/psychological counseling, women's center.

COSTS & FINANCIAL AID

Costs (2017–18) *Tuition:* state resident $12,016 full-time, $462 per credit part-time; nonresident $17,134 full-time, $659 per credit part-time. Full-time tuition and fees vary according to course load, program, and reciprocity agreements. Part-time tuition and fees vary according to course load, program, and reciprocity agreements. *Required fees:* $1328 full-time. *Room and board:* $7608. Room and board charges vary according to board plan and housing facility. *Payment plan:* installment. *Waivers:* children of alumni and employees or children of employees.

Financial Aid Of all full-time matriculated undergraduates who enrolled in 2016, 6,922 applied for aid, 4,894 were judged to have need, 1,321 had their need fully met. 499 Federal Work-Study jobs (averaging $814). 1,340 state and other part-time jobs (averaging $647). In 2016, 1289 non-need-based awards were made. *Average percent of need met:* 72. *Average financial aid package:* $12,652. *Average need-based loan:* $6501. *Average need-based gift aid:* $8032. *Average non-need-based aid:* $2316. *Average indebtedness upon graduation:* $30,445.

APPLYING

Standardized Tests *Required:* SAT or ACT (for admission).

Options: electronic application.

Application fee: $40.

Required: high school transcript. *Required for some:* interview. *Recommended:* essay or personal statement.

Application deadlines: 6/15 (freshmen), 6/15 (transfers).

Notification: continuous until 9/15 (freshmen), continuous (transfers).

CONTACT

Office of Admissions, University of Minnesota, Duluth, 25 Solon Campus Center, 1117 University Drive, Duluth, MN 55812-3000. *Phone:* 218-726-7171. *Toll-free phone:* 800-232-1339. *Fax:* 218-726-7040. *E-mail:* umdadmis@d.umn.edu.

University of Minnesota, Morris

Morris, Minnesota

http://www.morris.umn.edu/

- **State-supported** 4-year, founded 1959, part of University of Minnesota System
- **Rural** 130-acre campus
- **Endowment** $14.6 million
- **Coed** 1,627 undergraduate students, 94% full-time, 56% women, 44% men
- **Moderately difficult** entrance level, 64% of applicants were admitted

UNDERGRAD STUDENTS

1,526 full-time, 101 part-time. Students come from 32 states and territories; 24 other countries; 17% are from out of state; 2% Black or African American, non-Hispanic/Latino; 5% Hispanic/Latino; 3% Asian, non-Hispanic/Latino; 7% American Indian or Alaska Native, non-Hispanic/Latino; 12% Two or more races, non-Hispanic/Latino; 0.7% Race/ethnicity unknown; 12% international; 6% transferred in; 52% live on campus.

Freshmen:

Admission: 3,211 applied, 2,048 admitted, 356 enrolled. *Average high school GPA:* 3.6. *Test scores:* SAT evidence-based reading and writing scores over 500: 96%; SAT math scores over 500: 96%; ACT scores over 18: 97%; SAT evidence-based reading and writing scores over 600: 52%; SAT math scores over 600: 60%; ACT scores over 24: 61%; SAT evidence-based reading and writing scores over 700: 20%; SAT math scores over 700: 40%; ACT scores over 30: 16%.

Retention: 80% of full-time freshmen returned.

FACULTY

Total: 165, 76% full-time, 82% with terminal degrees.

Student/faculty ratio: 11:1.

ACADEMICS

Calendar: semesters. *Degree:* bachelor's.

Special study options: advanced placement credit, distance learning, double majors, English as a second language, freshman honors college, honors programs, independent study, internships, off-campus study, part-time degree program, services for LD students, student-designed majors, study abroad, summer session for credit.

Unusual degree programs: 3-2 engineering with University of Minnesota, Twin Cities Campus.

Computers: 350 computers/terminals and 548 ports are available on campus for general student use. Students can access the following: campus intranet, computer help desk, free student e-mail accounts, online (class) grades, online (class) registration, online (class) schedules. Campuswide network is available. 100% of college-owned or -operated housing units are wired for high-speed Internet access. Wireless service is available via classrooms, computer labs, dorm rooms, learning centers, libraries, student centers.

Library: Rodney A. Briggs Library plus 1 other. *Books:* 227,324 (physical), 184,220 (digital/electronic); *Serial titles:* 145 (physical), 81,647 (digital/electronic); *Databases:* 154. Weekly public service hours: 99.

STUDENT LIFE

Housing options: coed, special housing for students with disabilities. Campus housing is university owned. Freshman campus housing is guaranteed.

Activities and organizations: drama/theater group, student-run newspaper, radio station, choral group, Student Radio Station, Inter-Varsity Christian Fellowship, Jazz Ensemble/Concert Choir, Big Friend, Little Friend, Student Newspaper.

Athletics Member NCAA. All Division III. *Intercollegiate sports:* baseball M, basketball M/W, cross-country running M/W, football M, golf M/W, soccer M/W, softball W, swimming and diving W, tennis M/W, track and field M/W, volleyball W. *Intramural sports:* baseball M/W, basketball M/W, bowling M/W, cheerleading M(c)/W(c), equestrian sports M(c)/W(c), fencing M(c)/W(c), football M/W, racquetball M(c)/W(c), rugby M(c)/W(c), skiing (cross-country) M/W, soccer M(c)/W(c), softball M/W, swimming and diving M(c)/W(c), table tennis M/W, triathlon M(c)/W(c), ultimate Frisbee M(c)/W(c), volleyball M/W, weight lifting M(c)/W(c).

Campus security: 24-hour emergency response devices and patrols, late-night transport/escort service, controlled dormitory access.

Student services: health clinic, personal/psychological counseling, women's center, legal services.

COSTS & FINANCIAL AID

Costs (2017–18) *Tuition:* state resident $12,016 full-time, $462 per credit hour part-time; nonresident $14,036 full-time, $540 per credit hour part-time. Full-time tuition and fees vary according to reciprocity agreements. Part-time tuition and fees vary according to course load and reciprocity agreements. *Required fees:* $1056 full-time. *Room and board:* $8150; room only: $3864. Room and board charges vary according to board plan and housing facility. *Payment plan:* installment. *Waivers:* senior citizens.

Financial Aid Of all full-time matriculated undergraduates who enrolled in 2016, 1,256 applied for aid, 1,019 were judged to have need, 257 had their need fully met. 307 Federal Work-Study jobs (averaging $1317). 96 state and other part-time jobs (averaging $1515). In 2016, 188 non-need-based awards were made. *Average percent of need met:* 75. *Average financial aid package:* $12,633. *Average need-based loan:* $3730. *Average need-based gift aid:* $10,095. *Average non-need-based aid:* $4187. *Average indebtedness upon graduation:* $25,732.

APPLYING

Standardized Tests *Required:* SAT or ACT (for admission).

Options: electronic application, deferred entrance.

Application fee: $35.

Required: high school transcript. *Required for some:* essay or personal statement, 1 letter of recommendation, interview.

Application deadlines: 3/15 (freshmen), 5/1 (transfers).

Notification: continuous (freshmen), continuous (transfers).

CONTACT

University of Minnesota, Morris, 600 East 4th Street, Morris, MN 56267-2134. *Phone:* 320-539-6035. *Toll-free phone:* 888-866-3382. *Fax:* 320-589-6051. *E-mail:* admissions@morris.umn.edu.

University of Minnesota Rochester
Rochester, Minnesota
http://www.r.umn.edu/

CONTACT
University of Minnesota Rochester, 111 South Broadway, Suite 300, Rochester, MN 55904.

University of Minnesota, Twin Cities Campus
Minneapolis, Minnesota
http://www.twin-cities.umn.edu/

- **State-supported** university, founded 1851, part of University of Minnesota System
- **Urban** 2000-acre campus with easy access to Minneapolis-St. Paul
- **Coed** 35,433 undergraduate students, 85% full-time, 53% women, 47% men
- **Moderately difficult** entrance level, 50% of applicants were admitted

UNDERGRAD STUDENTS

29,991 full-time, 5,442 part-time. Students come from 51 states and territories; 101 other countries; 27% are from out of state; 5% Black or African American, non-Hispanic/Latino; 4% Hispanic/Latino; 10% Asian, non-Hispanic/Latino; 0.1% Native Hawaiian or other Pacific Islander, non-Hispanic/Latino; 0.3% American Indian or Alaska Native, non-Hispanic/Latino; 4% Two or more races, non-Hispanic/Latino; 0.8% Race/ethnicity unknown; 9% international; 6% transferred in; 23% live on campus.

Freshmen:
Admission: 43,720 applied, 21,681 admitted, 6,195 enrolled. *Test scores:* SAT evidence-based reading and writing scores over 500: 99%; SAT math scores over 500: 99%; ACT scores over 18: 100%; SAT evidence-based reading and writing scores over 600: 81%; SAT math scores over 600: 90%; ACT scores over 24: 91%; SAT evidence-based reading and writing scores over 700: 35%; SAT math scores over 700: 58%; ACT scores over 30: 40%.

Retention: 93% of full-time freshmen returned.

FACULTY

Total: 3,706, 70% full-time, 70% with terminal degrees.

Student/faculty ratio: 17:1.

ACADEMICS

Calendar: semesters. *Degrees:* certificates, diplomas, bachelor's, master's, doctoral, post-master's, and postbachelor's certificates.

Special study options: academic remediation for entering students, accelerated degree program, adult/continuing education programs, advanced placement credit, cooperative education, distance learning, double majors, English as a second language, external degree program, freshman honors college, honors programs, independent study, internships, off-campus study, part-time degree program, services for LD students, student-designed majors, study abroad, summer session for credit. *ROTC:* Army (b), Navy (b), Air Force (b).

Computers: Students can access the following: computer help desk, free student e-mail accounts, online (class) grades, online (class) registration, online (class) schedules. Campuswide network is available. Wireless service is available via entire campus.

Library: Wilson Library plus 17 others. *Books:* 3.5 million (physical), 1.0 million (digital/electronic); *Serial titles:* 150,445 (physical), 211,166 (digital/electronic); *Databases:* 891. Students can reserve study rooms.

STUDENT LIFE

Housing options: coed, cooperative, special housing for students with disabilities. Campus housing is university owned. Freshman campus housing is guaranteed.

Activities and organizations: drama/theater group, student-run newspaper, radio and television station, choral group, marching band, Student Government, national fraternities, national sororities.

Athletics Member NCAA. All Division I except football (Division I-A). *Intercollegiate sports:* baseball M(s), basketball M(s)/W(s), cross-country running M(s)/W(s), golf M(s)/W(s), gymnastics M(s)/W(s), ice hockey M(s)/W(s), soccer W(s), softball W(s), swimming and diving M(s)/W(s), tennis M(s)/W(s), track and field M(s)/W(s), volleyball W(s), wrestling M(s). *Intramural sports:* baseball M/W, basketball M/W, bowling M/W, crew M/W, football M/W, golf M/W, ice hockey M/W, rugby M/W, skiing (cross-country) M/W, skiing (downhill) M/W, soccer M/W, softball M/W, tennis M/W, volleyball M/W, water polo M/W, wrestling M/W.

Campus security: 24-hour emergency response devices and patrols, student patrols, late-night transport/escort service, controlled dormitory access, safety/security orientation, security lighting.

Student services: health clinic, personal/psychological counseling, women's center, legal services.

COSTS & FINANCIAL AID
Costs (2017–18) *Tuition:* state resident $12,800 full-time, $492 per credit hour part-time; nonresident $24,986 full-time, $884 per credit hour part-time. Full-time tuition and fees vary according to program and reciprocity agreements. Part-time tuition and fees vary according to course load, program, and reciprocity agreements. *Required fees:* $1617 full-time. *Room and board:* $9852; room only: $5586. Room and board charges vary according to board plan, housing facility, and location. *Payment plan:* installment. *Waivers:* senior citizens.

Financial Aid Of all full-time matriculated undergraduates who enrolled in 2017, 19,869 applied for aid, 14,293 were judged to have need, 3,068 had their need fully met. In 2017, 2238 non-need-based awards were made. *Average percent of need met:* 72. *Average financial aid package:* $13,381. *Average need-based loan:* $4734. *Average need-based gift aid:* $10,444. *Average non-need-based aid:* $5006. *Average indebtedness upon graduation:* $26,568.

APPLYING
Standardized Tests *Required:* SAT or ACT (for admission).
Options: electronic application, early admission, deferred entrance.
Application fee: $55.
Required: high school transcript. *Recommended:* minimum 2.0 GPA.
Application deadlines: rolling (freshmen), rolling (out-of-state freshmen), rolling (transfers).
Notification: continuous (freshmen), continuous (out-of-state freshmen), continuous (transfers).

CONTACT
Heidi Meyer, Executive Director of Admissions, University of Minnesota, Twin Cities Campus, 240 Williamson, Minneapolis, MN 55455-0213. *Phone:* 612-625-2008. *Toll-free phone:* 800-752-1000. *Fax:* 612-626-1693. *E-mail:* admissions@tc.umn.edu.

University of Northwestern–St. Paul
St. Paul, Minnesota
http://www.unwsp.edu/

CONTACT
Admissions, University of Northwestern–St. Paul, Officer of Admissions, 3003 Snelling Avenue North, 212 Nazareth Hall, St. Paul, MN 55113-1598. *Phone:* 651-631-5111. *Toll-free phone:* 800-827-6827. *Fax:* 651-631-5680. *E-mail:* admissions@unwsp.edu.

University of St. Thomas
St. Paul, Minnesota
http://www.stthomas.edu/
- **Independent Roman Catholic** university, founded 1885
- **Urban** 78-acre campus with easy access to Minneapolis-St. Paul
- **Endowment** $447.5 million
- **Coed** 6,199 undergraduate students, 96% full-time, 46% women, 54% men
- **Moderately difficult** entrance level, 85% of applicants were admitted

UNDERGRAD STUDENTS
5,945 full-time, 254 part-time. Students come from 46 states and territories; 78 other countries; 19% are from out of state; 3% Black or African American, non-Hispanic/Latino; 5% Hispanic/Latino; 4% Asian, non-Hispanic/Latino; 0.2% American Indian or Alaska Native, non-Hispanic/Latino; 3% Two or more races, non-Hispanic/Latino; 1% Race/ethnicity unknown; 3% international; 4% transferred in; 40% live on campus.

Freshmen:
Admission: 6,255 applied, 5,300 admitted, 1,498 enrolled. *Average high school GPA:* 3.6.
Retention: 88% of full-time freshmen returned.

FACULTY
Total: 810, 55% full-time, 62% with terminal degrees.
Student/faculty ratio: 14:1.

ACADEMICS
Calendar: 4-1-4. *Degrees:* certificates, associate, bachelor's, master's, doctoral, post-master's, and postbachelor's certificates.

Special study options: accelerated degree program, advanced placement credit, cooperative education, distance learning, double majors, English as a second language, honors programs, independent study, internships, off-campus study, part-time degree program, services for LD students, student-designed majors, study abroad, summer session for credit. *ROTC:* Army (c), Navy (c), Air Force (b).

Unusual degree programs: 3-2 engineering with University of Notre Dame; University of Minnesota, Twin Cities Campus.

Computers: Students can access the following: campus intranet, computer help desk, free student e-mail accounts, online (class) grades, online (class) registration, online (class) schedules. Campuswide network is available. 100% of college-owned or -operated housing units are wired for high-speed Internet access. Wireless service is available via entire campus.

Library: O'Shaughnessy-Frey Library plus 7 others. *Books:* 502,033 (physical), 251,462 (digital/electronic); *Serial titles:* 16,463 (physical), 118,059 (digital/electronic); *Databases:* 406. Students can reserve study rooms.

STUDENT LIFE
Housing options: coed, men-only, women-only, special housing for students with disabilities. Campus housing is university owned. Freshman applicants given priority for college housing.

Activities and organizations: drama/theater group, student-run newspaper, radio and television station, choral group.

Athletics Member NCAA. All Division III. *Intercollegiate sports:* baseball M, basketball M/W, cross-country running M/W, football M, golf M/W, ice hockey M/W, lacrosse M(c)/W(c), soccer M/W, softball W, swimming and diving M/W, tennis M/W, volleyball W. *Intramural sports:* badminton M/W, basketball M/W, crew M(c)/W(c), golf M/W, racquetball M/W, sailing M(c)/W, skiing (downhill) M(c)/W(c), soccer M/W, table tennis M/W, tennis M/W, track and field M(c)/W(c), volleyball M/W.

Campus security: 24-hour emergency response devices and patrols, late-night transport/escort service, controlled dormitory access.

Student services: health clinic, personal/psychological counseling, women's center.

COSTS & FINANCIAL AID
Costs (2017–18) *Comprehensive fee:* $51,187 includes full-time tuition ($40,224), mandatory fees ($909), and room and board ($10,054). Part-time tuition: $1257 per credit. *College room only:* $6304. Room and board charges vary according to board plan and housing facility. *Payment plans:* installment, deferred payment. *Waivers:* senior citizens and employees or children of employees.

Financial Aid Of all full-time matriculated undergraduates who enrolled in 2017, 3,991 applied for aid, 3,227 were judged to have need, 674 had their need fully met. 1,033 Federal Work-Study jobs (averaging $3041). 903 state and other part-time jobs (averaging $3017). In 2017, 632 non-need-based awards were made. *Average percent of need met:* 84. *Average financial aid package:* $28,746. *Average need-based loan:* $8121. *Average need-based gift aid:* $22,068. *Average non-need-based aid:* $19,563. *Average indebtedness upon graduation:* $40,983.

APPLYING
Standardized Tests *Required:* SAT or ACT (for admission).
Options: electronic application, early action, deferred entrance.
Required: essay or personal statement, high school transcript. *Recommended:* interview.
Application deadlines: rolling (freshmen), rolling (transfers), 11/1 (early action).

Notification: continuous (freshmen), continuous (transfers), 12/15 (early action).

CONTACT
University of St. Thomas, 2115 Summit Avenue, St. Paul, MN 55105-1096. *Toll-free phone:* 800-328-6819. *E-mail:* admissions@stthomas.edu.

Walden University
Minneapolis, Minnesota
http://www.waldenu.edu/

CONTACT
Walden University, 100 Washington South, Suite 900, Minneapolis, MN 55401. *Toll-free phone:* 866-492-5336.

Winona State University
Winona, Minnesota
http://www.winona.edu/

- **State-supported** comprehensive, founded 1858, part of Minnesota State Colleges and Universities System
- **Small-town** 125-acre campus with easy access to Minneapolis-St.Paul
- **Endowment** $22.6 million
- **Coed** 7,437 undergraduate students, 87% full-time, 63% women, 37% men
- **Moderately difficult** entrance level, 66% of applicants were admitted

UNDERGRAD STUDENTS
6,501 full-time, 936 part-time. Students come from 37 states and territories; 45 other countries; 29% are from out of state; 3% Black or African American, non-Hispanic/Latino; 3% Hispanic/Latino; 2% Asian, non-Hispanic/Latino; 0.1% Native Hawaiian or other Pacific Islander, non-Hispanic/Latino; 0.2% American Indian or Alaska Native, non-Hispanic/Latino; 3% Two or more races, non-Hispanic/Latino; 0.6% Race/ethnicity unknown; 2% international; 8% transferred in; 29% live on campus.

Freshmen:
Admission: 7,468 applied, 4,966 admitted, 1,610 enrolled. *Average high school GPA:* 3.4. *Test scores:* ACT scores over 18: 97%; ACT scores over 24: 37%; ACT scores over 30: 3%.
Retention: 78% of full-time freshmen returned.

FACULTY
Total: 526, 64% full-time, 59% with terminal degrees.
Student/faculty ratio: 18:1.

ACADEMICS
Calendar: semesters. *Degrees:* associate, bachelor's, master's, doctoral, post-master's, and postbachelor's certificates.
Special study options: academic remediation for entering students, adult/continuing education programs, advanced placement credit, distance learning, double majors, English as a second language, independent study, internships, off-campus study, part-time degree program, services for LD students, student-designed majors, study abroad, summer session for credit. *ROTC:* Army (c).
Unusual degree programs: 3-2 athletic training.
Computers: 50 computers/terminals and 19,500 ports are available on campus for general student use. Students can access the following: campus intranet, computer help desk, free student e-mail accounts, online (class) grades, online (class) registration, online (class) schedules. Campuswide network is available. 100% of college-owned or -operated housing units are wired for high-speed Internet access. Wireless service is available via entire campus.
Library: Darrel W. Krueger Library. *Books:* 242,347 (physical), 59,498 (digital/electronic); *Serial titles:* 2,097 (physical), 34,000 (digital/electronic); *Databases:* 138. Weekly public service hours: 99; students can reserve study rooms.

STUDENT LIFE
Housing options: coed, men-only, women-only, special housing for students with disabilities. Campus housing is university owned and leased by the school. Freshman campus housing is guaranteed.
Activities and organizations: drama/theater group, student-run newspaper, radio station, choral group, University Program Activities Committee, Student Senate, Residence Hall Association, Inter Varsity, national fraternities, national sororities.

Athletics Member NCAA. All Division II except gymnastics (Division III). *Intercollegiate sports:* baseball M(s), basketball M(s)/W(s), cross-country running M(s)/W(s), football M(s), golf M(s)/W(s), gymnastics W, soccer W(s), softball W(s), tennis W(s), track and field W(s), volleyball W(s). *Intramural sports:* badminton M(c)/W(c), baseball M(c)/W(c), basketball M/W, cheerleading M(c)/W(c), cross-country running M(c)/W(c), fencing M(c)/W(c), lacrosse M(c)/W(c), rugby M(c)/W(c), skiing (cross-country) M(c)/W(c), skiing (downhill) M(c)/W(c), soccer M/W, softball M/W, swimming and diving M(c)/W(c), table tennis M(c)/W(c), tennis M(c)/W(c), ultimate Frisbee M(c)/W(c), volleyball M/W, wrestling M(c)/W(c).

Campus security: 24-hour emergency response devices and patrols, student patrols, late-night transport/escort service, controlled dormitory access, security cameras.
Student services: health clinic, personal/psychological counseling.

COSTS & FINANCIAL AID
Costs (2017–18) *Tuition:* state resident $7377 full-time, $244 per credit hour part-time; nonresident $13,300 full-time, $443 per credit hour part-time. Full-time tuition and fees vary according to location, program, and reciprocity agreements. Part-time tuition and fees vary according to course load, location, program, and reciprocity agreements. *Required fees:* $2002 full-time, $39 per credit hour part-time, $485 per term part-time. *Room and board:* $8730. Room and board charges vary according to board plan, housing facility, and location. *Payment plan:* installment. *Waivers:* employees or children of employees.

Financial Aid Of all full-time matriculated undergraduates who enrolled in 2016, 5,306 applied for aid, 3,847 were judged to have need, 456 had their need fully met. 284 Federal Work-Study jobs (averaging $2750). 521 state and other part-time jobs (averaging $1750). In 2016, 849 non-need-based awards were made. *Average percent of need met:* 53. *Average financial aid package:* $7250. *Average need-based loan:* $4152. *Average need-based gift aid:* $5581. *Average non-need-based aid:* $1900. *Average indebtedness upon graduation:* $33,873.

APPLYING
Standardized Tests *Required:* SAT or ACT (for admission).
Options: electronic application, deferred entrance.
Application fee: $20.
Required: high school transcript, 16 high school preparation requirements and either minimum composite ACT of 21 with top two-thirds of high school class rank or minimum cumulative GPA of 2.75 or, minimum composite ACT of 18 with either top half of high school class rank or minimum cumulative high school GPA of 3.0.
Application deadlines: 7/1 (freshmen), 7/4 (out-of-state freshmen), 7/1 (transfers).
Notification: continuous (freshmen), continuous (out-of-state freshmen), continuous (transfers).

CONTACT
Brian Jicinsky, Director of Admissions, Winona State University, 175 West Mark Street, Winona, MN 55987. *Phone:* 507-457-5100. *Toll-free phone:* 800-DIAL WSU. *Fax:* 507-457-5620. *E-mail:* admissions@winona.edu.

MISSISSIPPI

Alcorn State University
Lorman, Mississippi
http://www.alcorn.edu/

- **State-supported** comprehensive, founded 1871, part of Mississippi Institutions of Higher Learning
- **Rural** 1756-acre campus
- **Endowment** $17.3 million
- **Coed** 3,172 undergraduate students, 91% full-time, 64% women, 36% men
- **Moderately difficult** entrance level, 79% of applicants were admitted

UNDERGRAD STUDENTS

2,893 full-time, 279 part-time. Students come from 35 states and territories; 31 other countries; 28% are from out of state; 91% Black or African American, non-Hispanic/Latino; 0.5% Hispanic/Latino; 0.1% Asian, non-Hispanic/Latino; 0.2% American Indian or Alaska Native, non-Hispanic/Latino; 2% Two or more races, non-Hispanic/Latino; 3% international; 5% transferred in; 63% live on campus.

Freshmen:
Admission: 3,464 applied, 2,723 admitted, 742 enrolled. *Average high school GPA:* 3.2. *Test scores:* ACT scores over 18: 61%; ACT scores over 24: 19%.

Retention: 75% of full-time freshmen returned.

FACULTY

Total: 221, 68% full-time, 66% with terminal degrees.
Student/faculty ratio: 19:1.

ACADEMICS

Calendar: semesters. *Degrees:* associate, bachelor's, master's, and post-master's certificates.

Special study options: academic remediation for entering students, accelerated degree program, adult/continuing education programs, advanced placement credit, cooperative education, distance learning, double majors, honors programs, independent study, internships, off-campus study, part-time degree program, study abroad, summer session for credit. *ROTC:* Army (b).

Computers: 500 computers/terminals and 2,500 ports are available on campus for general student use. Students can access the following: campus intranet, computer help desk, free student e-mail accounts, online (class) grades, online (class) registration, online (class) schedules, online payment; online transcript request. Campuswide network is available. 100% of college-owned or -operated housing units are wired for high-speed Internet access. Wireless service is available via entire campus.
Library: John Dewey Boyd Library plus 1 other. *Books:* 412,321 (physical), 441,114 (digital/electronic); *Serial titles:* 312 (physical), 75,805 (digital/electronic); *Databases:* 91. Weekly public service hours: 88; study areas open 24 hours, 5–7 days a week; students can reserve study rooms.

STUDENT LIFE

Housing options: men-only, women-only. Campus housing is university owned. Freshman campus housing is guaranteed.

Activities and organizations: drama/theater group, student-run newspaper, radio and television station, choral group, marching band, marching band, Gospel Choir, inter-faith choir, national fraternities, national sororities.

Athletics Member NCAA. All Division I. *Intercollegiate sports:* baseball M(s), basketball M(s)/W(s), cross-country running M(s)/W(s), football M(s), golf M(s)/W(s), soccer W(s), softball W(s), tennis M(s)/W(s), track and field M(s)/W(s), volleyball W(s). *Intramural sports:* basketball M/W, football M.

Campus security: 24-hour emergency response devices and patrols, late-night transport/escort service, controlled dormitory access.

Student services: health clinic, personal/psychological counseling.

COSTS & FINANCIAL AID

Costs (2017–18) *Tuition:* state resident $6888 full-time, $574 per credit hour part-time; nonresident $6888 full-time, $574 per credit hour part-time. Full-time tuition and fees vary according to course load. Part-time tuition and fees vary according to course load. *Room and board:* $9731; room only: $6639. Room and board charges vary according to board plan and housing facility. *Payment plan:* installment. *Waivers:* employees or children of employees.

Financial Aid Of all full-time matriculated undergraduates who enrolled in 2016, 1,337 applied for aid, 1,284 were judged to have need, 129 had their need fully met. 281 Federal Work-Study jobs (averaging $1111). In 2016, 721 non-need-based awards were made. *Average percent of need met:* 49. *Average financial aid package:* $15,032. *Average need-based loan:* $3892. *Average need-based gift aid:* $5902. *Average non-need-based aid:* $8158. *Average indebtedness upon graduation:* $35,077.

APPLYING

Standardized Tests *Required:* SAT or ACT (for admission).
Options: electronic application, deferred entrance.

Required: high school transcript, minimum 2.0 GPA.
Application deadlines: rolling (freshmen), rolling (transfers).
Notification: continuous (freshmen), continuous (transfers).

CONTACT

Mrs. Kantangelia Tenner, Director of Admissions, Alcorn State University, 1000 ASU Drive, #300, Alcorn State, MS 39096-7500. *Phone:* 601-877-6147. *Toll-free phone:* 800-222-6790. *Fax:* 601-877-6347. *E-mail:* ksampson@alcorn.edu.

Belhaven University
Jackson, Mississippi
http://www.belhaven.edu/

- **Independent Presbyterian** comprehensive, founded 1883
- **Urban** 46-acre campus
- **Endowment** $5.6 million
- **Coed** 2,482 undergraduate students, 50% full-time, 66% women, 34% men
- **Moderately difficult** entrance level, 59% of applicants were admitted

UNDERGRAD STUDENTS

1,248 full-time, 1,234 part-time. Students come from 47 states and territories; 25 other countries; 33% are from out of state; 45% Black or African American, non-Hispanic/Latino; 5% Hispanic/Latino; 0.9% Asian, non-Hispanic/Latino; 0.4% American Indian or Alaska Native, non-Hispanic/Latino; 3% Two or more races, non-Hispanic/Latino; 6% Race/ethnicity unknown; 2% international; 15% transferred in; 22% live on campus.

Freshmen:
Admission: 2,324 applied, 1,374 admitted, 240 enrolled. *Average high school GPA:* 3.4. *Test scores:* SAT evidence-based reading and writing scores over 500: 83%; SAT math scores over 500: 83%; ACT scores over 18: 97%; SAT evidence-based reading and writing scores over 600: 38%; SAT math scores over 600: 23%; ACT scores over 24: 35%; SAT evidence-based reading and writing scores over 700: 5%; SAT math scores over 700: 2%; ACT scores over 30: 4%.

Retention: 63% of full-time freshmen returned.

FACULTY

Total: 456, 21% full-time, 45% with terminal degrees.
Student/faculty ratio: 15:1.

ACADEMICS

Calendar: semesters. *Degrees:* certificates, associate, bachelor's, master's, doctoral, and postbachelor's certificates.

Special study options: academic remediation for entering students, accelerated degree program, adult/continuing education programs, advanced placement credit, distance learning, double majors, English as a second language, honors programs, independent study, internships, off-campus study, part-time degree program, student-designed majors, study abroad, summer session for credit. *ROTC:* Army (c), Air Force (c).

Unusual degree programs: 3-2 business administration; engineering with University of Mississippi; nursing; social work.

Computers: 36 computers/terminals are available on campus for general student use. Students can access the following: campus intranet, computer help desk, free student e-mail accounts, online (class) grades, online (class) registration, online (class) schedules. Campuswide network is available. 100% of college-owned or -operated housing units are wired for high-speed Internet access. Wireless service is available via classrooms, computer labs, dorm rooms, libraries, student centers.
Library: Warren A. Hood Library plus 1 other. *Books:* 42,425 (physical), 106,114 (digital/electronic); *Serial titles:* 160 (physical), 75,718 (digital/electronic); *Databases:* 96. Weekly public service hours: 104.

STUDENT LIFE

Housing options: men-only, women-only. Campus housing is university owned. Freshman campus housing is guaranteed.

Activities and organizations: drama/theater group, student-run newspaper, choral group, marching band, Belhaven Activities Team, Fellowship of Christian Athletes, Reformed University Fellowship, Phi Beta Lambda, Belhaven University New Music Society.

Athletics Member NCAA. All Division III. *Intercollegiate sports:* baseball M, basketball M/W, cheerleading W, cross-country running M/W, football M, golf M/W, soccer M/W, softball W, tennis M/W, volleyball W. *Intramural sports:* basketball M/W, football M/W, soccer M/W, softball M/W, volleyball M/W.

Campus security: 24-hour emergency response devices and patrols, late-night transport/escort service, controlled dormitory access.

Student services: health clinic, personal/psychological counseling.

COSTS & FINANCIAL AID

Costs (2018–19) *Comprehensive fee:* $33,800 includes full-time tuition ($24,950), mandatory fees ($350), and room and board ($8500). Full-time tuition and fees vary according to location and program. Part-time tuition: $425 per credit hour. Part-time tuition and fees vary according to course load, location, and program. *Room and board:* Room and board charges vary according to housing facility. *Payment plan:* installment. *Waivers:* employees or children of employees.

Financial Aid Of all full-time matriculated undergraduates who enrolled in 2015, 1,136 applied for aid, 1,057 were judged to have need, 59 had their need fully met. 215 Federal Work-Study jobs (averaging $1500). 42 state and other part-time jobs (averaging $2000). In 2015, 279 non-need-based awards were made. *Average percent of need met:* 59. *Average financial aid package:* $15,764. *Average need-based loan:* $4298. *Average need-based gift aid:* $12,671. *Average non-need-based aid:* $14,171. *Average indebtedness upon graduation:* $29,738.

APPLYING

Standardized Tests *Required:* SAT or ACT (for admission).

Options: electronic application, early admission, deferred entrance.

Application fee: $25.

Required: high school transcript, minimum 2.0 GPA, 1 letter of recommendation. *Required for some:* essay or personal statement, interview.

Application deadlines: rolling (freshmen), rolling (transfers).

Notification: continuous (freshmen), continuous (transfers).

CONTACT

Ms. Suzanne T. Sullivan, Assistant Vice President for Traditional and Online Admissions, Belhaven University, 1500 Peachtree Street, Jackson, MS 39202. *Phone:* 601-968-5940. *Toll-free phone:* 800-960-5940. *Fax:* 601-968-8946. *E-mail:* admission@belhaven.edu.

Blue Mountain College

Blue Mountain, Mississippi

http://www.bmc.edu/

- **Independent Southern Baptist** comprehensive, founded 1873
- **Rural** 190-acre campus with easy access to Memphis
- **Endowment** $15.6 million
- **Coed** 588 undergraduate students, 90% full-time, 55% women, 45% men
- **Moderately difficult** entrance level, 100% of applicants were admitted

UNDERGRAD STUDENTS

531 full-time, 57 part-time. Students come from 14 states and territories; 11 other countries; 19% are from out of state; 12% Black or African American, non-Hispanic/Latino; 2% Hispanic/Latino; 0.3% Asian, non-Hispanic/Latino; 0.5% American Indian or Alaska Native, non-Hispanic/Latino; 1% Two or more races, non-Hispanic/Latino; 2% international; 21% transferred in; 59% live on campus.

Freshmen:

Admission: 207 applied, 206 admitted, 127 enrolled. *Average high school GPA:* 3.4. *Test scores:* SAT evidence-based reading and writing scores over 500: 100%; SAT math scores over 500: 100%; ACT scores over 18: 84%; ACT scores over 24: 28%; ACT scores over 30: 3%.

Retention: 65% of full-time freshmen returned.

FACULTY

Total: 54, 65% full-time, 63% with terminal degrees.

Student/faculty ratio: 14:1.

ACADEMICS

Calendar: semesters. *Degrees:* bachelor's and master's.

Special study options: academic remediation for entering students, accelerated degree program, adult/continuing education programs, advanced placement credit, distance learning, double majors, honors programs, internships, part-time degree program, services for LD students, summer session for credit.

Unusual degree programs: 3-2 nursing with Union University.

Computers: 95 computers/terminals are available on campus for general student use. Students can access the following: computer help desk, free student e-mail accounts, online (class) grades, online (class) schedules. Campuswide network is available. 100% of college-owned or -operated housing units are wired for high-speed Internet access. Wireless service is available via entire campus.

Library: Guyton Library plus 1 other. *Books:* 41,725 (physical), 35,897 (digital/electronic); *Serial titles:* 143 (physical); *Databases:* 24. Weekly public service hours: 70.

STUDENT LIFE

Housing options: men-only, women-only. Campus housing is university owned.

Activities and organizations: drama/theater group, student-run newspaper, choral group, marching band, Baptist Student Union, Student Body Association, Intramural Association, Ministerial Association, Mississippi Association of Educators/Student Program.

Athletics Member NAIA. *Intercollegiate sports:* archery M(s)(c)/W(s)(c), baseball M(s), basketball M(s)/W(s), bowling M(s)(c)/W(s)(c), cheerleading M(s)(c)/W(s)(c), cross-country running M(s)/W(s), golf M(s)/W(s), softball W(s), tennis M(s)/W(s). *Intramural sports:* basketball M/W, football M, softball W, swimming and diving W, table tennis M/W, tennis W, track and field M/W, ultimate Frisbee M, volleyball M/W.

Campus security: 24-hour emergency response devices and patrols, controlled dormitory access.

COSTS & FINANCIAL AID

Costs (2017–18) *Comprehensive fee:* $17,885 includes full-time tuition ($9990), mandatory fees ($1770), and room and board ($6125). Full-time tuition and fees vary according to course load, degree level, and program. Part-time tuition: $333 per semester hour. Part-time tuition and fees vary according to course load, degree level, and program. *Required fees:* $50 per semester part-time. *Room and board:* Room and board charges vary according to gender, housing facility, and location. *Payment plans:* installment, deferred payment. *Waivers:* employees or children of employees.

Financial Aid Of all full-time matriculated undergraduates who enrolled in 2017, 526 applied for aid, 449 were judged to have need, 87 had their need fully met. In 2017, 39 non-need-based awards were made. *Average percent of need met:* 67. *Average financial aid package:* $11,919. *Average need-based loan:* $3581. *Average need-based gift aid:* $9950. *Average non-need-based aid:* $5966. *Average indebtedness upon graduation:* $19,084.

APPLYING

Standardized Tests *Required:* SAT or ACT (for admission).

Options: electronic application, early decision, deferred entrance.

Required for some: high school transcript. *Recommended:* minimum 2.0 GPA.

Application deadlines: rolling (freshmen), rolling (out-of-state freshmen), rolling (transfers).

Notification: continuous (freshmen), continuous (out-of-state freshmen), continuous (transfers).

CONTACT

Mr. Lynn Gibson, Vice President for Enrollment Services, Blue Mountain College, PO Box 160, Blue Mountain, MS 38610-0160. *Phone:* 662-685-4771 Ext. 176. *Toll-free phone:* 800-235-0136. *Fax:* 662-685-4776. *E-mail:* lgibson@bmc.edu.

Delta State University

Cleveland, Mississippi

http://www.deltastate.edu/

CONTACT

Mr. Chris Gaines, Director of Recruiting, Delta State University, 1003 West Sunflower Road, Kent Wyatt Hall, Office of Admissions, Cleveland, MS 38733. *Phone:* 662-846-4020. *Toll-free phone:* 800-468-6378. *E-mail:* admissions@deltastate.edu.

Jackson State University

Jackson, Mississippi

http://www.jsums.edu/

- **State-supported** university, founded 1877, part of Mississippi Institutions of Higher Learning
- **Urban** 250-acre campus
- **Endowment** $38.9 million
- **Coed** 6,500 undergraduate students, 91% full-time, 63% women, 37% men
- **Minimally difficult** entrance level, 72% of applicants were admitted

UNDERGRAD STUDENTS

5,935 full-time, 565 part-time. Students come from 60 other countries; 26% are from out of state; 91% Black or African American, non-Hispanic/Latino; 0.8% Hispanic/Latino; 0.2% Asian, non-Hispanic/Latino; 0.3% American Indian or Alaska Native, non-Hispanic/Latino; 1% Two or more races, non-Hispanic/Latino; 2% international; 9% transferred in; 36% live on campus.

Freshmen:

Admission: 6,282 applied, 4,506 admitted, 933 enrolled. *Average high school GPA:* 2.9. *Test scores:* ACT scores over 18: 66%; ACT scores over 24: 12%; ACT scores over 30: 1%.

Retention: 61% of full-time freshmen returned.

FACULTY

Total: 575, 64% full-time.

Student/faculty ratio: 17:1.

ACADEMICS

Calendar: semesters. *Degrees:* bachelor's, master's, doctoral, and post-master's certificates.

Special study options: academic remediation for entering students, accelerated degree program, adult/continuing education programs, advanced placement credit, cooperative education, distance learning, double majors, English as a second language, honors programs, independent study, internships, off-campus study, part-time degree program, services for LD students, study abroad, summer session for credit. *ROTC:* Army (b), Air Force (b).

Computers: 2,000 computers/terminals are available on campus for general student use. Students can access the following: computer help desk, free student e-mail accounts, online (class) grades, online (class) registration, online (class) schedules. Campuswide network is available. 100% of college-owned or -operated housing units are wired for high-speed Internet access. Wireless service is available via entire campus.

Library: H. T. Sampson Library plus 4 others. *Books:* 1.4 million (digital/electronic); *Serial titles:* 318,928 (digital/electronic).

STUDENT LIFE

Housing options: men-only, women-only, special housing for students with disabilities. Campus housing is university owned and leased by the school. Freshman applicants given priority for college housing.

Activities and organizations: drama/theater group, student-run newspaper, choral group, marching band, Student Government Association, Sonic Boom of the South, MADDRAMA, Interfaith, NAACP, national fraternities, national sororities.

Athletics Member NCAA. All Division I except football (Division I-AA). *Intercollegiate sports:* baseball M(s), basketball M(s)/W(s), bowling W(s), cheerleading M/W, cross-country running M(s)/W(s), golf M(s)/W(s), soccer W(s), softball W(s), tennis M(s)/W(s), track and field M(s)/W(s), volleyball W(s). *Intramural sports:* basketball M/W, football M/W, softball M/W, volleyball M/W.

Campus security: 24-hour emergency response devices and patrols, controlled dormitory access.

Student services: health clinic, personal/psychological counseling.

COSTS & FINANCIAL AID

Costs (2018–19) *Tuition:* state resident $7876 full-time, $329 per hour part-time; nonresident $19,104 full-time, $797 per hour part-time. Full-time tuition and fees vary according to course level, course load, degree level, and student level. Part-time tuition and fees vary according to course level, degree level, and student level. *Required fees:* $70 full-time. *Room and board:* $9552; room only: $5784. Room and board charges vary according to housing facility. *Payment plan:* installment. *Waivers:* children of alumni and employees or children of employees.

Financial Aid Of all full-time matriculated undergraduates who enrolled in 2017, 5,548 applied for aid, 5,036 were judged to have need, 453 had their need fully met. 1,104 Federal Work-Study jobs (averaging $2097). In 2017, 141 non-need-based awards were made. *Average percent of need met:* 51. *Average financial aid package:* $11,286. *Average need-based loan:* $4200. *Average need-based gift aid:* $5179. *Average non-need-based aid:* $9903. *Average indebtedness upon graduation:* $29,864.

APPLYING

Standardized Tests *Required:* SAT or ACT (for admission).

Options: electronic application.

Required: high school transcript, immunization record, minimum ACT Composite score of 16.

Application deadlines: 9/5 (freshmen), rolling (transfers), rolling (early action).

Notification: continuous (freshmen), continuous (transfers).

CONTACT

Ms. Latoysha Smith, Interim Director of Undergraduate Recruitment, Jackson State University, PO Box 18389, 1400 John R. Lynch Street, Jackson, MS 39217. *Phone:* 601-979-2914. *Toll-free phone:* 800-848-6817. *Fax:* 601-979-0360. *E-mail:* laytoysha.smith@jsums.edu.

Millsaps College

Jackson, Mississippi

http://www.millsaps.edu/

- **Independent United Methodist** comprehensive, founded 1890
- **Urban** 100-acre campus
- **Endowment** $100.8 million
- **Coed** 807 undergraduate students, 99% full-time, 49% women, 51% men
- **Moderately difficult** entrance level, 49% of applicants were admitted

UNDERGRAD STUDENTS

796 full-time, 11 part-time. Students come from 23 states and territories; 29 other countries; 56% are from out of state; 16% Black or African American, non-Hispanic/Latino; 5% Hispanic/Latino; 3% Asian, non-Hispanic/Latino; 0.1% Native Hawaiian or other Pacific Islander, non-Hispanic/Latino; 1% American Indian or Alaska Native, non-Hispanic/Latino; 2% Race/ethnicity unknown; 5% international; 2% transferred in; 89% live on campus.

Freshmen:

Admission: 4,276 applied, 2,093 admitted, 229 enrolled. *Average high school GPA:* 3.7. *Test scores:* SAT evidence-based reading and writing scores over 500: 92%; SAT math scores over 500: 92%; ACT scores over 18: 100%; SAT evidence-based reading and writing scores over 600: 63%; SAT math scores over 600: 66%; ACT scores over 24: 64%; SAT evidence-based reading and writing scores over 700: 10%; SAT math scores over 700: 15%; ACT scores over 30: 19%.

Retention: 75% of full-time freshmen returned.

FACULTY

Total: 110, 77% full-time, 53% with terminal degrees.

Student/faculty ratio: 9:1.

ACADEMICS

Calendar: semesters. *Degrees:* bachelor's and master's.

Special study options: accelerated degree program, advanced placement credit, double majors, honors programs, independent study, internships, off-campus study, part-time degree program, services for LD students, student-designed majors, study abroad, summer session for credit. *ROTC:* Army (c), Air Force (c).

Unusual degree programs: 3-2 engineering with Auburn University, Columbia University, Vanderbilt University; nursing with University of Mississippi Medical Center, Vanderbilt University.

Computers: 150 computers/terminals are available on campus for general student use. Students can access the following: campus intranet, computer help desk, free student e-mail accounts, online (class) grades, online (class) registration, online (class) schedules, online transcripts. Campuswide network is available. 100% of college-owned or -operated

housing units are wired for high-speed Internet access. Wireless service is available via entire campus.
Library: Millsaps-Wilson Library.

STUDENT LIFE

Housing options: on-campus residence required through sophomore year; coed, men-only, women-only, special housing for students with disabilities. Campus housing is university owned. Freshman campus housing is guaranteed.

Activities and organizations: drama/theater group, student-run newspaper, choral group, Campus Ministry Team, Student Body Association, SAPS (Campus Programming Board), Inter-fraternity/Panhellenic Councils, intramural sports, national fraternities, national sororities.

Athletics Member NCAA. All Division III. *Intercollegiate sports:* baseball M, basketball M/W, cross-country running M/W, football M, golf M/W, lacrosse M/W, soccer M/W, softball W, tennis M/W, track and field M/W, volleyball W. *Intramural sports:* basketball M/W, cheerleading W(c), fencing M(c)/W(c), football M/W, lacrosse W(c), soccer M/W, softball M/W, swimming and diving M(c)/W(c), ultimate Frisbee M(c)/W(c), volleyball M/W.

Campus security: 24-hour emergency response devices and patrols, student patrols, late-night transport/escort service, controlled dormitory access, self-defense education, lighted pathways.

Student services: health clinic, personal/psychological counseling.

COSTS & FINANCIAL AID

Costs (2018–19) *Comprehensive fee:* $53,640 includes full-time tuition ($37,290), mandatory fees ($2620), and room and board ($13,730). Part-time tuition: $1150 per semester hour. *Required fees:* $38 per semester hour part-time. *College room only:* $7680. Room and board charges vary according to board plan and housing facility. *Waivers:* employees or children of employees.

Financial Aid Of all full-time matriculated undergraduates who enrolled in 2016, 586 applied for aid, 517 were judged to have need, 103 had their need fully met. In 2016, 269 non-need-based awards were made. *Average percent of need met:* 77. *Average financial aid package:* $34,823. *Average need-based loan:* $4671. *Average need-based gift aid:* $28,403. *Average non-need-based aid:* $24,511. *Average indebtedness upon graduation:* $33,569.

APPLYING

Standardized Tests *Required:* SAT or ACT (for admission).

Options: electronic application, early admission, early action, deferred entrance.

Required: essay or personal statement, high school transcript, minimum 2.5 GPA, 1 letter of recommendation, secondary school report. *Required for some:* interview.

Application deadlines: 2/1 (freshmen), rolling (out-of-state freshmen), 7/1 (transfers), 11/15 (early action).

Notification: continuous until 3/15 (freshmen), continuous until 3/15 (out-of-state freshmen), continuous until 3/15 (transfers), 1/15 (early action).

CONTACT

Dr. Robert Alexander, Vice President of Enrollment and Communications, Millsaps College, 1701 North State Street, Jackson, MS 39210-0001. *Phone:* 601-974-1050. *Toll-free phone:* 800-352-1050. *Fax:* 601-974-1059. *E-mail:* admissions@millsaps.edu.

Mississippi College
Clinton, Mississippi
http://www.mc.edu/

CONTACT

Mr. William Kyle Brantley, Director of Admissions, Mississippi College, Box 4026, 200 South Capitol Street, Clinton, MS 39058-0001. *Phone:* 601-925-7634. *Toll-free phone:* 800-738-1236. *Fax:* 601-925-3950. *E-mail:* enrollment-services@mc.edu.

Mississippi State University
Mississippi State, Mississippi
http://www.msstate.edu/

- **State-supported** university, founded 1878, part of Mississippi Institutions of Higher Learning
- **Small-town** 4200-acre campus
- **Endowment** $472.0 million
- **Coed** 18,312 undergraduate students, 92% full-time, 50% women, 50% men
- **Moderately difficult** entrance level, 73% of applicants were admitted

UNDERGRAD STUDENTS

16,803 full-time, 1,509 part-time. Students come from 52 states and territories; 49 other countries; 30% are from out of state; 20% Black or African American, non-Hispanic/Latino; 3% Hispanic/Latino; 1% Asian, non-Hispanic/Latino; 0.1% Native Hawaiian or other Pacific Islander, non-Hispanic/Latino; 0.5% American Indian or Alaska Native, non-Hispanic/Latino; 2% Two or more races, non-Hispanic/Latino; 0.5% Race/ethnicity unknown; 1% international; 11% transferred in; 27% live on campus.

Freshmen:
Admission: 13,817 applied, 10,144 admitted, 3,435 enrolled. *Average high school GPA:* 3.4. *Test scores:* ACT scores over 18: 96%; ACT scores over 24: 56%; ACT scores over 30: 17%.

Retention: 79% of full-time freshmen returned.

FACULTY

Total: 1,142, 85% full-time, 76% with terminal degrees.

Student/faculty ratio: 20:1.

ACADEMICS

Calendar: semesters. *Degrees:* associate, bachelor's, master's, doctoral, and post-master's certificates.

Special study options: academic remediation for entering students, accelerated degree program, adult/continuing education programs, advanced placement credit, cooperative education, distance learning, double majors, English as a second language, freshman honors college, honors programs, independent study, internships, off-campus study, part-time degree program, services for LD students, student-designed majors, study abroad, summer session for credit. *ROTC:* Army (b), Air Force (b).

Computers: 1,000 computers/terminals and 1,000 ports are available on campus for general student use. Students can access the following: campus intranet, computer help desk, free student e-mail accounts, online (class) grades, online (class) registration, online (class) schedules. Campuswide network is available. 100% of college-owned or -operated housing units are wired for high-speed Internet access. Wireless service is available via entire campus.

Library: Mitchell Memorial Library plus 2 others. *Books:* 257,296 (physical), 56,456 (digital/electronic); *Serial titles:* 1,646 (physical), 231,031 (digital/electronic); *Databases:* 185. Weekly public service hours: 110; students can reserve study rooms.

STUDENT LIFE

Housing options: on-campus residence required for freshman year; coed, men-only, women-only, special housing for students with disabilities. Campus housing is university owned. Freshman applicants given priority for college housing.

Activities and organizations: drama/theater group, student-run newspaper, radio and television station, choral group, marching band, Student Association, Black Student Alliance, Residence Hall Association, Fashion Board, Campus Activities Board, national fraternities, national sororities.

Athletics Member NCAA. All Division I except football (Division I-A). *Intercollegiate sports:* baseball M(s), basketball M(s)/W(s), cheerleading M(s)/W(s), cross-country running M/W(s), golf M(s)/W(s), soccer W(s), softball W(s), tennis M(s)/W(s), track and field M(s)/W(s), volleyball W(s). *Intramural sports:* archery M(c)/W(c), badminton M(c)/W(c), basketball M/W, bowling M/W, cross-country running W(c), equestrian sports M/W, fencing M(c)/W(c), football M/W, golf M/W, ice hockey M(c)/W(c), lacrosse M(c)/W(c), racquetball M/W, riflery M/W, rugby M(c), soccer M(c)/W(c), softball M(c)/W(c), swimming and diving M(c)/W(c), table tennis M(c)/W(c), tennis M(c)/W(c), ultimate Frisbee M/W, volleyball M(c)/W(c), water polo M/W, weight lifting M/W.

Campus security: 24-hour emergency response devices and patrols, late-night transport/escort service, controlled dormitory access, bicycle patrols, crime prevention program, RAD program, general law enforcement services.

Student services: health clinic, personal/psychological counseling.

COSTS & FINANCIAL AID

Costs (2017–18) *One-time required fee:* $55. *Tuition:* state resident $8318 full-time, $347 per credit hour part-time; nonresident $22,358 full-time, $932 per credit hour part-time. Full-time tuition and fees vary according to degree level and location. Part-time tuition and fees vary according to course load, degree level, and location. *Room and board:* $9614; room only: $6044. Room and board charges vary according to board plan, housing facility, and student level. *Payment plans:* tuition prepayment, installment. *Waivers:* children of alumni, senior citizens, and employees or children of employees.

Financial Aid Of all full-time matriculated undergraduates who enrolled in 2016, 12,236 applied for aid, 10,519 were judged to have need, 2,540 had their need fully met. 950 Federal Work-Study jobs (averaging $3450). In 2016, 3735 non-need-based awards were made. *Average percent of need met:* 60. *Average financial aid package:* $14,785. *Average need-based loan:* $3871. *Average need-based gift aid:* $6091. *Average non-need-based aid:* $4568. *Average indebtedness upon graduation:* $30,721.

APPLYING

Standardized Tests *Required:* SAT or ACT (for admission).

Options: electronic application.

Application fee: $40.

Required: high school transcript, minimum 2.0 GPA.

Application deadlines: 8/1 (freshmen), 8/1 (transfers).

Notification: continuous (freshmen), continuous (transfers).

CONTACT

Ms. Lori Ball, Director of Undergraduate Admissions, Mississippi State University, PO Box 6334, Mississippi State, MS 39762. *Phone:* 662-325-2224. *Fax:* 662-325-1MSU. *E-mail:* admit@msstate.edu.

Mississippi University for Women

Columbus, Mississippi

http://www.muw.edu/

CONTACT

Mississippi University for Women, 1100 College Street, MUW-1600, Columbus, MS 39701-9998. *Phone:* 662-329-7106. *Toll-free phone:* 877-GO 2 THE W.

Mississippi Valley State University

Itta Bena, Mississippi

http://www.mvsu.edu/

- **State-supported** comprehensive, founded 1946, part of Mississippi Institutions of Higher Learning
- **Small-town** 450-acre campus
- **Endowment** $1.6 million
- **Coed**
- **Minimally difficult** entrance level

FACULTY
Student/faculty ratio: 15:1.

ACADEMICS
Calendar: semesters. *Degrees:* bachelor's and master's.
Library: James Herbert White Library. *Books:* 127,541 (physical), 53,358 (digital/electronic); *Databases:* 62. Weekly public service hours: 84; students can reserve study rooms.

STUDENT LIFE
Housing options: men-only, women-only. Campus housing is university owned.

Activities and organizations: drama/theater group, student-run newspaper, radio and television station, choral group, marching band, Student Government Association, Baptist Student Union, Black Student

Fellowship, National Education Association, national fraternities, national sororities.

Athletics Member NCAA. All Division I except football (Division I-AA).

Campus security: 24-hour emergency response devices and patrols, controlled dormitory access.

Student services: health clinic, personal/psychological counseling.

COSTS
Costs (2017–18) *Tuition:* state resident $6422 full-time, $267 per credit hour part-time; nonresident $6422 full-time, $267 per credit hour part-time. *Required fees:* $20 full-time. *Room and board:* $7764; room only: $4258.

APPLYING
Standardized Tests *Required:* SAT or ACT (for admission).

Options: deferred entrance.

Required: high school transcript. *Required for some:* 2.5 letters of recommendation. *Recommended:* interview.

CONTACT
Mississippi Valley State University, 14000 Highway 82 West, Itta Bena, MS 38941-1400. *Phone:* 662-254-3345. *Toll-free phone:* 800-844-6885.

Rust College

Holly Springs, Mississippi

http://www.rustcollege.edu/

- **Independent United Methodist** 4-year, founded 1866
- **Small-town** 126-acre campus with easy access to Memphis
- **Endowment** $41.7 million
- **Coed** 1,004 undergraduate students, 87% full-time, 60% women, 40% men
- **Minimally difficult** entrance level, 7% of applicants were admitted

UNDERGRAD STUDENTS
873 full-time, 131 part-time. Students come from 22 states and territories; 6 other countries; 58% are from out of state; 95% Black or African American, non-Hispanic/Latino; 0.1% Asian, non-Hispanic/Latino; 2% Race/ethnicity unknown; 2% international; 7% transferred in; 76% live on campus.

Freshmen:
Admission: 5,337 applied, 360 admitted, 360 enrolled. *Average high school GPA:* 2.7.
Retention: 59% of full-time freshmen returned.

FACULTY
Total: 51, 94% full-time, 53% with terminal degrees.
Student/faculty ratio: 20:1.

ACADEMICS
Calendar: semesters. *Degrees:* associate and bachelor's.

Special study options: academic remediation for entering students, accelerated degree program, adult/continuing education programs, advanced placement credit, double majors, honors programs, independent study, internships, part-time degree program, study abroad, summer session for credit.

Computers: 339 computers/terminals are available on campus for general student use. Students can access the following: campus intranet, computer help desk, free student e-mail accounts, online (class) grades. Campuswide network is available. 100% of college-owned or -operated housing units are wired for high-speed Internet access. Wireless service is available via computer centers, computer labs, dorm rooms, libraries.
Library: Leontyne Price Library. *Books:* 126,854 (physical), 438 (digital/electronic); *Serial titles:* 279 (physical); *Databases:* 6. Weekly public service hours: 90; students can reserve study rooms.

STUDENT LIFE
Housing options: on-campus residence required for freshman year; men-only, women-only. Campus housing is university owned. Freshman campus housing is guaranteed.

Activities and organizations: drama/theater group, student-run radio and television station, choral group, marching band, National Sororities, National Fraternities, Choral Group, Television Station, Radio Station, national fraternities, national sororities.

Athletics Member NCAA. All Division III. *Intercollegiate sports:* baseball M, basketball M/W, cheerleading M/W, cross-country running M/W, softball W, tennis M/W, track and field M/W, volleyball M/W. *Intramural sports:* badminton M/W, basketball M/W, swimming and diving M/W, table tennis M/W, tennis M/W, volleyball M/W.

Campus security: 24-hour emergency response devices and patrols, controlled dormitory access.

Student services: health clinic, women's center.

COSTS & FINANCIAL AID

Costs (2018–19) *Comprehensive fee:* $14,200 includes full-time tuition ($9900) and room and board ($4300). Full-time tuition and fees vary according to course load. Part-time tuition and fees vary according to course load. *Payment plan:* installment. *Waivers:* senior citizens and employees or children of employees.

Financial Aid Of all full-time matriculated undergraduates who enrolled in 2004, 806 applied for aid, 806 were judged to have need, 481 had their need fully met. 492 Federal Work-Study jobs (averaging $714). 189 state and other part-time jobs (averaging $546). In 2004, 112 non-need-based awards were made. *Average percent of need met:* 60. *Average financial aid package:* $5067. *Average need-based loan:* $2158. *Average need-based gift aid:* $4281. *Average non-need-based aid:* $2795. *Average indebtedness upon graduation:* $9314.

APPLYING

Standardized Tests *Required:* ACT (for admission).

Application fee: $10.

Required: high school transcript, minimum 2.5 GPA, 2 letters of recommendation.

Application deadlines: rolling (freshmen), rolling (transfers).

Notification: continuous (freshmen), continuous (transfers).

CONTACT
Mr. Braque Talley, Dean of Enrollment, Rust College, 150 Rust Avenue, Holly Springs, MS 38635-2328. *Phone:* 601-252-8000 Ext. 4059. *Toll-free phone:* 888-886-8492 Ext. 4065. *Fax:* 662-252-8895. *E-mail:* btalley@rustcollege.edu.

Southeastern Baptist College

Laurel, Mississippi

http://www.southeasternbaptist.edu/

CONTACT
Mrs. Emma Bond, Director of Admissions, Southeastern Baptist College, 4229 Highway 15 North, Laurel, MS 39440-1096. *Phone:* 601-426-6346.

Strayer University–Jackson Campus

Jackson, Mississippi

http://www.strayer.edu/mississippi/jackson/

CONTACT
Strayer University–Jackson Campus, 460 Briarwood Drive, Suite 200, Jackson, MS 39206. *Toll-free phone:* 888-311-0355.

Tougaloo College

Tougaloo, Mississippi

http://www.tougaloo.edu/

CONTACT
Dr. Juno Jacobs, Director of Admissions, Tougaloo College, 500 West County Line Road, Tougaloo, MS 39174. *Phone:* 601-977-7765. *Toll-free phone:* 888-42GALOO. *Fax:* 601-977-4501. *E-mail:* jjacobs@tougaloo.edu.

University of Mississippi

Oxford, Mississippi

http://www.olemiss.edu/

CONTACT
Ms. Martina Brewer, Associate Director of Admissions, University of Mississippi, 128 Martindale Student Services Center, University, MS

38677. *Phone:* 662-915-7226. *Toll-free phone:* 800-653-6477. *Fax:* 662-915-5869. *E-mail:* admissions@olemiss.edu.

University of Mississippi Medical Center

Jackson, Mississippi

http://www.umc.edu/

CONTACT
Ms. Barbara Westerfield, Director of Student Records and Registrar, University of Mississippi Medical Center, 2500 North State Street, Jackson, MS 39216-4505. *Phone:* 601-984-1080. *Fax:* 601-984-1079.

University of Southern Mississippi

Hattiesburg, Mississippi

http://www.usm.edu/

- **State-supported** university, founded 1910, part of Mississippi Institutions of Higher Learning
- **Suburban** 1090-acre campus
- **Endowment** $82.7 million
- **Coed** 11,815 undergraduate students, 88% full-time, 63% women, 37% men
- **Moderately difficult** entrance level, 98% of applicants were admitted

UNDERGRAD STUDENTS
10,384 full-time, 1,431 part-time. 18% are from out of state; 28% Black or African American, non-Hispanic/Latino; 3% Hispanic/Latino; 1% Asian, non-Hispanic/Latino; 0.1% Native Hawaiian or other Pacific Islander, non-Hispanic/Latino; 0.5% American Indian or Alaska Native, non-Hispanic/Latino; 3% Two or more races, non-Hispanic/Latino; 1% Race/ethnicity unknown; 2% international; 15% transferred in; 28% live on campus.

Freshmen:
Admission: 6,405 applied, 6,306 admitted, 1,903 enrolled. *Average high school GPA:* 3.3. *Test scores:* ACT scores over 18: 91%; ACT scores over 24: 41%; ACT scores over 30: 10%.

Retention: 72% of full-time freshmen returned.

FACULTY
Total: 899, 79% full-time, 68% with terminal degrees.

Student/faculty ratio: 17:1.

ACADEMICS
Calendar: semesters. *Degrees:* certificates, bachelor's, master's, doctoral, post-master's, and postbachelor's certificates.

Special study options: academic remediation for entering students, accelerated degree program, adult/continuing education programs, advanced placement credit, cooperative education, distance learning, double majors, English as a second language, honors programs, independent study, internships, off-campus study, part-time degree program, services for LD students, study abroad, summer session for credit. *ROTC:* Army (c), Air Force (b).

Computers: 436 computers/terminals are available on campus for general student use. Students can access the following: campus intranet, computer help desk, free student e-mail accounts, online (class) grades, online (class) registration, online (class) schedules. Campuswide network is available. 100% of college-owned or -operated housing units are wired for high-speed Internet access. Wireless service is available via entire campus.

Library: Cook Memorial Library plus 4 others. *Books:* 1.4 million (physical), 331,932 (digital/electronic); *Serial titles:* 27,243 (physical), 118,798 (digital/electronic); *Databases:* 200. Weekly public service hours: 117; students can reserve study rooms.

STUDENT LIFE
Housing options: men-only, women-only, special housing for students with disabilities. Campus housing is university owned. Freshman applicants given priority for college housing.

Activities and organizations: drama/theater group, student-run newspaper, radio station, choral group, marching band, national fraternities, national sororities.

Athletics Member NCAA. All Division I. *Intercollegiate sports:* baseball M(s), basketball M(s)/W(s), cheerleading M/W, cross-country running W(s), football M(s), golf M(s)/W(s), soccer W(s), softball W(s), tennis M(s)/W(s), track and field M(s)/W(s), volleyball W(s). *Intramural sports:* badminton M/W, basketball M/W, bowling M/W, racquetball M/W, rugby M, soccer M/W, softball W, tennis M/W, track and field M/W, ultimate Frisbee M/W, volleyball M/W.

Campus security: 24-hour emergency response devices and patrols, late-night transport/escort service, controlled dormitory access.

Student services: health clinic, personal/psychological counseling, women's center, legal services.

COSTS & FINANCIAL AID

Costs (2018–19) *Tuition:* state resident $8108 full-time, $338 per credit hour part-time; nonresident $10,108 full-time, $338 per credit hour part-time. Part-time tuition and fees vary according to course load and degree level. *Room and board:* $10,638; room only: $6598. Room and board charges vary according to board plan and housing facility. *Payment plan:* installment. *Waivers:* children of alumni, senior citizens, and employees or children of employees.

Financial Aid Of all full-time matriculated undergraduates who enrolled in 2016, 8,547 applied for aid, 7,550 were judged to have need, 1,702 had their need fully met. In 2016, 700 non-need-based awards were made. *Average percent of need met:* 69. *Average financial aid package:* $11,603. *Average need-based loan:* $5029. *Average need-based gift aid:* $4589. *Average non-need-based aid:* $5788. *Average indebtedness upon graduation:* $27,859.

APPLYING

Standardized Tests *Required:* SAT or ACT (for admission).

Options: electronic application, early admission.

Application fee: $40.

Required: minimum 2.0 GPA. *Required for some:* high school transcript, statement of good standing from prior institutions, college transcripts.

Application deadlines: 6/30 (freshmen), 8/19 (transfers).

CONTACT

University of Southern Mississippi, 118 College Drive, Hattiesburg, MS 39406-0001. *Phone:* 601-266-5000.

William Carey University

Hattiesburg, Mississippi
http://www.wmcarey.edu/

CONTACT
Mr. William N. Curry, Dean of Enrollment Management, William Carey University, 710 William Carey Parkway, Hattiesburg, MS 39401. *Phone:* 601-318-6051. *Toll-free phone:* 800-962-5991. *Fax:* 601-318-6154. *E-mail:* admissions@wmcarey.edu.

MISSOURI

American Business & Technology University

Saint Joseph, Missouri
http://www.abtu.edu/

CONTACT
Richard Lingle, Lead Admission Coordinator, American Business & Technology University, 1018 West St.Maartens Drive, Saint Joseph, MO 64506. *Phone:* 800-908-9329 Ext. 13. *Toll-free phone:* 800-804-1388. *E-mail:* ricahrd@acot.edu.

Avila University

Kansas City, Missouri
http://www.avila.edu/
- **Independent Roman Catholic** comprehensive, founded 1916
- **Suburban** 50-acre campus
- **Coed** 1,372 undergraduate students, 78% full-time, 55% women, 37% men
- **Minimally difficult** entrance level, 41% of applicants were admitted

UNDERGRAD STUDENTS
1,077 full-time, 195 part-time. Students come from 33 states and territories; 22 other countries; 28% are from out of state; 21% Black or African American, non-Hispanic/Latino; 8% Hispanic/Latino; 2% Asian, non-Hispanic/Latino; 0.2% Native Hawaiian or other Pacific Islander, non-Hispanic/Latino; 0.3% American Indian or Alaska Native, non-Hispanic/Latino; 4% Two or more races, non-Hispanic/Latino; 10% international; 13% transferred in; 31% live on campus.

Freshmen:
Admission: 2,040 applied, 836 admitted, 183 enrolled. *Average high school GPA:* 3.2. *Test scores:* SAT evidence-based reading and writing scores over 500: 75%; SAT math scores over 500: 58%; ACT scores over 18: 92%; SAT math scores over 600: 8%; ACT scores over 24: 23%; ACT scores over 30: 2%.
Retention: 69% of full-time freshmen returned.

FACULTY
Total: 238, 31% full-time, 49% with terminal degrees.
Student/faculty ratio: 13:1.

ACADEMICS
Calendar: semesters. *Degrees:* bachelor's, master's, and postbachelor's certificates.

Special study options: academic remediation for entering students, accelerated degree program, adult/continuing education programs, advanced placement credit, cooperative education, distance learning, double majors, English as a second language, independent study, internships, off-campus study, part-time degree program, services for LD students, study abroad, summer session for credit. *ROTC:* Army (c).

Unusual degree programs: 3-2 occupational therapy, physical therapy, law with Rockhurst University, University of Missouri–Kansas City.

Computers: 141 computers/terminals and 225 ports are available on campus for general student use. Students can access the following: campus intranet, computer help desk, free student e-mail accounts, online (class) grades, online (class) registration, online (class) schedules, laptop checkout through library. Campuswide network is available. 100% of college-owned or -operated housing units are wired for high-speed Internet access. Wireless service is available via entire campus.

Library: Hooley-Bundshu Library plus 1 other. *Books:* 39,963 (physical), 309,288 (digital/electronic); *Serial titles:* 205 (physical), 389,497 (digital/electronic); *Databases:* 72. Weekly public service hours: 91; students can reserve study rooms.

STUDENT LIFE
Housing options: on-campus residence required through sophomore year; coed, men-only, women-only. Campus housing is university owned. Freshman campus housing is guaranteed.

Activities and organizations: drama/theater group, student-run newspaper, choral group, Avila Ambassadors, Avila Student Nurses Association, Campus Ministries, Saudi Arabian Student Association, Avila University Theatre Company.

Athletics Member NAIA. *Intercollegiate sports:* baseball M(s), basketball M(s)/W(s), cheerleading W(s), cross-country running M(s)/W(s), football M(s), golf M(s)/W(s), soccer M(s)/W(s), softball W(s), track and field M(s)/W(s), volleyball W(s). *Intramural sports:* bowling M/W, table tennis M/W.

Campus security: 24-hour emergency response devices and patrols, student patrols, late-night transport/escort service, controlled dormitory access.

Student services: health clinic, personal/psychological counseling.

COSTS & FINANCIAL AID
Costs (2018–19) *Comprehensive fee:* $27,100 includes full-time tuition ($19,900) and room and board ($7200). Full-time tuition and fees vary

according to course load and program. Part-time tuition: $778 per credit hour. Part-time tuition and fees vary according to course load and program. No tuition increase for student's term of enrollment. *College room only:* $3300. Room and board charges vary according to board plan and housing facility. *Payment plans:* installment, deferred payment. *Waivers:* children of alumni, senior citizens, and employees or children of employees.

Financial Aid Of all full-time matriculated undergraduates who enrolled in 2008, 1,927 applied for aid, 1,852 were judged to have need, 1,846 had their need fully met. 161 Federal Work-Study jobs (averaging $903). 55 state and other part-time jobs (averaging $885). In 2008, 60 non-need-based awards were made. *Average percent of need met:* 35. *Average financial aid package:* $12,976. *Average need-based loan:* $5465. *Average need-based gift aid:* $7854. *Average non-need-based aid:* $9152. *Average indebtedness upon graduation:* $16,508.

APPLYING

Standardized Tests *Required:* SAT or ACT (for admission).

Options: electronic application, early admission.

Required: high school transcript, minimum 2.5 GPA, secondary school report. *Required for some:* essay or personal statement. *Recommended:* interview.

Application deadlines: 8/15 (freshmen), 8/15 (transfers).

Notification: 8/15 (freshmen), 8/15 (transfers).

CONTACT
Josh Parisse, Director of Undergraduate Admissions, Avila University, 11901 Wornall Road, Kansas City, MO 64145. *Phone:* 816-501-2400. *Toll-free phone:* 800-GO-AVILA. *Fax:* 816-501-2453. *E-mail:* josh.parisse@avila.edu.

Baptist Bible College

Springfield, Missouri
http://www.gobbc.edu/

CONTACT
Mr. Terry Allcorn, Director of Admissions, Baptist Bible College, 628 East Kearney Street, Springfield, MO 65803-3498. *Phone:* 417-268-6000. *Toll-free phone:* 800-228-5754. *Fax:* 417-268-6694.

Bryan University

Springfield, Missouri
http://www.bryanu.edu/

CONTACT
Bryan University, 4255 South Nature Center Way, Springfield, MO 65804. *Toll-free phone:* 855-566-0650.

Calvary University

Kansas City, Missouri
http://www.calvary.edu/

- **Independent nondenominational** comprehensive, founded 1932
- **Suburban** 55-acre campus with easy access to Kansas City
- **Endowment** $1.2 million
- **Coed** 231 undergraduate students, 60% full-time, 48% women, 52% men
- **Noncompetitive** entrance level, 98% of applicants were admitted

UNDERGRAD STUDENTS
138 full-time, 93 part-time. Students come from 18 states and territories; 1 other country; 49% are from out of state; 10% Black or African American, non-Hispanic/Latino; 1% Hispanic/Latino; 3% Asian, non-Hispanic/Latino; 0.4% Native Hawaiian or other Pacific Islander, non-Hispanic/Latino; 1% American Indian or Alaska Native, non-Hispanic/Latino; 5% Two or more races, non-Hispanic/Latino; 0.4% Race/ethnicity unknown; 12% transferred in; 41% live on campus.

Freshmen:
Admission: 44 applied, 43 admitted, 32 enrolled. *Average high school GPA:* 3.5. *Test scores:* ACT scores over 18: 95%; ACT scores over 24: 45%; ACT scores over 30: 15%.

Retention: 53% of full-time freshmen returned.

FACULTY
Total: 44, 25% full-time, 36% with terminal degrees.

Student/faculty ratio: 7:1.

ACADEMICS
Calendar: semesters. *Degrees:* certificates, associate, bachelor's, and master's.

Special study options: accelerated degree program, adult/continuing education programs, advanced placement credit, cooperative education, distance learning, double majors, independent study, internships, off-campus study, part-time degree program, services for LD students, student-designed majors, summer session for credit. *ROTC:* Army (c).

Computers: 32 computers/terminals are available on campus for general student use. Students can access the following: computer help desk, free student e-mail accounts, online (class) grades, online (class) registration, online (class) schedules. Campuswide network is available. 100% of college-owned or -operated housing units are wired for high-speed Internet access. Wireless service is available via classrooms, computer centers, computer labs, dorm rooms, learning centers, libraries, student centers.

Library: Hilda Kroeker Library. *Books:* 41,841 (physical), 420 (digital/electronic); *Serial titles:* 268 (physical); *Databases:* 4.

STUDENT LIFE
Housing options: men-only, women-only. Campus housing is university owned. Freshman campus housing is guaranteed.

Activities and organizations: drama/theater group, choral group, Missions Encounter, Masterworks (Fine Arts).

Athletics Member NCCAA. *Intercollegiate sports:* basketball M/W, soccer M, volleyball W.

Campus security: 24-hour emergency response devices and patrols, late-night transport/escort service, controlled dormitory access, night patrols by trained security personnel, monitored closed circuit cameras.

Student services: personal/psychological counseling.

COSTS & FINANCIAL AID
Costs (2018–19) *One-time required fee:* $100. *Comprehensive fee:* $19,387 includes full-time tuition ($10,276), mandatory fees ($876), and room and board ($8235). Full-time tuition and fees vary according to location and program. Part-time tuition: $367 per credit hour. Part-time tuition and fees vary according to location and program. *Required fees:* $63 per credit hour part-time, $438 per term part-time. *College room only:* $3900. Room and board charges vary according to board plan and housing facility. *Payment plan:* installment. *Waivers:* employees or children of employees.

Financial Aid Of all full-time matriculated undergraduates who enrolled in 2016, 101 applied for aid, 95 were judged to have need, 7 had their need fully met. 8 Federal Work-Study jobs (averaging $1687). In 2016, 4 non-need-based awards were made. *Average percent of need met:* 66. *Average financial aid package:* $12,774. *Average need-based loan:* $4265. *Average need-based gift aid:* $5694. *Average non-need-based aid:* $2543. *Average indebtedness upon graduation:* $19,246.

APPLYING
Standardized Tests *Required:* SAT or ACT (for admission).

Options: electronic application.

Required: essay or personal statement, minimum 2.0 GPA, 2 letters of recommendation. *Required for some:* high school transcript. *Recommended:* interview.

Application deadlines: rolling (freshmen), rolling (transfers), rolling (early action).

Notification: continuous (freshmen), continuous (transfers).

CONTACT
Ms. Ann Rogers, Admissions Secretary, Calvary University, 15800 Calvary Road, Kansas City, MO 64147-1341. *Phone:* 816-322-0110 Ext. 1323. *Toll-free phone:* 800-326-3960. *Fax:* 816-331-4474. *E-mail:* ann.rogers@cavalry.edu.

Central Christian College of the Bible
Moberly, Missouri
http://www.cccb.edu/

CONTACT
Mr. Aaron Merritt, Director of Admissions, Central Christian College of the Bible, 911 Urbandale Drive East, Moberly, MO 65270-1997. *Phone:* 660-263-3900. *Toll-free phone:* 888-263-3900. *Fax:* 660-263-3936. *E-mail:* admissions@cccb.edu.

Central Methodist University
Fayette, Missouri
http://www.centralmethodist.edu/
- **Independent Methodist** comprehensive, founded 1854
- **Small-town** 80-acre campus
- **Endowment** $45.5 million
- **Coed** 1,060 undergraduate students, 98% full-time, 53% women, 47% men
- **Moderately difficult** entrance level, 63% of applicants were admitted

UNDERGRAD STUDENTS
1,034 full-time, 26 part-time. Students come from 24 states and territories; 29 other countries; 15% are from out of state; 8% Black or African American, non-Hispanic/Latino; 4% Hispanic/Latino; 0.3% Asian, non-Hispanic/Latino; 0.1% Native Hawaiian or other Pacific Islander, non-Hispanic/Latino; 0.5% American Indian or Alaska Native, non-Hispanic/Latino; 4% Two or more races, non-Hispanic/Latino; 2% Race/ethnicity unknown; 6% international; 8% transferred in; 60% live on campus.

Freshmen:
Admission: 1,357 applied, 850 admitted, 279 enrolled. *Average high school GPA:* 3.5. *Test scores:* ACT scores over 18: 96%; ACT scores over 24: 32%; ACT scores over 30: 4%.
Retention: 68% of full-time freshmen returned.

FACULTY
Total: 118, 58% full-time, 44% with terminal degrees.
Student/faculty ratio: 12:1.

ACADEMICS
Calendar: semesters. *Degrees:* associate, bachelor's, and master's.
Special study options: academic remediation for entering students, advanced placement credit, cooperative education, double majors, honors programs, independent study, internships, part-time degree program, services for LD students, student-designed majors, study abroad, summer session for credit. *ROTC:* Army (c), Air Force (c).
Unusual degree programs: 3-2 engineering with Missouri University of Science and Technology.
Computers: 100 computers/terminals and 816 ports are available on campus for general student use. Students can access the following: computer help desk, free student e-mail accounts, online (class) grades, online (class) registration, online (class) schedules. Campuswide network is available. 100% of college-owned or -operated housing units are wired for high-speed Internet access. Wireless service is available via entire campus.
Library: Smiley Library. *Books:* 67,581 (physical), 127,545 (digital/electronic); *Serial titles:* 96 (physical), 38,528 (digital/electronic); *Databases:* 35. Students can reserve study rooms.

STUDENT LIFE
Housing options: on-campus residence required through senior year; coed, men-only, women-only. Campus housing is university owned. Freshman applicants given priority for college housing.
Activities and organizations: drama/theater group, student-run newspaper, radio and television station, choral group, marching band, Student Government Association, Enactus, Alpha Phi Omega, Beta Beta Beta, Campus Ministries, national fraternities, national sororities.
Athletics Member NAIA. *Intercollegiate sports:* baseball M(s), basketball M(s)/W(s), cheerleading M(s)/W(s), cross-country running M(s)/W(s), football M(s), soccer M(s)/W(s), softball W(s), track and field M(s)/W(s), volleyball W(s). *Intramural sports:* basketball M/W, football

M/W, racquetball M/W, soccer M/W, softball M/W, tennis M/W, track and field M/W, volleyball M/W, water polo M/W.
Campus security: 24-hour emergency response devices, late-night transport/escort service, controlled dormitory access.
Student services: health clinic, personal/psychological counseling.

COSTS & FINANCIAL AID
Costs (2018–19) *One-time required fee:* $100. *Comprehensive fee:* $32,360 includes full-time tuition ($23,650), mandatory fees ($770), and room and board ($7940). Full-time tuition and fees vary according to program and reciprocity agreements. Part-time tuition: $210 per credit hour. Part-time tuition and fees vary according to course load and program. *Required fees:* $31 per credit hour part-time. *College room only:* $3890. Room and board charges vary according to board plan and housing facility. *Payment plan:* installment. *Waivers:* children of alumni and employees or children of employees.
Financial Aid Of all full-time matriculated undergraduates who enrolled in 2017, 904 applied for aid, 834 were judged to have need, 178 had their need fully met. In 2017, 138 non-need-based awards were made. *Average percent of need met:* 75. *Average financial aid package:* $20,911. *Average need-based loan:* $4246. *Average need-based gift aid:* $5303. *Average non-need-based aid:* $11,700.

APPLYING
Standardized Tests *Required:* SAT or ACT (for admission).
Options: electronic application, deferred entrance.
Required: high school transcript, minimum 2.5 GPA. *Required for some:* 2 letters of recommendation.
Application deadlines: rolling (freshmen), rolling (out-of-state freshmen), rolling (transfers).
Notification: continuous (freshmen), continuous (out-of-state freshmen), continuous (transfers).

CONTACT
Central Methodist University, 411 Central Methodist Square, Fayette, MO 65248-1198. *Toll-free phone:* 888-CMU-1854 (in-state); 877-CMU-1854 (out-of-state).

Chamberlain College of Nursing
St. Louis, Missouri
http://www.chamberlain.edu/
- **Proprietary** 4-year, founded 1889, part of DeVry University
- **Urban** campus
- **Coed**
- **Moderately difficult** entrance level

FACULTY
Student/faculty ratio: 7:1.

ACADEMICS
Calendar: semesters. *Degree:* bachelor's.

STUDENT LIFE
Housing options: college housing not available.
Campus security: 24-hour patrols, late-night transport/escort service, controlled dormitory access.

COSTS
Costs (2017–18) *Tuition:* $18,900 full-time. *Required fees:* $600 full-time.

APPLYING
Standardized Tests *Required:* SAT or ACT (for admission).
Options: deferred entrance.
Application fee: $95.
Required: essay or personal statement, high school transcript. *Required for some:* interview.

CONTACT
Admissions, Chamberlain College of Nursing, 11830 Westline Industrial Drive, Suite 106, St. Louis, MO 63146. *Phone:* 314-991-6200. *Toll-free phone:* 877-751-5783.

City Vision University

Kansas City, Missouri

http://www.cityvision.edu/

- **Independent Christian** comprehensive, founded 1998
- **Coed**
- **Noncompetitive** entrance level

FACULTY
Student/faculty ratio: 5:1.

ACADEMICS
Calendar: 5 terms that are 8 week long course offerings. *Degrees:* associate, bachelor's, and master's.
Library: http://www.cityvision.edu/library.

COSTS & FINANCIAL AID
Costs (2017–18) *One-time required fee:* $50. *Tuition:* $7000 full-time, $3500 per year part-time. Full-time tuition and fees vary according to course load and degree level. Part-time tuition and fees vary according to course load and degree level.

Financial Aid Of all full-time matriculated undergraduates who enrolled in 2014, 60 applied for aid, 60 were judged to have need, 40 had their need fully met. In 2014, 9 non-need-based awards were made. *Average percent of need met:* 100. *Average financial aid package:* $3806. *Average need-based loan:* $4054. *Average need-based gift aid:* $2548. *Average non-need-based aid:* $850.

APPLYING
Options: electronic application.
Required: high school transcript.

CONTACT
Mrs. Nancy Young, Director of Admissions, City Vision University, 3101 Troost Avenue, Suite 200, Kansas City, MO 64109-1845. *Phone:* 816-960-2008 Ext. 3. *Fax:* 816-256-8471. *E-mail:* newstudents@cityvision.edu.

College of the Ozarks

Point Lookout, Missouri

http://www.cofo.edu/

- **Independent Presbyterian** 4-year, founded 1906
- **Rural** 1000-acre campus
- **Endowment** $459.3 million
- **Coed** 1,508 undergraduate students, 98% full-time, 55% women, 45% men
- **Moderately difficult** entrance level, 16% of applicants were admitted

UNDERGRAD STUDENTS
1,477 full-time, 31 part-time. Students come from 24 states and territories; 17 other countries; 24% are from out of state; 0.7% Black or African American, non-Hispanic/Latino; 2% Hispanic/Latino; 0.7% Asian, non-Hispanic/Latino; 0.1% Native Hawaiian or other Pacific Islander, non-Hispanic/Latino; 0.4% American Indian or Alaska Native, non-Hispanic/Latino; 2% Two or more races, non-Hispanic/Latino; 2% Race/ethnicity unknown; 1% international; 1% transferred in; 90% live on campus.

Freshmen:
Admission: 2,879 applied, 447 admitted, 368 enrolled. *Average high school GPA:* 3.7. *Test scores:* SAT evidence-based reading and writing scores over 500: 100%; ACT scores over 18: 99%; SAT evidence-based reading and writing scores over 600: 42%; ACT scores over 24: 49%; ACT scores over 30: 6%.
Retention: 73% of full-time freshmen returned.

FACULTY
Total: 143, 64% full-time, 44% with terminal degrees.
Student/faculty ratio: 14:1.

ACADEMICS
Calendar: semesters. *Degree:* bachelor's.
Special study options: academic remediation for entering students, advanced placement credit, double majors, English as a second language, independent study, internships, off-campus study, services for LD

students, student-designed majors, summer session for credit. *ROTC:* Army (b).

Unusual degree programs: medical technology with Cox Medical Center Springfield, MO.

Computers: 402 computers/terminals and 1,771 ports are available on campus for general student use. Students can access the following: campus intranet, computer help desk, free student e-mail accounts, online (class) grades, online (class) registration, online (class) schedules. Campuswide network is available. 100% of college-owned or -operated housing units are wired for high-speed Internet access. Wireless service is available via classrooms, dorm rooms, libraries, student centers.
Library: Lyons Memorial Library plus 2 others. *Books:* 98,400 (physical), 400,000 (digital/electronic); *Serial titles:* 300 (physical), 52,500 (digital/electronic); *Databases:* 45. Weekly public service hours: 77.

STUDENT LIFE
Housing options: on-campus residence required through senior year; men-only, women-only. Campus housing is university owned.

Activities and organizations: drama/theater group, student-run newspaper, radio station, choral group, Young Americans for Freedom, Chi Alpha, Baptist Student Union, Agriculture Club, FCA.

Athletics Member NCAA, NAIA. All NCAA Division II. *Intercollegiate sports:* baseball M(s), basketball M(s)/W(s), cheerleading M/W, cross-country running M/W, golf M/W, track and field M/W, volleyball W(s). *Intramural sports:* basketball M/W, football M/W, racquetball M/W, softball M/W, volleyball M/W.

Campus security: 24-hour emergency response devices and patrols, student patrols, late-night transport/escort service, controlled dormitory access, front gate closed 6 pm to 5 am, security checks cars for proper credentials for entry.
Student services: health clinic, personal/psychological counseling.

COSTS & FINANCIAL AID
Costs (2018–19) *Comprehensive fee:* includes mandatory fees ($460) and room and board ($7400). Part-time tuition: $310 per credit hour. Part-time tuition and fees vary according to course load. Each student participates in the on-campus work program for 15 hours per week and two forty-hour work weeks. Earnings from participation in the work program, plus any federal and/or state aid for which students qualify, plus a College of the Ozarks Cost of Education Scholarship combine to meet each student's full tuition charge. *College room only:* $3700. *Payment plan:* installment.

Financial Aid Of all full-time matriculated undergraduates who enrolled in 2016, 1,531 applied for aid, 1,366 were judged to have need. *Average financial aid package:* $18,500. *Average need-based gift aid:* $14,188.

APPLYING
Standardized Tests *Required:* SAT or ACT (for admission). *Recommended:* ACT (for admission).
Options: electronic application.
Required: high school transcript, 2 letters of recommendation, interview, medical history, financial statement. *Recommended:* minimum 3.0 GPA.
Application deadlines: 12/31 (freshmen), 12/31 (transfers).
Notification: continuous (freshmen), continuous (transfers).

CONTACT
Mrs. Kim Williams, Admissions Secretary, College of the Ozarks, PO Box 17, Point Lookout, MO 65726. *Phone:* 417-690-2636. *Toll-free phone:* 800-222-0525. *Fax:* 417-335-2618. *E-mail:* admissions@cofo.edu.

Columbia College

Columbia, Missouri

http://www.ccis.edu/

- **Independent** comprehensive, founded 1851, affiliated with Christian Church (Disciples of Christ)
- **Urban** 33-acre campus with easy access to St. Louis and Kansas City
- **Endowment** $163.3 million
- **Coed** 1,041 undergraduate students, 82% full-time, 58% women, 42% men
- **Minimally difficult** entrance level, 52% of applicants were admitted

UNDERGRAD STUDENTS

856 full-time, 185 part-time. Students come from 28 states and territories; 14 other countries; 12% are from out of state; 5% Black or African American, non-Hispanic/Latino; 4% Hispanic/Latino; 1% Asian, non-Hispanic/Latino; 0.3% American Indian or Alaska Native, non-Hispanic/Latino; 6% Two or more races, non-Hispanic/Latino; 3% Race/ethnicity unknown; 6% international; 13% transferred in; 37% live on campus.

Freshmen:
Admission: 1,589 applied, 831 admitted, 174 enrolled. *Average high school GPA:* 3.4. *Test scores:* SAT evidence-based reading and writing scores over 500: 90%; SAT math scores over 500: 95%; ACT scores over 18: 96%; SAT evidence-based reading and writing scores over 600: 37%; SAT math scores over 600: 48%; ACT scores over 24: 46%; SAT math scores over 700: 11%; ACT scores over 30: 7%.

Retention: 78% of full-time freshmen returned.

FACULTY
Total: 135, 55% full-time, 29% with terminal degrees.
Student/faculty ratio: 11:1.

ACADEMICS
Calendar: semesters. *Degrees:* certificates, associate, bachelor's, and master's (offers continuing education program with significant enrollment not reflected in profile).

Special study options: adult/continuing education programs, advanced placement credit, cooperative education, distance learning, double majors, English as a second language, honors programs, independent study, internships, off-campus study, part-time degree program, services for LD students, student-designed majors, study abroad, summer session for credit. *ROTC:* Army (c), Navy (c), Air Force (c).

Unusual degree programs: 3-2 nursing; education.

Computers: 134 computers/terminals and 1,000 ports are available on campus for general student use. Students can access the following: campus intranet, computer help desk, free student e-mail accounts, online (class) grades, online (class) registration, online (class) schedules. Campuswide network is available. 100% of college-owned or -operated housing units are wired for high-speed Internet access. Wireless service is available via entire campus.
Library: J. W. and Lois Stafford Library. *Books:* 61,727 (physical), 212,036 (digital/electronic); *Serial titles:* 108 (physical), 93,017 (digital/electronic); *Databases:* 61. Weekly public service hours: 94; students can reserve study rooms.

STUDENT LIFE
Housing options: on-campus residence required through sophomore year; coed, women-only, special housing for students with disabilities. Campus housing is university owned and leased by the school. Freshman campus housing is guaranteed.

Activities and organizations: drama/theater group, choral group, International Club, Honor Student Association, Black Student Coalition, Pre-Healthcare Professionals, Commited and Serving Together.

Athletics Member NAIA. *Intercollegiate sports:* baseball M(s), basketball M(s)/W(s), cross-country running M(s)/W(s), golf M(s)/W(s), soccer M(s)/W(s), softball W(s), volleyball W(s). *Intramural sports:* basketball M/W, football M/W, soccer M/W, softball M/W, volleyball M/W.

Campus security: 24-hour emergency response devices and patrols, late-night transport/escort service, controlled dormitory access, building monitor patrols off-campus site.
Student services: health clinic, personal/psychological counseling.

COSTS & FINANCIAL AID
Costs (2018–19) *Tuition:* $22,704 full-time, $487 per credit hour part-time. Full-time tuition and fees vary according to class time, course load, program, reciprocity agreements, and student level. Part-time tuition and fees vary according to class time, course load, location, and reciprocity agreements. No tuition increase for student's term of enrollment. *Room only:* Room and board charges vary according to housing facility. *Payment plans:* installment, deferred payment. *Waivers:* children of alumni, senior citizens, and employees or children of employees.

Financial Aid Of all full-time matriculated undergraduates who enrolled in 2016, 633 applied for aid, 552 were judged to have need, 92 had their need fully met. 156 Federal Work-Study jobs (averaging $2805). 34 state and other part-time jobs (averaging $1709). In 2016, 94 non-need-based awards were made. *Average percent of need met:* 62. *Average financial aid package:* $16,156. *Average need-based loan:* $3438. *Average need-based gift aid:* $4977. *Average non-need-based aid:* $8988. *Average indebtedness upon graduation:* $26,312.

APPLYING
Standardized Tests *Required:* SAT or ACT (for admission).
Options: electronic application, deferred entrance.
Application fee: $35.
Required: high school transcript, minimum 2.5 GPA. *Required for some:* essay or personal statement, interview.
Notification: continuous (freshmen), continuous (out-of-state freshmen), continuous (transfers).

CONTACT
Admissions Office, Columbia College, 1001 Rogers Street, Columbia, MO 65216. Phone: 573-875-7352. *Toll-free phone:* 800-231-2391. *Fax:* 573-875-7506. *E-mail:* admissions@ccis.edu.

Conception Seminary College
Conception, Missouri
http://www.conception.edu/
- **Independent Roman Catholic** 4-year, founded 1886
- **Rural** 30-acre campus
- **Men only** 67 undergraduate students, 100% full-time
- **Noncompetitive** entrance level, 100% of applicants were admitted

UNDERGRAD STUDENTS
67 full-time. Students come from 58 states and territories; 4 other countries; 76% are from out of state; 18% Hispanic/Latino; 7% Asian, non-Hispanic/Latino; 21% transferred in.

Freshmen:
Admission: 28 applied, 28 admitted, 14 enrolled.
Retention: 45% of full-time freshmen returned.

FACULTY
Student/faculty ratio: 4:1.

ACADEMICS
Calendar: semesters. *Degrees:* bachelor's and postbachelor's certificates.
Special study options: academic remediation for entering students, advanced placement credit, cooperative education, English as a second language, independent study, off-campus study, services for LD students.
Computers: 20 computers/terminals and 20 ports are available on campus for general student use. Students can access the following: free student e-mail accounts. Campuswide network is available. 100% of college-owned or -operated housing units are wired for high-speed Internet access. Wireless service is available via entire campus.
Library: Conception Seminary College Library.

STUDENT LIFE
Housing options: on-campus residence required through senior year; men-only. Campus housing is university owned.
Activities and organizations: drama/theater group, choral group, national fraternities.
Campus security: 24-hour emergency response devices.
Student services: health clinic, personal/psychological counseling.

COSTS & FINANCIAL AID
Costs (2018–19) *Comprehensive fee:* $34,385 includes full-time tuition ($21,326), mandatory fees ($250), and room and board ($12,809). Part-time tuition: $200 per credit hour. *College room only:* $5358. *Payment plan:* installment. *Waivers:* employees or children of employees.

Financial Aid Of all full-time matriculated undergraduates who enrolled in 2016, 35 applied for aid, 24 were judged to have need, 1 had their need fully met. 20 Federal Work-Study jobs (averaging $876). 34 state and other part-time jobs (averaging $977). In 2016, 22 non-need-based awards were made. *Average percent of need met:* 90. *Average financial aid package:* $30,220. *Average need-based loan:* $4941. *Average need-based gift aid:* $6347. *Average non-need-based aid:* $2016. *Average indebtedness upon graduation:* $31,817.

APPLYING

Standardized Tests *Required:* SAT or ACT (for admission).

Options: early admission, deferred entrance.

Required: essay or personal statement, high school transcript, minimum 2.0 GPA, 2 letters of recommendation, church certificate, medical history.

CONTACT

Mrs. Jeanette Schieber, Director of Admissions, Conception Seminary College, 37174 State Highway VV, Conception, MO 64433. *Phone:* 660-944-2886. *Fax:* 660-944-2829. *E-mail:* admissions@conception.edu.

Cottey College

Nevada, Missouri

http://www.cottey.edu/

- **Independent** primarily 2-year, founded 1884
- **Small-town** 51-acre campus
- **Endowment** $108.8 million
- **Women only** 265 undergraduate students, 98% full-time
- **Moderately difficult** entrance level, 64% of applicants were admitted

UNDERGRAD STUDENTS

260 full-time, 5 part-time. Students come from 32 states and territories; 18 other countries; 85% are from out of state; 5% Black or African American, non-Hispanic/Latino; 8% Hispanic/Latino; 0.4% Asian, non-Hispanic/Latino; 0.4% Native Hawaiian or other Pacific Islander, non-Hispanic/Latino; 2% American Indian or Alaska Native, non-Hispanic/Latino; 5% Two or more races, non-Hispanic/Latino; 15% international; 4% transferred in; 90% live on campus.

Freshmen:

Admission: 525 applied, 338 admitted, 82 enrolled. *Average high school GPA:* 3.4. *Test scores:* SAT evidence-based reading and writing scores over 500: 73%; SAT math scores over 500: 52%; SAT evidence-based reading and writing scores over 600: 18%; SAT math scores over 600: 9%; SAT math scores over 700: 3%.

Retention: 70% of full-time freshmen returned.

FACULTY

Total: 52, 79% full-time, 75% with terminal degrees.

Student/faculty ratio: 7:1.

ACADEMICS

Calendar: semesters. *Degrees:* associate and bachelor's.

Special study options: advanced placement credit, distance learning, independent study, internships, part-time degree program, services for LD students, study abroad.

Computers: 70 computers/terminals are available on campus for general student use. Students can access the following: campus intranet, computer help desk, free student e-mail accounts. Campuswide network is available. 100% of college-owned or -operated housing units are wired for high-speed Internet access. Wireless service is available via entire campus.

Library: Blanche Skiff Ross Memorial Library plus 1 other. Weekly public service hours: 88.

STUDENT LIFE

Housing options: women-only. Campus housing is university owned.

Activities and organizations: drama/theater group, choral group, Inter-Society, Golden Key, French Club, Student Government, Global Citizens.

Athletics Member NJCAA. *Intercollegiate sports:* basketball W(s), cross-country running W(s), golf W(s), softball W(s), track and field W, volleyball W(s).

Campus security: 24-hour emergency response devices and patrols, late-night transport/escort service, controlled dormitory access.

Student services: health clinic, personal/psychological counseling.

COSTS & FINANCIAL AID

Costs (2018–19) *Comprehensive fee:* $28,850 includes full-time tuition ($19,900), mandatory fees ($1250), and room and board ($7700). Part-time tuition: $125 per credit hour. Part-time tuition and fees vary according to course load. *Required fees:* $22 per credit hour part-time, $88 per term part-time. *College room only:* $4200. Room and board

charges vary according to housing facility. *Payment plan:* installment. *Waivers:* employees or children of employees.

Financial Aid Of all full-time matriculated undergraduates who enrolled in 2017, 208 applied for aid, 190 were judged to have need, 64 had their need fully met. 20 Federal Work-Study jobs (averaging $2071). In 2017, 69 non-need-based awards were made. *Average percent of need met:* 84. *Average financial aid package:* $20,620. *Average need-based loan:* $3241. *Average need-based gift aid:* $16,929. *Average non-need-based aid:* $14,729. *Average indebtedness upon graduation:* $26,427.

APPLYING

Standardized Tests *Required:* SAT or ACT (for admission). *Required for some:* TOEFL, IELTS.

Options: electronic application, early admission, deferred entrance.

Application fee: $20.

Required: essay or personal statement, high school transcript, 1 letter of recommendation. *Recommended:* minimum 2.6 GPA, interview.

Application deadlines: rolling (freshmen), rolling (out-of-state freshmen), rolling (transfers).

Notification: continuous (freshmen), continuous (out-of-state freshmen), continuous (transfers).

CONTACT

Mrs. Angela Moore, Enrollment Office, Cottey College, 1000 West Austin Boulevard, Nevada, MO 64772. *Phone:* 417-667-8181. *Toll-free phone:* 888-526-8839. *Fax:* 417-667-8103. *E-mail:* amoore@cottey.edu.

Cox College

Springfield, Missouri

http://www.coxcollege.edu/

- **Independent** comprehensive, founded 1907
- **Urban** campus
- **Coed, primarily women**
- 59% of applicants were admitted

FACULTY

Student/faculty ratio: 9:1.

ACADEMICS

Calendar: semesters. *Degrees:* certificates, associate, bachelor's, master's, post-master's, and postbachelor's certificates.

Library: The Cox Health Systems Libraries plus 2 others. Weekly public service hours: 60.

STUDENT LIFE

Housing options: college housing not available.

Campus security: 24-hour emergency response devices and patrols, late-night transport/escort service, controlled dormitory access.

Student services: personal/psychological counseling.

COSTS & FINANCIAL AID

Costs (2017–18) *One-time required fee:* $225. *Tuition:* $8800 full-time, $400 per credit hour part-time. Full-time tuition and fees vary according to course load, degree level, and program. Part-time tuition and fees vary according to course load, degree level, and program. *Required fees:* $1470 full-time.

Financial Aid Of all full-time matriculated undergraduates who enrolled in 2016, 205 applied for aid, 205 were judged to have need. 22 Federal Work-Study jobs (averaging $2061). *Average financial aid package:* $3422. *Average need-based loan:* $3422. *Average need-based gift aid:* $4390.

APPLYING

Standardized Tests *Recommended:* SAT or ACT (for admission).

Options: electronic application, early decision.

Application fee: $50.

Required: high school transcript, minimum 2.5 GPA.

CONTACT

Cox College, 1423 North Jefferson, Springfield, MO 65802. *Phone:* 417-269-3083. *Toll-free phone:* 866-898-5355.

Culver-Stockton College

Canton, Missouri
http://www.culver.edu/
- **Independent** comprehensive, founded 1853, affiliated with Christian Church (Disciples of Christ)
- **Rural** 143-acre campus
- **Endowment** $21.7 million
- **Coed** 1,093 undergraduate students, 89% full-time, 50% women, 50% men
- **Moderately difficult** entrance level, 55% of applicants were admitted

UNDERGRAD STUDENTS
969 full-time, 124 part-time. Students come from 38 states and territories; 20 other countries; 46% are from out of state; 12% Black or African American, non-Hispanic/Latino; 6% Hispanic/Latino; 0.3% Asian, non-Hispanic/Latino; 0.2% Native Hawaiian or other Pacific Islander, non-Hispanic/Latino; 0.5% American Indian or Alaska Native, non-Hispanic/Latino; 3% Two or more races, non-Hispanic/Latino; 7% international; 6% transferred in; 76% live on campus.

Freshmen:
Admission: 3,308 applied, 1,808 admitted, 305 enrolled. *Average high school GPA:* 3.3. *Test scores:* SAT evidence-based reading and writing scores over 500: 68%; SAT math scores over 500: 56%; ACT scores over 18: 89%; SAT evidence-based reading and writing scores over 600: 6%; SAT math scores over 600: 10%; ACT scores over 24: 20%; ACT scores over 30: 2%.
Retention: 68% of full-time freshmen returned.

FACULTY
Total: 103, 50% full-time, 39% with terminal degrees.
Student/faculty ratio: 15:1.

ACADEMICS
Calendar: semesters. *Degrees:* bachelor's and master's.

Special study options: academic remediation for entering students, accelerated degree program, adult/continuing education programs, advanced placement credit, distance learning, double majors, honors programs, independent study, internships, part-time degree program, services for LD students, student-designed majors, study abroad, summer session for credit.

Unusual degree programs: 3-2 occupational therapy with Washington University in St. Louis.

Computers: 125 computers/terminals and 50 ports are available on campus for general student use. Students can access the following: campus intranet, computer help desk, free student e-mail accounts, online (class) grades, online (class) registration, online (class) schedules. Campuswide network is available. 100% of college-owned or -operated housing units are wired for high-speed Internet access. Wireless service is available via entire campus.
Library: Carl Johann Memorial Library. *Books:* 110,983 (physical), 177,943 (digital/electronic); *Serial titles:* 80 (physical), 164,151 (digital/electronic); *Databases:* 26. Weekly public service hours: 86; students can reserve study rooms.

STUDENT LIFE
Housing options: on-campus residence required through senior year; coed, men-only, women-only. Campus housing is university owned. Freshman campus housing is guaranteed.

Activities and organizations: drama/theater group, student-run newspaper, radio and television station, choral group, Campus Programming Council (CPC), The Black Student Union (BSU), Student Government Association (SGA), Health Outreach Peer Educators (HOPE), Institute of Management Accountants (IMA), national fraternities, national sororities.

Athletics Member NAIA. *Intercollegiate sports:* baseball M(s), basketball M(s)/W(s), bowling M(s)/W(s), cheerleading M(s)/W(s), cross-country running M(s)/W(s), football M(s), golf M(s)/W(s), soccer M(s)/W(s), softball W(s), track and field M(s)/W(s), volleyball M(s)/W(s). *Intramural sports:* baseball M/W, basketball M/W, football M/W, soccer M/W, softball M/W, volleyball M/W.

Campus security: 24-hour emergency response devices and patrols, late-night transport/escort service, controlled dormitory access, lighted pathways/sidewalks, self defense education.
Student services: personal/psychological counseling.

COSTS & FINANCIAL AID
Costs (2018–19) *One-time required fee:* $210. *Comprehensive fee:* $35,200 includes full-time tuition ($26,255), mandatory fees ($425), and room and board ($8520). Part-time tuition: $600 per credit hour. *Required fees:* $18 per credit hour part-time. *College room only:* $3815. Room and board charges vary according to board plan and housing facility. *Payment plan:* installment. *Waivers:* senior citizens and employees or children of employees.

Financial Aid Of all full-time matriculated undergraduates who enrolled in 2017, 851 applied for aid, 789 were judged to have need, 130 had their need fully met. 72 Federal Work-Study jobs (averaging $1146). 383 state and other part-time jobs (averaging $1117). In 2017, 153 non-need-based awards were made. *Average percent of need met:* 72. *Average financial aid package:* $21,033. *Average need-based loan:* $4259. *Average need-based gift aid:* $17,185. *Average non-need-based aid:* $9964. *Average indebtedness upon graduation:* $29,105. *Financial aid deadline:* 6/1.

APPLYING
Standardized Tests *Required:* SAT or ACT (for admission).
Options: electronic application, deferred entrance.
Required: high school transcript, minimum 2.0 GPA. *Recommended:* essay or personal statement, 1 letter of recommendation, interview.
Application deadlines: rolling (freshmen), rolling (transfers).
Notification: continuous (freshmen), continuous (transfers).

CONTACT
Misty McBee, Executive Director of Admission and Marketing, Culver-Stockton College, One College Hill, Canton, MO 63435-1299. *Phone:* 573-288-6331. *Toll-free phone:* 800-537-1883. *Fax:* 573-288-6618. *E-mail:* admission@culver.edu.

DeVry University–Kansas City Campus

Kansas City, Missouri
http://www.devry.edu/
- **Proprietary** comprehensive, founded 1931, part of DeVry University
- **Urban** campus
- **Coed**
- **Minimally difficult** entrance level

FACULTY
Student/faculty ratio: 14:1.

ACADEMICS
Calendar: semesters. *Degrees:* associate, bachelor's, master's, and postbachelor's certificates.

COSTS & FINANCIAL AID
Costs (2017–18) *Tuition:* $14,308 full-time. *Required fees:* $500 full-time.

Financial Aid Of all full-time matriculated undergraduates who enrolled in 2007, 294 applied for aid, 281 were judged to have need, 12 had their need fully met. In 2007, 30 non-need-based awards were made. *Average percent of need met:* 40. *Average financial aid package:* $11,948. *Average need-based loan:* $8396. *Average need-based gift aid:* $5419. *Average non-need-based aid:* $13,609. *Average indebtedness upon graduation:* $8969.

APPLYING
Options: deferred entrance.
Application fee: $30.

CONTACT
Admissions Office, DeVry University–Kansas City Campus, 11224 Holmes Road, Kansas City, MO 64131. *Phone:* 816-943-7300. *Toll-free phone:* 866-338-7934.

Drury University

Springfield, Missouri

http://www.drury.edu/

- **Independent** comprehensive, founded 1873
- **Urban** 80-acre campus
- **Endowment** $88.8 million
- **Coed** 1,425 undergraduate students, 98% full-time, 56% women, 44% men
- **Moderately difficult** entrance level, 72% of applicants were admitted

UNDERGRAD STUDENTS

1,398 full-time, 27 part-time. Students come from 30 states and territories; 55 other countries; 25% are from out of state; 3% Black or African American, non-Hispanic/Latino; 3% Hispanic/Latino; 2% Asian, non-Hispanic/Latino; 0.1% Native Hawaiian or other Pacific Islander, non-Hispanic/Latino; 0.6% American Indian or Alaska Native, non-Hispanic/Latino; 4% Two or more races, non-Hispanic/Latino; 9% international; 5% transferred in; 65% live on campus.

Freshmen:

Admission: 1,474 applied, 1,067 admitted, 360 enrolled. *Average high school GPA:* 3.8. *Test scores:* ACT scores over 18: 98%; ACT scores over 24: 72%; ACT scores over 30: 15%.

Retention: 86% of full-time freshmen returned.

FACULTY

Total: 131, 84% full-time, 82% with terminal degrees.

Student/faculty ratio: 13:1.

ACADEMICS

Calendar: semesters. *Degrees:* bachelor's and master's (also offers evening program with significant enrollment not reflected in profile).

Special study options: academic remediation for entering students, accelerated degree program, adult/continuing education programs, advanced placement credit, cooperative education, distance learning, double majors, English as a second language, freshman honors college, honors programs, independent study, internships, off-campus study, part-time degree program, services for LD students, student-designed majors, study abroad, summer session for credit. *ROTC:* Army (c).

Unusual degree programs: 3-2 engineering with Washington University in St. Louis; international management with American Graduate School of International Management, occupational therapy with Washington University in St. Louis.

Computers: 385 computers/terminals are available on campus for general student use. Students can access the following: campus intranet, computer help desk, free student e-mail accounts, online (class) grades, online (class) registration, online (class) schedules, digital imaging lab, online bill payment/student information. Campuswide network is available. 100% of college-owned or -operated housing units are wired for high-speed Internet access. Wireless service is available via entire campus.

Library: F. W. Olin Library plus 1 other. *Books:* 149,706 (physical), 185,811 (digital/electronic); *Serial titles:* 751 (physical), 38 (digital/electronic); *Databases:* 44. Weekly public service hours: 92; students can reserve study rooms.

STUDENT LIFE

Housing options: on-campus residence required through junior year; coed, men-only, women-only. Campus housing is university owned and leased by the school. Freshman campus housing is guaranteed.

Activities and organizations: drama/theater group, student-run newspaper, radio and television station, choral group, Drury Volunteer Corps (DVC), International Student Association, Fanthers, Drury Allies, Commuter Student Association, national fraternities, national sororities.

Athletics Member NCAA. All Division II. *Intercollegiate sports:* baseball M(s), basketball M(s)/W(s), cheerleading M(s)/W(s), cross-country running M(s)/W(s), golf M(s)/W(s), riflery M/W, soccer M(s)/W(s), softball W(s), swimming and diving M(s)/W(s), tennis M(s)/W(s), track and field M(s)/W(s), triathlon M(s)/W(s), volleyball W(s), wrestling M(s). *Intramural sports:* basketball M/W, bowling M(c)/W(c), football M/W, ice hockey M(c), soccer M/W, softball M/W, ultimate Frisbee M(c)/W(c), volleyball M/W.

Campus security: 24-hour emergency response devices and patrols, student patrols, late-night transport/escort service, controlled dormitory access, security cameras in parking areas, police substation on campus, well-lit campus.

Student services: health clinic, personal/psychological counseling.

COSTS & FINANCIAL AID

Costs (2018–19) *One-time required fee:* $150. *Comprehensive fee:* $37,405 includes full-time tuition ($27,350), mandatory fees ($1015), and room and board ($9040). Full-time tuition and fees vary according to class time. Part-time tuition and fees vary according to class time. *Required fees:* $911 per credit hour part-time. *College room only:* $6774. Room and board charges vary according to board plan and housing facility. *Payment plans:* installment, deferred payment. *Waivers:* minority students, children of alumni, and employees or children of employees.

Financial Aid Of all full-time matriculated undergraduates who enrolled in 2016, 1,007 applied for aid, 881 were judged to have need, 191 had their need fully met. 108 Federal Work-Study jobs (averaging $2720). 340 state and other part-time jobs (averaging $1265). In 2016, 410 non-need-based awards were made. *Average percent of need met:* 75. *Average financial aid package:* $20,254. *Average need-based loan:* $4447. *Average need-based gift aid:* $16,645. *Average non-need-based aid:* $9409. *Average indebtedness upon graduation:* $31,137.

APPLYING

Standardized Tests *Required:* SAT or ACT (for admission).

Options: electronic application, deferred entrance.

Required: essay or personal statement, high school transcript, minimum 2.7 GPA, 1 letter of recommendation. *Recommended:* interview.

Application deadlines: rolling (freshmen), rolling (transfers).

Notification: continuous (freshmen), continuous (transfers).

CONTACT

Mr. Kevin Kropf, Dean of Enrollment, Drury University, 900 North Benton Avenue, Springfield, MO 65802. *Phone:* 417-873-7205. *Toll-free phone:* 800-922-2274. *Fax:* 417-866-3873. *E-mail:* druryad@drury.edu.

Evangel University

Springfield, Missouri

http://www.evangel.edu/

- **Independent** comprehensive, founded 1955, affiliated with Assemblies of God
- **Urban** 80-acre campus
- **Coed** 1,631 undergraduate students, 90% full-time, 55% women, 45% men
- **Moderately difficult** entrance level

UNDERGRAD STUDENTS

1,461 full-time, 170 part-time. 4% Black or African American, non-Hispanic/Latino; 5% Hispanic/Latino; 2% Asian, non-Hispanic/Latino; 0.2% Native Hawaiian or other Pacific Islander, non-Hispanic/Latino; 0.6% American Indian or Alaska Native, non-Hispanic/Latino; 2% Two or more races, non-Hispanic/Latino; 5% Race/ethnicity unknown; 0.8% international; 5% transferred in.

Freshmen:

Admission: 918 applied, 400 enrolled. *Test scores:* SAT evidence-based reading and writing scores over 500: 76%; SAT math scores over 500: 66%; ACT scores over 18: 85%; SAT evidence-based reading and writing scores over 600: 30%; SAT math scores over 600: 14%; ACT scores over 24: 38%; SAT evidence-based reading and writing scores over 700: 6%; SAT math scores over 700: 2%; ACT scores over 30: 5%.

Retention: 79% of full-time freshmen returned.

FACULTY

Student/faculty ratio: 14:1.

ACADEMICS

Calendar: semesters. *Degrees:* associate, bachelor's, master's, and doctoral.

ROTC: Army (c).

Computers: Students can access the following: computer help desk, free student e-mail accounts, online (class) grades, online (class) registration, online (class) schedules, online payment. Campuswide network is available. Wireless service is available via classrooms, computer labs, learning centers, libraries, student centers.

Library: Claude Kendrick Library.

STUDENT LIFE
Housing options: on-campus residence required through senior year; coed, men-only, women-only. Campus housing is university owned.

Activities and organizations: drama/theater group, student-run newspaper, radio and television station, choral group, marching band, Activities Board, student government, CrossWalk Student Ministries, Honor Societies, Music Ensembles.

Athletics Member NAIA. *Intercollegiate sports:* baseball M(s), basketball M(s)/W(s), cross-country running M(s)/W(s), football M(s), golf M(s)/W(s), softball W(s), tennis M(s)/W(s), track and field M(s)/W(s), volleyball W(s). *Intramural sports:* baseball M, basketball M/W, football M, golf M/W, soccer M/W, softball W, tennis M/W, volleyball W.

Campus security: 24-hour emergency response devices and patrols, student patrols, late-night transport/escort service, controlled dormitory access.

Student services: health clinic, personal/psychological counseling.

COSTS & FINANCIAL AID
Costs (2018–19) *Tuition:* $22,146 full-time, $896 per credit hour part-time. Full-time tuition and fees vary according to course load. Part-time tuition and fees vary according to course load. *Required fees:* $1275 full-time. *Room only:* $4304. Room and board charges vary according to board plan. *Payment plan:* installment. *Waivers:* employees or children of employees.

Financial Aid Of all full-time matriculated undergraduates who enrolled in 2016, 1,384 applied for aid, 1,220 were judged to have need, 156 had their need fully met. 964 Federal Work-Study jobs (averaging $1835). In 2016, 191 non-need-based awards were made. *Average percent of need met:* 70. *Average financial aid package:* $18,255. *Average need-based loan:* $4622. *Average need-based gift aid:* $13,273. *Average non-need-based aid:* $8215. *Average indebtedness upon graduation:* $30,443.

APPLYING
Standardized Tests *Required:* SAT or ACT (for admission).

Options: electronic application, deferred entrance.

Required: essay or personal statement, high school transcript, interview. *Recommended:* minimum 2.0 GPA.

CONTACT
Evangel University, 1111 North Glenstone, Springfield, MO 65802. *Phone:* 417-865-2811 Ext. 7205. *Toll-free phone:* 800-382-6435. *Fax:* 417-865-9599. *E-mail:* admissions@evangel.edu.

Fontbonne University
St. Louis, Missouri
http://www.fontbonne.edu/
CONTACT
Mr. Michelle Palumbo, Associate Vice President of Undergraduate Admissions, Fontbonne University, 6800 Wydown Boulevard, St. Louis, MO 63105. *Phone:* 314-889-1400. *Toll-free phone:* 800-205-5862. *Fax:* 314-889-1451. *E-mail:* fbyou@fontbonne.edu.

Global University
Springfield, Missouri
http://www.globaluniversity.edu/
- **Independent** comprehensive, founded 1948, affiliated with Assemblies of God
- **Small-town** campus
- **Coed**
- **Noncompetitive** entrance level

FACULTY
Student/faculty ratio: 11:1.

ACADEMICS
Calendar: continuous. *Degrees:* certificates, diplomas, associate, bachelor's, master's, doctoral, and postbachelor's certificates (offers only external degree programs).

Library: Global University Library.

STUDENT LIFE
Campus security: 24-hour emergency response devices.

APPLYING
Application fee: $50.

Required: high school transcript. *Required for some:* 1 letter of recommendation. *Recommended:* essay or personal statement.

CONTACT
Rev. Todd Waggoner, Enrollment and International Student Services Director, Global University, 1211 South Glenstone Avenue, Springfield, MO 65804. *Phone:* 417-862-9533 Ext. 2335. *Toll-free phone:* 800-443-1083. *Fax:* 417-863-9621. *E-mail:* twaggoner@globaluniversity.edu.

Goldfarb School of Nursing at Barnes-Jewish College
St. Louis, Missouri
http://www.barnesjewishcollege.edu/
- **Independent** comprehensive, founded 1902
- **Urban** 2-acre campus with easy access to St. Louis, Missouri
- **Endowment** $25.2 million
- **Coed, primarily women** 630 undergraduate students, 90% full-time, 90% women, 10% men
- **Moderately difficult** entrance level, 84% of applicants were admitted

UNDERGRAD STUDENTS
569 full-time, 61 part-time. Students come from 11 states and territories; 2 other countries; 27% are from out of state; 7% Black or African American, non-Hispanic/Latino; 3% Hispanic/Latino; 2% Asian, non-Hispanic/Latino; 0.3% Native Hawaiian or other Pacific Islander, non-Hispanic/Latino; 0.5% American Indian or Alaska Native, non-Hispanic/Latino; 3% Two or more races, non-Hispanic/Latino; 2% Race/ethnicity unknown; 0.3% international; 100% transferred in.

Freshmen:
Admission: 429 applied, 361 admitted.

FACULTY
Total: 97, 47% full-time, 24% with terminal degrees.

Student/faculty ratio: 11:1.

ACADEMICS
Calendar: trimesters. *Degrees:* bachelor's, master's, doctoral, and post-master's certificates.

Special study options: accelerated degree program, advanced placement credit, independent study, off-campus study, services for LD students, summer session for credit.

Computers: 160 computers/terminals are available on campus for general student use. Students can access the following: campus intranet, computer help desk, free student e-mail accounts, software, research databases. Campuswide network is available. Wireless service is available via entire campus.

Library: Goldfarb School of Nursing Library plus 2 others. *Books:* 1,100 (physical), 20,000 (digital/electronic); *Serial titles:* 62 (digital/electronic); *Databases:* 14.

STUDENT LIFE
Housing options: college housing not available.

Activities and organizations: student-run newspaper, Student Nurses Association, Student Council, GSON Men Excelling in Nursing, Veterans and Supporters Together.

Campus security: 24-hour patrols, late-night transport/escort service.

Student services: personal/psychological counseling, legal services.

COSTS & FINANCIAL AID
Costs (2018–19) *Tuition:* $19,058 full-time, $733 per credit hour part-time. Full-time tuition and fees vary according to course load and degree level. Part-time tuition and fees vary according to course load and degree level. *Required fees:* $1130 full-time, $615 per term part-time. *Payment plan:* installment.

Financial Aid Of all full-time matriculated undergraduates who enrolled in 2016, 465 applied for aid, 441 were judged to have need. 29 Federal Work-Study jobs (averaging $33,757). In 2016, 2 non-need-based awards were made. *Average financial aid package:* $4027. *Average need-based* *loan:* $4850. *Average need-based gift aid:* $2750. *Average non-need-based aid:* $6250.

APPLYING

Options: electronic application, deferred entrance.

Application fee: $50.

Notification: continuous (transfers).

CONTACT

Goldfarb School of Nursing at Barnes-Jewish College, 4483 Duncan Avenue, St. Louis, MO 63110. *Phone:* 314-362-9155. *Toll-free phone:* 800-832-9009.

Graceland University

Independence, Missouri

http://www.graceland.edu/

CONTACT

Admissions, Graceland University, 1401 West Truman Road, Independence, MO 64050-3434. *Phone:* 816-833-0524. *Toll-free phone:* 866-GRACELAND. *E-mail:* gic@graceland.edu.

Hannibal-LaGrange University

Hannibal, Missouri

http://www.hlg.edu/

- **Independent Southern Baptist** comprehensive, founded 1858
- **Small-town** 110-acre campus
- **Endowment** $8.4 million
- **Coed** 911 undergraduate students, 78% full-time, 59% women, 41% men
- **Minimally difficult** entrance level

UNDERGRAD STUDENTS

707 full-time, 204 part-time. Students come from 26 states and territories; 25 other countries; 16% are from out of state; 4% Black or African American, non-Hispanic/Latino; 3% Hispanic/Latino; 0.4% Asian, non-Hispanic/Latino; 0.3% Native Hawaiian or other Pacific Islander, non-Hispanic/Latino; 0.3% American Indian or Alaska Native, non-Hispanic/Latino; 3% Two or more races, non-Hispanic/Latino; 2% Race/ethnicity unknown; 6% international; 59% live on campus.

FACULTY

Total: 138, 45% full-time.

Student/faculty ratio: 14:1.

ACADEMICS

Calendar: semesters. *Degrees:* certificates, associate, bachelor's, and master's.

Special study options: academic remediation for entering students, accelerated degree program, adult/continuing education programs, advanced placement credit, distance learning, double majors, English as a second language, honors programs, independent study, internships, off-campus study, part-time degree program, services for LD students, student-designed majors, study abroad, summer session for credit.

Computers: 258 computers/terminals are available on campus for general student use. Students can access the following: free student e-mail accounts, online (class) grades, online (class) registration, online (class) schedules. Campuswide network is available. 100% of college-owned or -operated housing units are wired for high-speed Internet access. Wireless service is available via classrooms, computer centers, computer labs, dorm rooms, learning centers, libraries, student centers.

Library: Roland Library plus 1 other. *Books:* 113,238 (physical), 11,053 (digital/electronic); *Databases:* 77. Students can reserve study rooms.

STUDENT LIFE

Housing options: on-campus residence required through junior year; men-only, women-only. Campus housing is university owned. Freshman applicants given priority for college housing.

Activities and organizations: drama/theater group, student-run newspaper, choral group, Phi Beta Lambda, Student Nursing Association, Student Teachers Organization, Phi Beta Delta, Alpha Tau Beta.

Athletics Member NAIA. *Intercollegiate sports:* baseball M(s), basketball M(s)/W(s), cheerleading M(s)/W(s), cross-country running M(s)/W(s), golf M(s)/W(s), soccer M(s)/W(s), softball W(s), track and field M(s)/W(s), volleyball W(s), wrestling M(s). *Intramural sports:* archery M/W, basketball M/W, bowling M/W, racquetball M/W, table tennis M/W, ultimate Frisbee M/W, volleyball M/W.

Campus security: 24-hour emergency response devices and patrols, student patrols, late-night transport/escort service, controlled dormitory access, camera surveillance, alert system.

COSTS & FINANCIAL AID

Costs (2017–18) *One-time required fee:* $150. *Comprehensive fee:* $29,818 includes full-time tuition ($20,610), mandatory fees ($1100), and room and board ($8108). Full-time tuition and fees vary according to course load, degree level, location, program, and student level. Part-time tuition and fees vary according to course load, degree level, location, program, and student level. *Required fees:* $687 per credit hour part-time. *Room and board:* Room and board charges vary according to housing facility. *Payment plan:* installment. *Waivers:* employees or children of employees.

Financial Aid Of all full-time matriculated undergraduates who enrolled in 2016, 80 Federal Work-Study jobs (averaging $750).

APPLYING

Standardized Tests *Required:* SAT or ACT (for admission).

Options: electronic application, early admission, deferred entrance.

Application fee: $25.

Required: high school transcript, minimum 2.0 GPA.

Application deadlines: rolling (freshmen), 8/10 (out-of-state freshmen), rolling (transfers).

Notification: continuous until 9/10 (freshmen), 9/10 (out-of-state freshmen), continuous (transfers).

CONTACT

Dr. Ray Carty, Vice President for Enrollment Management, Hannibal-LaGrange University, 2800 Palmyra Road, Hannibal, MO 63401-1999. *Phone:* 573-629-3094. *Toll-free phone:* 800-HLG-1119. *E-mail:* admissions@hlg.edu.

Harris-Stowe State University

St. Louis, Missouri

http://www.hssu.edu/

- **State-supported** 4-year, founded 1857, part of Missouri Coordinating Board for Higher Education
- **Urban** 22-acre campus with easy access to St. Louis
- **Coed** 1,442 undergraduate students, 81% full-time, 66% women, 34% men
- **Noncompetitive** entrance level, 40% of applicants were admitted

UNDERGRAD STUDENTS

1,163 full-time, 279 part-time. 24% are from out of state; 80% Black or African American, non-Hispanic/Latino; 3% Hispanic/Latino; 0.5% Asian, non-Hispanic/Latino; 0.1% American Indian or Alaska Native, non-Hispanic/Latino; 3% Two or more races, non-Hispanic/Latino; 6% Race/ethnicity unknown; 1% international; 12% transferred in; 29% live on campus.

Freshmen:

Admission: 4,414 applied, 1,749 admitted, 270 enrolled. *Average high school GPA:* 2.7. *Test scores:* ACT scores over 18: 40%; ACT scores over 24: 3%.

Retention: 55% of full-time freshmen returned.

FACULTY

Total: 170, 17% full-time, 36% with terminal degrees.

Student/faculty ratio: 16:1.

ACADEMICS

Calendar: semesters. *Degree:* certificates and bachelor's.

Special study options: academic remediation for entering students, accelerated degree program, advanced placement credit, cooperative education, distance learning, honors programs, internships, off-campus study, part-time degree program, services for LD students, student-designed majors, study abroad, summer session for credit. *ROTC:* Army (c).

Unusual degree programs: 3-2 engineering with Saint Louis University.

Computers: Students can access the following: computer help desk, free student e-mail accounts, online (class) grades, online (class) registration, online (class) schedules. Campuswide network is available. 100% of college-owned or -operated housing units are wired for high-speed Internet access. Wireless service is available via entire campus.

Library: AT&T Library and Technology Center plus 1 other.

STUDENT LIFE

Housing options: coed. Campus housing is university owned. Freshman applicants given priority for college housing.

Activities and organizations: drama/theater group, choral group, Drama Club, Concert chorale, Student Government Association, Multicultural Council, Student Ambassadors, national fraternities, national sororities.

Athletics Member NAIA. *Intercollegiate sports:* baseball M(s), basketball M(s)/W(s), cheerleading M(s)/W(s), soccer M(s)/W(s), softball W(s), volleyball W(s). *Intramural sports:* basketball M/W, sand volleyball M/W.

Campus security: 24-hour emergency response devices and patrols, late-night transport/escort service, controlled dormitory access.

Student services: health clinic, personal/psychological counseling.

COSTS & FINANCIAL AID

Costs (2017–18) *Tuition:* state resident $4896 full-time, $204 per credit hour part-time; nonresident $9529 full-time, $397 per credit hour part-time. Full-time tuition and fees vary according to course load. *Required fees:* $444 full-time, $222 per term part-time. *Room only:* $6500. Room and board charges vary according to housing facility. *Payment plan:* installment. *Waivers:* employees or children of employees.

Financial Aid Of all full-time matriculated undergraduates who enrolled in 2016, 1,157 applied for aid, 1,006 were judged to have need, 572 had their need fully met. In 2016, 52 non-need-based awards were made. *Average percent of need met:* 76. *Average financial aid package:* $9247. *Average need-based loan:* $4016. *Average need-based gift aid:* $5198. *Average non-need-based aid:* $2462.

APPLYING

Standardized Tests *Required:* SAT or ACT (for admission).

Options: electronic application, early admission, deferred entrance.

Application fee: $20.

Required: high school transcript.

Notification: continuous (freshmen), continuous (transfers).

CONTACT

Dr. Chauvette McElmurry-Green, Registrar, Harris-Stowe State University, 3026 Laclede Avenue, St. Louis, MO 63103. *Phone:* 314-340-3300. *Fax:* 314-340-3555. *E-mail:* admissions@hssu.edu.

Kansas City Art Institute

Kansas City, Missouri
http://www.kcai.edu/

- **Independent** 4-year, founded 1885
- **Urban** 18-acre campus with easy access to Kansas City, MO
- **Coed** 663 undergraduate students, 99% full-time, 72% women, 28% men
- **Moderately difficult** entrance level, 67% of applicants were admitted

UNDERGRAD STUDENTS

656 full-time, 7 part-time. 64% are from out of state; 5% Black or African American, non-Hispanic/Latino; 8% Hispanic/Latino; 3% Asian, non-Hispanic/Latino; 0.4% American Indian or Alaska Native, non-Hispanic/Latino; 10% Two or more races, non-Hispanic/Latino; 8% Race/ethnicity unknown; 1% international; 8% transferred in; 37% live on campus.

Freshmen:

Admission: 669 applied, 447 admitted, 171 enrolled. *Test scores:* SAT evidence-based reading and writing scores over 500: 97%; SAT math scores over 500: 72%; ACT scores over 18: 89%; SAT evidence-based reading and writing scores over 600: 47%; SAT math scores over 600: 31%; ACT scores over 24: 49%; SAT evidence-based reading and writing scores over 700: 9%; ACT scores over 30: 11%.

Retention: 77% of full-time freshmen returned.

FACULTY
Total: 56.

Student/faculty ratio: 9:1.

ACADEMICS

Calendar: semesters. *Degree:* certificates and bachelor's.

Special study options: double majors, independent study, internships, off-campus study, part-time degree program, services for LD students, study abroad, summer session for credit.

Computers: Students can access the following: campus intranet, computer help desk, free student e-mail accounts, online (class) grades, online (class) registration, online (class) schedules. Campuswide network is available. 100% of college-owned or -operated housing units are wired for high-speed Internet access. Wireless service is available via entire campus.

Library: Jannes Library. Weekly public service hours: 84; students can reserve study rooms.

STUDENT LIFE

Housing options: on-campus residence required for freshman year; coed. Campus housing is university owned. Freshman applicants given priority for college housing.

Activities and organizations: student-run radio station.

Campus security: 24-hour emergency response devices and patrols, late-night transport/escort service, controlled dormitory access.

Student services: personal/psychological counseling.

COSTS & FINANCIAL AID

Costs (2017–18) *Comprehensive fee:* $47,950 includes full-time tuition ($37,400), mandatory fees ($150), and room and board ($10,400). Full-time tuition and fees vary according to reciprocity agreements. Part-time tuition: $1510 per credit hour. Part-time tuition and fees vary according to reciprocity agreements. *Payment plan:* installment. *Waivers:* employees or children of employees.

Financial Aid Of all full-time matriculated undergraduates who enrolled in 2017, 605 applied for aid, 554 were judged to have need, 66 had their need fully met. In 2017, 94 non-need-based awards were made. *Average percent of need met:* 64. *Average financial aid package:* $27,003. *Average need-based loan:* $4780. *Average need-based gift aid:* $22,499. *Average non-need-based aid:* $18,295. *Average indebtedness upon graduation:* $25,000.

APPLYING

Standardized Tests *Required:* SAT or ACT (for admission). *Required for some:* TOEFL.

Options: electronic application, early admission, deferred entrance.

Application fee: $45.

Required: essay or personal statement, high school transcript, 1 letter of recommendation, portfolio. *Recommended:* minimum 2.5 GPA, interview.

Application deadlines: 8/15 (freshmen), 8/15 (transfers).

CONTACT

Mr. Gerald Valet, Director of Admission Technology, Kansas City Art Institute, 4415 Warwick Boulevard, Kansas City, MO 64111-1874. *Phone:* 816-474-5224. *Toll-free phone:* 800-522-5224. *Fax:* 816-802-3309. *E-mail:* admiss@kcai.edu.

Lincoln University

Jefferson City, Missouri
http://www.lincolnu.edu/

- **State-supported** comprehensive, founded 1866
- **Small-town** 174-acre campus
- **Endowment** $1.6 million
- **Coed** 2,512 undergraduate students, 72% full-time, 58% women, 42% men
- **Noncompetitive** entrance level, 52% of applicants were admitted

UNDERGRAD STUDENTS

1,804 full-time, 708 part-time. Students come from 30 states and territories; 4 other countries; 30% are from out of state; 57% Black or African American, non-Hispanic/Latino; 2% Hispanic/Latino; 0.6% Asian, non-Hispanic/Latino; 0.1% Native Hawaiian or other Pacific Islander, non-Hispanic/Latino; 0.3% American Indian or Alaska Native, non-Hispanic/Latino; 3% Two or more races, non-Hispanic/Latino; 5%

Race/ethnicity unknown; 2% international; 5% transferred in; 48% live on campus.

Freshmen:
Admission: 3,423 applied, 1,796 admitted, 475 enrolled. *Average high school GPA:* 2.6. *Test scores:* SAT evidence-based reading and writing scores over 500: 14%; SAT math scores over 500: 23%; ACT scores over 18: 42%; SAT evidence-based reading and writing scores over 600: 3%; ACT scores over 24: 6%; ACT scores over 30: 1%.

Retention: 53% of full-time freshmen returned.

FACULTY
Total: 153, 69% full-time, 50% with terminal degrees.
Student/faculty ratio: 17:1.

ACADEMICS
Calendar: semesters. *Degrees:* associate, bachelor's, master's, and postbachelor's certificates.

Special study options: accelerated degree program, adult/continuing education programs, advanced placement credit, cooperative education, distance learning, double majors, freshman honors college, honors programs, independent study, internships, off-campus study, part-time degree program, services for LD students, study abroad, summer session for credit. *ROTC:* Army (b).

Computers: 365 computers/terminals and 1,100 ports are available on campus for general student use. Students can access the following: campus intranet, computer help desk, free student e-mail accounts, online (class) grades, online (class) registration, online (class) schedules. Campuswide network is available. 100% of college-owned or -operated housing units are wired for high-speed Internet access. Wireless service is available via entire campus.
Library: Inman E. Page Library. *Books:* 99,126 (physical), 197,476 (digital/electronic); *Serial titles:* 1,194 (physical), 19,000 (digital/electronic); *Databases:* 39. Weekly public service hours: 88.

STUDENT LIFE
Housing options: on-campus residence required through sophomore year; coed, men-only, women-only. Campus housing is university owned.

Activities and organizations: student-run newspaper, choral group, marching band, Student Government Association (SGA), Lincoln University Band, Alpha Kappa Mu, Army ROTC, International Student Association, national fraternities, national sororities.

Athletics Member NCAA. All Division II. *Intercollegiate sports:* basketball M(s)/W(s), bowling W(s), cross-country running W(s), football M(s), golf M(s)/W(s), softball W(s), track and field M(s)/W(s). *Intramural sports:* basketball M/W, bowling M/W, cheerleading W(c), soccer M/W, table tennis M/W, volleyball M/W.

Campus security: 24-hour emergency response devices and patrols, student patrols, late-night transport/escort service, controlled dormitory access, Rape Aggression Defense class upon request, Operation ID-ent, timely warnings, text message safety alerts, Webpage with helpful tips.

Student services: health clinic, personal/psychological counseling, women's center.

COSTS & FINANCIAL AID
Costs (2017–18) *Tuition:* state resident $6270 full-time, $209 per credit hour part-time; nonresident $12,810 full-time, $427 per credit hour part-time. Full-time tuition and fees vary according to course load, location, and reciprocity agreements. Part-time tuition and fees vary according to course load, location, and reciprocity agreements. *Required fees:* $1362 full-time, $10 per credit hour part-time, $531 per term part-time. *Room and board:* $6770; room only: $3510. Room and board charges vary according to board plan and housing facility. *Payment plans:* installment, deferred payment. *Waivers:* senior citizens and employees or children of employees.

Financial Aid Of all full-time matriculated undergraduates who enrolled in 2017, 1,621 applied for aid, 1,445 were judged to have need, 52 had their need fully met. 188 Federal Work-Study jobs (averaging $984). 33 state and other part-time jobs (averaging $1780). In 2017, 3 non-need-based awards were made. *Average percent of need met:* 68. *Average financial aid package:* $14,660. *Average need-based loan:* $4112. *Average need-based gift aid:* $4024. *Average non-need-based aid:* $3000. *Average indebtedness upon graduation:* $32,928.

APPLYING
Standardized Tests *Required:* SAT or ACT (for admission).
Options: electronic application, deferred entrance.
Required: high school transcript. *Required for some:* minimum 2.0 GPA.
Application deadlines: rolling (freshmen), rolling (out-of-state freshmen), rolling (transfers).
Notification: continuous (freshmen), continuous (out-of-state freshmen), continuous (transfers).

CONTACT
Liz Morrow, Director of Admissions/Registrar, Lincoln University, Office of Admissions, 820 Chestnut Street, B-7 Young Hall, Jefferson City, MO 65101. *Phone:* 573-681-5102. *Fax:* 573-681-5889. *E-mail:* admissions@lincolnu.edu.

Lindenwood University
St. Charles, Missouri
http://www.lindenwood.edu/
- **Independent Presbyterian** comprehensive, founded 1827
- **Suburban** 550-acre campus with easy access to St. Louis
- **Endowment** $160.3 million
- **Coed** 6,948 undergraduate students, 90% full-time, 54% women, 46% men
- **Moderately difficult** entrance level, 74% of applicants were admitted

UNDERGRAD STUDENTS
6,235 full-time, 713 part-time. Students come from 49 states and territories; 88 other countries; 39% are from out of state; 12% Black or African American, non-Hispanic/Latino; 4% Hispanic/Latino; 0.7% Asian, non-Hispanic/Latino; 0.3% Native Hawaiian or other Pacific Islander, non-Hispanic/Latino; 0.3% American Indian or Alaska Native, non-Hispanic/Latino; 2% Two or more races, non-Hispanic/Latino; 18% Race/ethnicity unknown; 12% international; 10% transferred in; 55% live on campus.

Freshmen:
Admission: 2,895 applied, 2,135 admitted, 949 enrolled. *Average high school GPA:* 3.3. *Test scores:* SAT evidence-based reading and writing scores over 500: 69%; SAT math scores over 500: 79%; ACT scores over 18: 95%; SAT evidence-based reading and writing scores over 600: 20%; SAT math scores over 600: 21%; ACT scores over 24: 36%; SAT evidence-based reading and writing scores over 700: 1%; SAT math scores over 700: 6%; ACT scores over 30: 5%.

Retention: 73% of full-time freshmen returned.

FACULTY
Total: 1,330, 22% full-time, 49% with terminal degrees.
Student/faculty ratio: 13:1.

ACADEMICS
Calendar: 4-1-4 for daytime programs; quarters and trimesters for evening programs. *Degrees:* bachelor's, master's, doctoral, post-master's, and postbachelor's certificates.

Special study options: academic remediation for entering students, accelerated degree program, adult/continuing education programs, advanced placement credit, distance learning, double majors, English as a second language, external degree program, freshman honors college, honors programs, independent study, internships, off-campus study, part-time degree program, services for LD students, student-designed majors, study abroad, summer session for credit. *ROTC:* Army (c), Air Force (c).

Unusual degree programs: 3-2 engineering with University of Missouri–Columbia, University of Missouri–St. Louis, Washington University in St. Louis; nursing with Golfarb School of Nursing at Barnes-Jewish College.

Computers: Students can access the following: campus intranet, computer help desk, free student e-mail accounts, online (class) grades, online (class) registration, online (class) schedules. Campuswide network is available. 100% of college-owned or -operated housing units are wired for high-speed Internet access. Wireless service is available via classrooms, computer centers, computer labs, dorm rooms, learning centers, libraries, student centers.
Library: Library and Academic Resource Center plus 1 other. *Books:* 82,506 (physical), 225,902 (digital/electronic); *Serial titles:* 197

(physical), 87 (digital/electronic); *Databases:* 140. Students can reserve study rooms.

STUDENT LIFE
Housing options: coed, men-only, women-only. Campus housing is university owned and leased by the school. Freshman applicants given priority for college housing.

Activities and organizations: drama/theater group, student-run newspaper, radio and television station, choral group, marching band, Kappa Delta Pi, Athletes in Action, Black Student Union, Lindenwood Gender Sexualities Alliance, Psychology Interest Club, national fraternities, national sororities.

Athletics Member NCAA, NAIA, USCAA. All NCAA Division II. *Intercollegiate sports:* baseball M(s), basketball M(s)/W(s), bowling M(s)/W(s), cheerleading M(s)/W(s), cross-country running M(s)/W(s), field hockey W(s), football M(s), golf M(s)/W(s), gymnastics W(s), ice hockey M(s)/W(s), lacrosse M(s)/W(s), riflery M(s)/W(s), rugby M(s)/W(s), soccer M(s)/W(s), softball W(s), swimming and diving M(s)/W(s), table tennis M(s)/W(s), tennis M(s)/W(s), track and field M(s)/W(s), volleyball M(s)/W(s), water polo M(s)/W(s), weight lifting M(s)/W(s), wrestling M(s)/W(s). *Intramural sports:* basketball M/W, sand volleyball M/W, soccer M/W, softball M/W, volleyball M/W.

Campus security: 24-hour emergency response devices and patrols, late-night transport/escort service, controlled dormitory access, surveillance cameras throughout the campus and facilities.

Student services: health clinic, personal/psychological counseling.

COSTS & FINANCIAL AID
Costs (2017–18) *Comprehensive fee:* $25,760 includes full-time tuition ($16,300), mandatory fees ($660), and room and board ($8800). Full-time tuition and fees vary according to class time. Part-time tuition: $460 per credit hour. Part-time tuition and fees vary according to course load. *Required fees:* $305 per term part-time. *Room and board:* Room and board charges vary according to board plan. *Payment plans:* installment, deferred payment. *Waivers:* senior citizens and employees or children of employees.

Financial Aid Of all full-time matriculated undergraduates who enrolled in 2017, 6,081 applied for aid, 3,757 were judged to have need, 331 had their need fully met. 169 Federal Work-Study jobs (averaging $2850). In 2017, 1925 non-need-based awards were made. *Average percent of need met:* 42. *Average financial aid package:* $12,478. *Average need-based loan:* $4138. *Average need-based gift aid:* $4974. *Average non-need-based aid:* $7185. *Average indebtedness upon graduation:* $32,774.

APPLYING
Standardized Tests *Required for some:* SAT or ACT (for admission).

Options: electronic application, deferred entrance.

Application fee: $30.

Required: minimum 2.5 GPA, personal resumé indicating community service, youth leadership, clubs, organizations, and non-academic experience. *Required for some:* essay or personal statement, high school transcript. *Recommended:* 3 letters of recommendation, interview.

Application deadlines: rolling (freshmen), rolling (transfers).

Notification: continuous (freshmen), continuous (transfers).

CONTACT
Mrs. Lucy Cohen, Interim Director of Day Admissions, Lindenwood University, 209 South Kings Highway, St. Charles, MO 63301. *Phone:* 636-949-4367. *Fax:* 636-949-4989. *E-mail:* LCohen@lindenwood.edu.

Logan University
Chesterfield, Missouri
http://www.logan.edu/

- **Independent** upper-level, founded 1935
- **Suburban** 112-acre campus with easy access to St. Louis
- **Endowment** $15.6 million
- **Coed** 126 undergraduate students, 40% full-time, 63% women, 37% men
- **100% of applicants were admitted**

UNDERGRAD STUDENTS
51 full-time, 75 part-time. Students come from 2 other countries; 61% are from out of state; 3% Hispanic/Latino; 0.8% Asian, non-Hispanic/Latino;

6% Two or more races, non-Hispanic/Latino; 67% Race/ethnicity unknown; 0.8% international; 25% transferred in.

Freshmen:
Admission: 8 applied, 8 admitted.

FACULTY
Total: 114, 43% full-time, 73% with terminal degrees.
Student/faculty ratio: 9:1.

ACADEMICS
Calendar: trimesters. *Degrees:* bachelor's, master's, and doctoral.

Special study options: accelerated degree program, adult/continuing education programs, advanced placement credit, cooperative education, distance learning, external degree program, independent study, part-time degree program, services for LD students, summer session for credit.

Computers: 100 computers/terminals are available on campus for general student use. Students can access the following: computer help desk, free student e-mail accounts, online (class) grades, online (class) registration, online (class) schedules, student portal, learning management system, online storage, specialty health care software, high-speed printing. Campuswide network is available. Wireless service is available via entire campus.

Library: Learning Resources Center. *Books:* 11,773 (physical), 3,679 (digital/electronic); *Serial titles:* 23 (physical), 64 (digital/electronic); *Databases:* 94. Weekly public service hours: 84.

STUDENT LIFE
Housing options: college housing not available.

Activities and organizations: Chiropractic on Purpose, SOT Club, Rehab2Performance, Family Wellness, Gonstead Club, national fraternities, national sororities.

Athletics *Intercollegiate sports:* basketball M(c)/W(c), golf M(c), soccer M(c), tennis M(c). *Intramural sports:* basketball M/W, football M, ice hockey M, softball M/W, volleyball M/W.

Campus security: 24-hour patrols, late-night transport/escort service.

Student services: health clinic, personal/psychological counseling.

COSTS & FINANCIAL AID
Costs (2017–18) *Tuition:* $8250 full-time, $275 per credit hour part-time. Full-time tuition and fees vary according to course load, degree level, and program. Part-time tuition and fees vary according to course load, degree level, and program. *Required fees:* $150 full-time, $80 per term part-time. *Waivers:* employees or children of employees.

Financial Aid Of all full-time matriculated undergraduates who enrolled in 2016, 45 applied for aid, 44 were judged to have need, 2 had their need fully met. 7 Federal Work-Study jobs (averaging $2603). *Average percent of need met:* 28. *Average financial aid package:* $10,203. *Average need-based loan:* $7216. *Average need-based gift aid:* $4616.

APPLYING
Options: electronic application.

Application fee: $25.

Required: minimum cumulative 2.0 GPA for transfer students.

CONTACT
Ms. Natach Douglas, Director of Admissions, Logan University, 1851 Schoettler Road, Chesterfield, MO 63017. *Phone:* 636-227-2100 Ext. 1718. *Toll-free phone:* 800-533-9210. *Fax:* 636-207-2425. *E-mail:* admissions@logan.edu.

Maryville University of Saint Louis
St. Louis, Missouri
http://www.maryville.edu/

- **Independent** university, founded 1872
- **Suburban** 130-acre campus with easy access to St. Louis
- **Endowment** $47.8 million
- **Coed** 3,183 undergraduate students, 75% full-time, 66% women, 34% men
- **Moderately difficult** entrance level, 92% of applicants were admitted

UNDERGRAD STUDENTS
2,375 full-time, 808 part-time. Students come from 45 states and territories; 45 other countries; 26% are from out of state; 8% Black or

African American, non-Hispanic/Latino; 4% Hispanic/Latino; 3% Asian, non-Hispanic/Latino; 0.1% Native Hawaiian or other Pacific Islander, non-Hispanic/Latino; 0.3% American Indian or Alaska Native, non-Hispanic/Latino; 3% Two or more races, non-Hispanic/Latino; 5% Race/ethnicity unknown; 4% international; 8% transferred in; 11% live on campus.

Freshmen:
Admission: 2,241 applied, 2,059 admitted, 604 enrolled. *Average high school GPA:* 3.6. *Test scores:* ACT scores over 18: 94%; ACT scores over 24: 53%; ACT scores over 30: 8%.
Retention: 83% of full-time freshmen returned.

FACULTY
Total: 667, 22% full-time, 44% with terminal degrees.
Student/faculty ratio: 14:1.

ACADEMICS
Calendar: semesters. *Degrees:* bachelor's, master's, doctoral, post-master's, and postbachelor's certificates.

Special study options: accelerated degree program, adult/continuing education programs, advanced placement credit, cooperative education, distance learning, double majors, English as a second language, external degree program, honors programs, independent study, internships, off-campus study, part-time degree program, services for LD students, study abroad, summer session for credit. *ROTC:* Army (c).

Unusual degree programs: 3-2 business administration; engineering with Washington University in St. Louis; social work with Saint Louis University; education.

Computers: 563 computers/terminals are available on campus for general student use. Students can access the following: campus intranet, computer help desk, free student e-mail accounts, online (class) grades, online (class) registration, online (class) schedules, specialized software, university catalog. Campuswide network is available. 100% of college-owned or -operated housing units are wired for high-speed Internet access. Wireless service is available via entire campus.
Library: University Library. *Books:* 59,580 (physical), 231,310 (digital/electronic); *Serial titles:* 60,067 (digital/electronic); *Databases:* 129. Weekly public service hours: 101; study areas open 24 hours, 5–7 days a week.

STUDENT LIFE
Housing options: coed. Campus housing is university owned.

Activities and organizations: drama/theater group, student-run newspaper, choral group, Campus Activities Board, Physical Therapy Club, Student Nurses Association, Community Service Club, Green Maryville Student Association.

Athletics Member NCAA. All Division II. *Intercollegiate sports:* baseball M(s), basketball M(s)/W(s), bowling W(s), cross-country running M(s)/W(s), golf M(s)/W(s), lacrosse M(s)/W(s), soccer M(s)/W(s), softball W(s), swimming and diving M(s)/W(s), tennis M(s)/W(s), track and field M(s)/W(s), volleyball W(s), wrestling M(s). *Intramural sports:* basketball M/W, cheerleading M/W, lacrosse M/W, rugby M, soccer M/W, softball W, table tennis M/W, tennis M/W, ultimate Frisbee M/W, volleyball M/W.

Campus security: 24-hour emergency response devices and patrols, late-night transport/escort service, controlled dormitory access, video security system in residence halls, self-defense and education programs.
Student services: health clinic, personal/psychological counseling.

COSTS & FINANCIAL AID
Costs (2018–19) *Comprehensive fee:* $38,558 includes full-time tuition ($26,070), mandatory fees ($2400), and room and board ($10,088). Full-time tuition and fees vary according to course load, degree level, and program. Part-time tuition: $781 per credit hour. Part-time tuition and fees vary according to class time, degree level, and program. *Required fees:* $450 per term part-time. *Room and board:* Room and board charges vary according to board plan and housing facility. *Payment plans:* installment, deferred payment. *Waivers:* senior citizens and employees or children of employees.

Financial Aid Of all full-time matriculated undergraduates who enrolled in 2017, 2,217 applied for aid, 1,988 were judged to have need, 181 had their need fully met. 361 Federal Work-Study jobs (averaging $945). 350 state and other part-time jobs (averaging $490). In 2017, 484 non-need-based awards were made. *Average percent of need met:* 54. *Average financial aid package:* $15,811. *Average need-based loan:* $3841. *Average need-based gift aid:* $13,542. *Average non-need-based aid:* $15,421. *Average indebtedness upon graduation:* $29,849.

APPLYING
Standardized Tests *Required for some:* SAT or ACT (for admission).
Options: electronic application, deferred entrance.
Required: high school transcript, minimum 2.5 GPA. *Required for some:* essay or personal statement, interview, audition, portfolio.
Application deadlines: 8/15 (freshmen), rolling (out-of-state freshmen), rolling (transfers).
Notification: continuous (freshmen), continuous (out-of-state freshmen), continuous (transfers).

CONTACT
Ms. Shani Lenore-Jenkins, Associate Vice President of Enrollment, Maryville University of Saint Louis, 650 Maryville University Drive, St. Louis, MO 63141-7299. *Phone:* 314-529-9350. *Toll-free phone:* 800-627-9855. *Fax:* 314-529-9927. *E-mail:* admissions@maryville.edu.

Metro Business College
Cape Girardeau, Missouri
http://www.metrobusinesscollege.edu/

CONTACT
Ms. Kyla Evans, Admissions Director, Metro Business College, 1732 North Kingshighway, Cape Girardeau, MO 63701. *Phone:* 573-334-9181, *Toll-free phone:* 888-206-4545. *Fax:* 573-334-0617.

Midwest University
Wentzville, Missouri
http://www.midwest.edu/

CONTACT
Jeoung H. Ham, Registrar/Director of Admissions, Midwest University, 851 Parr Road, Wentzville, MO 63385. *Phone:* 636-327-4645. *Fax:* 636-327-4715. *E-mail:* usa@midwest.edu.

Missouri Baptist University
St. Louis, Missouri
http://www.mobap.edu/
- **Independent Southern Baptist** comprehensive, founded 1964
- **Suburban** 65-acre campus with easy access to St. Louis
- **Endowment** $5.0 million
- **Coed** 4,508 undergraduate students, 34% full-time, 61% women, 39% men
- **Moderately difficult** entrance level, 55% of applicants were admitted

UNDERGRAD STUDENTS
1,519 full-time, 2,989 part-time. Students come from 38 states and territories; 16 other countries; 30% are from out of state; 13% Black or African American, non-Hispanic/Latino; 0.9% Hispanic/Latino; 1% Asian, non-Hispanic/Latino; 0.3% Native Hawaiian or other Pacific Islander, non-Hispanic/Latino; 1% American Indian or Alaska Native, non-Hispanic/Latino; 2% Two or more races, non-Hispanic/Latino; 7% Race/ethnicity unknown; 2% international; 8% transferred in; 33% live on campus.

Freshmen:
Admission: 1,000 applied, 545 admitted, 283 enrolled. *Average high school GPA:* 3.2.
Retention: 59% of full-time freshmen returned.

FACULTY
Total: 286, 26% full-time, 36% with terminal degrees.
Student/faculty ratio: 19:1.

ACADEMICS
Calendar: semesters. *Degrees:* certificates, associate, bachelor's, master's, doctoral, post-master's, and postbachelor's certificates.

Special study options: academic remediation for entering students, accelerated degree program, adult/continuing education programs,

advanced placement credit, distance learning, double majors, honors programs, independent study, internships, off-campus study, part-time degree program, services for LD students, student-designed majors, study abroad, summer session for credit. *ROTC:* Army (c).

Computers: 100 computers/terminals are available on campus for general student use. Students can access the following: campus intranet, computer help desk, free student e-mail accounts, online (class) grades, online (class) registration, online (class) schedules. Campuswide network is available. 100% of college-owned or -operated housing units are wired for high-speed Internet access. Wireless service is available via entire campus.

Library: Jung-Kellogg Library. *Books:* 54,840 (physical), 209,509 (digital/electronic); *Serial titles:* 549 (physical), 106 (digital/electronic); *Databases:* 91. Weekly public service hours: 76.

STUDENT LIFE

Housing options: men-only, women-only, special housing for students with disabilities. Campus housing is university owned. Freshman applicants given priority for college housing.

Activities and organizations: drama/theater group, student-run radio station, choral group, Enactus: Students in Free Enterprise, Amp Ministries, Student Missouri State Teacher's Association, Gamma Delta Sigma, Ministerial Alliance, national fraternities, national sororities.

Athletics Member NAIA. *Intercollegiate sports:* baseball M(s), basketball M(s)/W(s), bowling M(s)(c)/W(s)(c), cheerleading M(s)/W(s), cross-country running M(s)/W(s), football M(s), golf M(s)/W(s), lacrosse M(s)(c)/W(s)(c), soccer M(s)/W(s), softball W(s), tennis M(s)/W(s), track and field M(s)/W(s), volleyball M(s)/W(s), wrestling M(s)/W(s). *Intramural sports:* basketball M/W, bowling M/W, football M/W, soccer M/W, softball M/W, volleyball M/W.

Campus security: 24-hour emergency response devices and patrols, late-night transport/escort service, controlled dormitory access, self-defense classes.

Student services: health clinic, personal/psychological counseling.

COSTS & FINANCIAL AID

Costs (2017–18) *Comprehensive fee:* $36,400 includes full-time tuition ($24,764), mandatory fees ($1256), and room and board ($10,380). Full-time tuition and fees vary according to course load and location. Part-time tuition: $857 per credit hour. Part-time tuition and fees vary according to course load and location. *Required fees:* $27 per credit hour part-time. *Room and board:* Room and board charges vary according to board plan and housing facility. *Payment plan:* installment. *Waivers:* children of alumni, senior citizens, and employees or children of employees.

Financial Aid Of all full-time matriculated undergraduates who enrolled in 2017, 1,332 applied for aid, 1,207 were judged to have need, 324 had their need fully met. 516 Federal Work-Study jobs (averaging $2148). In 2017, 42 non-need-based awards were made. *Average financial aid package:* $18,252. *Average need-based loan:* $4353. *Average need-based gift aid:* $5197. *Average non-need-based aid:* $8179. *Average indebtedness upon graduation:* $27,951.

APPLYING

Standardized Tests *Required:* SAT or ACT (for admission).

Options: electronic application.

Application fee: $35.

Required: high school transcript, minimum 2.0 GPA, 1 letter of recommendation.

Application deadlines: rolling (freshmen), rolling (transfers).

Notification: continuous (freshmen), continuous (transfers).

CONTACT

Mrs. Cynthia Sutton, Director of Admissions, Missouri Baptist University, One College Park Drive, St. Louis, MO 63141-8660. *Phone:* 877-434-1115. *Toll-free phone:* 877-434-1115 Ext. 2290. *Fax:* 314-434-7596. *E-mail:* admissions@mobap.edu.

Missouri Southern State University
Joplin, Missouri
http://www.mssu.edu/

CONTACT
Mr. Derek Skaggs, Director of Enrollment Services, Missouri Southern State University, 3950 East Newman Road, Hearnes 106B, Joplin, MO 64801-1595. *Phone:* 417-625-9537. *Toll-free phone:* 866-818-MSSU. *Fax:* 417-659-4429. *E-mail:* admissions@mssu.edu.

Missouri State University
Springfield, Missouri
http://www.missouristate.edu/
- **State-supported** comprehensive, founded 1905
- **Suburban** 225-acre campus
- **Coed** 20,364 undergraduate students, 75% full-time, 58% women, 42% men
- **Moderately difficult** entrance level, 84% of applicants were admitted

UNDERGRAD STUDENTS
15,363 full-time, 5,001 part-time. 11% are from out of state; 5% Black or African American, non-Hispanic/Latino; 4% Hispanic/Latino; 1% Asian, non-Hispanic/Latino; 0.1% Native Hawaiian or other Pacific Islander, non-Hispanic/Latino; 0.4% American Indian or Alaska Native, non-Hispanic/Latino; 4% Two or more races, non-Hispanic/Latino; 0.7% Race/ethnicity unknown; 4% international; 8% transferred in; 23% live on campus.

Freshmen:
Admission: 9,453 applied, 7,944 admitted, 3,238 enrolled. *Average high school GPA:* 3.6. *Test scores:* SAT evidence-based reading and writing scores over 500: 83%; SAT math scores over 500: 78%; ACT scores over 18: 98%; SAT evidence-based reading and writing scores over 600: 35%; SAT math scores over 600: 31%; ACT scores over 24: 50%; SAT math scores over 700: 3%; ACT scores over 30: 8%.
Retention: 77% of full-time freshmen returned.

FACULTY
Total: 1,123, 67% full-time, 61% with terminal degrees.
Student/faculty ratio: 21:1.

ACADEMICS
Calendar: semesters. *Degrees:* certificates, bachelor's, master's, doctoral, post-master's, and postbachelor's certificates.

Special study options: accelerated degree program, advanced placement credit, cooperative education, distance learning, double majors, English as a second language, freshman honors college, honors programs, independent study, internships, off-campus study, part-time degree program, services for LD students, student-designed majors, study abroad, summer session for credit. *ROTC:* Army (b).

Computers: Students can access the following: campus intranet, computer help desk, free student e-mail accounts, online (class) grades, online (class) registration, online (class) schedules. Campuswide network is available. 100% of college-owned or -operated housing units are wired for high-speed Internet access. Wireless service is available via classrooms, computer centers, computer labs, learning centers, libraries, student centers.

Library: Meyer Library.

STUDENT LIFE
Housing options: on-campus residence required for freshman year; coed, special housing for students with disabilities. Campus housing is university owned. Freshman campus housing is guaranteed.

Activities and organizations: drama/theater group, student-run newspaper, radio and television station, choral group, marching band, Residence Hall Association, Campus Ministries, Fraternity and Sorority Life, Student Government Association, Student Activities Council, national fraternities, national sororities.

Athletics Member NCAA. All Division I except football (Division I-AA). *Intercollegiate sports:* baseball M(s), basketball M(s)/W(s), bowling M(c)/W(c), cross-country running W(s), equestrian sports M(c)/W(c), field hockey W(s), golf M(s)/W(s), ice hockey M(c), lacrosse M(c), racquetball M(c)/W(c), soccer M(s)/W(s), softball W(s), swimming and diving M(s)/W(s), track and field W(s), ultimate Frisbee M(c)/W(c), volleyball M(c)/W(s), wrestling M(c). *Intramural sports:* basketball M/W, bowling M/W, football M/W, golf M/W, racquetball M/W, soccer M/W, softball M/W, table tennis M/W, tennis M/W, track and field W, ultimate Frisbee M/W, volleyball M/W, weight lifting M/W.

Campus security: 24-hour emergency response devices and patrols, late-night transport/escort service, controlled dormitory access, on-campus police substation.

Student services: health clinic, personal/psychological counseling, legal services.

COSTS & FINANCIAL AID

Costs (2017–18) *Tuition:* state resident $6300 full-time, $210 per credit hour part-time; nonresident $13,740 full-time, $458 per credit hour part-time. Full-time tuition and fees vary according to course level, course load, and program. Part-time tuition and fees vary according to course level, course load, and program. *Required fees:* $1006 full-time. *Room and board:* $8537. Room and board charges vary according to board plan, housing facility, and location. *Payment plan:* deferred payment. *Waivers:* children of alumni, senior citizens, and employees or children of employees.

Financial Aid Of all full-time matriculated undergraduates who enrolled in 2017, 11,947 applied for aid, 9,284 were judged to have need, 1,326 had their need fully met. In 2017, 1811 non-need-based awards were made. *Average percent of need met:* 55. *Average financial aid package:* $9224. *Average need-based loan:* $4203. *Average need-based gift aid:* $5942. *Average non-need-based aid:* $3302. *Average indebtedness upon graduation:* $25,714.

APPLYING

Standardized Tests *Required:* SAT or ACT (for admission).

Options: electronic application.

Application fee: $35.

Required: high school transcript. *Required for some:* essay or personal statement, interview.

CONTACT

Mr. Andrew Wright, Director of Admissions, Missouri State University, 901 South National Avenue, Springfield, MO 65897. *Phone:* 417-836-5517. *Toll-free phone:* 800-492-7900. *Fax:* 417-836-5137. *E-mail:* info@missouristate.edu.

Missouri University of Science and Technology

Rolla, Missouri

http://www.mst.edu/

- **State-supported** university, founded 1870, part of University of Missouri System
- **Small-town** 284-acre campus
- **Endowment** $160.2 million
- **Coed** 6,920 undergraduate students, 89% full-time, 24% women, 76% men
- **Very difficult** entrance level, 84% of applicants were admitted

UNDERGRAD STUDENTS

6,128 full-time, 792 part-time. Students come from 50 states and territories; 38 other countries; 17% are from out of state; 3% Black or African American, non-Hispanic/Latino; 4% Hispanic/Latino; 4% Asian, non-Hispanic/Latino; 0.3% American Indian or Alaska Native, non-Hispanic/Latino; 3% Two or more races, non-Hispanic/Latino; 2% Race/ethnicity unknown; 3% international; 6% transferred in; 30% live on campus.

Freshmen:

Admission: 3,876 applied, 3,237 admitted, 1,426 enrolled. *Average high school GPA:* 3.6. *Test scores:* SAT evidence-based reading and writing scores over 500: 86%; SAT math scores over 500: 100%; ACT scores over 18: 98%; SAT evidence-based reading and writing scores over 600: 43%; SAT math scores over 600: 71%; ACT scores over 24: 88%; SAT evidence-based reading and writing scores over 700: 5%; SAT math scores over 700: 29%; ACT scores over 30: 38%.

Retention: 81% of full-time freshmen returned.

FACULTY

Total: 453, 82% full-time, 84% with terminal degrees.

Student/faculty ratio: 20:1.

ACADEMICS

Calendar: semesters. *Degrees:* bachelor's, master's, doctoral, and postbachelor's certificates.

Special study options: accelerated degree program, adult/continuing education programs, advanced placement credit, cooperative education, distance learning, double majors, English as a second language, freshman honors college, honors programs, independent study, internships, off-campus study, part-time degree program, services for LD students, study abroad, summer session for credit. *ROTC:* Army (b), Air Force (b).

Computers: 980 computers/terminals and 5,720 ports are available on campus for general student use. Students can access the following: campus intranet, computer help desk, free student e-mail accounts, online (class) grades, online (class) registration, online (class) schedules. Campuswide network is available. 100% of college-owned or -operated housing units are wired for high-speed Internet access. Wireless service is available via entire campus.

Library: Curtis Laws Wilson Library. *Books:* 305,834 (physical), 447,868 (digital/electronic); *Serial titles:* 14,178 (physical), 79,586 (digital/electronic); *Databases:* 180. Weekly public service hours: 112; students can reserve study rooms.

STUDENT LIFE

Housing options: on-campus residence required through sophomore year; coed, cooperative, special housing for students with disabilities. Campus housing is university owned and leased by the school. Freshman campus housing is guaranteed.

Activities and organizations: drama/theater group, student-run newspaper, radio station, choral group, marching band, Academic Organizations, Honor Society, Special Interest Group, Greek Organizations, Recreational and Sports Club, national fraternities, national sororities.

Athletics Member NCAA. All Division II. *Intercollegiate sports:* baseball M(s), basketball M(s)/W(s), cross-country running M(s)/W(s), football M(s), soccer M(s)/W(s), softball W(s), swimming and diving M(s), track and field M(s)/W(s), volleyball W(s). *Intramural sports:* badminton M/W, basketball M/W, bowling M/W, football M/W, golf M/W, racquetball M/W, soccer M/W, softball M/W, swimming and diving M/W, table tennis M/W, tennis M/W, track and field M/W, ultimate Frisbee M/W, volleyball M/W, water polo M/W, weight lifting M/W.

Campus security: 24-hour emergency response devices and patrols, student patrols, late-night transport/escort service, controlled dormitory access, crime prevention programs.

Student services: health clinic, personal/psychological counseling, women's center.

COSTS & FINANCIAL AID

Costs (2018–19) *Tuition:* state resident $8460 full-time, $282 per credit hour part-time; nonresident $26,322 full-time, $877 per credit hour part-time. Full-time tuition and fees vary according to course load, degree level, program, and student level. Part-time tuition and fees vary according to course load, degree level, program, and student level. *Room and board:* $10,094. Room and board charges vary according to board plan, housing facility, and location. *Payment plan:* installment. *Waivers:* employees or children of employees.

Financial Aid Of all full-time matriculated undergraduates who enrolled in 2015, 3,545 applied for aid, 3,375 were judged to have need, 980 had their need fully met. 156 Federal Work-Study jobs (averaging $1675). 17 state and other part-time jobs (averaging $639). In 2015, 703 non-need-based awards were made. *Average percent of need met:* 35. *Average financial aid package:* $14,980. *Average need-based loan:* $7472. *Average need-based gift aid:* $7931. *Average non-need-based aid:* $5583. *Average indebtedness upon graduation:* $28,259.

APPLYING

Standardized Tests *Required:* SAT or ACT (for admission). *Recommended:* ACT (for admission).

Options: electronic application, deferred entrance.

Application fee: $50.

Required: high school transcript. *Required for some:* essay or personal statement, interview.

Application deadlines: 7/1 (freshmen), rolling (out-of-state freshmen), 8/20 (transfers).

Notification: continuous until 10/1 (freshmen), continuous until 10/1 (out-of-state freshmen), continuous (transfers).

CONTACT
Ms. Lynn Stichnote, Admissions Office, Missouri University of Science and Technology, 300 West 13th Street, 106 Parker Hall, Rolla, MO 65409. *Phone:* 573-341-4075. *Toll-free phone:* 800-522-0938. *Fax:* 573-341-4082. *E-mail:* admissions@mst.edu.

Missouri Valley College
Marshall, Missouri
http://www.moval.edu/

- **Independent** comprehensive, founded 1889, affiliated with Presbyterian Church
- **Small-town** 140-acre campus with easy access to Kansas City
- **Coed** 1,798 undergraduate students, 72% full-time, 45% women, 55% men
- **Minimally difficult** entrance level, 54% of applicants were admitted

UNDERGRAD STUDENTS
1,296 full-time, 502 part-time. 53% are from out of state; 20% Black or African American, non-Hispanic/Latino; 10% Hispanic/Latino; 0.8% Asian, non-Hispanic/Latino; 0.5% Native Hawaiian or other Pacific Islander, non-Hispanic/Latino; 0.8% American Indian or Alaska Native, non-Hispanic/Latino; 4% Two or more races, non-Hispanic/Latino; 2% Race/ethnicity unknown; 16% international; 9% transferred in; 75% live on campus.

Freshmen:
Admission: 2,300 applied, 1,234 admitted, 392 enrolled. *Average high school GPA:* 2.9. *Test scores:* SAT evidence-based reading and writing scores over 500: 44%; SAT math scores over 500: 46%; ACT scores over 18: 60%; SAT evidence-based reading and writing scores over 600: 7%; SAT math scores over 600: 9%; ACT scores over 24: 8%; SAT math scores over 700: 2%.
Retention: 45% of full-time freshmen returned.

FACULTY
Total: 147, 59% full-time, 28% with terminal degrees.
Student/faculty ratio: 14:1.

ACADEMICS
Calendar: semesters plus 2 summer sessions. *Degrees:* associate, bachelor's, and master's.

Special study options: academic remediation for entering students, adult/continuing education programs, advanced placement credit, cooperative education, distance learning, double majors, English as a second language, honors programs, independent study, internships, part-time degree program, services for LD students, student-designed majors, study abroad, summer session for credit. *ROTC:* Army (c).

Computers: 300 computers/terminals are available on campus for general student use. Students can access the following: campus intranet, computer help desk, free student e-mail accounts, online (class) grades, online (class) registration, online (class) schedules. Campuswide network is available. 100% of college-owned or -operated housing units are wired for high-speed Internet access. Wireless service is available via entire campus.
Library: Murrell Memorial Library plus 1 other. *Databases:* 37.

STUDENT LIFE
Housing options: men-only, women-only. Campus housing is university owned. Freshman campus housing is guaranteed.

Activities and organizations: drama/theater group, student-run newspaper, radio and television station, choral group, national fraternities, national sororities.

Athletics Member NAIA. *Intercollegiate sports:* baseball M(s), basketball M(s)/W(s), cheerleading M(s)/W(s), cross-country running M(s)/W(s), football M(s), golf M(s)/W(s), lacrosse M(s)/W(s), soccer M(s)/W(s), softball W(s), tennis M(s)/W(s), track and field M(s)/W(s), volleyball M(s)/W(s), wrestling M(s)/W(s). *Intramural sports:* badminton M/W, baseball M, basketball M/W, bowling M/W, football M/W, soccer M/W, softball M/W, table tennis M/W, tennis M/W, volleyball M/W.

Campus security: 24-hour emergency response devices, student patrols, late-night transport/escort service, evening to 4 am patrol by trained security personnel.
Student services: health clinic, personal/psychological counseling.

COSTS & FINANCIAL AID
Costs (2018–19) *Comprehensive fee:* $29,750 includes full-time tuition ($19,300), mandatory fees ($1300), and room and board ($9150). Full-time tuition and fees vary according to program. Part-time tuition: $350 per credit hour. Part-time tuition and fees vary according to program. *College room only:* $4850. Room and board charges vary according to board plan, gender, housing facility, location, and student level. *Payment plans:* tuition prepayment, installment. *Waivers:* children of alumni and employees or children of employees.

Financial Aid Of all full-time matriculated undergraduates who enrolled in 2014, 1,150 applied for aid, 1,127 were judged to have need, 452 had their need fully met. 119 Federal Work-Study jobs (averaging $1860). 450 state and other part-time jobs (averaging $1860). In 2014, 452 non-need-based awards were made. *Average percent of need met:* 85. *Average financial aid package:* $12,850. *Average need-based loan:* $3750. *Average need-based gift aid:* $12,850. *Average non-need-based aid:* $12,850. *Average indebtedness upon graduation:* $25,200.

APPLYING
Standardized Tests *Required:* SAT or ACT (for admission).
Options: electronic application, early admission, deferred entrance.
Required: high school transcript. *Required for some:* essay or personal statement, 3 letters of recommendation, interview. *Recommended:* minimum 2.0 GPA, interview.
Application deadlines: 9/1 (freshmen), rolling (transfers).
Notification: continuous (freshmen), continuous (transfers).

CONTACT
Ms. Jessica Green, Admissions and Student Visit Coordinator, Missouri Valley College, 500 East College, Marshall, MO 65340-3197. *Phone:* 660-831-4114. *Fax:* 660-831-4233. *E-mail:* admissions@moval.edu.

Missouri Western State University
St. Joseph, Missouri
http://www.missouriwestern.edu/

- **State-supported** comprehensive, founded 1915
- **Suburban** 744-acre campus with easy access to Kansas City
- **Coed** 5,292 undergraduate students, 66% full-time, 59% women, 41% men
- **Noncompetitive** entrance level, 74% of applicants were admitted

UNDERGRAD STUDENTS
3,498 full-time, 1,794 part-time. Students come from 37 states and territories; 27 other countries; 14% are from out of state; 11% Black or African American, non-Hispanic/Latino; 1% Hispanic/Latino; 1% Asian, non-Hispanic/Latino; 0.3% Native Hawaiian or other Pacific Islander, non-Hispanic/Latino; 0.5% American Indian or Alaska Native, non-Hispanic/Latino; 4% Two or more races, non-Hispanic/Latino; 4% Race/ethnicity unknown; 1% international; 6% transferred in; 21% live on campus.

Freshmen:
Admission: 5,390 applied, 3,981 admitted, 979 enrolled. *Average high school GPA:* 3.3. *Test scores:* ACT scores over 18: 80%; ACT scores over 24: 22%; ACT scores over 30: 1%.
Retention: 66% of full-time freshmen returned.

FACULTY
Total: 343, 60% full-time, 57% with terminal degrees.
Student/faculty ratio: 17:1.

ACADEMICS
Calendar: semesters. *Degrees:* certificates, associate, bachelor's, master's, and postbachelor's certificates.

Special study options: academic remediation for entering students, accelerated degree program, adult/continuing education programs, advanced placement credit, distance learning, double majors, English as a second language, freshman honors college, honors programs, independent study, internships, off-campus study, part-time degree program, services for LD students, student-designed majors, study abroad, summer session for credit. *ROTC:* Army (b).

Computers: Students can access the following: campus intranet, computer help desk, free student e-mail accounts, online (class) grades, online (class) registration, online (class) schedules, personal online storage. Campuswide network is available. 100% of college-owned or -operated housing units are wired for high-speed Internet access. Wireless service is available via entire campus.

Library: Missouri Western State University Library. *Books:* 166,649 (physical), 215,083 (digital/electronic); *Serial titles:* 1,585 (physical), 57,298 (digital/electronic); *Databases:* 65.

STUDENT LIFE

Housing options: on-campus residence required for freshman year; coed, special housing for students with disabilities. Campus housing is university owned.

Activities and organizations: drama/theater group, student-run newspaper, television station, choral group, marching band, national fraternities, national sororities.

Athletics Member NCAA. All Division II. *Intercollegiate sports:* baseball M(s), basketball M(s)/W(s), cross-country running M(s)/W(s), football M(s), golf M(s)/W(s), soccer W(s), softball W(s), tennis W(s), track and field M(s)/W(s), volleyball W(s). *Intramural sports:* basketball M/W, football M/W, soccer M/W, softball M/W, table tennis M/W, tennis M/W, volleyball M/W.

Campus security: 24-hour patrols, student patrols, late-night transport/escort service, controlled dormitory access.

Student services: health clinic, personal/psychological counseling, women's center.

COSTS & FINANCIAL AID

Costs (2017–18) *Tuition:* state resident $6124 full-time, $204 per credit hour part-time; nonresident $12,632 full-time, $421 per credit hour part-time. Full-time tuition and fees vary according to course load and program. Part-time tuition and fees vary according to course load and program. *Required fees:* $718 full-time, $99 per credit hour part-time. *Room and board:* $8102; room only: $4644. Room and board charges vary according to board plan and housing facility. *Payment plan:* installment. *Waivers:* senior citizens and employees or children of employees.

Financial Aid Of all full-time matriculated undergraduates who enrolled in 2017, 325 Federal Work-Study jobs (averaging $1428). 664 state and other part-time jobs (averaging $2071).

APPLYING

Standardized Tests *Required:* SAT or ACT (for admission).

Options: electronic application.

Required: high school transcript.

Application deadlines: 5/1 (freshmen), 6/1 (transfers).

Notification: continuous (freshmen), continuous (transfers).

CONTACT

Mrs. Jamie Sweiger, Assistant Director of Admissions, Missouri Western State University, 4525 Downs Drive, St. Joseph, MO 64507-2294. *Phone:* 816-271-4183. *Toll-free phone:* 800-662-7041. *E-mail:* admission@ missouriwestern.edu.

National American University

Independence, Missouri
http://www.national.edu/

CONTACT
National American University, 3620 Arowhead Avenue, Independence, MO 64057. *Toll-free phone:* 866-628-1288.

National American University

Kansas City, Missouri
http://www.national.edu/

CONTACT
Admissions Office, National American University, 7490 Northwest 87th Street, Kansas City, MO 64153. *Phone:* 816-412-5500. *Toll-free phone:* 866-628-1288. *E-mail:* zradmissions@national.edu.

National American University

Lee's Summit, Missouri
http://www.national.edu/

CONTACT
National American University, 401 NW Murray Road, Lee's Summit, MO 64081. *Toll-free phone:* 866-628-1288.

Northwest Missouri State University

Maryville, Missouri
http://www.nwmissouri.edu/

- **State-supported** comprehensive, founded 1905, part of Missouri Coordinating Board for Higher Education
- **Small-town** 370-acre campus with easy access to Kansas City
- **Endowment** $27.3 million
- **Coed** 5,474 undergraduate students, 88% full-time, 57% women, 43% men
- **Moderately difficult** entrance level, 74% of applicants were admitted

UNDERGRAD STUDENTS
4,806 full-time, 668 part-time. Students come from 36 states and territories; 31 other countries; 30% are from out of state; 5% Black or African American, non-Hispanic/Latino; 4% Hispanic/Latino; 0.9% Asian, non-Hispanic/Latino; 0.2% Native Hawaiian or other Pacific Islander, non-Hispanic/Latino; 0.3% American Indian or Alaska Native, non-Hispanic/Latino; 3% Two or more races, non-Hispanic/Latino; 2% Race/ethnicity unknown; 4% international; 5% transferred in; 33% live on campus.

Freshmen:
Admission: 5,129 applied, 3,801 admitted, 1,216 enrolled. *Average high school GPA:* 3.4. *Test scores:* ACT scores over 18: 93%; ACT scores over 24: 38%; ACT scores over 30: 5%.
Retention: 73% of full-time freshmen returned.

FACULTY
Total: 302, 80% full-time, 62% with terminal degrees.
Student/faculty ratio: 21:1.

ACADEMICS
Calendar: trimesters. *Degrees:* certificates, bachelor's, master's, post-master's, and postbachelor's certificates.

Special study options: academic remediation for entering students, advanced placement credit, distance learning, double majors, honors programs, independent study, internships, off-campus study, part-time degree program, services for LD students, study abroad, summer session for credit.

Computers: 253 computers/terminals and 1,143 ports are available on campus for general student use. Students can access the following: campus intranet, computer help desk, free student e-mail accounts, online (class) grades, online (class) registration, online (class) schedules, online courses with library and databases. Campuswide network is available. 100% of college-owned or -operated housing units are wired for high-speed Internet access. Wireless service is available via classrooms, computer centers, computer labs, dorm rooms, learning centers, libraries, student centers.

Library: Owens Library. *Books:* 172,234 (physical), 1,506 (digital/electronic); *Serial titles:* 31 (physical), 15 (digital/electronic); *Databases:* 103. Weekly public service hours: 95; students can reserve study rooms.

STUDENT LIFE

Housing options: on-campus residence required for freshman year; coed, special housing for students with disabilities. Campus housing is university owned. Freshman campus housing is guaranteed.

Activities and organizations: drama/theater group, student-run newspaper, radio and television station, choral group, marching band, Indian Student Association, ACM, National Society of Leadership and Success, Student Senate, Resident Hall Association (RHA), national fraternities, national sororities.

Athletics Member NCAA. All Division II. *Intercollegiate sports:* baseball M, basketball M(s)/W(s), cheerleading M(s)/W(s), cross-country running M/W, football M(s), golf W, soccer W, softball W, tennis M(s)/W(s), track and field M(s)/W(s), volleyball W(s). *Intramural sports:* badminton M/W, basketball M/W, cross-country running M/W, football M/W, golf M/W, racquetball M/W, sand volleyball M/W, skiing (cross-country) M/W, soccer M(c)/W(c), softball W, swimming and diving M/W, table tennis M/W, tennis M/W, track and field M/W, volleyball M/W, wrestling M(c).

Campus security: 24-hour emergency response devices and patrols, student patrols, late-night transport/escort service, controlled dormitory access, security personnel are all police officers.

Student services: health clinic, personal/psychological counseling, women's center.

COSTS & FINANCIAL AID

Costs (2017–18) *Tuition:* state resident $5627 full-time, $188 per credit hour part-time; nonresident $12,191 full-time, $406 per credit hour part-time. Full-time tuition and fees vary according to course load, location, program, and reciprocity agreements. Part-time tuition and fees vary according to course load and location. *Required fees:* $3945 full-time, $132 per credit hour part-time. *Room and board:* $9770; room only: $6200. Room and board charges vary according to board plan and housing facility. *Payment plans:* installment, deferred payment. *Waivers:* senior citizens and employees or children of employees.

Financial Aid Of all full-time matriculated undergraduates who enrolled in 2016, 4,157 applied for aid, 3,283 were judged to have need, 960 had their need fully met. 386 Federal Work-Study jobs (averaging $1253). 1,048 state and other part-time jobs (averaging $1661). In 2016, 413 non-need-based awards were made. *Average percent of need met:* 62. *Average financial aid package:* $9727. *Average need-based loan:* $3880. *Average need-based gift aid:* $5951. *Average non-need-based aid:* $2910. *Average indebtedness upon graduation:* $28,332.

APPLYING

Standardized Tests *Required:* SAT or ACT (for admission).

Options: electronic application, deferred entrance.

Application fee: $25.

Required: high school transcript, minimum 2.0 GPA, 21 ACT composite (SAT 980). *Required for some:* interview.

Application deadlines: rolling (freshmen), rolling (transfers).

Notification: continuous (freshmen), continuous (transfers).

CONTACT

Mrs. Tammi Grow, Associate Director of Admissions, Northwest Missouri State University, 800 University Drive, Maryville, MO 64468-6001. *Phone:* 660-562-1146. *Toll-free phone:* 800-633-1175. *Fax:* 660-562-1337. *E-mail:* admissions@nwmissouri.edu.

Ozark Christian College

Joplin, Missouri
http://www.occ.edu/

CONTACT
Mr. Bob Witte, Executive Director of Admissions, Ozark Christian College, 1111 North Main Street, Joplin, MO 64801-4804. *Phone:* 417-624-2518. *Toll-free phone:* 800-299-4622. *Fax:* 417-624-0090. *E-mail:* occadmin@occ.edu.

Park University

Parkville, Missouri
http://www.park.edu/

CONTACT
Mr. Eric Blair, Director of Undergraduate Admissions, Park University, 8700 NW River Park Drive, Campus Box 1, Parkville, MO 64152. *Phone:* 816-584-6858. *Toll-free phone:* 800-745-7275. *Fax:* 816-741-4462. *E-mail:* admissions@mail.park.edu.

Ranken Technical College

St. Louis, Missouri
http://www.ranken.edu/

CONTACT
Ranken Technical College, 4431 Finney Avenue, St. Louis, MO 63113. *Phone:* 314-371-0233 Ext. 4811. *Toll-free phone:* 866-4-RANKEN.

Research College of Nursing

Kansas City, Missouri
http://www.researchcollege.edu/

- **Independent** comprehensive, founded 1980, part of Rockhurst University
- **Urban** 66-acre campus with easy access to Kansas City
- **Coed, primarily women** 264 undergraduate students, 100% full-time, 92% women, 8% men
- **Moderately difficult** entrance level, 73% of applicants were admitted

UNDERGRAD STUDENTS
264 full-time. Students come from 7 states and territories; 20% are from out of state; 3% Black or African American, non-Hispanic/Latino; 4% Hispanic/Latino; 2% Asian, non-Hispanic/Latino; 0.4% American Indian or Alaska Native, non-Hispanic/Latino; 3% Two or more races, non-Hispanic/Latino; 11% Race/ethnicity unknown; 2% transferred in.

Freshmen:
Admission: 339 applied, 249 admitted, 78 enrolled. *Average high school GPA:* 3.5. *Test scores:* ACT scores over 18: 100%; ACT scores over 24: 56%; ACT scores over 30: 4%.

FACULTY
Total: 29, 90% full-time, 14% with terminal degrees.
Student/faculty ratio: 7:1.

ACADEMICS
Calendar: semesters. *Degrees:* bachelor's, master's, and post-master's certificates (bachelor's degree offered jointly with Rockhurst College).

Special study options: accelerated degree program, advanced placement credit, double majors, honors programs, independent study, services for LD students, study abroad, summer session for credit. *ROTC:* Army (c).

Computers: 125 computers/terminals are available on campus for general student use. Students can access the following: online (class) registration. Campuswide network is available.
Library: Greenlease Library.

STUDENT LIFE
Housing options: coed, men-only, women-only. Campus housing is university owned. Freshman campus housing is guaranteed.

Activities and organizations: drama/theater group, student-run newspaper, radio station, choral group, national fraternities, national sororities.

Athletics Member NCAA. All Division II. *Intercollegiate sports:* baseball M(s), basketball M(s)/W(s), golf M(s)/W(s), soccer M(s)/W(s), softball W(s), tennis M(s)/W(s), volleyball W(s). *Intramural sports:* badminton M/W, basketball M/W, cross-country running M/W, field hockey M/W, golf M/W, lacrosse M/W, racquetball M/W, rugby M/W, soccer M/W, softball M/W, table tennis M/W, tennis M/W, volleyball M/W, weight lifting M.

Campus security: 24-hour emergency response devices and patrols, late-night transport/escort service, controlled dormitory access.

Student services: health clinic, personal/psychological counseling.

COSTS & FINANCIAL AID

Costs (2017–18) *One-time required fee:* $150. *Comprehensive fee:* $46,685 includes full-time tuition ($35,800), mandatory fees ($915), and room and board ($9970). Part-time tuition: $1194 per credit hour. Part-time tuition and fees vary according to class time. *Required fees:* $35 per credit hour part-time. *College room only:* $6120. Room and board charges vary according to board plan, housing facility, and location. *Payment plans:* installment, deferred payment. *Waivers:* senior citizens and employees or children of employees.

Financial Aid Of all full-time matriculated undergraduates who enrolled in 2015, 138 applied for aid, 102 were judged to have need, 52 had their need fully met. In 2015, 162 non-need-based awards were made. *Average percent of need met:* 78. *Average financial aid package:* $28,500. *Average need-based loan:* $5500. *Average need-based gift aid:* $9200. *Average non-need-based aid:* $34,800.

APPLYING

Standardized Tests *Required:* SAT or ACT (for admission).

Options: electronic application, deferred entrance.

Required: high school transcript, 1 letter of recommendation. *Recommended:* minimum 2.8 GPA, interview.

Application deadlines: 6/30 (freshmen), 2/15 (transfers).

Notification: 8/15 (freshmen), 6/20 (out-of-state freshmen), 3/15 (transfers).

CONTACT

Mr. Kyle Johnson, Director of Admission, Research College of Nursing, 1100 Rockhurst Road, Kansas City, MO 64110. *Phone:* 816-501-4000. *E-mail:* kyle.johnson@rockhurst.edu.

Rockhurst University

Kansas City, Missouri

http://www.rockhurst.edu/

- **Independent Roman Catholic (Jesuit)** comprehensive, founded 1910
- **Urban** 35-acre campus
- **Endowment** $35.7 million
- **Coed** 2,208 undergraduate students, 65% full-time, 61% women, 39% men
- **Moderately difficult** entrance level, 72% of applicants were admitted

UNDERGRAD STUDENTS

1,445 full-time, 763 part-time. Students come from 39 states and territories; 17 other countries; 33% are from out of state; 5% Black or African American, non-Hispanic/Latino; 9% Hispanic/Latino; 3% Asian, non-Hispanic/Latino; 0.7% American Indian or Alaska Native, non-Hispanic/Latino; 3% Two or more races, non-Hispanic/Latino; 6% Race/ethnicity unknown; 1% international; 4% transferred in; 49% live on campus.

Freshmen:
Admission: 3,115 applied, 2,257 admitted, 430 enrolled. *Average high school GPA:* 3.6. *Test scores:* ACT scores over 18: 98%; ACT scores over 24: 61%; ACT scores over 30: 13%.
Retention: 86% of full-time freshmen returned.

FACULTY

Total: 239, 54% full-time, 59% with terminal degrees.
Student/faculty ratio: 13:1.

ACADEMICS

Calendar: semesters. *Degrees:* certificates, bachelor's, master's, doctoral, and postbachelor's certificates.

Special study options: academic remediation for entering students, accelerated degree program, advanced placement credit, cooperative education, distance learning, double majors, freshman honors college, honors programs, independent study, internships, off-campus study, part-time degree program, services for LD students, study abroad, summer session for credit. *ROTC:* Army (c).

Computers: 235 computers/terminals are available on campus for general student use. Students can access the following: computer help desk, free student e-mail accounts, online (class) grades, online (class) registration, online (class) schedules, campus portal. Campuswide network is available. 100% of college-owned or -operated housing units are wired for high-speed Internet access. Wireless service is available via entire campus.

Library: Greenlease Library. *Books:* 112,979 (physical), 180,624 (digital/electronic); *Serial titles:* 798 (physical), 103,252 (digital/electronic); *Databases:* 110. Weekly public service hours: 85.

STUDENT LIFE

Housing options: on-campus residence required through sophomore year; coed, men-only, women-only, special housing for students with disabilities. Campus housing is university owned. Freshman campus housing is guaranteed.

Activities and organizations: drama/theater group, student-run newspaper, choral group, Student Activities Board, Student Senate, Voices for Justice, Panhellenic Sororities, IFC Fraternities, national fraternities, national sororities.

Athletics Member NCAA. All Division II. *Intercollegiate sports:* baseball M(s), basketball M(s)/W(s), cross-country running W(s), golf M(s)/W(s), lacrosse M(s)/W(s), soccer M(s)/W(s), softball W(s), tennis M(s)/W(s), volleyball W(s). *Intramural sports:* basketball M/W, bowling M/W, cheerleading M(c)/W(c), ultimate Frisbee M(c)/W(c).

Campus security: 24-hour emergency response devices and patrols, late-night transport/escort service, controlled dormitory access, closed-circuit TV monitors.

Student services: health clinic, personal/psychological counseling.

COSTS & FINANCIAL AID

Costs (2017–18) *Comprehensive fee:* $46,560 includes full-time tuition ($35,800), mandatory fees ($790), and room and board ($9970). Full-time tuition and fees vary according to class time and course load. Part-time tuition: $597 per credit hour. Part-time tuition and fees vary according to class time and course load. *Required fees:* $25 per credit hour part-time. *College room only:* $6120. Room and board charges vary according to board plan and housing facility. *Payment plans:* installment, deferred payment. *Waivers:* senior citizens and employees or children of employees.

Financial Aid Of all full-time matriculated undergraduates who enrolled in 2016, 1,393 applied for aid, 973 were judged to have need, 268 had their need fully met. In 2016, 224 non-need-based awards were made. *Average percent of need met:* 89. *Average financial aid package:* $35,475. *Average need-based loan:* $5021. *Average need-based gift aid:* $22,241. *Average non-need-based aid:* $20,682. *Average indebtedness upon graduation:* $32,157.

APPLYING

Standardized Tests *Required:* SAT or ACT (for admission).

Options: electronic application, deferred entrance.

Required: high school transcript, minimum 2.0 GPA, 1 letter of recommendation. *Required for some:* essay or personal statement, interview.

Application deadlines: 6/30 (freshmen), rolling (transfers).

Notification: continuous (freshmen), continuous (transfers).

CONTACT

Kyle Johnson, Director of Freshman Admissions, Rockhurst University, 1100 Rockhurst Road, Kansas City, MO 64110-2561. *Phone:* 816-501-4100. *Toll-free phone:* 800-842-6776. *Fax:* 816-501-4142. *E-mail:* admission@rockhurst.edu.

Saint Louis Christian College

Florissant, Missouri

http://www.stlchristian.edu/

- **Independent Christian** 4-year, founded 1956
- **Suburban** 30-acre campus with easy access to St. Louis
- **Endowment** $1.1 million
- **Coed**
- **Minimally difficult** entrance level

FACULTY

Student/faculty ratio: 9:1.

ACADEMICS

Calendar: semesters. *Degrees:* associate and bachelor's.
Library: St. Louis Christian College Library. *Books:* 30,076 (physical); *Serial titles:* 332 (physical).

Phone: 314-446-8328. *Toll-free phone:* 800-278-5267. *Fax:* 314-446-8310. *E-mail:* connie.horrall@stlcop.edu.

Saint Louis University

St. Louis, Missouri
http://www.slu.edu/

- **Independent Roman Catholic (Jesuit)** university, founded 1818
- **Urban** 281-acre campus
- **Endowment** $1.1 billion
- **Coed** 7,411 undergraduate students, 91% full-time, 60% women, 40% men
- **Very difficult** entrance level, 64% of applicants were admitted

UNDERGRAD STUDENTS
6,725 full-time, 686 part-time. Students come from 50 states and territories; 75 other countries; 59% are from out of state; 6% Black or African American, non-Hispanic/Latino; 6% Hispanic/Latino; 10% Asian, non-Hispanic/Latino; 0.2% American Indian or Alaska Native, non-Hispanic/Latino; 3% Two or more races, non-Hispanic/Latino; 0.8% Race/ethnicity unknown; 7% international; 4% transferred in; 51% live on campus.

Freshmen:
Admission: 13,431 applied, 8,653 admitted, 1,633 enrolled. *Average high school GPA:* 3.9. *Test scores:* SAT evidence-based reading and writing scores over 500: 95%; SAT math scores over 500: 95%; ACT scores over 18: 100%; SAT evidence-based reading and writing scores over 600: 72%; SAT math scores over 600: 70%; ACT scores over 24: 90%; SAT evidence-based reading and writing scores over 700: 24%; SAT math scores over 700: 27%; ACT scores over 30: 39%.
Retention: 90% of full-time freshmen returned.

FACULTY
Total: 1,134, 62% full-time, 69% with terminal degrees.
Student/faculty ratio: 9:1.

ACADEMICS
Calendar: semesters. *Degrees:* certificates, bachelor's, master's, doctoral, post-master's, and postbachelor's certificates.

Special study options: academic remediation for entering students, accelerated degree program, adult/continuing education programs, advanced placement credit, cooperative education, distance learning, double majors, English as a second language, honors programs, independent study, internships, part-time degree program, services for LD students, student-designed majors, study abroad, summer session for credit. *ROTC:* Army (c), Air Force (b).

Unusual degree programs: 3-2 engineering with Washington University in St. Louis; American studies, bioinformatics and comparative biology, theological studies, women's and gender studies, computer science, political science, Sociology, Software Engineering, Engineering, Health Administration, Public Health, Accounting.

Computers: 150 computers/terminals and 2,100 ports are available on campus for general student use. Students can access the following: campus intranet, computer help desk, free student e-mail accounts, online (class) grades, online (class) registration, online (class) schedules. Campuswide network is available. 100% of college-owned or -operated housing units are wired for high-speed Internet access. Wireless service is available via entire campus.

Library: Pius XII Memorial Library plus 2 others. *Books:* 1.3 million (physical), 339,573 (digital/electronic); *Serial titles:* 124,266 (physical), 121,743 (digital/electronic); *Databases:* 448. Weekly public service hours: 141; study areas open 24 hours, 5–7 days a week; students can reserve study rooms.

STUDENT LIFE
Housing options: on-campus residence required through sophomore year; coed, special housing for students with disabilities. Campus housing is university owned. Freshman campus housing is guaranteed.

Activities and organizations: drama/theater group, student-run newspaper, radio and television station, choral group, Alpha Phi Omega, Alpha Epsilon Delta, Habitat for Humanity, Interfraternity Council, Panhellenic Council, national fraternities, national sororities.

Athletics Member NCAA. All Division I. *Intercollegiate sports:* badminton M(c)/W(c), baseball M(s), basketball M(s)/W(s), bowling

M(c)/W(c), crew M(c)/W(c), cross-country running M(s)/W(s), equestrian sports M(c)/W(c), fencing M(c)/W(c), field hockey W(s), golf M(c)/W(c), ice hockey M(c), lacrosse M(c)/W(c), racquetball M(c)/W(c), rugby M(c), soccer M(s)/W(s), softball W(s), swimming and diving M(s)/W(s), table tennis M(c)/W(c), tennis M(s)/W(s), track and field M(s)/W(s), ultimate Frisbee M(c)/W(c), volleyball M(c)/W(s), water polo M(c)/W(c).
Intramural sports: badminton M/W, basketball M/W, bowling M/W, football M/W, golf M/W, racquetball M/W, sand volleyball M/W, soccer M/W, softball M/W, squash M/W, table tennis M/W, triathlon M/W, ultimate Frisbee M/W, volleyball M/W.

Campus security: 24-hour emergency response devices and patrols, late-night transport/escort service, controlled dormitory access, Self-defense education, shuttle buses, foot and vehicle patrols, video cameras, identification of valuables (bike registration).
Student services: health clinic, personal/psychological counseling.

COSTS & FINANCIAL AID
Costs (2017–18) *Comprehensive fee:* $53,162 includes full-time tuition ($41,540), mandatory fees ($626), and room and board ($10,996). Full-time tuition and fees vary according to course load, degree level, location, and program. Part-time tuition: $1450 per credit hour. Part-time tuition and fees vary according to course load, degree level, location, and program. *Required fees:* $198 per term part-time. *College room only:* $6124. Room and board charges vary according to board plan, housing facility, and location. *Payment plans:* installment, deferred payment. *Waivers:* employees or children of employees.

Financial Aid Of all full-time matriculated undergraduates who enrolled in 2016, 4,715 applied for aid, 3,989 were judged to have need, 1,361 had their need fully met. 638 Federal Work-Study jobs (averaging $1762). 231 state and other part-time jobs (averaging $2337). In 2016, 2543 non-need-based awards were made. *Average percent of need met:* 78. *Average financial aid package:* $29,810. *Average need-based loan:* $5303. *Average need-based gift aid:* $27,300. *Average non-need-based aid:* $17,447. *Average indebtedness upon graduation:* $21,292.

APPLYING
Standardized Tests *Required:* SAT or ACT (for admission).
Options: electronic application, early admission, deferred entrance.
Required: essay or personal statement, high school transcript, minimum 2.5 GPA. *Recommended:* 2 letters of recommendation, interview, Health exam.
Application deadlines: 8/15 (freshmen), 8/15 (transfers).
Notification: continuous until 11/1 (freshmen), continuous until 2/1 (transfers).

CONTACT
Jean M. Cox, Assistant Vice President, Office of Admission, Saint Louis University, One North Grand Boulevard, DuBourg Hall, Room 119, St. Louis, MO 63103. *Phone:* 314-977-2500. *Toll-free phone:* 800-758-3678. *Fax:* 314-977-7136. *E-mail:* admission@slu.edu.

Saint Luke's College of Health Sciences

Kansas City, Missouri
http://www.saintlukescollege.edu/

CONTACT
Mrs. Jennifer Wright, Student Services Associate, Saint Luke's College of Health Sciences, 624 Westport Road, Kansas City, MO 64111. *Phone:* 816-932-8629. *Fax:* 816-932-9064.

Southeast Missouri State University

Cape Girardeau, Missouri
http://www.semo.edu/

- **State-supported** comprehensive, founded 1873, part of Missouri Coordinating Board for Higher Education
- **Small-town** 400-acre campus
- **Endowment** $74.9 million
- **Coed** 10,458 undergraduate students, 74% full-time, 58% women, 42% men
- **Moderately difficult** entrance level, 85% of applicants were admitted

UNDERGRAD STUDENTS

7,779 full-time, 2,679 part-time. Students come from 43 states and territories; 56 other countries; 20% are from out of state; 9% Black or African American, non-Hispanic/Latino; 2% Hispanic/Latino; 1% Asian, non-Hispanic/Latino; 0.3% American Indian or Alaska Native, non-Hispanic/Latino; 0.9% Two or more races, non-Hispanic/Latino; 1% Race/ethnicity unknown; 5% international; 6% transferred in; 34% live on campus.

Freshmen:
Admission: 4,977 applied, 4,208 admitted, 1,803 enrolled. *Average high school GPA:* 3.4. *Test scores:* ACT scores over 18: 95%; ACT scores over 24: 40%; ACT scores over 30: 6%.
Retention: 75% of full-time freshmen returned.

FACULTY
Total: 578, 71% full-time, 60% with terminal degrees.
Student/faculty ratio: 20:1.

ACADEMICS
Calendar: semesters. *Degrees:* certificates, associate, bachelor's, master's, post-master's, and postbachelor's certificates.

Special study options: academic remediation for entering students, accelerated degree program, adult/continuing education programs, advanced placement credit, distance learning, double majors, English as a second language, honors programs, independent study, internships, off-campus study, part-time degree program, services for LD students, student-designed majors, study abroad, summer session for credit. *ROTC:* Air Force (b).

Computers: 1,550 computers/terminals are available on campus for general student use. Students can access the following: campus intranet, computer help desk, free student e-mail accounts, online (class) grades, online (class) registration, online (class) schedules. Campuswide network is available. 100% of college-owned or -operated housing units are wired for high-speed Internet access. Wireless service is available via classrooms, computer centers, computer labs, dorm rooms, learning centers, libraries, student centers.

Library: Kent Library. *Books:* 368,983 (physical), 198,866 (digital/electronic); *Serial titles:* 4,166 (physical), 81,800 (digital/electronic); *Databases:* 152. Weekly public service hours: 92.

STUDENT LIFE
Housing options: on-campus residence required through sophomore year; coed, special housing for students with disabilities. Campus housing is university owned. Freshman campus housing is guaranteed.

Activities and organizations: drama/theater group, student-run newspaper, radio and television station, choral group, marching band, Student Government, Student Activities Council, Greek Life, Residence Hall Association, International Students Association, national fraternities, national sororities.

Athletics Member NCAA. All Division I. *Intercollegiate sports:* baseball M(s), basketball M(s)/W(s), cheerleading M(s)/W(s), cross-country running M(s)/W(s), football M(s), gymnastics W(s), soccer W(s), softball W(s), tennis M(s), track and field M(s)/W(s), volleyball W(s). *Intramural sports:* archery M, basketball M/W, bowling M/W, equestrian sports M(c)/W(c), fencing M/W, football M/W, lacrosse M, riflery M/W, rock climbing M/W, rugby M/W, soccer M/W, softball M/W, table tennis M/W, tennis M/W, ultimate Frisbee M/W, volleyball M/W, weight lifting M/W.

Campus security: 24-hour emergency response devices and patrols, late-night transport/escort service, controlled dormitory access.

Student services: health clinic, personal/psychological counseling.

COSTS & FINANCIAL AID
Costs (2017–18) *Tuition:* state resident $6183 full-time, $206 per credit hour part-time; nonresident $11,718 full-time, $391 per credit hour part-time. Full-time tuition and fees vary according to course load and location. Part-time tuition and fees vary according to course load and location. *Required fees:* $1002 full-time, $33 per credit hour part-time. *Room and board:* $8715. Room and board charges vary according to board plan and housing facility. *Payment plans:* installment, deferred payment. *Waivers:* senior citizens and employees or children of employees.

Financial Aid Of all full-time matriculated undergraduates who enrolled in 2016, 6,069 applied for aid, 4,705 were judged to have need, 686 had their need fully met. 216 Federal Work-Study jobs (averaging $1671).

1,695 state and other part-time jobs (averaging $2084). In 2016, 1482 non-need-based awards were made. *Average percent of need met:* 59. *Average financial aid package:* $9234. *Average need-based loan:* $4167. *Average need-based gift aid:* $6269. *Average non-need-based aid:* $4188. *Average indebtedness upon graduation:* $27,991.

APPLYING
Standardized Tests *Required:* SAT or ACT (for admission).
Options: electronic application, deferred entrance.
Application fee: $30.
Required: high school transcript, minimum 2.0 GPA.
Application deadlines: 7/1 (freshmen), rolling (out-of-state freshmen), 7/1 (transfers).
Notification: 9/1 (freshmen), continuous until 9/1 (transfers).

CONTACT
Southeast Missouri State University, One University Plaza, Cape Girardeau, MO 63701-4799. *Phone:* 573-651-2590.

Southwest Baptist University
Bolivar, Missouri
http://www.sbuniv.edu/

- **Independent Southern Baptist** comprehensive, founded 1878
- **Small-town** 152-acre campus
- **Endowment** $24.4 million
- **Coed** 2,822 undergraduate students, 65% full-time, 64% women, 36% men
- **Moderately difficult** entrance level, 74% of applicants were admitted

UNDERGRAD STUDENTS
1,835 full-time, 987 part-time. Students come from 30 states and territories; 22 other countries; 14% are from out of state; 6% Black or African American, non-Hispanic/Latino; 3% Hispanic/Latino; 0.7% Asian, non-Hispanic/Latino; 0.2% Native Hawaiian or other Pacific Islander, non-Hispanic/Latino; 0.9% American Indian or Alaska Native, non-Hispanic/Latino; 1% Two or more races, non-Hispanic/Latino; 4% Race/ethnicity unknown; 2% international; 7% transferred in; 51% live on campus.

Freshmen:
Admission: 1,754 applied, 1,298 admitted, 474 enrolled. *Average high school GPA:* 3.5. *Test scores:* SAT evidence-based reading and writing scores over 500: 63%; SAT math scores over 500: 69%; ACT scores over 18: 89%; SAT evidence-based reading and writing scores over 600: 24%; SAT math scores over 600: 32%; ACT scores over 24: 42%; SAT evidence-based reading and writing scores over 700: 5%; SAT math scores over 700: 3%; ACT scores over 30: 7%.
Retention: 64% of full-time freshmen returned.

FACULTY
Total: 333, 47% full-time, 28% with terminal degrees.
Student/faculty ratio: 11:1.

ACADEMICS
Calendar: 4-1-4. *Degrees:* associate, bachelor's, master's, doctoral, and post-master's certificates.

Special study options: academic remediation for entering students, advanced placement credit, cooperative education, distance learning, double majors, honors programs, independent study, internships, off-campus study, part-time degree program, services for LD students, student-designed majors, study abroad, summer session for credit. *ROTC:* Army (c).

Unusual degree programs: 3-2 engineering with Missouri University of Science and Technology.

Computers: 345 computers/terminals are available on campus for general student use. Students can access the following: campus intranet, computer help desk, free student e-mail accounts, online (class) grades, online (class) registration, online (class) schedules. Campuswide network is available. 100% of college-owned or -operated housing units are wired for high-speed Internet access. Wireless service is available via entire campus.

Library: Harriett K. Hutchens Library. Weekly public service hours: 85; students can reserve study rooms.

STUDENT LIFE

Housing options: on-campus residence required through junior year; men-only, women-only, special housing for students with disabilities. Campus housing is university owned. Freshman campus housing is guaranteed.

Activities and organizations: drama/theater group, student-run newspaper, choral group, Enactus, Student Government Association, Fellowship of Christian Athletes, Student Missouri State Teachers Association, PSY CHI.

Athletics Member NCAA. All Division II. *Intercollegiate sports:* baseball M(s), basketball M(s)/W(s), cheerleading M/W, cross-country running M(s)/W(s), football M(s), golf M(s)/W(s), soccer M(s)/W(s), softball W(s), tennis M(s)/W(s), track and field M(s)/W(s), volleyball W(s). *Intramural sports:* basketball M/W, football M/W, sand volleyball M/W, soccer M/W, softball M/W, table tennis M/W, volleyball M/W.

Campus security: 24-hour emergency response devices and patrols, controlled dormitory access.

Student services: health clinic, personal/psychological counseling.

COSTS & FINANCIAL AID

Costs (2018–19) *Comprehensive fee:* $31,730 includes full-time tuition ($23,100), mandatory fees ($910), and room and board ($7720). Full-time tuition and fees vary according to course load, degree level, and location. Part-time tuition: $870 per credit hour. Part-time tuition and fees vary according to course load and location. *Required fees:* $185 per term part-time. *College room only:* $3400. Room and board charges vary according to board plan and housing facility. *Payment plan:* installment. *Waivers:* employees or children of employees.

Financial Aid Of all full-time matriculated undergraduates who enrolled in 2017, 1,608 applied for aid, 1,475 were judged to have need, 273 had their need fully met. 342 Federal Work-Study jobs (averaging $1880). In 2017, 237 non-need-based awards were made. *Average percent of need met:* 71. *Average financial aid package:* $19,846. *Average need-based loan:* $3391. *Average need-based gift aid:* $6299. *Average non-need-based aid:* $9933. *Average indebtedness upon graduation:* $29,429.

APPLYING

Standardized Tests *Required:* SAT or ACT (for admission).

Options: electronic application.

Application fee: $30.

Required: high school transcript, minimum 2.5 GPA. *Required for some:* 3 letters of recommendation. *Recommended:* essay or personal statement, interview.

Application deadlines: rolling (freshmen), rolling (transfers).

Notification: continuous (freshmen), continuous (transfers).

CONTACT

Becky Van Stavern, Director of Admissions, Southwest Baptist University, 1600 University Avenue, Bolivar, MO 65613-2597. *Phone:* 417-328-1815. *Toll-free phone:* 800-526-5859. *Fax:* 417-328-1808. *E-mail:* bvanstavern@sbuniv.edu.

Stephens College

Columbia, Missouri

http://www.stephens.edu/

- **Independent** comprehensive, founded 1833
- **Urban** 48-acre campus
- **Endowment** $46.8 million
- **Undergraduate: women only; graduate: coed**
- **Moderately difficult** entrance level

FACULTY

Student/faculty ratio: 8:1.

ACADEMICS

Calendar: semesters. *Degrees:* certificates, associate, bachelor's, master's, post-master's, and postbachelor's certificates.

Library: Hugh Stephens Library.

STUDENT LIFE

Housing options: on-campus residence required through senior year; women-only. Campus housing is university owned and is provided by a third party. Freshman campus housing is guaranteed.

Activities and organizations: drama/theater group, student-run newspaper, television station, choral group, Innovative Fashion Association, Warehouse Theatre, Student Government Association, American Marketing Association (AMA), national sororities.

Athletics Member NAIA.

Campus security: 24-hour emergency response devices and patrols, student patrols, late-night transport/escort service, controlled dormitory access.

Student services: health clinic, personal/psychological counseling.

FINANCIAL AID

Financial Aid Of all full-time matriculated undergraduates who enrolled in 2015, 521 applied for aid, 521 were judged to have need. In 2015, 58 non-need-based awards were made. *Average percent of need met:* 70. *Average financial aid package:* $10,000. *Average need-based gift aid:* $14,000. *Average non-need-based aid:* $8000.

APPLYING

Standardized Tests *Required:* SAT or ACT (for admission).

Options: electronic application, deferred entrance.

Application fee: $25.

Required: essay or personal statement, high school transcript, minimum 2.0 GPA. *Required for some:* 1 letter of recommendation, audition for dance, audition recommended for theater. *Recommended:* minimum 2.5 GPA, interview.

CONTACT

Tiffany Goalder, Director of Undergraduate Admissions, Stephens College, 1200 East Broadway, Box 2121, Columbia, MO 65215-0002. *Phone:* 573-876-7239. *Toll-free phone:* 800-876-7207. *Fax:* 573-876-7237. *E-mail:* apply@stephens.edu.

Stevens–The Institute of Business & Arts

St. Louis, Missouri

http://www.siba.edu/

- **Proprietary** 4-year, founded 1947
- **Urban** campus
- **Coed** 121 undergraduate students, 88% full-time, 81% women, 19% men
- **Moderately difficult** entrance level, 71% of applicants were admitted

UNDERGRAD STUDENTS

107 full-time, 14 part-time. Students come from 5 states and territories; 25% are from out of state; 65% Black or African American, non-Hispanic/Latino; 3% Hispanic/Latino; 0.8% Asian, non-Hispanic/Latino; 0.8% Two or more races, non-Hispanic/Latino; 2% Race/ethnicity unknown.

Freshmen:

Admission: 45 applied, 32 admitted. *Average high school GPA:* 2.8.

Retention: 69% of full-time freshmen returned.

FACULTY

Total: 17, 29% full-time.

Student/faculty ratio: 9:1.

ACADEMICS

Calendar: quarters. *Degrees:* associate and bachelor's.

Special study options: academic remediation for entering students, accelerated degree program, adult/continuing education programs, independent study, internships, part-time degree program, summer session for credit.

Computers: 45 computers/terminals are available on campus for general student use. Students can access the following: campus intranet, free student e-mail accounts, online (class) schedules. Campuswide network is available. Wireless service is available via entire campus.

Library: St. Louis Public Library.

STUDENT LIFE

Housing options: college housing not available.

Activities and organizations: Student Government.

Campus security: late-night transport/escort service, 24-hour controlled entrances.

COSTS

Costs (2018–19) *Tuition:* $12,720 full-time, $265 per credit hour part-time. Full-time tuition and fees vary according to course load and program. Part-time tuition and fees vary according to course load and program. No tuition increase for student's term of enrollment. *Required fees:* $600 full-time, $200 per term part-time. *Payment plan:* installment. *Waivers:* employees or children of employees.

APPLYING

Standardized Tests *Required for some:* SAT or ACT (for admission).

Options: electronic application, early admission, deferred entrance.

Application fee: $25.

Required: essay or personal statement, high school transcript, interview.

Application deadlines: rolling (freshmen), rolling (out-of-state freshmen), rolling (transfers), rolling (early action).

Early decision deadline: rolling (for plan 1), rolling (for plan 2).

Notification: continuous (freshmen), continuous (out-of-state freshmen), continuous (transfers), rolling (early decision plan 1), rolling (early decision plan 2), rolling (early action).

CONTACT

Sara Dorn, Director of Admissions, Stevens–The Institute of Business & Arts, 1521 Washington Avenue, St. Louis, MO 63103. *Phone:* 314-421-0949 Ext. 1118. *Toll-free phone:* 800-871-0949. *Fax:* 314-421-0304. *E-mail:* admission@siba.edu.

Truman State University

Kirksville, Missouri

http://www.truman.edu/

- **State-supported** comprehensive, founded 1867
- **Small-town** 140-acre campus
- **Endowment** $45.9 million
- **Coed** 5,898 undergraduate students, 87% full-time, 59% women, 41% men
- **Moderately difficult** entrance level, 67% of applicants were admitted

UNDERGRAD STUDENTS

5,134 full-time, 764 part-time. Students come from 42 states and territories; 45 other countries; 29% are from out of state; 3% Black or African American, non-Hispanic/Latino; 3% Hispanic/Latino; 3% Asian, non-Hispanic/Latino; 0.1% Native Hawaiian or other Pacific Islander, non-Hispanic/Latino; 0.3% American Indian or Alaska Native, non-Hispanic/Latino; 3% Two or more races, non-Hispanic/Latino; 1% Race/ethnicity unknown; 7% international; 3% transferred in; 42% live on campus.

Freshmen:

Admission: 5,263 applied, 3,552 admitted, 1,328 enrolled. *Average high school GPA:* 3.8. *Test scores:* SAT evidence-based reading and writing scores over 500: 95%; SAT math scores over 500: 97%; ACT scores over 18: 100%; SAT evidence-based reading and writing scores over 600: 78%; SAT math scores over 600: 68%; ACT scores over 24: 80%; SAT evidence-based reading and writing scores over 700: 30%; SAT math scores over 700: 33%; ACT scores over 30: 28%.

Retention: 86% of full-time freshmen returned.

FACULTY

Total: 398, 81% full-time, 75% with terminal degrees.

Student/faculty ratio: 16:1.

ACADEMICS

Calendar: semesters. *Degrees:* bachelor's and master's.

Special study options: accelerated degree program, advanced placement credit, cooperative education, double majors, honors programs, independent study, internships, off-campus study, part-time degree program, services for LD students, student-designed majors, study abroad, summer session for credit. *ROTC:* Army (b).

Unusual degree programs: 3-2 engineering with Missouri University of Science and Technology; University of Missouri, Columbia; chiropractic with Logan University.

Computers: 1,056 computers/terminals and 3,690 ports are available on campus for general student use. Students can access the following: campus intranet, computer help desk, free student e-mail accounts, online (class) grades, online (class) registration, online (class) schedules. Campuswide network is available. 100% of college-owned or -operated housing units are wired for high-speed Internet access. Wireless service is available via entire campus.

Library: Pickler Memorial Library. *Books:* 498,179 (physical), 359,767 (digital/electronic); *Serial titles:* 459 (physical), 2,638 (digital/electronic); *Databases:* 107. Weekly public service hours: 105; students can reserve study rooms.

STUDENT LIFE

Housing options: on-campus residence required for freshman year; coed, special housing for students with disabilities. Campus housing is university owned. Freshman campus housing is guaranteed.

Activities and organizations: drama/theater group, student-run newspaper, radio and television station, choral group, marching band, Alpha Phi Omega (co-ed service fraternity), Nursing Students Association, Alpha Sigma Gamma (service sorority), Beta Beta Beta (biology honors), National Society of Collegiate Scholars, national fraternities, national sororities.

Athletics Member NCAA. All Division II. *Intercollegiate sports:* baseball M(s), basketball M(s)/W(s), bowling M(c)/W(c), cheerleading M(c)/W(c), cross-country running M(s)/W(s), equestrian sports M(c)/W(c), football M(s), golf W(s), lacrosse W(c), riflery M(c)/W(c), rock climbing M(c)/W(c), rugby M(c)/W(c), soccer M(s)/W(s), softball W(s), swimming and diving M/W(s), tennis M(s)/W(s), track and field M(s)/W(s), ultimate Frisbee M(c)/W(c), volleyball M(c)/W(s), weight lifting M(c)/W(c), wrestling M(s). *Intramural sports:* badminton M/W, basketball M/W, cross-country running M/W, football M/W, skiing (cross-country) M(c)/W(c), skiing (downhill) M(c)/W(c), soccer M/W, softball M/W, swimming and diving M/W, table tennis M/W, tennis M/W, track and field M/W, ultimate Frisbee M/W, volleyball M/W.

Campus security: 24-hour emergency response devices and patrols, student patrols, late-night transport/escort service, controlled dormitory access, patrols by commissioned officers, perimeter access system, dual 911 call center for campus/community, emergency text messaging system.

Student services: health clinic, personal/psychological counseling, women's center.

COSTS & FINANCIAL AID

Costs (2017–18) *One-time required fee:* $350. *Tuition:* state resident $7352 full-time, $306 per credit hour part-time; nonresident $14,136 full-time, $589 per credit hour part-time. Full-time tuition and fees vary according to course load, degree level, and program. Part-time tuition and fees vary according to course load, degree level, and program. *Required fees:* $304 full-time, $304 per year part-time. *Room and board:* $8630; room only: $5730. Room and board charges vary according to board plan and housing facility. *Payment plan:* installment. *Waivers:* children of alumni, senior citizens, and employees or children of employees.

Financial Aid Of all full-time matriculated undergraduates who enrolled in 2016, 3,666 applied for aid, 2,593 were judged to have need, 933 had their need fully met. 449 Federal Work-Study jobs (averaging $1491). 1,399 state and other part-time jobs (averaging $1129). In 2016, 1960 non-need-based awards were made. *Average percent of need met:* 84. *Average financial aid package:* $12,518. *Average need-based loan:* $4431. *Average need-based gift aid:* $7824. *Average non-need-based aid:* $5992. *Average indebtedness upon graduation:* $24,938.

APPLYING

Options: electronic application, deferred entrance.

Required: essay or personal statement, high school transcript. *Recommended:* minimum 3.0 GPA, interview, activities list/resume.

Application deadlines: rolling (freshmen), rolling (transfers).

Notification: continuous until 9/1 (freshmen), continuous (transfers).

CONTACT

Melody Chambers, Director of Admission, Truman State University, Ruth Towne Museum and Visitors Center, 100 East Normal Avenue, Kirksville, MO 63501-4221. *Phone:* 660-785-4114. *Toll-free phone:* 800-892-7792. *Fax:* 660-785-7456. *E-mail:* mchamber@truman.edu.

University of Central Missouri

Warrensburg, Missouri

http://www.ucmo.edu/

- **State-supported** comprehensive, founded 1871
- **Small-town** 1561-acre campus with easy access to Kansas City
- **Coed** 9,801 undergraduate students, 79% full-time, 56% women, 44% men
- **Moderately difficult** entrance level, 84% of applicants were admitted

UNDERGRAD STUDENTS

7,701 full-time, 2,100 part-time. Students come from 46 states and territories; 42 other countries; 11% are from out of state; 10% Black or African American, non-Hispanic/Latino; 5% Hispanic/Latino; 0.9% Asian, non-Hispanic/Latino; 0.3% Native Hawaiian or other Pacific Islander, non-Hispanic/Latino; 0.3% American Indian or Alaska Native, non-Hispanic/Latino; 4% Two or more races, non-Hispanic/Latino; 2% Race/ethnicity unknown; 3% international; 9% transferred in; 34% live on campus.

Freshmen:

Admission: 4,748 applied, 3,982 admitted, 1,691 enrolled. *Average high school GPA:* 3.4. *Test scores:* ACT scores over 18: 91%; ACT scores over 24: 33%; ACT scores over 30: 4%.

Retention: 72% of full-time freshmen returned.

FACULTY

Total: 655, 75% full-time, 57% with terminal degrees.

Student/faculty ratio: 18:1.

ACADEMICS

Calendar: semesters. *Degrees:* certificates, bachelor's, master's, post-master's, and postbachelor's certificates.

Special study options: academic remediation for entering students, accelerated degree program, adult/continuing education programs, advanced placement credit, distance learning, double majors, English as a second language, honors programs, internships, off-campus study, part-time degree program, services for LD students, student-designed majors, study abroad, summer session for credit. *ROTC:* Army (b), Air Force (c).

Unusual degree programs: 3-2 engineering with University of Missouri–Columbia, Missouri University of Science and Technology, University of Missouri–Kansas City; law, medicine.

Computers: 6,395 computers/terminals and 19,008 ports are available on campus for general student use. Students can access the following: campus intranet, computer help desk, free student e-mail accounts, online (class) grades, online (class) registration, online (class) schedules. Campuswide network is available. 100% of college-owned or -operated housing units are wired for high-speed Internet access. Wireless service is available via classrooms, computer centers, computer labs, dorm rooms, learning centers, libraries, student centers.

Library: James C. Kirkpatrick Library plus 1 other. *Books:* 499,982 (physical), 268,431 (digital/electronic); *Serial titles:* 1,579 (physical), 89,008 (digital/electronic); *Databases:* 97. Weekly public service hours: 96; students can reserve study rooms.

STUDENT LIFE

Housing options: on-campus residence required through sophomore year; coed, women-only, special housing for students with disabilities. Campus housing is university owned. Freshman campus housing is guaranteed.

Activities and organizations: drama/theater group, student-run newspaper, radio and television station, choral group, marching band, Roaring Red (Student Booster Club), Greek Organization, Campus Christian House, BSU (Baptist Student Union), International Student Organization, national fraternities, national sororities.

Athletics Member NCAA. All Division II. *Intercollegiate sports:* baseball M(s), basketball M(s)/W(s), bowling M(s)(c)/W(s)(c), cheerleading M/W, cross-country running M(s)/W(s), football M(s), golf M(s)/W(s), rugby M(c)/W(c), soccer M(c)/W(s), softball W(s), track and field M(s)/W(s), volleyball M(c)/W(s), wrestling M(s). *Intramural sports:* archery M/W, badminton M/W, basketball M/W, bowling M/W, cheerleading M/W, fencing M/W, football M/W, golf M/W, racquetball M/W, riflery M/W, rock climbing M/W, sand volleyball M/W, soccer M/W, softball M/W, swimming and diving M/W, table tennis M/W, tennis M/W, track and field M/W, ultimate Frisbee M(c)/W(c), volleyball M/W.

Campus security: 24-hour emergency response devices and patrols, student patrols, late-night transport/escort service, controlled dormitory access, canine patrol.

Student services: health clinic, personal/psychological counseling, women's center.

COSTS & FINANCIAL AID

Costs (2017–18) *Tuition:* state resident $6630 full-time, $221 per credit hour part-time; nonresident $13,260 full-time, $442 per credit hour part-time. Full-time tuition and fees vary according to course load and location. Part-time tuition and fees vary according to location. *Required fees:* $890 full-time, $30 per credit hour part-time. *Room and board:* $8536; room only: $5394. Room and board charges vary according to board plan, housing facility, and student level. *Payment plans:* installment, deferred payment. *Waivers:* employees or children of employees.

Financial Aid Of all full-time matriculated undergraduates who enrolled in 2016, 4,949 applied for aid, 3,701 were judged to have need, 355 had their need fully met. 87 Federal Work-Study jobs (averaging $1522). 1,690 state and other part-time jobs. In 2016, 1728 non-need-based awards were made. *Average percent of need met:* 62. *Average financial aid package:* $8622. *Average need-based gift aid:* $2833. *Average non-need-based aid:* $3474. *Average indebtedness upon graduation:* $27,481.

APPLYING

Standardized Tests *Required:* SAT or ACT (for admission).

Options: electronic application, deferred entrance.

Application fee: $30.

Required: high school transcript, rank in upper two-thirds of high school class.

Application deadlines: rolling (freshmen), rolling (transfers).

Notification: continuous (freshmen), continuous (transfers).

CONTACT

Mr. J. D. Gragg, Director of Admissions, University of Central Missouri, 1400 Ward Edwards, Warrensburg, MO 64093. *Phone:* 660-543-4290. *Toll-free phone:* 800-729-8266. *Fax:* 660-543-8517. *E-mail:* admit@ucmo.edu.

University of Missouri

Columbia, Missouri

http://www.missouri.edu/

- **State-supported** university, founded 1839, part of University of Missouri System
- **Suburban** 1262-acre campus
- **Endowment** $947.5 million
- **Coed** 23,817 undergraduate students, 93% full-time, 52% women, 48% men
- **Moderately difficult** entrance level, 78% of applicants were admitted

UNDERGRAD STUDENTS

22,197 full-time, 1,620 part-time. Students come from 50 states and territories; 67 other countries; 21% are from out of state; 7% Black or African American, non-Hispanic/Latino; 4% Hispanic/Latino; 3% Asian, non-Hispanic/Latino; 0.2% American Indian or Alaska Native, non-Hispanic/Latino; 3% Two or more races, non-Hispanic/Latino; 0.7% Race/ethnicity unknown; 4% international; 4% transferred in; 21% live on campus.

Freshmen:

Admission: 16,373 applied, 12,787 admitted, 4,134 enrolled. *Test scores:* SAT evidence-based reading and writing scores over 500: 94%; SAT math scores over 500: 94%; ACT scores over 18: 100%; SAT evidence-based reading and writing scores over 600: 67%; SAT math scores over 600: 53%; ACT scores over 24: 71%; SAT evidence-based reading and writing scores over 700: 17%; SAT math scores over 700: 14%; ACT scores over 30: 19%.

Retention: 87% of full-time freshmen returned.

FACULTY

Total: 1,314, 95% full-time, 91% with terminal degrees.

Student/faculty ratio: 18:1.

ACADEMICS

Calendar: semesters. *Degrees:* bachelor's, master's, doctoral, and post-master's certificates.

Special study options: accelerated degree program, adult/continuing education programs, advanced placement credit, cooperative education, distance learning, double majors, English as a second language, external degree program, freshman honors college, honors programs, independent study, internships, off-campus study, part-time degree program, services for LD students, student-designed majors, study abroad, summer session for credit. *ROTC:* Army (b), Navy (b), Air Force (b).

Unusual degree programs: 3-2 accountancy, occupational therapy.

Computers: 1,200 computers/terminals are available on campus for general student use. Students can access the following: computer help desk, free student e-mail accounts, online (class) grades, online (class) registration, online (class) schedules. Campuswide network is available. 95% of college-owned or -operated housing units are wired for high-speed Internet access. Wireless service is available via entire campus.

Library: Ellis Library plus 10 others. *Books:* 4.7 million (physical), 1.4 million (digital/electronic). Students can reserve study rooms.

STUDENT LIFE

Housing options: on-campus residence required for freshman year; coed, men-only, women-only, special housing for students with disabilities. Campus housing is university owned. Freshman campus housing is guaranteed.

Activities and organizations: drama/theater group, student-run newspaper, radio and television station, choral group, marching band, Academic organizations, Greek organizations, Religious/Spiritual organizations, Sports clubs, Student Governance, national fraternities, national sororities.

Athletics Member NCAA. All Division I except football (Division I-A). *Intercollegiate sports:* baseball M(s), basketball M(s)/W(s), cheerleading M/W, cross-country running M(s)/W(s), golf M(s)/W(s), gymnastics W(s), soccer W(s), softball W(s), swimming and diving M(s)/W(s), tennis W(s), track and field M(s)/W(s), volleyball W(s), wrestling M(s). *Intramural sports:* archery M(c)/W(c), badminton W(c), baseball M(c), basketball M(c)/W(c), fencing M(c)/W(c), field hockey W(c), golf M(c)/W(c), ice hockey M(c), lacrosse M(c)/W(c), racquetball M(c)/W(c), rugby M(c)/W(c), soccer M(c)/W(c), softball W(c), swimming and diving M(c)/W(c), table tennis M(c)/W(c), tennis M(c)/W(c), ultimate Frisbee M(c)/W(c), volleyball M(c)/W(c), water polo M(c)/W(c), weight lifting M(c)/W(c).

Campus security: 24-hour emergency response devices and patrols, late-night transport/escort service, controlled dormitory access.

Student services: health clinic, personal/psychological counseling, women's center, legal services.

COSTS & FINANCIAL AID

Costs (2017–18) *Tuition:* state resident $8460 full-time, $282 per credit hour part-time; nonresident $25,179 full-time, $839 per credit hour part-time. Full-time tuition and fees vary according to course load, program, and reciprocity agreements. Part-time tuition and fees vary according to course load, program, and reciprocity agreements. *Required fees:* $1327 full-time. *Room and board:* $10,676; room only: $7641. Room and board charges vary according to board plan and housing facility. *Payment plan:* installment. *Waivers:* senior citizens and employees or children of employees.

Financial Aid Of all full-time matriculated undergraduates who enrolled in 2016, 15,683 applied for aid, 11,344 were judged to have need, 1,556 had their need fully met. In 2016, 4276 non-need-based awards were made. *Average percent of need met:* 59. *Average financial aid package:* $11,696. *Average need-based loan:* $5032. *Average need-based gift aid:* $9807. *Average non-need-based aid:* $6104. *Average indebtedness upon graduation:* $26,685.

APPLYING

Standardized Tests *Required:* SAT or ACT (for admission). *Recommended:* ACT (for admission).

Options: electronic application, deferred entrance.

Application fee: $65.

Required: high school transcript, specific high school curriculum.

Application deadlines: rolling (freshmen), rolling (transfers).

Notification: continuous (freshmen), continuous (transfers).

CONTACT

Mr. Charles May, Director of Admissions, University of Missouri, 230 Jesse Hall, Columbia, MO 65211. *Phone:* 573-882-7786. *Toll-free phone:* 800-225-6075. *Fax:* 573-882-7887. *E-mail:* mu4u@missouri.edu.

University of Missouri–Kansas City

Kansas City, Missouri

http://www.umkc.edu/

- **State-supported** university, founded 1929, part of University of Missouri System
- **Urban** 191-acre campus with easy access to Kansas City
- **Endowment** $305.8 million
- **Coed**
- **Moderately difficult** entrance level

FACULTY

Student/faculty ratio: 14:1.

ACADEMICS

Calendar: semesters. *Degrees:* bachelor's, master's, doctoral, and post-master's certificates.

Library: Miller-Nichols Library plus 3 others. Students can reserve study rooms.

STUDENT LIFE

Housing options: coed, special housing for students with disabilities. Campus housing is university owned.

Activities and organizations: drama/theater group, student-run newspaper, radio station, choral group, Union Programming Board, International Student Council, Alpha Phi Omega, Omicron Delta Kappa, Greek Organizations, national fraternities, national sororities.

Athletics Member NCAA. All Division I.

Campus security: 24-hour emergency response devices and patrols, late-night transport/escort service, controlled dormitory access.

Student services: health clinic, personal/psychological counseling, women's center, legal services.

COSTS & FINANCIAL AID

Costs (2017–18) *Tuition:* state resident $8340 full-time, $278 per credit hour part-time; nonresident $23,067 full-time, $769 per credit hour part-time. Full-time tuition and fees vary according to course load and program. Part-time tuition and fees vary according to course load and program. *Required fees:* $1424 full-time, $102 per credit hour part-time. *Room and board:* $10,383; room only: $6884. Room and board charges vary according to board plan and housing facility.

Financial Aid Of all full-time matriculated undergraduates who enrolled in 2016, 5,942 applied for aid, 4,998 were judged to have need, 413 had their need fully met. 632 Federal Work-Study jobs (averaging $4144). In 2016, 1022 non-need-based awards were made. *Average percent of need met:* 54. *Average financial aid package:* $9810. *Average need-based loan:* $7966. *Average need-based gift aid:* $7152. *Average non-need-based aid:* $5397. *Average indebtedness upon graduation:* $25,912.

APPLYING

Standardized Tests *Required:* SAT or ACT (for admission).

Options: electronic application, deferred entrance.

Application fee: $45.

Required: high school transcript. *Required for some:* essay or personal statement, interview.

CONTACT

Ms. Tamera Byland, Director of Admissions, University of Missouri–Kansas City, Office of Admissions, 5100 Rockhill Road, Kansas City, MO 64110-2499. *Phone:* 816-235-1111. *Toll-free phone:* 800-775-8652. *Fax:* 816-235-5544. *E-mail:* admit@umkc.edu.

University of Missouri–St. Louis

St. Louis, Missouri

http://www.umsl.edu/

- **State-supported** university, founded 1963, part of University of Missouri System
- **Suburban** 350-acre campus with easy access to St. Louis
- **Endowment** $83.5 million
- **Coed** 13,842 undergraduate students, 40% full-time, 57% women, 43% men
- **Moderately difficult** entrance level, 76% of applicants were admitted

UNDERGRAD STUDENTS

5,492 full-time, 8,350 part-time. Students come from 34 states and territories; 44 other countries; 11% are from out of state; 17% Black or African American, non-Hispanic/Latino; 3% Hispanic/Latino; 5% Asian, non-Hispanic/Latino; 0.1% Native Hawaiian or other Pacific Islander, non-Hispanic/Latino; 0.4% American Indian or Alaska Native, non-Hispanic/Latino; 3% Two or more races, non-Hispanic/Latino; 4% Race/ethnicity unknown; 3% international; 10% transferred in; 9% live on campus.

Freshmen:

Admission: 1,970 applied, 1,496 admitted, 482 enrolled. **Test scores:** SAT evidence-based reading and writing scores over 500: 97%; ACT scores over 18: 98%; SAT evidence-based reading and writing scores over 600: 27%; ACT scores over 24: 58%; SAT evidence-based reading and writing scores over 700: 12%; ACT scores over 30: 10%.

Retention: 74% of full-time freshmen returned.

FACULTY

Total: 825, 52% full-time, 56% with terminal degrees.

Student/faculty ratio: 18:1.

ACADEMICS

Calendar: semesters. *Degrees:* bachelor's, master's, doctoral, post-master's, and postbachelor's certificates.

Special study options: accelerated degree program, adult/continuing education programs, advanced placement credit, cooperative education, distance learning, double majors, English as a second language, freshman honors college, honors programs, independent study, internships, off-campus study, part-time degree program, services for LD students, student-designed majors, study abroad, summer session for credit. **ROTC:** Army (b), Air Force (c).

Unusual degree programs: 3-2 engineering with Washington University in St. Louis; economics, history, philosophy, political science, sociology.

Computers: 1,391 computers/terminals and 1,391 ports are available on campus for general student use. Students can access the following: campus intranet, computer help desk, free student e-mail accounts, online (class) grades, online (class) registration, online (class) schedules. Campuswide network is available. 90% of college-owned or -operated housing units are wired for high-speed Internet access. Wireless service is available via classrooms, computer centers, computer labs, dorm rooms, learning centers, libraries, student centers.

Library: Thomas Jefferson Library plus 1 other. *Books:* 1.3 million (physical), 206,616 (digital/electronic); *Serial titles:* 990 (physical), 1,295 (digital/electronic); *Databases:* 195. Weekly public service hours: 82; students can reserve study rooms.

STUDENT LIFE

Housing options: coed, men-only, women-only, special housing for students with disabilities. Campus housing is university owned and is provided by a third party.

Activities and organizations: drama/theater group, student-run newspaper, radio station, choral group, Student Government Association, Associated Black Collegians, Pierre laclede Honors College Student Association, Residence Hall Association, UMSL Radio Station, national fraternities, national sororities.

Athletics Member NCAA. All Division II. *Intercollegiate sports:* baseball M(s), basketball M(s)/W(s), cheerleading W, golf M(s)/W(s), ice hockey M(c), soccer M(s)/W(s), softball W(s), swimming and diving M(s)/W(s), table tennis M(c)/W(c), tennis M(s)/W(s), volleyball W(s). *Intramural sports:* badminton M/W, basketball M/W, bowling M/W, football M/W, golf M/W, racquetball M/W, rock climbing M/W, sand volleyball M/W, skiing (downhill) M/W, soccer M/W, softball M/W, table tennis M/W, tennis M/W, ultimate Frisbee M/W, volleyball M/W, weight lifting M/W.

Campus security: 24-hour emergency response devices and patrols, late-night transport/escort service, controlled dormitory access, criminal investigations.

Student services: health clinic, personal/psychological counseling, women's center.

COSTS & FINANCIAL AID

Costs (2017–18) *Tuition:* state resident $10,275 full-time, $343 per credit hour part-time; nonresident $27,327 full-time, $911 per credit hour part-time. Full-time tuition and fees vary according to course level, course load, location, program, and reciprocity agreements. Part-time tuition and fees vary according to course level, course load, location, program, and reciprocity agreements. *Room and board:* $9363; room only: $5340. Room and board charges vary according to board plan and housing facility. *Payment plan:* installment. *Waivers:* senior citizens and employees or children of employees.

Financial Aid Of all full-time matriculated undergraduates who enrolled in 2017, 4,245 applied for aid, 3,682 were judged to have need, 721 had their need fully met. 83 Federal Work-Study jobs (averaging $4307). In 2017, 502 non-need-based awards were made. *Average percent of need met:* 66. *Average financial aid package:* $11,989. *Average need-based loan:* $4450. *Average need-based gift aid:* $8292. *Average non-need-based aid:* $5614. *Average indebtedness upon graduation:* $25,873.

APPLYING

Standardized Tests *Required:* SAT or ACT (for admission).

Options: electronic application.

Application fee: $35.

Required: high school transcript, minimum 2.0 GPA, CBHE core requirements. *Required for some:* essay or personal statement, 2 letters of recommendation, interview.

Application deadlines: rolling (freshmen), rolling (transfers).

Notification: continuous (freshmen), continuous (transfers).

CONTACT

Mr. Andrew L. Griffin, Dean of Admissions, University of Missouri–St. Louis, 351 Millennium Student Center, One University Boulevard, St. Louis, MO 63121-4400. *Phone:* 314-516-6941. *Toll-free phone:* 888-GO2-UMSL (in-state); 888-GO2-USML (out-of-state). *Fax:* 314-516-5310. *E-mail:* askdrew@umsl.edu.

Vatterott College

Berkeley, Missouri

http://www.vatterott.edu/

CONTACT

Ann Farajallah, Director of Admissions, Vatterott College, 8580 Evans Avenue, Berkeley, MO 63134. *Phone:* 314-264-1020. *Toll-free phone:* 888-553-6627.

Vatterott College

Sunset Hills, Missouri

http://www.vatterott.edu/

CONTACT

Director of Admission, Vatterott College, 12900 Maurer Industrial Drive, Sunset Hills, MO 63127. *Phone:* 314-843-4200. *Toll-free phone:* 888-553-6627. *Fax:* 314-843-1709.

Washington University in St. Louis

St. Louis, Missouri

http://www.wustl.edu/

- **Independent** university, founded 1853
- **Suburban** 169-acre campus with easy access to St. Louis
- **Endowment** $7.2 billion
- **Coed** 7,675 undergraduate students, 92% full-time, 54% women, 46% men
- **Most difficult** entrance level, 16% of applicants were admitted

UNDERGRAD STUDENTS
7,074 full-time, 601 part-time. Students come from 53 states and territories; 50 other countries; 91% are from out of state; 8% Black or African American, non-Hispanic/Latino; 9% Hispanic/Latino; 17% Asian, non-Hispanic/Latino; 0.1% American Indian or Alaska Native, non-Hispanic/Latino; 5% Two or more races, non-Hispanic/Latino; 2% Race/ethnicity unknown; 7% international; 1% transferred in; 74% live on campus.

Freshmen:
Admission: 30,463 applied, 4,863 admitted, 1,778 enrolled. *Test scores:* SAT evidence-based reading and writing scores over 500: 100%; SAT math scores over 500: 100%; ACT scores over 18: 100%; SAT evidence-based reading and writing scores over 600: 100%; SAT math scores over 600: 100%; ACT scores over 24: 100%; SAT evidence-based reading and writing scores over 700: 85%; SAT math scores over 700: 92%; ACT scores over 30: 94%.

Retention: 97% of full-time freshmen returned.

FACULTY
Total: 1,300, 73% full-time.
Student/faculty ratio: 8:1.

ACADEMICS
Calendar: semesters. *Degrees:* certificates, bachelor's, master's, doctoral, post-master's, and postbachelor's certificates.

Special study options: accelerated degree program, adult/continuing education programs, advanced placement credit, cooperative education, double majors, English as a second language, independent study, internships, off-campus study, part-time degree program, services for LD students, student-designed majors, study abroad, summer session for credit. *ROTC:* Army (b), Air Force (c).

Unusual degree programs: 3-2 business administration; engineering; social work; art, occupational therapy, physical therapy.

Computers: 2,500 computers/terminals and 3,500 ports are available on campus for general student use. Students can access the following: campus intranet, computer help desk, free student e-mail accounts, online (class) grades, online (class) registration, online (class) schedules. Campuswide network is available. 95% of college-owned or -operated housing units are wired for high-speed Internet access. Wireless service is available via classrooms, computer centers, computer labs, dorm rooms, learning centers, libraries, student centers.

Library: John M. Olin Library plus 12 others. *Books:* 2.6 million (physical), 1.8 million (digital/electronic); *Serial titles:* 992 (physical), 151,613 (digital/electronic); *Databases:* 693. Weekly public service hours: 130; study areas open 24 hours, 5–7 days a week; students can reserve study rooms.

STUDENT LIFE
Housing options: on-campus residence required for freshman year; coed, men-only, women-only, cooperative. Campus housing is university owned. Freshman campus housing is guaranteed.

Activities and organizations: drama/theater group, student-run newspaper, radio and television station, choral group, national fraternities, national sororities.

Athletics Member NCAA. All Division III. *Intercollegiate sports:* archery M(c)/W(c), badminton M(c)/W(c), baseball M, basketball M/W, cross-country running M/W, equestrian sports M(c)/W(c), fencing M(c)/W(c), field hockey W(c), football M, golf M(c)/W, gymnastics M(c)/W(c), ice hockey M(c), lacrosse M(c)/W(c), racquetball M(c)/W(c), rowing M(c)/W(c), rugby M(c)/W(c), sailing M(c)/W(c), soccer M/W, softball W, squash M(c)/W(c), swimming and diving M/W, table tennis M(c)/W(c), tennis M/W, track and field M/W, triathlon M(c)/W(c), ultimate Frisbee M(c)/W(c), volleyball M(c)/W, water polo M(c)/W(c), weight lifting M(c)/W(c), wrestling M(c). *Intramural sports:* archery M/W, badminton M/W, baseball M(c), basketball M(c)/W(c), bowling M/W, cross-country running M(c)/W(c), football M/W, golf M/W(c), racquetball M/W, rock climbing M/W, sand volleyball M/W, soccer M(c)/W(c), softball M/W(c), squash M/W, swimming and diving M(c)/W(c), table tennis M/W, tennis M(c)/W(c), track and field M/W, ultimate Frisbee M/W, volleyball M/W(c), water polo M/W, weight lifting M/W.

Campus security: 24-hour emergency response devices and patrols, student patrols, late-night transport/escort service, controlled dormitory access, SafeTrek app for reporting emergencies.

Student services: health clinic, personal/psychological counseling.

COSTS & FINANCIAL AID
Costs (2018–19) *Comprehensive fee:* $69,839 includes full-time tuition ($52,400), mandatory fees ($999), and room and board ($16,440). *College room only:* $11,310. Room and board charges vary according to board plan and housing facility. *Payment plans:* tuition prepayment, installment. *Waivers:* employees or children of employees.

Financial Aid Of all full-time matriculated undergraduates who enrolled in 2017, 3,204 applied for aid, 2,926 were judged to have need, 2,891 had their need fully met. 1,374 Federal Work-Study jobs (averaging $2304). In 2017, 553 non-need-based awards were made. *Average percent of need met:* 100. *Average financial aid package:* $46,638. *Average need-based loan:* $4698. *Average need-based gift aid:* $43,745. *Average non-need-based aid:* $5305. *Average indebtedness upon graduation:* $22,592. *Financial aid deadline:* 2/1.

APPLYING
Standardized Tests *Required:* SAT or ACT (for admission).

Options: electronic application, early admission, early decision, deferred entrance.

Application fee: $75.

Required: essay or personal statement, high school transcript, 2 letters of recommendation. *Required for some:* portfolio for the College of Art and the College of Architecture. *Recommended:* minimum 3.5 GPA.

Application deadlines: 1/2 (freshmen), 3/15 (transfers).

Early decision deadline: 11/1 (for plan 1), 1/2 (for plan 2).

Notification: 4/1 (freshmen), 5/15 (transfers), 12/15 (early decision plan 1), 2/15 (early decision plan 2).

CONTACT
Ms. Julie Shimabukuro, Director of Admissions, Washington University in St. Louis, Campus Box 1089, One Brookings Drive, St. Louis, MO 63130-4899. *Phone:* 314-935-6000. *Toll-free phone:* 800-638-0700. *Fax:* 314-935-4290. *E-mail:* admissions@wustl.edu.

Webster University
St. Louis, Missouri
http://www.webster.edu/

- **Independent** comprehensive, founded 1915
- **Suburban** 47-acre campus with easy access to St. Louis
- **Coed** 2,544 undergraduate students, 87% full-time, 55% women, 45% men
- **Moderately difficult** entrance level, 47% of applicants were admitted

UNDERGRAD STUDENTS
2,212 full-time, 332 part-time. 27% are from out of state; 12% Black or African American, non-Hispanic/Latino; 6% Hispanic/Latino; 2% Asian, non-Hispanic/Latino; 0.1% American Indian or Alaska Native, non-Hispanic/Latino; 4% Two or more races, non-Hispanic/Latino; 7% Race/ethnicity unknown; 3% international; 9% transferred in.

Freshmen:
Admission: 2,585 applied, 1,205 admitted, 514 enrolled. *Average high school GPA:* 3.5. *Test scores:* ACT scores over 18: 95%; ACT scores over 24: 51%; ACT scores over 30: 10%.

Retention: 79% of full-time freshmen returned.

FACULTY
Total: 198.
Student/faculty ratio: 9:1.

ACADEMICS
Calendar: semesters. *Degrees:* certificates, bachelor's, master's, doctoral, post-master's, and postbachelor's certificates.

Special study options: accelerated degree program, adult/continuing education programs, advanced placement credit, cooperative education, distance learning, double majors, English as a second language, independent study, internships, off-campus study, part-time degree program, services for LD students, student-designed majors, study abroad, summer session for credit. *ROTC:* Army (c), Air Force (c).

Unusual degree programs: 3-2 engineering with Washington University in St. Louis; occupational therapy with Washington University in St. Louis.

Computers: Students can access the following: campus intranet, computer help desk, free student e-mail accounts, online (class) grades, online (class) registration, online (class) schedules. Campuswide network is available. 100% of college-owned or -operated housing units are wired for high-speed Internet access. Wireless service is available via entire campus.

Library: Emerson Library. Study areas open 24 hours, 5–7 days a week; students can reserve study rooms.

STUDENT LIFE

Housing options: on-campus residence required through sophomore year; coed, special housing for students with disabilities. Campus housing is university owned and leased by the school. Freshman applicants given priority for college housing.

Activities and organizations: drama/theater group, student-run newspaper, radio and television station, choral group, national sororities.

Athletics Member NCAA. All Division III. *Intercollegiate sports:* baseball M, basketball M/W, cross-country running M/W, golf M, soccer M/W, softball W, tennis M/W, track and field M/W, volleyball W. *Intramural sports:* basketball M/W, bowling M/W, cheerleading M(c)/W(c), football M/W, soccer M(c)/W(c), swimming and diving M(c)/W(c), volleyball M/W.

Campus security: 24-hour emergency response devices and patrols, student patrols, late-night transport/escort service, controlled dormitory access.

Student services: health clinic, personal/psychological counseling.

COSTS & FINANCIAL AID

Costs (2017–18) *One-time required fee:* $125. *Comprehensive fee:* $38,150 includes full-time tuition ($26,900), mandatory fees ($200), and room and board ($11,050). Full-time tuition and fees vary according to program. Part-time tuition: $690 per credit hour. *College room only:* $6050. Room and board charges vary according to board plan and housing facility. *Payment plan:* deferred payment. *Waivers:* employees or children of employees.

Financial Aid Of all full-time matriculated undergraduates who enrolled in 2017, 1,846 applied for aid, 1,500 were judged to have need, 283 had their need fully met. 1,291 Federal Work-Study jobs (averaging $2738). In 2017, 122 non-need-based awards were made. *Average percent of need met:* 63. *Average financial aid package:* $23,727. *Average need-based loan:* $4629. *Average need-based gift aid:* $8574. *Average non-need-based aid:* $13,621. *Average indebtedness upon graduation:* $29,867.

APPLYING

Standardized Tests *Required:* SAT or ACT (for admission).

Options: electronic application, early admission, deferred entrance.

Application fee: $35.

Required: essay or personal statement, high school transcript, minimum 2.5 GPA, 1 letter of recommendation. *Required for some:* interview, audition, portfolio review, and/or interview. *Recommended:* minimum 3.0 GPA.

Application deadlines: 8/1 (freshmen), 8/1 (transfers).

Notification: continuous (freshmen), continuous (out-of-state freshmen), continuous (transfers).

CONTACT

Webster University, 470 East Lockwood Avenue, St. Louis, MO 63119-3194. *Phone:* 314-246-7910. *Toll-free phone:* 800-753-6765.

Westminster College

Fulton, Missouri

http://www.westminster-mo.edu/

CONTACT

Robert Andrews, Vice President and Dean of Enrollment Management, Westminster College, 501 Westminster Avenue, Fulton, MO 65251-1299. *Phone:* 573-592-5251. *Toll-free phone:* 800-475-3361. *Fax:* 573-592-5255. *E-mail:* admissions@westminster-mo.edu.

William Jewell College

Liberty, Missouri

http://www.jewell.edu/

- **Independent** comprehensive, founded 1849
- **Suburban** 200-acre campus with easy access to Kansas City
- **Endowment** $62.3 million
- **Coed** 928 undergraduate students, 98% full-time, 59% women, 41% men
- **Moderately difficult** entrance level, 48% of applicants were admitted

UNDERGRAD STUDENTS

909 full-time, 19 part-time. Students come from 34 states and territories; 19 other countries; 42% are from out of state; 5% Black or African American, non-Hispanic/Latino; 4% Hispanic/Latino; 1% Asian, non-Hispanic/Latino; 0.1% Native Hawaiian or other Pacific Islander, non-Hispanic/Latino; 0.1% American Indian or Alaska Native, non-Hispanic/Latino; 5% Two or more races, non-Hispanic/Latino; 2% Race/ethnicity unknown; 4% international; 5% transferred in; 85% live on campus.

Freshmen:

Admission: 1,644 applied, 783 admitted, 198 enrolled. *Average high school GPA:* 3.7. *Test scores:* SAT evidence-based reading and writing scores over 500: 71%; SAT math scores over 500: 86%; ACT scores over 18: 98%; SAT evidence-based reading and writing scores over 600: 21%; SAT math scores over 600: 36%; ACT scores over 24: 68%; SAT evidence-based reading and writing scores over 700: 7%; ACT scores over 30: 16%.

Retention: 77% of full-time freshmen returned.

FACULTY

Total: 129, 64% full-time, 59% with terminal degrees.

Student/faculty ratio: 10:1.

ACADEMICS

Calendar: semesters. *Degrees:* bachelor's, master's, and postbachelor's certificates (also offers evening program with significant enrollment not reflected in profile).

Special study options: accelerated degree program, advanced placement credit, cooperative education, distance learning, double majors, English as a second language, honors programs, independent study, internships, off-campus study, services for LD students, student-designed majors, study abroad, summer session for credit. *ROTC:* Army (c).

Unusual degree programs: 3-2 engineering with Washington University in St. Louis, University of Kansas, Vanderbilt University, Columbia University, Missouri University of Science and Technology; forestry with Duke University; occupational therapy with Washington University in St. Louis.

Computers: 25 computers/terminals and 900 ports are available on campus for general student use. Students can access the following: campus intranet, computer help desk, free student e-mail accounts, online (class) grades, online (class) registration, online (class) schedules, all students provided with an iPad and support service. Campuswide network is available. 100% of college-owned or -operated housing units are wired for high-speed Internet access. Wireless service is available via entire campus.

Library: Charles F. Curry Library. *Books:* 129,403 (physical), 364,504 (digital/electronic); *Serial titles:* 71 (physical), 57,096 (digital/electronic); *Databases:* 63. Weekly public service hours: 90; study areas open 24 hours, 5–7 days a week; students can reserve study rooms.

STUDENT LIFE

Housing options: on-campus residence required through senior year; coed, men-only, women-only, special housing for students with disabilities. Campus housing is university owned. Freshman campus housing is guaranteed.

Activities and organizations: drama/theater group, student-run newspaper, choral group, College Union Activities, Intramurals, Mosaic, Student Senate, Black Student Association, national fraternities, national sororities.

Athletics Member NCAA. All Division II. *Intercollegiate sports:* baseball M(s), basketball M(s)/W(s), cheerleading M(s)/W(s), cross-country running M(s)/W(s), football M(s), golf M(s)/W(s), soccer M(s)/W(s), softball W(s), swimming and diving M(s)/W(s), tennis M(s)/W(s), track and field M(s)/W(s), volleyball W(s). *Intramural* *sports:* basketball M/W, racquetball M/W, sand volleyball M/W, soccer M/W, softball M/W, tennis M/W, ultimate Frisbee M/W, volleyball M/W.

Campus security: 24-hour emergency response devices and patrols, late-night transport/escort service, controlled dormitory access.

Student services: health clinic, personal/psychological counseling.

COSTS & FINANCIAL AID
Costs (2018–19) *Comprehensive fee:* $44,330 includes full-time tuition ($33,500), mandatory fees ($900), and room and board ($9930). Full-time tuition and fees vary according to program. Part-time tuition: $980 per credit hour. *Room and board:* Room and board charges vary according to board plan and housing facility. *Payment plan:* installment. *Waivers:* employees or children of employees.

Financial Aid Of all full-time matriculated undergraduates who enrolled in 2017, 719 applied for aid, 620 were judged to have need, 167 had their need fully met. 427 Federal Work-Study jobs (averaging $2349). 117 state and other part-time jobs (averaging $444). In 2017, 138 non-need-based awards were made. *Average percent of need met:* 72. *Average financial aid package:* $30,556. *Average need-based loan:* $5582. *Average need-based gift aid:* $24,739. *Average non-need-based aid:* $19,039. *Average indebtedness upon graduation:* $33,326.

APPLYING
Standardized Tests *Recommended:* SAT or ACT (for admission).

Options: electronic application, deferred entrance.

Required: essay or personal statement, high school transcript. *Required for some:* interview.

Application deadlines: rolling (freshmen), rolling (transfers).

Notification: 11/1 (freshmen), continuous (transfers).

CONTACT
Mr. Brian Haines, Director of Admission Services, William Jewell College, 500 College Hill, Liberty, MO 64068. *Phone:* 816-415-7871. *Toll-free phone:* 888-2JEWELL. *Fax:* 816-415-5040. *E-mail:* hainesb@william.jewell.edu.

William Woods University
Fulton, Missouri
http://www.williamwoods.edu/
- **Independent** comprehensive, founded 1870, affiliated with Christian Church (Disciples of Christ)
- **Small-town** 200-acre campus with easy access to St. Louis, Kansas City
- **Endowment** $18.5 million
- **Coed** 958 undergraduate students, 83% full-time, 73% women, 27% men
- **Moderately difficult** entrance level, 75% of applicants were admitted

UNDERGRAD STUDENTS
796 full-time, 162 part-time. Students come from 31 states and territories; 19 other countries; 39% are from out of state; 5% Black or African American, non-Hispanic/Latino; 3% Hispanic/Latino; 0.7% Asian, non-Hispanic/Latino; 0.5% American Indian or Alaska Native, non-Hispanic/Latino; 2% Two or more races, non-Hispanic/Latino; 3% Race/ethnicity unknown; 5% international; 6% transferred in; 63% live on campus.

Freshmen:
Admission: 892 applied, 668 admitted, 195 enrolled. *Average high school GPA:* 3.4. *Test scores:* SAT math scores over 500: 70%; ACT scores over 18: 89%; SAT math scores over 600: 20%; ACT scores over 24: 43%; ACT scores over 30: 8%.

Retention: 72% of full-time freshmen returned.

FACULTY
Total: 240, 25% full-time, 43% with terminal degrees.

Student/faculty ratio: 16:1.

ACADEMICS
Calendar: semesters. *Degrees:* associate, bachelor's, master's, doctoral, and post-master's certificates.

Special study options: academic remediation for entering students, accelerated degree program, advanced placement credit, distance learning, double majors, honors programs, independent study, internships, off-

campus study, part-time degree program, services for LD students, student-designed majors, study abroad, summer session for credit. *ROTC:* Army (c), Navy (c), Air Force (c).

Unusual degree programs: 3-2 business administration.

Computers: 197 computers/terminals and 1,339 ports are available on campus for general student use. Students can access the following: campus intranet, computer help desk, free student e-mail accounts, online (class) grades, online (class) registration, online (class) schedules. Campuswide network is available. 100% of college-owned or -operated housing units are wired for high-speed Internet access. Wireless service is available via entire campus.

Library: Dulany Library. *Books:* 75,506 (physical), 274,700 (digital/electronic); *Serial titles:* 821 (physical), 122,059 (digital/electronic); *Databases:* 57. Weekly public service hours: 87; students can reserve study rooms.

STUDENT LIFE
Housing options: on-campus residence required through senior year; coed, men-only, women-only, special housing for students with disabilities. Campus housing is university owned. Freshman campus housing is guaranteed.

Activities and organizations: drama/theater group, student-run radio station, choral group, DECA, Students of Social Work, Campus Activities Board, Hands Up , Campus Crusade for Christ, national fraternities, national sororities.

Athletics Member NAIA. *Intercollegiate sports:* baseball M(s), basketball M(s)/W(s), cheerleading W(s), cross-country running M(s)/W(s), golf M(s)/W(s), soccer M(s)/W(s), softball W(s), tennis M(s)/W(s), track and field M(s)/W(s), volleyball W(s). *Intramural sports:* basketball M/W, equestrian sports M/W, tennis M/W.

Campus security: 24-hour emergency response devices and patrols, late-night transport/escort service, controlled dormitory access.

Student services: health clinic, personal/psychological counseling.

COSTS
Costs (2018–19) *Comprehensive fee:* $33,885 includes full-time tuition ($23,230), mandatory fees ($955), and room and board ($9700). Full-time tuition and fees vary according to course load and program. Part-time tuition: $425 per credit hour. Part-time tuition and fees vary according to course load and program. *Required fees:* $50 per term part-time. *College room only:* $5050. Room and board charges vary according to board plan and housing facility. *Payment plan:* installment. *Waivers:* children of alumni, senior citizens, and employees or children of employees.

APPLYING
Standardized Tests *Required:* SAT or ACT (for admission).

Options: electronic application, deferred entrance.

Required: high school transcript, minimum 2.5 GPA, 16 hours college preparatory unit.

Application deadlines: 8/15 (freshmen), rolling (transfers).

Notification: continuous (freshmen), continuous (transfers).

CONTACT
Mrs. Ashley Sundin, Admissions Office Coordinator, William Woods University, One University Avenue, Fulton, MO 65251. *Phone:* 573-592-4400. *Toll-free phone:* 800-995-3159 Ext. 4221. *Fax:* 573-592-1146. *E-mail:* ashley.sundin@williamwoods.edu.

MONTANA

Carroll College
Helena, Montana
http://www.carroll.edu/
- **Independent Roman Catholic** 4-year, founded 1909
- **Small-town** 61-acre campus
- **Endowment** $36.0 million
- **Coed** 1,352 undergraduate students, 95% full-time, 59% women, 41% men
- **Moderately difficult** entrance level, 71% of applicants were admitted

UNDERGRAD STUDENTS

1,287 full-time, 65 part-time. Students come from 35 states and territories; 14 other countries; 5% are from out of state; 0.4% Black or African American, non-Hispanic/Latino; 6% Hispanic/Latino; 1% Asian, non-Hispanic/Latino; 0.1% Native Hawaiian or other Pacific Islander, non-Hispanic/Latino; 0.9% American Indian or Alaska Native, non-Hispanic/Latino; 3% Two or more races, non-Hispanic/Latino; 9% Race/ethnicity unknown; 2% international; 3% transferred in; 57% live on campus.

Freshmen:

Admission: 3,005 applied, 2,148 admitted, 294 enrolled. *Average high school GPA:* 3.6. *Test scores:* ACT scores over 18: 97%; ACT scores over 24: 63%; ACT scores over 30: 11%.

Retention: 79% of full-time freshmen returned.

FACULTY

Total: 163, 56% full-time.
Student/faculty ratio: 12:1.

ACADEMICS

Calendar: semesters. *Degrees:* certificates, associate, and bachelor's.

Special study options: accelerated degree program, adult/continuing education programs, advanced placement credit, cooperative education, double majors, English as a second language, freshman honors college, honors programs, independent study, internships, part-time degree program, student-designed majors, study abroad, summer session for credit. *ROTC:* Army (b).

Unusual degree programs: 3-2 engineering with Columbia University, University of Southern California, University of Notre Dame, Montana State University, Gonzaga University, Montana College of Mineral Science and Technology, University of Minnesota.

Computers: Students can access the following: campus intranet, computer help desk, free student e-mail accounts, online (class) grades, online (class) registration, online (class) schedules, online book order. Campuswide network is available. 100% of college-owned or -operated housing units are wired for high-speed Internet access. Wireless service is available via entire campus.

Library: Corette Library plus 1 other. *Books:* 76,993 (physical), 230,000 (digital/electronic); *Databases:* 79. Study areas open 24 hours, 5–7 days a week; students can reserve study rooms.

STUDENT LIFE

Housing options: on-campus residence required through sophomore year; coed. Campus housing is university owned. Freshman campus housing is guaranteed.

Activities and organizations: drama/theater group, student-run newspaper, radio station, choral group, Student Government, Carroll Outreach Team, Carroll Adventure and Mountaineering Program, Up &'Til Dawn, Engineers Without Borders.

Athletics Member NAIA. *Intercollegiate sports:* basketball M(s)/W(s), cheerleading M(s)/W(s), cross-country running M(s)/W(s), football M(s), golf M(s)/W(s), soccer M(s)/W(s), softball W(s), track and field M(s)/W(s), volleyball W(s). *Intramural sports:* ice hockey M(c).

Campus security: 24-hour emergency response devices, late-night transport/escort service, controlled dormitory access.

Student services: health clinic, personal/psychological counseling.

COSTS & FINANCIAL AID

Costs (2017–18) *Comprehensive fee:* $44,088 includes full-time tuition ($33,500), mandatory fees ($980), and room and board ($9608). Full-time tuition and fees vary according to program. Part-time tuition: $1395 per credit hour. Part-time tuition and fees vary according to program. *Required fees:* $490 per year part-time. *Room and board:* Room and board charges vary according to board plan. *Payment plan:* installment. *Waivers:* senior citizens and employees or children of employees.

Financial Aid Of all full-time matriculated undergraduates who enrolled in 2015, 1,063 applied for aid, 927 were judged to have need, 178 had their need fully met. 209 Federal Work-Study jobs (averaging $1175). In 2015, 442 non-need-based awards were made. *Average percent of need met:* 75. *Average financial aid package:* $22,667. *Average need-based loan:* $4079. *Average need-based gift aid:* $17,608. *Average non-need-based aid:* $12,983. *Average indebtedness upon graduation:* $32,768.

APPLYING

Standardized Tests *Required:* SAT or ACT (for admission). *Required for some:* SAT Subject Tests (for admission).

Options: electronic application, deferred entrance.

Application fee: $35.

Required: essay or personal statement, high school transcript. *Required for some:* interview. *Recommended:* interview.

Application deadlines: 2/15 (freshmen), 6/15 (transfers).

Notification: continuous (freshmen), continuous (out-of-state freshmen), continuous (transfers).

CONTACT

Director of Admission, Carroll College, 1601 North Benton Avenue, Helena, MT 59625-0002. *Phone:* 406-447-4384. *Toll-free phone:* 800-992-3648. *E-mail:* admission@carroll.edu.

Montana Bible College

Bozeman, Montana

http://www.montanabiblecollege.edu/

- **Independent Christian** 4-year
- **Urban** campus
- **Coed**

ACADEMICS

Calendar: semesters. *Degree:* certificates and bachelor's.
Library: Gail Horton Library plus 1 other.

STUDENT LIFE

Housing options: Campus housing is university owned.

COSTS

Costs (2017–18) *Tuition:* $7040 full-time, $220 per credit hour part-time. Full-time tuition and fees vary according to location. Part-time tuition and fees vary according to course load and location. *Required fees:* $600 full-time. *Room only:* $3000. Room and board charges vary according to housing facility. *Payment plan:* installment.

APPLYING

Standardized Tests *Required:* SAT or ACT (for admission).

Options: electronic application.

Required: essay or personal statement, 4 letters of recommendation. *Required for some:* high school transcript, college transcript.

CONTACT

Montana Bible College, 3625 South 19th Avenue, Bozeman, MT 59718. *Toll-free phone:* 888-462-2463.

Montana State University

Bozeman, Montana

http://www.montana.edu/

- **State-supported** university, founded 1893, part of Montana University System
- **Small-town** 1850-acre campus
- **Endowment** $126.5 million
- **Coed**
- **Moderately difficult** entrance level

FACULTY

Student/faculty ratio: 19:1.

ACADEMICS

Calendar: semesters. *Degrees:* certificates, associate, bachelor's, master's, doctoral, post-master's, and postbachelor's certificates.
Library: Renne Library plus 2 others. Students can reserve study rooms.

STUDENT LIFE

Housing options: on-campus residence required for freshman year; coed, men-only, women-only, special housing for students with disabilities. Campus housing is university owned. Freshman campus housing is guaranteed.

Activities and organizations: drama/theater group, student-run newspaper, radio and television station, choral group, marching band, Spurs, Inter-Varsity Christian Fellowship, Campus Crusade for Christ, Fangs, Mortar Board, national fraternities, national sororities.

Athletics Member NCAA. All Division I except football (Division I-AA).

Campus security: 24-hour emergency response devices and patrols, student patrols, late-night transport/escort service, 24-hour residence hall monitoring.

Student services: health clinic, personal/psychological counseling, women's center, legal services.

COSTS & FINANCIAL AID

Costs (2017–18) *Tuition:* state resident $5490 full-time, $229 per credit hour part-time; nonresident $22,194 full-time, $925 per credit hour part-time. Full-time tuition and fees vary according to course load, degree level, location, and program. Part-time tuition and fees vary according to course load, degree level, location, and program. *Required fees:* $1733 full-time, $113 per credit hour part-time. *Room and board:* $9250. Room and board charges vary according to board plan and housing facility. *Payment plans:* installment, deferred payment.

Financial Aid Of all full-time matriculated undergraduates who enrolled in 2016, 7,706 applied for aid, 5,393 were judged to have need, 1,649 had their need fully met. In 2016, 1230 non-need-based awards were made. *Average percent of need met:* 74. *Average financial aid package:* $11,308. *Average need-based loan:* $7269. *Average need-based gift aid:* $4905. *Average non-need-based aid:* $2012. *Average indebtedness upon graduation:* $27,254.

APPLYING

Standardized Tests *Required:* SAT or ACT (for admission).

Options: electronic application, early admission, deferred entrance.

Application fee: $30.

Required: high school transcript, minimum 2.5 GPA.

CONTACT

Ms. Ronda Russell, Director of Admissions, Montana State University, PO Box 172190, Bozeman, MT 59717-2190. *Phone:* 406-994-2452. *Toll-free phone:* 888-MSU-CATS. *Fax:* 406-994-1923. *E-mail:* admissions@montana.edu.

Montana State University Billings

Billings, Montana

http://www.msubillings.edu/

- **State-supported** comprehensive, founded 1927, part of Montana University System
- **Urban** 92-acre campus
- **Endowment** $21.9 million
- **Coed**
- **Minimally difficult** entrance level

FACULTY
Student/faculty ratio: 17:1.

ACADEMICS
Calendar: semesters. *Degrees:* certificates, associate, bachelor's, and master's.
Library: Montana State University Billings Library plus 2 others. *Books:* 138,650 (physical), 351,351 (digital/electronic); *Serial titles:* 1,368 (physical), 669,204 (digital/electronic); *Databases:* 170. Weekly public service hours: 82; students can reserve study rooms.

STUDENT LIFE
Housing options: on-campus residence required for freshman year; coed, women-only, special housing for students with disabilities. Campus housing is university owned. Freshman applicants given priority for college housing.

Activities and organizations: drama/theater group, student-run newspaper, radio station, choral group, Art Student League, Band Club, Inter-Varsity Christian Fellowship, Residence Hall Association, Student Council for Exceptional Children.

Athletics Member NCAA. All Division II.

Campus security: 24-hour emergency response devices and patrols, late-night transport/escort service, controlled dormitory access.

Student services: health clinic, personal/psychological counseling, women's center, legal services.

COSTS & FINANCIAL AID

Costs (2017–18) *Tuition:* state resident $4397 full-time, $183 per credit hour part-time; nonresident $16,662 full-time, $715 per credit hour part-time. Full-time tuition and fees vary according to course load, location, and program. Part-time tuition and fees vary according to course load, location, and program. *Required fees:* $1429 full-time. *Room and board:* $7510. Room and board charges vary according to board plan, housing facility, and location.

Financial Aid Of all full-time matriculated undergraduates who enrolled in 2015, 1,570 applied for aid, 1,570 were judged to have need, 440 had their need fully met. In 2015, 172 non-need-based awards were made. *Average percent of need met:* 72. *Average financial aid package:* $6981. *Average need-based loan:* $6241. *Average need-based gift aid:* $4513. *Average non-need-based aid:* $2671. *Average indebtedness upon graduation:* $28,337.

APPLYING

Standardized Tests *Required for some:* SAT or ACT (for admission).

Options: electronic application.

Application fee: $30.

Required: high school transcript.

CONTACT

Ms. Tammi Watson, Associate Director of Admissions, Montana State University Billings, 1500 University Drive, Billings, MT 59101. *Phone:* 406-657-2158. *Toll-free phone:* 800-565-6782. *Fax:* 406-657-2302. *E-mail:* tammi.watson@msubillings.edu.

Montana State University–Northern

Havre, Montana

http://www.msun.edu/

- **State-supported** comprehensive, founded 1929, part of Montana University System
- **Small-town** 10-acre campus
- **Coed**
- **Moderately difficult** entrance level

FACULTY
Student/faculty ratio: 15:1.

ACADEMICS
Calendar: semesters. *Degrees:* certificates, diplomas, associate, bachelor's, and master's.
Library: Vande Bogart Libraries.

STUDENT LIFE
Housing options: on-campus residence required for freshman year; coed. Campus housing is university owned.

Athletics Member NAIA.

COSTS & FINANCIAL AID

Costs (2017–18) *Tuition:* state resident $5480 full-time; nonresident $17,312 full-time. *Room and board:* $7500.

Financial Aid Of all full-time matriculated undergraduates who enrolled in 2012, 772 applied for aid, 686 were judged to have need, 21 had their need fully met. 61 Federal Work-Study jobs (averaging $1382). 25 state and other part-time jobs (averaging $1644). In 2012, 7 non-need-based awards were made. *Average percent of need met:* 60. *Average financial aid package:* $10,291. *Average need-based loan:* $3522. *Average need-based gift aid:* $4826. *Average non-need-based aid:* $715. *Average indebtedness upon graduation:* $21,365.

APPLYING

Options: early admission, deferred entrance.

Application fee: $30.

Required: high school transcript. *Required for some:* minimum 2.0 GPA.

CONTACT

Montana State University–Northern, PO Box 7751, Havre, MT 59501-7751. *Phone:* 406-265-3704. *Toll-free phone:* 800-662-6132.

Montana Tech of The University of Montana

Butte, Montana

http://www.mtech.edu/

- **State-supported** comprehensive, founded 1895, part of Montana University System
- **Small-town** 56-acre campus
- **Endowment** $32.9 million
- **Coed** 2,428 undergraduate students, 79% full-time, 38% women, 62% men
- **Moderately difficult** entrance level, 92% of applicants were admitted

UNDERGRAD STUDENTS

1,924 full-time, 504 part-time. Students come from 39 states and territories; 10 other countries; 14% are from out of state; 0.9% Black or African American, non-Hispanic/Latino; 2% Hispanic/Latino; 0.5% Asian, non-Hispanic/Latino; 2% American Indian or Alaska Native, non-Hispanic/Latino; 0.3% Two or more races, non-Hispanic/Latino; 6% Race/ethnicity unknown; 10% international; 6% transferred in; 12% live on campus.

Freshmen:

Admission: 981 applied, 898 admitted, 384 enrolled. *Average high school GPA:* 3.6. *Test scores:* SAT evidence-based reading and writing scores over 500: 95%; SAT math scores over 500: 94%; ACT scores over 18: 99%; SAT evidence-based reading and writing scores over 600: 39%; SAT math scores over 600: 58%; ACT scores over 24: 55%; SAT evidence-based reading and writing scores over 700: 11%; SAT math scores over 700: 8%; ACT scores over 30: 9%.

Retention: 76% of full-time freshmen returned.

FACULTY

Total: 213, 70% full-time, 44% with terminal degrees.

Student/faculty ratio: 13:1.

ACADEMICS

Calendar: semesters. *Degrees:* certificates, diplomas, associate, bachelor's, master's, doctoral, and postbachelor's certificates.

Special study options: academic remediation for entering students, adult/continuing education programs, advanced placement credit, cooperative education, distance learning, double majors, external degree program, honors programs, independent study, internships, part-time degree program, services for LD students, student-designed majors, summer session for credit.

Unusual degree programs: engineering.

Computers: 660 computers/terminals are available on campus for general student use. Students can access the following: campus intranet, computer help desk, free student e-mail accounts, online (class) grades, online (class) registration, online (class) schedules. Campuswide network is available. 100% of college-owned or -operated housing units are wired for high-speed Internet access. Wireless service is available via entire campus.

Library: Montana Tech Library. *Books:* 80,864 (physical), 91,830 (digital/electronic); *Serial titles:* 1,859 (physical), 67,191 (digital/electronic); *Databases:* 148. Weekly public service hours: 80; students can reserve study rooms.

STUDENT LIFE

Housing options: on-campus residence required for freshman year; coed, special housing for students with disabilities. Campus housing is university owned. Freshman campus housing is guaranteed.

Activities and organizations: student-run newspaper, radio station, choral group, Circle K, Ski/Snowboard Club, BSU, Hockey Club, Dance Club.

Athletics Member NAIA. *Intercollegiate sports:* basketball M(s)/W(s), football M(s), golf M(s)/W(s), volleyball W(s). *Intramural sports:* basketball M/W, cheerleading M(c)/W(c), football M/W, ice hockey M(c)/W(c), racquetball M/W, rugby M(c)/W(c), skiing (cross-country) M(c)/W(c), skiing (downhill) M(c)/W(c), softball M/W, volleyball M/W.

Campus security: 24-hour patrols, controlled dormitory access.

Student services: health clinic, personal/psychological counseling.

COSTS & FINANCIAL AID

Costs (2018–19) *Tuition:* state resident $5707 full-time; nonresident $20,870 full-time. Full-time tuition and fees vary according to course load, degree level, location, and program. Part-time tuition and fees vary according to course load, degree level, location, and program. *Required fees:* $1704 full-time. *Room and board:* $9828; room only: $4366. Room and board charges vary according to board plan. *Payment plan:* installment. *Waivers:* minority students, senior citizens, and employees or children of employees.

Financial Aid Of all full-time matriculated undergraduates who enrolled in 2016, 1,421 applied for aid, 1,119 were judged to have need, 146 had their need fully met. In 2016, 271 non-need-based awards were made. *Average percent of need met:* 59. *Average financial aid package:* $11,025. *Average need-based loan:* $3992. *Average need-based gift aid:* $5768. *Average non-need-based aid:* $3784. *Average indebtedness upon graduation:* $27,926.

APPLYING

Standardized Tests *Required:* SAT or ACT (for admission).

Options: electronic application, deferred entrance.

Application fee: $30.

Required: high school transcript, proof of immunization. *Required for some:* minimum 2.5 GPA.

Application deadlines: rolling (freshmen), rolling (transfers).

Notification: continuous (freshmen), continuous (transfers).

CONTACT

Stephanie Crowe, Montana Tech of The University of Montana, 1300 West Park Street, Butte, MT 59701-8997. *Phone:* 406-496-4568. *Toll-free phone:* 800-445-TECH. *Fax:* 406-496-4705. *E-mail:* scrowe@mtech.edu.

Rocky Mountain College

Billings, Montana

http://www.rocky.edu/

- **Independent interdenominational** comprehensive, founded 1878
- **Suburban** 60-acre campus
- **Endowment** $29.7 million
- **Coed** 899 undergraduate students, 97% full-time, 49% women, 51% men
- **Moderately difficult** entrance level, 64% of applicants were admitted

UNDERGRAD STUDENTS

869 full-time, 30 part-time. Students come from 41 states and territories; 16 other countries; 48% are from out of state; 3% Black or African American, non-Hispanic/Latino; 5% Hispanic/Latino; 0.6% Asian, non-Hispanic/Latino; 0.9% Native Hawaiian or other Pacific Islander, non-Hispanic/Latino; 2% American Indian or Alaska Native, non-Hispanic/Latino; 6% Two or more races, non-Hispanic/Latino; 2% Race/ethnicity unknown; 4% international; 6% transferred in; 49% live on campus.

Freshmen:

Admission: 1,238 applied, 797 admitted, 247 enrolled. *Average high school GPA:* 3.3. *Test scores:* SAT evidence-based reading and writing scores over 500: 64%; SAT math scores over 500: 64%; ACT scores over 18: 90%; SAT evidence-based reading and writing scores over 600: 21%; SAT math scores over 600: 13%; ACT scores over 24: 34%; SAT evidence-based reading and writing scores over 700: 4%; ACT scores over 30: 4%.

Retention: 67% of full-time freshmen returned.

FACULTY

Total: 111, 57% full-time, 55% with terminal degrees.

Student/faculty ratio: 11:1.

ACADEMICS

Calendar: semesters. *Degrees:* associate, bachelor's, and master's.

Special study options: academic remediation for entering students, accelerated degree program, adult/continuing education programs, advanced placement credit, double majors, English as a second language, honors programs, independent study, internships, off-campus study, part-time degree program, services for LD students, student-designed majors, study abroad, summer session for credit. *ROTC:* Army (c).

Unusual degree programs: 3-2 athletic training with Montana State University Billings, accountancy.

Computers: 113 computers/terminals are available on campus for general student use. Students can access the following: campus intranet, free student e-mail accounts, online (class) grades, online (class) registration, online (class) schedules. Campuswide network is available. 100% of college-owned or -operated housing units are wired for high-speed Internet access. Wireless service is available via entire campus.

Library: Paul M. Adams Memorial Library. *Books:* 46,075 (physical), 41,042 (digital/electronic); *Serial titles:* 388 (physical), 61,207 (digital/electronic); *Databases:* 65. Weekly public service hours: 89.

STUDENT LIFE

Housing options: on-campus residence required through sophomore year; coed, special housing for students with disabilities. Campus housing is university owned. Freshman campus housing is guaranteed.

Activities and organizations: drama/theater group, student-run newspaper, choral group, Outdoor Recreation, Enactus, Flight Team/Club, Environmental Club, InterVarsity Christian Fellowship.

Athletics Member NAIA. *Intercollegiate sports:* basketball M(s)/W(s), cheerleading M(s)/W(s), cross-country running M(s)/W(s), equestrian sports M(c)/W(c), football M(s), golf M(s)/W(s), skiing (downhill) M(s)/W(s), soccer M(s)/W(s), track and field M(s)/W(s), volleyball W(s). *Intramural sports:* basketball M/W, fencing M(c)/W(c), football M/W, golf M/W, ice hockey M(c)/W(c), racquetball M/W, rock climbing M/W, skiing (downhill) M/W, soccer M/W, softball M/W, swimming and diving M/W, table tennis M/W, ultimate Frisbee M/W, volleyball M/W, weight lifting M(c)/W(c), wrestling M(c)/W(c).

Campus security: 24-hour emergency response devices, student patrols, late-night transport/escort service, controlled dormitory access, security cameras.

Student services: health clinic, personal/psychological counseling.

COSTS & FINANCIAL AID

Costs (2018–19) *Comprehensive fee:* $36,842 includes full-time tuition ($27,982), mandatory fees ($530), and room and board ($8330). Full-time tuition and fees vary according to course load, degree level, and program. Part-time tuition: $1166 per credit. Part-time tuition and fees vary according to course load, degree level, and program. *Required fees:* $160 per term part-time. *College room only:* $4018. Room and board charges vary according to board plan and housing facility. *Payment plan:* installment. *Waivers:* employees or children of employees.

Financial Aid Of all full-time matriculated undergraduates who enrolled in 2017, 722 applied for aid, 659 were judged to have need, 119 had their need fully met. 315 Federal Work-Study jobs (averaging $462). 188 state and other part-time jobs (averaging $878). In 2017, 36 non-need-based awards were made. *Average percent of need met:* 77. *Average financial aid package:* $24,480. *Average need-based loan:* $3894. *Average need-based gift aid:* $19,625. *Average non-need-based aid:* $13,358. *Average indebtedness upon graduation:* $29,452.

APPLYING

Standardized Tests *Required:* SAT or ACT (for admission).

Options: electronic application, deferred entrance.

Application fee: $35.

Required: high school transcript, minimum 2.5 GPA. *Required for some:* essay or personal statement, 2 letters of recommendation, interview.

Application deadlines: rolling (freshmen), rolling (transfers).

Notification: continuous (freshmen), continuous (transfers).

CONTACT

Austin Mapston, Dean for Enrollment Services, Rocky Mountain College, 1511 Poly Drive, Billings, MT 59102. *Phone:* 406-657-1026. *Toll-free phone:* 800-877-6259. *Fax:* 406-259-9751. *E-mail:* admissions@ rocky.edu.

Salish Kootenai College
Pablo, Montana
http://www.skc.edu/

CONTACT
Ms. Jackie Moran, Admissions Officer, Salish Kootenai College, PO Box 70, Pablo, MT 59855-0117. *Phone:* 406-275-4866. *Fax:* 406-275-4810. *E-mail:* jackie_moran@skc.edu.

University of Montana
Missoula, Montana
http://www.umt.edu/

- **State-supported** university, founded 1893, part of Montana University System
- **Urban** 220-acre campus
- **Endowment** $166.4 million
- **Coed** 9,323 undergraduate students, 80% full-time, 55% women, 45% men
- **Moderately difficult** entrance level, 93% of applicants were admitted

UNDERGRAD STUDENTS
7,444 full-time, 1,879 part-time. Students come from 56 states and territories; 68 other countries; 28% are from out of state; 1% Black or African American, non-Hispanic/Latino; 5% Hispanic/Latino; 1% Asian, non-Hispanic/Latino; 0.2% Native Hawaiian or other Pacific Islander, non-Hispanic/Latino; 3% American Indian or Alaska Native, non-Hispanic/Latino; 4% Two or more races, non-Hispanic/Latino; 7% Race/ethnicity unknown; 2% international; 9% transferred in; 35% live on campus.

Freshmen:
Admission: 6,182 applied, 5,727 admitted, 1,681 enrolled. *Average high school GPA:* 3.6. *Test scores:* SAT evidence-based reading and writing scores over 500: 87%; SAT math scores over 500: 85%; ACT scores over 18: 92%; SAT evidence-based reading and writing scores over 600: 48%; SAT math scores over 600: 38%; ACT scores over 24: 50%; SAT evidence-based reading and writing scores over 700: 9%; SAT math scores over 700: 3%; ACT scores over 30: 10%.
Retention: 69% of full-time freshmen returned.

FACULTY
Total: 728, 72% full-time, 69% with terminal degrees.
Student/faculty ratio: 17:1.

ACADEMICS
Calendar: semesters. *Degrees:* certificates, associate, bachelor's, master's, doctoral, post-master's, and postbachelor's certificates.

Special study options: academic remediation for entering students, advanced placement credit, cooperative education, distance learning, double majors, English as a second language, external degree program, freshman honors college, honors programs, independent study, internships, off-campus study, part-time degree program, services for LD students, study abroad, summer session for credit. *ROTC:* Army (b).

Computers: Students can access the following: computer help desk, free student e-mail accounts, online (class) registration, online (class) schedules. Campuswide network is available. 100% of college-owned or -operated housing units are wired for high-speed Internet access. Wireless service is available via entire campus.

Library: Maureen and Mike Mansfield Library plus 2 others. *Books:* 139,763 (physical), 602,331 (digital/electronic); *Serial titles:* 15,019 (physical), 62,294 (digital/electronic); *Databases:* 202. Students can reserve study rooms.

STUDENT LIFE
Housing options: on-campus residence required for freshman year; coed, men-only, women-only, special housing for students with disabilities. Campus housing is university owned. Freshman campus housing is guaranteed.

Activities and organizations: drama/theater group, student-run newspaper, radio station, choral group, marching band, national fraternities, national sororities.

Athletics Member NCAA. All Division I except football (Division I-AA). *Intercollegiate sports:* baseball M(c), basketball M(s)/W(s), crew

M(c)/W(c), cross-country running M(s)/W(s), equestrian sports M(c)/W(c), fencing M(c)/W(c), field hockey W(c), golf W(s), gymnastics W(c), ice hockey M(c)/W(c), lacrosse M(c)/W(c), rugby M(c)/W(c), skiing (downhill) M(c)/W(c), soccer W(s), softball W(s), tennis M(s)/W(s), track and field M(s)/W(s), ultimate Frisbee M(c)/W(c), volleyball W(s). *Intramural sports:* archery M/W, badminton M/W, baseball M, basketball M/W, bowling M/W, cross-country running M/W, football M/W, ice hockey M, racquetball M/W, rugby M/W, skiing (cross-country) M/W, soccer W, softball M/W, swimming and diving M/W, table tennis M/W, tennis M/W, track and field M/W, volleyball M/W, water polo M/W, weight lifting M/W.

Campus security: 24-hour emergency response devices and patrols, student patrols, late-night transport/escort service, controlled dormitory access.

Student services: health clinic, personal/psychological counseling, women's center, legal services.

COSTS & FINANCIAL AID

Costs (2018–19) *Tuition:* state resident $5347 full-time, $223 per credit hour part-time; nonresident $23,062 full-time, $961 per credit hour part-time. Full-time tuition and fees vary according to degree level, location, program, reciprocity agreements, and student level. Part-time tuition and fees vary according to course load, degree level, location, and student level. *Required fees:* $1897 full-time, $115 per credit hour part-time. *Room and board:* $9544. Room and board charges vary according to board plan and housing facility. *Payment plan:* installment. *Waivers:* minority students, senior citizens, and employees or children of employees.

Financial Aid Of all full-time matriculated undergraduates who enrolled in 2017, 5,478 applied for aid, 4,453 were judged to have need, 419 had their need fully met. 2,286 Federal Work-Study jobs (averaging $2952). 10 state and other part-time jobs (averaging $2810). In 2017, 1353 non-need-based awards were made. *Average percent of need met:* 62. *Average financial aid package:* $11,594. *Average need-based loan:* $4698. *Average need-based gift aid:* $5094. *Average non-need-based aid:* $4509. *Average indebtedness upon graduation:* $30,000.

APPLYING

Standardized Tests *Required:* SAT or ACT (for admission).

Options: electronic application, early admission, deferred entrance.

Application fee: $36.

Required: high school transcript, minimum 2.5 GPA.

Application deadlines: rolling (freshmen), rolling (transfers).

CONTACT

University of Montana, Missoula, MT 59812-0002. *Phone:* 406-243-6266. *Toll-free phone:* 800-462-8636. *Fax:* 406-243-5711. *E-mail:* admiss@umontana.edu.

The University of Montana Western
Dillon, Montana
http://www.umwestern.edu/

- **State-supported** 4-year, founded 1893, part of Montana University System
- **Small-town** 30-acre campus
- **Endowment** $4.3 million
- **Coed**
- **Minimally difficult** entrance level

FACULTY
Student/faculty ratio: 17:1.

ACADEMICS
Calendar: semesters. *Degrees:* certificates, associate, and bachelor's.
Library: Lucy Carson Memorial Library. *Books:* 90,019 (physical), 583,775 (digital/electronic); *Serial titles:* 109 (physical); *Databases:* 117. Weekly public service hours: 85; students can reserve study rooms.

STUDENT LIFE
Housing options: on-campus residence required for freshman year; coed, men-only, women-only, special housing for students with disabilities. Campus housing is university owned. Freshman campus housing is guaranteed.

Activities and organizations: drama/theater group, student-run radio station, choral group, Biology Club, Rodeo Club, YoungLife Club, Education Club, Social Club.

Athletics Member NAIA.

Campus security: 24-hour emergency response devices and patrols, student patrols, late-night transport/escort service.

Student services: health clinic, personal/psychological counseling.

COSTS & FINANCIAL AID

Costs (2017–18) *Tuition:* state resident $4308 full-time, $183 per credit hour part-time; nonresident $15,450 full-time, $644 per course part-time. Full-time tuition and fees vary according to course load, location, program, reciprocity agreements, and student level. Part-time tuition and fees vary according to course load, location, program, reciprocity agreements, and student level. *Required fees:* $1194 full-time. *Room and board:* $7744; room only: $2944. Room and board charges vary according to housing facility. *Payment plans:* installment, deferred payment.

Financial Aid Of all full-time matriculated undergraduates who enrolled in 2016, 1,117 applied for aid, 922 were judged to have need, 1 had their need fully met. 107 Federal Work-Study jobs (averaging $2000). 24 state and other part-time jobs (averaging $2000). In 2016, 16 non-need-based awards were made. *Average percent of need met:* 16. *Average financial aid package:* $3423. *Average need-based loan:* $3954. *Average need-based gift aid:* $3514. *Average non-need-based aid:* $1261. *Average indebtedness upon graduation:* $29,779.

APPLYING

Standardized Tests *Required:* SAT or ACT (for admission).

Options: electronic application, deferred entrance.

Application fee: $30.

Required: high school transcript, MMR immunization record.

CONTACT

Mrs. Janet Jones, Admissions Evaluator, The University of Montana Western, 710 South Atlantic, Dillon, MT 59725. *Phone:* 406-683-7331. *Toll-free phone:* 877-683-7331. *E-mail:* janet.jones@umwestern.edu.

University of Providence
Great Falls, Montana
http://www.uprovidence.edu/

- **Independent Roman Catholic** comprehensive, founded 1932
- **Urban** 40-acre campus
- **Coed** 927 undergraduate students, 51% full-time, 70% women, 30% men
- **Noncompetitive** entrance level, 76% of applicants were admitted

UNDERGRAD STUDENTS
469 full-time, 458 part-time. 70% are from out of state; 3% Black or African American, non-Hispanic/Latino; 6% Hispanic/Latino; 4% Asian, non-Hispanic/Latino; 0.6% Native Hawaiian or other Pacific Islander, non-Hispanic/Latino; 1% American Indian or Alaska Native, non-Hispanic/Latino; 0.1% Two or more races, non-Hispanic/Latino; 8% Race/ethnicity unknown; 11% transferred in; 38% live on campus.

Freshmen:
Admission: 805 applied, 610 admitted, 101 enrolled. *Average high school GPA:* 3.3. *Test scores:* SAT math scores over 500: 100%; ACT scores over 18: 69%; SAT math scores over 600: 50%; ACT scores over 24: 18%; SAT math scores over 700: 50%.

Retention: 59% of full-time freshmen returned.

FACULTY
Total: 123, 41% full-time, 44% with terminal degrees.
Student/faculty ratio: 10:1.

ACADEMICS
Calendar: semesters. *Degrees:* certificates, associate, bachelor's, and master's.

Special study options: adult/continuing education programs, part-time degree program.

Computers: Students can access the following: campus intranet, computer help desk, free student e-mail accounts, online (class) grades, online (class) registration, online (class) schedules. Campuswide network is available. Wireless service is available via classrooms, computer

centers, computer labs, dorm rooms, learning centers, libraries, student centers.
Library: University of Great Falls Library.

STUDENT LIFE
Housing options: on-campus residence required through sophomore year; coed. Campus housing is university owned and leased by the school. Freshman campus housing is guaranteed.

Athletics Member NAIA. *Intercollegiate sports:* basketball M(s)/W(s), cheerleading M(s)/W(s), cross-country running M/W, equestrian sports M(s)/W(s), golf M(s)/W(s), soccer M(s)/W(s), softball W, track and field M(s)/W(s), volleyball W(s), wrestling M(s). *Intramural sports:* basketball M/W, equestrian sports M/W(c), football M/W, golf M/W, skiing (downhill) M/W, soccer M/W, softball W, table tennis M/W, track and field M/W, ultimate Frisbee M/W, volleyball M/W, wrestling M.

Campus security: 24-hour emergency response devices and patrols, late-night transport/escort service, controlled dormitory access.

COSTS & FINANCIAL AID
Costs (2018–19) *Comprehensive fee:* $34,518 includes full-time tuition ($24,968), mandatory fees ($350), and room and board ($9200). Full-time tuition and fees vary according to course load. Part-time tuition: $814 per credit hour. Part-time tuition and fees vary according to course load. *College room only:* $4800. Room and board charges vary according to board plan. *Payment plan:* deferred payment. *Waivers:* employees or children of employees.

Financial Aid Of all full-time matriculated undergraduates who enrolled in 2017, 401 applied for aid, 355 were judged to have need, 8 had their need fully met. In 2017, 43 non-need-based awards were made. *Average percent of need met:* 68. *Average financial aid package:* $20,968. *Average need-based loan:* $3929. *Average need-based gift aid:* $10,611. *Average non-need-based aid:* $9270. *Average indebtedness upon graduation:* $31,642.

APPLYING
Standardized Tests *Required:* SAT or ACT (for admission). *Recommended:* SAT and SAT Subject Tests or ACT (for admission), SAT Subject Tests (for admission).
Options: electronic application, early admission, deferred entrance.
Application fee: $35.
Required: high school transcript. *Recommended:* essay or personal statement, interview.
Notification: continuous (freshmen), continuous (transfers).

CONTACT
Kelly Braun, Assistant Director of Admissions, University of Providence, 1301 20th Street South, Great Falls, MT 59405. *Phone:* 406-791-5202 Ext. 5211. *Toll-free phone:* 800-856-9544. *Fax:* 406-791-5209. *E-mail:* admissions@uprovidence.edu.

NEBRASKA

Bellevue University
Bellevue, Nebraska
http://www.bellevue.edu/

CONTACT
Nick Baker, Director of Undergraduate Enrollment, Bellevue University, 1000 Galvin Road South, Bellevue, NE 68005-3098. *Phone:* 402-557-7250. *Toll-free phone:* 800-756-7920. *E-mail:* nick.baker@bellevue.edu.

Bryan College of Health Sciences
Lincoln, Nebraska
http://www.bryanhealthcollege.edu/
• **Independent** comprehensive
• **Coed**
• 52% of applicants were admitted

Freshmen:
Admission: 107 applied, 56 admitted.

ACADEMICS
Degrees: associate, bachelor's, and master's.

COSTS
Costs (2017–18) *One-time required fee:* $175. *Tuition:* $17,760 full-time. Full-time tuition and fees vary according to course load. Part-time tuition and fees vary according to course load. *Required fees:* $960 full-time. *Payment plans:* installment, deferred payment.

APPLYING
Standardized Tests *Required:* SAT or ACT (for admission).
Options: electronic application.
Required: high school transcript, 2 letters of recommendation. *Required for some:* essay or personal statement, minimum 2.8 GPA, interview.

CONTACT
Bryan College of Health Sciences, 5035 Everett Street, Lincoln, NE 68506-1398.

Chadron State College
Chadron, Nebraska
http://www.csc.edu/

CONTACT
Ms. Tena Cook, Director of Admissions, Chadron State College, 1000 Main Street, Chadron, NE 69337-2690. *Phone:* 308-432-6263. *Toll-free phone:* 800-242-3766. *Fax:* 308-432-6229. *E-mail:* inquire@csc.edu.

Clarkson College
Omaha, Nebraska
http://www.clarksoncollege.edu/

CONTACT
Clarkson College, 101 South 42nd Street, Omaha, NE 68131-2739. *Phone:* 402-552-3100. *Toll-free phone:* 800-647-5500.

College of Saint Mary
Omaha, Nebraska
http://www.csm.edu/
• **Independent Roman Catholic** comprehensive, founded 1923
• **Urban** 25-acre campus
• **Endowment** $18.1 million
• **Women only** 832 undergraduate students, 91% full-time
• **Minimally difficult** entrance level, 56% of applicants were admitted

UNDERGRAD STUDENTS
761 full-time, 71 part-time. Students come from 24 states and territories; 8 other countries; 24% are from out of state; 8% Black or African American, non-Hispanic/Latino; 14% Hispanic/Latino; 3% Asian, non-Hispanic/Latino; 0.4% Native Hawaiian or other Pacific Islander, non-Hispanic/Latino; 1% American Indian or Alaska Native, non-Hispanic/Latino; 3% Two or more races, non-Hispanic/Latino; 0.9% international; 17% transferred in; 38% live on campus.

Freshmen:
Admission: 378 applied, 212 admitted, 102 enrolled. *Average high school GPA:* 3.4. *Test scores:* ACT scores over 18: 93%; ACT scores over 24: 30%; ACT scores over 30: 1%.
Retention: 84% of full-time freshmen returned.

FACULTY
Total: 176, 39% full-time, 48% with terminal degrees.
Student/faculty ratio: 10:1.

ACADEMICS
Calendar: semesters. *Degrees:* certificates, associate, bachelor's, master's, doctoral, and postbachelor's certificates.

Special study options: academic remediation for entering students, accelerated degree program, advanced placement credit, distance learning, double majors, honors programs, independent study, internships, part-time degree program, services for LD students, study abroad, summer session for credit. *ROTC:* Army (c), Air Force (c).

Computers: 215 computers/terminals and 320 ports are available on campus for general student use. Students can access the following: campus intranet, computer help desk, free student e-mail accounts, online (class) grades, online (class) registration, online (class) schedules. Campuswide network is available. 100% of college-owned or -operated housing units are wired for high-speed Internet access. Wireless service is available via entire campus.

Library: College of Saint Mary Library. *Books:* 57,635 (physical), 29,889 (digital/electronic); *Serial titles:* 35 (physical), 107 (digital/electronic); *Databases:* 30. Weekly public service hours: 81; study areas open 24 hours, 5–7 days a week.

STUDENT LIFE
Housing options: on-campus residence required through sophomore year; women-only. Campus housing is university owned. Freshman campus housing is guaranteed.

Activities and organizations: drama/theater group, choral group, Residence Hall Council, Campus Activities Board, Student Education Association of Nebraska, Student Occupational Therapy Club, Student Nurses Association.

Athletics Member NAIA. *Intercollegiate sports:* basketball W(s), bowling W(s), cross-country running W(s), golf W(s), soccer W(s), softball W(s), swimming and diving W(s), tennis W(s), volleyball W(s).

Campus security: 24-hour emergency response devices and patrols, late-night transport/escort service, controlled dormitory access, surveillance cameras at residence hall entrances; CSM Alert Text Message System.

Student services: health clinic, personal/psychological counseling.

COSTS & FINANCIAL AID
Costs (2018–19) *Comprehensive fee:* $28,050 includes full-time tuition ($20,350) and room and board ($7700). Full-time tuition and fees vary according to program. Part-time tuition: $750 per credit. Part-time tuition and fees vary according to course load and program. *Payment plans:* installment, deferred payment. *Waivers:* senior citizens and employees or children of employees.

Financial Aid Of all full-time matriculated undergraduates who enrolled in 2017, 670 applied for aid, 592 were judged to have need, 81 had their need fully met. 159 Federal Work-Study jobs (averaging $2851). 14 state and other part-time jobs (averaging $6575). In 2017, 126 non-need-based awards were made. *Average percent of need met:* 59. *Average financial aid package:* $14,824. *Average need-based loan:* $5123. *Average need-based gift aid:* $9748. *Average non-need-based aid:* $10,316. *Average indebtedness upon graduation:* $35,259.

APPLYING
Standardized Tests *Required:* SAT or ACT (for admission). *Required for some:* ACT (for admission).

Options: electronic application.

Application fee: $30.

Required: high school transcript, minimum 2.0 GPA. *Required for some:* essay or personal statement, 3 letters of recommendation, interview.

Application deadlines: rolling (freshmen), rolling (transfers).

Notification: continuous (freshmen), continuous (transfers).

CONTACT
Enrollment Services, College of Saint Mary, 7000 Mercy Road, Omaha, NE 68106. *Phone:* 402-399-2355. *Toll-free phone:* 800-926-5534. *Fax:* 402-399-2412. *E-mail:* enroll@csm.edu.

Concordia University, Nebraska
Seward, Nebraska
http://www.cune.edu/

- **Independent** comprehensive, founded 1894, affiliated with Lutheran Church–Missouri Synod
- **Small-town** 120-acre campus with easy access to Omaha
- **Endowment** $51.0 million
- **Coed** 1,684 undergraduate students, 73% full-time, 54% women, 46% men
- **Moderately difficult** entrance level, 75% of applicants were admitted

UNDERGRAD STUDENTS
1,231 full-time, 453 part-time. Students come from 40 states and territories; 9 other countries; 52% are from out of state; 4% Black or African American, non-Hispanic/Latino; 6% Hispanic/Latino; 1% Asian, non-Hispanic/Latino; 0.2% Native Hawaiian or other Pacific Islander, non-Hispanic/Latino; 0.2% American Indian or Alaska Native, non-Hispanic/Latino; 0.8% Two or more races, non-Hispanic/Latino; 9% Race/ethnicity unknown; 2% international; 2% transferred in; 57% live on campus.

Freshmen:
Admission: 1,537 applied, 1,152 admitted, 348 enrolled. *Average high school GPA:* 3.5. *Test scores:* SAT evidence-based reading and writing scores over 500: 65%; SAT math scores over 500: 39%; ACT scores over 18: 97%; SAT evidence-based reading and writing scores over 600: 8%; SAT math scores over 600: 12%; ACT scores over 24: 45%; SAT evidence-based reading and writing scores over 700: 1%; ACT scores over 30: 6%.

Retention: 74% of full-time freshmen returned.

FACULTY
Total: 253, 24% full-time, 54% with terminal degrees.
Student/faculty ratio: 14:1.

ACADEMICS
Calendar: 4-4-1. *Degrees:* bachelor's and master's.

Special study options: academic remediation for entering students, accelerated degree program, adult/continuing education programs, advanced placement credit, distance learning, double majors, independent study, internships, off-campus study, part-time degree program, services for LD students, study abroad, summer session for credit. *ROTC:* Army (c), Air Force (c).

Computers: 220 computers/terminals and 1,508 ports are available on campus for general student use. Students can access the following: campus intranet, computer help desk, free student e-mail accounts, online (class) grades, online (class) registration, online (class) schedules, academic plans, human resource data. Campuswide network is available. 100% of college-owned or -operated housing units are wired for high-speed Internet access. Wireless service is available via entire campus.

Library: Link Library plus 1 other. *Books:* 124,354 (physical), 38,136 (digital/electronic); *Serial titles:* 711 (physical), 82 (digital/electronic); *Databases:* 22. Weekly public service hours: 89; students can reserve study rooms.

STUDENT LIFE
Housing options: on-campus residence required through junior year; men-only, women-only, special housing for students with disabilities. Campus housing is university owned. Freshman campus housing is guaranteed.

Activities and organizations: drama/theater group, student-run newspaper, choral group, Student Activities Council, Musical Groups, Curtain/Drama Club, Student Senate, Concordia Youth Ministry.

Athletics Member NAIA. *Intercollegiate sports:* baseball M(s), basketball M(s)/W(s), cheerleading M(s)/W(s), cross-country running M(s)/W(s), football M(s), golf M(s)/W(s), riflery M(s)(c)/W(s)(c), soccer M(s)/W(s), softball W(s), tennis M(s)/W(s), track and field M(s)/W(s), volleyball W(s), wrestling M(s). *Intramural sports:* basketball M/W, sand volleyball M/W, soccer M/W, softball M/W, table tennis M/W, tennis M/W, ultimate Frisbee M/W, volleyball M/W.

Campus security: 24-hour emergency response devices and patrols, controlled dormitory access.

Student services: health clinic, personal/psychological counseling.

COSTS & FINANCIAL AID
Costs (2018–19) *Comprehensive fee:* $40,690 includes full-time tuition ($31,620), mandatory fees ($600), and room and board ($8470). Part-time tuition: $925 per credit hour. *Required fees:* $150 per term part-time. *College room only:* $3570. Room and board charges vary according to board plan and housing facility. *Payment plan:* installment. *Waivers:* employees or children of employees.

Financial Aid Of all full-time matriculated undergraduates who enrolled in 2017, 1,057 applied for aid, 943 were judged to have need, 244 had their need fully met. In 2017, 97 non-need-based awards were made. *Average percent of need met:* 82. *Average financial aid package:* $25,229. *Average need-based loan:* $4392. *Average need-based gift aid:* $20,584. *Average non-need-based aid:* $16,989. *Average indebtedness upon graduation:* $27,722.

APPLYING

Standardized Tests *Required:* SAT or ACT (for admission).

Options: electronic application, deferred entrance.

Required: high school transcript. *Required for some:* essay or personal statement, 2 letters of recommendation.

Application deadlines: 8/1 (freshmen), 8/1 (transfers).

Notification: continuous (freshmen), continuous (transfers).

CONTACT

Mr. Aaron W. Roberts, Director of Undergraduate Admissions, Concordia University, Nebraska, 800 North Columbia Avenue, Seward, NE 68434-1556. *Phone:* 800-535-5494 Ext. 7233. *Toll-free phone:* 800-535-5494. *Fax:* 402-643-4073. *E-mail:* admiss@cune.edu.

Creative Center

Omaha, Nebraska

http://www.creativecenter.edu/

- **Proprietary** 4-year, founded 1993
- **Urban** 2-acre campus with easy access to Omaha
- **Coed** 51 undergraduate students, 98% full-time, 69% women, 31% men

UNDERGRAD STUDENTS

50 full-time, 1 part-time.

Freshmen:

Admission: 11 enrolled.

Retention: 80% of full-time freshmen returned.

FACULTY

Total: 12, 17% full-time, 25% with terminal degrees.

Student/faculty ratio: 10:1.

ACADEMICS

Calendar: semesters. *Degrees:* associate and bachelor's.

Special study options: accelerated degree program, advanced placement credit, part-time degree program, services for LD students.

Computers: 8 computers/terminals are available on campus for general student use. Students can access the following: campus intranet, computer help desk, all students own a laptop computer as part of tuition and fees. Campuswide network is available. Wireless service is available via entire campus.

Library: Student Library plus 1 other.

STUDENT LIFE

Housing options: college housing not available.

COSTS

Costs (2018–19) *One-time required fee:* $2800. *Tuition:* $25,600 full-time, $2560 per course part-time. Full-time tuition and fees vary according to course load, degree level, program, and student level. Part-time tuition and fees vary according to course load, degree level, program, and student level. *Required fees:* $2055 full-time, $200 per course part-time.

APPLYING

Required: essay or personal statement, high school transcript, 1 letter of recommendation, interview, portfolio, letter of recommendation. *Recommended:* minimum 2.0 GPA.

CONTACT

Mr. Richard Caldwell, Director of Admissions, Creative Center, 10850 Emmet Street, Omaha, NE 68164. *Phone:* 402-898-1000 Ext. 216. *Toll-free phone:* 888-898-1789. *Fax:* 402-898-1301. *E-mail:* rich_c@creativecenter.edu.

Creighton University

Omaha, Nebraska

http://www.creighton.edu/

- **Independent Roman Catholic (Jesuit)** university, founded 1878
- **Urban** 139-acre campus with easy access to Omaha
- **Endowment** $525.6 million
- **Coed** 4,255 undergraduate students, 94% full-time, 56% women, 44% men
- **Moderately difficult** entrance level, 72% of applicants were admitted

UNDERGRAD STUDENTS

4,011 full-time, 244 part-time. Students come from 51 states and territories; 27 other countries; 77% are from out of state; 3% Black or African American, non-Hispanic/Latino; 8% Hispanic/Latino; 9% Asian, non-Hispanic/Latino; 0.4% Native Hawaiian or other Pacific Islander, non-Hispanic/Latino; 0.4% American Indian or Alaska Native, non-Hispanic/Latino; 5% Two or more races, non-Hispanic/Latino; 1% Race/ethnicity unknown; 3% international; 1% transferred in; 57% live on campus.

Freshmen:

Admission: 9,727 applied, 7,004 admitted, 1,120 enrolled. *Average high school GPA:* 3.8. *Test scores:* SAT evidence-based reading and writing scores over 500: 87%; SAT math scores over 500: 92%; ACT scores over 18: 100%; SAT evidence-based reading and writing scores over 600: 33%; SAT math scores over 600: 56%; ACT scores over 24: 82%; SAT evidence-based reading and writing scores over 700: 8%; SAT math scores over 700: 12%; ACT scores over 30: 25%.

Retention: 89% of full-time freshmen returned.

FACULTY

Total: 890, 64% full-time, 77% with terminal degrees.

Student/faculty ratio: 11:1.

ACADEMICS

Calendar: semesters. *Degrees:* certificates, associate, bachelor's, master's, doctoral, post-master's, and postbachelor's certificates.

Special study options: accelerated degree program, adult/continuing education programs, advanced placement credit, distance learning, double majors, English as a second language, honors programs, independent study, internships, off-campus study, part-time degree program, services for LD students, study abroad, summer session for credit. *ROTC:* Army (b), Air Force (c).

Computers: 404 computers/terminals are available on campus for general student use. Students can access the following: campus intranet, computer help desk, free student e-mail accounts, online (class) grades, online (class) registration, online (class) schedules, financial aid information. Campuswide network is available. 100% of college-owned or -operated housing units are wired for high-speed Internet access. Wireless service is available via entire campus.

Library: Reinert Alumni Memorial Library plus 2 others. Study areas open 24 hours, 5–7 days a week.

STUDENT LIFE

Housing options: on-campus residence required through sophomore year; coed, special housing for students with disabilities. Campus housing is university owned. Freshman campus housing is guaranteed.

Activities and organizations: drama/theater group, student-run newspaper, radio station, choral group, Birdcage, Hui O Hawaii, Pre-Med Society, Partners Against Cancer, American Pharmacists Association Academy of Student Pharmacist, national fraternities, national sororities.

Athletics Member NCAA. All Division I. *Intercollegiate sports:* baseball M(s), basketball M(s)/W(s), crew W(s), cross-country running M(s)/W(s), golf M(s)/W(s), soccer M(s)/W(s), softball W(s), tennis M(s)/W(s), volleyball W(s). *Intramural sports:* badminton M(c)/W(c), basketball M/W, crew M(c), football M/W, golf M/W, ice hockey M(c), lacrosse M(c)/W(c), racquetball M/W, rugby M(c), skiing (downhill) M(c)/W(c), soccer M/W, softball M/W, table tennis M/W, tennis M/W, ultimate Frisbee M/W, volleyball M/W.

Campus security: 24-hour emergency response devices and patrols, student patrols, late-night transport/escort service, controlled dormitory access, shuttle buses, lighted pathway/sidewalks, self-defense education, crime prevention officer, violence intervention and prevention center.

Student services: health clinic, personal/psychological counseling, women's center.

COSTS & FINANCIAL AID

Costs (2018–19) *Comprehensive fee:* $50,952 includes full-time tuition ($38,200), mandatory fees ($1716), and room and board ($11,036). Full-time tuition and fees vary according to program. Part-time tuition: $1195 per credit hour. Part-time tuition and fees vary according to course load and program. *Required fees:* $168 per term part-time. *Room and board:* Room and board charges vary according to housing facility. *Payment plan:* installment. *Waivers:* adult students, senior citizens, and employees or children of employees.

Financial Aid Of all full-time matriculated undergraduates who enrolled in 2017, 2,693 applied for aid, 2,159 were judged to have need, 560 had their need fully met. 839 Federal Work-Study jobs (averaging $2177). In 2017, 1606 non-need-based awards were made. *Average percent of need met:* 79. *Average financial aid package:* $28,732. *Average need-based loan:* $6411. *Average need-based gift aid:* $21,635. *Average non-need-based aid:* $16,224. *Average indebtedness upon graduation:* $35,766.

APPLYING

Standardized Tests *Required:* SAT or ACT (for admission).

Options: electronic application, early action, deferred entrance.

Application fee: $40.

Required: essay or personal statement, high school transcript, 1 letter of recommendation. *Recommended:* minimum 3.0 GPA.

Application deadlines: 2/15 (freshmen), 8/1 (transfers), 11/1 (early action).

Notification: continuous (freshmen), continuous (transfers), rolling (early action).

CONTACT

Ms. Sarah Richardson, Director of Admissions and Scholarships, Creighton University, 2500 California Plaza, Omaha, NE 68178-0001. *Phone:* 402-280-2703. *Toll-free phone:* 800-282-5835. *Fax:* 402-280-2685. *E-mail:* admissions@creighton.edu.

Doane University
Crete, Nebraska
http://www.doane.edu/

- **Independent** comprehensive, founded 1872, affiliated with United Church of Christ
- **Small-town** 300-acre campus with easy access to Omaha
- **Endowment** $112.9 million
- **Coed** 1,069 undergraduate students, 99% full-time, 47% women, 53% men

UNDERGRAD STUDENTS

1,062 full-time, 7 part-time. Students come from 31 states and territories; 11 other countries; 23% are from out of state; 2% Black or African American, non-Hispanic/Latino; 7% Hispanic/Latino; 1% Asian, non-Hispanic/Latino; 0.2% Native Hawaiian or other Pacific Islander, non-Hispanic/Latino; 0.4% American Indian or Alaska Native, non-Hispanic/Latino; 4% Two or more races, non-Hispanic/Latino; 0.9% Race/ethnicity unknown; 2% international; 3% transferred in; 82% live on campus.

Freshmen:

Admission: 299 enrolled. *Average high school GPA:* 3.5. *Test scores:* ACT scores over 18: 95%; ACT scores over 24: 42%; ACT scores over 30: 5%.

Retention: 78% of full-time freshmen returned.

FACULTY

Total: 124, 71% full-time, 72% with terminal degrees.

Student/faculty ratio: 11:1.

ACADEMICS

Calendar: 4-1-4. *Degrees:* bachelor's, master's, doctoral, and post-master's certificates (non-traditional undergraduate programs and graduate programs offered at Lincoln campus).

Special study options: advanced placement credit, cooperative education, double majors, English as a second language, honors programs, independent study, internships, off-campus study, student-designed majors, study abroad, summer session for credit. *ROTC:* Army (c), Air Force (c).

Unusual degree programs: 3-2 engineering with Columbia University, Washington University in St. Louis; forestry with Duke University; environmental studies with Duke University.

Computers: 250 computers/terminals and 1,000 ports are available on campus for general student use. Students can access the following: campus intranet, computer help desk, free student e-mail accounts, online (class) grades, online (class) registration, online (class) schedules. Campuswide network is available. 100% of college-owned or -operated housing units are wired for high-speed Internet access. Wireless service is available via entire campus.

Library: Perkins Library plus 1 other. Study areas open 24 hours, 5–7 days a week; students can reserve study rooms.

STUDENT LIFE

Housing options: on-campus residence required through senior year; coed, women-only. Campus housing is university owned. Freshman campus housing is guaranteed.

Activities and organizations: drama/theater group, student-run newspaper, radio and television station, choral group, marching band, Student Activities Council, Hansen Leadership Program, band/choir, Doane Ambassadors, Doane Art League.

Athletics Member NAIA. *Intercollegiate sports:* baseball M(s), basketball M(s)/W(s), cross-country running M(s)/W(s), football M(s), golf M(s)/W(s), soccer M(s)/W(s), softball W(s), tennis M/W, track and field M(s)/W(s), volleyball W(s). *Intramural sports:* baseball M(c)/W(c), basketball M/W, bowling M/W, football M/W, golf M/W, ice hockey M, racquetball M(c)/W(c), softball M/W, swimming and diving M/W, table tennis M(c)/W(c), tennis M/W, volleyball M/W, water polo M/W.

Campus security: 24-hour emergency response devices and patrols, student patrols, late-night transport/escort service, controlled dormitory access, evening patrols by trained security personnel.

Student services: health clinic, personal/psychological counseling.

COSTS & FINANCIAL AID

Costs (2017–18) *Comprehensive fee:* $41,340 includes full-time tuition ($31,450), mandatory fees ($800), and room and board ($9090). Full-time tuition and fees vary according to location. Part-time tuition: $1048 per credit hour. Part-time tuition and fees vary according to course load and location. *Room and board:* Room and board charges vary according to board plan, housing facility, and location. *Payment plan:* installment. *Waivers:* senior citizens and employees or children of employees.

Financial Aid Of all full-time matriculated undergraduates who enrolled in 2017, 912 applied for aid, 804 were judged to have need, 298 had their need fully met. In 2017, 82 non-need-based awards were made. *Average percent of need met:* 87. *Average financial aid package:* $25,179. *Average need-based loan:* $4554. *Average need-based gift aid:* $21,182. *Average non-need-based aid:* $17,710. *Average indebtedness upon graduation:* $28,240.

APPLYING

Standardized Tests *Required:* SAT or ACT (for admission).

Required: high school transcript, 2 letters of recommendation. *Required for some:* interview. *Recommended:* minimum 2.0 GPA.

CONTACT

Mr. Kyle McMurray, Director of Admission, Doane University, 1014 Boswell Avenue, Crete, NE 68333. *Phone:* 402-826-8222. *Toll-free phone:* 800-333-6263. *E-mail:* kyle.mcmurray@doane.edu.

Hastings College
Hastings, Nebraska
http://www.hastings.edu/

CONTACT

Mr. Chris Schukei, Director of Admissions, Hastings College, 710 North Turner Avenue, Hastings, NE 68901-7621. *Phone:* 402-461-7341. *Toll-free phone:* 800-532-7642. *Fax:* 402-461-7490. *E-mail:* cschukei@hastings.edu.

Kaplan University, Lincoln
Lincoln, Nebraska
http://www.kaplanuniversity.edu/

CONTACT

Kaplan University, Lincoln, 1821 K Street, Lincoln, NE 68508. *Phone:* 402-474-5315. *Toll-free phone:* 800-987-7734.

Kaplan University, Omaha
Omaha, Nebraska
http://www.kaplanuniversity.edu/

CONTACT
Kaplan University, Omaha, 5425 North 103rd Street, Omaha, NE 68134. *Phone:* 402-572-8500. *Toll-free phone:* 800-987-7734.

Midland University
Fremont, Nebraska
http://www.midlandu.edu/

CONTACT
Danielle Oliver, Associate Director of Admissions, Midland University, Fremont, NE 68025-4200. *Phone:* 402-941-6501. *Toll-free phone:* 800-642-8382 Ext. 6501. *E-mail:* oliver@midlandu.edu.

National American University
Bellevue, Nebraska
http://www.national.edu/

CONTACT
National American University, 3604 Summit Plaza Drive, Bellevue, NE 68123.

Nebraska Christian College of Hope International University
Papillion, Nebraska
http://www.nechristian.edu/

- **Independent** comprehensive, founded 1944, affiliated with Christian Churches and Churches of Christ
- **Small-town** 85-acre campus with easy access to Omaha, NE
- **Endowment** $1.3 million
- **Coed** 145 undergraduate students, 99% full-time, 41% women, 59% men

UNDERGRAD STUDENTS
144 full-time, 1 part-time. 52% are from out of state; 9% Black or African American, non-Hispanic/Latino; 14% Hispanic/Latino; 1% Asian, non-Hispanic/Latino; 1% American Indian or Alaska Native, non-Hispanic/Latino; 7% Two or more races, non-Hispanic/Latino; 3% Race/ethnicity unknown; 19% transferred in; 73% live on campus.

Freshmen:
Admission: 46 enrolled. *Average high school GPA:* 2.9. *Test scores:* SAT math scores over 500: 50%; ACT scores over 18: 62%; ACT scores over 24: 10%.

Retention: 63% of full-time freshmen returned.

FACULTY
Total: 27, 19% full-time, 15% with terminal degrees.
Student/faculty ratio: 12:1.

ACADEMICS
Calendar: semesters. *Degrees:* certificates, associate, bachelor's, master's, and postbachelor's certificates.

Special study options: academic remediation for entering students, distance learning, double majors, independent study, internships, off-campus study, part-time degree program, study abroad.

Computers: Students can access the following: campus intranet, free student e-mail accounts, online (class) grades, online (class) registration, online (class) schedules. Campuswide network is available. 100% of college-owned or -operated housing units are wired for high-speed Internet access. Wireless service is available via entire campus.
Library: Swedberg Library.

STUDENT LIFE
Housing options: on-campus residence required through junior year; men-only, women-only. Campus housing is university owned. Freshman campus housing is guaranteed.

Activities and organizations: choral group, Global Gospel Group, Running Club, Minority Students Organization, Spiritual Life Group, Writing Club.

Athletics Member NCCAA. *Intercollegiate sports:* basketball M. *Intramural sports:* basketball M/W, football M/W, table tennis M/W, ultimate Frisbee M/W.
Campus security: student patrols, controlled dormitory access.

COSTS & FINANCIAL AID
Costs (2017–18) Comprehensive fee: $25,960 includes full-time tuition ($16,530), mandatory fees ($300), and room and board ($9130). Full-time tuition and fees vary according to course load. Part-time tuition: $710 per credit hour. Part-time tuition and fees vary according to course load.
Room and board: Room and board charges vary according to board plan and housing facility. *Payment plans:* installment, deferred payment. *Waivers:* employees or children of employees.

Financial Aid Of all full-time matriculated undergraduates who enrolled in 2014, 119 applied for aid.

APPLYING
Standardized Tests *Required:* ACT (for admission).

Required: essay or personal statement, high school transcript, 2 letters of recommendation. *Required for some:* interview, minimum ACT score of 18 for recent high school graduates.

CONTACT
Mr. D. J. Perkey, Associate Director of Admissions, Nebraska Christian College of Hope International University, 12550 S. 114th Street, Papillion, NE 68046. *Phone:* 402-935-9439. *E-mail:* dj.parkey@nechristian.edu.

Nebraska Methodist College
Omaha, Nebraska
http://www.methodistcollege.edu/

- **Independent** comprehensive, founded 1891, affiliated with United Methodist Church
- **Urban** 8-acre campus
- **Coed** 881 undergraduate students, 49% full-time, 90% women, 10% men
- **Moderately difficult** entrance level, 68% of applicants were admitted

UNDERGRAD STUDENTS
434 full-time, 447 part-time. Students come from 17 states and territories; 5 other countries; 14% are from out of state; 4% Black or African American, non-Hispanic/Latino; 6% Hispanic/Latino; 2% Asian, non-Hispanic/Latino; 0.1% American Indian or Alaska Native, non-Hispanic/Latino; 2% Two or more races, non-Hispanic/Latino; 3% Race/ethnicity unknown; 20% transferred in; 7% live on campus.

Freshmen:
Admission: 88 applied, 60 admitted, 45 enrolled. *Average high school GPA:* 3.5.

Retention: 77% of full-time freshmen returned.

FACULTY
Total: 72, 88% full-time, 31% with terminal degrees.
Student/faculty ratio: 12:1.

ACADEMICS
Calendar: semesters. *Degrees:* certificates, associate, bachelor's, master's, doctoral, post-master's, and postbachelor's certificates.

Special study options: academic remediation for entering students, accelerated degree program, adult/continuing education programs, advanced placement credit, cooperative education, distance learning, external degree program, independent study, services for LD students, summer session for credit. *ROTC:* Air Force (c).

Computers: 50 computers/terminals and 25 ports are available on campus for general student use. Students can access the following: campus intranet, computer help desk, online (class) grades, online (class) registration, online (class) schedules. Campuswide network is available. 100% of college-owned or -operated housing units are wired for high-speed Internet access. Wireless service is available via entire campus.
Library: John Moritz Library. *Books:* 2,146 (physical), 21 (digital/electronic); *Serial titles:* 369 (physical); *Databases:* 23. Weekly public service hours: 65.

STUDENT LIFE
Housing options: coed. Campus housing is university owned.

Activities and organizations: Student Nurses Association, Methodist Allied Health Student Association, Student Government, Student Ambassadors, Residence Hall Council.

Campus security: 24-hour emergency response devices and patrols, late-night transport/escort service, controlled dormitory access.

Student services: health clinic, personal/psychological counseling.

COSTS & FINANCIAL AID
Costs (2018–19) *Tuition:* $15,660 full-time, $580 per credit hour part-time. Full-time tuition and fees vary according to course load, degree level, and program. Part-time tuition and fees vary according to course load, degree level, and program. *Required fees:* $320 full-time, $160 per term part-time. *Room only:* $6300. *Payment plan:* installment. *Waivers:* employees or children of employees.

Financial Aid Of all full-time matriculated undergraduates who enrolled in 2017, 414 applied for aid, 365 were judged to have need, 15 had their need fully met. 22 Federal Work-Study jobs (averaging $2050). In 2017, 55 non-need-based awards were made. *Average percent of need met:* 34. *Average financial aid package:* $9579. *Average need-based loan:* $4690. *Average need-based gift aid:* $6117. *Average non-need-based aid:* $4390. *Average indebtedness upon graduation:* $37,215.

APPLYING
Standardized Tests *Required:* SAT or ACT (for admission).

Options: electronic application, deferred entrance.

Application fee: $25.

Required: essay or personal statement, high school transcript, minimum 2.5 GPA.

Application deadlines: rolling (freshmen), rolling (transfers).

CONTACT
Ms. Megan Maryott, Director of Enrollment Services, Nebraska Methodist College, 720 North 87th Street, Omaha, NE 68114. *Phone:* 402-354-7111. *Toll-free phone:* 800-335-5510. *Fax:* 402-354-7020. *E-mail:* megan.maryott@methodistcollege.edu.

Nebraska Wesleyan University
Lincoln, Nebraska
http://www.nebrwesleyan.edu/

- **Independent United Methodist** comprehensive, founded 1887
- **Suburban** 50-acre campus with easy access to Omaha
- **Endowment** $50.9 million
- **Coed**
- **Moderately difficult** entrance level

FACULTY
Student/faculty ratio: 12:1.

ACADEMICS
Calendar: semesters. *Degrees:* certificates, bachelor's, master's, post-master's, and postbachelor's certificates.
Library: Cochrane Woods Library. *Books:* 316,222 (physical), 185,022 (digital/electronic); *Serial titles:* 1,711 (physical), 16,353 (digital/electronic); *Databases:* 69. Weekly public service hours: 91; students can reserve study rooms.

STUDENT LIFE
Housing options: on-campus residence required through junior year; coed, women-only. Campus housing is university owned. Freshman campus housing is guaranteed.

Activities and organizations: drama/theater group, student-run newspaper, radio station, choral group, marching band, national fraternities, national sororities.

Athletics Member NCAA. All Division III.

Campus security: 24-hour emergency response devices and patrols, late-night transport/escort service, controlled dormitory access.

Student services: health clinic, personal/psychological counseling, women's center.

COSTS & FINANCIAL AID
Costs (2017–18) *Comprehensive fee:* $42,044 includes full-time tuition ($31,974), mandatory fees ($920), and room and board ($9150). Part-time tuition: $1160 per credit hour. Part-time tuition and fees vary according to class time, degree level, location, and program. *College room only:*

$5200. Room and board charges vary according to board plan and housing facility.

Financial Aid Of all full-time matriculated undergraduates who enrolled in 2012, 1,172 applied for aid, 1,008 were judged to have need, 178 had their need fully met. In 2012, 415 non-need-based awards were made. *Average percent of need met:* 69. *Average financial aid package:* $17,992. *Average need-based loan:* $4729. *Average need-based gift aid:* $13,077. *Average non-need-based aid:* $8867. *Average indebtedness upon graduation:* $28,077.

APPLYING
Standardized Tests *Required:* SAT or ACT (for admission).

Options: electronic application, early decision, deferred entrance.

Required: high school transcript. *Required for some:* essay or personal statement.

CONTACT
Mr. Gordie Coffin, Director of Admissions, Nebraska Wesleyan University, 5000 Saint Paul Avenue, Lincoln, NE 68504. *Phone:* 402-465-2218. *Toll-free phone:* 800-541-3818. *Fax:* 402-465-2177. *E-mail:* admissions@nebrwesleyan.edu.

Peru State College
Peru, Nebraska
http://www.peru.edu/

CONTACT
Ms. Micki Willis, Vice President for Enrollment Management and Student Affairs, Peru State College, PO Box 10, Peru, NE 68421. *Phone:* 402-872-2221. *Toll-free phone:* 800-742-4412 (in-state); 800-741-4412 (out-of-state). *Fax:* 402-872-2296. *E-mail:* mwillis@peru.edu.

St. Gregory the Great Seminary
Seward, Nebraska
http://www.stgregoryseminary.edu/

CONTACT
Rev. Peter M. Mitchell, Dean of Men, St. Gregory the Great Seminary, 800 Fletcher Road, Seward, NE 68434. *Phone:* 402-643-4052. *Fax:* 402-643-6964. *E-mail:* sggs@stgregoryseminary.edu.

Union College
Lincoln, Nebraska
http://www.ucollege.edu/

- **Independent Seventh-day Adventist** comprehensive, founded 1891
- **Suburban** 26-acre campus with easy access to Omaha
- **Coed** 781 undergraduate students, 91% full-time, 58% women, 42% men
- **Moderately difficult** entrance level, 60% of applicants were admitted

UNDERGRAD STUDENTS
707 full-time, 74 part-time. Students come from 45 states and territories; 29 other countries; 80% are from out of state; 8% Black or African American, non-Hispanic/Latino; 22% Hispanic/Latino; 5% Asian, non-Hispanic/Latino; 0.5% Native Hawaiian or other Pacific Islander, non-Hispanic/Latino; 0.4% American Indian or Alaska Native, non-Hispanic/Latino; 3% Two or more races, non-Hispanic/Latino; 0.5% Race/ethnicity unknown; 8% international; 11% transferred in; 75% live on campus.

Freshmen:
Admission: 1,573 applied, 943 admitted, 157 enrolled. *Average high school GPA:* 3.3. *Test scores:* SAT evidence-based reading and writing scores over 500: 76%; SAT math scores over 500: 62%; ACT scores over 18: 82%; SAT evidence-based reading and writing scores over 600: 31%; SAT math scores over 600: 7%; ACT scores over 24: 30%; SAT evidence-based reading and writing scores over 700: 3%; ACT scores over 30: 5%.
Retention: 80% of full-time freshmen returned.

FACULTY
Total: 118, 54% full-time, 39% with terminal degrees.
Student/faculty ratio: 9:1.

ACADEMICS

Calendar: semesters. *Degrees:* associate, bachelor's, and master's.

Special study options: accelerated degree program, adult/continuing education programs, advanced placement credit, cooperative education, double majors, honors programs, independent study, internships, off-campus study, part-time degree program, services for LD students, student-designed majors, study abroad, summer session for credit.

Computers: Students can access the following: free student e-mail accounts, online (class) grades, online (class) registration, online (class) schedules. Campuswide network is available. 100% of college-owned or - operated housing units are wired for high-speed Internet access. Wireless service is available via entire campus.

Library: Ella Johnson Crandall Library. *Books:* 143,808 (physical), 187,159 (digital/electronic); *Serial titles:* 136 (physical), 136 (digital/electronic); *Databases:* 61. Students can reserve study rooms.

STUDENT LIFE

Housing options: on-campus residence required through junior year; men-only, women-only, special housing for students with disabilities. Campus housing is university owned. Freshman campus housing is guaranteed.

Activities and organizations: drama/theater group, student-run newspaper, choral group, Business and Computer Science Club, Math and Science Club, Nursing Club, Amnesty International, International Club.

Athletics *Intercollegiate sports:* basketball M/W, golf M, volleyball W. *Intramural sports:* basketball M/W, football M/W, gymnastics M(c)/W(c), soccer M(c), softball M/W, volleyball M/W.

Campus security: 24-hour emergency response devices, student patrols, late-night transport/escort service.

Student services: health clinic, personal/psychological counseling.

COSTS & FINANCIAL AID

Costs (2018–19) *Comprehensive fee:* $30,850 includes full-time tuition ($22,680), mandatory fees ($1100), and room and board ($7070). Full-time tuition and fees vary according to course load, degree level, and program. Part-time tuition: $945 per credit hour. Part-time tuition and fees vary according to program. *Required fees:* $550 per term part-time. *College room only:* $4020. Room and board charges vary according to board plan and housing facility. *Payment plan:* installment. *Waivers:* employees or children of employees.

Financial Aid Of all full-time matriculated undergraduates who enrolled in 2015, 590 applied for aid, 520 were judged to have need, 63 had their need fully met. In 2015, 196 non-need-based awards were made. *Average percent of need met:* 62. *Average financial aid package:* $16,149. *Average need-based loan:* $4998. *Average need-based gift aid:* $11,588. *Average non-need-based aid:* $6746. *Average indebtedness upon graduation:* $35,893.

APPLYING

Standardized Tests *Required:* SAT or ACT (for admission).

Options: electronic application.

Required: high school transcript, minimum 2.5 GPA, 3 letters of recommendation. *Required for some:* essay or personal statement, interview.

CONTACT

Kristina Hammer, Assistant Director of Admissions, Union College, 3800 South 48th Street, Lincoln, NE 68506. *Phone:* 402-486-2969 Ext. 2052. *Toll-free phone:* 800-228-4600. *Fax:* 402-486-2895. *E-mail:* enroll@ucollege.edu.

University of Nebraska at Kearney

Kearney, Nebraska

http://www.unk.edu/

- **State-supported** comprehensive, founded 1903, part of University of Nebraska System
- **Small-town** 235-acre campus
- **Coed** 4,843 undergraduate students, 84% full-time, 57% women, 43% men
- **Moderately difficult** entrance level, 82% of applicants were admitted

UNDERGRAD STUDENTS

4,063 full-time, 780 part-time. 8% are from out of state; 2% Black or African American, non-Hispanic/Latino; 11% Hispanic/Latino; 0.8% Asian, non-Hispanic/Latino; 0.1% Native Hawaiian or other Pacific Islander, non-Hispanic/Latino; 0.1% American Indian or Alaska Native, non-Hispanic/Latino; 2% Two or more races, non-Hispanic/Latino; 0.3% Race/ethnicity unknown; 5% international; 6% transferred in; 35% live on campus.

Freshmen:

Admission: 5,911 applied, 4,832 admitted, 904 enrolled. *Average high school GPA:* 3.5. *Test scores:* SAT evidence-based reading and writing scores over 500: 80%; SAT math scores over 500: 80%; ACT scores over 18: 90%; SAT evidence-based reading and writing scores over 600: 10%; SAT math scores over 600: 20%; ACT scores over 24: 39%; ACT scores over 30: 6%.

Retention: 79% of full-time freshmen returned.

FACULTY

Total: 457, 71% full-time, 59% with terminal degrees.

Student/faculty ratio: 14:1.

ACADEMICS

Calendar: semesters. *Degrees:* certificates, bachelor's, master's, and post-master's certificates.

Special study options: distance learning, double majors, honors programs, independent study, internships, part-time degree program, services for LD students, study abroad. *ROTC:* Army (b).

Computers: Students can access the following: computer help desk, free student e-mail accounts, online (class) grades, online (class) registration, online (class) schedules, online degree audit, online personal information update, online bill viewing and payment, online financial aid awards and acceptance. Campuswide network is available. Wireless service is available via entire campus.

Library: Calvin T. Ryan Library.

STUDENT LIFE

Housing options: on-campus residence required for freshman year; coed. Campus housing is university owned. Freshman campus housing is guaranteed.

Activities and organizations: drama/theater group, student-run newspaper, radio and television station, marching band, national fraternities, national sororities.

Athletics Member NCAA. All Division II. *Intercollegiate sports:* baseball M(s), basketball M(s)/W(s), cross-country running M(s)/W(s), football M(s), golf M(s)/W(s), soccer W(s), softball W(s), swimming and diving W(s), tennis M(s)/W(s), track and field M(s)/W(s), volleyball W(s), wrestling M(s). *Intramural sports:* badminton M/W, basketball M/W, cross-country running M/W, football M/W, golf M/W, racquetball M/W, soccer M/W, softball M/W, tennis M/W, volleyball M/W, water polo M/W, wrestling M/W.

Campus security: 24-hour emergency response devices and patrols, late-night transport/escort service.

Student services: health clinic, personal/psychological counseling.

COSTS & FINANCIAL AID

Costs (2017–18) *Tuition:* state resident $5753 full-time, $192 per credit hour part-time; nonresident $12,533 full-time, $418 per credit hour part-time. Full-time tuition and fees vary according to course level, course load, degree level, location, and program. Part-time tuition and fees vary according to course level, course load, degree level, location, and program. *Required fees:* $1573 full-time. *Room and board:* $9688; room only: $4962. Room and board charges vary according to board plan and housing facility. *Payment plan:* installment. *Waivers:* employees or children of employees.

Financial Aid Of all full-time matriculated undergraduates who enrolled in 2016, 3,287 applied for aid, 2,744 were judged to have need, 642 had their need fully met. In 2016, 696 non-need-based awards were made. *Average percent of need met:* 68. *Average financial aid package:* $10,769. *Average need-based loan:* $4001. *Average need-based gift aid:* $7946. *Average non-need-based aid:* $4975. *Average indebtedness upon graduation:* $19,538.

APPLYING

Standardized Tests *Required:* SAT or ACT (for admission).

Options: electronic application.

Application fee: $45.

Required: high school transcript, rank in upper 50% of high school class.

Notification: continuous until 9/1 (freshmen), continuous (transfers).

CONTACT
Mr. Dusty Newton, Director of Admissions, University of Nebraska at Kearney, 905 West 25th Street, Kearney, NE 68849-0001. *Phone:* 308-865-8702. *Toll-free phone:* 800-532-7639. *Fax:* 308-865-8987. *E-mail:* admissionsug@unk.edu.

University of Nebraska at Omaha
Omaha, Nebraska
http://www.unomaha.edu/

CONTACT
University of Nebraska at Omaha, 6001 Dodge Street, Omaha, NE 68182. *Phone:* 402-554-3520. *Toll-free phone:* 800-858-8648.

University of Nebraska–Lincoln
Lincoln, Nebraska
http://www.unl.edu/

- **State-supported** university, founded 1869, part of University of Nebraska System
- **Urban** 623-acre campus with easy access to Omaha
- **Endowment** $1.6 billion
- **Coed** 20,954 undergraduate students, 93% full-time, 48% women, 52% men
- **Moderately difficult** entrance level, 64% of applicants were admitted

UNDERGRAD STUDENTS
19,534 full-time, 1,420 part-time. Students come from 53 states and territories; 107 other countries; 23% are from out of state; 3% Black or African American, non-Hispanic/Latino; 6% Hispanic/Latino; 3% Asian, non-Hispanic/Latino; 0.1% Native Hawaiian or other Pacific Islander, non-Hispanic/Latino; 0.2% American Indian or Alaska Native, non-Hispanic/Latino; 3% Two or more races, non-Hispanic/Latino; 1% Race/ethnicity unknown; 9% international; 4% transferred in; 37% live on campus.

Freshmen:
Admission: 14,947 applied, 9,623 admitted, 4,905 enrolled. *Average high school GPA:* 3.6. *Test scores:* ACT scores over 18: 98%; ACT scores over 24: 62%; ACT scores over 30: 20%.
Retention: 83% of full-time freshmen returned.

FACULTY
Total: 1,129, 99% full-time, 90% with terminal degrees.
Student/faculty ratio: 21:1.

ACADEMICS
Calendar: semesters. *Degrees:* bachelor's, master's, doctoral, post-master's, and postbachelor's certificates.

Special study options: accelerated degree program, adult/continuing education programs, advanced placement credit, cooperative education, distance learning, double majors, English as a second language, honors programs, independent study, internships, off-campus study, part-time degree program, services for LD students, student-designed majors, study abroad, summer session for credit. *ROTC:* Army (b), Navy (b), Air Force (b).

Unusual degree programs: 3-2 design/architecture with University of Nebraska-Lincoln, animal science/veterinary science with Iowa State University.

Computers: 455 computers/terminals are available on campus for general student use. Students can access the following: campus intranet, computer help desk, free student e-mail accounts, online (class) grades, online (class) registration, online (class) schedules. Campuswide network is available. 100% of college-owned or -operated housing units are wired for high-speed Internet access. Wireless service is available via entire campus.

Library: Love Memorial Library plus 7 others. *Books:* 1.6 million (physical), 738,095 (digital/electronic); *Serial titles:* 92,670 (physical), 77,142 (digital/electronic); *Databases:* 462. Weekly public service hours: 109; students can reserve study rooms.

STUDENT LIFE
Housing options: on-campus residence required for freshman year; coed, women-only, cooperative, special housing for students with disabilities. Campus housing is university owned. Freshman campus housing is guaranteed.

Activities and organizations: drama/theater group, student-run newspaper, radio station, choral group, marching band, Student Alumni Association, University Ambassadors, University Program Council, eSAB (College of Engineering Student Advisory Board), ASUN (Association of Students of the University of Nebraska, student body government), national fraternities, national sororities.

Athletics Member NCAA. All Division I except football (Division I-A). *Intercollegiate sports:* baseball M(s), basketball M(s)/W(s), bowling W(s), cross-country running M(s)/W(s), golf M(s)/W(s), gymnastics M(s)/W(s), riflery W(s), sand volleyball W(s), soccer W(s), softball W(s), swimming and diving W(s), tennis M(s)/W(s), track and field M(s)/W(s), volleyball W(s), wrestling M(s). *Intramural sports:* badminton M/W, baseball M(c), basketball M/W, bowling M(c)/W, crew M(c)/W(c), cross-country running M(c)/W(c), equestrian sports M(c)/W(c), golf M/W, ice hockey M(c)/W(c), lacrosse M(c)/W(c), racquetball M/W, riflery M(c)/W(c), rock climbing M/W, rowing M(c)/W(c), rugby M(c)/W(c), sand volleyball M/W, soccer M(c)/W(c), softball M(c)/W(c), swimming and diving M(c)/W(c), table tennis M(c)/W(c), tennis M(c)/W(c), track and field M/W, ultimate Frisbee M(c)/W(c), volleyball M(c)/W(c), water polo M(c)/W(c), weight lifting M(c)/W(c), wrestling M/W.

Campus security: 24-hour emergency response devices and patrols, late-night transport/escort service, controlled dormitory access, CCTV surveillance; Public weapons storage for students/faculty/staff.

Student services: health clinic, personal/psychological counseling, women's center, legal services.

COSTS & FINANCIAL AID
Costs (2017–18) *Tuition:* state resident $7125 full-time, $238 per credit hour part-time; nonresident $22,425 full-time, $748 per credit hour part-time. Full-time tuition and fees vary according to course load, location, program, and reciprocity agreements. Part-time tuition and fees vary according to course load, location, program, and reciprocity agreements. *Required fees:* $1762 full-time, $17 per credit hour part-time, $375 per term part-time. *Room and board:* $11,044. Room and board charges vary according to board plan and housing facility. *Payment plan:* installment. *Waivers:* employees or children of employees.

Financial Aid Of all full-time matriculated undergraduates who enrolled in 2016, 11,534 applied for aid, 8,810 were judged to have need, 1,490 had their need fully met. 1,332 Federal Work-Study jobs (averaging $2688). In 2016, 1268 non-need-based awards were made. *Average percent of need met:* 74. *Average financial aid package:* $14,021. *Average need-based loan:* $4386. *Average need-based gift aid:* $7482. *Average non-need-based aid:* $7438. *Average indebtedness upon graduation:* $22,918.

APPLYING
Standardized Tests *Required:* SAT or ACT (for admission). *Recommended:* ACT (for admission).

Options: electronic application.

Application fee: $45.

Required: high school transcript, minimum ACT score of 20 or combined total of 1030 or higher on the SAT Evidence-Based Reading & Writing and SAT Math sections or rank in upper 50% of high school class.

Application deadlines: 5/1 (freshmen), 5/1 (transfers).

Notification: continuous (freshmen), continuous (out-of-state freshmen), continuous (transfers).

CONTACT
Ms. Abby Freeman, Director of Admissions, University of Nebraska–Lincoln, 1410 Q Street, Lincoln, NE 68588-0417. *Phone:* 402-472-2023. *Toll-free phone:* 800-742-8800. *Fax:* 402-472-0670. *E-mail:* admissions@unl.edu.

University of Nebraska Medical Center

Omaha, Nebraska

http://www.unmc.edu/

CONTACT
University of Nebraska Medical Center, Nebraska Medical Center, Omaha, NE 68198. *Toll-free phone:* 800-626-8431 Ext. 6468.

Wayne State College

Wayne, Nebraska

http://www.wsc.edu/

- **State-supported** comprehensive, founded 1910, part of Nebraska State College System
- **Small-town** 128-acre campus
- **Endowment** $22.0 million
- **Coed** 2,757 undergraduate students, 87% full-time, 58% women, 42% men
- **Noncompetitive** entrance level, 100% of applicants were admitted

UNDERGRAD STUDENTS
2,404 full-time, 353 part-time. Students come from 36 states and territories; 25 other countries; 15% are from out of state; 3% Black or African American, non-Hispanic/Latino; 9% Hispanic/Latino; 0.7% Asian, non-Hispanic/Latino; 0.1% Native Hawaiian or other Pacific Islander, non-Hispanic/Latino; 1% American Indian or Alaska Native, non-Hispanic/Latino; 3% Two or more races, non-Hispanic/Latino; 2% Race/ethnicity unknown; 1% international; 8% transferred in; 40% live on campus.

Freshmen:
Admission: 1,706 applied, 1,706 admitted, 606 enrolled. *Average high school GPA:* 3.3.
Retention: 69% of full-time freshmen returned.

FACULTY
Total: 204, 58% full-time, 54% with terminal degrees.
Student/faculty ratio: 19:1.

ACADEMICS
Calendar: semesters. *Degrees:* bachelor's, master's, and post-master's certificates.

Special study options: adult/continuing education programs, advanced placement credit, cooperative education, distance learning, double majors, honors programs, independent study, internships, off-campus study, part-time degree program, services for LD students, student-designed majors, study abroad, summer session for credit. *ROTC:* Army (b).

Computers: 365 computers/terminals are available on campus for general student use. Students can access the following: campus intranet, computer help desk, free student e-mail accounts, online (class) grades, online (class) registration, online (class) schedules. Campuswide network is available. 100% of college-owned or -operated housing units are wired for high-speed Internet access. Wireless service is available via entire campus.
Library: U. S. Conn Library. *Books:* 145,315 (physical), 290,865 (digital/electronic); *Serial titles:* 1,045 (physical), 66 (digital/electronic); *Databases:* 49.

STUDENT LIFE
Housing options: on-campus residence required for freshman year; coed. Campus housing is university owned. Freshman campus housing is guaranteed.
Activities and organizations: drama/theater group, student-run newspaper, radio and television station, choral group, marching band, national fraternities, national sororities.
Athletics Member NCAA. All Division II. *Intercollegiate sports:* baseball M(s), basketball M(s)/W(s), cheerleading M(c)/W(c), cross-country running M(s)/W(s), football M(s), rugby M(c)/W(c), soccer M(c)/W(s), softball W(s), track and field M(s)/W(s), volleyball W(s), wrestling M(c). *Intramural sports:* archery M/W, badminton M/W, basketball M/W, bowling M/W, football M/W, golf M/W, racquetball M/W, softball M/W, swimming and diving M/W, table tennis M/W, tennis M/W, track and field M/W, volleyball M/W, weight lifting M/W, wrestling M.
Campus security: 24-hour emergency response devices and patrols, student patrols, late-night transport/escort service, controlled dormitory access.
Student services: health clinic, personal/psychological counseling.

COSTS & FINANCIAL AID
Costs (2017–18) *Tuition:* state resident $5160 full-time, $172 per credit hour part-time; nonresident $10,320 full-time, $344 per credit hour part-time. Full-time tuition and fees vary according to course level, course load, and location. Part-time tuition and fees vary according to course level, course load, and location. *Required fees:* $1664 full-time, $64 per credit hour part-time. *Room and board:* $7430; room only: $3640. Room and board charges vary according to board plan and housing facility. *Payment plan:* installment. *Waivers:* employees or children of employees.
Financial Aid Of all full-time matriculated undergraduates who enrolled in 2017, 2,180 applied for aid, 1,705 were judged to have need, 738 had their need fully met. In 2017, 92 non-need-based awards were made. *Average percent of need met:* 61. *Average financial aid package:* $9494. *Average need-based loan:* $3893. *Average need-based gift aid:* $5464. *Average non-need-based aid:* $2470.

APPLYING
Options: electronic application, deferred entrance.
Required: high school transcript.
Application deadlines: rolling (freshmen), rolling (transfers).
Notification: continuous (freshmen), continuous (transfers).

CONTACT
Mr. Kevin Halle, Director of Admissions, Wayne State College, 1111 Main Street, Wayne, NE 68787. *Phone:* 402-375-7234. *Toll-free phone:* 866-WSC-CATS. *Fax:* 402-375-7204. *E-mail:* admit1@wsc.edu.

York College

York, Nebraska

http://www.york.edu/

CONTACT
Ms. Janae Parsons, York College, 1125 East 8th Street, York, NE 68467-2699. *Phone:* 402-363-5627. *Toll-free phone:* 800-950-9675. *Fax:* 402-363-5623. *E-mail:* enroll@york.edu.

NEVADA

Arizona College–Las Vegas

Las Vegas, Nevada

http://www.arizonacollege.edu/

CONTACT
Arizona College–Las Vegas, 2320 South Rancho Drive, Las Vegas, NV 89102.

The Art Institute of Las Vegas

Henderson, Nevada

http://www.artinstitutes.edu/lasvegas/

CONTACT
The Art Institute of Las Vegas, 2350 Corporate Circle Drive, Henderson, NV 89074. *Phone:* 702-369-9944. *Toll-free phone:* 800-833-2678.

Chamberlain College of Nursing

Las Vegas, Nevada

http://www.chamberlain.edu/

- **Proprietary** 4-year
- **Coed**

FACULTY
Student/faculty ratio: 12:1.

ACADEMICS
Degree: bachelor's.

STUDENT LIFE
Housing options: college housing not available.

COSTS
Costs (2017–18) *Tuition:* $18,900 full-time. *Required fees:* $600 full-time.

APPLYING
Standardized Tests *Required:* SAT or ACT (for admission).
Options: deferred entrance.
Application fee: $95.

CONTACT
Chamberlain College of Nursing, 9901 Covington Cross Drive, Las Vegas, NV 89144. *Toll-free phone:* 877-751-5783.

College of Southern Nevada
Las Vegas, Nevada
http://www.csn.edu/

CONTACT
Admissions and Records, College of Southern Nevada, 6375 West Charleston Boulevard, Las Vegas, NV 89146. *Phone:* 702-651-4060.

DeVry University–Henderson Campus
Henderson, Nevada
http://www.devry.edu/

CONTACT
Admissions Office, DeVry University–Henderson Campus, 2490 Paseo Verde Parkway, Suite 150, Henderson, NV 89074-7120. *Phone:* 702-933-9700. *Toll-free phone:* 866-338-7934.

Great Basin College
Elko, Nevada
http://www.gbcnv.edu/
- **State-supported** primarily 2-year, founded 1967, part of Nevada System of Higher Education
- **Small-town** 45-acre campus
- **Endowment** $6.7 million
- **Coed**
- **Noncompetitive** entrance level

ACADEMICS
Calendar: semesters. *Degrees:* certificates, associate, bachelor's, and postbachelor's certificates.
Library: Learning Resource Center. *Books:* 94,193 (physical), 250,157 (digital/electronic); *Serial titles:* 2,946 (physical), 230,872 (digital/electronic); *Databases:* 80. Weekly public service hours: 46; students can reserve study rooms.

STUDENT LIFE
Housing options: coed, special housing for students with disabilities. Campus housing is university owned.
Campus security: late-night transport/escort service, evening patrols by trained security personnel.
Student services: personal/psychological counseling.

COSTS & FINANCIAL AID
Costs (2017–18) *Tuition:* state resident $2850 full-time, $1330 per year part-time; nonresident $9628 full-time, $2383 per year part-time. *Required fees:* $165 full-time, $6 per unit part-time. *Room only:* $3150. Room and board charges vary according to housing facility.
Financial Aid Of all full-time matriculated undergraduates who enrolled in 2017, 395 applied for aid, 349 were judged to have need, 32 had their need fully met. In 2017, 91 non-need-based awards were made. *Average financial aid package:* $2590. *Average need-based loan:* $3134. *Average need-based gift aid:* $2866. *Average non-need-based aid:* $1027.

APPLYING
Options: electronic application, early admission, deferred entrance.

Application fee: $10.

CONTACT
Ms. Jan King, Director of Admissions and Registrar, Great Basin College, 1500 College Parkway, Elko, NV 89801. *Phone:* 775-753-2102. *E-mail:* jan.king@gbcnv.edu.

Nevada State College
Henderson, Nevada
http://www.nsc.edu/
- **State-supported** 4-year, founded 2002, part of Nevada System of Higher Education
- **Suburban** 520-acre campus with easy access to Las Vegas
- **Endowment** $1.0 million
- **Coed**
- **Minimally difficult** entrance level

FACULTY
Student/faculty ratio: 18:1.

ACADEMICS
Calendar: semesters. *Degree:* bachelor's.
Library: Nevada State College Library plus 1 other. *Books:* 15,768 (physical), 206,855 (digital/electronic); *Serial titles:* 53,083 (digital/electronic); *Databases:* 98. Students can reserve study rooms.

STUDENT LIFE
Housing options: college housing not available.
Activities and organizations: student-run newspaper, Nevada State Student Alliance (Student Government), Pre-Professional Club, American Sign Language Club, Student Nurses Association, Circle K International.
Campus security: private contracted security patrols.
Student services: health clinic, personal/psychological counseling.

COSTS
Costs (2017–18) *Tuition:* state resident $4830 full-time, $161 per credit part-time; nonresident $11,113 full-time, $322 per credit part-time. Full-time tuition and fees vary according to program. Part-time tuition and fees vary according to program. *Payment plans:* installment, deferred payment.

APPLYING
Options: electronic application.
Application fee: $30.
Required: high school transcript, minimum 2.0 GPA.

CONTACT
Adelfa Sullivan, Registrar, Nevada State College, Office of Admissions and Records, 1300 Nevada State Drive, Henderson, NV 89002. *Phone:* 702-992-2115. *Fax:* 702-992-2111. *E-mail:* admissions@nsc.edu.

Pima Medical Institute
Las Vegas, Nevada
http://www.pmi.edu/

CONTACT
Admissions Office, Pima Medical Institute, 3333 East Flamingo Road, Las Vegas, NV 89121. *Phone:* 702-458-9650 Ext. 202. *Toll-free phone:* 800-477-PIMA.

Sierra Nevada College
Incline Village, Nevada
http://www.sierranevada.edu/
- **Independent** comprehensive, founded 1969
- **Small-town** 20-acre campus with easy access to Reno
- **Endowment** $4.3 million
- **Coed** 433 undergraduate students, 95% full-time, 43% women, 57% men
- **Moderately difficult** entrance level, 69% of applicants were admitted

UNDERGRAD STUDENTS
410 full-time, 23 part-time. Students come from 19 states and territories; 7 other countries; 82% are from out of state; 3% Black or African American, non-Hispanic/Latino; 4% Hispanic/Latino; 3% Asian, non-Hispanic/Latino; 2% Native Hawaiian or other Pacific Islander, non-

Hispanic/Latino; 3% American Indian or Alaska Native, non-Hispanic/Latino; 6% Race/ethnicity unknown; 12% transferred in; 40% live on campus.

Freshmen:
Admission: 735 applied, 507 admitted, 72 enrolled. *Average high school GPA:* 3.2. *Test scores:* SAT evidence-based reading and writing scores over 500: 59%; SAT math scores over 500: 54%; ACT scores over 18: 83%; SAT evidence-based reading and writing scores over 600: 18%; SAT math scores over 600: 18%; ACT scores over 24: 33%; SAT evidence-based reading and writing scores over 700: 3%.
Retention: 68% of full-time freshmen returned.

FACULTY
Total: 130, 32% full-time, 39% with terminal degrees.
Student/faculty ratio: 10:1.

ACADEMICS
Calendar: semesters. *Degrees:* certificates, diplomas, bachelor's, and master's.

Special study options: academic remediation for entering students, accelerated degree program, adult/continuing education programs, advanced placement credit, cooperative education, distance learning, double majors, English as a second language, honors programs, independent study, internships, part-time degree program, services for LD students, student-designed majors, study abroad, summer session for credit.

Unusual degree programs: 3-2 education.

Computers: 50 computers/terminals are available on campus for general student use. Students can access the following: campus intranet, computer help desk, free student e-mail accounts, online (class) grades, online (class) schedules. Campuswide network is available. 100% of college-owned or -operated housing units are wired for high-speed Internet access. Wireless service is available via entire campus.
Library: Prim Library. *Books:* 27,716 (physical), 7,520 (digital/electronic); *Serial titles:* 1,106 (physical); *Databases:* 35. Weekly public service hours: 40.

STUDENT LIFE
Housing options: on-campus residence required through sophomore year; coed, special housing for students with disabilities. Campus housing is university owned. Freshman campus housing is guaranteed.

Activities and organizations: student-run newspaper, choral group, Film Club, International Club, Sustainability Club, Rock Climbing Club, First Generation Club.

Athletics Member NAIA. *Intercollegiate sports:* cross-country running M(s)/W(s), golf M(s)/W(s), lacrosse M(s)/W(s), rock climbing M/W, skiing (downhill) M(s)/W(s), soccer M(s)/W(s). *Intramural sports:* rock climbing M/W, skiing (downhill) M/W, soccer M/W, softball M/W, volleyball M/W.

Campus security: 24-hour emergency response devices and patrols, student patrols, controlled dormitory access.

Student services: personal/psychological counseling.

COSTS
Costs (2017–18) *Comprehensive fee:* $45,403 includes full-time tuition ($31,685), mandatory fees ($954), and room and board ($12,764). Full-time tuition and fees vary according to course load, degree level, location, program, and reciprocity agreements. Part-time tuition: $1348 per credit hour. Part-time tuition and fees vary according to course load, degree level, location, program, and reciprocity agreements. *College room only:* $6382. Room and board charges vary according to board plan. *Payment plan:* installment. *Waivers:* employees or children of employees.

APPLYING
Standardized Tests *Required:* SAT or ACT (for admission).
Options: electronic application, deferred entrance.
Required: minimum 2.6 GPA. *Required for some:* high school transcript, 1 letter of recommendation. *Recommended:* essay or personal statement, interview.
Application deadlines: rolling (freshmen), rolling (transfers).

CONTACT
Ms. Julie Hernandez, Sierra Nevada College, 999 Tahoe Boulevard, Incline Village, NV 89451. *Phone:* 866-412-4636. *Fax:* 775-831-6223. *E-mail:* admissions@sierranevada.edu.

Truckee Meadows Community College
Reno, Nevada
http://www.tmcc.edu/

- **State-supported** primarily 2-year, founded 1971, part of Nevada System of Higher Education
- **Suburban** 63-acre campus
- **Endowment** $9.4 million
- **Coed** 10,720 undergraduate students, 26% full-time, 54% women, 46% men
- **Noncompetitive** entrance level, 100% of applicants were admitted

UNDERGRAD STUDENTS
2,816 full-time, 7,904 part-time. Students come from 24 states and territories; 19 other countries; 7% are from out of state; 2% Black or African American, non-Hispanic/Latino; 29% Hispanic/Latino; 6% Asian, non-Hispanic/Latino; 0.1% Native Hawaiian or other Pacific Islander, non-Hispanic/Latino; 1% American Indian or Alaska Native, non-Hispanic/Latino; 4% Two or more races, non-Hispanic/Latino; 2% Race/ethnicity unknown; 0.4% international; 5% transferred in.

Freshmen:
Admission: 1,888 applied, 1,888 admitted, 1,459 enrolled.
Retention: 63% of full-time freshmen returned.

FACULTY
Total: 530, 29% full-time.
Student/faculty ratio: 21:1.

ACADEMICS
Calendar: semesters. *Degrees:* certificates, associate, and bachelor's.

Special study options: academic remediation for entering students, accelerated degree program, adult/continuing education programs, advanced placement credit, cooperative education, distance learning, double majors, English as a second language, independent study, internships, part-time degree program, services for LD students, summer session for credit. *ROTC:* Army (c).

Computers: Students can access the following: computer help desk, free student e-mail accounts, online (class) grades, online (class) registration, online (class) schedules. Campuswide network is available. Wireless service is available via entire campus.
Library: Elizabeth Sturm Library.

STUDENT LIFE
Housing options: college housing not available.

Activities and organizations: drama/theater group, student-run newspaper, Entrepreneurship Club, International Club, Phi Theta Kappa, Student Government Association, Student Media and Broadcasting Club.

Campus security: 24-hour emergency response devices and patrols, late-night transport/escort service.

Student services: personal/psychological counseling.

COSTS & FINANCIAL AID
Costs (2017–18) *Tuition:* state resident $95 per credit hour part-time; nonresident $200 per credit hour part-time. Full-time tuition and fees vary according to course level, course load, degree level, and program. Part-time tuition and fees vary according to course level, course load, degree level, and program. *Required fees:* $8 per credit hour part-time. *Payment plan:* installment. *Waivers:* employees or children of employees.

Financial Aid Of all full-time matriculated undergraduates who enrolled in 2016, 126 Federal Work-Study jobs (averaging $5000). 368 state and other part-time jobs (averaging $5000).

APPLYING
Options: electronic application, early admission.
Application fee: $10.
Application deadlines: rolling (freshmen), rolling (out-of-state freshmen), rolling (transfers).

Notification: continuous (freshmen), continuous (out-of-state freshmen), continuous (transfers).

CONTACT
Truckee Meadows Community College, 7000 Dandini Boulevard, Reno, NV 89512-3901. *Phone:* 775-673-7240.

University of Nevada, Las Vegas
Las Vegas, Nevada
http://www.unlv.edu/

- **State-supported** university, founded 1957, part of Nevada System of Higher Education
- **Urban** 332-acre campus with easy access to Las Vegas
- **Endowment** $49.7 million
- **Coed** 25,279 undergraduate students, 75% full-time, 57% women, 43% men
- **Moderately difficult** entrance level, 81% of applicants were admitted

UNDERGRAD STUDENTS
18,958 full-time, 6,321 part-time. Students come from 54 states and territories; 11% are from out of state; 8% Black or African American, non-Hispanic/Latino; 29% Hispanic/Latino; 16% Asian, non-Hispanic/Latino; 0.9% Native Hawaiian or other Pacific Islander, non-Hispanic/Latino; 0.2% American Indian or Alaska Native, non-Hispanic/Latino; 10% Two or more races, non-Hispanic/Latino; 1% Race/ethnicity unknown; 4% international; 10% transferred in; 7% live on campus.

Freshmen:
Admission: 9,872 applied, 8,003 admitted, 3,958 enrolled. *Average high school GPA:* 3.4. *Test scores:* SAT evidence-based reading and writing scores over 500: 83%; SAT math scores over 500: 80%; ACT scores over 18: 85%; SAT evidence-based reading and writing scores over 600: 35%; SAT math scores over 600: 33%; ACT scores over 24: 32%; SAT evidence-based reading and writing scores over 700: 4%; SAT math scores over 700: 6%; ACT scores over 30: 4%.
Retention: 74% of full-time freshmen returned.

FACULTY
Total: 1,778, 54% full-time, 49% with terminal degrees.
Student/faculty ratio: 21:1.

ACADEMICS
Calendar: semesters. *Degrees:* certificates, bachelor's, master's, doctoral, post-master's, and postbachelor's certificates.
Special study options: academic remediation for entering students, adult/continuing education programs, advanced placement credit, cooperative education, distance learning, double majors, English as a second language, honors programs, independent study, internships, part-time degree program, services for LD students, study abroad, summer session for credit. *ROTC:* Army (b), Air Force (b).
Computers: 2,100 computers/terminals and 8,000 ports are available on campus for general student use. Students can access the following: campus intranet, computer help desk, free student e-mail accounts, online (class) grades, online (class) registration, online (class) schedules. Campuswide network is available. 100% of college-owned or -operated housing units are wired for high-speed Internet access. Wireless service is available via entire campus.
Library: Lied Library. *Books:* 939,652 (physical), 1.3 million (digital/electronic); *Serial titles:* 20,453 (physical), 59,248 (digital/electronic); *Databases:* 320. Weekly public service hours: 101; students can reserve study rooms.

STUDENT LIFE
Housing options: coed, special housing for students with disabilities. Campus housing is university owned. Freshman applicants given priority for college housing.
Activities and organizations: drama/theater group, student-run newspaper, radio and television station, choral group, marching band, National Society of Leadership and Success, National Society of Minorities in Hospitality, Residential Hall Association, Social sororities and fraternities, `Ewalu Club, national fraternities, national sororities.
Athletics Member NCAA. All Division I except football (Division I-A). *Intercollegiate sports:* baseball M(s), basketball M(s)/W(s), cheerleading M(s)/W(s), cross-country running W(s), golf M(s), soccer M(s)/W(s),

softball W(s), swimming and diving M(s)/W(s), tennis M(s)/W(s), track and field W(s), volleyball W(s). *Intramural sports:* badminton M/W, basketball M/W, bowling M/W, football M/W, golf M/W, racquetball M/W, soccer M/W, softball M/W, swimming and diving M/W, tennis M/W, volleyball M/W.
Campus security: 24-hour emergency response devices and patrols, late-night transport/escort service, controlled dormitory access.
Student services: health clinic, personal/psychological counseling, women's center, legal services.

COSTS & FINANCIAL AID
Costs (2018–19) *One-time required fee:* $120. *Tuition:* state resident $7154 full-time, $224 per credit hour part-time; nonresident $21,626 full-time, $471 per credit hour part-time. Full-time tuition and fees vary according to course level, program, and reciprocity agreements. Part-time tuition and fees vary according to course level, program, and reciprocity agreements. *Required fees:* $646 full-time, $14 per credit hour part-time, $323 per term part-time. *Room and board:* $10,780; room only: $5880. Room and board charges vary according to board plan and housing facility. *Payment plans:* installment, deferred payment. *Waivers:* employees or children of employees.
Financial Aid Of all full-time matriculated undergraduates who enrolled in 2016, 13,793 applied for aid, 11,648 were judged to have need, 902 had their need fully met. In 2016, 1380 non-need-based awards were made. *Average percent of need met:* 54. *Average financial aid package:* $8335. *Average need-based loan:* $4218. *Average need-based gift aid:* $6006. *Average non-need-based aid:* $3987. *Average indebtedness upon graduation:* $25,374.

APPLYING
Standardized Tests *Required:* SAT or ACT (for admission).
Options: electronic application, early admission, deferred entrance.
Application fee: $60.
Required: high school transcript, minimum 3.0 GPA.
Application deadlines: 7/1 (freshmen), 7/1 (transfers).
Notification: continuous (freshmen), continuous (transfers).

CONTACT
University of Nevada, Las Vegas, 4505 South Maryland Parkway, Las Vegas, NV 89154.

University of Nevada, Reno
Reno, Nevada
http://www.unr.edu/

- **State-supported** university, founded 1874, part of Nevada System of Higher Education
- **Urban** 200-acre campus
- **Endowment** $302.7 million
- **Coed** 18,348 undergraduate students, 85% full-time, 53% women, 47% men
- **Moderately difficult** entrance level, 88% of applicants were admitted

UNDERGRAD STUDENTS
15,572 full-time, 2,776 part-time. Students come from 45 states and territories; 60 other countries; 28% are from out of state; 3% Black or African American, non-Hispanic/Latino; 21% Hispanic/Latino; 8% Asian, non-Hispanic/Latino; 0.6% Native Hawaiian or other Pacific Islander, non-Hispanic/Latino; 0.7% American Indian or Alaska Native, non-Hispanic/Latino; 7% Two or more races, non-Hispanic/Latino; 2% Race/ethnicity unknown; 2% international; 7% transferred in; 16% live on campus.

Freshmen:
Admission: 9,721 applied, 8,557 admitted, 3,354 enrolled. *Average high school GPA:* 3.4. *Test scores:* SAT evidence-based reading and writing scores over 500: 90%; SAT math scores over 500: 88%; ACT scores over 18: 93%; SAT evidence-based reading and writing scores over 600: 44%; SAT math scores over 600: 41%; ACT scores over 24: 46%; SAT evidence-based reading and writing scores over 700: 6%; SAT math scores over 700: 7%; ACT scores over 30: 9%.
Retention: 81% of full-time freshmen returned.

FACULTY
Total: 1,274, 56% full-time, 64% with terminal degrees.

Student/faculty ratio: 20:1.

ACADEMICS

Calendar: semesters. *Degrees:* certificates, bachelor's, master's, doctoral, post-master's, and postbachelor's certificates.

Special study options: academic remediation for entering students, adult/continuing education programs, advanced placement credit, distance learning, double majors, English as a second language, honors programs, independent study, internships, off-campus study, part-time degree program, services for LD students, study abroad, summer session for credit. *ROTC:* Army (b).

Unusual degree programs: 3-2 biotechnology.

Computers: Students can access the following: computer help desk, free student e-mail accounts, online (class) grades, online (class) registration, online (class) schedules. Campuswide network is available. 100% of college-owned or -operated housing units are wired for high-speed Internet access. Wireless service is available via entire campus.

Library: Mathewson-IGT Knowledge Center plus 2 others. *Books:* 1.4 million (physical), 588,940 (digital/electronic). Students can reserve study rooms.

STUDENT LIFE

Housing options: coed, men-only, women-only, special housing for students with disabilities. Campus housing is university owned. Freshman applicants given priority for college housing.

Activities and organizations: drama/theater group, student-run newspaper, radio station, choral group, marching band, Intervarsity Christian Fellowship, Student Ambassadors, Young Democrats, Asian American Association, Blue Crew, national fraternities, national sororities.

Athletics Member NCAA. All Division I except football (Division I-A). *Intercollegiate sports:* baseball M(s), basketball M(s)/W(s), cheerleading M(c)/W(c), cross-country running W(s), golf M(s)/W(s), riflery M(s)/W(s), soccer W(s), softball W(s), swimming and diving W(s), tennis M(s)/W(s), track and field W(s), volleyball W(s). *Intramural sports:* basketball M/W, bowling M/W, cross-country running M/W, equestrian sports M/W, football M, golf M/W, racquetball M/W, rock climbing M/W, rugby M/W, skiing (cross-country) M/W, skiing (downhill) M/W, soccer M/W, softball M/W, swimming and diving M/W, table tennis M/W, tennis M/W, track and field M/W, ultimate Frisbee M/W, volleyball M/W, water polo M/W.

Campus security: 24-hour emergency response devices and patrols, late-night transport/escort service, controlled dormitory access.

Student services: health clinic, personal/psychological counseling, women's center, legal services.

COSTS & FINANCIAL AID

Costs (2018–19) *Tuition:* state resident $6990 full-time, $224 per credit part-time; nonresident $21,462 full-time, $729 per credit part-time. Full-time tuition and fees vary according to course level, course load, degree level, and program. Part-time tuition and fees vary according to course level, course load, degree level, and program. *Required fees:* $774 full-time, $282 per term part-time. *Room and board:* $10,868; room only: $6100. Room and board charges vary according to board plan and housing facility. *Payment plan:* installment. *Waivers:* senior citizens and employees or children of employees.

Financial Aid Of all full-time matriculated undergraduates who enrolled in 2015, 10,201 applied for aid, 7,911 were judged to have need, 729 had their need fully met. In 2015, 1968 non-need-based awards were made. *Average percent of need met:* 61. *Average financial aid package:* $8756. *Average need-based loan:* $4095. *Average need-based gift aid:* $5080. *Average non-need-based aid:* $2250. *Average indebtedness upon graduation:* $23,110.

APPLYING

Standardized Tests *Required:* SAT or ACT (for admission).

Options: electronic application, early admission, early action, deferred entrance.

Application fee: $60.

Required: high school transcript, minimum 3.0 GPA.

Application deadlines: 4/7 (freshmen), 7/1 (transfers), 11/1 (early action).

Notification: continuous (freshmen), continuous (out-of-state freshmen), continuous (transfers), rolling (early action).

CONTACT

Dr. Steve Maples, Director of Undergraduate Admissions, University of Nevada, Reno, Mail Stop 120, Reno, NV 89557. *Phone:* 775-784-4700. *Toll-free phone:* 866-263-8232. *Fax:* 775-784-4283. *E-mail:* asknevada@unr.edu.

University of Phoenix–Las Vegas Campus
Las Vegas, Nevada
http://www.phoenix.edu/

CONTACT

Marc Booker, Sr. Director, Office of Admissions and Evaluation, University of Phoenix–Las Vegas Campus, 4305 South Riverpoint Parkway, Mail Stop CF-L101, Phoenix, AZ 85040. *Phone:* 602-557-4609. *Toll-free phone:* 866-766-0766. *Fax:* 480-643-1156.

Western Nevada College
Carson City, Nevada
http://www.wnc.edu/

- **State-supported** primarily 2-year, founded 1971, part of Nevada System of Higher Education
- **Small-town** 200-acre campus
- **Endowment** $250,000
- **Coed**
- **Noncompetitive** entrance level

FACULTY
Student/faculty ratio: 18:1.

ACADEMICS

Calendar: semesters. *Degrees:* certificates, associate, and bachelor's.

Library: Western Nevada College Library and Media Services plus 1 other. *Books:* 35,923 (physical), 4,544 (digital/electronic); *Serial titles:* 2,725 (physical); *Databases:* 33. Weekly public service hours: 61; students can reserve study rooms.

STUDENT LIFE

Housing options: college housing not available.

Activities and organizations: drama/theater group, choral group, Associated Students of Western Nevada, Soccer Club, Veterans Club, National Student Nurses Association, American Sign Language Club.

Campus security: late-night transport/escort service.

Student services: personal/psychological counseling.

COSTS & FINANCIAL AID

Costs (2017–18) *Tuition:* state resident $3015 full-time; nonresident $9793 full-time. Full-time tuition and fees vary according to degree level. Part-time tuition and fees vary according to degree level. *Payment plans:* tuition prepayment, installment.

Financial Aid Of all full-time matriculated undergraduates who enrolled in 2017, 412 applied for aid, 386 were judged to have need, 21 had their need fully met. In 2017, 41 non-need-based awards were made. *Average financial aid package:* $2460. *Average need-based loan:* $3302. *Average need-based gift aid:* $2681.

APPLYING

Options: electronic application, early admission.

Application fee: $15.

Required for some: high school transcript. *Recommended:* high school transcript.

CONTACT

Admissions and Records, Western Nevada College, 2201 West College Parkway, Carson City, NV 89703. *Phone:* 775-445-2377. *Fax:* 775-445-3147. *E-mail:* wncc_aro@wncc.edu.

NEW HAMPSHIRE

Colby-Sawyer College

New London, New Hampshire

http://www.colby-sawyer.edu/

- **Independent** 4-year, founded 1837
- **Small-town** 200-acre campus
- **Endowment** $36.0 million
- **Coed**
- **Moderately difficult** entrance level

FACULTY
Student/faculty ratio: 14:1.

ACADEMICS
Calendar: semesters. *Degrees:* certificates, associate, and bachelor's.
Library: Susan Colgate Cleveland Library Learning Center. *Books:*
83,409 (physical), 144,473 (digital/electronic); *Serial titles:* 486
(physical); *Databases:* 119. Weekly public service hours: 100; students
can reserve study rooms.

STUDENT LIFE
Housing options: on-campus residence required through sophomore year;
coed, women-only. Campus housing is university owned and leased by the
school. Freshman campus housing is guaranteed.

Activities and organizations: drama/theater group, student-run
newspaper, choral group, Campus Activities Board, Student Government
Association, Dance Club, Colby-Sawyer Players (Theater), Student
Nurses Association.

Athletics Member NCAA. All Division III.

Campus security: 24-hour emergency response devices and patrols, late-
night transport/escort service, controlled dormitory access, awareness
seminars.

Student services: health clinic, personal/psychological counseling.

COSTS & FINANCIAL AID
Costs (2017–18) *Comprehensive fee:* $54,836 includes full-time tuition
($40,386), mandatory fees ($800), and room and board ($13,650). Part-
time tuition: $1346 per credit. Part-time tuition and fees vary according to
course load. *Room and board:* Room and board charges vary according to
board plan and housing facility.

Financial Aid *Financial aid deadline:* 3/1.

APPLYING
Options: electronic application, early admission, early action, deferred
entrance.

Application fee: $45.

Required: essay or personal statement, high school transcript, minimum
2.5 GPA, college preparatory courses: 4 years of English, 3 years of math,
3 years of lab science, 3 years of social science and 2 years of the same
language. *Recommended:* 1 letter of recommendation, interview.

CONTACT
Ms. Jaimee Hofstetter, Director of Enrollment Operations, Colby-Sawyer
College, 541 Main Street, New London, NH 03257-4648. *Phone:* 603-
526-3887. *Toll-free phone:* 800-272-1015. *Fax:* 603-526-3452. *E-mail:*
admissions@colby-sawyer.edu.

Dartmouth College

Hanover, New Hampshire

http://www.dartmouth.edu/

- **Independent** university, founded 1769
- **Small-town** 269-acre campus
- **Endowment** $5.0 million
- **Coed** 4,410 undergraduate students, 99% full-time, 49% women, 51%
  men
- **Most difficult** entrance level, 10% of applicants were admitted

UNDERGRAD STUDENTS
4,360 full-time, 50 part-time. Students come from 50 states and territories;
81 other countries; 97% are from out of state; 7% Black or African
American, non-Hispanic/Latino; 10% Hispanic/Latino; 15% Asian, non-
Hispanic/Latino; 0.3% Native Hawaiian or other Pacific Islander, non-
Hispanic/Latino; 2% American Indian or Alaska Native, non-
Hispanic/Latino; 5% Two or more races, non-Hispanic/Latino; 2%
Race/ethnicity unknown; 9% international; 0.1% transferred in; 85% live
on campus.

Freshmen:
Admission: 20,035 applied, 2,093 admitted, 1,215 enrolled. *Test scores:*
SAT evidence-based reading and writing scores over 500: 100%; SAT
math scores over 500: 100%; ACT scores over 18: 100%; SAT evidence-
based reading and writing scores over 600: 98%; SAT math scores over
600: 98%; ACT scores over 24: 99%; SAT evidence-based reading and
writing scores over 700: 81%; SAT math scores over 700: 83%; ACT
scores over 30: 79%.
Retention: 97% of full-time freshmen returned.

FACULTY
Total: 781, 78% full-time, 93% with terminal degrees.
Student/faculty ratio: 7:1.

ACADEMICS
Calendar: quarters. *Degrees:* bachelor's, master's, and doctoral.

Special study options: advanced placement credit, double majors, honors
programs, independent study, internships, off-campus study, services for
LD students, student-designed majors, study abroad, summer session for
credit. *ROTC:* Army (c).

Unusual degree programs: 3-2 engineering.

Computers: 200 computers/terminals are available on campus for general
student use. Students can access the following: campus intranet, computer
help desk, free student e-mail accounts, online (class) grades, online
(class) registration, online (class) schedules. Campuswide network is
available. 100% of college-owned or -operated housing units are wired for
high-speed Internet access. Wireless service is available via entire
campus.
Library: Baker-Berry Library plus 8 others. *Books:* 2.6 million
(physical), 880,374 (digital/electronic); *Serial titles:* 75,548 (physical).
Study areas open 24 hours, 5–7 days a week; students can reserve study
rooms.

STUDENT LIFE
Housing options: on-campus residence required for freshman year; coed,
cooperative. Campus housing is university owned. Freshman campus
housing is guaranteed.

Activities and organizations: drama/theater group, student-run
newspaper, radio and television station, choral group, marching band,
Dartmouth Student Assembly, Dartmouth Outing Club, Collis After Dark,
Green Key Society, GLOS - Greek Letter Organizations and Societies,
national fraternities, national sororities.

Athletics Member NCAA. All Division I except football (Division I-AA).
Intercollegiate sports: badminton M(c)/W(c), baseball M, basketball
M/W, cheerleading M(c)/W(c), crew M/W, cross-country running M/W,
equestrian sports M/W, fencing M(c)/W(c), field hockey W, golf M/W,
gymnastics M(c)/W(c), ice hockey M/W, lacrosse M/W, rowing M/W,
rugby M(c)/W, sailing M/W, skiing (cross-country) M/W, skiing
(downhill) M/W, soccer M/W, softball W, squash M/W, swimming and
diving M/W, table tennis M(c)/W(c), tennis M/W, track and field M/W,
ultimate Frisbee M(c)/W(c), volleyball M(c)/W, water polo M(c)/W(c),
wrestling M(c). *Intramural sports:* baseball M, basketball M/W, cross-
country running M/W, football M/W, golf M/W, ice hockey M/W, lacrosse
M/W, rugby M/W, skiing (cross-country) M/W, skiing (downhill) M/W,
soccer M/W, softball M/W, squash M/W, swimming and diving M/W,
table tennis M/W, tennis M/W, track and field M/W, volleyball M/W,
water polo M/W, weight lifting M/W, wrestling M.

Campus security: 24-hour emergency response devices and patrols, late-
night transport/escort service, controlled dormitory access.

Student services: health clinic, personal/psychological counseling,
women's center.

COSTS & FINANCIAL AID
Costs (2017–18) *One-time required fee:* $418. *Comprehensive fee:*
$68,109 includes full-time tuition ($51,468), mandatory fees ($1482), and
room and board ($15,159). *College room only:* $9144. Room and board
charges vary according to board plan. *Payment plans:* tuition prepayment,
installment.

Financial Aid Of all full-time matriculated undergraduates who enrolled in 2017, 2,494 applied for aid, 2,236 were judged to have need, 2,236 had their need fully met. 1,397 Federal Work-Study jobs (averaging $2199). 547 state and other part-time jobs (averaging $2404). *Average percent of need met:* 100. *Average financial aid package:* $50,665. *Average need-based loan:* $4569. *Average need-based gift aid:* $48,772. *Average indebtedness upon graduation:* $19,571. *Financial aid deadline:* 2/1.

APPLYING
Standardized Tests *Required:* SAT or ACT (for admission). *Recommended:* SAT Subject Tests (for admission).

Options: electronic application, early admission, early decision, deferred entrance.

Application fee: $80.

Required: essay or personal statement, high school transcript, 2 letters of recommendation, peer evaluation. *Recommended:* interview.

Application deadlines: 1/1 (freshmen), 3/1 (transfers).

Early decision deadline: 11/1.

Notification: 4/10 (freshmen), 5/15 (transfers), 12/15 (early decision).

CONTACT
Paul Sunde, Director of Admissions, Dartmouth College, 6016 McNutt Hall, Hanover, NH 03755. *Phone:* 603-646-2875. *E-mail:* admissions.reply@dartmouth.edu.

Franklin Pierce University
Rindge, New Hampshire
http://www.franklinpierce.edu/
- **Independent** university, founded 1962
- **Rural** 1200-acre campus
- **Endowment** $10.1 million
- **Coed** 1,711 undergraduate students, 91% full-time, 56% women, 44% men
- **Minimally difficult** entrance level, 76% of applicants were admitted

UNDERGRAD STUDENTS
1,564 full-time, 147 part-time. Students come from 27 states and territories; 15 other countries; 81% are from out of state; 7% Black or African American, non-Hispanic/Latino; 7% Hispanic/Latino; 1% Asian, non-Hispanic/Latino; 0.1% Native Hawaiian or other Pacific Islander, non-Hispanic/Latino; 0.4% American Indian or Alaska Native, non-Hispanic/Latino; 1% Two or more races, non-Hispanic/Latino; 7% Race/ethnicity unknown; 3% international; 2% transferred in; 92% live on campus.

Freshmen:
Admission: 5,642 applied, 4,312 admitted, 466 enrolled. *Average high school GPA:* 2.8.
Retention: 62% of full-time freshmen returned.

FACULTY
Total: 327, 29% full-time, 41% with terminal degrees.
Student/faculty ratio: 13:1.

ACADEMICS
Calendar: differs by branch and program. *Degrees:* certificates, associate, bachelor's, master's, doctoral, and postbachelor's certificates (profile does not reflect significant enrollment at 6 continuing education sites; master's degree is only offered at these sites).

Special study options: academic remediation for entering students, accelerated degree program, adult/continuing education programs, advanced placement credit, distance learning, double majors, English as a second language, external degree program, freshman honors college, honors programs, independent study, internships, off-campus study, part-time degree program, services for LD students, student-designed majors, study abroad, summer session for credit. *ROTC:* Army (c), Air Force (c).

Computers: 100 computers/terminals are available on campus for general student use. Students can access the following: campus intranet, computer help desk, free student e-mail accounts, online (class) grades, online (class) registration, online (class) schedules. Campuswide network is available. 100% of college-owned or -operated housing units are wired for high-speed Internet access. Wireless service is available via entire campus.

Library: Frank S. DiPietro Library plus 1 other. *Books:* 110,827 (physical), 192,113 (digital/electronic); *Serial titles:* 107 (physical), 68,000 (digital/electronic); *Databases:* 68. Weekly public service hours: 95.

STUDENT LIFE
Housing options: on-campus residence required for freshman year; coed. Campus housing is university owned. Freshman campus housing is guaranteed.

Activities and organizations: drama/theater group, student-run newspaper, radio and television station, choral group, Outing Club, WFPR Radio, Student Senate, Law Club, Business Club.

Athletics Member NCAA. All Division II. *Intercollegiate sports:* baseball M(s), basketball M(s)/W(s), cross-country running M(s)/W(s), field hockey W(s), golf M(s)/W(s), ice hockey M, lacrosse M(s)/W(s), soccer M(s)/W(s), softball W(s), tennis M(s)/W(s), track and field M(s)/W(s), volleyball W(s). *Intramural sports:* baseball M, basketball M/W, cheerleading W(c), cross-country running M/W, field hockey W, football M, golf M/W, ice hockey M, lacrosse M/W, rugby M(c)/W(c), soccer M/W, softball W, tennis M/W, track and field M/W, volleyball W.

Campus security: 24-hour emergency response devices and patrols, student patrols, late-night transport/escort service, controlled dormitory access.

Student services: health clinic, personal/psychological counseling.

COSTS & FINANCIAL AID
Costs (2017–18) *Comprehensive fee:* $48,077 includes full-time tuition ($32,445), mandatory fees ($2550), and room and board ($13,082). Full-time tuition and fees vary according to course load, degree level, location, and program. Part-time tuition: $1082 per credit hour. Part-time tuition and fees vary according to course load, degree level, location, and program. *College room only:* $7622. Room and board charges vary according to board plan, housing facility, and student level. *Payment plan:* installment. *Waivers:* senior citizens and employees or children of employees.

Financial Aid Of all full-time matriculated undergraduates who enrolled in 2017, 1,193 applied for aid, 1,112 were judged to have need, 225 had their need fully met. In 2017, 190 non-need-based awards were made. *Average percent of need met:* 75. *Average financial aid package:* $27,928. *Average need-based loan:* $4652. *Average need-based gift aid:* $23,562. *Average non-need-based aid:* $18,494. *Average indebtedness upon graduation:* $41,661.

APPLYING
Standardized Tests *Required for some:* SAT or ACT (for admission).
Options: electronic application, early admission, deferred entrance.
Application fee: $40.
Required: essay or personal statement, high school transcript, 1 letter of recommendation. *Required for some:* minimum 2.0 GPA. *Recommended:* minimum 2.2 GPA, interview.
Application deadlines: rolling (freshmen), rolling (transfers).
Notification: continuous (freshmen), continuous (transfers).

CONTACT
Office of Admissions, Franklin Pierce University, 40 University Drive, Rindge, NH 03461. *Phone:* 603-899-4050. *Toll-free phone:* 800-437-0048. *Fax:* 603-899-4394. *E-mail:* admissions@franklinpierce.edu.

Granite State College
Concord, New Hampshire
http://www.granite.edu/
- **State and locally supported** comprehensive, founded 1972, part of University System of New Hampshire
- **Suburban** campus
- **Endowment** $6.7 million
- **Coed** 1,758 undergraduate students, 46% full-time, 73% women, 27% men
- **Noncompetitive** entrance level, 100% of applicants were admitted

UNDERGRAD STUDENTS
807 full-time, 951 part-time. Students come from 42 states and territories; 1 other country; 18% are from out of state; 3% Black or African American, non-Hispanic/Latino; 4% Hispanic/Latino; 1% Asian, non-

Hispanic/Latino; 0.4% American Indian or Alaska Native, non-Hispanic/Latino; 2% Two or more races, non-Hispanic/Latino; 6% Race/ethnicity unknown; 0.1% international; 18% transferred in.

Freshmen:
Admission: 272 applied, 272 admitted, 73 enrolled.
Retention: 46% of full-time freshmen returned.

FACULTY
Total: 272, 3% full-time, 42% with terminal degrees.
Student/faculty ratio: 11:1.

ACADEMICS
Calendar: trimesters. *Degrees:* associate, bachelor's, master's, and postbachelor's certificates (offers primarily part-time degree programs; courses offered at 50 locations in New Hampshire).

Special study options: academic remediation for entering students, accelerated degree program, adult/continuing education programs, advanced placement credit, cooperative education, distance learning, double majors, independent study, internships, off-campus study, part-time degree program, services for LD students, student-designed majors, summer session for credit. *ROTC:* Army (c), Air Force (c).

Computers: 120 computers/terminals are available on campus for general student use. Students can access the following: campus intranet, computer help desk, free student e-mail accounts, online (class) grades, online (class) registration, online (class) schedules. Campuswide network is available. Wireless service is available via classrooms, computer centers, computer labs, learning centers.

Library: GSC Library and Information Commons. *Books:* 200,000 (digital/electronic); *Serial titles:* 23,000 (digital/electronic); *Databases:* 20. Weekly public service hours: 126.

STUDENT LIFE
Activities and organizations: Alumni Learner Association, Green Team.
Campus security: UNH Alert system provides emergency notifications via text and voice messages.
Student services: personal/psychological counseling.

COSTS
Costs (2017–18) *Tuition:* state resident $7368 full-time, $307 per credit part-time; nonresident $8280 full-time, $345 per credit part-time. *Required fees:* $225 full-time, $75 per term part-time. *Payment plan:* installment. *Waivers:* senior citizens and employees or children of employees.

APPLYING
Options: electronic application.
Required for some: high school transcript, associate degree for some BS programs.
Application deadlines: rolling (freshmen), rolling (transfers).
Notification: continuous (freshmen), continuous (transfers).

CONTACT
Ms. Christine Williams, Director of Admissions Operations, Granite State College, 25 Hall Street, Concord, NH 03301. *Phone:* 603-228-3000. *Toll-free phone:* 888-228-3000. *Fax:* 603-513-1386. *E-mail:* gsc.admissions@granite.edu.

Hellenic American University
Nashua, New Hampshire
http://www.hauniv.edu/

CONTACT
Hellenic American University, 505 Amherst Street, Nashua, NH 03063.

Keene State College
Keene, New Hampshire
http://www.keene.edu/

- **State-supported** comprehensive, founded 1909, part of University System of New Hampshire
- **Small-town** 150-acre campus
- **Coed** 3,780 undergraduate students, 96% full-time, 55% women, 45% men
- **Moderately difficult** entrance level, 83% of applicants were admitted

UNDERGRAD STUDENTS
3,624 full-time, 156 part-time. Students come from 27 states and territories; 8 other countries; 57% are from out of state; 2% Black or African American, non-Hispanic/Latino; 4% Hispanic/Latino; 1% Asian, non-Hispanic/Latino; 0.1% Native Hawaiian or other Pacific Islander, non-Hispanic/Latino; 0.2% American Indian or Alaska Native, non-Hispanic/Latino; 2% Two or more races, non-Hispanic/Latino; 6% Race/ethnicity unknown; 0.1% international; 3% transferred in; 55% live on campus.

Freshmen:
Admission: 5,580 applied, 4,613 admitted, 931 enrolled. *Average high school GPA:* 3.0. *Test scores:* SAT evidence-based reading and writing scores over 500: 69%; SAT math scores over 500: 61%; ACT scores over 18: 80%; SAT evidence-based reading and writing scores over 600: 18%; SAT math scores over 600: 11%; ACT scores over 24: 29%; SAT evidence-based reading and writing scores over 700: 1%; SAT math scores over 700: 1%; ACT scores over 30: 4%.
Retention: 71% of full-time freshmen returned.

ACADEMICS
Calendar: semesters. *Degrees:* certificates, bachelor's, master's, post-master's, and postbachelor's certificates.

Special study options: accelerated degree program, adult/continuing education programs, advanced placement credit, cooperative education, distance learning, double majors, English as a second language, freshman honors college, honors programs, independent study, internships, off-campus study, part-time degree program, services for LD students, student-designed majors, study abroad, summer session for credit. *ROTC:* Army (c), Air Force (c).

Unusual degree programs: 3-2 engineering with Clarkson University.

Computers: 600 computers/terminals are available on campus for general student use. Students can access the following: campus intranet, computer help desk, free student e-mail accounts, online (class) grades, online (class) registration, online (class) schedules. Campuswide network is available. 100% of college-owned or -operated housing units are wired for high-speed Internet access. Wireless service is available via entire campus.

Library: Mason Library. *Books:* 247,720 (physical), 319,081 (digital/electronic); *Serial titles:* 142 (physical), 73,114 (digital/electronic); *Databases:* 92. Weekly public service hours: 102; students can reserve study rooms.

STUDENT LIFE
Housing options: on-campus residence required through sophomore year; coed, women-only. Campus housing is university owned. Freshman campus housing is guaranteed.

Activities and organizations: drama/theater group, student-run newspaper, radio and television station, choral group, Environmental Outing Club, Social Activities Council, Student Government, Chock Full O Notes, The Equinox student newspaper, national fraternities, national sororities.

Athletics Member NCAA. All Division III. *Intercollegiate sports:* baseball M, basketball M/W, cheerleading W, cross-country running M/W, field hockey W, ice hockey M(c)/W(c), lacrosse M/W, rugby M(c)/W(c), soccer M/W, softball W, swimming and diving M/W, track and field M/W, ultimate Frisbee M(c)/W(c), volleyball W. *Intramural sports:* badminton M/W, basketball M/W, bowling M/W, fencing M(c)/W(c), football M/W, soccer M/W, softball M/W, table tennis M/W, tennis M/W, volleyball M/W, weight lifting M(c)/W(c).

Campus security: 24-hour emergency response devices and patrols, late-night transport/escort service, controlled dormitory access, Emergency Notification System.

Student services: health clinic, personal/psychological counseling, women's center.

COSTS & FINANCIAL AID
Costs (2017–18) *Tuition:* state resident $11,188 full-time, $466 per credit hour part-time; nonresident $19,934 full-time, $514 per credit hour part-time. Part-time tuition and fees vary according to course load. *Required fees:* $2680 full-time, $106 per credit hour part-time. *Room and board:* $10,736. Room and board charges vary according to board plan and housing facility. *Payment plan:* installment. *Waivers:* senior citizens and employees or children of employees.

Financial Aid Of all full-time matriculated undergraduates who enrolled in 2016, 3,312 applied for aid, 2,620 were judged to have need, 364 had their need fully met. 1,061 Federal Work-Study jobs (averaging $2311). 608 state and other part-time jobs (averaging $1246). In 2016, 676 non-need-based awards were made. *Average percent of need met:* 65. *Average financial aid package:* $12,701. *Average need-based loan:* $4241. *Average need-based gift aid:* $7089. *Average non-need-based aid:* $4677. *Average indebtedness upon graduation:* $40,195. *Financial aid deadline:* 3/1.

APPLYING
Options: electronic application, deferred entrance.

Application fee: $50.

Required: essay or personal statement, high school transcript. *Recommended:* 1 letter of recommendation.

Application deadlines: 4/1 (freshmen), rolling (transfers).

Notification: continuous (freshmen), continuous (transfers).

CONTACT
Ms. Peggy Richmond, Director of Admissions, Keene State College, 229 Main Street, Keene, NH 03435-2604. *Phone:* 603-358-2273. *Toll-free phone:* 800-KSC-1909. *Fax:* 603-358-2767. *E-mail:* mrichmon@keene.edu.

New England College
Henniker, New Hampshire
http://www.nec.edu/
- **Independent** comprehensive, founded 1946
- **Small-town** 225-acre campus with easy access to Boston
- **Endowment** $11.9 million
- **Coed**
- **Minimally difficult** entrance level

FACULTY
Student/faculty ratio: 16:1.

ACADEMICS
Calendar: semesters for residential undergraduates; 7-week terms for online undergraduate and graduate programs. *Degrees:* associate, bachelor's, master's, and doctoral.

Library: Danforth Library. *Books:* 98,000 (physical), 152,000 (digital/electronic); *Serial titles:* 101 (physical), 100,000 (digital/electronic); *Databases:* 22. Weekly public service hours: 126; study areas open 24 hours, 5–7 days a week; students can reserve study rooms.

STUDENT LIFE
Housing options: on-campus residence required through junior year; coed. Campus housing is university owned. Freshman campus housing is guaranteed.

Activities and organizations: drama/theater group, student-run newspaper, radio station, Student Senate, Campus Activities Board, Role Playing Association, International Student Association, Political Science Club, national fraternities, national sororities.

Athletics Member NCAA. All Division III.

Campus security: 24-hour emergency response devices and patrols, student patrols, late-night transport/escort service, controlled dormitory access, emergency text system.

Student services: health clinic, personal/psychological counseling, women's center.

COSTS & FINANCIAL AID
Costs (2017–18) *Comprehensive fee:* $50,828 includes full-time tuition ($35,858), mandatory fees ($1096), and room and board ($13,874). Full-time tuition and fees vary according to class time, course load, location, program, and reciprocity agreements. Part-time tuition: $439 per credit hour. Part-time tuition and fees vary according to class time, course load, location, and program. *College room only:* $6274. Room and board charges vary according to board plan and housing facility.

Financial Aid Of all full-time matriculated undergraduates who enrolled in 2017, 1,585 applied for aid, 1,564 were judged to have need, 95 had their need fully met. In 2017, 114 non-need-based awards were made. *Average percent of need met:* 57. *Average financial aid package:* $23,463. *Average need-based loan:* $4616. *Average need-based gift aid:*

$17,182. *Average non-need-based aid:* $19,847. *Average indebtedness upon graduation:* $37,450.

APPLYING
Options: electronic application, deferred entrance.

Application fee: $35.

Required: essay or personal statement, high school transcript, 2 letters of recommendation. *Recommended:* interview.

CONTACT
Kay Reynolds, Associate Director of Undergraduate Admissions, New England College, 102 Bridge Street, Henniker, NH 03242. *Phone:* 603-428-2341. *Toll-free phone:* 800-521-7642. *Fax:* 603-428 3155. *E-mail:* klucier@nec.edu.

New Hampshire Institute of Art
Manchester, New Hampshire
http://www.nhia.edu/
- **Independent** comprehensive, founded 1898
- **Urban** campus with easy access to Boston
- **Endowment** $22.8 million
- **Coed** 342 undergraduate students, 92% full-time, 67% women, 33% men
- **Moderately difficult** entrance level, 58% of applicants were admitted

UNDERGRAD STUDENTS
316 full-time, 26 part-time. Students come from 14 states and territories; 48% are from out of state; 1% Black or African American, non-Hispanic/Latino; 9% Hispanic/Latino; 1% Asian, non-Hispanic/Latino; 0.6% Native Hawaiian or other Pacific Islander, non-Hispanic/Latino; 0.6% American Indian or Alaska Native, non-Hispanic/Latino; 2% Two or more races, non-Hispanic/Latino; 25% Race/ethnicity unknown; 4% transferred in; 52% live on campus.

Freshmen:
Admission: 356 applied, 206 admitted, 66 enrolled.

Retention: 73% of full-time freshmen returned.

FACULTY
Total: 73, 25% full-time.

Student/faculty ratio: 10:1.

ACADEMICS
Calendar: semesters. *Degrees:* certificates, bachelor's, and master's.

Special study options: accelerated degree program, adult/continuing education programs, advanced placement credit, cooperative education, independent study, internships, part-time degree program, services for LD students, study abroad, summer session for credit.

Computers: 100 computers/terminals and 32 ports are available on campus for general student use. Students can access the following: computer help desk, free student e-mail accounts, online (class) grades, online (class) registration, online (class) schedules. Campuswide network is available. 100% of college-owned or -operated housing units are wired for high-speed Internet access. Wireless service is available via entire campus.

Library: Teti Library. *Books:* 17,000 (physical), 144,463 (digital/electronic); *Serial titles:* 80 (physical), 7,800 (digital/electronic); *Databases:* 30. Weekly public service hours: 63.

STUDENT LIFE
Housing options: on-campus residence required through sophomore year; coed. Campus housing is university owned and leased by the school. Freshman applicants given priority for college housing.

Activities and organizations: student-run newspaper, radio station, Student Leadership Council, Comic/Arts Club, Neo-Victorian Club, Design Ink, Gay/Straight Alliance.

Campus security: late-night transport/escort service, controlled dormitory access.

Student services: health clinic, personal/psychological counseling.

COSTS
Costs (2018–19) *Comprehensive fee:* $39,740 includes full-time tuition ($25,590), mandatory fees ($2690), and room and board ($11,460). Full-time tuition and fees vary according to degree level. Part-time tuition: $3285 per course. Part-time tuition and fees vary according to course load and degree level. *Required fees:* $95 per credit hour part-time, $100 per

term part-time. **Room and board:** Room and board charges vary according to board plan. **Payment plan:** installment. **Waivers:** employees or children of employees.

APPLYING

Standardized Tests *Required for some:* SAT or ACT (for admission).

Options: electronic application, early action, deferred entrance.

Application fee: $30.

Required: essay or personal statement, high school transcript, portfolio. **Recommended:** minimum 2.0 GPA, 2 letters of recommendation.

Application deadlines: rolling (freshmen), rolling (out-of-state freshmen), rolling (transfers), 12/15 (early action).

Notification: continuous (freshmen), continuous (out-of-state freshmen), continuous (transfers), 1/15 (early action).

CONTACT

Mr. Scott Ramon, Director of Student Recruitment, New Hampshire Institute of Art, 148 Concord Street, Manchester, NH 03104-4158. *Phone:* 603-836-2148. *Toll-free phone:* 866-241-4918. *E-mail:* admissions@ nhia.edu.

Northeast Catholic College

Warner, New Hampshire

http://www.magdalen.edu/

CONTACT

Admissions Director, Northeast Catholic College, 511 Kearsarge Mountain Road, Warner, NH 03278. *Phone:* 603-456-2656. *Toll-free phone:* 877-498-1723. *Fax:* 603-456-2660. *E-mail:* admissions@ magdalen.edu.

Plymouth State University

Plymouth, New Hampshire

http://www.plymouth.edu/

- **State-supported** comprehensive, founded 1871, part of University System of New Hampshire
- **Small-town** 170-acre campus with easy access to Manchester
- **Endowment** $19.3 million
- **Coed**
- **Moderately difficult** entrance level

FACULTY

Student/faculty ratio: 17:1.

ACADEMICS

Calendar: semesters. *Degrees:* certificates, bachelor's, master's, doctoral, post-master's, and postbachelor's certificates.

Library: Lamson Learning Commons. *Books:* 344,605 (physical), 155,000 (digital/electronic); *Serial titles:* 790 (physical), 1,500 (digital/electronic); *Databases:* 87. Weekly public service hours: 94.

STUDENT LIFE

Housing options: on-campus residence required through sophomore year; coed, cooperative, special housing for students with disabilities. Campus housing is university owned. Freshman campus housing is guaranteed.

Activities and organizations: drama/theater group, student-run newspaper, radio station, choral group, Pre Medical Professional Society, Student Nurse Association, Marketing Association of Plymouth State, Gaming Club, Programing Activities in a Campus Environment, national sororities.

Athletics Member NCAA. All Division III.

Campus security: 24-hour emergency response devices and patrols, late-night transport/escort service, controlled dormitory access, shuttle bus service, crime prevention programs, self-defense education.

Student services: health clinic, personal/psychological counseling, women's center.

FINANCIAL AID

Financial Aid Of all full-time matriculated undergraduates who enrolled in 2016, 3,355 applied for aid, 2,743 were judged to have need, 471 had their need fully met. 1,858 Federal Work-Study jobs (averaging $2273). In 2016, 783 non-need-based awards were made. *Average percent of need met:* 58. *Average financial aid package:* $11,652. *Average need-based*

loan: $3971. *Average need-based gift aid:* $6988. *Average non-need-based aid:* $4352. *Average indebtedness upon graduation:* $39,319.

APPLYING

Options: electronic application, deferred entrance.

Application fee: $50.

Required: essay or personal statement, 1 letter of recommendation. *Required for some:* high school transcript, interview. *Recommended:* minimum 2.5 GPA.

CONTACT

Mr. Tony Trodella, Director of Undergraduate Recruitment, Plymouth State University, Plymouth, NH 03264-1595. *Phone:* 603-535-2237. *Toll-free phone:* 800-842-6900. *Fax:* 603-535-2714. *E-mail:* admissions@ plymouth.edu.

Rivier University

Nashua, New Hampshire

http://www.rivier.edu/

- **Independent Roman Catholic** comprehensive, founded 1933
- **Suburban** 68-acre campus with easy access to Boston
- **Coed** 1,349 undergraduate students, 64% full-time, 81% women, 19% men
- **Moderately difficult** entrance level, 68% of applicants were admitted

UNDERGRAD STUDENTS

863 full-time, 486 part-time. Students come from 27 states and territories; 17 other countries; 45% are from out of state; 4% Black or African American, non-Hispanic/Latino; 4% Hispanic/Latino; 3% Asian, non-Hispanic/Latino; 0.2% Native Hawaiian or other Pacific Islander, non-Hispanic/Latino; 0.4% American Indian or Alaska Native, non-Hispanic/Latino; 4% Two or more races, non-Hispanic/Latino; 9% Race/ethnicity unknown; 9% transferred in; 48% live on campus.

Freshmen:

Admission: 2,271 applied, 1,546 admitted, 252 enrolled. *Test scores:* SAT evidence-based reading and writing scores over 500: 69%; SAT math scores over 500: 66%; ACT scores over 18: 90%; SAT evidence-based reading and writing scores over 600: 12%; SAT math scores over 600: 11%; ACT scores over 24: 25%; SAT evidence-based reading and writing scores over 700: 1%; SAT math scores over 700: 1%.

Retention: 73% of full-time freshmen returned.

FACULTY

Total: 209, 29% full-time, 34% with terminal degrees.

Student/faculty ratio: 13:1.

ACADEMICS

Calendar: semesters. *Degrees:* certificates, associate, bachelor's, master's, doctoral, post-master's, and postbachelor's certificates.

Special study options: advanced placement credit, distance learning, double majors, independent study, internships, off-campus study, part-time degree program, services for LD students, study abroad, summer session for credit. *ROTC:* Army (c), Air Force (c).

Computers: 175 computers/terminals and 200 ports are available on campus for general student use. Students can access the following: campus intranet, computer help desk, free student e-mail accounts, online (class) grades, online (class) registration, online (class) schedules. Campuswide network is available. 100% of college-owned or -operated housing units are wired for high-speed Internet access. Wireless service is available via entire campus.

Library: Regina Library plus 1 other.

STUDENT LIFE

Housing options: coed. Campus housing is university owned. Freshman campus housing is guaranteed.

Activities and organizations: drama/theater group, choral group, Student Government Association, Campus Activities Board, Campus Ministry, Student Nurses Association, Theater Club.

Athletics Member NCAA. All Division III. *Intercollegiate sports:* baseball M, basketball M/W, cross-country running M/W, field hockey W, lacrosse M/W, soccer M/W, softball W, volleyball M/W. *Intramural sports:* basketball M/W, volleyball M/W.

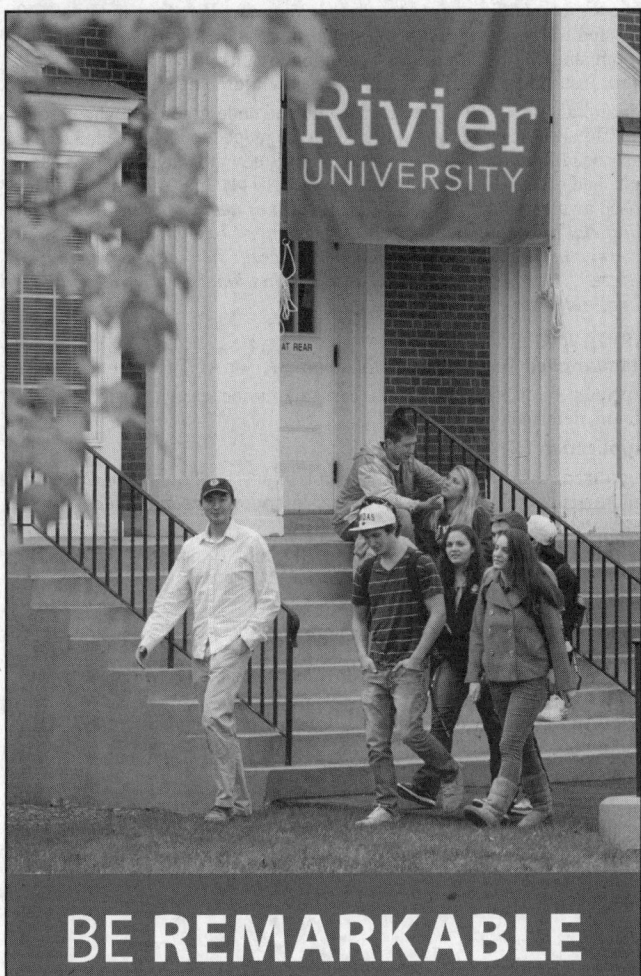

BE **REMARKABLE**

Top reasons why you should make **Rivier University** *your* university:

- Innovative Employment Promise Program: Find out more at **www.rivier.edu/employmentpromise**

- Distinctive Journeys of Transformation Core Curriculum

- Global Scholars Honors Program

- Internship and study abroad options

- Championship athletic teams

- Competitive merit scholarships and grants

Associate, Bachelor's, Master's and Doctoral degree programs

420 S. Main Street, Nashua, N.H. • www.rivier.edu
(603) 897-8507 • admissions@rivier.edu

Campus security: 24-hour emergency response devices and patrols, late-night transport/escort service, controlled dormitory access.

Student services: health clinic, personal/psychological counseling.

FINANCIAL AID

Financial Aid Of all full-time matriculated undergraduates who enrolled in 2010, 888 applied for aid, 822 were judged to have need, 70 had their need fully met. In 2010, 105 non-need-based awards were made. *Average percent of need met:* 59. *Average financial aid package:* $14,850. *Average need-based loan:* $4378. *Average need-based gift aid:* $10,806. *Average non-need-based aid:* $5066. *Average indebtedness upon graduation:* $43,189.

APPLYING

Standardized Tests *Required for some:* SAT or ACT (for admission), nursing exam. *Recommended:* SAT or ACT (for admission).

Options: electronic application, deferred entrance.

Application fee: $25.

Required: essay or personal statement, high school transcript, 1 letter of recommendation. *Recommended:* minimum 2.3 GPA, interview.

Application deadlines: rolling (freshmen), rolling (out-of-state freshmen), rolling (transfers).

Notification: continuous (freshmen), continuous (out-of-state freshmen), continuous (transfers).

CONTACT

Valerie Leclair, Executive Director of Undergraduate & Graduate Admissions, Rivier University, 420 South Main Street, Nashua, NH 03060. *Phone:* 603-897-8515. *Toll-free phone:* 800-44RIVIER. *Fax:* 603-891-1799. *E-mail:* rivadmit@rivier.edu.

See this page for display ad and page 1400 for the College Close-Up.

★ Saint Anselm College
Manchester, New Hampshire
http://www.anselm.edu/

- **Independent Roman Catholic** 4-year, founded 1889
- **Suburban** 380-acre campus with easy access to Boston
- **Endowment** $134.6 million
- **Coed** 1,964 undergraduate students, 98% full-time, 61% women, 39% men
- **Moderately difficult** entrance level, 76% of applicants were admitted

UNDERGRAD STUDENTS

1,926 full-time, 38 part-time. Students come from 35 states and territories; 7 other countries; 78% are from out of state; 2% Black or African American, non-Hispanic/Latino; 4% Hispanic/Latino; 1% Asian, non-Hispanic/Latino; 0.1% Native Hawaiian or other Pacific Islander, non-Hispanic/Latino; 0.1% American Indian or Alaska Native, non-Hispanic/Latino; 2% Two or more races, non-Hispanic/Latino; 3% Race/ethnicity unknown; 0.6% international; 0.6% transferred in; 92% live on campus.

Freshmen:

Admission: 3,892 applied, 2,960 admitted, 546 enrolled. *Average high school GPA:* 3.3. *Test scores:* SAT evidence-based reading and writing scores over 500: 99%; SAT math scores over 500: 98%; ACT scores over 18: 100%; SAT evidence-based reading and writing scores over 600: 64%; SAT math scores over 600: 60%; ACT scores over 24: 78%; SAT evidence-based reading and writing scores over 700: 7%; SAT math scores over 700: 5%; ACT scores over 30: 14%.

Retention: 88% of full-time freshmen returned.

FACULTY

Total: 225, 68% full-time, 74% with terminal degrees.

Student/faculty ratio: 11:1.

ACADEMICS

Calendar: semesters. *Degree:* bachelor's.

Special study options: accelerated degree program, advanced placement credit, double majors, honors programs, independent study, internships, off-campus study, part-time degree program, services for LD students, study abroad, summer session for credit. *ROTC:* Army (c).

Unusual degree programs: 3-2 engineering with University of Massachusetts Lowell, The Catholic University of America, University of

Notre Dame, Manhattan College; pharmacy, optometry, physical therapy, physician assistant with Massachusetts College of Pharmacy and Health Sciences.

Computers: 400 computers/terminals are available on campus for general student use. Students can access the following: campus intranet, computer help desk, free student e-mail accounts, online (class) registration, online (class) schedules. Campuswide network is available. 100% of college-owned or -operated housing units are wired for high-speed Internet access. Wireless service is available via entire campus.

Library: Geisel Library plus 2 others. Students can reserve study rooms.

STUDENT LIFE

Housing options: coed, men-only, women-only, special housing for students with disabilities. Campus housing is university owned. Freshman campus housing is guaranteed.

Activities and organizations: drama/theater group, student-run newspaper, choral group, Meelia Center for Community Engagement, Anselmian Abbey Players, Club Sports, Service and Solidarity Mission Trips, Saint Anselm College Crier (School Newspaper).

Athletics Member NCAA. All Division II. *Intercollegiate sports:* baseball M, basketball M/W, cross-country running M/W, field hockey W, football M, golf M, ice hockey M/W, lacrosse M/W, skiing (downhill) M/W, soccer M/W, softball W, tennis M/W, volleyball W. *Intramural sports:* basketball M/W, football M/W, ice hockey M/W, racquetball M(c)/W(c), soccer M/W, softball M/W, table tennis M(c)/W(c), tennis M/W, track and field M(c)/W(c), ultimate Frisbee M/W, volleyball M/W.

Campus security: 24-hour emergency response devices and patrols, student patrols, late-night transport/escort service, controlled dormitory access.

Student services: health clinic, personal/psychological counseling.

COSTS & FINANCIAL AID

Costs (2018–19) *Comprehensive fee:* $55,700 includes full-time tuition ($39,900), mandatory fees ($1300), and room and board ($14,500). Full-time tuition and fees vary according to program. Part-time tuition: $1000 per credit. *Required fees:* $600 per term part-time. *Room and board:* Room and board charges vary according to housing facility. *Payment plan:* installment. *Waivers:* employees or children of employees.

Financial Aid Of all full-time matriculated undergraduates who enrolled in 2017, 1,597 applied for aid, 1,403 were judged to have need, 328 had their need fully met. 1,084 Federal Work-Study jobs (averaging $1482). 9 state and other part-time jobs (averaging $1944). In 2017, 451 non-need-based awards were made. *Average percent of need met:* 79. *Average financial aid package:* $28,108. *Average need-based loan:* $4152. *Average need-based gift aid:* $23,682. *Average non-need-based aid:* $15,587. *Average indebtedness upon graduation:* $36,567. *Financial aid deadline:* 2/15.

APPLYING

Standardized Tests *Required for some:* SAT or ACT (for admission).

Options: electronic application, early admission, early decision, early action, deferred entrance.

Application fee: $50.

Required: essay or personal statement, high school transcript, 2 letters of recommendation. *Required for some:* interview. *Recommended:* interview.

Application deadlines: 2/1 (freshmen), rolling (transfers), 11/15 (early action).

Early decision deadline: 12/1.

Notification: 3/15 (freshmen), continuous (transfers), 12/31 (early decision), 1/15 (early action).

CONTACT

Saint Anselm College, 100 Saint Anselm Drive, Manchester, NH 03102. *Phone:* 603-641-7500. *Toll-free phone:* 888-4ANSELM. *Fax:* 603-641-7550. *E-mail:* admission@anselm.edu.

See below for display ad and page 1406 for the College Close-Up.

Southern New Hampshire University

Manchester, New Hampshire
http://www.snhu.edu/

- **Independent** university, founded 1932
- **Suburban** 317-acre campus with easy access to Boston
- **Coed**
- **Moderately difficult** entrance level

FACULTY
Student/faculty ratio: 13:1.

ACADEMICS
Calendar: semesters. *Degrees:* certificates, associate, bachelor's, master's, doctoral, post-master's, and postbachelor's certificates.
Library: Shapiro Library and Learning Commons. Students can reserve study rooms.

STUDENT LIFE
Housing options: coed, special housing for students with disabilities. Campus housing is university owned.

Activities and organizations: drama/theater group, student-run newspaper, radio and television station, choral group, Coordinators of Activities and Programming Events (CAPE), Psychology Club, Economics/Finance Association, Gaming Club, Outing Club, national fraternities, national sororities.

Athletics Member NCAA. All Division II.

Campus security: 24-hour emergency response devices and patrols, student patrols, late-night transport/escort service, controlled dormitory access.

Student services: health clinic, women's center.

COSTS & FINANCIAL AID
Costs (2017–18) *Comprehensive fee:* $43,414 includes full-time tuition ($30,756), mandatory fees ($380), and room and board ($12,278). Full-time tuition and fees vary according to course load. Part-time tuition: $1282 per credit hour. *College room only:* $8799. Room and board charges vary according to board plan and housing facility. *Payment plans:* installment, deferred payment.

Financial Aid Of all full-time matriculated undergraduates who enrolled in 2016, 2,322 applied for aid, 2,106 were judged to have need, 325 had their need fully met. In 2016, 588 non-need-based awards were made. *Average percent of need met:* 63. *Average financial aid package:* $22,185. *Average need-based loan:* $4138. *Average need-based gift aid:* $6130. *Average non-need-based aid:* $12,451. *Average indebtedness upon graduation:* $40,327. *Financial aid deadline:* 6/30.

APPLYING
Options: electronic application, early action, deferred entrance.

Application fee: $40.

Required: essay or personal statement, high school transcript, minimum 2.0 GPA, 1 letter of recommendation. *Recommended:* interview.

CONTACT
Mr. Tim Whittum, Director of Freshman Admission, Southern New Hampshire University, 2500 North River Road, Manchester, NH 03106-1045. *Phone:* 603-645-9611. *Toll-free phone:* 888-327-7648. *Fax:* 603-645-9693. *E-mail:* t.whittum@snhu.edu.

See below for display ad and page 1432 for the College Close-Up.

Thomas More College of Liberal Arts

Merrimack, New Hampshire
http://www.thomasmorecollege.edu/

- **Independent** 4-year, founded 1978, affiliated with Roman Catholic Church
- **Small-town** 14-acre campus with easy access to Boston
- **Endowment** $551,325
- **Coed** 90 undergraduate students, 100% full-time, 53% women, 47% men
- **Moderately difficult** entrance level, 41% of applicants were admitted

UNDERGRAD STUDENTS
90 full-time. Students come from 23 states and territories; 1 other country; 89% are from out of state; 1% Black or African American, non-Hispanic/Latino; 4% Hispanic/Latino; 1% American Indian or Alaska

Native, non-Hispanic/Latino; 2% Race/ethnicity unknown; 2% international; 8% transferred in; 98% live on campus.

Freshmen:
Admission: 32 applied, 13 admitted, 13 enrolled.
Retention: 100% of full-time freshmen returned.

FACULTY
Student/faculty ratio: 9:1.

ACADEMICS
Calendar: semesters. *Degree:* bachelor's.

Special study options: independent study, study abroad.

Computers: 4 computers/terminals are available on campus for general student use. Students can access the following: free student e-mail accounts, online (class) registration.

Library: Warren Memorial Library plus 1 other. *Books:* 44,075 (physical); *Serial titles:* 43,515 (physical).

STUDENT LIFE
Housing options: on-campus residence required through senior year; men-only, women-only. Campus housing is university owned. Freshman campus housing is guaranteed.

Activities and organizations: drama/theater group, choral group.

Campus security: 24-hour emergency response devices, student patrols, late-night transport/escort service, on-site staff member.

COSTS & FINANCIAL AID
Costs (2018–19) *Comprehensive fee:* $31,300 includes full-time tuition ($21,600) and room and board ($9700). Full-time tuition and fees vary according to course load, program, and reciprocity agreements. Part-time tuition: $900 per credit hour. Part-time tuition and fees vary according to course load, program, and reciprocity agreements. *Room and board:* Room and board charges vary according to board plan. *Payment plan:* installment. *Waivers:* employees or children of employees.

Financial Aid Of all full-time matriculated undergraduates who enrolled in 2016, 81 applied for aid, 80 were judged to have need, 17 had their need fully met. In 2016, 33 non-need-based awards were made. *Average percent of need met:* 75. *Average financial aid package:* $18,718. *Average need-based loan:* $4490. *Average need-based gift aid:* $16,730. *Average non-need-based aid:* $6643. *Average indebtedness upon graduation:* $26,828.

APPLYING
Standardized Tests *Recommended:* SAT or ACT (for admission).

Options: electronic application.

Required: essay or personal statement, high school transcript, 2 letters of recommendation. *Required for some:* interview.

Application deadlines: rolling (freshmen), rolling (transfers).

Notification: continuous (freshmen), continuous (out-of-state freshmen), continuous (transfers).

CONTACT
Mr. Jonathan Rensch, Director of Admissions, Thomas More College of Liberal Arts, 6 Manchester Street, Merrimack, NH 03054-4818. *Phone:* 603-8808308 Ext. 14. *Toll-free phone:* 800-880-8308. *Fax:* 603-5460034. *E-mail:* jrensch@thomasmorecollege.edu.

University of New Hampshire
Durham, New Hampshire
http://www.unh.edu/

- **State-supported** university, founded 1866, part of University System of New Hampshire
- **Small-town** 2600-acre campus with easy access to Boston
- **Endowment** $365.4 million
- **Coed** 12,967 undergraduate students, 98% full-time, 55% women, 45% men
- **Moderately difficult** entrance level, 77% of applicants were admitted

UNDERGRAD STUDENTS
12,646 full-time, 321 part-time. Students come from 45 states and territories; 41 other countries; 53% are from out of state; 1% Black or African American, non-Hispanic/Latino; 3% Hispanic/Latino; 3% Asian, non-Hispanic/Latino; 0.2% American Indian or Alaska Native, non-

Hispanic/Latino; 2% Two or more races, non-Hispanic/Latino; 5% Race/ethnicity unknown; 4% international; 4% transferred in; 54% live on campus.

Freshmen:
Admission: 19,966 applied, 15,275 admitted, 3,018 enrolled. *Average high school GPA:* 3.5. *Test scores:* SAT evidence-based reading and writing scores over 500: 93%; SAT math scores over 500: 90%; ACT scores over 18: 99%; SAT evidence-based reading and writing scores over 600: 45%; SAT math scores over 600: 41%; ACT scores over 24: 67%; SAT evidence-based reading and writing scores over 700: 5%; SAT math scores over 700: 7%; ACT scores over 30: 14%.
Retention: 86% of full-time freshmen returned.

FACULTY
Total: 1,059, 62% full-time, 67% with terminal degrees.
Student/faculty ratio: 18:1.

ACADEMICS
Calendar: semesters. *Degrees:* associate, bachelor's, master's, doctoral, post-master's, and postbachelor's certificates.

Special study options: accelerated degree program, advanced placement credit, distance learning, double majors, English as a second language, honors programs, independent study, internships, off-campus study, part-time degree program, services for LD students, student-designed majors, study abroad, summer session for credit. *ROTC:* Army (b), Air Force (b).

Unusual degree programs: 3-2 business administration; social work; accounting, biochemistry, occupational therapy, education, kinesiology.

Computers: 320 computers/terminals and 7,500 ports are available on campus for general student use. Students can access the following: campus intranet, computer help desk, free student e-mail accounts, online (class) grades, online (class) registration, online (class) schedules. Campuswide network is available. 100% of college-owned or -operated housing units are wired for high-speed Internet access. Wireless service is available via entire campus.

Library: Dimond Library plus 4 others. *Books:* 1.1 million (physical), 889,664 (digital/electronic); *Serial titles:* 749 (physical), 90,600 (digital/electronic); *Databases:* 456. Weekly public service hours: 117; students can reserve study rooms.

STUDENT LIFE
Housing options: coed, special housing for students with disabilities. Campus housing is university owned. Freshman campus housing is guaranteed.

Activities and organizations: drama/theater group, student-run newspaper, radio station, choral group, marching band, Campus Activity Board, The Outing Club, Resident Hall Association, Alpha Phi Omega, Memorial Union Student Organization, national fraternities, national sororities.

Athletics Member NCAA. All Division I except football (Division I-AA). *Intercollegiate sports:* archery M(c)/W(c), baseball M(c), basketball M(s)/W(s), crew M(c)/W(c), cross-country running M(s)/W(s), fencing M(c)/W(c), field hockey W(s), golf M(c)/W(c), gymnastics W(s), ice hockey M(s)/W(s), lacrosse M(c)/W(s), riflery M(c)/W(c), rock climbing M(c)/W(c), rugby M(c)/W(c), sailing M(c)/W(c), skiing (cross-country) M(s)/W(s), skiing (downhill) M(s)/W(s), soccer M(s)/W(s), softball W(c), swimming and diving W(s), tennis M(c)/W(c), track and field M(s)/W(s), ultimate Frisbee M(c)/W(c), volleyball M(c)/W(s), wrestling M(c)/W(c). *Intramural sports:* basketball M/W, football M/W, ice hockey M/W, sand volleyball M/W, soccer M/W, softball M/W, table tennis M/W, tennis M/W, ultimate Frisbee M/W, volleyball M/W.

Campus security: 24-hour emergency response devices and patrols, student patrols, late-night transport/escort service, controlled dormitory access, lighted pathways and sidewalks.

Student services: health clinic, personal/psychological counseling, women's center.

COSTS & FINANCIAL AID
Costs (2018–19) *Tuition:* state resident $15,140 full-time; nonresident $30,520 full-time. Full-time tuition and fees vary according to program. Part-time tuition and fees vary according to course load and program. *Required fees:* $3359 full-time. *Room and board:* $11,588; room only: $7220. Room and board charges vary according to board plan and housing facility. *Payment plan:* installment. *Waivers:* employees or children of employees.

Financial Aid Of all full-time matriculated undergraduates who enrolled in 2016, 9,820 applied for aid, 8,084 were judged to have need, 1,243 had their need fully met. 5,723 Federal Work-Study jobs (averaging $2477). 4,114 state and other part-time jobs (averaging $1629). In 2016, 1973 non-need-based awards were made. *Average percent of need met:* 75. *Average financial aid package:* $23,953. *Average need-based loan:* $3295. *Average need-based gift aid:* $6124. *Average non-need-based aid:* $6651. *Average indebtedness upon graduation:* $33,013.

APPLYING
Standardized Tests *Required:* SAT or ACT (for admission).
Options: electronic application, early action, deferred entrance.
Application fee: $50.
Required: high school transcript, 1 letter of recommendation, Common Application, audition for some majors in music and theater, portfolio for art studio majors. *Recommended:* minimum 3.0 GPA.
Application deadlines: 2/1 (freshmen), 4/1 (transfers), 11/15 (early action).
Notification: continuous until 12/1 (freshmen), continuous until 4/15 (transfers), 12/1 (early action).

CONTACT
Admissions Office, University of New Hampshire, 3 Garrison Avenue, Durham, NH 03824. *Phone:* 603-862-1360. *Fax:* 603-862-0077. *E-mail:* admissions@unh.edu.

University of New Hampshire at Manchester

Manchester, New Hampshire
http://manchester.unh.edu/

- **State-supported** comprehensive, founded 1967, part of University of New Hampshire
- **Urban** campus with easy access to Boston
- **Coed**
- **Moderately difficult** entrance level

FACULTY
Student/faculty ratio: 11:1.

ACADEMICS
Calendar: semesters. *Degrees:* associate, bachelor's, and master's.
Library: UNH Manchester Library plus 1 other. *Books:* 30,000 (physical). Students can reserve study rooms.

STUDENT LIFE
Housing options: college housing not available.
Activities and organizations: student-run newspaper, choral group, Milling Around (A Cappella Group), Be Involved (Community Service), Common Ground (LGBT+), Our World (Environmental), Veterans and Allies Club.
Campus security: 24-hour emergency response devices, late-night transport/escort service.

COSTS & FINANCIAL AID
Costs (2017–18) *Tuition:* state resident $14,430 full-time, $437 per credit hour part-time; nonresident $28,990 full-time, $481 per credit hour part-time. Full-time tuition and fees vary according to course load and program. Part-time tuition and fees vary according to course load and program. *Required fees:* $430 full-time. *Room and board:* Room and board charges vary according to housing facility.
Financial Aid Of all full-time matriculated undergraduates who enrolled in 2016, 570 applied for aid, 470 were judged to have need, 46 had their need fully met. 206 Federal Work-Study jobs (averaging $2402). In 2016, 46 non-need-based awards were made. *Average percent of need met:* 60. *Average financial aid package:* $13,943. *Average need-based loan:* $3852. *Average need-based gift aid:* $1970. *Average non-need-based aid:* $2157. *Average indebtedness upon graduation:* $26,618.

APPLYING
Standardized Tests *Required:* SAT or ACT (for admission).
Options: electronic application, deferred entrance.

Application fee: $65.
Required: essay or personal statement, high school transcript, 1 letter of recommendation. *Recommended:* interview.

CONTACT
Erika Couture, Senior Associate Director of Admission, University of New Hampshire at Manchester, 88 Commerical Street, Manchester, NH 03101. *Phone:* 603-641-4150. *E-mail:* erika.couture@unh.edu.

NEW JERSEY

Bais Medrash Toras Chesed

Lakewood, New Jersey
http://www.bmtc.edu/

CONTACT
Bais Medrash Toras Chesed, 910 Monmouth Avenue, Lakewood, NJ 08701.

Berkeley College–Woodland Park Campus

Woodland Park, New Jersey
http://www.berkeleycollege.edu/

- **Proprietary** comprehensive, founded 1931
- **Suburban** 25-acre campus with easy access to New York City
- **Coed**
- **Minimally difficult** entrance level

FACULTY
Student/faculty ratio: 14:1.

ACADEMICS
Calendar: semesters. *Degrees:* certificates, associate, bachelor's, and master's.
Library: Walter A. Brower Library. *Books:* 150,121 (digital/electronic); *Serial titles:* 42,150 (digital/electronic); *Databases:* 81. Students can reserve study rooms.

STUDENT LIFE
Activities and organizations: student-run newspaper.
Athletics Member USCAA.
Campus security: 24-hour emergency response devices and patrols.
Student services: personal/psychological counseling.

COSTS
Costs (2017–18) *One-time required fee:* $100. *Tuition:* $23,600 full-time, $825 per credit hour part-time. Full-time tuition and fees vary according to course load. Part-time tuition and fees vary according to course load. No tuition increase for student's term of enrollment. *Required fees:* $1700 full-time, $425 per term part-time.

APPLYING
Options: electronic application, deferred entrance.
Application fee: $50.
Required: high school transcript. *Recommended:* interview.

CONTACT
Carol J Covino, Associate Vice President, High School Admissions, Berkeley College–Woodland Park Campus, 44 Rifle Camp Road, Woodland Park, NJ 07424. *Phone:* 973-278-5400. *Toll-free phone:* 800-446-5400. *E-mail:* info@berkeleycollege.edu.

Beth Medrash Govoha

Lakewood, New Jersey

CONTACT
Beth Medrash Govoha, 617 Sixth Street, Lakewood, NJ 08701-2797. *Phone:* 732-367-1060 Ext. 4224.

Bloomfield College

Bloomfield, New Jersey

http://www.bloomfield.edu/

- **Independent** comprehensive, founded 1868, affiliated with Presbyterian Church (U.S.A.)
- **Suburban** 12-acre campus with easy access to New York City
- **Endowment** $12.6 million
- **Coed**
- **Moderately difficult** entrance level

FACULTY

Student/faculty ratio: 15:1.

ACADEMICS

Calendar: semesters. *Degrees:* certificates, bachelor's, master's, and postbachelor's certificates.
Library: Bloomfield College Library plus 1 other. *Books:* 63,000 (physical), 127,000 (digital/electronic); *Serial titles:* 45 (physical); *Databases:* 50. Weekly public service hours: 92.

STUDENT LIFE

Housing options: coed. Campus housing is university owned.

Activities and organizations: drama/theater group, student-run radio and television station, First Ladies of Bloomfield, Green Hearts Environmental Club, Christian Fellowship, Team Infinite, Male Empowerment Network, national fraternities, national sororities.

Athletics Member NCAA. All Division II.

Campus security: 24-hour emergency response devices and patrols, late-night transport/escort service, controlled dormitory access, security cameras in high-traffic areas, controlled access to dormitories.

Student services: health clinic, personal/psychological counseling.

COSTS & FINANCIAL AID

Costs (2017–18) *Comprehensive fee:* $41,000 includes full-time tuition ($29,300) and room and board ($11,700). Full-time tuition and fees vary according to degree level. Part-time tuition: $3670 per course. Part-time tuition and fees vary according to course load and degree level. *College room only:* $5850. Room and board charges vary according to housing facility. *Payment plans:* installment, deferred payment.

Financial Aid Of all full-time matriculated undergraduates who enrolled in 2016, 1,767 applied for aid, 1,645 were judged to have need, 249 had their need fully met. 179 Federal Work-Study jobs (averaging $2169). In 2016, 81 non-need-based awards were made. *Average percent of need met:* 65. *Average financial aid package:* $27,426. *Average need-based loan:* $3896. *Average need-based gift aid:* $16,703. *Average non-need-based aid:* $14,208. *Financial aid deadline:* 4/15.

APPLYING

Standardized Tests *Required:* SAT or ACT (for admission).

Options: electronic application, early action, deferred entrance.

Application fee: $40.

Required: essay or personal statement, high school transcript, minimum 2.5 GPA, 2 letters of recommendation, graded essay/term paper or personal essay. *Recommended:* interview.

CONTACT

Ms. Nicole Cibelli, Director of Admissions, Bloomfield College, Office of Enrollment Management and Admission, Bloomfield, NJ 07003-9981. *Phone:* 973-748-9000 Ext. 1390. *Toll-free phone:* 800-848-4555 Ext. 230. *Fax:* 973-748-0916. *E-mail:* nicole_cibelli@bloomfield.edu.

Caldwell University

Caldwell, New Jersey

http://www.caldwell.edu/

- **Independent Roman Catholic** comprehensive, founded 1939
- **Suburban** 70-acre campus with easy access to New York City
- **Coed** 1,603 undergraduate students, 90% full-time, 68% women, 32% men
- **Moderately difficult** entrance level, 64% of applicants were admitted

UNDERGRAD STUDENTS

1,440 full-time, 163 part-time. Students come from 22 states and territories; 42 other countries; 8% are from out of state; 13% Black or African American, non-Hispanic/Latino; 23% Hispanic/Latino; 3% Asian, non-Hispanic/Latino; 0.1% Native Hawaiian or other Pacific Islander, non-Hispanic/Latino; 0.1% American Indian or Alaska Native, non-Hispanic/Latino; 0.9% Two or more races, non-Hispanic/Latino; 13% Race/ethnicity unknown; 12% international; 2% transferred in; 40% live on campus.

Freshmen:

Admission: 4,004 applied, 2,552 admitted, 361 enrolled. *Average high school GPA:* 3.3. *Test scores:* SAT evidence-based reading and writing scores over 500: 62%; SAT math scores over 500: 62%; ACT scores over 18: 71%; SAT evidence-based reading and writing scores over 600: 17%; SAT math scores over 600: 20%; ACT scores over 24: 19%; SAT evidence-based reading and writing scores over 700: 1%; SAT math scores over 700: 10%; ACT scores over 30: 7%.

Retention: 84% of full-time freshmen returned.

FACULTY

Total: 293, 29% full-time.

Student/faculty ratio: 12:1.

ACADEMICS

Calendar: semesters. *Degrees:* bachelor's, master's, doctoral, post-master's, and postbachelor's certificates.

Special study options: academic remediation for entering students, accelerated degree program, adult/continuing education programs, advanced placement credit, distance learning, double majors, honors programs, independent study, internships, part-time degree program, services for LD students, student-designed majors, study abroad, summer session for credit. *ROTC:* Army (c).

Unusual degree programs: 3-2 business administration; social work with Rutgers University; biology or psychology/occupational therapy with Columbia University, biology/athletic training with Seton Hall University, psychology/counseling psychology, psychology/applied behavior analysis, education/curriculum and instruction.

Computers: 286 computers/terminals and 796 ports are available on campus for general student use. Students can access the following: campus intranet, computer help desk, free student e-mail accounts, online (class) grades, online (class) registration, online (class) schedules. Campuswide network is available. 100% of college-owned or -operated housing units are wired for high-speed Internet access. Wireless service is available via entire campus.

Library: Jennings Library plus 1 other. *Books:* 143,853 (physical), 151,660 (digital/electronic); *Serial titles:* 104 (physical), 419,719 (digital/electronic); *Databases:* 68. Students can reserve study rooms.

STUDENT LIFE

Housing options: coed. Campus housing is university owned. Freshman applicants given priority for college housing.

Activities and organizations: drama/theater group, student-run newspaper, television station, choral group, marching band, International Student Organization, Latino American Student Organization, Circle K, Anime Club, Dance Team, national fraternities, national sororities.

Athletics Member NCAA. All Division II. *Intercollegiate sports:* baseball M(s), basketball M(s)/W(s), bowling W(s), cross-country running M(s)/W(s), football M(c), lacrosse W(s), soccer M(s)/W(s), softball W(s), tennis W(s), track and field M(s)/W(s), volleyball W(s).

Campus security: 24-hour emergency response devices and patrols, late-night transport/escort service, controlled dormitory access.

Student services: health clinic, personal/psychological counseling.

COSTS & FINANCIAL AID

Costs (2018–19) *Comprehensive fee:* $48,015 includes full-time tuition ($32,990), mandatory fees ($1725), and room and board ($13,300). Full-time tuition and fees vary according to course load, location, and program. Part-time tuition: $715 per credit hour. Part-time tuition and fees vary according to course load, location, and program. *Required fees:* $230 per term part-time. *Room and board:* Room and board charges vary according to board plan and housing facility. *Payment plan:* installment. *Waivers:* children of alumni, adult students, senior citizens, and employees or children of employees.

Financial Aid Of all full-time matriculated undergraduates who enrolled in 2017, 1,148 applied for aid, 1,085 were judged to have need, 113 had their need fully met. 135 Federal Work-Study jobs (averaging $1500). 100

state and other part-time jobs (averaging $2300). In 2017, 306 non-need-based awards were made. *Average percent of need met:* 75. *Average financial aid package:* $27,760. *Average need-based loan:* $4011. *Average need-based gift aid:* $24,508. *Average non-need-based aid:* $19,777. *Average indebtedness upon graduation:* $25,114.

APPLYING

Standardized Tests *Required:* SAT or ACT (for admission).

Options: electronic application, early admission, early decision, deferred entrance.

Application fee: $50.

Required: essay or personal statement, high school transcript, 2 letters of recommendation. *Required for some:* interview. *Recommended:* minimum 3.0 GPA, interview, 16 units of college preparatory coursework.

Application deadlines: 4/1 (freshmen), rolling (transfers).

Notification: 4/15 (freshmen), continuous (transfers).

CONTACT

Mr. Stephen Quinn, Assistant Vice President, Enrollment Management, Caldwell University, 120 Bloomfield Avenue, Caldwell, NJ 07006. *Phone:* 973-618-3320. *Fax:* 973-618-3600. *E-mail:* squinn@ caldwell.edu.

Centenary University

Hackettstown, New Jersey

http://www.centenaryuniversity.edu/

- **Independent** comprehensive, founded 1867, affiliated with United Methodist Church
- **Suburban** 105-acre campus with easy access to New York City
- **Endowment** $10.7 million
- **Coed**
- **Moderately difficult** entrance level

ACADEMICS

Calendar: semesters. *Degrees:* certificates, associate, bachelor's, master's, doctoral, and postbachelor's certificates.
Library: Taylor Memorial Library. *Books:* 45,025 (physical), 114 (digital/electronic); *Serial titles:* 2,710 (physical), 1,896 (digital/electronic); *Databases:* 85. Weekly public service hours: 82.

STUDENT LIFE

Housing options: coed, women-only. Campus housing is university owned. Freshman applicants given priority for college housing.

Activities and organizations: drama/theater group, student-run newspaper, First Year Leaders, Student Government, ENACTUS, Honor Societies, Fraternities and Sororities, national fraternities, national sororities.

Athletics Member NCAA. All Division III.

Campus security: 24-hour emergency response devices and patrols, late-night transport/escort service, controlled dormitory access.

Student services: health clinic, personal/psychological counseling.

COSTS & FINANCIAL AID

Costs (2017–18) *Comprehensive fee:* $43,690 includes full-time tuition ($31,156), mandatory fees ($1424), and room and board ($11,110). Full-time tuition and fees vary according to program. Part-time tuition: $600 per credit hour. Part-time tuition and fees vary according to program. *Required fees:* $11 per credit hour part-time, $18 per term part-time. *Room and board:* Room and board charges vary according to board plan.

Financial Aid Of all full-time matriculated undergraduates who enrolled in 2010, 1,219 applied for aid, 1,094 were judged to have need, 121 had their need fully met. In 2010, 303 non-need-based awards were made. *Average percent of need met:* 72. *Average financial aid package:* $19,967. *Average need-based loan:* $5414. *Average need-based gift aid:* $15,457. *Average non-need-based aid:* $9157. *Average indebtedness upon graduation:* $25,019.

APPLYING

Standardized Tests *Required:* SAT or ACT (for admission).

Options: electronic application, deferred entrance.

Application fee: $30.

Required: essay or personal statement, high school transcript. *Required for some:* interview. *Recommended:* interview.

CONTACT

Jenna Yount, Director of Admissions, Centenary University, 400 Jefferson Street, Hackettstown, NJ 07840. *Phone:* 908-852-1400 Ext. 2082. *Toll-free phone:* 800-236-8679. *E-mail:* yountj@centenaryuniversity.edu.

Chamberlain College of Nursing

North Brunswick, New Jersey

http://www.chamberlain.edu/

- **Proprietary** 4-year
- **Coed**

FACULTY

Student/faculty ratio: 12:1.

ACADEMICS

Degree: bachelor's.

STUDENT LIFE

Housing options: college housing not available.

COSTS

Costs (2017–18) *Tuition:* $18,900 full-time. *Required fees:* $600 full-time.

APPLYING

Standardized Tests *Required:* SAT or ACT (for admission).

Options: deferred entrance.

Application fee: $95.

CONTACT

Chamberlain College of Nursing, 630 U.S. Highway 1, North Brunswick, NJ 08902. *Toll-free phone:* 877-751-5783.

The College of New Jersey

Ewing, New Jersey

http://www.tcnj.edu/

- **State-supported** comprehensive, founded 1855
- **Suburban** 255-acre campus with easy access to Philadelphia
- **Coed** 6,955 undergraduate students, 97% full-time, 58% women, 42% men
- **Very difficult** entrance level, 48% of applicants were admitted

UNDERGRAD STUDENTS

6,728 full-time, 227 part-time. Students come from 24 states and territories; 4 other countries; 6% are from out of state; 6% Black or African American, non-Hispanic/Latino; 13% Hispanic/Latino; 12% Asian, non-Hispanic/Latino; 0.2% Native Hawaiian or other Pacific Islander, non-Hispanic/Latino; 0.1% American Indian or Alaska Native, non-Hispanic/Latino; 0.5% Two or more races, non-Hispanic/Latino; 3% Race/ethnicity unknown; 0.3% international; 3% transferred in; 58% live on campus.

Freshmen:

Admission: 12,898 applied, 6,130 admitted, 1,542 enrolled. *Test scores:* SAT evidence-based reading and writing scores over 500: 98%; SAT math scores over 500: 98%; ACT scores over 18: 100%; SAT evidence-based reading and writing scores over 600: 70%; SAT math scores over 600: 67%; ACT scores over 24: 87%; SAT evidence-based reading and writing scores over 700: 14%; SAT math scores over 700: 17%; ACT scores over 30: 28%.

Retention: 94% of full-time freshmen returned.

FACULTY

Total: 858, 43% full-time, 52% with terminal degrees.

Student/faculty ratio: 13:1.

ACADEMICS

Calendar: semesters. *Degrees:* certificates, bachelor's, master's, post-master's, and postbachelor's certificates.

Special study options: academic remediation for entering students, accelerated degree program, advanced placement credit, double majors, English as a second language, honors programs, independent study, internships, off-campus study, part-time degree program, services for LD students, student-designed majors, study abroad, summer session for credit. **ROTC:** Army (c), Air Force (c).

COLLEGES AT-A-GLANCE

Unusual degree programs: 3-2 education of the deaf and hard of hearing, elementary education, special education and urban education.

Computers: 631 computers/terminals are available on campus for general student use. Students can access the following: campus intranet, computer help desk, free student e-mail accounts, online (class) grades, online (class) registration, online (class) schedules. Campuswide network is available. 100% of college-owned or -operated housing units are wired for high-speed Internet access. Wireless service is available via classrooms, computer labs, learning centers, libraries, student centers.

Library: The College of New Jersey Library. *Books:* 694,461 (physical), 6,455 (digital/electronic); *Serial titles:* 44,898 (physical), 8,859 (digital/electronic); *Databases:* 114. Weekly public service hours: 98; students can reserve study rooms.

STUDENT LIFE

Housing options: on-campus residence required for freshman year; coed, special housing for students with disabilities. Campus housing is university owned. Freshman campus housing is guaranteed.

Activities and organizations: drama/theater group, student-run newspaper, radio and television station, choral group, Student Government Association, College Union Board, Inter-Greek Council, The Signal, national fraternities, national sororities.

Athletics Member NCAA. All Division III. *Intercollegiate sports:* baseball M, basketball M/W, cross-country running M/W, field hockey W, football M, lacrosse W, soccer M/W, softball W, swimming and diving M/W, tennis M/W, track and field M/W, wrestling M. *Intramural sports:* baseball M(c), basketball M(c)/W, bowling M(c)/W(c), cheerleading M(c)/W(c), crew M(c)/W(c), fencing M(c)/W(c), field hockey M/W, football M/W, golf M(c)/W(c), ice hockey M(c), lacrosse M(c)/W(c), racquetball M/W, rugby M(c)/W(c), skiing (cross-country) M(c)/W(c), skiing (downhill) M(c)/W(c), soccer M(c)/W(c), softball M/W(c), swimming and diving M(c)/W(c), table tennis M(c)/W(c), tennis M(c)/W(c), ultimate Frisbee M(c)/W(c), volleyball M(c)/W(c), water polo M(c)/W(c).

Campus security: 24-hour emergency response devices and patrols, student patrols, late-night transport/escort service, controlled dormitory access.

Student services: health clinic, personal/psychological counseling, women's center, legal services.

COSTS & FINANCIAL AID

Costs (2017–18) *Tuition:* state resident $12,632 full-time, $448 per credit hour part-time; nonresident $24,061 full-time, $772 per credit hour part-time. Full-time tuition and fees vary according to course load. Part-time tuition and fees vary according to course load. *Required fees:* $3517 full-time, $134 per credit hour part-time. *Room and board:* $13,200; room only: $8696. Room and board charges vary according to board plan. *Payment plan:* installment. *Waivers:* senior citizens and employees or children of employees.

Financial Aid Of all full-time matriculated undergraduates who enrolled in 2016, 4,588 applied for aid, 3,318 were judged to have need, 344 had their need fully met. In 2016, 496 non-need-based awards were made. *Average percent of need met:* 43. *Average financial aid package:* $10,955. *Average need-based loan:* $4564. *Average need-based gift aid:* $11,951. *Average non-need-based aid:* $5018. *Average indebtedness upon graduation:* $35,798. *Financial aid deadline:* 10/1.

APPLYING

Standardized Tests *Required:* SAT or ACT (for admission).

Options: electronic application, early decision, deferred entrance.

Application fee: $75.

Required: essay or personal statement, high school transcript. *Required for some:* interview, art portfolio or music audition. *Recommended:* minimum 2.5 GPA, 3 letters of recommendation.

Application deadlines: 2/1 (freshmen), 2/15 (transfers).

Early decision deadline: 11/1 (for plan 1), 1/1 (for plan 2).

Notification: continuous until 4/1 (freshmen), continuous until 4/1 (transfers), 12/1 (early decision plan 1), 2/1 (early decision plan 2).

CONTACT

The College of New Jersey, 2000 Pennington Road, PO Box 7718, Ewing, NJ 08628.

See below for display ad and page 1264 for the College Close-Up.

THE COLLEGE OF NEW JERSEY

The **No.1** Public Institution in the Northern Region of the Country.

www.tcnj.edu

TCNJ
THE COLLEGE OF NEW JERSEY

College of Saint Elizabeth
Morristown, New Jersey
http://www.cse.edu/

- **Independent Roman Catholic** comprehensive, founded 1899
- **Suburban** 200-acre campus with easy access to New York City
- **Endowment** $19.3 million
- **Coed** 765 undergraduate students, 77% full-time, 79% women, 21% men
- 65% of applicants were admitted

UNDERGRAD STUDENTS
587 full-time, 178 part-time. Students come from 12 states and territories; 14 other countries; 6% are from out of state; 32% Black or African American, non-Hispanic/Latino; 24% Hispanic/Latino; 4% Asian, non-Hispanic/Latino; 0.3% Native Hawaiian or other Pacific Islander, non-Hispanic/Latino; 0.4% American Indian or Alaska Native, non-Hispanic/Latino; 2% Two or more races, non-Hispanic/Latino; 10% Race/ethnicity unknown; 3% international; 4% transferred in; 48% live on campus.

Freshmen:
Admission: 1,969 applied, 1,271 admitted, 164 enrolled. *Average high school GPA:* 2.6. *Test scores:* SAT evidence-based reading and writing scores over 500: 26%; SAT math scores over 500: 22%; SAT evidence-based reading and writing scores over 600: 3%; SAT math scores over 600: 2%; SAT evidence-based reading and writing scores over 700: 1%.
Retention: 68% of full-time freshmen returned.

FACULTY
Total: 177, 28% full-time.
Student/faculty ratio: 10:1.

ACADEMICS
Calendar: semesters. *Degrees:* certificates, bachelor's, master's, doctoral, and postbachelor's certificates (also offers coed adult undergraduate degree program and coed graduate programs).

Special study options: academic remediation for entering students, accelerated degree program, adult/continuing education programs, advanced placement credit, distance learning, double majors, English as a second language, external degree program, honors programs, independent study, internships, off-campus study, part-time degree program, services for LD students, student-designed majors, study abroad, summer session for credit.

Unusual degree programs: 3-2 business administration; religious studies/theology, criminal justice/justice administration and public service, foods and nutrition, psychology.

Computers: 127 computers/terminals and 668 ports are available on campus for general student use. Students can access the following: computer help desk, free student e-mail accounts, online (class) grades, online (class) registration, online (class) schedules, online course evaluations; online system for registering for student activities, clubs, and events. Campuswide network is available. 100% of college-owned or -operated housing units are wired for high-speed Internet access. Wireless service is available via entire campus.
Library: Mahoney Library plus 1 other. *Books:* 113,292 (physical), 1.1 million (digital/electronic); *Serial titles:* 240 (physical), 26,767 (digital/electronic); *Databases:* 122. Weekly public service hours: 75.

STUDENT LIFE
Housing options: coed. Campus housing is university owned. Freshman campus housing is guaranteed.

Activities and organizations: drama/theater group, choral group, Student Government Association (SGA), Students Take Action Committee (STAC) Volunteer Organization, International/Intercultural Clubs, College Activities Board (CAB), Campus Ministry.

Athletics Member NCAA. All Division III. *Intercollegiate sports:* basketball M/W, cross-country running M/W, soccer M/W, softball W, tennis M/W, volleyball M/W.

Campus security: 24-hour emergency response devices and patrols, late-night transport/escort service, controlled dormitory access.

Student services: health clinic, personal/psychological counseling.

COSTS
Costs (2018–19) *Comprehensive fee:* $45,875 includes full-time tuition ($31,000), mandatory fees ($2131), and room and board ($12,744). Full-time tuition and fees vary according to course load and program. Part-time tuition: $800 per credit hour. Part-time tuition and fees vary according to course load, location, and program. *Room and board:* Room and board charges vary according to board plan. *Payment plan:* installment. *Waivers:* senior citizens and employees or children of employees.

APPLYING
Options: electronic application, deferred entrance.
Application fee: $35.
Required: essay or personal statement, high school transcript, minimum 2.0 GPA, 2 letters of recommendation. *Recommended:* interview.
Application deadlines: rolling (freshmen), rolling (transfers).
Notification: continuous (freshmen), continuous (transfers).

CONTACT
Ms. Adrianna Arroyo, Director of Undergraduate Admissions, College of Saint Elizabeth, 2 Convent Road, Morristown, NJ 07960-6989. *Phone:* 973-290-4700. *Toll-free phone:* 800-210-7900. *Fax:* 973-290-4710. *E-mail:* apply@cse.edu.

DeVry University–North Brunswick Campus
North Brunswick, New Jersey
http://www.devry.edu/

- **Proprietary** comprehensive, founded 1969, part of DeVry University
- **Urban** campus
- **Coed**
- **Minimally difficult** entrance level

FACULTY
Student/faculty ratio: 14:1.

ACADEMICS
Calendar: semesters. *Degrees:* associate, bachelor's, and master's.
Library: Learning Resource Center.

STUDENT LIFE
Housing options: college housing not available.

COSTS
Costs (2017–18) *Tuition:* $14,392 full-time. *Required fees:* $500 full-time.

APPLYING
Options: deferred entrance.
Application fee: $30.
Required: high school transcript, interview.

CONTACT
DeVry University–North Brunswick Campus, 630 US Highway 1, North Brunswick, NJ 08902. *Phone:* 732-729-3532. *Toll-free phone:* 866-338-7934.

Drew University
Madison, New Jersey
http://www.drew.edu/

- **Independent** university, founded 1867, affiliated with United Methodist Church
- **Suburban** 186-acre campus with easy access to New York City
- **Coed** 1,537 undergraduate students, 98% full-time, 57% women, 43% men
- **Moderately difficult** entrance level, 63% of applicants were admitted

UNDERGRAD STUDENTS
1,507 full-time, 30 part-time. Students come from 38 states and territories; 49 other countries; 35% are from out of state; 7% Black or African American, non-Hispanic/Latino; 13% Hispanic/Latino; 5% Asian, non-Hispanic/Latino; 5% Two or more races, non-Hispanic/Latino; 5% Race/ethnicity unknown; 10% international; 5% transferred in; 79% live on campus.

Freshmen:
Admission: 3,205 applied, 2,033 admitted, 371 enrolled. *Average high school GPA:* 3.5. *Test scores:* SAT evidence-based reading and writing

scores over 500: 96%; SAT math scores over 500: 93%; ACT scores over 18: 100%; SAT evidence-based reading and writing scores over 600: 58%; SAT math scores over 600: 47%; ACT scores over 24: 67%; SAT evidence-based reading and writing scores over 700: 9%; SAT math scores over 700: 10%; ACT scores over 30: 14%.

Retention: 85% of full-time freshmen returned.

FACULTY
Total: 257, 58% full-time.
Student/faculty ratio: 10:1.

ACADEMICS
Calendar: semesters. *Degrees:* bachelor's, master's, doctoral, post-master's, and postbachelor's certificates.

Special study options: accelerated degree program, adult/continuing education programs, advanced placement credit, double majors, English as a second language, freshman honors college, honors programs, independent study, internships, off-campus study, part-time degree program, services for LD students, student-designed majors, study abroad, summer session for credit. *ROTC:* Army (c).

Unusual degree programs: 3-2 engineering with Columbia University, Stevens Institute of Technology; forestry with Duke University; nursing with Drexel University; management with Wake Forest University, environmental management with Duke University, teaching.

Computers: Students can access the following: campus intranet, computer help desk, free student e-mail accounts, online (class) grades, online (class) registration, online (class) schedules. Campuswide network is available. 100% of college-owned or -operated housing units are wired for high-speed Internet access. Wireless service is available via entire campus.

Library: Rose Memorial Library plus 1 other. *Books:* 662,733 (physical), 288,268 (digital/electronic); *Serial titles:* 8,820 (physical), 121,021 (digital/electronic); *Databases:* 196. Weekly public service hours: 107; students can reserve study rooms.

STUDENT LIFE
Housing options: coed, special housing for students with disabilities. Campus housing is university owned. Freshman campus housing is guaranteed.

Activities and organizations: drama/theater group, student-run newspaper, radio station, choral group, Pre-Health Society, Coed Volleyball, Drew Organization of Anime, Drew Democrats, University Program Board.

Athletics Member NCAA. All Division III. *Intercollegiate sports:* baseball M, basketball M/W, cross-country running M/W, equestrian sports W, fencing M/W, field hockey W, golf M/W, lacrosse M/W, rugby M(c)/W(c), soccer M/W, softball W, swimming and diving M/W, tennis M/W, track and field M/W. *Intramural sports:* badminton M/W, basketball M/W, football M, racquetball M/W, soccer M/W, squash M/W, table tennis M/W, volleyball M/W.

Campus security: 24-hour emergency response devices and patrols, late-night transport/escort service, controlled dormitory access.

Student services: health clinic, personal/psychological counseling.

COSTS & FINANCIAL AID
Costs (2018–19) *Comprehensive fee:* $53,608 includes full-time tuition ($38,668), mandatory fees ($832), and room and board ($14,108). Part-time tuition: $1612 per credit. Part-time tuition and fees vary according to course load. *College room only:* $8909. Room and board charges vary according to board plan and housing facility. *Payment plans:* tuition prepayment, installment, deferred payment. *Waivers:* employees or children of employees.

Financial Aid Of all full-time matriculated undergraduates who enrolled in 2017, 1,054 applied for aid, 981 were judged to have need, 127 had their need fully met. 709 Federal Work-Study jobs (averaging $2000). In 2017, 340 non-need-based awards were made. *Average percent of need met:* 83. *Average financial aid package:* $44,512. *Average need-based loan:* $4519. *Average need-based gift aid:* $38,899. *Average non-need-based aid:* $22,610. *Average indebtedness upon graduation:* $24,058.

APPLYING
Options: electronic application, early admission, early decision, early action, deferred entrance.

Application fee: $40.

Required: essay or personal statement, high school transcript, 2 letters of recommendation. *Recommended:* interview.

Application deadlines: 2/1 (freshmen), 12/15 (transfers).

Early decision deadline: 11/15 (for plan 1), 1/15 (for plan 2).

Notification: 3/18 (freshmen), continuous (transfers), 12/15 (early decision plan 1), 2/15 (early decision plan 2).

CONTACT
Drew University, 36 Madison Avenue, Madison, NJ 07940-1493. *Phone:* 973-408-3739. *E-mail:* cadm@drew.edu.

Eastern International College
Belleville, New Jersey
http://www.eicollege.edu/

CONTACT
Eastern International College, 251 Washington Avenue, Belleville, NJ 07109.

Eastern International College
Jersey City, New Jersey
http://www.eicollege.edu/

CONTACT
Eastern International College, 684 Newark Avenue, Jersey City, NJ 07306.

Eastwick College
Ramsey, New Jersey
http://www.eastwickcollege.edu/

CONTACT
Eastwick College, 10 South Franklin Turnpike, Ramsey, NJ 07446.

Fairleigh Dickinson University, Florham Campus
Madison, New Jersey
http://www.fdu.edu/

- **Independent** comprehensive, founded 1942
- **Suburban** 178-acre campus with easy access to New York City
- **Coed** 2,747 undergraduate students, 96% full-time, 57% women, 43% men
- **Moderately difficult** entrance level, 84% of applicants were admitted

UNDERGRAD STUDENTS
2,640 full-time, 107 part-time. Students come from 25 states and territories; 9 other countries; 17% are from out of state; 8% Black or African American, non-Hispanic/Latino; 18% Hispanic/Latino; 5% Asian, non-Hispanic/Latino; 0.1% Native Hawaiian or other Pacific Islander, non-Hispanic/Latino; 0.2% American Indian or Alaska Native, non-Hispanic/Latino; 3% Two or more races, non-Hispanic/Latino; 8% Race/ethnicity unknown; 0.4% international; 4% transferred in; 61% live on campus.

Freshmen:
Admission: 4,175 applied, 3,503 admitted, 802 enrolled. *Average high school GPA:* 3.4. *Test scores:* SAT evidence-based reading and writing scores over 500: 86%; SAT math scores over 500: 84%; ACT scores over 18: 95%; SAT evidence-based reading and writing scores over 600: 33%; SAT math scores over 600: 28%; ACT scores over 24: 43%; SAT evidence-based reading and writing scores over 700: 2%; SAT math scores over 700: 3%; ACT scores over 30: 8%.

Retention: 81% of full-time freshmen returned.

FACULTY
Total: 453, 34% full-time, 54% with terminal degrees.
Student/faculty ratio: 13:1.

ACADEMICS
Calendar: semesters. *Degrees:* bachelor's, master's, doctoral, post-master's, and postbachelor's certificates.

Special study options: academic remediation for entering students, accelerated degree program, adult/continuing education programs, advanced placement credit, cooperative education, distance learning, double majors, honors programs, independent study, internships, off-campus study, part-time degree program, services for LD students, student-designed majors, study abroad, summer session for credit. *ROTC:* Army (c), Air Force (c).

Computers: Students can access the following: computer help desk, free student e-mail accounts, online (class) grades, online (class) registration, online (class) schedules. Campuswide network is available. 100% of college-owned or -operated housing units are wired for high-speed Internet access. Wireless service is available via entire campus.

Library: Monninger Center for Learning and Research. *Books:* 131,212 (physical), 158,628 (digital/electronic); *Serial titles:* 1,423 (physical), 126,248 (digital/electronic); *Databases:* 144. Weekly public service hours: 83.

STUDENT LIFE

Housing options: coed, special housing for students with disabilities. Campus housing is university owned. Freshman applicants given priority for college housing.

Activities and organizations: drama/theater group, student-run newspaper, choral group, national fraternities, national sororities.

Athletics Member NCAA. All Division III. *Intercollegiate sports:* baseball M, basketball M/W, cross-country running M/W, field hockey W, football M, golf M/W, lacrosse M/W, soccer M/W, softball W, swimming and diving M/W, tennis M/W, volleyball W. *Intramural sports:* basketball M/W, football M/W, soccer M/W, softball M/W, volleyball M/W, weight lifting M/W.

Campus security: 24-hour emergency response devices and patrols, late-night transport/escort service, controlled dormitory access, trained law enforcement personnel on staff.

Student services: health clinic, personal/psychological counseling.

COSTS & FINANCIAL AID

Costs (2017–18) *One-time required fee:* $810. *Comprehensive fee:* $54,910 includes full-time tuition ($40,752), mandatory fees ($1028), and room and board ($13,130). Full-time tuition and fees vary according to location and program. Part-time tuition: $987 per credit hour. Part-time tuition and fees vary according to location and program. *Required fees:* $414 per year part-time. *College room only:* $8636. Room and board charges vary according to board plan, housing facility, and location. *Payment plans:* installment, deferred payment. *Waivers:* senior citizens and employees or children of employees.

Financial Aid Of all full-time matriculated undergraduates who enrolled in 2017, 2,307 applied for aid, 2,151 were judged to have need, 283 had their need fully met. 2,732 Federal Work-Study jobs (averaging $1420). In 2017, 432 non-need-based awards were made. *Average percent of need met:* 73. *Average financial aid package:* $40,034. *Average need-based loan:* $4420. *Average need-based gift aid:* $29,076. *Average non-need-based aid:* $17,451. *Average indebtedness upon graduation:* $42,122. *Financial aid deadline:* 2/15.

APPLYING

Standardized Tests *Required:* SAT or ACT (for admission).

Options: electronic application.

Application fee: $40.

Required: high school transcript, 2 letters of recommendation.

Application deadlines: rolling (freshmen), rolling (out-of-state freshmen), 8/1 (transfers).

Notification: continuous (freshmen), continuous (out-of-state freshmen).

CONTACT

Fairleigh Dickinson University, Florham Campus, 285 Madison Avenue, Madison, NJ 07940-1099. *Toll-free phone:* 800-338-8803.

Fairleigh Dickinson University, Metropolitan Campus

Teaneck, New Jersey

http://www.fdu.edu/

- **Independent** university, founded 1942
- **Suburban** 88-acre campus with easy access to New York City
- **Coed** 5,467 undergraduate students, 43% full-time, 57% women, 43% men
- **Moderately difficult** entrance level, 88% of applicants were admitted

UNDERGRAD STUDENTS

2,374 full-time, 3,093 part-time. Students come from 31 states and territories; 50 other countries; 12% are from out of state; 7% Black or African American, non-Hispanic/Latino; 31% Hispanic/Latino; 6% Asian, non-Hispanic/Latino; 0.4% Native Hawaiian or other Pacific Islander, non-Hispanic/Latino; 0.4% American Indian or Alaska Native, non-Hispanic/Latino; 2% Two or more races, non-Hispanic/Latino; 12% Race/ethnicity unknown; 4% international; 5% transferred in; 22% live on campus.

Freshmen:

Admission: 3,777 applied, 3,306 admitted, 710 enrolled. *Average high school GPA:* 3.3. *Test scores:* SAT evidence-based reading and writing scores over 500: 78%; SAT math scores over 500: 79%; ACT scores over 18: 86%; SAT evidence-based reading and writing scores over 600: 27%; SAT math scores over 600: 25%; ACT scores over 24: 33%; SAT evidence-based reading and writing scores over 700: 3%; SAT math scores over 700: 3%; ACT scores over 30: 4%.

Retention: 74% of full-time freshmen returned.

FACULTY

Total: 682, 25% full-time, 45% with terminal degrees.

Student/faculty ratio: 14:1.

ACADEMICS

Calendar: semesters. *Degrees:* certificates, associate, bachelor's, master's, doctoral, post-master's, and postbachelor's certificates.

Special study options: academic remediation for entering students, accelerated degree program, adult/continuing education programs, advanced placement credit, cooperative education, distance learning, double majors, English as a second language, external degree program, honors programs, independent study, internships, off-campus study, part-time degree program, services for LD students, student-designed majors, study abroad, summer session for credit. *ROTC:* Army (c), Air Force (c).

Computers: Students can access the following: computer help desk, free student e-mail accounts, online (class) grades, online (class) registration, online (class) schedules. Campuswide network is available. 100% of college-owned or -operated housing units are wired for high-speed Internet access. Wireless service is available via entire campus.

Library: Giovatto Library. *Books:* 157,566 (physical); *Serial titles:* 1,217 (physical), 126,248 (digital/electronic); *Databases:* 144. Weekly public service hours: 87.

STUDENT LIFE

Housing options: coed, special housing for students with disabilities. Campus housing is university owned.

Activities and organizations: drama/theater group, student-run newspaper, radio station, choral group, national fraternities, national sororities.

Athletics Member NCAA. All Division I. *Intercollegiate sports:* baseball M(s), basketball M(s)/W(s), bowling W(s), cheerleading W, cross-country running M(s)/W(s), fencing W(s), golf M(s)/W(s), soccer M(s)/W(s), softball W(s), tennis M(s)/W(s), track and field M(s)/W(s), volleyball W(s). *Intramural sports:* badminton M/W, basketball M/W, football M/W, rugby M(c)/W(c), soccer M/W, table tennis M/W, tennis M/W, ultimate Frisbee M/W, volleyball M/W.

Campus security: 24-hour emergency response devices and patrols, late-night transport/escort service, controlled dormitory access, trained law enforcement personnel on staff.

Student services: health clinic, personal/psychological counseling, women's center.

COSTS & FINANCIAL AID

Costs (2017–18) *One-time required fee:* $810. *Comprehensive fee:* $52,532 includes full-time tuition ($38,418), mandatory fees ($1028), and room and board ($13,086). Full-time tuition and fees vary according to location and program. Part-time tuition: $987 per credit hour. Part-time tuition and fees vary according to location and program. *Required fees:* $414 per year part-time. *College room only:* $8592. Room and board charges vary according to board plan and housing facility. *Payment plans:* installment, deferred payment. *Waivers:* senior citizens and employees or children of employees.

Financial Aid Of all full-time matriculated undergraduates who enrolled in 2017, 2,019 applied for aid, 1,964 were judged to have need, 170 had their need fully met. 3,391 Federal Work-Study jobs (averaging $1416). In 2017, 258 non-need-based awards were made. *Average percent of need met:* 65. *Average financial aid package:* $36,702. *Average need-based loan:* $4152. *Average need-based gift aid:* $26,806. *Average non-need-based aid:* $15,540. *Average indebtedness upon graduation:* $40,151. *Financial aid deadline:* 2/15.

APPLYING

Standardized Tests *Required:* SAT or ACT (for admission).

Options: electronic application, early admission.

Application fee: $40.

Required: high school transcript, 2 letters of recommendation. *Required for some:* interview.

Application deadlines: rolling (freshmen), rolling (out-of-state freshmen), rolling (transfers).

Notification: continuous (freshmen), continuous (out-of-state freshmen), continuous (transfers).

CONTACT

Fairleigh Dickinson University, Metropolitan Campus, 1000 River Road, Teaneck, NJ 07666-1914. *Toll-free phone:* 800-338-8803.

Felician University

Lodi, New Jersey

http://www.felician.edu/

- **Independent Roman Catholic** comprehensive, founded 1942
- **Small-town** 37-acre campus with easy access to New York City
- **Endowment** $6.5 million
- **Coed** 1,626 undergraduate students, 88% full-time, 71% women, 29% men
- **Moderately difficult** entrance level, 79% of applicants were admitted

UNDERGRAD STUDENTS

1,430 full-time, 196 part-time. Students come from 14 states and territories; 18 other countries; 8% are from out of state; 24% Black or African American, non-Hispanic/Latino; 29% Hispanic/Latino; 5% Asian, non-Hispanic/Latino; 0.4% Native Hawaiian or other Pacific Islander, non-Hispanic/Latino; 0.4% American Indian or Alaska Native, non-Hispanic/Latino; 0.6% Two or more races, non-Hispanic/Latino; 9% Race/ethnicity unknown; 2% international; 10% transferred in; 30% live on campus.

Freshmen:

Admission: 2,249 applied, 1,786 admitted, 308 enrolled. *Average high school GPA:* 3.1. *Test scores:* SAT evidence-based reading and writing scores over 500: 55%; SAT math scores over 500: 53%; ACT scores over 18: 70%; SAT evidence-based reading and writing scores over 600: 8%; SAT math scores over 600: 9%; ACT scores over 24: 11%; SAT math scores over 700: 1%; ACT scores over 30: 2%.

Retention: 76% of full-time freshmen returned.

FACULTY

Total: 215, 37% full-time, 42% with terminal degrees.

Student/faculty ratio: 14:1.

ACADEMICS

Calendar: semesters. *Degrees:* certificates, associate, bachelor's, master's, doctoral, post-master's, and postbachelor's certificates.

Special study options: academic remediation for entering students, accelerated degree program, adult/continuing education programs, advanced placement credit, cooperative education, distance learning, double majors, English as a second language, external degree program, honors programs, independent study, internships, off-campus study, part-time degree program, services for LD students, student-designed majors, study abroad, summer session for credit. *ROTC:* Army (c), Air Force (c).

Unusual degree programs: business administration; psychology/counseling.

Computers: 190 computers/terminals and 50 ports are available on campus for general student use. Students can access the following: computer help desk, free student e-mail accounts, online (class) grades, online (class) registration, online (class) schedules. Campuswide network is available. 100% of college-owned or -operated housing units are wired for high-speed Internet access. Wireless service is available via entire campus.

Library: Felician University Library plus 1 other. *Books:* 68,565 (physical), 158,952 (digital/electronic); *Serial titles:* 178 (physical), 51,874 (digital/electronic); *Databases:* 56. Weekly public service hours: 137; students can reserve study rooms.

STUDENT LIFE

Housing options: coed, men-only, women-only, special housing for students with disabilities. Campus housing is university owned. Freshman applicants given priority for college housing.

Activities and organizations: drama/theater group, student-run radio station, choral group, Student Nurses Association, Zeta Alpha Zeta teaching sorority, Campus Activity Board, Students in Free Enterprise (SIFE), Student Government Association.

Athletics Member NCAA, NAIA. All NCAA Division II. *Intercollegiate sports:* baseball M(s), basketball M(s)/W(s), bowling W(s), cross-country running M(s)/W(s), golf M(s), soccer M(s)/W(s), softball W(s), volleyball W(s). *Intramural sports:* cheerleading W(c), soccer M/W, softball W, volleyball M/W, weight lifting M/W.

Campus security: 24-hour patrols, student patrols, late-night transport/escort service.

Student services: health clinic, personal/psychological counseling.

COSTS & FINANCIAL AID

Costs (2018–19) *Comprehensive fee:* $47,200 includes full-time tuition ($31,915), mandatory fees ($2400), and room and board ($12,885). Full-time tuition and fees vary according to program. Part-time tuition: $1055 per credit hour. Part-time tuition and fees vary according to course load and program. *Required fees:* $475 per term part-time. *Room and board:* Room and board charges vary according to housing facility. *Payment plan:* installment. *Waivers:* employees or children of employees.

Financial Aid Of all full-time matriculated undergraduates who enrolled in 2016, 1,345 applied for aid, 1,297 were judged to have need, 96 had their need fully met. 49 Federal Work-Study jobs (averaging $2236). In 2016, 78 non-need-based awards were made. *Average percent of need met:* 65. *Average financial aid package:* $26,743. *Average need-based loan:* $4279. *Average need-based gift aid:* $13,799. *Average non-need-based aid:* $13,431.

APPLYING

Standardized Tests *Required:* SAT or ACT (for admission). *Required for some:* SAT (for admission), ACT (for admission), SAT Subject Tests (for admission). *Recommended:* SAT and SAT Subject Tests or ACT (for admission).

Options: deferred entrance.

Application fee: $30.

Required: essay or personal statement, high school transcript, minimum 2.0 GPA, letters of recommendation. *Required for some:* interview.

Application deadlines: 5/1 (freshmen), 2/15 (out-of-state freshmen), rolling (transfers).

Notification: continuous (freshmen), continuous (out-of-state freshmen), continuous (transfers).

CONTACT

Colleen Fuller, Director of Undergraduate Admissions, Felician University, 262 South Main Street, Lodi, NJ 07644-2117. *Phone:* 201-355-1444. *E-mail:* fullerc@felician.edu.

Georgian Court University
Lakewood, New Jersey
http://www.georgian.edu/

- **Independent Roman Catholic** comprehensive, founded 1908
- **Suburban** 156-acre campus with easy access to New York City, Philadelphia
- **Endowment** $56.0 million
- **Coed** 1,613 undergraduate students, 83% full-time, 71% women, 29% men
- **Moderately difficult** entrance level, 69% of applicants were admitted

UNDERGRAD STUDENTS
1,343 full-time, 270 part-time. Students come from 19 states and territories; 16 other countries; 6% are from out of state; 12% Black or African American, non-Hispanic/Latino; 13% Hispanic/Latino; 3% Asian, non-Hispanic/Latino; 0.1% Native Hawaiian or other Pacific Islander, non-Hispanic/Latino; 0.5% American Indian or Alaska Native, non-Hispanic/Latino; 2% Two or more races, non-Hispanic/Latino; 8% Race/ethnicity unknown; 1% international; 19% transferred in; 27% live on campus.

Freshmen:
Admission: 1,946 applied, 1,340 admitted, 216 enrolled. *Average high school GPA:* 3.4. *Test scores:* SAT evidence-based reading and writing scores over 500: 58%; SAT math scores over 500: 51%; ACT scores over 18: 70%; SAT evidence-based reading and writing scores over 600: 14%; SAT math scores over 600: 8%; ACT scores over 24: 15%; SAT evidence-based reading and writing scores over 700: 1%; SAT math scores over 700: 1%.
Retention: 72% of full-time freshmen returned.

FACULTY
Total: 284, 31% full-time, 50% with terminal degrees.
Student/faculty ratio: 12:1.

ACADEMICS
Calendar: semesters. *Degrees:* certificates, bachelor's, master's, post-master's, and postbachelor's certificates.

Special study options: academic remediation for entering students, accelerated degree program, adult/continuing education programs, advanced placement credit, distance learning, double majors, English as a second language, honors programs, independent study, internships, off-campus study, part-time degree program, services for LD students, student-designed majors, study abroad, summer session for credit.

Computers: 221 computers/terminals and 300 ports are available on campus for general student use. Students can access the following: campus intranet, computer help desk, free student e-mail accounts, online (class) grades, online (class) registration, online (class) schedules. Campuswide network is available. 100% of college-owned or -operated housing units are wired for high-speed Internet access. Wireless service is available via entire campus.

Library: The Sister Mary Joseph Cunningham Library. *Books:* 129,447 (physical), 117,590 (digital/electronic); *Serial titles:* 2,898 (physical), 33,651 (digital/electronic); *Databases:* 115. Weekly public service hours: 85; students can reserve study rooms.

STUDENT LIFE
Housing options: coed. Campus housing is university owned. Freshman campus housing is guaranteed.

Activities and organizations: student-run newspaper, Basketball Club, Black Student Union, Math Club, Dance Theatre Club, History Club.

Athletics Member NCAA. All Division II. *Intercollegiate sports:* basketball M(s)/W(s), cross-country running M(s)/W(s), lacrosse M(s)/W(s), soccer M(s)/W(s), softball W(s), track and field M(s)/W(s), volleyball W(s).

Campus security: 24-hour emergency response devices and patrols, late-night transport/escort service, controlled dormitory access.

Student services: health clinic, personal/psychological counseling.

COSTS & FINANCIAL AID
Costs (2017–18) *Comprehensive fee:* $43,068 includes full-time tuition ($30,800), mandatory fees ($1460), and room and board ($10,808). Full-time tuition and fees vary according to location, program, and reciprocity agreements. Part-time tuition: $704 per credit hour. Part-time tuition and fees vary according to location, program, and reciprocity agreements. *Required fees:* $365 per term part-time. *Payment plan:* installment.

MAKE IT YOUR PLACE
- 2018 *U.S. News & World Report* "Best Colleges & Universities"
- 2017 *Washington Monthly* "Best Bang for the Buck"
- 2017 Strive for College Partner: First Generation College Students
- 2017 Catholic College of Distinction/College of Distinction
- 2017 Champion of Good Works
- 2017 Victory Media "Military-Friendly School"

GEORGIAN COURT UNIVERSITY Lakewood, NJ • georgian.edu • 732.987.2700
THE MERCY UNIVERSITY OF NEW JERSEY

Waivers: children of alumni, senior citizens, and employees or children of employees.

Financial Aid Of all full-time matriculated undergraduates who enrolled in 2017, 1,192 applied for aid, 1,130 were judged to have need, 226 had their need fully met. 206 Federal Work-Study jobs (averaging $1552). 15 state and other part-time jobs (averaging $1400). In 2017, 159 non-need-based awards were made. *Average percent of need met:* 74. *Average financial aid package:* $28,824. *Average need-based loan:* $6823. *Average need-based gift aid:* $19,530. *Average non-need-based aid:* $14,344. *Average indebtedness upon graduation:* $39,006. *Financial aid deadline:* 7/1.

APPLYING

Standardized Tests *Required:* SAT or ACT (for admission).

Options: electronic application, early action, deferred entrance.

Application fee: $40.

Required: high school transcript, minimum 2.5 GPA. *Required for some:* essay or personal statement, 2 letters of recommendation, interview.

Application deadlines: 8/1 (freshmen), 8/1 (transfers), 12/1 (early action).

Notification: continuous (transfers).

CONTACT

Director of Undergraduate Admissions, Georgian Court University, 900 Lakewood Avenue, Lakewood, NJ 08701-2697. *Phone:* 732-987-2745. *Toll-free phone:* 800-458-8422. *Fax:* 732-987-2000. *E-mail:* admissions@georgian.edu.

See previous page for display ad and page 1298 for the College Close-Up.

Kean University

Union, New Jersey

http://www.kean.edu/

- **State-supported** university, founded 1855, part of New Jersey State College System
- **Suburban** 185-acre campus with easy access to New York City
- **Endowment** $16.4 million
- **Coed** 11,984 undergraduate students, 79% full-time, 60% women, 40% men
- **Moderately difficult** entrance level, 82% of applicants were admitted

UNDERGRAD STUDENTS

9,516 full-time, 2,468 part-time. Students come from 21 states and territories; 43 other countries; 2% are from out of state; 19% Black or African American, non-Hispanic/Latino; 28% Hispanic/Latino; 5% Asian, non-Hispanic/Latino; 0.2% Native Hawaiian or other Pacific Islander, non-Hispanic/Latino; 0.2% American Indian or Alaska Native, non-Hispanic/Latino; 2% Two or more races, non-Hispanic/Latino; 8% Race/ethnicity unknown; 3% international; 12% transferred in; 16% live on campus.

Freshmen:

Admission: 8,851 applied, 7,277 admitted, 1,784 enrolled. *Average high school GPA:* 3.0. *Test scores:* SAT evidence-based reading and writing scores over 500: 47%; SAT math scores over 500: 47%; ACT scores over 18: 59%; SAT evidence-based reading and writing scores over 600: 7%; SAT math scores over 600: 6%; ACT scores over 24: 15%; ACT scores over 30: 1%.

Retention: 76% of full-time freshmen returned.

FACULTY

Total: 1,432, 23% full-time.

Student/faculty ratio: 17:1.

ACADEMICS

Calendar: semesters. *Degrees:* bachelor's, master's, doctoral, and post-master's certificates.

Special study options: academic remediation for entering students, accelerated degree program, adult/continuing education programs, advanced placement credit, cooperative education, distance learning, double majors, English as a second language, external degree program, independent study, internships, off-campus study, part-time degree program, services for LD students, study abroad, summer session for credit. *ROTC:* Army (c), Air Force (c).

Computers: 1,700 computers/terminals and 2,000 ports are available on campus for general student use. Students can access the following: free student e-mail accounts, online (class) grades, online (class) registration, online (class) schedules. Campuswide network is available. 100% of college-owned or -operated housing units are wired for high-speed Internet access. Wireless service is available via entire campus.

Library: Nancy Thompson Library. *Books:* 208,670 (physical), 11,430 (digital/electronic); *Serial titles:* 58,034 (digital/electronic); *Databases:* 249. Weekly public service hours: 102.

STUDENT LIFE

Housing options: coed, special housing for students with disabilities. Campus housing is university owned. Freshman applicants given priority for college housing.

Activities and organizations: drama/theater group, student-run newspaper, radio station, choral group, Kean University Council for Exceptional Children, American Sign Language Club, National Society of Collegiate Scholars, Speech, Language and Hearing Student Association, Outdoor Adventure and Recreation Club, national fraternities, national sororities.

Athletics Member NCAA. All Division III. *Intercollegiate sports:* baseball M, basketball M/W, field hockey W, football M, lacrosse M/W, soccer M/W, softball W, swimming and diving W, tennis W, volleyball M/W. *Intramural sports:* basketball M/W, sand volleyball M/W, soccer M/W, softball M/W, tennis M/W, ultimate Frisbee M/W, volleyball M/W, weight lifting M/W.

Campus security: 24-hour emergency response devices and patrols, student patrols, late-night transport/escort service, controlled dormitory access.

Student services: health clinic, personal/psychological counseling.

COSTS & FINANCIAL AID

Costs (2017–18) *Tuition:* state resident $7909 full-time, $308 per credit part-time; nonresident $14,811 full-time, $523 per credit part-time. Part-time tuition and fees vary according to course load. *Required fees:* $4198 full-time, $154 per credit part-time. *Room and board:* $13,513. Room and board charges vary according to board plan, housing facility, and location. *Payment plan:* installment. *Waivers:* senior citizens and employees or children of employees.

Financial Aid Of all full-time matriculated undergraduates who enrolled in 2017, 7,837 applied for aid, 6,945 were judged to have need, 57 had their need fully met. 288 Federal Work-Study jobs (averaging $2409). In 2017, 139 non-need-based awards were made. *Average percent of need met:* 84. *Average financial aid package:* $11,052. *Average need-based loan:* $4444. *Average need-based gift aid:* $8690. *Average non-need-based aid:* $3237. *Average indebtedness upon graduation:* $32,277.

APPLYING

Standardized Tests *Required:* SAT or ACT (for admission).

Options: electronic application, early action, deferred entrance.

Application fee: $75.

Required: high school transcript. *Required for some:* interview. *Recommended:* essay or personal statement, 2 letters of recommendation.

Application deadlines: 8/15 (freshmen), 8/1 (transfers), 12/1 (early action).

Notification: continuous until 11/1 (freshmen), continuous (transfers), 1/1 (early action).

CONTACT

Mr. Carlos Nazario, Director of Admissions, Kean University, 1000 Morris Avenue, Office of Admissions - Kean Hall, Union, NJ 07083. *Phone:* 908-737-7100. *Fax:* 908-737-7105. *E-mail:* admitme@kean.edu.

★ Monmouth University

West Long Branch, New Jersey

http://www.monmouth.edu/

- **Independent** comprehensive, founded 1933
- **Suburban** 159-acre campus with easy access to New York City, Philadelphia
- **Endowment** $77.8 million
- **Coed**
- **Moderately difficult** entrance level

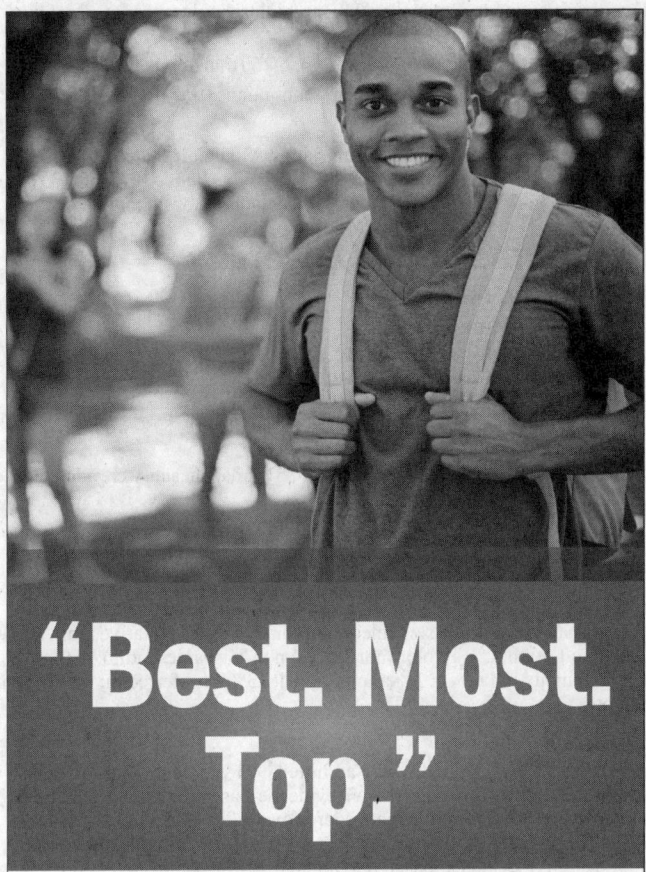

FACULTY
Student/faculty ratio: 13:1.

ACADEMICS
Calendar: semesters. *Degrees:* certificates, bachelor's, master's, doctoral, post-master's, and postbachelor's certificates.
Library: Monmouth University Library. *Books:* 275,000 (physical), 40,416 (digital/electronic); *Serial titles:* 1,622 (physical), 73,909 (digital/electronic); *Databases:* 189. Weekly public service hours: 111; students can reserve study rooms.

STUDENT LIFE
Housing options: coed. Campus housing is university owned and leased by the school. Freshman campus housing is guaranteed.

Activities and organizations: drama/theater group, student-run newspaper, radio and television station, choral group, Veterans Student Association, Student Government Association, Economics and Finance Club, Pre-Law Club, Colleges Against Cancer, national fraternities, national sororities.

Athletics Member NCAA. All Division I except football (Division I-AA).

Campus security: 24-hour emergency response devices and patrols, late-night transport/escort service, controlled dormitory access.

Student services: health clinic, personal/psychological counseling, women's center, legal services.

COSTS & FINANCIAL AID
Costs (2017–18) *One-time required fee:* $200. *Comprehensive fee:* $50,284 includes full-time tuition ($36,032), mandatory fees ($700), and room and board ($13,552). Part-time tuition: $1043 per credit hour. Part-time tuition and fees vary according to course load. *Required fees:* $175 per term part-time. *College room only:* $7784. Room and board charges vary according to board plan and housing facility.

Financial Aid Of all full-time matriculated undergraduates who enrolled in 2017, 3,719 applied for aid, 3,238 were judged to have need, 3,154 had their need fully met. 2,022 Federal Work-Study jobs (averaging $1965). 622 state and other part-time jobs (averaging $930). In 2017, 1204 non-need-based awards were made. *Average percent of need met:* 66. *Average financial aid package:* $27,389. *Average need-based loan:* $4689. *Average need-based gift aid:* $12,962. *Average non-need-based aid:* $9517. *Average indebtedness upon graduation:* $30,985.

APPLYING
Standardized Tests *Required:* SAT or ACT (for admission).

Options: electronic application, early action, deferred entrance.

Application fee: $50.

Required: essay or personal statement, high school transcript, 1 letter of recommendation. *Required for some:* interview. *Recommended:* resume of activities including community involvement and leadership positions.

CONTACT
Ms. Victoria Bobik, Director of Undergraduate Admission, Monmouth University, 400 Cedar Avenue, West Long Branch, NJ 07764-1898. *Phone:* 732-571-3456. *Toll-free phone:* 800-543-9671. *Fax:* 732-263-5166. *E-mail:* admission@monmouth.edu.

See this page for display ad and page 1350 for the College Close-Up.

Montclair State University
Montclair, New Jersey
http://www.montclair.edu/
- **State-supported** university, founded 1908
- **Suburban** 250-acre campus with easy access to New York City
- **Coed** 16,852 undergraduate students, 89% full-time, 61% women, 39% men
- **Moderately difficult** entrance level, 71% of applicants were admitted

UNDERGRAD STUDENTS
14,944 full-time, 1,908 part-time. 3% are from out of state; 13% Black or African American, non-Hispanic/Latino; 28% Hispanic/Latino; 6% Asian, non-Hispanic/Latino; 0.2% Native Hawaiian or other Pacific Islander, non-Hispanic/Latino; 0.1% American Indian or Alaska Native, non-Hispanic/Latino; 3% Two or more races, non-Hispanic/Latino; 7% Race/ethnicity unknown; 2% international; 9% transferred in; 32% live on campus.

Freshmen:
Admission: 13,384 applied, 9,457 admitted, 3,004 enrolled. *Average high school GPA:* 3.2.
Retention: 81% of full-time freshmen returned.

FACULTY
Total: 1,855, 34% full-time, 31% with terminal degrees.
Student/faculty ratio: 17:1.

ACADEMICS
Calendar: semesters. *Degrees:* certificates, bachelor's, master's, doctoral, and postbachelor's certificates.

Special study options: academic remediation for entering students, accelerated degree program, adult/continuing education programs, advanced placement credit, cooperative education, double majors, English as a second language, freshman honors college, honors programs, independent study, internships, off-campus study, part-time degree program, services for LD students, study abroad, summer session for credit.

Unusual degree programs: teaching, music, aquatic and coastal science, chemistry, mathematics, statistics.

Computers: 1,850 computers/terminals and 27,000 ports are available on campus for general student use. Students can access the following: campus intranet, computer help desk, free student e-mail accounts, online (class) grades, online (class) registration, online (class) schedules, online storage, online course delivery, online computing lab, student online portal. Campuswide network is available. 100% of college-owned or - operated housing units are wired for high-speed Internet access. Wireless service is available via entire campus.

Library: Sprague Library. *Books:* 441,470 (physical), 145,833 (digital/electronic); *Serial titles:* 9,751 (physical), 40,969 (digital/electronic); *Databases:* 165. Weekly public service hours: 93; students can reserve study rooms.

STUDENT LIFE
Housing options: coed. Campus housing is university owned and is provided by a third party. Freshman campus housing is guaranteed.

Activities and organizations: drama/theater group, student-run newspaper, radio and television station, choral group, Latin American Student Organization, Campus Recreation, MSU Players, Unified Asian American Student Organization, SLAM (Student Life At Montclair), national fraternities, national sororities.

Athletics Member NCAA. All Division III. *Intercollegiate sports:* baseball M, basketball M/W, field hockey W, football M, lacrosse M/W, soccer M/W, softball W, swimming and diving M/W, track and field M/W, volleyball W. *Intramural sports:* baseball M(c), basketball M/W, cheerleading W(c), field hockey M(c)/W(c), ice hockey M(c)/W(c), lacrosse M(c), racquetball M/W, rugby M(c)/W(c), soccer M/W, softball M/W, table tennis M/W, tennis M/W, track and field M(c)/W(c), volleyball M/W, water polo M/W, wrestling M(c)/W(c).

Campus security: 24-hour emergency response devices and patrols, late-night transport/escort service, controlled dormitory access, video surveillance, student escorts.

Student services: health clinic, personal/psychological counseling, women's center.

COSTS & FINANCIAL AID
Costs (2017–18) *Tuition:* state resident $10,808 full-time, $360 per credit part-time; nonresident $18,920 full-time, $631 per credit part-time. *Required fees:* $1647 full-time, $55 per credit part-time. *Room and board:* $13,466. Room and board charges vary according to board plan and housing facility. *Payment plan:* installment. *Waivers:* senior citizens and employees or children of employees.

Financial Aid Of all full-time matriculated undergraduates who enrolled in 2016, 12,347 applied for aid, 10,689 were judged to have need, 1,184 had their need fully met. 533 Federal Work-Study jobs (averaging $1362). In 2016, 445 non-need-based awards were made. *Average percent of need met:* 67. *Average financial aid package:* $9931. *Average need-based loan:* $4229. *Average need-based gift aid:* $8536. *Average non-need-based aid:* $4899. *Average indebtedness upon graduation:* $28,070.

APPLYING
Options: electronic application, deferred entrance.
Application fee: $65.

Required: essay or personal statement, high school transcript. *Required for some:* interview.
Application deadlines: 3/1 (freshmen), 6/15 (transfers).
Notification: continuous (freshmen), continuous (transfers).

CONTACT
Jeff Indiveri-Gant, Director of Admissions, Montclair State University, One Normal Avenue, Montclair, NJ 07043-1624. *Phone:* 973-655-3316. *Fax:* 973-655-7700. *E-mail:* undergraduate.admissions@montclair.edu.

New Jersey City University
Jersey City, New Jersey
http://www.njcu.edu/

- **State-supported** comprehensive, founded 1927
- **Urban** 51-acre campus with easy access to New York City
- **Endowment** $7.3 million
- **Coed** 6,509 undergraduate students, 80% full-time, 59% women, 41% men
- **Moderately difficult** entrance level, 85% of applicants were admitted

UNDERGRAD STUDENTS
5,211 full-time, 1,298 part-time. Students come from 23 states and territories; 16 other countries; 1% are from out of state; 23% Black or African American, non-Hispanic/Latino; 40% Hispanic/Latino; 8% Asian, non-Hispanic/Latino; 0.6% Native Hawaiian or other Pacific Islander, non-Hispanic/Latino; 0.3% American Indian or Alaska Native, non-Hispanic/Latino; 2% Two or more races, non-Hispanic/Latino; 4% Race/ethnicity unknown; 1% international; 13% transferred in; 9% live on campus.

Freshmen:
Admission: 3,987 applied, 3,391 admitted, 991 enrolled. *Average high school GPA:* 3.0. *Test scores:* SAT evidence-based reading and writing scores over 500: 42%; SAT math scores over 500: 45%; SAT evidence-based reading and writing scores over 600: 10%; SAT math scores over 600: 8%; SAT evidence-based reading and writing scores over 700: 1%; SAT math scores over 700: 1%.
Retention: 77% of full-time freshmen returned.

FACULTY
Total: 823, 31% full-time.
Student/faculty ratio: 15:1.

ACADEMICS
Calendar: semesters. *Degrees:* bachelor's, master's, doctoral, and post-master's certificates.

Special study options: academic remediation for entering students, accelerated degree program, adult/continuing education programs, advanced placement credit, cooperative education, distance learning, double majors, English as a second language, honors programs, independent study, internships, off-campus study, part-time degree program, services for LD students, study abroad, summer session for credit. *ROTC:* Army (c), Navy (c).

Computers: Students can access the following: free student e-mail accounts, online (class) grades, online (class) registration, online (class) schedules. Campuswide network is available. 100% of college-owned or - operated housing units are wired for high-speed Internet access. Wireless service is available via classrooms, computer centers, computer labs, dorm rooms, learning centers, libraries, student centers.

Library: Congressman Frank J. Guarini Library. *Books:* 300,000 (physical), 150,000 (digital/electronic); *Serial titles:* 150 (physical), 32,000 (digital/electronic); *Databases:* 152. Weekly public service hours: 82.

STUDENT LIFE
Housing options: coed. Campus housing is university owned.

Activities and organizations: drama/theater group, student-run newspaper, radio station, choral group, national fraternities, national sororities.

Athletics Member NCAA. All Division III. *Intercollegiate sports:* baseball M, basketball M/W, bowling W, cross-country running M/W, golf M, soccer M/W, softball W, volleyball M/W. *Intramural sports:* basketball M/W, bowling M/W, cheerleading M/W, cross-country running M/W, football M/W, golf M, racquetball M/W, soccer M/W, softball M/W, swimming and diving M/W, table tennis M/W, tennis W, track and field M/W, volleyball M/W.

Campus security: 24-hour emergency response devices and patrols, late-night transport/escort service.

Student services: health clinic, personal/psychological counseling, women's center, legal services.

COSTS & FINANCIAL AID
Costs (2017–18) *Tuition:* state resident $8115 full-time, $278 per credit hour part-time; nonresident $17,142 full-time, $588 per credit hour part-time. Part-time tuition and fees vary according to course load. *Required fees:* $3316 full-time, $111 per credit hour part-time. *Room and board:* $12,446. Room and board charges vary according to board plan and housing facility. *Payment plans:* installment, deferred payment. *Waivers:* senior citizens and employees or children of employees.

Financial Aid Of all full-time matriculated undergraduates who enrolled in 2015, 4,408 applied for aid, 4,191 were judged to have need, 125 had their need fully met. In 2015, 56 non-need-based awards were made. *Average percent of need met:* 50. *Average financial aid package:* $10,213. *Average need-based loan:* $4178. *Average need-based gift aid:* $8191. *Average non-need-based aid:* $7464. *Average indebtedness upon graduation:* $26,093.

APPLYING
Standardized Tests *Recommended:* SAT (for admission).

Options: electronic application, deferred entrance.

Application fee: $50.

Required: essay or personal statement, high school transcript, minimum 2.8 GPA. *Required for some:* interview. *Recommended:* 1 letter of recommendation.

Notification: continuous (freshmen).

CONTACT
Mr. Jose Balda, Director of Admissions, New Jersey City University, 2039 Kennedy Boulevard, Jersey City, NJ 07305. *Phone:* 201-200-3234. *Toll-free phone:* 888-441-NJCU. *E-mail:* admissions@nicu.edu.

New Jersey Institute of Technology
Newark, New Jersey
http://www.njit.edu/
- **State-supported** university, founded 1881, part of State of New Jersey Department of Education
- **Urban** 48-acre campus with easy access to New York City
- **Endowment** $104.6 million
- **Coed** 8,483 undergraduate students, 75% full-time, 26% women, 74% men
- **Moderately difficult** entrance level, 61% of applicants were admitted

UNDERGRAD STUDENTS
6,380 full-time, 2,103 part-time. Students come from 23 states and territories; 64 other countries; 3% are from out of state; 8% Black or African American, non-Hispanic/Latino; 20% Hispanic/Latino; 21% Asian, non-Hispanic/Latino; 0.1% American Indian or Alaska Native, non-Hispanic/Latino; 3% Two or more races, non-Hispanic/Latino; 12% Race/ethnicity unknown; 4% international; 10% transferred in; 53% live on campus.

Freshmen:
Admission: 7,254 applied, 4,453 admitted, 1,114 enrolled. *Average high school GPA:* 3.6. *Test scores:* SAT evidence-based reading and writing scores over 500: 99%; SAT math scores over 500: 100%; ACT scores over 18: 100%; SAT evidence-based reading and writing scores over 600: 66%; SAT math scores over 600: 84%; ACT scores over 24: 80%; SAT evidence-based reading and writing scores over 700: 16%; SAT math scores over 700: 28%; ACT scores over 30: 32%.

Retention: 88% of full-time freshmen returned.

FACULTY
Total: 776, 57% full-time.

Student/faculty ratio: 17:1.

ACADEMICS
Calendar: semesters. *Degrees:* bachelor's, master's, doctoral, and postbachelor's certificates.

Special study options: academic remediation for entering students, accelerated degree program, adult/continuing education programs, advanced placement credit, cooperative education, distance learning, double majors, English as a second language, freshman honors college, honors programs, independent study, internships, off-campus study, part-time degree program, services for LD students, study abroad, summer session for credit. *ROTC:* Army (c), Air Force (b).

Unusual degree programs: 3-2 business administration; engineering.

Computers: 1,938 computers/terminals are available on campus for general student use. Students can access the following: campus intranet, computer help desk, free student e-mail accounts, online (class) grades, online (class) registration, online (class) schedules. Campuswide network is available. 100% of college-owned or -operated housing units are wired for high-speed Internet access. Wireless service is available via entire campus.

Library: Van Houten Library plus 1 other. *Books:* 137,517 (physical), 177,107 (digital/electronic); *Serial titles:* 55,291 (physical), 55,291 (digital/electronic); *Databases:* 34. Weekly public service hours: 105; students can reserve study rooms.

STUDENT LIFE
Housing options: coed. Campus housing is university owned.

Activities and organizations: drama/theater group, student-run newspaper, radio station, Student Senate, Student Activities Council, Vector, Institute of Industrial Engineers, WJTB Geek Radio, national fraternities, national sororities.

Athletics Member NCAA. All Division I. *Intercollegiate sports:* baseball M(s), basketball M(s)/W(s), bowling M(c), cross-country running M(s)/W(s), fencing M(s)/W(s), ice hockey M(c), soccer M(s)/W(s), swimming and diving M(s)/W(s), tennis M(s)/W(s), track and field M/W, volleyball M(s)/W(s). *Intramural sports:* basketball M/W, bowling M/W, cheerleading M/W, ice hockey M, racquetball M/W, soccer M/W, softball M, swimming and diving M/W, tennis M/W, track and field M/W, ultimate Frisbee M/W, volleyball M/W, water polo M/W.

Campus security: 24-hour emergency response devices and patrols, late-night transport/escort service, controlled dormitory access, bicycle patrols.

Student services: health clinic, personal/psychological counseling, women's center.

COSTS & FINANCIAL AID
Costs (2017–18) *Tuition:* state resident $13,906 full-time, $529 per credit part-time; nonresident $28,926 full-time, $1237 per credit part-time. Full-time tuition and fees vary according to course load and degree level. Part-time tuition and fees vary according to course load and degree level. *Required fees:* $2992 full-time, $176 per credit part-time. *Room and board:* $13,300; room only: $8680. Room and board charges vary according to board plan and housing facility. *Payment plans:* installment, deferred payment. *Waivers:* employees or children of employees.

Financial Aid Of all full-time matriculated undergraduates who enrolled in 2016, 4,925 applied for aid, 4,365 were judged to have need, 392 had their need fully met. 276 Federal Work-Study jobs (averaging $472,008). 821 state and other part-time jobs (averaging $1.7 million). In 2016, 737 non-need-based awards were made. *Average percent of need met:* 41. *Average financial aid package:* $13,104. *Average need-based loan:* $4392. *Average need-based gift aid:* $12,484. *Average non-need-based aid:* $16,181. *Average indebtedness upon graduation:* $40,979. *Financial aid deadline:* 2/15.

APPLYING
Standardized Tests *Required:* SAT or ACT (for admission).

Options: electronic application, early admission, deferred entrance.

Application fee: $75.

Required: high school transcript. *Required for some:* essay or personal statement, interview. *Recommended:* 1 letter of recommendation.

Application deadlines: 3/1 (freshmen), 6/1 (transfers).

Notification: continuous (freshmen), continuous (transfers).

CONTACT
Mr. Stephen M. Eck, Executive Director of University Admissions, New Jersey Institute of Technology, University Heights, Newark, NJ 07102. *Phone:* 973-596-3306. *Toll-free phone:* 800-925-NJIT. *Fax:* 973-596-3461. *E-mail:* admissions@njit.edu.

Pillar College
Newark, New Jersey
http://www.pillar.edu/

CONTACT
Ms. Linda Aarni, Senior Admissions Counselor, Pillar College, 60 Park Place, Suite 701, Newark, NJ 07102. *Phone:* 973-803-5000. *Toll-free phone:* 800-234-9305. *Fax:* 732-356-4846. *E-mail:* info@pillar.edu.

Princeton University
Princeton, New Jersey
http://www.princeton.edu/

- **Independent** university, founded 1746
- **Suburban** 600-acre campus with easy access to New York City, Philadelphia
- **Endowment** $23.4 billion
- **Coed** 5,394 undergraduate students, 98% full-time, 49% women, 51% men
- **Most difficult** entrance level, 6% of applicants were admitted

UNDERGRAD STUDENTS
5,260 full-time, 134 part-time. Students come from 53 states and territories; 97 other countries; 82% are from out of state; 8% Black or African American, non-Hispanic/Latino; 10% Hispanic/Latino; 21% Asian, non-Hispanic/Latino; 0.2% Native Hawaiian or other Pacific Islander, non-Hispanic/Latino; 0.2% American Indian or Alaska Native, non-Hispanic/Latino; 4% Two or more races, non-Hispanic/Latino; 1% Race/ethnicity unknown; 12% international; 96% live on campus.

Freshmen:
Admission: 31,056 applied, 1,990 admitted, 1,305 enrolled. *Average high school GPA:* 3.9. *Test scores:* SAT evidence-based reading and writing scores over 500: 100%; SAT math scores over 500: 99%; ACT scores over 18: 100%; SAT evidence-based reading and writing scores over 600: 99%; SAT math scores over 600: 99%; ACT scores over 24: 99%; SAT evidence-based reading and writing scores over 700: 81%; SAT math scores over 700: 84%; ACT scores over 30: 88%.
Retention: 98% of full-time freshmen returned.

FACULTY
Total: 1,149, 83% full-time, 87% with terminal degrees.
Student/faculty ratio: 5:1.

ACADEMICS
Calendar: semesters. *Degrees:* bachelor's, master's, and doctoral.
Special study options: advanced placement credit, independent study, off-campus study, services for LD students, student-designed majors, study abroad. *ROTC:* Army (b), Navy (c), Air Force (c).
Computers: 500 computers/terminals and 17,000 ports are available on campus for general student use. Students can access the following: campus intranet, computer help desk, free student e-mail accounts, online (class) grades, online (class) registration, online (class) schedules, academic applications and courseware, printing, network file space, website hosting, media lab, broadcast center. Campuswide network is available. 100% of college-owned or -operated housing units are wired for high-speed Internet access. Wireless service is available via entire campus.
Library: Harvey S. Firestone Memorial Library plus 9 others. *Books:* 7.3 million (physical), 2.1 million (digital/electronic); *Serial titles:* 159,820 (physical), 291,025 (digital/electronic); *Databases:* 1,899. Weekly public service hours: 105.

STUDENT LIFE
Housing options: on-campus residence required through sophomore year; coed, men-only, women-only, special housing for students with disabilities. Campus housing is university owned. Freshman campus housing is guaranteed.
Activities and organizations: drama/theater group, student-run newspaper, radio and television station, choral group, marching band.
Athletics Member NCAA. All Division I except football (Division I-AA). *Intercollegiate sports:* baseball M, basketball M/W, crew M/W, cross-country running M/W, fencing M/W, field hockey W, golf M/W, ice hockey M/W, lacrosse M/W, soccer M/W, softball W, squash M/W, swimming and diving M/W, tennis M/W, track and field M/W, volleyball M/W, water polo M/W, wrestling M. *Intramural sports:* badminton M(c)/W(c), baseball M(c), basketball M(c)/W(c), cheerleading M(c)/W(c), cross-country running M(c)/W(c), equestrian sports M(c)/W(c), fencing M(c)/W(c), field hockey W(c), ice hockey M(c)/W(c), lacrosse M(c)/W(c), rugby M(c)/W(c), sailing M(c)/W(c), skiing (downhill) M(c)/W(c), soccer M(c)/W(c), softball W(c), squash M(c)/W(c), swimming and diving M(c)/W(c), table tennis M(c)/W(c), tennis M(c)/W(c), ultimate Frisbee M(c)/W(c), volleyball M(c)/W(c).

Campus security: 24-hour emergency response devices and patrols, student patrols, late-night transport/escort service, controlled dormitory access.

Student services: health clinic, personal/psychological counseling, women's center, legal services.

COSTS & FINANCIAL AID
Costs (2018–19) *One-time required fee:* $890. *Comprehensive fee:* $65,620 includes full-time tuition ($49,330) and room and board ($16,290). Part-time tuition: $5893 per year. *Required fees:* $25 per term part-time. *College room only:* $9450. Room and board charges vary according to board plan. *Payment plans:* installment, deferred payment. *Waivers:* employees or children of employees.
Financial Aid Of all full-time matriculated undergraduates who enrolled in 2017, 3,378 applied for aid, 3,155 were judged to have need, 3,155 had their need fully met. *Average percent of need met:* 100. *Average financial aid package:* $53,415. *Average need-based gift aid:* $51,365. *Average indebtedness upon graduation:* $9005.

APPLYING
Standardized Tests *Required:* SAT or ACT (for admission). *Recommended:* SAT Subject Tests (for admission).
Options: electronic application, early action, deferred entrance.
Application fee: $65.
Required: essay or personal statement, high school transcript, 3 letters of recommendation. *Recommended:* interview.
Application deadlines: 1/1 (freshmen), 11/1 (early action).
Notification: 4/1 (freshmen), 12/15 (early action).

CONTACT
Office of Admission, Princeton University, PO Box 430, Princeton, NJ 08542-0430. *Phone:* 609-258-3060. *Fax:* 609-258-6743. *E-mail:* uaoffice@princeton.edu.

Rabbi Jacob Joseph School
Edison, New Jersey

CONTACT
Rabbi Jacob Joseph School, One Plainfield Ave, Edison, NJ 08817.

Rabbinical College of America
Morristown, New Jersey
http://www.rca.edu/

CONTACT
Shoshana Solomon, Registrar, Rabbinical College of America, 226 Sussex Avenue, PO Box 1996, Morristown, NJ 07962-1996. *Phone:* 973-267-9404. *E-mail:* rca079@aol.com.

Ramapo College of New Jersey
Mahwah, New Jersey
http://www.ramapo.edu/

- **State-supported** comprehensive, founded 1969, part of New Jersey State College System
- **Suburban** 300-acre campus with easy access to New York City
- **Coed** 5,618 undergraduate students, 87% full-time, 55% women, 45% men
- **Moderately difficult** entrance level, 57% of applicants were admitted

UNDERGRAD STUDENTS
4,910 full-time, 708 part-time. 6% are from out of state; 5% Black or African American, non-Hispanic/Latino; 16% Hispanic/Latino; 8% Asian, non-Hispanic/Latino; 0.1% Native Hawaiian or other Pacific Islander,

non-Hispanic/Latino; 0.5% American Indian or Alaska Native, non-Hispanic/Latino; 0.5% Two or more races, non-Hispanic/Latino; 5% Race/ethnicity unknown; 2% international; 9% transferred in; 46% live on campus.

Freshmen:
Admission: 6,695 applied, 3,840 admitted, 913 enrolled. *Average high school GPA:* 3.4. *Test scores:* SAT evidence-based reading and writing scores over 500: 86%; SAT math scores over 500: 86%; ACT scores over 18: 95%; SAT evidence-based reading and writing scores over 600: 39%; SAT math scores over 600: 30%; ACT scores over 24: 45%; SAT evidence-based reading and writing scores over 700: 3%; SAT math scores over 700: 7%; ACT scores over 30: 11%.
Retention: 86% of full-time freshmen returned.

FACULTY
Total: 491, 44% full-time, 41% with terminal degrees.
Student/faculty ratio: 18:1.

ACADEMICS
Calendar: semesters. *Degrees:* certificates, bachelor's, master's, post-master's, and postbachelor's certificates.

Special study options: academic remediation for entering students, accelerated degree program, adult/continuing education programs, advanced placement credit, cooperative education, distance learning, double majors, external degree program, freshman honors college, honors programs, independent study, internships, off-campus study, part-time degree program, services for LD students, student-designed majors, study abroad, summer session for credit. *ROTC:* Army (c), Air Force (c).

Unusual degree programs: 3-2 biology, chemistry with Rutgers, The State University of New Jersey; dentistry with New York University; optometry with SUNY State College of Optometry.

Computers: Students can access the following: campus intranet, computer help desk, free student e-mail accounts, online (class) grades, online (class) registration, online (class) schedules. Campuswide network is available. 100% of college-owned or -operated housing units are wired for high-speed Internet access. Wireless service is available via classrooms, computer centers, computer labs, learning centers, libraries, student centers.
Library: George T. Potter Library.

STUDENT LIFE
Housing options: coed. Campus housing is university owned. Freshman campus housing is guaranteed.

Activities and organizations: drama/theater group, student-run newspaper, radio and television station, choral group, NORML, 1 Step, Biology & Biochemistry Club, Campus Crusade for Christ, Culture Club, national fraternities, national sororities.

Athletics Member NCAA. All Division III. *Intercollegiate sports:* baseball M, basketball M/W, cross-country running M/W, field hockey W, lacrosse W, soccer M/W, softball W, swimming and diving M/W, tennis M/W, track and field M/W, volleyball M/W. *Intramural sports:* basketball M/W, bowling M/W, football M/W, rock climbing M/W, soccer M/W, softball M/W, table tennis M/W, ultimate Frisbee M/W, volleyball M/W.

Campus security: 24-hour emergency response devices and patrols, late-night transport/escort service, controlled dormitory access, surveillance cameras, patrols by trained security personnel.

Student services: health clinic, personal/psychological counseling, women's center.

COSTS & FINANCIAL AID
Costs (2017–18) *Tuition:* state resident $11,640 full-time, $364 per credit hour part-time; nonresident $20,774 full-time, $649 per credit hour part-time. Full-time tuition and fees vary according to reciprocity agreements. Part-time tuition and fees vary according to reciprocity agreements. *Required fees:* $2440 full-time, $76 per credit hour part-time. *Room and board:* $12,180; room only: $8460. Room and board charges vary according to board plan and housing facility. *Payment plan:* installment. *Waivers:* senior citizens and employees or children of employees.

Financial Aid Of all full-time matriculated undergraduates who enrolled in 2016, 4,063 applied for aid, 2,707 were judged to have need, 129 had their need fully met. In 2016, 540 non-need-based awards were made. *Average percent of need met:* 53. *Average financial aid package:* $10,489. *Average need-based loan:* $4298. *Average need-based gift aid:*

$9240. *Average non-need-based aid:* $10,394. *Average indebtedness upon graduation:* $10,082.

APPLYING
Standardized Tests *Required:* SAT or ACT (for admission).
Options: electronic application, early admission, early decision, deferred entrance.
Application fee: $65.
Required: essay or personal statement, high school transcript. *Recommended:* minimum 3.0 GPA.

CONTACT
Michael, Associate Director for Freshmen Admissions, Ramapo College of New Jersey, Office of Admissions, 505 Ramapo Valley Road, Mahwah, NJ 07430-1680. *Phone:* 201-684-7300. *Toll-free phone:* 800-9RAMAPO. *Fax:* 201-684-7964. *E-mail:* admissions@ramapo.edu.

Rider University
Lawrenceville, New Jersey
http://www.rider.edu/
- **Independent** comprehensive, founded 1865
- **Suburban** 280-acre campus with easy access to New York City, Philadelphia
- **Endowment** $56.3 million
- **Coed** 4,094 undergraduate students, 91% full-time, 58% women, 42% men
- **Moderately difficult** entrance level, 67% of applicants were admitted

UNDERGRAD STUDENTS
3,711 full-time, 383 part-time. Students come from 44 states and territories; 46 other countries; 25% are from out of state; 13% Black or African American, non-Hispanic/Latino; 15% Hispanic/Latino; 5% Asian, non-Hispanic/Latino; 0.0% Native Hawaiian or other Pacific Islander, non-Hispanic/Latino; 0.1% American Indian or Alaska Native, non-Hispanic/Latino; 3% Two or more races, non-Hispanic/Latino; 1% Race/ethnicity unknown; 3% international; 54% live on campus.

Freshmen:
Admission: 9,519 applied, 6,389 admitted. *Average high school GPA:* 3.4. *Test scores:* SAT evidence-based reading and writing scores over 500: 77%; SAT math scores over 500: 73%; ACT scores over 18: 87%; SAT evidence-based reading and writing scores over 600: 27%; SAT math scores over 600: 23%; ACT scores over 24: 39%; SAT evidence-based reading and writing scores over 700: 4%; SAT math scores over 700: 4%; ACT scores over 30: 9%.
Retention: 80% of full-time freshmen returned.

FACULTY
Total: 602, 41% full-time, 72% with terminal degrees.
Student/faculty ratio: 11:1.

ACADEMICS
Calendar: semesters. *Degrees:* certificates, associate, bachelor's, master's, doctoral, post-master's, and postbachelor's certificates.

Special study options: academic remediation for entering students, adult/continuing education programs, advanced placement credit, cooperative education, distance learning, double majors, English as a second language, honors programs, independent study, internships, part-time degree program, services for LD students, study abroad, summer session for credit. *ROTC:* Army (c).

Computers: 300 computers/terminals are available on campus for general student use. Students can access the following: computer help desk, free student e-mail accounts, online (class) grades, online (class) registration, online (class) schedules. Campuswide network is available. 100% of college-owned or -operated housing units are wired for high-speed Internet access. Wireless service is available via entire campus.
Library: Franklin F. Moore Library plus 1 other. *Books:* 311,400 (physical), 150,000 (digital/electronic); *Serial titles:* 882 (physical), 44,599 (digital/electronic); *Databases:* 148. Study areas open 24 hours, 5–7 days a week; students can reserve study rooms.

STUDENT LIFE
Housing options: coed, women-only, special housing for students with disabilities. Campus housing is university owned. Freshman applicants given priority for college housing.

Activities and organizations: drama/theater group, student-run newspaper, radio and television station, choral group, Student Government Association, Greek Council, Association of Commuter Students, Black Student Union, Residence Hall Association, national fraternities, national sororities.

Athletics Member NCAA. All Division I. *Intercollegiate sports:* baseball M(s), basketball M(s)/W(s), cheerleading M/W, cross-country running M(s)/W(s), field hockey W(s), golf M(s), soccer M(s)/W(s), softball W(s), swimming and diving M(s)/W(s), tennis M(s)/W(s), track and field M(s)/W(s), volleyball M/W(s), wrestling M(s). *Intramural sports:* baseball M, basketball M/W, cheerleading M/W, cross-country running W, equestrian sports M/W(c), golf M, ice hockey M(c), lacrosse M(c)/W, soccer M/W, softball W, tennis M/W, track and field M/W, volleyball M/W, water polo M/W.

Campus security: 24-hour emergency response devices and patrols, student patrols, late-night transport/escort service, controlled dormitory access.

Student services: health clinic, personal/psychological counseling.

COSTS & FINANCIAL AID

Costs (2018–19) *Comprehensive fee:* $56,010 includes full-time tuition ($40,570), mandatory fees ($740), and room and board ($14,700). *College room only:* $9640.

Financial Aid Of all full-time matriculated undergraduates who enrolled in 2017, 3,084 applied for aid, 2,828 were judged to have need, 421 had their need fully met. In 2017, 702 non-need-based awards were made. *Average percent of need met:* 75. *Average financial aid package:* $30,642. *Average need-based loan:* $3705. *Average need-based gift aid:* $26,595. *Average non-need-based aid:* $18,887. *Average indebtedness upon graduation:* $35,332.

APPLYING

Standardized Tests *Required:* SAT or ACT (for admission).

Options: electronic application, early admission, early action, deferred entrance.

Application fee: $50.

Required: essay or personal statement, high school transcript, 2 letters of recommendation. *Required for some:* interview.

Application deadlines: rolling (freshmen), rolling (transfers), 11/15 (early action).

Notification: continuous (freshmen), continuous (transfers), 12/15 (early action).

CONTACT
Mr. William Larrousse, Director of Admissions, Rider University, 2083 Lawrenceville Road, Lawrenceville, NJ 08648. *Phone:* 609-896-5177. *Toll-free phone:* 800-257-9026. *Fax:* 609-895-6645. *E-mail:* wlarrousse@rider.edu.

See below for display ad and page 1396 for the College Close-Up.

Rowan University
Glassboro, New Jersey
http://www.rowan.edu/

- **State-supported** comprehensive, founded 1923, part of New Jersey State College System
- **Suburban** 921-acre campus with easy access to Philadelphia
- **Endowment** $173.2 million
- **Coed** 15,401 undergraduate students, 89% full-time, 46% women, 54% men
- **Moderately difficult** entrance level, 59% of applicants were admitted

UNDERGRAD STUDENTS

13,635 full-time, 1,766 part-time. Students come from 28 states and territories; 22 other countries; 5% are from out of state; 10% Black or African American, non-Hispanic/Latino; 10% Hispanic/Latino; 5% Asian, non-Hispanic/Latino; 0.1% Native Hawaiian or other Pacific Islander, non-Hispanic/Latino; 0.1% American Indian or Alaska Native, non-Hispanic/Latino; 3% Two or more races, non-Hispanic/Latino; 6% Race/ethnicity unknown; 0.8% international; 13% transferred in; 37% live on campus.

Freshmen:
Admission: 13,900 applied, 8,159 admitted, 2,387 enrolled. *Average high school GPA:* 3.5. *Test scores:* SAT evidence-based reading and writing scores over 500: 84%; SAT math scores over 500: 85%; ACT scores over 18: 94%; SAT evidence-based reading and writing scores over 600: 35%;

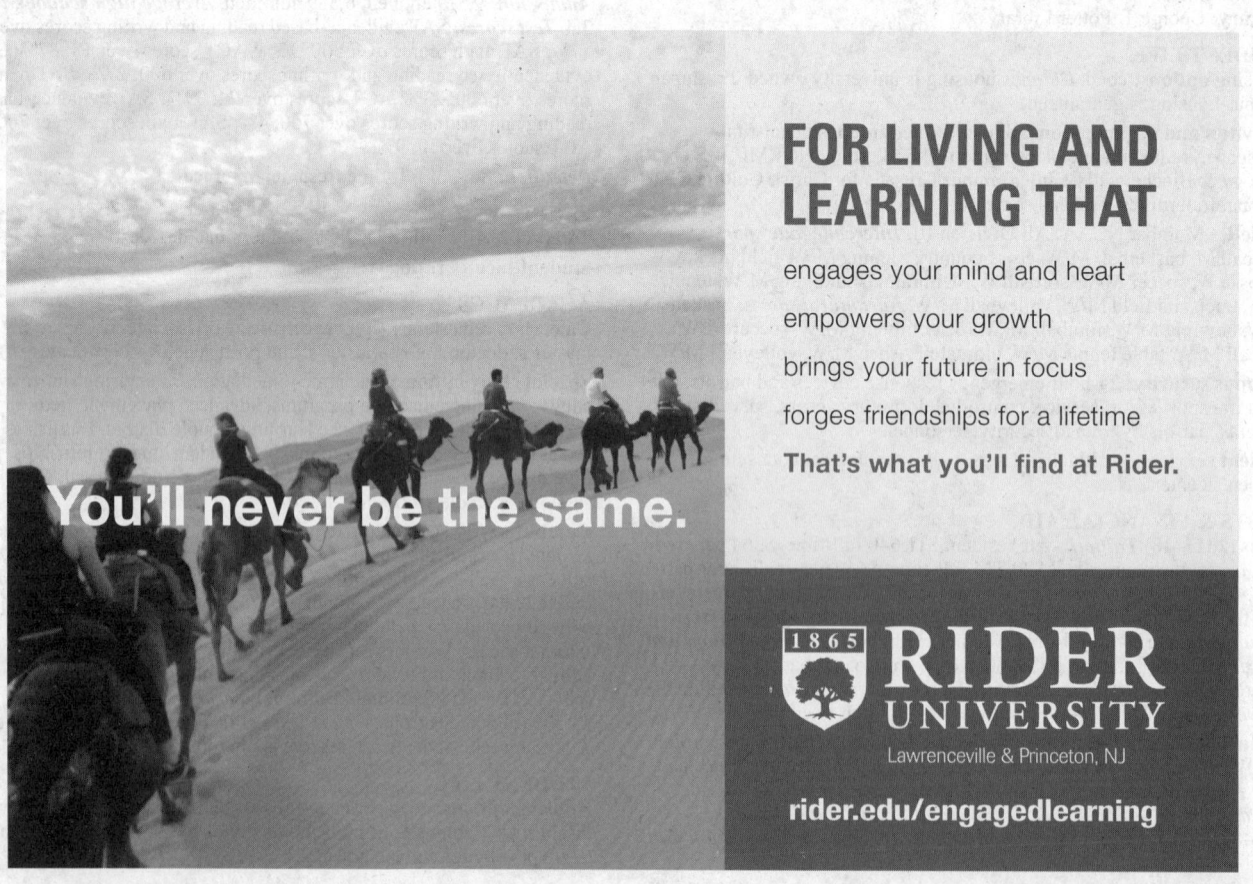

FOR LIVING AND LEARNING THAT

engages your mind and heart

empowers your growth

brings your future in focus

forges friendships for a lifetime

That's what you'll find at Rider.

You'll never be the same.

RIDER UNIVERSITY
Lawrenceville & Princeton, NJ

rider.edu/engagedlearning

SAT math scores over 600: 35%; ACT scores over 24: 51%; SAT evidence-based reading and writing scores over 700: 5%; SAT math scores over 700: 7%; ACT scores over 30: 13%.
Retention: 85% of full-time freshmen returned.

FACULTY
Total: 1,593, 29% full-time, 37% with terminal degrees.
Student/faculty ratio: 17:1.

ACADEMICS
Calendar: semesters. *Degrees:* certificates, bachelor's, master's, doctoral, post-master's, and postbachelor's certificates.

Special study options: academic remediation for entering students, accelerated degree program, adult/continuing education programs, advanced placement credit, cooperative education, distance learning, double majors, English as a second language, freshman honors college, honors programs, independent study, internships, off-campus study, part-time degree program, services for LD students, study abroad, summer session for credit. *ROTC:* Army (c).

Unusual degree programs: 3-2 mathematics and computer science.

Computers: 836 computers/terminals and 2,500 ports are available on campus for general student use. Students can access the following: campus intranet, computer help desk, free student e-mail accounts, online (class) grades, online (class) registration, online (class) schedules. Campuswide network is available. 100% of college-owned or -operated housing units are wired for high-speed Internet access. Wireless service is available via entire campus.

Library: Keith and Shirley Campbell Library plus 4 others. *Books:* 328,891 (physical), 494,739 (digital/electronic); *Serial titles:* 129,972 (digital/electronic); *Databases:* 846. Students can reserve study rooms.

STUDENT LIFE
Housing options: on-campus residence required through sophomore year; coed, special housing for students with disabilities. Campus housing is university owned and leased by the school. Freshman campus housing is guaranteed.

Activities and organizations: drama/theater group, student-run newspaper, radio and television station, choral group, Kappa Delta Pi, Public Relations Student Society of America, Student University Programmes, Rowan Television Network, Elementary Education Club, national fraternities, national sororities.

Athletics Member NCAA. All Division III. *Intercollegiate sports:* baseball M, basketball M/W, cross-country running M/W, field hockey W, football M, lacrosse M/W, rugby M/W, soccer M/W, softball M, swimming and diving M/W, track and field M/W, volleyball W. *Intramural sports:* basketball M/W, cheerleading M/W(c), field hockey W(c), football M/W, golf M/W, racquetball M/W, rock climbing M(c)/W, skiing (downhill) M(c)/W(c), soccer M/W, softball M/W, table tennis M/W, tennis M(c)/W(c), ultimate Frisbee M(c)/W(c), volleyball M/W, water polo M/W, weight lifting M/W, wrestling M(c).

Campus security: 24-hour emergency response devices and patrols, student patrols, late-night transport/escort service, controlled dormitory access, EMS service including 2 ambulances, security and campus police trained as police officers in NJ.

Student services: health clinic, personal/psychological counseling, legal services.

COSTS & FINANCIAL AID
Costs (2017–18) *Tuition:* state resident $9434 full-time, $362 per credit hour part-time; nonresident $17,704 full-time, $682 per credit hour part-time. Full-time tuition and fees vary according to course load, degree level, location, and program. Part-time tuition and fees vary according to course load, degree level, location, and program. *Required fees:* $3674 full-time, $157 per credit hour part-time. *Room and board:* $11,688; room only: $7608. Room and board charges vary according to board plan and housing facility. *Payment plans:* installment, deferred payment. *Waivers:* employees or children of employees.

Financial Aid Of all full-time matriculated undergraduates who enrolled in 2016, 10,428 applied for aid, 8,305 were judged to have need, 1,393 had their need fully met. 437 Federal Work-Study jobs (averaging $1587). In 2016, 1182 non-need-based awards were made. *Average percent of need met:* 68. *Average financial aid package:* $10,064. *Average need-based loan:* $4272. *Average need-based gift aid:* $8598. *Average non-need-based aid:* $8105. *Average indebtedness upon graduation:* $31,900.

APPLYING
Standardized Tests *Required:* SAT or ACT (for admission).
Options: electronic application, early admission, deferred entrance.
Application fee: $65.
Required: high school transcript, minimum 2.0 GPA. *Required for some:* interview.
Application deadlines: 3/1 (freshmen), 3/1 (transfers).
Notification: continuous (freshmen), continuous (transfers).

CONTACT
Rowan University, 201 Mullica Hill Road, Glassboro, NJ 08028-1701.
Toll-free phone: 800-447-1165 (in-state); 800-447-1165N (out-of-state).

Rutgers University–Camden
Camden, New Jersey
http://www.camden.rutgers.edu/
- **State-supported** university, founded 1926
- **Urban** 29-acre campus with easy access to Philadelphia
- **Endowment** $1.2 million
- **Coed** 5,489 undergraduate students, 82% full-time, 59% women, 41% men
- **Moderately difficult** entrance level, 69% of applicants were admitted

UNDERGRAD STUDENTS
4,493 full-time, 996 part-time. Students come from 29 states and territories; 24 other countries; 2% are from out of state; 18% Black or African American, non-Hispanic/Latino; 15% Hispanic/Latino; 10% Asian, non-Hispanic/Latino; 0.1% Native Hawaiian or other Pacific Islander, non-Hispanic/Latino; 0.1% American Indian or Alaska Native, non-Hispanic/Latino; 4% Two or more races, non-Hispanic/Latino; 2% Race/ethnicity unknown; 2% international; 16% transferred in; 17% live on campus.

Freshmen:
Admission: 11,338 applied, 7,861 admitted, 758 enrolled. *Test scores:* SAT evidence-based reading and writing scores over 500: 76%; SAT math scores over 500: 77%; SAT evidence-based reading and writing scores over 600: 23%; SAT math scores over 600: 22%; SAT evidence-based reading and writing scores over 700: 3%; SAT math scores over 700: 3%.
Retention: 88% of full-time freshmen returned.

FACULTY
Total: 700, 45% full-time, 99% with terminal degrees.
Student/faculty ratio: 11:1.

ACADEMICS
Calendar: semesters. *Degrees:* bachelor's, master's, doctoral, post-master's, and postbachelor's certificates.

Special study options: academic remediation for entering students, accelerated degree program, adult/continuing education programs, advanced placement credit, cooperative education, distance learning, double majors, English as a second language, freshman honors college, honors programs, independent study, internships, off-campus study, part-time degree program, services for LD students, student-designed majors, study abroad, summer session for credit. *ROTC:* Army (c), Air Force (c).

Unusual degree programs: 3-2 business administration; engineering; nursing; social work; medical technology, African-American studies, general science, childhood studies, English, history, liberal studies, psychology, biology, chemistry, mathematics.

Computers: Students can access the following: campus intranet, computer help desk, free student e-mail accounts, online (class) grades, online (class) registration, online (class) schedules. Campuswide network is available. 100% of college-owned or -operated housing units are wired for high-speed Internet access. Wireless service is available via classrooms, computer centers, computer labs, dorm rooms, learning centers, libraries, student centers.
Library: Paul Robeson Library plus 1 other. Weekly public service hours: 90; students can reserve study rooms.

STUDENT LIFE

Housing options: coed, special housing for students with disabilities. Campus housing is university owned.

Activities and organizations: drama/theater group, student-run newspaper, radio station, choral group, national fraternities, national sororities.

Athletics Member NCAA. All Division III. *Intercollegiate sports:* baseball M, basketball M/W, crew M/W, cross-country running W, golf M, lacrosse W, soccer M/W, softball W, track and field M/W, volleyball W. *Intramural sports:* cheerleading M(c)/W(c), crew M, football M, ice hockey M(c), soccer M/W, tennis M, ultimate Frisbee M/W, volleyball M/W.

Campus security: 24-hour emergency response devices and patrols, student patrols, late-night transport/escort service, controlled dormitory access.

Student services: health clinic, personal/psychological counseling, women's center, legal services.

COSTS & FINANCIAL AID

Costs (2017–18) *Tuition:* state resident $11,619 full-time, $374 per credit hour part-time; nonresident $27,042 full-time, $878 per credit hour part-time. Full-time tuition and fees vary according to program. Part-time tuition and fees vary according to course load and program. *Required fees:* $2882 full-time, $591 per term part-time. *Room and board:* $12,094; room only: $8422. Room and board charges vary according to board plan and housing facility. *Payment plan:* installment. *Waivers:* employees or children of employees.

Financial Aid Of all full-time matriculated undergraduates who enrolled in 2016, 3,533 applied for aid, 3,269 were judged to have need, 76 had their need fully met. 277 Federal Work-Study jobs (averaging $1858). 588 state and other part-time jobs (averaging $2759). In 2016, 61 non-need-based awards were made. *Average percent of need met:* 47. *Average financial aid package:* $12,663. *Average need-based loan:* $4590. *Average need-based gift aid:* $9796. *Average non-need-based aid:* $3905. *Average indebtedness upon graduation:* $32,781.

APPLYING

Standardized Tests *Required:* SAT or ACT (for admission).

Options: electronic application, early action, deferred entrance.

Application fee: $70.

Required: essay or personal statement. *Required for some:* high school transcript, interview.

Notification: 4/15 (transfers), 1/31 (early action).

CONTACT

Office of Graduate and Undergraduate Admissions, Rutgers University–Camden, 330 Cooper Street, Camden, NJ 08102. *Phone:* 856-225-6104. *E-mail:* admissions@camden.rutgers.edu.

Rutgers University–Newark

Newark, New Jersey

http://www.newark.rutgers.edu/

- **State-supported** university, founded 1908
- **Urban** 40-acre campus with easy access to New York City
- **Endowment** $1.2 million
- **Coed** 8,551 undergraduate students, 84% full-time, 55% women, 45% men
- **Moderately difficult** entrance level, 64% of applicants were admitted

UNDERGRAD STUDENTS

7,162 full-time, 1,389 part-time. Students come from 26 states and territories; 57 other countries; 1% are from out of state; 20% Black or African American, non-Hispanic/Latino; 29% Hispanic/Latino; 18% Asian, non-Hispanic/Latino; 0.3% Native Hawaiian or other Pacific Islander, non-Hispanic/Latino; 0.1% American Indian or Alaska Native, non-Hispanic/Latino; 3% Two or more races, non-Hispanic/Latino; 2% Race/ethnicity unknown; 5% international; 13% transferred in; 22% live on campus.

Freshmen:

Admission: 13,435 applied, 8,631 admitted, 1,325 enrolled. *Test scores:* SAT evidence-based reading and writing scores over 500: 78%; SAT math scores over 500: 80%; SAT evidence-based reading and writing scores over 600: 19%; SAT math scores over 600: 22%; SAT evidence-based reading and writing scores over 700: 1%; SAT math scores over 700: 3%.

Retention: 84% of full-time freshmen returned.

FACULTY

Total: 1,023, 54% full-time, 99% with terminal degrees.

Student/faculty ratio: 10:1.

ACADEMICS

Calendar: semesters. *Degrees:* bachelor's, master's, doctoral, post-master's, and postbachelor's certificates.

Special study options: academic remediation for entering students, accelerated degree program, adult/continuing education programs, advanced placement credit, cooperative education, distance learning, double majors, English as a second language, freshman honors college, honors programs, independent study, internships, off-campus study, part-time degree program, services for LD students, student-designed majors, study abroad, summer session for credit. *ROTC:* Army (b), Navy (b), Air Force (b).

Unusual degree programs: 3-2 business administration; engineering; nursing; social work.

Computers: Students can access the following: campus intranet, computer help desk, free student e-mail accounts, online (class) grades, online (class) registration, online (class) schedules. Campuswide network is available. 100% of college-owned or -operated housing units are wired for high-speed Internet access. Wireless service is available via classrooms, computer centers, computer labs, dorm rooms, learning centers, libraries, student centers.

Library: John Cotton Dana Library plus 4 others. Weekly public service hours: 91; students can reserve study rooms.

STUDENT LIFE

Housing options: coed. Campus housing is university owned.

Activities and organizations: drama/theater group, student-run newspaper, radio station, choral group, marching band, national fraternities, national sororities.

Athletics Member NCAA. All Division III. *Intercollegiate sports:* baseball M, basketball M/W, cross-country running M/W, soccer M/W, softball W, tennis M/W, track and field M/W, volleyball M/W. *Intramural sports:* basketball M/W, cross-country running M/W, football M/W, racquetball M/W, soccer M/W, tennis M/W, volleyball M/W, water polo M/W.

Campus security: 24-hour emergency response devices and patrols, student patrols, late-night transport/escort service, controlled dormitory access.

Student services: health clinic, personal/psychological counseling, women's center, legal services.

COSTS & FINANCIAL AID

Costs (2017–18) *Tuition:* state resident $11,619 full-time, $374 per credit hour part-time; nonresident $27,560 full-time, $894 per credit hour part-time. Full-time tuition and fees vary according to program. Part-time tuition and fees vary according to course load and program. *Required fees:* $2466 full-time, $475 per term part-time. *Room and board:* $13,266; room only: $8216. Room and board charges vary according to board plan and housing facility. *Payment plan:* installment. *Waivers:* employees or children of employees.

Financial Aid Of all full-time matriculated undergraduates who enrolled in 2016, 5,463 applied for aid, 5,181 were judged to have need, 99 had their need fully met. 563 Federal Work-Study jobs (averaging $2018). 948 state and other part-time jobs (averaging $2617). In 2016, 33 non-need-based awards were made. *Average percent of need met:* 51. *Average financial aid package:* $13,928. *Average need-based loan:* $4594. *Average need-based gift aid:* $11,465. *Average non-need-based aid:* $8046. *Average indebtedness upon graduation:* $29,077.

APPLYING

Standardized Tests *Required:* SAT or ACT (for admission).

Options: electronic application, early action, deferred entrance.

Application fee: $70.

Required: essay or personal statement. *Required for some:* high school transcript.

Notification: 4/15 (transfers), 1/31 (early action).

CONTACT
Office of Undergraduate and Graduate Admissions, Rutgers University–Newark, 190 University Avenue, Room 101, Newark, NJ 07102. *Phone:* 973-353-5205. *E-mail:* newarkadmissions@ugadm.rutgers.edu.

Rutgers University–New Brunswick
Piscataway, New Jersey
http://newbrunswick.rutgers.edu/

- **State-supported** university, founded 1766
- **Urban** 2685-acre campus with easy access to New York City
- **Endowment** $1.2 million
- **Coed** 35,641 undergraduate students, 94% full-time, 50% women, 50% men
- **Moderately difficult** entrance level, 58% of applicants were admitted

UNDERGRAD STUDENTS
33,677 full-time, 1,964 part-time. Students come from 51 states and territories; 92 other countries; 6% are from out of state; 7% Black or African American, non-Hispanic/Latino; 13% Hispanic/Latino; 27% Asian, non-Hispanic/Latino; 0.3% Native Hawaiian or other Pacific Islander, non-Hispanic/Latino; 3% Two or more races, non-Hispanic/Latino; 2% Race/ethnicity unknown; 9% international; 8% transferred in; 43% live on campus.

Freshmen:
Admission: 38,384 applied, 22,186 admitted, 6,268 enrolled. *Test scores:* SAT evidence-based reading and writing scores over 500: 97%; SAT math scores over 500: 98%; SAT evidence-based reading and writing scores over 600: 71%; SAT math scores over 600: 77%; SAT evidence-based reading and writing scores over 700: 21%; SAT math scores over 700: 36%.

Retention: 93% of full-time freshmen returned.

FACULTY
Total: 4,525, 46% full-time, 99% with terminal degrees.
Student/faculty ratio: 13:1.

ACADEMICS
Calendar: semesters. *Degrees:* certificates, diplomas, associate, bachelor's, master's, doctoral, post-master's, and postbachelor's certificates.
Special study options: academic remediation for entering students, accelerated degree program, adult/continuing education programs, advanced placement credit, cooperative education, distance learning, double majors, English as a second language, freshman honors college, honors programs, independent study, internships, off-campus study, part-time degree program, services for LD students, student-designed majors, study abroad, summer session for credit. *ROTC:* Army (b), Navy (b), Air Force (b).
Unusual degree programs: 3-2 business administration; engineering; nursing; social work; medicine with Rutgers University, New Jersey Medical School and Robert Wood Johnson Medical School.
Computers: Students can access the following: campus intranet, computer help desk, free student e-mail accounts, online (class) grades, online (class) registration, online (class) schedules. Campuswide network is available. 100% of college-owned or -operated housing units are wired for high-speed Internet access. Wireless service is available via classrooms, computer centers, computer labs, dorm rooms, learning centers, libraries, student centers.
Library: Archibald S. Alexander Library plus 15 others. Study areas open 24 hours, 5–7 days a week; students can reserve study rooms.

STUDENT LIFE
Housing options: coed, men-only, women-only, cooperative. Campus housing is university owned.
Activities and organizations: drama/theater group, student-run newspaper, radio and television station, choral group, marching band, national fraternities, national sororities.
Athletics Member NCAA. All Division I except football (Division I-A). *Intercollegiate sports:* baseball M(s), basketball M(s)/W(s), crew W(s), cross-country running M(s)/W(s), field hockey W(s), golf M(s)/W(s), gymnastics W(s), lacrosse M(s)/W(s), soccer M(s)/W(s), softball W(s), swimming and diving W(s), tennis M(s)/W(s), track and field M(s)/W(s), volleyball W(s), wrestling M(s). *Intramural sports:* badminton M/W, baseball M, basketball M/W, crew M(c), cross-country running M(c)/W(c), equestrian sports M(c)/W(c), fencing M(c)/W(c), football M/W, golf M/W, gymnastics W(c), ice hockey M(c)/W(c), lacrosse M(c)/W(c), racquetball M/W, rugby M(c)/W(c), sailing M(c)/W(c), skiing (downhill) M(c)/W(c), soccer M/W, softball M/W, squash M(c)/W(c), swimming and diving M/W, table tennis M/W, tennis M/W, track and field M/W, triathlon M(c)/W(c), ultimate Frisbee M/W, volleyball M/W, water polo M/W, weight lifting M(c), wrestling M.
Campus security: 24-hour emergency response devices and patrols, student patrols, late-night transport/escort service, controlled dormitory access.
Student services: health clinic, personal/psychological counseling, women's center, legal services.

COSTS & FINANCIAL AID
Costs (2017–18) *Tuition:* state resident $11,619 full-time, $374 per credit hour part-time; nonresident $27,560 full-time, $894 per credit hour part-time. Full-time tuition and fees vary according to program. Part-time tuition and fees vary according to course load and program. *Required fees:* $3019 full-time, $434 per term part-time. *Room and board:* $12,452; room only: $7602. Room and board charges vary according to board plan and housing facility. *Payment plan:* installment. *Waivers:* employees or children of employees.
Financial Aid Of all full-time matriculated undergraduates who enrolled in 2016, 21,143 applied for aid, 18,102 were judged to have need, 717 had their need fully met. 3,163 Federal Work-Study jobs (averaging $1952). 7,461 state and other part-time jobs (averaging $2026). In 2016, 758 non-need-based awards were made. *Average percent of need met:* 48. *Average financial aid package:* $13,747. *Average need-based loan:* $4688. *Average need-based gift aid:* $11,124. *Average non-need-based aid:* $10,461. *Average indebtedness upon graduation:* $32,601.

APPLYING
Standardized Tests *Required:* SAT or ACT (for admission).
Options: electronic application, early action, deferred entrance.
Application fee: $70.
Required: essay or personal statement. *Required for some:* high school transcript, interview.
Notification: 4/15 (transfers), 1/31 (early action).

CONTACT
Undergraduate Admissions Office, Rutgers University–New Brunswick, 65 Davidson Road, Room 202, Piscataway, NJ 08854. *Phone:* 732-445-1000. *E-mail:* admissions@ugadm.rutgers.edu.

Saint Peter's University
Jersey City, New Jersey
http://www.saintpeters.edu/

- **Independent Roman Catholic (Jesuit)** comprehensive, founded 1872
- **Urban** 15-acre campus with easy access to New York City
- **Coed** 2,637 undergraduate students, 91% full-time, 64% women, 36% men
- **Moderately difficult** entrance level, 91% of applicants were admitted

UNDERGRAD STUDENTS
2,387 full-time, 250 part-time. 9% are from out of state; 22% Black or African American, non-Hispanic/Latino; 45% Hispanic/Latino; 7% Asian, non-Hispanic/Latino; 0.7% Native Hawaiian or other Pacific Islander, non-Hispanic/Latino; 0.4% American Indian or Alaska Native, non-Hispanic/Latino; 2% Two or more races, non-Hispanic/Latino; 6% Race/ethnicity unknown; 2% international; 5% transferred in; 31% live on campus.

Freshmen:
Admission: 3,626 applied, 3,310 admitted, 651 enrolled. *Average high school GPA:* 3.3. *Test scores:* SAT evidence-based reading and writing scores over 500: 58%; SAT math scores over 500: 58%; ACT scores over 18: 73%; SAT evidence-based reading and writing scores over 600: 12%; SAT math scores over 600: 11%; ACT scores over 24: 13%; SAT evidence-based reading and writing scores over 700: 1%; SAT math scores over 700: 1%; ACT scores over 30: 4%.

Retention: 82% of full-time freshmen returned.

FACULTY
Total: 322, 37% full-time, 57% with terminal degrees.
Student/faculty ratio: 13:1.

ACADEMICS
Calendar: semesters. *Degrees:* certificates, associate, bachelor's, master's, doctoral, post-master's, and postbachelor's certificates.

Special study options: academic remediation for entering students, accelerated degree program, adult/continuing education programs, advanced placement credit, cooperative education, distance learning, double majors, English as a second language, honors programs, independent study, internships, off-campus study, part-time degree program, services for LD students, student-designed majors, study abroad, summer session for credit. *ROTC:* Army (c).

Unusual degree programs: 3-2 pharmacy, clinical and laboratory sciences with Rutgers, The State University of New Jersey; physician's assistant, physical therapy with Seton Hall University.

Computers: Students can access the following: computer help desk, free student e-mail accounts, online (class) grades, online (class) registration, online (class) schedules. Campuswide network is available. Wireless service is available via entire campus.
Library: Theresa and Edward O'Toole Library plus 2 others.

STUDENT LIFE
Housing options: coed, special housing for students with disabilities. Campus housing is university owned. Freshman campus housing is guaranteed.

Activities and organizations: drama/theater group, student-run newspaper, radio station, choral group.

Athletics Member NCAA. All Division I. *Intercollegiate sports:* baseball M(s), basketball M(s)/W(s), bowling M/W, cross-country running M(s)/W(s), golf M(s), soccer M(s)/W(s), softball W(s), swimming and diving M(s)/W(s), tennis M(s)/W(s), track and field M(s)/W(s), volleyball W(s). *Intramural sports:* badminton M/W, basketball M/W, bowling M/W, football M/W, golf M/W, racquetball M/W, soccer M/W, softball M/W, squash M/W, swimming and diving M/W, table tennis M/W, tennis M/W, track and field M/W, volleyball M/W, water polo M/W, weight lifting M/W.

Campus security: 24-hour emergency response devices and patrols, late-night transport/escort service, controlled dormitory access, ID checks at residence halls and library.

Student services: health clinic, personal/psychological counseling.

FINANCIAL AID
Financial Aid Of all full-time matriculated undergraduates who enrolled in 2017, 2,257 applied for aid, 2,075 were judged to have need, 132 had their need fully met. In 2017, 178 non-need-based awards were made. *Average percent of need met:* 79. *Average financial aid package:* $32,097. *Average need-based loan:* $4048. *Average need-based gift aid:* $29,853. *Average non-need-based aid:* $21,252. *Average indebtedness upon graduation:* $22,317.

APPLYING
Standardized Tests *Required for some:* SAT or ACT (for admission).

Options: early action, deferred entrance.

Required: essay or personal statement, high school transcript, minimum 2.0 GPA, 2 letters of recommendation. *Required for some:* interview. *Recommended:* interview.

Notification: continuous until 11/7 (freshmen).

CONTACT
Miss Kacey Tillotson, Director of Undergraduate Admissions, Saint Peter's University, Office of Admission, Lee House, Jersey City 07306. *Phone:* 201-761-7100. *Toll-free phone:* 888-SPC-9933. *E-mail:* ktillotson@saintpeters.edu.

★ Seton Hall University
South Orange, New Jersey
http://www.shu.edu/

CONTACT
Mary Clare Cullum, Director of Undergraduate Admissions, Seton Hall University, Enrollment Management Office, 400 South Orange Avenue, South Orange, NJ 07079-2697. *Phone:* 973-275-2589. *Toll-free phone:*

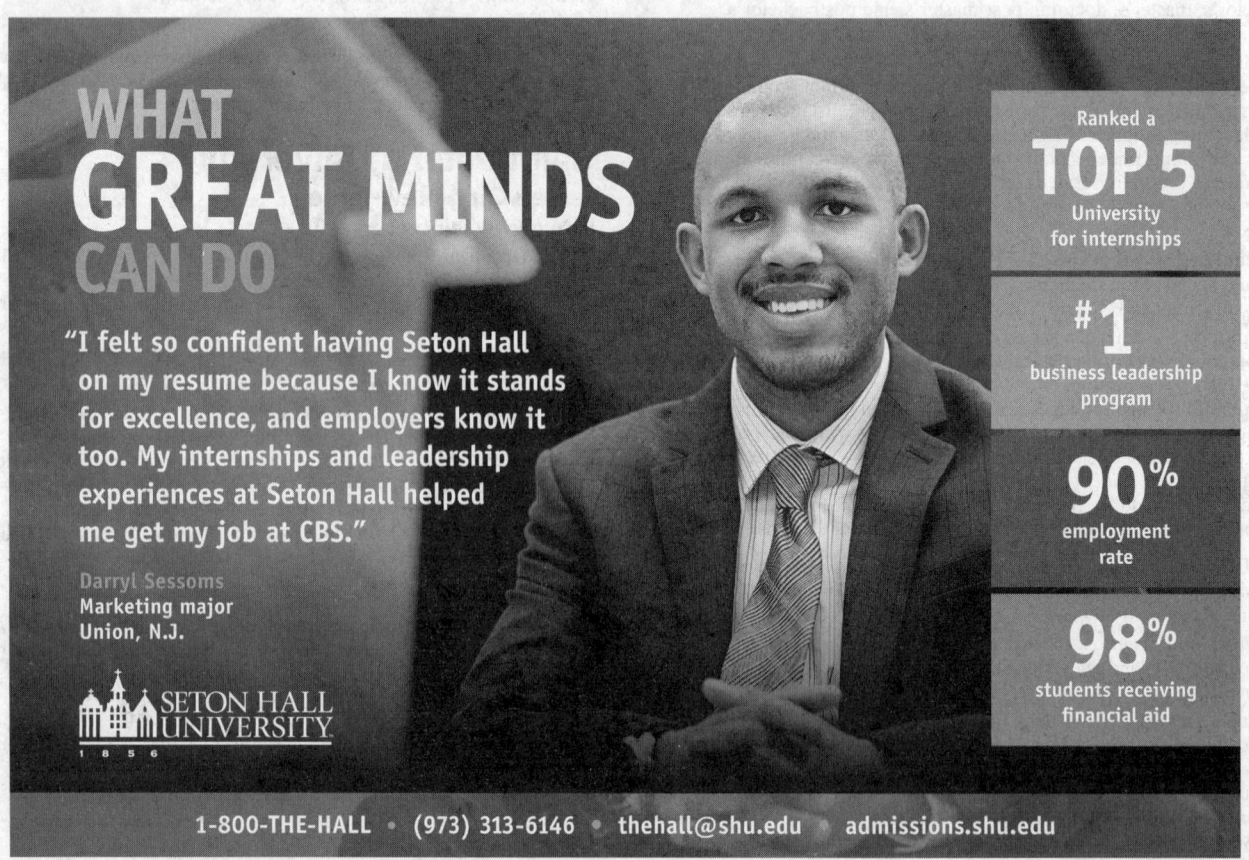

800-THE HALL. *Fax:* 973-275-2321. *E-mail:* maryclare.cullum@ shu.edu.

See previous page for display ad and page 1422 for the College Close-Up.

Stevens Institute of Technology
Hoboken, New Jersey
http://www.stevens.edu/

- **Independent** university, founded 1870
- **Urban** 55-acre campus with easy access to New York City
- **Coed** 3,123 undergraduate students, 100% full-time, 30% women, 70% men
- **Very difficult** entrance level, 44% of applicants were admitted

UNDERGRAD STUDENTS
3,113 full-time, 10 part-time. Students come from 37 states and territories; 39 other countries; 39% are from out of state; 2% Black or African American, non-Hispanic/Latino; 10% Hispanic/Latino; 12% Asian, non-Hispanic/Latino; 0.1% American Indian or Alaska Native, non-Hispanic/Latino; 4% Race/ethnicity unknown; 4% international; 0.8% transferred in; 64% live on campus.

Freshmen:
Admission: 8,335 applied, 3,657 admitted, 762 enrolled. *Average high school GPA:* 3.8. *Test scores:* SAT evidence-based reading and writing scores over 500: 100%; SAT math scores over 500: 100%; ACT scores over 18: 100%; SAT evidence-based reading and writing scores over 600: 94%; SAT math scores over 600: 97%; ACT scores over 24: 100%; SAT evidence-based reading and writing scores over 700: 33%; SAT math scores over 700: 63%; ACT scores over 30: 73%.

Retention: 94% of full-time freshmen returned.

FACULTY
Total: 415, 62% full-time, 80% with terminal degrees.
Student/faculty ratio: 10:1.

ACADEMICS
Calendar: semesters. *Degrees:* bachelor's, master's, doctoral, and postbachelor's certificates.
Special study options: accelerated degree program, advanced placement credit, cooperative education, distance learning, double majors, honors programs, independent study, internships, off-campus study, services for LD students, study abroad, summer session for credit. *ROTC:* Army (c), Air Force (c).
Computers: 500 computers/terminals and 3,800 ports are available on campus for general student use. Students can access the following: campus intranet, computer help desk, free student e-mail accounts, online (class) grades, online (class) registration, online (class) schedules, online account information, debit dining program, laundry status. Campuswide network is available. 100% of college-owned or -operated housing units are wired for high-speed Internet access. Wireless service is available via entire campus.
Library: Samuel C. Williams Library. *Books:* 66,492 (physical), 210,243 (digital/electronic); *Serial titles:* 898 (physical), 35,353 (digital/electronic); *Databases:* 71. Students can reserve study rooms.

STUDENT LIFE
Housing options: on-campus residence required for freshman year; coed, women-only. Campus housing is university owned and leased by the school. Freshman campus housing is guaranteed.
Activities and organizations: drama/theater group, student-run newspaper, radio and television station, choral group, Alpha Phi Omega, Computer & Gaming Society (C2GS), Society of Women Engineers, American Society of Mechanical Engineers (ASME), Ethnic Student Council, national fraternities, national sororities.
Athletics Member NCAA. All Division III. *Intercollegiate sports:* baseball M, basketball M/W, cross-country running M/W, equestrian sports W, fencing M/W, field hockey W, golf M, lacrosse M/W, soccer M/W, softball W, swimming and diving M/W, tennis M/W, track and field M/W, volleyball M/W, wrestling M. *Intramural sports:* archery M(c)/W(c), baseball M(c), basketball M, bowling M(c)/W(c), crew M(c)/W(c), field hockey M, football M/W(c), ice hockey M(c), lacrosse M(c), sailing M(c)/W(c), skiing (cross-country) M(c)/W(c), skiing (downhill) M(c)/W(c), soccer M(c)/W(c), softball W, squash M, ultimate Frisbee M(c), volleyball M(c)/W(c).

Campus security: 24-hour emergency response devices and patrols, late-night transport/escort service, controlled dormitory access.
Student services: health clinic, personal/psychological counseling, women's center.

COSTS & FINANCIAL AID
Costs (2018–19) *Comprehensive fee:* $67,446 includes full-time tuition ($50,370), mandatory fees ($1832), and room and board ($15,244). Full-time tuition and fees vary according to course load. Part-time tuition: $1679 per credit. Part-time tuition and fees vary according to course load. *Required fees:* $916 per term part-time. *Room and board:* Room and board charges vary according to board plan and housing facility. *Payment plan:* installment. *Waivers:* employees or children of employees.
Financial Aid Of all full-time matriculated undergraduates who enrolled in 2016, 2,948 applied for aid, 2,027 were judged to have need, 355 had their need fully met. 443 Federal Work-Study jobs (averaging $1139). In 2016, 1047 non-need-based awards were made. *Average percent of need met:* 69. *Average financial aid package:* $29,336. *Average need-based loan:* $4466. *Average need-based gift aid:* $12,741. *Average non-need-based aid:* $18,074. *Average indebtedness upon graduation:* $38,402.

APPLYING
Standardized Tests *Required for some:* SAT or ACT (for admission), SAT and SAT Subject Tests or ACT (for admission), Applicants to Music and Technology or Visual Arts and Technology may submit a digital portfolio in place of standardized test scores. International applicants may submit 2 SAT II scores, 2 AP scores, or 2 IB scores in place of standardized test scores.
Options: electronic application, early admission, early decision, deferred entrance.
Application fee: $70.
Required: essay or personal statement, high school transcript, 2 letters of recommendation. *Required for some:* digital portfolio for music and technology or visual arts and technology programs. *Recommended:* interview.
Application deadlines: 1/15 (freshmen), 1/15 (out-of-state freshmen), 6/1 (transfers).
Early decision deadline: 11/15 (for plan 1), 1/15 (for plan 2).
Notification: 4/1 (freshmen), 4/1 (out-of-state freshmen), continuous until 6/30 (transfers), 12/15 (early decision plan 1), 2/15 (early decision plan 2).

CONTACT
Jackie Williams, Dean of Undergraduate Admissions, Stevens Institute of Technology, Castle Point on Hudson, Hoboken, NJ 07030. *Phone:* 201-216-5207. *Toll-free phone:* 800-458-5323. *E-mail:* jackie.williams@ stevens.edu.

★ Stockton University
Galloway, New Jersey
http://www.stockton.edu/

- **State-supported** comprehensive, founded 1969, part of New Jersey State College System
- **Suburban** 2000-acre campus with easy access to Philadelphia
- **Endowment** $28.9 million
- **Coed** 8,275 undergraduate students, 94% full-time, 59% women, 41% men
- **Very difficult** entrance level, 82% of applicants were admitted

UNDERGRAD STUDENTS
7,809 full-time, 466 part-time. Students come from 19 states and territories; 10 other countries; 2% are from out of state; 8% Black or African American, non-Hispanic/Latino; 13% Hispanic/Latino; 6% Asian, non-Hispanic/Latino; 0.2% Native Hawaiian or other Pacific Islander, non-Hispanic/Latino; 0.1% American Indian or Alaska Native, non-Hispanic/Latino; 2% Two or more races, non-Hispanic/Latino; 2% Race/ethnicity unknown; 0.5% international; 12% transferred in; 37% live on campus.

Freshmen:
Admission: 5,706 applied, 4,652 admitted, 1,569 enrolled. *Test scores:* SAT evidence-based reading and writing scores over 500: 83%; SAT math scores over 500: 79%; ACT scores over 18: 89%; SAT evidence-based reading and writing scores over 600: 30%; SAT math scores over 600:

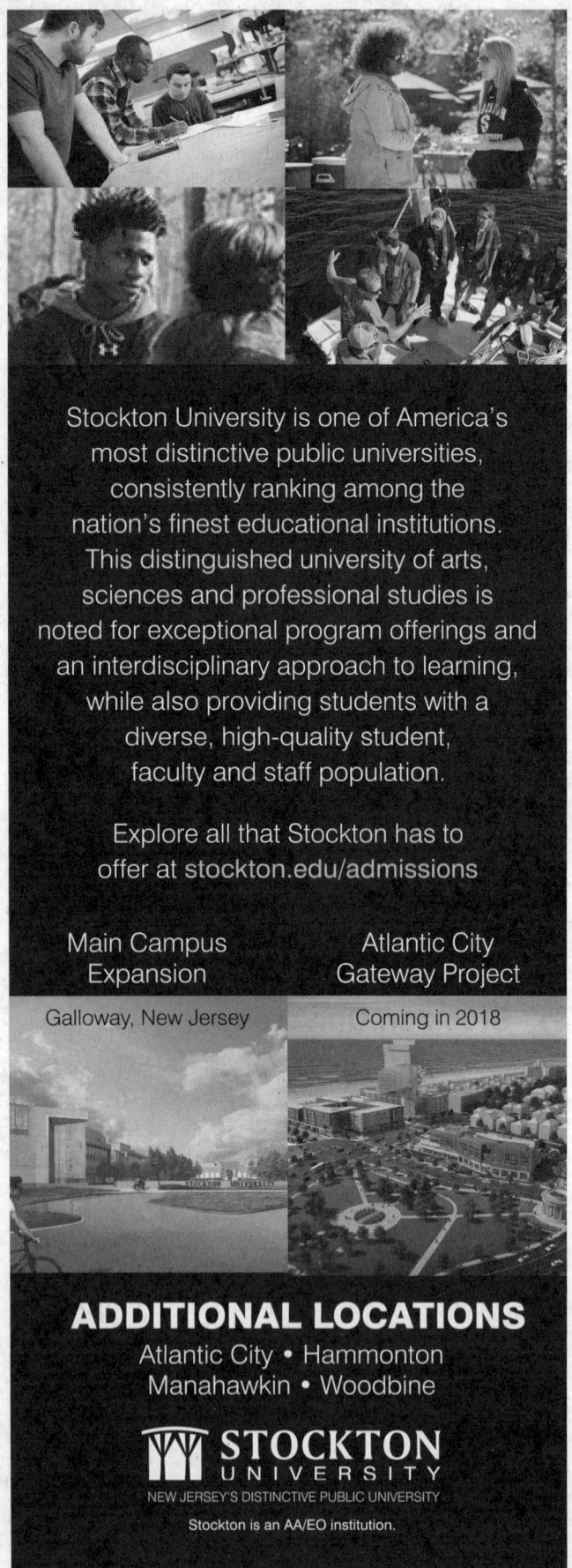

24%; ACT scores over 24: 39%; SAT evidence-based reading and writing scores over 700: 3%; SAT math scores over 700: 3%; ACT scores over 30: 4%.
Retention: 87% of full-time freshmen returned.

FACULTY
Total: 719, 46% full-time, 61% with terminal degrees.
Student/faculty ratio: 17:1.

ACADEMICS
Calendar: semesters. *Degrees:* bachelor's, master's, doctoral, and postbachelor's certificates.

Special study options: academic remediation for entering students, accelerated degree program, adult/continuing education programs, advanced placement credit, distance learning, double majors, English as a second language, honors programs, independent study, internships, off-campus study, part-time degree program, services for LD students, student-designed majors, study abroad, summer session for credit. *ROTC:* Army (c).

Unusual degree programs: 3-2 business administration; engineering with New Jersey Institute of Technology; Rutgers, The State University of New Jersey; Rowan University; public health with Rutgers University, medical technology with University of Delaware.

Computers: 1,224 computers/terminals are available on campus for general student use. Students can access the following: campus intranet, computer help desk, free student e-mail accounts, online (class) grades, online (class) registration, online (class) schedules. Campuswide network is available. 100% of college-owned or -operated housing units are wired for high-speed Internet access. Wireless service is available via entire campus.

Library: Richard E. Bjork Library. *Books:* 222,477 (physical), 142,000 (digital/electronic); *Serial titles:* 127 (physical), 132,055 (digital/electronic); *Databases:* 176. Weekly public service hours: 91.

STUDENT LIFE
Housing options: coed, special housing for students with disabilities. Campus housing is university owned. Freshman campus housing is guaranteed.

Activities and organizations: drama/theater group, student-run newspaper, radio and television station, choral group, Occupational Therapy Club, Sign Language Club, Animal Friendly Organization, Commuters on the Go, Archery Recreational Club of Stockton, national fraternities, national sororities.

Athletics Member NCAA. All Division III. *Intercollegiate sports:* baseball M, basketball M/W, crew W, cross-country running M/W, field hockey W, lacrosse M/W, soccer M/W, softball W, tennis W, track and field M/W, volleyball W. *Intramural sports:* basketball M/W, bowling M(c)/W(c), crew M(c), fencing M(c)/W(c), golf M(c)/W(c), ice hockey M(c)/W(c), soccer M/W, softball M/W, table tennis M(c)/W(c), tennis M(c)/W(c), ultimate Frisbee M(c)/W(c), volleyball M(c).

Campus security: 24-hour emergency response devices and patrols, late-night transport/escort service, controlled dormitory access, on-campus sworn/commissioned police force.

Student services: health clinic, personal/psychological counseling, women's center.

COSTS & FINANCIAL AID
Costs (2017–18) *Tuition:* state resident $8646 full-time, $333 per credit part-time; nonresident $15,599 full-time, $600 per credit part-time. Part-time tuition and fees vary according to course load. *Required fees:* $4758 full-time, $183 per credit part-time, $110 per term part-time. *Room and board:* $12,120; room only: $8070. Room and board charges vary according to board plan and housing facility. *Payment plans:* installment, deferred payment. *Waivers:* senior citizens and employees or children of employees.

Financial Aid Of all full-time matriculated undergraduates who enrolled in 2017, 6,838 applied for aid, 5,672 were judged to have need, 1,435 had their need fully met. 260 Federal Work-Study jobs (averaging $1780). 911 state and other part-time jobs (averaging $1837). In 2017, 517 non-need-based awards were made. *Average percent of need met:* 67. *Average financial aid package:* $16,756. *Average need-based loan:* $4467. *Average need-based gift aid:* $9059. *Average non-need-based aid:* $6175. *Average indebtedness upon graduation:* $33,629.

APPLYING

Standardized Tests *Required:* SAT or ACT (for admission).

Options: electronic application, early admission.

Application fee: $50.

Required: high school transcript, minimum 2.0 GPA. *Recommended:* essay or personal statement, minimum 3.0 GPA, 3 letters of recommendation.

Application deadlines: 5/1 (freshmen), 6/1 (transfers).

Notification: 5/15 (freshmen), continuous until 6/15 (transfers).

CONTACT

Stockton University, 101 Vera King Farris Drive, Galloway, NJ 08205-9441. *Phone:* 609-652-4261.

See previous page for display ad and page 1442 for the College Close-Up.

Strayer University–Cherry Hill Campus

Cherry Hill, New Jersey

http://www.strayer.edu/new-jersey/cherry-hill/

CONTACT

Strayer University–Cherry Hill Campus, 2201 Route 38, Suite 100, Cherry Hill, NJ 08002. *Toll-free phone:* 888-311-0355.

Strayer University–Piscataway Campus

Piscataway, New Jersey

http://www.strayer.edu/new-jersey/piscataway/

CONTACT

Strayer University–Piscataway Campus, 242 Old New Brunswick Road, Suite 220, Piscataway, NJ 08854. *Toll-free phone:* 888-311-0355.

Strayer University–Willingboro Campus

Willingboro, New Jersey

http://www.strayer.edu/new-jersey/willingboro/

CONTACT

Strayer University–Willingboro Campus, 300 Willingboro Parkway, Willingboro Town Center, Suite 125, Willingboro, NJ 08046. *Toll-free phone:* 888-311-0355.

Talmudical Academy of New Jersey

Adelphia, New Jersey

CONTACT

Director of Admissions, Talmudical Academy of New Jersey, 868 Route 524, Adelphia, NJ 07710. *Phone:* 201-431-1600.

Thomas Edison State University

Trenton, New Jersey

http://www.tesu.edu/

- **State-supported** comprehensive, founded 1972
- **Urban** 2-acre campus with easy access to Philadelphia
- **Coed** 15,238 undergraduate students, 43% women, 57% men
- **Noncompetitive** entrance level

UNDERGRAD STUDENTS

49 full-time, 15,189 part-time. 15% Black or African American, non-Hispanic/Latino; 10% Hispanic/Latino; 4% Asian, non-Hispanic/Latino; 0.6% Native Hawaiian or other Pacific Islander, non-Hispanic/Latino; 0.5% American Indian or Alaska Native, non-Hispanic/Latino; 2% Two or more races, non-Hispanic/Latino; 16% Race/ethnicity unknown; 1% international.

ACADEMICS

Calendar: continuous. *Degrees:* certificates, associate, bachelor's, master's, doctoral, and postbachelor's certificates (offers only distance learning degree programs).

Special study options: accelerated degree program, adult/continuing education programs, advanced placement credit, distance learning, double majors, external degree program, independent study, part-time degree program, services for LD students, student-designed majors, summer session for credit.

Computers: Students can access the following: online (class) grades, online (class) registration, online (class) schedules, undergraduate and Nursing students are able to schedule appointments online with their advisors. Campuswide network is available. Wireless service is available via entire campus.

STUDENT LIFE

Housing options: college housing not available.

Campus security: 24-hour emergency response devices and patrols, late-night transport/escort service, security officer from 7 am to 11 pm, local police patrol.

COSTS

Costs (2017–18) *Tuition:* state resident $7300 full-time, $396 per credit hour part-time; nonresident $9820 full-time, $499 per credit hour part-time. *Payment plan:* installment. *Waivers:* employees or children of employees.

APPLYING

Options: electronic application.

Application fee: $75.

Required: must be 21 or older and a high school graduate.

Application deadlines: rolling (freshmen), rolling (transfers).

CONTACT

Ms. Juliette Punchello, Senior Director, Admissions and Enrollment Services, Thomas Edison State University, 111 West State Street, Trenton, NJ 08608. *Phone:* 888-442-8372. *Toll-free phone:* 888-442-8372. *Fax:* 609-984-8447. *E-mail:* admissions@tesu.edu.

William Paterson University of New Jersey

Wayne, New Jersey

http://www.wpunj.edu/

- **State-supported** comprehensive, founded 1855
- **Suburban** 370-acre campus with easy access to New York City
- **Coed** 8,838 undergraduate students, 82% full-time, 54% women, 45% men
- **Moderately difficult** entrance level, 92% of applicants were admitted

UNDERGRAD STUDENTS

7,282 full-time, 1,550 part-time. Students come from 24 states and territories; 37 other countries; 2% are from out of state; 17% Black or African American, non-Hispanic/Latino; 32% Hispanic/Latino; 7% Asian, non-Hispanic/Latino; 0.1% American Indian or Alaska Native, non-Hispanic/Latino; 3% Two or more races, non-Hispanic/Latino; 3% Race/ethnicity unknown; 0.5% international; 11% transferred in; 24% live on campus.

Freshmen:

Admission: 7,933 applied, 7,330 admitted, 1,317 enrolled. *Average high school GPA:* 3.1. *Test scores:* SAT evidence-based reading and writing scores over 500: 61%; SAT math scores over 500: 60%; ACT scores over 18: 76%; SAT evidence-based reading and writing scores over 600: 15%; SAT math scores over 600: 12%; ACT scores over 24: 30%; SAT evidence-based reading and writing scores over 700: 1%; SAT math scores over 700: 1%; ACT scores over 30: 2%.

Retention: 77% of full-time freshmen returned.

FACULTY

Total: 1,042, 39% full-time, 47% with terminal degrees.

Student/faculty ratio: 14:1.

ACADEMICS

Calendar: semesters. *Degrees:* bachelor's, master's, doctoral, post-master's, and postbachelor's certificates.

Special study options: academic remediation for entering students, accelerated degree program, adult/continuing education programs, advanced placement credit, distance learning, double majors, English as a second language, freshman honors college, honors programs, independent study, internships, off-campus study, part-time degree program, services for LD students, study abroad, summer session for credit. *ROTC:* Air Force (c).

Computers: 1,271 computers/terminals and 3,000 ports are available on campus for general student use. Students can access the following: campus intranet, computer help desk, free student e-mail accounts, online (class) grades, online (class) registration, online (class) schedules. Campuswide network is available. 100% of college-owned or -operated housing units are wired for high-speed Internet access. Wireless service is available via entire campus.

Library: David and Lorraine Cheng Library. *Books:* 369,216 (physical), 116,597 (digital/electronic); *Serial titles:* 3,772 (physical), 164,249 (digital/electronic); *Databases:* 126. Weekly public service hours: 102; students can reserve study rooms.

STUDENT LIFE

Housing options: coed, special housing for students with disabilities. Campus housing is university owned. Freshman campus housing is guaranteed.

Activities and organizations: drama/theater group, student-run newspaper, radio and television station, choral group, Student Activities Programming Board (SAPB), Students for Awareness Black Leadership and Equality (SABLE), Student Government Association (SGA), The B.A.B.Y. Dolls (Community Service org.), Pioneer Players (drama), national fraternities, national sororities.

Athletics Member NCAA. All Division III. *Intercollegiate sports:* baseball M, basketball M/W, field hockey W, football M, golf M, soccer M/W, softball W, swimming and diving M/W, tennis W, volleyball W. *Intramural sports:* basketball M/W, bowling M(c), cheerleading M(c)/W(c), equestrian sports M(c)/W(c), field hockey W, ice hockey M(c), racquetball M/W, rugby M(c), soccer W, softball M/W, volleyball M/W.

Campus security: 24-hour emergency response devices and patrols, student patrols, late-night transport/escort service, controlled dormitory access.

Student services: health clinic, personal/psychological counseling, women's center, legal services.

COSTS & FINANCIAL AID

Costs (2017–18) *Tuition:* state resident $12,680 full-time, $406 per credit part-time; nonresident $20,718 full-time, $671 per credit part-time. Full-time tuition and fees vary according to course load. Part-time tuition and fees vary according to course load. *Required fees:* $124 full-time, $4 per credit part-time. *Room and board:* $11,218; room only: $6998. Room and board charges vary according to board plan, housing facility, and location. *Payment plan:* installment. *Waivers:* senior citizens and employees or children of employees.

Financial Aid Of all full-time matriculated undergraduates who enrolled in 2017, 6,620 applied for aid, 5,497 were judged to have need, 1,627 had their need fully met. 210 Federal Work-Study jobs (averaging $1800). In 2017, 510 non-need-based awards were made. *Average financial aid package:* $11,535. *Average need-based loan:* $4330. *Average need-based gift aid:* $8781. *Average non-need-based aid:* $5441. *Average indebtedness upon graduation:* $33,355.

APPLYING

Standardized Tests *Required:* SAT or ACT (for admission).

Options: electronic application.

Application fee: $50.

Required: high school transcript, minimum 2.0 GPA. *Required for some:* essay or personal statement, 1 letter of recommendation, interview, portfolio for art, audition for music.

Application deadlines: 6/1 (freshmen), 8/1 (transfers).

Notification: continuous (freshmen), continuous (transfers).

CONTACT

Mr. Anthony Leckey, Senior Associate Director of Admissions, William Paterson University of New Jersey, Undergraduate Admissions, 300 Pompton Road, Wayne, NJ 07470. *Phone:* 973-720-2900. *Toll-free phone:* 877-WPU-EXCEL. *Fax:* 973-720-2910. *E-mail:* leckeya@wpunj.edu.

Yeshiva Gedolah Shaarei Shmuel
Lakewood, New Jersey
http://www.yeshivagedolahshaareishmuel.com/

CONTACT
Yeshiva Gedolah Shaarei Shmuel, 511 Ocean Avenue, Lakewood, NJ 08701.

Yeshiva Gedolah Zichron Leyma
Linden, New Jersey

CONTACT
Yeshiva Gedolah Zichron Leyma, 1000 Orchard Terrace, Linden, NJ 07036.

Yeshivas Be'er Yitzchok
Elizabeth, New Jersey
http://www.elizabethkollel.org/

CONTACT
Yeshivas Be'er Yitzchok, 1391 North Avenue, Elizabeth, NJ 07208.

Yeshiva Toras Chaim
Lakewood, New Jersey

CONTACT
Yeshiva Toras Chaim, 999 Ridge Avenue, Lakewood, NJ 08701.

NEW MEXICO

Brookline College
Albuquerque, New Mexico
http://brooklinecollege.edu/

CONTACT
Mr. Andrew Webb, Campus Director, Brookline College, 4201 Central Avenue NW, Suite J, Albuquerque, NM 87105. *Phone:* 505-880-2877. *Toll-free phone:* 888-660-2428. *Fax:* 505-352-0199. *E-mail:* awebb@brooklinecollege.edu.

Eastern New Mexico University
Portales, New Mexico
http://www.enmu.edu/

- **State-supported** comprehensive, founded 1934
- **Rural** 344-acre campus
- **Endowment** $9.8 million
- **Coed** 4,599 undergraduate students, 56% full-time, 56% women, 44% men
- **Noncompetitive** entrance level, 60% of applicants were admitted

UNDERGRAD STUDENTS
2,590 full-time, 2,009 part-time. Students come from 48 states and territories; 22 other countries; 22% are from out of state; 6% Black or African American, non-Hispanic/Latino; 42% Hispanic/Latino; 0.9% Asian, non-Hispanic/Latino; 0.7% Native Hawaiian or other Pacific Islander, non-Hispanic/Latino; 2% American Indian or Alaska Native, non-Hispanic/Latino; 3% Two or more races, non-Hispanic/Latino; 2% Race/ethnicity unknown; 2% international; 10% transferred in; 16% live on campus.

Freshmen:
Admission: 2,635 applied, 1,594 admitted, 630 enrolled. *Average high school GPA:* 3.3. *Test scores:* SAT evidence-based reading and writing scores over 500: 52%; SAT math scores over 500: 45%; ACT scores over 18: 70%; SAT evidence-based reading and writing scores over 600: 6%; SAT math scores over 600: 10%; ACT scores over 24: 18%; ACT scores over 30: 1%.
Retention: 59% of full-time freshmen returned.

FACULTY
Total: 330, 47% full-time, 44% with terminal degrees.
Student/faculty ratio: 19:1.

ACADEMICS
Calendar: semesters. *Degrees:* certificates, associate, bachelor's, master's, and postbachelor's certificates.

Special study options: academic remediation for entering students, accelerated degree program, adult/continuing education programs, advanced placement credit, cooperative education, distance learning, double majors, English as a second language, independent study, internships, part-time degree program, services for LD students, student-designed majors, summer session for credit.

Unusual degree programs: 3-2 chemistry.

Computers: 453 computers/terminals are available on campus for general student use. Students can access the following: campus intranet, computer help desk, free student e-mail accounts, online (class) grades, online (class) registration, online (class) schedules. Campuswide network is available. 100% of college-owned or -operated housing units are wired for high-speed Internet access. Wireless service is available via entire campus.
Library: Golden Library plus 2 others.

STUDENT LIFE
Housing options: on-campus residence required for freshman year; coed, women-only, special housing for students with disabilities. Campus housing is university owned. Freshman campus housing is guaranteed.

Activities and organizations: drama/theater group, student-run newspaper, radio and television station, choral group, marching band, Student Government, Student Activities Board, Residence Hall Association, IFC (Inter-Fraternity Council)Panhellenic Council, national fraternities, national sororities.

Athletics Member NCAA. All Division II. *Intercollegiate sports:* baseball M(s), basketball M(s)/W(s), cross-country running M(s)/W(s), football M(s), soccer M(s)/W(s), softball W(s), track and field M(s)/W(s), volleyball W(s). *Intramural sports:* badminton M/W, basketball M/W, cross-country running M/W, football M/W, racquetball M/W, soccer M/W, softball M/W, tennis M/W, volleyball M/W, water polo M/W.

Campus security: 24-hour emergency response devices and patrols, late-night transport/escort service, controlled dormitory access, University Emergency Notification System, security cameras, security lights.

Student services: health clinic, personal/psychological counseling.

FINANCIAL AID
Financial Aid Of all full-time matriculated undergraduates who enrolled in 2014, 1,617 applied for aid, 1,616 were judged to have need, 1,616 had their need fully met. In 2014, 45 non-need-based awards were made. *Average percent of need met:* 40. *Average financial aid package:* $10,675. *Average need-based loan:* $3904. *Average need-based gift aid:* $4301. *Average non-need-based aid:* $4803. *Average indebtedness upon graduation:* $4895.

APPLYING
Standardized Tests *Required for some:* SAT (for admission), ACT (for admission).

Options: electronic application.

Required: official transcripts from any post-secondary institution attended, good standing with all previous institutions. *Required for some:* high school transcript, minimum 2.5 GPA.

Application deadlines: 8/24 (freshmen), rolling (out-of-state freshmen), 8/24 (transfers).

Notification: continuous until 8/1 (freshmen), continuous until 8/1 (out-of-state freshmen), continuous until 8/1 (transfers).

CONTACT
Eastern New Mexico University, 1500 South Avenue K, Portales, NM 88130. *Toll-free phone:* 800-367-3668.

EC-Council University
Albuquerque, New Mexico
http://www.eccu.edu/
- **Proprietary** upper-level, founded 2003
- **Coed**

FACULTY
Student/faculty ratio: 5:1.

ACADEMICS
Degrees: bachelor's and master's.

Special study options: academic remediation for entering students, distance learning, internships, part-time degree program, services for LD students.

STUDENT LIFE
Housing options: college housing not available.

APPLYING
Options: electronic application, early admission, deferred entrance.

CONTACT
EC-Council University, 101 C Sun Avenue NE, Albuquerque, NM 87109.

Institute of American Indian Arts
Santa Fe, New Mexico
http://www.iaia.edu/
- **Federally supported** comprehensive, founded 1962
- **Suburban** 140-acre campus with easy access to Albuquerque
- **Coed** 607 undergraduate students, 49% full-time, 55% women, 45% men

UNDERGRAD STUDENTS
299 full-time, 308 part-time. 0.3% Black or African American, non-Hispanic/Latino; 14% Hispanic/Latino; 1% Asian, non-Hispanic/Latino; 68% American Indian or Alaska Native, non-Hispanic/Latino; 2% Two or more races, non-Hispanic/Latino; 7% Race/ethnicity unknown; 0.5% international.

Freshmen:
Admission: 80 enrolled.

FACULTY
Student/faculty ratio: 7:1.

ACADEMICS
Calendar: semesters. *Degrees:* certificates, associate, bachelor's, and master's.

Special study options: academic remediation for entering students, advanced placement credit, distance learning, double majors, independent study, internships, off-campus study, part-time degree program, services for LD students, study abroad, summer session for credit.

Computers: 100 computers/terminals are available on campus for general student use. Students can access the following: campus intranet, computer help desk, free student e-mail accounts, online (class) grades, online (class) registration, online (class) schedules. Campuswide network is available. 100% of college-owned or -operated housing units are wired for high-speed Internet access. Wireless service is available via entire campus.
Library: IAIA Library plus 1 other. Students can reserve study rooms.

STUDENT LIFE
Housing options: on-campus residence required for freshman year; coed, special housing for students with disabilities. Campus housing is university owned. Freshman campus housing is guaranteed.

Activities and organizations: drama/theater group, student-run newspaper, television station.

Athletics *Intramural sports:* archery M/W.

Campus security: 24-hour patrols, late-night transport/escort service, controlled dormitory access.

Student services: personal/psychological counseling.

COSTS & FINANCIAL AID

Costs (2017–18) *Tuition:* state resident $4700 full-time, $196 per semester hour part-time; nonresident $4700 full-time, $196 per semester hour part-time. *Required fees:* $260 full-time, $130 per term part-time. *Room and board:* $9100; room only: $3910. Room and board charges vary according to board plan and housing facility. *Payment plan:* installment. *Waivers:* employees or children of employees.

Financial Aid Of all full-time matriculated undergraduates who enrolled in 2011, 263 applied for aid, 261 were judged to have need, 201 had their need fully met. 2 Federal Work-Study jobs (averaging $2300). 3 state and other part-time jobs (averaging $2300). In 2011, 58 non-need-based awards were made. *Average percent of need met:* 71. *Average financial aid package:* $5005. *Average need-based gift aid:* $2500. *Average non-need-based aid:* $2500.

APPLYING

Required: high school transcript. *Required for some:* essay or personal statement, interview. *Recommended:* interview.

CONTACT

Ms. Mary Silentwalker, Director, Admissions and Recruitment, Institute of American Indian Arts, 83 Avan Nu Po Road, Santa Fe, NM 87508. *Phone:* 505-424-2307. *Fax:* 505-424-0909. *E-mail:* mary.silentwalker@iaia.edu.

National American University

Albuquerque, New Mexico

http://www.national.edu/

CONTACT

Admissions Office, National American University, 10131 Coors Boulevard NW, Suite I-01, Albuquerque, NM 87114. *Toll-free phone:* 800-895-9904.

National American University

Albuquerque, New Mexico

http://www.national.edu/

CONTACT

National American University, 4775 Indian School Road NE, Suite 200, Albuquerque, NM 87110. *Phone:* 505-265-7517. *Toll-free phone:* 800-895-9904.

National College of Midwifery

Taos, New Mexico

http://www.midwiferycollege.org/

CONTACT

Ms. Beth Enson, Dean of Students, National College of Midwifery, 1041 Reed Street, Suite C, Taos, NM 87571. *Phone:* 505-758-8914. *E-mail:* info@midwiferycollege.org.

Navajo Technical University

Crownpoint, New Mexico

http://www.navajotech.edu/

CONTACT

Director of Admission, Navajo Technical University, PO Box 849, Crownpoint, NM 87313. *Phone:* 505-786-4100.

New Mexico Highlands University

Las Vegas, New Mexico

http://www.nmhu.edu/

- **State-supported** comprehensive, founded 1893
- **Small-town** campus
- **Coed** 2,181 undergraduate students, 66% full-time, 63% women, 37% men
- **Minimally difficult** entrance level, 100% of applicants were admitted

UNDERGRAD STUDENTS

1,442 full-time, 739 part-time. 15% are from out of state; 5% Black or African American, non-Hispanic/Latino; 58% Hispanic/Latino; 0.6% Asian, non-Hispanic/Latino; 0.6% Native Hawaiian or other Pacific Islander, non-Hispanic/Latino; 8% American Indian or Alaska Native, non-Hispanic/Latino; 2% Two or more races, non-Hispanic/Latino; 1% Race/ethnicity unknown; 5% international; 18% transferred in; 22% live on campus.

Freshmen:
Admission: 1,158 applied, 1,158 admitted, 316 enrolled. *Average high school GPA:* 3.0.
Retention: 53% of full-time freshmen returned.

FACULTY

Total: 249, 55% full-time, 43% with terminal degrees.
Student/faculty ratio: 15:1.

ACADEMICS

Calendar: semesters. *Degrees:* bachelor's, master's, post-master's, and postbachelor's certificates.

Special study options: academic remediation for entering students, accelerated degree program, adult/continuing education programs, advanced placement credit, cooperative education, distance learning, double majors, honors programs, independent study, internships, off-campus study, part-time degree program, services for LD students, summer session for credit.

Computers: Students can access the following: online (class) registration. Campuswide network is available.
Library: Thomas C. Donnelly Library.

STUDENT LIFE

Housing options: coed, special housing for students with disabilities. Campus housing is university owned.

Activities and organizations: drama/theater group, student-run radio station, choral group, marching band, Vatos Rugby, Fire Escape Club, MeChA, NMHU Cheerleaders, NMHU Student Ambassadors, national fraternities, national sororities.

Athletics Member NCAA. All Division II. *Intercollegiate sports:* baseball M(s), basketball M(s)/W(s), cross-country running M(s)/W(s), football M(s), soccer W(s), softball W(s), track and field M/W, volleyball W(s). *Intramural sports:* badminton M/W, basketball M/W, football M, golf M/W, racquetball M/W, rugby M, skiing (cross-country) M/W, skiing (downhill) M/W, softball W, swimming and diving M/W, table tennis M/W, tennis M/W, volleyball M/W, weight lifting M/W.

Campus security: 24-hour emergency response devices and patrols, late-night transport/escort service, controlled dormitory access.

Student services: health clinic, personal/psychological counseling, women's center.

COSTS & FINANCIAL AID

Costs (2017–18) *One-time required fee:* $15. *Tuition:* state resident $4748 full-time, $177 per credit hour part-time; nonresident $8117 full-time, $316 per credit hour part-time. Full-time tuition and fees vary according to course load and location. Part-time tuition and fees vary according to course load and location. *Required fees:* $1706 full-time, $65 per term part-time. *Room and board:* $7654; room only: $3740. Room and board charges vary according to board plan and housing facility. *Payment plan:* installment. *Waivers:* senior citizens and employees or children of employees.

Financial Aid Of all full-time matriculated undergraduates who enrolled in 2015, 1,299 applied for aid, 1,136 were judged to have need, 96 had their need fully met. In 2015, 506 non-need-based awards were made. *Average percent of need met:* 19. *Average financial aid package:* $1811. *Average need-based loan:* $2531. *Average need-based gift aid:* $1945. *Average non-need-based aid:* $2229. *Average indebtedness upon graduation:* $17,312.

APPLYING

Options: electronic application, early admission, deferred entrance.
Required: high school transcript, minimum 2.0 GPA. *Required for some:* 2 letters of recommendation, interview.

CONTACT

Ms. Jessica Jaramillo, Director of Recruitment and Admissions, New Mexico Highlands University, Box 9000, Las Vegas, NM 87701. *Phone:* 505-454-3394. *Toll-free phone:* 800-338-6648. *E-mail:* admissions@nmhu.edu.

New Mexico Institute of Mining and Technology

Socorro, New Mexico

http://www.nmt.edu/

- **State-supported** university, founded 1889
- **Small-town** 320-acre campus with easy access to Albuquerque
- **Endowment** $45.0 million
- **Coed** 1,471 undergraduate students, 88% full-time, 30% women, 70% men
- **Moderately difficult** entrance level, 22% of applicants were admitted

UNDERGRAD STUDENTS

1,294 full-time, 177 part-time. Students come from 30 states and territories; 7 other countries; 11% are from out of state; 2% Black or African American, non-Hispanic/Latino; 30% Hispanic/Latino; 4% Asian, non-Hispanic/Latino; 0.1% Native Hawaiian or other Pacific Islander, non-Hispanic/Latino; 4% American Indian or Alaska Native, non-Hispanic/Latino; 5% Two or more races, non-Hispanic/Latino; 1% Race/ethnicity unknown; 2% international; 5% transferred in; 50% live on campus.

Freshmen:

Admission: 1,513 applied, 328 admitted, 240 enrolled. *Average high school GPA:* 3.7. *Test scores:* SAT evidence-based reading and writing scores over 500: 86%; SAT math scores over 500: 84%; ACT scores over 18: 100%; SAT evidence-based reading and writing scores over 600: 86%; SAT math scores over 600: 67%; ACT scores over 24: 74%; SAT evidence-based reading and writing scores over 700: 43%; SAT math scores over 700: 17%; ACT scores over 30: 24%.

Retention: 74% of full-time freshmen returned.

FACULTY

Total: 188, 70% full-time.

Student/faculty ratio: 11:1.

ACADEMICS

Calendar: semesters. *Degrees:* associate, bachelor's, master's, and doctoral.

Special study options: accelerated degree program, advanced placement credit, cooperative education, distance learning, double majors, independent study, internships, services for LD students, student-designed majors, summer session for credit.

Unusual degree programs: 3-2 earth science, biology, math, physics.

Computers: 225 computers/terminals are available on campus for general student use. Students can access the following: computer help desk, free student e-mail accounts, online (class) registration, online (class) schedules. Campuswide network is available. Wireless service is available via computer centers, learning centers, student centers.

Library: The Skeen Library. Students can reserve study rooms.

STUDENT LIFE

Housing options: coed, men-only, women-only. Campus housing is university owned.

Activities and organizations: drama/theater group, student-run newspaper, radio station, choral group.

Athletics *Intercollegiate sports:* rugby M(c)/W(c), soccer M(c)/W(c). *Intramural sports:* badminton M/W, basketball M/W, soccer M/W, softball M/W, volleyball M/W.

Campus security: 24-hour emergency response devices and patrols, late-night transport/escort service.

Student services: health clinic, personal/psychological counseling.

COSTS & FINANCIAL AID

Costs (2017–18) *Tuition:* state resident $6133 full-time, $256 per credit hour part-time; nonresident $19,941 full-time, $831 per credit hour part-time. Full-time tuition and fees vary according to reciprocity agreements. Part-time tuition and fees vary according to course load. *Required fees:* $1050 full-time, $17 per credit hour part-time, $309 per term part-time. *Room and board:* $8202. Room and board charges vary according to board plan and housing facility. *Waivers:* senior citizens and employees or children of employees.

Financial Aid Of all full-time matriculated undergraduates who enrolled in 2017, 1,159 applied for aid, 691 were judged to have need, 141 had

their need fully met. In 2017, 418 non-need-based awards were made. *Average percent of need met:* 78. *Average financial aid package:* $12,524. *Average need-based loan:* $4408. *Average need-based gift aid:* $6059. *Average non-need-based aid:* $5656. *Average indebtedness upon graduation:* $26,817.

APPLYING

Standardized Tests *Required:* SAT or ACT (for admission). *Recommended:* ACT (for admission).

Options: electronic application, deferred entrance.

Application fee: $15.

Required: high school transcript, minimum 2.5 GPA. *Required for some:* 2 letters of recommendation. *Recommended:* interview.

Application deadlines: 8/1 (freshmen), 8/1 (transfers).

Notification: continuous (freshmen), continuous (transfers).

CONTACT

Mr. Anthony Ortiz, Director of Admissions, New Mexico Institute of Mining and Technology, 801 Leroy Place, Socorro, NM 87801. *Phone:* 575-835-5424. *Toll-free phone:* 800-428-TECH. *Fax:* 575-835-5989. *E-mail:* admission@nmt.edu.

New Mexico State University

Las Cruces, New Mexico

http://www.nmsu.edu/

- **State-supported** university, founded 1888, part of New Mexico State University System
- **Suburban** 900-acre campus with easy access to El Paso, TX
- **Endowment** $167.5 million
- **Coed** 11,713 undergraduate students, 83% full-time, 55% women, 45% men
- **Moderately difficult** entrance level, 64% of applicants were admitted

UNDERGRAD STUDENTS

9,703 full-time, 2,010 part-time. Students come from 54 states and territories; 50 other countries; 26% are from out of state; 3% Black or African American, non-Hispanic/Latino; 59% Hispanic/Latino; 1% Asian, non-Hispanic/Latino; 0.1% Native Hawaiian or other Pacific Islander, non-Hispanic/Latino; 2% American Indian or Alaska Native, non-Hispanic/Latino; 2% Two or more races, non-Hispanic/Latino; 1% Race/ethnicity unknown; 4% international; 5% transferred in; 20% live on campus.

Freshmen:

Admission: 8,192 applied, 5,230 admitted, 2,042 enrolled. *Average high school GPA:* 3.5. *Test scores:* SAT evidence-based reading and writing scores over 500: 59%; SAT math scores over 500: 62%; ACT scores over 18: 79%; SAT evidence-based reading and writing scores over 600: 20%; SAT math scores over 600: 16%; ACT scores over 24: 24%; SAT evidence-based reading and writing scores over 700: 2%; SAT math scores over 700: 2%; ACT scores over 30: 3%.

Retention: 74% of full-time freshmen returned.

FACULTY

Total: 976, 65% full-time, 74% with terminal degrees.

Student/faculty ratio: 16:1.

ACADEMICS

Calendar: semesters. *Degrees:* certificates, associate, bachelor's, master's, doctoral, post-master's, and postbachelor's certificates.

Special study options: academic remediation for entering students, accelerated degree program, advanced placement credit, cooperative education, distance learning, double majors, English as a second language, freshman honors college, honors programs, independent study, internships, off-campus study, part-time degree program, services for LD students, student-designed majors, study abroad, summer session for credit. *ROTC:* Army (b), Air Force (b).

Unusual degree programs: engineering; pharmacy with University of New Mexico, accountancy and physics.

Computers: 708 computers/terminals and 600 ports are available on campus for general student use. Students can access the following: campus intranet, computer help desk, free student e-mail accounts, online (class) grades, online (class) registration, online (class) schedules, antivirus software; student portal online with file share/storage space, student employee clock-in, payments system, hardware rentals, short-term tablet checkout, software discounts. Campuswide network is available. 100% of college-owned or -operated housing units are wired for high-speed Internet access. Wireless service is available via entire campus. **Library:** New Mexico State University Library - Zuhl plus 1 other. *Books:* 1.2 million (physical), 160,068 (digital/electronic); *Serial titles:* 23,730 (physical), 135,113 (digital/electronic); *Databases:* 410. Weekly public service hours: 112; students can reserve study rooms.

STUDENT LIFE

Housing options: on-campus residence required for freshman year; coed. Campus housing is university owned. Freshman campus housing is guaranteed.

Activities and organizations: drama/theater group, student-run newspaper, radio and television station, choral group, marching band, national fraternities, national sororities.

Athletics Member NCAA. All Division I except football (Division I-A). *Intercollegiate sports:* baseball M(s), basketball M(s)/W(s), cross-country running M(s)/W(s), golf M(s)/W(s), soccer W(s), softball W(s), swimming and diving W(s), tennis M(s)/W(s), track and field W(s), volleyball W(s). *Intramural sports:* badminton M(c)/W(c), basketball M/W, cheerleading M/W, fencing M(c)/W(c), football M/W, golf M/W, racquetball M/W, rugby M(c)/W(c), soccer M(c)/W(c), softball M/W, table tennis M/W, tennis M(c)/W(c), ultimate Frisbee M(c)/W(c), volleyball M(c)/W(c), water polo M/W, weight lifting M(c)/W(c).

Campus security: 24-hour emergency response devices and patrols, late-night transport/escort service, controlled dormitory access.

Student services: health clinic, personal/psychological counseling, legal services.

COSTS & FINANCIAL AID

Costs (2017–18) *One-time required fee:* $165. *Tuition:* state resident $5323 full-time, $222 per credit hour part-time; nonresident $19,884 full-time, $829 per credit hour part-time. Full-time tuition and fees vary according to course load and reciprocity agreements. Part-time tuition and fees vary according to course load and reciprocity agreements. *Required fees:* $1138 full-time, $47 per credit hour part-time. *Room and board:* $8686; room only: $4886. Room and board charges vary according to board plan and housing facility. *Payment plan:* installment. *Waivers:* senior citizens and employees or children of employees.

Financial Aid Of all full-time matriculated undergraduates who enrolled in 2016, 7,186 applied for aid, 6,283 were judged to have need, 592 had their need fully met. 247 Federal Work-Study jobs (averaging $2734). 338 state and other part-time jobs (averaging $5916). In 2016, 1307 non-need-based awards were made. *Average percent of need met:* 65. *Average financial aid package:* $12,018. *Average need-based loan:* $3507. *Average need-based gift aid:* $9202. *Average non-need-based aid:* $2578. *Average indebtedness upon graduation:* $21,019. *Financial aid deadline:* 6/30.

APPLYING

Standardized Tests *Required:* SAT or ACT (for admission).

Options: electronic application.

Application fee: $20.

Required: high school transcript, high school course requirements: 4 units of English, 4 of math, 2 of science beyond general science, and 1 foreign language/fine art; must have 2.75 HS GPA, rank in the top 20% of graduating class, or ACT composite score of 21 (SAT of 1060 new format). *Required for some:* 3 letters of recommendation.

Application deadlines: rolling (freshmen), rolling (transfers).

Notification: continuous (freshmen), continuous (transfers).

CONTACT

Danielle Staley, Interim Director of Admissions, New Mexico State University, Box 30001, MSC 3A, Las Cruces, NM 88003-8001. *Phone:* 575-646-3121. *Toll-free phone:* 800-662-6678. *Fax:* 575-646-6330. *E-mail:* admssions@nmsu.edu.

Northern New Mexico College
Española, New Mexico
http://www.nnmc.edu/

CONTACT
Mr. Mike L. Costello, Registrar, Northern New Mexico College, 921 Paseo de Oñate, Española, NM 87532. *Phone:* 505-747-2193. *Fax:* 505-747-2191. *E-mail:* dms@nnmc.edu.

Pima Medical Institute
Albuquerque, New Mexico
http://www.pmi.edu/

CONTACT
Admissions Office, Pima Medical Institute, 4400 Cutler Avenue NE, Albuquerque, NM 87110. *Phone:* 505-881-1234. *Toll-free phone:* 800-477-PIMA. *Fax:* 505-881-5329.

St. John's College
Santa Fe, New Mexico
http://www.sjc.edu/

- **Independent** comprehensive, founded 1964
- **Small-town** 250-acre campus with easy access to Albuquerque, NM
- **Endowment** $168.5 million
- **Coed** 322 undergraduate students, 96% full-time, 44% women, 56% men
- **Moderately difficult** entrance level, 63% of applicants were admitted

UNDERGRAD STUDENTS
309 full-time, 13 part-time. Students come from 42 states and territories; 28 other countries; 87% are from out of state; 0.9% Black or African American, non-Hispanic/Latino; 9% Hispanic/Latino; 2% Asian, non-Hispanic/Latino; 6% Two or more races, non-Hispanic/Latino; 0.9% Race/ethnicity unknown; 26% international; 5% transferred in; 83% live on campus.

Freshmen:

Admission: 342 applied, 216 admitted, 70 enrolled. *Average high school GPA:* 3.5. *Test scores:* SAT evidence-based reading and writing scores over 500: 100%; SAT math scores over 500: 100%; ACT scores over 18: 95%; SAT evidence-based reading and writing scores over 600: 80%; SAT math scores over 600: 59%; ACT scores over 24: 81%; SAT evidence-based reading and writing scores over 700: 52%; SAT math scores over 700: 28%; ACT scores over 30: 45%.

Retention: 68% of full-time freshmen returned.

FACULTY
Total: 54, 80% full-time, 87% with terminal degrees.

Student/faculty ratio: 8:1.

ACADEMICS
Calendar: semesters. *Degrees:* bachelor's and master's.

Special study options: English as a second language, internships, off-campus study, services for LD students, study abroad, summer session for credit.

Computers: 16 computers/terminals and 425 ports are available on campus for general student use. Students can access the following: campus intranet, computer help desk, free student e-mail accounts, Support for &"bring your own"; mobile devices. Campuswide network is available. 100% of college-owned or -operated housing units are wired for high-speed Internet access. Wireless service is available via entire campus.

Library: Meem Library. *Books:* 70,251 (physical); *Serial titles:* 69 (physical); *Databases:* 9. Weekly public service hours: 82; study areas open 24 hours, 5–7 days a week.

STUDENT LIFE
Housing options: on-campus residence required through senior year; coed, men-only, women-only, special housing for students with disabilities. Campus housing is university owned. Freshman campus housing is guaranteed.

Activities and organizations: drama/theater group, student-run newspaper, choral group, Student Government (Polity), Iron Bookworm Workout, Intramural sports, PiYo , International Student Association.

Athletics *Intramural sports:* archery M(c)/W(c), basketball M(c)/W(c), fencing M(c)/W(c), field hockey M/W, ice hockey M(c)/W(c), rock climbing M/W, skiing (cross-country) M/W, skiing (downhill) M/W, soccer M(c)/W(c), softball M(c)/W, squash M/W, swimming and diving M/W, table tennis M(c)/W(c), tennis M/W, ultimate Frisbee M/W, volleyball M/W, weight lifting M(c)/W(c).

Campus security: 24-hour emergency response devices and patrols, late-night transport/escort service, controlled dormitory access, Crime Prevention Education and Awareness.

Student services: health clinic, personal/psychological counseling.

COSTS & FINANCIAL AID
Costs (2018–19) *Comprehensive fee:* $65,366 includes full-time tuition ($52,734), mandatory fees ($484), and room and board ($12,148). Full-time tuition and fees vary according to location. Part-time tuition: $1551 per credit. *Room and board:* Room and board charges vary according to board plan, housing facility, and location. *Payment plan:* installment. *Waivers:* employees or children of employees.

Financial Aid Of all full-time matriculated undergraduates who enrolled in 2017, 309 applied for aid, 303 were judged to have need, 132 had their need fully met. 76 Federal Work-Study jobs (averaging $2791). 100 state and other part-time jobs (averaging $2827). In 2017, 41 non-need-based awards were made. *Average percent of need met:* 89. *Average financial aid package:* $42,100. *Average need-based loan:* $7450. *Average need-based gift aid:* $33,500. *Average non-need-based aid:* $19,583. *Average indebtedness upon graduation:* $26,990.

APPLYING
Standardized Tests *Required for some:* SAT or ACT (for admission), SAT/ACT, TOEFL/IELTS or interview for international applicants; SAT/ACT/CLT for homeschooled students and applicants who have not and will not graduate high school.

Options: electronic application, early admission, early action, deferred entrance.

Required: essay or personal statement, high school transcript, 2 letters of recommendation. *Required for some:* outline of curriculum for home-schooled applicants. *Recommended:* interview.

Application deadlines: rolling (freshmen), rolling (transfers), 11/15 (early action).

Notification: continuous (freshmen), continuous (transfers), 12/15 (early action).

CONTACT
Ms. Yvette Sobky Shaffer, Director of Admissions, St. John's College, 1160 Camino Cruz Blanca, Santa Fe, NM 87505. *Phone:* 505-984-6060. *Toll-free phone:* 800-331-5232. *E-mail:* santafe.admissions@sjc.edu.

University of New Mexico
Albuquerque, New Mexico
http://www.unm.edu/
- **State-supported** university, founded 1889
- **Urban** 769-acre campus with easy access to Albuquerque
- **Endowment** $400.8 million
- **Coed** 19,516 undergraduate students, 77% full-time, 56% women, 44% men
- **Moderately difficult** entrance level, 49% of applicants were admitted

UNDERGRAD STUDENTS
15,060 full-time, 4,456 part-time. 13% are from out of state; 2% Black or African American, non-Hispanic/Latino; 49% Hispanic/Latino; 4% Asian, non-Hispanic/Latino; 0.2% Native Hawaiian or other Pacific Islander, non-Hispanic/Latino; 6% American Indian or Alaska Native, non-Hispanic/Latino; 4% Two or more races, non-Hispanic/Latino; 1% Race/ethnicity unknown; 2% international; 9% transferred in; 6% live on campus.

Freshmen:
Admission: 11,347 applied, 5,604 admitted, 3,221 enrolled. *Average high school GPA:* 3.4. *Test scores:* SAT evidence-based reading and writing scores over 500: 84%; SAT math scores over 500: 84%; ACT scores over 18: 87%; SAT evidence-based reading and writing scores over 600: 45%; SAT math scores over 600: 37%; ACT scores over 24: 36%; SAT

evidence-based reading and writing scores over 700: 9%; SAT math scores over 700: 8%; ACT scores over 30: 6%.

FACULTY
Total: 1,451, 76% full-time, 64% with terminal degrees.
Student/faculty ratio: 16:1.

ACADEMICS
Calendar: semesters. *Degrees:* certificates, associate, bachelor's, master's, doctoral, and post-master's certificates.

Special study options: academic remediation for entering students, accelerated degree program, adult/continuing education programs, advanced placement credit, cooperative education, distance learning, double majors, English as a second language, freshman honors college, honors programs, independent study, internships, off-campus study, part-time degree program, services for LD students, student-designed majors, study abroad, summer session for credit. *ROTC:* Army (b), Navy (b), Air Force (b).

Unusual degree programs: 3-2 business administration; engineering; Latin American studies, business.

Computers: 990 computers/terminals and 56,000 ports are available on campus for general student use. Students can access the following: campus intranet, computer help desk, free student e-mail accounts, online (class) grades, online (class) registration, online (class) schedules. Campuswide network is available. 100% of college-owned or -operated housing units are wired for high-speed Internet access. Wireless service is available via entire campus.

Library: College of University Libraries and Learning Sciences plus 7 others. Students can reserve study rooms.

STUDENT LIFE
Housing options: coed, special housing for students with disabilities. Campus housing is university owned and is provided by a third party.

Activities and organizations: drama/theater group, student-run newspaper, radio and television station, choral group, marching band, Associated Students of UNM, Graduate and Professional Students Association, Golden Key National Honor Society, national fraternities, national sororities.

Athletics Member NCAA. All Division I except football (Division I-A). *Intercollegiate sports:* baseball M(s), basketball M(s)/W(s), cross-country running M(s)/W(s), golf M(s)/W(s), skiing (cross-country) M(s)/W(s), skiing (downhill) M(s)/W(s), soccer M(s)/W(s), softball W(s), swimming and diving M/W(s), tennis M(s)/W(s), track and field M(s)/W(s), volleyball W(s). *Intramural sports:* archery M/W, badminton M/W, basketball M/W, bowling M(c)/W(c), cheerleading M(c)/W(c), fencing M/W, football M, golf M/W, ice hockey M(c)/W(c), lacrosse M(c)/W(c), racquetball M/W, rugby M(c)/W(c), skiing (cross-country) M/W, skiing (downhill) M/W, soccer M/W, softball M/W, swimming and diving W, table tennis M/W, tennis M/W, ultimate Frisbee M(c)/W(c), volleyball M/W, water polo M/W, wrestling M(c).

Campus security: 24-hour emergency response devices and patrols, student patrols, late-night transport/escort service, controlled dormitory access.

Student services: health clinic, personal/psychological counseling, women's center.

COSTS
Costs (2017–18) *Tuition:* state resident $5286 full-time, $248 per credit hour part-time; nonresident $20,549 full-time, $856 per credit hour part-time. Full-time tuition and fees vary according to course level and program. Part-time tuition and fees vary according to course level, course load, and program. *Required fees:* $1860 full-time, $62 per credit hour part-time. *Room and board:* $9662. Room and board charges vary according to board plan and housing facility. *Payment plan:* installment. *Waivers:* senior citizens and employees or children of employees.

APPLYING
Standardized Tests *Required:* SAT or ACT (for admission).
Options: electronic application, early admission, deferred entrance.
Application fee: $25.
Required: high school transcript, minimum 2.5 GPA. *Required for some:* essay or personal statement, interview.
Application deadlines: rolling (freshmen), rolling (transfers).
Notification: continuous (freshmen), continuous (transfers).

CONTACT
Mr. Matthew Hulett, Director of Admissions and Recruitment Services, University of New Mexico, Office of Admissions, PO Box 4895, Albuquerque, NM 87196-4895. *Phone:* 505-277-8900. *Toll-free phone:* 800-CALL-UNM. *Fax:* 505-277-6686. *E-mail:* apply@unm.edu.

University of the Southwest
Hobbs, New Mexico
http://www.usw.edu/
- **Independent Christian** comprehensive, founded 1962
- **Small-town** 162-acre campus
- **Endowment** $5.6 million
- **Coed**
- **Moderately difficult** entrance level

FACULTY
Student/faculty ratio: 17:1.

ACADEMICS
Calendar: semesters. *Degrees:* bachelor's and master's.
Library: Scarborough Memorial Library.

STUDENT LIFE
Housing options: on-campus residence required through sophomore year; coed. Campus housing is university owned. Freshman applicants given priority for college housing.

Activities and organizations: Student Government Association (SGA), Students in Free Enterprise (SIFE), Southwest Association of Future Educators, Fellowship of Christian Athletes, BEST.

Athletics Member NAIA.

Campus security: student patrols, controlled dormitory access, night security.

Student services: personal/psychological counseling.

FINANCIAL AID
Financial Aid Of all full-time matriculated undergraduates who enrolled in 2016, 36 Federal Work-Study jobs (averaging $1500). 17 state and other part-time jobs (averaging $1500).

APPLYING
Standardized Tests *Required:* minimum ACT score of 18 or SAT of 940, top 50% of graduating class (for admission).

Options: electronic application, early admission.

Required: high school transcript, minimum 2.0 GPA. *Required for some:* essay or personal statement.

CONTACT
Lissete Terrazas, Director of Admissions, University of the Southwest, 6610 North Lovington Highway, Hobbs, NM 88240. *Phone:* 575-492-2122. *Toll-free phone:* 800-530-4400. *Fax:* 575-392-6006. *E-mail:* lterrazas@usw.edu.

Western New Mexico University
Silver City, New Mexico
http://www.wnmu.edu/

CONTACT
Mr. Matthew Lara, Director of Admissions, Western New Mexico University, PO Box 680, Silver City, NM 88062-0680. *Phone:* 505-538-6106. *Toll-free phone:* 800-872-WNMU. *Fax:* 505-538-6127. *E-mail:* tresslerd@wnmu.edu.

NEW YORK

Adelphi University
Garden City, New York
http://www.adelphi.edu/
- **Independent** university, founded 1896
- **Suburban** 75-acre campus with easy access to New York City
- **Endowment** $175.8 million
- **Coed** 5,266 undergraduate students, 93% full-time, 68% women, 32% men
- **Moderately difficult** entrance level, 73% of applicants were admitted

UNDERGRAD STUDENTS
4,874 full-time, 392 part-time. Students come from 36 states and territories; 46 other countries; 6% are from out of state; 9% Black or African American, non-Hispanic/Latino; 17% Hispanic/Latino; 11% Asian, non-Hispanic/Latino; 0.2% American Indian or Alaska Native, non-Hispanic/Latino; 2% Two or more races, non-Hispanic/Latino; 7% Race/ethnicity unknown; 4% international; 8% transferred in; 22% live on campus.

Freshmen:
Admission: 11,851 applied, 8,666 admitted, 1,131 enrolled. *Average high school GPA:* 3.5. *Test scores:* SAT evidence-based reading and writing scores over 500: 92%; SAT math scores over 500: 91%; ACT scores over 18: 99%; SAT evidence-based reading and writing scores over 600: 37%; SAT math scores over 600: 36%; ACT scores over 24: 61%; SAT evidence-based reading and writing scores over 700: 5%; SAT math scores over 700: 7%; ACT scores over 30: 13%.

Retention: 80% of full-time freshmen returned.

FACULTY
Total: 1,062, 32% full-time, 43% with terminal degrees.
Student/faculty ratio: 12:1.

ACADEMICS
Calendar: semesters. *Degrees:* certificates, associate, bachelor's, master's, doctoral, post-master's, and postbachelor's certificates.

Special study options: accelerated degree program, adult/continuing education programs, advanced placement credit, distance learning, double majors, English as a second language, honors programs, independent study, internships, part-time degree program, services for LD students, student-designed majors, study abroad, summer session for credit. *ROTC:* Army (c), Air Force (c).

Unusual degree programs: 3-2 engineering with Columbia University; physical therapy with New York Medical Coll, New York Institute of Tech; dentistry with NYU Coll of Dentistry; medicine with Philadelphia Coll of Osteopathic Medicine, Lake Erie Coll of Osteopathic Medicine; optometry with SUNY State Coll of Optometry; podiatry with NYCPM.

Computers: 880 computers/terminals are available on campus for general student use. Students can access the following: campus intranet, computer help desk, free student e-mail accounts, online (class) grades, online (class) registration, online (class) schedules, payment, drop/add classes, check application status. Campuswide network is available. 100% of college-owned or -operated housing units are wired for high-speed Internet access. Wireless service is available via entire campus.
Library: Swirbul Library. *Books:* 488,954 (physical), 29,258 (digital/electronic); *Serial titles:* 614 (physical); *Databases:* 272. Students can reserve study rooms.

STUDENT LIFE
Housing options: coed, special housing for students with disabilities. Campus housing is university owned. Freshman applicants given priority for college housing.

Activities and organizations: drama/theater group, student-run newspaper, radio station, choral group, Student Activities Board, C. A. L. I. B. E. R. (Cause to Achieve Leadership, Intelligence, Brotherhood, Excellence, and Respect), Commuter Student Organization, Christian Fellowship, Circle K International, national fraternities, national sororities.

Athletics Member NCAA. All Division II. *Intercollegiate sports:* baseball M(s), basketball M(s)/W(s), bowling W(s), cross-country running M(s)/W(s), field hockey W(s), golf M(s)/W(s), lacrosse

M(s)/W(s), soccer M(s)/W(s), softball W(s), swimming and diving M(s)/W(s), tennis M(s)/W(s), track and field M(s)/W(s), volleyball W(s). *Intramural sports:* badminton M(c)/W(c), baseball M(c)/W(c), basketball M/W, cheerleading W, equestrian sports M(c)/W(c), fencing M(c)/W(c), soccer M/W, ultimate Frisbee M(c)/W(c), volleyball M/W.

Campus security: 24-hour emergency response devices and patrols, late-night transport/escort service, controlled dormitory access.

Student services: health clinic, personal/psychological counseling.

COSTS & FINANCIAL AID

Costs (2017–18) *Comprehensive fee:* $52,670 includes full-time tuition ($35,430), mandatory fees ($1740), and room and board ($15,500). Full-time tuition and fees vary according to course level, course load, location, program, and student level. Part-time tuition: $1080 per credit hour. Part-time tuition and fees vary according to course level, course load, location, program, and student level. *Required fees:* $463 per term part-time. *Room and board:* Room and board charges vary according to board plan and housing facility. *Payment plans:* tuition prepayment, installment, deferred payment. *Waivers:* senior citizens and employees or children of employees.

Financial Aid Of all full-time matriculated undergraduates who enrolled in 2017, 3,910 applied for aid, 3,400 were judged to have need, 461 had their need fully met. 364 Federal Work-Study jobs (averaging $1835). 1,241 state and other part-time jobs (averaging $2641). In 2017, 985 non-need-based awards were made. *Average percent of need met:* 45. *Average financial aid package:* $21,500. *Average need-based loan:* $4181. *Average need-based gift aid:* $17,300. *Average non-need-based aid:* $15,523. *Average indebtedness upon graduation:* $35,285.

APPLYING

Standardized Tests *Required for some:* SAT or ACT (for admission).

Options: electronic application, early action, deferred entrance.

Application fee: $40.

Required: essay or personal statement, high school transcript, . *Required for some:* interview, auditions/portfolios for performing and fine arts.

Application deadlines: rolling (freshmen), rolling (transfers), 12/1 (early action).

Notification: continuous (freshmen), continuous (transfers), 12/31 (early action).

CONTACT

Ms. Stephanie Espina, Director of Freshman Admissions, Adelphi University, Nexus Building, Room 110, 1 South Avenue, PO Box 701, Garden City, NY 11530-0701. *Phone:* 516-877-3056. *Toll-free phone:* 800-ADELPHI. *Fax:* 516-877-3039. *E-mail:* admissions@adelphi.edu.

Albany College of Pharmacy and Health Sciences

Albany, New York

http://www.acphs.edu/

CONTACT

Mr. Matthew Stever, Director of Admissions, Albany College of Pharmacy and Health Sciences, 106 New Scotland Avenue, Albany, NY 12208. *Phone:* 518-694-7221. *Toll-free phone:* 888-203-8010. *Fax:* 518-694-7322. *E-mail:* admissions@acphs.edu.

Alfred University

Alfred, New York

http://www.alfred.edu/

- **Independent** university, founded 1836
- **Rural** 232-acre campus with easy access to Rochester
- **Endowment** $118.6 million
- **Coed** 1,707 undergraduate students, 94% full-time, 48% women, 52% men
- **Moderately difficult** entrance level, 63% of applicants were admitted

UNDERGRAD STUDENTS

1,600 full-time, 107 part-time. Students come from 40 states and territories; 14 other countries; 18% are from out of state; 10% Black or African American, non-Hispanic/Latino; 8% Hispanic/Latino; 2% Asian, non-Hispanic/Latino; 0.3% American Indian or Alaska Native, non-

Hispanic/Latino; 3% Two or more races, non-Hispanic/Latino; 12% Race/ethnicity unknown; 2% international; 4% transferred in; 75% live on campus.

Freshmen:

Admission: 3,566 applied, 2,237 admitted, 418 enrolled. *Average high school GPA:* 3.0. *Test scores:* SAT evidence-based reading and writing scores over 500: 77%; SAT math scores over 500: 76%; ACT scores over 18: 87%; SAT evidence-based reading and writing scores over 600: 27%; SAT math scores over 600: 27%; ACT scores over 24: 26%; SAT evidence-based reading and writing scores over 700: 7%; SAT math scores over 700: 6%; ACT scores over 30: 1%.

Retention: 68% of full-time freshmen returned.

FACULTY

Total: 193, 79% full-time, 83% with terminal degrees.

Student/faculty ratio: 11:1.

ACADEMICS

Calendar: semesters. *Degrees:* bachelor's, master's, doctoral, and post-master's certificates.

Special study options: advanced placement credit, cooperative education, double majors, honors programs, independent study, internships, off-campus study, part-time degree program, services for LD students, student-designed majors, study abroad, summer session for credit. *ROTC:* Army (c).

Computers: Students can access the following: computer help desk, free student e-mail accounts, online (class) grades, online (class) registration, online (class) schedules, online bill pay. Campuswide network is available. 100% of college-owned or -operated housing units are wired for high-speed Internet access. Wireless service is available via entire campus.

Library: Herrick Memorial Library plus 1 other. *Books:* 217,226 (physical), 530,999 (digital/electronic); *Serial titles:* 243 (physical), 114,188 (digital/electronic); *Databases:* 279. Study areas open 24 hours, 5–7 days a week; students can reserve study rooms.

STUDENT LIFE

Housing options: on-campus residence required through junior year; coed, cooperative. Campus housing is university owned. Freshman campus housing is guaranteed.

Activities and organizations: drama/theater group, student-run newspaper, radio station, choral group, Student Senate, Habitat for Humanity, Drawn to Diversity, Student Activities Board.

Athletics Member NCAA. All Division III. *Intercollegiate sports:* basketball M/W, cross-country running M/W, equestrian sports M/W, football M, lacrosse M/W, skiing (downhill) M/W, soccer M/W, softball W, swimming and diving M/W, tennis M/W, track and field M/W, volleyball W. *Intramural sports:* baseball M(c), basketball M/W, cheerleading W(c), football M/W, golf M/W, ice hockey M(c), lacrosse M/W, racquetball M/W, rugby M(c)/W(c), skiing (cross-country) M/W, soccer M/W, softball M/W, squash M/W, tennis M/W, ultimate Frisbee M(c)/W(c), volleyball M/W.

Campus security: 24-hour emergency response devices, student patrols, late-night transport/escort service, controlled dormitory access, key-only access to dormitories.

Student services: health clinic, personal/psychological counseling, women's center.

COSTS & FINANCIAL AID

Costs (2018–19) *Comprehensive fee:* $46,000 includes full-time tuition ($32,494), mandatory fees ($990), and room and board ($12,516). Full-time tuition and fees vary according to program. Part-time tuition: $998 per credit hour. *Required fees:* $84 per term part-time. *College room only:* $6340. Room and board charges vary according to board plan and housing facility. *Payment plan:* installment. *Waivers:* employees or children of employees.

Financial Aid Of all full-time matriculated undergraduates who enrolled in 2017, 1,456 applied for aid, 1,326 were judged to have need, 271 had their need fully met. 936 Federal Work-Study jobs (averaging $1861). In 2017, 89 non-need-based awards were made. *Average percent of need met:* 83. *Average financial aid package:* $27,889. *Average need-based loan:* $5940. *Average need-based gift aid:* $21,500. *Average non-need-based aid:* $12,114. *Average indebtedness upon graduation:* $35,987. *Financial aid deadline:* 3/15.

APPLYING

Standardized Tests *Required:* SAT or ACT (for admission).

Options: electronic application, early admission, early decision, deferred entrance.

Application fee: $50.

Required: essay or personal statement, high school transcript, 1 letter of recommendation. *Required for some:* interview, portfolio for applicants to the School of Art and Design. *Recommended:* interview.

Application deadlines: 8/1 (freshmen), 8/1 (transfers).

Early decision deadline: 12/1.

Notification: continuous (freshmen), continuous (transfers), 12/15 (early decision).

CONTACT

Mr. Jake Yale, Director of Admissions, Alfred University, Alumni Hall, Alfred, NY 14802-1205. *Phone:* 607-871-2115. *Toll-free phone:* 800-541-9229. *Fax:* 607-871-2198. *E-mail:* admissions@alfred.edu.

Bard College

Annandale-on-Hudson, New York

http://www.bard.edu/

- **Independent** comprehensive, founded 1860
- **Rural** 1000-acre campus
- **Coed** 1,930 undergraduate students, 96% full-time, 59% women, 41% men
- **Moderately difficult** entrance level, 58% of applicants were admitted

UNDERGRAD STUDENTS

1,855 full-time, 75 part-time. Students come from 46 states and territories; 55 other countries; 66% are from out of state; 7% Black or African American, non-Hispanic/Latino; 6% Hispanic/Latino; 4% Asian, non-Hispanic/Latino; 0.1% American Indian or Alaska Native, non-Hispanic/Latino; 5% Two or more races, non-Hispanic/Latino; 7% Race/ethnicity unknown; 11% international; 3% transferred in; 75% live on campus.

Freshmen:

Admission: 4,922 applied, 2,865 admitted, 470 enrolled.

Retention: 82% of full-time freshmen returned.

FACULTY

Total: 297, 52% full-time, 76% with terminal degrees.

Student/faculty ratio: 9:1.

ACADEMICS

Calendar: semesters. *Degrees:* bachelor's, master's, and doctoral.

Special study options: adult/continuing education programs, advanced placement credit, double majors, independent study, internships, off-campus study, part-time degree program, services for LD students, student-designed majors, study abroad.

Unusual degree programs: 3-2 business administration; engineering with Columbia University, Washington University in St. Louis, Dartmouth College; forestry with Duke University; social work; teaching.

Computers: Students can access the following: campus intranet, computer help desk, free student e-mail accounts, online (class) grades, online (class) registration, online (class) schedules. Campuswide network is available. 100% of college-owned or -operated housing units are wired for high-speed Internet access. Wireless service is available via classrooms, computer centers, computer labs, dorm rooms, learning centers, libraries, student centers.

Library: Stevenson Library plus 3 others. Weekly public service hours: 75; students can reserve study rooms.

STUDENT LIFE

Housing options: on-campus residence required through sophomore year; coed, women-only, cooperative, special housing for students with disabilities. Campus housing is university owned. Freshman campus housing is guaranteed.

Activities and organizations: drama/theater group, student-run newspaper, radio station, choral group.

Athletics Member NCAA, NAIA. All NCAA Division III. *Intercollegiate sports:* baseball M, basketball M/W, cross-country running M/W, lacrosse M/W, soccer M/W, squash M, swimming and diving M/W, tennis M/W, track and field M/W, volleyball M/W. *Intramural sports:* badminton M/W, basketball M/W, bowling M/W, equestrian sports M(c)/W(c), fencing M(c)/W(c), golf M/W, rugby M(c)/W(c), softball M/W, squash M/W, table tennis M/W, tennis M/W, ultimate Frisbee M(c)/W(c), volleyball M/W.

Campus security: 24-hour emergency response devices and patrols, student patrols, late-night transport/escort service, controlled dormitory access.

Student services: health clinic, personal/psychological counseling, legal services.

COSTS & FINANCIAL AID

Costs (2017–18) *One-time required fee:* $1635. *Comprehensive fee:* $67,981 includes full-time tuition ($52,226), mandatory fees ($689), and room and board ($15,066). Full-time tuition and fees vary according to degree level and location. Part-time tuition: $1635 per credit hour. Part-time tuition and fees vary according to degree level and location. *Room and board:* Room and board charges vary according to location. *Payment plans:* tuition prepayment, installment. *Waivers:* employees or children of employees.

Financial Aid Of all full-time matriculated undergraduates who enrolled in 2017, 1,340 applied for aid, 1,270 were judged to have need, 318 had their need fully met. 873 Federal Work-Study jobs (averaging $1687). In 2017, 33 non-need-based awards were made. *Average percent of need met:* 83. *Average financial aid package:* $46,810. *Average need-based loan:* $5815. *Average need-based gift aid:* $41,498. *Average non-need-based aid:* $21,100. *Average indebtedness upon graduation:* $26,904. *Financial aid deadline:* 2/15.

APPLYING

Options: electronic application, early admission, early decision, early action, deferred entrance.

Application fee: $50.

Required: essay or personal statement, high school transcript, minimum 3.0 GPA, 3 letters of recommendation.

Application deadlines: 1/1 (freshmen), 11/1 (early action).

Early decision deadline: 11/1.

Notification: 4/1 (freshmen), 1/1 (early action).

CONTACT

Ms. Mackie Siebens, Director of Admissions, Bard College, PO Box 5000, 30 Campus Road, Annandale-on-Hudson, NY 12504-5000. *Phone:* 845-758-7472. *Fax:* 845-758-5208. *E-mail:* admission@bard.edu.

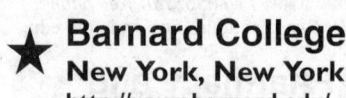

★ Barnard College

New York, New York

http://www.barnard.edu/

- **Independent** 4-year, founded 1889
- **Urban** 4-acre campus
- **Endowment** $327.2 million
- **Women only** 2,604 undergraduate students, 99% full-time
- **Most difficult** entrance level, 15% of applicants were admitted

UNDERGRAD STUDENTS

2,574 full-time, 30 part-time. Students come from 50 states and territories; 66 other countries; 73% are from out of state; 6% Black or African American, non-Hispanic/Latino; 12% Hispanic/Latino; 15% Asian, non-Hispanic/Latino; 0.1% Native Hawaiian or other Pacific Islander, non-Hispanic/Latino; 0.2% American Indian or Alaska Native, non-Hispanic/Latino; 6% Two or more races, non-Hispanic/Latino; 0.3% Race/ethnicity unknown; 9% international; 3% transferred in; 91% live on campus.

Freshmen:

Admission: 7,716 applied, 1,190 admitted, 603 enrolled. *Average high school GPA:* 4.0. *Test scores:* SAT evidence-based reading and writing scores over 500: 99%; SAT math scores over 500: 99%; ACT scores over 18: 100%; SAT evidence-based reading and writing scores over 600: 92%; SAT math scores over 600: 90%; ACT scores over 24: 99%; SAT evidence-based reading and writing scores over 700: 64%; SAT math scores over 700: 53%; ACT scores over 30: 77%.

Retention: 95% of full-time freshmen returned.

FACULTY
Total: 363, 62% full-time, 84% with terminal degrees.
Student/faculty ratio: 10:1.

ACADEMICS
Calendar: semesters. *Degree:* bachelor's.

Special study options: accelerated degree program, advanced placement credit, double majors, independent study, internships, off-campus study, services for LD students, student-designed majors, study abroad. *ROTC:* Army (c), Navy (c), Air Force (c).

Unusual degree programs: 3-2 engineering with Columbia University; international affairs, public administration with Columbia University; music with The Juilliard School; religion with Jewish Theological Seminary; music with Manhattan School of Music; law; dentistry.

Computers: 165 computers/terminals are available on campus for general student use. Students can access the following: campus intranet, computer help desk, free student e-mail accounts, online (class) grades, online (class) registration, online (class) schedules. Campuswide network is available. 100% of college-owned or -operated housing units are wired for high-speed Internet access. Wireless service is available via entire campus.

Library: Lefrak Center plus 20 others. Study areas open 24 hours, 5–7 days a week.

STUDENT LIFE
Housing options: women-only, special housing for students with disabilities. Campus housing is university owned and leased by the school. Freshman campus housing is guaranteed.

Activities and organizations: drama/theater group, student-run newspaper, radio and television station, choral group, marching band, Community Impact (community service), Student Government Association, Take Back the Night, Student Activities Council, Musical Theater Society, national sororities.

Athletics Member NCAA. All Division I. *Intercollegiate sports:* archery W, basketball W, crew W, cross-country running W, equestrian sports W(c), fencing W, field hockey W, golf W, ice hockey W(c), lacrosse W, rugby W(c), sailing W(c), skiing (downhill) W(c), soccer W, softball W, squash W, swimming and diving W, tennis W, track and field W, volleyball W, water polo W(c). *Intramural sports:* archery W, badminton W, basketball W, equestrian sports W, ice hockey W, rugby W, sailing W, soccer W, squash W, table tennis W, tennis W, volleyball W, water polo W.

Campus security: 24-hour emergency response devices and patrols, late-night transport/escort service, controlled dormitory access, gated campus with permanent security posts.

Student services: health clinic, personal/psychological counseling, women's center.

COSTS & FINANCIAL AID
Costs (2017–18) *Comprehensive fee:* $68,762 includes full-time tuition ($50,882), mandatory fees ($1780), and room and board ($16,100). Part-time tuition: $1697 per credit hour. *College room only:* $9510. Room and board charges vary according to board plan and housing facility. *Payment plans:* tuition prepayment, installment, deferred payment. *Waivers:* employees or children of employees.

Financial Aid Of all full-time matriculated undergraduates who enrolled in 2017, 1,124 applied for aid, 994 were judged to have need, 978 had their need fully met. 238 Federal Work-Study jobs (averaging $2332). 642 state and other part-time jobs (averaging $2252). *Average percent of need met:* 100. *Average financial aid package:* $50,194. *Average need-based loan:* $4431. *Average need-based gift aid:* $43,984. *Average indebtedness upon graduation:* $23,276. *Financial aid deadline:* 2/1.

APPLYING
Standardized Tests *Required:* SAT or ACT (for admission).

Options: electronic application, early admission, early decision, deferred entrance.

Application fee: $75.

Required: essay or personal statement, high school transcript, 3 letters of recommendation, Common Application with Barnard Supplement. *Recommended:* interview.

Application deadlines: 1/1 (freshmen), 3/15 (transfers).

Early decision deadline: 11/1.

Notification: 4/1 (freshmen), 5/15 (transfers), 12/15 (early decision).

CONTACT
Ms. Jennifer Gill Fondiller, Vice President for Enrollment, Barnard College, Barnard College, 3009 Broadway, New York, NY 10027. *Phone:* 212-854-2014. *Fax:* 212-854-6220. *E-mail:* admissions@barnard.edu.

See previous page for display ad and page 1240 for the College Close-Up.

Baruch College of the City University of New York
New York, New York
http://www.baruch.cuny.edu/
- **State and locally supported** comprehensive, founded 1919, part of City University of New York System
- **Urban** 4-acre campus
- **Coed** 15,253 undergraduate students, 76% full-time, 49% women, 51% men
- **Very difficult** entrance level, 29% of applicants were admitted

UNDERGRAD STUDENTS
11,598 full-time, 3,655 part-time. Students come from 26 states and territories; 3% are from out of state; 9% Black or African American, non-Hispanic/Latino; 26% Hispanic/Latino; 31% Asian, non-Hispanic/Latino; 0.2% Native Hawaiian or other Pacific Islander, non-Hispanic/Latino; 0.1% American Indian or Alaska Native, non-Hispanic/Latino; 1% Two or more races, non-Hispanic/Latino; 11% international; 11% transferred in; 2% live on campus.

Freshmen:
Admission: 21,432 applied, 6,268 admitted, 1,605 enrolled. *Average high school GPA:* 3.3. *Test scores:* SAT evidence-based reading and writing scores over 500: 97%; SAT math scores over 500: 100%; SAT evidence-based reading and writing scores over 600: 67%; SAT math scores over 600: 82%; SAT evidence-based reading and writing scores over 700: 10%; SAT math scores over 700: 24%.

Retention: 90% of full-time freshmen returned.

FACULTY
Total: 1,129, 44% full-time, 62% with terminal degrees.
Student/faculty ratio: 18:1.

ACADEMICS
Calendar: semesters. *Degrees:* bachelor's, master's, and post-master's certificates.

Special study options: accelerated degree program, adult/continuing education programs, advanced placement credit, distance learning, double majors, English as a second language, freshman honors college, honors programs, independent study, internships, part-time degree program, services for LD students, student-designed majors, study abroad, summer session for credit. *ROTC:* Army (c).

Computers: 1,300 computers/terminals are available on campus for general student use. Students can access the following: campus intranet, computer help desk, free student e-mail accounts, online (class) grades, online (class) registration, online (class) schedules. Campuswide network is available. 100% of college-owned or -operated housing units are wired for high-speed Internet access. Wireless service is available via classrooms, computer centers, computer labs, learning centers, libraries, student centers.
Library: The William and Anita Newman Library. *Books:* 626,753 (physical), 2.1 million (digital/electronic); *Serial titles:* 89,951 (physical), 52,020 (digital/electronic). Students can reserve study rooms.

STUDENT LIFE
Housing options: coed. Campus housing is provided by a third party.
Activities and organizations: drama/theater group, student-run newspaper, radio station, choral group, Accounting Society, Caribbean Students Association, Association of Latino Professionals in Finance and Accounting, Golden Key International Honor Society, Helpline, national fraternities, national sororities.
Athletics Member NCAA. All Division III. *Intercollegiate sports:* baseball M, basketball M/W, cheerleading M/W, cross-country running M/W, soccer M, softball W, swimming and diving M/W, tennis M/W, volleyball M/W. *Intramural sports:* archery M(c)/W(c), badminton M/W, basketball M/W, cross-country running M/W, racquetball M/W, swimming and diving M/W, table tennis M/W, volleyball M/W.

Campus security: 24-hour emergency response devices and patrols, late-night transport/escort service, controlled access by ID card.
Student services: health clinic, personal/psychological counseling, legal services.

COSTS & FINANCIAL AID
Costs (2018–19) *Tuition:* state resident $6530 full-time, $285 per credit hour part-time; nonresident $17,400 full-time, $580 per credit hour part-time. Full-time tuition and fees vary according to course load. Part-time tuition and fees vary according to course load. *Required fees:* $585 full-time, $163 per term part-time. *Room and board:* Room and board charges vary according to housing facility. *Payment plans:* installment, deferred payment. *Waivers:* senior citizens and employees or children of employees.

Financial Aid Of all full-time matriculated undergraduates who enrolled in 2016, 9,529 applied for aid, 8,559 were judged to have need, 835 had their need fully met. 481 Federal Work-Study jobs (averaging $2988). In 2016, 1796 non-need-based awards were made. *Average percent of need met:* 24. *Average financial aid package:* $5836. *Average need-based loan:* $3842. *Average need-based gift aid:* $5330. *Average non-need-based aid:* $5003. *Average indebtedness upon graduation:* $5642.

APPLYING
Standardized Tests *Required:* SAT or ACT (for admission).
Options: electronic application, early admission, early decision, deferred entrance.

Application fee: $65.
Required: high school transcript, minimum 2.5 GPA, 16 academic units. *Required for some:* interview.
Application deadlines: 2/1 (freshmen), 2/1 (transfers).
Notification: 5/15 (freshmen), continuous until 5/1 (transfers).

CONTACT
Baruch College of the City University of New York, 1 Bernard Baruch Way, New York, NY 10010-5585. *Phone:* 646-312-1383.

Be'er Yaakov Talmudic Seminary
Spring Valley, New York

CONTACT
Be'er Yaakov Talmudic Seminary, 12 Jefferson Avenue, Spring Valley, NY 10977.

Beis Medrash Heichal Dovid
Far Rockaway, New York

CONTACT
Beis Medrash Heichal Dovid, 257 Beach 17th Street, Far Rockaway, NY 11691.

Berkeley College–New York City Campus
New York, New York
http://www.berkeleycollege.edu/
- **Proprietary** 4-year, founded 1936
- **Urban** campus with easy access to New York City
- **Coed**
- **Minimally difficult** entrance level

FACULTY
Student/faculty ratio: 23:1.

ACADEMICS
Calendar: semesters. *Degrees:* certificates, associate, and bachelor's.
Library:Books: 150,230 (digital/electronic); *Serial titles:* 42,150 (digital/electronic); *Databases:* 78.

STUDENT LIFE
Housing options: college housing not available.
Activities and organizations: student-run newspaper.
Athletics Member USCAA.
Campus security: 24-hour emergency response devices.

Student services: personal/psychological counseling.

COSTS
Costs (2017–18) *One-time required fee:* $100. *Tuition:* $23,600 full-time, $810 per credit part-time. Full-time tuition and fees vary according to course load. Part-time tuition and fees vary according to course load. No tuition increase for student's term of enrollment. *Required fees:* $1700 full-time, $425 per term part-time.

APPLYING
Options: electronic application, deferred entrance.
Application fee: $50.
Required: high school transcript. *Recommended:* interview.

CONTACT
Michelle Gomez, Director, High School Admissions, Berkeley College–New York City Campus, 3 East 43 Street, New York, NY 1007. *Phone:* 212-986-4343. *Toll-free phone:* 800-446-5400. *E-mail:* info@berkeleycollege.edu.

Berkeley College–White Plains Campus
White Plains, New York
http://www.berkeleycollege.edu/
- **Proprietary** 4-year, founded 1945
- **Suburban** campus with easy access to New York City
- **Coed**
- **Minimally difficult** entrance level

FACULTY
Student/faculty ratio: 23:1.

ACADEMICS
Calendar: semesters. *Degrees:* associate and bachelor's.
Library:Books: 150,230 (digital/electronic); *Serial titles:* 42,150 (digital/electronic); *Databases:* 81.

STUDENT LIFE
Housing options: coed. Campus housing is university owned.
Activities and organizations: student-run newspaper.
Athletics Member USCAA.
Campus security: 24-hour emergency response devices, controlled dormitory access, monitored entrance with front desk security guard.
Student services: personal/psychological counseling.

COSTS
Costs (2017–18) *One-time required fee:* $100. *Tuition:* $23,600 full-time, $825 per credit hour part-time. Full-time tuition and fees vary according to course load. Part-time tuition and fees vary according to course load. No tuition increase for student's term of enrollment. *Required fees:* $1700 full-time, $425 per term part-time. *Room only:* $9000.

APPLYING
Options: electronic application, deferred entrance.
Application fee: $50.
Required: high school transcript. *Recommended:* interview.

CONTACT
Lynn Ovimeleh, Director of High School Admissions, Berkeley College–White Plains Campus, 99 Church Street, White Plains, NY 10601. *Phone:* 914-694-1122. *Toll-free phone:* 800-446-5400. *E-mail:* info@berkeleycollege.edu.

Beth HaMedrash Shaarei Yosher Institute
Brooklyn, New York
CONTACT
Director of Admissions, Beth HaMedrash Shaarei Yosher Institute, 4102-10 Sixteenth Avenue, Brooklyn, NY 11204. *Phone:* 718-854-2290.

Beth Hatalmud Rabbinical College
Brooklyn, New York
CONTACT
Rabbi Osina, Director of Admissions, Beth Hatalmud Rabbinical College, 2127 Eighty-second Street, Brooklyn, NY 11214. *Phone:* 718-259-2525.

Beth Medrash Meor Yitzchok
Monsey, New York
CONTACT
Beth Medrash Meor Yitzchok, 85 Dykstras Way East, Monsey, NY 10952.

Bet Medrash Gadol Ateret Torah
Brooklyn, New York
CONTACT
Bet Medrash Gadol Ateret Torah, 1750 East Fourth Street, Brooklyn, NY 11223.

Binghamton University, State University of New York
Binghamton, New York
http://www.binghamton.edu/
- **State-supported** university, founded 1946, part of State University of New York System
- **Suburban** 930-acre campus
- **Endowment** $109.3 million
- **Coed** 13,708 undergraduate students, 97% full-time, 49% women, 51% men
- **Very difficult** entrance level, 40% of applicants were admitted

UNDERGRAD STUDENTS
13,337 full-time, 371 part-time. Students come from 48 states and territories; 97 other countries; 6% are from out of state; 5% Black or African American, non-Hispanic/Latino; 11% Hispanic/Latino; 14% Asian, non-Hispanic/Latino; 0.1% Native Hawaiian or other Pacific Islander, non-Hispanic/Latino; 0.1% American Indian or Alaska Native, non-Hispanic/Latino; 2% Two or more races, non-Hispanic/Latino; 2% Race/ethnicity unknown; 8% international; 8% transferred in; 52% live on campus.

Freshmen:
Admission: 33,467 applied, 13,507 admitted, 2,736 enrolled. *Average high school GPA:* 3.7. *Test scores:* SAT evidence-based reading and writing scores over 500: 99%; SAT math scores over 500: 100%; ACT scores over 18: 100%; SAT evidence-based reading and writing scores over 600: 92%; SAT math scores over 600: 94%; ACT scores over 24: 97%; SAT evidence-based reading and writing scores over 700: 39%; SAT math scores over 700: 45%; ACT scores over 30: 50%.
Retention: 91% of full-time freshmen returned.

FACULTY
Total: 1,047, 72% full-time, 82% with terminal degrees.
Student/faculty ratio: 19:1.

ACADEMICS
Calendar: semesters. *Degrees:* bachelor's, master's, doctoral, and post-master's certificates.
Special study options: accelerated degree program, adult/continuing education programs, advanced placement credit, distance learning, double majors, English as a second language, honors programs, independent study, internships, off-campus study, part-time degree program, services for LD students, student-designed majors, study abroad, summer session for credit. *ROTC:* Army (c), Air Force (c).
Unusual degree programs: 3-2 business administration; engineering; anthropology; art history; Asian/AsianAmerican studies; biology; chemistry; computer science; economics; education; French; geography; geology; Italian; math; material science; philosophy, politics & law; physics; political science; public administration; sociology; Spanish; systems science; theatre.

Computers: 1,184 computers/terminals and 13,200 ports are available on campus for general student use. Students can access the following: campus intranet, computer help desk, free student e-mail accounts, online (class) registration, online (class) schedules, course management system, personal Web space, wiki, virtual desktop. Campuswide network is available. 100% of college-owned or -operated housing units are wired for high-speed Internet access. Wireless service is available via entire campus.

Library: Glenn G. Bartle Library plus 4 others. *Books:* 2.3 million (physical), 1.1 million (digital/electronic); *Serial titles:* 683 (physical), 125,064 (digital/electronic); *Databases:* 358. Weekly public service hours: 136; study areas open 24 hours, 5–7 days a week; students can reserve study rooms.

STUDENT LIFE

Housing options: on-campus residence required for freshman year; coed, special housing for students with disabilities. Campus housing is university owned. Freshman campus housing is guaranteed.

Activities and organizations: drama/theater group, student-run newspaper, radio and television station, choral group, Finance Society, Student Volunteer Center, Habitat for Humanity, Pre-Medical Association, Sno-Cats Ski and Snowboard Club, national fraternities, national sororities.

Athletics Member NCAA. All Division I. *Intercollegiate sports:* baseball M(s), basketball M(s)/W(s), cross-country running M(s)/W(s), golf M(s), lacrosse M(s)/W(s), soccer M(s)/W(s), softball W(s), swimming and diving M(s)/W(s), tennis M(s)/W(s), track and field M(s)/W(s), volleyball W(s), wrestling M(s). *Intramural sports:* badminton M(c)/W(c), baseball M(c), basketball M/W, bowling M/W, crew M(c)/W(c), cross-country running M(c)/W(c), equestrian sports M(c)/W(c), fencing M(c)/W(c), field hockey M(c)/W(c), golf M(c)/W(c), gymnastics M(c)/W(c), ice hockey M(c)/W(c), lacrosse M(c)/W(c), racquetball M/W, rugby M(c)/W(c), skiing (downhill) M(c)/W(c), soccer M/W, softball M/W, swimming and diving M(c)/W(c), table tennis M(c)/W(c), tennis M/W, ultimate Frisbee M(c)/W(c), volleyball M/W, water polo M(c)/W(c).

Campus security: 24-hour emergency response devices and patrols, student patrols, late-night transport/escort service, controlled dormitory access, only main gate open to traffic 12-5 am, emergency text system,self-defense workshops.

Student services: health clinic, personal/psychological counseling, women's center, legal services.

COSTS & FINANCIAL AID

Costs (2017–18) *Tuition:* state resident $6670 full-time, $278 per credit hour part-time; nonresident $21,550 full-time, $898 per credit hour part-time. Full-time tuition and fees vary according to program. Part-time tuition and fees vary according to course load and program. *Required fees:* $2853 full-time, $116 per credit hour part-time, $22 per term part-time. *Room and board:* $14,577; room only: $9567. Room and board charges vary according to board plan and housing facility. *Payment plan:* installment.

Financial Aid Of all full-time matriculated undergraduates who enrolled in 2017, 9,510 applied for aid, 6,895 were judged to have need, 981 had their need fully met. 312 Federal Work-Study jobs (averaging $1483). In 2017, 366 non-need-based awards were made. *Average percent of need met:* 69. *Average financial aid package:* $13,677. *Average need-based loan:* $5001. *Average need-based gift aid:* $9356. *Average non-need-based aid:* $7980. *Average indebtedness upon graduation:* $27,022.

APPLYING

Standardized Tests *Required:* SAT or ACT (for admission).

Options: electronic application, early admission, early action, deferred entrance.

Application fee: $50.

Required: essay or personal statement, high school transcript, 1 letter of recommendation. *Required for some:* portfolio, audition.

Application deadlines: rolling (freshmen), rolling (transfers), 11/1 (early action).

Notification: 4/1 (freshmen), continuous (transfers), 1/15 (early action).

CONTACT

Krista Medionte-Phillips, Director of Undergraduate Admissions, Binghamton University, State University of New York, PO Box 6001, Binghamton, NY 13902-6001. *Phone:* 607-777-2171. *Fax:* 607-777-4445. *E-mail:* admit@binghamton.edu.

Boricua College
New York, New York
http://www.boricuacollege.edu/

CONTACT

Mrs. Miriam Pfeffer, Director of Student Services, Boricua College, 186 North 6th Street, Brooklyn, NY 11211. *Phone:* 718-782-2200. *Fax:* 718-782-2025. *E-mail:* mpfeffer@boricuacollege.edu.

Brooklyn College of the City University of New York
Brooklyn, New York
http://www.brooklyn.cuny.edu/

- **State and locally supported** comprehensive, founded 1930, part of City University of New York System
- **Urban** 35-acre campus with easy access to Manhattan
- **Coed**
- **Moderately difficult** entrance level

FACULTY
Student/faculty ratio: 17:1.

ACADEMICS
Calendar: semesters. *Degrees:* certificates, bachelor's, master's, post-master's, and postbachelor's certificates.

Library: Brooklyn College Library plus 1 other. Students can reserve study rooms.

STUDENT LIFE
Housing options: college housing not available.

Activities and organizations: drama/theater group, student-run newspaper, radio and television station, choral group, Academic Club Association, Kingsman and Excelsior Newspaper, NY Public Interest Group (NYPIRG), Student Government CIAS, SGS, and GSO, Student Forensics, national fraternities, national sororities.

Athletics Member NCAA. All Division III.

Campus security: 24-hour emergency response devices and patrols, late-night transport/escort service.

Student services: health clinic, personal/psychological counseling, women's center.

FINANCIAL AID
Financial Aid Of all full-time matriculated undergraduates who enrolled in 2015, 9,770 applied for aid, 9,156 were judged to have need, 6,501 had their need fully met. 407 Federal Work-Study jobs (averaging $2613). In 2015, 310 non-need-based awards were made. *Average percent of need met:* 89. *Average financial aid package:* $7500. *Average need-based loan:* $3000. *Average need-based gift aid:* $3400. *Average non-need-based aid:* $2500. *Average indebtedness upon graduation:* $15,235. *Financial aid deadline:* 5/1.

APPLYING
Standardized Tests *Required:* SAT or ACT (for admission).

Application fee: $65.

Required: high school transcript, minimum 3.1 GPA, combined SAT or ACT scores of 1000.

CONTACT
Office of Admissions, Brooklyn College of the City University of New York, 2900 Bedford Avenue, West Quad Building, Room 222, Brooklyn, NY 11210-2889. *Phone:* 718-951-5001. *Fax:* 718-951-4506. *E-mail:* adminqry@brooklyn.cuny.edu.

Bryant & Stratton College–Amherst Campus

Clarence, New York
http://www.bryantstratton.edu/

CONTACT
Mr. Brian K. Dioguardi, Director of Admissions, Bryant & Stratton College–Amherst Campus, Audubon Business Center, 40 Hazelwood Drive, Amherst, NY 14228. *Phone:* 716-691-0012. *Fax:* 716-691-0012. *E-mail:* bkdioguardi@bryantstratton.edu.

Bryant & Stratton College–Buffalo Campus

Buffalo, New York
http://www.bryantstratton.edu/

CONTACT
Mr. Philip J. Struebel, Director of Admissions, Bryant & Stratton College–Buffalo Campus, 465 Main Street, Suite 400, Buffalo, NY 14203. *Phone:* 716-884-9120. *Fax:* 716-884-0091. *E-mail:* pjstruebel@bryantstratton.edu.

Bryant & Stratton College–Orchard Park Campus

Orchard Park, New York
http://www.bryantstratton.edu/

CONTACT
Bryant & Stratton College–Orchard Park Campus, 200 Redtail Road, Orchard Park, NY 14127. *Phone:* 716-677-9500.

Buffalo State College, State University of New York

Buffalo, New York
http://www.buffalostate.edu/

- **State-supported** comprehensive, founded 1867, part of State University of New York System
- **Urban** 115-acre campus
- **Endowment** $42.9 million
- **Coed** 8,572 undergraduate students, 89% full-time, 56% women, 44% men
- **Moderately difficult** entrance level, 60% of applicants were admitted

UNDERGRAD STUDENTS
7,665 full-time, 862 part-time. Students come from 27 states and territories; 35 other countries; 1% are from out of state; 33% Black or African American, non-Hispanic/Latino; 13% Hispanic/Latino; 3% Asian, non-Hispanic/Latino; 0.1% Native Hawaiian or other Pacific Islander, non-Hispanic/Latino; 0.5% American Indian or Alaska Native, non-Hispanic/Latino; 3% Two or more races, non-Hispanic/Latino; 0.1% Race/ethnicity unknown; 1% international; 10% transferred in; 29% live on campus.

Freshmen:
Admission: 14,663 applied, 8,793 admitted, 1,425 enrolled. *Average high school GPA:* 3.1. *Test scores:* SAT evidence-based reading and writing scores over 500: 50%; SAT math scores over 500: 44%; SAT evidence-based reading and writing scores over 600: 9%; SAT math scores over 600: 10%; SAT evidence-based reading and writing scores over 700: 1%; SAT math scores over 700: 1%.
Retention: 66% of full-time freshmen returned.

FACULTY
Total: 816, 46% full-time, 53% with terminal degrees.
Student/faculty ratio: 16:1.

ACADEMICS
Calendar: semesters. *Degrees:* bachelor's, master's, and post-master's certificates.
Special study options: academic remediation for entering students, adult/continuing education programs, advanced placement credit, cooperative education, distance learning, double majors, English as a second language, freshman honors college, honors programs, independent study, internships, off-campus study, part-time degree program, services for LD students, study abroad, summer session for credit. *ROTC:* Army (c).
Unusual degree programs: 3-2 engineering with Binghamton University, State University of New York; Clarkson University; University at Buffalo, the State University of New York.
Computers: 1,700 computers/terminals are available on campus for general student use. Students can access the following: computer help desk, free student e-mail accounts, online (class) registration, online (class) schedules. Campuswide network is available. 100% of college-owned or -operated housing units are wired for high-speed Internet access. Wireless service is available via entire campus.
Library: E. H. Butler Library plus 1 other.

STUDENT LIFE
Housing options: on-campus residence required through sophomore year; coed. Campus housing is university owned. Freshman campus housing is guaranteed.
Activities and organizations: drama/theater group, student-run newspaper, radio station, choral group, United Student Government, African-American Student Organization, Caribbean Student Organization, The Record, WBNY radio, national fraternities, national sororities.
Athletics Member NCAA. All Division III. *Intercollegiate sports:* baseball M(c), basketball M/W, bowling M(c)/W(c), cheerleading W(c), cross-country running M/W, fencing M(c), football M, ice hockey M/W, lacrosse M(c)/W, rugby M(c)/W(c), skiing (cross-country) M(c)/W(c), skiing (downhill) M(c)/W(c), soccer M/W, softball W, swimming and diving M/W, tennis W, track and field M/W, volleyball M(c)/W. *Intramural sports:* basketball M, football M, racquetball M/W, softball M/W, volleyball M/W, water polo M(c)/W(c).
Campus security: 24-hour emergency response devices and patrols, student patrols, late-night transport/escort service, controlled dormitory access.
Student services: health clinic, personal/psychological counseling, women's center, legal services.

COSTS & FINANCIAL AID
Costs (2017–18) *Tuition:* state resident $6670 full-time, $278 per semester hour part-time; nonresident $16,320 full-time, $680 per semester hour part-time. Part-time tuition and fees vary according to course load. *Required fees:* $1306 full-time, $55 per semester hour part-time. *Room and board:* $12,982; room only: $7782. Room and board charges vary according to board plan, housing facility, and student level. *Payment plan:* installment. *Waivers:* employees or children of employees.
Financial Aid Of all full-time matriculated undergraduates who enrolled in 2016, 253 Federal Work-Study jobs (averaging $3744). *Average indebtedness upon graduation:* $27,672. *Financial aid deadline:* 5/1.

APPLYING
Standardized Tests *Required:* SAT or ACT (for admission), SAT and SAT Subject Tests or ACT (for admission). *Recommended:* SAT (for admission).
Options: electronic application, early admission, deferred entrance.
Application fee: $50.
Required: high school transcript, minimum 3.0 GPA. *Required for some:* essay or personal statement, interview.
Application deadlines: rolling (freshmen), rolling (transfers).
Notification: continuous (freshmen), continuous (transfers).

CONTACT
Ms. Carmella Thompson, Director of Admissions, Buffalo State College, State University of New York, 110 Moot Hall, Buffalo, NY 14222. *Phone:* 716-878-4017. *Fax:* 716-878-6100. *E-mail:* admissions@buffalostate.edu.

Canisius College
Buffalo, New York
http://www.canisius.edu/

- **Independent Roman Catholic (Jesuit)** comprehensive, founded 1870
- **Urban** 72-acre campus with easy access to Buffalo-Niagara Falls
- **Endowment** $123.8 million
- **Coed** 2,398 undergraduate students, 96% full-time, 50% women, 50% men
- **Moderately difficult** entrance level, 78% of applicants were admitted

UNDERGRAD STUDENTS
2,303 full-time, 95 part-time. Students come from 36 states and territories; 18 other countries; 11% are from out of state; 8% Black or African American, non-Hispanic/Latino; 6% Hispanic/Latino; 3% Asian, non-Hispanic/Latino; 0.2% Native Hawaiian or other Pacific Islander, non-Hispanic/Latino; 0.3% American Indian or Alaska Native, non-Hispanic/Latino; 2% Two or more races, non-Hispanic/Latino; 3% Race/ethnicity unknown; 4% international; 4% transferred in; 44% live on campus.

Freshmen:
Admission: 4,488 applied, 3,509 admitted, 553 enrolled. *Test scores:* SAT evidence-based reading and writing scores over 500: 84%; SAT math scores over 500: 84%; ACT scores over 18: 96%; SAT evidence-based reading and writing scores over 600: 41%; SAT math scores over 600: 36%; ACT scores over 24: 65%; SAT evidence-based reading and writing scores over 700: 6%; SAT math scores over 700: 7%; ACT scores over 30: 15%.
Retention: 83% of full-time freshmen returned.

FACULTY
Total: 368, 47% full-time, 69% with terminal degrees.
Student/faculty ratio: 11:1.

ACADEMICS
Calendar: semesters. *Degrees:* associate, bachelor's, master's, post-master's, and postbachelor's certificates.
Special study options: academic remediation for entering students, adult/continuing education programs, advanced placement credit, cooperative education, distance learning, double majors, English as a second language, honors programs, independent study, internships, off-campus study, part-time degree program, services for LD students, study abroad, summer session for credit. *ROTC:* Army (b).
Unusual degree programs: 3-2 business administration; engineering with University at Buffalo, the State University of New York.
Computers: 700 computers/terminals are available on campus for general student use. Students can access the following: computer help desk, free student e-mail accounts, online (class) grades, online (class) registration, online (class) schedules, online accounts. Campuswide network is available. 100% of college-owned or -operated housing units are wired for high-speed Internet access. Wireless service is available via entire campus.
Library: Andrew L. Bouwhuis Library plus 1 other. *Books:* 222,252 (physical), 1.7 million (digital/electronic); *Serial titles:* 1,143 (physical), 303,210 (digital/electronic); *Databases:* 108. Weekly public service hours: 110; students can reserve study rooms.

STUDENT LIFE
Housing options: on-campus residence required through sophomore year; coed, special housing for students with disabilities. Campus housing is university owned. Freshman applicants given priority for college housing.
Activities and organizations: drama/theater group, student-run newspaper, radio and television station, choral group, Residence Hall Association, UNITY, Afro-American Society, Project Conservation, FUSION Gaming Society, national fraternities, national sororities.
Athletics Member NCAA. All Division I. *Intercollegiate sports:* baseball M(s), basketball M(s)/W(s), cross-country running M(s)/W(s), equestrian sports W(c), golf M(s), ice hockey M(s), lacrosse M(s)/W(s), rugby M(c)/W(c), soccer M(s)/W(s), softball W(s), swimming and diving M(s)/W(s), volleyball M(c)/W(s). *Intramural sports:* basketball M/W, bowling M(c)/W(c), cheerleading M(c)/W(c), crew M(c)/W(c), fencing M(c)/W(c), field hockey W(c), ice hockey M(c)/W(c), lacrosse M(c), racquetball M/W, riflery M(c)/W(c), skiing (downhill) M(c)/W(c), soccer

M/W, softball M/W, tennis M/W, track and field M(c)/W(c), ultimate Frisbee M(c)/W(c), volleyball M/W, wrestling M(c).
Campus security: 24-hour emergency response devices and patrols, late-night transport/escort service, controlled dormitory access, crime prevention programs, closed-circuit television monitors, emergency call boxes across campus.
Student services: health clinic, personal/psychological counseling.

COSTS & FINANCIAL AID
Costs (2018–19) *Comprehensive fee:* $39,788 includes full-time tuition ($27,000), mandatory fees ($1488), and room and board ($11,300). Part-time tuition: $999 per credit hour. *Required fees:* $21 per credit hour part-time, $83 per term part-time. *College room only:* $5764. Room and board charges vary according to board plan and housing facility. *Payment plans:* installment, deferred payment. *Waivers:* employees or children of employees.
Financial Aid Of all full-time matriculated undergraduates who enrolled in 2017, 1,909 applied for aid, 1,756 were judged to have need, 382 had their need fully met. 357 Federal Work-Study jobs (averaging $1802). In 2017, 484 non-need-based awards were made. *Average percent of need met:* 79. *Average financial aid package:* $30,770. *Average need-based loan:* $4698. *Average need-based gift aid:* $24,341. *Average non-need-based aid:* $18,008. *Average indebtedness upon graduation:* $33,694.

APPLYING
Standardized Tests *Required:* SAT or ACT (for admission).
Options: electronic application, early admission, deferred entrance.
Required: high school transcript, minimum 2.0 GPA. *Required for some:* interview. *Recommended:* essay or personal statement, 1 letter of recommendation, interview.
Application deadlines: 5/1 (freshmen), rolling (transfers).
Notification: continuous (freshmen), continuous (transfers).

CONTACT
Mr. Justin P. Rogers, Director of Admissions, Canisius College, 2001 Main Street, Buffalo, NY 14208-1098. *Phone:* 716-888-2200. *Toll-free phone:* 800-843-1517. *Fax:* 716-888-3230. *E-mail:* admissions@canisius.edu.

Cazenovia College
Cazenovia, New York
http://www.cazenovia.edu/

- **Independent** 4-year, founded 1824
- **Small-town** 40-acre campus with easy access to Syracuse
- **Coed** 893 undergraduate students, 80% full-time, 72% women, 28% men
- **Minimally difficult** entrance level, 92% of applicants were admitted

UNDERGRAD STUDENTS
713 full-time, 180 part-time. Students come from 3 other countries; 12% are from out of state; 9% Black or African American, non-Hispanic/Latino; 5% Hispanic/Latino; 1% Asian, non-Hispanic/Latino; 0.1% Native Hawaiian or other Pacific Islander, non-Hispanic/Latino; 1% American Indian or Alaska Native, non-Hispanic/Latino; 3% Two or more races, non-Hispanic/Latino; 13% Race/ethnicity unknown; 0.6% international; 4% transferred in; 81% live on campus.

Freshmen:
Admission: 1,802 applied, 1,665 admitted, 165 enrolled. *Average high school GPA:* 3.2. *Test scores:* SAT evidence-based reading and writing scores over 500: 65%; SAT math scores over 500: 57%; ACT scores over 18: 60%; SAT evidence-based reading and writing scores over 600: 10%; SAT math scores over 600: 5%; ACT scores over 24: 20%.
Retention: 68% of full-time freshmen returned.

FACULTY
Total: 118, 47% full-time.
Student/faculty ratio: 10:1.

ACADEMICS
Calendar: semesters. *Degrees:* certificates, associate, and bachelor's.
Special study options: academic remediation for entering students, accelerated degree program, adult/continuing education programs, advanced placement credit, distance learning, double majors, freshman honors college, honors programs, independent study, internships, off-

campus study, part-time degree program, services for LD students, study abroad, summer session for credit. *ROTC:* Army (c), Air Force (c).

Computers: Students can access the following: campus intranet, computer help desk, free student e-mail accounts, online (class) grades, online (class) schedules. Campuswide network is available. 100% of college-owned or -operated housing units are wired for high-speed Internet access. Wireless service is available via classrooms, computer centers, computer labs, dorm rooms, learning centers, libraries, student centers.

Library: Witheral Library. Students can reserve study rooms.

STUDENT LIFE

Housing options: on-campus residence required through junior year; coed, men-only, women-only, special housing for students with disabilities. Campus housing is university owned and leased by the school. Freshman campus housing is guaranteed.

Activities and organizations: drama/theater group, student-run newspaper, radio station, choral group, Activities Board, Multicultural Student Group, performing arts, student radio station, yearbook.

Athletics Member NCAA. All Division III. *Intercollegiate sports:* baseball M, basketball M/W, cross-country running M/W, equestrian sports M/W, lacrosse M/W, soccer M/W, softball W, swimming and diving M/W, volleyball W. *Intramural sports:* baseball M, basketball M/W, bowling M/W, cheerleading M(c)/W(c), crew M(c)/W(c), equestrian sports M/W, field hockey W(c), football M/W, skiing (downhill) M/W, soccer M/W, softball M/W, tennis M(c)/W(c), ultimate Frisbee M/W, volleyball M/W, weight lifting M/W.

Campus security: 24-hour emergency response devices and patrols, late-night transport/escort service, controlled dormitory access.

Student services: health clinic, personal/psychological counseling.

COSTS & FINANCIAL AID

Costs (2017–18) *Comprehensive fee:* $47,866 includes full-time tuition ($33,068), mandatory fees ($588), and room and board ($14,210). Full-time tuition and fees vary according to class time, course load, and program. Part-time tuition: $700 per credit hour. Part-time tuition and fees vary according to class time and course load. *College room only:* $7620. Room and board charges vary according to board plan and housing facility. *Payment plan:* installment. *Waivers:* employees or children of employees.

Financial Aid Of all full-time matriculated undergraduates who enrolled in 2015, 899 applied for aid, 858 were judged to have need, 157 had their need fully met. In 2015, 80 non-need-based awards were made. *Average percent of need met:* 80. *Average financial aid package:* $31,152. *Average need-based loan:* $4119. *Average need-based gift aid:* $27,096. *Average non-need-based aid:* $18,424. *Average indebtedness upon graduation:* $33,631.

APPLYING

Standardized Tests *Recommended:* SAT or ACT (for admission).

Options: electronic application, deferred entrance.

Required: high school transcript, 1 letter of recommendation. *Recommended:* essay or personal statement, minimum 2.0 GPA, interview, portfolio for art and design students.

Application deadlines: rolling (freshmen), rolling (transfers).

CONTACT

Office of Admission and Enrollment Services, Cazenovia College, 3 Sullivan Street, Cazenovia, NY 13035. *Phone:* 315-655-7208. *Toll-free phone:* 800-654-3210. *Fax:* 315-655-4860. *E-mail:* admission@cazenovia.edu.

Central Yeshiva Beth Joseph
Brooklyn, New York
http://www.centralyeshivabethjoseph.com

CONTACT

Central Yeshiva Beth Joseph, 1502 Avenue N, Brooklyn, NY 11230.

Central Yeshiva Tomchei Tmimim-Lubavitch
Brooklyn, New York

CONTACT

Director of Admissions, Central Yeshiva Tomchei Tmimim-Lubavitch, 841-853 Ocean Parkway, Brooklyn, NY 11230. *Phone:* 718-859-7600.

City College of the City University of New York
New York, New York
http://www.ccny.cuny.edu/

- **State and locally supported** comprehensive, founded 1847, part of City University of New York System
- **Urban** 35-acre campus with easy access to New York City
- **Coed** 13,411 undergraduate students, 76% full-time, 51% women, 49% men
- **Moderately difficult** entrance level, 41% of applicants were admitted

UNDERGRAD STUDENTS

10,151 full-time, 3,260 part-time. Students come from 155 other countries; 4% are from out of state; 15% Black or African American, non-Hispanic/Latino; 38% Hispanic/Latino; 24% Asian, non-Hispanic/Latino; 0.1% American Indian or Alaska Native, non-Hispanic/Latino; 2% Two or more races, non-Hispanic/Latino; 6% international; 1% live on campus.

Freshmen:
Admission: 25,378 applied, 10,340 admitted. *Average high school GPA:* 3.3. *Test scores:* SAT evidence-based reading and writing scores over 500: 68%; SAT evidence-based reading and writing scores over 600: 19%; SAT evidence-based reading and writing scores over 700: 6%.

Retention: 92% of full-time freshmen returned.

FACULTY

Total: 1,461, 34% full-time, 35% with terminal degrees.

Student/faculty ratio: 15:1.

ACADEMICS

Calendar: semesters. *Degrees:* bachelor's, master's, doctoral, and post-master's certificates.

Special study options: accelerated degree program, adult/continuing education programs, advanced placement credit, English as a second language, freshman honors college, honors programs, independent study, internships, off-campus study, part-time degree program, services for LD students, student-designed majors, study abroad, summer session for credit. *ROTC:* Army (b).

Computers: 3,000 computers/terminals are available on campus for general student use. Students can access the following: campus intranet, computer help desk, free student e-mail accounts, online (class) grades, online (class) registration, online (class) schedules. Campuswide network is available. 100% of college-owned or -operated housing units are wired for high-speed Internet access. Wireless service is available via entire campus.

Library: Morris Raphael Cohen Library plus 8 others. *Books:* 950,000 (physical), 980,000 (digital/electronic); *Serial titles:* 118,000 (digital/electronic); *Databases:* 308. Weekly public service hours: 99; students can reserve study rooms.

STUDENT LIFE

Housing options: coed. Campus housing is provided by a third party.

Activities and organizations: drama/theater group, student-run newspaper, radio station, choral group, Latin American Engineering Student Assoc./Society of Hispanic Professional Engineers, National Society of Black Engineers, Bangladesh Student Association, Salsa-Mambo, InterVarsity Christian Fellowship, national fraternities.

Athletics Member NCAA. All Division III. *Intercollegiate sports:* baseball M, basketball M/W, cross-country running M/W, fencing W, lacrosse M, soccer M/W, softball W, tennis M/W, track and field M/W, volleyball W. *Intramural sports:* basketball M/W, fencing W, soccer M, softball W, tennis M/W, track and field M/W, volleyball W.

Campus security: 24-hour patrols, late-night transport/escort service, controlled dormitory access.

Student services: health clinic, personal/psychological counseling.

FINANCIAL AID
Financial Aid Of all full-time matriculated undergraduates who enrolled in 2016, 9,399 applied for aid, 8,966 were judged to have need, 7,545 had their need fully met. In 2016, 756 non-need-based awards were made. *Average percent of need met:* 84. *Average financial aid package:* $9340. *Average need-based loan:* $4249. *Average need-based gift aid:* $8246. *Average non-need-based aid:* $4410.

APPLYING
Standardized Tests *Required:* SAT or ACT (for admission).

Options: early admission, deferred entrance.

Application fee: $65.

Required: high school transcript. *Required for some:* essay or personal statement, letters of recommendation, creative challenge for architecture, supplemental application for engineering.

Application deadlines: 2/1 (freshmen), 2/1 (transfers).

Notification: continuous until 2/1 (freshmen), continuous until 3/1 (transfers).

CONTACT
City College of the City University of New York, 160 Convent Avenue, New York, NY 10031-9198. *Phone:* 212-650-6977.

Clarkson University
Potsdam, New York
http://www.clarkson.edu/

- **Independent** university, founded 1896
- **Small-town** 640-acre campus
- **Endowment** $191.1 million
- **Coed** 3,090 undergraduate students, 98% full-time, 30% women, 70% men
- **Very difficult** entrance level, 66% of applicants were admitted

UNDERGRAD STUDENTS
3,021 full-time, 69 part-time. Students come from 43 states and territories; 38 other countries; 27% are from out of state; 2% Black or African American, non-Hispanic/Latino; 5% Hispanic/Latino; 4% Asian, non-Hispanic/Latino; 0.2% American Indian or Alaska Native, non-Hispanic/Latino; 3% Two or more races, non-Hispanic/Latino; 2% Race/ethnicity unknown; 3% international; 3% transferred in; 80% live on campus.

Freshmen:
Admission: 7,000 applied, 4,600 admitted, 677 enrolled. *Average high school GPA:* 3.6. *Test scores:* SAT evidence-based reading and writing scores over 500: 95%; SAT math scores over 500: 97%; ACT scores over 18: 100%; SAT evidence-based reading and writing scores over 600: 58%; SAT math scores over 600: 67%; ACT scores over 24: 82%; SAT evidence-based reading and writing scores over 700: 11%; SAT math scores over 700: 15%; ACT scores over 30: 24%.

Retention: 87% of full-time freshmen returned.

FACULTY
Total: 359, 70% full-time, 76% with terminal degrees.
Student/faculty ratio: 13:1.

ACADEMICS
Calendar: semesters. *Degrees:* bachelor's, master's, doctoral, and postbachelor's certificates.

Special study options: accelerated degree program, advanced placement credit, cooperative education, distance learning, double majors, English as a second language, honors programs, independent study, internships, off-campus study, part-time degree program, services for LD students, student-designed majors, study abroad, summer session for credit. *ROTC:* Army (b), Air Force (b).

Unusual degree programs: 3-2 engineering.

Computers: 350 computers/terminals and 6,000 ports are available on campus for general student use. Students can access the following: campus intranet, computer help desk, free student e-mail accounts, online (class) grades, online (class) registration, online (class) schedules. Campuswide network is available. 100% of college-owned or -operated housing units are wired for high-speed Internet access. Wireless service is available via entire campus.

Library: Harriet Call Burnap Memorial Library plus 1 other. *Books:* 104,973 (physical), 193,399 (digital/electronic); *Serial titles:* 1,948 (physical), 69,072 (digital/electronic); *Databases:* 148. Weekly public service hours: 97; students can reserve study rooms.

STUDENT LIFE
Housing options: on-campus residence required through senior year; coed, men-only, women-only, special housing for students with disabilities. Campus housing is university owned. Freshman campus housing is guaranteed.

Activities and organizations: drama/theater group, student-run newspaper, radio and television station, choral group, Outing Club, Ski & Snowboard Club, Society of Women Engineers, Pep Band, Student Association for Engineering Management, national fraternities, national sororities.

Athletics Member NCAA. All Division III except men's and women's ice hockey (Division I). *Intercollegiate sports:* baseball M, basketball M/W, cross-country running M/W, golf M, ice hockey M(s)/W(s), lacrosse M/W, skiing (cross-country) M/W, skiing (downhill) M/W, soccer M/W, softball W, swimming and diving M/W, volleyball W. *Intramural sports:* baseball M(c), basketball M/W, bowling M(c)/W(c), crew M(c)/W(c), equestrian sports M(c)/W(c), football M/W, golf M(c), ice hockey M/W, lacrosse M(c)/W(c), racquetball M(c)/W(c), rowing M(c)/W(c), rugby M(c)/W(c), skiing (cross-country) M(c)/W(c), skiing (downhill) M(c)/W(c), soccer M/W, softball M/W, tennis M(c)/W(c), ultimate Frisbee M(c)/W(c), volleyball M/W, wrestling M(c).

Campus security: 24-hour emergency response devices and patrols, controlled dormitory access.

Student services: health clinic, personal/psychological counseling, legal services.

COSTS & FINANCIAL AID
Costs (2018–19) *Comprehensive fee:* $64,352 includes full-time tuition ($48,194), mandatory fees ($1250), and room and board ($14,908). Full-time tuition and fees vary according to course load. Part-time tuition: $1606 per credit hour. Part-time tuition and fees vary according to course load. *College room only:* $8008. Room and board charges vary according to board plan and housing facility. *Payment plan:* installment. *Waivers:* employees or children of employees.

Financial Aid Of all full-time matriculated undergraduates who enrolled in 2017, 2,588 applied for aid, 2,416 were judged to have need, 501 had their need fully met. 1,528 Federal Work-Study jobs (averaging $1600). 58 state and other part-time jobs (averaging $11,135). In 2017, 484 non-need-based awards were made. *Average percent of need met:* 89. *Average financial aid package:* $43,666. *Average need-based loan:* $5365. *Average need-based gift aid:* $32,061. *Average non-need-based aid:* $22,996. *Average indebtedness upon graduation:* $24,500. *Financial aid deadline:* 3/1.

APPLYING
Standardized Tests *Required:* SAT or ACT (for admission). *Recommended:* SAT Subject Tests (for admission).

Options: electronic application, early admission, early decision, deferred entrance.

Application fee: $50.

Required: essay or personal statement, high school transcript, 2 letters of recommendation. *Recommended:* interview.

Application deadlines: 1/15 (freshmen), rolling (transfers).

Early decision deadline: 12/1.

Notification: continuous (freshmen), continuous (transfers), 1/1 (early decision).

CONTACT
Trish Dobbs, Director of Admissions, Clarkson University, 8 Clarkson Avenue, Box 5605, Potsdam, NY 13699. *Phone:* 315-268-6480. *Toll-free phone:* 800-527-6577. *Fax:* 315-268-7647. *E-mail:* admissions@clarkson.edu.

Colgate University

Hamilton, New York
http://www.colgate.edu/

- **Independent** comprehensive, founded 1819
- **Small-town** 575-acre campus with easy access to Syracuse, Utica
- **Endowment** $881.0 million
- **Coed** 2,873 undergraduate students, 99% full-time, 55% women, 45% men
- **Most difficult** entrance level, 28% of applicants were admitted

UNDERGRAD STUDENTS
2,854 full-time, 19 part-time. Students come from 48 states and territories; 50 other countries; 74% are from out of state; 5% Black or African American, non-Hispanic/Latino; 9% Hispanic/Latino; 4% Asian, non-Hispanic/Latino; 0.1% American Indian or Alaska Native, non-Hispanic/Latino; 4% Two or more races, non-Hispanic/Latino; 4% Race/ethnicity unknown; 9% international; 0.5% transferred in; 90% live on campus.

Freshmen:
Admission: 8,542 applied, 2,404 admitted, 771 enrolled. *Average high school GPA:* 3.7. *Test scores:* SAT evidence-based reading and writing scores over 500: 100%; SAT math scores over 500: 100%; ACT scores over 18: 100%; SAT evidence-based reading and writing scores over 600: 94%; SAT math scores over 600: 88%; ACT scores over 24: 99%; SAT evidence-based reading and writing scores over 700: 55%; SAT math scores over 700: 58%; ACT scores over 30: 84%.

Retention: 94% of full-time freshmen returned.

FACULTY
Total: 360, 82% full-time, 94% with terminal degrees.
Student/faculty ratio: 9:1.

ACADEMICS
Calendar: semesters. *Degrees:* bachelor's and master's.

Special study options: advanced placement credit, double majors, independent study, internships, off-campus study, services for LD students, student-designed majors, study abroad. *ROTC:* Army (c).

Unusual degree programs: 3-2 engineering with Columbia University, Rensselaer Polytechnic Institute, Washington University in St. Louis.

Computers: Students can access the following: campus intranet, computer help desk, free student e-mail accounts, online (class) registration, online (class) schedules, software applications. Campuswide network is available. 100% of college-owned or -operated housing units are wired for high-speed Internet access. Wireless service is available via entire campus.
Library: Case Library and Geyer Center for Information Technology plus 1 other. *Books:* 832,561 (physical), 668,260 (digital/electronic); *Serial titles:* 443 (physical), 5,859 (digital/electronic); *Databases:* 286. Study areas open 24 hours, 5–7 days a week; students can reserve study rooms.

STUDENT LIFE
Housing options: on-campus residence required through junior year; coed, cooperative, special housing for students with disabilities. Campus housing is university owned. Freshman campus housing is guaranteed.

Activities and organizations: drama/theater group, student-run newspaper, radio and television station, choral group, COVE (35+ community service groups), Student Government Association, Cultural/ethnic interest groups, Student communications/publications (including WCRU radio station), Club sports/Outdoor Education, national fraternities, national sororities.

Athletics Member NCAA. All Division I. *Intercollegiate sports:* badminton M(c)/W(c), baseball M(c), basketball M(s)/W(s), bowling M(c)/W(c), cheerleading M(c)/W(c), crew M/W, cross-country running M/W, equestrian sports M(c)/W(c), fencing M(c)/W(c), field hockey W(s), football M(s), golf M, ice hockey M(s)/W(s), lacrosse M(s)/W(s), rugby M(c)/W(c), sailing M(c)/W(c), skiing (downhill) M(c)/W(c), soccer M(s)/W(s), softball W(s), squash M(c)/W(c), swimming and diving M/W/W(s), table tennis M(c)/W(c), tennis M/W, track and field M/W, volleyball M(c)/W(s), water polo M(c)/W(c). *Intramural sports:* basketball M/W, cross-country running M(c)/W(c), football M, golf M(c), lacrosse M(c)/W(c), racquetball M(c)/W(c), riflery M(c)/W(c), rock climbing M(c)/W(c), skiing (cross-country) M(c)/W(c), soccer M/W,

softball M/W, swimming and diving M(c)/W(c), tennis M/W, triathlon M/W, ultimate Frisbee M/W, volleyball W.

Campus security: 24-hour emergency response devices and patrols, student patrols, late-night transport/escort service, controlled dormitory access.

Student services: health clinic, personal/psychological counseling, women's center, legal services.

COSTS & FINANCIAL AID
Costs (2017–18) *One-time required fee:* $50. *Comprehensive fee:* $67,500 includes full-time tuition ($53,650), mandatory fees ($330), and room and board ($13,520). *College room only:* $6525. Room and board charges vary according to board plan and housing facility. *Payment plans:* tuition prepayment, installment, deferred payment. *Waivers:* employees or children of employees.

Financial Aid Of all full-time matriculated undergraduates who enrolled in 2017, 1,142 applied for aid, 1,037 were judged to have need, 1,035 had their need fully met. 624 Federal Work-Study jobs (averaging $2271). 228 state and other part-time jobs (averaging $2121). *Average percent of need met:* 100. *Average financial aid package:* $52,488. *Average need-based loan:* $3475. *Average need-based gift aid:* $48,369. *Average indebtedness upon graduation:* $24,761. *Financial aid deadline:* 1/15.

APPLYING
Standardized Tests *Required:* SAT or ACT (for admission).

Options: electronic application, early decision, deferred entrance.

Application fee: $60.

Required: essay or personal statement, high school transcript, 3 letters of recommendation, Colgate supplement.

Application deadlines: 1/15 (freshmen), 3/15 (transfers).

Early decision deadline: 11/15 (for plan 1), 1/15 (for plan 2).

Notification: 4/1 (freshmen), 4/1 (out-of-state freshmen), 5/1 (transfers), 12/15 (early decision plan 1), rolling (early decision plan 2).

CONTACT
Mr. Gary L. Ross, Vice President and Dean of Admission and Financial Aid, Colgate University, Colgate Office of Admission, 13 Oak Drive, Hamilton, NY 13346-1383. *Phone:* 315-228-7401. *Fax:* 315-228-7544. *E-mail:* admission@colgate.edu.

The College at Brockport, State University of New York

Brockport, New York
http://www.brockport.edu/

- **State-supported** comprehensive, founded 1867, part of State University of New York System
- **Small-town** 464-acre campus with easy access to Rochester
- **Coed** 7,180 undergraduate students, 89% full-time, 57% women, 43% men
- **Moderately difficult** entrance level, 53% of applicants were admitted

UNDERGRAD STUDENTS
6,419 full-time, 761 part-time. Students come from 26 states and territories; 24 other countries; 2% are from out of state; 11% Black or African American, non-Hispanic/Latino; 7% Hispanic/Latino; 2% Asian, non-Hispanic/Latino; 0.1% Native Hawaiian or other Pacific Islander, non-Hispanic/Latino; 0.2% American Indian or Alaska Native, non-Hispanic/Latino; 3% Two or more races, non-Hispanic/Latino; 5% Race/ethnicity unknown; 0.9% international; 14% transferred in; 37% live on campus.

Freshmen:
Admission: 9,628 applied, 5,120 admitted, 1,262 enrolled. *Average high school GPA:* 2.9. *Test scores:* SAT evidence-based reading and writing scores over 500: 80%; SAT math scores over 500: 78%; ACT scores over 18: 94%; SAT evidence-based reading and writing scores over 600: 23%; SAT math scores over 600: 21%; ACT scores over 24: 37%; SAT evidence-based reading and writing scores over 700: 2%; SAT math scores over 700: 1%; ACT scores over 30: 5%.

Retention: 79% of full-time freshmen returned.

FACULTY
Total: 610, 61% full-time, 49% with terminal degrees.

Student/faculty ratio: 17:1.

ACADEMICS

Calendar: semesters. *Degrees:* bachelor's, master's, post-master's, and postbachelor's certificates.

Special study options: accelerated degree program, advanced placement credit, cooperative education, distance learning, double majors, English as a second language, freshman honors college, honors programs, independent study, internships, off-campus study, part-time degree program, services for LD students, student-designed majors, study abroad, summer session for credit. *ROTC:* Army (b), Navy (c), Air Force (c).

Unusual degree programs: 3-2 business administration; nursing; social work; biology, environmental science, environmental science and biology, pharmacy, history, mathematics, political science, sociology/public administration, psychology.

Computers: 1,000 computers/terminals are available on campus for general student use. Students can access the following: campus intranet, computer help desk, free student e-mail accounts, online (class) grades, online (class) registration, online (class) schedules. Campuswide network is available. 100% of college-owned or -operated housing units are wired for high-speed Internet access. Wireless service is available via entire campus.

Library: Drake Memorial Library. *Books:* 500,461 (physical), 185,000 (digital/electronic); *Serial titles:* 4,747 (physical), 113,396 (digital/electronic); *Databases:* 270. Weekly public service hours: 93; students can reserve study rooms.

STUDENT LIFE

Housing options: on-campus residence required through sophomore year; coed, special housing for students with disabilities. Campus housing is university owned. Freshman campus housing is guaranteed.

Activities and organizations: drama/theater group, student-run newspaper, radio and television station, choral group, Habitat for Humanity, Brockport Pre-Professional Health Club, Brockport Psychology Club, Student Nursing Organization, Caribbean Student Association, national fraternities, national sororities.

Athletics Member NCAA. All Division III. *Intercollegiate sports:* baseball M, basketball M/W, cross-country running M/W, field hockey W, football M, gymnastics W, ice hockey M, lacrosse M, soccer M/W, softball W, swimming and diving M/W, tennis W, track and field M/W, volleyball W, wrestling M. *Intramural sports:* baseball M(c), basketball M/W, cheerleading M(c)/W(c), cross-country running M(c)/W(c), equestrian sports M(c)/W(c), golf M(c)/W(c), gymnastics M(c)/W(c), ice hockey M(c)/W(c), lacrosse M(c)/W(c), rugby M(c)/W(c), soccer M/W, softball W(c), swimming and diving M(c)/W(c), tennis M(c)/W, track and field M(c)/W(c), ultimate Frisbee M(c)/W(c), volleyball M/W, weight lifting M(c)/W(c).

Campus security: 24-hour emergency response devices and patrols, student patrols, late-night transport/escort service, controlled dormitory access, Emergency Notification System, Community Policing Program.

Student services: health clinic, personal/psychological counseling, women's center, legal services.

COSTS & FINANCIAL AID

Costs (2018–19) *Tuition:* state resident $6670 full-time, $278 per credit hour part-time; nonresident $16,320 full-time, $680 per credit hour part-time. Part-time tuition and fees vary according to course load. *Required fees:* $1484 full-time, $61 per credit hour part-time, $1484 per year part-time. *Room and board:* $12,904; room only: $7974. Room and board charges vary according to board plan and housing facility. *Payment plans:* installment, deferred payment. *Waivers:* employees or children of employees.

Financial Aid Of all full-time matriculated undergraduates who enrolled in 2016, 4,706 applied for aid, 3,897 were judged to have need, 549 had their need fully met. 338 Federal Work-Study jobs (averaging $2475). 986 state and other part-time jobs (averaging $1818). In 2016, 132 non-need-based awards were made. *Average percent of need met:* 68. *Average financial aid package:* $10,755. *Average need-based loan:* $4852. *Average need-based gift aid:* $6852. *Average non-need-based aid:* $4898. *Average indebtedness upon graduation:* $30,416.

APPLYING

Standardized Tests *Required:* SAT or ACT (for admission). *Recommended:* SAT (for admission), ACT (for admission).

Options: electronic application, deferred entrance.

Application fee: $50.

Required: high school transcript, minimum 2.5 GPA, 1 letter of recommendation. *Required for some:* essay or personal statement, interview. *Recommended:* essay or personal statement, minimum 3.0 GPA.

Application deadlines: rolling (freshmen), rolling (out-of-state freshmen), 8/1 (transfers).

Notification: continuous (freshmen), continuous (out-of-state freshmen), continuous (transfers).

CONTACT

The College at Brockport, State University of New York, 350 New Campus Drive, Brockport, NY 14420-2997. *Phone:* 585-395-2751.

College of Mount Saint Vincent
Riverdale, New York
http://www.mountsaintvincent.edu/

- **Independent** comprehensive, founded 1911
- **Suburban** 70-acre campus with easy access to New York City
- **Coed** 1,695 undergraduate students, 94% full-time, 69% women, 31% men
- **Moderately difficult** entrance level, 91% of applicants were admitted

UNDERGRAD STUDENTS

1,585 full-time, 110 part-time. 12% are from out of state; 15% Black or African American, non-Hispanic/Latino; 42% Hispanic/Latino; 9% Asian, non-Hispanic/Latino; 0.1% American Indian or Alaska Native, non-Hispanic/Latino; 4% Two or more races, non-Hispanic/Latino; 4% Race/ethnicity unknown; 1% international; 6% transferred in; 49% live on campus.

Freshmen:
Admission: 2,740 applied, 2,496 admitted, 447 enrolled. *Average high school GPA:* 3.1. *Test scores:* SAT evidence-based reading and writing scores over 500: 51%; SAT math scores over 500: 46%; ACT scores over 18: 80%; SAT evidence-based reading and writing scores over 600: 9%; SAT math scores over 600: 8%; ACT scores over 24: 12%; SAT evidence-based reading and writing scores over 700: 1%; SAT math scores over 700: 1%.

FACULTY
Total: 226, 36% full-time, 55% with terminal degrees.
Student/faculty ratio: 13:1.

ACADEMICS
Calendar: semesters. *Degrees:* bachelor's, master's, and post-master's certificates.

Special study options: academic remediation for entering students, accelerated degree program, adult/continuing education programs, advanced placement credit, double majors, honors programs, independent study, internships, part-time degree program, services for LD students, study abroad, summer session for credit. *ROTC:* Army (c), Air Force (c).

Unusual degree programs: 3-2 occupational therapy with Columbia University, physical therapy with New York Medical College.

Computers: Students can access the following: campus intranet, computer help desk, free student e-mail accounts, online (class) grades, online (class) registration, online (class) schedules. Campuswide network is available. Wireless service is available via classrooms, computer centers, computer labs, dorm rooms, libraries, student centers.
Library: Elizabeth Seton Library.

STUDENT LIFE
Housing options: coed, special housing for students with disabilities. Campus housing is university owned. Freshman campus housing is guaranteed.

Activities and organizations: drama/theater group, student-run newspaper, radio and television station, choral group.

Athletics Member NCAA. All Division III. *Intercollegiate sports:* baseball M, basketball M/W, cheerleading W, cross-country running M/W, lacrosse M/W, soccer M/W, softball W, swimming and diving M/W, tennis M/W, track and field M/W, volleyball M/W, wrestling M. *Intramural sports:* basketball M.

Campus security: 24-hour emergency response devices and patrols, late-night transport/escort service, controlled dormitory access, emergency call boxes.

Student services: health clinic, personal/psychological counseling.

COSTS & FINANCIAL AID

Costs (2017–18) *Comprehensive fee:* $46,600 includes full-time tuition ($35,620), mandatory fees ($1480), and room and board ($9500). Full-time tuition and fees vary according to student level. Part-time tuition: $1020 per credit hour. *Required fees:* $45 per credit hour part-time. *Payment plan:* installment. *Waivers:* employees or children of employees.

Financial Aid Of all full-time matriculated undergraduates who enrolled in 2013, 1,362 applied for aid, 1,250 were judged to have need, 169 had their need fully met. In 2013, 112 non-need-based awards were made. *Average percent of need met:* 68. *Average financial aid package:* $19,829. *Average need-based loan:* $4333. *Average need-based gift aid:* $10,243. *Average non-need-based aid:* $12,904.

APPLYING

Standardized Tests *Required:* SAT or ACT (for admission).

Options: electronic application, early admission, early action, deferred entrance.

Required: essay or personal statement, high school transcript, minimum 2.0 GPA. *Required for some:* interview. *Recommended:* 2 letters of recommendation, interview.

Application deadlines: 7/29 (freshmen), 11/15 (early action).

Notification: 12/15 (early action).

CONTACT

College of Mount Saint Vincent, 6301 Riverdale Avenue, Riverdale, NY 10471-1093. *Phone:* 718-405-3268. *Toll-free phone:* 800-665-CMSV.

The College of New Rochelle
New Rochelle, New York
http://www.cnr.edu/

- **Independent** comprehensive, founded 1904
- **Suburban** 20-acre campus with easy access to New York City
- **Endowment** $2.3 million
- **Coed** 1,328 undergraduate students, 87% full-time, 83% women, 17% men
- **Moderately difficult** entrance level, 68% of applicants were admitted

UNDERGRAD STUDENTS

1,151 full-time, 177 part-time. Students come from 24 states and territories; 2 other countries; 9% are from out of state; 40% Black or African American, non-Hispanic/Latino; 30% Hispanic/Latino; 6% Asian, non-Hispanic/Latino; 0.3% Native Hawaiian or other Pacific Islander, non-Hispanic/Latino; 3% Two or more races, non-Hispanic/Latino; 6% Race/ethnicity unknown; 0.1% international; 14% transferred in; 32% live on campus.

Freshmen:
Admission: 1,675 applied, 1,145 admitted, 186 enrolled. *Test scores:* SAT evidence-based reading and writing scores over 500: 49%; SAT math scores over 500: 37%; ACT scores over 18: 95%; SAT evidence-based reading and writing scores over 600: 4%; SAT math scores over 600: 4%. *Retention:* 71% of full-time freshmen returned.

FACULTY

Total: 291, 21% full-time.

Student/faculty ratio: 10:1.

ACADEMICS

Calendar: semesters. *Degrees:* bachelor's, master's, post-master's, and postbachelor's certificates (also offers a non-traditional adult program with significant enrollment not reflected in profile).

Special study options: academic remediation for entering students, accelerated degree program, adult/continuing education programs, advanced placement credit, cooperative education, double majors, honors programs, independent study, internships, off-campus study, part-time degree program, services for LD students, student-designed majors, study abroad, summer session for credit.

Computers: 86 computers/terminals and 120 ports are available on campus for general student use. Students can access the following:

campus intranet, computer help desk, free student e-mail accounts, online (class) grades, online (class) registration, online (class) schedules. Campuswide network is available. 100% of college-owned or -operated housing units are wired for high-speed Internet access. Wireless service is available via entire campus.

Library: Gill Library plus 1 other. *Books:* 93,999 (physical), 153,914 (digital/electronic); *Serial titles:* 886 (physical), 94,336 (digital/electronic); *Databases:* 133. Weekly public service hours: 86; students can reserve study rooms.

STUDENT LIFE

Housing options: coed, special housing for students with disabilities. Campus housing is university owned. Freshman campus housing is guaranteed.

Activities and organizations: choral group, Music Ensembles, CNR Model United Nations, Student Nurses Association, Campus Ministry, Student Government.

Athletics Member NCAA. All Division III except soccer (Division II). *Intercollegiate sports:* basketball M/W, cross-country running M/W, soccer M/W, softball W, swimming and diving M/W, tennis M/W, volleyball W. *Intramural sports:* basketball M/W, cross-country running M/W(c), soccer M/W, swimming and diving M/W, table tennis M/W, volleyball M/W.

Campus security: 24-hour emergency response devices and patrols, late-night transport/escort service, controlled dormitory access, 24-hour monitored security cameras at residence hall entrances.

Student services: health clinic, personal/psychological counseling.

COSTS & FINANCIAL AID

Costs (2018–19) *Comprehensive fee:* $52,322 includes full-time tuition ($36,180), mandatory fees ($1580), and room and board ($14,562). Full-time tuition and fees vary according to course load, degree level, and program. Part-time tuition: $1206 per credit. Part-time tuition and fees vary according to course load, degree level, and program. *Room and board:* Room and board charges vary according to housing facility. *Payment plan:* installment. *Waivers:* employees or children of employees.

Financial Aid Of all full-time matriculated undergraduates who enrolled in 2015, 564 applied for aid, 526 were judged to have need, 11 had their need fully met. 400 Federal Work-Study jobs (averaging $2598). In 2015, 34 non-need-based awards were made. *Average percent of need met:* 57. *Average financial aid package:* $22,905. *Average need-based loan:* $5172. *Average need-based gift aid:* $9705. *Average non-need-based aid:* $13,685. *Average indebtedness upon graduation:* $35,430.

APPLYING

Standardized Tests *Required:* SAT or ACT (for admission).

Options: electronic application, deferred entrance.

Application fee: $35.

Required: high school transcript. *Recommended:* essay or personal statement, 1 letter of recommendation, interview.

Application deadlines: rolling (freshmen), rolling (transfers).

Notification: continuous (freshmen), continuous (transfers).

CONTACT

Mr. Brian Sondey, Admissions Director, The College of New Rochelle, 29 Castle Place, New Rochelle, NY 10805-2339. *Phone:* 914-654-5921. *Toll-free phone:* 800-933-5923. *Fax:* 914-654-5464. *E-mail:* bsondey@cnr.edu.

The College of Saint Rose
Albany, New York
http://www.strose.edu/

- **Independent** comprehensive, founded 1920
- **Urban** 49-acre campus
- **Endowment** $42.3 million
- **Coed** 2,523 undergraduate students, 96% full-time, 67% women, 33% men
- **Moderately difficult** entrance level, 83% of applicants were admitted

UNDERGRAD STUDENTS

2,426 full-time, 97 part-time. Students come from 31 states and territories; 33 other countries; 12% are from out of state; 15% Black or African American, non-Hispanic/Latino; 7% Hispanic/Latino; 3% Asian, non-

Hispanic/Latino; 0.2% Native Hawaiian or other Pacific Islander, non-Hispanic/Latino; 0.2% American Indian or Alaska Native, non-Hispanic/Latino; 10% Two or more races, non-Hispanic/Latino; 4% Race/ethnicity unknown; 2% international; 7% transferred in; 48% live on campus.

Freshmen:

Admission: 6,727 applied, 5,565 admitted, 577 enrolled. *Average high school GPA:* 3.2. *Test scores:* SAT evidence-based reading and writing scores over 500: 75%; SAT math scores over 500: 69%; ACT scores over 18: 93%; SAT evidence-based reading and writing scores over 600: 21%; SAT math scores over 600: 14%; ACT scores over 24: 38%; SAT evidence-based reading and writing scores over 700: 1%; SAT math scores over 700: 1%; ACT scores over 30: 7%.

Retention: 75% of full-time freshmen returned.

FACULTY
Total: 327, 52% full-time, 68% with terminal degrees.
Student/faculty ratio: 14:1.

ACADEMICS
Calendar: semesters. *Degrees:* certificates, bachelor's, master's, post-master's, and postbachelor's certificates.

Special study options: academic remediation for entering students, accelerated degree program, advanced placement credit, double majors, English as a second language, independent study, internships, off-campus study, part-time degree program, services for LD students, student-designed majors, study abroad, summer session for credit. *ROTC:* Army (c), Air Force (c).

Unusual degree programs: 3-2 engineering with Rensselaer Polytechnic Institute; clinical laboratory science, biology/cytotechnology with Albany College of Pharmacy.

Computers: 787 computers/terminals and 4,642 ports are available on campus for general student use. Students can access the following: computer help desk, free student e-mail accounts, online (class) grades, online (class) registration, online (class) schedules. Campuswide network is available. 100% of college-owned or -operated housing units are wired for high-speed Internet access. Wireless service is available via entire campus.

Library: Neil Hellman Library plus 2 others. *Books:* 241,000 (physical), 116,500 (digital/electronic); *Serial titles:* 1,201 (physical), 10 (digital/electronic); *Databases:* 104. Students can reserve study rooms.

STUDENT LIFE
Housing options: on-campus residence required for freshman year; coed, men-only, women-only, special housing for students with disabilities. Campus housing is university owned and leased by the school. Freshman campus housing is guaranteed.

Activities and organizations: drama/theater group, student-run newspaper, radio and television station, choral group, Student Association, Student Events Board, Spectrum-ALANA Student Union, Colleges Against Cancer, Music and Entertainment Industry Student Association.

Athletics Member NCAA. All Division II. *Intercollegiate sports:* baseball M(s), basketball M(s)/W(s), cross-country running M(s)/W(s), golf M(s)/W(s), lacrosse M(s), soccer M(s)/W(s), softball W(s), swimming and diving M(s)/W(s), tennis W(s), track and field M(s)/W(s), volleyball W(s). *Intramural sports:* basketball M/W, cheerleading M(c)/W(c), soccer M/W, ultimate Frisbee M/W, volleyball M/W.

Campus security: 24-hour emergency response devices and patrols, late-night transport/escort service, controlled dormitory access.

Student services: health clinic, personal/psychological counseling.

COSTS & FINANCIAL AID
Costs (2018–19) *One-time required fee:* $455. *Comprehensive fee:* $45,288 includes full-time tuition ($31,432), mandatory fees ($1142), and room and board ($12,714). Full-time tuition and fees vary according to course load. Part-time tuition: $1045 per credit hour. Part-time tuition and fees vary according to course load. *Required fees:* $33 per credit hour part-time, $139 per term part-time. *College room only:* $6394. Room and board charges vary according to board plan and housing facility. *Payment plan:* installment. *Waivers:* employees or children of employees.

Financial Aid Of all full-time matriculated undergraduates who enrolled in 2016, 2,286 applied for aid, 2,115 were judged to have need, 325 had

their need fully met. In 2016, 244 non-need-based awards were made. *Average percent of need met:* 77. *Average financial aid package:* $21,805. *Average need-based loan:* $4423. *Average need-based gift aid:* $7828. *Average non-need-based aid:* $13,269. *Average indebtedness upon graduation:* $37,506. *Financial aid deadline:* 5/1.

APPLYING
Standardized Tests *Required for some:* SAT or ACT (for admission).

Options: electronic application, early admission, early action, deferred entrance.

Required: high school transcript, 1 letter of recommendation. *Required for some:* interview. *Recommended:* essay or personal statement, minimum 2.5 GPA.

Application deadlines: 5/1 (freshmen), 8/1 (transfers), 12/1 (early action).

Notification: continuous (freshmen), continuous (transfers), 12/15 (early action).

CONTACT
Ms. Kathleen Lesko, Assistant Vice President of Undergraduate Admissions, The College of Saint Rose, 1001 Madison Avenue, Albany, NY 12203. *Phone:* 518-454-5154. *Toll-free phone:* 800-637-8556. *Fax:* 518-454-2013. *E-mail:* admit@strose.edu.

College of Staten Island of the City University of New York
Staten Island, New York
http://www.csi.cuny.edu/
- **State and locally supported** comprehensive, founded 1955, part of City University of New York
- **Urban** 204-acre campus with easy access to New York City
- **Endowment** $8.3 million
- **Coed** 12,509 undergraduate students, 78% full-time, 55% women, 45% men

UNDERGRAD STUDENTS
9,710 full-time, 2,799 part-time. Students come from 11 states and territories; 117 other countries; 1% are from out of state; 16% Black or African American, non-Hispanic/Latino; 19% Hispanic/Latino; 12% Asian, non-Hispanic/Latino; 0.2% American Indian or Alaska Native, non-Hispanic/Latino; 3% international; 6% transferred in; 3% live on campus.

Freshmen:
Admission: 2,729 enrolled. *Average high school GPA:* 3.0. *Test scores:* SAT math scores over 500: 54%; SAT math scores over 600: 14%; SAT math scores over 700: 1%.

Retention: 77% of full-time freshmen returned.

FACULTY
Total: 1,124, 32% full-time, 38% with terminal degrees.
Student/faculty ratio: 18:1.

ACADEMICS
Calendar: semesters. *Degrees:* certificates, associate, bachelor's, master's, doctoral, post-master's, and postbachelor's certificates.

Special study options: academic remediation for entering students, adult/continuing education programs, cooperative education, double majors, English as a second language, honors programs, independent study, internships, services for LD students, student-designed majors, study abroad, summer session for credit.

Computers: 1,700 computers/terminals and 1,400 ports are available on campus for general student use. Students can access the following: computer help desk, free student e-mail accounts, online (class) grades, online (class) registration, online (class) schedules, MyInfo app. Campuswide network is available. 100% of college-owned or -operated housing units are wired for high-speed Internet access. Wireless service is available via entire campus.

Library: College of Staten Island Library. Weekly public service hours: 112; students can reserve study rooms.

STUDENT LIFE
Housing options: coed, special housing for students with disabilities. Campus housing is university owned.

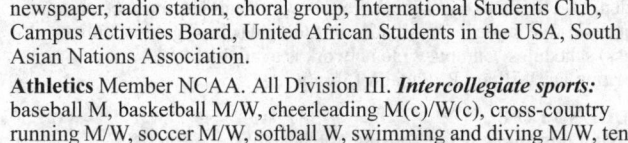

College of Staten Island/CUNY

Excellent academic programs.
Exciting research opportunities.
High-end on-campus living!

Choose from over 40 undergraduate areas of study:

Accounting (BS)
African and African Diaspora Studies (BA)
American Studies (BA)
Art (BA/BFA): Studio Art Concentration
Art/Photography (BA/BFA)
Biochemistry (BS)
Biology*(BS): Tracks: Bioinformatics; Ecology, Evolution and Behavioral Biology; Molecular, Cellular and Developmental Biology; Neuroscience; Health Science
Business (BS): Finance, International Business, Management, Marketing Concentrations
Chemistry*(BS)
Cinema Studies (BA): Critical Studies and Production Concentrations
Communications (BS): Journalism, Media Studies, Design and Digital Media, Corporate Communications Concentrations
Computer Science (BS)
Computer Sci./Mathematics (BS)
Drama (BS)
Earth and Environmental Science (BS)
Earth Science*(BS)
Economics (BA/BS): Business, Finance Specializations
Education: Early Childhood, Childhood and Adolescence Programs
Electrical Engineering (BS)
Engineering Science (BS): Computer, Electrical and Mechanical Specializations

English*(BA): Writing, Linguistics, Literature and Dramatic Literature Concentrations
Geography (BA)
History*(BA)
Information Systems and Informatics (BS)
International Studies (BA)
Italian Studies*(BA)
Mathematics*(BS): Pure, Applied Mathematics
Medical Technology (BS)
Music (BA/BS): Classical Performance, Literature and Theory, Music Technology, Jazz Studies and Performance Concentrations
Nursing (BS)
Philosophy (BA)
Philosophy and Political Science (BA): Dual major
Physics*(BS)
Political Science (BA)
Pre-Professional Preparation: Chiropractic, Dentistry, Law, Medicine, Optometry, Physical Therapy and Podiatry
Psychology (BA/BS)
Science Letters and Society (BA): Early Childhood Sequence (Birth–2), Childhood Sequence (1–6)
Social Work (BS)
Sociology-Anthropology (BA)
Spanish*(BA)
Women's, Gender & Sexuality Studies (BA)

* Adolescent Education Track Available (Grades 7–12)

THE CITY UNIVERSITY OF NEW YORK
College of Staten Island

College of Staten Island • *The City University of New York*
2800 Victory Boulevard • Staten Island, New York 10314
Office of Recruitment and Admissions • Bldg. 2A, Room 103
718.982.2010 • admissions@csi.cuny.edu • www.csi.cuny.edu

Activities and organizations: drama/theater group, student-run newspaper, radio station, choral group, International Students Club, Campus Activities Board, United African Students in the USA, South Asian Nations Association.

Athletics Member NCAA. All Division III. *Intercollegiate sports:* baseball M, basketball M/W, cheerleading M(c)/W(c), cross-country running M/W, soccer M/W, softball W, swimming and diving M/W, tennis M/W, track and field M(c)/W(c), volleyball M/W. *Intramural sports:* badminton M/W, basketball M/W, cheerleading M/W, golf M/W, soccer M/W, swimming and diving M/W, table tennis M/W, tennis M/W, track and field M/W, ultimate Frisbee M/W, volleyball M/W.

Campus security: 24-hour emergency response devices and patrols, student patrols, late-night transport/escort service, controlled dormitory access, radar-controlled traffic monitoring, vehicle and bicycle patrols, closed circuit video surveillance.

Student services: health clinic, personal/psychological counseling, women's center.

COSTS & FINANCIAL AID
Costs (2017–18) *Tuition:* state resident $6530 full-time, $285 per credit hour part-time; nonresident $17,400 full-time, $580 per credit hour part-time. *Required fees:* $559 full-time, $181 per term part-time. *Room only:* $13,900. Room and board charges vary according to housing facility. *Payment plan:* installment. *Waivers:* senior citizens and employees or children of employees.

Financial Aid Of all full-time matriculated undergraduates who enrolled in 2016, 7,704 applied for aid, 6,956 were judged to have need, 361 had their need fully met. In 2016, 240 non-need-based awards were made. *Average percent of need met:* 39. *Average financial aid package:* $8225. *Average need-based loan:* $8970. *Average need-based gift aid:* $7674. *Average non-need-based aid:* $3124.

APPLYING
Standardized Tests *Required:* SAT or ACT (for admission).

Required: high school transcript. *Required for some:* essay or personal statement, 2 letters of recommendation, interview.

CONTACT
College of Staten Island of the City University of New York, 2800 Victory Boulevard, 2A-103, Staten Island, NY 10314. *Phone:* 718-982-2010. *Fax:* 718-982-2500. *E-mail:* admissions@csi.cuny.edu.

See this page for display ad and page 1266 for the College Close-Up.

The College of Westchester
White Plains, New York
http://www.cw.edu/
- **Proprietary** primarily 2-year, founded 1915
- **Suburban** campus with easy access to New York City
- **Coed** 915 undergraduate students, 79% full-time, 64% women, 36% men
- **Minimally difficult** entrance level, 98% of applicants were admitted

UNDERGRAD STUDENTS
721 full-time, 194 part-time. Students come from 5 states and territories; 4% are from out of state; 38% Black or African American, non-Hispanic/Latino; 47% Hispanic/Latino; 2% Asian, non-Hispanic/Latino; 0.2% Native Hawaiian or other Pacific Islander, non-Hispanic/Latino; 0.1% American Indian or Alaska Native, non-Hispanic/Latino; 1% Two or more races, non-Hispanic/Latino; 3% Race/ethnicity unknown; 10% transferred in.

Freshmen:
Admission: 1,002 applied, 984 admitted, 161 enrolled.
Retention: 65% of full-time freshmen returned.

FACULTY
Total: 69, 46% full-time.
Student/faculty ratio: 20:1.

ACADEMICS
Calendar: semesters. *Degrees:* certificates, associate, and bachelor's.
Special study options: academic remediation for entering students, accelerated degree program, adult/continuing education programs, cooperative education, distance learning, double majors, honors programs, internships, part-time degree program, summer session for credit.

Computers: 271 computers/terminals are available on campus for general student use. Students can access the following: campus intranet, computer help desk, free student e-mail accounts, online (class) grades, online (class) schedules. Campuswide network is available.

Library: Dr. William R. Papallo Library.

STUDENT LIFE

Housing options: college housing not available.

Activities and organizations: student-run newspaper.

Student services: personal/psychological counseling.

COSTS

Costs (2017–18) *Tuition:* $20,115 full-time, $745 per credit part-time. *Required fees:* $900 full-time, $100 per course part-time. *Payment plan:* installment. *Waivers:* employees or children of employees.

APPLYING

Standardized Tests *Recommended:* SAT (for admission).

Options: electronic application, deferred entrance.

Application fee: $40.

Required: high school transcript, interview. *Required for some:* essay or personal statement.

Application deadlines: rolling (freshmen), rolling (transfers).

CONTACT

Mr. Matt Curtis, Vice President, Enrollment Management, The College of Westchester, 325 Central Avenue, PO Box 710, White Plains, NY 10602. *Phone:* 914-948-4442 Ext. 313. *Toll-free phone:* 855-403-7722. *Fax:* 914-948-5441. *E-mail:* admissions@cw.edu.

Columbia University
New York, New York
http://www.columbia.edu/

- **Independent** university, founded 1754
- **Urban** 36-acre campus
- **Endowment** $10.0 billion
- **Coed** 6,231 undergraduate students, 100% full-time, 48% women, 52% men
- **Most difficult** entrance level, 6% of applicants were admitted

UNDERGRAD STUDENTS

6,231 full-time. Students come from 52 states and territories; 93 other countries; 78% are from out of state; 12% Black or African American, non-Hispanic/Latino; 12% Hispanic/Latino; 22% Asian, non-Hispanic/Latino; 2% American Indian or Alaska Native, non-Hispanic/Latino; 2% Race/ethnicity unknown; 16% international; 2% transferred in; 93% live on campus.

Freshmen:

Admission: 37,389 applied, 2,263 admitted, 1,405 enrolled. *Test scores:* SAT evidence-based reading and writing scores over 500: 100%; SAT math scores over 500: 100%; ACT scores over 18: 100%; SAT evidence-based reading and writing scores over 600: 98%; SAT math scores over 600: 99%; ACT scores over 24: 100%; SAT evidence-based reading and writing scores over 700: 84%; SAT math scores over 700: 88%; ACT scores over 30: 92%.

Retention: 99% of full-time freshmen returned.

FACULTY
Student/faculty ratio: 6:1.

ACADEMICS

Calendar: semesters. *Degrees:* bachelor's, master's, and doctoral.

Special study options: accelerated degree program, advanced placement credit, double majors, English as a second language, independent study, internships, off-campus study, services for LD students, student-designed majors, study abroad, summer session for credit. *ROTC:* Army (c), Navy (b), Air Force (c).

Unusual degree programs: 3-2 engineering.

Computers: 460 computers/terminals are available on campus for general student use. Students can access the following: campus intranet, computer help desk, free student e-mail accounts, online (class) grades, online (class) registration, online (class) schedules. Campuswide network is available. Wireless service is available via entire campus.

Library: Butler plus 18 others. *Books:* 11.5 million (physical), 2.5 million (digital/electronic); *Databases:* 1,689. Weekly public service hours: 86; study areas open 24 hours, 5–7 days a week; students can reserve study rooms.

STUDENT LIFE

Housing options: on-campus residence required for freshman year; coed, cooperative, special housing for students with disabilities. Campus housing is university owned. Freshman campus housing is guaranteed.

Activities and organizations: drama/theater group, student-run newspaper, radio and television station, choral group, marching band, community service, cultural organizations, performing arts, athletics, publications, national fraternities, national sororities.

Athletics Member NCAA. All Division I except football (Division I-AA). *Intercollegiate sports:* archery W, baseball M, basketball M/W, crew M/W, cross-country running M/W, fencing M/W, field hockey W, golf M/W, ice hockey M(c)/W(c), lacrosse M(c)/W, rowing M/W, rugby M(c)/W(c), soccer M/W, softball W, squash M/W, swimming and diving M/W, tennis M/W, track and field M/W, ultimate Frisbee M(c)/W(c), volleyball W, water polo M(c)/W(c), wrestling M. *Intramural sports:* archery M(c)/W(c), badminton M(c)/W(c), basketball M/W, equestrian sports M(c)/W(c), football M/W, racquetball M/W, rock climbing M(c)/W(c), sailing M(c)/W(c), skiing (downhill) M(c)/W(c), soccer M/W, squash M/W, table tennis M(c)/W(c), tennis M(c)/W(c), triathlon M(c)/W(c), volleyball M(c)/W(c).

Campus security: 24-hour emergency response devices and patrols, late-night transport/escort service, controlled dormitory access.

Student services: health clinic, personal/psychological counseling, women's center.

COSTS & FINANCIAL AID

Costs (2017–18) *Comprehensive fee:* $70,826 includes full-time tuition ($54,504), mandatory fees ($2704), and room and board ($13,618). *Room and board:* Room and board charges vary according to board plan. *Payment plans:* tuition prepayment, installment. *Waivers:* employees or children of employees.

Financial Aid Of all full-time matriculated undergraduates who enrolled in 2017, 3,341 applied for aid, 3,143 were judged to have need, 2,943 had their need fully met. *Average percent of need met:* 100. *Average financial aid package:* $58,630. *Average need-based loan:* $3623. *Average need-based gift aid:* $53,879.

APPLYING

Standardized Tests *Required:* SAT or ACT (for admission).

Options: electronic application, early admission, early decision, deferred entrance.

Application fee: $85.

Required: essay or personal statement, high school transcript, 3 letters of recommendation.

Application deadlines: 1/1 (freshmen), 3/1 (transfers).

Early decision deadline: 11/1.

Notification: 4/1 (freshmen), 5/15 (transfers), 12/15 (early decision).

CONTACT

Columbia University, 116th Street and Broadway, New York, NY 10027. *Phone:* 212-854-1222.

See previous page for display ad and page 1268 for the College Close-Up.

Columbia University School of General Studies

New York, New York

http://www.gs.columbia.edu/

- **Independent** 4-year, founded 1754, part of Columbia University
- **Urban** 36-acre campus with easy access to New York City
- **Endowment** $9.0 billion
- **Coed**
- **Most difficult** entrance level

ACADEMICS

Calendar: semesters. *Degrees:* bachelor's and postbachelor's certificates. **Library:** Butler Library plus 20 others.

STUDENT LIFE

Housing options: coed, cooperative, special housing for students with disabilities. Campus housing is university owned, leased by the school and is provided by a third party.

Activities and organizations: drama/theater group, student-run newspaper, radio and television station, choral group, marching band, General Studies Student Council, national fraternities, national sororities.

Athletics Member NCAA. All Division I except football (Division I-AA).

Campus security: 24-hour emergency response devices and patrols, late-night transport/escort service.

Student services: health clinic, personal/psychological counseling, women's center.

COSTS & FINANCIAL AID

Costs (2017–18) *One-time required fee:* $105. *Comprehensive fee:* $69,428 includes full-time tuition ($52,680), mandatory fees ($2798), and room and board ($13,950). Full-time tuition and fees vary according to course load and program. Part-time tuition: $1756 per credit hour. Part-time tuition and fees vary according to course load and program. *College room only:* $8530. Room and board charges vary according to board plan and housing facility. *Payment plans:* tuition prepayment, installment.

Financial Aid Of all full-time matriculated undergraduates who enrolled in 2015, 950 applied for aid, 874 were judged to have need, 29 had their need fully met. In 2015, 65 non-need-based awards were made. *Average percent of need met:* 45. *Average financial aid package:* $30,819. *Average need-based loan:* $8359. *Average need-based gift aid:* $22,797. *Average non-need-based aid:* $12,545. *Financial aid deadline:* 6/1.

APPLYING

Standardized Tests *Required:* SAT or ACT (for admission).

Options: electronic application, early action, deferred entrance.

Application fee: $80.

Required: essay or personal statement, high school transcript, 2 letters of recommendation. *Required for some:* interview.

CONTACT

Mr. Curtis M. Rodgers, Vice Dean, Columbia University School of General Studies, 2970 Broadway, 408 Lewisohn Hall, MC 4101, New York, NY 10027. *Phone:* 212-854-2772. *Toll-free phone:* 800-895-1169. *Fax:* 212-854-6316. *E-mail:* gsdegree@columbia.edu.

See next page for display ad and page 1270 for the College Close-Up.

Concordia College–New York

Bronxville, New York

http://www.concordia-ny.edu/

- **Independent Lutheran** comprehensive, founded 1881, part of Concordia University System
- **Suburban** 33-acre campus with easy access to New York City
- **Endowment** $6.4 million
- **Coed** 1,129 undergraduate students, 91% full-time, 74% women, 26% men
- **Moderately difficult** entrance level, 78% of applicants were admitted

UNDERGRAD STUDENTS

1,024 full-time, 105 part-time. Students come from 14 states and territories; 31 other countries; 16% Black or African American, non-Hispanic/Latino; 22% Hispanic/Latino; 4% Asian, non-Hispanic/Latino; 0.2% Native Hawaiian or other Pacific Islander, non-Hispanic/Latino;

0.2% American Indian or Alaska Native, non-Hispanic/Latino; 2% Two or more races, non-Hispanic/Latino; 2% Race/ethnicity unknown; 11% international; 60% live on campus.

Freshmen:
Admission: 942 applied, 738 admitted. *Average high school GPA:* 3.2.
Test scores: ACT scores over 18: 56%; ACT scores over 24: 19%.
Retention: 78% of full-time freshmen returned.

FACULTY
Total: 148, 35% full-time.
Student/faculty ratio: 11:1.

ACADEMICS
Calendar: semesters. *Degrees:* certificates, diplomas, associate, bachelor's, and master's.

Special study options: academic remediation for entering students, accelerated degree program, adult/continuing education programs, cooperative education, double majors, English as a second language, honors programs, independent study, internships, off-campus study, part-time degree program, services for LD students, student-designed majors, study abroad.

Computers: Students can access the following: campus intranet, computer help desk, free student e-mail accounts, online (class) grades, online (class) registration, online (class) schedules. Campuswide network is available. 100% of college-owned or -operated housing units are wired for high-speed Internet access. Wireless service is available via entire campus.
Library: Scheele Memorial Library plus 1 other.

STUDENT LIFE
Housing options: men-only, women-only, special housing for students with disabilities. Campus housing is university owned.

Activities and organizations: drama/theater group, student-run newspaper, choral group, Student Government Association, Choral Groups, Campus Christian Ministries, International and Afro/Latin American Club, Yearbook and newspaper.

Athletics Member NCAA. All Division II. *Intercollegiate sports:* baseball M(s), basketball M(s)/W(s), cross-country running M(s)/W(s), golf M, soccer M(s)/W(s), softball W(s), tennis M(s)/W(s), volleyball W(s). *Intramural sports:* basketball M/W, cheerleading W, football M/W, racquetball M/W, sand volleyball M/W, softball W, squash M/W, table tennis M/W, tennis M/W, ultimate Frisbee M/W.

Campus security: 24-hour emergency response devices and patrols, controlled dormitory access.

Student services: health clinic, personal/psychological counseling.

COSTS & FINANCIAL AID
Costs (2018–19) *Comprehensive fee:* $45,590 includes full-time tuition ($31,500), mandatory fees ($1400), and room and board ($12,690). Full-time tuition and fees vary according to class time, course load, location, and program. Part-time tuition: $880 per credit. Part-time tuition and fees vary according to class time, course load, location, and program. *Room and board:* Room and board charges vary according to board plan. *Payment plan:* installment. *Waivers:* employees or children of employees.

Financial Aid Of all full-time matriculated undergraduates who enrolled in 2008, 533 applied for aid, 448 were judged to have need, 89 had their need fully met. In 2008, 100 non-need-based awards were made. *Average percent of need met:* 71. *Average financial aid package:* $22,309. *Average need-based loan:* $4133. *Average need-based gift aid:* $11,129. *Average non-need-based aid:* $6170. *Average indebtedness upon graduation:* $24,153.

APPLYING
Standardized Tests *Required for some:* SAT or ACT (for admission), TOEFL or IELTS for students for whom English is not their first language.

Options: electronic application, early admission, early action, deferred entrance.

Application fee: $60.

Required: essay or personal statement, high school transcript, 2 letters of recommendation. *Required for some:* interview. *Recommended:* minimum 2.5 GPA.

Application deadlines: 3/15 (freshmen), 7/15 (transfers), 11/15 (early action).

Notification: continuous (freshmen), continuous until 8/15 (transfers), 12/15 (early action).

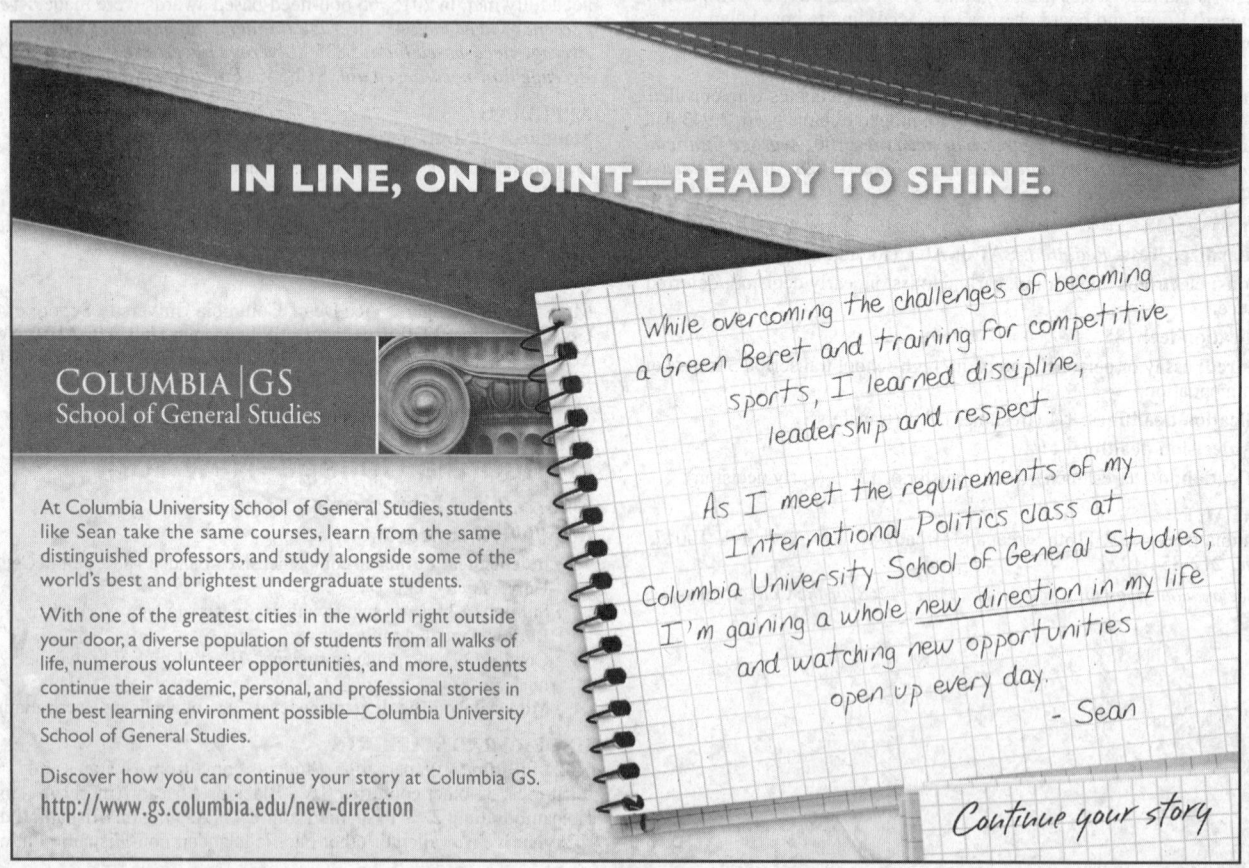

CONTACT
Ms. Toral Bhatt, Director of Recruitment, Concordia College–New York, 171 White Plains Road, Bronxville, NY 10708. *Phone:* 914-337-9300 Ext. 2124. *Toll-free phone:* 800-YES-COLLEGE. *Fax:* 914-395-4636. *E-mail:* toral.bhatt@concordia-ny.edu.

Cooper Union for the Advancement of Science and Art
New York, New York
http://www.cooper.edu/
- **Independent** comprehensive, founded 1859
- **Urban** campus with easy access to New York City
- **Endowment** $798.9 million
- **Coed** 867 undergraduate students, 99% full-time, 35% women, 65% men

UNDERGRAD STUDENTS
859 full-time, 8 part-time. Students come from 30 states and territories; 18 other countries; 50% are from out of state; 3% Black or African American, non-Hispanic/Latino; 10% Hispanic/Latino; 20% Asian, non-Hispanic/Latino; 7% Two or more races, non-Hispanic/Latino; 10% Race/ethnicity unknown; 20% international; 2% transferred in; 20% live on campus.

Freshmen:
Admission: 191 enrolled. *Average high school GPA:* 3.8. *Test scores:* SAT evidence-based reading and writing scores over 500: 98%; SAT math scores over 500: 94%; ACT scores over 18: 100%; SAT evidence-based reading and writing scores over 600: 85%; SAT math scores over 600: 81%; ACT scores over 24: 91%; SAT evidence-based reading and writing scores over 700: 53%; SAT math scores over 700: 71%; ACT scores over 30: 70%.

Retention: 95% of full-time freshmen returned.

FACULTY
Total: 206, 28% full-time.
Student/faculty ratio: 8:1.

ACADEMICS
Calendar: semesters. *Degrees:* certificates, bachelor's, and master's (also offers master's program primarily made up of currently-enrolled students).

Special study options: accelerated degree program, advanced placement credit, independent study, internships, off-campus study, services for LD students, student-designed majors, study abroad, summer session for credit.

Computers: 100 computers/terminals are available on campus for general student use. Students can access the following: computer help desk, free student e-mail accounts, online (class) grades, online (class) registration, online (class) schedules. Campuswide network is available. 100% of college-owned or -operated housing units are wired for high-speed Internet access. Wireless service is available via entire campus.
Library: Cooper Union Library. *Books:* 98,400 (physical), 213,578 (digital/electronic); *Serial titles:* 71 (physical), 40,306 (digital/electronic); *Databases:* 48. Weekly public service hours: 69.

STUDENT LIFE
Housing options: coed. Campus housing is university owned. Freshman applicants given priority for college housing.

Activities and organizations: drama/theater group, student-run newspaper, choral group, South Asian Society, Pro Musica, Chinese Student Association, Drama Society, Outdoors Club; Intervarsity Christian Fellowship, national fraternities, national sororities.

Athletics *Intercollegiate sports:* basketball M/W, cross-country running M/W, soccer M/W, tennis M/W, volleyball M/W. *Intramural sports:* badminton M(c)/W(c), basketball M/W, bowling M/W, fencing M(c)/W(c), golf M/W, skiing (downhill) M/W, soccer M(c)/W(c), swimming and diving M/W, table tennis M/W, tennis M/W, ultimate Frisbee M(c)/W(c), volleyball M/W.

Campus security: 24-hour emergency response devices and patrols, controlled dormitory access, security guards.

Student services: personal/psychological counseling.

COSTS & FINANCIAL AID
Costs (2018–19) *Tuition:* $1310 per credit hour part-time. Full-time tuition and fees vary according to degree level and reciprocity agreements. Part-time tuition and fees vary according to degree level and reciprocity agreements. *Required fees:* $1075 per term part-time. *Room only:* Room and board charges vary according to housing facility. *Payment plan:* installment. *Waivers:* employees or children of employees.

Financial Aid Of all full-time matriculated undergraduates who enrolled in 2017, 497 applied for aid, 413 were judged to have need, 162 had their need fully met. 37 Federal Work-Study jobs (averaging $902). In 2017, 438 non-need-based awards were made. *Average percent of need met:* 76. *Average financial aid package:* $47,735. *Average need-based loan:* $4529. *Average need-based gift aid:* $25,221. *Average non-need-based aid:* $24,338. *Average indebtedness upon graduation:* $17,037.

APPLYING
Standardized Tests *Required:* SAT or ACT (for admission), studio test for architecture, home test for art (for admission). *Required for some:* SAT Subject Tests (for admission).

Required: essay or personal statement, high school transcript. *Required for some:* minimum 3.5 GPA, 3 letters of recommendation, interview, portfolio for art, studio test for architecture. *Recommended:* minimum 3.0 GPA, 2 letters of recommendation.

CONTACT
Ms. Adrianne Greth, Associate Dean of Admissions, Cooper Union for the Advancement of Science and Art, 30 Cooper Square, New York, NY 10003. *Phone:* 212-353-4121. *Fax:* 212-353-4342. *E-mail:* admissions@cooper.edu.

Cornell University
Ithaca, New York
http://www.cornell.edu/
- **Independent** university, founded 1865, part of State University of New York System
- **Small-town** 745-acre campus with easy access to Syracuse
- **Endowment** $6.0 billion
- **Coed** 14,907 undergraduate students, 100% full-time, 52% women, 48% men
- **Most difficult** entrance level, 13% of applicants were admitted

UNDERGRAD STUDENTS
14,907 full-time. Students come from 56 states and territories; 88 other countries; 65% are from out of state; 7% Black or African American, non-Hispanic/Latino; 13% Hispanic/Latino; 19% Asian, non-Hispanic/Latino; 0.1% Native Hawaiian or other Pacific Islander, non-Hispanic/Latino; 0.4% American Indian or Alaska Native, non-Hispanic/Latino; 5% Two or more races, non-Hispanic/Latino; 8% Race/ethnicity unknown; 11% international; 4% transferred in; 54% live on campus.

Freshmen:
Admission: 47,039 applied, 5,962 admitted, 3,349 enrolled. *Test scores:* SAT evidence-based reading and writing scores over 500: 100%; ACT scores over 18: 100%; SAT evidence-based reading and writing scores over 600: 97%; ACT scores over 24: 99%; SAT evidence-based reading and writing scores over 700: 71%; ACT scores over 30: 89%.
Retention: 97% of full-time freshmen returned.

FACULTY
Total: 2,157, 81% full-time, 88% with terminal degrees.
Student/faculty ratio: 9:1.

ACADEMICS
Calendar: semesters. *Degrees:* bachelor's, master's, and doctoral.

Special study options: academic remediation for entering students, accelerated degree program, advanced placement credit, cooperative education, distance learning, double majors, English as a second language, honors programs, independent study, internships, off-campus study, services for LD students, student-designed majors, study abroad, summer session for credit. *ROTC:* Army (b), Navy (b), Air Force (b).

Computers: 2,650 computers/terminals and 2,500 ports are available on campus for general student use. Students can access the following: campus intranet, computer help desk, free student e-mail accounts, online (class) grades, online (class) registration. Campuswide network is available. 100% of college-owned or -operated housing units are wired for high-speed Internet access. Wireless service is available via entire campus.

Library: Main Library plus 16 others. *Books:* 8.1 million (physical), 1.6 million (digital/electronic); *Serial titles:* 236,248 (physical), 153,975 (digital/electronic); *Databases:* 4,125. Weekly public service hours: 146; study areas open 24 hours, 5–7 days a week; students can reserve study rooms.

STUDENT LIFE

Housing options: coed, women-only, cooperative, special housing for students with disabilities. Campus housing is university owned. Freshman campus housing is guaranteed.

Activities and organizations: drama/theater group, student-run newspaper, radio and television station, choral group, marching band, Student Assembly, Class Councils, Cornell Concert Commission, Interfraternity Council, Panhellenic Association, national fraternities, national sororities.

Athletics Member NCAA. All Division I. *Intercollegiate sports:* baseball M, basketball M/W, crew M/W, cross-country running M/W, equestrian sports W, fencing W, field hockey W, football M, golf M, gymnastics W, ice hockey M/W, lacrosse M/W, sailing W, soccer M/W, softball W, squash M/W, swimming and diving M/W, tennis M/W, track and field M/W, ultimate Frisbee M(c)/W(c), volleyball M(c)/W, water polo M(c)/W(c), wrestling M. *Intramural sports:* archery M(c)/W(c), badminton M/W, baseball M(c), basketball M/W, bowling M/W, cheerleading W(c), cross-country running M(c)/W(c), equestrian sports M(c)/W(c), fencing M(c)/W(c), field hockey W(c), football M(c)/W(c), golf M/W, gymnastics M(c)/W(c), ice hockey M(c)/W(c), lacrosse W(c), rugby M(c)/W(c), sailing M(c)/W(c), sand volleyball M(c)/W(c), skiing (cross-country) M(c)/W(c), skiing (downhill) M(c)/W(c), soccer M/W, softball M/W, squash M/W, table tennis M/W, tennis M/W, ultimate Frisbee M/W, volleyball M/W, water polo M/W, wrestling M(c)/W(c).

Campus security: 24-hour emergency response devices and patrols, late-night transport/escort service, controlled dormitory access, indoor/outdoor emergency phones, lighted pathways/sidewalks, shuttle buses, safety escorts, weekly safety messages to the community.

Student services: health clinic, personal/psychological counseling, women's center.

COSTS & FINANCIAL AID

Costs (2017–18) *Comprehensive fee:* $67,233 includes full-time tuition ($52,612), mandatory fees ($241), and room and board ($14,380). Full-time tuition and fees vary according to degree level. *College room only:* $8564. Room and board charges vary according to board plan and housing facility. *Payment plan:* installment. *Waivers:* employees or children of employees.

Financial Aid Of all full-time matriculated undergraduates who enrolled in 2017, 7,642 applied for aid, 7,031 were judged to have need, 7,031 had their need fully met. 5,318 Federal Work-Study jobs (averaging $2434). 743 state and other part-time jobs (averaging $2277). *Average percent of need met:* 100. *Average financial aid package:* $47,202. *Average need-based loan:* $5158. *Average need-based gift aid:* $40,540. *Average indebtedness upon graduation:* $25,542. *Financial aid deadline:* 2/15.

APPLYING

Standardized Tests *Required:* SAT or ACT (for admission). *Required for some:* SAT Subject Tests (for admission).

Options: electronic application, early decision, deferred entrance.

Application fee: $80.

Required: essay or personal statement, high school transcript, 2 letters of recommendation. *Required for some:* interview.

Application deadlines: 1/2 (freshmen), 3/15 (transfers).

Early decision deadline: 11/1.

Notification: 3/31 (freshmen), 6/15 (transfers), 12/15 (early decision).

CONTACT

Director of Undergraduate Admissions, Cornell University, 144 East Avenue, Ithaca, NY 14853. *Phone:* 607-255-5241. *Fax:* 607-255-0659. *E-mail:* admissions@cornell.edu.

The Culinary Institute of America
Hyde Park, New York
http://www.ciachef.edu/

- **Independent** 4-year, founded 1946
- **Suburban** 170-acre campus
- **Endowment** $128.6 million
- **Coed** 3,116 undergraduate students, 100% full-time, 50% women, 50% men
- **Moderately difficult** entrance level, 97% of applicants were admitted

UNDERGRAD STUDENTS

3,116 full-time. Students come from 53 states and territories; 46 other countries; 66% are from out of state; 6% Black or African American, non-Hispanic/Latino; 16% Hispanic/Latino; 7% Asian, non-Hispanic/Latino; 0.4% Native Hawaiian or other Pacific Islander, non-Hispanic/Latino; 0.4% American Indian or Alaska Native, non-Hispanic/Latino; 3% Two or more races, non-Hispanic/Latino; 3% Race/ethnicity unknown; 15% international; 8% transferred in.

Freshmen:
Admission: 1,170 applied, 1,137 admitted, 433 enrolled. *Average high school GPA:* 3.1. *Test scores:* SAT evidence-based reading and writing scores over 500: 75%; SAT math scores over 500: 68%; ACT scores over 18: 73%; SAT evidence-based reading and writing scores over 600: 28%; SAT math scores over 600: 22%; ACT scores over 24: 33%; SAT evidence-based reading and writing scores over 700: 1%; SAT math scores over 700: 4%; ACT scores over 30: 5%.

FACULTY
Total: 183, 77% full-time.
Student/faculty ratio: 20:1.

ACADEMICS

Calendar: semesters plus 18 or 21 week externship program. *Degrees:* certificates, associate, bachelor's, and postbachelor's certificates.

Special study options: academic remediation for entering students, double majors, internships, off-campus study, services for LD students, study abroad.

Computers: 227 computers/terminals are available on campus for general student use. Students can access the following: campus intranet, computer help desk, free student e-mail accounts, online (class) grades, online (class) registration, online (class) schedules, online course guides. Campuswide network is available. 100% of college-owned or -operated housing units are wired for high-speed Internet access. Wireless service is available via entire campus.

Library: Conrad N. Hilton Library. *Books:* 57,977 (physical), 1,149 (digital/electronic); *Serial titles:* 449 (physical), 22,228 (digital/electronic); *Databases:* 75. Weekly public service hours: 92; students can reserve study rooms.

STUDENT LIFE

Housing options: coed. Campus housing is university owned and is provided by a third party. Freshman campus housing is guaranteed.

Activities and organizations: student-run newspaper, Bacchus Wine Society, Tea Club, KACIA, Culinary Christian Fellowship, Black Culinarian Society.

Athletics *Intercollegiate sports:* basketball M/W, cross-country running M/W, soccer M/W, tennis M/W, volleyball M(c)/W. *Intramural sports:* basketball M/W, football M/W, soccer M/W, softball M/W, tennis M/W, volleyball M/W, weight lifting M/W.

Campus security: 24-hour emergency response devices and patrols, late-night transport/escort service, controlled dormitory access, CCTV & Nightly Visitor Screening.

Student services: health clinic, personal/psychological counseling.

COSTS & FINANCIAL AID

Costs (2017–18) *Comprehensive fee:* $42,486 includes full-time tuition ($29,380), mandatory fees ($2236), and room and board ($10,870). *College room only:* $7320. Room and board charges vary according to board plan, housing facility, and location. *Payment plan:* installment. *Waivers:* employees or children of employees.

Financial Aid Of all full-time matriculated undergraduates who enrolled in 2016, 1,924 applied for aid, 1,787 were judged to have need, 122 had their need fully met. 1,045 Federal Work-Study jobs (averaging $2238). In

2016, 132 non-need-based awards were made. *Average percent of need met:* 71. *Average financial aid package:* $16,541. *Average need-based loan:* $3825. *Average need-based gift aid:* $12,031. *Average non-need-based aid:* $6359. *Average indebtedness upon graduation:* $51,200.

APPLYING
Options: electronic application, early action, deferred entrance.

Application fee: $50.

Required: essay or personal statement, high school transcript, 1 letter of recommendation. *Required for some:* Affidavit of Support. *Recommended:* minimum 2.0 GPA.

Notification: continuous (transfers).

CONTACT
Ms. Rachel Birchwood, Sr. Director of Admissions, The Culinary Institute of America, 1946 Campus Drive, Hyde Park, NY 12538. *Phone:* 845-451-1459. *Toll-free phone:* 800-CULINARY. *Fax:* 845-451-1068. *E-mail:* admissions@culinary.edu.

Daemen College
Amherst, New York
http://www.daemen.edu/
- **Independent** comprehensive, founded 1947
- **Suburban** 35-acre campus with easy access to Buffalo
- **Endowment** $14.4 million
- **Coed** 1,802 undergraduate students, 87% full-time, 71% women, 29% men
- **Moderately difficult** entrance level, 49% of applicants were admitted

UNDERGRAD STUDENTS
1,559 full-time, 243 part-time. Students come from 18 other countries; 11% Black or African American, non-Hispanic/Latino; 7% Hispanic/Latino; 3% Asian, non-Hispanic/Latino; 0.1% Native Hawaiian or other Pacific Islander, non-Hispanic/Latino; 0.2% American Indian or Alaska Native, non-Hispanic/Latino; 0.9% Two or more races, non-Hispanic/Latino; 1% Race/ethnicity unknown; 2% international; 14% transferred in; 36% live on campus.

Freshmen:
Admission: 3,529 applied, 1,744 admitted, 387 enrolled. *Average high school GPA:* 3.6. *Test scores:* SAT evidence-based reading and writing scores over 500: 80%; SAT math scores over 500: 82%; ACT scores over 18: 98%; SAT evidence-based reading and writing scores over 600: 29%; SAT math scores over 600: 34%; ACT scores over 24: 52%; SAT evidence-based reading and writing scores over 700: 2%; SAT math scores over 700: 5%; ACT scores over 30: 9%.

Retention: 76% of full-time freshmen returned.

FACULTY
Total: 304, 48% full-time, 62% with terminal degrees.

Student/faculty ratio: 12:1.

ACADEMICS
Calendar: semesters. *Degrees:* certificates, bachelor's, master's, doctoral, post-master's, and postbachelor's certificates.

Special study options: academic remediation for entering students, accelerated degree program, adult/continuing education programs, advanced placement credit, distance learning, double majors, honors programs, independent study, internships, off-campus study, part-time degree program, services for LD students, student-designed majors, study abroad, summer session for credit. *ROTC:* Army (c).

Unusual degree programs: 3-2 business administration; pharmacy with D'Youville College or SUNY Buffalo, veterinary Medicine with Lincoln Memorial Univerity, osteopathic medicine with Nova Southeastern University.

Computers: 163 computers/terminals are available on campus for general student use. Students can access the following: campus intranet, computer help desk, free student e-mail accounts, online (class) grades, online (class) registration, online (class) schedules. Campuswide network is available. 100% of college-owned or -operated housing units are wired for high-speed Internet access. Wireless service is available via classrooms, computer labs, dorm rooms, learning centers, libraries, student centers.

Library: Research and Information Commons. *Books:* 85,205 (physical), 138,085 (digital/electronic); *Serial titles:* 488 (physical); *Databases:* 38. Weekly public service hours: 117; students can reserve study rooms.

STUDENT LIFE
Housing options: on-campus residence required for freshman year; coed, special housing for students with disabilities. Campus housing is university owned and leased by the school. Freshman campus housing is guaranteed.

Activities and organizations: drama/theater group, student-run newspaper, choral group, Game Club, Anime Club, Best Buddies, CRU, Pride Club.

Athletics Member NCAA. All Division II. *Intercollegiate sports:* basketball M(s)/W(s), bowling W(s), cross-country running M(s)/W(s), golf M(s), soccer M(s)/W(s), tennis M(s)/W(s), track and field M(s)/W(s), triathlon W(s), volleyball M(s)/W(s). *Intramural sports:* baseball M(c), basketball M/W, cheerleading M(c)/W(c), ice hockey M(c), lacrosse W(c), sand volleyball M/W, soccer M/W, ultimate Frisbee M/W, volleyball M(c)/W(c).

Campus security: 24-hour emergency response devices and patrols, late-night transport/escort service, controlled dormitory access, 24-hour security cameras.

Student services: personal/psychological counseling.

COSTS & FINANCIAL AID
Costs (2017–18) *Comprehensive fee:* $40,686 includes full-time tuition ($27,450), mandatory fees ($540), and room and board ($12,696). Full-time tuition and fees vary according to location and reciprocity agreements. Part-time tuition: $915 per credit hour. Part-time tuition and fees vary according to course load, location, and reciprocity agreements. *Required fees:* $7 per credit hour part-time, $80 per term part-time. *Room and board:* Room and board charges vary according to board plan and housing facility. *Payment plans:* installment, deferred payment. *Waivers:* senior citizens and employees or children of employees.

Financial Aid Of all full-time matriculated undergraduates who enrolled in 2016, 1,523 applied for aid, 1,025 were judged to have need, 133 had their need fully met. 713 Federal Work-Study jobs (averaging $2697). 90 state and other part-time jobs (averaging $4428). In 2016, 415 non-need-based awards were made. *Average percent of need met:* 81. *Average financial aid package:* $25,911. *Average need-based loan:* $4671. *Average need-based gift aid:* $11,070. *Average non-need-based aid:* $10,645. *Average indebtedness upon graduation:* $31,359.

APPLYING
Standardized Tests *Required for some:* SAT or ACT (for admission), SAT/ACT or high school course grades, show rigor of courses and teacher recommendations. *Recommended:* SAT or ACT (for admission).

Options: electronic application, early admission, deferred entrance.

Application fee: $25.

Required: essay or personal statement, high school transcript, 1 letter of recommendation. *Recommended:* interview.

Application deadlines: rolling (freshmen), rolling (transfers).

Notification: continuous (freshmen), continuous (transfers).

CONTACT
Ms. Caroline Marciszewski, Associate Director of Undergraduate Admissions, Daemen College, Daemen College, 4380 Main Street, Amherst, NY 14226-3592. *Phone:* 716-566-7856. *Toll-free phone:* 800-462-7652. *Fax:* 716-839-8229. *E-mail:* admissions@daemen.edu.

Davis College
Johnson City, New York
http://www.davisny.edu/
- **Independent nondenominational** 4-year, founded 1900
- **Suburban** 22-acre campus with easy access to Syracuse
- **Coed**
- **Minimally difficult** entrance level

FACULTY
Student/faculty ratio: 14:1.

ACADEMICS
Calendar: semesters. *Degrees:* certificates, diplomas, associate, and bachelor's.

Library: Alice E. Chatlos Library. Students can reserve study rooms.

STUDENT LIFE

Housing options: on-campus residence required for freshman year; men-only, women-only. Campus housing is university owned. Freshman campus housing is guaranteed.

Activities and organizations: drama/theater group, student-run newspaper, choral group, Student Missionary Fellowship, Student Wives Fellowship, Student Life Committee, Married Couples Fellowship.

Athletics Member NCCAA, USCAA.

Campus security: 24-hour emergency response devices and patrols, student patrols, late-night transport/escort service, controlled dormitory access.

Student services: health clinic, personal/psychological counseling.

COSTS & FINANCIAL AID

Costs (2017–18) *One-time required fee:* $150. *Comprehensive fee:* $24,000 includes full-time tuition ($15,000), mandatory fees ($1300), and room and board ($7700). Full-time tuition and fees vary according to course load and location. Part-time tuition: $500 per credit hour. Part-time tuition and fees vary according to course load and location. *Required fees:* $650 per year part-time. *Room and board:* Room and board charges vary according to board plan and housing facility.

Financial Aid Of all full-time matriculated undergraduates who enrolled in 2016, 178 applied for aid, 178 were judged to have need. 11 state and other part-time jobs (averaging $1000). *Average financial aid package:* $9924. *Average need-based gift aid:* $9924. *Average indebtedness upon graduation:* $9381. *Financial aid deadline:* 8/15.

APPLYING

Standardized Tests *Recommended:* SAT or ACT (for admission).

Options: electronic application, deferred entrance.

Application fee: $45.

Required: essay or personal statement, high school transcript, 1 letter of recommendation. *Recommended:* minimum 2.0 GPA, interview.

CONTACT

Ms. Hannah Hempstead, Assistant Director of Admissions for Communication, Davis College, 400 Riverside Drive, Johnson City, NY 13790. *Phone:* 607-729-1581 Ext. 341. *Toll-free phone:* 877-949-3248. *Fax:* 607-770-6886. *E-mail:* hhempstead@davisny.edu.

DeVry College of New York–Midtown Manhattan Campus

New York, New York

http://www.devry.edu/

CONTACT

DeVry College of New York–Midtown Manhattan Campus, 180 Madison Avenue, Suite 900, New York, NY 10016. *Phone:* 212-312-4300. *Toll-free phone:* 866-338-7934.

Dominican College

Orangeburg, New York

http://www.dc.edu/

- **Independent** comprehensive, founded 1952
- **Suburban** 70-acre campus with easy access to New York City
- **Endowment** $4.5 million
- **Coed** 1,425 undergraduate students, 89% full-time, 67% women, 33% men
- **Noncompetitive** entrance level, 75% of applicants were admitted

UNDERGRAD STUDENTS

1,271 full-time, 154 part-time. Students come from 28 states and territories; 16 other countries; 22% are from out of state; 15% Black or African American, non-Hispanic/Latino; 30% Hispanic/Latino; 6% Asian, non-Hispanic/Latino; 0.9% Native Hawaiian or other Pacific Islander, non-Hispanic/Latino; 3% Two or more races, non-Hispanic/Latino; 8% Race/ethnicity unknown; 1% international; 10% transferred in; 48% live on campus.

Freshmen:
Admission: 1,751 applied, 1,321 admitted, 229 enrolled. *Average high school GPA:* 3.0.
Retention: 74% of full-time freshmen returned.

FACULTY

Total: 237, 32% full-time, 40% with terminal degrees.

Student/faculty ratio: 15:1.

ACADEMICS

Calendar: semesters. *Degrees:* certificates, diplomas, associate, bachelor's, master's, doctoral, and postbachelor's certificates.

Special study options: academic remediation for entering students, accelerated degree program, adult/continuing education programs, advanced placement credit, cooperative education, distance learning, double majors, honors programs, independent study, internships, off-campus study, part-time degree program, services for LD students, study abroad, summer session for credit.

Unusual degree programs: 3-2 engineering with Manhattan College; occupational therapy.

Computers: 150 computers/terminals are available on campus for general student use. Students can access the following: campus intranet, computer help desk, free student e-mail accounts, online (class) registration, online (class) schedules, Web portal, learning management system. Campuswide network is available. 100% of college-owned or -operated housing units are wired for high-speed Internet access. Wireless service is available via entire campus.

Library: Sullivan Library plus 1 other. *Books:* 74,226 (physical), 117,187 (digital/electronic); *Serial titles:* 610 (physical), 75,067 (digital/electronic); *Databases:* 85. Weekly public service hours: 89; students can reserve study rooms.

STUDENT LIFE

Housing options: coed. Campus housing is university owned. Freshman campus housing is guaranteed.

Activities and organizations: drama/theater group, student-run radio station, choral group, Student Government Association, Business Club, Aquin Players Drama Society, Anime Magna and Videogame Club, Student Nursing Association.

Athletics Member NCAA. All Division II. *Intercollegiate sports:* baseball M(s), basketball M(s)/W(s), cross-country running M(s)/W(s), golf M(s), lacrosse M(s)/W(s), soccer M(s)/W(s), softball W(s), track and field M(s)/W(s), volleyball W(s). *Intramural sports:* basketball M/W, ultimate Frisbee M(c)/W(c), volleyball M/W.

Campus security: 24-hour emergency response devices and patrols, student patrols, late-night transport/escort service, controlled dormitory access.

Student services: health clinic, personal/psychological counseling.

COSTS & FINANCIAL AID

Costs (2018–19) *Comprehensive fee:* $42,150 includes full-time tuition ($28,140), mandatory fees ($860), and room and board ($13,150). Full-time tuition and fees vary according to course load and degree level. Part-time tuition: $851 per credit hour. Part-time tuition and fees vary according to course load, degree level, and program. *Required fees:* $200 per term part-time. *Room and board:* Room and board charges vary according to board plan and housing facility. *Payment plans:* installment, deferred payment. *Waivers:* senior citizens and employees or children of employees.

Financial Aid Of all full-time matriculated undergraduates who enrolled in 2016, 1,202 applied for aid, 1,082 were judged to have need, 133 had their need fully met. 305 Federal Work-Study jobs (averaging $701). In 2016, 189 non-need-based awards were made. *Average percent of need met:* 66. *Average financial aid package:* $21,434. *Average need-based loan:* $5165. *Average need-based gift aid:* $17,255. *Average non-need-based aid:* $9422. *Average indebtedness upon graduation:* $31,976.

APPLYING

Options: electronic application, deferred entrance.

Application fee: $35.

Required: high school transcript. *Required for some:* essay or personal statement, interview. *Recommended:* interview.

Application deadlines: rolling (freshmen), rolling (transfers).

Notification: continuous (freshmen), continuous (transfers).

CONTACT
Mr. Robert Tyrrell, Assistant Director of Freshman Admissions, Dominican College, 470 Western Highway, Orangeburg, NY 10962-1210. *Phone:* 845-359-7906. *Toll-free phone:* 866-432-4636. *Fax:* 845-365-3150. *E-mail:* rob.tyrrell@dc.edu.

D'Youville College
Buffalo, New York
http://www.dyc.edu/
- **Independent** comprehensive, founded 1908
- **Urban** 11-acre campus
- **Endowment** $43.3 million
- **Coed** 1,735 undergraduate students, 75% full-time, 74% women, 26% men
- **Moderately difficult** entrance level, 97% of applicants were admitted

UNDERGRAD STUDENTS
1,295 full-time, 440 part-time. Students come from 29 states and territories; 31 other countries; 9% are from out of state; 9% Black or African American, non-Hispanic/Latino; 4% Hispanic/Latino; 6% Asian, non-Hispanic/Latino; 0.1% Native Hawaiian or other Pacific Islander, non-Hispanic/Latino; 0.5% American Indian or Alaska Native, non-Hispanic/Latino; 2% Two or more races, non-Hispanic/Latino; 5% Race/ethnicity unknown; 1% international; 12% transferred in; 18% live on campus.

Freshmen:
Admission: 1,541 applied, 1,491 admitted, 277 enrolled. *Average high school GPA:* 3.4. *Test scores:* SAT evidence-based reading and writing scores over 500: 83%; SAT math scores over 500: 78%; ACT scores over 18: 96%; SAT evidence-based reading and writing scores over 600: 26%; SAT math scores over 600: 27%; ACT scores over 24: 48%; SAT evidence-based reading and writing scores over 700: 2%; SAT math scores over 700: 2%; ACT scores over 30: 3%.
Retention: 79% of full-time freshmen returned.

FACULTY
Total: 295, 64% full-time, 50% with terminal degrees.
Student/faculty ratio: 9:1.

ACADEMICS
Calendar: semesters plus summer session. *Degrees:* bachelor's, master's, doctoral, post-master's, and postbachelor's certificates.

Special study options: academic remediation for entering students, accelerated degree program, adult/continuing education programs, advanced placement credit, distance learning, double majors, independent study, internships, off-campus study, part-time degree program, services for LD students, study abroad, summer session for credit. *ROTC:* Army (c).

Unusual degree programs: 3-2 nursing; education, chiropractic, dietetics, occupational therapy, pharmacy, physical therapy, physician assistant.

Computers: 120 computers/terminals are available on campus for general student use. Students can access the following: computer help desk, free student e-mail accounts, online (class) grades, online (class) registration, online (class) schedules. Campuswide network is available. 100% of college-owned or -operated housing units are wired for high-speed Internet access. Wireless service is available via entire campus.
Library: Montante Family Library. *Books:* 69,415 (physical), 75,525 (digital/electronic); *Serial titles:* 572 (physical), 41,529 (digital/electronic); *Databases:* 84. Weekly public service hours: 87; study areas open 24 hours, 5–7 days a week; students can reserve study rooms.

STUDENT LIFE
Housing options: coed, men-only, women-only, special housing for students with disabilities. Campus housing is university owned. Freshman campus housing is guaranteed.

Activities and organizations: drama/theater group, student-run newspaper, choral group, Student Association, Occupational Therapy Student Association, Physical Therapy Student Association, Student Nurses Association, Black Student Union.

Athletics Member NCAA. All Division III. *Intercollegiate sports:* baseball M, basketball M/W, cheerleading W, cross-country running M/W, golf M/W, lacrosse W, soccer M/W, softball W, tennis M/W, volleyball M/W. *Intramural sports:* basketball M/W, crew W, ice hockey M, volleyball M/W.

Campus security: 24-hour emergency response devices and patrols, late-night transport/escort service, controlled dormitory access.
Student services: health clinic, personal/psychological counseling.

COSTS & FINANCIAL AID
Costs (2017–18) *Comprehensive fee:* $37,678 includes full-time tuition ($25,240), mandatory fees ($630), and room and board ($11,808). Full-time tuition and fees vary according to course load, degree level, and program. Part-time tuition: $788 per credit hour. Part-time tuition and fees vary according to course load, degree level, and program. No tuition increase for student's term of enrollment. *Required fees:* $3 per credit hour part-time, $55 per credit hour part-time. *Room and board:* Room and board charges vary according to board plan and housing facility. *Payment plans:* installment, deferred payment. *Waivers:* children of alumni, senior citizens, and employees or children of employees.

Financial Aid Of all full-time matriculated undergraduates who enrolled in 2015, 810 applied for aid, 720 were judged to have need, 158 had their need fully met. In 2015, 123 non-need-based awards were made. *Average percent of need met:* 73. *Average financial aid package:* $19,004. *Average need-based loan:* $4353. *Average need-based gift aid:* $15,177. *Average non-need-based aid:* $8739. *Average indebtedness upon graduation:* $34,593.

APPLYING
Standardized Tests *Required:* SAT or ACT (for admission).
Options: electronic application, deferred entrance.
Required: high school transcript, minimum 2.0 GPA. *Required for some:* essay or personal statement, minimum 3.0 GPA, interview.
Application deadlines: rolling (freshmen), rolling (transfers).
Notification: continuous (freshmen), continuous (transfers).

CONTACT
Meghan Harmon, Interim Director of Undergraduate Admissions, D'Youville College, 320 Porter Avenue, Buffalo, NY 14201. *Phone:* 716-829-7600. *Toll-free phone:* 800-777-3921. *Fax:* 716-829-7900. *E-mail:* harmonm@dyc.edu.

Elmira College
Elmira, New York
http://www.elmira.edu/
- **Independent** comprehensive, founded 1855
- **Small-town** 55-acre campus
- **Endowment** $38.0 million
- **Coed**
- **Moderately difficult** entrance level

FACULTY
Student/faculty ratio: 11:1.

ACADEMICS
Calendar: 4-4-1. *Degrees:* associate, bachelor's, master's, and postbachelor's certificates.
Library: Gannett-Tripp Library. *Books:* 122,814 (physical), 154,862 (digital/electronic); *Serial titles:* 646 (physical), 31,991 (digital/electronic); *Databases:* 94. Weekly public service hours: 110.

STUDENT LIFE
Housing options: on-campus residence required through senior year; coed, women-only, cooperative, special housing for students with disabilities. Campus housing is university owned. Freshman campus housing is guaranteed.

Activities and organizations: drama/theater group, student-run newspaper, radio station, choral group, SAB (Student Activities Board), Enactus, Colleges Against Cancer (Relay for Life), Orchesis, Habitat for Humanity.

Athletics Member NCAA. All Division III.

Campus security: 24-hour emergency response devices and patrols, student patrols, late-night transport/escort service, controlled dormitory access, 24-hour locked residence hall entrances.

Student services: health clinic, personal/psychological counseling.

COSTS & FINANCIAL AID

Costs (2017–18) *Comprehensive fee:* $53,900 includes full-time tuition ($41,900) and room and board ($12,000). Full-time tuition and fees vary according to degree level. Part-time tuition: $1200 per credit hour. Part-time tuition and fees vary according to course load and degree level. *College room only:* $6400. Room and board charges vary according to board plan and housing facility. *Payment plans:* tuition prepayment, installment.

Financial Aid Of all full-time matriculated undergraduates who enrolled in 2017, 738 applied for aid, 695 were judged to have need, 125 had their need fully met. 117 Federal Work-Study jobs (averaging $1200). 151 state and other part-time jobs (averaging $1100). In 2017, 128 non-need-based awards were made. *Average percent of need met:* 77. *Average financial aid package:* $32,512. *Average need-based loan:* $4592. *Average need-based gift aid:* $28,475. *Average non-need-based aid:* $23,911. *Average indebtedness upon graduation:* $29,601.

APPLYING

Options: electronic application, early action, deferred entrance.

Required: essay or personal statement, high school transcript, minimum 2.0 GPA, 1 letter of recommendation. *Required for some:* interview. *Recommended:* interview.

CONTACT

Mr. Christopher R. Coons, Vice President of Enrollment Management, Elmira College, 855 College Ave, Elmira, NY 14901. *Phone:* 607-735-1724. *Toll-free phone:* 800-935-6472. *Fax:* 607-735-1718. *E-mail:* admissions@elmira.edu.

Eugene Lang College of Liberal Arts
New York, New York
http://www.newschool.edu/lang

- **Independent** 4-year, founded 1975, part of The New School
- **Urban** campus with easy access to New York City
- **Endowment** $322.3 million
- **Coed** 1,738 undergraduate students, 96% full-time, 79% women, 21% men

UNDERGRAD STUDENTS

1,668 full-time, 70 part-time. Students come from 49 states and territories; 49 other countries; 74% are from out of state; 8% Black or African American, non-Hispanic/Latino; 17% Hispanic/Latino; 6% Asian, non-Hispanic/Latino; 0.2% Native Hawaiian or other Pacific Islander, non-Hispanic/Latino; 6% Two or more races, non-Hispanic/Latino; 7% Race/ethnicity unknown; 9% international; 7% transferred in; 32% live on campus.

Freshmen:

Admission: 464 enrolled. *Average high school GPA:* 3.4. *Test scores:* SAT evidence-based reading and writing scores over 500: 98%; SAT math scores over 500: 86%; ACT scores over 18: 100%; SAT evidence-based reading and writing scores over 600: 76%; SAT math scores over 600: 39%; ACT scores over 24: 77%; SAT evidence-based reading and writing scores over 700: 14%; ACT scores over 30: 17%.

Retention: 70% of full-time freshmen returned.

FACULTY

Total: 158, 45% full-time, 39% with terminal degrees.

Student/faculty ratio: 17:1.

ACADEMICS

Calendar: semesters. *Degree:* bachelor's.

Special study options: academic remediation for entering students, accelerated degree program, advanced placement credit, cooperative education, distance learning, double majors, English as a second language, independent study, internships, off-campus study, part-time degree program, services for LD students, student-designed majors, study abroad, summer session for credit.

Unusual degree programs: psychology.

Computers: 717 computers/terminals are available on campus for general student use. Students can access the following: campus intranet, computer help desk, free student e-mail accounts, online (class) grades, online (class) registration, online (class) schedules. Campuswide network is available. 100% of college-owned or -operated housing units are wired for high-speed Internet access. Wireless service is available via entire campus.

Library: New School Libraries & Archives plus 3 others. *Books:* 215,937 (physical), 840,933 (digital/electronic); *Serial titles:* 2,265 (physical), 113,452 (digital/electronic); *Databases:* 376. Weekly public service hours: 155; study areas open 24 hours, 5–7 days a week; students can reserve study rooms.

STUDENT LIFE

Housing options: coed, special housing for students with disabilities. Campus housing is university owned and leased by the school. Freshman applicants given priority for college housing.

Activities and organizations: drama/theater group, student-run newspaper, choral group.

Athletics *Intramural sports:* basketball M/W, cross-country running M/W, soccer M/W, tennis M/W.

Campus security: 24-hour emergency response devices, controlled dormitory access, 24-hour desk attendants in residence halls.

Student services: health clinic, personal/psychological counseling.

COSTS & FINANCIAL AID

Costs (2017–18) *Comprehensive fee:* $62,590 includes full-time tuition ($45,240), mandatory fees ($1100), and room and board ($16,250). Part-time tuition: $1540 per credit hour. Part-time tuition and fees vary according to course load. *Required fees:* $550 per term part-time. *College room only:* $15,000. Room and board charges vary according to housing facility and location. *Payment plan:* installment. *Waivers:* employees or children of employees.

Financial Aid Of all full-time matriculated undergraduates who enrolled in 2016, 1,001 applied for aid, 868 were judged to have need, 123 had their need fully met. 136 Federal Work-Study jobs (averaging $3360). In 2016, 404 non-need-based awards were made. *Average percent of need met:* 82. *Average financial aid package:* $39,799. *Average need-based loan:* $4167. *Average need-based gift aid:* $16,078. *Average non-need-based aid:* $11,242. *Average indebtedness upon graduation:* $62,290. *Financial aid deadline:* 2/1.

APPLYING

Standardized Tests *Required for some:* TOEFL, IELTS and PTE for some applicants whose first language is not English.

Required: essay or personal statement, high school transcript, 2 letters of recommendation, online application, 2 supplemental essays, counselor evaluation or teacher evaluation, academic paper (grade preferred). *Recommended:* minimum 3.0 GPA.

CONTACT

Ms. Candice MacLusky, Director of Admissions, Eugene Lang College of Liberal Arts, 65 West 11th Street, New York, NY 10011-8601. *Phone:* 212-229-5155 Ext. 4024. *Toll-free phone:* 800-292-3040. *E-mail:* macluskc@newschool.edu.

Excelsior College
Albany, New York
http://www.excelsior.edu/

- **Independent** comprehensive, founded 1970
- **Suburban** campus with easy access to Albany, NY
- **Coed** 28,384 undergraduate students, 50% women, 50% men

UNDERGRAD STUDENTS

28,384 part-time. Students come from 55 states and territories; 37 other countries; 84% are from out of state; 19% Black or African American, non-Hispanic/Latino; 11% Hispanic/Latino; 3% Asian, non-Hispanic/Latino; 0.6% Native Hawaiian or other Pacific Islander, non-Hispanic/Latino; 0.6% American Indian or Alaska Native, non-Hispanic/Latino; 3% Two or more races, non-Hispanic/Latino; 2% Race/ethnicity unknown; 0.8% international; 6% transferred in.

FACULTY

Total: 1,529, 35% with terminal degrees.

Student/faculty ratio: 10:1.

ACADEMICS

Calendar: continuous. *Degrees:* certificates, associate, bachelor's, master's, post-master's, and postbachelor's certificates (offers only external degree programs).

Special study options: adult/continuing education programs, distance learning, external degree program, independent study, part-time degree program, services for LD students, student-designed majors.

Unusual degree programs: 3-2 business administration; nursing; nuclear engineering technology, health care management, business, information technology/business administration; nursing; information technology/cybersecurity.

Computers: Students can access the following: computer help desk, online (class) grades, online (class) registration, online (class) schedules. Campuswide network is available.

Library: Excelsior College Library.

STUDENT LIFE
Housing options: college housing not available.

COSTS
Costs (2018–19) *Tuition:* $510 per credit part-time. Part-time tuition and fees vary according to reciprocity agreements. *Payment plan:* installment. *Waivers:* employees or children of employees.

APPLYING
Options: electronic application.
Application fee: $50.
Required for some: college transcripts.
Application deadlines: rolling (freshmen), rolling (transfers).
Notification: continuous (freshmen), continuous (transfers).

CONTACT
Admissions, Excelsior College, 7 Columbia Circle, Albany, NY 12203-5159. *Phone:* 518-464-8500. *Toll-free phone:* 888-647-2388. *Fax:* 518-464-8777. *E-mail:* admissions@excelsior.edu.

Farmingdale State College
Farmingdale, New York
http://www.farmingdale.edu/

- **State-supported** comprehensive, founded 1912, part of State University of New York System
- **Suburban** 380-acre campus with easy access to New York City
- **Endowment** $5.5 million
- **Coed** 9,552 undergraduate students, 78% full-time, 43% women, 57% men
- **Moderately difficult** entrance level, 59% of applicants were admitted

UNDERGRAD STUDENTS
7,407 full-time, 2,145 part-time. Students come from 12 states and territories; 72 other countries; 0.3% are from out of state; 10% Black or African American, non-Hispanic/Latino; 21% Hispanic/Latino; 8% Asian, non-Hispanic/Latino; 0.3% Native Hawaiian or other Pacific Islander, non-Hispanic/Latino; 0.2% American Indian or Alaska Native, non-Hispanic/Latino; 2% Two or more races, non-Hispanic/Latino; 0.3% Race/ethnicity unknown; 1% international; 13% transferred in; 7% live on campus.

Freshmen:
Admission: 6,063 applied, 3,579 admitted, 1,291 enrolled. *Average high school GPA:* 3.2. *Test scores:* SAT evidence-based reading and writing scores over 500: 73%; SAT math scores over 500: 73%; ACT scores over 18: 89%; SAT evidence-based reading and writing scores over 600: 16%; SAT math scores over 600: 15%; ACT scores over 24: 22%; SAT evidence-based reading and writing scores over 700: 1%; SAT math scores over 700: 1%; ACT scores over 30: 1%.
Retention: 83% of full-time freshmen returned.

FACULTY
Total: 743, 32% full-time.
Student/faculty ratio: 20:1.

ACADEMICS
Calendar: semesters. *Degrees:* certificates, associate, bachelor's, and master's.
Special study options: academic remediation for entering students, advanced placement credit, cooperative education, distance learning, double majors, independent study, internships, part-time degree program, services for LD students, study abroad, summer session for credit. *ROTC:* Army (c), Navy (c), Air Force (b).

Computers: 367 computers/terminals are available on campus for general student use. Students can access the following: computer help desk, free student e-mail accounts, online (class) grades, online (class) registration, online (class) schedules. Campuswide network is available. 100% of college-owned or -operated housing units are wired for high-speed Internet access. Wireless service is available via entire campus.
Library: Greenley Library. *Books:* 104,155 (physical), 100,000 (digital/electronic); *Databases:* 102. Weekly public service hours: 80.

STUDENT LIFE
Housing options: coed. Campus housing is university owned.
Activities and organizations: drama/theater group, student-run radio station, Campus Activities Board, Farmingdale Student Government, Ram Nation Radio, Greek Life, national fraternities, national sororities.
Athletics Member NCAA. All Division III. *Intercollegiate sports:* baseball M, basketball M/W, cross-country running M/W, golf M, ice hockey M(c), lacrosse M/W, soccer M/W, softball W, tennis M/W, track and field M/W, volleyball W. *Intramural sports:* badminton M/W, basketball M/W, football M, sand volleyball M/W, soccer M/W, softball M/W, ultimate Frisbee M/W, volleyball M/W.
Campus security: 24-hour emergency response devices and patrols, controlled dormitory access.
Student services: health clinic, personal/psychological counseling.

COSTS & FINANCIAL AID
Costs (2017–18) *Tuition:* state resident $6670 full-time, $278 per credit part-time; nonresident $16,320 full-time, $680 per credit part-time. Full-time tuition and fees vary according to program. Part-time tuition and fees vary according to course load and program. *Required fees:* $1406 full-time, $57 per credit part-time, $10 per term part-time. *Room and board:* $12,892; room only: $7852. Room and board charges vary according to board plan and housing facility. *Payment plan:* installment. *Waivers:* employees or children of employees.
Financial Aid Of all full-time matriculated undergraduates who enrolled in 2015, 4,444 applied for aid, 3,365 were judged to have need, 257 had their need fully met. In 2015, 55 non-need-based awards were made. *Average percent of need met:* 56. *Average financial aid package:* $7859. *Average need-based loan:* $3809. *Average need-based gift aid:* $6569. *Average non-need-based aid:* $1693.

APPLYING
Standardized Tests *Required:* SAT or ACT (for admission).
Options: electronic application, early admission, deferred entrance.
Application fee: $50.
Required: high school transcript, minimum 3.0 GPA. *Required for some:* interview.
Application deadlines: 6/1 (freshmen), 6/30 (transfers).
Notification: continuous (freshmen), continuous (out-of-state freshmen), continuous (transfers).

CONTACT
Farmingdale State College, 2350 Broadhollow Road, Farmingdale, NY 11735. *Phone:* 631-420-2200.

Fashion Institute of Technology
New York, New York
http://www.fitnyc.edu/

- **State and locally supported** comprehensive, founded 1944, part of State University of New York System
- **Urban** 5-acre campus with easy access to New York City
- **Coed, primarily women** 8,661 undergraduate students, 83% full-time, 85% women, 15% men
- **Moderately difficult** entrance level, 47% of applicants were admitted

UNDERGRAD STUDENTS
7,210 full-time, 1,451 part-time. 31% are from out of state; 9% Black or African American, non-Hispanic/Latino; 19% Hispanic/Latino; 11% Asian, non-Hispanic/Latino; 0.2% Native Hawaiian or other Pacific Islander, non-Hispanic/Latino; 0.1% American Indian or Alaska Native, non-Hispanic/Latino; 3% Two or more races, non-Hispanic/Latino; 0.7% Race/ethnicity unknown; 11% international; 9% transferred in; 21% live on campus.

Freshmen:
Admission: 4,739 applied, 2,229 admitted, 1,263 enrolled. *Average high school GPA:* 3.6.
Retention: 89% of full-time freshmen returned.

FACULTY
Total: 1,116, 21% full-time.
Student/faculty ratio: 15:1.

ACADEMICS
Calendar: semesters. *Degrees:* certificates, associate, bachelor's, and master's.

Special study options: academic remediation for entering students, advanced placement credit, distance learning, English as a second language, honors programs, independent study, internships, part-time degree program, services for LD students, study abroad, summer session for credit.

Computers: Campuswide network is available.
Library: Gladys Marcus Library.

STUDENT LIFE
Housing options: coed, women-only, special housing for students with disabilities. Campus housing is university owned. Freshman applicants given priority for college housing.

Activities and organizations: drama/theater group, student-run newspaper, radio and television station, choral group.

Athletics Member NJCAA. *Intercollegiate sports:* cross-country running M/W, soccer W, swimming and diving M/W, table tennis M/W, tennis M/W, track and field M/W, volleyball W.

Campus security: 24-hour emergency response devices and patrols, late-night transport/escort service, controlled dormitory access.

Student services: health clinic, personal/psychological counseling.

COSTS & FINANCIAL AID
Costs (2017–18) *Tuition:* state resident $6670 full-time, $278 per credit hour part-time; nonresident $20,192 full-time, $841 per credit hour part-time. Full-time tuition and fees vary according to degree level. Part-time tuition and fees vary according to degree level. *Required fees:* $793 full-time. *Room and board:* $13,945; room only: $9291. Room and board charges vary according to board plan and housing facility. *Waivers:* employees or children of employees.

Financial Aid Of all full-time matriculated undergraduates who enrolled in 2015, 4,591 applied for aid, 3,763 were judged to have need, 1,664 had their need fully met. In 2015, 230 non-need-based awards were made. *Average percent of need met:* 67. *Average financial aid package:* $11,804. *Average need-based loan:* $3135. *Average need-based gift aid:* $6078. *Average non-need-based aid:* $773. *Average indebtedness upon graduation:* $24,850.

APPLYING
Options: electronic application.

Application fee: $50.

Required: essay or personal statement, high school transcript. *Required for some:* portfolio for art and design programs.

Application deadlines: 1/1 (freshmen), 1/1 (transfers).
Notification: 4/1 (freshmen), 4/1 (transfers).

CONTACT
Ms. Magda Francois, Director of Admissions and Strategic Recruitment, Fashion Institute of Technology, Seventh Avenue at 27th Street, New York, NY 10001-5992. *E-mail:* fitinfo@fitnyc.edu.

See below for display ad and page 1292 for the College Close-Up.

Five Towns College
Dix Hills, New York
http://www.ftc.edu/

CONTACT
Ms. Cynthia Catalano, Admissions, Five Towns College, 305 North Service Road, Dix Hills, NY 11746-6055. *Phone:* 631-424-7000 Ext. 2107. *Fax:* 631-656-2107. *E-mail:* cynthia.catalano@ftc.edu.

★ Fordham University

New York, New York

http://www.fordham.edu/

- **Independent Roman Catholic (Jesuit)** university, founded 1841
- **Urban** 93-acre campus with easy access to New York City
- **Endowment** $665.5 million
- **Coed** 9,599 undergraduate students, 95% full-time, 58% women, 42% men
- **Very difficult** entrance level, 46% of applicants were admitted

UNDERGRAD STUDENTS

9,132 full-time, 467 part-time. Students come from 48 states and territories; 74 other countries; 57% are from out of state; 4% Black or African American, non-Hispanic/Latino; 14% Hispanic/Latino; 10% Asian, non-Hispanic/Latino; 0.1% Native Hawaiian or other Pacific Islander, non-Hispanic/Latino; 0.1% American Indian or Alaska Native, non-Hispanic/Latino; 3% Two or more races, non-Hispanic/Latino; 2% Race/ethnicity unknown; 9% international; 4% transferred in; 50% live on campus.

Freshmen:

Admission: 45,147 applied, 20,966 admitted, 2,283 enrolled. *Average high school GPA:* 3.7. *Test scores:* SAT evidence-based reading and writing scores over 500: 99%; SAT math scores over 500: 99%; ACT scores over 18: 100%; SAT evidence-based reading and writing scores over 600: 85%; SAT math scores over 600: 82%; ACT scores over 24: 96%; SAT evidence-based reading and writing scores over 700: 30%; SAT math scores over 700: 33%; ACT scores over 30: 49%.

Retention: 91% of full-time freshmen returned.

FACULTY

Total: 1,622, 45% full-time, 68% with terminal degrees.
Student/faculty ratio: 15:1.

ACADEMICS

Calendar: semesters. *Degrees:* bachelor's, master's, doctoral, post-master's, and postbachelor's certificates (branch locations at Rose Hill and Lincoln Center).

Special study options: accelerated degree program, adult/continuing education programs, advanced placement credit, double majors, English as a second language, honors programs, independent study, internships, off-campus study, part-time degree program, services for LD students, student-designed majors, study abroad, summer session for credit. *ROTC:* Army (b), Navy (c), Air Force (c).

Unusual degree programs: 3-2 engineering with Columbia University, Case Western Reserve University.

Computers: 2,400 computers/terminals and 2,400 ports are available on campus for general student use. Students can access the following: campus intranet, computer help desk, free student e-mail accounts, online (class) grades, online (class) registration, online (class) schedules. Campuswide network is available. 100% of college-owned or -operated housing units are wired for high-speed Internet access. Wireless service is available via entire campus.
Library: Walsh Library plus 3 others. *Books:* 2.0 million (physical), 575,000 (digital/electronic); *Serial titles:* 6,400 (physical), 76,000 (digital/electronic); *Databases:* 260. Weekly public service hours: 100; study areas open 24 hours, 5–7 days a week.

STUDENT LIFE

Housing options: coed, special housing for students with disabilities. Campus housing is university owned and leased by the school.

Activities and organizations: drama/theater group, student-run newspaper, radio and television station, choral group, marching band, United Student Government, Commuting Student Association, Residence Hall Association, Ambassador Program (Admission Department Student Tour Guides), Campus Activities Board.

Athletics Member NCAA. All Division I except football (Division I-AA). *Intercollegiate sports:* baseball M(s), basketball M(s)/W(s), bowling W, cheerleading W, cross-country running M(s)/W(s), golf M(s), ice hockey M(c), rowing W(s), sailing M(c)/W(c), soccer M(s)/W(s), softball W(s), squash M(s), swimming and diving M(s)/W(s), tennis M(s)/W(s), track and field M(s)/W(s), volleyball W(s), water polo M(s). *Intramural sports:* baseball M(c), basketball M(c)/W(c), crew M(c), lacrosse M(c)/W(c),

rugby M(c)/W(c), soccer M(c)/W(c), softball M/W, squash W(c), tennis W(c), ultimate Frisbee M(c)/W(c), volleyball M/W.

Campus security: 24-hour emergency response devices and patrols, student patrols, late-night transport/escort service, controlled dormitory access, security at each campus entrance and at residence halls.

Student services: health clinic, personal/psychological counseling.

COSTS & FINANCIAL AID

Costs (2017–18) *Comprehensive fee:* $68,431 includes full-time tuition ($49,645), mandatory fees ($1341), and room and board ($17,445). Part-time tuition: $1655 per credit hour. Part-time tuition and fees vary according to class time and course load. *Room and board:* Room and board charges vary according to board plan, housing facility, and location. *Payment plan:* installment. *Waivers:* employees or children of employees.

Financial Aid Of all full-time matriculated undergraduates who enrolled in 2016, 7,226 applied for aid, 5,406 were judged to have need, 1,449 had their need fully met. In 2016, 1642 non-need-based awards were made. *Average percent of need met:* 76. *Average financial aid package:* $34,723. *Average need-based loan:* $8514. *Average need-based gift aid:* $26,457. *Average non-need-based aid:* $17,059. *Average indebtedness upon graduation:* $35,735. *Financial aid deadline:* 2/1.

APPLYING

Standardized Tests *Required:* SAT or ACT (for admission).

Options: electronic application, early admission, early decision, early action, deferred entrance.

Application fee: $70.

Required: essay or personal statement, high school transcript, 1 letter of recommendation, Common Application. *Recommended:* 1 letter of recommendation.

Application deadlines: 1/1 (freshmen), 6/1 (transfers), 11/1 (early action).

Early decision deadline: 11/1.

Notification: 4/1 (freshmen), continuous (transfers), 12/20 (early decision), 12/20 (early action).

CONTACT

Dr. Patricia Peek, Dean of Undergraduate Admission, Fordham University, Office of Undergraduate Admission, Duane Library, 441 East Fordham Road, Bronx, NY 10458. *Phone:* 718-817-3706. *Toll-free phone:* 800-FORDHAM. *Fax:* 718-367-9404. *E-mail:* peek@fordham.edu.

Hamilton College

Clinton, New York

http://www.hamilton.edu/

- **Independent** 4-year, founded 1812
- **Small-town** 1300-acre campus
- **Endowment** $905.8 million
- **Coed** 1,897 undergraduate students, 99% full-time, 53% women, 47% men
- **Very difficult** entrance level, 24% of applicants were admitted

UNDERGRAD STUDENTS

1,886 full-time, 11 part-time. Students come from 47 states and territories; 45 other countries; 70% are from out of state; 4% Black or African American, non-Hispanic/Latino; 9% Hispanic/Latino; 7% Asian, non-Hispanic/Latino; 0.1% American Indian or Alaska Native, non-Hispanic/Latino; 4% Two or more races, non-Hispanic/Latino; 6% Race/ethnicity unknown; 6% international; 0.9% transferred in; 100% live on campus.

Freshmen:

Admission: 5,678 applied, 1,375 admitted, 480 enrolled. *Test scores:* SAT evidence-based reading and writing scores over 500: 100%; SAT math scores over 500: 100%; ACT scores over 18: 100%; SAT evidence-based reading and writing scores over 600: 95%; SAT math scores over 600: 89%; ACT scores over 24: 99%; SAT evidence-based reading and writing scores over 700: 67%; SAT math scores over 700: 67%; ACT scores over 30: 83%.

Retention: 96% of full-time freshmen returned.

FACULTY
Total: 226, 83% full-time, 92% with terminal degrees.
Student/faculty ratio: 9:1.

ACADEMICS
Calendar: semesters. *Degree:* bachelor's.

Special study options: accelerated degree program, adult/continuing education programs, advanced placement credit, double majors, English as a second language, independent study, internships, off-campus study, part-time degree program, services for LD students, student-designed majors, study abroad. *ROTC:* Army (c), Air Force (c).

Unusual degree programs: 3-2 engineering with Columbia University, Dartmouth College, Rensselaer Polytechnic Institute, Washington University in St. Louis.

Computers: 804 computers/terminals and 10,519 ports are available on campus for general student use. Students can access the following: campus intranet, computer help desk, free student e-mail accounts, online (class) grades, online (class) registration, online (class) schedules. Campuswide network is available. 100% of college-owned or -operated housing units are wired for high-speed Internet access. Wireless service is available via entire campus.

Library: Burke Library plus 1 other. *Books:* 482,004 (physical), 414,932 (digital/electronic); *Serial titles:* 3,424 (physical), 127,978 (digital/electronic); *Databases:* 182. Weekly public service hours: 114; study areas open 24 hours, 5–7 days a week; students can reserve study rooms.

STUDENT LIFE
Housing options: on-campus residence required through senior year; coed, cooperative, special housing for students with disabilities. Campus housing is university owned. Freshman campus housing is guaranteed.

Activities and organizations: drama/theater group, student-run newspaper, radio and television station, choral group, WHCL (Hamilton College Radio), Slow Food, Powder Club, Black & Latin Student Union (BLSU), Hamilton College Climbing Club, national fraternities.

Athletics Member NCAA. All Division III. *Intercollegiate sports:* baseball M, basketball M/W, crew M/W, cross-country running M/W, equestrian sports M(c)/W(c), fencing M(c)/W(c), field hockey W, football M, golf M/W, ice hockey M/W, lacrosse M/W, rugby M(c)/W(c), sailing M(c)/W(c), skiing (cross-country) M(c)/W(c), skiing (downhill) M(c)/W(c), soccer M/W, softball W, squash M/W, swimming and diving M/W, tennis M/W, track and field M/W, ultimate Frisbee M(c)/W(c), volleyball M(c)/W, water polo M(c). *Intramural sports:* badminton M/W, basketball M/W, football M/W, golf M/W, ice hockey M/W, racquetball M/W, skiing (cross-country) M/W, soccer M/W, softball M/W, squash M/W, tennis M/W, volleyball M/W, water polo M/W.

Campus security: 24-hour emergency response devices and patrols, late-night transport/escort service, controlled dormitory access, student safety program.

Student services: health clinic, personal/psychological counseling.

COSTS & FINANCIAL AID
Costs (2017–18) *Comprehensive fee:* $66,170 includes full-time tuition ($52,250), mandatory fees ($520), and room and board ($13,400). Part-time tuition: $6531 per course. *College room only:* $7320. Room and board charges vary according to board plan. *Payment plan:* installment. *Waivers:* employees or children of employees.

Financial Aid Of all full-time matriculated undergraduates who enrolled in 2016, 938 applied for aid, 892 were judged to have need, 892 had their need fully met. 563 Federal Work-Study jobs (averaging $1837). 52 state and other part-time jobs (averaging $1942). *Average percent of need met:* 100. *Average financial aid package:* $47,003. *Average need-based loan:* $4292. *Average need-based gift aid:* $41,825. *Average indebtedness upon graduation:* $21,491. *Financial aid deadline:* 2/15.

APPLYING
Standardized Tests *Required:* (for admission).

Options: electronic application, early decision, deferred entrance.

Application fee: $60.

Required: essay or personal statement, high school transcript, 1 letter of recommendation. *Recommended:* interview.

Application deadlines: 1/1 (freshmen), 4/1 (transfers).

Early decision deadline: 11/15 (for plan 1), 1/1 (for plan 2).

Notification: 4/1 (freshmen), 5/15 (transfers), 12/15 (early decision plan 1), 2/15 (early decision plan 2).

CONTACT
Ms. T. Peaches Valdes, Dean of Admission, Hamilton College, 198 College Hill Road, Clinton, NY 13323. *Phone:* 800-843-2655. *Toll-free phone:* 800-843-2655. *Fax:* 315-859-4457. *E-mail:* admission@hamilton.edu.

Hartwick College
Oneonta, New York
http://www.hartwick.edu/
- **Independent** 4-year, founded 1797
- **Small-town** 425-acre campus with easy access to Capital District, NY
- **Endowment** $74.3 million
- **Coed** 1,201 undergraduate students, 98% full-time, 59% women, 41% men
- **Moderately difficult** entrance level, 89% of applicants were admitted

UNDERGRAD STUDENTS
1,180 full-time, 21 part-time. Students come from 29 states and territories; 18 other countries; 20% are from out of state; 9% Black or African American, non-Hispanic/Latino; 9% Hispanic/Latino; 3% Asian, non-Hispanic/Latino; 0.1% Native Hawaiian or other Pacific Islander, non-Hispanic/Latino; 1% American Indian or Alaska Native, non-Hispanic/Latino; 12% Race/ethnicity unknown; 3% international; 3% transferred in; 80% live on campus.

Freshmen:
Admission: 3,019 applied, 2,674 admitted, 351 enrolled. *Average high school GPA:* 3.0. *Test scores:* SAT evidence-based reading and writing scores over 500: 55%; SAT math scores over 500: 58%; ACT scores over 18: 91%; SAT evidence-based reading and writing scores over 600: 8%; SAT math scores over 600: 13%; ACT scores over 24: 47%; SAT evidence-based reading and writing scores over 700: 1%; SAT math scores over 700: 1%; ACT scores over 30: 6%.

Retention: 70% of full-time freshmen returned.

FACULTY
Total: 174, 61% full-time, 55% with terminal degrees.
Student/faculty ratio: 11:1.

ACADEMICS
Calendar: 4-1-4. *Degree:* bachelor's.

Special study options: accelerated degree program, advanced placement credit, distance learning, double majors, honors programs, independent study, internships, off-campus study, part-time degree program, services for LD students, student-designed majors, study abroad, summer session for credit.

Unusual degree programs: 3-2 business administration; engineering with Clarkson University, Columbia University; nursing.

Computers: 80 computers/terminals are available on campus for general student use. Students can access the following: computer help desk, free student e-mail accounts, online (class) grades, online (class) registration, online (class) schedules. Campuswide network is available. 100% of college-owned or -operated housing units are wired for high-speed Internet access. Wireless service is available via entire campus.

Library: Stevens-German Library. *Books:* 209,006 (physical), 4,560 (digital/electronic); *Serial titles:* 1,392 (physical), 38,934 (digital/electronic); *Databases:* 59. Weekly public service hours: 96; students can reserve study rooms.

STUDENT LIFE
Housing options: on-campus residence required through senior year; coed. Campus housing is university owned. Freshman campus housing is guaranteed.

Activities and organizations: drama/theater group, student-run newspaper, radio station, choral group, Student Union, student radio station, Student Senate, Hilltops campus newspaper, Cardboard Alley Players (theater), national fraternities, national sororities.

Athletics Member NCAA. All Division III. *Intercollegiate sports:* basketball M/W, cheerleading W(c), cross-country running M/W, equestrian sports W, field hockey W, football M, lacrosse M/W, soccer M/W, swimming and diving M/W, tennis W, volleyball W. *Intramural* *sports:* basketball M/W, football M, riflery M(c)/W(c), rugby M(c), skiing (downhill) M(c)/W(c), soccer M/W, softball W(c), volleyball M/W.

Campus security: 24-hour emergency response devices and patrols, late-night transport/escort service, controlled dormitory access.

Student services: health clinic, personal/psychological counseling.

COSTS & FINANCIAL AID
Costs (2018–19) *One-time required fee:* $400. *Comprehensive fee:* $57,970 includes full-time tuition ($44,650), mandatory fees ($860), and room and board ($12,460). Full-time tuition and fees vary according to course load. Part-time tuition: $1435 per credit hour. Part-time tuition and fees vary according to course load. *College room only:* $6460. Room and board charges vary according to board plan and housing facility. *Payment plan:* installment. *Waivers:* employees or children of employees.

Financial Aid Of all full-time matriculated undergraduates who enrolled in 2016, 850 Federal Work-Study jobs (averaging $2000). *Average indebtedness upon graduation:* $27,653.

APPLYING
Standardized Tests *Required for some:* SAT or ACT (for admission).

Options: electronic application, early admission, early decision, deferred entrance.

Required: high school transcript. *Required for some:* audition for music program, portfolio for art majors. *Recommended:* minimum 2.5 GPA.

Application deadlines: rolling (freshmen), 8/1 (transfers).

Early decision deadline: 11/1.

Notification: continuous (freshmen), continuous until 8/15 (transfers), 12/1 (early decision plan 1), rolling (early decision plan 2).

CONTACT
Ms. Lisa Starkey-Wood, Director of Admissions, Hartwick College, PO Box 4022, Oneonta, NY 13820-4022. *Phone:* 607-431-4150. *Toll-free phone:* 888-HARTWICK. *Fax:* 607-431-4102. *E-mail:* admissions@ hartwick.edu.

Helene Fuld College of Nursing
New York, New York
http://www.helenefuld.edu/

CONTACT
Helene Fuld College of Nursing, 24 East 120th Street, New York, NY 10035. *Phone:* 212-616-7271.

Hilbert College
Hamburg, New York
http://www.hilbert.edu/
- **Independent Roman Catholic** comprehensive, founded 1957
- **Suburban** 40-acre campus with easy access to Buffalo
- **Endowment** $7.0 million
- **Coed** 746 undergraduate students, 91% full-time, 55% women, 45% men
- **Minimally difficult** entrance level, 81% of applicants were admitted

UNDERGRAD STUDENTS
680 full-time, 66 part-time. Students come from 22 states and territories; 2 other countries; 5% are from out of state; 6% Black or African American, non-Hispanic/Latino; 3% Hispanic/Latino; 0.4% Asian, non-Hispanic/Latino; 0.3% Native Hawaiian or other Pacific Islander, non-Hispanic/Latino; 2% American Indian or Alaska Native, non-Hispanic/Latino; 8% Two or more races, non-Hispanic/Latino; 7% Race/ethnicity unknown; 0.5% international; 655% transferred in; 31% live on campus.

Freshmen:
Admission: 968 applied, 785 admitted, 169 enrolled. *Average high school GPA:* 3.2. *Test scores:* SAT evidence-based reading and writing scores over 500: 60%; SAT math scores over 500: 59%; ACT scores over 18: 91%; SAT evidence-based reading and writing scores over 600: 12%; SAT math scores over 600: 14%; ACT scores over 24: 32%; ACT scores over 30: 9%.

Retention: 71% of full-time freshmen returned.

FACULTY
Total: 104, 37% full-time, 44% with terminal degrees.

Student/faculty ratio: 12:1.

ACADEMICS
Calendar: semesters. *Degrees:* associate, bachelor's, and master's.

Special study options: academic remediation for entering students, accelerated degree program, adult/continuing education programs, advanced placement credit, cooperative education, distance learning, honors programs, independent study, internships, services for LD students, study abroad, summer session for credit. *ROTC:* Army (c).

Computers: 146 computers/terminals are available on campus for general student use. Students can access the following: campus intranet, computer help desk, free student e-mail accounts, online (class) grades, online (class) registration, online (class) schedules. Campuswide network is available. 100% of college-owned or -operated housing units are wired for high-speed Internet access. Wireless service is available via entire campus.

Library: McGrath Library. *Books:* 36,902 (physical), 9,442 (digital/electronic); *Serial titles:* 172 (physical), 100,109 (digital/electronic); *Databases:* 49. Weekly public service hours: 77; students can reserve study rooms.

STUDENT LIFE
Housing options: coed. Campus housing is university owned and leased by the school. Freshman applicants given priority for college housing.

Activities and organizations: drama/theater group, student-run newspaper, radio station, Student Government Association, Student Business and Accounting Association, SADD, Students in Free Enterprise (SIFE), Criminal Justice Association.

Athletics Member NCAA. All Division III. *Intercollegiate sports:* baseball M, basketball M/W, bowling W, cross-country running M/W, golf M, lacrosse M/W, soccer M/W, softball W, track and field W, volleyball M/W. *Intramural sports:* baseball M, basketball M/W, bowling M/W, cheerleading W, football M/W, golf M, ice hockey M(c), lacrosse W(c), skiing (downhill) M(c)/W(c), soccer M/W, softball W, table tennis M/W, ultimate Frisbee M/W, volleyball M/W.

Campus security: 24-hour emergency response devices and patrols, student patrols, late-night transport/escort service, controlled dormitory access.

Student services: health clinic, personal/psychological counseling.

COSTS & FINANCIAL AID
Costs (2018–19) *One-time required fee:* $50. *Comprehensive fee:* $31,700 includes full-time tuition ($21,750), mandatory fees ($600), and room and board ($9350). Part-time tuition: $560 per credit hour. *Required fees:* $13 per credit hour part-time, $55 per term part-time. *Room and board:* Room and board charges vary according to board plan and housing facility. *Payment plan:* installment. *Waivers:* minority students, children of alumni, adult students, senior citizens, and employees or children of employees.

Financial Aid Of all full-time matriculated undergraduates who enrolled in 2017, 658 applied for aid, 599 were judged to have need, 121 had their need fully met. In 2017, 65 non-need-based awards were made. *Average percent of need met:* 74. *Average financial aid package:* $15,839. *Average need-based loan:* $4996. *Average need-based gift aid:* $11,962. *Average non-need-based aid:* $6024. *Average indebtedness upon graduation:* $19,613.

APPLYING
Standardized Tests *Recommended:* SAT or ACT (for admission).

Options: electronic application, deferred entrance.

Application fee: $25.

Required: high school transcript. *Required for some:* interview. *Recommended:* essay or personal statement, interview.

Application deadlines: rolling (freshmen), rolling (out-of-state freshmen), rolling (transfers).

Notification: continuous (freshmen), continuous (out-of-state freshmen), continuous (transfers).

CONTACT
Mr. Brian Filjones, Director, Admissions, Hilbert College, 5200 South Park Avenue, Hamburg, NY 14075-1597. *Phone:* 716-649-7900 Ext. 210. *Toll-free phone:* 800-649-8003. *Fax:* 716-649-1152. *E-mail:* bfiljones@ hilbert.edu.

Hobart and William Smith Colleges
Geneva, New York
http://www.hws.edu/

- **Independent** comprehensive, founded 1822
- **Small-town** 200-acre campus with easy access to Rochester, Syracuse
- **Endowment** $202.0 million
- **Coed** 2,237 undergraduate students, 99% full-time, 51% women, 49% men
- **Very difficult** entrance level, 61% of applicants were admitted

UNDERGRAD STUDENTS
2,220 full-time, 17 part-time. Students come from 40 states and territories; 27 other countries; 60% are from out of state; 6% Black or African American, non-Hispanic/Latino; 5% Hispanic/Latino; 3% Asian, non-Hispanic/Latino; 0.4% American Indian or Alaska Native, non-Hispanic/Latino; 5% Race/ethnicity unknown; 6% international; 0.8% transferred in; 90% live on campus.

Freshmen:
Admission: 4,409 applied, 2,696 admitted, 634 enrolled. *Average high school GPA:* 3.4.
Retention: 86% of full-time freshmen returned.

FACULTY
Total: 244, 91% full-time, 94% with terminal degrees.
Student/faculty ratio: 10:1.

ACADEMICS
Calendar: semesters. *Degrees:* bachelor's, master's, and postbachelor's certificates.

Special study options: accelerated degree program, adult/continuing education programs, advanced placement credit, double majors, English as a second language, honors programs, independent study, internships, off-campus study, services for LD students, student-designed majors, study abroad. *ROTC:* Army (c), Air Force (c).

Unusual degree programs: 3-2 business administration with Clarkson University, Rochester Institute of Technology; engineering with Columbia University, Rensselaer Polytechnic Institute, Dartmouth College; architecture with Washington University in St. Louis.

Computers: 247 computers/terminals and 10,215 ports are available on campus for general student use. Students can access the following: campus intranet, computer help desk, free student e-mail accounts, online (class) grades, online (class) registration, online (class) schedules. Campuswide network is available. 100% of college-owned or -operated housing units are wired for high-speed Internet access. Wireless service is available via entire campus.
Library: Warren Hunting Smith Library plus 1 other. *Books:* 389,139 (physical), 285,340 (digital/electronic); *Serial titles:* 1,485 (physical), 57,835 (digital/electronic); *Databases:* 134. Weekly public service hours: 114; study areas open 24 hours, 5–7 days a week; students can reserve study rooms.

STUDENT LIFE
Housing options: on-campus residence required through junior year; coed, men-only, women-only, cooperative. Campus housing is university owned. Freshman campus housing is guaranteed.

Activities and organizations: drama/theater group, student-run newspaper, radio station, choral group, Student Life and Leadership, student government, campus publications, Service Network, sports clubs, national fraternities, national sororities.

Athletics Member NCAA. All Division III except lacrosse (Division I). *Intercollegiate sports:* basketball M/W, crew M/W, cross-country running M/W, equestrian sports M(c)/W(c), field hockey W, football M, golf M/W, ice hockey M/W, lacrosse M/W, rock climbing M(c)/W(c), rugby M(c)/W(c), sailing M/W, skiing (downhill) M(c)/W(c), soccer M/W, squash M/W, swimming and diving W, tennis M/W, ultimate Frisbee M(c)/W(c). *Intramural sports:* badminton M/W, baseball M, basketball M/W, fencing M/W, football M, golf M/W, ice hockey M/W, lacrosse M/W, racquetball M/W, skiing (cross-country) M/W, skiing (downhill) M/W, soccer M/W, softball M/W, squash M/W, swimming and diving M/W, table tennis M/W, tennis M/W, track and field M/W, ultimate Frisbee M/W, volleyball M/W, water polo M/W, weight lifting M/W.

Campus security: 24-hour emergency response devices and patrols, late-night transport/escort service, controlled dormitory access.

Student services: health clinic, personal/psychological counseling, women's center.

COSTS & FINANCIAL AID
Costs (2018–19) *Comprehensive fee:* $69,290 includes full-time tuition ($54,060), mandatory fees ($1195), and room and board ($14,035). *Room and board:* Room and board charges vary according to board plan. *Payment plans:* tuition prepayment, installment. *Waivers:* employees or children of employees.

Financial Aid Of all full-time matriculated undergraduates who enrolled in 2016, 1,494 applied for aid, 1,278 were judged to have need, 855 had their need fully met. 864 Federal Work-Study jobs (averaging $1953). 485 state and other part-time jobs (averaging $1892). In 2016, 714 non-need-based awards were made. *Average percent of need met:* 78. *Average financial aid package:* $36,758. *Average need-based loan:* $3975. *Average need-based gift aid:* $32,528. *Average non-need-based aid:* $16,040. *Average indebtedness upon graduation:* $33,600. *Financial aid deadline:* 2/1.

APPLYING
Standardized Tests *Required for some:* SAT or ACT (for admission).
Options: electronic application, early admission, early decision, deferred entrance.
Required: essay or personal statement, high school transcript, 1 letter of recommendation. *Recommended:* interview.
Application deadlines: 2/1 (freshmen), 7/1 (transfers).
Early decision deadline: 11/15 (for plan 1), 1/1 (for plan 2).
Notification: 4/1 (freshmen), continuous (transfers), 12/15 (early decision plan 1), 2/1 (early decision plan 2).

CONTACT
Hobart and William Smith Colleges, 300 Pulteney Street, Geneva, NY 14456. *Phone:* 315-781-3622. *Toll-free phone:* 800-852-2256.

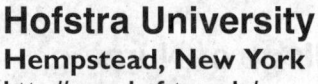

★ Hofstra University
Hempstead, New York
http://www.hofstra.edu/

- **Independent** university, founded 1935
- **Suburban** 244-acre campus with easy access to New York City
- **Endowment** $518.7 million
- **Coed** 6,861 undergraduate students, 95% full-time, 55% women, 45% men
- **Moderately difficult** entrance level, 64% of applicants were admitted

UNDERGRAD STUDENTS
6,494 full-time, 367 part-time. Students come from 47 states and territories; 76 other countries; 38% are from out of state; 9% Black or African American, non-Hispanic/Latino; 13% Hispanic/Latino; 10% Asian, non-Hispanic/Latino; 0.5% Native Hawaiian or other Pacific Islander, non-Hispanic/Latino; 0.4% American Indian or Alaska Native, non-Hispanic/Latino; 3% Two or more races, non-Hispanic/Latino; 3% Race/ethnicity unknown; 6% international; 4% transferred in; 45% live on campus.

Freshmen:
Admission: 26,808 applied, 17,143 admitted, 1,638 enrolled. *Average high school GPA:* 3.6. *Test scores:* SAT evidence-based reading and writing scores over 500: 97%; SAT math scores over 500: 97%; ACT scores over 18: 100%; SAT evidence-based reading and writing scores over 600: 61%; SAT math scores over 600: 56%; ACT scores over 24: 80%; SAT evidence-based reading and writing scores over 700: 10%; SAT math scores over 700: 11%; ACT scores over 30: 20%.

Retention: 81% of full-time freshmen returned.

FACULTY
Total: 1,236, 40% full-time, 64% with terminal degrees.
Student/faculty ratio: 13:1.

ACADEMICS
Calendar: semesters. *Degrees:* certificates, bachelor's, master's, doctoral, post-master's, and postbachelor's certificates.

Special study options: accelerated degree program, advanced placement credit, cooperative education, distance learning, double majors, English as a second language, external degree program, freshman honors college,

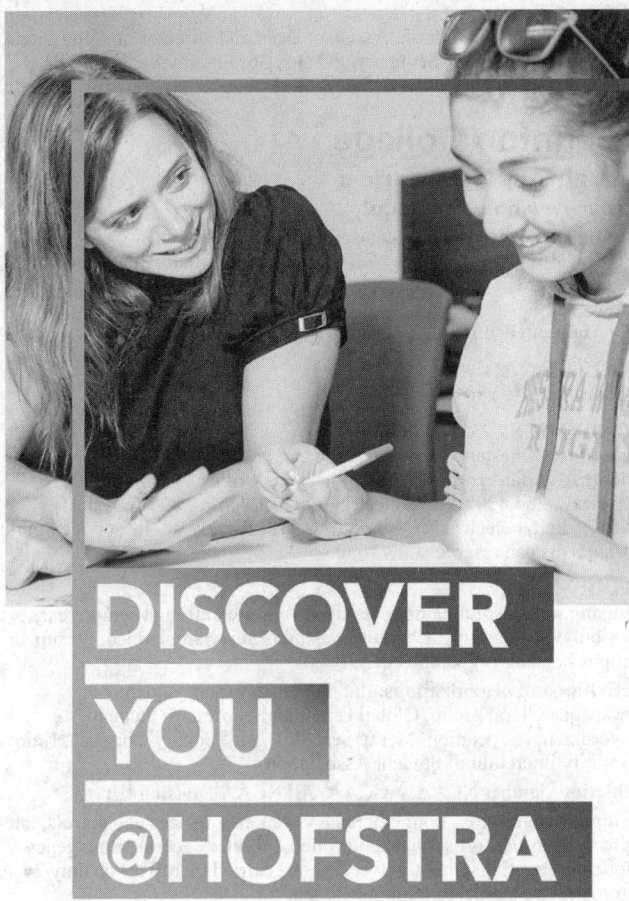

DISCOVER YOU @HOFSTRA

Seek, shape, and discover your own educational and career journey at Hofstra University. Small classes, tailored programs, and dedicated faculty help you pursue your passion in a dynamic learning environment that encourages collaboration, engagement, and interaction. And Hofstra's proximity to Manhattan offers a wide range of networking and internship opportunities.

Schedule a campus visit today:
Go to **hofstra.edu/visit**
or call **516-463-6700**.

HOFSTRA
UNIVERSITY®

honors programs, independent study, internships, off-campus study, part-time degree program, services for LD students, student-designed majors, study abroad, summer session for credit. *ROTC:* Army (b).

Unusual degree programs: 3-2 business administration; physician assistant studies, computer science, law.

Computers: 1,536 computers/terminals and 1,900 ports are available on campus for general student use. Students can access the following: campus intranet, computer help desk, free student e-mail accounts, online (class) grades, online (class) registration, online (class) schedules, Emergency alert system, online course management system, online card services balance update, online e-portfolio, software tutoring, support for specific tech-enhanced assignments, repair and rebuilding-after-virus services, and printing services. Campuswide network is available. 100% of college-owned or -operated housing units are wired for high-speed Internet access. Wireless service is available via entire campus.

Library: Axinn Library plus 3 others. *Books:* 1.1 million (physical), 199,044 (digital/electronic); *Serial titles:* 1,761 (physical), 17,415 (digital/electronic); *Databases:* 241. Weekly public service hours: 110; study areas open 24 hours, 5–7 days a week; students can reserve study rooms.

STUDENT LIFE

Housing options: coed, special housing for students with disabilities. Campus housing is university owned. Freshman applicants given priority for college housing.

Activities and organizations: drama/theater group, student-run newspaper, radio and television station, choral group, Hofstra Live Action Gaming Club, Masquerade, DanceWorks, Inter Fraternity Sorority Council, Student Government Association, national fraternities, national sororities.

Athletics Member NCAA. All Division I. *Intercollegiate sports:* baseball M(s), basketball M(s)/W(s), cross-country running M(s)/W(s), field hockey W(s), golf M(s)/W(s), lacrosse M(s)/W(s), soccer M(s)/W(s), softball W(s), tennis M(s)/W(s), volleyball W(s), wrestling M(s). *Intramural sports:* badminton M(c)/W(c), baseball M(c), basketball M/W, bowling M(c)/W(c), cheerleading M(c)/W(c), crew M(c)/W(c), cross-country running M(c)/W(c), equestrian sports M(c)/W(c), ice hockey M(c)/W(c), lacrosse M(c)/W(c), rock climbing M(c)/W(c), rugby M(c)/W(c), skiing (downhill) M(c)/W(c), soccer M(c)/W(c), softball M/W, table tennis M(c)/W(c), tennis M(c)/W(c), track and field M(c)/W(c), ultimate Frisbee M(c)/W(c), volleyball M(c)/W(c), weight lifting M(c)/W(c).

Campus security: 24-hour emergency response devices and patrols, student patrols, late-night transport/escort service, controlled dormitory access, security cameras monitoring residence hall entrances 24/7, bike patrol, motorist assistance program.

Student services: health clinic, personal/psychological counseling.

COSTS & FINANCIAL AID

Costs (2017–18) *Comprehensive fee:* $58,890 includes full-time tuition ($42,900), mandatory fees ($1060), and room and board ($14,930). Full-time tuition and fees vary according to course load. Part-time tuition: $1438 per credit hour. Part-time tuition and fees vary according to course load. No tuition increase for student's term of enrollment. *Required fees:* $155 per term part-time. *College room only:* $10,020. Room and board charges vary according to board plan and housing facility. *Payment plan:* installment. *Waivers:* employees or children of employees.

Financial Aid Of all full-time matriculated undergraduates who enrolled in 2016, 4,945 applied for aid, 4,160 were judged to have need, 1,019 had their need fully met. 1,749 Federal Work-Study jobs (averaging $3009). 1,513 state and other part-time jobs (averaging $3074). In 2016, 1591 non-need-based awards were made. *Average percent of need met:* 65. *Average financial aid package:* $29,000. *Average need-based loan:* $5000. *Average need-based gift aid:* $20,000. *Average non-need-based aid:* $17,000.

APPLYING

Standardized Tests *Required for some:* TOEFL for international students.

Options: electronic application, early admission, early action, deferred entrance.

Application fee: $70.

Required: essay or personal statement, high school transcript, 2 letters of recommendation. *Required for some:* interview.

Application deadlines: rolling (freshmen), 12/15 (early action).
Notification: 2/1 (freshmen), continuous (transfers), 1/15 (early action).

CONTACT
Sunil A. Samuel, Assistant Vice President of Admissions, Hofstra University, 100 Hofstra University, Hempstead, NY 11549. *Phone:* 516-463-6700. *Toll-free phone:* 800-HOFSTRA. *Fax:* 516-463-5100. *E-mail:* admission@hofstra.edu.

See previous page for display ad and page 1310 for the College Close-Up.

Holy Trinity Orthodox Seminary
Jordanville, New York
http://www.hts.edu/
- **Independent Russian Orthodox** 4-year, founded 1948
- **Rural** 900-acre campus
- **Men only** 77 undergraduate students, 25% full-time
- **Noncompetitive** entrance level

UNDERGRAD STUDENTS
19 full-time, 58 part-time. Students come from 8 states and territories; 8 other countries; 5% Black or African American, non-Hispanic/Latino; 5% Hispanic/Latino; 11% Asian, non-Hispanic/Latino; 42% international.

Freshmen:
Admission: 4 enrolled.

FACULTY
Total: 21, 38% full-time, 38% with terminal degrees.
Student/faculty ratio: 2:1.

ACADEMICS
Calendar: semesters. *Degree:* certificates and bachelor's.
Special study options: accelerated degree program, English as a second language, external degree program, independent study.
Computers: 2 computers/terminals are available on campus for general student use. Students can access the following: free student e-mail accounts, online (class) grades, online (class) schedules. Campuswide network is available. 1% of college-owned or -operated housing units are wired for high-speed Internet access. Wireless service is available via classrooms, computer labs, dorm rooms, libraries, student centers.
Library: Holy Trinity Orthodox Seminary Library. *Books:* 40,000 (physical). Weekly public service hours: 40.

STUDENT LIFE
Housing options: men-only. Campus housing is university owned. Freshman campus housing is guaranteed.
Activities and organizations: student-run newspaper, choral group, Student Union.
Campus security: 24-hour emergency response devices.
Student services: health clinic, personal/psychological counseling.

COSTS
Costs (2017–18) *Comprehensive fee:* $11,650 includes full-time tuition ($7250), mandatory fees ($300), and room and board ($4100). Full-time tuition and fees vary according to location and program. *College room only:* $4100. *Payment plan:* installment.

APPLYING
Options: electronic application, deferred entrance.
Application fee: $40.
Required: essay or personal statement, high school transcript, minimum 2.0 GPA, 1 letter of recommendation, Orthodoxy/Orthodox baptism, entrance exam, recommendation from spiritual father or parish priest.
Application deadlines: 6/1 (freshmen), 6/1 (transfers).

CONTACT
Rev. Fr. Ephraim Willmarth, Assistant Dean and Director of Admissions, Holy Trinity Orthodox Seminary, PO Box 36, Jordanville, NY 13361. *Phone:* 315-858-0945. *Fax:* 315-858-0945. *E-mail:* ejwillmarth@hts.edu.

Houghton College
Houghton, New York
http://www.houghton.edu/
- **Independent Wesleyan** comprehensive, founded 1883
- **Rural** 1300-acre campus with easy access to Buffalo, Rochester
- **Endowment** $46.4 million
- **Coed**
- **Moderately difficult** entrance level

FACULTY
Student/faculty ratio: 13:1.

ACADEMICS
Calendar: semesters. *Degrees:* associate, bachelor's, and master's.
Library: Willard J. Houghton Library plus 1 other. *Books:* 176,037 (physical), 284,490 (digital/electronic); *Serial titles:* 821 (physical), 58,547 (digital/electronic); *Databases:* 118. Weekly public service hours: 82; students can reserve study rooms.

STUDENT LIFE
Housing options: on-campus residence required through senior year; men-only, women-only. Campus housing is university owned. Freshman campus housing is guaranteed.
Activities and organizations: drama/theater group, student-run newspaper, choral group, Global Christian Fellowship, Student Government Association, Mercy Seat, Allegany County Outreach, Kairos (formerly Intercultural Student Association).
Athletics Member NCAA, NCCAA. All NCAA Division III.
Campus security: 24-hour emergency response devices and patrols, late-night transport/escort service, controlled dormitory access, Emergency phone number rings directly to cell phone carried by officer on duty 24/7, automatic fire alarms throughout campus.
Student services: health clinic, personal/psychological counseling.

COSTS & FINANCIAL AID
Costs (2017–18) *Comprehensive fee:* $40,558 includes full-time tuition ($31,040), mandatory fees ($500), and room and board ($9018). Full-time tuition and fees vary according to course load and location. Part-time tuition: $1305 per semester hour. Part-time tuition and fees vary according to course load and location. *College room only:* $4838. Room and board charges vary according to board plan and housing facility.
Financial Aid Of all full-time matriculated undergraduates who enrolled in 2016, 873 applied for aid, 802 were judged to have need, 133 had their need fully met. 477 Federal Work-Study jobs (averaging $1861). 123 state and other part-time jobs (averaging $1945). In 2016, 192 non-need-based awards were made. *Average percent of need met:* 80. *Average financial aid package:* $25,309. *Average need-based loan:* $5480. *Average need-based gift aid:* $19,457. *Average non-need-based aid:* $15,099. *Average indebtedness upon graduation:* $23,277.

APPLYING
Standardized Tests *Recommended:* SAT or ACT (for admission).
Options: electronic application, deferred entrance.
Application fee: $40.
Required: high school transcript, 1 letter of recommendation. *Required for some:* essay or personal statement. *Recommended:* essay or personal statement, minimum 3.0 GPA, interview.

CONTACT
Mr. Ryan Spear, Associate Director of Admission Operations, Houghton College, PO Box 128, Houghton, NY 14744. *Phone:* 585-567-9353. *Toll-free phone:* 800-777-2556. *Fax:* 585-567-9522. *E-mail:* admission@houghton.edu.

Hunter College of the City University of New York

New York, New York

http://www.hunter.cuny.edu/

- **State and locally supported** comprehensive, founded 1870, part of City University of New York System
- **Urban** campus
- **Endowment** $105.7 million
- **Coed** 16,844 undergraduate students, 75% full-time, 65% women, 35% men
- **Moderately difficult** entrance level, 40% of applicants were admitted

UNDERGRAD STUDENTS

12,612 full-time, 4,232 part-time. Students come from 41 states and territories; 162 other countries; 3% are from out of state; 12% Black or African American, non-Hispanic/Latino; 22% Hispanic/Latino; 30% Asian, non-Hispanic/Latino; 0.1% American Indian or Alaska Native, non-Hispanic/Latino; 5% international; 11% transferred in; 1% live on campus.

Freshmen:

Admission: 29,326 applied, 11,784 admitted, 2,337 enrolled. *Average high school GPA:* 3.4. *Test scores:* SAT evidence-based reading and writing scores over 500: 88%; SAT math scores over 500: 94%; SAT evidence-based reading and writing scores over 600: 30%; SAT math scores over 600: 48%; SAT evidence-based reading and writing scores over 700: 8%; SAT math scores over 700: 9%.

Retention: 83% of full-time freshmen returned.

FACULTY

Total: 2,144, 31% full-time, 60% with terminal degrees.

Student/faculty ratio: 14:1.

ACADEMICS

Calendar: semesters. *Degrees:* bachelor's, master's, doctoral, post-master's, and postbachelor's certificates.

Special study options: advanced placement credit, distance learning, double majors, English as a second language, freshman honors college, honors programs, independent study, internships, off-campus study, part-time degree program, services for LD students, student-designed majors, study abroad, summer session for credit.

Unusual degree programs: 3-2 nursing; social work; anthropology, economics, English, history, mathematics, music, physics, sociology.

Computers: 600 computers/terminals are available on campus for general student use. Students can access the following: computer help desk, free student e-mail accounts, online (class) registration, online (class) schedules. Campuswide network is available. 100% of college-owned or -operated housing units are wired for high-speed Internet access. Wireless service is available via entire campus.

Library: Hunter College Library plus 1 other. *Books:* 435,121 (physical), 498,891 (digital/electronic); *Serial titles:* 6,282 (physical), 96,375 (digital/electronic); *Databases:* 275.

STUDENT LIFE

Housing options: coed.

Activities and organizations: drama/theater group, student-run newspaper, radio and television station, choral group.

Athletics Member NCAA. All Division III. *Intercollegiate sports:* basketball M/W, cross-country running M/W, fencing M/W, gymnastics W, soccer M, swimming and diving W, tennis M/W, track and field M/W, volleyball M/W, wrestling M. *Intramural sports:* basketball M/W, cross-country running M/W, gymnastics M/W, racquetball M/W, rugby M, soccer M/W, swimming and diving M/W, tennis M/W, volleyball M/W.

Campus security: 24-hour emergency response devices and patrols.

Student services: personal/psychological counseling, women's center.

COSTS & FINANCIAL AID

Costs (2017–18) *Tuition:* state resident $6530 full-time, $285 per credit hour part-time; nonresident $17,400 full-time, $580 per credit hour part-time. Full-time tuition and fees vary according to course load, degree level, and program. Part-time tuition and fees vary according to course load, degree level, and program. *Required fees:* $450 full-time, $133 per

term part-time. *Room only:* $4857. Room and board charges vary according to housing facility and location. *Payment plan:* installment.

Financial Aid Of all full-time matriculated undergraduates who enrolled in 2017, 10,550 applied for aid, 9,509 were judged to have need, 5,041 had their need fully met. 1,067 Federal Work-Study jobs (averaging $1266). In 2017, 428 non-need-based awards were made. *Average percent of need met:* 79. *Average financial aid package:* $8126. *Average need-based loan:* $4068. *Average need-based gift aid:* $7789. *Average non-need-based aid:* $4179. *Average indebtedness upon graduation:* $12,122.

APPLYING

Standardized Tests *Required:* SAT or ACT (for admission).

Options: early admission.

Application fee: $65.

Required: high school transcript.

Application deadlines: 3/15 (freshmen), 3/15 (transfers).

Notification: continuous (freshmen), continuous (transfers).

CONTACT

Ms. Lori Janowski, Associate Director of Undergraduate Admissions, Hunter College of the City University of New York, 695 Park Avenue, New York, NY 10065-5085. *Phone:* 212-772-4490. *Fax:* 212-650-3472. *E-mail:* lori.janowski@hunter.cuny.edu.

Iona College

New Rochelle, New York

http://www.iona.edu/

- **Independent** comprehensive, founded 1940, affiliated with Roman Catholic Church
- **Suburban** 35-acre campus with easy access to New York City
- **Endowment** $130.8 million
- **Coed** 3,178 undergraduate students, 93% full-time, 51% women, 49% men
- **Moderately difficult** entrance level, 92% of applicants were admitted

UNDERGRAD STUDENTS

2,949 full-time, 229 part-time. Students come from 35 states and territories; 38 other countries; 24% are from out of state; 9% Black or African American, non-Hispanic/Latino; 23% Hispanic/Latino; 2% Asian, non-Hispanic/Latino; 0.1% Native Hawaiian or other Pacific Islander, non-Hispanic/Latino; 0.2% American Indian or Alaska Native, non-Hispanic/Latino; 2% Two or more races, non-Hispanic/Latino; 6% Race/ethnicity unknown; 3% international; 3% transferred in; 46% live on campus.

Freshmen:

Admission: 10,304 applied, 9,501 admitted, 860 enrolled. *Average high school GPA:* 3.0. *Test scores:* SAT evidence-based reading and writing scores over 500: 76%; SAT math scores over 500: 67%; ACT scores over 18: 94%; SAT evidence-based reading and writing scores over 600: 25%; SAT math scores over 600: 20%; ACT scores over 24: 43%; SAT evidence-based reading and writing scores over 700: 1%; SAT math scores over 700: 1%; ACT scores over 30: 6%.

Retention: 75% of full-time freshmen returned.

FACULTY

Total: 330, 52% full-time, 48% with terminal degrees.

Student/faculty ratio: 15:1.

ACADEMICS

Calendar: semesters. *Degrees:* certificates, bachelor's, master's, post-master's, and postbachelor's certificates.

Special study options: accelerated degree program, adult/continuing education programs, advanced placement credit, distance learning, double majors, English as a second language, honors programs, independent study, internships, part-time degree program, services for LD students, study abroad, summer session for credit. *ROTC:* Army (c), Air Force (c).

Unusual degree programs: 3-2 business administration.

Computers: 10,000 ports are available on campus for general student use. Students can access the following: campus intranet, computer help desk, free student e-mail accounts, online (class) grades, online (class) registration, online (class) schedules, bill payment. Campuswide network is available. 100% of college-owned or -operated housing units are wired for high-speed Internet access. Wireless service is available via entire campus.

Library: Ryan Library plus 1 other. *Books:* 268,290 (physical), 330,337 (digital/electronic); *Serial titles:* 112 (physical), 369 (digital/electronic); *Databases:* 160. Weekly public service hours: 101; students can reserve study rooms.

STUDENT LIFE

Housing options: coed, special housing for students with disabilities. Campus housing is university owned and leased by the school. Freshman campus housing is guaranteed.

Activities and organizations: drama/theater group, student-run newspaper, radio and television station, choral group, Student Government Association, Gaels Activities Board, Council for Greek Governance, Student Leader Alliance for Multiculturalism, The Ionian - Student Newspaper, national fraternities, national sororities.

Athletics Member NCAA. All Division I. *Intercollegiate sports:* baseball M(s), basketball M(s)/W(s), cross-country running M(s)/W(s), golf M(s), lacrosse W(s), rowing M/W, soccer M(s)/W(s), softball W(s), swimming and diving M(s)/W(s), track and field M(s)/W(s), volleyball W(s), water polo M/W(s). *Intramural sports:* basketball M/W, cheerleading M(c)/W(c), football M/W, rugby M(c), soccer M/W, table tennis M/W, volleyball M/W.

Campus security: 24-hour emergency response devices and patrols, controlled dormitory access.

Student services: health clinic, personal/psychological counseling.

COSTS & FINANCIAL AID

Costs (2017–18) *Comprehensive fee:* $52,514 includes full-time tuition ($35,482), mandatory fees ($2200), and room and board ($14,832). Part-time tuition: $1176 per credit hour. Part-time tuition and fees vary according to course load. *Required fees:* $540 per term part-time. *Room and board:* Room and board charges vary according to board plan. *Payment plan:* installment. *Waivers:* children of alumni and employees or children of employees.

Financial Aid Of all full-time matriculated undergraduates who enrolled in 2017, 2,890 applied for aid, 2,523 were judged to have need, 475 had their need fully met. 409 Federal Work-Study jobs (averaging $1412). In 2017, 360 non-need-based awards were made. *Average percent of need met:* 16. *Average financial aid package:* $26,300. *Average need-based loan:* $3835. *Average need-based gift aid:* $5720. *Average non-need-based aid:* $19,100. *Average indebtedness upon graduation:* $32,487. *Financial aid deadline:* 4/15.

APPLYING

Standardized Tests *Required:* SAT or ACT (for admission).

Options: electronic application, early action, deferred entrance.

Application fee: $50.

Required: high school transcript. *Required for some:* interview. *Recommended:* essay or personal statement, 2 letters of recommendation.

Application deadlines: 2/15 (freshmen), 8/15 (transfers), 12/1 (early action).

Notification: continuous (freshmen), continuous (transfers), 12/20 (early action).

CONTACT

Mr. Bryan Rothstein, Director of Undergraduate Admissions, Iona College, Admissions, 715 North Avenue, New Rochelle, NY 10801. *Phone:* 914-633-2502. *Toll-free phone:* 800-231-IONA. *Fax:* 914-633-2778. *E-mail:* admissions@iona.edu.

Ithaca College

Ithaca, New York

http://www.ithaca.edu/

- **Independent** comprehensive, founded 1892
- **Small-town** 669-acre campus with easy access to Syracuse
- **Endowment** $300.7 million
- **Coed** 6,059 undergraduate students, 98% full-time, 58% women, 42% men
- **Moderately difficult** entrance level, 71% of applicants were admitted

UNDERGRAD STUDENTS

5,936 full-time, 123 part-time. Students come from 45 states and territories; 42 other countries; 56% are from out of state; 6% Black or African American, non-Hispanic/Latino; 8% Hispanic/Latino; 4% Asian, non-Hispanic/Latino; 0.0% Native Hawaiian or other Pacific Islander, non-Hispanic/Latino; 0.1% American Indian or Alaska Native, non-Hispanic/Latino; 3% Two or more races, non-Hispanic/Latino; 4% Race/ethnicity unknown; 2% international; 2% transferred in; 70% live on campus.

Freshmen:

Admission: 14,152 applied, 9,980 admitted, 1,622 enrolled. *Test scores:* SAT evidence-based reading and writing scores over 500: 98%; SAT math scores over 500: 97%; ACT scores over 18: 99%; SAT evidence-based reading and writing scores over 600: 71%; SAT math scores over 600: 53%; ACT scores over 24: 85%; SAT evidence-based reading and writing scores over 700: 15%; SAT math scores over 700: 10%; ACT scores over 30: 23%.

Retention: 83% of full-time freshmen returned.

FACULTY

Total: 785, 66% full-time, 64% with terminal degrees.

Student/faculty ratio: 10:1.

ACADEMICS

Calendar: semesters. *Degrees:* certificates, bachelor's, master's, and doctoral.

Special study options: accelerated degree program, adult/continuing education programs, advanced placement credit, distance learning, double majors, freshman honors college, honors programs, independent study, internships, off-campus study, part-time degree program, services for LD students, student-designed majors, study abroad, summer session for credit. **ROTC:** Army (c), Air Force (c).

Unusual degree programs: 3-2 engineering with Cornell University, Rensselaer Polytechnic Institute, Clarkson University, Watson School of Engineering at Binghamton University.

Computers: 640 computers/terminals and 20 ports are available on campus for general student use. Students can access the following: campus intranet, computer help desk, free student e-mail accounts, online (class) grades, online (class) registration, online (class) schedules. Campuswide network is available. 100% of college-owned or -operated housing units are wired for high-speed Internet access. Wireless service is available via entire campus.

Library: Ithaca College Library. *Books:* 315,000 (physical), 165,000 (digital/electronic); *Serial titles:* 640 (physical), 68,858 (digital/electronic); *Databases:* 155. Weekly public service hours: 148; study areas open 24 hours, 5–7 days a week.

STUDENT LIFE

Housing options: on-campus residence required through junior year; coed, special housing for students with disabilities. Campus housing is university owned. Freshman campus housing is guaranteed.

Activities and organizations: drama/theater group, student-run newspaper, radio and television station, choral group, Student Governance Council, Colleges Against Cancer, Brothers 4 Brothers, International Club, Asian American Alliance, national fraternities.

Athletics Member NCAA. All Division III. *Intercollegiate sports:* baseball M, basketball M/W, crew M/W, cross-country running M/W, field hockey W, football M, golf W, gymnastics W, lacrosse M/W, soccer M/W, softball W, swimming and diving M/W, tennis M/W, track and field M/W, volleyball W, wrestling M. *Intramural sports:* basketball M/W, equestrian sports M(c)/W(c), fencing M(c)/W(c), football M, golf M/W, ice hockey M(c), lacrosse M(c)/W(c), rugby M(c)/W(c), skiing (downhill) M(c)/W(c), soccer M/W, softball M/W, squash M/W(c), table tennis M(c)/W(c), tennis M/W, ultimate Frisbee M(c)/W(c), volleyball M/W.

Campus security: 24-hour emergency response devices and patrols, student patrols, late-night transport/escort service, controlled dormitory access.

Student services: health clinic, personal/psychological counseling.

COSTS & FINANCIAL AID

Costs (2018–19) *Comprehensive fee:* $59,540 includes full-time tuition ($43,978) and room and board ($15,562). Part-time tuition: $1466 per credit hour. *College room only:* $8568. Room and board charges vary according to board plan and housing facility. *Payment plan:* installment. *Waivers:* children of alumni and employees or children of employees.

Financial Aid Of all full-time matriculated undergraduates who enrolled in 2017, 4,648 applied for aid, 4,044 were judged to have need, 1,659 had their need fully met. 1,677 state and other part-time jobs (averaging $2402). In 2017, 1482 non-need-based awards were made. *Average percent of need met:* 86. *Average financial aid package:* $37,506. *Average need-based loan:* $6512. *Average need-based gift aid:* $27,622. *Average non-need-based aid:* $15,712. *Average indebtedness upon graduation:* $42,016.

APPLYING

Options: electronic application, early admission, early decision, early action, deferred entrance.

Application fee: $60.

Required: essay or personal statement, high school transcript, 1 letter of recommendation. *Required for some:* audition for some programs. *Recommended:* minimum 3.0 GPA.

Application deadlines: 2/1 (freshmen), 3/1 (transfers), 12/1 (early action).

Early decision deadline: 11/1.

Notification: 4/15 (freshmen), continuous (transfers), 12/15 (early decision), 2/1 (early action).

CONTACT

Ithaca College, 953 Danby Road, Ithaca, NY 14850. *Toll-free phone:* 800-429-4274.

Jamestown Business College

Jamestown, New York
http://www.jbc.edu/

- **Proprietary** primarily 2-year, founded 1886
- **Small-town** 1-acre campus
- **Coed**
- **Minimally difficult** entrance level

FACULTY
Student/faculty ratio: 23:1.

ACADEMICS
Calendar: quarters. *Degrees:* certificates, associate, and bachelor's.
Library: James Prendergast Library. *Books:* 173,745 (physical), 12,508 (digital/electronic); *Serial titles:* 103 (physical), 70 (digital/electronic); *Databases:* 55. Weekly public service hours: 55; study areas open 24 hours, 5–7 days a week.

STUDENT LIFE
Housing options: college housing not available.
Campus security: 24-hour emergency response devices, student key card for building entrance.

APPLYING
Application fee: $25.
Required: essay or personal statement, high school transcript, interview.

CONTACT
Mrs. Brenda Salemme, Director of Admissions, Jamestown Business College, 7 Fairmount Avenue, Box 429, Jamestown, NY 14702-0429. *Phone:* 716-664-5100. *Fax:* 716-664-3144. *E-mail:* brendasalemme@jbc.edu.

The Jewish Theological Seminary

New York, New York
http://www.jtsa.edu/

CONTACT
Mr. Sergio Lineberge, List College Admissions Coordinator, The Jewish Theological Seminary, 3080 Broadway, New York, NY 10027. *Phone:* 212-678-8820. *E-mail:* lcadmissions@jtsa.edu.

John Jay College of Criminal Justice of the City University of New York

New York, New York
http://www.jjay.cuny.edu/

- **State and locally supported** comprehensive, founded 1964, part of City University of New York
- **Urban** campus with easy access to New York City
- **Coed** 12,916 undergraduate students, 80% full-time, 56% women, 44% men
- **Moderately difficult** entrance level, 55% of applicants were admitted

UNDERGRAD STUDENTS
10,276 full-time, 2,640 part-time. Students come from 21 states and territories; 36 other countries; 3% are from out of state; 20% Black or African American, non-Hispanic/Latino; 44% Hispanic/Latino; 12% Asian, non-Hispanic/Latino; 0.4% American Indian or Alaska Native, non-Hispanic/Latino; 3% international; 15% transferred in; 1% live on campus.

Freshmen:
Admission: 18,090 applied, 9,864 admitted, 1,844 enrolled. *Average high school GPA:* 2.9. *Test scores:* SAT evidence-based reading and writing scores over 500: 50%; SAT math scores over 500: 48%; SAT evidence-based reading and writing scores over 600: 6%; SAT math scores over 600: 9%; SAT evidence-based reading and writing scores over 700: 1%; SAT math scores over 700: 1%.

Retention: 77% of full-time freshmen returned.

ACADEMICS
Calendar: semesters. *Degrees:* certificates, bachelor's, and master's.

Special study options: academic remediation for entering students, advanced placement credit, cooperative education, distance learning, double majors, English as a second language, honors programs, independent study, internships, off-campus study, part-time degree program, services for LD students, study abroad, summer session for credit.

Unusual degree programs: 3-2 social work; public management, law enforcement.

Computers: 1,980 computers/terminals are available on campus for general student use. Students can access the following: campus intranet, computer help desk, free student e-mail accounts, online (class) grades, online (class) registration, online (class) schedules. Campuswide network is available. Wireless service is available via classrooms, computer centers, computer labs, dorm rooms, learning centers, libraries, student centers.

Library: Lloyd George Sealy Library. *Books:* 182,059 (physical), 631,447 (digital/electronic); *Serial titles:* 7,124 (physical), 101,219 (digital/electronic); *Databases:* 178. Weekly public service hours: 77; study areas open 24 hours, 5–7 days a week; students can reserve study rooms.

STUDENT LIFE
Housing options: coed. Campus housing is leased by the school.

Activities and organizations: drama/theater group, student-run newspaper, radio station, choral group, Auxiliary University Program, Student Athlete Advisory Community Club, Environmental Club, Law Society, Artists United.

Athletics Member NCAA. All Division III. *Intercollegiate sports:* baseball M, basketball M/W, cheerleading M/W, cross-country running M/W, riflery M/W, soccer M/W, softball W, swimming and diving W, tennis M/W, volleyball M/W. *Intramural sports:* basketball M/W, cheerleading M/W, riflery M/W, soccer M/W, swimming and diving M/W.

Campus security: 24-hour emergency response devices and patrols, controlled dormitory access.

Student services: health clinic, personal/psychological counseling, women's center, legal services.

COSTS & FINANCIAL AID
Costs (2017–18) *Tuition:* state resident $6530 full-time, $285 per credit hour part-time; nonresident $13,920 full-time, $580 per credit hour part-time. *Required fees:* $540 full-time, $183 per term part-time. *Room and board:* $20,007.

Financial Aid Of all full-time matriculated undergraduates who enrolled in 2016, 10,236 applied for aid, 9,861 were judged to have need. *Average percent of need met:* 85. *Average financial aid package:* $8610. *Average need-based loan:* $3903. *Average need-based gift aid:* $2693.

APPLYING
Standardized Tests *Required:* SAT or ACT (for admission).

Options: deferred entrance.

Application fee: $65.

Required: high school transcript, minimum 2.0 GPA, minimum SAT score of 1100.

Application deadlines: 5/31 (freshmen), 5/31 (transfers).

Notification: continuous until 2/15 (freshmen), continuous until 2/15 (transfers).

CONTACT
Mr. Vincent Papandrea, Director, John Jay College of Criminal Justice of the City University of New York, 524 West 59th Street, L.64.14NB, New York, NY 10019. *Phone:* 212-237-8864. *Toll-free phone:* 877-JOHNJAY. *E-mail:* vpapandrea@jjay.cuny.edu.

The Juilliard School
New York, New York
http://www.juilliard.edu/
- **Independent** comprehensive, founded 1905
- **Urban** campus with easy access to New York City
- **Coed** 566 undergraduate students, 86% full-time, 46% women, 54% men
- **Most difficult** entrance level, 6% of applicants were admitted

UNDERGRAD STUDENTS
486 full-time, 80 part-time. 79% are from out of state; 6% Black or African American, non-Hispanic/Latino; 8% Hispanic/Latino; 13% Asian, non-Hispanic/Latino; 0.2% Native Hawaiian or other Pacific Islander, non-Hispanic/Latino; 5% Two or more races, non-Hispanic/Latino; 8% Race/ethnicity unknown; 24% international; 3% transferred in.

Freshmen:
Admission: 2,753 applied, 163 admitted, 110 enrolled.

FACULTY
Total: 350, 37% full-time.

Student/faculty ratio: 4:1.

ACADEMICS
Calendar: semesters. *Degrees:* diplomas, bachelor's, master's, doctoral, post-master's, and postbachelor's certificates.

Special study options: adult/continuing education programs.

Computers: Campuswide network is available. Wireless service is available via entire campus.

Library: Lila Acheson Wallace Library.

STUDENT LIFE
Housing options: on-campus residence required for freshman year; coed. Campus housing is university owned. Freshman campus housing is guaranteed.

Activities and organizations: drama/theater group, student-run newspaper.

Campus security: 24-hour emergency response devices and patrols, controlled dormitory access, electronically operated main building entrances.

Student services: health clinic, personal/psychological counseling.

COSTS & FINANCIAL AID
Costs (2017–18) *Comprehensive fee:* $59,510 includes full-time tuition ($43,170), mandatory fees ($350), and room and board ($15,990). *Payment plan:* installment. *Waivers:* employees or children of employees.

Financial Aid Of all full-time matriculated undergraduates who enrolled in 2017, 421 applied for aid, 356 were judged to have need, 109 had their need fully met. 167 Federal Work-Study jobs (averaging $1921). 294 state and other part-time jobs (averaging $1993). In 2017, 56 non-need-based awards were made. *Average percent of need met:* 77. *Average financial aid package:* $35,281. *Average need-based loan:* $4802. *Average need-based gift aid:* $30,721. *Average non-need-based aid:* $21,139. *Average indebtedness upon graduation:* $33,025. *Financial aid deadline:* 3/1.

APPLYING
Standardized Tests *Required for some:* SAT or ACT (for admission).

Options: electronic application.

Application fee: $110.

Required: essay or personal statement, high school transcript, audition.

Application deadlines: 12/1 (freshmen), 12/1 (transfers).

Notification: 4/1 (freshmen), 4/1 (transfers).

CONTACT
Ms. Kathy Tesar, Associate Dean for Enrollment Management, The Juilliard School, 60 Lincoln Center Plaza, New York, NY 10023-6588. *Phone:* 212-799-5000 Ext. 223. *Fax:* 212-724-0263. *E-mail:* admissions@juilliard.edu.

Kehilath Yakov Rabbinical Seminary
Ossining, New York
http://kehilathyakov.com/

CONTACT
Admissions Officer, Kehilath Yakov Rabbinical Seminary, 340 Illington Road, Ossining, NY 10562. *Phone:* 718-963-1212.

Keuka College
Keuka Park, New York
http://www.keuka.edu/
- **Independent** comprehensive, founded 1890, affiliated with American Baptist Churches in the U.S.A.
- **Rural** 173-acre campus with easy access to Rochester
- **Endowment** $13.3 million
- **Coed**
- **Moderately difficult** entrance level

FACULTY
Student/faculty ratio: 11:1.

ACADEMICS
Calendar: 4-1-4. *Degrees:* bachelor's and master's.

Library: Lightner Library plus 1 other. *Books:* 79,009 (physical), 1,083 (digital/electronic); *Serial titles:* 687 (physical), 112 (digital/electronic); *Databases:* 89. Weekly public service hours: 96.

STUDENT LIFE
Housing options: on-campus residence required through senior year; coed, women-only, cooperative, special housing for students with disabilities. Campus housing is university owned. Freshman campus housing is guaranteed.

Activities and organizations: drama/theater group, student-run newspaper, choral group, Sigma Alpha Pi Honor Society, SOTA, ASL Club, Art Club, KC Chemistry Club.

Athletics Member NCAA. All Division III.

Campus security: 24-hour emergency response devices and patrols, late-night transport/escort service.

Student services: health clinic, personal/psychological counseling, women's center.

COSTS & FINANCIAL AID
Costs (2017–18) *One-time required fee:* $225. *Comprehensive fee:* $42,398 includes full-time tuition ($29,926), mandatory fees ($1020), and room and board ($11,452). Full-time tuition and fees vary according to course load, degree level, location, program, and reciprocity agreements. Part-time tuition: $999 per credit hour. Part-time tuition and fees vary according to course load, degree level, location, program, and reciprocity agreements. *Required fees:* $650 per year part-time. *College room only:* $5520. Room and board charges vary according to housing facility.

Financial Aid Of all full-time matriculated undergraduates who enrolled in 2017, 1,200 applied for aid, 1,100 were judged to have need, 100 had their need fully met. In 2017, 40 non-need-based awards were made. *Average financial aid package:* $20,000. *Average need-based loan:* $4300. *Average need-based gift aid:* $8000. *Average non-need-based aid:* $12,000.

APPLYING
Options: electronic application, early admission, deferred entrance.

Required: high school transcript. *Required for some:* interview. *Recommended:* minimum 2.8 GPA, 1 letter of recommendation, interview.

CONTACT
Mrs. Megan Perkins (Ryan), Keuka College, 141 Central Avenue, Keuka Park, NY 14478. *Phone:* 315-279-5254. *Toll-free phone:* 800-33-KEUKA. *Fax:* 315-279-5386. *E-mail:* admissions@keuka.edu.

The King's College
New York, New York
http://www.tkc.edu/

- **Independent nondenominational** 4-year, founded 1939
- **Urban** campus with easy access to New York City
- **Endowment** $488,024
- **Coed** 555 undergraduate students, 98% full-time, 64% women, 36% men
- **Moderately difficult** entrance level, 41% of applicants were admitted

UNDERGRAD STUDENTS
542 full-time, 13 part-time. Students come from 45 states and territories; 10 other countries; 93% are from out of state; 6% Black or African American, non-Hispanic/Latino; 7% Hispanic/Latino; 4% Asian, non-Hispanic/Latino; 0.4% Native Hawaiian or other Pacific Islander, non-Hispanic/Latino; 0.4% American Indian or Alaska Native, non-Hispanic/Latino; 0.2% Two or more races, non-Hispanic/Latino; 12% Race/ethnicity unknown; 3% international; 11% transferred in.

Freshmen:
Admission: 2,098 applied, 858 admitted, 149 enrolled. *Average high school GPA:* 3.8. *Test scores:* SAT evidence-based reading and writing scores over 500: 100%; SAT math scores over 500: 94%; ACT scores over 18: 100%; SAT evidence-based reading and writing scores over 600: 74%; SAT math scores over 600: 39%; ACT scores over 24: 82%; SAT evidence-based reading and writing scores over 700: 16%; SAT math scores over 700: 8%; ACT scores over 30: 21%.
Retention: 73% of full-time freshmen returned.

FACULTY
Total: 55, 55% full-time, 67% with terminal degrees.
Student/faculty ratio: 14:1.

ACADEMICS
Calendar: semesters. *Degree:* bachelor's.
Special study options: advanced placement credit, distance learning, double majors, independent study, internships, services for LD students, study abroad, summer session for credit. *ROTC:* Army (c).
Computers: Students can access the following: computer help desk, free student e-mail accounts, online (class) grades, online (class) registration, online (class) schedules. Campuswide network is available. 100% of college-owned or -operated housing units are wired for high-speed Internet access. Wireless service is available via entire campus.
Library: Battles Library.

STUDENT LIFE
Housing options: men-only, women-only. Campus housing is university owned and leased by the school. Freshman campus housing is guaranteed.
Activities and organizations: drama/theater group, student-run newspaper, choral group, The King's Players, King's Debate Society, Refuge, Empire State Tribune, The Kings of Swing.
Athletics Member NCCAA, USCAA. *Intercollegiate sports:* baseball M, basketball M/W, golf M/W, soccer M/W, volleyball W. *Intramural sports:* basketball M(c)/W(c), cheerleading W(c), fencing M(c)/W(c), football M(c), rugby M(c), ultimate Frisbee M(c)/W(c).
Campus security: 24-hour emergency response devices, 24-hour security/doormen, fire sprinklers, fire/evacuation emergency plan.
Student services: personal/psychological counseling.

COSTS & FINANCIAL AID
Costs (2018–19) *Tuition:* $36,000 full-time, $1460 per credit hour part-time. Part-time tuition and fees vary according to course load. *Required fees:* $450 full-time, $225 per term part-time. *Room only:* $16,840. Room and board charges vary according to location. *Payment plans:* installment, deferred payment. *Waivers:* employees or children of employees.

Financial Aid Of all full-time matriculated undergraduates who enrolled in 2016, 416 applied for aid, 362 were judged to have need, 53 had their need fully met. In 2016, 149 non-need-based awards were made. *Average percent of need met:* 67. *Average financial aid package:* $25,583. *Average need-based loan:* $3639. *Average need-based gift aid:* $20,736. *Average non-need-based aid:* $15,629. *Average indebtedness upon graduation:* $34,271.

APPLYING
Standardized Tests *Required:* SAT, ACT or CLT (for admission).
Options: electronic application, early action, deferred entrance.
Application fee: $30.
Required: high school transcript. *Recommended:* minimum 3.0 GPA, interview.
Application deadlines: rolling (freshmen), rolling (transfers).
Notification: continuous (freshmen), continuous (transfers).

CONTACT
Mr. Noah Hunter, Director of Admissions, The King's College, 56 Broadway, New York, NY 10004. *Phone:* 212-659-3615. *Toll-free phone:* 888-969-7200 Ext. 3610. *Fax:* 212-659-3611. *E-mail:* nhunter@tkc.edu.

Lehman College of the City University of New York
Bronx, New York
http://www.lehman.cuny.edu/

- **State and locally supported** comprehensive, founded 1931, part of City University of New York System
- **Urban** 37-acre campus with easy access to New York City
- **Endowment** $7.1 million
- **Coed** 11,671 undergraduate students, 60% full-time, 67% women, 33% men
- **Moderately difficult** entrance level, 35% of applicants were admitted

UNDERGRAD STUDENTS
7,048 full-time, 4,623 part-time. Students come from 15 states and territories; 99 other countries; 1% are from out of state; 30% Black or African American, non-Hispanic/Latino; 54% Hispanic/Latino; 7% Asian, non-Hispanic/Latino; 3% international.

Freshmen:
Admission: 15,138 applied, 5,298 admitted, 944 enrolled. *Test scores:* SAT math scores over 500: 31%; SAT math scores over 600: 5%; SAT math scores over 700: 1%.
Retention: 86% of full-time freshmen returned.

FACULTY
Total: 938, 40% full-time, 46% with terminal degrees.
Student/faculty ratio: 17:1.

ACADEMICS
Calendar: semesters. *Degrees:* certificates, bachelor's, master's, and post-master's certificates.
Special study options: adult/continuing education programs, advanced placement credit, cooperative education, distance learning, double majors, English as a second language, freshman honors college, honors programs, independent study, internships, off-campus study, part-time degree program, services for LD students, student-designed majors, study abroad, summer session for credit. *ROTC:* Army (c).
Unusual degree programs: 3-2 mathematics.
Computers: 800 computers/terminals are available on campus for general student use. Students can access the following: campus intranet, computer help desk, free student e-mail accounts, online (class) grades, online (class) registration, online (class) schedules. Campuswide network is available. Wireless service is available via entire campus.
Library: Leonard Lief Library plus 1 other. *Books:* 362,674 (physical); *Serial titles:* 299,414 (physical). Weekly public service hours: 40; students can reserve study rooms.

STUDENT LIFE
Housing options: Campus housing is university owned.
Activities and organizations: drama/theater group, student-run newspaper, radio and television station, choral group, Club Mac, African

Students Association, Dominican Student Association, The Sociology Club, Club Live.

Athletics Member NCAA. All Division III. *Intercollegiate sports:* baseball M, basketball M/W, cross-country running M/W, racquetball M/W, soccer M/W, softball M/W, swimming and diving M/W, table tennis M/W, tennis M/W, track and field M/W, volleyball M/W, water polo M, wrestling M. *Intramural sports:* badminton M/W, baseball M/W, basketball M/W, cross-country running M/W, racquetball M/W, soccer M, softball M/W, swimming and diving M/W, tennis M/W, volleyball M/W, wrestling M.

Campus security: 24-hour emergency response devices and patrols, student patrols, late-night transport/escort service.

Student services: health clinic, personal/psychological counseling, women's center.

COSTS & FINANCIAL AID

Costs (2017–18) *Tuition:* state resident $6330 full-time, $285 per credit hour part-time; nonresident $13,440 full-time, $580 per credit hour part-time. Full-time tuition and fees vary according to course load. Part-time tuition and fees vary according to course load. *Required fees:* $680 full-time, $130 per term part-time. *Waivers:* employees or children of employees.

Financial Aid Of all full-time matriculated undergraduates who enrolled in 2016, 6,096 applied for aid, 6,096 were judged to have need, 3,674 had their need fully met. 448 Federal Work-Study jobs (averaging $1846). In 2016, 116 non-need-based awards were made. *Average percent of need met:* 60. *Average financial aid package:* $9353. *Average need-based loan:* $3776. *Average need-based gift aid:* $8035. *Average non-need-based aid:* $3674.

APPLYING

Standardized Tests *Required:* SAT or ACT (for admission).

Options: deferred entrance.

Application fee: $65.

Required: high school transcript, minimum 3.0 GPA. *Required for some:* essay or personal statement, interview.

Application deadlines: rolling (freshmen), rolling (transfers).

Notification: continuous (freshmen), continuous (transfers).

CONTACT

Ms. Laurie Austin, Director of Admissions, Lehman College of the City University of New York, 250 Bedford Park Boulevard West, Bronx, NY 10468. *Phone:* 718-960-8706. *Toll-free phone:* 877-LEHMAN1. *Fax:* 718-960-8712. *E-mail:* enroll@lehman.cuny.edu.

 Le Moyne College

Syracuse, New York

http://www.lemoyne.edu/

- **Independent Roman Catholic (Jesuit)** comprehensive, founded 1946
- **Suburban** 161-acre campus
- **Endowment** $179.1 million
- **Coed** 2,788 undergraduate students, 86% full-time, 60% women, 40% men
- **Moderately difficult** entrance level, 64% of applicants were admitted

UNDERGRAD STUDENTS

2,410 full-time, 378 part-time. Students come from 23 states and territories; 46 other countries; 6% are from out of state; 6% Black or African American, non-Hispanic/Latino; 5% Hispanic/Latino; 3% Asian, non-Hispanic/Latino; 0.1% Native Hawaiian or other Pacific Islander, non-Hispanic/Latino; 0.3% American Indian or Alaska Native, non-Hispanic/Latino; 2% Two or more races, non-Hispanic/Latino; 4% Race/ethnicity unknown; 1% international; 4% transferred in; 58% live on campus.

Freshmen:

Admission: 7,429 applied, 4,751 admitted, 545 enrolled. *Average high school GPA:* 3.5. *Test scores:* SAT evidence-based reading and writing scores over 500: 94%; SAT math scores over 500: 93%; ACT scores over 18: 99%; SAT evidence-based reading and writing scores over 600: 40%; SAT math scores over 600: 41%; ACT scores over 24: 54%; SAT evidence-based reading and writing scores over 700: 4%; SAT math scores over 700: 4%; ACT scores over 30: 5%.

Retention: 84% of full-time freshmen returned.

FACULTY

Total: 335, 50% full-time, 65% with terminal degrees.

Student/faculty ratio: 13:1.

ACADEMICS

Calendar: semesters. *Degrees:* bachelor's, master's, post-master's, and postbachelor's certificates.

Special study options: academic remediation for entering students, accelerated degree program, adult/continuing education programs, advanced placement credit, distance learning, double majors, honors programs, independent study, internships, off-campus study, part-time degree program, services for LD students, study abroad, summer session for credit. *ROTC:* Army (c), Air Force (c).

Unusual degree programs: 3-2 engineering with Syracuse University.

Computers: 330 computers/terminals and 330 ports are available on campus for general student use. Students can access the following: campus intranet, computer help desk, free student e-mail accounts, online (class) grades, online (class) registration, online (class) schedules, ECHO (campus-wide portal), some virtual access from off campus. Campuswide network is available. 100% of college-owned or -operated housing units are wired for high-speed Internet access. Wireless service is available via entire campus.

Library: Noreen Reale Falcone Library. *Books:* 261,183 (physical), 206,330 (digital/electronic); *Serial titles:* 1,391 (physical), 508 (digital/electronic); *Databases:* 270. Weekly public service hours: 109; study areas open 24 hours, 5–7 days a week; students can reserve study rooms.

STUDENT LIFE

Housing options: on-campus residence required through senior year; coed, special housing for students with disabilities. Campus housing is university owned. Freshman campus housing is guaranteed.

Activities and organizations: drama/theater group, student-run newspaper, radio and television station, choral group, Student Programming Board, Outing Club, Performing Arts Groups, Cultural Groups, New Student Orientation Committee.

Athletics Member NCAA. All Division II. *Intercollegiate sports:* baseball M(s), basketball M(s)/W(s), cross-country running M(s)/W(s), golf M(s)/W(s), lacrosse M(s)/W(s), soccer M(s)/W(s), softball W(s), swimming and diving M(s)/W(s), tennis M(s)/W(s), track and field M(s)/W(s), volleyball W(s). *Intramural sports:* basketball M/W, bowling M(c)/W(c), cheerleading M(c)/W(c), equestrian sports M(c)/W(c), fencing M(c)/W(c), field hockey W(c), football M/W, ice hockey M(c), lacrosse M(c)/W(c), racquetball M/W, rowing M(c)/W(c), rugby M(c)/W(c), sailing M(c)/W(c), soccer M/W, softball M/W, ultimate Frisbee M(c)/W(c), volleyball M/W.

Campus security: 24-hour emergency response devices and patrols, late-night transport/escort service, controlled dormitory access, lighted pathways, closed-circuit security cameras, and emergency code blue phones.

Student services: health clinic, personal/psychological counseling.

COSTS & FINANCIAL AID

Costs (2018–19) *Comprehensive fee:* $48,405 includes full-time tuition ($33,560), mandatory fees ($1065), and room and board ($13,780). Part-time tuition: $704 per credit hour. Part-time tuition and fees vary according to class time and course load. *College room only:* $8590. Room and board charges vary according to board plan and housing facility. *Payment plans:* installment, deferred payment. *Waivers:* employees or children of employees.

Financial Aid Of all full-time matriculated undergraduates who enrolled in 2016, 2,292 applied for aid, 2,081 were judged to have need, 537 had their need fully met. 358 Federal Work-Study jobs (averaging $1405). 453 state and other part-time jobs (averaging $1658). In 2016, 335 non-need-based awards were made. *Average percent of need met:* 78. *Average financial aid package:* $26,170. *Average need-based loan:* $4676. *Average need-based gift aid:* $21,366. *Average non-need-based aid:* $14,365. *Average indebtedness upon graduation:* $35,209.

APPLYING

Standardized Tests *Required for some:* SAT or ACT (for admission).

Options: electronic application, early admission, early action, deferred entrance.

MEANINGFUL SUCCESS

At Le Moyne, **we look at success a little differently.** It's not just an outcome. It's a way of living. It's not simply what you do, but why, and for whom. Success means being slightly restless – fulfilled and challenged, absolutely – but always asking, "What else?" At Le Moyne, success is immersing yourself in an education that is **inspirational, forward thinking and timeless** to become the best possible version of you.

MEASURES OF *OUR* SUCCESS

Ranked among the **TOP 15%** of colleges and universities nationwide by The Princeton Review.

Lauded for academic excellence and value by *U.S. News and World Report* for **24 CONSECUTIVE YEARS** and included in the "**Great Schools, Great Prices**" and "**Best Colleges for Veterans**" categories.

You're going places. Start with a visit to Le Moyne.

lemoyne.edu/visit

LE MOYNE
Greatness meets Goodness

800-333-4733 | 315-445-4300 | admission@lemoyne.edu

Required: essay or personal statement, high school transcript, 3 letters of recommendation. *Recommended:* interview.

Application deadlines: 2/1 (freshmen), 8/1 (transfers), 11/15 (early action).

Notification: continuous until 1/1 (freshmen), continuous (transfers), 12/15 (early action).

CONTACT

Le Moyne College, 1419 Salt Springs Road, Syracuse, NY 13214. *Toll-free phone:* 800-333-4733.

See this page for display ad and page 1324 for the College Close-Up.

★ LIM College
New York, New York
http://www.limcollege.edu/

- **Proprietary** comprehensive, founded 1939
- **Urban** campus with easy access to New York City
- **Coed, primarily women** 1,402 undergraduate students, 93% full-time, 91% women, 9% men

UNDERGRAD STUDENTS

1,300 full-time, 102 part-time. Students come from 41 states and territories; 30 other countries; 65% are from out of state; 15% Black or African American, non-Hispanic/Latino; 8% Hispanic/Latino; 8% Asian, non-Hispanic/Latino; 0.5% Native Hawaiian or other Pacific Islander, non-Hispanic/Latino; 1% American Indian or Alaska Native, non-Hispanic/Latino; 8% Race/ethnicity unknown; 6% international; 12% transferred in; 26% live on campus.

Freshmen:

Admission: 253 enrolled. *Average high school GPA:* 3.0. *Test scores:* SAT evidence-based reading and writing scores over 500: 64%; SAT math scores over 500: 55%; ACT scores over 18: 81%; SAT evidence-based reading and writing scores over 600: 14%; SAT math scores over 600: 9%; ACT scores over 24: 27%; SAT evidence-based reading and writing scores over 700: 1%; ACT scores over 30: 2%.

Retention: 67% of full-time freshmen returned.

FACULTY

Total: 176, 15% full-time.

Student/faculty ratio: 8:1.

ACADEMICS

Calendar: semesters. *Degrees:* certificates, bachelor's, master's, post-master's, and postbachelor's certificates.

Special study options: academic remediation for entering students, accelerated degree program, advanced placement credit, cooperative education, distance learning, honors programs, internships, off-campus study, part-time degree program, services for LD students, study abroad, summer session for credit.

Computers: 352 computers/terminals are available on campus for general student use. Students can access the following: campus intranet, computer help desk, free student e-mail accounts, online (class) grades, online (class) registration, online (class) schedules. Campuswide network is available. 100% of college-owned or -operated housing units are wired for high-speed Internet access. Wireless service is available via entire campus.

Library: Adrian G. Marcuse Library. *Books:* 15,000 (physical), 700 (digital/electronic); *Serial titles:* 172 (physical); *Databases:* 55. Students can reserve study rooms.

STUDENT LIFE

Housing options: coed. Campus housing is leased by the school.

Activities and organizations: student-run newspaper, Fashion Show Production Club, Lexington Line Magazine, Student Life Activities Board, Dance Team, Black Retail Action Group.

Campus security: 24-hour patrols, controlled dormitory access.

Student services: personal/psychological counseling.

COSTS & FINANCIAL AID

Costs (2018–19) *Tuition:* $26,210 full-time, $870 per credit part-time. *Required fees:* $820 full-time, $419 per term part-time. *Room only:* Room and board charges vary according to housing facility. *Payment plan:* installment. *Waivers:* employees or children of employees.

Financial Aid Of all full-time matriculated undergraduates who enrolled in 2015, 1,363 applied for aid, 970 were judged to have need, 32 had their need fully met. In 2015, 158 non-need-based awards were made. *Average percent of need met:* 42. *Average financial aid package:* $10,246. *Average need-based loan:* $4425. *Average need-based gift aid:* $8338. *Average non-need-based aid:* $4975. *Average indebtedness upon graduation:* $34,717. *Financial aid deadline:* 11/15.

APPLYING

Required: essay or personal statement, high school transcript, 1 letter of recommendation. *Required for some:* interview. *Recommended:* minimum 2.0 GPA.

CONTACT

Ms. Adeline Affonso, Director of Admissions, LIM College, 12 East 53rd Street, New York, NY 10022. *Phone:* 212-310-0608 Ext. 238. *Toll-free phone:* 800-677-1323. *E-mail:* admissions@limcollege.edu.

Long Island University–LIU Brooklyn

Brooklyn, New York

http://www.liu.edu/

- **Independent** university, founded 1926
- **Urban** 11-acre campus with easy access to New York City
- **Endowment** $92.4 million
- **Coed** 3,945 undergraduate students, 86% full-time, 70% women, 30% men
- **84% of applicants were admitted**

UNDERGRAD STUDENTS

3,396 full-time, 549 part-time. Students come from 37 states and territories; 40 other countries; 13% are from out of state; 22% Black or African American, non-Hispanic/Latino; 15% Hispanic/Latino; 17% Asian, non-Hispanic/Latino; 0.2% Native Hawaiian or other Pacific Islander, non-Hispanic/Latino; 0.4% American Indian or Alaska Native, non-Hispanic/Latino; 2% Two or more races, non-Hispanic/Latino; 18% Race/ethnicity unknown; 3% international; 12% transferred in; 15% live on campus.

Freshmen:

Admission: 6,830 applied, 5,755 admitted, 674 enrolled. *Average high school GPA:* 3.2. *Test scores:* SAT evidence-based reading and writing scores over 500: 79%; SAT math scores over 500: 78%; ACT scores over 18: 88%; SAT evidence-based reading and writing scores over 600: 34%; SAT math scores over 600: 38%; ACT scores over 24: 47%; SAT evidence-based reading and writing scores over 700: 4%; SAT math scores over 700: 10%; ACT scores over 30: 9%.

Retention: 66% of full-time freshmen returned.

FACULTY

Total: 729, 39% full-time, 52% with terminal degrees.

Student/faculty ratio: 13:1.

ACADEMICS

Calendar: semesters. *Degrees:* associate, bachelor's, master's, doctoral, post-master's, and postbachelor's certificates.

Special study options: academic remediation for entering students, accelerated degree program, advanced placement credit, cooperative education, distance learning, double majors, English as a second language, freshman honors college, honors programs, independent study, internships, part-time degree program, services for LD students, student-designed majors, study abroad, summer session for credit. *ROTC:* Army (c).

Unusual degree programs: 3-2 nursing; accounting, athletic training, communications sciences and disorders/speech-language pathology, health science, occupational therapy.

Computers: 600 computers/terminals are available on campus for general student use. Students can access the following: campus intranet, computer help desk, free student e-mail accounts, online (class) grades, online (class) registration, online (class) schedules. Campuswide network is available. 100% of college-owned or -operated housing units are wired for high-speed Internet access. Wireless service is available via entire campus.

Library: Salena Library. *Books:* 257,706 (physical), 406,939 (digital/electronic); *Serial titles:* 27 (physical), 466,233 (digital/electronic); *Databases:* 495.

STUDENT LIFE

Housing options: coed, special housing for students with disabilities. Campus housing is university owned and leased by the school. Freshman campus housing is guaranteed.

Activities and organizations: drama/theater group, student-run newspaper, radio and television station, choral group, The Student Government Association, The American Pharmacists Association, Hillel Jewish Students Organization, Student Activities Board, Indo American Pharmaceutical Association, national fraternities, national sororities.

Athletics Member NCAA. All Division I. *Intercollegiate sports:* baseball M(s), basketball M(s)/W(s), bowling W(s), cross-country running W(s), field hockey W(s), golf M(s)/W(s), lacrosse W(s), soccer M(s)/W(s), softball W(s), swimming and diving W(s), tennis W(s), track and field M(s)/W(s), volleyball W(s). *Intramural sports:* basketball M(c)/W(c), soccer M(c)/W(c), volleyball M(c)/W(c).

Campus security: 24-hour emergency response devices and patrols, late-night transport/escort service, controlled dormitory access, lighted pathways/sidewalks.

Student services: health clinic, personal/psychological counseling.

COSTS & FINANCIAL AID

Costs (2017–18) *Comprehensive fee:* $50,698 includes full-time tuition ($35,038), mandatory fees ($1940), and room and board ($13,720). Part-time tuition: $1093 per credit. *Required fees:* $460 per term part-time. *Room and board:* Room and board charges vary according to board plan and housing facility. *Payment plan:* installment. *Waivers:* employees or children of employees.

Financial Aid Of all full-time matriculated undergraduates who enrolled in 2017, 3,128 applied for aid, 2,913 were judged to have need, 51 had their need fully met. 449 Federal Work-Study jobs (averaging $2602). In 2017, 120 non-need-based awards were made. *Average percent of need met:* 48. *Average financial aid package:* $20,824. *Average need-based loan:* $3447. *Average need-based gift aid:* $9976. *Average non-need-based aid:* $15,289. *Average indebtedness upon graduation:* $46,578.

APPLYING

Standardized Tests *Required:* SAT or ACT (for admission).

Options: electronic application, early action, deferred entrance.

Application fee: $50.

Required: essay or personal statement, high school transcript, letters of recommendation. *Required for some:* interview.

Application deadlines: rolling (freshmen), rolling (transfers), 12/1 (early action).

Notification: continuous (freshmen), continuous (transfers), 12/31 (early action).

CONTACT

Mr. Luis Santiago, Dean of Enrollment, Long Island University–LIU Brooklyn, 1 University Plaza, Brooklyn, NY 11201. *Phone:* 718-488-1011. *Toll-free phone:* 800-LIU-PLAN. *Fax:* 718-780-6110. *E-mail:* bkln-admissions@liu.edu.

Long Island University–LIU Post

Brookville, New York

http://www.liu.edu/

- **Independent** university, founded 1954
- **Suburban** 322-acre campus with easy access to New York City
- **Endowment** $100.1 million
- **Coed** 6,316 undergraduate students, 45% full-time, 59% women, 41% men
- **83% of applicants were admitted**

UNDERGRAD STUDENTS

2,845 full-time, 3,471 part-time. Students come from 38 states and territories; 28 other countries; 9% are from out of state; 11% Black or African American, non-Hispanic/Latino; 15% Hispanic/Latino; 4% Asian, non-Hispanic/Latino; 0.2% American Indian or Alaska Native, non-Hispanic/Latino; 2% Two or more races, non-Hispanic/Latino; 14% Race/ethnicity unknown; 6% international; 6% transferred in; 30% live on campus.

Freshmen:

Admission: 6,951 applied, 5,748 admitted, 694 enrolled. *Average high school GPA:* 3.2. *Test scores:* SAT evidence-based reading and writing scores over 500: 91%; SAT math scores over 500: 89%; ACT scores over 18: 98%; SAT evidence-based reading and writing scores over 600: 37%; SAT math scores over 600: 35%; ACT scores over 24: 50%; SAT evidence-based reading and writing scores over 700: 4%; SAT math scores over 700: 4%; ACT scores over 30: 4%.

Retention: 78% of full-time freshmen returned.

FACULTY

Total: 650, 40% full-time, 61% with terminal degrees.
Student/faculty ratio: 14:1.

ACADEMICS

Calendar: semesters. *Degrees:* associate, bachelor's, master's, doctoral, post-master's, and postbachelor's certificates.

Special study options: academic remediation for entering students, accelerated degree program, advanced placement credit, cooperative education, distance learning, double majors, English as a second language, freshman honors college, honors programs, independent study, internships, part-time degree program, services for LD students, student-designed majors, study abroad, summer session for credit. *ROTC:* Army (c).

Unusual degree programs: 3-2 business administration; accountancy, arts management, criminal justice, digital game design & development, health care administration, information systems, information management & technology, nutrition, political science, public administration.

Computers: 600 computers/terminals are available on campus for general student use. Students can access the following: campus intranet, computer help desk, free student e-mail accounts, online (class) grades, online (class) registration, online (class) schedules. Campuswide network is available. 100% of college-owned or -operated housing units are wired for high-speed Internet access. Wireless service is available via entire campus.

Library: B. Davis Schwartz Memorial Library. *Books:* 459,336 (physical), 203,430 (digital/electronic); *Serial titles:* 482 (physical), 466,233 (digital/electronic); *Databases:* 478.

STUDENT LIFE

Housing options: coed, special housing for students with disabilities. Campus housing is university owned. Freshman campus housing is guaranteed.

Activities and organizations: drama/theater group, student-run newspaper, radio and television station, choral group, marching band, Student Government Association, Student Activities Board, Resident Student Association, Commuter Student Association, Greek Programming Board, national fraternities, national sororities.

Athletics Member NCAA. All Division II. *Intercollegiate sports:* baseball M(s), basketball M(s)/W(s), bowling W(s), crew M(c)/W(c), cross-country running M(s)/W(s), equestrian sports W(s), fencing W, field hockey W(s), football M(s), golf W, ice hockey M(c), lacrosse M(s)/W(s), rugby W, soccer M(s)/W(s), softball W(s), swimming and diving W(s), tennis W(s), track and field M/W, volleyball W(s), wrestling M(s). *Intramural sports:* badminton M(c)/W(c), baseball M(c), basketball M(c)/W(c), cheerleading M(c)/W(c), equestrian sports M(c)/W(c), football M(c)/W(c), racquetball M(c)/W(c), soccer M(c)/W(c), softball M(c)/W(c), ultimate Frisbee M(c)/W(c), weight lifting M(c)/W(c).

Campus security: 24-hour emergency response devices and patrols, student patrols, late-night transport/escort service, controlled dormitory access, lighted pathways/sidewalks.

Student services: health clinic, personal/psychological counseling.

COSTS & FINANCIAL AID

Costs (2017–18) *Comprehensive fee:* $50,698 includes full-time tuition ($35,038), mandatory fees ($1940), and room and board ($13,720). Part-time tuition: $1093 per credit. *Required fees:* $460 per term part-time. *Room and board:* Room and board charges vary according to board plan and housing facility. *Payment plan:* installment. *Waivers:* employees or children of employees.

Financial Aid Of all full-time matriculated undergraduates who enrolled in 2017, 2,391 applied for aid, 2,063 were judged to have need, 84 had their need fully met. 535 Federal Work-Study jobs (averaging $2255). In 2017, 268 non-need-based awards were made. *Average percent of need*

met: 62. *Average financial aid package:* $24,166. *Average need-based loan:* $3097. *Average need-based gift aid:* $6177. *Average non-need-based aid:* $15,714. *Average indebtedness upon graduation:* $36,533.

APPLYING

Standardized Tests *Required:* SAT or ACT (for admission).
Options: electronic application, early action, deferred entrance.
Application fee: $50.
Required: essay or personal statement, high school transcript, 1 letter of recommendation. *Required for some:* interview.
Application deadlines: rolling (freshmen), rolling (transfers), 12/1 (early action).
Notification: continuous (freshmen), continuous (transfers), 12/31 (early action).

CONTACT

Ms. Anne Marie Caradonna, Director of Admissions Operations, Long Island University–LIU Post, 720 Northern Boulevard, Brookville, NY 11548-1300. *Phone:* 516-299-2900. *Toll-free phone:* 800-LIU-PLAN. *Fax:* 516-299-2137. *E-mail:* post-enroll@liu.edu.

Machzikei Hadath Rabbinical College
Brooklyn, New York

CONTACT
Rabbi Abraham M. Lezerowitz, Director of Admissions, Machzikei Hadath Rabbinical College, 5407 Sixteenth Avenue, Brooklyn, NY 11204-1805. *Phone:* 718-854-8777.

★ Manhattan College
Riverdale, New York
http://www.manhattan.edu/

- **Independent** comprehensive, founded 1853, affiliated with Roman Catholic Church
- **Urban** 31-acre campus with easy access to New York City
- **Endowment** $89.8 million
- **Coed** 3,664 undergraduate students, 95% full-time, 45% women, 55% men
- **Moderately difficult** entrance level, 67% of applicants were admitted

UNDERGRAD STUDENTS

3,479 full-time, 185 part-time. 31% are from out of state; 5% Black or African American, non-Hispanic/Latino; 22% Hispanic/Latino; 5% Asian, non-Hispanic/Latino; 0.1% American Indian or Alaska Native, non-Hispanic/Latino; 2% Two or more races, non-Hispanic/Latino; 8% Race/ethnicity unknown; 3% international; 5% transferred in; 67% live on campus.

Freshmen:

Admission: 8,313 applied, 5,557 admitted, 765 enrolled. *Average high school GPA:* 3.4. *Test scores:* SAT evidence-based reading and writing scores over 500: 89%; SAT math scores over 500: 85%; ACT scores over 18: 99%; SAT evidence-based reading and writing scores over 600: 42%; SAT math scores over 600: 36%; ACT scores over 24: 69%; SAT evidence-based reading and writing scores over 700: 3%; SAT math scores over 700: 3%; ACT scores over 30: 13%.

Retention: 89% of full-time freshmen returned.

FACULTY

Total: 436, 55% full-time, 75% with terminal degrees.
Student/faculty ratio: 13:1.

ACADEMICS

Calendar: semesters. *Degrees:* bachelor's, master's, and post-master's certificates.

Special study options: accelerated degree program, adult/continuing education programs, advanced placement credit, cooperative education, distance learning, double majors, English as a second language, honors programs, independent study, internships, off-campus study, part-time degree program, services for LD students, student-designed majors, study abroad, summer session for credit. *ROTC:* Army (c), Air Force (b).

Unusual degree programs: 3-2 business administration; engineering; education.

Computers: 450 computers/terminals and 3,000 ports are available on campus for general student use. Students can access the following: campus intranet, computer help desk, free student e-mail accounts, online (class) grades, online (class) registration, online (class) schedules, course management system, degree audit/planning tool, campus card access. Campuswide network is available. 100% of college-owned or -operated housing units are wired for high-speed Internet access. Wireless service is available via entire campus.

Library: Mary Alice and Tom OMalley Library. *Books:* 259,987 (physical), 191,706 (digital/electronic); *Serial titles:* 379 (physical), 186,500 (digital/electronic). Weekly public service hours: 168; study areas open 24 hours, 5–7 days a week.

STUDENT LIFE

Housing options: men-only, women-only, special housing for students with disabilities. Campus housing is university owned. Freshman campus housing is guaranteed.

Activities and organizations: drama/theater group, student-run newspaper, choral group, Society of Hispanic Professional Engineers, Singers, Student Government, Social Life Commission, Manhattan College Players (Theater/Drama group), national fraternities, national sororities.

Athletics Member NCAA. All Division I. *Intercollegiate sports:* baseball M(s), basketball M(s)/W(s), cheerleading W, crew M(c)/W, cross-country running M(s)/W(s), golf M(s), lacrosse M(s)/W(s), rugby M(c), soccer M(s)/W(s), softball W(s), swimming and diving M(s)/W(s), track and field M(s)/W(s), volleyball W(s). *Intramural sports:* baseball M, basketball M/W, cheerleading M/W, cross-country running M/W, football M/W, soccer M/W, softball M/W, swimming and diving W, track and field M/W, volleyball M/W.

Campus security: 24-hour emergency response devices and patrols, late-night transport/escort service, controlled dormitory access.

Student services: health clinic, personal/psychological counseling.

COSTS & FINANCIAL AID

Costs (2017–18) *Comprehensive fee:* $57,687 includes full-time tuition ($38,200), mandatory fees ($3887), and room and board ($15,600). Full-time tuition and fees vary according to course load, program, and student level. Part-time tuition: $980 per credit. Part-time tuition and fees vary according to course load. *Room and board:* Room and board charges vary according to board plan. *Payment plans:* installment, deferred payment. *Waivers:* employees or children of employees.

Financial Aid Of all full-time matriculated undergraduates who enrolled in 2016, 2,997 applied for aid, 2,693 were judged to have need. In 2016, 807 non-need-based awards were made. *Average percent of need met:* 65. *Average financial aid package:* $25,262. *Average need-based gift aid:* $17,892. *Average non-need-based aid:* $6585. *Average indebtedness upon graduation:* $39,443.

APPLYING

Standardized Tests *Required:* SAT (for admission), ACT (for admission), SAT or ACT (for admission).

Options: electronic application, early admission, early decision, deferred entrance.

Application fee: $60.

Required: essay or personal statement, high school transcript, minimum 2.5 GPA, 1 letter of recommendation. *Required for some:* interview. *Recommended:* minimum 3.0 GPA, interview.

Application deadlines: 4/15 (freshmen), 7/1 (transfers).

Early decision deadline: 11/15.

Notification: continuous until 4/15 (freshmen), continuous until 8/15 (transfers), 12/1 (early decision).

CONTACT

Dr. William Bisset, Vice President for Enrollment Management, Manhattan College, 4513 Manhattan College Parkway, Riverdale, NY 10471. *Phone:* 718-862-7200. *Toll-free phone:* 800-622-9235. *Fax:* 718-862-8019. *E-mail:* admit@manhattan.edu.

See below for display ad and page 1336 for the College Close-Up.

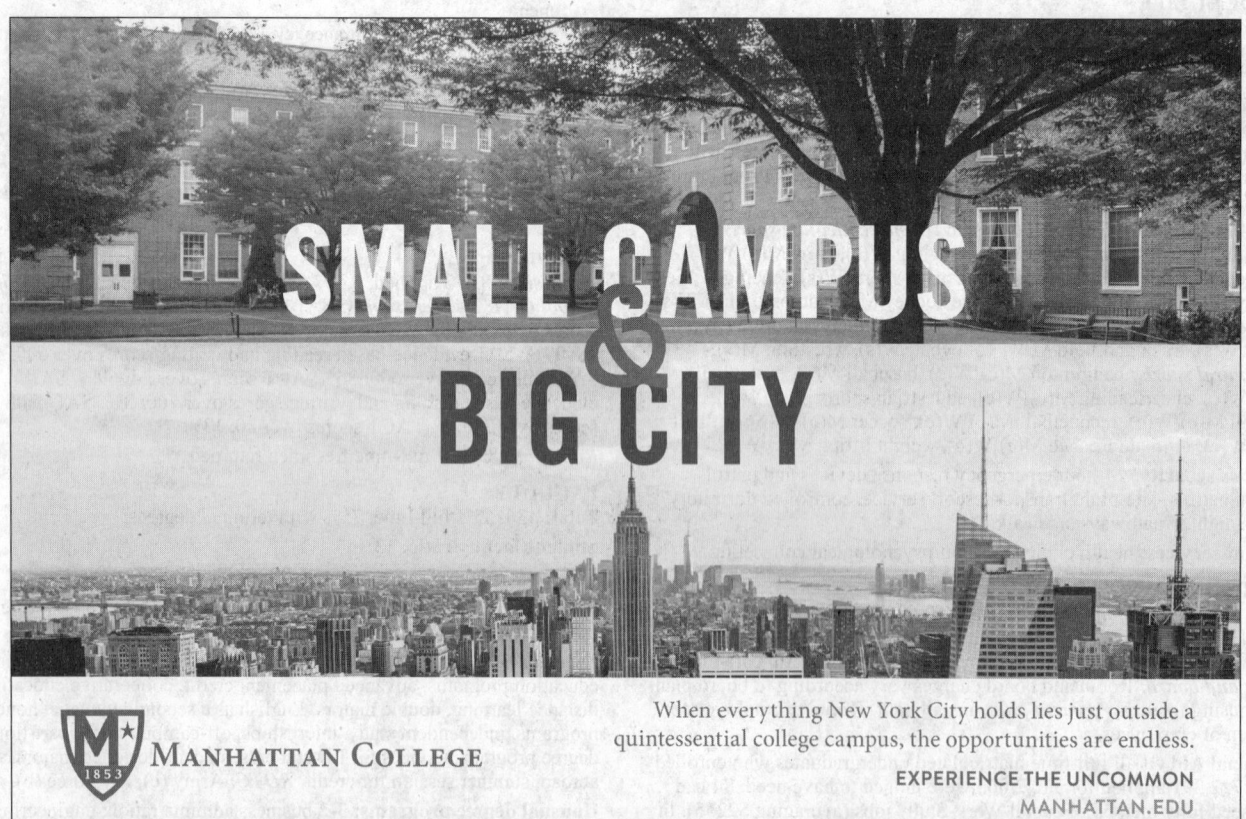

Manhattan School of Music

New York, New York

http://www.msmnyc.edu/

CONTACT
Ms. Amy Anderson, Dean of Enrollment Management, Manhattan School of Music, 120 Claremont Avenue, New York, NY 10027-4698. *Phone:* 917-493-4501. *Fax:* 212-749-3025. *E-mail:* aanderson@msmnyc.edu.

Manhattanville College

Purchase, New York

http://www.mville.edu/

- **Independent** comprehensive, founded 1841
- **Suburban** 100-acre campus with easy access to New York City
- **Endowment** $29.6 million
- **Coed** 1,725 undergraduate students, 95% full-time, 63% women, 37% men
- **Moderately difficult** entrance level, 82% of applicants were admitted

UNDERGRAD STUDENTS
1,633 full-time, 92 part-time. Students come from 34 states and territories; 47 other countries; 27% are from out of state; 9% Black or African American, non-Hispanic/Latino; 25% Hispanic/Latino; 2% Asian, non-Hispanic/Latino; 0.5% Native Hawaiian or other Pacific Islander, non-Hispanic/Latino; 0.2% American Indian or Alaska Native, non-Hispanic/Latino; 2% Two or more races, non-Hispanic/Latino; 7% Race/ethnicity unknown; 7% international; 3% transferred in; 60% live on campus.

Freshmen:
Admission: 3,841 applied, 3,152 admitted, 416 enrolled. *Average high school GPA:* 3.1. *Test scores:* SAT math scores over 500: 67%; ACT scores over 18: 84%; SAT math scores over 600: 17%; ACT scores over 24: 42%; SAT math scores over 700: 1%; ACT scores over 30: 2%.
Retention: 74% of full-time freshmen returned.

FACULTY
Total: 384, 31% full-time, 51% with terminal degrees.
Student/faculty ratio: 11:1.

ACADEMICS
Calendar: semesters. *Degrees:* bachelor's, master's, doctoral, and post-master's certificates.
Special study options: accelerated degree program, adult/continuing education programs, advanced placement credit, double majors, honors programs, independent study, internships, off-campus study, part-time degree program, services for LD students, student-designed majors, study abroad, summer session for credit.
Unusual degree programs: business administration; education.
Computers: 125 computers/terminals are available on campus for general student use. Students can access the following: campus intranet, computer help desk, free student e-mail accounts, online (class) grades, online (class) registration, online (class) schedules, Mobile Apps. Campuswide network is available. 100% of college-owned or -operated housing units are wired for high-speed Internet access. Wireless service is available via entire campus.
Library: Manhattanville College Library. *Books:* 229,036 (physical), 177,644 (digital/electronic); *Serial titles:* 927 (physical), 59,881 (digital/electronic); *Databases:* 118. Weekly public service hours: 108; study areas open 24 hours, 5–7 days a week.

STUDENT LIFE
Housing options: coed, special housing for students with disabilities. Campus housing is university owned. Freshman campus housing is guaranteed.
Activities and organizations: drama/theater group, student-run newspaper, radio station, choral group, Women's Rugby, Minds in Motion (MiMo), Manhattanville Dance Ensemble (MDE), Latin Fusion, Touchstone Newspaper.
Athletics Member NCAA. All Division III. *Intercollegiate sports:* baseball M, basketball M/W, cross-country running M/W, field hockey W, golf M/W, ice hockey M/W, lacrosse M/W, soccer M/W, softball W, track and field M/W, volleyball W.

Campus security: 24-hour emergency response devices and patrols, late-night transport/escort service, controlled dormitory access, officer at the main campus gate 24/7, emergency notification system, seminars on campus safety and security practices.
Student services: health clinic, personal/psychological counseling.

COSTS & FINANCIAL AID
Costs (2018–19) *Comprehensive fee:* $53,340 includes full-time tuition ($37,370), mandatory fees ($1450), and room and board ($14,520). Full-time tuition and fees vary according to course load. Part-time tuition: $845 per credit hour. Part-time tuition and fees vary according to course load and program. *Required fees:* $60 per course part-time. *College room only:* $8680. Room and board charges vary according to board plan. *Payment plan:* installment. *Waivers:* children of alumni and employees or children of employees.
Financial Aid Of all full-time matriculated undergraduates who enrolled in 2017, 1,316 applied for aid, 1,220 were judged to have need, 143 had their need fully met. 535 Federal Work-Study jobs (averaging $1665). In 2017, 385 non-need-based awards were made. *Average percent of need met:* 70. *Average financial aid package:* $28,326. *Average need-based loan:* $4619. *Average need-based gift aid:* $5526. *Average non-need-based aid:* $18,648. *Average indebtedness upon graduation:* $33,850.

APPLYING
Standardized Tests *Recommended:* SAT (for admission), ACT (for admission), SAT or ACT (for admission).
Options: electronic application, early action, deferred entrance.
Application fee: $50.
Required: essay or personal statement, high school transcript, minimum 2.5 GPA, 2 letters of recommendation. *Required for some:* interview.
Application deadlines: rolling (freshmen), rolling (out-of-state freshmen), rolling (transfers), 12/1 (early action).
Notification: continuous (freshmen), continuous (out-of-state freshmen), continuous (transfers), 12/20 (early action).

CONTACT
Mr. Joseph Cosentino, Director of Admissions, Undergraduate Admissions, Manhattanville College, 2900 Purchase Street, Purchase, NY 10577. *Phone:* 914-323-5125. *Toll-free phone:* 800-328-4553. *Fax:* 914-694-1732. *E-mail:* Joseph.Cosentino@mville.edu.

Maria College

Albany, New York

http://www.mariacollege.edu/

- **Independent** 4-year, founded 1958
- **Urban** 9-acre campus
- **Coed** 849 undergraduate students, 29% full-time, 86% women, 14% men
- **Minimally difficult** entrance level, 44% of applicants were admitted

UNDERGRAD STUDENTS
245 full-time, 604 part-time. Students come from 9 states and territories; 1 other country; 3% are from out of state; 10% Black or African American, non-Hispanic/Latino; 4% Hispanic/Latino; 4% Asian, non-Hispanic/Latino; 0.1% Native Hawaiian or other Pacific Islander, non-Hispanic/Latino; 1% Two or more races, non-Hispanic/Latino; 26% Race/ethnicity unknown; 16% transferred in.

Freshmen:
Admission: 265 applied, 116 admitted, 41 enrolled. *Average high school GPA:* 2.5. *Test scores:* ACT scores over 18: 83%; ACT scores over 24: 33%.
Retention: 68% of full-time freshmen returned.

FACULTY
Total: 72, 42% full-time, 15% with terminal degrees.
Student/faculty ratio: 10:1.

ACADEMICS
Calendar: semesters. *Degrees:* certificates, associate, and bachelor's.
Special study options: adult/continuing education programs, advanced placement credit, cooperative education, distance learning, English as a second language, honors programs, independent study, internships, off-campus study, part-time degree program, services for LD students, summer session for credit.

Application fee: $50.

Required: essay or personal statement, high school transcript, 2 letters of recommendation.

Application deadlines: 2/1 (freshmen), 6/1 (transfers), 11/15 (early action).

Early decision deadline: 11/15 (for plan 1), 2/1 (for plan 2).

Notification: continuous until 4/1 (freshmen), continuous (transfers), 12/15 (early decision plan 1), 2/15 (early decision plan 2), 1/15 (early action).

CONTACT
Mr. Kent Rinehart, Dean of Undergraduate Admissions, Marist College, 3399 North Road, Poughkeepsie, NY 12601. *Phone:* 845-575-3226. *Toll-free phone:* 800-436-5483. *Fax:* 845-575-3215. *E-mail:* admission@marist.edu.

Marymount Manhattan College

New York, New York

http://www.mmm.edu/

- **Independent** 4-year, founded 1936
- **Urban** campus
- **Endowment** $19.8 million
- **Coed** 2,150 undergraduate students, 89% full-time, 77% women, 23% men
- **Moderately difficult** entrance level, 79% of applicants were admitted

UNDERGRAD STUDENTS
1,915 full-time, 235 part-time. Students come from 49 states and territories; 44 other countries; 60% are from out of state; 8% Black or African American, non-Hispanic/Latino; 16% Hispanic/Latino; 3% Asian, non-Hispanic/Latino; 0.1% Native Hawaiian or other Pacific Islander, non-Hispanic/Latino; 0.3% American Indian or Alaska Native, non-Hispanic/Latino; 4% Two or more races, non-Hispanic/Latino; 7% Race/ethnicity unknown; 4% international; 5% transferred in; 35% live on campus.

Freshmen:
Admission: 5,532 applied, 4,363 admitted, 546 enrolled. *Average high school GPA:* 3.4. *Test scores:* SAT evidence-based reading and writing scores over 500: 51%; SAT math scores over 500: 58%; ACT scores over 18: 96%; SAT evidence-based reading and writing scores over 600: 23%; SAT math scores over 600: 28%; ACT scores over 24: 59%; SAT evidence-based reading and writing scores over 700: 4%; SAT math scores over 700: 9%; ACT scores over 30: 15%.
Retention: 76% of full-time freshmen returned.

FACULTY
Total: 369, 25% full-time.
Student/faculty ratio: 11:1.

ACADEMICS
Calendar: semesters plus summer and January mini-semesters. *Degrees:* associate and bachelor's.

Special study options: academic remediation for entering students, accelerated degree program, adult/continuing education programs, advanced placement credit, distance learning, double majors, honors programs, independent study, internships, off-campus study, part-time degree program, services for LD students, student-designed majors, study abroad, summer session for credit.

Computers: 120 computers/terminals are available on campus for general student use. Students can access the following: campus intranet, computer help desk, free student e-mail accounts, online (class) grades, online (class) registration, online (class) schedules, online payments, direct deposits. Campuswide network is available. 100% of college-owned or -operated housing units are wired for high-speed Internet access. Wireless service is available via entire campus.
Library: Thomas J. Shanahan Library. *Books:* 48,966 (physical), 108,552 (digital/electronic); *Serial titles:* 40,105 (physical), 40,105 (digital/electronic); *Databases:* 52. Weekly public service hours: 80.

STUDENT LIFE
Housing options: coed, men-only, women-only. Campus housing is university owned and leased by the school. Freshman applicants given priority for college housing.

Activities and organizations: drama/theater group, student-run newspaper, radio station, choral group, Student Government Association (SGA), Black and Latino Student Association (BLSA), The Monitor-Student Newspaper, Musical Theater Association (MTA), Christian Fellowship.

Campus security: 24-hour emergency response devices and patrols, student patrols, 24-hour security in residence halls.

Student services: health clinic, personal/psychological counseling.

COSTS & FINANCIAL AID
Costs (2018–19) *Comprehensive fee:* $50,610 includes full-time tuition ($32,210), mandatory fees ($1568), and room and board ($16,832). Full-time tuition and fees vary according to course load and program. Part-time tuition: $1075 per credit hour. Part-time tuition and fees vary according to course load and program. *Required fees:* $571 per term part-time. *College room only:* $14,832. Room and board charges vary according to board plan. *Payment plan:* installment. *Waivers:* senior citizens and employees or children of employees.

Financial Aid Of all full-time matriculated undergraduates who enrolled in 2016, 1,445 applied for aid, 1,260 were judged to have need, 109 had their need fully met. 123 Federal Work-Study jobs (averaging $3139). In 2016, 158 non-need-based awards were made. *Average percent of need met:* 54. *Average financial aid package:* $17,829. *Average need-based loan:* $4152. *Average need-based gift aid:* $14,526. *Average non-need-based aid:* $9243. *Average indebtedness upon graduation:* $26,742.

APPLYING
Standardized Tests *Required:* SAT or ACT (for admission).

Options: electronic application, deferred entrance.

Application fee: $60.

Required: essay or personal statement, high school transcript, 2 letters of recommendation. *Required for some:* interview.

Application deadlines: rolling (freshmen), rolling (out-of-state freshmen), rolling (transfers).

Notification: continuous (freshmen), continuous (out-of-state freshmen), continuous (transfers).

CONTACT
Jim Rogers, Dean of Admissions, Marymount Manhattan College, 221 East 71st Street, New York, NY 10021. *Phone:* 212-517-0430. *Toll-free phone:* 800-627-9668. *E-mail:* jrogers@mmm.edu.

Medaille College

Buffalo, New York

http://www.medaille.edu/

CONTACT
Christopher LaRusso, Vice President for Enrollment Management and Undergraduate Admissions, Medaille College, Office of Admissions, Buffalo, NY 14214. *Phone:* 716-880-2200. *Toll-free phone:* 800-292-1582. *Fax:* 716-880-2007. *E-mail:* admissionsug@medaille.edu.

Medgar Evers College of the City University of New York

Brooklyn, New York

http://www.mec.cuny.edu/

- **State and locally supported** 4-year, founded 1969, part of City University of New York System
- **Urban** 8-acre campus
- **Endowment** $515,142
- **Coed** 6,652 undergraduate students, 72% full-time, 72% women, 28% men
- **Noncompetitive** entrance level, 100% of applicants were admitted

UNDERGRAD STUDENTS
4,806 full-time, 1,846 part-time. Students come from 7 states and territories; 77 other countries; 1% are from out of state; 59% Black or African American, non-Hispanic/Latino; 14% Hispanic/Latino; 2% Asian, non-Hispanic/Latino; 0.3% American Indian or Alaska Native, non-Hispanic/Latino; 22% Race/ethnicity unknown; 0.8% international.

Freshmen:
Admission: 10,834 applied, 10,834 admitted, 1,186 enrolled. *Test scores:* SAT evidence-based reading and writing scores over 500: 14%; SAT math scores over 500: 6%.

FACULTY
Total: 534, 35% full-time, 40% with terminal degrees.
Student/faculty ratio: 18:1.

ACADEMICS
Calendar: semesters. *Degrees:* certificates, associate, and bachelor's.
Special study options: academic remediation for entering students, adult/continuing education programs, advanced placement credit, cooperative education, double majors, English as a second language, external degree program, honors programs, independent study, internships, off-campus study, part-time degree program, services for LD students, study abroad, summer session for credit.
Computers: 120 computers/terminals are available on campus for general student use. Students can access the following: free student e-mail accounts, online (class) grades, online (class) registration, online (class) schedules. Campuswide network is available. Wireless service is available via entire campus.
Library: Charles Evans Inniss Memorial Library plus 1 other.

STUDENT LIFE
Housing options: college housing not available.
Activities and organizations: drama/theater group, student-run newspaper, radio and television station, choral group, American Marketing Association, Drama Students Association, Rising Stars, Medgar Evers College Society of Public Administrators, National Society of Black Accountants.
Athletics Member NCAA. All Division III. *Intercollegiate sports:* basketball M/W, cross-country running M/W, soccer M/W, tennis W, track and field M/W, volleyball M/W. *Intramural sports:* basketball M/W, tennis W.
Campus security: 24-hour patrols.
Student services: women's center, legal services.

COSTS & FINANCIAL AID
Costs (2018–19) *Tuition:* state resident $6330 full-time, $275 per credit part-time; nonresident $16,800 full-time, $560 per credit part-time. Full-time tuition and fees vary according to course load. Part-time tuition and fees vary according to course load. *Required fees:* $320 full-time, $101 per term part-time. *Payment plans:* installment, deferred payment.
Financial Aid Of all full-time matriculated undergraduates who enrolled in 2016, 4,072 applied for aid, 4,072 were judged to have need. *Average financial aid package:* $9212. *Average need-based gift aid:* $7867. *Average non-need-based aid:* $3034.

APPLYING
Standardized Tests *Recommended:* SAT and SAT Subject Tests or ACT (for admission).
Options: electronic application, deferred entrance.
Application fee: $65.
Required: high school transcript.
Application deadlines: rolling (freshmen), rolling (transfers).
Notification: continuous (freshmen), continuous (transfers).

CONTACT
Dr. Shannon Clarke-Anderson, Director of Admissions, Medgar Evers College of the City University of New York, 1650 Bedford Avenue, Brooklyn, NY 11225. *Phone:* 718-270-5143. *Fax:* 718-270-6411. *E-mail:* shannon@mec.cuny.edu.

Mercy College
Dobbs Ferry, New York
http://www.mercy.edu/

- **Independent** comprehensive, founded 1951, affiliated with Roman Catholic Church
- **Suburban** 66-acre campus with easy access to New York City
- **Endowment** $224.4 million
- **Coed** 6,864 undergraduate students, 74% full-time, 66% women, 34% men
- **Moderately difficult** entrance level, 79% of applicants were admitted

UNDERGRAD STUDENTS
5,055 full-time, 1,809 part-time. Students come from 36 states and territories; 48 other countries; 8% are from out of state; 22% Black or African American, non-Hispanic/Latino; 39% Hispanic/Latino; 4% Asian, non-Hispanic/Latino; 0.3% Native Hawaiian or other Pacific Islander, non-Hispanic/Latino; 0.3% American Indian or Alaska Native, non-Hispanic/Latino; 2% Two or more races, non-Hispanic/Latino; 7% Race/ethnicity unknown; 1% international; 10% transferred in; 11% live on campus.

Freshmen:
Admission: 6,901 applied, 5,433 admitted, 910 enrolled. *Average high school GPA:* 3.4.
Retention: 73% of full-time freshmen returned.

FACULTY
Total: 944, 22% full-time, 18% with terminal degrees.
Student/faculty ratio: 16:1.

ACADEMICS
Calendar: semesters. *Degrees:* certificates, associate, bachelor's, master's, doctoral, post-master's, and postbachelor's certificates.
Special study options: accelerated degree program, adult/continuing education programs, advanced placement credit, cooperative education, distance learning, double majors, freshman honors college, honors programs, independent study, internships, off-campus study, part-time degree program, services for LD students, study abroad, summer session for credit. *ROTC:* Army (c), Air Force (c).
Unusual degree programs: 3-2 business administration; education, cybersecurity.
Computers: 1,100 computers/terminals and 300 ports are available on campus for general student use. Students can access the following: campus intranet, computer help desk, free student e-mail accounts, online (class) grades, online (class) registration, online (class) schedules. Campuswide network is available. 100% of college-owned or -operated housing units are wired for high-speed Internet access. Wireless service is available via entire campus.
Library: Mercy College Library plus 3 others. *Books:* 85,689 (digital/electronic); *Serial titles:* 21,126 (digital/electronic). Students can reserve study rooms.

STUDENT LIFE
Housing options: coed, special housing for students with disabilities. Campus housing is university owned and leased by the school. Freshman applicants given priority for college housing.
Activities and organizations: student-run newspaper, choral group, Model United Nations, Honors Club and 17 National Honor Societies, Mercy Gives Back, Maverick Society, ROTARACT Club for Community Volunteer Service.
Athletics Member NCAA. All Division II. *Intercollegiate sports:* baseball M(s), basketball M(s)/W(s), field hockey W(s), lacrosse M(s)/W(s), soccer M(s)/W(s), softball W(s), volleyball W(s). *Intramural sports:* baseball M, basketball M/W, softball W.
Campus security: 24-hour emergency response devices and patrols, late-night transport/escort service, controlled dormitory access.
Student services: health clinic, personal/psychological counseling.

COSTS & FINANCIAL AID
Costs (2017–18) *Comprehensive fee:* $32,613 includes full-time tuition ($18,083), mandatory fees ($630), and room and board ($13,900). Full-time tuition and fees vary according to course load. Part-time tuition: $761 per credit. Part-time tuition and fees vary according to course load. *Required fees:* $158 per term part-time. *College room only:* $9350. Room

and board charges vary according to board plan. **Payment plans:** installment, deferred payment. **Waivers:** senior citizens and employees or children of employees.

Financial Aid Of all full-time matriculated undergraduates who enrolled in 2016, 4,577 applied for aid, 4,322 were judged to have need, 80 had their need fully met. In 2016, 118 non-need-based awards were made. **Average percent of need met:** 50. **Average financial aid package:** $13,811. **Average need-based loan:** $4040. **Average need-based gift aid:** $10,218. **Average non-need-based aid:** $4684. **Average indebtedness upon graduation:** $30,258.

APPLYING

Options: electronic application, early action, deferred entrance.

Application fee: $40.

Required: high school transcript, minimum 2.5 GPA, 1 letter of recommendation. **Required for some:** essay or personal statement, interview. **Recommended:** interview.

Application deadlines: rolling (freshmen), rolling (transfers), 12/1 (early action).

Notification: continuous (freshmen), continuous (transfers), 1/2 (early action).

CONTACT

Mrs. Tara Fay-Reilly, Senior Director of Admissions, Mercy College, 555 Broadway, Dobbs Ferry, NY 10522-1189. *Phone:* 877-637-2946. *Toll-free phone:* 877-637-2946 (in-state); 877-MERCY-GO (out-of-state). *Fax:* 914-674-7382. *E-mail:* admissions@mercy.edu.

Mesivta of Eastern Parkway–Yeshiva Zichron Meilech
Brooklyn, New York

CONTACT

Mesivta of Eastern Parkway–Yeshiva Zichron Meilech, 510 Dahill Road, Brooklyn, NY 11218-5559. *Phone:* 718-438-1002.

Mesivta Torah Vodaath Rabbinical Seminary
Brooklyn, New York
http://www.torahvodaath.org/

CONTACT

Rabbi Issac Braun, Administrator, Mesivta Torah Vodaath Rabbinical Seminary, 425 East Ninth Street, Brooklyn, NY 11218-5299. *Phone:* 718-941-8000.

Mesivtha Tifereth Jerusalem of America
New York, New York

CONTACT

Rabbi Fishellis, Director of Admissions, Mesivtha Tifereth Jerusalem of America, 145 East Broadway, New York, NY 10002-6301. *Phone:* 212-964-2830.

Metropolitan College of New York
New York, New York
http://www.mcny.edu/
- **Independent** comprehensive, founded 1964
- **Urban** campus
- **Coed** 777 undergraduate students, 88% full-time, 70% women, 30% men
- **Moderately difficult** entrance level, 91% of applicants were admitted

UNDERGRAD STUDENTS

681 full-time, 96 part-time. Students come from 11 states and territories; 4% are from out of state; 55% Black or African American, non-Hispanic/Latino; 29% Hispanic/Latino; 3% Asian, non-Hispanic/Latino; 0.3% Native Hawaiian or other Pacific Islander, non-Hispanic/Latino; 0.6% American Indian or Alaska Native, non-Hispanic/Latino; 3% Two or more races, non-Hispanic/Latino; 5% Race/ethnicity unknown; 1% international; 29% transferred in.

Freshmen:
Admission: 126 applied, 115 admitted, 99 enrolled. **Average high school GPA:** 2.1.
Retention: 47% of full-time freshmen returned.

FACULTY
Total: 224, 10% full-time.
Student/faculty ratio: 11:1.

ACADEMICS
Calendar: 3 15-week semesters. *Degrees:* certificates, associate, bachelor's, and master's.

Special study options: academic remediation for entering students, accelerated degree program, adult/continuing education programs, cooperative education, distance learning, English as a second language, honors programs, independent study, internships, part-time degree program, services for LD students, study abroad, summer session for credit.

Computers: 120 computers/terminals are available on campus for general student use. Students can access the following: free student e-mail accounts, online (class) grades, online (class) registration, online (class) schedules. Campuswide network is available. Wireless service is available via entire campus.
Library: Main Library plus 1 other. *Books:* 26,191 (physical), 156,497 (digital/electronic); *Serial titles:* 29,206 (digital/electronic); *Databases:* 91. Weekly public service hours: 72.

STUDENT LIFE
Housing options: college housing not available.

Activities and organizations: student-run newspaper, Student Government, Student Newsletter, Networking Club, Yearbook Committee.

Campus security: 24-hour patrols.

Student services: personal/psychological counseling.

COSTS & FINANCIAL AID
Costs (2017–18) *Tuition:* $18,330 full-time, $766 per credit part-time. Full-time tuition and fees vary according to degree level and program. Part-time tuition and fees vary according to degree level and program. No tuition increase for student's term of enrollment. **Required fees:** $850 full-time. **Payment plans:** installment, deferred payment. **Waivers:** employees or children of employees.

Financial Aid Of all full-time matriculated undergraduates who enrolled in 2017, 638 applied for aid, 635 were judged to have need, 4 had their need fully met. In 2017, 16 non-need-based awards were made. **Average percent of need met:** 46. **Average financial aid package:** $17,286. **Average need-based loan:** $4917. **Average need-based gift aid:** $12,710. **Average non-need-based aid:** $2931.

APPLYING
Standardized Tests *Required for some:* ACCUPLACER. *Recommended:* SAT or ACT (for admission).

Options: electronic application, deferred entrance.

Application fee: $30.

Required: high school transcript, 2 letters of recommendation, interview. *Recommended:* essay or personal statement, minimum 3.0 GPA.

Application deadlines: 9/9 (freshmen), rolling (transfers).

Notification: continuous (freshmen), continuous (transfers).

CONTACT
Metropolitan College of New York, 60 West Street, New York, NY 10006. *Phone:* 212-343-1234 Ext. 2700. *Toll-free phone:* 800-33-THINK Ext. 5001. *Fax:* 212-343-8470.

Mirrer Yeshiva Central Institute
Brooklyn, New York

CONTACT
Director of Admissions, Mirrer Yeshiva Central Institute, 1791 Ocean Parkway, Brooklyn, NY 11223-2010. *Phone:* 718-645-0536.

★ Molloy College
Rockville Centre, New York
http://www.molloy.edu/

- **Independent** comprehensive, founded 1955
- **Suburban** 30-acre campus with easy access to New York City
- **Endowment** $36.1 million
- **Coed** 3,534 undergraduate students, 79% full-time, 75% women, 25% men
- **Moderately difficult** entrance level, 76% of applicants were admitted

UNDERGRAD STUDENTS
2,800 full-time, 734 part-time. Students come from 31 states and territories; 10 other countries; 4% are from out of state; 11% Black or African American, non-Hispanic/Latino; 17% Hispanic/Latino; 8% Asian, non-Hispanic/Latino; 0.2% Native Hawaiian or other Pacific Islander, non-Hispanic/Latino; 0.4% American Indian or Alaska Native, non-Hispanic/Latino; 2% Two or more races, non-Hispanic/Latino; 1% Race/ethnicity unknown; 0.4% international; 10% transferred in; 8% live on campus.

Freshmen:
Admission: 4,188 applied, 3,184 admitted, 514 enrolled. *Average high school GPA:* 3.0. *Test scores:* SAT evidence-based reading and writing scores over 500: 93%; SAT math scores over 500: 94%; ACT scores over 18: 100%; SAT evidence-based reading and writing scores over 600: 35%; SAT math scores over 600: 33%; ACT scores over 24: 50%; SAT evidence-based reading and writing scores over 700: 2%; SAT math scores over 700: 3%; ACT scores over 30: 9%.
Retention: 88% of full-time freshmen returned.

FACULTY
Total: 720, 27% full-time, 36% with terminal degrees.
Student/faculty ratio: 10:1.

ACADEMICS
Calendar: 4-1-4. *Degrees:* associate, bachelor's, master's, doctoral, post-master's, and postbachelor's certificates.

Special study options: academic remediation for entering students, accelerated degree program, adult/continuing education programs, advanced placement credit, distance learning, double majors, English as a second language, honors programs, independent study, internships, part-time degree program, services for LD students, student-designed majors, study abroad, summer session for credit. *ROTC:* Army (c), Navy (c).

Computers: 784 computers/terminals are available on campus for general student use. Students can access the following: computer help desk, free student e-mail accounts, online (class) grades, online (class) registration, online (class) schedules. Campuswide network is available. 100% of college-owned or -operated housing units are wired for high-speed Internet access. Wireless service is available via entire campus.
Library: James Edward Tobin Library plus 1 other. *Books:* 43,968 (physical), 262,675 (digital/electronic); *Serial titles:* 48 (physical), 67,340 (digital/electronic); *Databases:* 183.

STUDENT LIFE
Housing options: coed. Campus housing is university owned. Freshman applicants given priority for college housing.

Activities and organizations: drama/theater group, student-run newspaper, choral group, Molloy Student Government, Molloy Nursing Student Association, Molloy Performing Arts Club, Men's Rugby, MolloyLife Media.

Athletics Member NCAA. All Division II. *Intercollegiate sports:* baseball M(s), basketball M(s)/W(s), bowling W(s), cross-country running M(s)/W(s), field hockey W(s), lacrosse M(s)/W(s), rugby W(s), soccer M(s)/W(s), softball W(s), tennis W(s), track and field M(s)/W(s), volleyball W(s). *Intramural sports:* cheerleading M(c)/W(c), equestrian sports W(c), rugby M(c), ultimate Frisbee M(c)/W(c).

Campus security: 24-hour emergency response devices and patrols, late-night transport/escort service, controlled dormitory access.

Student services: health clinic, personal/psychological counseling, women's center.

COSTS & FINANCIAL AID
Costs (2017–18) *Comprehensive fee:* $45,022 includes full-time tuition ($29,110), mandatory fees ($1200), and room and board ($14,712). Full-time tuition and fees vary according to degree level. Part-time tuition:

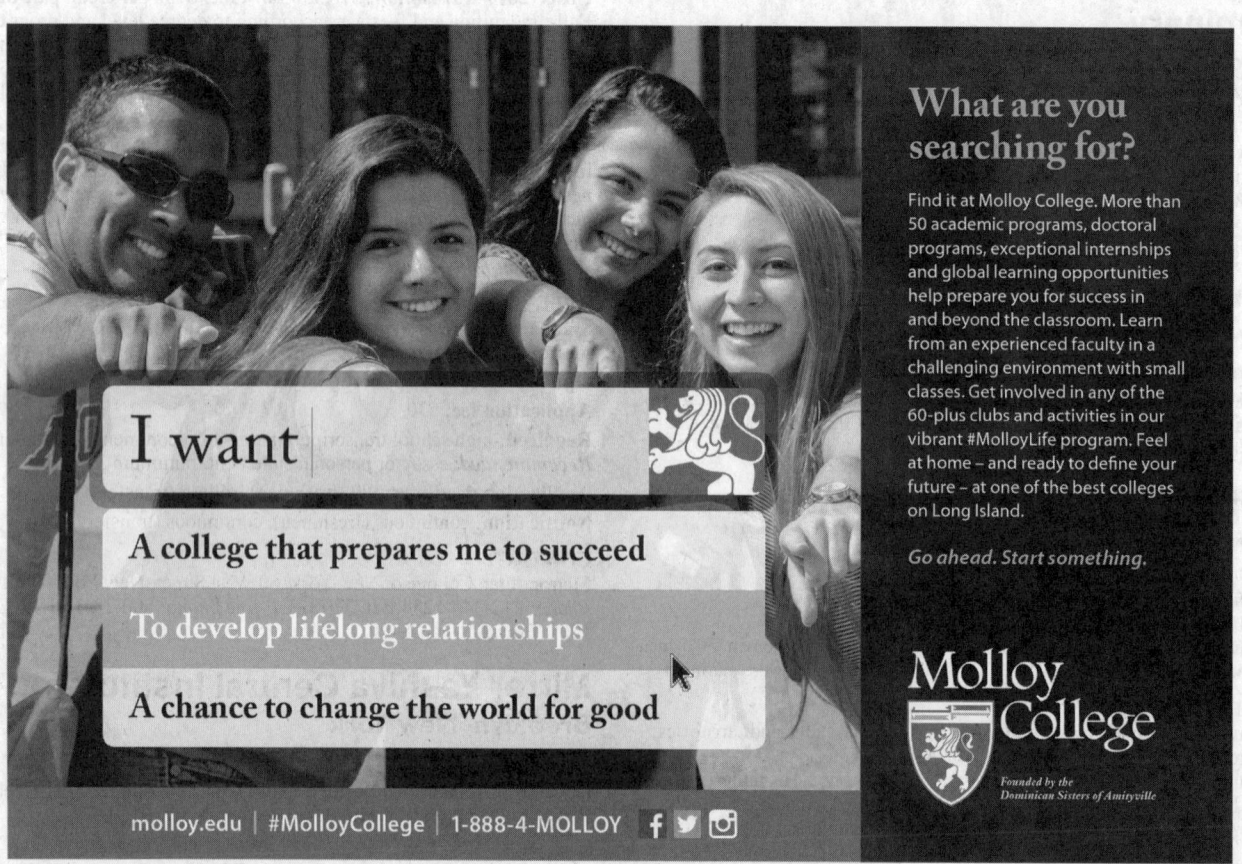

$965 per credit hour. Part-time tuition and fees vary according to degree level. *Room and board:* Room and board charges vary according to board plan. *Payment plans:* installment, deferred payment. *Waivers:* senior citizens and employees or children of employees.

Financial Aid Of all full-time matriculated undergraduates who enrolled in 2016, 2,630 applied for aid, 2,357 were judged to have need, 216 had their need fully met. 197 Federal Work-Study jobs (averaging $1501). In 2016, 218 non-need-based awards were made. *Average percent of need met:* 46. *Average financial aid package:* $16,123. *Average need-based loan:* $4152. *Average need-based gift aid:* $12,441. *Average non-need-based aid:* $9906. *Average indebtedness upon graduation:* $33,197. *Financial aid deadline:* 5/1.

APPLYING
Standardized Tests *Required:* SAT or ACT (for admission).

Options: electronic application, early action, deferred entrance.

Application fee: $40.

Required for some: essay or personal statement, high school transcript, 1 letter of recommendation. *Recommended:* interview.

Application deadlines: rolling (freshmen), rolling (transfers), 12/1 (early action).

Notification: continuous (freshmen), continuous (transfers), 12/15 (early action).

CONTACT
Mr. Marc Soevyn, Admissions Counselor, Molloy College, 1000 Hempstead Avenue, PO Box 5002, Rockville Centre, NY 11571-5002. *Phone:* 516-323-4000. *Toll-free phone:* 888-4MOLLOY. *E-mail:* admissions@molloy.edu.

See previous page for display ad and page 1348 for the College Close-Up.

Monroe College
Bronx, New York
http://www.monroecollege.edu/

CONTACT
Monroe College, 2501 Jerome Avenue, Bronx, NY 10468. *Phone:* 718-933-6700. *Toll-free phone:* 800-55MONROE.

Morrisville State College
Morrisville, New York
http://www.morrisville.edu/

- **State-supported** 4-year, founded 1908, part of State University of New York System
- **Rural** 185-acre campus with easy access to Syracuse
- **Coed**
- **Moderately difficult** entrance level

FACULTY
Student/faculty ratio: 11:1.

ACADEMICS
Calendar: semesters. *Degrees:* certificates, associate, and bachelor's.
Library: Morrisville State Library (Butcher Library) plus 1 other. Students can reserve study rooms.

STUDENT LIFE
Housing options: on-campus residence required through sophomore year; coed, special housing for students with disabilities. Campus housing is university owned. Freshman campus housing is guaranteed.

Activities and organizations: drama/theater group, student-run newspaper, radio station, Campus Activities Board, Conservation Tri Society, CASU, CollegiateFFA, Automotive Club.

Athletics Member NCAA. All Division III.

Campus security: 24-hour emergency response devices and patrols, student patrols, late-night transport/escort service, controlled dormitory access.

Student services: health clinic, personal/psychological counseling.

COSTS & FINANCIAL AID
Costs (2017–18) *Tuition:* state resident $6670 full-time, $278 per credit hour part-time; nonresident $11,300 full-time, $472 per credit hour part-time. Full-time tuition and fees vary according to course level, degree level, location, and program. Part-time tuition and fees vary according to class time, course level, course load, degree level, location, and program. *Required fees:* $1639 full-time, $67 per credit hour part-time. *Room and board:* $13,238; room only: $7648. Room and board charges vary according to board plan, housing facility, and location. *Payment plans:* installment, deferred payment.

Financial Aid Of all full-time matriculated undergraduates who enrolled in 2015, 2,335 applied for aid, 2,177 were judged to have need, 15 had their need fully met. In 2015, 263 non-need-based awards were made. *Average percent of need met:* 49. *Average financial aid package:* $9758. *Average need-based loan:* $3874. *Average need-based gift aid:* $6963. *Average non-need-based aid:* $1761. *Average indebtedness upon graduation:* $28,106.

APPLYING
Standardized Tests *Required for some:* SAT or ACT (for admission). *Recommended:* SAT or ACT (for admission).

Options: electronic application, deferred entrance.

Application fee: $50.

Required: essay or personal statement, high school transcript. *Required for some:* minimum 2.5 GPA, letters of recommendation. *Recommended:* minimum 2.0 GPA, letters of recommendation, interview.

CONTACT
Ms. Melissa Ward, Assistant Director of Enrollment Marketing, Morrisville State College, PO Box 901, Morrisville, NY 13408. *Phone:* 315-684-6046. *Toll-free phone:* 800-258-0111. *Fax:* 315-684-6427.

Mount Saint Mary College
Newburgh, New York
http://www.msmc.edu/

- **Independent** comprehensive, founded 1960
- **Suburban** 86-acre campus with easy access to New York City
- **Endowment** $72.9 million
- **Coed** 2,036 undergraduate students, 85% full-time, 70% women, 30% men
- **Moderately difficult** entrance level, 93% of applicants were admitted

UNDERGRAD STUDENTS
1,737 full-time, 299 part-time. Students come from 18 states and territories; 12% are from out of state; 7% Black or African American, non-Hispanic/Latino; 17% Hispanic/Latino; 2% Asian, non-Hispanic/Latino; 0.2% Native Hawaiian or other Pacific Islander, non-Hispanic/Latino; 0.5% American Indian or Alaska Native, non-Hispanic/Latino; 1% Two or more races, non-Hispanic/Latino; 9% Race/ethnicity unknown; 0.5% international; 9% transferred in; 48% live on campus.

Freshmen:
Admission: 3,824 applied, 3,571 admitted, 401 enrolled. *Average high school GPA:* 3.3. *Test scores:* SAT evidence-based reading and writing scores over 500: 78%; SAT math scores over 500: 75%; ACT scores over 18: 88%; SAT evidence-based reading and writing scores over 600: 19%; SAT math scores over 600: 16%; ACT scores over 24: 25%; SAT evidence-based reading and writing scores over 700: 1%; SAT math scores over 700: 2%; ACT scores over 30: 2%.
Retention: 78% of full-time freshmen returned.

FACULTY
Total: 269, 33% full-time, 39% with terminal degrees.
Student/faculty ratio: 13:1.

ACADEMICS
Calendar: semesters. *Degrees:* certificates, bachelor's, master's, and post-master's certificates.

Special study options: academic remediation for entering students, accelerated degree program, adult/continuing education programs, advanced placement credit, cooperative education, distance learning, double majors, freshman honors college, honors programs, independent study, internships, off-campus study, part-time degree program, services for LD students, student-designed majors, study abroad, summer session for credit. *ROTC:* Army (c).

COLLEGES AT-A-GLANCE

Unusual degree programs: 3-2 business administration; nursing; social work with Fordham University; publishing, counseling with Pace University.

Computers: 470 computers/terminals are available on campus for general student use. Students can access the following: campus intranet, computer help desk, free student e-mail accounts, online (class) grades, online (class) registration, online (class) schedules. Campuswide network is available. 100% of college-owned or -operated housing units are wired for high-speed Internet access. Wireless service is available via entire campus.

Library: Kaplan Family Library and Learning Center. *Books:* 87,924 (physical), 11,522 (digital/electronic); *Serial titles:* 202 (physical), 70,271 (digital/electronic); *Databases:* 87. Students can reserve study rooms.

STUDENT LIFE

Housing options: on-campus residence required through junior year; coed, men-only, women-only, special housing for students with disabilities. Campus housing is university owned. Freshman campus housing is guaranteed.

Activities and organizations: drama/theater group, student-run newspaper, radio station, choral group, Nursing Student Union, Colleges Against Cancer, Big Brothers/Big Sisters, Dance Team, Habitat for Humanity.

Athletics Member NCAA. All Division III. *Intercollegiate sports:* baseball M, basketball M/W, cheerleading W, cross-country running M/W, golf M, lacrosse M/W, soccer M/W, softball W, swimming and diving M/W, tennis M/W, track and field M/W, volleyball W. *Intramural sports:* basketball M/W, bowling M/W, football M, soccer M/W, softball M/W, swimming and diving M/W, table tennis M/W, volleyball M/W.

Campus security: 24-hour emergency response devices and patrols, student patrols, late-night transport/escort service, controlled dormitory access, monitored surveillance cameras in all residence halls.

Student services: health clinic, personal/psychological counseling.

COSTS & FINANCIAL AID

Costs (2018–19) Comprehensive fee: $46,226 includes full-time tuition ($30,046), mandatory fees ($1072), and room and board ($15,108). Full-time tuition and fees vary according to class time, course load, location, and program. Part-time tuition: $1002 per credit. Part-time tuition and fees vary according to class time, course load, location, and program. *Required fees:* $86 per year part-time. *College room only:* $8752. Room and board charges vary according to board plan and housing facility. *Payment plan:* installment. *Waivers:* employees or children of employees.

Financial Aid Of all full-time matriculated undergraduates who enrolled in 2017, 1,544 applied for aid, 1,378 were judged to have need, 215 had their need fully met. 360 Federal Work-Study jobs (averaging $1444). In 2017, 258 non-need-based awards were made. *Average percent of need met:* 64. *Average financial aid package:* $20,126. *Average need-based loan:* $4265. *Average need-based gift aid:* $15,747. *Average non-need-based aid:* $11,056. *Average indebtedness upon graduation:* $28,313. *Financial aid deadline:* 3/1.

APPLYING

Standardized Tests *Required:* SAT or ACT (for admission).

Options: electronic application, early admission, deferred entrance.

Application fee: $45.

Required: essay or personal statement, high school transcript. *Required for some:* 2 letters of recommendation, interview. *Recommended:* minimum 3.0 GPA, 2 letters of recommendation.

Notification: continuous (freshmen).

CONTACT

Ms. Nancy Scaffidi-Clark, Director of Admissions, Mount Saint Mary College, 330 Powell Avenue, Newburgh, NY 12550. *Phone:* 845-569-3254. *Toll-free phone:* 888-937-6762. *Fax:* 845-562-6762. *E-mail:* admissions@msmc.edu.

Nazareth College of Rochester
Rochester, New York
http://www.naz.edu/

- **Independent** comprehensive, founded 1924
- **Suburban** 150-acre campus
- **Endowment** $65.7 million
- **Coed** 2,194 undergraduate students, 96% full-time, 74% women, 26% men
- **Moderately difficult** entrance level, 63% of applicants were admitted

UNDERGRAD STUDENTS
2,099 full-time, 95 part-time. Students come from 33 states and territories; 33 other countries; 12% are from out of state; 6% Black or African American, non-Hispanic/Latino; 6% Hispanic/Latino; 3% Asian, non-Hispanic/Latino; 0.2% American Indian or Alaska Native, non-Hispanic/Latino; 2% Two or more races, non-Hispanic/Latino; 3% Race/ethnicity unknown; 1% international; 6% transferred in.

Freshmen:
Admission: 4,494 applied, 2,815 admitted, 550 enrolled. *Test scores:* SAT evidence-based reading and writing scores over 500: 91%; SAT math scores over 500: 86%; ACT scores over 18: 97%; SAT evidence-based reading and writing scores over 600: 43%; SAT math scores over 600: 41%; ACT scores over 24: 65%; SAT evidence-based reading and writing scores over 700: 5%; SAT math scores over 700: 4%; ACT scores over 30: 8%.

Retention: 79% of full-time freshmen returned.

FACULTY
Total: 508, 35% full-time, 44% with terminal degrees.

Student/faculty ratio: 9:1.

ACADEMICS
Calendar: semesters. *Degrees:* bachelor's, master's, doctoral, post-master's, and postbachelor's certificates.

Special study options: academic remediation for entering students, adult/continuing education programs, advanced placement credit, cooperative education, double majors, English as a second language, honors programs, independent study, internships, off-campus study, part-time degree program, services for LD students, study abroad, summer session for credit. *ROTC:* Army (c), Air Force (c).

Computers: 240 computers/terminals are available on campus for general student use. Students can access the following: computer help desk, free student e-mail accounts, online (class) grades, online (class) registration, online (class) schedules. Campuswide network is available. 100% of college-owned or -operated housing units are wired for high-speed Internet access. Wireless service is available via entire campus.

Library: Lorette Wilmot Library. *Books:* 45,000 (physical), 137,000 (digital/electronic); *Databases:* 137,000. Students can reserve study rooms.

STUDENT LIFE
Housing options: on-campus residence required through sophomore year; coed, special housing for students with disabilities. Campus housing is university owned. Freshman campus housing is guaranteed.

Activities and organizations: drama/theater group, student-run newspaper, radio station, choral group, Campus Activities Board, Center for Spirituality, Physical Therapy Club, Diversity Council, Intramurals.

Athletics Member NCAA. All Division III. *Intercollegiate sports:* basketball M/W, cross-country running M/W, equestrian sports M/W, field hockey W, golf M/W, ice hockey M, lacrosse M/W, soccer M/W, softball W, swimming and diving M/W, tennis M/W, track and field M/W, volleyball M/W. *Intramural sports:* basketball M/W, ice hockey M/W, racquetball M/W, rowing M/W, skiing (downhill) M/W, soccer M/W, ultimate Frisbee M/W, volleyball M/W.

Campus security: 24-hour emergency response devices and patrols, late-night transport/escort service, controlled dormitory access, alarm system, security beeper, lighted pathways, alert system.

Student services: health clinic, personal/psychological counseling, women's center.

COSTS & FINANCIAL AID
Costs (2018–19) One-time required fee: $550. **Comprehensive fee:** $46,734 includes full-time tuition ($31,924), mandatory fees ($1400), and

room and board ($13,410). Full-time tuition and fees vary according to course load, program, and reciprocity agreements. Part-time tuition: $760 per credit hour. *Room and board:* Room and board charges vary according to board plan and housing facility. *Payment plans:* installment, deferred payment. *Waivers:* minority students, children of alumni, and employees or children of employees.

Financial Aid Of all full-time matriculated undergraduates who enrolled in 2017, 1,926 applied for aid, 1,755 were judged to have need, 530 had their need fully met. 1,127 Federal Work-Study jobs (averaging $2148). In 2017, 333 non-need-based awards were made. *Average percent of need met:* 80. *Average financial aid package:* $27,685. *Average need-based loan:* $4570. *Average need-based gift aid:* $17,736. *Average non-need-based aid:* $18,299. *Average indebtedness upon graduation:* $40,958.

APPLYING
Standardized Tests *Required for some:* SAT or ACT (for admission).
Options: electronic application, early admission, early decision, deferred entrance.
Application fee: $45.
Required: essay or personal statement, high school transcript, 1 letter of recommendation. *Required for some:* audition/portfolio review. *Recommended:* interview.
Application deadlines: 2/1 (freshmen), rolling (transfers).
Early decision deadline: 11/15 (for plan 1), 1/10 (for plan 2).
Notification: continuous until 3/1 (freshmen), continuous (transfers), 12/15 (early decision plan 1), 1/25 (early decision plan 2).

CONTACT
Mr. Ian Mortimer, Vice President for Enrollment Management, Nazareth College of Rochester, 4245 East Avenue, Rochester, NY 14618-3790. *Phone:* 585-389-2830. *Toll-free phone:* 800-462-3944. *Fax:* 585-389-2826. *E-mail:* admissions@naz.edu.

The New School College of Performing Arts

New York, New York

http://www.newschool.edu/performing-arts/
- **Independent** comprehensive, part of The New School
- **Urban** campus with easy access to New York City
- **Endowment** $322.3 million
- **Coed** 594 undergraduate students, 98% full-time, 44% women, 56% men
- **Moderately difficult** entrance level, 51% of applicants were admitted

UNDERGRAD STUDENTS
580 full-time, 14 part-time. Students come from 38 states and territories; 47 other countries; 79% are from out of state; 9% Black or African American, non-Hispanic/Latino; 9% Hispanic/Latino; 4% Asian, non-Hispanic/Latino; 0.2% Native Hawaiian or other Pacific Islander, non-Hispanic/Latino; 0.2% American Indian or Alaska Native, non-Hispanic/Latino; 5% Two or more races, non-Hispanic/Latino; 4% Race/ethnicity unknown; 30% international; 8% transferred in; 30% live on campus.

Freshmen:
Admission: 1,259 applied, 644 admitted, 167 enrolled. *Average high school GPA:* 3.3. *Test scores:* ACT scores over 18: 90%; ACT scores over 24: 80%; ACT scores over 30: 40%.
Retention: 81% of full-time freshmen returned.

FACULTY
Total: 454, 4% full-time, 5% with terminal degrees.
Student/faculty ratio: 5:1.

ACADEMICS
Calendar: semesters. *Degrees:* diplomas, bachelor's, and master's.
Special study options: academic remediation for entering students, accelerated degree program, distance learning, double majors, English as a second language, independent study, internships, off-campus study, part-time degree program, services for LD students, student-designed majors, study abroad, summer session for credit.
Computers: 717 computers/terminals are available on campus for general student use. Students can access the following: campus intranet, computer help desk, free student e-mail accounts, online (class) grades, online

(class) registration, online (class) schedules. Campuswide network is available. 100% of college-owned or -operated housing units are wired for high-speed Internet access. Wireless service is available via entire campus.
Library: New School Libraries & Archives plus 3 others. *Books:* 215,937 (physical), 840,933 (digital/electronic); *Serial titles:* 2,265 (physical), 113,452 (digital/electronic); *Databases:* 376. Weekly public service hours: 155; study areas open 24 hours, 5–7 days a week; students can reserve study rooms.

STUDENT LIFE
Housing options: coed, special housing for students with disabilities. Campus housing is university owned and leased by the school. Freshman applicants given priority for college housing.
Activities and organizations: drama/theater group, student-run newspaper, choral group.
Athletics *Intramural sports:* basketball M/W, cross-country running M/W, soccer M/W, tennis M/W.
Campus security: 24-hour emergency response devices, controlled dormitory access, 24-hour desk attendants in residence halls.
Student services: health clinic, personal/psychological counseling.

COSTS & FINANCIAL AID
Costs (2017–18) *Comprehensive fee:* $62,590 includes full-time tuition ($45,240), mandatory fees ($1100), and room and board ($16,250). Part-time tuition: $1540 per credit hour. Part-time tuition and fees vary according to course load. *Required fees:* $550 per term part-time. *College room only:* $15,000. Room and board charges vary according to housing facility and location. *Payment plan:* installment. *Waivers:* employees or children of employees.

Financial Aid Of all full-time matriculated undergraduates who enrolled in 2016, 246 applied for aid, 217 were judged to have need, 28 had their need fully met. 36 Federal Work-Study jobs (averaging $3194). In 2016, 174 non-need-based awards were made. *Average percent of need met:* 78. *Average financial aid package:* $38,161. *Average need-based loan:* $4148. *Average need-based gift aid:* $7141. *Average non-need-based aid:* $17,173. *Average indebtedness upon graduation:* $77,353. *Financial aid deadline:* 2/1.

APPLYING
Options: electronic application, early action, deferred entrance.
Application fee: $50.
Required: essay or personal statement, high school transcript, 1 letter of recommendation. *Required for some:* interview, prescreening, live audition/interview. *Recommended:* minimum 3.0 GPA.
Application deadlines: 1/15 (freshmen), 4/1 (transfers), 11/1 (early action).
Notification: continuous until 3/15 (freshmen), continuous until 3/15 (transfers), 12/20 (early action).

CONTACT
Ms. Amanda Hosking, Director of Admission, The New School College of Performing Arts, 79 Fifth Avenue, New York, NY 10003. *Phone:* 212-229-5150 Ext. 4805. *Toll-free phone:* 800-292-3040. *E-mail:* hoskinga@newschool.edu.

The New School for Public Engagement

New York, New York

http://www.newschool.edu/public-engagement/
- **Independent** comprehensive, founded 1919, part of The New School
- **Urban** campus with easy access to New York City
- **Endowment** $322.3 million
- **Coed** 471 undergraduate students, 49% full-time, 65% women, 35% men

UNDERGRAD STUDENTS
231 full-time, 240 part-time. Students come from 38 states and territories; 33 other countries; 48% are from out of state; 9% Black or African American, non-Hispanic/Latino; 16% Hispanic/Latino; 3% Asian, non-Hispanic/Latino; 0.2% Native Hawaiian or other Pacific Islander, non-Hispanic/Latino; 6% Two or more races, non-Hispanic/Latino; 7% Race/ethnicity unknown; 11% international; 26% transferred in; 25% live on campus.

Freshmen:
Admission: 13 enrolled.

FACULTY
Total: 356, 23% full-time, 16% with terminal degrees.
Student/faculty ratio: 5:1.

ACADEMICS
Calendar: semesters. *Degrees:* certificates, bachelor's, master's, doctoral, post-master's, and postbachelor's certificates.

Special study options: accelerated degree program, adult/continuing education programs, advanced placement credit, distance learning, double majors, English as a second language, independent study, internships, off-campus study, part-time degree program, services for LD students, student-designed majors, study abroad, summer session for credit.

Unusual degree programs: psychology.

Computers: 717 computers/terminals are available on campus for general student use. Students can access the following: campus intranet, computer help desk, free student e-mail accounts, online (class) grades, online (class) registration, online (class) schedules. Campuswide network is available. 100% of college-owned or -operated housing units are wired for high-speed Internet access. Wireless service is available via entire campus.
Library: New School Libraries & Archives plus 3 others. *Books:* 215,937 (physical), 840,933 (digital/electronic); *Serial titles:* 2,265 (physical), 113,452 (digital/electronic); *Databases:* 376. Weekly public service hours: 155; study areas open 24 hours, 5–7 days a week; students can reserve study rooms.

STUDENT LIFE
Housing options: coed, special housing for students with disabilities. Campus housing is university owned and leased by the school. Freshman applicants given priority for college housing.
Activities and organizations: drama/theater group, student-run newspaper, choral group.
Athletics *Intramural sports:* basketball M/W, cross-country running M/W, soccer M/W, tennis M/W.
Campus security: 24-hour emergency response devices, controlled dormitory access, trained security personnel in central buildings and 24-hour desk attendants in residence halls.
Student services: health clinic, personal/psychological counseling.

COSTS & FINANCIAL AID
Costs (2017–18) *Comprehensive fee:* $47,110 includes full-time tuition ($29,760), mandatory fees ($1100), and room and board ($16,250). Part-time tuition: $1240 per credit hour. Part-time tuition and fees vary according to course load. *Required fees:* $550 per term part-time. *College room only:* $15,000. Room and board charges vary according to housing facility and location. *Payment plan:* installment. *Waivers:* employees or children of employees.
Financial Aid Of all full-time matriculated undergraduates who enrolled in 2016, 145 applied for aid, 129 were judged to have need, 9 had their need fully met. 6 Federal Work-Study jobs (averaging $3333). In 2016, 60 non-need-based awards were made. *Average percent of need met:* 65. *Average financial aid package:* $18,122. *Average need-based loan:* $4379. *Average need-based gift aid:* $11,648. *Average non-need-based aid:* $2950. *Financial aid deadline:* 2/1.

APPLYING
Required: essay or personal statement, high school transcript.
Recommended: 1 letter of recommendation.

CONTACT
Ms. Elizabeth Puleio, Associate Director of Admission, The New School for Public Engagement, 72 Fifth Avenue, New York, NY 10011. *Phone:* 212-229-5150 Ext. 3789. *Toll-free phone:* 800-292-3040. *E-mail:* puleioe@newschool.edu.

New York City College of Technology of the City University of New York
Brooklyn, New York
http://www.citytech.cuny.edu/

- **State and locally supported** 4-year, founded 1946, part of City University of New York System
- **Urban** campus with easy access to New York City
- **Endowment** $17.1 million
- **Coed**
- **Noncompetitive** entrance level

FACULTY
Student/faculty ratio: 17:1.

ACADEMICS
Calendar: semesters. *Degrees:* certificates, associate, and bachelor's.
Library: Ursula C. Schwerin Library. *Books:* 116,667 (physical), 487,902 (digital/electronic); *Serial titles:* 1,650 (physical), 95,329 (digital/electronic); *Databases:* 146. Weekly public service hours: 75; students can reserve study rooms.

STUDENT LIFE
Housing options: college housing not available.
Activities and organizations: drama/theater group, student-run newspaper, Art and Design Club, BMI Club, International Business Organization, SADHA (Dental Hygienists Club), National Society of Collegiate Scholars Club.
Campus security: 24-hour emergency response devices and patrols.
Student services: health clinic, personal/psychological counseling, women's center.

COSTS & FINANCIAL AID
Costs (2017–18) *Tuition:* state resident $6530 full-time, $285 per credit part-time; nonresident $17,400 full-time, $580 per credit part-time. Full-time tuition and fees vary according to course load and program. Part-time tuition and fees vary according to course load and program. *Required fees:* $320 full-time, $78 per term part-time.
Financial Aid Of all full-time matriculated undergraduates who enrolled in 2012, 8,718 applied for aid, 8,272 were judged to have need, 350 had their need fully met. In 2012, 128 non-need-based awards were made. *Average percent of need met:* 57. *Average financial aid package:* $8867. *Average need-based loan:* $4267. *Average need-based gift aid:* $8356. *Average non-need-based aid:* $233.

APPLYING
Standardized Tests *Required for some:* SAT or ACT (for admission).
Options: electronic application, deferred entrance.
Application fee: $65.
Required: high school transcript.

CONTACT
Alexis Chaconis, Director of Admissions, New York City College of Technology of the City University of New York, 300 Jay Street, Brooklyn, NY 11201-2983. *Phone:* 718-260-5500. *E-mail:* achaconis@citytech.cuny.edu.

New York College of Health Professions
Syosset, New York
http://www.nycollege.edu/

CONTACT
Ms. Mary Rodas, Associate Director of Admissions, New York College of Health Professions, 6801 Jericho Turnpike, Syosset, NY 11791-4413. *Toll-free phone:* 800-922-7337 Ext. 351. *E-mail:* rdodas@nycollege.edu.

New York Institute of Technology

Old Westbury, New York
http://www.nyit.edu/
- **Independent** comprehensive, founded 1955
- **Suburban** 215-acre campus with easy access to New York City
- **Endowment** $110.5 million
- **Coed** 3,688 undergraduate students, 88% full-time, 36% women, 64% men
- **Moderately difficult** entrance level, 77% of applicants were admitted

UNDERGRAD STUDENTS
3,239 full-time, 449 part-time. Students come from 40 states and territories; 64 other countries; 15% are from out of state; 9% Black or African American, non-Hispanic/Latino; 16% Hispanic/Latino; 18% Asian, non-Hispanic/Latino; 0.4% Native Hawaiian or other Pacific Islander, non-Hispanic/Latino; 0.3% American Indian or Alaska Native, non-Hispanic/Latino; 4% Two or more races, non-Hispanic/Latino; 12% Race/ethnicity unknown; 16% international; 7% transferred in; 14% live on campus.

Freshmen:
Admission: 9,945 applied, 7,651 admitted, 894 enrolled. *Average high school GPA:* 3.3. *Test scores:* SAT evidence-based reading and writing scores over 500: 83%; SAT math scores over 500: 90%; ACT scores over 18: 96%; SAT evidence-based reading and writing scores over 600: 31%; SAT math scores over 600: 38%; ACT scores over 24: 55%; SAT evidence-based reading and writing scores over 700: 2%; SAT math scores over 700: 6%; ACT scores over 30: 16%.
Retention: 77% of full-time freshmen returned.

FACULTY
Total: 900, 35% full-time, 33% with terminal degrees.
Student/faculty ratio: 13:1.

ACADEMICS
Calendar: semesters. *Degrees:* certificates, diplomas, associate, bachelor's, master's, doctoral, post-master's, and postbachelor's certificates.
Special study options: academic remediation for entering students, accelerated degree program, adult/continuing education programs, advanced placement credit, cooperative education, distance learning, double majors, English as a second language, honors programs, internships, off-campus study, part-time degree program, services for LD students, study abroad, summer session for credit. *ROTC:* Army (c), Air Force (c).
Unusual degree programs: 3-2 life sciences/osteopathic medicine, occupational therapy, physical therapy, physician assistant studies.
Computers: 1,250 computers/terminals are available on campus for general student use. Students can access the following: computer help desk, free student e-mail accounts, online (class) grades, online (class) registration, online (class) schedules. Campuswide network is available. 100% of college-owned or -operated housing units are wired for high-speed Internet access. Wireless service is available via entire campus.
Library: George and Gertrude Wisser Memorial Library plus 3 others. *Books:* 89,426 (physical), 70,248 (digital/electronic); *Serial titles:* 2,279 (physical), 23,926 (digital/electronic). Weekly public service hours: 78; students can reserve study rooms.

STUDENT LIFE
Housing options: coed. Campus housing is university owned and leased by the school. Freshman campus housing is guaranteed.
Activities and organizations: student-run newspaper, television station, national fraternities, national sororities.
Athletics Member NCAA. All Division II. *Intercollegiate sports:* baseball M(s), basketball M(s)/W(s), cheerleading W, cross-country running M(s)/W(s), lacrosse M(s)/W(s), soccer M(s)/W(s), softball W(s), tennis M(s)/W(s), volleyball W(s). *Intramural sports:* basketball M/W, cross-country running M(c)/W(c), soccer M/W, volleyball M/W.
Campus security: 24-hour emergency response devices and patrols, late-night transport/escort service, controlled dormitory access.
Student services: health clinic, personal/psychological counseling.

COSTS & FINANCIAL AID
Costs (2018–19) *Comprehensive fee:* $51,180 includes full-time tuition ($35,585), mandatory fees ($1305), and room and board ($14,290). Full-time tuition and fees vary according to program. Part-time tuition: $1205 per credit. Part-time tuition and fees vary according to course load and program. *Required fees:* $540 per term part-time. *College room only:* $9320. Room and board charges vary according to housing facility and location. *Payment plan:* installment. *Waivers:* senior citizens and employees or children of employees.
Financial Aid Of all full-time matriculated undergraduates who enrolled in 2016, 2,590 applied for aid, 2,361 were judged to have need. In 2016, 424 non-need-based awards were made. *Average financial aid package:* $21,916. *Average need-based loan:* $4298. *Average need-based gift aid:* $8131. *Average non-need-based aid:* $12,606.

APPLYING
Standardized Tests *Required:* SAT or ACT (for admission).
Options: electronic application, deferred entrance.
Application fee: $50.
Required: essay or personal statement, high school transcript, 2 letters of recommendation. *Required for some:* interview. *Recommended:* minimum 2.7 GPA.
Application deadlines: rolling (freshmen), rolling (transfers).
Notification: continuous (freshmen), continuous (transfers).

CONTACT
Ms. Marcelle Hicks, Senior Director, Undergraduate Admissions, New York Institute of Technology, Old Westbury, NY 11568. *Phone:* 516-686-1020. *Toll-free phone:* 800-345-NYIT. *E-mail:* admissions@nyit.edu.

New York School of Interior Design

New York, New York
http://www.nysid.edu/

CONTACT
Jaspreet Bains, Admissions Associate, New York School of Interior Design, 170 East 70th Street, New York, NY 10021-5110. *Phone:* 212-472-1500 Ext. 212. *Toll-free phone:* 800-336-9743 Ext. 205. *Fax:* 212-472-1867. *E-mail:* admissions@nysid.edu.

New York University

New York, New York
http://www.nyu.edu/
- **Independent** university, founded 1831
- **Urban** 230-acre campus with easy access to New York City
- **Coed** 26,417 undergraduate students, 96% full-time, 57% women, 43% men
- **Very difficult** entrance level, 28% of applicants were admitted

UNDERGRAD STUDENTS
25,347 full-time, 1,070 part-time. Students come from 52 states and territories; 140 other countries; 66% are from out of state; 6% Black or African American, non-Hispanic/Latino; 14% Hispanic/Latino; 20% Asian, non-Hispanic/Latino; 0.2% Native Hawaiian or other Pacific Islander, non-Hispanic/Latino; 0.1% American Indian or Alaska Native, non-Hispanic/Latino; 5% Two or more races, non-Hispanic/Latino; 6% Race/ethnicity unknown; 19% international; 4% transferred in; 43% live on campus.

Freshmen:
Admission: 64,007 applied, 17,707 admitted, 6,022 enrolled. *Average high school GPA:* 3.7. *Test scores:* SAT evidence-based reading and writing scores over 500: 100%; SAT math scores over 500: 100%; ACT scores over 18: 100%; SAT evidence-based reading and writing scores over 600: 93%; SAT math scores over 600: 89%; ACT scores over 24: 98%; SAT evidence-based reading and writing scores over 700: 46%; SAT math scores over 700: 54%; ACT scores over 30: 70%.
Retention: 93% of full-time freshmen returned.

FACULTY
Total: 6,498, 46% full-time, 71% with terminal degrees.
Student/faculty ratio: 10:1.

ACADEMICS

Calendar: semesters. *Degrees:* certificates, associate, bachelor's, master's, doctoral, post-master's, and postbachelor's certificates.

Special study options: accelerated degree program, adult/continuing education programs, advanced placement credit, cooperative education, distance learning, double majors, English as a second language, honors programs, independent study, internships, off-campus study, part-time degree program, services for LD students, student-designed majors, study abroad, summer session for credit. *ROTC:* Army (c), Air Force (c).

Unusual degree programs: 3-2 engineering with School of Engineering and College of Arts and Science; nursing.

Computers: Students can access the following: computer help desk, free student e-mail accounts, online (class) grades, online (class) registration, online (class) schedules. Campuswide network is available. 100% of college-owned or -operated housing units are wired for high-speed Internet access. Wireless service is available via entire campus.

Library: Elmer H. Bobst Library plus 12 others. *Books:* 3.3 million (physical), 1.1 million (digital/electronic); *Serial titles:* 51,029 (physical), 166,202 (digital/electronic); *Databases:* 1,320. Study areas open 24 hours, 5–7 days a week; students can reserve study rooms.

STUDENT LIFE

Housing options: coed, special housing for students with disabilities. Campus housing is university owned and leased by the school. Freshman campus housing is guaranteed.

Activities and organizations: drama/theater group, student-run newspaper, radio and television station, choral group, national fraternities, national sororities.

Athletics Member NCAA. All Division III. *Intercollegiate sports:* baseball M, basketball M/W, cross-country running M/W, fencing M/W, golf M/W, soccer M/W, softball W, swimming and diving M/W, tennis M/W, track and field M/W, volleyball M/W, wrestling M. *Intramural sports:* badminton M(c)/W(c), baseball M(c), basketball M/W, bowling M/W, cheerleading M(c)/W(c), crew M(c)/W(c), equestrian sports M(c)/W(c), football M/W, ice hockey M(c), lacrosse M(c)/W(c), racquetball M(c)/W(c), soccer M/W, softball M/W, squash M(c)/W(c), table tennis M(c)/W(c), tennis M/W, ultimate Frisbee M(c)/W(c), volleyball M(c)/W(c), water polo M/W(c).

Campus security: 24-hour emergency response devices and patrols, student patrols, late-night transport/escort service, controlled dormitory access, 24-hour security in residence halls.

Student services: health clinic, personal/psychological counseling, women's center.

COSTS & FINANCIAL AID

Costs (2017–18) *Tuition:* $47,942 full-time, $1412 per credit hour part-time. Full-time tuition and fees vary according to course load and program. Part-time tuition and fees vary according to program. *Required fees:* $2522 full-time, $479 per term part-time. *Room only:* Room and board charges vary according to board plan and housing facility. *Payment plans:* tuition prepayment, installment, deferred payment. *Waivers:* employees or children of employees.

Financial Aid Of all full-time matriculated undergraduates who enrolled in 2015, 15,702 applied for aid, 12,605 were judged to have need, 801 had their need fully met. In 2015, 1123 non-need-based awards were made. *Average percent of need met:* 60. *Average financial aid package:* $34,532. *Average need-based loan:* $5233. *Average need-based gift aid:* $29,971. *Average non-need-based aid:* $6167. *Average indebtedness upon graduation:* $31,210. *Financial aid deadline:* 2/15.

APPLYING

Standardized Tests *Required:* SAT and SAT Subject Tests or ACT (for admission), (for admission).

Options: electronic application, early admission, early decision, deferred entrance.

Application fee: $80.

Required: essay or personal statement, high school transcript, 1 letter of recommendation. *Required for some:* audition or a portfolio for some specific programs.

Application deadlines: 1/1 (freshmen), 4/1 (transfers).

Early decision deadline: 11/1 (for plan 1), 1/1 (for plan 2).

Notification: 4/1 (freshmen), 5/15 (transfers), 12/15 (early decision plan 1), 2/15 (early decision plan 2).

CONTACT

Kristy Materasso, Undergraduate Admissions Processing Center, New York University, 383 Lafayette Street, New York, NY 10003. *Phone:* 212-998-4500. *Fax:* 212-995-4902. *E-mail:* admissions@nyu.edu.

★ Niagara University
Niagara Falls, New York
http://www.niagara.edu/

- **Independent** comprehensive, founded 1856, affiliated with Roman Catholic Church
- **Suburban** 160-acre campus with easy access to Buffalo, NY and Toronto, Ontario (Canada)
- **Endowment** $98.0 million
- **Coed** 2,994 undergraduate students, 94% full-time, 62% women, 38% men
- **Moderately difficult** entrance level, 84% of applicants were admitted

UNDERGRAD STUDENTS

2,827 full-time, 167 part-time. Students come from 35 states and territories; 42 other countries; 8% are from out of state; 5% Black or African American, non-Hispanic/Latino; 4% Hispanic/Latino; 2% Asian, non-Hispanic/Latino; 0.6% American Indian or Alaska Native, non-Hispanic/Latino; 3% Two or more races, non-Hispanic/Latino; 2% Race/ethnicity unknown; 13% international; 4% transferred in; 40% live on campus.

Freshmen:
Admission: 3,101 applied, 2,611 admitted, 590 enrolled. *Average high school GPA:* 3.4. *Test scores:* SAT evidence-based reading and writing scores over 500: 82%; SAT math scores over 500: 81%; ACT scores over 18: 95%; SAT evidence-based reading and writing scores over 600: 29%; SAT math scores over 600: 26%; ACT scores over 24: 48%; SAT evidence-based reading and writing scores over 700: 1%; SAT math scores over 700: 2%; ACT scores over 30: 5%.

Retention: 83% of full-time freshmen returned.

FACULTY

Total: 442, 38% full-time, 48% with terminal degrees.
Student/faculty ratio: 11:1.

ACADEMICS

Calendar: semesters. *Degrees:* certificates, associate, bachelor's, master's, doctoral, post-master's, and postbachelor's certificates.

Special study options: academic remediation for entering students, accelerated degree program, advanced placement credit, cooperative education, distance learning, double majors, English as a second language, independent study, internships, off-campus study, part-time degree program, services for LD students, student-designed majors, study abroad, summer session for credit. *ROTC:* Army (b).

Computers: 81 computers/terminals are available on campus for general student use. Students can access the following: campus intranet, computer help desk, free student e-mail accounts, online (class) grades, online (class) registration, online (class) schedules. Campuswide network is available. 100% of college-owned or -operated housing units are wired for high-speed Internet access. Wireless service is available via entire campus.

Library: Our Lady of Angels Library. *Books:* 122,720 (physical), 348,406 (digital/electronic); *Serial titles:* 32,000 (digital/electronic); *Databases:* 111. Weekly public service hours: 107; study areas open 24 hours, 5–7 days a week; students can reserve study rooms.

STUDENT LIFE

Housing options: on-campus residence required through sophomore year; coed. Campus housing is university owned. Freshman campus housing is guaranteed.

Activities and organizations: drama/theater group, student-run newspaper, radio station, choral group, Student Nursing Association, Future Teachers Association, NY Players (theatre), Beta Alpha Psi, Hospitality & Tourism Association, national fraternities, national sororities.

Athletics Member NCAA. All Division I. *Intercollegiate sports:* baseball M(s), basketball M(s)/W(s), cross-country running M(s)/W(s), golf M(s)/W(s), ice hockey M(s), lacrosse W(s), soccer M(s)/W(s), softball

W(s), swimming and diving M(s)/W(s), tennis M(s)/W(s), track and field W(s), volleyball W(s). *Intramural sports:* badminton M(c)/W(c), baseball M(c), basketball M(c)/W(c), bowling M(c)/W(c), field hockey M(c)/W(c), golf M(c), ice hockey M(c)/W(c), lacrosse M(c)/W(c), racquetball M(c)/W(c), rugby M(c)/W(c), soccer M(c)/W(c), softball M/W(c), tennis M/W, volleyball M(c)/W(c), weight lifting M(c)/W(c), wrestling M(c).

Campus security: 24-hour emergency response devices and patrols, late-night transport/escort service, controlled dormitory access, 24-hour escort service, Emergency Notification System.

Student services: health clinic, personal/psychological counseling.

COSTS & FINANCIAL AID

Costs (2018–19) *Comprehensive fee:* $46,700 includes full-time tuition ($31,700), mandatory fees ($1800), and room and board ($13,200). Full-time tuition and fees vary according to program. Part-time tuition and fees vary according to program. *Room and board:* Room and board charges vary according to housing facility. *Payment plans:* installment, deferred payment. *Waivers:* employees or children of employees.

Financial Aid Of all full-time matriculated undergraduates who enrolled in 2017, 2,173 applied for aid, 1,985 were judged to have need, 1,016 had their need fully met. 377 Federal Work-Study jobs (averaging $3655). 39 state and other part-time jobs (averaging $6308). In 2017, 462 non-need-based awards were made. *Average percent of need met:* 82. *Average financial aid package:* $26,503. *Average need-based loan:* $4941. *Average need-based gift aid:* $22,246. *Average non-need-based aid:* $15,547. *Average indebtedness upon graduation:* $34,214.

APPLYING

Options: electronic application, early admission, early action, deferred entrance.

Required: high school transcript. *Recommended:* minimum 3.0 GPA, 3 letters of recommendation, interview.

Application deadlines: 8/1 (freshmen), 8/15 (transfers).

Notification: continuous (freshmen), continuous (transfers).

CONTACT

Mr. Mark Wojnowski, Director of Undergraduate Admissions, Niagara University, 5795 Lewiston Road, Gacioch Center, Niagara University, NY 14109. *Phone:* 716-286-8700. *Toll-free phone:* 800-462-2111. *Fax:* 716-286-8733. *E-mail:* admissions@niagara.edu.

See this page for display ad and page 1364 for the College Close-Up.

Nyack College

Nyack, New York

http://www.nyack.edu/

- **Independent** comprehensive, founded 1882, affiliated with The Christian and Missionary Alliance
- **Suburban** 125-acre campus with easy access to New York City
- **Coed** 1,398 undergraduate students, 81% full-time, 58% women, 42% men
- **Minimally difficult** entrance level, 98% of applicants were admitted

UNDERGRAD STUDENTS

1,131 full-time, 267 part-time. 35% are from out of state; 30% Black or African American, non-Hispanic/Latino; 29% Hispanic/Latino; 8% Asian, non-Hispanic/Latino; 0.6% Native Hawaiian or other Pacific Islander, non-Hispanic/Latino; 0.7% American Indian or Alaska Native, non-Hispanic/Latino; 2% Two or more races, non-Hispanic/Latino; 2% Race/ethnicity unknown; 6% international; 12% transferred in; 69% live on campus.

Freshmen:

Admission: 435 applied, 428 admitted, 201 enrolled. *Average high school GPA:* 2.9. *Test scores:* SAT evidence-based reading and writing scores over 500: 49%; SAT math scores over 500: 52%; ACT scores over 18: 74%; SAT evidence-based reading and writing scores over 600: 17%; SAT math scores over 600: 11%; ACT scores over 24: 9%; SAT evidence-based reading and writing scores over 700: 1%; SAT math scores over 700: 2%.

Retention: 59% of full-time freshmen returned.

FACULTY

Total: 262, 31% full-time, 46% with terminal degrees.

Student/faculty ratio: 12:1.

ACADEMICS

Calendar: semesters. *Degrees:* associate, bachelor's, master's, and doctoral.

Special study options: academic remediation for entering students, adult/continuing education programs, advanced placement credit, distance learning, double majors, honors programs, independent study, internships, off-campus study, part-time degree program, services for LD students, student-designed majors, study abroad, summer session for credit.

Unusual degree programs: 3-2 childhood special education.

Computers: Students can access the following: campus intranet, computer help desk, free student e-mail accounts, online (class) grades, online (class) registration, online (class) schedules. Campuswide network is available. 95% of college-owned or -operated housing units are wired for high-speed Internet access. Wireless service is available via classrooms, computer labs, dorm rooms, libraries, student centers.

Library: Bailey Library plus 3 others.

STUDENT LIFE

Housing options: on-campus residence required through sophomore year; men-only, women-only. Campus housing is university owned. Freshman campus housing is guaranteed.

Activities and organizations: drama/theater group, student-run newspaper, radio station, choral group, Student leadership, Choral groups, Lost & Found, Small group ministries, Intramurals.

Athletics Member NCAA. All Division II. *Intercollegiate sports:* baseball M(s), basketball M(s)/W(s), cross-country running M(s)/W(s), golf M(s), lacrosse W(s), soccer M(s)/W(s), softball W(s), volleyball W(s). *Intramural sports:* baseball M, basketball M/W, skiing (downhill) M/W, soccer M/W, softball W, ultimate Frisbee M/W, volleyball M/W.

Campus security: 24-hour emergency response devices and patrols.

Student services: health clinic, personal/psychological counseling.

COSTS & FINANCIAL AID

Costs (2018–19) *Comprehensive fee:* $34,800 includes full-time tuition ($25,000), mandatory fees ($350), and room and board ($9450). Part-time tuition: $1040 per credit hour. Part-time tuition and fees vary according to course load. *Room and board:* Room and board charges vary according to board plan and housing facility. *Payment plan:* installment. *Waivers:* employees or children of employees.

Financial Aid Of all full-time matriculated undergraduates who enrolled in 2014, 1,257 applied for aid, 1,172 were judged to have need, 107 had their need fully met. 184 Federal Work-Study jobs (averaging $1125). 73 state and other part-time jobs (averaging $1875). In 2014, 207 non-need-based awards were made. *Average percent of need met:* 64. *Average financial aid package:* $20,230. *Average need-based loan:* $4028. *Average need-based gift aid:* $9923. *Average non-need-based aid:* $10,808. *Average indebtedness upon graduation:* $34,670.

APPLYING

Standardized Tests *Required for some:* SAT or ACT (for admission), SAT and SAT Subject Tests or ACT (for admission).

Options: electronic application, early action, deferred entrance.

Application fee: $25.

Required: essay or personal statement, high school transcript, minimum 2.0 GPA, 1 letter of recommendation, signed statement of faith and community life form. *Required for some:* interview.

Application deadlines: rolling (freshmen), rolling (out-of-state freshmen), rolling (transfers).

Notification: continuous (freshmen), continuous (out-of-state freshmen), continuous (transfers).

CONTACT

Mr. Dan Bailey, Director of Admissions, Nyack College, 1 South Boulevard, Nyack, NY 10960-3698. *Phone:* 845-675-4401. *Toll-free phone:* 800-33-NYACK. *Fax:* 845-358-3047. *E-mail:* admissions@nyack.edu.

Ohr Hameir Theological Seminary
Cortlandt Manor, New York

CONTACT

Director of Admissions, Ohr Hameir Theological Seminary, 141 Furnace Woods Road, Cortlandt Manor, NY 10567. *Phone:* 914-736-1500.

Ohr Somayach/Joseph Tanenbaum Educational Center
Monsey, New York
http://ohr.edu/

- **Independent Jewish** comprehensive, founded 1979
- **Small-town** 7-acre campus with easy access to New York City
- **Men only** 40 undergraduate students, 100% full-time
- **Moderately difficult** entrance level, 60% of applicants were admitted

UNDERGRAD STUDENTS

40 full-time. Students come from 10 states and territories; 4 other countries; 60% are from out of state; 8% transferred in.

Freshmen:
Admission: 100 applied, 60 admitted, 10 enrolled.

FACULTY
Total: 12, 50% full-time.

ACADEMICS

Calendar: semesters. *Degree:* doctoral.

Special study options: academic remediation for entering students, adult/continuing education programs, honors programs, internships, part-time degree program, services for LD students, summer session for credit.

Library: Finer Library.

STUDENT LIFE

Housing options: on-campus residence required through senior year; men-only. Campus housing is university owned.

Campus security: 24-hour emergency response devices and patrols, controlled dormitory access.

Student services: personal/psychological counseling.

APPLYING

Options: early admission.

Required: interview. *Required for some:* essay or personal statement. *Recommended:* high school transcript.

Application deadlines: rolling (freshmen), rolling (transfers).

CONTACT

Ohr Somayach/Joseph Tanenbaum Educational Center, PO Box 334, 244 Route 306, Monsey, NY 10952-0334. *Phone:* 845-425-1370 Ext. 22.

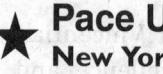 Pace University
New York, New York
http://www.pace.edu/nyc

- **Independent** university, founded 1906
- **Urban** campus with easy access to New York City
- **Endowment** $169.9 million
- **Coed** 6,400 undergraduate students, 87% full-time, 63% women, 37% men
- **Moderately difficult** entrance level, 82% of applicants were admitted

UNDERGRAD STUDENTS

5,538 full-time, 862 part-time. Students come from 51 states and territories; 115 other countries; 48% are from out of state; 9% Black or African American, non-Hispanic/Latino; 11% Hispanic/Latino; 9% Asian, non-Hispanic/Latino; 0.1% Native Hawaiian or other Pacific Islander, non-Hispanic/Latino; 0.2% American Indian or Alaska Native, non-Hispanic/Latino; 4% Two or more races, non-Hispanic/Latino; 3% Race/ethnicity unknown; 19% international; 3% transferred in; 36% live on campus.

Freshmen:
Admission: 16,217 applied, 13,255 admitted, 1,471 enrolled. *Average high school GPA:* 3.2. *Test scores:* SAT evidence-based reading and writing scores over 500: 90%; SAT math scores over 500: 83%; ACT scores over 18: 98%; SAT evidence-based reading and writing scores over 600: 42%; SAT math scores over 600: 31%; ACT scores over 24: 55%; SAT evidence-based reading and writing scores over 700: 5%; SAT math scores over 700: 6%; ACT scores over 30: 9%.

Retention: 78% of full-time freshmen returned.

FACULTY
Total: 840, 38% full-time, 55% with terminal degrees.

Student/faculty ratio: 16:1.

ACADEMICS
Calendar: semesters. *Degrees:* certificates, associate, bachelor's, master's, doctoral, post-master's, and postbachelor's certificates.

Special study options: accelerated degree program, adult/continuing education programs, advanced placement credit, cooperative education, distance learning, double majors, English as a second language, freshman honors college, honors programs, independent study, internships, part-time degree program, services for LD students, study abroad, summer session for credit. *ROTC:* Army (c), Air Force (c).

Unusual degree programs: 3-2 business administration; engineering with Manhattan College, Rensselaer Polytechnic Institute; occupational Therapy with Columbia University, optometry with SUNY College of Optometry, physical therapy with New York Medical College, podiatry with the New York College of Podiatric Medicine.

Computers: 209 computers/terminals are available on campus for general student use. Students can access the following: computer help desk, free student e-mail accounts, online (class) grades, online (class) registration, online (class) schedules, administrative functions (tuition, student records, financial aid, health insurance waiver). Campuswide network is available. 100% of college-owned or -operated housing units are wired for high-speed Internet access. Wireless service is available via entire campus.

Library: Henry Birnbaum Library. *Books:* 382,858 (physical), 224,418 (digital/electronic); *Serial titles:* 73 (physical), 576,860 (digital/electronic); *Databases:* 172. Weekly public service hours: 93; students can reserve study rooms.

STUDENT LIFE
Housing options: coed, special housing for students with disabilities. Campus housing is university owned and leased by the school. Freshman campus housing is guaranteed.

Activities and organizations: drama/theater group, student-run newspaper, radio and television station, choral group, Kappa Delta, Sigma Delta Tau, Beta Alpha Psi, Profashionals, Programming and Campus Entertainment Board, national fraternities, national sororities.

Athletics Member NCAA. All Division II. *Intercollegiate sports:* baseball M(s), basketball M(s)/W(s), cross-country running M(s)/W(s), field hockey W(s), football M(s), lacrosse M(s)/W(s), soccer W(s), softball W(s), swimming and diving M(s)/W(s), volleyball W(s). *Intramural sports:* badminton M/W, basketball M/W, soccer M/W, ultimate Frisbee M/W, volleyball M/W.

Campus security: 24-hour emergency response devices and patrols, late-night transport/escort service, controlled dormitory access.

Student services: health clinic, personal/psychological counseling.

COSTS & FINANCIAL AID
Costs (2018–19) *Comprehensive fee:* $64,480 includes full-time tuition ($43,624), mandatory fees ($1656), and room and board ($19,200). Full-time tuition and fees vary according to location. Part-time tuition: $1251 per credit hour. Part-time tuition and fees vary according to course load and location. *Room and board:* Room and board charges vary according to board plan, housing facility, location, and student level. *Payment plan:* installment. *Waivers:* senior citizens and employees or children of employees.

Financial Aid Of all full-time matriculated undergraduates who enrolled in 2014, 5,656 applied for aid, 5,240 were judged to have need, 583 had their need fully met. 1,123 Federal Work-Study jobs (averaging $2241). In 2014, 1533 non-need-based awards were made. *Average percent of need met:* 70. *Average financial aid package:* $29,194. *Average need-based loan:* $4582. *Average need-based gift aid:* $24,743. *Average non-need-based aid:* $15,903. *Average indebtedness upon graduation:* $35,442.

APPLYING
Standardized Tests *Required for some:* SAT or ACT (for admission).

Options: electronic application, early decision, early action, deferred entrance.

Application fee: $50.

Required: essay or personal statement, high school transcript, 2 letters of recommendation. *Recommended:* interview.

Application deadlines: 2/15 (freshmen), rolling (transfers), 12/1 (early action).

Notification: continuous (freshmen), continuous (transfers), 1/1 (early action).

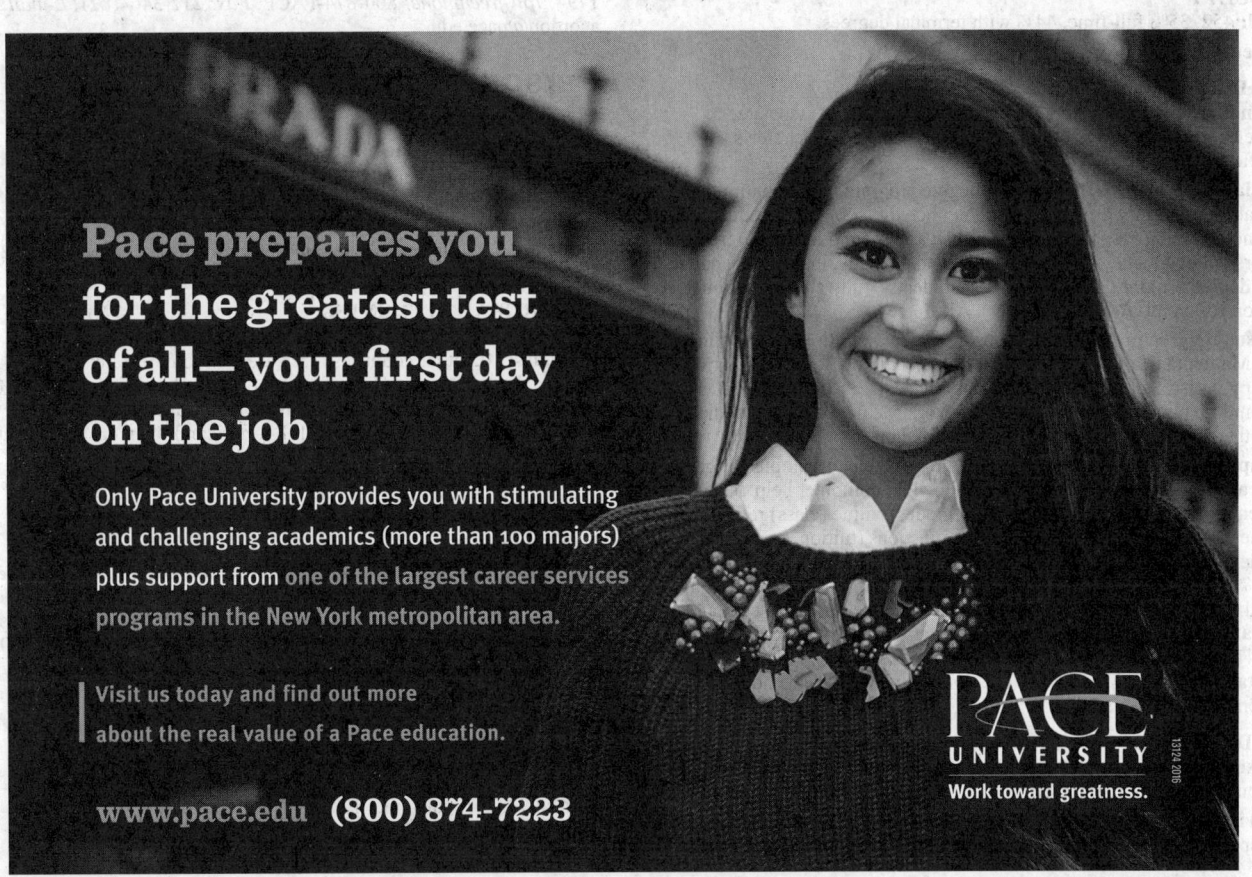

CONTACT
Mr. Andre Cordon, Dean of Admissions, Pace University, One Pace Plaza, 163 William Street, New York, NY 10038. *Phone:* 212-346-1794. *Toll-free phone:* 800-874-7223. *Fax:* 212-346-1821. *E-mail:* acordon@pace.edu.

See previous page for display ad and page 1380 for the College Close-Up.

Pace University, Pleasantville Campus

Pleasantville, New York

http://www.pace.edu/westchester

- **Independent** university, founded 1906
- **Suburban** campus with easy access to New York City
- **Endowment** $169.9 million
- **Coed** 2,600 undergraduate students, 90% full-time, 58% women, 42% men
- **Moderately difficult** entrance level, 72% of applicants were admitted

UNDERGRAD STUDENTS
2,340 full-time, 260 part-time. Students come from 49 states and territories; 68 other countries; 27% are from out of state; 13% Black or African American, non-Hispanic/Latino; 15% Hispanic/Latino; 5% Asian, non-Hispanic/Latino; 0.2% American Indian or Alaska Native, non-Hispanic/Latino; 3% Two or more races, non-Hispanic/Latino; 4% Race/ethnicity unknown; 2% international; 7% transferred in; 55% live on campus.

Freshmen:
Admission: 4,727 applied, 3,407 admitted, 574 enrolled. *Average high school GPA:* 3.2. *Test scores:* SAT evidence-based reading and writing scores over 500: 87%; SAT math scores over 500: 85%; ACT scores over 18: 97%; SAT evidence-based reading and writing scores over 600: 28%; SAT math scores over 600: 20%; ACT scores over 24: 50%; SAT evidence-based reading and writing scores over 700: 2%; SAT math scores over 700: 1%; ACT scores over 30: 5%.

Retention: 82% of full-time freshmen returned.

FACULTY
Total: 452, 35% full-time, 44% with terminal degrees.
Student/faculty ratio: 11:1.

ACADEMICS
Calendar: semesters. *Degrees:* certificates, diplomas, associate, bachelor's, master's, doctoral, post-master's, and postbachelor's certificates.

Special study options: accelerated degree program, adult/continuing education programs, advanced placement credit, cooperative education, distance learning, double majors, English as a second language, freshman honors college, honors programs, independent study, internships, part-time degree program, services for LD students, study abroad, summer session for credit. *ROTC:* Army (c), Air Force (c).

Unusual degree programs: 3-2 business administration; engineering with Manhattan College, Rensselaer Polytechnic Institute; occupational therapy with Columbia University, optometry with SUNY College of Optometry, physical therapy with New York Medical College, podiatry with the New York College of Podiatric Medicine.

Computers: 132 computers/terminals are available on campus for general student use. Students can access the following: computer help desk, free student e-mail accounts, online (class) grades, online (class) registration, online (class) schedules, administrative functions (tuition, student records, financial aid, health insurance waiver). Campuswide network is available. 100% of college-owned or -operated housing units are wired for high-speed Internet access. Wireless service is available via entire campus. **Library:** Edward and Doris Mortola Library. *Books:* 167,456 (physical), 224,418 (digital/electronic); *Serial titles:* 34 (physical), 576,860 (digital/electronic); *Databases:* 172. Weekly public service hours: 113; students can reserve study rooms.

STUDENT LIFE
Housing options: coed. Campus housing is university owned. Freshman campus housing is guaranteed.

Activities and organizations: drama/theater group, student-run newspaper, radio and television station, choral group, Lubin Business

Association, National Student Nurses Association, Future Leaders in Healthcare, Black Student Union, Accounting Society, national fraternities, national sororities.

Athletics Member NCAA. All Division II. *Intercollegiate sports:* baseball M(s), basketball M(s)/W(s), cross-country running M(s)/W(s), field hockey W(s), football M(s), lacrosse M(s)/W(s), soccer W(s), softball W(s), swimming and diving M(s)/W(s), volleyball W(s). *Intramural sports:* badminton M/W, basketball M/W, soccer M/W, softball M/W, tennis M/W, ultimate Frisbee M/W, volleyball M/W.

Campus security: 24-hour emergency response devices and patrols, late-night transport/escort service, controlled dormitory access.

Student services: health clinic, personal/psychological counseling.

COSTS
Costs (2018–19) *Comprehensive fee:* $61,880 includes full-time tuition ($43,624), mandatory fees ($1656), and room and board ($16,600). Full-time tuition and fees vary according to location. Part-time tuition: $1251 per credit hour. Part-time tuition and fees vary according to course load and location. *Room and board:* Room and board charges vary according to board plan, housing facility, location, and student level. *Payment plan:* installment. *Waivers:* senior citizens and employees or children of employees.

APPLYING
Standardized Tests *Required for some:* SAT or ACT (for admission).
Options: electronic application, early decision, early action, deferred entrance.
Application fee: $50.
Required: essay or personal statement, high school transcript, 2 letters of recommendation. *Recommended:* interview.
Application deadlines: 2/15 (freshmen), rolling (transfers), 12/1 (early action).
Notification: continuous (freshmen), continuous (transfers), 1/1 (early action).

CONTACT
Mr. Andre Cordon, Dean of Admission, Pace University, Pleasantville Campus, 861 Bedford Road, Pleasantville, NY 10570. *Phone:* 212-346-1794. *Toll-free phone:* 800-874-PACE. *Fax:* 212-346-1821. *E-mail:* acordon@pace.edu.

Parsons School of Design

New York, New York

http://www.newschool.edu/parsons/

- **Independent** comprehensive, founded 1896, part of The New School
- **Urban** campus with easy access to New York City
- **Endowment** $322.3 million
- **Coed** 4,291 undergraduate students, 90% full-time, 78% women, 22% men

UNDERGRAD STUDENTS
3,859 full-time, 432 part-time. Students come from 51 states and territories; 102 other countries; 75% are from out of state; 4% Black or African American, non-Hispanic/Latino; 10% Hispanic/Latino; 13% Asian, non-Hispanic/Latino; 0.1% Native Hawaiian or other Pacific Islander, non-Hispanic/Latino; 0.1% American Indian or Alaska Native, non-Hispanic/Latino; 3% Two or more races, non-Hispanic/Latino; 3% Race/ethnicity unknown; 44% international; 7% transferred in; 25% live on campus.

Freshmen:
Admission: 917 enrolled. *Average high school GPA:* 3.4. *Test scores:* SAT evidence-based reading and writing scores over 500: 94%; SAT math scores over 500: 91%; ACT scores over 18: 99%; SAT evidence-based reading and writing scores over 600: 53%; SAT math scores over 600: 52%; ACT scores over 24: 74%; SAT evidence-based reading and writing scores over 700: 8%; SAT math scores over 700: 16%; ACT scores over 30: 14%.

Retention: 88% of full-time freshmen returned.

FACULTY
Total: 993, 16% full-time, 12% with terminal degrees.
Student/faculty ratio: 11:1.

ACADEMICS

Calendar: semesters. *Degrees:* associate, bachelor's, master's, and postbachelor's certificates.

Special study options: academic remediation for entering students, accelerated degree program, advanced placement credit, cooperative education, distance learning, double majors, English as a second language, independent study, internships, off-campus study, part-time degree program, services for LD students, student-designed majors, study abroad, summer session for credit.

Computers: 717 computers/terminals are available on campus for general student use. Students can access the following: campus intranet, computer help desk, free student e-mail accounts, online (class) grades, online (class) registration, online (class) schedules. Campuswide network is available. 100% of college-owned or -operated housing units are wired for high-speed Internet access. Wireless service is available via entire campus.

Library: New School Libraries & Archives plus 3 others. *Books:* 215,937 (physical), 840,933 (digital/electronic); *Serial titles:* 2,265 (physical), 113,452 (digital/electronic); *Databases:* 376. Weekly public service hours: 155; study areas open 24 hours, 5–7 days a week; students can reserve study rooms.

STUDENT LIFE

Housing options: coed, special housing for students with disabilities. Campus housing is university owned and leased by the school. Freshman applicants given priority for college housing.

Activities and organizations: drama/theater group, student-run newspaper, choral group.

Athletics *Intramural sports:* basketball M/W, cross-country running M/W, soccer M/W, tennis M/W.

Campus security: 24-hour emergency response devices, controlled dormitory access, 24-hour security desk personnel.

Student services: health clinic, personal/psychological counseling.

COSTS & FINANCIAL AID

Costs (2017–18) *Comprehensive fee:* $62,920 includes full-time tuition ($46,820), mandatory fees ($1100), and room and board ($15,000). Full-time tuition and fees vary according to degree level and location. Part-time tuition: $1590 per credit hour. Part-time tuition and fees vary according to degree level and location. *Required fees:* $550 per term part-time. *College room only:* $16,250. Room and board charges vary according to board plan, housing facility, and location. *Payment plan:* installment. *Waivers:* employees or children of employees.

Financial Aid Of all full-time matriculated undergraduates who enrolled in 2016, 1,426 applied for aid, 1,255 were judged to have need, 198 had their need fully met. 146 Federal Work-Study jobs (averaging $3026). In 2016, 1834 non-need-based awards were made. *Average percent of need met:* 79. *Average financial aid package:* $23,941. *Average need-based loan:* $4281. *Average need-based gift aid:* $16,503. *Average non-need-based aid:* $7449. *Average indebtedness upon graduation:* $70,361. *Financial aid deadline:* 2/1.

APPLYING

Standardized Tests *Required for some:* TOEFL/IELTS /PTE for students whose native language is not English.

Required: essay or personal statement, high school transcript, 2 letters of recommendation, online application, Parsons Challenge portfolio, artist statement. *Recommended:* minimum 3.0 GPA.

CONTACT

Ms. Erin Stine, Director of Undergraduate Admissions for Parsons School of Design, Parsons School of Design, 72 Fifth Avenue at 13th Street, New York, NY 10011. *Phone:* 212-229-8989. *Toll-free phone:* 800-292-3040. *E-mail:* stinee@newschool.edu.

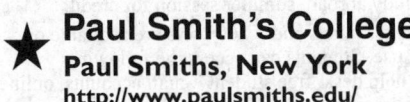

★ Paul Smith's College
Paul Smiths, New York
http://www.paulsmiths.edu/

CONTACT

Admissions Office, Paul Smith's College, Routes 86 and 30, PO Box 265, Paul Smiths, NY 12970. *Phone:* 518-327-6227. *Toll-free phone:* 800-421-2605. *Fax:* 518-327-6016. *E-mail:* admissions@paulsmiths.edu.

Phillips Beth Israel School of Nursing
New York, New York
http://www.mountsinai.org/locations/beth-israel/pson

CONTACT

Mrs. Bernice Pass-Stern, Assistant Dean, Phillips Beth Israel School of Nursing, 776 Sixth Avenue, 4th Floor, New York, NY 10010-6354. *Phone:* 212-614-6176. *Fax:* 212-614-6109. *E-mail:* bstern@chpnet.org.

Plaza College
Forest Hills, New York
http://www.plazacollege.edu/

CONTACT

Dean Vanessa Lopez, Dean of Admissions, Plaza College, 118-33 Queens Boulevard, Forest Hills, NY 11375. *Phone:* 718-779-1430. *E-mail:* info@plazacollege.edu.

★ Pratt Institute
Brooklyn, New York
http://www.pratt.edu/

- **Independent** comprehensive, founded 1887
- **Urban** 25-acre campus
- **Coed** 3,439 undergraduate students, 97% full-time, 70% women, 30% men
- **Very difficult** entrance level, 50% of applicants were admitted

UNDERGRAD STUDENTS

3,331 full-time, 108 part-time. 72% are from out of state; 4% Black or African American, non-Hispanic/Latino; 10% Hispanic/Latino; 13% Asian, non-Hispanic/Latino; 0.1% Native Hawaiian or other Pacific Islander, non-Hispanic/Latino; 4% Two or more races, non-Hispanic/Latino; 0.6% Race/ethnicity unknown; 30% international; 4% transferred in; 53% live on campus.

Freshmen:
Admission: 6,044 applied, 3,018 admitted, 693 enrolled. *Average high school GPA:* 3.8. *Test scores:* SAT evidence-based reading and writing scores over 500: 91%; SAT math scores over 500: 93%; ACT scores over 18: 100%; SAT evidence-based reading and writing scores over 600: 44%; SAT math scores over 600: 60%; ACT scores over 24: 87%; SAT evidence-based reading and writing scores over 700: 7%; SAT math scores over 700: 18%; ACT scores over 30: 25%.

Retention: 88% of full-time freshmen returned.

FACULTY

Total: 1,148, 14% full-time, 11% with terminal degrees.

Student/faculty ratio: 10:1.

ACADEMICS

Calendar: semesters plus optional May term and summer session. *Degrees:* associate, bachelor's, master's, and post-master's certificates.

Special study options: part-time degree program. *ROTC:* Army (c).

Computers: Students can access the following: online (class) registration. Campuswide network is available.

Library: Pratt Institute Library.

STUDENT LIFE

Housing options: coed, special housing for students with disabilities. Campus housing is university owned. Freshman campus housing is guaranteed.

Athletics Member NCAA. All Division III. *Intercollegiate sports:* basketball M, cross-country running M/W, soccer M/W, tennis M/W, track and field M/W, volleyball W. *Intramural sports:* badminton M/W, basketball M, field hockey M, football M, golf M, lacrosse M/W, volleyball M, weight lifting M/W.

Campus security: 24-hour emergency response devices and patrols, late-night transport/escort service.

COSTS & FINANCIAL AID

Costs (2018–19) *Comprehensive fee:* $64,492 includes full-time tuition ($49,810), mandatory fees ($2060), and room and board ($12,622). Part-

At Pratt, Talent Teaches Talent.

Study art, design, architecture or writing with successful and talented practicing professionals at Pratt Institute in New York City. Ranked one of the top design schools in the US by **Business Week,** Pratt offers students an outstanding professional education.

- Highly ranked majors in art and design, architecture, and writing.

- Strong connections to the professional world through the faculty, an outstanding internship program, and industry-based projects.

- Beautifully landscaped 25-acre campus just 25 minutes from Manhattan in a quiet residential neighborhood in Brooklyn.

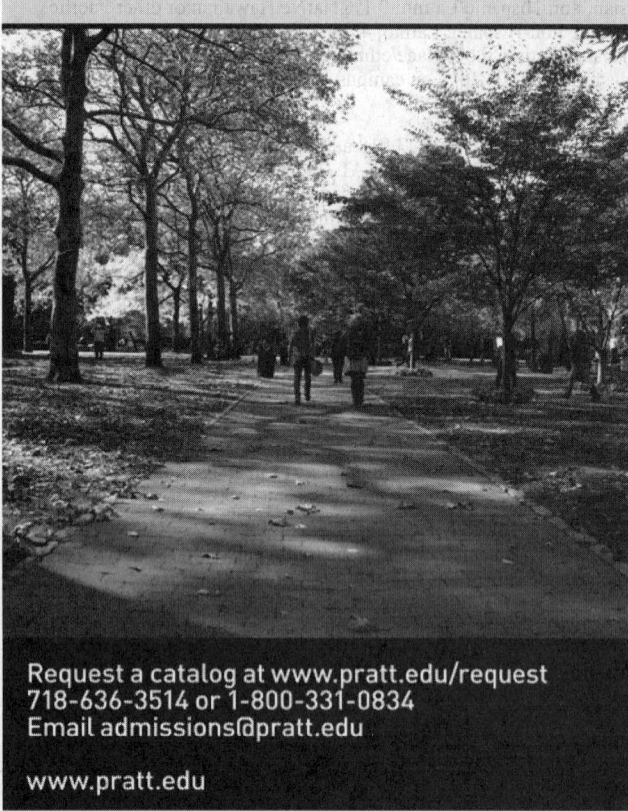

Request a catalog at www.pratt.edu/request
718-636-3514 or 1-800-331-0834
Email admissions@pratt.edu

www.pratt.edu

Pratt

DRAW IT, BUILD IT, MAKE IT

time tuition: $1607 per credit hour. *College room only:* $8862. Room and board charges vary according to board plan and housing facility.

Financial Aid Of all full-time matriculated undergraduates who enrolled in 2016, 1,712 applied for aid, 1,510 were judged to have need, 140 had their need fully met. In 2016, 1089 non-need-based awards were made. *Average percent of need met:* 57. *Average financial aid package:* $30,560. *Average need-based loan:* $10,133. *Average need-based gift aid:* $5790. *Average non-need-based aid:* $17,724. *Average indebtedness upon graduation:* $37,926. *Financial aid deadline:* 3/1.

APPLYING

Standardized Tests *Required:* SAT or ACT (for admission). *Required for some:* SAT Subject Tests (for admission).

Options: electronic application, early action, deferred entrance.

Application fee: $50.

Required: essay or personal statement, high school transcript, 1 letter of recommendation. *Required for some:* portfolio. *Recommended:* minimum 3.0 GPA.

CONTACT

Ms. Olga Burger, Visit Coordinator, Pratt Institute, 200 Willoughby Avenue, DeKalb Hall, Brooklyn, NY 11205. *Phone:* 718-636-3779. *Toll-free phone:* 800-331-0834. *Fax:* 718-636-3670. *E-mail:* visit@pratt.edu.

See this page for display ad and page 1388 for the College Close-Up.

Purchase College, State University of New York

Purchase, New York

http://www.purchase.edu/

- **State-supported** comprehensive, founded 1967, part of State University of New York System
- **Small-town** 500-acre campus with easy access to New York City
- **Coed** 4,121 undergraduate students, 91% full-time, 57% women, 43% men
- **Moderately difficult** entrance level, 44% of applicants were admitted

UNDERGRAD STUDENTS

3,755 full-time, 366 part-time. Students come from 42 states and territories; 30 other countries; 15% are from out of state; 11% Black or African American, non-Hispanic/Latino; 19% Hispanic/Latino; 4% Asian, non-Hispanic/Latino; 0.2% Native Hawaiian or other Pacific Islander, non-Hispanic/Latino; 0.3% American Indian or Alaska Native, non-Hispanic/Latino; 5% Two or more races, non-Hispanic/Latino; 6% Race/ethnicity unknown; 2% international; 10% transferred in; 67% live on campus.

Freshmen:

Admission: 6,762 applied, 2,942 admitted, 732 enrolled. *Average high school GPA:* 3.2. *Test scores:* ACT scores over 18: 94%; ACT scores over 24: 54%; ACT scores over 30: 12%.

Retention: 81% of full-time freshmen returned.

FACULTY

Total: 461, 36% full-time, 31% with terminal degrees.

Student/faculty ratio: 14:1.

ACADEMICS

Calendar: semesters. *Degrees:* certificates, bachelor's, master's, and post-master's certificates.

Special study options: academic remediation for entering students, adult/continuing education programs, advanced placement credit, double majors, English as a second language, independent study, internships, off-campus study, part-time degree program, services for LD students, student-designed majors, study abroad, summer session for credit.

Computers: 600 computers/terminals and 3,500 ports are available on campus for general student use. Students can access the following: campus intranet, computer help desk, free student e-mail accounts, online (class) grades, online (class) registration, online (class) schedules. Campuswide network is available. 100% of college-owned or -operated housing units are wired for high-speed Internet access. Wireless service is available via classrooms, computer centers, computer labs, learning centers, libraries, student centers.

Library: Purchase College Library. *Books:* 237,710 (physical), 11,422 (digital/electronic); *Serial titles:* 107 (physical), 65,714 (digital/electronic); *Databases:* 176.

STUDENT LIFE

Housing options: coed. Campus housing is university owned. Freshman applicants given priority for college housing.

Activities and organizations: drama/theater group, student-run newspaper, radio and television station, choral group, Student Union, WPUR radio station, Latinos Unidos, Gay/Lesbian/Bisexual/Transgender Union, Organization of African People in America.

Athletics Member NCAA. All Division III. *Intercollegiate sports:* baseball M, basketball M/W, cross-country running M/W, golf M, lacrosse M/W, soccer M/W, softball W, swimming and diving M/W, tennis M/W, volleyball M/W. *Intramural sports:* badminton M/W, basketball M/W, bowling M/W, cross-country running M/W, fencing M/W, football M/W, golf M/W, racquetball M/W, skiing (cross-country) M/W, skiing (downhill) M/W, soccer M/W, softball M/W, squash M/W, swimming and diving M/W, table tennis M/W, tennis M/W, volleyball M/W, water polo M/W, weight lifting M/W.

Campus security: 24-hour emergency response devices and patrols, late-night transport/escort service, controlled dormitory access, 24-hour patrols by police officers.

Student services: health clinic, personal/psychological counseling, women's center.

COSTS & FINANCIAL AID

Costs (2018–19) *Tuition:* state resident $6670 full-time, $278 per credit hour part-time; nonresident $16,320 full-time, $680 per credit hour part-time. Part-time tuition and fees vary according to course load. *Required fees:* $1828 full-time. *Room and board:* $13,334; room only: $8674. Room and board charges vary according to board plan and housing facility. *Payment plan:* installment. *Waivers:* employees or children of employees.

Financial Aid Of all full-time matriculated undergraduates who enrolled in 2016, 2,879 applied for aid, 2,214 were judged to have need, 14 had their need fully met. In 2016, 418 non-need-based awards were made. *Average percent of need met:* 49. *Average financial aid package:* $10,029. *Average need-based loan:* $4453. *Average need-based gift aid:* $9724. *Average non-need-based aid:* $2174. *Average indebtedness upon graduation:* $31,188.

APPLYING

Standardized Tests *Required:* SAT or ACT (for admission). *Recommended:* SAT (for admission).

Options: electronic application, early admission, early action, deferred entrance.

Application fee: $50.

Required: high school transcript, minimum 3.0 GPA. *Required for some:* essay or personal statement, 1 letter of recommendation, interview, audition, portfolio.

Application deadlines: 7/15 (freshmen), rolling (transfers), 11/15 (early action).

Notification: continuous until 5/1 (freshmen), continuous (transfers), 12/15 (early action).

CONTACT

Caitlin Read, Dean of Enrollment Management, Purchase College, State University of New York, 735 Anderson Hill Road, Purchase, NY 10577-1400. *Phone:* 914-251-6300. *Fax:* 914-251-6314. *E-mail:* admission@purchase.edu.

Queens College of the City University of New York

Queens, New York

http://www.qc.cuny.edu/

- **State and locally supported** comprehensive, founded 1937, part of City University of New York
- **Urban** 80-acre campus with easy access to New York City
- **Endowment** $50.4 million
- **Coed** 16,680 undergraduate students, 73% full-time, 55% women, 45% men
- **Very difficult** entrance level, 43% of applicants were admitted

UNDERGRAD STUDENTS

12,149 full-time, 4,531 part-time. Students come from 28 states and territories; 144 other countries; 2% are from out of state; 9% Black or African American, non-Hispanic/Latino; 28% Hispanic/Latino; 29% Asian, non-Hispanic/Latino; 0.4% Native Hawaiian or other Pacific Islander, non-Hispanic/Latino; 0.3% American Indian or Alaska Native, non-Hispanic/Latino; 1% Two or more races, non-Hispanic/Latino; 5% international; 15% transferred in; 2% live on campus.

Freshmen:

Admission: 18,180 applied, 7,769 admitted, 1,672 enrolled. *Average high school GPA:* 3.5. *Test scores:* SAT evidence-based reading and writing scores over 500: 85%; SAT math scores over 500: 97%; SAT evidence-based reading and writing scores over 600: 26%; SAT math scores over 600: 38%; SAT evidence-based reading and writing scores over 700: 2%; SAT math scores over 700: 4%.

Retention: 84% of full-time freshmen returned.

FACULTY

Total: 1,625, 36% full-time, 48% with terminal degrees.

Student/faculty ratio: 15:1.

ACADEMICS

Calendar: semesters. *Degrees:* bachelor's, master's, post-master's, and postbachelor's certificates.

Special study options: accelerated degree program, adult/continuing education programs, advanced placement credit, cooperative education, double majors, English as a second language, honors programs, independent study, internships, off-campus study, part-time degree program, services for LD students, study abroad, summer session for credit. *ROTC:* Army (c).

Unusual degree programs: biology, chemistry, computer science, history, music, philosophy, physics, political science, and urban studies, accounting, physics/photonics.

Computers: 2,480 computers/terminals are available on campus for general student use. Students can access the following: campus intranet, computer help desk, free student e-mail accounts, online (class) grades, online (class) registration, online (class) schedules. Campuswide network is available. 100% of college-owned or -operated housing units are wired for high-speed Internet access. Wireless service is available via entire campus.

Library: The Benjamin S. Rosenthal Library plus 1 other. *Books:* 1.1 million (physical), 404,708 (digital/electronic); *Serial titles:* 198 (physical), 125,145 (digital/electronic); *Databases:* 266. Weekly public service hours: 94; students can reserve study rooms.

STUDENT LIFE

Housing options: coed. Campus housing is university owned.

Activities and organizations: drama/theater group, student-run newspaper, radio station, choral group, Science Fiction and Animation, Chabad of QC, La Tertulia, PRISM: The Sexuality and Gender Alliance of QC, Muslim Students Association, national fraternities, national sororities.

Athletics Member NCAA. All Division II. *Intercollegiate sports:* baseball M(s), basketball M(s)/W(s), cross-country running M(s)/W(s), fencing W(s), lacrosse W(s), soccer M(s)/W(s), softball W(s), swimming and diving M(s)/W(s), tennis M(s)/W(s), track and field M(s)/W(s), volleyball W(s). *Intramural sports:* badminton M(c)/W(c), basketball M/W, cross-country running M(c)/W(c), football M/W, soccer M/W, swimming and diving M(c)/W(c), tennis M(c)/W(c), track and field M/W, ultimate Frisbee M(c)/W(c), volleyball M/W.

Campus security: 24-hour emergency response devices and patrols, controlled dormitory access.

Student services: health clinic, personal/psychological counseling.

COSTS & FINANCIAL AID

Costs (2017–18) *Tuition:* state resident $6530 full-time, $285 per credit part-time; nonresident $17,400 full-time, $580 per credit part-time. Full-time tuition and fees vary according to course load. Part-time tuition and fees vary according to course load. *Required fees:* $608 full-time, $209 per term part-time. *Room and board:* $15,352; room only: $12,020. Room and board charges vary according to board plan and housing facility. *Payment plan:* installment. *Waivers:* senior citizens and employees or children of employees.

Financial Aid Of all full-time matriculated undergraduates who enrolled in 2017, 9,400 applied for aid, 8,658 were judged to have need, 266 had their need fully met. 531 Federal Work-Study jobs (averaging $1733). In 2017, 119 non-need-based awards were made. *Average percent of need met:* 49. *Average financial aid package:* $6475. *Average need-based loan:* $4132. *Average need-based gift aid:* $7486. *Average non-need-based aid:* $3914. *Average indebtedness upon graduation:* $14,738.

APPLYING

Standardized Tests *Required:* SAT or ACT (for admission). *Required for some:* SAT Subject Tests (for admission).

Options: electronic application, deferred entrance.

Application fee: $65.

Required: high school transcript, minimum 3.0 GPA. *Required for some:* essay or personal statement.

Application deadlines: 2/1 (freshmen), 2/1 (transfers).

Notification: 2/1 (freshmen), continuous (transfers).

CONTACT
Ms. Chelsea Lavington, Director of Undergraduate Admissions, Queens College of the City University of New York, 65-30 Kissena Boulevard, Queens, NY 11367. *Phone:* 718-997-5600. *Fax:* 718-997-5617.

Rabbinical Academy Mesivta Rabbi Chaim Berlin

Brooklyn, New York

CONTACT
Executive Administrator, Rabbinical Academy Mesivta Rabbi Chaim Berlin, 1605 Coney Island Avenue, Brooklyn, NY 11230-4715. *Phone:* 718-377-0777. *Fax:* 718-338-5578.

Rabbinical College Beth Shraga

Monsey, New York

CONTACT
Rabbi Sydney Schiff, Director of Admissions, Rabbinical College Beth Shraga, 28 Saddle River Road, Monsey, NY 10952-3035.

Rabbinical College Bobover Yeshiva B'nei Zion

Brooklyn, New York

CONTACT
Director of Admissions, Rabbinical College Bobover Yeshiva B'nei Zion, 1577 Forty-eighth Street, Brooklyn, NY 11219. *Phone:* 718-438-2018.

Rabbinical College of Long Island

Long Beach, New York

CONTACT
Director of Admissions, Rabbinical College of Long Island, 205 West Beech Street, Long Beach, NY 11561-3305. *Phone:* 516-431-7414.

Rabbinical College of Ohr Shimon Yisroel

Brooklyn, New York

CONTACT
Rabbinical College of Ohr Shimon Yisroel, 215-217 Hewes Street, Brooklyn, NY 11211.

Rabbinical College Ohr Yisroel

Brooklyn, New York
http://www.rabbinicalcollegeohryisroel.com/

CONTACT
Rabbinical College Ohr Yisroel, 8800 Seaview Avenue, Brooklyn, NY 11236.

Rabbinical Seminary of America

Flushing, New York

CONTACT
Rabbi Abraham Semmel, Director of Admissions, Rabbinical Seminary of America, 76-01 147th Street, Flushing, NY 11367. *Phone:* 718-268-4700.

Rensselaer Polytechnic Institute

Troy, New York
http://www.rpi.edu/

- **Independent** university, founded 1824
- **Suburban** 284-acre campus with easy access to Albany, NY
- **Endowment** $673.7 million
- **Coed** 6,366 undergraduate students, 100% full-time, 32% women, 68% men
- **Very difficult** entrance level, 43% of applicants were admitted

UNDERGRAD STUDENTS

6,340 full-time, 26 part-time. Students come from 50 states and territories; 39 other countries; 67% are from out of state; 4% Black or African American, non-Hispanic/Latino; 9% Hispanic/Latino; 12% Asian, non-Hispanic/Latino; 0.1% American Indian or Alaska Native, non-Hispanic/Latino; 7% Two or more races, non-Hispanic/Latino; 1% Race/ethnicity unknown; 14% international; 2% transferred in; 57% live on campus.

Freshmen:
Admission: 19,505 applied, 8,420 admitted, 1,663 enrolled. *Average high school GPA:* 3.8. *Test scores:* SAT evidence-based reading and writing scores over 500: 100%; SAT math scores over 500: 100%; ACT scores over 18: 100%; SAT evidence-based reading and writing scores over 600: 90%; SAT math scores over 600: 97%; ACT scores over 24: 96%; SAT evidence-based reading and writing scores over 700: 43%; SAT math scores over 700: 69%; ACT scores over 30: 53%.

Retention: 93% of full-time freshmen returned.

FACULTY

Total: 517, 90% full-time, 89% with terminal degrees.

Student/faculty ratio: 13:1.

ACADEMICS

Calendar: semesters. *Degrees:* bachelor's, master's, and doctoral.

Special study options: accelerated degree program, adult/continuing education programs, advanced placement credit, cooperative education, double majors, English as a second language, honors programs, independent study, internships, off-campus study, part-time degree program, services for LD students, student-designed majors, study abroad, summer session for credit. *ROTC:* Army (b), Navy (b), Air Force (b).

Unusual degree programs: 3-2 engineering.

Computers: Students can access the following: campus intranet, computer help desk, free student e-mail accounts, online (class) grades, online (class) registration, online (class) schedules, billing, downloadable software, webpages. Campuswide network is available. 100% of college-owned or -operated housing units are wired for high-speed Internet access. Wireless service is available via entire campus.

Library: Folsom Library plus 2 others. Students can reserve study rooms.

STUDENT LIFE

Housing options: on-campus residence required through sophomore year; coed, special housing for students with disabilities. Campus housing is university owned. Freshman campus housing is guaranteed.

Activities and organizations: drama/theater group, student-run newspaper, radio and television station, choral group, Red Army Spirit Club, Outing Club, Indian Student Association, Chinese American Student Association, pep band, national fraternities, national sororities.

Athletics Member NCAA. All Division III except men's and women's ice hockey (Division I). *Intercollegiate sports:* archery M(c)/W(c), badminton M(c)/W(c), baseball M/W(c), basketball M/W, crew M(c)/W(c), cross-country running M/W, equestrian sports M(c)/W(c), fencing M(c)/W(c), field hockey W, football M, golf M, ice hockey M(s)/W(s), lacrosse M/W, racquetball M(c)/W(c), riflery M(c)/W(c), rugby M(c)/W(c), sailing M(c)/W(c), skiing (cross-country) M(c)/W(c), soccer M/W, softball W, squash M(c)/W(c), swimming and diving M/W, table tennis M(c)/W(c), tennis M/W, track and field M/W, ultimate Frisbee M(c)/W(c), volleyball M(c)/W(c), water polo M(c)/W(c), weight lifting M(c)/W(c). *Intramural sports:* basketball M/W, bowling M(c)/W(c), cheerleading W, ice hockey M/W, lacrosse M(c), racquetball M/W, rock climbing M(c)/W(c), skiing (downhill) M/W, soccer M/W, softball M/W, swimming and diving M(c)/W(c), table tennis M/W, tennis M(c)/W(c), ultimate Frisbee M/W, volleyball M/W, wrestling M.

Campus security: 24-hour emergency response devices and patrols, late-night transport/escort service, controlled dormitory access, campus foot patrols at night.

Student services: health clinic, personal/psychological counseling, women's center, legal services.

COSTS & FINANCIAL AID

Costs (2018–19) *Comprehensive fee:* $69,140 includes full-time tuition ($52,550), mandatory fees ($1330), and room and board ($15,260). Part-time tuition: $1640 per credit hour. *College room only:* $8650. Room and board charges vary according to board plan and location. *Payment plan:* installment. *Waivers:* employees or children of employees.

Financial Aid Of all full-time matriculated undergraduates who enrolled in 2016, 4,239 applied for aid, 3,760 were judged to have need, 725 had their need fully met. 795 Federal Work-Study jobs (averaging $1983). In 2016, 1631 non-need-based awards were made. *Average percent of need met:* 80. *Average financial aid package:* $38,742. *Average need-based loan:* $5398. *Average need-based gift aid:* $33,119. *Average non-need-based aid:* $17,920.

APPLYING

Standardized Tests *Required:* SAT or ACT (for admission). *Required for some:* SAT and SAT Subject Tests or ACT (for admission).

Options: electronic application, early admission, early decision, deferred entrance.

Application fee: $70.

Required for some: essay or personal statement, high school transcript, interview, portfolio for electronic arts. *Recommended:* minimum 3.0 GPA, 1 letter of recommendation.

Early decision deadline: 11/1 (for plan 1), 12/15 (for plan 2).

Notification: 3/12 (freshmen), continuous (transfers), 12/10 (early decision plan 1), 1/14 (early decision plan 2).

CONTACT

Ms. Karen Long, Director, Undergrad Admissions, Rensselaer Polytechnic Institute, 110 8th Street, Troy, NY 12180. *Phone:* 518-276-6216. *Fax:* 518-276-4072. *E-mail:* admissions@rpi.edu.

Roberts Wesleyan College

Rochester, New York

http://www.roberts.edu/

- **Independent** comprehensive, founded 1866, affiliated with Free Methodist Church of North America
- **Suburban** 188-acre campus with easy access to Rochester
- **Endowment** $24.2 million
- **Coed** 1,321 undergraduate students, 94% full-time, 69% women, 31% men
- **Moderately difficult** entrance level, 69% of applicants were admitted

UNDERGRAD STUDENTS

1,248 full-time, 73 part-time. Students come from 27 states and territories; 28 other countries; 8% are from out of state; 9% Black or African American, non-Hispanic/Latino; 6% Hispanic/Latino; 2% Asian, non-Hispanic/Latino; 0.2% Native Hawaiian or other Pacific Islander, non-Hispanic/Latino; 0.2% American Indian or Alaska Native, non-Hispanic/Latino; 3% Two or more races, non-Hispanic/Latino; 2% Race/ethnicity unknown; 4% international; 6% transferred in; 61% live on campus.

Freshmen:

Admission: 1,330 applied, 916 admitted, 219 enrolled. *Average high school GPA:* 3.5. *Test scores:* SAT evidence-based reading and writing scores over 500: 88%; SAT math scores over 500: 84%; ACT scores over 18: 98%; SAT evidence-based reading and writing scores over 600: 39%; SAT math scores over 600: 29%; ACT scores over 24: 60%; SAT evidence-based reading and writing scores over 700: 6%; SAT math scores over 700: 5%; ACT scores over 30: 12%.

Retention: 82% of full-time freshmen returned.

FACULTY

Total: 249, 36% full-time, 36% with terminal degrees.

Student/faculty ratio: 12:1.

ACADEMICS

Calendar: semesters. *Degrees:* bachelor's, master's, and doctoral.

Special study options: academic remediation for entering students, accelerated degree program, adult/continuing education programs, advanced placement credit, distance learning, double majors, English as a second language, honors programs, independent study, internships, off-campus study, services for LD students, student-designed majors, study abroad, summer session for credit. *ROTC:* Army (c), Air Force (c).

Unusual degree programs: 3-2 engineering with Clarkson University, Rensselaer Polytechnic Institute, Rochester Institute of Technology.

Computers: 140 computers/terminals are available on campus for general student use. Students can access the following: campus intranet, computer help desk, free student e-mail accounts, online (class) grades, online (class) registration, online (class) schedules. Campuswide network is available. 100% of college-owned or -operated housing units are wired for high-speed Internet access. Wireless service is available via entire campus.

Library: B. Thomas Golisano Library. *Books:* 128,708 (physical), 6,200 (digital/electronic); *Databases:* 105. Study areas open 24 hours, 5–7 days a week; students can reserve study rooms.

STUDENT LIFE

Housing options: on-campus residence required through senior year; men-only, women-only, special housing for students with disabilities. Campus housing is university owned. Freshman campus housing is guaranteed.

Activities and organizations: drama/theater group, student-run newspaper, choral group, Intramurals, Foot of the Cross, Fellowship of Christian Athletes, Nursing Club, Drama Club.

Athletics Member NCAA, NCCAA. All NCAA Division II. *Intercollegiate sports:* basketball M(s)/W(s), bowling W(s), cheerleading M(c)/W(c), cross-country running M(s)/W(s), golf M(s), lacrosse M(s)/W(s), soccer M(s)/W(s), swimming and diving M(s)/W(s), tennis M(s)/W(s), track and field M(s)/W(s), volleyball W(s). *Intramural sports:* basketball M/W, field hockey M/W, football M/W, racquetball M/W, skiing (downhill) M/W, soccer M/W, softball M/W, swimming and diving M/W, table tennis M/W, tennis M/W, ultimate Frisbee M/W, volleyball M/W, water polo M/W.

Campus security: 24-hour emergency response devices and patrols, student patrols, late-night transport/escort service, controlled dormitory access, 24-hour Resident Life staff on-call.

Student services: health clinic, personal/psychological counseling.

COSTS & FINANCIAL AID

Costs (2018–19) *One-time required fee:* $250. *Comprehensive fee:* $41,366 includes full-time tuition ($29,600), mandatory fees ($1336), and room and board ($10,430). Part-time tuition and fees vary according to course load. *College room only:* $6548. Room and board charges vary according to board plan and housing facility. *Payment plan:* installment. *Waivers:* senior citizens and employees or children of employees.

Financial Aid Of all full-time matriculated undergraduates who enrolled in 2017, 1,073 applied for aid, 1,005 were judged to have need, 130 had their need fully met. 618 Federal Work-Study jobs (averaging $479). 46 state and other part-time jobs (averaging $1891). In 2017, 173 non-need-based awards were made. *Average percent of need met:* 71. *Average financial aid package:* $22,228. *Average need-based loan:* $5738. *Average need-based gift aid:* $17,073. *Average non-need-based aid:* $11,437. *Average indebtedness upon graduation:* $34,679.

APPLYING

Standardized Tests *Required:* SAT or ACT (for admission).

Options: electronic application, early admission, early action, deferred entrance.

Required: essay or personal statement, high school transcript. *Recommended:* minimum 2.7 GPA, interview.

Application deadlines: 8/20 (freshmen), rolling (transfers), 11/15 (early action).

Notification: continuous until 9/1 (freshmen), continuous (transfers), 12/6 (early action).

CONTACT

Mr. J.P. Anderson, Associate Vice President of Undergraduate Admissions, Roberts Wesleyan College, 2301 Westside Drive, Rochester, NY 14624-1997. *Phone:* 585-594-6400. *Toll-free phone:* 800-777-4RWC. *Fax:* 585-594-6371. *E-mail:* admissions@roberts.edu.

Rochester Institute of Technology

Rochester, New York

http://www.rit.edu/

- **Independent** university, founded 1829
- **Suburban** 1300-acre campus with easy access to Rochester
- **Endowment** $847.2 million
- **Coed** 13,515 undergraduate students, 92% full-time, 32% women, 68% men
- **Moderately difficult** entrance level, 57% of applicants were admitted

UNDERGRAD STUDENTS

12,447 full-time, 1,068 part-time. Students come from 52 states and territories; 67 other countries; 46% are from out of state; 5% Black or African American, non-Hispanic/Latino; 7% Hispanic/Latino; 9% Asian, non-Hispanic/Latino; 0.2% American Indian or Alaska Native, non-Hispanic/Latino; 4% Two or more races, non-Hispanic/Latino; 6% Race/ethnicity unknown; 6% international; 4% transferred in; 52% live on campus.

Freshmen:

Admission: 20,451 applied, 11,599 admitted, 2,758 enrolled. *Average high school GPA:* 3.7. *Test scores:* SAT evidence-based reading and writing scores over 500: 98%; SAT math scores over 500: 99%; ACT scores over 18: 100%; SAT evidence-based reading and writing scores over 600: 71%; SAT math scores over 600: 79%; ACT scores over 24: 94%; SAT evidence-based reading and writing scores over 700: 17%; SAT math scores over 700: 30%; ACT scores over 30: 47%.

Retention: 90% of full-time freshmen returned.

FACULTY

Total: 1,459, 70% full-time, 50% with terminal degrees.

Student/faculty ratio: 13:1.

ACADEMICS

Calendar: semesters. *Degrees:* certificates, associate, bachelor's, master's, doctoral, and postbachelor's certificates.

Special study options: accelerated degree program, adult/continuing education programs, advanced placement credit, cooperative education, distance learning, double majors, English as a second language, honors programs, independent study, internships, off-campus study, part-time degree program, services for LD students, student-designed majors, study abroad, summer session for credit. *ROTC:* Army (b), Navy (c), Air Force (b).

Computers: 3,500 computers/terminals and 20,000 ports are available on campus for general student use. Students can access the following: campus intranet, computer help desk, free student e-mail accounts, online (class) grades, online (class) registration, online (class) schedules, student account information. Campuswide network is available. 100% of college-

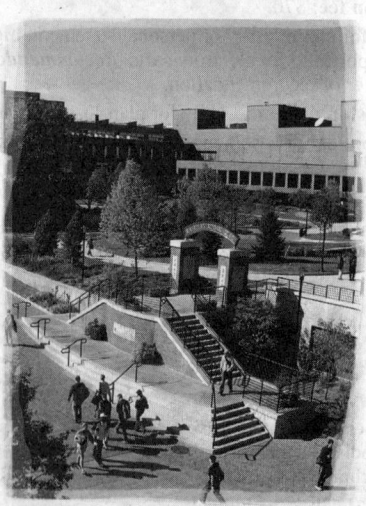

owned or -operated housing units are wired for high-speed Internet access. Wireless service is available via entire campus.

Library: Wallace Memorial Library. *Books:* 429,176 (physical), 240,712 (digital/electronic); *Serial titles:* 58,293 (digital/electronic); *Databases:* 113. Weekly public service hours: 147; study areas open 24 hours, 5–7 days a week; students can reserve study rooms.

STUDENT LIFE

Housing options: on-campus residence required for freshman year; coed, men-only, women-only, special housing for students with disabilities. Campus housing is university owned. Freshman campus housing is guaranteed.

Activities and organizations: drama/theater group, student-run newspaper, radio station, choral group, national fraternities, national sororities.

Athletics Member NCAA. All Division III except men's and women's ice hockey (Division I). *Intercollegiate sports:* baseball M, basketball M/W, bowling M(c)/W(c), cheerleading M(c)/W(c), crew M/W, cross-country running M/W, equestrian sports M(c)/W(c), fencing M(c)/W(c), field hockey W(c), ice hockey M/W, lacrosse M/W, skiing (downhill) M(c)/W(c), soccer M/W, softball W, swimming and diving M/W, tennis M/W, track and field M/W, ultimate Frisbee M(c)/W(c), volleyball M(c)/W, water polo M(c)/W(c), wrestling M. *Intramural sports:* badminton M/W, basketball M/W, bowling M/W, football M, golf M/W, ice hockey M/W, lacrosse M(c), racquetball M/W, rock climbing M(c)/W(c), soccer M/W, softball M/W, table tennis M/W, tennis M/W, volleyball M/W.

Campus security: 24-hour emergency response devices and patrols, student patrols, late-night transport/escort service, controlled dormitory access.

Student services: health clinic, personal/psychological counseling, women's center, legal services.

COSTS & FINANCIAL AID

Costs (2017–18) *Comprehensive fee:* $52,734 includes full-time tuition ($39,506), mandatory fees ($562), and room and board ($12,666). Full-time tuition and fees vary according to course load. Part-time tuition: $1463 per credit hour. Part-time tuition and fees vary according to class time and course load. *Required fees:* $70 per term part-time. *College room only:* $7376. Room and board charges vary according to board plan and housing facility. *Payment plans:* tuition prepayment, installment, deferred payment. *Waivers:* employees or children of employees.

Financial Aid Of all full-time matriculated undergraduates who enrolled in 2016, 10,091 applied for aid, 9,026 were judged to have need, 7,300 had their need fully met. In 2016, 1800 non-need-based awards were made. *Average percent of need met:* 87. *Average financial aid package:* $28,000. *Average need-based loan:* $6500. *Average need-based gift aid:* $22,200. *Average non-need-based aid:* $10,200. *Average indebtedness upon graduation:* $38,927.

APPLYING

Standardized Tests *Required:* SAT or ACT (for admission).

Options: electronic application, early admission, early decision, deferred entrance.

Application fee: $65.

Required: essay or personal statement, high school transcript. *Required for some:* portfolio of original artwork for School of Art, Design and Crafts; interview for BS/MS physician assistant program. *Recommended:* minimum 3.4 GPA, 1 letter of recommendation, interview.

Early decision deadline: 11/15.

Notification: continuous until 2/15 (freshmen), continuous (transfers), 12/15 (early decision).

CONTACT

Ms. Marian Nicoletti, Director of Admission, Rochester Institute of Technology, 60 Lomb Memorial Drive, Rochester, NY 14623-5604. *Phone:* 585-475-6631. *Fax:* 585-475-7424. *E-mail:* admissions@rit.edu.

See previous page for display ad and page 1404 for the College Close-Up.

The Sage Colleges
Troy, New York
http://www.sage.edu/

- **Independent** comprehensive, founded 1916
- **Urban** 23-acre campus
- **Endowment** $35.0 million
- **Coed** 1,320 undergraduate students, 88% full-time, 79% women, 21% men
- **Moderately difficult** entrance level, 56% of applicants were admitted

UNDERGRAD STUDENTS

1,159 full-time, 161 part-time. Students come from 18 states and territories; 2 other countries; 8% are from out of state; 13% Black or African American, non-Hispanic/Latino; 9% Hispanic/Latino; 3% Asian, non-Hispanic/Latino; 0.1% Native Hawaiian or other Pacific Islander, non-Hispanic/Latino; 0.2% American Indian or Alaska Native, non-Hispanic/Latino; 3% Two or more races, non-Hispanic/Latino; 7% Race/ethnicity unknown; 0.4% international; 13% transferred in; 52% live on campus.

Freshmen:
Admission: 1,813 applied, 1,008 admitted, 202 enrolled. *Average high school GPA:* 3.3. *Test scores:* ACT scores over 18: 93%; ACT scores over 24: 26%.

Retention: 79% of full-time freshmen returned.

FACULTY
Total: 297, 44% full-time, 52% with terminal degrees.

Student/faculty ratio: 13:1.

ACADEMICS

Calendar: semesters. *Degrees:* certificates, bachelor's, master's, doctoral, post-master's, and postbachelor's certificates.

Special study options: accelerated degree program, adult/continuing education programs, advanced placement credit, cooperative education, distance learning, double majors, honors programs, independent study, internships, off-campus study, part-time degree program, services for LD students, student-designed majors, study abroad, summer session for credit. *ROTC:* Army (c), Air Force (c).

Unusual degree programs: 3-2 business administration with Sage Graduate School; engineering with Rensselaer Polytechnic Institute; nursing with Sage Graduate School; occupational therapy, physical therapy with Sage Graduate School.

Computers: 441 computers/terminals are available on campus for general student use. Students can access the following: campus intranet, computer help desk, free student e-mail accounts, online (class) grades, online (class) registration, online (class) schedules. Campuswide network is available. 100% of college-owned or -operated housing units are wired for high-speed Internet access. Wireless service is available via classrooms, computer labs, learning centers, libraries, student centers.

Library: James Wheelock Clark Library plus 1 other. *Books:* 184,027 (physical), 190,703 (digital/electronic); *Serial titles:* 232 (physical), 65,180 (digital/electronic); *Databases:* 103. Weekly public service hours: 70; students can reserve study rooms.

STUDENT LIFE

Housing options: coed, women-only. Campus housing is university owned and leased by the school. Freshman campus housing is guaranteed.

Activities and organizations: drama/theater group, student-run newspaper, choral group, Dance Ensemble, SALANA (African American, Latino, Asian, Native American), BLSA (Black Latino), ASIC (Interior Design), AIGA (Graphic Design).

Athletics Member NCAA. All Division III. *Intercollegiate sports:* basketball M/W, cross-country running M/W, golf M, lacrosse M/W, soccer M/W, softball W, tennis M/W, track and field M/W, volleyball M/W. *Intramural sports:* football M/W, ice hockey M(c)/W(c), lacrosse W(c), skiing (downhill) M(c)/W(c).

Campus security: 24-hour emergency response devices and patrols, late-night transport/escort service, controlled dormitory access.

Student services: health clinic, personal/psychological counseling, women's center.

COSTS & FINANCIAL AID

Costs (2018–19) *Comprehensive fee:* $43,475 includes full-time tuition ($29,357), mandatory fees ($1500), and room and board ($12,618). *College room only:* $6430. Room and board charges vary according to board plan. *Payment plan:* installment. *Waivers:* employees or children of employees.

Financial Aid Of all full-time matriculated undergraduates who enrolled in 2017, 1,157 applied for aid, 1,092 were judged to have need. In 2017, 50 non-need-based awards were made. *Average need-based loan:* $4307. *Average need-based gift aid:* $12,243. *Average non-need-based aid:* $10,073. *Average indebtedness upon graduation:* $30,905.

APPLYING

Standardized Tests *Required for some:* SAT or ACT (for admission).

Options: electronic application, early admission, early action, deferred entrance.

Application fee: $30.

Required: essay or personal statement, high school transcript, minimum 2.5 GPA, 2 letters of recommendation. *Required for some:* portfolio for art and design programs. *Recommended:* interview.

Application deadlines: rolling (freshmen), rolling (transfers).

Notification: continuous (freshmen), continuous (transfers).

CONTACT

Ms. Kathryn Aviza, Senior Director of Undergraduate Admission, TSC, The Sage Colleges, 140 New Scotland Avenue, Albany, NY 12208. *Phone:* 518-292-1928. *Fax:* 518-292-1912. *E-mail:* avizak@sage.edu.

St. Bonaventure University

St. Bonaventure, New York

http://www.sbu.edu/

- **Independent** comprehensive, founded 1858, affiliated with Roman Catholic Church
- **Small-town** 500-acre campus
- **Endowment** $65.2 million
- **Coed** 1,627 undergraduate students, 98% full-time, 48% women, 52% men
- **Moderately difficult** entrance level, 71% of applicants were admitted

UNDERGRAD STUDENTS

1,591 full-time, 36 part-time. Students come from 33 states and territories; 17 other countries; 32% are from out of state; 6% Black or African American, non-Hispanic/Latino; 8% Hispanic/Latino; 4% Asian, non-Hispanic/Latino; 0.1% Native Hawaiian or other Pacific Islander, non-Hispanic/Latino; 0.4% American Indian or Alaska Native, non-Hispanic/Latino; 2% Two or more races, non-Hispanic/Latino; 7% Race/ethnicity unknown; 3% international; 4% transferred in; 80% live on campus.

Freshmen:

Admission: 2,986 applied, 2,106 admitted, 439 enrolled. *Average high school GPA:* 3.4. *Test scores:* SAT evidence-based reading and writing scores over 500: 80%; SAT math scores over 500: 78%; ACT scores over 18: 94%; SAT evidence-based reading and writing scores over 600: 32%; SAT math scores over 600: 31%; ACT scores over 24: 56%; SAT evidence-based reading and writing scores over 700: 3%; SAT math scores over 700: 6%; ACT scores over 30: 12%.

Retention: 84% of full-time freshmen returned.

FACULTY

Total: 239, 53% full-time, 53% with terminal degrees.

Student/faculty ratio: 11:1.

ACADEMICS

Calendar: semesters. *Degrees:* associate, bachelor's, master's, post-master's, and postbachelor's certificates.

Special study options: accelerated degree program, advanced placement credit, distance learning, double majors, honors programs, independent study, internships, off-campus study, part-time degree program, services

for LD students, student-designed majors, study abroad, summer session for credit. *ROTC:* Army (b).

Unusual degree programs: business administration.

Computers: 320 computers/terminals and 2,500 ports are available on campus for general student use. Students can access the following: campus intranet, computer help desk, free student e-mail accounts, online (class) grades, online (class) registration, online (class) schedules. Campuswide network is available. 100% of college-owned or -operated housing units are wired for high-speed Internet access. Wireless service is available via entire campus.

Library: Friedsam Memorial Library. *Books:* 371,691 (physical), 1.6 million (digital/electronic); *Serial titles:* 253 (physical), 269,989 (digital/electronic); *Databases:* 64. Weekly public service hours: 109; students can reserve study rooms.

STUDENT LIFE

Housing options: on-campus residence required through junior year; coed, special housing for students with disabilities. Campus housing is university owned. Freshman campus housing is guaranteed.

Activities and organizations: drama/theater group, student-run newspaper, radio and television station, choral group, Student Government Association, Bona Responds, BV newspaper, Students for the Mountain, Student Ambassadors.

Athletics Member NCAA. All Division I. *Intercollegiate sports:* baseball M(s), basketball M(s)/W(s), cross-country running M(s)/W(s), field hockey M(c)/W(c), golf M(s), ice hockey M(c), lacrosse M(s)/W(s), rugby M(c)/W(c), soccer M(s)/W(s), softball W(s), swimming and diving M(s)/W(s), tennis M(s)/W(s), track and field M/W, volleyball M(c)/W(c). *Intramural sports:* baseball M(c), basketball M(c)/W(c), football M/W, golf M/W, ice hockey M(c)/W(c), lacrosse M(c)/W(c), skiing (downhill) M(c)/W(c), soccer M(c)/W(c), softball W(c), tennis M/W, track and field M(c)/W(c), ultimate Frisbee M/W, volleyball M/W.

Campus security: 24-hour emergency response devices and patrols, late-night transport/escort service, controlled dormitory access.

Student services: health clinic, personal/psychological counseling.

COSTS & FINANCIAL AID

Costs (2017–18) *One-time required fee:* $100. *Comprehensive fee:* $45,146 includes full-time tuition ($32,366), mandatory fees ($965), and room and board ($11,815). Part-time tuition: $962 per credit hour. Part-time tuition and fees vary according to course load. *Required fees:* $962 per credit hour part-time. *College room only:* $6230. Room and board charges vary according to board plan and housing facility. *Waivers:* senior citizens and employees or children of employees.

Financial Aid Of all full-time matriculated undergraduates who enrolled in 2016, 1,340 applied for aid, 1,182 were judged to have need, 405 had their need fully met. 271 Federal Work-Study jobs (averaging $927). 374 state and other part-time jobs (averaging $910). In 2016, 715 non-need-based awards were made. *Average percent of need met:* 75. *Average financial aid package:* $22,673. *Average need-based loan:* $4338. *Average need-based gift aid:* $11,290. *Average non-need-based aid:* $2951. *Average indebtedness upon graduation:* $15,101.

APPLYING

Standardized Tests *Required:* SAT or ACT (for admission). *Required for some:* SAT and SAT Subject Tests or ACT (for admission).

Options: electronic application, deferred entrance.

Required: high school transcript, 1 letter of recommendation. *Required for some:* essay or personal statement. *Recommended:* essay or personal statement, minimum 3.0 GPA, 3 letters of recommendation, interview.

Application deadlines: 7/1 (freshmen), 8/15 (transfers).

Notification: continuous until 10/15 (freshmen), continuous until 10/1 (transfers).

CONTACT

Mr. Doug Brady, Director of Recruitment, St. Bonaventure University, PO Box D, 3261 West State Road, St. Bonaventure, NY 14778. *Phone:* 716-375-2455. *Toll-free phone:* 800-462-5050. *Fax:* 716-375-4005. *E-mail:* dbrady@sbu.edu.

St. Francis College
Brooklyn Heights, New York
http://www.sfc.edu/

CONTACT
Mrs. Lisa Randazzo, Associate Director of Admissions, St. Francis College, 180 Remsen Street, Brooklyn Heights, NY 11201-4398. *Phone:* 718-489-5336. *Fax:* 718-802-0453. *E-mail:* lrandazzo@sfc.edu.

St. John Fisher College
Rochester, New York
http://www.sjfc.edu/
- **Independent** comprehensive, founded 1948, affiliated with Roman Catholic Church
- **Suburban** 154-acre campus
- **Endowment** $83.8 million
- **Coed** 2,759 undergraduate students, 95% full-time, 60% women, 40% men
- **Moderately difficult** entrance level, 65% of applicants were admitted

UNDERGRAD STUDENTS
2,630 full-time, 129 part-time. Students come from 19 states and territories; 4 other countries; 3% are from out of state; 4% Black or African American, non-Hispanic/Latino; 5% Hispanic/Latino; 3% Asian, non-Hispanic/Latino; 0.3% American Indian or Alaska Native, non-Hispanic/Latino; 2% Two or more races, non-Hispanic/Latino; 2% Race/ethnicity unknown; 0.2% international; 7% transferred in; 51% live on campus.

Freshmen:
Admission: 4,432 applied, 2,860 admitted, 626 enrolled. *Average high school GPA:* 3.5. *Test scores:* SAT evidence-based reading and writing scores over 500: 89%; SAT math scores over 500: 90%; ACT scores over 18: 95%; SAT evidence-based reading and writing scores over 600: 34%; SAT math scores over 600: 37%; ACT scores over 24: 58%; SAT evidence-based reading and writing scores over 700: 2%; SAT math scores over 700: 2%; ACT scores over 30: 6%.
Retention: 85% of full-time freshmen returned.

FACULTY
Total: 449, 52% full-time, 47% with terminal degrees.
Student/faculty ratio: 12:1.

ACADEMICS
Calendar: semesters. *Degrees:* certificates, bachelor's, master's, doctoral, post-master's, and postbachelor's certificates.
Special study options: accelerated degree program, adult/continuing education programs, advanced placement credit, distance learning, double majors, honors programs, independent study, internships, off-campus study, part-time degree program, services for LD students, student-designed majors, study abroad, summer session for credit. *ROTC:* Army (c), Navy (c), Air Force (c).
Unusual degree programs: 3-2 engineering with Columbia University, Rensselaer Polytechnic Institute, University of Rochester.
Computers: 550 computers/terminals and 1,875 ports are available on campus for general student use. Students can access the following: campus intranet, computer help desk, free student e-mail accounts, online (class) grades, online (class) registration, online (class) schedules. Campuswide network is available. 100% of college-owned or -operated housing units are wired for high-speed Internet access. Wireless service is available via entire campus.
Library: Charles J. Lavery Library plus 1 other. *Books:* 162,694 (physical), 137,162 (digital/electronic); *Databases:* 197. Students can reserve study rooms.

STUDENT LIFE
Housing options: coed, women-only, special housing for students with disabilities. Campus housing is university owned. Freshman campus housing is guaranteed.
Activities and organizations: drama/theater group, student-run newspaper, television station, choral group, Student Government, Student Activities Board, Commuter Council, Resident Student Association, Teddi Dance for Love.

Athletics Member NCAA. All Division III. *Intercollegiate sports:* baseball M, basketball M/W, crew W, cross-country running M/W, field hockey W, football M, golf M/W, lacrosse M/W, soccer M/W, softball W, tennis M/W, track and field M/W, volleyball M/W. *Intramural sports:* basketball M/W, cheerleading W(c), crew M(c), equestrian sports M(c)/W(c), ice hockey M(c)/W(c), rugby M(c)/W(c), soccer M/W, volleyball M.
Campus security: 24-hour emergency response devices and patrols, late-night transport/escort service, controlled dormitory access.
Student services: health clinic, personal/psychological counseling.

COSTS & FINANCIAL AID
Costs (2017–18) *Comprehensive fee:* $45,270 includes full-time tuition ($32,540), mandatory fees ($580), and room and board ($12,150). Full-time tuition and fees vary according to program. Part-time tuition: $885 per credit hour. Part-time tuition and fees vary according to course load and program. *Required fees:* $10 per credit hour part-time. *College room only:* $7780. Room and board charges vary according to board plan. *Payment plans:* installment, deferred payment. *Waivers:* employees or children of employees.
Financial Aid Of all full-time matriculated undergraduates who enrolled in 2017, 2,337 applied for aid, 2,169 were judged to have need, 726 had their need fully met. 1,345 Federal Work-Study jobs (averaging $1500). In 2017, 457 non-need-based awards were made. *Average percent of need met:* 69. *Average financial aid package:* $23,140. *Average need-based loan:* $4810. *Average need-based gift aid:* $18,096. *Average non-need-based aid:* $12,151. *Average indebtedness upon graduation:* $38,639.

APPLYING
Standardized Tests *Required:* SAT or ACT (for admission).
Options: electronic application, early decision, deferred entrance.
Required: essay or personal statement, high school transcript, minimum 3.0 GPA, 1 letter of recommendation. *Recommended:* interview.
Application deadlines: rolling (freshmen), rolling (transfers).
Early decision deadline: 12/1.
Notification: continuous until 12/1 (freshmen), continuous until 9/1 (transfers), 12/15 (early decision).

CONTACT
Mrs. Stacy A. Ledermann, Director of Freshmen Admissions, St. John Fisher College, 3690 East Avenue, Rochester, NY 14618. *Phone:* 585-385-8064. *Toll-free phone:* 800-444-4640. *Fax:* 585-385-8386. *E-mail:* admissions@sjfc.edu.

St. John's University
Queens, New York
http://www.stjohns.edu/
- **Independent** university, founded 1870, affiliated with Roman Catholic Church
- **Urban** 102-acre campus with easy access to New York City
- **Endowment** $716.5 million
- **Coed** 16,766 undergraduate students, 69% full-time, 58% women, 42% men
- **Moderately difficult** entrance level, 68% of applicants were admitted

UNDERGRAD STUDENTS
11,531 full-time, 5,235 part-time. Students come from 47 states and territories; 101 other countries; 25% are from out of state; 13% Black or African American, non-Hispanic/Latino; 9% Hispanic/Latino; 14% Asian, non-Hispanic/Latino; 0.3% Native Hawaiian or other Pacific Islander, non-Hispanic/Latino; 0.5% American Indian or Alaska Native, non-Hispanic/Latino; 4% Two or more races, non-Hispanic/Latino; 8% Race/ethnicity unknown; 4% international; 2% transferred in; 26% live on campus.

Freshmen:
Admission: 27,179 applied, 18,408 admitted, 2,967 enrolled. *Average high school GPA:* 3.5. *Test scores:* SAT evidence-based reading and writing scores over 500: 91%; SAT math scores over 500: 88%; ACT scores over 18: 99%; SAT evidence-based reading and writing scores over 600: 39%; SAT math scores over 600: 37%; ACT scores over 24: 67%; SAT evidence-based reading and writing scores over 700: 5%; SAT math scores over 700: 9%; ACT scores over 30: 19%.

Retention: 84% of full-time freshmen returned.

FACULTY
Total: 1,460, 44% full-time, 53% with terminal degrees.
Student/faculty ratio: 17:1.

ACADEMICS
Calendar: semesters. *Degrees:* certificates, bachelor's, master's, doctoral, post-master's, and postbachelor's certificates.

Special study options: accelerated degree program, adult/continuing education programs, advanced placement credit, distance learning, double majors, English as a second language, honors programs, independent study, internships, off-campus study, part-time degree program, services for LD students, study abroad, summer session for credit. *ROTC:* Army (b).

Unusual degree programs: 3-2 business administration.

Computers: 12,702 computers/terminals and 12,754 ports are available on campus for general student use. Students can access the following: campus intranet, computer help desk, free student e-mail accounts, online (class) grades, online (class) registration, online (class) schedules. Campuswide network is available. 100% of college-owned or -operated housing units are wired for high-speed Internet access. Wireless service is available via entire campus.

Library: St. John's University Library plus 3 others. *Books:* 534,824 (physical), 608,270 (digital/electronic); *Serial titles:* 68,549 (physical), 88,058 (digital/electronic); *Databases:* 226. Weekly public service hours: 92; students can reserve study rooms.

STUDENT LIFE
Housing options: coed, special housing for students with disabilities. Campus housing is university owned and leased by the school.

Activities and organizations: drama/theater group, student-run newspaper, radio and television station, choral group, Student Government, Incorporated, Haraya (Pan-African Students Coalition), American Pharmaceutical Association, Muslim Students, Pare-Philippine- Americans Reaching Everyone, national fraternities, national sororities.

Athletics Member NCAA. All Division I. *Intercollegiate sports:* baseball M(s), basketball M(s)/W(s), cross-country running W(s), fencing M(s)/W(s), golf M(s)/W(s), lacrosse M(s), soccer M(s)/W(s), softball W(s), tennis M(s)/W(s), track and field W(s), volleyball W(s). *Intramural sports:* badminton M/W, basketball M/W, bowling M(c), cross-country running M(c)/W(c), football M/W, soccer M/W, softball M/W, tennis M/W, track and field M(c)/W(c), ultimate Frisbee M(c), volleyball M/W.

Campus security: 24-hour emergency response devices and patrols, late-night transport/escort service, controlled dormitory access, Emergency Notification System, CNS Boards, Public Address System.

Student services: health clinic, personal/psychological counseling.

COSTS & FINANCIAL AID
Costs (2017–18) *One-time required fee:* $250. *Comprehensive fee:* $57,540 includes full-time tuition ($39,690), mandatory fees ($830), and room and board ($17,020). Full-time tuition and fees vary according to course load, location, program, reciprocity agreements, and student level. Part-time tuition: $1323 per credit. Part-time tuition and fees vary according to course load, location, program, and student level. *Required fees:* $313 per term part-time. *College room only:* $10,670. Room and board charges vary according to board plan, housing facility, and location. *Payment plan:* installment. *Waivers:* adult students, senior citizens, and employees or children of employees.

Financial Aid Of all full-time matriculated undergraduates who enrolled in 2016, 9,639 applied for aid, 8,924 were judged to have need, 1,077 had their need fully met. 822 Federal Work-Study jobs (averaging $2484). In 2016, 696 non-need-based awards were made. *Average percent of need met:* 66. *Average financial aid package:* $28,656. *Average need-based loan:* $4609. *Average need-based gift aid:* $8725. *Average non-need-based aid:* $21,098. *Average indebtedness upon graduation:* $32,831.

APPLYING
Standardized Tests *Required for some:* SAT or ACT (for admission).

Options: electronic application, early admission, early decision, early action, deferred entrance.

Required: high school transcript, minimum 3.0 GPA. *Required for some:* essay or personal statement, 2 letters of recommendation, interview. *Recommended:* essay or personal statement, 2 letters of recommendation.

Application deadlines: rolling (freshmen), rolling (out-of-state freshmen), rolling (transfers), 12/15 (early action).

Early decision deadline: 11/15.

Notification: continuous (freshmen), continuous (out-of-state freshmen), continuous (transfers), 12/15 (early decision), 1/15 (early action).

CONTACT
St. John's University, 8000 Utopia Parkway, Queens, NY 11439. *Toll-free phone:* 888-9STJOHNS.

St. Joseph's College, Long Island Campus
Patchogue, New York
http://www.sjcny.edu/
- **Independent** comprehensive, founded 1916
- **Suburban** 32-acre campus with easy access to New York City
- **Endowment** $20.7 million
- **Coed** 3,059 undergraduate students, 85% full-time, 66% women, 34% men
- **Moderately difficult** entrance level, 71% of applicants were admitted

UNDERGRAD STUDENTS
2,613 full-time, 446 part-time. Students come from 14 states and territories; 8 other countries; 1% are from out of state; 5% Black or African American, non-Hispanic/Latino; 12% Hispanic/Latino; 2% Asian, non-Hispanic/Latino; 0.1% Native Hawaiian or other Pacific Islander, non-Hispanic/Latino; 0.2% American Indian or Alaska Native, non-Hispanic/Latino; 2% Two or more races, non-Hispanic/Latino; 13% Race/ethnicity unknown; 14% transferred in.

Freshmen:
Admission: 1,861 applied, 1,317 admitted, 402 enrolled. *Average high school GPA:* 3.5. *Test scores:* SAT evidence-based reading and writing scores over 500: 84%; SAT math scores over 500: 82%; ACT scores over 18: 97%; SAT evidence-based reading and writing scores over 600: 20%; SAT math scores over 600: 26%; ACT scores over 24: 51%; SAT math scores over 700: 1%; ACT scores over 30: 4%.
Retention: 80% of full-time freshmen returned.

FACULTY
Total: 422, 24% full-time, 32% with terminal degrees.
Student/faculty ratio: 14:1.

ACADEMICS
Calendar: 4-1-4. *Degrees:* certificates, bachelor's, master's, and postbachelor's certificates.

Special study options: accelerated degree program, adult/continuing education programs, advanced placement credit, distance learning, double majors, honors programs, independent study, internships, off-campus study, part-time degree program, services for LD students, study abroad, summer session for credit. *ROTC:* Army (c).

Computers: 258 computers/terminals are available on campus for general student use. Students can access the following: campus intranet, computer help desk, free student e-mail accounts, online (class) grades, online (class) registration, online (class) schedules, library databases, learning management system, course evaluations, print management, virtual application labs, office 365, student suggestion box. Campuswide network is available. Wireless service is available via entire campus.

Library: Callahan Library plus 1 other. *Books:* 95,272 (physical), 163,718 (digital/electronic); *Serial titles:* 224 (physical), 59,734 (digital/electronic); *Databases:* 116. Weekly public service hours: 80; students can reserve study rooms.

STUDENT LIFE
Housing options: college housing not available.

Activities and organizations: drama/theater group, student-run newspaper, radio station, choral group, STARS (Students Taking an Active Role in Society), All Greek Life (Alpha Phi Delta and Delta Kappa Epsilon Fraternities), Drama Society, Project Sunshine, SJC Sharps, national fraternities, national sororities.

Athletics Member NCAA. All Division III. *Intercollegiate sports:* baseball M, basketball M/W, cross-country running M/W, equestrian sports W(c), golf M, lacrosse M/W, soccer M/W, softball W, swimming and diving W, tennis M/W, track and field M/W, volleyball M/W.

Campus security: 24-hour emergency response devices and patrols, late-night transport/escort service, Emergency Notification System via cell phones, lighted pathways/sidewalks.

Student services: personal/psychological counseling.

COSTS & FINANCIAL AID

Costs (2017–18) *Tuition:* $25,930 full-time, $840 per credit part-time. Full-time tuition and fees vary according to course load, location, and program. Part-time tuition and fees vary according to course load, location, and program. *Required fees:* $630 full-time. *Payment plan:* installment. *Waivers:* employees or children of employees.

Financial Aid Of all full-time matriculated undergraduates who enrolled in 2016, 2,465 applied for aid, 1,965 were judged to have need, 547 had their need fully met. 93 Federal Work-Study jobs (averaging $2568). 89 state and other part-time jobs (averaging $3697). In 2016, 417 non-need-based awards were made. *Average percent of need met:* 63. *Average financial aid package:* $13,862. *Average need-based loan:* $4294. *Average need-based gift aid:* $11,540. *Average non-need-based aid:* $9494. *Average indebtedness upon graduation:* $30,358.

APPLYING

Standardized Tests *Required:* SAT or ACT (for admission).

Options: electronic application, deferred entrance.

Application fee: $25.

Required: essay or personal statement, high school transcript, minimum 3.0 GPA, 2 letters of recommendation. *Required for some:* RN for RN-BSN program. *Recommended:* interview.

Application deadlines: rolling (freshmen), rolling (transfers).

Notification: continuous until 11/1 (freshmen), continuous until 11/1 (transfers).

CONTACT

Ms. Gigi Lamens, Vice President for Enrollment Management, St. Joseph's College, Long Island Campus, 155 West Roe Boulevard, Patchogue, NY 11772. *Phone:* 631-687-4500. *E-mail:* glamens@ sjcny.edu.

St. Joseph's College, New York

Brooklyn, New York
http://www.sjcny.edu/

- **Independent** comprehensive, founded 1916
- **Urban** 5-acre campus with easy access to Manhattan
- **Endowment** $7.3 million
- **Coed** 929 undergraduate students, 86% full-time, 68% women, 32% men
- **Moderately difficult** entrance level, 68% of applicants were admitted

UNDERGRAD STUDENTS

798 full-time, 131 part-time. Students come from 18 states and territories; 35 other countries; 6% are from out of state; 22% Black or African American, non-Hispanic/Latino; 23% Hispanic/Latino; 8% Asian, non-Hispanic/Latino; 0.3% Native Hawaiian or other Pacific Islander, non-Hispanic/Latino; 0.3% American Indian or Alaska Native, non-Hispanic/Latino; 2% Two or more races, non-Hispanic/Latino; 8% Race/ethnicity unknown; 10% transferred in; 5% live on campus.

Freshmen:
Admission: 2,098 applied, 1,420 admitted, 172 enrolled. *Average high school GPA:* 3.2. *Test scores:* SAT evidence-based reading and writing scores over 500: 71%; SAT math scores over 500: 69%; ACT scores over 18: 75%; SAT evidence-based reading and writing scores over 600: 17%; SAT math scores over 600: 17%; ACT scores over 24: 18%; SAT evidence-based reading and writing scores over 700: 1%; SAT math scores over 700: 3%.

Retention: 82% of full-time freshmen returned.

FACULTY
Total: 158, 35% full-time, 37% with terminal degrees.
Student/faculty ratio: 11:1.

ACADEMICS
Calendar: semesters. *Degrees:* certificates, bachelor's, master's, and postbachelor's certificates.

Special study options: accelerated degree program, adult/continuing education programs, advanced placement credit, distance learning, double majors, English as a second language, honors programs, independent study, internships, off-campus study, part-time degree program, services for LD students, study abroad, summer session for credit.

Computers: 238 computers/terminals are available on campus for general student use. Students can access the following: campus intranet, computer help desk, free student e-mail accounts, online (class) grades, online (class) registration, online (class) schedules, library databases, learning management system, course evaluations, print management, virtual application labs, office software, student suggestion box. Campuswide network is available. 100% of college-owned or -operated housing units are wired for high-speed Internet access. Wireless service is available via entire campus.

Library: McEntegart Hall Library plus 1 other. *Books:* 84,227 (physical), 163,718 (digital/electronic); *Serial titles:* 36 (physical), 59,734 (digital/electronic); *Databases:* 116. Weekly public service hours: 83; students can reserve study rooms.

STUDENT LIFE
Housing options: coed. Campus housing is leased by the school.

Activities and organizations: drama/theater group, Campus Activities Board (C.A.B.), Student Senate, Chapel Players Drama Club, Council of Multicultural Organizations, Dance Club, national fraternities.

Athletics Member NCAA. All Division III. *Intercollegiate sports:* baseball M, basketball M/W, cross-country running M/W, soccer M/W, softball W, swimming and diving M/W, tennis M/W, track and field M(c)/W(c), volleyball M/W.

Campus security: 24-hour emergency response devices and patrols, late-night transport/escort service, controlled dormitory access, Emergency Notification System via cell phones, lighted pathways/sidewalks.

Student services: health clinic, personal/psychological counseling.

COSTS & FINANCIAL AID
Costs (2017–18) *Tuition:* $25,930 full-time, $840 per credit part-time. Full-time tuition and fees vary according to course load and program. Part-time tuition and fees vary according to course load and program. *Required fees:* $620 full-time. *Payment plan:* installment. *Waivers:* employees or children of employees.

Financial Aid Of all full-time matriculated undergraduates who enrolled in 2016, 761 applied for aid, 646 were judged to have need, 121 had their need fully met. 96 Federal Work-Study jobs (averaging $2594). In 2016, 99 non-need-based awards were made. *Average percent of need met:* 66. *Average financial aid package:* $17,201. *Average need-based loan:* $3825. *Average need-based gift aid:* $15,207. *Average non-need-based aid:* $11,591. *Average indebtedness upon graduation:* $21,123.

APPLYING
Standardized Tests *Required:* SAT or ACT (for admission).

Options: electronic application, early admission, deferred entrance.

Application fee: $25.

Required: essay or personal statement, high school transcript, minimum 2.7 GPA, 1 letter of recommendation. *Required for some:* RN license for the RN to BSN Program. *Recommended:* interview.

Application deadlines: 8/31 (freshmen), rolling (transfers).

Notification: continuous until 11/1 (freshmen), continuous (transfers).

CONTACT
Ms. Christine Murphy, Vice President for Enrollment Management, St. Joseph's College, New York, 245 Clinton Avenue, Brooklyn, NY 11205. *Phone:* 718-940-5820. *E-mail:* cmurphy@sjcny.edu.

★ St. Lawrence University
Canton, New York
http://www.stlawu.edu/

- **Independent** comprehensive, founded 1856
- **Small-town** 1100-acre campus
- **Endowment** $282.1 million
- **Coed** 2,414 undergraduate students, 98% full-time, 56% women, 44% men
- **Moderately difficult** entrance level, 48% of applicants were admitted

UNDERGRAD STUDENTS

2,372 full-time, 42 part-time. Students come from 43 states and territories; 53 other countries; 54% are from out of state; 3% Black or African American, non-Hispanic/Latino; 5% Hispanic/Latino; 1% Asian, non-Hispanic/Latino; 0.2% American Indian or Alaska Native, non-Hispanic/Latino; 2% Two or more races, non-Hispanic/Latino; 2% Race/ethnicity unknown; 9% international; 0.8% transferred in; 98% live on campus.

Freshmen:
Admission: 5,866 applied, 2,835 admitted, 695 enrolled. *Average high school GPA:* 3.6. *Test scores:* SAT evidence-based reading and writing scores over 500: 96%; SAT math scores over 500: 96%; ACT scores over 18: 99%; SAT evidence-based reading and writing scores over 600: 73%; SAT math scores over 600: 67%; ACT scores over 24: 87%; SAT evidence-based reading and writing scores over 700: 16%; SAT math scores over 700: 16%; ACT scores over 30: 30%.

Retention: 92% of full-time freshmen returned.

FACULTY
Total: 217, 81% full-time, 95% with terminal degrees.
Student/faculty ratio: 11:1.

ACADEMICS
Calendar: semesters. *Degrees:* bachelor's, master's, and post-master's certificates.
Special study options: advanced placement credit, double majors, English as a second language, independent study, internships, off-campus study, part-time degree program, services for LD students, student-designed majors, study abroad, summer session for credit. *ROTC:* Army (c), Air Force (c).

Unusual degree programs: 3-2 engineering with Columbia University, Clarkson University, Rensselaer Polytechnic Institute, University of Rochester, Dartmouth College; nursing with New York University; pharmacy with Buffalo State College, State University of New York; physical therapy, physicians assistant with Clarkson University.

Computers: 738 computers/terminals are available on campus for general student use. Students can access the following: computer help desk, free student e-mail accounts, online (class) grades, online (class) registration, online (class) schedules. Campuswide network is available. 100% of college-owned or -operated housing units are wired for high-speed Internet access. Wireless service is available via entire campus.
Library: Owen D. Young Library plus 2 others. *Books:* 602,154 (physical), 303,918 (digital/electronic); *Serial titles:* 98,010 (physical), 123,193 (digital/electronic); *Databases:* 170. Students can reserve study rooms.

STUDENT LIFE
Housing options: on-campus residence required through senior year; coed, women-only, cooperative. Campus housing is university owned. Freshman campus housing is guaranteed.

Activities and organizations: drama/theater group, student-run newspaper, radio station, choral group, The Thelomathesian Society (student government), Outing Club, Environmental Action Organization, Association for Campus Entertainment, La Sociedad Hispana, national fraternities, national sororities.

Athletics Member NCAA. All Division III except men's and women's ice hockey (Division I), men's and women's skiing (downhill) (Division I). *Intercollegiate sports:* baseball M, basketball M/W, cross-country running M/W, equestrian sports M(c)/W(c), field hockey W, football M, golf M/W, ice hockey M(s)/W(s), lacrosse M/W, rowing M/W, skiing (downhill) M/W, soccer M/W, softball W, squash M/W, swimming and diving M/W, tennis M/W, track and field M/W, volleyball W. *Intramural sports:* basketball M/W, rugby M/W, soccer M/W.

Campus security: 24-hour emergency response devices and patrols, student patrols, late-night transport/escort service, controlled dormitory access.

Student services: health clinic, personal/psychological counseling.

COSTS & FINANCIAL AID
Costs (2018–19) *Comprehensive fee:* $68,980 includes full-time tuition ($54,454), mandatory fees ($392), and room and board ($14,134). *College room only:* $7614. Room and board charges vary according to board plan. *Payment plans:* tuition prepayment, installment. *Waivers:* employees or children of employees.

Financial Aid Of all full-time matriculated undergraduates who enrolled in 2017, 1,813 applied for aid, 1,526 were judged to have need, 414 had their need fully met. 905 Federal Work-Study jobs (averaging $1633). 297 state and other part-time jobs (averaging $1640). In 2017, 774 non-need-based awards were made. *Average percent of need met:* 87. *Average financial aid package:* $44,793. *Average need-based loan:* $4492. *Average need-based gift aid:* $37,572. *Average non-need-based aid:* $18,912. *Average indebtedness upon graduation:* $32,627. *Financial aid deadline:* 2/1.

APPLYING
Options: electronic application, early admission, early decision, deferred entrance.

Application fee: $60.

Required: essay or personal statement, high school transcript, 2 letters of recommendation. *Recommended:* interview.

Application deadlines: 2/1 (freshmen), 3/1 (transfers).

Early decision deadline: 11/1.

Notification: 3/31 (freshmen), continuous (transfers), rolling (early decision).

CONTACT
Jeremy Freeman, Director of Admissions, St. Lawrence University, 23 Romoda Drive, Canton, NY 13617-1455. *Phone:* 315-229-5261. *Toll-free phone:* 800-285-1856. *Fax:* 315-229-5818. *E-mail:* jfreeman@stlawu.edu.

See next page for display ad and page 1412 for the College Close-Up.

★ St. Thomas Aquinas College
Sparkill, New York
http://www.stac.edu/

- **Independent** comprehensive, founded 1952
- **Suburban** 46-acre campus with easy access to New York City
- **Endowment** $30.6 million
- **Coed** 1,778 undergraduate students, 61% full-time, 54% women, 46% men
- **Moderately difficult** entrance level, 79% of applicants were admitted

UNDERGRAD STUDENTS

1,091 full-time, 687 part-time. Students come from 18 states and territories; 16 other countries; 21% are from out of state; 12% Black or African American, non-Hispanic/Latino; 23% Hispanic/Latino; 2% Asian, non-Hispanic/Latino; 0.1% Native Hawaiian or other Pacific Islander, non-Hispanic/Latino; 0.6% Two or more races, non-Hispanic/Latino; 6% Race/ethnicity unknown; 5% international; 5% transferred in; 52% live on campus.

Freshmen:
Admission: 1,953 applied, 1,546 admitted, 246 enrolled. *Average high school GPA:* 3.0. *Test scores:* SAT evidence-based reading and writing scores over 500: 52%; SAT math scores over 500: 53%; ACT scores over 18: 71%; SAT evidence-based reading and writing scores over 600: 11%; SAT math scores over 600: 13%; ACT scores over 24: 20%; SAT evidence-based reading and writing scores over 700: 2%; ACT scores over 30: 5%.

Retention: 74% of full-time freshmen returned.

FACULTY
Total: 157, 37% full-time, 48% with terminal degrees.
Student/faculty ratio: 12:1.

ACADEMICS

Calendar: semesters. *Degrees:* associate, bachelor's, master's, post-master's, and postbachelor's certificates.

Special study options: academic remediation for entering students, accelerated degree program, adult/continuing education programs, advanced placement credit, double majors, freshman honors college, honors programs, independent study, internships, off-campus study, part-time degree program, services for LD students, study abroad, summer session for credit. *ROTC:* Air Force (c).

Unusual degree programs: 3-2 engineering with George Washington University, Manhattan College; social work with New York University School of Social Work; physical therapy with New York Medical College.

Computers: 200 computers/terminals are available on campus for general student use. Students can access the following: campus intranet, computer help desk, free student e-mail accounts, online (class) grades, online (class) registration, online (class) schedules. Campuswide network is available. 100% of college-owned or -operated housing units are wired for high-speed Internet access. Wireless service is available via entire campus.

Library: Lougheed Library plus 1 other. *Books:* 50,000 (physical); *Serial titles:* 110 (physical), 75,000 (digital/electronic); *Databases:* 68. Weekly public service hours: 83; students can reserve study rooms.

STUDENT LIFE

Housing options: men-only, women-only, special housing for students with disabilities. Campus housing is university owned. Freshman campus housing is guaranteed.

Activities and organizations: drama/theater group, student-run newspaper, radio station, choral group, Spartan Volunteers, Campus Activities Board, WSTK campus radio, Bowling Club, Laetare Players, national fraternities.

Athletics Member NCAA, NAIA. All NCAA Division II. *Intercollegiate sports:* baseball M(s), basketball M(s)/W(s), bowling W, cross-country running M(s)/W(s), field hockey W, golf M/W, lacrosse M/W, soccer M(s)/W(s), softball W(s), tennis M/W, track and field M/W, triathlon W, volleyball W(s). *Intramural sports:* basketball M/W, ice hockey M(c), volleyball M/W.

Campus security: 24-hour emergency response devices and patrols, student patrols, late-night transport/escort service, controlled dormitory access.

Student services: health clinic, personal/psychological counseling.

COSTS & FINANCIAL AID

Costs (2017–18) *Comprehensive fee:* $43,500 includes full-time tuition ($29,950), mandatory fees ($800), and room and board ($12,750). Part-time tuition: $955 per credit hour. *Required fees:* $200 per term part-time. *College room only:* $6880. Room and board charges vary according to board plan and housing facility. *Payment plan:* installment. *Waivers:* employees or children of employees.

Financial Aid Of all full-time matriculated undergraduates who enrolled in 2017, 1,020 applied for aid, 833 were judged to have need, 172 had their need fully met. 114 Federal Work-Study jobs (averaging $1453). In 2017, 224 non-need-based awards were made. *Average percent of need met:* 38. *Average financial aid package:* $18,100. *Average need-based loan:* $4800. *Average need-based gift aid:* $11,500. *Average non-need-based aid:* $13,800. *Average indebtedness upon graduation:* $28,750.

APPLYING

Standardized Tests *Required:* SAT or ACT (for admission).

Options: electronic application, deferred entrance.

Application fee: $30.

Required: high school transcript, minimum 2.0 GPA. *Required for some:* 3 letters of recommendation. *Recommended:* essay or personal statement, 2 letters of recommendation, interview.

Application deadlines: rolling (freshmen), rolling (transfers).

Notification: continuous (transfers).

CONTACT

Mr. Samantha Bazile, Director of Admissions, St. Thomas Aquinas College, 125 Route 340, Sparkill, NY 10976. *Phone:* 845-398-4104. *Fax:* 845-398-4114. *E-mail:* sbazile@stac.edu.

See next page for display ad and page 1418 for the College Close-Up.

Sarah Lawrence College

Bronxville, New York

http://www.sarahlawrence.edu/

- **Independent** comprehensive, founded 1926
- **Suburban** 44-acre campus with easy access to New York City
- **Endowment** $105.2 million
- **Coed** 1,399 undergraduate students, 99% full-time, 71% women, 29% men
- **Very difficult** entrance level, 53% of applicants were admitted

UNDERGRAD STUDENTS

1,384 full-time, 15 part-time. Students come from 49 states and territories; 44 other countries; 78% are from out of state; 4% Black or African American, non-Hispanic/Latino; 9% Hispanic/Latino; 4% Asian, non-Hispanic/Latino; 0.1% American Indian or Alaska Native, non-Hispanic/Latino; 7% Two or more races, non-Hispanic/Latino; 8% Race/ethnicity unknown; 13% international; 3% transferred in; 84% live on campus.

Freshmen:

Admission: 3,463 applied, 1,842 admitted, 393 enrolled. *Average high school GPA:* 3.7. *Test scores:* SAT evidence-based reading and writing scores over 500: 99%; SAT math scores over 500: 96%; ACT scores over 18: 99%; SAT evidence-based reading and writing scores over 600: 88%; SAT math scores over 600: 68%; ACT scores over 24: 95%; SAT evidence-based reading and writing scores over 700: 45%; SAT math scores over 700: 21%; ACT scores over 30: 48%.

Retention: 82% of full-time freshmen returned.

FACULTY

Total: 311, 38% full-time, 70% with terminal degrees.
Student/faculty ratio: 9:1.

ACADEMICS

Calendar: semesters. *Degrees:* bachelor's and master's.
Special study options: accelerated degree program, advanced placement credit, double majors, independent study, internships, off-campus study, services for LD students, student-designed majors, study abroad, summer session for credit. *ROTC:* Air Force (c).

Unusual degree programs: 3-2 engineering with Columbia University; teaching, child development, women's history.

Computers: 143 computers/terminals are available on campus for general student use. Students can access the following: campus intranet, computer help desk, free student e-mail accounts, online (class) grades, online (class) schedules. Campuswide network is available. 100% of college-owned or -operated housing units are wired for high-speed Internet access. Wireless service is available via entire campus.

Library: Esther Rauschenbush Library plus 2 others. *Books:* 339,102 (physical), 338,028 (digital/electronic); *Serial titles:* 4,113 (physical), 30,722 (digital/electronic); *Databases:* 137. Weekly public service hours: 109; study areas open 24 hours, 5–7 days a week; students can reserve study rooms.

STUDENT LIFE

Housing options: on-campus residence required for freshman year; coed, men-only, women-only, cooperative, special housing for students with disabilities. Campus housing is university owned. Freshman campus housing is guaranteed.

Activities and organizations: drama/theater group, student-run newspaper, radio station, choral group, Outdoor Adventure Club, VOX: Voices of Planned Parenthood, Figure Drawing Club, Sarah Lawrence Yoga Collective, Environmental Awareness Organization.

Athletics Member NCAA. All Division III. *Intercollegiate sports:* basketball M/W, crew W, cross-country running M/W, equestrian sports M/W, soccer M/W, softball W, swimming and diving M/W, tennis M/W, volleyball M/W. *Intramural sports:* basketball M/W, soccer M/W, squash M/W, table tennis M/W, ultimate Frisbee M/W, volleyball M/W.

Campus security: 24-hour emergency response devices and patrols, late-night transport/escort service, controlled dormitory access.

Student services: health clinic, personal/psychological counseling.

COSTS & FINANCIAL AID

Costs (2017–18) *Comprehensive fee:* $68,866 includes full-time tuition ($52,600), mandatory fees ($1410), and room and board ($14,856). Full-time tuition and fees vary according to course load. Part-time tuition:

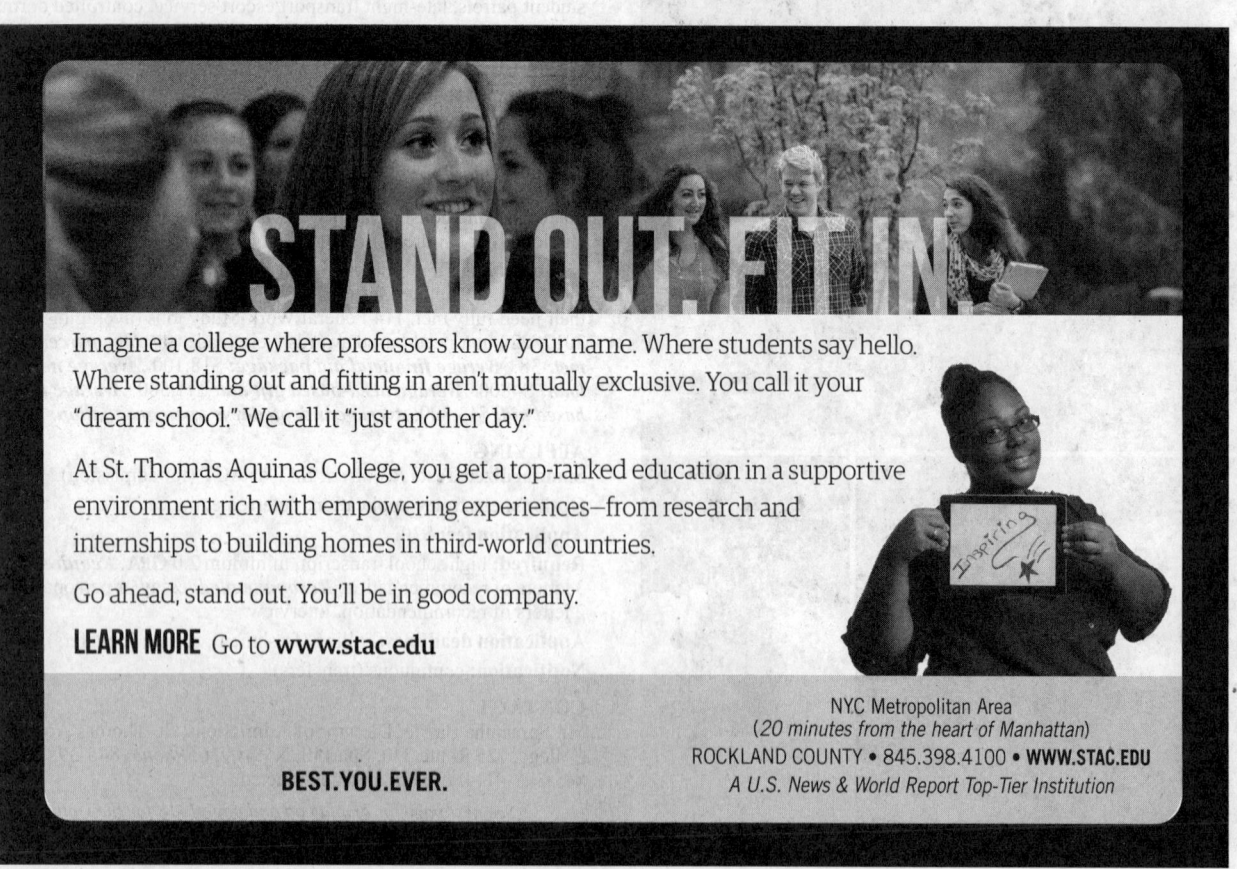

$1753 per credit hour. Part-time tuition and fees vary according to course load. *Required fees:* $570 per term part-time. *College room only:* $9830. Room and board charges vary according to board plan. *Payment plan:* installment. *Waivers:* employees or children of employees.

Financial Aid Of all full-time matriculated undergraduates who enrolled in 2016, 958 applied for aid, 822 were judged to have need, 134 had their need fully met. 604 Federal Work-Study jobs (averaging $1663). 43 state and other part-time jobs (averaging $1724). In 2016, 286 non-need-based awards were made. *Average percent of need met:* 76. *Average financial aid package:* $37,319. *Average need-based loan:* $2690. *Average need-based gift aid:* $34,799. *Average non-need-based aid:* $15,178. *Average indebtedness upon graduation:* $19,772. *Financial aid deadline:* 2/1.

APPLYING
Options: electronic application, early admission, early decision, early action, deferred entrance.

Application fee: $60.

Required: essay or personal statement, high school transcript, 2 letters of recommendation, counselor recommendation, school report. *Recommended:* minimum 3.0 GPA, interview.

Application deadlines: 1/15 (freshmen), 3/1 (transfers), 11/1 (early action).

Early decision deadline: 11/1 (for plan 1), 1/2 (for plan 2).

Notification: 3/15 (freshmen), 6/1 (transfers), 12/15 (early decision plan 1), 2/15 (early decision plan 2), 12/15 (early action).

CONTACT
Ms. Jennifer Gayles, Director of Admission and Multicultural Recruitment, Sarah Lawrence College, 1 Mead Way, Bronxville, NY 10708-5999. *Phone:* 914-395-2510. *Toll-free phone:* 800-888-2858. *Fax:* 914-395-2515. *E-mail:* slcadmit@sarahlawrence.edu.

★ School of Visual Arts
New York, New York
http://www.sva.edu/
- **Proprietary** comprehensive, founded 1947
- **Urban** 1-acre campus
- **Coed** 3,752 undergraduate students, 93% full-time, 69% women, 31% men
- **Moderately difficult** entrance level, 74% of applicants were admitted

UNDERGRAD STUDENTS
3,506 full-time, 246 part-time. 53% are from out of state; 4% Black or African American, non-Hispanic/Latino; 11% Hispanic/Latino; 14% Asian, non-Hispanic/Latino; 0.1% American Indian or Alaska Native, non-Hispanic/Latino; 0.6% Two or more races, non-Hispanic/Latino; 2% Race/ethnicity unknown; 43% international; 8% transferred in; 31% live on campus.

Freshmen:
Admission: 3,648 applied, 2,697 admitted, 699 enrolled. *Average high school GPA:* 3.3. *Test scores:* SAT evidence-based reading and writing scores over 500: 82%; SAT math scores over 500: 78%; ACT scores over 18: 94%; SAT evidence-based reading and writing scores over 600: 37%; SAT math scores over 600: 31%; ACT scores over 24: 51%; SAT evidence-based reading and writing scores over 700: 4%; SAT math scores over 700: 10%; ACT scores over 30: 12%.
Retention: 87% of full-time freshmen returned.

FACULTY
Total: 1,179, 18% full-time, 34% with terminal degrees.
Student/faculty ratio: 9:1.

ACADEMICS
Calendar: semesters. *Degrees:* bachelor's and master's.
Special study options: academic remediation for entering students, adult/continuing education programs, advanced placement credit, English as a second language, freshman honors college, honors programs, independent study, internships, services for LD students, study abroad, summer session for credit.
Computers: Students can access the following: campus intranet, computer help desk, free student e-mail accounts, online (class) grades, online (class) schedules. Campuswide network is available. Wireless

service is available via classrooms, computer centers, computer labs, dorm rooms, libraries, student centers.
Library: School of Visual Arts Library.

STUDENT LIFE
Housing options: coed, women-only. Campus housing is university owned, leased by the school and is provided by a third party. Freshman applicants given priority for college housing.
Activities and organizations: student-run newspaper, radio station.
Athletics *Intramural sports:* baseball M/W, softball M/W.
Campus security: 24-hour patrols.
Student services: health clinic, personal/psychological counseling.

COSTS & FINANCIAL AID
Costs (2018–19) *Comprehensive fee:* $60,300 includes full-time tuition ($39,900) and room and board ($20,400). Part-time tuition: $1335 per credit hour. *College room only:* $17,500. Room and board charges vary according to housing facility.

Financial Aid Of all full-time matriculated undergraduates who enrolled in 2016, 1,581 applied for aid, 1,477 were judged to have need, 16 had their need fully met. In 2016, 272 non-need-based awards were made. *Average percent of need met:* 36. *Average financial aid package:* $17,121. *Average need-based loan:* $4253. *Average need-based gift aid:* $13,772. *Average non-need-based aid:* $12,192. *Average indebtedness upon graduation:* $46,328. *Financial aid deadline:* 3/1.

APPLYING
Standardized Tests *Required:* SAT or ACT (for admission).
Options: electronic application, deferred entrance.
Application fee: $50.
Required: essay or personal statement, high school transcript, minimum 2.5 GPA, portfolio. *Recommended:* interview.
Application deadlines: rolling (freshmen), rolling (transfers).
Notification: continuous (freshmen), continuous (transfers).

CONTACT
Admissions Office, School of Visual Arts, 209 East 23rd Street, New York, NY 10010. *Phone:* 212-592-2100. *Toll-free phone:* 800-436-4204. *Fax:* 212-592-2116. *E-mail:* admissions@sva.edu.

Sh'or Yoshuv Rabbinical College
Lawrence, New York

CONTACT
Rabbi Moshe Rubin, Registrar, Sh'or Yoshuv Rabbinical College, 1 Cedarlawn Avenue, Lawrence, NY 11559-1714. *Phone:* 516-239-9002 Ext. 124. *Fax:* 516-977-1282. *E-mail:* mrubin@shoryoshuv.org.

Siena College
Loudonville, New York
http://www.siena.edu/
- **Independent Roman Catholic** comprehensive, founded 1937
- **Suburban** 175-acre campus with easy access to Albany, NY
- **Endowment** $129.3 million
- **Coed** 3,174 undergraduate students, 96% full-time, 53% women, 47% men
- **Moderately difficult** entrance level, 78% of applicants were admitted

UNDERGRAD STUDENTS
3,039 full-time, 135 part-time. Students come from 35 states and territories; 32 other countries; 20% are from out of state; 3% Black or African American, non-Hispanic/Latino; 8% Hispanic/Latino; 4% Asian, non-Hispanic/Latino; 0.1% American Indian or Alaska Native, non-Hispanic/Latino; 2% Two or more races, non-Hispanic/Latino; 0.9% Race/ethnicity unknown; 2% international; 5% transferred in; 78% live on campus.

Freshmen:
Admission: 7,626 applied, 5,937 admitted, 776 enrolled. *Average high school GPA:* 3.5. *Test scores:* SAT evidence-based reading and writing scores over 500: 89%; SAT math scores over 500: 90%; ACT scores over 18: 98%; SAT evidence-based reading and writing scores over 600: 37%; SAT math scores over 600: 39%; ACT scores over 24: 58%; SAT

evidence-based reading and writing scores over 700: 5%; SAT math scores over 700: 4%; ACT scores over 30: 13%.

Retention: 88% of full-time freshmen returned.

FACULTY
Total: 332, 61% full-time, 70% with terminal degrees.
Student/faculty ratio: 12:1.

ACADEMICS
Calendar: semesters. *Degrees:* certificates, bachelor's, and master's.

Special study options: advanced placement credit, cooperative education, double majors, English as a second language, honors programs, independent study, internships, off-campus study, part-time degree program, services for LD students, student-designed majors, study abroad, summer session for credit. *ROTC:* Army (b), Air Force (c).

Unusual degree programs: 3-2 engineering with Binghamton University, Clarkson University, Manhattan College, Rensselaer Polytechnic Institute, Western New England College.

Computers: 402 computers/terminals and 5,341 ports are available on campus for general student use. Students can access the following: campus intranet, computer help desk, free student e-mail accounts, online (class) grades, online (class) registration, online (class) schedules. Campuswide network is available. 100% of college-owned or -operated housing units are wired for high-speed Internet access. Wireless service is available via entire campus.

Library: J. Spencer and Patricia Standish Library. *Books:* 281,429 (physical), 301,497 (digital/electronic); *Serial titles:* 29,000 (digital/electronic); *Databases:* 172. Weekly public service hours: 102; students can reserve study rooms.

STUDENT LIFE
Housing options: on-campus residence required through senior year; coed, special housing for students with disabilities. Campus housing is university owned. Freshman applicants given priority for college housing.

Activities and organizations: drama/theater group, student-run newspaper, radio and television station, choral group, Outing Club, Best Buddies, Make-a-Wish Wishmakers on Campus, Fitness Club, Psychology Club.

Athletics Member NCAA. All Division I. *Intercollegiate sports:* baseball M(s), basketball M(s)/W(s), cross-country running M(s)/W(s), golf M(s)/W(s), lacrosse M(s)/W(s), soccer M(s)/W(s), softball W(s), swimming and diving W(s), tennis M(s)/W(s), track and field M/W, volleyball W(s), water polo W(s). *Intramural sports:* basketball M/W, cheerleading W(c), equestrian sports W(c), football M/W, ice hockey M, rugby M(c)/W(c), soccer M/W, softball M/W, squash M(c), tennis M(c)/W(c), track and field M(c)/W(c), ultimate Frisbee M(c), volleyball M/W.

Campus security: 24-hour emergency response devices and patrols, late-night transport/escort service, controlled dormitory access.

Student services: health clinic, personal/psychological counseling, women's center.

COSTS & FINANCIAL AID
Costs (2018–19) *One-time required fee:* $625. *Comprehensive fee:* $51,975 includes full-time tuition ($36,675), mandatory fees ($300), and room and board ($15,000). Full-time tuition and fees vary according to course load. Part-time tuition: $675 per credit hour. Part-time tuition and fees vary according to course load. *Required fees:* $80 per term part-time. *College room only:* $8895. Room and board charges vary according to board plan and housing facility. *Payment plan:* installment. *Waivers:* employees or children of employees.

Financial Aid Of all full-time matriculated undergraduates who enrolled in 2016, 2,558 applied for aid, 2,292 were judged to have need, 612 had their need fully met. 380 Federal Work-Study jobs (averaging $1000). In 2016, 525 non-need-based awards were made. *Average percent of need met:* 75. *Average financial aid package:* $29,350. *Average need-based loan:* $4419. *Average need-based gift aid:* $22,275. *Average non-need-based aid:* $11,837. *Average indebtedness upon graduation:* $35,827. *Financial aid deadline:* 2/15.

APPLYING
Standardized Tests *Required for some:* SAT or ACT (for admission).
Options: electronic application, early admission, early decision, early action, deferred entrance.

Application fee: $50.
Required: essay or personal statement, high school transcript, 1 letter of recommendation. *Required for some:* interview. *Recommended:* interview.

Application deadlines: 2/15 (freshmen), 8/15 (transfers), 12/1 (early action).

Early decision deadline: 12/1.

Notification: 3/15 (freshmen), continuous (transfers), 1/1 (early decision), 1/7 (early action).

CONTACT
Ms. Katie Szalda, Director of Admissions, Siena College, 515 Loudon Road, Loudonville, NY 12211-1462. *Phone:* 518-782-6767. *Toll-free phone:* 888-AT-SIENA. *Fax:* 518-783-2436. *E-mail:* admissions@siena.edu.

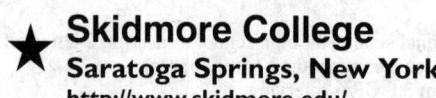

★ Skidmore College
Saratoga Springs, New York
http://www.skidmore.edu/

- **Independent** 4-year, founded 1903
- **Small-town** 890-acre campus with easy access to Albany, NY
- **Endowment** $367.2 million
- **Coed** 2,680 undergraduate students, 98% full-time, 60% women, 40% men
- **Very difficult** entrance level, 25% of applicants were admitted

UNDERGRAD STUDENTS
2,636 full-time, 44 part-time. Students come from 40 states and territories; 61 other countries; 66% are from out of state; 5% Black or African American, non-Hispanic/Latino; 9% Hispanic/Latino; 5% Asian, non-Hispanic/Latino; 4% Two or more races, non-Hispanic/Latino; 3% Race/ethnicity unknown; 11% international; 1% transferred in; 89% live on campus.

Freshmen:
Admission: 10,053 applied, 2,465 admitted, 661 enrolled. *Test scores:* SAT evidence-based reading and writing scores over 500: 98%; SAT math scores over 500: 99%; ACT scores over 18: 100%; SAT evidence-based reading and writing scores over 600: 82%; SAT math scores over 600: 75%; ACT scores over 24: 96%; SAT evidence-based reading and writing scores over 700: 30%; SAT math scores over 700: 28%; ACT scores over 30: 45%.

Retention: 93% of full-time freshmen returned.

FACULTY
Total: 384, 72% full-time, 71% with terminal degrees.
Student/faculty ratio: 8:1.

ACADEMICS
Calendar: semesters plus optional 6-week internship period. *Degree:* bachelor's.

Special study options: accelerated degree program, advanced placement credit, distance learning, double majors, honors programs, independent study, internships, off-campus study, services for LD students, student-designed majors, study abroad, summer session for credit. *ROTC:* Army (c), Air Force (c).

Unusual degree programs: 3-2 business administration with Clarkson University, Rochester Institute of Technology, Syracuse University; engineering with Dartmouth College, Clarkson University, Rensselaer Polytechnic Institute; nursing with New York University; finance or accounting with Syracuse University, physical or occupational therapy with Sage Graduate School, accounting with Wake Forest.

Computers: Students can access the following: campus intranet, computer help desk, free student e-mail accounts, online (class) grades, online (class) registration, online (class) schedules. Campuswide network is available. 100% of college-owned or -operated housing units are wired for high-speed Internet access. Wireless service is available via classrooms, computer centers, computer labs, dorm rooms, learning centers, libraries, student centers.

Library: Scribner Library. *Books:* 413,844 (physical), 85,590 (digital/electronic); *Serial titles:* 2,151 (physical); *Databases:* 393. Weekly public service hours: 109; students can reserve study rooms.

STUDENT LIFE

Housing options: on-campus residence required through sophomore year; coed, women-only, special housing for students with disabilities. Campus housing is university owned. Freshman campus housing is guaranteed.

Activities and organizations: drama/theater group, student-run newspaper, radio and television station, choral group, Student Government Association, Student radio station (WSPN), Benefaction (Student Volunteer), Outing Club, UJIMA.

Athletics Member NCAA. All Division III. *Intercollegiate sports:* baseball M, basketball M/W, crew M/W, equestrian sports W, field hockey W, golf M, ice hockey M, lacrosse M/W, soccer M/W, softball W, swimming and diving M/W, tennis M/W, volleyball W. *Intramural sports:* basketball M/W, ice hockey M(c)/W(c), racquetball M/W, soccer M/W, softball M/W, tennis M/W, volleyball M/W.

Campus security: 24-hour emergency response devices and patrols, late-night transport/escort service, controlled dormitory access, well-lit campus.

Student services: health clinic, personal/psychological counseling.

COSTS & FINANCIAL AID

Costs (2017–18) *One-time required fee:* $150. *Comprehensive fee:* $66,450 includes full-time tuition ($51,456), mandatory fees ($990), and room and board ($14,004). Full-time tuition and fees vary according to course load. Part-time tuition: $1715 per credit. Part-time tuition and fees vary according to course load. *Required fees:* $25 per term part-time. *College room only:* $8278. Room and board charges vary according to board plan and housing facility. *Payment plans:* tuition prepayment, installment. *Waivers:* senior citizens and employees or children of employees.

Financial Aid Of all full-time matriculated undergraduates who enrolled in 2017, 1,360 applied for aid, 1,111 were judged to have need, 1,044 had their need fully met. In 2017, 12 non-need-based awards were made. *Average percent of need met:* 94. *Average financial aid package:* $49,300. *Average need-based loan:* $4200. *Average need-based gift aid:* $44,600. *Average non-need-based aid:* $13,250. *Average indebtedness upon graduation:* $23,916. *Financial aid deadline:* 2/1.

APPLYING

Standardized Tests *Required for some:* SAT or ACT (for admission).

Options: electronic application, early admission, early decision, deferred entrance.

Application fee: $65.

Required: essay or personal statement, high school transcript, 2 letters of recommendation. *Recommended:* interview.

Application deadlines: 1/15 (freshmen), 4/1 (transfers).

Early decision deadline: 11/15 (for plan 1), 1/15 (for plan 2).

Notification: 4/1 (freshmen), 4/22 (transfers), 12/15 (early decision plan 1), 2/15 (early decision plan 2).

CONTACT

Ms. Mary Lou Bates, Vice President and Dean of Admissions and Financial Aid, Skidmore College, 815 North Broadway, Saratoga Springs, NY 12866-1632. *Phone:* 518-580-5570. *Toll-free phone:* 800-867-6007. *Fax:* 518-580-5584. *E-mail:* admissions@skidmore.edu.

See below for display ad and page 1426 for the College Close-Up.

State University of New York at Fredonia

Fredonia, New York
http://www.fredonia.edu/

- **State-supported** comprehensive, founded 1826, part of State University of New York System
- **Small-town** 249-acre campus with easy access to Buffalo
- **Endowment** $31.1 million
- **Coed** 4,392 undergraduate students, 97% full-time, 58% women, 42% men
- **Moderately difficult** entrance level, 65% of applicants were admitted

UNDERGRAD STUDENTS

4,279 full-time, 113 part-time. Students come from 30 states and territories; 12 other countries; 3% are from out of state; 8% Black or African American, non-Hispanic/Latino; 9% Hispanic/Latino; 2% Asian, non-Hispanic/Latino; 0.5% American Indian or Alaska Native, non-

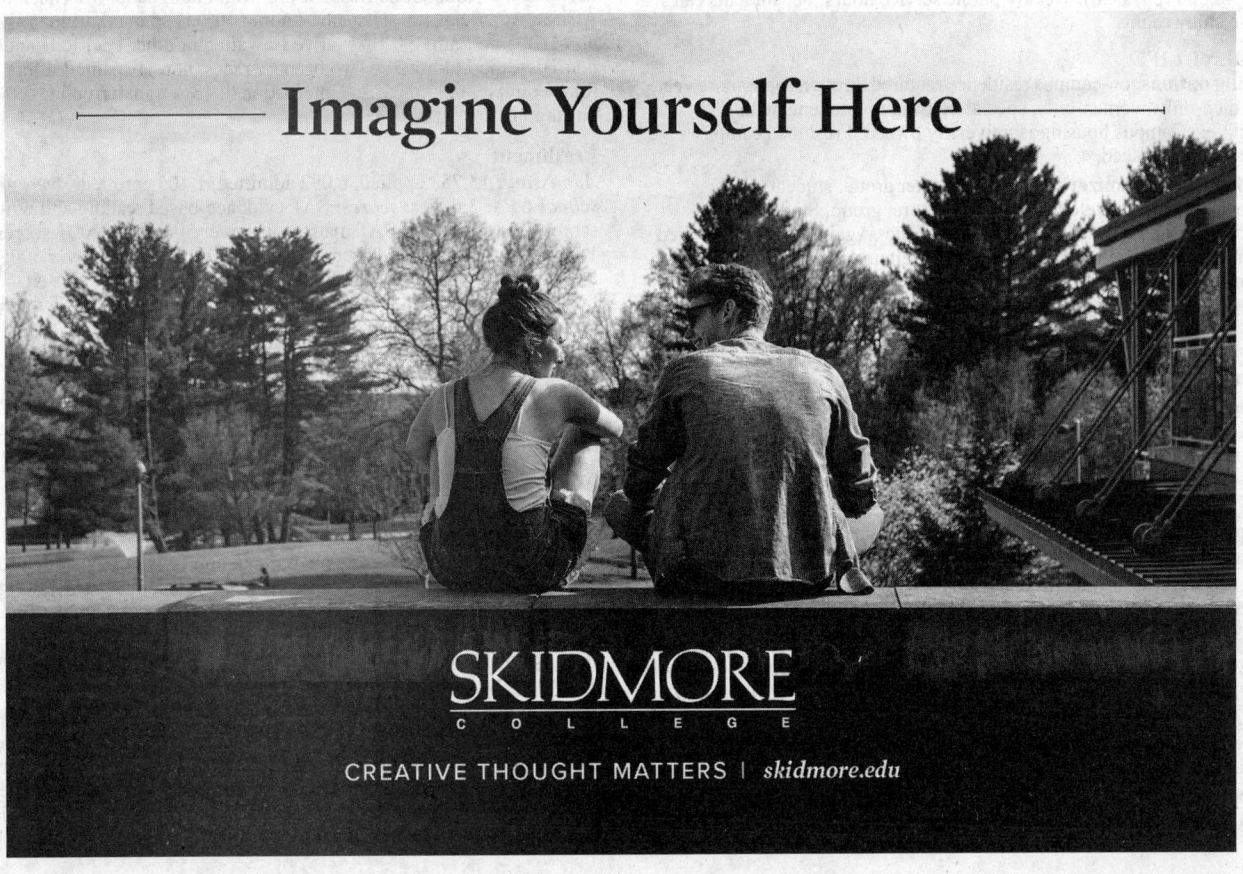

Hispanic/Latino; 3% Two or more races, non-Hispanic/Latino; 2% Race/ethnicity unknown; 2% international; 7% transferred in; 53% live on campus.

Freshmen:
Admission: 5,474 applied, 3,553 admitted, 1,129 enrolled. *Average high school GPA:* 3.2. *Test scores:* SAT evidence-based reading and writing scores over 500: 75%; SAT math scores over 500: 69%; ACT scores over 18: 82%; SAT evidence-based reading and writing scores over 600: 28%; SAT math scores over 600: 21%; ACT scores over 24: 39%; SAT evidence-based reading and writing scores over 700: 4%; SAT math scores over 700: 1%; ACT scores over 30: 6%.
Retention: 79% of full-time freshmen returned.

FACULTY
Total: 442, 57% full-time, 58% with terminal degrees.
Student/faculty ratio: 14:1.

ACADEMICS
Calendar: semesters. *Degrees:* bachelor's, master's, and post-master's certificates.

Special study options: accelerated degree program, adult/continuing education programs, advanced placement credit, distance learning, double majors, English as a second language, honors programs, independent study, internships, off-campus study, part-time degree program, services for LD students, student-designed majors, study abroad, summer session for credit.

Unusual degree programs: 3-2 engineering with Clarkson University, State University of New York at Buffalo, Case Western Reserve, Columbia University, Louisiana Technical University, New York State College of Ceramics at Alfred, Ohio State University.

Computers: 500 computers/terminals are available on campus for general student use. Students can access the following: campus intranet, computer help desk, free student e-mail accounts, online (class) grades, online (class) registration, online (class) schedules. Campuswide network is available. 100% of college-owned or -operated housing units are wired for high-speed Internet access. Wireless service is available via entire campus.
Library: Daniel A. Reed Library. *Books:* 18.0 million (physical); *Serial titles:* 48,000 (physical). Weekly public service hours: 68; students can reserve study rooms.

STUDENT LIFE
Housing options: on-campus residence required through sophomore year; coed, men-only, women-only, special housing for students with disabilities. Campus housing is university owned. Freshman campus housing is guaranteed.

Activities and organizations: drama/theater group, student-run newspaper, radio and television station, choral group, Student Association, Fredonia Radio Systems, Colleges Against Cancer, Applied Communication Association, Spectrum Entertainment Board, national fraternities, national sororities.

Athletics Member NCAA. All Division III. *Intercollegiate sports:* baseball M, basketball M/W, cheerleading M/W, cross-country running M/W, field hockey M(c)/W(c), ice hockey M, lacrosse M(c)/W, rugby M(c)/W(c), soccer M/W, softball W, swimming and diving M/W, tennis W, track and field M/W, volleyball W. *Intramural sports:* basketball M/W, fencing M(c)/W(c), ice hockey M(c), racquetball M/W, rock climbing M/W, sand volleyball M/W, skiing (downhill) M/W, soccer M/W, softball M/W, squash M/W, tennis M/W, ultimate Frisbee M/W, volleyball M/W, water polo M/W.

Campus security: 24-hour emergency response devices and patrols, late-night transport/escort service, controlled dormitory access.

Student services: health clinic, personal/psychological counseling, legal services.

COSTS & FINANCIAL AID
Costs (2018–19) *Tuition:* state resident $6670 full-time, $278 per credit hour part-time; nonresident $16,320 full-time, $680 per credit hour part-time. *Required fees:* $1618 full-time, $67 per credit hour part-time. *Room and board:* $12,490; room only: $7500. Room and board charges vary according to board plan and housing facility. *Payment plan:* installment.

Financial Aid Of all full-time matriculated undergraduates who enrolled in 2017, 3,765 applied for aid, 3,129 were judged to have need, 580 had

their need fully met. 173 Federal Work-Study jobs (averaging $2025). In 2017, 404 non-need-based awards were made. *Average percent of need met:* 66. *Average financial aid package:* $11,791. *Average need-based loan:* $5448. *Average need-based gift aid:* $6752. *Average non-need-based aid:* $3352. *Average indebtedness upon graduation:* $27,586.

APPLYING
Standardized Tests *Required:* SAT or ACT (for admission).
Options: electronic application, early admission, deferred entrance.
Application fee: $50.
Required: essay or personal statement, high school transcript, 1 letter of recommendation. *Required for some:* interview, audition for music, dance and theater programs: portfolio for visual arts and technical theatre programs.
Application deadlines: rolling (freshmen), rolling (transfers).
Notification: continuous (freshmen), continuous (transfers).

CONTACT
Mr. Cory M. Bezek, Office of Admissions, State University of New York at Fredonia, 178 Central Avenue, Fredonia, NY 14063. *Phone:* 716-673-3251. *Toll-free phone:* 800-252-1212. *Fax:* 716-673-3249. *E-mail:* admissions@fredonia.edu.

State University of New York at New Paltz

New Paltz, New York
http://www.newpaltz.edu/

- **State-supported** comprehensive, founded 1828, part of State University of New York System
- **Small-town** 216-acre campus
- **Endowment** $20.4 million
- **Coed** 6,733 undergraduate students, 93% full-time, 61% women, 39% men
- **Very difficult** entrance level, 44% of applicants were admitted

UNDERGRAD STUDENTS
6,235 full-time, 498 part-time. Students come from 24 states and territories; 37 other countries; 3% are from out of state; 6% Black or African American, non-Hispanic/Latino; 19% Hispanic/Latino; 5% Asian, non-Hispanic/Latino; 0.1% Native Hawaiian or other Pacific Islander, non-Hispanic/Latino; 3% Two or more races, non-Hispanic/Latino; 3% Race/ethnicity unknown; 2% international; 13% transferred in; 46% live on campus.

Freshmen:
Admission: 13,753 applied, 6,092 admitted, 1,105 enrolled. *Average high school GPA:* 3.6. *Test scores:* SAT evidence-based reading and writing scores over 500: 91%; SAT math scores over 500: 90%; ACT scores over 18: 99%; SAT evidence-based reading and writing scores over 600: 51%; SAT math scores over 600: 38%; ACT scores over 24: 71%; SAT evidence-based reading and writing scores over 700: 6%; SAT math scores over 700: 4%; ACT scores over 30: 13%.
Retention: 87% of full-time freshmen returned.

FACULTY
Total: 624, 56% full-time, 60% with terminal degrees.
Student/faculty ratio: 16:1.

ACADEMICS
Calendar: semesters. *Degrees:* bachelor's, master's, post-master's, and postbachelor's certificates.

Special study options: academic remediation for entering students, advanced placement credit, cooperative education, distance learning, double majors, English as a second language, external degree program, honors programs, independent study, internships, off-campus study, part-time degree program, services for LD students, student-designed majors, study abroad, summer session for credit.

Unusual degree programs: 3-2 business administration; engineering.

Computers: 800 computers/terminals are available on campus for general student use. Students can access the following: campus intranet, computer help desk, free student e-mail accounts, online (class) grades, online (class) registration, online (class) schedules. Campuswide network is available. 100% of college-owned or -operated housing units are wired for

high-speed Internet access. Wireless service is available via entire campus.

Library: Sojourner Truth Library. *Books:* 455,728 (physical), 149,851 (digital/electronic); *Serial titles:* 234 (physical), 85,306 (digital/electronic); *Databases:* 98. Weekly public service hours: 103; students can reserve study rooms.

STUDENT LIFE
Housing options: on-campus residence required for freshman year; coed, special housing for students with disabilities. Campus housing is university owned. Freshman campus housing is guaranteed.

Activities and organizations: drama/theater group, student-run newspaper, radio and television station, choral group, Student Association, Residence Hall Student Association, Outing Club, The Oracle Newspaper, United Greek Association, national fraternities, national sororities.

Athletics Member NCAA. All Division III. *Intercollegiate sports:* baseball M, basketball M/W, cross-country running M/W, field hockey W, lacrosse W, soccer M/W, swimming and diving M/W, tennis W, volleyball M/W. *Intramural sports:* basketball M/W, cheerleading M(c)/W(c), equestrian sports M(c)/W(c), lacrosse M(c)/W(c), racquetball M/W, rugby M(c)/W(c), soccer M/W, swimming and diving M(c)/W(c), table tennis M(c)/W(c), tennis M/W, track and field M(c)/W(c), ultimate Frisbee M(c)/W(c), volleyball M/W, water polo M/W, wrestling M(c).

Campus security: 24-hour emergency response devices and patrols, late-night transport/escort service, controlled dormitory access, safety seminars, RAD Women's Self Defense.

Student services: health clinic, personal/psychological counseling, legal services.

COSTS & FINANCIAL AID
Costs (2018–19) *Tuition:* state resident $6670 full-time; nonresident $16,320 full-time. *Required fees:* $1305 full-time. *Room and board:* $12,642; room only: $8480. Room and board charges vary according to board plan. *Payment plan:* installment.

Financial Aid Of all full-time matriculated undergraduates who enrolled in 2017, 4,918 applied for aid, 3,813 were judged to have need, 284 had

their need fully met. In 2017, 39 non-need-based awards were made. *Average percent of need met:* 58. *Average financial aid package:* $11,568. *Average need-based loan:* $4252. *Average need-based gift aid:* $5106. *Average non-need-based aid:* $3653. *Average indebtedness upon graduation:* $26,385.

APPLYING
Standardized Tests *Required:* SAT or ACT (for admission).
Options: electronic application, early admission, early action.
Application fee: $50.
Required: essay or personal statement, high school transcript, 1 letter of recommendation. *Required for some:* portfolio for art program, audition for music and theater programs.
Application deadlines: 5/1 (freshmen), 5/1 (transfers), 11/15 (early action).
Notification: continuous (freshmen), continuous (transfers), rolling (early action).

CONTACT
Ms. Kimberly A. Strano, Director of Freshman Admissions, State University of New York at New Paltz, 1 Hawk Drive, New Paltz, NY 12561-2499. *Phone:* 845-257-3200. *Toll-free phone:* 877-MY-NP-411. *Fax:* 845-257-3209. *E-mail:* admissions@newpaltz.edu.

 State University of New York at Oswego
Oswego, New York
http://www.oswego.edu/

- **State-supported** comprehensive, founded 1861, part of State University of New York System
- **Small-town** 696-acre campus with easy access to Syracuse
- **Endowment** $28.8 million
- **Coed** 7,125 undergraduate students, 96% full-time, 49% women, 51% men
- **Moderately difficult** entrance level, 54% of applicants were admitted

UNDERGRAD STUDENTS

6,836 full-time, 289 part-time. Students come from 28 states and territories; 35 other countries; 3% are from out of state; 9% Black or African American, non-Hispanic/Latino; 12% Hispanic/Latino; 3% Asian, non-Hispanic/Latino; 0.2% American Indian or Alaska Native, non-Hispanic/Latino; 3% Two or more races, non-Hispanic/Latino; 0.2% Race/ethnicity unknown; 3% international; 11% transferred in; 62% live on campus.

Freshmen:

Admission: 10,715 applied, 5,824 admitted, 1,463 enrolled. *Average high school GPA:* 3.5. *Test scores:* ACT scores over 18: 100%; ACT scores over 24: 49%; ACT scores over 30: 4%.

Retention: 78% of full-time freshmen returned.

FACULTY

Total: 578, 65% full-time, 65% with terminal degrees.
Student/faculty ratio: 17:1.

ACADEMICS

Calendar: semesters. *Degrees:* bachelor's, master's, post-master's, and postbachelor's certificates.

Special study options: accelerated degree program, adult/continuing education programs, advanced placement credit, cooperative education, distance learning, double majors, English as a second language, freshman honors college, honors programs, independent study, internships, off-campus study, part-time degree program, services for LD students, study abroad, summer session for credit. *ROTC:* Army (c), Air Force (c).

Unusual degree programs: 3-2 engineering with Clarkson University, Case Western Reserve University, State University of New York at Binghamton.

Computers: 1,250 computers/terminals are available on campus for general student use. Students can access the following: campus intranet, computer help desk, free student e-mail accounts, online (class) grades, online (class) registration, online (class) schedules. Campuswide network is available. 100% of college-owned or -operated housing units are wired for high-speed Internet access. Wireless service is available via entire campus.

Library: Penfield Library. *Books:* 331,049 (physical), 154,207 (digital/electronic); *Serial titles:* 1,932 (physical), 55,500 (digital/electronic); *Databases:* 139. Weekly public service hours: 96; study areas open 24 hours, 5–7 days a week; students can reserve study rooms.

STUDENT LIFE

Housing options: on-campus residence required through sophomore year; coed, special housing for students with disabilities. Campus housing is university owned. Freshman campus housing is guaranteed.

Activities and organizations: drama/theater group, student-run newspaper, radio and television station, choral group, club/intramural sports, student radio/television stations (WNYO and WTOP), Outdoor Club, Dance Organization (Del Sarte), Accounting Society, national fraternities, national sororities.

Athletics Member NCAA. All Division III. *Intercollegiate sports:* baseball M, basketball M/W, crew M(c)/W(c), cross-country running M/W, field hockey W, golf M, ice hockey M/W, lacrosse M/W, soccer M/W, softball W, swimming and diving M/W, tennis M/W, track and field M/W, volleyball W, wrestling M. *Intramural sports:* badminton M/W, basketball M/W, cheerleading W(c), equestrian sports M(c)/W(c), fencing M(c)/W(c), field hockey W(c), football M/W, golf M/W, gymnastics M(c)/W(c), ice hockey M(c)/W(c), lacrosse M(c), racquetball M/W, rock climbing M(c)/W(c), rugby M(c)/W(c), skiing (cross-country) M(c)/W(c), skiing (downhill) M(c)/W(c), soccer M/W, softball M/W, swimming and diving M/W, table tennis M/W, tennis M/W, ultimate Frisbee M(c)/W(c), volleyball M(c)/W, water polo M/W.

Campus security: 24-hour emergency response devices and patrols, controlled dormitory access, Oswego Guardian.

Student services: health clinic, personal/psychological counseling, women's center, legal services.

COSTS & FINANCIAL AID

Costs (2017–18) *Tuition:* state resident $6670 full-time, $278 per credit hour part-time; nonresident $16,320 full-time, $680 per credit hour part-time. Part-time tuition and fees vary according to course load. *Required fees:* $1521 full-time, $48 per credit hour part-time. *Room and board:*

$13,740; room only: $8590. Room and board charges vary according to board plan and housing facility. *Payment plan:* installment.

Financial Aid Of all full-time matriculated undergraduates who enrolled in 2016, 5,670 applied for aid, 4,522 were judged to have need, 406 had their need fully met. 457 Federal Work-Study jobs (averaging $1250). In 2016, 796 non-need-based awards were made. *Average percent of need met:* 80. *Average financial aid package:* $11,290. *Average need-based loan:* $4602. *Average need-based gift aid:* $7538. *Average non-need-based aid:* $2529. *Average indebtedness upon graduation:* $28,676.

APPLYING

Standardized Tests *Required:* SAT or ACT (for admission).

Options: electronic application, early admission, early action, deferred entrance.

Application fee: $50.

Required: essay or personal statement, high school transcript, 1 letter of recommendation. *Recommended:* minimum 2.7 GPA, interview.

Application deadlines: rolling (freshmen), rolling (transfers), 11/5 (early action).

Notification: 1/15 (freshmen), 1/15 (transfers), 12/15 (early action).

CONTACT

Mr. Daniel Griffin, Director of Admissions, State University of New York at Oswego, 7060 State Route 104, Oswego, NY 13126. *Phone:* 315-312-2250. *Fax:* 315-312-3260. *E-mail:* admiss@oswego.edu.

See previous page for display ad and page 1436 for the College Close-Up.

State University of New York at Plattsburgh
Plattsburgh, New York
http://www.plattsburgh.edu/

- **State-supported** comprehensive, founded 1889, part of State University of New York System
- **Small-town** 265-acre campus with easy access to Montreal
- **Endowment** $19.9 million
- **Coed** 5,351 undergraduate students, 91% full-time, 58% women, 43% men
- **Moderately difficult** entrance level, 53% of applicants were admitted

UNDERGRAD STUDENTS

4,894 full-time, 457 part-time. Students come from 30 states and territories; 65 other countries; 4% are from out of state; 9% Black or African American, non-Hispanic/Latino; 12% Hispanic/Latino; 3% Asian, non-Hispanic/Latino; 0.1% Native Hawaiian or other Pacific Islander, non-Hispanic/Latino; 0.4% American Indian or Alaska Native, non-Hispanic/Latino; 2% Two or more races, non-Hispanic/Latino; 3% Race/ethnicity unknown; 7% international; 10% transferred in; 50% live on campus.

Freshmen:

Admission: 9,643 applied, 5,101 admitted, 1,110 enrolled. *Average high school GPA:* 3.3. *Test scores:* SAT evidence-based reading and writing scores over 500: 66%; SAT math scores over 500: 76%; ACT scores over 18: 99%; SAT evidence-based reading and writing scores over 600: 20%; SAT math scores over 600: 17%; ACT scores over 24: 39%; SAT evidence-based reading and writing scores over 700: 1%; SAT math scores over 700: 2%; ACT scores over 30: 3%.

Retention: 82% of full-time freshmen returned.

FACULTY

Total: 451, 60% full-time, 58% with terminal degrees.
Student/faculty ratio: 16:1.

ACADEMICS

Calendar: semesters plus 2 5-week summer sessions and 1 winter session. *Degrees:* certificates, bachelor's, master's, and post-master's certificates.

Special study options: academic remediation for entering students, advanced placement credit, cooperative education, distance learning, double majors, English as a second language, honors programs, independent study, internships, off-campus study, part-time degree program, services for LD students, student-designed majors, study abroad, summer session for credit.

Computers: 450 computers/terminals are available on campus for general student use. Students can access the following: campus intranet, computer help desk, free student e-mail accounts, online (class) grades, online (class) registration, online (class) schedules. Campuswide network is available. 100% of college-owned or -operated housing units are wired for high-speed Internet access.

Library: Feinberg Library. *Books:* 265,921 (physical), 183,957 (digital/electronic); *Serial titles:* 153 (physical), 538 (digital/electronic); *Databases:* 112. Weekly public service hours: 100; students can reserve study rooms.

STUDENT LIFE

Housing options: on-campus residence required through sophomore year; coed, special housing for students with disabilities. Campus housing is university owned. Freshman campus housing is guaranteed.

Activities and organizations: drama/theater group, student-run newspaper, radio and television station, choral group, Student Association, Honor Societies, Student Media Organizations, service/leadership organizations, intramural and recreational sports, national fraternities, national sororities.

Athletics Member NCAA. All Division III. *Intercollegiate sports:* baseball M, basketball M/W, cross-country running M/W, ice hockey M/W, lacrosse M, soccer M/W, softball W, tennis W, track and field M/W, volleyball W. *Intramural sports:* basketball M/W, cheerleading M(c)/W(c), field hockey M/W, football M, ice hockey M(c)/W(c), racquetball M/W, rock climbing M(c)/W(c), rugby M(c)/W(c), sand volleyball M/W, soccer M/W, softball M/W, tennis M/W, ultimate Frisbee M/W, volleyball M/W.

Campus security: 24-hour emergency response devices and patrols, late-night transport/escort service, controlled dormitory access.

Student services: health clinic, personal/psychological counseling, women's center, legal services.

COSTS & FINANCIAL AID

Costs (2018–19) *Tuition:* state resident $6670 full-time, $278 per credit hour part-time; nonresident $16,320 full-time, $680 per credit hour part-time. Full-time tuition and fees vary according to course load and location. Part-time tuition and fees vary according to course load and location. *Required fees:* $1494 full-time, $64 per credit hour part-time. *Room and board:* $12,988; room only: $8258. Room and board charges vary according to board plan and housing facility. *Payment plans:* installment, deferred payment.

Financial Aid Of all full-time matriculated undergraduates who enrolled in 2016, 3,838 applied for aid, 3,080 were judged to have need, 600 had their need fully met. 358 Federal Work-Study jobs (averaging $2684). In 2016, 731 non-need-based awards were made. *Average percent of need met:* 76. *Average financial aid package:* $13,822. *Average need-based loan:* $8065. *Average need-based gift aid:* $7694. *Average non-need-based aid:* $5261. *Average indebtedness upon graduation:* $29,865.

APPLYING

Standardized Tests *Required:* SAT or ACT (for admission).

Options: electronic application, early admission, deferred entrance.

Application fee: $50.

Required: essay or personal statement, high school transcript, minimum 2.5 GPA, 1 letter of recommendation. *Required for some:* minimum 3.4 GPA. *Recommended:* minimum 3.0 GPA, interview.

Application deadlines: rolling (freshmen), rolling (transfers).

Notification: continuous (freshmen), continuous (transfers).

CONTACT

Mrs. Erin Peters, Assistant Director of Admissions, State University of New York at Plattsburgh, 101 Broad Street, Plattsburgh, NY 12901. *Phone:* 888-673-0012. *Toll-free phone:* 888-673-0012. *Fax:* 518-564-2045. *E-mail:* hamm1417@plattsburgh.edu.

State University of New York College at Cortland
Cortland, New York
http://www.cortland.edu/

- **State-supported** comprehensive, founded 1868, part of State University of New York System
- **Small-town** 191-acre campus with easy access to Syracuse
- **Coed** 6,346 undergraduate students, 98% full-time, 56% women, 44% men
- **Moderately difficult** entrance level, 48% of applicants were admitted

UNDERGRAD STUDENTS

6,196 full-time, 150 part-time. 4% are from out of state; 6% Black or African American, non-Hispanic/Latino; 13% Hispanic/Latino; 1% Asian, non-Hispanic/Latino; 0.1% Native Hawaiian or other Pacific Islander, non-Hispanic/Latino; 0.2% American Indian or Alaska Native, non-Hispanic/Latino; 2% Two or more races, non-Hispanic/Latino; 4% Race/ethnicity unknown; 0.7% international; 10% transferred in.

Freshmen:
Admission: 11,909 applied, 5,708 admitted, 1,288 enrolled. *Average high school GPA:* 3.4. *Test scores:* SAT evidence-based reading and writing scores over 500: 91%; SAT math scores over 500: 94%; ACT scores over 18: 100%; SAT evidence-based reading and writing scores over 600: 26%; SAT math scores over 600: 28%; ACT scores over 24: 64%; SAT evidence-based reading and writing scores over 700: 1%; SAT math scores over 700: 1%; ACT scores over 30: 5%.
Retention: 80% of full-time freshmen returned.

FACULTY
Total: 619, 50% full-time, 45% with terminal degrees.
Student/faculty ratio: 16:1.

ACADEMICS
Calendar: semesters. *Degrees:* bachelor's, master's, post-master's, and postbachelor's certificates.

Special study options: adult/continuing education programs, off-campus study. *ROTC:* Army (c), Air Force (c).

Unusual degree programs: 3-2 engineering with State University of New York at Buffalo, State University of New York at Stony Brook, Alfred University, Clarkson University, State University of New York at Binghamton, Case Western Reserve University; forestry with Duke University, State University of New York College of Environmental Science and Forestry.

Computers: Campuswide network is available.
Library: Memorial Library.

STUDENT LIFE
Housing options: coed, cooperative, special housing for students with disabilities. Campus housing is university owned.

Activities and organizations: drama/theater group, student-run newspaper, radio and television station, choral group.

Athletics Member NCAA. All Division III. *Intercollegiate sports:* baseball M, basketball M/W, cross-country running M/W, field hockey W, football M/W(c), golf W, gymnastics W, ice hockey M/W(c), lacrosse M/W, racquetball M(c)/W(c), rugby M(c)/W(c), soccer M/W, softball W, swimming and diving M/W, tennis W, track and field M/W, volleyball M(c)/W, wrestling M. *Intramural sports:* archery M/W, badminton M/W, baseball M, basketball M/W, bowling M/W, cross-country running M/W, fencing M/W, field hockey W, football M/W, golf M/W, gymnastics W, ice hockey M, lacrosse M/W, racquetball M/W, rugby M/W, skiing (cross-country) M/W, skiing (downhill) M/W, soccer M/W, softball M/W, squash M/W, swimming and diving M/W, table tennis M/W, tennis M/W, track and field M/W, volleyball M/W, weight lifting M/W, wrestling M.

Campus security: 24-hour emergency response devices and patrols, late-night transport/escort service.

COSTS & FINANCIAL AID
Costs (2017–18) *Tuition:* state resident $6670 full-time, $278 per credit hour part-time; nonresident $16,320 full-time, $680 per credit hour part-time. Full-time tuition and fees vary according to course load and degree level. Part-time tuition and fees vary according to course load and degree level. *Required fees:* $1630 full-time. *Room and board:* $12,410; room

only: $7900. Room and board charges vary according to board plan and housing facility. *Payment plan:* installment. *Waivers:* employees or children of employees.

Financial Aid Of all full-time matriculated undergraduates who enrolled in 2016, 4,882 applied for aid, 3,699 were judged to have need, 393 had their need fully met. In 2016, 270 non-need-based awards were made. *Average percent of need met:* 67. *Average financial aid package:* $14,832. *Average need-based loan:* $3616. *Average need-based gift aid:* $5854. *Average non-need-based aid:* $3616. *Average indebtedness upon graduation:* $29,111.

APPLYING
Standardized Tests *Required for some:* SAT or ACT (for admission).

Options: electronic application, early admission, early action, deferred entrance.

Application fee: $50.

Required: essay or personal statement, high school transcript, minimum 2.3 GPA, 1 letter of recommendation. *Recommended:* minimum 3.0 GPA, 3 letters of recommendation, interview.

CONTACT
Director of Admission, State University of New York College at Cortland, PO Box 2000, Cortland, NY 13045. *Phone:* 607-753-4711. *Fax:* 607-753-5998. *E-mail:* admissions@cortland.edu.

State University of New York College at Geneseo

Geneseo, New York
http://www.geneseo.edu/

- **State-supported** comprehensive, founded 1871, part of State University of New York
- **Small-town** 220-acre campus with easy access to Rochester
- **Endowment** $33.5 million
- **Coed** 5,495 undergraduate students, 98% full-time, 60% women, 40% men
- **Moderately difficult** entrance level, 72% of applicants were admitted

UNDERGRAD STUDENTS
5,391 full-time, 104 part-time. Students come from 26 states and territories; 33 other countries; 2% are from out of state; 3% Black or African American, non-Hispanic/Latino; 8% Hispanic/Latino; 6% Asian, non-Hispanic/Latino; 0.1% American Indian or Alaska Native, non-Hispanic/Latino; 3% Two or more races, non-Hispanic/Latino; 3% Race/ethnicity unknown; 2% international; 5% transferred in; 54% live on campus.

Freshmen:
Admission: 8,789 applied, 6,360 admitted, 1,340 enrolled. *Average high school GPA:* 3.6. *Test scores:* SAT evidence-based reading and writing scores over 500: 96%; SAT math scores over 500: 94%; ACT scores over 18: 100%; SAT evidence-based reading and writing scores over 600: 58%; SAT math scores over 600: 54%; ACT scores over 24: 82%; SAT evidence-based reading and writing scores over 700: 10%; SAT math scores over 700: 9%; ACT scores over 30: 17%.

Retention: 86% of full-time freshmen returned.

FACULTY
Total: 365, 70% full-time, 73% with terminal degrees.
Student/faculty ratio: 19:1.

ACADEMICS
Calendar: semesters. *Degrees:* bachelor's and master's.
Special study options: advanced placement credit, distance learning, double majors, English as a second language, honors programs, independent study, internships, off-campus study, part-time degree program, services for LD students, study abroad, summer session for credit. *ROTC:* Army (c), Air Force (c).

Unusual degree programs: 3-2 business administration with Alfred University; Binghamton University, State University of New York; Clarkson University; Rochester Institute of Technology; Union College; engineering with Case Western Reserve; Clarkson University; Columbia University; University at Buffalo, State University of New York;

optometry with SUNY College of Optometry, dentistry with SUNY at Buffalo, physical therapy with SUNY Upstate Medical University, osteopathy with New York Institute of Technology College of Osteopathic Medicine.

Computers: 409 computers/terminals and 3,000 ports are available on campus for general student use. Students can access the following: campus intranet, computer help desk, free student e-mail accounts, online (class) grades, online (class) registration, online (class) schedules. Campuswide network is available. 100% of college-owned or -operated housing units are wired for high-speed Internet access. Wireless service is available via entire campus.

Library: Milne Library plus 1 other. *Books:* 333,883 (physical), 151,724 (digital/electronic); *Serial titles:* 1,420 (physical), 213,056 (digital/electronic); *Databases:* 430. Weekly public service hours: 109; students can reserve study rooms.

STUDENT LIFE
Housing options: on-campus residence required through sophomore year; coed, special housing for students with disabilities. Campus housing is university owned. Freshman campus housing is guaranteed.

Activities and organizations: drama/theater group, student-run newspaper, radio station, choral group, Phi Alpha Delta, Orchesis, Newman Catholic Community, Golden Key, Alpha Phi Omega, national fraternities, national sororities.

Athletics Member NCAA. All Division III. *Intercollegiate sports:* baseball M(c), basketball M/W, cheerleading M(c)/W(c), crew M(c)/W(c), cross-country running M/W, equestrian sports W, fencing M(c)/W(c), field hockey W, ice hockey M/W(c), lacrosse M/W, rugby M(c)/W(c), skiing (downhill) M(c)/W(c), soccer M/W, softball W, swimming and diving M/W, tennis M(c)/W, track and field M/W, ultimate Frisbee M(c)/W(c), volleyball M(c)/W, water polo M(c). *Intramural sports:* badminton M/W, basketball M/W, racquetball M/W, soccer M/W, softball M/W, table tennis M/W, tennis M/W, volleyball M/W.

Campus security: 24-hour emergency response devices and patrols, student patrols, late-night transport/escort service, controlled dormitory access.

Student services: health clinic, personal/psychological counseling, legal services.

COSTS & FINANCIAL AID
Costs (2017–18) *Tuition:* state resident $6670 full-time, $278 per credit hour part-time; nonresident $16,320 full-time, $680 per credit hour part-time. Part-time tuition and fees vary according to course load. *Required fees:* $1738 full-time, $72 per credit hour part-time. *Room and board:* $13,214; room only: $7890. Room and board charges vary according to board plan and housing facility. *Payment plans:* installment, deferred payment.

Financial Aid Of all full-time matriculated undergraduates who enrolled in 2017, 4,037 applied for aid, 2,812 were judged to have need, 372 had their need fully met. 408 Federal Work-Study jobs (averaging $1539). In 2017, 363 non-need-based awards were made. *Average percent of need met:* 36. *Average financial aid package:* $9946. *Average need-based loan:* $3663. *Average need-based gift aid:* $2398. *Average non-need-based aid:* $2773. *Average indebtedness upon graduation:* $25,148.

APPLYING
Standardized Tests *Required:* SAT or ACT (for admission).

Options: electronic application, early admission, early decision, deferred entrance.

Application fee: $50.

Required: high school transcript. *Recommended:* essay or personal statement, 1 letter of recommendation.

Application deadlines: 1/1 (freshmen), rolling (transfers).

Early decision deadline: 11/15.

Notification: 3/1 (freshmen), 12/15 (early decision).

CONTACT
Mr. Kevin J. Reed, Assistant Director of Admissions, State University of New York College at Geneseo, Doty Hall 200, Geneseo, NY 14454-1401. *Phone:* 585-245-5571. *Toll-free phone:* 866-245-5211. *Fax:* 585-245-5550. *E-mail:* admissions@geneseo.edu.

State University of New York College at Old Westbury
Old Westbury, New York
http://www.oldwestbury.edu/

- **State-supported** comprehensive, founded 1965, part of State University of New York System
- **Suburban** 604-acre campus with easy access to New York City
- **Coed** 4,242 undergraduate students, 86% full-time, 59% women, 41% men
- **Moderately difficult** entrance level, 69% of applicants were admitted

UNDERGRAD STUDENTS
3,632 full-time, 610 part-time. Students come from 14 states and territories; 11 other countries; 1% are from out of state; 27% Black or African American, non-Hispanic/Latino; 24% Hispanic/Latino; 11% Asian, non-Hispanic/Latino; 0.3% Native Hawaiian or other Pacific Islander, non-Hispanic/Latino; 0.3% American Indian or Alaska Native, non-Hispanic/Latino; 3% Two or more races, non-Hispanic/Latino; 2% Race/ethnicity unknown; 0.1% international; 20% transferred in; 19% live on campus.

Freshmen:
Admission: 3,545 applied, 2,432 admitted, 501 enrolled. *Average high school GPA:* 3.1.
Retention: 81% of full-time freshmen returned.

FACULTY
Total: 351, 47% full-time, 57% with terminal degrees.
Student/faculty ratio: 16:1.

ACADEMICS
Calendar: semesters. *Degrees:* certificates, bachelor's, master's, and post-master's certificates.
Special study options: academic remediation for entering students, advanced placement credit, distance learning, double majors, freshman honors college, honors programs, independent study, internships, off-campus study, part-time degree program, services for LD students, study abroad, summer session for credit. *ROTC:* Army (c), Air Force (c).
Unusual degree programs: 3-2 engineering with Stony Brook University, State University of New York; biological sciences/osteopathic medicine with New York College of Osteopathic Medicine.
Computers: 480 computers/terminals and 700 ports are available on campus for general student use. Students can access the following: campus intranet, free student e-mail accounts, online (class) grades, online (class) registration, financial aid, billing information. Campuswide network is available. 100% of college-owned or -operated housing units are wired for high-speed Internet access. Wireless service is available via entire campus.
Library: SUNY College at Old Westbury Library plus 1 other. *Books:* 156,872 (physical), 144,263 (digital/electronic); *Databases:* 138. Weekly public service hours: 99.

STUDENT LIFE
Housing options: coed. Campus housing is university owned. Freshman campus housing is guaranteed.
Activities and organizations: drama/theater group, student-run newspaper, radio station, choral group, Student Government Association, Alianza Latina, PRIDE, Step Tunes, Anime Magna Games Club, national fraternities, national sororities.
Athletics Member NCAA. All Division III. *Intercollegiate sports:* baseball M, basketball M/W, cross-country running M/W, golf M, lacrosse W, soccer M/W, softball W, swimming and diving M/W, volleyball W. *Intramural sports:* badminton M/W, basketball M/W, cheerleading M(c)/W(c), equestrian sports M(c)/W(c), football M/W, racquetball M/W, soccer M/W, softball W, squash M/W, ultimate Frisbee M/W, weight lifting M/W.
Campus security: 24-hour emergency response devices and patrols, student patrols, late-night transport/escort service, controlled dormitory access.
Student services: health clinic, personal/psychological counseling, women's center.

COSTS & FINANCIAL AID
Costs (2017–18) *Tuition:* state resident $6670 full-time, $278 per credit hour part-time; nonresident $16,320 full-time, $680 per credit hour part-time. Part-time tuition and fees vary according to course load. *Required fees:* $1213 full-time, $24 per credit hour part-time, $163 per term part-time. *Room and board:* $11,020; room only: $7300. Room and board charges vary according to housing facility. *Payment plan:* installment. *Waivers:* senior citizens.
Financial Aid Of all full-time matriculated undergraduates who enrolled in 2015, 2,853 applied for aid, 2,509 were judged to have need, 182 had their need fully met. 245 Federal Work-Study jobs (averaging $975). In 2015, 26 non-need-based awards were made. *Average percent of need met:* 60. *Average financial aid package:* $10,395. *Average need-based loan:* $3960. *Average need-based gift aid:* $6876. *Average non-need-based aid:* $5636.

APPLYING
Standardized Tests *Required:* SAT or ACT (for admission).
Options: electronic application, early admission, early decision, deferred entrance.
Application fee: $50.
Required: essay or personal statement, high school transcript, 2 letters of recommendation. *Required for some:* interview.
Application deadlines: rolling (freshmen), 12/15 (transfers).
Early decision deadline: 11/1.
Notification: continuous (freshmen), continuous (transfers), 12/15 (early decision).

CONTACT
State University of New York College at Old Westbury, PO Box 307, Old Westbury, NY 11568. *Phone:* 516-876-3073. *Fax:* 516-876-3307. *E-mail:* enroll@oldwestbury.edu.

State University of New York College at Oneonta
Oneonta, New York
http://www.oneonta.edu/

- **State-supported** comprehensive, founded 1889, part of State University of New York System
- **Small-town** 250-acre campus
- **Endowment** $49.1 million
- **Coed** 5,940 undergraduate students, 98% full-time, 60% women, 40% men
- **Very difficult** entrance level, 60% of applicants were admitted

UNDERGRAD STUDENTS
5,828 full-time, 112 part-time. Students come from 18 states and territories; 32 other countries; 1% are from out of state; 4% Black or African American, non-Hispanic/Latino; 14% Hispanic/Latino; 2% Asian, non-Hispanic/Latino; 0.1% Native Hawaiian or other Pacific Islander, non-Hispanic/Latino; 0.3% American Indian or Alaska Native, non-Hispanic/Latino; 2% Two or more races, non-Hispanic/Latino; 1% Race/ethnicity unknown; 0.8% international; 10% transferred in; 59% live on campus.

Freshmen:
Admission: 11,100 applied, 6,607 admitted, 1,381 enrolled. *Average high school GPA:* 3.4. *Test scores:* SAT evidence-based reading and writing scores over 500: 87%; SAT math scores over 500: 86%; ACT scores over 18: 98%; SAT evidence-based reading and writing scores over 600: 26%; SAT math scores over 600: 24%; ACT scores over 24: 44%; SAT evidence-based reading and writing scores over 700: 1%; SAT math scores over 700: 2%; ACT scores over 30: 2%.
Retention: 85% of full-time freshmen returned.

FACULTY
Total: 490, 58% full-time.
Student/faculty ratio: 17:1.

ACADEMICS
Calendar: semesters. *Degrees:* bachelor's, master's, post-master's, and postbachelor's certificates.

Special study options: academic remediation for entering students, adult/continuing education programs, advanced placement credit, distance learning, double majors, English as a second language, honors programs, independent study, internships, off-campus study, part-time degree program, services for LD students, study abroad, summer session for credit.

Unusual degree programs: 3-2 business administration with State University of New York at Binghamton, Clarkson University, Rochester Institute of Technology, Union College; engineering with University at Buffalo, the State University of New York; Alfred University; Clarkson University; Rensselaer Polytechnic Institute; Syracuse University; accounting at State University of New York at Binghamton, fashion with Fashion Institute of Technology, American Intercontinental University in London.

Computers: 700 computers/terminals are available on campus for general student use. Students can access the following: campus intranet, computer help desk, free student e-mail accounts, online (class) grades, online (class) registration, online (class) schedules, digital video/audio editing suites, presentation rehearsal room using lecture capture software, large format printing, network file storage space. Campuswide network is available. 100% of college-owned or -operated housing units are wired for high-speed Internet access. Wireless service is available via entire campus.

Library: Milne Library. *Books:* 394,015 (physical), 417,737 (digital/electronic); *Serial titles:* 60 (physical), 119,484 (digital/electronic); *Databases:* 251. Students can reserve study rooms.

STUDENT LIFE

Housing options: on-campus residence required through sophomore year; coed. Campus housing is university owned. Freshman campus housing is guaranteed.

Activities and organizations: drama/theater group, student-run newspaper, radio and television station, choral group, Center for Social Responsibility and Community, Music Industry Club, Terpsichorean Dance Company, Student Government, Zombie Defense Corps, national fraternities, national sororities.

Athletics Member NCAA. All Division III. *Intercollegiate sports:* baseball M, basketball M/W, cheerleading W(c), cross-country running M/W, fencing M(c)/W(c), field hockey W, ice hockey M(c), lacrosse M/W, rugby W(c), soccer M/W, softball W, swimming and diving M/W, tennis M/W, track and field M/W, volleyball W, wrestling M. *Intramural sports:* badminton M(c)/W(c), basketball M/W, equestrian sports M(c)/W(c), football M, racquetball M(c)/W(c), skiing (downhill) M(c)/W(c), soccer M/W, softball M/W, ultimate Frisbee M/W, volleyball M/W.

Campus security: 24-hour emergency response devices and patrols, late-night transport/escort service, controlled dormitory access, Oneonta Emergency Squad: an organization of student volunteers with first responder credential.

Student services: health clinic, personal/psychological counseling, women's center.

COSTS & FINANCIAL AID

Costs (2018–19) *Tuition:* state resident $6670 full-time, $278 per credit hour part-time; nonresident $16,320 full-time, $680 per credit hour part-time. Part-time tuition and fees vary according to course load. *Required fees:* $1466 full-time, $42 per credit hour part-time. *Room and board:* $12,658; room only: $8350. Room and board charges vary according to housing facility. *Payment plan:* installment. *Waivers:* employees or children of employees.

Financial Aid Of all full-time matriculated undergraduates who enrolled in 2016, 4,164 applied for aid, 3,220 were judged to have need, 1,559 had their need fully met. In 2016, 242 non-need-based awards were made. *Average percent of need met:* 65. *Average financial aid package:* $9837. *Average need-based loan:* $4810. *Average need-based gift aid:* $7239. *Average non-need-based aid:* $4046. *Average indebtedness upon graduation:* $27,045.

APPLYING

Standardized Tests *Required:* SAT or ACT (for admission).

Options: electronic application, early admission, early action, deferred entrance.

Application fee: $50.

Required: essay or personal statement, high school transcript. *Recommended:* minimum 3.0 GPA, 3 letters of recommendation.

Application deadlines: rolling (freshmen), rolling (transfers), 11/15 (early action).

Notification: continuous (freshmen), continuous (transfers), 12/1 (early action).

CONTACT
Ms. Karen Brown, Director of Admissions, State University of New York College at Oneonta, Alumni Hall 116, Oneonta, NY 13820-4015. *Phone:* 607-436-2524. *Toll-free phone:* 800-SUNY-123. *Fax:* 607-436-3074. *E-mail:* admissions@oneonta.edu.

State University of New York College at Potsdam
Potsdam, New York
http://www.potsdam.edu/

- **State-supported** comprehensive, founded 1816, part of State University of New York System
- **Small-town** 240-acre campus
- **Endowment** $29.6 million
- **Coed** 3,321 undergraduate students, 96% full-time, 58% women, 42% men
- **Moderately difficult** entrance level, 67% of applicants were admitted

UNDERGRAD STUDENTS
3,196 full-time, 125 part-time. Students come from 30 states and territories; 6 other countries; 4% are from out of state; 13% Black or African American, non-Hispanic/Latino; 15% Hispanic/Latino; 2% Asian, non-Hispanic/Latino; 0.1% Native Hawaiian or other Pacific Islander, non-Hispanic/Latino; 2% American Indian or Alaska Native, non-Hispanic/Latino; 2% Two or more races, non-Hispanic/Latino; 4% Race/ethnicity unknown; 0.5% international; 8% transferred in; 58% live on campus.

Freshmen:
Admission: 5,581 applied, 3,717 admitted, 783 enrolled.
Retention: 75% of full-time freshmen returned.

FACULTY
Total: 366, 71% full-time, 67% with terminal degrees.
Student/faculty ratio: 11:1.

ACADEMICS
Calendar: semesters. *Degrees:* bachelor's, master's, and post-master's certificates.

Special study options: advanced placement credit, distance learning, double majors, honors programs, independent study, internships, off-campus study, part-time degree program, services for LD students, student-designed majors, study abroad, summer session for credit. *ROTC:* Army (c), Air Force (c).

Unusual degree programs: 3-2 engineering with Clarkson University; Binghamton University, State University of New York; physics, computer science, chemistry, engineering; mathematics with Clarkson University.

Computers: 608 computers/terminals and 80 ports are available on campus for general student use. Students can access the following: campus intranet, computer help desk, free student e-mail accounts, online (class) grades, online (class) registration, online (class) schedules, online access to financial aid status, unofficial transcripts, billing, meal plan and housing sign-up. Campuswide network is available. 100% of college-owned or -operated housing units are wired for high-speed Internet access. Wireless service is available via classrooms, computer centers, computer labs, dorm rooms, learning centers, libraries, student centers.

Library: F. W. Crumb Memorial Library plus 1 other. *Books:* 258,039 (physical), 45,425 (digital/electronic); *Serial titles:* 3,227 (physical), 100,736 (digital/electronic); *Databases:* 144. Weekly public service hours: 119; study areas open 24 hours, 5–7 days a week; students can reserve study rooms.

STUDENT LIFE
Housing options: on-campus residence required through sophomore year; coed, special housing for students with disabilities. Campus housing is university owned. Freshman campus housing is guaranteed.

Activities and organizations: drama/theater group, student-run newspaper, radio station, choral group, Student Government Association, Crane Student Association, Black Student Alliance, SOCO LOCO, Musical Theatre Organization, national fraternities, national sororities.

Athletics Member NCAA. All Division III. *Intercollegiate sports:* basketball M/W, cross-country running M/W, golf M, ice hockey M/W, lacrosse M/W, soccer M/W, swimming and diving M/W, track and field M/W, volleyball W. *Intramural sports:* basketball M/W, bowling M(c)/W(c), cheerleading M(c)/W(c), ice hockey M(c)/W(c), racquetball M/W, rugby M(c)/W(c), skiing (downhill) M(c)/W(c), soccer M/W, softball M/W, track and field M(c)/W(c), triathlon M/W, ultimate Frisbee M(c)/W(c), volleyball M/W.

Campus security: 24-hour emergency response devices and patrols, late-night transport/escort service, controlled dormitory access, 24 hr. foot patrol, RAVE Guardian, Video Surveillance System, security escort service,self-defense education,controlled access to dorms.

Student services: health clinic, personal/psychological counseling, women's center, legal services.

COSTS & FINANCIAL AID
Costs (2017–18) *Tuition:* state resident $6670 full-time, $278 per credit hour part-time; nonresident $16,320 full-time, $680 per credit hour part-time. Full-time tuition and fees vary according to course load. Part-time tuition and fees vary according to course load. *Required fees:* $1551 full-time, $83 per credit hour part-time. *Room and board:* $12,830; room only: $7360. Room and board charges vary according to board plan and housing facility. *Payment plan:* installment. *Waivers:* employees or children of employees.

Financial Aid Of all full-time matriculated undergraduates who enrolled in 2017, 3,040 applied for aid, 2,501 were judged to have need, 189 had their need fully met. 165 Federal Work-Study jobs (averaging $1652). In 2017, 281 non-need-based awards were made. *Average percent of need met:* 94. *Average financial aid package:* $16,750. *Average need-based loan:* $4597. *Average need-based gift aid:* $8424. *Average non-need-based aid:* $3178. *Average indebtedness upon graduation:* $28,797.

APPLYING
Options: electronic application, early admission, deferred entrance.
Application fee: $50.
Required: high school transcript, minimum 2.5 GPA, 1 letter of recommendation. *Required for some:* essay or personal statement, minimum 2.0 GPA, DVD audition for music.
Application deadlines: rolling (freshmen), rolling (transfers).
Notification: continuous (freshmen), continuous (transfers).

CONTACT
Mr. Thomas Nesbitt, Director of Admissions, State University of New York College at Potsdam, 44 Pierrepont Avenue, Potsdam, NY 13676. *Phone:* 315-267-2180. *Toll-free phone:* 877-POTSDAM. *Fax:* 315-267-2163. *E-mail:* admissions@potsdam.edu.

State University of New York College of Agriculture and Technology at Cobleskill
Cobleskill, New York
http://www.cobleskill.edu/
- **State-supported** 4-year, founded 1916, part of State University of New York System
- **Small-town** 950-acre campus with easy access to Albany, NY
- **Endowment** $2.5 million
- **Coed**
- **Minimally difficult** entrance level

FACULTY
Student/faculty ratio: 17:1.

ACADEMICS
Calendar: semesters. *Degrees:* certificates, associate, and bachelor's.
Library: Jared van Wagenen Library. *Books:* 53,260 (physical), 54,322 (digital/electronic); *Serial titles:* 200 (physical), 91,655 (digital/electronic); *Databases:* 60. Weekly public service hours: 76; students can reserve study rooms.

STUDENT LIFE
Housing options: on-campus residence required through sophomore year; coed, men-only, women-only, special housing for students with disabilities. Campus housing is university owned.

Activities and organizations: drama/theater group, student-run newspaper, choral group, Dairy Cattle Club, Wildlife Society, Canine Club, Woodsmen's Club, American Fisheries Society.

Athletics Member NCAA. All Division III.

Campus security: 24-hour emergency response devices and patrols, student patrols, late-night transport/escort service, controlled dormitory access, bicycle patrols, horse-mounted patrols.

Student services: health clinic, personal/psychological counseling.

COSTS & FINANCIAL AID
Costs (2017–18) *Tuition:* state resident $6670 full-time, $278 per credit hour part-time; nonresident $16,320 full-time, $680 per credit hour part-time. Full-time tuition and fees vary according to course level and degree level. Part-time tuition and fees vary according to course level and degree level. *Required fees:* $1469 full-time, $63 per credit hour part-time. *Room and board:* $13,182; room only: $7878. Room and board charges vary according to board plan and housing facility. *Payment plans:* installment, deferred payment.

Financial Aid Of all full-time matriculated undergraduates who enrolled in 2016, 2,058 applied for aid, 1,861 were judged to have need, 13 had their need fully met. 97 Federal Work-Study jobs (averaging $1166). 353 state and other part-time jobs (averaging $1506). In 2016, 61 non-need-based awards were made. *Average percent of need met:* 60. *Average financial aid package:* $7614. *Average need-based loan:* $2279. *Average need-based gift aid:* $4333. *Average non-need-based aid:* $2623. *Average indebtedness upon graduation:* $29,645.

APPLYING
Standardized Tests *Required for some:* SAT or ACT (for admission).
Options: electronic application, early admission, deferred entrance.
Application fee: $50.
Required: high school transcript. *Required for some:* essay or personal statement, minimum 2.0 GPA, 3 letters of recommendation, interview. *Recommended:* minimum 1.8 GPA.

CONTACT
Lisa Starr-DeCarlo, Office Assistant 1, State University of New York College of Agriculture and Technology at Cobleskill, 213 Knapp Hall, Cobleskill, NY 12043. *Phone:* 518-255-5525. *Toll-free phone:* 800-295-8988. *Fax:* 518-255-6769. *E-mail:* admissions@cobleskill.edu.

State University of New York College of Environmental Science and Forestry
Syracuse, New York
http://www.esf.edu/
- **State-supported** university, founded 1911, part of State University of New York System
- **Urban** 17-acre campus with easy access to Syracuse
- **Endowment** $34.2 million
- **Coed** 1,796 undergraduate students, 97% full-time, 47% women, 53% men
- **Very difficult** entrance level, 52% of applicants were admitted

UNDERGRAD STUDENTS
1,738 full-time, 58 part-time. Students come from 27 states and territories; 9 other countries; 15% are from out of state; 2% Black or African American, non-Hispanic/Latino; 6% Hispanic/Latino; 4% Asian, non-Hispanic/Latino; 0.2% American Indian or Alaska Native, non-Hispanic/Latino; 3% Two or more races, non-Hispanic/Latino; 4% Race/ethnicity unknown; 2% international; 13% transferred in; 35% live on campus.

Freshmen:
Admission: 1,815 applied, 948 admitted, 328 enrolled. *Average high school GPA:* 3.8. *Test scores:* SAT evidence-based reading and writing scores over 500: 98%; SAT math scores over 500: 98%; ACT scores over

18: 100%; SAT evidence-based reading and writing scores over 600: 69%; SAT math scores over 600: 62%; ACT scores over 24: 86%; SAT evidence-based reading and writing scores over 700: 10%; SAT math scores over 700: 8%; ACT scores over 30: 22%.
Retention: 83% of full-time freshmen returned.

FACULTY
Total: 159, 73% full-time, 70% with terminal degrees.
Student/faculty ratio: 13:1.

ACADEMICS
Calendar: semesters. *Degrees:* associate, bachelor's, master's, doctoral, and postbachelor's certificates.

Special study options: accelerated degree program, advanced placement credit, cooperative education, distance learning, double majors, English as a second language, freshman honors college, honors programs, independent study, internships, off-campus study, part-time degree program, services for LD students, study abroad, summer session for credit. *ROTC:* Army (c), Air Force (c).

Computers: 350 computers/terminals and 2,250 ports are available on campus for general student use. Students can access the following: campus intranet, computer help desk, free student e-mail accounts, online (class) grades, online (class) registration, online (class) schedules. Campuswide network is available. 100% of college-owned or -operated housing units are wired for high-speed Internet access. Wireless service is available via classrooms, computer centers, computer labs, dorm rooms, libraries, student centers.

Library: F. Franklin Moon Library plus 1 other. *Books:* 137,535 (physical), 348,596 (digital/electronic); *Serial titles:* 1,741 (physical), 241,084 (digital/electronic); *Databases:* 171. Weekly public service hours: 97.

STUDENT LIFE
Housing options: on-campus residence required for freshman year; coed, special housing for students with disabilities. Campus housing is university owned and is provided by a third party. Freshman campus housing is guaranteed.

Activities and organizations: drama/theater group, student-run newspaper, choral group, marching band, Bob Marshall/Outing Club, Forestry Club, Student Environmental Action Coalition, Student Green Campus Initiative, Alpha Phi Omega (Service).

Athletics Member USCAA. *Intercollegiate sports:* basketball M, cross-country running M/W, golf M/W, soccer M/W, track and field M/W. *Intramural sports:* archery M/W, badminton M/W, baseball M, basketball M/W, bowling M/W, cheerleading M/W, crew M/W, cross-country running M/W, equestrian sports M/W, fencing M/W, field hockey W, football M, gymnastics M/W, ice hockey M/W, lacrosse M/W, racquetball M/W, riflery M, rugby M/W, sailing M/W, skiing (downhill) M/W, soccer M/W, softball M/W, squash M/W, swimming and diving M/W, table tennis M/W, tennis M/W, track and field M/W, ultimate Frisbee M/W, volleyball M/W.

Campus security: 24-hour emergency response devices and patrols, late-night transport/escort service, controlled dormitory access.

Student services: health clinic, personal/psychological counseling, women's center, legal services.

COSTS & FINANCIAL AID
Costs (2018–19) *One-time required fee:* $278. *Tuition:* state resident $6670 full-time, $278 per credit hour part-time; nonresident $16,320 full-time, $680 per credit hour part-time. Full-time tuition and fees vary according to location. Part-time tuition and fees vary according to course load and location. *Required fees:* $1898 full-time, $76 per credit hour part-time, $15 per term part-time. *Room and board:* $16,140; room only: $8300. Room and board charges vary according to board plan, housing facility, and location. *Payment plan:* installment.

Financial Aid Of all full-time matriculated undergraduates who enrolled in 2017, 1,467 applied for aid, 1,069 were judged to have need, 512 had their need fully met. 180 Federal Work-Study jobs (averaging $1790). 217 state and other part-time jobs (averaging $886). In 2017, 369 non-need-based awards were made. *Average percent of need met:* 66. *Average financial aid package:* $10,160. *Average need-based loan:* $4675. *Average need-based gift aid:* $6648. *Average non-need-based aid:* $3246. *Average indebtedness upon graduation:* $26,679.

APPLYING

Standardized Tests *Required:* SAT or ACT (for admission).

Options: electronic application, early admission, early decision, deferred entrance.

Application fee: $50.

Required: essay or personal statement, high school transcript, minimum 2.5 GPA. *Recommended:* 1 letter of recommendation, interview.

Application deadlines: 2/1 (freshmen), rolling (out-of-state freshmen), 3/1 (transfers).

Early decision deadline: 12/1.

Notification: continuous until 2/1 (freshmen), continuous (out-of-state freshmen), continuous (transfers), 1/15 (early decision).

CONTACT

Ms. Susan Sanford, Director of Admissions, State University of New York College of Environmental Science and Forestry, Office of Undergraduate Admissions, Gateway Center 1 Forestry Drive, Syracuse, NY 13210-2779. *Phone:* 315-470-6600. *Fax:* 315-470-6933. *E-mail:* esfinfo@esf.edu.

See previous page for display ad and page 1438 for the College Close-Up.

State University of New York College of Technology at Alfred

Alfred, New York

http://www.alfredstate.edu/

- **State-supported** primarily 2-year, founded 1908, part of State University of New York System
- **Rural** 1084-acre campus with easy access to Rochester, Buffalo
- **Endowment** $4.5 million
- **Coed** 3,686 undergraduate students, 92% full-time, 36% women, 64% men
- **Moderately difficult** entrance level, 68% of applicants were admitted

UNDERGRAD STUDENTS

3,396 full-time, 290 part-time. Students come from 27 states and territories; 14 other countries; 4% are from out of state; 13% Black or African American, non-Hispanic/Latino; 9% Hispanic/Latino; 1% Asian, non-Hispanic/Latino; 0.1% Native Hawaiian or other Pacific Islander, non-Hispanic/Latino; 0.3% American Indian or Alaska Native, non-Hispanic/Latino; 3% Two or more races, non-Hispanic/Latino; 0.8% Race/ethnicity unknown; 1% international; 8% transferred in; 65% live on campus.

Freshmen:

Admission: 5,395 applied, 3,650 admitted, 1,120 enrolled. *Average high school GPA:* 3.0. *Test scores:* SAT evidence-based reading and writing scores over 500: 57%; SAT math scores over 500: 61%; ACT scores over 18: 85%; SAT evidence-based reading and writing scores over 600: 16%; SAT math scores over 600: 15%; ACT scores over 24: 43%; SAT evidence-based reading and writing scores over 700: 2%; SAT math scores over 700: 2%; ACT scores over 30: 6%.

Retention: 65% of full-time freshmen returned.

FACULTY

Total: 249, 67% full-time, 33% with terminal degrees.

Student/faculty ratio: 18:1.

ACADEMICS

Calendar: semesters. *Degrees:* certificates, associate, and bachelor's.

Special study options: academic remediation for entering students, accelerated degree program, adult/continuing education programs, advanced placement credit, cooperative education, distance learning, double majors, English as a second language, honors programs, independent study, internships, off-campus study, part-time degree program, services for LD students, student-designed majors, study abroad, summer session for credit. *ROTC:* Army (c).

Computers: 108 computers/terminals are available on campus for general student use. Students can access the following: campus intranet, computer help desk, free student e-mail accounts, online (class) grades, online (class) registration, online (class) schedules. Campuswide network is available. 100% of college-owned or -operated housing units are wired for high-speed Internet access. Wireless service is available via entire campus.

Library: Walter C. Hinkle Memorial Library plus 1 other. *Books:* 54,671 (physical), 49,782 (digital/electronic); *Serial titles:* 253 (physical), 164,768 (digital/electronic); *Databases:* 193. Weekly public service hours: 88.

STUDENT LIFE

Housing options: coed, men-only, women-only, special housing for students with disabilities. Campus housing is university owned. Freshman campus housing is guaranteed.

Activities and organizations: drama/theater group, student-run newspaper, radio station, choral group, Outdoor Recreation Club, Caribbean Student Association, Alfred Programming Board, Pioneer Woodsmen, Disaster Relief Team.

Athletics Member NCAA, USCAA. All Division III. *Intercollegiate sports:* baseball M, basketball M/W, cross-country running M/W, equestrian sports M/W, football M, lacrosse M, soccer M/W, softball W, swimming and diving M/W, track and field M/W, volleyball W, wrestling M. *Intramural sports:* basketball M/W, equestrian sports M(c)/W(c), football M, golf M/W, ice hockey M(c), rock climbing M/W, soccer M/W, softball M/W, swimming and diving M/W, tennis M/W, ultimate Frisbee M/W, volleyball M/W.

Campus security: 24-hour emergency response devices and patrols, late-night transport/escort service, controlled dormitory access, residence hall entrance guards.

Student services: health clinic, personal/psychological counseling.

COSTS & FINANCIAL AID

Costs (2018–19) *One-time required fee:* $110. *Tuition:* state resident $6670 full-time, $278 per credit hour part-time; nonresident $9740 full-time, $406 per credit hour part-time. Full-time tuition and fees vary according to course load and degree level. Part-time tuition and fees vary according to course load and degree level. *Required fees:* $1657 full-time, $66 per credit hour part-time, $10 per credit hour part-time. *Room and board:* $12,250; room only: $7500. Room and board charges vary according to board plan and housing facility. *Payment plan:* installment. *Waivers:* employees or children of employees.

Financial Aid Of all full-time matriculated undergraduates who enrolled in 2016, 3,170 applied for aid, 2,762 were judged to have need, 219 had their need fully met. In 2016, 162 non-need-based awards were made. *Average percent of need met:* 58. *Average financial aid package:* $10,778. *Average need-based loan:* $3916. *Average need-based gift aid:* $6709. *Average non-need-based aid:* $5675. *Average indebtedness upon graduation:* $32,017.

APPLYING

Standardized Tests *Required for some:* SAT or ACT (for admission). *Recommended:* SAT or ACT (for admission).

Options: electronic application.

Application fee: $50.

Required: high school transcript, minimum 2.0 GPA, Common Application with essay on supplemental application. *Recommended:* essay or personal statement, interview.

Application deadlines: rolling (freshmen), rolling (transfers).

Notification: continuous (freshmen), continuous (transfers).

CONTACT

Mrs. Deborah Goodrich, Associate Vice President for Enrollment Management, State University of New York College of Technology at Alfred, Huntington Administration Building, 10 Upper College Drive, Alfred, NY 14802. *Phone:* 607-587-3945. *Toll-free phone:* 800-4-ALFRED. *Fax:* 607-587-4299. *E-mail:* admissions@alfredstate.edu.

State University of New York College of Technology at Canton

Canton, New York

http://www.canton.edu/

- **State-supported** 4-year, founded 1906, part of State University of New York System
- **Small-town** 555-acre campus
- **Endowment** $11.9 million
- **Coed** 3,180 undergraduate students, 84% full-time, 59% women, 41% men
- **Minimally difficult** entrance level, 79% of applicants were admitted

UNDERGRAD STUDENTS

2,657 full-time, 523 part-time. Students come from 33 states and territories; 17 other countries; 3% are from out of state; 15% Black or African American, non-Hispanic/Latino; 11% Hispanic/Latino; 1% Asian, non-Hispanic/Latino; 0.1% Native Hawaiian or other Pacific Islander, non-Hispanic/Latino; 1% American Indian or Alaska Native, non-Hispanic/Latino; 3% Two or more races, non-Hispanic/Latino; 2% Race/ethnicity unknown; 2% international; 10% transferred in; 45% live on campus.

Freshmen:
Admission: 3,672 applied, 2,886 admitted, 692 enrolled. *Average high school GPA:* 2.9. *Test scores:* SAT evidence-based reading and writing scores over 500: 48%; SAT math scores over 500: 46%; ACT scores over 18: 68%; SAT evidence-based reading and writing scores over 600: 9%; SAT math scores over 600: 7%; ACT scores over 24: 12%.

Retention: 77% of full-time freshmen returned.

FACULTY

Total: 238, 54% full-time, 41% with terminal degrees.
Student/faculty ratio: 17:1.

ACADEMICS

Calendar: semesters. *Degrees:* certificates, associate, and bachelor's.

Special study options: academic remediation for entering students, advanced placement credit, cooperative education, distance learning, honors programs, independent study, internships, off-campus study, services for LD students, study abroad, summer session for credit. *ROTC:* Army (c), Air Force (c).

Computers: 825 computers/terminals are available on campus for general student use. Students can access the following: campus intranet, computer help desk, free student e-mail accounts, online (class) grades, online (class) registration, online (class) schedules, online bill payment. Campuswide network is available. 100% of college-owned or -operated housing units are wired for high-speed Internet access. Wireless service is available via classrooms, computer centers, computer labs, learning centers, libraries, student centers.

Library: Southworth Library. *Books:* 23,958 (physical), 168,143 (digital/electronic); *Serial titles:* 14 (physical), 5,928 (digital/electronic); *Databases:* 84. Weekly public service hours: 125.

STUDENT LIFE

Housing options: on-campus residence required through sophomore year; coed, special housing for students with disabilities. Campus housing is university owned. Freshman applicants given priority for college housing.

Activities and organizations: drama/theater group, choral group, Student Government Alliance, College Activities Board, Greek Council, Brother to Brother, Sister to Sister.

Athletics Member NCAA, USCAA. All Division III. *Intercollegiate sports:* baseball M, basketball M/W, cross-country running M/W, golf M/W, ice hockey M/W, lacrosse M/W, soccer M/W, softball W, volleyball W. *Intramural sports:* basketball M/W, cheerleading M(c)/W(c), football M/W, ice hockey M(c), soccer M/W, softball M/W, ultimate Frisbee M(c)/W(c), volleyball M/W.

Campus security: 24-hour emergency response devices and patrols, late-night transport/escort service, controlled dormitory access, student EMS group.

Student services: health clinic, personal/psychological counseling.

COSTS & FINANCIAL AID

Costs (2017–18) *One-time required fee:* $120. *Tuition:* state resident $6670 full-time, $278 per credit hour part-time; nonresident $16,320 full-time, $680 per credit hour part-time. Full-time tuition and fees vary according to degree level. Part-time tuition and fees vary according to degree level. *Required fees:* $1459 full-time, $59 per credit hour part-time, $5 per term part-time. *Room and board:* $12,450; room only: $7350. Room and board charges vary according to board plan and housing facility. *Payment plans:* installment, deferred payment. *Waivers:* employees or children of employees.

Financial Aid Of all full-time matriculated undergraduates who enrolled in 2016, 2,438 applied for aid, 2,195 were judged to have need, 347 had their need fully met. 190 Federal Work-Study jobs (averaging $1280). 12 state and other part-time jobs (averaging $1050). In 2016, 44 non-need-based awards were made. *Average percent of need met:* 16. *Average financial aid package:* $10,650. *Average need-based loan:* $3904. *Average need-based gift aid:* $7852. *Average non-need-based aid:* $2071. *Average indebtedness upon graduation:* $31,499.

APPLYING

Standardized Tests *Required for some:* SAT or ACT (for admission).

Options: electronic application, deferred entrance.

Application fee: $50.

Required: high school transcript. *Required for some:* essay or personal statement, interview. *Recommended:* minimum 2.0 GPA.

Application deadlines: 8/30 (freshmen), rolling (out-of-state freshmen), 8/30 (transfers).

Notification: continuous (freshmen), continuous (out-of-state freshmen), continuous (transfers).

CONTACT

Melissa Evans, Director of Admissions, State University of New York College of Technology at Canton, 34 Cornell Drive, Canton, NY 13617. *Phone:* 315-386-7123. *Toll-free phone:* 800-388-7123. *Fax:* 315-386-7929. *E-mail:* admissions@canton.edu.

State University of New York College of Technology at Delhi

Delhi, New York

http://www.delhi.edu/

- **State-supported** comprehensive, founded 1913, part of State University of New York System
- **Rural** 405-acre campus
- **Endowment** $6.9 million
- **Coed** 3,469 undergraduate students, 78% full-time, 56% women, 44% men
- **Moderately difficult** entrance level, 63% of applicants were admitted

UNDERGRAD STUDENTS

2,704 full-time, 765 part-time. Students come from 26 states and territories; 5 other countries; 3% are from out of state; 17% Black or African American, non-Hispanic/Latino; 21% Hispanic/Latino; 2% Asian, non-Hispanic/Latino; 0.7% American Indian or Alaska Native, non-Hispanic/Latino; 3% Race/ethnicity unknown; 3% international; 10% transferred in; 52% live on campus.

Freshmen:
Admission: 6,206 applied, 3,889 admitted, 966 enrolled. *Average high school GPA:* 2.8.

Retention: 65% of full-time freshmen returned.

FACULTY

Total: 250, 62% full-time, 28% with terminal degrees.
Student/faculty ratio: 16:1.

ACADEMICS

Calendar: semesters. *Degrees:* certificates, associate, bachelor's, and master's.

Special study options: academic remediation for entering students, accelerated degree program, adult/continuing education programs, advanced placement credit, distance learning, double majors, English as a second language, honors programs, independent study, internships, off-campus study, part-time degree program, services for LD students, study abroad, summer session for credit.

Computers: 102 computers/terminals are available on campus for general student use. Students can access the following: computer help desk, free student e-mail accounts, online (class) grades, online (class) registration, online (class) schedules. Campuswide network is available. 100% of college-owned or -operated housing units are wired for high-speed Internet access. Wireless service is available via entire campus.

Library: Resnick Library. *Books:* 37,908 (physical), 152,584 (digital/electronic); *Serial titles:* 350,364 (physical), 350,364 (digital/electronic); *Databases:* 68. Weekly public service hours: 93; students can reserve study rooms.

STUDENT LIFE

Housing options: on-campus residence required through sophomore year; coed. Campus housing is university owned. Freshman applicants given priority for college housing.

Activities and organizations: drama/theater group, student-run newspaper, radio and television station, choral group, New York State Association for Veterinary Technicians, National Student Nursing Association, Black Student Union, Bronco's Finest, Equine Club, national fraternities, national sororities.

Athletics Member NCAA. All Division III. *Intercollegiate sports:* basketball M/W, cross-country running M/W, golf M/W, lacrosse M, soccer M/W, softball W, swimming and diving M/W, tennis M/W, track and field M/W, volleyball W. *Intramural sports:* badminton M/W, basketball M, bowling M/W, ultimate Frisbee M/W, volleyball M/W.

Campus security: 24-hour emergency response devices and patrols, late-night transport/escort service, controlled dormitory access.

Student services: health clinic, personal/psychological counseling.

COSTS & FINANCIAL AID

Costs (2017–18) *Tuition:* state resident $6670 full-time, $278 per credit hour part-time; nonresident $10,840 full-time, $452 per credit hour part-time. Full-time tuition and fees vary according to location. Part-time tuition and fees vary according to course load and location. *Required fees:* $1450 full-time, $60 per credit hour part-time, $5 per term part-time. *Room and board:* $11,980; room only: $6900. Room and board charges vary according to board plan and housing facility. *Payment plan:* installment.

Financial Aid Of all full-time matriculated undergraduates who enrolled in 2015, 72 Federal Work-Study jobs (averaging $1188). *Average indebtedness upon graduation:* $28,367.

APPLYING

Standardized Tests *Recommended:* SAT or ACT (for admission).

Options: electronic application, deferred entrance.

Application fee: $50.

Required: high school transcript. *Required for some:* minimum 2.0 GPA, 2 letters of recommendation, associate degree for some bachelor programs, RN license for BSN program. Letters of recommendation required at the graduate level. *Recommended:* interview.

Application deadlines: rolling (freshmen), rolling (transfers).

Notification: continuous (freshmen), continuous (transfers).

CONTACT
State University of New York College of Technology at Delhi, 454 Delhi Drive, Delhi, NY 13753. *Phone:* 607-746-4550. *Toll-free phone:* 800-96-DELHI. *Fax:* 607-746-4104. *E-mail:* enroll@delhi.edu.

State University of New York Downstate Medical Center

Brooklyn, New York
http://www.downstate.edu/

CONTACT
Admissions Office, State University of New York Downstate Medical Center, 450 Clarkson Avenue, Brooklyn, NY 11203-2446. *Phone:* 718-270-2446. *Fax:* 718-270-7592. *E-mail:* admissions@downstate.edu.

State University of New York Empire State College

Saratoga Springs, New York
http://www.esc.edu/

- **State-supported** comprehensive, founded 1971, part of State University of New York System
- **Small-town** campus
- **Endowment** $19.8 million
- **Coed** 9,839 undergraduate students, 38% full-time, 62% women, 38% men
- **Noncompetitive** entrance level, 84% of applicants were admitted

UNDERGRAD STUDENTS
3,773 full-time, 6,066 part-time. 5% are from out of state; 15% Black or African American, non-Hispanic/Latino; 13% Hispanic/Latino; 3% Asian, non-Hispanic/Latino; 0.2% Native Hawaiian or other Pacific Islander, non-Hispanic/Latino; 0.4% American Indian or Alaska Native, non-Hispanic/Latino; 2% Two or more races, non-Hispanic/Latino; 4% Race/ethnicity unknown; 0.5% international; 12% transferred in.

Freshmen:
Admission: 1,081 applied, 907 admitted, 443 enrolled.

FACULTY
Total: 913, 19% full-time.
Student/faculty ratio: 15:1.

ACADEMICS
Calendar: 5 terms. *Degrees:* certificates, associate, bachelor's, master's, and postbachelor's certificates (branch locations at 7 regional centers with 35 auxiliary units).

Special study options: accelerated degree program, adult/continuing education programs, advanced placement credit, distance learning, double majors, external degree program, independent study, off-campus study, part-time degree program, services for LD students, student-designed majors, summer session for credit.

Computers: 300 computers/terminals are available on campus for general student use. Students can access the following: computer help desk, free student e-mail accounts, online (class) grades, online (class) registration, online (class) schedules. Campuswide network is available.

Library:*Books:* 229,000 (digital/electronic); *Databases:* 94.

STUDENT LIFE
Housing options: college housing not available.

COSTS
Costs (2018–19) *Tuition:* state resident $6670 full-time, $278 per credit part-time; nonresident $16,134 full-time, $680 per credit part-time. Full-time tuition and fees vary according to program. Part-time tuition and fees vary according to program. *Required fees:* $535 full-time. *Payment plan:* installment.

APPLYING
Options: electronic application, deferred entrance.

Application fee: $50.

Required: essay or personal statement, high school transcript.

CONTACT
Ms. Jennifer D'Agostino, Senior Director of Admissions, State University of New York Empire State College, Two Union Avenue, Saratoga Springs, NY 12866. *Phone:* 518-587-2100. *Toll-free phone:* 800-847-3000. *E-mail:* admissions@esc.edu.

State University of New York Maritime College

Throggs Neck, New York

http://www.sunymaritime.edu/

- **State-supported** comprehensive, founded 1874, part of State University of New York System
- **Urban** 55-acre campus with easy access to New York City
- **Endowment** $7.0 million
- **Coed** 1,641 undergraduate students, 96% full-time, 12% women, 88% men
- **Very difficult** entrance level, 69% of applicants were admitted

UNDERGRAD STUDENTS

1,581 full-time, 60 part-time. Students come from 30 states and territories; 11 other countries; 24% are from out of state; 4% Black or African American, non-Hispanic/Latino; 13% Hispanic/Latino; 5% Asian, non-Hispanic/Latino; 0.1% American Indian or Alaska Native, non-Hispanic/Latino; 3% Two or more races, non-Hispanic/Latino; 3% Race/ethnicity unknown; 2% international; 5% transferred in; 83% live on campus.

Freshmen:

Admission: 1,274 applied, 884 admitted, 342 enrolled. *Average high school GPA:* 3.3. *Test scores:* SAT evidence-based reading and writing scores over 500: 94%; SAT math scores over 500: 93%; ACT scores over 18: 98%; SAT evidence-based reading and writing scores over 600: 46%; SAT math scores over 600: 51%; ACT scores over 24: 63%; SAT evidence-based reading and writing scores over 700: 3%; SAT math scores over 700: 5%; ACT scores over 30: 11%.

Retention: 85% of full-time freshmen returned.

FACULTY

Total: 149, 62% full-time, 35% with terminal degrees.

Student/faculty ratio: 15:1.

ACADEMICS

Calendar: semesters plus 2-month summer sea term. *Degrees:* certificates, associate, bachelor's, master's, and postbachelor's certificates.

Special study options: academic remediation for entering students, advanced placement credit, distance learning, double majors, independent study, internships, off-campus study, part-time degree program, services for LD students, study abroad, summer session for credit. *ROTC:* Army (c), Navy (b).

Computers: 160 computers/terminals and 650 ports are available on campus for general student use. Students can access the following: computer help desk, free student e-mail accounts, online (class) grades, online (class) registration, online (class) schedules. Campuswide network is available. 100% of college-owned or -operated housing units are wired for high-speed Internet access. Wireless service is available via classrooms, computer centers, computer labs, dorm rooms, learning centers, libraries, student centers.

Library: Stephen B. Luce Library. *Books:* 43,000 (physical), 60,309 (digital/electronic); *Serial titles:* 125 (physical), 322,940 (digital/electronic); *Databases:* 69. Weekly public service hours: 111; students can reserve study rooms.

STUDENT LIFE

Housing options: on-campus residence required through senior year; coed. Campus housing is university owned.

Activities and organizations: choral group, marching band, Student Government, Maritime Activities and Programs, The Cultural Club, Campus Crusade for Christ, The Maritime Divers Association.

Athletics Member NCAA. All Division III. *Intercollegiate sports:* baseball M, basketball M, crew M/W, cross-country running M/W, football M, ice hockey M(c), lacrosse M/W, riflery M(c)/W(c), sailing M/W, soccer M/W, swimming and diving M/W, volleyball W. *Intramural sports:* basketball M/W, football M/W, soccer M/W, softball M/W, volleyball M/W, water polo M/W.

Campus security: 24-hour emergency response devices and patrols, student patrols, late-night transport/escort service, controlled dormitory access.

Student services: health clinic, personal/psychological counseling.

COSTS & FINANCIAL AID

Costs (2017–18) *Tuition:* state resident $6670 full-time, $278 per credit hour part-time; nonresident $16,320 full-time, $680 per credit hour part-time. Full-time tuition and fees vary according to course load. Part-time tuition and fees vary according to course load. *Required fees:* $1404 full-time. *Room and board:* $12,134; room only: $7714. Room and board charges vary according to board plan and housing facility. *Payment plan:* installment.

Financial Aid Of all full-time matriculated undergraduates who enrolled in 2015, 1,261 applied for aid, 894 were judged to have need, 122 had their need fully met. 101 Federal Work-Study jobs (averaging $352). 235 state and other part-time jobs (averaging $1600). In 2015, 94 non-need-based awards were made. *Average percent of need met:* 20. *Average financial aid package:* $4446. *Average need-based loan:* $2160. *Average need-based gift aid:* $3553. *Average non-need-based aid:* $1399.

APPLYING

Standardized Tests *Required:* SAT or ACT (for admission).

Options: electronic application, early decision, deferred entrance.

Application fee: $50.

Required: essay or personal statement. *Recommended:* high school transcript, interview.

Application deadlines: 1/31 (freshmen), rolling (transfers).

Early decision deadline: 11/1.

Notification: 3/1 (freshmen), continuous (transfers), 12/15 (early decision).

CONTACT

Mr. Rohan Howell, Dean of Admissions, State University of New York Maritime College, 6 Pennyfield Avenue, Throggs Neck, NY 10465. *Phone:* 718-409-2220. *Fax:* 718-409-7465. *E-mail:* rhowell@sunymaritime.edu.

State University of New York Polytechnic Institute

Utica, New York

http://www.sunypoly.edu/

- **State-supported** comprehensive, founded 1966, part of State University of New York System
- **Suburban** 850-acre campus
- **Endowment** $5.5 million
- **Coed** 2,184 undergraduate students, 85% full-time, 34% women, 66% men
- **Moderately difficult** entrance level, 62% of applicants were admitted

UNDERGRAD STUDENTS

1,860 full-time, 324 part-time. Students come from 15 states and territories; 16 other countries; 2% are from out of state; 6% Black or African American, non-Hispanic/Latino; 9% Hispanic/Latino; 6% Asian, non-Hispanic/Latino; 0.2% Native Hawaiian or other Pacific Islander, non-Hispanic/Latino; 0.2% American Indian or Alaska Native, non-Hispanic/Latino; 3% Two or more races, non-Hispanic/Latino; 0.3% Race/ethnicity unknown; 1% international; 14% transferred in; 44% live on campus.

Freshmen:

Admission: 2,984 applied, 1,863 admitted, 463 enrolled. *Average high school GPA:* 3.7. *Test scores:* SAT evidence-based reading and writing scores over 500: 84%; SAT math scores over 500: 88%; ACT scores over 18: 94%; SAT evidence-based reading and writing scores over 600: 30%; SAT math scores over 600: 38%; ACT scores over 24: 41%; SAT evidence-based reading and writing scores over 700: 3%; SAT math scores over 700: 7%; ACT scores over 30: 9%.

Retention: 80% of full-time freshmen returned.

FACULTY

Total: 274, 50% full-time, 59% with terminal degrees.

Student/faculty ratio: 13:1.

ACADEMICS

Calendar: semesters. *Degrees:* bachelor's, master's, doctoral, post-master's, and postbachelor's certificates.

Special study options: accelerated degree program, advanced placement credit, cooperative education, distance learning, double majors, independent study, internships, off-campus study, part-time degree program, services for LD students, study abroad, summer session for credit. *ROTC:* Army (c), Air Force (c).

Computers: 380 computers/terminals and 144 ports are available on campus for general student use. Students can access the following: campus intranet, computer help desk, free student e-mail accounts, online (class) grades, online (class) registration, online (class) schedules. Campuswide network is available. 100% of college-owned or -operated housing units are wired for high-speed Internet access. Wireless service is available via entire campus.

Library: Peter J. Cayan Library. *Books:* 139,500 (physical), 108,500 (digital/electronic); *Serial titles:* 2,175 (physical), 49,045 (digital/electronic); *Databases:* 50. Weekly public service hours: 87; students can reserve study rooms.

STUDENT LIFE

Housing options: on-campus residence required through sophomore year; coed, special housing for students with disabilities. Campus housing is university owned and leased by the school. Freshman campus housing is guaranteed.

Activities and organizations: student-run newspaper, radio and television station, International Student Association, SUNY Tech Gamers Club, Black and Latino American Student Union, Colleges Against Cancer, BAJA SAE (Society of Automotive Engineers).

Athletics Member NCAA. All Division III. *Intercollegiate sports:* baseball M, basketball M/W, cross-country running M/W, lacrosse M/W, soccer M/W, softball W, volleyball M/W. *Intramural sports:* badminton M/W, basketball M/W, bowling M/W, cross-country running M/W, football M, racquetball M/W, soccer M/W, softball M/W, volleyball M/W.

Campus security: 24-hour emergency response devices and patrols, student patrols, late-night transport/escort service, controlled dormitory access, closed-circuit TV monitors, 24-hour police department.

Student services: health clinic, personal/psychological counseling, legal services.

COSTS & FINANCIAL AID

Costs (2017–18) *Tuition:* state resident $6670 full-time, $278 per credit hour part-time; nonresident $16,320 full-time, $680 per credit hour part-time. Full-time tuition and fees vary according to course load, degree level, and location. Part-time tuition and fees vary according to course load, degree level, and location. *Required fees:* $1328 full-time, $55 per credit hour part-time. *Room and board:* $12,440. Room and board charges vary according to board plan and location. *Payment plan:* installment.

Financial Aid Of all full-time matriculated undergraduates who enrolled in 2016, 1,402 applied for aid, 1,138 were judged to have need, 1,126 had their need fully met. 126 Federal Work-Study jobs (averaging $1500). In 2016, 236 non-need-based awards were made. *Average percent of need met:* 99. *Average financial aid package:* $10,449. *Average need-based loan:* $4309. *Average need-based gift aid:* $7506. *Average non-need-based aid:* $4137.

APPLYING

Standardized Tests *Required:* SAT or ACT (for admission).

Options: electronic application, early admission, early action, deferred entrance.

Application fee: $50.

Required: essay or personal statement, high school transcript, minimum 3.0 GPA, 2 letters of recommendation. *Recommended:* interview.

Application deadlines: 6/1 (freshmen), 6/1 (transfers), 11/15 (early action).

Notification: continuous until 1/15 (freshmen), continuous until 12/1 (transfers), 12/15 (early action).

CONTACT

Ms. Gina Liscio, Director of Admissions, State University of New York Polytechnic Institute, 100 Seymour Road, Utica, NY 13502. *Phone:* 315-792-7500. *Toll-free phone:* 866-278-6948. *Fax:* 315-792-7837. *E-mail:* admissions@sunyit.edu.

State University of New York Upstate Medical University
Syracuse, New York
http://www.upstate.edu/

CONTACT
Mrs. Donna L. Vavonese, Associate Director of Admissions, State University of New York Upstate Medical University, Weiskotten Hall, 766 Irving Avenue, Syracuse, NY 13210. *Phone:* 315-464-4570. *Toll-free phone:* 800-736-2171. *Fax:* 315-464-8867. *E-mail:* admiss@upstate.edu.

Stony Brook University, State University of New York
Stony Brook, New York
http://www.stonybrook.edu/

- **State-supported** university, founded 1957, part of State University of New York System
- **Suburban** 1450-acre campus with easy access to New York City
- **Endowment** $234.0 million
- **Coed** 17,364 undergraduate students, 93% full-time, 47% women, 53% men
- **Very difficult** entrance level, 42% of applicants were admitted

UNDERGRAD STUDENTS
16,212 full-time, 1,152 part-time. Students come from 44 states and territories; 130 other countries; 6% are from out of state; 7% Black or African American, non-Hispanic/Latino; 12% Hispanic/Latino; 24% Asian, non-Hispanic/Latino; 0.1% Native Hawaiian or other Pacific Islander, non-Hispanic/Latino; 0.2% American Indian or Alaska Native, non-Hispanic/Latino; 3% Two or more races, non-Hispanic/Latino; 6% Race/ethnicity unknown; 14% international; 9% transferred in; 53% live on campus.

Freshmen:
Admission: 35,313 applied, 14,899 admitted, 3,167 enrolled. *Average high school GPA:* 3.8. *Test scores:* SAT evidence-based reading and writing scores over 500: 97%; SAT math scores over 500: 99%; ACT scores over 18: 100%; SAT evidence-based reading and writing scores over 600: 73%; SAT math scores over 600: 83%; ACT scores over 24: 90%; SAT evidence-based reading and writing scores over 700: 18%; SAT math scores over 700: 41%; ACT scores over 30: 41%.

Retention: 90% of full-time freshmen returned.

FACULTY
Total: 1,566, 69% full-time, 76% with terminal degrees.
Student/faculty ratio: 18:1.

ACADEMICS
Calendar: semesters. *Degrees:* bachelor's, master's, doctoral, post-master's, and postbachelor's certificates.

Special study options: academic remediation for entering students, accelerated degree program, adult/continuing education programs, advanced placement credit, cooperative education, distance learning, double majors, English as a second language, freshman honors college, honors programs, independent study, internships, off-campus study, part-time degree program, services for LD students, student-designed majors, study abroad, summer session for credit. *ROTC:* Army (b), Navy (c), Air Force (c).

Unusual degree programs: 3-2 business administration; engineering; nursing; social work; education.

Computers: 1,590 computers/terminals are available on campus for general student use. Students can access the following: campus intranet, computer help desk, free student e-mail accounts, online (class) grades, online (class) registration, online (class) schedules. Campuswide network is available. 100% of college-owned or -operated housing units are wired for high-speed Internet access. Wireless service is available via entire campus.

Library: Frank Melville, Jr. Memorial Library plus 7 others. *Books:* 1.9 million (physical), 348,868 (digital/electronic); *Serial titles:* 1,225 (physical), 190,674 (digital/electronic); *Databases:* 679. Weekly public service hours: 131; study areas open 24 hours, 5–7 days a week; students can reserve study rooms.

STUDENT LIFE

Housing options: coed. Campus housing is university owned. Freshman campus housing is guaranteed.

Activities and organizations: drama/theater group, student-run newspaper, radio and television station, choral group, marching band, Community Service Organization, Residence Hall Association, Commuter Student Association, Asian Students Alliance, Chinese Association at Stony Brook, national fraternities, national sororities.

Athletics Member NCAA. All Division I. *Intercollegiate sports:* baseball M(s), basketball M(s)/W(s), cross-country running M(s)/W(s), football M(s), lacrosse M(s)/W(s), soccer M(s)/W(s), softball W(s), swimming and diving W(s), tennis M/W(s), track and field M(s)/W(s), volleyball W(s). *Intramural sports:* archery M(c)/W(c), badminton M(c)/W(c), basketball M/W, bowling M(c)/W(c), cheerleading W, crew M(c), equestrian sports M(c)/W(c), fencing M(c)/W(c), field hockey W(c), golf M(c)/W(c), ice hockey M(c), lacrosse M(c)/W(c), racquetball M/W, rugby M(c)/W(c), sailing M(c)/W(c), soccer M/W, softball W, swimming and diving M(c)/W(c), table tennis M(c)/W(c), tennis M(c)/W(c), ultimate Frisbee M(c)/W(c), volleyball M/W, weight lifting M(c)/W(c), wrestling M(c).

Campus security: 24-hour emergency response devices and patrols, late-night transport/escort service, controlled dormitory access.

Student services: health clinic, personal/psychological counseling, women's center, legal services.

COSTS & FINANCIAL AID

Costs (2017–18) *Tuition:* state resident $6670 full-time, $278 per credit hour part-time; nonresident $24,180 full-time, $1008 per credit hour part-time. Full-time tuition and fees vary according to course load and program. Part-time tuition and fees vary according to course load and program. *Required fees:* $2587 full-time, $128 per credit hour part-time. *Room and board:* $13,446; room only: $8402. Room and board charges vary according to board plan, housing facility, and location. *Payment plan:* installment.

Financial Aid Of all full-time matriculated undergraduates who enrolled in 2016, 10,468 applied for aid, 8,577 were judged to have need, 1,579 had their need fully met. 382 Federal Work-Study jobs (averaging $2584). 2,687 state and other part-time jobs (averaging $3703). In 2016, 1592 non-need-based awards were made. *Average percent of need met:* 67. *Average financial aid package:* $13,292. *Average need-based loan:* $4763. *Average need-based gift aid:* $8641. *Average non-need-based aid:* $5378. *Average indebtedness upon graduation:* $26,219.

APPLYING

Standardized Tests *Required:* SAT or ACT (for admission).

Options: electronic application, deferred entrance.

Application fee: $50.

Required: essay or personal statement, high school transcript, 1 letter of recommendation. *Required for some:* interview, audition. *Recommended:* minimum 3.5 GPA.

Application deadlines: 1/15 (freshmen), 3/1 (transfers).

Notification: 4/1 (freshmen), continuous until 4/1 (transfers).

CONTACT

Ms. Judith Burke-Berhanan, Dean of Undergraduate Admissions, Stony Brook University, State University of New York, Admissions Office, 118 Administration Building, Stony Brook, NY 11794-1901. *Phone:* 631-632-6868. *Fax:* 631-632-9898. *E-mail:* enroll@stonybrook.edu.

Swedish Institute, College of Health Sciences

New York, New York

http://www.swedishinstitute.edu/

CONTACT

Admissions Advisor, Swedish Institute, College of Health Sciences, 226 West 26th Street, New York, NY 10001. *Phone:* 212-914-5900 Ext. 125. *E-mail:* admissions@swedishinstitute.edu.

Syracuse University

Syracuse, New York

http://www.syracuse.edu/

- **Independent** university, founded 1870
- **Urban** 721-acre campus with easy access to Syracuse, NY
- **Endowment** $1.3 billion
- **Coed** 15,252 undergraduate students, 96% full-time, 54% women, 46% men
- **Very difficult** entrance level, 47% of applicants were admitted

UNDERGRAD STUDENTS

14,675 full-time, 577 part-time. Students come from 50 states and territories; 86 other countries; 60% are from out of state; 7% Black or African American, non-Hispanic/Latino; 9% Hispanic/Latino; 7% Asian, non-Hispanic/Latino; 0.1% Native Hawaiian or other Pacific Islander, non-Hispanic/Latino; 0.6% American Indian or Alaska Native, non-Hispanic/Latino; 3% Two or more races, non-Hispanic/Latino; 3% Race/ethnicity unknown; 13% international; 2% transferred in; 53% live on campus.

Freshmen:

Admission: 33,099 applied, 15,517 admitted, 3,649 enrolled. *Average high school GPA:* 3.6. *Test scores:* SAT evidence-based reading and writing scores over 500: 96%; SAT math scores over 500: 97%; ACT scores over 18: 100%; SAT evidence-based reading and writing scores over 600: 68%; SAT math scores over 600: 68%; ACT scores over 24: 86%; SAT evidence-based reading and writing scores over 700: 12%; SAT math scores over 700: 21%; ACT scores over 30: 25%.

Retention: 91% of full-time freshmen returned.

FACULTY

Total: 1,691, 67% full-time, 66% with terminal degrees.

Student/faculty ratio: 15:1.

ACADEMICS

Calendar: semesters. *Degrees:* certificates, bachelor's, master's, doctoral, post-master's, and postbachelor's certificates.

Special study options: accelerated degree program, adult/continuing education programs, advanced placement credit, cooperative education, distance learning, double majors, English as a second language, freshman honors college, honors programs, independent study, internships, off-campus study, part-time degree program, services for LD students, student-designed majors, study abroad, summer session for credit. *ROTC:* Army (b), Air Force (b).

Unusual degree programs: 3-2 education.

Computers: 3,500 computers/terminals and 678 ports are available on campus for general student use. Students can access the following: campus intranet, computer help desk, free student e-mail accounts, online (class) grades, online (class) registration, online (class) schedules, web conferencing, learning management system, blogging service, personal Websites, "View My Advising Report" digital asset management system, office software, online video training. Campuswide network is available. 100% of college-owned or -operated housing units are wired for high-speed Internet access. Wireless service is available via classrooms, computer centers, computer labs, dorm rooms, learning centers, libraries, student centers.

Library: E. S. Bird Library plus 4 others. *Books:* 2.2 million (physical), 508,060 (digital/electronic); *Serial titles:* 33,629 (physical), 112,830 (digital/electronic); *Databases:* 544. Weekly public service hours: 146; study areas open 24 hours, 5–7 days a week; students can reserve study rooms.

STUDENT LIFE

Housing options: on-campus residence required through sophomore year; coed, special housing for students with disabilities. Campus housing is university owned. Freshman campus housing is guaranteed.

Activities and organizations: drama/theater group, student-run newspaper, radio and television station, choral group, marching band, First Year Players, Ottothon, Otto, Goon Squad, University Union, national fraternities, national sororities.

Athletics Member NCAA. All Division I except football (Division I-A). *Intercollegiate sports:* badminton M(c)/W(c), baseball M(c), basketball M(s)/W(s), bowling M(c)/W(c), cheerleading M/W, crew M(s)/W(s), cross-country running M(s)/W(s), equestrian sports M(c)/W(c), fencing

M(c)/W(c), field hockey W(s), gymnastics M(c)/W(c), ice hockey M(c)/W(s), lacrosse M(s)/W(s), rugby M(c)/W(c), sailing M(c)/W(c), skiing (downhill) M(c)/W(c), soccer M(s)/W(s), softball W(s), tennis M(c)/W(s), track and field M(s)/W(s), volleyball M(c)/W(s), water polo M(c)/W(c), wrestling M(c). *Intramural sports:* basketball M/W, field hockey W(c), golf M(c)/W(c), ice hockey M/W, lacrosse M(c)/W(c), racquetball M/W, soccer M/W, softball M/W, swimming and diving M(c)/W(c), table tennis M(c)/W(c), tennis M/W, ultimate Frisbee M(c)/W(c), volleyball M/W.

Campus security: 24-hour emergency response devices and patrols, student patrols, late-night transport/escort service, controlled dormitory access, crisis alert notification system, off-campus patrols in student rental neighborhoods.

Student services: health clinic, personal/psychological counseling, women's center, legal services.

COSTS & FINANCIAL AID
Costs (2017–18) *Comprehensive fee:* $62,313 includes full-time tuition ($45,150), mandatory fees ($1605), and room and board ($15,558). Full-time tuition and fees vary according to course load. Part-time tuition: $1966 per credit hour. Part-time tuition and fees vary according to course load. *College room only:* $8268. Room and board charges vary according to board plan and housing facility. *Payment plans:* tuition prepayment, installment. *Waivers:* employees or children of employees.

Financial Aid Of all full-time matriculated undergraduates who enrolled in 2017, 8,860 applied for aid, 6,698 were judged to have need, 3,025 had their need fully met. 5,292 Federal Work-Study jobs (averaging $2585). In 2017, 2874 non-need-based awards were made. *Average percent of need met:* 93. *Average financial aid package:* $38,870. *Average need-based loan:* $5750. *Average need-based gift aid:* $31,062. *Average non-need-based aid:* $12,470. *Average indebtedness upon graduation:* $38,918. *Financial aid deadline:* 1/1.

APPLYING
Standardized Tests *Required:* SAT or ACT (for admission).

Options: electronic application, early admission, early decision, deferred entrance.

Application fee: $75.

Required: essay or personal statement, high school transcript, 2 letters of recommendation. *Recommended:* interview.

Application deadlines: 1/1 (freshmen), 7/1 (transfers).

Early decision deadline: 11/15.

Notification: 3/15 (freshmen), 12/15 (early decision).

CONTACT
Office of Admissions, Syracuse University, 100 Crouse-Hinds Hall, 900 South Crouse Avenue, Syracuse, NY 13244-2130. *Phone:* 315-443-3611. *Fax:* 315-443-4226. *E-mail:* orange@syr.edu.

Talmudical Institute of Upstate New York
Rochester, New York
http://www.tiuny.org/

CONTACT
Rabbi Menachem Davidowitz, Director of Admissions, Talmudical Institute of Upstate New York, 769 Park Avenue, Rochester, NY 14607-3046. *Phone:* 716-473-2810. *E-mail:* yeshiva@tiuny.org.

Talmudical Seminary of Bobov
Brooklyn, New York

CONTACT
Talmudical Seminary of Bobov, 5120 New Utrecht Avenue, Brooklyn, NY 11219.

Talmudical Seminary Oholei Torah
Brooklyn, New York

CONTACT
Rabbi Yisroel Friedman, Director of Academic Affairs, Talmudical Seminary Oholei Torah, 667 Eastern Parkway, Brooklyn, NY 11213-3310. *Phone:* 718-363-2034. *E-mail:* info@oholeitorah.com.

Torah Temimah Talmudical Seminary
Brooklyn, New York

CONTACT
Principal, Torah Temimah Talmudical Seminary, 507 Ocean Parkway, Brooklyn, NY 11218-5913. *Phone:* 718-853-8500.

Touro College
New York, New York
http://www.touro.edu/

CONTACT
Mr. David Luk, Associate Director of Admissions, Touro College, 27-33 West 23rd Street, New York, NY 10010. *Phone:* 212-463-0400 Ext. 5644. *Fax:* 212-627-9542. *E-mail:* david.luk@touro.edu.

Trocaire College
Buffalo, New York
http://www.trocaire.edu/

CONTACT
Trocaire College, 360 Choate Avenue, Buffalo, NY 14220-2094. *Phone:* 716-826-2558.

Union College
Schenectady, New York
http://www.union.edu/

- **Independent** 4-year, founded 1795
- **Urban** 100-acre campus
- **Endowment** $427.6 million
- **Coed** 2,272 undergraduate students, 96% full-time, 46% women, 54% men
- **Very difficult** entrance level, 37% of applicants were admitted

UNDERGRAD STUDENTS
2,176 full-time, 96 part-time. Students come from 40 states and territories; 36 other countries; 62% are from out of state; 4% Black or African American, non-Hispanic/Latino; 7% Hispanic/Latino; 6% Asian, non-Hispanic/Latino; 0.1% American Indian or Alaska Native, non-Hispanic/Latino; 3% Two or more races, non-Hispanic/Latino; 0.2% Race/ethnicity unknown; 7% international; 0.8% transferred in; 90% live on campus.

Freshmen:
Admission: 6,676 applied, 2,495 admitted, 570 enrolled. *Average high school GPA:* 3.4. *Test scores:* SAT evidence-based reading and writing scores over 500: 100%; SAT math scores over 500: 100%; ACT scores over 18: 100%; SAT evidence-based reading and writing scores over 600: 92%; SAT math scores over 600: 91%; ACT scores over 24: 97%; SAT evidence-based reading and writing scores over 700: 32%; SAT math scores over 700: 40%; ACT scores over 30: 61%.
Retention: 92% of full-time freshmen returned.

FACULTY
Total: 229, 92% full-time, 95% with terminal degrees.
Student/faculty ratio: 10:1.

ACADEMICS
Calendar: trimesters. *Degree:* bachelor's.

Special study options: accelerated degree program, advanced placement credit, double majors, honors programs, independent study, internships, off-campus study, student-designed majors, study abroad, summer session for credit. *ROTC:* Army (c), Navy (c), Air Force (c).

Computers: 554 computers/terminals and 3,032 ports are available on campus for general student use. Students can access the following: campus intranet, computer help desk, free student e-mail accounts, online (class) grades, online (class) registration, online (class) schedules, Digital Studio and Learning Commons. Campuswide network is available. 100% of college-owned or -operated housing units are wired for high-speed Internet access. Wireless service is available via entire campus.

Library: Schaffer Library. Study areas open 24 hours, 5–7 days a week; students can reserve study rooms.

STUDENT LIFE

Housing options: on-campus residence required through junior year; coed. Campus housing is university owned. Freshman campus housing is guaranteed.

Activities and organizations: drama/theater group, student-run newspaper, radio and television station, choral group, U-Program (Programming Board), speaker's forum, student newspaper, Concert Committee, ski club, national fraternities, national sororities.

Athletics Member NCAA. All Division III except men's and women's ice hockey (Division I). *Intercollegiate sports:* baseball M, basketball M/W, cheerleading M(c)/W(c), crew M/W, cross-country running M/W, equestrian sports W, field hockey W, football M, golf W, ice hockey M/W, lacrosse M/W, rugby M(c)/W(c), soccer M/W, softball W, swimming and diving M/W, tennis M/W, track and field M/W, ultimate Frisbee M(c)/W(c), volleyball W. *Intramural sports:* badminton M(c)/W(c), basketball M/W, bowling M(c)/W(c), equestrian sports M(c)/W(c), fencing M(c)/W(c), football M/W, golf M(c)/W(c), ice hockey M(c)/W(c), lacrosse M(c)/W, racquetball M/W, rock climbing M(c)/W(c), skiing (downhill) M(c)/W(c), soccer M/W, softball M/W, squash M/W, tennis M/W, volleyball M/W, water polo M/W.

Campus security: 24-hour emergency response devices and patrols, late-night transport/escort service, controlled dormitory access, awareness programs, bicycle patrol, shuttle service.

Student services: health clinic, personal/psychological counseling, women's center.

COSTS & FINANCIAL AID

Costs (2017–18) *Comprehensive fee:* $66,609 includes full-time tuition ($53,019), mandatory fees ($471), and room and board ($13,119). *College room only:* $7194. *Payment plan:* installment. *Waivers:* senior citizens and employees or children of employees.

Financial Aid Of all full-time matriculated undergraduates who enrolled in 2017, 1,176 applied for aid, 1,055 were judged to have need, 1,055 had their need fully met. In 2017, 632 non-need-based awards were made. *Average percent of need met:* 100. *Average financial aid package:* $44,649. *Average need-based loan:* $5067. *Average need-based gift aid:* $37,748. *Average non-need-based aid:* $11,741. *Average indebtedness upon graduation:* $34,221. *Financial aid deadline:* 1/15.

APPLYING

Standardized Tests *Required for some:* SAT (for admission), SAT and SAT Subject Tests or ACT (for admission), SAT I and two SAT II tests or ACT for leadership in medicine program, SAT or ACT for law and public policy program.

Options: electronic application, early admission, early decision, deferred entrance.

Required: essay or personal statement, high school transcript, 2 letters of recommendation. *Recommended:* interview.

Application deadlines: 1/15 (freshmen), 4/15 (transfers).

Early decision deadline: 11/15 (for plan 1), 1/15 (for plan 2).

Notification: 4/1 (freshmen), continuous (transfers), 12/15 (early decision plan 1), 2/8 (early decision plan 2).

CONTACT

Union College, Grant Hall, 807 Union Street, Schenectady, NY 12308. *Phone:* 518-388-6112. *Toll-free phone:* 888-843-6688. *Fax:* 518-388-6986. *E-mail:* admissions@union.edu.

★ United States Merchant Marine Academy
Kings Point, New York
http://www.usmma.edu/

- **Federally supported** comprehensive, founded 1943
- **Suburban** 82-acre campus with easy access to New York City
- **Coed** 954 undergraduate students, 100% full-time, 17% women, 83% men
- **Very difficult** entrance level, 22% of applicants were admitted

UNDERGRAD STUDENTS

954 full-time. Students come from 47 states and territories; 4 other countries; 93% are from out of state; 3% Black or African American, non-Hispanic/Latino; 10% Hispanic/Latino; 8% Asian, non-Hispanic/Latino; 0.2% Native Hawaiian or other Pacific Islander, non-Hispanic/Latino; 1% American Indian or Alaska Native, non-Hispanic/Latino; 3% Race/ethnicity unknown; 0.9% international; 0.9% transferred in; 100% live on campus.

Freshmen:
Admission: 1,855 applied, 411 admitted, 263 enrolled. *Average high school GPA:* 3.6. *Test scores:* ACT scores over 18: 100%; ACT scores over 24: 98%; ACT scores over 30: 24%.
Retention: 94% of full-time freshmen returned.

FACULTY
Total: 132, 86% full-time.
Student/faculty ratio: 8:1.

ACADEMICS
Calendar: trimesters. *Degrees:* bachelor's and master's.

Special study options: academic remediation for entering students, advanced placement credit, distance learning, honors programs, independent study, internships, off-campus study.

Computers: Students can access the following: campus intranet, computer help desk, free student e-mail accounts, engineering and economics software. Campuswide network is available.
Library: Schuyler Otis Bland Memorial Library. *Books:* 176,485 (physical), 2,791 (digital/electronic); *Serial titles:* 1,511 (physical), 505 (digital/electronic); *Databases:* 17. Weekly public service hours: 84.

STUDENT LIFE
Housing options: on-campus residence required through senior year; coed. Campus housing is university owned. Freshman campus housing is guaranteed.

Activities and organizations: drama/theater group, student-run newspaper, choral group, marching band, Regimental Band, CFC, Neuman Club, Honor Guard.

Athletics Member NCAA. All Division III. *Intercollegiate sports:* baseball M, basketball M/W, crew M/W, cross-country running M/W, football M, lacrosse M/W, sailing M/W, soccer M, swimming and diving M/W, tennis M, track and field M/W, volleyball W, wrestling M. *Intramural sports:* basketball M/W, golf M(c), ice hockey M(c), racquetball M/W, riflery M(c)/W(c), rugby M(c), soccer W(c), ultimate Frisbee M(c), volleyball M(c), water polo M(c), weight lifting M(c)/W(c).

Campus security: 24-hour emergency response devices and patrols, controlled dormitory access.

Student services: health clinic, personal/psychological counseling.

COSTS
Costs (2017–18) *Comprehensive fee:* includes mandatory fees ($1020). Midshipmen at the United States Merchant Marine Academy receive from the Federal Government their education, room and board, uniforms, and books. However, midshipmen are responsible for the payment of fees for mandatory educational supplies not provided by the government. *Payment plan:* installment.

APPLYING
Standardized Tests *Required:* SAT or ACT (for admission).
Options: electronic application.
Required: essay or personal statement, high school transcript, 3 letters of recommendation. *Recommended:* interview.
Application deadlines: 3/1 (freshmen), 3/1 (transfers).

Notification: continuous until 4/1 (freshmen), continuous until 4/1 (transfers).

CONTACT
Lt. Cdr. Keith L. Watson, Assistant Director of Admissions and Financial Aid, United States Merchant Marine Academy, 300 Steamboat Road, Kings Point, NY 11024-1699. *Phone:* 516-726-5642. *Toll-free phone:* 866-546-4778. *Fax:* 516-773-5390. *E-mail:* admissions@usmma.edu.

See page 1450 for the College Close-Up.

United States Military Academy
West Point, New York
http://www.usma.edu/
- **Federally supported** 4-year, founded 1802
- **Small-town** 16,080-acre campus with easy access to New York City
- **Endowment** $348.2 million
- **Coed** 4,491 undergraduate students, 100% full-time, 22% women, 78% men

UNDERGRAD STUDENTS
4,491 full-time. Students come from 30 other countries; 94% are from out of state; 12% Black or African American, non-Hispanic/Latino; 10% Hispanic/Latino; 8% Asian, non-Hispanic/Latino; 0.3% Native Hawaiian or other Pacific Islander, non-Hispanic/Latino; 1% American Indian or Alaska Native, non-Hispanic/Latino; 3% Two or more races, non-Hispanic/Latino; 1% Race/ethnicity unknown; 1% international; 100% live on campus.

Freshmen:
Admission: 1,210 enrolled. *Test scores:* SAT evidence-based reading and writing scores over 500: 98%; SAT math scores over 500: 100%; ACT scores over 18: 100%; SAT evidence-based reading and writing scores over 600: 69%; SAT math scores over 600: 75%; ACT scores over 24: 71%; SAT evidence-based reading and writing scores over 700: 22%; SAT math scores over 700: 29%; ACT scores over 30: 16%.
Retention: 96% of full-time freshmen returned.

FACULTY
Total: 611, 100% full-time, 52% with terminal degrees.
Student/faculty ratio: 7:1.

ACADEMICS
Calendar: semesters. *Degree:* bachelor's.
Special study options: academic remediation for entering students, advanced placement credit, double majors, honors programs, independent study, off-campus study, student-designed majors, study abroad.
Computers: Students can access the following: campus intranet, computer help desk, free student e-mail accounts, online (class) grades, online (class) registration, online (class) schedules, all cadets will receive a tablet, printer, PDA, and portable memory device; learning management system access. Campuswide network is available. 100% of college-owned or -operated housing units are wired for high-speed Internet access. Wireless service is available via classrooms, dorm rooms, learning centers, libraries, student centers.
Library: United States Military Academy Library at West Point. *Books:* 422,671 (physical), 931,618 (digital/electronic); *Serial titles:* 110 (physical), 113,741 (digital/electronic); *Databases:* 270. Weekly public service hours: 100.

STUDENT LIFE
Housing options: on-campus residence required through senior year; coed. Campus housing is university owned. Freshman campus housing is guaranteed.
Activities and organizations: drama/theater group, student-run radio station, choral group, Spirit Clubs, Big Brother/Big Sister, Cadet Fine Arts Forum, Film Forum, Philosophy Forum.
Athletics Member NCAA. All Division I except football (Division I-A). *Intercollegiate sports:* baseball M, basketball M/W, cheerleading M/W, crew M(c)/W(c), cross-country running M/W, equestrian sports M(c)/W(c), fencing M(c)/W(c), golf M, gymnastics M, ice hockey M, lacrosse M/W, riflery M/W, rugby M/W, soccer M/W, softball W, swimming and diving M/W, tennis M/W, track and field M/W, volleyball M(c)/W, water polo M(c), wrestling M. *Intramural sports:* basketball M/W, bowling M(c), racquetball M(c)/W(c), sailing M(c)/W(c), skiing (downhill) M(c)/W(c), soccer M/W, swimming and diving M/W, ultimate Frisbee M/W, wrestling M/W.
Campus security: 24-hour emergency response devices and patrols, late-night transport/escort service, controlled dormitory access.
Student services: health clinic, personal/psychological counseling, legal services.

COSTS
Costs (2018–19) *Comprehensive fee:* Cadets receive a full scholarship and an annual salary. There is no tuition charge, but there is a requirement for an initial deposit. Room, board, and medical and dental care are provided by the US Government. A portion of the cadet pay is deposited to a "Cadet Account" to help pay for uniforms, books, a laptop computer, and incidentals. The only cost is a one-time deposit upon admission to defray the initial issue of uniforms, books, supplies, and equipment. If needed, loans of $100 to $2,000 are available for the deposit. Upon graduation, cadets incur a 5-year Active Duty service obligation and 3 years of reserve duty in the US Army.

APPLYING
Standardized Tests *Required:* SAT or ACT (for admission).
Required: essay or personal statement, high school transcript, 4 letters of recommendation, Service Academies Pre-candidate Questionnaire. *Recommended:* interview.

CONTACT
United States Military Academy, 600 Thayer Road, West Point, NY 10996. *Phone:* 845-938-4041. *E-mail:* admissions@usma.edu.

United Talmudical Seminary
Brooklyn, New York
CONTACT
Director of Admissions, United Talmudical Seminary, 191 Rodney Street, Brooklyn, NY 11211. *Phone:* 718-963-9770.

University at Albany, State University of New York
Albany, New York
http://www.albany.edu/
- **State-supported** university, founded 1844, part of State University of New York System
- **Suburban** 560-acre campus
- **Endowment** $59.8 million
- **Coed** 13,508 undergraduate students, 94% full-time, 51% women, 49% men
- **Very difficult** entrance level, 54% of applicants were admitted

UNDERGRAD STUDENTS
12,740 full-time, 768 part-time. Students come from 36 states and territories; 25 other countries; 5% are from out of state; 18% Black or African American, non-Hispanic/Latino; 17% Hispanic/Latino; 8% Asian, non-Hispanic/Latino; 0.1% Native Hawaiian or other Pacific Islander, non-Hispanic/Latino; 0.2% American Indian or Alaska Native, non-Hispanic/Latino; 3% Two or more races, non-Hispanic/Latino; 3% Race/ethnicity unknown; 5% international; 11% transferred in; 56% live on campus.

Freshmen:
Admission: 24,887 applied, 13,442 admitted, 2,815 enrolled. *Average high school GPA:* 3.2. *Test scores:* SAT evidence-based reading and writing scores over 500: 92%; SAT math scores over 500: 92%; ACT scores over 18: 98%; SAT evidence-based reading and writing scores over 600: 35%; SAT math scores over 600: 34%; ACT scores over 24: 51%; SAT evidence-based reading and writing scores over 700: 3%; SAT math scores over 700: 4%; ACT scores over 30: 6%.
Retention: 83% of full-time freshmen returned.

FACULTY
Total: 1,185, 57% full-time, 75% with terminal degrees.
Student/faculty ratio: 19:1.

ACADEMICS

Calendar: semesters. *Degrees:* bachelor's, master's, doctoral, post-master's, and postbachelor's certificates.

Special study options: accelerated degree program, advanced placement credit, distance learning, double majors, English as a second language, freshman honors college, honors programs, independent study, internships, off-campus study, part-time degree program, services for LD students, student-designed majors, study abroad, summer session for credit. *ROTC:* Army (b), Air Force (c).

Unusual degree programs: 3-2 business administration; engineering.

Computers: 500 computers/terminals are available on campus for general student use. Students can access the following: campus intranet, computer help desk, free student e-mail accounts, online (class) grades, online (class) registration, online (class) schedules. Campuswide network is available. 100% of college-owned or -operated housing units are wired for high-speed Internet access. Wireless service is available via classrooms, computer centers, computer labs, dorm rooms, libraries, student centers.

Library: University Library plus 2 others. *Books:* 2.3 million (physical), 342,263 (digital/electronic); *Serial titles:* 97,614 (digital/electronic). Weekly public service hours: 113; students can reserve study rooms.

STUDENT LIFE

Housing options: on-campus residence required through sophomore year; coed. Campus housing is university owned. Freshman campus housing is guaranteed.

Activities and organizations: drama/theater group, student-run newspaper, radio and television station, choral group, intramural athletics, cultural organizations, political organizations, community service, honor societies, national fraternities, national sororities.

Athletics Member NCAA. All Division I. *Intercollegiate sports:* baseball M(s), basketball M(s)/W(s), crew M/W, cross-country running M(s)/W(s), field hockey W(s), football M(s), golf W(s), lacrosse M(s)/W(s), rock climbing M/W, soccer M(s)/W(s), softball W(s), tennis W(s), track and field M(s)/W(s), volleyball W(s). *Intramural sports:* badminton M/W, baseball M, basketball M/W, equestrian sports W, fencing M/W, football M/W, ice hockey M, lacrosse M/W, racquetball M/W, rugby M/W, skiing (cross-country) M/W, skiing (downhill) M/W, soccer M/W, softball W, tennis M/W, track and field M/W, ultimate Frisbee M/W, volleyball M/W, wrestling M.

Campus security: 24-hour emergency response devices and patrols, late-night transport/escort service, controlled dormitory access, Five Quad Ambulance Service, on-campus car battery assistance.

Student services: health clinic, personal/psychological counseling, legal services.

COSTS & FINANCIAL AID

Costs (2018–19) *Tuition:* state resident $6670 full-time, $278 per credit hour part-time; nonresident $21,550 full-time, $898 per credit hour part-time. Part-time tuition and fees vary according to course load. *Required fees:* $2820 full-time, $76 per credit hour part-time. *Room and board:* $13,864; room only: $8364. Room and board charges vary according to board plan and housing facility.

Financial Aid Of all full-time matriculated undergraduates who enrolled in 2016, 9,827 applied for aid, 8,118 were judged to have need, 489 had their need fully met. 610 Federal Work-Study jobs (averaging $1434). 234 state and other part-time jobs (averaging $7502). In 2016, 646 non-need-based awards were made. *Average percent of need met:* 58. *Average financial aid package:* $11,046. *Average need-based loan:* $4702. *Average need-based gift aid:* $7760. *Average non-need-based aid:* $4414. *Average indebtedness upon graduation:* $21,217.

APPLYING

Standardized Tests *Required:* SAT or ACT (for admission).

Options: electronic application, early admission, early action, deferred entrance.

Application fee: $50.

Required: essay or personal statement, high school transcript, 1 letter of recommendation. *Required for some:* portfolio, audition.

Application deadlines: 3/16 (freshmen), 7/16 (transfers), 11/1 (early action).

Notification: continuous (freshmen), continuous (transfers), 1/15 (early action).

CONTACT

University at Albany, State University of New York, Office of Undergraduate Admissions, 1400 Washington Avenue, Albany, NY 12222. *Phone:* 518-442-5435. *Fax:* 518-442-5383. *E-mail:* ugadmissions@albany.edu.

University at Buffalo, the State University of New York

Buffalo, New York

http://www.buffalo.edu/

- **State-supported** university, founded 1846, part of State University of New York System
- **Suburban** 1350-acre campus
- **Endowment** $659.2 million
- **Coed** 21,020 undergraduate students, 93% full-time, 43% women, 57% men
- **Moderately difficult** entrance level, 57% of applicants were admitted

UNDERGRAD STUDENTS

19,453 full-time, 1,567 part-time. Students come from 39 states and territories; 85 other countries; 2% are from out of state; 8% Black or African American, non-Hispanic/Latino; 7% Hispanic/Latino; 15% Asian, non-Hispanic/Latino; 0.1% Native Hawaiian or other Pacific Islander, non-Hispanic/Latino; 0.3% American Indian or Alaska Native, non-Hispanic/Latino; 2% Two or more races, non-Hispanic/Latino; 4% Race/ethnicity unknown; 16% international; 9% transferred in; 35% live on campus.

Freshmen:

Admission: 28,088 applied, 16,128 admitted, 4,179 enrolled. *Average high school GPA:* 3.6. *Test scores:* SAT evidence-based reading and writing scores over 500: 96%; SAT math scores over 500: 98%; ACT scores over 18: 99%; SAT evidence-based reading and writing scores over 600: 53%; SAT math scores over 600: 64%; ACT scores over 24: 78%; SAT evidence-based reading and writing scores over 700: 7%; SAT math scores over 700: 14%; ACT scores over 30: 13%.

Retention: 87% of full-time freshmen returned.

FACULTY

Total: 1,839, 70% full-time, 90% with terminal degrees.

Student/faculty ratio: 13:1.

ACADEMICS

Calendar: semesters. *Degrees:* certificates, bachelor's, master's, doctoral, and post-master's certificates.

Special study options: academic remediation for entering students, accelerated degree program, advanced placement credit, cooperative education, distance learning, double majors, English as a second language, freshman honors college, honors programs, independent study, internships, off-campus study, part-time degree program, services for LD students, student-designed majors, study abroad, summer session for credit. *ROTC:* Army (c).

Unusual degree programs: 3-2 business administration; engineering; nursing; social work; law.

Computers: 3,061 computers/terminals are available on campus for general student use. Students can access the following: campus intranet, computer help desk, free student e-mail accounts, online (class) grades, online (class) registration, online (class) schedules. Campuswide network is available. 100% of college-owned or -operated housing units are wired for high-speed Internet access. Wireless service is available via entire campus.

Library: Lockwood Memorial Library plus 11 others. *Books:* 3.4 million (physical), 826,650 (digital/electronic); *Serial titles:* 2,352 (physical), 175,278 (digital/electronic); *Databases:* 383. Weekly public service hours: 168; study areas open 24 hours, 5–7 days a week; students can reserve study rooms.

STUDENT LIFE

Housing options: coed, special housing for students with disabilities. Campus housing is university owned. Freshman campus housing is guaranteed.

Activities and organizations: drama/theater group, student-run newspaper, radio and television station, choral group, marching band, national fraternities, national sororities.

Athletics Member NCAA. All Division I. *Intercollegiate sports:* basketball M(s)/W(s), cross-country running M(s)/W(s), football M(s), soccer M, softball W(s), swimming and diving M, tennis M(s)/W(s), track and field M(s)/W(s), volleyball W(s), wrestling M(s). *Intramural sports:* baseball M(c), basketball M/W(c), crew M(c)/W(c), cross-country running M(c)/W(c), equestrian sports M(c)/W(c), fencing M(c)/W(c), field hockey M(c)/W(c), golf M(c)/W(c), gymnastics M(c)/W(c), ice hockey M(c)/W(c), lacrosse M(c)/W(c), rugby M(c)/W(c), sailing M(c)/W(c), skiing (downhill) M(c)/W(c), soccer M(c)/W(c), swimming and diving M(c)/W(c), table tennis M(c)/W(c), tennis M(c)/W(c), track and field M(c)/W(c), ultimate Frisbee M(c)/W(c), volleyball M(c)/W(c), water polo M(c)/W(c), wrestling M(c).

Campus security: 24-hour emergency response devices and patrols, student patrols, late-night transport/escort service, controlled dormitory access, self-defense and awareness programs, security cameras.

Student services: health clinic, personal/psychological counseling, women's center, legal services.

COSTS & FINANCIAL AID

Costs (2017–18) *Tuition:* state resident $6670 full-time, $278 per credit hour part-time; nonresident $24,180 full-time, $1008 per credit hour part-time. Part-time tuition and fees vary according to course load. *Required fees:* $3158 full-time, $136 per credit hour part-time. *Room and board:* $13,782; room only: $8032. Room and board charges vary according to board plan and housing facility. *Payment plan:* installment. *Waivers:* minority students.

Financial Aid Of all full-time matriculated undergraduates who enrolled in 2016, 13,326 applied for aid, 10,109 were judged to have need, 9,579 had their need fully met. 848 Federal Work-Study jobs (averaging $1139); 962 state and other part-time jobs (averaging $14,693). In 2016, 731 non-need-based awards were made. *Average percent of need met:* 50. *Average financial aid package:* $10,466. *Average need-based loan:* $4519. *Average need-based gift aid:* $7389. *Average non-need-based aid:* $4253. *Average indebtedness upon graduation:* $25,598.

APPLYING

Standardized Tests *Required:* SAT or ACT (for admission).

Options: electronic application, early admission, early action.

Application fee: $50.

Required: essay or personal statement, high school transcript, 1 letter of recommendation. *Required for some:* portfolio for architecture; audition for dance, music theatre, theatre and music.

Notification: continuous (freshmen), continuous (transfers), 1/15 (early action).

CONTACT

Mr. Lee Melvin, Vice Provost for Enrollment Management, University at Buffalo, the State University of New York, 1 Capen Hall, North Campus, Buffalo, NY 14260-1660. *Phone:* 716-645-6900. *Toll-free phone:* 888-UB-ADMIT. *E-mail:* ub-admissions@buffalo.edu.

University of Rochester

Rochester, New York

http://www.rochester.edu/

- **Independent** university, founded 1850
- **Suburban** 655-acre campus
- **Endowment** $2.1 billion
- **Coed** 5,796 undergraduate students, 96% full-time, 49% women, 51% men
- **Very difficult** entrance level, 31% of applicants were admitted

UNDERGRAD STUDENTS

5,570 full-time, 226 part-time. Students come from 52 states and territories; 101 other countries; 59% are from out of state; 5% Black or African American, non-Hispanic/Latino; 7% Hispanic/Latino; 11% Asian, non-Hispanic/Latino; 0.1% American Indian or Alaska Native, non-Hispanic/Latino; 3% Two or more races, non-Hispanic/Latino; 6% Race/ethnicity unknown; 26% international; 2% transferred in; 90% live on campus.

Freshmen:
Admission: 18,066 applied, 5,591 admitted, 1,432 enrolled. *Average high school GPA:* 3.8.
Retention: 96% of full-time freshmen returned.

FACULTY
Total: 368.
Student/faculty ratio: 10:1.

ACADEMICS
Calendar: semesters plus optional summer term. *Degrees:* bachelor's, master's, doctoral, post-master's, and postbachelor's certificates.

Special study options: accelerated degree program, advanced placement credit, cooperative education, double majors, English as a second language, honors programs, independent study, internships, off-campus study, part-time degree program, services for LD students, student-designed majors, study abroad, summer session for credit. *ROTC:* Army (c), Navy (b), Air Force (c).

Unusual degree programs: 3-2 business administration; nursing; business, computer science, engineering, neuroscience, physics, physics and astronomy, public health.

Computers: 700 computers/terminals and 4,000 ports are available on campus for general student use. Students can access the following: computer help desk, free student e-mail accounts, online (class) grades, online (class) registration, online (class) schedules. Campuswide network is available. 100% of college-owned or -operated housing units are wired for high-speed Internet access. Wireless service is available via entire campus.

Library: Rush Rhees Library plus 7 others. Study areas open 24 hours, 5–7 days a week; students can reserve study rooms.

STUDENT LIFE
Housing options: on-campus residence required through sophomore year; coed. Campus housing is university owned and leased by the school. Freshman campus housing is guaranteed.

Activities and organizations: drama/theater group, student-run newspaper, radio and television station, choral group, marching band, Campus Activities Board, Black Students'; Union, Grassroots (environmental group), Women's Caucus, American Sign Language Club, national fraternities, national sororities.

Athletics Member NCAA. All Division III except squash (Division I). *Intercollegiate sports:* archery M(c)/W(c), badminton M(c)/W(c), baseball M, basketball M/W, bowling M(c)/W(c), cheerleading M(c)/W(c), crew M(c)/W, cross-country running M/W, equestrian sports M(c)/W(c), fencing M(c)/W(c), field hockey W, football M, golf M, ice hockey M(c)/W(c), lacrosse M(c)/W, rugby M(c)/W(c), sailing M(c)/W(c), skiing (downhill) M(c)/W(c), soccer M/W, softball W, squash M(s), swimming and diving M/W, tennis M/W, track and field M/W, ultimate Frisbee M(c)/W(c), volleyball M(c)/W, water polo M(c)/W(c). *Intramural sports:* basketball M/W, football M/W, soccer M/W, tennis M(c)/W(c), ultimate Frisbee M/W, volleyball M/W.

Campus security: 24-hour emergency response devices and patrols, student patrols, late-night transport/escort service, controlled dormitory access.

Student services: health clinic, personal/psychological counseling, women's center, legal services.

COSTS & FINANCIAL AID
Costs (2018–19) *Comprehensive fee:* $69,685 includes full-time tuition ($52,867), mandatory fees ($958), and room and board ($15,860). Part-time tuition: $1652 per credit hour. Part-time tuition and fees vary according to course load. *Room and board:* Room and board charges vary according to board plan and housing facility. *Payment plan:* installment. *Waivers:* employees or children of employees.

Financial Aid Of all full-time matriculated undergraduates who enrolled in 2017, 3,803 applied for aid, 3,222 were judged to have need, 2,922 had their need fully met. In 2017, 1832 non-need-based awards were made. *Average percent of need met:* 96. *Average financial aid package:* $47,340. *Average need-based loan:* $4492. *Average need-based gift aid:* $42,106. *Average non-need-based aid:* $15,124. *Average indebtedness upon graduation:* $29,013.

APPLYING

Standardized Tests *Required for some:* SAT and SAT Subject Tests or ACT (for admission). *Recommended:* SAT or ACT (for admission), SAT Subject Tests (for admission).

Options: electronic application, early decision, deferred entrance.

Application fee: $50.

Required: essay or personal statement, high school transcript. *Required for some:* audition for Eastman School of Music. *Recommended:* 2 letters of recommendation, interview.

Application deadlines: 1/5 (freshmen), 3/15 (transfers).

Early decision deadline: 11/1.

Notification: 4/1 (freshmen), 4/1 (out-of-state freshmen), 3/1 (transfers), 12/15 (early decision).

CONTACT

Office of Admissions, University of Rochester, PO Box 270251, 300 Wilson Boulevard, Rochester, NY 14627-0251. *Phone:* 585-275-3221. *Toll-free phone:* 888-822-2256. *Fax:* 585-461-4595. *E-mail:* admit@admissions.rochester.edu.

U.T.A. Mesivta of Kiryas Joel
Monroe, New York

CONTACT
U.T.A. Mesivta of Kiryas Joel, 48 Bakertown Road, Suite 501, Monroe, NY 10950.

Utica College
Utica, New York
http://www.utica.edu/

- **Independent** comprehensive, founded 1946
- **Suburban** 128-acre campus
- **Endowment** $24.6 million
- **Coed** 3,685 undergraduate students, 79% full-time, 60% women, 40% men
- **Moderately difficult** entrance level, 84% of applicants were admitted

UNDERGRAD STUDENTS

2,901 full-time, 784 part-time. Students come from 48 states and territories; 28 other countries; 19% are from out of state; 12% Black or African American, non-Hispanic/Latino; 9% Hispanic/Latino; 4% Asian, non-Hispanic/Latino; 0.1% Native Hawaiian or other Pacific Islander, non-Hispanic/Latino; 0.4% American Indian or Alaska Native, non-Hispanic/Latino; 2% Two or more races, non-Hispanic/Latino; 4% Race/ethnicity unknown; 1% international; 5% transferred in; 34% live on campus.

Freshmen:
Admission: 5,656 applied, 4,732 admitted, 548 enrolled. *Average high school GPA:* 3.1. *Test scores:* SAT evidence-based reading and writing scores over 500: 79%; SAT math scores over 500: 69%; ACT scores over 18: 90%; SAT evidence-based reading and writing scores over 600: 20%; SAT math scores over 600: 22%; ACT scores over 24: 45%; SAT evidence-based reading and writing scores over 700: 3%; SAT math scores over 700: 2%; ACT scores over 30: 2%.

Retention: 76% of full-time freshmen returned.

FACULTY
Total: 452, 33% full-time, 39% with terminal degrees.

Student/faculty ratio: 13:1.

ACADEMICS
Calendar: semesters. *Degrees:* certificates, bachelor's, master's, doctoral, and postbachelor's certificates.

Special study options: academic remediation for entering students, accelerated degree program, adult/continuing education programs, advanced placement credit, cooperative education, distance learning, double majors, English as a second language, honors programs, independent study, internships, off-campus study, part-time degree program, services for LD students, study abroad, summer session for credit. *ROTC:* Army (b), Air Force (c).

Unusual degree programs: 3-2 engineering with Syracuse University.

Computers: 430 computers/terminals are available on campus for general student use. Students can access the following: computer help desk, free student e-mail accounts, online (class) grades, online (class) registration,

online (class) schedules. Campuswide network is available. 100% of college-owned or -operated housing units are wired for high-speed Internet access. Wireless service is available via entire campus.
Library: Frank E. Gannett Memorial Library. *Books:* 307,523 (physical); *Serial titles:* 267,023 (physical). Students can reserve study rooms.

STUDENT LIFE
Housing options: on-campus residence required through sophomore year; coed, special housing for students with disabilities. Campus housing is university owned. Freshman campus housing is guaranteed.

Activities and organizations: drama/theater group, student-run newspaper, radio station, choral group, Physical Therapy Society, Student Nurses Association, Kappa Delta Pi, Student Senate, Utica College Honor Association, national fraternities, national sororities.

Athletics Member NCAA. All Division III. *Intercollegiate sports:* baseball M, basketball M/W, cross-country running M/W, field hockey W, football M, golf M/W, ice hockey M/W, lacrosse M/W, soccer M/W, softball W, swimming and diving M/W, tennis M/W, track and field M/W, volleyball W, water polo W. *Intramural sports:* basketball M/W, bowling M/W, cheerleading M(c)/W(c), fencing M(c)/W(c), racquetball M/W, soccer M/W, softball M/W, tennis M/W, volleyball M/W, water polo M/W.

Campus security: 24-hour emergency response devices and patrols, late-night transport/escort service, controlled dormitory access.

Student services: health clinic, personal/psychological counseling, women's center.

COSTS & FINANCIAL AID
Costs (2017–18) *Comprehensive fee:* $31,510 includes full-time tuition ($20,126), mandatory fees ($550), and room and board ($10,834). Full-time tuition and fees vary according to course load, degree level, and location. Part-time tuition: $671 per credit hour. Part-time tuition and fees vary according to course load, degree level, and location. *Required fees:* $50 per term part-time. *Room and board:* Room and board charges vary according to board plan. *Waivers:* employees or children of employees.

Financial Aid Of all full-time matriculated undergraduates who enrolled in 2017, 2,655 applied for aid, 2,404 were judged to have need, 170 had their need fully met. In 2017, 248 non-need-based awards were made. *Average percent of need met:* 51. *Average financial aid package:* $13,958. *Average need-based loan:* $4403. *Average need-based gift aid:* $4805. *Average non-need-based aid:* $4896. *Average indebtedness upon graduation:* $31,694.

APPLYING
Standardized Tests *Required for some:* SAT or ACT (for admission).

Options: electronic application, early decision, early action, deferred entrance.

Application fee: $40.

Required: essay or personal statement, high school transcript, minimum 2.0 GPA, 1 letter of recommendation. *Required for some:* minimum 3.0 GPA. *Recommended:* interview.

Application deadlines: rolling (freshmen), rolling (transfers).

Notification: 9/1 (freshmen), continuous (transfers).

CONTACT
Utica College, 1600 Burrstone Road, Utica, NY 13502-4892. *Phone:* 315-792-3006. *Toll-free phone:* 800-782-8884.

See previous page for display ad and page 1486 for the College Close-Up.

Vassar College
Poughkeepsie, New York
http://www.vassar.edu/

- **Independent** 4-year, founded 1861
- **Suburban** 1000-acre campus with easy access to New York City
- **Endowment** $948.6 million
- **Coed** 2,353 undergraduate students, 99% full-time, 59% women, 41% men
- **Very difficult** entrance level, 24% of applicants were admitted

UNDERGRAD STUDENTS
2,334 full-time, 19 part-time. Students come from 53 states and territories; 40 other countries; 75% are from out of state; 4% Black or African American, non-Hispanic/Latino; 11% Hispanic/Latino; 13% Asian, non-Hispanic/Latino; 0.1% American Indian or Alaska Native, non-Hispanic/Latino; 7% Two or more races, non-Hispanic/Latino; 0.3% Race/ethnicity unknown; 8% international; 0.3% transferred in; 95% live on campus.

Freshmen:
Admission: 7,746 applied, 1,842 admitted, 624 enrolled. *Test scores:* SAT evidence-based reading and writing scores over 500: 100%; SAT math scores over 500: 99%; ACT scores over 18: 101%; SAT evidence-based reading and writing scores over 600: 98%; SAT math scores over 600: 97%; ACT scores over 24: 101%; SAT evidence-based reading and writing scores over 700: 72%; SAT math scores over 700: 63%; ACT scores over 30: 90%.
Retention: 96% of full-time freshmen returned.

FACULTY
Total: 336, 84% full-time, 85% with terminal degrees.
Student/faculty ratio: 8:1.

ACADEMICS
Calendar: semesters. *Degrees:* bachelor's and master's.

Special study options: advanced placement credit, cooperative education, double majors, independent study, internships, off-campus study, part-time degree program, services for LD students, student-designed majors, study abroad.

Unusual degree programs: 3-2 engineering with Dartmouth College.

Computers: 135 computers/terminals are available on campus for general student use. Students can access the following: campus intranet, computer help desk, free student e-mail accounts, online (class) grades, online (class) registration, online (class) schedules, Ethernet. Campuswide network is available. 100% of college-owned or -operated housing units are wired for high-speed Internet access. Wireless service is available via entire campus.

Library: Vassar College Library plus 2 others. *Books:* 1.1 million (physical), 520,203 (digital/electronic); *Serial titles:* 15,914 (physical), 98,004 (digital/electronic); *Databases:* 847. Weekly public service hours: 145; study areas open 24 hours, 5–7 days a week; students can reserve study rooms.

STUDENT LIFE
Housing options: on-campus residence required through senior year; coed, women-only, cooperative, special housing for students with disabilities. Campus housing is university owned. Freshman campus housing is guaranteed.

Activities and organizations: drama/theater group, student-run newspaper, radio station, choral group, Student Association, WVKR radio station, VICE (programming social events), Vassar Greens, Ultimate Frisbee.

Athletics Member NCAA. All Division III. *Intercollegiate sports:* baseball M, basketball M/W, crew M(c)/W(c), cross-country running M/W, fencing M/W, field hockey W, golf W, lacrosse M/W, rugby M(c)/W(c), soccer M/W, squash M/W, swimming and diving M/W, tennis M/W, track and field M/W, volleyball M/W. *Intramural sports:* badminton M(c)/W(c), basketball M(c)/W(c), soccer M(c)/W(c), table tennis M(c)/W(c), tennis M(c)/W(c), ultimate Frisbee M(c)/W(c), volleyball M(c)/W(c).

Campus security: 24-hour emergency response devices and patrols, student patrols, late-night transport/escort service, controlled dormitory access.

Student services: health clinic, personal/psychological counseling, women's center.

COSTS & FINANCIAL AID
Costs (2017–18) *One-time required fee:* $80. *Comprehensive fee:* $68,110 includes full-time tuition ($54,410), mandatory fees ($800), and room and board ($12,900). Part-time tuition: $6480 per unit. *College room only:* $9000. Room and board charges vary according to housing facility. *Payment plan:* installment. *Waivers:* employees or children of employees.

Financial Aid Of all full-time matriculated undergraduates who enrolled in 2017, 1,621 applied for aid, 1,448 were judged to have need, 1,448 had their need fully met. 1,119 Federal Work-Study jobs (averaging $2539). 346 state and other part-time jobs (averaging $2521). *Average percent of need met:* 100. *Average financial aid package:* $53,642. *Average need-

based loan: $3462. *Average need-based gift aid:* $48,194. *Average indebtedness upon graduation:* $19,439. *Financial aid deadline:* 2/1.

APPLYING
Standardized Tests *Required:* SAT or ACT (for admission).

Options: electronic application, early decision, deferred entrance.

Application fee: $70.

Required: essay or personal statement, high school transcript, 2 letters of recommendation.

Application deadlines: 1/1 (freshmen), 3/15 (transfers).

Early decision deadline: 11/15.

Notification: 4/1 (freshmen), 5/10 (transfers), 12/15 (early decision).

CONTACT
Dean Art D. Rodriguez, Dean of Admission and Financial Aid, Vassar College, 124 Raymond Avenue, Poughkeepsie, NY 12604. *Phone:* 845-437-7300. *Toll-free phone:* 800-827-7270. *Fax:* 845-437-7063. *E-mail:* admissions@vassar.edu.

Vaughn College of Aeronautics and Technology

Flushing, New York
http://www.vaughn.edu/

- **Independent** comprehensive, founded 1932
- **Urban** 6-acre campus with easy access to New York City
- **Coed, primarily men** 1,496 undergraduate students, 82% full-time, 13% women, 87% men
- **Moderately difficult** entrance level, 90% of applicants were admitted

UNDERGRAD STUDENTS
1,228 full-time, 268 part-time. 12% are from out of state; 18% Black or African American, non-Hispanic/Latino; 33% Hispanic/Latino; 11% Asian, non-Hispanic/Latino; 0.9% Native Hawaiian or other Pacific Islander, non-Hispanic/Latino; 0.5% American Indian or Alaska Native, non-Hispanic/Latino; 2% Two or more races, non-Hispanic/Latino; 17% Race/ethnicity unknown; 5% international; 12% transferred in; 11% live on campus.

Freshmen:
Admission: 711 applied, 643 admitted, 253 enrolled. *Average high school GPA:* ####. *Test scores:* SAT evidence-based reading and writing scores over 500: 70%; SAT math scores over 500: 77%; ACT scores over 18: 100%; SAT evidence-based reading and writing scores over 600: 11%; SAT math scores over 600: 11%; ACT scores over 24: 43%; SAT evidence-based reading and writing scores over 700: 1%; SAT math scores over 700: 1%.

FACULTY
Total: 189, 19% full-time, 17% with terminal degrees.
Student/faculty ratio: 15:1.

ACADEMICS
Calendar: semesters. *Degrees:* certificates, diplomas, associate, bachelor's, and master's.

Special study options: academic remediation for entering students, advanced placement credit, distance learning, double majors, English as a second language, internships, part-time degree program, services for LD students, summer session for credit. *ROTC:* Army (c), Air Force (c).

Computers: Students can access the following: campus intranet, computer help desk, free student e-mail accounts, online (class) grades, online (class) registration, online (class) schedules, Vaughn Student Portal. Campuswide network is available. 100% of college-owned or -operated housing units are wired for high-speed Internet access. Wireless service is available via entire campus.

Library: Library and Learning Commons.

STUDENT LIFE
Housing options: coed, special housing for students with disabilities. Campus housing is university owned. Freshman applicants given priority for college housing.

Athletics Member USCAA. *Intercollegiate sports:* basketball M/W, cross-country running M/W, soccer M, tennis M/W. *Intramural sports:* basketball M/W, cross-country running M/W, soccer M, tennis M/W.

Campus security: 24-hour emergency response devices and patrols, controlled dormitory access.

Student services: personal/psychological counseling.

COSTS & FINANCIAL AID
Costs (2017–18) *One-time required fee:* $160. *Comprehensive fee:* $39,062 includes full-time tuition ($23,877), mandatory fees ($1000), and room and board ($14,185). Full-time tuition and fees vary according to course load, degree level, and program. Part-time tuition: $800 per credit hour. Part-time tuition and fees vary according to course load, degree level, and program. *Required fees:* $400 per term part-time. *College room only:* $10,983. Room and board charges vary according to board plan. *Payment plan:* installment. *Waivers:* employees or children of employees.

Financial Aid Of all full-time matriculated undergraduates who enrolled in 2008, 704 applied for aid, 704 were judged to have need, 476 had their need fully met. 25 Federal Work-Study jobs (averaging $3000). In 2008, 145 non-need-based awards were made. *Average percent of need met:* 82. *Average financial aid package:* $18,030. *Average need-based loan:* $1770. *Average need-based gift aid:* $2950. *Average non-need-based aid:* $2000. *Average indebtedness upon graduation:* $17,125.

APPLYING
Standardized Tests *Required:* SAT or ACT (for admission). *Recommended:* SAT and SAT Subject Tests or ACT (for admission), SAT Subject Tests (for admission).

Options: electronic application.

Application fee: $40.

Required: high school transcript. *Recommended:* essay or personal statement, 2 letters of recommendation, interview.

Application deadlines: rolling (freshmen), rolling (out-of-state freshmen), rolling (transfers).

Notification: continuous (freshmen), continuous (out-of-state freshmen), continuous (transfers).

CONTACT
Mr. David Sookdeo, Acting Director of Admissions, Vaughn College of Aeronautics and Technology, 8601 23rd Avenue, Flushing, NY 11369. *Phone:* 718-429.6600 Ext. 192. *Toll-free phone:* 866-6VAUGHN. *Fax:* 718-779.2231. *E-mail:* david.sookdeo@vaughn.edu.

Villa Maria College

Buffalo, New York
http://www.villa.edu/

- **Independent** 4-year, founded 1960, affiliated with Roman Catholic Church
- **Suburban** 9-acre campus with easy access to Buffalo-Niagara
- **Endowment** $1.9 million
- **Coed** 596 undergraduate students, 82% full-time, 62% women, 38% men

UNDERGRAD STUDENTS
490 full-time, 106 part-time. Students come from 9 states and territories; 2 other countries; 3% are from out of state; 33% Black or African American, non-Hispanic/Latino; 6% Hispanic/Latino; 2% Asian, non-Hispanic/Latino; 0.5% American Indian or Alaska Native, non-Hispanic/Latino; 5% Two or more races, non-Hispanic/Latino; 0.3% international; 13% transferred in.

Freshmen:
Admission: 133 enrolled. *Average high school GPA:* 2.6.
Retention: 61% of full-time freshmen returned.

FACULTY
Total: 103, 33% full-time, 39% with terminal degrees.
Student/faculty ratio: 9:1.

ACADEMICS
Calendar: semesters. *Degrees:* certificates, associate, and bachelor's.

Special study options: advanced placement credit, cooperative education, distance learning, honors programs, independent study, internships, off-campus study, part-time degree program, services for LD students, study abroad.

Computers: 275 computers/terminals are available on campus for general student use. Students can access the following: computer help desk, free student e-mail accounts, online (class) grades, online (class) registration,

online (class) schedules. Campuswide network is available. Wireless service is available via entire campus.
Library: Villa Maria College Library. *Books:* 17,213 (physical), 153,087 (digital/electronic); *Serial titles:* 82 (physical); *Databases:* 45.

STUDENT LIFE
Housing options: college housing not available.
Activities and organizations: choral group.
Athletics Member USCAA. *Intercollegiate sports:* basketball M/W, bowling W, cross-country running M/W, golf M, soccer M/W.
Campus security: 24-hour emergency response devices, late-night transport/escort service, security guard during hours of operation.
Student services: health clinic, personal/psychological counseling.

COSTS & FINANCIAL AID
Costs (2017–18) *Tuition:* $20,830 full-time, $695 per credit hour part-time. Full-time tuition and fees vary according to degree level, program, and reciprocity agreements. Part-time tuition and fees vary according to course load, degree level, program, and reciprocity agreements. *Required fees:* $1250 full-time. *Payment plan:* installment. *Waivers:* employees or children of employees.
Financial Aid *Average indebtedness upon graduation:* $22,658.

APPLYING
Required: high school transcript. *Required for some:* interview, health forms, essay, portfolio and interview for Art programs, audition for music programs. *Recommended:* essay or personal statement.

CONTACT
Mr. Brian Emerson, Vice President for Enrollment and Student Services, Villa Maria College, 240 Pine Ridge Road, Buffalo, NY 14225. *Phone:* 716-896-0700 Ext. 1838. *Fax:* 716-896-0705. *E-mail:* admissions@villa.edu.

Wagner College
Staten Island, New York
http://www.wagner.edu/
- **Independent** comprehensive, founded 1883
- **Urban** 105-acre campus with easy access to New York City
- **Endowment** $88.5 million
- **Coed** 1,812 undergraduate students, 96% full-time, 64% women, 36% men

UNDERGRAD STUDENTS
1,745 full-time, 67 part-time. Students come from 41 states and territories; 43 other countries; 54% are from out of state; 8% Black or African American, non-Hispanic/Latino; 12% Hispanic/Latino; 4% Asian, non-Hispanic/Latino; 0.2% Native Hawaiian or other Pacific Islander, non-Hispanic/Latino; 0.1% American Indian or Alaska Native, non-Hispanic/Latino; 3% Two or more races, non-Hispanic/Latino; 5% Race/ethnicity unknown; 4% international; 7% transferred in; 71% live on campus.

Freshmen:
Admission: 432 enrolled. *Average high school GPA:* 3.6. *Test scores:* SAT evidence-based reading and writing scores over 500: 94%; SAT math scores over 500: 93%; ACT scores over 18: 95%; SAT evidence-based reading and writing scores over 600: 47%; SAT math scores over 600: 40%; ACT scores over 24: 71%; SAT evidence-based reading and writing scores over 700: 8%; SAT math scores over 700: 4%; ACT scores over 30: 27%.
Retention: 85% of full-time freshmen returned.

FACULTY
Total: 265, 42% full-time, 45% with terminal degrees.
Student/faculty ratio: 13:1.

ACADEMICS
Calendar: semesters. *Degrees:* bachelor's, master's, doctoral, and post-master's certificates.
Special study options: accelerated degree program, adult/continuing education programs, advanced placement credit, cooperative education, double majors, honors programs, independent study, internships, off-campus study, part-time degree program, services for LD students,

student-designed majors, study abroad, summer session for credit. *ROTC:* Army (c).
Unusual degree programs: 3-2 business administration; physician assistant.
Computers: 230 computers/terminals are available on campus for general student use. Students can access the following: campus intranet, computer help desk, free student e-mail accounts, online (class) grades, online (class) registration, online (class) schedules. Campuswide network is available. 100% of college-owned or -operated housing units are wired for high-speed Internet access. Wireless service is available via entire campus.
Library: August Horrmann Library. *Books:* 70,465 (physical), 180,000 (digital/electronic); *Serial titles:* 79,532 (physical); *Databases:* 61. Weekly public service hours: 120; students can reserve study rooms.

STUDENT LIFE
Housing options: coed. Campus housing is university owned and leased by the school. Freshman campus housing is guaranteed.
Activities and organizations: drama/theater group, student-run newspaper, radio station, choral group, marching band, Student Government Association, Student Activities Board, Wagner College Theatre, Wagner College Choir, student newspaper, national fraternities, national sororities.
Athletics Member NCAA. All Division I except football (Division I-AA). *Intercollegiate sports:* baseball M(s), basketball M(s)/W(s), cheerleading W(c), cross-country running M(s)/W(s), fencing W(s), golf M(s)/W(s), ice hockey M(c), lacrosse M(s)/W(s), soccer W(s), softball W(s), swimming and diving W(s), tennis M(s)/W(s), track and field M(s)/W(s), water polo M(s)/W(s). *Intramural sports:* basketball M/W, bowling M/W, football M, rugby M(c), soccer M/W, softball M/W.
Campus security: 24-hour emergency response devices and patrols, late-night transport/escort service, controlled dormitory access.
Student services: health clinic, personal/psychological counseling.

COSTS & FINANCIAL AID
Costs (2017–18) *Comprehensive fee:* $59,030 includes full-time tuition ($44,800), mandatory fees ($580), and room and board ($13,650). Full-time tuition and fees vary according to program. Part-time tuition: $5600 per course. *Payment plan:* installment. *Waivers:* employees or children of employees.
Financial Aid Of all full-time matriculated undergraduates who enrolled in 2016, 1,324 applied for aid, 1,149 were judged to have need, 255 had their need fully met. In 2016, 422 non-need-based awards were made. *Average percent of need met:* 70. *Average financial aid package:* $29,515. *Average need-based loan:* $4937. *Average need-based gift aid:* $22,748. *Average non-need-based aid:* $17,988.

APPLYING
Standardized Tests *Required for some:* SAT or ACT (for admission).
Required: essay or personal statement, high school transcript, minimum 2.5 GPA, 2 letters of recommendation. *Required for some:* interview. *Recommended:* minimum 3.0 GPA, interview.

CONTACT
Mr. James Gibbons, Director of Admissions, Wagner College, One Campus Road, Pape Admissions Building, Staten Island, NY 10301. *Phone:* 718-390-3180. *Toll-free phone:* 800-221-1010. *Fax:* 718-390-3105. *E-mail:* jgibbons@wagner.edu.

Webb Institute
Glen Cove, New York
http://www.webb.edu/
- **Independent** 4-year, founded 1889
- **Suburban** 26-acre campus with easy access to New York City
- **Endowment** $66.3 million
- **Coed** 98 undergraduate students, 100% full-time, 20% women, 80% men
- **Most difficult** entrance level, 35% of applicants were admitted

UNDERGRAD STUDENTS
98 full-time. Students come from 27 states and territories; 2 other countries; 72% are from out of state; 1% Hispanic/Latino; 11% Asian, non-Hispanic/Latino; 5% Two or more races, non-Hispanic/Latino; 2% Race/ethnicity unknown; 2% transferred in; 100% live on campus.

Freshmen:

Admission: 106 applied, 37 admitted, 26 enrolled. *Average high school GPA:* 4.0. *Test scores:* SAT evidence-based reading and writing scores over 500: 100%; SAT math scores over 500: 100%; ACT scores over 18: 100%; SAT evidence-based reading and writing scores over 600: 95%; SAT math scores over 600: 100%; ACT scores over 24: 100%; SAT evidence-based reading and writing scores over 700: 57%; SAT math scores over 700: 93%; ACT scores over 30: 96%.

Retention: 93% of full-time freshmen returned.

FACULTY

Total: 14, 71% full-time, 71% with terminal degrees.
Student/faculty ratio: 9:1.

ACADEMICS

Calendar: semesters. *Degree:* bachelor's.

Special study options: double majors, independent study, internships, services for LD students, study abroad.

Computers: 25 computers/terminals are available on campus for general student use. Students can access the following: campus intranet, computer help desk, free student e-mail accounts, online (class) grades. Campuswide network is available. 100% of college-owned or -operated housing units are wired for high-speed Internet access. Wireless service is available via entire campus.

Library: Livingston Library. *Books:* 44,800 (physical), 4,190 (digital/electronic); *Serial titles:* 817 (physical), 43,658 (digital/electronic); *Databases:* 62. Weekly public service hours: 35; study areas open 24 hours, 5–7 days a week.

STUDENT LIFE

Housing options: on-campus residence required through senior year; coed, men-only, women-only. Campus housing is university owned. Freshman campus housing is guaranteed.

Activities and organizations: choral group, Student Organization, Society of Naval Architects and Marine Engineers, American Society of Naval Engineers, Society of Women Engineers, Marine Technology Society.

Athletics *Intercollegiate sports:* basketball M/W, cross-country running M(c)/W(c), sailing M/W, soccer M/W, tennis M/W, volleyball M/W. *Intramural sports:* crew M/W, cross-country running M/W, ultimate Frisbee M/W.

Campus security: 24-hour emergency response devices and patrols, controlled dormitory access.

Student services: personal/psychological counseling.

COSTS & FINANCIAL AID

Costs (2018–19) *One-time required fee:* $3000. *Comprehensive fee:* $65,225 includes full-time tuition ($49,750), mandatory fees ($425), and room and board ($15,050). Webb provides scholarships that will fully cover the tuition expenses of U.S. citizens and permanent residents. One-time required fee is for a laptop charged in the first year only.

Financial Aid Of all full-time matriculated undergraduates who enrolled in 2016, 29 applied for aid, 29 were judged to have need. In 2016, 62 non-need-based awards were made. *Average percent of need met:* 95. *Average financial aid package:* $52,750. *Average need-based loan:* $4710. *Average need-based gift aid:* $1950. *Average non-need-based aid:* $47,000. *Average indebtedness upon graduation:* $17,870. *Financial aid deadline:* 5/1.

APPLYING

Standardized Tests *Required:* SAT or ACT (for admission), SAT Subject Tests (for admission).

Options: electronic application, early decision, deferred entrance.

Application fee: $60.

Required: essay or personal statement, high school transcript, minimum 3.5 GPA, 2 letters of recommendation, interview, proof of U.S. citizenship or permanent residency status.

Application deadlines: 2/1 (freshmen), 2/1 (transfers).

Early decision deadline: 10/15.

Notification: 3/15 (freshmen), 3/15 (transfers), 12/15 (early decision).

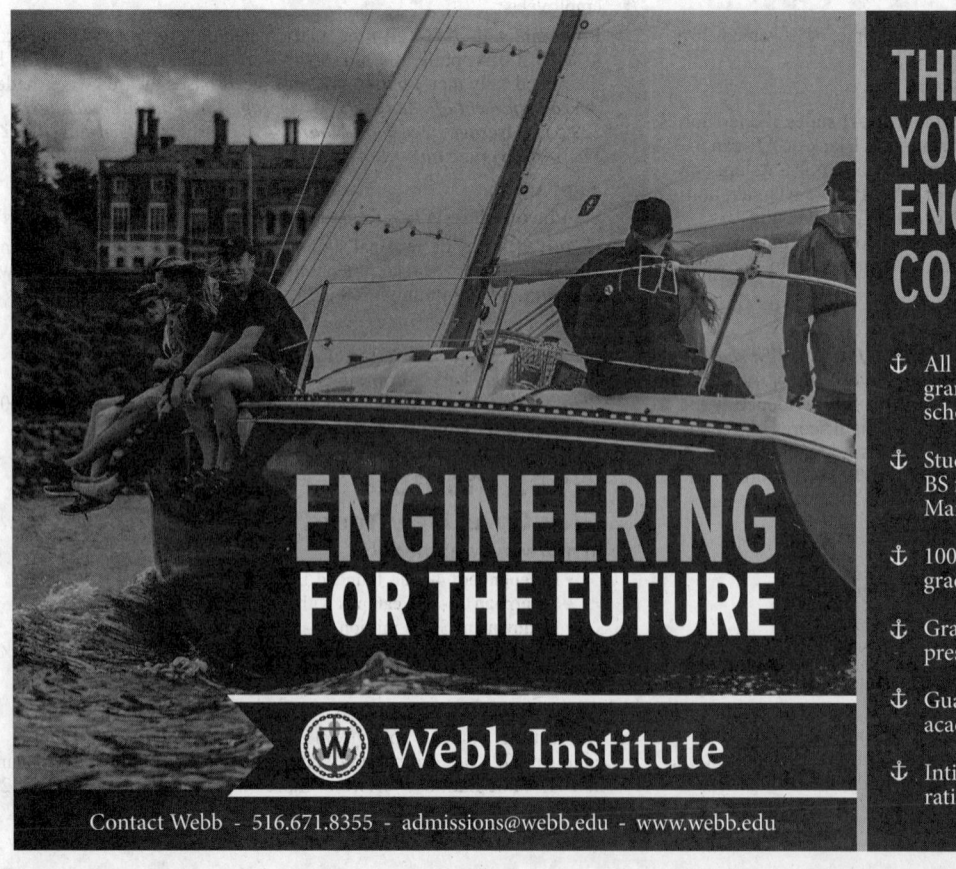

CONTACT

Lauren Carballo, Director of Admissions and Student Services, Webb Institute, 298 Crescent Beach Road, Glen Cove, NY 11542. *Phone:* 516-671-8355. *Fax:* 516-674-9838. *E-mail:* admissions@webb.edu.

See previous page for display ad and page 1492 for the College Close-Up.

Wells College

Aurora, New York

http://www.wells.edu/

- **Independent** 4-year, founded 1868
- **Rural** 365-acre campus with easy access to Syracuse
- **Endowment** $23.5 million
- **Coed** 488 undergraduate students, 99% full-time, 64% women, 36% men
- **Moderately difficult** entrance level, 80% of applicants were admitted

UNDERGRAD STUDENTS

481 full-time, 7 part-time. 23% are from out of state; 13% Black or African American, non-Hispanic/Latino; 14% Hispanic/Latino; 2% Asian, non-Hispanic/Latino; 1% American Indian or Alaska Native, non-Hispanic/Latino; 2% Two or more races, non-Hispanic/Latino; 7% Race/ethnicity unknown; 3% transferred in; 95% live on campus.

Freshmen:

Admission: 1,693 applied, 1,350 admitted, 137 enrolled. *Average high school GPA:* 3.1. *Test scores:* ACT scores over 18: 66%; ACT scores over 24: 33%; ACT scores over 30: 11%.

Retention: 70% of full-time freshmen returned.

FACULTY

Total: 58, 69% full-time, 79% with terminal degrees.

Student/faculty ratio: 10:1.

ACADEMICS

Calendar: semesters. *Degree:* bachelor's.

Special study options: adult/continuing education programs, advanced placement credit, double majors, English as a second language, independent study, internships, off-campus study, part-time degree program, services for LD students, student-designed majors, study abroad.

Unusual degree programs: 3-2 business administration with Clarkson University; engineering with Columbia University, Clarkson University, Cornell University; nursing; education with University of Rochester.

Computers: 96 computers/terminals and 1,224 ports are available on campus for general student use. Students can access the following: campus intranet, computer help desk, free student e-mail accounts, online (class) grades, online (class) registration, online (class) schedules. Campuswide network is available. 100% of college-owned or -operated housing units are wired for high-speed Internet access. Wireless service is available via classrooms, dorm rooms, learning centers, libraries, student centers.

Library: Louis Jefferson Long Library. Students can reserve study rooms.

STUDENT LIFE

Housing options: on-campus residence required through junior year; coed, women-only, special housing for students with disabilities. Campus housing is university owned. Freshman campus housing is guaranteed.

Activities and organizations: drama/theater group, choral group, Umoja, Prodigy, Red Cross Club, Campus Greens, Programming Board.

Athletics Member NCAA. All Division III. *Intercollegiate sports:* baseball M, basketball M/W, cross-country running M/W, field hockey W, lacrosse M/W, soccer M/W, softball W, swimming and diving M/W, volleyball M/W. *Intramural sports:* rugby M(c)/W(c).

Campus security: 24-hour emergency response devices and patrols, late-night transport/escort service, controlled dormitory access.

Student services: health clinic, personal/psychological counseling, women's center.

COSTS & FINANCIAL AID

Costs (2018–19) *Comprehensive fee:* $53,330 includes full-time tuition ($38,100), mandatory fees ($1500), and room and board ($13,730). Part-time tuition: $800 per credit hour. Part-time tuition and fees vary according to course load. *Room and board:* Room and board charges vary according to housing facility. *Payment plan:* installment. *Waivers:* senior citizens and employees or children of employees.

Financial Aid Of all full-time matriculated undergraduates who enrolled in 2016, 491 applied for aid, 474 were judged to have need, 87 had their need fully met. 68 Federal Work-Study jobs (averaging $1850). 175 state and other part-time jobs (averaging $1850). In 2016, 29 non-need-based awards were made. *Average percent of need met:* 82. *Average financial aid package:* $34,750. *Average need-based loan:* $3783. *Average need-based gift aid:* $29,240. *Average non-need-based aid:* $19,731. *Average indebtedness upon graduation:* $35,287.

APPLYING

Options: electronic application, early admission, early decision, early action, deferred entrance.

Required: essay or personal statement, high school transcript, 2 letters of recommendation. *Recommended:* minimum 3.0 GPA, interview.

Application deadlines: 3/1 (freshmen), rolling (transfers), 12/15 (early action).

Early decision deadline: 12/15.

Notification: continuous until 4/1 (freshmen), continuous (transfers), 1/15 (early decision), 2/1 (early action).

CONTACT

Wells College, 170 Main Street, Aurora, NY 13026. *Toll-free phone:* 800-952-9355.

Yeshiva and Kolel Bais Medrash Elyon

Monsey, New York

CONTACT

Yeshiva and Kolel Bais Medrash Elyon, 73 Main Street, Monsey, NY 10952.

Yeshiva and Kollel Harbotzas Torah

Brooklyn, New York

CONTACT

Yeshiva and Kollel Harbotzas Torah, 1049 East 15th Street, Brooklyn, NY 11230.

Yeshiva Derech Chaim

Brooklyn, New York

CONTACT

Yeshiva Derech Chaim, 1573 39th Street, Brooklyn, NY 11218.

Yeshiva D'Monsey Rabbinical College

Monsey, New York

CONTACT

Yeshiva D'Monsey Rabbinical College, 2 Roman Boulevard, Monsey, NY 10952.

Yeshiva Gedolah Imrei Yosef D'Spinka

Brooklyn, New York

CONTACT

Yeshiva Gedolah Imrei Yosef D'Spinka, 1466 56th Street, Brooklyn, NY 11219.

Yeshiva Gedola Ohr Yisrael

Brooklyn, New York

http://www.ohryisroel.org/

CONTACT

Yeshiva Gedola Ohr Yisrael, 2899 Nostrand Avenue, Brooklyn, NY 11229.

Yeshiva Karlin Stolin
Brooklyn, New York

CONTACT
Director of Admissions, Yeshiva Karlin Stolin, 1818 54th Street, Brooklyn, NY 11204. *Phone:* 718-232-7800 Ext. 26.

Yeshiva of Far Rockaway Derech Ayson Rabbinical Seminary
Far Rockaway, New York
http://www.yofr.org/

CONTACT
Yeshiva of Far Rockaway Derech Ayson Rabbinical Seminary, 802 Hicksville Road, Far Rockaway, NY 11691.

Yeshiva of Machzikai Hadas
Brooklyn, New York

CONTACT
Yeshiva of Machzikai Hadas, 1321 43rd Street, Brooklyn, NY 11219.

Yeshiva of Nitra Rabbinical College
Mount Kisco, New York

CONTACT
Administrator, Yeshiva of Nitra Rabbinical College, Croton Lake Road, Mount Kisco, NY 10549. *Phone:* 718-384-5460. *Fax:* 718-387-9400.

Yeshiva of the Telshe Alumni
Riverdale, New York

CONTACT
Yeshiva of the Telshe Alumni, 4904 Independence Avenue, Riverdale, NY 10471.

Yeshiva Shaarei Torah of Rockland
Suffern, New York

CONTACT
Yeshiva Shaarei Torah of Rockland, 91 West Carlton Road, Suffern, NY 10901.

Yeshiva Shaar Hatorah Talmudic Research Institute
Kew Gardens, New York

CONTACT
Assistant Dean, Yeshiva Shaar Hatorah Talmudic Research Institute, 117-06 84th Avenue, Kew Gardens, NY 11418-1469. *Phone:* 718-846-1940.

Yeshivas Maharit D'Satmar
Monroe, New York
http://www.yeshivasmaharit.com/

CONTACT
Yeshivas Maharit D'Satmar, 475 County Route 105, Monroe, NY 10950.

Yeshivas Novominsk
Brooklyn, New York

CONTACT
Yeshivas Novominsk, 1569 47th Street, Brooklyn, NY 11219.

Yeshivath Viznitz
Monsey, New York

CONTACT
Registrar, Yeshivath Viznitz, 15 Elyon Road, Monsey, NY 10952. *Phone:* 914-356-1010.

Yeshivath Zichron Moshe
South Fallsburg, New York

CONTACT
Rabbi Abba Gorelick, Dean, Yeshivath Zichron Moshe, Laurel Park Road, South Fallsburg, NY 12779. *Phone:* 914-434-5240.

Yeshivat Mikdash Melech
Brooklyn, New York

CONTACT
Rabbi S. Beyda, Director of Admissions, Yeshivat Mikdash Melech, 1326 Ocean Parkway, Brooklyn, NY 11230-5601. *Phone:* 718-339-1090. *E-mail:* mikdashmelech@verizon.net.

Yeshiva University
New York, New York
http://www.yu.edu/

CONTACT
Yeshiva University, 500 West 185th Street, New York, NY 10033-3201. *Phone:* 212-960-5277.

Yeshiva Zichron Aryeh
Far Rockaway, New York
http://www.yeshivazichronaryeh.com/

CONTACT
Yeshiva Zichron Aryeh, 1213 Bay 25th Street, Far Rockaway, NY 11691.

York College of the City University of New York
Jamaica, New York
http://www.york.cuny.edu/

- **State and locally supported** comprehensive, founded 1967, part of City University of New York System
- **Urban** 50-acre campus with easy access to New York City
- **Endowment** $890,940
- **Coed**
- **Moderately difficult** entrance level

FACULTY
Student/faculty ratio: 23:1.

ACADEMICS
Calendar: semesters. *Degrees:* bachelor's and master's.
Library: Main Library plus 1 other. *Books:* 150,914 (physical), 473,723 (digital/electronic).

STUDENT LIFE
Housing options: college housing not available.

Activities and organizations: drama/theater group, student-run newspaper, television station, choral group, Haitian Students Association, Caribbean Students Association, Haitian Cultural Association, Latin Caucus, Muslim Student Association.

Athletics Member NCAA. All Division III.

Campus security: 24-hour emergency response devices and patrols, late-night transport/escort service.

Student services: health clinic, personal/psychological counseling, women's center.

COSTS & FINANCIAL AID

Costs (2017–18) *Tuition:* state resident $6530 full-time, $285 per credit part-time; nonresident $17,400 full-time, $580 per credit part-time. *Required fees:* $427 full-time, $131 per term part-time.

Financial Aid Of all full-time matriculated undergraduates who enrolled in 2016, 4,269 applied for aid, 4,269 were judged to have need, 79 had their need fully met. In 2016, 61 non-need-based awards were made. *Average percent of need met:* 60. *Average financial aid package:* $7738. *Average need-based loan:* $3931. *Average need-based gift aid:* $8254. *Average non-need-based aid:* $4914. *Average indebtedness upon graduation:* $4614. *Financial aid deadline:* 6/30.

APPLYING

Standardized Tests *Required:* SAT (for admission), SAT or ACT (for admission).

Options: electronic application, early admission, deferred entrance.

Application fee: $65.

Required: high school transcript, minimum 2.8 GPA. *Required for some:* minimum 2.5 GPA. *Recommended:* minimum 3.0 GPA.

CONTACT

Dr. La Toro Yates, Director of Admissions, York College of the City University of New York, 94-20 Guy R. Brewer Boulevard, Jamaica, NY 11451. *Phone:* 718-262-2165. *Fax:* 718-262-2601. *E-mail:* lyates@york.cuny.edu.

NORTH CAROLINA

Apex School of Theology

Durham, North Carolina

http://www.apexsot.edu/

CONTACT

Dr. Henry D. Wells Jr., Registrar, Apex School of Theology, 1701 T.W. Alexander Drive, Durham, NC 27703. *Phone:* 919-572-1625. *Fax:* 919-572-1762. *E-mail:* registrar@apexsot.edu.

Appalachian State University

Boone, North Carolina

http://www.appstate.edu/

- **State-supported** comprehensive, founded 1899, part of University of North Carolina System
- **Small-town** 489-acre campus
- **Endowment** $105.7 million
- **Coed** 17,017 undergraduate students, 94% full-time, 55% women, 45% men
- **Moderately difficult** entrance level, 70% of applicants were admitted

UNDERGRAD STUDENTS

16,071 full-time, 946 part-time. Students come from 47 states and territories; 83 other countries; 8% are from out of state; 4% Black or African American, non-Hispanic/Latino; 6% Hispanic/Latino; 2% Asian, non-Hispanic/Latino; 0.1% Native Hawaiian or other Pacific Islander, non-Hispanic/Latino; 0.3% American Indian or Alaska Native, non-Hispanic/Latino; 4% Two or more races, non-Hispanic/Latino; 1% Race/ethnicity unknown; 0.8% international; 9% transferred in; 33% live on campus.

Freshmen:

Admission: 14,009 applied, 9,813 admitted, 3,306 enrolled. *Average high school GPA:* 4.2. *Test scores:* SAT evidence-based reading and writing scores over 500: 94%; SAT math scores over 500: 94%; ACT scores over 18: 100%; SAT evidence-based reading and writing scores over 600: 50%; SAT math scores over 600: 40%; ACT scores over 24: 74%; SAT evidence-based reading and writing scores over 700: 5%; SAT math scores over 700: 3%; ACT scores over 30: 12%.

Retention: 89% of full-time freshmen returned.

FACULTY

Total: 1,330, 73% full-time, 93% with terminal degrees.

Student/faculty ratio: 16:1.

ACADEMICS

Calendar: semesters. *Degrees:* bachelor's, master's, doctoral, post-master's, and postbachelor's certificates.

Special study options: academic remediation for entering students, adult/continuing education programs, advanced placement credit, distance learning, double majors, English as a second language, honors programs, independent study, internships, off-campus study, part-time degree program, services for LD students, student-designed majors, study abroad, summer session for credit. *ROTC:* Army (b).

Unusual degree programs: 3-2 engineering with Auburn University, Clemson University, North Carolina State University.

Computers: 2,280 computers/terminals are available on campus for general student use. Students can access the following: campus intranet, computer help desk, free student e-mail accounts, online (class) grades, online (class) registration, online (class) schedules. Campuswide network is available. 100% of college-owned or -operated housing units are wired for high-speed Internet access. Wireless service is available via entire campus.

Library: Carol Grotnes Belk Library plus 1 other. *Books:* 670,241 (physical), 1.2 million (digital/electronic); *Serial titles:* 14,157 (physical), 124,939 (digital/electronic); *Databases:* 478. Weekly public service hours: 137; students can reserve study rooms.

STUDENT LIFE

Housing options: on-campus residence required for freshman year; coed, women-only, special housing for students with disabilities. Campus housing is university owned. Freshman campus housing is guaranteed.

Activities and organizations: drama/theater group, student-run newspaper, radio and television station, choral group, marching band, Health Professions Club, National Society of Leadership and Success, Appalachian Educators, National Society of Collegiate Scholars, App Sits Meditation Club, national fraternities, national sororities.

Athletics Member NCAA, NAIA. All NCAA Division I except football (Division I-A). *Intercollegiate sports:* archery M(c)/W(c), baseball M(s), basketball M(s)/W(s), cross-country running M(s)/W(s), equestrian sports W(c), fencing M(c)/W(c), field hockey W(s), golf M(s)/W(s), ice hockey M(c)/W(c), lacrosse M(c)/W(c), racquetball M(c)/W(c), rock climbing M(c)/W(c), rugby M(c)/W(c), skiing (downhill) M(c)/W(c), soccer M(s)/W(s), softball W(s), swimming and diving M(c)/W(c), tennis M(s)/W(s), track and field M(s)/W(s), triathlon M(c)/W(c), ultimate Frisbee M(c)/W(c), volleyball M(c)/W(c), wrestling M(s). *Intramural sports:* badminton M/W, basketball M/W, bowling M/W, cross-country running M/W, golf M/W, racquetball M/W, soccer M/W, softball M/W, swimming and diving M/W, table tennis M/W, tennis M/W, ultimate Frisbee M/W, volleyball M/W, weight lifting M/W.

Campus security: 24-hour emergency response devices and patrols, late-night transport/escort service, controlled dormitory access, Campus Alert System.

Student services: health clinic, personal/psychological counseling, women's center, legal services.

COSTS & FINANCIAL AID

Costs (2017–18) *Tuition:* state resident $4242 full-time, $143 per credit hour part-time; nonresident $19,049 full-time, $644 per credit hour part-time. Part-time tuition and fees vary according to course load. No tuition increase for student's term of enrollment. *Required fees:* $3061 full-time, $19 per credit hour part-time. *Room and board:* $8174; room only: $4340. Room and board charges vary according to board plan and housing facility. *Payment plan:* installment. *Waivers:* employees or children of employees.

Financial Aid Of all full-time matriculated undergraduates who enrolled in 2015, 10,616 applied for aid, 7,870 were judged to have need, 1,285 had their need fully met. In 2015, 527 non-need-based awards were made. *Average percent of need met:* 71. *Average financial aid package:* $9759. *Average need-based loan:* $4201. *Average need-based gift aid:* $8238. *Average non-need-based aid:* $2806. *Average indebtedness upon graduation:* $22,696.

APPLYING

Standardized Tests *Required:* SAT or ACT (for admission).

Options: electronic application, early action, deferred entrance.

Application fee: $65.

COLLEGES AT-A-GLANCE

Required: high school transcript. *Recommended:* essay or personal statement.

Application deadlines: 3/15 (freshmen), rolling (transfers).

Notification: continuous until 1/25 (freshmen), continuous (transfers).

CONTACT
Mr. Alexis Pope, Director of Admissions, Appalachian State University, ASU Box 32004, Boone, NC 28608. *Phone:* 828-262-2120. *Fax:* 828-262-3296. *E-mail:* admissions@appstate.edu.

The Art Institute of Charlotte, a branch of Miami International University of Art & Design

Charlotte, North Carolina
http://www.artinstitutes.edu/charlotte/

CONTACT
The Art Institute of Charlotte, a branch of Miami International University of Art & Design, Three LakePointe Plaza, 2110 Water Ridge Parkway, Charlotte, NC 28217. *Phone:* 704-357-8020. *Toll-free phone:* 800-872-4417.

The Art Institute of Raleigh-Durham, a branch of Miami International University of Art & Design

Durham, North Carolina
http://www.artinstitutes.edu/raleigh-durham

CONTACT
The Art Institute of Raleigh-Durham, a branch of Miami International University of Art & Design, 410 Blackwell Street, Suite 200, Durham, NC 27701. *Phone:* 919-317-3050. *Toll-free phone:* 888-245-9593.

Barton College

Wilson, North Carolina
http://www.barton.edu/

- **Independent** comprehensive, founded 1902, affiliated with Christian Church (Disciples of Christ)
- **Small-town** 76-acre campus with easy access to Raleigh-Durham
- **Endowment** $28.2 million
- **Coed** 887 undergraduate students, 94% full-time, 69% women, 31% men
- **Minimally difficult** entrance level, 39% of applicants were admitted

UNDERGRAD STUDENTS
830 full-time, 57 part-time. Students come from 31 states and territories; 17 other countries; 18% are from out of state; 23% Black or African American, non-Hispanic/Latino; 8% Hispanic/Latino; 1% Asian, non-Hispanic/Latino; 0.7% American Indian or Alaska Native, non-Hispanic/Latino; 3% Two or more races, non-Hispanic/Latino; 5% Race/ethnicity unknown; 5% international; 9% transferred in; 45% live on campus.

Freshmen:
Admission: 2,632 applied, 1,024 admitted, 198 enrolled. *Average high school GPA:* 3.2. *Test scores:* SAT evidence-based reading and writing scores over 500: 69%; SAT math scores over 500: 67%; ACT scores over 18: 83%; SAT evidence-based reading and writing scores over 600: 12%; SAT math scores over 600: 14%; ACT scores over 24: 19%; SAT math scores over 700: 1%.
Retention: 63% of full-time freshmen returned.

FACULTY
Total: 124, 58% full-time, 56% with terminal degrees.
Student/faculty ratio: 10:1.

ACADEMICS
Calendar: semesters. *Degrees:* bachelor's and master's.
Special study options: academic remediation for entering students, accelerated degree program, adult/continuing education programs, advanced placement credit, distance learning, double majors, honors programs, independent study, internships, part-time degree program, services for LD students, student-designed majors, study abroad, summer session for credit.

Unusual degree programs: 3-2 business administration.

Computers: Students can access the following: campus intranet, computer help desk, free student e-mail accounts, online (class) grades, online (class) registration, online (class) schedules, student picture directory. Campuswide network is available. 100% of college-owned or -operated housing units are wired for high-speed Internet access. Wireless service is available via classrooms, computer centers, computer labs, learning centers, libraries, student centers.

Library: Willis N. Hackney Library. *Books:* 124,260 (physical), 326,162 (digital/electronic); *Serial titles:* 78,676 (digital/electronic); *Databases:* 128. Weekly public service hours: 96; students can reserve study rooms.

STUDENT LIFE
Housing options: on-campus residence required through sophomore year; coed, women-only. Campus housing is university owned and leased by the school. Freshman campus housing is guaranteed.

Activities and organizations: drama/theater group, student-run newspaper, radio and television station, choral group, Student Ambassador Program, Barton College Association of Nursing, Barton College Orientation Team, Barton College Catholic Campus Ministries, Minority Student Association, national fraternities, national sororities.

Athletics Member NCAA. All Division II. *Intercollegiate sports:* baseball M(s), basketball M(s)/W(s), cross-country running M(s)/W(s), golf M(s)/W(s), lacrosse W(s), soccer M(s)/W(s), softball W(s), swimming and diving M(s)/W(s), tennis M(s)/W(s), track and field M(s)/W(s), volleyball M(s)/W(s). *Intramural sports:* basketball M/W, football M/W, soccer M/W, softball M/W, volleyball M/W.

Campus security: 24-hour emergency response devices and patrols, late-night transport/escort service, controlled dormitory access, city police substation on campus.

Student services: health clinic, personal/psychological counseling, women's center.

COSTS & FINANCIAL AID
Costs (2018–19) *Comprehensive fee:* $41,000 includes full-time tuition ($30,880) and room and board ($10,120). Full-time tuition and fees vary according to class time, course load, and program. Part-time tuition: $600 per credit hour. Part-time tuition and fees vary according to class time, course load, and program. *College room only:* $4360. Room and board charges vary according to board plan and housing facility. *Payment plan:* installment. *Waivers:* adult students and employees or children of employees.

Financial Aid Of all full-time matriculated undergraduates who enrolled in 2017, 759 applied for aid, 719 were judged to have need, 91 had their need fully met. In 2017, 103 non-need-based awards were made. *Average percent of need met:* 63. *Average financial aid package:* $22,703. *Average need-based loan:* $4168. *Average need-based gift aid:* $18,982. *Average non-need-based aid:* $11,553. *Average indebtedness upon graduation:* $26,477.

APPLYING
Standardized Tests *Required:* SAT or ACT (for admission).

Options: electronic application.

Required: high school transcript, minimum 2.0 GPA. *Required for some:* essay or personal statement, letters of recommendation, interview.

Application deadlines: rolling (freshmen), rolling (out-of-state freshmen), rolling (transfers).

Notification: continuous (freshmen), continuous (transfers).

CONTACT
Barton College, PO Box 5000, Wilson, NC 27893-7000. *Phone:* 800-345-4973. *Toll-free phone:* 800-345-4973.

Belmont Abbey College

Belmont, North Carolina
http://www.belmontabbeycollege.edu/

- **Independent Roman Catholic** 4-year, founded 1876
- **Small-town** 650-acre campus with easy access to Charlotte
- **Coed**
- **Moderately difficult** entrance level

ACADEMICS
Calendar: semesters. *Degree:* bachelor's.
Library: Abbot Vincent Taylor Library plus 1 other.

STUDENT LIFE
Housing options: men-only, women-only. Campus housing is university owned. Freshman campus housing is guaranteed.

Activities and organizations: drama/theater group, student-run newspaper, choral group, Crusaders for Life, Improv Troupe, Abbey Volunteers, International Club, Green Team, national fraternities, national sororities.

Athletics Member NCAA. All Division II.

Campus security: 24-hour emergency response devices and patrols.

Student services: health clinic, personal/psychological counseling.

FINANCIAL AID
Financial Aid Of all full-time matriculated undergraduates who enrolled in 2016, 1,181 applied for aid, 1,015 were judged to have need, 99 had their need fully met. 83 Federal Work-Study jobs (averaging $2000). In 2016, 307 non-need-based awards were made. *Average percent of need met:* 52. *Average financial aid package:* $12,389. *Average need-based loan:* $4398. *Average need-based gift aid:* $8458. *Average non-need-based aid:* $4619. *Average indebtedness upon graduation:* $25,610.

APPLYING
Options: electronic application, deferred entrance.

Required: high school transcript, minimum 2.3 GPA. *Required for some:* essay or personal statement. *Recommended:* interview.

CONTACT
Ms. Nicole Focareto, Executive Director of Admissions, Belmont Abbey College, 100 Belmont-Mt. Holly Road, Belmont, NC 28012. *Phone:* 704-461-6214. *Toll-free phone:* 888-BAC-0110. *Fax:* 704-461-6220. *E-mail:* nicolefocareto@bac.edu.

Bennett College
Greensboro, North Carolina
http://www.bennett.edu/

- **Independent United Methodist** 4-year, founded 1873
- **Urban** 60-acre campus
- **Endowment** $12.6 million
- **Women only** 493 undergraduate students, 81% full-time
- **Minimally difficult** entrance level, 89% of applicants were admitted

UNDERGRAD STUDENTS
400 full-time, 93 part-time. Students come from 24 states and territories; 3 other countries; 49% are from out of state; 85% Black or African American, non-Hispanic/Latino; 3% Hispanic/Latino; 0.2% Asian, non-Hispanic/Latino; 0.2% American Indian or Alaska Native, non-Hispanic/Latino; 4% Two or more races, non-Hispanic/Latino; 7% Race/ethnicity unknown; 0.6% international; 0.8% transferred in; 69% live on campus.

Freshmen:
Admission: 2,150 applied, 1,912 admitted, 174 enrolled. *Average high school GPA:* 2.8.
Retention: 44% of full-time freshmen returned.

FACULTY
Total: 56, 59% full-time, 68% with terminal degrees.
Student/faculty ratio: 10:1.

ACADEMICS
Calendar: semesters. *Degree:* bachelor's.
Special study options: academic remediation for entering students, advanced placement credit, cooperative education, distance learning, double majors, English as a second language, honors programs, independent study, internships, off-campus study, part-time degree program, services for LD students, student-designed majors, study abroad, summer session for credit. *ROTC:* Army (c), Air Force (c).
Unusual degree programs: 3-2 engineering with North Carolina Agricultural and Technical State University.
Computers: 225 computers/terminals are available on campus for general student use. Students can access the following: campus intranet, computer

help desk, free student e-mail accounts, online (class) grades, online (class) registration, online (class) schedules, wireless capability is in all buildings except Steele and Shell halls. Campuswide network is available. 100% of college-owned or -operated housing units are wired for high-speed Internet access. Wireless service is available via entire campus.
Library: Holgate Library. *Books:* 68,203 (physical), 193,780 (digital/electronic); *Serial titles:* 10 (physical); *Databases:* 78. Weekly public service hours: 83.

STUDENT LIFE
Housing options: on-campus residence required through sophomore year; women-only. Campus housing is university owned. Freshman campus housing is guaranteed.

Activities and organizations: drama/theater group, choral group, Student Government Association, Pre-Alumnae Council, Senior Class, Junior Class, Sophomore Class, national sororities.

Campus security: 24-hour emergency response devices and patrols, late-night transport/escort service, controlled dormitory access, alerts and educational programs are offered.

Student services: health clinic, personal/psychological counseling.

COSTS & FINANCIAL AID
Costs (2017–18) *Comprehensive fee:* $26,627 includes full-time tuition ($15,964), mandatory fees ($2549), and room and board ($8114). Full-time tuition and fees vary according to course load. Part-time tuition: $665 per credit hour. Part-time tuition and fees vary according to course load. *Required fees:* $1067 per term part-time. *College room only:* $4040. Room and board charges vary according to board plan. *Payment plan:* installment. *Waivers:* employees or children of employees.

Financial Aid Of all full-time matriculated undergraduates who enrolled in 2011, 664 applied for aid, 643 were judged to have need, 22 had their need fully met. In 2011, 7 non-need-based awards were made. *Average percent of need met:* 47. *Average financial aid package:* $13,092. *Average need-based loan:* $4170. *Average need-based gift aid:* $9402. *Average non-need-based aid:* $4714. *Financial aid deadline:* 3/15.

APPLYING
Standardized Tests *Required:* SAT or ACT (for admission).
Options: electronic application, deferred entrance.
Application fee: $35.
Required: high school transcript, minimum 2.5 GPA, 2 letters of recommendation. *Recommended:* essay or personal statement.
Application deadlines: rolling (freshmen), rolling (out-of-state freshmen), rolling (transfers).

CONTACT
Mr. James Crawford, Director, Admissions, Bennett College, 900 East Washington Street, Enrollment Management Center, Greensboro, NC 27401. *Phone:* 336-517-1818. *Toll-free phone:* 800-413-5323. *E-mail:* jcrawford@bennett.edu.

Brevard College
Brevard, North Carolina
http://www.brevard.edu/

CONTACT
Mr. David Volrath, Admissions, Brevard College, One Brevard College Drive, Brevard, NC 28712. *Phone:* 828-884-8367. *Toll-free phone:* 800-527-9090. *Fax:* 828-884-3790. *E-mail:* admissions@brevard.edu.

Cabarrus College of Health Sciences
Concord, North Carolina
http://www.cabarruscollege.edu/

- **Independent** comprehensive, founded 1942
- **Suburban** 5-acre campus with easy access to Charlotte
- **Endowment** $2.0 million
- **Coed, primarily women**
- **Moderately difficult** entrance level

ACADEMICS
Calendar: semesters. *Degrees:* certificates, diplomas, associate, bachelor's, and master's.

Library: Cabarrus College Information Resource Center plus 1 other. Study areas open 24 hours, 5–7 days a week.

STUDENT LIFE
Housing options: college housing not available.
Activities and organizations: Rotaract Service Club, Cabarrus College Association of Nursing Students, Student Government Association, Honor Society, Christian Student Union.
Campus security: 24-hour emergency response devices and patrols.
Student services: health clinic, personal/psychological counseling.

COSTS
Costs (2017–18) *Tuition:* $12,306 full-time, $395 per credit hour part-time. Full-time tuition and fees vary according to course load. Part-time tuition and fees vary according to course load. *Required fees:* $320 full-time, $125 per term part-time.

APPLYING
Standardized Tests *Required:* SAT or ACT (for admission).
Options: electronic application.
Application fee: $50.
Required: essay or personal statement, high school transcript, minimum 2.0 GPA, 2 letters of recommendation. *Required for some:* interview. *Recommended:* minimum 3.0 GPA.

CONTACT
McKenzie Allen, Admissions Representative, Cabarrus College of Health Sciences, 401 Medical Park Drive, Concord, NC 28025-2077. *Phone:* 704-403-2589. *Fax:* 704-403-2077. *E-mail:* mckenzie.allen@ cabarruscollege.edu.

Campbell University
Buies Creek, North Carolina
http://www.campbell.edu/

CONTACT
Ms. Peggy Mason, Director of Admissions, Campbell University, PO Box 546, 450 Leslie Campbell Avenue, Buies Creek, NC 27506. *Phone:* 910-893-1290. *Toll-free phone:* 800-334-4111. *Fax:* 910-893-1288. *E-mail:* adm@mailcenter.campbell.edu.

Carolina Christian College
Winston-Salem, North Carolina
http://www.carolina.edu/
- **Independent nondenominational** comprehensive, founded 1945
- **Small-town** 2-acre campus
- **Endowment** $250,000
- **Coed** 47 undergraduate students, 100% full-time, 45% women, 55% men
- **Noncompetitive** entrance level, 75% of applicants were admitted

UNDERGRAD STUDENTS
47 full-time. Students come from 5 states and territories; 10% are from out of state; 87% Black or African American, non-Hispanic/Latino; 2% Hispanic/Latino; 2% Two or more races, non-Hispanic/Latino; 9% transferred in.

Freshmen:
Admission: 12 applied, 9 admitted, 9 enrolled. *Average high school GPA:* 2.6.
Retention: 83% of full-time freshmen returned.

FACULTY
Total: 12, 17% full-time, 8% with terminal degrees.
Student/faculty ratio: 11:1.

ACADEMICS
Calendar: semesters. *Degrees:* associate, bachelor's, and master's.
Special study options: accelerated degree program, adult/continuing education programs, external degree program, part-time degree program.
Computers: 8 computers/terminals and 8 ports are available on campus for general student use. Students can access the following: free student e-mail accounts, online (class) registration. Campuswide network is available. Wireless service is available via entire campus.

Library: Aubrey Payne. *Books:* 14,200 (physical), 3,900 (digital/electronic); *Serial titles:* 1,006 (digital/electronic); *Databases:* 4. Weekly public service hours: 2.

STUDENT LIFE
Housing options: college housing not available.
Athletics Member NCCAA. except basketball (Division I-AA)
Campus security: 24-hour emergency response devices.
Student services: personal/psychological counseling.

COSTS & FINANCIAL AID
Costs (2018–19) *One-time required fee:* $75. *Tuition:* $12,500 full-time, $2750 per term part-time. *Required fees:* $1450 full-time, $600 per term part-time. *Payment plan:* installment. *Waivers:* employees or children of employees.
Financial Aid Of all full-time matriculated undergraduates who enrolled in 2017, 35 applied for aid, 35 were judged to have need, 32 had their need fully met. *Average percent of need met:* 95. *Average financial aid package:* $9500. *Average need-based loan:* $2000. *Average need-based gift aid:* $5290.

APPLYING
Options: electronic application.
Application fee: $50.
Required: essay or personal statement, high school transcript, 2 letters of recommendation, interview.
Application deadlines: rolling (freshmen), rolling (out-of-state freshmen), rolling (transfers).
Notification: continuous (freshmen), continuous (out-of-state freshmen), continuous (transfers).

CONTACT
Garriell Lucas, Admission Officer, Carolina Christian College, 4209 Indiana Ave., Winston-Salem, NC 27105. *Phone:* 336-744-0900.

Carolina College of Biblical Studies
Fayetteville, North Carolina
http://carolinabiblecollege.org/

CONTACT
Carolina College of Biblical Studies, 817 South McPherson Church Road, Fayetteville, NC 28303.

Catawba College
Salisbury, North Carolina
http://www.catawba.edu/
- **Independent** comprehensive, founded 1851, affiliated with United Church of Christ
- **Small-town** 276-acre campus with easy access to Charlotte, NC
- **Endowment** $61.9 million
- **Coed** 1,325 undergraduate students, 96% full-time, 53% women, 47% men
- **Moderately difficult** entrance level, 42% of applicants were admitted

UNDERGRAD STUDENTS
1,267 full-time, 58 part-time. Students come from 37 states and territories; 19 other countries; 19% are from out of state; 19% Black or African American, non-Hispanic/Latino; 7% Hispanic/Latino; 0.8% Asian, non-Hispanic/Latino; 0.1% Native Hawaiian or other Pacific Islander, non-Hispanic/Latino; 0.3% American Indian or Alaska Native, non-Hispanic/Latino; 3% Two or more races, non-Hispanic/Latino; 0.2% Race/ethnicity unknown; 4% international; 5% transferred in; 57% live on campus.

Freshmen:
Admission: 3,125 applied, 1,325 admitted, 332 enrolled. *Average high school GPA:* 3.8.
Retention: 73% of full-time freshmen returned.

FACULTY
Total: 159, 54% full-time, 50% with terminal degrees.
Student/faculty ratio: 12:1.

ACADEMICS

Calendar: semesters. *Degrees:* bachelor's and master's.

Special study options: advanced placement credit, double majors, honors programs, independent study, internships, part-time degree program, services for LD students, student-designed majors, study abroad, summer session for credit. *ROTC:* Army (c), Air Force (c).

Computers: 175 computers/terminals are available on campus for general student use. Students can access the following: campus intranet, computer help desk, free student e-mail accounts, online (class) grades, online (class) registration, online (class) schedules. Campuswide network is available. 100% of college-owned or -operated housing units are wired for high-speed Internet access. Wireless service is available via entire campus.

Library: Corriher-Linn-Black Memorial Library plus 1 other. *Books:* 149,877 (physical), 228,252 (digital/electronic); *Serial titles:* 12,505 (physical), 112,726 (digital/electronic); *Databases:* 100. Weekly public service hours: 83; students can reserve study rooms.

STUDENT LIFE

Housing options: on-campus residence required for freshman year; coed, men-only, women-only. Campus housing is university owned. Freshman campus housing is guaranteed.

Activities and organizations: drama/theater group, student-run newspaper, radio station, choral group, marching band, Volunteer Catawba, Catawba Ambassadors (admissions guides), Blue Masque (drama), Fellowship of Christian Athletes, Wigwam Productions (student activities board).

Athletics Member NCAA. All Division II. *Intercollegiate sports:* baseball M(s), basketball M(s)/W(s), cheerleading M(c)/W(c), cross-country running M(s)/W(s), football M(s), golf M(s)/W(s), lacrosse M(s)/W(s), soccer M(s)/W(s), softball W(s), swimming and diving M(s)/W(s), tennis M(s)/W(s), track and field M/W, volleyball W(s). *Intramural sports:* badminton M/W, basketball M/W, bowling M/W, football M, racquetball M/W, soccer M/W, softball M, table tennis M/W, tennis M/W, ultimate Frisbee M/W, volleyball M/W.

Campus security: 24-hour emergency response devices and patrols, late-night transport/escort service, controlled dormitory access.

Student services: health clinic, personal/psychological counseling.

COSTS & FINANCIAL AID

Costs (2018–19) *Comprehensive fee:* $41,008 includes full-time tuition ($30,520) and room and board ($10,488). Full-time tuition and fees vary according to class time, course load, and degree level. Part-time tuition and fees vary according to class time, course load, and degree level. *College room only:* $6188. *Payment plan:* installment. *Waivers:* employees or children of employees.

Financial Aid Of all full-time matriculated undergraduates who enrolled in 2016, 1,107 applied for aid, 1,020 were judged to have need, 269 had their need fully met. 115 Federal Work-Study jobs (averaging $1589). 124 state and other part-time jobs (averaging $1420). In 2016, 190 non-need-based awards were made. *Average percent of need met:* 78. *Average financial aid package:* $24,637. *Average need-based loan:* $4290. *Average need-based gift aid:* $6930. *Average non-need-based aid:* $15,130. *Average indebtedness upon graduation:* $31,471.

APPLYING

Options: electronic application, early admission, deferred entrance.

Required: essay or personal statement, high school transcript, minimum 2.0 GPA, 2 letters of recommendation. *Recommended:* interview.

Application deadlines: rolling (freshmen), rolling (transfers).

Notification: continuous (freshmen), continuous (transfers).

CONTACT

Catawba College, 2300 West Innes Street, Salisbury, NC 28144-2488. *Phone:* 704-645-4584. *Toll-free phone:* 800-CATAWBA.

Chamberlain College of Nursing
Charlotte, North Carolina
http://www.chamberlain.edu/

CONTACT

Chamberlain College of Nursing, 2015 Ayrsley Town Boulevard, Charlotte, NC 28273.

Charlotte Christian College and Theological Seminary
Charlotte, North Carolina
http://www.charlottechristian.edu/

- **Independent Christian** comprehensive, founded 1996
- **Urban** 3-acre campus with easy access to Charlotte, NC
- **Coed** 65 undergraduate students, 37% full-time, 66% women, 34% men

UNDERGRAD STUDENTS

24 full-time, 41 part-time. Students come from 9 states and territories; 8 other countries; 10% are from out of state; 83% Black or African American, non-Hispanic/Latino; 3% Asian, non-Hispanic/Latino; 4% international; 20% transferred in.

Freshmen:
Admission: 2 enrolled.
Retention: 67% of full-time freshmen returned.

FACULTY

Total: 24, 29% full-time, 75% with terminal degrees.
Student/faculty ratio: 5:1.

ACADEMICS

Calendar: quarters. *Degrees:* associate, bachelor's, master's, and doctoral.

Special study options: adult/continuing education programs, cooperative education, distance learning, double majors, independent study, off-campus study, part-time degree program, services for LD students, summer session for credit.

Computers: 2 ports are available on campus for general student use. Students can access the following: campus intranet, free student e-mail accounts, online (class) grades, online (class) registration, online (class) schedules, class syllabi. Campuswide network is available. Wireless service is available via entire campus.

Library: CCCTS Library. *Books:* 26,489 (physical), 1,100 (digital/electronic); *Serial titles:* 30 (physical). Weekly public service hours: 50.

STUDENT LIFE

Housing options: college housing not available.

Campus security: 24-hour emergency response devices.

COSTS & FINANCIAL AID

Costs (2018–19) *Tuition:* $10,048 full-time, $454 per credit hour part-time. Full-time tuition and fees vary according to course load and program. Part-time tuition and fees vary according to course load and program. No tuition increase for student's term of enrollment. *Required fees:* $420 full-time, $420 per year part-time. *Payment plan:* installment. *Waivers:* employees or children of employees.

Financial Aid Of all full-time matriculated undergraduates who enrolled in 2016, 3 applied for aid, 3 were judged to have need, 3 had their need fully met. 2 Federal Work-Study jobs (averaging $4714). *Average percent of need met:* 100. *Average financial aid package:* $5092. *Average need-based loan:* $3500. *Average need-based gift aid:* $2960. *Average indebtedness upon graduation:* $33,034.

APPLYING

Options: electronic application.

Application fee: $50.

Required: essay or personal statement, high school transcript, letters of recommendation, certification of Church membership and involvement.

Application deadlines: rolling (freshmen), rolling (out-of-state freshmen), rolling (transfers).

Notification: continuous (freshmen), continuous (out-of-state freshmen), continuous (transfers).

CONTACT

Mr. George Shears, Director of Admissions, Charlotte Christian College and Theological Seminary, P.O. Box 790106, Charlotte, NC 28206. *Phone:* 704-334-6882 Ext. 115. *Fax:* 704-334-6885. *E-mail:* gshears@charlottechristian.edu.

Chowan University

Murfreesboro, North Carolina

http://www.chowan.edu/

- **Independent Baptist** comprehensive, founded 1848
- **Small-town** 300-acre campus with easy access to Norfolk
- **Endowment** $26.1 million
- **Coed** 1,498 undergraduate students, 96% full-time, 53% women, 47% men
- **Minimally difficult** entrance level, 60% of applicants were admitted

UNDERGRAD STUDENTS

1,440 full-time, 58 part-time. Students come from 31 states and territories; 22 other countries; 41% are from out of state; 70% Black or African American, non-Hispanic/Latino; 4% Hispanic/Latino; 0.3% Asian, non-Hispanic/Latino; 0.3% Native Hawaiian or other Pacific Islander, non-Hispanic/Latino; 0.7% American Indian or Alaska Native, non-Hispanic/Latino; 2% Two or more races, non-Hispanic/Latino; 3% Race/ethnicity unknown; 3% international; 4% transferred in; 89% live on campus.

Freshmen:
Admission: 4,379 applied, 2,629 admitted, 526 enrolled. *Average high school GPA:* 2.7. *Test scores:* SAT evidence-based reading and writing scores over 500: 20%; SAT math scores over 500: 18%; ACT scores over 18: 24%; SAT evidence-based reading and writing scores over 600: 2%; SAT math scores over 600: 1%; ACT scores over 24: 4%.
Retention: 48% of full-time freshmen returned.

FACULTY
Total: 132, 51% full-time, 39% with terminal degrees.
Student/faculty ratio: 16:1.

ACADEMICS
Calendar: semesters. *Degrees:* associate, bachelor's, and master's.
Special study options: academic remediation for entering students, advanced placement credit, cooperative education, double majors, freshman honors college, honors programs, independent study, internships, part-time degree program, services for LD students, student-designed majors, study abroad, summer session for credit.
Computers: 251 computers/terminals and 13 ports are available on campus for general student use. Students can access the following: campus intranet, computer help desk, free student e-mail accounts, online (class) grades, online (class) registration, online (class) schedules. Campuswide network is available. 100% of college-owned or -operated housing units are wired for high-speed Internet access. Wireless service is available via entire campus.
Library: Whitaker Library plus 1 other. *Books:* 163,497 (physical), 405,678 (digital/electronic); *Serial titles:* 1,310 (physical), 69,556 (digital/electronic); *Databases:* 135. Weekly public service hours: 84; students can reserve study rooms.

STUDENT LIFE
Housing options: on-campus residence required through sophomore year; men-only, women-only. Campus housing is university owned. Freshman campus housing is guaranteed.
Activities and organizations: drama/theater group, student-run newspaper, choral group, Honors Societies, Rotaract, Campus Ministry, Psychology Club, Science Club, national fraternities, national sororities.
Athletics Member NCAA, NCCAA. All NCAA Division II.
Intercollegiate sports: baseball M(s), basketball M(s)/W(s), bowling W(s), cheerleading M/W, cross-country running M(s)/W(s), football M(s), golf M(s)/W(s), lacrosse M(s)/W(s), soccer M(s)/W(s), softball W(s), swimming and diving W(s), tennis M(s)/W(s), volleyball W(s).
Intramural sports: basketball M/W, football M/W, racquetball M/W, soccer M/W, softball M/W, table tennis M/W, tennis M/W, volleyball M/W.
Campus security: 24-hour emergency response devices and patrols, late-night transport/escort service, controlled dormitory access.
Student services: health clinic, personal/psychological counseling.

COSTS & FINANCIAL AID
Costs (2018–19) *Comprehensive fee:* $34,380 includes full-time tuition ($24,980) and room and board ($9400). Part-time tuition: $400 per credit hour. *Room and board:* Room and board charges vary according to board plan. *Payment plan:* installment. *Waivers:* employees or children of employees.
Financial Aid Of all full-time matriculated undergraduates who enrolled in 2017, 1,427 applied for aid, 1,379 were judged to have need, 114 had their need fully met. 271 Federal Work-Study jobs (averaging $1449). 194 state and other part-time jobs (averaging $2669). In 2017, 48 non-need-based awards were made. *Average percent of need met:* 66. *Average financial aid package:* $21,151. *Average need-based loan:* $3295. *Average need-based gift aid:* $16,993. *Average non-need-based aid:* $6088. *Average indebtedness upon graduation:* $38,443.

APPLYING
Standardized Tests *Required:* SAT or ACT (for admission).
Options: electronic application.
Application fee: $20.
Required: high school transcript. *Required for some:* essay or personal statement, interview. *Recommended:* minimum 2.0 GPA, 2 letters of recommendation.
Application deadlines: rolling (freshmen), rolling (transfers).
Notification: continuous (freshmen), continuous (transfers).

CONTACT
Mr. Scott Parker Esq., Director of Admissions Information, Chowan University, One University Place, Murfreesboro, NC 27855. *Phone:* 252-398-6314. *Toll-free phone:* 888-4-CHOWAN. *Fax:* 252-398-1190. *E-mail:* parkes@chowan.edu.

Davidson College

Davidson, North Carolina

http://www.davidson.edu/

- **Independent Presbyterian** 4-year, founded 1837
- **Small-town** 665-acre campus with easy access to Charlotte
- **Endowment** $730.4 million
- **Coed** 1,796 undergraduate students, 100% full-time, 49% women, 51% men
- **Very difficult** entrance level, 20% of applicants were admitted

UNDERGRAD STUDENTS

1,796 full-time. Students come from 49 states and territories; 49 other countries; 77% are from out of state; 7% Black or African American, non-Hispanic/Latino; 7% Hispanic/Latino; 5% Asian, non-Hispanic/Latino; 0.7% American Indian or Alaska Native, non-Hispanic/Latino; 4% Two or more races, non-Hispanic/Latino; 2% Race/ethnicity unknown; 7% international; 0.7% transferred in; 98% live on campus.

Freshmen:
Admission: 5,618 applied, 1,130 admitted, 514 enrolled. *Average high school GPA:* 3.9. *Test scores:* ACT scores over 18: 100%; ACT scores over 24: 99%; ACT scores over 30: 64%.
Retention: 94% of full-time freshmen returned.

FACULTY
Total: 189, 98% full-time, 97% with terminal degrees.
Student/faculty ratio: 10:1.

ACADEMICS
Calendar: semesters. *Degree:* bachelor's.
Special study options: advanced placement credit, double majors, independent study, internships, off-campus study, services for LD students, student-designed majors, study abroad. *ROTC:* Army (b), Air Force (c).
Unusual degree programs: 3-2 engineering with Columbia University, Washington University in St. Louis.
Computers: 180 computers/terminals are available on campus for general student use. Students can access the following: campus intranet, computer help desk, free student e-mail accounts, online (class) grades, online (class) registration, online (class) schedules. Campuswide network is available. 100% of college-owned or -operated housing units are wired for high-speed Internet access. Wireless service is available via entire campus.
Library: E. H. Little Library plus 1 other. Study areas open 24 hours, 5–7 days a week; students can reserve study rooms.

STUDENT LIFE

Housing options: on-campus residence required through senior year; coed, cooperative. Campus housing is university owned. Freshman campus housing is guaranteed.

Activities and organizations: drama/theater group, student-run newspaper, radio station, choral group, Inter-Varsity Christian Fellowship, Dean Rusk Program Student Advisory Council, music organizations, Community Service Council, Student Government Association, national fraternities, national sororities.

Athletics Member NCAA. All Division I except football (Division I-AA). *Intercollegiate sports:* baseball M(s), basketball M(s)/W(s), crew M(c)/W(c), cross-country running M(s)/W(s), fencing M(c)/W(c), field hockey W(s), golf M(s), lacrosse W(s), rugby M(c), sailing M(c)/W(c), soccer M(s)/W(s), swimming and diving M(s)/W(s), tennis M(s)/W(s), track and field M(s)/W(s), ultimate Frisbee M(c)/W(c), volleyball W(s), weight lifting M(c)/W(c), wrestling M(s). *Intramural sports:* basketball M/W, equestrian sports W(c), field hockey M(c)/W(c), football M/W, lacrosse M(c)/W(c), soccer M(c)/W(c), softball M/W, swimming and diving M(c)/W(c), tennis M(c)/W(c), volleyball M/W(c), water polo M(c).

Campus security: 24-hour emergency response devices and patrols, late-night transport/escort service, controlled dormitory access.

Student services: health clinic, personal/psychological counseling, women's center.

COSTS & FINANCIAL AID

Costs (2017–18) *Comprehensive fee:* $63,903 includes full-time tuition ($49,454), mandatory fees ($495), and room and board ($13,954). *College room only:* $7102. Room and board charges vary according to board plan. *Payment plan:* installment. *Waivers:* employees or children of employees.

Financial Aid Of all full-time matriculated undergraduates who enrolled in 2017, 1,079 applied for aid, 904 were judged to have need, 904 had their need fully met. 348 Federal Work-Study jobs (averaging $2059). 194 state and other part-time jobs (averaging $1729). In 2017, 118 non-need-based awards were made. *Average percent of need met:* 100. *Average financial aid package:* $47,803. *Average need-based loan:* $3770. *Average need-based gift aid:* $44,434. *Average non-need-based aid:* $24,739. *Average indebtedness upon graduation:* $20,431. *Financial aid deadline:* 2/15.

APPLYING

Standardized Tests *Required:* SAT or ACT (for admission). *Recommended:* SAT and SAT Subject Tests or ACT (for admission).

Options: electronic application, early admission, early decision, deferred entrance.

Application fee: $50.

Required: essay or personal statement, high school transcript, 3 letters of recommendation. *Recommended:* interview.

Application deadlines: 1/2 (freshmen), 3/15 (transfers).

Early decision deadline: 11/15 (for plan 1), 1/2 (for plan 2).

Notification: 4/1 (freshmen), 5/15 (transfers), 12/15 (early decision plan 1), 2/1 (early decision plan 2).

CONTACT

Mr. Christopher J. Gruber, Vice President and Dean of Admission and Financial Aid, Davidson College, Box 7156, Davidson, NC 28035-7156. *Phone:* 704-894-2230. *Toll-free phone:* 800-768-0380. *Fax:* 704-894-2016. *E-mail:* admission@davidson.edu.

DeVry University–Charlotte Campus
Charlotte, North Carolina
http://www.devry.edu/

CONTACT

Admissions Office, DeVry University–Charlotte Campus, 2015 Ayrsley Town Boulevard, Suite 109, Charlotte, NC 28273-4068. *Phone:* 704-362-2345. *Toll-free phone:* 866-338-7934.

Duke University
Durham, North Carolina
http://www.duke.edu/

- **Independent** university, founded 1838, affiliated with United Methodist Church
- **Suburban** 8500-acre campus
- **Coed**
- **Most difficult** entrance level

FACULTY

Student/faculty ratio: 6:1.

ACADEMICS

Calendar: semesters. *Degrees:* bachelor's, master's, doctoral, post-master's, and postbachelor's certificates.

Library: Perkins Library.

STUDENT LIFE

Housing options: on-campus residence required through junior year; coed, men-only, women-only. Campus housing is university owned. Freshman campus housing is guaranteed.

Activities and organizations: drama/theater group, student-run newspaper, radio and television station, choral group, marching band, national fraternities, national sororities.

Athletics Member NCAA. All Division I except football (Division I-A).

Campus security: 24-hour emergency response devices and patrols, late-night transport/escort service, controlled dormitory access.

Student services: health clinic, personal/psychological counseling, women's center, legal services.

COSTS & FINANCIAL AID

Costs (2017–18) *Comprehensive fee:* $68,298 includes full-time tuition ($51,720), mandatory fees ($1780), and room and board ($14,798). Part-time tuition: $1616 per credit hour. *College room only:* $8494. Room and board charges vary according to board plan and housing facility. *Payment plans:* tuition prepayment, installment.

Financial Aid Of all full-time matriculated undergraduates who enrolled in 2017, 3,461 applied for aid, 2,932 were judged to have need, 2,932 had their need fully met. 1,917 Federal Work-Study jobs (averaging $2045). 540 state and other part-time jobs (averaging $1933). In 2017, 215 non-need-based awards were made. *Average percent of need met:* 100. *Average financial aid package:* $52,745. *Average need-based loan:* $3289. *Average need-based gift aid:* $47,556. *Average non-need-based aid:* $69,506. *Average indebtedness upon graduation:* $23,819. *Financial aid deadline:* 2/1.

APPLYING

Standardized Tests *Required:* SAT and SAT Subject Tests or ACT (for admission).

Options: electronic application, early decision.

Application fee: $85.

Required: essay or personal statement, high school transcript. *Required for some:* audition tape for dance, drama, or music; slides of work for art. *Recommended:* interview.

CONTACT

Mr. Christoph Guttentag, Director of Admissions, Duke University, Durham, NC 27708-0586. *Phone:* 919-684-3214. *E-mail:* askduke@admiss.duke.edu.

East Carolina University
Greenville, North Carolina
http://www.ecu.edu/

- **State-supported** university, founded 1907, part of University of North Carolina System
- **Urban** 1402-acre campus
- **Endowment** $185.8 million
- **Coed** 23,265 undergraduate students, 86% full-time, 57% women, 43% men
- **Moderately difficult** entrance level, 79% of applicants were admitted

UNDERGRAD STUDENTS

19,999 full-time, 3,266 part-time. Students come from 44 states and territories; 41 other countries; 10% are from out of state; 16% Black or African American, non-Hispanic/Latino; 7% Hispanic/Latino; 3% Asian, non-Hispanic/Latino; 0.1% Native Hawaiian or other Pacific Islander, non-Hispanic/Latino; 0.7% American Indian or Alaska Native, non-Hispanic/Latino; 4% Two or more races, non-Hispanic/Latino; 3% Race/ethnicity unknown; 0.6% international; 8% transferred in; 29% live on campus.

Freshmen:

Admission: 16,007 applied, 12,615 admitted, 4,362 enrolled. *Average high school GPA:* 3.8. *Test scores:* SAT evidence-based reading and writing scores over 500: 90%; SAT math scores over 500: 88%; ACT scores over 18: 99%; SAT evidence-based reading and writing scores over 600: 22%; SAT math scores over 600: 20%; ACT scores over 24: 28%; SAT evidence-based reading and writing scores over 700: 1%; SAT math scores over 700: 1%; ACT scores over 30: 3%.

Retention: 83% of full-time freshmen returned.

FACULTY

Total: 1,502, 79% full-time, 75% with terminal degrees.
Student/faculty ratio: 19:1.

ACADEMICS

Calendar: semesters. *Degrees:* bachelor's, master's, doctoral, post-master's, and postbachelor's certificates.

Special study options: academic remediation for entering students, accelerated degree program, adult/continuing education programs, advanced placement credit, cooperative education, distance learning, double majors, English as a second language, freshman honors college, honors programs, independent study, internships, off-campus study, part-time degree program, services for LD students, student-designed majors, study abroad, summer session for credit. *ROTC:* Army (b), Air Force (b).

Unusual degree programs: 3-2 business administration.

Computers: 2,760 computers/terminals and 2,760 ports are available on campus for general student use. Students can access the following: campus intranet, computer help desk, free student e-mail accounts, online (class) grades, online (class) registration, online (class) schedules. Campuswide network is available. 100% of college-owned or -operated housing units are wired for high-speed Internet access. Wireless service is available via entire campus.

Library: Joyner Library plus 1 other. *Books:* 1.2 million (physical), 827,747 (digital/electronic); *Serial titles:* 8,311 (physical), 91,772 (digital/electronic); *Databases:* 507. Weekly public service hours: 143; study areas open 24 hours, 5–7 days a week; students can reserve study rooms.

STUDENT LIFE

Housing options: on-campus residence required for freshman year; coed, women-only, special housing for students with disabilities. Campus housing is university owned. Freshman campus housing is guaranteed.

Activities and organizations: drama/theater group, student-run newspaper, radio and television station, choral group, marching band, Student Government Association, Student Activities Board, Residence Hall Association, Student Pirate Club, Black Student Union, national fraternities, national sororities.

Athletics Member NCAA. All Division I. *Intercollegiate sports:* baseball M(s), basketball M(s)/W(s), cross-country running M(s)/W(s), football M(s), golf M(s)/W(s), lacrosse W(s), soccer W(s), softball W(s), swimming and diving M(s)/W(s), tennis M(s)/W(s), track and field M(s)/W(s), volleyball W(s). *Intramural sports:* badminton M(c)/W(c), baseball M(c), basketball M/W, bowling M/W, cheerleading W(c), cross-country running M(c)/W(c), equestrian sports M(c)/W(c), fencing M(c)/W(c), field hockey M(c)/W(c), football M/W, golf M(c)/W(c), ice hockey M(c)/W(c), lacrosse M(c)/W(c), racquetball M/W, rock climbing M(c)/W(c), rugby M(c)/W(c), skiing (downhill) M(c)/W(c), soccer M/W, softball M/W, swimming and diving M(c)/W(c), table tennis M/W, tennis M/W, ultimate Frisbee M(c)/W(c), volleyball M/W, weight lifting M(c)/W(c), wrestling M(c)/W(c).

Campus security: 24-hour emergency response devices and patrols, student patrols, late-night transport/escort service, controlled dormitory access, Operation ID, Staff and Faculty Eyes, ECU Alert, self-defense classes, ECU CARES.

Student services: health clinic, personal/psychological counseling, women's center, legal services.

COSTS & FINANCIAL AID

Costs (2017–18) *Tuition:* state resident $4452 full-time, $247 per credit hour part-time; nonresident $20,729 full-time, $1151 per credit hour part-time. Full-time tuition and fees vary according to location and program. Part-time tuition and fees vary according to course load, location, and program. No tuition increase for student's term of enrollment. *Required fees:* $2691 full-time. *Room and board:* $9835; room only: $5623. Room and board charges vary according to board plan and housing facility. *Payment plans:* installment, deferred payment. *Waivers:* employees or children of employees.

Financial Aid Of all full-time matriculated undergraduates who enrolled in 2017, 14,796 applied for aid, 12,079 were judged to have need, 1,044 had their need fully met. 436 Federal Work-Study jobs (averaging $3189). In 2017, 274 non-need-based awards were made. *Average percent of need met:* 61. *Average financial aid package:* $10,383. *Average need-based loan:* $7040. *Average need-based gift aid:* $7702. *Average non-need-based aid:* $3884. *Average indebtedness upon graduation:* $28,918.

APPLYING

Standardized Tests *Required:* SAT or ACT (for admission).

Options: electronic application, deferred entrance.

Application fee: $75.

Required: high school transcript, minimum 2.5 GPA.

Application deadlines: 3/1 (freshmen), 6/4 (transfers).

Notification: continuous (freshmen), continuous (transfers).

CONTACT

Undergraduate Admission, East Carolina University, Whichard Building 106, East Fifth Street, Greenville, NC 27858-4353. *Phone:* 252-328-6640. *E-mail:* admis@ecu.edu.

Elizabeth City State University

Elizabeth City, North Carolina

http://www.ecsu.edu/

- **State-supported** comprehensive, founded 1891, part of University of North Carolina System
- **Small-town** 200-acre campus with easy access to Norfolk
- **Endowment** $6.0 million
- **Coed**
- **Moderately difficult** entrance level

FACULTY

Student/faculty ratio: 14:1.

ACADEMICS

Calendar: semesters. *Degrees:* bachelor's and master's.
Library: G. R. Little Library plus 1 other. *Books:* 231,406 (physical), 184,579 (digital/electronic); *Serial titles:* 1,923 (physical), 22,828 (digital/electronic); *Databases:* 101. Weekly public service hours: 82.

STUDENT LIFE

Housing options: coed, men-only, women-only. Campus housing is university owned and leased by the school. Freshman campus housing is guaranteed.

Activities and organizations: drama/theater group, student-run newspaper, choral group, marching band, Vans (Vikings Assisting New Students), Student Activities Committee, Vike Nu' Fashion Troupe, Pep Squad, Essence of Praise, national fraternities, national sororities.

Athletics Member NCAA. All Division II.

Campus security: 24-hour emergency response devices and patrols, controlled dormitory access.

Student services: health clinic, personal/psychological counseling.

COSTS & FINANCIAL AID

Costs (2017–18) *Tuition:* state resident $2856 full-time, $357 per credit hour part-time; nonresident $16,000 full-time, $2000 per credit hour part-time. Full-time tuition and fees vary according to degree level. Part-time tuition and fees vary according to degree level. *Required fees:* $2284 full-time, $277 per term part-time. *Room and board:* $7948; room only: $4610. Room and board charges vary according to housing facility.

Financial Aid Of all full-time matriculated undergraduates who enrolled in 2016, 1,365 applied for aid, 1,277 were judged to have need, 11 had their need fully met. In 2016, 46 non-need-based awards were made. *Average percent of need met:* 59. *Average financial aid package:* $7833. *Average need-based loan:* $3949. *Average need-based gift aid:* $7143. *Average non-need-based aid:* $4540. *Average indebtedness upon graduation:* $19,631. *Financial aid deadline:* 6/1.

APPLYING
Standardized Tests *Required:* SAT or ACT (for admission).

Options: electronic application, deferred entrance.

Application fee: $30.

Required: high school transcript, minimum 2.3 GPA.

CONTACT
Mr. Darius Eure, Assistant Director, Admissions and Recruitment, Elizabeth City State University, 131 Marion D. Thorpe Administration Building Box 901, 1704 Weeksville Road, Elizabeth City, NC 27909. *Phone:* 252-335-8530. *Toll-free phone:* 800-347-3278. *Fax:* 252-335-3537. *E-mail:* ddeure@ecsu.edu.

Elon University
Elon, North Carolina
http://www.elon.edu/

- **Independent** comprehensive, founded 1889, affiliated with United Church of Christ
- **Suburban** 656-acre campus with easy access to Raleigh
- **Endowment** $230.4 million
- **Coed** 6,045 undergraduate students, 97% full-time, 60% women, 40% men
- **Moderately difficult** entrance level, 67% of applicants were admitted

UNDERGRAD STUDENTS
5,885 full-time, 160 part-time. Students come from 52 states and territories; 58 other countries; 82% are from out of state; 5% Black or African American, non-Hispanic/Latino; 6% Hispanic/Latino; 2% Asian, non-Hispanic/Latino; 0.1% American Indian or Alaska Native, non-Hispanic/Latino; 3% Two or more races, non-Hispanic/Latino; 0.3% Race/ethnicity unknown; 2% international; 1% transferred in; 64% live on campus.

Freshmen:
Admission: 9,623 applied, 6,402 admitted, 1,573 enrolled. *Average high school GPA:* 4.0. *Test scores:* SAT evidence-based reading and writing scores over 500: 98%; SAT math scores over 500: 97%; ACT scores over 18: 99%; SAT evidence-based reading and writing scores over 600: 66%; SAT math scores over 600: 56%; ACT scores over 24: 85%; SAT evidence-based reading and writing scores over 700: 13%; SAT math scores over 700: 9%; ACT scores over 30: 23%.

Retention: 89% of full-time freshmen returned.

FACULTY
Total: 599, 72% full-time, 76% with terminal degrees.

Student/faculty ratio: 12:1.

ACADEMICS
Calendar: semesters 3-week winter term. *Degrees:* bachelor's, master's, and doctoral.

Special study options: accelerated degree program, advanced placement credit, distance learning, double majors, English as a second language, honors programs, independent study, internships, off-campus study, part-time degree program, services for LD students, student-designed majors, study abroad, summer session for credit. *ROTC:* Army (b), Air Force (c).

Unusual degree programs: 3-2 engineering with East Carolina University, North Carolina State University, Georgia Tech, Penn State, Virginia Tech, University of Notre Dame, Columbia University, Washington University in St. Louis, North Carolina A&T State University, University of South Carolina.

Computers: 1,200 computers/terminals and 10,000 ports are available on campus for general student use. Students can access the following: computer help desk, free student e-mail accounts, online (class) grades, online (class) registration, online (class) schedules. Campuswide network is available. 100% of college-owned or -operated housing units are wired for high-speed Internet access. Wireless service is available via entire campus.

Library: Carol Grotnes Belk. *Books:* 401,760 (physical), 1.3 million (digital/electronic); *Serial titles:* 217 (physical), 64,848 (digital/electronic); *Databases:* 179. Weekly public service hours: 143; study areas open 24 hours, 5–7 days a week; students can reserve study rooms.

STUDENT LIFE
Housing options: on-campus residence required through sophomore year; coed, men-only, women-only. Campus housing is university owned and leased by the school. Freshman campus housing is guaranteed.

Activities and organizations: drama/theater group, student-run newspaper, radio and television station, choral group, marching band, Elon Volunteers, Student Media, Intramural Athletics, Religious Life, Habitat for Humanity, national fraternities, national sororities.

Athletics Member NCAA. All Division I except football (Division I-AA). *Intercollegiate sports:* baseball M(s), basketball M(s)/W(s), cheerleading M/W, cross-country running M(s)/W(s), equestrian sports M(c)/W(c), field hockey W(c), golf M(s)/W(s), ice hockey M(c), lacrosse M(c)/W(s), rock climbing M(c), rugby M(c)/W(c), soccer M(s)/W(s), softball W(s), swimming and diving M(c)/W(c), tennis M(s)/W(s), track and field W(s), triathlon M(c)/W(c), ultimate Frisbee M(c)/W(c), volleyball M(s)(c)/W(s). *Intramural sports:* basketball M/W, bowling M/W, fencing M/W, field hockey W, football M/W, golf M/W, lacrosse M/W, racquetball M/W, rock climbing M/W, sand volleyball M/W, soccer M/W, softball W, squash M/W, table tennis M/W, ultimate Frisbee M/W, volleyball M/W.

Campus security: 24-hour emergency response devices and patrols, late-night transport/escort service, controlled dormitory access, Student Transport Service (Safe Rides).

Student services: health clinic, personal/psychological counseling, women's center.

COSTS & FINANCIAL AID
Costs (2018–19) *Comprehensive fee:* $47,548 includes full-time tuition ($34,850), mandatory fees ($468), and room and board ($12,230). Part-time tuition: $1110 per credit hour. Part-time tuition and fees vary according to course load. *College room only:* $6020. Room and board charges vary according to board plan and housing facility. *Payment plan:* installment. *Waivers:* employees or children of employees.

Financial Aid Of all full-time matriculated undergraduates who enrolled in 2017, 2,685 applied for aid, 1,928 were judged to have need, 337 had their need fully met. 1,341 Federal Work-Study jobs (averaging $2369). In 2017, 1335 non-need-based awards were made. *Average percent of need met:* 62. *Average financial aid package:* $20,060. *Average need-based loan:* $4378. *Average need-based gift aid:* $15,476. *Average non-need-based aid:* $7889. *Average indebtedness upon graduation:* $30,458.

APPLYING
Standardized Tests *Required:* SAT or ACT (for admission).

Options: electronic application, early admission, early decision, early action, deferred entrance.

Application fee: $50.

Required: essay or personal statement, high school transcript, counselor evaluation form. *Required for some:* interview.

Application deadlines: 1/10 (freshmen), rolling (transfers), 11/10 (early action).

Early decision deadline: 11/1.

Notification: 3/20 (freshmen), continuous (transfers), 12/1 (early decision), 12/20 (early action).

CONTACT
Ms. Melinda Wood, Senior Associate Dean of Admissions, Elon University, 2700 Campus Box, Elon, NC 27244. *Phone:* 336-278-3566. *Toll-free phone:* 800-334-8448. *Fax:* 336-278-7699. *E-mail:* admissions@elon.edu.

Fayetteville State University

Fayetteville, North Carolina
http://www.uncfsu.edu/

- **State-supported** comprehensive, founded 1867, part of University of North Carolina System
- **Urban** 156-acre campus with easy access to Raleigh
- **Endowment** $21.2 million
- **Coed** 5,393 undergraduate students, 72% full-time, 60% women, 40% men
- **Minimally difficult** entrance level, 67% of applicants were admitted

UNDERGRAD STUDENTS

3,905 full-time, 1,488 part-time. Students come from 40 states and territories; 13 other countries; 7% are from out of state; 63% Black or African American, non-Hispanic/Latino; 7% Hispanic/Latino; 2% Asian, non-Hispanic/Latino; 0.2% Native Hawaiian or other Pacific Islander, non-Hispanic/Latino; 3% American Indian or Alaska Native, non-Hispanic/Latino; 2% Two or more races, non-Hispanic/Latino; 5% Race/ethnicity unknown; 0.3% international; 15% transferred in; 28% live on campus.

Freshmen:
Admission: 3,882 applied, 2,620 admitted, 670 enrolled. *Average high school GPA:* 3.3.
Retention: 78% of full-time freshmen returned.

FACULTY
Total: 333, 80% full-time, 71% with terminal degrees.
Student/faculty ratio: 15:1.

ACADEMICS
Calendar: semesters. *Degrees:* bachelor's, master's, and doctoral.

Special study options: academic remediation for entering students, accelerated degree program, adult/continuing education programs, advanced placement credit, cooperative education, distance learning, double majors, honors programs, independent study, internships, part-time degree program, services for LD students, study abroad, summer session for credit. *ROTC:* Army (c), Air Force (b).

Unusual degree programs: 3-2 engineering with North Carolina State University.

Computers: 600 computers/terminals and 2,400 ports are available on campus for general student use. Students can access the following: campus intranet, computer help desk, free student e-mail accounts, online (class) grades, online (class) registration, online (class) schedules. Campuswide network is available. 100% of college-owned or -operated housing units are wired for high-speed Internet access. Wireless service is available via classrooms, computer centers, computer labs, learning centers, libraries, student centers.
Library: Charles W. Chestnut Library. *Books:* 218,500 (physical), 225,740 (digital/electronic); *Serial titles:* 298 (physical), 30,747 (digital/electronic); *Databases:* 427. Weekly public service hours: 97; students can reserve study rooms.

STUDENT LIFE
Housing options: coed, men-only, women-only, special housing for students with disabilities. Campus housing is university owned. Freshman applicants given priority for college housing.

Activities and organizations: drama/theater group, student-run newspaper, radio station, choral group, marching band, Student Government Association, Student Activities Council, Pan-Hellenic Council, Residence Hall Association, Illusions and Black Millennium Modeling Clubs, national fraternities, national sororities.

Athletics Member NCAA. All Division II. *Intercollegiate sports:* basketball M(s)/W(s), bowling W, cross-country running M(s)/W(s), football M(s), golf M(s)/W, softball W(s), tennis M/W(s), track and field M/W(s), volleyball W(s). *Intramural sports:* baseball M, basketball M/W, bowling M/W, football M, golf M/W, gymnastics M/W, swimming and diving M/W, tennis M, volleyball M/W.

Campus security: 24-hour emergency response devices and patrols, late-night transport/escort service, controlled dormitory access.

Student services: health clinic, personal/psychological counseling.

COSTS & FINANCIAL AID
Costs (2017–18) *Tuition:* state resident $2982 full-time; nonresident $14,590 full-time. Full-time tuition and fees vary according to course level, course load, degree level, location, and program. Part-time tuition and fees vary according to course level, course load, degree level, location, and program. *Required fees:* $2226 full-time. *Room and board:* $7996; room only: $4173. Room and board charges vary according to board plan and housing facility. *Payment plan:* installment. *Waivers:* senior citizens and employees or children of employees.

Financial Aid Of all full-time matriculated undergraduates who enrolled in 2014, 3,562 applied for aid, 3,380 were judged to have need, 373 had their need fully met. In 2014, 2 non-need-based awards were made. *Average percent of need met:* 70. *Average financial aid package:* $10,632. *Average need-based loan:* $4232. *Average need-based gift aid:* $7083. *Average non-need-based aid:* $750. *Average indebtedness upon graduation:* $25,215. *Financial aid deadline:* 3/1.

APPLYING
Standardized Tests *Required:* SAT or ACT (for admission).

Options: electronic application, early admission, early decision, early action, deferred entrance.

Application fee: $40.

Required: high school transcript, minimum 2.5 GPA. *Recommended:* essay or personal statement.

Application deadlines: 6/30 (freshmen), 6/30 (transfers).

Notification: continuous (freshmen), continuous (transfers).

CONTACT
Fayetteville State University, 1200 Murchison Road, Fayetteville, NC 28301-4298. *Phone:* 910-672-1371. *Toll-free phone:* 800-222-2594. *Fax:* 910-672-1414.

Gardner-Webb University

Boiling Springs, North Carolina
http://www.gardner-webb.edu/

- **Independent Baptist** university, founded 1905
- **Small-town** 250-acre campus with easy access to Charlotte
- **Endowment** $51.1 million
- **Coed**
- **Moderately difficult** entrance level

FACULTY
Student/faculty ratio: 13:1.

ACADEMICS
Calendar: semesters. *Degrees:* certificates, associate, bachelor's, master's, and doctoral.
Library: Dover Memorial Library plus 1 other.

STUDENT LIFE
Housing options: on-campus residence required through junior year; men-only, women-only, special housing for students with disabilities. Campus housing is university owned. Freshman campus housing is guaranteed.

Activities and organizations: drama/theater group, student-run newspaper, radio station, choral group, marching band, Campus Ministries United, Student Government Association, Dawg Pound, Honors Student Association, International Club.

Athletics Member NCAA. All Division I except football (Division I-AA).

Campus security: 24-hour emergency response devices and patrols, student patrols, late-night transport/escort service, controlled dormitory access.

Student services: personal/psychological counseling.

COSTS & FINANCIAL AID
Costs (2017–18) *Comprehensive fee:* $35,830 includes full-time tuition ($30,310), mandatory fees ($420), and room and board ($5100). Part-time tuition: $482 per hour. *College room only:* $4980. Room and board charges vary according to board plan and housing facility.

Financial Aid Of all full-time matriculated undergraduates who enrolled in 2017, 1,180 applied for aid, 1,068 were judged to have need, 215 had their need fully met. 297 Federal Work-Study jobs (averaging $1341). 26 state and other part-time jobs (averaging $1402). In 2017, 325 non-need-based awards were made. *Average percent of need met:* 75. *Average financial aid package:* $25,228. *Average need-based loan:* $4097. *Average need-based gift aid:* $8063. *Average non-need-based aid:* $12,416. *Average indebtedness upon graduation:* $31,926.

APPLYING

Standardized Tests *Required:* SAT or ACT (for admission).

Options: electronic application.

Application fee: $40.

Required: high school transcript, minimum 2.5 GPA. *Required for some:* 2 letters of recommendation, interview. *Recommended:* essay or personal statement, 2 letters of recommendation.

CONTACT

Associate Vice President of Undergraduate Admissions, Gardner-Webb University, PO Box 817, 110 South Main Street, Boiling Springs, NC 28017. *Phone:* 704-406-4491. *Toll-free phone:* 800-253-6472. *Fax:* 704-406-4488. *E-mail:* admissions@gardner-webb.edu.

Grace College of Divinity

Fayetteville, North Carolina

http://www.gcd.edu/

CONTACT

Grace College of Divinity, 5117 Cliffdale Road, Fayetteville, NC 28314.

Greensboro College

Greensboro, North Carolina

http://www.greensboro.edu/

- **Independent United Methodist** comprehensive, founded 1838
- **Urban** 75-acre campus with easy access to Charlotte
- **Endowment** $20.5 million
- **Coed** 894 undergraduate students
- **Minimally difficult** entrance level, 41% of applicants were admitted

UNDERGRAD STUDENTS

Students come from 17 states and territories; 11 other countries; 4% are from out of state; 32% Black or African American, non-Hispanic/Latino; 2% Hispanic/Latino; 0.9% Asian, non-Hispanic/Latino; 0.1% Native Hawaiian or other Pacific Islander, non-Hispanic/Latino; 0.2% American Indian or Alaska Native, non-Hispanic/Latino; 5% Two or more races, non-Hispanic/Latino; 7% Race/ethnicity unknown; 73% live on campus.

Freshmen:

Admission: 2,192 applied, 892 admitted. *Average high school GPA:* 3.4. *Test scores:* SAT evidence-based reading and writing scores over 500: 59%; SAT math scores over 500: 59%; ACT scores over 18: 64%; SAT evidence-based reading and writing scores over 600: 17%; SAT math scores over 600: 18%; ACT scores over 24: 19%; SAT evidence-based reading and writing scores over 700: 2%; SAT math scores over 700: 2%.

Retention: 55% of full-time freshmen returned.

FACULTY

Total: 84, 75% full-time.

Student/faculty ratio: 12:1.

ACADEMICS

Calendar: semesters. *Degrees:* certificates, bachelor's, master's, and postbachelor's certificates.

Special study options: academic remediation for entering students, accelerated degree program, adult/continuing education programs, advanced placement credit, double majors, English as a second language, freshman honors college, honors programs, independent study, internships, off-campus study, part-time degree program, services for LD students, student-designed majors, study abroad, summer session for credit. *ROTC:* Army (c), Air Force (c).

Computers: 180 computers/terminals and 325 ports are available on campus for general student use. Students can access the following: campus intranet, computer help desk, free student e-mail accounts, online (class) grades, online (class) schedules. Campuswide network is available. 100% of college-owned or -operated housing units are wired for high-speed Internet access. Wireless service is available via entire campus.

Library: James Addison Jones Library. *Books:* 77,657 (physical), 194,596 (digital/electronic). Weekly public service hours: 60; students can reserve study rooms.

STUDENT LIFE

Housing options: on-campus residence required through sophomore year; coed, men-only, women-only. Campus housing is university owned. Freshman campus housing is guaranteed.

Activities and organizations: drama/theater group, student-run newspaper, choral group, marching band, Pheta VI, Alpha Z Delta, Student Athletic Advisor Counsel, Pride Productions, United African American Society, national fraternities, national sororities.

Athletics Member NCAA. All Division III. *Intercollegiate sports:* baseball M, basketball M/W, cheerleading M/W, football M, golf M/W, lacrosse M/W, soccer M/W, softball W, swimming and diving M/W, tennis M/W, volleyball W, wrestling M. *Intramural sports:* basketball M/W, bowling M/W, football M/W, racquetball M/W, skiing (downhill) M/W, ultimate Frisbee M/W.

Campus security: 24-hour patrols, late-night transport/escort service, controlled dormitory access.

Student services: health clinic, personal/psychological counseling.

COSTS & FINANCIAL AID

Costs (2018–19) *Comprehensive fee:* $39,940 includes full-time tuition ($28,440), mandatory fees ($700), and room and board ($10,800). Full-time tuition and fees vary according to degree level and program. Part-time tuition and fees vary according to course load, degree level, and program. *Required fees:* $700 per year part-time. *Room and board:* Room and board charges vary according to housing facility. *Payment plan:* installment. *Waivers:* adult students, senior citizens, and employees or children of employees.

Financial Aid Of all full-time matriculated undergraduates who enrolled in 2015, 692 applied for aid, 673 were judged to have need, 54 had their need fully met. 131 Federal Work-Study jobs (averaging $717). In 2015, 24 non-need-based awards were made. *Average percent of need met:* 82. *Average financial aid package:* $20,493. *Average need-based loan:* $7623. *Average need-based gift aid:* $8148. *Average non-need-based aid:* $10,703. *Average indebtedness upon graduation:* $43,509.

APPLYING

Standardized Tests *Required:* SAT or ACT (for admission).

Options: electronic application, early admission, deferred entrance.

Required: high school transcript. *Required for some:* interview. *Recommended:* essay or personal statement.

Application deadlines: rolling (freshmen), rolling (transfers).

Notification: continuous (freshmen), continuous (transfers).

CONTACT

Greensboro College, 815 West Market Street, Greensboro, NC 27401-1875. *Toll-free phone:* 800-346-8226.

Guilford College

Greensboro, North Carolina

http://www.guilford.edu/

- **Independent** comprehensive, founded 1837, affiliated with Society of Friends
- **Suburban** 351-acre campus
- **Endowment** $74.5 million
- **Coed** 1,674 undergraduate students, 85% full-time, 53% women, 47% men
- **Moderately difficult** entrance level, 91% of applicants were admitted

UNDERGRAD STUDENTS

1,429 full-time, 245 part-time. Students come from 39 states and territories; 10 other countries; 29% are from out of state; 25% Black or African American, non-Hispanic/Latino; 9% Hispanic/Latino; 3% Asian, non-Hispanic/Latino; 0.1% Native Hawaiian or other Pacific Islander, non-Hispanic/Latino; 0.5% American Indian or Alaska Native, non-Hispanic/Latino; 4% Two or more races, non-Hispanic/Latino; 1% Race/ethnicity unknown; 1% international; 6% transferred in; 74% live on campus.

Freshmen:

Admission: 1,865 applied, 1,692 admitted, 343 enrolled. *Average high school GPA:* 3.2. *Test scores:* SAT evidence-based reading and writing scores over 500: 55%; SAT math scores over 500: 59%; ACT scores over 18: 86%; SAT evidence-based reading and writing scores over 600: 18%; SAT math scores over 600: 9%; ACT scores over 24: 38%; SAT evidence-based reading and writing scores over 700: 5%; ACT scores over 30: 9%.

Retention: 66% of full-time freshmen returned.

FACULTY

Total: 185, 55% full-time, 58% with terminal degrees.

Student/faculty ratio: 12:1.

ACADEMICS

Calendar: 4-1-4. *Degrees:* bachelor's, master's, and postbachelor's certificates.

Special study options: accelerated degree program, adult/continuing education programs, advanced placement credit, cooperative education, distance learning, double majors, honors programs, independent study, internships, off-campus study, part-time degree program, services for LD students, student-designed majors, study abroad, summer session for credit. *ROTC:* Army (c), Air Force (c).

Unusual degree programs: engineering; law with Elon University.

Computers: 275 computers/terminals are available on campus for general student use. Students can access the following: campus intranet, computer help desk, free student e-mail accounts, online (class) grades, online (class) registration, online (class) schedules, network storage. Campuswide network is available. 100% of college-owned or -operated housing units are wired for high-speed Internet access. Wireless service is available via entire campus.

Library: Hege Library. *Books:* 164,946 (physical), 326,808 (digital/electronic); *Serial titles:* 4,301 (physical), 45,891 (digital/electronic); *Databases:* 169. Weekly public service hours: 93; students can reserve study rooms.

STUDENT LIFE

Housing options: on-campus residence required through junior year; coed, women-only, cooperative, special housing for students with disabilities. Campus housing is university owned. Freshman campus housing is guaranteed.

Activities and organizations: drama/theater group, student-run newspaper, radio station, choral group, Student Government, Student Radio Station, Student Newspaper.

Athletics Member NCAA. All Division III. *Intercollegiate sports:* baseball M, basketball M/W, cross-country running M/W, football M, golf M, lacrosse M/W, soccer M/W, softball W, swimming and diving W, tennis M/W, track and field M/W, volleyball W. *Intramural sports:* badminton M(c)/W(c), basketball M(c), football M(c), rugby M(c)/W(c), soccer M(c)/W(c), table tennis M(c)/W(c), tennis M(c)/W(c), ultimate Frisbee M(c)/W(c), volleyball M(c)/W(c).

Campus security: 24-hour emergency response devices and patrols, student patrols, late-night transport/escort service, controlled dormitory access.

Student services: health clinic, personal/psychological counseling.

COSTS & FINANCIAL AID

Costs (2017–18) *Comprehensive fee:* $44,437 includes full-time tuition ($33,710), mandatory fees ($505), and room and board ($10,222). Full-time tuition and fees vary according to degree level and program. Part-time tuition: $1032 per credit hour. Part-time tuition and fees vary according to degree level and program. No tuition increase for student's term of enrollment. *Required fees:* $205 per term part-time. *College room only:* $5000. Room and board charges vary according to board plan and housing facility. *Payment plan:* installment. *Waivers:* employees or children of employees.

Financial Aid Of all full-time matriculated undergraduates who enrolled in 2016, 1,206 applied for aid, 1,073 were judged to have need, 597 had their need fully met. In 2016, 131 non-need-based awards were made. *Average percent of need met:* 74. *Average financial aid package:* $25,481. *Average need-based loan:* $3773. *Average need-based gift aid:* $4418. *Average non-need-based aid:* $9961. *Average indebtedness upon graduation:* $35,392.

APPLYING

Standardized Tests *Recommended:* SAT or ACT (for admission).

Options: electronic application, early admission, early decision, early action, deferred entrance.

Required: essay or personal statement, minimum 2.0 GPA. *Required for some:* high school transcript, 1 letter of recommendation. *Recommended:* minimum 3.0 GPA, interview.

Application deadlines: rolling (freshmen), rolling (out-of-state freshmen), rolling (transfers), 12/1 (early action).

Early decision deadline: 11/1.

Notification: continuous (freshmen), continuous (out-of-state freshmen), continuous (transfers), 11/15 (early decision), 12/15 (early action).

CONTACT
Mr. Kyle Wooden, Interim Director of Admission, Guilford College, 5800 West Friendly Avenue, Greensboro, NC 27410. *Phone:* 336-316-2000. *Toll-free phone:* 800-992-7759. *Fax:* 336-316-2954. *E-mail:* admission@guilford.edu.

Heritage Bible College
Dunn, North Carolina
http://www.heritagebiblecollege.edu/

- **Independent Pentecostal Free Will Baptist** 4-year, founded 1971
- **Small-town** 82-acre campus with easy access to Raleigh-Durham
- **Endowment** $53,446
- **Coed**
- **Minimally difficult** entrance level

ACADEMICS
Calendar: semesters. *Degrees:* associate and bachelor's.
Library: Alphin Ellis Learning Center plus 1 other. Students can reserve study rooms.

STUDENT LIFE
Housing options: coed. Campus housing is university owned.
Activities and organizations: choral group.

COSTS & FINANCIAL AID
Costs (2017–18) *One-time required fee:* $35. *Tuition:* $7560 full-time, $12 per credit hour part-time. *Required fees:* $768 full-time, $315 per credit hour part-time. *Room only:* $3100.

Financial Aid Of all full-time matriculated undergraduates who enrolled in 2015, 36 applied for aid, 36 were judged to have need, 3 had their need fully met. 3 Federal Work-Study jobs (averaging $1872). *Average percent of need met:* 54. *Average financial aid package:* $2739. *Average need-based loan:* $1712. *Average need-based gift aid:* $200. *Average indebtedness upon graduation:* $15,000. *Financial aid deadline:* 7/1.

APPLYING
Options: electronic application.
Application fee: $35.
Required: essay or personal statement, high school transcript, medical history required for all, immunization record required for some. *Required for some:* interview.

CONTACT
Ms. Iris Prince, Admissions Director, Heritage Bible College, PO Box 1628, Dunn, NC 28335-1628. *Phone:* 910-892-3178 Ext. 239. *Toll-free phone:* 800-297-6351. *Fax:* 910-891-1660. *E-mail:* iprince@heritagebiblecollege.edu.

★ High Point University
High Point, North Carolina
http://www.highpoint.edu/

- **Independent United Methodist** university, founded 1924
- **Suburban** 380-acre campus with easy access to Charlotte
- **Endowment** $49.8 million
- **Coed** 4,467 undergraduate students, 99% full-time, 59% women, 41% men
- **Moderately difficult** entrance level, 81% of applicants were admitted

UNDERGRAD STUDENTS

4,418 full-time, 49 part-time. Students come from 47 states and territories; 35 other countries; 78% are from out of state; 5% Black or African American, non-Hispanic/Latino; 5% Hispanic/Latino; 2% Asian, non-Hispanic/Latino; 0.2% American Indian or Alaska Native, non-Hispanic/Latino; 7% Two or more races, non-Hispanic/Latino; 2% Race/ethnicity unknown; 2% international; 1% transferred in; 94% live on campus.

Freshmen:

Admission: 8,936 applied, 7,208 admitted, 1,111 enrolled. *Average high school GPA:* 3.3. *Test scores:* SAT evidence-based reading and writing scores over 500: 89%; SAT math scores over 500: 88%; ACT scores over 18: 96%; SAT evidence-based reading and writing scores over 600: 36%; SAT math scores over 600: 37%; ACT scores over 24: 50%; SAT evidence-based reading and writing scores over 700: 3%; SAT math scores over 700: 5%; ACT scores over 30: 8%.

Retention: 79% of full-time freshmen returned.

FACULTY

Total: 462, 66% full-time, 63% with terminal degrees.
Student/faculty ratio: 14:1.

ACADEMICS

Calendar: semesters. *Degrees:* bachelor's, master's, doctoral, and postbachelor's certificates.

Special study options: accelerated degree program, advanced placement credit, cooperative education, double majors, English as a second language, honors programs, independent study, internships, services for LD students, student-designed majors, study abroad, summer session for credit. *ROTC:* Army (c), Air Force (c).

Unusual degree programs: 3-2 elementary education, strategic communication, athletic training.

Computers: 749 computers/terminals are available on campus for general student use. Students can access the following: campus intranet, computer help desk, free student e-mail accounts, online (class) grades, online (class) registration, online (class) schedules. Campuswide network is available. 100% of college-owned or -operated housing units are wired for high-speed Internet access. Wireless service is available via entire campus.

Library: Smith Library plus 1 other. *Books:* 181,000 (physical), 404,000 (digital/electronic); *Serial titles:* 56 (physical), 32,000 (digital/electronic); *Databases:* 195. Weekly public service hours: 168; study areas open 24 hours, 5–7 days a week; students can reserve study rooms.

STUDENT LIFE

Housing options: on-campus residence required through junior year; coed, men-only, women-only, cooperative, special housing for students with disabilities. Campus housing is university owned. Freshman campus housing is guaranteed.

Activities and organizations: drama/theater group, student-run newspaper, radio and television station, choral group, Big Brothers Big Sisters, Campus Activities Team, Purple Reign, Entrepreneurship Club, Volunteer Center, national fraternities, national sororities.

Athletics Member NCAA. All Division I. *Intercollegiate sports:* baseball M(s), basketball M(s)/W(s), cheerleading W, cross-country running M(s)/W(s), golf M(s)/W(s), lacrosse M(s)/W(s), soccer M(s)/W(s), track and field M(s)/W(s), volleyball W(s). *Intramural sports:* badminton M/W, baseball M(c), basketball M(c)/W(c), bowling M/W, crew M(c)/W(c), cross-country running M(c)/W(c), equestrian sports M(c)/W(c), field hockey W(c), football M/W, golf M(c)/W(c), ice hockey M(c), lacrosse M(c)/W(c), racquetball M/W, rowing M(c)/W(c), soccer M(c)/W(c), softball W(c), swimming and diving M(c)/W(c), tennis M(c)/W(c), ultimate Frisbee M(c), volleyball M(c)/W(c), water polo M/W, weight lifting M(c)/W(c).

Campus security: 24-hour emergency response devices and patrols, student patrols, late-night transport/escort service, controlled dormitory access.

Student services: health clinic, personal/psychological counseling.

COSTS & FINANCIAL AID

Costs (2018–19) *Comprehensive fee:* $49,248 includes full-time tuition ($30,748), mandatory fees ($4370), and room and board ($14,130). Full-time tuition and fees vary according to course load and reciprocity agreements. Part-time tuition: $955 per credit hour. Part-time tuition and fees vary according to course load and reciprocity agreements. *Required*

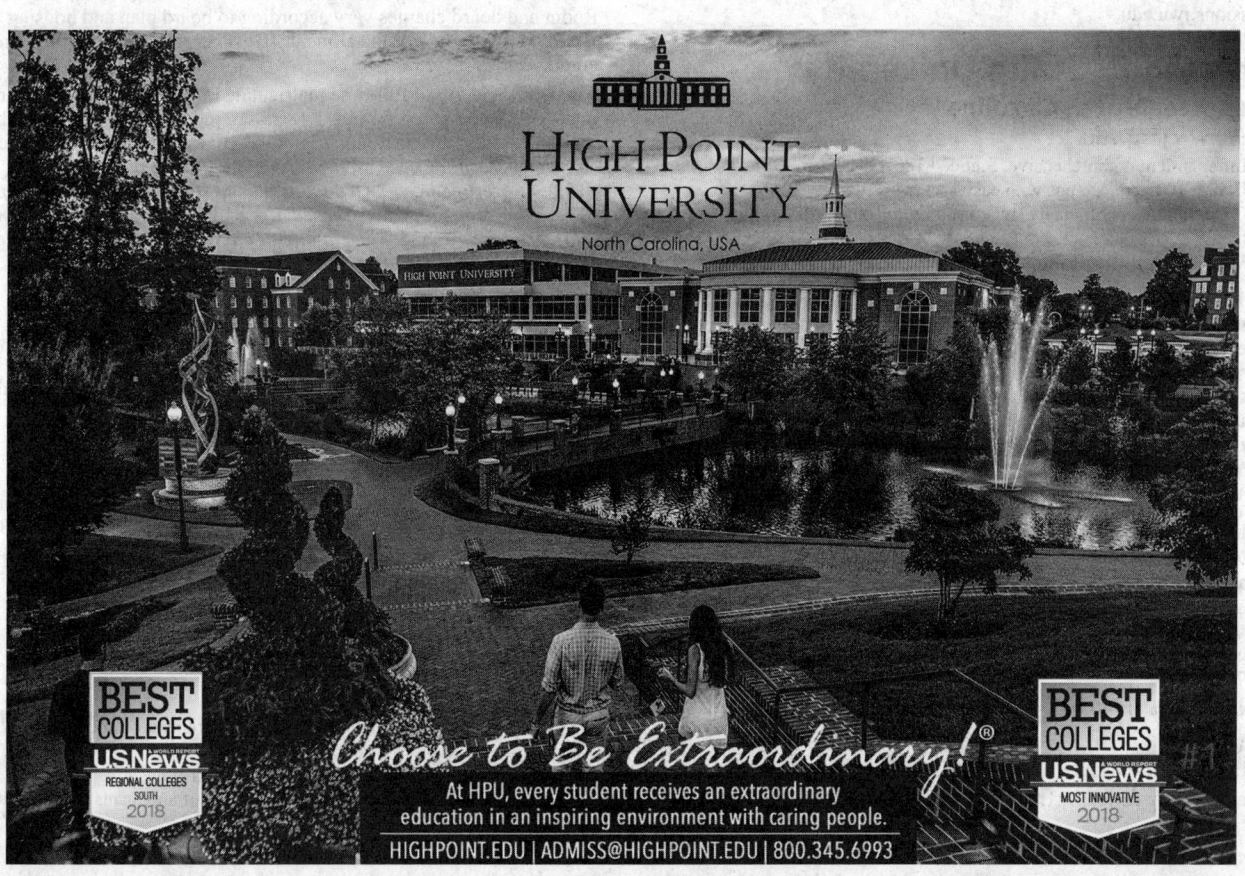

fees: $2102 per term part-time. ***Room and board:*** Room and board charges vary according to board plan and housing facility. ***Payment plan:*** installment. *Waivers:* employees or children of employees.

Financial Aid Of all full-time matriculated undergraduates who enrolled in 2016, 2,417 applied for aid, 1,861 were judged to have need, 190 had their need fully met. 228 Federal Work-Study jobs (averaging $1128). In 2016, 1488 non-need-based awards were made. ***Average percent of need met:*** 51. ***Average financial aid package:*** $15,723. ***Average need-based loan:*** $4252. ***Average need-based gift aid:*** $11,884. ***Average non-need-based aid:*** $7416. ***Average indebtedness upon graduation:*** $37,025.

APPLYING

Options: electronic application, early decision, early action, deferred entrance.

Application fee: $50.

Required: essay or personal statement, high school transcript, 1 letter of recommendation. ***Recommended:*** interview.

Application deadlines: 3/15 (freshmen), 7/1 (transfers), 11/15 (early action).

Early decision deadline: 11/1 (for plan 1), 2/1 (for plan 2).

Notification: continuous (freshmen), continuous (transfers), 11/27 (early decision plan 1), rolling (early decision plan 2), 12/15 (early action).

CONTACT

Dr. Kerr Ramsay, Associate Vice President of Admissions, High Point University, Office of Undergraduate Admissions, One University Parkway, High Point, NC 27268. *Phone:* 336-841-9176. *Toll-free phone:* 800-345-6993. *Fax:* 336-888-6382. *E-mail:* kramsay@highpoint.edu.

See previous page for display ad and page 1306 for the College Close-Up.

Johnson & Wales University

Charlotte, North Carolina

http://www.jwu.edu/charlotte/

CONTACT

Joseph Campos, Director of Admissions, Johnson & Wales University, 801 West Trade Street, Charlotte, NC 28202. *Phone:* 980-598-1100. *Toll-free phone:* 866-598-2427. *Fax:* 980-598-1111. *E-mail:* clt@admissions.jwu.edu.

Johnson C. Smith University

Charlotte, North Carolina

http://www.jcsu.edu/

- **Independent** comprehensive, founded 1867
- **Urban** 100-acre campus with easy access to Atlanta
- **Coed** 1,394 undergraduate students, 95% full-time, 61% women, 39% men
- **Moderately difficult** entrance level, 38% of applicants were admitted

UNDERGRAD STUDENTS

1,329 full-time, 65 part-time. Students come from 32 states and territories; 8 other countries; 40% are from out of state; 84% Black or African American, non-Hispanic/Latino; 4% Hispanic/Latino; 0.1% Asian, non-Hispanic/Latino; 0.1% Native Hawaiian or other Pacific Islander, non-Hispanic/Latino; 0.2% American Indian or Alaska Native, non-Hispanic/Latino; 1% Two or more races, non-Hispanic/Latino; 8% Race/ethnicity unknown; 1% international; 4% transferred in; 62% live on campus.

Freshmen:

Admission: 6,657 applied, 2,536 admitted, 339 enrolled. ***Average high school GPA:*** 2.8. ***Test scores:*** SAT evidence-based reading and writing scores over 500: 19%; SAT math scores over 500: 12%; ACT scores over 18: 36%; SAT evidence-based reading and writing scores over 600: 4%; ACT scores over 24: 4%; SAT evidence-based reading and writing scores over 700: 4%.

Retention: 69% of full-time freshmen returned.

FACULTY

Total: 173, 54% full-time, 63% with terminal degrees.

Student/faculty ratio: 12:1.

ACADEMICS

Calendar: semesters. *Degrees:* bachelor's and master's.

Special study options: accelerated degree program, adult/continuing education programs, advanced placement credit, cooperative education, distance learning, double majors, English as a second language, independent study, internships, part-time degree program, services for LD students, student-designed majors, study abroad, summer session for credit.

Computers: 125 computers/terminals are available on campus for general student use. Students can access the following: campus intranet, computer help desk, free student e-mail accounts, online (class) grades, online (class) registration, online (class) schedules. Campuswide network is available. 100% of college-owned or -operated housing units are wired for high-speed Internet access. Wireless service is available via entire campus.

Library: James B. Duke Library. *Books:* 114,150 (physical), 184,548 (digital/electronic); *Serial titles:* 257 (physical); *Databases:* 78. Weekly public service hours: 79; study areas open 24 hours, 5–7 days a week; students can reserve study rooms.

STUDENT LIFE

Housing options: coed, men-only, women-only. Campus housing is university owned and leased by the school. Freshman campus housing is guaranteed.

Activities and organizations: drama/theater group, choral group, marching band, national fraternities, national sororities.

Athletics Member NCAA. All Division II. ***Intercollegiate sports:*** basketball M(s)/W(s), bowling W(s), cheerleading W, cross-country running M(s)/W(s), football M(s), golf M(s), softball W(s), tennis M(s)/W(s), track and field M(s)/W(s), volleyball W(s).

Campus security: 24-hour emergency response devices and patrols, late-night transport/escort service, controlled dormitory access.

Student services: health clinic, personal/psychological counseling.

COSTS & FINANCIAL AID

Costs (2017–18) *Comprehensive fee:* $25,336 includes full-time tuition ($18,236) and room and board ($7100). Full-time tuition and fees vary according to course load. Part-time tuition: $418 per credit hour. Part-time tuition and fees vary according to course load. *College room only:* $4086. Room and board charges vary according to board plan and housing facility. ***Payment plan:*** installment. *Waivers:* employees or children of employees.

Financial Aid Of all full-time matriculated undergraduates who enrolled in 2016, 1,222 applied for aid, 1,180 were judged to have need, 57 had their need fully met. In 2016, 76 non-need-based awards were made. ***Average percent of need met:*** 58. ***Average financial aid package:*** $15,658. ***Average need-based loan:*** $4036. ***Average need-based gift aid:*** $11,855. ***Average non-need-based aid:*** $14,336. ***Average indebtedness upon graduation:*** $35,769. ***Financial aid deadline:*** 4/1.

APPLYING

Standardized Tests *Required:* SAT or ACT (for admission).

Options: electronic application, deferred entrance.

Application fee: $25.

Required: high school transcript. ***Recommended:*** essay or personal statement, 1 letter of recommendation.

Notification: continuous (freshmen), continuous (transfers).

CONTACT

Mr. Vory Billups, Director of Admissions, Johnson C. Smith University, 100 Beatties Ford Road, Charlotte, NC 28216. *Phone:* 704-378-1081. *Toll-free phone:* 800-782-7303. *Fax:* 704-378-1242. *E-mail:* vbillups@jcsu.edu.

John Wesley University

High Point, North Carolina

http://www.johnwesley.edu/

- **Independent interdenominational** comprehensive, founded 1932
- **Urban** 24-acre campus
- **Coed** 136 undergraduate students, 90% full-time, 43% women, 57% men
- **Moderately difficult** entrance level, 18% of applicants were admitted

UNDERGRAD STUDENTS
122 full-time, 14 part-time. Students come from 10 states and territories; 2 other countries; 6% are from out of state; 26% Black or African American, non-Hispanic/Latino; 15% Hispanic/Latino; 0.7% Asian, non-Hispanic/Latino; 3% American Indian or Alaska Native, non-Hispanic/Latino; 3% Two or more races, non-Hispanic/Latino; 1% international; 7% transferred in; 47% live on campus.

Freshmen:
Admission: 168 applied, 31 admitted, 31 enrolled. *Average high school GPA:* 3.0.
Retention: 38% of full-time freshmen returned.

FACULTY
Total: 19, 21% full-time, 79% with terminal degrees.
Student/faculty ratio: 15:1.

ACADEMICS
Calendar: semesters. *Degrees:* certificates, associate, bachelor's, master's, and doctoral.
Special study options: academic remediation for entering students, adult/continuing education programs, advanced placement credit, distance learning, double majors, independent study, internships, off-campus study, part-time degree program, summer session for credit.
Computers: 7 computers/terminals and 7 ports are available on campus for general student use. Students can access the following: free student e-mail accounts, online (class) grades, online (class) registration, online (class) schedules. 100% of college-owned or -operated housing units are wired for high-speed Internet access. Wireless service is available via entire campus.
Library: Temple Library. *Books:* 3,885 (physical), 26 (digital/electronic); *Serial titles:* 38 (physical), 164 (digital/electronic); *Databases:* 4.

STUDENT LIFE
Housing options: men-only, women-only. Campus housing is university owned.
Activities and organizations: choral group, Student Government, Choir, Praise Band, Ambassadors Club, Men and Womens Leadership.
Athletics Member NCCAA. *Intercollegiate sports:* soccer M(s)/W(s), softball W(s), volleyball W(s).
Campus security: 24-hour emergency response devices, full-time retired Police Officer on campus.

FINANCIAL AID
Financial Aid Of all full-time matriculated undergraduates who enrolled in 2016, 117 applied for aid, 117 were judged to have need, 3 had their need fully met. 7 Federal Work-Study jobs (averaging $1671). 13 state and other part-time jobs (averaging $1610). In 2016, 2 non-need-based awards were made. *Average percent of need met:* 51. *Average financial aid package:* $8343. *Average need-based loan:* $4106. *Average need-based gift aid:* $5781. *Average non-need-based aid:* $1125. *Average indebtedness upon graduation:* $28,217. *Financial aid deadline:* 8/1.

APPLYING
Standardized Tests *Required:* SAT or ACT (for admission).
Options: electronic application, early admission, deferred entrance.
Application fee: $20.
Required: essay or personal statement, high school transcript, 2 letters of recommendation. *Recommended:* minimum 2.0 GPA, interview.
Application deadlines: 8/1 (freshmen), 8/1 (transfers).
Notification: continuous (freshmen), continuous (out-of-state freshmen), continuous (transfers).

CONTACT
Jake Smith, Admissions, John Wesley University, 1215 Eastchester Drive, High Point, NC 27265-3197. *Phone:* 336-821-2486. *Toll-free phone:* 855-528-7358.

Lees-McRae College
Banner Elk, North Carolina
http://www.lmc.edu/
- **Independent** 4-year, founded 1900, affiliated with Presbyterian Church (U.S.A.)
- **Rural** 460-acre campus
- **Endowment** $12.2 million
- **Coed**
- **Minimally difficult** entrance level

FACULTY
Student/faculty ratio: 13:1.

ACADEMICS
Calendar: semesters. *Degree:* bachelor's.
Library: Dotti M. Shelton Learning Commons. *Books:* 70,132 (physical), 173,083 (digital/electronic); *Serial titles:* 225 (physical), 146,361 (digital/electronic); *Databases:* 143. Students can reserve study rooms.

STUDENT LIFE
Housing options: coed, men-only, women-only, special housing for students with disabilities. Campus housing is university owned. Freshman campus housing is guaranteed.
Activities and organizations: drama/theater group, choral group.
Athletics Member NCAA. All Division II.
Campus security: 24-hour emergency response devices and patrols, controlled dormitory access.
Student services: health clinic, personal/psychological counseling.

COSTS & FINANCIAL AID
Costs (2017–18) *Comprehensive fee:* $36,956 includes full-time tuition ($24,878), mandatory fees ($1320), and room and board ($10,758). Full-time tuition and fees vary according to course load, location, and reciprocity agreements. Part-time tuition: $710 per credit hour. Part-time tuition and fees vary according to course load, location, and reciprocity agreements. No tuition increase for student's term of enrollment. *College room only:* $5142. Room and board charges vary according to housing facility.
Financial Aid Of all full-time matriculated undergraduates who enrolled in 2017, 748 applied for aid, 681 were judged to have need, 6 had their need fully met. In 2017, 82 non-need-based awards were made. *Average percent of need met:* 73. *Average financial aid package:* $25,260. *Average need-based loan:* $4180. *Average need-based gift aid:* $8625. *Average non-need-based aid:* $5910.

APPLYING
Standardized Tests *Required for some:* SAT or ACT (for admission), SAT or ACT scores for prospective intercollegiate athletes and honors program students.
Options: electronic application, early action.
Application fee: $35.
Required: high school transcript, minimum 2.0 GPA. *Required for some:* essay or personal statement, interview.

CONTACT
Mrs. Candace Silver, Director of Admissions, Lees-McRae College, PO Box 128, Banner Elk, NC 28604. *Phone:* 800-280-4562. *Toll-free phone:* 800-280-4562. *Fax:* 828-898-8707. *E-mail:* admissions@lmc.edu.

Lenoir-Rhyne University
Hickory, North Carolina
http://www.lr.edu/
- **Independent Lutheran** comprehensive, founded 1891
- **Small-town** 100-acre campus with easy access to Charlotte
- **Endowment** $106.3 million
- **Coed** 1,699 undergraduate students, 85% full-time, 59% women, 41% men
- **Moderately difficult** entrance level, 74% of applicants were admitted

UNDERGRAD STUDENTS
1,441 full-time, 258 part-time. Students come from 30 states and territories; 24 other countries; 19% are from out of state; 12% Black or African American, non-Hispanic/Latino; 6% Hispanic/Latino; 2% Asian,

non-Hispanic/Latino; 0.4% American Indian or Alaska Native, non-Hispanic/Latino; 4% Two or more races, non-Hispanic/Latino; 8% Race/ethnicity unknown; 3% international; 6% transferred in; 51% live on campus.

Freshmen:
Admission: 5,356 applied, 3,958 admitted, 408 enrolled. *Average high school GPA:* 3.3. *Test scores:* SAT evidence-based reading and writing scores over 500: 67%; SAT math scores over 500: 71%; SAT evidence-based reading and writing scores over 600: 16%; SAT math scores over 600: 16%; SAT evidence-based reading and writing scores over 700: 2%.
Retention: 73% of full-time freshmen returned.

FACULTY
Total: 271, 48% full-time, 63% with terminal degrees.
Student/faculty ratio: 13:1.

ACADEMICS
Calendar: semesters. *Degrees:* bachelor's, master's, and doctoral.
Special study options: academic remediation for entering students, accelerated degree program, adult/continuing education programs, advanced placement credit, distance learning, double majors, freshman honors college, honors programs, independent study, internships, off-campus study, part-time degree program, services for LD students, study abroad, summer session for credit.

Unusual degree programs: 3-2 engineering with North Carolina Agricultural and Technical State University, North Carolina State University, University of North Carolina at Charlotte; forestry with Duke University.

Computers: 150 computers/terminals and 150 ports are available on campus for general student use. Students can access the following: campus intranet, computer help desk, free student e-mail accounts, online (class) grades, online (class) registration, online (class) schedules. Campuswide network is available. 100% of college-owned or -operated housing units are wired for high-speed Internet access. Wireless service is available via entire campus.
Library: Carl Rudisill Library. *Books:* 121,005 (physical), 537,443 (digital/electronic); *Serial titles:* 49 (physical), 28,271 (digital/electronic); *Databases:* 135. Weekly public service hours: 89.

STUDENT LIFE
Housing options: on-campus residence required through junior year; coed. Campus housing is university owned. Freshman campus housing is guaranteed.

Activities and organizations: drama/theater group, student-run newspaper, radio station, choral group, marching band, Circle K, CAB, Nu Generation, Greek Organizations, Sign Troupe, national sororities.

Athletics Member NCAA. All Division II. *Intercollegiate sports:* baseball M(s), basketball M(s)/W(s), cheerleading M(s)/W(s), cross-country running M(s)/W(s), football M(s), golf M(s)/W(s), lacrosse M(s)/W(s), soccer M(s)/W(s), softball W(s), swimming and diving M(s)/W(s), tennis M(s)/W(s), track and field M(s)/W(s), volleyball W(s). *Intramural sports:* baseball M, basketball M/W, equestrian sports M(c)/W(c), football M/W, racquetball M/W, sand volleyball M/W, soccer M/W, ultimate Frisbee M/W, volleyball M/W.

Campus security: 24-hour emergency response devices and patrols, late-night transport/escort service, controlled dormitory access.

Student services: health clinic, personal/psychological counseling.

COSTS & FINANCIAL AID
Costs (2017–18) *Comprehensive fee:* $47,500 includes full-time tuition ($35,350) and room and board ($12,150). Part-time tuition: $1460 per credit. *Room and board:* Room and board charges vary according to board plan. *Waivers:* senior citizens and employees or children of employees.

Financial Aid Of all full-time matriculated undergraduates who enrolled in 2015, 1,261 applied for aid, 1,181 were judged to have need, 175 had their need fully met. In 2015, 172 non-need-based awards were made. *Average percent of need met:* 71. *Average financial aid package:* $27,008. *Average need-based loan:* $4282. *Average need-based gift aid:* $22,559. *Average non-need-based aid:* $15,825. *Average indebtedness upon graduation:* $28,294.

APPLYING
Standardized Tests *Required:* SAT or ACT (for admission).

Options: electronic application, early admission, early action, deferred entrance.
Application fee: $35.
Required: high school transcript, minimum 2.5 GPA. *Recommended:* essay or personal statement, letters of recommendation.
Application deadlines: rolling (freshmen), rolling (transfers), 11/7 (early action).
Notification: continuous (freshmen), continuous (transfers), 11/21 (early action).

CONTACT
Lenoir-Rhyne University, 625 7th Avenue NE, Hickory, NC 28601. *Phone:* 828-328-7392. *Toll-free phone:* 800-277-5721.

Living Arts College
Raleigh, North Carolina
http://www.living-arts-college.edu/

CONTACT
Julie Wenta, Director of Admissions, Living Arts College, 3000 Wakefield Crossing Drive, Raleigh, NC 27614. *Phone:* 919-488-5902. *Toll-free phone:* 800-288-7442. *Fax:* 919-488-8490. *E-mail:* jwenta@living-arts-college.edu.

Livingstone College
Salisbury, North Carolina
http://www.livingstone.edu/

CONTACT
Mr. Tony Baldwin, Livingstone College, 701 West Monroe Street, Salisbury, NC 28144. *Phone:* 704-216-6001. *Toll-free phone:* 800-835-3435. *Fax:* 704-216-6215. *E-mail:* admissions@livingstone.edu.

Mars Hill University
Mars Hill, North Carolina
http://www.mhu.edu/

CONTACT
Kristie Vance, Director of Admissions, Mars Hill University, PO Box 370, Mars Hill, NC 28754. *Phone:* 828-689-1201. *Toll-free phone:* 866-648-4968. *Fax:* 828-689-1473. *E-mail:* admissions@mhu.edu.

★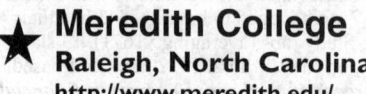
Meredith College
Raleigh, North Carolina
http://www.meredith.edu/
- **Independent** comprehensive, founded 1891
- **Urban** 225-acre campus
- **Undergraduate: women only; graduate: coed** 1,682 undergraduate students, 95% full-time, 100% women, 0% men
- **Moderately difficult** entrance level, 69% of applicants were admitted

UNDERGRAD STUDENTS
1,600 full-time, 82 part-time. Students come from 31 states and territories; 33 other countries; 12% are from out of state; 8% Black or African American, non-Hispanic/Latino; 8% Hispanic/Latino; 3% Asian, non-Hispanic/Latino; 0.1% Native Hawaiian or other Pacific Islander, non-Hispanic/Latino; 0.8% American Indian or Alaska Native, non-Hispanic/Latino; 4% Two or more races, non-Hispanic/Latino; 4% Race/ethnicity unknown; 2% international; 5% transferred in; 54% live on campus.

Freshmen:
Admission: 1,737 applied, 1,197 admitted, 395 enrolled. *Average high school GPA:* 3.4. *Test scores:* SAT evidence-based reading and writing scores over 500: 81%; SAT math scores over 500: 71%; ACT scores over 18: 88%; SAT evidence-based reading and writing scores over 600: 32%; SAT math scores over 600: 19%; ACT scores over 24: 39%; SAT evidence-based reading and writing scores over 700: 2%; SAT math scores over 700: 2%; ACT scores over 30: 4%.
Retention: 80% of full-time freshmen returned.

FACULTY
Total: 222, 59% full-time, 62% with terminal degrees.
Student/faculty ratio: 12:1.

ACADEMICS
Calendar: semesters. *Degrees:* bachelor's, master's, and postbachelor's certificates.

Special study options: academic remediation for entering students, accelerated degree program, advanced placement credit, cooperative education, double majors, honors programs, independent study, internships, off-campus study, part-time degree program, services for LD students, student-designed majors, study abroad, summer session for credit. *ROTC:* Army (c), Air Force (c).

Unusual degree programs: 3-2 engineering with North Carolina State University.

Computers: Students can access the following: free student e-mail accounts, online (class) registration. Campuswide network is available. 100% of college-owned or -operated housing units are wired for high-speed Internet access. Wireless service is available via classrooms, computer centers, computer labs, dorm rooms, learning centers, libraries, student centers.
Library: Carlyle Campbell Library.

STUDENT LIFE
Housing options: on-campus residence required through sophomore year; women-only. Campus housing is university owned. Freshman campus housing is guaranteed.

Activities and organizations: drama/theater group, student-run newspaper, choral group, Student Government Association, Entertainment Association, Recreation Association, Class Organizations, choral groups.

Athletics Member NCAA. All Division III. *Intercollegiate sports:* basketball W, cross-country running W, lacrosse W, soccer W, softball W, tennis W, track and field W, volleyball W.

Campus security: 24-hour emergency response devices and patrols, late-night transport/escort service, controlled dormitory access.

Student services: health clinic, personal/psychological counseling.

COSTS & FINANCIAL AID
Costs (2017–18) *Comprehensive fee:* $46,634 includes full-time tuition ($35,816), mandatory fees ($100), and room and board ($10,718). Full-time tuition and fees vary according to course load. Part-time tuition: $889 per credit hour. Part-time tuition and fees vary according to course load. *Required fees:* $100 per year part-time. *Room and board:* Room and board charges vary according to board plan and housing facility. *Waivers:* employees or children of employees.

Financial Aid Of all full-time matriculated undergraduates who enrolled in 2016, 1,347 applied for aid, 1,204 were judged to have need, 195 had their need fully met. In 2016, 131 non-need-based awards were made. *Average percent of need met:* 72. *Average financial aid package:* $24,977. *Average need-based loan:* $4348. *Average need-based gift aid:* $20,935. *Average non-need-based aid:* $13,427. *Average indebtedness upon graduation:* $33,993.

APPLYING
Standardized Tests *Required:* SAT or ACT (for admission).

Options: electronic application, early admission, early decision, deferred entrance.

Application fee: $40.

Required: high school transcript, minimum 2.0 GPA, 2 letters of recommendation. *Required for some:* essay or personal statement, interview. *Recommended:* essay or personal statement.

Application deadlines: 2/15 (freshmen), 2/15 (transfers).

Early decision deadline: 10/15.

Notification: continuous (freshmen), continuous (transfers), 11/1 (early decision).

CONTACT
Shery Boyles, Director of Admissions, Meredith College, 3800 Hillsborough Street, Raleigh, NC 27807-5298. *Phone:* 919-760-8026. *Toll-free phone:* 800-MEREDITH. *Fax:* 919-760-2298. *E-mail:* admissions@meredith.edu.

Methodist University
Fayetteville, North Carolina
http://www.methodist.edu/

CONTACT
Mr. Jamie Legg, Director of Admissions, Methodist University, 5400 Ramset Street, Fayetteville, NC 28311-1496. *Phone:* 910-630-7027. *Toll-free phone:* 800-488-7110 Ext. 7027. *Fax:* 910-630-7285. *E-mail:* admissions@methodist.edu.

Mid-Atlantic Christian University
Elizabeth City, North Carolina
http://www.macuniversity.edu/
- **Independent Christian** 4-year, founded 1948
- **Small-town** 19-acre campus with easy access to Norfolk
- **Endowment** $3.1 million
- **Coed** 192 undergraduate students, 86% full-time, 55% women, 45% men
- **Minimally difficult** entrance level, 53% of applicants were admitted

UNDERGRAD STUDENTS
166 full-time, 26 part-time. Students come from 17 states and territories; 3 other countries; 34% are from out of state; 19% Black or African American, non-Hispanic/Latino; 6% Hispanic/Latino; 0.5% Asian, non-Hispanic/Latino; 0.5% American Indian or Alaska Native, non-Hispanic/Latino; 2% Two or more races, non-Hispanic/Latino; 0.5% Race/ethnicity unknown; 2% international; 5% transferred in; 64% live on campus.

Freshmen:
Admission: 189 applied, 101 admitted, 54 enrolled. *Average high school GPA:* 3.1. *Test scores:* SAT evidence-based reading and writing scores over 500: 52%; SAT math scores over 500: 48%; ACT scores over 18: 75%; SAT evidence-based reading and writing scores over 600: 13%; SAT math scores over 600: 6%; ACT scores over 24: 6%.
Retention: 63% of full-time freshmen returned.

FACULTY
Total: 33, 36% full-time, 48% with terminal degrees.
Student/faculty ratio: 11:1.

ACADEMICS
Calendar: semesters. *Degrees:* certificates, associate, bachelor's, and postbachelor's certificates.

Special study options: academic remediation for entering students, adult/continuing education programs, advanced placement credit, distance learning, double majors, internships, part-time degree program, summer session for credit. *ROTC:* Army (c).

Computers: 24 computers/terminals are available on campus for general student use. Students can access the following: free student e-mail accounts, online (class) grades, online (class) registration, online (class) schedules. Campuswide network is available. 100% of college-owned or -operated housing units are wired for high-speed Internet access. Wireless service is available via entire campus.
Library: Watson-Griffith Library. *Books:* 33,941 (physical), 1,572 (digital/electronic). Students can reserve study rooms.

STUDENT LIFE
Housing options: on-campus residence required through senior year; men-only, women-only. Campus housing is university owned. Freshman campus housing is guaranteed.

Activities and organizations: national sororities.

Athletics Member USCAA. *Intercollegiate sports:* basketball M/W, golf M, soccer M, volleyball W. *Intramural sports:* basketball M/W, softball M/W, table tennis M/W, tennis M/W, volleyball M/W.

Campus security: 24-hour emergency response devices, controlled dormitory access.

Student services: personal/psychological counseling.

COSTS & FINANCIAL AID
Costs (2018–19) *Comprehensive fee:* $23,450 includes full-time tuition ($14,400), mandatory fees ($450), and room and board ($8600). Full-time tuition and fees vary according to program. Part-time tuition: $450 per credit hour. Part-time tuition and fees vary according to program.

Required fees: $55 per credit hour part-time. *Room and board:* Room and board charges vary according to housing facility. *Payment plan:* deferred payment. *Waivers:* children of alumni, senior citizens, and employees or children of employees.

Financial Aid Of all full-time matriculated undergraduates who enrolled in 2015, 170 applied for aid, 156 were judged to have need, 10 had their need fully met. In 2015, 17 non-need-based awards were made. *Average percent of need met:* 55. *Average financial aid package:* $11,333. *Average need-based loan:* $3758. *Average need-based gift aid:* $6671. *Average non-need-based aid:* $3478. *Average indebtedness upon graduation:* $26,414. *Financial aid deadline:* 3/1.

APPLYING
Standardized Tests *Required for some:* SAT or ACT (for admission).

Options: electronic application, early admission, deferred entrance.

Application fee: $50.

Required: essay or personal statement, high school transcript, minimum 2.0 GPA, 1 letter of recommendation, reference from church or character reference. *Required for some:* interview.

Application deadlines: 8/1 (freshmen), 8/1 (transfers).

Notification: continuous (freshmen), continuous (transfers).

CONTACT
Mid-Atlantic Christian University, 715 North Poindexter Street, Elizabeth City, NC 27909-4054. *Toll-free phone:* 866-996-MACU.

Montreat College
Montreat, North Carolina
http://www.montreat.edu/

CONTACT
Miss Mandi Pike, Senior Admissions Specialist, Montreat College, PO Box 1267, Montreat, NC 28757. *Phone:* 828-669-8012 Ext. 3789. *Toll-free phone:* 800-622-6968. *Fax:* 828-669-0120. *E-mail:* admissions@ montreat.edu.

North Carolina Agricultural and Technical State University
Greensboro, North Carolina
http://www.ncat.edu/

CONTACT
Ms. Cheryl Pollard-Burns, Director of Admissions, North Carolina Agricultural and Technical State University, North Carolina Agricultural & Technical State University (Webb Hall), 1601 East Market Street, Greensboro, NC 27411. *Phone:* 336-334-7946. *Toll-free phone:* 800-443-8964. *Fax:* 336-334-7478. *E-mail:* uadmit@ncat.edu.

North Carolina Central University
Durham, North Carolina
http://www.nccu.edu/

- **State-supported** comprehensive, founded 1910, part of University of North Carolina System
- **Urban** 115-acre campus with easy access to Raleigh
- **Endowment** $22.9 million
- **Coed** 6,355 undergraduate students, 84% full-time, 67% women, 33% men
- **Minimally difficult** entrance level, 83% of applicants were admitted

UNDERGRAD STUDENTS
5,363 full-time, 992 part-time. Students come from 39 states and territories; 47 other countries; 10% are from out of state; 79% Black or African American, non-Hispanic/Latino; 6% Hispanic/Latino; 1% Asian, non-Hispanic/Latino; 0.4% American Indian or Alaska Native, non-Hispanic/Latino; 5% Two or more races, non-Hispanic/Latino; 3% Race/ethnicity unknown; 0.2% international; 8% transferred in; 40% live on campus.

Freshmen:
Admission: 6,671 applied, 5,524 admitted, 1,275 enrolled. *Average high school GPA:* 3.2. *Test scores:* ACT scores over 18: 49%; ACT scores over 24: 8%; ACT scores over 30: 1%.

Retention: 77% of full-time freshmen returned.

FACULTY
Total: 564, 68% full-time.

Student/faculty ratio: 16:1.

ACADEMICS
Calendar: semesters. *Degrees:* bachelor's, master's, and doctoral.

Special study options: academic remediation for entering students, accelerated degree program, adult/continuing education programs, advanced placement credit, cooperative education, distance learning, double majors, English as a second language, external degree program, honors programs, independent study, internships, off-campus study, part-time degree program, services for LD students, study abroad, summer session for credit. *ROTC:* Army (b), Air Force (b).

Computers: 1,262 computers/terminals and 3,700 ports are available on campus for general student use. Students can access the following: campus intranet, computer help desk, free student e-mail accounts, online (class) grades, online (class) registration, online (class) schedules. Campuswide network is available. 100% of college-owned or -operated housing units are wired for high-speed Internet access. Wireless service is available via entire campus.

Library: Shepherd Library plus 2 others. Study areas open 24 hours, 5–7 days a week; students can reserve study rooms.

STUDENT LIFE
Housing options: coed. Campus housing is university owned and leased by the school. Freshman applicants given priority for college housing.

Activities and organizations: drama/theater group, student-run newspaper, choral group, marching band, national fraternities, national sororities.

Athletics Member NCAA, NAIA. All NCAA Division I. *Intercollegiate sports:* baseball M(s), basketball M(s)/W(s), bowling W(s), cross-country running M(s)/W(s), football M(s), golf M(s), softball W(s), tennis M(s)/W(s), track and field M(s)/W(s), volleyball W(s). *Intramural sports:* basketball M/W, football M, golf M, soccer M, volleyball W.

Campus security: 24-hour emergency response devices and patrols, student patrols, late-night transport/escort service, controlled dormitory access.

Student services: health clinic, personal/psychological counseling, women's center.

COSTS & FINANCIAL AID
Costs (2018–19) *Tuition:* state resident $3728 full-time, $466 per credit hour part-time; nonresident $16,435 full-time, $2054 per credit hour part-time. Part-time tuition and fees vary according to course load. *Required fees:* $2838 full-time, $600 per term part-time. *Room and board:* $8446. Room and board charges vary according to board plan, housing facility, and location. *Payment plan:* installment. *Waivers:* employees or children of employees.

Financial Aid Of all full-time matriculated undergraduates who enrolled in 2014, 4,987 applied for aid, 4,684 were judged to have need, 222 had their need fully met. In 2014, 45 non-need-based awards were made. *Average percent of need met:* 58. *Average financial aid package:* $11,745. *Average need-based loan:* $4225. *Average need-based gift aid:* $7918. *Average non-need-based aid:* $13,302. *Average indebtedness upon graduation:* $35,017.

APPLYING
Standardized Tests *Required:* SAT or ACT (for admission).

Options: electronic application, deferred entrance.

Application fee: $40.

Required: high school transcript, minimum 2.5 GPA, University of North Carolina System minimum course requirements.

Application deadlines: 8/1 (freshmen), 8/1 (transfers).

Notification: continuous until 10/15 (freshmen), continuous until 10/15 (transfers).

CONTACT
North Carolina Central University, 1801 Fayetteville Street, Durham, NC 27707-3129. *Toll-free phone:* 877-667-7533.

North Carolina State University
Raleigh, North Carolina
http://www.ncsu.edu/

- **State-supported** university, founded 1887, part of University of North Carolina System
- **Urban** 2100-acre campus with easy access to Raleigh-Durham
- **Endowment** $1.1 billion
- **Coed** 24,150 undergraduate students, 89% full-time, 45% women, 55% men
- **Very difficult** entrance level, 51% of applicants were admitted

UNDERGRAD STUDENTS
21,384 full-time, 2,766 part-time. Students come from 53 states and territories; 109 other countries; 10% are from out of state; 6% Black or African American, non-Hispanic/Latino; 5% Hispanic/Latino; 6% Asian, non-Hispanic/Latino; 0.1% Native Hawaiian or other Pacific Islander, non-Hispanic/Latino; 0.4% American Indian or Alaska Native, non-Hispanic/Latino; 4% Two or more races, non-Hispanic/Latino; 5% Race/ethnicity unknown; 5% international; 5% transferred in; 41% live on campus.

Freshmen:
Admission: 26,859 applied, 13,690 admitted, 4,799 enrolled. *Average high school GPA:* 3.7. *Test scores:* SAT evidence-based reading and writing scores over 500: 99%; SAT math scores over 500: 99%; ACT scores over 18: 100%; SAT evidence-based reading and writing scores over 600: 84%; SAT math scores over 600: 85%; ACT scores over 24: 96%; SAT evidence-based reading and writing scores over 700: 20%; SAT math scores over 700: 31%; ACT scores over 30: 39%.
Retention: 94% of full-time freshmen returned.

FACULTY
Total: 2,607, 86% full-time, 90% with terminal degrees.
Student/faculty ratio: 13:1.

ACADEMICS
Calendar: semesters. *Degrees:* associate, bachelor's, master's, doctoral, post-master's, and postbachelor's certificates.

Special study options: academic remediation for entering students, accelerated degree program, adult/continuing education programs, advanced placement credit, cooperative education, distance learning, double majors, English as a second language, honors programs, independent study, internships, off-campus study, part-time degree program, services for LD students, student-designed majors, study abroad, summer session for credit. *ROTC:* Army (b), Navy (b), Air Force (b).

Unusual degree programs: business administration; engineering; nursing with North Carolina Central University; agriculture, life sciences, physical sciences, communication, computer science, economics, foreign languages, history, mathematics, education, statistics, textiles.

Computers: 3,125 computers/terminals are available on campus for general student use. Students can access the following: campus intranet, computer help desk, free student e-mail accounts, online (class) grades, online (class) registration, online (class) schedules, online course materials, homework submission, testing/quizzes, financial aid/cashier's office account balances, blogging service, Web space, unlimited cloud storage, on site hardware and virus removal support. Campuswide network is available. 100% of college-owned or -operated housing units are wired for high-speed Internet access. Wireless service is available via entire campus.
Library: D. H. Hill Library plus 5 others. *Books:* 2.6 million (physical), 1.1 million (digital/electronic); *Serial titles:* 47,100 (physical), 58,263 (digital/electronic); *Databases:* 620. Weekly public service hours: 146; study areas open 24 hours, 5–7 days a week; students can reserve study rooms.

STUDENT LIFE
Housing options: on-campus residence required for freshman year; coed, men-only, women-only, special housing for students with disabilities. Campus housing is university owned. Freshman campus housing is guaranteed.

Activities and organizations: drama/theater group, student-run newspaper, radio and television station, choral group, marching band, Student Alumni Association, Student Wolfpack Club, Finance Club, National Society of Leadership and Success, Collegiate Shag Association, national fraternities, national sororities.

Athletics Member NCAA. All Division I. *Intercollegiate sports:* baseball M(s), basketball M(s)/W(s), bowling M(c)/W(c), cheerleading M(s)/W(s), crew M(c)/W(c), cross-country running M(s)/W(s), equestrian sports M(c)/W(c), fencing M(c)/W(c), field hockey M(c)/W(c), football M(s), golf M(s)/W(s), gymnastics M(c)/W(s), ice hockey M(c), lacrosse M(c)/W(c), racquetball M(c)/W(c), riflery M(s)/W(s), rugby M(c)/W(c), sailing M(c)/W(c), skiing (downhill) M(c)/W(c), soccer M(s)/W(s), softball W(s), swimming and diving M(s)/W(s), table tennis M(c)/W(c), tennis M(s)/W(s), track and field M(s)/W(s), ultimate Frisbee M(c)/W(c), volleyball M(c)/W(s), water polo M(c)/W(c), wrestling M(s). *Intramural sports:* badminton M/W, basketball M/W, bowling M/W, football M/W, golf M/W, racquetball M/W, soccer M/W, softball M/W, swimming and diving M/W, table tennis M/W, tennis M/W, track and field M/W, ultimate Frisbee M/W, volleyball M/W.

Campus security: 24-hour emergency response devices and patrols, late-night transport/escort service, controlled dormitory access, mounted police.

Student services: health clinic, personal/psychological counseling, women's center, legal services.

COSTS & FINANCIAL AID
Costs (2018–19) *Tuition:* state resident $6535 full-time; nonresident $25,879 full-time. Full-time tuition and fees vary according to course level, degree level, location, program, and reciprocity agreements. Part-time tuition and fees vary according to course level, course load, degree level, location, program, and reciprocity agreements. No tuition increase for student's term of enrollment. *Required fees:* $2565 full-time. *Room and board:* $11,078; room only: $6714. Room and board charges vary according to board plan and housing facility. *Payment plan:* installment. *Waivers:* employees or children of employees.

Financial Aid Of all full-time matriculated undergraduates who enrolled in 2017, 14,729 applied for aid, 10,508 were judged to have need, 2,263 had their need fully met. 873 Federal Work-Study jobs (averaging $1608). 5,702 state and other part-time jobs (averaging $1869). In 2017, 1093 non-need-based awards were made. *Average percent of need met:* 75. *Average financial aid package:* $13,108. *Average need-based loan:* $4033. *Average need-based gift aid:* $9974. *Average non-need-based aid:* $5591. *Average indebtedness upon graduation:* $24,053.

APPLYING
Standardized Tests *Required:* SAT or ACT (for admission).
Options: electronic application, early action, deferred entrance.
Application fee: $85.
Required: high school transcript. *Required for some:* interview. *Recommended:* essay or personal statement.
Application deadlines: 1/15 (freshmen), 2/15 (transfers), 10/15 (early action).
Notification: 3/30 (freshmen), 4/15 (transfers), 1/30 (early action).

CONTACT
Mr. Thomas Griffin, Director of Undergraduate Admissions, North Carolina State University, Box 7103, Raleigh, NC 27695. *Phone:* 919-515-2434. *Fax:* 919-515-5039. *E-mail:* undergrad-admissions@ncsu.edu.

North Carolina Wesleyan College
Rocky Mount, North Carolina
http://www.ncwc.edu/

- **Independent** 4-year, founded 1956, affiliated with United Methodist Church
- **Suburban** 200-acre campus
- **Endowment** $10.6 million
- **Coed** 2,093 undergraduate students, 84% full-time, 58% women, 42% men
- **Moderately difficult** entrance level, 98% of applicants were admitted

UNDERGRAD STUDENTS
1,754 full-time, 339 part-time. Students come from 23 states and territories; 31 other countries; 13% are from out of state; 42% Black or

African American, non-Hispanic/Latino; 3% Hispanic/Latino; 0.7% Asian, non-Hispanic/Latino; 1% American Indian or Alaska Native, non-Hispanic/Latino; 3% Two or more races, non-Hispanic/Latino; 13% Race/ethnicity unknown; 5% international; 7% transferred in; 72% live on campus.

Freshmen:
Admission: 1,666 applied, 1,629 admitted, 329 enrolled. *Average high school GPA:* 3.2. *Test scores:* SAT evidence-based reading and writing scores over 500: 46%; SAT math scores over 500: 42%; ACT scores over 18: 57%; SAT evidence-based reading and writing scores over 600: 8%; SAT math scores over 600: 5%; ACT scores over 24: 14%; SAT math scores over 700: 1%.

Retention: 60% of full-time freshmen returned.

FACULTY
Total: 313.

Student/faculty ratio: 16:1.

ACADEMICS
Calendar: semesters. *Degrees:* bachelor's (also offers adult part-time degree program with significant enrollment not reflected in profile).

Special study options: academic remediation for entering students, accelerated degree program, adult/continuing education programs, advanced placement credit, cooperative education, distance learning, double majors, honors programs, independent study, internships, part-time degree program, services for LD students, summer session for credit. *ROTC:* Army (c).

Computers: 223 computers/terminals are available on campus for general student use. Students can access the following: campus intranet, computer help desk, free student e-mail accounts, online (class) grades, online (class) schedules. Campuswide network is available. Wireless service is available via entire campus.

Library: Elizabeth Braswell Pearsall Library. *Books:* 78,800 (physical), 44,751 (digital/electronic); *Serial titles:* 4,326 (physical), 4,329 (digital/electronic); *Databases:* 86. Students can reserve study rooms.

STUDENT LIFE
Housing options: on-campus residence required through sophomore year; coed, men-only, women-only, special housing for students with disabilities. Campus housing is university owned. Freshman campus housing is guaranteed.

Activities and organizations: drama/theater group, student-run newspaper, choral group, marching band, Refuge Campus Ministry, NCWC Cheerleaders, Voices of Triumph, Campus Crusade for Christ, Visions of Beauty, national fraternities, national sororities.

Athletics Member NCAA. All Division III. *Intercollegiate sports:* baseball M, basketball M/W, cheerleading M/W, cross-country running M/W, football M, golf M, lacrosse W, soccer M/W, softball W, tennis M/W, volleyball W. *Intramural sports:* basketball M/W, football M/W, lacrosse M/W, softball M/W, table tennis M/W, tennis M/W, ultimate Frisbee M/W, volleyball M/W.

Campus security: 24-hour emergency response devices and patrols, late-night transport/escort service, controlled dormitory access.

Student services: health clinic, personal/psychological counseling.

COSTS & FINANCIAL AID
Costs (2018–19) *Comprehensive fee:* $40,200 includes full-time tuition ($29,750), mandatory fees ($400), and room and board ($10,050). Full-time tuition and fees vary according to location. Part-time tuition: $500 per semester hour. Part-time tuition and fees vary according to course load and location. *College room only:* $4650. Room and board charges vary according to housing facility. *Payment plan:* installment. *Waivers:* employees or children of employees.

Financial Aid Of all full-time matriculated undergraduates who enrolled in 2008, 956 applied for aid, 788 were judged to have need, 360 had their need fully met. 323 Federal Work-Study jobs (averaging $1438). 67 state and other part-time jobs (averaging $565). In 2008, 46 non-need-based awards were made. *Average percent of need met:* 70. *Average financial aid package:* $12,524. *Average need-based loan:* $3898. *Average need-based gift aid:* $6696. *Average non-need-based aid:* $7876. *Average indebtedness upon graduation:* $7269.

APPLYING
Standardized Tests *Required:* SAT or ACT (for admission).

Options: electronic application.

Required: high school transcript. *Required for some:* essay or personal statement, interview. *Recommended:* minimum 2.0 GPA, 2 letters of recommendation, interview.

Application deadlines: rolling (freshmen), 7/15 (transfers).

Notification: continuous (freshmen), continuous (transfers).

CONTACT
Mr. Ben Lilley, Assistant Director of Admissions, North Carolina Wesleyan College, 3400 North Wesleyan Boulevard, Rocky Mount, NC 27804. *Phone:* 252-985-5113. *Toll-free phone:* 800-488-6292. *Fax:* 252-985-5295. *E-mail:* blilley@ncwc.edu.

Pfeiffer University
Misenheimer, North Carolina
http://www.pfeiffer.edu/

- **Independent United Methodist** comprehensive, founded 1885
- **Rural** 300-acre campus with easy access to Charlotte
- **Coed** 813 undergraduate students, 90% full-time, 52% women, 48% men
- **Moderately difficult** entrance level, 66% of applicants were admitted

UNDERGRAD STUDENTS
732 full-time, 81 part-time. 19% are from out of state; 23% Black or African American, non-Hispanic/Latino; 7% Hispanic/Latino; 1% Asian, non-Hispanic/Latino; 0.2% Native Hawaiian or other Pacific Islander, non-Hispanic/Latino; 0.5% American Indian or Alaska Native, non-Hispanic/Latino; 3% Two or more races, non-Hispanic/Latino; 0.4% Race/ethnicity unknown; 2% international; 7% transferred in; 59% live on campus.

Freshmen:
Admission: 1,860 applied, 1,228 admitted, 277 enrolled. *Average high school GPA:* 3.2. *Test scores:* SAT evidence-based reading and writing scores over 500: 56%; SAT math scores over 500: 53%; ACT scores over 18: 66%; SAT evidence-based reading and writing scores over 600: 12%; SAT math scores over 600: 12%; ACT scores over 24: 15%; SAT evidence-based reading and writing scores over 700: 1%; SAT math scores over 700: 1%; ACT scores over 30: 3%.

Retention: 61% of full-time freshmen returned.

FACULTY
Total: 126, 64% full-time, 69% with terminal degrees.

Student/faculty ratio: 12:1.

ACADEMICS
Calendar: semesters. *Degrees:* bachelor's, master's, post-master's, and postbachelor's certificates.

Special study options: academic remediation for entering students, accelerated degree program, advanced placement credit, cooperative education, double majors, English as a second language, honors programs, independent study, internships, part-time degree program, services for LD students, study abroad, summer session for credit. *ROTC:* Army (c).

Unusual degree programs: 3-2 business administration; engineering with Auburn University.

Computers: Students can access the following: campus intranet, computer help desk, free student e-mail accounts, online (class) grades, online (class) registration, online (class) schedules. Campuswide network is available. 100% of college-owned or -operated housing units are wired for high-speed Internet access. Wireless service is available via classrooms, computer centers, student centers.

Library: Gustavus A. Pfeiffer Library.

STUDENT LIFE
Housing options: on-campus residence required through senior year; coed, women-only. Campus housing is university owned. Freshman applicants given priority for college housing.

Activities and organizations: drama/theater group, student-run newspaper, choral group, Student Government Association, Religious Life Council, Commuter Student Association, Programming Activities Council, Residence Hall Association.

Athletics Member NCAA. All Division II. *Intercollegiate sports:* baseball M(s), basketball M(s)/W(s), cheerleading M(s)/W(s), cross-country running M(s)/W(s), golf M(s)/W(s), lacrosse M(s)/W(s), soccer

M(s)/W(s), softball W(s), swimming and diving M(s)/W(s), tennis M(s)/W(s), volleyball W(s). *Intramural sports:* badminton M/W, basketball M/W, football M/W, soccer M/W, softball M/W, tennis M/W, ultimate Frisbee M/W, volleyball M/W, water polo M/W.

Campus security: 24-hour emergency response devices and patrols, late-night transport/escort service, controlled dormitory access.

Student services: health clinic, personal/psychological counseling, women's center.

COSTS & FINANCIAL AID
Costs (2017–18) *Comprehensive fee:* $40,532 includes full-time tuition ($28,560), mandatory fees ($1014), and room and board ($10,958). Full-time tuition and fees vary according to course load. Part-time tuition: $450 per semester hour. Part-time tuition and fees vary according to course load. *Required fees:* $210 per term part-time. *College room only:* $5836. Room and board charges vary according to board plan and housing facility. *Payment plan:* installment. *Waivers:* employees or children of employees.

Financial Aid Of all full-time matriculated undergraduates who enrolled in 2016, 567 applied for aid, 527 were judged to have need, 79 had their need fully met. In 2016, 109 non-need-based awards were made. *Average percent of need met:* 72. *Average financial aid package:* $23,786. *Average need-based loan:* $3795. *Average need-based gift aid:* $20,281. *Average non-need-based aid:* $12,602. *Average indebtedness upon graduation:* $15,939. *Financial aid deadline:* 7/1.

APPLYING
Options: electronic application, early admission, deferred entrance.
Required: high school transcript. *Required for some:* 2 letters of recommendation. *Recommended:* minimum 2.0 GPA, interview.
Application deadlines: rolling (freshmen), rolling (transfers).
Notification: continuous (freshmen), continuous (transfers).

CONTACT
Pfeiffer University, PO Box 960, Misenheimer, NC 28109-0960. *Toll-free phone:* 800-338-2060.

Piedmont International University
Winston-Salem, North Carolina
http://www.piedmontu.edu/
- **Independent Baptist** university, founded 1947
- **Urban** 12-acre campus
- **Coed**
- **Noncompetitive** entrance level

FACULTY
Student/faculty ratio: 10:1.

ACADEMICS
Calendar: semesters. *Degrees:* certificates, associate, bachelor's, master's, and doctoral.
Library: George Manuel Memorial Library.

STUDENT LIFE
Housing options: on-campus residence required through sophomore year; men-only, women-only. Campus housing is university owned.
Activities and organizations: drama/theater group, choral group.
Athletics Member NCCAA.
Campus security: 24-hour emergency response devices, student patrols, late-night transport/escort service, controlled dormitory access, security guards on duty from dusk until dawn.

COSTS & FINANCIAL AID
Costs (2017–18) *Comprehensive fee:* $17,285 includes full-time tuition ($9300), mandatory fees ($800), and room and board ($7185). Full-time tuition and fees vary according to location and program. Part-time tuition: $325 per credit hour. Part-time tuition and fees vary according to program. *Required fees:* $60 per course part-time, $100 per term part-time. *Room and board:* Room and board charges vary according to board plan.

Financial Aid Of all full-time matriculated undergraduates who enrolled in 2016, 174 applied for aid, 161 were judged to have need, 6 had their need fully met. In 2016, 12 non-need-based awards were made. *Average percent of need met:* 42. *Average financial aid package:* $9317. *Average need-based loan:* $4283. *Average need-based gift aid:* $6843. *Average*

non-need-based aid: $4605. *Average indebtedness upon graduation:* $19,784.

APPLYING
Standardized Tests *Required:* SAT or ACT (for admission).
Options: electronic application.
Application fee: $55.
Required: essay or personal statement, high school transcript, 2 letters of recommendation, medical history, proof of immunization. *Recommended:* minimum 2.0 GPA, interview.

CONTACT
Mr. Joe Edgerton, Undergraduate Admissions Counselor, Piedmont International University, 420 South Broad Street, Winston-Salem, NC 27101. *Phone:* 336-714-7933. *Toll-free phone:* 800-937-5097. *Fax:* 336-725-5522. *E-mail:* stevensons@piedmontU.edu.

Queens University of Charlotte
Charlotte, North Carolina
http://www.queens.edu/

CONTACT
Evan Sprinkle, Senior Assistant Director, Queens University of Charlotte, 1900 Selwyn Avenue, Harris Welcome Center, MSC 1428, Charlotte, NC 28274. *Phone:* 704-337-2212. *Toll-free phone:* 800-849-0202. *Fax:* 704-337-2403. *E-mail:* admissions@queens.edu.

St. Andrews University
Laurinburg, North Carolina
http://www.sa.edu/
- **Independent Presbyterian** comprehensive, founded 1958
- **Small-town** 600-acre campus
- **Coed** 627 undergraduate students, 95% full-time, 46% women, 54% men
- **Moderately difficult** entrance level, 41% of applicants were admitted

UNDERGRAD STUDENTS
593 full-time, 34 part-time. Students come from 31 states and territories; 30 other countries; 40% are from out of state; 24% Black or African American, non-Hispanic/Latino; 4% Hispanic/Latino; 0.5% Asian, non-Hispanic/Latino; 1% American Indian or Alaska Native, non-Hispanic/Latino; 3% Two or more races, non-Hispanic/Latino; 8% Race/ethnicity unknown; 13% international; 9% transferred in; 85% live on campus.

Freshmen:
Admission: 1,104 applied, 454 admitted, 187 enrolled. *Average high school GPA:* 3.1. *Test scores:* ACT scores over 18: 53%; ACT scores over 24: 9%.
Retention: 42% of full-time freshmen returned.

FACULTY
Total: 73, 41% full-time, 62% with terminal degrees.
Student/faculty ratio: 14:1.

ACADEMICS
Calendar: semesters. *Degrees:* diplomas, bachelor's, and master's.
Special study options: adult/continuing education programs, advanced placement credit, distance learning, double majors, English as a second language, honors programs, independent study, internships, part-time degree program, services for LD students, student-designed majors, study abroad, summer session for credit.
Computers: 100 computers/terminals are available on campus for general student use. Students can access the following: campus intranet, computer help desk, free student e-mail accounts, online (class) grades, online (class) schedules. Campuswide network is available. 100% of college-owned or -operated housing units are wired for high-speed Internet access. Wireless service is available via entire campus.
Library: DeTamble Library. *Books:* 83,851 (physical), 345,661 (digital/electronic); *Serial titles:* 1,165 (physical), 31,450 (digital/electronic); *Databases:* 90.

STUDENT LIFE
Housing options: on-campus residence required through senior year; coed, men-only, women-only. Campus housing is university owned.

Activities and organizations: drama/theater group, choral group.

Athletics Member NCAA, NAIA. All NCAA Division II. *Intercollegiate sports:* baseball M(s), basketball M(s)/W(s), cross-country running M(s)/W(s), equestrian sports M(s)/W(s), golf M(s)/W(s), lacrosse M(s)/W(s), soccer M(s)/W(s), softball W(s), wrestling M. *Intramural sports:* basketball M/W, football M, rugby M(c)/W(c), softball M/W, volleyball M/W.

Campus security: 24-hour emergency response devices and patrols, late-night transport/escort service.

COSTS & FINANCIAL AID
Costs (2018–19) *Tuition:* $25,618 full-time, $288 per credit part-time. Full-time tuition and fees vary according to course load and location. Part-time tuition and fees vary according to location. *Room only:* Room and board charges vary according to housing facility. *Payment plan:* installment. *Waivers:* adult students, senior citizens, and employees or children of employees.

Financial Aid Of all full-time matriculated undergraduates who enrolled in 2016, 482 applied for aid, 454 were judged to have need, 47 had their need fully met. In 2016, 86 non-need-based awards were made. *Average percent of need met:* 71. *Average financial aid package:* $21,033. *Average need-based loan:* $4456. *Average need-based gift aid:* $17,118. *Average non-need-based aid:* $10,580. *Average indebtedness upon graduation:* $25,327.

APPLYING
Standardized Tests *Recommended:* SAT (for admission), ACT (for admission), SAT or ACT (for admission), SAT and SAT Subject Tests or ACT (for admission), SAT Subject Tests (for admission).

Options: electronic application, deferred entrance.

Application fee: $35.

Required: high school transcript. *Required for some:* essay or personal statement, interview. *Recommended:* minimum 2.0 GPA.

CONTACT
Erin Balduf, Director of Admissions, St. Andrews University, 1700 Dogwood Mile, Laurinburg, NC 28352. *Phone:* 910-277-5555. *Toll-free phone:* 800-763-0198. *Fax:* 910-277-5087. *E-mail:* admission@sapc.edu.

Saint Augustine's University
Raleigh, North Carolina
http://www.st-aug.edu/

- **Independent Episcopal** 4-year, founded 1867
- **Urban** 122-acre campus
- **Coed** 944 undergraduate students, 97% full-time, 46% women, 54% men
- **Moderately difficult** entrance level, 71% of applicants were admitted

UNDERGRAD STUDENTS
920 full-time, 24 part-time. Students come from 13 states and territories; 3 other countries; 338% are from out of state; 89% Black or African American, non-Hispanic/Latino; 1% Hispanic/Latino; 0.1% Asian, non-Hispanic/Latino; 0.6% American Indian or Alaska Native, non-Hispanic/Latino; 6% Race/ethnicity unknown; 1% international; 8% transferred in; 76% live on campus.

Freshmen:
Admission: 4,040 applied, 2,853 admitted, 347 enrolled.
Retention: 55% of full-time freshmen returned.

FACULTY
Total: 96, 61% full-time, 44% with terminal degrees.
Student/faculty ratio: 13:1.

ACADEMICS
Calendar: semesters. *Degree:* bachelor's.

Special study options: accelerated degree program, adult/continuing education programs, advanced placement credit, cooperative education, double majors, freshman honors college, honors programs, independent study, internships, off-campus study, part-time degree program, services for LD students, study abroad, summer session for credit. *ROTC:* Army (b), Air Force (c).

Computers: 183 computers/terminals and 1,670 ports are available on campus for general student use. Students can access the following:

campus intranet, computer help desk, free student e-mail accounts, online (class) grades, online (class) registration, online (class) schedules. Campuswide network is available. 100% of college-owned or -operated housing units are wired for high-speed Internet access. Wireless service is available via entire campus.

Library: Prezell R. Robinson Library. Students can reserve study rooms.

STUDENT LIFE
Housing options: on-campus residence required through sophomore year; men-only, women-only. Campus housing is university owned and leased by the school. Freshman campus housing is guaranteed.

Activities and organizations: drama/theater group, student-run newspaper, radio and television station, choral group, marching band, Campus Activity Board, Christian Fellowship Organization, Collegiate 100 Black Men of America, Student Government Association/Student Leaders, Falcon Fanatic Pep Squad, national fraternities, national sororities.

Athletics Member NCAA. All Division II. *Intercollegiate sports:* baseball M(s), basketball M(s)/W(s), bowling W(s), cheerleading W(s), cross-country running M(s)/W(s), football M(s), golf M(s), softball W(s), track and field M(s)/W(s), volleyball W(s).

Campus security: 24-hour emergency response devices and patrols, RAVE: Emergency Notification System.

Student services: health clinic, personal/psychological counseling, women's center.

COSTS & FINANCIAL AID
Costs (2017–18) *Comprehensive fee:* $25,582 includes full-time tuition ($12,890), mandatory fees ($5000), and room and board ($7692). Full-time tuition and fees vary according to course load. Part-time tuition: $537 per credit hour. Part-time tuition and fees vary according to course load. *Required fees:* $208 per credit hour part-time. *College room only:* $3182. Room and board charges vary according to housing facility. *Payment plan:* deferred payment. *Waivers:* children of alumni and employees or children of employees.

Financial Aid *Average indebtedness upon graduation:* $19,500.

APPLYING
Standardized Tests *Required:* SAT or ACT (for admission).

Options: electronic application, deferred entrance.

Application fee: $50.

Required: high school transcript, minimum 2.0 GPA, 2 letters of recommendation, medical history, background check. *Required for some:* essay or personal statement, interview. *Recommended:* minimum 2.5 GPA.

Application deadlines: rolling (freshmen), rolling (transfers).

Notification: continuous (freshmen), continuous (transfers).

CONTACT
Mr. Chris J. Withers, Director of Admissions, Saint Augustine's University, 1315 Oakwood Avenue, Raleigh, NC 27610-2298. *Phone:* 919-516-4012. *Toll-free phone:* 800-948-1126. *Fax:* 919-516-5804. *E-mail:* jesousa@st-aug.edu.

Salem College
Winston-Salem, North Carolina
http://www.salem.edu/

CONTACT
Dean Katherine Knapp Watts, Dean of Admissions and Financial Aid, Salem College, Single Sisters House, 601 South Church Street, Winston-Salem, NC 27101. *Phone:* 336-721-2621. *Toll-free phone:* 800-327-2536. *Fax:* 336-917-5572. *E-mail:* admissions@salem.edu.

Shaw University
Raleigh, North Carolina
http://www.shawu.edu/

- **Independent Baptist** comprehensive, founded 1865
- **Urban** 30-acre campus
- **Coed** 1,546 undergraduate students, 95% full-time, 58% women, 42% men
- **Minimally difficult** entrance level, 53% of applicants were admitted

UNDERGRAD STUDENTS

1,466 full-time, 80 part-time. Students come from 38 states and territories; 19 other countries; 37% are from out of state; 74% Black or African American, non-Hispanic/Latino; 0.1% Hispanic/Latino; 1% Asian, non-Hispanic/Latino; 1% Native Hawaiian or other Pacific Islander, non-Hispanic/Latino; 0.3% American Indian or Alaska Native, non-Hispanic/Latino; 3% Two or more races, non-Hispanic/Latino; 15% Race/ethnicity unknown; 4% international; 6% transferred in; 58% live on campus.

Freshmen:
Admission: 12,060 applied, 6,375 admitted, 493 enrolled. *Average high school GPA:* 2.6. *Test scores:* SAT evidence-based reading and writing scores over 500: 15%; SAT math scores over 500: 13%; ACT scores over 18: 17%; SAT evidence-based reading and writing scores over 600: 1%; SAT math scores over 600: 1%; ACT scores over 24: 3%; ACT scores over 30: 1%.
Retention: 43% of full-time freshmen returned.

FACULTY
Total: 139, 55% full-time.
Student/faculty ratio: 17:1.

ACADEMICS
Calendar: semesters. *Degrees:* certificates, bachelor's, and master's.
Special study options: academic remediation for entering students, accelerated degree program, adult/continuing education programs, advanced placement credit, distance learning, double majors, honors programs, independent study, internships, off-campus study, part-time degree program, services for LD students, student-designed majors, study abroad, summer session for credit. *ROTC:* Army (c), Air Force (c).
Computers: Students can access the following: computer help desk, free student e-mail accounts, online (class) grades, online (class) registration, online (class) schedules. Campuswide network is available. Wireless service is available via classrooms, computer centers, computer labs, learning centers, libraries, student centers.
Library: James E. Cheek Learning Resources Center.

STUDENT LIFE
Housing options: on-campus residence required for freshman year; men-only, women-only. Campus housing is university owned. Freshman applicants given priority for college housing.
Activities and organizations: drama/theater group, student-run newspaper, radio station, choral group, marching band, Student Government Association, choir, University band, academic clubs, International Student Organization, national fraternities, national sororities.
Athletics Member NCAA. All Division II. *Intercollegiate sports:* basketball M(s)/W(s), bowling W(s), cross-country running M(s)/W(s), football M(s), soccer M(s)/W(s), softball W(s), tennis M(s)/W(s), track and field M(s)/W(s), volleyball W(s). *Intramural sports:* basketball M/W, football M, tennis M/W, volleyball M/W.
Campus security: 24-hour emergency response devices and patrols, late-night transport/escort service, 24-hour electronic surveillance cameras.
Student services: health clinic, personal/psychological counseling.

COSTS & FINANCIAL AID
Costs (2017–18) *Comprehensive fee:* $24,638 includes full-time tuition ($11,808), mandatory fees ($4672), and room and board ($8158). Part-time tuition: $492 per credit hour. *College room only:* $3842. *Payment plans:* installment, deferred payment. *Waivers:* employees or children of employees.
Financial Aid Of all full-time matriculated undergraduates who enrolled in 2005, 2,197 applied for aid, 2,068 were judged to have need, 201 had their need fully met. 347 Federal Work-Study jobs (averaging $1120). In 2005, 117 non-need-based awards were made. *Average percent of need met:* 63. *Average financial aid package:* $8992. *Average need-based loan:* $3394. *Average need-based gift aid:* $5898. *Average non-need-based aid:* $9333. *Average indebtedness upon graduation:* $15,982. *Financial aid deadline:* 6/1.

APPLYING
Standardized Tests *Required:* SAT or ACT (for admission).
Options: electronic application, early admission, deferred entrance.
Application fee: $25.
Required: high school transcript, minimum 2.0 GPA.
Application deadlines: 7/30 (freshmen), 7/30 (transfers).
Notification: continuous (freshmen), continuous (transfers).

CONTACT
Shaw University, 118 East South Street, Raleigh, NC 27601-2399. *Toll-free phone:* 800-214-6683.

Southeastern Baptist Theological Seminary
Wake Forest, North Carolina
http://www.sebts.edu/
- **Independent Southern Baptist** comprehensive, founded 1950
- **Suburban** 300-acre campus with easy access to Raleigh
- **Coed**
- **Noncompetitive** entrance level

FACULTY
Student/faculty ratio: 15:1.

ACADEMICS
Calendar: semesters. *Degrees:* certificates, associate, bachelor's, master's, and doctoral.
Library: The Library at Southeastern plus 1 other. *Books:* 195,926 (physical), 135,058 (digital/electronic); *Databases:* 5. Weekly public service hours: 71; students can reserve study rooms.

STUDENT LIFE
Housing options: on-campus residence required for freshman year; men-only, women-only. Campus housing is university owned and leased by the school. Freshman applicants given priority for college housing.
Activities and organizations: drama/theater group, choral group.
Campus security: 24-hour emergency response devices and patrols, late-night transport/escort service.
Student services: health clinic, personal/psychological counseling, women's center.

COSTS
Costs (2017–18) *One-time required fee:* $130. *Tuition:* $10,440 full-time, $348 per credit hour part-time. Full-time tuition and fees vary according to degree level, location, and program. Part-time tuition and fees vary according to degree level, location, and program. *Required fees:* $580 full-time, $290 per term part-time. *Room only:* $3265. Room and board charges vary according to housing facility.

APPLYING
Standardized Tests *Required:* SAT or ACT (for admission).
Options: electronic application.
Application fee: $40.
Required: essay or personal statement, high school transcript, minimum 2.0 GPA, 3 letters of recommendation.

CONTACT
Mr. Sean Robinson, Admissions Counselor, Southeastern Baptist Theological Seminary, 120 South Wingate Street, Wake Forest, NC 27587. *Phone:* 919-761-2281. *Toll-free phone:* 800-284-6317.

South University
High Point, North Carolina
http://www.southuniversity.edu/high-point.aspx
CONTACT
South University, 3975 Premier Drive, High Point, NC 27265. *Phone:* 336-812-7200. *Toll-free phone:* 855-268-2187.

Strayer University–Greensboro Campus

Greensboro, North Carolina
http://www.strayer.edu/north-carolina/greensboro/

CONTACT
Strayer University–Greensboro Campus, 4900 Koger Boulevard, Suite 400, Greensboro, NC 27407. *Toll-free phone:* 888-311-0355.

Strayer University–Huntersville Campus

Huntersville, North Carolina
http://www.strayer.edu/north-carolina/huntersville/

CONTACT
Strayer University–Huntersville Campus, 13620 Reese Boulevard, Suite 310, Huntersville, NC 28078. *Toll-free phone:* 888-311-0355.

Strayer University–Morrisville Campus

Morrisville, North Carolina
http://www.strayer.edu/north-carolina/morrisville

CONTACT
Strayer University–Morrisville Campus, 4 Copley Parkway, Morrisville, NC 27560. *Toll-free phone:* 888-311-0355.

Strayer University–North Charlotte Campus

Concord, North Carolina
http://www.strayer.edu/north-carolina/north-charlotte/

CONTACT
Strayer University–North Charlotte Campus, 7870 Commons Park Circle NW, Concord, NC 28027. *Toll-free phone:* 888-311-0355.

Strayer University–North Raleigh Campus

Raleigh, North Carolina
http://www.strayer.edu/north-carolina/north-raleigh/

CONTACT
Strayer University–North Raleigh Campus, 8701 Wadford Drive, Raleigh, NC 27616. *Toll-free phone:* 888-311-0355.

Strayer University–South Charlotte Campus

Charlotte, North Carolina
http://www.strayer.edu/north-carolina/south-charlotte/

CONTACT
Strayer University–South Charlotte Campus, 9101 Kings Parade Boulevard, Suite 200, Charlotte, NC 28273. *Toll-free phone:* 888-311-0355.

Strayer University–South Raleigh Campus

Raleigh, North Carolina
http://www.strayer.edu/north-carolina/south-raleigh/

CONTACT
Strayer University–South Raleigh Campus, 3421 Olympia Drive, Raleigh, NC 27603. *Toll-free phone:* 888-311-0355.

University of Mount Olive

Mount Olive, North Carolina
http://www.umo.edu/

CONTACT
University of Mount Olive, 634 Henderson Street, Mount Olive, NC 28365. *Phone:* 919-658-2502 Ext. 3009. *Toll-free phone:* 800-653-0854.

University of North Carolina at Asheville

Asheville, North Carolina
http://www.unca.edu/

- **State-supported** comprehensive, founded 1927, part of University of North Carolina System
- **Urban** 365-acre campus
- **Endowment** $44.2 million
- **Coed** 3,826 undergraduate students, 86% full-time, 57% women, 43% men
- **Moderately difficult** entrance level, 81% of applicants were admitted

UNDERGRAD STUDENTS
3,285 full-time, 541 part-time. Students come from 44 states and territories; 26 other countries; 11% are from out of state; 5% Black or African American, non-Hispanic/Latino; 6% Hispanic/Latino; 2% Asian, non-Hispanic/Latino; 0.1% Native Hawaiian or other Pacific Islander, non-Hispanic/Latino; 0.6% American Indian or Alaska Native, non-Hispanic/Latino; 4% Two or more races, non-Hispanic/Latino; 3% Race/ethnicity unknown; 1% international; 9% transferred in; 38% live on campus.

Freshmen:
Admission: 3,358 applied, 2,730 admitted, 648 enrolled. *Average high school GPA:* 3.4. *Test scores:* SAT evidence-based reading and writing scores over 500: 93%; SAT math scores over 500: 90%; ACT scores over 18: 97%; SAT evidence-based reading and writing scores over 600: 56%; SAT math scores over 600: 35%; ACT scores over 24: 60%; SAT evidence-based reading and writing scores over 700: 11%; SAT math scores over 700: 5%; ACT scores over 30: 11%.
Retention: 75% of full-time freshmen returned.

FACULTY
Total: 324, 69% full-time, 76% with terminal degrees.
Student/faculty ratio: 13:1.

ACADEMICS
Calendar: semesters. *Degrees:* bachelor's, master's, and postbachelor's certificates.
Special study options: adult/continuing education programs, advanced placement credit, cooperative education, distance learning, double majors, honors programs, independent study, internships, off-campus study, part-time degree program, services for LD students, student-designed majors, study abroad, summer session for credit.
Computers: 500 computers/terminals and 1,900 ports are available on campus for general student use. Students can access the following: campus intranet, computer help desk, free student e-mail accounts, online (class) grades, online (class) registration, online (class) schedules. Campuswide network is available. 100% of college-owned or -operated housing units are wired for high-speed Internet access. Wireless service is available via classrooms, computer centers, computer labs, dorm rooms, learning centers, libraries, student centers.
Library: D. Hiden Ramsey Library. *Books:* 279,970 (physical), 670,018 (digital/electronic); *Serial titles:* 199 (physical), 76,919 (digital/electronic); *Databases:* 178. Students can reserve study rooms.

STUDENT LIFE
Housing options: on-campus residence required for freshman year; coed, special housing for students with disabilities. Campus housing is university owned. Freshman campus housing is guaranteed.
Activities and organizations: drama/theater group, student-run newspaper, radio station, choral group, Student Government Association, Alliance, Black Student Association, Gaming Club, Underdog Productions, national fraternities, national sororities.

Athletics Member NCAA. All Division I. *Intercollegiate sports:* archery M(c)/W(c), baseball M(s), basketball M(s)/W(s), cross-country running M(s)/W(s), equestrian sports M(c)/W(c), fencing M(c)/W(c), golf W(s), rugby M(c)/W(c), soccer M(s)/W(s), swimming and diving W(s), tennis M(s)/W(s), track and field M(s)/W(s), volleyball W(s). *Intramural sports:* badminton M/W, basketball M/W, football M(c)/W(c), racquetball M/W, soccer M/W, ultimate Frisbee M(c)/W(c), volleyball M/W, water polo M/W.

Campus security: 24-hour emergency response devices and patrols, late-night transport/escort service, controlled dormitory access.

Student services: health clinic, personal/psychological counseling.

COSTS & FINANCIAL AID
Costs (2018–19) *One-time required fee:* $150. *Tuition:* state resident $4122 full-time, $139 per credit hour part-time; nonresident $20,845 full-time, $704 per credit hour part-time. Full-time tuition and fees vary according to course load and degree level. Part-time tuition and fees vary according to course load and degree level. *Required fees:* $3023 full-time, $16 per credit hour part-time. *Room and board:* $9106; room only: $5134. Room and board charges vary according to board plan and housing facility. *Payment plans:* installment, deferred payment. *Waivers:* employees or children of employees.

Financial Aid Of all full-time matriculated undergraduates who enrolled in 2016, 2,471 applied for aid, 1,799 were judged to have need, 483 had their need fully met. 55 Federal Work-Study jobs (averaging $2572). 1,921 state and other part-time jobs (averaging $1289). In 2016, 263 non-need-based awards were made. *Average percent of need met:* 75. *Average financial aid package:* $12,231. *Average need-based loan:* $4625. *Average need-based gift aid:* $7071. *Average non-need-based aid:* $2248. *Average indebtedness upon graduation:* $23,824.

APPLYING
Standardized Tests *Required:* SAT or ACT (for admission).

Options: electronic application, early action, deferred entrance.

Application fee: $75.

Required: essay or personal statement, high school transcript, 1 letter of recommendation, minimum course requirement.

Application deadlines: 2/15 (freshmen), 4/15 (transfers), 11/15 (early action).

Notification: continuous until 12/15 (freshmen), continuous (transfers), 12/15 (early action).

CONTACT
Steve McKellips, Senior Director of Admissions and Financial Aid, University of North Carolina at Asheville, Brown Hall, CPO # 1320, Asheville, NC 28804-8510. *Phone:* 828-250-3829. *Toll-free phone:* 800-531-9842. *Fax:* 828-251-6482. *E-mail:* admissions@unca.edu.

The University of North Carolina at Chapel Hill
Chapel Hill, North Carolina
http://www.unc.edu/
- **State-supported** university, founded 1789, part of University of North Carolina System
- **Suburban** 729-acre campus with easy access to Raleigh-Durham
- **Endowment** $2.9 billion
- **Coed** 18,862 undergraduate students, 97% full-time, 59% women, 41% men
- **Very difficult** entrance level, 24% of applicants were admitted

UNDERGRAD STUDENTS
18,303 full-time, 559 part-time. Students come from 52 states and territories; 93 other countries; 16% are from out of state; 8% Black or African American, non-Hispanic/Latino; 8% Hispanic/Latino; 11% Asian, non-Hispanic/Latino; 0.1% Native Hawaiian or other Pacific Islander, non-Hispanic/Latino; 0.4% American Indian or Alaska Native, non-Hispanic/Latino; 4% Two or more races, non-Hispanic/Latino; 4% Race/ethnicity unknown; 3% international; 4% transferred in; 51% live on campus.

Freshmen:
Admission: 40,919 applied, 9,709 admitted, 4,356 enrolled. *Average high school GPA:* 4.7. *Test scores:* SAT evidence-based reading and writing scores over 500: 100%; SAT math scores over 500: 100%; ACT scores over 18: 100%; SAT evidence-based reading and writing scores over 600: 90%; SAT math scores over 600: 85%; ACT scores over 24: 94%; SAT evidence-based reading and writing scores over 700: 39%; SAT math scores over 700: 36%; ACT scores over 30: 55%.

Retention: 97% of full-time freshmen returned.

FACULTY
Total: 2,187, 76% full-time, 77% with terminal degrees.
Student/faculty ratio: 13:1.

ACADEMICS
Calendar: semesters. *Degrees:* certificates, bachelor's, master's, doctoral, post-master's, and postbachelor's certificates.

Special study options: advanced placement credit, distance learning, double majors, honors programs, independent study, internships, off-campus study, part-time degree program, services for LD students, student-designed majors, study abroad, summer session for credit. *ROTC:* Army (b), Navy (b), Air Force (b).

Computers: 867 computers/terminals and 9,999 ports are available on campus for general student use. Students can access the following: computer help desk, free student e-mail accounts, online (class) grades, online (class) registration, online (class) schedules. Campuswide network is available. 100% of college-owned or -operated housing units are wired for high-speed Internet access. Wireless service is available via entire campus.

Library: Davis Library plus 12 others. *Books:* 7.7 million (physical), 1.7 million (digital/electronic); *Serial titles:* 180,757 (digital/electronic); *Databases:* 1,288. Weekly public service hours: 137; study areas open 24 hours, 5–7 days a week; students can reserve study rooms.

STUDENT LIFE
Housing options: on-campus residence required for freshman year; coed, men-only, women-only, special housing for students with disabilities. Campus housing is university owned. Freshman campus housing is guaranteed.

Activities and organizations: drama/theater group, student-run newspaper, radio and television station, choral group, marching band, Residence Hall Association, Carolina Fever, Campus Y, UNC-CH Habitat for Humanity, Carolina for the Kids Foundation (Dance Marathon), national fraternities, national sororities.

Athletics Member NCAA. All Division I except football (Division I-A). *Intercollegiate sports:* badminton M(c)/W(c), baseball M(s), basketball M(s)/W(s), cheerleading W(c), crew M(c)/W(s), cross-country running M(s)/W(s), equestrian sports M(c)/W(c), fencing M(s)/W(s), field hockey M(c)/W(s), golf M(s)/W(s), gymnastics M(c)/W(s), ice hockey M(c), lacrosse M(s)/W(s), racquetball M(c)/W(c), rugby M(c)/W(c), sailing M(c)/W(c), skiing (downhill) M(c)/W(c), soccer M(s)/W(s), softball W(s), swimming and diving M(s)/W(s), tennis M(s)/W(s), track and field M(s)/W(s), triathlon M(c)/W(c), ultimate Frisbee M(c)/W(c), volleyball M(c)/W(s), water polo M(c)/W(s), wrestling M(s). *Intramural sports:* badminton M/W, baseball M(c), basketball M(c)/W(c), crew W(c), cross-country running M(c)/W(c), field hockey W(c), football M(c), golf M(c)/W(c), gymnastics W(c), lacrosse W(c), racquetball M/W, soccer M(c)/W(c), softball M/W(c), swimming and diving M(c)/W(c), table tennis M/W, tennis M(c)/W(c), track and field M(c)/W(c), triathlon M/W, ultimate Frisbee M/W, volleyball M/W(c), water polo M/W.

Campus security: 24-hour emergency response devices and patrols, late-night transport/escort service, controlled dormitory access, crime prevention initiatives, campus-wide emergency alert system, cell phone/GPS security options.

Student services: health clinic, personal/psychological counseling, women's center, legal services.

COSTS & FINANCIAL AID
Costs (2018–19) *Tuition:* state resident $7019 full-time; nonresident $33,202 full-time. Full-time tuition and fees vary according to program. Part-time tuition and fees vary according to course load and program. *Required fees:* $1967 full-time. *Room and board:* $11,190; room only: $6610. Room and board charges vary according to board plan, housing facility, and location. *Payment plan:* installment. *Waivers:* employees or children of employees.

Financial Aid Of all full-time matriculated undergraduates who enrolled in 2016, 10,433 applied for aid, 8,072 were judged to have need, 6,495 had their need fully met. 2,134 Federal Work-Study jobs (averaging $1767). In 2016, 798 non-need-based awards were made. *Average percent of need met:* 100. *Average financial aid package:* $19,626. *Average need-based loan:* $4993. *Average need-based gift aid:* $17,607. *Average non-need-based aid:* $7924. *Average indebtedness upon graduation:* $22,214.

APPLYING

Standardized Tests *Required:* SAT or ACT (for admission).

Options: electronic application, early action, deferred entrance.

Application fee: $80.

Required: essay or personal statement, high school transcript, 1 letter of recommendation, counselor's statement.

Application deadlines: 1/15 (freshmen), 2/15 (transfers), 10/15 (early action).

Notification: 3/31 (freshmen), 4/15 (transfers), 1/31 (early action).

CONTACT

The University of North Carolina at Chapel Hill, Chapel Hill, NC 27599. *Phone:* 919-966-3932.

The University of North Carolina at Charlotte

Charlotte, North Carolina

http://www.uncc.edu/

- **State-supported** university, founded 1946, part of University of North Carolina System
- **Suburban** 1000-acre campus with easy access to Charlotte
- **Endowment** $77.6 million
- **Coed** 23,914 undergraduate students, 86% full-time, 47% women, 53% men
- **Moderately difficult** entrance level, 66% of applicants were admitted

UNDERGRAD STUDENTS

20,597 full-time, 3,317 part-time. Students come from 41 states and territories; 92 other countries; 4% are from out of state; 17% Black or African American, non-Hispanic/Latino; 10% Hispanic/Latino; 7% Asian, non-Hispanic/Latino; 0.1% Native Hawaiian or other Pacific Islander, non-Hispanic/Latino; 0.3% American Indian or Alaska Native, non-Hispanic/Latino; 4% Two or more races, non-Hispanic/Latino; 2% Race/ethnicity unknown; 3% international; 12% transferred in; 24% live on campus.

Freshmen:

Admission: 16,743 applied, 11,061 admitted, 3,373 enrolled. *Average high school GPA:* 4.0. *Test scores:* SAT evidence-based reading and writing scores over 500: 98%; SAT math scores over 500: 98%; ACT scores over 18: 99%; SAT evidence-based reading and writing scores over 600: 46%; SAT math scores over 600: 48%; ACT scores over 24: 48%; SAT evidence-based reading and writing scores over 700: 4%; SAT math scores over 700: 6%; ACT scores over 30: 5%.

Retention: 83% of full-time freshmen returned.

FACULTY

Total: 1,666, 70% full-time, 70% with terminal degrees.

Student/faculty ratio: 19:1.

ACADEMICS

Calendar: semesters. *Degrees:* bachelor's, master's, doctoral, post-master's, and postbachelor's certificates.

Special study options: accelerated degree program, adult/continuing education programs, advanced placement credit, cooperative education, distance learning, double majors, English as a second language, freshman honors college, honors programs, independent study, internships, off-campus study, part-time degree program, services for LD students, study abroad, summer session for credit. *ROTC:* Army (b), Air Force (b).

Computers: 1,600 computers/terminals are available on campus for general student use. Students can access the following: computer help desk, free student e-mail accounts, online (class) grades, online (class) registration, online (class) schedules. Campuswide network is available. 100% of college-owned or -operated housing units are wired for high-speed Internet access. Wireless service is available via entire campus.

Library: J. Murrey Atkins Library plus 1 other. *Books:* 812,959 (physical), 980,416 (digital/electronic); *Serial titles:* 4,578 (physical), 92,904 (digital/electronic); *Databases:* 675. Study areas open 24 hours, 5–7 days a week; students can reserve study rooms.

STUDENT LIFE

Housing options: coed, special housing for students with disabilities. Campus housing is university owned.

Activities and organizations: drama/theater group, student-run newspaper, radio station, choral group, marching band, Triveni (Indian Students Association), eSports Club, Kinesiology Student Organization, National Society of Collegiate Scholars, National Society of Leadership and Success, national fraternities, national sororities.

Athletics Member NCAA. All Division I. *Intercollegiate sports:* baseball M(s), basketball M(s)/W(s), cheerleading M(s)/W(s), cross-country running M(s)/W(s), football M(s), golf M(s)/W(s), soccer M(s)/W(s), softball W(s), tennis M(s)/W(s), track and field M(s)/W(s), volleyball W(s). *Intramural sports:* archery M(c)/W(c), badminton M/W, baseball M(c), basketball M/W, bowling M/W, equestrian sports M(c)/W(c), fencing M(c)/W(c), football M/W, golf M(c), ice hockey M(c), lacrosse M(c)/W(c), rock climbing M/W, rugby M(c)/W(c), sailing M(c)/W(c), soccer M/W, softball M/W, table tennis M/W, ultimate Frisbee M(c)/W(c), volleyball M/W, water polo M/W, weight lifting M(c)/W(c), wrestling M(c)/W(c).

Campus security: 24-hour emergency response devices and patrols, late-night transport/escort service, controlled dormitory access.

Student services: health clinic, personal/psychological counseling.

COSTS & FINANCIAL AID

Costs (2017–18) *Tuition:* state resident $3812 full-time; nonresident $17,246 full-time. Full-time tuition and fees vary according to course load and program. Part-time tuition and fees vary according to course load and program. *Required fees:* $3211 full-time. *Room and board:* $10,780; room only: $6150. Room and board charges vary according to board plan and housing facility. *Payment plan:* installment. *Waivers:* employees or children of employees.

Financial Aid Of all full-time matriculated undergraduates who enrolled in 2017, 16,417 applied for aid, 13,354 were judged to have need, 1,390 had their need fully met. 766 Federal Work-Study jobs (averaging $2352). In 2017, 255 non-need-based awards were made. *Average percent of need met:* 55. *Average financial aid package:* $9124. *Average need-based loan:* $4144. *Average need-based gift aid:* $6414. *Average non-need-based aid:* $8248. *Average indebtedness upon graduation:* $27,453.

APPLYING

Standardized Tests *Required:* SAT or ACT (for admission).

Options: electronic application, early action.

Application fee: $60.

Required: high school transcript, minimum 2.0 GPA.

Application deadlines: 6/1 (freshmen), 6/1 (transfers), 11/1 (early action).

Notification: continuous (freshmen), continuous (out-of-state freshmen), continuous (transfers), 1/30 (early action).

CONTACT

Ms. Claire Kirby, Director of Admissions, The University of North Carolina at Charlotte, 9201 University City Boulevard, 1st Floor, Cato Hall, Charlotte, NC 28223-0001. *Phone:* 704-687-5507. *Fax:* 704-687-6483. *E-mail:* admissions@uncc.edu.

The University of North Carolina at Greensboro

Greensboro, North Carolina

http://www.uncg.edu/

- **State-supported** university, founded 1891, part of University of North Carolina System
- **Urban** 250-acre campus
- **Endowment** $275.0 million
- **Coed** 16,439 undergraduate students, 86% full-time, 66% women, 34% men
- **Moderately difficult** entrance level, 78% of applicants were admitted

UNDERGRAD STUDENTS

14,136 full-time, 2,303 part-time. Students come from 43 states and territories; 38 other countries; 5% are from out of state; 28% Black or African American, non-Hispanic/Latino; 9% Hispanic/Latino; 5% Asian, non-Hispanic/Latino; 0.1% Native Hawaiian or other Pacific Islander, non-Hispanic/Latino; 0.4% American Indian or Alaska Native, non-Hispanic/Latino; 5% Two or more races, non-Hispanic/Latino; 2% Race/ethnicity unknown; 2% international; 11% transferred in; 32% live on campus.

Freshmen:

Admission: 8,524 applied, 6,645 admitted, 2,791 enrolled. *Average high school GPA:* 3.7. *Test scores:* SAT evidence-based reading and writing scores over 500: 87%; SAT math scores over 500: 83%; ACT scores over 18: 100%; SAT evidence-based reading and writing scores over 600: 27%; SAT math scores over 600: 18%; ACT scores over 24: 39%; SAT evidence-based reading and writing scores over 700: 3%; SAT math scores over 700: 2%; ACT scores over 30: 4%.

Retention: 76% of full-time freshmen returned.

FACULTY

Total: 1,077, 74% full-time, 70% with terminal degrees.
Student/faculty ratio: 18:1.

ACADEMICS

Calendar: semesters. *Degrees:* bachelor's, master's, doctoral, post-master's, and postbachelor's certificates.

Special study options: academic remediation for entering students, accelerated degree program, adult/continuing education programs, advanced placement credit, distance learning, double majors, English as a second language, freshman honors college, honors programs, independent study, internships, off-campus study, part-time degree program, services for LD students, student-designed majors, study abroad, summer session for credit. *ROTC:* Army (c), Air Force (c).

Unusual degree programs: 3-2 accounting, biology/chemistry, chemistry, computer science, economics/public affairs, kinesiology/athletic training, political science/public affairs.

Computers: 474 computers/terminals are available on campus for general student use. Students can access the following: computer help desk, free student e-mail accounts, online (class) grades, online (class) registration, online (class) schedules, wireless printing services, cloud storage services. Campuswide network is available. 100% of college-owned or -operated housing units are wired for high-speed Internet access. Wireless service is available via entire campus.

Library: Walter Clinton Jackson Library plus 4 others. *Books:* 1.2 million (physical), 844,669 (digital/electronic); *Serial titles:* 19,514 (physical), 90,815 (digital/electronic); *Databases:* 671. Weekly public service hours: 138; study areas open 24 hours, 5–7 days a week; students can reserve study rooms.

STUDENT LIFE

Housing options: coed, special housing for students with disabilities. Campus housing is university owned.

Activities and organizations: drama/theater group, student-run newspaper, radio station, choral group, Alpha Lamda Delta, Beta Gamma Sigma, Sigma Theta Tau, Gamma Zeta, Golden Key, UNCG Leadership Challenge - Bronze, national fraternities, national sororities.

Athletics Member NCAA. All Division I. *Intercollegiate sports:* baseball M(s), basketball M(s)/W(s), cross-country running M(s)/W(s), golf M(s)/W(s), soccer M(s)/W(s), softball W(s), tennis M(s)/W(s), track and field M(s)/W(s), volleyball W(s). *Intramural sports:* badminton M/W, basketball M/W, cross-country running M(c)/W(c), equestrian sports M(c)/W(c), fencing M(c)/W(c), field hockey M/W, football M(c)/W(c), lacrosse M(c)/W(c), racquetball M/W, rock climbing M/W, rugby M(c)/W(c), sand volleyball M/W, soccer M/W, softball M(c)/W(c), swimming and diving M(c)/W(c), table tennis M/W, tennis M(c)/W(c), ultimate Frisbee M/W, volleyball M(c)/W(c), water polo M/W.

Campus security: 24-hour emergency response devices and patrols, student patrols, late-night transport/escort service, controlled dormitory access.

Student services: health clinic, personal/psychological counseling, women's center.

COSTS & FINANCIAL AID

Costs (2018–19) *Tuition:* state resident $4336 full-time, $553 per credit hour part-time; nonresident $19,582 full-time, $2448 per credit hour part-time. Part-time tuition and fees vary according to course load. *Required fees:* $2828 full-time, $105 per credit hour part-time. *Room and board:* $8834; room only: $5250. Room and board charges vary according to board plan and housing facility. *Payment plan:* installment. *Waivers:* senior citizens and employees or children of employees.

Financial Aid Of all full-time matriculated undergraduates who enrolled in 2017, 12,019 applied for aid, 11,837 were judged to have need, 1,856 had their need fully met. 321 Federal Work-Study jobs (averaging $2204). In 2017, 218 non-need-based awards were made. *Average percent of need met:* 72. *Average financial aid package:* $11,508. *Average need-based loan:* $4220. *Average need-based gift aid:* $6224. *Average non-need-based aid:* $3728. *Average indebtedness upon graduation:* $26,841.

APPLYING

Standardized Tests *Required:* SAT or ACT (for admission).
Options: electronic application.
Application fee: $65.
Required: high school transcript, minimum 2.3 GPA.
Application deadlines: 3/1 (freshmen), 7/15 (transfers).
Notification: continuous until 9/15 (freshmen), continuous (transfers).

CONTACT

The University of North Carolina at Greensboro, Armfield-Preyer Admissions and Visitor Center, 1400 Spring Garden Street, Greensboro, NC 27412. *Phone:* 336-334-5243. *Fax:* 336-334-5051. *E-mail:* admissions@uncg.edu.

The University of North Carolina at Pembroke

Pembroke, North Carolina

http://www.uncp.edu/

- **State-supported** comprehensive, founded 1887, part of University of North Carolina System
- **Rural** 264-acre campus
- **Endowment** $20.4 million
- **Coed** 5,481 undergraduate students, 82% full-time, 61% women, 39% men
- **Moderately difficult** entrance level, 81% of applicants were admitted

UNDERGRAD STUDENTS

4,483 full-time, 998 part-time. Students come from 35 states and territories; 15 other countries; 3% are from out of state; 34% Black or African American, non-Hispanic/Latino; 5% Hispanic/Latino; 2% Asian, non-Hispanic/Latino; 16% American Indian or Alaska Native, non-Hispanic/Latino; 3% Two or more races, non-Hispanic/Latino; 2% Race/ethnicity unknown; 0.7% international; 10% transferred in; 37% live on campus.

Freshmen:

Admission: 4,549 applied, 3,666 admitted, 1,033 enrolled. *Average high school GPA:* 3.5. *Test scores:* SAT evidence-based reading and writing scores over 500: 52%; SAT math scores over 500: 47%; ACT scores over 18: 70%; SAT evidence-based reading and writing scores over 600: 9%; SAT math scores over 600: 6%; ACT scores over 24: 11%.

Retention: 69% of full-time freshmen returned.

FACULTY

Total: 387, 74% full-time, 68% with terminal degrees.
Student/faculty ratio: 16:1.

ACADEMICS

Calendar: semesters. *Degrees:* bachelor's and master's.

Special study options: academic remediation for entering students, accelerated degree program, adult/continuing education programs, advanced placement credit, cooperative education, distance learning, double majors, English as a second language, honors programs, internships, off-campus study, part-time degree program, services for LD students, study abroad, summer session for credit. *ROTC:* Army (b), Air Force (b).

Computers: 501 computers/terminals are available on campus for general student use. Students can access the following: campus intranet, computer help desk, free student e-mail accounts, online (class) grades, online (class) registration, online (class) schedules, commuter/off campus connection to network, discounted computer software/hardware. Campuswide network is available. 100% of college-owned or -operated housing units are wired for high-speed Internet access. Wireless service is available via classrooms, computer centers, computer labs, dorm rooms, learning centers, libraries, student centers.

Library: Livermore Library. *Books:* 409,000 (physical), 172,000 (digital/electronic); *Serial titles:* 425 (physical), 52,000 (digital/electronic). Weekly public service hours: 92; students can reserve study rooms.

STUDENT LIFE

Housing options: on-campus residence required for freshman year; coed, men-only, women-only. Campus housing is university owned and is provided by a third party. Freshman applicants given priority for college housing.

Activities and organizations: drama/theater group, student-run newspaper, radio and television station, choral group, marching band, Health Careers Club, Spectrum, Graduate Student Organization, Phi Alpha, National Association for the Advancement of Colored People, national fraternities, national sororities.

Athletics Member NCAA. All Division II. *Intercollegiate sports:* baseball M(s), basketball M(s)/W(s), cheerleading M/W, cross-country running M(s)/W(s), football M(s), golf W(s), soccer M(s)/W(s), softball W(s), swimming and diving W, track and field M(s)/W(s), volleyball W(s), wrestling M(s). *Intramural sports:* basketball M/W, bowling M/W, cheerleading M/W, football M, golf M, racquetball M/W, rugby M, sand volleyball M/W, soccer M, softball M/W, swimming and diving M/W, tennis M/W, ultimate Frisbee M/W, volleyball M/W, weight lifting M/W, wrestling M.

Campus security: 24-hour emergency response devices and patrols, late-night transport/escort service, controlled dormitory access.

Student services: health clinic, personal/psychological counseling.

COSTS & FINANCIAL AID

Costs (2018–19) *Tuition:* state resident $3602 full-time, $132 per credit hour part-time; nonresident $15,193 full-time, $502 per credit hour part-time. Full-time tuition and fees vary according to course load, location, and program. Part-time tuition and fees vary according to course load, location, and program. *Required fees:* $2353 full-time. *Room and board:* $8782; room only: $4890. Room and board charges vary according to board plan, housing facility, and location. *Payment plans:* tuition prepayment, installment. *Waivers:* employees or children of employees.

Financial Aid Of all full-time matriculated undergraduates who enrolled in 2017, 4,080 applied for aid, 3,689 were judged to have need, 250 had their need fully met. 82 Federal Work-Study jobs (averaging $2000). In 2017, 46 non-need-based awards were made. *Average percent of need met:* 62. *Average financial aid package:* $10,050. *Average need-based loan:* $4221. *Average need-based gift aid:* $6683. *Average non-need-based aid:* $1819. *Average indebtedness upon graduation:* $25,831.

APPLYING

Standardized Tests *Required:* SAT or ACT (for admission). *Required for some:* TOEFL.

Options: electronic application, deferred entrance.

Application fee: $45.

Required: high school transcript. *Required for some:* 1 letter of recommendation, interview. *Recommended:* essay or personal statement, minimum 2.0 GPA.

Application deadlines: 6/30 (freshmen), 6/30 (transfers).

Notification: continuous (freshmen), continuous (transfers).

CONTACT

The University of North Carolina at Pembroke, One University Drive, PO Box 1510, Pembroke, NC 28372-1510. *Phone:* 910-522-5800. *Toll-free phone:* 800-949-UNCP.

University of North Carolina School of the Arts

Winston-Salem, North Carolina

http://www.uncsa.edu/

- **State-supported** comprehensive, founded 1963, part of University of North Carolina system
- **Urban** 74-acre campus
- **Endowment** $56.5 million
- **Coed** 873 undergraduate students, 97% full-time, 53% women, 47% men

UNDERGRAD STUDENTS

847 full-time, 26 part-time. Students come from 46 states and territories; 14 other countries; 48% are from out of state; 10% Black or African American, non-Hispanic/Latino; 6% Hispanic/Latino; 2% Asian, non-Hispanic/Latino; 0.1% Native Hawaiian or other Pacific Islander, non-Hispanic/Latino; 1% American Indian or Alaska Native, non-Hispanic/Latino; 5% Two or more races, non-Hispanic/Latino; 2% Race/ethnicity unknown; 2% international; 7% transferred in; 58% live on campus.

Freshmen:

Admission: 173 enrolled. *Average high school GPA:* 3.7. *Test scores:* ACT scores over 18: 97%; ACT scores over 24: 63%; ACT scores over 30: 17%.

Retention: 91% of full-time freshmen returned.

FACULTY

Total: 188, 76% full-time, 43% with terminal degrees.

Student/faculty ratio: 6:1.

ACADEMICS

Calendar: semesters. *Degrees:* certificates, bachelor's, master's, and post-master's certificates.

Special study options: advanced placement credit, English as a second language, independent study, internships, services for LD students, summer session for credit.

Computers: 86 computers/terminals and 1,000 ports are available on campus for general student use. Students can access the following: computer help desk, free student e-mail accounts, online (class) grades, online (class) registration, online (class) schedules. Campuswide network is available. 100% of college-owned or -operated housing units are wired for high-speed Internet access. Wireless service is available via entire campus.

Library: UNCSA Library. *Books:* 101,494 (physical), 26,321 (digital/electronic); *Serial titles:* 437 (physical), 57,650 (digital/electronic); *Databases:* 123. Weekly public service hours: 90; students can reserve study rooms.

STUDENT LIFE

Housing options: on-campus residence required through sophomore year; coed. Campus housing is university owned. Freshman campus housing is guaranteed.

Activities and organizations: drama/theater group, student-run newspaper, choral group, A.R.T.S. Club (awareness on social issues through artistic expression), The Artist Underground, Art & Soul, UNCSA Artists of Color.

Campus security: 24-hour emergency response devices and patrols, late-night transport/escort service, controlled dormitory access.

Student services: health clinic, personal/psychological counseling.

COSTS & FINANCIAL AID

Costs (2018–19) *Tuition:* state resident $271 per credit hour part-time; nonresident $927 per credit hour part-time. No tuition increase for student's term of enrollment. *Room and board:* $9021; room only: $4502. Room and board charges vary according to board plan and housing facility. *Payment plan:* installment. *Waivers:* employees or children of employees.

Financial Aid Of all full-time matriculated undergraduates who enrolled in 2016, 672 applied for aid, 546 were judged to have need, 53 had their need fully met. 146 Federal Work-Study jobs (averaging $800). In 2016, 37 non-need-based awards were made. *Average percent of need met:* 63. *Average financial aid package:* $13,596. *Average need-based loan:*

$4538. *Average need-based gift aid:* $8575. *Average non-need-based aid:* $2070. *Average indebtedness upon graduation:* $28,551.

APPLYING
Standardized Tests *Required:* SAT or ACT (for admission).
Required: essay or personal statement, high school transcript, minimum 2.5 GPA, 2 letters of recommendation, interview, audition.

CONTACT
University of North Carolina School of the Arts, 1533 South Main Street, PO Box 12189, Winston-Salem, NC 27127-2738. *Phone:* 336-770-3290.

The University of North Carolina Wilmington
Wilmington, North Carolina
http://www.uncw.edu/

- **State-supported** comprehensive, founded 1947, part of University of North Carolina System
- **Urban** 661-acre campus
- **Endowment** $83.4 million
- **Coed** 14,502 undergraduate students, 85% full-time, 62% women, 38% men
- **Moderately difficult** entrance level, 67% of applicants were admitted

UNDERGRAD STUDENTS
12,346 full-time, 2,156 part-time. Students come from 51 states and territories; 53 other countries; 12% are from out of state; 4% Black or African American, non-Hispanic/Latino; 7% Hispanic/Latino; 2% Asian, non-Hispanic/Latino; 0.1% Native Hawaiian or other Pacific Islander, non-Hispanic/Latino; 0.5% American Indian or Alaska Native, non-Hispanic/Latino; 4% Two or more races, non-Hispanic/Latino; 3% Race/ethnicity unknown; 2% international; 13% transferred in; 22% live on campus.

Freshmen:
Admission: 11,677 applied, 7,767 admitted, 2,145 enrolled. *Average high school GPA:* 4.2. *Test scores:* SAT evidence-based reading and writing scores over 500: 99%; SAT math scores over 500: 100%; ACT scores over 18: 100%; SAT evidence-based reading and writing scores over 600: 76%; SAT math scores over 600: 66%; ACT scores over 24: 63%; SAT evidence-based reading and writing scores over 700: 10%; SAT math scores over 700: 6%; ACT scores over 30: 7%.
Retention: 87% of full-time freshmen returned.

FACULTY
Total: 1,067, 61% full-time, 61% with terminal degrees.
Student/faculty ratio: 18:1.

ACADEMICS
Calendar: semesters. *Degrees:* bachelor's, master's, doctoral, post-master's, and postbachelor's certificates.

Special study options: academic remediation for entering students, accelerated degree program, advanced placement credit, cooperative education, distance learning, double majors, English as a second language, honors programs, independent study, internships, off-campus study, services for LD students, study abroad, summer session for credit.

Unusual degree programs: 3-2 English, Mathematics, Spanish.

Computers: 1,423 computers/terminals and 6,024 ports are available on campus for general student use. Students can access the following: campus intranet, computer help desk, free student e-mail accounts, online (class) grades, online (class) registration, online (class) schedules. Campuswide network is available. 100% of college-owned or -operated housing units are wired for high-speed Internet access. Wireless service is available via entire campus.

Library: William Madison Randall Library. *Books:* 573,457 (physical), 272,920 (digital/electronic); *Serial titles:* 4,761 (physical), 71,907 (digital/electronic); *Databases:* 305. Weekly public service hours: 110; study areas open 24 hours, 5–7 days a week; students can reserve study rooms.

STUDENT LIFE
Housing options: on-campus residence required for freshman year; coed, special housing for students with disabilities. Campus housing is university owned and is provided by a third party. Freshman applicants given priority for college housing.

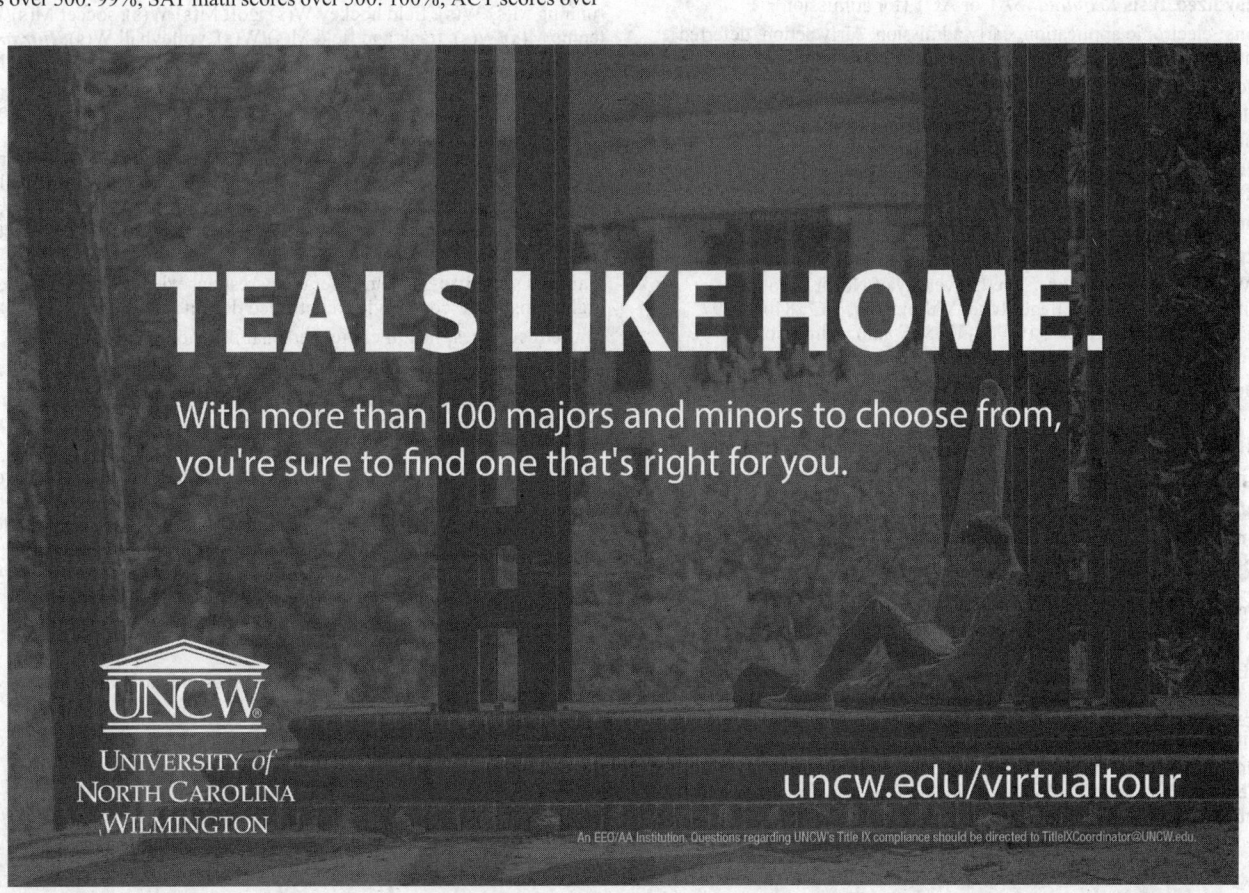

Activities and organizations: drama/theater group, student-run newspaper, radio station, choral group, Student Government Association, Association of Campus Entertainment, Residence Hall Association, Sports Club Council, Graduate Student Association, national fraternities, national sororities.

Athletics Member NCAA. All Division I. *Intercollegiate sports:* baseball M(s), basketball M(s)/W(s), cheerleading M/W, cross-country running M(s)/W(s), golf M(s)/W(s), soccer M(s)/W(s), softball W(s), swimming and diving M(s)/W(s), tennis M(s)/W(s), track and field M(s)/W(s), volleyball W(s). *Intramural sports:* badminton M/W, baseball M(c), basketball M/W, crew M(c)/W(c), equestrian sports W(c), field hockey W(c), football M/W, golf M(c)/W(c), gymnastics M(c)/W(c), ice hockey M(c), lacrosse M(c)/W(c), racquetball M/W, rugby M(c)/W(c), sailing M(c)/W(c), sand volleyball M/W, soccer M/W, softball M(c)/W(c), swimming and diving M(c)/W(c), tennis M/W, triathlon M(c)/W(c), ultimate Frisbee M(c)/W(c), volleyball M/W, water polo M/W.

Campus security: 24-hour emergency response devices and patrols, late-night transport/escort service, controlled dormitory access.

Student services: health clinic, personal/psychological counseling, women's center.

COSTS & FINANCIAL AID

Costs (2017–18) *Tuition:* state resident $4400 full-time, $160 per credit hour part-time; nonresident $18,416 full-time, $668 per credit hour part-time. Full-time tuition and fees vary according to course load and location. Part-time tuition and fees vary according to course load and location. *Required fees:* $2648 full-time, $77 per credit hour part-time. *Room and board:* $9736; room only: $6056. Room and board charges vary according to board plan and housing facility. *Payment plan:* installment. *Waivers:* employees or children of employees.

Financial Aid Of all full-time matriculated undergraduates who enrolled in 2016, 8,578 applied for aid, 6,794 were judged to have need, 914 had their need fully met. In 2016, 146 non-need-based awards were made. *Average financial aid package:* $9398. *Average need-based loan:* $4622. *Average need-based gift aid:* $6020. *Average non-need-based aid:* $3096. *Average indebtedness upon graduation:* $24,605.

APPLYING

Standardized Tests *Required:* SAT or ACT (for admission).

Options: electronic application, early admission, early action, deferred entrance.

Application fee: $80.

Required: essay or personal statement, high school transcript, 1 letter of recommendation.

Application deadlines: 2/1 (freshmen), 3/1 (transfers), 11/1 (early action).

Notification: 4/1 (freshmen), continuous (transfers), 1/20 (early action).

CONTACT

UNCW Office of Admissions, The University of North Carolina Wilmington, 601 South College Road, Wilmington, NC 28403-3297. *Phone:* 910-962-3243. *Fax:* 910-962-3038. *E-mail:* admissions@uncw.edu.

See previous page for display ad and page 1474 for the College Close-Up.

Wake Forest University

Winston-Salem, North Carolina

http://www.wfu.edu/

- **Independent** university, founded 1834
- **Suburban** 340-acre campus
- **Coed** 5,102 undergraduate students, 99% full-time, 54% women, 46% men
- **Very difficult** entrance level, 28% of applicants were admitted

UNDERGRAD STUDENTS

5,046 full-time, 56 part-time. 78% are from out of state; 7% Black or African American, non-Hispanic/Latino; 7% Hispanic/Latino; 4% Asian, non-Hispanic/Latino; 0.1% American Indian or Alaska Native, non-Hispanic/Latino; 3% Two or more races, non-Hispanic/Latino; 0.1% Race/ethnicity unknown; 10% international; 0.8% transferred in; 75% live on campus.

Freshmen:
Admission: 13,071 applied, 3,604 admitted, 1,349 enrolled. *Test scores:* SAT evidence-based reading and writing scores over 500: 98%; SAT math scores over 500: 97%; ACT scores over 18: 100%; SAT evidence-based reading and writing scores over 600: 88%; SAT math scores over 600: 83%; ACT scores over 24: 94%; SAT evidence-based reading and writing scores over 700: 33%; SAT math scores over 700: 46%; ACT scores over 30: 61%.

Retention: 94% of full-time freshmen returned.

FACULTY
Total: 579.

Student/faculty ratio: 11:1.

ACADEMICS
Calendar: semesters. *Degrees:* bachelor's, master's, doctoral, and postbachelor's certificates.

Special study options: advanced placement credit, distance learning, double majors, honors programs, independent study, internships, part-time degree program, services for LD students, study abroad, summer session for credit. *ROTC:* Army (b).

Unusual degree programs: 3-2 engineering.

Computers: Students can access the following: campus intranet, computer help desk, free student e-mail accounts, online (class) grades, online (class) registration, online (class) schedules, financial information online, drop-add, transcript requests. Campuswide network is available. Wireless service is available via entire campus.

Library: Z. Smith Reynolds Library.

STUDENT LIFE
Housing options: on-campus residence required through sophomore year; coed. Campus housing is university owned. Freshman campus housing is guaranteed.

Activities and organizations: drama/theater group, student-run newspaper, radio and television station, choral group, marching band, national fraternities, national sororities.

Athletics Member NCAA. All Division I except football (Division I-A). *Intercollegiate sports:* baseball M(s), basketball M(s)/W(s), cross-country running M(s)/W(s), field hockey W(s), golf M(s)/W(s), soccer M(s)/W(s), tennis M(s)/W(s), track and field M(s)/W(s), volleyball W(s). *Intramural sports:* archery M(c)/W(c), baseball M(c), basketball M/W, bowling M/W, cheerleading M(c)/W(c), crew M(c)/W(c), cross-country running M(c)/W(c), equestrian sports M(c)/W(c), fencing M(c)/W(c), field hockey W(c), football M, golf M(c)/W(c), ice hockey M(c)/W(c), lacrosse M(c)/W(c), racquetball M/W, rugby M(c)/W(c), skiing (cross-country) M(c)/W(c), skiing (downhill) M(c)/W(c), soccer M(c)/W(c), softball M/W(c), swimming and diving M/W, table tennis M/W, tennis M/W, ultimate Frisbee M/W, volleyball M/W, water polo M(c)/W(c), wrestling M(c).

Campus security: 24-hour emergency response devices and patrols, late-night transport/escort service, controlled dormitory access.

Student services: health clinic, personal/psychological counseling.

COSTS & FINANCIAL AID
Costs (2018–19) *Comprehensive fee:* $69,354 includes full-time tuition ($52,348), mandatory fees ($974), and room and board ($16,032). Part-time tuition: $2170 per credit hour. *College room only:* $9282.

Financial Aid Of all full-time matriculated undergraduates who enrolled in 2017, 1,910 applied for aid, 1,558 were judged to have need, 1,558 had their need fully met. In 2017, 468 non-need-based awards were made. *Average percent of need met:* 100. *Average financial aid package:* $49,309. *Average need-based loan:* $10,118. *Average need-based gift aid:* $44,338. *Average non-need-based aid:* $12,792. *Average indebtedness upon graduation:* $35,434. *Financial aid deadline:* 1/1.

APPLYING
Options: electronic application, early admission, early decision.

Application fee: $65.

Required: essay or personal statement, high school transcript, 1 letter of recommendation. *Recommended:* interview.

Early decision deadline: 11/15.

Notification: continuous (freshmen), rolling (early decision).

CONTACT
Wake Forest University, 1834 Wake Forest Road, PO Box 7373 Reynolda Station, Winston-Salem, NC 27109. *Phone:* 336-758-5201.

Warren Wilson College
Swannanoa, North Carolina
http://www.warren-wilson.edu/

CONTACT
Monique Cote, Campus Visit Coordinator, Warren Wilson College, PO Box 9000, Asheville, NC 28815-9000. *Phone:* 828-771-2073. *Toll-free phone:* 800-934-3536. *Fax:* 828-298-1440. *E-mail:* admit@warren-wilson.edu.

Western Carolina University
Cullowhee, North Carolina
http://www.wcu.edu/
- **State-supported** university, founded 1889, part of University of North Carolina System
- **Rural** 682-acre campus
- **Coed**
- **Moderately difficult** entrance level

FACULTY
Student/faculty ratio: 17:1.

ACADEMICS
Calendar: semesters. *Degrees:* bachelor's, master's, doctoral, post-master's, and postbachelor's certificates.
Library: Hunter Library. Weekly public service hours: 96; study areas open 24 hours, 5–7 days a week; students can reserve study rooms.

STUDENT LIFE
Housing options: on-campus residence required for freshman year; coed, men-only, women-only, special housing for students with disabilities. Campus housing is university owned, leased by the school and is provided by a third party. Freshman campus housing is guaranteed.
Activities and organizations: drama/theater group, student-run newspaper, radio and television station, choral group, marching band, national fraternities, national sororities.
Athletics Member NCAA. All Division I except football (Division I-AA).
Campus security: 24-hour emergency response devices and patrols, late-night transport/escort service, controlled dormitory access.
Student services: health clinic, personal/psychological counseling, women's center.

COSTS & FINANCIAL AID
Costs (2017–18) *Tuition:* state resident $3971 full-time; nonresident $14,364 full-time. Full-time tuition and fees vary according to degree level. Part-time tuition and fees vary according to course load and degree level. *Required fees:* $3220 full-time. *Room and board:* $9164; room only: $4616. Room and board charges vary according to board plan and housing facility.
Financial Aid Of all full-time matriculated undergraduates who enrolled in 2016, 6,554 applied for aid, 5,327 were judged to have need, 651 had their need fully met. In 2016, 350 non-need-based awards were made. *Average percent of need met:* 65. *Average financial aid package:* $11,395. *Average need-based loan:* $6375. *Average need-based gift aid:* $6131. *Average non-need-based aid:* $2601. *Average indebtedness upon graduation:* $15,669.

APPLYING
Standardized Tests *Required:* SAT or ACT (for admission). *Recommended:* ACT (for admission).
Options: electronic application, early admission, early action.
Application fee: $65.
Required: high school transcript.

CONTACT
Office of Undergraduate Admission, Western Carolina University, 102 Camp Building, Cullowhee, NC 28723. *Phone:* 828-227-7317. *Toll-free phone:* 877-WCU4YOU. *E-mail:* admiss@email.wcu.edu.

William Peace University
Raleigh, North Carolina
http://www.peace.edu/
- **Independent** 4-year, founded 1857, affiliated with Presbyterian Church (U.S.A.)
- **Urban** 21-acre campus with easy access to Raleigh-Cary
- **Endowment** $35.6 million
- **Coed** 930 undergraduate students, 88% full-time, 52% women, 48% men
- **Moderately difficult** entrance level, 59% of applicants were admitted

UNDERGRAD STUDENTS
814 full-time, 116 part-time. Students come from 12 states and territories; 2 other countries; 8% are from out of state; 28% Black or African American, non-Hispanic/Latino; 9% Hispanic/Latino; 2% Asian, non-Hispanic/Latino; 0.2% Native Hawaiian or other Pacific Islander, non-Hispanic/Latino; 1% American Indian or Alaska Native, non-Hispanic/Latino; 1% Two or more races, non-Hispanic/Latino; 12% Race/ethnicity unknown; 0.3% international; 11% transferred in; 50% live on campus.

Freshmen:
Admission: 1,569 applied, 927 admitted, 203 enrolled. *Average high school GPA:* 3.4. *Test scores:* SAT evidence-based reading and writing scores over 500: 53%; SAT math scores over 500: 53%; ACT scores over 18: 73%; SAT evidence-based reading and writing scores over 600: 9%; SAT math scores over 600: 9%; ACT scores over 24: 21%; ACT scores over 30: 2%.
Retention: 61% of full-time freshmen returned.

FACULTY
Total: 121, 28% full-time, 41% with terminal degrees.
Student/faculty ratio: 14:1.

ACADEMICS
Calendar: semesters. *Degree:* bachelor's.
Special study options: academic remediation for entering students, accelerated degree program, adult/continuing education programs, advanced placement credit, cooperative education, distance learning, double majors, honors programs, independent study, internships, off-campus study, part-time degree program, services for LD students, study abroad, summer session for credit. *ROTC:* Army (c), Air Force (c).
Computers: 101 computers/terminals are available on campus for general student use. Students can access the following: campus intranet, computer help desk, free student e-mail accounts, online (class) grades, online (class) registration, online (class) schedules. Campuswide network is available. 100% of college-owned or -operated housing units are wired for high-speed Internet access. Wireless service is available via entire campus.
Library: Lucy Cooper Finch Library. *Books:* 48,196 (physical), 250,000 (digital/electronic); *Serial titles:* 13 (physical), 25,000 (digital/electronic); *Databases:* 94. Weekly public service hours: 90; students can reserve study rooms.

STUDENT LIFE
Housing options: on-campus residence required through junior year; coed, women-only. Campus housing is university owned, leased by the school and is provided by a third party. Freshman applicants given priority for college housing.
Activities and organizations: drama/theater group, student-run newspaper, choral group, Campus Activities Board, Phi Beta Lambda, Gamma Sigma Sigma, Ambassadors for Christ, Class Councils.
Athletics Member NCAA. All Division III. *Intercollegiate sports:* baseball M, basketball M/W, cross-country running M/W, golf M, lacrosse M/W, soccer M/W, softball W, swimming and diving M/W, tennis M/W, volleyball W. *Intramural sports:* basketball M/W, cheerleading M(c)/W(c), football M/W, lacrosse M/W, soccer M/W, tennis M/W, ultimate Frisbee M(c)/W(c), volleyball M/W.
Campus security: 24-hour emergency response devices and patrols, late-night transport/escort service, controlled dormitory access.
Student services: health clinic, personal/psychological counseling.

COSTS & FINANCIAL AID
Costs (2017–18) *Comprehensive fee:* $39,500 includes full-time tuition ($28,500), mandatory fees ($200), and room and board ($10,800). Full-

time tuition and fees vary according to class time and course load. Part-time tuition: $950 per credit hour. Part-time tuition and fees vary according to class time and course load. *College room only:* $7200. Room and board charges vary according to board plan. *Payment plan:* installment. *Waivers:* employees or children of employees.

Financial Aid Of all full-time matriculated undergraduates who enrolled in 2016, 828 applied for aid, 758 were judged to have need, 8 had their need fully met. 93 Federal Work-Study jobs (averaging $2000). In 2016, 60 non-need-based awards were made. *Average percent of need met:* 64. *Average financial aid package:* $18,464. *Average need-based loan:* $4095. *Average need-based gift aid:* $8612. *Average non-need-based aid:* $3171. *Average indebtedness upon graduation:* $20,921.

APPLYING
Standardized Tests *Required:* SAT or ACT (for admission).
Options: electronic application, early admission, deferred entrance.
Application fee: $35.
Required: high school transcript, minimum 2.5 GPA. *Required for some:* essay or personal statement. *Recommended:* essay or personal statement, letters of recommendation, interview.
Application deadlines: rolling (freshmen), rolling (out-of-state freshmen), rolling (transfers).
Notification: continuous (freshmen), continuous (out-of-state freshmen), continuous (transfers).

CONTACT
Josh Bistromowitz, Director of Admissions, William Peace University, 15 East Peace Street, Raleigh, NC 27604. *Phone:* 919-508-2000. *E-mail:* admission@peace.edu.

Wingate University
Wingate, North Carolina
http://www.wingate.edu/
- **Independent Baptist** comprehensive, founded 1896
- **Small-town** 400-acre campus with easy access to Charlotte
- **Coed**
- **Moderately difficult** entrance level

FACULTY
Student/faculty ratio: 14:1.

ACADEMICS
Calendar: semesters. *Degrees:* bachelor's, master's, doctoral, and post-master's certificates.
Library: Ethel K. Smith Library. *Books:* 96,673 (physical); *Databases:* 110. Students can reserve study rooms.

STUDENT LIFE
Housing options: on-campus residence required through senior year; coed, men-only, women-only, cooperative, special housing for students with disabilities. Campus housing is university owned. Freshman campus housing is guaranteed.
Activities and organizations: drama/theater group, student-run newspaper, television station, choral group, University and Community Assistance Network (UCAN), Bulldog Activities Resource Committee, Fellowship of Christian Athletes, Student Bulldog Club, Student Government Association, national fraternities, national sororities.
Athletics Member NCAA. All Division II.
Campus security: 24-hour emergency response devices and patrols, late-night transport/escort service, controlled dormitory access.
Student services: health clinic, personal/psychological counseling.

COSTS & FINANCIAL AID
Costs (2017–18) *Comprehensive fee:* $41,900 includes full-time tuition ($31,120) and room and board ($10,780). Part-time tuition: $1035 per credit hour. Part-time tuition and fees vary according to course load.
Financial Aid Of all full-time matriculated undergraduates who enrolled in 2015, 1,731 applied for aid, 1,594 were judged to have need, 397 had their need fully met. In 2015, 406 non-need-based awards were made. *Average percent of need met:* 75. *Average financial aid package:* $24,280. *Average need-based loan:* $3914. *Average need-based gift aid:* $20,912. *Average non-need-based aid:* $15,467. *Average indebtedness upon graduation:* $31,997.

APPLYING
Standardized Tests *Required:* SAT or ACT (for admission).
Options: electronic application, deferred entrance.
Required: high school transcript, minimum 2.7 GPA. *Required for some:* essay or personal statement. *Recommended:* interview.

CONTACT
Mr. Gabe Hollingsworth, Director of Admissions, Wingate University, PO Box 159, Wingate, NC 28174. *Phone:* 704-233-8000. *Toll-free phone:* 800-755-5550. *Fax:* 704-233-8110. *E-mail:* admit@wingate.edu.

Winston-Salem State University
Winston-Salem, North Carolina
http://www.wssu.edu/

CONTACT
Ms. Tomikia LeGrande, Assistant Vice Chancellor for Enrollment Services, Winston-Salem State University, 601 Martin Luther King, Jr. Drive, Thompson Center, Winston-Salem, NC 27110. *Phone:* 336-750-2070. *Toll-free phone:* 800-257-4052. *Fax:* 336-750-2079. *E-mail:* legrandet@wssu.edu.

NORTH DAKOTA

Bismarck State College
Bismarck, North Dakota
http://www.bismarckstate.edu/
- **State-supported** primarily 2-year, founded 1939, part of North Dakota University System
- **Urban** 120-acre campus
- **Endowment** $16.3 million
- **Coed**
- **Noncompetitive** entrance level

FACULTY
Student/faculty ratio: 14:1.

ACADEMICS
Calendar: semesters. *Degrees:* certificates, diplomas, associate, and bachelor's.
Library: Bismarck State College Library. *Books:* 61,059 (physical), 16,804 (digital/electronic); *Serial titles:* 121 (physical), 114 (digital/electronic); *Databases:* 88. Weekly public service hours: 67; students can reserve study rooms.

STUDENT LIFE
Housing options: coed, men-only, women-only, special housing for students with disabilities. Campus housing is university owned.
Activities and organizations: drama/theater group, student-run newspaper, radio station, choral group, Intramural Sports, Campus Crusade, Student Government Association, Concert/Chamber Choir, Drama Club.
Athletics Member NJCAA.
Campus security: late-night transport/escort service, controlled dormitory access.
Student services: personal/psychological counseling.

COSTS & FINANCIAL AID
Costs (2017–18) *Tuition:* state resident $3791 full-time, $126 per credit hour part-time; nonresident $10,121 full-time, $337 per credit hour part-time. Full-time tuition and fees vary according to course level, course load, degree level, location, program, and reciprocity agreements. Part-time tuition and fees vary according to course level, course load, degree level, location, program, and reciprocity agreements. *Required fees:* $800 full-time, $33 per credit hour part-time. *Room and board:* $6992; room only: $2892. Room and board charges vary according to board plan and housing facility.
Financial Aid Of all full-time matriculated undergraduates who enrolled in 2015, 1,507 applied for aid, 906 were judged to have need, 341 had their need fully met. In 2015, 230 non-need-based awards were made. *Average percent of need met:* 67. *Average financial aid package:* $8283.

Average need-based loan: $4493. *Average need-based gift aid:* $4696. *Average non-need-based aid:* $1388.

APPLYING
Standardized Tests *Recommended:* ACT (for admission).
Options: electronic application, early admission, deferred entrance.
Application fee: $35.
Required: high school transcript. *Required for some:* interview.

CONTACT
Karen Erickson, Director of Admissions and Enrollment Services, Bismarck State College, PO Box 5587, Bismarck, ND 58506. *Phone:* 701-224-5424. *Toll-free phone:* 800-445-5073. *Fax:* 701-224-5643. *E-mail:* karen.erickson@bismarckstate.edu.

Dickinson State University
Dickinson, North Dakota
http://www.dickinsonstate.edu/

- **State-supported** comprehensive, founded 1918, part of North Dakota University System
- **Small-town** 132-acre campus
- **Coed** 1,525 undergraduate students, 60% full-time, 62% women, 38% men
- **Minimally difficult** entrance level, 99% of applicants were admitted

UNDERGRAD STUDENTS
922 full-time, 603 part-time. Students come from 36 states and territories; 30 other countries; 29% are from out of state; 4% Black or African American, non-Hispanic/Latino; 5% Hispanic/Latino; 0.8% Asian, non-Hispanic/Latino; 0.4% Native Hawaiian or other Pacific Islander, non-Hispanic/Latino; 0.9% American Indian or Alaska Native, non-Hispanic/Latino; 3% Two or more races, non-Hispanic/Latino; 4% Race/ethnicity unknown; 5% international; 12% transferred in; 21% live on campus.

Freshmen:
Admission: 388 applied, 384 admitted, 194 enrolled. *Average high school GPA:* 3.3. *Test scores:* ACT scores over 18: 88%; ACT scores over 24: 18%.
Retention: 64% of full-time freshmen returned.

FACULTY
Total: 169, 57% full-time, 30% with terminal degrees.
Student/faculty ratio: 9:1.

ACADEMICS
Calendar: semesters. *Degrees:* certificates, associate, bachelor's, and master's.
Special study options: academic remediation for entering students, adult/continuing education programs, advanced placement credit, cooperative education, distance learning, double majors, English as a second language, external degree program, honors programs, independent study, internships, off-campus study, part-time degree program, services for LD students, study abroad, summer session for credit.
Computers: 250 computers/terminals and 300 ports are available on campus for general student use. Students can access the following: campus intranet, computer help desk, free student e-mail accounts, online (class) grades, online (class) registration, online (class) schedules. Campuswide network is available. 100% of college-owned or -operated housing units are wired for high-speed Internet access. Wireless service is available via entire campus.
Library: Stoxen Library plus 1 other. *Books:* 73,571 (physical), 23,355 (digital/electronic); *Serial titles:* 119 (physical), 107,800 (digital/electronic); *Databases:* 71. Weekly public service hours: 56.

STUDENT LIFE
Housing options: on-campus residence required through sophomore year; coed. Campus housing is university owned. Freshman campus housing is guaranteed.
Activities and organizations: drama/theater group, choral group, Rodeo Club, Blue Hawk Brigade, chorale, Business Club, Navigators, national fraternities.
Athletics Member NAIA. *Intercollegiate sports:* baseball M(s), basketball M(s)/W(s), cross-country running M(s)/W(s), football M(s), golf M(s)/W(s), softball W(s), track and field M(s)/W(s), volleyball W(s), wrestling M(s). *Intramural sports:* basketball M/W, soccer M/W, softball M/W, squash M/W, table tennis M/W, tennis M/W, ultimate Frisbee M/W, volleyball M/W.
Campus security: 24-hour emergency response devices and patrols, late-night transport/escort service, controlled dormitory access, Crisis Manager App. for Phones, Automated Mass Notification System.
Student services: health clinic, personal/psychological counseling.

COSTS & FINANCIAL AID
Costs (2018–19) *Tuition:* state resident $5555 full-time, $232 per credit hour part-time; nonresident $8334 full-time, $347 per credit hour part-time. Full-time tuition and fees vary according to course load, location, and reciprocity agreements. Part-time tuition and fees vary according to course load, location, and reciprocity agreements. *Required fees:* $1210 full-time, $50 per credit hour part-time, $302 per term part-time. *Room and board:* $6898; room only: $2900. Room and board charges vary according to board plan, housing facility, and location. *Payment plan:* installment. *Waivers:* senior citizens and employees or children of employees.
Financial Aid Of all full-time matriculated undergraduates who enrolled in 2015, 645 applied for aid, 445 were judged to have need, 160 had their need fully met. 79 Federal Work-Study jobs (averaging $2153). In 2015, 28 non-need-based awards were made. *Average percent of need met:* 54. *Average financial aid package:* $10,663. *Average need-based loan:* $5539. *Average need-based gift aid:* $5358. *Average non-need-based aid:* $2227. *Average indebtedness upon graduation:* $25,936.

APPLYING
Standardized Tests *Required:* SAT or ACT (for admission).
Options: electronic application, early admission, early action, deferred entrance.
Application fee: $35.
Required: high school transcript, minimum 2.0 GPA. *Required for some:* essay or personal statement, medical history, proof of measles-rubella shot.
Application deadlines: 8/15 (freshmen), 8/15 (transfers).
Notification: continuous (freshmen), continuous (transfers).

CONTACT
Ms. Heidi Kippenhan, Assistant Dean, Enrollment Management, Dickinson State University, Dickinson, ND 58601. *Phone:* 701-483-2566. *Toll-free phone:* 800-279-4295. *E-mail:* Heidi.Kippenhan@dickinsonstate.edu.

Mayville State University
Mayville, North Dakota
http://www.mayvillestate.edu/

CONTACT
Jim Morowski, Director of Freshmen Enrollment Services, Mayville State University, 330 3rd Street, NE, Mayville, ND 58257-1299. *Phone:* 701-788-4842. *Toll-free phone:* 800-437-4104. *Fax:* 701-788-4748. *E-mail:* james.morowski@mayvillestate.edu.

Minot State University
Minot, North Dakota
http://www.minotstateu.edu/

- **State-supported** comprehensive, founded 1913, part of North Dakota University System
- **Small-town** 103-acre campus
- **Coed** 2,956 undergraduate students, 66% full-time, 60% women, 40% men
- **Moderately difficult** entrance level, 69% of applicants were admitted

UNDERGRAD STUDENTS
1,952 full-time, 1,004 part-time. 19% are from out of state; 5% Black or African American, non-Hispanic/Latino; 7% Hispanic/Latino; 2% Asian, non-Hispanic/Latino; 0.3% Native Hawaiian or other Pacific Islander, non-Hispanic/Latino; 2% American Indian or Alaska Native, non-Hispanic/Latino; 4% Two or more races, non-Hispanic/Latino; 2% Race/ethnicity unknown; 9% international; 11% transferred in; 15% live on campus.

Freshmen:
Admission: 709 applied, 489 admitted, 373 enrolled. *Average high school GPA:* 3.2.
Retention: 69% of full-time freshmen returned.

FACULTY
Total: 291, 54% full-time, 19% with terminal degrees.
Student/faculty ratio: 12:1.

ACADEMICS
Calendar: semesters. *Degrees:* certificates, associate, bachelor's, master's, and postbachelor's certificates.

Special study options: academic remediation for entering students, accelerated degree program, advanced placement credit, cooperative education, distance learning, double majors, English as a second language, honors programs, independent study, internships, part-time degree program, services for LD students, student-designed majors, study abroad, summer session for credit.

Computers: Students can access the following: campus intranet, computer help desk, free student e-mail accounts, online (class) grades, online (class) registration, online (class) schedules. Campuswide network is available. Wireless service is available via entire campus.
Library: Gordon B. Olson Library.

STUDENT LIFE
Housing options: on-campus residence required for freshman year; coed, men-only, women-only, special housing for students with disabilities. Campus housing is university owned. Freshman campus housing is guaranteed.

Activities and organizations: drama/theater group, student-run newspaper, radio and television station, choral group, marching band, Residence Hall Association, Student Government Association, Beavers on Business, Student Social Work Organization, National Student Speech and Hearing Association.

Athletics Member NCAA, NAIA, NCCAA. All NCAA Division II. *Intercollegiate sports:* baseball M(s), basketball M(s)/W(s), cheerleading W, cross-country running M(s)/W(s), football M(s), golf M/W, ice hockey M(c), soccer W, softball W(s), track and field M(s)/W(s), volleyball W(s), wrestling M. *Intramural sports:* basketball M/W, racquetball M/W, softball M/W, volleyball M/W.

Campus security: controlled dormitory access, patrols by trained security personnel.

Student services: health clinic, personal/psychological counseling, women's center.

COSTS & FINANCIAL AID
Costs (2017–18) *Tuition:* state resident $5400 full-time, $225 per credit hour part-time; nonresident $5400 full-time, $225 per credit hour part-time. Full-time tuition and fees vary according to class time, course load, degree level, location, program, and reciprocity agreements. Part-time tuition and fees vary according to class time, course load, degree level, location, program, and reciprocity agreements. *Required fees:* $1410 full-time, $59 per credit hour part-time. *Room and board:* $6140; room only: $2246. Room and board charges vary according to board plan and housing facility. *Payment plan:* installment. *Waivers:* minority students, children of alumni, senior citizens, and employees or children of employees.

Financial Aid Of all full-time matriculated undergraduates who enrolled in 2016, 1,324 applied for aid, 904 were judged to have need, 299 had their need fully met. 77 Federal Work-Study jobs (averaging $1532). In 2016, 315 non-need-based awards were made. *Average percent of need met:* 68. *Average financial aid package:* $10,424. *Average need-based loan:* $6045. *Average need-based gift aid:* $5412. *Average non-need-based aid:* $1372. *Average indebtedness upon graduation:* $23,400.

APPLYING
Standardized Tests *Required:* SAT or ACT (for admission).
Options: electronic application, deferred entrance.
Application fee: $35.
Required: high school transcript. *Required for some:* minimum 2.5 GPA.

CONTACT
Mr. Kevin Harmon, Vice President of Enrollment Management, Minot State University, 500 University Avenue West, Minot, ND 58707-0002.

Phone: 701-858-3126. *Toll-free phone:* 800-777-0750 Ext. 3350. *Fax:* 701-858-3825. *E-mail:* askmsu@minotstateu.edu.

North Dakota State University
Fargo, North Dakota
http://www.ndsu.edu/
- **State-supported** university, founded 1890, part of North Dakota University System
- **Urban** 2100-acre campus
- **Endowment** $512,215
- **Coed** 11,984 undergraduate students, 90% full-time, 46% women, 54% men
- **Moderately difficult** entrance level, 92% of applicants were admitted

UNDERGRAD STUDENTS
10,782 full-time, 1,202 part-time. Students come from 39 states and territories; 52 other countries; 58% are from out of state; 3% Black or African American, non-Hispanic/Latino; 2% Hispanic/Latino; 1% Asian, non-Hispanic/Latino; 0.1% Native Hawaiian or other Pacific Islander, non-Hispanic/Latino; 0.6% American Indian or Alaska Native, non-Hispanic/Latino; 3% Two or more races, non-Hispanic/Latino; 2% Race/ethnicity unknown; 2% international; 6% transferred in; 39% live on campus.

Freshmen:
Admission: 6,424 applied, 5,884 admitted, 2,633 enrolled. *Average high school GPA:* 3.5. *Test scores:* SAT evidence-based reading and writing scores over 500: 79%; SAT math scores over 500: 92%; ACT scores over 18: 97%; SAT evidence-based reading and writing scores over 600: 50%; SAT math scores over 600: 52%; ACT scores over 24: 53%; SAT evidence-based reading and writing scores over 700: 19%; SAT math scores over 700: 19%; ACT scores over 30: 9%.
Retention: 79% of full-time freshmen returned.

FACULTY
Total: 776, 87% full-time, 81% with terminal degrees.
Student/faculty ratio: 18:1.

ACADEMICS
Calendar: semesters. *Degrees:* certificates, bachelor's, master's, doctoral, post-master's, and postbachelor's certificates.

Special study options: accelerated degree program, advanced placement credit, cooperative education, distance learning, double majors, honors programs, independent study, internships, off-campus study, part-time degree program, services for LD students, student-designed majors, study abroad, summer session for credit. *ROTC:* Army (b), Air Force (b).

Computers: 601 computers/terminals are available on campus for general student use. Students can access the following: campus intranet, computer help desk, free student e-mail accounts, online (class) grades, online (class) registration, online (class) schedules, online course content (e.g., learning management system, lecture capture video recordings). Campuswide network is available. 100% of college-owned or -operated housing units are wired for high-speed Internet access. Wireless service is available via entire campus.
Library: North Dakota State University Library plus 6 others. *Books:* 662,884 (physical), 162,977 (digital/electronic); *Serial titles:* 171,924 (physical), 99,565 (digital/electronic); *Databases:* 232. Weekly public service hours: 93; students can reserve study rooms.

STUDENT LIFE
Housing options: on-campus residence required for freshman year; coed, men-only, women-only, special housing for students with disabilities. Campus housing is university owned. Freshman campus housing is guaranteed.

Activities and organizations: drama/theater group, student-run newspaper, radio and television station, choral group, marching band, Saddle and Sirloin, Students Today, Leaders Forever, Chi Alpha Christian Organization, fraternities/sororities, CRU, national fraternities, national sororities.

Athletics Member NCAA. All Division I. *Intercollegiate sports:* baseball M(s), basketball M(s)/W(s), cross-country running M(s)/W(s), equestrian sports M(c)/W(c), football M(s), golf M/W(s), ice hockey M(c)/W(c), lacrosse M(c)/W(c), riflery M(c)/W(c), rock climbing M(c)/W(c), rugby M(c)/W(c), skiing (cross-country) M(c)/W(c), soccer M(c)/W(s), softball

W(s), tennis M(c)/W(c), track and field M(s)/W(s), volleyball M(c)/W(s), water polo M(c)/W(c), wrestling M(s). *Intramural sports:* baseball M(c), basketball M/W, football M/W, racquetball M/W, soccer M/W, softball M/W, swimming and diving M(c)/W(c), table tennis M/W, tennis M(c)/W(c), ultimate Frisbee M(c)/W(c), volleyball M/W(c), water polo M(c)/W(c).

Campus security: 24-hour emergency response devices and patrols, late-night transport/escort service, controlled dormitory access, Pathlight app.

Student services: health clinic, personal/psychological counseling.

COSTS & FINANCIAL AID
Costs (2017–18) *One-time required fee:* $120. *Tuition:* state resident $7201 full-time, $317 per credit hour part-time; nonresident $19,227 full-time, $846 per credit hour part-time. Full-time tuition and fees vary according to course load, program, and reciprocity agreements. Part-time tuition and fees vary according to course load, program, and reciprocity agreements. *Required fees:* $1345 full-time, $56 per credit hour part-time. *Room and board:* $8356; room only: $3830. Room and board charges vary according to board plan and housing facility. *Waivers:* minority students, children of alumni, senior citizens, and employees or children of employees.

Financial Aid Of all full-time matriculated undergraduates who enrolled in 2007, 7,109 applied for aid, 4,917 were judged to have need, 980 had their need fully met. In 2007, 1763 non-need-based awards were made. *Average percent of need met:* 3. *Average financial aid package:* $7030. *Average need-based loan:* $4378. *Average need-based gift aid:* $3419. *Average non-need-based aid:* $1533.

APPLYING
Standardized Tests *Required:* SAT or ACT (for admission).
Options: electronic application.
Application fee: $35.
Required: high school transcript, minimum 2.8 GPA.
Application deadlines: 8/1 (freshmen), 8/1 (transfers).
Notification: continuous (freshmen), continuous (transfers).

CONTACT
Ms. Merideth Sherlin, Director of Admission, North Dakota State University, NDSU Department 2832, PO Box 6050, Fargo, ND 58108-6050. *Phone:* 701-231-8643. *Toll-free phone:* 800-488-6378. *Fax:* 701-231-8802. *E-mail:* ndsu.admission@ndsu.edu.

Rasmussen College Fargo
Fargo, North Dakota
http://www.rasmussen.edu/
- **Proprietary** 4-year, founded 1902, part of Rasmussen College System
- **Suburban** campus
- **Coed** 391 undergraduate students, 72% full-time, 74% women, 26% men
- **Minimally difficult** entrance level, 86% of applicants were admitted

UNDERGRAD STUDENTS
280 full-time, 111 part-time.

Freshmen:
Admission: 22 applied, 19 admitted, 19 enrolled.

FACULTY
Total: 8, 50% full-time.
Student/faculty ratio: 22:1.

ACADEMICS
Calendar: quarters. *Degrees:* certificates, diplomas, associate, and bachelor's.
Special study options: academic remediation for entering students, accelerated degree program, adult/continuing education programs, distance learning, double majors, internships, part-time degree program, summer session for credit.
Computers: 87 computers/terminals are available on campus for general student use. Students can access the following: computer help desk, free student e-mail accounts, online (class) grades, online (class) schedules. Campuswide network is available. Wireless service is available via entire campus.
Library: Rasmussen College Library - Fargo.

STUDENT LIFE
Housing options: college housing not available.

COSTS
Costs (2017–18) *Tuition:* $11,055 full-time, $290 per credit hour part-time. Full-time tuition and fees vary according to course level, course load, degree level, location, and program. Part-time tuition and fees vary according to course level, course load, degree level, location, and program. No tuition increase for student's term of enrollment. *Required fees:* $1695 full-time, $44 per credit hour part-time. *Payment plans:* installment, deferred payment. *Waivers:* employees or children of employees.

APPLYING
Standardized Tests *Required:* institutional exam (for admission).
Options: electronic application, early admission, deferred entrance.
Required: high school transcript, minimum 2.0 GPA. *Required for some:* interview.
Application deadlines: rolling (freshmen), rolling (transfers).

CONTACT
Dwayne Bertotto, Vice President of Admissions and Student Experience, Rasmussen College Fargo, 8300 Norman Center Drive, Suite 300, Bloomington, MN 55437. *Phone:* 952-806-3958. *Toll-free phone:* 888-549-6755. *E-mail:* dwayne.bertotto@rasmussen.edu.

Sitting Bull College
Fort Yates, North Dakota
http://www.sittingbull.edu/
CONTACT
Ms. Melody Silk, Director of Registration and Admissions, Sitting Bull College, 1341 92nd Street, Fort Yates, ND 58538-9701. *Phone:* 701-854-3864. *Fax:* 701-854-3403. *E-mail:* melodys@sbcl.edu.

Trinity Bible College and Graduate School
Ellendale, North Dakota
http://www.trinitybiblecollege.edu/
CONTACT
Trinity Bible College and Graduate School, 50 Sixth Avenue South, Ellendale, ND 58436. *Phone:* 701-349-5399. *Toll-free phone:* 800-523-1603. *E-mail:* admissions@trinitybiblecollege.edu.

University of Jamestown
Jamestown, North Dakota
http://www.uj.edu/
- **Independent Presbyterian** comprehensive, founded 1883
- **Small-town** 110-acre campus
- **Endowment** $35.6 million
- **Coed** 915 undergraduate students, 95% full-time, 50% women, 50% men
- **Minimally difficult** entrance level, 65% of applicants were admitted

UNDERGRAD STUDENTS
869 full-time, 46 part-time. Students come from 36 states and territories; 20 other countries; 49% are from out of state; 4% Black or African American, non-Hispanic/Latino; 7% Hispanic/Latino; 0.7% Asian, non-Hispanic/Latino; 1% Native Hawaiian or other Pacific Islander, non-Hispanic/Latino; 0.5% American Indian or Alaska Native, non-Hispanic/Latino; 1% Race/ethnicity unknown; 10% international; 5% transferred in; 74% live on campus.

Freshmen:
Admission: 1,154 applied, 753 admitted, 235 enrolled. *Average high school GPA:* 3.4. *Test scores:* SAT evidence-based reading and writing scores over 500: 50%; SAT math scores over 500: 66%; ACT scores over 18: 92%; SAT evidence-based reading and writing scores over 600: 12%; SAT math scores over 600: 8%; ACT scores over 24: 33%; SAT evidence-based reading and writing scores over 700: 4%; ACT scores over 30: 3%.
Retention: 72% of full-time freshmen returned.

COLLEGES AT-A-GLANCE

FACULTY

Total: 111, 65% full-time, 53% with terminal degrees.
Student/faculty ratio: 12:1.

ACADEMICS

Calendar: semesters. *Degrees:* bachelor's, master's, and doctoral.

Special study options: advanced placement credit, cooperative education, double majors, honors programs, independent study, internships, part-time degree program, services for LD students, student-designed majors, study abroad, summer session for credit.

Unusual degree programs: 3-2 engineering with North Dakota State University, University of North Dakota, South Dakota State University, Washington University in St. Louis.

Computers: 200 computers/terminals and 570 ports are available on campus for general student use. Students can access the following: campus intranet, computer help desk, free student e-mail accounts, online (class) grades, online (class) registration, online (class) schedules. Campuswide network is available. 100% of college-owned or -operated housing units are wired for high-speed Internet access. Wireless service is available via entire campus.

Library: Raugust Library. *Books:* 94,318 (physical), 15,565 (digital/electronic); *Serial titles:* 822 (physical), 343 (digital/electronic); *Databases:* 87. Weekly public service hours: 89; students can reserve study rooms.

STUDENT LIFE

Housing options: on-campus residence required through junior year; coed, special housing for students with disabilities. Campus housing is university owned and leased by the school. Freshman campus housing is guaranteed.

Activities and organizations: drama/theater group, student-run newspaper, choral group, Cru-Ignite, Student Senate, Relay for Life, Habitat for Humanity, Fellowship of Athletes in Christ.

Athletics Member NAIA. *Intercollegiate sports:* baseball M(s), basketball M(s)/W(s), cheerleading M(s)/W(s), cross-country running M(s)/W(s), football M(s), golf M(s)/W(s), ice hockey M(c), soccer M(s)/W(s), softball W(s), track and field M(s)/W(s), volleyball W(s), wrestling M(s)/W(s). *Intramural sports:* basketball M/W, football M/W, volleyball M/W.

Campus security: 24-hour emergency response devices, late-night transport/escort service, controlled dormitory access, campus security cameras.

Student services: personal/psychological counseling.

COSTS & FINANCIAL AID

Costs (2018–19) *Comprehensive fee:* $29,546 includes full-time tuition ($21,196), mandatory fees ($780), and room and board ($7570). Full-time tuition and fees vary according to course load, degree level, and program. Part-time tuition: $435 per credit hour. Part-time tuition and fees vary according to course load, degree level, and program. *College room only:* $3570. Room and board charges vary according to housing facility. *Payment plan:* installment. *Waivers:* employees or children of employees.

Financial Aid Of all full-time matriculated undergraduates who enrolled in 2016, 705 applied for aid, 576 were judged to have need, 149 had their need fully met. 259 Federal Work-Study jobs (averaging $669). 81 state and other part-time jobs (averaging $472). In 2016, 324 non-need-based awards were made. *Average percent of need met:* 75. *Average financial aid package:* $15,700. *Average need-based loan:* $3926. *Average need-based gift aid:* $12,546. *Average non-need-based aid:* $8618. *Average indebtedness upon graduation:* $27,238.

APPLYING

Standardized Tests *Required:* SAT or ACT (for admission).

Options: electronic application, deferred entrance.

Required: high school transcript, minimum 2.5 GPA. *Required for some:* interview.

Application deadlines: rolling (freshmen), rolling (transfers).

CONTACT

Mr. Mike Heitkamp, Vice President of Enrollment Management, University of Jamestown, 6081 College Lane, Jamestown, ND 58401. *Phone:* 701-252-3467 Ext. 5512. *Toll-free phone:* 800-336-2554. *Fax:* 701-253-4318. *E-mail:* admissions@uj.edu.

University of Mary
Bismarck, North Dakota
http://www.umary.edu/

CONTACT
Mr. Curtis Ray DeGraw, University of Mary, 7500 University Drive, Bismarck, ND 58504-9652. *Phone:* 701-355-8191. *Toll-free phone:* 800-288-6279. *Fax:* 701-255-7687. *E-mail:* mcheitkamp@umary.edu.

University of North Dakota
Grand Forks, North Dakota
http://www.und.edu/

- **State-supported** university, founded 1883, part of North Dakota University System
- **Urban** 521-acre campus
- **Endowment** $23.6 million
- **Coed** 11,000 undergraduate students, 78% full-time, 44% women, 56% men
- **Minimally difficult** entrance level, 83% of applicants were admitted

UNDERGRAD STUDENTS
8,525 full-time, 2,475 part-time. Students come from 57 states and territories; 72 other countries; 61% are from out of state; 2% Black or African American, non-Hispanic/Latino; 3% Hispanic/Latino; 2% Asian, non-Hispanic/Latino; 0.1% Native Hawaiian or other Pacific Islander, non-Hispanic/Latino; 1% American Indian or Alaska Native, non-Hispanic/Latino; 3% Two or more races, non-Hispanic/Latino; 1% Race/ethnicity unknown; 5% international; 8% transferred in; 28% live on campus.

Freshmen:
Admission: 5,230 applied, 4,366 admitted, 1,939 enrolled. *Average high school GPA:* 3.5. *Test scores:* ACT scores over 18: 97%; ACT scores over 24: 54%; ACT scores over 30: 8%.
Retention: 81% of full-time freshmen returned.

FACULTY
Total: 715, 95% full-time, 72% with terminal degrees.
Student/faculty ratio: 21:1.

ACADEMICS
Calendar: semesters. *Degrees:* certificates, bachelor's, master's, doctoral, post-master's, and postbachelor's certificates.

Special study options: accelerated degree program, adult/continuing education programs, advanced placement credit, cooperative education, distance learning, double majors, English as a second language, external degree program, honors programs, independent study, internships, off-campus study, part-time degree program, services for LD students, student-designed majors, study abroad, summer session for credit. *ROTC:* Army (b), Air Force (b).

Unusual degree programs: 3-2 engineering; applied economics, counseling, chemistry, public administration.

Computers: 1,000 computers/terminals and 400 ports are available on campus for general student use. Students can access the following: campus intranet, computer help desk, free student e-mail accounts, online (class) grades, online (class) registration, online (class) schedules. Campuswide network is available. 100% of college-owned or -operated housing units are wired for high-speed Internet access. Wireless service is available via classrooms, computer centers, computer labs, dorm rooms, learning centers, libraries, student centers.

Library: Chester Fritz Library plus 2 others. *Books:* 571,458 (physical), 146,797 (digital/electronic); *Serial titles:* 26,062 (physical), 62,508 (digital/electronic); *Databases:* 90. Weekly public service hours: 99.

STUDENT LIFE
Housing options: coed, men-only, women-only, special housing for students with disabilities. Campus housing is university owned.

Activities and organizations: drama/theater group, student-run newspaper, radio and television station, choral group, marching band, NODAK NATION, Cru, Volunteers Together, Nursing Student Association, Sororities/Fraternities, national fraternities, national sororities.

Athletics Member NCAA. All Division I. *Intercollegiate sports:* basketball M(s)/W(s), cross-country running M(s)/W(s), football M(s), golf M(s)/W(s), ice hockey M(s), soccer W(s), softball W(s), tennis M(s)/W(s), track and field M(s)/W(s), volleyball W(s). *Intramural sports:* basketball M/W, ice hockey M/W, soccer M/W, softball M/W, ultimate Frisbee M/W, volleyball M/W.

Campus security: 24-hour emergency response devices and patrols, late-night transport/escort service, controlled dormitory access, in room safes,virtual escort service (safety app),work/study alone monitoring service.

Student services: health clinic, personal/psychological counseling, women's center, legal services.

COSTS & FINANCIAL AID
Costs (2017–18) *Tuition:* state resident $6946 full-time, $289 per credit hour part-time; nonresident $18,546 full-time, $773 per credit hour part-time. Full-time tuition and fees vary according to degree level, program, and reciprocity agreements. Part-time tuition and fees vary according to course load, degree level, program, and reciprocity agreements. *Required fees:* $1501 full-time. *Room and board:* $8226. Room and board charges vary according to board plan and housing facility. *Payment plan:* deferred payment. *Waivers:* minority students and employees or children of employees.

Financial Aid Of all full-time matriculated undergraduates who enrolled in 2016, 6,413 applied for aid, 4,171 were judged to have need, 1,816 had their need fully met. In 2016, 883 non-need-based awards were made. *Average percent of need met:* 60. *Average financial aid package:* $13,661. *Average need-based loan:* $7607. *Average need-based gift aid:* $5293. *Average non-need-based aid:* $2068.

APPLYING
Standardized Tests *Required for some:* SAT or ACT (for admission), SAT and SAT Subject Tests or ACT (for admission).

Options: electronic application, deferred entrance.

Application fee: $35.

Required: high school transcript. *Recommended:* minimum 2.5 GPA.

Notification: continuous (transfers).

CONTACT
Mr. Jason Trainer, Director of Admissions, University of North Dakota, Gorecki Alumni Center, 3501 University Avenue, Stop 8357, Grand Forks, ND 58202. *Phone:* 701-777-3000. *Toll-free phone:* 800-CALL-UND. *Fax:* 701-777-2721. *E-mail:* und.admissions@und.edu.

Valley City State University
Valley City, North Dakota
http://www.vcsu.edu/

- **State-supported** comprehensive, founded 1890, part of North Dakota University System
- **Small-town** 55-acre campus
- **Endowment** $6.8 million
- **Coed** 1,372 undergraduate students, 61% full-time, 57% women, 43% men
- **Noncompetitive** entrance level, 99% of applicants were admitted

UNDERGRAD STUDENTS
834 full-time, 538 part-time. Students come from 38 states and territories; 10 other countries; 38% are from out of state; 3% Black or African American, non-Hispanic/Latino; 5% Hispanic/Latino; 0.8% Asian, non-Hispanic/Latino; 0.1% Native Hawaiian or other Pacific Islander, non-Hispanic/Latino; 1% American Indian or Alaska Native, non-Hispanic/Latino; 4% Two or more races, non-Hispanic/Latino; 0.8% Race/ethnicity unknown; 2% international; 7% transferred in; 32% live on campus.

Freshmen:
Admission: 384 applied, 380 admitted, 190 enrolled. *Average high school GPA:* 3.2. *Test scores:* SAT math scores over 500: 77%; ACT scores over 18: 80%; SAT math scores over 600: 18%; ACT scores over 24: 18%; ACT scores over 30: 2%.
Retention: 72% of full-time freshmen returned.

FACULTY
Total: 106, 62% full-time, 46% with terminal degrees.
Student/faculty ratio: 11:1.

ACADEMICS
Calendar: semesters. *Degrees:* bachelor's and master's.

Special study options: academic remediation for entering students, cooperative education, distance learning, double majors, internships, off-campus study, part-time degree program, services for LD students, student-designed majors, study abroad, summer session for credit.

Computers: 1,200 computers/terminals are available on campus for general student use. Students can access the following: campus intranet, computer help desk, free student e-mail accounts, online (class) grades, online (class) registration, online (class) schedules. Campuswide network is available. 100% of college-owned or -operated housing units are wired for high-speed Internet access. Wireless service is available via entire campus.

Library: Allen Memorial Library. *Books:* 77,906 (physical), 140,050 (digital/electronic); *Serial titles:* 1,301 (physical), 29,378 (digital/electronic); *Databases:* 86. Weekly public service hours: 61; students can reserve study rooms.

STUDENT LIFE
Housing options: on-campus residence required for freshman year; coed, men-only, women-only. Campus housing is university owned. Freshman campus housing is guaranteed.

Activities and organizations: choral group, departmental clubs, Fellowship of Christian Athletes, VCAB, Viking Ambassadors, local fraternities/sororities.

Athletics Member NAIA. *Intercollegiate sports:* baseball M(s), basketball M(s)/W(s), cross-country running M(s)/W(s), football M(s), golf M(s)/W(s), softball W(s), tennis M(c)/W(c), track and field M(s)/W(s), volleyball W(s). *Intramural sports:* basketball M/W, bowling M/W, cross-country running M/W, football M/W, golf M/W, ice hockey M/W, racquetball M/W, skiing (cross-country) M/W, soccer M/W, softball M/W, tennis M/W, track and field M/W, volleyball M/W.

Campus security: controlled dormitory access, security cameras throughout campus.

Student services: health clinic, personal/psychological counseling.

COSTS & FINANCIAL AID
Costs (2017–18) *Tuition:* state resident $5493 full-time, $183 per semester hour part-time; nonresident $14,666 full-time, $489 per semester hour part-time. Full-time tuition and fees vary according to course load, location, program, and reciprocity agreements. Part-time tuition and fees vary according to course load, location, program, and reciprocity agreements. *Required fees:* $1913 full-time, $80 per semester hour part-time. *Room and board:* $6328; room only: $2378. Room and board charges vary according to board plan and housing facility. *Payment plan:* installment. *Waivers:* employees or children of employees.

Financial Aid Of all full-time matriculated undergraduates who enrolled in 2017, 617 applied for aid, 439 were judged to have need, 217 had their need fully met. 40 Federal Work-Study jobs (averaging $2143). In 2017, 158 non-need-based awards were made. *Average percent of need met:* 82. *Average financial aid package:* $12,648. *Average need-based loan:* $6008. *Average need-based gift aid:* $6379. *Average non-need-based aid:* $2699. *Average indebtedness upon graduation:* $27,050.

APPLYING
Standardized Tests *Required:* SAT or ACT (for admission).

Options: electronic application.

Application fee: $35.

Required: high school transcript.

Application deadlines: rolling (freshmen), rolling (out-of-state freshmen), rolling (transfers).

Notification: continuous (freshmen), continuous (out-of-state freshmen), continuous (transfers).

CONTACT
Ms. Kaleen Peterson, Admission Counselor, Valley City State University, 101 College Street Southwest, Valley City, ND 58072. *Phone:* 701-845-7115. *Toll-free phone:* 800-532-8641 Ext. 7101. *Fax:* 701-845-7299. *E-mail:* kaleen.peterson@vcsu.edu.

OHIO

AIC College of Design
Cincinnati, Ohio
http://www.aic-arts.edu/
- **Independent** primarily 2-year, founded 1976
- **Urban** 3-acre campus with easy access to Cincinnati
- **Coed** 34 undergraduate students, 88% full-time, 65% women, 35% men
- **Noncompetitive** entrance level, 67% of applicants were admitted

UNDERGRAD STUDENTS
30 full-time, 4 part-time. Students come from 3 states and territories; 27% are from out of state; 18% Black or African American, non-Hispanic/Latino.

Freshmen:
Admission: 36 applied, 24 admitted, 6 enrolled. *Average high school GPA:* 3.3.
Retention: 90% of full-time freshmen returned.

FACULTY
Total: 11, 36% full-time, 18% with terminal degrees.
Student/faculty ratio: 5:1.

ACADEMICS
Degrees: associate and bachelor's.

Special study options: academic remediation for entering students, accelerated degree program, adult/continuing education programs, advanced placement credit, cooperative education, part-time degree program, services for LD students.

Computers: 20 computers/terminals and 50 ports are available on campus for general student use. Students can access the following: campus intranet, free student e-mail accounts, online (class) grades, online (class) registration, online (class) schedules. Campuswide network is available. Wireless service is available via entire campus.
Library: AIC College of Design Library plus 1 other.

STUDENT LIFE
Housing options: college housing not available.
Activities and organizations: AIGA Student Chapter.
Campus security: 24-hour emergency response devices, SMS.
Student services: personal/psychological counseling.

COSTS
Costs (2017–18) *Tuition:* $511 per credit hour part-time. Full-time tuition and fees vary according to course load. Part-time tuition and fees vary according to course load. No tuition increase for student's term of enrollment. *Payment plan:* installment. *Waivers:* employees or children of employees.

APPLYING
Standardized Tests *Recommended:* SAT or ACT (for admission).
Options: early admission, early decision, deferred entrance.
Application fee: $100.
Required: essay or personal statement, high school transcript, interview. *Recommended:* minimum 2.0 GPA, letters of recommendation.
Application deadlines: rolling (freshmen), rolling (transfers).
Notification: continuous (freshmen), continuous (transfers).

CONTACT
Megan Orsburn, Admissions Assistant, AIC College of Design, 1171 E. Kemper Road, Cincinnati, OH 45246. *Phone:* 513-751-1206.

Allegheny Wesleyan College
Salem, Ohio
http://www.awc.edu/

CONTACT
Admissions Office, Allegheny Wesleyan College, 2161 Woodsdale Road, Salem, OH 44460. *Phone:* 330-337-6403. *Toll-free phone:* 800-292-3153. *E-mail:* college@awc.edu.

Antioch College
Yellow Springs, Ohio
http://www.antiochcollege.edu/
- **Independent** 4-year, founded 2011
- **Rural** 1100-acre campus with easy access to Columbus
- **Endowment** $9.9 million
- **Coed** 133 undergraduate students, 100% full-time, 62% women, 38% men
- 97% of applicants were admitted

UNDERGRAD STUDENTS
133 full-time. Students come from 25 states and territories; 11 other countries; 63% are from out of state; 10% Black or African American, non-Hispanic/Latino; 13% Hispanic/Latino; 4% Asian, non-Hispanic/Latino; 0.8% Native Hawaiian or other Pacific Islander, non-Hispanic/Latino; 9% Two or more races, non-Hispanic/Latino; 5% Race/ethnicity unknown; 7% transferred in; 56% live on campus.

Freshmen:
Admission: 152 applied, 147 admitted, 19 enrolled. *Average high school GPA:* 3.1.
Retention: 53% of full-time freshmen returned.

FACULTY
Total: 35, 89% full-time, 74% with terminal degrees.
Student/faculty ratio: 4:1.

ACADEMICS
Calendar: quarters. *Degree:* bachelor's.

Special study options: academic remediation for entering students, advanced placement credit, cooperative education, independent study, off-campus study, services for LD students, student-designed majors, study abroad, summer session for credit.

Computers: Students can access the following: campus intranet, computer help desk, free student e-mail accounts, online (class) grades, online (class) registration, online (class) schedules. Campuswide network is available. 100% of college-owned or -operated housing units are wired for high-speed Internet access. Wireless service is available via entire campus.
Library: Olive Kettering Library plus 1 other. *Books:* 305,000 (physical), 10,600 (digital/electronic); *Serial titles:* 30,500 (physical), 30,500 (digital/electronic); *Databases:* 195. Weekly public service hours: 72.

STUDENT LIFE
Housing options: on-campus residence required through sophomore year; coed. Campus housing is university owned.
Activities and organizations: drama/theater group, student-run newspaper, radio station, People of Color Group, Queer Center, Outdoors Club, Antioch Creative Collective, ei@A (Entrepreneurs & Innovation @ Antioch).
Athletics *Intramural sports:* basketball M/W, volleyball M/W.
Campus security: 24-hour emergency response devices and patrols, controlled dormitory access.
Student services: health clinic, personal/psychological counseling.

COSTS
Costs (2018–19) *One-time required fee:* $150. *Comprehensive fee:* $43,208 includes full-time tuition ($34,568), mandatory fees ($1000), and room and board ($7640). Part-time tuition: $500 per credit hour. *College room only:* $4622. *Payment plan:* installment. *Waivers:* employees or children of employees.

APPLYING
Options: electronic application, early admission, deferred entrance.
Required: essay or personal statement, high school transcript, 2 letters of recommendation. *Required for some:* interview.
Application deadlines: 7/1 (freshmen), 7/1 (out-of-state freshmen).
Notification: continuous (freshmen), continuous (out-of-state freshmen).

CONTACT
Mr. Shane Creepingbear, Associate Director of Admission, Antioch College, South Hall, Antioch College, Yellow Springs, OH 45387. *Phone:* 937-284-0830. *E-mail:* screepingbear@antiochcollege.edu.

Antioch University Midwest

Yellow Springs, Ohio
http://www.antioch.edu/midwest/
- **Independent** upper-level, founded 1988, part of Antioch University
- **Small-town** 100-acre campus with easy access to Dayton
- **Coed** 41 undergraduate students, 49% full-time, 73% women, 27% men
- **Noncompetitive** entrance level

UNDERGRAD STUDENTS
20 full-time, 21 part-time. Students come from 13 states and territories; 1% are from out of state; 13% Black or African American, non-Hispanic/Latino; 8% Hispanic/Latino; 3% Race/ethnicity unknown.

ACADEMICS
Calendar: semesters. *Degrees:* certificates, bachelor's, master's, post-master's, and postbachelor's certificates.

Special study options: accelerated degree program, adult/continuing education programs, advanced placement credit, cooperative education, distance learning, double majors, independent study, internships, off-campus study, part-time degree program, services for LD students, student-designed majors, summer session for credit.

Computers: 10 computers/terminals are available on campus for general student use. Students can access the following: campus intranet, computer help desk, free student e-mail accounts, online (class) grades, online (class) registration, online (class) schedules, online bill pay and view/acceptance of financial aid award letter, narrative evaluations. Campuswide network is available. Wireless service is available via entire campus.
Library: Midwest Library.

STUDENT LIFE
Housing options: college housing not available.
Campus security: 24-hour emergency response devices.
Student services: personal/psychological counseling.

COSTS
Costs (2017–18) *Tuition:* $18,972 full-time, $527 per credit part-time. *Required fees:* $400 full-time, $200 per term part-time. *Payment plan:* installment. *Waivers:* employees or children of employees.

APPLYING
Options: electronic application, deferred entrance.
Application fee: $45.

CONTACT
Antioch University Midwest, 900 Dayton Street, Yellow Springs, OH 45387-1609. *Phone:* 937-769-1823.

Art Academy of Cincinnati

Cincinnati, Ohio
http://www.artacademy.edu/

CONTACT
Mr. John J. Wadell, Director of Admissions, Art Academy of Cincinnati, 1212 Jackson Street, Cincinnati, OH 45202-7106. *Phone:* 513-562-8744. *Toll-free phone:* 800-323-5692. *Fax:* 513-562-8778. *E-mail:* admissions@artacademy.edu.

Ashland University

Ashland, Ohio
http://www.ashland.edu/
- **Independent** comprehensive, founded 1878, affiliated with Brethren Church
- **Small-town** 135-acre campus with easy access to Cleveland, Akron
- **Endowment** $36.8 million
- **Coed** 4,536 undergraduate students, 75% full-time, 47% women, 53% men
- **Moderately difficult** entrance level, 76% of applicants were admitted

UNDERGRAD STUDENTS
3,414 full-time, 1,122 part-time. Students come from 31 states and territories; 19 other countries; 7% are from out of state; 13% Black or African American, non-Hispanic/Latino; 3% Hispanic/Latino; 0.6%

Asian, non-Hispanic/Latino; 0.1% Native Hawaiian or other Pacific Islander, non-Hispanic/Latino; 0.5% American Indian or Alaska Native, non-Hispanic/Latino; 2% Two or more races, non-Hispanic/Latino; 3% Race/ethnicity unknown; 2% international; 4% transferred in.

Freshmen:
Admission: 3,121 applied, 2,367 admitted, 623 enrolled. *Average high school GPA:* 3.4. *Test scores:* ACT scores over 18: 97%; ACT scores over 24: 35%; ACT scores over 30: 4%.
Retention: 80% of full-time freshmen returned.

FACULTY
Total: 392, 44% full-time, 50% with terminal degrees.
Student/faculty ratio: 12:1.

ACADEMICS
Calendar: semesters. *Degrees:* certificates, diplomas, associate, bachelor's, master's, doctoral, post-master's, and postbachelor's certificates.

Special study options: academic remediation for entering students, accelerated degree program, adult/continuing education programs, advanced placement credit, cooperative education, distance learning, double majors, English as a second language, external degree program, honors programs, independent study, internships, off-campus study, part-time degree program, services for LD students, student-designed majors, study abroad, summer session for credit.

Unusual degree programs: 3-2 business administration.

Computers: 760 computers/terminals are available on campus for general student use. Students can access the following: campus intranet, computer help desk, free student e-mail accounts, online (class) grades, online (class) registration, online (class) schedules. Campuswide network is available. 100% of college-owned or -operated housing units are wired for high-speed Internet access. Wireless service is available via entire campus.
Library: Ashland University Library plus 2 others. *Books:* 223,607 (physical), 255,789 (digital/electronic); *Serial titles:* 1,070 (physical), 114,001 (digital/electronic); *Databases:* 200. Weekly public service hours: 102; students can reserve study rooms.

STUDENT LIFE
Housing options: on-campus residence required through junior year; coed, women-only. Campus housing is university owned. Freshman campus housing is guaranteed.

Activities and organizations: drama/theater group, student-run newspaper, radio and television station, choral group, marching band, Campus Activity Board, Fellowship of Christian Athletes, The Well Campus Ministry, intramurals, Sororities, national fraternities, national sororities.

Athletics Member NCAA. All Division II. *Intercollegiate sports:* baseball M(s), basketball M(s)/W(s), cheerleading W(s), cross-country running M(s)/W(s), football M(s), golf M(s)/W(s), lacrosse W(s), soccer M(s)/W(s), softball W(s), swimming and diving M(s)/W(s), tennis M(s)/W(s), track and field M(s)/W(s), volleyball W(s), wrestling M(s). *Intramural sports:* badminton M/W, baseball M(c), basketball M/W, bowling M/W, cross-country running M/W, field hockey M/W, football M, golf M/W, lacrosse M(c)/W(c), racquetball M/W, rock climbing M/W, rugby M(c)/W(c), skiing (downhill) M(c)/W(c), soccer M/W, softball M(c)/W(c), swimming and diving M/W, table tennis M/W, tennis M/W, track and field M/W, triathlon M/W, ultimate Frisbee M/W, volleyball M(c)/W(c), weight lifting M(c)/W(c), wrestling M.

Campus security: 24-hour emergency response devices and patrols, student patrols, late-night transport/escort service, controlled dormitory access.

Student services: health clinic, personal/psychological counseling.

COSTS & FINANCIAL AID
Costs (2017–18) *Comprehensive fee:* $30,430 includes full-time tuition ($19,740), mandatory fees ($944), and room and board ($9746). Full-time tuition and fees vary according to location and program. Part-time tuition: $899 per credit hour. Part-time tuition and fees vary according to course load, location, and program. *Required fees:* $23 per credit hour part-time. *College room only:* $5250. Room and board charges vary according to board plan, housing facility, and location. *Payment plan:* installment. *Waivers:* children of alumni, senior citizens, and employees or children of employees.

Financial Aid Of all full-time matriculated undergraduates who enrolled in 2014, 2,191 applied for aid, 1,924 were judged to have need. 1,380 Federal Work-Study jobs (averaging $2589). In 2014, 264 non-need-based awards were made. *Average financial aid package:* $17,689. *Average need-based loan:* $4836. *Average need-based gift aid:* $10,445. *Average non-need-based aid:* $5248. *Average indebtedness upon graduation:* $36,779.

APPLYING

Standardized Tests *Required:* SAT or ACT (for admission).

Options: electronic application, deferred entrance.

Required: high school transcript, minimum 2.5 GPA, minimum 18 ACT or 860 SAT.

Application deadlines: rolling (freshmen), rolling (transfers).

Notification: continuous (freshmen), continuous (transfers).

CONTACT

Mr. W.C. Vance, Director of Admissions, Ashland University, 401 College Avenue, Ashland, OH 44805. *Phone:* 419-289-5052. *Toll-free phone:* 800-882-1548. *Fax:* 419-289-5999. *E-mail:* enrollme@ashland.edu.

Aultman College of Nursing and Health Sciences

Canton, Ohio

http://www.aultmancollege.edu/

- **Independent** 4-year, founded 2004
- **Urban** 5-acre campus with easy access to Cleveland
- **Endowment** $1.4 million
- **Coed** 394 undergraduate students, 27% full-time, 90% women, 10% men
- **Moderately difficult** entrance level, 88% of applicants were admitted

UNDERGRAD STUDENTS

108 full-time, 286 part-time. Students come from 1 other state; 4% Black or African American, non-Hispanic/Latino; 2% Hispanic/Latino; 0.5% Asian, non-Hispanic/Latino; 0.3% Native Hawaiian or other Pacific Islander, non-Hispanic/Latino; 1% American Indian or Alaska Native, non-Hispanic/Latino; 2% Two or more races, non-Hispanic/Latino; 0.3% Race/ethnicity unknown; 25% transferred in.

Freshmen:

Admission: 51 applied, 45 admitted, 36 enrolled. *Average high school GPA:* 3.3. *Test scores:* ACT scores over 18: 100%; ACT scores over 24: 18%; ACT scores over 30: 3%.

FACULTY

Total: 66, 18% full-time, 29% with terminal degrees.
Student/faculty ratio: 7:1.

ACADEMICS

Calendar: semesters. *Degrees:* associate and bachelor's.

Special study options: academic remediation for entering students, advanced placement credit, cooperative education, distance learning, internships, part-time degree program, services for LD students.

Computers: 198 computers/terminals are available on campus for general student use. Students can access the following: campus intranet, computer help desk, free student e-mail accounts, online (class) grades, online (class) registration, online (class) schedules. Campuswide network is available. Wireless service is available via entire campus.

Library: Aultman Health Sciences Library plus 1 other. *Books:* 2,448 (physical), 81,000 (digital/electronic); *Serial titles:* 129 (physical), 10,007 (digital/electronic); *Databases:* 145. Study areas open 24 hours, 5–7 days a week.

STUDENT LIFE

Housing options: college housing not available.

Activities and organizations: Aultman College Student Nurse Association, Radiography Club, Aultman College Campus Ministry, Aultman College Veterans Association, Men in Nursing Association.

Campus security: 24-hour emergency response devices and patrols, late-night transport/escort service.

Student services: health clinic.

COSTS

Costs (2018–19) *One-time required fee:* $200. *Tuition:* $17,000 full-time, $725 per credit hour part-time. Full-time tuition and fees vary according to course load, degree level, and program. Part-time tuition and fees vary according to course load, degree level, and program. *Required fees:* $1000 full-time, $500 per term part-time. *Payment plan:* installment. *Waivers:* employees or children of employees.

APPLYING

Standardized Tests *Required for some:* SAT or ACT (for admission). *Recommended:* SAT or ACT (for admission).

Options: electronic application.

Application fee: $45.

Required: high school transcript. *Required for some:* minimum 3.0 GPA, interview.

Notification: continuous until 10/1 (freshmen).

CONTACT

Mrs. Kelsey Binsley, Enrollment Specialist, Aultman College of Nursing and Health Sciences, 2600 6th Street SW, Canton, OH 44710. *Phone:* 330-363-6773. *Fax:* 330-5806654. *E-mail:* Admissions@aultmancollege.edu.

Baldwin Wallace University

Berea, Ohio

http://www.bw.edu/

- **Independent Methodist** comprehensive, founded 1845
- **Suburban** 153-acre campus with easy access to Cleveland
- **Endowment** $164.5 million
- **Coed** 3,204 undergraduate students, 93% full-time, 55% women, 45% men
- **Moderately difficult** entrance level, 78% of applicants were admitted

UNDERGRAD STUDENTS

2,979 full-time, 225 part-time. Students come from 41 states and territories; 23 other countries; 24% are from out of state; 9% Black or African American, non-Hispanic/Latino; 5% Hispanic/Latino; 2% Asian, non-Hispanic/Latino; 0.1% Native Hawaiian or other Pacific Islander, non-Hispanic/Latino; 0.1% American Indian or Alaska Native, non-Hispanic/Latino; 5% Two or more races, non-Hispanic/Latino; 0.2% Race/ethnicity unknown; 0.7% international; 5% transferred in; 61% live on campus.

Freshmen:

Admission: 3,576 applied, 2,791 admitted, 685 enrolled. *Average high school GPA:* 3.5. *Test scores:* SAT evidence-based reading and writing scores over 500: 87%; SAT math scores over 500: 85%; ACT scores over 18: 95%; SAT evidence-based reading and writing scores over 600: 52%; SAT math scores over 600: 41%; ACT scores over 24: 54%; SAT evidence-based reading and writing scores over 700: 10%; SAT math scores over 700: 8%; ACT scores over 30: 8%.

Retention: 78% of full-time freshmen returned.

FACULTY

Total: 474, 47% full-time, 40% with terminal degrees.
Student/faculty ratio: 11:1.

ACADEMICS

Calendar: semesters. *Degrees:* certificates, bachelor's, and master's.

Special study options: academic remediation for entering students, accelerated degree program, adult/continuing education programs, advanced placement credit, distance learning, double majors, English as a second language, honors programs, independent study, internships, off-campus study, part-time degree program, services for LD students, student-designed majors, study abroad, summer session for credit. *ROTC:* Army (c), Air Force (c).

Unusual degree programs: 3-2 engineering with Case Western Reserve University; social work with Case Western Reserve University; accounting, computer information systems, computer science, or human resources/business administration.

Computers: 500 computers/terminals and 100 ports are available on campus for general student use. Students can access the following: campus intranet, computer help desk, free student e-mail accounts, online (class) grades, online (class) registration, online (class) schedules.

Campuswide network is available. 100% of college-owned or -operated housing units are wired for high-speed Internet access. Wireless service is available via entire campus.

Library: Ritter Library plus 2 others. *Books:* 109,038 (physical), 387,882 (digital/electronic); *Serial titles:* 174 (physical), 73,946 (digital/electronic); *Databases:* 265. Weekly public service hours: 90; study areas open 24 hours, 5–7 days a week; students can reserve study rooms.

STUDENT LIFE

Housing options: on-campus residence required through sophomore year; coed, special housing for students with disabilities. Campus housing is university owned. Freshman applicants given priority for college housing.

Activities and organizations: drama/theater group, student-run newspaper, radio and television station, choral group, marching band, Dance Marathon, Mid-Night Madness (MNM), Ohio Collegiate Music Educators Association (OCMEA), Sport Management Club, Student Ambassadors, national fraternities, national sororities.

Athletics Member NCAA. All Division III. *Intercollegiate sports:* baseball M, basketball M/W, cross-country running M/W, football M, golf M/W, lacrosse M/W, soccer M/W, softball W, swimming and diving M/W, tennis M/W, track and field M/W, volleyball W, wrestling M. *Intramural sports:* archery M(c)/W(c), badminton M/W, basketball M/W, cheerleading W(c), crew M(c)/W(c), football M, golf M/W, racquetball M/W, riflery M(c)/W(c), rowing M(c)/W(c), rugby M(c)/W(c), sailing M(c)/W(c), skiing (cross-country) M(c)/W(c), skiing (downhill) M(c)/W(c), soccer M/W, softball M/W, table tennis M/W, tennis M/W, ultimate Frisbee M/W, volleyball M/W, wrestling M.

Campus security: 24-hour emergency response devices and patrols, student patrols, late-night transport/escort service, controlled dormitory access, emergency text messaging.

Student services: health clinic, personal/psychological counseling.

COSTS & FINANCIAL AID

Costs (2018–19) *Comprehensive fee:* $42,140 includes full-time tuition ($32,586) and room and board ($9554). Full-time tuition and fees vary according to class time, course level, course load, degree level, program, and reciprocity agreements. Part-time tuition: $1013 per credit hour. Part-time tuition and fees vary according to class time, course level, course load, degree level, program, and reciprocity agreements. *College room only:* $5518. Room and board charges vary according to housing facility. *Payment plans:* installment, deferred payment. *Waivers:* children of alumni and employees or children of employees.

Financial Aid Of all full-time matriculated undergraduates who enrolled in 2017, 2,586 applied for aid, 2,345 were judged to have need, 867 had their need fully met. 960 Federal Work-Study jobs (averaging $1330). 550 state and other part-time jobs (averaging $1511). In 2017, 540 non-need-based awards were made. *Average percent of need met:* 87. *Average financial aid package:* $26,990. *Average need-based loan:* $4699. *Average need-based gift aid:* $20,876. *Average non-need-based aid:* $13,504. *Average indebtedness upon graduation:* $36,426.

APPLYING

Standardized Tests *Required for some:* SAT or ACT (for admission).

Options: electronic application, deferred entrance.

Application fee: $25.

Required: essay or personal statement, high school transcript. *Required for some:* minimum 3.0 cum GPA and recently graded paper in lieu of ACT or SAT scores for Test Optional applicants. *Recommended:* minimum 3.0 GPA, 1 letter of recommendation, interview.

Application deadlines: 5/1 (freshmen), 8/1 (transfers).

Notification: continuous (freshmen), continuous (out-of-state freshmen), continuous (transfers).

CONTACT

Joyce J Cendroski, Director of First Year RCMT and Admission, Baldwin Wallace University, Durst Welcome Center, 115 Tressel Street, Berea, OH 44017. *Phone:* 440-826-2222. *Toll-free phone:* 877-BW-APPLY. *Fax:* 440-826-3830. *E-mail:* admission@bw.edu.

See below for display ad and page 1238 for the College Close-Up.

Bluffton University
Bluffton, Ohio
http://www.bluffton.edu/

- **Independent Mennonite** comprehensive, founded 1899
- **Small-town** 65-acre campus with easy access to Dayton
- **Endowment** $24.2 million
- **Coed** 748 undergraduate students, 89% full-time, 50% women, 50% men
- **Moderately difficult** entrance level, 49% of applicants were admitted

UNDERGRAD STUDENTS
669 full-time, 79 part-time. Students come from 15 states and territories; 8 other countries; 12% are from out of state; 9% Black or African American, non-Hispanic/Latino; 4% Hispanic/Latino; 0.5% Asian, non-Hispanic/Latino; 0.3% American Indian or Alaska Native, non-Hispanic/Latino; 4% Two or more races, non-Hispanic/Latino; 2% Race/ethnicity unknown; 1% international; 2% transferred in; 80% live on campus.

Freshmen:
Admission: 1,767 applied, 863 admitted, 211 enrolled. *Average high school GPA:* 3.3. *Test scores:* ACT scores over 18: 84%; ACT scores over 24: 31%; ACT scores over 30: 3%.
Retention: 67% of full-time freshmen returned.

FACULTY
Total: 99, 51% full-time, 54% with terminal degrees.
Student/faculty ratio: 11:1.

ACADEMICS
Calendar: semesters. *Degrees:* bachelor's, master's, and postbachelor's certificates.

Special study options: academic remediation for entering students, accelerated degree program, adult/continuing education programs, advanced placement credit, distance learning, double majors, English as a second language, honors programs, independent study, internships, off-campus study, part-time degree program, services for LD students, student-designed majors, study abroad, summer session for credit.

Computers: 175 computers/terminals and 1,600 ports are available on campus for general student use. Students can access the following: campus intranet, computer help desk, free student e-mail accounts, online (class) grades, online (class) registration, online (class) schedules. Campuswide network is available. 100% of college-owned or -operated housing units are wired for high-speed Internet access. Wireless service is available via classrooms, computer centers, computer labs, dorm rooms, libraries, student centers.

Library: Musselman Library plus 1 other. *Books:* 73,648 (physical), 283,031 (digital/electronic); *Serial titles:* 1,001 (physical), 46,672 (digital/electronic); *Databases:* 258. Weekly public service hours: 74; students can reserve study rooms.

STUDENT LIFE
Housing options: on-campus residence required through senior year; coed, men-only, women-only. Campus housing is university owned. Freshman campus housing is guaranteed.

Activities and organizations: drama/theater group, student-run newspaper, radio station, choral group, Marbeck Center Board, Multicultural Student Organization, Bluffton Education Association, Fellowship of Christian Athletes, Bluffton University Business Leaders.

Athletics Member NCAA. All Division III. *Intercollegiate sports:* baseball M, basketball M/W, cross-country running M/W, football M, golf M/W, soccer M/W, softball W, track and field M/W, volleyball W. *Intramural sports:* basketball M/W, bowling M/W, football M/W, golf M/W, softball M/W, tennis M/W, ultimate Frisbee M, volleyball M/W.

Campus security: 24-hour emergency response devices, controlled dormitory access, night security guards.

Student services: health clinic, personal/psychological counseling.

COSTS & FINANCIAL AID
Costs (2018–19) *Comprehensive fee:* $43,566 includes full-time tuition ($32,316), mandatory fees ($450), and room and board ($10,800). Full-time tuition and fees vary according to course load, degree level, and program. Part-time tuition: $1347 per credit hour. Part-time tuition and fees vary according to course load, degree level, and program. *Required fees:* $113 per term part-time. *College room only:* $5316. Room and board charges vary according to board plan and housing facility. *Payment plan:* installment. *Waivers:* employees or children of employees.

Financial Aid Of all full-time matriculated undergraduates who enrolled in 2017, 614 applied for aid, 575 were judged to have need, 80 had their need fully met. 442 Federal Work-Study jobs (averaging $2306). 188 state and other part-time jobs (averaging $2907). In 2017, 86 non-need-based awards were made. *Average percent of need met:* 75. *Average financial aid package:* $27,173. *Average need-based loan:* $4551. *Average need-based gift aid:* $21,925. *Average non-need-based aid:* $16,395. *Average indebtedness upon graduation:* $36,796. *Financial aid deadline:* 10/1.

APPLYING
Standardized Tests *Required:* SAT or ACT (for admission).
Options: electronic application, deferred entrance.
Required: high school transcript, minimum 2.3 GPA, 1 letter of recommendation, rank in upper 50% of high school class or minimum ACT score of 19. *Required for some:* essay or personal statement. *Recommended:* interview.
Application deadlines: rolling (freshmen), rolling (transfers).
Notification: continuous (freshmen), continuous (transfers).

CONTACT
Ms. Emily Warner, Admissions Operation Manager, Bluffton University, 1 University Drive, Bluffton, OH 45817. *Phone:* 419-358-3255. *Toll-free phone:* 800-488-3257. *Fax:* 419-358-3081. *E-mail:* admissions@bluffton.edu.

Bowling Green State University
Bowling Green, Ohio
http://www.bgsu.edu/

- **State-supported** university, founded 1910
- **Small-town** 1338-acre campus with easy access to Toledo
- **Endowment** $156.0 million
- **Coed** 14,680 undergraduate students, 89% full-time, 56% women, 44% men
- **Moderately difficult** entrance level, 68% of applicants were admitted

UNDERGRAD STUDENTS
13,104 full-time, 1,576 part-time. Students come from 50 states and territories; 57 other countries; 12% are from out of state; 9% Black or African American, non-Hispanic/Latino; 4% Hispanic/Latino; 0.9% Asian, non-Hispanic/Latino; 0.1% Native Hawaiian or other Pacific Islander, non-Hispanic/Latino; 0.1% American Indian or Alaska Native, non-Hispanic/Latino; 3% Two or more races, non-Hispanic/Latino; 2% Race/ethnicity unknown; 3% international; 4% transferred in; 42% live on campus.

Freshmen:
Admission: 16,739 applied, 11,438 admitted, 3,344 enrolled. *Average high school GPA:* 3.4. *Test scores:* SAT evidence-based reading and writing scores over 500: 82%; SAT math scores over 500: 80%; ACT scores over 18: 95%; SAT evidence-based reading and writing scores over 600: 34%; SAT math scores over 600: 29%; ACT scores over 24: 40%; SAT evidence-based reading and writing scores over 700: 6%; SAT math scores over 700: 6%; ACT scores over 30: 5%.
Retention: 77% of full-time freshmen returned.

FACULTY
Total: 1,134, 66% full-time, 58% with terminal degrees.
Student/faculty ratio: 18:1.

ACADEMICS
Calendar: semesters. *Degrees:* bachelor's, master's, doctoral, post-master's, and postbachelor's certificates.

Special study options: academic remediation for entering students, accelerated degree program, adult/continuing education programs, advanced placement credit, cooperative education, distance learning, double majors, English as a second language, freshman honors college, honors programs, independent study, internships, off-campus study, part-time degree program, services for LD students, student-designed majors, study abroad, summer session for credit. *ROTC:* Army (b), Air Force (b).

Computers: 1,500 computers/terminals and 500 ports are available on campus for general student use. Students can access the following: campus intranet, computer help desk, free student e-mail accounts, online (class) grades, online (class) registration, online (class) schedules, wireless networking, OneDrive, Bursar billing information and payment, online mid-term grade reporting, view and change personal information, order official and unofficial transcripts, check meal plan balance, apply for graduation. Campuswide network is available. 100% of college-owned or -operated housing units are wired for high-speed Internet access. Wireless service is available via entire campus.

Library: William T. Jerome Library. *Books:* 1.6 million (physical), 194,293 (digital/electronic); *Serial titles:* 774 (physical), 12,510 (digital/electronic); *Databases:* 300. Weekly public service hours: 110; students can reserve study rooms.

STUDENT LIFE
Housing options: on-campus residence required through sophomore year; coed, men-only, women-only, special housing for students with disabilities. Campus housing is university owned and leased by the school. Freshman campus housing is guaranteed.

Activities and organizations: drama/theater group, student-run newspaper, radio and television station, choral group, marching band, Dance Marathon, Undergraduate Student Government, University Activities Organization, Alpha Phi Omega, Athletic Training Student Organization, national fraternities, national sororities.

Athletics Member NCAA. All Division I. *Intercollegiate sports:* baseball M(s), basketball M(s)/W(s), cross-country running M(s)/W(s), football M(s), golf M(s)/W(s), gymnastics W(s), ice hockey M(s), soccer M(s)/W(s), softball W(s), swimming and diving W(s), tennis W(s), track and field W(s), volleyball W(s). *Intramural sports:* badminton M/W, baseball M(c), basketball M/W, bowling M(c)/W(c), cross-country running M(c)/W(c), equestrian sports W(c), football M, golf M/W, gymnastics W(c), ice hockey M, lacrosse M(c)/W(c), rugby M(c)/W(c), soccer M/W, softball W(c), swimming and diving M(c)/W(c), tennis M(c)/W(c), track and field M(c)/W(c), ultimate Frisbee M/W, volleyball M/W, water polo M(c)/W(c).

Campus security: 24-hour emergency response devices and patrols, late-night transport/escort service, controlled dormitory access.

Student services: health clinic, personal/psychological counseling, women's center, legal services.

COSTS & FINANCIAL AID
Costs (2017–18) *Tuition:* state resident $9096 full-time, $379 per credit hour part-time; nonresident $16,632 full-time, $693 per credit hour part-time. Full-time tuition and fees vary according to course load and location. Part-time tuition and fees vary according to course load and location. *Required fees:* $1961 full-time, $81 per credit hour part-time. *Room and board:* $8918. Room and board charges vary according to board plan and housing facility. *Payment plan:* installment. *Waivers:* senior citizens and employees or children of employees.

Financial Aid Of all full-time matriculated undergraduates who enrolled in 2017, 10,783 applied for aid, 8,580 were judged to have need, 1,253 had their need fully met. 351 Federal Work-Study jobs (averaging $1207). In 2017, 2660 non-need-based awards were made. *Average percent of need met:* 80. *Average financial aid package:* $14,097. *Average need-based loan:* $4107. *Average need-based gift aid:* $7209. *Average non-need-based aid:* $5075. *Average indebtedness upon graduation:* $30,814.

APPLYING
Standardized Tests *Required:* SAT or ACT (for admission).

Options: electronic application, deferred entrance.

Application fee: $45.

Required: high school transcript. *Required for some:* interview.

Application deadlines: 7/15 (freshmen), 8/1 (transfers).

Notification: continuous until 8/1 (freshmen), continuous (transfers).

CONTACT
Bowling Green State University, Admissions Office, 200 University Hall, Bowling Green State University, Bowling Green, OH 43403-0085. *Phone:* 419-372-2478. *Fax:* 419-372-6955. *E-mail:* choosebgsu@bgsu.edu.

Bowling Green State University–Firelands College
Huron, Ohio
http://www.firelands.bgsu.edu/
- **State-supported** primarily 2-year, founded 1968, part of Bowling Green State University System
- **Rural** 216-acre campus with easy access to Cleveland, Toledo
- **Coed** 1,970 undergraduate students, 48% full-time, 64% women, 36% men
- **Noncompetitive** entrance level

UNDERGRAD STUDENTS
936 full-time, 1,034 part-time. Students come from 6 states and territories; 1 other country; 1% are from out of state; 6% Black or African American, non-Hispanic/Latino; 5% Hispanic/Latino; 0.8% Asian, non-Hispanic/Latino; 0.2% American Indian or Alaska Native, non-Hispanic/Latino; 4% Two or more races, non-Hispanic/Latino; 5% Race/ethnicity unknown; 0.1% international.

Freshmen:
Admission: 419 enrolled. *Average high school GPA:* 2.8.
Retention: 53% of full-time freshmen returned.

FACULTY
Total: 102, 43% full-time.
Student/faculty ratio: 20:1.

ACADEMICS
Calendar: semesters. *Degrees:* certificates, associate, and bachelor's (also offers some upper-level and graduate courses).

Special study options: academic remediation for entering students, adult/continuing education programs, advanced placement credit, cooperative education, distance learning, double majors, honors programs, independent study, internships, part-time degree program, services for LD students, student-designed majors, study abroad, summer session for credit. *ROTC:* Army (c), Air Force (c).

Computers: 300 computers/terminals are available on campus for general student use. Students can access the following: computer help desk, free student e-mail accounts, online (class) grades, online (class) registration, online (class) schedules. Campuswide network is available. Wireless service is available via entire campus.
Library: BGSU Firelands College Library.

STUDENT LIFE
Housing options: college housing not available.

Activities and organizations: drama/theater group, choral group, Society of Fandom and Gaming, Student Government, Student Theater Guild, Safe Space, Society of Leadership and Success.

Athletics *Intramural sports:* basketball M/W, bowling M/W, football M, table tennis M/W, volleyball M/W.

Campus security: 24-hour emergency response devices, late-night transport/escort service, patrols by trained security personnel.

COSTS
Costs (2018–19) *Tuition:* state resident $4706 full-time, $196 per credit hour part-time; nonresident $12,014 full-time, $510 per credit hour part-time. Full-time tuition and fees vary according to location and reciprocity agreements. Part-time tuition and fees vary according to location and reciprocity agreements. *Required fees:* $240 full-time, $9 per credit hour part-time, $120 per term part-time. *Payment plan:* installment. *Waivers:* children of alumni, senior citizens, and employees or children of employees.

APPLYING
Options: electronic application, early admission, deferred entrance.
Application fee: $45.
Required: high school transcript.
Application deadlines: 8/6 (freshmen), 8/6 (transfers).
Notification: continuous (freshmen), continuous (transfers).

CONTACT
Dr. Megan Zahler, Assistant Dean for Strategic Enrollment Planning, Bowling Green State University–Firelands College, One University

Drive, Huron, OH 44839-9791. *Phone:* 419-433-5560. *Toll-free phone:* 800-322-4787. *Fax:* 419-372-0604. *E-mail:* mzahler@bgsu.edu.

Bryant & Stratton College–Akron Campus

Akron, Ohio
http://www.bryantstratton.edu/

CONTACT
Bryant & Stratton College–Akron Campus, 190 Montrose West Avenue, Akron, OH 44321.

Bryant & Stratton College–Cleveland Campus

Cleveland, Ohio
http://www.bryantstratton.edu/

CONTACT
Bryant & Stratton College–Cleveland Campus, Cleveland, OH 44114-3203. *Phone:* 216-771-1700. *Fax:* 216-771-7787.

Bryant & Stratton College–Eastlake Campus

Eastlake, Ohio
http://www.bryantstratton.edu/

CONTACT
Ms. Melanie Pettit, Director of Admissions, Bryant & Stratton College–Eastlake Campus, 35350 Curtis Boulevard, Eastlake, OH 44095. *Phone:* 440-510-1112.

Bryant & Stratton College–Parma Campus

Parma, Ohio
http://www.bryantstratton.edu/

CONTACT
Bryant & Stratton College–Parma Campus, 12955 Snow Road, Parma, OH 44130-1005. *Phone:* 216-265-3151. *Toll-free phone:* 866-948-0571.

Capital University

Columbus, Ohio
http://www.capital.edu/

- **Independent** comprehensive, founded 1830, affiliated with Evangelical Lutheran Church in America
- **Suburban** 48-acre campus with easy access to Columbus
- **Endowment** $78.0 million
- **Coed** 2,699 undergraduate students, 92% full-time, 61% women, 39% men
- **Moderately difficult** entrance level, 69% of applicants were admitted

UNDERGRAD STUDENTS
2,493 full-time, 206 part-time. Students come from 34 states and territories; 22 other countries; 9% are from out of state; 10% Black or African American, non-Hispanic/Latino; 4% Hispanic/Latino; 1% Asian, non-Hispanic/Latino; 0.2% Native Hawaiian or other Pacific Islander, non-Hispanic/Latino; 0.2% American Indian or Alaska Native, non-Hispanic/Latino; 5% Two or more races, non-Hispanic/Latino; 3% Race/ethnicity unknown; 2% international; 3% transferred in; 59% live on campus.

Freshmen:
Admission: 4,208 applied, 2,889 admitted, 595 enrolled. *Average high school GPA:* 3.6. *Test scores:* SAT evidence-based reading and writing scores over 500: 93%; SAT math scores over 500: 86%; ACT scores over 18: 97%; SAT evidence-based reading and writing scores over 600: 49%; SAT math scores over 600: 33%; ACT scores over 24: 59%; SAT

evidence-based reading and writing scores over 700: 4%; SAT math scores over 700: 3%; ACT scores over 30: 9%.
Retention: 78% of full-time freshmen returned.

FACULTY
Total: 409, 40% full-time, 47% with terminal degrees.
Student/faculty ratio: 11:1.

ACADEMICS
Calendar: semesters. *Degrees:* bachelor's, master's, doctoral, and postbachelor's certificates.
Special study options: accelerated degree program, adult/continuing education programs, advanced placement credit, cooperative education, double majors, English as a second language, external degree program, freshman honors college, honors programs, independent study, internships, off-campus study, part-time degree program, services for LD students, student-designed majors, study abroad, summer session for credit. *ROTC:* Army (b), Air Force (c).
Unusual degree programs: 3-2 engineering with Washington University in St. Louis, Case Western Reserve University.
Computers: 457 computers/terminals and 1,400 ports are available on campus for general student use. Students can access the following: campus intranet, computer help desk, free student e-mail accounts, online (class) grades, online (class) registration, online (class) schedules. Campuswide network is available. 100% of college-owned or -operated housing units are wired for high-speed Internet access. Wireless service is available via entire campus.
Library: Blackmore Library.

STUDENT LIFE
Housing options: on-campus residence required through sophomore year; coed, special housing for students with disabilities. Campus housing is university owned. Freshman campus housing is guaranteed.
Activities and organizations: drama/theater group, student-run newspaper, radio and television station, choral group, Campus Crusade for Christ, student government, University Programming, College Republicans, American Marketing Association, national fraternities, national sororities.
Athletics Member NCAA. All Division III. *Intercollegiate sports:* baseball M, basketball M/W, cross-country running M/W, football M, golf M/W, lacrosse M/W, soccer M/W, softball W, tennis M/W, track and field M/W, volleyball W. *Intramural sports:* basketball M/W, cheerleading M(c)/W(c), fencing M(c)/W(c), football M/W, racquetball M/W, ultimate Frisbee M/W, volleyball M/W.
Campus security: 24-hour emergency response devices and patrols, late-night transport/escort service, controlled dormitory access.
Student services: health clinic, personal/psychological counseling.

COSTS & FINANCIAL AID
Costs (2018–19) *Comprehensive fee:* $46,308 includes full-time tuition ($35,146), mandatory fees ($320), and room and board ($10,842). Full-time tuition and fees vary according to course load. Part-time tuition: $1172 per credit hour. Part-time tuition and fees vary according to course load. *Room and board:* Room and board charges vary according to board plan and housing facility. *Payment plan:* installment. *Waivers:* senior citizens and employees or children of employees.
Financial Aid Of all full-time matriculated undergraduates who enrolled in 2016, 2,150 applied for aid, 1,955 were judged to have need, 577 had their need fully met. In 2016, 494 non-need-based awards were made. *Average percent of need met:* 80. *Average financial aid package:* $28,438. *Average need-based loan:* $4665. *Average need-based gift aid:* $23,427. *Average non-need-based aid:* $20,185. *Average indebtedness upon graduation:* $32,515.

APPLYING
Standardized Tests *Required:* SAT or ACT (for admission).
Options: electronic application, deferred entrance.
Application fee: $25.
Required: high school transcript, minimum 2.6 GPA. *Required for some:* 1 letter of recommendation, audition for Conservatory of Music. *Recommended:* interview.
Application deadlines: 5/1 (freshmen), rolling (transfers).
Notification: 9/30 (freshmen), continuous (transfers).

CONTACT

Mr. Garien Hudson, Director of Admission, Capital University, 1 College and Main, Columbus, OH 43209. *Phone:* 614-236-6232. *Toll-free phone:* 866-544-6175. *Fax:* 614-236-6926. *E-mail:* ghudson@capital.edu.

Case Western Reserve University

Cleveland, Ohio

http://www.case.edu/

- **Independent** university, founded 1826
- **Urban** 267-acre campus
- **Endowment** $1.8 billion
- **Coed** 5,150 undergraduate students, 97% full-time, 45% women, 55% men
- **Very difficult** entrance level, 33% of applicants were admitted

UNDERGRAD STUDENTS

4,978 full-time, 172 part-time. Students come from 47 states and territories; 46 other countries; 72% are from out of state; 4% Black or African American, non-Hispanic/Latino; 7% Hispanic/Latino; 21% Asian, non-Hispanic/Latino; 0.1% Native Hawaiian or other Pacific Islander, non-Hispanic/Latino; 0.1% American Indian or Alaska Native, non-Hispanic/Latino; 5% Two or more races, non-Hispanic/Latino; 2% Race/ethnicity unknown; 13% international; 0.7% transferred in; 80% live on campus.

Freshmen:

Admission: 25,380 applied, 8,405 admitted, 1,309 enrolled. *Test scores:* SAT evidence-based reading and writing scores over 500: 100%; SAT math scores over 500: 100%; ACT scores over 18: 100%; SAT evidence-based reading and writing scores over 600: 96%; SAT math scores over 600: 97%; ACT scores over 24: 99%; SAT evidence-based reading and writing scores over 700: 52%; SAT math scores over 700: 75%; ACT scores over 30: 76%.

Retention: 93% of full-time freshmen returned.

FACULTY

Total: 1,007, 78% full-time, 84% with terminal degrees.
Student/faculty ratio: 11:1.

ACADEMICS

Calendar: semesters. *Degrees:* bachelor's, master's, doctoral, post-master's, and postbachelor's certificates.

Special study options: accelerated degree program, adult/continuing education programs, advanced placement credit, cooperative education, double majors, English as a second language, honors programs, independent study, internships, off-campus study, part-time degree program, services for LD students, student-designed majors, study abroad, summer session for credit. *ROTC:* Army (b), Air Force (c).

Unusual degree programs: 3-2 engineering.

Computers: 357 computers/terminals and 50,000 ports are available on campus for general student use. Students can access the following: campus intranet, free student e-mail accounts, online (class) grades, online (class) registration, online (class) schedules, software library, online reference databases, electronic books and journals, research computing, training. Campuswide network is available. 100% of college-owned or -operated housing units are wired for high-speed Internet access. Wireless service is available via entire campus.

Library: Kelvin Smith Library plus 6 others. *Books:* 3.4 million (physical); *Serial titles:* 196,361 (physical); *Databases:* 470. Students can reserve study rooms.

STUDENT LIFE

Housing options: on-campus residence required through sophomore year; coed. Campus housing is university owned. Freshman campus housing is guaranteed.

Activities and organizations: drama/theater group, student-run newspaper, radio station, choral group, marching band, SpartaTHON, Quidditch Team, Spartans for Special Olympics, Undergraduate Indian Student Association, Footlighters, national fraternities, national sororities.

Athletics Member NCAA. All Division III. *Intercollegiate sports:* baseball M, basketball M/W, cross-country running M/W, football M, soccer M/W, softball W, swimming and diving M/W, tennis M/W, track and field M/W, volleyball W, wrestling M. *Intramural sports:* badminton M/W, basketball M/W, bowling M/W, football M/W, golf M/W,

racquetball M/W, soccer M/W, softball M/W, swimming and diving M/W, table tennis M/W, tennis M/W, ultimate Frisbee M/W, volleyball M/W, water polo M/W, weight lifting M/W.

Campus security: 24-hour emergency response devices and patrols, student patrols, late-night transport/escort service, controlled dormitory access, crime prevention programs.

Student services: health clinic, personal/psychological counseling, women's center, legal services.

COSTS & FINANCIAL AID

Costs (2017–18) *One-time required fee:* $540. *Comprehensive fee:* $62,284 includes full-time tuition ($47,074), mandatory fees ($426), and room and board ($14,784). Part-time tuition: $1962 per credit hour. Part-time tuition and fees vary according to course load. *College room only:* $8570. Room and board charges vary according to board plan, housing facility, and student level. *Payment plan:* installment. *Waivers:* employees or children of employees.

Financial Aid Of all full-time matriculated undergraduates who enrolled in 2017, 2,945 applied for aid, 2,474 were judged to have need, 1,599 had their need fully met. 1,509 Federal Work-Study jobs (averaging $2613). 86 state and other part-time jobs (averaging $2344). In 2017, 1623 non-need-based awards were made. *Average percent of need met:* 89. *Average financial aid package:* $44,122. *Average need-based loan:* $6996. *Average need-based gift aid:* $30,713. *Average non-need-based aid:* $23,582. *Average indebtedness upon graduation:* $32,377. *Financial aid deadline:* 2/1.

APPLYING

Standardized Tests *Required:* SAT or ACT (for admission).

Options: electronic application, early admission, early decision, early action, deferred entrance.

Application fee: $70.

Required: essay or personal statement, high school transcript, 2 letters of recommendation, school report, including a counselor recommendation. *Recommended:* interview.

Application deadlines: 1/15 (freshmen), 5/1 (transfers), 11/1 (early action).

Early decision deadline: 11/1 (for plan 1), 1/15 (for plan 2).

Notification: 3/20 (freshmen), continuous until 6/1 (transfers), 12/17 (early decision plan 1), 2/1 (early decision plan 2), 12/15 (early action).

CONTACT

Robert McCullough, Director of Undergraduate Admission, Case Western Reserve University, 10900 Euclid Avenue, Cleveland, OH 44106. *Phone:* 216-368-4450. *Fax:* 216-368-5111. *E-mail:* admission@case.edu.

Cedarville University

Cedarville, Ohio

http://www.cedarville.edu/

- **Independent Baptist** comprehensive, founded 1887
- **Small-town** 441-acre campus with easy access to Columbus, Dayton
- **Endowment** $28.8 million
- **Coed** 3,535 undergraduate students, 88% full-time, 53% women, 47% men
- **Moderately difficult** entrance level, 71% of applicants were admitted

UNDERGRAD STUDENTS

3,109 full-time, 426 part-time. Students come from 49 states and territories; 39 other countries; 57% are from out of state; 1% Black or African American, non-Hispanic/Latino; 2% Hispanic/Latino; 2% Asian, non-Hispanic/Latino; 0.3% American Indian or Alaska Native, non-Hispanic/Latino; 3% Two or more races, non-Hispanic/Latino; 6% Race/ethnicity unknown; 1% international; 3% transferred in; 73% live on campus.

Freshmen:

Admission: 4,039 applied, 2,886 admitted, 872 enrolled. *Average high school GPA:* 3.7. *Test scores:* SAT evidence-based reading and writing scores over 500: 96%; SAT math scores over 500: 94%; ACT scores over 18: 100%; SAT evidence-based reading and writing scores over 600: 71%; SAT math scores over 600: 54%; ACT scores over 24: 74%; SAT evidence-based reading and writing scores over 700: 19%; SAT math scores over 700: 15%; ACT scores over 30: 19%.

COLLEGES AT-A-GLANCE

Retention: 84% of full-time freshmen returned.

FACULTY
Total: 385, 47% full-time, 54% with terminal degrees.
Student/faculty ratio: 14:1.

ACADEMICS
Calendar: semesters. *Degrees:* certificates, bachelor's, master's, doctoral, post-master's, and postbachelor's certificates.

Special study options: academic remediation for entering students, adult/continuing education programs, advanced placement credit, cooperative education, distance learning, double majors, honors programs, independent study, internships, off-campus study, part-time degree program, services for LD students, student-designed majors, study abroad, summer session for credit. *ROTC:* Army (c), Air Force (c).

Computers: 1,500 computers/terminals and 4,000 ports are available on campus for general student use. Students can access the following: campus intranet, computer help desk, free student e-mail accounts, online (class) grades, online (class) registration, online (class) schedules, over 70 software packages. Campuswide network is available. 100% of college-owned or -operated housing units are wired for high-speed Internet access. Wireless service is available via entire campus.
Library: Centennial Library. *Books:* 182,543 (physical), 128,348 (digital/electronic); *Serial titles:* 737 (physical), 26,199 (digital/electronic); *Databases:* 199. Weekly public service hours: 91; students can reserve study rooms.

STUDENT LIFE
Housing options: on-campus residence required through senior year; men-only, women-only, special housing for students with disabilities. Campus housing is university owned. Freshman campus housing is guaranteed.

Activities and organizations: drama/theater group, student-run newspaper, radio station, choral group, Student Nurses Association, Tau Delta Kappa, Mu Kappa, AYO, MISO (Multicultural International Student Org).

Athletics Member NCAA, NCCAA. All NCAA Division II. *Intercollegiate sports:* baseball M(s), basketball M(s)/W(s), cheerleading M/W, cross-country running M(s)/W(s), golf M(s), soccer M(s)/W(s), softball W(s), tennis M(s)/W(s), track and field M(s)/W(s), volleyball W(s). *Intramural sports:* badminton M/W, basketball M/W, football M/W, golf M/W, racquetball M/W, riflery M(c)/W(c), rock climbing M/W, rugby M(c)/W(c), soccer M/W, swimming and diving M(c)/W(c), table tennis M/W, tennis M/W, ultimate Frisbee M(c)/W(c), volleyball M/W.

Campus security: 24-hour emergency response devices and patrols, late-night transport/escort service, controlled dormitory access.

Student services: health clinic, personal/psychological counseling.

COSTS & FINANCIAL AID
Costs (2018–19) *Comprehensive fee:* $37,630 includes full-time tuition ($30,070), mandatory fees ($200), and room and board ($7360). Part-time tuition: $1138 per credit. Part-time tuition and fees vary according to course load. *Required fees:* $50 per term part-time. *College room only:* $4172. Room and board charges vary according to board plan and housing facility. *Payment plan:* installment. *Waivers:* adult students, senior citizens, and employees or children of employees.

Financial Aid Of all full-time matriculated undergraduates who enrolled in 2017, 2,521 applied for aid, 2,165 were judged to have need, 708 had their need fully met. 240 Federal Work-Study jobs (averaging $2291). 1,439 state and other part-time jobs (averaging $1374). In 2017, 572 non-need-based awards were made. *Average percent of need met:* 31. *Average financial aid package:* $21,864. *Average need-based loan:* $5346. *Average need-based gift aid:* $4707. *Average non-need-based aid:* $21,005. *Average indebtedness upon graduation:* $29,582.

APPLYING
Standardized Tests *Required:* SAT or ACT (for admission).
Options: electronic application, early admission, deferred entrance.
Application fee: $30.

Required: essay or personal statement, high school transcript, minimum 3.0 GPA, 1 letter of recommendation, clear testimony of faith in Jesus Christ and evidence of a consistent Christian lifestyle, minimum ACT score of 22 or SAT score of 1020, minimum 3.0 unweighted, cumulative GPA in college prep course work. *Required for some:* interview.

Application deadlines: rolling (freshmen), rolling (transfers).
Notification: continuous (freshmen), continuous (transfers).

CONTACT
Ms. Becky Hayes, Director of Enrollment Services, Cedarville University, 251 North Main Street, Cedarville, OH 45314-0601. *Phone:* 937-766-7700. *Toll-free phone:* 800-233-2784. *E-mail:* admissions@cedarville.edu.

Central State University
Wilberforce, Ohio
http://www.centralstate.edu/

- **State-supported** 4-year, founded 1887, part of Ohio Board of Regents
- **Rural** 60-acre campus with easy access to Dayton
- **Endowment** $3.7 million
- **Coed** 1,784 undergraduate students, 96% full-time, 59% women, 41% men
- **Minimally difficult** entrance level, 48% of applicants were admitted

UNDERGRAD STUDENTS
1,710 full-time, 74 part-time. Students come from 29 states and territories; 12 other countries; 38% are from out of state; 92% Black or African American, non-Hispanic/Latino; 0.6% Hispanic/Latino; 0.1% American Indian or Alaska Native, non-Hispanic/Latino; 2% Two or more races, non-Hispanic/Latino; 2% Race/ethnicity unknown; 2% international; 6% transferred in; 36% live on campus.

Freshmen:
Admission: 12,517 applied, 6,010 admitted, 664 enrolled. *Average high school GPA:* 2.7.
Retention: 47% of full-time freshmen returned.

FACULTY
Total: 213, 46% full-time, 41% with terminal degrees.
Student/faculty ratio: 13:1.

ACADEMICS
Calendar: semesters. *Degree:* bachelor's.

Special study options: adult/continuing education programs, cooperative education, double majors, honors programs, independent study, internships, off-campus study, part-time degree program, services for LD students, study abroad, summer session for credit. *ROTC:* Army (b).

Computers: 780 computers/terminals and 2,600 ports are available on campus for general student use. Students can access the following: campus intranet, computer help desk, free student e-mail accounts, online (class) grades, online (class) registration, online (class) schedules. Campuswide network is available. 100% of college-owned or -operated housing units are wired for high-speed Internet access. Wireless service is available via entire campus.
Library: Hallie Q. Brown Memorial Library plus 1 other. *Books:* 312,636 (physical), 8,242 (digital/electronic); *Serial titles:* 69 (physical); *Databases:* 179. Weekly public service hours: 77.

STUDENT LIFE
Housing options: on-campus residence required for freshman year; coed, men-only, women-only. Campus housing is university owned. Freshman campus housing is guaranteed.

Activities and organizations: drama/theater group, student-run newspaper, radio and television station, choral group, marching band, Student Ambassadors, student government, Make it Happen (Inter-Faith), Daughters of Nia Anaya (Social Group), Evolutions (Modeling Troupe), national fraternities, national sororities.

Athletics Member NCAA. All Division II. *Intercollegiate sports:* basketball M(s)/W(s), cheerleading M(s)/W(s), cross-country running M(s)/W(s), golf M(s)/W(s), tennis M(s)/W(s), track and field M(s)/W(s), volleyball W(s). *Intramural sports:* basketball M/W, bowling M/W, softball M/W, tennis M/W.

Campus security: 24-hour emergency response devices and patrols, controlled dormitory access.

Student services: health clinic, personal/psychological counseling.

COSTS & FINANCIAL AID
Costs (2017–18) *Tuition:* state resident $3926 full-time, $275 per credit hour part-time; nonresident $5776 full-time, $625 per credit hour part-

time. Full-time tuition and fees vary according to course load and reciprocity agreements. Part-time tuition and fees vary according to course load and reciprocity agreements. *Required fees:* $2320 full-time. *Room and board:* $9934; room only: $5340. Room and board charges vary according to board plan and housing facility. *Payment plan:* installment. *Waivers:* senior citizens and employees or children of employees.

Financial Aid Of all full-time matriculated undergraduates who enrolled in 2012, 1,820 applied for aid, 1,820 were judged to have need. 337 Federal Work-Study jobs (averaging $1216). *Average financial aid package:* $6373. *Average need-based loan:* $2103. *Average need-based gift aid:* $3269.

APPLYING
Options: electronic application.
Application fee: $20.
Required: essay or personal statement, high school transcript. *Required for some:* minimum 2.2 GPA, 2 letters of recommendation.
Application deadlines: 6/15 (freshmen), 6/15 (transfers).
Notification: continuous (freshmen), continuous (transfers).

CONTACT
Mr. Stephen Williams, Director, Admissions, Central State University, PO Box 1004, 1400 Blush Row Road, Wilberforce, OH 45384. *Phone:* 937-376-6218. *Toll-free phone:* 800-388-CSU1 (in-state); 800-388-2781 (out-of-state). *Fax:* 937-376-6648. *E-mail:* admissions@centralstate.edu.

Chamberlain College of Nursing
Cleveland, Ohio
http://www.chamberlain.edu/
- **Proprietary** 4-year
- **Coed**

FACULTY
Student/faculty ratio: 6:1.

ACADEMICS
Degree: bachelor's.

COSTS
Costs (2017–18) *Tuition:* $18,900 full-time. *Required fees:* $600 full-time.

APPLYING
Standardized Tests *Required:* SAT or ACT (for admission).
Options: deferred entrance.
Application fee: $95.

CONTACT
Chamberlain College of Nursing, 6700 Euclid Avenue, Cleveland, OH 44103. *Toll-free phone:* 877-751-5783.

Chamberlain College of Nursing
Columbus, Ohio
http://www.chamberlain.edu/
- **Proprietary** 4-year
- **Coed**

FACULTY
Student/faculty ratio: 10:1.

ACADEMICS
Calendar: semesters. *Degree:* bachelor's.

STUDENT LIFE
Housing options: college housing not available.

COSTS
Costs (2017–18) *Tuition:* $18,900 full-time. *Required fees:* $600 full-time.

APPLYING
Standardized Tests *Required:* SAT or ACT (for admission).
Options: deferred entrance.
Application fee: $95.

CONTACT
Admissions, Chamberlain College of Nursing, 1350 Alum Creek Drive, Columbus, OH 43209. *Phone:* 614-252-8890. *Toll-free phone:* 877-751-5783.

Cincinnati Christian University
Cincinnati, Ohio
http://www.ccuniversity.edu/

CONTACT
Cincinnati Christian University, 2700 Glenway Avenue, PO Box 04320, Cincinnati, OH 45204-3200. *Phone:* 513-244-8110. *Toll-free phone:* 800-949-4228 (in-state); 800-949-4CCU (out-of-state).

Cincinnati College of Mortuary Science
Cincinnati, Ohio
http://www.ccms.edu/

CONTACT
Cincinnati College of Mortuary Science, 645 West North Bend Road, Cincinnati, OH 45224-1462. *Phone:* 513-761-2020. *Toll-free phone:* 888-377-8433. *Fax:* 513-761-3333.

Cleveland Institute of Art
Cleveland, Ohio
http://www.cia.edu/
- **Independent** 4-year, founded 1882
- **Urban** 2-acre campus with easy access to Cleveland
- **Endowment** $25.3 million
- **Coed**
- **Moderately difficult** entrance level

FACULTY
Student/faculty ratio: 9:1.

ACADEMICS
Calendar: semesters. *Degree:* bachelor's.
Library: Gund Library. *Books:* 47,638 (physical), 150,000 (digital/electronic); *Serial titles:* 415 (physical), 11 (digital/electronic); *Databases:* 73. Weekly public service hours: 74; students can reserve study rooms.

STUDENT LIFE
Housing options: on-campus residence required for freshman year; coed. Campus housing is leased by the school. Freshman applicants given priority for college housing.

Activities and organizations: drama/theater group, choral group, marching band, Campus Activities Board, Student Independent Exhibition, International Interior Design Association, Student Leadership Council, Community Service Club, national fraternities, national sororities.

Campus security: 24-hour emergency response devices and patrols, controlled dormitory access.

Student services: health clinic, personal/psychological counseling, women's center.

COSTS & FINANCIAL AID
Costs (2017–18) *Comprehensive fee:* $51,455 includes full-time tuition ($37,980), mandatory fees ($2675), and room and board ($10,800). Full-time tuition and fees vary according to reciprocity agreements. Part-time tuition: $1585 per credit. Part-time tuition and fees vary according to course load and reciprocity agreements. *Required fees:* $73 per semester hour part-time, $115 per semester part-time. *College room only:* $8150. Room and board charges vary according to board plan and housing facility.

Financial Aid Of all full-time matriculated undergraduates who enrolled in 2015, 504 applied for aid, 474 were judged to have need, 33 had their need fully met. 139 Federal Work-Study jobs (averaging $1203). In 2015, 94 non-need-based awards were made. *Average percent of need met:* 61. *Average financial aid package:* $27,354. *Average need-based loan:*

$4627. *Average need-based gift aid:* $22,663. *Average non-need-based aid:* $13,768. *Average indebtedness upon graduation:* $35,136.

APPLYING

Standardized Tests *Required:* SAT or ACT (for admission).

Options: electronic application, early admission, early action.

Application fee: $40.

Required: essay or personal statement, high school transcript, minimum 2.0 GPA, 1 letter of recommendation, portfolio. *Recommended:* interview.

CONTACT

Office of Admissions, Cleveland Institute of Art, 11610 Euclid Avenue, Cleveland, OH 44106. *Phone:* 216-421-7418. *Toll-free phone:* 800-223-4700. *Fax:* 216-754-3634. *E-mail:* admissions@cia.edu.

Cleveland Institute of Music

Cleveland, Ohio

http://www.cim.edu/

CONTACT

Mr. William Fay, Director of Admission, Cleveland Institute of Music, 11021 East Boulevard, Cleveland, OH 44106-1776. *Phone:* 216-795-3107. *Fax:* 216-791-1530. *E-mail:* william.fay@case.edu.

Cleveland State University

Cleveland, Ohio

http://www.csuohio.edu/

- **State-supported** university, founded 1964, part of University System of Ohio
- **Urban** 85-acre campus with easy access to Cleveland, OH
- **Endowment** $66.2 million
- **Coed** 12,306 undergraduate students, 75% full-time, 54% women, 46% men
- **Moderately difficult** entrance level, 88% of applicants were admitted

UNDERGRAD STUDENTS

9,268 full-time, 3,038 part-time. Students come from 33 states and territories; 96 other countries; 4% are from out of state; 16% Black or African American, non-Hispanic/Latino; 6% Hispanic/Latino; 3% Asian, non-Hispanic/Latino; 0.1% Native Hawaiian or other Pacific Islander, non-Hispanic/Latino; 0.2% American Indian or Alaska Native, non-Hispanic/Latino; 4% Two or more races, non-Hispanic/Latino; 1% Race/ethnicity unknown; 5% international; 11% transferred in; 6% live on campus.

Freshmen:

Admission: 8,351 applied, 7,359 admitted, 1,955 enrolled. *Average high school GPA:* 3.4. *Test scores:* ACT scores over 18: 86%; ACT scores over 24: 33%; ACT scores over 30: 4%.

Retention: 70% of full-time freshmen returned.

FACULTY

Total: 1,178, 46% full-time.

Student/faculty ratio: 17:1.

ACADEMICS

Calendar: semesters. *Degrees:* bachelor's, master's, doctoral, post-master's, and postbachelor's certificates.

Special study options: academic remediation for entering students, accelerated degree program, adult/continuing education programs, advanced placement credit, cooperative education, distance learning, double majors, English as a second language, freshman honors college, honors programs, independent study, internships, off-campus study, part-time degree program, services for LD students, study abroad, summer session for credit. *ROTC:* Army (c), Air Force (c).

Computers: 736 computers/terminals are available on campus for general student use. Students can access the following: campus intranet, computer help desk, free student e-mail accounts, online (class) grades, online (class) registration, online (class) schedules, each general purpose computer lab has a scanner and printer, students are allowed free black and white printing up to 2,000 pages per semester. Campuswide network is available. 100% of college-owned or -operated housing units are wired

for high-speed Internet access. Wireless service is available via entire campus.

Library: Michael Schwartz Library plus 1 other. *Books:* 524,556 (physical), 228,146 (digital/electronic); *Serial titles:* 6,155 (physical), 194 (digital/electronic); *Databases:* 733. Students can reserve study rooms.

STUDENT LIFE

Housing options: coed, special housing for students with disabilities. Campus housing is university owned. Freshman campus housing is guaranteed.

Activities and organizations: drama/theater group, student-run newspaper, radio station, choral group, Black Student Union, Chinese Students and Scholars Association, Through the Cross Campus Ministries, Student Nurses Association, Joint Engineering Council, national fraternities, national sororities.

Athletics Member NCAA. All Division I. *Intercollegiate sports:* basketball M(s)/W(s), cheerleading M/W, cross-country running W(s), fencing M(s)/W(s), golf M(s)/W, lacrosse M, soccer M(s)/W, softball W(s), swimming and diving M(s)/W(s), tennis M/W(s), track and field W(s), volleyball W(s), wrestling M(s). *Intramural sports:* baseball M(c), basketball M/W, crew M(c)/W(c), cross-country running M/W, fencing M/W, golf M/W, ice hockey M(c), rock climbing M(c)/W(c), rugby M(c), soccer M(c)/W(c), track and field M/W, ultimate Frisbee M/W, volleyball W, wrestling M.

Campus security: 24-hour emergency response devices and patrols, late-night transport/escort service, controlled dormitory access, Campus Watch, CSU Alert Notification System, Community Emergency and Response Team (CERT).

Student services: health clinic, personal/psychological counseling, women's center.

COSTS & FINANCIAL AID

Costs (2017–18) *Tuition:* state resident $9636 full-time, $402 per credit hour part-time; nonresident $13,687 full-time, $570 per credit hour part-time. Full-time tuition and fees vary according to course load, degree level, location, and program. Part-time tuition and fees vary according to course load, degree level, location, and program. *Required fees:* $60 full-time, $49 per credit hour part-time, $35 per term part-time. *Room and board:* $12,000. Room and board charges vary according to board plan and housing facility. *Payment plan:* installment. *Waivers:* senior citizens and employees or children of employees.

Financial Aid Of all full-time matriculated undergraduates who enrolled in 2017, 7,508 applied for aid, 6,579 were judged to have need, 409 had their need fully met. 259 Federal Work-Study jobs (averaging $3378). In 2017, 735 non-need-based awards were made. *Average percent of need met:* 47. *Average financial aid package:* $8932. *Average need-based loan:* $4046. *Average need-based gift aid:* $6903. *Average non-need-based aid:* $4951. *Average indebtedness upon graduation:* $39,380.

APPLYING

Standardized Tests *Required:* SAT or ACT (for admission).

Options: electronic application, early action, deferred entrance.

Application fee: $30.

Required: high school transcript, minimum 2.3 GPA.

Application deadlines: 5/15 (freshmen), 5/15 (transfers), 5/1 (early action).

Notification: continuous (freshmen), continuous (transfers).

CONTACT

Undergraduate Admissions Office, Cleveland State University, 2121 Euclid Avenue, EC 100, Cleveland, OH 44115. *Phone:* 216-523-7416. *Toll-free phone:* 888-CSU-OHIO. *E-mail:* admissions@csuohio.edu.

The College of Wooster

Wooster, Ohio

http://www.wooster.edu/

- **Independent** 4-year, founded 1866, affiliated with Presbyterian Church (U.S.A.)
- **Small-town** 240-acre campus with easy access to Cleveland
- **Endowment** $280.5 million
- **Coed** 1,980 undergraduate students, 99% full-time, 55% women, 45% men
- **Moderately difficult** entrance level, 56% of applicants were admitted

UNDERGRAD STUDENTS

1,962 full-time, 18 part-time. Students come from 43 states and territories; 37 other countries; 63% are from out of state; 9% Black or African American, non-Hispanic/Latino; 5% Hispanic/Latino; 5% Asian, non-Hispanic/Latino; 1% American Indian or Alaska Native, non-Hispanic/Latino; 1% Race/ethnicity unknown; 13% international; 0.6% transferred in; 99% live on campus.

Freshmen:

Admission: 5,615 applied, 3,169 admitted, 568 enrolled. *Average high school GPA:* 3.7. *Test scores:* SAT evidence-based reading and writing scores over 500: 81%; SAT math scores over 500: 91%; ACT scores over 18: 99%; SAT evidence-based reading and writing scores over 600: 46%; SAT math scores over 600: 49%; ACT scores over 24: 78%; SAT evidence-based reading and writing scores over 700: 9%; SAT math scores over 700: 9%; ACT scores over 30: 26%.

Retention: 86% of full-time freshmen returned.

FACULTY

Total: 212, 78% full-time, 85% with terminal degrees.

Student/faculty ratio: 11:1.

ACADEMICS

Calendar: semesters. *Degree:* bachelor's.

Special study options: advanced placement credit, double majors, independent study, internships, off-campus study, services for LD students, student-designed majors, study abroad.

Unusual degree programs: 3-2 engineering with Case Western Reserve University, Washington University in St. Louis, University of Michigan; forestry with Duke University; nursing with Case Western Reserve University; social work with Case Western Reserve University; dentistry with Case Western Reserve University, architecture with Washington University in St. Louis.

Computers: 450 computers/terminals are available on campus for general student use. Students can access the following: campus intranet, computer help desk, free student e-mail accounts, online (class) grades, online (class) registration, online (class) schedules, learning management system, campus blogging site, campus wiki site. Campuswide network is available. 100% of college-owned or -operated housing units are wired for high-speed Internet access. Wireless service is available via entire campus.

Library: The College of Wooster Libraries plus 3 others. *Books:* 453,145 (physical), 719,794 (digital/electronic); *Serial titles:* 2,693 (physical), 102,227 (digital/electronic); *Databases:* 568. Weekly public service hours: 112; students can reserve study rooms.

STUDENT LIFE

Housing options: on-campus residence required through senior year; coed, women-only. Campus housing is university owned. Freshman campus housing is guaranteed.

Activities and organizations: drama/theater group, student-run newspaper, radio station, choral group, marching band, Volunteer Network, International Student Association, Inter-Greek Council, Wooster Activities Crew, Women's Athletic and Recreation Association.

Athletics Member NCAA. All Division III. *Intercollegiate sports:* baseball M, basketball M/W, cheerleading W(c), cross-country running M/W, field hockey W, football M, golf M/W, lacrosse M/W, rugby W(c), soccer M/W, softball W, swimming and diving M/W, tennis M/W, track and field M/W, volleyball W. *Intramural sports:* badminton M/W, equestrian sports M(c)/W(c), ice hockey M(c)/W(c), table tennis M/W, ultimate Frisbee M(c)/W(c), volleyball M(c).

Campus security: 24-hour emergency response devices and patrols, student patrols, late-night transport/escort service, controlled dormitory access.

Student services: health clinic, personal/psychological counseling, women's center.

COSTS & FINANCIAL AID

Costs (2017–18) *Comprehensive fee:* $60,000 includes full-time tuition ($48,160), mandatory fees ($440), and room and board ($11,400). Full-time tuition and fees vary according to course load. Part-time tuition: $1494 per credit hour. Part-time tuition and fees vary according to course load. *College room only:* $5500. Room and board charges vary according to board plan and housing facility. *Payment plan:* installment. *Waivers:* employees or children of employees.

Financial Aid Of all full-time matriculated undergraduates who enrolled in 2017, 1,246 applied for aid, 1,093 were judged to have need, 537 had their need fully met. 835 Federal Work-Study jobs (averaging $2045). 159 state and other part-time jobs (averaging $3468). In 2017, 826 non-need-based awards were made. *Average percent of need met:* 93. *Average financial aid package:* $43,407. *Average need-based loan:* $5017. *Average need-based gift aid:* $32,621. *Average non-need-based aid:* $24,652. *Average indebtedness upon graduation:* $30,053.

APPLYING

Standardized Tests *Required:* SAT or ACT (for admission).

Options: electronic application, early admission, early decision, early action, deferred entrance.

Required: essay or personal statement, high school transcript. *Recommended:* letters of recommendation, interview.

Application deadlines: 2/15 (freshmen), 7/15 (transfers), 11/15 (early action).

Early decision deadline: 11/1 (for plan 1), 1/15 (for plan 2).

Notification: 4/1 (freshmen), continuous (transfers), 11/15 (early decision plan 1), 2/1 (early decision plan 2), 12/31 (early action).

CONTACT

Ms. Jennifer Winge, Dean of Admissions, The College of Wooster, 1189 Beall Avenue, Wooster, OH 44691-2363. *Phone:* 330-263-2270. *Toll-free phone:* 800-877-9905. *Fax:* 330-263-2621. *E-mail:* admissions@wooster.edu.

Columbus College of Art & Design

Columbus, Ohio

http://www.ccad.edu/

- **Independent** comprehensive, founded 1879
- **Urban** 17-acre campus
- **Endowment** $11.7 million
- **Coed**
- **Moderately difficult** entrance level

FACULTY

Student/faculty ratio: 10:1.

ACADEMICS

Calendar: semesters. *Degrees:* bachelor's and master's.

Library: Packard Library. *Books:* 40,836 (physical), 28,701 (digital/electronic); *Serial titles:* 434 (physical), 253,828 (digital/electronic).

STUDENT LIFE

Housing options: on-campus residence required for freshman year; coed, special housing for students with disabilities. Campus housing is university owned. Freshman campus housing is guaranteed.

Activities and organizations: Student Government Association, Student Collective, Student Programming Board, CCAD Battle Alliance.

Campus security: 24-hour emergency response devices and patrols, late-night transport/escort service, controlled dormitory access.

Student services: personal/psychological counseling.

COSTS & FINANCIAL AID

Costs (2017–18) *Comprehensive fee:* $44,745 includes full-time tuition ($33,960), mandatory fees ($1415), and room and board ($9370). Full-time tuition and fees vary according to course load. Part-time tuition: $1415 per credit hour. Part-time tuition and fees vary according to course load. *Room and board:* Room and board charges vary according to board plan, housing facility, location, and student level. *Payment plans:* installment, deferred payment.

Financial Aid Of all full-time matriculated undergraduates who enrolled in 2017, 873 applied for aid, 817 were judged to have need, 84 had their need fully met. 142 Federal Work-Study jobs (averaging $3550). 292 state and other part-time jobs (averaging $3550). In 2017, 185 non-need-based awards were made. *Average percent of need met:* 62. *Average financial aid package:* $24,992. *Average need-based loan:* $6805. *Average need-based gift aid:* $18,632. *Average non-need-based aid:* $13,415. *Average indebtedness upon graduation:* $32,258.

APPLYING

Standardized Tests *Recommended:* SAT or ACT (for admission).

Options: electronic application, deferred entrance.

Application fee: $50.

Required: essay or personal statement, high school transcript, minimum 3.0 GPA, 2 letters of recommendation, portfolio. *Required for some:* interview.

CONTACT
Columbus College of Art & Design, 60 Cleveland Avenue, Columbus, OH 43215-1758. *Phone:* 614-224-9101. *Toll-free phone:* 877-997-2223. *Fax:* 614-232-8344. *E-mail:* admissions@ccad.edu.

Defiance College

Defiance, Ohio
http://www.defiance.edu/

- **Independent** comprehensive, founded 1850, affiliated with United Church of Christ
- **Small-town** 150-acre campus with easy access to Toledo
- **Endowment** $15.2 million
- **Coed** 599 undergraduate students, 88% full-time, 46% women, 54% men
- **Moderately difficult** entrance level, 56% of applicants were admitted

UNDERGRAD STUDENTS
525 full-time, 74 part-time. Students come from 23 states and territories; 4 other countries; 30% are from out of state; 12% Black or African American, non-Hispanic/Latino; 7% Hispanic/Latino; 0.8% Asian, non-Hispanic/Latino; 0.3% American Indian or Alaska Native, non-Hispanic/Latino; 3% Two or more races, non-Hispanic/Latino; 0.8% Race/ethnicity unknown; 2% international; 6% transferred in; 50% live on campus.

Freshmen:
Admission: 1,257 applied, 710 admitted, 151 enrolled. *Average high school GPA:* 3.1.
Retention: 60% of full-time freshmen returned.

FACULTY
Total: 77, 47% full-time, 39% with terminal degrees.
Student/faculty ratio: 11:1.

ACADEMICS
Calendar: semesters. *Degrees:* associate, bachelor's, and master's.

Special study options: academic remediation for entering students, adult/continuing education programs, advanced placement credit, double majors, honors programs, independent study, internships, off-campus study, services for LD students, student-designed majors, study abroad, summer session for credit.

Computers: 200 computers/terminals and 300 ports are available on campus for general student use. Students can access the following: campus intranet, computer help desk, free student e-mail accounts, online (class) grades, online (class) registration, online (class) schedules. Campuswide network is available. 100% of college-owned or -operated housing units are wired for high-speed Internet access. Wireless service is available via entire campus.
Library: Pilgrim Library plus 1 other. *Books:* 62,576 (physical), 271,510 (digital/electronic); *Serial titles:* 308 (physical), 79,914 (digital/electronic); *Databases:* 162. Weekly public service hours: 90; students can reserve study rooms.

STUDENT LIFE
Housing options: on-campus residence required through junior year; coed. Campus housing is university owned. Freshman campus housing is guaranteed.
Activities and organizations: drama/theater group, student-run newspaper, choral group, marching band, Campus Activities Board, Criminal Justice Society, Student Senate, Black Action Student Association, Tau Kappa Epsilon, national fraternities, national sororities.
Athletics Member NCAA. All Division III. *Intercollegiate sports:* baseball M, basketball M/W, cross-country running M/W, football M, golf M/W, soccer M/W, softball W, tennis M/W, track and field M/W, volleyball W, wrestling M. *Intramural sports:* basketball M/W, cheerleading M/W, football M/W, volleyball M/W, weight lifting M/W, wrestling M.
Campus security: late-night transport/escort service, controlled dormitory access.

Student services: personal/psychological counseling.

COSTS & FINANCIAL AID
Costs (2018–19) *Comprehensive fee:* $42,950 includes full-time tuition ($31,990), mandatory fees ($740), and room and board ($10,220). Full-time tuition and fees vary according to course load. Part-time tuition: $495 per credit hour. Part-time tuition and fees vary according to course load. *Required fees:* $100 per term part-time. *College room only:* $5500. Room and board charges vary according to board plan and housing facility. *Payment plan:* installment. *Waivers:* employees or children of employees.
Financial Aid Of all full-time matriculated undergraduates who enrolled in 2016, 481 applied for aid, 469 were judged to have need, 60 had their need fully met. In 2016, 43 non-need-based awards were made. *Average percent of need met:* 67. *Average financial aid package:* $23,603. *Average need-based loan:* $4590. *Average need-based gift aid:* $18,809. *Average non-need-based aid:* $17,479.

APPLYING
Standardized Tests *Required:* SAT or ACT (for admission).
Options: electronic application, deferred entrance.
Application fee: $25.
Required: high school transcript, minimum 2.3 GPA. *Required for some:* essay or personal statement, 1 letter of recommendation, interview.
Application deadlines: 8/15 (freshmen), 8/15 (transfers).
Notification: continuous (freshmen), continuous (out-of-state freshmen), continuous (transfers).

CONTACT
Mrs. Brenda Averesch, Assistant Dean of Admissions and Financial Aid, Defiance College, 701 North Clinton Street, Defiance, OH 43512. *Phone:* 419-783-2352. *Toll-free phone:* 800-520-4632. *Fax:* 419-783-2468. *E-mail:* baveresch@defiance.edu.

Denison University

Granville, Ohio
http://www.denison.edu/

- **Independent** 4-year, founded 1831
- **Suburban** 931-acre campus with easy access to Columbus
- **Coed** 2,341 undergraduate students, 99% full-time, 55% women, 45% men
- **Very difficult** entrance level, 37% of applicants were admitted

UNDERGRAD STUDENTS
2,319 full-time, 22 part-time. 74% are from out of state; 7% Black or African American, non-Hispanic/Latino; 9% Hispanic/Latino; 4% Asian, non-Hispanic/Latino; 0.1% Native Hawaiian or other Pacific Islander, non-Hispanic/Latino; 3% Two or more races, non-Hispanic/Latino; 2% Race/ethnicity unknown; 10% international; 0.8% transferred in; 99% live on campus.

Freshmen:
Admission: 7,540 applied, 2,808 admitted, 617 enrolled. *Test scores:* SAT evidence-based reading and writing scores over 500: 100%; SAT math scores over 500: 100%; ACT scores over 18: 100%; SAT evidence-based reading and writing scores over 600: 78%; SAT math scores over 600: 76%; ACT scores over 24: 100%; SAT evidence-based reading and writing scores over 700: 20%; SAT math scores over 700: 24%; ACT scores over 30: 43%.
Retention: 91% of full-time freshmen returned.

FACULTY
Total: 254, 86% full-time, 90% with terminal degrees.
Student/faculty ratio: 9:1.

ACADEMICS
Calendar: semesters plus optional May term. *Degree:* bachelor's.
Special study options: advanced placement credit, double majors, honors programs, independent study, internships, off-campus study, part-time degree program, services for LD students, student-designed majors, study abroad. *ROTC:* Army (c).
Unusual degree programs: engineering with Case Western Reserve University, Columbia University, Rensselaer Polytechnic Institute, Washington University in St. Louis; forestry with Duke University; natural resources with University of Michigan; occupational therapy with

Washington University in St. Louis; environmental management, dentistry with Case Western Reserve University; medical technology with Rochester General Hospital.

Computers: 650 computers/terminals are available on campus for general student use. Students can access the following: campus intranet, computer help desk, free student e-mail accounts, online (class) grades, online (class) registration, online (class) schedules, eClassrooms; eSpaces; special purpose rooms and computer labs with specialized software; computers, digital video, audio and other media equipment may be checked out; software downloads. Campuswide network is available. 100% of college-owned or -operated housing units are wired for high-speed Internet access. Wireless service is available via entire campus.

Library: William Howard Doane Library. *Books:* 1.4 million (physical), 912,952 (digital/electronic); *Serial titles:* 540 (physical), 653 (digital/electronic); *Databases:* 464. Weekly public service hours: 104; students can reserve study rooms.

STUDENT LIFE
Housing options: on-campus residence required through senior year; coed, men-only, women-only, cooperative. Campus housing is university owned. Freshman campus housing is guaranteed.

Activities and organizations: drama/theater group, student-run newspaper, radio and television station, choral group, national fraternities, national sororities.

Athletics Member NCAA. All Division III. *Intercollegiate sports:* baseball M, basketball M/W, crew M(c), cross-country running M/W, equestrian sports M(c)/W(c), field hockey W, football M, golf M, ice hockey M(c), lacrosse M/W, riflery M(c)/W(c), rugby M(c)/W(c), sailing M(c)/W(c), skiing (downhill) M(c)/W(c), soccer M/W, softball W, squash M(c)/W(c), swimming and diving M/W, tennis M/W, track and field M/W, volleyball W. *Intramural sports:* badminton M(c)/W(c), basketball M/W, cheerleading M/W, crew W(c), fencing M(c)/W(c), football M/W, golf M/W, lacrosse M(c), racquetball M/W, soccer M/W, softball M/W, squash M/W, table tennis M/W, tennis M/W, ultimate Frisbee M/W, volleyball M(c)/W, water polo M/W, weight lifting M/W.

Campus security: 24-hour emergency response devices and patrols, student patrols, late-night transport/escort service, controlled dormitory access, security lighting, escort.

Student services: health clinic, personal/psychological counseling, women's center.

COSTS & FINANCIAL AID
Costs (2017–18) *Comprehensive fee:* $62,770 includes full-time tuition ($49,310), mandatory fees ($1130), and room and board ($12,330). Part-time tuition: $1541 per credit hour. Part-time tuition and fees vary according to course load. *College room only:* $6790. Room and board charges vary according to board plan and housing facility. *Payment plans:* installment, deferred payment. *Waivers:* employees or children of employees.

Financial Aid Of all full-time matriculated undergraduates who enrolled in 2017, 1,497 applied for aid, 1,259 were judged to have need, 588 had their need fully met. In 2017, 955 non-need-based awards were made. *Average percent of need met:* 91. *Average financial aid package:* $44,138. *Average need-based loan:* $5161. *Average need-based gift aid:* $38,832. *Average non-need-based aid:* $21,862. *Average indebtedness upon graduation:* $27,823.

APPLYING
Options: early admission, early decision, deferred entrance.

Required: essay or personal statement, high school transcript, 2 letters of recommendation. *Recommended:* interview.

Early decision deadline: 11/15 (for plan 1), 1/15 (for plan 2).

Notification: 4/1 (freshmen), continuous (transfers), 12/15 (early decision plan 1), 2/15 (early decision plan 2).

CONTACT
Mr. Michael S. Hills, Director of Admissions, Denison University, 100 West College Street, Granville, OH 43023. *Phone:* 740-587-6627. *Toll-free phone:* 800-DENISON. *E-mail:* hills@denison.edu.

DeVry University–Columbus Campus
Columbus, Ohio
http://www.devry.edu/

- **Proprietary** comprehensive, founded 1952
- **Urban** campus
- **Coed**
- **Minimally difficult** entrance level

FACULTY
Student/faculty ratio: 35:1.

ACADEMICS
Calendar: semesters. *Degrees:* associate, bachelor's, master's, and postbachelor's certificates.

COSTS
Costs (2017–18) *Tuition:* $14,504 full-time. *Required fees:* $500 full-time.

APPLYING
Application fee: $30.

CONTACT
Admissions Office, DeVry University–Columbus Campus, 1350 Alum Creek Drive, Columbus, OH 43209. *Phone:* 614-253-7291. *Toll-free phone:* 866-338-7934.

DeVry University–Seven Hills Campus
Seven Hills, Ohio
http://www.devry.edu/

CONTACT
Admissions Office, DeVry University–Seven Hills Campus, 4141 Rockside Road, Suite 110, Seven Hills, OH 44131. *Phone:* 216-328-8754. *Toll-free phone:* 866-338-7934.

Franciscan University of Steubenville
Steubenville, Ohio
http://www.franciscan.edu/

- **Independent Roman Catholic** comprehensive, founded 1946
- **Suburban** 235-acre campus with easy access to Pittsburg, PA
- **Endowment** $54.5 million
- **Coed**
- **Moderately difficult** entrance level

FACULTY
Student/faculty ratio: 14:1.

ACADEMICS
Calendar: semesters. *Degrees:* associate, bachelor's, and master's.
Library: St. John Paul II Library. *Books:* 143,662 (physical), 254,496 (digital/electronic); *Serial titles:* 590 (physical), 51,894 (digital/electronic); *Databases:* 131. Weekly public service hours: 93.

STUDENT LIFE
Housing options: on-campus residence required through junior year; men-only, women-only. Campus housing is university owned. Freshman applicants given priority for college housing.

Activities and organizations: drama/theater group, student-run newspaper, radio station, choral group.

Athletics Member NCAA. All Division III.

Campus security: 24-hour emergency response devices and patrols, student patrols, late-night transport/escort service, controlled dormitory access.

Student services: health clinic, personal/psychological counseling.

COSTS & FINANCIAL AID
Costs (2017–18) *Comprehensive fee:* $34,830 includes full-time tuition ($25,970), mandatory fees ($460), and room and board ($8400). Part-time tuition and fees vary according to class time and course load. *College room only:* $4800. Room and board charges vary according to board plan.

Financial Aid Of all full-time matriculated undergraduates who enrolled in 2016, 1,501 applied for aid, 1,237 were judged to have need, 204 had

their need fully met. In 2016, 629 non-need-based awards were made. *Average percent of need met:* 62. *Average financial aid package:* $15,628. *Average need-based loan:* $4456. *Average need-based gift aid:* $11,640. *Average non-need-based aid:* $6363.

APPLYING
Standardized Tests *Required:* SAT or ACT (for admission).
Options: electronic application, deferred entrance.
Application fee: $20.
Required: high school transcript, minimum 2.4 GPA. *Required for some:* essay or personal statement, 3 letters of recommendation. *Recommended:* interview.

CONTACT
Miss Victoria Kubicz, Assistant Director of Admissions, Franciscan University of Steubenville, 1235 University Boulevard, Steubenville, OH 43952-1763. *Phone:* 740-284-5863. *Toll-free phone:* 800-783-6220. *Fax:* 740-284-5456. *E-mail:* admissions@franciscan.edu.

Franklin University
Columbus, Ohio
http://www.franklin.edu/

CONTACT
Mrs. Lynne Hull, Director of New Student Enrollment, Franklin University, 201 South Grant Avenue, Columbus, OH 43215. *Phone:* 614-947-6046. *Toll-free phone:* 877-341-6300. *E-mail:* hulll@franklin.edu.

Galen College of Nursing
Cincinnati, Ohio
http://www.galencollege.edu/

CONTACT
Galen College of Nursing, 100 East Business Way, Suite 200, Cincinnati, OH 45241. *Toll-free phone:* 877-223-7040.

God's Bible School and College
Cincinnati, Ohio
http://www.gbs.edu/

CONTACT
Heather Couch, Director of Financial Aid and Admissions, God's Bible School and College, 1810 Young Street, Cincinnati, OH 45202-6838. *Phone:* 513-721-7944 Ext. 1161. *Toll-free phone:* 800-486-4637. *Fax:* 513-763-6649. *E-mail:* hcouch@gbs.edu.

Good Samaritan College of Nursing and Health Science
Cincinnati, Ohio
http://www.gscollege.edu/

CONTACT
Admissions Office, Good Samaritan College of Nursing and Health Science, 375 Dixmyth Avenue, Cincinnati, OH 45220. *Phone:* 513-862-2743. *Fax:* 513-862-3572.

Harrison College
Grove City, Ohio
http://www.harrison.edu/

CONTACT
Mr. Jason Howanec, Vice President of Enrollment, Harrison College, 500 N. Meridian Street, Indianapolis, IN 46204. *Phone:* 888-544-4422. *Toll-free phone:* 888-544-4422. *E-mail:* admissions@harrison.edu.

Heidelberg University
Tiffin, Ohio
http://www.heidelberg.edu/
- **Independent** comprehensive, founded 1850, affiliated with United Church of Christ
- **Small-town** 115-acre campus with easy access to Toledo, Cleveland, Columbus
- **Endowment** $48.9 million
- **Coed** 1,059 undergraduate students, 98% full-time, 46% women, 54% men
- **Moderately difficult** entrance level, 76% of applicants were admitted

UNDERGRAD STUDENTS
1,041 full-time, 18 part-time. Students come from 26 states and territories; 2 other countries; 19% are from out of state; 10% Black or African American, non-Hispanic/Latino; 3% Hispanic/Latino; 0.9% Asian, non-Hispanic/Latino; 0.1% Native Hawaiian or other Pacific Islander, non-Hispanic/Latino; 0.1% American Indian or Alaska Native, non-Hispanic/Latino; 3% Two or more races, non-Hispanic/Latino; 4% Race/ethnicity unknown; 2% transferred in; 79% live on campus.

Freshmen:
Admission: 1,721 applied, 1,309 admitted, 319 enrolled. *Average high school GPA:* 3.3. *Test scores:* ACT scores over 18: 92%; ACT scores over 24: 35%; ACT scores over 30: 5%.
Retention: 67% of full-time freshmen returned.

FACULTY
Total: 124, 47% full-time, 52% with terminal degrees.
Student/faculty ratio: 13:1.

ACADEMICS
Calendar: semesters. *Degrees:* bachelor's and master's.
Special study options: academic remediation for entering students, advanced placement credit, double majors, English as a second language, honors programs, independent study, internships, off-campus study, part-time degree program, services for LD students, student-designed majors, study abroad, summer session for credit. *ROTC:* Army (c), Air Force (c).
Unusual degree programs: 3-2 engineering with Case Western Reserve University; nursing with Ursuline College.
Computers: 125 computers/terminals are available on campus for general student use. Students can access the following: campus intranet, computer help desk, free student e-mail accounts, online (class) grades, online (class) registration, online (class) schedules. Campuswide network is available. 100% of college-owned or -operated housing units are wired for high-speed Internet access. Wireless service is available via entire campus.
Library: Beeghly Library plus 1 other. *Books:* 86,891 (physical), 279,499 (digital/electronic); *Serial titles:* 1,293 (physical), 61,058 (digital/electronic); *Databases:* 198. Weekly public service hours: 83.

STUDENT LIFE
Housing options: on-campus residence required through junior year; coed, women-only, cooperative. Campus housing is university owned and leased by the school. Freshman campus housing is guaranteed.
Activities and organizations: drama/theater group, student-run newspaper, radio and television station, choral group, Alpha Phi Omega, BERG Events Council, Student Senate, Campus Fellowship, Black Student Union/World Student Union.
Athletics Member NCAA. All Division III. *Intercollegiate sports:* baseball M, basketball M/W, cheerleading M/W, cross-country running M/W, football M, golf M/W, lacrosse M/W, soccer M/W, softball W, tennis M/W, track and field M/W, volleyball M/W, wrestling M. *Intramural sports:* archery M/W, badminton M/W, football M/W, golf M/W, soccer M/W, softball M/W, table tennis M/W, volleyball M/W, weight lifting M/W.
Campus security: 24-hour emergency response devices and patrols, student patrols, late-night transport/escort service, controlled dormitory access.
Student services: health clinic, personal/psychological counseling.

COSTS & FINANCIAL AID
Costs (2018–19) *Comprehensive fee:* $41,400 includes full-time tuition ($30,400), mandatory fees ($600), and room and board ($10,400). Part-

time tuition: $900 per contact hour. *College room only:* $5300. Room and board charges vary according to board plan and housing facility. *Payment plan:* installment. *Waivers:* employees or children of employees.

Financial Aid *Average indebtedness upon graduation:* $35,872.

APPLYING
Standardized Tests *Required:* SAT or ACT (for admission).

Options: electronic application, deferred entrance.

Required: high school transcript. *Required for some:* essay or personal statement, 2 letters of recommendation. *Recommended:* essay or personal statement, minimum 2.5 GPA, 1 letter of recommendation.

Application deadlines: rolling (freshmen), 8/15 (transfers).

Notification: continuous (freshmen), 8/15 (transfers).

CONTACT
Mr. Mike Brown, Director of Admission, Heidelberg University, 310 East Market Street, Tiffin, OH 44883. *Phone:* 419-448-2507. *Toll-free phone:* 800-434-3352. *Fax:* 419-448-2334. *E-mail:* mbrown@heidelberg.edu.

Herzing University
Akron, Ohio
http://www.herzing.edu/akron

CONTACT
Herzing University, 1600 South Arlington Street, Suite 100, Akron, OH 44306. *Toll-free phone:* 800-596-0724.

Herzing University
Toledo, Ohio
http://www.herzing.edu/toledo

CONTACT
Herzing University, 5212 Hill Avenue, Toledo, OH 43615. *Toll-free phone:* 800-596-0724.

Hiram College
Hiram, Ohio
http://www.hiram.edu/

- **Independent** comprehensive, founded 1850, affiliated with Christian Church (Disciples of Christ)
- **Rural** 110-acre campus with easy access to Cleveland
- **Endowment** $72.8 million
- **Coed** 1,210 undergraduate students, 70% full-time, 54% women, 46% men
- **Moderately difficult** entrance level, 64% of applicants were admitted

UNDERGRAD STUDENTS
853 full-time, 357 part-time. Students come from 33 states and territories; 12 other countries; 18% are from out of state; 16% Black or African American, non-Hispanic/Latino; 4% Hispanic/Latino; 1% Asian, non-Hispanic/Latino; 0.4% Native Hawaiian or other Pacific Islander, non-Hispanic/Latino; 3% Two or more races, non-Hispanic/Latino; 9% Race/ethnicity unknown; 1% international; 3% transferred in; 84% live on campus.

Freshmen:
Admission: 2,761 applied, 1,754 admitted, 258 enrolled. *Average high school GPA:* 3.4. *Test scores:* SAT evidence-based reading and writing scores over 500: 65%; SAT math scores over 500: 62%; ACT scores over 18: 81%; SAT evidence-based reading and writing scores over 600: 29%; SAT math scores over 600: 24%; ACT scores over 24: 30%; SAT evidence-based reading and writing scores over 700: 11%; SAT math scores over 700: 4%; ACT scores over 30: 7%.
Retention: 70% of full-time freshmen returned.

FACULTY
Total: 142, 56% full-time.
Student/faculty ratio: 10:1.

ACADEMICS
Calendar: semesters. *Degrees:* bachelor's and master's.

Special study options: accelerated degree program, adult/continuing education programs, advanced placement credit, cooperative education, distance learning, double majors, English as a second language, honors programs, independent study, internships, off-campus study, part-time degree program, services for LD students, student-designed majors, study abroad, summer session for credit. *ROTC:* Army (c), Air Force (c).

Unusual degree programs: 3-2 engineering with Case Western Reserve University, Washington University in St. Louis; social work with Case Western Reserve University.

Computers: 75 computers/terminals and 3,500 ports are available on campus for general student use. Students can access the following: campus intranet, computer help desk, free student e-mail accounts, online (class) grades, online (class) registration, online (class) schedules. Campuswide network is available. 100% of college-owned or -operated housing units are wired for high-speed Internet access. Wireless service is available via entire campus.
Library: Hiram College Library. *Books:* 180,596 (physical), 165,681 (digital/electronic); *Serial titles:* 85 (physical), 11,187 (digital/electronic); *Databases:* 141. Weekly public service hours: 97.

STUDENT LIFE
Housing options: on-campus residence required through sophomore year; coed, men-only, women-only, special housing for students with disabilities. Campus housing is university owned. Freshman campus housing is guaranteed.

Activities and organizations: drama/theater group, choral group, Black Students United, Intercultural Forum, Terrier Activities Board, Student-Athlete Advisory Committee, H-ART Hiram Art Renaissance Troops.

Athletics Member NCAA. All Division III. *Intercollegiate sports:* baseball M, basketball M/W, cheerleading W, football M, golf M/W, lacrosse M/W, soccer M/W, softball W, swimming and diving M/W, volleyball M/W. *Intramural sports:* basketball M/W, cross-country running M/W, equestrian sports M/W, football M/W, rugby M/W, skiing (downhill) M/W, soccer M/W, ultimate Frisbee M/W, volleyball M/W.

Campus security: 24-hour emergency response devices, student patrols, late-night transport/escort service, controlled dormitory access, daytime services available M-F 8am-5pm and evenings 5pm-3am, weekend services from 5pm-3am.

Student services: health clinic, personal/psychological counseling.

COSTS & FINANCIAL AID
Costs (2017–18) *Comprehensive fee:* $44,590 includes full-time tuition ($32,700), mandatory fees ($1600), and room and board ($10,290). Part-time tuition: $475 per credit hour. No tuition increase for student's term of enrollment. *Required fees:* $125 per term part-time. *College room only:* $5150. Room and board charges vary according to housing facility. *Payment plan:* installment. *Waivers:* employees or children of employees.

Financial Aid Of all full-time matriculated undergraduates who enrolled in 2002, 790 applied for aid, 736 were judged to have need, 699 had their need fully met. 587 Federal Work-Study jobs (averaging $1600). 18 state and other part-time jobs (averaging $1580). In 2002, 114 non-need-based awards were made. *Average percent of need met:* 95. *Average financial aid package:* $21,218. *Average need-based loan:* $6960. *Average need-based gift aid:* $8163. *Average non-need-based aid:* $8635. *Average indebtedness upon graduation:* $17,125.

APPLYING
Standardized Tests *Required for some:* SAT or ACT (for admission), SAT or ACT for applicants with cumulative GPA below 2.8, nursing or education applicants, or Trustee and/or President's Scholarships applicants.

Options: electronic application, deferred entrance.

Application fee: $25.

Required: essay or personal statement, high school transcript. *Recommended:* minimum 2.8 GPA, interview.

Application deadlines: rolling (freshmen), rolling (transfers).

Notification: continuous (freshmen), continuous (transfers).

CONTACT
Sherman C. Dean II, Director of Admission, Hiram College, PO Box 96, Hiram, OH 44234. *Phone:* 330-569-5169. *Toll-free phone:* 800-362-5280. *Fax:* 330-569-5944. *E-mail:* admission@hiram.edu.

John Carroll University
University Heights, Ohio
http://www.jcu.edu/

- **Independent Roman Catholic (Jesuit)** comprehensive, founded 1886
- **Suburban** 60-acre campus with easy access to Cleveland
- **Endowment** $211.0 million
- **Coed** 3,026 undergraduate students, 97% full-time, 49% women, 51% men
- **Moderately difficult** entrance level, 85% of applicants were admitted

UNDERGRAD STUDENTS
2,935 full-time, 91 part-time. Students come from 36 states and territories; 30 other countries; 31% are from out of state; 5% Black or African American, non-Hispanic/Latino; 4% Hispanic/Latino; 2% Asian, non-Hispanic/Latino; 0.1% American Indian or Alaska Native, non-Hispanic/Latino; 2% Two or more races, non-Hispanic/Latino; 1% Race/ethnicity unknown; 2% international; 2% transferred in; 53% live on campus.

Freshmen:
Admission: 3,840 applied, 3,265 admitted, 717 enrolled. *Average high school GPA:* 3.6. *Test scores:* SAT evidence-based reading and writing scores over 500: 79%; SAT math scores over 500: 69%; ACT scores over 18: 98%; SAT evidence-based reading and writing scores over 600: 12%; SAT math scores over 600: 12%; ACT scores over 24: 61%; SAT math scores over 700: 2%; ACT scores over 30: 13%.
Retention: 84% of full-time freshmen returned.

FACULTY
Total: 442, 40% full-time, 67% with terminal degrees.
Student/faculty ratio: 12:1.

ACADEMICS
Calendar: semesters. *Degrees:* bachelor's, master's, post-master's, and postbachelor's certificates.

Special study options: advanced placement credit, distance learning, double majors, honors programs, independent study, internships, off-campus study, part-time degree program, services for LD students, student-designed majors, study abroad, summer session for credit. *ROTC:* Army (b).

Unusual degree programs: 3-2 business administration; engineering with Case Western Reserve University; nursing with Ursuline College.

Computers: 396 computers/terminals are available on campus for general student use. Students can access the following: campus intranet, computer help desk, free student e-mail accounts, online (class) grades, online (class) registration, online (class) schedules, campus student online registration, billing, advising system, JCU mobile app, course management site (BlackBoard), online financial aid and billing; online course sites; online housing selection. Campuswide network is available. 100% of college-owned or -operated housing units are wired for high-speed Internet access. Wireless service is available via entire campus.
Library: Grasselli Library. *Books:* 456,260 (physical), 91,554 (digital/electronic); *Serial titles:* 459,633 (physical), 115,548 (digital/electronic); *Databases:* 279. Weekly public service hours: 111; students can reserve study rooms.

STUDENT LIFE
Housing options: on-campus residence required through sophomore year; coed, women-only, special housing for students with disabilities. Campus housing is university owned. Freshman campus housing is guaranteed.

Activities and organizations: drama/theater group, student-run newspaper, radio and television station, choral group, Community Outreach/Volunteer Service Organization, Student Union, Club Sports, Fraternities and Sororities, Carroll News, national fraternities, national sororities.

Athletics Member NCAA. All Division III. *Intercollegiate sports:* baseball M, basketball M/W, cross-country running M/W, football M, golf M/W, ice hockey M(c), lacrosse M/W, rowing M(c)/W(c), rugby M(c), sailing M(c)/W(c), soccer M/W, softball W, swimming and diving M/W, tennis M/W, track and field M/W, ultimate Frisbee M(c)/W(c), volleyball M(c)/W, wrestling M. *Intramural sports:* badminton M/W, basketball M/W, cheerleading W, football M/W, soccer M/W, softball M/W, volleyball M/W.

Campus security: 24-hour emergency response devices and patrols, late-night transport/escort service, controlled dormitory access, student-led EMS program.
Student services: health clinic, personal/psychological counseling, women's center.

COSTS & FINANCIAL AID
Costs (2017–18) *One-time required fee:* $325. *Comprehensive fee:* $51,370 includes full-time tuition ($38,490), mandatory fees ($1300), and room and board ($11,580). Full-time tuition and fees vary according to degree level. Part-time tuition: $1283 per credit hour. Part-time tuition and fees vary according to course load and degree level. *Room and board:* Room and board charges vary according to board plan and housing facility. *Payment plan:* installment. *Waivers:* senior citizens and employees or children of employees.

Financial Aid Of all full-time matriculated undergraduates who enrolled in 2016, 2,441 applied for aid, 2,056 were judged to have need, 563 had their need fully met. In 2016, 754 non-need-based awards were made. *Average percent of need met:* 82. *Average financial aid package:* $30,799. *Average need-based loan:* $3981. *Average need-based gift aid:* $24,502. *Average non-need-based aid:* $19,475. *Average indebtedness upon graduation:* $31,993. *Financial aid deadline:* 3/15.

APPLYING
Standardized Tests *Required:* SAT or ACT (for admission).
Options: electronic application, early admission, early action, deferred entrance.
Required: essay or personal statement, high school transcript, 1 letter of recommendation. *Required for some:* 2 letters of recommendation, interview.
Application deadlines: rolling (freshmen), 8/15 (transfers), 12/1 (early action).
Notification: continuous until 12/1 (freshmen), continuous (transfers), 12/15 (early action).

CONTACT
Mr. Steven P. Vitatoe, Assistant Vice President of Undergraduate Admission, John Carroll University, 1 John Carroll Boulevard, University Heights, OH 44118. *Phone:* 216-397-4277. *Toll-free phone:* 888-335-6800. *E-mail:* svitatoe@jcu.edu.

Kent State University
Kent, Ohio
http://www.kent.edu/

- **State-supported** university, founded 1910, part of Kent State University System
- **Suburban** 866-acre campus with easy access to Cleveland, Akron, Canton
- **Endowment** $129.1 million
- **Coed** 23,178 undergraduate students, 88% full-time, 61% women, 39% men
- **Moderately difficult** entrance level, 88% of applicants were admitted

UNDERGRAD STUDENTS
20,509 full-time, 2,669 part-time. Students come from 51 states and territories; 96 other countries; 16% are from out of state; 9% Black or African American, non-Hispanic/Latino; 4% Hispanic/Latino; 2% Asian, non-Hispanic/Latino; 0.1% Native Hawaiian or other Pacific Islander, non-Hispanic/Latino; 0.2% American Indian or Alaska Native, non-Hispanic/Latino; 4% Two or more races, non-Hispanic/Latino; 3% Race/ethnicity unknown; 5% international; 5% transferred in.

Freshmen:
Admission: 15,538 applied, 13,598 admitted, 4,292 enrolled. *Average high school GPA:* 3.4. *Test scores:* SAT evidence-based reading and writing scores over 500: 89%; SAT math scores over 500: 83%; ACT scores over 18: 99%; SAT evidence-based reading and writing scores over 600: 36%; SAT math scores over 600: 27%; ACT scores over 24: 41%; SAT evidence-based reading and writing scores over 700: 5%; SAT math scores over 700: 4%; ACT scores over 30: 6%.
Retention: 80% of full-time freshmen returned.

FACULTY
Total: 1,846, 55% full-time.

Student/faculty ratio: 20:1.

ACADEMICS

Calendar: semesters. *Degrees:* certificates, bachelor's, master's, doctoral, post-master's, and postbachelor's certificates.

Special study options: academic remediation for entering students, accelerated degree program, adult/continuing education programs, advanced placement credit, cooperative education, distance learning, double majors, English as a second language, freshman honors college, honors programs, independent study, internships, off-campus study, part-time degree program, services for LD students, student-designed majors, study abroad, summer session for credit. *ROTC:* Army (b), Air Force (b).

Unusual degree programs: 3-2 business administration; nursing; speech pathology and audiology, fashion merchandising.

Computers: Students can access the following: computer help desk, free student e-mail accounts, online (class) grades, online (class) registration, online (class) schedules. Campuswide network is available. 100% of college-owned or -operated housing units are wired for high-speed Internet access. Wireless service is available via entire campus.

Library: Kent State University Main Library plus 4 others. *Books:* 3.0 million (physical), 1.2 million (digital/electronic); *Serial titles:* 35,857 (physical), 14,996 (digital/electronic); *Databases:* 355. Weekly public service hours: 146; study areas open 24 hours, 5–7 days a week; students can reserve study rooms.

STUDENT LIFE

Housing options: on-campus residence required through sophomore year; coed, men-only, women-only, cooperative, special housing for students with disabilities. Freshman applicants given priority for college housing.

Activities and organizations: drama/theater group, student-run newspaper, radio and television station, choral group, marching band, Black United Students, Running Club, National Society of Leadership and Success, Kent Inter-hall Council, Kent Indian Association, national fraternities, national sororities.

Athletics Member NCAA. All Division I. *Intercollegiate sports:* baseball M(s), basketball M(s)/W(s), cross-country running M(s)/W(s), field hockey W(s), football M(s), golf M(s)/W(s), gymnastics W(s), soccer W(s), softball W(s), track and field M(s)/W(s), volleyball W(s), wrestling M(s). *Intramural sports:* baseball M(c)/W(c), basketball M/W, bowling M(c)/W(c), equestrian sports M(c)/W(c), fencing M(c)/W(c), field hockey M(c)/W(c), golf M/W, gymnastics M(c)/W(c), ice hockey M(c)/W(c), lacrosse M(c)/W(c), rugby M(c)/W(c), sand volleyball M/W, soccer M/W, ultimate Frisbee M/W, volleyball M/W.

Campus security: 24-hour emergency response devices and patrols, student patrols, late-night transport/escort service, controlled dormitory access, campus police and fire department, electronic locks on computer labs, studios and laboratory research areas.

Student services: health clinic, personal/psychological counseling, women's center, legal services.

COSTS & FINANCIAL AID

Costs (2018–19) One-time required fee: $150. *Tuition:* state resident $10,012 full-time, $456 per credit hour part-time; nonresident $18,544 full-time, $818 per credit hour part-time. Full-time tuition and fees vary according to course load. Part-time tuition and fees vary according to course load. *Room and board:* $10,916; room only: $6876. Room and board charges vary according to board plan and housing facility. *Payment plan:* installment. *Waivers:* senior citizens and employees or children of employees.

Financial Aid Of all full-time matriculated undergraduates who enrolled in 2017, 15,181 applied for aid, 12,488 were judged to have need, 1,574 had their need fully met. 371 Federal Work-Study jobs (averaging $3140). In 2017, 1905 non-need-based awards were made. *Average percent of need met:* 59. *Average financial aid package:* $10,715. *Average need-based loan:* $4664. *Average need-based gift aid:* $5472. *Average non-need-based aid:* $5348. *Average indebtedness upon graduation:* $32,790.

APPLYING

Standardized Tests *Required:* SAT or ACT (for admission).

Options: electronic application, deferred entrance.

Application fee: $50.

Required: high school transcript. *Required for some:* ACT/new SAT score (Not required if you have been out of high school for 3 or more years or if you are over the age of 21.).

Application deadlines: 5/1 (freshmen), rolling (transfers).

Notification: continuous (freshmen), continuous (transfers).

CONTACT

Mr. Christopher Buttenschon, Senior Assistant Director of Admissions, Kent State University, 161 Michael Schwartz Center, Admissions Office, Kent, OH 44242-0001. *Phone:* 330-672-2444. *Toll-free phone:* 800-988-KENT. *Fax:* 330-672-2499. *E-mail:* cbuttens@kent.edu.

Kent State University at Ashtabula
Ashtabula, Ohio
http://www.ashtabula.kent.edu/

- **State-supported** primarily 2-year, founded 1958, part of Kent State University System
- **Small-town** 83-acre campus with easy access to Cleveland
- **Coed** 1,971 undergraduate students, 52% full-time, 64% women, 36% men
- **Noncompetitive** entrance level, 99% of applicants were admitted

UNDERGRAD STUDENTS

1,027 full-time, 944 part-time. Students come from 25 states and territories; 3 other countries; 5% are from out of state; 5% Black or African American, non-Hispanic/Latino; 5% Hispanic/Latino; 1% Asian, non-Hispanic/Latino; 0.2% Native Hawaiian or other Pacific Islander, non-Hispanic/Latino; 0.2% American Indian or Alaska Native, non-Hispanic/Latino; 3% Two or more races, non-Hispanic/Latino; 2% Race/ethnicity unknown; 0.4% international; 4% transferred in.

Freshmen:
Admission: 375 applied, 370 admitted, 232 enrolled. *Average high school GPA:* 2.8. *Test scores:* SAT evidence-based reading and writing scores over 500: 83%; SAT math scores over 500: 50%; ACT scores over 18: 64%; SAT evidence-based reading and writing scores over 600: 33%; ACT scores over 24: 10%; SAT evidence-based reading and writing scores over 700: 17%; ACT scores over 30: 1%.
Retention: 51% of full-time freshmen returned.

FACULTY
Total: 99, 51% full-time.
Student/faculty ratio: 20:1.

ACADEMICS
Calendar: semesters. *Degrees:* certificates, associate, and bachelor's (also offers some upper-level and graduate courses).

Special study options: academic remediation for entering students, advanced placement credit, distance learning, double majors, independent study, internships, part-time degree program, services for LD students, student-designed majors, study abroad, summer session for credit. *ROTC:* Army (c), Air Force (c).

Computers: Students can access the following: computer help desk, free student e-mail accounts, online (class) grades, online (class) registration, online (class) schedules. Campuswide network is available. Wireless service is available via entire campus.

Library: Kent State at Ashtabula Library. Weekly public service hours: 56.

STUDENT LIFE
Housing options: college housing not available.

Activities and organizations: Student Government, Student Veterans Association, Student Nurses Association, Student Occupational Therapy Association, Media Club.

Athletics *Intramural sports:* volleyball M(c)/W(c).

Campus security: 24-hour emergency response devices.

COSTS & FINANCIAL AID
Costs (2018–19) One-time required fee: $150. *Tuition:* state resident $5664 full-time, $258 per credit hour part-time; nonresident $14,196 full-time, $620 per credit hour part-time. Full-time tuition and fees vary according to course level and course load. Part-time tuition and fees vary according to course level and course load. *Payment plan:* installment. *Waivers:* senior citizens and employees or children of employees.

Financial Aid Of all full-time matriculated undergraduates who enrolled in 2017, 453 applied for aid, 401 were judged to have need, 21 had their need fully met. 13 Federal Work-Study jobs (averaging $3234). In 2017, 19 non-need-based awards were made. *Average percent of need met:* 57. *Average financial aid package:* $7604. *Average need-based loan:* $3887. *Average need-based gift aid:* $5044. *Average non-need-based aid:* $1544.

APPLYING

Standardized Tests *Recommended:* SAT or ACT (for admission).

Options: electronic application, deferred entrance.

Application fee: $40.

Required: high school transcript. *Required for some:* ACT/new SAT scores (unless 21 and over or out of school for 3 years).

Application deadlines: 8/1 (freshmen), rolling (transfers).

Notification: continuous (freshmen), continuous (transfers).

CONTACT

Megan Krippel, Admissions Coordinator, Kent State University at Ashtabula, 3300 Lake Road West, Ashtabula, OH 44004. *Phone:* 440-964-4277. *Fax:* 440-964-4269. *E-mail:* ashtabula_admissions@kent.edu.

Kent State University at East Liverpool

East Liverpool, Ohio

http://www.eliv.kent.edu/

- **State-supported** primarily 2-year, founded 1967, part of Kent State University System
- **Small-town** 3-acre campus with easy access to Pittsburgh, Youngstown
- **Coed** 1,174 undergraduate students, 54% full-time, 68% women, 32% men
- **Noncompetitive** entrance level, 99% of applicants were admitted

UNDERGRAD STUDENTS

635 full-time, 539 part-time. Students come from 13 states and territories; 10 other countries; 6% are from out of state; 5% Black or African American, non-Hispanic/Latino; 2% Hispanic/Latino; 0.6% Asian, non-Hispanic/Latino; 0.2% American Indian or Alaska Native, non-Hispanic/Latino; 4% Two or more races, non-Hispanic/Latino; 2% Race/ethnicity unknown; 0.6% international; 4% transferred in.

Freshmen:

Admission: 83 applied, 82 admitted, 66 enrolled. *Average high school GPA:* 2.8. *Test scores:* ACT scores over 18: 83%; ACT scores over 24: 7%.

Retention: 65% of full-time freshmen returned.

FACULTY

Total: 55, 38% full-time.

Student/faculty ratio: 25:1.

ACADEMICS

Calendar: semesters. *Degrees:* certificates, associate, and bachelor's.

Special study options: academic remediation for entering students, accelerated degree program, adult/continuing education programs, advanced placement credit, distance learning, double majors, freshman honors college, honors programs, independent study, internships, part-time degree program, services for LD students, student-designed majors, study abroad, summer session for credit. *ROTC:* Army (c), Air Force (c).

Computers: Students can access the following: computer help desk, free student e-mail accounts, online (class) grades, online (class) registration, online (class) schedules. Campuswide network is available. Wireless service is available via entire campus.

Library: Paul Blair Memorial Library. Weekly public service hours: 46.

STUDENT LIFE

Housing options: college housing not available.

Activities and organizations: Undergraduate Student Government, Student Nurses Association, Environmental Club, Student Occupational Therapist Assistants, Physical Therapist Assistant Club.

Campus security: 24-hour emergency response devices, student patrols, late-night transport/escort service.

Student services: personal/psychological counseling.

COSTS & FINANCIAL AID

Costs (2018–19) *One-time required fee:* $150. *Tuition:* state resident $5664 full-time, $258 per credit hour part-time; nonresident $14,196 full-time, $620 per credit hour part-time. Full-time tuition and fees vary according to course level and course load. Part-time tuition and fees vary according to course level and course load. *Payment plan:* installment. *Waivers:* senior citizens and employees or children of employees.

Financial Aid Of all full-time matriculated undergraduates who enrolled in 2017, 172 applied for aid, 152 were judged to have need, 8 had their need fully met. 4 Federal Work-Study jobs (averaging $2941). In 2017, 10 non-need-based awards were made. *Average percent of need met:* 56. *Average financial aid package:* $7507. *Average need-based loan:* $3723. *Average need-based gift aid:* $4569. *Average non-need-based aid:* $2755.

APPLYING

Standardized Tests *Recommended:* SAT or ACT (for admission).

Options: electronic application, deferred entrance.

Application fee: $40.

Required: high school transcript. *Required for some:* ACT/new SAT scores (not required if over 21 or have been out of school for 3 years).

Application deadlines: 8/1 (freshmen), rolling (transfers).

Notification: continuous (freshmen), continuous (transfers).

CONTACT

Office of Admissions, Kent State University at East Liverpool, 400 East 4th Street, East Liverpool, OH 43920-3497. *Phone:* 330-385-3805.

Kent State University at Geauga

Burton, Ohio

http://www.geauga.kent.edu/

- **State-supported** comprehensive, founded 1964, part of Kent State University System
- **Rural** 87-acre campus with easy access to Cleveland, Akron, Youngstown
- **Coed** 2,247 undergraduate students, 58% full-time, 62% women, 38% men
- **Noncompetitive** entrance level, 98% of applicants were admitted

UNDERGRAD STUDENTS

1,308 full-time, 939 part-time. Students come from 5 states and territories; 4 other countries; 3% are from out of state; 11% Black or African American, non-Hispanic/Latino; 3% Hispanic/Latino; 2% Asian, non-Hispanic/Latino; 0.1% Native Hawaiian or other Pacific Islander, non-Hispanic/Latino; 0.3% American Indian or Alaska Native, non-Hispanic/Latino; 3% Two or more races, non-Hispanic/Latino; 3% Race/ethnicity unknown; 0.5% international; 6% transferred in.

Freshmen:

Admission: 782 applied, 766 admitted, 265 enrolled. *Average high school GPA:* 2.7. *Test scores:* SAT evidence-based reading and writing scores over 500: 60%; SAT math scores over 500: 57%; ACT scores over 18: 70%; SAT evidence-based reading and writing scores over 600: 13%; ACT scores over 24: 11%.

Retention: 58% of full-time freshmen returned.

FACULTY

Total: 132, 29% full-time, 3% with terminal degrees.

Student/faculty ratio: 23:1.

ACADEMICS

Calendar: semesters. *Degrees:* certificates, associate, bachelor's, and master's.

Special study options: academic remediation for entering students, advanced placement credit, distance learning, internships, part-time degree program, services for LD students, student-designed majors, summer session for credit.

Computers: Students can access the following: computer help desk, free student e-mail accounts, online (class) grades, online (class) registration, online (class) schedules. Campuswide network is available. Wireless service is available via entire campus.

Library: Kent State University at Geauga Library. *Books:* 12,083 (physical); *Serial titles:* 43 (physical). Weekly public service hours: 53.

STUDENT LIFE

Housing options: college housing not available.

Activities and organizations: National Student Nurse Association Twinsburg, Geauga Student Nurses Association, Alpha Delta Nu-Gamma Sigma Chapter, Kent State University Geauga College Republicans, Undergraduate Student Government.

Campus security: 24-hour emergency response devices.

COSTS & FINANCIAL AID

Costs (2017–18) *One-time required fee:* $150. *Tuition:* state resident $5664 full-time, $258 per credit hour part-time; nonresident $14,028 full-time, $620 per credit hour part-time. Full-time tuition and fees vary according to course level and course load. Part-time tuition and fees vary according to course level and course load. *Payment plan:* installment. *Waivers:* senior citizens and employees or children of employees.

Financial Aid Of all full-time matriculated undergraduates who enrolled in 2017, 441 applied for aid, 350 were judged to have need, 21 had their need fully met. 15 Federal Work-Study jobs (averaging $2260). In 2017, 18 non-need-based awards were made. *Average percent of need met:* 57. *Average financial aid package:* $6911. *Average need-based loan:* $3816. *Average need-based gift aid:* $4848. *Average non-need-based aid:* $1175.

APPLYING

Standardized Tests *Recommended:* SAT or ACT (for admission).

Options: electronic application, deferred entrance.

Application fee: $40.

Required: high school transcript.

Application deadlines: 8/15 (freshmen), 8/15 (transfers).

Notification: continuous (freshmen), continuous (transfers).

CONTACT

Kent State University at Geauga, 14111 Claridon-Troy Road, Burton, OH 44021. *Phone:* 440-834-4187. *Fax:* 440-834-3786. *E-mail:* geaugaadmissions@kent.edu.

Kent State University at Salem

Salem, Ohio

http://www.salem.kent.edu/

- **State-supported** primarily 2-year, founded 1966, part of Kent State University System
- **Rural** 100-acre campus with easy access to Youngstown
- **Coed** 1,694 undergraduate students, 63% full-time, 70% women, 30% men
- **Noncompetitive** entrance level, 100% of applicants were admitted

UNDERGRAD STUDENTS

1,062 full-time, 632 part-time. Students come from 7 states and territories; 2% are from out of state; 4% Black or African American, non-Hispanic/Latino; 2% Hispanic/Latino; 0.9% Asian, non-Hispanic/Latino; 0.1% American Indian or Alaska Native, non-Hispanic/Latino; 2% Two or more races, non-Hispanic/Latino; 3% Race/ethnicity unknown; 0.1% international; 6% transferred in.

Freshmen:

Admission: 264 applied, 264 admitted, 175 enrolled. *Average high school GPA:* 2.9. *Test scores:* ACT scores over 18: 69%; ACT scores over 24: 13%.

Retention: 53% of full-time freshmen returned.

FACULTY

Total: 115, 36% full-time.

Student/faculty ratio: 19:1.

ACADEMICS

Calendar: semesters. *Degrees:* certificates, associate, and bachelor's (also offers some upper-level and graduate courses).

Special study options: academic remediation for entering students, accelerated degree program, adult/continuing education programs, advanced placement credit, cooperative education, distance learning, double majors, freshman honors college, honors programs, independent study, part-time degree program, services for LD students, student-designed majors, study abroad, summer session for credit. *ROTC:* Army (c), Air Force (c).

Computers: 85 computers/terminals are available on campus for general student use. Students can access the following: free student e-mail accounts, online (class) grades, online (class) registration, online (class) schedules. Campuswide network is available. Wireless service is available via entire campus.

Library: Kent State Salem Library. *Books:* 23,500 (physical); *Serial titles:* 4,500 (physical).

STUDENT LIFE

Housing options: college housing not available.

Campus security: 24-hour emergency response devices, late-night transport/escort service.

Student services: personal/psychological counseling.

COSTS & FINANCIAL AID

Costs (2017–18) *One-time required fee:* $150. *Tuition:* state resident $5664 full-time, $258 per credit hour part-time; nonresident $14,028 full-time, $620 per credit hour part-time. Full-time tuition and fees vary according to course level and course load. Part-time tuition and fees vary according to course level and course load. *Payment plan:* installment. *Waivers:* senior citizens and employees or children of employees.

Financial Aid Of all full-time matriculated undergraduates who enrolled in 2017, 539 applied for aid, 447 were judged to have need, 37 had their need fully met. 18 Federal Work-Study jobs (averaging $1756). In 2017, 28 non-need-based awards were made. *Average percent of need met:* 59. *Average financial aid package:* $7407. *Average need-based loan:* $3954. *Average need-based gift aid:* $4835. *Average non-need-based aid:* $1257.

APPLYING

Standardized Tests *Required for some:* SAT or ACT (for admission). *Recommended:* SAT or ACT (for admission).

Options: electronic application, deferred entrance.

Application fee: $40.

Required: high school transcript. *Required for some:* essay or personal statement.

Application deadlines: 12/15 (freshmen), 12/15 (transfers).

Notification: continuous (freshmen), continuous (transfers).

CONTACT

Office of Admissions, Kent State University at Salem, 2491 State Route 45 South, Salem, OH 44460-9412. *Phone:* 330-332-0361.

Kent State University at Stark

Canton, Ohio

http://www.stark.kent.edu/

- **State-supported** comprehensive, founded 1946, part of Kent State University System
- **Suburban** 200-acre campus with easy access to Cleveland, Akron, Canton
- **Coed** 4,995 undergraduate students, 63% full-time, 60% women, 40% men
- **Noncompetitive** entrance level, 100% of applicants were admitted

UNDERGRAD STUDENTS

3,157 full-time, 1,838 part-time. Students come from 11 states and territories; 4 other countries; 2% are from out of state; 6% Black or African American, non-Hispanic/Latino; 2% Hispanic/Latino; 1% Asian, non-Hispanic/Latino; 0.4% American Indian or Alaska Native, non-Hispanic/Latino; 4% Two or more races, non-Hispanic/Latino; 3% Race/ethnicity unknown; 0.4% international; 6% transferred in.

Freshmen:

Admission: 1,127 applied, 1,127 admitted, 652 enrolled. *Average high school GPA:* 2.9. *Test scores:* SAT evidence-based reading and writing scores over 500: 60%; SAT math scores over 500: 53%; ACT scores over 18: 76%; SAT evidence-based reading and writing scores over 600: 20%; SAT math scores over 600: 7%; ACT scores over 24: 17%; ACT scores over 30: 2%.

Retention: 66% of full-time freshmen returned.

FACULTY

Total: 276, 39% full-time, 5% with terminal degrees.

Student/faculty ratio: 23:1.

ACADEMICS

Calendar: semesters. *Degrees:* associate, bachelor's, and master's.

Special study options: academic remediation for entering students, adult/continuing education programs, advanced placement credit, distance learning, double majors, honors programs, independent study, internships, off-campus study, part-time degree program, services for LD students, student-designed majors, study abroad, summer session for credit. *ROTC:* Army (c), Air Force (c).

Computers: 605 computers/terminals are available on campus for general student use. Students can access the following: computer help desk, free student e-mail accounts, online (class) grades, online (class) registration, online (class) schedules. Campuswide network is available. Wireless service is available via entire campus.

Library: Kent State Stark Library. *Serial titles:* 600 (physical). Weekly public service hours: 72; students can reserve study rooms.

STUDENT LIFE

Housing options: college housing not available.

Activities and organizations: drama/theater group, choral group, Music Technology Club, Biology Club, SCRUBS (Nursing Organization), HDFS (Human Development Family Studies), Revive (Faith Based).

Athletics *Intramural sports:* basketball M/W, table tennis M/W, volleyball M/W.

Campus security: 24-hour emergency response devices, student patrols, late-night transport/escort service.

Student services: personal/psychological counseling.

COSTS & FINANCIAL AID

Costs (2017–18) *One-time required fee:* $150. *Tuition:* state resident $5664 full-time, $258 per credit hour part-time; nonresident $14,028 full-time, $620 per credit hour part-time. Full-time tuition and fees vary according to course level and course load. Part-time tuition and fees vary according to course level and course load. *Payment plan:* installment. *Waivers:* senior citizens and employees or children of employees.

Financial Aid Of all full-time matriculated undergraduates who enrolled in 2017, 1,765 applied for aid, 1,471 were judged to have need, 170 had their need fully met. 57 Federal Work-Study jobs (averaging $2390). In 2017, 99 non-need-based awards were made. *Average percent of need met:* 62. *Average financial aid package:* $7045. *Average need-based loan:* $3878. *Average need-based gift aid:* $4636. *Average non-need-based aid:* $2465.

APPLYING

Standardized Tests *Recommended:* SAT or ACT (for admission).

Options: electronic application, deferred entrance.

Application fee: $40.

Required: high school transcript.

Application deadlines: 8/15 (freshmen), 8/15 (transfers).

CONTACT

Office of Admissions, Kent State University at Stark, 6000 Frank Avenue NW, North Canton, OH 44720. *Phone:* 330-244-3251. *Fax:* 330-499-0301. *E-mail:* starkadmissions@kent.edu.

Kent State University at Trumbull

Warren, Ohio

http://www.trumbull.kent.edu/

- **State-supported** primarily 2-year, founded 1954, part of Kent State University System
- **Suburban** 438-acre campus with easy access to Akron, Youngstown
- **Coed** 2,889 undergraduate students, 67% full-time, 62% women, 38% men
- **Noncompetitive** entrance level, 100% of applicants were admitted

UNDERGRAD STUDENTS

1,940 full-time, 949 part-time. Students come from 6 states and territories; 3% are from out of state; 8% Black or African American, non-Hispanic/Latino; 3% Hispanic/Latino; 0.9% Asian, non-Hispanic/Latino; 0.1% Native Hawaiian or other Pacific Islander, non-Hispanic/Latino; 0.2% American Indian or Alaska Native, non-Hispanic/Latino; 3% Two or more races, non-Hispanic/Latino; 3% Race/ethnicity unknown; 0.4% international; 4% transferred in.

Freshmen:

Admission: 388 applied, 388 admitted, 243 enrolled. *Average high school GPA:* 2.7. *Test scores:* SAT evidence-based reading and writing scores over 500: 50%; SAT math scores over 500: 50%; ACT scores over 18: 68%; ACT scores over 24: 9%.

Retention: 60% of full-time freshmen returned.

FACULTY

Total: 106, 48% full-time.

Student/faculty ratio: 25:1.

ACADEMICS

Calendar: semesters. *Degrees:* associate, bachelor's, and master's (also offers some upper-level and graduate courses).

Special study options: academic remediation for entering students, adult/continuing education programs, advanced placement credit, distance learning, double majors, freshman honors college, honors programs, independent study, internships, part-time degree program, services for LD students, student-designed majors, summer session for credit. *ROTC:* Army (c), Air Force (c).

Computers: 300 computers/terminals are available on campus for general student use. Students can access the following: computer help desk, free student e-mail accounts, online (class) grades, online (class) registration, online (class) schedules. Campuswide network is available. Wireless service is available via entire campus.

Library: Gelbke Library at Kent State Trumbull. *Books:* 40,000 (physical), 100,000 (digital/electronic); *Serial titles:* 40 (physical); *Databases:* 459. Weekly public service hours: 56.

STUDENT LIFE

Housing options: college housing not available.

Activities and organizations: drama/theater group, The National Society for Leadership and Success, Sigma Alpha Pi, Jurisprudence Organization, Student Nurses Association, Pride Alliance, S.E.E.D.S..

Athletics *Intramural sports:* cross-country running M(c)/W(c).

Campus security: 24-hour emergency response devices, late-night transport/escort service, patrols by trained security personnel during hours of operation.

Student services: personal/psychological counseling.

COSTS & FINANCIAL AID

Costs (2017–18) *One-time required fee:* $150. *Tuition:* state resident $5664 full-time, $258 per credit hour part-time; nonresident $14,028 full-time, $620 per credit hour part-time. Full-time tuition and fees vary according to course level and course load. Part-time tuition and fees vary according to course level and course load. *Payment plan:* installment. *Waivers:* senior citizens and employees or children of employees.

Financial Aid Of all full-time matriculated undergraduates who enrolled in 2017, 725 applied for aid, 638 were judged to have need, 36 had their need fully met. 20 Federal Work-Study jobs (averaging $2713). In 2017, 27 non-need-based awards were made. *Average percent of need met:* 59. *Average financial aid package:* $7668. *Average need-based loan:* $3896. *Average need-based gift aid:* $4965. *Average non-need-based aid:* $2303.

APPLYING

Standardized Tests *Recommended:* SAT or ACT (for admission).

Options: electronic application, deferred entrance.

Application fee: $40.

Required: high school transcript.

Application deadlines: 8/15 (freshmen), 8/15 (transfers).

CONTACT

Office of Enrollment Management, Kent State University at Trumbull, 4314 Mahoning Avenue, NW, Warren, OH 44483-1998. *Phone:* 330-675-8860. *E-mail:* trumbullinfo@kent.edu.

Kent State University at Tuscarawas
New Philadelphia, Ohio
http://www.tusc.kent.edu/

- **State-supported** primarily 2-year, founded 1962, part of Kent State University System
- **Small-town** 180-acre campus with easy access to Akron, Canton
- **Coed** 2,131 undergraduate students, 61% full-time, 57% women, 43% men
- **Noncompetitive** entrance level, 100% of applicants were admitted

UNDERGRAD STUDENTS
1,299 full-time, 832 part-time. Students come from 8 states and territories; 3 other countries; 2% are from out of state; 4% Black or African American, non-Hispanic/Latino; 2% Hispanic/Latino; 0.7% Asian, non-Hispanic/Latino; 0.4% American Indian or Alaska Native, non-Hispanic/Latino; 2% Two or more races, non-Hispanic/Latino; 2% Race/ethnicity unknown; 0.5% international; 6% transferred in.

Freshmen:
Admission: 415 applied, 414 admitted, 288 enrolled. *Average high school GPA:* 3.0. *Test scores:* ACT scores over 18: 76%; ACT scores over 24: 16%; ACT scores over 30: 2%.
Retention: 62% of full-time freshmen returned.

FACULTY
Total: 122, 39% full-time.
Student/faculty ratio: 22:1.

ACADEMICS
Calendar: semesters. *Degrees:* certificates, diplomas, associate, and bachelor's (also offers some upper-level and graduate courses).

Special study options: academic remediation for entering students, accelerated degree program, adult/continuing education programs, advanced placement credit, distance learning, double majors, freshman honors college, honors programs, independent study, internships, part-time degree program, services for LD students, student-designed majors, study abroad, summer session for credit. *ROTC:* Army (c), Air Force (c).

Computers: 194 computers/terminals are available on campus for general student use. Students can access the following: computer help desk, free student e-mail accounts, online (class) grades, online (class) registration, online (class) schedules. Campuswide network is available. Wireless service is available via entire campus.
Library: Kent State Tuscarawas Library. *Books:* 52,500 (physical), 12 (digital/electronic); *Serial titles:* 540 (physical).

STUDENT LIFE
Housing options: college housing not available.
Activities and organizations: choral group, Student Nurses Association, Technology Club, Vet Tech Student Chapter, Realms of Roleplay, Vision.
Athletics Member USCAA. *Intercollegiate sports:* baseball M, basketball M/W, cross-country running M/W, golf M/W, softball W, track and field M/W, volleyball W, wrestling M.
Campus security: 24-hour emergency response devices.

COSTS & FINANCIAL AID
Costs (2017–18) *One-time required fee:* $150. *Tuition:* state resident $5664 full-time, $258 per credit hour part-time; nonresident $14,028 full-time, $620 per credit hour part-time. Full-time tuition and fees vary according to course level and course load. Part-time tuition and fees vary according to course level and course load. *Payment plan:* installment. *Waivers:* senior citizens and employees or children of employees.
Financial Aid Of all full-time matriculated undergraduates who enrolled in 2017, 643 applied for aid, 542 were judged to have need, 65 had their need fully met. 21 Federal Work-Study jobs (averaging $2495). In 2017, 43 non-need-based awards were made. *Average percent of need met:* 63. *Average financial aid package:* $6767. *Average need-based loan:* $3651. *Average need-based gift aid:* $4391. *Average non-need-based aid:* $2398.

APPLYING
Standardized Tests *Recommended:* SAT or ACT (for admission).
Options: electronic application, deferred entrance.
Application fee: $40.
Required: high school transcript.

Application deadlines: 8/15 (freshmen), 8/15 (transfers).
Notification: continuous (freshmen), continuous (transfers).
CONTACT
Office of Admissions, Kent State University at Tuscarawas, 330 University Drive NE, New Philadelphia, OH 44663-9403. *Phone:* 330-339-3391. *E-mail:* infotusc@kent.edu.

Kenyon College
Gambier, Ohio
http://www.kenyon.edu/

- **Independent** 4-year, founded 1824
- **Rural** 1000-acre campus with easy access to Columbus
- **Endowment** $208.9 million
- **Coed** 1,677 undergraduate students, 99% full-time, 56% women, 44% men
- **Most difficult** entrance level, 34% of applicants were admitted

UNDERGRAD STUDENTS
1,661 full-time, 16 part-time. Students come from 47 states and territories; 46 other countries; 85% are from out of state; 3% Black or African American, non-Hispanic/Latino; 6% Hispanic/Latino; 3% Asian, non-Hispanic/Latino; 7% Two or more races, non-Hispanic/Latino; 3% Race/ethnicity unknown; 6% international; 0.8% transferred in; 100% live on campus.

Freshmen:
Admission: 5,603 applied, 1,896 admitted, 453 enrolled. *Average high school GPA:* 3.9. *Test scores:* SAT evidence-based reading and writing scores over 500: 100%; SAT math scores over 500: 99%; ACT scores over 18: 100%; SAT evidence-based reading and writing scores over 600: 93%; SAT math scores over 600: 85%; ACT scores over 24: 97%; SAT evidence-based reading and writing scores over 700: 47%; SAT math scores over 700: 39%; ACT scores over 30: 68%.
Retention: 93% of full-time freshmen returned.

FACULTY
Total: 214, 78% full-time, 86% with terminal degrees.
Student/faculty ratio: 9:1.

ACADEMICS
Calendar: semesters. *Degree:* bachelor's.
Special study options: accelerated degree program, advanced placement credit, double majors, honors programs, independent study, internships, off-campus study, services for LD students, student-designed majors, study abroad.
Unusual degree programs: 3-2 engineering with Washington University in St. Louis, Case Western Reserve University, Rensselaer Polytechnic Institute; environmental science with Duke University, education with The Bank Street College of Education.
Computers: 715 computers/terminals are available on campus for general student use. Students can access the following: campus intranet, computer help desk, free student e-mail accounts, online (class) grades, online (class) registration, online (class) schedules, commercial databases. Campuswide network is available. 99% of college-owned or -operated housing units are wired for high-speed Internet access. Wireless service is available via entire campus.
Library: Olin Library plus 1 other. *Books:* 495,501 (physical), 42,965 (digital/electronic); *Serial titles:* 1,670 (physical), 43,534 (digital/electronic); *Databases:* 332. Weekly public service hours: 131; students can reserve study rooms.

STUDENT LIFE
Housing options: on-campus residence required through senior year; coed, women-only, special housing for students with disabilities. Campus housing is university owned. Freshman campus housing is guaranteed.
Activities and organizations: drama/theater group, student-run newspaper, radio station, choral group, student advisory groups, student radio station, musical groups, intramural sports and clubs, outdoors club, national fraternities, national sororities.
Athletics Member NCAA. All Division III. *Intercollegiate sports:* baseball M, basketball M/W, cross-country running M/W, equestrian sports M(c)/W(c), field hockey W, football M, golf M, lacrosse M/W, rugby M(c)/W(c), soccer M/W, softball W, squash M(c)/W(c), swimming

and diving M/W, tennis M/W, track and field M/W, ultimate Frisbee M(c)/W(c), volleyball W. *Intramural sports:* archery M(c)/W(c), basketball M/W, fencing M(c)/W(c), racquetball M/W, soccer M(c)/W(c), tennis M(c)/W(c), volleyball M/W.

Campus security: 24-hour emergency response devices and patrols, student patrols, late-night transport/escort service, controlled dormitory access.

Student services: health clinic, personal/psychological counseling, women's center.

COSTS & FINANCIAL AID

Costs (2018–19) *Comprehensive fee:* $68,440 includes full-time tuition ($53,830), mandatory fees ($2100), and room and board ($12,510). Full-time tuition and fees vary according to reciprocity agreements. Part-time tuition and fees vary according to reciprocity agreements. *College room only:* $5470. Room and board charges vary according to housing facility and student level. *Payment plan:* installment. *Waivers:* employees or children of employees.

Financial Aid Of all full-time matriculated undergraduates who enrolled in 2017, 865 applied for aid, 729 were judged to have need, 729 had their need fully met. 324 Federal Work-Study jobs (averaging $1797). 196 state and other part-time jobs (averaging $1811). In 2017, 208 non-need-based awards were made. *Average percent of need met:* 100. *Average financial aid package:* $46,069. *Average need-based loan:* $4164. *Average need-based gift aid:* $42,031. *Average non-need-based aid:* $16,649. *Average indebtedness upon graduation:* $21,404.

APPLYING

Standardized Tests *Required:* SAT or ACT (for admission).

Options: electronic application, early admission, early decision, deferred entrance.

Required: essay or personal statement, high school transcript, counselor recommendation. *Recommended:* 2 letters of recommendation, interview.

Application deadlines: 1/15 (freshmen), 4/1 (transfers).

Early decision deadline: 11/15 (for plan 1), 1/15 (for plan 2).

Notification: 4/1 (freshmen), 5/15 (transfers), 12/15 (early decision plan 1), 2/1 (early decision plan 2).

CONTACT

Ms. Diane Anci, Vice President of Enrollment Management and Dean of Admissions and Financial Aid, Kenyon College, Ransom Hall, Gambier, OH 43022. *Phone:* 740-427-5776. *Toll-free phone:* 800-848-2468. *Fax:* 740-427-5770. *E-mail:* admissions@kenyon.edu.

Kettering College

Kettering, Ohio
http://www.kc.edu/

CONTACT

Mrs. Becky McDonald, Director of Enrollment Services, Kettering College, 3737 Southern Boulevard, Kettering, OH 45429-1299. *Phone:* 937-395-8628. *Toll-free phone:* 800-433-5262. *Fax:* 937-296-4238.

Lake Erie College

Painesville, Ohio
http://www.lec.edu/

- **Independent** comprehensive, founded 1856
- **Suburban** 46-acre campus with easy access to Cleveland
- **Endowment** $32.7 million
- **Coed**
- **Moderately difficult** entrance level

FACULTY
Student/faculty ratio: 14:1.

ACADEMICS
Calendar: semesters. *Degrees:* bachelor's, master's, and postbachelor's certificates.
Library: Lincoln Library. *Books:* 38,463 (physical), 299,340 (digital/electronic); *Serial titles:* 18,188 (digital/electronic); *Databases:* 107. Weekly public service hours: 56; students can reserve study rooms.

STUDENT LIFE

Housing options: on-campus residence required through sophomore year; coed, men-only, women-only. Campus housing is university owned and leased by the school. Freshman applicants given priority for college housing.

Activities and organizations: drama/theater group, choral group, Student Athlete Advisory Committee, Intercollegiate Horse Show Association, Gamma Phi Beta Sorority, Spanish Club, Student Government Association, national fraternities, national sororities.

Athletics Member NCAA. All Division II.

Campus security: 24-hour emergency response devices and patrols, late-night transport/escort service.

COSTS & FINANCIAL AID

Costs (2017–18) *One-time required fee:* $350. *Comprehensive fee:* $40,322 includes full-time tuition ($29,426), mandatory fees ($1436), and room and board ($9460). Full-time tuition and fees vary according to course load, degree level, and program. Part-time tuition: $780 per credit hour. Part-time tuition and fees vary according to course load, degree level, and program. *Required fees:* $51 per credit hour part-time. *College room only:* $4508. Room and board charges vary according to board plan and housing facility.

Financial Aid Of all full-time matriculated undergraduates who enrolled in 2016, 633 applied for aid, 585 were judged to have need, 109 had their need fully met. In 2016, 91 non-need-based awards were made. *Average percent of need met:* 75. *Average financial aid package:* $23,882. *Average need-based loan:* $4342. *Average need-based gift aid:* $19,849. *Average non-need-based aid:* $13,855. *Average indebtedness upon graduation:* $38,234.

APPLYING

Standardized Tests *Required for some:* SAT or ACT (for admission), SAT and SAT Subject Tests or ACT (for admission). *Recommended:* AP, CLEP, institutional exam.

Options: electronic application, early action, deferred entrance.

Application fee: $30.

Required: high school transcript, minimum 2.5 GPA. *Required for some:* essay or personal statement, letters of recommendation. *Recommended:* essay or personal statement, interview.

CONTACT

Mrs. Liz Sellers, Director of Admissions, Lake Erie College, 391 West Washington Street, Painesville, OH 44077-3389. *Phone:* 440-375-7251. *Toll-free phone:* 800-916-0904. *Fax:* 440-375-7058. *E-mail:* admissions@lec.edu.

Lourdes University

Sylvania, Ohio
http://www.lourdes.edu/

- **Independent Roman Catholic** comprehensive, founded 1958
- **Suburban** 113-acre campus with easy access to Toledo
- **Endowment** $11.0 million
- **Coed**
- **Moderately difficult** entrance level

FACULTY
Student/faculty ratio: 12:1.

ACADEMICS
Calendar: semesters. *Degrees:* certificates, associate, bachelor's, master's, and postbachelor's certificates.
Library: Duns Scotus Library plus 1 other. *Books:* 54,138 (physical), 325,641 (digital/electronic); *Serial titles:* 486 (physical), 2,057 (digital/electronic). Study areas open 24 hours, 5–7 days a week.

STUDENT LIFE

Housing options: on-campus residence required through senior year; coed. Campus housing is university owned. Freshman applicants given priority for college housing.

Activities and organizations: drama/theater group, choral group, Student Government Association, Student Nurses Association, Orbis Ars, Future Doctors of America, Active Minds.

Athletics Member NAIA.

Campus security: 24-hour emergency response devices and patrols, late-night transport/escort service, controlled dormitory access.

Student services: health clinic, personal/psychological counseling.

COSTS & FINANCIAL AID
Costs (2017–18) *One-time required fee:* $250. *Comprehensive fee:* $31,240 includes full-time tuition ($20,800), mandatory fees ($740), and room and board ($9700). Full-time tuition and fees vary according to course load. Part-time tuition: $695 per credit hour. Part-time tuition and fees vary according to course load. *Required fees:* $220 per term part-time. *College room only:* $5100. Room and board charges vary according to board plan and housing facility. *Payment plans:* installment, deferred payment.

Financial Aid Of all full-time matriculated undergraduates who enrolled in 2013, 1,091 applied for aid, 938 were judged to have need. 68 Federal Work-Study jobs (averaging $1872). 128 state and other part-time jobs (averaging $1500). *Average financial aid package:* $13,172. *Average need-based loan:* $3988. *Average need-based gift aid:* $6089.

APPLYING
Standardized Tests *Required:* SAT or ACT (for admission).

Options: electronic application, early admission, deferred entrance.

Application fee: $25.

Required: high school transcript, minimum 2.5 GPA.

CONTACT
Amy Houston, Associate Director of Admissions, Lourdes University, 6832 Convent Boulevard, Sylvania, OH 43560. *Phone:* 419-885-5291. *Toll-free phone:* 800-878-3210.

Malone University
Canton, Ohio
http://www.malone.edu/

- **Independent** comprehensive, founded 1892, affiliated with Evangelical Friends Church–Eastern Region
- **Suburban** 96-acre campus with easy access to Cleveland
- **Endowment** $19.4 million
- **Coed** 1,333 undergraduate students, 82% full-time, 58% women, 42% men
- **Moderately difficult** entrance level, 66% of applicants were admitted

UNDERGRAD STUDENTS
1,099 full-time, 234 part-time. Students come from 25 states and territories; 11 other countries; 14% are from out of state; 11% Black or African American, non-Hispanic/Latino; 3% Hispanic/Latino; 0.5% Asian, non-Hispanic/Latino; 0.1% American Indian or Alaska Native, non-Hispanic/Latino; 4% Two or more races, non-Hispanic/Latino; 1% Race/ethnicity unknown; 1% international; 3% transferred in; 63% live on campus.

Freshmen:
Admission: 1,864 applied, 1,230 admitted, 338 enrolled. *Average high school GPA:* 3.3. *Test scores:* SAT evidence-based reading and writing scores over 500: 62%; SAT math scores over 500: 67%; ACT scores over 18: 91%; SAT evidence-based reading and writing scores over 600: 20%; SAT math scores over 600: 20%; ACT scores over 24: 28%; SAT evidence-based reading and writing scores over 700: 6%; SAT math scores over 700: 6%; ACT scores over 30: 3%.
Retention: 70% of full-time freshmen returned.

FACULTY
Total: 175, 46% full-time, 51% with terminal degrees.

Student/faculty ratio: 12:1.

ACADEMICS
Calendar: semesters. *Degrees:* bachelor's and master's.

Special study options: academic remediation for entering students, accelerated degree program, adult/continuing education programs, advanced placement credit, distance learning, double majors, honors programs, independent study, internships, off-campus study, part-time

degree program, services for LD students, student-designed majors, study abroad, summer session for credit.

Unusual degree programs: 3-2 engineering with The University of Akron.

Computers: 254 computers/terminals and 3,900 ports are available on campus for general student use. Students can access the following: campus intranet, free student e-mail accounts, online (class) grades, online (class) registration, online (class) schedules, online advising, online financial aid information, and online credit card payments. Campuswide network is available. 100% of college-owned or -operated housing units are wired for high-speed Internet access. Wireless service is available via entire campus.

Library: Everett L. Cattell Library plus 1 other. *Books:* 169,479 (physical), 312,753 (digital/electronic); *Serial titles:* 2,035 (physical), 39,854 (digital/electronic); *Databases:* 176. Weekly public service hours: 88.

STUDENT LIFE
Housing options: on-campus residence required through junior year; men-only, women-only, special housing for students with disabilities. Campus housing is university owned. Freshman applicants given priority for college housing.

Activities and organizations: drama/theater group, student-run newspaper, choral group, marching band, Celebration Worship Services (and other Spiritual Formation activities), Student Activities Council, Student Senate, FCA (Fellowship of Christian Athletes), intramural athletics.

Athletics Member NCAA. All Division II. *Intercollegiate sports:* baseball M(s), basketball M(s)/W(s), cheerleading M/W, cross-country running M(s)/W(s), football M(s), golf M(s)/W(s), soccer M(s)/W(s), softball W(s), swimming and diving M(s)/W(s), track and field M(s)/W(s), volleyball W(s). *Intramural sports:* basketball M/W, football M/W, soccer M/W, tennis M/W, ultimate Frisbee M/W, volleyball M/W.

Campus security: 24-hour emergency response devices and patrols, late-night transport/escort service, controlled dormitory access.

Student services: health clinic, personal/psychological counseling.

COSTS & FINANCIAL AID
Costs (2018–19) *Comprehensive fee:* $40,360 includes full-time tuition ($29,900), mandatory fees ($960), and room and board ($9500). Part-time tuition: $500 per credit hour. Part-time tuition and fees vary according to course load. *Required fees:* $240 per term part-time. *College room only:* $4700. Room and board charges vary according to board plan. *Payment plan:* installment. *Waivers:* senior citizens and employees or children of employees.

Financial Aid Of all full-time matriculated undergraduates who enrolled in 2017, 956 applied for aid, 901 were judged to have need, 176 had their need fully met. 363 Federal Work-Study jobs (averaging $1862). 106 state and other part-time jobs (averaging $1922). In 2017, 135 non-need-based awards were made. *Average percent of need met:* 80. *Average financial aid package:* $25,724. *Average need-based loan:* $4212. *Average need-based gift aid:* $21,814. *Average non-need-based aid:* $12,106. *Average indebtedness upon graduation:* $33,330. *Financial aid deadline:* 7/31.

APPLYING
Standardized Tests *Required:* SAT or ACT (for admission).

Options: electronic application, early admission, deferred entrance.

Application fee: $20.

Required: high school transcript, minimum 2.0 GPA. *Required for some:* essay or personal statement. *Recommended:* interview.

Application deadlines: rolling (freshmen), rolling (out-of-state freshmen), rolling (transfers).

Notification: continuous (freshmen), continuous (transfers).

CONTACT
Mrs. Anissa D. Scott, Assistant Director, Admissions, Malone University, 2600 Cleveland Avenue NW, Canton, OH 44709-3308. *Phone:* 330-471-8153. *Toll-free phone:* 800-521-1146. *Fax:* 330-471-8149. *E-mail:* admissions@malone.edu.

Marietta College

Marietta, Ohio
http://www.marietta.edu/

- **Independent** comprehensive, founded 1835
- **Small-town** 90-acre campus
- **Endowment** $70.3 million
- **Coed** 1,065 undergraduate students, 90% full-time, 39% women, 61% men
- **Moderately difficult** entrance level, 93% of applicants were admitted

UNDERGRAD STUDENTS

954 full-time, 111 part-time. Students come from 31 states and territories; 8 other countries; 33% are from out of state; 5% Black or African American, non-Hispanic/Latino; 2% Hispanic/Latino; 0.8% Asian, non-Hispanic/Latino; 0.2% American Indian or Alaska Native, non-Hispanic/Latino; 4% Two or more races, non-Hispanic/Latino; 7% Race/ethnicity unknown; 17% international; 3% transferred in; 70% live on campus.

Freshmen:
Admission: 1,308 applied, 1,217 admitted, 272 enrolled. *Average high school GPA:* 3.4. *Test scores:* SAT evidence-based reading and writing scores over 500: 73%; SAT math scores over 500: 71%; ACT scores over 18: 93%; SAT evidence-based reading and writing scores over 600: 33%; SAT math scores over 600: 33%; ACT scores over 24: 38%; SAT evidence-based reading and writing scores over 700: 6%; SAT math scores over 700: 8%; ACT scores over 30: 4%.
Retention: 67% of full-time freshmen returned.

FACULTY

Total: 171, 57% full-time, 50% with terminal degrees.
Student/faculty ratio: 9:1.

ACADEMICS

Calendar: semesters. *Degrees:* certificates, associate, bachelor's, and master's.
Special study options: academic remediation for entering students, adult/continuing education programs, advanced placement credit, double majors, English as a second language, honors programs, independent study, internships, off-campus study, part-time degree program, services for LD students, student-designed majors, study abroad, summer session for credit.
Unusual degree programs: 3-2 engineering with Columbia University, Case Western Reserve University, Ohio University; forestry with Duke University.
Computers: 475 computers/terminals and 450 ports are available on campus for general student use. Students can access the following: campus intranet, computer help desk, free student e-mail accounts, online (class) grades, online (class) registration, online (class) schedules. Campuswide network is available. 100% of college-owned or -operated housing units are wired for high-speed Internet access. Wireless service is available via classrooms, computer centers, computer labs, dorm rooms, learning centers, libraries, student centers.
Library: Legacy Library. *Books:* 183,103 (physical), 137,587 (digital/electronic); *Serial titles:* 230 (physical), 15,786 (digital/electronic); *Databases:* 186. Weekly public service hours: 95; students can reserve study rooms.

STUDENT LIFE

Housing options: on-campus residence required through senior year; coed, men-only, women-only, special housing for students with disabilities. Campus housing is university owned, leased by the school and is provided by a third party. Freshman campus housing is guaranteed.
Activities and organizations: drama/theater group, student-run newspaper, radio and television station, choral group, Pioneer Activities Council, student government, Panhellenic Council, Inter-Varsity Christian Fellowship, Inter Fraternity Council, national fraternities, national sororities.
Athletics Member NCAA. All Division III. *Intercollegiate sports:* baseball M, basketball M/W, cheerleading M(c)/W(c), crew M/W, cross-country running M/W, football M, golf M/W, lacrosse M/W, soccer M/W, softball W, tennis M/W, track and field M/W, volleyball W. *Intramural sports:* badminton M/W, basketball M/W, bowling M/W, cross-country running M/W, football M/W, golf M/W, racquetball M/W, rock climbing

M/W, sand volleyball M/W, soccer M/W, softball M/W, swimming and diving M/W, tennis M/W, ultimate Frisbee M/W, volleyball M/W, weight lifting M/W.
Campus security: 24-hour emergency response devices and patrols, student patrols, late-night transport/escort service, controlled dormitory access.
Student services: health clinic, personal/psychological counseling.

COSTS & FINANCIAL AID

Costs (2018–19) *Comprehensive fee:* $47,360 includes full-time tuition ($35,030), mandatory fees ($1010), and room and board ($11,320). Full-time tuition and fees vary according to course load. Part-time tuition: $1170 per credit hour. Part-time tuition and fees vary according to course load. *Room and board:* Room and board charges vary according to board plan and housing facility. *Payment plan:* installment. *Waivers:* employees or children of employees.
Financial Aid Of all full-time matriculated undergraduates who enrolled in 2016, 721 applied for aid, 666 were judged to have need, 288 had their need fully met. 706 Federal Work-Study jobs (averaging $1909). In 2016, 130 non-need-based awards were made. *Average percent of need met:* 79. *Average financial aid package:* $31,373. *Average need-based loan:* $5840. *Average need-based gift aid:* $2909. *Average non-need-based aid:* $19,323. *Average indebtedness upon graduation:* $40,196.

APPLYING

Standardized Tests *Required:* SAT or ACT (for admission). *Recommended:* SAT Subject Tests (for admission).
Options: electronic application, early admission, deferred entrance.
Required: essay or personal statement, high school transcript, minimum 2.5 GPA. *Recommended:* minimum 3.4 GPA, letters of recommendation, interview.
Application deadlines: 7/1 (freshmen), rolling (transfers).
Notification: continuous until 7/1 (freshmen), continuous (transfers).

CONTACT

Mr. Stephen Lazowski, Vice President for Enrollment Management, Marietta College, 215 Fifth Street, Marietta, OH 45750. *Phone:* 740-376-4503. *Toll-free phone:* 800-331-7896. *Fax:* 740-376-8888. *E-mail:* admit@marietta.edu.

Mercy College of Ohio

Toledo, Ohio
http://www.mercycollege.edu/

- **Independent** comprehensive, founded 1993, affiliated with Roman Catholic Church
- **Urban** campus with easy access to Toledo, OH
- **Endowment** $14.8 million
- **Coed, primarily women** 1,404 undergraduate students, 31% full-time, 85% women, 15% men
- **Moderately difficult** entrance level, 57% of applicants were admitted

UNDERGRAD STUDENTS

439 full-time, 965 part-time. Students come from 28 states and territories; 30% are from out of state; 12% Black or African American, non-Hispanic/Latino; 4% Hispanic/Latino; 2% Asian, non-Hispanic/Latino; 0.3% American Indian or Alaska Native, non-Hispanic/Latino; 4% Two or more races, non-Hispanic/Latino; 0.8% Race/ethnicity unknown; 26% transferred in; 2% live on campus.

Freshmen:
Admission: 221 applied, 127 admitted, 66 enrolled. *Test scores:* ACT scores over 18: 72%; ACT scores over 24: 14%.
Retention: 89% of full-time freshmen returned.

FACULTY

Total: 210, 28% full-time, 14% with terminal degrees.
Student/faculty ratio: 7:1.

ACADEMICS

Calendar: semesters. *Degrees:* certificates, associate, bachelor's, and master's.
Special study options: academic remediation for entering students, accelerated degree program, advanced placement credit, distance learning,

double majors, independent study, internships, part-time degree program, services for LD students, summer session for credit.

Computers: 127 computers/terminals and 127 ports are available on campus for general student use. Students can access the following: computer help desk, free student e-mail accounts, online (class) grades, online (class) registration, online (class) schedules. Campuswide network is available. Wireless service is available via classrooms, computer centers, computer labs, learning centers, libraries, student centers.

Library: Mercy College of Ohio Library. *Books:* 7,502 (physical), 70,294 (digital/electronic); *Serial titles:* 65 (physical), 40,683 (digital/electronic); *Databases:* 15. Students can reserve study rooms.

STUDENT LIFE
Housing options: college housing not availableCampus housing is leased by the school.

Activities and organizations: American Assembly of Men in Nursing, National Student Nurses Association, Student Government Association, Gay Straight Alliance, Hoffman Ambassadors.

Campus security: 24-hour emergency response devices and patrols, late-night transport/escort service.

Student services: personal/psychological counseling.

COSTS & FINANCIAL AID
Costs (2017–18) *One-time required fee:* $250. *Tuition:* $12,360 full-time, $454 per credit hour part-time. Full-time tuition and fees vary according to course load and program. Part-time tuition and fees vary according to course load and program. *Required fees:* $2250 full-time, $55 per credit hour part-time, $300 per term part-time. *Room only:* $5460. *Payment plan:* installment. *Waivers:* employees or children of employees.

Financial Aid Of all full-time matriculated undergraduates who enrolled in 2015, 24 Federal Work-Study jobs (averaging $1744).

APPLYING
Standardized Tests *Required for some:* SAT or ACT (for admission). *Recommended:* SAT or ACT (for admission).

Options: electronic application, deferred entrance.

Application fee: $25.

Required: high school transcript, minimum 2.0 GPA.

Application deadlines: rolling (freshmen), rolling (transfers).

Notification: continuous (freshmen), continuous (transfers).

CONTACT
Ms. Kristen Porter, Admissions Officer, Mercy College of Ohio, 2221 Madison Avenue, Toledo, OH 43604. *Phone:* 419-251-1313. *Toll-free phone:* 888-80-MERCY. *Fax:* 419-251-1462. *E-mail:* kristen.porter@mercycollege.edu.

Miami University
Oxford, Ohio
http://miamioh.edu/
- **State-related** university, founded 1809, part of Miami University System
- **Small-town** 2100-acre campus with easy access to Cincinnati
- **Endowment** $512.4 million
- **Coed** 17,147 undergraduate students, 97% full-time, 50% women, 50% men
- **Moderately difficult** entrance level, 68% of applicants were admitted

UNDERGRAD STUDENTS
16,619 full-time, 528 part-time. Students come from 50 states and territories; 92 other countries; 36% are from out of state; 3% Black or African American, non-Hispanic/Latino; 4% Hispanic/Latino; 2% Asian, non-Hispanic/Latino; 0.1% Native Hawaiian or other Pacific Islander, non-Hispanic/Latino; 0.2% American Indian or Alaska Native, non-Hispanic/Latino; 3% Two or more races, non-Hispanic/Latino; 0.4% Race/ethnicity unknown; 15% international; 1% transferred in; 45% live on campus.

Freshmen:
Admission: 30,255 applied, 20,635 admitted, 3,822 enrolled. *Average high school GPA:* 3.8. *Test scores:* SAT evidence-based reading and writing scores over 500: 96%; SAT math scores over 500: 99%; ACT scores over 18: 100%; SAT evidence-based reading and writing scores over 600: 68%; SAT math scores over 600: 80%; ACT scores over 24:

95%; SAT evidence-based reading and writing scores over 700: 14%; SAT math scores over 700: 30%; ACT scores over 30: 38%.

Retention: 91% of full-time freshmen returned.

FACULTY
Total: 1,281, 76% full-time, 73% with terminal degrees.
Student/faculty ratio: 17:1.

ACADEMICS
Calendar: semesters. *Degrees:* certificates, associate, bachelor's, master's, doctoral, and post-master's certificates.

Special study options: advanced placement credit, cooperative education, distance learning, double majors, English as a second language, honors programs, independent study, internships, off-campus study, services for LD students, student-designed majors, study abroad, summer session for credit. *ROTC:* Army (c), Navy (b), Air Force (b).

Unusual degree programs: 3-2 engineering with Case Western Reserve University, Columbia University.

Computers: Students can access the following: campus intranet, computer help desk, free student e-mail accounts, online (class) grades, online (class) registration, online (class) schedules. Campuswide network is available. 100% of college-owned or -operated housing units are wired for high-speed Internet access. Wireless service is available via entire campus.

Library: King Library plus 3 others. *Books:* 2.4 million (physical), 727,667 (digital/electronic); *Serial titles:* 1,019 (physical), 25,772 (digital/electronic); *Databases:* 743. Weekly public service hours: 168; study areas open 24 hours, 5–7 days a week; students can reserve study rooms.

STUDENT LIFE
Housing options: on-campus residence required through sophomore year; coed, men-only, women-only, special housing for students with disabilities. Campus housing is university owned. Freshman campus housing is guaranteed.

Activities and organizations: drama/theater group, student-run newspaper, radio and television station, choral group, marching band, CRU (formerly Campus Crusade for Christ), Alpha Phi Omega, College Republicans, 4 Paws for Ability, Best Buddies, national fraternities, national sororities.

Athletics Member NCAA. All Division I except football (Division I-A). *Intercollegiate sports:* baseball M(s)/W(c), basketball M(s)/W(s), cross-country running M(s)/W(s), equestrian sports M(c)/W(c), fencing M(c)/W(c), field hockey M(c)/W(s), golf M(s), gymnastics M(c)/W(c), ice hockey M(s)/W(c), lacrosse M(c)/W(c), rugby M(c)/W(c), sailing M(c)/W(c), soccer M(c)/W(s), softball M(c)/W(s), swimming and diving M(s)/W(s), tennis M(c)/W(s), track and field M(s)/W(s), ultimate Frisbee M(c)/W(c), volleyball M(c)/W(s), water polo M(c)/W(c), weight lifting M(c)/W(c), wrestling M(c)/W(c). *Intramural sports:* badminton M(c)/W(c), baseball M/W, basketball M/W, golf M(c)/W(c), ice hockey M/W, racquetball M/W, soccer M/W, softball M/W, ultimate Frisbee M/W, volleyball M/W.

Campus security: 24-hour emergency response devices and patrols, student patrols, late-night transport/escort service, controlled dormitory access.

Student services: health clinic, personal/psychological counseling, women's center.

COSTS & FINANCIAL AID
Costs (2017–18) *Tuition:* state resident $13,772 full-time; nonresident $31,962 full-time. Full-time tuition and fees vary according to location, program, and student level. Part-time tuition and fees vary according to course load, location, program, and student level. No tuition increase for student's term of enrollment. *Required fees:* $806 full-time. *Room and board:* $12,725; room only: $7833. Room and board charges vary according to board plan, housing facility, and student level. *Payment plan:* installment. *Waivers:* employees or children of employees.

Financial Aid Of all full-time matriculated undergraduates who enrolled in 2017, 8,490 applied for aid, 5,583 were judged to have need, 1,311 had their need fully met. 2,623 Federal Work-Study jobs (averaging $1087). In 2017, 4998 non-need-based awards were made. *Average percent of need met:* 64. *Average financial aid package:* $15,056. *Average need-based loan:* $5187. *Average need-based gift aid:* $11,276. *Average non-need-based aid:* $8931. *Average indebtedness upon graduation:* $29,434.

COLLEGES AT-A-GLANCE

APPLYING

Standardized Tests *Required:* SAT or ACT (for admission).

Options: electronic application, early decision, early action, deferred entrance.

Application fee: $50.

Required: essay or personal statement, high school transcript, 1 letter of recommendation.

Application deadlines: 2/1 (freshmen), 6/1 (transfers), 12/1 (early action).

Early decision deadline: 11/15.

Notification: 3/15 (freshmen), continuous (transfers), 12/15 (early decision), 2/1 (early action).

CONTACT

Office of Admissions, Miami University, 301 South Campus Avenue, Oxford, OH 45056. *Phone:* 513-529-2531. *E-mail:* admission@miamioh.edu.

Miami University Hamilton

Hamilton, Ohio

http://regionals.miamioh.edu/

CONTACT

Mr. Archie Nelson, Director of Admission and Financial Aid, Miami University Hamilton, 1601 Peck Boulevard, Hamilton, OH 45011-3399. *Phone:* 513-785-3111. *Fax:* 513-785-1807. *E-mail:* nelsona3@muohio.edu.

Miami University Middletown

Middletown, Ohio

http://regionals.miamioh.edu/

CONTACT

Diane Cantonwine, Assistant Director of Admission and Financial Aid, Miami University Middletown, 4200 East University Boulevard, Middletown, OH 45042-3497. *Phone:* 513-727-3346. *Toll-free phone:* 866-426-4643. *Fax:* 513-727-3223. *E-mail:* cantondm@muohio.edu.

Mount Carmel College of Nursing

Columbus, Ohio

http://www.mccn.edu/

- **Independent** comprehensive, founded 1903
- **Urban** campus with easy access to Columbus
- **Endowment** $1.9 million
- **Coed, primarily women** 880 undergraduate students, 73% full-time, 90% women, 10% men
- **Moderately difficult** entrance level, 63% of applicants were admitted

UNDERGRAD STUDENTS

638 full-time, 242 part-time. 1% are from out of state; 10% Black or African American, non-Hispanic/Latino; 1% Hispanic/Latino; 2% Asian, non-Hispanic/Latino; 0.1% Native Hawaiian or other Pacific Islander, non-Hispanic/Latino; 0.2% American Indian or Alaska Native, non-Hispanic/Latino; 2% Two or more races, non-Hispanic/Latino; 0.9% Race/ethnicity unknown; 11% transferred in; 9% live on campus.

Freshmen:
Admission: 235 applied, 149 admitted, 95 enrolled. *Average high school GPA:* 3.6. *Test scores:* ACT scores over 18: 98%; ACT scores over 24: 17%; ACT scores over 30: 1%.
Retention: 69% of full-time freshmen returned.

FACULTY

Total: 116, 45% full-time, 24% with terminal degrees.
Student/faculty ratio: 11:1.

ACADEMICS

Calendar: semesters. *Degrees:* bachelor's, master's, doctoral, and post-master's certificates.

Special study options: accelerated degree program, adult/continuing education programs, advanced placement credit, distance learning, honors

programs, off-campus study, summer session for credit. *ROTC:* Army (c), Navy (c), Air Force (c).

Computers: 25 computers/terminals are available on campus for general student use. Students can access the following: campus intranet, computer help desk, free student e-mail accounts, online (class) grades, online (class) registration, online (class) schedules. Campuswide network is available. 100% of college-owned or -operated housing units are wired for high-speed Internet access. Wireless service is available via entire campus.

Library: The Mount Carmel Health Sciences Library plus 1 other. *Books:* 8,163 (physical), 297,441 (digital/electronic); *Serial titles:* 683 (physical), 48,768 (digital/electronic); *Databases:* 178. Weekly public service hours: 61; study areas open 24 hours, 5–7 days a week; students can reserve study rooms.

STUDENT LIFE

Housing options: on-campus residence required through sophomore year; coed. Campus housing is leased by the school. Freshman applicants given priority for college housing.

Activities and organizations: Campus Ministry, Student Nurses Association of Mount Carmel (SNAM), Mount Carmel Rho Omicron Chapter of Sigma Theta Tau International Honor Society, Student Government Association (SGA), Student Ambassador Program.

Athletics *Intramural sports:* basketball W(c), softball W(c), volleyball M(c)/W(c).

Campus security: 24-hour emergency response devices and patrols, late-night transport/escort service, controlled dormitory access.

Student services: health clinic, personal/psychological counseling.

COSTS & FINANCIAL AID

Costs (2017–18) *One-time required fee:* $225. *Tuition:* $12,927 full-time, $417 per semester hour part-time. Full-time tuition and fees vary according to course level, course load, program, and student level. Part-time tuition and fees vary according to course level, course load, program, and student level. *Required fees:* $515 full-time, $417 per semester hour part-time. *Room only:* $5000. *Payment plan:* installment. *Waivers:* employees or children of employees.

Financial Aid Of all full-time matriculated undergraduates who enrolled in 2017, 575 applied for aid, 509 were judged to have need, 29 had their need fully met. In 2017, 35 non-need-based awards were made. *Average percent of need met:* 40. *Average financial aid package:* $10,326. *Average need-based loan:* $4332. *Average need-based gift aid:* $8995. *Average non-need-based aid:* $2950. *Average indebtedness upon graduation:* $36,309.

APPLYING

Standardized Tests *Required for some:* SAT or ACT (for admission).

Options: electronic application.

Application fee: $30.

Required: essay or personal statement, high school transcript, activities/interests resumé. *Required for some:* interview. *Recommended:* minimum 3.0 GPA.

Application deadlines: 4/1 (freshmen), 4/1 (transfers).

Notification: continuous (freshmen), continuous (out-of-state freshmen), continuous (transfers).

CONTACT

Dr. Kim Campbell, Director, Admissions and Recruitment, Mount Carmel College of Nursing, 127 South Davis Avenue, Columbus, OH 43222-1504. *Phone:* 614-234-5144. *Toll-free phone:* 800-556-6942. *Fax:* 614-234-5427. *E-mail:* kcampbell@mccn.edu.

Mount St. Joseph University

Cincinnati, Ohio

http://www.msj.edu/

- **Independent Roman Catholic** comprehensive, founded 1920
- **Suburban** 92-acre campus with easy access to Cincinnati, Ohio
- **Endowment** $36.2 million
- **Coed** 1,318 undergraduate students, 76% full-time, 61% women, 39% men
- **Minimally difficult** entrance level, 73% of applicants were admitted

812 Peterson's® Four-Year Colleges 2019

UNDERGRAD STUDENTS

1,000 full-time, 318 part-time. Students come from 20 states and territories; 3 other countries; 17% are from out of state; 13% Black or African American, non-Hispanic/Latino; 1% Hispanic/Latino; 0.5% Asian, non-Hispanic/Latino; 0.2% Native Hawaiian or other Pacific Islander, non-Hispanic/Latino; 0.2% American Indian or Alaska Native, non-Hispanic/Latino; 5% Two or more races, non-Hispanic/Latino; 2% Race/ethnicity unknown; 0.3% international; 3% transferred in; 27% live on campus.

Freshmen:

Admission: 983 applied, 720 admitted, 277 enrolled. *Average high school GPA:* 3.5. *Test scores:* ACT scores over 18: 92%; ACT scores over 24: 30%; ACT scores over 30: 4%.

Retention: 72% of full-time freshmen returned.

FACULTY

Total: 206, 46% full-time, 35% with terminal degrees.
Student/faculty ratio: 11:1.

ACADEMICS

Calendar: semesters. *Degrees:* certificates, associate, bachelor's, master's, doctoral, and postbachelor's certificates.

Special study options: academic remediation for entering students, accelerated degree program, advanced placement credit, cooperative education, distance learning, double majors, honors programs, independent study, internships, off-campus study, part-time degree program, services for LD students, study abroad, summer session for credit. *ROTC:* Army (c), Air Force (c).

Computers: 172 computers/terminals are available on campus for general student use. Students can access the following: computer help desk, free student e-mail accounts, online (class) grades, online (class) registration, online (class) schedules, wireless printing, storage space. Campuswide network is available. Wireless service is available via entire campus.
Library: Archbishop Alter Library. *Books:* 58,795 (physical), 132,030 (digital/electronic); *Serial titles:* 41 (physical), 29,902 (digital/electronic); *Databases:* 150. Weekly public service hours: 82.

STUDENT LIFE

Housing options: on-campus residence required through sophomore year; coed, special housing for students with disabilities. Campus housing is university owned. Freshman applicants given priority for college housing.

Activities and organizations: drama/theater group, student-run newspaper, choral group, marching band, Black Student Union, Campus Activities Board, Student Government Association, Group Fitness, Residence Hall Council, national fraternities.

Athletics Member NCAA. All Division III. *Intercollegiate sports:* baseball M, basketball M/W, cheerleading W, cross-country running M/W, football M, golf M/W, lacrosse M/W, soccer M/W, softball W, tennis M/W, track and field M/W, volleyball M, wrestling M. *Intramural sports:* basketball M/W, racquetball M/W, soccer M/W, volleyball M/W.

Campus security: 24-hour emergency response devices and patrols, late-night transport/escort service.

Student services: health clinic, personal/psychological counseling.

COSTS & FINANCIAL AID

Costs (2018–19) *Comprehensive fee:* $39,542 includes full-time tuition ($29,100), mandatory fees ($1000), and room and board ($9442). Full-time tuition and fees vary according to course load, location, and reciprocity agreements. Part-time tuition: $540 per credit hour. Part-time tuition and fees vary according to course load, location, and reciprocity agreements. *Required fees:* $540 per credit hour part-time. *Room and board:* Room and board charges vary according to board plan, housing facility, and location. *Payment plans:* installment, deferred payment. *Waivers:* senior citizens and employees or children of employees.

Financial Aid Of all full-time matriculated undergraduates who enrolled in 2017, 914 applied for aid, 826 were judged to have need, 133 had their need fully met. 235 Federal Work-Study jobs (averaging $1488). 138 state and other part-time jobs (averaging $1468). In 2017, 151 non-need-based awards were made. *Average percent of need met:* 77. *Average financial aid package:* $22,394. *Average need-based loan:* $4125. *Average need-based gift aid:* $17,776. *Average non-need-based aid:* $11,293.

APPLYING

Standardized Tests *Required:* SAT or ACT (for admission).

Options: electronic application, deferred entrance.
Application fee: $25.
Required: high school transcript. *Recommended:* minimum 3.0 GPA.
Application deadlines: 8/18 (freshmen), rolling (transfers).
Notification: continuous (freshmen), continuous (transfers).

CONTACT

Peggy Minnich, Director of Admission, Mount St. Joseph University, 5701 Delhi Road, Cincinnati, OH 45233-1670. *Phone:* 513-244-4531. *Toll-free phone:* 800-654-9314. *Fax:* 513-244-4629. *E-mail:* admissions@msj.edu.

Mount Vernon Nazarene University
Mount Vernon, Ohio
http://www.mvnu.edu/

- **Independent Nazarene** comprehensive, founded 1968
- **Small-town** 332-acre campus with easy access to Columbus
- **Endowment** $19.7 million
- **Coed** 1,828 undergraduate students, 79% full-time, 63% women, 37% men
- **Moderately difficult** entrance level, 77% of applicants were admitted

UNDERGRAD STUDENTS

1,439 full-time, 389 part-time. Students come from 31 states and territories; 13 other countries; 8% are from out of state; 3% Black or African American, non-Hispanic/Latino; 2% Hispanic/Latino; 0.6% Asian, non-Hispanic/Latino; 0.1% Native Hawaiian or other Pacific Islander, non-Hispanic/Latino; 0.1% American Indian or Alaska Native, non-Hispanic/Latino; 3% Two or more races, non-Hispanic/Latino; 6% Race/ethnicity unknown; 0.3% international; 1% transferred in; 71% live on campus.

Freshmen:

Admission: 1,187 applied, 910 admitted, 344 enrolled. *Average high school GPA:* 3.5. *Test scores:* ACT scores over 18: 92%; ACT scores over 24: 39%; ACT scores over 30: 3%.

Retention: 79% of full-time freshmen returned.

FACULTY

Total: 251, 30% full-time, 40% with terminal degrees.
Student/faculty ratio: 14:1.

ACADEMICS

Calendar: semesters. *Degrees:* associate, bachelor's, and master's.

Special study options: academic remediation for entering students, adult/continuing education programs, advanced placement credit, distance learning, double majors, honors programs, independent study, internships, off-campus study, part-time degree program, services for LD students, study abroad, summer session for credit.

Unusual degree programs: pre-occupational therapy/physician assistant with Chatham University.

Computers: 250 computers/terminals and 915 ports are available on campus for general student use. Students can access the following: campus intranet, computer help desk, free student e-mail accounts, online (class) grades, online (class) registration, online (class) schedules. Campuswide network is available. 100% of college-owned or -operated housing units are wired for high-speed Internet access. Wireless service is available via entire campus.
Library: Thorne Library/Learning Resource Center. *Books:* 100,952 (physical), 790 (digital/electronic); *Serial titles:* 900 (physical), 29,195 (digital/electronic); *Databases:* 242. Weekly public service hours: 93; study areas open 24 hours, 5–7 days a week; students can reserve study rooms.

STUDENT LIFE

Housing options: coed, men-only, women-only, special housing for students with disabilities. Campus housing is university owned. Freshman campus housing is guaranteed.

Activities and organizations: drama/theater group, student-run newspaper, radio station, choral group, Campus Ministry Groups, Student Government Association, Student Education Association, Drama Club, Music Department Ensembles.

Athletics Member NAIA. *Intercollegiate sports:* baseball M(s), basketball M(s)/W(s), cross-country running M(s)/W(s), golf M(s)/W(s), soccer M(s)/W(s), softball W(s), tennis M(s)/W(s), track and field M(s)/W(s), volleyball W(s). *Intramural sports:* basketball M/W, cheerleading M(c)/W(c), football M/W, soccer M/W, softball M/W, ultimate Frisbee M/W, volleyball M/W.

Campus security: 24-hour emergency response devices and patrols, late-night transport/escort service, controlled dormitory access.

Student services: health clinic, personal/psychological counseling.

COSTS & FINANCIAL AID
Costs (2018–19) *Comprehensive fee:* $37,364 includes full-time tuition ($28,944), mandatory fees ($250), and room and board ($8170). Full-time tuition and fees vary according to program. Part-time tuition: $803 per credit hour. Part-time tuition and fees vary according to course load and program. *College room only:* $4564. *Payment plan:* installment. *Waivers:* senior citizens and employees or children of employees.

Financial Aid Of all full-time matriculated undergraduates who enrolled in 2016, 1,456 applied for aid, 1,266 were judged to have need, 530 had their need fully met. In 2016, 427 non-need-based awards were made. *Average percent of need met:* 63. *Average financial aid package:* $18,251. *Average need-based loan:* $3783. *Average need-based gift aid:* $16,247. *Average non-need-based aid:* $12,652. *Average indebtedness upon graduation:* $21,564.

APPLYING
Standardized Tests *Required:* SAT or ACT (for admission).

Options: electronic application, deferred entrance.

Application fee: $25.

Required: essay or personal statement, high school transcript, minimum 2.5 GPA, 2 letters of recommendation.

Notification: 9/1 (freshmen), continuous (transfers).

CONTACT
Mr. Tracy Waal, Director of Admissions and Student Recruitment, Mount Vernon Nazarene University, 800 Martinsburg Road, Mount Vernon, OH 43050. *Phone:* 740-392-6868 Ext. 4514. *Toll-free phone:* 866-462-6868. *Fax:* 740-393-0511. *E-mail:* admissions@mvnu.edu.

Muskingum University
New Concord, Ohio
http://www.muskingum.edu/

- **Independent** comprehensive, founded 1837, affiliated with Presbyterian Church (U.S.A.)
- **Small-town** 245-acre campus with easy access to Columbus
- **Endowment** $73.6 million
- **Coed** 1,557 undergraduate students, 88% full-time, 55% women, 45% men
- **Moderately difficult** entrance level, 74% of applicants were admitted

UNDERGRAD STUDENTS
1,363 full-time, 194 part-time. Students come from 24 states and territories; 8 other countries; 8% are from out of state; 5% Black or African American, non-Hispanic/Latino; 3% Hispanic/Latino; 0.8% Asian, non-Hispanic/Latino; 0.1% American Indian or Alaska Native, non-Hispanic/Latino; 4% Two or more races, non-Hispanic/Latino; 6% Race/ethnicity unknown; 5% international; 5% transferred in; 68% live on campus.

Freshmen:
Admission: 1,850 applied, 1,376 admitted, 383 enrolled. *Average high school GPA:* 3.2. *Test scores:* SAT evidence-based reading and writing scores over 500: 53%; SAT math scores over 500: 48%; ACT scores over 18: 81%; SAT evidence-based reading and writing scores over 600: 17%; SAT math scores over 600: 10%; ACT scores over 24: 27%; ACT scores over 30: 3%.

Retention: 75% of full-time freshmen returned.

FACULTY
Total: 154, 64% full-time, 66% with terminal degrees.

Student/faculty ratio: 12:1.

ACADEMICS
Calendar: semesters. *Degrees:* bachelor's and master's.

Special study options: accelerated degree program, adult/continuing education programs, advanced placement credit, distance learning, double majors, English as a second language, external degree program, independent study, internships, off-campus study, part-time degree program, services for LD students, student-designed majors, study abroad, summer session for credit.

Unusual degree programs: engineering with Case Western Reserve University.

Computers: 266 computers/terminals are available on campus for general student use. Students can access the following: campus intranet, computer help desk, free student e-mail accounts, online (class) grades, online (class) registration, online (class) schedules. Campuswide network is available. 100% of college-owned or -operated housing units are wired for high-speed Internet access. Wireless service is available via entire campus.

Library: Roberta A. Smith Library. *Books:* 100,959 (physical), 312,835 (digital/electronic); *Serial titles:* 1,254 (physical), 63,193 (digital/electronic); *Databases:* 271. Weekly public service hours: 89; students can reserve study rooms.

STUDENT LIFE
Housing options: on-campus residence required through junior year; coed, men-only, women-only. Campus housing is university owned. Freshman campus housing is guaranteed.

Activities and organizations: drama/theater group, student-run newspaper, radio and television station, choral group, marching band, Campus Crusade for Christ (CRU), Greek Life, Muskingum Programming Board, Game Club, Multicultural Association:Black Student Union, national fraternities, national sororities.

Athletics Member NCAA. All Division III. *Intercollegiate sports:* baseball M, basketball M/W, bowling M/W, cheerleading M(c)/W(c), cross-country running M/W, football M, golf M/W, lacrosse M/W, soccer M/W, softball M, tennis M/W, track and field M/W, ultimate Frisbee M(c)/W(c), volleyball W, wrestling M. *Intramural sports:* badminton M/W, basketball M/W, cross-country running M/W, football M/W, golf M/W, racquetball M/W, sand volleyball M/W, soccer M/W, softball M/W, swimming and diving M/W, table tennis M/W, tennis M/W, track and field M/W, volleyball M/W, water polo M/W, weight lifting M/W, wrestling M.

Campus security: 24-hour emergency response devices and patrols, late-night transport/escort service, controlled dormitory access.

Student services: health clinic, personal/psychological counseling, women's center.

COSTS & FINANCIAL AID
Costs (2018–19) *One-time required fee:* $250. *Comprehensive fee:* $39,996 includes full-time tuition ($27,500), mandatory fees ($1016), and room and board ($11,480). Part-time tuition: $610 per credit hour. Part-time tuition and fees vary according to course load. *College room only:* $5860. *Payment plan:* installment. *Waivers:* children of alumni and employees or children of employees.

Financial Aid Of all full-time matriculated undergraduates who enrolled in 2016, 1,156 applied for aid, 1,094 were judged to have need, 186 had their need fully met. 394 Federal Work-Study jobs (averaging $1000). In 2016, 177 non-need-based awards were made. *Average percent of need met:* 77. *Average financial aid package:* $24,239. *Average need-based loan:* $5331. *Average need-based gift aid:* $19,222. *Average non-need-based aid:* $13,018. *Average indebtedness upon graduation:* $33,490.

APPLYING
Standardized Tests *Required:* SAT or ACT (for admission).

Options: electronic application, early admission, deferred entrance.

Required: high school transcript, minimum 2.0 GPA. *Recommended:* essay or personal statement, minimum 3.0 GPA, 1 letter of recommendation, interview.

Application deadlines: 6/1 (freshmen), 8/1 (transfers).

Notification: continuous (freshmen), continuous (transfers).

CONTACT
Mrs. Beth DaLonzo, Senior Director of Admission, Muskingum University, 163 Stormont Street, New Concord, OH 43762. *Phone:* 740-826-8137. *Toll-free phone:* 800-752-6082. *Fax:* 740-826-8100. *E-mail:* adminfo@muskingum.edu.

Notre Dame College
South Euclid, Ohio
http://www.notredamecollege.edu/

CONTACT
Mr. David Armstrong, Dean of Admissions, Notre Dame College, 4545 College Road, South Euclid, OH 44121-4293. *Phone:* 216-373-5214. *Toll-free phone:* 877-NDC-OHIO. *Fax:* 216-381-3802. *E-mail:* admissinos@ndc.edu.

Oberlin College
Oberlin, Ohio
http://www.oberlin.edu/

- **Independent** comprehensive, founded 1833
- **Small-town** 440-acre campus with easy access to Cleveland
- **Endowment** $820.3 million
- **Coed** 2,827 undergraduate students, 99% full-time, 58% women, 42% men
- **Very difficult** entrance level, 34% of applicants were admitted

UNDERGRAD STUDENTS
2,793 full-time, 34 part-time. Students come from 52 states and territories; 46 other countries; 94% are from out of state; 5% Black or African American, non-Hispanic/Latino; 8% Hispanic/Latino; 4% Asian, non-Hispanic/Latino; 0.1% Native Hawaiian or other Pacific Islander, non-Hispanic/Latino; 8% Two or more races, non-Hispanic/Latino; 0.8% Race/ethnicity unknown; 10% international; 0.5% transferred in; 93% live on campus.

Freshmen:
Admission: 7,762 applied, 2,617 admitted, 728 enrolled. *Average high school GPA:* 3.6. *Test scores:* SAT evidence-based reading and writing scores over 500: 100%; SAT math scores over 500: 98%; ACT scores over 18: 100%; SAT evidence-based reading and writing scores over 600: 94%; SAT math scores over 600: 85%; ACT scores over 24: 97%; SAT evidence-based reading and writing scores over 700: 44%; SAT math scores over 700: 40%; ACT scores over 30: 64%.
Retention: 91% of full-time freshmen returned.

FACULTY
Total: 381.
Student/faculty ratio: 10:1.

ACADEMICS
Calendar: 4-1-4. *Degrees:* diplomas, bachelor's, master's, and postbachelor's certificates.
Special study options: advanced placement credit, double majors, English as a second language, honors programs, independent study, internships, off-campus study, part-time degree program, services for LD students, student-designed majors, study abroad.
Unusual degree programs: 3-2 engineering with Washington University in St. Louis, Case Western Reserve University, California Institute of Technology, Columbia University.
Computers: 250 computers/terminals are available on campus for general student use. Students can access the following: campus intranet, computer help desk, free student e-mail accounts, online (class) grades, online (class) registration, online (class) schedules. Campuswide network is available. 100% of college-owned or -operated housing units are wired for high-speed Internet access. Wireless service is available via entire campus.
Library: Mudd Center Library plus 3 others. *Books:* 1.4 million (physical), 676,883 (digital/electronic); *Serial titles:* 188,472 (physical). Students can reserve study rooms.

STUDENT LIFE
Housing options: on-campus residence required through senior year; coed, women-only, cooperative, special housing for students with disabilities. Campus housing is university owned. Freshman campus housing is guaranteed.
Activities and organizations: drama/theater group, student-run newspaper, radio station, choral group, Experimental College, Community Outreach, Student Government, Student Cooperative Association, student radio station.

Athletics Member NCAA. All Division III. *Intercollegiate sports:* badminton M(c)/W(c), baseball M, basketball M/W, bowling M(c)/W(c), cross-country running M/W, equestrian sports M(c)/W(c), fencing M(c)/W(c), field hockey W, football M, golf M(c)/W(c), gymnastics M(c)/W(c), ice hockey M(c)/W(c), lacrosse M/W, rugby M(c)/W(c), soccer M/W, softball W, swimming and diving M/W, table tennis M(c)/W(c), tennis M/W, track and field M/W, ultimate Frisbee M(c)/W(c), volleyball W. *Intramural sports:* baseball M/W, basketball M/W, bowling M/W, cross-country running M/W, football M/W, gymnastics M(c)/W(c), racquetball M/W, rock climbing M/W, rugby M, soccer M/W, softball M/W, squash M/W, table tennis M(c)/W, tennis M/W, track and field M/W, volleyball M/W, water polo M/W, weight lifting M/W.
Campus security: 24-hour emergency response devices and patrols, student patrols, late-night transport/escort service, controlled dormitory access, crime prevention programs.
Student services: health clinic, personal/psychological counseling, women's center.

COSTS & FINANCIAL AID
Costs (2017–18) *Comprehensive fee:* $67,862 includes full-time tuition ($52,762), mandatory fees ($698), and room and board ($14,402). Part-time tuition: $2220 per credit. Part-time tuition and fees vary according to course load. *College room only:* $7482. Room and board charges vary according to board plan and housing facility. *Payment plan:* installment. *Waivers:* employees or children of employees.
Financial Aid Of all full-time matriculated undergraduates who enrolled in 2016, 1,596 applied for aid, 1,356 were judged to have need, 1,356 had their need fully met. 600 state and other part-time jobs (averaging $2400). In 2016, 1188 non-need-based awards were made. *Average percent of need met:* 100. *Average financial aid package:* $41,836. *Average need-based loan:* $5102. *Average need-based gift aid:* $37,059. *Average non-need-based aid:* $14,434. *Average indebtedness upon graduation:* $27,114.

APPLYING
Standardized Tests *Required:* SAT or ACT (for admission). *Required for some:* SAT and SAT Subject Tests or ACT (for admission).
Options: electronic application, early admission, early decision, deferred entrance.
Required: essay or personal statement, high school transcript, 2 letters of recommendation. *Required for some:* interview, audition for the Conservatory of Music, detailed portfolio for homeschooled students. *Recommended:* interview.
Application deadlines: 1/15 (freshmen), 3/15 (transfers).
Early decision deadline: 11/15 (for plan 1), 1/2 (for plan 2).
Notification: 4/1 (freshmen), 5/15 (transfers), 12/15 (early decision plan 1), 2/1 (early decision plan 2).

CONTACT
Manuel Carballo, Vice President and Dean of Admissions and Financial Aid, Oberlin College, College of Arts and Sciences Admissions, 38 East College Street, Oberlin, OH 44074. *Phone:* 440-775-8411. *Toll-free phone:* 800-622-OBIE. *Fax:* 440-775-6905. *E-mail:* college.admissions@oberlin.edu.

Ohio Christian University
Circleville, Ohio
http://www.ohiochristian.edu/

- **Independent** comprehensive, founded 1948, affiliated with Churches of Christ in Christian Union
- **Small-town** 40-acre campus with easy access to Columbus
- **Endowment** $4.1 million
- **Coed** 4,213 undergraduate students, 59% full-time, 64% women, 36% men
- **Minimally difficult** entrance level

UNDERGRAD STUDENTS
2,481 full-time, 1,732 part-time. 27% Black or African American, non-Hispanic/Latino; 2% Hispanic/Latino; 0.5% Asian, non-Hispanic/Latino; 0.3% American Indian or Alaska Native, non-Hispanic/Latino; 3% Two or more races, non-Hispanic/Latino; 19% Race/ethnicity unknown; 0.3% international; 7% transferred in; 8% live on campus.

Freshmen:
Admission: 653 enrolled.

FACULTY
Total: 368, 40% full-time, 17% with terminal degrees.
Student/faculty ratio: 12:1.

ACADEMICS
Calendar: semesters. *Degrees:* associate, bachelor's, and master's.

Special study options: academic remediation for entering students, adult/continuing education programs, advanced placement credit, double majors, honors programs, independent study, internships, off-campus study, part-time degree program, services for LD students, student-designed majors, summer session for credit. *ROTC:* Air Force (c).

Computers: 68 computers/terminals are available on campus for general student use. Students can access the following: campus intranet, computer help desk, free student e-mail accounts, online (class) grades, online (class) registration, online (class) schedules. Campuswide network is available. 100% of college-owned or -operated housing units are wired for high-speed Internet access. Wireless service is available via entire campus.

Library: Melvin Maxwell Memorial Library. *Books:* 59,755 (physical), 96,276 (digital/electronic); *Serial titles:* 143 (physical), 6,473 (digital/electronic). Weekly public service hours: 88; students can reserve study rooms.

STUDENT LIFE
Housing options: men-only, women-only. Campus housing is university owned.

Activities and organizations: drama/theater group, choral group.

Athletics Member NAIA. *Intercollegiate sports:* baseball M(s), basketball M(s)/W(s), cross-country running M/W, golf M/W, soccer M, softball W, tennis M/W, volleyball W. *Intramural sports:* basketball M/W, soccer M/W, table tennis M/W, volleyball M/W.

Campus security: controlled dormitory access, security checks after midnight.

Student services: personal/psychological counseling, legal services.

COSTS & FINANCIAL AID
Costs (2017–18) *Comprehensive fee:* $19,597 includes full-time tuition ($10,849), mandatory fees ($1250), and room and board ($7498). Full-time tuition and fees vary according to class time, course load, degree level, location, and program. Part-time tuition and fees vary according to class time, location, and program. *Required fees:* $860 per semester hour part-time. *Room and board:* Room and board charges vary according to board plan. *Waivers:* employees or children of employees.

Financial Aid Of all full-time matriculated undergraduates who enrolled in 2007, 480 applied for aid, 415 were judged to have need, 100 had their need fully met. 50 Federal Work-Study jobs (averaging $1700). In 2007, 80 non-need-based awards were made. *Average percent of need met:* 50. *Average financial aid package:* $9500. *Average need-based loan:* $4500. *Average need-based gift aid:* $4000. *Average non-need-based aid:* $1500. *Average indebtedness upon graduation:* $30,000.

APPLYING
Standardized Tests *Required for some:* ACT (for admission). *Recommended:* SAT (for admission).

Options: electronic application, early admission.

Application fee: $25.

Required: essay or personal statement, high school transcript, 4 letters of recommendation, medical form. *Required for some:* interview.

Application deadlines: rolling (freshmen), rolling (transfers).

Notification: continuous (freshmen), continuous (transfers).

CONTACT
Ohio Christian University, 1476 Lancaster Pike, Circleville, OH 43113. *Phone:* 740-477-7741. *Toll-free phone:* 877-762-8669.

★ Ohio Dominican University

Columbus, Ohio
http://www.ohiodominican.edu/

- **Independent Roman Catholic** comprehensive, founded 1911
- **Urban** 92-acre campus with easy access to Columbus, OH
- **Endowment** $24.1 million
- **Coed** 1,177 undergraduate students, 81% full-time, 55% women, 45% men
- **Moderately difficult** entrance level, 77% of applicants were admitted

UNDERGRAD STUDENTS
957 full-time, 220 part-time. Students come from 27 states and territories; 20 other countries; 5% are from out of state; 22% Black or African American, non-Hispanic/Latino; 4% Hispanic/Latino; 1% Asian, non-Hispanic/Latino; 0.3% American Indian or Alaska Native, non-Hispanic/Latino; 5% Two or more races, non-Hispanic/Latino; 10% Race/ethnicity unknown; 2% international; 7% transferred in; 43% live on campus.

Freshmen:
Admission: 1,238 applied, 956 admitted, 244 enrolled. *Average high school GPA:* 3.3. *Test scores:* SAT evidence-based reading and writing scores over 500: 64%; SAT math scores over 500: 84%; SAT evidence-based reading and writing scores over 600: 32%; SAT math scores over 600: 36%; SAT evidence-based reading and writing scores over 700: 4%; SAT math scores over 700: 4%.
Retention: 62% of full-time freshmen returned.

FACULTY
Total: 169, 36% full-time, 54% with terminal degrees.
Student/faculty ratio: 14:1.

ACADEMICS
Calendar: semesters. *Degrees:* certificates, associate, bachelor's, master's, and postbachelor's certificates.

Special study options: academic remediation for entering students, accelerated degree program, adult/continuing education programs, advanced placement credit, distance learning, double majors, honors programs, independent study, internships, off-campus study, part-time degree program, services for LD students, student-designed majors, study abroad, summer session for credit. *ROTC:* Army (c), Air Force (c).

Unusual degree programs: 3-2 business administration; sport management.

Computers: 350 computers/terminals and 2,300 ports are available on campus for general student use. Students can access the following: campus intranet, computer help desk, free student e-mail accounts, online (class) grades, online (class) registration, online (class) schedules. Campuswide network is available. 100% of college-owned or -operated housing units are wired for high-speed Internet access. Wireless service is available via classrooms, computer centers, computer labs, dorm rooms, learning centers, libraries, student centers.

Library: Ohio Dominican Library. *Books:* 76,769 (physical), 149,371 (digital/electronic); *Serial titles:* 5,325 (physical), 29,438 (digital/electronic); *Databases:* 261. Students can reserve study rooms.

STUDENT LIFE
Housing options: on-campus residence required through sophomore year; coed. Campus housing is university owned. Freshman campus housing is guaranteed.

Activities and organizations: drama/theater group, student-run radio station, choral group, marching band, Panther Activities Council, Student Athletic Advisory Committee, Black Student Union, World Student Club, Panther Players.

Athletics Member NCAA. All Division II except golf (Division I). *Intercollegiate sports:* baseball M(s), basketball M(s)/W(s), cross-country running M(s)/W(s), football M(s), golf M(s)/W(s), soccer M(s)/W(s), softball W(s), track and field M/W, volleyball W(s). *Intramural sports:* basketball M/W, sand volleyball M/W, table tennis M/W, ultimate Frisbee M/W.

Campus security: 24-hour emergency response devices and patrols, late-night transport/escort service, controlled dormitory access.

Student services: health clinic, personal/psychological counseling.

COSTS & FINANCIAL AID

Costs (2018–19) *Comprehensive fee:* $42,028 includes full-time tuition ($30,500), mandatory fees ($580), and room and board ($10,948). Part-time tuition: $720 per credit hour. Part-time tuition and fees vary according to course load. *Required fees:* $175 per term part-time. *Room and board:* Room and board charges vary according to board plan and housing facility. *Payment plan:* installment. *Waivers:* senior citizens and employees or children of employees.

Financial Aid Of all full-time matriculated undergraduates who enrolled in 2016, 200 Federal Work-Study jobs (averaging $2000). *Average percent of need met:* 92. *Average financial aid package:* $12,467. *Average indebtedness upon graduation:* $13,500.

APPLYING

Standardized Tests *Required for some:* SAT or ACT (for admission).

Options: electronic application, deferred entrance.

Required: high school transcript, minimum 2.3 GPA. *Required for some:* essay or personal statement. *Recommended:* interview.

Application deadlines: rolling (freshmen), rolling (out-of-state freshmen), rolling (transfers).

Notification: continuous (freshmen), continuous (out-of-state freshmen), continuous (transfers).

CONTACT

Mr. Michael Halligan, Director of Undergraduate Admissions, Ohio Dominican University, 1216 Sunbury Road, Columbus, OH 43219. *Phone:* 614-251-4500. *Toll-free phone:* 800-955-6446. *Fax:* 614-251-0156. *E-mail:* admissions@ohiodominican.edu.

Ohio Northern University

Ada, Ohio

http://www.onu.edu/

- **Independent** comprehensive, founded 1871, affiliated with United Methodist Church
- **Small-town** 342-acre campus
- **Endowment** $162.0 million
- **Coed** 2,312 undergraduate students, 90% full-time, 44% women, 56% men
- **Moderately difficult** entrance level, 66% of applicants were admitted

UNDERGRAD STUDENTS

2,092 full-time, 220 part-time. Students come from 38 states and territories; 23 other countries; 17% are from out of state; 4% Black or African American, non-Hispanic/Latino; 1% Hispanic/Latino; 2% Asian, non-Hispanic/Latino; 0.1% Native Hawaiian or other Pacific Islander, non-Hispanic/Latino; 0.1% American Indian or Alaska Native, non-Hispanic/Latino; 2% Two or more races, non-Hispanic/Latino; 11% Race/ethnicity unknown; 3% international; 3% transferred in; 75% live on campus.

Freshmen:

Admission: 4,159 applied, 2,749 admitted, 640 enrolled. *Average high school GPA:* 3.7. *Test scores:* SAT evidence-based reading and writing scores over 500: 90%; SAT math scores over 500: 97%; ACT scores over 18: 99%; SAT evidence-based reading and writing scores over 600: 48%; SAT math scores over 600: 53%; ACT scores over 24: 65%; SAT evidence-based reading and writing scores over 700: 6%; SAT math scores over 700: 9%; ACT scores over 30: 14%.

Retention: 82% of full-time freshmen returned.

FACULTY

Total: 286, 78% full-time, 74% with terminal degrees.

Student/faculty ratio: 11:1.

ACADEMICS

Calendar: semesters. *Degrees:* certificates, bachelor's, master's, doctoral, and postbachelor's certificates.

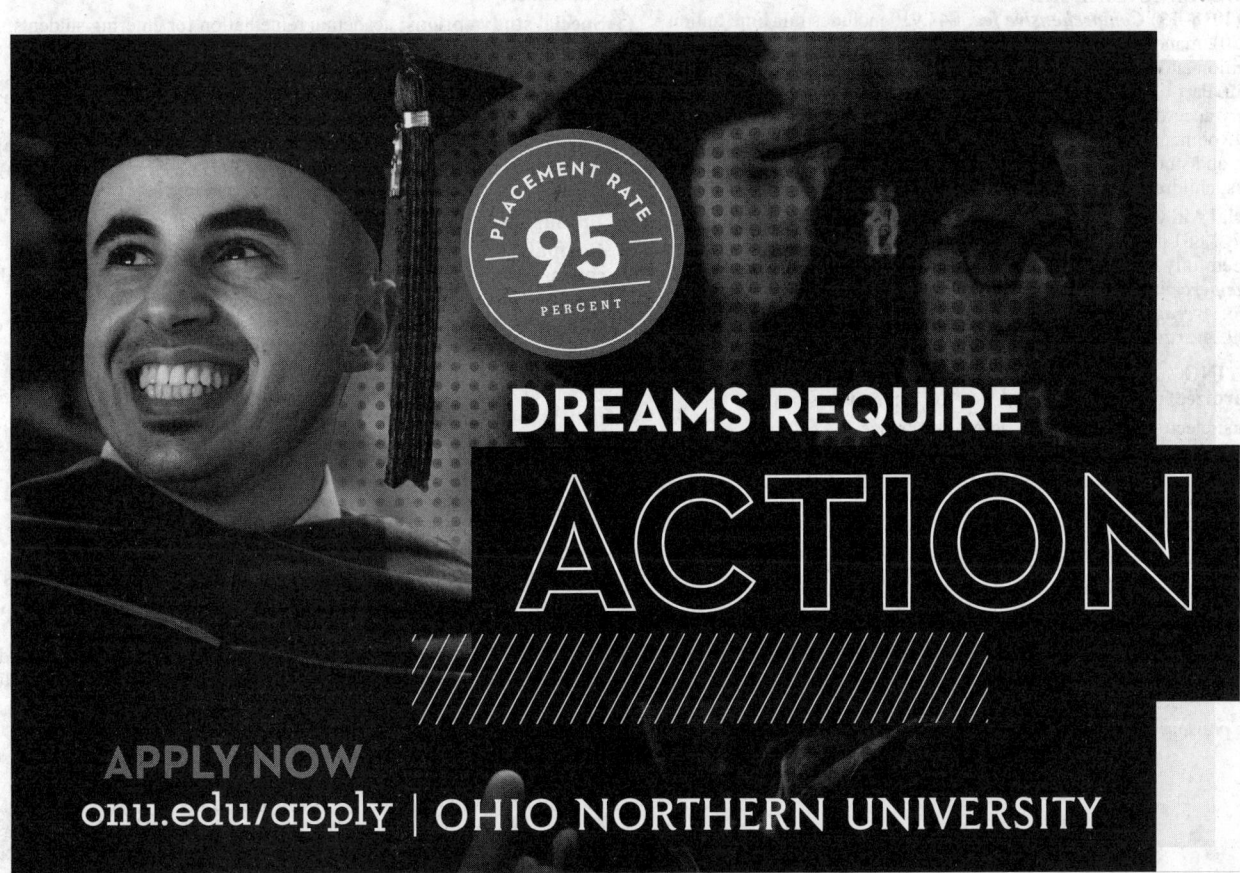

Special study options: academic remediation for entering students, advanced placement credit, cooperative education, distance learning, double majors, English as a second language, honors programs, independent study, internships, off-campus study, part-time degree program, services for LD students, study abroad, summer session for credit. *ROTC:* Army (c), Air Force (c).

Computers: Students can access the following: campus intranet, computer help desk, free student e-mail accounts, online (class) grades, online (class) registration, online (class) schedules. Campuswide network is available. 100% of college-owned or -operated housing units are wired for high-speed Internet access. Wireless service is available via entire campus.

Library: Heterick Memorial Library plus 1 other. Students can reserve study rooms.

STUDENT LIFE

Housing options: on-campus residence required through junior year; coed, men-only, women-only, special housing for students with disabilities. Campus housing is university owned. Freshman campus housing is guaranteed.

Activities and organizations: drama/theater group, student-run newspaper, radio and television station, choral group, marching band, Habitat for Humanity, Student Planning Committee, Student Senate, Northern Christian Fellowship, Marching Band, national fraternities, national sororities.

Athletics Member NCAA. All Division III. *Intercollegiate sports:* baseball M, basketball M/W, cross-country running M/W, football M, golf M/W, lacrosse M/W, soccer M/W, softball W, swimming and diving M/W, tennis M/W, track and field M/W, volleyball W, wrestling M. *Intramural sports:* badminton M/W, basketball M/W, cheerleading M(c)/W(c), fencing M(c)/W(c), ice hockey M(c), rugby M(c)/W(c), soccer M(c)/W(c), softball M/W(c), table tennis M/W, tennis M/W, ultimate Frisbee M(c)/W(c), volleyball M(c)/W, water polo W(c).

Campus security: 24-hour emergency response devices and patrols, controlled dormitory access.

Student services: health clinic, personal/psychological counseling, legal services.

COSTS & FINANCIAL AID

Costs (2018–19) *Comprehensive fee:* $43,910 includes full-time tuition ($31,350), mandatory fees ($910), and room and board ($11,650). Full-time tuition and fees vary according to course load, degree level, and program. Part-time tuition: $1310 per credit hour. Part-time tuition and fees vary according to course load, degree level, and program. *Room and board:* Room and board charges vary according to board plan, housing facility, and student level. *Payment plan:* installment. *Waivers:* minority students, children of alumni, and employees or children of employees.

Financial Aid Of all full-time matriculated undergraduates who enrolled in 2017, 1,881 applied for aid, 1,685 were judged to have need, 384 had their need fully met. In 2017, 343 non-need-based awards were made. *Average percent of need met:* 23. *Average financial aid package:* $27,756. *Average need-based loan:* $5458. *Average need-based gift aid:* $23,399. *Average non-need-based aid:* $14,791.

APPLYING

Standardized Tests *Required:* SAT or ACT (for admission).

Options: electronic application, deferred entrance.

Required: high school transcript. *Required for some:* essay or personal statement, 1 letter of recommendation, interview. *Recommended:* essay or personal statement.

Application deadlines: 8/15 (freshmen), 8/15 (transfers).

Notification: continuous (freshmen), continuous (transfers).

CONTACT

Ms. Deborah Miller, Director of Admissions, Ohio Northern University, 525 South Main Street, Ada, OH 45810-1599. *Phone:* 419-772-2260 Ext. 2464. *Toll-free phone:* 888-408-4ONU. *Fax:* 419-772-2821. *E-mail:* admissions-ug@onu.edu.

See previous page for display ad and page 1374 for the College Close-Up.

The Ohio State University
Columbus, Ohio
http://www.osu.edu/

- **State-supported** university, founded 1870, part of The Ohio State University
- **Urban** 1665-acre campus with easy access to Columbus
- **Endowment** $4.2 billion
- **Coed** 45,946 undergraduate students, 91% full-time, 48% women, 52% men
- **Very difficult** entrance level, 48% of applicants were admitted

UNDERGRAD STUDENTS

42,003 full-time, 3,943 part-time. Students come from 58 states and territories; 69 other countries; 19% are from out of state; 6% Black or African American, non-Hispanic/Latino; 4% Hispanic/Latino; 7% Asian, non-Hispanic/Latino; 0.1% Native Hawaiian or other Pacific Islander, non-Hispanic/Latino; 0.1% American Indian or Alaska Native, non-Hispanic/Latino; 3% Two or more races, non-Hispanic/Latino; 3% Race/ethnicity unknown; 8% international; 6% transferred in; 32% live on campus.

Freshmen:

Admission: 47,782 applied, 22,964 admitted, 7,209 enrolled. *Test scores:* SAT evidence-based reading and writing scores over 500: 99%; SAT math scores over 500: 98%; ACT scores over 18: 99%; SAT evidence-based reading and writing scores over 600: 82%; SAT math scores over 600: 87%; ACT scores over 24: 93%; SAT evidence-based reading and writing scores over 700: 27%; SAT math scores over 700: 52%; ACT scores over 30: 51%.

Retention: 94% of full-time freshmen returned.

FACULTY

Total: 5,589, 71% full-time, 71% with terminal degrees.

Student/faculty ratio: 19:1.

ACADEMICS

Calendar: semesters. *Degrees:* certificates, diplomas, associate, bachelor's, master's, doctoral, post-master's, and postbachelor's certificates.

Special study options: academic remediation for entering students, accelerated degree program, adult/continuing education programs, advanced placement credit, cooperative education, distance learning, double majors, English as a second language, freshman honors college, honors programs, independent study, internships, off-campus study, part-time degree program, services for LD students, student-designed majors, study abroad, summer session for credit. *ROTC:* Army (b), Navy (b), Air Force (b).

Unusual degree programs: 3-2 business administration.

Computers: Students can access the following: campus intranet, computer help desk, free student e-mail accounts, online (class) grades, online (class) registration, online (class) schedules, admission applications, fee payment. Campuswide network is available. 100% of college-owned or -operated housing units are wired for high-speed Internet access. Wireless service is available via entire campus.

Library: William Oxley Thompson Library plus 10 others. *Books:* 5.0 million (physical), 1.3 million (digital/electronic); *Serial titles:* 664,616 (physical), 55,339 (digital/electronic); *Databases:* 2,046. Study areas open 24 hours, 5–7 days a week; students can reserve study rooms.

STUDENT LIFE

Housing options: on-campus residence required through sophomore year; coed, women-only, cooperative, special housing for students with disabilities. Campus housing is university owned. Freshman campus housing is guaranteed.

Activities and organizations: drama/theater group, student-run newspaper, radio and television station, choral group, marching band, Artificial Intelligence Club, International Friendships, Pre-Dental Club of The Ohio State University, Rubik's Cube Club, Smiles With Style, national fraternities, national sororities.

Athletics Member NCAA. All Division I. *Intercollegiate sports:* baseball M(s), basketball M(s)/W(s), cheerleading M(s)/W(s), cross-country running M(s)/W(s), fencing M(s)/W(s), field hockey W(s), football M(s), golf M(s)/W(s), gymnastics M(s)/W(s), ice hockey M(s)/W(s), lacrosse M(s)/W(s), riflery M(s)/W(s), rowing W(s), soccer M(s)/W(s), softball

W(s), swimming and diving M(s)/W(s), tennis M(s)/W(s), track and field M(s)/W(s), volleyball M(s)/W(s), wrestling M(s). *Intramural sports:* archery M(c)/W(c), badminton M(c)/W(c), baseball M(c), basketball M(c)/W(c), bowling M(c)/W(c), cheerleading W(c), crew M(c)/W(c), equestrian sports M(c)/W(c), fencing M(c)/W(c), field hockey M(c)/W, football M(c)/W, golf M(c)/W(c), gymnastics M(c)/W(c), ice hockey M(c)/W(c), lacrosse M(c)/W(c), racquetball M(c)/W(c), rugby M(c)/W(c), sailing M(c)/W(c), sand volleyball M/W, skiing (downhill) M(c)/W(c), soccer M(c)/W(c), softball M/W(c), squash M(c)/W(c), swimming and diving M(c)/W(c), table tennis M/W, tennis M/W, triathlon M(c)/W(c), ultimate Frisbee M(c)/W(c), volleyball M(c)/W(c), water polo M(c)/W(c).

Campus security: 24-hour emergency response devices and patrols, student patrols, late-night transport/escort service, controlled dormitory access, dorm entrances locked 24-hrs a day, lighted pathways and sidewalks, self-defense education.

Student services: health clinic, personal/psychological counseling, legal services.

COSTS & FINANCIAL AID

Costs (2017–18) *Tuition:* state resident $10,591 full-time, $480 per credit hour part-time; nonresident $29,695 full-time, $1276 per credit hour part-time. Full-time tuition and fees vary according to course load, degree level, location, program, reciprocity agreements, and student level. Part-time tuition and fees vary according to course load, degree level, location, program, reciprocity agreements, and student level. No tuition increase for student's term of enrollment. *Room and board:* $12,252. Room and board charges vary according to board plan, housing facility, and location. *Payment plan:* installment. *Waivers:* senior citizens and employees or children of employees.

Financial Aid Of all full-time matriculated undergraduates who enrolled in 2017, 27,918 applied for aid, 19,942 were judged to have need, 3,778 had their need fully met. 1,821 Federal Work-Study jobs (averaging $2889). 1 state and other part-time job (averaging $2500). In 2017, 8114 non-need-based awards were made. *Average percent of need met:* 70. *Average financial aid package:* $13,960. *Average need-based loan:* $4767. *Average need-based gift aid:* $10,325. *Average non-need-based aid:* $7189. *Average indebtedness upon graduation:* $28,158.

APPLYING

Standardized Tests *Required:* SAT or ACT (for admission).

Options: electronic application, early action, deferred entrance.

Application fee: $60.

Required: essay or personal statement, high school transcript.

Application deadlines: 2/1 (freshmen), 5/1 (transfers), 11/1 (early action).

Notification: 3/31 (freshmen), continuous (transfers), 1/15 (early action).

CONTACT

The Ohio State University, Student Academic Services Building, 281 West Lane Avenue, Columbus, OH 43210. *Phone:* 614-292-3980. *Fax:* 614-292-4818. *E-mail:* askabuckeye@osu.edu.

The Ohio State University at Lima

Lima, Ohio

http://lima.osu.edu/

- **State-supported** comprehensive, founded 1960, part of The Ohio State University
- **Suburban** 562-acre campus
- **Endowment** $5.1 million
- **Coed** 1,007 undergraduate students, 84% full-time, 57% women, 43% men
- **Noncompetitive** entrance level, 99% of applicants were admitted

UNDERGRAD STUDENTS

844 full-time, 163 part-time. Students come from 8 states and territories; 1 other country; 0.8% are from out of state; 5% Black or African American, non-Hispanic/Latino; 4% Hispanic/Latino; 2% Asian, non-Hispanic/Latino; 4% Two or more races, non-Hispanic/Latino; 3% Race/ethnicity unknown; 0.2% international; 6% transferred in.

Freshmen:

Admission: 1,294 applied, 1,282 admitted, 325 enrolled. *Test scores:* SAT evidence-based reading and writing scores over 500: 80%; SAT math scores over 500: 80%; ACT scores over 18: 91%; SAT evidence-based reading and writing scores over 600: 20%; SAT math scores over 600: 40%; ACT scores over 24: 42%; ACT scores over 30: 3%.

Retention: 65% of full-time freshmen returned.

FACULTY

Total: 79, 41% full-time.

Student/faculty ratio: 19:1.

ACADEMICS

Calendar: semesters. *Degrees:* associate, bachelor's, and master's.

Special study options: academic remediation for entering students, accelerated degree program, adult/continuing education programs, advanced placement credit, cooperative education, distance learning, double majors, English as a second language, freshman honors college, honors programs, independent study, internships, off-campus study, part-time degree program, services for LD students, student-designed majors, study abroad, summer session for credit.

Computers: Students can access the following: campus intranet, computer help desk, free student e-mail accounts, online (class) grades, online (class) registration, online (class) schedules. Campuswide network is available. 100% of college-owned or -operated housing units are wired for high-speed Internet access. Wireless service is available via entire campus.

Library: Lima Campus Library. *Books:* 69,584 (physical), 1.3 million (digital/electronic); *Serial titles:* 50 (physical), 55,339 (digital/electronic); *Databases:* 2,046. Weekly public service hours: 57; students can reserve study rooms.

STUDENT LIFE

Housing options: college housing not available.

Activities and organizations: drama/theater group, choral group, United Way Club, Campus Activities Board, Nert Club, Student Senate, Psych Club.

Athletics *Intercollegiate sports:* baseball M(c), basketball M(c)/W(c), golf M(c)/W(c), volleyball W(c). *Intramural sports:* basketball M/W, bowling M/W, football M/W, soccer M/W, ultimate Frisbee M/W, volleyball M/W.

Campus security: 24-hour emergency response devices and patrols, student patrols, late-night transport/escort service, lighted pathways/sidewalks.

Student services: personal/psychological counseling.

COSTS

Costs (2017–18) *Tuition:* state resident $7553 full-time, $315 per credit hour part-time; nonresident $26,657 full-time, $1111 per credit hour part-time. Full-time tuition and fees vary according to course load, location, program, reciprocity agreements, and student level. Part-time tuition and fees vary according to course load, location, program, reciprocity agreements, and student level. No tuition increase for student's term of enrollment. *Payment plan:* installment. *Waivers:* senior citizens and employees or children of employees.

APPLYING

Standardized Tests *Required for some:* SAT or ACT (for admission).

Options: electronic application.

Application fee: $60.

Required: high school transcript.

Application deadlines: 6/1 (freshmen), 6/1 (transfers).

Notification: continuous (freshmen), continuous (transfers).

CONTACT

The Ohio State University at Lima, OH. *Phone:* 419-995-8434. *Fax:* 419-995-8483. *E-mail:* askabuckeye@osu.edu.

The Ohio State University at Mansfield
Mansfield, Ohio
http://www.mansfield.osu.edu/

- **State-supported** comprehensive, founded 1958, part of The Ohio State University
- **Small-town** 620-acre campus with easy access to Columbus, Cleveland
- **Endowment** $2.3 million
- **Coed** 1,189 undergraduate students, 83% full-time, 54% women, 46% men
- **Noncompetitive** entrance level, 99% of applicants were admitted

UNDERGRAD STUDENTS
990 full-time, 199 part-time. Students come from 8 states and territories; 3 other countries; 1% are from out of state; 11% Black or African American, non-Hispanic/Latino; 3% Hispanic/Latino; 2% Asian, non-Hispanic/Latino; 0.1% American Indian or Alaska Native, non-Hispanic/Latino; 3% Two or more races, non-Hispanic/Latino; 2% Race/ethnicity unknown; 4% transferred in; 17% live on campus.

Freshmen:
Admission: 1,607 applied, 1,595 admitted, 522 enrolled. *Test scores:* ACT scores over 18: 86%; ACT scores over 24: 40%; ACT scores over 30: 3%.
Retention: 69% of full-time freshmen returned.

FACULTY
Total: 92, 41% full-time.
Student/faculty ratio: 19:1.

ACADEMICS
Calendar: semesters. *Degrees:* associate and bachelor's.

Special study options: academic remediation for entering students, adult/continuing education programs, advanced placement credit, cooperative education, distance learning, double majors, English as a second language, freshman honors college, honors programs, independent study, internships, off-campus study, part-time degree program, services for LD students, student-designed majors, study abroad, summer session for credit. *ROTC:* Army (c), Navy (c), Air Force (c).

Computers: Students can access the following: campus intranet, computer help desk, free student e-mail accounts, online (class) grades, online (class) registration, online (class) schedules. Campuswide network is available. 100% of college-owned or -operated housing units are wired for high-speed Internet access. Wireless service is available via entire campus.
Library: Bromfield Library & Information Commons. *Books:* 43,140 (physical), 1.3 million (digital/electronic); *Serial titles:* 55,339 (digital/electronic); *Databases:* 2,046. Weekly public service hours: 63; students can reserve study rooms.

STUDENT LIFE
Housing options: coed, special housing for students with disabilities. Campus housing is university owned. Freshman applicants given priority for college housing.

Activities and organizations: drama/theater group, choral group, Campus Activities Board, Best Buddies, Awakening, College Democrats, College Republicans.

Athletics *Intercollegiate sports:* baseball M(c), basketball M(c)/W(c), volleyball W(c). *Intramural sports:* baseball M, basketball M/W, cheerleading M(c)/W(c), football M/W, soccer M/W, tennis M/W, volleyball M/W.

Campus security: 24-hour emergency response devices and patrols.
Student services: personal/psychological counseling.

COSTS
Costs (2017–18) *Tuition:* state resident $7553 full-time, $315 per credit hour part-time; nonresident $26,657 full-time, $1111 per credit hour part-time. Full-time tuition and fees vary according to course load, location, program, reciprocity agreements, and student level. Part-time tuition and fees vary according to course load, location, program, reciprocity agreements, and student level. No tuition increase for student's term of enrollment. *Room and board:* $7976; room only: $6328. Room and board charges vary according to board plan, housing facility, and location.

Payment plan: installment. **Waivers:** senior citizens and employees or children of employees.

APPLYING
Standardized Tests *Required for some:* SAT or ACT (for admission).
Options: electronic application.
Application fee: $60.
Required: high school transcript.
Application deadlines: 6/1 (freshmen), 6/1 (transfers).
Notification: continuous (freshmen), continuous (transfers).

CONTACT
The Ohio State University at Mansfield, OH. *Phone:* 419-755-4224. *E-mail:* askabuckeye@osu.edu.

The Ohio State University at Marion
Marion, Ohio
http://osumarion.osu.edu/

- **State-supported** comprehensive, founded 1958, part of The Ohio State University
- **Small-town** 188-acre campus with easy access to Columbus
- **Endowment** $5.2 million
- **Coed** 1,198 undergraduate students, 82% full-time, 52% women, 48% men
- **Noncompetitive** entrance level, 99% of applicants were admitted

UNDERGRAD STUDENTS
978 full-time, 220 part-time. Students come from 6 states and territories; 3 other countries; 0.5% are from out of state; 4% Black or African American, non-Hispanic/Latino; 4% Hispanic/Latino; 4% Asian, non-Hispanic/Latino; 0.1% Native Hawaiian or other Pacific Islander, non-Hispanic/Latino; 0.5% American Indian or Alaska Native, non-Hispanic/Latino; 3% Two or more races, non-Hispanic/Latino; 3% Race/ethnicity unknown; 0.4% international; 4% transferred in.

Freshmen:
Admission: 1,025 applied, 1,012 admitted, 437 enrolled. *Test scores:* SAT evidence-based reading and writing scores over 500: 93%; SAT math scores over 500: 90%; ACT scores over 18: 88%; SAT evidence-based reading and writing scores over 600: 52%; SAT math scores over 600: 48%; ACT scores over 24: 39%; SAT evidence-based reading and writing scores over 700: 7%; SAT math scores over 700: 10%; ACT scores over 30: 2%.
Retention: 70% of full-time freshmen returned.

FACULTY
Total: 94, 38% full-time.
Student/faculty ratio: 19:1.

ACADEMICS
Calendar: semesters. *Degrees:* associate and bachelor's.

Special study options: academic remediation for entering students, adult/continuing education programs, advanced placement credit, cooperative education, distance learning, double majors, English as a second language, freshman honors college, honors programs, independent study, internships, off-campus study, part-time degree program, services for LD students, student-designed majors, study abroad, summer session for credit. *ROTC:* Air Force (c).

Computers: Students can access the following: campus intranet, computer help desk, free student e-mail accounts, online (class) grades, online (class) registration, online (class) schedules. Campuswide network is available. Wireless service is available via classrooms, libraries.
Library: Marion Campus Library. *Books:* 46,288 (physical), 1.3 million (digital/electronic); *Serial titles:* 4,903 (physical), 55,339 (digital/electronic); *Databases:* 2,046. Weekly public service hours: 57; students can reserve study rooms.

STUDENT LIFE
Housing options: college housing not available.

Activities and organizations: drama/theater group, choral group.

Athletics Member USCAA. *Intramural sports:* volleyball M/W.
Campus security: 24-hour emergency response devices.
Student services: personal/psychological counseling.

COSTS

Costs (2017–18) *Tuition:* state resident $7553 full-time, $315 per credit hour part-time; nonresident $26,657 full-time, $1111 per credit hour part-time. Full-time tuition and fees vary according to course load, location, program, reciprocity agreements, and student level. Part-time tuition and fees vary according to course load, location, program, reciprocity agreements, and student level. No tuition increase for student's term of enrollment. *Payment plan:* installment. *Waivers:* senior citizens and employees or children of employees.

APPLYING

Standardized Tests *Required for some:* SAT or ACT (for admission).

Options: electronic application.

Application fee: $60.

Required: high school transcript.

Application deadlines: 6/1 (freshmen), 6/1 (transfers).

Notification: continuous (freshmen), continuous (transfers).

CONTACT

Mr. Mathieu Moreau, Admissions and Financial Aid Coordinator, The Ohio State University at Marion, 1461 Mount Vernon Avenue, Marion, OH 43302. *Phone:* 740-725-6389. *E-mail:* moreau.1@osu.edu.

The Ohio State University at Newark
Newark, Ohio
http://www.newark.osu.edu/

- **State-supported** comprehensive, founded 1957, part of The Ohio State University
- **Small-town** 111-acre campus with easy access to Columbus
- **Endowment** $3.8 million
- **Coed** 2,607 undergraduate students, 85% full-time, 50% women, 50% men
- **Noncompetitive** entrance level, 99% of applicants were admitted

UNDERGRAD STUDENTS

2,218 full-time, 389 part-time. Students come from 9 states and territories; 2 other countries; 0.6% are from out of state; 15% Black or African American, non-Hispanic/Latino; 3% Hispanic/Latino; 4% Asian, non-Hispanic/Latino; 0.2% American Indian or Alaska Native, non-Hispanic/Latino; 4% Two or more races, non-Hispanic/Latino; 4% Race/ethnicity unknown; 0.1% international; 4% transferred in; 12% live on campus.

Freshmen:
Admission: 3,665 applied, 3,632 admitted, 1,369 enrolled. *Test scores:* SAT evidence-based reading and writing scores over 500: 79%; SAT math scores over 500: 81%; ACT scores over 18: 87%; SAT evidence-based reading and writing scores over 600: 32%; SAT math scores over 600: 27%; ACT scores over 24: 37%; SAT evidence-based reading and writing scores over 700: 2%; SAT math scores over 700: 2%; ACT scores over 30: 2%.

Retention: 68% of full-time freshmen returned.

FACULTY

Total: 158, 30% full-time.

Student/faculty ratio: 28:1.

ACADEMICS

Calendar: semesters. *Degrees:* associate, bachelor's, and master's.

Special study options: academic remediation for entering students, adult/continuing education programs, advanced placement credit, cooperative education, distance learning, double majors, English as a second language, freshman honors college, honors programs, independent study, internships, off-campus study, part-time degree program, services for LD students, student-designed majors, study abroad, summer session for credit. *ROTC:* Army (b), Air Force (c).

Computers: Students can access the following: campus intranet, computer help desk, free student e-mail accounts, online (class) grades, online (class) registration, online (class) schedules. Campuswide network is available. 100% of college-owned or -operated housing units are wired for high-speed Internet access. Wireless service is available via entire campus.

Library: John L. and Christine Warner library. Weekly public service hours: 69; students can reserve study rooms.

STUDENT LIFE

Housing options: coed, special housing for students with disabilities. Campus housing is university owned. Freshman applicants given priority for college housing.

Activities and organizations: drama/theater group, choral group, Campus Activities Board, Ebonye Horizons, Journay Campus Ministry, Collegiate 4 - H, American Sign Language.

Athletics *Intramural sports:* badminton M/W, basketball M/W, football M/W, golf M/W, soccer M/W, softball M/W, table tennis M(c)/W(c), volleyball M/W, weight lifting M/W.

Campus security: 24-hour emergency response devices and patrols, late-night transport/escort service, self-defense education.

Student services: personal/psychological counseling, legal services.

COSTS

Costs (2017–18) *Tuition:* state resident $7553 full-time, $315 per credit hour part-time; nonresident $26,657 full-time, $1111 per credit hour part-time. Full-time tuition and fees vary according to course load, location, program, reciprocity agreements, and student level. Part-time tuition and fees vary according to course load, location, program, reciprocity agreements, and student level. No tuition increase for student's term of enrollment. *Room and board:* $9132; room only: $7484. Room and board charges vary according to board plan, housing facility, and location. *Payment plan:* installment. *Waivers:* senior citizens and employees or children of employees.

APPLYING

Standardized Tests *Required for some:* SAT or ACT (for admission).

Options: electronic application.

Application fee: $60.

Required: high school transcript.

Application deadlines: 6/1 (freshmen), 6/1 (transfers).

Notification: continuous (freshmen), continuous (transfers).

CONTACT

Ms. Diane Kanney, Director of Enrollment, The Ohio State University at Newark, 1179 University Drive, Newark, OH 43055. *Phone:* 740-366-9333. *E-mail:* kanney.24@osu.edu.

Ohio University
Athens, Ohio
http://www.ohio.edu/

- **State-supported** university, founded 1804, part of Ohio Board of Regents
- **Small-town** 1800-acre campus
- **Endowment** $536.2 million
- **Coed** 23,323 undergraduate students, 76% full-time, 60% women, 40% men
- **Moderately difficult** entrance level, 74% of applicants were admitted

UNDERGRAD STUDENTS

17,802 full-time, 5,521 part-time. Students come from 44 states and territories; 72 other countries; 15% are from out of state; 6% Black or African American, non-Hispanic/Latino; 3% Hispanic/Latino; 1% Asian, non-Hispanic/Latino; 0.1% Native Hawaiian or other Pacific Islander, non-Hispanic/Latino; 0.2% American Indian or Alaska Native, non-Hispanic/Latino; 3% Two or more races, non-Hispanic/Latino; 2% Race/ethnicity unknown; 2% international; 2% transferred in; 40% live on campus.

Freshmen:
Admission: 26,263 applied, 19,416 admitted, 4,056 enrolled. *Average high school GPA:* 3.5. *Test scores:* SAT evidence-based reading and writing scores over 500: 91%; SAT math scores over 500: 90%; ACT scores over 18: 99%; SAT evidence-based reading and writing scores over 600: 48%; SAT math scores over 600: 38%; ACT scores over 24: 54%; SAT evidence-based reading and writing scores over 700: 6%; SAT math scores over 700: 5%; ACT scores over 30: 8%.

Retention: 80% of full-time freshmen returned.

FACULTY

Total: 1,370, 73% full-time, 65% with terminal degrees.

Student/faculty ratio: 17:1.

ACADEMICS

Calendar: semesters. *Degrees:* certificates, associate, bachelor's, master's, and doctoral.

Special study options: academic remediation for entering students, accelerated degree program, adult/continuing education programs, advanced placement credit, cooperative education, distance learning, double majors, English as a second language, external degree program, freshman honors college, honors programs, independent study, internships, off-campus study, part-time degree program, services for LD students, student-designed majors, study abroad, summer session for credit. *ROTC:* Army (b), Air Force (b).

Computers: 1,000 computers/terminals and 22,000 ports are available on campus for general student use. Students can access the following: campus intranet, computer help desk, free student e-mail accounts, online (class) grades, online (class) registration, online (class) schedules. Campuswide network is available. 100% of college-owned or -operated housing units are wired for high-speed Internet access. Wireless service is available via entire campus.

Library: Alden Library plus 3 others. *Books:* 2.3 million (physical), 1.1 million (digital/electronic); *Serial titles:* 72,438 (physical), 81,627 (digital/electronic); *Databases:* 545. Weekly public service hours: 146; study areas open 24 hours, 5–7 days a week; students can reserve study rooms.

STUDENT LIFE

Housing options: on-campus residence required through sophomore year; coed, women-only, special housing for students with disabilities. Campus housing is university owned. Freshman campus housing is guaranteed.

Activities and organizations: drama/theater group, student-run newspaper, radio and television station, choral group, marching band, Student Senate, Student Alumni Board, International Student Union, University Program Council, Black Student Cultural Programming Board, national fraternities, national sororities.

Athletics Member NCAA. All Division I except football (Division I-A). *Intercollegiate sports:* baseball M(s), basketball M(s)/W(s), cheerleading M/W, cross-country running M(s)/W(s), field hockey W(s), golf M(s)/W(s), ice hockey M(c), soccer W(s), softball W(s), swimming and diving W(s), track and field W(s), volleyball W(s), wrestling M(s). *Intramural sports:* archery M(c)/W(c), badminton M/W, baseball M(c), basketball M/W, bowling M/W, crew M(c)/W(c), equestrian sports M(c)/W(c), fencing M(c)/W(c), golf M(c)/W(c), gymnastics M(c)/W(c), lacrosse M(c)/W(c), racquetball M/W, rugby M(c)/W(c), soccer M(c)/W(c), softball M(c)/W(c), swimming and diving M(c)/W(c), tennis M/W, ultimate Frisbee M/W(c), volleyball M(c)/W(c), water polo M(c)/W(c).

Campus security: 24-hour emergency response devices and patrols, student patrols, late-night transport/escort service, controlled dormitory access, electronic access to some dorms; fully sworn, 24/7 police department.

Student services: health clinic, personal/psychological counseling, women's center, legal services.

COSTS & FINANCIAL AID

Costs (2017–18) *Tuition:* state resident $11,896 full-time, $563 per semester hour part-time; nonresident $21,360 full-time, $1029 per semester hour part-time. Full-time tuition and fees vary according to degree level, location, program, and reciprocity agreements. Part-time tuition and fees vary according to course load, degree level, location, program, and reciprocity agreements. No tuition increase for student's term of enrollment. *Room and board:* $11,498; room only: $6822. Room and board charges vary according to board plan. *Payment plan:* installment. *Waivers:* senior citizens and employees or children of employees.

Financial Aid Of all full-time matriculated undergraduates who enrolled in 2017, 12,550 applied for aid, 10,100 were judged to have need, 3,630 had their need fully met. 681 Federal Work-Study jobs (averaging $1839). In 2017, 1583 non-need-based awards were made. *Average percent of need met:* 48. *Average financial aid package:* $8870. *Average need-based loan:* $3064. *Average need-based gift aid:* $6200. *Average non-need-based aid:* $4432. *Average indebtedness upon graduation:* $27,993.

APPLYING

Standardized Tests *Required:* SAT or ACT (for admission).

Options: electronic application, early admission, early action, deferred entrance.

Application fee: $50.

Required for some: essay or personal statement, high school transcript, 2 letters of recommendation, audition for music and dance and portfolio, advising for visual communications, interview for Honors Tutorial College. *Recommended:* 2 letters of recommendation.

Application deadlines: 12/1 (freshmen), 6/15 (transfers), 12/1 (early action).

Notification: continuous (freshmen), continuous (transfers), rolling (early action).

CONTACT

Undergraduate Admissions, Ohio University, Athens, OH 45701-2979. *Phone:* 740-593-4100. *Fax:* 740-593-0560. *E-mail:* admissions@ohio.edu.

Ohio University–Chillicothe

Chillicothe, Ohio

http://www.chillicothe.ohiou.edu/

CONTACT

Neeley Allen, Coordinator, Recruitment, Ohio University–Chillicothe, 101 University Drive, Chillicothe, OH 45601. *Phone:* 740-774-7241. *Toll-free phone:* 877-462-6824. *Fax:* 740-774-7214. *E-mail:* evelandt@ohio.edu.

Ohio University–Eastern

St. Clairsville, Ohio

http://www.eastern.ohiou.edu/

- **State-supported** comprehensive, founded 1957, part of Ohio Board of Regents
- **Rural** 300-acre campus
- **Coed**
- **Noncompetitive** entrance level

ACADEMICS

Calendar: semesters. *Degrees:* associate, bachelor's, and master's (also offers some graduate courses).

Library: The Library and Learning Commons. Weekly public service hours: 75; students can reserve study rooms.

STUDENT LIFE

Housing options: college housing not available.

Activities and organizations: drama/theater group.

Campus security: late-night transport/escort service.

Student services: personal/psychological counseling.

COSTS & FINANCIAL AID

Costs (2017–18) *Tuition:* state resident $4984 full-time, $219 per credit hour part-time; nonresident $6652 full-time, $305 per credit hour part-time. Full-time tuition and fees vary according to course load, location, program, reciprocity agreements, and student level. Part-time tuition and fees vary according to course load, location, program, reciprocity agreements, and student level. *Required fees:* $66 full-time, $3 per credit hour part-time.

Financial Aid Of all full-time matriculated undergraduates who enrolled in 2017, 243 applied for aid, 193 were judged to have need, 25 had their need fully met. 11 Federal Work-Study jobs (averaging $1467). *Average percent of need met:* 42. *Average financial aid package:* $6031. *Average need-based loan:* $3025. *Average need-based gift aid:* $4637. *Average indebtedness upon graduation:* $27,993.

APPLYING

Options: electronic application, early admission, deferred entrance.

Application fee: $20.

Required: high school transcript.

CONTACT

Ms. Lisa Jeffries, Recruitment Coordinator, Ohio University–Eastern, 45425 National Road, St. Clairsville, OH 43950-9724. *Phone:* 740-699-2504. *Toll-free phone:* 800-648-3331. *E-mail:* jeffriee@ohio.edu.

Ohio University–Lancaster

Lancaster, Ohio

http://www.ohiou.edu/lancaster/

CONTACT
Pat Fox, Enrollment Manager, Ohio University–Lancaster, 1570 Granville Pike, Lancaster, OH 43130-1097. *Phone:* 740-654-6711 Ext. 215. *Toll-free phone:* 888-446-4468. *E-mail:* fox@ohio.edu.

Ohio University–Southern Campus

Ironton, Ohio

http://www.ohiou.edu/

CONTACT
Linda Harlow, Admission, Registration and Records Coordinator, Ohio University–Southern Campus, 1804 Liberty Avenue, Ironton, OH 45638-2214. *Phone:* 740-533-4584. *Toll-free phone:* 800-626-0513. *E-mail:* harlow@ohio.edu.

Ohio University–Zanesville

Zanesville, Ohio

http://www.ohio.edu/zanesville/

- **State-supported** 4-year, founded 1946
- **Rural** 179-acre campus with easy access to Columbus
- **Coed** 1,878 undergraduate students, 74% full-time, 70% women, 30% men
- **Noncompetitive** entrance level, 90% of applicants were admitted

UNDERGRAD STUDENTS
1,388 full-time, 490 part-time. 1% are from out of state; 3% Black or African American, non-Hispanic/Latino; 1% Hispanic/Latino; 0.6% Asian, non-Hispanic/Latino; 0.3% American Indian or Alaska Native, non-Hispanic/Latino; 4% Two or more races, non-Hispanic/Latino; 2% Race/ethnicity unknown; 0.6% international.

Freshmen:
Admission: 468 applied, 421 admitted, 228 enrolled.

FACULTY
Total: 130, 24% full-time, 25% with terminal degrees.
Student/faculty ratio: 18:1.

ACADEMICS
Calendar: semesters. *Degrees:* associate and bachelor's (offers first 2 years of most bachelor's degree programs available at the main campus in Athens; also offers several bachelor's degree programs that can be completed at this campus; also offers some graduate courses).
Special study options: academic remediation for entering students, accelerated degree program, adult/continuing education programs, advanced placement credit, distance learning, double majors, external degree program, independent study, off-campus study, part-time degree program, services for LD students, student-designed majors, study abroad, summer session for credit.
Computers: 200 computers/terminals are available on campus for general student use. Students can access the following: computer help desk, free student e-mail accounts, online (class) grades, online (class) registration, online (class) schedules. Campuswide network is available. Wireless service is available via entire campus.
Library: Zanesville Campus Library plus 1 other. Students can reserve study rooms.

STUDENT LIFE
Housing options: college housing not available.
Activities and organizations: student-run radio station, Student Senate, Student Nurses Association, Good Intentions Group, Green Bobcats, Habitat for Humanity Club.
Athletics *Intercollegiate sports:* baseball M, basketball M/W, softball W.
Campus security: student patrols, late-night transport/escort service, night security.
Student services: personal/psychological counseling, legal services.

COSTS & FINANCIAL AID
Costs (2017–18) *Tuition:* state resident $4984 full-time, $234 per semester hour part-time; nonresident $8624 full-time, $413 per semester hour part-time. Full-time tuition and fees vary according to course load and student level. Part-time tuition and fees vary according to course load and student level. *Required fees:* $92 full-time. *Payment plan:* installment. *Waivers:* senior citizens and employees or children of employees.
Financial Aid Of all full-time matriculated undergraduates who enrolled in 2017, 633 applied for aid, 513 were judged to have need, 73 had their need fully met. 8 Federal Work-Study jobs (averaging $1579). *Average percent of need met:* 43. *Average financial aid package:* $5805. *Average need-based loan:* $2911. *Average need-based gift aid:* $4478. *Average indebtedness upon graduation:* $27,993.

APPLYING
Standardized Tests *Required for some:* SAT or ACT (for admission).
Options: electronic application.
Application fee: $20.
Required: high school transcript.
Application deadlines: rolling (freshmen), rolling (transfers).

CONTACT
Ohio University–Zanesville, Office of Student Services, 1425 Newark Road, Zanesville, OH 43701. *Phone:* 740-588-1440. *Fax:* 740-588-1444. *E-mail:* ouzservices@ohio.edu.

Ohio Wesleyan University

Delaware, Ohio

http://www.owu.edu/

- **Independent United Methodist** 4-year, founded 1842
- **Small-town** 200-acre campus with easy access to Columbus
- **Coed** 1,565 undergraduate students, 99% full-time, 53% women, 47% men
- **Very difficult** entrance level, 71% of applicants were admitted

UNDERGRAD STUDENTS
1,550 full-time, 15 part-time. 54% are from out of state; 10% Black or African American, non-Hispanic/Latino; 6% Hispanic/Latino; 3% Asian, non-Hispanic/Latino; 0.1% Native Hawaiian or other Pacific Islander, non-Hispanic/Latino; 0.1% American Indian or Alaska Native, non-Hispanic/Latino; 5% Two or more races, non-Hispanic/Latino; 2% Race/ethnicity unknown; 5% international; 2% transferred in; 86% live on campus.

Freshmen:
Admission: 4,160 applied, 2,970 admitted, 453 enrolled. *Average high school GPA:* 3.4. *Test scores:* SAT evidence-based reading and writing scores over 500: 87%; SAT math scores over 500: 88%; ACT scores over 18: 98%; SAT evidence-based reading and writing scores over 600: 49%; SAT math scores over 600: 39%; ACT scores over 24: 70%; SAT evidence-based reading and writing scores over 700: 7%; SAT math scores over 700: 7%; ACT scores over 30: 17%.
Retention: 78% of full-time freshmen returned.

FACULTY
Total: 208, 66% full-time.
Student/faculty ratio: 9:1.

ACADEMICS
Calendar: semesters. *Degree:* bachelor's.
Special study options: double majors, honors programs, internships, off-campus study, services for LD students, student-designed majors, study abroad, summer session for credit. *ROTC:* Army (c), Air Force (c).
Unusual degree programs: 3-2 engineering with Alfred University, California Institute of Technology, Case Western Reserve University, Polytechnic University, Rensselaer Polytechnic Institute, Washington University in St. Louis.
Computers: Students can access the following: campus intranet, computer help desk, free student e-mail accounts, online (class) grades, online (class) registration, online (class) schedules. Campuswide network is available. 100% of college-owned or -operated housing units are wired

for high-speed Internet access. Wireless service is available via entire campus.

Library: L. A. Beeghly Library.

STUDENT LIFE

Housing options: on-campus residence required through senior year; coed, women-only. Campus housing is university owned. Freshman campus housing is guaranteed.

Activities and organizations: drama/theater group, student-run newspaper, radio station, choral group, national fraternities, national sororities.

Athletics Member NCAA. All Division III. *Intercollegiate sports:* baseball M, basketball M/W, cross-country running M/W, equestrian sports M(c)/W(c), field hockey W, football M, golf M, ice hockey M(c)/W(c), lacrosse M/W, rugby M(c)/W(c), sailing M(c)/W(c), soccer M/W, softball W, swimming and diving M/W, tennis M/W, track and field M/W, ultimate Frisbee M(c)/W(c), volleyball M(c)/W. *Intramural sports:* badminton M/W, basketball M/W, football M/W, golf M/W, lacrosse M/W, racquetball M/W, skiing (cross-country) M/W, skiing (downhill) M/W, soccer M/W, softball M/W, squash M/W, swimming and diving M/W, tennis M/W, track and field M/W, volleyball M/W, water polo M/W.

Campus security: 24-hour emergency response devices and patrols, late-night transport/escort service, controlled dormitory access.

Student services: health clinic, personal/psychological counseling, women's center.

COSTS & FINANCIAL AID

Costs (2018–19) *Comprehensive fee:* $58,170 includes full-time tuition ($45,500), mandatory fees ($240), and room and board ($12,430). Full-time tuition and fees vary according to course load. Part-time tuition: $2720 per credit hour. Part-time tuition and fees vary according to course load. *College room only:* $6800. Room and board charges vary according to board plan and housing facility. *Payment plan:* installment. *Waivers:* employees or children of employees.

Financial Aid Of all full-time matriculated undergraduates who enrolled in 2016, 1,294 applied for aid, 1,156 were judged to have need, 229 had their need fully met. In 2016, 461 non-need-based awards were made. *Average percent of need met:* 79. *Average financial aid package:*

$36,326. *Average need-based loan:* $4850. *Average need-based gift aid:* $30,716. *Average non-need-based aid:* $23,369. *Average indebtedness upon graduation:* $35,221.

APPLYING

Standardized Tests *Required for some:* SAT or ACT (for admission).

Options: electronic application, early admission, early decision, early action, deferred entrance.

Required: essay or personal statement, high school transcript, minimum 2.5 GPA, 1 letter of recommendation. *Recommended:* 2 letters of recommendation, interview.

Application deadlines: 3/1 (freshmen), rolling (transfers), 12/15 (early action).

Early decision deadline: 11/15.

Notification: continuous (freshmen), continuous (out-of-state freshmen), continuous (transfers), 12/1 (early decision), 1/15 (early action).

CONTACT

Ms. Alisha Couch, Director of Admission, Ohio Wesleyan University, 61 South Sandusky Street, Delaware, OH 43015. *Phone:* 740-368-3099. *Toll-free phone:* 800-922-8953. *Fax:* 740-368-3314. *E-mail:* amcouch@owu.edu.

See below for display ad and page 1376 for the College Close-Up.

Otterbein University
Westerville, Ohio
http://www.otterbein.edu/

- **Independent United Methodist** comprehensive, founded 1847
- **Suburban** 142-acre campus with easy access to Columbus
- **Endowment** $91.5 million
- **Coed** 2,480 undergraduate students, 93% full-time, 62% women, 38% men
- **Moderately difficult** entrance level, 76% of applicants were admitted

UNDERGRAD STUDENTS

2,294 full-time, 186 part-time. Students come from 38 states and territories; 8 other countries; 13% are from out of state; 6% Black or

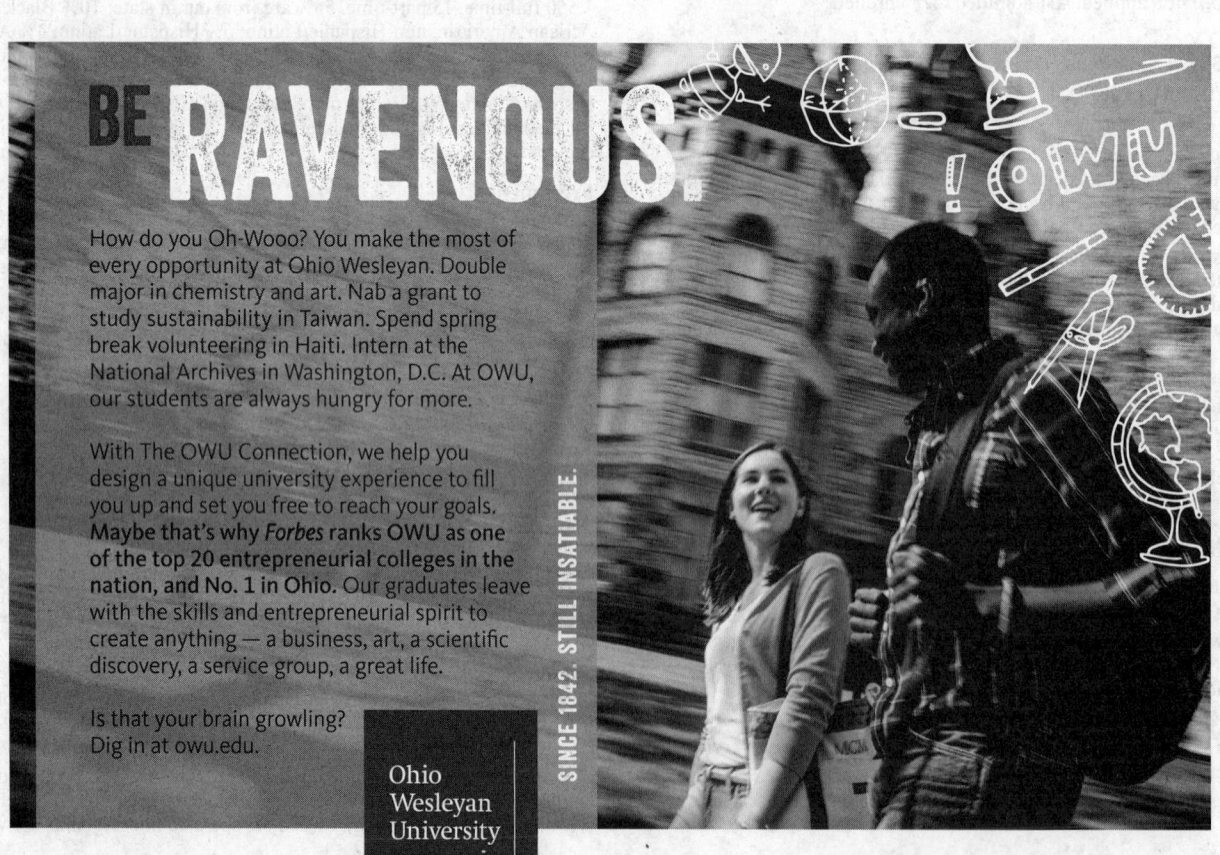

African American, non-Hispanic/Latino; 3% Hispanic/Latino; 2% Asian, non-Hispanic/Latino; 0.3% American Indian or Alaska Native, non-Hispanic/Latino; 5% Two or more races, non-Hispanic/Latino; 5% Race/ethnicity unknown; 2% international; 3% transferred in; 60% live on campus.

Freshmen:
Admission: 3,119 applied, 2,383 admitted, 609 enrolled. *Average high school GPA:* 3.6. *Test scores:* SAT evidence-based reading and writing scores over 500: 84%; SAT math scores over 500: 87%; ACT scores over 18: 97%; SAT evidence-based reading and writing scores over 600: 55%; SAT math scores over 600: 44%; ACT scores over 24: 59%; SAT evidence-based reading and writing scores over 700: 13%; SAT math scores over 700: 8%; ACT scores over 30: 9%.
Retention: 81% of full-time freshmen returned.

FACULTY
Total: 328, 53% full-time, 50% with terminal degrees.
Student/faculty ratio: 12:1.

ACADEMICS
Calendar: semesters. *Degrees:* bachelor's, master's, doctoral, and post-master's certificates.
Special study options: academic remediation for entering students, adult/continuing education programs, advanced placement credit, cooperative education, distance learning, double majors, English as a second language, honors programs, internships, off-campus study, part-time degree program, services for LD students, student-designed majors, study abroad, summer session for credit. *ROTC:* Army (c), Air Force (c).
Computers: 198 computers/terminals are available on campus for general student use. Students can access the following: campus intranet, computer help desk, free student e-mail accounts, online (class) grades, online (class) registration, online (class) schedules. Campuswide network is available. 100% of college-owned or -operated housing units are wired for high-speed Internet access. Wireless service is available via entire campus.
Library: Courtright Memorial Library. *Books:* 281,721 (physical), 243,407 (digital/electronic); *Serial titles:* 15,441 (physical), 7,204 (digital/electronic). Weekly public service hours: 102; students can reserve study rooms.

STUDENT LIFE
Housing options: on-campus residence required through junior year; coed, men-only, women-only. Campus housing is university owned. Freshman campus housing is guaranteed.
Activities and organizations: drama/theater group, student-run newspaper, radio and television station, choral group, marching band, Musical groups, Honoraries, Academic interest clubs, Governance, national fraternities.
Athletics Member NCAA. All Division III. *Intercollegiate sports:* baseball M, basketball M/W, cheerleading M/W, cross-country running M/W, equestrian sports M/W, football M, golf M/W, lacrosse M/W, soccer M/W, softball W, tennis M/W, track and field M/W, volleyball W, wrestling M. *Intramural sports:* basketball M/W, football M, racquetball M/W, soccer M/W, softball M/W, ultimate Frisbee M/W, volleyball M/W, wrestling M.
Campus security: 24-hour emergency response devices and patrols, student patrols, late-night transport/escort service, controlled dormitory access, 24-hour locked residence hall entrances.
Student services: health clinic, personal/psychological counseling.

COSTS & FINANCIAL AID
Costs (2018–19) *Tuition:* $31,424 full-time, $564 per credit hour part-time. *Required fees:* $450 full-time, $250 per year part-time. *Room only:* Room and board charges vary according to board plan and housing facility. *Waivers:* employees or children of employees.
Financial Aid Of all full-time matriculated undergraduates who enrolled in 2015, 1,803 applied for aid, 1,604 were judged to have need, 297 had their need fully met. 868 Federal Work-Study jobs (averaging $1511). In 2015, 444 non-need-based awards were made. *Average percent of need met:* 75. *Average financial aid package:* $23,544. *Average need-based loan:* $4177. *Average need-based gift aid:* $17,851. *Average non-need-based aid:* $17,222. *Average indebtedness upon graduation:* $40,397.

APPLYING
Standardized Tests *Required:* SAT or ACT (for admission).
Options: electronic application, deferred entrance.
Application fee: $35.
Required: high school transcript. *Required for some:* essay or personal statement, 1 letter of recommendation. *Recommended:* minimum 2.5 GPA, interview.
Application deadlines: 3/1 (freshmen), rolling (transfers).
Notification: continuous (freshmen), continuous (transfers).
CONTACT
Mr. Mark Moffit, Director of Admissions, Otterbein University, 1 South Grove Street, Office of Admission, Westerville, OH 43081-9924. *Phone:* 614-823-1500. *Toll-free phone:* 800-488-8144. *Fax:* 614-823-1200. *E-mail:* uotterb@otterbein.edu.

Pontifical College Josephinum
Columbus, Ohio
http://www.pcj.edu/
CONTACT
Mrs. Arminda Crawford, Secretary for Admissions, Pontifical College Josephinum, 7825 North High Street, Columbus, OH 43235. *Phone:* 614-985-2241. *Toll-free phone:* 888-252-5812. *Fax:* 614-885-2307. *E-mail:* acrawford@pcj.edu.

Rabbinical College of Telshe
Wickliffe, Ohio
CONTACT
Admissions Office, Rabbinical College of Telshe, 28400 Euclid Avenue, Wickliffe, OH 44092-2523. *Phone:* 440-943-5300.

Ross College
Canton, Ohio
http://www.rosseducation.edu/
CONTACT
Ross College, 4300 Munson Street NW, Canton, OH 44718. *Phone:* 330-494-1214. *Toll-free phone:* 866-815-5578.

Shawnee State University
Portsmouth, Ohio
http://www.shawnee.edu/
- **State-supported** comprehensive, founded 1986, part of Ohio Higher Educational System
- **Small-town** 62-acre campus with easy access to Charleston-Huntington-Ashland Area
- **Endowment** $19.3 million
- **Coed** 3,406 undergraduate students, 83% full-time, 54% women, 46% men
- **Noncompetitive** entrance level, 70% of applicants were admitted

UNDERGRAD STUDENTS
2,832 full-time, 574 part-time. Students come from 27 states and territories; 18 other countries; 12% are from out of state; 5% Black or African American, non-Hispanic/Latino; 0.6% Hispanic/Latino; 0.7% Asian, non-Hispanic/Latino; 0.1% Native Hawaiian or other Pacific Islander, non-Hispanic/Latino; 0.6% American Indian or Alaska Native, non-Hispanic/Latino; 2% Two or more races, non-Hispanic/Latino; 5% Race/ethnicity unknown; 1% international; 5% transferred in; 28% live on campus.

Freshmen:
Admission: 2,860 applied, 2,000 admitted, 700 enrolled. *Average high school GPA:* 3.3.
Retention: 68% of full-time freshmen returned.

FACULTY
Total: 314, 48% full-time, 27% with terminal degrees.
Student/faculty ratio: 13:1.

ACADEMICS

Calendar: semesters. *Degrees:* certificates, associate, bachelor's, and master's.

Special study options: academic remediation for entering students, accelerated degree program, adult/continuing education programs, advanced placement credit, distance learning, double majors, English as a second language, honors programs, independent study, internships, off-campus study, part-time degree program, services for LD students, student-designed majors, study abroad, summer session for credit.

Unusual degree programs: 3-2 psychology/occupational therapy.

Computers: 620 computers/terminals are available on campus for general student use. Students can access the following: campus intranet, computer help desk, free student e-mail accounts, online (class) grades, online (class) registration, online (class) schedules, financial aid, student billing, courses, student service portal. Campuswide network is available. 100% of college-owned or -operated housing units are wired for high-speed Internet access. Wireless service is available via entire campus.

Library: Clark Memorial Library. *Books:* 122,670 (physical), 103,584 (digital/electronic); *Serial titles:* 140 (physical), 672 (digital/electronic); *Databases:* 543. Weekly public service hours: 91; study areas open 24 hours, 5–7 days a week; students can reserve study rooms.

STUDENT LIFE

Housing options: on-campus residence required for freshman year; coed. Campus housing is university owned, leased by the school and is provided by a third party. Freshman applicants given priority for college housing.

Activities and organizations: drama/theater group, student-run newspaper, choral group, campus ministry, Health Executives and Administrators Learning Society, Student Programming Board, Student Government Association, national fraternities, national sororities.

Athletics Member NAIA. *Intercollegiate sports:* baseball M(s), basketball M(s)/W(s), bowling M/W, cross-country running M(s)/W(s), golf M(s)/W(s), soccer M(s)/W(s), softball W(s), tennis W(s), track and field M(s)/W(s), volleyball W(s). *Intramural sports:* basketball M/W, bowling M/W, golf M/W, racquetball M/W, softball M, swimming and diving M/W, table tennis M/W, tennis M/W, volleyball M/W.

Campus security: 24-hour emergency response devices and patrols.

Student services: health clinic, personal/psychological counseling, women's center.

COSTS & FINANCIAL AID

Costs (2018–19) *Tuition:* state resident $8556 full-time, $260 per credit hour part-time; nonresident $14,714 full-time, $502 per credit hour part-time. Full-time tuition and fees vary according to course load, program, and reciprocity agreements. Part-time tuition and fees vary according to course load, program, and reciprocity agreements. No tuition increase for student's term of enrollment. *Required fees:* $46 per credit hour part-time. *Room and board:* $10,864; room only: $6896. Room and board charges vary according to board plan and housing facility. *Payment plan:* installment. *Waivers:* senior citizens and employees or children of employees.

Financial Aid Of all full-time matriculated undergraduates who enrolled in 2016, 2,874 applied for aid, 1,900 were judged to have need, 99 had their need fully met. 60 Federal Work-Study jobs (averaging $1854). In 2016, 404 non-need-based awards were made. *Average percent of need met:* 45. *Average financial aid package:* $8972. *Average need-based loan:* $3964. *Average need-based gift aid:* $5855. *Average non-need-based aid:* $3875. *Average indebtedness upon graduation:* $30,554.

APPLYING

Options: electronic application.

Required: high school transcript. *Required for some:* essay or personal statement, minimum 2.7 GPA, interview, ACT/SAT scores if student is under 21.

Application deadlines: rolling (freshmen), rolling (transfers).

Notification: continuous (freshmen), continuous (transfers).

CONTACT

Amanda Means, Director of Admissions, Shawnee State University, 940 Second St, Portsmouth, OH 45662. *Phone:* 740-351-3229. *Toll-free phone:* 800-959-2778. *Fax:* 740-351-3111. *E-mail:* ameans@shawnee.edu.

South University

Cleveland, Ohio

http://www.southuniversity.edu/cleveland.aspx

CONTACT

South University, 4743 Richmond Road, Cleveland, OH 44128. *Phone:* 216-755-5000. *Toll-free phone:* 855-398-9280.

Tiffin University

Tiffin, Ohio

http://www.tiffin.edu/

- **Independent** comprehensive, founded 1888
- **Small-town** 135-acre campus with easy access to Toledo
- **Endowment** $9.1 million
- **Coed** 2,243 undergraduate students, 79% full-time, 46% women, 54% men
- **Moderately difficult** entrance level, 69% of applicants were admitted

UNDERGRAD STUDENTS

1,772 full-time, 471 part-time. Students come from 47 states and territories; 22 other countries; 26% are from out of state; 10% Black or African American, non-Hispanic/Latino; 3% Hispanic/Latino; 0.2% Asian, non-Hispanic/Latino; 2% Two or more races, non-Hispanic/Latino; 33% Race/ethnicity unknown; 13% international; 9% transferred in; 42% live on campus.

Freshmen:

Admission: 3,808 applied, 2,621 admitted, 452 enrolled. *Average high school GPA:* 3.0. *Test scores:* SAT evidence-based reading and writing scores over 500: 49%; SAT math scores over 500: 47%; ACT scores over 18: 73%; SAT evidence-based reading and writing scores over 600: 10%; SAT math scores over 600: 9%; ACT scores over 24: 17%; ACT scores over 30: 1%.

Retention: 65% of full-time freshmen returned.

FACULTY

Total: 361, 20% full-time.

Student/faculty ratio: 14:1.

ACADEMICS

Calendar: semesters. *Degrees:* certificates, associate, bachelor's, master's, post-master's, and postbachelor's certificates.

Special study options: academic remediation for entering students, accelerated degree program, adult/continuing education programs, advanced placement credit, distance learning, double majors, English as a second language, freshman honors college, independent study, internships, off-campus study, services for LD students, study abroad, summer session for credit. *ROTC:* Army (c), Air Force (c).

Computers: 280 computers/terminals are available on campus for general student use. Students can access the following: campus intranet, computer help desk, free student e-mail accounts, online (class) grades, online (class) registration, online (class) schedules. Campuswide network is available. 100% of college-owned or -operated housing units are wired for high-speed Internet access. Wireless service is available via classrooms, computer centers, computer labs, dorm rooms, learning centers, libraries, student centers.

Library: Pfeiffer Library plus 1 other. *Books:* 40,849 (physical), 125,971 (digital/electronic); *Serial titles:* 120 (physical), 25,420 (digital/electronic); *Databases:* 187. Weekly public service hours: 73.

STUDENT LIFE

Housing options: on-campus residence required through sophomore year; coed, men-only, women-only, special housing for students with disabilities. Campus housing is university owned and leased by the school. Freshman campus housing is guaranteed.

Activities and organizations: drama/theater group, student-run newspaper, choral group, marching band, Student Government Association, H2O, International Student Association, Global Affairs Organization, Circle K, national fraternities, national sororities.

Athletics Member NCAA. All Division II. *Intercollegiate sports:* baseball M(s), basketball M(s)/W(s), cross-country running M(s)/W(s), football M(s), golf M(s)/W(s), lacrosse W(s), soccer M(s)/W(s), softball W(s), swimming and diving M(s)/W(s), tennis M(s)/W(s), track and field

M(s)/W(s), volleyball W(s), wrestling M(s). *Intramural sports:* basketball M/W, bowling M/W, equestrian sports M(c)/W(c), football M, rugby M(c), soccer M/W, softball M/W, table tennis M/W, tennis M/W, ultimate Frisbee M/W, volleyball M/W, weight lifting M/W.

Campus security: 24-hour emergency response devices, student patrols, late-night transport/escort service, controlled dormitory access.

Student services: health clinic, personal/psychological counseling, women's center.

COSTS & FINANCIAL AID

Costs (2018–19) *Comprehensive fee:* $36,200 includes full-time tuition ($24,600), mandatory fees ($400), and room and board ($11,200). Full-time tuition and fees vary according to course load, degree level, location, program, and reciprocity agreements. Part-time tuition: $820 per credit hour. Part-time tuition and fees vary according to course load, degree level, location, program, and reciprocity agreements. *College room only:* $6000. Room and board charges vary according to board plan and housing facility. *Payment plans:* installment, deferred payment. *Waivers:* senior citizens and employees or children of employees.

Financial Aid Of all full-time matriculated undergraduates who enrolled in 2017, 1,398 applied for aid, 1,280 were judged to have need, 212 had their need fully met. *Average percent of need met:* 67. *Average financial aid package:* $18,067. *Average need-based loan:* $3960. *Average need-based gift aid:* $14,483. *Average indebtedness upon graduation:* $36,819.

APPLYING

Standardized Tests *Required for some:* SAT or ACT (for admission).

Options: electronic application.

Application fee: $20.

Required: high school transcript. *Required for some:* essay or personal statement, interview. *Recommended:* minimum 3.0 GPA.

Application deadlines: rolling (freshmen), rolling (transfers).

Notification: continuous (freshmen), continuous (transfers).

CONTACT

Mrs. Sarah Johnson, Director of Undergraduate Admissions, Tiffin University, 155 Miami Street, Tiffin, OH 44883. *Phone:* 419-448-3014. *Toll-free phone:* 800-968-6446. *Fax:* 419-443-5006. *E-mail:* depughst@tiffin.edu.

Tri-State Bible College
South Point, Ohio
http://www.tsbc.edu/

CONTACT

Tri-State Bible College, 506 Margaret Street, PO Box 445, South Point, OH 45680-8402. *Phone:* 740-377-2520.

Union Institute & University
Cincinnati, Ohio
http://www.myunion.edu/

- **Independent** university, founded 1964
- **Urban** 5-acre campus with easy access to Cincinnati
- **Endowment** $793,428
- **Coed**
- **Noncompetitive** entrance level

FACULTY
Student/faculty ratio: 8:1.

ACADEMICS
Calendar: trimesters some programs offer split (8-week) sessions; some programs have two 6-month semesters. *Degrees:* bachelor's, master's, doctoral, and post-master's certificates.
Library: Union Institute & University Library. *Books:* 3.0 million (digital/electronic); *Serial titles:* 77,317 (digital/electronic); *Databases:* 171. Weekly public service hours: 50.

STUDENT LIFE
Housing options: college housing not available.

Campus security: 24-hour emergency response devices, late-night transport/escort service, security personnel on site during business and class hours.

COSTS
Costs (2017–18) *Tuition:* $12,240 full-time, $530 per credit hour part-time. Full-time tuition and fees vary according to course load and program. Part-time tuition and fees vary according to course load and program. *Required fees:* $176 full-time, $88 per term part-time.

APPLYING
Options: electronic application, deferred entrance.

Required: essay or personal statement, recommendation from program faculty. *Required for some:* high school transcript, 1 letter of recommendation. *Recommended:* interview.

CONTACT
Union Institute & University, 440 East McMillan Street, Cincinnati, OH 45206-1925. *Phone:* 513-487-1173. *Toll-free phone:* 800-486-3116.

The University of Akron
Akron, Ohio
http://www.uakron.edu/

- **State-supported** university, founded 1870
- **Urban** 223-acre campus with easy access to Cleveland
- **Endowment** $191.4 million
- **Coed** 16,871 undergraduate students, 80% full-time, 47% women, 53% men
- **Moderately difficult** entrance level, 93% of applicants were admitted

UNDERGRAD STUDENTS
13,562 full-time, 3,309 part-time. Students come from 38 states and territories; 67 other countries; 6% are from out of state; 12% Black or African American, non-Hispanic/Latino; 3% Hispanic/Latino; 3% Asian, non-Hispanic/Latino; 0.1% American Indian or Alaska Native, non-Hispanic/Latino; 5% Two or more races, non-Hispanic/Latino; 2% Race/ethnicity unknown; 2% international; 3% transferred in; 17% live on campus.

Freshmen:
Admission: 15,109 applied, 13,983 admitted, 3,440 enrolled. *Average high school GPA:* 3.5. *Test scores:* SAT evidence-based reading and writing scores over 500: 79%; SAT math scores over 500: 73%; ACT scores over 18: 84%; SAT evidence-based reading and writing scores over 600: 39%; SAT math scores over 600: 39%; ACT scores over 24: 42%; SAT evidence-based reading and writing scores over 700: 9%; SAT math scores over 700: 15%; ACT scores over 30: 9%.

Retention: 73% of full-time freshmen returned.

FACULTY
Total: 1,452, 48% full-time.
Student/faculty ratio: 18:1.

ACADEMICS
Calendar: semesters. *Degrees:* certificates, associate, bachelor's, master's, doctoral, post-master's, and postbachelor's certificates.

Special study options: academic remediation for entering students, accelerated degree program, adult/continuing education programs, advanced placement credit, cooperative education, distance learning, double majors, English as a second language, external degree program, freshman honors college, honors programs, independent study, internships, part-time degree program, services for LD students, student-designed majors, study abroad, summer session for credit. *ROTC:* Army (b), Air Force (c).

Unusual degree programs: 3-2 business administration; engineering; medicine, polymer chemistry.

Computers: 3,150 computers/terminals and 16,000 ports are available on campus for general student use. Students can access the following: campus intranet, computer help desk, free student e-mail accounts, online (class) grades, online (class) registration, online (class) schedules, library laptops for student checkout. Campuswide network is available. 100% of college-owned or -operated housing units are wired for high-speed Internet access. Wireless service is available via entire campus.

Library: Bierce Library plus 2 others. *Books:* 1.1 million (physical); *Serial titles:* 25,089 (physical). Study areas open 24 hours, 5–7 days a week; students can reserve study rooms.

STUDENT LIFE

Housing options: on-campus residence required for freshman year; coed, special housing for students with disabilities. Campus housing is university owned. Freshman applicants given priority for college housing.

Activities and organizations: drama/theater group, student-run newspaper, radio and television station, choral group, marching band, AK-Rowdies, Akron Animation Association, National Society of Leadership and Success, Golden Key International Honor Society, Alpha Phi Omega, national fraternities, national sororities.

Athletics Member NCAA. All Division I except football (Division I-A). *Intercollegiate sports:* basketball M(s)/W(s), cheerleading M/W, cross-country running M(s)/W(s), golf M(s)/W(s), riflery M/W(s), soccer M(s)/W(s), softball W(s), swimming and diving W(s), tennis W(s), track and field M(s)/W(s), volleyball W(s). *Intramural sports:* badminton M/W, basketball M/W, bowling M/W, cross-country running M/W, golf M/W, racquetball M/W, skiing (cross-country) M/W, skiing (downhill) M/W, soccer M/W, softball M/W, swimming and diving M/W, table tennis M/W, track and field M/W, volleyball W, wrestling M.

Campus security: 24-hour emergency response devices and patrols, student patrols, late-night transport/escort service, controlled dormitory access.

Student services: health clinic, personal/psychological counseling, women's center, legal services.

COSTS & FINANCIAL AID

Costs (2018–19) *Tuition:* state resident $8618 full-time, $359 per credit hour part-time; nonresident $17,149 full-time, $715 per credit hour part-time. Full-time tuition and fees vary according to course load, degree level, location, and program. Part-time tuition and fees vary according to course load, degree level, location, and program. *Required fees:* $1652 full-time. *Room and board:* $12,296; room only: $8026. Room and board charges vary according to board plan and housing facility. *Payment plan:* installment. *Waivers:* senior citizens and employees or children of employees.

Financial Aid Of all full-time matriculated undergraduates who enrolled in 2017, 11,799 applied for aid, 9,312 were judged to have need, 986 had their need fully met. 302 Federal Work-Study jobs. In 2017, 1777 non-need-based awards were made. *Average percent of need met:* 52. *Average financial aid package:* $7811. *Average need-based loan:* $3927. *Average need-based gift aid:* $5276. *Average non-need-based aid:* $5150. *Average indebtedness upon graduation:* $32,033.

APPLYING

Standardized Tests *Required:* SAT or ACT (for admission).

Options: electronic application, early action, deferred entrance.

Application fee: $45.

Required: high school transcript. *Required for some:* essay or personal statement, 3 letters of recommendation, interview.

Application deadlines: 8/11 (freshmen), rolling (transfers), 11/1 (early action).

Notification: 9/15 (freshmen), continuous (transfers).

CONTACT

Ms. Kimberley Gentile, Senior Associate Director of Admissions Outreach, The University of Akron, Office of Admissions, Simmons Hall 109N. *Phone:* 330-972-6345. *Toll-free phone:* 800-655-4884. *E-mail:* gentile@uakron.edu.

The University of Akron Wayne College

Orrville, Ohio
http://www.wayne.uakron.edu/

CONTACT

Ms. Alicia Broadus, Student Services Counselor, The University of Akron Wayne College, Orrville, OH 44667. *Phone:* 800-221-8308 Ext. 8901. *Toll-free phone:* 800-221-8308. *Fax:* 330-684-8989. *E-mail:* wayneadmissions@uakron.edu.

University of Cincinnati

Cincinnati, Ohio
http://www.uc.edu/

- **State-supported** university, founded 1819
- **Urban** 137-acre campus with easy access to Cincinnati
- **Endowment** $1.3 billion
- **Coed** 26,608 undergraduate students, 85% full-time, 49% women, 51% men
- **Moderately difficult** entrance level, 78% of applicants were admitted

UNDERGRAD STUDENTS

22,671 full-time, 3,937 part-time. Students come from 51 states and territories; 138 other countries; 15% are from out of state; 7% Black or African American, non-Hispanic/Latino; 3% Hispanic/Latino; 4% Asian, non-Hispanic/Latino; 0.1% Native Hawaiian or other Pacific Islander, non-Hispanic/Latino; 0.1% American Indian or Alaska Native, non-Hispanic/Latino; 4% Two or more races, non-Hispanic/Latino; 3% Race/ethnicity unknown; 4% international; 7% transferred in; 26% live on campus.

Freshmen:
Admission: 21,161 applied, 16,517 admitted, 5,400 enrolled. *Average high school GPA:* 3.6. *Test scores:* SAT evidence-based reading and writing scores over 500: 95%; SAT math scores over 500: 95%; ACT scores over 18: 99%; SAT evidence-based reading and writing scores over 600: 60%; SAT math scores over 600: 60%; ACT scores over 24: 70%; SAT evidence-based reading and writing scores over 700: 15%; SAT math scores over 700: 19%; ACT scores over 30: 18%.

Retention: 86% of full-time freshmen returned.

FACULTY

Total: 3,511, 63% full-time.
Student/faculty ratio: 17:1.

ACADEMICS

Calendar: semesters. *Degrees:* certificates, associate, bachelor's, master's, doctoral, post-master's, and postbachelor's certificates.

Special study options: academic remediation for entering students, accelerated degree program, adult/continuing education programs, advanced placement credit, cooperative education, distance learning, double majors, English as a second language, honors programs, independent study, internships, off-campus study, services for LD students, study abroad, summer session for credit. *ROTC:* Army (b), Air Force (b).

Computers: 499 computers/terminals are available on campus for general student use. Students can access the following: campus intranet, computer help desk, free student e-mail accounts, online (class) grades, online (class) registration, online (class) schedules. Campuswide network is available. 100% of college-owned or -operated housing units are wired for high-speed Internet access. Wireless service is available via entire campus.

Library: Walter C. Langsam Library plus 13 others. *Books:* 2.7 million (physical), 1.6 million (digital/electronic); *Serial titles:* 98,491 (physical), 2.1 million (digital/electronic); *Databases:* 1,270. Study areas open 24 hours, 5–7 days a week; students can reserve study rooms.

STUDENT LIFE

Housing options: on-campus residence required for freshman year; coed, men-only, women-only. Campus housing is university owned, leased by the school and is provided by a third party. Freshman campus housing is guaranteed.

Activities and organizations: drama/theater group, student-run newspaper, radio station, choral group, marching band, Serve Beyond Cincinnati, University of Cincinnati Mountaineering Club, Rally Cats, Engineers Without Borders, UC League of Legends, national fraternities, national sororities.

Athletics Member NCAA. All Division I except football (Division I-A). *Intercollegiate sports:* baseball M(s), basketball M(s)/W(s), cheerleading M/W, cross-country running M(s)/W(s), golf M(s)/W(s), lacrosse W(s), soccer M(s)/W(s), swimming and diving M(s)/W(s), tennis W(s), track and field M(s)/W(s), volleyball W(s). *Intramural sports:* badminton M(c)/W(c), baseball M(c), basketball M/W, bowling M(c)/W(c), crew M(c)/W(c), cross-country running M(c)/W(c), equestrian sports M(c)/W(c), fencing M(c)/W(c), football M/W, golf M(c)/W(c), gymnastics M(c)/W(c), ice hockey M(c), lacrosse M(c)/W(c), racquetball M(c)/W(c), rugby M(c)/W(c), soccer M(c)/W(c), softball W(c), swimming and diving M(c)/W(c), table tennis M(c)/W(c), tennis M(c)/W(c), triathlon M(c)/W(c), ultimate Frisbee M(c)/W(c), volleyball M(c)/W(c), water polo M(c)/W(c), wrestling M(c).

Campus security: 24-hour emergency response devices and patrols, student patrols, late-night transport/escort service, controlled dormitory access.

Student services: health clinic, personal/psychological counseling, women's center.

COSTS & FINANCIAL AID

Costs (2018–19) *Tuition:* state resident $9322 full-time, $389 per credit hour part-time; nonresident $24,656 full-time, $1098 per credit hour part-time. Full-time tuition and fees vary according to course load, location, program, and reciprocity agreements. Part-time tuition and fees vary according to course load, location, program, and reciprocity agreements. *Required fees:* $1678 full-time, $70 per credit hour part-time. *Room and board:* $11,118; room only: $6624. Room and board charges vary according to board plan and housing facility. *Payment plan:* installment. *Waivers:* employees or children of employees.

Financial Aid Of all full-time matriculated undergraduates who enrolled in 2016, 14,728 applied for aid, 11,674 were judged to have need, 520 had their need fully met. 1,366 Federal Work-Study jobs (averaging $3243). In 2016, 4018 non-need-based awards were made. *Average percent of need met:* 39. *Average financial aid package:* $8514. *Average need-based loan:* $4472. *Average need-based gift aid:* $6116. *Average non-need-based aid:* $4549. *Average indebtedness upon graduation:* $25,877.

APPLYING

Standardized Tests *Required:* SAT or ACT (for admission).

Options: electronic application, early action, deferred entrance.

Application fee: $50.

Required: essay or personal statement, high school transcript. *Required for some:* 1 letter of recommendation, audition for performing arts majors.

Application deadlines: 3/1 (freshmen), 7/1 (transfers), 12/1 (early action).

Notification: continuous until 5/1 (freshmen), continuous (transfers), rolling (early action).

CONTACT

Dr. Caroline Miller, Vice Provost for Enrollment Management, University of Cincinnati, Office of Admissions, PO Box210091, Cincinnati, OH 45221-0091. *Phone:* 513-556-1100. *Fax:* 513-556-1105. *E-mail:* admissions@uc.edu.

University of Cincinnati Blue Ash College

Cincinnati, Ohio

http://www.ucblueash.edu/

- **State-supported** primarily 2-year, founded 1967, part of Ohio Department of Higher Education
- **Suburban** 120-acre campus with easy access to Cincinnati
- **Endowment** $457,000
- **Coed**
- **Noncompetitive** entrance level

FACULTY

Student/faculty ratio: 16:1.

ACADEMICS

Calendar: semesters. *Degrees:* certificates, associate, bachelor's, and postbachelor's certificates.
Library: UC Blue Ash College Library. *Books:* 19,690 (physical). Weekly public service hours: 50; students can reserve study rooms.

STUDENT LIFE

Housing options: college housing not available.

Campus security: 24-hour emergency response devices and patrols, student patrols, late-night transport/escort service.

Student services: personal/psychological counseling.

COSTS & FINANCIAL AID

Costs (2017–18) *Tuition:* state resident $6010 full-time, $251 per credit hour part-time; nonresident $14,808 full-time, $617 per credit hour part-time. Full-time tuition and fees vary according to course load, degree level, location, program, and reciprocity agreements. Part-time tuition and fees vary according to course load, degree level, location, and reciprocity agreements. *Required fees:* $736 full-time.

Financial Aid Of all full-time matriculated undergraduates who enrolled in 2016, 285 Federal Work-Study jobs (averaging $2903).

APPLYING

Options: electronic application, deferred entrance.

Application fee: $50.

Required: high school transcript.

CONTACT

University of Cincinnati Blue Ash College, 9555 Plainfield Road, Cincinnati, OH 45236-1007. *Phone:* 513-745-5700.

University of Cincinnati Clermont College

Batavia, Ohio

http://www.ucclermont.edu/

- **State-supported** primarily 2-year, founded 1972, part of University of Cincinnati System
- **Rural** 91-acre campus with easy access to Cincinnati
- **Coed**
- **Noncompetitive** entrance level

FACULTY

Student/faculty ratio: 13:1.

ACADEMICS

Calendar: semesters. *Degrees:* certificates, associate, bachelor's, and postbachelor's certificates.
Library: UC Clermont College Library. Students can reserve study rooms.

STUDENT LIFE

Housing options: college housing not available.

Activities and organizations: student-run newspaper, Active Minds, PACE (Professionalism Academics Character Experiences), Phi Theta Kappa, Association of Paralegal Students, Cheerleading.

Athletics Member USCAA.

Campus security: 24-hour emergency response devices and patrols.

Student services: personal/psychological counseling.

COSTS

Costs (2017–18) *Tuition:* state resident $5316 full-time, $222 per credit part-time; nonresident $12,548 full-time, $523 per credit part-time. Full-time tuition and fees vary according to course level, degree level, program, and reciprocity agreements. Part-time tuition and fees vary according to course level, degree level, program, and reciprocity agreements.

APPLYING

Options: electronic application, deferred entrance.

Application fee: $50.

Required: high school transcript.

CONTACT

Mrs. Jamie Adkins, University Services Associate, University of Cincinnati Clermont College, 4200 Clermont College Drive, Batavia, OH 45103. *Phone:* 513-732-5294. *Toll-free phone:* 866-446-2822. *Fax:* 513-732-5303. *E-mail:* jamie.adkins@uc.edu.

University of Dayton
Dayton, Ohio
http://www.udayton.edu/

- **Independent Roman Catholic** university, founded 1850
- **Suburban** 388-acre campus with easy access to Cincinnati
- **Coed** 8,499 undergraduate students, 95% full-time, 48% women, 52% men
- **Moderately difficult** entrance level, 72% of applicants were admitted

UNDERGRAD STUDENTS
8,079 full-time, 420 part-time. Students come from 50 states and territories; 39 other countries; 52% are from out of state; 3% Black or African American, non-Hispanic/Latino; 5% Hispanic/Latino; 1% Asian, non-Hispanic/Latino; 0.1% Native Hawaiian or other Pacific Islander, non-Hispanic/Latino; 0.1% American Indian or Alaska Native, non-Hispanic/Latino; 3% Two or more races, non-Hispanic/Latino; 1% Race/ethnicity unknown; 7% international; 1% transferred in; 75% live on campus.

Freshmen:
Admission: 15,942 applied, 11,427 admitted, 2,226 enrolled. *Average high school GPA:* 3.7. *Test scores:* SAT evidence-based reading and writing scores over 500: 94%; SAT math scores over 500: 94%; ACT scores over 18: 100%; SAT evidence-based reading and writing scores over 600: 53%; SAT math scores over 600: 52%; ACT scores over 24: 79%; SAT evidence-based reading and writing scores over 700: 9%; SAT math scores over 700: 12%; ACT scores over 30: 25%.

Retention: 90% of full-time freshmen returned.

FACULTY
Total: 1,034, 54% full-time, 48% with terminal degrees.

Student/faculty ratio: 15:1.

ACADEMICS
Calendar: semesters plus 2 6-week summer terms. *Degrees:* bachelor's, master's, doctoral, post-master's, and postbachelor's certificates.

Special study options: academic remediation for entering students, accelerated degree program, adult/continuing education programs, advanced placement credit, cooperative education, distance learning, double majors, English as a second language, honors programs, independent study, internships, off-campus study, part-time degree program, services for LD students, student-designed majors, study abroad, summer session for credit. *ROTC:* Army (b), Air Force (c).

Unusual degree programs: 3-2 business administration; engineering.

Computers: 7,675 computers/terminals and 19,337 ports are available on campus for general student use. Students can access the following: campus intranet, computer help desk, free student e-mail accounts, online (class) grades, online (class) registration, online (class) schedules, applications, admission/enrollment status, virtual orientation, online digital resources, online courses, assistive technology, learning management system, multimedia labs, payment, cyber cafes, centrally-licensed, downloadable software and training. Campuswide network is available. 100% of college-owned or -operated housing units are wired for high-speed Internet access. Wireless service is available via entire campus.

Library: Roesch Library plus 3 others. *Books:* 881,689 (physical), 972,137 (digital/electronic); *Serial titles:* 2,325 (physical), 96,661 (digital/electronic); *Databases:* 316. Weekly public service hours: 134; students can reserve study rooms.

STUDENT LIFE
Housing options: on-campus residence required through sophomore year; coed, men-only, women-only, special housing for students with disabilities. Campus housing is university owned. Freshman campus housing is guaranteed.

Activities and organizations: drama/theater group, student-run newspaper, radio and television station, choral group, marching band, Student Government Association, Marching Band, Red Scare (basketball student cheering section), Campus Connection, Habitat for Humanity, national fraternities, national sororities.

Athletics Member NCAA. All Division I except football (Division I-AA). *Intercollegiate sports:* baseball M(s), basketball M(s)/W(s), cheerleading M/W, crew W, cross-country running M(s)/W(s), golf M(s)/W, soccer M(s)/W(s), softball W(s), tennis M(s)/W(s), track and field W(s), volleyball W(s). *Intramural sports:* baseball M(c), basketball M(c)/W(c), bowling M/W, crew M(c), cross-country running M(c)/W(c), field hockey M(c)/W(c), football M/W, golf M(c)/W(c), gymnastics M(c)/W(c), ice hockey M(c), lacrosse M(c)/W(c), racquetball M(c)/W(c), rugby M(c)/W(c), soccer M(c)/W(c), softball M/W(c), swimming and diving M(c)/W(c), tennis M(c)/W(c), ultimate Frisbee M(c)/W(c), volleyball M(c)/W(c), water polo M(c)/W(c), weight lifting M(c)/W(c), wrestling M(c)/W(c).

Campus security: 24-hour emergency response devices and patrols, student patrols, late-night transport/escort service, controlled dormitory access, approximately 1000 recording video cameras, automated external defibrillators in high density residential facilities and other areas.

Student services: health clinic, personal/psychological counseling, women's center.

COSTS & FINANCIAL AID
Costs (2018–19) *Tuition:* No tuition increase for student's term of enrollment. *Room and board:* $13,580; room only: $8140. Room and board charges vary according to housing facility and student level. *Payment plan:* installment. *Waivers:* employees or children of employees.

Financial Aid Of all full-time matriculated undergraduates who enrolled in 2017, 6,359 applied for aid, 4,780 were judged to have need, 4,585 had their need fully met. In 2017, 3153 non-need-based awards were made. *Average percent of need met:* 83. *Average financial aid package:* $31,029. *Average need-based loan:* $3325. *Average need-based gift aid:* $27,594. *Average non-need-based aid:* $18,131. *Average indebtedness upon graduation:* $35,689. *Financial aid deadline:* 5/1.

APPLYING
Standardized Tests *Required:* SAT or ACT (for admission).

Options: electronic application, early action, deferred entrance.

Required: essay or personal statement, high school transcript, 1 letter of recommendation. *Required for some:* audition for music, music therapy, music education programs.

Application deadlines: 6/15 (transfers), 11/1 (early action).

Notification: continuous (transfers), 2/1 (early action).

CONTACT
Mr. Robert Durkle, Dean of Admission and Financial Aid, University of Dayton, 300 College Park, Dayton, OH 45469-1310. *Phone:* 937-229-4411. *Toll-free phone:* 800-837-7433. *Fax:* 937-229-4729. *E-mail:* admission@udayton.edu.

 # The University of Findlay
Findlay, Ohio
http://www.findlay.edu/

- **Independent** comprehensive, founded 1882, affiliated with Church of God
- **Small-town** 390-acre campus
- **Coed** 3,562 undergraduate students, 70% full-time, 65% women, 35% men
- **Moderately difficult** entrance level, 75% of applicants were admitted

UNDERGRAD STUDENTS
2,499 full-time, 1,063 part-time. Students come from 45 states and territories; 28 other countries; 19% are from out of state; 3% Black or African American, non-Hispanic/Latino; 2% Hispanic/Latino; 1% Asian, non-Hispanic/Latino; 0.1% Native Hawaiian or other Pacific Islander, non-Hispanic/Latino; 0.1% American Indian or Alaska Native, non-Hispanic/Latino; 3% Two or more races, non-Hispanic/Latino; 2% Race/ethnicity unknown; 5% international; 2% transferred in; 45% live on campus.

Freshmen:
Admission: 3,611 applied, 2,711 admitted, 595 enrolled. *Average high school GPA:* 3.6. *Test scores:* SAT evidence-based reading and writing scores over 500: 66%; SAT math scores over 500: 74%; ACT scores over 18: 98%; SAT evidence-based reading and writing scores over 600: 24%; SAT math scores over 600: 34%; ACT scores over 24: 54%; SAT evidence-based reading and writing scores over 700: 5%; SAT math scores over 700: 4%; ACT scores over 30: 11%.

Retention: 80% of full-time freshmen returned.

FACULTY
Total: 274, 79% full-time, 60% with terminal degrees.
Student/faculty ratio: 16:1.

ACADEMICS
Calendar: semesters. *Degrees:* certificates, associate, bachelor's, master's, and doctoral.

Special study options: academic remediation for entering students, accelerated degree program, adult/continuing education programs, advanced placement credit, cooperative education, distance learning, double majors, English as a second language, honors programs, independent study, internships, off-campus study, part-time degree program, services for LD students, student-designed majors, study abroad, summer session for credit. *ROTC:* Army (c), Air Force (c).

Unusual degree programs: 3-2 athletic training.

Computers: 151 computers/terminals are available on campus for general student use. Students can access the following: campus intranet, computer help desk, free student e-mail accounts, online (class) grades, online (class) registration, online (class) schedules. Campuswide network is available. 100% of college-owned or -operated housing units are wired for high-speed Internet access. Wireless service is available via entire campus.

Library: Shafer Library plus 4 others. *Books:* 98,272 (physical), 325,566 (digital/electronic); *Serial titles:* 361 (physical), 78,798 (digital/electronic); *Databases:* 173. Weekly public service hours: 94; study areas open 24 hours, 5–7 days a week.

STUDENT LIFE
Housing options: on-campus residence required through sophomore year; coed, women-only. Campus housing is university owned. Freshman campus housing is guaranteed.

Activities and organizations: drama/theater group, student-run newspaper, radio and television station, choral group, marching band, Habitat for Humanity, Pre-Vet Club, Horse Club, Stride, Black Student Union, national fraternities, national sororities.

Athletics Member NCAA. All Division II. *Intercollegiate sports:* baseball M(s), basketball M(s)/W(s), cheerleading M/W, cross-country running M(s)/W(s), equestrian sports M/W, football M(s), golf M(s)/W(s), lacrosse W(s), soccer M(s)/W(s), softball W(s), swimming and diving M(s)/W(s), tennis M(s)/W(s), track and field M(s)/W(s), volleyball W(s), wrestling M(s). *Intramural sports:* basketball M/W, bowling M/W, golf M/W, soccer M/W, volleyball M/W.

Campus security: 24-hour emergency response devices and patrols, student patrols, late-night transport/escort service, controlled dormitory access, parking lot and building cameras (over 500), campus police.

Student services: health clinic, personal/psychological counseling, women's center.

COSTS & FINANCIAL AID
Costs (2017–18) *Comprehensive fee:* $43,040 includes full-time tuition ($32,330), mandatory fees ($990), and room and board ($9720). Full-time tuition and fees vary according to program. Part-time tuition: $715 per semester hour. Part-time tuition and fees vary according to course load and program. *Required fees:* $430 per term part-time. *College room only:* $4850. Room and board charges vary according to board plan and housing facility. *Payment plan:* installment. *Waivers:* senior citizens and employees or children of employees.

Financial Aid Of all full-time matriculated undergraduates who enrolled in 2016, 2,212 applied for aid, 1,909 were judged to have need, 512 had their need fully met. In 2016, 2000 non-need-based awards were made. *Average percent of need met:* 79. *Average financial aid package:* $29,186. *Average need-based loan:* $4146. *Average need-based gift aid:* $25,592. *Average non-need-based aid:* $21,595. *Average indebtedness upon graduation:* $37,424. *Financial aid deadline:* 9/1.

APPLYING
Standardized Tests *Required:* SAT or ACT (for admission).
Options: electronic application, deferred entrance.
Required: high school transcript, minimum 2.5 GPA. *Required for some:* essay or personal statement, 1 letter of recommendation. *Recommended:* interview.
Application deadlines: rolling (freshmen), rolling (transfers).
Notification: continuous (freshmen), continuous (transfers).

CONTACT
Ms. Shawn Jordan, Assistant Director of Undergraduate Admissions, The University of Findlay, 1000 North Main Street, Findlay, OH 45840-3653. *Phone:* 419-434-4890. *Toll-free phone:* 800-548-0932. *Fax:* 419-434-4898. *E-mail:* jordan@findlay.edu.

University of Mount Union
Alliance, Ohio
http://www.mountunion.edu/
- **Independent United Methodist** comprehensive, founded 1846
- **Suburban** 123-acre campus with easy access to Cleveland
- **Endowment** $138.8 million
- **Coed** 2,095 undergraduate students, 98% full-time, 48% women, 52% men
- **Moderately difficult** entrance level, 81% of applicants were admitted

UNDERGRAD STUDENTS
2,046 full-time, 49 part-time. Students come from 32 states and territories; 12 other countries; 17% are from out of state; 6% Black or African American, non-Hispanic/Latino; 3% Hispanic/Latino; 0.7% Asian, non-Hispanic/Latino; 0.7% American Indian or Alaska Native, non-Hispanic/Latino; 3% Two or more races, non-Hispanic/Latino; 6% Race/ethnicity unknown; 0.1% international; 3% transferred in; 67% live on campus.

Freshmen:
Admission: 2,020 applied, 1,638 admitted, 540 enrolled. *Average high school GPA:* 3.4. *Test scores:* ACT scores over 18: 92%; ACT scores over 24: 39%; ACT scores over 30: 5%.
Retention: 75% of full-time freshmen returned.

FACULTY
Total: 255, 55% full-time, 59% with terminal degrees.
Student/faculty ratio: 13:1.

ACADEMICS
Calendar: semesters. *Degrees:* bachelor's, master's, and doctoral.

Special study options: accelerated degree program, adult/continuing education programs, advanced placement credit, cooperative education, distance learning, double majors, English as a second language, honors programs, independent study, internships, off-campus study, part-time degree program, services for LD students, student-designed majors, study abroad, summer session for credit. *ROTC:* Army (c).

Computers: 265 computers/terminals and 6,000 ports are available on campus for general student use. Students can access the following: campus intranet, computer help desk, free student e-mail accounts, online (class) grades, online (class) registration, online (class) schedules. Campuswide network is available. 100% of college-owned or -operated housing units are wired for high-speed Internet access. Wireless service is available via entire campus.

Library: University of Mount Union Library plus 1 other. *Books:* 327,033 (physical), 423,723 (digital/electronic); *Serial titles:* 2,492 (physical), 60,137 (digital/electronic); *Databases:* 226. Study areas open 24 hours, 5–7 days a week; students can reserve study rooms.

STUDENT LIFE
Housing options: on-campus residence required through sophomore year; coed, men-only, women-only, special housing for students with disabilities. Campus housing is university owned. Freshman campus housing is guaranteed.

Activities and organizations: drama/theater group, student-run newspaper, radio and television station, choral group, marching band, Alpha Phi Omega, Student Senate, FCA Fellowship of Christian Athletes, Black Student Union, Raider Programming Board, national fraternities, national sororities.

Athletics Member NCAA. All Division III. *Intercollegiate sports:* baseball M, basketball M/W, cheerleading W, cross-country running M/W, football M, golf M/W, lacrosse M/W, soccer M/W, softball W, swimming and diving M/W, tennis M/W, track and field M/W, volleyball W, wrestling M. *Intramural sports:* archery M/W, badminton M/W, basketball M/W, bowling M/W, football M, golf M/W, gymnastics M/W, racquetball M/W, soccer M/W, softball M/W, swimming and diving M/W, tennis M/W, track and field M/W, volleyball M/W, weight lifting M/W.

Campus security: 24-hour emergency response devices and patrols, late-night transport/escort service, controlled dormitory access, 24-hour locked residence hall entrances, outside phones.

Student services: health clinic, personal/psychological counseling.

COSTS & FINANCIAL AID
Costs (2018–19) *Comprehensive fee:* $41,060 includes full-time tuition ($30,460), mandatory fees ($400), and room and board ($10,200). Full-time tuition and fees vary according to course load. Part-time tuition: $1300 per credit hour. Part-time tuition and fees vary according to course load. *Room and board:* Room and board charges vary according to board plan and housing facility. *Payment plans:* tuition prepayment, installment. *Waivers:* children of alumni, senior citizens, and employees or children of employees.

Financial Aid Of all full-time matriculated undergraduates who enrolled in 2015, 1,778 applied for aid, 1,602 were judged to have need, 224 had their need fully met. 1,257 Federal Work-Study jobs (averaging $1074). 328 state and other part-time jobs (averaging $1487). In 2015, 367 non-need-based awards were made. *Average percent of need met:* 78. *Average financial aid package:* $22,577. *Average need-based loan:* $5877. *Average need-based gift aid:* $16,946. *Average non-need-based aid:* $12,016. *Average indebtedness upon graduation:* $32,680.

APPLYING
Standardized Tests *Required:* SAT or ACT (for admission).

Options: electronic application, early admission, deferred entrance.

Required: essay or personal statement, high school transcript, minimum 2.0 GPA, 1 letter of recommendation. *Recommended:* interview.

Application deadlines: rolling (freshmen), rolling (transfers).

Notification: continuous (freshmen), continuous (transfers).

CONTACT
Mr. Eric Young, Director of Admission, University of Mount Union, 1972 Clark Avenue, Alliance, OH 44601. *Phone:* 330-829-8238. *Toll-free phone:* 800-334-6682. *Fax:* 330-823-5097. *E-mail:* admission@ mountunion.edu.

University of Northwestern Ohio
Lima, Ohio
http://www.unoh.edu/
- **Independent** comprehensive, founded 1920
- **Small-town** 200-acre campus with easy access to Dayton, Toledo
- **Coed**
- **Noncompetitive** entrance level

FACULTY
Student/faculty ratio: 20:1.

ACADEMICS
Calendar: quarters. *Degrees:* certificates, diplomas, associate, bachelor's, and master's.
Library: Dr. Cheryl Mueller Library. Students can reserve study rooms.

STUDENT LIFE
Housing options: men-only, women-only, special housing for students with disabilities. Campus housing is university owned and leased by the school. Freshman campus housing is guaranteed.

Activities and organizations: Business Professionals of America, ROTORAC, American Marketing Association, Optimist Club, Drag Club.

Athletics Member NAIA.

Campus security: 24-hour emergency response devices and patrols, late-night transport/escort service.

Student services: personal/psychological counseling.

COSTS & FINANCIAL AID
Costs (2017–18) *Tuition:* $10,350 full-time, $230 per credit hour part-time. Full-time tuition and fees vary according to class time, course load, and program. Part-time tuition and fees vary according to class time, course load, and program. *Required fees:* $300 full-time, $300 per term part-time. *Room only:* $2850. Room and board charges vary according to board plan and housing facility.

Financial Aid Of all full-time matriculated undergraduates who enrolled in 2016, 40 Federal Work-Study jobs (averaging $2000).

APPLYING
Options: electronic application, early admission, deferred entrance.

Application fee: $20.

Required: high school transcript.

CONTACT
Mr. Don Lowden, Director of Admissions, University of Northwestern Ohio, 1441 North Cable Road, Lima, OH 45805-1498. *Phone:* 419-998-3120. *E-mail:* dmlowden@unoh.edu.

University of Rio Grande
Rio Grande, Ohio
http://www.rio.edu/

CONTACT
Kristie Russell, Assistant Director of Admissions, University of Rio Grande, PO Box 500, Rio Grande, OH 45674. *Phone:* 740-245-7208. *Toll-free phone:* 800-282-7201. *Fax:* 740-245-7260. *E-mail:* admissions@ rio.edu.

The University of Toledo
Toledo, Ohio
http://www.utoledo.edu/
- **State-supported** university, founded 1872
- **Urban** 858-acre campus with easy access to Detroit
- **Endowment** $294.1 million
- **Coed** 16,194 undergraduate students, 81% full-time, 49% women, 51% men
- **Noncompetitive** entrance level, 94% of applicants were admitted

UNDERGRAD STUDENTS
13,056 full-time, 3,138 part-time. Students come from 52 states and territories; 68 other countries; 20% are from out of state; 11% Black or African American, non-Hispanic/Latino; 5% Hispanic/Latino; 2% Asian, non-Hispanic/Latino; 0.1% Native Hawaiian or other Pacific Islander, non-Hispanic/Latino; 0.1% American Indian or Alaska Native, non-Hispanic/Latino; 3% Two or more races, non-Hispanic/Latino; 4% Race/ethnicity unknown; 6% international; 6% transferred in; 21% live on campus.

Freshmen:
Admission: 10,946 applied, 10,328 admitted, 3,228 enrolled. *Average high school GPA:* 3.4. *Test scores:* ACT scores over 18: 87%; ACT scores over 24: 43%; ACT scores over 30: 7%.
Retention: 75% of full-time freshmen returned.

FACULTY
Total: 1,080, 72% full-time, 66% with terminal degrees.
Student/faculty ratio: 21:1.

ACADEMICS
Calendar: semesters. *Degrees:* certificates, bachelor's, master's, doctoral, post-master's, and postbachelor's certificates.

Special study options: academic remediation for entering students, accelerated degree program, adult/continuing education programs, advanced placement credit, cooperative education, distance learning, double majors, English as a second language, freshman honors college, honors programs, independent study, internships, off-campus study, part-time degree program, services for LD students, student-designed majors, study abroad, summer session for credit. *ROTC:* Army (b), Air Force (c).

Unusual degree programs: 3-2 business administration; engineering; nursing; social work; environmental sciences/public health.

Computers: 5,000 computers/terminals and 10,000 ports are available on campus for general student use. Students can access the following: campus intranet, computer help desk, free student e-mail accounts, online (class) grades, online (class) registration, online (class) schedules, online transcripts, student account. Campuswide network is available. 100% of college-owned or -operated housing units are wired for high-speed Internet access. Wireless service is available via entire campus.

Library: Carlson Library plus 3 others. *Books:* 563,687 (physical), 339,697 (digital/electronic); *Serial titles:* 5,602 (physical), 74,382 (digital/electronic); *Databases:* 340. Weekly public service hours: 107; students can reserve study rooms.

STUDENT LIFE

Housing options: on-campus residence required through sophomore year; coed, special housing for students with disabilities. Campus housing is university owned and is provided by a third party. Freshman campus housing is guaranteed.

Activities and organizations: drama/theater group, student-run newspaper, radio and television station, choral group, marching band, Student Government, University YMCA, Newman Club, International Student Association, Campus Activities and Programming, national fraternities, national sororities.

Athletics Member NCAA. All Division I except football (Division I-A). *Intercollegiate sports:* baseball M(s), basketball M(s)/W(s), cross-country running M(s)/W(s), golf M(s)/W(s), soccer W(s), softball W(s), swimming and diving W(s), tennis M(s)/W(s), track and field W(s), volleyball W(s). *Intramural sports:* badminton M/W, basketball M/W, bowling M/W, cheerleading W, crew M(c)/W(c), fencing M(c)/W(c), football M/W, golf M/W, lacrosse M/W, racquetball M/W, sailing M(c)/W(c), skiing (cross-country) M(c)/W(c), skiing (downhill) M(c)/W(c), soccer M(c)/W(c), softball M/W, swimming and diving M/W, table tennis M/W, tennis M/W, track and field M/W, volleyball M/W, water polo M/W, weight lifting M/W, wrestling M.

Campus security: 24-hour emergency response devices and patrols, student patrols, late-night transport/escort service, controlled dormitory access, bicycle patrols by security staff, crime prevention officer.

Student services: health clinic, personal/psychological counseling, women's center, legal services.

COSTS & FINANCIAL AID

Costs (2017–18) *Tuition:* state resident $8050 full-time, $335 per credit hour part-time; nonresident $17,388 full-time, $725 per credit hour part-time. Full-time tuition and fees vary according to course load, program, reciprocity agreements, and student level. Part-time tuition and fees vary according to course load, program, reciprocity agreements, and student level. *Required fees:* $1190 full-time, $50 per credit hour part-time. *Room and board:* $11,151; room only: $7471. Room and board charges vary according to board plan and housing facility. *Payment plan:* installment. *Waivers:* employees or children of employees.

Financial Aid Of all full-time matriculated undergraduates who enrolled in 2017, 10,240 applied for aid, 8,238 were judged to have need, 770 had their need fully met. In 2017, 2990 non-need-based awards were made. *Average percent of need met:* 57. *Average financial aid package:* $10,938. *Average need-based loan:* $4106. *Average need-based gift aid:* $8810. *Average non-need-based aid:* $5995. *Average indebtedness upon graduation:* $28,260.

APPLYING

Standardized Tests *Required:* SAT or ACT (for admission).

Options: electronic application, deferred entrance.

Application fee: $40.

Required: high school transcript. *Required for some:* minimum 2.0 GPA, core high school curriculum.

Application deadlines: rolling (freshmen), rolling (out-of-state freshmen), rolling (transfers).

Notification: continuous (freshmen), continuous (out-of-state freshmen), continuous (transfers).

CONTACT

William Pierce, Director of Undergraduate Admissions, The University of Toledo, 2801 West Bancroft, Toledo, OH 43606-3390. *Phone:* 419-530-5445. *Toll-free phone:* 800-5TOLEDO. *Fax:* 419-530-5713. *E-mail:* william.pierce@utoledo.edu.

Urbana University–A Branch Campus of Franklin University

Urbana, Ohio
http://www.urbana.edu/

CONTACT

Mr. Donnel W. Wiggins, Director of Admissions, Urbana University–A Branch Campus of Franklin University, 579 College Way, Urbana, OH 43078. *Toll-free phone:* 800-7-URBANA. *E-mail:* admiss@urbana.edu.

Ursuline College

Pepper Pike, Ohio
http://www.ursuline.edu/

- **Independent Roman Catholic** comprehensive, founded 1871
- **Suburban** 62-acre campus with easy access to Cleveland
- **Endowment** $43.5 million
- **Coed, primarily women** 621 undergraduate students, 73% full-time, 92% women, 8% men
- **Minimally difficult** entrance level, 93% of applicants were admitted

UNDERGRAD STUDENTS

455 full-time, 166 part-time. Students come from 17 states and territories; 11 other countries; 8% are from out of state; 21% Black or African American, non-Hispanic/Latino; 2% Hispanic/Latino; 2% Asian, non-Hispanic/Latino; 4% Two or more races, non-Hispanic/Latino; 6% Race/ethnicity unknown; 2% international; 12% transferred in; 25% live on campus.

Freshmen:

Admission: 525 applied, 490 admitted, 79 enrolled. *Average high school GPA:* 3.3. *Test scores:* SAT evidence-based reading and writing scores over 500: 75%; ACT scores over 18: 75%; SAT evidence-based reading and writing scores over 600: 25%; ACT scores over 24: 29%; ACT scores over 30: 1%.

Retention: 71% of full-time freshmen returned.

FACULTY

Total: 170, 35% full-time, 41% with terminal degrees.

Student/faculty ratio: 8:1.

ACADEMICS

Calendar: semesters. *Degrees:* certificates, bachelor's, master's, doctoral, post-master's, and postbachelor's certificates (applications from men are also accepted).

Special study options: academic remediation for entering students, accelerated degree program, adult/continuing education programs, advanced placement credit, distance learning, double majors, independent study, internships, off-campus study, part-time degree program, services for LD students, student-designed majors, summer session for credit. *ROTC:* Army (c).

Unusual degree programs: 3-2 pharmacy with University of Toledo.

Computers: 72 computers/terminals are available on campus for general student use. Students can access the following: campus intranet, computer help desk, online (class) grades, online (class) registration, online (class) schedules. Campuswide network is available. 100% of college-owned or -operated housing units are wired for high-speed Internet access. Wireless service is available via entire campus.

Library: Ralph M. Besse Library. *Books:* 132,089 (physical), 137,533 (digital/electronic); *Serial titles:* 902 (physical), 14,413 (digital/electronic); *Databases:* 162. Weekly public service hours: 91; students can reserve study rooms.

STUDENT LIFE

Housing options: coed, women-only, special housing for students with disabilities. Campus housing is university owned. Freshman campus housing is guaranteed.

Activities and organizations: drama/theater group, Programming Board, Student Nurses of Ursuline College, U-Earth, Women's Circle, Anime Club.

Athletics Member NCAA. All Division II. *Intercollegiate sports:* basketball W(s), bowling W(s), cross-country running W(s), golf W(s), lacrosse W(s), soccer W(s), softball W(s), swimming and diving W(s), tennis W(s), track and field W(s), volleyball W(s).

Campus security: 24-hour emergency response devices and patrols, late-night transport/escort service, controlled dormitory access.

Student services: personal/psychological counseling.

COSTS & FINANCIAL AID

Costs (2018–19) *Comprehensive fee:* $43,166 includes full-time tuition ($32,070), mandatory fees ($320), and room and board ($10,776). Full-time tuition and fees vary according to class time, course load, degree level, location, and program. Part-time tuition: $1069 per credit hour. Part-time tuition and fees vary according to class time, course load, degree level, location, and program. *Required fees:* $120 per term part-time.

Room and board: Room and board charges vary according to housing facility. **Payment plan:** installment. **Waivers:** employees or children of employees.

Financial Aid Of all full-time matriculated undergraduates who enrolled in 2016, 410 applied for aid, 382 were judged to have need, 47 had their need fully met. In 2016, 51 non-need-based awards were made. **Average percent of need met:** 70. **Average financial aid package:** $22,926. **Average need-based loan:** $5302. **Average need-based gift aid:** $19,054. **Average non-need-based aid:** $8531. **Average indebtedness upon graduation:** $32,375.

APPLYING

Standardized Tests *Required:* SAT or ACT (for admission).

Options: electronic application, deferred entrance.

Required: essay or personal statement, high school transcript, 1 letter of recommendation. **Recommended:** minimum 2.5 GPA, interview.

Application deadlines: 2/1 (freshmen), rolling (transfers).

Notification: continuous (freshmen), continuous (out-of-state freshmen), continuous (transfers).

CONTACT

Ms. Emily Haggerty, Associate Director, Admission and Recruitment, Ursuline College, 2550 Lander Road, Pepper Pike, OH 44124. *Phone:* 440-684-6107. *Toll-free phone:* 888-URSULINE. *E-mail:* esmith2@ursuline.edu.

Virginia Marti College of Art and Design

Lakewood, Ohio

http://www.vmcad.edu/

- **Proprietary** 4-year, founded 1966
- **Urban** campus with easy access to Cleveland
- **Coed**
- **Moderately difficult** entrance level

FACULTY

Student/faculty ratio: 12:1.

ACADEMICS

Calendar: quarters. *Degrees:* certificates, associate, and bachelor's. **Library:** VMCAD Library.

STUDENT LIFE

Housing options: college housing not available.

Campus security: 24-hour emergency response devices.

Student services: personal/psychological counseling.

COSTS

Costs (2017–18) *One-time required fee:* $125. *Tuition:* $18,900 full-time, $420 per credit hour part-time. Full-time tuition and fees vary according to course load and program. Part-time tuition and fees vary according to course load and program. *Required fees:* $1155 full-time, $1155 per year part-time.

APPLYING

Standardized Tests *Required:* SAT or ACT (for admission). *Required for some:* Wonderlic aptitude test.

Options: electronic application, early admission, deferred entrance.

Required: essay or personal statement, high school transcript, minimum 2.0 GPA. *Required for some:* entrance evaluation test. *Recommended:* 1 letter of recommendation, interview.

CONTACT

Regina Reihard, Admissions Representative, Virginia Marti College of Art and Design, 11724 Detroit Ave, Lakewood, OH 44107. *Phone:* 216-221-8584 Ext. 113. *E-mail:* rreihard@vmcad.edu.

Walsh University

North Canton, Ohio

http://www.walsh.edu/

- **Independent Roman Catholic** comprehensive, founded 1958
- **Small-town** 134-acre campus with easy access to Cleveland
- **Endowment** $22.6 million
- **Coed** 2,009 undergraduate students, 87% full-time, 59% women, 41% men
- **Moderately difficult** entrance level, 78% of applicants were admitted

UNDERGRAD STUDENTS

1,744 full-time, 265 part-time. Students come from 34 states and territories; 24 other countries; 9% are from out of state; 7% Black or African American, non-Hispanic/Latino; 4% Hispanic/Latino; 0.6% Asian, non-Hispanic/Latino; 0.0% Native Hawaiian or other Pacific Islander, non-Hispanic/Latino; 0.2% American Indian or Alaska Native, non-Hispanic/Latino; 2% Two or more races, non-Hispanic/Latino; 15% Race/ethnicity unknown; 4% international; 4% transferred in; 48% live on campus.

Freshmen:

Admission: 1,693 applied, 1,315 admitted, 462 enrolled. **Average high school GPA:** 3.5. **Test scores:** ACT scores over 18: 93%; ACT scores over 24: 43%; ACT scores over 30: 7%.

Retention: 74% of full-time freshmen returned.

FACULTY

Total: 242, 54% full-time, 43% with terminal degrees.

Student/faculty ratio: 14:1.

ACADEMICS

Calendar: semesters. *Degrees:* certificates, associate, bachelor's, master's, and doctoral.

Special study options: academic remediation for entering students, accelerated degree program, adult/continuing education programs, advanced placement credit, distance learning, double majors, English as a second language, external degree program, honors programs, independent study, internships, off-campus study, part-time degree program, services for LD students, study abroad, summer session for credit.

Unusual degree programs: 3-2 engineering with University of Dayton; behavioral science/counseling, biology/physical therapy.

Computers: 336 computers/terminals and 1,622 ports are available on campus for general student use. Students can access the following: campus intranet, computer help desk, free student e-mail accounts, online (class) grades, online (class) registration, online (class) schedules. Campuswide network is available. 100% of college-owned or -operated housing units are wired for high-speed Internet access. Wireless service is available via entire campus.

Library: Brother Edmond Drouin Library. *Books:* 97,575 (physical), 254,114 (digital/electronic); *Serial titles:* 995 (physical), 82,413 (digital/electronic); *Databases:* 167. Weekly public service hours: 79.

STUDENT LIFE

Housing options: on-campus residence required through senior year; coed, cooperative, special housing for students with disabilities. Campus housing is university owned. Freshman campus housing is guaranteed.

Activities and organizations: drama/theater group, student-run newspaper, radio station, choral group, marching band, Student Government, University Programming Board, Business and Communication Club, Behavioral Science Club, Education Club.

Athletics Member NCAA. All Division II. *Intercollegiate sports:* baseball M(s), basketball M(s)/W(s), cheerleading W(c), cross-country running M(s)/W(s), football M(s), golf M(s)/W(s), lacrosse M(s)/W(s), soccer M(s)/W(s), softball W(s), tennis M(s)/W(s), track and field M(s)/W(s), volleyball W(s). *Intramural sports:* basketball M/W, bowling M/W, football M, golf M/W, skiing (downhill) M(c)/W(c), soccer M/W, table tennis M/W, tennis M/W, ultimate Frisbee M(c)/W(c), volleyball M/W.

Campus security: 24-hour emergency response devices and patrols, late-night transport/escort service, controlled dormitory access.

Student services: health clinic, personal/psychological counseling.

COSTS & FINANCIAL AID

Costs (2017–18) *Comprehensive fee:* $39,680 includes full-time tuition ($27,650), mandatory fees ($1500), and room and board ($10,530). Full-time tuition and fees vary according to location. Part-time tuition: $920 per credit hour. Part-time tuition and fees vary according to location. *Required fees:* $50 per credit hour part-time. *College room only:* $5770. Room and board charges vary according to board plan and housing facility. *Payment plan:* installment. *Waivers:* children of alumni, senior citizens, and employees or children of employees.

Financial Aid Of all full-time matriculated undergraduates who enrolled in 2010, 1,726 applied for aid, 1,661 were judged to have need, 798 had their need fully met. In 2010, 180 non-need-based awards were made. *Average percent of need met:* 71. *Average financial aid package:* $18,133. *Average need-based loan:* $4850. *Average need-based gift aid:* $6844. *Average non-need-based aid:* $9372. *Average indebtedness upon graduation:* $24,753.

APPLYING

Standardized Tests *Required for some:* SAT or ACT (for admission).

Options: electronic application, early admission, deferred entrance.

Application fee: $25.

Required: high school transcript, minimum 2.4 GPA. *Required for some:* essay or personal statement, minimum 3.0 GPA, 2 letters of recommendation. *Recommended:* interview.

Application deadlines: rolling (freshmen), rolling (transfers).

Notification: continuous (freshmen), continuous (transfers).

CONTACT

Ms. Melissa Schoeppner, Campus Visit Coordinator, Walsh University, 2020 East Maple, North Canton, OH 44720. *Phone:* 330-490-7172. *Toll-free phone:* 800-362-9846 (in-state); 800-362-8846 (out-of-state). *Fax:* 330-490-7165. *E-mail:* admissions@walsh.edu.

Wilberforce University

Wilberforce, Ohio

http://www.wilberforce.edu/

CONTACT

Ms. Dadra Driscoll, Director, Office of Admissions, Wilberforce University, 1055 N. Bickett Road, PO Box 1001, Wolfe Administration, Wilberforce, OH 45384. *Phone:* 937-708-5556. *Toll-free phone:* 800-367-8568. *E-mail:* ddriscoll@wilberforce.edu.

Wilmington College

Wilmington, Ohio

http://www.wilmington.edu/

CONTACT

Ms. Tina Garland, Director of Admission and Financial Aid, Wilmington College, 1870 Quaker Way, Wilmington, OH 45177. *Phone:* 937-382-6661 Ext. 426. *Toll-free phone:* 800-341-9318. *Fax:* 937-383-8542. *E-mail:* admissions@wilmington.edu.

Wittenberg University

Springfield, Ohio

http://www.wittenberg.edu/

- **Independent** comprehensive, founded 1845, affiliated with Evangelical Lutheran Church
- **Suburban** 114-acre campus with easy access to Columbus, Dayton
- **Coed** 1,857 undergraduate students, 96% full-time, 54% women, 46% men
- **Moderately difficult** entrance level, 72% of applicants were admitted

UNDERGRAD STUDENTS

1,775 full-time, 82 part-time. Students come from 38 states and territories; 11 other countries; 25% are from out of state; 10% Black or African American, non-Hispanic/Latino; 4% Hispanic/Latino; 1% Asian, non-Hispanic/Latino; 0.1% Native Hawaiian or other Pacific Islander, non-Hispanic/Latino; 0.2% American Indian or Alaska Native, non-Hispanic/Latino; 6% Two or more races, non-Hispanic/Latino; 1% Race/ethnicity unknown; 1% international; 2% transferred in; 85% live on campus.

Freshmen:

Admission: 7,249 applied, 5,232 admitted, 539 enrolled. *Average high school GPA:* 3.4. *Test scores:* SAT evidence-based reading and writing scores over 500: 88%; SAT math scores over 500: 80%; ACT scores over 18: 97%; SAT evidence-based reading and writing scores over 600: 50%; SAT math scores over 600: 45%; ACT scores over 24: 61%; SAT evidence-based reading and writing scores over 700: 14%; SAT math scores over 700: 10%; ACT scores over 30: 14%.

Retention: 72% of full-time freshmen returned.

FACULTY

Total: 185, 62% full-time, 75% with terminal degrees.

Student/faculty ratio: 13:1.

ACADEMICS

Calendar: semesters. *Degrees:* bachelor's and master's.

Special study options: academic remediation for entering students, adult/continuing education programs, advanced placement credit, cooperative education, double majors, freshman honors college, honors programs, independent study, internships, off-campus study, part-time degree program, student-designed majors, study abroad, summer session for credit. *ROTC:* Army (c), Air Force (c).

Unusual degree programs: 3-2 engineering with Georgia Institute of Technology, Washington University in St. Louis, Case Western Reserve University; forestry with Duke University; nursing with Case Western Reserve University, Johns Hopkins University; occupational therapy with Washington University in St. Louis.

Computers: 900 computers/terminals and 1,200 ports are available on campus for general student use. Students can access the following: computer help desk, free student e-mail accounts, online (class) grades, online (class) registration, online (class) schedules. Campuswide network is available. Wireless service is available via entire campus.

Library: Thomas Library plus 1 other. *Books:* 135,595 (digital/electronic); *Serial titles:* 163,369 (digital/electronic); *Databases:* 209. Weekly public service hours: 93.

STUDENT LIFE

Housing options: on-campus residence required through sophomore year; coed, women-only. Campus housing is university owned, leased by the school and is provided by a third party. Freshman campus housing is guaranteed.

Activities and organizations: drama/theater group, student-run newspaper, radio station, choral group, Student Senate, Union Board, Choirs, Weaver Chapel Association, national fraternities, national sororities.

Athletics Member NCAA. All Division III. *Intercollegiate sports:* baseball M, basketball M/W, crew M(c)/W(c), cross-country running M/W, field hockey W, football M, golf M/W, lacrosse M/W, rugby M(c)/W(c), soccer M/W, softball W, swimming and diving M/W, tennis M/W, track and field M/W, volleyball M/W. *Intramural sports:* basketball M/W, bowling M(c)/W(c), cheerleading M(c)/W(c), football M, golf M/W, ice hockey M(c)/W(c), sailing M/W, soccer M/W, softball M/W, swimming and diving M/W, tennis M/W, track and field M/W, volleyball M/W.

Campus security: 24-hour emergency response devices and patrols, student patrols, late-night transport/escort service, controlled dormitory access, crime prevention programs.

Student services: health clinic, personal/psychological counseling, women's center.

COSTS & FINANCIAL AID

Costs (2018–19) *Comprehensive fee:* $49,856 includes full-time tuition ($38,680), mandatory fees ($820), and room and board ($10,356). Part-time tuition: $1289 per credit hour. Part-time tuition and fees vary according to course load. *College room only:* $5288. Room and board charges vary according to board plan and housing facility. *Payment plan:* installment. *Waivers:* minority students, children of alumni, adult students, senior citizens, and employees or children of employees.

Financial Aid Of all full-time matriculated undergraduates who enrolled in 2017, 1,652 applied for aid, 1,453 were judged to have need, 391 had their need fully met. In 2017, 315 non-need-based awards were made. *Average percent of need met:* 83. *Average financial aid package:* $32,409. *Average need-based loan:* $4444. *Average need-based gift aid:*

$26,551. *Average non-need-based aid:* $20,649. *Average indebtedness upon graduation:* $35,242.

APPLYING
Standardized Tests *Recommended:* Test score optional.

Options: electronic application, early admission, early decision, early action, deferred entrance.

Application fee: $40.

Required: high school transcript, interview. *Recommended:* essay or personal statement.

Application deadlines: rolling (transfers), 12/1 (early action).

Early decision deadline: 11/15.

Notification: continuous (freshmen), continuous (transfers), 12/15 (early decision), 1/1 (early action).

CONTACT
Ms. Karen Hunt, Director of Admission, Wittenberg University, PO Box 720, Springfield, OH 45501-0720. *Phone:* 877-206-0332 Ext. 6377. *Toll-free phone:* 800-677-7558 Ext. 6314. *Fax:* 937-327-6379. *E-mail:* admission@wittenberg.edu.

Wright State University
Dayton, Ohio
http://www.wright.edu/

- **State-supported** university, founded 1964, part of University System of Ohio
- **Suburban** 557-acre campus with easy access to Dayton, Columbus, Cincinnati
- **Coed** 12,115 undergraduate students, 78% full-time, 52% women, 48% men
- **Minimally difficult** entrance level, 97% of applicants were admitted

UNDERGRAD STUDENTS
9,423 full-time, 2,692 part-time. 5% are from out of state; 11% Black or African American, non-Hispanic/Latino; 4% Hispanic/Latino; 3% Asian, non-Hispanic/Latino; 0.1% Native Hawaiian or other Pacific Islander, non-Hispanic/Latino; 0.1% American Indian or Alaska Native, non-Hispanic/Latino; 4% Two or more races, non-Hispanic/Latino; 0.5% Race/ethnicity unknown; 3% international; 8% transferred in; 19% live on campus.

Freshmen:
Admission: 5,826 applied, 5,638 admitted, 2,281 enrolled. *Average high school GPA:* 3.3. *Test scores:* SAT evidence-based reading and writing scores over 500: 73%; SAT math scores over 500: 74%; ACT scores over 18: 82%; SAT evidence-based reading and writing scores over 600: 41%; SAT math scores over 600: 35%; ACT scores over 24: 38%; SAT evidence-based reading and writing scores over 700: 7%; SAT math scores over 700: 6%; ACT scores over 30: 7%.

Retention: 63% of full-time freshmen returned.

ACADEMICS
Calendar: semesters. *Degrees:* certificates, bachelor's, master's, doctoral, post-master's, and postbachelor's certificates.

Special study options: academic remediation for entering students, adult/continuing education programs, advanced placement credit, cooperative education, distance learning, double majors, English as a second language, freshman honors college, honors programs, independent study, internships, off-campus study, part-time degree program, services for LD students, student-designed majors, study abroad, summer session for credit. *ROTC:* Army (b), Air Force (b).

Computers: Students can access the following: campus intranet, computer help desk, free student e-mail accounts, online (class) grades, online (class) registration, online (class) schedules, student webpages, Lap tops 2 Go, office software programs. Campuswide network is available. 100% of college-owned or -operated housing units are wired for high-speed Internet access. Wireless service is available via entire campus.

Library: Paul Laurence Dunbar Library plus 1 other. Students can reserve study rooms.

STUDENT LIFE
Housing options: coed, special housing for students with disabilities. Campus housing is university owned and leased by the school.

Activities and organizations: drama/theater group, student-run newspaper, radio and television station, choral group, national fraternities, national sororities.

Athletics Member NCAA. All Division I. *Intercollegiate sports:* baseball M(s), basketball M(s)/W(s), cheerleading M(s)/W(s), cross-country running M(s)/W(s), golf M(s), soccer M(s)/W(s), softball W(s), swimming and diving M(s)/W(s), tennis M(s)/W(s), track and field W(s), volleyball W(s). *Intramural sports:* baseball M(c), basketball M, football M(c)/W(c), gymnastics M(c)/W(c), ice hockey M(c), rugby M(c)/W(c), skiing (downhill) M(c)/W(c), soccer M/W, softball M/W, swimming and diving M(c)/W(c), table tennis M, track and field M(c)/W(c), ultimate Frisbee M(c)/W(c), volleyball W, water polo M/W, wrestling M(c).

Campus security: 24-hour emergency response devices and patrols, student patrols, late-night transport/escort service, controlled dormitory access.

Student services: health clinic, personal/psychological counseling, women's center, legal services.

COSTS & FINANCIAL AID
Costs (2017–18) *Tuition:* state resident $8730 full-time, $394 per credit hour part-time; nonresident $17,608 full-time, $803 per credit hour part-time. Full-time tuition and fees vary according to course load, location, and reciprocity agreements. Part-time tuition and fees vary according to course load, location, and reciprocity agreements. *Room and board:* $11,376; room only: $6380. Room and board charges vary according to board plan, housing facility, and location. *Payment plan:* installment. *Waivers:* senior citizens and employees or children of employees.

Financial Aid Of all full-time matriculated undergraduates who enrolled in 2017, 7,246 applied for aid, 5,862 were judged to have need, 975 had their need fully met. In 2017, 1720 non-need-based awards were made. *Average percent of need met:* 62. *Average financial aid package:* $10,526. *Average need-based loan:* $4024. *Average need-based gift aid:* $6586. *Average non-need-based aid:* $4185. *Average indebtedness upon graduation:* $30,677.

APPLYING
Standardized Tests *Required:* SAT or ACT (for admission).

Options: electronic application, early admission, deferred entrance.

Application fee: $30.

Required: high school transcript. *Recommended:* minimum 2.0 GPA.

Application deadlines: 8/20 (freshmen), rolling (transfers).

Notification: 9/1 (freshmen), continuous (transfers).

CONTACT
Wright State University, 3640 Colonel Glenn Highway, E147 Student Union, Dayton, OH 45435. *Phone:* 937-775-5700. *Toll-free phone:* 800-247-1770. *Fax:* 937-775-5795. *E-mail:* admissions@wright.edu.

Wright State University–Lake Campus
Celina, Ohio
http://www.wright.edu/lake/

- **State-supported** comprehensive, founded 1969
- **Small-town** 211-acre campus
- **Coed** 1,037 undergraduate students, 67% full-time, 55% women, 45% men
- **Minimally difficult** entrance level, 99% of applicants were admitted

UNDERGRAD STUDENTS
699 full-time, 338 part-time. 1% are from out of state; 2% Black or African American, non-Hispanic/Latino; 3% Hispanic/Latino; 0.7% Asian, non-Hispanic/Latino; 1% Two or more races, non-Hispanic/Latino; 1% Race/ethnicity unknown; 0.1% international; 5% transferred in; 7% live on campus.

Freshmen:
Admission: 372 applied, 370 admitted, 242 enrolled. *Average high school GPA:* 3.1. *Test scores:* SAT evidence-based reading and writing scores over 500: 62%; SAT math scores over 500: 31%; ACT scores over 18: 80%; SAT evidence-based reading and writing scores over 600: 8%; SAT math scores over 600: 8%; ACT scores over 24: 21%; ACT scores over 30: 1%.

Retention: 75% of full-time freshmen returned.

ACADEMICS

Calendar: semesters. *Degrees:* certificates, associate, and bachelor's.

Special study options: academic remediation for entering students, accelerated degree program, adult/continuing education programs, advanced placement credit, cooperative education, distance learning, double majors, honors programs, independent study, internships, off-campus study, part-time degree program, services for LD students, student-designed majors, study abroad, summer session for credit.

Computers: Students can access the following: campus intranet, computer help desk, free student e-mail accounts, online (class) grades, online (class) registration, online (class) schedules. Campuswide network is available. 100% of college-owned or -operated housing units are wired for high-speed Internet access. Wireless service is available via entire campus.

Library: Lake Campus Library & Technology Center plus 1 other.

STUDENT LIFE

Housing options: coed. Campus housing is leased by the school.

Athletics Member USCAA. *Intercollegiate sports:* baseball M, basketball M/W, softball W, volleyball W.

Campus security: 24-hour emergency response devices, WSU-Police Department presence, 40 hours per week.

Student services: health clinic, personal/psychological counseling.

COSTS & FINANCIAL AID

Costs (2017–18) *Tuition:* state resident $5842 full-time, $265 per credit hour part-time; nonresident $14,720 full-time, $674 per credit hour part-time. Full-time tuition and fees vary according to course load, location, and reciprocity agreements. Part-time tuition and fees vary according to course load, location, and reciprocity agreements. *Room and board:* $10,584; room only: $4996. Room and board charges vary according to board plan, housing facility, and location. *Payment plan:* installment. *Waivers:* senior citizens and employees or children of employees.

Financial Aid Of all full-time matriculated undergraduates who enrolled in 2016, 555 applied for aid, 418 were judged to have need, 102 had their need fully met. In 2016, 127 non-need-based awards were made. *Average percent of need met:* 69. *Average financial aid package:* $7922. *Average need-based loan:* $3658. *Average need-based gift aid:* $4609. *Average non-need-based aid:* $2567. *Average indebtedness upon graduation:* $22,549.

APPLYING

Standardized Tests *Required:* SAT or ACT (for admission).

Options: electronic application, deferred entrance.

Application fee: $30.

Required: high school transcript. *Recommended:* minimum 2.0 GPA.

Application deadlines: rolling (freshmen), rolling (transfers).

Notification: continuous (freshmen), continuous (transfers).

CONTACT

Ms. Jill Puthoff, Admissions/Communications Coordinator, Wright State University–Lake Campus, 174 Dwyer Hall, Celina, OH 45822. *Phone:* 419-586-0363. *Toll-free phone:* 800-237-1477. *E-mail:* jill.puthoff@wright.edu.

Xavier University

Cincinnati, Ohio

http://www.xavier.edu/

CONTACT

Xavier University, 3800 Victory Parkway, Cincinnati, OH 45207-5311. *Phone:* 513-745-3301. *Toll-free phone:* 877-XUADMIT. *E-mail:* xuadmit@xavier.edu.

Youngstown State University

Youngstown, Ohio

http://www.ysu.edu/

- **State-supported** comprehensive, founded 1908
- **Urban** 160-acre campus with easy access to Cleveland, Pittsburgh
- **Endowment** $241.4 million
- **Coed** 11,386 undergraduate students, 78% full-time, 52% women, 48% men
- **Minimally difficult** entrance level, 65% of applicants were admitted

UNDERGRAD STUDENTS

8,880 full-time, 2,506 part-time. Students come from 71 other countries; 15% are from out of state; 10% Black or African American, non-Hispanic/Latino; 4% Hispanic/Latino; 1% Asian, non-Hispanic/Latino; 0.1% Native Hawaiian or other Pacific Islander, non-Hispanic/Latino; 0.1% American Indian or Alaska Native, non-Hispanic/Latino; 3% Two or more races, non-Hispanic/Latino; 4% Race/ethnicity unknown; 3% international; 5% transferred in; 21% live on campus.

Freshmen:
Admission: 9,765 applied, 6,379 admitted, 2,215 enrolled. *Average high school GPA:* 3.3. *Test scores:* SAT evidence-based reading and writing scores over 500: 71%; SAT math scores over 500: 73%; ACT scores over 18: 84%; SAT evidence-based reading and writing scores over 600: 26%; SAT math scores over 600: 34%; ACT scores over 24: 31%; SAT evidence-based reading and writing scores over 700: 4%; SAT math scores over 700: 7%; ACT scores over 30: 5%.

Retention: 76% of full-time freshmen returned.

FACULTY

Total: 1,044, 38% full-time.

Student/faculty ratio: 17:1.

ACADEMICS

Calendar: semesters. *Degrees:* certificates, diplomas, associate, bachelor's, master's, doctoral, post-master's, and postbachelor's certificates.

Special study options: academic remediation for entering students, accelerated degree program, adult/continuing education programs, advanced placement credit, cooperative education, distance learning, double majors, English as a second language, freshman honors college, honors programs, independent study, internships, off-campus study, part-time degree program, services for LD students, student-designed majors, study abroad, summer session for credit. *ROTC:* Army (b), Air Force (c).

Unusual degree programs: 3-2 chemistry, medicine.

Computers: 500 computers/terminals are available on campus for general student use. Students can access the following: campus intranet, computer help desk, free student e-mail accounts, online (class) grades, online (class) registration, online (class) schedules. Campuswide network is available. 100% of college-owned or -operated housing units are wired for high-speed Internet access. Wireless service is available via entire campus.

Library: William F. Maag, Jr. Library plus 1 other. *Books:* 773,051 (physical), 100,530 (digital/electronic); *Serial titles:* 71,715 (physical), 51,515 (digital/electronic); *Databases:* 251. Weekly public service hours: 84; students can reserve study rooms.

STUDENT LIFE

Housing options: coed, women-only. Campus housing is university owned and is provided by a third party. Freshman applicants given priority for college housing.

Activities and organizations: drama/theater group, student-run newspaper, radio station, choral group, marching band, American Society of Mechanical Engineers, Society for Human Resource Management, Black Student Union, Fraternities/Sororities (IFC, NPHC and Panhellenic Council), STEM Leadership Society, national fraternities, national sororities.

Athletics Member NCAA. All Division I except football (Division I-AA). *Intercollegiate sports:* baseball M(s), basketball M(s)/W(s), bowling W, cross-country running M(s)/W(s), golf M(s)/W(s), soccer W(s), softball W(s), swimming and diving W(s), tennis M(s)/W(s), track and field M(s)/W(s), volleyball W(s). *Intramural sports:* basketball M/W, bowling M(c)/W(c), cross-country running M/W, equestrian sports M(c)/W(c), fencing M(c)/W(c), football M, ice hockey M(c), lacrosse M(c)/W(c), racquetball M(c)/W(c), riflery M(c), rock climbing M/W, rugby W(c), sand volleyball M/W, soccer M/W, table tennis M/W, track and field M(c)/W(c), ultimate Frisbee M(c)/W(c), volleyball M/W, weight lifting M/W, wrestling M(c)/W(c).

Campus security: 24-hour emergency response devices and patrols, student patrols, late-night transport/escort service, controlled dormitory access, residence hall patrols.

Student services: health clinic, personal/psychological counseling.

COSTS & FINANCIAL AID
Costs (2018–19) *Tuition:* state resident $8899 full-time, $371 per credit hour part-time; nonresident $14,899 full-time, $621 per credit hour part-time. Full-time tuition and fees vary according to course load. Part-time tuition and fees vary according to course load. *Room and board:* Room and board charges vary according to board plan and housing facility. *Payment plans:* installment, deferred payment. *Waivers:* senior citizens and employees or children of employees.

Financial Aid Of all full-time matriculated undergraduates who enrolled in 2016, 7,411 applied for aid, 6,243 were judged to have need, 556 had their need fully met. In 2016, 1116 non-need-based awards were made. *Average percent of need met:* 33. *Average financial aid package:* $9147. *Average need-based loan:* $3760. *Average need-based gift aid:* $5362. *Average non-need-based aid:* $3587. *Average indebtedness upon graduation:* $31,759.

APPLYING
Standardized Tests *Required:* SAT or ACT (for admission).

Options: electronic application, early admission, deferred entrance.

Application fee: $45.

Required: high school transcript, minimum 2.0 GPA, minimum ACT composite score of 17 or combined SAT score of 910 from evidence-based writing and reading test and math test.

Application deadlines: 8/1 (freshmen), 8/1 (transfers).

Notification: continuous (freshmen), continuous (out-of-state freshmen), continuous (transfers).

CONTACT
Ms. Sue Davis, Director of Admissions, Youngstown State University, One University Plaza, Youngstown, OH 44555-0001. *Phone:* 330-941-2000. *Toll-free phone:* 877-468-6978. *Fax:* 330-941-3674. *E-mail:* enroll@ysu.edu.

OKLAHOMA

Bacone College
Muskogee, Oklahoma
http://www.bacone.edu/

CONTACT
Bacone College, 2299 Old Bacone Road, Muskogee, OK 74403-1597. *Phone:* 918-781-7342. *Toll-free phone:* 888-682-5514 Ext. 7340.

Cameron University
Lawton, Oklahoma
http://www.cameron.edu/

- **State-supported** comprehensive, founded 1908, part of Oklahoma State Regents for Higher Education
- **Small-town** 360-acre campus
- **Endowment** $18.2 million
- **Coed** 4,150 undergraduate students, 68% full-time, 60% women, 40% men
- **Noncompetitive** entrance level, 100% of applicants were admitted

UNDERGRAD STUDENTS
2,814 full-time, 1,336 part-time. Students come from 46 states and territories; 42 other countries; 12% are from out of state; 13% Black or African American, non-Hispanic/Latino; 13% Hispanic/Latino; 2% Asian, non-Hispanic/Latino; 0.6% Native Hawaiian or other Pacific Islander, non-Hispanic/Latino; 5% American Indian or Alaska Native, non-Hispanic/Latino; 9% Two or more races, non-Hispanic/Latino; 3%

Race/ethnicity unknown; 4% international; 7% transferred in; 8% live on campus.

Freshmen:
Admission: 1,093 applied, 1,093 admitted, 638 enrolled. *Average high school GPA:* 3.1. *Test scores:* ACT scores over 18: 70%; ACT scores over 24: 20%; ACT scores over 30: 2%.
Retention: 65% of full-time freshmen returned.

FACULTY
Total: 249, 56% full-time, 51% with terminal degrees.
Student/faculty ratio: 20:1.

ACADEMICS
Calendar: semesters. *Degrees:* associate, bachelor's, and master's.

Special study options: academic remediation for entering students, accelerated degree program, adult/continuing education programs, advanced placement credit, distance learning, double majors, honors programs, independent study, internships, off-campus study, part-time degree program, services for LD students, student-designed majors, summer session for credit. *ROTC:* Army (b).

Computers: 240 computers/terminals are available on campus for general student use. Students can access the following: computer help desk, free student e-mail accounts, online (class) grades, online (class) registration, online (class) schedules, online courses. Campuswide network is available. 100% of college-owned or -operated housing units are wired for high-speed Internet access. Wireless service is available via classrooms, computer centers, computer labs, dorm rooms, learning centers, libraries, student centers.

Library: Cameron University Library. *Books:* 91,153 (physical), 269,279 (digital/electronic); *Serial titles:* 10 (physical), 37,786 (digital/electronic); *Databases:* 67. Weekly public service hours: 34; students can reserve study rooms.

STUDENT LIFE
Housing options: men-only, women-only, special housing for students with disabilities. Campus housing is university owned.

Activities and organizations: drama/theater group, student-run newspaper, television station, choral group, Student Government Association, International Club, Nigerian Student Association, Greek Life, Nepalese Association, national fraternities, national sororities.

Athletics Member NCAA. All Division II. *Intercollegiate sports:* baseball M(s), basketball M(s)/W(s), cross-country running M(s), golf M(s)/W(s), softball W(s), tennis M(s)/W(s), volleyball W(s). *Intramural sports:* badminton M/W, basketball M/W, bowling M/W, racquetball M/W, soccer M/W, softball M/W, table tennis M/W, tennis M/W, volleyball M/W, weight lifting M/W.

Campus security: 24-hour emergency response devices and patrols, late-night transport/escort service, controlled dormitory access.

Student services: health clinic, personal/psychological counseling.

COSTS & FINANCIAL AID
Costs (2017–18) *Tuition:* state resident $4470 full-time, $149 per credit hour part-time; nonresident $13,800 full-time, $460 per credit hour part-time. Full-time tuition and fees vary according to course level, course load, location, program, and student level. Part-time tuition and fees vary according to course level, course load, location, program, and student level. *Required fees:* $1710 full-time, $57 per credit hour part-time. *Room and board:* $5452; room only: $2222. Room and board charges vary according to board plan and housing facility. *Payment plan:* installment. *Waivers:* senior citizens and employees or children of employees.

Financial Aid Of all full-time matriculated undergraduates who enrolled in 2016, 2,344 applied for aid, 2,102 were judged to have need, 120 had their need fully met. 57 Federal Work-Study jobs (averaging $2069). 261 state and other part-time jobs (averaging $2986). In 2016, 255 non-need-based awards were made. *Average percent of need met:* 55. *Average financial aid package:* $8706. *Average need-based loan:* $3708. *Average need-based gift aid:* $6240. *Average non-need-based aid:* $3184. *Average indebtedness upon graduation:* $23,961.

APPLYING
Standardized Tests *Required for some:* SAT or ACT (for admission).
Options: electronic application, deferred entrance.
Application fee: $25.

Required for some: high school transcript.

Application deadlines: rolling (freshmen), rolling (out-of-state freshmen), rolling (transfers).

Notification: continuous (freshmen), continuous (out-of-state freshmen), continuous (transfers).

CONTACT
Ms. Teresa Briggs, Administrative Assistant II, Cameron University, Admissions, 2800 West Gore Boulevard, Lawton, OK 73505-6377. *Phone:* 580-581-2987. *Toll-free phone:* 888-454-7600. *Fax:* 580-581-5416. *E-mail:* tbriggs@cameron.edu.

DeVry University–Oklahoma City Campus

Oklahoma City, Oklahoma
http://www.devry.edu/

CONTACT
Admissions Office, DeVry University–Oklahoma City Campus, Lakepointe Towers, 4013 Northwest Expressway Street, Suite 100, Oklahoma City, OK 73116. *Phone:* 405-767-9516. *Toll-free phone:* 866-338-7934.

East Central University

Ada, Oklahoma
http://www.ecok.edu/

- **State-supported** comprehensive, founded 1909, part of Oklahoma State Regents for Higher Education
- **Small-town** 144-acre campus with easy access to Oklahoma City
- **Endowment** $31.3 million
- **Coed** 3,029 undergraduate students, 78% full-time, 60% women, 40% men
- **Minimally difficult** entrance level, 48% of applicants were admitted

UNDERGRAD STUDENTS
2,372 full-time, 657 part-time. Students come from 22 states and territories; 32 other countries; 7% are from out of state; 4% Black or African American, non-Hispanic/Latino; 6% Hispanic/Latino; 0.3% Asian, non-Hispanic/Latino; 0.3% Native Hawaiian or other Pacific Islander, non-Hispanic/Latino; 15% American Indian or Alaska Native, non-Hispanic/Latino; 8% Two or more races, non-Hispanic/Latino; 2% Race/ethnicity unknown; 7% international; 9% transferred in; 31% live on campus.

Freshmen:
Admission: 1,847 applied, 887 admitted, 471 enrolled. *Average high school GPA:* 3.4. *Test scores:* SAT evidence-based reading and writing scores over 500: 59%; SAT math scores over 500: 74%; ACT scores over 18: 79%; SAT evidence-based reading and writing scores over 600: 9%; SAT math scores over 600: 26%; ACT scores over 24: 18%; ACT scores over 30: 2%.
Retention: 34% of full-time freshmen returned.

FACULTY
Total: 223, 68% full-time, 55% with terminal degrees.
Student/faculty ratio: 18:1.

ACADEMICS
Calendar: semesters. *Degrees:* bachelor's, master's, post-master's, and postbachelor's certificates.
Special study options: academic remediation for entering students, adult/continuing education programs, advanced placement credit, double majors, English as a second language, honors programs, independent study, internships, off-campus study, part-time degree program, services for LD students, student-designed majors, study abroad, summer session for credit.
Computers: 800 computers/terminals are available on campus for general student use. Students can access the following: campus intranet, computer help desk, free student e-mail accounts, online (class) grades, online (class) registration, online (class) schedules. Campuswide network is available. 100% of college-owned or -operated housing units are wired for high-speed Internet access. Wireless service is available via entire campus.
Library: Linscheid Library. *Books:* 159,582 (physical), 25,548 (digital/electronic); *Serial titles:* 24,879 (physical), 825 (digital/electronic); *Databases:* 73. Weekly public service hours: 71; students can reserve study rooms.

STUDENT LIFE
Housing options: on-campus residence required for freshman year; coed. Campus housing is university owned.
Activities and organizations: drama/theater group, choral group, marching band, Campus Connection, F.A.T.E., GSA, ECU Wesley, Tigers for Tigers, national fraternities, national sororities.
Athletics Member NCAA. All Division II. *Intercollegiate sports:* baseball M(s), basketball M(s)/W(s), cross-country running M(s)/W(s), football M(s), soccer W(s), softball W(s), track and field M/W, volleyball W(s). *Intramural sports:* basketball M/W, cheerleading M/W, football M/W, racquetball M/W, soccer M/W, softball M/W, tennis M/W, ultimate Frisbee M/W, volleyball M/W, weight lifting M/W.
Campus security: 24-hour emergency response devices and patrols, student patrols, late-night transport/escort service, controlled dormitory access, agreements with all local, state, federal, and tribal police departments for added crime and violation prevention.
Student services: health clinic, personal/psychological counseling.

COSTS & FINANCIAL AID
Costs (2017–18) *Tuition:* state resident $5301 full-time, $177 per semester hour part-time; nonresident $14,421 full-time, $481 per semester hour part-time. No tuition increase for student's term of enrollment. *Required fees:* $1299 full-time, $43 per semester hour part-time. *Room and board:* $6730; room only: $3516. Room and board charges vary according to board plan and housing facility. *Waivers:* employees or children of employees.
Financial Aid Of all full-time matriculated undergraduates who enrolled in 2016, 2,228 applied for aid, 1,962 were judged to have need, 745 had their need fully met. In 2016, 17 non-need-based awards were made. *Average financial aid package:* $6226. *Average need-based loan:* $7097. *Average need-based gift aid:* $3976. *Average non-need-based aid:* $1082. *Average indebtedness upon graduation:* $24,171.

APPLYING
Standardized Tests *Required:* ACT (for admission). *Recommended:* SAT or ACT (for admission).
Options: electronic application, early admission.
Application fee: $20.
Required: high school transcript. *Required for some:* minimum 2.7 GPA, rank in upper 50% of high school class.
Application deadlines: rolling (freshmen), rolling (transfers).
Notification: continuous (freshmen), continuous (transfers).

CONTACT
Ms. Kylie Stephens, Admissions Counselor, East Central University, 1100 East 14th Street, PMB R-8, Ada, OK 74820-6999. *Phone:* 580-559-5209. *E-mail:* kstephens@ecok.edu.

Family of Faith Christian University

Shawnee, Oklahoma
http://www.familyoffaith.edu/

CONTACT
Family of Faith Christian University, 30 Kinville, Shawnee, OK 74802.

Langston University

Langston, Oklahoma
http://www.langston.edu/

- **State-supported** comprehensive, founded 1897, part of Oklahoma A&M System
- **Rural** 40-acre campus with easy access to Oklahoma City
- **Endowment** $1.6 million
- **Coed** 2,013 undergraduate students, 83% full-time, 63% women, 37% men
- **Moderately difficult** entrance level, 61% of applicants were admitted

UNDERGRAD STUDENTS
1,664 full-time, 349 part-time. Students come from 37 states and territories; 12 other countries; 38% are from out of state; 79% Black or African American, non-Hispanic/Latino; 2% Hispanic/Latino; 0.7% Native Hawaiian or other Pacific Islander, non-Hispanic/Latino; 2% American Indian or Alaska Native, non-Hispanic/Latino; 4% Race/ethnicity unknown; 0.7% international; 9% transferred in; 67% live on campus.

Freshmen:
Admission: 9,244 applied, 5,635 admitted, 633 enrolled. *Average high school GPA:* 2.8.
Retention: 47% of full-time freshmen returned.

FACULTY
Total: 221, 64% full-time, 33% with terminal degrees.
Student/faculty ratio: 22:1.

ACADEMICS
Calendar: semesters. *Degrees:* associate, bachelor's, master's, and doctoral.

Special study options: academic remediation for entering students, accelerated degree program, adult/continuing education programs, advanced placement credit, cooperative education, distance learning, double majors, English as a second language, external degree program, honors programs, independent study, internships, part-time degree program, services for LD students, study abroad, summer session for credit. *ROTC:* Army (c).

Computers: 300 computers/terminals and 1,600 ports are available on campus for general student use. Students can access the following: campus intranet, computer help desk, free student e-mail accounts, online (class) grades, online (class) registration, online (class) schedules. Campuswide network is available. 100% of college-owned or -operated housing units are wired for high-speed Internet access. Wireless service is available via entire campus.
Library: G. Lamar Harrison Library plus 2 others. *Books:* 44,337 (physical), 189,180 (digital/electronic); *Serial titles:* 111 (physical), 20,763 (digital/electronic); *Databases:* 61. Students can reserve study rooms.

STUDENT LIFE
Housing options: coed, special housing for students with disabilities. Campus housing is university owned and is provided by a third party. Freshman campus housing is guaranteed.

Activities and organizations: drama/theater group, student-run newspaper, radio station, choral group, marching band, Student Government Association, Student Senate, Sorority and Fraternity (Greek Letter), NAACP, Pre- Alumni Council, national fraternities, national sororities.

Athletics Member NAIA. *Intercollegiate sports:* basketball M(s)/W(s), cheerleading W, cross-country running M/W, football M(s), softball W, track and field M(s)/W(s), volleyball W. *Intramural sports:* archery M/W, badminton M/W, basketball M/W, football M/W, golf M/W, soccer M, swimming and diving M/W, table tennis M/W, tennis M/W, track and field M/W, volleyball M/W.

Campus security: 24-hour emergency response devices and patrols, student patrols, late-night transport/escort service, controlled dormitory access.

Student services: health clinic, personal/psychological counseling, women's center.

COSTS & FINANCIAL AID
Costs (2017–18) *Tuition:* state resident $3944 full-time, $131 per credit hour part-time; nonresident $11,294 full-time, $131 per credit hour part-time. Full-time tuition and fees vary according to degree level, location, and program. Part-time tuition and fees vary according to degree level, location, and program. No tuition increase for student's term of enrollment. *Required fees:* $2006 full-time, $48 per credit hour part-time, $284 per term part-time. *Room and board:* $10,094; room only: $6952. Room and board charges vary according to board plan and housing facility. *Payment plans:* tuition prepayment, installment. *Waivers:* children of alumni and employees or children of employees.

Financial Aid Of all full-time matriculated undergraduates who enrolled in 2015, 1,939 applied for aid, 1,814 were judged to have need, 334 had their need fully met. In 2015, 197 non-need-based awards were made.

Average percent of need met: 54. *Average financial aid package:* $10,893. *Average need-based gift aid:* $5109. *Average non-need-based aid:* $6138. *Average indebtedness upon graduation:* $39,681.

APPLYING
Standardized Tests *Required:* SAT or ACT (for admission).
Options: electronic application, deferred entrance.
Required: high school transcript, minimum 2.7 GPA.
Application deadlines: rolling (freshmen), rolling (transfers).

CONTACT
Mr. Jeremy Lane, Director of Admissions, Langston University, Box 1550, Langston, OK 73052. *Phone:* 405-466-3428. *Fax:* 405-466-2915. *E-mail:* jlane@langston.edu.

Mid-America Christian University
Oklahoma City, Oklahoma
http://www.macu.edu/

- **Independent** comprehensive, founded 1953, affiliated with Church of God
- **Suburban** 145-acre campus with easy access to Oklahoma City, Oklahoma
- **Endowment** $2.6 million
- **Coed** 869 undergraduate students
- **Noncompetitive** entrance level

FACULTY
Student/faculty ratio: 11:1.

ACADEMICS
Calendar: semesters. *Degrees:* certificates, associate, bachelor's, master's, and post-master's certificates.

Special study options: academic remediation for entering students, accelerated degree program, adult/continuing education programs, advanced placement credit, distance learning, double majors, internships, part-time degree program, services for LD students, summer session for credit.

Computers: 24 computers/terminals and 60 ports are available on campus for general student use. Students can access the following: campus intranet, computer help desk, free student e-mail accounts, online (class) grades, online (class) registration, online (class) schedules. Campuswide network is available. 100% of college-owned or -operated housing units are wired for high-speed Internet access. Wireless service is available via entire campus.
Library: Charles Ewing Brown Library. Weekly public service hours: 70; study areas open 24 hours, 5–7 days a week; students can reserve study rooms.

STUDENT LIFE
Housing options: on-campus residence required through sophomore year; men-only, women-only, special housing for students with disabilities. Campus housing is university owned. Freshman campus housing is guaranteed.

Activities and organizations: student-run newspaper, choral group.

Athletics Member NAIA. *Intercollegiate sports:* baseball M(s), basketball M(s)/W(s), cheerleading M/W, golf M(s)/W(s), soccer M(s)/W(s), softball W(s), volleyball W(s). *Intramural sports:* basketball M/W, golf M/W, soccer M, softball M/W, table tennis M/W, volleyball M/W.

Campus security: 24-hour patrols, student patrols.

Student services: personal/psychological counseling.

COSTS & FINANCIAL AID
Costs (2017–18) *Comprehensive fee:* $25,612 includes full-time tuition ($16,560), mandatory fees ($1270), and room and board ($7782). Full-time tuition and fees vary according to course load, location, and program. Part-time tuition: $690 per credit hour. Part-time tuition and fees vary according to course load, location, and program. *Required fees:* $635 per term part-time. *College room only:* $4166. Room and board charges vary according to board plan. *Payment plans:* installment, deferred payment. *Waivers:* employees or children of employees.

Financial Aid Of all full-time matriculated undergraduates who enrolled in 2001, 589 applied for aid, 581 were judged to have need, 68 had their need fully met. In 2001, 41 non-need-based awards were made. *Average* *percent of need met:* 75. *Average financial aid package:* $6682. *Average need-based loan:* $3617. *Average need-based gift aid:* $2734. *Average non-need-based aid:* $5214.

APPLYING
Standardized Tests *Recommended:* SAT or ACT (for admission).
Options: early admission.
Application fee: $25.
Required: high school transcript. *Required for some:* 2 letters of recommendation, interview.
Application deadlines: rolling (freshmen), rolling (transfers).

CONTACT
Mid-America Christian University, 3500 Southwest 119th Street, Oklahoma City, OK 73170-4504. *Phone:* 405-692-3281. *Toll-free phone:* 888-436-3035.

National American University
Tulsa, Oklahoma
http://www.national.edu/

CONTACT
National American University, 8040 South Sheridan Road, Tulsa, OK 74133. *Toll-free phone:* 800-209-0338.

Northeastern State University
Tahlequah, Oklahoma
http://www.nsuok.edu/

- **State-supported** comprehensive, founded 1846, part of Regional University System of Oklahoma
- **Small-town** 200-acre campus with easy access to Tulsa
- **Endowment** $5.0 million
- **Coed** 6,818 undergraduate students, 70% full-time, 60% women, 40% men
- **Moderately difficult** entrance level, 90% of applicants were admitted

UNDERGRAD STUDENTS
4,787 full-time, 2,031 part-time. Students come from 35 states and territories; 54 other countries; 6% are from out of state; 4% Black or African American, non-Hispanic/Latino; 6% Hispanic/Latino; 2% Asian, non-Hispanic/Latino; 18% American Indian or Alaska Native, non-Hispanic/Latino; 20% Two or more races, non-Hispanic/Latino; 0.6% Race/ethnicity unknown; 3% international; 12% transferred in; 18% live on campus.

Freshmen:
Admission: 1,767 applied, 1,598 admitted, 840 enrolled. *Average high school GPA:* 3.4. *Test scores:* ACT scores over 18: 86%; ACT scores over 24: 27%; ACT scores over 30: 2%.
Retention: 63% of full-time freshmen returned.

FACULTY
Total: 448, 65% full-time, 57% with terminal degrees.
Student/faculty ratio: 18:1.

ACADEMICS
Calendar: semesters. *Degrees:* bachelor's, master's, doctoral, post-master's, and postbachelor's certificates.

Special study options: academic remediation for entering students, adult/continuing education programs, advanced placement credit, cooperative education, distance learning, double majors, honors programs, independent study, internships, part-time degree program, services for LD students, student-designed majors, summer session for credit. *ROTC:* Army (b).

Computers: 1,160 computers/terminals and 1,200 ports are available on campus for general student use. Students can access the following: campus intranet, computer help desk, free student e-mail accounts, online (class) grades, online (class) registration, online (class) schedules. Campuswide network is available. 100% of college-owned or -operated housing units are wired for high-speed Internet access. Wireless service is available via entire campus.

Library: John Vaughn Library. *Books:* 411,595 (physical), 60,775 (digital/electronic); *Serial titles:* 29,909 (physical), 77,542 (digital/electronic); *Databases:* 141. Weekly public service hours: 114.

STUDENT LIFE
Housing options: on-campus residence required for freshman year; coed, women-only, special housing for students with disabilities. Campus housing is university owned. Freshman applicants given priority for college housing.

Activities and organizations: drama/theater group, student-run newspaper, television station, choral group, marching band, national fraternities, national sororities.

Athletics Member NCAA. All Division II. *Intercollegiate sports:* baseball M(s), basketball M(s)/W(s), football M(s), golf M(s)/W(s), soccer M(s)/W(s), softball W(s), tennis W(s). *Intramural sports:* basketball M/W, football M/W, golf M/W, racquetball M/W, soccer M/W, softball M/W, tennis M/W, volleyball M/W.

Campus security: 24-hour emergency response devices and patrols, late-night transport/escort service, controlled dormitory access.

Student services: health clinic, personal/psychological counseling.

COSTS & FINANCIAL AID
Costs (2017–18) *Tuition:* state resident $5213 full-time, $174 per credit hour part-time; nonresident $12,900 full-time, $430 per credit hour part-time. Full-time tuition and fees vary according to course load and program. Part-time tuition and fees vary according to course load and program. No tuition increase for student's term of enrollment. *Required fees:* $1122 full-time, $37 per credit hour part-time. *Room and board:* $7020; room only: $3100. Room and board charges vary according to board plan and housing facility. *Payment plan:* installment. *Waivers:* employees or children of employees.

Financial Aid Of all full-time matriculated undergraduates who enrolled in 2017, 4,066 applied for aid, 3,237 were judged to have need, 2,139 had their need fully met. 272 Federal Work-Study jobs (averaging $2726). 430 state and other part-time jobs (averaging $1711). In 2017, 210 non-need-based awards were made. *Average percent of need met:* 94. *Average financial aid package:* $12,937. *Average need-based loan:* $7412. *Average need-based gift aid:* $7011. *Average non-need-based aid:* $2886. *Average indebtedness upon graduation:* $21,268.

APPLYING
Standardized Tests *Required:* ACT (for admission).
Options: electronic application, deferred entrance.
Application fee: $25.
Required: high school transcript, minimum 2.7 GPA, upper 50% of class or minimum ACT composite of 20. *Required for some:* interview.
Application deadlines: 8/1 (freshmen), 8/1 (transfers).
Notification: continuous (freshmen), continuous (transfers).

CONTACT
Ms. Jennifer McClendon, Director, Admissions and Recruitment, Northeastern State University, Case Building Room 220, 701 N Grand Avenue, Tahlequah, OK 74464. *Phone:* 918-449-6192. *Toll-free phone:* 800-722-9614. *E-mail:* mcclendo@nsuok.edu.

Northwestern Oklahoma State University
Alva, Oklahoma
http://www.nwosu.edu/

- **State-supported** comprehensive, founded 1897, part of Oklahoma State Regents for Higher Education
- **Rural** 70-acre campus
- **Endowment** $34.0 million
- **Coed** 1,873 undergraduate students, 71% full-time, 59% women, 41% men
- **Moderately difficult** entrance level, 94% of applicants were admitted

UNDERGRAD STUDENTS
1,322 full-time, 551 part-time. Students come from 39 states and territories; 21 other countries; 23% are from out of state; 8% Black or African American, non-Hispanic/Latino; 10% Hispanic/Latino; 0.5% Asian, non-Hispanic/Latino; 0.3% Native Hawaiian or other Pacific Islander, non-Hispanic/Latino; 7% American Indian or Alaska Native,

non-Hispanic/Latino; 1% Two or more races, non-Hispanic/Latino; 6% Race/ethnicity unknown; 3% international; 11% transferred in; 30% live on campus.

Freshmen:
Admission: 762 applied, 715 admitted, 358 enrolled. *Average high school GPA:* 3.3.

Retention: 54% of full-time freshmen returned.

FACULTY
Total: 156, 57% full-time, 46% with terminal degrees.
Student/faculty ratio: 15:1.

ACADEMICS
Calendar: semesters. *Degrees:* certificates, bachelor's, master's, and doctoral.

Special study options: academic remediation for entering students, adult/continuing education programs, advanced placement credit, cooperative education, distance learning, honors programs, independent study, internships, off-campus study, part-time degree program, services for LD students, study abroad, summer session for credit.

Computers: 260 computers/terminals are available on campus for general student use. Students can access the following: campus intranet, free student e-mail accounts, online (class) grades, online (class) registration, online (class) schedules. Campuswide network is available. 100% of college-owned or -operated housing units are wired for high-speed Internet access. Wireless service is available via classrooms, computer centers, computer labs, learning centers, libraries, student centers.
Library: J. W. Martin Library plus 1 other. *Books:* 96,306 (physical), 177,000 (digital/electronic); *Serial titles:* 9 (physical), 34,500 (digital/electronic); *Databases:* 39. Weekly public service hours: 84; students can reserve study rooms.

STUDENT LIFE
Housing options: on-campus residence required for freshman year; men-only, women-only. Campus housing is university owned. Freshman campus housing is guaranteed.

Activities and organizations: drama/theater group, student-run newspaper, radio and television station, choral group, marching band, Student Government Association, Aggie Club, Delta Mu Delta, Baptist Student Union, SOEA.

Athletics Member NCAA. All Division II. *Intercollegiate sports:* baseball M(s), basketball M(s)/W(s), cheerleading M(s)/W(s), cross-country running M(s)/W(s), football M(s), golf M(s)/W(s), soccer W(s), softball W(s), volleyball W(s). *Intramural sports:* basketball M/W, football M, racquetball M/W, softball M/W, ultimate Frisbee M/W, volleyball M/W.

Campus security: 24-hour emergency response devices and patrols, late-night transport/escort service.

Student services: personal/psychological counseling.

COSTS & FINANCIAL AID
Costs (2018–19) *Tuition:* state resident $6705 full-time; nonresident $13,823 full-time. Full-time tuition and fees vary according to course load, degree level, location, program, and student level. Part-time tuition and fees vary according to course load, degree level, location, program, and student level. *Required fees:* $653 full-time. *Room and board:* $4480; room only: $1780. Room and board charges vary according to board plan. *Payment plan:* installment. *Waivers:* senior citizens and employees or children of employees.

Financial Aid Of all full-time matriculated undergraduates who enrolled in 2014, 1,149 applied for aid, 950 were judged to have need. *Average indebtedness upon graduation:* $16,932.

APPLYING
Standardized Tests *Required:* SAT or ACT (for admission).
Options: electronic application, early admission.
Application fee: $15.
Required: high school transcript. *Required for some:* essay or personal statement, minimum 2.7 GPA, 3 letters of recommendation.
Application deadlines: rolling (freshmen), rolling (transfers).
Notification: continuous (freshmen), continuous (transfers).

CONTACT
Ms. Paige Fischer, Director of Recruitment, Northwestern Oklahoma State University, 709 Oklahoma Boulevard, Alva, OK 73717-2799. *Phone:* 580-327-8545. *Fax:* 580-327-8699. *E-mail:* plfischer@nwosu.edu.

Oklahoma Baptist University
Shawnee, Oklahoma
http://www.okbu.edu/

- **Independent Southern Baptist** comprehensive, founded 1910
- **Small-town** 125-acre campus with easy access to Oklahoma City
- **Endowment** $116.2 million
- **Coed** 1,972 undergraduate students, 96% full-time, 59% women, 41% men
- **Moderately difficult** entrance level, 65% of applicants were admitted

UNDERGRAD STUDENTS
1,888 full-time, 84 part-time. Students come from 38 states and territories; 40 other countries; 31% are from out of state; 5% Black or African American, non-Hispanic/Latino; 2% Hispanic/Latino; 1% Asian, non-Hispanic/Latino; 0.2% Native Hawaiian or other Pacific Islander, non-Hispanic/Latino; 5% American Indian or Alaska Native, non-Hispanic/Latino; 12% Two or more races, non-Hispanic/Latino; 4% Race/ethnicity unknown; 4% international; 4% transferred in; 76% live on campus.

Freshmen:
Admission: 4,070 applied, 2,634 admitted, 570 enrolled. *Average high school GPA:* 3.6. *Test scores:* ACT scores over 18: 94%; ACT scores over 24: 44%; ACT scores over 30: 8%.

Retention: 78% of full-time freshmen returned.

FACULTY
Total: 175, 73% full-time, 52% with terminal degrees.
Student/faculty ratio: 11:1.

ACADEMICS
Calendar: 4-1-4. *Degrees:* associate, bachelor's, and master's.

Special study options: academic remediation for entering students, advanced placement credit, cooperative education, double majors, honors programs, independent study, internships, off-campus study, part-time degree program, services for LD students, student-designed majors, study abroad, summer session for credit. *ROTC:* Air Force (c).

Unusual degree programs: medicine.

Computers: 175 computers/terminals are available on campus for general student use. Students can access the following: computer help desk, free student e-mail accounts, online (class) grades, online (class) registration, online (class) schedules, campus portal, online course work. Campuswide network is available. 100% of college-owned or -operated housing units are wired for high-speed Internet access. Wireless service is available via entire campus.
Library: Mabee Learning Center. *Books:* 162,334 (physical), 188,606 (digital/electronic); *Serial titles:* 1,140 (physical); *Databases:* 60. Weekly public service hours: 91; students can reserve study rooms.

STUDENT LIFE
Housing options: on-campus residence required through junior year; men-only, women-only. Campus housing is university owned. Freshman campus housing is guaranteed.

Activities and organizations: drama/theater group, student-run newspaper, television station, choral group, marching band, Campus Activities Board, University Concert Series, Student Foundation, Blitz Week Activities, Canterbury.

Athletics Member NCAA, NCCAA. All NCAA Division II except cross-country running (Division I), men's and women's swimming and diving (Division I). *Intercollegiate sports:* baseball M(s), basketball M(s)/W(s), cross-country running M(s)/W(s), football M(s), golf M(s)/W(s), lacrosse W(s), soccer M(s)/W(s), softball W(s), swimming and diving M(s)/W(s), tennis M(s)/W(s), track and field M(s)/W(s), volleyball W(s). *Intramural sports:* archery M/W, basketball M/W, bowling M/W, cheerleading W, football M/W, racquetball M/W, riflery M/W, rock climbing M/W, sand volleyball M/W, soccer M/W, softball M/W, table tennis M/W, tennis M/W, ultimate Frisbee M/W, volleyball M/W.

Campus security: 24-hour emergency response devices and patrols, late-night transport/escort service, controlled dormitory access, CLEET certified police officers.

Student services: health clinic, personal/psychological counseling.

COSTS & FINANCIAL AID

Costs (2018–19) *Comprehensive fee:* $35,608 includes full-time tuition ($25,138), mandatory fees ($3120), and room and board ($7350). Part-time tuition and fees vary according to course load. *College room only:* $3310. Room and board charges vary according to housing facility. *Payment plan:* installment. *Waivers:* senior citizens and employees or children of employees.

Financial Aid Of all full-time matriculated undergraduates who enrolled in 2016, 1,486 applied for aid, 1,366 were judged to have need, 323 had their need fully met. In 2016, 426 non-need-based awards were made. *Average percent of need met:* 81. *Average financial aid package:* $23,506. *Average need-based loan:* $4542. *Average need-based gift aid:* $6904. *Average non-need-based aid:* $10,725. *Average indebtedness upon graduation:* $24,451.

APPLYING

Standardized Tests *Required:* SAT or ACT (for admission).

Options: electronic application, early admission, deferred entrance.

Required: high school transcript, minimum 3.0 GPA. *Required for some:* essay or personal statement, interview.

Application deadlines: rolling (freshmen), 8/1 (transfers).

Notification: continuous until 9/1 (freshmen), continuous until 9/1 (transfers).

CONTACT

Oklahoma Baptist University, 500 West University, Shawnee, OK 74804. *Phone:* 405-585-5000. *Toll-free phone:* 800-654-3285.

Oklahoma Christian University
Oklahoma City, Oklahoma
http://www.oc.edu/

- **Independent** comprehensive, founded 1950, affiliated with Church of Christ
- **Suburban** 200-acre campus with easy access to Oklahoma City
- **Coed** 1,986 undergraduate students, 94% full-time, 49% women, 51% men
- **Moderately difficult** entrance level, 51% of applicants were admitted

UNDERGRAD STUDENTS

1,870 full-time, 116 part-time. Students come from 42 states and territories; 36 other countries; 54% are from out of state; 5% Black or African American, non-Hispanic/Latino; 6% Hispanic/Latino; 1% Asian, non-Hispanic/Latino; 0.1% Native Hawaiian or other Pacific Islander, non-Hispanic/Latino; 2% American Indian or Alaska Native, non-Hispanic/Latino; 7% Two or more races, non-Hispanic/Latino; 0.1% Race/ethnicity unknown; 6% international; 4% transferred in; 81% live on campus.

Freshmen:

Admission: 2,530 applied, 1,289 admitted, 515 enrolled. *Average high school GPA:* 3.5. *Test scores:* ACT scores over 18: 92%; ACT scores over 24: 52%; ACT scores over 30: 14%.

Retention: 79% of full-time freshmen returned.

FACULTY

Total: 211, 44% full-time, 48% with terminal degrees.

Student/faculty ratio: 14:1.

ACADEMICS

Calendar: semesters. *Degrees:* certificates, bachelor's, master's, and postbachelor's certificates.

Special study options: academic remediation for entering students, accelerated degree program, advanced placement credit, cooperative education, distance learning, double majors, English as a second language, honors programs, independent study, internships, off-campus study, services for LD students, student-designed majors, study abroad, summer session for credit. *ROTC:* Army (c), Air Force (c).

Computers: 101 computers/terminals and 450 ports are available on campus for general student use. Students can access the following: campus intranet, computer help desk, free student e-mail accounts, online (class) grades, online (class) registration, online (class) schedules. Campuswide network is available. 100% of college-owned or -operated housing units are wired for high-speed Internet access. Wireless service is available via entire campus.

Library: Tom and Ada Beam Library. *Books:* 107,521 (physical), 66,800 (digital/electronic); *Serial titles:* 1,610 (physical), 42,377 (digital/electronic); *Databases:* 74. Weekly public service hours: 82; students can reserve study rooms.

STUDENT LIFE

Housing options: on-campus residence required through senior year; men-only, women-only, special housing for students with disabilities. Campus housing is university owned. Freshman campus housing is guaranteed.

Activities and organizations: drama/theater group, student-run newspaper, radio and television station, choral group, Outreach, Wishing Well Project, Student Government Association, Young Republicans, College Democrats.

Athletics Member NCAA. All Division II. *Intercollegiate sports:* baseball M(s), basketball M(s)/W(s), bowling M(c)/W(c), cross-country running M(s)/W(s), golf M(s)/W(s), soccer M(s)/W(s), softball W(s), swimming and diving M(s)/W(s), track and field M(s)/W(s). *Intramural sports:* basketball M/W, bowling M/W, cross-country running M/W, football M/W, golf M/W, soccer M/W, softball M/W, swimming and diving M/W, table tennis M/W, tennis M/W, track and field M/W, volleyball M/W.

Campus security: 24-hour emergency response devices and patrols, late-night transport/escort service, controlled dormitory access.

Student services: health clinic, personal/psychological counseling.

COSTS & FINANCIAL AID

Costs (2018–19) *Comprehensive fee:* $30,950 includes full-time tuition ($22,460), mandatory fees ($300), and room and board ($8190). Full-time tuition and fees vary according to course load and reciprocity agreements. Part-time tuition: $935 per credit hour. Part-time tuition and fees vary according to course load and reciprocity agreements. *Room and board:* Room and board charges vary according to board plan and housing facility. *Payment plan:* installment. *Waivers:* employees or children of employees.

Financial Aid Of all full-time matriculated undergraduates who enrolled in 2015, 1,421 applied for aid, 1,209 were judged to have need, 468 had their need fully met. In 2015, 579 non-need-based awards were made. *Average percent of need met:* 73. *Average financial aid package:* $22,287. *Average need-based loan:* $2349. *Average need-based gift aid:* $3217. *Average non-need-based aid:* $7609. *Average indebtedness upon graduation:* $27,793. *Financial aid deadline:* 8/31.

APPLYING

Standardized Tests *Required:* SAT or ACT (for admission).

Options: electronic application, early admission, deferred entrance.

Application fee: $25.

Required: high school transcript. *Required for some:* interview.

Application deadlines: rolling (freshmen), rolling (transfers).

Notification: continuous (freshmen), continuous (transfers).

CONTACT

Ms. Bonnie Howard, Director of Admissions and International Records, Oklahoma Christian University, Box 11000, Oklahoma City, OK 73136-1100. *Phone:* 405-425-5000. *Toll-free phone:* 800-877-5010. *Fax:* 405-425-5208. *E-mail:* admissions@oc.edu.

Oklahoma City University
Oklahoma City, Oklahoma
http://www.okcu.edu/

- **Independent United Methodist** comprehensive, founded 1904
- **Urban** 104-acre campus with easy access to Oklahoma City
- **Endowment** $104.5 million
- **Coed** 1,692 undergraduate students, 91% full-time, 68% women, 32% men

COLLEGES AT-A-GLANCE

UNDERGRAD STUDENTS
1,542 full-time, 150 part-time. Students come from 47 states and territories; 51 other countries; 50% are from out of state; 5% Black or African American, non-Hispanic/Latino; 9% Hispanic/Latino; 2% Asian, non-Hispanic/Latino; 2% American Indian or Alaska Native, non-Hispanic/Latino; 8% Two or more races, non-Hispanic/Latino; 0.1% Race/ethnicity unknown; 11% international; 13% transferred in; 53% live on campus.

Freshmen:
Admission: 296 enrolled. *Average high school GPA:* 3.8. *Test scores:* SAT evidence-based reading and writing scores over 500: 95%; SAT math scores over 500: 91%; ACT scores over 18: 98%; SAT evidence-based reading and writing scores over 600: 58%; SAT math scores over 600: 47%; ACT scores over 24: 69%; SAT evidence-based reading and writing scores over 700: 10%; SAT math scores over 700: 10%; ACT scores over 30: 13%.
Retention: 82% of full-time freshmen returned.

FACULTY
Total: 268, 72% full-time, 56% with terminal degrees.
Student/faculty ratio: 11:1.

ACADEMICS
Calendar: semesters. *Degrees:* bachelor's, master's, and doctoral.
Special study options: accelerated degree program, adult/continuing education programs, advanced placement credit, cooperative education, distance learning, double majors, English as a second language, honors programs, independent study, internships, off-campus study, part-time degree program, services for LD students, study abroad, summer session for credit. *ROTC:* Army (c), Air Force (c).
Unusual degree programs: 3-2 business administration; nursing.
Computers: 368 computers/terminals are available on campus for general student use. Students can access the following: campus intranet, computer help desk, free student e-mail accounts, online (class) grades, online (class) registration, online (class) schedules. Campuswide network is available. 100% of college-owned or -operated housing units are wired for high-speed Internet access. Wireless service is available via entire campus.
Library: Dulaney Browne Library plus 1 other. *Books:* 279,046 (physical), 372,318 (digital/electronic); *Serial titles:* 5,543 (physical), 621,360 (digital/electronic); *Databases:* 114. Weekly public service hours: 99; students can reserve study rooms.

STUDENT LIFE
Housing options: coed, special housing for students with disabilities. Campus housing is university owned and is provided by a third party. Freshman applicants given priority for college housing.
Activities and organizations: drama/theater group, student-run newspaper, television station, choral group, Tri-Beta, Multicultural Student Association, Student Nursing Associate, Fellowship of Christian Athletes, national fraternities, national sororities.
Athletics Member NAIA. *Intercollegiate sports:* baseball M(s), basketball M(s)/W(s), cheerleading M(s)/W(s), crew M(s)/W(s), golf M(s)/W(s), sailing M(c)/W(c), soccer M(s)/W(s), softball W(s), track and field M(s)/W(s), volleyball W(s), wrestling M(s)/W(s). *Intramural sports:* basketball M/W, golf M/W, softball M/W, table tennis M/W, volleyball M/W.
Campus security: 24-hour emergency response devices and patrols, late-night transport/escort service, controlled dormitory access.
Student services: health clinic, personal/psychological counseling.

COSTS & FINANCIAL AID
Costs (2018–19) One-time required fee: $360. *Comprehensive fee:* $39,922 includes full-time tuition ($27,276), mandatory fees ($3750), and room and board ($8896). Full-time tuition and fees vary according to course level, course load, and program. Part-time tuition: $925 per credit hour. Part-time tuition and fees vary according to course level and program. *Required fees:* $125 per credit hour part-time. *College room only:* $4100. Room and board charges vary according to board plan and housing facility. *Payment plans:* installment, deferred payment. *Waivers:* employees or children of employees.
Financial Aid Of all full-time matriculated undergraduates who enrolled in 2017, 749 applied for aid, 663 were judged to have need, 525 had their need fully met. 227 Federal Work-Study jobs (averaging $1407). 256 state and other part-time jobs (averaging $1383). In 2017, 73 non-need-based awards were made. *Average percent of need met:* 59. *Average financial aid package:* $21,635. *Average need-based loan:* $4338. *Average need-based gift aid:* $17,773. *Average non-need-based aid:* $14,043. *Average indebtedness upon graduation:* $27,209.

APPLYING
Standardized Tests Required: SAT or ACT (for admission).
Required: essay or personal statement, high school transcript. *Required for some:* interview.

CONTACT
Ms. Michelle Cook, Senior Director of Admissions, Oklahoma City University, 2501 North Blackwelder, Oklahoma City, OK 73106. *Phone:* 405-208-5055. *Toll-free phone:* 800-633-7242. *Fax:* 405-208-5916. *E-mail:* michelle.cook@okcu.edu.

Oklahoma Panhandle State University
Goodwell, Oklahoma
http://www.opsu.edu/

CONTACT
Mr. Bobby Jenkins, Registrar and Director of Admissions, Oklahoma Panhandle State University, PO Box 430, 323 Eagle Boulevard, Goodwell, OK 73939-0430. *Phone:* 580-349-1376. *Toll-free phone:* 800-664-6778. *Fax:* 580-349-1371. *E-mail:* opsu@opsu.edu.

Oklahoma State University
Stillwater, Oklahoma
http://www.okstate.edu/

- **State-supported** university, founded 1890, part of Oklahoma State University
- **Small-town** 840-acre campus with easy access to Oklahoma City, Tulsa
- **Endowment** $794.8 million
- **Coed** 20,978 undergraduate students, 87% full-time, 49% women, 51% men
- **Moderately difficult** entrance level, 74% of applicants were admitted

UNDERGRAD STUDENTS
18,167 full-time, 2,811 part-time. Students come from 58 states and territories; 67 other countries; 27% are from out of state; 5% Black or African American, non-Hispanic/Latino; 8% Hispanic/Latino; 2% Asian, non-Hispanic/Latino; 0.1% Native Hawaiian or other Pacific Islander, non-Hispanic/Latino; 5% American Indian or Alaska Native, non-Hispanic/Latino; 10% Two or more races, non-Hispanic/Latino; 0.2% Race/ethnicity unknown; 4% international; 7% transferred in; 45% live on campus.

Freshmen:
Admission: 13,635 applied, 10,123 admitted, 4,220 enrolled. *Average high school GPA:* 3.6. *Test scores:* SAT evidence-based reading and writing scores over 500: 90%; SAT math scores over 500: 88%; ACT scores over 18: 97%; SAT evidence-based reading and writing scores over 600: 47%; SAT math scores over 600: 43%; ACT scores over 24: 61%; SAT evidence-based reading and writing scores over 700: 7%; SAT math scores over 700: 7%; ACT scores over 30: 14%.
Retention: 81% of full-time freshmen returned.

FACULTY
Total: 1,321, 77% full-time, 73% with terminal degrees.
Student/faculty ratio: 20:1.

ACADEMICS
Calendar: semesters. *Degrees:* bachelor's, master's, doctoral, post-master's, and postbachelor's certificates.
Special study options: accelerated degree program, advanced placement credit, distance learning, double majors, English as a second language, freshman honors college, honors programs, independent study, internships, off-campus study, part-time degree program, services for LD students, student-designed majors, study abroad, summer session for credit. *ROTC:* Army (b), Air Force (b).
Unusual degree programs: 3-2 business administration; accounting, special education, biochemistry, early childhood education.

Financial Aid Of all full-time matriculated undergraduates who enrolled in 2017, 1,479 applied for aid, 1,316 were judged to have need, 234 had their need fully met. In 2017, 32 non-need-based awards were made. *Average percent of need met:* 45. *Average financial aid package:* $8193. *Average need-based loan:* $3582. *Average need-based gift aid:* $5104. *Average non-need-based aid:* $1849. *Financial aid deadline:* 6/30.

APPLYING
Standardized Tests *Required for some:* SAT or ACT (for admission). *Recommended:* ACT (for admission).

Options: deferred entrance.

Required: high school transcript.

Application deadlines: rolling (freshmen), rolling (transfers).

CONTACT
Kyle Gregorio, Assistant Registrar, Oklahoma State University Institute of Technology, 1801 E. 4th Street, Okmulgee, OK 74447. *Phone:* 918-293-5274. *Toll-free phone:* 800-722-4471. *Fax:* 918-293-4643. *E-mail:* kyleg@okstate.edu.

Oklahoma State University–Oklahoma City

Oklahoma City, Oklahoma
http://www.osuokc.edu/

- **State-supported** primarily 2-year, founded 1961, part of Oklahoma State University
- **Urban** 110-acre campus with easy access to Oklahoma City
- **Coed** 5,839 undergraduate students, 30% full-time, 62% women, 38% men
- **Noncompetitive** entrance level, 34% of applicants were admitted

UNDERGRAD STUDENTS
1,728 full-time, 4,111 part-time. Students come from 28 states and territories; 12 other countries; 4% are from out of state; 11% Black or African American, non-Hispanic/Latino; 16% Hispanic/Latino; 3% Asian, non-Hispanic/Latino; 0.2% Native Hawaiian or other Pacific Islander, non-Hispanic/Latino; 4% American Indian or Alaska Native, non-Hispanic/Latino; 7% Two or more races, non-Hispanic/Latino; 4% Race/ethnicity unknown; 2% international; 13% transferred in.

Freshmen:
Admission: 3,765 applied, 1,267 admitted, 1,007 enrolled. *Average high school GPA:* 2.8.

Retention: 51% of full-time freshmen returned.

FACULTY
Total: 355, 24% full-time.

Student/faculty ratio: 16:1.

ACADEMICS
Calendar: semesters. *Degrees:* certificates, associate, and bachelor's.

Special study options: academic remediation for entering students, advanced placement credit, distance learning, double majors, honors programs, independent study, internships, part-time degree program, services for LD students, study abroad, summer session for credit.

Computers: 715 computers/terminals are available on campus for general student use. Students can access the following: campus intranet, computer help desk, free student e-mail accounts, online (class) grades, online (class) registration, online (class) schedules. Campuswide network is available. Wireless service is available via entire campus.
Library: Oklahoma State University, Oklahoma City Library. *Books:* 34,772 (physical), 198,662 (digital/electronic); *Serial titles:* 229 (physical); *Databases:* 72. Weekly public service hours: 75.

STUDENT LIFE
Housing options: college housing not available.

Activities and organizations: OSU-OKC Chapter of the OK Student Nurse Association, Veterinary Technician Association, Hispanic Student Association, Phi Theta Kappa, Student Government Association.

Campus security: 24-hour patrols, late-night transport/escort service.

COSTS & FINANCIAL AID
Costs (2017–18) *Tuition:* state resident $2938 full-time, $122 per credit hour part-time; nonresident $8171 full-time, $340 per credit hour part-time. Full-time tuition and fees vary according to class time, course level, and degree level. Part-time tuition and fees vary according to class time, course level, and degree level. No tuition increase for student's term of enrollment. *Required fees:* $70 full-time, $35 per term part-time. *Payment plans:* tuition prepayment, installment. *Waivers:* senior citizens and employees or children of employees.

Financial Aid Of all full-time matriculated undergraduates who enrolled in 2017, 1,116 applied for aid, 1,116 were judged to have need, 856 had their need fully met. 192 Federal Work-Study jobs (averaging $52,801). In 2017, 611 non-need-based awards were made. *Average percent of need met:* 81. *Average financial aid package:* $1757. *Average need-based gift aid:* $2293. *Average non-need-based aid:* $1025. *Average indebtedness upon graduation:* $2195.

APPLYING
Options: electronic application.

Required for some: high school transcript.

Application deadlines: rolling (freshmen), rolling (transfers).

Notification: continuous (freshmen), continuous (transfers).

CONTACT
Mr. Kyle Williams, Senior Director of Enrollment Management, Oklahoma State University–Oklahoma City, 900 North Portland Avenue, AD202, Oklahoma City, OK 73107. *Phone:* 405-945-9152. *Toll-free phone:* 800-560-4099. *E-mail:* wilkylw@osuokc.edu.

Oklahoma Wesleyan University

Bartlesville, Oklahoma
http://www.okwu.edu/

CONTACT
Samantha Peterson, Assistant Vice President of Enrollment, Oklahoma Wesleyan University, 2201 Silver Lake Road, Bartlesville, OK 74006. *Phone:* 866-222-8226. *Toll-free phone:* 866-222-8226. *Fax:* 918-335-6229. *E-mail:* admissions@okwu.edu.

Oral Roberts University

Tulsa, Oklahoma
http://www.oru.edu/

- **Independent interdenominational** comprehensive, founded 1963
- **Urban** 263-acre campus
- **Coed** 3,381 undergraduate students, 85% full-time, 59% women, 41% men
- **Moderately difficult** entrance level, 93% of applicants were admitted

UNDERGRAD STUDENTS
2,866 full-time, 515 part-time. 56% are from out of state; 13% Black or African American, non-Hispanic/Latino; 13% Hispanic/Latino; 2% Asian, non-Hispanic/Latino; 3% American Indian or Alaska Native, non-Hispanic/Latino; 5% Two or more races, non-Hispanic/Latino; 10% Race/ethnicity unknown; 10% international; 6% transferred in; 61% live on campus.

Freshmen:
Admission: 2,433 applied, 2,271 admitted, 622 enrolled. *Average high school GPA:* 3.6. *Test scores:* SAT evidence-based reading and writing scores over 500: 80%; SAT math scores over 500: 73%; ACT scores over 18: 91%; SAT evidence-based reading and writing scores over 600: 35%; SAT math scores over 600: 21%; ACT scores over 24: 39%; SAT evidence-based reading and writing scores over 700: 8%; SAT math scores over 700: 6%; ACT scores over 30: 9%.

Retention: 84% of full-time freshmen returned.

FACULTY
Total: 296, 53% full-time, 53% with terminal degrees.

Student/faculty ratio: 14:1.

ACADEMICS
Calendar: semesters. *Degrees:* certificates, diplomas, bachelor's, master's, and doctoral.

Special study options: adult/continuing education programs, part-time degree program. *ROTC:* Air Force (c).

Computers: Students can access the following: free student e-mail accounts, online (class) registration. Campuswide network is available.
Library: John D. Messick Resources Center.

STUDENT LIFE
Housing options: on-campus residence required through senior year; men-only, women-only, special housing for students with disabilities.

Athletics Member NCAA. All Division I. *Intercollegiate sports:* baseball M(s), basketball M(s)/W(s), cross-country running M(s)/W(s), golf M(s)/W(s), soccer M(s)/W(s), tennis M(s)/W(s), track and field M(s)/W(s), volleyball W(s), wrestling M. *Intramural sports:* badminton M/W, basketball M/W, bowling M/W, cross-country running M/W, football M/W, golf M/W, racquetball M/W, softball M/W, swimming and diving M/W, table tennis M/W, tennis M/W, volleyball M/W.

Campus security: 24-hour emergency response devices and patrols, late-night transport/escort service.

COSTS & FINANCIAL AID
Costs (2018–19) *Comprehensive fee:* $37,178 includes full-time tuition ($26,700), mandatory fees ($1028), and room and board ($9450). Full-time tuition and fees vary according to course load, degree level, and location. Part-time tuition: $1115 per contact hour. Part-time tuition and fees vary according to course load, degree level, and location. *College room only:* $4390. Room and board charges vary according to board plan and housing facility. *Payment plan:* installment. *Waivers:* employees or children of employees.

Financial Aid Of all full-time matriculated undergraduates who enrolled in 2017, 2,264 applied for aid, 2,057 were judged to have need, 882 had their need fully met. In 2017, 667 non-need-based awards were made. *Average percent of need met:* 90. *Average financial aid package:* $25,595. *Average need-based loan:* $7891. *Average need-based gift aid:* $17,721. *Average non-need-based aid:* $13,540. *Average indebtedness upon graduation:* $32,745.

APPLYING
Standardized Tests *Required:* SAT or ACT (for admission).
Options: deferred entrance.
Application fee: $35.
Required: essay or personal statement, high school transcript, minimum 2.0 GPA, 1 letter of recommendation, proof of immunization. *Required for some:* interview. *Recommended:* interview.
Notification: continuous until 8/15 (freshmen).

CONTACT
Director of Enrollment, Oral Roberts University, 7777 South Lewis Avenue, Tulsa, OK 74171. *Phone:* 918-495-6529. *Toll-free phone:* 800-678-8876. *Fax:* 918-495-6222. *E-mail:* admissions@oru.edu.

Randall University
Moore, Oklahoma
http://www.hc.edu/

CONTACT
Randall University, PO Box 7208, Moore, OK 73160. *Phone:* 405-912-9007. *Fax:* 405-912-9050. *E-mail:* recruitment@hc.edu.

Rogers State University
Claremore, Oklahoma
http://www.rsu.edu/

- **State-supported** comprehensive, founded 1909, part of Oklahoma State Regents for Higher Education
- **Small-town** 40-acre campus with easy access to Tulsa
- **Endowment** $13.1 million
- **Coed** 3,694 undergraduate students, 59% full-time, 60% women, 40% men
- **Noncompetitive** entrance level, 14% of applicants were admitted

UNDERGRAD STUDENTS
2,180 full-time, 1,514 part-time. Students come from 26 states and territories; 9 other countries; 5% are from out of state; 4% Black or African American, non-Hispanic/Latino; 6% Hispanic/Latino; 2% Asian, non-Hispanic/Latino; 0.2% Native Hawaiian or other Pacific Islander, non-Hispanic/Latino; 8% American Indian or Alaska Native, non-

Hispanic/Latino; 21% Two or more races, non-Hispanic/Latino; 2% Race/ethnicity unknown; 9% transferred in; 20% live on campus.

Freshmen:
Admission: 7,241 applied, 1,032 admitted, 524 enrolled. *Average high school GPA:* 3.1. *Test scores:* ACT scores over 18: 73%; ACT scores over 24: 18%; ACT scores over 30: 1%.
Retention: 46% of full-time freshmen returned.

FACULTY
Total: 236, 43% full-time, 38% with terminal degrees.
Student/faculty ratio: 11:1.

ACADEMICS
Calendar: semesters. *Degrees:* associate, bachelor's, and master's.
Special study options: academic remediation for entering students, adult/continuing education programs, advanced placement credit, cooperative education, distance learning, double majors, honors programs, independent study, internships, off-campus study, part-time degree program, services for LD students, study abroad, summer session for credit.

Computers: 251 computers/terminals are available on campus for general student use. Students can access the following: computer help desk, free student e-mail accounts, online (class) grades, online (class) registration, online (class) schedules, software to support courses. Campuswide network is available. 100% of college-owned or -operated housing units are wired for high-speed Internet access. Wireless service is available via classrooms, computer labs, dorm rooms, learning centers, libraries, student centers.
Library: Stratton Taylor Library. *Books:* 80,238 (physical), 298,063 (digital/electronic); *Serial titles:* 491 (physical), 67,126 (digital/electronic); *Databases:* 81. Weekly public service hours: 86; students can reserve study rooms.

STUDENT LIFE
Housing options: coed. Campus housing is university owned.
Activities and organizations: drama/theater group, student-run radio station, choral group, Student Government Association, Student Nurses Association, President's Leadership Class, Pre-Professional Health Club (Pre-SOMA), Student Athlete Advisory Committee, national fraternities, national sororities.

Athletics Member NCAA. All Division II. *Intercollegiate sports:* baseball M(s), basketball M(s)/W(s), cheerleading M(s)/W(s), cross-country running M(s)/W(s), golf M(s)/W(s), soccer M(s)/W(s), softball W(s), track and field M(s)/W(s). *Intramural sports:* basketball M/W, soccer M/W, softball M/W, volleyball M/W.

Campus security: 24-hour patrols, student patrols, late-night transport/escort service, controlled dormitory access, state-certified law enforcement officers, comprehensive camera surveillance system.
Student services: health clinic, personal/psychological counseling.

COSTS & FINANCIAL AID
Costs (2017–18) *Tuition:* state resident $4170 full-time; nonresident $12,510 full-time. Full-time tuition and fees vary according to course level, course load, location, program, and student level. Part-time tuition and fees vary according to course level, course load, location, program, and student level. *Required fees:* $2700 full-time. *Room and board:* $8050; room only: $4600. Room and board charges vary according to housing facility. *Payment plan:* installment. *Waivers:* senior citizens and employees or children of employees.

Financial Aid Of all full-time matriculated undergraduates who enrolled in 2017, 1,755 applied for aid, 1,510 were judged to have need, 168 had their need fully met. In 2017, 154 non-need-based awards were made. *Average percent of need met:* 52. *Average financial aid package:* $9771. *Average need-based loan:* $3762. *Average need-based gift aid:* $7294. *Average non-need-based aid:* $6019. *Average indebtedness upon graduation:* $16,164.

APPLYING
Standardized Tests *Required:* SAT or ACT (for admission). *Recommended:* ACT (for admission).
Options: electronic application.
Application fee: $20.

Required: high school transcript. *Required for some:* minimum 2.7 GPA, minimum ACT composite of 20 or 2.70, GPA and top 50% rank for baccalaureate programs.

Application deadlines: rolling (freshmen), rolling (transfers).

CONTACT
Ms. Joy Lin Hall, Director of Admissions, Rogers State University, 1701 West Will Rogers Boulevard, Claremore, OK 74017. *Phone:* 918-343-7546. *Toll-free phone:* 800-256-7511. *Fax:* 918-343-7595. *E-mail:* admissions@rsu.edu.

Southeastern Oklahoma State University
Durant, Oklahoma
http://www.se.edu/

- **State-supported** comprehensive, founded 1909, part of Oklahoma State Regents for Higher Education
- **Small-town** 276-acre campus
- **Endowment** $23.2 million
- **Coed** 3,132 undergraduate students, 77% full-time, 54% women, 46% men
- **Moderately difficult** entrance level, 72% of applicants were admitted

UNDERGRAD STUDENTS
2,411 full-time, 721 part-time. Students come from 28 states and territories; 36 other countries; 25% are from out of state; 6% Black or African American, non-Hispanic/Latino; 6% Hispanic/Latino; 0.7% Asian, non-Hispanic/Latino; 0.3% Native Hawaiian or other Pacific Islander, non-Hispanic/Latino; 30% American Indian or Alaska Native, non-Hispanic/Latino; 3% Race/ethnicity unknown; 11% transferred in; 18% live on campus.

Freshmen:
Admission: 1,174 applied, 851 admitted, 517 enrolled. *Average high school GPA:* 3.4. *Test scores:* ACT scores over 18: 80%; ACT scores over 24: 22%; ACT scores over 30: 2%.

Retention: 55% of full-time freshmen returned.

FACULTY
Total: 251, 53% full-time, 47% with terminal degrees.
Student/faculty ratio: 18:1.

ACADEMICS
Calendar: semesters. *Degrees:* bachelor's, master's, and post-master's certificates.

Special study options: academic remediation for entering students, accelerated degree program, adult/continuing education programs, advanced placement credit, distance learning, double majors, honors programs, independent study, internships, off-campus study, part-time degree program, services for LD students, summer session for credit.

Computers: 598 computers/terminals and 598 ports are available on campus for general student use. Students can access the following: campus intranet, free student e-mail accounts, online (class) grades, online (class) registration, online (class) schedules, campus learning management system classes. Campuswide network is available. 100% of college-owned or -operated housing units are wired for high-speed Internet access. Wireless service is available via classrooms, computer labs, dorm rooms, learning centers, libraries, student centers.

Library: Henry G. Bennett Memorial Library plus 1 other. *Books:* 192,351 (physical), 17,845 (digital/electronic); *Serial titles:* 83 (physical), 2,534 (digital/electronic); *Databases:* 108. Weekly public service hours: 79; students can reserve study rooms.

STUDENT LIFE
Housing options: on-campus residence required for freshman year; coed, men-only, women-only, special housing for students with disabilities. Campus housing is university owned. Freshman campus housing is guaranteed.

Activities and organizations: drama/theater group, student-run newspaper, radio station, choral group, marching band, Baptist Collegiate Ministries, Greek Community, Student Government Association, Kappa Kappa Psi, Psychology Club, national fraternities, national sororities.

Athletics Member NCAA. All Division II. *Intercollegiate sports:* baseball M(s), basketball M(s)/W(s), cross-country running W(s), football M(s), golf M(s), softball W(s), tennis M(s)/W(s), volleyball W(s). *Intramural sports:* basketball M/W, football M.

Campus security: 24-hour emergency response devices and patrols, late-night transport/escort service, controlled dormitory access.

Student services: health clinic, personal/psychological counseling.

COSTS & FINANCIAL AID
Costs (2017–18) *Tuition:* state resident $6240 full-time, $208 per credit hour part-time; nonresident $14,880 full-time, $496 per credit hour part-time. Full-time tuition and fees vary according to course level, course load, degree level, location, and program. Part-time tuition and fees vary according to course level, course load, degree level, location, and program. No tuition increase for student's term of enrollment. *Required fees:* $510 full-time, $17 per credit hour part-time. *Room and board:* $6568; room only: $3368. Room and board charges vary according to board plan, housing facility, and student level. *Payment plan:* installment. *Waivers:* minority students, children of alumni, adult students, senior citizens, and employees or children of employees.

Financial Aid Of all full-time matriculated undergraduates who enrolled in 2016, 1,713 applied for aid, 1,530 were judged to have need, 151 had their need fully met. In 2016, 28 non-need-based awards were made. *Average percent of need met:* 6. *Average financial aid package:* $11,735. *Average need-based loan:* $2093. *Average need-based gift aid:* $2002. *Average non-need-based aid:* $720. *Average indebtedness upon graduation:* $16,542.

APPLYING
Standardized Tests *Required:* SAT or ACT (for admission).
Options: electronic application.
Application fee: $20.
Required: high school transcript. *Required for some:* interview.
Application deadlines: rolling (freshmen), rolling (transfers).
Notification: continuous (freshmen), continuous (transfers).

CONTACT
Southeastern Oklahoma State University, 1405 North 4th Avenue, Durant, OK 74701-0609. *Toll-free phone:* 800-435-1327.

Southern Nazarene University
Bethany, Oklahoma
http://www.snu.edu/

CONTACT
Dr. Linda Cantwell, Director of Recruitment, Southern Nazarene University, 6729 Northwest 39th Expressway, Bethany, OK 73008. *Phone:* 405-491-6324. *Toll-free phone:* 800-648-9899. *Fax:* 405-491-6320. *E-mail:* admiss@snu.edu.

Southwestern Christian University
Bethany, Oklahoma
http://www.swcu.edu/

CONTACT
Ms. Jessie Burpo, Admissions Counselor, Southwestern Christian University, PO Box 340, Bethany, OK 73008-0340. *Phone:* 405-789-7661 Ext. 3432. *Fax:* 405-495-0078. *E-mail:* admissions@swcu.edu.

Southwestern Oklahoma State University
Weatherford, Oklahoma
http://www.swosu.edu/

- **State-supported** comprehensive, founded 1901
- **Small-town** 73-acre campus with easy access to Oklahoma City
- **Endowment** $22.3 million
- **Coed**
- **Minimally difficult** entrance level

FACULTY
Student/faculty ratio: 19:1.

ACADEMICS

Calendar: semesters. *Degrees:* certificates, associate, bachelor's, master's, and doctoral.

Library: Al Harris Library plus 1 other. *Books:* 303,978 (physical), 364,203 (digital/electronic); *Serial titles:* 128 (physical), 47,086 (digital/electronic); *Databases:* 99. Weekly public service hours: 84; students can reserve study rooms.

STUDENT LIFE

Housing options: men-only, women-only. Campus housing is university owned.

Activities and organizations: drama/theater group, student-run newspaper, choral group, marching band, Collegiate Activities Board, Southwestern International Student Association, Saudi Arabian Student Organization, SWOSU Computer Club, Kappa Epsilon and Sigma Sigma Chi, national fraternities, national sororities.

Athletics Member NCAA. All Division II.

Campus security: late-night transport/escort service, police available 24 hours a day.

Student services: health clinic, personal/psychological counseling, legal services.

COSTS & FINANCIAL AID

Costs (2017–18) *One-time required fee:* $100. *Tuition:* state resident $5610 full-time, $187 per credit hour part-time; nonresident $12,510 full-time, $417 per credit hour part-time. Full-time tuition and fees vary according to degree level, location, and program. Part-time tuition and fees vary according to degree level, location, and program. *Required fees:* $1395 full-time, $47 per credit hour part-time. *Room and board:* $5500; room only: $2300. Room and board charges vary according to board plan and housing facility. *Payment plans:* installment, deferred payment.

Financial Aid Of all full-time matriculated undergraduates who enrolled in 2017, 3,173 applied for aid, 2,475 were judged to have need, 419 had their need fully met. In 2017, 420 non-need-based awards were made. *Average percent of need met:* 62. *Average financial aid package:* $5333. *Average need-based loan:* $1990. *Average need-based gift aid:* $3557. *Average non-need-based aid:* $1540. *Average indebtedness upon graduation:* $18,520. *Financial aid deadline:* 3/1.

APPLYING

Standardized Tests *Required:* SAT or ACT (for admission). *Recommended:* ACT (for admission).

Options: electronic application, deferred entrance.

Application fee: $15.

Required: high school transcript. *Required for some:* minimum 2.7 GPA, minimum ACT score of 20 (940 SAT) or rank in the upper 50% of high school graduating class or have a high school GPA of 2.7 in the 15-unit core curriculum.

CONTACT

Ms. Cassie Jones, Admissions Coordinator, Southwestern Oklahoma State University, Southwestern Oklahoma State University, John Hays Administration Building, Room 108-C, Weatherford, OK 73096. *Phone:* 580-774-3009. *Fax:* 580-774-3795. *E-mail:* cassie.jones@swosu.edu.

Spartan College of Aeronautics and Technology

Tulsa, Oklahoma

http://www.spartan.edu/

CONTACT

Mr. Mark Fowler, Vice President of Student Records and Finance, Spartan College of Aeronautics and Technology, 8820 East Pine Street, Tulsa, OK 74115. *Phone:* 918-836-6886. *Toll-free phone:* 800-331-1204.

University of Central Oklahoma

Edmond, Oklahoma

http://www.uco.edu/

- **State-supported** comprehensive, founded 1890, part of Oklahoma State Regents for Higher Education
- **Suburban** 210-acre campus with easy access to Oklahoma City
- **Endowment** $25.7 million
- **Coed** 14,337 undergraduate students, 73% full-time, 59% women, 41% men
- **Minimally difficult** entrance level, 81% of applicants were admitted

UNDERGRAD STUDENTS

10,449 full-time, 3,888 part-time. Students come from 43 states and territories; 88 other countries; 10% are from out of state; 9% Black or African American, non-Hispanic/Latino; 10% Hispanic/Latino; 4% Asian, non-Hispanic/Latino; 0.2% Native Hawaiian or other Pacific Islander, non-Hispanic/Latino; 4% American Indian or Alaska Native, non-Hispanic/Latino; 10% Two or more races, non-Hispanic/Latino; 0.9% Race/ethnicity unknown; 6% international; 10% transferred in; 11% live on campus.

Freshmen:
Admission: 4,722 applied, 3,831 admitted, 2,250 enrolled. *Average high school GPA:* 3.4. *Test scores:* ACT scores over 18: 87%; ACT scores over 24: 29%; ACT scores over 30: 4%.
Retention: 64% of full-time freshmen returned.

FACULTY

Total: 1,030, 53% full-time, 54% with terminal degrees.

Student/faculty ratio: 18:1.

ACADEMICS

Calendar: semesters. *Degrees:* certificates, associate, bachelor's, and master's.

Special study options: academic remediation for entering students, accelerated degree program, advanced placement credit, distance learning, double majors, English as a second language, independent study, internships, part-time degree program, services for LD students, study abroad, summer session for credit. *ROTC:* Army (b).

Unusual degree programs: 3-2 engineering.

Computers: 650 computers/terminals and 12,774 ports are available on campus for general student use. Students can access the following: computer help desk, free student e-mail accounts, online (class) grades, online (class) registration, online (class) schedules. Campuswide network is available. 100% of college-owned or -operated housing units are wired for high-speed Internet access. Wireless service is available via entire campus.

Library: Max Chambers Library plus 1 other. *Books:* 555,825 (physical), 296,818 (digital/electronic); *Serial titles:* 23,218 (physical), 124,803 (digital/electronic); *Databases:* 239. Weekly public service hours: 107; students can reserve study rooms.

STUDENT LIFE

Housing options: coed, men-only, women-only. Campus housing is university owned and leased by the school.

Activities and organizations: drama/theater group, student-run newspaper, radio and television station, choral group, marching band, Student Government Association, Student Programming Board, International Student Council, Panhellenic Council, Interfraternity Council, national fraternities, national sororities.

Athletics Member NCAA. All Division II. *Intercollegiate sports:* baseball M(s), basketball M(s)/W(s), cross-country running W(s), football M(s), golf M(s)/W(s), rowing W(s), soccer W(s), softball W(s), tennis W(s), track and field W(s), volleyball W(s), wrestling M(s). *Intramural sports:* badminton M/W, basketball M/W, field hockey M/W, football M/W, golf M/W, ice hockey M(c), sand volleyball M/W, soccer M/W, softball M/W, table tennis M/W, tennis M/W, ultimate Frisbee M/W, volleyball M/W, water polo M/W, wrestling M.

Campus security: 24-hour emergency response devices and patrols, late-night transport/escort service.

Student services: health clinic, personal/psychological counseling, women's center.

COSTS & FINANCIAL AID

Costs (2017–18) *Tuition:* state resident $6161 full-time, $206 per credit hour part-time; nonresident $16,508 full-time, $582 per credit hour part-time. Full-time tuition and fees vary according to course level, course load, degree level, location, and program. Part-time tuition and fees vary according to course level, course load, degree level, location, and program. No tuition increase for student's term of enrollment. *Required fees:* $939 full-time, $31 per credit hour part-time. *Room and board:* $8050; room only: $3900. Room and board charges vary according to board plan and housing facility. *Payment plan:* deferred payment. *Waivers:* employees or children of employees.

Financial Aid Of all full-time matriculated undergraduates who enrolled in 2016, 7,448 applied for aid, 6,334 were judged to have need, 621 had their need fully met. 3,125 Federal Work-Study jobs (averaging $4739). In 2016, 396 non-need-based awards were made. *Average percent of need met:* 52. *Average financial aid package:* $9809. *Average need-based loan:* $3959. *Average need-based gift aid:* $6245. *Average non-need-based aid:* $1541. *Average indebtedness upon graduation:* $26,939.

APPLYING

Standardized Tests *Required:* SAT or ACT (for admission). *Required for some:* SAT and SAT Subject Tests or ACT (for admission). *Recommended:* SAT (for admission), ACT (for admission).

Options: electronic application, deferred entrance.

Application fee: $50.

Required: high school transcript, minimum 2.7 GPA, rank in upper 50% of high school class; composite ACT score of 20; 2.7 GPA in core curriculum classes.

Application deadlines: rolling (freshmen), rolling (out-of-state freshmen), rolling (transfers).

Notification: continuous (freshmen), continuous (out-of-state freshmen), continuous (transfers).

CONTACT

Mr. John Stephens, Director of Undergraduate Admissions, University of Central Oklahoma, Office of Undergraduate Admissions, 100 North University Drive, Box 151, Edmond, OK 73034-5209. *Phone:* 405-974-2727. *Fax:* 405-974-3841. *E-mail:* onestop@uco.edu.

University of Oklahoma
Norman, Oklahoma
http://www.ou.edu/

- **State-supported** university, founded 1890
- **Suburban** 3955-acre campus with easy access to Oklahoma City
- **Endowment** $1.1 billion
- **Coed** 22,032 undergraduate students, 86% full-time, 50% women, 50% men
- **Moderately difficult** entrance level, 69% of applicants were admitted

UNDERGRAD STUDENTS

19,054 full-time, 2,978 part-time. Students come from 56 states and territories; 120 other countries; 36% are from out of state; 5% Black or African American, non-Hispanic/Latino; 10% Hispanic/Latino; 6% Asian, non-Hispanic/Latino; 0.1% Native Hawaiian or other Pacific Islander, non-Hispanic/Latino; 4% American Indian or Alaska Native, non-Hispanic/Latino; 8% Two or more races, non-Hispanic/Latino; 2% Race/ethnicity unknown; 4% international; 5% transferred in; 32% live on campus.

Freshmen:

Admission: 16,777 applied, 11,552 admitted, 4,473 enrolled. *Average high school GPA:* 3.6. *Test scores:* SAT evidence-based reading and writing scores over 500: 96%; SAT math scores over 500: 96%; ACT scores over 18: 100%; SAT evidence-based reading and writing scores over 600: 66%; SAT math scores over 600: 63%; ACT scores over 24: 73%; SAT evidence-based reading and writing scores over 700: 25%; SAT math scores over 700: 25%; ACT scores over 30: 23%.

Retention: 92% of full-time freshmen returned.

FACULTY

Total: 1,454, 83% full-time, 81% with terminal degrees.

Student/faculty ratio: 18:1.

ACADEMICS

Calendar: semesters. *Degrees:* certificates, bachelor's, master's, doctoral, and postbachelor's certificates.

Special study options: academic remediation for entering students, accelerated degree program, adult/continuing education programs, advanced placement credit, cooperative education, distance learning, double majors, English as a second language, external degree program, freshman honors college, honors programs, independent study, internships, off-campus study, part-time degree program, services for LD students, student-designed majors, study abroad, summer session for credit. *ROTC:* Army (b), Navy (b), Air Force (b).

Unusual degree programs: 3-2 business administration; engineering; nursing; social work; English, mathematics/biostatistics, computer science, international studies, political science/public administration.

Computers: 4,500 computers/terminals and 2,200 ports are available on campus for general student use. Students can access the following: campus intranet, computer help desk, free student e-mail accounts, online (class) grades, online (class) registration, online (class) schedules. Campuswide network is available. 100% of college-owned or -operated housing units are wired for high-speed Internet access. Wireless service is available via entire campus.

Library: Bizzell Memorial Library plus 5 others. *Books:* 4.4 million (physical), 1.4 million (digital/electronic); *Serial titles:* 71,289 (physical), 128,934 (digital/electronic); *Databases:* 311. Weekly public service hours: 114; students can reserve study rooms.

STUDENT LIFE

Housing options: on-campus residence required for freshman year; coed, men-only, women-only, special housing for students with disabilities. Campus housing is university owned. Freshman campus housing is guaranteed.

Activities and organizations: drama/theater group, student-run newspaper, radio and television station, choral group, marching band, Campus Activities Council Soonerthon, Campus Activities Council Homecoming, Engineers Club, Relay For Life, The Big Event, national fraternities, national sororities.

Athletics Member NCAA. All Division I except football (Division I-A). *Intercollegiate sports:* baseball M(s), basketball M(s)/W(s), cheerleading M(s)/W(s), crew W(s), cross-country running M(s)/W(s), golf M(s)/W(s), gymnastics M(s)/W(s), rowing W(s), soccer W(s), softball W(s), tennis M(s)/W(s), track and field M(s)/W(s), volleyball W(s), wrestling M(s). *Intramural sports:* badminton M(c)/W(c), basketball M/W, crew M(c)/W(c), cross-country running M/W, equestrian sports W(c), field hockey M(c)/W(c), golf M(c)/W(c), ice hockey M(c), lacrosse M(c), racquetball M/W, rowing M(c)/W(c), rugby M(c)/W(c), sand volleyball M/W, soccer M(c)/W, softball M/W, table tennis M/W, tennis M/W, triathlon M(c)/W(c), ultimate Frisbee M(c)/W(c), volleyball M(c)/W(c).

Campus security: 24-hour emergency response devices and patrols, late-night transport/escort service, controlled dormitory access, crime prevention programs, police bicycle patrols, self-defense classes, emergency notification system, lighted pathways/sidewalks.

Student services: health clinic, personal/psychological counseling, women's center, legal services.

COSTS & FINANCIAL AID

Costs (2017–18) *Tuition:* state resident $4788 full-time, $160 per credit hour part-time; nonresident $20,169 full-time, $672 per credit hour part-time. Full-time tuition and fees vary according to course load, location, and program. Part-time tuition and fees vary according to course load, location, and program. No tuition increase for student's term of enrollment. *Required fees:* $4275 full-time, $134 per credit hour part-time, $127 per term part-time. *Room and board:* $10,588; room only: $6192. Room and board charges vary according to board plan and housing facility. *Payment plan:* installment. *Waivers:* senior citizens and employees or children of employees.

Financial Aid Of all full-time matriculated undergraduates who enrolled in 2016, 10,648 applied for aid, 8,230 were judged to have need, 6,721 had their need fully met. 539 Federal Work-Study jobs (averaging $3225). 99 state and other part-time jobs (averaging $10,145). In 2016, 2478 non-need-based awards were made. *Average percent of need met:* 83. *Average financial aid package:* $13,031. *Average need-based loan:* $4427. *Average need-based gift aid:* $6142. *Average non-need-based aid:* $2464. *Average indebtedness upon graduation:* $29,283.

APPLYING

Standardized Tests *Required:* SAT or ACT (for admission).

Options: electronic application.

Application fee: $40.

Required: essay or personal statement, high school transcript, 15 specified curricular units.

Application deadlines: 2/1 (freshmen), 6/1 (transfers).

Notification: continuous (freshmen), continuous (transfers).

CONTACT

Mr. Jeff Blahnik, Director of Admissions, University of Oklahoma, 1000 Asp Avenue, Room 127, Norman, OK 73019-3032. *Phone:* 405-325-2151. *Toll-free phone:* 800-234-6868. *Fax:* 405-325-7478. *E-mail:* admissions@ou.edu.

University of Oklahoma Health Sciences Center

Oklahoma City, Oklahoma

http://www.ouhsc.edu/

- **State-supported** upper-level, founded 1890, part of University of Oklahoma
- **Urban** 300-acre campus with easy access to Oklahoma City
- **Endowment** $312.6 million
- **Coed** 786 undergraduate students, 94% full-time, 88% women, 12% men

UNDERGRAD STUDENTS

737 full-time, 49 part-time. Students come from 43 states and territories; 14 other countries; 17% are from out of state; 3% Black or African American, non-Hispanic/Latino; 9% Hispanic/Latino; 6% Asian, non-Hispanic/Latino; 0.1% Native Hawaiian or other Pacific Islander, non-Hispanic/Latino; 4% American Indian or Alaska Native, non-Hispanic/Latino; 2% Two or more races, non-Hispanic/Latino; 8% Race/ethnicity unknown; 0.3% international; 38% transferred in.

FACULTY

Total: 408, 73% full-time, 71% with terminal degrees.

Student/faculty ratio: 10:1.

ACADEMICS

Calendar: semesters. *Degrees:* bachelor's, master's, doctoral, post-master's, and postbachelor's certificates.

Special study options: advanced placement credit, distance learning, honors programs, internships, part-time degree program, summer session for credit. *ROTC:* Army (c), Air Force (c).

Computers: 140 computers/terminals are available on campus for general student use. Students can access the following: campus intranet, computer help desk, free student e-mail accounts, online (class) grades, online (class) registration, online (class) schedules, online bursar bill and payment. Campuswide network is available. 100% of college-owned or -operated housing units are wired for high-speed Internet access. Wireless service is available via classrooms, computer centers, computer labs, learning centers, libraries, student centers.

Library: Robert M. Bird Health Sciences Library plus 1 other. *Books:* 286,469 (physical), 19,136 (digital/electronic); *Serial titles:* 158 (physical), 26,678 (digital/electronic); *Databases:* 157. Weekly public service hours: 111.

STUDENT LIFE

Housing options: coed. Campus housing is university owned.

Activities and organizations: student-run radio station, OU Health Sciences Center Student Association, OU College of Nursing Student Association, OU College of Medicine Student Association, OU College of Pharmacy Student Counsel, OU College of Allied Health Student Association.

Campus security: 24-hour emergency response devices and patrols, late-night transport/escort service.

Student services: health clinic, personal/psychological counseling, women's center.

COSTS

Costs (2018–19) *Tuition:* state resident $4788 full-time, $160 per credit hour part-time; nonresident $20,169 full-time, $672 per credit hour part-time. Full-time tuition and fees vary according to course level, course load, degree level, location, program, and student level. Part-time tuition and fees vary according to course level, course load, degree level, location, program, and student level. *Required fees:* $2365 full-time, $62 per credit hour part-time, $250 per term part-time. *Room and board:* Room and board charges vary according to location. *Payment plan:* installment. *Waivers:* employees or children of employees.

APPLYING

Options: electronic application, deferred entrance.

Notification: continuous (transfers).

CONTACT

University of Oklahoma Health Sciences Center, PO Box 26901, Oklahoma City, OK 73190. *Phone:* 405-271-2347 Ext. 48916.

University of Science and Arts of Oklahoma

Chickasha, Oklahoma

http://www.usao.edu/

- **State-supported** 4-year, founded 1908, part of Oklahoma State Regents for Higher Education
- **Small-town** 75-acre campus with easy access to Oklahoma City
- **Endowment** $13.1 million
- **Coed** 888 undergraduate students, 89% full-time, 66% women, 34% men
- **Moderately difficult** entrance level, 66% of applicants were admitted

UNDERGRAD STUDENTS

787 full-time, 101 part-time. Students come from 16 states and territories; 22 other countries; 14% are from out of state; 5% Black or African American, non-Hispanic/Latino; 7% Hispanic/Latino; 0.9% Asian, non-Hispanic/Latino; 14% American Indian or Alaska Native, non-Hispanic/Latino; 2% Race/ethnicity unknown; 8% international; 9% transferred in; 44% live on campus.

Freshmen:

Admission: 706 applied, 466 admitted, 223 enrolled. *Average high school GPA:* 3.4. *Test scores:* ACT scores over 18: 81%; ACT scores over 24: 23%; ACT scores over 30: 4%.

Retention: 77% of full-time freshmen returned.

FACULTY

Total: 87, 62% full-time, 60% with terminal degrees.

Student/faculty ratio: 12:1.

ACADEMICS

Calendar: trimesters. *Degree:* bachelor's.

Special study options: academic remediation for entering students, accelerated degree program, advanced placement credit, double majors, independent study, internships, off-campus study, part-time degree program, services for LD students, student-designed majors, summer session for credit.

Computers: 185 computers/terminals are available on campus for general student use. Students can access the following: computer help desk, free student e-mail accounts, online (class) schedules. Campuswide network is available. 100% of college-owned or -operated housing units are wired for high-speed Internet access. Wireless service is available via entire campus.

Library: Nash Library plus 1 other. *Books:* 87,603 (physical), 4,798 (digital/electronic); *Serial titles:* 22 (physical), 10,500 (digital/electronic); *Databases:* 60. Weekly public service hours: 81.

STUDENT LIFE

Housing options: on-campus residence required for freshman year; coed. Campus housing is university owned. Freshman campus housing is guaranteed.

Activities and organizations: drama/theater group, student-run newspaper, television station, choral group, Student Activities Board, Volunteer Action Council, Psychology Club, Young Democrats, Young Conservatives, national fraternities.

Athletics Member NAIA. *Intercollegiate sports:* baseball M(s), basketball M(s)/W(s), cheerleading M(s)/W(s), cross-country running M/W, soccer M(s)/W(s), softball W(s), volleyball W. *Intramural sports:* basketball M/W, football M/W, golf M/W, softball M/W, volleyball M/W.

Campus security: 24-hour emergency response devices and patrols, controlled dormitory access.

Student services: health clinic, personal/psychological counseling.

COSTS & FINANCIAL AID

Costs (2017–18) Tuition: state resident $6030 full-time, $201 per credit hour part-time; nonresident $16,380 full-time, $546 per credit hour part-time. No tuition increase for student's term of enrollment. *Required fees:* $1170 full-time, $39 per credit hour part-time. *Room and board:* Room and board charges vary according to board plan and housing facility. *Payment plan:* installment. *Waivers:* senior citizens and employees or children of employees.

Financial Aid Of all full-time matriculated undergraduates who enrolled in 2017, 612 applied for aid, 536 were judged to have need, 86 had their need fully met. 157 state and other part-time jobs (averaging $1399). In 2017, 105 non-need-based awards were made. *Average percent of need met:* 68. *Average financial aid package:* $11,420. *Average need-based loan:* $2906. *Average need-based gift aid:* $9417. *Average non-need-based aid:* $2805. *Average indebtedness upon graduation:* $22,351.

APPLYING

Standardized Tests *Required:* SAT or ACT (for admission).

Options: electronic application, deferred entrance.

Application fee: $40.

Required for some: high school transcript, minimum 3.0 GPA, minimum ACT score of 24 and 3.0 GPA/top 50% high school class, 3.0 GPA and top 25% high school class, or minimum ACT score of 22 and 3.0 GPA in 15-unit high school core. *Recommended:* minimum ACT score of 24 and 3.0 GPA/top 50% high school class, 3.0 GPA and top 25% high school class, or minimum ACT score of 22 and 3.0 GPA in 15-unit high school core.

Application deadlines: 9/2 (freshmen), rolling (out-of-state freshmen), 9/2 (transfers).

Notification: continuous until 1/2 (freshmen), continuous until 1/2 (out-of-state freshmen), continuous (transfers).

CONTACT

Mrs. Laura Coponiti, Dean of Admissions and Financial Aid, University of Science and Arts of Oklahoma, 1727 West Alabama, Chickasha, OK 73018-5322. *Phone:* 405-574-1350. *Toll-free phone:* 800-933-8726. *Fax:* 405-574-1220. *E-mail:* usao-admissions@usao.edu.

See below for display ad and page 1482 for the College Close-Up.

The University of Tulsa
Tulsa, Oklahoma
http://www.utulsa.edu/

- **Independent** university, founded 1894, affiliated with Presbyterian Church (U.S.A.)
- **Urban** 209-acre campus with easy access to Tulsa
- **Endowment** $1.1 billion
- **Coed** 3,343 undergraduate students, 96% full-time, 44% women, 56% men
- **Very difficult** entrance level, 39% of applicants were admitted

UNDERGRAD STUDENTS

3,203 full-time, 140 part-time. Students come from 41 states and territories; 56 other countries; 41% are from out of state; 5% Black or African American, non-Hispanic/Latino; 6% Hispanic/Latino; 5% Asian, non-Hispanic/Latino; 0.1% Native Hawaiian or other Pacific Islander, non-Hispanic/Latino; 3% American Indian or Alaska Native, non-Hispanic/Latino; 3% Two or more races, non-Hispanic/Latino; 2% Race/ethnicity unknown; 20% international; 4% transferred in; 65% live on campus.

Freshmen:

Admission: 7,869 applied, 3,065 admitted, 743 enrolled. *Average high school GPA:* 3.9. *Test scores:* SAT evidence-based reading and writing scores over 500: 93%; SAT math scores over 500: 91%; ACT scores over 18: 99%; SAT evidence-based reading and writing scores over 600: 74%; SAT math scores over 600: 66%; ACT scores over 24: 86%; SAT evidence-based reading and writing scores over 700: 32%; SAT math scores over 700: 34%; ACT scores over 30: 46%.

Retention: 88% of full-time freshmen returned.

FACULTY

Total: 456, 77% full-time, 94% with terminal degrees.

Student/faculty ratio: 11:1.

YOUR FUTURE STARTS HERE.

APPLY NOW!

USAO

UNIVERSITY OF SCIENCE AND ARTS OF OKLAHOMA

USAO.EDU | 405.224.3140

ACADEMICS

Calendar: semesters. *Degrees:* bachelor's, master's, doctoral, and postbachelor's certificates.

Special study options: accelerated degree program, adult/continuing education programs, advanced placement credit, double majors, English as a second language, honors programs, independent study, internships, part-time degree program, services for LD students, student-designed majors, study abroad, summer session for credit. *ROTC:* Air Force (c).

Unusual degree programs: 3-2 business administration; engineering; accountancy, mathematics, athletic training, biochemistry, biology, chemistry, computer science, cyber security, geosciences, geophysics, history, physics, women's and gender studies.

Computers: 710 computers/terminals and 250 ports are available on campus for general student use. Students can access the following: campus intranet, computer help desk, free student e-mail accounts, online (class) grades, online (class) registration, online (class) schedules. Campuswide network is available. 100% of college-owned or -operated housing units are wired for high-speed Internet access. Wireless service is available via entire campus.

Library: McFarlin Library plus 1 other. *Books:* 1.2 million (physical), 460,240 (digital/electronic); *Serial titles:* 59,171 (digital/electronic); *Databases:* 289. Weekly public service hours: 94; study areas open 24 hours, 5–7 days a week; students can reserve study rooms.

STUDENT LIFE

Housing options: on-campus residence required through sophomore year; coed, men-only, women-only, special housing for students with disabilities. Campus housing is university owned. Freshman campus housing is guaranteed.

Activities and organizations: drama/theater group, student-run newspaper, radio and television station, choral group, marching band, Student Association, Residence Hall Association, Pre-Professional organizations, intramural sports, Greek life, national fraternities, national sororities.

Athletics Member NCAA. All Division I except football (Division I-A). *Intercollegiate sports:* basketball M(s)/W(s), cheerleading M/W, crew W(s), cross-country running M(s)/W(s), golf W(s), soccer M(s)/W(s), softball W(s), tennis M(s)/W(s), track and field M(s)/W(s), volleyball

W(s). *Intramural sports:* badminton M/W, basketball M/W, bowling M/W, crew M(c), cross-country running M/W, football M/W, golf W, lacrosse M(c), racquetball M/W, rugby M(c), soccer M/W, softball M/W, squash M/W, table tennis M/W, tennis M/W, track and field M/W, volleyball M/W, weight lifting M/W.

Campus security: 24-hour emergency response devices and patrols, late-night transport/escort service, controlled dormitory access.

Student services: health clinic, personal/psychological counseling, legal services.

COSTS & FINANCIAL AID

Costs (2018–19) *One-time required fee:* $485. *Comprehensive fee:* $52,140 includes full-time tuition ($40,484), mandatory fees ($540), and room and board ($11,116). Full-time tuition and fees vary according to course load and program. Part-time tuition: $1453 per credit hour. Part-time tuition and fees vary according to course load and program. *College room only:* $6394. Room and board charges vary according to board plan and housing facility. *Payment plan:* installment. *Waivers:* employees or children of employees.

Financial Aid Of all full-time matriculated undergraduates who enrolled in 2017, 1,752 applied for aid, 1,507 were judged to have need, 531 had their need fully met. 335 Federal Work-Study jobs (averaging $2481). In 2017, 1262 non-need-based awards were made. *Average percent of need met:* 82. *Average financial aid package:* $31,580. *Average need-based loan:* $5820. *Average need-based gift aid:* $7945. *Average non-need-based aid:* $21,531. *Average indebtedness upon graduation:* $34,869.

APPLYING

Standardized Tests *Required:* SAT or ACT (for admission).

Options: electronic application, early admission, early action, deferred entrance.

Application fee: $50.

Required: essay or personal statement, high school transcript, 1 letter of recommendation. *Recommended:* minimum 3.0 GPA, interview.

Application deadlines: rolling (freshmen), rolling (transfers), 11/1 (early action).

Notification: continuous (freshmen), continuous (transfers), 12/15 (early action).

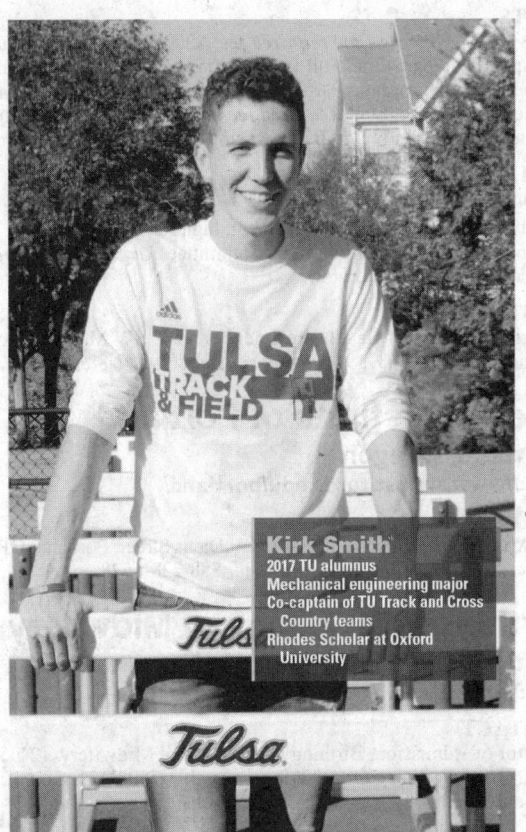

CONTACT
Ms. Casey Reed, Dean of Admission, The University of Tulsa, 800 South Tucker Drive, Tulsa, OK 74104. *Phone:* 918-631-2307. *Toll-free phone:* 800-331-3050. *Fax:* 918-631-5003. *E-mail:* admission@utulsa.edu.

See previous page for display ad and page 1484 for the College Close-Up.

OREGON

American College of Healthcare Sciences
Portland, Oregon
http://www.achs.edu/
- **Independent** comprehensive
- **Coed**
- 50% of applicants were admitted

UNDERGRAD STUDENTS
Students come from 63 other countries.

Freshmen:
Admission: 2 applied, 1 admitted.

ACADEMICS
Degrees: certificates, diplomas, associate, bachelor's, master's, and postbachelor's certificates.

Special study options: academic remediation for entering students, accelerated degree program, adult/continuing education programs, distance learning, double majors, honors programs, off-campus study, part-time degree program, services for LD students, student-designed majors, study abroad, summer session for credit.

Computers: Students can access the following: computer help desk, free student e-mail accounts, online (class) grades, online (class) registration, online (class) schedules. Wireless service is available via entire campus.
Library: ACHS Virtual Library. *Books:* 2,971 (digital/electronic); *Serial titles:* 17,514 (digital/electronic); *Databases:* 70.

COSTS
Costs (2017–18) *One-time required fee:* $200. *Tuition:* $7800 full-time, $325 per credit part-time. Full-time tuition and fees vary according to course load and program. Part-time tuition and fees vary according to course load and program. *Required fees:* $350 per course part-time. *Payment plan:* installment. *Waivers:* employees or children of employees.

APPLYING
Options: electronic application.

Required: essay or personal statement, high school transcript, recommendation from Admissions Committee. *Required for some:* letters of recommendation, interview.

CONTACT
American College of Healthcare Sciences, 5005 SW Macadam Avenue, Portland, OR 97239-3719. *Toll-free phone:* 800-487-8839.

The Art Institute of Portland
Portland, Oregon
http://www.artinstitutes.edu/portland/

CONTACT
The Art Institute of Portland, 1122 NW Davis Street, Portland, OR 97209. *Phone:* 503-228-6528. *Toll-free phone:* 888-228-6528.

Birthingway College of Midwifery
Portland, Oregon
http://www.birthingway.edu/

CONTACT
Director of Admission, Birthingway College of Midwifery, 12113 SE Foster Road, Portland, OR 97299. *Phone:* 503-760-3131. *E-mail:* info@birthingway.edu.

Concordia University
Portland, Oregon
http://www.cu-portland.edu/

CONTACT
Ms. Bobi Swan, Dean of Admission, Concordia University, 2811 Northeast Holman, Portland, OR 97211-6099. *Phone:* 503-493-6526. *Toll-free phone:* 800-321-9371. *Fax:* 503-280-8531. *E-mail:* admissions@cu-portland.edu.

Corban University
Salem, Oregon
http://www.corban.edu/
- **Independent Christian** comprehensive, founded 1935
- **Suburban** 145-acre campus with easy access to Portland
- **Coed** 1,021 undergraduate students, 92% full-time, 61% women, 39% men
- **Moderately difficult** entrance level, 33% of applicants were admitted

UNDERGRAD STUDENTS
936 full-time, 85 part-time. 46% are from out of state; 1% Black or African American, non-Hispanic/Latino; 2% Hispanic/Latino; 2% Asian, non-Hispanic/Latino; 0.6% Native Hawaiian or other Pacific Islander, non-Hispanic/Latino; 1% American Indian or Alaska Native, non-Hispanic/Latino; 8% Two or more races, non-Hispanic/Latino; 5% Race/ethnicity unknown; 5% international; 6% transferred in; 49% live on campus.

Freshmen:
Admission: 1,943 applied, 641 admitted, 197 enrolled. *Average high school GPA:* 3.6. *Test scores:* SAT evidence-based reading and writing scores over 500: 87%; SAT math scores over 500: 79%; ACT scores over 18: 97%; SAT evidence-based reading and writing scores over 600: 46%; SAT math scores over 600: 25%; ACT scores over 24: 49%; SAT evidence-based reading and writing scores over 700: 9%; SAT math scores over 700: 7%; ACT scores over 30: 6%.

Retention: 79% of full-time freshmen returned.

FACULTY
Total: 134, 37% full-time, 40% with terminal degrees.
Student/faculty ratio: 14:1.

ACADEMICS
Calendar: semesters. *Degrees:* associate, bachelor's, master's, and doctoral.

Special study options: accelerated degree program, adult/continuing education programs, advanced placement credit, cooperative education, distance learning, double majors, English as a second language, external degree program, honors programs, independent study, internships, off-campus study, services for LD students, student-designed majors, study abroad, summer session for credit. *ROTC:* Army (c), Air Force (c).

Computers: 54 computers/terminals and 700 ports are available on campus for general student use. Students can access the following: campus intranet, computer help desk, free student e-mail accounts, online (class) grades, online (class) registration, online (class) schedules. Campuswide network is available. 100% of college-owned or -operated housing units are wired for high-speed Internet access. Wireless service is available via entire campus.
Library: Corban University Library. *Books:* 81,025 (physical), 126,255 (digital/electronic); *Databases:* 14. Students can reserve study rooms.

STUDENT LIFE
Housing options: on-campus residence required through junior year; men-only, women-only. Campus housing is university owned. Freshman campus housing is guaranteed.

Activities and organizations: drama/theater group, student-run newspaper, choral group, Corban Recreation, Corban Community Garden, Stories of Glory, Dens and Leviathans, Corban Students for LIfe.

Athletics Member NAIA, NCCAA. *Intercollegiate sports:* baseball M(s), basketball M(s)/W(s), cross-country running M(s)/W(s), golf M(s)/W(s), soccer M(s)/W(s), softball W(s), track and field M(s)/W(s), volleyball W(s). *Intramural sports:* basketball M/W, football M, soccer M/W, table tennis M/W, ultimate Frisbee M/W, volleyball M/W.

Campus security: 24-hour emergency response devices and patrols, student patrols, late-night transport/escort service, controlled dormitory access.

Student services: health clinic, personal/psychological counseling.

COSTS & FINANCIAL AID
Costs (2018–19) *One-time required fee:* $150. *Comprehensive fee:* $43,271 includes full-time tuition ($32,380), mandatory fees ($660), and room and board ($10,231). Full-time tuition and fees vary according to course load, degree level, program, and reciprocity agreements. Part-time tuition: $1350 per credit hour. Part-time tuition and fees vary according to course load, degree level, program, and reciprocity agreements. *Required fees:* $330 per term part-time. *College room only:* $5852. Room and board charges vary according to board plan. *Payment plan:* installment. *Waivers:* children of alumni, senior citizens, and employees or children of employees.

Financial Aid Of all full-time matriculated undergraduates who enrolled in 2016, 838 applied for aid, 765 were judged to have need, 132 had their need fully met. 226 Federal Work-Study jobs (averaging $1494). In 2016, 93 non-need-based awards were made. *Average percent of need met:* 70. *Average financial aid package:* $22,273. *Average need-based loan:* $4289. *Average need-based gift aid:* $18,636. *Average non-need-based aid:* $10,522. *Average indebtedness upon graduation:* $31,408.

APPLYING
Standardized Tests *Required:* SAT or ACT (for admission).

Options: electronic application.

Application fee: $40.

Required: essay or personal statement, high school transcript, minimum 2.7 GPA, 2 letters of recommendation.

Application deadlines: 8/1 (freshmen), 8/1 (transfers).

Notification: continuous (freshmen), continuous (transfers).

CONTACT
Jordan Lindsey, Associate Director of Admissions, Corban University, 5000 Deer Park Drive, SE, Salem, OR 97301-9392. *Phone:* 503-375-7156. *Toll-free phone:* 800-845-3005. *Fax:* 503-585-4316. *E-mail:* admissions@corban.edu.

Eastern Oregon University
La Grande, Oregon
http://www.eou.edu/

- **State-supported** comprehensive, founded 1929
- **Rural** 121-acre campus
- **Endowment** $10.7 million
- **Coed** 2,737 undergraduate students, 61% full-time, 61% women, 39% men
- **Minimally difficult** entrance level, 98% of applicants were admitted

UNDERGRAD STUDENTS
1,668 full-time, 1,069 part-time. 31% are from out of state; 2% Black or African American, non-Hispanic/Latino; 12% Hispanic/Latino; 1% Asian, non-Hispanic/Latino; 4% Native Hawaiian or other Pacific Islander, non-Hispanic/Latino; 2% American Indian or Alaska Native, non-Hispanic/Latino; 4% Two or more races, non-Hispanic/Latino; 3% Race/ethnicity unknown; 2% international; 15% transferred in; 15% live on campus.

Freshmen:
Admission: 1,011 applied, 988 admitted, 327 enrolled. *Average high school GPA:* 3.4. *Test scores:* SAT evidence-based reading and writing scores over 500: 65%; SAT math scores over 500: 68%; ACT scores over 18: 81%; SAT evidence-based reading and writing scores over 600: 18%; SAT math scores over 600: 15%; ACT scores over 24: 25%; SAT evidence-based reading and writing scores over 700: 2%; SAT math scores over 700: 1%; ACT scores over 30: 3%.

FACULTY
Total: 170, 64% full-time, 31% with terminal degrees.
Student/faculty ratio: 17:1.

ACADEMICS
Calendar: quarters. *Degrees:* certificates, associate, bachelor's, master's, and postbachelor's certificates.

Special study options: academic remediation for entering students, adult/continuing education programs, advanced placement credit, cooperative education, distance learning, double majors, external degree program, honors programs, independent study, internships, off-campus study, part-time degree program, services for LD students, student-designed majors, study abroad, summer session for credit. *ROTC:* Army (b).

Computers: Students can access the following: free student e-mail accounts, online (class) grades, online (class) registration, online (class) schedules. Campuswide network is available. Wireless service is available via entire campus.

Library: Pierce Library. Students can reserve study rooms.

STUDENT LIFE
Housing options: on-campus residence required for freshman year; coed, special housing for students with disabilities. Campus housing is university owned. Freshman applicants given priority for college housing.

Activities and organizations: drama/theater group, student-run newspaper, radio station, choral group, Outdoor Program, Pre-Professional Health Club, Student Government, International Student Association, Chemistry Club.

Athletics Member NAIA. *Intercollegiate sports:* basketball M(s)/W(s), cross-country running M(s)/W(s), football M(s), soccer M(s)/W(s), softball W(s), track and field M(s)/W(s), volleyball W(s). *Intramural sports:* basketball M/W, football M, rock climbing M(c)/W(c), soccer M/W, softball M/W, volleyball M/W.

Campus security: 24-hour emergency response devices, late-night transport/escort service, controlled dormitory access.

Student services: health clinic, personal/psychological counseling, women's center.

COSTS & FINANCIAL AID
Costs (2017–18) *One-time required fee:* $350. *Tuition:* state resident $6928 full-time, $154 per credit hour part-time; nonresident $18,248 full-time, $406 per credit hour part-time. Full-time tuition and fees vary according to course load, location, and reciprocity agreements. Part-time tuition and fees vary according to course load, location, and reciprocity agreements. *Required fees:* $1434 full-time, $466 per term part-time. *Room and board:* $9250; room only: $5500. Room and board charges vary according to board plan and housing facility. *Payment plans:* installment, deferred payment. *Waivers:* senior citizens and employees or children of employees.

Financial Aid Of all full-time matriculated undergraduates who enrolled in 2016, 1,567 applied for aid, 1,352 were judged to have need, 170 had their need fully met. In 2016, 138 non-need-based awards were made. *Average percent of need met:* 56. *Average financial aid package:* $9696. *Average need-based loan:* $4227. *Average need-based gift aid:* $8126. *Average non-need-based aid:* $2112. *Average indebtedness upon graduation:* $31,314.

APPLYING
Standardized Tests *Required:* SAT or ACT (for admission). *Required for some:* SAT and SAT Subject Tests or ACT (for admission).

Options: electronic application, early admission, early action, deferred entrance.

Application fee: $50.

Required: high school transcript, minimum 2.8 GPA. *Required for some:* essay or personal statement, 2 letters of recommendation.

Application deadlines: 9/1 (freshmen), 9/1 (transfers), 2/1 (early action).

Notification: continuous (freshmen), continuous (out-of-state freshmen), continuous (transfers), rolling (early action).

CONTACT
Admissions Department, Eastern Oregon University, One University Boulevard, La Grande, OR. *Phone:* 800-452-8639. *Toll-free phone:* 800-452-8639. *Fax:* 541-962-3418. *E-mail:* admissions@eou.edu.

George Fox University

Newberg, Oregon

http://www.georgefox.edu/

- **Independent Friends** university, founded 1891
- **Small-town** 108-acre campus with easy access to Portland
- **Coed**
- **Moderately difficult** entrance level

FACULTY

Student/faculty ratio: 14:1.

ACADEMICS

Calendar: semesters. *Degrees:* bachelor's, master's, doctoral, post-master's, and postbachelor's certificates.
Library: Murdock Learning Resource Center plus 1 other. *Books:* 463,450 (physical); *Serial titles:* 101,027 (digital/electronic); *Databases:* 209. Weekly public service hours: 93; study areas open 24 hours, 5–7 days a week; students can reserve study rooms.

STUDENT LIFE

Housing options: on-campus residence required through junior year; men-only, women-only, cooperative, special housing for students with disabilities. Campus housing is university owned. Freshman applicants given priority for college housing.

Activities and organizations: drama/theater group, student-run newspaper, radio station, choral group, Student Government, Christian Ministries, Orientation Committee, Outdoor Club and Bruin Ambassadors, Blue Zone.

Athletics Member NCAA. All Division III.

Campus security: 24-hour emergency response devices and patrols, student patrols, late-night transport/escort service, controlled dormitory access, parking lot cameras, video surveillance of key buildings.

Student services: health clinic, personal/psychological counseling.

COSTS & FINANCIAL AID

Costs (2017–18) *Comprehensive fee:* $45,752 includes full-time tuition ($34,500), mandatory fees ($366), and room and board ($10,886). Full-time tuition and fees vary according to reciprocity agreements. Part-time tuition and fees vary according to course load. *Room and board:* Room and board charges vary according to board plan.

Financial Aid Of all full-time matriculated undergraduates who enrolled in 2017, 2,092 applied for aid, 1,861 were judged to have need, 659 had their need fully met. 1,399 Federal Work-Study jobs (averaging $2214). In 2017, 590 non-need-based awards were made. *Average percent of need met:* 84. *Average financial aid package:* $22,230. *Average need-based loan:* $3989. *Average need-based gift aid:* $18,195. *Average non-need-based aid:* $13,374. *Average indebtedness upon graduation:* $29,207.

APPLYING

Standardized Tests *Required:* SAT or ACT (for admission).

Options: electronic application, early action, deferred entrance.

Application fee: $40.

Required: essay or personal statement, 1 letter of recommendation. *Required for some:* high school transcript. *Recommended:* high school transcript.

CONTACT

Ms. Lindsay Knox, Director of Undergraduate Admissions, George Fox University, 414 North Meridian Street, Newberg, OR 97132. *Phone:* 503-554-2240. *Toll-free phone:* 800-765-4369. *Fax:* 503-554-3110. *E-mail:* admissions@georgefox.edu.

Gutenberg College

Eugene, Oregon

http://www.gutenberg.edu/

- **Independent Christian** 4-year
- **Urban** campus
- **Coed** 13 undergraduate students, 100% full-time, 69% women, 31% men
- **Moderately difficult** entrance level

UNDERGRAD STUDENTS

13 full-time. 88% live on campus.

Freshmen:
Admission: 2 enrolled.
Retention: 75% of full-time freshmen returned.

FACULTY

Total: 8, 50% full-time, 50% with terminal degrees.
Student/faculty ratio: 2:1.

ACADEMICS

Degree: bachelor's.

Computers: 2 computers/terminals are available on campus for general student use. Students can access the following: free student e-mail accounts. Campuswide network is available. Wireless service is available via entire campus.

STUDENT LIFE

Housing options: cooperative. Campus housing is university owned and leased by the school. Freshman applicants given priority for college housing.

Student services: personal/psychological counseling, legal services.

COSTS

Costs (2018–19) *Comprehensive fee:* $18,500 includes full-time tuition ($13,000), mandatory fees ($500), and room and board ($5000). *Room and board:* Room and board charges vary according to housing facility. *Payment plan:* installment. *Waivers:* employees or children of employees.

APPLYING

Standardized Tests *Required:* SAT or ACT (for admission), CLT (for admission).

Options: electronic application, early decision.

Application fee: $40.

Required: essay or personal statement, high school transcript, 2 letters of recommendation, interview.

Early decision deadline: 1/1.

CONTACT

Dr. Eliot Grasso, Director of Admissions and Development, Gutenberg College, 1883 University Street, Eugene, OR 97403. *Phone:* 541-683-5141. *Fax:* 541-683-6997. *E-mail:* egrasso@gutenberg.edu.

Lewis & Clark College

Portland, Oregon

http://www.lclark.edu/

- **Independent** comprehensive, founded 1867
- **Urban** 137-acre campus with easy access to Portland
- **Endowment** $202.3 million
- **Coed**
- **Very difficult** entrance level

FACULTY

Student/faculty ratio: 11:1.

ACADEMICS

Calendar: semesters. *Degrees:* bachelor's, master's, doctoral, and post-master's certificates.
Library: Aubrey Watzek Library plus 1 other. *Books:* 523,517 (physical), 275,318 (digital/electronic); *Serial titles:* 7,568 (physical), 6,299 (digital/electronic); *Databases:* 327. Weekly public service hours: 141; study areas open 24 hours, 5–7 days a week; students can reserve study rooms.

STUDENT LIFE

Housing options: on-campus residence required through sophomore year; coed, women-only. Campus housing is university owned. Freshman campus housing is guaranteed.

Activities and organizations: drama/theater group, student-run newspaper, radio station, choral group, International Students of Lewis & Clark, Campus Activities Board, MOSAIC (Multicultural Organizations Seeking An Inclusive Community), Bacchus Men's Ultimate Frisbee, Hillel.

Athletics Member NCAA. All Division III.

Campus security: 24-hour emergency response devices and patrols, late-night transport/escort service, controlled dormitory access.

Student services: health clinic, personal/psychological counseling.

COSTS & FINANCIAL AID
Costs (2017–18) *Comprehensive fee:* $61,084 includes full-time tuition ($48,628), mandatory fees ($360), and room and board ($12,096). Part-time tuition: $2431 per credit hour. Part-time tuition and fees vary according to course load. *Required fees:* $18 per credit hour part-time. *College room only:* $6728. Room and board charges vary according to board plan and housing facility.

Financial Aid Of all full-time matriculated undergraduates who enrolled in 2017, 1,412 applied for aid, 1,208 were judged to have need, 496 had their need fully met. 944 Federal Work-Study jobs (averaging $2455). 156 state and other part-time jobs (averaging $2140). In 2017, 673 non-need-based awards were made. *Average percent of need met:* 87. *Average financial aid package:* $40,854. *Average need-based loan:* $4381. *Average need-based gift aid:* $33,162. *Average non-need-based aid:* $16,695. *Average indebtedness upon graduation:* $27,591.

APPLYING
Standardized Tests *Required:* SAT or ACT scores or Test-Optional Portfolio Path materials (for admission).

Options: electronic application, early decision, early action, deferred entrance.

Required: essay or personal statement, high school transcript, 1 letter of recommendation. *Required for some:* 2 letters of recommendation, graded writing sample, math or science sample, 2 letters of recommendation for Test Optional Portfolio Path. *Recommended:* interview.

CONTACT
Erica Johnson, Director of Admissions, Lewis & Clark College, 0615 SW Palatine Hill Road, Portland, OR 97219. *Phone:* 503-768-7040. *Toll-free phone:* 800-444-4111. *Fax:* 503-768-7055. *E-mail:* admissions@lclark.edu.

★ Linfield College
McMinnville, Oregon
http://www.linfield.edu/

- **Independent American Baptist Churches in the USA** 4-year, founded 1858, part of Linfield College
- **Small-town** 189-acre campus with easy access to Portland
- **Endowment** $113.8 million
- **Coed** 1,535 undergraduate students, 98% full-time, 60% women, 40% men
- **Moderately difficult** entrance level, 81% of applicants were admitted

UNDERGRAD STUDENTS
1,505 full-time, 30 part-time. Students come from 21 states and territories; 22 other countries; 42% are from out of state; 2% Black or African American, non-Hispanic/Latino; 16% Hispanic/Latino; 5% Asian, non-Hispanic/Latino; 0.8% Native Hawaiian or other Pacific Islander, non-Hispanic/Latino; 0.7% American Indian or Alaska Native, non-Hispanic/Latino; 10% Two or more races, non-Hispanic/Latino; 3% Race/ethnicity unknown; 4% international; 4% transferred in; 74% live on campus.

Freshmen:
Admission: 2,325 applied, 1,878 admitted, 400 enrolled. *Average high school GPA:* 3.6. *Test scores:* SAT evidence-based reading and writing scores over 500: 81%; SAT math scores over 500: 82%; ACT scores over 18: 94%; SAT evidence-based reading and writing scores over 600: 34%; SAT math scores over 600: 34%; ACT scores over 24: 44%; SAT evidence-based reading and writing scores over 700: 4%; SAT math scores over 700: 3%; ACT scores over 30: 7%.

Retention: 81% of full-time freshmen returned.

FACULTY
Total: 204, 60% full-time, 72% with terminal degrees.
Student/faculty ratio: 10:1.

ACADEMICS
Calendar: 4-1-4. *Degrees:* bachelor's and postbachelor's certificates (Linfield College includes the Linfield College McMinnville Campus in

McMinnville, Oregon; the Linfield-Good Samaritan School of Nursing in Portland, Oregon(Portland Campus) and the Linfield College Adult Degree Program online).

Special study options: accelerated degree program, adult/continuing education programs, advanced placement credit, distance learning, double majors, English as a second language, external degree program, independent study, internships, off-campus study, part-time degree program, services for LD students, student-designed majors, study abroad, summer session for credit. *ROTC:* Air Force (c).

Unusual degree programs: 3-2 engineering with Washington State University, Oregon State University, University of Southern California.

Computers: 250 computers/terminals are available on campus for general student use. Students can access the following: computer help desk, free student e-mail accounts, online (class) grades, online (class) registration, online (class) schedules. Campuswide network is available. 100% of college-owned or -operated housing units are wired for high-speed Internet access. Wireless service is available via entire campus.

Library: Jereld R. Nicholson Library. *Books:* 154,091 (physical), 5,719 (digital/electronic); *Serial titles:* 30,997 (physical), 2 (digital/electronic); *Databases:* 186. Weekly public service hours: 95.

STUDENT LIFE

Housing options: on-campus residence required through junior year; coed, men-only, women-only, special housing for students with disabilities. Campus housing is university owned. Freshman campus housing is guaranteed.

Activities and organizations: drama/theater group, student-run newspaper, radio station, choral group, marching band, Fellowship of Christian Athletes, Linfield Ultimate Players Association, Hawaiian Club, International Club, Outdoor Club, national fraternities, national sororities.

Athletics Member NCAA. All Division III. *Intercollegiate sports:* baseball M, basketball M/W, cross-country running M/W, football M, golf M/W, lacrosse W, soccer M/W, softball W, swimming and diving M/W, tennis M/W, track and field M/W, volleyball W. *Intramural sports:* basketball M/W, bowling M/W, football M/W, soccer M/W, softball M/W, tennis M/W, ultimate Frisbee M/W, volleyball M/W.

Campus security: 24-hour emergency response devices and patrols, late-night transport/escort service, controlled dormitory access.

Student services: health clinic, personal/psychological counseling.

COSTS & FINANCIAL AID

Costs (2017–18) *Comprehensive fee:* $53,346 includes full-time tuition ($41,100), mandatory fees ($476), and room and board ($11,770). Full-time tuition and fees vary according to course load, location, and program. Part-time tuition: $1285 per semester hour. Part-time tuition and fees vary according to course load, location, and program. *Required fees:* $132 per term part-time. *College room only:* $6400. Room and board charges vary according to board plan, housing facility, and location. *Payment plan:* installment. *Waivers:* senior citizens and employees or children of employees.

Financial Aid Of all full-time matriculated undergraduates who enrolled in 2017, 1,289 applied for aid, 1,156 were judged to have need, 268 had their need fully met. 557 Federal Work-Study jobs (averaging $1379). 340 state and other part-time jobs (averaging $1114). In 2017, 300 non-need-based awards were made. *Average percent of need met:* 82. *Average financial aid package:* $34,716. *Average need-based loan:* $4497. *Average need-based gift aid:* $28,935. *Average non-need-based aid:* $19,043. *Average indebtedness upon graduation:* $34,244.

APPLYING

Standardized Tests *Required:* SAT or ACT (for admission).

Options: electronic application, early action, deferred entrance.

Required: essay or personal statement, high school transcript, 1 letter of recommendation. *Recommended:* interview.

Application deadlines: 2/1 (freshmen), 4/15 (transfers), 11/1 (early action).

Notification: 4/1 (freshmen), 5/15 (transfers), 12/1 (early action).

CONTACT

Ms. Lisa Knodle-Bragiel, Director of Admission, Linfield College, 900 SE Baker Street, McMinnville, OR 97128. *Phone:* 503-883-2213. *Toll-free phone:* 800-640-2287. *Fax:* 503-883-2472. *E-mail:* admission@linfield.edu.

See previous page for display ad and page 1328 for the College Close-Up.

Marylhurst University
Marylhurst, Oregon
http://www.marylhurst.edu/

- **Independent Roman Catholic** comprehensive, founded 1893
- **Suburban** 63-acre campus with easy access to Portland
- **Coed** 364 undergraduate students, 34% full-time, 71% women, 29% men
- **Noncompetitive** entrance level

UNDERGRAD STUDENTS

124 full-time, 240 part-time. Students come from 32 states and territories; 7 other countries; 20% are from out of state; 3% Black or African American, non-Hispanic/Latino; 9% Hispanic/Latino; 2% Asian, non-Hispanic/Latino; 0.8% American Indian or Alaska Native, non-Hispanic/Latino; 4% Two or more races, non-Hispanic/Latino; 15% Race/ethnicity unknown; 3% international.

FACULTY

Total: 143, 26% full-time.

Student/faculty ratio: 7:1.

ACADEMICS

Calendar: quarters. *Degrees:* certificates, bachelor's, master's, post-master's, and postbachelor's certificates.

Special study options: accelerated degree program, adult/continuing education programs, advanced placement credit, distance learning, double majors, English as a second language, honors programs, independent study, internships, off-campus study, part-time degree program, services for LD students, student-designed majors, study abroad, summer session for credit.

Computers: Students can access the following: campus intranet, computer help desk, free student e-mail accounts, online (class) grades, online (class) registration, online (class) schedules. Campuswide network is available. Wireless service is available via entire campus.

Library: Shoen Library. *Books:* 105,578 (physical), 271,865 (digital/electronic). Students can reserve study rooms.

STUDENT LIFE

Activities and organizations: choral group, Creative Counseling Therapies Student Group, Alpha Phi Tau, English Honors Society, Marylhurst LGBTQ Alliance, Student Organization for Sustainability (SOS), Student Veterans Club.

Campus security: security is available during campus hours.

Student services: personal/psychological counseling.

COSTS & FINANCIAL AID

Costs (2018–19) *Tuition:* $20,835 full-time, $463 per credit hour part-time. Full-time tuition and fees vary according to program. Part-time tuition and fees vary according to program. *Payment plan:* installment. *Waivers:* employees or children of employees.

Financial Aid Of all full-time matriculated undergraduates who enrolled in 2017, 115 applied for aid, 111 were judged to have need, 1 had their need fully met. 16 Federal Work-Study jobs (averaging $5312). In 2017, 17 non-need-based awards were made. *Average percent of need met:* 45. *Average financial aid package:* $15,152. *Average need-based loan:* $4746. *Average need-based gift aid:* $11,247. *Average non-need-based aid:* $5282.

APPLYING

Options: electronic application, deferred entrance.

Required: essay or personal statement, high school transcript. *Required for some:* 2 letters of recommendation, interview.

Application deadlines: rolling (freshmen), rolling (transfers).

Notification: continuous (freshmen), continuous (transfers).

CONTACT

Marylhurst University, 17600 Pacific Highway, PO Box 261, Marylhurst, OR 97036-0261. *Phone:* 503-503.534.7029. *Toll-free phone:* 800-634-9982.

Mount Angel Seminary

Saint Benedict, Oregon

http://www.mountangelabbey.org/seminary/

CONTACT
Registrar/Admissions Officer, Mount Angel Seminary, Saint Benedict, OR 97373. *Phone:* 503-845-3951 Ext. 14. *E-mail:* admissions@mtangel.edu.

Multnomah University

Portland, Oregon

http://www.multnomah.edu/

- **Independent interdenominational** comprehensive, founded 1936
- **Urban** 22-acre campus with easy access to Portland, OR
- **Endowment** $6.9 million
- **Coed** 417 undergraduate students, 87% full-time, 48% women, 52% men
- **Moderately difficult** entrance level, 70% of applicants were admitted

UNDERGRAD STUDENTS
364 full-time, 53 part-time. Students come from 18 states and territories; 57% are from out of state; 3% Black or African American, non-Hispanic/Latino; 8% Hispanic/Latino; 1% Asian, non-Hispanic/Latino; 1% Native Hawaiian or other Pacific Islander, non-Hispanic/Latino; 0.7% American Indian or Alaska Native, non-Hispanic/Latino; 9% Two or more races, non-Hispanic/Latino; 1% Race/ethnicity unknown; 14% transferred in; 48% live on campus.

Freshmen:
Admission: 198 applied, 139 admitted, 72 enrolled. *Average high school GPA:* 3.2. *Test scores:* ACT scores over 18: 100%; ACT scores over 24: 45%; ACT scores over 30: 18%.
Retention: 63% of full-time freshmen returned.

FACULTY
Total: 100, 26% full-time, 42% with terminal degrees.
Student/faculty ratio: 12:1.

ACADEMICS
Calendar: semesters. *Degrees:* bachelor's, master's, doctoral, and postbachelor's certificates.

Special study options: academic remediation for entering students, adult/continuing education programs, advanced placement credit, distance learning, double majors, internships, part-time degree program, services for LD students, summer session for credit.

Computers: 36 computers/terminals are available on campus for general student use. Students can access the following: campus intranet, computer help desk, free student e-mail accounts, online (class) grades, online (class) registration, online (class) schedules. Campuswide network is available. 80% of college-owned or -operated housing units are wired for high-speed Internet access. Wireless service is available via entire campus.
Library: John Mitchell Library. *Books:* 120,106 (physical), 152,698 (digital/electronic); *Serial titles:* 548 (physical), 20,000 (digital/electronic); *Databases:* 45. Weekly public service hours: 82; students can reserve study rooms.

STUDENT LIFE
Housing options: on-campus residence required through sophomore year; men-only, women-only, special housing for students with disabilities. Campus housing is university owned. Freshman campus housing is guaranteed.
Activities and organizations: choral group, Student Government, Commuter Life, Poetry Club, Brunch Chats, Res Life.
Athletics Member NAIA. *Intercollegiate sports:* basketball M(s)/W(s), cross-country running M(s)/W(s), golf M(s)/W(s), soccer M(s), track and field M(s)/W(s), volleyball W. *Intramural sports:* basketball M/W, softball M/W, table tennis M/W, ultimate Frisbee M/W, volleyball M/W.
Campus security: 24-hour emergency response devices and patrols, controlled dormitory access.
Student services: personal/psychological counseling.

COSTS & FINANCIAL AID
Costs (2017–18) *Comprehensive fee:* $33,240 includes full-time tuition ($24,100), mandatory fees ($580), and room and board ($8560). Full-time tuition and fees vary according to course load, degree level, location, and program. Part-time tuition: $760 per credit hour. Part-time tuition and fees vary according to course load, degree level, location, and program. *Required fees:* $145 per term part-time. *Room and board:* Room and board charges vary according to board plan and housing facility. *Payment plan:* installment. *Waivers:* employees or children of employees.

Financial Aid Of all full-time matriculated undergraduates who enrolled in 2009, 503 applied for aid, 441 were judged to have need, 11 had their need fully met. 75 Federal Work-Study jobs (averaging $1500). In 2009, 36 non-need-based awards were made. *Average percent of need met:* 50. *Average financial aid package:* $9211. *Average need-based loan:* $4094. *Average need-based gift aid:* $5846. *Average non-need-based aid:* $1848. *Average indebtedness upon graduation:* $21,020.

APPLYING
Standardized Tests *Recommended:* SAT or ACT (for admission).
Options: electronic application, deferred entrance.
Application fee: $40.
Required: essay or personal statement, high school transcript, minimum 2.5 GPA, 2 letters of recommendation.
Notification: continuous (freshmen), continuous (transfers).

CONTACT
Ms. Jenae Johnson, Admissions Counselor, Multnomah University, 8435 Northeast Glisan Street, Portland, OR 97220-5898. *Phone:* 503-251-6467. *Toll-free phone:* 877-251-6560. *Fax:* 503-254-1268. *E-mail:* admiss@multnomah.edu.

New Hope Christian College

Eugene, Oregon

http://www.newhope.edu/

CONTACT
Sarah Slater, Director of Admissions, New Hope Christian College, 2155 Bailey Hill Road, Eugene, OR 97405. *Phone:* 541-485-1780 Ext. 3115. *Toll-free phone:* 800-322-2638. *Fax:* 541-343-5801. *E-mail:* sarahslater@newhope.edu.

Northwest Christian University

Eugene, Oregon

http://www.nwcu.edu/

- **Independent Christian** comprehensive, founded 1895
- **Urban** 8-acre campus with easy access to Portland
- **Endowment** $13.5 million
- **Coed** 605 undergraduate students, 73% full-time, 61% women, 39% men
- **Minimally difficult** entrance level, 69% of applicants were admitted

UNDERGRAD STUDENTS
443 full-time, 162 part-time. Students come from 16 states and territories; 4 other countries; 25% are from out of state; 5% Black or African American, non-Hispanic/Latino; 6% Hispanic/Latino; 6% Asian, non-Hispanic/Latino; 1% Native Hawaiian or other Pacific Islander, non-Hispanic/Latino; 3% American Indian or Alaska Native, non-Hispanic/Latino; 6% Two or more races, non-Hispanic/Latino; 1% Race/ethnicity unknown; 1% international; 6% transferred in; 68% live on campus.

Freshmen:
Admission: 407 applied, 280 admitted, 102 enrolled. *Average high school GPA:* 3.4. *Test scores:* SAT evidence-based reading and writing scores over 500: 68%; SAT math scores over 500: 65%; ACT scores over 18: 68%; SAT evidence-based reading and writing scores over 600: 15%; SAT math scores over 600: 11%; ACT scores over 24: 22%; ACT scores over 30: 5%.
Retention: 62% of full-time freshmen returned.

FACULTY
Total: 82, 40% full-time, 24% with terminal degrees.
Student/faculty ratio: 15:1.

ACADEMICS

Calendar: quarters. *Degrees:* associate, bachelor's, master's, and postbachelor's certificates.

Special study options: academic remediation for entering students, accelerated degree program, adult/continuing education programs, advanced placement credit, cooperative education, distance learning, double majors, English as a second language, independent study, internships, part-time degree program, services for LD students, study abroad, summer session for credit.

Computers: 16 computers/terminals are available on campus for general student use. Students can access the following: campus intranet, computer help desk, free student e-mail accounts, online (class) grades, online (class) registration, online (class) schedules. Campuswide network is available. Wireless service is available via entire campus.

Library: Edward P. Kellenberger Library. *Books:* 59,536 (physical), 14 (digital/electronic); *Serial titles:* 156 (physical), 105,706 (digital/electronic); *Databases:* 105. Weekly public service hours: 70.

STUDENT LIFE

Housing options: on-campus residence required through senior year; men-only, women-only. Campus housing is university owned. Freshman campus housing is guaranteed.

Activities and organizations: student-run newspaper, choral group, Embrace the City (community service), FeMystique (Social justice club), Beacon Boards (game board club), History Club, Psychology Club.

Athletics Member NAIA. *Intercollegiate sports:* basketball M(s)/W(s), cross-country running M(s)/W(s), golf M(s)/W(s), soccer M(s)/W(s), softball W(s), track and field M(s)/W(s), volleyball W(s). *Intramural sports:* basketball M/W, volleyball M/W.

Campus security: 24-hour emergency response devices and patrols, late-night transport/escort service, controlled dormitory access.

Student services: personal/psychological counseling.

COSTS & FINANCIAL AID

Costs (2017–18) *Comprehensive fee:* $37,480 includes full-time tuition ($28,500), mandatory fees ($180), and room and board ($8800). Full-time tuition and fees vary according to course load. Part-time tuition: $950 per credit hour. Part-time tuition and fees vary according to course load. *Required fees:* $180 per year part-time. *Room and board:* Room and board charges vary according to housing facility. *Payment plan:* installment. *Waivers:* employees or children of employees.

Financial Aid Of all full-time matriculated undergraduates who enrolled in 2017, 397 applied for aid, 356 were judged to have need, 56 had their need fully met. 118 Federal Work-Study jobs (averaging $2750). 8 state and other part-time jobs (averaging $2750). In 2017, 68 non-need-based awards were made. *Average percent of need met:* 70. *Average financial aid package:* $21,511. *Average need-based loan:* $4245. *Average need-based gift aid:* $17,800. *Average non-need-based aid:* $9148. *Average indebtedness upon graduation:* $28,740.

APPLYING

Standardized Tests *Required:* SAT or ACT (for admission).

Options: electronic application, deferred entrance.

Required: essay or personal statement, minimum 2.5 GPA. *Required for some:* high school transcript. *Recommended:* interview.

Application deadlines: rolling (freshmen), rolling (out-of-state freshmen), rolling (transfers).

Notification: continuous (freshmen), continuous (out-of-state freshmen), continuous (transfers).

CONTACT

Kassia Galick, Assistant Director of Undergraduate Admissions, Northwest Christian University, 828 E. 11th Avenue, Eugene, OR 97401-3745. *Phone:* 541-684-7334. *Toll-free phone:* 877-463-6622. *Fax:* 541-684-7317. *E-mail:* kgalick@nwcu.edu.

Oregon College of Art and Craft

Portland, Oregon

http://www.ocac.edu/

- **Independent** comprehensive, founded 1907
- **Urban** 10-acre campus with easy access to Portland
- **Endowment** $1.9 million
- **Coed**
- **Moderately difficult** entrance level

FACULTY

Student/faculty ratio: 7:1.

ACADEMICS

Calendar: semesters. *Degrees:* certificates, bachelor's, master's, and postbachelor's certificates.

Library: Oregon College of Art and Craft Library plus 1 other. *Books:* 11,673 (physical); *Serial titles:* 111 (physical); *Databases:* 3. Weekly public service hours: 40.

STUDENT LIFE

Housing options: coed. Campus housing is university owned. Freshman applicants given priority for college housing.

Activities and organizations: Student Commonwealth, Ceramics Club, Photo Society, Film Club, Figure Drawing Club.

Campus security: 24-hour emergency response devices.

Student services: personal/psychological counseling.

COSTS & FINANCIAL AID

Costs (2017–18) *One-time required fee:* $40. *Comprehensive fee:* $43,060 includes full-time tuition ($31,500), mandatory fees ($1660), and room and board ($9900). Full-time tuition and fees vary according to course load and degree level. Part-time tuition: $1315 per credit hour. Part-time tuition and fees vary according to course load and degree level. *Required fees:* $47 per credit hour part-time, $365 per term part-time. *College room only:* $6400. Room and board charges vary according to board plan and housing facility.

Financial Aid Of all full-time matriculated undergraduates who enrolled in 2015, 83 applied for aid, 69 were judged to have need, 6 had their need fully met. In 2015, 25 non-need-based awards were made. *Average percent of need met:* 58. *Average financial aid package:* $19,960. *Average need-based loan:* $3891. *Average need-based gift aid:* $15,856. *Average non-need-based aid:* $9639. *Average indebtedness upon graduation:* $20,793.

APPLYING

Standardized Tests *Recommended:* SAT (for admission), ACT (for admission).

Options: electronic application, deferred entrance.

Application fee: $45.

Required: essay or personal statement, high school transcript, minimum 2.0 GPA, portfolio including 12 to 20 pieces of studio artwork. *Required for some:* interview. *Recommended:* letters of recommendation.

CONTACT

Oregon College of Art and Craft, 8245 Southwest Barnes Road, Portland, OR 97225. *Phone:* 971-255-4192. *Toll-free phone:* 800-390-0632.

Oregon Health & Science University

Portland, Oregon

http://www.ohsu.edu/

CONTACT

Oregon Health & Science University, 3181 Southwest Sam Jackson Park Road, Portland, OR 97239-3098. *Phone:* 503-494-0954.

Oregon Institute of Technology

Klamath Falls, Oregon

http://www.oit.edu/

- **State-supported** comprehensive, founded 1947
- **Small-town** 190-acre campus
- **Endowment** $7.9 million
- **Coed** 5,384 undergraduate students, 42% full-time, 49% women, 51% men
- **Moderately difficult** entrance level, 61% of applicants were admitted

UNDERGRAD STUDENTS

2,284 full-time, 3,100 part-time. Students come from 44 states and territories; 19 other countries; 25% are from out of state; 2% Black or African American, non-Hispanic/Latino; 11% Hispanic/Latino; 7% Asian, non-Hispanic/Latino; 0.7% Native Hawaiian or other Pacific Islander, non-Hispanic/Latino; 1% American Indian or Alaska Native, non-Hispanic/Latino; 5% Two or more races, non-Hispanic/Latino; 4% Race/ethnicity unknown; 2% international; 11% transferred in; 15% live on campus.

Freshmen:

Admission: 1,314 applied, 807 admitted, 334 enrolled. *Average high school GPA:* 3.5. *Test scores:* SAT evidence-based reading and writing scores over 500: 84%; SAT math scores over 500: 84%; ACT scores over 18: 95%; SAT evidence-based reading and writing scores over 600: 38%; SAT math scores over 600: 35%; ACT scores over 24: 45%; SAT evidence-based reading and writing scores over 700: 5%; SAT math scores over 700: 5%; ACT scores over 30: 4%.

Retention: 80% of full-time freshmen returned.

FACULTY

Total: 305, 55% full-time.
Student/faculty ratio: 16:1.

ACADEMICS

Calendar: quarters. *Degrees:* certificates, associate, bachelor's, master's, and postbachelor's certificates.

Special study options: academic remediation for entering students, advanced placement credit, cooperative education, distance learning, double majors, external degree program, honors programs, internships, off-campus study, part-time degree program, services for LD students, student-designed majors, study abroad, summer session for credit. *ROTC:* Army (c).

Computers: Students can access the following: online (class) registration. Campuswide network is available. Wireless service is available via entire campus.

Library:Books: 140,000 (physical); *Databases:* 70. Students can reserve study rooms.

STUDENT LIFE

Housing options: coed. Campus housing is university owned.

Activities and organizations: student-run newspaper, radio and television station, choral group, Phi Delta Theta, Christian Fellowship, International Club, Society of Women Engineers, Association of Student Mechanical Engineers, national fraternities.

Athletics Member NAIA. *Intercollegiate sports:* baseball M(s), basketball M(s)/W(s), cross-country running M(s)/W(s), golf M(s)/W(s), soccer M(s)/W(s), softball W, track and field M(s)/W(s), volleyball W(s). *Intramural sports:* basketball M/W, bowling M/W, cheerleading M/W, cross-country running M/W, rugby M/W, soccer W, softball W, track and field M/W, volleyball W.

Campus security: 24-hour emergency response devices and patrols, late-night transport/escort service.

Student services: health clinic, personal/psychological counseling, women's center.

COSTS & FINANCIAL AID

Costs (2017–18) *Tuition:* state resident $8422 full-time, $176 per credit hour part-time; nonresident $26,807 full-time, $560 per credit hour part-time. Full-time tuition and fees vary according to course load, location, program, and reciprocity agreements. Part-time tuition and fees vary according to course load, location, program, and reciprocity agreements. *Required fees:* $1560 full-time, $206 per credit hour part-time, $540 per term part-time. *Room and board:* $9206; room only: $5576. Room and board charges vary according to board plan and housing facility. *Payment plan:* installment. *Waivers:* employees or children of employees.

Financial Aid Of all full-time matriculated undergraduates who enrolled in 2013, 1,966 applied for aid, 1,722 were judged to have need, 512 had their need fully met. *Average percent of need met:* 23. *Average financial aid package:* $8064. *Average need-based loan:* $4613. *Average need-based gift aid:* $5912. *Average indebtedness upon graduation:* $29,685.

APPLYING

Standardized Tests *Required:* SAT or ACT (for admission).

Options: electronic application, deferred entrance.

Application fee: $50.

Required: high school transcript, minimum 3.0 GPA.

Notification: continuous (freshmen).

CONTACT

Oregon Institute of Technology, 3201 Campus Drive, Klamath Falls, OR 97601-8801. *Toll-free phone:* 800-422-2017.

Oregon State University

Corvallis, Oregon

http://www.oregonstate.edu/

- **State-supported** university, founded 1868
- **Small-town** 422-acre campus
- **Endowment** $624.5 million
- **Coed** 25,838 undergraduate students, 73% full-time, 46% women, 54% men
- **Moderately difficult** entrance level, 77% of applicants were admitted

UNDERGRAD STUDENTS

18,829 full-time, 7,009 part-time. Students come from 58 states and territories; 81 other countries; 32% are from out of state; 1% Black or African American, non-Hispanic/Latino; 10% Hispanic/Latino; 8% Asian, non-Hispanic/Latino; 0.3% Native Hawaiian or other Pacific Islander, non-Hispanic/Latino; 0.5% American Indian or Alaska Native, non-Hispanic/Latino; 7% Two or more races, non-Hispanic/Latino; 2% Race/ethnicity unknown; 7% international; 8% transferred in; 17% live on campus.

Freshmen:

Admission: 14,595 applied, 11,308 admitted, 3,819 enrolled. *Test scores:* SAT evidence-based reading and writing scores over 500: 89%; SAT math scores over 500: 88%; ACT scores over 18: 96%; SAT evidence-based reading and writing scores over 600: 51%; SAT math scores over 600: 47%; ACT scores over 24: 61%; SAT evidence-based reading and writing scores over 700: 11%; SAT math scores over 700: 11%; ACT scores over 30: 17%.

Retention: 85% of full-time freshmen returned.

FACULTY

Total: 1,697, 70% full-time, 77% with terminal degrees.
Student/faculty ratio: 18:1.

ACADEMICS

Calendar: quarters. *Degrees:* certificates, bachelor's, master's, doctoral, post-master's, and postbachelor's certificates.

Special study options: academic remediation for entering students, accelerated degree program, advanced placement credit, cooperative education, distance learning, double majors, English as a second language, freshman honors college, honors programs, independent study, internships, off-campus study, part-time degree program, services for LD students, student-designed majors, study abroad, summer session for credit. *ROTC:* Army (b), Navy (b), Air Force (b).

Computers: 2,179 computers/terminals are available on campus for general student use. Students can access the following: campus intranet, computer help desk, free student e-mail accounts, online (class) grades, online (class) registration, online (class) schedules. Campuswide network is available. 100% of college-owned or -operated housing units are wired for high-speed Internet access. Wireless service is available via entire campus.

Library: Valley Library plus 2 others. *Books:* 1.7 million (physical), 481,665 (digital/electronic); *Serial titles:* 2,376 (physical), 74,203 (digital/electronic); *Databases:* 150. Weekly public service hours: 138;

study areas open 24 hours, 5–7 days a week; students can reserve study rooms.

STUDENT LIFE

Housing options: on-campus residence required for freshman year; coed, special housing for students with disabilities. Campus housing is university owned. Freshman applicants given priority for college housing.

Activities and organizations: drama/theater group, student-run newspaper, radio and television station, choral group, marching band, Ballroom Dance Club, Gaming Club, Organic Growers Club, Blood Drive Association, Residence Hall Association, national fraternities, national sororities.

Athletics Member NCAA. All Division I except football (Division I-A). *Intercollegiate sports:* baseball M(s), basketball M(s)/W(s), crew M/W, cross-country running W(s), golf M(s)/W(s), gymnastics W(s), soccer M(s)/W(s), softball W(s), swimming and diving W(s), track and field W(s), volleyball W(s), wrestling M(s). *Intramural sports:* archery M/W, badminton M/W, baseball M, basketball M/W, bowling M/W, cheerleading M/W, crew M/W, cross-country running M/W, equestrian sports M(c)/W(c), fencing M(c)/W(c), football M, golf M/W, gymnastics M(c)/W(c), lacrosse M(c)/W(c), racquetball M/W, riflery M(c)/W(c), rock climbing M/W, rugby M(c)/W(c), sailing M(c)/W(c), sand volleyball M/W, skiing (cross-country) M(c)/W(c), skiing (downhill) M(c)/W(c), soccer M/W, softball M/W, squash M(c), swimming and diving M/W, table tennis M(c)/W(c), tennis M/W, track and field M/W, triathlon M(c)/W(c), ultimate Frisbee M/W, volleyball M/W, water polo M(c)/W(c), wrestling M.

Campus security: 24-hour emergency response devices and patrols, student patrols, late-night transport/escort service, controlled dormitory access, crime prevention office.

Student services: health clinic, personal/psychological counseling, women's center, legal services.

COSTS & FINANCIAL AID

Costs (2017–18) *One-time required fee:* $350. *Tuition:* state resident $9075 full-time, $195 per credit hour part-time; nonresident $27,735 full-time, $594 per credit hour part-time. Full-time tuition and fees vary according to course load, location, and program. Part-time tuition and fees vary according to course load, location, and program. *Required fees:* $1722 full-time, $529 per term part-time. *Room and board:* $12,540; room only: $8610. Room and board charges vary according to board plan and housing facility. *Waivers:* employees or children of employees.

Financial Aid Of all full-time matriculated undergraduates who enrolled in 2016, 12,517 applied for aid, 9,760 were judged to have need, 857 had their need fully met. 553 Federal Work-Study jobs (averaging $2951). In 2016, 2866 non-need-based awards were made. *Average percent of need met:* 66. *Average financial aid package:* $13,177. *Average need-based loan:* $4940. *Average need-based gift aid:* $7366. *Average non-need-based aid:* $4952. *Average indebtedness upon graduation:* $26,749.

APPLYING

Standardized Tests *Required:* SAT or ACT (for admission). *Required for some:* SAT Subject Tests (for admission).

Options: electronic application, early action, deferred entrance.

Application fee: $60.

Required: essay or personal statement, high school transcript, minimum 3.0 GPA.

Application deadlines: 2/1 (freshmen), 6/1 (transfers), 11/1 (early action).

Notification: continuous (freshmen), continuous (transfers), 12/20 (early action).

CONTACT

Oregon State University, Corvallis, OR 97331. *Phone:* 541-737-4411. *Toll-free phone:* 800-291-4192.

Oregon State University–Cascades
Bend, Oregon
http://www.osucascades.edu/

CONTACT
Admissions Department, Oregon State University–Cascades, 2600 Northwest College Way, Bend, OR 97701. *Phone:* 541-322-3150. *E-mail:* cascadeadmit@osucascades.edu.

Pacific Northwest College of Art
Portland, Oregon
http://www.pnca.edu/

- **Independent** comprehensive, founded 1909
- **Urban** 2-acre campus with easy access to Portland
- **Endowment** $12.9 million
- **Coed** 405 undergraduate students, 90% full-time, 68% women, 32% men
- **Noncompetitive** entrance level, 95% of applicants were admitted

UNDERGRAD STUDENTS
363 full-time, 42 part-time. Students come from 41 states and territories; 4 other countries; 54% are from out of state; 2% Black or African American, non-Hispanic/Latino; 5% Hispanic/Latino; 4% Asian, non-Hispanic/Latino; 0.5% Native Hawaiian or other Pacific Islander, non-Hispanic/Latino; 1% American Indian or Alaska Native, non-Hispanic/Latino; 11% Two or more races, non-Hispanic/Latino; 12% Race/ethnicity unknown; 2% international; 11% transferred in; 25% live on campus.

Freshmen:
Admission: 312 applied, 297 admitted, 81 enrolled.
Retention: 61% of full-time freshmen returned.

FACULTY
Total: 98, 27% full-time, 27% with terminal degrees.
Student/faculty ratio: 9:1.

ACADEMICS
Calendar: semesters. *Degrees:* bachelor's and master's.

Special study options: advanced placement credit, cooperative education, independent study, internships, off-campus study, part-time degree program, services for LD students, student-designed majors, study abroad, summer session for credit.

Computers: 300 computers/terminals are available on campus for general student use. Students can access the following: campus intranet, computer help desk, free student e-mail accounts, online (class) grades, online (class) registration, online (class) schedules. Campuswide network is available. 100% of college-owned or -operated housing units are wired for high-speed Internet access. Wireless service is available via entire campus.

Library: Albert Solheim Library. *Books:* 34,806 (physical); *Serial titles:* 270 (physical); *Databases:* 52. Weekly public service hours: 87; students can reserve study rooms.

STUDENT LIFE
Housing options: on-campus residence required for freshman year; coed, men-only, women-only, special housing for students with disabilities. Campus housing is provided by a third party. Freshman campus housing is guaranteed.

Campus security: 24-hour emergency response devices, late-night transport/escort service, controlled dormitory access, entrance security guards and patrols during hours of operation.

Student services: personal/psychological counseling.

COSTS & FINANCIAL AID
Costs (2017–18) *Comprehensive fee:* $49,510 includes full-time tuition ($35,740), mandatory fees ($700), and room and board ($13,070). Full-time tuition and fees vary according to degree level. Part-time tuition: $1489 per credit hour. Part-time tuition and fees vary according to course load and degree level. *Required fees:* $17 per credit hour part-time, $150 per year part-time. *Payment plan:* installment. *Waivers:* employees or children of employees.

Financial Aid Of all full-time matriculated undergraduates who enrolled in 2006, 264 applied for aid, 238 were judged to have need, 13 had their need fully met. 33 Federal Work-Study jobs (averaging $1200). 33 state and other part-time jobs (averaging $1200). In 2006, 10 non-need-based awards were made. *Average percent of need met:* 54. *Average financial aid package:* $11,845. *Average need-based loan:* $4040. *Average need-based gift aid:* $4699. *Average non-need-based aid:* $2442. *Average indebtedness upon graduation:* $22,155.

APPLYING
Options: electronic application, early admission, deferred entrance.

Application fee: $45.

Required: essay or personal statement, portfolio of artwork. *Required for some:* high school transcript. *Recommended:* minimum 2.3 GPA.

Application deadlines: rolling (freshmen), rolling (transfers).

Notification: continuous (freshmen), continuous (transfers).

CONTACT
Pacific Northwest College of Art, 511 NW Broadway, Portland, OR 97209.

★ Pacific University
Forest Grove, Oregon
http://www.pacificu.edu/

CONTACT
Ms. Karen Dunston, Executive Director, Pacific University, 2043 College Way, Forest Grove, OR 97116-1797. *Phone:* 503-352-2218. *Toll-free phone:* 877-722-8648. *Fax:* 503-352-2975. *E-mail:* admissions@pacificu.edu.

See below for display ad and page 1382 for the College Close-Up.

Pioneer Pacific College
Wilsonville, Oregon
http://www.pioneerpacific.edu/

CONTACT
Ms. Juli Lau, Vice President of Admissions, Pioneer Pacific College, 27375 Southwest Parkway Avenue, Wilsonville, OR 97070. *Phone:* 503-682-1862. *Toll-free phone:* 866-PPC-INFO. *Fax:* 503-682-1514. *E-mail:* info@pioneerpacific.edu.

Portland State University
Portland, Oregon
http://www.pdx.edu/

- **State-supported** university, founded 1946
- **Urban** 49-acre campus with easy access to Portland
- **Endowment** $81.3 million
- **Coed** 21,725 undergraduate students, 64% full-time, 54% women, 46% men
- **Moderately difficult** entrance level, 92% of applicants were admitted

UNDERGRAD STUDENTS
13,991 full-time, 7,734 part-time. Students come from 50 states and territories; 89 other countries; 15% are from out of state; 4% Black or African American, non-Hispanic/Latino; 14% Hispanic/Latino; 9% Asian, non-Hispanic/Latino; 0.6% Native Hawaiian or other Pacific Islander, non-Hispanic/Latino; 1% American Indian or Alaska Native, non-Hispanic/Latino; 6% Two or more races, non-Hispanic/Latino; 5% Race/ethnicity unknown; 6% international; 11% transferred in; 10% live on campus.

Freshmen:
Admission: 6,815 applied, 6,300 admitted, 1,827 enrolled. *Average high school GPA:* 3.4. *Test scores:* SAT evidence-based reading and writing scores over 500: 87%; ACT scores over 18: 70%; SAT evidence-based reading and writing scores over 600: 60%; ACT scores over 24: 25%; SAT evidence-based reading and writing scores over 700: 22%.

Retention: 71% of full-time freshmen returned.

FACULTY
Total: 1,603, 53% full-time, 54% with terminal degrees.

Student/faculty ratio: 18:1.

ACADEMICS
Calendar: quarters. *Degrees:* certificates, bachelor's, master's, doctoral, and postbachelor's certificates.

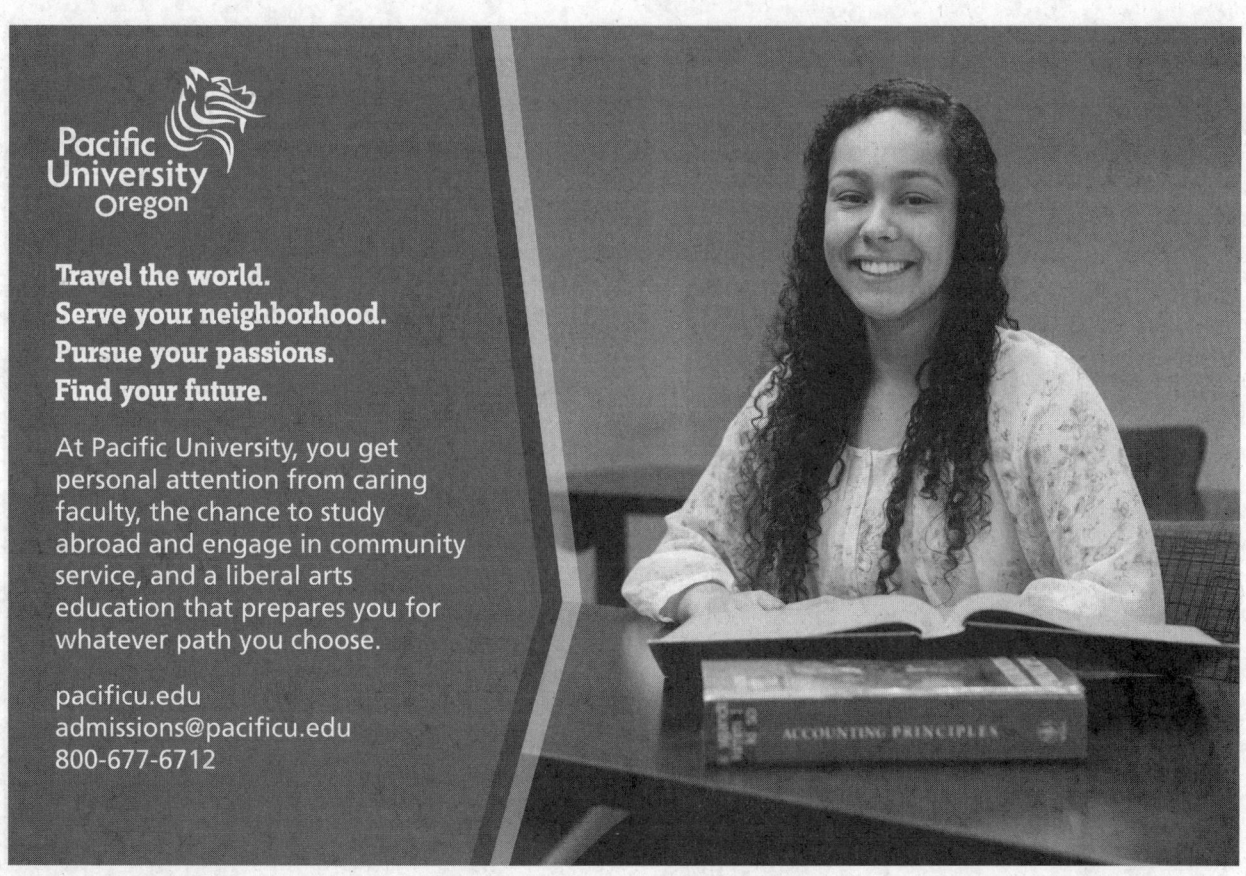

Special study options: academic remediation for entering students, accelerated degree program, adult/continuing education programs, advanced placement credit, cooperative education, distance learning, double majors, English as a second language, freshman honors college, honors programs, independent study, internships, off-campus study, part-time degree program, services for LD students, study abroad, summer session for credit. *ROTC:* Army (c), Air Force (c).

Computers: Students can access the following: campus intranet, computer help desk, free student e-mail accounts, online (class) grades, online (class) registration, online (class) schedules. Campuswide network is available. Wireless service is available via entire campus.

Library: Branford P. Millar Library plus 1 other. Students can reserve study rooms.

STUDENT LIFE

Housing options: coed, cooperative, special housing for students with disabilities. Campus housing is university owned. Freshman campus housing is guaranteed.

Activities and organizations: drama/theater group, student-run newspaper, radio station, choral group, national fraternities, national sororities.

Athletics Member NCAA. All Division I except football (Division I-AA). *Intercollegiate sports:* basketball M/W, cross-country running M/W, golf W, soccer W, softball W, tennis M/W, track and field M/W, volleyball W.

Campus security: 24-hour emergency response devices and patrols, late-night transport/escort service, controlled dormitory access.

Student services: health clinic, personal/psychological counseling, women's center, legal services.

COSTS & FINANCIAL AID

Costs (2017–18) *Tuition:* state resident $7403 full-time, $165 per credit hour part-time; nonresident $24,750 full-time, $550 per credit hour part-time. Full-time tuition and fees vary according to program and reciprocity agreements. Part-time tuition and fees vary according to program and reciprocity agreements. *Required fees:* $1380 full-time, $136 per credit hour part-time, $460 per term part-time. *Room and board:* $12,831; room only: $9204. Room and board charges vary according to board plan and housing facility. *Payment plan:* installment. *Waivers:* senior citizens and employees or children of employees.

Financial Aid Of all full-time matriculated undergraduates who enrolled in 2017, 10,347 applied for aid, 9,264 were judged to have need, 410 had their need fully met. In 2017, 72 non-need-based awards were made. *Average percent of need met:* 51. *Average financial aid package:* $10,562. *Average need-based loan:* $4513. *Average need-based gift aid:* $7066. *Average non-need-based aid:* $3337. *Average indebtedness upon graduation:* $26,867.

APPLYING

Standardized Tests *Required for some:* SAT or ACT (for admission).

Options: electronic application, early admission, deferred entrance.

Application fee: $50.

Required: high school transcript, minimum 3.0 GPA.

Application deadlines: rolling (freshmen), rolling (transfers).

Notification: continuous (freshmen), continuous (transfers).

CONTACT

Shannon Carr, Executive Director, Admissions and New Student Programs, Portland State University, PO Box 751, Portland, OR 97207. *Phone:* 503-725-3511. *Toll-free phone:* 800-547-8887. *Fax:* 503-725-5525. *E-mail:* shannon.carr@pdx.edu.

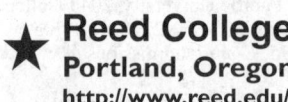

★ Reed College
Portland, Oregon
http://www.reed.edu/

- **Independent** comprehensive, founded 1908
- **Urban** 116-acre campus with easy access to Portland
- **Coed** 1,447 undergraduate students, 97% full-time, 54% women, 46% men
- **Very difficult** entrance level, 36% of applicants were admitted

UNDERGRAD STUDENTS

1,408 full-time, 39 part-time. 93% are from out of state; 2% Black or African American, non-Hispanic/Latino; 10% Hispanic/Latino; 6% Asian, non-Hispanic/Latino; 0.2% Native Hawaiian or other Pacific Islander,

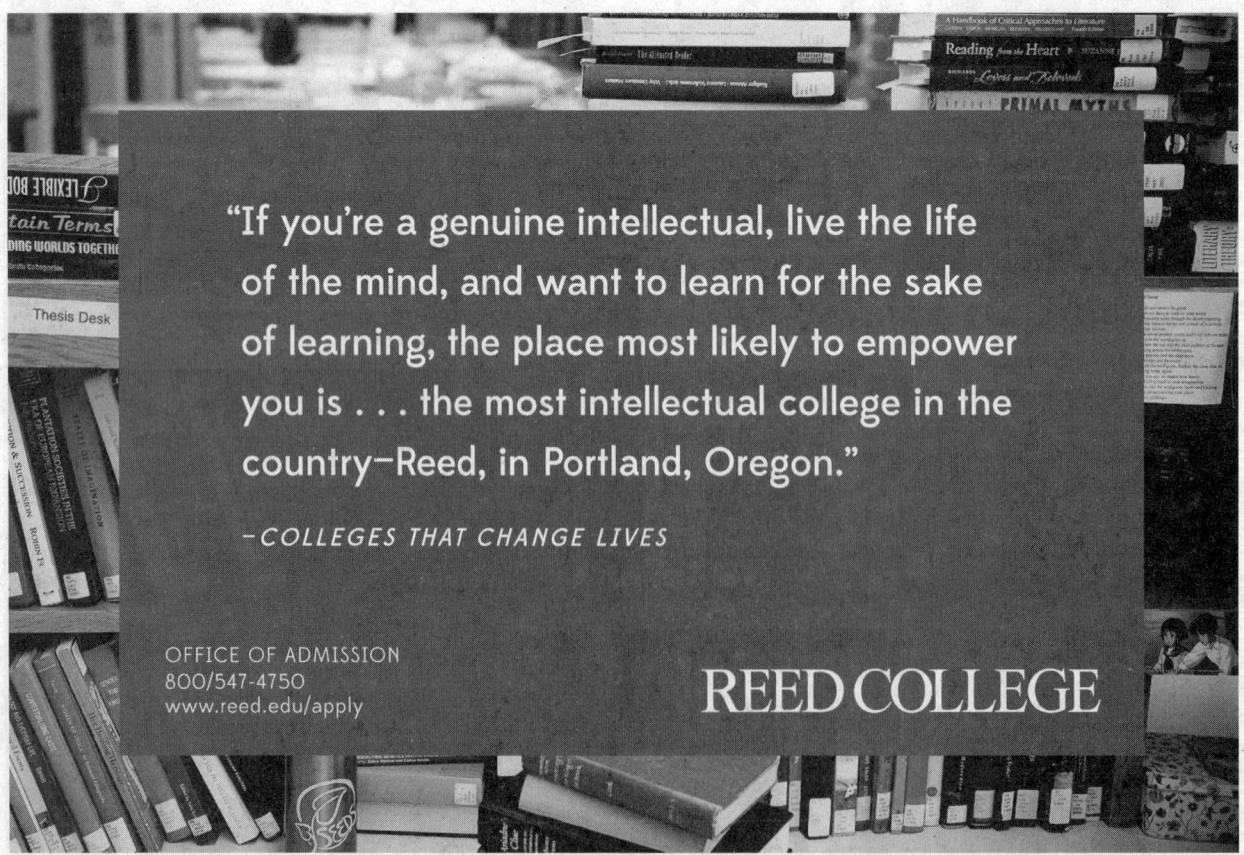

non-Hispanic/Latino; 0.3% American Indian or Alaska Native, non-Hispanic/Latino; 8% Two or more races, non-Hispanic/Latino; 3% Race/ethnicity unknown; 11% international; 1% transferred in; 65% live on campus.

Freshmen:
Admission: 5,652 applied, 2,014 admitted, 411 enrolled. *Average high school GPA:* 3.9. *Test scores:* SAT evidence-based reading and writing scores over 500: 100%; SAT math scores over 500: 99%; ACT scores over 18: 100%; SAT evidence-based reading and writing scores over 600: 96%; SAT math scores over 600: 90%; ACT scores over 24: 99%; SAT evidence-based reading and writing scores over 700: 60%; SAT math scores over 700: 48%; ACT scores over 30: 79%.
Retention: 88% of full-time freshmen returned.

FACULTY
Total: 156, 93% full-time, 94% with terminal degrees.
Student/faculty ratio: 10:1.

ACADEMICS
Calendar: semesters. *Degrees:* bachelor's and master's.
Special study options: academic remediation for entering students, advanced placement credit, cooperative education, double majors, independent study, internships, off-campus study, services for LD students, student-designed majors, study abroad.
Unusual degree programs: 3-2 forestry with Duke University; visual arts with the Pacific Northwest College of Art, engineering with California Institute of Technology, Columbia University, Rensselaer Polytechnic Institute.
Computers: 434 computers/terminals are available on campus for general student use. Students can access the following: campus intranet, computer help desk, free student e-mail accounts, online (class) registration, online (class) schedules. Campuswide network is available. 100% of college-owned or -operated housing units are wired for high-speed Internet access. Wireless service is available via entire campus.
Library: Eric V. Hauser Memorial Library plus 1 other. Study areas open 24 hours, 5–7 days a week.

STUDENT LIFE
Housing options: coed, women-only, cooperative, special housing for students with disabilities. Campus housing is university owned. Freshman campus housing is guaranteed.
Activities and organizations: drama/theater group, student-run newspaper, radio station, choral group.
Athletics *Intramural sports:* basketball M/W, rugby M/W, soccer M/W, ultimate Frisbee M/W.
Campus security: 24-hour emergency response devices and patrols, student patrols, late-night transport/escort service, controlled dormitory access.
Student services: health clinic, personal/psychological counseling, women's center, legal services.

COSTS & FINANCIAL AID
Costs (2017–18) *Comprehensive fee:* $67,870 includes full-time tuition ($53,900), mandatory fees ($300), and room and board ($13,670). Full-time tuition and fees vary according to degree level. Part-time tuition and fees vary according to course load and degree level. *Room and board:* Room and board charges vary according to board plan and housing facility. *Payment plan:* installment. *Waivers:* employees or children of employees.
Financial Aid Of all full-time matriculated undergraduates who enrolled in 2017, 819 applied for aid, 746 were judged to have need, 619 had their need fully met. *Average percent of need met:* 100. *Average financial aid package:* $43,875. *Average need-based loan:* $3124. *Average need-based gift aid:* $38,994. *Average indebtedness upon graduation:* $17,467. *Financial aid deadline:* 2/1.

APPLYING
Standardized Tests *Required:* SAT or ACT (for admission).
Options: electronic application, early admission, early decision, early action, deferred entrance.
Required: essay or personal statement, high school transcript, 2 letters of recommendation. *Recommended:* interview.

Application deadlines: 1/1 (freshmen), 3/1 (transfers), 11/15 (early action).
Early decision deadline: 11/15 (for plan 1), 12/20 (for plan 2).
Notification: 4/1 (freshmen), 5/1 (transfers), 12/15 (early decision plan 1), 2/1 (early decision plan 2), 1/31 (early action).

CONTACT
Office of Admission, Reed College, 3203 Southeast Woodstock Boulevard, Portland, OR 97202-8199. *Phone:* 800-547-4750. *Toll-free phone:* 800-547-4750. *Fax:* 503-777-7553. *E-mail:* admission@reed.edu.
See previous page for display ad and page 1392 for the College Close-Up.

Southern Oregon University
Ashland, Oregon
http://www.sou.edu/
- **State-supported** comprehensive, founded 1926
- **Small-town** 175-acre campus
- **Endowment** $24.6 million
- **Coed**
- **Moderately difficult** entrance level

FACULTY
Student/faculty ratio: 21:1.

ACADEMICS
Calendar: quarters. *Degrees:* certificates, bachelor's, master's, and postbachelor's certificates.
Library: Lenn and Dixie Hannon Library. *Books:* 340,015 (physical), 135,298 (digital/electronic); *Databases:* 80. Students can reserve study rooms.

STUDENT LIFE
Housing options: on-campus residence required for freshman year; coed, special housing for students with disabilities. Campus housing is university owned. Freshman campus housing is guaranteed.
Activities and organizations: drama/theater group, student-run newspaper, radio and television station, choral group, Native American Student Union, International Student Association, Impact (religious club), Ho`opa`a Hawaii Club, Omicron Delta Kappa.
Athletics Member NAIA.
Campus security: 24-hour emergency response devices and patrols, student patrols, late-night transport/escort service, controlled dormitory access.
Student services: health clinic, personal/psychological counseling, women's center, legal services.

COSTS & FINANCIAL AID
Costs (2017–18) *Tuition:* state resident $7426 full-time, $165 per credit hour part-time; nonresident $22,770 full-time, $506 per credit hour part-time. Full-time tuition and fees vary according to course load, program, and reciprocity agreements. Part-time tuition and fees vary according to course load, program, and reciprocity agreements. *Required fees:* $1860 full-time, $76 per credit hour part-time. *Room and board:* $12,831; room only: $7191. Room and board charges vary according to board plan and housing facility. *Payment plans:* installment, deferred payment.
Financial Aid Of all full-time matriculated undergraduates who enrolled in 2016, 2,729 applied for aid, 2,129 were judged to have need, 495 had their need fully met. 195 Federal Work-Study jobs (averaging $2977). *Average percent of need met:* 77. *Average financial aid package:* $11,131. *Average need-based loan:* $7371. *Average need-based gift aid:* $6825. *Average indebtedness upon graduation:* $27,375.

APPLYING
Standardized Tests *Required:* SAT or ACT (for admission). *Required for some:* SAT and SAT Subject Tests or ACT (for admission), SAT Subject Tests (for admission).
Options: electronic application, early admission, deferred entrance.
Application fee: $60.
Required: high school transcript, minimum 3.0 GPA. *Required for some:* essay or personal statement.

CONTACT
Mr. Kelly Moutsatson, Director of Admissions, Southern Oregon University, 1250 Siskiyou Boulevard, Ashland, OR 97520. *Phone:* 541-

552-6411. *Toll-free phone:* 855-470-3377. *Fax:* 541-552-6614. *E-mail:* admissions@sou.edu.

University of Oregon

Eugene, Oregon
http://www.uoregon.edu/

- **State-supported** university, founded 1876
- **Suburban** 295-acre campus with easy access to Portland, Oregon
- **Endowment** $828.5 million
- **Coed** 19,340 undergraduate students, 92% full-time, 54% women, 46% men
- **Moderately difficult** entrance level, 83% of applicants were admitted

UNDERGRAD STUDENTS

17,801 full-time, 1,539 part-time. Students come from 51 states and territories; 80 other countries; 43% are from out of state; 2% Black or African American, non-Hispanic/Latino; 12% Hispanic/Latino; 6% Asian, non-Hispanic/Latino; 0.3% Native Hawaiian or other Pacific Islander, non-Hispanic/Latino; 0.6% American Indian or Alaska Native, non-Hispanic/Latino; 8% Two or more races, non-Hispanic/Latino; 1% Race/ethnicity unknown; 12% international; 6% transferred in; 21% live on campus.

Freshmen:

Admission: 20,317 applied, 16,824 admitted, 3,938 enrolled. *Average high school GPA:* 3.6. *Test scores:* SAT evidence-based reading and writing scores over 500: 91%; SAT math scores over 500: 87%; ACT scores over 18: 95%; SAT evidence-based reading and writing scores over 600: 51%; SAT math scores over 600: 41%; ACT scores over 24: 63%; SAT evidence-based reading and writing scores over 700: 9%; SAT math scores over 700: 7%; ACT scores over 30: 12%.

Retention: 86% of full-time freshmen returned.

FACULTY

Total: 1,666, 68% full-time, 91% with terminal degrees.

Student/faculty ratio: 17:1.

ACADEMICS

Calendar: quarters. *Degrees:* bachelor's, master's, doctoral, post-master's, and postbachelor's certificates.

Special study options: advanced placement credit, cooperative education, distance learning, double majors, English as a second language, honors programs, independent study, internships, off-campus study, part-time degree program, services for LD students, student-designed majors, study abroad, summer session for credit. *ROTC:* Army (b), Air Force (c).

Unusual degree programs: 3-2 engineering with Oregon State University.

Computers: 497 computers/terminals are available on campus for general student use. Students can access the following: campus intranet, computer help desk, free student e-mail accounts, online (class) grades, online (class) registration, online (class) schedules. Campuswide network is available. 100% of college-owned or -operated housing units are wired for high-speed Internet access. Wireless service is available via entire campus.

Library: Knight Library plus 6 others. *Books:* 2.3 million (physical), 851,235 (digital/electronic); *Serial titles:* 74,066 (physical), 162,481 (digital/electronic); *Databases:* 469. Weekly public service hours: 124; students can reserve study rooms.

STUDENT LIFE

Housing options: on-campus residence required for freshman year; coed, cooperative. Campus housing is university owned. Freshman applicants given priority for college housing.

Activities and organizations: drama/theater group, student-run newspaper, radio and television station, choral group, marching band, political and environmental action, cultural organizations, major-specific organizations, community service organizations, club sports, national fraternities, national sororities.

Athletics Member NCAA. All Division I except football (Division I-A). *Intercollegiate sports:* baseball M(s), basketball M(s)/W(s), cross-country running M(s)/W(s), golf M(s)/W(s), lacrosse W(s), sand volleyball W(s), soccer W(s), softball W(s), tennis M(s)/W(s), track and field M(s)/W(s), volleyball W(s). *Intramural sports:* badminton M(c)/W(c), baseball M(c), basketball M/W, cross-country running M(c)/W(c), equestrian sports

M(c)/W(c), fencing M(c)/W(c), football M/W, golf M(c)/W(c), ice hockey M(c)/W(c), lacrosse M(c)/W(c), rock climbing M(c)/W(c), rowing M(c)/W(c), rugby M(c)/W(c), sailing M(c)/W(c), skiing (downhill) M(c)/W(c), soccer M(c)/W(c), softball M(c)/W(c), squash M(c)/W(c), swimming and diving M(c)/W(c), table tennis M(c)/W(c), tennis M/W, track and field M/W, triathlon M(c)/W(c), ultimate Frisbee M(c)/W(c), volleyball M(c)/W(c), water polo M(c)/W(c), weight lifting M(c)/W(c).

Campus security: 24-hour emergency response devices and patrols, late-night transport/escort service, controlled dormitory access, Lighted pathways, emergency phones, self-defense classes.

Student services: health clinic, personal/psychological counseling, women's center, legal services.

COSTS & FINANCIAL AID

Costs (2017–18) *One-time required fee:* $430. *Tuition:* state resident $9495 full-time, $211 per credit hour part-time; nonresident $32,535 full-time, $723 per credit hour part-time. Full-time tuition and fees vary according to course load. Part-time tuition and fees vary according to course load. *Required fees:* $2076 full-time. *Room and board:* $12,450. Room and board charges vary according to board plan and housing facility. *Payment plan:* installment. *Waivers:* employees or children of employees.

Financial Aid Of all full-time matriculated undergraduates who enrolled in 2016, 10,804 applied for aid, 8,214 were judged to have need, 530 had their need fully met. 2,364 Federal Work-Study jobs (averaging $1762). 78 state and other part-time jobs (averaging $3295). In 2016, 2482 non-need-based awards were made. *Average percent of need met:* 59. *Average financial aid package:* $11,187. *Average need-based loan:* $4764. *Average need-based gift aid:* $8886. *Average non-need-based aid:* $6140. *Average indebtedness upon graduation:* $26,164.

APPLYING

Standardized Tests *Required:* SAT or ACT (for admission). *Required for some:* SAT and SAT Subject Tests or ACT (for admission).

Options: electronic application, early action, deferred entrance.

Application fee: $65.

Required: essay or personal statement, high school transcript, C+ or better in 15 college preparatory units. *Required for some:* 2 letters of recommendation.

Application deadlines: 1/15 (freshmen), 6/30 (transfers), 11/1 (early action).

Notification: 4/1 (freshmen), 12/15 (early action).

CONTACT

University of Oregon, Eugene, OR 97403. *Phone:* 541-346-3201. *Toll-free phone:* 800-232-3825.

University of Portland

Portland, Oregon
http://www.up.edu/

CONTACT

Mr. Jason McDonald, Dean of Admissions, University of Portland, 5000 North Willamette Boulevard, Portland, OR 97203-5798. *Phone:* 503-943-7147. *Toll-free phone:* 888-627-5601. *Fax:* 503-943-7315. *E-mail:* admissions@up.edu.

Warner Pacific College

Portland, Oregon
http://www.warnerpacific.edu/

- **Independent** comprehensive, founded 1937, affiliated with Church of God
- **Urban** 15-acre campus with easy access to Portland
- **Endowment** $10.2 million
- **Coed** 400 undergraduate students, 99% full-time, 60% women, 41% men
- **Moderately difficult** entrance level, 63% of applicants were admitted

UNDERGRAD STUDENTS

396 full-time, 4 part-time. 10% Black or African American, non-Hispanic/Latino; 34% Hispanic/Latino; 5% Asian, non-Hispanic/Latino; 2% Native Hawaiian or other Pacific Islander, non-Hispanic/Latino; 1% American Indian or Alaska Native, non-Hispanic/Latino; 10% Two or

more races, non-Hispanic/Latino; 3% Race/ethnicity unknown; 0.5% international; 13% transferred in; 41% live on campus.

Freshmen:
Admission: 476 applied, 299 admitted, 58 enrolled. *Average high school GPA:* 3.3. *Test scores:* SAT evidence-based reading and writing scores over 500: 52%; SAT math scores over 500: 56%; ACT scores over 18: 54%; SAT evidence-based reading and writing scores over 600: 15%; SAT math scores over 600: 4%; ACT scores over 24: 3%.
Retention: 62% of full-time freshmen returned.

FACULTY
Total: 33, 100% with terminal degrees.
Student/faculty ratio: 7:1.

ACADEMICS
Calendar: semesters. *Degrees:* certificates, associate, bachelor's, master's, and post-master's certificates.

Special study options: academic remediation for entering students, accelerated degree program, adult/continuing education programs, advanced placement credit, cooperative education, double majors, honors programs, independent study, internships, off-campus study, part-time degree program, services for LD students, student-designed majors, study abroad, summer session for credit. *ROTC:* Air Force (c).

Computers: 90 computers/terminals are available on campus for general student use. Students can access the following: campus intranet, computer help desk, free student e-mail accounts, online (class) grades, online (class) registration, online (class) schedules. Campuswide network is available. 100% of college-owned or -operated housing units are wired for high-speed Internet access. Wireless service is available via classrooms, computer centers, computer labs, dorm rooms, learning centers, libraries, student centers.
Library: Otto F. Linn Library. *Books:* 65,397 (physical), 164,990 (digital/electronic); *Serial titles:* 257 (physical), 139,309 (digital/electronic); *Databases:* 478. Weekly public service hours: 7.

STUDENT LIFE
Housing options: on-campus residence required through junior year; men-only, women-only, special housing for students with disabilities. Campus housing is university owned. Freshman applicants given priority for college housing.

Activities and organizations: drama/theater group, student-run newspaper, choral group.

Athletics Member NAIA, NCCAA. *Intercollegiate sports:* basketball M(s)/W(s), cross-country running M(s)/W(s), golf M(s)/W(s), soccer M(s)/W(s), track and field M(s)/W(s), volleyball W(s), wrestling M/W. *Intramural sports:* basketball M/W, volleyball M/W.

Campus security: 24-hour emergency response devices and patrols, student patrols, late-night transport/escort service, controlled dormitory access.

Student services: personal/psychological counseling.

COSTS & FINANCIAL AID
Costs (2017–18) *Comprehensive fee:* $33,800 includes full-time tuition ($23,840), mandatory fees ($660), and room and board ($9300). Part-time tuition: $1085 per semester hour. Part-time tuition and fees vary according to course load. *Required fees:* $330 per term part-time. *College room only:* $3870. Room and board charges vary according to board plan and housing facility. *Payment plans:* installment, deferred payment. *Waivers:* children of alumni and employees or children of employees.

Financial Aid Of all full-time matriculated undergraduates who enrolled in 2017, 354 applied for aid, 334 were judged to have need, 61 had their need fully met. 270 Federal Work-Study jobs (averaging $2391). In 2017, 47 non-need-based awards were made. *Average percent of need met:* 66. *Average financial aid package:* $21,056. *Average need-based loan:* $3823. *Average need-based gift aid:* $7072. *Average non-need-based aid:* $7065. *Average indebtedness upon graduation:* $28,471.

APPLYING
Standardized Tests *Required:* SAT or ACT (for admission).
Options: electronic application.
Application fee: $25.

Required: essay or personal statement, high school transcript, minimum 2.5 GPA. *Required for some:* 1 letter of recommendation, interview. *Recommended:* minimum 3.0 GPA, interview.
Application deadlines: rolling (freshmen), rolling (transfers).
Notification: continuous (freshmen), continuous (transfers).

CONTACT
Dale Seipp, Vice President for Enrollment Management, Warner Pacific College, 2219 Southeast 68th Avenue, Portland, OR 97215. *Phone:* 503-517-1020. *Toll-free phone:* 800-804-1510. *Fax:* 503-517-1540. *E-mail:* admiss@warnerpacific.edu.

Western Oregon University
Monmouth, Oregon
http://www.wou.edu/
- **State-supported** comprehensive, founded 1856
- **Rural** 157-acre campus with easy access to Portland
- **Coed** 4,776 undergraduate students, 85% full-time, 62% women, 38% men
- **Moderately difficult** entrance level, 81% of applicants were admitted

UNDERGRAD STUDENTS
4,042 full-time, 734 part-time. Students come from 33 states and territories; 22 other countries; 23% are from out of state; 4% Black or African American, non-Hispanic/Latino; 16% Hispanic/Latino; 5% Asian, non-Hispanic/Latino; 3% Native Hawaiian or other Pacific Islander, non-Hispanic/Latino; 2% American Indian or Alaska Native, non-Hispanic/Latino; 0.4% Two or more races, non-Hispanic/Latino; 4% Race/ethnicity unknown; 6% international; 13% transferred in; 24% live on campus.

Freshmen:
Admission: 2,942 applied, 2,371 admitted, 727 enrolled. *Average high school GPA:* 3.3. *Test scores:* ACT scores over 18: 72%; ACT scores over 24: 20%; ACT scores over 30: 3%.
Retention: 72% of full-time freshmen returned.

FACULTY
Total: 378, 76% full-time, 56% with terminal degrees.
Student/faculty ratio: 15:1.

ACADEMICS
Calendar: quarters. *Degrees:* certificates, bachelor's, master's, and postbachelor's certificates.

Special study options: academic remediation for entering students, advanced placement credit, distance learning, double majors, English as a second language, freshman honors college, honors programs, independent study, internships, off-campus study, part-time degree program, services for LD students, student-designed majors, study abroad, summer session for credit. *ROTC:* Army (c).

Unusual degree programs: nursing.

Computers: 411 computers/terminals are available on campus for general student use. Students can access the following: computer help desk, free student e-mail accounts, online (class) grades, online (class) registration, online (class) schedules. Campuswide network is available. 100% of college-owned or -operated housing units are wired for high-speed Internet access. Wireless service is available via entire campus.
Library: Wayne and Lynn Hamersly Library. *Books:* 164,610 (physical), 193,700 (digital/electronic); *Serial titles:* 33,400 (physical), 223,223 (digital/electronic); *Databases:* 291. Study areas open 24 hours, 5–7 days a week; students can reserve study rooms.

STUDENT LIFE
Housing options: on-campus residence required for freshman year; coed, men-only, women-only, special housing for students with disabilities. Campus housing is university owned. Freshman campus housing is guaranteed.

Activities and organizations: drama/theater group, student-run newspaper, radio station, choral group, Model United Nations, Multicultural Student Union, Oregon Student Association, Alternative Spring Break (community service), M.E.Ch.A, national fraternities, national sororities.

Athletics Member NCAA. All Division II. *Intercollegiate sports:* baseball M(s), basketball M(s)/W(s), cross-country running M(s)/W(s), football M(s), soccer W(s), softball W(s), track and field M(s)/W(s), volleyball W(s). *Intramural sports:* badminton M/W, basketball M/W, bowling M/W, cross-country running M(c)/W(c), football M/W, golf M/W, lacrosse M(c), racquetball M(c)/W(c), rugby M(c)/W(c), soccer M(c)/W(c), softball M/W, swimming and diving M(c)/W(c), tennis M/W, track and field M/W, volleyball M(c)/W(c), water polo M(c)/W(c).

Campus security: 24-hour emergency response devices and patrols, late-night transport/escort service, controlled dormitory access.

Student services: health clinic, personal/psychological counseling, women's center.

COSTS & FINANCIAL AID
Costs (2017–18) *Tuition:* state resident $7440 full-time, $171 per credit hour part-time; nonresident $23,895 full-time, $531 per credit hour part-time. Full-time tuition and fees vary according to course load. Part-time tuition and fees vary according to course load. No tuition increase for student's term of enrollment. *Required fees:* $1758 full-time. *Room and board:* $10,203; room only: $8148. Room and board charges vary according to board plan and housing facility.

Financial Aid Of all full-time matriculated undergraduates who enrolled in 2016, 3,087 applied for aid, 2,597 were judged to have need, 221 had their need fully met. 283 Federal Work-Study jobs (averaging $953). In 2016, 219 non-need-based awards were made. *Average percent of need met:* 55. *Average financial aid package:* $9865. *Average need-based loan:* $4030. *Average need-based gift aid:* $7374. *Average non-need-based aid:* $2317. *Average indebtedness upon graduation:* $29,565.

APPLYING
Options: electronic application.

Application fee: $60.

Required: high school transcript, minimum 2.8 GPA, general college preparatory program completion.

Application deadlines: rolling (freshmen), rolling (transfers).

Notification: continuous (freshmen), continuous (transfers).

CONTACT
Mr. David Compton, Assistant Director of Admissions for Recruitment, Western Oregon University, 345 North Monmouth Avenue, Monmouth, OR 97361. *Phone:* 503-838-8211. *Toll-free phone:* 877-877-1593. *Fax:* 503-838-8067. *E-mail:* wolfgram@wou.edu.

Willamette University
Salem, Oregon
http://www.willamette.edu/
- **Independent United Methodist** comprehensive, founded 1842
- **Urban** 72-acre campus with easy access to Portland
- **Endowment** $225.3 million
- **Coed** 2,112 undergraduate students, 85% full-time, 58% women, 42% men
- **Very difficult** entrance level, 89% of applicants were admitted

UNDERGRAD STUDENTS
1,786 full-time, 326 part-time. Students come from 39 states and territories; 14 other countries; 77% are from out of state; 2% Black or African American, non-Hispanic/Latino; 12% Hispanic/Latino; 8% Asian, non-Hispanic/Latino; 0.3% Native Hawaiian or other Pacific Islander, non-Hispanic/Latino; 0.6% American Indian or Alaska Native, non-Hispanic/Latino; 8% Two or more races, non-Hispanic/Latino; 5% Race/ethnicity unknown; 8% international; 1% transferred in; 62% live on campus.

Freshmen:
Admission: 4,484 applied, 3,995 admitted, 440 enrolled. *Average high school GPA:* 3.8. *Test scores:* SAT evidence-based reading and writing scores over 500: 95%; SAT math scores over 500: 92%; ACT scores over 18: 97%; SAT evidence-based reading and writing scores over 600: 66%; SAT math scores over 600: 51%; ACT scores over 24: 85%; SAT evidence-based reading and writing scores over 700: 16%; SAT math scores over 700: 7%; ACT scores over 30: 35%.

Retention: 86% of full-time freshmen returned.

FACULTY
Total: 250, 80% full-time, 90% with terminal degrees.

Student/faculty ratio: 11:1.

ACADEMICS
Calendar: semesters. *Degrees:* bachelor's, master's, and doctoral.

Special study options: accelerated degree program, advanced placement credit, double majors, independent study, internships, off-campus study, part-time degree program, services for LD students, student-designed majors, study abroad. *ROTC:* Army (c), Air Force (c).

Unusual degree programs: 3-2 engineering with University of Southern California, Washington University in St. Louis, Columbia University; forestry with Duke University.

Computers: Students can access the following: computer help desk, free student e-mail accounts, online (class) grades, online (class) registration, online (class) schedules. Campuswide network is available. 100% of college-owned or -operated housing units are wired for high-speed Internet access. Wireless service is available via entire campus.

Library: Mark O. Hatfield Library plus 1 other. Study areas open 24 hours, 5–7 days a week; students can reserve study rooms.

STUDENT LIFE
Housing options: on-campus residence required through sophomore year; coed. Campus housing is university owned. Freshman campus housing is guaranteed.

Activities and organizations: drama/theater group, student-run newspaper, radio station, choral group, national fraternities, national sororities.

Athletics Member NCAA. All Division III. *Intercollegiate sports:* baseball M, basketball M/W, crew M/W, cross-country running M/W, football M, golf M/W, lacrosse M(c), soccer M/W, softball W, swimming and diving M/W, tennis M/W, track and field M/W, volleyball W. *Intramural sports:* badminton M/W, basketball M/W, bowling M/W, cross-country running M/W, football M/W, golf M/W, racquetball M/W, skiing (cross-country) M(c)/W(c), skiing (downhill) M(c)/W(c), soccer M/W, softball M/W, table tennis M/W, tennis M/W, ultimate Frisbee M/W, volleyball M/W, water polo M/W, weight lifting M/W.

Campus security: 24-hour emergency response devices and patrols, student patrols, late-night transport/escort service, controlled dormitory access.

Student services: health clinic, personal/psychological counseling, women's center.

COSTS & FINANCIAL AID
Costs (2018–19) *Comprehensive fee:* $62,514 includes full-time tuition ($49,750), mandatory fees ($324), and room and board ($12,440). Full-time tuition and fees vary according to course load. Part-time tuition: $6219 per credit. Part-time tuition and fees vary according to course load. *Room and board:* Room and board charges vary according to board plan and housing facility. *Payment plans:* tuition prepayment, installment. *Waivers:* employees or children of employees.

Financial Aid Of all full-time matriculated undergraduates who enrolled in 2017, 1,283 applied for aid, 1,107 were judged to have need, 238 had their need fully met. In 2017, 617 non-need-based awards were made. *Average percent of need met:* 79. *Average financial aid package:* $36,235. *Average need-based loan:* $5054. *Average need-based gift aid:* $30,571. *Average non-need-based aid:* $21,358. *Average indebtedness upon graduation:* $32,117.

APPLYING
Standardized Tests *Recommended:* SAT or ACT (for admission), SAT and SAT Subject Tests or ACT (for admission), SAT Subject Tests (for admission).

Options: electronic application, early action, deferred entrance.

Application fee: $50.

Required: essay or personal statement, high school transcript, minimum 2.0 GPA, 1 letter of recommendation. *Required for some:* interview. *Recommended:* interview.

Application deadlines: 1/15 (freshmen), 2/1 (transfers), 11/15 (early action).

Notification: continuous until 5/1 (freshmen), 3/15 (transfers), 12/31 (early action).

CONTACT
Sue Corner, Senior Associate Director of Admission, Willamette University, 900 State Street, Salem, OR 97301. *Phone:* 503-375-5337. *Toll-free phone:* 877-542-2787. *E-mail:* bearcat@willamette.edu.

PENNSYLVANIA

Albright College
Reading, Pennsylvania
http://www.albright.edu/
- **Independent** comprehensive, founded 1856, affiliated with United Methodist Church
- **Suburban** 118-acre campus with easy access to Philadelphia
- **Endowment** $67.7 million
- **Coed** 2,015 undergraduate students, 99% full-time, 59% women, 41% men
- **Moderately difficult** entrance level, 50% of applicants were admitted

UNDERGRAD STUDENTS
1,993 full-time, 22 part-time. Students come from 28 states and territories; 14 other countries; 40% are from out of state; 21% Black or African American, non-Hispanic/Latino; 12% Hispanic/Latino; 3% Asian, non-Hispanic/Latino; 0.9% American Indian or Alaska Native, non-Hispanic/Latino; 2% Two or more races, non-Hispanic/Latino; 9% Race/ethnicity unknown; 2% international; 2% transferred in; 68% live on campus.

Freshmen:
Admission: 8,332 applied, 4,169 admitted, 465 enrolled. *Average high school GPA:* 3.2. *Test scores:* SAT evidence-based reading and writing scores over 500: 78%; SAT math scores over 500: 74%; ACT scores over 18: 91%; SAT evidence-based reading and writing scores over 600: 24%; SAT math scores over 600: 18%; ACT scores over 24: 44%; SAT evidence-based reading and writing scores over 700: 1%; SAT math scores over 700: 1%; ACT scores over 30: 6%.
Retention: 69% of full-time freshmen returned.

FACULTY
Total: 156, 66% full-time, 65% with terminal degrees.
Student/faculty ratio: 14:1.

ACADEMICS
Calendar: 4-1-4. *Degrees:* certificates, bachelor's, and master's.
Special study options: accelerated degree program, adult/continuing education programs, advanced placement credit, distance learning, double majors, honors programs, independent study, internships, off-campus study, services for LD students, student-designed majors, study abroad, summer session for credit.
Computers: 450 computers/terminals are available on campus for general student use. Students can access the following: campus intranet, computer help desk, free student e-mail accounts, online (class) grades, online (class) registration, online (class) schedules, online financial statements, housing choices, course management systems. Campuswide network is available. 100% of college-owned or -operated housing units are wired for high-speed Internet access. Wireless service is available via entire campus.
Library: F. W. Gingrich Library. *Books:* 210,904 (physical), 296,145 (digital/electronic); *Serial titles:* 1,210 (physical), 35,708 (digital/electronic); *Databases:* 70. Students can reserve study rooms.

STUDENT LIFE
Housing options: on-campus residence required through senior year; coed, special housing for students with disabilities. Campus housing is university owned and leased by the school. Freshman campus housing is guaranteed.
Activities and organizations: drama/theater group, student-run newspaper, radio and television station, choral group, Greek Organizations (combined), Alpha Phi Omega (service organization), Student Government Association, Albright College Activities Council, Albrightian (newspaper), national fraternities, national sororities.
Athletics Member NCAA. All Division III. *Intercollegiate sports:* badminton M(c)/W(c), baseball M, basketball M/W, cheerleading M/W, cross-country running M/W, field hockey W, football M, golf M/W, lacrosse M/W, rugby M(c)/W(c), soccer M/W, softball W, swimming and diving M/W, tennis M/W, track and field M/W, triathlon M/W, ultimate Frisbee M(c)/W(c), volleyball W. *Intramural sports:* basketball M/W, bowling M/W, lacrosse M(c)/W(c), soccer M/W, softball M/W, volleyball M/W.

Campus security: 24-hour emergency response devices and patrols, student patrols, late-night transport/escort service, controlled dormitory access, E2 Campus Text messaging, Rape Aggression Defense Training, marked patrol cars, partnership with local and state police.
Student services: health clinic, personal/psychological counseling, women's center.

COSTS & FINANCIAL AID
Costs (2018–19) *Comprehensive fee:* $57,372 includes full-time tuition ($44,202), mandatory fees ($1100), and room and board ($12,070). Full-time tuition and fees vary according to degree level. Part-time tuition: $5526 per course. Part-time tuition and fees vary according to degree level. *College room only:* $6664. Room and board charges vary according to board plan and housing facility. *Payment plan:* installment. *Waivers:* adult students, senior citizens, and employees or children of employees.
Financial Aid Of all full-time matriculated undergraduates who enrolled in 2017, 1,575 applied for aid, 1,515 were judged to have need, 152 had their need fully met. In 2017, 128 non-need-based awards were made. *Average percent of need met:* 80. *Average financial aid package:* $38,880. *Average need-based loan:* $5532. *Average need-based gift aid:* $32,813. *Average non-need-based aid:* $22,066. *Average indebtedness upon graduation:* $38,599.

APPLYING
Options: electronic application, deferred entrance.
Application fee: $35.
Required: high school transcript, minimum 2.5 GPA. *Required for some:* essay or personal statement, 1 letter of recommendation, interview, secondary school report (guidance department), interview for students applying test-optional.
Application deadlines: rolling (freshmen), rolling (transfers).
Notification: continuous (freshmen), continuous (transfers).

CONTACT
Mr. Paul Cramer, Vice President for Enrollment Management, Albright College, PO Box 15234, 13th and Bern Streets, Reading, PA 19612-5234. *Phone:* 610-921-7260. *Toll-free phone:* 800-252-1856. *Fax:* 610-921-7294. *E-mail:* admission@albright.edu.

★ Allegheny College
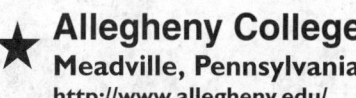
Meadville, Pennsylvania
http://www.allegheny.edu/
- **Independent** 4-year, founded 1815
- **Suburban** 566-acre campus
- **Endowment** $204.5 million
- **Coed** 1,802 undergraduate students, 97% full-time, 54% women, 46% men
- **Very difficult** entrance level, 68% of applicants were admitted

UNDERGRAD STUDENTS
1,752 full-time, 50 part-time. Students come from 47 states and territories; 50 other countries; 50% are from out of state; 9% Black or African American, non-Hispanic/Latino; 9% Hispanic/Latino; 3% Asian, non-Hispanic/Latino; 0.1% Native Hawaiian or other Pacific Islander, non-Hispanic/Latino; 0.1% American Indian or Alaska Native, non-Hispanic/Latino; 4% Two or more races, non-Hispanic/Latino; 3% Race/ethnicity unknown; 3% international; 0.8% transferred in; 94% live on campus.

Freshmen:
Admission: 5,114 applied, 3,472 admitted, 484 enrolled. *Average high school GPA:* 3.5. *Test scores:* SAT evidence-based reading and writing scores over 500: 95%; SAT math scores over 500: 95%; ACT scores over 18: 96%; SAT evidence-based reading and writing scores over 600: 68%; SAT math scores over 600: 57%; ACT scores over 24: 71%; SAT evidence-based reading and writing scores over 700: 15%; SAT math scores over 700: 6%; ACT scores over 30: 21%.
Retention: 81% of full-time freshmen returned.

FACULTY
Total: 200, 84% full-time, 84% with terminal degrees.
Student/faculty ratio: 10:1.

ACADEMICS

Calendar: semesters. *Degree:* bachelor's.

Special study options: advanced placement credit, double majors, English as a second language, honors programs, independent study, internships, off-campus study, services for LD students, student-designed majors, study abroad. *ROTC:* Army (c).

Unusual degree programs: 3-2 engineering with Columbia University, Case Western Reserve University, Duke University, Washington University, University of Pittsburgh; arts management, public policy and management, health care policy and management, information systems management with Carnegie Mellon University; physician assistant and occupational therapy with Chatham University.

Computers: 207 computers/terminals and 200 ports are available on campus for general student use. Students can access the following: campus intranet, computer help desk, free student e-mail accounts, online (class) grades, online (class) registration, online (class) schedules, placement testing, course catalog, class lists, repair service, transcript review and ordering, billing, payroll time cards, internet kiosks, dataports for laptops, education applications, campus organizations, financial aid, room draw. Campuswide network is available. 100% of college-owned or -operated housing units are wired for high-speed Internet access. Wireless service is available via entire campus.

Library: Lawrence Lee Pelletier Library. *Books:* 357,901 (physical), 497,973 (digital/electronic); *Serial titles:* 72 (physical), 56,506 (digital/electronic). Weekly public service hours: 115; students can reserve study rooms.

STUDENT LIFE

Housing options: on-campus residence required through senior year; coed, men-only, women-only, special housing for students with disabilities. Campus housing is university owned and leased by the school. Freshman campus housing is guaranteed.

Activities and organizations: drama/theater group, student-run newspaper, radio and television station, choral group, Student Government, Gators Activity Programming, Alpha Phi Omega (service fraternity), Outing Club, Greek life, national fraternities, national sororities.

Athletics Member NCAA. All Division III. *Intercollegiate sports:* baseball M, basketball M/W, cheerleading M(c)/W(c), cross-country running M/W, equestrian sports M(c)/W(c), fencing M(c)/W(c), field hockey W, football M, golf M/W, ice hockey M(c), lacrosse M/W, rugby M(c)/W(c), soccer M/W, softball W, swimming and diving M/W, tennis M/W, track and field M/W, ultimate Frisbee M(c)/W(c), volleyball M(c)/W. *Intramural sports:* basketball M/W, soccer M/W, volleyball M/W.

Campus security: 24-hour emergency response devices and patrols, student patrols, late-night transport/escort service, controlled dormitory access, local police patrol, emergency alert system, property engraving, CCTV system for parking lots.

Student services: health clinic, personal/psychological counseling.

COSTS & FINANCIAL AID

Costs (2018–19) *Comprehensive fee:* $59,680 includes full-time tuition ($47,040), mandatory fees ($500), and room and board ($12,140). Part-time tuition: $1960 per credit hour. Part-time tuition and fees vary according to course load. *Required fees:* $250 per term part-time. *College room only:* $6410. Room and board charges vary according to board plan and housing facility. *Payment plan:* installment. *Waivers:* employees or children of employees.

Financial Aid Of all full-time matriculated undergraduates who enrolled in 2017, 1,493 applied for aid, 1,365 were judged to have need, 370 had their need fully met. 917 Federal Work-Study jobs (averaging $2475). 116 state and other part-time jobs (averaging $4885). In 2017, 354 non-need-based awards were made. *Average percent of need met:* 90. *Average financial aid package:* $41,669. *Average need-based loan:* $5145. *Average need-based gift aid:* $34,310. *Average non-need-based aid:* $21,604.

APPLYING

Options: electronic application, early admission, early decision, early action, deferred entrance.

Required: essay or personal statement, high school transcript, 2 letters of recommendation, college preparatory program. *Recommended:* interview.

Application deadlines: 2/15 (freshmen), 7/1 (transfers), 12/1 (early action).

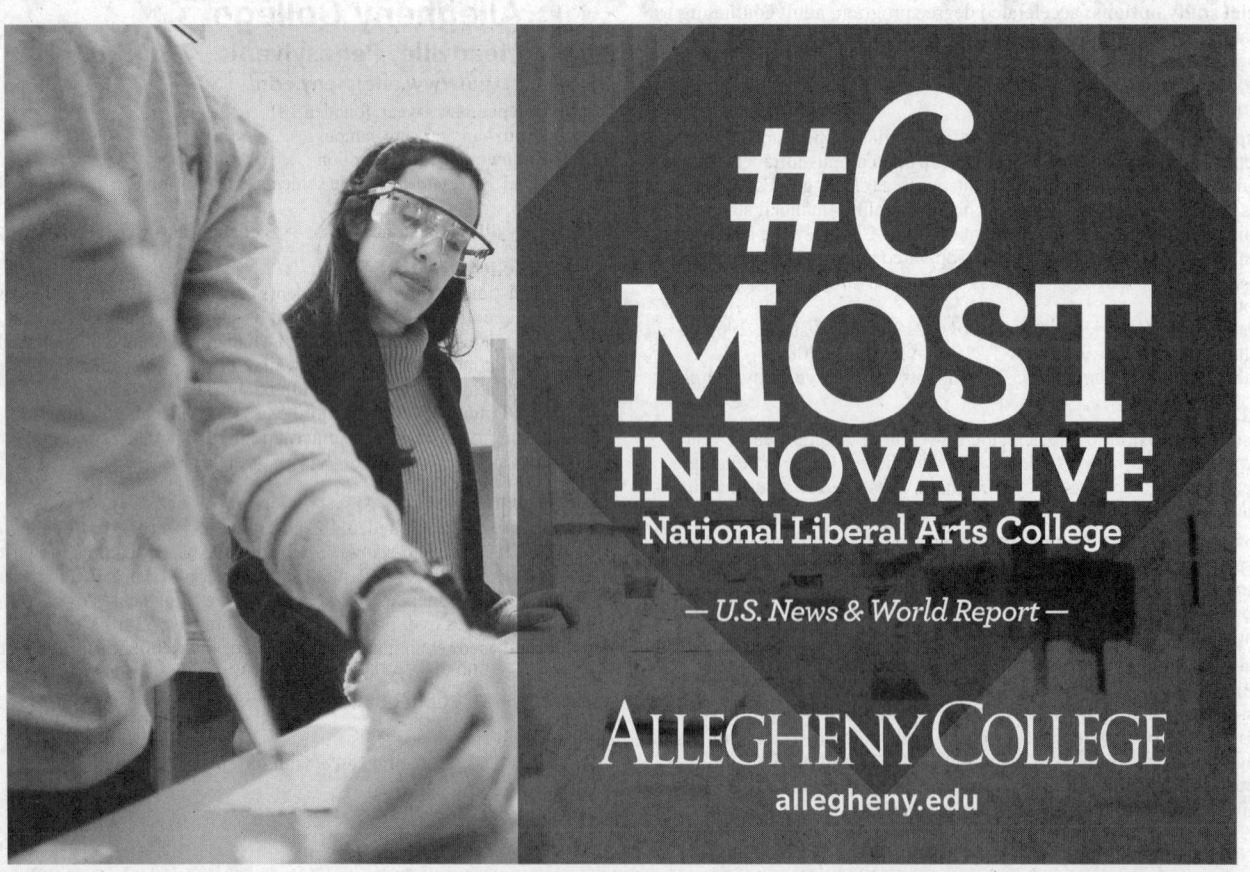

Early decision deadline: 11/1 (for plan 1), 2/1 (for plan 2).

Notification: 3/15 (freshmen), 8/1 (transfers), 11/15 (early decision plan 1), 2/15 (early decision plan 2), 1/1 (early action).

CONTACT
Ms. Linda Clune, Senior Associate Director of Admissions, Allegheny College, 520 North Main Street, Box 5, Meadville, PA 16335. *Phone:* 814-332-4351. *Toll-free phone:* 800-521-5293. *Fax:* 814-337-0431. *E-mail:* admissions@allegheny.edu.

See previous page for display ad and page 1230 for the College Close-Up.

Alvernia University
Reading, Pennsylvania
http://www.alvernia.edu/
- **Independent Roman Catholic** comprehensive, founded 1958
- **Suburban** 121-acre campus with easy access to Philadelphia
- **Endowment** $22.4 million
- **Coed**
- **Moderately difficult** entrance level

FACULTY
Student/faculty ratio: 12:1.

ACADEMICS
Calendar: semesters. *Degrees:* associate, bachelor's, master's, and doctoral.
Library: Dr. Frank A. Franco Library Learning Center. *Books:* 90,227 (physical), 7,907 (digital/electronic); *Serial titles:* 599 (physical), 45,037 (digital/electronic); *Databases:* 39. Weekly public service hours: 107; students can reserve study rooms.

STUDENT LIFE
Housing options: on-campus residence required for freshman year; coed, special housing for students with disabilities. Campus housing is university owned. Freshman campus housing is guaranteed.

Activities and organizations: drama/theater group, student-run newspaper, choral group, Student Government Association, Student Nurses Association of Alvernia (ASNA), Criminal Justice Association (CJA), Sport Management Association (SMA), Science Association.

Athletics Member NCAA. All Division III.

Campus security: 24-hour patrols, late-night transport/escort service, controlled dormitory access.

Student services: health clinic, personal/psychological counseling.

COSTS & FINANCIAL AID
Costs (2017–18) *Comprehensive fee:* $45,530 includes full-time tuition ($32,840), mandatory fees ($800), and room and board ($11,890). Full-time tuition and fees vary according to class time and reciprocity agreements. Part-time tuition: $900 per credit. Part-time tuition and fees vary according to class time and course load. *College room only:* $6030. Room and board charges vary according to board plan and housing facility.

Financial Aid Of all full-time matriculated undergraduates who enrolled in 2016, 1,582 applied for aid, 1,434 were judged to have need, 192 had their need fully met. 981 Federal Work-Study jobs (averaging $1592). In 2016, 207 non-need-based awards were made. *Average percent of need met:* 65. *Average financial aid package:* $20,349. *Average need-based loan:* $4113. *Average need-based gift aid:* $16,212. *Average non-need-based aid:* $13,054. *Average indebtedness upon graduation:* $51,958.

APPLYING
Standardized Tests *Required:* SAT or ACT (for admission).
Options: electronic application, deferred entrance.
Application fee: $25.
Required: essay or personal statement, high school transcript. *Required for some:* 2 letters of recommendation, interview. *Recommended:* minimum 2.0 GPA, 1 letter of recommendation.

CONTACT
Mr. Dan Hartzman, Director of Undergraduate Admissions, Alvernia University, 400 Saint Bernardine Street, Reading, PA 19607-1799. *Phone:* 610-568-1530. *Toll-free phone:* 888-ALVERNIA. *Fax:* 610-796-2873. *E-mail:* admissions@alvernia.edu.

Arcadia University
Glenside, Pennsylvania
http://www.arcadia.edu/
- **Independent** comprehensive, founded 1853, affiliated with Presbyterian Church (U.S.A.)
- **Suburban** 76-acre campus with easy access to Philadelphia
- **Coed** 2,390 undergraduate students, 91% full-time, 69% women, 31% men
- **Moderately difficult** entrance level, 62% of applicants were admitted

UNDERGRAD STUDENTS
2,177 full-time, 213 part-time. Students come from 42 states and territories; 13 other countries; 38% are from out of state; 10% Black or African American, non-Hispanic/Latino; 9% Hispanic/Latino; 5% Asian, non-Hispanic/Latino; 0.2% Native Hawaiian or other Pacific Islander, non-Hispanic/Latino; 0.2% American Indian or Alaska Native, non-Hispanic/Latino; 4% Two or more races, non-Hispanic/Latino; 4% Race/ethnicity unknown; 3% international; 4% transferred in; 49% live on campus.

Freshmen:
Admission: 8,931 applied, 5,564 admitted, 565 enrolled. *Average high school GPA:* 3.6. *Test scores:* SAT evidence-based reading and writing scores over 500: 89%; SAT math scores over 500: 85%; ACT scores over 18: 96%; SAT evidence-based reading and writing scores over 600: 43%; SAT math scores over 600: 34%; ACT scores over 24: 60%; SAT evidence-based reading and writing scores over 700: 5%; SAT math scores over 700: 5%; ACT scores over 30: 11%.
Retention: 78% of full-time freshmen returned.

FACULTY
Total: 477, 38% full-time.
Student/faculty ratio: 11:1.

ACADEMICS
Calendar: semesters. *Degrees:* certificates, bachelor's, master's, doctoral, post-master's, and postbachelor's certificates.

Special study options: accelerated degree program, advanced placement credit, cooperative education, distance learning, double majors, English as a second language, honors programs, independent study, internships, off-campus study, part-time degree program, services for LD students, student-designed majors, study abroad, summer session for credit.

Unusual degree programs: 3-2 engineering with Columbia University, University of Pittsburgh, and Washington University in Saint Louis; forensic science, international peace and conflict resolution.

Computers: Students can access the following: campus intranet, computer help desk, free student e-mail accounts, online (class) grades, online (class) registration, online (class) schedules. Campuswide network is available. 100% of college-owned or -operated housing units are wired for high-speed Internet access. Wireless service is available via entire campus.
Library: Bette E. Landman Library. Students can reserve study rooms.

STUDENT LIFE
Housing options: coed, women-only. Campus housing is university owned and leased by the school. Freshman applicants given priority for college housing.

Activities and organizations: drama/theater group, student-run newspaper, radio station, choral group, Student Program Board, Residence Hall Council, Student Government, Arcadia Christian Fellowship, Student Alumni Association.

Athletics Member NCAA. All Division III. *Intercollegiate sports:* baseball M, basketball M/W, cross-country running M/W, field hockey W, golf M/W, lacrosse M/W, soccer M/W, softball W, swimming and diving M/W, tennis M/W, volleyball M/W. *Intramural sports:* basketball M/W, cheerleading M(c)/W(c), equestrian sports M/W, soccer M/W, volleyball M/W.

Campus security: 24-hour emergency response devices and patrols, student patrols, late-night transport/escort service, controlled dormitory access.

Student services: health clinic, personal/psychological counseling.

COSTS & FINANCIAL AID

Costs (2017–18) *Comprehensive fee:* $55,990 includes full-time tuition ($41,630), mandatory fees ($700), and room and board ($13,660). Part-time tuition: $700 per credit hour. *College room only:* $9000. Room and board charges vary according to board plan and housing facility. *Payment plan:* installment. *Waivers:* employees or children of employees.

Financial Aid Of all full-time matriculated undergraduates who enrolled in 2016, 2,054 applied for aid, 1,863 were judged to have need, 558 had their need fully met. 140 state and other part-time jobs (averaging $1671). In 2016, 354 non-need-based awards were made. *Average percent of need met:* 83. *Average financial aid package:* $30,072. *Average need-based loan:* $3894. *Average need-based gift aid:* $26,516. *Average non-need-based aid:* $17,060.

APPLYING

Standardized Tests *Required:* SAT or ACT (for admission).

Options: electronic application, deferred entrance.

Application fee: $30.

Required: essay or personal statement, high school transcript, 2 letters of recommendation. *Required for some:* portfolio, audition. *Recommended:* minimum 3.0 GPA.

Application deadlines: 3/1 (freshmen), 6/15 (transfers).

Notification: continuous until 9/1 (freshmen), continuous until 9/1 (transfers).

CONTACT

Colleen Pernicello, Director of Undergraduate Admissions, Arcadia University, 450 South Easton Road, Glenside, PA 19038. *Phone:* 215-572-2910. *Toll-free phone:* 877-ARCADIA. *Fax:* 215-572-4049. *E-mail:* admiss@arcadia.edu.

The Art Institute of Philadelphia

Philadelphia, Pennsylvania
http://www.artinstitutes.edu/philadelphia/

CONTACT

The Art Institute of Philadelphia, 1622 Chestnut Street, Philadelphia, PA 19103. *Phone:* 215-567-7080. *Toll-free phone:* 800-275-2474.

The Art Institute of Pittsburgh

Pittsburgh, Pennsylvania
http://www.artinstitutes.edu/pittsburgh/

CONTACT

The Art Institute of Pittsburgh, 420 Boulevard of the Allies, Pittsburgh, PA 15219. *Phone:* 412-263-6600. *Toll-free phone:* 800-275-2470.

Bloomsburg University of Pennsylvania

Bloomsburg, Pennsylvania
http://www.bloomu.edu/

- **State-supported** comprehensive, founded 1839, part of Pennsylvania State System of Higher Education
- **Small-town** 366-acre campus
- **Endowment** $45.0 million
- **Coed** 8,606 undergraduate students, 91% full-time, 57% women, 43% men
- **Minimally difficult** entrance level, 73% of applicants were admitted

UNDERGRAD STUDENTS

7,863 full-time, 743 part-time. Students come from 22 states and territories; 30 other countries; 9% are from out of state; 9% Black or African American, non-Hispanic/Latino; 7% Hispanic/Latino; 1% Asian, non-Hispanic/Latino; 0.1% Native Hawaiian or other Pacific Islander, non-Hispanic/Latino; 0.2% American Indian or Alaska Native, non-Hispanic/Latino; 3% Two or more races, non-Hispanic/Latino; 1% Race/ethnicity unknown; 0.5% international; 5% transferred in; 41% live on campus.

Freshmen:

Admission: 9,683 applied, 7,093 admitted, 1,861 enrolled. *Average high school GPA:* 3.3. *Test scores:* SAT evidence-based reading and writing scores over 500: 72%; SAT math scores over 500: 67%; ACT scores over 18: 85%; SAT evidence-based reading and writing scores over 600: 19%; SAT math scores over 600: 15%; ACT scores over 24: 32%; SAT evidence-based reading and writing scores over 700: 1%; SAT math scores over 700: 1%; ACT scores over 30: 1%.

Retention: 74% of full-time freshmen returned.

FACULTY

Total: 519, 81% full-time, 73% with terminal degrees.

Student/faculty ratio: 19:1.

ACADEMICS

Calendar: semesters. *Degrees:* certificates, bachelor's, master's, doctoral, and postbachelor's certificates.

Special study options: academic remediation for entering students, advanced placement credit, cooperative education, distance learning, double majors, English as a second language, honors programs, independent study, internships, off-campus study, part-time degree program, services for LD students, student-designed majors, study abroad, summer session for credit. *ROTC:* Army (b), Air Force (c).

Unusual degree programs: 3-2 engineering with Penn State University.

Computers: 1,571 computers/terminals are available on campus for general student use. Students can access the following: computer help desk, free student e-mail accounts, online (class) grades, online (class) registration, online (class) schedules. Campuswide network is available. 100% of college-owned or -operated housing units are wired for high-speed Internet access. Wireless service is available via entire campus.

Library: Andruss Library. *Books:* 374,393 (physical), 269,435 (digital/electronic); *Serial titles:* 5,838 (physical), 84,065 (digital/electronic); *Databases:* 165. Weekly public service hours: 98; students can reserve study rooms.

STUDENT LIFE

Housing options: on-campus residence required for freshman year; coed. Campus housing is university owned and leased by the school. Freshman campus housing is guaranteed.

Activities and organizations: drama/theater group, student-run newspaper, radio and television station, choral group, marching band, Living and Learning Communities, Band and Music Groups, Greek Organizations, Residence Hall Councils, Club Sports, national fraternities, national sororities.

Athletics Member NCAA. All Division II except wrestling (Division I). *Intercollegiate sports:* baseball M(s), basketball M(s)/W(s), cross-country running M(s)/W(s), field hockey W(s), football M(s), lacrosse W(s), soccer M(s)/W(s), softball W(s), swimming and diving M(s)/W(s), tennis M(s)/W(s), track and field M(s)/W(s), volleyball W, wrestling M(s). *Intramural sports:* baseball M(c), basketball M/W, cheerleading M(c)/W(c), equestrian sports M(c)/W(c), field hockey W, football M, ice hockey M(c), lacrosse M(c)/W(c), racquetball M/W, rugby M(c)/W(c), sand volleyball M/W, skiing (downhill) M(c)/W(c), soccer M(c)/W(c), softball M/W, swimming and diving M(c)/W(c), table tennis M(c)/W(c), tennis M(c)/W(c), ultimate Frisbee M(c)/W(c), volleyball M(c)/W(c), wrestling M(c).

Campus security: 24-hour emergency response devices and patrols, late-night transport/escort service, controlled dormitory access, monitored surveillance cameras.

Student services: health clinic, personal/psychological counseling, women's center, legal services.

COSTS & FINANCIAL AID

Costs (2017–18) *Tuition:* state resident $7492 full-time, $312 per credit part-time; nonresident $18,730 full-time, $780 per credit part-time. Full-time tuition and fees vary according to course load and location. Part-time tuition and fees vary according to course load and location. *Required fees:* $3008 full-time, $110 per credit part-time, $75 per term part-time. *Room and board:* $9430; room only: $6080. Room and board charges vary according to board plan and housing facility. *Payment plan:* installment. *Waivers:* senior citizens and employees or children of employees.

Financial Aid Of all full-time matriculated undergraduates who enrolled in 2017, 7,058 applied for aid, 5,258 were judged to have need, 617 had their need fully met. 873 Federal Work-Study jobs (averaging $2923).

1,222 state and other part-time jobs (averaging $3801). In 2017, 243 non-need-based awards were made. *Average percent of need met:* 56. *Average financial aid package:* $9310. *Average need-based loan:* $4157. *Average need-based gift aid:* $5867. *Average non-need-based aid:* $2450. *Average indebtedness upon graduation:* $35,407.

APPLYING

Standardized Tests *Required:* SAT or ACT (for admission).

Options: electronic application, early admission, early action, deferred entrance.

Application fee: $35.

Required: high school transcript.

Application deadlines: rolling (freshmen), rolling (transfers).

Notification: continuous until 9/18 (freshmen), continuous (transfers), 5/1 (early action).

CONTACT

Bloomsburg University of Pennsylvania, 400 East Second Street, Bloomsburg, PA 17815-1301.

Bryn Athyn College of the New Church

Bryn Athyn, Pennsylvania

http://www.brynathyn.edu/

- **Independent Christian** comprehensive, founded 1877, affiliated with Church of the New Jerusalem, part of The Academy of the New Church
- **Suburban** 130-acre campus with easy access to Philadelphia
- **Endowment** $58.8 million
- **Coed** 326 undergraduate students, 96% full-time, 51% women, 49% men
- **Minimally difficult** entrance level, 88% of applicants were admitted

UNDERGRAD STUDENTS

314 full-time, 12 part-time. Students come from 23 states and territories; 5 other countries; 30% are from out of state; 15% Black or African American, non-Hispanic/Latino; 7% Hispanic/Latino; 2% Asian, non-Hispanic/Latino; 0.6% Native Hawaiian or other Pacific Islander, non-Hispanic/Latino; 2% American Indian or Alaska Native, non-Hispanic/Latino; 2% Two or more races, non-Hispanic/Latino; 0.9% Race/ethnicity unknown; 2% international; 10% transferred in; 62% live on campus.

Freshmen:

Admission: 241 applied, 211 admitted, 106 enrolled. *Average high school GPA:* 3.3. *Test scores:* SAT evidence-based reading and writing scores over 500: 67%; SAT math scores over 500: 59%; ACT scores over 18: 77%; SAT evidence-based reading and writing scores over 600: 22%; SAT math scores over 600: 17%; ACT scores over 24: 22%; SAT evidence-based reading and writing scores over 700: 4%; SAT math scores over 700: 3%; ACT scores over 30: 4%.

Retention: 76% of full-time freshmen returned.

FACULTY

Total: 85, 44% full-time, 53% with terminal degrees.

Student/faculty ratio: 6:1.

ACADEMICS

Calendar: trimesters. *Degrees:* associate, bachelor's, and master's.

Special study options: academic remediation for entering students, accelerated degree program, advanced placement credit, cooperative education, English as a second language, independent study, internships, part-time degree program, services for LD students, student-designed majors, study abroad. *ROTC:* Army (c), Air Force (c).

Computers: 18 computers/terminals are available on campus for general student use. Students can access the following: campus intranet, computer help desk, free student e-mail accounts, online (class) grades, online (class) registration, online (class) schedules. Campuswide network is available. 100% of college-owned or -operated housing units are wired for high-speed Internet access. Wireless service is available via entire campus.

Library: Swedenborg Library plus 1 other. *Books:* 70,742 (physical), 252 (digital/electronic); *Serial titles:* 834 (physical), 74 (digital/electronic); *Databases:* 13.

STUDENT LIFE

Housing options: men-only, women-only. Campus housing is university owned. Freshman applicants given priority for college housing.

Activities and organizations: drama/theater group, choral group, C.A.R.E. (Community Service), Social council, International Student Organization, Peer Advisory Council, Student Government.

Athletics Member NCAA. All Division III. *Intercollegiate sports:* basketball M/W, cross-country running M/W, field hockey W, golf M, ice hockey M, lacrosse M/W, soccer M/W, tennis M/W, volleyball W.

Campus security: 24-hour emergency response devices, controlled dormitory access, 18-hour patrols by trained personnel.

Student services: health clinic, personal/psychological counseling.

COSTS & FINANCIAL AID

Costs (2017–18) *Comprehensive fee:* $32,664 includes full-time tuition ($19,671), mandatory fees ($1455), and room and board ($11,538). Part-time tuition: $810 per credit hour. *Required fees:* $55 per credit hour part-time. *College room only:* $5769. *Payment plan:* installment. *Waivers:* senior citizens.

Financial Aid Of all full-time matriculated undergraduates who enrolled in 2008, 92 applied for aid, 66 were judged to have need, 30 had their need fully met. In 2008, 22 non-need-based awards were made. *Average percent of need met:* 95. *Average financial aid package:* $9987. *Average need-based loan:* $3329. *Average need-based gift aid:* $8358. *Average non-need-based aid:* $2232. *Average indebtedness upon graduation:* $8299. *Financial aid deadline:* 7/1.

APPLYING

Standardized Tests *Required:* SAT or ACT (for admission).

Options: electronic application, deferred entrance.

Required: essay or personal statement, high school transcript, minimum 2.0 GPA, 1 letter of recommendation. *Required for some:* interview.

Application deadlines: rolling (freshmen), rolling (out-of-state freshmen), rolling (transfers).

Notification: continuous (freshmen), continuous (out-of-state freshmen), continuous (transfers).

CONTACT

Ms. Nicole D'Amico, Admissions Office, Bryn Athyn College of the New Church, 2945 College Drive, Box 717, Bryn Athyn, PA 19009. *Phone:* 267-502-6000. *Toll-free phone:* 800-767-9552. *Fax:* 267-502-2593. *E-mail:* admissions@brynathyn.edu.

★ Bryn Mawr College

Bryn Mawr, Pennsylvania

http://www.brynmawr.edu/

- **Independent** university, founded 1885
- **Suburban** 135-acre campus with easy access to Philadelphia
- **Endowment** $852.7 million
- **Undergraduate: women only; graduate: coed** 1,334 undergraduate students, 99% full-time, 100% women, 0% men
- **Most difficult** entrance level, 38% of applicants were admitted

UNDERGRAD STUDENTS

1,325 full-time, 9 part-time. Students come from 48 states and territories; 58 other countries; 82% are from out of state; 6% Black or African American, non-Hispanic/Latino; 9% Hispanic/Latino; 12% Asian, non-Hispanic/Latino; 0.1% Native Hawaiian or other Pacific Islander, non-Hispanic/Latino; 6% Two or more races, non-Hispanic/Latino; 7% Race/ethnicity unknown; 23% international; 0.4% transferred in; 91% live on campus.

Freshmen:

Admission: 2,936 applied, 1,116 admitted, 354 enrolled. *Test scores:* SAT evidence-based reading and writing scores over 500: 100%; SAT math scores over 500: 100%; ACT scores over 18: 100%; SAT evidence-based reading and writing scores over 600: 92%; SAT math scores over 600: 93%; ACT scores over 24: 99%; SAT evidence-based reading and writing scores over 700: 53%; SAT math scores over 700: 56%; ACT scores over 30: 67%.

Retention: 92% of full-time freshmen returned.

FACULTY
Total: 201, 79% full-time, 85% with terminal degrees.
Student/faculty ratio: 8:1.

ACADEMICS
Calendar: semesters. *Degrees:* bachelor's, master's, doctoral, and postbachelor's certificates.

Special study options: academic remediation for entering students, accelerated degree program, advanced placement credit, double majors, independent study, internships, off-campus study, services for LD students, student-designed majors, study abroad, summer session for credit. *ROTC:* Air Force (c).

Unusual degree programs: 3-2 engineering with California Institute of Technology, Columbia University.

Computers: 125 computers/terminals are available on campus for general student use. Students can access the following: computer help desk, free student e-mail accounts, online (class) grades, online (class) registration, online (class) schedules. Campuswide network is available. 100% of college-owned or -operated housing units are wired for high-speed Internet access. Wireless service is available via entire campus.

Library: Canaday Library plus 2 others. *Books:* 740,887 (physical), 754,968 (digital/electronic); *Serial titles:* 9,146 (physical), 123,010 (digital/electronic); *Databases:* 170. Weekly public service hours: 105; study areas open 24 hours, 5–7 days a week.

STUDENT LIFE
Housing options: on-campus residence required for freshman year; coed, women-only, cooperative. Campus housing is university owned. Freshman campus housing is guaranteed.

Activities and organizations: drama/theater group, student-run newspaper, radio station, choral group, Student Government Association.

Athletics Member NCAA. All Division III. *Intercollegiate sports:* badminton W, basketball W, crew W, cross-country running W, field hockey W, lacrosse W, soccer W, swimming and diving W, tennis W, track and field W, volleyball W.

Campus security: 24-hour emergency response devices and patrols, late-night transport/escort service, controlled dormitory access, shuttle bus service, awareness programs, bicycle registration, security Web site.

Student services: health clinic, personal/psychological counseling, women's center.

COSTS & FINANCIAL AID
Costs (2017–18) *Comprehensive fee:* $66,410 includes full-time tuition ($49,310), mandatory fees ($1190), and room and board ($15,910). Part-time tuition: $6165 per course. *College room only:* $9080. *Payment plan:* installment.

Financial Aid Of all full-time matriculated undergraduates who enrolled in 2017, 774 applied for aid, 697 were judged to have need, 692 had their need fully met. In 2017, 226 non-need-based awards were made. *Average percent of need met:* 100. *Average financial aid package:* $47,906. *Average need-based loan:* $3545. *Average need-based gift aid:* $42,244. *Average non-need-based aid:* $17,307. *Average indebtedness upon graduation:* $25,448. *Financial aid deadline:* 1/15.

APPLYING
Standardized Tests *Required for some:* SAT and SAT Subject Tests or ACT (for admission).

Options: electronic application, early admission, early decision, deferred entrance.

Application fee: $50.

Required: essay or personal statement, high school transcript, 3 letters of recommendation. *Recommended:* interview.

Application deadlines: 1/15 (freshmen), 3/1 (transfers).

Early decision deadline: 11/15 (for plan 1), 1/1 (for plan 2).

Notification: 4/1 (freshmen), 6/1 (transfers), 12/15 (early decision plan 1), 2/1 (early decision plan 2).

CONTACT
Dr. Cheryl Lynn Horsey, Chief Enrollment Officer, Bryn Mawr College, 101 North Merion Avenue, Bryn Mawr, PA 19010. *Phone:* 610-526-6522. *Toll-free phone:* 800-BMC-1885. *Fax:* 610-526-7471. *E-mail:* chorsey@brynmawr.edu.

See below for display ad and page 1252 for the College Close-Up.

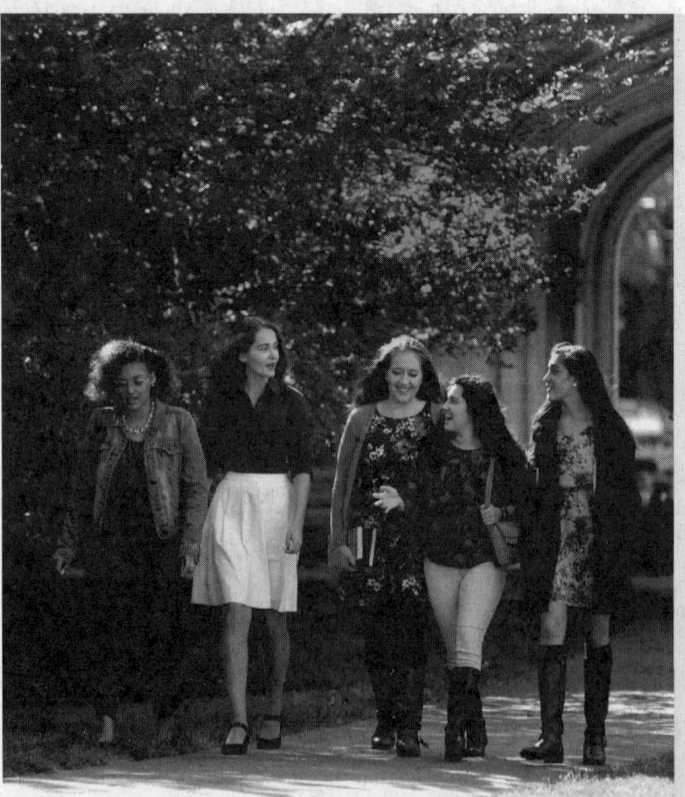

Bucknell University

Lewisburg, Pennsylvania

http://www.bucknell.edu/

- **Independent** comprehensive, founded 1846
- **Small-town** 446-acre campus
- **Endowment** $800.8 million
- **Coed** 3,611 undergraduate students, 99% full-time, 51% women, 49% men
- **Most difficult** entrance level, 31% of applicants were admitted

UNDERGRAD STUDENTS
3,585 full-time, 26 part-time. Students come from 42 states and territories; 45 other countries; 78% are from out of state; 4% Black or African American, non-Hispanic/Latino; 7% Hispanic/Latino; 5% Asian, non-Hispanic/Latino; 4% Two or more races, non-Hispanic/Latino; 0.2% Race/ethnicity unknown; 6% international; 0.8% transferred in; 91% live on campus.

Freshmen:
Admission: 10,253 applied, 3,187 admitted, 973 enrolled. *Average high school GPA:* 3.6. *Test scores:* SAT evidence-based reading and writing scores over 500: 99%; SAT math scores over 500: 100%; ACT scores over 18: 100%; SAT evidence-based reading and writing scores over 600: 84%; SAT math scores over 600: 85%; ACT scores over 24: 98%; SAT evidence-based reading and writing scores over 700: 27%; SAT math scores over 700: 40%; ACT scores over 30: 54%.
Retention: 94% of full-time freshmen returned.

FACULTY
Total: 434, 88% full-time, 92% with terminal degrees.
Student/faculty ratio: 9:1.

ACADEMICS
Calendar: semesters. *Degrees:* bachelor's and master's.
Special study options: advanced placement credit, double majors, honors programs, independent study, internships, off-campus study, part-time degree program, services for LD students, student-designed majors, study abroad, summer session for credit. *ROTC:* Army (b).
Unusual degree programs: 3-2 engineering; biology, chemistry.
Computers: 1,031 computers/terminals and 190 ports are available on campus for general student use. Students can access the following: campus intranet, computer help desk, free student e-mail accounts, online (class) grades, online (class) registration, online (class) schedules. Campuswide network is available. 100% of college-owned or -operated housing units are wired for high-speed Internet access. Wireless service is available via entire campus.
Library: Ellen Clarke Bertrand Library. *Books:* 708,581 (physical), 659,133 (digital/electronic); *Serial titles:* 288 (physical), 46,902 (digital/electronic); *Databases:* 221. Weekly public service hours: 125.

STUDENT LIFE
Housing options: on-campus residence required through senior year; coed, women-only, cooperative, special housing for students with disabilities. Campus housing is university owned. Freshman campus housing is guaranteed.
Activities and organizations: drama/theater group, student-run newspaper, radio station, choral group, Black Student Union, Outing Club, Activities and Campus Events, Catholic Campus Ministries, CALVIN and HOBBES, national fraternities, national sororities.
Athletics Member NCAA. All Division I except football (Division I-AA). *Intercollegiate sports:* baseball M, basketball M(s)/W(s), cheerleading M(c)/W(c), crew M(c)/W, cross-country running M/W(s), equestrian sports M(c)/W(c), field hockey W(s), golf M/W, ice hockey M(c), lacrosse M(s)/W(s), rock climbing M(c)/W(c), rugby M(c)/W(c), sailing M(c)/W(c), skiing (downhill) M(c)/W(c), soccer M(s)/W, softball W(s), squash M(c)/W(c), swimming and diving M(s)/W, tennis M/W, track and field M/W(s), ultimate Frisbee M(c)/W(c), volleyball M(c)/W(s), water polo M/W, weight lifting M(c)/W(c), wrestling M(s). *Intramural sports:* basketball M/W, cross-country running M/W, golf M/W, racquetball M/W, soccer M/W, softball M/W, squash M/W, table tennis M/W, tennis M/W, ultimate Frisbee M/W, volleyball M/W, weight lifting M, wrestling M.
Campus security: 24-hour emergency response devices and patrols, student patrols, late-night transport/escort service, controlled dormitory access, well-lit pathways, self-defense education, safety/security orientation.
Student services: health clinic, personal/psychological counseling, women's center.

COSTS & FINANCIAL AID
Costs (2017–18) *Comprehensive fee:* $67,136 includes full-time tuition ($53,692), mandatory fees ($294), and room and board ($13,150). Part-time tuition: $5892 per course. *College room only:* $8020. Room and board charges vary according to board plan and housing facility. *Payment plans:* tuition prepayment, installment. *Waivers:* employees or children of employees.
Financial Aid Of all full-time matriculated undergraduates who enrolled in 2017, 1,406 applied for aid, 1,295 were judged to have need. 600 Federal Work-Study jobs (averaging $1500). 50 state and other part-time jobs (averaging $1500). In 2017, 416 non-need-based awards were made. *Average percent of need met:* 91. *Average financial aid package:* $33,500. *Average need-based loan:* $5500. *Average need-based gift aid:* $29,000. *Average non-need-based aid:* $11,898. *Average indebtedness upon graduation:* $33,000. *Financial aid deadline:* 1/15.

APPLYING
Standardized Tests *Required:* SAT or ACT (for admission).
Options: electronic application, early decision, deferred entrance.
Application fee: $40.
Required: essay or personal statement, high school transcript, 1 letter of recommendation.
Application deadlines: 1/15 (freshmen), 3/15 (transfers).
Early decision deadline: 11/15 (for plan 1), 1/15 (for plan 2).
Notification: 4/1 (freshmen), 5/1 (transfers), 12/15 (early decision plan 1), 2/15 (early decision plan 2).

CONTACT
Dean Kevin Mathes, Dean of Admissions, Bucknell University, 1 Dent Drive, Lewisburg, PA 17837. *Phone:* 570-577-3000. *Fax:* 570-577-3538. *E-mail:* admissions@bucknell.edu.

Cabrini University

Radnor, Pennsylvania

http://www.cabrini.edu/

- **Independent Roman Catholic** comprehensive, founded 1957
- **Suburban** 112-acre campus with easy access to Philadelphia
- **Endowment** $43.7 million
- **Coed**
- **Moderately difficult** entrance level

FACULTY
Student/faculty ratio: 13:1.

ACADEMICS
Calendar: semesters. *Degrees:* bachelor's, master's, and doctoral.
Library: Holy Spirit Library. *Books:* 143,980 (digital/electronic); *Serial titles:* 67 (physical), 68,500 (digital/electronic); *Databases:* 47. Weekly public service hours: 97.

STUDENT LIFE
Housing options: coed, women-only, special housing for students with disabilities. Campus housing is university owned and leased by the school. Freshman applicants given priority for college housing.
Activities and organizations: drama/theater group, student-run newspaper, radio and television station, choral group, Campus Activities and Programming (CAP) Board, Student Government Association (SGA), Black Student Union, Catholic Relief Services (CRS) Ambassadors, Cabrini Friends of Exceptional Children (CFEC), national fraternities, national sororities.
Athletics Member NCAA. All Division III.
Campus security: 24-hour emergency response devices and patrols, student patrols, late-night transport/escort service, controlled dormitory access, Resident Assistants and Directors on nightly duty.
Student services: health clinic, personal/psychological counseling.

COSTS & FINANCIAL AID
Costs (2017–18) *Comprehensive fee:* $43,490 includes full-time tuition ($30,400), mandatory fees ($950), and room and board ($12,140). Part-

time tuition: $550 per credit hour. Part-time tuition and fees vary according to course load. *Required fees:* $45 per term part-time. *Room and board:* Room and board charges vary according to board plan and housing facility.

Financial Aid Of all full-time matriculated undergraduates who enrolled in 2015, 1,197 applied for aid, 1,006 were judged to have need, 258 had their need fully met. 226 Federal Work-Study jobs (averaging $1141). In 2015, 221 non-need-based awards were made. *Average financial aid package:* $16,988. *Average need-based loan:* $3257. *Average need-based gift aid:* $7627. *Average non-need-based aid:* $10,210. *Average indebtedness upon graduation:* $43,437.

APPLYING
Standardized Tests *Recommended:* SAT or ACT (for admission).

Options: electronic application, deferred entrance.

Application fee: $20.

Required: essay or personal statement, high school transcript, minimum 2.0 GPA. *Recommended:* minimum 2.0 GPA, 1 letter of recommendation, interview.

CONTACT
Ms. Shannon Zottola, Assistant Vice President for Enrollment Management, Cabrini University, 610 King of Prussia Road, Radnor, PA 19087-3698. *Phone:* 610-902-1027. *Toll-free phone:* 800-848-1003. *Fax:* 610-902-8508. *E-mail:* admit@cabrini.edu.

Cairn University
Langhorne, Pennsylvania
http://cairn.edu/

- **Independent nondenominational** comprehensive, founded 1913
- **Suburban** 115-acre campus with easy access to Philadelphia
- **Endowment** $11.0 million
- **Coed** 762 undergraduate students, 95% full-time, 56% women, 44% men
- **Moderately difficult** entrance level, 99% of applicants were admitted

UNDERGRAD STUDENTS
726 full-time, 36 part-time. Students come from 29 states and territories; 20 other countries; 46% are from out of state; 13% Black or African American, non-Hispanic/Latino; 6% Hispanic/Latino; 4% Asian, non-Hispanic/Latino; 0.3% American Indian or Alaska Native, non-Hispanic/Latino; 2% Two or more races, non-Hispanic/Latino; 3% international; 9% transferred in; 62% live on campus.

Freshmen:
Admission: 345 applied, 340 admitted, 154 enrolled. *Average high school GPA:* 3.3. *Test scores:* SAT evidence-based reading and writing scores over 500: 61%; SAT math scores over 500: 48%; ACT scores over 18: 73%; SAT evidence-based reading and writing scores over 600: 17%; SAT math scores over 600: 15%; ACT scores over 24: 18%; SAT evidence-based reading and writing scores over 700: 4%; SAT math scores over 700: 1%; ACT scores over 30: 3%.
Retention: 74% of full-time freshmen returned.

FACULTY
Total: 123, 37% full-time, 43% with terminal degrees.
Student/faculty ratio: 12:1.

ACADEMICS
Calendar: semesters. *Degrees:* bachelor's, master's, and postbachelor's certificates.
Special study options: academic remediation for entering students, accelerated degree program, adult/continuing education programs, advanced placement credit, double majors, honors programs, independent study, internships, off-campus study, part-time degree program, services for LD students, study abroad, summer session for credit. *ROTC:* Air Force (c).
Computers: 55 computers/terminals are available on campus for general student use. Students can access the following: campus intranet, computer help desk, free student e-mail accounts, online (class) grades, online (class) registration, online (class) schedules. Campuswide network is available. 100% of college-owned or -operated housing units are wired for high-speed Internet access. Wireless service is available via entire campus.

Library: Masland Learning Resource Center. *Books:* 104,860 (physical), 421,604 (digital/electronic); *Serial titles:* 945 (physical), 53,295 (digital/electronic); *Databases:* 177. Weekly public service hours: 86; students can reserve study rooms.

STUDENT LIFE
Housing options: on-campus residence required through senior year; men-only, women-only, special housing for students with disabilities. Campus housing is university owned. Freshman campus housing is guaranteed.

Activities and organizations: drama/theater group, student-run newspaper, choral group, Ascend (outdoor adventure club), Chi Beta Sigma (Social Work Club), Enactus (Business), Mu Kappa (Missionary Kids Association), Student Visual Arts Society.

Athletics Member NCAA, NCCAA. All NCAA Division III.
Intercollegiate sports: baseball M, basketball M/W, cross-country running M/W, golf M, soccer M/W, softball W, tennis W, volleyball M/W.
Intramural sports: badminton M/W, basketball M/W, soccer M/W, table tennis M/W, tennis M/W, ultimate Frisbee M/W, volleyball M/W.

Campus security: 24-hour emergency response devices and patrols, student patrols, late-night transport/escort service, controlled dormitory access.

Student services: health clinic, personal/psychological counseling.

COSTS & FINANCIAL AID
Costs (2018–19) *Comprehensive fee:* $37,573 includes full-time tuition ($26,979), mandatory fees ($300), and room and board ($10,294). Full-time tuition and fees vary according to course load. Part-time tuition: $800 per credit. Part-time tuition and fees vary according to course load. *College room only:* $5389. Room and board charges vary according to board plan and location. *Payment plan:* installment. *Waivers:* employees or children of employees.

Financial Aid Of all full-time matriculated undergraduates who enrolled in 2017, 640 applied for aid, 585 were judged to have need, 71 had their need fully met. In 2017, 117 non-need-based awards were made. *Average percent of need met:* 75. *Average financial aid package:* $21,885. *Average need-based loan:* $5057. *Average need-based gift aid:* $16,755. *Average non-need-based aid:* $12,008. *Average indebtedness upon graduation:* $35,717.

APPLYING
Standardized Tests *Required:* SAT or ACT (for admission).

Options: electronic application, early admission, deferred entrance.

Application fee: $25.

Required: essay or personal statement, high school transcript, minimum 2.0 GPA, interview.

Application deadlines: rolling (freshmen), rolling (transfers).

Notification: continuous (freshmen), continuous (transfers).

CONTACT
Mr. Thomas Sherf, Director of Undergraduate Admissions, Cairn University, 200 Manor Avenue, Langhorne, PA 19047. *Phone:* 215-702-4248. *Toll-free phone:* 800-366-0049. *Fax:* 215-702-4248. *E-mail:* admissions@cairn.edu.

California University of Pennsylvania
California, Pennsylvania
http://www.calu.edu/

- **State-supported** comprehensive, founded 1852, part of Pennsylvania State System of Higher Education
- **Rural** 188-acre campus with easy access to Pittsburgh
- **Endowment** $31.3 million
- **Coed** 5,557 undergraduate students, 82% full-time, 53% women, 47% men
- **Moderately difficult** entrance level, 94% of applicants were admitted

UNDERGRAD STUDENTS
4,534 full-time, 1,023 part-time. Students come from 51 states and territories; 23 other countries; 11% are from out of state; 13% Black or African American, non-Hispanic/Latino; 3% Hispanic/Latino; 1% Asian, non-Hispanic/Latino; 0.1% Native Hawaiian or other Pacific Islander, non-Hispanic/Latino; 0.3% American Indian or Alaska Native, non-

Hispanic/Latino; 4% Two or more races, non-Hispanic/Latino; 2% Race/ethnicity unknown; 0.8% international; 13% transferred in; 33% live on campus.

Freshmen:
Admission: 3,324 applied, 3,133 admitted, 993 enrolled. *Average high school GPA:* 3.1. *Test scores:* SAT evidence-based reading and writing scores over 500: 64%; SAT math scores over 500: 57%; ACT scores over 18: 66%; SAT evidence-based reading and writing scores over 600: 17%; SAT math scores over 600: 11%; ACT scores over 24: 24%; SAT evidence-based reading and writing scores over 700: 1%; SAT math scores over 700: 1%; ACT scores over 30: 2%.
Retention: 73% of full-time freshmen returned.

FACULTY
Total: 383, 66% full-time, 72% with terminal degrees.
Student/faculty ratio: 20:1.

ACADEMICS
Calendar: semesters. *Degrees:* certificates, associate, bachelor's, master's, doctoral, post-master's, and postbachelor's certificates.

Special study options: academic remediation for entering students, accelerated degree program, adult/continuing education programs, advanced placement credit, cooperative education, distance learning, double majors, English as a second language, honors programs, independent study, internships, off-campus study, part-time degree program, services for LD students, study abroad, summer session for credit. *ROTC:* Army (b).

Computers: 1,300 computers/terminals and 18,000 ports are available on campus for general student use. Students can access the following: campus intranet, computer help desk, free student e-mail accounts, online (class) grades, online (class) registration, online (class) schedules. 100% of college-owned or -operated housing units are wired for high-speed Internet access. Wireless service is available via entire campus.
Library: Manderino Library. *Books:* 219,774 (physical), 273,898 (digital/electronic); *Serial titles:* 22,098 (physical), 48,610 (digital/electronic); *Databases:* 97. Students can reserve study rooms.

STUDENT LIFE
Housing options: on-campus residence required for freshman year; coed, special housing for students with disabilities. Campus housing is university owned, leased by the school and is provided by a third party. Freshman campus housing is guaranteed.

Activities and organizations: drama/theater group, student-run newspaper, radio and television station, choral group, marching band, national fraternities, national sororities.

Athletics Member NCAA. All Division II. *Intercollegiate sports:* baseball M, basketball M/W, cross-country running M/W, football M, golf M/W, soccer M/W, softball W, swimming and diving W, tennis W, track and field M/W, volleyball W.

Campus security: 24-hour emergency response devices and patrols, student patrols, late-night transport/escort service, controlled dormitory access, residence hall entrances staffed 24/7, fire suppression and smoke detection systems, security staff are trained police officers.

Student services: health clinic, personal/psychological counseling, women's center, legal services.

COSTS & FINANCIAL AID
Costs (2018–19) *Tuition:* state resident $312 per credit hour part-time; nonresident $468 per credit hour part-time. Full-time tuition and fees vary according to course load, location, and student level. Part-time tuition and fees vary according to course load, location, and student level. *Room and board:* $10,344; room only: $6592. Room and board charges vary according to board plan and housing facility. *Payment plan:* installment. *Waivers:* employees or children of employees.

Financial Aid Of all full-time matriculated undergraduates who enrolled in 2016, 4,243 applied for aid, 3,563 were judged to have need, 262 had their need fully met. 666 Federal Work-Study jobs (averaging $580). 1,116 state and other part-time jobs (averaging $1154). In 2016, 89 non-need-based awards were made. *Average percent of need met:* 51. *Average financial aid package:* $9213. *Average need-based loan:* $4142. *Average need-based gift aid:* $5997. *Average non-need-based aid:* $4361. *Average indebtedness upon graduation:* $26,242.

APPLYING
Standardized Tests *Required:* SAT or ACT (for admission).

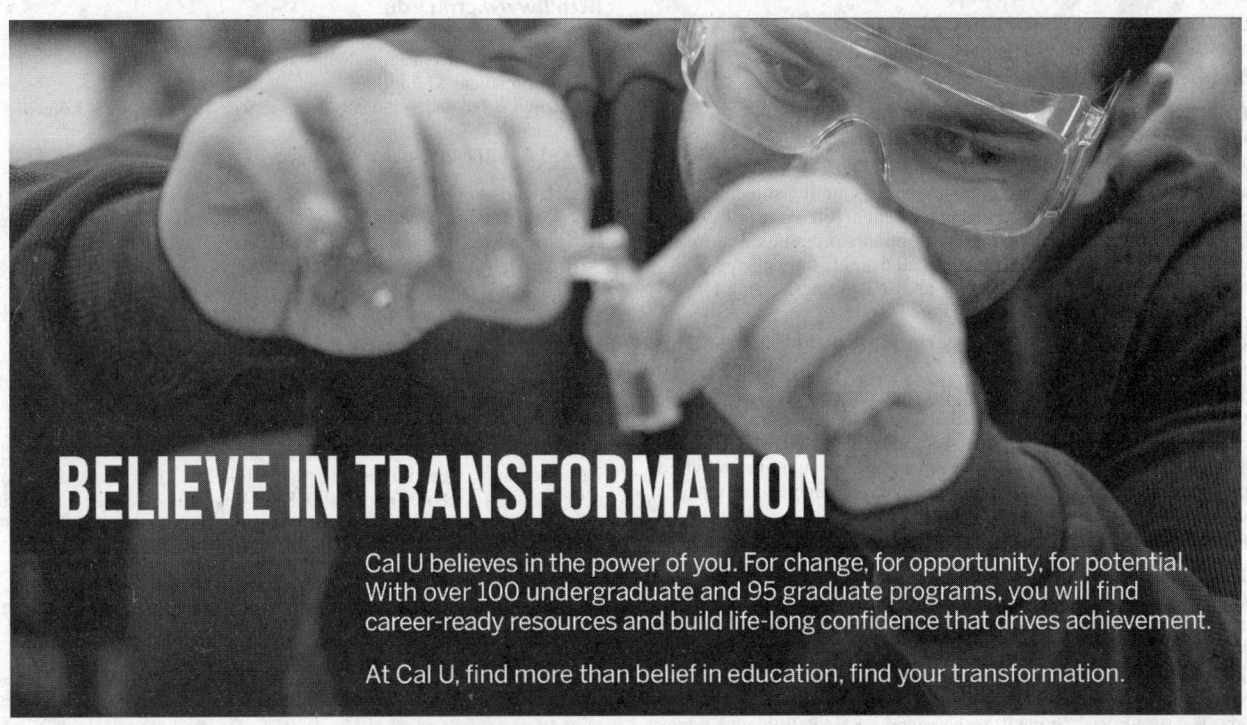

Options: electronic application, deferred entrance.
Application fee: $25.
Required: high school transcript.
Application deadlines: rolling (freshmen), rolling (transfers).
Notification: continuous (freshmen), continuous (transfers).

CONTACT
Dr. Tracey Sheetz, Dean of Undergraduate Admissions, California University of Pennsylvania, 250 University Avenue, California, PA 15419. *Phone:* 724-938-4404. *Toll-free phone:* 888-412-0479. *Fax:* 724-938-4564.

See previous page for display ad and page 1254 for the College Close-Up.

Carlow University
Pittsburgh, Pennsylvania
http://www.carlow.edu/

- **Independent Roman Catholic** comprehensive, founded 1929
- **Urban** 13-acre campus with easy access to Pittsburgh
- **Coed, primarily women** 1,365 undergraduate students, 79% full-time, 84% women, 16% men
- **Minimally difficult** entrance level, 91% of applicants were admitted

UNDERGRAD STUDENTS
1,075 full-time, 290 part-time. 5% are from out of state; 18% Black or African American, non-Hispanic/Latino; 2% Hispanic/Latino; 2% Asian, non-Hispanic/Latino; 0.1% Native Hawaiian or other Pacific Islander, non-Hispanic/Latino; 0.2% American Indian or Alaska Native, non-Hispanic/Latino; 4% Two or more races, non-Hispanic/Latino; 6% Race/ethnicity unknown; 0.2% international; 14% transferred in; 32% live on campus.

Freshmen:
Admission: 877 applied, 802 admitted, 241 enrolled. *Average high school GPA:* 3.5. *Test scores:* SAT evidence-based reading and writing scores over 500: 60%; SAT math scores over 500: 47%; ACT scores over 18: 89%; SAT evidence-based reading and writing scores over 600: 9%; SAT math scores over 600: 11%; ACT scores over 24: 30%; SAT evidence-based reading and writing scores over 700: 1%; ACT scores over 30: 6%.

FACULTY
Total: 260, 37% full-time, 49% with terminal degrees.
Student/faculty ratio: 12:1.

ACADEMICS
Calendar: semesters. *Degrees:* certificates, bachelor's, master's, doctoral, post-master's, and postbachelor's certificates.
Special study options: academic remediation for entering students, accelerated degree program, advanced placement credit, cooperative education, distance learning, double majors, honors programs, independent study, internships, off-campus study, part-time degree program, services for LD students, study abroad, summer session for credit. *ROTC:* Army (c), Navy (c), Air Force (c).
Unusual degree programs: 3-2 biology/environmental science and Management with Duquesne University.
Computers: Students can access the following: campus intranet, computer help desk, free student e-mail accounts, online (class) grades, online (class) registration, online (class) schedules. Campuswide network is available. 100% of college-owned or -operated housing units are wired for high-speed Internet access. Wireless service is available via entire campus.
Library: Grace Library.

STUDENT LIFE
Housing options: coed, men-only, women-only, special housing for students with disabilities. Campus housing is university owned. Freshman applicants given priority for college housing.
Activities and organizations: drama/theater group, student-run newspaper, choral group, Student Government Association, Campus Activities Board, SPiRiT (Student Ambassadors), SNAP (Student Nursing Association), PSEA (School Education Association), national fraternities.
Athletics Member NAIA, USCAA. *Intercollegiate sports:* basketball M(s)/W(s), cross-country running M(s)/W(s), soccer W(s), softball W(s), tennis W(s), volleyball W(s).

Campus security: 24-hour emergency response devices and patrols, late-night transport/escort service, controlled dormitory access.
Student services: health clinic, personal/psychological counseling.

COSTS & FINANCIAL AID
Costs (2017–18) *Comprehensive fee:* $39,704 includes full-time tuition ($27,950), mandatory fees ($646), and room and board ($11,108). Full-time tuition and fees vary according to course load, program, and reciprocity agreements. Part-time tuition: $889 per credit hour. Part-time tuition and fees vary according to course load, program, and reciprocity agreements. *Required fees:* $13 per credit hour part-time. *College room only:* $5680. Room and board charges vary according to board plan. *Payment plan:* installment. *Waivers:* children of alumni, adult students, and employees or children of employees.
Financial Aid Of all full-time matriculated undergraduates who enrolled in 2016, 1,085 applied for aid, 1,018 were judged to have need, 226 had their need fully met. *Average percent of need met:* 62. *Average financial aid package:* $18,975. *Average need-based loan:* $3342. *Average need-based gift aid:* $4160. *Financial aid deadline:* 5/1.

APPLYING
Standardized Tests *Required:* SAT or ACT (for admission). *Recommended:* SAT (for admission), SAT and SAT Subject Tests or ACT (for admission).
Options: electronic application, deferred entrance.
Required: high school transcript. *Recommended:* essay or personal statement, minimum 2.5 GPA, interview.
Application deadlines: rolling (freshmen), rolling (transfers).
Notification: continuous (freshmen), continuous (transfers).

CONTACT
Ms. Wivina Chmura, Director of Undergraduate Admissions, Carlow University, 3333 Fifth Avenue, Pittsburgh, PA 15213. *Phone:* 412-578-8762. *Toll-free phone:* 800-333-CARLOW. *Fax:* 412-578-6668. *E-mail:* admissions@carlow.edu.

Carnegie Mellon University
Pittsburgh, Pennsylvania
http://www.cmu.edu/

- **Independent** university, founded 1900
- **Urban** 153-acre campus with easy access to Pittsburgh
- **Endowment** $1.7 billion
- **Coed** 6,896 undergraduate students, 97% full-time, 49% women, 51% men
- **Most difficult** entrance level, 22% of applicants were admitted

UNDERGRAD STUDENTS
6,664 full-time, 232 part-time. Students come from 50 states and territories; 57 other countries; 85% are from out of state; 4% Black or African American, non-Hispanic/Latino; 8% Hispanic/Latino; 29% Asian, non-Hispanic/Latino; 4% Two or more races, non-Hispanic/Latino; 5% Race/ethnicity unknown; 23% international; 0.4% transferred in; 60% live on campus.

Freshmen:
Admission: 20,497 applied, 4,550 admitted, 1,784 enrolled. *Average high school GPA:* 3.8. *Test scores:* SAT evidence-based reading and writing scores over 500: 100%; SAT math scores over 500: 100%; SAT evidence-based reading and writing scores over 600: 98%; SAT math scores over 600: 97%; ACT scores over 24: 99%; SAT evidence-based reading and writing scores over 700: 77%; SAT math scores over 700: 85%; ACT scores over 30: 86%.
Retention: 96% of full-time freshmen returned.

FACULTY
Total: 1,074, 95% full-time, 91% with terminal degrees.
Student/faculty ratio: 13:1.

ACADEMICS
Calendar: semesters. *Degrees:* bachelor's, master's, doctoral, post-master's, and postbachelor's certificates.
Special study options: accelerated degree program, advanced placement credit, cooperative education, distance learning, double majors, independent study, internships, off-campus study, part-time degree

program, services for LD students, student-designed majors, study abroad, summer session for credit. *ROTC:* Army (c), Navy (b), Air Force (c).

Unusual degree programs: 3-2 business administration; engineering; public management and policy.

Computers: 462 computers/terminals are available on campus for general student use. Students can access the following: campus intranet, computer help desk, free student e-mail accounts, online (class) grades, online (class) registration, online (class) schedules. Campuswide network is available. 100% of college-owned or -operated housing units are wired for high-speed Internet access. Wireless service is available via entire campus.

Library: Hunt Library plus 2 others. Weekly public service hours: 168; study areas open 24 hours, 5–7 days a week; students can reserve study rooms.

STUDENT LIFE
Housing options: on-campus residence required for freshman year; coed, men-only, women-only, special housing for students with disabilities. Campus housing is university owned. Freshman campus housing is guaranteed.

Activities and organizations: drama/theater group, student-run newspaper, radio station, choral group, marching band, national fraternities, national sororities.

Athletics Member NCAA. All Division III. *Intercollegiate sports:* baseball M(c), basketball M/W, cross-country running M/W, fencing M(c)/W(c), football M, golf M/W, ice hockey M(c)/W(c), lacrosse M(c)/W(c), rowing M(c)/W(c), rugby M(c)/W(c), skiing (downhill) M(c)/W(c), soccer M/W, swimming and diving M/W, tennis M/W, track and field M/W, ultimate Frisbee M(c)/W(c), volleyball M(c)/W, water polo M(c)/W(c). *Intramural sports:* badminton M/W, basketball M/W, racquetball M/W, soccer M/W, softball M/W, squash M/W, table tennis M/W, tennis M/W, ultimate Frisbee M/W, volleyball M/W, water polo M/W.

Campus security: 24-hour emergency response devices and patrols, late-night transport/escort service, controlled dormitory access, Safe Walk.

Student services: health clinic, personal/psychological counseling, legal services.

COSTS & FINANCIAL AID
Costs (2018–19) *Comprehensive fee:* $69,883 includes full-time tuition ($54,244), mandatory fees ($1221), and room and board ($14,418). Part-time tuition: $753 per unit. *College room only:* $8450. Room and board charges vary according to board plan and housing facility. *Payment plan:* installment. *Waivers:* employees or children of employees.

Financial Aid Of all full-time matriculated undergraduates who enrolled in 2017, 3,206 applied for aid, 2,603 were judged to have need, 1,739 had their need fully met. In 2017, 350 non-need-based awards were made. *Average percent of need met:* 94. *Average financial aid package:* $43,182. *Average need-based loan:* $6071. *Average need-based gift aid:* $37,531. *Average non-need-based aid:* $15,142. *Average indebtedness upon graduation:* $31,077.

APPLYING
Standardized Tests *Required:* SAT or ACT (for admission). *Recommended:* SAT Subject Tests (for admission).

Options: electronic application, early admission, early decision, deferred entrance.

Application fee: $75.

Required: essay or personal statement, high school transcript. *Required for some:* audition/portfolio for fine arts. *Recommended:* interview.

Application deadlines: 1/1 (freshmen), 2/15 (transfers).

Early decision deadline: 11/1.

Notification: 4/15 (freshmen), 5/15 (transfers), 12/15 (early decision).

CONTACT
Mr. Greg Edleman, Director of Admission, Carnegie Mellon University, 5000 Forbes Avenue, Pittsburgh, PA 15213. *Phone:* 412-268-2082. *Fax:* 412-268-7838. *E-mail:* admission@andrew.cmu.edu.

Cedar Crest College
Allentown, Pennsylvania
http://www.cedarcrest.edu/
- **Independent** comprehensive, founded 1867, affiliated with United Church of Christ
- **Suburban** 84-acre campus with easy access to Philadelphia
- **Coed, primarily women** 1,433 undergraduate students, 65% full-time, 88% women, 12% men
- **Moderately difficult** entrance level, 63% of applicants were admitted

UNDERGRAD STUDENTS
931 full-time, 502 part-time. 15% are from out of state; 9% Black or African American, non-Hispanic/Latino; 3% Hispanic/Latino; 9% Asian, non-Hispanic/Latino; 1% Native Hawaiian or other Pacific Islander, non-Hispanic/Latino; 0.1% American Indian or Alaska Native, non-Hispanic/Latino; 3% Two or more races, non-Hispanic/Latino; 59% Race/ethnicity unknown; 0.4% international; 3% transferred in; 32% live on campus.

Freshmen:
Admission: 1,208 applied, 765 admitted, 213 enrolled. *Average high school GPA:* 3.4. *Test scores:* SAT evidence-based reading and writing scores over 500: 70%; SAT math scores over 500: 61%; ACT scores over 18: 80%; SAT evidence-based reading and writing scores over 600: 26%; SAT math scores over 600: 15%; ACT scores over 24: 46%; SAT evidence-based reading and writing scores over 700: 3%; SAT math scores over 700: 2%; ACT scores over 30: 8%.

Retention: 82% of full-time freshmen returned.

FACULTY
Total: 221, 35% full-time, 43% with terminal degrees.

Student/faculty ratio: 10:1.

ACADEMICS
Calendar: semesters. *Degrees:* certificates, bachelor's, master's, post-master's, and postbachelor's certificates.

Special study options: academic remediation for entering students, advanced placement credit, double majors, honors programs, independent study, internships, off-campus study, part-time degree program, services for LD students, student-designed majors, summer session for credit.

Computers: Students can access the following: campus intranet, computer help desk, free student e-mail accounts, online (class) grades, online (class) registration, online (class) schedules. Campuswide network is available. 100% of college-owned or -operated housing units are wired for high-speed Internet access. Wireless service is available via entire campus.

Library: Frank M. Cressman Library.

STUDENT LIFE
Housing options: women-only. Campus housing is university owned. Freshman campus housing is guaranteed.

Activities and organizations: drama/theater group, student-run newspaper, radio station, choral group, Student Activities Board, Student Government Association, Commuter Awareness Board, Student Nurse Association, Forensic Student Science organization.

Athletics Member NCAA. All Division III. *Intercollegiate sports:* basketball W, cross-country running W, equestrian sports W(c), field hockey W, lacrosse W, soccer W, softball W, swimming and diving W, tennis W, track and field W(c), volleyball W. *Intramural sports:* badminton W, basketball W, soccer W, softball W, tennis W, volleyball W.

Campus security: 24-hour emergency response devices and patrols, late-night transport/escort service, controlled dormitory access, crime prevention programs.

Student services: health clinic, personal/psychological counseling.

COSTS & FINANCIAL AID
Costs (2018–19) *Comprehensive fee:* $50,760 includes full-time tuition ($38,616), mandatory fees ($600), and room and board ($11,544). Full-time tuition and fees vary according to class time, course load, and program. Part-time tuition and fees vary according to class time, course load, and program. *College room only:* $5420. Room and board charges vary according to board plan and housing facility. *Payment plans:* installment, deferred payment. *Waivers:* employees or children of employees.

Financial Aid Of all full-time matriculated undergraduates who enrolled in 2017, 693 applied for aid, 662 were judged to have need, 88 had their need fully met. In 2017, 4 non-need-based awards were made. *Average percent of need met:* 76. *Average financial aid package:* $29,602. *Average need-based loan:* $4519. *Average need-based gift aid:* $25,512. *Average non-need-based aid:* $19,374. *Average indebtedness upon graduation:* $44,032.

APPLYING
Standardized Tests *Required:* SAT or ACT (for admission).

Options: electronic application, early admission, deferred entrance.

Required: essay or personal statement, high school transcript. *Required for some:* 2 letters of recommendation. *Recommended:* minimum 2.0 GPA, interview.

Application deadlines: rolling (freshmen), rolling (transfers).

Notification: continuous (freshmen), continuous (transfers).

CONTACT
Mary Alice Ozechoski, Vice President of Student Affairs and Traditional Enrollment, Cedar Crest College, 100 College Drive, Allentown, PA 18104. *Phone:* 610-606-4666. *Toll-free phone:* 800-360-1222. *E-mail:* admissions@cedarcrest.edu.

Central Penn College

Summerdale, Pennsylvania
http://www.centralpenn.edu/

- **Proprietary** comprehensive, founded 1881
- **Small-town** 35-acre campus with easy access to Harrisburg
- **Coed** 1,196 undergraduate students, 26% full-time, 65% women, 35% men
- **Minimally difficult** entrance level, 79% of applicants were admitted

UNDERGRAD STUDENTS
316 full-time, 880 part-time. Students come from 19 states and territories; 5% are from out of state; 21% Black or African American, non-Hispanic/Latino; 4% Hispanic/Latino; 3% Asian, non-Hispanic/Latino; 0.3% Native Hawaiian or other Pacific Islander, non-Hispanic/Latino; 3% American Indian or Alaska Native, non-Hispanic/Latino; 3% Two or more races, non-Hispanic/Latino; 3% Race/ethnicity unknown; 0.7% international; 14% transferred in; 23% live on campus.

Freshmen:
Admission: 436 applied, 344 admitted, 164 enrolled.
Retention: 47% of full-time freshmen returned.

FACULTY
Total: 102, 43% full-time, 18% with terminal degrees.
Student/faculty ratio: 10:1.

ACADEMICS
Calendar: quarters. *Degrees:* associate, bachelor's, and master's.

Special study options: academic remediation for entering students, adult/continuing education programs, advanced placement credit, distance learning, honors programs, independent study, internships, part-time degree program, services for LD students, summer session for credit.

Computers: 100 computers/terminals are available on campus for general student use. Students can access the following: campus intranet, computer help desk, free student e-mail accounts, online (class) grades, online (class) registration, online (class) schedules. Campuswide network is available. 100% of college-owned or -operated housing units are wired for high-speed Internet access. Wireless service is available via entire campus.

Library: Charles T Jones Leadership Library plus 1 other. *Books:* 24,566 (physical), 140,336 (digital/electronic); *Serial titles:* 67 (physical), 2 (digital/electronic); *Databases:* 34. Weekly public service hours: 74.

STUDENT LIFE
Housing options: coed, men-only, women-only, special housing for students with disabilities. Campus housing is university owned. Freshman applicants given priority for college housing.

Activities and organizations: drama/theater group, student-run newspaper, PTA Club, Student Government Association, Central Penn Players, Student Ambassadors, Colleges Against Cancer.

Athletics Member USCAA. *Intercollegiate sports:* baseball M, basketball M/W, cross-country running M/W, soccer M/W, volleyball W. *Intramural sports:* basketball M/W, cheerleading W, football M/W, sand volleyball M/W, soccer M/W.

Campus security: 24-hour emergency response devices and patrols, student patrols, late-night transport/escort service, controlled dormitory access.

Student services: personal/psychological counseling.

COSTS & FINANCIAL AID
Costs (2018–19) *One-time required fee:* $100. *Comprehensive fee:* $26,130 includes full-time tuition ($17,784), mandatory fees ($930), and room and board ($7416). Part-time tuition: $494 per credit hour. *Required fees:* $310 per term part-time. *College room only:* $5346. Room and board charges vary according to board plan and housing facility. *Payment plan:* installment. *Waivers:* employees or children of employees.

Financial Aid *Financial aid deadline:* 5/1.

APPLYING
Standardized Tests *Required for some:* SAT or ACT (for admission).

Options: electronic application.

Required: high school transcript, minimum 2.0 GPA. *Required for some:* 1 letter of recommendation, interview. *Recommended:* essay or personal statement, 1 letter of recommendation.

Application deadlines: rolling (freshmen), rolling (transfers).

Notification: continuous (freshmen), continuous (transfers).

CONTACT
Central Penn College, College Hill & Valley Roads, Summerdale, PA 17093-0309. *Toll-free phone:* 800-759-2727.

Chatham University

Pittsburgh, Pennsylvania
http://www.chatham.edu/

- **Independent** university, founded 1869
- **Urban** 427-acre campus
- **Endowment** $77.7 million
- **Coed, primarily women** 1,208 undergraduate students, 79% full-time, 76% women, 24% men
- **Moderately difficult** entrance level, 55% of applicants were admitted

UNDERGRAD STUDENTS
951 full-time, 257 part-time. Students come from 39 states and territories; 25 other countries; 21% are from out of state; 5% Black or African American, non-Hispanic/Latino; 3% Hispanic/Latino; 2% Asian, non-Hispanic/Latino; 0.2% Native Hawaiian or other Pacific Islander, non-Hispanic/Latino; 0.4% American Indian or Alaska Native, non-Hispanic/Latino; 1% Two or more races, non-Hispanic/Latino; 17% Race/ethnicity unknown; 6% international; 7% transferred in; 60% live on campus.

Freshmen:
Admission: 2,231 applied, 1,217 admitted, 284 enrolled. *Average high school GPA:* 3.7. *Test scores:* SAT evidence-based reading and writing scores over 500: 93%; SAT math scores over 500: 85%; ACT scores over 18: 98%; SAT evidence-based reading and writing scores over 600: 46%; SAT math scores over 600: 28%; ACT scores over 24: 54%; SAT evidence-based reading and writing scores over 700: 6%; SAT math scores over 700: 1%; ACT scores over 30: 9%.
Retention: 85% of full-time freshmen returned.

FACULTY
Total: 339, 35% full-time, 54% with terminal degrees.
Student/faculty ratio: 10:1.

ACADEMICS
Calendar: 4-4-1. *Degrees:* bachelor's, master's, doctoral, post-master's, and postbachelor's certificates.

Special study options: accelerated degree program, adult/continuing education programs, advanced placement credit, cooperative education, distance learning, double majors, English as a second language, honors programs, independent study, internships, off-campus study, part-time degree program, services for LD students, student-designed majors, study abroad, summer session for credit. *ROTC:* Army (c), Navy (c), Air Force (c).

Unusual degree programs: 3-2 business administration; engineering with Carnegie Mellon University, Penn State University, University of Pittsburgh; nursing; social work; arts management with Carnegie Mellon, biology, counseling psychology, film/digital technology, leadership/organizational transformation, occupational therapy, physician assistant studies, business, teaching, writing and creative writing, architecture (landscape and interior), global/public policy.

Computers: 202 computers/terminals and 500 ports are available on campus for general student use. Students can access the following: campus intranet, computer help desk, free student e-mail accounts, online (class) grades, online (class) registration, online (class) schedules. Campuswide network is available. 100% of college-owned or -operated housing units are wired for high-speed Internet access. Wireless service is available via entire campus.

Library: Jennie King Mellon Library. *Books:* 88,368 (physical), 1,200 (digital/electronic); *Serial titles:* 92 (physical), 32,874 (digital/electronic); *Databases:* 65. Weekly public service hours: 99; study areas open 24 hours, 5–7 days a week; students can reserve study rooms.

STUDENT LIFE
Housing options: on-campus residence required through sophomore year; coed, women-only. Campus housing is university owned. Freshman campus housing is guaranteed.

Activities and organizations: drama/theater group, student-run newspaper, choral group, Chatham Student Government, Residence Hall Council, Student Athletic Advisory Council (SAAC), Creative Writing Club and MFA Writing Council, Graduate Student Assembly.

Athletics Member NCAA. All Division III. *Intercollegiate sports:* baseball M, basketball M/W, cross-country running M/W, ice hockey M/W, lacrosse M/W, soccer W, softball W, swimming and diving M/W, track and field M/W, volleyball W. *Intramural sports:* basketball W, bowling M/W, cheerleading M/W, soccer M/W, squash M/W, volleyball M/W.

Campus security: 24-hour emergency response devices and patrols, late-night transport/escort service, controlled dormitory access, self-defense education, well-lighted pathways and sidewalks.

Student services: health clinic, personal/psychological counseling, women's center.

COSTS & FINANCIAL AID
Costs (2018–19) *Comprehensive fee:* $49,701 includes full-time tuition ($36,276), mandatory fees ($1335), and room and board ($12,090). Part-time tuition: $880 per credit hour. Part-time tuition and fees vary according to course load. *College room only:* $6240. Room and board charges vary according to board plan and housing facility. *Payment plan:* installment. *Waivers:* employees or children of employees.

Financial Aid Of all full-time matriculated undergraduates who enrolled in 2017, 865 applied for aid, 812 were judged to have need, 109 had their need fully met. 338 Federal Work-Study jobs (averaging $2200). In 2017, 89 non-need-based awards were made. *Average percent of need met:* 63. *Average financial aid package:* $26,138. *Average need-based loan:* $3963. *Average need-based gift aid:* $9112. *Average non-need-based aid:* $16,089. *Average indebtedness upon graduation:* $35,303.

APPLYING
Options: electronic application, early admission, deferred entrance.

Application fee: $35.

Required: essay or personal statement, high school transcript, minimum 2.0 GPA, 1 letter of recommendation. *Recommended:* interview.

Application deadlines: 8/1 (freshmen), rolling (transfers).

Notification: continuous (freshmen), continuous (transfers).

CONTACT
Ms. Amy M. Becher, Vice President for Enrollment Management, Chatham University, Woodland, Berry Hall, Pittsburgh, PA 15232. *Phone:* 800-837-1290. *Toll-free phone:* 800-837-1290. *Fax:* 412-365-1609. *E-mail:* admission@chatham.edu.

Chestnut Hill College
Philadelphia, Pennsylvania
http://www.chc.edu/
- **Independent Roman Catholic** comprehensive, founded 1924
- **Suburban** 75-acre campus with easy access to Philadelphia
- **Endowment** $9.4 million
- **Coed** 1,364 undergraduate students, 82% full-time, 63% women, 37% men
- **Moderately difficult** entrance level, 96% of applicants were admitted

UNDERGRAD STUDENTS
1,118 full-time, 246 part-time. Students come from 27 states and territories; 39 other countries; 22% are from out of state; 34% Black or African American, non-Hispanic/Latino; 9% Hispanic/Latino; 2% Asian, non-Hispanic/Latino; 0.1% Native Hawaiian or other Pacific Islander, non-Hispanic/Latino; 0.1% American Indian or Alaska Native, non-Hispanic/Latino; 4% Two or more races, non-Hispanic/Latino; 11% Race/ethnicity unknown; 2% international; 5% transferred in; 52% live on campus.

Freshmen:
Admission: 1,286 applied, 1,231 admitted, 207 enrolled. *Average high school GPA:* 3.2. *Test scores:* ACT scores over 18: 65%; ACT scores over 24: 11%; ACT scores over 30: 2%.

Retention: 79% of full-time freshmen returned.

FACULTY
Total: 297, 28% full-time, 44% with terminal degrees.

Student/faculty ratio: 10:1.

ACADEMICS
Calendar: semesters. *Degrees:* certificates, associate, bachelor's, master's, doctoral, post-master's, and postbachelor's certificates (profile includes figures from both traditional and accelerated (part-time) programs).

Special study options: academic remediation for entering students, accelerated degree program, adult/continuing education programs, advanced placement credit, cooperative education, double majors, English as a second language, honors programs, independent study, internships, off-campus study, part-time degree program, services for LD students, student-designed majors, study abroad, summer session for credit.

Unusual degree programs: 3-2 computer science/instructional technology, early education, biology/chemistry with Thomas Jefferson University; biology/chemistry and physician assistant with Arcadia University; human services administration; counseling psychology; international business, language, and culture.

Computers: 70 computers/terminals and 150 ports are available on campus for general student use. Students can access the following: campus intranet, computer help desk, free student e-mail accounts, online (class) grades, online (class) registration, online (class) schedules. Campuswide network is available. 90% of college-owned or -operated housing units are wired for high-speed Internet access. Wireless service is available via classrooms, dorm rooms.

Library: Logue Library. *Books:* 120,908 (physical), 226,691 (digital/electronic); *Serial titles:* 670 (physical), 271,184 (digital/electronic); *Databases:* 433. Weekly public service hours: 99; students can reserve study rooms.

STUDENT LIFE
Housing options: coed. Campus housing is university owned and leased by the school.

Activities and organizations: drama/theater group, student-run newspaper, radio and television station, choral group, Student Government, Mask and Foil Drama Club, Association for Musical Performance, Campus Ministry Community Service Group, Business Club.

Athletics Member NCAA. All Division II. *Intercollegiate sports:* baseball M(s), basketball M(s)/W(s), bowling W(s), cross-country running M(s)/W(s), football M(s)(c), golf M(s)(c)/W(c), lacrosse M(s)/W(s), soccer M(s)/W(s), softball W(s), tennis M(s)/W(s), track and field M(s)/W(s), volleyball W(s).

Campus security: 24-hour emergency response devices and patrols, late-night transport/escort service, controlled dormitory access.

Student services: health clinic, personal/psychological counseling.

COSTS & FINANCIAL AID

Costs (2018–19) *One-time required fee:* $475. *Comprehensive fee:* $47,180 includes full-time tuition ($35,950), mandatory fees ($230), and room and board ($11,000). Part-time tuition: $745 per credit hour. Part-time tuition and fees vary according to class time. *Required fees:* $230 per year part-time. *Room and board:* Room and board charges vary according to housing facility. *Payment plans:* installment, deferred payment. *Waivers:* senior citizens and employees or children of employees.

Financial Aid Of all full-time matriculated undergraduates who enrolled in 2017, 885 applied for aid, 885 were judged to have need, 262 had their need fully met. In 2017, 133 non-need-based awards were made. *Average percent of need met:* 92. *Average financial aid package:* $24,523. *Average need-based loan:* $4468. *Average need-based gift aid:* $8336. *Average non-need-based aid:* $14,146. *Average indebtedness upon graduation:* $42,527. *Financial aid deadline:* 6/30.

APPLYING

Standardized Tests *Required:* SAT or ACT (for admission).

Options: electronic application, deferred entrance.

Application fee: $35.

Required: high school transcript. *Required for some:* interview. *Recommended:* essay or personal statement, .

Application deadlines: rolling (freshmen), rolling (transfers).

Notification: continuous (freshmen), continuous (transfers).

CONTACT

Ms. Stephanie Williams, Chestnut Hill College, 9601 Germantown Avenue, Philadelphia, PA 19118-2693. *Phone:* 215-248-7001. *Toll-free phone:* 800-248-0052. *Fax:* 215-248-7082. *E-mail:* williamss@chc.edu.

Cheyney University of Pennsylvania

Cheyney, Pennsylvania

http://www.cheyney.edu/

CONTACT

Shon Jeffery, Associate Director of Enrollment Management, Cheyney University of Pennsylvania, 1837 University Circle, PO Box 200, Cheyney, PA 19319. *Phone:* 610-399-2255. *Toll-free phone:* 800-CHEYNEY. *E-mail:* spjeffery@cheyney.edu.

Clarion University of Pennsylvania

Clarion, Pennsylvania

http://www.clarion.edu/

- **State-supported** comprehensive, founded 1867, part of Pennsylvania State System of Higher Education
- **Rural** 201-acre campus
- **Endowment** $34.9 million
- **Coed** 4,321 undergraduate students, 81% full-time, 64% women, 36% men

UNDERGRAD STUDENTS

3,481 full-time, 840 part-time. Students come from 38 states and territories; 8 other countries; 8% are from out of state; 8% Black or African American, non-Hispanic/Latino; 3% Hispanic/Latino; 0.9% Asian, non-Hispanic/Latino; 0.1% Native Hawaiian or other Pacific Islander, non-Hispanic/Latino; 0.1% American Indian or Alaska Native, non-Hispanic/Latino; 3% Two or more races, non-Hispanic/Latino; 4% Race/ethnicity unknown; 0.3% international; 8% transferred in; 42% live on campus.

Freshmen:

Admission: 875 enrolled. *Average high school GPA:* 3.3. *Test scores:* SAT evidence-based reading and writing scores over 500: 62%; SAT math scores over 500: 59%; ACT scores over 18: 76%; SAT evidence-based reading and writing scores over 600: 15%; SAT math scores over 600: 9%; ACT scores over 24: 20%; SAT evidence-based reading and writing scores over 700: 1%; SAT math scores over 700: 1%; ACT scores over 30: 3%.

Retention: 74% of full-time freshmen returned.

FACULTY

Total: 294, 69% full-time.

Student/faculty ratio: 18:1.

ACADEMICS

Calendar: semesters. *Degrees:* certificates, associate, bachelor's, master's, doctoral, post-master's, and postbachelor's certificates.

Special study options: academic remediation for entering students, accelerated degree program, adult/continuing education programs, advanced placement credit, cooperative education, distance learning, double majors, English as a second language, honors programs, independent study, internships, off-campus study, part-time degree program, services for LD students, study abroad, summer session for credit. *ROTC:* Army (b).

Unusual degree programs: 3-2 engineering with University of Pittsburgh, Case Western Reserve University.

Computers: 950 computers/terminals and 24 ports are available on campus for general student use. Students can access the following: campus intranet, computer help desk, free student e-mail accounts, online (class) grades, online (class) registration, online (class) schedules, Online Learning Management System, web-based personal disk space, other online student services (financial aid, billing etc.). Campuswide network is available. 100% of college-owned or -operated housing units are wired for high-speed Internet access. Wireless service is available via entire campus.

Library: Carlson Library plus 1 other. *Books:* 447,921 (physical), 250,647 (digital/electronic); *Serial titles:* 177 (physical), 53,762 (digital/electronic); *Databases:* 102. Weekly public service hours: 94; students can reserve study rooms.

STUDENT LIFE

Housing options: on-campus residence required through sophomore year; coed, special housing for students with disabilities. Campus housing is university owned. Freshman campus housing is guaranteed.

Activities and organizations: drama/theater group, student-run newspaper, radio and television station, choral group, marching band, The National Student Speech-Language Hearing Association, Phi Eta Sigma freshman honor society, Allies, Black Student Union, Cru, national fraternities, national sororities.

Athletics Member NCAA. All Division II except wrestling (Division I). *Intercollegiate sports:* baseball M(s), basketball M(s)/W(s), cross-country running W(s), football M(s), golf M(s)/W(s), soccer W(s), softball W(s), swimming and diving M(s)/W(s), tennis W(s), track and field W(s), volleyball W, wrestling M(s). *Intramural sports:* badminton M/W, basketball M/W, equestrian sports M(c)/W(c), golf M/W, racquetball M/W, rock climbing M(c)/W(c), rugby M(c)/W(c), sand volleyball M/W, soccer M/W, softball M/W, table tennis M/W, tennis M/W, track and field M(c)/W(c), ultimate Frisbee M(c)/W(c), volleyball M/W, weight lifting M/W, wrestling M/W.

Campus security: 24-hour emergency response devices and patrols, student patrols, late-night transport/escort service, controlled dormitory access.

Student services: health clinic, personal/psychological counseling, women's center.

COSTS & FINANCIAL AID

Costs (2017–18) *One-time required fee:* $50. *Tuition:* state resident $7492 full-time, $312 per credit hour part-time; nonresident $11,238 full-time, $468 per credit hour part-time. Full-time tuition and fees vary according to course load, location, and program. Part-time tuition and fees vary according to location and program. *Required fees:* $3398 full-time. *Room and board:* $11,058; room only: $7350. Room and board charges vary according to board plan and housing facility. *Payment plans:* installment, deferred payment. *Waivers:* senior citizens and employees or children of employees.

Financial Aid Of all full-time matriculated undergraduates who enrolled in 2017, 3,198 applied for aid, 2,837 were judged to have need, 134 had their need fully met. 299 Federal Work-Study jobs (averaging $1085). 734 state and other part-time jobs (averaging $1329). In 2017, 202 non-need-based awards were made. *Average percent of need met:* 43. *Average financial aid package:* $9478. *Average need-based loan:* $4173. *Average need-based gift aid:* $5628. *Average non-need-based aid:* $2177. *Average indebtedness upon graduation:* $35,277.

APPLYING

Standardized Tests *Required:* SAT or ACT (for admission). *Required for some:* TOEFL, TSE or IELTS for international students.

Required: high school transcript, minimum 2.0 GPA. *Required for some:* essay or personal statement, interview, NLN Test for ASN program. *Recommended:* essay or personal statement, 2 letters of recommendation, interview.

CONTACT

Clarion University of Pennsylvania, 840 Wood Street, Clarion, PA 16214. *Phone:* 814-393-2306. *Toll-free phone:* 800-672-7171.

Clarks Summit University

South Abington Township, Pennsylvania
http://www.clarkssummitu.edu/

CONTACT

Ms. Kellyn Lovell, Supervisor, Support Services, Clarks Summit University, 538 Venard Road, Clarks Summit, PA 18411-1297. *Phone:* 800-451-7664. *Toll-free phone:* 800-451-7664. *Fax:* 570-585-9271. *E-mail:* admissions@bbc.edu.

Curtis Institute of Music

Philadelphia, Pennsylvania
http://www.curtis.edu/

CONTACT

Mr. Christopher Hodges, Admissions Officer, Curtis Institute of Music, 1726 Locust Street, Philadelphia, PA 19103-6107. *Phone:* 215-893-5262. *E-mail:* chris.hodges@curtis.edu.

Delaware Valley University

Doylestown, Pennsylvania
http://www.delval.edu/

- **Independent** comprehensive, founded 1896
- **Suburban** 571-acre campus with easy access to Philadelphia
- **Endowment** $32.4 million
- **Coed** 1,992 undergraduate students, 88% full-time, 60% women, 40% men
- **Minimally difficult** entrance level, 66% of applicants were admitted

UNDERGRAD STUDENTS

1,756 full-time, 236 part-time. Students come from 26 states and territories; 7 other countries; 38% are from out of state; 9% Black or African American, non-Hispanic/Latino; 8% Hispanic/Latino; 2% Asian, non-Hispanic/Latino; 0.2% Native Hawaiian or other Pacific Islander, non-Hispanic/Latino; 0.6% American Indian or Alaska Native, non-Hispanic/Latino; 1% Two or more races, non-Hispanic/Latino; 10% Race/ethnicity unknown; 0.8% international; 7% transferred in; 66% live on campus.

Freshmen:

Admission: 2,405 applied, 1,597 admitted, 412 enrolled. *Average high school GPA:* 3.3. *Test scores:* SAT evidence-based reading and writing scores over 500: 72%; SAT math scores over 500: 70%; ACT scores over 18: 86%; SAT evidence-based reading and writing scores over 600: 25%; SAT math scores over 600: 16%; ACT scores over 24: 36%; SAT evidence-based reading and writing scores over 700: 1%; SAT math scores over 700: 1%; ACT scores over 30: 4%.

Retention: 71% of full-time freshmen returned.

FACULTY

Total: 266, 35% full-time, 24% with terminal degrees.

Student/faculty ratio: 14:1.

ACADEMICS

Calendar: semesters. *Degrees:* certificates, bachelor's, master's, doctoral, and postbachelor's certificates.

Special study options: academic remediation for entering students, accelerated degree program, adult/continuing education programs, advanced placement credit, cooperative education, distance learning, double majors, honors programs, independent study, internships, part-time degree program, services for LD students, study abroad, summer session for credit.

Computers: 160 computers/terminals are available on campus for general student use. Students can access the following: campus intranet, computer help desk, free student e-mail accounts, online (class) grades, online (class) registration, online (class) schedules. Campuswide network is available. 100% of college-owned or -operated housing units are wired for high-speed Internet access. Wireless service is available via entire campus.

Library: Joseph Krauskopf Memorial Library. *Books:* 45,855 (physical), 7,258 (digital/electronic); *Serial titles:* 79 (physical), 104,133 (digital/electronic); *Databases:* 51. Weekly public service hours: 92.

STUDENT LIFE

Housing options: coed, special housing for students with disabilities. Campus housing is university owned. Freshman campus housing is guaranteed.

Activities and organizations: drama/theater group, choral group, Dairy Society, Pre-Vet club, Equestrian Team, American Association of Zookeepers, FFA, national fraternities, national sororities.

Athletics Member NCAA. All Division III. *Intercollegiate sports:* baseball M, basketball M/W, cross-country running M/W, equestrian sports W, field hockey W, football M, golf M/W, lacrosse M/W, soccer M/W, softball W, tennis M/W, track and field M/W, volleyball W, wrestling M. *Intramural sports:* basketball M/W, cheerleading W, soccer M/W, softball M/W, volleyball M/W.

Campus security: 24-hour emergency response devices and patrols, late-night transport/escort service, controlled dormitory access.

Student services: health clinic, personal/psychological counseling.

COSTS & FINANCIAL AID

Costs (2017–18) *Comprehensive fee:* $51,950 includes full-time tuition ($35,610), mandatory fees ($2390), and room and board ($13,950). Full-time tuition and fees vary according to class time and program. Part-time tuition: $982 per credit hour. Part-time tuition and fees vary according to class time, course load, and program. *Required fees:* $116 per course part-time. *College room only:* $6648. Room and board charges vary according to board plan and housing facility. *Payment plan:* installment. *Waivers:* employees or children of employees.

Financial Aid Of all full-time matriculated undergraduates who enrolled in 2017, 1,552 applied for aid, 1,413 were judged to have need, 129 had their need fully met. 150 Federal Work-Study jobs (averaging $1642). In 2017, 312 non-need-based awards were made. *Average percent of need met:* 66. *Average financial aid package:* $27,782. *Average need-based loan:* $4578. *Average need-based gift aid:* $23,360. *Average non-need-based aid:* $18,122. *Average indebtedness upon graduation:* $45,953.

APPLYING

Standardized Tests *Required:* SAT or ACT (for admission). *Required for some:* TOEFL.

Options: electronic application, deferred entrance.

Application fee: $50.

Required: essay or personal statement, high school transcript, 1 letter of recommendation. *Recommended:* interview.

Application deadlines: rolling (freshmen), rolling (out-of-state freshmen), rolling (transfers).

Notification: continuous (freshmen), continuous (out-of-state freshmen), continuous (transfers).

CONTACT

Mr. Dwayne Walker, Interim Vice President for Enrollment Management and Director of Admissions, Delaware Valley University, 700 E. Butler Avenue, Doylestown, PA 18901. *Phone:* 215-489-2372. *Toll-free phone:* 800-2DELVAL. *Fax:* 215-230-2968. *E-mail:* dwayne.walker@delval.edu.

DeSales University
Center Valley, Pennsylvania
http://www.desales.edu/

- **Independent Roman Catholic** comprehensive, founded 1964
- **Suburban** 480-acre campus with easy access to Philadelphia, PA
- **Endowment** $80.1 million
- **Coed** 2,345 undergraduate students, 77% full-time, 61% women, 39% men
- **Moderately difficult** entrance level, 74% of applicants were admitted

UNDERGRAD STUDENTS
1,811 full-time, 534 part-time. Students come from 29 states and territories; 3 other countries; 24% are from out of state; 5% Black or African American, non-Hispanic/Latino; 14% Hispanic/Latino; 3% Asian, non-Hispanic/Latino; 3% Two or more races, non-Hispanic/Latino; 5% Race/ethnicity unknown; 0.1% international; 3% transferred in; 46% live on campus.

Freshmen:
Admission: 3,033 applied, 2,238 admitted, 475 enrolled. *Average high school GPA:* 3.3. *Test scores:* SAT evidence-based reading and writing scores over 500: 81%; SAT math scores over 500: 77%; ACT scores over 18: 95%; SAT evidence-based reading and writing scores over 600: 37%; SAT math scores over 600: 30%; ACT scores over 24: 65%; SAT evidence-based reading and writing scores over 700: 6%; SAT math scores over 700: 4%; ACT scores over 30: 10%.
Retention: 81% of full-time freshmen returned.

FACULTY
Total: 346, 36% full-time.
Student/faculty ratio: 12:1.

ACADEMICS
Calendar: semesters. *Degrees:* certificates, bachelor's, master's, doctoral, post-master's, and postbachelor's certificates.

Special study options: academic remediation for entering students, accelerated degree program, adult/continuing education programs, advanced placement credit, cooperative education, distance learning, double majors, external degree program, honors programs, independent study, internships, off-campus study, part-time degree program, services for LD students, student-designed majors, study abroad, summer session for credit. *ROTC:* Army (c).

Unusual degree programs: 3-2 medical studies/physician assistant studies.

Computers: 245 computers/terminals are available on campus for general student use. Students can access the following: campus intranet, computer help desk, free student e-mail accounts, online (class) grades, online (class) registration, online (class) schedules. Campuswide network is available. 100% of college-owned or -operated housing units are wired for high-speed Internet access. Wireless service is available via entire campus.

Library: Trexler Library. *Books:* 155,243 (physical), 135,000 (digital/electronic); *Serial titles:* 260 (physical), 19,000 (digital/electronic); *Databases:* 87. Weekly public service hours: 102; students can reserve study rooms.

STUDENT LIFE
Housing options: coed, men-only, women-only, special housing for students with disabilities. Campus housing is university owned. Freshman campus housing is guaranteed.

Activities and organizations: drama/theater group, student-run newspaper, radio and television station, choral group, marching band, College Against Cancer, Outdoor Adventure Club, Student Nursing Association, Criminal Justice Association, Natural Science Club.

Athletics Member NCAA. All Division III. *Intercollegiate sports:* baseball M, basketball M/W, cross-country running M/W, field hockey W, golf M, lacrosse M, soccer M/W, softball W, tennis M/W, track and field M/W, volleyball W. *Intramural sports:* cheerleading M(c)/W(c), ice hockey M(c), rugby M(c), swimming and diving M(c)/W(c), tennis M(c)/W(c), volleyball M(c).

Campus security: 24-hour emergency response devices and patrols, late-night transport/escort service, controlled dormitory access.

Student services: health clinic, personal/psychological counseling.

COSTS & FINANCIAL AID
Costs (2017–18) *Comprehensive fee:* $48,900 includes full-time tuition ($34,500), mandatory fees ($1600), and room and board ($12,800). Full-time tuition and fees vary according to class time and course load. Part-time tuition: $1440 per credit hour. Part-time tuition and fees vary according to class time and course load. *Room and board:* Room and board charges vary according to board plan and housing facility. *Payment plans:* installment, deferred payment. *Waivers:* adult students, senior citizens, and employees or children of employees.

Financial Aid Of all full-time matriculated undergraduates who enrolled in 2017, 1,550 applied for aid, 1,394 were judged to have need, 292 had their need fully met. 440 Federal Work-Study jobs (averaging $1988). 329 state and other part-time jobs (averaging $1997). In 2017, 347 non-need-based awards were made. *Average percent of need met:* 72. *Average financial aid package:* $25,821. *Average need-based loan:* $4671. *Average need-based gift aid:* $20,163. *Average non-need-based aid:* $16,682. *Average indebtedness upon graduation:* $42,536.

APPLYING
Standardized Tests *Required:* SAT or ACT (for admission).

Options: electronic application, early admission, deferred entrance.

Required: essay or personal statement, high school transcript, letters of recommendation. *Recommended:* interview.

Notification: continuous until 10/6 (freshmen).

CONTACT
Mr. Derrick Wetzel, Director of Admissions, DeSales University, 2755 Station Avenue, Center Valley, PA 18034-9568. *Phone:* 610-282-4443. *Fax:* 610-282-0131. *E-mail:* derrick.wetzell@desales.edu.

DeVry University–Ft. Washington Campus
Fort Washington, Pennsylvania
http://www.devry.edu/

CONTACT
DeVry University–Ft. Washington Campus, 1140 Virginia Drive, Fort Washington, PA 19034. *Phone:* 215-591-5700. *Toll-free phone:* 866-338-7934.

Dickinson College
Carlisle, Pennsylvania
http://www.dickinson.edu/

- **Independent** 4-year, founded 1773
- **Suburban** 144-acre campus with easy access to Harrisburg
- **Endowment** $412.8 million
- **Coed** 2,382 undergraduate students, 98% full-time, 58% women, 42% men
- **Very difficult** entrance level, 49% of applicants were admitted

UNDERGRAD STUDENTS
2,346 full-time, 36 part-time. Students come from 40 states and territories; 44 other countries; 79% are from out of state; 5% Black or African American, non-Hispanic/Latino; 8% Hispanic/Latino; 4% Asian, non-Hispanic/Latino; 0.1% Native Hawaiian or other Pacific Islander, non-Hispanic/Latino; 0.1% American Indian or Alaska Native, non-Hispanic/Latino; 4% Two or more races, non-Hispanic/Latino; 0.9% Race/ethnicity unknown; 13% international; 0.3% transferred in; 95% live on campus.

Freshmen:
Admission: 5,941 applied, 2,894 admitted, 607 enrolled. *Test scores:* SAT evidence-based reading and writing scores over 500: 100%; SAT math scores over 500: 99%; ACT scores over 18: 100%; SAT evidence-based reading and writing scores over 600: 88%; SAT math scores over 600: 82%; ACT scores over 24: 96%; SAT evidence-based reading and writing scores over 700: 27%; SAT math scores over 700: 33%; ACT scores over 30: 51%.
Retention: 90% of full-time freshmen returned.

FACULTY
Total: 283, 80% full-time, 88% with terminal degrees.
Student/faculty ratio: 9:1.

ACADEMICS

Calendar: semesters. *Degree:* bachelor's.

Special study options: accelerated degree program, adult/continuing education programs, advanced placement credit, double majors, English as a second language, independent study, internships, off-campus study, part-time degree program, services for LD students, student-designed majors, study abroad. *ROTC:* Army (b).

Unusual degree programs: 3-2 engineering with Case Western Reserve University, Rensselaer Polytechnic Institute, Columbia University; international studies with Johns Hopkins University.

Computers: 1,750 computers/terminals and 5,000 ports are available on campus for general student use. Students can access the following: campus intranet, computer help desk, free student e-mail accounts, online (class) grades, online (class) registration, online (class) schedules. Campuswide network is available. 100% of college-owned or -operated housing units are wired for high-speed Internet access. Wireless service is available via classrooms, computer centers, computer labs, dorm rooms, libraries, student centers.

Library: Waidner-Spahr Library. *Books:* 526,367 (physical), 667,635 (digital/electronic); *Serial titles:* 3,846 (physical), 93,067 (digital/electronic); *Databases:* 504. Weekly public service hours: 114; students can reserve study rooms.

STUDENT LIFE

Housing options: on-campus residence required through senior year; coed, special housing for students with disabilities. Campus housing is university owned. Freshman campus housing is guaranteed.

Activities and organizations: drama/theater group, student-run newspaper, radio station, choral group, Multi-Organization Board, Outing Club, Student Senate, Admissions Volunteers, WDCV Radio Station, national fraternities, national sororities.

Athletics Member NCAA. All Division III. *Intercollegiate sports:* baseball M, basketball M/W, cheerleading M(c)/W(c), cross-country running M/W, equestrian sports M(c)/W(c), fencing M(c)/W(c), field hockey W, football M, golf M/W, ice hockey M(c)/W(c), lacrosse M/W, rock climbing M(c)/W(c), skiing (downhill) M(c)/W(c), soccer M/W, softball W, squash M/W, swimming and diving M/W, tennis M/W, track and field M/W, ultimate Frisbee M(c)/W(c), volleyball M(c)/W. *Intramural sports:* badminton M/W, basketball M/W, field hockey M/W, football M/W, lacrosse M(c)/W(c), racquetball M/W, sand volleyball M/W, soccer M/W, softball M, squash M/W, tennis M/W, volleyball M/W.

Campus security: 24-hour emergency response devices and patrols, student patrols, late-night transport/escort service, controlled dormitory access.

Student services: health clinic, personal/psychological counseling, women's center.

COSTS & FINANCIAL AID

Costs (2017–18) *One-time required fee:* $25. *Comprehensive fee:* $66,166 includes full-time tuition ($52,480), mandatory fees ($450), and room and board ($13,236). Part-time tuition: $6560 per course. *Required fees:* $56 per course part-time. *College room only:* $6826. Room and board charges vary according to board plan and housing facility. *Payment plan:* installment. *Waivers:* senior citizens and employees or children of employees.

Financial Aid Of all full-time matriculated undergraduates who enrolled in 2017, 1,428 applied for aid, 1,331 were judged to have need, 1,020 had their need fully met. 992 Federal Work-Study jobs (averaging $2277). 217 state and other part-time jobs (averaging $3678). In 2017, 359 non-need-based awards were made. *Average percent of need met:* 98. *Average financial aid package:* $45,710. *Average need-based loan:* $4933. *Average need-based gift aid:* $39,595. *Average non-need-based aid:* $10,287. *Average indebtedness upon graduation:* $25,881. *Financial aid deadline:* 1/15.

APPLYING

Standardized Tests *Recommended:* SAT or ACT (for admission).

Options: electronic application, early decision, early action, deferred entrance.

Application fee: $65.

Required: essay or personal statement, high school transcript, 2 letters of recommendation. *Recommended:* minimum 3.0 GPA, interview.

Application deadlines: 1/15 (freshmen), 4/1 (transfers), 12/1 (early action).

Early decision deadline: 11/15 (for plan 1), 1/15 (for plan 2).

Notification: 3/23 (freshmen), continuous until 5/15 (transfers), 12/15 (early decision plan 1), 2/15 (early decision plan 2), 2/15 (early action).

CONTACT

Catherine Davenport, Dean of Admissions, Dickinson College, PO Box 1773, Admissions Office, Carlisle, PA 17013-2896. *Phone:* 717-245-1231. *Toll-free phone:* 800-644-1773. *Fax:* 717-245-1442. *E-mail:* admissions@dickinson.edu.

★ Drexel University
Philadelphia, Pennsylvania
http://www.drexel.edu/

- **Independent** university, founded 1891
- **Urban** 96-acre campus with easy access to Philadelphia
- **Endowment** $650.3 million
- **Coed** 15,498 undergraduate students, 88% full-time, 48% women, 52% men
- **Moderately difficult** entrance level, 79% of applicants were admitted

UNDERGRAD STUDENTS

13,569 full-time, 1,929 part-time. Students come from 48 states and territories; 117 other countries; 48% are from out of state; 7% Black or African American, non-Hispanic/Latino; 6% Hispanic/Latino; 16% Asian, non-Hispanic/Latino; 0.4% Native Hawaiian or other Pacific Islander, non-Hispanic/Latino; 0.1% American Indian or Alaska Native, non-Hispanic/Latino; 4% Two or more races, non-Hispanic/Latino; 2% Race/ethnicity unknown; 12% international; 5% transferred in; 22% live on campus.

Freshmen:

Admission: 28,454 applied, 22,489 admitted, 3,275 enrolled. *Average high school GPA:* 3.7. *Test scores:* SAT evidence-based reading and writing scores over 500: 98%; SAT math scores over 500: 98%; ACT scores over 18: 99%; SAT evidence-based reading and writing scores over 600: 65%; SAT math scores over 600: 65%; ACT scores over 24: 79%; SAT evidence-based reading and writing scores over 700: 14%; SAT math scores over 700: 22%; ACT scores over 30: 27%.

Retention: 89% of full-time freshmen returned.

FACULTY

Total: 2,017, 55% full-time, 50% with terminal degrees.

Student/faculty ratio: 11:1.

ACADEMICS

Calendar: quarters. *Degrees:* certificates, bachelor's, master's, doctoral, post-master's, and postbachelor's certificates.

Special study options: academic remediation for entering students, accelerated degree program, adult/continuing education programs, advanced placement credit, cooperative education, distance learning, double majors, English as a second language, freshman honors college, honors programs, independent study, internships, part-time degree program, services for LD students, student-designed majors, study abroad, summer session for credit. *ROTC:* Army (b), Navy (c), Air Force (c).

Unusual degree programs: 3-2 business administration; engineering; nursing.

Computers: Students can access the following: campus intranet, computer help desk, free student e-mail accounts, online (class) grades, online (class) registration, online (class) schedules. Campuswide network is available. 100% of college-owned or -operated housing units are wired for high-speed Internet access. Wireless service is available via entire campus.

Library: W. W. Hagerty Library plus 3 others. *Books:* 286,613 (physical), 215,379 (digital/electronic); *Serial titles:* 126 (physical), 51,775 (digital/electronic); *Databases:* 465. Weekly public service hours: 87; study areas open 24 hours, 5–7 days a week; students can reserve study rooms.

STUDENT LIFE

Housing options: on-campus residence required for freshman year; coed, special housing for students with disabilities. Campus housing is university owned. Freshman campus housing is guaranteed.

Activities and organizations: drama/theater group, student-run newspaper, radio and television station, choral group, Student Government, Black Student Union, Society of Hispanic Professional Engineers, Society of Minority Engineers and Scientists, Campus Activities Board, national fraternities, national sororities.

Athletics Member NCAA. All Division I. *Intercollegiate sports:* basketball M(s)/W(s), crew M(s)/W(s), field hockey W(s), golf M(s), lacrosse M(s)/W(s), soccer M(s)/W(s), softball W(s), squash M(s)/W(s), swimming and diving M(s)/W(s), tennis M(s)/W(s), wrestling M(s). *Intramural sports:* basketball M/W, fencing M/W, football M, ice hockey M, riflery M/W, sailing M/W, soccer M/W, softball M/W, squash M/W, table tennis M/W, tennis M/W, volleyball M/W, water polo M/W.

Campus security: 24-hour emergency response devices and patrols, late-night transport/escort service, controlled dormitory access.

Student services: health clinic, personal/psychological counseling, women's center.

COSTS & FINANCIAL AID

Costs (2018–19) *Comprehensive fee:* $65,892 includes full-time tuition ($49,632), mandatory fees ($2370), and room and board ($13,890). Full-time tuition and fees vary according to course load, location, program, and student level. Part-time tuition: $1116 per credit hour. Part-time tuition and fees vary according to course load and program. *Required fees:* $150 per term part-time. *College room only:* $8205. Room and board charges vary according to board plan and housing facility. *Payment plan:* installment. *Waivers:* employees or children of employees.

Financial Aid Of all full-time matriculated undergraduates who enrolled in 2017, 9,584 applied for aid, 8,603 were judged to have need, 1,981 had their need fully met. In 2017, 4137 non-need-based awards were made. *Average percent of need met:* 73. *Average financial aid package:* $37,744. *Average need-based loan:* $11,000. *Average need-based gift aid:* $27,694. *Average non-need-based aid:* $15,018. *Financial aid deadline:* 2/15.

APPLYING

Standardized Tests *Required:* SAT or ACT (for admission).

Options: electronic application, early admission, early decision, early action, deferred entrance.

Application fee: $50.

Required: essay or personal statement, high school transcript, minimum 2.0 GPA. *Recommended:* 2 letters of recommendation, interview.

Application deadlines: 1/15 (freshmen), rolling (transfers), 11/1 (early action).

Early decision deadline: 11/1.

Notification: continuous until 4/1 (freshmen), continuous (transfers), 12/15 (early decision), 12/15 (early action).

CONTACT
Evelyn Thimba, Vice President, Dean of Admissions, Drexel University, 3141 Chestnut Street, Philadelphia, PA 19104-2875. *Phone:* 215-895-6712. *Toll-free phone:* 800-2-DREXEL. *E-mail:* evelyn.k.thimba@drexel.edu.

See below for display ad and page 1274 for the College Close-Up.

Duquesne University
Pittsburgh, Pennsylvania
http://www.duq.edu/

- **Independent Roman Catholic** university, founded 1878
- **Urban** 50-acre campus with easy access to Pittsburgh
- **Endowment** $307.9 million
- **Coed** 5,942 undergraduate students, 98% full-time, 64% women, 36% men
- **Moderately difficult** entrance level, 72% of applicants were admitted

UNDERGRAD STUDENTS

5,826 full-time, 116 part-time. Students come from 44 states and territories; 48 other countries; 28% are from out of state; 5% Black or African American, non-Hispanic/Latino; 4% Hispanic/Latino; 3% Asian, non-Hispanic/Latino; 0.1% Native Hawaiian or other Pacific Islander, non-Hispanic/Latino; 0.1% American Indian or Alaska Native, non-Hispanic/Latino; 3% Two or more races, non-Hispanic/Latino; 1% Race/ethnicity unknown; 4% international; 4% transferred in; 60% live on campus.

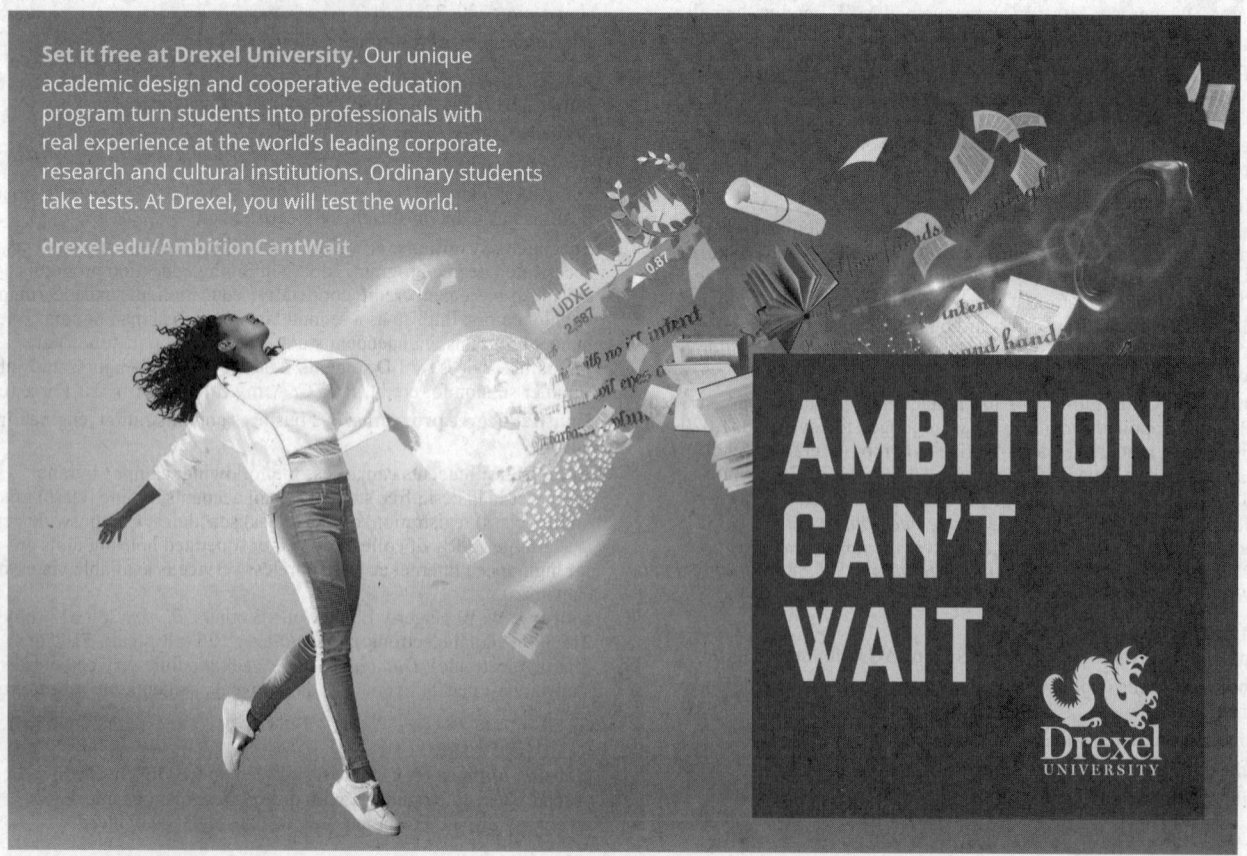

Set it free at Drexel University. Our unique academic design and cooperative education program turn students into professionals with real experience at the world's leading corporate, research and cultural institutions. Ordinary students take tests. At Drexel, you will test the world.

drexel.edu/AmbitionCantWait

AMBITION CAN'T WAIT

Drexel UNIVERSITY

Freshmen:
Admission: 7,336 applied, 5,260 admitted, 1,562 enrolled. *Average high school GPA:* 3.7. *Test scores:* SAT evidence-based reading and writing scores over 500: 99%; SAT math scores over 500: 98%; ACT scores over 18: 100%; SAT evidence-based reading and writing scores over 600: 57%; SAT math scores over 600: 47%; ACT scores over 24: 79%; SAT evidence-based reading and writing scores over 700: 6%; SAT math scores over 700: 5%; ACT scores over 30: 20%.
Retention: 86% of full-time freshmen returned.

FACULTY
Total: 974, 52% full-time.
Student/faculty ratio: 14:1.

ACADEMICS
Calendar: semesters. *Degrees:* bachelor's, master's, doctoral, post-master's, and postbachelor's certificates.
Special study options: academic remediation for entering students, accelerated degree program, adult/continuing education programs, advanced placement credit, distance learning, double majors, English as a second language, external degree program, freshman honors college, honors programs, independent study, internships, off-campus study, part-time degree program, services for LD students, student-designed majors, study abroad, summer session for credit. *ROTC:* Army (b), Navy (c), Air Force (c).
Unusual degree programs: 3-2 engineering with Case Western Reserve University, University of Pittsburgh.
Computers: 1,000 computers/terminals are available on campus for general student use. Students can access the following: campus intranet, computer help desk, free student e-mail accounts, online (class) grades, online (class) registration, online (class) schedules. Campuswide network is available. 100% of college-owned or -operated housing units are wired for high-speed Internet access. Wireless service is available via entire campus.
Library: Gumberg Library plus 1 other. *Books:* 562,257 (physical), 305,837 (digital/electronic); *Serial titles:* 142 (physical), 83,995 (digital/electronic); *Databases:* 205. Weekly public service hours: 112; students can reserve study rooms.

STUDENT LIFE
Housing options: on-campus residence required through sophomore year; coed, men-only, women-only, special housing for students with disabilities. Campus housing is university owned. Freshman campus housing is guaranteed.
Activities and organizations: drama/theater group, student-run newspaper, radio and television station, choral group, marching band, Duquesne University Volunteers (DUV), Red and Blue Crew, Student Government Association, Duquesne Program Council, Residence Hall Association, national fraternities, national sororities.
Athletics Member NCAA. All Division I except football (Division I-AA). *Intercollegiate sports:* basketball M(s)/W(s), bowling W(s), crew W(s), cross-country running M(s)/W(s), lacrosse W(s), soccer M(s)/W(s), swimming and diving W(s), tennis M(s)/W(s), track and field M(s)/W(s), volleyball W(s). *Intramural sports:* baseball M(c)/W(c), basketball M/W, crew W(c), equestrian sports M(c)/W(c), golf M(c)/W(c), ice hockey M(c)/W(c), lacrosse M(c)/W(c), racquetball M/W, rugby M(c)/W(c), soccer M/W, tennis M(c)/W(c), ultimate Frisbee M/W, volleyball M/W.
Campus security: 24-hour emergency response devices and patrols, late-night transport/escort service, controlled dormitory access, cameras monitor exterior 24-hours/day, card access for buildings, outside warning siren system.
Student services: health clinic, personal/psychological counseling.

COSTS & FINANCIAL AID
Costs (2017–18) *Comprehensive fee:* $48,508 includes full-time tuition ($36,394) and room and board ($12,114). Full-time tuition and fees vary according to course load and program. Part-time tuition: $1206 per credit hour. Part-time tuition and fees vary according to course load and program. *College room only:* $6658. Room and board charges vary according to board plan and housing facility. *Payment plans:* installment, deferred payment. *Waivers:* senior citizens and employees or children of employees.
Financial Aid Of all full-time matriculated undergraduates who enrolled in 2016, 4,620 applied for aid, 3,931 were judged to have need, 785 had

their need fully met. 1,765 Federal Work-Study jobs (averaging $2400). In 2016, 1640 non-need-based awards were made. *Average percent of need met:* 72. *Average financial aid package:* $24,570. *Average need-based loan:* $4628. *Average need-based gift aid:* $21,218. *Average non-need-based aid:* $13,180. *Average indebtedness upon graduation:* $43,637. *Financial aid deadline:* 5/1.

APPLYING
Standardized Tests *Required for some:* SAT or ACT (for admission).
Options: electronic application, early admission, early decision, early action, deferred entrance.
Application fee: $50.
Required: high school transcript. *Required for some:* essay or personal statement, 1 letter of recommendation, audition for School of Music; 40 hours of volunteer, paid, or shadowing experience for physical therapy. *Recommended:* minimum 3.0 GPA, interview.
Application deadlines: 7/1 (freshmen), 7/1 (transfers), 12/1 (early action).
Early decision deadline: 11/1.
Notification: continuous until 10/1 (freshmen), 11/15 (early decision), 1/15 (early action).

CONTACT
Ms. Debra Zugates, Director of Admissions, Duquesne University, Administration Building, 600 Forbes Avenue, Pittsburgh, PA 15282-0201. *Phone:* 412-396-5211. *Toll-free phone:* 800-456-0590. *Fax:* 412-396-5644. *E-mail:* admissions@duq.edu.

Eastern University
St. Davids, Pennsylvania
http://www.eastern.edu/
- **Independent Christian** university, founded 1952
- **Suburban** 114-acre campus with easy access to Philadelphia
- **Endowment** $29.0 million
- **Coed** 1,887 undergraduate students, 77% full-time, 69% women, 31% men
- **Moderately difficult** entrance level, 66% of applicants were admitted

UNDERGRAD STUDENTS
1,462 full-time, 425 part-time. Students come from 35 states and territories; 9 other countries; 43% are from out of state; 20% Black or African American, non-Hispanic/Latino; 19% Hispanic/Latino; 2% Asian, non-Hispanic/Latino; 0.1% Native Hawaiian or other Pacific Islander, non-Hispanic/Latino; 2% Two or more races, non-Hispanic/Latino; 5% Race/ethnicity unknown; 2% international; 10% transferred in; 80% live on campus.

Freshmen:
Admission: 1,759 applied, 1,154 admitted, 381 enrolled. *Average high school GPA:* 3.4. *Test scores:* SAT evidence-based reading and writing scores over 500: 79%; SAT math scores over 500: 74%; ACT scores over 18: 90%; SAT evidence-based reading and writing scores over 600: 32%; SAT math scores over 600: 22%; ACT scores over 24: 46%; SAT evidence-based reading and writing scores over 700: 4%; SAT math scores over 700: 3%; ACT scores over 30: 10%.
Retention: 75% of full-time freshmen returned.

FACULTY
Total: 484, 26% full-time, 29% with terminal degrees.
Student/faculty ratio: 10:1.

ACADEMICS
Calendar: semesters. *Degrees:* certificates, diplomas, associate, bachelor's, master's, doctoral, and post-master's certificates.
Special study options: academic remediation for entering students, accelerated degree program, adult/continuing education programs, advanced placement credit, distance learning, double majors, English as a second language, external degree program, honors programs, independent study, internships, off-campus study, part-time degree program, services for LD students, student-designed majors, study abroad, summer session for credit. *ROTC:* Army (c), Air Force (c).
Computers: 98 computers/terminals and 300 ports are available on campus for general student use. Students can access the following:

campus intranet, computer help desk, free student e-mail accounts, online (class) grades, online (class) registration, online (class) schedules, BRIGHTSPACE. Campuswide network is available. 100% of college-owned or -operated housing units are wired for high-speed Internet access. Wireless service is available via entire campus.

Library: Warner Memorial Library plus 1 other. *Books:* 172,820 (physical), 1.5 million (digital/electronic); *Serial titles:* 94 (physical), 48,564 (digital/electronic); *Databases:* 155. Weekly public service hours: 83; students can reserve study rooms.

STUDENT LIFE

Housing options: on-campus residence required through senior year; men-only, women-only, special housing for students with disabilities. Campus housing is university owned and leased by the school. Freshman campus housing is guaranteed.

Activities and organizations: drama/theater group, student-run newspaper, choral group, Wednesday Night Worship, Super Smash Bros Club, Student Athletic Training Club, Blaze Step Team, Political Activism Club.

Athletics Member NCAA. All Division III. *Intercollegiate sports:* baseball M, basketball M/W, cross-country running M/W, field hockey W, golf M/W, lacrosse M/W, soccer M/W, softball W, tennis M/W, track and field M/W, volleyball W. *Intramural sports:* basketball M/W, soccer M/W, volleyball M/W.

Campus security: 24-hour emergency response devices and patrols, late-night transport/escort service, controlled dormitory access.

Student services: health clinic, personal/psychological counseling.

COSTS & FINANCIAL AID

Costs (2018–19) *One-time required fee:* $65. *Comprehensive fee:* $44,136 includes full-time tuition ($32,492), mandatory fees ($390), and room and board ($11,254). Full-time tuition and fees vary according to course load, degree level, and program. Part-time tuition: $712 per credit. Part-time tuition and fees vary according to course load, degree level, and program. *Required fees:* $195 per term part-time. *College room only:* $5986. Room and board charges vary according to housing facility and location. *Payment plan:* installment. *Waivers:* children of alumni and employees or children of employees.

Financial Aid Of all full-time matriculated undergraduates who enrolled in 2016, 1,740 applied for aid, 1,610 were judged to have need, 415 had their need fully met. 337 Federal Work-Study jobs (averaging $1088). In 2016, 101 non-need-based awards were made. *Average percent of need met:* 81. *Average financial aid package:* $20,817. *Average need-based loan:* $4134. *Average need-based gift aid:* $7123. *Average non-need-based aid:* $13,445. *Average indebtedness upon graduation:* $37,225.

APPLYING

Standardized Tests *Required for some:* SAT or ACT (for admission).

Options: electronic application, early admission, deferred entrance.

Application fee: $35.

Required: essay or personal statement, high school transcript, minimum 2.0 GPA, 1 letter of recommendation. *Recommended:* 2 letters of recommendation, interview.

Application deadlines: rolling (freshmen), rolling (transfers).

Notification: continuous (freshmen), continuous (transfers).

CONTACT

Mr. Michael Dziedziak, Executive Director of Enrollment, Eastern University, 1300 Eagle Road, St Davids, PA 19087-3696. *Phone:* 610-341-1376. *Toll-free phone:* 800-452-0996. *Fax:* 610-341-1723. *E-mail:* ugadm@eastern.edu.

East Stroudsburg University of Pennsylvania

East Stroudsburg, Pennsylvania

http://www.esu.edu/

- **State-supported** comprehensive, founded 1893, part of Pennsylvania State System of Higher Education
- **Rural** 258-acre campus
- **Endowment** $14,323
- **Coed** 6,051 undergraduate students, 92% full-time, 56% women, 44% men
- **Moderately difficult** entrance level, 79% of applicants were admitted

UNDERGRAD STUDENTS

5,552 full-time, 499 part-time. 20% are from out of state; 18% Black or African American, non-Hispanic/Latino; 13% Hispanic/Latino; 2% Asian, non-Hispanic/Latino; 0.1% Native Hawaiian or other Pacific Islander, non-Hispanic/Latino; 0.2% American Indian or Alaska Native, non-Hispanic/Latino; 4% Two or more races, non-Hispanic/Latino; 2% Race/ethnicity unknown; 0.4% international; 9% transferred in; 43% live on campus.

Freshmen:

Admission: 9,997 applied, 7,849 admitted, 1,282 enrolled. *Average high school GPA:* 3.2. *Test scores:* SAT evidence-based reading and writing scores over 500: 57%; SAT math scores over 500: 56%; ACT scores over 18: 72%; SAT evidence-based reading and writing scores over 600: 12%; SAT math scores over 600: 9%; ACT scores over 24: 17%; SAT evidence-based reading and writing scores over 700: 1%; ACT scores over 30: 1%.

Retention: 70% of full-time freshmen returned.

FACULTY

Total: 354, 75% full-time, 47% with terminal degrees.

Student/faculty ratio: 19:1.

ACADEMICS

Calendar: semesters. *Degrees:* certificates, bachelor's, master's, doctoral, post-master's, and postbachelor's certificates.

Special study options: academic remediation for entering students, accelerated degree program, adult/continuing education programs, advanced placement credit, distance learning, double majors, honors programs, independent study, internships, off-campus study, part-time degree program, services for LD students, student-designed majors, study abroad, summer session for credit. *ROTC:* Army (b), Air Force (c).

Unusual degree programs: 3-2 engineering with Penn State University Park.

Computers: 500 computers/terminals and 1,500 ports are available on campus for general student use. Students can access the following: campus intranet, computer help desk, free student e-mail accounts, online (class) grades, online (class) registration, online (class) schedules, online classes. Campuswide network is available. 100% of college-owned or -operated housing units are wired for high-speed Internet access. Wireless service is available via classrooms, computer labs, dorm rooms, libraries, student centers.

Library: Kemp Library. *Books:* 306,633 (physical), 408,082 (digital/electronic); *Serial titles:* 4,066 (physical) 22,666 (digital/electronic); *Databases:* 93. Weekly public service hours: 99.

STUDENT LIFE

Housing options: on-campus residence required for freshman year; coed, special housing for students with disabilities. Campus housing is university owned and is provided by a third party. Freshman campus housing is guaranteed.

Activities and organizations: drama/theater group, student-run newspaper, radio station, choral group, marching band, Student Senate, Stage II, Council for Exceptional Children, Environmental Club, National Speech/Hearing/Language Association, national fraternities, national sororities.

Athletics Member NCAA. All Division II. *Intercollegiate sports:* baseball M(s), basketball M(s)/W(s), cheerleading M/W, cross-country running M(s)/W(s), equestrian sports M(c)/W(c), field hockey W(s), football M(s), golf M(c)/W, ice hockey M(c)/W(c), lacrosse M(c)/W(s), rugby M(c)/W(c), soccer M(s)/W(s), softball W(s), swimming and diving W(s), tennis M(c)/W(s), track and field M(s)/W(s), ultimate Frisbee

M(c)/W(c), volleyball M(c)/W(s), wrestling M(s). *Intramural sports:* basketball M/W, racquetball M(c)/W(c), soccer M(c)/W(c), softball M/W.

Campus security: 24-hour emergency response devices and patrols, late-night transport/escort service, controlled dormitory access, self-defense education, shuttle buses, lighted pathways/sidewalks, controlled building access.

Student services: health clinic, personal/psychological counseling, women's center, legal services.

COSTS & FINANCIAL AID

Costs (2017–18) *Tuition:* state resident $7492 full-time, $312 per credit hour part-time; nonresident $18,730 full-time, $780 per credit hour part-time. Full-time tuition and fees vary according to course load, location, and program. Part-time tuition and fees vary according to location and program. *Required fees:* $2806 full-time, $151 per credit hour part-time, $716 per term part-time. *Room and board:* $8672; room only: $6000. Room and board charges vary according to board plan and housing facility. *Payment plan:* installment. *Waivers:* senior citizens and employees or children of employees.

Financial Aid Of all full-time matriculated undergraduates who enrolled in 2016, 3,838 applied for aid, 3,215 were judged to have need, 1,525 had their need fully met. 1,539 Federal Work-Study jobs (averaging $1091). *Average percent of need met:* 68. *Average financial aid package:* $8857. *Average need-based loan:* $4116. *Average need-based gift aid:* $8374. *Average indebtedness upon graduation:* $24,182.

APPLYING

Standardized Tests *Required for some:* SAT or ACT (for admission).

Options: electronic application, deferred entrance.

Application fee: $25.

Required: high school transcript.

Application deadlines: 5/1 (freshmen), 6/1 (transfers).

Notification: 5/1 (freshmen), continuous (transfers).

CONTACT

Ms. Donna Tatarka, Director of Admissions and Orientation, East Stroudsburg University of Pennsylvania, 200 Prospect Street, East Stroudsburg, PA 18301. *Phone:* 570-422-3542. *Toll-free phone:* 877-230-5547. *Fax:* 570-422-3933. *E-mail:* undergrads@po-box.esu.edu.

Edinboro University of Pennsylvania

Edinboro, Pennsylvania

http://www.edinboro.edu/

CONTACT

Ms. Melissa Manning, Associate Director of Undergraduate Admissions, Edinboro University of Pennsylvania, Academy Hall, Edinboro, PA 16444. *Phone:* 814-732-2761. *Toll-free phone:* 888-846-2676. *Fax:* 814-732-2420. *E-mail:* eup_admissions@edinboro.edu.

Elizabethtown College

Elizabethtown, Pennsylvania

http://www.etown.edu/

- **Independent** comprehensive, founded 1899, affiliated with Church of the Brethren
- **Small-town** 203-acre campus with easy access to Philadelphia, Baltimore, Harrisburg, Lancaster
- **Endowment** $79.1 million
- **Coed** 1,671 undergraduate students, 98% full-time, 62% women, 38% men
- **Moderately difficult** entrance level, 74% of applicants were admitted

UNDERGRAD STUDENTS

1,636 full-time, 35 part-time. Students come from 28 states and territories; 23 other countries; 32% are from out of state; 3% Black or African American, non-Hispanic/Latino; 4% Hispanic/Latino; 3% Asian, non-Hispanic/Latino; 0.1% Native Hawaiian or other Pacific Islander, non-

BE A JAY

SOAR HIGHER THAN YOU EVER DREAMED.

Where is life taking you? The Blue Jay experience at Elizabethtown is unique. It's personal. And finding your way academically and socially is all part of the plan. At the heart of the plan is **Signature Learning**, guaranteed for every one of our students. You will select two of the five **Signature Learning Experiences**. Your signature selections include: supervised research, cross-cultural experiences, community-based learning, internships, and capstone courses.

The Blue Jay experience is about more than life in the classroom. It's about life on the outside.

Fly with us at Elizabethtown.

Elizabethtown College
ELIZABETHTOWN, PA

www.etown.edu

Hispanic/Latino; 0.1% American Indian or Alaska Native, non-Hispanic/Latino; 2% Two or more races, non-Hispanic/Latino; 0.4% Race/ethnicity unknown; 2% international; 1% transferred in; 84% live on campus.

Freshmen:

Admission: 3,030 applied, 2,243 admitted, 411 enrolled. *Test scores:* SAT evidence-based reading and writing scores over 500: 92%; SAT math scores over 500: 86%; ACT scores over 18: 95%; SAT evidence-based reading and writing scores over 600: 45%; SAT math scores over 600: 44%; ACT scores over 24: 59%; SAT evidence-based reading and writing scores over 700: 7%; SAT math scores over 700: 8%; ACT scores over 30: 14%.

Retention: 87% of full-time freshmen returned.

FACULTY
Total: 183, 70% full-time, 76% with terminal degrees.
Student/faculty ratio: 11:1.

ACADEMICS
Calendar: semesters. *Degrees:* bachelor's and master's.

Special study options: advanced placement credit, distance learning, double majors, English as a second language, honors programs, independent study, internships, off-campus study, services for LD students, study abroad, summer session for credit.

Unusual degree programs: 3-2 forestry with Duke University; allied health with Thomas Jefferson University, Widener University; environmental management with Duke University.

Computers: 230 computers/terminals and 200 ports are available on campus for general student use. Students can access the following: campus intranet, computer help desk, free student e-mail accounts, online (class) grades, online (class) registration, online (class) schedules, file space, personal Web page, financial aid, student billing, residence hall selection, personal and group blogs. Campuswide network is available. 100% of college-owned or -operated housing units are wired for high-speed Internet access. Wireless service is available via entire campus.
Library: High Library plus 1 other. *Books:* 253,054 (physical), 5,306 (digital/electronic); *Serial titles:* 1,628 (physical), 7,972 (digital/electronic); *Databases:* 73. Weekly public service hours: 102; students can reserve study rooms.

STUDENT LIFE
Housing options: on-campus residence required through senior year; coed, women-only, special housing for students with disabilities. Campus housing is university owned and leased by the school. Freshman campus housing is guaranteed.

Activities and organizations: drama/theater group, student-run newspaper, radio and television station, choral group, Professional Organizations, Emotion Dance Club, Student Senate, A cappella groups, Religious groups.

Athletics Member NCAA. All Division III. *Intercollegiate sports:* baseball M, basketball M/W, cross-country running M/W, field hockey W, golf M/W, lacrosse M/W, soccer M/W, softball W, swimming and diving M/W, tennis M/W, track and field M/W, volleyball W, wrestling M. *Intramural sports:* basketball M/W, bowling M/W, equestrian sports M(c)/W(c), golf M/W, ice hockey M(c), soccer M/W, softball M/W, tennis M/W, triathlon M(c)/W(c), ultimate Frisbee M(c)/W(c), volleyball M(c)/W(c).

Campus security: 24-hour emergency response devices and patrols, student patrols, late-night transport/escort service, controlled dormitory access, self-defense workshops, crime prevention program.

Student services: health clinic, personal/psychological counseling.

COSTS & FINANCIAL AID
Costs (2018–19) *Comprehensive fee:* $58,310 includes full-time tuition ($46,940) and room and board ($11,370). Full-time tuition and fees vary according to course load. Part-time tuition: $1100 per credit hour. Part-time tuition and fees vary according to course load. *College room only:* $5630. Room and board charges vary according to board plan and housing facility. *Payment plan:* installment. *Waivers:* employees or children of employees.

Financial Aid Of all full-time matriculated undergraduates who enrolled in 2017, 1,375 applied for aid, 1,260 were judged to have need, 287 had their need fully met. 679 Federal Work-Study jobs (averaging $1263). In 2017, 350 non-need-based awards were made. *Average percent of need met:* 80. *Average financial aid package:* $33,166. *Average need-based loan:* $4567. *Average need-based gift aid:* $28,603. *Average non-need-based aid:* $22,579. *Average indebtedness upon graduation:* $42,316.

APPLYING
Standardized Tests *Required:* SAT or ACT (for admission).
Options: electronic application, deferred entrance.
Application fee: $30.
Required: essay or personal statement, high school transcript, minimum 2.0 GPA, 2 letters of recommendation. *Required for some:* interview. *Recommended:* minimum 3.0 GPA, interview.
Application deadlines: 3/1 (freshmen), 8/1 (transfers).
Notification: continuous (freshmen), continuous (transfers).

CONTACT
Ms. Lauren Deibler, Director of Admissions and Coordinator of International Recruitment, Elizabethtown College, One Alpha Drive, Elizabethtown, PA 17022. *Phone:* 717-361-1400. *Fax:* 717-361-1365. *E-mail:* admissions@etown.edu.

See previous page for display ad and page 1278 for the College Close-Up.

Elizabethtown College School of Continuing and Professional Studies
Elizabethtown, Pennsylvania
http://www.etowndegrees.com/

CONTACT
Ms. Barbara A. Randazzo, Assistant Dean of Enrollment Management, Elizabethtown College School of Continuing and Professional Studies, One Alpha Drive, Elizabethtown College, PA 17022. *Phone:* 717-361-3750. *Toll-free phone:* 800-877-2694. *Fax:* 717-361-1466. *E-mail:* randazzob@etown.edu.

Franklin & Marshall College
Lancaster, Pennsylvania
http://www.fandm.edu/
- **Independent** 4-year, founded 1787
- **Suburban** 209-acre campus with easy access to Philadelphia
- **Coed** 2,289 undergraduate students, 99% full-time, 54% women, 46% men
- **Very difficult** entrance level, 34% of applicants were admitted

UNDERGRAD STUDENTS
2,263 full-time, 26 part-time. Students come from 47 states and territories; 47 other countries; 77% are from out of state; 6% Black or African American, non-Hispanic/Latino; 10% Hispanic/Latino; 5% Asian, non-Hispanic/Latino; 0.1% American Indian or Alaska Native, non-Hispanic/Latino; 2% Two or more races, non-Hispanic/Latino; 4% Race/ethnicity unknown; 16% international; 0.9% transferred in; 99% live on campus.

Freshmen:
Admission: 6,720 applied, 2,292 admitted, 645 enrolled. *Test scores:* SAT evidence-based reading and writing scores over 500: 100%; SAT math scores over 500: 100%; ACT scores over 18: 100%; SAT evidence-based reading and writing scores over 600: 90%; SAT math scores over 600: 93%; ACT scores over 24: 100%; SAT evidence-based reading and writing scores over 700: 25%; SAT math scores over 700: 38%; ACT scores over 30: 59%.

Retention: 92% of full-time freshmen returned.

FACULTY
Total: 273, 89% full-time, 89% with terminal degrees.
Student/faculty ratio: 9:1.

ACADEMICS
Calendar: semesters. *Degree:* bachelor's.

Special study options: accelerated degree program, advanced placement credit, double majors, independent study, internships, off-campus study, services for LD students, student-designed majors, study abroad, summer session for credit.

Unusual degree programs: 3-2 engineering with Rensselaer Polytechnic Institute, Washington University in St. Louis, Columbia University, Case Western Reserve University, Penn State University College of Engineering; forestry with Duke University; environmental studies with Duke University.

Computers: 125 computers/terminals are available on campus for general student use. Students can access the following: campus intranet, computer help desk, free student e-mail accounts, online (class) grades, online (class) registration, online (class) schedules, online degree audit, unofficial transcripts, course material. Campuswide network is available. 100% of college-owned or -operated housing units are wired for high-speed Internet access. Wireless service is available via entire campus.

Library: Shadek-Fackenthal Library plus 1 other. *Books:* 468,748 (physical), 135,071 (digital/electronic); *Serial titles:* 2,680 (physical), 167,874 (digital/electronic). Weekly public service hours: 110; students can reserve study rooms.

STUDENT LIFE

Housing options: on-campus residence required through senior year; coed, men-only, women-only, cooperative, special housing for students with disabilities. Campus housing is university owned and is provided by a third party. Freshman campus housing is guaranteed.

Activities and organizations: drama/theater group, student-run newspaper, radio station, choral group, Intervarsity, Hillel, Mi Gente Latina, Cia Bella, F&M Players, national fraternities, national sororities.

Athletics Member NCAA. All Division III except wrestling (Division I). *Intercollegiate sports:* baseball M, basketball M/W, crew M(c)/W, cross-country running M/W, equestrian sports W(c), field hockey W, football M, golf M/W, ice hockey M(c), lacrosse M/W, rugby M(c)/W(c), soccer M/W, softball W, squash M/W, swimming and diving M/W, tennis M/W, track and field M/W, ultimate Frisbee M(c)/W(c), volleyball M(c)/W, wrestling M. *Intramural sports:* basketball M/W, football M, soccer M/W, softball M/W, squash M/W, tennis M/W, volleyball M/W, wrestling M.

Campus security: 24-hour emergency response devices and patrols, late-night transport/escort service, controlled dormitory access, residence hall security, campus security connected to city police and fire company.

Student services: health clinic, personal/psychological counseling, women's center.

COSTS & FINANCIAL AID

Costs (2017–18) *One-time required fee:* $200. *Comprehensive fee:* $67,960 includes full-time tuition ($54,280), mandatory fees ($100), and room and board ($13,580). Part-time tuition: $6785 per course. Part-time tuition and fees vary according to course load. *College room only:* $8030. Room and board charges vary according to board plan and housing facility. *Payment plans:* installment, deferred payment. *Waivers:* employees or children of employees.

Financial Aid Of all full-time matriculated undergraduates who enrolled in 2017, 1,400 applied for aid, 1,239 were judged to have need, 1,239 had their need fully met. In 2017, 21 non-need-based awards were made. *Average percent of need met:* 100. *Average financial aid package:* $50,865. *Average need-based loan:* $4107. *Average need-based gift aid:* $46,102. *Average non-need-based aid:* $12,125. *Average indebtedness upon graduation:* $27,011. *Financial aid deadline:* 2/1.

APPLYING

Options: electronic application, early admission, early decision, deferred entrance.

Application fee: $60.

Required: essay or personal statement, high school transcript, 2 letters of recommendation, Common Application Supplement. *Required for some:* interview.

Application deadlines: 1/15 (freshmen), 5/15 (transfers).

Early decision deadline: 11/15 (for plan 1), 1/15 (for plan 2).

Notification: 4/1 (freshmen), 12/15 (early decision plan 1), 2/15 (early decision plan 2).

CONTACT

Julie Kerich, Director of Admissions, Franklin & Marshall College, PO Box 3003, Lancaster, PA 17604-3003. *Phone:* 717-358-47433. *Toll-free phone:* 877-678-9111. *Fax:* 717-358-4389. *E-mail:* julie.kerich@fandm.edu.

★ Gannon University
Erie, Pennsylvania
http://www.gannon.edu/

- **Independent Roman Catholic** university, founded 1925
- **Urban** 38-acre campus with easy access to Cleveland, Buffalo, Pittsburgh
- **Coed** 3,076 undergraduate students, 82% full-time, 57% women, 43% men
- **Moderately difficult** entrance level, 80% of applicants were admitted

UNDERGRAD STUDENTS

2,530 full-time, 546 part-time. Students come from 31 states and territories; 39 other countries; 29% are from out of state; 5% Black or African American, non-Hispanic/Latino; 3% Hispanic/Latino; 1% Asian, non-Hispanic/Latino; 0.1% American Indian or Alaska Native, non-Hispanic/Latino; 3% Two or more races, non-Hispanic/Latino; 6% Race/ethnicity unknown; 9% international; 3% transferred in; 46% live on campus.

Freshmen:
Admission: 4,642 applied, 3,709 admitted, 645 enrolled. *Average high school GPA:* 3.5. *Test scores:* SAT evidence-based reading and writing scores over 500: 78%; SAT math scores over 500: 75%; ACT scores over 18: 91%; SAT evidence-based reading and writing scores over 600: 32%; SAT math scores over 600: 29%; ACT scores over 24: 48%; SAT evidence-based reading and writing scores over 700: 3%; SAT math scores over 700: 4%; ACT scores over 30: 8%.
Retention: 85% of full-time freshmen returned.

FACULTY

Total: 403, 59% full-time, 57% with terminal degrees.
Student/faculty ratio: 12:1.

ACADEMICS

Calendar: semesters plus 2 summer sessions. *Degrees:* certificates, associate, bachelor's, master's, doctoral, post-master's, and postbachelor's certificates.

Special study options: academic remediation for entering students, accelerated degree program, adult/continuing education programs, advanced placement credit, cooperative education, distance learning, double majors, English as a second language, honors programs, independent study, internships, off-campus study, part-time degree program, services for LD students, study abroad, summer session for credit. *ROTC:* Army (b).

Unusual degree programs: 3-2 business administration; engineering with University of Pittsburgh; occupational therapy, physician assistant, sport and exercise science.

Computers: 386 computers/terminals and 1,425 ports are available on campus for general student use. Students can access the following: campus intranet, computer help desk, free student e-mail accounts, online (class) grades, online (class) registration, online (class) schedules. Campuswide network is available. 100% of college-owned or -operated housing units are wired for high-speed Internet access. Wireless service is available via entire campus.

Library: Nash Library. *Books:* 213,041 (physical), 252,244 (digital/electronic); *Serial titles:* 37 (physical), 52,805 (digital/electronic); *Databases:* 45. Weekly public service hours: 97; students can reserve study rooms.

STUDENT LIFE

Housing options: on-campus residence required through sophomore year; coed, special housing for students with disabilities. Campus housing is university owned and leased by the school. Freshman campus housing is guaranteed.

Activities and organizations: drama/theater group, student-run newspaper, radio station, choral group, GU Society of Physician Assistant, GU Habitat for Humanity, Activities Programming Board, Student Occupational Therapy Association, Organization of Women Leaders, national fraternities, national sororities.

Athletics Member NCAA. All Division II. *Intercollegiate sports:* baseball M(s), basketball M(s)/W(s), cheerleading W(s)(c), cross-country running M(s)/W(s), football M(s), golf M(s)/W(s), gymnastics W(s)(c), lacrosse W(s), rugby M(c), soccer M(s)/W(s), softball W(s), swimming

A CATHOLIC UNIVERSITY WITH A
90-YEAR
SUCCESS RECORD

- A University built on Catholic Tradition
- Generous scholarships and financial aid packages available ensuring a high-quality education is within everyone's reach
- Our faculty experts provide real-world experience and lead you to internships that prepare you to become a professional in the field
- Over 100 academic programs including certificate, accelerated and online options mean countless possibilities
- Small class sizes with 13:1 student-to-faculty ratio
- Located in Erie, Pa., Gannon offers small-town friendliness with big-city attractions

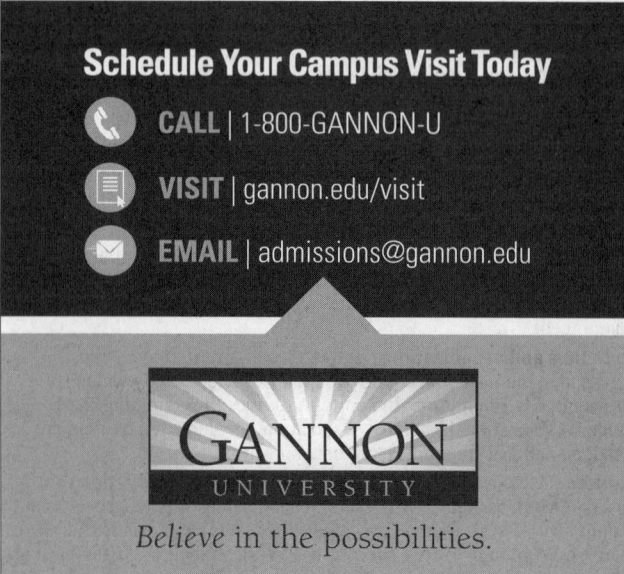

Schedule Your Campus Visit Today

CALL | 1-800-GANNON-U

VISIT | gannon.edu/visit

EMAIL | admissions@gannon.edu

GANNON
UNIVERSITY

Believe in the possibilities.

and diving M(s)/W(s), volleyball W(s), water polo M(s)/W(s), wrestling M(s). *Intramural sports:* basketball M/W, football M/W, ice hockey M(c), lacrosse M(c), racquetball M/W, rugby M(c)/W(c), sailing M(c)/W(c), soccer M/W(c), ultimate Frisbee M(c)/W(c), volleyball M(c)/W(c).

Campus security: 24-hour emergency response devices and patrols, late-night transport/escort service, controlled dormitory access, security cameras in and outside of campus facilities, including streets and sidewalks.

Student services: health clinic, personal/psychological counseling.

FINANCIAL AID
Financial Aid Of all full-time matriculated undergraduates who enrolled in 2016, 2,091 applied for aid, 1,915 were judged to have need, 467 had their need fully met. In 2016, 390 non-need-based awards were made. *Average percent of need met:* 73. *Average financial aid package:* $24,832. *Average need-based loan:* $4322. *Average need-based gift aid:* $20,924. *Average non-need-based aid:* $14,266.

APPLYING
Standardized Tests *Required:* SAT or ACT (for admission).

Options: electronic application, deferred entrance.

Application fee: $25.

Required: high school transcript, minimum 2.0 GPA, counselor's recommendation. *Required for some:* minimum 3.0 GPA, 2 letters of recommendation, interview. *Recommended:* essay or personal statement.

Application deadlines: rolling (freshmen), rolling (transfers).

Notification: continuous (freshmen), continuous (transfers).

CONTACT
Office of Admissions, Gannon University, 109 University Square, Erie, PA 16541. *Phone:* 814-871-7240. *Toll-free phone:* 800-GANNONU. *Fax:* 814-871-5803. *E-mail:* admissions@gannon.edu.

See this page for display ad and page 1296 for the College Close-Up.

Geneva College
Beaver Falls, Pennsylvania
http://www.geneva.edu/
- **Independent** comprehensive, founded 1848, affiliated with Reformed Presbyterian Church of North America
- **Small-town** 55-acre campus with easy access to Pittsburgh
- **Endowment** $37.0 million
- **Coed** 1,418 undergraduate students, 88% full-time, 50% women, 50% men
- **Moderately difficult** entrance level, 69% of applicants were admitted

UNDERGRAD STUDENTS
1,248 full-time, 170 part-time. Students come from 36 states and territories; 9 other countries; 26% are from out of state; 8% Black or African American, non-Hispanic/Latino; 1% Hispanic/Latino; 1% Asian, non-Hispanic/Latino; 0.1% Native Hawaiian or other Pacific Islander, non-Hispanic/Latino; 0.1% American Indian or Alaska Native, non-Hispanic/Latino; 3% Two or more races, non-Hispanic/Latino; 3% Race/ethnicity unknown; 2% international; 2% transferred in; 68% live on campus.

Freshmen:
Admission: 1,691 applied, 1,167 admitted, 303 enrolled. *Average high school GPA:* 3.5. *Test scores:* SAT evidence-based reading and writing scores over 500: 71%; SAT math scores over 500: 74%; ACT scores over 18: 88%; SAT evidence-based reading and writing scores over 600: 29%; SAT math scores over 600: 29%; ACT scores over 24: 46%; SAT evidence-based reading and writing scores over 700: 5%; SAT math scores over 700: 5%; ACT scores over 30: 7%.

Retention: 80% of full-time freshmen returned.

FACULTY
Total: 209, 33% full-time, 48% with terminal degrees.

Student/faculty ratio: 12:1.

ACADEMICS
Calendar: semesters. *Degrees:* associate, bachelor's, and master's (also offers non-traditional programs in Philadelphia and western Pennsylvania with significant enrollment not reflected in profile).

Special study options: academic remediation for entering students, accelerated degree program, adult/continuing education programs, advanced placement credit, cooperative education, distance learning, double majors, English as a second language, honors programs, independent study, internships, off-campus study, part-time degree program, services for LD students, student-designed majors, study abroad, summer session for credit. *ROTC:* Army (c).

Unusual degree programs: 3-2 divinity with Reformed Presbyterian Theological Seminary.

Computers: 150 computers/terminals and 400 ports are available on campus for general student use. Students can access the following: campus intranet, computer help desk, free student e-mail accounts, online (class) grades, online (class) registration, online (class) schedules. Campuswide network is available. 100% of college-owned or -operated housing units are wired for high-speed Internet access. Wireless service is available via entire campus.

Library: McCartney Library plus 3 others. *Books:* 139,301 (physical), 12,739 (digital/electronic); *Serial titles:* 438 (physical), 20 (digital/electronic); *Databases:* 53. Weekly public service hours: 84.

STUDENT LIFE

Housing options: men-only, women-only. Campus housing is university owned. Freshman campus housing is guaranteed.

Activities and organizations: drama/theater group, student-run newspaper, choral group, marching band, marching band, Genevans Choir, Intramural sports, ministry groups, discipleship groups.

Athletics Member NCAA, NCCAA. All NCAA Division III. *Intercollegiate sports:* baseball M, basketball M/W, cross-country running M/W, football M, soccer M/W, softball W, tennis M/W, track and field M/W, volleyball M(c)/W. *Intramural sports:* basketball M/W, cheerleading W(c), football M/W, ice hockey M(c), racquetball M/W, rugby M(c)/W(c), skiing (downhill) M(c)/W(c), soccer M/W, softball M/W, table tennis M/W, ultimate Frisbee M/W, volleyball M/W.

Campus security: 24-hour emergency response devices and patrols, late-night transport/escort service, controlled dormitory access.

Student services: health clinic, personal/psychological counseling.

COSTS & FINANCIAL AID

Costs (2018–19) *Comprehensive fee:* $37,150 includes full-time tuition ($26,730), mandatory fees ($250), and room and board ($10,170). Full-time tuition and fees vary according to course load. Part-time tuition: $900 per credit hour. Part-time tuition and fees vary according to course load. *Room and board:* Room and board charges vary according to board plan. *Payment plan:* installment. *Waivers:* employees or children of employees.

Financial Aid Of all full-time matriculated undergraduates who enrolled in 2016, 1,037 applied for aid, 943 were judged to have need, 219 had their need fully met. 198 Federal Work-Study jobs (averaging $765). In 2016, 195 non-need-based awards were made. *Average percent of need met:* 80. *Average financial aid package:* $20,943. *Average need-based loan:* $4400. *Average need-based gift aid:* $16,549. *Average non-need-based aid:* $10,965. *Average indebtedness upon graduation:* $35,440.

APPLYING

Standardized Tests *Required:* SAT or ACT (for admission).

Options: electronic application, early admission, deferred entrance.

Application fee: $40.

Required: essay or personal statement, high school transcript, minimum 2.0 GPA. *Required for some:* interview, 1 unit of chemistry and physics and 4 units of college-prep mathematics (including trigonometry and pre-calculus) for engineering. *Recommended:* minimum 3.0 GPA, 2 letters of recommendation, interview.

Application deadlines: rolling (freshmen), rolling (transfers).

Notification: continuous (freshmen), continuous (transfers).

CONTACT

Mr. David Layton, Associate Vice President for Enrollment, Geneva College, 3200 College Avenue, Beaver Falls, PA 15010-3599. *Phone:* 724-847-6500. *Toll-free phone:* 800-847-8255. *E-mail:* admissions@geneva.edu.

Gettysburg College

Gettysburg, Pennsylvania

http://www.gettysburg.edu/

- **Independent** 4-year, founded 1832, affiliated with Evangelical Lutheran Church in America
- **Suburban** 200-acre campus with easy access to Baltimore and Washington, D.C.
- **Endowment** $313.8 million
- **Coed** 2,409 undergraduate students, 100% full-time, 53% women, 47% men
- **Most difficult** entrance level, 46% of applicants were admitted

UNDERGRAD STUDENTS

2,400 full-time, 9 part-time. Students come from 38 states and territories; 38 other countries; 74% are from out of state; 4% Black or African American, non-Hispanic/Latino; 8% Hispanic/Latino; 2% Asian, non-Hispanic/Latino; 0.1% American Indian or Alaska Native, non-Hispanic/Latino; 3% Two or more races, non-Hispanic/Latino; 2% Race/ethnicity unknown; 7% international; 0.4% transferred in; 94% live on campus.

Freshmen:
Admission: 6,384 applied, 2,924 admitted, 720 enrolled. *Test scores:* SAT evidence-based reading and writing scores over 500: 100%; SAT math scores over 500: 100%; SAT evidence-based reading and writing scores over 600: 97%; SAT math scores over 600: 96%; SAT evidence-based reading and writing scores over 700: 31%; SAT math scores over 700: 33%.

Retention: 90% of full-time freshmen returned.

FACULTY

Total: 305, 74% full-time, 84% with terminal degrees.

Student/faculty ratio: 9:1.

ACADEMICS

Calendar: semesters. *Degree:* bachelor's.

Special study options: adult/continuing education programs, advanced placement credit, double majors, independent study, internships, off-campus study, student-designed majors, study abroad. *ROTC:* Army (c).

Unusual degree programs: 3-2 engineering with Rensselaer Polytechnic Institute, Washington University, Columbia University, University of Pittsburgh; forestry with Duke University; nursing with Johns Hopkins University; optometry with Pennsylvania College of Optometry.

Computers: 350 computers/terminals are available on campus for general student use. Students can access the following: campus intranet, computer help desk, free student e-mail accounts, online (class) grades, online (class) registration, online (class) schedules. Campuswide network is available. 100% of college-owned or -operated housing units are wired for high-speed Internet access. Wireless service is available via entire campus.

Library: Musselman Library. *Books:* 370,500 (physical), 350,000 (digital/electronic); *Databases:* 299. Study areas open 24 hours, 5–7 days a week.

STUDENT LIFE

Housing options: on-campus residence required through senior year; coed, men-only, women-only. Campus housing is university owned. Freshman campus housing is guaranteed.

Activities and organizations: drama/theater group, student-run newspaper, radio and television station, choral group, marching band, community service, music, athletics, student government, national fraternities, national sororities.

Athletics Member NCAA. All Division III. *Intercollegiate sports:* baseball M, basketball M/W, cheerleading M/W, cross-country running M/W, equestrian sports M(c)/W(c), field hockey W, football M, golf M/W, ice hockey M(c), lacrosse M/W, rugby M(c)/W(c), soccer M/W, softball W, swimming and diving M/W, tennis M/W, track and field M/W, ultimate Frisbee M(c)/W(c), volleyball W, wrestling M. *Intramural sports:* basketball M/W, fencing M(c)/W(c), football M/W, soccer M/W, softball M/W, squash M(c), volleyball M/W, water polo M/W.

Campus security: 24-hour emergency response devices and patrols, student patrols, late-night transport/escort service, controlled dormitory access.

Student services: health clinic, personal/psychological counseling, women's center.

COSTS & FINANCIAL AID

Costs (2017–18) *Comprehensive fee:* $65,210 includes full-time tuition ($52,640) and room and board ($12,570). *College room only:* $6740. Room and board charges vary according to board plan and housing facility. *Payment plan:* installment. *Waivers:* employees or children of employees.

Financial Aid Of all full-time matriculated undergraduates who enrolled in 2017, 1,837 applied for aid, 1,631 were judged to have need, 1,431 had their need fully met. 376 Federal Work-Study jobs (averaging $958). 1,180 state and other part-time jobs (averaging $1048). In 2017, 475 non-need-based awards were made. *Average percent of need met:* 90. *Average financial aid package:* $40,700. *Average need-based loan:* $4702. *Average need-based gift aid:* $36,153. *Average non-need-based aid:* $13,256. *Average indebtedness upon graduation:* $31,323. *Financial aid deadline:* 1/15.

APPLYING

Standardized Tests *Required for some:* SAT or ACT (for admission).

Options: electronic application, early admission, early decision, deferred entrance.

Application fee: $60.

Required: essay or personal statement, high school transcript, 2 letters of recommendation. *Recommended:* minimum 3.0 GPA, interview, extracurricular activities.

Application deadlines: 1/15 (freshmen), 11/1 (transfers).

Early decision deadline: 11/15 (for plan 1), 1/15 (for plan 2).

Notification: 4/1 (freshmen), continuous (transfers), 12/15 (early decision plan 1), 2/15 (early decision plan 2).

CONTACT

Ms. Gail Sweezey, Director of Admissions, Gettysburg College, 300 North Washington Street, Gettysburg, PA 17325. *Phone:* 717-337-6100. *Toll-free phone:* 800-431-0803. *Fax:* 717-337-6145. *E-mail:* admiss@gettysburg.edu.

Grove City College

Grove City, Pennsylvania

http://www.gcc.edu/

- **Independent Presbyterian** 4-year, founded 1876
- **Small-town** 180-acre campus with easy access to Pittsburgh
- **Endowment** $112.8 million
- **Coed** 2,373 undergraduate students, 98% full-time, 49% women, 51% men
- **Moderately difficult** entrance level, 80% of applicants were admitted

UNDERGRAD STUDENTS

2,315 full-time, 58 part-time. Students come from 44 states and territories; 13 other countries; 44% are from out of state; 1% Black or African American, non-Hispanic/Latino; 1% Hispanic/Latino; 2% Asian, non-Hispanic/Latino; 3% Two or more races, non-Hispanic/Latino; 1% international; 1% transferred in; 95% live on campus.

Freshmen:

Admission: 1,783 applied, 1,424 admitted, 636 enrolled. *Average high school GPA:* 3.7. *Test scores:* SAT evidence-based reading and writing scores over 500: 97%; SAT math scores over 500: 94%; ACT scores over 18: 99%; SAT evidence-based reading and writing scores over 600: 64%; SAT math scores over 600: 54%; ACT scores over 24: 76%; SAT evidence-based reading and writing scores over 700: 19%; SAT math scores over 700: 13%; ACT scores over 30: 27%.

Retention: 89% of full-time freshmen returned.

FACULTY

Total: 246, 63% full-time, 59% with terminal degrees.

Student/faculty ratio: 13:1.

ACADEMICS

Calendar: semesters. *Degree:* bachelor's.

Special study options: accelerated degree program, advanced placement credit, distance learning, double majors, independent study, internships, off-campus study, services for LD students, study abroad, summer session for credit.

Computers: 50 computers/terminals and 8,000 ports are available on campus for general student use. Students can access the following: campus intranet, computer help desk, free student e-mail accounts, online (class) grades, online (class) registration, online (class) schedules. Campuswide network is available. 100% of college-owned or -operated housing units are wired for high-speed Internet access. Wireless service is available via entire campus.

Library: Henry Buhl Library plus 1 other. *Books:* 149,450 (physical), 231,000 (digital/electronic); *Serial titles:* 25 (physical), 33,037 (digital/electronic); *Databases:* 107. Weekly public service hours: 103.

STUDENT LIFE

Housing options: on-campus residence required through senior year; men-only, women-only. Campus housing is university owned. Freshman campus housing is guaranteed.

Activities and organizations: drama/theater group, student-run newspaper, radio and television station, choral group, marching band, Warriors for Christ, Orchesis, Orientation Board, Association for Women Students (AWS), Young Life.

Athletics Member NCAA. All Division III. *Intercollegiate sports:* baseball M, basketball M/W, cross-country running M/W, fencing M(c)/W(c), football M, golf M/W, lacrosse M/W(c), rugby M(c)/W(c), soccer M/W, softball W, swimming and diving M/W, tennis M/W, track and field M/W, volleyball M(c)/W, water polo M(c)/W. *Intramural sports:* badminton M/W, basketball M/W, bowling M/W, football M/W, racquetball M/W, soccer M/W, softball M, tennis M/W, ultimate Frisbee M/W, volleyball M/W.

Campus security: 24-hour emergency response devices and patrols, student patrols, late-night transport/escort service, controlled dormitory access, security cameras located around campus and in parking lots.

Student services: health clinic, personal/psychological counseling.

COSTS & FINANCIAL AID

Costs (2017–18) *Comprehensive fee:* $26,654 includes full-time tuition ($17,254) and room and board ($9400). Part-time tuition: $560 per credit hour. *Room and board:* Room and board charges vary according to housing facility. *Waivers:* employees or children of employees.

Financial Aid Of all full-time matriculated undergraduates who enrolled in 2017, 1,337 applied for aid, 1,072 were judged to have need, 96 had their need fully met. In 2017, 406 non-need-based awards were made. *Average percent of need met:* 50. *Average financial aid package:* $7424. *Average need-based gift aid:* $7424. *Average non-need-based aid:* $2936. *Average indebtedness upon graduation:* $40,747. *Financial aid deadline:* 4/15.

APPLYING

Standardized Tests *Required:* SAT or ACT (for admission), SAT, ACT, and/or CLT test scores (for admission).

Options: electronic application, early admission, early decision, deferred entrance.

Application fee: $50.

Required: essay or personal statement, high school transcript, 2 letters of recommendation. *Recommended:* interview.

Application deadlines: 1/20 (freshmen), 8/15 (transfers).

Early decision deadline: 11/1 (for plan 1), 12/1 (for plan 2).

Notification: 2/20 (freshmen), continuous (transfers), 12/15 (early decision plan 1), 1/15 (early decision plan 2).

CONTACT

Sarah E. Gibbs, Director of Admissions, Grove City College, 100 Campus Drive, Grove City, PA 16127-2104. *Phone:* 724-458-2100. *Fax:* 724-458-3395. *E-mail:* admissions@gcc.edu.

Gwynedd Mercy University
Gwynedd Valley, Pennsylvania
http://www.gmercyu.edu/

- **Independent Roman Catholic** comprehensive, founded 1948
- **Suburban** 170-acre campus with easy access to Philadelphia
- **Endowment** $23.3 million
- **Coed** 2,081 undergraduate students, 93% full-time, 78% women, 22% men
- **Moderately difficult** entrance level, 94% of applicants were admitted

UNDERGRAD STUDENTS
1,934 full-time, 147 part-time. Students come from 18 states and territories; 32 other countries; 13% are from out of state; 23% Black or African American, non-Hispanic/Latino; 5% Hispanic/Latino; 6% Asian, non-Hispanic/Latino; 0.3% American Indian or Alaska Native, non-Hispanic/Latino; 1% Two or more races, non-Hispanic/Latino; 5% Race/ethnicity unknown; 12% transferred in; 19% live on campus.

Freshmen:
Admission: 1,043 applied, 978 admitted, 266 enrolled. *Average high school GPA:* 3.2. *Test scores:* SAT evidence-based reading and writing scores over 500: 58%; SAT math scores over 500: 59%; ACT scores over 18: 73%; SAT evidence-based reading and writing scores over 600: 14%; SAT math scores over 600: 11%; ACT scores over 24: 25%; SAT math scores over 700: 1%; ACT scores over 30: 6%.

Retention: 84% of full-time freshmen returned.

FACULTY
Total: 303, 27% full-time, 27% with terminal degrees.
Student/faculty ratio: 11:1.

ACADEMICS
Calendar: semesters. *Degrees:* bachelor's, master's, doctoral, and post-master's certificates.

Special study options: academic remediation for entering students, accelerated degree program, adult/continuing education programs, advanced placement credit, cooperative education, distance learning, double majors, external degree program, honors programs, independent study, internships, part-time degree program, services for LD students, study abroad, summer session for credit.

Computers: 250 computers/terminals and 1,000 ports are available on campus for general student use. Students can access the following: campus intranet, computer help desk, free student e-mail accounts, online (class) grades, online (class) registration, online (class) schedules. Campuswide network is available. 100% of college-owned or -operated housing units are wired for high-speed Internet access. Wireless service is available via entire campus.

Library: Keiss Library plus 1 other. *Books:* 84,372 (physical), 150,948 (digital/electronic); *Serial titles:* 172 (physical), 32,373 (digital/electronic); *Databases:* 45. Weekly public service hours: 76; students can reserve study rooms.

STUDENT LIFE
Housing options: coed, special housing for students with disabilities. Campus housing is university owned. Freshman applicants given priority for college housing.

Activities and organizations: student-run newspaper, choral group, Voices of Gwynedd, Athletic Association, Student Government, Program Board, Peer Mentors.

Athletics Member NCAA. All Division III. *Intercollegiate sports:* baseball M, basketball M/W, cheerleading M/W, cross-country running M/W, field hockey W, lacrosse M/W, soccer M/W, softball W, tennis M/W, track and field M/W, volleyball W. *Intramural sports:* basketball M/W, soccer M/W, softball M/W.

Campus security: 24-hour emergency response devices and patrols, late-night transport/escort service, controlled dormitory access.

Student services: health clinic, personal/psychological counseling.

COSTS & FINANCIAL AID
Costs (2018–19) *Comprehensive fee:* $45,500 includes full-time tuition ($32,820), mandatory fees ($700), and room and board ($11,980). Full-time tuition and fees vary according to location and program. Part-time tuition: $725 per credit hour. Part-time tuition and fees vary according to location and program. *College room only:* $5360. Room and board charges vary according to board plan and housing facility. *Payment plan:* installment. *Waivers:* employees or children of employees.

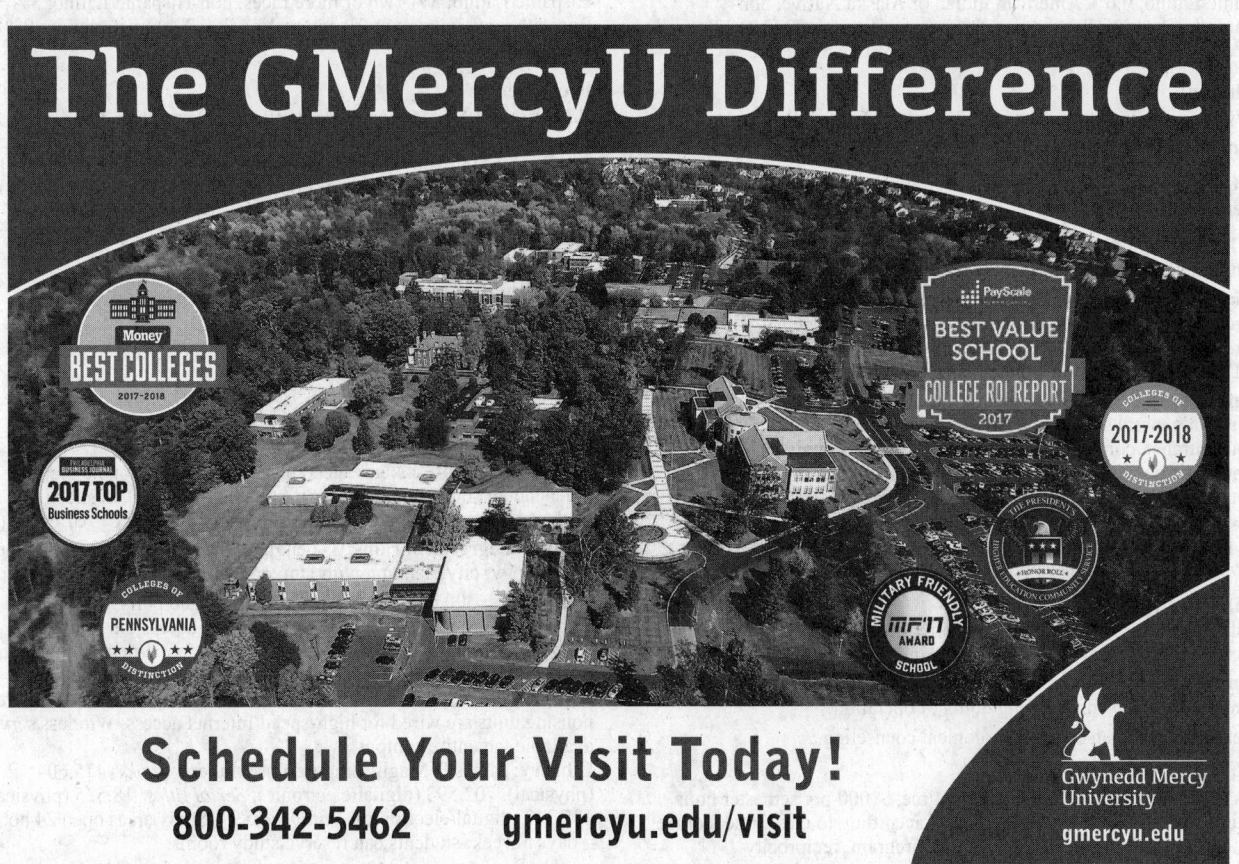

The GMercyU Difference

Schedule Your Visit Today!
800-342-5462   gmercyu.edu/visit

Gwynedd Mercy University
gmercyu.edu

Financial Aid Of all full-time matriculated undergraduates who enrolled in 2017, 1,551 applied for aid, 1,429 were judged to have need, 161 had their need fully met. 397 Federal Work-Study jobs (averaging $1418). In 2017, 150 non-need-based awards were made. *Average percent of need met:* 60. *Average financial aid package:* $22,116. *Average need-based loan:* $4172. *Average need-based gift aid:* $19,869. *Average non-need-based aid:* $13,795. *Average indebtedness upon graduation:* $46,139. *Financial aid deadline:* 5/1.

APPLYING
Standardized Tests *Required:* SAT or ACT (for admission).

Options: electronic application, deferred entrance.

Required: high school transcript. *Required for some:* essay or personal statement, interview. *Recommended:* letters of recommendation.

Application deadlines: rolling (freshmen), 8/20 (transfers).

Notification: continuous (freshmen), continuous (transfers).

CONTACT
Ms. Michelle Diehl, Director of Admissions, Gwynedd Mercy University, 1325 Sumneytown Pike, Gwynedd Valley, PA 19437-0901. *Phone:* 215-646-7300. *Toll-free phone:* 800-342-5462. *Fax:* 215-641-5556. *E-mail:* admissions@gmercyu.edu.

See previous page for display ad and page 1302 for the College Close-Up.

Harrisburg University of Science and Technology
Harrisburg, Pennsylvania
http://www.HarrisburgU.edu/
- **Independent** comprehensive, founded 2005
- **Urban** campus
- **Coed** 511 undergraduate students, 86% full-time, 49% women, 51% men
- **Minimally difficult** entrance level

UNDERGRAD STUDENTS
441 full-time, 70 part-time. Students come from 6 states and territories; 4 other countries; 28% are from out of state; 38% Black or African American, non-Hispanic/Latino; 13% Hispanic/Latino; 4% Asian, non-Hispanic/Latino; 0.6% American Indian or Alaska Native, non-Hispanic/Latino; 5% Two or more races, non-Hispanic/Latino; 1% Race/ethnicity unknown; 1% international; 6% transferred in.

Freshmen:
Admission: 178 enrolled. *Average high school GPA:* 2.9.
Retention: 54% of full-time freshmen returned.

FACULTY
Student/faculty ratio: 34:1.

ACADEMICS
Calendar: semesters. *Degrees:* bachelor's, master's, and doctoral.

Special study options: academic remediation for entering students, adult/continuing education programs, advanced placement credit, double majors, independent study, internships, part-time degree program, services for LD students, student-designed majors, summer session for credit.

Computers: 10 computers/terminals and 240 ports are available on campus for general student use. Students can access the following: campus intranet, computer help desk, free student e-mail accounts. Campuswide network is available. Wireless service is available via entire campus.

Library: Information Commons. *Books:* 4,130 (physical), 26 (digital/electronic); *Serial titles:* 103 (physical), 126 (digital/electronic); *Databases:* 24. Study areas open 24 hours, 5–7 days a week.

STUDENT LIFE
Housing options: Campus housing is provided by a third party. Freshman applicants given priority for college housing.

Campus security: 24-hour emergency response devices and patrols, trained security personnel during hours of operation.

Student services: personal/psychological counseling.

COSTS & FINANCIAL AID
Costs (2018–19) *Tuition:* $23,900 full-time, $1000 per semester hour part-time. Full-time tuition and fees vary according to class time, course level, course load, degree level, location, program, reciprocity

agreements, and student level. Part-time tuition and fees vary according to class time, course level, course load, degree level, location, program, reciprocity agreements, and student level. *Room only:* $6800. Room and board charges vary according to housing facility. *Payment plans:* installment, deferred payment.

Financial Aid Of all full-time matriculated undergraduates who enrolled in 2016, 335 applied for aid, 320 were judged to have need, 56 had their need fully met. 15 Federal Work-Study jobs (averaging $2000). In 2016, 22 non-need-based awards were made. *Average percent of need met:* 65. *Average financial aid package:* $19,814. *Average need-based loan:* $3923. *Average need-based gift aid:* $16,857. *Average non-need-based aid:* $15,789. *Average indebtedness upon graduation:* $34,547.

APPLYING
Options: electronic application.

Required: high school transcript. *Recommended:* essay or personal statement, interview.

Notification: continuous (freshmen).

CONTACT
Harrisburg University of Science and Technology, 326 Market Street, Harrisburg, PA 17101. *Phone:* 717-901-5150. *Toll-free phone:* 866-HBG-UNIV.

Haverford College
Haverford, Pennsylvania
http://www.haverford.edu/
- **Independent** 4-year, founded 1833
- **Suburban** 216-acre campus with easy access to Philadelphia
- **Endowment** $502.9 million
- **Coed** 1,296 undergraduate students, 100% full-time, 52% women, 48% men
- **Most difficult** entrance level, 20% of applicants were admitted

UNDERGRAD STUDENTS
1,294 full-time, 2 part-time. Students come from 43 states and territories; 39 other countries; 86% are from out of state; 7% Black or African American, non-Hispanic/Latino; 9% Hispanic/Latino; 12% Asian, non-Hispanic/Latino; 3% Two or more races, non-Hispanic/Latino; 3% Race/ethnicity unknown; 9% international; 0.7% transferred in; 98% live on campus.

Freshmen:
Admission: 4,408 applied, 884 admitted, 349 enrolled. *Test scores:* SAT evidence-based reading and writing scores over 500: 100%; SAT math scores over 500: 100%; ACT scores over 18: 100%; SAT evidence-based reading and writing scores over 600: 99%; SAT math scores over 600: 98%; ACT scores over 24: 100%; SAT evidence-based reading and writing scores over 700: 80%; SAT math scores over 700: 70%; ACT scores over 30: 89%.
Retention: 97% of full-time freshmen returned.

FACULTY
Total: 165, 83% full-time, 99% with terminal degrees.
Student/faculty ratio: 9:1.

ACADEMICS
Calendar: semesters. *Degree:* bachelor's.

Special study options: advanced placement credit, double majors, independent study, internships, off-campus study, services for LD students, student-designed majors, study abroad. *ROTC:* Air Force (c).

Unusual degree programs: 3-2 engineering with California Institute of Technology; city planning with University of Pennsylvania.

Computers: 300 computers/terminals and 1,600 ports are available on campus for general student use. Students can access the following: campus intranet, computer help desk, free student e-mail accounts, online (class) grades, online (class) registration, online (class) schedules. Campuswide network is available. 100% of college-owned or -operated housing units are wired for high-speed Internet access. Wireless service is available via entire campus.

Library: James P. Magill Library plus 3 others. *Books:* 475,604 (physical), 702,593 (digital/electronic); *Serial titles:* 18,525 (physical), 135,312 (digital/electronic); *Databases:* 91. Study areas open 24 hours, 5–7 days a week; students can reserve study rooms.

STUDENT LIFE

Housing options: on-campus residence required for freshman year; coed, men-only, women-only, special housing for students with disabilities. Campus housing is university owned. Freshman campus housing is guaranteed.

Activities and organizations: drama/theater group, student-run newspaper, radio station, choral group, Volunteer Programs, Student government, Choral groups, Multicultural Groups, Orientation Team/Residential Life Leaders.

Athletics Member NCAA. All Division III. *Intercollegiate sports:* badminton W(c), baseball M, basketball M/W, crew M(c)/W(c), cross-country running M/W, fencing M/W, field hockey W, golf M(c)/W(c), lacrosse M/W, rugby M(c), soccer M/W, softball W, squash M/W, tennis M/W, track and field M/W, ultimate Frisbee M(c)/W(c), volleyball M(c)/W, wrestling M(c). *Intramural sports:* basketball M/W, ice hockey M(c)/W(c), sailing M(c)/W(c), soccer M/W, softball M/W, tennis M/W, volleyball W.

Campus security: 24-hour emergency response devices and patrols, late-night transport/escort service, controlled dormitory access.

Student services: health clinic, personal/psychological counseling, women's center.

COSTS & FINANCIAL AID

Costs (2017–18) *One-time required fee:* $240. *Comprehensive fee:* $68,712 includes full-time tuition ($52,278), mandatory fees ($476), and room and board ($15,958). *College room only:* $9120. *Payment plan:* installment. *Waivers:* employees or children of employees.

Financial Aid Of all full-time matriculated undergraduates who enrolled in 2017, 663 applied for aid, 609 were judged to have need, 609 had their need fully met. *Average percent of need met:* 100. *Average financial aid package:* $51,271. *Average need-based loan:* $3418. *Average need-based gift aid:* $48,895. *Average indebtedness upon graduation:* $15,000.

APPLYING

Standardized Tests *Required:* SAT or ACT (for admission).

Options: electronic application, early admission, early decision, deferred entrance.

Application fee: $65.

Required: essay or personal statement. *Required for some:* high school transcript. *Recommended:* interview.

Application deadlines: 1/15 (freshmen), 3/31 (transfers).

Early decision deadline: 11/15 (for plan 1), 1/1 (for plan 2).

Notification: 4/1 (freshmen), 5/15 (transfers), 12/15 (early decision plan 1), 2/15 (early decision plan 2).

CONTACT

Mr. Jess Lord, Dean of Admissions and Financial Aid, Haverford College, 370 Lancaster Avenue, Haverford, PA 19041-1392. *Phone:* 610-896-1350. *Fax:* 610-896-1338. *E-mail:* admission@haverford.edu.

Holy Family University
Philadelphia, Pennsylvania
http://www.holyfamily.edu/

- **Independent Roman Catholic** comprehensive, founded 1954
- **Suburban** 47-acre campus with easy access to Philadelphia
- **Endowment** $18.5 million
- **Coed** 2,093 undergraduate students, 77% full-time, 74% women, 26% men
- **Minimally difficult** entrance level, 71% of applicants were admitted

UNDERGRAD STUDENTS

1,621 full-time, 472 part-time. Students come from 25 states and territories; 6 other countries; 14% are from out of state; 12% Black or African American, non-Hispanic/Latino; 4% Hispanic/Latino; 5% Asian, non-Hispanic/Latino; 0.4% Native Hawaiian or other Pacific Islander, non-Hispanic/Latino; 0.2% American Indian or Alaska Native, non-Hispanic/Latino; 20% Race/ethnicity unknown; 0.2% international; 8% transferred in; 15% live on campus.

Freshmen:
Admission: 1,429 applied, 1,011 admitted, 361 enrolled. *Average high school GPA:* 3.1.

Retention: 78% of full-time freshmen returned.

FACULTY

Total: 310, 25% full-time, 19% with terminal degrees.

Student/faculty ratio: 15:1.

ACADEMICS

Calendar: semesters. *Degrees:* certificates, associate, bachelor's, master's, doctoral, post-master's, and postbachelor's certificates.

Special study options: academic remediation for entering students, accelerated degree program, adult/continuing education programs, advanced placement credit, cooperative education, distance learning, double majors, honors programs, independent study, internships, off-campus study, part-time degree program, services for LD students, study abroad, summer session for credit. *ROTC:* Army (c).

Unusual degree programs: 3-2 criminal justice; psychology, sociology/criminal justice; business administration/human resources management, information systems management.

Computers: 300 computers/terminals and 388 ports are available on campus for general student use. Students can access the following: campus intranet, computer help desk, free student e-mail accounts, online (class) grades, online (class) registration, online (class) schedules, online course syllabi, online course evaluations. Campuswide network is available. 100% of college-owned or -operated housing units are wired for high-speed Internet access. Wireless service is available via entire campus.

Library: Holy Family University Library plus 1 other. *Books:* 75,943 (physical), 27,681 (digital/electronic); *Serial titles:* 1,106 (physical), 22,214 (digital/electronic); *Databases:* 42. Weekly public service hours: 116; students can reserve study rooms.

STUDENT LIFE

Housing options: coed, special housing for students with disabilities. Campus housing is university owned. Freshman campus housing is guaranteed.

Activities and organizations: drama/theater group, student-run newspaper, choral group, Students at Your Service (S.A.Y.S.), Green Team, Campus Ministry Team, Habitat for Humanity, Student Nurses Association of Holy Family.

Athletics Member NCAA. All Division II. *Intercollegiate sports:* basketball M(s)/W(s), cross-country running M(s)/W(s), lacrosse W(s), soccer M(s)/W(s), softball W(s), tennis W(s), track and field M(s)/W(s), volleyball W(s). *Intramural sports:* baseball M(c), basketball M/W, cheerleading M(c)/W(c), rugby M(c), volleyball M/W.

Campus security: 24-hour emergency response devices and patrols, late-night transport/escort service, controlled dormitory access, video surveillance.

Student services: health clinic, personal/psychological counseling.

COSTS & FINANCIAL AID

Costs (2018–19) *One-time required fee:* $504. *Comprehensive fee:* $43,922 includes full-time tuition ($29,338), mandatory fees ($1008), and room and board ($13,576). Full-time tuition and fees vary according to class time, course level, course load, degree level, program, and reciprocity agreements. Part-time tuition: $627 per credit hour. Part-time tuition and fees vary according to class time, course level, course load, degree level, program, and reciprocity agreements. *Required fees:* $112 per term part-time. *College room only:* $7140. Room and board charges vary according to board plan and housing facility. *Payment plans:* installment, deferred payment. *Waivers:* senior citizens and employees or children of employees.

Financial Aid Of all full-time matriculated undergraduates who enrolled in 2017, 1,371 applied for aid, 1,265 were judged to have need, 159 had their need fully met. 293 Federal Work-Study jobs (averaging $1069). In 2017, 171 non-need-based awards were made. *Average percent of need met:* 72. *Average financial aid package:* $21,883. *Average need-based loan:* $3756. *Average need-based gift aid:* $17,716. *Average non-need-based aid:* $12,972. *Average indebtedness upon graduation:* $36,609.

APPLYING

Standardized Tests *Required:* SAT or ACT (for admission).

Options: electronic application, deferred entrance.

Application fee: $25.

Required: essay or personal statement, high school transcript, minimum 2.0 GPA, 2 letters of recommendation. *Recommended:* interview.

Application deadlines: rolling (freshmen), rolling (transfers).
Notification: continuous (freshmen), continuous (transfers).

CONTACT
Ms. Lauren Campbell, Director of Admissions, Holy Family University, 9801 Frankford Avenue, Philadelphia, PA 19114-2009. *Phone:* 215-637-3050. *Fax:* 215-281-1022. *E-mail:* admissions@holyfamily.edu.

Hussian College, School of Art
Philadelphia, Pennsylvania
http://www.hussiancollege.edu/

CONTACT
Mr. Mark Cernero, Director of Admissions, Hussian College, School of Art, The Bourse, Suite 300, 111 South Independence Mall East, Philadelphia, PA 19106. *Phone:* 215-574-9600. *Fax:* 215-574-9800. *E-mail:* mcernero@hussianart.edu.

Immaculata University
Immaculata, Pennsylvania
http://www.immaculata.edu/

- **Independent Roman Catholic** university, founded 1920
- **Suburban** 373-acre campus with easy access to Philadelphia
- **Endowment** $17.0 million
- **Coed** 1,482 undergraduate students, 60% full-time, 75% women, 25% men
- **Moderately difficult** entrance level, 83% of applicants were admitted

UNDERGRAD STUDENTS
885 full-time, 597 part-time. 27% are from out of state; 15% Black or African American, non-Hispanic/Latino; 6% Hispanic/Latino; 2% Asian, non-Hispanic/Latino; 0.1% Native Hawaiian or other Pacific Islander, non-Hispanic/Latino; 0.1% American Indian or Alaska Native, non-Hispanic/Latino; 2% Two or more races, non-Hispanic/Latino; 4% Race/ethnicity unknown; 1% international; 3% transferred in.

Freshmen:
Admission: 1,550 applied, 1,293 admitted, 201 enrolled. *Average high school GPA:* 3.3. *Test scores:* SAT evidence-based reading and writing scores over 500: 70%; SAT math scores over 500: 65%; ACT scores over 18: 74%; SAT evidence-based reading and writing scores over 600: 26%; SAT math scores over 600: 17%; ACT scores over 24: 21%; SAT evidence-based reading and writing scores over 700: 3%; SAT math scores over 700: 1%; ACT scores over 30: 3%.
Retention: 78% of full-time freshmen returned.

FACULTY
Total: 308, 28% full-time.
Student/faculty ratio: 9:1.

ACADEMICS
Calendar: semesters. *Degrees:* certificates, associate, bachelor's, master's, and doctoral.
Special study options: academic remediation for entering students, accelerated degree program, adult/continuing education programs, advanced placement credit, distance learning, double majors, honors programs, independent study, internships, off-campus study, part-time degree program, services for LD students, study abroad, summer session for credit. *ROTC:* Army (c).
Unusual degree programs: 3-2 business administration with DeSales University; occupational therapy with Thomas Jefferson University.
Computers: 600 computers/terminals are available on campus for general student use. Students can access the following: campus intranet, computer help desk, free student e-mail accounts, online (class) grades, online (class) registration, online (class) schedules. Campuswide network is available. Wireless service is available via entire campus.
Library: Gabriele Library. *Books:* 117,104 (physical), 10,441 (digital/electronic); *Databases:* 53. Students can reserve study rooms.

STUDENT LIFE
Housing options: coed, men-only, women-only, special housing for students with disabilities. Campus housing is university owned. Freshman campus housing is guaranteed.

Activities and organizations: drama/theater group, student-run newspaper, choral group, National Society of Leadership and Success, Student Dietetic Association, Immaculata University Chorale, College of Undergraduate Studies Honor Society, Immaculata University Pre-Med.
Athletics Member NCAA. All Division III. *Intercollegiate sports:* baseball M, basketball M/W, cross-country running M/W, field hockey W, golf M/W, lacrosse M/W, soccer M/W, softball W, tennis M/W, track and field M/W, volleyball W. *Intramural sports:* basketball M/W, cheerleading W(c), soccer M/W, softball M/W, volleyball M/W.
Campus security: 24-hour emergency response devices and patrols, late-night transport/escort service, controlled dormitory access.
Student services: health clinic, personal/psychological counseling.

COSTS
Costs (2018–19) *Comprehensive fee:* $39,970 includes full-time tuition ($26,500), mandatory fees ($850), and room and board ($12,620). Full-time tuition and fees vary according to course load. Part-time tuition: $540 per credit hour. Part-time tuition and fees vary according to course load. *College room only:* $6390. Room and board charges vary according to board plan and housing facility. *Payment plan:* installment. *Waivers:* employees or children of employees.

APPLYING
Standardized Tests *Required for some:* SAT or ACT (for admission).
Options: electronic application, deferred entrance.
Application fee: $35.
Required: essay or personal statement, high school transcript, minimum 2.0 GPA, 1 letter of recommendation. *Required for some:* 2 letters of recommendation, audition for music students. *Recommended:* minimum 3.0 GPA, interview.
Application deadlines: rolling (freshmen), rolling (transfers).
Notification: continuous (freshmen), continuous (transfers).

CONTACT
Ms. Christine Esbensen, Assistant Director of Admissions, Immaculata University, 1145 King Road, Immaculata, PA 19345-0702. *Phone:* 610-647-4400 Ext. 3044. *Toll-free phone:* 877-428-6329. *Fax:* 610-640-0836. *E-mail:* admiss@immaculata.edu.

Indiana University of Pennsylvania
Indiana, Pennsylvania
http://www.iup.edu/

- **State-supported** university, founded 1875, part of Pennsylvania State System of Higher Education
- **Small-town** 374-acre campus with easy access to Pittsburgh
- **Endowment** $67.2 million
- **Coed** 10,143 undergraduate students, 92% full-time, 57% women, 43% men
- **Minimally difficult** entrance level, 91% of applicants were admitted

UNDERGRAD STUDENTS
9,350 full-time, 793 part-time. Students come from 26 states and territories; 39 other countries; 5% are from out of state; 12% Black or African American, non-Hispanic/Latino; 4% Hispanic/Latino; 1% Asian, non-Hispanic/Latino; 0.0% American Indian or Alaska Native, non-Hispanic/Latino; 4% Two or more races, non-Hispanic/Latino; 1% Race/ethnicity unknown; 4% international; 5% transferred in; 32% live on campus.

Freshmen:
Admission: 9,880 applied, 8,973 admitted, 2,333 enrolled. *Test scores:* SAT evidence-based reading and writing scores over 500: 59%; SAT math scores over 500: 52%; SAT evidence-based reading and writing scores over 600: 14%; SAT math scores over 600: 8%; SAT evidence-based reading and writing scores over 700: 1%.
Retention: 71% of full-time freshmen returned.

FACULTY
Total: 678, 84% full-time.
Student/faculty ratio: 16:1.

ACADEMICS
Calendar: semesters. *Degrees:* certificates, associate, bachelor's, master's, doctoral, post-master's, and postbachelor's certificates.

Special study options: academic remediation for entering students, accelerated degree program, adult/continuing education programs, advanced placement credit, cooperative education, distance learning, double majors, English as a second language, external degree program, freshman honors college, honors programs, independent study, internships, off-campus study, part-time degree program, services for LD students, student-designed majors, study abroad, summer session for credit. *ROTC:* Army (b).

Unusual degree programs: 3-2 engineering with Drexel University, University of Pittsburgh; chiropractic with Logan College of Chiropractic, New York Chiropractic College, Parker College, Sherman College of Straight Chiropractic; dentistry with Temple University School of Dentistry; optometry with Pennsylvania College of Optometry.

Computers: 2,363 computers/terminals and 5,000 ports are available on campus for general student use. Students can access the following: computer help desk, free student e-mail accounts, online (class) grades, online (class) registration, online (class) schedules. Campuswide network is available. 100% of college-owned or -operated housing units are wired for high-speed Internet access. Wireless service is available via entire campus.

Library: Stapleton Library. *Books:* 508,667 (physical), 79,230 (digital/electronic); *Serial titles:* 130,318 (physical). Weekly public service hours: 101; study areas open 24 hours, 5–7 days a week; students can reserve study rooms.

STUDENT LIFE

Housing options: on-campus residence required for freshman year; coed, women-only, special housing for students with disabilities. Campus housing is university owned and is provided by a third party. Freshman campus housing is guaranteed.

Activities and organizations: drama/theater group, student-run newspaper, radio and television station, choral group, marching band, Student Government Association, Panhellenic Association, Interfraternity Council, Student Association of Nutrition and Dietetics, Saudi Student Association, national fraternities, national sororities.

Athletics Member NCAA. All Division II. *Intercollegiate sports:* baseball M(s), basketball M(s)/W(s), cross-country running M(s)/W(s), field hockey W(s), football M(s), golf M(s), lacrosse W(s), soccer W(s), softball W(s), swimming and diving M(s)/W(s), tennis W(s), track and field M(s)/W(s), volleyball W(s). *Intramural sports:* baseball M(c), basketball M/W, cheerleading M(c)/W(c), equestrian sports M(c)/W(c), fencing M(c)/W(c), golf M(c)/W(c), ice hockey M(c)/W(c), lacrosse M(c)/W(c), riflery M(c)/W(c), rugby M(c)/W(c), sailing M(c)/W(c), soccer M(c)/W(c), swimming and diving M(c)/W(c), tennis M(c)/W(c), ultimate Frisbee M(c)/W(c), volleyball M(c)/W.

Campus security: 24-hour emergency response devices and patrols, late-night transport/escort service, controlled dormitory access.

Student services: health clinic, personal/psychological counseling, legal services.

COSTS & FINANCIAL AID

Costs (2017–18) *Tuition:* state resident $9000 full-time, $300 per credit hour part-time; nonresident $18,720 full-time, $780 per credit hour part-time. Full-time tuition and fees vary according to course load and reciprocity agreements. Part-time tuition and fees vary according to course load and reciprocity agreements. *Required fees:* $3146 full-time, $116 per credit hour part-time, $50 per term part-time. *Room and board:* $12,488; room only: $8950. Room and board charges vary according to board plan, housing facility, and location. *Payment plans:* installment, deferred payment. *Waivers:* senior citizens and employees or children of employees.

Financial Aid Of all full-time matriculated undergraduates who enrolled in 2016, 8,468 applied for aid, 7,068 were judged to have need, 561 had their need fully met. 953 Federal Work-Study jobs (averaging $1876). 1,397 state and other part-time jobs (averaging $2795). In 2016, 344 non-need-based awards were made. *Average percent of need met:* 55. *Average financial aid package:* $10,314. *Average need-based loan:* $4236. *Average need-based gift aid:* $6170. *Average non-need-based aid:* $2452. *Average indebtedness upon graduation:* $39,833.

APPLYING

Standardized Tests *Required:* SAT or ACT (for admission).

Options: electronic application, early admission, deferred entrance.

Application fee: $25.

Required: high school transcript. *Recommended:* essay or personal statement, 2 letters of recommendation.

Application deadlines: rolling (freshmen), rolling (transfers).

Notification: 9/1 (freshmen), continuous (transfers).

CONTACT

Office of Admissions, Indiana University of Pennsylvania, 1011 South Drive, Sutton Hall, Suite120, Indiana, PA 15705. *Phone:* 724-357-2230. *Toll-free phone:* 800-442-6830. *Fax:* 724-357-6281. *E-mail:* admissions-inquiry@iup.edu.

Juniata College

Huntingdon, Pennsylvania

http://www.juniata.edu/

- **Independent** comprehensive, founded 1876, affiliated with Church of the Brethren
- **Small-town** 110-acre campus
- **Endowment** $112.0 million
- **Coed** 1,485 undergraduate students, 94% full-time, 56% women, 44% men
- **Moderately difficult** entrance level, 71% of applicants were admitted

UNDERGRAD STUDENTS

1,400 full-time, 85 part-time. Students come from 36 states and territories; 35 other countries; 34% are from out of state; 5% Black or African American, non-Hispanic/Latino; 3% Hispanic/Latino; 3% Asian, non-Hispanic/Latino; 0.1% American Indian or Alaska Native, non-Hispanic/Latino; 2% Two or more races, non-Hispanic/Latino; 3% Race/ethnicity unknown; 9% international; 2% transferred in; 82% live on campus.

Freshmen:

Admission: 2,289 applied, 1,620 admitted, 341 enrolled. *Average high school GPA:* 3.7. *Test scores:* SAT evidence-based reading and writing scores over 500: 93%; SAT math scores over 500: 94%; ACT scores over 18: 97%; SAT evidence-based reading and writing scores over 600: 49%; SAT math scores over 600: 49%; ACT scores over 24: 67%; SAT evidence-based reading and writing scores over 700: 9%; SAT math scores over 700: 8%; ACT scores over 30: 19%.

Retention: 81% of full-time freshmen returned.

FACULTY

Total: 156, 76% full-time, 75% with terminal degrees.

Student/faculty ratio: 11:1.

ACADEMICS

Calendar: semesters. *Degrees:* bachelor's and master's.

Special study options: advanced placement credit, double majors, English as a second language, honors programs, independent study, internships, off-campus study, part-time degree program, services for LD students, student-designed majors, study abroad, summer session for credit.

Unusual degree programs: 3-2 engineering with Columbia University, Penn State University, Washington University in St. Louis, Clarkson University; nursing with Case Western University, Johns Hopkins University.

Computers: 150 computers/terminals and 257 ports are available on campus for general student use. Students can access the following: computer help desk, free student e-mail accounts, online (class) grades, online (class) registration, online (class) schedules, access to bills. Campuswide network is available. 100% of college-owned or -operated housing units are wired for high-speed Internet access. Wireless service is available via classrooms, computer centers, computer labs, dorm rooms, learning centers, libraries, student centers.

Library: Beeghly Library. *Books:* 170,000 (physical); *Serial titles:* 241 (physical). Weekly public service hours: 107.

STUDENT LIFE

Housing options: on-campus residence required through senior year; coed, women-only. Campus housing is university owned. Freshman campus housing is guaranteed.

Activities and organizations: drama/theater group, student-run radio station, choral group, Student Government Association, Juniata Activities

Board (JAB), Habitat for Humanity, National Society of Leadership and Success.

Athletics Member NCAA. All Division III. *Intercollegiate sports:* baseball M, basketball M/W, cross-country running M/W, field hockey W, football M, golf M/W, lacrosse W, rugby M(c)/W(c), soccer M/W, softball W, swimming and diving W, tennis M/W, track and field M/W, ultimate Frisbee M(c)/W(c), volleyball M/W. *Intramural sports:* basketball M/W, cheerleading W(c), equestrian sports M(c)/W(c), field hockey M(c)/W(c), racquetball M/W, skiing (downhill) M(c)/W(c), soccer M/W, swimming and diving M/W, table tennis M(c)/W(c), tennis M(c)/W(c), volleyball M(c)/W(c).

Campus security: 24-hour emergency response devices and patrols, student patrols, late-night transport/escort service, controlled dormitory access, fire safety training, adopt-an-officer program, security Website, weather/terror alerts, travel forecast, crime statistics.

Student services: health clinic, personal/psychological counseling, women's center.

COSTS & FINANCIAL AID
Costs (2018–19) *Comprehensive fee:* $58,118 includes full-time tuition ($44,772), mandatory fees ($825), and room and board ($12,521). Full-time tuition and fees vary according to course load, degree level, and program. Part-time tuition and fees vary according to course load and degree level. *College room only:* $6666. Room and board charges vary according to board plan and housing facility. *Payment plan:* installment. *Waivers:* senior citizens and employees or children of employees.

Financial Aid Of all full-time matriculated undergraduates who enrolled in 2017, 1,137 applied for aid, 1,041 were judged to have need, 177 had their need fully met. 334 Federal Work-Study jobs (averaging $480). 739 state and other part-time jobs (averaging $875). In 2017, 327 non-need-based awards were made. *Average percent of need met:* 83. *Average financial aid package:* $36,787. *Average need-based loan:* $5950. *Average need-based gift aid:* $30,389. *Average non-need-based aid:* $22,987. *Average indebtedness upon graduation:* $38,478.

APPLYING
Standardized Tests *Recommended:* SAT or ACT (for admission).

Options: electronic application, early admission, early decision, early action, deferred entrance.
Required: essay or personal statement, high school transcript, minimum 3.0 GPA, 1 letter of recommendation. *Recommended:* interview.
Application deadlines: 2/15 (freshmen), 6/15 (transfers).
Early decision deadline: 11/15 (for plan 1), 2/15 (for plan 2).
Notification: 2/1 (freshmen), continuous (transfers), 12/23 (early decision plan 1), rolling (early decision plan 2).

CONTACT
Terri Bollman-Dalansky, Senior Associate Dean of Admission, Juniata College, 1700 Moore Street, Huntingdon, PA 16652-2119. *Phone:* 814-641-3424. *Toll-free phone:* 877-JUNIATA. *Fax:* 814-641-3100. *E-mail:* bollmat@juniata.edu.

Keystone College
La Plume, Pennsylvania
http://www.keystone.edu/

CONTACT
Jessica Lopez, Senior Administrative Assistant, Keystone College, One College Green, PO Box 50, La Plume, PA 18440-1099. *Phone:* 570-945-8111. *Toll-free phone:* 877-4-COLLEGE. *Fax:* 570-945-7916. *E-mail:* admissions@keystone.edu.

King's College
Wilkes-Barre, Pennsylvania
http://www.kings.edu/

- **Independent Roman Catholic** comprehensive, founded 1946
- **Urban** 48-acre campus
- **Endowment** $75.4 million
- **Coed** 2,197 undergraduate students, 92% full-time, 46% women, 54% men
- **Moderately difficult** entrance level, 71% of applicants were admitted

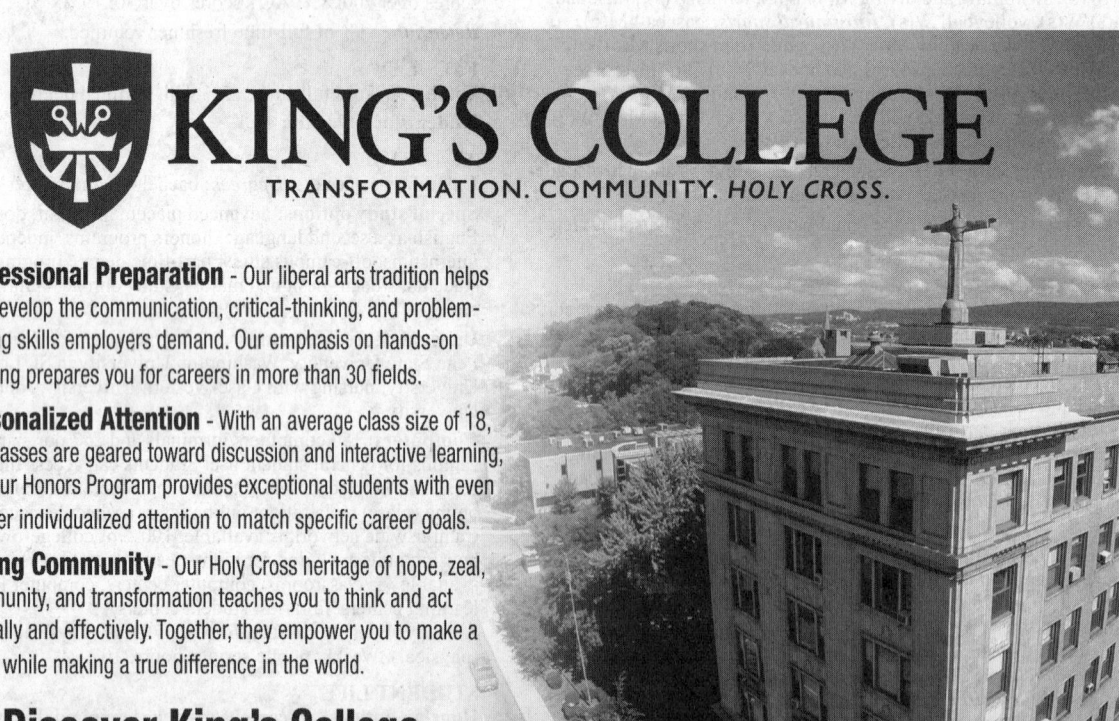

UNDERGRAD STUDENTS

2,025 full-time, 172 part-time. Students come from 26 states and territories; 6 other countries; 30% are from out of state; 4% Black or African American, non-Hispanic/Latino; 7% Hispanic/Latino; 2% Asian, non-Hispanic/Latino; 0.1% American Indian or Alaska Native, non-Hispanic/Latino; 3% Two or more races, non-Hispanic/Latino; 4% Race/ethnicity unknown; 8% international; 5% transferred in; 48% live on campus.

Freshmen:

Admission: 4,354 applied, 3,080 admitted, 624 enrolled. *Average high school GPA:* 3.4. *Test scores:* SAT evidence-based reading and writing scores over 500: 74%; SAT math scores over 500: 75%; ACT scores over 18: 93%; SAT evidence-based reading and writing scores over 600: 25%; SAT math scores over 600: 28%; ACT scores over 24: 55%; SAT evidence-based reading and writing scores over 700: 2%; SAT math scores over 700: 2%; ACT scores over 30: 8%.

Retention: 73% of full-time freshmen returned.

FACULTY

Total: 225, 60% full-time, 61% with terminal degrees.

Student/faculty ratio: 13:1.

ACADEMICS

Calendar: semesters. *Degrees:* bachelor's, master's, and postbachelor's certificates.

Special study options: accelerated degree program, adult/continuing education programs, advanced placement credit, distance learning, double majors, English as a second language, honors programs, independent study, internships, off-campus study, part-time degree program, services for LD students, student-designed majors, study abroad, summer session for credit. *ROTC:* Army (b), Air Force (c).

Unusual degree programs: 3-2 engineering with University of Notre Dame.

Computers: 470 computers/terminals are available on campus for general student use. Students can access the following: computer help desk, free student e-mail accounts, online (class) grades, online (class) registration, online (class) schedules. Campuswide network is available. 100% of college-owned or -operated housing units are wired for high-speed Internet access. Wireless service is available via classrooms, computer labs, dorm rooms, libraries, student centers.

Library: D. Leonard Corgan Library. *Books:* 182,499 (physical); *Databases:* 54. Weekly public service hours: 89; study areas open 24 hours, 5–7 days a week.

STUDENT LIFE

Housing options: on-campus residence required through sophomore year; coed, men-only, women-only, cooperative, special housing for students with disabilities. Campus housing is university owned. Freshman campus housing is guaranteed.

Activities and organizations: drama/theater group, student-run newspaper, radio station, choral group, Association of Campus Events, Student Government Association, Accounting Association, International/Multicultural Club, Biology Club.

Athletics Member NCAA. All Division III. *Intercollegiate sports:* baseball M, basketball M/W, cross-country running M/W, field hockey W, football M, golf M, ice hockey M/W, lacrosse M/W, soccer M/W, softball W, swimming and diving M/W, tennis M/W, track and field M/W, volleyball W, wrestling M. *Intramural sports:* basketball M/W, rugby M, soccer M/W.

Campus security: 24-hour emergency response devices and patrols, late-night transport/escort service, controlled dormitory access.

Student services: health clinic, personal/psychological counseling.

COSTS & FINANCIAL AID

Costs (2017–18) *Comprehensive fee:* $48,240 includes full-time tuition ($34,630), mandatory fees ($1200), and room and board ($12,410). Part-time tuition: $566 per credit hour. *College room only:* $6240. Room and board charges vary according to board plan. *Payment plan:* installment. *Waivers:* senior citizens and employees or children of employees.

Financial Aid Of all full-time matriculated undergraduates who enrolled in 2017, 1,757 applied for aid, 1,590 were judged to have need, 301 had their need fully met. 269 Federal Work-Study jobs (averaging $1910). 253 state and other part-time jobs (averaging $1046). In 2017, 298 non-need-based awards were made. *Average percent of need met:* 73. *Average financial aid package:* $25,469. *Average need-based loan:* $5059. *Average need-based gift aid:* $19,645. *Average non-need-based aid:* $16,259. *Average indebtedness upon graduation:* $38,625.

APPLYING

Standardized Tests *Recommended:* SAT or ACT (for admission).

Options: electronic application, early action, deferred entrance.

Application fee: $30.

Required: essay or personal statement, high school transcript. *Recommended:* interview.

Application deadlines: rolling (freshmen), rolling (transfers), 12/1 (early action).

Notification: continuous (freshmen), continuous (transfers), 12/15 (early action).

CONTACT

Mr. Corry Unis, Vice President for Enrollment Management, King's College, 133 North River Street, Wilkes-Barre, PA 18711-0801. *Phone:* 570-208-5858. *Toll-free phone:* 888-KINGSPA. *Fax:* 570-208-5971. *E-mail:* admissions@kings.edu.

See previous page for display ad and page 1320 for the College Close-Up.

Kutztown University of Pennsylvania
Kutztown, Pennsylvania
http://www.kutztown.edu/

- **State-supported** comprehensive, founded 1866, part of Pennsylvania State System of Higher Education
- **Rural** 289-acre campus with easy access to Philadelphia
- **Endowment** $22.2 million
- **Coed** 7,489 undergraduate students, 94% full-time, 53% women, 47% men
- **Moderately difficult** entrance level, 74% of applicants were admitted

UNDERGRAD STUDENTS

7,053 full-time, 436 part-time. Students come from 27 states and territories; 32 other countries; 12% are from out of state; 7% Black or African American, non-Hispanic/Latino; 9% Hispanic/Latino; 1% Asian, non-Hispanic/Latino; 0.1% Native Hawaiian or other Pacific Islander, non-Hispanic/Latino; 0.2% American Indian or Alaska Native, non-Hispanic/Latino; 3% Two or more races, non-Hispanic/Latino; 1% Race/ethnicity unknown; 0.9% international; 8% transferred in; 45% live on campus.

Freshmen:

Admission: 8,073 applied, 5,965 admitted, 1,605 enrolled. *Average high school GPA:* 3.2. *Test scores:* SAT evidence-based reading and writing scores over 500: 71%; SAT math scores over 500: 68%; ACT scores over 18: 83%; SAT evidence-based reading and writing scores over 600: 20%; SAT math scores over 600: 13%; ACT scores over 24: 27%; SAT evidence-based reading and writing scores over 700: 2%; SAT math scores over 700: 1%; ACT scores over 30: 4%.

Retention: 74% of full-time freshmen returned.

FACULTY

Total: 445, 87% full-time, 79% with terminal degrees.

Student/faculty ratio: 18:1.

ACADEMICS

Calendar: semesters. *Degrees:* bachelor's, master's, doctoral, post-master's, and postbachelor's certificates.

Special study options: academic remediation for entering students, accelerated degree program, adult/continuing education programs, advanced placement credit, distance learning, double majors, honors programs, independent study, internships, off-campus study, part-time degree program, services for LD students, student-designed majors, study abroad, summer session for credit. *ROTC:* Army (c).

Unusual degree programs: business administration; social work.

Computers: 1,075 computers/terminals and 100 ports are available on campus for general student use. Students can access the following: computer help desk, free student e-mail accounts, online (class) grades, online (class) registration, online (class) schedules. Campuswide network is available. 100% of college-owned or -operated housing units are wired for high-speed Internet access. Wireless service is available via classrooms, computer centers, computer labs, dorm rooms, learning centers, libraries, student centers.

Library: Rohrbach Library. *Books:* 317,044 (physical), 299,170 (digital/electronic); *Serial titles:* 88,613 (digital/electronic); *Databases:* 134. Weekly public service hours: 92; students can reserve study rooms.

STUDENT LIFE

Housing options: coed, women-only, cooperative. Campus housing is university owned and leased by the school. Freshman campus housing is guaranteed.

Activities and organizations: drama/theater group, student-run newspaper, radio and television station, choral group, marching band, Marching Unit, Honors Club, American Marketing Association Kutztown Chapter, Humans versus Zombies: Kutztown Chapter, Paws for Love, national fraternities, national sororities.

Athletics Member NCAA. All Division II. *Intercollegiate sports:* baseball M(s), basketball M(s)/W(s), bowling W(s), cheerleading W(c), cross-country running M(s)/W(s), equestrian sports M(c)/W(c), fencing M(c)/W(c), field hockey W(s), football M(s), golf M(c)/W(s), ice hockey M(c), lacrosse M(c)/W(s), rugby M(c)/W(c), soccer M(c)/W(s), softball W(s), swimming and diving W(s), tennis M(s)/W(s), track and field M(s)/W(s), ultimate Frisbee M(c)/W(c), volleyball M(c)/W(s), wrestling M(s). *Intramural sports:* basketball M/W, football M/W, racquetball M/W, rock climbing M/W, soccer M/W, softball M/W, table tennis M/W, tennis M/W, volleyball M/W.

Campus security: 24-hour emergency response devices and patrols, student patrols, late-night transport/escort service, controlled dormitory access, secondary door electronic alarm system in residence halls, 24-hour student desk personnel at main entrance of residence halls.

Student services: health clinic, personal/psychological counseling, women's center.

COSTS & FINANCIAL AID

Costs (2017–18) *One-time required fee:* $108. *Tuition:* state resident $7492 full-time, $312 per credit part-time; nonresident $11,238 full-time, $468 per credit part-time. Full-time tuition and fees vary according to course load. Part-time tuition and fees vary according to course load. *Required fees:* $2495 full-time, $105 per credit part-time. *Room and board:* $10,282. Room and board charges vary according to board plan and housing facility. *Payment plans:* installment, deferred payment. *Waivers:* senior citizens and employees or children of employees.

Financial Aid Of all full-time matriculated undergraduates who enrolled in 2016, 6,321 applied for aid, 5,213 were judged to have need, 349 had their need fully met. 468 Federal Work-Study jobs (averaging $2572). In 2016, 287 non-need-based awards were made. *Average percent of need met:* 46. *Average financial aid package:* $8860. *Average need-based loan:* $4172. *Average need-based gift aid:* $5741. *Average non-need-based aid:* $1169. *Average indebtedness upon graduation:* $40,084.

APPLYING

Standardized Tests *Required:* SAT or ACT (for admission). *Required for some:* SAT Subject Tests (for admission).

Options: electronic application, early admission, deferred entrance.

Application fee: $35.

Required: high school transcript, minimum 2.0 GPA. *Required for some:* audition for music, portfolio and/or art test for arts.

Application deadlines: rolling (freshmen), rolling (transfers).

Notification: continuous (freshmen), continuous (transfers).

CONTACT

Kutztown University of Pennsylvania, 15200 Kutztown Road, Kutztown, PA 19530-0730. *Phone:* 484-646-4144. *Toll-free phone:* 877-628-1915.

See below for display ad and page 1322 for the College Close-Up.

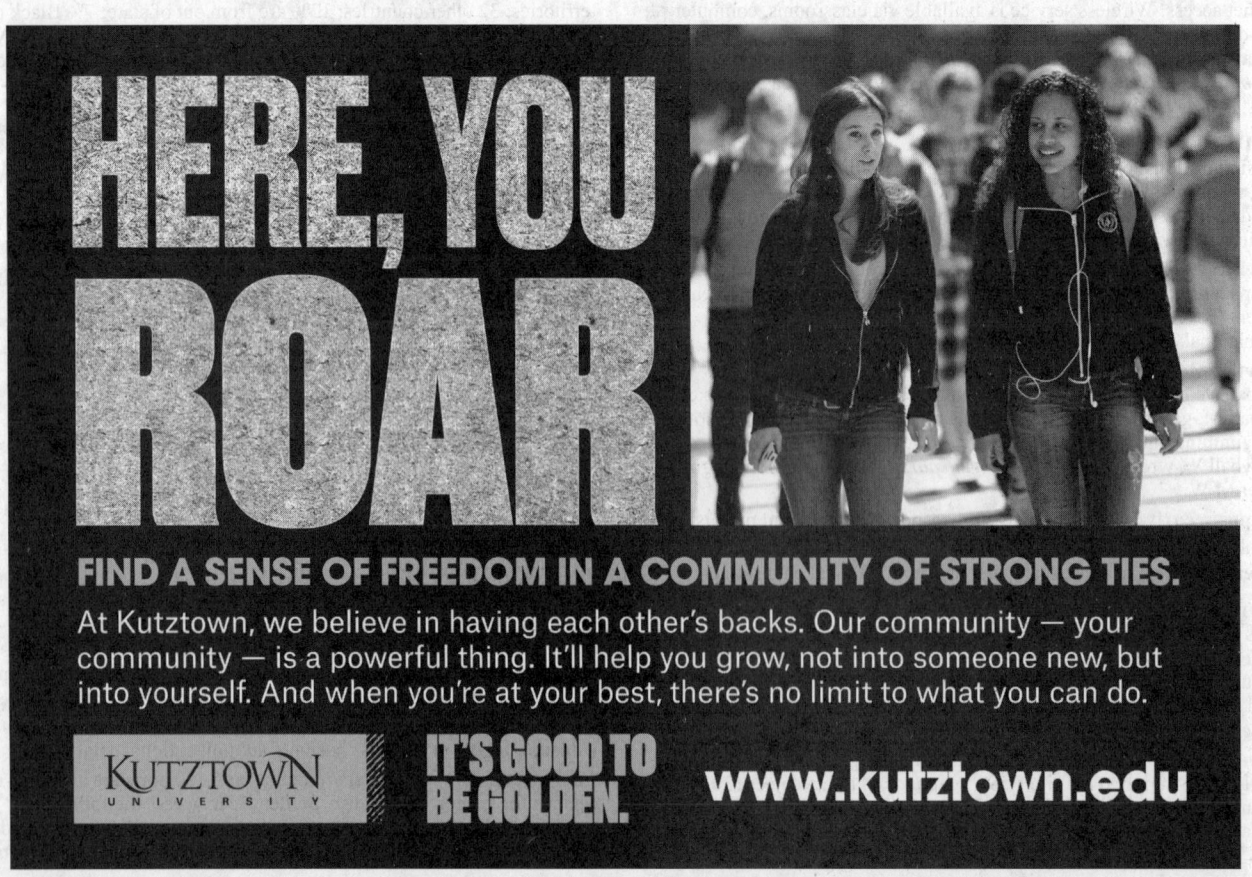

Lafayette College

Easton, Pennsylvania
http://www.lafayette.edu/

- **Independent** 4-year, founded 1826, affiliated with Presbyterian Church (U.S.A.)
- **Suburban** 340-acre campus with easy access to New York City, Philadelphia
- **Endowment** $833.1 million
- **Coed** 2,594 undergraduate students, 98% full-time, 52% women, 48% men

UNDERGRAD STUDENTS
2,551 full-time, 43 part-time. Students come from 44 states and territories; 61 other countries; 81% are from out of state; 5% Black or African American, non-Hispanic/Latino; 7% Hispanic/Latino; 4% Asian, non-Hispanic/Latino; 3% Two or more races, non-Hispanic/Latino; 6% Race/ethnicity unknown; 10% international; 0.6% transferred in; 93% live on campus.

Freshmen:
Admission: 680 enrolled. *Test scores:* SAT evidence-based reading and writing scores over 500: 99%; SAT math scores over 500: 99%; ACT scores over 18: 100%; SAT evidence-based reading and writing scores over 600: 86%; SAT math scores over 600: 87%; ACT scores over 24: 96%; SAT evidence-based reading and writing scores over 700: 33%; SAT math scores over 700: 41%; ACT scores over 30: 53%.
Retention: 95% of full-time freshmen returned.

FACULTY
Total: 293, 81% full-time, 90% with terminal degrees.
Student/faculty ratio: 10:1.

ACADEMICS
Calendar: semesters plus interim January program. *Degree:* bachelor's.
Special study options: academic remediation for entering students, accelerated degree program, advanced placement credit, double majors, honors programs, independent study, internships, off-campus study, part-time degree program, services for LD students, student-designed majors, study abroad, summer session for credit. *ROTC:* Army (c).
Computers: 690 computers/terminals and 690 ports are available on campus for general student use. Students can access the following: campus intranet, computer help desk, free student e-mail accounts, online (class) grades, online (class) registration, online (class) schedules. Campuswide network is available. 100% of college-owned or -operated housing units are wired for high-speed Internet access. Wireless service is available via entire campus.
Library: Skillman Library plus 2 others. *Books:* 603,599 (physical), 344,469 (digital/electronic); *Serial titles:* 306 (physical), 68,298 (digital/electronic); *Databases:* 132. Weekly public service hours: 106.

STUDENT LIFE
Housing options: on-campus residence required through senior year; coed, men-only, women-only, special housing for students with disabilities. Campus housing is university owned. Freshman campus housing is guaranteed.
Activities and organizations: drama/theater group, student-run newspaper, radio station, choral group, LAF (Lafayette Activities Forum), Student Government, Crew, International Students Association, Leopards Lair, national fraternities, national sororities.
Athletics Member NCAA. All Division I except football (Division I-AA). *Intercollegiate sports:* baseball M, basketball M/W, crew M(c)/W(c), cross-country running M/W, equestrian sports M(c)/W(c), fencing M/W, field hockey W, golf M, ice hockey M(c), lacrosse M/W, rugby M(c)/W(c), skiing (downhill) M(c)/W(c), soccer M/W, softball W, squash M(c), swimming and diving M/W, tennis M/W, track and field M/W, volleyball W, weight lifting M(c)/W(c), wrestling M(c). *Intramural sports:* badminton M/W, baseball M, basketball M/W, bowling M/W, cross-country running M/W, fencing M/W, field hockey W, football M, golf M/W, lacrosse M/W, racquetball M/W, sailing M(c)/W(c), skiing (cross-country) M(c)/W(c), soccer M/W, softball M/W, squash M/W, swimming and diving M/W, table tennis M/W, tennis M/W, track and field M/W, volleyball M/W, weight lifting M/W, wrestling M.

Campus security: 24-hour emergency response devices and patrols, student patrols, late-night transport/escort service, controlled dormitory access.
Student services: health clinic, personal/psychological counseling, women's center.

COSTS & FINANCIAL AID
Costs (2017–18) *One-time required fee:* $740. *Comprehensive fee:* $65,890 includes full-time tuition ($50,400), mandatory fees ($450), and room and board ($15,040). *College room only:* $9300. *Payment plan:* installment. *Waivers:* employees or children of employees.
Financial Aid Of all full-time matriculated undergraduates who enrolled in 2017, 1,339 applied for aid, 762 were judged to have need, 759 had their need fully met. 516 Federal Work-Study jobs (averaging $1258). In 2017, 210 non-need-based awards were made. *Average percent of need met:* 100. *Average financial aid package:* $49,361. *Average need-based loan:* $4099. *Average need-based gift aid:* $43,399. *Average non-need-based aid:* $28,900. *Average indebtedness upon graduation:* $32,974. *Financial aid deadline:* 1/15.

APPLYING
Standardized Tests *Required:* SAT or ACT (for admission). *Recommended:* SAT Subject Tests (for admission).
Required: essay or personal statement, high school transcript, 1 letter of recommendation. *Recommended:* interview.

CONTACT
Mr. Matthew Hyde, Director of Admissions, Lafayette College, 118 Markle Hall, 730 High Street, Easton, PA 18042-1798. *Phone:* 610-330-5100. *Fax:* 610-330-5355. *E-mail:* hydem@lafayette.edu.

Lancaster Bible College

Lancaster, Pennsylvania
http://www.lbc.edu/

CONTACT
Mrs. Joanne M. Roper, Associate Vice President for Admissions, Lancaster Bible College, PO Box 83403, Lancaster, PA 17608. *Phone:* 717-560-8271. *Toll-free phone:* 800-544-7335. *Fax:* 717-560-8213. *E-mail:* admissions@lbc.edu.

La Roche College

Pittsburgh, Pennsylvania
http://www.laroche.edu/

- **Independent** comprehensive, founded 1963, affiliated with Roman Catholic Church
- **Suburban** 43-acre campus
- **Endowment** $5.7 million
- **Coed** 1,378 undergraduate students, 84% full-time, 55% women, 45% men
- **Minimally difficult** entrance level, 97% of applicants were admitted

UNDERGRAD STUDENTS
1,163 full-time, 215 part-time. Students come from 18 states and territories; 27 other countries; 10% are from out of state; 10% Black or African American, non-Hispanic/Latino; 3% Hispanic/Latino; 2% Asian, non-Hispanic/Latino; 0.1% Native Hawaiian or other Pacific Islander, non-Hispanic/Latino; 0.4% American Indian or Alaska Native, non-Hispanic/Latino; 2% Two or more races, non-Hispanic/Latino; 4% Race/ethnicity unknown; 15% international; 12% transferred in; 37% live on campus.

Freshmen:
Admission: 1,197 applied, 1,156 admitted, 227 enrolled. *Average high school GPA:* 3.3. *Test scores:* SAT evidence-based reading and writing scores over 500: 66%; SAT math scores over 500: 58%; ACT scores over 18: 77%; SAT evidence-based reading and writing scores over 600: 20%; SAT math scores over 600: 10%; ACT scores over 24: 24%; SAT evidence-based reading and writing scores over 700: 1%; ACT scores over 30: 4%.
Retention: 68% of full-time freshmen returned.

FACULTY
Total: 210, 31% full-time, 38% with terminal degrees.

Student/faculty ratio: 12:1.

ACADEMICS

Calendar: semesters plus summer term. *Degrees:* certificates, associate, bachelor's, master's, doctoral, and postbachelor's certificates.

Special study options: academic remediation for entering students, accelerated degree program, adult/continuing education programs, advanced placement credit, distance learning, double majors, English as a second language, freshman honors college, honors programs, independent study, internships, off-campus study, part-time degree program, services for LD students, student-designed majors, study abroad, summer session for credit. *ROTC:* Army (c), Air Force (c).

Unusual degree programs: engineering with University of Pittsburgh; physical therapy, physician's assistant, speech language pathologist, athletic trainer, occupational therapy with Duquesne University; pharmacy, dental and medical with Lake Erie College of Osteopathic Medicine; software engineering with Gannon University.

Computers: Students can access the following: campus intranet, computer help desk, free student e-mail accounts, online (class) grades, online (class) registration, online (class) schedules. Campuswide network is available. 100% of college-owned or -operated housing units are wired for high-speed Internet access. Wireless service is available via classrooms, computer labs, learning centers, libraries, student centers.

Library: John J. Wright Library plus 1 other. *Books:* 75,803 (physical), 221,000 (digital/electronic); *Databases:* 1,248.

STUDENT LIFE

Housing options: coed. Campus housing is university owned. Freshman campus housing is guaranteed.

Activities and organizations: student-run newspaper, radio station, American Society of Interior Design, student government, Visions (environmental club).

Athletics Member NCAA. All Division III. *Intercollegiate sports:* baseball M, basketball M/W, cross-country running M/W, golf M, lacrosse M/W, soccer M/W, softball W, tennis W, volleyball W. *Intramural sports:* basketball M/W, weight lifting M/W.

Campus security: 24-hour emergency response devices and patrols, student patrols, late-night transport/escort service, controlled dormitory access.

Student services: health clinic, personal/psychological counseling.

COSTS & FINANCIAL AID

Costs (2018–19) *Comprehensive fee:* $40,120 includes full-time tuition ($27,714), mandatory fees ($850), and room and board ($11,556). Part-time tuition: $700 per credit hour. *Required fees:* $40 per term part-time. *College room only:* $7316. Room and board charges vary according to board plan and housing facility. *Payment plan:* installment. *Waivers:* senior citizens and employees or children of employees.

Financial Aid Of all full-time matriculated undergraduates who enrolled in 2017, 850 applied for aid, 800 were judged to have need, 298 had their need fully met. 136 Federal Work-Study jobs (averaging $1544). In 2017, 50 non-need-based awards were made. *Average percent of need met:* 94. *Average financial aid package:* $30,310. *Average need-based loan:* $7400. *Average need-based gift aid:* $8593. *Average non-need-based aid:* $19,408. *Average indebtedness upon graduation:* $27,298.

APPLYING

Standardized Tests *Required:* SAT or ACT (for admission).

Options: electronic application, early admission, deferred entrance.

Application fee: $50.

Required: high school transcript, minimum 2.0 GPA, 2 letters of recommendation. *Recommended:* essay or personal statement, minimum 3.0 GPA, interview.

Application deadlines: rolling (freshmen), rolling (transfers).

Notification: 9/15 (freshmen).

CONTACT

La Roche College, 9000 Babcock Boulevard, Pittsburgh, PA 15237. *Phone:* 412-536-1272. *Toll-free phone:* 800-838-4LRC. *Fax:* 412-536-1048. *E-mail:* admissions@laroche.edu.

La Salle University

Philadelphia, Pennsylvania

http://www.lasalle.edu/

- **Independent Roman Catholic** comprehensive, founded 1863
- **Urban** 133-acre campus with easy access to Philadelphia
- **Endowment** $82.0 million
- **Coed** 3,821 undergraduate students, 87% full-time, 61% women, 39% men
- **Moderately difficult** entrance level, 79% of applicants were admitted

UNDERGRAD STUDENTS

3,322 full-time, 499 part-time. Students come from 37 states and territories; 31 other countries; 31% are from out of state; 20% Black or African American, non-Hispanic/Latino; 18% Hispanic/Latino; 5% Asian, non-Hispanic/Latino; 0.2% Native Hawaiian or other Pacific Islander, non-Hispanic/Latino; 0.2% American Indian or Alaska Native, non-Hispanic/Latino; 3% Two or more races, non-Hispanic/Latino; 2% Race/ethnicity unknown; 2% international; 4% transferred in; 53% live on campus.

Freshmen:
Admission: 6,566 applied, 5,205 admitted, 1,052 enrolled. *Average high school GPA:* 3.3. *Test scores:* SAT evidence-based reading and writing scores over 500: 76%; SAT math scores over 500: 69%; SAT evidence-based reading and writing scores over 600: 25%; SAT math scores over 600: 18%; SAT evidence-based reading and writing scores over 700: 3%; SAT math scores over 700: 2%.

Retention: 76% of full-time freshmen returned.

FACULTY

Total: 547, 40% full-time.

Student/faculty ratio: 11:1.

ACADEMICS

Calendar: semesters. *Degrees:* associate, bachelor's, master's, doctoral, post-master's, and postbachelor's certificates.

Special study options: academic remediation for entering students, accelerated degree program, adult/continuing education programs, advanced placement credit, cooperative education, distance learning, double majors, English as a second language, freshman honors college, honors programs, independent study, internships, off-campus study, part-time degree program, services for LD students, student-designed majors, study abroad, summer session for credit. *ROTC:* Army (c), Air Force (c).

Unusual degree programs: 3-2 business administration; communication sciences and disorders/speech language pathology, communication/professional business communication, computer information science, history, elementary/special education, occupational therapy program with Thomas Jefferson University.

Computers: 1,100 computers/terminals are available on campus for general student use. Students can access the following: campus intranet, computer help desk, free student e-mail accounts, online (class) grades, online (class) registration, online (class) schedules, course management system. Campuswide network is available. 100% of college-owned or -operated housing units are wired for high-speed Internet access. Wireless service is available via classrooms, computer centers, computer labs, dorm rooms, learning centers, libraries, student centers.

Library: Connelly Library. *Books:* 274,998 (physical), 172,068 (digital/electronic); *Serial titles:* 1,470 (physical), 127,163 (digital/electronic); *Databases:* 88. Weekly public service hours: 96; students can reserve study rooms.

STUDENT LIFE

Housing options: on-campus residence required through sophomore year; coed, men-only, women-only, special housing for students with disabilities. Campus housing is university owned. Freshman campus housing is guaranteed.

Activities and organizations: drama/theater group, student-run newspaper, radio and television station, choral group, Student Government Association, community service organization, La Salle Entertainment Organization, The Explorer (yearbook), The Masque (theater group), national fraternities, national sororities.

Athletics Member NCAA. All Division I. *Intercollegiate sports:* baseball M(s), basketball M(s)/W(s), cheerleading M/W, crew M(s)/W(s), cross-country running M(s)/W(s), field hockey W(s), golf M(s)/W(s), lacrosse

W(s), soccer M(s)/W(s), softball W(s), swimming and diving M(s)/W(s), tennis M(s)/W(s), track and field M(s)/W(s), volleyball W(s), water polo M(s)/W(s). *Intramural sports:* basketball M/W, football M/W, ice hockey M(c), lacrosse M(c), rugby M(c)/W(c), softball M/W, ultimate Frisbee M(c)/W(c), volleyball M/W.

Campus security: 24-hour emergency response devices and patrols, student patrols, late-night transport/escort service, controlled dormitory access.

Student services: health clinic, personal/psychological counseling, women's center.

COSTS & FINANCIAL AID
Costs (2018–19) *One-time required fee:* $250. *Comprehensive fee:* $44,190 includes full-time tuition ($28,800), mandatory fees ($700), and room and board ($14,690). Full-time tuition and fees vary according to course load and program. Part-time tuition: $585 per credit hour. Part-time tuition and fees vary according to course load and program. *Required fees:* $250 per term part-time. *College room only:* $7530. Room and board charges vary according to board plan and housing facility. *Payment plans:* installment, deferred payment. *Waivers:* employees or children of employees.

Financial Aid Of all full-time matriculated undergraduates who enrolled in 2016, 2,765 applied for aid, 2,605 were judged to have need, 366 had their need fully met. 364 Federal Work-Study jobs (averaging $1837). In 2016, 471 non-need-based awards were made. *Average percent of need met:* 75. *Average financial aid package:* $32,236. *Average need-based loan:* $4822. *Average need-based gift aid:* $25,432. *Average non-need-based aid:* $19,520. *Average indebtedness upon graduation:* $37,002.

APPLYING
Standardized Tests *Required for some:* SAT or ACT (for admission).

Options: electronic application, early admission, early action, deferred entrance.

Required: essay or personal statement, high school transcript, 1 letter of recommendation. *Recommended:* interview.

Application deadlines: 8/15 (transfers), 11/15 (early action).

Notification: continuous (freshmen), continuous (transfers), 12/15 (early action).

CONTACT
Mr. James Plunkett, Executive Director of Undergraduate Admission, La Salle University, 1900 West Olney Avenue, Philadelphia, PA 19141-1199. *Phone:* 215-951-1500. *Toll-free phone:* 800-328-1910. *Fax:* 215-951-1656. *E-mail:* admiss@lasalle.edu.

Lebanon Valley College
Annville, Pennsylvania
http://www.lvc.edu/
- **Independent United Methodist** comprehensive, founded 1866
- **Small-town** 357-acre campus
- **Endowment** $67.5 million
- **Coed** 1,756 undergraduate students, 92% full-time, 55% women, 45% men
- **Moderately difficult** entrance level, 73% of applicants were admitted

UNDERGRAD STUDENTS
1,624 full-time, 132 part-time. Students come from 22 states and territories; 12 other countries; 20% are from out of state; 4% Black or African American, non-Hispanic/Latino; 6% Hispanic/Latino; 2% Asian, non-Hispanic/Latino; 0.1% Native Hawaiian or other Pacific Islander, non-Hispanic/Latino; 0.1% American Indian or Alaska Native, non-Hispanic/Latino; 3% Two or more races, non-Hispanic/Latino; 4% Race/ethnicity unknown; 1% international; 3% transferred in; 80% live on campus.

Freshmen:
Admission: 2,833 applied, 2,068 admitted, 466 enrolled. *Average high school GPA:* 3.7. *Test scores:* SAT evidence-based reading and writing scores over 500: 90%; SAT math scores over 500: 93%; ACT scores over 18: 95%; SAT evidence-based reading and writing scores over 600: 41%; SAT math scores over 600: 37%; ACT scores over 24: 60%; SAT evidence-based reading and writing scores over 700: 4%; SAT math scores over 700: 7%; ACT scores over 30: 10%.

Retention: 81% of full-time freshmen returned.

FACULTY
Total: 285, 41% full-time, 55% with terminal degrees.
Student/faculty ratio: 10:1.

ACADEMICS
Calendar: semesters. *Degrees:* bachelor's, master's, doctoral, and postbachelor's certificates.

Special study options: academic remediation for entering students, accelerated degree program, adult/continuing education programs, advanced placement credit, distance learning, double majors, English as a second language, independent study, internships, off-campus study, part-time degree program, services for LD students, student-designed majors, study abroad, summer session for credit.

Unusual degree programs: 3-2 business administration; engineering with Case Western Reserve University, The Penn State University; athletic training, speech language pathology, medical technology.

Computers: 202 computers/terminals are available on campus for general student use. Students can access the following: campus intranet, computer help desk, free student e-mail accounts, online (class) grades, online (class) registration, online (class) schedules. Campuswide network is available. 100% of college-owned or -operated housing units are wired for high-speed Internet access. Wireless service is available via entire campus.

Library: Vernon and Doris Bishop Library. *Books:* 152,349 (physical), 204,880 (digital/electronic); *Serial titles:* 3,047 (physical), 59,331 (digital/electronic); *Databases:* 256. Weekly public service hours: 101; students can reserve study rooms.

STUDENT LIFE
Housing options: on-campus residence required through senior year; coed, special housing for students with disabilities. Campus housing is university owned. Freshman campus housing is guaranteed.

Activities and organizations: drama/theater group, student-run newspaper, choral group, marching band, Mini-THON, Student Government, Colleges Against Cancer, Wig and Buckle Theater Group, Valleyfest, national fraternities, national sororities.

Athletics Member NCAA. All Division III. *Intercollegiate sports:* baseball M, basketball M/W, cross-country running M/W, field hockey W, football M, golf M/W, ice hockey M/W, lacrosse M/W, soccer M/W, softball W, swimming and diving M/W, tennis M/W, track and field M/W, volleyball W. *Intramural sports:* archery M(c)/W(c), basketball M/W, cheerleading W(c), equestrian sports M(c)/W(c), football M/W, soccer M(c)/W(c), ultimate Frisbee M(c)/W(c), volleyball M/W, weight lifting W(c).

Campus security: 24-hour emergency response devices and patrols, late-night transport/escort service, controlled dormitory access.

Student services: health clinic, personal/psychological counseling, women's center.

COSTS & FINANCIAL AID
Costs (2018–19) *Comprehensive fee:* $55,510 includes full-time tuition ($42,420), mandatory fees ($1230), and room and board ($11,860). Part-time tuition: $698 per credit hour. Part-time tuition and fees vary according to class time and degree level. *College room only:* $5720. Room and board charges vary according to board plan and housing facility. *Payment plan:* installment. *Waivers:* senior citizens and employees or children of employees.

Financial Aid Of all full-time matriculated undergraduates who enrolled in 2016, 1,486 applied for aid, 1,367 were judged to have need, 324 had their need fully met. 986 Federal Work-Study jobs (averaging $1475). In 2016, 218 non-need-based awards were made. *Average percent of need met:* 79. *Average financial aid package:* $31,829. *Average need-based loan:* $4466. *Average need-based gift aid:* $25,805. *Average non-need-based aid:* $19,319. *Average indebtedness upon graduation:* $46,346.

APPLYING
Options: electronic application, early decision.

Required: high school transcript. *Required for some:* audition for music majors, specific requirements for physical therapy and athletic training programs. *Recommended:* 2 letters of recommendation, interview.

Application deadlines: rolling (freshmen), rolling (transfers).

Early decision deadline: 11/1.

Notification: continuous until 11/15 (freshmen), continuous (transfers), 11/1 (early decision).

CONTACT
Mr. Edwin Wright, Vice President of Enrollment Management, Lebanon Valley College, 101 North College Avenue, Annville, PA 17003. *Phone:* 717-867-6181. *Toll-free phone:* 866-LVC-4ADM. *Fax:* 717-867-6026. *E-mail:* admission@lvc.edu.

Lehigh University
Bethlehem, Pennsylvania
http://www.lehigh.edu/

- **Independent** university, founded 1865
- **Suburban** 2355-acre campus with easy access to Philadelphia
- **Endowment** $1.3 billion
- **Coed** 5,075 undergraduate students, 99% full-time, 45% women, 55% men
- **Most difficult** entrance level, 25% of applicants were admitted

UNDERGRAD STUDENTS
5,013 full-time, 62 part-time. Students come from 52 states and territories; 62 other countries; 73% are from out of state; 4% Black or African American, non-Hispanic/Latino; 9% Hispanic/Latino; 8% Asian, non-Hispanic/Latino; 0.1% Native Hawaiian or other Pacific Islander, non-Hispanic/Latino; 0.2% American Indian or Alaska Native, non-Hispanic/Latino; 3% Two or more races, non-Hispanic/Latino; 4% Race/ethnicity unknown; 9% international; 0.6% transferred in; 65% live on campus.

Freshmen:
Admission: 13,871 applied, 3,489 admitted, 1,234 enrolled. *Test scores:* SAT evidence-based reading and writing scores over 500: 100%; SAT math scores over 500: 100%; ACT scores over 18: 100%; SAT evidence-based reading and writing scores over 600: 86%; SAT math scores over 600: 91%; ACT scores over 24: 97%; SAT evidence-based reading and writing scores over 700: 29%; SAT math scores over 700: 48%; ACT scores over 30: 66%.
Retention: 96% of full-time freshmen returned.

FACULTY
Total: 699, 78% full-time, 83% with terminal degrees.
Student/faculty ratio: 9:1.

ACADEMICS
Calendar: semesters. *Degrees:* bachelor's, master's, doctoral, post-master's, and postbachelor's certificates.

Special study options: accelerated degree program, advanced placement credit, cooperative education, distance learning, double majors, English as a second language, external degree program, honors programs, independent study, internships, off-campus study, services for LD students, study abroad, summer session for credit. *ROTC:* Army (b).

Unusual degree programs: 3-2 engineering; education.

Computers: 597 computers/terminals are available on campus for general student use. Students can access the following: campus intranet, computer help desk, free student e-mail accounts, online (class) grades, online (class) registration, online (class) schedules. Campuswide network is available. 100% of college-owned or -operated housing units are wired for high-speed Internet access. Wireless service is available via classrooms, computer centers, computer labs, dorm rooms, learning centers, libraries, student centers.

Library: E. W. Fairchild-Martindale Library plus 1 other. *Books:* 798,207 (physical), 402,504 (digital/electronic); *Serial titles:* 2,050 (physical), 61,205 (digital/electronic); *Databases:* 191. Weekly public service hours: 83; students can reserve study rooms.

STUDENT LIFE
Housing options: on-campus residence required through sophomore year; coed, special housing for students with disabilities. Campus housing is university owned. Freshman campus housing is guaranteed.

Activities and organizations: drama/theater group, student-run newspaper, radio station, choral group, marching band, Marching 97, Indian Student Association, Accounting Club, Student Senate, Phi Sigma Pi, national fraternities, national sororities.

Athletics Member NCAA. All Division I. *Intercollegiate sports:* baseball M(s), basketball M(s)/W(s), crew M(c)/W(s), cross-country running M(s)/W(s), equestrian sports M(c)/W(c), fencing M(c)/W(c), field hockey W(s), football M(s), golf M(s)/W(s), ice hockey M(c), lacrosse M(s)/W(s), rugby M(c)/W(c), skiing (downhill) M(c)/W(c), soccer M(s)/W(s), softball W(s), squash M(c)/W(c), swimming and diving M(s)/W(s), tennis M(s)/W(s), track and field M(s)/W(s), ultimate Frisbee M(c)/W(c), volleyball M(c)/W(c), water polo M(c)/W(c), wrestling M(s). *Intramural sports:* badminton M(c)/W(c), baseball M(c), basketball M/W, cheerleading M(c)/W(c), cross-country running M/W, field hockey W(c), football M/W, golf M(c)/W(c), gymnastics M(c)/W(c), lacrosse M(c)/W(c), skiing (downhill) M(c)/W(c), soccer M/W, softball M/W, volleyball M/W, wrestling M(c).

Campus security: 24-hour emergency response devices and patrols, student patrols, late-night transport/escort service, controlled dormitory access, self defense training.

Student services: health clinic, personal/psychological counseling, women's center.

COSTS & FINANCIAL AID
Costs (2017–18) *Comprehensive fee:* $63,860 includes full-time tuition ($50,320), mandatory fees ($420), and room and board ($13,120). Part-time tuition: $2100 per credit hour. *College room only:* $7590. Room and board charges vary according to board plan and housing facility. *Payment plans:* tuition prepayment, installment. *Waivers:* employees or children of employees.

Financial Aid Of all full-time matriculated undergraduates who enrolled in 2017, 2,699 applied for aid, 2,098 were judged to have need, 1,603 had their need fully met. 1,233 Federal Work-Study jobs (averaging $1930). 89 state and other part-time jobs (averaging $1696). In 2017, 246 non-need-based awards were made. *Average percent of need met:* 97. *Average financial aid package:* $46,861. *Average need-based loan:* $4073. *Average need-based gift aid:* $40,472. *Average non-need-based aid:* $12,724. *Average indebtedness upon graduation:* $35,440. *Financial aid deadline:* 2/15.

APPLYING
Standardized Tests *Required:* SAT or ACT (for admission). *Recommended:* SAT (for admission), ACT (for admission).

Options: electronic application, early admission, early decision, deferred entrance.

Application fee: $70.

Required: essay or personal statement, high school transcript, 2 letters of recommendation.

Application deadlines: 1/1 (freshmen), 2/15 (transfers).

Early decision deadline: 11/15 (for plan 1), 1/1 (for plan 2).

Notification: 3/31 (freshmen), 4/15 (transfers), 12/15 (early decision plan 1), 2/15 (early decision plan 2).

CONTACT
Krista Evans, Interim Director of Admissions, Lehigh University, 27 Memorial Drive West, Bethlehem, PA 18015. *Phone:* 610-758-3100. *Fax:* 610-758-4361. *E-mail:* admissions@lehigh.edu.

★ Lincoln University
Lincoln University, Pennsylvania
http://www.lincoln.edu/

- **State-related** comprehensive, founded 1854
- **Rural** 422-acre campus with easy access to Philadelphia
- **Endowment** $38.6 million
- **Coed** 2,002 undergraduate students, 91% full-time, 66% women, 34% men
- **Minimally difficult** entrance level, 80% of applicants were admitted

UNDERGRAD STUDENTS
1,826 full-time, 176 part-time. Students come from 30 states and territories; 13 other countries; 54% are from out of state; 84% Black or African American, non-Hispanic/Latino; 3% Hispanic/Latino; 0.1% Asian, non-Hispanic/Latino; 0.2% American Indian or Alaska Native, non-Hispanic/Latino; 2% Two or more races, non-Hispanic/Latino; 6% Race/ethnicity unknown; 3% international; 5% transferred in; 79% live on campus.

Freshmen:
Admission: 3,587 applied, 2,858 admitted, 664 enrolled. *Average high school GPA:* 3.1. *Test scores:* SAT evidence-based reading and writing scores over 500: 47%; SAT math scores over 500: 40%; ACT scores over 18: 54%; SAT evidence-based reading and writing scores over 600: 6%; SAT math scores over 600: 7%; ACT scores over 24: 4%; SAT math scores over 700: 1%.
Retention: 68% of full-time freshmen returned.

FACULTY
Total: 207, 47% full-time.
Student/faculty ratio: 15:1.

ACADEMICS
Calendar: semesters. *Degrees:* certificates, bachelor's, and master's.
Special study options: academic remediation for entering students, accelerated degree program, adult/continuing education programs, advanced placement credit, double majors, external degree program, honors programs, independent study, internships, part-time degree program, services for LD students, study abroad, summer session for credit. *ROTC:* Army (c).
Computers: 280 computers/terminals are available on campus for general student use. Students can access the following: campus intranet, computer help desk, free student e-mail accounts, online (class) grades, online (class) registration, online (class) schedules. Campuswide network is available. 60% of college-owned or -operated housing units are wired for high-speed Internet access. Wireless service is available via entire campus.
Library: Langston Hughes Memorial Library. Weekly public service hours: 80; study areas open 24 hours, 5–7 days a week; students can reserve study rooms.

STUDENT LIFE
Housing options: on-campus residence required for freshman year; coed, men-only, women-only, special housing for students with disabilities. Campus housing is university owned. Freshman applicants given priority for college housing.
Activities and organizations: drama/theater group, student-run newspaper, radio and television station, choral group, marching band,
Student Government: Class sections, We R "1" Family, Residence Hall Association, International Students Association, Onyx Dance Troupe, national fraternities, national sororities.
Athletics Member NCAA. All Division II. *Intercollegiate sports:* baseball M(s), basketball M(s)/W(s), cheerleading W(s), cross-country running M/W, football M(s), soccer W(s), softball W(s), track and field M(s)/W(s), volleyball W(s). *Intramural sports:* basketball M/W, bowling M/W, football M, swimming and diving M/W, volleyball W.
Campus security: 24-hour emergency response devices and patrols, late-night transport/escort service, controlled dormitory access, 24-hour command center, gated entrance/exit, medical transports.
Student services: health clinic, personal/psychological counseling, women's center.

COSTS & FINANCIAL AID
Costs (2018–19) *One-time required fee:* $216. *Tuition:* state resident $7866 full-time; nonresident $13,002 full-time. Full-time tuition and fees vary according to course load, degree level, location, program, and student level. Part-time tuition and fees vary according to course load, degree level, location, program, and student level. No tuition increase for student's term of enrollment. *Required fees:* $2770 full-time. *Room and board:* $9738. Room and board charges vary according to board plan and housing facility. *Payment plans:* installment, deferred payment. *Waivers:* children of alumni and employees or children of employees.
Financial Aid Of all full-time matriculated undergraduates who enrolled in 2016, 1,598 applied for aid, 1,501 were judged to have need, 96 had their need fully met. 202 Federal Work-Study jobs (averaging $1037). In 2016, 54 non-need-based awards were made. *Average percent of need met:* 38. *Average financial aid package:* $12,397. *Average need-based loan:* $4192. *Average need-based gift aid:* $6797. *Average non-need-based aid:* $5821. *Average indebtedness upon graduation:* $41,630.

APPLYING
Standardized Tests *Required:* SAT or ACT (for admission).
Options: electronic application, deferred entrance.
Required: high school transcript, minimum 2.0 GPA. *Recommended:* essay or personal statement, 2 letters of recommendation, interview.
Application deadlines: 5/1 (freshmen), 6/15 (transfers).

Notification: continuous (freshmen), continuous (transfers).

CONTACT
Ms. Nikoia Forde, Associate Director, Undergraduate Admissions, Lincoln University, 1570 Baltimore Pike, Lincoln University, PA 19352. *Phone:* 484-365-7275. *Toll-free phone:* 800-790-0191. *Fax:* 484-365-8109. *E-mail:* nfredericksen@lincoln.edu.

See previous page for display ad and page 1326 for the College Close-Up.

Lock Haven University of Pennsylvania
Lock Haven, Pennsylvania
http://www.lockhaven.edu/
- **State-supported** comprehensive, founded 1870, part of Pennsylvania State System of Higher Education
- **Rural** 165-acre campus
- **Endowment** $10.7 million
- **Coed** 3,472 undergraduate students, 91% full-time, 58% women, 42% men
- **Moderately difficult** entrance level, 89% of applicants were admitted

UNDERGRAD STUDENTS
3,176 full-time, 296 part-time. Students come from 29 states and territories; 20 other countries; 5% are from out of state; 10% Black or African American, non-Hispanic/Latino; 2% Hispanic/Latino; 1% Asian, non-Hispanic/Latino; 0.1% Native Hawaiian or other Pacific Islander, non-Hispanic/Latino; 0.7% American Indian or Alaska Native, non-Hispanic/Latino; 0.7% Two or more races, non-Hispanic/Latino; 4% Race/ethnicity unknown; 1% international; 5% transferred in; 34% live on campus.

Freshmen:
Admission: 3,020 applied, 2,689 admitted, 790 enrolled. *Average high school GPA:* 3.3. *Test scores:* SAT evidence-based reading and writing scores over 500: 53%; SAT math scores over 500: 55%; ACT scores over 18: 59%; SAT evidence-based reading and writing scores over 600: 12%; SAT math scores over 600: 12%; ACT scores over 24: 16%.
Retention: 70% of full-time freshmen returned.

FACULTY
Total: 232, 88% full-time, 84% with terminal degrees.
Student/faculty ratio: 17:1.

ACADEMICS
Calendar: semesters. *Degrees:* associate, bachelor's, and master's.
Special study options: academic remediation for entering students, adult/continuing education programs, advanced placement credit, cooperative education, distance learning, double majors, English as a second language, freshman honors college, honors programs, independent study, internships, off-campus study, part-time degree program, services for LD students, student-designed majors, study abroad, summer session for credit. *ROTC:* Army (b).
Unusual degree programs: 3-2 engineering with Penn State University Park.
Computers: 290 computers/terminals are available on campus for general student use. Students can access the following: online (class) registration. Campuswide network is available.
Library: Stevenson Library plus 1 other. *Books:* 238,440 (physical), 18,458 (digital/electronic); *Serial titles:* 37,709 (physical), 60,878 (digital/electronic); *Databases:* 5. Weekly public service hours: 87; students can reserve study rooms.

STUDENT LIFE
Housing options: on-campus residence required through sophomore year; coed. Campus housing is university owned and is provided by a third party. Freshman applicants given priority for college housing.
Activities and organizations: drama/theater group, student-run newspaper, radio and television station, choral group, marching band, Student Government, Residence Hall Association, national fraternities, national sororities.
Athletics Member NCAA. All Division II except field hockey (Division I), wrestling (Division I). *Intercollegiate sports:* baseball M(s), basketball M(s)/W(s), cross-country running M(s)/W(s), field hockey W(s), football

M(s), lacrosse W(s), soccer M(s)/W(s), softball W(s), swimming and diving W(s), track and field M(s)/W(s), volleyball W(s), wrestling M(s). *Intramural sports:* badminton M/W, basketball M/W, cross-country running M/W, fencing M/W, field hockey W, football M, golf M/W, ice hockey M, lacrosse M/W, racquetball M/W, rugby M/W, skiing (cross-country) M/W, skiing (downhill) M/W, soccer M/W, softball M/W, swimming and diving M/W, tennis M/W, track and field M/W, ultimate Frisbee M/W, volleyball M/W, water polo M, weight lifting M/W, wrestling M.
Campus security: 24-hour emergency response devices and patrols, late-night transport/escort service, controlled dormitory access.
Student services: health clinic, personal/psychological counseling, women's center.

COSTS & FINANCIAL AID
Costs (2017–18) *Tuition:* state resident $7492 full-time, $312 per credit hour part-time; nonresident $16,730 full-time, $697 per credit hour part-time. Full-time tuition and fees vary according to course load, location, and program. Part-time tuition and fees vary according to course load, location, and program. *Required fees:* $3084 full-time, $163 per credit hour part-time. *Room and board:* $9968; room only: $6328. Room and board charges vary according to board plan and housing facility. *Payment plan:* installment. *Waivers:* minority students, senior citizens, and employees or children of employees.
Financial Aid Of all full-time matriculated undergraduates who enrolled in 2017, 2,704 applied for aid, 2,447 were judged to have need, 2,213 had their need fully met. In 2017, 34 non-need-based awards were made. *Average percent of need met:* 73. *Average financial aid package:* $4791. *Average need-based loan:* $4397. *Average need-based gift aid:* $6103. *Average non-need-based aid:* $1377. *Average indebtedness upon graduation:* $34,863.

APPLYING
Standardized Tests *Required:* SAT or ACT (for admission).
Options: electronic application, deferred entrance.
Application fee: $25.
Required: high school transcript. *Required for some:* essay or personal statement. *Recommended:* interview.
Application deadlines: rolling (freshmen), rolling (transfers).
Notification: continuous (freshmen), continuous (transfers).

CONTACT
Lock Haven University of Pennsylvania, Office of Admission, DACC, Lock Haven, PA 17745. *Phone:* 570-484-2109. *Toll-free phone:* 800-332-8900 (in-state); 800-233-8978 (out-of-state). *Fax:* 570-484-2201. *E-mail:* admissions@lockhaven.edu.

Lycoming College
Williamsport, Pennsylvania
http://www.lycoming.edu/
- **Independent United Methodist** 4-year, founded 1812
- **Small-town** 35-acre campus
- **Endowment** $200.8 million
- **Coed** 1,223 undergraduate students, 98% full-time, 50% women, 50% men
- **Moderately difficult** entrance level, 64% of applicants were admitted

UNDERGRAD STUDENTS
1,199 full-time, 24 part-time. Students come from 30 states and territories; 21 other countries; 41% are from out of state; 12% Black or African American, non-Hispanic/Latino; 10% Hispanic/Latino; 1% Asian, non-Hispanic/Latino; 0.1% Native Hawaiian or other Pacific Islander, non-Hispanic/Latino; 0.2% American Indian or Alaska Native, non-Hispanic/Latino; 3% Two or more races, non-Hispanic/Latino; 6% Race/ethnicity unknown; 5% international; 2% transferred in; 87% live on campus.

Freshmen:
Admission: 1,924 applied, 1,232 admitted, 282 enrolled. *Average high school GPA:* 3.4. *Test scores:* SAT evidence-based reading and writing scores over 500: 75%; SAT math scores over 500: 75%; ACT scores over 18: 96%; SAT evidence-based reading and writing scores over 600: 30%; SAT math scores over 600: 27%; ACT scores over 24: 43%; SAT

evidence-based reading and writing scores over 700: 2%; SAT math scores over 700: 3%; ACT scores over 30: 3%.

Retention: 80% of full-time freshmen returned.

FACULTY
Total: 124, 72% full-time, 81% with terminal degrees.
Student/faculty ratio: 12:1.

ACADEMICS
Calendar: semesters. *Degree:* bachelor's.

Special study options: adult/continuing education programs, advanced placement credit, cooperative education, double majors, honors programs, independent study, internships, off-campus study, part-time degree program, services for LD students, student-designed majors, study abroad, summer session for credit. *ROTC:* Army (c).

Unusual degree programs: 3-2 engineering with Binghamton University, State University of New York; forestry with Duke University; environmental management with Duke University, clinical laboratory science with Susquehanna Health, Robert Packer, Lancaster, and Abington Hospitals.

Computers: 188 computers/terminals and 3,408 ports are available on campus for general student use. Students can access the following: campus intranet, computer help desk, free student e-mail accounts, online (class) grades, online (class) registration, online financial aid, free printing up to a limit, password management. Campuswide network is available. 100% of college-owned or -operated housing units are wired for high-speed Internet access. Wireless service is available via entire campus.
Library: Snowden Library. *Books:* 133,910 (physical), 135,327 (digital/electronic); *Serial titles:* 1,005 (physical), 15,136 (digital/electronic); *Databases:* 89. Weekly public service hours: 107.

STUDENT LIFE
Housing options: on-campus residence required through senior year; coed, women-only. Campus housing is university owned. Freshman campus housing is guaranteed.

Activities and organizations: drama/theater group, student-run newspaper, radio station, choral group, Campus Activities Board, Lycoming Dance Club, Habitat for Humanity, Circle K, United Campus Ministry, national fraternities, national sororities.

Athletics Member NCAA. All Division III. *Intercollegiate sports:* badminton M(c)/W(c), basketball M/W, cheerleading M(c)/W(c), crew M(c)/W(c), cross-country running M/W, equestrian sports M(c)/W(c), fencing M(c)/W(c), football M, golf M/W, lacrosse M/W, rugby M(c), soccer M/W, softball W, swimming and diving M/W, tennis M/W, ultimate Frisbee M(c)/W(c), volleyball W, water polo M(c)/W(c), wrestling M. *Intramural sports:* basketball M/W, football M/W, soccer M/W, softball M/W, table tennis M/W, volleyball M/W.

Campus security: 24-hour emergency response devices and patrols, student patrols, late-night transport/escort service, controlled dormitory access.

Student services: health clinic, personal/psychological counseling.

COSTS & FINANCIAL AID
Costs (2018–19) *One-time required fee:* $225. *Comprehensive fee:* $52,658 includes full-time tuition ($39,360), mandatory fees ($730), and room and board ($12,568). Part-time tuition: $1230 per credit hour. Part-time tuition and fees vary according to course load. *Room and board:* Room and board charges vary according to board plan and housing facility. *Payment plan:* installment. *Waivers:* employees or children of employees.

Financial Aid Of all full-time matriculated undergraduates who enrolled in 2017, 1,065 applied for aid, 1,009 were judged to have need, 266 had their need fully met. In 2017, 174 non-need-based awards were made. *Average percent of need met:* 84. *Average financial aid package:* $37,279. *Average need-based loan:* $4751. *Average need-based gift aid:* $31,590. *Average non-need-based aid:* $24,770.

APPLYING
Standardized Tests *Recommended:* SAT or ACT (for admission).

Options: electronic application, early decision, early action, deferred entrance.

Required: essay or personal statement, high school transcript, 2 letters of recommendation. *Recommended:* minimum 2.3 GPA, interview.

Application deadlines: 8/1 (freshmen), 7/1 (transfers), 12/1 (early action).

Early decision deadline: 11/15.

Notification: continuous until 12/15 (freshmen), continuous until 12/15 (transfers), 12/1 (early decision), 12/15 (early action).

CONTACT
Jessica Hess, Director of Admissions, Lycoming College, 700 College Place, Williamsport, PA 17701. *Phone:* 570-321-4318. *Toll-free phone:* 800-345-3920 Ext. 4026. *Fax:* 570-321-4317. *E-mail:* admissions@lycoming.edu.

Mansfield University of Pennsylvania
Mansfield, Pennsylvania
http://www.mansfield.edu/
- **State-supported** comprehensive, founded 1857, part of Pennsylvania State System of Higher Education
- **Small-town** 174-acre campus
- **Coed** 1,836 undergraduate students, 90% full-time, 59% women, 41% men
- **Moderately difficult** entrance level, 68% of applicants were admitted

UNDERGRAD STUDENTS
1,655 full-time, 181 part-time. 17% are from out of state; 10% Black or African American, non-Hispanic/Latino; 4% Hispanic/Latino; 0.7% Asian, non-Hispanic/Latino; 0.1% Native Hawaiian or other Pacific Islander, non-Hispanic/Latino; 0.1% American Indian or Alaska Native, non-Hispanic/Latino; 2% Two or more races, non-Hispanic/Latino; 2% Race/ethnicity unknown; 0.7% international; 4% transferred in; 49% live on campus.

Freshmen:
Admission: 2,501 applied, 1,703 admitted, 406 enrolled. *Average high school GPA:* 3.4. *Test scores:* SAT evidence-based reading and writing scores over 500: 62%; SAT math scores over 500: 63%; SAT evidence-based reading and writing scores over 600: 14%; SAT math scores over 600: 12%; SAT evidence-based reading and writing scores over 700: 1%.
Retention: 71% of full-time freshmen returned.

FACULTY
Total: 145, 69% full-time, 68% with terminal degrees.
Student/faculty ratio: 15:1.

ACADEMICS
Calendar: semesters. *Degrees:* associate, bachelor's, master's, and postbachelor's certificates.

Special study options: adult/continuing education programs, part-time degree program. *ROTC:* Army (c).

Computers: Students can access the following: campus intranet, computer help desk, free student e-mail accounts, online (class) grades, online (class) registration, online (class) schedules. Campuswide network is available. 100% of college-owned or -operated housing units are wired for high-speed Internet access. Wireless service is available via classrooms, computer centers, computer labs, dorm rooms, learning centers, libraries, student centers.
Library: North Hall Library.

STUDENT LIFE
Housing options: on-campus residence required through sophomore year; coed. Campus housing is university owned. Freshman campus housing is guaranteed.

Activities and organizations: drama/theater group, student-run newspaper, radio and television station, choral group, marching band, national fraternities, national sororities.

Athletics Member NCAA. All Division II. *Intercollegiate sports:* baseball M(s), basketball M(s)/W(s), cross-country running M(s)/W(s), field hockey W(s), football M(c), soccer W(s), softball W(s), swimming and diving W, track and field M(s)/W(s). *Intramural sports:* badminton M/W, basketball M/W, bowling M/W, cheerleading W, cross-country running M/W, equestrian sports M/W, football M/W, golf M/W, racquetball M/W, skiing (cross-country) M/W, skiing (downhill) M/W, soccer M/W, softball M/W, swimming and diving M/W, tennis M/W, track and field M/W, volleyball M/W, water polo M/W, weight lifting M/W.

Campus security: 24-hour emergency response devices and patrols, student patrols, late-night transport/escort service, controlled dormitory access.

Student services: health clinic, personal/psychological counseling, women's center.

COSTS & FINANCIAL AID

Costs (2017–18) *Tuition:* state resident $9450 full-time, $315 per credit hour part-time; nonresident $18,900 full-time, $630 per credit hour part-time. *Required fees:* $2866 full-time. *Room and board:* $11,928; room only: $8468. Room and board charges vary according to board plan. *Payment plans:* installment, deferred payment. *Waivers:* senior citizens and employees or children of employees.

Financial Aid Of all full-time matriculated undergraduates who enrolled in 2016, 1,808 applied for aid, 1,155 were judged to have need, 559 had their need fully met. In 2016, 149 non-need-based awards were made. *Average percent of need met:* 43. *Average financial aid package:* $10,205. *Average need-based loan:* $4433. *Average need-based gift aid:* $6658. *Average non-need-based aid:* $2046. *Average indebtedness upon graduation:* $36,624. *Financial aid deadline:* 6/30.

APPLYING

Standardized Tests *Required for some:* SAT or ACT (for admission).

Options: electronic application, early admission, deferred entrance.

Application fee: $25.

Required: high school transcript. *Required for some:* interview. *Recommended:* essay or personal statement, minimum 2.5 GPA.

CONTACT

Ms. Rachel Green, Director of Admissions, Mansfield University of Pennsylvania, Academy Street, Mansfield, PA 16933. *Phone:* 570-662-4813. *Toll-free phone:* 800-577-6826. *E-mail:* admissions@mnsfld.edu.

Marywood University
Scranton, Pennsylvania
http://www.marywood.edu/

- **Independent Roman Catholic** comprehensive, founded 1915
- **Suburban** 123-acre campus
- **Endowment** $35.4 million
- **Coed** 1,964 undergraduate students, 89% full-time, 69% women, 31% men
- **Moderately difficult** entrance level, 75% of applicants were admitted

UNDERGRAD STUDENTS

1,756 full-time, 208 part-time. Students come from 21 states and territories; 10 other countries; 31% are from out of state; 3% Black or African American, non-Hispanic/Latino; 7% Hispanic/Latino; 2% Asian, non-Hispanic/Latino; 0.1% Native Hawaiian or other Pacific Islander, non-Hispanic/Latino; 0.2% American Indian or Alaska Native, non-Hispanic/Latino; 2% Two or more races, non-Hispanic/Latino; 11% Race/ethnicity unknown; 2% international; 5% transferred in; 37% live on campus.

Freshmen:

Admission: 2,268 applied, 1,700 admitted, 449 enrolled. *Average high school GPA:* 3.4. *Test scores:* SAT evidence-based reading and writing scores over 500: 80%; SAT math scores over 500: 76%; SAT evidence-based reading and writing scores over 600: 29%; SAT math scores over 600: 22%; SAT evidence-based reading and writing scores over 700: 3%; SAT math scores over 700: 2%.

Retention: 86% of full-time freshmen returned.

FACULTY

Total: 394, 37% full-time.

Student/faculty ratio: 12:1.

ACADEMICS

Calendar: semesters. *Degrees:* certificates, bachelor's, master's, doctoral, post-master's, and postbachelor's certificates.

Special study options: adult/continuing education programs, advanced placement credit, double majors, English as a second language, honors

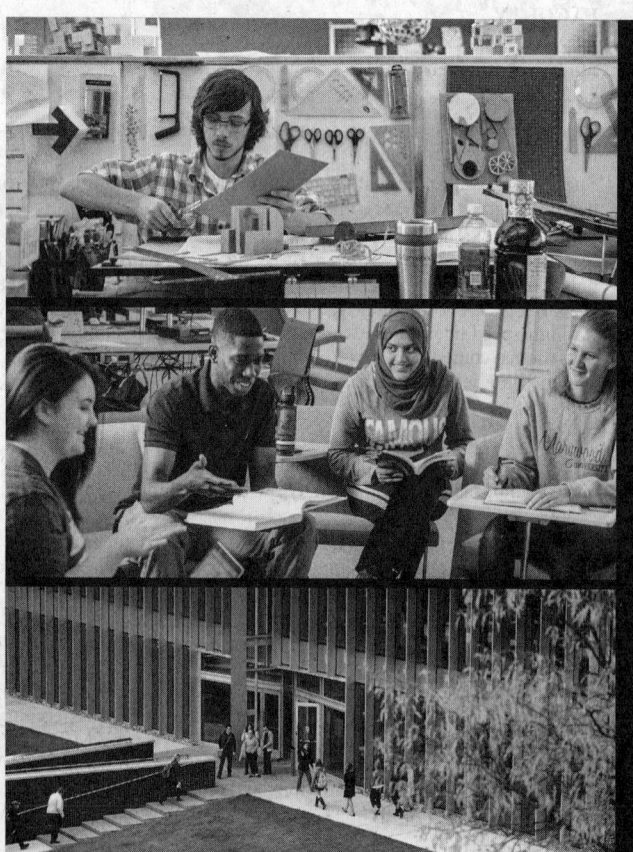

programs, independent study, internships, off-campus study, part-time degree program, services for LD students, student-designed majors, study abroad, summer session for credit. *ROTC:* Army (c), Air Force (c).

Unusual degree programs: 3-2 physician assistant, communication sciences disorders, criminal justice, biotechnology, health services administration.

Computers: 359 computers/terminals are available on campus for general student use. Students can access the following: computer help desk, free student e-mail accounts, online (class) grades, online (class) registration, online (class) schedules, degree audit, student account management, financial aid self-service, student planning. Campuswide network is available. 100% of college-owned or -operated housing units are wired for high-speed Internet access. Wireless service is available via entire campus.

Library: Learning Commons plus 2 others. *Books:* 204,320 (physical), 50,560 (digital/electronic); *Serial titles:* 97 (physical), 31,831 (digital/electronic); *Databases:* 54. Weekly public service hours: 111; students can reserve study rooms.

STUDENT LIFE

Housing options: on-campus residence required through sophomore year; men-only, women-only, special housing for students with disabilities. Campus housing is university owned. Freshman campus housing is guaranteed.

Activities and organizations: drama/theater group, student-run newspaper, radio and television station, choral group, Student Nurses Association, Health Professions Club, Speech and Hearing Club, Volunteers in Action (VIA), American Institute of Architects.

Athletics Member NCAA. All Division III. *Intercollegiate sports:* baseball M, basketball M/W, cross-country running M/W, field hockey W, golf M, lacrosse M/W, soccer M/W, softball W, swimming and diving M/W, tennis M/W, track and field M/W, volleyball W. *Intramural sports:* badminton M/W, basketball M/W, cheerleading M(c)/W(c), football M/W, golf W(c), racquetball M/W, rock climbing M(c)/W(c), soccer M/W, softball M/W, swimming and diving M/W, table tennis M/W, tennis M/W, volleyball M/W, water polo M/W.

Campus security: 24-hour emergency response devices and patrols, late-night transport/escort service, controlled dormitory access, apartments with deadbolts, self-defense education, lighted pathways, seminars on safety.

Student services: health clinic, personal/psychological counseling.

COSTS & FINANCIAL AID

Costs (2018–19) *Comprehensive fee:* $48,810 includes full-time tuition ($33,160), mandatory fees ($1750), and room and board ($13,900). Full-time tuition and fees vary according to course load. Part-time tuition and fees vary according to course load. *College room only:* $7822. Room and board charges vary according to board plan and housing facility. *Payment plans:* installment, deferred payment. *Waivers:* senior citizens and employees or children of employees.

Financial Aid Of all full-time matriculated undergraduates who enrolled in 2016, 1,561 applied for aid, 1,427 were judged to have need, 235 had their need fully met. 584 Federal Work-Study jobs (averaging $1917). In 2016, 251 non-need-based awards were made. *Average percent of need met:* 69. *Average financial aid package:* $24,643. *Average need-based loan:* $4509. *Average need-based gift aid:* $19,504. *Average non-need-based aid:* $13,963. *Average indebtedness upon graduation:* $42,603.

APPLYING

Standardized Tests *Required:* SAT or ACT (for admission).

Options: electronic application, early admission, deferred entrance.

Application fee: $35.

Required: essay or personal statement, high school transcript, minimum 2.5 GPA, 1 letter of recommendation. *Required for some:* interview, portfolio for art majors, audition for music majors. *Recommended:* interview.

Application deadlines: rolling (freshmen), rolling (transfers).

Notification: continuous (freshmen), continuous (transfers).

CONTACT

Mr. Christian DiGregorio, Director of University Admissions, Marywood University, 2300 Adams Avenue, Scranton, PA 18509. *Phone:* 570-348-6234. *Toll-free phone:* 866-279-9663. *Fax:* 570-961-4763. *E-mail:* yourfuture@marywood.edu.

See previous page for display ad and page 1340 for the College Close-Up.

Mercyhurst North East
North East, Pennsylvania
http://northeast.mercyhurst.edu/

CONTACT
Travis Lindahl, Director of Admissions, Mercyhurst North East, 16 West Division Street, North East, PA 16428. *Phone:* 814-725-6217. *Toll-free phone:* 866-846-6042. *Fax:* 814-725-6251. *E-mail:* neadmiss@ mercyhurst.edu.

Mercyhurst University
Erie, Pennsylvania
http://www.mercyhurst.edu/

- **Independent Roman Catholic** comprehensive, founded 1926
- **Suburban** 88-acre campus with easy access to Buffalo
- **Endowment** $31.6 million
- **Coed** 2,470 undergraduate students, 96% full-time, 58% women, 42% men
- **Moderately difficult** entrance level, 75% of applicants were admitted

UNDERGRAD STUDENTS
2,383 full-time, 87 part-time. Students come from 42 states and territories; 31 other countries; 48% are from out of state; 6% Black or African American, non-Hispanic/Latino; 4% Hispanic/Latino; 2% Asian, non-Hispanic/Latino; 0.1% Native Hawaiian or other Pacific Islander, non-Hispanic/Latino; 1% American Indian or Alaska Native, non-Hispanic/Latino; 8% Race/ethnicity unknown; 9% international; 2% transferred in; 68% live on campus.

Freshmen:
Admission: 3,254 applied, 2,448 admitted, 589 enrolled. *Average high school GPA:* 3.4.

Retention: 80% of full-time freshmen returned.

FACULTY
Total: 146.

Student/faculty ratio: 15:1.

ACADEMICS
Calendar: semesters. *Degrees:* bachelor's, master's, and postbachelor's certificates.

Special study options: academic remediation for entering students, accelerated degree program, adult/continuing education programs, advanced placement credit, distance learning, double majors, honors programs, independent study, internships, off-campus study, part-time degree program, services for LD students, student-designed majors, study abroad, summer session for credit. *ROTC:* Army (b), Air Force (c).

Unusual degree programs: 3-2 business administration.

Computers: 350 computers/terminals and 150 ports are available on campus for general student use. Students can access the following: campus intranet, computer help desk, free student e-mail accounts, online (class) grades, online (class) registration, online (class) schedules. Campuswide network is available. 100% of college-owned or -operated housing units are wired for high-speed Internet access. Wireless service is available via entire campus.

Library: Hammermill Library. *Books:* 108,088 (physical), 134,244 (digital/electronic); *Serial titles:* 500 (physical), 122,471 (digital/electronic); *Databases:* 66. Study areas open 24 hours, 5–7 days a week; students can reserve study rooms.

STUDENT LIFE
Housing options: on-campus residence required through sophomore year; coed, men-only, women-only, special housing for students with disabilities. Campus housing is university owned and leased by the school. Freshman campus housing is guaranteed.

Activities and organizations: drama/theater group, student-run newspaper, choral group, marching band, Student Government, chorus, Admission Ambassadors, Amnesty International, The Merciad (student newspaper).

Athletics Member NCAA. All Division II except men's and women's ice hockey (Division I). *Intercollegiate sports:* baseball M(s), basketball M(s)/W(s), crew M(s)/W(s), cross-country running M(s)/W(s), field hockey W(s), football M(s), golf M(s)/W(s), ice hockey M(s)/W(s), lacrosse M(s)/W(s), soccer M(s)/W(s), softball W(s), tennis M(s)/W(s), volleyball W(s), water polo M(s)/W(s), wrestling M(s). *Intramural sports:* basketball M/W, football M, skiing (cross-country) M/W, skiing (downhill) M/W, volleyball M/W.

Campus security: 24-hour emergency response devices and patrols, campus-wide camera system.

Student services: health clinic, personal/psychological counseling.

COSTS & FINANCIAL AID

Costs (2017–18) *Comprehensive fee:* $48,530 includes full-time tuition ($34,050), mandatory fees ($2270), and room and board ($12,210). Full-time tuition and fees vary according to class time, course load, degree level, location, and program. Part-time tuition: $3405 per course. Part-time tuition and fees vary according to class time, course load, degree level, location, and program. *Required fees:* $715 per term part-time. *College room only:* $6190. Room and board charges vary according to board plan, housing facility, and location. *Payment plan:* installment. *Waivers:* adult students and employees or children of employees.

Financial Aid Of all full-time matriculated undergraduates who enrolled in 2015, 1,866 applied for aid, 1,686 were judged to have need, 104 had their need fully met. In 2015, 411 non-need-based awards were made. *Average percent of need met:* 50. *Average financial aid package:* $26,019. *Average need-based loan:* $4360. *Average need-based gift aid:* $16,089. *Average non-need-based aid:* $15,583. *Average indebtedness upon graduation:* $24,739. *Financial aid deadline:* 5/1.

APPLYING

Options: electronic application, deferred entrance.

Required: essay or personal statement, high school transcript. *Required for some:* 1 letter of recommendation. *Recommended:* interview.

Application deadlines: rolling (freshmen), rolling (transfers).

Notification: continuous until 11/1 (freshmen), continuous until 12/1 (transfers).

CONTACT

Mercyhurst University, 501 East 38th Street, Erie, PA 16546. *Toll-free phone:* 800-825-1926.

Messiah College

Mechanicsburg, Pennsylvania

http://www.messiah.edu/

- **Independent interdenominational** comprehensive, founded 1909
- **Small-town** 485-acre campus
- **Endowment** $134.2 million
- **Coed** 2,759 undergraduate students, 96% full-time, 60% women, 40% men
- **Moderately difficult** entrance level, 77% of applicants were admitted

UNDERGRAD STUDENTS

2,637 full-time, 122 part-time. Students come from 37 states and territories; 32 other countries; 36% are from out of state; 2% Black or African American, non-Hispanic/Latino; 5% Hispanic/Latino; 2% Asian, non-Hispanic/Latino; 3% Two or more races, non-Hispanic/Latino; 1% Race/ethnicity unknown; 5% international; 3% transferred in; 87% live on campus.

Freshmen:

Admission: 2,558 applied, 1,970 admitted, 665 enrolled. *Average high school GPA:* 3.8. *Test scores:* SAT evidence-based reading and writing scores over 500: 95%; SAT math scores over 500: 92%; ACT scores over 18: 99%; SAT evidence-based reading and writing scores over 600: 56%; SAT math scores over 600: 48%; ACT scores over 24: 68%; SAT evidence-based reading and writing scores over 700: 14%; SAT math scores over 700: 11%; ACT scores over 30: 17%.

Retention: 88% of full-time freshmen returned.

FACULTY

Total: 368, 54% full-time, 50% with terminal degrees.

Student/faculty ratio: 12:1.

ACADEMICS

Calendar: semesters. *Degrees:* bachelor's, master's, doctoral, post-master's, and postbachelor's certificates.

Special study options: academic remediation for entering students, accelerated degree program, adult/continuing education programs, advanced placement credit, cooperative education, distance learning, double majors, English as a second language, freshman honors college, honors programs, independent study, internships, off-campus study, part-time degree program, services for LD students, student-designed majors, study abroad, summer session for credit.

Unusual degree programs: 3-2 applied health science or biopsychology/occupational therapy with Thomas Jefferson University, biochemistry/pharmacy with the University of the Sciences in Philadelphia, politics/public policy and management with Carnegie Mellon University.

Computers: 571 computers/terminals are available on campus for general student use. Students can access the following: campus intranet, computer help desk, free student e-mail accounts, online (class) grades, online (class) registration, online (class) schedules, access to software. Campuswide network is available. 100% of college-owned or -operated housing units are wired for high-speed Internet access. Wireless service is available via entire campus.

Library: Murray Library. *Books:* 249,852 (physical), 603,562 (digital/electronic); *Serial titles:* 160 (physical), 115,500 (digital/electronic); *Databases:* 108. Weekly public service hours: 96; students can reserve study rooms.

STUDENT LIFE

Housing options: on-campus residence required through senior year; coed, men-only, women-only, special housing for students with disabilities. Campus housing is university owned. Freshman campus housing is guaranteed.

Activities and organizations: drama/theater group, student-run newspaper, radio station, choral group, Outreach teams, student government, choral groups and ensembles, Small Group Program, Outdoors Club.

Athletics Member NCAA. All Division III. *Intercollegiate sports:* baseball M, basketball M/W, cross-country running M/W, field hockey W, lacrosse M/W, soccer M/W, softball W, swimming and diving M/W, tennis M/W, track and field M/W, volleyball M/W, wrestling M. *Intramural sports:* basketball M/W, field hockey W(c), football M/W, ice hockey M(c), soccer M/W, softball M/W, ultimate Frisbee M(c)/W(c), volleyball M/W.

Campus security: 24-hour emergency response devices and patrols, student patrols, late-night transport/escort service, controlled dormitory access, bicycle patrols, security lighting, self-defense classes, prevention/awareness programs.

Student services: health clinic, personal/psychological counseling.

COSTS & FINANCIAL AID

Costs (2018–19) *Comprehensive fee:* $45,680 includes full-time tuition ($34,320), mandatory fees ($840), and room and board ($10,520). Part-time tuition: $1430 per credit hour. *College room only:* $5570. Room and board charges vary according to board plan and housing facility. *Payment plan:* installment. *Waivers:* adult students, senior citizens, and employees or children of employees.

Financial Aid Of all full-time matriculated undergraduates who enrolled in 2017, 2,185 applied for aid, 1,944 were judged to have need, 334 had their need fully met. 711 Federal Work-Study jobs (averaging $2181). 932 state and other part-time jobs (averaging $1965). In 2017, 703 non-need-based awards were made. *Average percent of need met:* 71. *Average financial aid package:* $24,287. *Average need-based loan:* $4763. *Average need-based gift aid:* $18,561. *Average non-need-based aid:* $14,659. *Average indebtedness upon graduation:* $37,399.

APPLYING

Standardized Tests *Required:* SAT or ACT (for admission).

Options: electronic application.

Application fee: $50.

Required: essay or personal statement, high school transcript. *Required for some:* interview.

Application deadlines: rolling (freshmen), rolling (transfers).

Notification: continuous (freshmen), continuous (transfers).

CONTACT

Dr. John Chopka, Vice President for Enrollment Management, Messiah College, One College Avenue, Suite 3005, Mechanicsburg, PA 17055. *Phone:* 717-691-6000. *Toll-free phone:* 800-233-4220. *Fax:* 717-691-2307. *E-mail:* admiss@messiah.edu.

Millersville University of Pennsylvania

Millersville, Pennsylvania
http://www.millersville.edu/

- **State-supported** comprehensive, founded 1855, part of Pennsylvania State System of Higher Education
- **Small-town** 250-acre campus
- **Endowment** $10.8 million
- **Coed** 6,758 undergraduate students, 84% full-time, 57% women, 43% men
- **Moderately difficult** entrance level, 79% of applicants were admitted

UNDERGRAD STUDENTS

5,666 full-time, 1,092 part-time. Students come from 34 states and territories; 57 other countries; 6% are from out of state; 9% Black or African American, non-Hispanic/Latino; 11% Hispanic/Latino; 3% Asian, non-Hispanic/Latino; 0.1% Native Hawaiian or other Pacific Islander, non-Hispanic/Latino; 0.3% American Indian or Alaska Native, non-Hispanic/Latino; 2% Two or more races, non-Hispanic/Latino; 1% Race/ethnicity unknown; 0.7% international; 7% transferred in; 32% live on campus.

Freshmen:

Admission: 6,717 applied, 5,340 admitted, 1,351 enrolled. *Average high school GPA:* 3.3. *Test scores:* SAT evidence-based reading and writing scores over 500: 73%; SAT math scores over 500: 68%; ACT scores over 18: 83%; SAT evidence-based reading and writing scores over 600: 21%; SAT math scores over 600: 17%; ACT scores over 24: 34%; SAT evidence-based reading and writing scores over 700: 2%; SAT math scores over 700: 2%; ACT scores over 30: 6%.

Retention: 77% of full-time freshmen returned.

FACULTY

Total: 497, 62% full-time, 70% with terminal degrees.
Student/faculty ratio: 18:1.

ACADEMICS

Calendar: 4-1-4. *Degrees:* certificates, associate, bachelor's, master's, doctoral, post-master's, and postbachelor's certificates.

Special study options: academic remediation for entering students, accelerated degree program, adult/continuing education programs, advanced placement credit, cooperative education, distance learning, double majors, English as a second language, freshman honors college, honors programs, independent study, internships, off-campus study, part-time degree program, services for LD students, student-designed majors, study abroad, summer session for credit. *ROTC:* Army (b).

Unusual degree programs: 3-2 engineering with Penn State University, University of Delaware.

Computers: 430 computers/terminals and 2,500 ports are available on campus for general student use. Students can access the following: campus intranet, computer help desk, free student e-mail accounts, online (class) grades, online (class) registration, online (class) schedules. Campuswide network is available. 100% of college-owned or -operated housing units are wired for high-speed Internet access. Wireless service is available via entire campus.

Library: The Francine G. McNairy Library and Learning Forum at Ganser Hall. *Books:* 315,441 (physical), 54,392 (digital/electronic); *Serial titles:* 4,191 (physical), 391,998 (digital/electronic); *Databases:* 179. Weekly public service hours: 94; students can reserve study rooms.

STUDENT LIFE

Housing options: on-campus residence required through sophomore year; coed, special housing for students with disabilities. Campus housing is university owned and leased by the school. Freshman campus housing is guaranteed.

Activities and organizations: drama/theater group, student-run newspaper, radio and television station, choral group, marching band, University Activities Board, Honors College Student Association, Mini-THON, Graduate Student Organization, Helping Paws, national fraternities, national sororities.

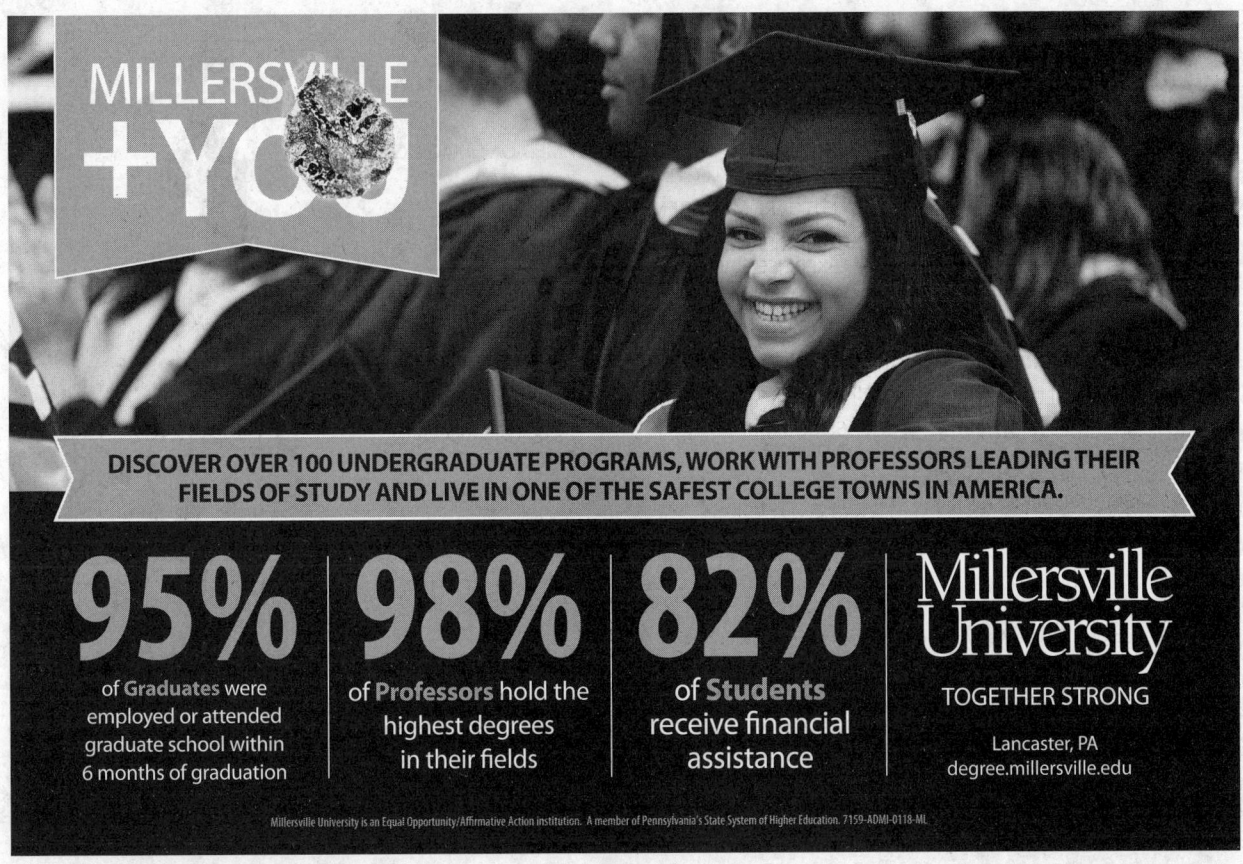

A ★ *indicates that the school has detailed information with a Premium Profile on Petersons.com.*

Athletics Member NCAA. All Division II. *Intercollegiate sports:* baseball M(s), basketball M(s)/W(s), cross-country running W(s), field hockey W(s), football M(s), golf M(s)/W(s), lacrosse W(s), soccer M(s)/W(s), softball W(s), swimming and diving W(s), tennis M(s)/W(s), track and field W(s), volleyball W(s), wrestling M(s). *Intramural sports:* badminton M/W, baseball M(c), basketball M/W, bowling M(c)/W(c), cheerleading M(c)/W(c), cross-country running M(c)/W(c), equestrian sports M(c)/W(c), fencing M(c)/W(c), football M/W, ice hockey M(c)/W(c), lacrosse M(c), rugby M(c)/W(c), soccer M/W, softball M/W, table tennis M/W, tennis M/W, ultimate Frisbee M/W, volleyball M/W, water polo M(c)/W(c).

Campus security: 24-hour emergency response devices and patrols, student patrols, late-night transport/escort service, controlled dormitory access, ENS; crime awareness programs, warning alerts; self-defense educ.; shuttle buses; lighted pathways, TAT, LiveSafe app.

Student services: health clinic, personal/psychological counseling, women's center.

COSTS & FINANCIAL AID
Costs (2017–18) *Tuition:* state resident $9270 full-time, $309 per credit part-time; nonresident $18,730 full-time, $780 per credit part-time. Full-time tuition and fees vary according to course load. Part-time tuition and fees vary according to course load. *Required fees:* $2588 full-time, $89 per credit part-time, $20 per credit part-time. *Room and board:* $13,440. Room and board charges vary according to board plan and housing facility. *Payment plan:* installment. *Waivers:* senior citizens and employees or children of employees.

Financial Aid Of all full-time matriculated undergraduates who enrolled in 2016, 4,918 applied for aid, 4,068 were judged to have need, 176 had their need fully met. 231 Federal Work-Study jobs (averaging $1367). 1,452 state and other part-time jobs (averaging $1377). In 2016, 239 non-need-based awards were made. *Average percent of need met:* 58. *Average financial aid package:* $8467. *Average need-based loan:* $4085. *Average need-based gift aid:* $5884. *Average non-need-based aid:* $2867. *Average indebtedness upon graduation:* $31,476.

APPLYING
Standardized Tests *Required:* SAT or ACT (for admission).

Options: electronic application, early admission, deferred entrance.
Application fee: $50.
Required: essay or personal statement, high school transcript, minimum 2.0 GPA. *Required for some:* 1 letter of recommendation, interview, health examination, audition for music applicants, portfolio for art applicants, Associate degree in Nursing or Diploma and RN license for nursing program. *Recommended:* minimum 3.0 GPA, 2 letters of recommendation.

Application deadlines: rolling (freshmen), rolling (out-of-state freshmen), rolling (transfers).
Notification: continuous (freshmen), continuous (out-of-state freshmen), continuous (transfers).

CONTACT
Ms. Katy A. Ferrier, Director of Admissions, Millersville University of Pennsylvania, PO Box 1002, Millersville, PA 17551-0302. *Phone:* 717-871-4625. *Toll-free phone:* 800-MU-ADMIT. *Fax:* 717-871-2147. *E-mail:* admissions@millersville.edu.

See previous page for display ad and page 1342 for the College Close-Up.

Misericordia University
Dallas, Pennsylvania
http://www.misericordia.edu/
- **Independent Roman Catholic** comprehensive, founded 1924
- **Small-town** 120-acre campus
- **Endowment** $49.2 million
- **Coed** 2,146 undergraduate students, 77% full-time, 67% women, 33% men
- **Moderately difficult** entrance level, 74% of applicants were admitted

UNDERGRAD STUDENTS
1,660 full-time, 486 part-time. Students come from 28 states and territories; 1 other country; 27% are from out of state; 3% Black or African American, non-Hispanic/Latino; 3% Hispanic/Latino; 1% Asian, non-Hispanic/Latino; 0.1% Native Hawaiian or other Pacific Islander, non-Hispanic/Latino; 0.3% American Indian or Alaska Native, non-Hispanic/Latino; 3% Two or more races, non-Hispanic/Latino; 2%

DEGREE PROGRAMS

ACCOUNTING

BIOCHEMISTRY*

BIOLOGY*†

BUSINESS ADMINISTRATION

CHEMISTRY*†

CLINICAL LAB. SCIENCE

COMPUTER SCIENCE

DIAGNOSTIC MEDICAL SONOGRAPHY

EDUCATION
- EARLY CHILDHOOD AND SPECIAL EDUCATION
- MIDDLE LEVEL

ENGLISH †§

GOVERNMENT, LAW AND NATIONAL SECURITY

HEALTH CARE MANAGEMENT

HEALTH SCIENCE:
- EXERCISE SCIENCE
- MEDICAL SCIENCE
- PATIENT NAVIGATION

HISTORY †§

INFORMATION TECHNOLOGY

MASS COMMUNICATIONS AND DESIGN

MATHEMATICS †

MEDICAL AND HEALTH HUMANITIES*

MEDICAL IMAGING

NURSING

OCCUPATIONAL THERAPY

PHILOSOPHY

PHYSICAL THERAPY

PROFESSIONAL STUDIES

PSYCHOLOGY §

SOCIAL WORK

SPEECH-LANGUAGE PATHOLOGY

SPORT MANAGEMENT

STATISTICS

* Pre-medicine, Pre-dentistry, Pre-optometry, Pre-veterinary option
† Secondary Education option   § Pre-law option

MISERICORDIA
UNIVERSITY.

Dallas, Pennsylvania
Founded by the Sisters of Mercy
admissions.misericordia.edu

Race/ethnicity unknown; 0.1% international; 4% transferred in; 43% live on campus.

Freshmen:
Admission: 1,823 applied, 1,357 admitted, 440 enrolled. *Average high school GPA:* 3.4. *Test scores:* ACT scores over 18: 96%; ACT scores over 24: 54%; ACT scores over 30: 6%.
Retention: 85% of full-time freshmen returned.

FACULTY
Total: 304, 46% full-time, 46% with terminal degrees.
Student/faculty ratio: 12:1.

ACADEMICS
Calendar: semesters. *Degrees:* certificates, bachelor's, master's, doctoral, post-master's, and postbachelor's certificates.

Special study options: accelerated degree program, adult/continuing education programs, advanced placement credit, cooperative education, distance learning, double majors, honors programs, independent study, internships, off-campus study, part-time degree program, services for LD students, student-designed majors, study abroad, summer session for credit. *ROTC:* Army (c), Air Force (c).

Computers: 150 computers/terminals and 1,000 ports are available on campus for general student use. Students can access the following: campus intranet, computer help desk, free student e-mail accounts, online (class) grades, online (class) registration, online (class) schedules. Campuswide network is available. 100% of college-owned or -operated housing units are wired for high-speed Internet access. Wireless service is available via entire campus.
Library: Mary Kintz Bevevino Library. *Books:* 80,036 (physical), 13,154 (digital/electronic); *Serial titles:* 8,153 (physical), 28,230 (digital/electronic); *Databases:* 111. Students can reserve study rooms.

STUDENT LIFE
Housing options: coed. Campus housing is university owned and is provided by a third party. Freshman applicants given priority for college housing.

Activities and organizations: drama/theater group, student-run newspaper, radio station, choral group, Physical Therapy club, MSOTA, Colleges against Cancer, Dance Ensemble, Medical Imaging club.

Athletics Member NCAA. All Division III except tennis (Division II). *Intercollegiate sports:* baseball M, basketball M/W, cross-country running M/W, field hockey W, football M, golf M/W, lacrosse M/W, soccer M/W, softball W, swimming and diving M/W, tennis M/W, track and field M/W, volleyball M/W. *Intramural sports:* basketball M/W, football M/W, soccer M/W, softball M/W, tennis M/W, ultimate Frisbee M/W, volleyball M/W.

Campus security: 24-hour emergency response devices and patrols, late-night transport/escort service, controlled dormitory access.

Student services: health clinic, personal/psychological counseling, women's center.

COSTS & FINANCIAL AID
Costs (2018–19) *Comprehensive fee:* $47,200 includes full-time tuition ($31,530), mandatory fees ($1710), and room and board ($13,960). Full-time tuition and fees vary according to degree level. Part-time tuition: $610 per credit. Part-time tuition and fees vary according to class time and location. *College room only:* $7600. Room and board charges vary according to board plan and housing facility. *Payment plans:* installment, deferred payment. *Waivers:* employees or children of employees.
Financial Aid Of all full-time matriculated undergraduates who enrolled in 2017, 1,534 applied for aid, 1,361 were judged to have need, 347 had their need fully met. In 2017, 172 non-need-based awards were made. *Average percent of need met:* 81. *Average financial aid package:* $24,313. *Average need-based loan:* $8593. *Average need-based gift aid:* $17,695. *Average non-need-based aid:* $14,098. *Average indebtedness upon graduation:* $47,764. *Financial aid deadline:* 5/1.

APPLYING
Standardized Tests *Required:* SAT or ACT (for admission).
Options: electronic application, early admission, deferred entrance.
Application fee: $35.

Required: high school transcript. *Required for some:* essay or personal statement, minimum 2.5 GPA, 2 letters of recommendation. *Recommended:* interview.
Application deadlines: rolling (freshmen), rolling (transfers).
Notification: continuous (freshmen), continuous (transfers).

CONTACT
Mr. Glenn Bozinski, Director of Admissions, Misericordia University, 301 Lake Street, Dallas, PA 18612-1098. *Phone:* 570-675-6264. *Toll-free phone:* 866-262-6363. *Fax:* 570-674-6232. *E-mail:* admiss@ misericordia.edu.

See previous page for display ad and page 1346 for the College Close-Up.

Moore College of Art & Design
Philadelphia, Pennsylvania
http://www.moore.edu/

CONTACT
Ms. Jasmine Zateeny, Assistant Director of Admissions, Recruitment Coordinator, Moore College of Art & Design, 20th and The Parkway, Philadelphia, PA 19103. *Phone:* 215-965-4015. *Toll-free phone:* 800-523-2025. *Fax:* 215-965-8544. *E-mail:* enroll@moore.edu.

Moravian College
Bethlehem, Pennsylvania
http://www.moravian.edu/
- **Independent** comprehensive, founded 1742, affiliated with Moravian Church
- **Suburban** 85-acre campus with easy access to Philadelphia
- **Endowment** $111.3 million
- **Coed** 2,033 undergraduate students, 91% full-time, 59% women, 41% men
- **Moderately difficult** entrance level, 76% of applicants were admitted

UNDERGRAD STUDENTS
1,840 full-time, 193 part-time. Students come from 22 states and territories; 16 other countries; 31% are from out of state; 5% Black or African American, non-Hispanic/Latino; 10% Hispanic/Latino; 2% Asian, non-Hispanic/Latino; 0.2% American Indian or Alaska Native, non-Hispanic/Latino; 2% Two or more races, non-Hispanic/Latino; 5% Race/ethnicity unknown; 6% international; 4% transferred in; 65% live on campus.

Freshmen:
Admission: 3,059 applied, 2,324 admitted, 477 enrolled. *Average high school GPA:* 3.5. *Test scores:* SAT evidence-based reading and writing scores over 500: 82%; SAT math scores over 500: 78%; ACT scores over 18: 92%; SAT evidence-based reading and writing scores over 600: 26%; SAT math scores over 600: 25%; ACT scores over 24: 50%; SAT evidence-based reading and writing scores over 700: 3%; SAT math scores over 700: 2%; ACT scores over 30: 5%.
Retention: 82% of full-time freshmen returned.

FACULTY
Total: 294, 48% full-time, 60% with terminal degrees.
Student/faculty ratio: 11:1.

ACADEMICS
Calendar: semesters. *Degrees:* bachelor's, master's, doctoral, post-master's, and postbachelor's certificates.

Special study options: accelerated degree program, adult/continuing education programs, advanced placement credit, cooperative education, distance learning, double majors, honors programs, independent study, internships, off-campus study, part-time degree program, services for LD students, student-designed majors, study abroad, summer session for credit. *ROTC:* Army (c).

Unusual degree programs: 3-2 engineering with Lehigh University, Washington University in St. Louis.

Computers: 230 computers/terminals and 1,700 ports are available on campus for general student use. Students can access the following: campus intranet, computer help desk, free student e-mail accounts, online (class) grades, online (class) registration, online (class) schedules. Campuswide network is available. 100% of college-owned or -operated

housing units are wired for high-speed Internet access. Wireless service is available via entire campus.

Library: Reeves Library. *Books:* 198,012 (physical), 168,981 (digital/electronic); *Serial titles:* 2,490 (physical), 183 (digital/electronic); *Databases:* 67. Weekly public service hours: 86.

STUDENT LIFE

Housing options: on-campus residence required through senior year; coed, men-only, women-only, special housing for students with disabilities. Campus housing is university owned. Freshman campus housing is guaranteed.

Activities and organizations: drama/theater group, student-run newspaper, radio station, choral group, marching band, Moravian Activities Council, Black Student Union, Habitat for Humanity, Commuter Student Union, American Association of University Women, national fraternities, national sororities.

Athletics Member NCAA. All Division III. *Intercollegiate sports:* baseball M, basketball M/W, cheerleading W(c), cross-country running M/W, equestrian sports W(c), field hockey W, football M, golf M, ice hockey M(c), lacrosse M/W, rugby M(c), soccer M/W, softball W, tennis M/W, track and field M/W, volleyball W. *Intramural sports:* basketball M/W, football M/W, soccer M/W, softball M/W, table tennis M/W, tennis M/W, volleyball M/W.

Campus security: 24-hour emergency response devices and patrols, late-night transport/escort service, controlled dormitory access.

Student services: health clinic, personal/psychological counseling.

COSTS & FINANCIAL AID

Costs (2018–19) *One-time required fee:* $140. *Comprehensive fee:* $57,014 includes full-time tuition ($41,905), mandatory fees ($1731), and room and board ($13,378). Full-time tuition and fees vary according to class time and program. Part-time tuition: $1548 per credit. Part-time tuition and fees vary according to class time. *College room only:* $7538. Room and board charges vary according to board plan and housing facility. *Payment plan:* installment. *Waivers:* employees or children of employees.

Financial Aid Of all full-time matriculated undergraduates who enrolled in 2017, 1,585 applied for aid, 1,482 were judged to have need, 216 had

their need fully met. In 2017, 339 non-need-based awards were made. *Average percent of need met:* 73. *Average financial aid package:* $30,834. *Average need-based loan:* $4433. *Average need-based gift aid:* $25,346. *Average non-need-based aid:* $14,331. *Average indebtedness upon graduation:* $33,096.

APPLYING

Standardized Tests *Required:* SAT or ACT (for admission).

Options: electronic application, deferred entrance.

Required: essay or personal statement, high school transcript, 1 letter of recommendation. *Required for some:* portfolio for art majors; audition for music majors; 3.3 high school GPA, minimum SAT combined score of 1500 (with no section less than 500) or ACT score of 23 for nursing.

Application deadlines: 3/1 (freshmen), 5/1 (transfers).

Notification: continuous until 11/15 (freshmen).

CONTACT

Mr. Scott Myers, Director of Undergraduate Admission, Moravian College, 1200 Main Street, Bethlehem, PA 18018. *Phone:* 610-861-1320 Ext. 7115. *Toll-free phone:* 800-441-3191. *Fax:* 610-625-7930. *E-mail:* myersj02@moravian.edu.

★ Mount Aloysius College
Cresson, Pennsylvania
http://www.mtaloy.edu/

• **Independent Roman Catholic** comprehensive, founded 1939
• **Small-town** 193-acre campus
• **Coed** 1,688 undergraduate students, 59% full-time, 67% women, 33% men
• **Minimally difficult** entrance level, 61% of applicants were admitted

UNDERGRAD STUDENTS

999 full-time, 689 part-time. 6% are from out of state; 3% Black or African American, non-Hispanic/Latino; 1% Hispanic/Latino; 0.7% Asian, non-Hispanic/Latino; 0.3% American Indian or Alaska Native, non-Hispanic/Latino; 12% Race/ethnicity unknown; 6% international; 5% transferred in; 38% live on campus.

Freshmen:

Admission: 1,748 applied, 1,064 admitted, 267 enrolled. *Average high school GPA:* 3.4. *Test scores:* SAT evidence-based reading and writing scores over 500: 61%; SAT math scores over 500: 62%; ACT scores over 18: 85%; SAT evidence-based reading and writing scores over 600: 14%; SAT math scores over 600: 9%; ACT scores over 24: 13%; SAT evidence-based reading and writing scores over 700: 1%.

FACULTY

Total: 160, 44% full-time.

Student/faculty ratio: 11:1.

ACADEMICS

Calendar: semesters. *Degrees:* certificates, associate, bachelor's, and master's.

Special study options: academic remediation for entering students, accelerated degree program, advanced placement credit, distance learning, double majors, honors programs, independent study, internships, part-time degree program, student-designed majors, study abroad, summer session for credit.

Computers: Students can access the following: campus intranet, computer help desk, free student e-mail accounts, online (class) grades, online (class) registration, online (class) schedules. Campuswide network is available. 100% of college-owned or -operated housing units are wired for high-speed Internet access. Wireless service is available via entire campus.

Library: Mount Aloysius College Library.

STUDENT LIFE

Housing options: on-campus residence required through sophomore year; coed. Campus housing is university owned. Freshman campus housing is guaranteed.

Activities and organizations: drama/theater group, student-run newspaper, choral group, Student Government, Campus Activity Board, Student Athletic Advisory Committee, Spirit Team, Dance Team.

Athletics Member NCAA. All Division III. *Intercollegiate sports:* baseball M, basketball M/W, cross-country running M/W, golf M/W, soccer M/W, softball W, tennis M/W, volleyball W. *Intramural sports:* basketball M/W, bowling M/W, cheerleading M(c)/W(c), football M/W, skiing (cross-country) M/W, skiing (downhill) M/W, table tennis M/W, ultimate Frisbee M/W, volleyball M/W, weight lifting M/W.

Campus security: 24-hour emergency response devices and patrols, student patrols, late-night transport/escort service, controlled dormitory access.

Student services: health clinic, personal/psychological counseling.

COSTS & FINANCIAL AID

Costs (2017–18) *Comprehensive fee:* $32,768 includes full-time tuition ($21,230), mandatory fees ($1200), and room and board ($10,338). Part-time tuition: $800 per credit hour. *College room only:* $5200.

Financial Aid Of all full-time matriculated undergraduates who enrolled in 2017, 990 applied for aid, 776 were judged to have need. In 2017, 214 non-need-based awards were made. *Average percent of need met:* 36. *Average financial aid package:* $13,500. *Average need-based loan:* $4200. *Average need-based gift aid:* $2800. *Average non-need-based aid:* $5000. *Average indebtedness upon graduation:* $36,899.

APPLYING

Standardized Tests *Required:* SAT or ACT (for admission). *Recommended:* SAT (for admission), ACT (for admission).

Options: electronic application, early admission, deferred entrance.

Application fee: $30.

Required: high school transcript. *Required for some:* essay or personal statement, interview. *Recommended:* interview.

Application deadlines: rolling (freshmen), rolling (transfers).

Notification: continuous (freshmen), continuous (transfers).

CONTACT

Mr. Frank C. Crouse Jr., Vice President for Enrollment Management/Dean of Admissions, Mount Aloysius College, 7373 Admiral Peary Highway, Cresson, PA 16630-1999. *Phone:* 814-886-6383. *Toll-free phone:* 888-823-2220. *Fax:* 814-886-6441. *E-mail:* admissions@mtaloy.edu.

See previous page for display ad and page 1352 for the College Close-Up.

Muhlenberg College
Allentown, Pennsylvania
http://www.muhlenberg.edu/

- **Independent** 4-year, founded 1848, affiliated with Lutheran Church
- **Suburban** 75-acre campus with easy access to Philadelphia
- **Endowment** $246.9 million
- **Coed** 2,408 undergraduate students, 96% full-time, 60% women, 40% men
- **Very difficult** entrance level, 48% of applicants were admitted

UNDERGRAD STUDENTS

2,318 full-time, 90 part-time. Students come from 35 states and territories; 13 other countries; 76% are from out of state; 3% Black or African American, non-Hispanic/Latino; 7% Hispanic/Latino; 3% Asian, non-Hispanic/Latino; 1% Two or more races, non-Hispanic/Latino; 6% Race/ethnicity unknown; 3% international; 0.8% transferred in; 92% live on campus.

Freshmen:

Admission: 4,636 applied, 2,242 admitted, 593 enrolled. *Average high school GPA:* 3.3. *Test scores:* SAT evidence-based reading and writing scores over 500: 97%; SAT math scores over 500: 95%; ACT scores over 18: 100%; SAT evidence-based reading and writing scores over 600: 66%; SAT math scores over 600: 55%; ACT scores over 24: 87%; SAT evidence-based reading and writing scores over 700: 16%; SAT math scores over 700: 15%; ACT scores over 30: 29%.

Retention: 90% of full-time freshmen returned.

FACULTY

Total: 297, 62% full-time, 64% with terminal degrees.

Student/faculty ratio: 10:1.

ACADEMICS

Calendar: semesters. *Degrees:* certificates, associate, and bachelor's.

Special study options: accelerated degree program, adult/continuing education programs, advanced placement credit, double majors, honors programs, independent study, internships, off-campus study, part-time degree program, services for LD students, student-designed majors, study abroad, summer session for credit. *ROTC:* Army (c).

Unusual degree programs: 3-2 engineering with Columbia University; forestry with Duke University; dentistry with University of Pennsylvania, medicine with Drexel University, optometry with State University of New York (SUNY) State College of Optometry, occupational and physical therapy with Thomas Jefferson University.

Computers: 450 computers/terminals and 100 ports are available on campus for general student use. Students can access the following: campus intranet, computer help desk, free student e-mail accounts, online (class) grades, online (class) registration, online (class) schedules. Campuswide network is available. 100% of college-owned or -operated housing units are wired for high-speed Internet access. Wireless service is available via entire campus.

Library: Trexler Library. *Books:* 228,069 (physical), 515,579 (digital/electronic); *Serial titles:* 1,183 (physical), 40,276 (digital/electronic); *Databases:* 99. Weekly public service hours: 105; students can reserve study rooms.

STUDENT LIFE

Housing options: on-campus residence required through senior year; coed, women-only, special housing for students with disabilities. Campus housing is university owned and leased by the school. Freshman campus housing is guaranteed.

Activities and organizations: drama/theater group, student-run newspaper, radio and television station, choral group, Theater Association, Environmental Action Team, Jefferson School Partnership, Select Choir, Habitat for Humanity, national fraternities, national sororities.

Athletics Member NCAA. All Division III. *Intercollegiate sports:* baseball M, basketball M/W, cheerleading M/W, cross-country running M/W, field hockey W, football M, golf M/W, lacrosse M/W, soccer M/W, softball W, tennis M/W, track and field M/W, volleyball W, wrestling M. *Intramural sports:* basketball M/W, cross-country running M/W, football M/W, racquetball M/W, rugby M/W, soccer M/W, softball M, swimming and diving M/W, tennis M/W, ultimate Frisbee M/W, volleyball M/W.

Campus security: 24-hour emergency response devices and patrols, late-night transport/escort service, controlled dormitory access.

Student services: health clinic, personal/psychological counseling.

COSTS & FINANCIAL AID

Costs (2017–18) *One-time required fee:* $120. *Comprehensive fee:* $62,250 includes full-time tuition ($50,095), mandatory fees ($735), and room and board ($11,420). Part-time tuition: $5890 per course. Part-time tuition and fees vary according to program. *Required fees:* $368 per term part-time. *College room only:* $6205. Room and board charges vary according to board plan, housing facility, and location. *Payment plan:* installment. *Waivers:* employees or children of employees.

Financial Aid Of all full-time matriculated undergraduates who enrolled in 2017, 1,503 applied for aid, 1,293 were judged to have need, 318 had their need fully met. In 2017, 733 non-need-based awards were made. *Average percent of need met:* 87. *Average financial aid package:* $36,168. *Average need-based loan:* $4634. *Average need-based gift aid:* $32,257. *Average non-need-based aid:* $13,264. *Average indebtedness upon graduation:* $32,241. *Financial aid deadline:* 3/1.

APPLYING

Standardized Tests *Required for some:* SAT or ACT (for admission).

Options: electronic application, early admission, early decision, deferred entrance.

Application fee: $50.

Required: essay or personal statement, high school transcript, 2 letters of recommendation. *Required for some:* interview, graded paper. *Recommended:* interview.

Application deadlines: 2/1 (freshmen), 6/15 (transfers).

Early decision deadline: 11/15 (for plan 1), 2/1 (for plan 2).

Notification: 3/20 (freshmen), continuous until 7/1 (transfers), 12/15 (early decision plan 1), 2/15 (early decision plan 2).

CONTACT

Muhlenberg College, 2400 Chew Street, Allentown, PA 18104-5586.

See below for display ad and page 1356 for the College Close-Up.

★ Neumann University
Aston, Pennsylvania
http://www.neumann.edu/

- **Independent Roman Catholic** comprehensive, founded 1965
- **Suburban** 68-acre campus with easy access to Philadelphia
- **Endowment** $30.8 million
- **Coed** 2,085 undergraduate students, 70% full-time, 66% women, 34% men
- **Minimally difficult** entrance level, 96% of applicants were admitted

UNDERGRAD STUDENTS

1,462 full-time, 623 part-time. Students come from 30 states and territories; 9 other countries; 31% are from out of state; 24% Black or African American, non-Hispanic/Latino; 6% Hispanic/Latino; 1% Asian, non-Hispanic/Latino; 0.1% Native Hawaiian or other Pacific Islander, non-Hispanic/Latino; 0.1% American Indian or Alaska Native, non-Hispanic/Latino; 2% Two or more races, non-Hispanic/Latino; 12% Race/ethnicity unknown; 1% international; 4% transferred in; 35% live on campus.

Freshmen:

Admission: 1,505 applied, 1,449 admitted, 360 enrolled. *Average high school GPA:* 3.1. *Test scores:* SAT evidence-based reading and writing scores over 500: 53%; SAT math scores over 500: 48%; ACT scores over 18: 53%; SAT evidence-based reading and writing scores over 600: 10%; SAT math scores over 600: 7%; ACT scores over 24: 8%; SAT math scores over 700: 1%.

Retention: 77% of full-time freshmen returned.

FACULTY

Total: 241, 40% full-time, 54% with terminal degrees.

Student/faculty ratio: 15:1.

ACADEMICS

Calendar: semesters. *Degrees:* associate, bachelor's, master's, doctoral, post-master's, and postbachelor's certificates.

Special study options: academic remediation for entering students, accelerated degree program, adult/continuing education programs,

advanced placement credit, cooperative education, distance learning, double majors, honors programs, independent study, internships, off-campus study, part-time degree program, services for LD students, study abroad, summer session for credit. *ROTC:* Army (c), Air Force (c).

Computers: 275 computers/terminals and 1,500 ports are available on campus for general student use. Students can access the following: campus intranet, computer help desk, free student e-mail accounts, online (class) grades, online (class) registration, online (class) schedules. Campuswide network is available. 100% of college-owned or -operated housing units are wired for high-speed Internet access. Wireless service is available via entire campus.

Library: Neumann University Library plus 1 other. *Books:* 51,000 (physical), 161,000 (digital/electronic); *Serial titles:* 20 (physical), 100,000 (digital/electronic); *Databases:* 45. Weekly public service hours: 80; students can reserve study rooms.

STUDENT LIFE

Housing options: coed, special housing for students with disabilities. Campus housing is university owned and leased by the school. Freshman applicants given priority for college housing.

Activities and organizations: drama/theater group, student-run newspaper, radio and television station, choral group, Student Nurses Association, Student Activities Board, Boogie Nights, Knights for Education, Neumann Media.

Athletics Member NCAA. All Division III. *Intercollegiate sports:* baseball M, basketball M/W, cross-country running M/W, field hockey W, golf M/W, ice hockey M/W, lacrosse M/W, rugby M(c)/W(c), soccer M/W, softball W, swimming and diving W, tennis M/W, track and field M/W, volleyball M/W. *Intramural sports:* baseball M(c), basketball M(c)/W, cheerleading W(c), ice hockey M(c), soccer M/W, softball M/W, table tennis M/W, volleyball M/W.

Campus security: 24-hour emergency response devices and patrols, late-night transport/escort service, controlled dormitory access.

Student services: health clinic, personal/psychological counseling.

COSTS & FINANCIAL AID

Costs (2017–18) *One-time required fee:* $100. *Comprehensive fee:* $42,570 includes full-time tuition ($28,710), mandatory fees ($1340), and room and board ($12,520). Full-time tuition and fees vary according to degree level. Part-time tuition: $655 per credit hour. Part-time tuition and fees vary according to degree level and program. *Required fees:* $90 per term part-time. *College room only:* $7530. Room and board charges vary according to board plan and housing facility. *Payment plans:* installment, deferred payment. *Waivers:* employees or children of employees.

Financial Aid Of all full-time matriculated undergraduates who enrolled in 2016, 1,495 applied for aid, 1,338 were judged to have need. In 2016, 239 non-need-based awards were made. *Average percent of need met:* 70. *Average financial aid package:* $16,971. *Average need-based loan:* $4462. *Average need-based gift aid:* $7460. *Average non-need-based aid:* $9707.

APPLYING

Standardized Tests *Required:* SAT or ACT (for admission).

Options: electronic application, deferred entrance.

Application fee: $35.

Required: high school transcript, minimum 2.5 GPA. *Required for some:* 1 letter of recommendation. *Recommended:* essay or personal statement, interview.

Application deadlines: rolling (freshmen), rolling (out-of-state freshmen), rolling (transfers).

Notification: continuous (freshmen), continuous (out-of-state freshmen), continuous (transfers).

CONTACT

Mr. Edward P. Wright, Director of Undergraduate Admissions, Neumann University, One Neumann Drive, Aston, PA 19014-1298. *Phone:* 610-558-5616. *Toll-free phone:* 800-963-8626. *Fax:* 610-361-2548. *E-mail:* wrighte@neumann.edu.

See below for display ad and page 1358 for the College Close-Up.

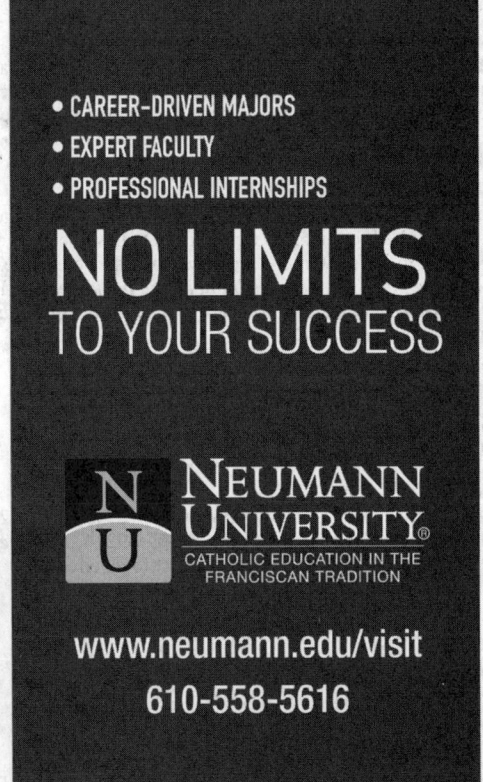

Peirce College
Philadelphia, Pennsylvania
http://www.peirce.edu/
- **Independent** comprehensive, founded 1865
- **Urban** 1-acre campus
- **Coed, primarily women** 1,389 undergraduate students, 23% full-time, 72% women, 28% men
- **Noncompetitive** entrance level

UNDERGRAD STUDENTS
315 full-time, 1,074 part-time. 9% are from out of state; 65% Black or African American, non-Hispanic/Latino; 8% Hispanic/Latino; 2% Asian, non-Hispanic/Latino; 0.1% Native Hawaiian or other Pacific Islander, non-Hispanic/Latino; 0.1% American Indian or Alaska Native, non-Hispanic/Latino; 1% Two or more races, non-Hispanic/Latino; 5% Race/ethnicity unknown; 0.3% international.

Freshmen:
Admission: 87 enrolled.

Retention: 50% of full-time freshmen returned.

FACULTY
Total: 99, 28% full-time, 46% with terminal degrees.

Student/faculty ratio: 14:1.

ACADEMICS
Calendar: semesters. *Degrees:* certificates, associate, bachelor's, and master's.

Special study options: accelerated degree program, adult/continuing education programs, advanced placement credit, cooperative education, distance learning, internships, part-time degree program, services for LD students, summer session for credit.

Computers: Students can access the following: campus intranet, computer help desk, free student e-mail accounts, online (class) grades, online (class) registration, online (class) schedules. Campuswide network is available. Wireless service is available via entire campus.

Library: Peirce College Library.

STUDENT LIFE
Housing options: college housing not available.

Campus security: 24-hour emergency response devices and patrols, late-night transport/escort service, 24-hour security cameras.

COSTS & FINANCIAL AID
Costs (2017–18) *Tuition:* $14,400 full-time, $600 per credit part-time. Full-time tuition and fees vary according to course load and reciprocity agreements. Part-time tuition and fees vary according to course load and reciprocity agreements. *Required fees:* $660 full-time. *Payment plans:* installment, deferred payment. *Waivers:* children of alumni and employees or children of employees.

Financial Aid Of all full-time matriculated undergraduates who enrolled in 2015, 286 applied for aid, 280 were judged to have need, 11 had their need fully met. In 2015, 10 non-need-based awards were made. *Average percent of need met:* 63. *Average financial aid package:* $12,116. *Average need-based loan:* $4250. *Average need-based gift aid:* $7911. *Average non-need-based aid:* $4457.

APPLYING
Options: electronic application.

Application fee: $50.

Required: high school transcript.

CONTACT
Mr. Paul Ballentine, Manager, Admissions, Peirce College, 1420 Pine Street, Philadelphia, PA 19102. *Phone:* 215-670-9214. *Toll-free phone:* 888-467-3472. *Fax:* 215-670-9366. *E-mail:* info@peirce.edu.

Penn State Abington
Abington, Pennsylvania
http://www.abington.psu.edu/
- **State-related** 4-year, founded 1950, part of Pennsylvania State University
- **Small-town** campus
- **Coed** 3,888 undergraduate students, 85% full-time, 51% women, 49% men
- **Very difficult** entrance level, 85% of applicants were admitted

UNDERGRAD STUDENTS
3,312 full-time, 576 part-time. 8% are from out of state; 13% Black or African American, non-Hispanic/Latino; 11% Hispanic/Latino; 16% Asian, non-Hispanic/Latino; 0.1% American Indian or Alaska Native, non-Hispanic/Latino; 3% Two or more races, non-Hispanic/Latino; 2% Race/ethnicity unknown; 10% international; 4% transferred in; 1% live on campus.

Freshmen:
Admission: 5,145 applied, 4,385 admitted, 1,056 enrolled. *Average high school GPA:* 3.2. *Test scores:* SAT evidence-based reading and writing scores over 500: 67%; SAT math scores over 500: 72%; ACT scores over 18: 99%; SAT evidence-based reading and writing scores over 600: 21%; SAT math scores over 600: 31%; ACT scores over 24: 54%; SAT evidence-based reading and writing scores over 700: 1%; SAT math scores over 700: 14%; ACT scores over 30: 9%.

Retention: 83% of full-time freshmen returned.

FACULTY
Total: 320, 46% full-time, 47% with terminal degrees.

Student/faculty ratio: 17:1.

ACADEMICS
Calendar: semesters. *Degrees:* certificates, associate, bachelor's, and postbachelor's certificates (enrollment figures include students enrolled at The Graduate School at Penn State who are taking courses at this location).

Special study options: adult/continuing education programs, external degree program, part-time degree program. *ROTC:* Army (c), Air Force (c).

Computers: Students can access the following: campus intranet, computer help desk, free student e-mail accounts, online (class) grades, online (class) registration, online (class) schedules. Campuswide network is available.

Library: Penn State Abington Library.

STUDENT LIFE
Housing options: coed, special housing for students with disabilities.

Athletics *Intercollegiate sports:* baseball M, basketball M/W, golf M, soccer M/W, softball W, tennis M/W, volleyball W. *Intramural sports:* basketball M/W, cross-country running M/W, football M, soccer M/W, softball M, tennis M/W, volleyball M/W.

Campus security: 24-hour emergency response devices and patrols.

COSTS & FINANCIAL AID
Costs (2017–18) *Tuition:* state resident $13,540 full-time, $557 per credit hour part-time; nonresident $21,582 full-time, $899 per credit hour part-time. Full-time tuition and fees vary according to course level, degree level, location, program, and student level. Part-time tuition and fees vary according to course level, course load, degree level, location, program, and student level. *Required fees:* $976 full-time. *Payment plans:* installment, deferred payment. *Waivers:* senior citizens and employees or children of employees.

Financial Aid Of all full-time matriculated undergraduates who enrolled in 2016, 2,465 applied for aid, 2,160 were judged to have need, 264 had their need fully met. In 2016, 181 non-need-based awards were made. *Average percent of need met:* 56. *Average financial aid package:* $10,195. *Average need-based loan:* $4016. *Average need-based gift aid:* $5482. *Average non-need-based aid:* $4134. *Average indebtedness upon graduation:* $31,007.

APPLYING
Standardized Tests *Required:* SAT or ACT (for admission).

Options: electronic application, early admission, deferred entrance.

Application fee: $65.

Required: high school transcript. *Required for some:* interview. *Recommended:* essay or personal statement.

Application deadlines: rolling (freshmen), rolling (transfers).

Notification: continuous (freshmen), continuous (transfers).

CONTACT
Admissions Office, Penn State Abington, 1600 Woodland Road, Abington, PA 19001. *Phone:* 215-881-7600. *Fax:* 215-881-7655. *E-mail:* abingtonadmissions@psu.edu.

Penn State Altoona

Altoona, Pennsylvania
http://www.altoona.psu.edu/

- **State-related** 4-year, founded 1939, part of Pennsylvania State University
- **Suburban** campus
- **Coed** 3,482 undergraduate students, 97% full-time, 45% women, 55% men
- **Very difficult** entrance level, 92% of applicants were admitted

UNDERGRAD STUDENTS
3,374 full-time, 108 part-time. 16% are from out of state; 6% Black or African American, non-Hispanic/Latino; 5% Hispanic/Latino; 3% Asian, non-Hispanic/Latino; 0.1% American Indian or Alaska Native, non-Hispanic/Latino; 3% Two or more races, non-Hispanic/Latino; 1% Race/ethnicity unknown; 8% international; 2% transferred in; 27% live on campus.

Freshmen:
Admission: 5,430 applied, 5,009 admitted, 1,274 enrolled. *Average high school GPA:* 3.1. *Test scores:* SAT evidence-based reading and writing scores over 500: 76%; SAT math scores over 500: 76%; ACT scores over 18: 96%; SAT evidence-based reading and writing scores over 600: 23%; SAT math scores over 600: 25%; ACT scores over 24: 46%; SAT evidence-based reading and writing scores over 700: 2%; SAT math scores over 700: 7%; ACT scores over 30: 5%.
Retention: 82% of full-time freshmen returned.

FACULTY
Total: 288, 68% full-time, 51% with terminal degrees.
Student/faculty ratio: 15:1.

ACADEMICS
Calendar: semesters. *Degrees:* certificates, associate, and bachelor's (enrollment figures include students enrolled at The Graduate School at Penn State who are taking courses at this location).
Special study options: independent study. *ROTC:* Army (c), Air Force (c).
Computers: Students can access the following: campus intranet, computer help desk, free student e-mail accounts, online (class) grades, online (class) registration, online (class) schedules.
Library: Robert E. Eiche Library.

STUDENT LIFE
Housing options: coed, cooperative, special housing for students with disabilities. Campus housing is university owned.
Athletics Member NCAA. All Division III. *Intercollegiate sports:* baseball M, basketball M/W, cross-country running M/W, golf M/W, soccer M/W, softball W, swimming and diving M/W, tennis M/W. *Intramural sports:* badminton M/W, baseball M/W, basketball M/W, football M/W, golf M/W, racquetball M/W, soccer M/W, softball M/W, table tennis M/W, tennis M/W, track and field M/W, volleyball M/W, weight lifting M/W.
Campus security: 24-hour emergency response devices and patrols, late-night transport/escort service.

COSTS & FINANCIAL AID
Costs (2017–18) *Tuition:* state resident $14,214 full-time, $592 per credit hour part-time; nonresident $22,716 full-time, $947 per credit hour part-time. Full-time tuition and fees vary according to course level, degree level, location, program, and student level. Part-time tuition and fees vary according to course level, course load, degree level, location, program, and student level. *Required fees:* $976 full-time. *Room and board:*

$11,280; room only: $6180. Room and board charges vary according to board plan, housing facility, and location. *Payment plans:* installment, deferred payment. *Waivers:* senior citizens and employees or children of employees.

Financial Aid Of all full-time matriculated undergraduates who enrolled in 2016, 2,656 applied for aid, 2,236 were judged to have need, 511 had their need fully met. In 2016, 219 non-need-based awards were made. *Average percent of need met:* 63. *Average financial aid package:* $9995. *Average need-based loan:* $3997. *Average need-based gift aid:* $5479. *Average non-need-based aid:* $3299. *Average indebtedness upon graduation:* $41,629.

APPLYING
Standardized Tests *Required:* SAT or ACT (for admission).
Options: electronic application, early admission, deferred entrance.
Application fee: $65.
Required: high school transcript. *Required for some:* interview. *Recommended:* essay or personal statement.
Application deadlines: rolling (freshmen), rolling (transfers).
Notification: continuous (freshmen), continuous (transfers).

CONTACT
Admissions Office, Penn State Altoona, 3000 Ivyside Park, Altoona, PA 16601. *Phone:* 814-949-5466. *Toll-free phone:* 800-848-9843. *Fax:* 814-949-5564. *E-mail:* aaadmit@psu.edu.

Penn State Beaver

Monaca, Pennsylvania
http://www.br.psu.edu/

- **State-related** 4-year, founded 1964, part of Pennsylvania State University
- **Small-town** campus
- **Coed** 655 undergraduate students, 86% full-time, 42% women, 58% men
- **Moderately difficult** entrance level, 88% of applicants were admitted

UNDERGRAD STUDENTS
563 full-time, 92 part-time. 12% are from out of state; 8% Black or African American, non-Hispanic/Latino; 5% Hispanic/Latino; 4% Asian, non-Hispanic/Latino; 0.2% American Indian or Alaska Native, non-Hispanic/Latino; 5% Two or more races, non-Hispanic/Latino; 0.2% Race/ethnicity unknown; 4% international; 5% transferred in; 22% live on campus.

Freshmen:
Admission: 792 applied, 694 admitted, 184 enrolled. *Average high school GPA:* 3.2. *Test scores:* SAT evidence-based reading and writing scores over 500: 72%; SAT math scores over 500: 75%; ACT scores over 18: 84%; SAT evidence-based reading and writing scores over 600: 25%; SAT math scores over 600: 28%; ACT scores over 24: 53%; SAT evidence-based reading and writing scores over 700: 1%; SAT math scores over 700: 4%; ACT scores over 30: 16%.
Retention: 76% of full-time freshmen returned.

FACULTY
Total: 66, 52% full-time, 41% with terminal degrees.
Student/faculty ratio: 14:1.

ACADEMICS
Calendar: semesters. *Degree:* certificates and bachelor's.
Special study options: adult/continuing education programs.

STUDENT LIFE
Housing options: coed, special housing for students with disabilities. Campus housing is university owned. Freshman campus housing is guaranteed.
Athletics Member NJCAA. *Intercollegiate sports:* baseball M, basketball M, softball M/W, volleyball W. *Intramural sports:* basketball M/W, cheerleading M(c)/W(c), cross-country running M/W, football M, golf M/W, soccer M/W, softball M/W, table tennis M/W.

COSTS & FINANCIAL AID
Costs (2017–18) *Tuition:* state resident $12,718 full-time, $524 per credit hour part-time; nonresident $20,352 full-time, $848 per credit hour part-time. Full-time tuition and fees vary according to course level, degree

level, location, program, and student level. Part-time tuition and fees vary according to course level, course load, degree level, location, program, and student level. *Required fees:* $976 full-time. *Room and board:* $11,280; room only: $6180. Room and board charges vary according to board plan, housing facility, and location. *Payment plans:* installment, deferred payment. *Waivers:* senior citizens and employees or children of employees.

Financial Aid Of all full-time matriculated undergraduates who enrolled in 2016, 565 applied for aid, 474 were judged to have need, 131 had their need fully met. In 2016, 75 non-need-based awards were made. *Average percent of need met:* 70. *Average financial aid package:* $10,943. *Average need-based loan:* $3984. *Average need-based gift aid:* $5679. *Average non-need-based aid:* $4185. *Average indebtedness upon graduation:* $35,924.

APPLYING
Standardized Tests *Required:* SAT or ACT (for admission).

Options: electronic application, early admission, deferred entrance.

Application fee: $65.

Required: high school transcript. *Required for some:* interview. *Recommended:* essay or personal statement.

Application deadlines: rolling (freshmen), rolling (transfers).

Notification: continuous (freshmen), continuous (transfers).

CONTACT
Admissions Office, Penn State Beaver, 100 University Drive, Monaca, PA 15061. *Phone:* 724-773-3800. *Fax:* 724-773-3658. *E-mail:* br-admissions@psu.edu.

Penn State Berks
Reading, Pennsylvania
http://www.bk.psu.edu/

- **State-related** 4-year, founded 1924, part of Pennsylvania State University
- **Suburban** campus
- **Coed** 2,719 undergraduate students, 89% full-time, 41% women, 59% men
- **Very difficult** entrance level, 86% of applicants were admitted

UNDERGRAD STUDENTS
2,411 full-time, 308 part-time. 7% are from out of state; 8% Black or African American, non-Hispanic/Latino; 13% Hispanic/Latino; 5% Asian, non-Hispanic/Latino; 0.1% Native Hawaiian or other Pacific Islander, non-Hispanic/Latino; 0.1% American Indian or Alaska Native, non-Hispanic/Latino; 3% Two or more races, non-Hispanic/Latino; 1% Race/ethnicity unknown; 4% international; 4% transferred in; 28% live on campus.

Freshmen:
Admission: 2,447 applied, 2,097 admitted, 694 enrolled. *Average high school GPA:* 3.1. *Test scores:* SAT evidence-based reading and writing scores over 500: 72%; SAT math scores over 500: 75%; ACT scores over 18: 91%; SAT evidence-based reading and writing scores over 600: 22%; SAT math scores over 600: 26%; ACT scores over 24: 49%; SAT evidence-based reading and writing scores over 700: 2%; SAT math scores over 700: 7%; ACT scores over 30: 3%.

Retention: 78% of full-time freshmen returned.

FACULTY
Total: 227, 60% full-time, 51% with terminal degrees.

Student/faculty ratio: 15:1.

ACADEMICS
Calendar: semesters. *Degrees:* certificates, associate, bachelor's, and postbachelor's certificates (enrollment figures include students enrolled at The Graduate School at Penn State who are taking courses at this location).

Special study options: adult/continuing education programs, part-time degree program. *ROTC:* Army (c).

Computers: Students can access the following: campus intranet, computer help desk, free student e-mail accounts, online (class) grades, online (class) registration, online (class) schedules. Campuswide network is available.

Library: Thun Library.

STUDENT LIFE
Housing options: coed, special housing for students with disabilities. Campus housing is university owned.

Athletics Member NJCAA. *Intercollegiate sports:* baseball M, basketball M/W, cheerleading M/W, cross-country running M/W, golf M, soccer M/W, softball W, tennis M/W, volleyball W. *Intramural sports:* badminton M/W, basketball M/W, football M/W, golf M/W, table tennis M/W, volleyball M/W.

Campus security: 24-hour emergency response devices and patrols, late-night transport/escort service, controlled dormitory access.

COSTS & FINANCIAL AID
Costs (2017–18) *Tuition:* state resident $14,214 full-time, $592 per credit hour part-time; nonresident $22,716 full-time, $947 per credit hour part-time. Full-time tuition and fees vary according to course level, degree level, location, program, and student level. Part-time tuition and fees vary according to course level, course load, degree level, location, program, and student level. *Required fees:* $976 full-time. *Room and board:* $12,400; room only: $7300. Room and board charges vary according to board plan, housing facility, and location. *Payment plans:* installment, deferred payment. *Waivers:* senior citizens and employees or children of employees.

Financial Aid Of all full-time matriculated undergraduates who enrolled in 2016, 2,168 applied for aid, 1,841 were judged to have need, 422 had their need fully met. In 2016, 123 non-need-based awards were made. *Average percent of need met:* 62. *Average financial aid package:* $9706. *Average need-based loan:* $4187. *Average need-based gift aid:* $5269. *Average non-need-based aid:* $3186. *Average indebtedness upon graduation:* $39,022.

APPLYING
Standardized Tests *Required:* SAT or ACT (for admission).

Options: electronic application, early admission, deferred entrance.

Application fee: $65.

Required: high school transcript. *Required for some:* interview. *Recommended:* essay or personal statement.

Application deadlines: rolling (freshmen), rolling (transfers).

Notification: continuous (freshmen), continuous (transfers).

CONTACT
Admissions Office, Penn State Berks, Tulpehocken Road, PO Box 7009, Reading, PA 19610. *Phone:* 610-396-6060. *Fax:* 610-396-6077. *E-mail:* admissionsbk@psu.edu.

Penn State Brandywine
Media, Pennsylvania
http://www.brandywine.psu.edu/

- **State-related** 4-year, founded 1966, part of Pennsylvania State University
- **Small-town** campus
- **Coed** 1,438 undergraduate students, 87% full-time, 42% women, 58% men
- **Moderately difficult** entrance level, 87% of applicants were admitted

UNDERGRAD STUDENTS
1,245 full-time, 193 part-time. 10% are from out of state; 17% Black or African American, non-Hispanic/Latino; 6% Hispanic/Latino; 13% Asian, non-Hispanic/Latino; 0.1% Native Hawaiian or other Pacific Islander, non-Hispanic/Latino; 0.3% American Indian or Alaska Native, non-Hispanic/Latino; 3% Two or more races, non-Hispanic/Latino; 5% Race/ethnicity unknown; 2% international; 3% transferred in; 15% live on campus.

Freshmen:
Admission: 1,627 applied, 1,416 admitted, 430 enrolled. *Average high school GPA:* 3.0. *Test scores:* SAT evidence-based reading and writing scores over 500: 67%; SAT math scores over 500: 70%; ACT scores over 18: 80%; SAT evidence-based reading and writing scores over 600: 23%; SAT math scores over 600: 28%; ACT scores over 24: 48%; SAT evidence-based reading and writing scores over 700: 2%; SAT math scores over 700: 8%; ACT scores over 30: 11%.

Retention: 74% of full-time freshmen returned.

FACULTY
Total: 134, 49% full-time, 48% with terminal degrees.
Student/faculty ratio: 15:1.

ACADEMICS
Calendar: semesters. *Degrees:* certificates, associate, and bachelor's.
Special study options: adult/continuing education programs. *ROTC:* Army (c), Air Force (c).
Computers: Students can access the following: online (class) registration. Campuswide network is available.

STUDENT LIFE
Housing options: coed.
Athletics Member NJCAA. *Intercollegiate sports:* baseball M, basketball M/W, soccer M/W, tennis M/W, volleyball W. *Intramural sports:* basketball M/W, cheerleading M(c)/W(c), golf M/W, ice hockey M(c)/W(c), lacrosse M/W, soccer M/W, softball W(c), tennis M/W, volleyball M(c)/W.
Campus security: late-night transport/escort service, part-time trained security personnel.

COSTS & FINANCIAL AID
Costs (2017–18) *Tuition:* state resident $13,484 full-time, $555 per credit hour part-time; nonresident $21,402 full-time, $892 per credit hour part-time. Full-time tuition and fees vary according to course level, degree level, location, program, and student level. Part-time tuition and fees vary according to course level, course load, degree level, location, program, and student level. *Required fees:* $976 full-time. *Room and board:* $11,860; room only: $6760. Room and board charges vary according to board plan. *Payment plans:* installment, deferred payment. *Waivers:* senior citizens and employees or children of employees.
Financial Aid Of all full-time matriculated undergraduates who enrolled in 2016, 947 applied for aid, 783 were judged to have need, 120 had their need fully met. In 2016, 88 non-need-based awards were made. *Average percent of need met:* 58. *Average financial aid package:* $10,446. *Average need-based loan:* $3945. *Average need-based gift aid:* $5587. *Average non-need-based aid:* $4510. *Average indebtedness upon graduation:* $34,353.

APPLYING
Standardized Tests *Required:* SAT or ACT (for admission).
Options: electronic application, early admission, deferred entrance.
Application fee: $65.
Required: high school transcript.
Application deadlines: rolling (freshmen), rolling (transfers).
Notification: continuous (freshmen), continuous (transfers).

CONTACT
Admissions Office, Penn State Brandywine, 25 Yearsley Mill Road, Media, PA 19063. *Phone:* 610-892-1200. *Fax:* 610-892-1320. *E-mail:* bwadmissions@psu.edu.

Penn State DuBois

DuBois, Pennsylvania
http://www.ds.psu.edu/
- **State-related** primarily 2-year, founded 1935, part of Pennsylvania State University
- **Small-town** campus
- **Coed** 585 undergraduate students, 79% full-time, 39% women, 61% men
- **Moderately difficult** entrance level, 84% of applicants were admitted

UNDERGRAD STUDENTS
464 full-time, 121 part-time. 3% are from out of state; 2% Black or African American, non-Hispanic/Latino; 2% Hispanic/Latino; 2% Asian, non-Hispanic/Latino; 1% Two or more races, non-Hispanic/Latino; 0.6% Race/ethnicity unknown; 1% international; 4% transferred in.

Freshmen:
Admission: 465 applied, 390 admitted, 132 enrolled. *Average high school GPA:* 3.2. *Test scores:* SAT evidence-based reading and writing scores over 500: 70%; SAT math scores over 500: 76%; ACT scores over 18: 100%; SAT evidence-based reading and writing scores over 600: 21%; SAT math scores over 600: 29%; ACT scores over 24: 50%; SAT math scores over 700: 3%; ACT scores over 30: 50%.

Retention: 80% of full-time freshmen returned.

FACULTY
Total: 54, 70% full-time, 50% with terminal degrees.
Student/faculty ratio: 12:1.

ACADEMICS
Calendar: semesters. *Degrees:* certificates, associate, and bachelor's.
Special study options: adult/continuing education programs, external degree program.
Computers: Students can access the following: online (class) registration. Campuswide network is available.

STUDENT LIFE
Housing options: college housing not available.
Athletics Member NJCAA. *Intercollegiate sports:* basketball M, cross-country running M/W, golf M/W, volleyball W. *Intramural sports:* basketball M/W, football M, soccer M/W, table tennis M/W, volleyball M/W.

COSTS & FINANCIAL AID
Costs (2017–18) *Tuition:* state resident $12,718 full-time, $524 per credit hour part-time; nonresident $20,352 full-time, $848 per credit hour part-time. Full-time tuition and fees vary according to course level, degree level, location, program, and student level. Part-time tuition and fees vary according to course level, course load, degree level, location, program, and student level. *Required fees:* $914 full-time. *Payment plans:* installment, deferred payment. *Waivers:* senior citizens and employees or children of employees.
Financial Aid Of all full-time matriculated undergraduates who enrolled in 2016, 429 applied for aid, 378 were judged to have need, 71 had their need fully met. In 2016, 21 non-need-based awards were made. *Average percent of need met:* 60. *Average financial aid package:* $9917. *Average need-based loan:* $3892. *Average need-based gift aid:* $4702. *Average non-need-based aid:* $3244. *Average indebtedness upon graduation:* $34,309.

APPLYING
Standardized Tests *Required:* SAT or ACT (for admission).
Options: electronic application, early admission, deferred entrance.
Application fee: $65.
Required: high school transcript. *Required for some:* interview. *Recommended:* essay or personal statement.
Application deadlines: rolling (freshmen), rolling (transfers).
Notification: continuous (freshmen), continuous (transfers).

CONTACT
Admissions Office, Penn State DuBois, 1 College Place, DuBois, PA 15801. *Phone:* 814-375-4720. *Toll-free phone:* 800-346-7627. *Fax:* 814-375-4784. *E-mail:* duboisinfo@psi.edu.

Penn State Erie, The Behrend College

Erie, Pennsylvania
http://www.psbehrend.psu.edu/
- **State-related** comprehensive, founded 1948, part of Pennsylvania State University
- **Suburban** 725-acre campus
- **Coed** 4,345 undergraduate students, 95% full-time, 33% women, 67% men
- **Very difficult** entrance level, 89% of applicants were admitted

UNDERGRAD STUDENTS
4,138 full-time, 207 part-time. 9% are from out of state; 3% Black or African American, non-Hispanic/Latino; 3% Hispanic/Latino; 3% Asian, non-Hispanic/Latino; 0.1% Native Hawaiian or other Pacific Islander, non-Hispanic/Latino; 0.1% American Indian or Alaska Native, non-Hispanic/Latino; 3% Two or more races, non-Hispanic/Latino; 1% Race/ethnicity unknown; 9% international; 2% transferred in; 37% live on campus.

Freshmen:
Admission: 4,076 applied, 3,624 admitted, 1,052 enrolled. *Average high school GPA:* 3.3. *Test scores:* SAT evidence-based reading and writing scores over 500: 86%; SAT math scores over 500: 88%; ACT scores over

---

18: 95%; SAT evidence-based reading and writing scores over 600: 34%; SAT math scores over 600: 44%; ACT scores over 24: 64%; SAT evidence-based reading and writing scores over 700: 3%; SAT math scores over 700: 10%; ACT scores over 30: 9%.
Retention: 84% of full-time freshmen returned.

FACULTY
Total: 339, 80% full-time, 57% with terminal degrees.
Student/faculty ratio: 15:1.

ACADEMICS
Calendar: semesters. *Degrees:* certificates, associate, bachelor's, and master's.

Special study options: adult/continuing education programs, part-time degree program. *ROTC:* Army (c).

Computers: Students can access the following: campus intranet, computer help desk, free student e-mail accounts, online (class) grades, online (class) registration, online (class) schedules. Campuswide network is available.
Library: John M. Lilley Library.

STUDENT LIFE
Housing options: coed, men-only, women-only, special housing for students with disabilities. Campus housing is university owned.

Athletics Member NCAA. All Division III. *Intercollegiate sports:* baseball M, basketball M/W, cheerleading M/W, cross-country running M/W, golf M/W, ice hockey M(c), lacrosse M(c), skiing (downhill) M(c)/W(c), soccer M/W, softball W, swimming and diving M/W, tennis M/W, track and field M/W, volleyball M(c)/W, water polo M/W.
Intramural sports: badminton M/W, basketball M/W, bowling M/W, cross-country running M/W, football M/W, golf M/W, skiing (downhill) M/W, soccer M/W, softball M/W, swimming and diving M/W, table tennis M/W, tennis M/W, volleyball M/W.

Campus security: 24-hour emergency response devices and patrols, student patrols, late-night transport/escort service, controlled dormitory access.

COSTS & FINANCIAL AID
Costs (2017–18) *Tuition:* state resident $14,214 full-time, $592 per credit hour part-time; nonresident $22,716 full-time, $947 per credit hour part-time. Full-time tuition and fees vary according to course level, degree level, location, program, and student level. Part-time tuition and fees vary according to course level, course load, degree level, location, program, and student level. *Required fees:* $976 full-time. *Room and board:* $11,280; room only: $6180. Room and board charges vary according to board plan, housing facility, and location. *Payment plans:* installment, deferred payment. *Waivers:* senior citizens and employees or children of employees.

Financial Aid Of all full-time matriculated undergraduates who enrolled in 2016, 3,227 applied for aid, 2,765 were judged to have need, 762 had their need fully met. In 2016, 240 non-need-based awards were made. *Average percent of need met:* 67. *Average financial aid package:* $10,632. *Average need-based loan:* $4418. *Average need-based gift aid:* $5687. *Average non-need-based aid:* $3891. *Average indebtedness upon graduation:* $39,977.

APPLYING
Standardized Tests *Required:* SAT or ACT (for admission).
Options: electronic application, early admission, deferred entrance.
Application fee: $65.
Required: high school transcript. *Required for some:* interview.
Recommended: essay or personal statement.
Application deadlines: rolling (freshmen), rolling (transfers).
Notification: continuous (freshmen), continuous (transfers).

CONTACT
Admissions Office, Penn State Erie, The Behrend College, 4701 College Drive, Erie, PA 16563. *Phone:* 814-898-6100. *Toll-free phone:* 866-374-3378. *Fax:* 814-898-6044. *E-mail:* behrend.admissions@psu.edu.

Penn State Fayette, The Eberly Campus
Lemont Furnace, Pennsylvania
http://www.fe.psu.edu/

- **State-related** primarily 2-year, founded 1934, part of Pennsylvania State University
- **Small-town** campus
- **Coed** 652 undergraduate students, 90% full-time, 57% women, 43% men
- **Moderately difficult** entrance level, 82% of applicants were admitted

UNDERGRAD STUDENTS
589 full-time, 63 part-time. 5% are from out of state; 4% Black or African American, non-Hispanic/Latino; 3% Hispanic/Latino; 0.8% Asian, non-Hispanic/Latino; 0.2% Native Hawaiian or other Pacific Islander, non-Hispanic/Latino; 0.3% American Indian or Alaska Native, non-Hispanic/Latino; 4% Two or more races, non-Hispanic/Latino; 0.9% Race/ethnicity unknown; 1% international; 5% transferred in.

Freshmen:
Admission: 728 applied, 598 admitted, 182 enrolled. *Average high school GPA:* 3.2. *Test scores:* SAT evidence-based reading and writing scores over 500: 66%; SAT math scores over 500: 58%; ACT scores over 18: 50%; SAT evidence-based reading and writing scores over 600: 18%; SAT math scores over 600: 13%; ACT scores over 24: 17%; SAT evidence-based reading and writing scores over 700: 1%; SAT math scores over 700: 1%; ACT scores over 30: 17%.
Retention: 78% of full-time freshmen returned.

FACULTY
Total: 69, 57% full-time, 38% with terminal degrees.
Student/faculty ratio: 12:1.

ACADEMICS
Calendar: semesters. *Degrees:* certificates, associate, and bachelor's.
Special study options: adult/continuing education programs, external degree program.
Computers: Students can access the following: online (class) registration. Campuswide network is available.

STUDENT LIFE
Housing options: college housing not available.
Athletics Member NJCAA. *Intercollegiate sports:* baseball M, basketball M, softball W, volleyball W. *Intramural sports:* badminton M/W, basketball M/W, cheerleading M(c)/W(c), equestrian sports M(c)/W(c), football M/W, golf M(c)/W(c), softball M/W, tennis M/W, volleyball M/W, weight lifting M/W.

Campus security: student patrols, 8-hour patrols by trained security personnel.

COSTS & FINANCIAL AID
Costs (2017–18) *Tuition:* state resident $12,718 full-time, $524 per credit hour part-time; nonresident $20,352 full-time, $848 per credit hour part-time. Full-time tuition and fees vary according to course level, degree level, location, program, and student level. Part-time tuition and fees vary according to course level, course load, degree level, location, program, and student level. *Required fees:* $914 full-time. *Payment plans:* installment, deferred payment. *Waivers:* senior citizens and employees or children of employees.

Financial Aid Of all full-time matriculated undergraduates who enrolled in 2016, 503 applied for aid, 436 were judged to have need, 101 had their need fully met. In 2016, 51 non-need-based awards were made. *Average percent of need met:* 63. *Average financial aid package:* $10,993. *Average need-based loan:* $3877. *Average need-based gift aid:* $5349. *Average non-need-based aid:* $3248. *Average indebtedness upon graduation:* $37,496.

APPLYING
Standardized Tests *Required:* SAT or ACT (for admission).
Options: electronic application, early admission, deferred entrance.
Application fee: $65.
Required: high school transcript. *Required for some:* interview.
Recommended: essay or personal statement.
Application deadlines: rolling (freshmen), rolling (transfers).

Notification: continuous (freshmen), continuous (transfers).

CONTACT
Admissions Office, Penn State Fayette, The Eberly Campus, 2201 University Drive, Lemont Furnace, PA 15456. *Phone:* 724-430-4130. *Toll-free phone:* 877-568-4130. *Fax:* 724-430-4175. *E-mail:* feadm@psu.edu.

Penn State Greater Allegheny
McKeesport, Pennsylvania
http://www.ga.psu.edu/

- **State-related** comprehensive, founded 1947, part of Pennsylvania State University
- **Small-town** campus
- **Coed** 497 undergraduate students, 91% full-time, 36% women, 64% men
- **Moderately difficult** entrance level, 82% of applicants were admitted

UNDERGRAD STUDENTS
453 full-time, 44 part-time. 7% are from out of state; 19% Black or African American, non-Hispanic/Latino; 4% Hispanic/Latino; 6% Asian, non-Hispanic/Latino; 5% Two or more races, non-Hispanic/Latino; 0.8% Race/ethnicity unknown; 3% international; 5% transferred in; 20% live on campus.

Freshmen:
Admission: 579 applied, 474 admitted, 115 enrolled. *Average high school GPA:* 3.2. *Test scores:* SAT evidence-based reading and writing scores over 500: 62%; SAT math scores over 500: 73%; ACT scores over 18: 83%; SAT evidence-based reading and writing scores over 600: 24%; SAT math scores over 600: 26%; ACT scores over 24: 33%; SAT evidence-based reading and writing scores over 700: 4%; SAT math scores over 700: 6%.
Retention: 73% of full-time freshmen returned.

FACULTY
Total: 65, 52% full-time, 51% with terminal degrees.
Student/faculty ratio: 11:1.

ACADEMICS
Calendar: semesters. *Degrees:* certificates, associate, and bachelor's.
Special study options: adult/continuing education programs.
Computers: Students can access the following: online (class) registration. Campuswide network is available.

STUDENT LIFE
Housing options: coed, special housing for students with disabilities. Campus housing is university owned. Freshman campus housing is guaranteed.
Athletics Member NJCAA. *Intercollegiate sports:* baseball M, basketball M, softball W, volleyball W. *Intramural sports:* basketball M/W, cheerleading M(c)/W(c), football M/W, ice hockey M(c), racquetball M/W, skiing (cross-country) M(c)/W(c), skiing (downhill) M(c)/W(c), soccer M(c)/W(c), softball M/W, tennis M/W, volleyball M/W.
Campus security: 24-hour patrols, controlled dormitory access.

COSTS & FINANCIAL AID
Costs (2017–18) *Tuition:* state resident $12,718 full-time, $524 per credit hour part-time; nonresident $20,352 full-time, $848 per credit hour part-time. Full-time tuition and fees vary according to course level, degree level, location, program, and student level. Part-time tuition and fees vary according to course level, course load, degree level, location, program, and student level. *Required fees:* $976 full-time. *Room and board:* $11,280; room only: $6180. Room and board charges vary according to board plan, housing facility, and location. *Payment plans:* installment, deferred payment. *Waivers:* senior citizens and employees or children of employees.
Financial Aid Of all full-time matriculated undergraduates who enrolled in 2016, 439 applied for aid, 390 were judged to have need, 80 had their need fully met. In 2016, 38 non-need-based awards were made. *Average percent of need met:* 68. *Average financial aid package:* $12,245. *Average need-based loan:* $3970. *Average need-based gift aid:* $5631. *Average non-need-based aid:* $4918. *Average indebtedness upon graduation:* $37,163.

APPLYING
Standardized Tests *Required:* SAT or ACT (for admission).
Options: electronic application, early admission, deferred entrance.
Application fee: $65.
Required: high school transcript.
Application deadlines: rolling (freshmen), rolling (transfers).
Notification: continuous (freshmen), continuous (transfers).

CONTACT
Admissions Office, Penn State Greater Allegheny, 4000 University Drive, McKeesport, PA 15132. *Phone:* 412-675-9010. *Fax:* 412-675-9046. *E-mail:* psuga@psu.edu.

Penn State Harrisburg
Middletown, Pennsylvania
http://www.harrisburg.psu.edu/

- **State-related** comprehensive, founded 1966, part of Pennsylvania State University
- **Small-town** campus
- **Coed** 4,286 undergraduate students, 92% full-time, 39% women, 61% men
- **Very difficult** entrance level, 84% of applicants were admitted

UNDERGRAD STUDENTS
3,960 full-time, 326 part-time. 17% are from out of state; 9% Black or African American, non-Hispanic/Latino; 7% Hispanic/Latino; 9% Asian, non-Hispanic/Latino; 0.1% Native Hawaiian or other Pacific Islander, non-Hispanic/Latino; 0.1% American Indian or Alaska Native, non-Hispanic/Latino; 3% Two or more races, non-Hispanic/Latino; 2% Race/ethnicity unknown; 15% international; 6% transferred in; 10% live on campus.

Freshmen:
Admission: 5,574 applied, 4,668 admitted, 962 enrolled. *Average high school GPA:* 3.2. *Test scores:* SAT evidence-based reading and writing scores over 500: 81%; SAT math scores over 500: 83%; ACT scores over 18: 97%; SAT evidence-based reading and writing scores over 600: 31%; SAT math scores over 600: 42%; ACT scores over 24: 59%; SAT evidence-based reading and writing scores over 700: 3%; SAT math scores over 700: 14%; ACT scores over 30: 7%.
Retention: 88% of full-time freshmen returned.

FACULTY
Total: 372, 61% full-time, 65% with terminal degrees.
Student/faculty ratio: 16:1.

ACADEMICS
Calendar: semesters. *Degrees:* certificates, associate, bachelor's, master's, doctoral, and postbachelor's certificates.
Special study options: adult/continuing education programs, part-time degree program. *ROTC:* Army (c).
Computers: Students can access the following: campus intranet, computer help desk, free student e-mail accounts, online (class) grades, online (class) registration, online (class) schedules. Campuswide network is available.
Library: Penn State Harrisburg Library.

STUDENT LIFE
Housing options: special housing for students with disabilities. Campus housing is university owned.
Athletics *Intercollegiate sports:* baseball M, basketball M/W, cross-country running M/W, golf M/W, soccer M/W, softball W, tennis M/W, volleyball W. *Intramural sports:* badminton M/W, basketball M/W, racquetball M/W, tennis M/W.
Campus security: 24-hour emergency response devices and patrols, student patrols, late-night transport/escort service, controlled dormitory access.

COSTS & FINANCIAL AID
Costs (2017–18) *Tuition:* state resident $14,214 full-time, $592 per credit hour part-time; nonresident $22,716 full-time, $947 per credit hour part-time. Full-time tuition and fees vary according to course level, degree level, location, program, and student level. Part-time tuition and fees vary according to course level, course load, degree level, location, program,

and student level. *Required fees:* $976 full-time. *Room and board:* $12,940; room only: $7840. Room and board charges vary according to board plan, housing facility, and location. *Payment plans:* installment, deferred payment. *Waivers:* senior citizens and employees or children of employees.

Financial Aid Of all full-time matriculated undergraduates who enrolled in 2016, 2,688 applied for aid, 2,313 were judged to have need, 432 had their need fully met. In 2016, 289 non-need-based awards were made. *Average percent of need met:* 59. *Average financial aid package:* $9771. *Average need-based loan:* $4372. *Average need-based gift aid:* $5437. *Average non-need-based aid:* $2404. *Average indebtedness upon graduation:* $42,315.

APPLYING

Standardized Tests *Required:* SAT or ACT (for admission).

Options: electronic application, early admission, deferred entrance.

Application fee: $65.

Required: high school transcript. *Required for some:* interview. *Recommended:* essay or personal statement.

Application deadlines: rolling (freshmen), rolling (transfers).

Notification: continuous (freshmen), continuous (transfers).

CONTACT

Admissions Office, Penn State Harrisburg, 777 West Harrisburg Pike, Middletown, PA 17057. *Phone:* 717-948-6250. *Toll-free phone:* 800-222-2056. *Fax:* 717-948-6325. *E-mail:* hbgadmit@psu.edu.

Penn State Hazleton

Hazleton, Pennsylvania

http://www.hn.psu.edu/

- **State-related** 4-year, founded 1934, part of Pennsylvania State University
- **Small-town** campus
- **Coed** 755 undergraduate students, 87% full-time, 49% women, 51% men
- **Moderately difficult** entrance level, 94% of applicants were admitted

UNDERGRAD STUDENTS

656 full-time, 99 part-time. 14% are from out of state; 9% Black or African American, non-Hispanic/Latino; 17% Hispanic/Latino; 3% Asian, non-Hispanic/Latino; 0.3% Native Hawaiian or other Pacific Islander, non-Hispanic/Latino; 0.1% American Indian or Alaska Native, non-Hispanic/Latino; 2% Two or more races, non-Hispanic/Latino; 0.9% Race/ethnicity unknown; 0.3% international; 4% transferred in; 27% live on campus.

Freshmen:

Admission: 602 applied, 563 admitted, 204 enrolled. *Average high school GPA:* 3.2. *Test scores:* SAT evidence-based reading and writing scores over 500: 60%; SAT math scores over 500: 61%; ACT scores over 18: 78%; SAT evidence-based reading and writing scores over 600: 17%; SAT math scores over 600: 17%; ACT scores over 24: 33%; SAT evidence-based reading and writing scores over 700: 1%; SAT math scores over 700: 2%; ACT scores over 30: 11%.

Retention: 83% of full-time freshmen returned.

FACULTY

Total: 62, 73% full-time, 55% with terminal degrees.

Student/faculty ratio: 14:1.

ACADEMICS

Calendar: semesters. *Degrees:* certificates, associate, bachelor's, and postbachelor's certificates.

Special study options: adult/continuing education programs. *ROTC:* Air Force (c).

Computers: Students can access the following: online (class) registration. Campuswide network is available.

STUDENT LIFE

Housing options: coed. Campus housing is university owned. Freshman campus housing is guaranteed.

Athletics Member NJCAA. *Intercollegiate sports:* baseball M, basketball M/W, cheerleading M/W, soccer M, softball W(s), tennis M/W, volleyball M/W. *Intramural sports:* basketball M/W, skiing (downhill) M(c)/W(c), soccer M/W, volleyball M/W.

Campus security: 24-hour patrols, late-night transport/escort service, controlled dormitory access.

COSTS & FINANCIAL AID

Costs (2017–18) *Tuition:* state resident $13,484 full-time, $555 per credit hour part-time; nonresident $21,402 full-time, $892 per credit hour part-time. Full-time tuition and fees vary according to course level, degree level, location, program, and student level. Part-time tuition and fees vary according to course level, course load, degree level, location, program, and student level. *Required fees:* $976 full-time. *Room and board:* $11,280; room only: $6180. Room and board charges vary according to board plan, housing facility, and location. *Payment plans:* installment, deferred payment. *Waivers:* senior citizens and employees or children of employees.

Financial Aid Of all full-time matriculated undergraduates who enrolled in 2016, 682 applied for aid, 618 were judged to have need, 137 had their need fully met. In 2016, 61 non-need-based awards were made. *Average percent of need met:* 67. *Average financial aid package:* $11,673. *Average need-based loan:* $3903. *Average need-based gift aid:* $5862. *Average non-need-based aid:* $4771. *Average indebtedness upon graduation:* $45,703.

APPLYING

Standardized Tests *Required:* SAT or ACT (for admission).

Options: electronic application, early admission, deferred entrance.

Application fee: $65.

Required: high school transcript. *Required for some:* interview. *Recommended:* essay or personal statement.

Application deadlines: rolling (freshmen), rolling (transfers).

Notification: continuous (freshmen), continuous (transfers).

CONTACT

Admissions Office, Penn State Hazleton, 76 University Drive, Hazleton, PA 18202. *Phone:* 570-450-3142. *Toll-free phone:* 800-279-8495. *Fax:* 570-450-3182. *E-mail:* admissions-hn@psu.edu.

Penn State Lehigh Valley

Center Valley, Pennsylvania

http://www.lv.psu.edu/

- **State-related** 4-year, founded 1912, part of Pennsylvania State University
- **Rural** campus
- **Coed** 900 undergraduate students, 82% full-time, 44% women, 56% men
- **Moderately difficult** entrance level, 85% of applicants were admitted

UNDERGRAD STUDENTS

739 full-time, 161 part-time. 7% are from out of state; 6% Black or African American, non-Hispanic/Latino; 15% Hispanic/Latino; 9% Asian, non-Hispanic/Latino; 0.2% American Indian or Alaska Native, non-Hispanic/Latino; 4% Two or more races, non-Hispanic/Latino; 2% Race/ethnicity unknown; 3% international; 6% transferred in.

Freshmen:

Admission: 1,262 applied, 1,077 admitted, 247 enrolled. *Average high school GPA:* 3.2. *Test scores:* SAT evidence-based reading and writing scores over 500: 73%; SAT math scores over 500: 73%; ACT scores over 18: 93%; SAT evidence-based reading and writing scores over 600: 25%; SAT math scores over 600: 36%; ACT scores over 24: 67%; SAT evidence-based reading and writing scores over 700: 3%; SAT math scores over 700: 6%; ACT scores over 30: 13%.

Retention: 81% of full-time freshmen returned.

FACULTY

Total: 85, 49% full-time, 41% with terminal degrees.

Student/faculty ratio: 14:1.

ACADEMICS

Calendar: semesters. *Degrees:* certificates, associate, bachelor's, and postbachelor's certificates (enrollment figures include students enrolled at The Graduate School at Penn State who are taking courses at this location).

Special study options: adult/continuing education programs, external degree program, part-time degree program. *ROTC:* Army (c).

Computers: Students can access the following: online (class) registration. Campuswide network is available.

STUDENT LIFE
Housing options: college housing not available.

Athletics *Intercollegiate sports:* baseball M, basketball M/W, bowling M(c)/W(c), cheerleading M/W, cross-country running M/W, football M(c), golf M(c)/W(c), ice hockey M(c)/W(c), skiing (downhill) M(c)/W(c), soccer M(c)/W, tennis M/W, volleyball M(c)/W. *Intramural sports:* badminton M/W, basketball M/W, football M/W, golf M/W, soccer M/W, volleyball M/W.

COSTS & FINANCIAL AID
Costs (2017–18) *Tuition:* state resident $13,484 full-time, $555 per credit hour part-time; nonresident $21,402 full-time, $892 per credit hour part-time. Full-time tuition and fees vary according to course level, degree level, location, program, and student level. Part-time tuition and fees vary according to course level, course load, degree level, location, program, and student level. *Required fees:* $976 full-time. *Payment plans:* installment, deferred payment. *Waivers:* senior citizens and employees or children of employees.

Financial Aid Of all full-time matriculated undergraduates who enrolled in 2016, 560 applied for aid, 465 were judged to have need, 61 had their need fully met. In 2016, 64 non-need-based awards were made. *Average percent of need met:* 57. *Average financial aid package:* $10,598. *Average need-based loan:* $4055. *Average need-based gift aid:* $5490. *Average non-need-based aid:* $3106. *Average indebtedness upon graduation:* $38,922.

APPLYING
Standardized Tests *Required:* SAT or ACT (for admission).

Options: electronic application, early admission, deferred entrance.

Application fee: $65.

Required: high school transcript.

CONTACT
Admissions Office, Penn State Lehigh Valley, 2809 Saucon Valley Road, Center Valley, PA 18034. *Phone:* 610-285-5000. *Fax:* 610-285-5220. *E-mail:* admissions-lv@psu.edu.

Penn State Mont Alto
Mont Alto, Pennsylvania
http://www.ma.psu.edu/

- **State-related** primarily 2-year, founded 1929, part of Pennsylvania State University
- **Small-town** campus
- **Coed** 917 undergraduate students, 71% full-time, 54% women, 46% men
- **Moderately difficult** entrance level, 78% of applicants were admitted

UNDERGRAD STUDENTS
653 full-time, 264 part-time. 15% are from out of state; 5% Black or African American, non-Hispanic/Latino; 8% Hispanic/Latino; 3% Asian, non-Hispanic/Latino; 4% Two or more races, non-Hispanic/Latino; 0.8% Race/ethnicity unknown; 0.5% international; 3% transferred in; 24% live on campus.

Freshmen:
Admission: 711 applied, 552 admitted, 203 enrolled. *Average high school GPA:* 3.2. *Test scores:* ACT scores over 18: 96%; ACT scores over 24: 46%; ACT scores over 30: 17%.

Retention: 83% of full-time freshmen returned.

FACULTY
Total: 95, 60% full-time, 34% with terminal degrees.

Student/faculty ratio: 11:1.

ACADEMICS
Calendar: semesters. *Degrees:* certificates, associate, and bachelor's.

Special study options: adult/continuing education programs, external degree program. *ROTC:* Army (c).

Computers: Students can access the following: online (class) registration. Campuswide network is available.

STUDENT LIFE
Housing options: coed, special housing for students with disabilities. Campus housing is university owned. Freshman campus housing is guaranteed.

Athletics Member NJCAA. *Intercollegiate sports:* basketball M/W, cheerleading M/W, cross-country running M/W, golf M/W, soccer M/W, softball W, tennis M/W, volleyball W. *Intramural sports:* badminton M/W, basketball M/W, cheerleading M(c)/W(c), racquetball M/W, soccer M/W, softball W, volleyball M/W.

Campus security: 24-hour patrols, controlled dormitory access.

COSTS & FINANCIAL AID
Costs (2017–18) *Tuition:* state resident $12,718 full-time, $524 per credit hour part-time; nonresident $20,352 full-time, $848 per credit hour part-time. Full-time tuition and fees vary according to course level, degree level, location, program, and student level. Part-time tuition and fees vary according to course level, course load, degree level, location, program, and student level. *Required fees:* $976 full-time. *Room and board:* $11,280; room only: $6180. Room and board charges vary according to board plan, housing facility, and location. *Payment plans:* installment, deferred payment. *Waivers:* senior citizens and employees or children of employees.

Financial Aid Of all full-time matriculated undergraduates who enrolled in 2016, 616 applied for aid, 536 were judged to have need, 139 had their need fully met. In 2016, 38 non-need-based awards were made. *Average percent of need met:* 66. *Average financial aid package:* $10,905. *Average need-based loan:* $3980. *Average need-based gift aid:* $4930. *Average non-need-based aid:* $5036. *Average indebtedness upon graduation:* $43,874.

APPLYING
Standardized Tests *Required:* SAT or ACT (for admission).

Options: electronic application, early admission, deferred entrance.

Application fee: $65.

Required: high school transcript. *Required for some:* interview. *Recommended:* essay or personal statement.

Application deadlines: rolling (freshmen), rolling (transfers).

Notification: continuous (freshmen), continuous (transfers).

CONTACT
Admissions Office, Penn State Mont Alto, 1 Campus Drive, Mont Alto, PA 17237. *Phone:* 717-749-6130. *Toll-free phone:* 800-392-6173. *Fax:* 717-749-6132. *E-mail:* psuma@psu.edu.

Penn State New Kensington
New Kensington, Pennsylvania
http://www.nk.psu.edu/

- **State-related** 4-year, founded 1958, part of Pennsylvania State University
- **Small-town** campus
- **Coed** 595 undergraduate students, 81% full-time, 40% women, 60% men
- **Moderately difficult** entrance level, 77% of applicants were admitted

UNDERGRAD STUDENTS
484 full-time, 111 part-time. 3% are from out of state; 3% Black or African American, non-Hispanic/Latino; 3% Hispanic/Latino; 1% Asian, non-Hispanic/Latino; 4% Two or more races, non-Hispanic/Latino; 2% Race/ethnicity unknown; 0.3% international; 6% transferred in.

Freshmen:
Admission: 555 applied, 426 admitted, 132 enrolled. *Average high school GPA:* 3.2. *Test scores:* SAT evidence-based reading and writing scores over 500: 74%; SAT math scores over 500: 76%; ACT scores over 18: 100%; SAT evidence-based reading and writing scores over 600: 19%; SAT math scores over 600: 27%; ACT scores over 24: 50%; SAT math scores over 700: 5%.

Retention: 78% of full-time freshmen returned.

FACULTY
Total: 68, 54% full-time, 50% with terminal degrees.

Student/faculty ratio: 11:1.

ACADEMICS
Calendar: semesters. *Degrees:* certificates, associate, and bachelor's.

Special study options: adult/continuing education programs, external degree program. *ROTC:* Air Force (c).

Computers: Students can access the following: online (class) registration. Campuswide network is available.

STUDENT LIFE

Athletics Member NJCAA. *Intercollegiate sports:* baseball M, basketball M/W, cheerleading M/W, golf M/W, softball W, volleyball W. *Intramural sports:* badminton M/W, basketball M/W, bowling M/W, cheerleading M(c)/W(c), football M/W, ice hockey M(c)/W(c), racquetball M/W, skiing (downhill) M(c)/W(c), soccer M/W, softball W, volleyball M/W.

Campus security: part-time trained security personnel.

COSTS & FINANCIAL AID

Costs (2017–18) *Tuition:* state resident $12,718 full-time, $524 per credit hour part-time; nonresident $20,352 full-time, $848 per credit hour part-time. Full-time tuition and fees vary according to course level, degree level, location, program, and student level. Part-time tuition and fees vary according to course level, course load, degree level, location, program, and student level. *Required fees:* $976 full-time. *Payment plans:* installment, deferred payment. *Waivers:* senior citizens and employees or children of employees.

Financial Aid Of all full-time matriculated undergraduates who enrolled in 2016, 449 applied for aid, 374 were judged to have need, 79 had their need fully met. In 2016, 46 non-need-based awards were made. *Average percent of need met:* 64. *Average financial aid package:* $9896. *Average need-based loan:* $3889. *Average need-based gift aid:* $5227. *Average non-need-based aid:* $3406. *Average indebtedness upon graduation:* $38,989.

APPLYING

Standardized Tests *Required:* SAT or ACT (for admission).

Options: electronic application, early admission, deferred entrance.

Application fee: $65.

Required: high school transcript. *Required for some:* interview. *Recommended:* essay or personal statement.

Application deadlines: rolling (freshmen), rolling (transfers).

Notification: continuous (freshmen), continuous (transfers).

CONTACT

Admissions Office, Penn State New Kensington, 3550 Seventh Street Road, New Kensington, PA 15068. *Phone:* 724-334-5466. *Toll-free phone:* 888-968-7297. *Fax:* 724-334-6111. *E-mail:* nkadmissions@psu.edu.

Penn State Schuylkill

Schuylkill Haven, Pennsylvania

http://www.sl.psu.edu/

- **State-related** 4-year, founded 1934, part of Pennsylvania State University
- **Small-town** campus
- **Coed** 732 undergraduate students, 81% full-time, 58% women, 42% men
- **Moderately difficult** entrance level, 76% of applicants were admitted

UNDERGRAD STUDENTS

595 full-time, 137 part-time. 12% are from out of state; 14% Black or African American, non-Hispanic/Latino; 8% Hispanic/Latino; 2% Asian, non-Hispanic/Latino; 0.1% Native Hawaiian or other Pacific Islander, non-Hispanic/Latino; 0.1% American Indian or Alaska Native, non-Hispanic/Latino; 2% Two or more races, non-Hispanic/Latino; 1% Race/ethnicity unknown; 0.9% international; 5% transferred in; 24% live on campus.

Freshmen:

Admission: 642 applied, 485 admitted, 178 enrolled. *Average high school GPA:* 2.9. *Test scores:* SAT evidence-based reading and writing scores over 500: 54%; SAT math scores over 500: 53%; ACT scores over 18: 63%; SAT evidence-based reading and writing scores over 600: 15%; SAT math scores over 600: 10%; ACT scores over 24: 38%; SAT evidence-based reading and writing scores over 700: 1%; SAT math scores over 700: 1%.

Retention: 83% of full-time freshmen returned.

FACULTY

Total: 60, 57% full-time, 53% with terminal degrees.

Student/faculty ratio: 15:1.

ACADEMICS

Calendar: semesters. *Degrees:* certificates, associate, and bachelor's (bachelor's degree programs completed at the Harrisburg campus).

Special study options: adult/continuing education programs, external degree program.

Computers: Students can access the following: online (class) registration. Campuswide network is available.

STUDENT LIFE

Housing options: special housing for students with disabilities.

Athletics Member NJCAA. *Intercollegiate sports:* basketball M, cross-country running M/W, golf M, soccer M, softball W, volleyball W. *Intramural sports:* basketball M/W, football M, soccer M/W, softball M/W, table tennis M/W, volleyball M/W.

Campus security: 24-hour patrols, controlled dormitory access.

COSTS & FINANCIAL AID

Costs (2017–18) *Tuition:* state resident $13,484 full-time, $555 per credit hour part-time; nonresident $21,402 full-time, $892 per credit hour part-time. Full-time tuition and fees vary according to course level, degree level, location, program, and student level. Part-time tuition and fees vary according to course level, course load, degree level, location, program, and student level. *Required fees:* $914 full-time. *Room and board:* $8426; room only: $6426. Room and board charges vary according to board plan, housing facility, and location. *Payment plans:* installment, deferred payment. *Waivers:* senior citizens and employees or children of employees.

Financial Aid Of all full-time matriculated undergraduates who enrolled in 2016, 586 applied for aid, 546 were judged to have need, 115 had their need fully met. In 2016, 31 non-need-based awards were made. *Average percent of need met:* 67. *Average financial aid package:* $11,387. *Average need-based loan:* $4032. *Average need-based gift aid:* $5436. *Average non-need-based aid:* $4421. *Average indebtedness upon graduation:* $38,360.

APPLYING

Standardized Tests *Required:* SAT or ACT (for admission).

Options: electronic application, early admission, deferred entrance.

Application fee: $65.

Required: high school transcript.

Application deadlines: rolling (freshmen), rolling (transfers).

Notification: continuous (freshmen), continuous (transfers).

CONTACT

Admissions Office, Penn State Schuylkill, 200 University Drive, Schuylkill Haven, PA 17972. *Phone:* 570-385-6252. *Fax:* 570-385-6272. *E-mail:* sl-admissions@psu.edu.

Penn State Shenango

Sharon, Pennsylvania

http://www.shenango.psu.edu/

- **State-related** 4-year, founded 1965, part of Pennsylvania State University
- **Small-town** campus
- **Coed** 490 undergraduate students, 49% full-time, 72% women, 28% men
- **Moderately difficult** entrance level, 74% of applicants were admitted

UNDERGRAD STUDENTS

241 full-time, 249 part-time. 21% are from out of state; 9% Black or African American, non-Hispanic/Latino; 3% Hispanic/Latino; 0.9% Asian, non-Hispanic/Latino; 3% Two or more races, non-Hispanic/Latino; 1% Race/ethnicity unknown; 7% transferred in.

Freshmen:

Admission: 276 applied, 205 admitted, 65 enrolled. *Average high school GPA:* 3.1. *Test scores:* SAT evidence-based reading and writing scores over 500: 73%; SAT math scores over 500: 61%; ACT scores over 18: 67%; SAT evidence-based reading and writing scores over 600: 18%; SAT math scores over 600: 18%; ACT scores over 24: 17%; SAT math scores over 700: 3%.

Retention: 55% of full-time freshmen returned.

FACULTY
Total: 47, 55% full-time, 34% with terminal degrees.
Student/faculty ratio: 10:1.

ACADEMICS
Calendar: semesters. *Degrees:* certificates, associate, and bachelor's.
Special study options: adult/continuing education programs, external degree program.
Computers: Students can access the following: online (class) registration. Campuswide network is available.

STUDENT LIFE
Housing options: college housing not available.
Athletics *Intramural sports:* basketball M(c)/W, bowling M/W, football M(c), golf M/W, softball M/W, tennis M/W, volleyball M/W.

COSTS & FINANCIAL AID
Costs (2017–18) *Tuition:* state resident $12,474 full-time, $504 per credit hour part-time; nonresident $19,960 full-time, $832 per credit hour part-time. Full-time tuition and fees vary according to course level, degree level, location, program, and student level. Part-time tuition and fees vary according to course level, course load, degree level, location, program, and student level. *Required fees:* $850 full-time. *Payment plans:* installment, deferred payment. *Waivers:* senior citizens and employees or children of employees.

Financial Aid Of all full-time matriculated undergraduates who enrolled in 2016, 214 applied for aid, 201 were judged to have need, 28 had their need fully met. In 2016, 17 non-need-based awards were made. *Average percent of need met:* 57. *Average financial aid package:* $13,129. *Average need-based loan:* $3856. *Average need-based gift aid:* $5934. *Average non-need-based aid:* $4055. *Average indebtedness upon graduation:* $45,746.

APPLYING
Standardized Tests *Required:* SAT or ACT (for admission).
Options: electronic application, early admission, deferred entrance.
Application fee: $65.
Required: high school transcript.
Application deadlines: rolling (freshmen), rolling (transfers).
Notification: continuous (freshmen), continuous (transfers).

CONTACT
Admissions Office, Penn State Shenango, 147 Shenango Avenue, Sharon, PA 16146. *Phone:* 724-983-2803. *Fax:* 724-983-2820. *E-mail:* psushenango@psu.edu.

Penn State University Park

State College, Pennsylvania
http://www.psu.edu/

- **State-related** university, founded 1855, part of The Pennsylvania State University
- **Small-town** 7958-acre campus with easy access to Harrisburg
- **Endowment** $2.8 billion
- **Coed** 40,835 undergraduate students, 97% full-time, 47% women, 53% men
- **Very difficult** entrance level, 50% of applicants were admitted

UNDERGRAD STUDENTS
39,785 full-time, 1,050 part-time. Students come from 55 states and territories; 133 other countries; 34% are from out of state; 4% Black or African American, non-Hispanic/Latino; 7% Hispanic/Latino; 6% Asian, non-Hispanic/Latino; 0.1% Native Hawaiian or other Pacific Islander, non-Hispanic/Latino; 0.1% American Indian or Alaska Native, non-Hispanic/Latino; 3% Two or more races, non-Hispanic/Latino; 2% Race/ethnicity unknown; 12% international; 0.7% transferred in; 35% live on campus.

Freshmen:
Admission: 56,114 applied, 28,233 admitted, 7,863 enrolled. *Average high school GPA:* 3.6. *Test scores:* SAT evidence-based reading and writing scores over 500: 97%; SAT math scores over 500: 97%; ACT scores over 18: 100%; SAT evidence-based reading and writing scores

over 600: 66%; SAT math scores over 600: 66%; ACT scores over 24: 89%; SAT evidence-based reading and writing scores over 700: 11%; SAT math scores over 700: 19%; ACT scores over 30: 28%.
Retention: 93% of full-time freshmen returned.

FACULTY
Total: 3,066, 87% full-time, 77% with terminal degrees.
Student/faculty ratio: 16:1.

ACADEMICS
Calendar: semesters. *Degrees:* certificates, associate, bachelor's, master's, doctoral, and postbachelor's certificates.
Special study options: academic remediation for entering students, accelerated degree program, adult/continuing education programs, advanced placement credit, cooperative education, distance learning, double majors, English as a second language, external degree program, freshman honors college, honors programs, independent study, internships, off-campus study, part-time degree program, services for LD students, student-designed majors, study abroad, summer session for credit. *ROTC:* Army (b), Navy (b), Air Force (b).
Unusual degree programs: 3-2 engineering; geoscience.
Computers: 3,154 computers/terminals are available on campus for general student use. Students can access the following: campus intranet, computer help desk, free student e-mail accounts, online (class) grades, online (class) registration, online (class) schedules. Campuswide network is available. 100% of college-owned or -operated housing units are wired for high-speed Internet access. Wireless service is available via classrooms, computer centers, computer labs, dorm rooms, learning centers, libraries, student centers.
Library: Pattee and Paterno Libraries plus 4 others. *Books:* 5.0 million (physical), 2.1 million (digital/electronic); *Serial titles:* 84,993 (physical), 160,000 (digital/electronic); *Databases:* 828. Weekly public service hours: 148; study areas open 24 hours, 5–7 days a week; students can reserve study rooms.

STUDENT LIFE
Housing options: on-campus residence required for freshman year; coed, women-only, special housing for students with disabilities. Campus housing is university owned. Freshman campus housing is guaranteed.
Activities and organizations: drama/theater group, student-run newspaper, radio and television station, choral group, marching band, national fraternities, national sororities.
Athletics Member NCAA, USCAA. All Division I except football (Division I-A). *Intercollegiate sports:* baseball M(s), basketball M(s)/W(s), cross-country running M(s)/W(s), fencing M(s)/W(s), field hockey W(s), golf M(s)/W(s), gymnastics M(s)/W(s), ice hockey M(s)(c)/W(s)(c), lacrosse M(s)/W(s), soccer M(s)/W(s), softball W(s), swimming and diving M(s)/W(s), tennis M(s)/W(s), track and field M(s)/W(s), volleyball M(s)/W(s), wrestling M(s). *Intramural sports:* archery M(c)/W(c), badminton M(c)/W(c), baseball M/W(c), basketball M/W, bowling M(c)/W(c), cheerleading M(c)/W(c), crew M(c)/W(c), cross-country running M/W, equestrian sports M(c)/W(c), fencing M/W, field hockey M(c)/W(c), football M, golf M/W, gymnastics M/W, ice hockey M/W, lacrosse M(c)/W(c), riflery M(c)/W(c), rowing M(c)/W(c), rugby M(c)/W(c), sailing M(c)/W(c), skiing (downhill) M(c)/W(c), soccer M/W, softball M(c)/W, squash M(c)/W(c), swimming and diving M/W, table tennis M(c)/W(c), tennis M/W, track and field M/W, triathlon M(c)/W(c), ultimate Frisbee M(c)/W(c), volleyball M/W, water polo M(c)/W(c), weight lifting M(c)/W(c), wrestling M/W(c).
Campus security: 24-hour emergency response devices and patrols, student patrols, late-night transport/escort service, controlled dormitory access.
Student services: health clinic, personal/psychological counseling, women's center, legal services.

COSTS & FINANCIAL AID
Costs (2017–18) *Tuition:* state resident $17,416 full-time, $726 per credit hour part-time; nonresident $32,644 full-time, $1360 per credit hour part-time. Full-time tuition and fees vary according to course level, degree level, location, program, and student level. Part-time tuition and fees vary according to course level, course load, degree level, location, program, and student level. *Required fees:* $1020 full-time. *Room and board:* $11,280; room only: $6180. Room and board charges vary according to board plan, housing facility, and location. *Payment plans:* installment,

deferred payment. *Waivers:* senior citizens and employees or children of employees.

Financial Aid Of all full-time matriculated undergraduates who enrolled in 2016, 23,987 applied for aid, 18,378 were judged to have need, 5,234 had their need fully met. 557 Federal Work-Study jobs (averaging $2200). In 2016, 3562 non-need-based awards were made. *Average percent of need met:* 63. *Average financial aid package:* $10,783. *Average need-based loan:* $4681. *Average need-based gift aid:* $6629. *Average non-need-based aid:* $5195. *Average indebtedness upon graduation:* $37,307.

APPLYING

Standardized Tests *Required:* SAT or ACT (for admission).

Options: electronic application, early admission, deferred entrance.

Application fee: $65.

Required: high school transcript. *Recommended:* essay or personal statement.

Application deadlines: rolling (freshmen), rolling (transfers).

Notification: continuous (freshmen), continuous (transfers).

CONTACT

Clark V. Brigger, Executive Director for Undergraduate Admissions, Penn State University Park, 201 Shields Building, University Park, PA 16802. *Phone:* 814-865-5471. *Fax:* 814-863-7590. *E-mail:* admissions@psu.edu.

Penn State Wilkes-Barre

Lehman, Pennsylvania

http://www.wb.psu.edu/

- **State-related** 4-year, founded 1916, part of Pennsylvania State University
- **Rural** campus
- **Coed** 456 undergraduate students, 85% full-time, 32% women, 68% men
- **Moderately difficult** entrance level, 82% of applicants were admitted

UNDERGRAD STUDENTS

387 full-time, 69 part-time. 7% are from out of state; 6% Black or African American, non-Hispanic/Latino; 5% Hispanic/Latino; 1% Asian, non-Hispanic/Latino; 0.3% Native Hawaiian or other Pacific Islander, non-Hispanic/Latino; 0.3% American Indian or Alaska Native, non-Hispanic/Latino; 4% Two or more races, non-Hispanic/Latino; 2% Race/ethnicity unknown; 0.3% international; 5% transferred in.

Freshmen:

Admission: 433 applied, 357 admitted, 103 enrolled. *Average high school GPA:* 3.2. *Test scores:* SAT evidence-based reading and writing scores over 500: 73%; SAT math scores over 500: 75%; ACT scores over 18: 83%; SAT evidence-based reading and writing scores over 600: 20%; SAT math scores over 600: 20%; ACT scores over 24: 33%; SAT evidence-based reading and writing scores over 700: 2%; SAT math scores over 700: 3%.

Retention: 81% of full-time freshmen returned.

FACULTY

Total: 51, 63% full-time, 41% with terminal degrees.

Student/faculty ratio: 11:1.

ACADEMICS

Calendar: semesters. *Degrees:* certificates, associate, bachelor's, and postbachelor's certificates (enrollment figures include students enrolled at The Graduate School at Penn State who are taking courses at this location).

Special study options: adult/continuing education programs, external degree program. *ROTC:* Army (c), Air Force (c).

Computers: Students can access the following: online (class) registration. Campuswide network is available.

STUDENT LIFE

Housing options: college housing not available.

Athletics Member NJCAA. *Intercollegiate sports:* baseball M, basketball M, cross-country running M/W, golf M/W, soccer M/W, volleyball W. *Intramural sports:* basketball M/W, bowling M(c)/W(c), cheerleading M(c)/W(c), football M, racquetball M/W, softball W, volleyball M(c)/W.

COSTS & FINANCIAL AID

Costs (2017–18) *Tuition:* state resident $12,718 full-time, $524 per credit hour part-time; nonresident $20,352 full-time, $848 per credit hour part-time. Full-time tuition and fees vary according to course level, degree level, location, program, and student level. Part-time tuition and fees vary according to course level, course load, degree level, location, program, and student level. *Required fees:* $850 full-time. *Payment plans:* installment, deferred payment. *Waivers:* senior citizens and employees or children of employees.

Financial Aid Of all full-time matriculated undergraduates who enrolled in 2016, 378 applied for aid, 317 were judged to have need, 75 had their need fully met. In 2016, 35 non-need-based awards were made. *Average percent of need met:* 62. *Average financial aid package:* $9665. *Average need-based loan:* $3991. *Average need-based gift aid:* $5606. *Average non-need-based aid:* $2933. *Average indebtedness upon graduation:* $34,805.

APPLYING

Standardized Tests *Required:* SAT or ACT (for admission).

Options: electronic application, early admission, deferred entrance.

Application fee: $65.

Required: high school transcript.

Application deadlines: rolling (freshmen), rolling (transfers).

Notification: continuous (freshmen), continuous (transfers).

CONTACT

Admissions Office, Penn State Wilkes-Barre, Old Route 115, PO Box PSU, Lehman, PA 18627. *Phone:* 570-675-9238. *Fax:* 570-675-9113. *E-mail:* wbadmissions@psu.edu.

Penn State Worthington Scranton

Dunmore, Pennsylvania

http://www.sn.psu.edu/

- **State-related** 4-year, founded 1923, part of Pennsylvania State University
- **Small-town** campus
- **Coed** 1,029 undergraduate students, 88% full-time, 49% women, 51% men
- **Moderately difficult** entrance level, 78% of applicants were admitted

UNDERGRAD STUDENTS

904 full-time, 125 part-time. 5% are from out of state; 4% Black or African American, non-Hispanic/Latino; 7% Hispanic/Latino; 7% Asian, non-Hispanic/Latino; 3% Two or more races, non-Hispanic/Latino; 1% Race/ethnicity unknown; 0.6% international; 3% transferred in.

Freshmen:

Admission: 883 applied, 688 admitted, 261 enrolled. *Average high school GPA:* 3.1. *Test scores:* SAT evidence-based reading and writing scores over 500: 66%; SAT math scores over 500: 65%; ACT scores over 18: 71%; SAT evidence-based reading and writing scores over 600: 16%; SAT math scores over 600: 17%; ACT scores over 24: 50%; SAT evidence-based reading and writing scores over 700: 3%.

Retention: 77% of full-time freshmen returned.

FACULTY

Total: 85, 59% full-time, 46% with terminal degrees.

Student/faculty ratio: 16:1.

ACADEMICS

Calendar: semesters. *Degrees:* certificates, associate, and bachelor's.

Special study options: adult/continuing education programs, external degree program. *ROTC:* Army (c), Air Force (c).

Computers: Students can access the following: online (class) registration. Campuswide network is available.

STUDENT LIFE

Housing options: college housing not available.

Athletics *Intercollegiate sports:* baseball M, basketball M/W, cheerleading M/W, cross-country running M/W, soccer M, softball W, volleyball W. *Intramural sports:* basketball M/W, bowling M(c)/W(c), skiing (downhill) M(c)/W(c), soccer M/W, softball M/W, volleyball M/W(c), weight lifting M(c)/W(c).

COSTS & FINANCIAL AID
Costs (2017–18) *Tuition:* state resident $13,484 full-time, $555 per credit hour part-time; nonresident $21,402 full-time, $892 per credit hour part-time. Full-time tuition and fees vary according to course level, degree level, location, program, and student level. Part-time tuition and fees vary according to course level, course load, degree level, location, program, and student level. *Required fees:* $976 full-time. *Payment plans:* installment, deferred payment. *Waivers:* senior citizens and employees or children of employees.

Financial Aid Of all full-time matriculated undergraduates who enrolled in 2016, 774 applied for aid, 704 were judged to have need, 117 had their need fully met. In 2016, 34 non-need-based awards were made. *Average percent of need met:* 59. *Average financial aid package:* $10,309. *Average need-based loan:* $3916. *Average need-based gift aid:* $5201. *Average non-need-based aid:* $3869. *Average indebtedness upon graduation:* $41,945.

APPLYING
Standardized Tests *Required:* SAT or ACT (for admission).

Options: electronic application, early admission, deferred entrance.

Application fee: $65.

Required: high school transcript. *Required for some:* interview. *Recommended:* essay or personal statement.

Application deadlines: rolling (freshmen), rolling (transfers).

Notification: continuous (freshmen), continuous (transfers).

CONTACT
Admissions Office, Penn State Worthington Scranton, 120 Ridge View Drive, Dunmore, PA 18512. *Phone:* 570-963-2500. *Fax:* 570-963-2524. *E-mail:* wsadmissions@psu.edu.

Penn State York
York, Pennsylvania
http://www.york.psu.edu/

- **State-related** comprehensive, founded 1926, part of Pennsylvania State University
- **Suburban** campus
- **Coed** 967 undergraduate students, 82% full-time, 42% women, 58% men
- **Moderately difficult** entrance level, 82% of applicants were admitted

UNDERGRAD STUDENTS
793 full-time, 174 part-time. 9% are from out of state; 6% Black or African American, non-Hispanic/Latino; 7% Hispanic/Latino; 6% Asian, non-Hispanic/Latino; 0.1% Native Hawaiian or other Pacific Islander, non-Hispanic/Latino; 3% Two or more races, non-Hispanic/Latino; 1% Race/ethnicity unknown; 20% international; 4% transferred in.

Freshmen:
Admission: 1,474 applied, 1,216 admitted, 287 enrolled. *Average high school GPA:* 3.1. *Test scores:* SAT evidence-based reading and writing scores over 500: 75%; SAT math scores over 500: 81%; ACT scores over 18: 94%; SAT evidence-based reading and writing scores over 600: 29%; SAT math scores over 600: 53%; ACT scores over 24: 66%; SAT evidence-based reading and writing scores over 700: 3%; SAT math scores over 700: 22%; ACT scores over 30: 9%.

Retention: 77% of full-time freshmen returned.

FACULTY
Total: 87, 55% full-time, 51% with terminal degrees.
Student/faculty ratio: 14:1.

ACADEMICS
Calendar: semesters. *Degrees:* certificates, associate, bachelor's, master's, and postbachelor's certificates (also offers up to 2 years of most bachelor's degree programs offered at University Park campus).

Special study options: adult/continuing education programs.

Computers: Students can access the following: online (class) registration. Campuswide network is available.

STUDENT LIFE
Housing options: college housing not available.

COSTS & FINANCIAL AID
Costs (2017–18) *Tuition:* state resident $13,484 full-time, $555 per credit hour part-time; nonresident $21,402 full-time, $892 per credit hour part-time. Full-time tuition and fees vary according to course level, degree level, location, program, and student level. Part-time tuition and fees vary according to course level, course load, degree level, location, program, and student level. *Required fees:* $976 full-time. *Payment plans:* installment, deferred payment. *Waivers:* senior citizens and employees or children of employees.

Financial Aid Of all full-time matriculated undergraduates who enrolled in 2016, 587 applied for aid, 470 were judged to have need, 80 had their need fully met. In 2016, 104 non-need-based awards were made. *Average percent of need met:* 58. *Average financial aid package:* $9753. *Average need-based loan:* $3864. *Average need-based gift aid:* $5197. *Average non-need-based aid:* $3147. *Average indebtedness upon graduation:* $39,091.

APPLYING
Standardized Tests *Required:* SAT or ACT (for admission).

Options: electronic application, early admission, deferred entrance.

Application fee: $65.

Required: high school transcript.

Application deadlines: rolling (freshmen), rolling (transfers).

Notification: continuous (freshmen), continuous (transfers).

CONTACT
Admissions Office, Penn State York, 1031 Edgecomb Avenue, York, PA 17403. *Phone:* 717-771-4040. *Toll-free phone:* 800-778-6227. *Fax:* 717-771-4005. *E-mail:* ykadmission@psu.edu.

Pennsylvania Academy of the Fine Arts
Philadelphia, Pennsylvania
http://www.pafa.edu/

CONTACT
André van de Putte, Dean of Enrollment, Pennsylvania Academy of the Fine Arts, 128 North Broad Street, Philadelphia, PA 19102. *E-mail:* avandeputte@pafa.edu.

Pennsylvania College of Art & Design
Lancaster, Pennsylvania
http://www.pcad.edu/

- **Independent** 4-year, founded 1982
- **Urban** campus with easy access to Philadelphia, Baltimore
- **Coed** 260 undergraduate students, 96% full-time, 68% women, 32% men
- **Moderately difficult** entrance level, 50% of applicants were admitted

UNDERGRAD STUDENTS
250 full-time, 10 part-time. 23% are from out of state; 6% Black or African American, non-Hispanic/Latino; 4% Hispanic/Latino; 5% Asian, non-Hispanic/Latino; 0.4% American Indian or Alaska Native, non-Hispanic/Latino; 6% Two or more races, non-Hispanic/Latino; 5% Race/ethnicity unknown; 5% transferred in.

Freshmen:
Admission: 344 applied, 172 admitted, 72 enrolled. *Average high school GPA:* 3.0.
Retention: 79% of full-time freshmen returned.

FACULTY
Total: 51, 20% full-time, 41% with terminal degrees.
Student/faculty ratio: 13:1.

ACADEMICS
Calendar: semesters. *Degree:* certificates and bachelor's.

Special study options: advanced placement credit, internships.

Computers: 90 computers/terminals are available on campus for general student use. Students can access the following: campus intranet, computer help desk, free student e-mail accounts, online (class) grades, online (class) registration, online (class) schedules. Campuswide network is available. Wireless service is available via entire campus.

Library: Pennsylvania College of Art & Design Library.

STUDENT LIFE

Housing options: college housing not available.

Activities and organizations: Student Council, Anime Club, Student AIGA, Society of Illustrators - Student Group.

Campus security: late-night transport/escort service, trained evening/weekend security personnel.

COSTS

Costs (2018–19) *Tuition:* $24,250 full-time, $1010 per credit part-time. Full-time tuition and fees vary according to course load and program. Part-time tuition and fees vary according to course load and program. *Required fees:* $1500 full-time, $1500 per year part-time. *Payment plan:* installment. *Waivers:* employees or children of employees.

APPLYING

Options: electronic application, deferred entrance.

Application fee: $40.

Required: essay or personal statement, high school transcript, minimum 2.5 GPA, portfolio. *Required for some:* 2 letters of recommendation, interview. *Recommended:* interview.

Application deadlines: rolling (freshmen), rolling (transfers).

Notification: continuous (freshmen), continuous (transfers).

CONTACT

Admissions Department, Pennsylvania College of Art & Design, 204 North Prince Street, PO Box 59, Lancaster, PA 17608. *Phone:* 717-396-7833. *Toll-free phone:* 800-689-0379 Ext. 1001. *Fax:* 717-396-1339. *E-mail:* admissions@pcad.edu.

Pennsylvania College of Health Sciences

Lancaster, Pennsylvania

http://www.pacollege.edu/

- **Independent** comprehensive, founded 1903
- **Suburban** 25-acre campus with easy access to Harrisburg
- **Endowment** $5.0 million
- **Coed** 1,686 undergraduate students, 31% full-time, 86% women, 14% men
- **Moderately difficult** entrance level, 67% of applicants were admitted

UNDERGRAD STUDENTS

527 full-time, 1,159 part-time. Students come from 16 states and territories; 3% are from out of state; 4% Black or African American, non-Hispanic/Latino; 8% Hispanic/Latino; 3% Asian, non-Hispanic/Latino; 0.1% American Indian or Alaska Native, non-Hispanic/Latino; 2% Two or more races, non-Hispanic/Latino; 5% Race/ethnicity unknown; 20% transferred in.

Freshmen:

Admission: 404 applied, 269 admitted, 183 enrolled.

Retention: 64% of full-time freshmen returned.

FACULTY

Total: 213, 35% full-time.

Student/faculty ratio: 12:1.

ACADEMICS

Calendar: semesters. *Degrees:* certificates, associate, bachelor's, master's, and doctoral.

Special study options: accelerated degree program, adult/continuing education programs, advanced placement credit, distance learning, part-time degree program, services for LD students, summer session for credit.

Computers: 200 computers/terminals are available on campus for general student use. Students can access the following: campus intranet, computer help desk, free student e-mail accounts, online (class) grades, online (class) registration, online (class) schedules. Campuswide network is available. Wireless service is available via entire campus.

Library: Health Sciences Library. *Books:* 1,185 (physical), 598 (digital/electronic); *Serial titles:* 93 (physical), 13,436 (digital/electronic); *Databases:* 43. Students can reserve study rooms.

STUDENT LIFE

Housing options: college housing not available.

Campus security: 24-hour emergency response devices and patrols, late-night transport/escort service.

Student services: health clinic, personal/psychological counseling.

COSTS

Costs (2017–18) *Tuition:* $27,084 full-time, $576 per credit hour part-time. Full-time tuition and fees vary according to course load, degree level, and program. Part-time tuition and fees vary according to course load, degree level, and program. *Payment plans:* installment, deferred payment.

APPLYING

Standardized Tests *Required for some:* SAT or ACT (for admission).

Options: electronic application, deferred entrance.

Application fee: $35.

Required: minimum 3.0 GPA, 2 letters of recommendation, transcripts of all institutions attended. *Required for some:* essay or personal statement.

Notification: continuous (freshmen).

CONTACT

Pennsylvania College of Health Sciences, 850 Greenfield Road, Lancaster, PA 17601. *Toll-free phone:* 800-622-5443.

Pennsylvania College of Technology

Williamsport, Pennsylvania

http://www.pct.edu/

- **State-related** 4-year, founded 1965
- **Suburban** 994-acre campus
- **Coed** 5,382 undergraduate students, 85% full-time, 36% women, 64% men
- **Noncompetitive** entrance level, 79% of applicants were admitted

UNDERGRAD STUDENTS

4,577 full-time, 805 part-time. Students come from 27 states and territories; 12 other countries; 11% are from out of state; 3% Black or African American, non-Hispanic/Latino; 4% Hispanic/Latino; 1% Asian, non-Hispanic/Latino; 0.1% Native Hawaiian or other Pacific Islander, non-Hispanic/Latino; 0.2% American Indian or Alaska Native, non-Hispanic/Latino; 2% Two or more races, non-Hispanic/Latino; 0.7% Race/ethnicity unknown; 0.6% international; 8% transferred in; 31% live on campus.

Freshmen:

Admission: 6,115 applied, 4,805 admitted, 1,225 enrolled. *Average high school GPA:* 3.1.

Retention: 75% of full-time freshmen returned.

FACULTY

Total: 448, 65% full-time.

Student/faculty ratio: 14:1.

ACADEMICS

Calendar: semesters. *Degrees:* certificates, associate, bachelor's, and master's.

Special study options: academic remediation for entering students, advanced placement credit, cooperative education, distance learning, English as a second language, independent study, internships, off-campus study, part-time degree program, services for LD students, student-designed majors, study abroad, summer session for credit. *ROTC:* Army (b).

Computers: 1,800 computers/terminals are available on campus for general student use. Students can access the following: campus intranet, computer help desk, free student e-mail accounts, online (class) grades, online (class) registration, online (class) schedules. Campuswide network is available. 100% of college-owned or -operated housing units are wired for high-speed Internet access. Wireless service is available via entire campus.

Library: Penn College Madigan Library plus 1 other. *Books:* 89,117 (physical), 27,388 (digital/electronic); *Serial titles:* 9,342 (physical), 88,304 (digital/electronic); *Databases:* 169. Weekly public service hours: 86; students can reserve study rooms.

STUDENT LIFE

Housing options: coed, special housing for students with disabilities. Campus housing is university owned.

Activities and organizations: Student Government Association, Residence Hall Association, Wildcats Event Board, Association of Computing Machinery, Campus Ministry International, national fraternities.

Athletics Member NCAA, USCAA. All Division III. *Intercollegiate sports:* archery M/W, baseball M, basketball M/W, bowling M/W, cross-country running M/W, golf M/W, soccer M/W, softball W, tennis M/W, volleyball M/W, wrestling M. *Intramural sports:* archery M/W, badminton M/W, basketball M/W, bowling M/W, football M, golf M/W, lacrosse M, soccer M/W, softball M/W, table tennis M/W, tennis M/W, ultimate Frisbee M/W, volleyball M/W, weight lifting M/W.

Campus security: 24-hour emergency response devices and patrols, late-night transport/escort service, controlled dormitory access.

Student services: health clinic, personal/psychological counseling.

COSTS & FINANCIAL AID

Costs (2018–19) *Tuition:* state resident $16,350 full-time; nonresident $23,280 full-time. Full-time tuition and fees vary according to course load and program. Part-time tuition and fees vary according to course load and program. *Required fees:* $2490 full-time. *Room and board:* $11,340; room only: $6456. Room and board charges vary according to board plan and housing facility. *Payment plan:* deferred payment. *Waivers:* employees or children of employees.

Financial Aid Of all full-time matriculated undergraduates who enrolled in 2016, 4,330 applied for aid, 4,171 were judged to have need. 113 Federal Work-Study jobs (averaging $1537). *Average percent of need met:* 23. *Average financial aid package:* $12,768. *Average need-based loan:* $2267. *Average need-based gift aid:* $8452. *Average indebtedness upon graduation:* $7218.

APPLYING

Standardized Tests *Required for some:* SAT (for admission).

Options: electronic application, early admission, deferred entrance.

Required for some: high school transcript, college transcripts for transfers.

Application deadlines: 7/1 (freshmen), rolling (transfers).

CONTACT

Ashley Murphy, Director of Admissions, Pennsylvania College of Technology, One College Avenue, DIF #119, Williamsport, PA 17701. *Phone:* 570-327-4761 Ext. 7337. *Toll-free phone:* 800-367-9222. *Fax:* 570-321-5551. *E-mail:* admissions@pct.edu.

Pittsburgh Technical College

Oakdale, Pennsylvania
http://www.ptcollege.edu/

- **Proprietary** primarily 2-year, founded 1946
- **Suburban** 180-acre campus with easy access to Pittsburgh
- **Coed** 1,835 undergraduate students, 100% full-time, 42% women, 58% men
- 87% of applicants were admitted

UNDERGRAD STUDENTS

1,835 full-time. Students come from 17 states and territories; 2 other countries; 17% are from out of state; 7% Black or African American, non-Hispanic/Latino; 0.4% Hispanic/Latino; 0.7% Asian, non-Hispanic/Latino; 0.1% Native Hawaiian or other Pacific Islander, non-Hispanic/Latino; 0.3% American Indian or Alaska Native, non-Hispanic/Latino; 4% Two or more races, non-Hispanic/Latino; 21% Race/ethnicity unknown; 11% transferred in; 44% live on campus.

Freshmen:

Admission: 1,608 applied, 1,402 admitted, 516 enrolled. *Average high school GPA:* 2.6.

Retention: 55% of full-time freshmen returned.

FACULTY

Total: 153, 51% full-time, 6% with terminal degrees.

Student/faculty ratio: 12:1.

ACADEMICS

Calendar: quarters. *Degrees:* certificates, associate, and bachelor's.

Special study options: academic remediation for entering students, adult/continuing education programs, advanced placement credit, cooperative education, distance learning, double majors, internships, services for LD students.

Computers: 316 computers/terminals are available on campus for general student use. Students can access the following: campus intranet, computer help desk, free student e-mail accounts, online (class) grades, online (class) schedules. Campuswide network is available. 100% of college-owned or -operated housing units are wired for high-speed Internet access. Wireless service is available via entire campus.

Library: Library Resource Center. *Books:* 7,378 (physical), 46,000 (digital/electronic); *Serial titles:* 116 (physical), 6 (digital/electronic); *Databases:* 12. Weekly public service hours: 58.

STUDENT LIFE

Housing options: coed. Campus housing is university owned and leased by the school.

Activities and organizations: drama/theater group, Software Development Club, Drama Club, DECA, Gay-Straight Alliance, Magic Club.

Athletics *Intramural sports:* basketball M/W, sand volleyball M/W, soccer M/W, softball M/W, ultimate Frisbee M/W, volleyball M/W.

Campus security: 24-hour emergency response devices and patrols, student patrols, late-night transport/escort service, controlled dormitory access.

Student services: personal/psychological counseling.

COSTS

Costs (2018–19) *Comprehensive fee:* $26,847 includes full-time tuition ($16,920) and room and board ($9927). Full-time tuition and fees vary according to degree level and program. No tuition increase for student's term of enrollment. *College room only:* $7344. Room and board charges vary according to housing facility. *Payment plans:* installment, deferred payment. *Waivers:* children of alumni and employees or children of employees.

APPLYING

Standardized Tests *Required:* entrance exams for practical nursing certificate and nursing and surgical technology Associate degrees (for admission). *Required for some:* SAT or ACT (for admission).

Options: electronic application, deferred entrance.

Required: high school transcript. *Required for some:* essay or personal statement, criminal background check, minimum rank in top 80% of class. *Recommended:* interview.

Application deadlines: rolling (freshmen), rolling (out-of-state freshmen), rolling (transfers).

Notification: continuous (freshmen), continuous (out-of-state freshmen), continuous (transfers).

CONTACT

Ms. Nancy Goodlin, Admissions Office Assistant, Pittsburgh Technical College, 1111 McKee Road, Oakdale, PA 15071. *Phone:* 412-809-5100. *Toll-free phone:* 800-784-9675. *Fax:* 412-809-5351. *E-mail:* goodlin.nancy@ptcollege.edu.

Point Park University

Pittsburgh, Pennsylvania
http://www.pointpark.edu/

- **Independent** university, founded 1960
- **Urban** campus
- **Endowment** $33.5 million
- **Coed** 3,281 undergraduate students, 84% full-time, 59% women, 41% men
- **Moderately difficult** entrance level, 65% of applicants were admitted

UNDERGRAD STUDENTS

2,758 full-time, 523 part-time. Students come from 44 states and territories; 40 other countries; 24% are from out of state; 15% Black or African American, non-Hispanic/Latino; 2% Hispanic/Latino; 2% Asian, non-Hispanic/Latino; 0.3% Native Hawaiian or other Pacific Islander, non-Hispanic/Latino; 0.2% American Indian or Alaska Native, non-

Hispanic/Latino; 5% Two or more races, non-Hispanic/Latino; 0.8% Race/ethnicity unknown; 4% international; 10% transferred in; 25% live on campus.

Freshmen:
Admission: 4,860 applied, 3,152 admitted, 640 enrolled. *Average high school GPA:* 3.4. *Test scores:* SAT evidence-based reading and writing scores over 500: 79%; SAT math scores over 500: 69%; ACT scores over 18: 89%; SAT evidence-based reading and writing scores over 600: 30%; SAT math scores over 600: 15%; ACT scores over 24: 41%; SAT evidence-based reading and writing scores over 700: 4%; SAT math scores over 700: 1%; ACT scores over 30: 2%.

Retention: 78% of full-time freshmen returned.

FACULTY
Total: 519, 29% full-time.
Student/faculty ratio: 13:1.

ACADEMICS
Calendar: semesters. *Degrees:* certificates, associate, bachelor's, master's, doctoral, and postbachelor's certificates.

Special study options: academic remediation for entering students, accelerated degree program, adult/continuing education programs, advanced placement credit, cooperative education, distance learning, double majors, English as a second language, honors programs, independent study, internships, off-campus study, part-time degree program, services for LD students, student-designed majors, study abroad, summer session for credit. *ROTC:* Army (c), Air Force (c).

Computers: 309 computers/terminals and 112 ports are available on campus for general student use. Students can access the following: campus intranet, computer help desk, free student e-mail accounts, online (class) grades, online (class) registration. Campuswide network is available. 100% of college-owned or -operated housing units are wired for high-speed Internet access. Wireless service is available via entire campus.
Library: Point Park University Library.

STUDENT LIFE
Housing options: coed, women-only, special housing for students with disabilities. Campus housing is university owned and leased by the school. Freshman campus housing is guaranteed.

Activities and organizations: drama/theater group, student-run newspaper, radio and television station, WPPJ student radio station, The Body Christian Fellowship, Dance Club, Campus Activities Board, Action Sports Club.

Athletics Member NAIA. *Intercollegiate sports:* baseball M(s), basketball M(s)/W(s), cheerleading W(s), cross-country running M(s)/W(s), golf M(s)/W(s), soccer M(s)/W(s), softball W(s), track and field M(s)/W(s), volleyball W(s). *Intramural sports:* basketball M, bowling M/W, football M, golf M, tennis M/W, volleyball M/W, weight lifting M/W.

Campus security: 24-hour emergency response devices and patrols, late-night transport/escort service, controlled dormitory access, campus patrolled by Accredited Law Enforcement Agency, 24-hour security desk, video security.
Student services: health clinic, personal/psychological counseling.

COSTS & FINANCIAL AID
Costs (2017–18) *Comprehensive fee:* $42,090 includes full-time tuition ($28,860), mandatory fees ($1270), and room and board ($11,960). Full-time tuition and fees vary according to program. Part-time tuition: $819 per credit. Part-time tuition and fees vary according to program. *Required fees:* $55 per credit part-time. *College room only:* $5220. Room and board charges vary according to board plan and housing facility. *Payment plans:* installment, deferred payment. *Waivers:* employees or children of employees.

Financial Aid Of all full-time matriculated undergraduates who enrolled in 2016, 2,367 applied for aid, 2,197 were judged to have need, 302 had their need fully met. In 2016, 161 non-need-based awards were made. *Average percent of need met:* 69. *Average financial aid package:* $23,782. *Average need-based loan:* $5235. *Average need-based gift aid:* $18,277. *Average non-need-based aid:* $11,847. *Average indebtedness upon graduation:* $26,729.

APPLYING
Standardized Tests *Required:* SAT or ACT (for admission).
Options: electronic application, deferred entrance.
Application fee: $40.
Required: high school transcript. *Required for some:* essay or personal statement, 2 letters of recommendation, interview, audition. *Recommended:* minimum 2.5 GPA.
Application deadlines: rolling (freshmen), rolling (transfers).
Notification: continuous (freshmen), continuous (transfers).

CONTACT
Point Park University, 201 Wood Street, Pittsburgh, PA 15222-1984. *Phone:* 412-392-3430. *Toll-free phone:* 800-321-0129.

The Restaurant School at Walnut Hill College
Philadelphia, Pennsylvania
http://www.walnuthillcollege.edu/

CONTACT
Mr. John English, Director of Admissions, The Restaurant School at Walnut Hill College, 4207 Walnut Street, Philadelphia, PA 19104-3518. *Phone:* 267-295-2353. *Fax:* 215-222-4219. *E-mail:* jenglish@walnuthillcollege.edu.

Robert Morris University
Moon Township, Pennsylvania
http://www.rmu.edu/
- **Independent** university, founded 1921
- **Suburban** 230-acre campus with easy access to Pittsburgh
- **Endowment** $33.6 million
- **Coed** 4,243 undergraduate students, 91% full-time, 43% women, 57% men
- **Minimally difficult** entrance level, 83% of applicants were admitted

UNDERGRAD STUDENTS
3,840 full-time, 403 part-time. Students come from 43 states and territories; 37 other countries; 13% are from out of state; 6% Black or African American, non-Hispanic/Latino; 2% Hispanic/Latino; 1% Asian, non-Hispanic/Latino; 0.1% Native Hawaiian or other Pacific Islander, non-Hispanic/Latino; 0.1% American Indian or Alaska Native, non-Hispanic/Latino; 3% Two or more races, non-Hispanic/Latino; 2% Race/ethnicity unknown; 12% international; 6% transferred in; 46% live on campus.

Freshmen:
Admission: 6,407 applied, 5,338 admitted, 871 enrolled. *Average high school GPA:* 3.5. *Test scores:* SAT evidence-based reading and writing scores over 500: 82%; SAT math scores over 500: 82%; ACT scores over 18: 98%; SAT evidence-based reading and writing scores over 600: 28%; SAT math scores over 600: 27%; ACT scores over 24: 50%; SAT evidence-based reading and writing scores over 700: 3%; SAT math scores over 700: 4%; ACT scores over 30: 12%.

Retention: 81% of full-time freshmen returned.

FACULTY
Total: 438, 46% full-time, 59% with terminal degrees.
Student/faculty ratio: 15:1.

ACADEMICS
Calendar: semesters. *Degrees:* bachelor's, master's, doctoral, and postbachelor's certificates.

Special study options: academic remediation for entering students, accelerated degree program, adult/continuing education programs, cooperative education, distance learning, double majors, honors programs, independent study, internships, off-campus study, part-time degree program, services for LD students, study abroad, summer session for credit. *ROTC:* Army (b), Navy (c), Air Force (c).

Computers: 375 computers/terminals are available on campus for general student use. Students can access the following: campus intranet, computer help desk, free student e-mail accounts, online (class) grades, online

(class) registration, online (class) schedules, online payment. Campuswide network is available. 100% of college-owned or -operated housing units are wired for high-speed Internet access. Wireless service is available via entire campus.
Library: Robert Morris University Library. *Books:* 97,693 (physical), 172,931 (digital/electronic); *Serial titles:* 244 (physical), 47,791 (digital/electronic); *Databases:* 104. Weekly public service hours: 101; study areas open 24 hours, 5–7 days a week; students can reserve study rooms.

STUDENT LIFE
Housing options: on-campus residence required for freshman year; coed, men-only, women-only, special housing for students with disabilities. Campus housing is university owned. Freshman applicants given priority for college housing.

Activities and organizations: drama/theater group, student-run newspaper, radio and television station, choral group, marching band, Student Government Association, Residence Hall Association, The Saudi Student Club, National Society of Collegiate Scholars, Top Secret Colonials, national fraternities, national sororities.

Athletics Member NCAA. All Division I. *Intercollegiate sports:* basketball M(s)/W(s), crew W(s), cross-country running W(s), football M(s), golf M(s), ice hockey M(s)/W, lacrosse M(s)/W, rowing W(s), soccer M(s)/W(s), softball W(s), track and field W(s), volleyball W(s). *Intramural sports:* baseball M(c), basketball M(c), bowling M(c)/W(c), golf M(c), ice hockey M(c), rugby M(c)/W(c), soccer M(c)/W(c), table tennis M(c)/W(c), tennis M(c)/W(c), ultimate Frisbee M(c)/W(c), volleyball M(c)/W(c), weight lifting M(c)/W(c), wrestling M(c).

Campus security: 24-hour emergency response devices and patrols, late-night transport/escort service, controlled dormitory access.

Student services: health clinic, personal/psychological counseling.

COSTS & FINANCIAL AID
Costs (2017–18) *Comprehensive fee:* $40,600 includes full-time tuition ($28,210), mandatory fees ($1210), and room and board ($11,180). Full-time tuition and fees vary according to degree level and program. Part-time tuition: $905 per credit hour. Part-time tuition and fees vary according to course load, degree level, and program. *Required fees:* $80 per credit hour part-time. *College room only:* $6220. Room and board charges vary according to board plan and housing facility. *Payment plans:* installment, deferred payment. *Waivers:* employees or children of employees.

Financial Aid Of all full-time matriculated undergraduates who enrolled in 2017, 2,996 applied for aid, 2,707 were judged to have need, 347 had their need fully met. In 2017, 670 non-need-based awards were made. *Average percent of need met:* 71. *Average financial aid package:* $22,897. *Average need-based loan:* $6650. *Average need-based gift aid:* $16,555. *Average non-need-based aid:* $12,841. *Average indebtedness upon graduation:* $39,856.

APPLYING
Standardized Tests *Required:* SAT or ACT (for admission).

Options: electronic application, deferred entrance.

Application fee: $30.

Required: high school transcript, minimum 2.0 GPA. *Required for some:* interview. *Recommended:* essay or personal statement, minimum 3.0 GPA, interview.

Application deadlines: rolling (freshmen), rolling (transfers).

Notification: continuous until 8/1 (freshmen), continuous (transfers).

CONTACT
Enrollment Services Department, Robert Morris University, 6001 University Boulevard, Moon Township, PA 15108-1189. *Phone:* 412-397-5200. *Toll-free phone:* 800-762-0097. *Fax:* 412-397-2425. *E-mail:* admissionsoffice@rmu.edu.

See this page for display ad and page 1402 for the College Close-Up.

Rosemont College

Rosemont, Pennsylvania

http://www.rosemont.edu/

- **Independent Roman Catholic** comprehensive, founded 1921
- **Suburban** 56-acre campus with easy access to Philadelphia
- **Coed** 635 undergraduate students, 82% full-time, 63% women, 37% men
- **Moderately difficult** entrance level, 70% of applicants were admitted

UNDERGRAD STUDENTS

520 full-time, 115 part-time. 25% are from out of state; 40% Black or African American, non-Hispanic/Latino; 6% Hispanic/Latino; 3% Asian, non-Hispanic/Latino; 0.3% Native Hawaiian or other Pacific Islander, non-Hispanic/Latino; 0.5% American Indian or Alaska Native, non-Hispanic/Latino; 3% Two or more races, non-Hispanic/Latino; 8% Race/ethnicity unknown; 4% international; 7% transferred in; 67% live on campus.

Freshmen:

Admission: 1,315 applied, 916 admitted, 143 enrolled. *Average high school GPA:* 3.2. *Test scores:* SAT evidence-based reading and writing scores over 500: 60%; SAT math scores over 500: 56%; ACT scores over 18: 50%; SAT evidence-based reading and writing scores over 600: 15%; SAT math scores over 600: 7%; ACT scores over 24: 9%; SAT evidence-based reading and writing scores over 700: 4%; SAT math scores over 700: 2%; ACT scores over 30: 2%.

Retention: 64% of full-time freshmen returned.

FACULTY

Total: 164, 15% full-time, 54% with terminal degrees.

Student/faculty ratio: 11:1.

ACADEMICS

Calendar: semesters. *Degrees:* bachelor's, master's, and postbachelor's certificates.

Special study options: accelerated degree program, adult/continuing education programs, advanced placement credit, distance learning, double majors, external degree program, honors programs, independent study, internships, off-campus study, part-time degree program, services for LD students, student-designed majors, study abroad, summer session for credit.

Computers: Students can access the following: campus intranet, computer help desk, free student e-mail accounts, online (class) grades, online (class) registration, online (class) schedules. Campuswide network is available. 100% of college-owned or -operated housing units are wired for high-speed Internet access. Wireless service is available via classrooms, computer centers, computer labs, dorm rooms, learning centers, libraries, student centers.

Library: Gertrude Kistler Memorial Library plus 1 other. *Books:* 143,162 (physical), 11,582 (digital/electronic); *Serial titles:* 20 (physical), 17,350 (digital/electronic); *Databases:* 40. Students can reserve study rooms.

STUDENT LIFE

Housing options: coed. Campus housing is university owned. Freshman campus housing is guaranteed.

Activities and organizations: drama/theater group, student-run newspaper, choral group.

Athletics Member NCAA. All Division III. *Intercollegiate sports:* basketball M/W, cross-country running M/W, golf M, lacrosse M/W, soccer M/W, softball W, tennis M/W, volleyball W.

Campus security: 24-hour emergency response devices and patrols, late-night transport/escort service, controlled dormitory access.

Student services: health clinic, personal/psychological counseling.

COSTS & FINANCIAL AID

Costs (2017–18) *Comprehensive fee:* $31,446 includes full-time tuition ($18,500), mandatory fees ($986), and room and board ($11,960). Full-time tuition and fees vary according to course load and degree level. Part-time tuition: $700 per credit hour. Part-time tuition and fees vary according to course load and degree level. *Required fees:* $342 per term part-time. *Room and board:* Room and board charges vary according to board plan and housing facility. *Payment plan:* installment. *Waivers:* employees or children of employees.

Financial Aid Of all full-time matriculated undergraduates who enrolled in 2016, 466 applied for aid, 433 were judged to have need, 34 had their need fully met. 123 Federal Work-Study jobs (averaging $849). 13 state and other part-time jobs (averaging $950). In 2016, 66 non-need-based awards were made. *Average percent of need met:* 72. *Average financial aid package:* $18,852. *Average need-based loan:* $4082. *Average need-based gift aid:* $14,887. *Average non-need-based aid:* $4789. *Average indebtedness upon graduation:* $30,437.

APPLYING

Standardized Tests *Required:* SAT or ACT (for admission).

Options: electronic application, deferred entrance.

Required: high school transcript, minimum 2.0 GPA. *Required for some:* essay or personal statement. *Recommended:* interview.

Application deadlines: rolling (freshmen), rolling (transfers).

Notification: continuous (transfers).

CONTACT

Ms. Bettsy Thommen, Director of Admissions, Undergraduate College, Rosemont College, 1400 Montgomery Avenue, Rosemont, PA 19010. *Phone:* 610-527-0200 Ext. 2601. *Toll-free phone:* 888-2-ROSEMONT. *Fax:* 610-520-4399. *E-mail:* bettsy.thommen@rosemont.edu.

Saint Charles Borromeo Seminary, Overbrook

Wynnewood, Pennsylvania

http://www.scs.edu/

- **Independent Roman Catholic** comprehensive, founded 1832
- **Suburban** 77-acre campus with easy access to Philadelphia
- **Coed, primarily men** 98 undergraduate students, 76% full-time, 17% women, 83% men
- **Moderately difficult** entrance level, 100% of applicants were admitted

UNDERGRAD STUDENTS

74 full-time, 24 part-time. Students come from 6 states and territories; 13% are from out of state; 9% Hispanic/Latino; 2% Asian, non-Hispanic/Latino; 5% transferred in; 100% live on campus.

Freshmen:

Admission: 8 applied, 8 admitted, 7 enrolled.

Retention: 78% of full-time freshmen returned.

FACULTY

Total: 33, 48% full-time, 48% with terminal degrees.

Student/faculty ratio: 6:1.

ACADEMICS

Calendar: semesters. *Degrees:* certificates, bachelor's, master's, and postbachelor's certificates (also offers coed part-time programs; students do not apply directly to the Seminary, but instead apply through their local Diocese).

Special study options: academic remediation for entering students, accelerated degree program, adult/continuing education programs, advanced placement credit, English as a second language, independent study, summer session for credit.

Computers: 60 computers/terminals are available on campus for general student use. Students can access the following: campus intranet, free student e-mail accounts, online (class) grades, online (class) schedules. Campuswide network is available. Wireless service is available via classrooms, computer centers, computer labs, libraries.

Library: Ryan Memorial Library.

STUDENT LIFE

Housing options: on-campus residence required through senior year; men-only. Campus housing is university owned. Freshman campus housing is guaranteed.

Activities and organizations: drama/theater group, student-run newspaper, choral group, Seminarians for Life, Student Council.

Athletics *Intramural sports:* basketball M, football M, soccer M, volleyball M.

Campus security: 24-hour emergency response devices and patrols.

Student services: health clinic, personal/psychological counseling.

COSTS & FINANCIAL AID

Costs (2017–18) *Comprehensive fee:* $33,970 includes full-time tuition ($19,420), mandatory fees ($1235), and room and board ($13,315). Full-time tuition and fees vary according to degree level, program, and student level. Part-time tuition: $100 per term. Part-time tuition and fees vary according to course level. *Required fees:* $317 per credit hour part-time, $100 per term part-time. *College room only:* $4350. *Payment plan:* installment.

Financial Aid Of all full-time matriculated undergraduates who enrolled in 2012, 22 applied for aid, 10 were judged to have need, 6 had their need fully met. *Average percent of need met:* 60. *Average financial aid package:* $20,000. *Average need-based loan:* $5500. *Average need-based gift aid:* $5000. *Average indebtedness upon graduation:* $19,000.

APPLYING

Options: deferred entrance.

Required: essay or personal statement, high school transcript, minimum 2.0 GPA, 3 letters of recommendation, interview, sponsorship by diocese or religious community.

Application deadlines: 7/15 (freshmen), 7/15 (transfers).

Notification: continuous (freshmen), continuous (transfers).

CONTACT

Rev. Joseph Shenosky, Vice Rector, Saint Charles Borromeo Seminary, Overbrook, 100 East Wynnewood Road, Wynnewood, PA 19096. *Phone:* 610-785-6520. *E-mail:* jshenosky@scs.edu.

Saint Francis University
Loretto, Pennsylvania
http://www.francis.edu/

- **Independent Roman Catholic** comprehensive, founded 1847
- **Rural** 600-acre campus
- **Endowment** $48.8 million
- **Coed** 1,661 undergraduate students, 88% full-time, 65% women, 35% men
- **Moderately difficult** entrance level, 76% of applicants were admitted

UNDERGRAD STUDENTS

1,462 full-time, 199 part-time. Students come from 39 states and territories; 38 other countries; 24% are from out of state; 7% Black or African American, non-Hispanic/Latino; 2% Hispanic/Latino; 1% Asian, non-Hispanic/Latino; 0.1% Native Hawaiian or other Pacific Islander, non-Hispanic/Latino; 0.3% American Indian or Alaska Native, non-Hispanic/Latino; 1% Two or more races, non-Hispanic/Latino; 3% Race/ethnicity unknown; 0.8% international; 2% transferred in; 88% live on campus.

Freshmen:
Admission: 1,704 applied, 1,288 admitted, 359 enrolled. *Average high school GPA:* 3.6. *Test scores:* SAT evidence-based reading and writing scores over 500: 56%; SAT math scores over 500: 64%; ACT scores over 18: 94%; SAT evidence-based reading and writing scores over 600: 9%; SAT math scores over 600: 14%; ACT scores over 24: 50%; ACT scores over 30: 9%.

Retention: 85% of full-time freshmen returned.

FACULTY

Total: 237, 55% full-time, 43% with terminal degrees.

Student/faculty ratio: 14:1.

ACADEMICS

Calendar: semesters. *Degrees:* certificates, associate, bachelor's, master's, and doctoral.

Special study options: academic remediation for entering students, accelerated degree program, adult/continuing education programs, advanced placement credit, cooperative education, distance learning, double majors, English as a second language, external degree program, freshman honors college, honors programs, independent study, internships, off-campus study, part-time degree program, services for LD students, student-designed majors, study abroad, summer session for credit. *ROTC:* Army (b).

Unusual degree programs: 3-2 engineering with Penn State University Park, University of Pittsburgh, Clarkson University; forestry with Duke University; optometry with Pennsylvania College of Optometry, osteopathic medicine with Lake Erie College of Osteopathic Medicine.

Computers: 75 computers/terminals are available on campus for general student use. Students can access the following: campus intranet, computer help desk, free student e-mail accounts, online (class) grades, online (class) registration, online (class) schedules. Campuswide network is available. 95% of college-owned or -operated housing units are wired for high-speed Internet access. Wireless service is available via entire campus.

Library: Saint Francis University Library. *Books:* 76,787 (physical), 153,616 (digital/electronic); *Databases:* 74.

STUDENT LIFE

Housing options: on-campus residence required through junior year; men-only, women-only. Campus housing is university owned and leased by the school. Freshman campus housing is guaranteed.

Activities and organizations: drama/theater group, student-run newspaper, radio station, choral group, marching band, Student Activities Organization, Club Baseball, Student Government Association, Best Buddies, Ultimate Frisbee Club, national fraternities, national sororities.

Athletics Member NCAA. All Division I. *Intercollegiate sports:* basketball M(s)/W(s), bowling W, cross-country running M(s)/W(s), field hockey W(s), football M, golf M(s)/W(s), lacrosse W(s), soccer M(s)/W(s), softball W(s), swimming and diving M(s)/W(s), tennis M(s)/W(s), track and field M(s)/W(s), volleyball M(s)/W(s). *Intramural sports:* baseball M(c), basketball M/W, cheerleading M/W, cross-country running M/W, football M, golf M/W, ice hockey M(c), lacrosse W, racquetball M/W, skiing (cross-country) M/W, skiing (downhill) M/W, soccer M/W, softball W, swimming and diving M/W, table tennis M/W, tennis M/W, track and field M/W, ultimate Frisbee M/W, volleyball M/W.

Campus security: 24-hour emergency response devices and patrols, late-night transport/escort service, controlled dormitory access.

Student services: health clinic, personal/psychological counseling.

COSTS & FINANCIAL AID

Costs (2017–18) *One-time required fee:* $110. *Comprehensive fee:* $46,884 includes full-time tuition ($33,856), mandatory fees ($1100), and room and board ($11,928). Full-time tuition and fees vary according to course load, degree level, program, and student level. Part-time tuition: $1057 per credit hour. Part-time tuition and fees vary according to class time, degree level, and program. *College room only:* $5906. Room and board charges vary according to board plan and housing facility. *Payment plan:* installment. *Waivers:* employees or children of employees.

Financial Aid Of all full-time matriculated undergraduates who enrolled in 2015, 1,497 applied for aid, 1,247 were judged to have need, 347 had their need fully met. 285 Federal Work-Study jobs (averaging $1000). 780 state and other part-time jobs (averaging $1000). In 2015, 289 non-need-based awards were made. *Average percent of need met:* 52. *Average financial aid package:* $20,018. *Average need-based loan:* $4207. *Average need-based gift aid:* $16,858. *Average non-need-based aid:* $17,963. *Average indebtedness upon graduation:* $36,656.

APPLYING

Standardized Tests *Required:* SAT or ACT (for admission).

Options: electronic application, deferred entrance.

Application fee: $30.

Required: essay or personal statement, high school transcript, 1 letter of recommendation. *Required for some:* interview. *Recommended:* interview.

Application deadlines: rolling (freshmen), rolling (transfers).

Notification: continuous (transfers).

CONTACT

Robert Beener, Dean for Enrollment Management, Saint Francis University, 117 Evergreen Drive, PO Box 600, Loretto, PA 15940-0600. *Phone:* 814-472-3100. *Toll-free phone:* 866-DIAL-SFU. *E-mail:* rbeener@francis.edu.

See previous page for display ad and page 1408 for the College Close-Up.

Saint Joseph's University
Philadelphia, Pennsylvania
http://www.sju.edu/

- **Independent Roman Catholic (Jesuit)** comprehensive, founded 1851
- **Suburban** 114-acre campus with easy access to Philadelphia
- **Endowment** $234.1 million
- **Coed** 5,145 undergraduate students, 87% full-time, 54% women, 46% men
- **Moderately difficult** entrance level, 77% of applicants were admitted

UNDERGRAD STUDENTS

4,482 full-time, 663 part-time. Students come from 40 states and territories; 37 other countries; 53% are from out of state; 6% Black or African American, non-Hispanic/Latino; 7% Hispanic/Latino; 2% Asian, non-Hispanic/Latino; 0.1% Native Hawaiian or other Pacific Islander, non-Hispanic/Latino; 2% Two or more races, non-Hispanic/Latino; 2% Race/ethnicity unknown; 2% international; 2% transferred in; 54% live on campus.

Freshmen:

Admission: 8,972 applied, 6,925 admitted, 1,077 enrolled. *Average high school GPA:* 3.6. *Test scores:* SAT evidence-based reading and writing scores over 500: 97%; SAT math scores over 500: 96%; ACT scores over 18: 100%; SAT evidence-based reading and writing scores over 600: 56%; SAT math scores over 600: 49%; ACT scores over 24: 75%; SAT evidence-based reading and writing scores over 700: 6%; SAT math scores over 700: 6%; ACT scores over 30: 16%.

Retention: 91% of full-time freshmen returned.

FACULTY

Total: 704, 44% full-time.

Student/faculty ratio: 11:1.

ACADEMICS

Calendar: semesters. *Degrees:* associate, bachelor's, master's, doctoral, post-master's, and postbachelor's certificates.

Special study options: accelerated degree program, adult/continuing education programs, advanced placement credit, cooperative education, distance learning, double majors, English as a second language, honors programs, independent study, internships, off-campus study, part-time degree program, services for LD students, student-designed majors, study abroad, summer session for credit. *ROTC:* Army (c), Navy (c), Air Force (b).

Computers: 682 computers/terminals are available on campus for general student use. Students can access the following: campus intranet, computer help desk, free student e-mail accounts, online (class) grades, online (class) registration, online (class) schedules. Campuswide network is available. 100% of college-owned or -operated housing units are wired for high-speed Internet access. Wireless service is available via entire campus.

Library: Post Learning Commons and Drexel Library. *Books:* 278,990 (physical), 557,060 (digital/electronic); *Serial titles:* 483 (physical), 71,735 (digital/electronic); *Databases:* 175. Weekly public service hours: 99; students can reserve study rooms.

STUDENT LIFE

Housing options: on-campus residence required through sophomore year; coed, men-only, women-only, special housing for students with disabilities. Campus housing is university owned, leased by the school and is provided by a third party. Freshman campus housing is guaranteed.

Activities and organizations: drama/theater group, student-run newspaper, radio station, choral group, Student Union Board, Hand-in-Hand, 54th Airborne / Booster Club, Appalachian Experience, Weekly Service, national fraternities, national sororities.

Athletics Member NCAA. All Division I. *Intercollegiate sports:* baseball M(s), basketball M(s)/W(s), cheerleading M(c)/W(c), crew M(s)/W(s), cross-country running M(s)/W(s), field hockey W(s), golf M(s), lacrosse M(s)/W(s), soccer M(s)/W(s), softball W(s), tennis M(s)/W(s), track and field M(s)/W(s). *Intramural sports:* baseball M(c), basketball M(c)/W(c), field hockey W(c), football M/W, golf M(c)/W(c), ice hockey M(c)/W(c), lacrosse M(c)/W(c), rugby M(c)/W(c), soccer M(c)/W(c), softball W, swimming and diving M(c)/W(c), tennis M(c)/W(c), ultimate Frisbee M(c)/W(c), volleyball M(c)/W(c), water polo M(c)/W(c).

Campus security: 24-hour emergency response devices and patrols, late-night transport/escort service, controlled dormitory access, 24-hour shuttle/escort service, bicycle patrols.

Student services: health clinic, personal/psychological counseling.

COSTS & FINANCIAL AID

Costs (2017–18) *Comprehensive fee:* $58,720 includes full-time tuition ($43,700), mandatory fees ($180), and room and board ($14,840). Full-time tuition and fees vary according to course load. Part-time tuition: $584 per credit. Part-time tuition and fees vary according to course load. *College room only:* $9424. Room and board charges vary according to board plan and housing facility. *Payment plan:* installment. *Waivers:* employees or children of employees.

Financial Aid Of all full-time matriculated undergraduates who enrolled in 2017, 3,138 applied for aid, 2,641 were judged to have need, 597 had their need fully met. In 2017, 1470 non-need-based awards were made. *Average percent of need met:* 76. *Average financial aid package:* $29,634. *Average need-based loan:* $4441. *Average need-based gift aid:* $23,091. *Average non-need-based aid:* $13,435.

APPLYING

Options: electronic application, early decision, early action, deferred entrance.

Application fee: $50.

Required: essay or personal statement, high school transcript, 1 letter of recommendation.

Application deadlines: 2/1 (freshmen), 3/1 (transfers), 11/1 (early action).

Early decision deadline: 11/1 (for plan 1), 1/15 (for plan 2).

Notification: 3/15 (freshmen), 12/20 (early decision plan 1), 2/15 (early decision plan 2), 12/20 (early action).

CONTACT

Office of Admissions, Saint Joseph's University, 5600 City Avenue, Philadelphia, PA 19131-1395. *Phone:* 610-660-1300. *Toll-free phone:* 888-BE-A-HAWK (in-state); 800-BE-A-HAWK (out-of-state). *Fax:* 610-660-1314. *E-mail:* admit@sju.edu.

See below for display ad and page 1410 for the College Close-Up.

Saint Vincent College
Latrobe, Pennsylvania
http://www.stvincent.edu/

- **Independent Roman Catholic** comprehensive, founded 1846
- **Suburban** 200-acre campus with easy access to Pittsburgh
- **Endowment** $98.8 million
- **Coed** 1,666 undergraduate students, 97% full-time, 45% women, 55% men
- **Moderately difficult** entrance level, 62% of applicants were admitted

UNDERGRAD STUDENTS

1,616 full-time, 50 part-time. Students come from 35 states and territories; 6 other countries; 22% are from out of state; 6% Black or African American, non-Hispanic/Latino; 4% Hispanic/Latino; 1% Asian, non-Hispanic/Latino; 0.1% Native Hawaiian or other Pacific Islander, non-Hispanic/Latino; 0.3% American Indian or Alaska Native, non-Hispanic/Latino; 2% Two or more races, non-Hispanic/Latino; 4% Race/ethnicity unknown; 0.3% international; 2% transferred in; 75% live on campus.

Freshmen:

Admission: 2,490 applied, 1,542 admitted, 456 enrolled. *Average high school GPA:* 3.5. *Test scores:* ACT scores over 18: 93%; ACT scores over 24: 45%; ACT scores over 30: 9%.

Retention: 83% of full-time freshmen returned.

FACULTY

Total: 227, 46% full-time, 61% with terminal degrees.
Student/faculty ratio: 11:1.

ACADEMICS

Calendar: semesters. *Degrees:* certificates, bachelor's, master's, doctoral, and postbachelor's certificates.

Special study options: advanced placement credit, cooperative education, distance learning, double majors, external degree program, honors programs, independent study, internships, part-time degree program, services for LD students, student-designed majors, study abroad, summer session for credit. *ROTC:* Army (c), Air Force (c).

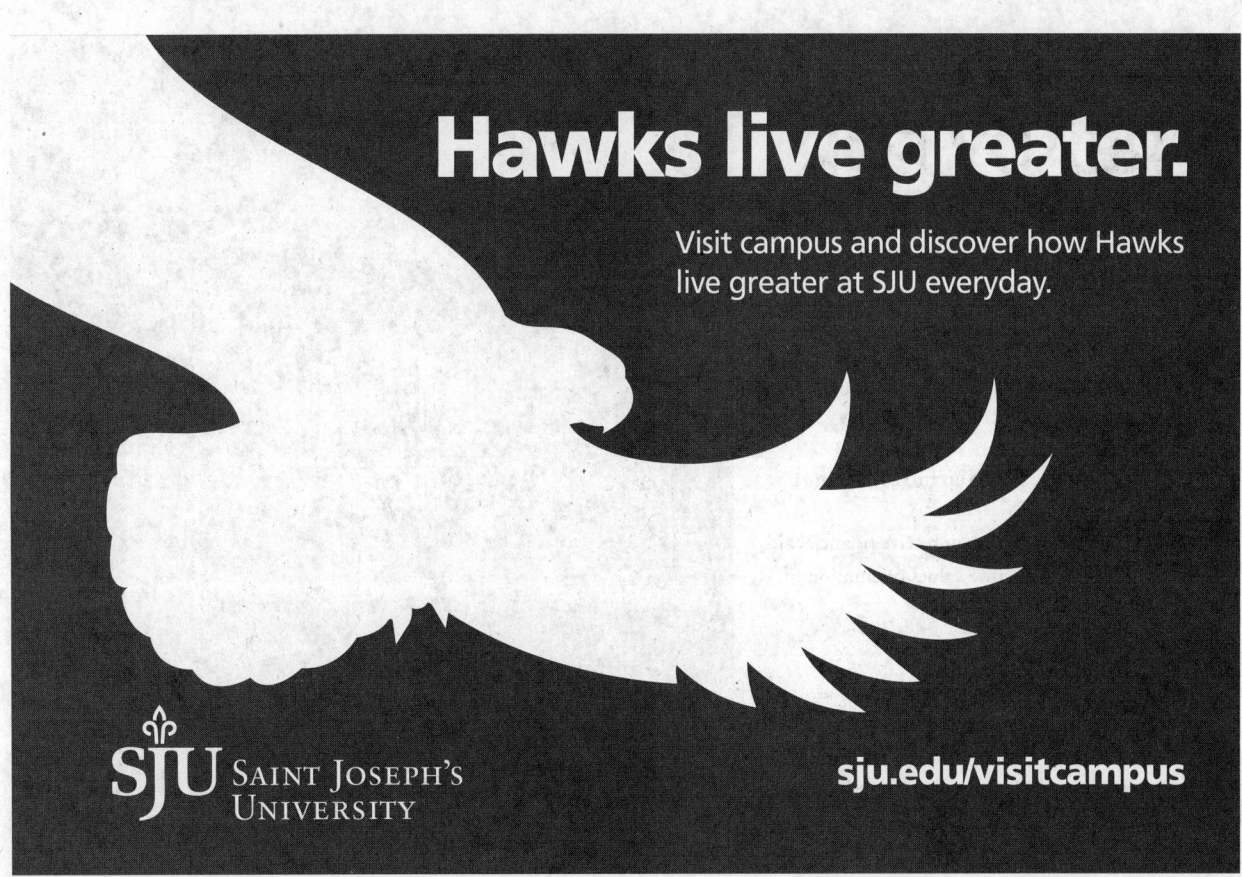

Hawks live greater.

Visit campus and discover how Hawks live greater at SJU everyday.

SJU SAINT JOSEPH'S UNIVERSITY

sju.edu/visitcampus

Unusual degree programs: 3-2 engineering with University of Pittsburgh, Penn State University, The Catholic University of America.

Computers: 313 computers/terminals are available on campus for general student use. Students can access the following: campus intranet, computer help desk, free student e-mail accounts, online (class) grades, online (class) registration, online (class) schedules, program requirement evaluation. Campuswide network is available. 100% of college-owned or -operated housing units are wired for high-speed Internet access. Wireless service is available via entire campus.

Library: Latimer Family Library plus 1 other. *Books:* 288,601 (physical); *Serial titles:* 249 (physical). Weekly public service hours: 84.

STUDENT LIFE

Housing options: coed. Campus housing is university owned. Freshman applicants given priority for college housing.

Activities and organizations: drama/theater group, student-run newspaper, choral group, marching band, Activities Programming Board, Orientation Committee, Campus Ministry, Visionaries of Hope.

Athletics Member NCAA. All Division III. *Intercollegiate sports:* baseball M, basketball M/W, cheerleading W(c), cross-country running M/W, equestrian sports M(c)/W(c), fencing M(c)/W(c), football M, golf M/W, ice hockey M(c), lacrosse M/W, rugby M(c)/W(c), soccer M/W, softball W, swimming and diving M/W, tennis M/W, track and field M/W, volleyball W. *Intramural sports:* basketball M/W, bowling W, football M/W, ultimate Frisbee M/W, volleyball M/W.

Campus security: 24-hour emergency response devices and patrols, late-night transport/escort service, controlled dormitory access, limited access to residence halls on weekends.

Student services: health clinic, personal/psychological counseling.

COSTS & FINANCIAL AID

Costs (2017–18) *Comprehensive fee:* $46,229 includes full-time tuition ($33,516), mandatory fees ($1314), and room and board ($11,399). Full-time tuition and fees vary according to course load and degree level. Part-time tuition: $1048 per credit hour. Part-time tuition and fees vary according to course load and degree level. *College room only:* $6113. Room and board charges vary according to board plan and housing

facility. *Payment plan:* installment. *Waivers:* employees or children of employees.

Financial Aid Of all full-time matriculated undergraduates who enrolled in 2017, 1,389 applied for aid, 1,372 were judged to have need, 322 had their need fully met. In 2017, 301 non-need-based awards were made. *Average percent of need met:* 85. *Average financial aid package:* $29,423. *Average need-based loan:* $4667. *Average need-based gift aid:* $6688. *Average non-need-based aid:* $19,173. *Average indebtedness upon graduation:* $46,794.

APPLYING

Standardized Tests *Required:* SAT or ACT (for admission).

Options: electronic application, early admission, deferred entrance.

Application fee: $25.

Required: essay or personal statement, high school transcript, minimum 2.5 GPA. *Required for some:* interview. *Recommended:* minimum 3.2 GPA, 3 letters of recommendation, interview.

Application deadlines: 5/1 (freshmen), 7/1 (transfers).

Notification: continuous until 10/1 (freshmen), continuous until 12/1 (transfers).

CONTACT

Mr. Stephen Neitz, Dean of Admission, Saint Vincent College, 300 Fraser Purchase Road, Latrobe, PA 15650-2690. *Phone:* 800-782-5549. *Toll-free phone:* 800-782-5549. *Fax:* 724-532-5069. *E-mail:* admission@ stvincent.edu.

See below for display ad and page 1420 for the College Close-Up.

Seton Hill University
Greensburg, Pennsylvania
http://www.setonhill.edu/

- **Independent Roman Catholic** comprehensive, founded 1883
- **Small-town** 200-acre campus with easy access to Pittsburgh
- **Coed** 1,676 undergraduate students, 92% full-time, 64% women, 36% men
- **Moderately difficult** entrance level, 74% of applicants were admitted

UNDERGRAD STUDENTS

1,548 full-time, 128 part-time. Students come from 33 states and territories; 16 other countries; 23% are from out of state; 8% Black or African American, non-Hispanic/Latino; 4% Hispanic/Latino; 1% Asian, non-Hispanic/Latino; 0.1% Native Hawaiian or other Pacific Islander, non-Hispanic/Latino; 0.1% American Indian or Alaska Native, non-Hispanic/Latino; 3% Two or more races, non-Hispanic/Latino; 0.6% Race/ethnicity unknown; 2% international; 4% transferred in; 47% live on campus.

Freshmen:
Admission: 2,573 applied, 1,902 admitted, 427 enrolled. *Average high school GPA:* 3.7. *Test scores:* SAT evidence-based reading and writing scores over 500: 81%; SAT math scores over 500: 78%; ACT scores over 18: 96%; SAT evidence-based reading and writing scores over 600: 32%; SAT math scores over 600: 29%; ACT scores over 24: 52%; SAT evidence-based reading and writing scores over 700: 4%; SAT math scores over 700: 2%; ACT scores over 30: 6%.
Retention: 84% of full-time freshmen returned.

FACULTY

Total: 199, 50% full-time, 59% with terminal degrees.
Student/faculty ratio: 14:1.

ACADEMICS

Calendar: semesters. *Degrees:* certificates, bachelor's, master's, and postbachelor's certificates.

Special study options: academic remediation for entering students, adult/continuing education programs, advanced placement credit, distance learning, double majors, English as a second language, honors programs, independent study, internships, off-campus study, part-time degree program, services for LD students, student-designed majors, study abroad, summer session for credit. *ROTC:* Army (c).

Unusual degree programs: 3-2 engineering with University of Pittsburgh, Penn State University Park, Georgia Institute of Technology; physician assistant with Seton Hill University, osteopathic medicine or pharmacy with Lake Erie College of Osteopathic Medicine.

Computers: 66 computers/terminals and 66 ports are available on campus for general student use. Students can access the following: campus intranet, computer help desk, free student e-mail accounts, online (class) grades, online (class) registration, online (class) schedules. Campuswide network is available. 100% of college-owned or -operated housing units are wired for high-speed Internet access. Wireless service is available via entire campus.
Library: Reeves Memorial Library. *Books:* 72,274 (physical), 127,160 (digital/electronic); *Serial titles:* 2,919 (physical); *Databases:* 37. Students can reserve study rooms.

STUDENT LIFE

Housing options: on-campus residence required for freshman year; coed. Campus housing is university owned. Freshman campus housing is guaranteed.

Activities and organizations: drama/theater group, student-run newspaper, choral group, marching band, Student Body Activities Council, Future Greek leaders, Dietetics Club, Biology Club, intramurals.

Athletics Member NCAA. All Division II. *Intercollegiate sports:* baseball M(s), basketball M(s)/W(s), cross-country running M(s)/W(s), equestrian sports W(s), field hockey W(s), football M(s), golf W(s), lacrosse M(s)/W(s), soccer M(s)/W(s), softball W(s), tennis W(s), track and field M(s)/W(s), volleyball W(s), wrestling M(s).

Campus security: 24-hour emergency response devices and patrols, late-night transport/escort service, controlled dormitory access, emergency phones throughout camps, campus alert system, safety committee.

Student services: health clinic, personal/psychological counseling.

COSTS & FINANCIAL AID

Costs (2017–18) *Comprehensive fee:* $45,940 includes full-time tuition ($33,910), mandatory fees ($750), and room and board ($11,280). Full-time tuition and fees vary according to course load, degree level, and program. Part-time tuition: $910 per credit. Part-time tuition and fees vary according to course load, degree level, and program. *Required fees:* $25 per credit part-time. *Room and board:* Room and board charges vary according to board plan and housing facility. *Payment plan:* installment. *Waivers:* employees or children of employees.

Financial Aid Of all full-time matriculated undergraduates who enrolled in 2016, 1,370 applied for aid, 1,262 were judged to have need, 223 had their need fully met. In 2016, 225 non-need-based awards were made. *Average percent of need met:* 71. *Average financial aid package:* $24,918. *Average need-based loan:* $6154. *Average need-based gift aid:* $19,632. *Average non-need-based aid:* $13,974. *Average indebtedness upon graduation:* $35,356.

APPLYING

Standardized Tests *Recommended:* SAT or ACT (for admission).
Options: electronic application, deferred entrance.
Application fee: $35.
Required: essay or personal statement, high school transcript, 1 letter of recommendation. *Required for some:* portfolio for art, audition for music and theatre. *Recommended:* interview.
Application deadlines: rolling (freshmen), rolling (transfers).
Notification: continuous (freshmen), continuous (transfers).

CONTACT

Mrs. Allison Sasso, Assistant Director of Admissions, Seton Hill University, Seton Hill Drive, Greensburg, PA 15601. *Phone:* 724-838-4255. *Toll-free phone:* 800-826-6234. *Fax:* 724-830-1294. *E-mail:* admit@setonhill.edu.

Shippensburg University of Pennsylvania
Shippensburg, Pennsylvania
http://www.ship.edu/

- **State-supported** comprehensive, founded 1871, part of Pennsylvania State System of Higher Education
- **Rural** 200-acre campus
- **Endowment** $38.9 million
- **Coed** 5,585 undergraduate students, 92% full-time, 50% women, 50% men
- **84%** of applicants were admitted

UNDERGRAD STUDENTS

5,160 full-time, 425 part-time. Students come from 23 states and territories; 19 other countries; 7% are from out of state; 10% Black or African American, non-Hispanic/Latino; 6% Hispanic/Latino; 2% Asian, non-Hispanic/Latino; 0.2% American Indian or Alaska Native, non-Hispanic/Latino; 4% Two or more races, non-Hispanic/Latino; 0.8% Race/ethnicity unknown; 0.7% international; 5% transferred in; 30% live on campus.

Freshmen:
Admission: 5,248 applied, 4,385 admitted, 1,219 enrolled. *Average high school GPA:* 3.2. *Test scores:* SAT evidence-based reading and writing scores over 500: 66%; SAT math scores over 500: 67%; ACT scores over 18: 77%; SAT evidence-based reading and writing scores over 600: 19%; SAT math scores over 600: 16%; ACT scores over 24: 22%; SAT evidence-based reading and writing scores over 700: 2%; SAT math scores over 700: 2%; ACT scores over 30: 2%.
Retention: 71% of full-time freshmen returned.

FACULTY

Total: 372, 80% full-time, 76% with terminal degrees.
Student/faculty ratio: 19:1.

ACADEMICS

Calendar: semesters. *Degrees:* certificates, bachelor's, master's, doctoral, post-master's, and postbachelor's certificates.

Special study options: academic remediation for entering students, accelerated degree program, advanced placement credit, cooperative education, distance learning, double majors, honors programs, independent study, internships, off-campus study, part-time degree program, services for LD students, study abroad, summer session for credit. *ROTC:* Army (b).

Unusual degree programs: 3-2 engineering with Penn State University Park, Penn State Harrisburg.

Computers: 1,100 computers/terminals are available on campus for general student use. Students can access the following: campus intranet, computer help desk, free student e-mail accounts, online (class) grades, online (class) registration, online (class) schedules, personal Web pages. Campuswide network is available. 100% of college-owned or -operated housing units are wired for high-speed Internet access. Wireless service is available via classrooms, computer centers, computer labs, dorm rooms, learning centers, libraries, student centers.

Library: Ezra Lehman Memorial Library plus 1 other. *Books:* 359,138 (physical), 189,092 (digital/electronic); *Serial titles:* 50 (physical), 255 (digital/electronic); *Databases:* 106. Weekly public service hours: 97.

STUDENT LIFE

Housing options: on-campus residence required for freshman year; coed. Campus housing is provided by a third party. Freshman campus housing is guaranteed.

Activities and organizations: drama/theater group, student-run newspaper, radio and television station, choral group, marching band, national fraternities, national sororities.

Athletics Member NCAA. All Division II. *Intercollegiate sports:* baseball M(s), basketball M(s)/W(s), cross-country running M(s)/W(s), field hockey W(s), football M(s), lacrosse W(s), soccer M(s)/W(s), softball W(s), swimming and diving M(s)/W(s), tennis W(s), track and field M(s)/W(s), volleyball W(s), wrestling M(s). *Intramural sports:* basketball M/W, equestrian sports M(c)/W(c), fencing M(c), ice hockey M(c), lacrosse M(c), soccer M/W, softball M/W, ultimate Frisbee M(c)/W(c), volleyball M/W, weight lifting M(c).

Campus security: 24-hour emergency response devices and patrols, late-night transport/escort service, controlled dormitory access, surveillance cameras in certain parking lots and buildings; foot, vehicular and bicycle patrols by security officers.

Student services: health clinic, personal/psychological counseling, women's center.

COSTS & FINANCIAL AID

Costs (2017–18) *Tuition:* state resident $9000 full-time, $300 per credit hour part-time; nonresident $16,858 full-time, $702 per credit hour part-time. *Required fees:* $3086 full-time, $129 per credit hour part-time. *Room and board:* $12,010; room only: $7880. Room and board charges vary according to board plan and housing facility. *Payment plan:* installment. *Waivers:* senior citizens and employees or children of employees.

Financial Aid Of all full-time matriculated undergraduates who enrolled in 2017, 4,448 applied for aid, 3,675 were judged to have need, 352 had their need fully met. 111 Federal Work-Study jobs (averaging $1300). 578 state and other part-time jobs (averaging $1726). In 2017, 364 non-need-based awards were made. *Average percent of need met:* 55. *Average financial aid package:* $9429. *Average need-based loan:* $4058. *Average need-based gift aid:* $6963. *Average non-need-based aid:* $5376. *Average indebtedness upon graduation:* $33,839.

APPLYING

Standardized Tests *Required:* SAT or ACT (for admission).

Options: electronic application, early admission, early action, deferred entrance.

Application fee: $45.

Required: high school transcript. *Required for some:* interview. *Recommended:* essay or personal statement, class rank, letters of recommendation.

Application deadlines: rolling (freshmen), rolling (transfers).

Notification: continuous (freshmen), continuous (transfers).

CONTACT

Mr. William H. Washabaugh, Associate Dean of Admissions, Shippensburg University of Pennsylvania, 1871 Old Main Drive, Shippensburg, PA 17257-2299. *Phone:* 717-477-1231. *Toll-free phone:* 800-822-8028. *Fax:* 717-477-4016. *E-mail:* admiss@ship.edu.

Slippery Rock University of Pennsylvania
Slippery Rock, Pennsylvania
http://www.sru.edu/

- **State-supported** university, founded 1889, part of Pennsylvania State System of Higher Education
- **Small-town** 660-acre campus with easy access to Pittsburgh
- **Endowment** $30.6 million
- **Coed** 7,638 undergraduate students, 93% full-time, 57% women, 43% men
- **Moderately difficult** entrance level, 71% of applicants were admitted

UNDERGRAD STUDENTS

7,125 full-time, 513 part-time. Students come from 47 states and territories; 33 other countries; 10% are from out of state; 5% Black or African American, non-Hispanic/Latino; 2% Hispanic/Latino; 0.9% Asian, non-Hispanic/Latino; 0.1% Native Hawaiian or other Pacific Islander, non-Hispanic/Latino; 0.2% American Indian or Alaska Native, non-Hispanic/Latino; 4% Two or more races, non-Hispanic/Latino; 0.9% Race/ethnicity unknown; 1% international; 7% transferred in; 36% live on campus.

Freshmen:
Admission: 5,836 applied, 4,172 admitted, 1,597 enrolled. *Average high school GPA:* 3.4. *Test scores:* SAT evidence-based reading and writing scores over 500: 79%; SAT math scores over 500: 76%; ACT scores over 18: 89%; SAT evidence-based reading and writing scores over 600: 20%; SAT math scores over 600: 16%; ACT scores over 24: 30%; SAT evidence-based reading and writing scores over 700: 1%; SAT math scores over 700: 1%; ACT scores over 30: 2%.
Retention: 81% of full-time freshmen returned.

FACULTY
Total: 419, 83% full-time, 78% with terminal degrees.
Student/faculty ratio: 21:1.

ACADEMICS
Calendar: semesters. *Degrees:* certificates, bachelor's, master's, doctoral, and postbachelor's certificates.

Special study options: academic remediation for entering students, adult/continuing education programs, advanced placement credit, distance learning, double majors, English as a second language, honors programs, independent study, internships, off-campus study, part-time degree program, services for LD students, student-designed majors, study abroad, summer session for credit. *ROTC:* Army (b).

Unusual degree programs: 3-2 engineering with Penn State University Park, Youngstown State University, West Virginia University, University of Pittsburg.

Computers: 1,654 computers/terminals and 75 ports are available on campus for general student use. Students can access the following: computer help desk, free student e-mail accounts, online (class) grades, online (class) registration, online (class) schedules. Campuswide network is available. 100% of college-owned or -operated housing units are wired for high-speed Internet access. Wireless service is available via entire campus.

Library: Bailey Library. *Books:* 282,009 (physical), 286,118 (digital/electronic); *Serial titles:* 248 (physical), 49,191 (digital/electronic); *Databases:* 134. Weekly public service hours: 98; students can reserve study rooms.

STUDENT LIFE

Housing options: on-campus residence required for freshman year; coed, special housing for students with disabilities. Campus housing is university owned. Freshman campus housing is guaranteed.

Activities and organizations: drama/theater group, student-run newspaper, radio and television station, choral group, marching band, University Program Board, Interfraternity Council/Panhellenic Council, State Government Association, Black Action Society, Gamer's Guild, national fraternities, national sororities.

Athletics Member NCAA. All Division II. *Intercollegiate sports:* baseball M(s), basketball M(s)/W(s), cheerleading M(c)/W(c), cross-country running M(s)/W(s), equestrian sports M(c)/W(c), field hockey W(s), football M(s), ice hockey M(c)/W(c), lacrosse M(c)/W(s), rugby

M(c)/W(c), soccer M(s)/W(s), softball W(s), tennis M(c)/W(s), track and field M(s)/W(s), volleyball M(c)/W(s). *Intramural sports:* badminton M/W, baseball M(c), basketball M/W, football M/W, golf M(c)/W(c), gymnastics M(c)/W(c), soccer M/W, softball M/W, swimming and diving M(c)/W(c), ultimate Frisbee M/W, volleyball M/W, water polo M/W, wrestling M(c).

Campus security: 24-hour emergency response devices and patrols, late-night transport/escort service, controlled dormitory access.

Student services: health clinic, personal/psychological counseling, women's center, legal services.

COSTS & FINANCIAL AID

Costs (2017–18) *Tuition:* state resident $7492 full-time, $312 per credit hour part-time; nonresident $11,238 full-time, $468 per credit hour part-time. Full-time tuition and fees vary according to course load. Part-time tuition and fees vary according to course load. *Required fees:* $2713 full-time, $113 per credit hour part-time. *Room and board:* $10,312; room only: $6742. Room and board charges vary according to board plan and housing facility. *Payment plan:* installment. *Waivers:* minority students, senior citizens, and employees or children of employees.

Financial Aid Of all full-time matriculated undergraduates who enrolled in 2017, 6,224 applied for aid, 4,987 were judged to have need, 350 had their need fully met. 584 Federal Work-Study jobs (averaging $1589). 957 state and other part-time jobs (averaging $1889). In 2017, 570 non-need-based awards were made. *Average percent of need met:* 58. *Average financial aid package:* $9352. *Average need-based loan:* $4497. *Average need-based gift aid:* $6066. *Average non-need-based aid:* $2713. *Average indebtedness upon graduation:* $34,300.

APPLYING

Standardized Tests *Required:* SAT or ACT (for admission).

Options: electronic application, deferred entrance.

Application fee: $30.

Required: high school transcript. *Recommended:* minimum 3.0 GPA.

Application deadlines: rolling (freshmen), rolling (out-of-state freshmen), rolling (transfers).

Notification: continuous until 6/15 (freshmen), continuous until 6/15 (out-of-state freshmen), continuous until 6/15 (transfers).

CONTACT

Slippery Rock University of Pennsylvania, 1 Morrow Way, Slippery Rock, PA 16057-1383. *Phone:* 724-738-2015. *Toll-free phone:* 800-SRU-9111.

Strayer University–Allentown Campus

Center Valley, Pennsylvania

http://www.strayer.edu/pennsylvania/allentown/

CONTACT

Strayer University–Allentown Campus, 3800 Sierra Circle, Suite 300, Center Valley, PA 18034. *Toll-free phone:* 888-311-0355.

Strayer University–Center City Campus

Philadelphia, Pennsylvania

http://www.strayer.edu/pennsylvania/center-city/

CONTACT

Strayer University–Center City Campus, 1601 Cherry Street, Suite 100, Philadelphia, PA 19102. *Toll-free phone:* 888-311-0355.

Strayer University–Delaware County Campus

Springfield, Pennsylvania

http://www.strayer.edu/pennsylvania/delaware-county/

CONTACT

Strayer University–Delaware County Campus, 760 West Sproul Road, Suite 200, Springfield, PA 19064. *Toll-free phone:* 888-311-0355.

Strayer University–Lower Bucks County Campus

Trevose, Pennsylvania

http://www.strayer.edu/pennsylvania/lower-bucks-county/

CONTACT

Strayer University–Lower Bucks County Campus, 3800 Horizon Boulevard, Suite 100, Trevose, PA 19053. *Toll-free phone:* 888-311-0355.

Strayer University–Warrendale Campus

Warrendale, Pennsylvania

http://www.strayer.edu/pennsylvania/warrendale/

CONTACT

Strayer University–Warrendale Campus, 802 Warrendale Village Drive, Warrendale, PA 15086. *Toll-free phone:* 888-311-0355.

Susquehanna University

Selinsgrove, Pennsylvania

http://www.susqu.edu/

- **Independent** 4-year, founded 1858, affiliated with Evangelical Lutheran Church in America
- **Small-town** 325-acre campus
- **Endowment** $143.2 million
- **Coed** 2,267 undergraduate students, 97% full-time, 56% women, 44% men
- **Moderately difficult** entrance level, 85% of applicants were admitted

UNDERGRAD STUDENTS

2,198 full-time, 69 part-time. Students come from 38 states and territories; 21 other countries; 42% are from out of state; 6% Black or African American, non-Hispanic/Latino; 7% Hispanic/Latino; 2% Asian, non-Hispanic/Latino; 0.3% American Indian or Alaska Native, non-Hispanic/Latino; 3% Two or more races, non-Hispanic/Latino; 3% Race/ethnicity unknown; 2% international; 0.9% transferred in; 93% live on campus.

Freshmen:

Admission: 4,896 applied, 4,159 admitted, 634 enrolled. *Average high school GPA:* 3.6. *Test scores:* SAT evidence-based reading and writing scores over 500: 93%; SAT math scores over 500: 90%; ACT scores over 18: 96%; SAT evidence-based reading and writing scores over 600: 44%; SAT math scores over 600: 34%; ACT scores over 24: 65%; SAT evidence-based reading and writing scores over 700: 5%; SAT math scores over 700: 3%; ACT scores over 30: 12%.

Retention: 87% of full-time freshmen returned.

FACULTY

Total: 260, 53% full-time, 63% with terminal degrees.

Student/faculty ratio: 12:1.

ACADEMICS

Calendar: semesters. *Degrees:* bachelor's (also offers evening associate degree program limited to local adult students).

Special study options: accelerated degree program, advanced placement credit, distance learning, double majors, English as a second language, honors programs, independent study, internships, off-campus study, part-time degree program, services for LD students, student-designed majors, study abroad, summer session for credit. *ROTC:* Army (c).

Unusual degree programs: 3-2 engineering with Columbia University.

Computers: 183 computers/terminals are available on campus for general student use. Students can access the following: campus intranet, computer help desk, free student e-mail accounts, online (class) grades, online (class) registration, online (class) schedules, online voting booth. Campuswide network is available. 100% of college-owned or -operated housing units are wired for high-speed Internet access. Wireless service is available via entire campus.

Library: Blough-Weis Library. *Books:* 161,900 (physical), 370,171 (digital/electronic); *Serial titles:* 612 (physical), 94,180 (digital/electronic); *Databases:* 137. Weekly public service hours: 106; students can reserve study rooms.

STUDENT LIFE
Housing options: on-campus residence required through senior year; coed. Campus housing is university owned. Freshman campus housing is guaranteed.

Activities and organizations: drama/theater group, student-run newspaper, radio station, choral group, Student Government Association, Alpha Phi Omega, Student Activities Committee, SU Dance Corps, Intramural Sports, national fraternities, national sororities.

Athletics Member NCAA. All Division III. *Intercollegiate sports:* baseball M, basketball M/W, cheerleading M(c)/W(c), crew M(c)/W(c), cross-country running M/W, equestrian sports M(c)/W(c), field hockey W, football M, golf M/W, lacrosse M/W, rugby M(c)/W(c), soccer M/W, softball M, swimming and diving M/W, tennis M/W, track and field M/W, volleyball M(c)/W. *Intramural sports:* basketball M/W, racquetball M/W, soccer M/W, softball M/W, tennis M/W, volleyball M/W.

Campus security: 24-hour emergency response devices and patrols, late-night transport/escort service, controlled dormitory access.

Student services: health clinic, personal/psychological counseling, women's center.

COSTS & FINANCIAL AID
Costs (2017–18) *Comprehensive fee:* $57,560 includes full-time tuition ($44,890), mandatory fees ($580), and room and board ($12,090). Part-time tuition: $1430 per credit hour. *College room only:* $6320. Room and board charges vary according to board plan. *Payment plans:* tuition prepayment, installment. *Waivers:* employees or children of employees.

Financial Aid Of all full-time matriculated undergraduates who enrolled in 2017, 1,961 applied for aid, 1,796 were judged to have need, 324 had their need fully met. 1,265 Federal Work-Study jobs (averaging $2023). In 2017, 456 non-need-based awards were made. *Average percent of need met:* 82. *Average financial aid package:* $36,552. *Average need-based loan:* $4314. *Average need-based gift aid:* $31,799. *Average non-need-based aid:* $22,119. *Average indebtedness upon graduation:* $33,757. *Financial aid deadline:* 2/1.

APPLYING
Options: electronic application, early admission, early decision, early action, deferred entrance.

Required: essay or personal statement, high school transcript, minimum 2.5 GPA, 1 letter of recommendation. *Required for some:* writing portfolio, audition for music programs. *Recommended:* minimum 3.0 GPA, interview.

Application deadlines: rolling (freshmen), rolling (out-of-state freshmen), 8/1 (transfers), 11/1 (early action).

Early decision deadline: 11/15.

Notification: continuous (freshmen), continuous (out-of-state freshmen), continuous (transfers), 12/1 (early decision), 12/1 (early action).

CONTACT
Mr. Philip Betz, Director of Admissions, Susquehanna University, 514 University Avenue, Selinsgrove, PA 17870. *Phone:* 570-372-4260. *Toll-free phone:* 800-326-9672. *Fax:* 570-372-2722. *E-mail:* suadmiss@susqu.edu.

Swarthmore College
Swarthmore, Pennsylvania
http://www.swarthmore.edu/
- **Independent** 4-year, founded 1864
- **Suburban** 425-acre campus with easy access to Philadelphia
- **Endowment** $1.7 million
- **Coed**

FACULTY
Student/faculty ratio: 8:1.

ACADEMICS
Calendar: semesters. *Degree:* bachelor's.
Library: McCabe Library plus 6 others.

STUDENT LIFE
Housing options: on-campus residence required for freshman year; coed, men-only, women-only, special housing for students with disabilities. Campus housing is university owned. Freshman campus housing is guaranteed.

Activities and organizations: drama/theater group, student-run newspaper, radio station, choral group, Boy Meets Tractor (sketch comedy troupe), Rhythm N' Motion (performing dance styles of the African Diaspora), Multi (community for people who self-identify as multiracial, multiethnic, multicultural, and/or multireligious), Mixed Company (a cappella group), national fraternities, national sororities.

Athletics Member NCAA. All Division III.

Campus security: 24-hour emergency response devices and patrols, late-night transport/escort service.

Student services: health clinic, personal/psychological counseling, women's center.

COSTS & FINANCIAL AID
Costs (2017–18) *Comprehensive fee:* $65,774 includes full-time tuition ($50,424), mandatory fees ($398), and room and board ($14,952). *College room only:* $7670. Room and board charges vary according to board plan.

Financial Aid Of all full-time matriculated undergraduates who enrolled in 2017, 981 applied for aid, 905 were judged to have need, 905 had their need fully met. 781 Federal Work-Study jobs (averaging $1970). In 2017, 16 non-need-based awards were made. *Average percent of need met:* 100. *Average financial aid package:* $50,361. *Average need-based gift aid:* $48,661. *Average non-need-based aid:* $50,424. *Average indebtedness upon graduation:* $20,209. *Financial aid deadline:* 1/1.

APPLYING
Standardized Tests *Required:* SAT or ACT (for admission).

Required: essay or personal statement, high school transcript, 3 letters of recommendation.

CONTACT
Swarthmore College, 500 College Avenue, Swarthmore, PA 19081-1397. *Toll-free phone:* 800-667-3110.

Talmudical Yeshiva of Philadelphia
Philadelphia, Pennsylvania

CONTACT
Rabbi Shmuel Kamenetsky, Co-Dean, Talmudical Yeshiva of Philadelphia, 6063 Drexel Road, Philadelphia, PA 19131-1296. *Phone:* 215-473-1212.

Temple University
Philadelphia, Pennsylvania
http://www.temple.edu/
- **State-related** university, founded 1884, part of Commonwealth System of Higher Education
- **Urban** 384-acre campus with easy access to Philadelphia
- **Endowment** $585.1 million
- **Coed** 29,550 undergraduate students, 90% full-time, 53% women, 47% men
- **Moderately difficult** entrance level, 57% of applicants were admitted

UNDERGRAD STUDENTS
26,613 full-time, 2,937 part-time. Students come from 50 states and territories; 128 other countries; 21% are from out of state; 13% Black or African American, non-Hispanic/Latino; 7% Hispanic/Latino; 11% Asian, non-Hispanic/Latino; 0.1% Native Hawaiian or other Pacific Islander, non-Hispanic/Latino; 0.1% American Indian or Alaska Native, non-Hispanic/Latino; 3% Two or more races, non-Hispanic/Latino; 4% Race/ethnicity unknown; 7% international; 8% transferred in; 6% live on campus.

Freshmen:
Admission: 35,880 applied, 20,332 admitted, 5,171 enrolled. *Average high school GPA:* 3.5. *Test scores:* SAT evidence-based reading and writing scores over 500: 96%; SAT math scores over 500: 96%; ACT scores over 18: 99%; SAT evidence-based reading and writing scores over 600: 62%; SAT math scores over 600: 53%; ACT scores over 24: 79%;

RELENTLESS PURSUITS.

REMARKABLE CHANGE.

Temple is ranked No. 7 among urban research universities driving innovation.

NEXTSTOP.TEMPLE.EDU

TEMPLE
UNIVERSITY

SAT evidence-based reading and writing scores over 700: 11%; SAT math scores over 700: 11%; ACT scores over 30: 23%.
Retention: 90% of full-time freshmen returned.

FACULTY
Total: 2,831, 52% full-time, 47% with terminal degrees.
Student/faculty ratio: 14:1.

ACADEMICS
Calendar: semesters. *Degrees:* certificates, diplomas, associate, bachelor's, master's, doctoral, post-master's, and postbachelor's certificates.

Special study options: academic remediation for entering students, accelerated degree program, adult/continuing education programs, advanced placement credit, cooperative education, distance learning, double majors, English as a second language, honors programs, independent study, internships, off-campus study, part-time degree program, services for LD students, study abroad, summer session for credit. *ROTC:* Army (b), Navy (c), Air Force (c).

Computers: 15,100 computers/terminals and 68,799 ports are available on campus for general student use. Students can access the following: campus intranet, computer help desk, free student e-mail accounts, online (class) grades, online (class) registration, online (class) schedules, student accounts, Web hosting. Campuswide network is available. 100% of college-owned or -operated housing units are wired for high-speed Internet access. Wireless service is available via entire campus.
Library: Paley Library plus 6 others. *Books:* 4.0 million (physical), 1.4 million (digital/electronic); *Serial titles:* 37,998 (physical), 117,699 (digital/electronic); *Databases:* 760. Students can reserve study rooms.

STUDENT LIFE
Housing options: coed, special housing for students with disabilities. Campus housing is university owned, leased by the school and is provided by a third party.

Activities and organizations: drama/theater group, student-run newspaper, radio and television station, choral group, marching band, Habitat for Humanity, Queer Student Union, Temple University Community Service Association, American Medical Student Association, Temple Outdoors Club, national fraternities, national sororities.

Athletics Member NCAA. All Division I except football (Division I-A). *Intercollegiate sports:* basketball M(s)/W(s), crew M(s)/W(s), cross-country running M(s)/W(s), fencing W(s), field hockey W(s), golf M(s), gymnastics W(s), lacrosse W(s), soccer M(s)/W(s), tennis M(s)/W(s), track and field W(s), volleyball W(s). *Intramural sports:* archery M(c), baseball M(c), basketball M/W, bowling M(c)/W(c), equestrian sports M(c)/W(c), fencing M(c)/W(c), field hockey W(c), football M/W, gymnastics M(c)/W(c), ice hockey M(c), lacrosse M(c)/W(c), racquetball M(c)/W(c), rugby M(c)/W(c), skiing (downhill) M(c)/W(c), soccer M/W, softball M/W, swimming and diving M(c)/W(c), tennis M(c)/W(c), track and field M(c), ultimate Frisbee M(c)/W(c), volleyball M/W, weight lifting M(c)/W(c), wrestling M(c).

Campus security: 24-hour emergency response devices and patrols, late-night transport/escort service, controlled dormitory access.

Student services: health clinic, personal/psychological counseling, women's center, legal services.

COSTS & FINANCIAL AID
Costs (2017–18) *Tuition:* state resident $15,768 full-time, $657 per credit hour part-time; nonresident $27,528 full-time, $1147 per credit hour part-time. Full-time tuition and fees vary according to course load, degree level, location, program, reciprocity agreements, and student level. Part-time tuition and fees vary according to course load, degree level, location, program, reciprocity agreements, and student level. *Required fees:* $890 full-time. *Room and board:* $11,566; room only: $7752. Room and board charges vary according to board plan and housing facility. *Payment plan:* installment. *Waivers:* employees or children of employees.

Financial Aid Of all full-time matriculated undergraduates who enrolled in 2016, 20,385 applied for aid, 17,777 were judged to have need, 4,271 had their need fully met. 1,163 Federal Work-Study jobs (averaging $1461). In 2016, 4678 non-need-based awards were made. *Average percent of need met:* 64. *Average financial aid package:* $18,627. *Average need-based loan:* $4500. *Average need-based gift aid:* $6439. *Average non-need-based aid:* $6557. *Average indebtedness upon graduation:* $38,108.

APPLYING

Options: electronic application, early action, deferred entrance.

Application fee: $55.

Required: essay or personal statement, high school transcript. *Recommended:* minimum 3.0 GPA, 1 letter of recommendation.

Application deadlines: 3/1 (freshmen), 6/1 (transfers).

Notification: continuous (freshmen), continuous (transfers).

CONTACT

Temple University, 1801 North Broad Street, Philadelphia, PA 19122-6096. *Phone:* 215-204-7200. *Toll-free phone:* 888-340-2222.

See previous page for display ad and page 1444 for the College Close-Up.

Thiel College

Greenville, Pennsylvania

http://www.thiel.edu/

CONTACT

Mr. Stephen Lazowski, Vice President for Enrollment Management, Thiel College, 75 College Avenue, Greenville, PA 16125. *Phone:* 724-589-2182. *Toll-free phone:* 800-248-4435. *Fax:* 724-589-2013. *E-mail:* admissions@thiel.edu.

 # Thomas Jefferson University

Philadelphia, Pennsylvania

http://www.jefferson.edu/university.html

- **Independent** university, founded 1824
- **Urban** 13-acre campus
- **Coed** 1,131 undergraduate students
- **Moderately difficult** entrance level

FACULTY

Total: 215, 69% full-time, 55% with terminal degrees.

Student/faculty ratio: 15:1.

ACADEMICS

Calendar: semesters. *Degrees:* associate, bachelor's, master's, doctoral, and postbachelor's certificates.

Special study options: academic remediation for entering students, accelerated degree program, adult/continuing education programs, advanced placement credit, cooperative education, distance learning, double majors, honors programs, independent study, internships, off-campus study, part-time degree program, services for LD students, study abroad. *ROTC:* Air Force (c).

Computers: Students can access the following: campus intranet, computer help desk, free student e-mail accounts, online (class) grades, online (class) registration, online (class) schedules. Campuswide network is available. Wireless service is available via entire campus.

Library: Scott Memorial Library plus 1 other. Study areas open 24 hours, 5–7 days a week; students can reserve study rooms.

STUDENT LIFE

Housing options: coed, men-only, women-only. Campus housing is university owned and is provided by a third party. Freshman campus housing is guaranteed.

Activities and organizations: choral group.

Athletics *Intercollegiate sports:* rugby M(c). *Intramural sports:* basketball M/W, fencing M(c)/W(c), racquetball M(c)/W(c), soccer M(c)/W(c), softball M/W, swimming and diving M/W, tennis W, volleyball M/W, water polo M(c)/W(c).

Campus security: 24-hour emergency response devices and patrols, late-night transport/escort service, controlled dormitory access.

Student services: health clinic, personal/psychological counseling.

FINANCIAL AID

Financial Aid *Average indebtedness upon graduation:* $55,363.

APPLYING

Standardized Tests *Required for some:* NET. *Recommended:* SAT or ACT (for admission).

Options: deferred entrance.

Application fee: $50.

Required: essay or personal statement, minimum 3.0 GPA, 2 letters of recommendation, interview. *Required for some:* high school transcript.

Application deadlines: rolling (freshmen), rolling (transfers).

Notification: continuous (freshmen), continuous (transfers).

CONTACT

Ms. Karen Jacobs, Director of Admissions, Thomas Jefferson University, Edison Building, 130 South Ninth Street, Philadelphia, PA 19107. *Phone:* 215-503-8890. *Toll-free phone:* 877-533-3247. *Fax:* 215-503-7241. *E-mail:* chpadmissions@mail.tju.edu.

See next page for display ad and page 1446 for the College Close-Up.

University of Pennsylvania

Philadelphia, Pennsylvania

http://www.upenn.edu/

- **Independent** university, founded 1740
- **Urban** 299-acre campus
- **Endowment** $12.2 billion
- **Coed** 10,033 undergraduate students, 97% full-time, 51% women, 49% men
- **Most difficult** entrance level, 9% of applicants were admitted

UNDERGRAD STUDENTS

9,782 full-time, 251 part-time. Students come from 54 states and territories; 102 other countries; 81% are from out of state; 7% Black or African American, non-Hispanic/Latino; 10% Hispanic/Latino; 21% Asian, non-Hispanic/Latino; 0.1% American Indian or Alaska Native, non-Hispanic/Latino; 5% Two or more races, non-Hispanic/Latino; 2% Race/ethnicity unknown; 13% international; 1% transferred in; 54% live on campus.

Freshmen:

Admission: 40,413 applied, 3,757 admitted, 2,412 enrolled. *Average high school GPA:* 3.9. *Test scores:* SAT evidence-based reading and writing scores over 500: 100%; SAT math scores over 500: 100%; ACT scores over 18: 100%; SAT evidence-based reading and writing scores over 600: 98%; SAT math scores over 600: 99%; ACT scores over 24: 100%; SAT evidence-based reading and writing scores over 700: 80%; SAT math scores over 700: 84%; ACT scores over 30: 92%.

Retention: 98% of full-time freshmen returned.

FACULTY

Total: 2,028, 75% full-time, 100% with terminal degrees.

Student/faculty ratio: 6:1.

ACADEMICS

Calendar: semesters plus 2 5-week summer sessions. *Degrees:* certificates, associate, bachelor's, master's, doctoral, post-master's, and postbachelor's certificates (also offers evening program with significant enrollment not reflected in profile).

Special study options: academic remediation for entering students, accelerated degree program, adult/continuing education programs, advanced placement credit, cooperative education, distance learning, double majors, English as a second language, honors programs, independent study, internships, off-campus study, part-time degree program, services for LD students, student-designed majors, study abroad, summer session for credit. *ROTC:* Army (c), Navy (b), Air Force (c).

Computers: Students can access the following: campus intranet, computer help desk, free student e-mail accounts, online (class) grades, online (class) registration, online (class) schedules, billing information, financial aid application, status, academic records, student services. Campuswide network is available. 100% of college-owned or -operated housing units are wired for high-speed Internet access. Wireless service is available via entire campus.

Library: Van Pelt Library plus 14 others. *Books:* 6.4 million (physical); *Serial titles:* 188,604 (physical). Study areas open 24 hours, 5–7 days a week; students can reserve study rooms.

STUDENT LIFE

Housing options: coed, special housing for students with disabilities. Campus housing is university owned. Freshman campus housing is guaranteed.

2800 UNDERGRADS

ON EAST FALLS CAMPUS

AVERAGE **18** **14:1** STUDENT to
class size FACULTY ratio

ACADEMIC MAJORS

Accounting

Animation and Digital Media

Architectural Studies

Concentrations available:

• *Architectural Design*
Technology

• *Historic Preservation*

Architecture (Five-year B.Arch.)

Biochemistry

Biology

Biopsychology

Chemistry

Communication

Construction Management

Engineering, B.S.E.

Minors available:

• *Architectural*

• *Composites*

• *Industrial and Systems*

• *Textile*

Fashion Design

Fashion Merchandising and
Management

Finance

Graphic Design Communication

Health Sciences

Health Sciences, B.S.
Athletic Training, M.S.

Health Sciences, B.S.
Community and Trauma
Counseling, M.S.

Health Sciences, B.S.
Occupational Therapy, M.S.
(Combined B.S./M.S.)

Health Sciences

Physician Assistant Studies
5-year Accelerated B.S./M.S.
Assured Admission Option

Health Sciences

Physician Assistant Studies
4+2 B.S./M.S.
Preferred Admission Option

Industrial Design

Interior Design

International Business

Landscape Architecture, B.L.A.

Law and Society

Management

Marketing

Mechanical Engineering, B.S.E.

Pre-Medical Studies

Pre-Nursing (Health Sciences
entry)

Pre-Pharmacy (Health Sciences
entry)

Psychology

Psychology, B.S.
Community and Trauma
Counseling, M.S.

Psychology, B.S.
Occupational Therapy, M.S.
(Combined B.S./M.S.)

Textile Design

Textile Materials Technology

Web Design and Development

Undecided

JOB SUCCESS and GRADUATE SCHOOL ACCEPTANCE RATE **96%**

LEARN MORE AND APPLY NOW
at EastFalls.Jefferson.edu/undergrad

Activities and organizations: drama/theater group, student-run newspaper, radio and television station, choral group, marching band, Kite and Key Society, Social Planning and Events Committee, Hillel at Penn, Sports Club Council, Interfraternity Council, national fraternities, national sororities.

Athletics Member NCAA. All Division I except football (Division I-AA). *Intercollegiate sports:* baseball M, basketball M/W, crew M/W, cross-country running M/W, fencing M/W, field hockey W, golf M/W, gymnastics W, lacrosse M/W, soccer M/W, softball W, squash M/W, swimming and diving M/W, tennis M/W, track and field M/W, volleyball W, wrestling M. *Intramural sports:* badminton M(c)/W(c), baseball M(c)/W(c), basketball M(c)/W(c), cheerleading M/W, equestrian sports M(c)/W(c), field hockey M(c)/W(c), golf M(c)/W(c), gymnastics M(c)/W(c), ice hockey M(c)/W(c), lacrosse M/W, rugby M(c)/W(c), sailing M(c)/W(c), skiing (downhill) M(c)/W(c), soccer M/W, softball M/W, squash M/W, swimming and diving M/W, table tennis M/W, tennis M/W, ultimate Frisbee M(c)/W(c), volleyball M/W, water polo M(c)/W(c).

Campus security: 24-hour emergency response devices and patrols, late-night transport/escort service, controlled dormitory access.

Student services: health clinic, personal/psychological counseling, women's center, legal services.

COSTS & FINANCIAL AID
Costs (2018–19) *Comprehensive fee:* $71,200 includes full-time tuition ($49,220), mandatory fees ($6364), and room and board ($15,616). Part-time tuition and fees vary according to course load. *Room and board:* Room and board charges vary according to board plan and housing facility. *Payment plans:* tuition prepayment, installment. *Waivers:* employees or children of employees.

Financial Aid Of all full-time matriculated undergraduates who enrolled in 2016, 4,851 applied for aid, 4,478 were judged to have need, 4,478 had their need fully met. *Average percent of need met:* 100. *Average financial aid package:* $48,971. *Average need-based loan:* $3922. *Average need-based gift aid:* $46,177. *Average indebtedness upon graduation:* $23,224.

APPLYING
Standardized Tests *Required:* SAT or ACT (for admission). *Recommended:* SAT Subject Tests (for admission).

Options: electronic application, early admission, early decision, deferred entrance.

Application fee: $75.

Required: essay or personal statement, high school transcript, 2 letters of recommendation.

Application deadlines: 1/5 (freshmen), 3/15 (transfers).

Early decision deadline: 11/1.

Notification: continuous until 4/1 (freshmen), 5/15 (transfers), 12/15 (early decision).

CONTACT
Office of Undergraduate Admissions, University of Pennsylvania, 1 College Hall, Room 1, Philadelphia, PA 19104. *Phone:* 215-898-7507.

University of Pittsburgh
Pittsburgh, Pennsylvania
http://www.pitt.edu/

• **State-related** university, founded 1787, part of Commonwealth System of Higher Education
• **Urban** 145-acre campus with easy access to Pittsburgh
• **Endowment** $4.0 billion
• **Coed** 19,326 undergraduate students, 95% full-time, 51% women, 49% men
• **Very difficult** entrance level, 60% of applicants were admitted

UNDERGRAD STUDENTS
18,390 full-time, 936 part-time. Students come from 50 states and territories; 56 other countries; 28% are from out of state; 5% Black or African American, non-Hispanic/Latino; 4% Hispanic/Latino; 10% Asian, non-Hispanic/Latino; 0.1% American Indian or Alaska Native, non-Hispanic/Latino; 4% Two or more races, non-Hispanic/Latino; 1% Race/ethnicity unknown; 4% international; 4% transferred in; 43% live on campus.

A ★ *indicates that the school has detailed information with a Premium Profile on Petersons.com.*

Freshmen:
Admission: 27,679 applied, 16,528 admitted, 4,019 enrolled. *Average high school GPA:* 4.1. *Test scores:* SAT evidence-based reading and writing scores over 500: 99%; SAT math scores over 500: 99%; ACT scores over 18: 100%; SAT evidence-based reading and writing scores over 600: 88%; SAT math scores over 600: 88%; ACT scores over 24: 99%; SAT evidence-based reading and writing scores over 700: 26%; SAT math scores over 700: 35%; ACT scores over 30: 51%.

Retention: 93% of full-time freshmen returned.

FACULTY
Total: 2,317, 76% full-time.
Student/faculty ratio: 15:1.

ACADEMICS
Calendar: semesters plus summer term. *Degrees:* certificates, associate, bachelor's, master's, doctoral, post-master's, and postbachelor's certificates.

Special study options: academic remediation for entering students, accelerated degree program, adult/continuing education programs, advanced placement credit, cooperative education, distance learning, double majors, English as a second language, external degree program, freshman honors college, honors programs, independent study, internships, off-campus study, part-time degree program, services for LD students, student-designed majors, study abroad, summer session for credit. *ROTC:* Army (b), Navy (c), Air Force (b).

Unusual degree programs: 3-2 engineering; computer science/statistics, pharmaceutical sciences, public health.

Computers: 1,156 computers/terminals and 18,250 ports are available on campus for general student use. Students can access the following: campus intranet, computer help desk, free student e-mail accounts, online (class) grades, online (class) registration, online (class) schedules, online class listings, online tuition payment. Campuswide network is available. 100% of college-owned or -operated housing units are wired for high-speed Internet access. Wireless service is available via entire campus.

Library: Hillman Library plus 16 others. *Books:* 5.8 million (physical), 1.7 million (digital/electronic); *Serial titles:* 109,160 (physical), 228,331 (digital/electronic); *Databases:* 571. Weekly public service hours: 145; study areas open 24 hours, 5–7 days a week; students can reserve study rooms.

STUDENT LIFE
Housing options: coed, cooperative, special housing for students with disabilities. Campus housing is university owned. Freshman campus housing is guaranteed.

Activities and organizations: drama/theater group, student-run newspaper, radio and television station, choral group, marching band, Resident Student Association, Black Action Society, Pitt Program Council, Interfraternity Council, Panhellenic Association, national fraternities, national sororities.

Athletics Member NCAA. All Division I except football (Division I-A). *Intercollegiate sports:* baseball M(s), basketball M(s)/W(s), cross-country running M(s)/W(s), gymnastics W(s), soccer M(s)/W(s), softball W(s), swimming and diving M(s)/W(s), tennis W(s), track and field M(s)/W(s), volleyball W(s), wrestling M(s). *Intramural sports:* archery M(c)/W(c), badminton M/W, baseball M(c)/W(c), basketball M/W, crew M(c)/W(c), cross-country running M(c)/W(c), equestrian sports M(c)/W(c), fencing M(c)/W(c), field hockey M(c)/W(c), football M, golf M(c)/W(c), gymnastics M(c)/W(c), ice hockey M(c)/W(c), lacrosse M(c)/W(c), racquetball M(c)/W(c), rowing M(c)/W(c), rugby M(c)/W(c), sailing M(c)/W(c), skiing (downhill) M(c)/W(c), soccer M/W, softball W(c), squash M/W, swimming and diving M(c)/W(c), table tennis M/W, tennis M(c)/W(c), triathlon M(c)/W(c), ultimate Frisbee M/W, volleyball M/W, water polo M(c)/W(c), wrestling M(c)/W(c).

Campus security: 24-hour emergency response devices and patrols, late-night transport/escort service, controlled dormitory access, on-call van transportation.

Student services: health clinic, personal/psychological counseling.

COSTS & FINANCIAL AID
Costs (2017–18) *Tuition:* state resident $18,130 full-time, $755 per credit hour part-time; nonresident $29,692 full-time, $1237 per credit hour part-time. Full-time tuition and fees vary according to location and program. Part-time tuition and fees vary according to location and program.

Required fees: $950 full-time, $279 per term part-time. *Room and board:* $10,950; room only: $6300. Room and board charges vary according to board plan, housing facility, and location. *Payment plans:* installment, deferred payment. *Waivers:* employees or children of employees.

Financial Aid Of all full-time matriculated undergraduates who enrolled in 2016, 12,404 applied for aid, 9,496 were judged to have need, 1,152 had their need fully met. In 2016, 598 non-need-based awards were made. *Average percent of need met:* 53. *Average financial aid package:* $12,192. *Average need-based loan:* $4718. *Average need-based gift aid:* $9771. *Average non-need-based aid:* $11,092. *Average indebtedness upon graduation:* $38,322.

APPLYING
Standardized Tests *Required:* SAT or ACT (for admission).
Options: electronic application.
Application fee: $45.
Required: high school transcript. *Recommended:* essay or personal statement, interview.
Application deadlines: rolling (freshmen), rolling (transfers).
Notification: continuous (freshmen), continuous (transfers).

CONTACT
Marc L. Harding, Chief Enrollment Officer, University of Pittsburgh, 4227 Fifth Avenue, First Floor, Alumni Hall, Pittsburgh, PA 15260. *Phone:* 412-624-7488. *Fax:* 412-648-8815. *E-mail:* oafa@pitt.edu.

University of Pittsburgh at Bradford
Bradford, Pennsylvania
http://www.upb.pitt.edu/

- **State-related** 4-year, founded 1963, part of University of Pittsburgh System
- **Small-town** 317-acre campus with easy access to Buffalo
- **Endowment** $24.8 million
- **Coed** 1,340 undergraduate students, 92% full-time, 55% women, 45% men
- **Minimally difficult** entrance level, 49% of applicants were admitted

UNDERGRAD STUDENTS
1,233 full-time, 107 part-time. Students come from 27 states and territories; 16 other countries; 24% are from out of state; 12% Black or African American, non-Hispanic/Latino; 5% Hispanic/Latino; 2% Asian, non-Hispanic/Latino; 0.1% Native Hawaiian or other Pacific Islander, non-Hispanic/Latino; 0.4% American Indian or Alaska Native, non-Hispanic/Latino; 3% Two or more races, non-Hispanic/Latino; 5% Race/ethnicity unknown; 3% international; 5% transferred in; 74% live on campus.

Freshmen:
Admission: 2,852 applied, 1,389 admitted, 348 enrolled. *Average high school GPA:* 3.3. *Test scores:* SAT evidence-based reading and writing scores over 500: 72%; SAT math scores over 500: 72%; ACT scores over 18: 91%; SAT evidence-based reading and writing scores over 600: 23%; SAT math scores over 600: 16%; ACT scores over 24: 30%; SAT evidence-based reading and writing scores over 700: 1%; SAT math scores over 700: 3%; ACT scores over 30: 7%.

Retention: 69% of full-time freshmen returned.

FACULTY
Total: 154, 49% full-time, 40% with terminal degrees.
Student/faculty ratio: 16:1.

ACADEMICS
Calendar: semesters. *Degrees:* associate and bachelor's.

Special study options: academic remediation for entering students, accelerated degree program, adult/continuing education programs, advanced placement credit, cooperative education, distance learning, double majors, independent study, internships, off-campus study, part-time degree program, services for LD students, student-designed majors, study abroad, summer session for credit. *ROTC:* Army (c).

Computers: 136 computers/terminals and 1,200 ports are available on campus for general student use. Students can access the following: computer help desk, free student e-mail accounts, online (class) grades, online (class) registration, online (class) schedules, online bills.

Campuswide network is available. 100% of college-owned or -operated housing units are wired for high-speed Internet access. Wireless service is available via entire campus.

Library: T. Edward and Tullah Hanley Library. *Books:* 105,844 (physical), 1.3 million (digital/electronic); *Serial titles:* 75 (physical), 10,000 (digital/electronic); *Databases:* 550. Weekly public service hours: 86; students can reserve study rooms.

STUDENT LIFE

Housing options: on-campus residence required for freshman year; coed, special housing for students with disabilities. Campus housing is university owned. Freshman campus housing is guaranteed.

Activities and organizations: drama/theater group, student-run radio station, choral group, Student Government Association, Student Activities Board, The Source (student newspaper), Alpha Phi Omega, WDRQ (student radio station), national fraternities, national sororities.

Athletics Member NCAA. All Division III. *Intercollegiate sports:* baseball M, basketball M/W, bowling W, golf M, ice hockey M, soccer M/W, softball W, swimming and diving M/W, tennis M/W, volleyball W. *Intramural sports:* basketball M/W, cheerleading W(c), football M/W, golf M/W, ice hockey M/W, rock climbing M/W, sand volleyball M/W, skiing (downhill) M/W, soccer M/W, softball M/W, swimming and diving M/W, tennis M/W, ultimate Frisbee M/W, volleyball M/W, water polo M/W, wrestling M(c).

Campus security: 24-hour emergency response devices and patrols, late-night transport/escort service, controlled dormitory access, Resident Assistants do nightly rounds of residence halls.

Student services: health clinic, personal/psychological counseling.

COSTS & FINANCIAL AID

Costs (2017–18) *One-time required fee:* $90. *Tuition:* state resident $12,940 full-time, $539 per credit hour part-time; nonresident $24,184 full-time, $1007 per credit hour part-time. Full-time tuition and fees vary according to course load and program. Part-time tuition and fees vary according to course load and program. *Required fees:* $960 full-time, $165 per term part-time. *Room and board:* $9058; room only: $5490. Room and board charges vary according to board plan and housing facility. *Payment plan:* installment. *Waivers:* employees or children of employees.

Financial Aid Of all full-time matriculated undergraduates who enrolled in 2016, 1,236 applied for aid, 1,138 were judged to have need, 116 had their need fully met. 165 Federal Work-Study jobs (averaging $1980). 67 state and other part-time jobs (averaging $1978). In 2016, 73 non-need-based awards were made. *Average percent of need met:* 61. *Average financial aid package:* $13,763. *Average need-based loan:* $4373. *Average need-based gift aid:* $10,081. *Average non-need-based aid:* $5890. *Average indebtedness upon graduation:* $36,250.

APPLYING

Standardized Tests *Required:* SAT or ACT (for admission).

Options: electronic application, deferred entrance.

Required: high school transcript, minimum 2.0 GPA. *Required for some:* minimum 3.0 GPA. *Recommended:* essay or personal statement, 2 letters of recommendation, interview.

Application deadlines: rolling (freshmen), rolling (transfers).

Notification: continuous (freshmen), continuous (transfers).

CONTACT

Ms. Vicky Pingie, Associate Director of Admissions, University of Pittsburgh at Bradford, 300 Campus Drive, Bradford, PA 16701. *Phone:* 814-362-7552. *Toll-free phone:* 800-872-1787. *Fax:* 814-362-5150. *E-mail:* monti@pitt.edu.

See below for display ad and page 1476 for the College Close-Up.

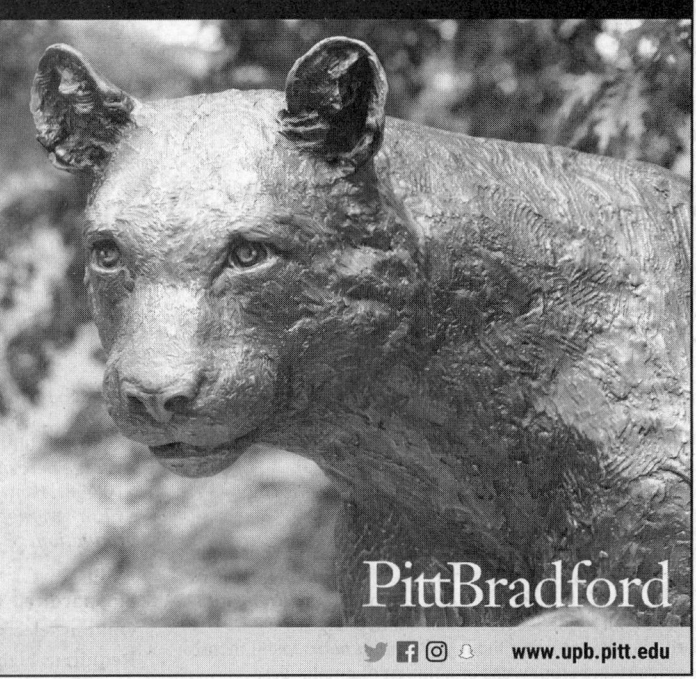

University of Pittsburgh at Greensburg

Greensburg, Pennsylvania

http://www.greensburg.pitt.edu/

- **State-related** 4-year, founded 1963, part of University of Pittsburgh System
- **Small-town** 219-acre campus with easy access to Pittsburgh
- **Coed** 1,523 undergraduate students, 94% full-time, 54% women, 46% men
- **Moderately difficult** entrance level, 73% of applicants were admitted

UNDERGRAD STUDENTS

1,436 full-time, 87 part-time. 4% are from out of state; 6% Black or African American, non-Hispanic/Latino; 6% Hispanic/Latino; 5% Asian, non-Hispanic/Latino; 0.1% Native Hawaiian or other Pacific Islander, non-Hispanic/Latino; 0.1% American Indian or Alaska Native, non-Hispanic/Latino; 3% Two or more races, non-Hispanic/Latino; 3% Race/ethnicity unknown; 1% international; 7% transferred in; 43% live on campus.

Freshmen:

Admission: 2,518 applied, 1,845 admitted, 433 enrolled. *Average high school GPA:* 3.4. *Test scores:* SAT evidence-based reading and writing scores over 500: 83%; SAT math scores over 500: 85%; ACT scores over 18: 85%; SAT evidence-based reading and writing scores over 600: 25%; SAT math scores over 600: 22%; ACT scores over 24: 38%; SAT evidence-based reading and writing scores over 700: 2%; SAT math scores over 700: 2%; ACT scores over 30: 5%.

Retention: 76% of full-time freshmen returned.

ACADEMICS

Calendar: semesters. *Degree:* certificates and bachelor's.

Special study options: academic remediation for entering students, accelerated degree program, adult/continuing education programs, advanced placement credit, distance learning, double majors, independent study, internships, off-campus study, part-time degree program, services for LD students, student-designed majors, study abroad, summer session for credit. *ROTC:* Army (b), Air Force (c).

Computers: Students can access the following: campus intranet, computer help desk, free student e-mail accounts, online (class) grades, online (class) registration, online (class) schedules. Campuswide network is available. 100% of college-owned or -operated housing units are wired for high-speed Internet access. Wireless service is available via classrooms, computer centers, computer labs, dorm rooms, learning centers, libraries, student centers.

Library: Millstein Library.

STUDENT LIFE

Housing options: coed. Campus housing is university owned.

Activities and organizations: drama/theater group, student-run newspaper, choral group, Habitat for Humanity, Student Government Association, Student Activities Board, Outdoor Adventure and Community Service, Freshmen Honor Society - Phi Eta Sigma.

Athletics Member NCAA. All Division III. *Intercollegiate sports:* baseball M, basketball M/W, cross-country running M/W, golf M, soccer M/W, softball W, tennis M/W, volleyball W. *Intramural sports:* baseball M, basketball M/W, bowling M/W, football M/W, golf M/W, racquetball M/W, skiing (cross-country) M/W, skiing (downhill) M/W, soccer M/W, softball M/W, table tennis M/W, tennis M/W, volleyball M/W, weight lifting M/W.

Campus security: 24-hour emergency response devices and patrols, late-night transport/escort service, controlled dormitory access.

Student services: health clinic, personal/psychological counseling.

COSTS & FINANCIAL AID

Costs (2017–18) *Tuition:* state resident $12,940 full-time, $539 per credit hour part-time; nonresident $24,184 full-time, $1007 per credit hour part-time. *Required fees:* $930 full-time, $174 per term part-time. *Room and board:* $10,270; room only: $6280. Room and board charges vary according to board plan and housing facility. *Payment plan:* installment. *Waivers:* senior citizens and employees or children of employees.

Financial Aid Of all full-time matriculated undergraduates who enrolled in 2016, 1,246 applied for aid, 1,079 were judged to have need, 110 had their need fully met. In 2016, 77 non-need-based awards were made. *Average percent of need met:* 60. *Average financial aid package:* $11,618. *Average need-based loan:* $4433. *Average need-based gift aid:* $8667. *Average non-need-based aid:* $5533. *Average indebtedness upon graduation:* $36,358.

APPLYING

Standardized Tests *Required:* SAT or ACT (for admission).

Options: electronic application, early admission, deferred entrance.

Application fee: $45.

Required: high school transcript, minimum 2.5 GPA. *Recommended:* essay or personal statement, interview.

Application deadlines: rolling (freshmen), rolling (out-of-state freshmen), rolling (transfers).

Notification: continuous (freshmen), continuous (transfers).

CONTACT

Ms. Heather Kabala, Director of Admissions, University of Pittsburgh at Greensburg, 150 Finoli Drive, Greensburg, PA 15601. *Phone:* 724-836-9880. *Fax:* 724-836-7471. *E-mail:* upgadmit@pitt.edu.

University of Pittsburgh at Johnstown

Johnstown, Pennsylvania

http://www.upj.pitt.edu/

- **State-related** 4-year, founded 1927, part of University of Pittsburgh System
- **Suburban** 655-acre campus with easy access to Pittsburgh
- **Coed**
- **Moderately difficult** entrance level

FACULTY

Student/faculty ratio: 20:1.

ACADEMICS

Calendar: semesters. *Degrees:* certificates, associate, and bachelor's.

Library: Owen Library. Study areas open 24 hours, 5–7 days a week.

STUDENT LIFE

Housing options: coed, special housing for students with disabilities. Campus housing is university owned. Freshman campus housing is guaranteed.

Activities and organizations: drama/theater group, student-run newspaper, radio and television station, choral group, Dance Ensemble, Student Senate, Programming Board, academic clubs, national fraternities, national sororities.

Athletics Member NCAA. All Division II.

Campus security: 24-hour emergency response devices and patrols, late-night transport/escort service, controlled dormitory access.

Student services: health clinic, personal/psychological counseling.

COSTS & FINANCIAL AID

Costs (2017–18) *Tuition:* state resident $12,452 full-time, $518 per credit part-time; nonresident $23,268 full-time, $969 per credit part-time. Full-time tuition and fees vary according to program. Part-time tuition and fees vary according to program. *Required fees:* $936 full-time, $127 per term part-time. *Room and board:* $9684; room only: $5470. Room and board charges vary according to board plan and housing facility.

Financial Aid Of all full-time matriculated undergraduates who enrolled in 2016, 2,398 applied for aid, 2,017 were judged to have need, 293 had their need fully met. In 2016, 160 non-need-based awards were made. *Average percent of need met:* 59. *Average financial aid package:* $10,434. *Average need-based loan:* $4139. *Average need-based gift aid:* $7762. *Average non-need-based aid:* $3513. *Average indebtedness upon graduation:* $37,239.

APPLYING

Standardized Tests *Required:* SAT or ACT (for admission).

Options: electronic application, early admission, deferred entrance.

Required: high school transcript, minimum 2.0 GPA. *Recommended:* essay or personal statement, 3 letters of recommendation, interview.

CONTACT

Mr. Ryan Clancy, Office of Admissions, University of Pittsburgh at Johnstown, 157 Blackington Hall, Johnstown, PA 15904. *Phone:* 814-269-7050. *Toll-free phone:* 800-765-4875. *E-mail:* upjadmit@pitt.edu.

The University of Scranton

Scranton, Pennsylvania

http://www.scranton.edu/

- **Independent Roman Catholic (Jesuit)** comprehensive, founded 1888
- **Urban** 50-acre campus
- **Endowment** $187.2 million
- **Coed** 3,810 undergraduate students, 95% full-time, 58% women, 42% men
- **Moderately difficult** entrance level, 76% of applicants were admitted

UNDERGRAD STUDENTS

3,630 full-time, 180 part-time. Students come from 25 states and territories; 25 other countries; 61% are from out of state; 2% Black or African American, non-Hispanic/Latino; 9% Hispanic/Latino; 2% Asian, non-Hispanic/Latino; 0.2% Native Hawaiian or other Pacific Islander, non-Hispanic/Latino; 0.2% American Indian or Alaska Native, non-Hispanic/Latino; 2% Two or more races, non-Hispanic/Latino; 2% Race/ethnicity unknown; 1% international; 1% transferred in; 65% live on campus.

Freshmen:

Admission: 10,002 applied, 7,580 admitted, 903 enrolled. *Average high school GPA:* 3.5. *Test scores:* SAT evidence-based reading and writing scores over 500: 95%; SAT math scores over 500: 94%; ACT scores over 18: 99%; SAT evidence-based reading and writing scores over 600: 50%; SAT math scores over 600: 43%; ACT scores over 24: 72%; SAT evidence-based reading and writing scores over 700: 7%; SAT math scores over 700: 6%; ACT scores over 30: 12%.

Retention: 87% of full-time freshmen returned.

FACULTY

Total: 468, 60% full-time, 62% with terminal degrees.

Student/faculty ratio: 12:1.

ACADEMICS

Calendar: semesters. *Degrees:* certificates, bachelor's, master's, doctoral, post-master's, and postbachelor's certificates.

Special study options: academic remediation for entering students, accelerated degree program, adult/continuing education programs, advanced placement credit, distance learning, double majors, honors programs, independent study, internships, off-campus study, part-time degree program, services for LD students, student-designed majors, study abroad, summer session for credit. *ROTC:* Army (b), Air Force (c).

Computers: 988 computers/terminals are available on campus for general student use. Students can access the following: computer help desk, free student e-mail accounts, online (class) grades, online (class) registration, online (class) schedules. Campuswide network is available. 100% of college-owned or -operated housing units are wired for high-speed Internet access. Wireless service is available via classrooms, computer centers, computer labs, dorm rooms, learning centers, libraries, student centers.

Library: Harry and Jeanette Weinberg Memorial Library. *Books:* 331,804 (physical), 212,028 (digital/electronic); *Serial titles:* 2,677 (physical), 53,194 (digital/electronic); *Databases:* 120. Weekly public service hours: 95; study areas open 24 hours, 5–7 days a week; students can reserve study rooms.

STUDENT LIFE

Housing options: on-campus residence required through sophomore year; coed, men-only, women-only, special housing for students with disabilities. Campus housing is university owned. Freshman campus housing is guaranteed.

Activities and organizations: drama/theater group, student-run newspaper, radio and television station, choral group, Service-oriented student clubs, United Colors, Retreat Programs, Biology/Pre-Medicine clubs, Pre-Law Society.

Athletics Member NCAA. All Division III. *Intercollegiate sports:* baseball M, basketball M/W, crew M(c)/W(c), cross-country running M/W, equestrian sports M(c)/W(c), fencing M(c)/W(c), field hockey W, golf M/W, ice hockey M(c), lacrosse M/W, rugby M(c)/W(c), soccer M/W, softball W, swimming and diving M/W, tennis M/W, track and field M/W, ultimate Frisbee M(c)/W(c), volleyball M(c)/W, wrestling M. *Intramural sports:* archery M(c)/W(c), badminton M/W, basketball M/W, cheerleading M(c)/W(c), football M/W, skiing (downhill) M(c)/W(c), soccer M/W, softball M/W, ultimate Frisbee M/W, volleyball M/W.

Campus security: 24-hour emergency response devices and patrols, student patrols, late-night transport/escort service, controlled dormitory access, sprinkler systems in all University-owned housing.

Student services: health clinic, personal/psychological counseling, women's center.

COSTS & FINANCIAL AID

Costs (2017–18) *Comprehensive fee:* $57,928 includes full-time tuition ($42,910), mandatory fees ($400), and room and board ($14,618). *College room only:* $8562. Room and board charges vary according to board plan and housing facility. *Payment plan:* installment. *Waivers:* senior citizens and employees or children of employees.

Financial Aid Of all full-time matriculated undergraduates who enrolled in 2014, 3,169 applied for aid, 2,768 were judged to have need, 321 had their need fully met. 892 Federal Work-Study jobs (averaging $1959). 543 state and other part-time jobs (averaging $2018). In 2014, 687 non-need-based awards were made. *Average percent of need met:* 68. *Average financial aid package:* $25,053. *Average need-based loan:* $8363. *Average need-based gift aid:* $21,367. *Average non-need-based aid:* $13,699. *Average indebtedness upon graduation:* $40,640.

APPLYING

Standardized Tests *Required:* SAT or ACT (for admission).

Options: electronic application, early admission, early action, deferred entrance.

Required: essay or personal statement, high school transcript, 1 letter of recommendation. *Required for some:* interview.

Application deadlines: 3/1 (freshmen), rolling (transfers), 11/15 (early action).

Notification: continuous until 1/5 (freshmen), continuous (transfers), 12/15 (early action).

CONTACT

Mr. Joseph Roback, Associate Vice Provost, Admissions and Enrollment, The University of Scranton, The Estate Room 208, Scranton, PA 18510-4501. *Phone:* 570-941-7540. *Toll-free phone:* 888-SCRANTON. *Fax:* 570-941-5928. *E-mail:* admissions@scranton.edu.

The University of the Arts

Philadelphia, Pennsylvania

http://www.uarts.edu/

- **Independent** comprehensive, founded 1876
- **Urban** 21-acre campus with easy access to Philadelphia
- **Coed** 1,681 undergraduate students, 98% full-time, 62% women, 38% men
- **Moderately difficult** entrance level, 74% of applicants were admitted

UNDERGRAD STUDENTS

1,653 full-time, 28 part-time. Students come from 44 states and territories; 25 other countries; 58% are from out of state; 17% Black or African American, non-Hispanic/Latino; 11% Hispanic/Latino; 2% Asian, non-Hispanic/Latino; 0.1% Native Hawaiian or other Pacific Islander, non-Hispanic/Latino; 0.4% American Indian or Alaska Native, non-Hispanic/Latino; 4% Two or more races, non-Hispanic/Latino; 4% Race/ethnicity unknown; 4% international; 6% transferred in.

Freshmen:

Admission: 1,714 applied, 1,269 admitted, 410 enrolled.

Retention: 82% of full-time freshmen returned.

FACULTY

Total: 467, 23% full-time.

Student/faculty ratio: 8:1.

ACADEMICS

Calendar: semesters. *Degrees:* diplomas, bachelor's, master's, doctoral, and postbachelor's certificates.

Special study options: academic remediation for entering students, advanced placement credit, double majors, English as a second language, honors programs, independent study, internships, off-campus study, part-time degree program, services for LD students, study abroad, summer session for credit.

Computers: Students can access the following: campus intranet, computer help desk, free student e-mail accounts, online (class) grades, online (class) registration, online (class) schedules. Campuswide network is available. 100% of college-owned or -operated housing units are wired for high-speed Internet access. Wireless service is available via entire campus.

Library: Albert M. Greenfield Library plus 1 other.

STUDENT LIFE

Housing options: coed. Campus housing is university owned and leased by the school. Freshman applicants given priority for college housing.

Activities and organizations: drama/theater group, choral group.

Athletics *Intramural sports:* basketball M/W, fencing M/W.

Campus security: 24-hour emergency response devices and patrols, crime prevention workshops and seminars.

Student services: health clinic, personal/psychological counseling.

COSTS & FINANCIAL AID

Costs (2018–19) *Comprehensive fee:* $61,102 includes full-time tuition ($44,780) and room and board ($16,322). Part-time tuition: $1866 per credit hour. Part-time tuition and fees vary according to course load. *College room only:* $10,540. Room and board charges vary according to board plan and housing facility. *Payment plan:* installment. *Waivers:* children of alumni and employees or children of employees.

Financial Aid Of all full-time matriculated undergraduates who enrolled in 2017, 1,305 applied for aid, 1,305 were judged to have need, 149 had their need fully met. In 2017, 334 non-need-based awards were made. *Average percent of need met:* 62. *Average financial aid package:* $29,310. *Average need-based loan:* $4103. *Average need-based gift aid:* $24,377. *Average non-need-based aid:* $16,427. *Average indebtedness upon graduation:* $17,000.

APPLYING

Options: electronic application, early admission, deferred entrance.

Application fee: $60.

Required: high school transcript. *Required for some:* interview, audition or portfolio required for performing arts programs; portfolio for design, visual arts, film programs. *Recommended:* minimum 2.0 GPA.

Application deadlines: rolling (freshmen), rolling (out-of-state freshmen), rolling (transfers).

Notification: continuous (freshmen), continuous (out-of-state freshmen), continuous (transfers).

CONTACT

Ms. Kaitlyn Arillo, Director of Undergraduate Recruitment, The University of the Arts, 320 South Broad Street, Philadelphia, PA 19102-4944. *Phone:* 215-717-6017. *Toll-free phone:* 800-616-ARTS. *Fax:* 215-717-6045. *E-mail:* admissions@uarts.edu.

University of the Sciences
Philadelphia, Pennsylvania
http://www.usciences.edu/

CONTACT

Executive Director of Admission and Enrollment Services, University of the Sciences, 600 South 43rd Street, Philadelphia, PA 19104-4495. *Phone:* 888-996-8747. *Toll-free phone:* 888-996-8747. *Fax:* 215-596-8821. *E-mail:* admit@usciences.edu.

University of Valley Forge
Phoenixville, Pennsylvania
http://www.valleyforge.edu/

- **Independent Assemblies of God** comprehensive, founded 1939
- **Small-town** 150-acre campus with easy access to Philadelphia
- **Endowment** $2.6 million
- **Coed** 705 undergraduate students, 83% full-time, 53% women, 47% men
- **Minimally difficult** entrance level, 53% of applicants were admitted

UNDERGRAD STUDENTS

588 full-time, 116 part-time. Students come from 37 states and territories; 13 other countries; 56% are from out of state; 16% Black or African American, non-Hispanic/Latino; 17% Hispanic/Latino; 2% Asian, non-Hispanic/Latino; 0.3% American Indian or Alaska Native, non-Hispanic/Latino; 5% Two or more races, non-Hispanic/Latino; 4% Race/ethnicity unknown; 1% international; 7% transferred in; 70% live on campus.

Freshmen:
Admission: 498 applied, 265 admitted, 81 enrolled. *Average high school GPA:* 3.1.
Retention: 69% of full-time freshmen returned.

FACULTY

Total: 117, 21% full-time, 30% with terminal degrees.
Student/faculty ratio: 12:1.

ACADEMICS

Calendar: semesters. *Degrees:* associate, bachelor's, and master's.

Special study options: academic remediation for entering students, accelerated degree program, adult/continuing education programs, advanced placement credit, distance learning, double majors, external degree program, honors programs, independent study, internships, part-time degree program, services for LD students, study abroad, summer session for credit.

Computers: 59 computers/terminals and 3,000 ports are available on campus for general student use. Students can access the following: campus intranet, computer help desk, free student e-mail accounts, online (class) grades, online (class) registration, online (class) schedules. Campuswide network is available. 100% of college-owned or -operated housing units are wired for high-speed Internet access. Wireless service is available via entire campus.

Library: Storms Research Center. *Books:* 56,000 (physical), 175,000 (digital/electronic); *Serial titles:* 44 (physical); *Databases:* 48. Weekly public service hours: 81; students can reserve study rooms.

STUDENT LIFE

Housing options: on-campus residence required through senior year; men-only, women-only. Campus housing is university owned. Freshman campus housing is guaranteed.

Activities and organizations: drama/theater group, choral group, Homeless Ministry, The Art Of, Noteworthy, Inspire India, Audience of One.

Athletics Member NCAA, USCAA. All Division III. *Intercollegiate sports:* baseball M, basketball M/W, cross-country running M/W, golf M, soccer M/W, softball W, volleyball W. *Intramural sports:* basketball M/W, soccer M/W, table tennis M/W, ultimate Frisbee M/W, volleyball M/W.

Campus security: 24-hour emergency response devices and patrols, student patrols, late-night transport/escort service, controlled dormitory access.

Student services: health clinic, personal/psychological counseling.

COSTS & FINANCIAL AID

Costs (2018–19) *Comprehensive fee:* $31,324 includes full-time tuition ($20,266), mandatory fees ($1172), and room and board ($9886). Full-time tuition and fees vary according to course load and location. Part-time tuition and fees vary according to course load and location. *College room only:* $5386. Room and board charges vary according to board plan, housing facility, and location. *Payment plan:* installment. *Waivers:* employees or children of employees.

Financial Aid Of all full-time matriculated undergraduates who enrolled in 2016, 640 applied for aid, 583 were judged to have need, 69 had their need fully met. 18 Federal Work-Study jobs (averaging $2671). In 2016, 64 non-need-based awards were made. *Average percent of need met:* 56. *Average financial aid package:* $13,961. *Average need-based loan:* $4059. *Average need-based gift aid:* $10,584. *Average non-need-based aid:* $8222. *Average indebtedness upon graduation:* $34,920.

APPLYING

Standardized Tests *Recommended:* SAT or ACT (for admission).

Options: electronic application, deferred entrance.

Application fee: $25.

Required: essay or personal statement, high school transcript. *Required for some:* interview. *Recommended:* minimum 2.0 GPA.

Application deadlines: 8/1 (freshmen), 8/1 (transfers).

Notification: continuous (freshmen), continuous (transfers).

CONTACT
Claire M. Eiler, Director of Admissions, University of Valley Forge, 1401 Charlestown Road, Phoenixville, PA 19460. *Phone:* 610-610-917-1487 Ext. 1487. *Toll-free phone:* 800-432-8322. *Fax:* 610-610-917-2069 Ext. 2069. *E-mail:* admissions@valleyforge.edu.

Ursinus College

Collegeville, Pennsylvania

http://www.ursinus.edu/

- **Independent** 4-year, founded 1869
- **Suburban** 170-acre campus with easy access to Philadelphia
- **Endowment** $136.8 million
- **Coed** 1,507 undergraduate students, 99% full-time, 53% women, 47% men
- **Moderately difficult** entrance level, 78% of applicants were admitted

UNDERGRAD STUDENTS
1,489 full-time, 18 part-time. Students come from 31 states and territories; 20 other countries; 40% are from out of state; 7% Black or African American, non-Hispanic/Latino; 7% Hispanic/Latino; 4% Asian, non-Hispanic/Latino; 0.1% Native Hawaiian or other Pacific Islander, non-Hispanic/Latino; 0.1% American Indian or Alaska Native, non-Hispanic/Latino; 3% Two or more races, non-Hispanic/Latino; 2% Race/ethnicity unknown; 2% international; 1% transferred in; 94% live on campus.

Freshmen:
Admission: 3,488 applied, 2,728 admitted, 402 enrolled. *Average high school GPA:* 3.3. *Test scores:* SAT evidence-based reading and writing scores over 500: 93%; SAT math scores over 500: 95%; ACT scores over 18: 98%; SAT evidence-based reading and writing scores over 600: 57%; SAT math scores over 600: 54%; ACT scores over 24: 78%; SAT evidence-based reading and writing scores over 700: 12%; SAT math scores over 700: 8%; ACT scores over 30: 28%.

Retention: 85% of full-time freshmen returned.

FACULTY
Total: 171, 71% full-time, 80% with terminal degrees.

Student/faculty ratio: 11:1.

ACADEMICS
Calendar: semesters. *Degree:* bachelor's.

Special study options: advanced placement credit, cooperative education, double majors, English as a second language, honors programs, independent study, internships, off-campus study, services for LD students, student-designed majors, study abroad, summer session for credit.

Unusual degree programs: 3-2 engineering with Columbia University.

Computers: Students can access the following: campus intranet, computer help desk, free student e-mail accounts, online (class) grades, online (class) registration, online (class) schedules. Campuswide network is available. 100% of college-owned or -operated housing units are wired for high-speed Internet access. Wireless service is available via entire campus.

Library: Myrin Library. *Books:* 179,000 (physical), 220,588 (digital/electronic); *Serial titles:* 821 (physical), 22,371 (digital/electronic); *Databases:* 47. Weekly public service hours: 113.

STUDENT LIFE
Housing options: on-campus residence required through senior year; coed, men-only, women-only, special housing for students with disabilities. Campus housing is university owned. Freshman campus housing is guaranteed.

Activities and organizations: drama/theater group, student-run newspaper, radio and television station, choral group, Campus Activities Board, Ursinus College Student Government, Best Buddies, The Grizzly student newspaper, Gender Sexuality Alliance, national fraternities, national sororities.

Athletics Member NCAA. All Division III. *Intercollegiate sports:* baseball M, basketball M/W, cross-country running M/W, field hockey W, football M, golf M/W, gymnastics W, lacrosse M/W, soccer M/W, softball W, swimming and diving M/W, tennis M/W, track and field M/W, volleyball W, wrestling M. *Intramural sports:* badminton M/W, cheerleading M(c)/W(c), cross-country running M(c)/W(c), fencing M(c)/W(c), field hockey M/W, football M/W, rugby M(c)/W(c), sand volleyball M/W, soccer M(c)/W, triathlon M/W, ultimate Frisbee M(c)/W(c), volleyball M(c).

Campus security: 24-hour emergency response devices and patrols, student patrols, late-night transport/escort service, controlled dormitory access.

Student services: health clinic, personal/psychological counseling.

COSTS & FINANCIAL AID
Costs (2018–19) *Comprehensive fee:* $64,800 includes full-time tuition ($52,050) and room and board ($12,750). Part-time tuition: $1626 per credit hour. *Payment plan:* installment. *Waivers:* employees or children of employees.

Financial Aid Of all full-time matriculated undergraduates who enrolled in 2017, 1,256 applied for aid, 1,121 were judged to have need, 284 had their need fully met. 623 Federal Work-Study jobs (averaging $1879). In 2017, 345 non-need-based awards were made. *Average percent of need met:* 83. *Average financial aid package:* $40,845. *Average need-based loan:* $4792. *Average need-based gift aid:* $34,433. *Average non-need-based aid:* $24,065. *Average indebtedness upon graduation:* $39,026. *Financial aid deadline:* 2/1.

APPLYING
Standardized Tests *Required for some:* SAT or ACT (for admission).

Options: electronic application, early decision, early action, deferred entrance.

Required: essay or personal statement, high school transcript, 1 letter of recommendation. *Required for some:* home schooled students must include detailed information about the depth of their curriculum, including reading lists and standardized tests. *Recommended:* interview.

Application deadlines: rolling (freshmen), 8/1 (transfers), 11/1 (early action).

Early decision deadline: 12/1 (for plan 1), 2/1 (for plan 2).

Notification: continuous (freshmen), continuous (transfers), 12/15 (early decision plan 1), 3/15 (early decision plan 2), 12/15 (early action).

CONTACT
Scott Myers, Director of Admission, Ursinus College, 601 E. Main Street, Collegeville, PA 19426. *Phone:* 610-409-3200. *Fax:* 610-409-3197. *E-mail:* admissions@ursinus.edu.

 # Villanova University

Villanova, Pennsylvania

http://www.villanova.edu/

- **Independent Roman Catholic** comprehensive, founded 1842
- **Suburban** 254-acre campus with easy access to Philadelphia
- **Endowment** $640.0 million
- **Coed** 6,966 undergraduate students, 94% full-time, 53% women, 47% men
- **Very difficult** entrance level, 36% of applicants were admitted

UNDERGRAD STUDENTS
6,525 full-time, 441 part-time. Students come from 51 states and territories; 44 other countries; 79% are from out of state; 5% Black or African American, non-Hispanic/Latino; 8% Hispanic/Latino; 6% Asian, non-Hispanic/Latino; 0.1% American Indian or Alaska Native, non-Hispanic/Latino; 3% Two or more races, non-Hispanic/Latino; 2% Race/ethnicity unknown; 2% international; 2% transferred in; 66% live on campus.

Freshmen:
Admission: 21,112 applied, 7,594 admitted, 1,725 enrolled. *Average high school GPA:* 4.1. *Test scores:* SAT evidence-based reading and writing scores over 500: 99%; SAT math scores over 500: 99%; ACT scores over 18: 100%; SAT evidence-based reading and writing scores over 600: 87%; SAT math scores over 600: 86%; ACT scores over 24: 99%; SAT

evidence-based reading and writing scores over 700: 31%; SAT math scores over 700: 43%; ACT scores over 30: 81%.

Retention: 95% of full-time freshmen returned.

FACULTY
Total: 1,039, 59% full-time.
Student/faculty ratio: 11:1.

ACADEMICS
Calendar: semesters. *Degrees:* bachelor's, master's, doctoral, post-master's, and postbachelor's certificates.

Special study options: accelerated degree program, adult/continuing education programs, advanced placement credit, cooperative education, distance learning, double majors, English as a second language, external degree program, honors programs, independent study, internships, off-campus study, part-time degree program, services for LD students, study abroad, summer session for credit. *ROTC:* Army (b), Navy (b), Air Force (c).

Unusual degree programs: 3-2 engineering; arts/liberal studies, classical studies, communication, criminal justice, political science, psychology, Spanish, religious studies, computer science, biology, chemistry, mathematics, mathematics/applied statistics, human resources development, business information systems/software engineering.

Computers: 700 computers/terminals and 15,000 ports are available on campus for general student use. Students can access the following: campus intranet, computer help desk, free student e-mail accounts, online (class) grades, online (class) registration, online (class) schedules, learning management system with anti-plagiarism software, testing software, online faculty hours, videoconferencing, electronic portfolios, data vaulting/backup service, software. Campuswide network is available. 100% of college-owned or -operated housing units are wired for high-speed Internet access. Wireless service is available via entire campus.
Library: Falvey Memorial Library plus 1 other. Study areas open 24 hours, 5–7 days a week; students can reserve study rooms.

STUDENT LIFE
Housing options: coed, women-only, special housing for students with disabilities. Campus housing is university owned. Freshman campus housing is guaranteed.

Activities and organizations: drama/theater group, student-run newspaper, radio and television station, choral group, marching band, Blue Key Society, New Student Orientation Counselor Program, Special Olympics, Campus Activities Team, Student Government Association, national fraternities, national sororities.

Athletics Member NCAA. All Division I except football (Division I-AA). *Intercollegiate sports:* baseball M(s), basketball M(s)/W(s), cheerleading M/W, crew M(c)/W, cross-country running M(s)/W(s), equestrian sports W(c), field hockey W(s), golf M, ice hockey M(c)/W(c), lacrosse M(s)/W(s), sailing M(c)/W(c), skiing (downhill) M(c)/W(c), soccer M(s)/W(s), softball W(s), swimming and diving M/W(s), tennis M/W, track and field M(s)/W(s), volleyball M(c)/W(s), water polo M(c)/W. *Intramural sports:* badminton M(c)/W(c), baseball M(c), basketball M(c)/W(c), crew M(c), cross-country running M(c)/W(c), equestrian sports W(c), field hockey W(c), football M, golf M(c)/W(c), ice hockey M(c)/W(c), lacrosse M(c)/W(c), rugby M(c), sailing M(c)/W(c), skiing (downhill) M(c)/W(c), soccer M(c)/W(c), softball M/W, swimming and diving M(c)/W(c), tennis M(c)/W(c), ultimate Frisbee M(c)/W(c), volleyball M(c)/W(c), water polo M(c).

Campus security: 24-hour emergency response devices and patrols, late-night transport/escort service, controlled dormitory access, Nova Alert: email, text messaging for emergency situations.

Student services: health clinic, personal/psychological counseling.

COSTS & FINANCIAL AID
Costs (2017–18) *Comprehensive fee:* $64,832 includes full-time tuition ($50,554), mandatory fees ($730), and room and board ($13,548). Full-time tuition and fees vary according to degree level, location, and student level. Part-time tuition: $2809 per credit hour. Part-time tuition and fees vary according to class time, course load, degree level, location, and program. *Required fees:* $20 per credit hour part-time. *College room only:* $7218. Room and board charges vary according to board plan and housing facility. *Payment plan:* installment. *Waivers:* senior citizens and employees or children of employees.

Financial Aid Of all full-time matriculated undergraduates who enrolled in 2017, 3,919 applied for aid, 3,223 were judged to have need, 312 had their need fully met. 2,059 Federal Work-Study jobs (averaging $2842). 46 state and other part-time jobs (averaging $2967). In 2017, 498 non-need-based awards were made. *Average percent of need met:* 75. *Average financial aid package:* $36,683. *Average need-based loan:* $5104. *Average need-based gift aid:* $32,405. *Average non-need-based aid:* $16,497. *Average indebtedness upon graduation:* $34,752. *Financial aid deadline:* 1/15.

APPLYING
Standardized Tests *Required:* SAT or ACT (for admission).

Options: electronic application, early admission, early action, deferred entrance.

Application fee: $80.

Required: essay or personal statement, high school transcript, 1 letter of recommendation.

Application deadlines: 1/15 (freshmen), 6/1 (transfers), 11/1 (early action).

Notification: 4/1 (freshmen), continuous (transfers), 12/20 (early action).

CONTACT
Villanova University, 800 Lancaster Avenue, Villanova, PA 19085-1699.

Washington & Jefferson College
Washington, Pennsylvania
http://www.washjeff.edu/

- **Independent** comprehensive, founded 1781
- **Suburban** 60-acre campus with easy access to Pittsburgh
- **Endowment** $137.2 million
- **Coed** 1,405 undergraduate students, 100% full-time, 48% women, 52% men
- **Very difficult** entrance level, 48% of applicants were admitted

UNDERGRAD STUDENTS
1,398 full-time, 7 part-time. Students come from 32 states and territories; 37 other countries; 23% are from out of state; 5% Black or African American, non-Hispanic/Latino; 5% Hispanic/Latino; 2% Asian, non-Hispanic/Latino; 0.1% Native Hawaiian or other Pacific Islander, non-Hispanic/Latino; 0.2% American Indian or Alaska Native, non-Hispanic/Latino; 4% Two or more races, non-Hispanic/Latino; 5% Race/ethnicity unknown; 5% international; 0.6% transferred in; 94% live on campus.

Freshmen:
Admission: 5,358 applied, 2,564 admitted, 339 enrolled. *Average high school GPA:* 3.7. *Test scores:* SAT evidence-based reading and writing scores over 500: 96%; SAT math scores over 500: 95%; ACT scores over 18: 100%; SAT evidence-based reading and writing scores over 600: 62%; SAT math scores over 600: 46%; ACT scores over 24: 73%; SAT evidence-based reading and writing scores over 700: 6%; SAT math scores over 700: 12%; ACT scores over 30: 15%.
Retention: 87% of full-time freshmen returned.

FACULTY
Total: 162, 69% full-time, 77% with terminal degrees.
Student/faculty ratio: 11:1.

ACADEMICS
Calendar: 4-1-4. *Degrees:* bachelor's, master's, and postbachelor's certificates.

Special study options: academic remediation for entering students, accelerated degree program, advanced placement credit, double majors, English as a second language, freshman honors college, honors programs, independent study, internships, off-campus study, part-time degree program, services for LD students, student-designed majors, study abroad, summer session for credit. *ROTC:* Army (b), Air Force (c).

Unusual degree programs: 3-2 engineering with Columbia University, Case Western Reserve University, Washington University in St. Louis.

Computers: 450 computers/terminals and 2,000 ports are available on campus for general student use. Students can access the following: campus intranet, computer help desk, free student e-mail accounts, online (class) grades, online (class) registration, online (class) schedules.

Campuswide network is available. 100% of college-owned or -operated housing units are wired for high-speed Internet access. Wireless service is available via entire campus.

Library: U. Grant Miller Library plus 4 others. *Books:* 128,645 (physical), 6,440 (digital/electronic); *Serial titles:* 238 (physical), 47,598 (digital/electronic); *Databases:* 77. Weekly public service hours: 107.

STUDENT LIFE

Housing options: on-campus residence required through senior year; coed, men-only, women-only, special housing for students with disabilities. Campus housing is university owned. Freshman campus housing is guaranteed.

Activities and organizations: drama/theater group, student-run newspaper, radio station, choral group, Student Government Association, Student Activities Board, Black Student Union, Mock Trial, Latino Culture Association, national fraternities, national sororities.

Athletics Member NCAA. All Division III. *Intercollegiate sports:* baseball M, basketball M/W, cheerleading M(c)/W(c), cross-country running M/W, equestrian sports M(c)/W(c), field hockey W, football M, golf M/W, ice hockey M(c), lacrosse M/W, rugby M(c)/W(c), soccer M/W, softball W, swimming and diving M/W, tennis M/W, track and field M/W, ultimate Frisbee M(c)/W(c), volleyball M(c)/W, water polo M/W, wrestling M. *Intramural sports:* basketball M/W, soccer M/W, tennis M/W, triathlon M/W, volleyball M/W.

Campus security: 24-hour emergency response devices and patrols, late-night transport/escort service, controlled dormitory access, security cameras monitored 24/7 throughout campus.

Student services: health clinic, personal/psychological counseling, women's center.

COSTS & FINANCIAL AID

Costs (2017–18) *Comprehensive fee:* $58,946 includes full-time tuition ($46,048), mandatory fees ($580), and room and board ($12,318). Full-time tuition and fees vary according to reciprocity agreements. Part-time tuition: $1155 per credit hour. Part-time tuition and fees vary according to course load. *College room only:* $7228. Room and board charges vary according to board plan and housing facility. *Payment plans:* tuition prepayment, installment. *Waivers:* employees or children of employees.

Financial Aid Of all full-time matriculated undergraduates who enrolled in 2017, 1,178 applied for aid, 1,079 were judged to have need, 109 had their need fully met. 672 Federal Work-Study jobs (averaging $1579). 195 state and other part-time jobs (averaging $1476). In 2017, 275 non-need-based awards were made. *Average percent of need met:* 77. *Average financial aid package:* $37,503. *Average need-based loan:* $4631. *Average need-based gift aid:* $12,202. *Average non-need-based aid:* $20,989. *Average indebtedness upon graduation:* $54,184.

APPLYING

Options: electronic application, early admission, early decision, early action, deferred entrance.

Application fee: $25.

Required: essay or personal statement, high school transcript, 1 letter of recommendation. *Required for some:* interview. *Recommended:* interview.

Application deadlines: 3/1 (freshmen), 1/15 (early action).

Early decision deadline: 12/1.

Notification: 4/1 (freshmen), 12/15 (early decision), 2/15 (early action).

CONTACT

Mr. Robert J. Gould, Vice President for Enrollment, Washington & Jefferson College, 60 South Lincoln Street, Washington, PA 15301. *Phone:* 724-223-6025. *Toll-free phone:* 888-WANDJAY. *Fax:* 724-223-6534. *E-mail:* admission@washjeff.edu.

Waynesburg University

Waynesburg, Pennsylvania

http://www.waynesburg.edu/

- **Independent** comprehensive, founded 1849, affiliated with Presbyterian Church (U.S.A.)
- **Small-town** 30-acre campus with easy access to Pittsburgh
- **Coed** 1,376 undergraduate students, 97% full-time, 59% women, 41% men
- **Moderately difficult** entrance level, 95% of applicants were admitted

UNDERGRAD STUDENTS

1,330 full-time, 46 part-time. Students come from 33 states and territories; 4 other countries; 21% are from out of state; 4% Black or African American, non-Hispanic/Latino; 2% Hispanic/Latino; 0.8% Asian, non-Hispanic/Latino; 0.2% American Indian or Alaska Native, non-Hispanic/Latino; 3% Two or more races, non-Hispanic/Latino; 4% Race/ethnicity unknown; 0.1% international; 2% transferred in; 79% live on campus.

Freshmen:
Admission: 1,608 applied, 1,533 admitted, 400 enrolled. *Average high school GPA:* 3.6.
Retention: 76% of full-time freshmen returned.

FACULTY

Total: 211, 37% full-time, 40% with terminal degrees.
Student/faculty ratio: 13:1.

ACADEMICS

Calendar: semesters. *Degrees:* bachelor's, master's, and doctoral.

Special study options: accelerated degree program, adult/continuing education programs, advanced placement credit, distance learning, double majors, honors programs, independent study, internships, part-time degree program, services for LD students, study abroad, summer session for credit. *ROTC:* Army (c).

Unusual degree programs: 3-2 engineering with Penn State University Park.

Computers: 160 computers/terminals are available on campus for general student use. Students can access the following: campus intranet, computer help desk, free student e-mail accounts, online (class) grades, online (class) registration, online (class) schedules. Campuswide network is available. 100% of college-owned or -operated housing units are wired for high-speed Internet access. Wireless service is available via classrooms, computer labs, dorm rooms, learning centers, libraries, student centers.

Library: Eberly Library. *Books:* 72,027 (physical), 149,845 (digital/electronic); *Serial titles:* 144 (physical), 101,518 (digital/electronic); *Databases:* 55.

STUDENT LIFE

Housing options: on-campus residence required through junior year; men-only, women-only, special housing for students with disabilities. Campus housing is university owned. Freshman campus housing is guaranteed.

Activities and organizations: drama/theater group, student-run newspaper, radio and television station, choral group, Student-Pennsylvania State Education Association, Lamplighter Choir, Student Nurses Association, Christian Fellowship.

Athletics Member NCAA. All Division III. *Intercollegiate sports:* baseball M, basketball M/W, cross-country running M/W, football M, golf M/W, lacrosse W, soccer M/W, softball W, tennis M/W, track and field M/W, volleyball W, wrestling M. *Intramural sports:* basketball M/W, bowling M/W, racquetball M/W, softball M/W, table tennis M/W, volleyball M/W.

Campus security: 24-hour emergency response devices and patrols, late-night transport/escort service, controlled dormitory access.

Student services: health clinic, personal/psychological counseling.

COSTS & FINANCIAL AID

Costs (2017–18) *Comprehensive fee:* $33,830 includes full-time tuition ($23,160), mandatory fees ($850), and room and board ($9820). Full-time tuition and fees vary according to class time. Part-time tuition: $960 per credit hour. Part-time tuition and fees vary according to class time, course load, and location. *Required fees:* $16 per credit hour part-time. *College room only:* $4970. Room and board charges vary according to board plan and housing facility. *Payment plan:* installment. *Waivers:* employees or children of employees.

Financial Aid Of all full-time matriculated undergraduates who enrolled in 2017, 1,242 applied for aid, 1,110 were judged to have need, 327 had their need fully met. 600 Federal Work-Study jobs (averaging $1500). In 2017, 219 non-need-based awards were made. *Average percent of need met:* 80. *Average financial aid package:* $19,900. *Average need-based loan:* $5000. *Average need-based gift aid:* $15,250. *Average non-need-based aid:* $11,200. *Average indebtedness upon graduation:* $31,000.

APPLYING

Standardized Tests *Required:* SAT or ACT (for admission).

Options: electronic application, early admission.

Application fee: $20.

Required: high school transcript, minimum 2.8 GPA. *Required for some:* essay or personal statement, 2 letters of recommendation. *Recommended:* minimum 3.0 GPA, interview.

Application deadlines: rolling (freshmen), rolling (transfers).

Notification: continuous (freshmen), continuous (transfers).

CONTACT

Mrs. Jacqueline Palko, Director of Admissions, Waynesburg University, 51 West College Street, Waynesburg, PA 15370. *Phone:* 724-852-3216. *Toll-free phone:* 800-225-7393. *Fax:* 724-627-8124. *E-mail:* admissions@waynesburg.edu.

West Chester University of Pennsylvania

West Chester, Pennsylvania

http://www.wcupa.edu/

- **State-supported** comprehensive, founded 1871, part of Pennsylvania State System of Higher Education
- **Suburban** 409-acre campus with easy access to Philadelphia
- **Endowment** $23.5 million
- **Coed** 14,451 undergraduate students, 90% full-time, 59% women, 41% men
- **Moderately difficult** entrance level, 69% of applicants were admitted

UNDERGRAD STUDENTS

13,020 full-time, 1,431 part-time. Students come from 35 states and territories; 82 other countries; 11% are from out of state; 11% Black or African American, non-Hispanic/Latino; 6% Hispanic/Latino; 2% Asian, non-Hispanic/Latino; 0.1% Native Hawaiian or other Pacific Islander, non-Hispanic/Latino; 0.1% American Indian or Alaska Native, non-Hispanic/Latino; 3% Two or more races, non-Hispanic/Latino; 1% Race/ethnicity unknown; 0.4% international; 9% transferred in; 36% live on campus.

Freshmen:

Admission: 12,667 applied, 8,677 admitted, 2,630 enrolled. *Average high school GPA:* 3.4. *Test scores:* SAT evidence-based reading and writing scores over 500: 89%; SAT math scores over 500: 85%; ACT scores over 18: 97%; SAT evidence-based reading and writing scores over 600: 32%; SAT math scores over 600: 27%; ACT scores over 24: 49%; SAT evidence-based reading and writing scores over 700: 3%; SAT math scores over 700: 2%; ACT scores over 30: 6%.

Retention: 85% of full-time freshmen returned.

FACULTY

Total: 952, 73% full-time, 69% with terminal degrees.

Student/faculty ratio: 19:1.

ACADEMICS

Calendar: semesters. *Degrees:* bachelor's, master's, doctoral, and postbachelor's certificates.

Special study options: academic remediation for entering students, accelerated degree program, adult/continuing education programs, advanced placement credit, distance learning, double majors, English as a second language, freshman honors college, honors programs, independent study, internships, off-campus study, part-time degree program, services for LD students, student-designed majors, study abroad, summer session for credit. *ROTC:* Army (b), Air Force (c).

Unusual degree programs: 3-2 engineering with Pennsylvania State University, Philadelphia University.

Computers: 2,700 computers/terminals are available on campus for general student use. Students can access the following: campus intranet, computer help desk, free student e-mail accounts, online (class) grades, online (class) registration, online (class) schedules, virtual software. Campuswide network is available. 100% of college-owned or -operated housing units are wired for high-speed Internet access. Wireless service is available via entire campus.

Library: Francis Harvey Green Library plus 1 other. *Books:* 719,762 (physical), 1.0 million (digital/electronic); *Serial titles:* 1,952 (physical), 101,028 (digital/electronic); *Databases:* 208. Weekly public service hours: 107; study areas open 24 hours, 5–7 days a week.

STUDENT LIFE

Housing options: coed, special housing for students with disabilities. Campus housing is university owned and is provided by a third party. Freshman applicants given priority for college housing.

Activities and organizations: drama/theater group, student-run newspaper, radio and television station, choral group, marching band, Student Government Association, Residence Hall Association, Fraternal Programming Board, Sports Club Council, CRU, national fraternities, national sororities.

Athletics Member NCAA. All Division II. *Intercollegiate sports:* baseball M(s), basketball M(s)/W(s), bowling M(c)/W(c), cheerleading W, equestrian sports M(c)/W(c), fencing M(c)/W(c), field hockey W(s), football M(s), golf M(s)/W(s), gymnastics W(s), ice hockey M(c)/W(c), lacrosse M(c)/W(s), rugby M(c)/W(s), skiing (downhill) M(c)/W(c), soccer M(s)/W(s), softball W(s), swimming and diving M(s)/W(s), tennis M(s)/W(s), track and field M(s)/W(s), volleyball M(c)/W(s), water polo M/W(c), wrestling M(c). *Intramural sports:* badminton M/W, basketball M/W, football M/W, racquetball M/W, rock climbing M/W, sand volleyball M/W, soccer M/W, softball M/W, table tennis M/W, tennis M/W, ultimate Frisbee M/W, volleyball M/W.

Campus security: 24-hour emergency response devices and patrols, late-night transport/escort service, controlled dormitory access, camera systems in campus residence halls, recreational and classroom facilities and outdoor areas.

Student services: health clinic, personal/psychological counseling, women's center, legal services.

COSTS & FINANCIAL AID

Costs (2017–18) *Tuition:* state resident $7492 full-time, $312 per credit part-time; nonresident $18,730 full-time, $780 per credit part-time. Full-time tuition and fees vary according to location. Part-time tuition and fees vary according to location. *Required fees:* $2619 full-time, $110 per credit part-time. *Room and board:* $9060; room only: $5408. Room and board charges vary according to board plan and housing facility. *Payment plan:* installment. *Waivers:* senior citizens and employees or children of employees.

Financial Aid Of all full-time matriculated undergraduates who enrolled in 2016, 10,070 applied for aid, 7,575 were judged to have need, 670 had their need fully met. 295 Federal Work-Study jobs (averaging $1644). In 2016, 205 non-need-based awards were made. *Average percent of need met:* 49. *Average financial aid package:* $8180. *Average need-based loan:* $4227. *Average need-based gift aid:* $5651. *Average non-need-based aid:* $4265. *Average indebtedness upon graduation:* $34,160.

APPLYING

Standardized Tests *Required:* SAT or ACT (for admission).

Options: electronic application.

Application fee: $45.

Required: essay or personal statement, high school transcript. *Required for some:* interview. *Recommended:* minimum 3.0 GPA.

Application deadlines: rolling (freshmen), rolling (out-of-state freshmen), rolling (transfers).

Notification: continuous (freshmen), continuous (out-of-state freshmen), continuous (transfers).

CONTACT

West Chester University of Pennsylvania, University Avenue and High Street, West Chester, PA 19383. *Phone:* 610-436-3411. *Toll-free phone:* 877-315-2165.

Westminster College

New Wilmington, Pennsylvania
http://www.westminster.edu/

- **Independent** comprehensive, founded 1852, affiliated with Presbyterian Church (U.S.A.)
- **Small-town** 350-acre campus with easy access to Pittsburgh
- **Endowment** $110.1 million
- **Coed** 1,192 undergraduate students, 98% full-time, 53% women, 47% men
- **Moderately difficult** entrance level, 72% of applicants were admitted

UNDERGRAD STUDENTS
1,171 full-time, 21 part-time. Students come from 32 states and territories; 2 other countries; 34% are from out of state; 5% Black or African American, non-Hispanic/Latino; 2% Hispanic/Latino; 0.9% Asian, non-Hispanic/Latino; 0.1% Native Hawaiian or other Pacific Islander, non-Hispanic/Latino; 0.3% American Indian or Alaska Native, non-Hispanic/Latino; 0.8% Two or more races, non-Hispanic/Latino; 21% Race/ethnicity unknown; 0.6% international; 1% transferred in; 75% live on campus.

Freshmen:
Admission: 2,874 applied, 2,083 admitted, 332 enrolled. *Average high school GPA:* 3.6. *Test scores:* SAT evidence-based reading and writing scores over 500: 77%; SAT math scores over 500: 73%; ACT scores over 18: 89%; SAT evidence-based reading and writing scores over 600: 36%; SAT math scores over 600: 25%; ACT scores over 24: 53%; SAT evidence-based reading and writing scores over 700: 4%; SAT math scores over 700: 3%; ACT scores over 30: 10%.

Retention: 78% of full-time freshmen returned.

FACULTY
Total: 144, 63% full-time, 65% with terminal degrees.
Student/faculty ratio: 11:1.

ACADEMICS
Calendar: semesters. *Degrees:* bachelor's and master's.

Special study options: adult/continuing education programs, advanced placement credit, distance learning, double majors, honors programs, independent study, internships, off-campus study, part-time degree program, services for LD students, student-designed majors, study abroad, summer session for credit. *ROTC:* Army (c).

Unusual degree programs: 3-2 engineering with Penn State University Park, Washington University in St. Louis, Case Western Reserve University.

Computers: 144 computers/terminals and 1,175 ports are available on campus for general student use. Students can access the following: campus intranet, computer help desk, free student e-mail accounts, online (class) grades, online (class) registration, online (class) schedules. Campuswide network is available. 100% of college-owned or -operated housing units are wired for high-speed Internet access. Wireless service is available via entire campus.

Library: McGill Memorial Library plus 1 other. *Books:* 160,296 (physical), 771,138 (digital/electronic); *Serial titles:* 89 (physical), 30,100 (digital/electronic); *Databases:* 70. Weekly public service hours: 104; students can reserve study rooms.

STUDENT LIFE
Housing options: on-campus residence required through junior year; coed, men-only, women-only. Campus housing is university owned. Freshman campus housing is guaranteed.

Activities and organizations: drama/theater group, student-run newspaper, radio and television station, choral group, marching band, Student Government Association, Interfraternity Council/Panhellenic Council, Dance Theatre, Habitat for Humanity, Campus Programming Council, national fraternities, national sororities.

Athletics Member NCAA. All Division III. *Intercollegiate sports:* baseball M, basketball M/W, cross-country running M/W, equestrian sports M(c)/W(c), football M, golf M/W, ice hockey M(c), lacrosse M/W, rock climbing M(c)/W(c), skiing (downhill) M(c)/W(c), soccer M/W, softball M, swimming and diving M/W, tennis M/W, track and field M/W, ultimate Frisbee M(c)/W(c), volleyball W. *Intramural sports:* archery M/W, badminton M/W, basketball M/W, cross-country running M/W, football M, golf M/W, racquetball M/W, skiing (cross-country) M/W,

skiing (downhill) M/W, softball M, swimming and diving M/W, tennis M/W, track and field W, volleyball W, weight lifting M/W.

Campus security: 24-hour emergency response devices and patrols, late-night transport/escort service, controlled dormitory access.

Student services: health clinic, personal/psychological counseling.

COSTS & FINANCIAL AID
Costs (2017–18) *Comprehensive fee:* $47,250 includes full-time tuition ($34,830), mandatory fees ($1400), and room and board ($11,020). Part-time tuition: $1125 per credit hour. *Room and board:* Room and board charges vary according to board plan and housing facility. *Payment plan:* installment. *Waivers:* employees or children of employees.

Financial Aid Of all full-time matriculated undergraduates who enrolled in 2016, 1,047 applied for aid, 969 were judged to have need, 185 had their need fully met. 304 Federal Work-Study jobs (averaging $1711). 77 state and other part-time jobs (averaging $1706). In 2016, 168 non-need-based awards were made. *Average percent of need met:* 83. *Average financial aid package:* $29,959. *Average need-based loan:* $4508. *Average need-based gift aid:* $25,465. *Average non-need-based aid:* $18,337. *Average indebtedness upon graduation:* $43,241.

APPLYING
Standardized Tests *Required:* SAT or ACT (for admission).

Options: electronic application, deferred entrance.

Application fee: $35.

Required: essay or personal statement, high school transcript, minimum 2.0 GPA, 2 letters of recommendation. *Recommended:* minimum 3.0 GPA, interview.

Application deadlines: 5/1 (freshmen), rolling (transfers).

Notification: continuous (freshmen), continuous (transfers).

CONTACT
Dr. Thomas H. Stein, Vice President for Enrollment Management, Westminster College, Remick House, 319 S. Market Street, New Wilmington, PA 16172. *Phone:* 724-946-7105. *Toll-free phone:* 800-942-8033. *Fax:* 724-946-7171. *E-mail:* steinth@westminster.edu.

Widener University

Chester, Pennsylvania
http://www.widener.edu/

- **Independent** comprehensive, founded 1821
- **Suburban** 110-acre campus with easy access to Philadelphia
- **Endowment** $87.1 million
- **Coed** 3,427 undergraduate students, 85% full-time, 57% women, 43% men
- **Moderately difficult** entrance level, 65% of applicants were admitted

UNDERGRAD STUDENTS
2,919 full-time, 508 part-time. 40% are from out of state; 13% Black or African American, non-Hispanic/Latino; 5% Hispanic/Latino; 4% Asian, non-Hispanic/Latino; 0.1% American Indian or Alaska Native, non-Hispanic/Latino; 3% Two or more races, non-Hispanic/Latino; 2% Race/ethnicity unknown; 3% international; 3% transferred in; 55% live on campus.

Freshmen:
Admission: 6,045 applied, 3,955 admitted, 787 enrolled. *Average high school GPA:* 3.5. *Test scores:* SAT evidence-based reading and writing scores over 500: 80%; SAT math scores over 500: 80%; ACT scores over 18: 93%; SAT evidence-based reading and writing scores over 600: 22%; SAT math scores over 600: 23%; ACT scores over 24: 40%; SAT evidence-based reading and writing scores over 700: 3%; SAT math scores over 700: 3%; ACT scores over 30: 5%.

Retention: 80% of full-time freshmen returned.

FACULTY
Total: 622, 44% full-time, 58% with terminal degrees.
Student/faculty ratio: 14:1.

ACADEMICS
Calendar: semesters. *Degrees:* associate, bachelor's, master's, doctoral, and post-master's certificates.

Special study options: academic remediation for entering students, accelerated degree program, adult/continuing education programs,

advanced placement credit, cooperative education, distance learning, double majors, English as a second language, honors programs, independent study, internships, off-campus study, part-time degree program, services for LD students, student-designed majors, study abroad, summer session for credit. *ROTC:* Army (b), Navy (c), Air Force (c).

Unusual degree programs: 3-2 business administration; engineering; social work; physical therapy, education.

Computers: Students can access the following: campus intranet, computer help desk, free student e-mail accounts, online (class) grades, online (class) registration, online (class) schedules. Campuswide network is available. 100% of college-owned or -operated housing units are wired for high-speed Internet access. Wireless service is available via classrooms, computer centers, computer labs, dorm rooms, learning centers, libraries, student centers.
Library: Wolfgram Memorial Library.

STUDENT LIFE
Housing options: on-campus residence required through junior year; coed, men-only, women-only, cooperative. Campus housing is university owned. Freshman campus housing is guaranteed.

Activities and organizations: drama/theater group, student-run television station, choral group, marching band, national fraternities, national sororities.

Athletics Member NCAA. All Division III. *Intercollegiate sports:* baseball M, basketball M/W, cheerleading W, cross-country running M/W, field hockey W, football M, golf M/W, lacrosse M/W, soccer M/W, softball W, swimming and diving M/W, track and field M/W, volleyball M/W. *Intramural sports:* ice hockey M(c), rugby M(c)/W(c), soccer M(c), volleyball M(c).

Campus security: 24-hour emergency response devices and patrols, late-night transport/escort service, controlled dormitory access.

Student services: health clinic, personal/psychological counseling.

COSTS & FINANCIAL AID
Costs (2017–18) *Comprehensive fee:* $58,190 includes full-time tuition ($43,296), mandatory fees ($870), and room and board ($14,024). Full-time tuition and fees vary according to class time, course load, and program. Part-time tuition: $1442 per credit hour. *College room only:*

$7300. Room and board charges vary according to board plan and housing facility. *Payment plan:* installment. *Waivers:* senior citizens and employees or children of employees.

Financial Aid Of all full-time matriculated undergraduates who enrolled in 2017, 2,543 applied for aid, 2,324 were judged to have need, 526 had their need fully met. 1,574 Federal Work-Study jobs (averaging $1950). In 2017, 439 non-need-based awards were made. *Average percent of need met:* 79. *Average financial aid package:* $33,521. *Average need-based loan:* $4815. *Average need-based gift aid:* $27,827. *Average non-need-based aid:* $23,211.

APPLYING
Standardized Tests *Required:* SAT or ACT (for admission).

Options: electronic application, deferred entrance.

Required: essay or personal statement, high school transcript. *Required for some:* minimum 2.9 GPA. *Recommended:* interview.

Application deadlines: rolling (freshmen), rolling (transfers).

Notification: continuous (freshmen), continuous (transfers).

CONTACT
Office of Admissions, Widener University, One University Place, Chester, PA 19013. *Phone:* 610-499-4126. *Toll-free phone:* 888-WIDENER. *Fax:* 610-499-4676. *E-mail:* admissions.office@widener.edu.

Wilkes University
Wilkes-Barre, Pennsylvania
http://www.wilkes.edu/

- **Independent** comprehensive, founded 1933
- **Urban** 25-acre campus
- **Endowment** $47.7 million
- **Coed** 2,491 undergraduate students, 90% full-time, 47% women, 53% men
- **Moderately difficult** entrance level, 75% of applicants were admitted

UNDERGRAD STUDENTS
2,233 full-time, 258 part-time. Students come from 23 states and territories; 12 other countries; 19% are from out of state; 5% Black or

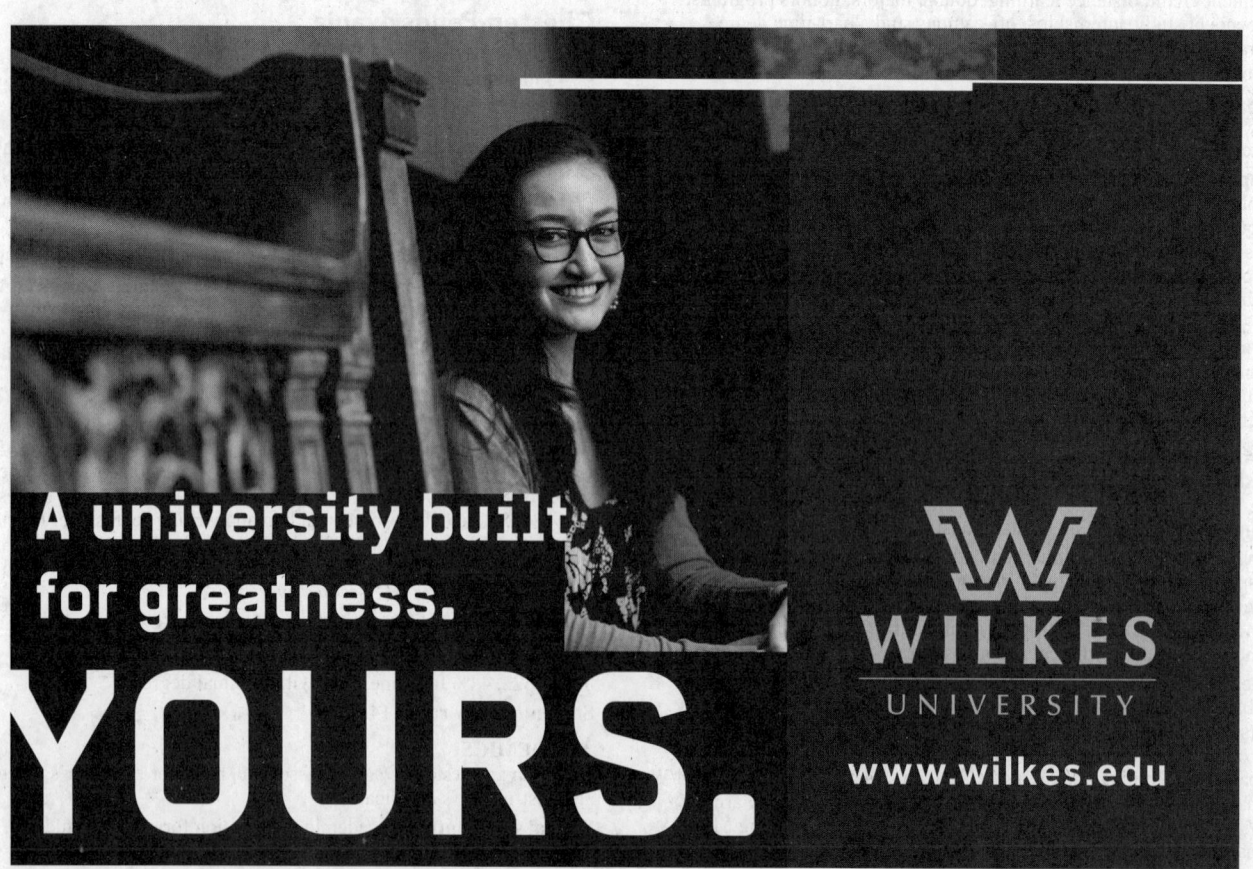

African American, non-Hispanic/Latino; 6% Hispanic/Latino; 2% Asian, non-Hispanic/Latino; 0.1% Native Hawaiian or other Pacific Islander, non-Hispanic/Latino; 0.4% American Indian or Alaska Native, non-Hispanic/Latino; 3% Two or more races, non-Hispanic/Latino; 3% Race/ethnicity unknown; 9% international; 7% transferred in; 41% live on campus.

Freshmen:
Admission: 4,067 applied, 3,063 admitted, 607 enrolled. *Average high school GPA:* 3.5. *Test scores:* SAT evidence-based reading and writing scores over 500: 86%; SAT math scores over 500: 84%; ACT scores over 18: 91%; SAT evidence-based reading and writing scores over 600: 33%; SAT math scores over 600: 31%; ACT scores over 24: 53%; SAT evidence-based reading and writing scores over 700: 2%; SAT math scores over 700: 4%; ACT scores over 30: 7%.
Retention: 76% of full-time freshmen returned.

FACULTY
Total: 416, 43% full-time.
Student/faculty ratio: 14:1.

ACADEMICS
Calendar: semesters. *Degrees:* bachelor's, master's, and doctoral.
Special study options: academic remediation for entering students, accelerated degree program, adult/continuing education programs, advanced placement credit, cooperative education, distance learning, double majors, English as a second language, honors programs, independent study, internships, off-campus study, part-time degree program, services for LD students, student-designed majors, study abroad, summer session for credit. *ROTC:* Army (c), Air Force (b).
Computers: 860 computers/terminals are available on campus for general student use. Students can access the following: campus intranet, computer help desk, free student e-mail accounts, online (class) grades, online (class) registration, online (class) schedules. Campuswide network is available. Wireless service is available via classrooms, dorm rooms, libraries, student centers.
Library: Eugene S. Farley Library. *Books:* 184,565 (physical), 8,000 (digital/electronic); *Serial titles:* 60,000 (digital/electronic); *Databases:* 88. Students can reserve study rooms.

STUDENT LIFE
Housing options: on-campus residence required through sophomore year; coed, men-only, women-only. Campus housing is university owned. Freshman campus housing is guaranteed.
Activities and organizations: drama/theater group, student-run newspaper, radio and television station, choral group, marching band.
Athletics Member NCAA. All Division III. *Intercollegiate sports:* baseball M, basketball M/W, cross-country running M/W, field hockey W, football M, golf M/W, ice hockey M/W, lacrosse M/W, soccer M/W, softball W, swimming and diving M/W, tennis M/W, volleyball M/W, wrestling M. *Intramural sports:* basketball M/W, cheerleading W(c), cross-country running M(c)/W(c), football M, racquetball M(c)/W(c), rock climbing M(c)/W(c), skiing (downhill) M(c)/W(c), softball M/W, ultimate Frisbee M(c)/W(c), volleyball M/W.
Campus security: 24-hour emergency response devices and patrols, late-night transport/escort service, controlled dormitory access.
Student services: health clinic, personal/psychological counseling.

COSTS & FINANCIAL AID
Costs (2017–18) *Comprehensive fee:* $49,166 includes full-time tuition ($33,208), mandatory fees ($1688), and room and board ($14,270). Part-time tuition: $922 per credit hour. *Required fees:* $74 per credit hour part-time. *College room only:* $8600. Room and board charges vary according to board plan and housing facility. *Payment plans:* installment, deferred payment. *Waivers:* employees or children of employees.
Financial Aid Of all full-time matriculated undergraduates who enrolled in 2017, 1,887 applied for aid, 1,782 were judged to have need, 231 had their need fully met. In 2017, 216 non-need-based awards were made. *Average percent of need met:* 71. *Average financial aid package:* $25,457. *Average need-based loan:* $4348. *Average need-based gift aid:* $21,706. *Average non-need-based aid:* $14,482. *Average indebtedness upon graduation:* $47,907.

APPLYING
Standardized Tests *Required:* SAT or ACT (for admission).

Options: electronic application, early admission, deferred entrance.
Application fee: $40.
Required: high school transcript. *Recommended:* interview.
Application deadlines: rolling (freshmen), rolling (transfers).
Notification: 8/30 (freshmen), continuous until 8/30 (transfers).

CONTACT
Terese Wignot, Associate Provost Enrollment, Wilkes University, 84 West South Street, Wilkes-Barre, PA 18766. *Phone:* 570-408-4400. *Toll-free phone:* 800-945-5378 Ext. 4400. *Fax:* 570-408-4904. *E-mail:* admissions@wilkes.edu.

See previous page for display ad and page 1506 for the College Close-Up.

Wilson College
Chambersburg, Pennsylvania
http://www.wilson.edu/
- **Independent** comprehensive, founded 1869, affiliated with Presbyterian Church (U.S.A.)
- **Small-town** 300-acre campus
- **Endowment** $51.3 million
- **Coed, primarily women**
- **Moderately difficult** entrance level

FACULTY
Student/faculty ratio: 8:1.

ACADEMICS
Calendar: 4-1-4. *Degrees:* associate, bachelor's, and master's.
Library: Stewart Library. Weekly public service hours: 88; students can reserve study rooms.

STUDENT LIFE
Housing options: on-campus residence required through junior year; women-only. Campus housing is university owned. Freshman campus housing is guaranteed.
Activities and organizations: drama/theater group, student-run newspaper, choral group, Muhibbah Club, Orchesis Club, student newspaper, Student Government, Campus Activity Board.
Athletics Member NCAA. All Division III.
Campus security: 24-hour emergency response devices and patrols, late-night transport/escort service, controlled dormitory access.
Student services: health clinic, personal/psychological counseling, women's center.

COSTS & FINANCIAL AID
Costs (2017–18) *Comprehensive fee:* $35,816 includes full-time tuition ($23,745), mandatory fees ($707), and room and board ($11,364). Full-time tuition and fees vary according to location and program. Part-time tuition: $792 per semester hour. Part-time tuition and fees vary according to course load, location, and program. *Required fees:* $40 per semester hour part-time. *College room only:* $5390. Room and board charges vary according to board plan and housing facility.
Financial Aid Of all full-time matriculated undergraduates who enrolled in 2015, 449 applied for aid, 422 were judged to have need, 68 had their need fully met. 37 Federal Work-Study jobs (averaging $2000). 140 state and other part-time jobs (averaging $2000). In 2015, 14 non-need-based awards were made. *Average percent of need met:* 75. *Average financial aid package:* $21,589. *Average need-based loan:* $4857. *Average need-based gift aid:* $17,520. *Average non-need-based aid:* $9367. *Average indebtedness upon graduation:* $31,613.

APPLYING
Standardized Tests *Required for some:* SAT or ACT (for admission), TOEFL/IELTS/STEP for international students.
Options: electronic application, early admission, deferred entrance.
Required: essay or personal statement, high school transcript, 1 letter of recommendation, college preparatory program that includes 4 units of English, 4 units of history/civics, 3 units of mathematics, 2 units of same foreign language, and 2 units of natural sciences with lab. *Recommended:* minimum 2.8 GPA, interview.

CONTACT
Mr. Michael Montana, Director of Admissions, Wilson College, 1015 Philadelphia Avenue, Chambersburg, PA 17201. *Phone:* 717-262-2002

Ext. 3197. *Toll-free phone:* 800-421-8402. *Fax:* 717-262-2546. *E-mail:* admissions@wilson.edu.

Yeshiva Beth Moshe
Scranton, Pennsylvania

CONTACT
Dean, Yeshiva Beth Moshe, 930 Hickory Street, PO Box 1141, Scranton, PA 18505-2124. *Phone:* 717-346-1747.

York College of Pennsylvania
York, Pennsylvania
http://www.ycp.edu/

- **Independent** comprehensive, founded 1787
- **Suburban** 190-acre campus with easy access to Baltimore
- **Coed** 4,171 undergraduate students, 91% full-time, 54% women, 46% men
- **Moderately difficult** entrance level, 70% of applicants were admitted

UNDERGRAD STUDENTS
3,814 full-time, 357 part-time. 40% are from out of state; 5% Black or African American, non-Hispanic/Latino; 6% Hispanic/Latino; 2% Asian, non-Hispanic/Latino; 0.1% Native Hawaiian or other Pacific Islander, non-Hispanic/Latino; 0.1% American Indian or Alaska Native, non-Hispanic/Latino; 3% Two or more races, non-Hispanic/Latino; 4% Race/ethnicity unknown; 0.6% international; 4% transferred in; 58% live on campus.

Freshmen:
Admission: 5,209 applied, 3,637 admitted, 990 enrolled. *Average high school GPA:* 3.5. *Test scores:* SAT evidence-based reading and writing scores over 500: 77%; SAT math scores over 500: 76%; ACT scores over 18: 91%; SAT evidence-based reading and writing scores over 600: 24%; SAT math scores over 600: 26%; ACT scores over 24: 35%; SAT evidence-based reading and writing scores over 700: 2%; SAT math scores over 700: 2%; ACT scores over 30: 5%.
Retention: 81% of full-time freshmen returned.

FACULTY
Total: 470, 38% full-time, 46% with terminal degrees.
Student/faculty ratio: 15:1.

ACADEMICS
Calendar: semesters. *Degrees:* associate, bachelor's, master's, doctoral, and post-master's certificates.
Special study options: academic remediation for entering students, advanced placement credit, cooperative education, double majors, honors programs, independent study, internships, part-time degree program, services for LD students, student-designed majors, study abroad, summer session for credit.
Unusual degree programs: 3-2 business administration.
Computers: Students can access the following: campus intranet, computer help desk, free student e-mail accounts, online (class) grades, online (class) registration, online (class) schedules. Campuswide network is available. 100% of college-owned or -operated housing units are wired for high-speed Internet access. Wireless service is available via entire campus.
Library: Schmidt Library.

STUDENT LIFE
Housing options: on-campus residence required through senior year; coed, special housing for students with disabilities. Campus housing is university owned. Freshman campus housing is guaranteed.
Activities and organizations: drama/theater group, student-run newspaper, radio and television station, choral group, Pre-Med Society, Ski and Outdoor Club, Habitat for Humanity, Students in Free Enterprise (SIFE), WVYC Radio Station, national fraternities, national sororities.
Athletics Member NCAA. All Division III. *Intercollegiate sports:* baseball M, basketball M/W, cheerleading M/W, cross-country running M/W, field hockey W, golf M, lacrosse M/W, soccer M/W, softball W, swimming and diving M/W, tennis M/W, track and field M/W, volleyball W, wrestling M. *Intramural sports:* badminton M/W, basketball M/W, equestrian sports M(c)/W(c), football M/W, lacrosse M(c)/W(c),

racquetball M/W, rugby M(c)/W(c), soccer M/W, softball M/W, table tennis M/W, tennis M/W, ultimate Frisbee M(c)/W(c), volleyball M/W.
Campus security: 24-hour emergency response devices and patrols, student patrols, late-night transport/escort service, controlled dormitory access.
Student services: health clinic, personal/psychological counseling.

COSTS & FINANCIAL AID
Costs (2018–19) *Comprehensive fee:* $31,300 includes full-time tuition ($18,180), mandatory fees ($1920), and room and board ($11,200). Full-time tuition and fees vary according to program. Part-time tuition: $555 per credit hour. *College room only:* $6330. Room and board charges vary according to board plan and housing facility. *Payment plan:* installment. *Waivers:* employees or children of employees.
Financial Aid Of all full-time matriculated undergraduates who enrolled in 2016, 3,192 applied for aid, 2,561 were judged to have need, 388 had their need fully met. In 2016, 1050 non-need-based awards were made. *Average percent of need met:* 55. *Average financial aid package:* $12,251. *Average need-based loan:* $4107. *Average need-based gift aid:* $5424. *Average non-need-based aid:* $5321. *Average indebtedness upon graduation:* $40,617.

APPLYING
Standardized Tests *Required:* SAT or ACT (for admission).
Options: electronic application, deferred entrance.
Required: high school transcript, minimum 2.0 GPA. *Required for some:* interview. *Recommended:* essay or personal statement, 1 letter of recommendation.
Notification: continuous (freshmen), continuous (transfers).

CONTACT
York College of Pennsylvania, 441 Country Club Road, York, PA 17403-3651. *Phone:* 717-815-2257. *Toll-free phone:* 800-455-8018.

RHODE ISLAND

Brown University
Providence, Rhode Island
http://www.brown.edu/

- **Independent** university, founded 1764
- **Urban** 154-acre campus with easy access to Boston
- **Endowment** $3.0 billion
- **Coed**
- **Most difficult** entrance level

FACULTY
Student/faculty ratio: 7:1.

ACADEMICS
Calendar: semesters. *Degrees:* bachelor's, master's, and doctoral.
Library: John D. Rockefeller Library plus 7 others. *Books:* 2.6 million (physical), 1.8 million (digital/electronic); *Serial titles:* 1,667 (physical), 112,138 (digital/electronic); *Databases:* 415. Study areas open 24 hours, 5–7 days a week; students can reserve study rooms.

STUDENT LIFE
Housing options: on-campus residence required through junior year; coed, cooperative, special housing for students with disabilities. Campus housing is university owned. Freshman campus housing is guaranteed.
Activities and organizations: drama/theater group, student-run newspaper, radio and television station, choral group, marching band, national fraternities, national sororities.
Athletics Member NCAA. All Division I.
Campus security: 24-hour emergency response devices and patrols, student patrols, late-night transport/escort service, controlled dormitory access.
Student services: health clinic, personal/psychological counseling, women's center.

COSTS & FINANCIAL AID
Costs (2017–18) *Comprehensive fee:* $67,439 includes full-time tuition ($52,231), mandatory fees ($1188), and room and board ($14,020). Part-

time tuition: $6529 per course. Part-time tuition and fees vary according to course load. *College room only:* $8784. Room and board charges vary according to board plan.

Financial Aid Of all full-time matriculated undergraduates who enrolled in 2017, 3,302 applied for aid, 2,929 were judged to have need, 2,929 had their need fully met. 1,670 Federal Work-Study jobs (averaging $2628). 316 state and other part-time jobs (averaging $2740). In 2017, 8 non-need-based awards were made. *Average percent of need met:* 100. *Average financial aid package:* $49,269. *Average need-based loan:* $6328. *Average need-based gift aid:* $45,644. *Average non-need-based aid:* $8458. *Average indebtedness upon graduation:* $25,471. *Financial aid deadline:* 2/1.

APPLYING
Standardized Tests *Required:* SAT or ACT (for admission). *Recommended:* SAT Subject Tests (for admission).

Options: electronic application, early decision, deferred entrance.

Application fee: $75.

Required: essay or personal statement, high school transcript, 2 letters of recommendation, Common Application, Brown Supplemental Questions, Alumni Interview if convenient for the applicant. *Recommended:* interview.

CONTACT
Mr. Logan Powell, Dean of Admission, Brown University, Box 1876, Providence, RI 02912. *Phone:* 401-863-2378. *Fax:* 401-863-9300. *E-mail:* admission_undergraduate@brown.edu.

Bryant University
Smithfield, Rhode Island
http://www.bryant.edu/

- **Independent** comprehensive, founded 1863
- **Suburban** 428-acre campus with easy access to Boston, Providence
- **Endowment** $174.2 million
- **Coed** 3,477 undergraduate students, 98% full-time, 39% women, 61% men
- **Moderately difficult** entrance level, 73% of applicants were admitted

UNDERGRAD STUDENTS
3,418 full-time, 59 part-time. Students come from 38 states and territories; 53 other countries; 86% are from out of state; 4% Black or African American, non-Hispanic/Latino; 7% Hispanic/Latino; 4% Asian, non-Hispanic/Latino; 0.1% Native Hawaiian or other Pacific Islander, non-Hispanic/Latino; 0.3% American Indian or Alaska Native, non-Hispanic/Latino; 1% Two or more races, non-Hispanic/Latino; 2% Race/ethnicity unknown; 8% international; 3% transferred in; 80% live on campus.

Freshmen:
Admission: 7,242 applied, 5,285 admitted, 892 enrolled. *Average high school GPA:* 3.4. *Test scores:* SAT evidence-based reading and writing scores over 500: 96%; SAT math scores over 500: 97%; ACT scores over 18: 100%; SAT evidence-based reading and writing scores over 600: 51%; SAT math scores over 600: 55%; ACT scores over 24: 81%; SAT evidence-based reading and writing scores over 700: 4%; SAT math scores over 700: 9%; ACT scores over 30: 22%.
Retention: 90% of full-time freshmen returned.

FACULTY
Total: 300, 56% full-time, 57% with terminal degrees.
Student/faculty ratio: 13:1.

ACADEMICS
Calendar: semesters. *Degrees:* bachelor's, master's, and postbachelor's certificates.

Special study options: adult/continuing education programs, advanced placement credit, double majors, English as a second language, honors programs, independent study, internships, off-campus study, part-time degree program, services for LD students, study abroad, summer session for credit. *ROTC:* Army (c).

Computers: 526 computers/terminals and 4,932 ports are available on campus for general student use. Students can access the following:

campus intranet, computer help desk, free student e-mail accounts, online (class) grades, online (class) registration, online (class) schedules, e-mail, online library, student Web hosts. Campuswide network is available. 100% of college-owned or -operated housing units are wired for high-speed Internet access. Wireless service is available via entire campus.
Library: Douglas and Judith Krupp Library plus 1 other. *Books:* 121,623 (physical), 16,854 (digital/electronic); *Serial titles:* 3,183 (physical), 299 (digital/electronic); *Databases:* 80. Weekly public service hours: 107; students can reserve study rooms.

STUDENT LIFE
Housing options: coed, special housing for students with disabilities. Campus housing is university owned. Freshman campus housing is guaranteed.

Activities and organizations: drama/theater group, student-run newspaper, radio and television station, choral group, CALO Community Activism & Leadership Organization, Linked Through Leadership, Technology & Applied Analytics Club, Dawg Pound, Enactus, national fraternities, national sororities.

Athletics Member NCAA. All Division I except football (Division I-AA). *Intercollegiate sports:* baseball M(s), basketball M(s)/W(s), bowling M(c)/W(c), cheerleading W(c), crew W(c), cross-country running M(s)/W(s), field hockey W(s), golf M(s), ice hockey M(s), lacrosse M(s)/W(s), racquetball M(c)/W(c), rowing W(c), rugby M(c)/W(c), soccer M(s)/W(s), softball W(s), squash M(c)/W(c), swimming and diving M(s)/W(s), tennis M(s)/W(s), track and field M(s)/W(s), ultimate Frisbee M(c)/W(c), volleyball M(c)/W(c). *Intramural sports:* badminton M/W, basketball M/W, field hockey W, sand volleyball M/W, soccer M/W, softball M/W, table tennis M/W, tennis M(c)/W(c).

Campus security: 24-hour emergency response devices and patrols, late-night transport/escort service, controlled dormitory access, 25 staff who patrol on foot, bike, golf cart, and car; Entry Control Station staffed 24/7 at only campus entry point.

Student services: health clinic, personal/psychological counseling, women's center.

COSTS & FINANCIAL AID
Costs (2018–19) *Comprehensive fee:* $59,675 includes full-time tuition ($43,076), mandatory fees ($897), and room and board ($15,702). Part-time tuition: $1067 per credit hour. Part-time tuition and fees vary according to course load. *College room only:* $9217. Room and board charges vary according to board plan and housing facility. *Payment plan:* installment. *Waivers:* employees or children of employees.

Financial Aid Of all full-time matriculated undergraduates who enrolled in 2015, 2,390 applied for aid, 2,106 were judged to have need, 477 had their need fully met. In 2015, 816 non-need-based awards were made. *Average percent of need met:* 51. *Average financial aid package:* $24,591. *Average need-based loan:* $4998. *Average need-based gift aid:* $9864. *Average non-need-based aid:* $14,240. *Average indebtedness upon graduation:* $39,283.

APPLYING
Options: electronic application, early decision, early action, deferred entrance.

Application fee: $50.

Required: essay or personal statement, high school transcript, 1 letter of recommendation, senior year first-quarter grades, three short essay questions in place of test scores. *Recommended:* minimum 3.3 GPA, 2 letters of recommendation, interview.

Application deadlines: 2/1 (freshmen), 5/1 (transfers), 12/1 (early action).

Early decision deadline: 11/15 (for plan 1), 1/15 (for plan 2).

Notification: 3/15 (freshmen), 3/15 (out-of-state freshmen), continuous (transfers), 12/15 (early decision plan 1), 2/15 (early decision plan 2), 1/15 (early action).

CONTACT
Ms. Michelle Cloutier, Vice President for Enrollment Management, Bryant University, 1150 Douglas Pike, Smithfield, RI 02917. *Phone:* 401-232-6100. *Toll-free phone:* 800-622-7001. *Fax:* 401-232-6741. *E-mail:* admission@bryant.edu.

Johnson & Wales University

Providence, Rhode Island

http://www.jwu.edu/providence/

CONTACT

Amy Podbelski, Dean of Undergraduate Admissions, Johnson & Wales University, 8 Abbott Park Place, Providence, RI 02903-3703. *Phone:* 401-598-2310. *Toll-free phone:* 800-342-5598. *Fax:* 401-598-2948. *E-mail:* pvd@admissions.jwu.edu.

New England Institute of Technology

East Greenwich, Rhode Island

http://www.neit.edu/

- **Independent** comprehensive, founded 1940
- **Suburban** 225-acre campus with easy access to Boston
- **Coed** 2,658 undergraduate students, 82% full-time, 34% women, 66% men
- **Minimally difficult** entrance level

UNDERGRAD STUDENTS

2,190 full-time, 468 part-time. Students come from 10 states and territories; 5 other countries; 54% are from out of state; 3% Black or African American, non-Hispanic/Latino; 12% Hispanic/Latino; 2% Asian, non-Hispanic/Latino; 0.4% American Indian or Alaska Native, non-Hispanic/Latino; 3% Two or more races, non-Hispanic/Latino; 38% Race/ethnicity unknown; 3% international; 10% live on campus.

Freshmen:

Admission: 523 enrolled.

FACULTY

Total: 329, 40% full-time, 14% with terminal degrees.

Student/faculty ratio: 16:1.

ACADEMICS

Calendar: quarters. *Degrees:* associate, bachelor's, and master's.

Special study options: academic remediation for entering students, accelerated degree program, adult/continuing education programs, advanced placement credit, cooperative education, distance learning, double majors, English as a second language, internships, part-time degree program, services for LD students, student-designed majors, summer session for credit.

Computers: 1,300 computers/terminals are available on campus for general student use. Students can access the following: campus intranet, computer help desk, free student e-mail accounts, online (class) grades, online (class) registration, online (class) schedules. Campuswide network is available. 100% of college-owned or -operated housing units are wired for high-speed Internet access. Wireless service is available via entire campus.

Library: New England Institute of Technology Library. *Books:* 48,657 (physical), 25,463 (digital/electronic); *Serial titles:* 316 (physical), 92,321 (digital/electronic); *Databases:* 68. Weekly public service hours: 65; students can reserve study rooms.

STUDENT LIFE

Housing options: coed. Campus housing is university owned. Freshman applicants given priority for college housing.

Activities and organizations: student-run radio station, Rotaract Club, Student Physical Therapist Assistant Club, Student Nurses Association, Video Club, Criminal Justice Club.

Athletics *Intramural sports:* basketball M(c)/W(c), golf M(c)/W(c), soccer M(c)/W(c).

Campus security: 24-hour emergency response devices and patrols, late-night transport/escort service, controlled dormitory access.

Student services: health clinic, personal/psychological counseling.

COSTS & FINANCIAL AID

Costs (2018–19) *Comprehensive fee:* $41,580 includes full-time tuition ($28,200), mandatory fees ($1740), and room and board ($11,640). Full-time tuition and fees vary according to program. Part-time tuition: $14,100 per year. Part-time tuition and fees vary according to program. No tuition increase for student's term of enrollment. *Required fees:* $1740 per year part-time. *Room and board:* Room and board charges vary according to board plan. *Payment plans:* tuition prepayment, installment. *Waivers:* employees or children of employees.

Financial Aid Of all full-time matriculated undergraduates who enrolled in 2016, 250 Federal Work-Study jobs (averaging $2290).

APPLYING

Standardized Tests *Recommended:* SAT or ACT (for admission).

Options: electronic application, early admission, deferred entrance.

Application fee: $25.

Required: high school transcript, interview. *Required for some:* portfolio for advanced standing.

Application deadlines: rolling (freshmen), rolling (out-of-state freshmen), rolling (transfers).

Notification: continuous (freshmen), continuous (out-of-state freshmen), continuous (transfers).

CONTACT

Mr. Michael Caruso, Director of Admissions, New England Institute of Technology, One New England Tech Boulevard, East Greenwich, RI 02818. *Phone:* 401-739-5000 Ext. 3411. *Toll-free phone:* 800-736-7744. *Fax:* 401-886-0868. *E-mail:* mcaruso@neit.edu.

Providence College

Providence, Rhode Island

http://www.providence.edu/

- **Independent Roman Catholic** comprehensive, founded 1917
- **Suburban** 105-acre campus with easy access to Boston
- **Endowment** $221.1 million
- **Coed** 4,306 undergraduate students, 94% full-time, 55% women, 45% men

UNDERGRAD STUDENTS

4,049 full-time, 257 part-time. Students come from 41 states and territories; 25 other countries; 91% are from out of state; 4% Black or African American, non-Hispanic/Latino; 9% Hispanic/Latino; 1% Asian, non-Hispanic/Latino; 0.3% Native Hawaiian or other Pacific Islander, non-Hispanic/Latino; 0.2% American Indian or Alaska Native, non-Hispanic/Latino; 2% Two or more races, non-Hispanic/Latino; 4% Race/ethnicity unknown; 2% international; 2% transferred in; 80% live on campus.

Freshmen:

Admission: 1,064 enrolled. *Average high school GPA:* 3.4. *Test scores:* SAT evidence-based reading and writing scores over 500: 98%; SAT math scores over 500: 98%; ACT scores over 18: 100%; SAT evidence-based reading and writing scores over 600: 69%; SAT math scores over 600: 64%; ACT scores over 24: 92%; SAT evidence-based reading and writing scores over 700: 11%; SAT math scores over 700: 11%; ACT scores over 30: 29%.

Retention: 92% of full-time freshmen returned.

FACULTY

Total: 535, 56% full-time, 69% with terminal degrees.

Student/faculty ratio: 12:1.

ACADEMICS

Calendar: semesters. *Degrees:* certificates, bachelor's, master's, and postbachelor's certificates.

Special study options: adult/continuing education programs, advanced placement credit, distance learning, double majors, honors programs, independent study, internships, off-campus study, part-time degree program, services for LD students, student-designed majors, study abroad, summer session for credit. *ROTC:* Army (b).

Unusual degree programs: 3-2 engineering with Columbia University, Washington University in St. Louis; biology/optometry with New England School of Optometry.

Computers: 440 computers/terminals and 5,000 ports are available on campus for general student use. Students can access the following: campus intranet, computer help desk, free student e-mail accounts, online (class) grades, online (class) registration, online (class) schedules. Campuswide network is available. 100% of college-owned or -operated housing units are wired for high-speed Internet access. Wireless service is available via entire campus.

Library: Phillips Memorial Library. *Books:* 320,000 (physical), 1.5 million (digital/electronic); *Serial titles:* 555 (physical), 62,209 (digital/electronic); *Databases:* 397. Weekly public service hours: 116; students can reserve study rooms.

STUDENT LIFE
Housing options: on-campus residence required through junior year; coed, men-only, women-only, special housing for students with disabilities. Campus housing is university owned. Freshman campus housing is guaranteed.

Activities and organizations: drama/theater group, student-run newspaper, radio and television station, choral group, Student Congress, Board of Multicultural Student Affairs, Campus Ministry, Dance Club, Board of Programmers.

Athletics Member NCAA. All Division I. *Intercollegiate sports:* basketball M(s)/W(s), cross-country running M(s)/W(s), field hockey W(s), ice hockey M(s)/W(s), lacrosse M(s), soccer M(s)/W(s), softball W(s), swimming and diving M/W, tennis W, track and field M(s)/W(s), volleyball W(s). *Intramural sports:* badminton M/W, basketball M(c)/W(c), cheerleading M(c)/W(c), cross-country running M/W, field hockey W, football M/W, golf M(c)/W(c), ice hockey M(c)/W, lacrosse M/W(c), racquetball M(c)/W(c), rugby M(c)/W(c), sailing M(c)/W(c), soccer M/W, softball M/W, table tennis M/W, track and field M/W, ultimate Frisbee M(c)/W(c), volleyball M(c)/W(c), water polo M/W, wrestling M(c)/W(c).

Campus security: 24-hour emergency response devices and patrols, late-night transport/escort service, controlled dormitory access.

Student services: health clinic, personal/psychological counseling, legal services.

COSTS & FINANCIAL AID
Costs (2017–18) *Comprehensive fee:* $63,004 includes full-time tuition ($47,870), mandatory fees ($894), and room and board ($14,240). Full-time tuition and fees vary according to class time and degree level. Part-time tuition: $1710 per credit hour. Part-time tuition and fees vary according to class time and degree level. *College room only:* $8210. Room and board charges vary according to board plan and housing facility. *Payment plan:* installment. *Waivers:* employees or children of employees.

Financial Aid Of all full-time matriculated undergraduates who enrolled in 2017, 2,579 applied for aid, 1,894 were judged to have need, 430 had their need fully met. In 2017, 792 non-need-based awards were made. *Average percent of need met:* 83. *Average financial aid package:* $31,565. *Average need-based loan:* $5084. *Average need-based gift aid:* $27,621. *Average non-need-based aid:* $17,350. *Average indebtedness upon graduation:* $41,383. *Financial aid deadline:* 2/1.

APPLYING
Standardized Tests *Required for some:* TOEFL or IELTS if English is not the applicant's first language.

Required: essay or personal statement, high school transcript, 2 letters of recommendation.

CONTACT
Providence College, 1 Cunningham Square, Providence, RI 02918. *Phone:* 401-865-2535. *Toll-free phone:* 800-721-6444.

Rhode Island College
Providence, Rhode Island
http://www.ric.edu/
- **State-supported** comprehensive, founded 1854
- **Suburban** 180-acre campus with easy access to Boston
- **Endowment** $18.2 million
- **Coed** 7,080 undergraduate students, 77% full-time, 68% women, 32% men
- **Moderately difficult** entrance level, 74% of applicants were admitted

UNDERGRAD STUDENTS
5,464 full-time, 1,616 part-time. Students come from 27 states and territories; 2 other countries; 14% are from out of state; 10% Black or African American, non-Hispanic/Latino; 19% Hispanic/Latino; 3% Asian, non-Hispanic/Latino; 0.1% Native Hawaiian or other Pacific Islander, non-Hispanic/Latino; 0.5% American Indian or Alaska Native, non-Hispanic/Latino; 2% Two or more races, non-Hispanic/Latino; 7%

Race/ethnicity unknown; 0.2% international; 9% transferred in; 15% live on campus.

Freshmen:
Admission: 4,846 applied, 3,566 admitted, 1,040 enrolled. *Test scores:* SAT evidence-based reading and writing scores over 500: 53%; SAT math scores over 500: 47%; ACT scores over 18: 59%; SAT evidence-based reading and writing scores over 600: 12%; SAT math scores over 600: 8%; ACT scores over 24: 17%; SAT evidence-based reading and writing scores over 700: 1%; ACT scores over 30: 3%.
Retention: 75% of full-time freshmen returned.

FACULTY
Total: 756, 44% full-time, 40% with terminal degrees.
Student/faculty ratio: 14:1.

ACADEMICS
Calendar: semesters. *Degrees:* certificates, bachelor's, master's, doctoral, post-master's, and postbachelor's certificates.

Special study options: academic remediation for entering students, adult/continuing education programs, advanced placement credit, double majors, English as a second language, honors programs, independent study, internships, off-campus study, part-time degree program, services for LD students, student-designed majors, study abroad, summer session for credit. *ROTC:* Army (c).

Unusual degree programs: 3-2 public administration with University of Rhode Island.

Computers: 250 computers/terminals are available on campus for general student use. Students can access the following: computer help desk, free student e-mail accounts, online (class) grades, online (class) registration, online (class) schedules. Campuswide network is available. 100% of college-owned or -operated housing units are wired for high-speed Internet access. Wireless service is available via classrooms, computer centers, computer labs, dorm rooms, learning centers, libraries, student centers.

Library: Adams Library. *Books:* 306,080 (physical), 302,387 (digital/electronic); *Serial titles:* 3,081 (physical), 52,652 (digital/electronic); *Databases:* 123. Weekly public service hours: 80.

STUDENT LIFE
Housing options: coed, special housing for students with disabilities. Campus housing is university owned. Freshman applicants given priority for college housing.

Activities and organizations: drama/theater group, student-run newspaper, radio and television station, choral group, Theta Phi Alpha, Delta Phi Epsilon, Alpha Sigma Tau, Sojourn Collegiate Ministries, Student Community Government, national fraternities, national sororities.

Athletics Member NCAA. All Division III. *Intercollegiate sports:* baseball M, basketball M/W, cross-country running M/W, golf M/W, gymnastics W, lacrosse W, soccer M/W, softball W, swimming and diving W, tennis M/W, track and field M/W, volleyball W, wrestling M. *Intramural sports:* badminton M/W, basketball M/W, football M, soccer M/W, softball M/W, swimming and diving M/W, tennis M/W, volleyball M/W, water polo M/W.

Campus security: 24-hour emergency response devices and patrols, late-night transport/escort service, controlled dormitory access.

Student services: health clinic, personal/psychological counseling, women's center, legal services.

COSTS & FINANCIAL AID
Costs (2017–18) *Tuition:* state resident $7637 full-time, $300 per credit part-time; nonresident $20,150 full-time, $740 per credit part-time. Part-time tuition and fees vary according to course load. *Required fees:* $1139 full-time, $39 per credit part-time. *Room and board:* $11,335; room only: $6582. Room and board charges vary according to housing facility. *Payment plan:* installment. *Waivers:* employees or children of employees.

Financial Aid Of all full-time matriculated undergraduates who enrolled in 2017, 4,584 applied for aid, 3,834 were judged to have need, 722 had their need fully met. In 2017, 131 non-need-based awards were made. *Average percent of need met:* 68. *Average financial aid package:* $9745. *Average need-based loan:* $3958. *Average need-based gift aid:* $7016. *Average non-need-based aid:* $2441. *Average indebtedness upon graduation:* $25,791.

APPLYING

Standardized Tests *Required:* SAT or ACT (for admission).

Options: electronic application, early admission.

Application fee: $50.

Required: essay or personal statement, high school transcript, 1 letter of recommendation, 1 letter from guidance counselor. ***Required for some:*** interview. *Recommended:* minimum 3.0 GPA.

Application deadlines: 3/15 (freshmen), 6/1 (transfers).

Notification: continuous until 12/15 (freshmen), continuous (out-of-state freshmen), continuous (transfers).

CONTACT

Jason Anthony, Director of Admissions, Rhode Island College, 600 Mount Pleasant Avenue, Providence, RI 02908-1927. *Phone:* 401-456-8234. *Toll-free phone:* 800-669-5760. *Fax:* 401-456-8817. *E-mail:* admissions@ric.edu.

Rhode Island School of Design

Providence, Rhode Island

http://www.risd.edu/

- **Independent** comprehensive, founded 1877
- **Urban** 19-acre campus with easy access to Boston, MA
- **Endowment** $329.6 million
- **Coed** 1,976 undergraduate students, 100% full-time, 68% women, 32% men

UNDERGRAD STUDENTS

1,976 full-time. Students come from 48 states and territories; 46 other countries; 95% are from out of state; 3% Black or African American, non-Hispanic/Latino; 8% Hispanic/Latino; 19% Asian, non-Hispanic/Latino; 0.2% American Indian or Alaska Native, non-Hispanic/Latino; 5% Two or more races, non-Hispanic/Latino; 4% Race/ethnicity unknown; 30% international; 3% transferred in; 60% live on campus.

Freshmen:

Admission: 450 enrolled.

Retention: 95% of full-time freshmen returned.

FACULTY

Total: 438, 37% full-time, 67% with terminal degrees.

Student/faculty ratio: 10:1.

ACADEMICS

Calendar: 4-1-4. *Degrees:* bachelor's and master's.

Special study options: advanced placement credit, double majors, honors programs, independent study, internships, off-campus study, services for LD students, study abroad. *ROTC:* Army (c).

Computers: 65 computers/terminals and 400 ports are available on campus for general student use. Students can access the following: campus intranet, computer help desk, free student e-mail accounts, online (class) grades, online (class) registration, online (class) schedules. Campuswide network is available. 100% of college-owned or -operated housing units are wired for high-speed Internet access. Wireless service is available via entire campus.

Library: Fleet Library. *Books:* 160,296 (physical), 144,887 (digital/electronic); *Serial titles:* 1,200 (digital/electronic); *Databases:* 62. Weekly public service hours: 89; students can reserve study rooms.

STUDENT LIFE

Housing options: on-campus residence required through sophomore year; coed, special housing for students with disabilities. Campus housing is university owned and leased by the school. Freshman campus housing is guaranteed.

Activities and organizations: drama/theater group, student-run newspaper, radio station, choral group, athletic clubs, Religious clubs, South Asian Student Association, RISD Global Initiative, Community Service Club.

Athletics *Intramural sports:* badminton M(c)/W(c), basketball M(c)/W(c), equestrian sports M(c)/W(c), fencing M(c)/W(c), football M(c)/W(c), ice hockey M(c)/W(c), sailing M(c)/W(c), skiing (downhill) M(c)/W(c), soccer M(c)/W(c), softball M(c)/W(c), squash M(c)/W(c), swimming and diving M(c)/W(c), tennis M(c)/W(c), ultimate Frisbee M(c)/W(c), volleyball M(c)/W(c), water polo M(c)/W(c).

Campus security: 24-hour emergency response devices and patrols, late-night transport/escort service, controlled dormitory access.

Student services: health clinic, personal/psychological counseling, legal services.

COSTS & FINANCIAL AID

Costs (2017–18) *Comprehensive fee:* $61,520 includes full-time tuition ($48,210), mandatory fees ($260), and room and board ($13,050). *College room only:* $7550. Room and board charges vary according to board plan and housing facility. *Payment plan:* installment. *Waivers:* employees or children of employees.

Financial Aid Of all full-time matriculated undergraduates who enrolled in 2016, 900 applied for aid, 774 were judged to have need, 10 had their need fully met. In 2016, 20 non-need-based awards were made. *Average percent of need met:* 65. *Average financial aid package:* $29,371. *Average need-based loan:* $5216. *Average need-based gift aid:* $22,934. *Average non-need-based aid:* $7500. *Average indebtedness upon graduation:* $31,037. *Financial aid deadline:* 2/15.

APPLYING

Standardized Tests *Required:* SAT or ACT (for admission).

Required: essay or personal statement, high school transcript, portfolio, drawing assignments. *Recommended:* 3 letters of recommendation.

CONTACT

Mr. James O'Hara, Vice President for Enrollment, Rhode Island School of Design, 2 College Street, Providence, RI 02903-2784. *Phone:* 401-454-6300. *Toll-free phone:* 800-364-7473. *Fax:* 401-454-6309. *E-mail:* admissions@risd.edu.

Roger Williams University

Bristol, Rhode Island

http://www.rwu.edu/

- **Independent** comprehensive, founded 1956
- **Small-town** 140-acre campus with easy access to Boston
- **Endowment** $67.6 million
- **Coed** 4,703 undergraduate students, 86% full-time, 53% women, 47% men
- **82%** of applicants were admitted

UNDERGRAD STUDENTS

4,042 full-time, 661 part-time. Students come from 42 states and territories; 56 other countries; 79% are from out of state; 2% Black or African American, non-Hispanic/Latino; 6% Hispanic/Latino; 2% Asian, non-Hispanic/Latino; 0.1% Native Hawaiian or other Pacific Islander, non-Hispanic/Latino; 0.1% American Indian or Alaska Native, non-Hispanic/Latino; 2% Two or more races, non-Hispanic/Latino; 12% Race/ethnicity unknown; 2% international; 1% transferred in; 76% live on campus.

Freshmen:

Admission: 9,515 applied, 7,830 admitted, 1,135 enrolled. *Average high school GPA:* 3.3. *Test scores:* SAT evidence-based reading and writing scores over 500: 96%; SAT math scores over 500: 95%; ACT scores over 18: 99%; SAT evidence-based reading and writing scores over 600: 49%; SAT math scores over 600: 41%; ACT scores over 24: 79%; SAT evidence-based reading and writing scores over 700: 4%; SAT math scores over 700: 5%; ACT scores over 30: 15%.

Retention: 79% of full-time freshmen returned.

FACULTY

Total: 538, 40% full-time, 37% with terminal degrees.

Student/faculty ratio: 14:1.

ACADEMICS

Calendar: semesters. *Degrees:* certificates, associate, bachelor's, master's, doctoral, and postbachelor's certificates.

Special study options: accelerated degree program, adult/continuing education programs, advanced placement credit, cooperative education, distance learning, double majors, English as a second language, freshman honors college, honors programs, independent study, internships, part-time degree program, services for LD students, student-designed majors, study abroad, summer session for credit. *ROTC:* Army (b).

Computers: 100 computers/terminals and 300 ports are available on campus for general student use. Students can access the following:

campus intranet, computer help desk, free student e-mail accounts, online (class) grades, online (class) registration, online (class) schedules. Campuswide network is available. 20% of college-owned or -operated housing units are wired for high-speed Internet access. Wireless service is available via entire campus.

Library: Roger Williams University Library plus 1 other. *Books:* 219,429 (physical), 448,637 (digital/electronic); *Serial titles:* 493 (physical), 52,585 (digital/electronic); *Databases:* 189. Weekly public service hours: 111; students can reserve study rooms.

STUDENT LIFE
Housing options: on-campus residence required through sophomore year; coed, special housing for students with disabilities. Campus housing is university owned. Freshman campus housing is guaranteed.

Activities and organizations: drama/theater group, student-run newspaper, radio station, choral group, Campus Entertainment Network, Dance Club, WQRI 88.3 Radio Station, Habitat for Humanity.

Athletics Member NCAA. All Division III. *Intercollegiate sports:* baseball M, basketball M/W, crew M(c)/W(c), cross-country running M/W, equestrian sports M/W, field hockey W, golf M, ice hockey M(c), lacrosse M/W, rugby M(c)/W(c), sailing M/W, soccer M/W, softball W, swimming and diving M/W, tennis M/W, track and field M/W, ultimate Frisbee M(c)/W(c), volleyball M(c)/W, wrestling M. *Intramural sports:* basketball M/W, cheerleading M(c)/W(c), football M/W, lacrosse M(c), soccer M/W, softball M/W, volleyball M/W.

Campus security: 24-hour emergency response devices and patrols, late-night transport/escort service, controlled dormitory access, Rave Guardian Emergency Communication App.

Student services: health clinic, personal/psychological counseling, women's center.

COSTS & FINANCIAL AID
Costs (2018–19) *Comprehensive fee:* $48,074 includes full-time tuition ($30,326), mandatory fees ($2184), and room and board ($15,564). Full-time tuition and fees vary according to class time, course load, degree level, and program. Part-time tuition and fees vary according to class time, course load, degree level, and program. No tuition increase for student's term of enrollment. *College room only:* $8310. Room and board charges vary according to board plan and housing facility. *Payment plan:* deferred payment. *Waivers:* employees or children of employees.

Financial Aid Of all full-time matriculated undergraduates who enrolled in 2017, 3,168 applied for aid, 2,596 were judged to have need, 308 had their need fully met. 1,522 Federal Work-Study jobs (averaging $1974). In 2017, 537 non-need-based awards were made. *Average percent of need met:* 88. *Average financial aid package:* $22,130. *Average need-based loan:* $4533. *Average need-based gift aid:* $14,413. *Average non-need-based aid:* $12,898. *Average indebtedness upon graduation:* $44,225. *Financial aid deadline:* 2/1.

APPLYING
Standardized Tests *Required for some:* SAT or ACT (for admission).

Options: electronic application, early action, deferred entrance.

Application fee: $50.

Required: essay or personal statement, 1 letter of recommendation. *Required for some:* high school transcript, portfolio review, audition, specific preparatory courses for visual arts studies, graphic design communications, architecture, creative writing, dance and theater.

Application deadlines: 2/1 (freshmen), rolling (transfers), 11/15 (early action).

Notification: continuous (freshmen), continuous (out-of-state freshmen), continuous (transfers).

CONTACT
Roger Williams University, 1 Old Ferry Road, Bristol, RI 02809. *Toll-free phone:* 800-458-7144.

Salve Regina University
Newport, Rhode Island
http://www.salve.edu/
- **Independent Roman Catholic** comprehensive, founded 1934
- **Suburban** 80-acre campus with easy access to Boston, Providence
- **Endowment** $59.9 million
- **Coed** 2,180 undergraduate students, 96% full-time, 67% women, 33% men
- 72% of applicants were admitted

UNDERGRAD STUDENTS
2,087 full-time, 93 part-time. Students come from 34 states and territories; 22 other countries; 80% are from out of state; 2% Black or African American, non-Hispanic/Latino; 7% Hispanic/Latino; 1% Asian, non-Hispanic/Latino; 0.3% American Indian or Alaska Native, non-Hispanic/Latino; 3% Two or more races, non-Hispanic/Latino; 4% Race/ethnicity unknown; 2% international; 2% transferred in; 59% live on campus.

Freshmen:
Admission: 4,991 applied, 3,588 admitted, 603 enrolled. *Average high school GPA:* 3.4.
Retention: 84% of full-time freshmen returned.

FACULTY
Total: 289, 44% full-time, 48% with terminal degrees.
Student/faculty ratio: 14:1.

ACADEMICS
Calendar: semesters. *Degrees:* certificates, associate, bachelor's, master's, doctoral, post-master's, and postbachelor's certificates.

Special study options: accelerated degree program, adult/continuing education programs, advanced placement credit, double majors, English as a second language, honors programs, independent study, internships, off-campus study, part-time degree program, services for LD students, study abroad, summer session for credit. *ROTC:* Army (c).

Unusual degree programs: 3-2 business administration; nursing; administration of justice, holistic counseling, international relations, MBA, management, rehabilitation counseling.

Computers: 163 computers/terminals are available on campus for general student use. Students can access the following: campus intranet, computer help desk, free student e-mail accounts, online (class) grades, online (class) registration, online (class) schedules. Campuswide network is available. 100% of college-owned or -operated housing units are wired for high-speed Internet access. Wireless service is available via entire campus.

Library: McKillop Library. *Books:* 160,888 (physical), 290,188 (digital/electronic); *Serial titles:* 193 (physical), 67,608 (digital/electronic); *Databases:* 53. Weekly public service hours: 58; students can reserve study rooms.

STUDENT LIFE
Housing options: on-campus residence required through sophomore year; coed, men-only, women-only. Campus housing is university owned and leased by the school. Freshman campus housing is guaranteed.

Activities and organizations: drama/theater group, student-run newspaper, radio station, choral group, Orpheus Musical Society, Student Government Association, Student Outdoor Adventures, Student Nurse Organization, Stagefright Theatre Company.

Athletics Member NCAA. All Division III. *Intercollegiate sports:* baseball M, basketball M/W, cross-country running M/W, field hockey W, football M, ice hockey M/W, lacrosse M/W, rugby M(c)/W(c), sailing M/W, soccer M/W, softball W, tennis M/W, track and field M/W, volleyball W. *Intramural sports:* baseball M, basketball M/W, cheerleading W(c), equestrian sports W(c), football M/W, golf M/W, ice hockey M, lacrosse M, rugby M(c)/W(c), soccer M/W, softball M/W, swimming and diving M(c)/W(c), tennis M/W, ultimate Frisbee M/W, volleyball M/W, weight lifting M/W.

Campus security: 24-hour emergency response devices and patrols, late-night transport/escort service, controlled dormitory access.

Student services: health clinic, personal/psychological counseling.

COSTS & FINANCIAL AID

Costs (2017–18) *Comprehensive fee:* $53,046 includes full-time tuition ($38,386), mandatory fees ($600), and room and board ($14,060). Full-time tuition and fees vary according to course load and location. Part-time tuition: $1280 per credit. Part-time tuition and fees vary according to course load and location. *Required fees:* $60 per term part-time. *Room and board:* Room and board charges vary according to board plan and housing facility. *Payment plan:* installment. *Waivers:* employees or children of employees.

Financial Aid Of all full-time matriculated undergraduates who enrolled in 2017, 1,685 applied for aid, 1,533 were judged to have need, 177 had their need fully met. In 2017, 396 non-need-based awards were made. *Average percent of need met:* 67. *Average financial aid package:* $27,756. *Average need-based loan:* $4436. *Average need-based gift aid:* $22,799. *Average non-need-based aid:* $14,854. *Average indebtedness upon graduation:* $37,464.

APPLYING

Standardized Tests *Required for some:* SAT or ACT (for admission).

Options: electronic application, early action, deferred entrance.

Application fee: $50.

Required: essay or personal statement, high school transcript, 2 letters of recommendation. *Recommended:* minimum 2.7 GPA.

Application deadlines: 2/1 (freshmen), rolling (transfers), 11/1 (early action).

Notification: 12/25 (freshmen), continuous (transfers), 12/25 (early action).

CONTACT

Dean Colleen Emerson, Dean of Undergraduate Admissions, Salve Regina University, 100 Ochre Point Avenue, Newport, RI 02840-4192. *Phone:* 401-341-2908. *Toll-free phone:* 888-GO SALVE. *Fax:* 401-848-2823. *E-mail:* emersonc@salve.edu.

University of Rhode Island

Kingston, Rhode Island

http://www.uri.edu/

- **State-supported** university, founded 1892
- **Small-town** 1200-acre campus
- **Endowment** $107.8 million
- **Coed** 15,092 undergraduate students, 84% full-time, 56% women, 44% men
- **Moderately difficult** entrance level, 69% of applicants were admitted

UNDERGRAD STUDENTS

12,615 full-time, 2,477 part-time. Students come from 43 states and territories; 38 other countries; 46% are from out of state; 5% Black or African American, non-Hispanic/Latino; 10% Hispanic/Latino; 3% Asian, non-Hispanic/Latino; 0.1% Native Hawaiian or other Pacific Islander, non-Hispanic/Latino; 0.2% American Indian or Alaska Native, non-Hispanic/Latino; 3% Two or more races, non-Hispanic/Latino; 6% Race/ethnicity unknown; 2% international; 4% transferred in; 41% live on campus.

Freshmen:
Admission: 22,667 applied, 15,618 admitted, 3,172 enrolled. *Average high school GPA:* 3.5. *Test scores:* SAT evidence-based reading and writing scores over 500: 95%; SAT math scores over 500: 91%; ACT scores over 18: 99%; SAT evidence-based reading and writing scores over 600: 45%; SAT math scores over 600: 38%; ACT scores over 24: 69%; SAT evidence-based reading and writing scores over 700: 4%; SAT math scores over 700: 4%; ACT scores over 30: 10%.

Retention: 85% of full-time freshmen returned.

FACULTY

Total: 1,146, 66% full-time, 61% with terminal degrees.

Student/faculty ratio: 17:1.

ACADEMICS

Calendar: semesters. *Degrees:* bachelor's, master's, doctoral, and postbachelor's certificates.

Special study options: academic remediation for entering students, accelerated degree program, adult/continuing education programs,

advanced placement credit, cooperative education, distance learning, double majors, English as a second language, honors programs, independent study, internships, off-campus study, part-time degree program, services for LD students, study abroad, summer session for credit. *ROTC:* Army (b).

Unusual degree programs: 3-2 engineering; nursing; accounting, pharmacy, chemistry, education, psychology.

Computers: 2,500 computers/terminals are available on campus for general student use. Students can access the following: campus intranet, computer help desk, free student e-mail accounts, online (class) grades, online (class) registration, online (class) schedules. Campuswide network is available. 100% of college-owned or -operated housing units are wired for high-speed Internet access. Wireless service is available via entire campus.

Library: Robert L. Carothers Library and Learning Commons plus 3 others. Study areas open 24 hours, 5–7 days a week; students can reserve study rooms.

STUDENT LIFE

Housing options: coed, cooperative, special housing for students with disabilities. Campus housing is university owned and leased by the school. Freshman campus housing is guaranteed.

Activities and organizations: drama/theater group, student-run newspaper, radio and television station, choral group, marching band, Student Entertainment Committee, student radio station, Intramural sport clubs, Student Alumni Association, student newspaper, national fraternities, national sororities.

Athletics Member NCAA. All Division I. *Intercollegiate sports:* baseball M(s), basketball M(s), cheerleading M/W, crew W, cross-country running M(s)/W(s), football M(s), golf M(s), soccer M(s)/W(s), softball W(s), swimming and diving W(s), tennis W(s), track and field M(s)/W(s), volleyball W(s). *Intramural sports:* equestrian sports M(c)/W(c), gymnastics W(c), ice hockey M(c)/W(c), lacrosse M(c)/W(c), rugby M(c)/W(c), sailing M(c)/W(c), skiing (downhill) M(c)/W(c), swimming and diving M(c), ultimate Frisbee M(c)/W(c), volleyball M(c), wrestling M(c).

Campus security: 24-hour emergency response devices and patrols, student patrols, late-night transport/escort service, controlled dormitory access.

Student services: health clinic, personal/psychological counseling, women's center.

COSTS & FINANCIAL AID

Costs (2017–18) *Tuition:* state resident $12,002 full-time, $500 per credit hour part-time; nonresident $28,252 full-time, $1177 per credit hour part-time. Full-time tuition and fees vary according to course load, location, and reciprocity agreements. Part-time tuition and fees vary according to course load, location, and reciprocity agreements. *Required fees:* $1790 full-time, $44 per credit hour part-time, $58 per term part-time. *Room and board:* $7774; room only: $4500. Room and board charges vary according to board plan and housing facility. *Payment plan:* installment. *Waivers:* minority students, senior citizens, and employees or children of employees.

Financial Aid Of all full-time matriculated undergraduates who enrolled in 2017, 12,831 applied for aid, 11,112 were judged to have need, 4,945 had their need fully met. In 2017, 1038 non-need-based awards were made. *Average percent of need met:* 56. *Average financial aid package:* $16,362. *Average need-based loan:* $6366. *Average need-based gift aid:* $10,371. *Average non-need-based aid:* $6673. *Average indebtedness upon graduation:* $33,335.

APPLYING

Standardized Tests *Required:* SAT or ACT (for admission).

Options: electronic application, early admission, early action, deferred entrance.

Application fee: $65.

Required: essay or personal statement, high school transcript, 1 letter of recommendation, list of senior courses. *Required for some:* 2 letters of recommendation.

Application deadlines: 2/1 (freshmen), 6/1 (transfers), 12/1 (early action).

Notification: 3/31 (freshmen), continuous (transfers), 1/31 (early action).

CONTACT

Ms. Joanne Lynch, Assistant Dean of Admissions, University of Rhode Island, Undergraduate Admission Office, Newman Hall, 14 Upper College Road, Kingston, RI 02881. *Phone:* 401-874-7110. *Fax:* 401-874-5523. *E-mail:* lynch@uri.edu.

SOUTH CAROLINA

Allen University

Columbia, South Carolina

http://www.allenuniversity.edu/

CONTACT

Terri Parker, Director of Admission, Allen University, 1530 Harden Street, Columbia, SC 29204. *Phone:* 803-376-5733. *Toll-free phone:* 877-625-5368. *E-mail:* tparker@allenuniversity.edu.

Anderson University

Anderson, South Carolina

http://www.andersonuniversity.edu/

- **Independent Baptist** comprehensive, founded 1911
- **Urban** 271-acre campus with easy access to Greenville
- **Endowment** $44.7 million
- **Coed** 2,986 undergraduate students, 85% full-time, 69% women, 31% men
- **Minimally difficult** entrance level, 79% of applicants were admitted

UNDERGRAD STUDENTS

2,550 full-time, 433 part-time. Students come from 35 states and territories; 20 other countries; 19% are from out of state; 6% Black or African American, non-Hispanic/Latino; 3% Hispanic/Latino; 0.5% Asian, non-Hispanic/Latino; 0.1% American Indian or Alaska Native, non-Hispanic/Latino; 3% Two or more races, non-Hispanic/Latino; 2% Race/ethnicity unknown; 1% international; 5% transferred in; 46% live on campus.

Freshmen:

Admission: 2,322 applied, 1,836 admitted, 681 enrolled. *Average high school GPA:* 3.6. *Test scores:* SAT evidence-based reading and writing scores over 500: 92%; SAT math scores over 500: 82%; ACT scores over 18: 97%; SAT evidence-based reading and writing scores over 600: 40%; SAT math scores over 600: 30%; ACT scores over 24: 43%; SAT evidence-based reading and writing scores over 700: 6%; SAT math scores over 700: 2%; ACT scores over 30: 6%.
Retention: 75% of full-time freshmen returned.

FACULTY

Total: 341, 43% full-time, 46% with terminal degrees.

Student/faculty ratio: 14:1.

ACADEMICS

Calendar: semesters. *Degrees:* bachelor's, master's, and doctoral.

Special study options: academic remediation for entering students, accelerated degree program, adult/continuing education programs, advanced placement credit, cooperative education, distance learning, double majors, honors programs, independent study, internships, part-time degree program, services for LD students, study abroad, summer session for credit. *ROTC:* Army (c), Air Force (c).

Computers: 192 computers/terminals are available on campus for general student use. Students can access the following: campus intranet, computer help desk, free student e-mail accounts, online (class) grades, online (class) registration, online (class) schedules. Campuswide network is available. 100% of college-owned or -operated housing units are wired for high-speed Internet access. Wireless service is available via entire campus.

Library: Thrift Library. *Books:* 90,729 (physical), 99,204 (digital/electronic); *Serial titles:* 14,268 (physical), 174,052 (digital/electronic); *Databases:* 200. Weekly public service hours: 88; students can reserve study rooms.

STUDENT LIFE

Housing options: on-campus residence required through sophomore year; men-only, women-only. Campus housing is university owned. Freshman campus housing is guaranteed.

Activities and organizations: drama/theater group, student-run newspaper, choral group, Baptist Collegiate Ministries, Gamma Beta Phi, Anderson University Education Club, Ducks Unlimited, Council of Exceptional Children.

Athletics Member NCAA. All Division II. *Intercollegiate sports:* baseball M(s), basketball M(s)/W(s), cheerleading W(s), cross-country running M(s)/W(s), golf M(s)/W(s), soccer M(s)/W(s), softball W(s), tennis M(s)/W(s), track and field M(s)/W(s), volleyball W(s). *Intramural sports:* basketball M/W, football M/W, racquetball M/W, softball M/W, table tennis M/W, ultimate Frisbee M/W, volleyball M/W, weight lifting M.

Campus security: 24-hour emergency response devices and patrols, late-night transport/escort service, controlled dormitory access.

Student services: health clinic, personal/psychological counseling.

COSTS & FINANCIAL AID

Costs (2017–18) *Comprehensive fee:* $36,650 includes full-time tuition ($24,290), mandatory fees ($2680), and room and board ($9680). Full-time tuition and fees vary according to course load and program. Part-time tuition: $605 per credit hour. Part-time tuition and fees vary according to course load and program. *College room only:* $5030. Room and board charges vary according to board plan and housing facility. *Payment plan:* installment. *Waivers:* employees or children of employees.

Financial Aid Of all full-time matriculated undergraduates who enrolled in 2017, 3,350 applied for aid, 2,828 were judged to have need, 598 had their need fully met. 161 Federal Work-Study jobs (averaging $2000). 243 state and other part-time jobs (averaging $1088). In 2017, 579 non-need-based awards were made. *Average percent of need met:* 53. *Average financial aid package:* $16,957. *Average need-based loan:* $4308. *Average need-based gift aid:* $14,718. *Average non-need-based aid:* $11,293. *Average indebtedness upon graduation:* $30,860. *Financial aid deadline:* 7/30.

APPLYING

Standardized Tests *Required:* SAT or ACT (for admission).

Options: electronic application, deferred entrance.

Application fee: $25.

Required: high school transcript. *Required for some:* essay or personal statement, 2 letters of recommendation, interview. *Recommended:* minimum 2.9 GPA.

Notification: continuous (freshmen), continuous (transfers).

CONTACT

Mr. Jacob Queen, Director of Admission, Anderson University, 316 Boulevard, Anderson, SC 29621. *Phone:* 864-231-5795. *Toll-free phone:* 800-542-3594. *E-mail:* jqueen@andersonuniversity.edu.

The Art Institute of Charleston, a branch of The Art Institute of Atlanta

Charleston, South Carolina

http://www.artinstitutes.edu/charleston/

CONTACT

The Art Institute of Charleston, a branch of The Art Institute of Atlanta, 24 North Market Street, Charleston, SC 29401. *Phone:* 843-727-3500. *Toll-free phone:* 866-211-0107.

Benedict College

Columbia, South Carolina

http://www.benedict.edu/

CONTACT

Benedict College, 1600 Harden Street, Columbia, SC 29204. *Phone:* 803-705-4491. *Toll-free phone:* 800-868-6598.

COLLEGES AT-A-GLANCE

Bob Jones University

Greenville, South Carolina
http://www.bju.edu/

- **Independent Christian** university, founded 1927
- **Urban** 225-acre campus
- **Coed** 2,606 undergraduate students, 88% full-time, 55% women, 45% men
- **Minimally difficult** entrance level, 86% of applicants were admitted

UNDERGRAD STUDENTS

2,306 full-time, 300 part-time. Students come from 55 states and territories; 40 other countries; 68% are from out of state; 2% Black or African American, non-Hispanic/Latino; 6% Hispanic/Latino; 2% Asian, non-Hispanic/Latino; 0.5% Native Hawaiian or other Pacific Islander, non-Hispanic/Latino; 0.4% American Indian or Alaska Native, non-Hispanic/Latino; 3% Two or more races, non-Hispanic/Latino; 3% Race/ethnicity unknown; 6% international; 3% transferred in; 69% live on campus.

Freshmen:
Admission: 1,062 applied, 915 admitted, 596 enrolled. *Average high school GPA:* 3.2. *Test scores:* ACT scores over 18: 87%; ACT scores over 24: 50%; ACT scores over 30: 7%.
Retention: 82% of full-time freshmen returned.

FACULTY
Total: 217, 86% full-time, 63% with terminal degrees.
Student/faculty ratio: 13:1.

ACADEMICS
Calendar: semesters. *Degrees:* associate, bachelor's, master's, doctoral, and post-master's certificates.

Special study options: accelerated degree program, adult/continuing education programs, advanced placement credit, distance learning, double majors, English as a second language, internships, off-campus study, part-time degree program, services for LD students, student-designed majors, summer session for credit.

Computers: 450 computers/terminals and 500 ports are available on campus for general student use. Students can access the following: campus intranet, computer help desk, free student e-mail accounts, online (class) grades, online (class) registration, online (class) schedules. Campuswide network is available. 100% of college-owned or -operated housing units are wired for high-speed Internet access. Wireless service is available via classrooms, computer labs, dorm rooms, learning centers, libraries, student centers.
Library: Mack Library plus 2 others.

STUDENT LIFE
Housing options: on-campus residence required through senior year; men-only, women-only, special housing for students with disabilities. Campus housing is university owned. Freshman campus housing is guaranteed.

Activities and organizations: drama/theater group, student-run newspaper, radio and television station, choral group, Community Service Council, Missions Advance, Societies, Mission Prayer Band, University Business Association.

Athletics Member NCCAA. *Intercollegiate sports:* basketball M/W, cross-country running M/W, golf M/W, riflery M, soccer M/W, track and field M/W. *Intramural sports:* badminton M/W, basketball M/W, cheerleading W, racquetball M, soccer M/W, softball M/W, table tennis M/W, tennis M/W, volleyball M/W, water polo W.

Campus security: 24-hour patrols, student patrols, late-night transport/escort service, controlled dormitory access, 24/7 emergency dispatcher.

Student services: health clinic, personal/psychological counseling.

COSTS & FINANCIAL AID
Costs (2018–19) *Comprehensive fee:* $25,126 includes full-time tuition ($17,250), mandatory fees ($900), and room and board ($6976). Full-time tuition and fees vary according to course load and program. Part-time tuition: $860 per credit hour. Part-time tuition and fees vary according to course load and program. *Required fees:* $488 per degree program part-

time. *Payment plan:* installment. *Waivers:* employees or children of employees.

Financial Aid Of all full-time matriculated undergraduates who enrolled in 2017, 1,862 applied for aid, 1,653 were judged to have need, 269 had their need fully met. In 2017, 470 non-need-based awards were made. *Average percent of need met:* 61. *Average financial aid package:* $12,290. *Average need-based loan:* $3814. *Average need-based gift aid:* $10,486. *Average non-need-based aid:* $5069. *Average indebtedness upon graduation:* $21,153.

APPLYING
Options: electronic application.

Required: essay or personal statement, high school transcript, 3 letters of recommendation.

Application deadlines: 8/1 (freshmen), 8/1 (transfers).

Notification: continuous (freshmen), continuous (transfers).

CONTACT
Mr. Gary Deedrick, Director of Admission, Bob Jones University, 1700 Wade Hampton Boulevard, Greenville, SC 29614. *Phone:* 864-242-5100. *Toll-free phone:* 800-252-6363. *Fax:* 800-232-9258. *E-mail:* admission@bju.edu.

Charleston Southern University

Charleston, South Carolina
http://www.charlestonsouthern.edu/

- **Independent Baptist** comprehensive, founded 1964
- **Suburban** 500-acre campus
- **Endowment** $18.2 million
- **Coed** 3,062 undergraduate students, 92% full-time, 62% women, 38% men
- **Moderately difficult** entrance level, 56% of applicants were admitted

UNDERGRAD STUDENTS

2,804 full-time, 258 part-time. Students come from 41 states and territories; 17 other countries; 16% are from out of state; 24% Black or African American, non-Hispanic/Latino; 4% Hispanic/Latino; 2% Asian, non-Hispanic/Latino; 0.2% Native Hawaiian or other Pacific Islander, non-Hispanic/Latino; 0.6% American Indian or Alaska Native, non-Hispanic/Latino; 3% Two or more races, non-Hispanic/Latino; 4% Race/ethnicity unknown; 0.7% international; 9% transferred in; 42% live on campus.

Freshmen:
Admission: 4,125 applied, 2,323 admitted, 632 enrolled.
Retention: 66% of full-time freshmen returned.

FACULTY
Total: 315, 57% full-time.
Student/faculty ratio: 15:1.

ACADEMICS
Calendar: 4-4-1. *Degrees:* bachelor's, master's, and post-master's certificates.

Special study options: academic remediation for entering students, accelerated degree program, advanced placement credit, double majors, honors programs, internships, off-campus study, part-time degree program, services for LD students, summer session for credit. *ROTC:* Army (b), Air Force (b).

Unusual degree programs: 3-2 engineering with University of South Carolina.

Computers: 250 computers/terminals are available on campus for general student use. Students can access the following: computer help desk, free student e-mail accounts, online (class) grades, online (class) registration, online (class) schedules, online course work. Campuswide network is available. 100% of college-owned or -operated housing units are wired for high-speed Internet access. Wireless service is available via entire campus.
Library: L. Mendel Rivers Library plus 1 other. *Books:* 117,095 (physical), 303,641 (digital/electronic); *Serial titles:* 4,761 (physical), 53,688 (digital/electronic); *Databases:* 177. Weekly public service hours: 83; students can reserve study rooms.

STUDENT LIFE

Housing options: on-campus residence required for freshman year; men-only, women-only. Campus housing is university owned. Freshman applicants given priority for college housing.

Activities and organizations: drama/theater group, student-run newspaper, choral group, marching band, Student Government, Baptist Student Union, Fellowship of Christian Athletes, national fraternities, national sororities.

Athletics Member NCAA. All Division I except football (Division I-AA). *Intercollegiate sports:* baseball M(s), basketball M(s)/W(s), cheerleading M/W, cross-country running M(s)/W(s), golf M(s)/W(s), soccer W(s), softball W(s), tennis W(s), track and field M(s)/W(s), volleyball W(s). *Intramural sports:* basketball M/W, football M/W, soccer M/W, softball M/W, volleyball M/W.

Campus security: 24-hour emergency response devices and patrols, late-night transport/escort service, controlled dormitory access.

Student services: personal/psychological counseling.

COSTS & FINANCIAL AID

Costs (2017–18) *Comprehensive fee:* $34,730 includes full-time tuition ($24,800), mandatory fees ($30), and room and board ($9900). Full-time tuition and fees vary according to course load and program. Part-time tuition: $470 per credit hour. Part-time tuition and fees vary according to course load and program. *Required fees:* $30 per year part-time. *Waivers:* employees or children of employees.

Financial Aid Of all full-time matriculated undergraduates who enrolled in 2007, 1,968 applied for aid, 1,749 were judged to have need, 421 had their need fully met. 614 Federal Work-Study jobs (averaging $1406). In 2007, 306 non-need-based awards were made. *Average percent of need met:* 73. *Average financial aid package:* $15,036. *Average need-based loan:* $4804. *Average need-based gift aid:* $11,008. *Average non-need-based aid:* $10,832. *Average indebtedness upon graduation:* $20,252.

APPLYING

Standardized Tests *Required:* SAT or ACT (for admission).

Options: electronic application.

Application fee: $40.

Required: high school transcript, minimum 2.0 GPA. *Required for some:* essay or personal statement, 1 letter of recommendation, interview.

Application deadlines: rolling (freshmen), rolling (transfers).

Notification: continuous (freshmen), continuous (transfers).

CONTACT

Mr. Jim Rhoden, Director of Enrollment Management, Charleston Southern University, Charleston, SC 29423-8087. *Phone:* 843-863-7050. *Toll-free phone:* 800-947-7474. *E-mail:* enroll@csuniv.edu.

The Citadel, The Military College of South Carolina

Charleston, South Carolina

http://www.citadel.edu/

- **State-supported** comprehensive, founded 1842
- **Suburban** 300-acre campus
- **Endowment** $254.3 million
- **Coed, primarily men** 2,837 undergraduate students, 90% full-time, 11% women, 89% men
- **Moderately difficult** entrance level, 81% of applicants were admitted

UNDERGRAD STUDENTS

2,559 full-time, 278 part-time. Students come from 42 states and territories; 8 other countries; 33% are from out of state; 9% Black or African American, non-Hispanic/Latino; 7% Hispanic/Latino; 2% Asian, non-Hispanic/Latino; 0.3% Native Hawaiian or other Pacific Islander, non-Hispanic/Latino; 0.4% American Indian or Alaska Native, non-Hispanic/Latino; 4% Two or more races, non-Hispanic/Latino; 0.8% Race/ethnicity unknown; 0.8% international; 5% transferred in; 100% live on campus.

Freshmen:

Admission: 2,642 applied, 2,142 admitted, 687 enrolled. *Average high school GPA:* 3.7. *Test scores:* SAT evidence-based reading and writing scores over 500: 82%; SAT math scores over 500: 80%; ACT scores over

18: 97%; SAT evidence-based reading and writing scores over 600: 34%; SAT math scores over 600: 27%; ACT scores over 24: 43%; SAT evidence-based reading and writing scores over 700: 2%; SAT math scores over 700: 4%; ACT scores over 30: 9%.

Retention: 85% of full-time freshmen returned.

FACULTY

Total: 317, 63% full-time, 73% with terminal degrees.

Student/faculty ratio: 12:1.

ACADEMICS

Calendar: semesters. *Degrees:* bachelor's, master's, post-master's, and postbachelor's certificates.

Special study options: adult/continuing education programs, advanced placement credit, cooperative education, distance learning, double majors, English as a second language, honors programs, independent study, internships, off-campus study, part-time degree program, services for LD students, study abroad, summer session for credit. *ROTC:* Army (b), Navy (b), Air Force (b).

Computers: 350 computers/terminals are available on campus for general student use. Students can access the following: campus intranet, computer help desk, free student e-mail accounts, online (class) grades, online (class) registration, online (class) schedules. Campuswide network is available. 100% of college-owned or -operated housing units are wired for high-speed Internet access. Wireless service is available via entire campus.

Library: Daniel Library. *Books:* 182,744 (physical), 225,852 (digital/electronic); *Serial titles:* 97 (physical); *Databases:* 250. Students can reserve study rooms.

STUDENT LIFE

Housing options: on-campus residence required through senior year; coed. Campus housing is university owned. Freshman campus housing is guaranteed.

Activities and organizations: student-run newspaper, choral group, marching band, The Republican Society, Semper Fi Society, American Society of Civil Engineers, Campus Outreach, Criminal Justice Society.

Athletics Member NCAA. All Division I except football (Division I-AA). *Intercollegiate sports:* baseball M(s), basketball M(s), cross-country running M(s)/W(s), golf W(s), riflery M(s)/W(s), soccer W(s), tennis M(s), track and field M(s)/W(s), volleyball W(s), wrestling M(s). *Intramural sports:* badminton M/W, basketball M/W, fencing M(c)/W(c), football M/W, golf M(c), ice hockey M(c)/W(c), lacrosse M(c), racquetball M/W, riflery M/W, rugby M(c)/W(c), sailing M(c)/W(c), sand volleyball M/W, soccer M/W, softball M/W, swimming and diving M/W, table tennis M/W, tennis M/W, track and field M/W, triathlon M(c)/W(c), ultimate Frisbee M/W, volleyball M(c)/W(c), weight lifting M/W, wrestling M/W.

Campus security: 24-hour patrols.

Student services: health clinic, personal/psychological counseling.

COSTS & FINANCIAL AID

Costs (2017–18) *Tuition:* state resident $12,056 full-time, $470 per credit hour part-time; nonresident $33,819 full-time, $874 per credit hour part-time. Full-time tuition and fees vary according to class time, degree level, program, and student level. Part-time tuition and fees vary according to class time and program. *Required fees:* $2312 full-time. *Room and board:* $6600. *Payment plan:* installment. *Waivers:* senior citizens and employees or children of employees.

Financial Aid Of all full-time matriculated undergraduates who enrolled in 2017, 1,921 applied for aid, 1,512 were judged to have need, 387 had their need fully met. In 2017, 589 non-need-based awards were made. *Average percent of need met:* 62. *Average financial aid package:* $17,136. *Average need-based loan:* $4191. *Average need-based gift aid:* $16,862. *Average non-need-based aid:* $15,228. *Average indebtedness upon graduation:* $32,039.

APPLYING

Standardized Tests *Required:* SAT or ACT (for admission).

Options: electronic application.

Application fee: $40.

Required: high school transcript. *Recommended:* interview.

Application deadlines: rolling (freshmen), rolling (transfers).

Notification: continuous (freshmen), continuous (transfers).

CONTACT
Lt. Col. John W. Powell Jr., Director of Admissions, The Citadel, The Military College of South Carolina, 171 Moultrie Street, Charleston, SC 29409. *Phone:* 843-953-5230. *Toll-free phone:* 800-868-1842. *Fax:* 843-953-7036. *E-mail:* john.powell@citadel.edu.

Claflin University
Orangeburg, South Carolina
http://www.claflin.edu/

CONTACT
Claflin University, 400 Magnolia Street, Orangeburg, SC 29115. *Phone:* 803-535-5340. *Toll-free phone:* 800-922-1276.

Clemson University
Clemson, South Carolina
http://www.clemson.edu/

- **State-supported** university, founded 1889
- **Small-town** 1400-acre campus
- **Endowment** $518.6 million
- **Coed** 19,402 undergraduate students, 96% full-time, 49% women, 51% men
- **Very difficult** entrance level, 47% of applicants were admitted

UNDERGRAD STUDENTS
18,642 full-time, 760 part-time. Students come from 53 states and territories; 84 other countries; 29% are from out of state; 7% Black or African American, non-Hispanic/Latino; 4% Hispanic/Latino; 2% Asian, non-Hispanic/Latino; 0.2% American Indian or Alaska Native, non-Hispanic/Latino; 3% Two or more races, non-Hispanic/Latino; 0.3% Race/ethnicity unknown; 0.9% international; 8% transferred in; 37% live on campus.

Freshmen:
Admission: 26,241 applied, 12,380 admitted, 3,649 enrolled. *Test scores:* SAT evidence-based reading and writing scores over 500: 98%; SAT math scores over 500: 98%; ACT scores over 18: 99%; SAT evidence-based reading and writing scores over 600: 84%; SAT math scores over 600: 79%; ACT scores over 24: 95%; SAT evidence-based reading and writing scores over 700: 22%; SAT math scores over 700: 28%; ACT scores over 30: 49%.

Retention: 93% of full-time freshmen returned.

FACULTY
Total: 1,648, 76% full-time, 77% with terminal degrees.
Student/faculty ratio: 16:1.

ACADEMICS
Calendar: semesters. *Degrees:* bachelor's, master's, doctoral, and post-master's certificates.

Special study options: academic remediation for entering students, advanced placement credit, cooperative education, distance learning, double majors, English as a second language, freshman honors college, honors programs, independent study, internships, off-campus study, part-time degree program, services for LD students, study abroad, summer session for credit. *ROTC:* Army (b), Air Force (b).

Computers: 1,250 computers/terminals are available on campus for general student use. Students can access the following: campus intranet, computer help desk, free student e-mail accounts, online (class) grades, online (class) registration, online (class) schedules. Campuswide network is available. 100% of college-owned or -operated housing units are wired for high-speed Internet access. Wireless service is available via entire campus.

Library: Robert Muldrow Cooper Library plus 1 other. Study areas open 24 hours, 5–7 days a week; students can reserve study rooms.

STUDENT LIFE
Housing options: on-campus residence required for freshman year; coed, men-only, women-only. Campus housing is university owned. Freshman campus housing is guaranteed.

Activities and organizations: drama/theater group, student-run newspaper, radio and television station, choral group, marching band, Student Government, Fellowship of Christian Athletes, Tiger Band, national fraternities, national sororities.

Athletics Member NCAA. All Division I except football (Division I-A). *Intercollegiate sports:* baseball M(s), basketball M(s)/W(s), bowling M(c)/W(c), cheerleading M/W, crew M(c)/W(s), cross-country running M(s)/W(s), equestrian sports M(c)/W(c), fencing M(c)/W(c), field hockey M(c)/W(c), golf M(s), ice hockey M(c)/W(c), lacrosse M(c)/W(c), riflery M(c)/W(c), rugby M(c)/W(c), sailing M(c)/W(c), soccer M(s)/W(s), softball W(s)(c), tennis M(s)/W(s), track and field M(s)/W(s), ultimate Frisbee M(c)/W(c), volleyball M(c)/W(s), weight lifting M(c)/W(c), wrestling M(c). *Intramural sports:* basketball M/W, golf M/W, racquetball M/W, soccer M/W, softball M/W, swimming and diving M(c)/W(c), table tennis M/W, tennis M(c)/W(c), volleyball M/W, water polo M/W.

Campus security: 24-hour emergency response devices and patrols, late-night transport/escort service, controlled dormitory access.

Student services: health clinic, personal/psychological counseling, legal services.

COSTS & FINANCIAL AID

Costs (2017–18) *Tuition:* state resident $13,520 full-time, $630 per credit hour part-time; nonresident $34,132 full-time, $1540 per credit hour part-time. Full-time tuition and fees vary according to course level, course load, location, program, and student level. Part-time tuition and fees vary according to course level, course load, location, program, and student level. *Required fees:* $1192 full-time. *Room and board:* $9592. Room and board charges vary according to board plan, housing facility, and location. *Payment plan:* installment. *Waivers:* senior citizens.

Financial Aid Of all full-time matriculated undergraduates who enrolled in 2017, 12,307 applied for aid, 8,958 were judged to have need, 1,409 had their need fully met. 584 state and other part-time jobs (averaging $1541). In 2017, 5332 non-need-based awards were made. *Average percent of need met:* 54. *Average financial aid package:* $11,582. *Average need-based loan:* $4531. *Average need-based gift aid:* $9183. *Average non-need-based aid:* $5071. *Average indebtedness upon graduation:* $30,201.

APPLYING

Standardized Tests *Required:* SAT or ACT (for admission).

Options: electronic application.

Application fee: $70.

Required: high school transcript. *Recommended:* essay or personal statement.

Application deadlines: 5/1 (freshmen), 7/1 (transfers).

Notification: continuous (freshmen), continuous (transfers).

CONTACT

Clemson University, Clemson, SC 29634.

See previous page for display ad and page 1260 for the College Close-Up.

Coastal Carolina University

Conway, South Carolina

http://www.coastal.edu/

- **State-supported** comprehensive, founded 1954
- **Suburban** 633-acre campus
- **Endowment** $39.4 million
- **Coed** 9,898 undergraduate students, 91% full-time, 54% women, 46% men
- **Moderately difficult** entrance level, 61% of applicants were admitted

UNDERGRAD STUDENTS

9,021 full-time, 877 part-time. Students come from 49 states and territories; 63 other countries; 51% are from out of state; 19% Black or African American, non-Hispanic/Latino; 4% Hispanic/Latino; 0.7% Asian, non-Hispanic/Latino; 0.1% Native Hawaiian or other Pacific Islander, non-Hispanic/Latino; 0.2% American Indian or Alaska Native, non-Hispanic/Latino; 5% Two or more races, non-Hispanic/Latino; 1% Race/ethnicity unknown; 2% international; 8% transferred in; 44% live on campus.

Freshmen:

Admission: 18,563 applied, 11,359 admitted, 2,390 enrolled. *Average high school GPA:* 3.6. *Test scores:* SAT evidence-based reading and writing scores over 500: 86%; SAT math scores over 500: 83%; ACT scores over 18: 96%; SAT evidence-based reading and writing scores over 600: 23%; SAT math scores over 600: 19%; ACT scores over 24: 32%; SAT evidence-based reading and writing scores over 700: 1%; SAT math scores over 700: 1%; ACT scores over 30: 2%.

Retention: 67% of full-time freshmen returned.

FACULTY

Total: 787, 57% full-time, 56% with terminal degrees.

Student/faculty ratio: 17:1.

ACADEMICS

Calendar: semesters. *Degrees:* certificates, bachelor's, master's, doctoral, post-master's, and postbachelor's certificates.

Special study options: accelerated degree program, adult/continuing education programs, advanced placement credit, cooperative education, distance learning, double majors, honors programs, independent study, internships, part-time degree program, services for LD students, student-designed majors, study abroad, summer session for credit. *ROTC:* Army (b).

Computers: 1,322 computers/terminals are available on campus for general student use. Students can access the following: computer help desk, free student e-mail accounts, online (class) grades, online (class) registration, online (class) schedules. Campuswide network is available. Wireless service is available via classrooms, computer centers, computer labs, dorm rooms, learning centers, libraries, student centers.

Library: Kimbel Library. *Books:* 137,543 (physical), 417,526 (digital/electronic); *Serial titles:* 588 (physical), 127,240 (digital/electronic); *Databases:* 175. Weekly public service hours: 168; study areas open 24 hours, 5–7 days a week.

STUDENT LIFE

Housing options: on-campus residence required through sophomore year; coed, special housing for students with disabilities. Campus housing is university owned. Freshman campus housing is guaranteed.

Activities and organizations: drama/theater group, student-run newspaper, radio station, choral group, marching band, National Society of Leadership and Success, Outdoor Adventure Club, Alpha Delta Pi, Salt Water Anglers, Aqua League (Scuba Club), national fraternities, national sororities.

Athletics Member NCAA. All Division I. *Intercollegiate sports:* baseball M(s), basketball M(s)/W(s), cheerleading M(c)/W(c), cross-country running M(s)/W(s), equestrian sports M(c)/W(c), field hockey M(c)/W(c), football M(s), golf M(s)/W(s), lacrosse M(c)/W(s), rugby M(c)/W(c), sailing M(c)/W(c), sand volleyball W(s), soccer M(s)/W(s), softball W(s), swimming and diving M(c)/W(c), tennis M(s)/W(s), track and field M(s)/W(s), volleyball M(c)/W(s), weight lifting M(c)/W(c), wrestling M(c). *Intramural sports:* badminton M/W, basketball M/W, sand volleyball M/W, soccer M/W, softball M/W, table tennis M/W, tennis M/W, volleyball M/W.

Campus security: 24-hour emergency response devices and patrols, late-night transport/escort service.

Student services: health clinic, personal/psychological counseling, women's center.

COSTS & FINANCIAL AID

Costs (2017–18) *Tuition:* state resident $11,020 full-time, $469 per credit hour part-time; nonresident $25,692 full-time, $1075 per credit hour part-time. Full-time tuition and fees vary according to course load, degree level, and reciprocity agreements. Part-time tuition and fees vary according to course load, degree level, and reciprocity agreements. *Required fees:* $180 full-time, $5 per credit hour part-time. *Room and board:* $9140; room only: $5440. Room and board charges vary according to board plan and housing facility. *Payment plan:* installment. *Waivers:* senior citizens and employees or children of employees.

Financial Aid Of all full-time matriculated undergraduates who enrolled in 2016, 7,333 applied for aid, 6,190 were judged to have need, 185 had their need fully met. 176 Federal Work-Study jobs (averaging $1890). 1,448 state and other part-time jobs (averaging $1820). In 2016, 1605 non-need-based awards were made. *Average percent of need met:* 46. *Average financial aid package:* $10,256. *Average need-based loan:* $9057. *Average need-based gift aid:* $4826. *Average non-need-based aid:* $14,432. *Average indebtedness upon graduation:* $37,373.

APPLYING

Standardized Tests *Required:* SAT or ACT (for admission).

Options: electronic application, deferred entrance.

Application fee: $45.

Required: high school transcript, minimum 2.0 GPA. *Recommended:* essay or personal statement, 1 letter of recommendation, interview.

Application deadlines: rolling (freshmen), rolling (transfers).

Notification: continuous until 10/1 (freshmen), continuous until 10/1 (transfers).

CONTACT
Coastal Carolina University, PO Box 261954, Conway, SC 29528-6054. *Phone:* 843-349-2170. *Toll-free phone:* 800-277-7000.

Coker College
Hartsville, South Carolina
http://www.coker.edu/

- **Independent** comprehensive, founded 1908
- **Small-town** 37-acre campus with easy access to Charlotte
- **Endowment** $29.2 million
- **Coed** 1,022 undergraduate students, 83% full-time, 60% women, 40% men
- **Moderately difficult** entrance level, 62% of applicants were admitted

UNDERGRAD STUDENTS
845 full-time, 177 part-time. Students come from 33 states and territories; 15 other countries; 24% are from out of state; 33% Black or African American, non-Hispanic/Latino; 3% Hispanic/Latino; 0.5% Asian, non-Hispanic/Latino; 0.1% Native Hawaiian or other Pacific Islander, non-Hispanic/Latino; 0.6% American Indian or Alaska Native, non-Hispanic/Latino; 6% Two or more races, non-Hispanic/Latino; 0.9% Race/ethnicity unknown; 3% international; 10% transferred in; 56% live on campus.

Freshmen:
Admission: 1,389 applied, 857 admitted, 210 enrolled. *Average high school GPA:* ####. *Test scores:* SAT evidence-based reading and writing scores over 500: 65%; SAT math scores over 500: 53%; ACT scores over 18: 69%; SAT evidence-based reading and writing scores over 600: 13%; SAT math scores over 600: 11%; ACT scores over 24: 14%; SAT math scores over 700: 1%; ACT scores over 30: 2%.

Retention: 61% of full-time freshmen returned.

FACULTY
Total: 95, 63% full-time, 69% with terminal degrees.
Student/faculty ratio: 13:1.

ACADEMICS
Calendar: semesters. *Degrees:* bachelor's and master's (also offers evening program with significant enrollment not reflected in profile).

Special study options: adult/continuing education programs, advanced placement credit, distance learning, double majors, honors programs, independent study, internships, off-campus study, part-time degree program, services for LD students, student-designed majors, study abroad, summer session for credit.

Computers: 116 computers/terminals and 400 ports are available on campus for general student use. Students can access the following: campus intranet, computer help desk, free student e-mail accounts, online (class) grades, online (class) registration, online (class) schedules. Campuswide network is available. 100% of college-owned or -operated housing units are wired for high-speed Internet access. Wireless service is available via entire campus.
Library: The Charles W. and Joan S. Coker Library-Information Technology Center plus 1 other. *Books:* 81,626 (physical), 15,760 (digital/electronic). Weekly public service hours: 87; students can reserve study rooms.

STUDENT LIFE
Housing options: coed, special housing for students with disabilities. Campus housing is university owned. Freshman campus housing is guaranteed.

Activities and organizations: drama/theater group, choral group, Student Government Association.

Athletics Member NCAA. All Division II except lacrosse (Division I). *Intercollegiate sports:* baseball M(s), basketball M(s)/W(s), cross-country running M(s)/W(s), golf M(s)/W(s), lacrosse M(s)/W(s), soccer M(s)/W(s), softball W(s), tennis M(s)/W(s), track and field M(s)/W(s), volleyball M(s)/W(s), wrestling M(s). *Intramural sports:* basketball M/W, football M/W, table tennis M/W, track and field M/W, volleyball M/W, weight lifting M/W.

Campus security: 24-hour patrols, late-night transport/escort service, controlled dormitory access.

Student services: health clinic, personal/psychological counseling.

COSTS & FINANCIAL AID
Costs (2017–18) *Comprehensive fee:* $37,508 includes full-time tuition ($28,464), mandatory fees ($220), and room and board ($8824). Full-time tuition and fees vary according to course load, degree level, location, and program. Part-time tuition: $1186 per credit hour. Part-time tuition and fees vary according to course load, degree level, location, and program. *College room only:* $4068. Room and board charges vary according to board plan and housing facility. *Payment plan:* installment. *Waivers:* employees or children of employees.

Financial Aid Of all full-time matriculated undergraduates who enrolled in 2016, 886 applied for aid, 822 were judged to have need, 162 had their need fully met. In 2016, 114 non-need-based awards were made. *Average percent of need met:* 70. *Average financial aid package:* $21,502. *Average need-based loan:* $4277. *Average need-based gift aid:* $21,502. *Average non-need-based aid:* $10,836. *Average indebtedness upon graduation:* $20,494.

APPLYING
Standardized Tests *Required:* SAT or ACT (for admission).

Options: electronic application, early action, deferred entrance.

Required: high school transcript. *Required for some:* essay or personal statement, interview, audition or portfolio for certain programs.

Application deadlines: rolling (freshmen), rolling (transfers), 12/1 (early action).

Notification: continuous (freshmen), continuous (out-of-state freshmen), continuous (transfers), 12/15 (early action).

CONTACT
Mr. Adam Connolly, Vice President for Enrollment Management, Coker College, 300 E. College Avenue, Hartsville, SC 29550. *Phone:* 843-383-8050. *Toll-free phone:* 800-950-1908. *Fax:* 843-383-8056. *E-mail:* admissions@coker.edu.

College of Charleston
Charleston, South Carolina
http://www.cofc.edu/

- **State-supported** comprehensive, founded 1770
- **Urban** 66-acre campus
- **Endowment** $80.1 million
- **Coed** 9,895 undergraduate students, 92% full-time, 63% women, 37% men
- **Moderately difficult** entrance level, 80% of applicants were admitted

UNDERGRAD STUDENTS
9,083 full-time, 812 part-time. Students come from 52 states and territories; 61 other countries; 40% are from out of state; 8% Black or African American, non-Hispanic/Latino; 5% Hispanic/Latino; 2% Asian, non-Hispanic/Latino; 0.2% Native Hawaiian or other Pacific Islander, non-Hispanic/Latino; 0.3% American Indian or Alaska Native, non-Hispanic/Latino; 4% Two or more races, non-Hispanic/Latino; 2% Race/ethnicity unknown; 1% international; 6% transferred in; 31% live on campus.

Freshmen:
Admission: 11,900 applied, 9,574 admitted, 1,840 enrolled. *Average high school GPA:* 3.9. *Test scores:* SAT evidence-based reading and writing scores over 500: 96%; SAT math scores over 500: 89%; ACT scores over 18: 99%; SAT evidence-based reading and writing scores over 600: 48%; SAT math scores over 600: 29%; ACT scores over 24: 61%; SAT evidence-based reading and writing scores over 700: 6%; SAT math scores over 700: 4%; ACT scores over 30: 11%.

Retention: 78% of full-time freshmen returned.

FACULTY
Total: 939, 58% full-time, 69% with terminal degrees.
Student/faculty ratio: 15:1.

ACADEMICS

Calendar: semesters. *Degrees:* bachelor's, master's, post-master's, and postbachelor's certificates (also offers graduate degree programs through University of Charleston, South Carolina).

Special study options: accelerated degree program, adult/continuing education programs, advanced placement credit, cooperative education, distance learning, double majors, English as a second language, honors programs, independent study, internships, off-campus study, part-time degree program, services for LD students, study abroad, summer session for credit. *ROTC:* Air Force (c).

Unusual degree programs: 3-2 computer science, mathematics.

Computers: Students can access the following: campus intranet, computer help desk, free student e-mail accounts, online (class) grades, online (class) registration, online (class) schedules. Campuswide network is available. 80% of college-owned or -operated housing units are wired for high-speed Internet access. Wireless service is available via entire campus.

Library: Marlene and Nathan Addlestone Library plus 3 others. *Books:* 700,910 (physical), 573,884 (digital/electronic); *Serial titles:* 2,721 (physical), 84,039 (digital/electronic); *Databases:* 328. Weekly public service hours: 121; students can reserve study rooms.

STUDENT LIFE

Housing options: coed, men-only, women-only, special housing for students with disabilities. Campus housing is university owned and leased by the school. Freshman applicants given priority for college housing.

Activities and organizations: drama/theater group, student-run newspaper, radio and television station, choral group, Student Government Association, Cougar Activities Board, Intramural Basketball, Black Student Union, Committed to Charleston Society, national fraternities, national sororities.

Athletics Member NCAA. All Division I. *Intercollegiate sports:* baseball M(s), basketball M(s)/W(s), cheerleading M/W, cross-country running M(s)/W(s), equestrian sports W, golf M(s)/W(s), sailing M/W, sand volleyball W(s), soccer M(s)/W(s), softball W(s), tennis M(s)/W(s), volleyball W(s). *Intramural sports:* badminton M/W, basketball M/W, crew M(c)/W(c), fencing M(c)/W(c), golf M(c)/W(c), gymnastics M(c)/W(c), ice hockey M(c)/W(c), lacrosse M(c)/W(c), rock climbing M/W, rowing M(c)/W(c), rugby M(c)/W(c), soccer M/W, softball M/W, squash M(c)/W(c), swimming and diving M(c)/W(c), table tennis M/W, tennis M(c)/W(c), ultimate Frisbee M(c)/W(c), volleyball M(c)/W(c), weight lifting M/W.

Campus security: 24-hour emergency response devices and patrols, student patrols, late-night transport/escort service, controlled dormitory access, shuttle service.

Student services: health clinic, personal/psychological counseling, women's center.

COSTS & FINANCIAL AID

Costs (2017–18) *Tuition:* state resident $11,998 full-time, $500 per credit hour part-time; nonresident $30,386 full-time, $1266 per credit hour part-time. Full-time tuition and fees vary according to student level. Part-time tuition and fees vary according to course load and student level. *Required fees:* $460 full-time, $16 per term part-time, $16 per term part-time. *Room and board:* $12,048; room only: $7828. Room and board charges vary according to board plan and housing facility. *Payment plan:* installment. *Waivers:* senior citizens and employees or children of employees.

Financial Aid Of all full-time matriculated undergraduates who enrolled in 2017, 5,879 applied for aid, 4,562 were judged to have need, 701 had their need fully met. In 2017, 1764 non-need-based awards were made. *Average percent of need met:* 53. *Average financial aid package:* $13,716. *Average need-based loan:* $3561. *Average need-based gift aid:* $3184. *Average non-need-based aid:* $11,798. *Average indebtedness upon graduation:* $27,256.

APPLYING

Standardized Tests *Required:* SAT or ACT (for admission).

Options: electronic application, early decision, early action, deferred entrance.

Application fee: $50.

Required: essay or personal statement, high school transcript. *Required for some:* letters of recommendation for Honors College.

Application deadlines: 2/15 (freshmen), 6/1 (transfers), 12/1 (early action).

Early decision deadline: 11/1.

Notification: 4/1 (freshmen), continuous (transfers), 1/1 (early action).

CONTACT
Ms. Suzette Stille, Executive Director of Admissions, College of Charleston, 66 George Street, Charleston, SC 29424-0001. *Phone:* 843-953-5670. *Fax:* 843-953-6322. *E-mail:* admissions@cofc.edu.

Columbia College
Columbia, South Carolina
http://www.columbiasc.edu/

- **Independent United Methodist** comprehensive, founded 1854
- **Suburban** 59-acre campus
- **Endowment** $25.6 million
- **Coed, primarily women** 1,400 undergraduate students, 57% full-time, 75% women, 25% men
- **Moderately difficult** entrance level, 87% of applicants were admitted

UNDERGRAD STUDENTS
802 full-time, 598 part-time. Students come from 27 states and territories; 21 other countries; 11% are from out of state; 33% Black or African American, non-Hispanic/Latino; 4% Hispanic/Latino; 0.7% Asian, non-Hispanic/Latino; 0.1% Native Hawaiian or other Pacific Islander, non-Hispanic/Latino; 0.8% American Indian or Alaska Native, non-Hispanic/Latino; 3% Two or more races, non-Hispanic/Latino; 1% Race/ethnicity unknown; 3% international; 15% transferred in; 29% live on campus.

Freshmen:
Admission: 880 applied, 764 admitted, 159 enrolled. *Average high school GPA:* 3.7. *Test scores:* SAT evidence-based reading and writing scores over 500: 66%; SAT math scores over 500: 50%; ACT scores over 18: 73%; SAT evidence-based reading and writing scores over 600: 16%; SAT math scores over 600: 3%; ACT scores over 24: 17%; ACT scores over 30: 3%.

Retention: 71% of full-time freshmen returned.

FACULTY
Total: 109, 50% full-time, 58% with terminal degrees.

Student/faculty ratio: 15:1.

ACADEMICS
Calendar: semesters. *Degrees:* bachelor's and master's.

Special study options: academic remediation for entering students, adult/continuing education programs, advanced placement credit, distance learning, double majors, honors programs, independent study, internships, off-campus study, part-time degree program, services for LD students, student-designed majors, study abroad, summer session for credit. *ROTC:* Army (c).

Computers: 165 computers/terminals are available on campus for general student use. Students can access the following: campus intranet, computer help desk, free student e-mail accounts, online (class) grades, online (class) registration, online (class) schedules. Campuswide network is available. 100% of college-owned or -operated housing units are wired for high-speed Internet access. Wireless service is available via entire campus.

Library: J. Edens Drake Library. *Books:* 128,000 (physical), 92 (digital/electronic); *Serial titles:* 310 (physical); *Databases:* 84. Weekly public service hours: 70; students can reserve study rooms.

STUDENT LIFE
Housing options: on-campus residence required through sophomore year; women-only. Campus housing is university owned. Freshman campus housing is guaranteed.

Activities and organizations: drama/theater group, student-run newspaper, choral group.

Athletics Member NAIA. *Intercollegiate sports:* basketball W(s), cross-country running W(s), golf W(s), lacrosse W(s), soccer W(s), softball W(s), swimming and diving W(s), tennis W(s), track and field W(s), volleyball W(s).

Campus security: 24-hour emergency response devices and patrols, late-night transport/escort service, controlled dormitory access.

Student services: health clinic, personal/psychological counseling, women's center.

COSTS & FINANCIAL AID

Costs (2018–19) *One-time required fee:* $150. *Comprehensive fee:* $27,400 includes full-time tuition ($19,500) and room and board ($7900). Full-time tuition and fees vary according to class time and location. Part-time tuition: $650 per semester hour. Part-time tuition and fees vary according to class time and location. *College room only:* $3900. Room and board charges vary according to board plan and housing facility. *Payment plan:* installment. *Waivers:* employees or children of employees.

Financial Aid Of all full-time matriculated undergraduates who enrolled in 2005, 794 applied for aid, 698 were judged to have need, 310 had their need fully met. 200 Federal Work-Study jobs (averaging $1000). In 2005, 152 non-need-based awards were made. *Average percent of need met:* 70. *Average financial aid package:* $20,052. *Average need-based loan:* $3810. *Average need-based gift aid:* $8495. *Average non-need-based aid:* $7775. *Average indebtedness upon graduation:* $25,333.

APPLYING

Options: electronic application.

Required: high school transcript. *Required for some:* interview. *Recommended:* essay or personal statement.

Application deadlines: 8/1 (freshmen), 8/1 (transfers).

CONTACT

Mr. Ryan Longe, Director of Admissions Operations, Columbia College, 1301 Columbia College Drive, Columbia, SC 29203. *Phone:* 803-786-3871. *Toll-free phone:* 800-277-1301. *E-mail:* rlonge@columbiasc.edu.

Columbia International University

Columbia, South Carolina

http://www.ciu.edu/

- **Independent nondenominational** university, founded 1923
- **Suburban** 400-acre campus with easy access to Columbia, SC
- **Endowment** $21.1 million
- **Coed**
- **Moderately difficult** entrance level

FACULTY

Student/faculty ratio: 16:1.

ACADEMICS

Calendar: semesters. *Degrees:* certificates, associate, bachelor's, master's, doctoral, post-master's, and postbachelor's certificates.

Library: G. Allen Fleece Library. *Books:* 32,000 (physical), 100,000 (digital/electronic); *Databases:* 133. Weekly public service hours: 81; students can reserve study rooms.

STUDENT LIFE

Housing options: on-campus residence required through senior year; men-only, women-only. Campus housing is university owned. Freshman campus housing is guaranteed.

Activities and organizations: drama/theater group, student-run newspaper, choral group, Student Union, Mu Kappa, Student Missions Connection, GradLife, African American Fellowship Ministries.

Athletics Member NCCAA.

Campus security: 24-hour emergency response devices and patrols, late-night transport/escort service, controlled dormitory access.

Student services: health clinic, personal/psychological counseling, legal services.

COSTS & FINANCIAL AID

Costs (2017–18) *Comprehensive fee:* $30,380 includes full-time tuition ($21,720), mandatory fees ($670), and room and board ($7990). Full-time tuition and fees vary according to course load, program, and reciprocity agreements. Part-time tuition: $905 per semester hour. Part-time tuition and fees vary according to course load, program, and reciprocity agreements. *Required fees:* $10 per semester hour part-time, $185 per term part-time. *Room and board:* Room and board charges vary according to board plan and housing facility.

Financial Aid Of all full-time matriculated undergraduates who enrolled in 2016, 391 applied for aid, 336 were judged to have need, 47 had their need fully met. In 2016, 91 non-need-based awards were made. *Average*

percent of need met: 69. *Average financial aid package:* $18,497. *Average need-based loan:* $4176. *Average need-based gift aid:* $14,494. *Average non-need-based aid:* $6922. *Average indebtedness upon graduation:* $24,132.

APPLYING

Standardized Tests *Required:* SAT or ACT (for admission).

Options: electronic application, deferred entrance.

Required: essay or personal statement, minimum 2.0 GPA, 1 letter of recommendation. *Required for some:* interview. *Recommended:* high school transcript.

CONTACT

Ms. Jen Johnson, Undergraduate Admissions Office, Columbia International University, Columbia, SC 29230-3122. *Phone:* 803-777-2227. *Toll-free phone:* 800-777-2227 Ext. 5024. *Fax:* 803-786-4041. *E-mail:* yesciu@ciu.edu.

Converse College

Spartanburg, South Carolina

http://www.converse.edu/

- **Independent** comprehensive, founded 1889
- **Urban** 70-acre campus
- **Undergraduate: women only; graduate: coed** 870 undergraduate students, 94% full-time, 100% women
- **Moderately difficult** entrance level, 60% of applicants were admitted

UNDERGRAD STUDENTS

815 full-time, 55 part-time. 24% are from out of state; 9% Black or African American, non-Hispanic/Latino; 4% Hispanic/Latino; 0.6% Asian, non-Hispanic/Latino; 4% Two or more races, non-Hispanic/Latino; 13% Race/ethnicity unknown; 2% international; 6% transferred in; 73% live on campus.

Freshmen:

Admission: 1,359 applied, 821 admitted, 242 enrolled. *Average high school GPA:* 4.0. *Test scores:* SAT evidence-based reading and writing scores over 500: 66%; SAT math scores over 500: 54%; ACT scores over 18: 95%; SAT evidence-based reading and writing scores over 600: 23%; SAT math scores over 600: 10%; ACT scores over 24: 43%; SAT evidence-based reading and writing scores over 700: 1%; SAT math scores over 700: 3%; ACT scores over 30: 4%.

Retention: 70% of full-time freshmen returned.

FACULTY

Total: 84, 96% full-time, 95% with terminal degrees.

Student/faculty ratio: 13:1.

ACADEMICS

Calendar: 4-1-4. *Degrees:* bachelor's, master's, and post-master's certificates.

Special study options: adult/continuing education programs, advanced placement credit, cooperative education, double majors, honors programs, independent study, internships, off-campus study, part-time degree program, student-designed majors, study abroad, summer session for credit. *ROTC:* Army (c).

Computers: 140 computers/terminals are available on campus for general student use. Students can access the following: campus intranet, computer help desk, free student e-mail accounts, online (class) grades, online (class) registration, online (class) schedules. Campuswide network is available. 100% of college-owned or -operated housing units are wired for high-speed Internet access. Wireless service is available via entire campus.

Library: Mickel Library. *Books:* 165,873 (physical), 252,047 (digital/electronic); *Databases:* 30.

STUDENT LIFE

Housing options: on-campus residence required through senior year; women-only. Campus housing is university owned. Freshman campus housing is guaranteed.

Activities and organizations: drama/theater group, student-run newspaper, choral group, Student Government, student volunteer services, Student Christian Organization, Student Activities Committee, Athletic Association.

Athletics Member NCAA. All Division II. *Intercollegiate sports:* basketball W(s), cross-country running W(s), equestrian sports W(s), golf W(s), lacrosse W(s), soccer W(s), swimming and diving W(s), tennis W(s), track and field W(s), volleyball W(s). *Intramural sports:* archery W, basketball W, bowling W, equestrian sports W, fencing W, field hockey W, soccer W, softball W, swimming and diving W, tennis W, volleyball W, weight lifting W.

Campus security: 24-hour emergency response devices and patrols, late-night transport/escort service, controlled dormitory access.

Student services: health clinic, personal/psychological counseling, women's center.

COSTS & FINANCIAL AID
Costs (2018–19) *Comprehensive fee:* $28,640 includes full-time tuition ($17,680), mandatory fees ($350), and room and board ($10,610). Full-time tuition and fees vary according to course load and program. Part-time tuition: $875 per credit. Part-time tuition and fees vary according to course load and program. *Room and board:* Room and board charges vary according to board plan. *Payment plan:* installment. *Waivers:* employees or children of employees.

Financial Aid Of all full-time matriculated undergraduates who enrolled in 2016, 772 applied for aid, 655 were judged to have need, 114 had their need fully met. 62 Federal Work-Study jobs (averaging $1339). 90 state and other part-time jobs (averaging $1653). In 2016, 131 non-need-based awards were made. *Average percent of need met:* 62. *Average financial aid package:* $14,724. *Average need-based loan:* $4352. *Average need-based gift aid:* $11,504. *Average non-need-based aid:* $5532. *Average indebtedness upon graduation:* $29,814.

APPLYING
Standardized Tests *Required:* SAT or ACT (for admission).

Options: electronic application, deferred entrance.

Required: high school transcript. *Recommended:* essay or personal statement, minimum 3.0 GPA.

Application deadlines: 8/1 (freshmen), rolling (out-of-state freshmen), 8/1 (transfers).

Notification: continuous until 9/1 (freshmen), continuous (out-of-state freshmen), continuous until 8/15 (transfers).

CONTACT
Admissions, Converse College, 580 East Main Street, Spartanburg, SC 29302. *Phone:* 864-596-9040. *Toll-free phone:* 800-766-1125. *E-mail:* admissions@converse.edu.

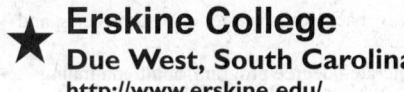

★ Erskine College
Due West, South Carolina
http://www.erskine.edu/

CONTACT
Ms. Tobe Frierson, Senior Admissions Specialist, Erskine College, 2 Washington Street, PO Box 338, Due West, SC 29639. *Phone:* 864-379-8838. *Toll-free phone:* 800-241-8721.

See next page for display ad and page 1288 for the College Close-Up.

Francis Marion University
Florence, South Carolina
http://www.fmarion.edu/

- **State-supported** comprehensive, founded 1970
- **Rural** 400-acre campus
- **Endowment** $25.7 million
- **Coed** 3,560 undergraduate students, 84% full-time, 67% women, 31% men
- **Moderately difficult** entrance level, 62% of applicants were admitted

UNDERGRAD STUDENTS
3,006 full-time, 454 part-time. Students come from 21 states and territories; 21 other countries; 3% are from out of state; 41% Black or African American, non-Hispanic/Latino; 2% Hispanic/Latino; 1% Asian, non-Hispanic/Latino; 0.1% Native Hawaiian or other Pacific Islander, non-Hispanic/Latino; 0.5% American Indian or Alaska Native, non-Hispanic/Latino; 3% Two or more races, non-Hispanic/Latino; 0.3%

Race/ethnicity unknown; 2% international; 7% transferred in; 50% live on campus.

Freshmen:
Admission: 3,738 applied, 2,301 admitted, 690 enrolled. *Average high school GPA:* 3.9. *Test scores:* ACT scores over 18: 69%; ACT scores over 24: 17%.

Retention: 65% of full-time freshmen returned.

FACULTY
Total: 258, 71% full-time, 62% with terminal degrees.

Student/faculty ratio: 16:1.

ACADEMICS
Calendar: semesters. *Degrees:* bachelor's, master's, and post-master's certificates.

Special study options: accelerated degree program, adult/continuing education programs, advanced placement credit, distance learning, double majors, honors programs, independent study, internships, off-campus study, part-time degree program, services for LD students, study abroad, summer session for credit. *ROTC:* Army (b).

Unusual degree programs: 3-2 engineering with Clemson University; forestry with Clemson University; wildlife and fisheries with Clemson University.

Computers: 634 computers/terminals are available on campus for general student use. Students can access the following: computer help desk, free student e-mail accounts, online (class) grades, online (class) registration, online (class) schedules, learning management system. Campuswide network is available. 100% of college-owned or -operated housing units are wired for high-speed Internet access. Wireless service is available via entire campus.

Library: James A. Rogers Library plus 1 other. *Books:* 343,000 (digital/electronic).

STUDENT LIFE
Housing options: men-only, women-only, special housing for students with disabilities. Campus housing is university owned and is provided by a third party. Freshman applicants given priority for college housing.

Activities and organizations: drama/theater group, student-run newspaper, choral group, Baptist Collegiate Ministries, University Programming Board, Psychology Club, Student Alumni Association, Young Gifted and Blessed Chorus, national fraternities, national sororities.

Athletics Member NCAA. All Division II except golf (Division I), soccer (Division I). *Intercollegiate sports:* baseball M(s), basketball M(s)/W(s), cheerleading W, cross-country running M(s)/W(s), golf M(s), soccer M(s)/W(s), softball W(s), tennis M(s)/W(s), track and field M/W, volleyball W(s). *Intramural sports:* basketball M/W, football M, racquetball M/W, soccer M/W, softball M/W, table tennis M/W, tennis M/W, volleyball M/W.

Campus security: 24-hour emergency response devices and patrols, late-night transport/escort service, controlled dormitory access.

Student services: health clinic, personal/psychological counseling.

COSTS & FINANCIAL AID
Costs (2017–18) *Tuition:* state resident $10,178 full-time, $509 per credit hour part-time; nonresident $20,354 full-time, $1018 per credit hour part-time. Full-time tuition and fees vary according to degree level and program. Part-time tuition and fees vary according to course load, degree level, and program. *Required fees:* $564 full-time, $15 per credit hour part-time, $88 per term part-time. *Room and board:* $7948; room only: $4490. Room and board charges vary according to board plan and housing facility. *Payment plan:* installment. *Waivers:* senior citizens and employees or children of employees.

Financial Aid Of all full-time matriculated undergraduates who enrolled in 2017, 2,572 applied for aid, 2,316 were judged to have need, 222 had their need fully met. In 2017, 364 non-need-based awards were made. *Average percent of need met:* 64. *Average financial aid package:* $12,465. *Average need-based loan:* $4154. *Average need-based gift aid:* $7675. *Average non-need-based aid:* $1798. *Average indebtedness upon graduation:* $36,021.

APPLYING
Standardized Tests *Required:* SAT or ACT (for admission).

Options: electronic application, deferred entrance.

Application fee: $39.

Required: minimum 2.0 GPA. *Required for some:* essay or personal statement, high school transcript.

Application deadlines: 8/15 (freshmen), rolling (transfers).

Notification: 9/1 (freshmen).

CONTACT

Jamie Hunt, Director of Admissions, Francis Marion University, PO Box 100547, Florence, SC 29502-0547. *Phone:* 843-661-1231. *Toll-free phone:* 800-368-7551. *Fax:* 843-661-4635. *E-mail:* admissions@ fmarion.edu.

Furman University

Greenville, South Carolina

http://www.furman.edu/

- **Independent** comprehensive, founded 1826
- **Suburban** 800-acre campus
- **Coed** 2,746 undergraduate students, 97% full-time, 59% women, 41% men
- **Moderately difficult** entrance level, 61% of applicants were admitted

UNDERGRAD STUDENTS

2,658 full-time, 88 part-time. Students come from 42 states and territories; 27 other countries; 69% are from out of state; 6% Black or African American, non-Hispanic/Latino; 5% Hispanic/Latino; 2% Asian, non-Hispanic/Latino; 0.2% American Indian or Alaska Native, non-Hispanic/Latino; 3% Two or more races, non-Hispanic/Latino; 3% Race/ethnicity unknown; 5% international; 0.7% transferred in; 96% live on campus.

Freshmen:

Admission: 5,002 applied, 3,060 admitted, 702 enrolled. *Test scores:* SAT evidence-based reading and writing scores over 500: 98%; SAT math scores over 500: 97%; SAT evidence-based reading and writing scores over 600: 76%; SAT math scores over 600: 68%; SAT evidence-based reading and writing scores over 700: 23%; SAT math scores over 700: 21%.

Retention: 93% of full-time freshmen returned.

FACULTY

Total: 327, 72% full-time, 86% with terminal degrees.

Student/faculty ratio: 10:1.

ACADEMICS

Calendar: semesters. *Degrees:* bachelor's, master's, post-master's, and postbachelor's certificates.

Special study options: accelerated degree program, adult/continuing education programs, advanced placement credit, double majors, independent study, internships, part-time degree program, services for LD students, student-designed majors, study abroad, summer session for credit. *ROTC:* Army (b).

Unusual degree programs: 3-2 engineering with Georgia Institute of Technology, Clemson University, Auburn University, North Carolina State University, Washington University in St. Louis.

Computers: 500 computers/terminals are available on campus for general student use. Students can access the following: campus intranet, computer help desk, free student e-mail accounts, online (class) grades, online (class) registration, online (class) schedules. Campuswide network is available. Wireless service is available via entire campus.

Library: James Buchanan Duke Library plus 3 others. Study areas open 24 hours, 5–7 days a week.

STUDENT LIFE

Housing options: on-campus residence required through senior year; coed, men-only, women-only, special housing for students with disabilities. Campus housing is university owned. Freshman campus housing is guaranteed.

Activities and organizations: drama/theater group, student-run newspaper, radio and television station, choral group, marching band, national fraternities, national sororities.

Athletics Member NCAA. All Division I except football (Division I-AA). *Intercollegiate sports:* baseball M(s), basketball M(s)/W(s), cheerleading M/W, crew M(c)/W(c), cross-country running M(s)/W(s), equestrian sports W(c), fencing M(c)/W(c), golf M(c)/W(s), ice hockey M(c), lacrosse M/W, rugby M(c)/W(c), soccer M(s)/W(s), softball W(s), swimming and diving M(c)/W(c), tennis M(s)/W(s), track and field M(s)/W(s), ultimate Frisbee M(c)/W(c), volleyball W(s), weight lifting M(c)/W(c), wrestling M(c). *Intramural sports:* basketball M/W, bowling M/W, cross-country running M/W, football M/W, golf M/W, racquetball M/W, soccer M/W, softball M/W, swimming and diving M/W, tennis M/W, track and field M/W, volleyball M/W.

Campus security: 24-hour emergency response devices and patrols, student patrols, late-night transport/escort service, controlled dormitory access.

Student services: health clinic, personal/psychological counseling, women's center.

COSTS & FINANCIAL AID

Costs (2017–18) *Comprehensive fee:* $60,506 includes full-time tuition ($47,968), mandatory fees ($380), and room and board ($12,158). Part-time tuition: $1499 per credit. Part-time tuition and fees vary according to course load. *College room only:* $6540. Room and board charges vary according to board plan and housing facility. *Payment plan:* installment. *Waivers:* employees or children of employees.

Financial Aid Of all full-time matriculated undergraduates who enrolled in 2016, 1,521 applied for aid, 1,255 were judged to have need, 434 had their need fully met. 598 Federal Work-Study jobs (averaging $1530). In 2016, 1176 non-need-based awards were made. *Average percent of need met:* 79. *Average financial aid package:* $39,063. *Average need-based loan:* $4884. *Average need-based gift aid:* $35,508. *Average non-need-based aid:* $20,472. *Average indebtedness upon graduation:* $36,846. *Financial aid deadline:* 1/15.

APPLYING

Options: electronic application, early decision, early action.

Application fee: $50.

Required: essay or personal statement, high school transcript.

Application deadlines: 1/15 (freshmen), 1/15 (transfers), 11/1 (early action).

Early decision deadline: 11/1.

Notification: 3/1 (freshmen), 3/1 (transfers), 11/15 (early decision), 12/20 (early action).

CONTACT

Mr. Brad Pochard, Dean of Admission, Furman University, 3300 Poinsett Highway, Greenville, SC 29613. *Phone:* 864-294-2034. *Fax:* 864-294-2018. *E-mail:* admissions@furman.edu.

Lander University

Greenwood, South Carolina

http://www.lander.edu/

CONTACT

Ms. Jennifer M. Mathis, Director of Admissions, Lander University, 320 Stanley Avenue, Greenwood, SC 29649. *Phone:* 864-388-8307. *Toll-free phone:* 888-452-6337. *Fax:* 864-388-8125. *E-mail:* admissions@lander.edu.

Limestone College

Gaffney, South Carolina

http://www.limestone.edu/

- **Independent** comprehensive, founded 1845
- **Suburban** 123-acre campus with easy access to Charlotte
- **Endowment** $17.0 million
- **Coed** 1,135 undergraduate students, 99% full-time, 39% women, 61% men
- **Minimally difficult** entrance level, 52% of applicants were admitted

UNDERGRAD STUDENTS

1,123 full-time, 12 part-time. Students come from 30 states and territories; 31 other countries; 42% are from out of state; 35% Black or African American, non-Hispanic/Latino; 4% Hispanic/Latino; 0.3% Asian, non-Hispanic/Latino; 0.3% American Indian or Alaska Native, non-Hispanic/Latino; 4% Two or more races, non-Hispanic/Latino; 2% Race/ethnicity unknown; 8% international; 3% transferred in; 74% live on campus.

Freshmen:

Admission: 3,070 applied, 1,582 admitted, 450 enrolled. *Average high school GPA:* 3.3. *Test scores:* SAT evidence-based reading and writing scores over 500: 68%; SAT math scores over 500: 71%; SAT evidence-based reading and writing scores over 600: 16%; SAT math scores over 600: 13%; SAT math scores over 700: 2%.

Retention: 51% of full-time freshmen returned.

FACULTY

Total: 121, 70% full-time, 57% with terminal degrees.

Student/faculty ratio: 10:1.

ACADEMICS

Calendar: semesters. *Degrees:* associate, bachelor's, and master's.

Special study options: academic remediation for entering students, accelerated degree program, adult/continuing education programs, advanced placement credit, distance learning, double majors, honors programs, independent study, internships, part-time degree program, services for LD students, student-designed majors, summer session for credit.

Computers: 137 computers/terminals are available on campus for general student use. Students can access the following: campus intranet, computer help desk, free student e-mail accounts, online (class) grades, online (class) registration, online (class) schedules. Campuswide network is available. 100% of college-owned or -operated housing units are wired for high-speed Internet access. Wireless service is available via classrooms, dorm rooms, learning centers, libraries, student centers.

Library: A. J. Eastwood Library plus 1 other. *Books:* 67,000 (physical), 239,537 (digital/electronic); *Serial titles:* 111 (physical), 482,082 (digital/electronic); *Databases:* 156. Weekly public service hours: 70.

STUDENT LIFE

Housing options: on-campus residence required through junior year; men-only, women-only. Campus housing is university owned. Freshman applicants given priority for college housing.

Activities and organizations: drama/theater group, choral group, marching band, Fellowship of Christian Athletes, Student Government Association, Student Alumni Leadership Council, Campus Crusade (CRU), Limestone Activities Board (LAB), national fraternities, national sororities.

Athletics Member NCAA. All Division II. *Intercollegiate sports:* baseball M(s), basketball M(s)/W(s), cheerleading M(s)/W(s), cross-country running M(s)/W(s), field hockey W(s), football M(s), golf M(s)/W(s), gymnastics W(s), lacrosse M(s)/W(s), soccer M(s)/W(s), softball W(s), swimming and diving M(s)/W(s), tennis M(s)/W(s), track and field M(s)/W(s), volleyball M(s)/W(s), wrestling M(s). *Intramural sports:* badminton M/W, basketball M/W, bowling M/W, racquetball M/W, soccer M/W, table tennis M/W, ultimate Frisbee M/W, volleyball M/W, weight lifting M/W.

Campus security: 24-hour emergency response devices and patrols, late-night transport/escort service, controlled dormitory access.

Student services: health clinic, personal/psychological counseling.

COSTS & FINANCIAL AID

Costs (2018–19) *Comprehensive fee:* $35,765 includes full-time tuition ($24,900), mandatory fees ($1100), and room and board ($9765). Full-time tuition and fees vary according to class time and course load. Part-time tuition: $1038 per credit hour. Part-time tuition and fees vary according to class time. *Required fees:* $1038 per credit hour part-time. *Room and board:* Room and board charges vary according to board plan and housing facility. *Payment plan:* installment. *Waivers:* employees or children of employees.

Financial Aid Of all full-time matriculated undergraduates who enrolled in 2015, 819 applied for aid, 749 were judged to have need, 117 had their need fully met. 105 Federal Work-Study jobs (averaging $1101). 90 state and other part-time jobs (averaging $673). In 2015, 192 non-need-based awards were made. *Average percent of need met:* 66. *Average financial aid package:* $19,841. *Average need-based loan:* $3850. *Average need-based gift aid:* $16,403. *Average non-need-based aid:* $5980. *Average indebtedness upon graduation:* $30,856.

APPLYING

Standardized Tests *Required:* SAT or ACT (for admission). *Required for some:* minimum score of 500 on TOEFL or proof of successfully completed ESL program for students whose native language is not English.

Options: electronic application.

Application fee: $25.

Required: high school transcript, minimum 2.0 GPA. *Recommended:* 2 letters of recommendation, interview.

Application deadlines: rolling (freshmen), rolling (transfers).

Notification: continuous (freshmen), continuous (transfers).

CONTACT
Ms. Lisa Hobbs, Admissions Office Manager, Limestone College, 1115 College Drive, Gaffney, SC 29340-3799. *Phone:* 864-488-4554. *Toll-free phone:* 800-795-7151. *Fax:* 864-487-8706. *E-mail:* lhobbs@ limestone.edu.

Medical University of South Carolina
Charleston, South Carolina
http://www.musc.edu/

CONTACT
Lyla E. Hudson, Director of Admissions, Medical University of South Carolina, 41 Bee Street MSC203, Charleston, SC 29425-2030. *Phone:* 843-792-7408. *E-mail:* hudsonly@musc.edu.

Morris College
Sumter, South Carolina
http://www.morris.edu/

- **Independent** 4-year, founded 1908, affiliated with Baptist Educational and Missionary Convention of South Carolina
- **Urban** 34-acre campus with easy access to Columbia, SC
- **Endowment** $10.9 million
- **Coed** 746 undergraduate students, 98% full-time, 55% women, 45% men
- **Noncompetitive** entrance level, 79% of applicants were admitted

UNDERGRAD STUDENTS
730 full-time, 16 part-time. Students come from 21 states and territories; 17% are from out of state; 98% Black or African American, non-Hispanic/Latino; 0.7% Hispanic/Latino; 0.1% Asian, non-Hispanic/Latino; 0.1% American Indian or Alaska Native, non-Hispanic/Latino; 1% Two or more races, non-Hispanic/Latino; 6% transferred in; 78% live on campus.

Freshmen:
Admission: 2,616 applied, 2,076 admitted, 236 enrolled. *Average high school GPA:* 2.6.
Retention: 55% of full-time freshmen returned.

FACULTY
Total: 56, 68% full-time, 59% with terminal degrees.
Student/faculty ratio: 13:1.

ACADEMICS
Calendar: semesters. *Degree:* bachelor's.

Special study options: academic remediation for entering students, accelerated degree program, adult/continuing education programs, advanced placement credit, cooperative education, double majors, honors programs, internships, study abroad, summer session for credit. *ROTC:* Army (b).

Unusual degree programs: 3-2 engineering with North Carolina Agricultural and Technical State University.

Computers: 292 computers/terminals are available on campus for general student use. Students can access the following: free student e-mail accounts, online (class) grades, online (class) schedules, online financial aid Information, learning management system. Campuswide network is available. 100% of college-owned or -operated housing units are wired for high-speed Internet access. Wireless service is available via entire campus.

Library: Richardson-Johnson Learning Resources Center plus 1 other. *Books:* 95,133 (physical), 37,342 (digital/electronic); *Serial titles:* 427 (physical), 4 (digital/electronic); *Databases:* 74. Weekly public service hours: 76.

STUDENT LIFE
Housing options: men-only, women-only. Campus housing is university owned. Freshman campus housing is guaranteed.

Activities and organizations: drama/theater group, student-run radio station, choral group, Student Government Association, New Emphasis on Nontraditional Students (NEONS), Block M Club, Pre Alumni Council, Baptist Student Union.

Athletics Member NAIA. *Intercollegiate sports:* baseball M(s), basketball M(s)/W(s), cheerleading M(s)/W(s), cross-country running M(s)/W(s), softball W(s), track and field M(s)/W(s), volleyball W(s). *Intramural sports:* basketball M/W, table tennis M/W.

Campus security: 24-hour emergency response devices and patrols.

Student services: health clinic, personal/psychological counseling.

COSTS & FINANCIAL AID
Costs (2017–18) *Comprehensive fee:* $19,195 includes full-time tuition ($12,100), mandatory fees ($1358), and room and board ($5737). Part-time tuition: $504 per credit hour. *College room only:* $2500. *Payment plan:* installment.

Financial Aid Of all full-time matriculated undergraduates who enrolled in 2016, 887 applied for aid, 859 were judged to have need, 10 had their need fully met. 300 Federal Work-Study jobs (averaging $818). *Average percent of need met:* 85. *Average financial aid package:* $12,100. *Average need-based loan:* $3900. *Average need-based gift aid:* $7400. *Average indebtedness upon graduation:* $17,125.

APPLYING
Options: electronic application, deferred entrance.

Required: high school transcript. *Required for some:* interview.

Application deadlines: rolling (freshmen), rolling (transfers).

Notification: continuous (freshmen), continuous (transfers).

CONTACT
Ms. Gloria Scriven, Assistant Director of Admissions and Records, Morris College, 100 West College Street, Sumter, SC 29150-3502. *Phone:* 803-934-3239. *Toll-free phone:* 866-853-1345. *Fax:* 803-773-8241. *E-mail:* gscriven@morris.edu.

Newberry College
Newberry, South Carolina
http://www.newberry.edu/

- **Independent Evangelical Lutheran** 4-year, founded 1856
- **Small-town** 90-acre campus with easy access to Columbia and Greenville, SC
- **Endowment** $18.8 million
- **Coed** 1,181 undergraduate students, 98% full-time, 44% women, 56% men
- **Moderately difficult** entrance level, 82% of applicants were admitted

UNDERGRAD STUDENTS
1,159 full-time, 22 part-time. Students come from 30 states and territories; 25 other countries; 21% are from out of state; 25% Black or African American, non-Hispanic/Latino; 4% Hispanic/Latino; 0.4% Asian, non-Hispanic/Latino; 0.3% Native Hawaiian or other Pacific Islander, non-Hispanic/Latino; 0.5% American Indian or Alaska Native, non-Hispanic/Latino; 4% Two or more races, non-Hispanic/Latino; 5% Race/ethnicity unknown; 5% international; 7% transferred in; 82% live on campus.

Freshmen:
Admission: 1,573 applied, 1,288 admitted, 353 enrolled. *Average high school GPA:* 3.5. *Test scores:* SAT evidence-based reading and writing scores over 500: 49%; SAT math scores over 500: 44%; ACT scores over 18: 74%; SAT evidence-based reading and writing scores over 600: 6%; SAT math scores over 600: 8%; ACT scores over 24: 18%; SAT evidence-based reading and writing scores over 700: 1%; ACT scores over 30: 2%.
Retention: 65% of full-time freshmen returned.

FACULTY
Total: 133, 46% full-time, 53% with terminal degrees.
Student/faculty ratio: 14:1.

ACADEMICS
Calendar: semesters. *Degree:* bachelor's.

Special study options: academic remediation for entering students, adult/continuing education programs, advanced placement credit, double majors, honors programs, independent study, internships, part-time degree program, services for LD students, student-designed majors, study abroad, summer session for credit. *ROTC:* Army (b).

Unusual degree programs: 3-2 engineering with Clemson University; forestry with Duke University; pharmacy with Presbyterian College.

Computers: 21 computers/terminals are available on campus for general student use. Students can access the following: campus intranet, computer help desk, free student e-mail accounts, online (class) grades, online (class) registration, online (class) schedules. Campuswide network is available. 100% of college-owned or -operated housing units are wired for high-speed Internet access. Wireless service is available via entire campus.

Library: Wessels Library. *Books:* 36,525 (physical), 295,982 (digital/electronic); *Serial titles:* 33 (physical), 10,000 (digital/electronic); *Databases:* 108. Weekly public service hours: 91.

STUDENT LIFE

Housing options: on-campus residence required through senior year; coed, men-only, women-only. Campus housing is university owned and is provided by a third party. Freshman applicants given priority for college housing.

Activities and organizations: drama/theater group, student-run radio station, choral group, marching band, National Society of Leadership and Success, Kappa Delta, Sigma Sigma Sigma, Alpha Xi Delta, Kappa Alpha Order, national fraternities, national sororities.

Athletics Member NCAA. All Division II. *Intercollegiate sports:* baseball M(s), basketball M(s)/W(s), cheerleading M(s)/W(s), cross-country running M(s)/W(s), field hockey W(s), football M(s), golf M(s)/W(s), lacrosse M(s)/W(s), soccer M(s)/W(s), softball W(s), tennis M(s)/W(s), track and field M(s)/W(s), volleyball W(s), wrestling M(s). *Intramural sports:* basketball M/W, football M/W, softball M/W, volleyball M/W.

Campus security: 24-hour emergency response devices and patrols, late-night transport/escort service, controlled dormitory access.

Student services: health clinic, personal/psychological counseling.

COSTS & FINANCIAL AID

Costs (2018–19) *Comprehensive fee:* $37,090 includes full-time tuition ($24,174), mandatory fees ($2250), and room and board ($10,666). Full-time tuition and fees vary according to course load. Part-time tuition: $820 per credit hour. Part-time tuition and fees vary according to course load. *Required fees:* $70 per credit hour part-time. *Room and board:* Room and board charges vary according to board plan and housing facility. *Payment plan:* installment. *Waivers:* employees or children of employees.

Financial Aid Of all full-time matriculated undergraduates who enrolled in 2016, 986 applied for aid, 897 were judged to have need, 149 had their need fully met. In 2016, 157 non-need-based awards were made. *Average percent of need met:* 74. *Average financial aid package:* $22,269. *Average need-based loan:* $3846. *Average need-based gift aid:* $19,229. *Average non-need-based aid:* $10,686. *Average indebtedness upon graduation:* $22,380.

APPLYING

Standardized Tests *Required:* SAT or ACT (for admission).

Options: electronic application, deferred entrance.

Required: high school transcript, minimum 2.0 GPA. *Required for some:* essay or personal statement, interview.

Application deadlines: rolling (freshmen), rolling (transfers).

Notification: continuous (freshmen), continuous (transfers).

CONTACT

Mr. Joel Vander Horst, Dean of Enrollment Management, Newberry College, 2100 College Street, Newberry, SC 29108. *Phone:* 803-947-2110. *Toll-free phone:* 800-845-4955. *Fax:* 803-321-5138. *E-mail:* admissions@newberry.edu.

North Greenville University
Tigerville, South Carolina
http://www.ngu.edu/

- **Independent Southern Baptist** comprehensive, founded 1892
- **Rural** 380-acre campus with easy access to Greenville
- **Endowment** $258.4 million
- **Coed** 2,363 undergraduate students, 88% full-time, 52% women, 48% men
- **Minimally difficult** entrance level, 60% of applicants were admitted

UNDERGRAD STUDENTS

2,083 full-time, 280 part-time. Students come from 37 states and territories; 26 other countries; 20% are from out of state; 8% Black or African American, non-Hispanic/Latino; 3% Hispanic/Latino; 1% Asian, non-Hispanic/Latino; 0.1% Native Hawaiian or other Pacific Islander, non-Hispanic/Latino; 0.5% American Indian or Alaska Native, non-Hispanic/Latino; 3% Two or more races, non-Hispanic/Latino; 8% Race/ethnicity unknown; 0.1% international; 4% transferred in; 63% live on campus.

Freshmen:
Admission: 1,701 applied, 1,019 admitted, 540 enrolled. *Average high school GPA:* 3.5. *Test scores:* SAT evidence-based reading and writing scores over 500: 77%; SAT math scores over 500: 69%; ACT scores over 18: 92%; SAT evidence-based reading and writing scores over 600: 24%; SAT math scores over 600: 22%; ACT scores over 24: 52%; SAT evidence-based reading and writing scores over 700: 3%; SAT math scores over 700: 4%; ACT scores over 30: 9%.
Retention: 71% of full-time freshmen returned.

FACULTY
Total: 218, 66% full-time, 51% with terminal degrees.
Student/faculty ratio: 14:1.

ACADEMICS
Calendar: semesters. *Degrees:* bachelor's, master's, and doctoral.

Special study options: academic remediation for entering students, accelerated degree program, adult/continuing education programs, advanced placement credit, cooperative education, distance learning, double majors, English as a second language, freshman honors college, honors programs, independent study, internships, part-time degree program, services for LD students, student-designed majors, study abroad, summer session for credit. *ROTC:* Army (c).

Unusual degree programs: 3-2 engineering with Clemson University.

Computers: 95 computers/terminals and 6 ports are available on campus for general student use. Students can access the following: campus intranet, computer help desk, free student e-mail accounts, online (class) grades, online (class) schedules. Campuswide network is available. 100% of college-owned or -operated housing units are wired for high-speed Internet access. Wireless service is available via entire campus.

Library: Hester Memorial Library. *Books:* 70,000 (physical), 250,000 (digital/electronic); *Serial titles:* 250 (physical), 150 (digital/electronic); *Databases:* 103. Weekly public service hours: 85.

STUDENT LIFE
Housing options: on-campus residence required through sophomore year; men-only, women-only. Campus housing is university owned. Freshman campus housing is guaranteed.

Activities and organizations: drama/theater group, student-run radio station, choral group, marching band, Baptist Student Union, Fellowship of Christians in Service, Fellowship of Christian Athletes, Black Student Fellowship, Education Club.

Athletics Member NCAA, NCCAA. All NCAA Division II. *Intercollegiate sports:* baseball M(s), basketball M(s)/W(s), cheerleading M(s)/W(s), cross-country running M(s)/W(s), football M(s), golf M(s)/W(s), lacrosse M(s)/W(s), soccer M(s)/W(s), softball W(s), tennis M(s)/W(s), track and field M(s)/W(s), volleyball M(s)/W(s). *Intramural sports:* basketball M/W, bowling M/W, football M, golf M/W, sand volleyball M/W, soccer M/W, softball M/W, table tennis M/W, tennis M/W, ultimate Frisbee M/W, volleyball W, weight lifting M/W.

Campus security: 24-hour emergency response devices and patrols, late-night transport/escort service, controlled dormitory access.

Student services: personal/psychological counseling.

COSTS & FINANCIAL AID

Costs (2017–18) *Comprehensive fee:* $29,390 includes full-time tuition ($18,750), mandatory fees ($400), and room and board ($10,240). Full-time tuition and fees vary according to course load. Part-time tuition: $455 per credit hour. *Required fees:* $200 per year part-time. *Room and board:* Room and board charges vary according to housing facility. *Payment plan:* installment. *Waivers:* employees or children of employees.

Financial Aid Of all full-time matriculated undergraduates who enrolled in 2015, 1,143 applied for aid, 1,143 were judged to have need, 1,143 had their need fully met. In 2015, 1989 non-need-based awards were made. *Average financial aid package:* $5783. *Average need-based gift aid:* $5783. *Average non-need-based aid:* $7081.

APPLYING

Standardized Tests *Required:* SAT or ACT (for admission). *Required for some:* CPT. *Recommended:* CPT.

Options: electronic application, early admission, deferred entrance.

Application fee: $30.

Required: high school transcript. *Required for some:* interview. *Recommended:* minimum 2.0 GPA.

Application deadlines: 8/22 (freshmen), 8/26 (transfers).

Notification: continuous (freshmen), continuous (transfers).

CONTACT

North Greenville University, PO Box 1892, Tigerville, SC 29688-1892. *Phone:* 864-977-7052. *Toll-free phone:* 800-468-6642 Ext. 7001.

Presbyterian College

Clinton, South Carolina

http://www.presby.edu/

- **Independent** comprehensive, founded 1880, affiliated with Presbyterian Church (U.S.A.)
- **Small-town** 240-acre campus with easy access to Greenville, Spartanburg
- **Endowment** $90.2 million
- **Coed** 1,016 undergraduate students, 96% full-time, 51% women, 49% men
- **Very difficult** entrance level, 63% of applicants were admitted

UNDERGRAD STUDENTS

976 full-time, 40 part-time. Students come from 31 states and territories; 24 other countries; 27% are from out of state; 12% Black or African American, non-Hispanic/Latino; 3% Hispanic/Latino; 0.8% Asian, non-Hispanic/Latino; 0.4% American Indian or Alaska Native, non-Hispanic/Latino; 3% Two or more races, non-Hispanic/Latino; 0.7% Race/ethnicity unknown; 5% international; 2% transferred in; 99% live on campus.

Freshmen:

Admission: 2,277 applied, 1,434 admitted, 276 enrolled. *Average high school GPA:* 3.5. *Test scores:* SAT evidence-based reading and writing scores over 500: 86%; SAT math scores over 500: 87%; ACT scores over 18: 96%; SAT evidence-based reading and writing scores over 600: 35%; SAT math scores over 600: 36%; ACT scores over 24: 47%; SAT evidence-based reading and writing scores over 700: 1%; SAT math scores over 700: 5%; ACT scores over 30: 10%.

Retention: 82% of full-time freshmen returned.

FACULTY

Total: 104, 71% full-time, 79% with terminal degrees.

Student/faculty ratio: 13:1.

ACADEMICS

Calendar: semesters. *Degrees:* bachelor's and doctoral.

Special study options: advanced placement credit, distance learning, double majors, English as a second language, honors programs, independent study, internships, off-campus study, services for LD students, study abroad, summer session for credit. *ROTC:* Army (b).

Unusual degree programs: 3-2 engineering with Auburn University, Clemson University, Vanderbilt University, University of South Carolina.

Computers: 100 computers/terminals and 275 ports are available on campus for general student use. Students can access the following: campus intranet, free student e-mail accounts, online (class) grades, online (class) registration, online (class) schedules. Campuswide network is available. 100% of college-owned or -operated housing units are wired for high-speed Internet access. Wireless service is available via entire campus.

Library: James H. Thomason Library. *Books:* 108,925 (physical), 227,396 (digital/electronic); *Serial titles:* 702 (physical), 16,342 (digital/electronic); *Databases:* 71. Study areas open 24 hours, 5–7 days a week; students can reserve study rooms.

STUDENT LIFE

Housing options: on-campus residence required through senior year; coed, men-only, women-only. Campus housing is university owned. Freshman campus housing is guaranteed.

Activities and organizations: drama/theater group, student-run newspaper, choral group, Student Volunteer Services, Intramural sports, Student Union Board, Fellowship of Christian Athletes, Student Government Association, national fraternities, national sororities.

Athletics Member NCAA. All Division I. *Intercollegiate sports:* baseball M(s), basketball M(s)/W(s), cheerleading M(s)/W(s), cross-country running M(s)/W(s), football M, golf M(s)/W(s), lacrosse W(s), soccer M(s)/W(s), softball W(s), tennis M(s)/W(s), volleyball W(s). *Intramural sports:* basketball M/W, football M/W, golf M/W, rock climbing M/W, skiing (cross-country) M/W, soccer M/W, softball M/W, table tennis M/W, tennis M/W, ultimate Frisbee M/W, volleyball M/W.

Campus security: 24-hour emergency response devices and patrols, late-night transport/escort service, controlled dormitory access.

Student services: health clinic, personal/psychological counseling.

COSTS & FINANCIAL AID

Costs (2017–18) *Comprehensive fee:* $48,140 includes full-time tuition ($34,982), mandatory fees ($2860), and room and board ($10,298). Full-time tuition and fees vary according to course load and reciprocity agreements. Part-time tuition: $1457 per credit hour. Part-time tuition and fees vary according to course load and program. *Required fees:* $27 per credit hour part-time, $25 per term part-time. *College room only:* $4992. Room and board charges vary according to board plan and housing facility. *Payment plan:* installment. *Waivers:* senior citizens and employees or children of employees.

Financial Aid Of all full-time matriculated undergraduates who enrolled in 2017, 812 applied for aid, 709 were judged to have need, 274 had their need fully met. In 2017, 224 non-need-based awards were made. *Average percent of need met:* 86. *Average financial aid package:* $36,465. *Average need-based loan:* $4408. *Average need-based gift aid:* $29,804. *Average non-need-based aid:* $16,805.

APPLYING

Standardized Tests *Required for some:* SAT or ACT (for admission).

Options: electronic application, early decision, early action, deferred entrance.

Required: essay or personal statement, high school transcript, minimum 2.0 GPA, 1 letter of recommendation. *Recommended:* interview.

Application deadlines: 6/30 (freshmen), 7/1 (transfers), 11/15 (early action).

Early decision deadline: 11/1.

Notification: 3/15 (freshmen), 3/15 (out-of-state freshmen), 7/15 (transfers), 12/1 (early decision), 12/15 (early action).

CONTACT

Mr. Mark O. Fox, Director of Admissions, Presbyterian College, 503 South Broad Street, Clinton, SC 29325. *Phone:* 864-833-8232. *Toll-free phone:* 800-476-7272. *Fax:* 864-833-8195. *E-mail:* mfox@presby.edu.

South Carolina State University

Orangeburg, South Carolina

http://www.scsu.edu/

- **State-supported** comprehensive, founded 1896, part of South Carolina Commission on Higher Education
- **Small-town** 160-acre campus
- **Coed**
- **Minimally difficult** entrance level

FACULTY

Student/faculty ratio: 17:1.

ACADEMICS
Calendar: semesters. *Degrees:* bachelor's, master's, doctoral, and postbachelor's certificates.
Library: Miller F. Whittaker Library. *Books:* 317,233 (physical), 195,578 (digital/electronic); *Serial titles:* 18,334 (digital/electronic); *Databases:* 114. Weekly public service hours: 74; students can reserve study rooms.

STUDENT LIFE
Housing options: coed, men-only, women-only, special housing for students with disabilities. Campus housing is university owned, leased by the school and is provided by a third party. Freshman applicants given priority for college housing.

Activities and organizations: drama/theater group, student-run newspaper, radio station, choral group, marching band, Student Government Association, Campus Activity Board, NAACP, United Voices of Christ, Student Media, national fraternities, national sororities.

Athletics Member NCAA. All Division I except football (Division I-AA).

Campus security: 24-hour emergency response devices and patrols, late-night transport/escort service, controlled dormitory access.

Student services: health clinic, personal/psychological counseling.

COSTS
Costs (2017–18) *Tuition:* state resident $9208 full-time, $448 per credit hour part-time; nonresident $19,588 full-time, $880 per credit hour part-time. Full-time tuition and fees vary according to course load and reciprocity agreements. Part-time tuition and fees vary according to course load and reciprocity agreements. *Required fees:* $1532 full-time. *Room and board:* $9890; room only: $6600. Room and board charges vary according to board plan and housing facility.

APPLYING
Standardized Tests *Required:* SAT or ACT (for admission).
Options: electronic application, deferred entrance.
Application fee: $25.
Required: high school transcript, minimum 2.0 GPA.

CONTACT
Mrs. Gennifer Bookhardt, South Carolina State University, PO Box 7127, 300 College Street NE, Orangeburg, SC 29117. *Phone:* 803-536-7186. *Toll-free phone:* 800-260-5956. *Fax:* 803-536-8990. *E-mail:* admissions@scsu.edu.

Southern Wesleyan University
Central, South Carolina
http://www.swu.edu/

CONTACT
Mrs. Beth Roe, Director of First Year Experience, Southern Wesleyan University, PO Box 1020, 907 Wesleyan Drive, Central, SC 29630-1020. *Phone:* 864-644-5149. *Toll-free phone:* 800-CU-AT-SWU. *Fax:* 864-644-5901. *E-mail:* broe@swu.edu.

South University
Columbia, South Carolina
http://www.southuniversity.edu/columbia/

CONTACT
South University, 9 Science Court, Columbia, SC 29203. *Phone:* 803-799-9082. *Toll-free phone:* 866-629-3031.

Strayer University–Charleston Campus
North Charleston, South Carolina
http://www.strayer.edu/south-carolina/charleston/

CONTACT
Strayer University–Charleston Campus, 5010 Wetland Crossing, North Charleston, SC 29418. *Toll-free phone:* 888-311-0355.

Strayer University–Columbia Campus
Columbia, South Carolina
http://www.strayer.edu/south-carolina/columbia/

CONTACT
Strayer University–Columbia Campus, 200 Center Point Circle, Suite 300, Columbia, SC 29210. *Toll-free phone:* 888-311-0355.

Strayer University–Greenville Campus
Greenville, South Carolina
http://www.strayer.edu/south-carolina/greenville/

CONTACT
Strayer University–Greenville Campus, 555 North Pleasantburg Drive, Suite 300, Greenville, SC 29607. *Toll-free phone:* 888-311-0355.

University of South Carolina
Columbia, South Carolina
http://www.sc.edu/
- **State-supported** university, founded 1801, part of University of South Carolina System
- **Urban** 444-acre campus
- **Coed** 26,362 undergraduate students, 94% full-time, 54% women, 46% men
- **Moderately difficult** entrance level, 72% of applicants were admitted

UNDERGRAD STUDENTS
24,772 full-time, 1,590 part-time. 40% are from out of state; 9% Black or African American, non-Hispanic/Latino; 5% Hispanic/Latino; 3% Asian, non-Hispanic/Latino; 0.1% Native Hawaiian or other Pacific Islander, non-Hispanic/Latino; 0.2% American Indian or Alaska Native, non-Hispanic/Latino; 4% Two or more races, non-Hispanic/Latino; 1% Race/ethnicity unknown; 3% international; 8% transferred in; 27% live on campus.

Freshmen:
Admission: 26,019 applied, 18,811 admitted, 5,879 enrolled. *Average high school GPA:* 4.1. *Test scores:* ACT scores over 18: 100%; ACT scores over 24: 87%; ACT scores over 30: 26%.
Retention: 89% of full-time freshmen returned.

FACULTY
Total: 2,200, 69% full-time, 73% with terminal degrees.
Student/faculty ratio: 17:1.

ACADEMICS
Calendar: semesters. *Degrees:* associate, bachelor's, master's, doctoral, post-master's, and postbachelor's certificates.

Special study options: accelerated degree program, adult/continuing education programs, advanced placement credit, cooperative education, distance learning, double majors, English as a second language, freshman honors college, honors programs, independent study, internships, part-time degree program, services for LD students, student-designed majors, study abroad, summer session for credit. *ROTC:* Army (b), Navy (b), Air Force (b).

Computers: Students can access the following: computer help desk, free student e-mail accounts, online (class) grades, online (class) registration, online (class) schedules. Campuswide network is available. Wireless service is available via entire campus.
Library: Thomas Cooper Library plus 6 others. *Books:* 1.8 million (physical), 1.1 million (digital/electronic); *Serial titles:* 72,412 (physical), 18,860 (digital/electronic); *Databases:* 574.

STUDENT LIFE
Housing options: on-campus residence required for freshman year; coed, men-only, women-only, special housing for students with disabilities. Campus housing is university owned. Freshman campus housing is guaranteed.

Activities and organizations: drama/theater group, student-run newspaper, radio and television station, choral group, marching band, national fraternities, national sororities.

COLLEGES AT-A-GLANCE

Athletics Member NCAA. All Division I except football (Division I-A). *Intercollegiate sports:* baseball M(s), basketball M(s)/W(s), cross-country running W(s), equestrian sports W(s), golf M(s)/W(s), soccer M(s)/W(s), softball W(s), swimming and diving M(s)/W(s), tennis M(s)/W(s), track and field M(s)/W(s), volleyball W(s). *Intramural sports:* badminton M(c)/W(c), baseball M(c), basketball M/W, bowling M/W, equestrian sports M(c)/W(c), fencing M(c)/W(c), field hockey W(c), football M/W, golf M/W, gymnastics W(c), ice hockey M(c), lacrosse M(c)/W(c), racquetball M/W, rock climbing M(c)/W(c), rugby M(c)/W(c), sailing M(c)/W(c), soccer M/W, softball M/W, swimming and diving M/W, table tennis M/W, tennis M/W, ultimate Frisbee M(c)/W(c), volleyball M/W, water polo M(c)/W(c), weight lifting M/W, wrestling M(c).

Campus security: 24-hour emergency response devices and patrols, student patrols, late-night transport/escort service, controlled dormitory access, Rave Guardian Safety App.

Student services: health clinic, personal/psychological counseling, women's center.

COSTS & FINANCIAL AID
Costs (2017–18) *Tuition:* state resident $11,862 full-time, $494 per credit hour part-time; nonresident $31,962 full-time, $1331 per credit hour part-time. Full-time tuition and fees vary according to program and reciprocity agreements. Part-time tuition and fees vary according to course load. *Required fees:* $400 full-time, $17 per term part-time. *Room and board:* $11,200; room only: $7500. Room and board charges vary according to board plan, housing facility, and location. *Payment plan:* deferred payment. *Waivers:* senior citizens and employees or children of employees.

Financial Aid Of all full-time matriculated undergraduates who enrolled in 2017, 15,867 applied for aid, 11,915 were judged to have need, 3,005 had their need fully met. In 2017, 8407 non-need-based awards were made. *Average percent of need met:* 71. *Average financial aid package:* $9482. *Average need-based loan:* $4476. *Average need-based gift aid:* $5189. *Average non-need-based aid:* $6586. *Average indebtedness upon graduation:* $28,972.

APPLYING
Standardized Tests *Required:* SAT or ACT (for admission).

Options: electronic application, early action.

Application fee: $65.

Required: high school transcript, minimum 2.0 GPA.

CONTACT
Dr. Mary Wagner, Director, Undergraduate Admissions, University of South Carolina, Columbia, SC 29208. *Phone:* 803-777-7700. *Toll-free phone:* 800-868-5872. *Fax:* 803-777-0101. *E-mail:* wagnermt@ mailbox.sc.edu.

University of South Carolina Aiken
Aiken, South Carolina
http://www.usca.edu/

- **State-supported** comprehensive, founded 1961, part of University of South Carolina System
- **Suburban** 453-acre campus with easy access to Columbia
- **Endowment** $25.4 million
- **Coed** 3,354 undergraduate students, 81% full-time, 64% women, 36% men
- **Moderately difficult** entrance level, 53% of applicants were admitted

UNDERGRAD STUDENTS
2,718 full-time, 636 part-time. Students come from 29 states and territories; 29 other countries; 10% are from out of state; 28% Black or African American, non-Hispanic/Latino; 4% Hispanic/Latino; 1% Asian, non-Hispanic/Latino; 0.1% Native Hawaiian or other Pacific Islander, non-Hispanic/Latino; 0.3% American Indian or Alaska Native, non-Hispanic/Latino; 4% Two or more races, non-Hispanic/Latino; 2% Race/ethnicity unknown; 3% international; 10% transferred in; 27% live on campus.

Freshmen:
Admission: 3,075 applied, 1,628 admitted, 573 enrolled. *Average high school GPA:* 3.8. *Test scores:* SAT evidence-based reading and writing scores over 500: 63%; SAT math scores over 500: 56%; ACT scores over 18: 79%; SAT evidence-based reading and writing scores over 600: 17%;

SAT math scores over 600: 11%; ACT scores over 24: 20%; SAT evidence-based reading and writing scores over 700: 2%; ACT scores over 30: 1%.

Retention: 68% of full-time freshmen returned.

FACULTY
Total: 288, 54% full-time, 54% with terminal degrees.

Student/faculty ratio: 15:1.

ACADEMICS
Calendar: semesters. *Degrees:* bachelor's and master's.

Special study options: adult/continuing education programs, advanced placement credit, cooperative education, distance learning, double majors, English as a second language, honors programs, independent study, internships, off-campus study, part-time degree program, services for LD students, student-designed majors, study abroad, summer session for credit.

Computers: 550 computers/terminals and 1,400 ports are available on campus for general student use. Students can access the following: computer help desk, free student e-mail accounts, online (class) grades, online (class) registration, online (class) schedules. Campuswide network is available. 100% of college-owned or -operated housing units are wired for high-speed Internet access. Wireless service is available via entire campus.

Library: Gregg-Graniteville Library. *Books:* 138,003 (physical), 382,370 (digital/electronic); *Serial titles:* 15,842 (physical), 110,572 (digital/electronic); *Databases:* 236. Weekly public service hours: 78; students can reserve study rooms.

STUDENT LIFE
Housing options: coed, special housing for students with disabilities. Campus housing is university owned. Freshman applicants given priority for college housing.

Activities and organizations: drama/theater group, student-run newspaper, choral group, National Society of Leadership and Success, Pacer Fanatics, Alpha Omicron Pi, Zeta Tau Alpha, Phi Mu, national fraternities, national sororities.

Athletics Member NCAA. All Division II. *Intercollegiate sports:* baseball M(s), basketball M(s)/W(s), cross-country running W(s), golf M(s), soccer M(s)/W(s), softball W(s), tennis M(s)/W(s), volleyball W(s). *Intramural sports:* basketball M/W, cheerleading M(c)/W(c), equestrian sports M(c)/W(c), rugby M(c)/W(c), soccer M/W, swimming and diving M(c)/W(c), table tennis M(c)/W(c), ultimate Frisbee M/W, volleyball M/W.

Campus security: 24-hour emergency response devices and patrols, late-night transport/escort service, controlled dormitory access.

Student services: health clinic, personal/psychological counseling.

COSTS & FINANCIAL AID
Costs (2017–18) *Tuition:* state resident $10,164 full-time, $424 per credit hour part-time; nonresident $20,364 full-time, $849 per credit hour part-time. Full-time tuition and fees vary according to reciprocity agreements. Part-time tuition and fees vary according to course load and reciprocity agreements. *Required fees:* $338 full-time, $12 per credit hour part-time, $25 per term part-time. *Room and board:* $7592; room only: $4942. Room and board charges vary according to board plan and housing facility. *Payment plan:* deferred payment. *Waivers:* senior citizens and employees or children of employees.

Financial Aid Of all full-time matriculated undergraduates who enrolled in 2016, 2,815 applied for aid, 1,986 were judged to have need, 318 had their need fully met. 71 Federal Work-Study jobs (averaging $1769). 433 state and other part-time jobs (averaging $1553). In 2016, 158 non-need-based awards were made. *Average percent of need met:* 60. *Average financial aid package:* $11,155. *Average need-based loan:* $3957. *Average need-based gift aid:* $6841. *Average non-need-based aid:* $2163. *Average indebtedness upon graduation:* $27,739.

APPLYING
Standardized Tests *Required:* SAT or ACT (for admission).

Options: electronic application, early admission, deferred entrance.

Application fee: $45.

Required: high school transcript.

Application deadlines: 8/1 (freshmen), 8/1 (transfers).

Notification: continuous (freshmen), continuous (out-of-state freshmen), continuous (transfers).

CONTACT
Mr. Andrew Hendrix, Director of Admissions, University of South Carolina Aiken, 471 University Parkway, Aiken, SC 29801-6309. *Phone:* 803-641-3366. *Toll-free phone:* 888-WOW-USCA. *Fax:* 803-641-3727. *E-mail:* admit@usca.edu.

University of South Carolina Beaufort
Bluffton, South Carolina
http://www.uscb.edu/

CONTACT
Ms. Monica Williams, University of South Carolina Beaufort, 1 University Boulevard, Bluffton, SC 29909. *Phone:* 843-208-8112. *Fax:* 843-208-8015. *E-mail:* monicaw@sc.edu.

University of South Carolina Union
Union, South Carolina
http://uscunion.sc.edu/
- **State-supported** primarily 2-year, founded 1965, part of University of South Carolina System
- **Small-town** 7-acre campus with easy access to Charlotte, North Carolina
- **Endowment** $1.2 million
- **Coed** 905 undergraduate students, 54% full-time, 53% women, 47% men
- **Minimally difficult** entrance level, 67% of applicants were admitted

UNDERGRAD STUDENTS
487 full-time, 418 part-time. Students come from 3 states and territories; 1 other country; 2% are from out of state; 43% Black or African American, non-Hispanic/Latino; 3% Hispanic/Latino.

Freshmen:
Admission: 1,378 applied, 930 admitted. *Average high school GPA:* 3.3. *Test scores:* ACT scores over 18: 75%; ACT scores over 24: 5%.

FACULTY
Total: 42, 29% full-time.
Student/faculty ratio: 18:1.

ACADEMICS
Calendar: semesters. *Degrees:* associate and bachelor's.
Special study options: advanced placement credit, cooperative education, distance learning, double majors, independent study, internships, part-time degree program, study abroad, summer session for credit.
Computers: 100 computers/terminals are available on campus for general student use. Students can access the following: campus intranet, computer help desk, free student e-mail accounts, online (class) grades, online (class) registration, online (class) schedules. Campuswide network is available. Wireless service is available via entire campus.
Library: USC Union Campus Library plus 1 other. Study areas open 24 hours, 5–7 days a week.

STUDENT LIFE
Housing options: college housing not available.
Activities and organizations: drama/theater group, choral group.
Athletics Member NJCAA. *Intramural sports:* baseball M, soccer M/W, softball W.
Campus security: 24-hour emergency response devices.
Student services: personal/psychological counseling.

COSTS & FINANCIAL AID
Costs (2018–19) *Tuition:* state resident $285 per credit hour part-time; nonresident $721 per credit hour part-time. Full-time tuition and fees vary according to class time, course load, degree level, location, program, and student level. Part-time tuition and fees vary according to class time, location, program, and student level. *Payment plan:* deferred payment. *Waivers:* senior citizens.
Financial Aid Of all full-time matriculated undergraduates who enrolled in 2016, 16 Federal Work-Study jobs (averaging $3400).

APPLYING
Standardized Tests *Required:* SAT or ACT (for admission).

Options: electronic application.
Application fee: $40.
Required: high school transcript.
Application deadlines: rolling (freshmen), rolling (out-of-state freshmen), rolling (transfers), rolling (early action).
Early decision deadline: rolling (for plan 1), rolling (for plan 2).
Notification: continuous (freshmen), continuous (out-of-state freshmen), continuous (transfers), rolling (early decision plan 1), rolling (early decision plan 2), rolling (early action).

CONTACT
Mr. Michael B. Greer, Director of Enrollment Services, University of South Carolina Union, PO Drawer 729, Union, SC 29379-0729. *Phone:* 864-424-8039. *E-mail:* greerm@mailbox.sc.edu.

University of South Carolina Upstate
Spartanburg, South Carolina
http://www.uscupstate.edu/

CONTACT
Ms. Donette Stewart, Associate Vice Chancellor for Enrollment Services, University of South Carolina Upstate, 800 University Way, Spartanburg, SC 29303. *Phone:* 864-503-5280. *Toll-free phone:* 800-277-8727. *Fax:* 864-503-5727. *E-mail:* dstewart@uscupstate.edu.

Voorhees College
Denmark, South Carolina
http://www.voorhees.edu/

CONTACT
Adrain West, Dean of Enrollment Management, Voorhees College, PO Box 678, Denmark, SC 29042. *Phone:* 803-780-1269. *Toll-free phone:* 866-237-4570. *E-mail:* west@voorhees.edu.

Winthrop University
Rock Hill, South Carolina
http://www.winthrop.edu/
- **State-supported** comprehensive, founded 1886, part of South Carolina Commission on Higher Education
- **Suburban** 456-acre campus with easy access to Charlotte
- **Coed** 5,014 undergraduate students, 90% full-time, 70% women, 30% men
- **Moderately difficult** entrance level, 73% of applicants were admitted

UNDERGRAD STUDENTS
4,488 full-time, 526 part-time. Students come from 40 states and territories; 69 other countries; 9% are from out of state; 29% Black or African American, non-Hispanic/Latino; 5% Hispanic/Latino; 1% Asian, non-Hispanic/Latino; 0.3% American Indian or Alaska Native, non-Hispanic/Latino; 4% Two or more races, non-Hispanic/Latino; 0.1% Race/ethnicity unknown; 1% international; 7% transferred in; 48% live on campus.

Freshmen:
Admission: 4,573 applied, 3,356 admitted, 1,050 enrolled. *Average high school GPA:* 4.0. *Test scores:* SAT evidence-based reading and writing scores over 500: 77%; SAT math scores over 500: 69%; ACT scores over 18: 87%; SAT evidence-based reading and writing scores over 600: 32%; SAT math scores over 600: 18%; ACT scores over 24: 37%; SAT evidence-based reading and writing scores over 700: 5%; SAT math scores over 700: 2%; ACT scores over 30: 5%.
Retention: 77% of full-time freshmen returned.

FACULTY
Total: 561, 50% full-time, 59% with terminal degrees.
Student/faculty ratio: 14:1.

ACADEMICS
Calendar: semesters. *Degrees:* certificates, bachelor's, master's, post-master's, and postbachelor's certificates.
Special study options: adult/continuing education programs, advanced placement credit, cooperative education, distance learning, double majors,

honors programs, independent study, internships, off-campus study, part-time degree program, services for LD students, student-designed majors, study abroad, summer session for credit. *ROTC:* Army (c), Air Force (c).

Computers: 620 computers/terminals are available on campus for general student use. Students can access the following: campus intranet, computer help desk, free student e-mail accounts, online (class) grades, online (class) registration, online (class) schedules, university services. Campuswide network is available. 100% of college-owned or -operated housing units are wired for high-speed Internet access. Wireless service is available via entire campus.

Library: Dacus Library plus 1 other. *Books:* 361,941 (physical), 288,136 (digital/electronic); *Serial titles:* 540 (physical), 36,003 (digital/electronic); *Databases:* 133. Weekly public service hours: 49; study areas open 24 hours, 5–7 days a week; students can reserve study rooms.

STUDENT LIFE

Housing options: on-campus residence required through sophomore year; coed, women-only, special housing for students with disabilities. Campus housing is university owned. Freshman campus housing is guaranteed.

Activities and organizations: drama/theater group, student-run newspaper, radio station, choral group, Association of Ebonites, WU Crew, Greek Life, DiGiorgio Student Union, Campus Ministries, national fraternities, national sororities.

Athletics Member NCAA. All Division I. *Intercollegiate sports:* baseball M(s), basketball M(s)/W(s), cheerleading M(c)/W(c), cross-country running M(s)/W(s), fencing M(c)/W(c), golf M(s)/W(s), lacrosse M(c)/W, rugby M(c), soccer M(s)/W(s), softball W(s), tennis M(s)/W(s), track and field M(s)/W(s), volleyball W(s). *Intramural sports:* badminton M/W, basketball M/W, cross-country running M/W, equestrian sports M(c)/W(c), football M/W, golf M/W, racquetball M/W, soccer M/W, softball M/W, swimming and diving M/W, table tennis M/W, tennis M/W, ultimate Frisbee M/W, volleyball M/W, water polo M/W, weight lifting M/W.

Campus security: 24-hour emergency response devices and patrols, late-night transport/escort service, controlled dormitory access.

Student services: health clinic, personal/psychological counseling.

COSTS & FINANCIAL AID

Costs (2017–18) *Tuition:* state resident $14,870 full-time, $620 per credit hour part-time; nonresident $28,786 full-time, $1200 per credit hour part-time. Full-time tuition and fees vary according to degree level, reciprocity agreements, and student level. Part-time tuition and fees vary according to degree level and student level. *Required fees:* $480 full-time. *Room and board:* $8740; room only: $5290. Room and board charges vary according to board plan and housing facility. *Payment plan:* installment. *Waivers:* senior citizens and employees or children of employees.

Financial Aid Of all full-time matriculated undergraduates who enrolled in 2017, 3,884 applied for aid, 3,390 were judged to have need, 443 had their need fully met. 148 Federal Work-Study jobs (averaging $1987). In 2017, 566 non-need-based awards were made. *Average percent of need met:* 57. *Average financial aid package:* $13,569. *Average need-based loan:* $4348. *Average need-based gift aid:* $9187. *Average non-need-based aid:* $4788. *Average indebtedness upon graduation:* $36,147.

APPLYING

Standardized Tests *Required:* SAT or ACT (for admission).

Options: electronic application, deferred entrance.

Application fee: $40.

Required: high school transcript, minimum 3.0 GPA. *Required for some:* essay or personal statement.

Application deadlines: 5/1 (freshmen), 5/1 (transfers).

Notification: continuous (freshmen), continuous (transfers).

CONTACT

Winthrop University, 701 Oakland Avenue, Rock Hill, SC 29733. *Phone:* 803-323-2191. *Toll-free phone:* 800-763-0230.

Wofford College

Spartanburg, South Carolina
http://www.wofford.edu/

- **Independent** 4-year, founded 1854, affiliated with United Methodist Church
- **Urban** 170-acre campus
- **Endowment** $194.0 million
- **Coed** 1,592 undergraduate students, 99% full-time, 53% women, 47% men
- **Very difficult** entrance level, 69% of applicants were admitted

UNDERGRAD STUDENTS

1,572 full-time, 20 part-time. Students come from 41 states and territories; 31 other countries; 46% are from out of state; 8% Black or African American, non-Hispanic/Latino; 4% Hispanic/Latino; 2% Asian, non-Hispanic/Latino; 0.2% Native Hawaiian or other Pacific Islander, non-Hispanic/Latino; 0.3% American Indian or Alaska Native, non-Hispanic/Latino; 4% Two or more races, non-Hispanic/Latino; 0.4% Race/ethnicity unknown; 2% international; 1% transferred in; 93% live on campus.

Freshmen:
Admission: 3,092 applied, 2,142 admitted, 452 enrolled. *Average high school GPA:* 3.7. *Test scores:* SAT evidence-based reading and writing scores over 500: 94%; SAT math scores over 500: 94%; ACT scores over 18: 98%; SAT evidence-based reading and writing scores over 600: 56%; SAT math scores over 600: 65%; ACT scores over 24: 71%; SAT evidence-based reading and writing scores over 700: 10%; SAT math scores over 700: 14%; ACT scores over 30: 17%.

Retention: 90% of full-time freshmen returned.

FACULTY

Total: 173, 84% full-time, 83% with terminal degrees.

Student/faculty ratio: 10:1.

ACADEMICS

Calendar: 4-1-4. *Degree:* bachelor's.

Special study options: accelerated degree program, advanced placement credit, double majors, independent study, internships, off-campus study, part-time degree program, student-designed majors, study abroad, summer session for credit. *ROTC:* Army (b).

Unusual degree programs: engineering with Clemson University.

Computers: 233 computers/terminals are available on campus for general student use. Students can access the following: campus intranet, computer help desk, free student e-mail accounts, online (class) grades, online (class) registration, online (class) schedules. Campuswide network is available. Wireless service is available via entire campus.

Library: Sandor Teszler Library. *Books:* 590,175 (digital/electronic).

STUDENT LIFE

Housing options: on-campus residence required through senior year; coed. Campus housing is university owned. Freshman applicants given priority for college housing.

Activities and organizations: drama/theater group, student-run newspaper, radio station, choral group, W.A.R. - Wofford Athletics and Recreation, W.A.C. - Wofford Activities Council, Twin Towers - Service Organization, Math Academy, Arcadia Volunteer Corp, national fraternities, national sororities.

Athletics Member NCAA. All Division I except football (Division I-AA). *Intercollegiate sports:* baseball M(s), basketball M(s)/W(s), cheerleading W, cross-country running M(s)/W(s), golf M(s)/W(s), lacrosse W(s), riflery M(s)/W(s), soccer M(s)/W(s), tennis M(s)/W(s), track and field M(s)/W(s), volleyball W(s). *Intramural sports:* basketball M/W, football M/W, soccer M/W, softball M/W, table tennis M/W, tennis M/W, ultimate Frisbee M/W.

Campus security: 24-hour emergency response devices and patrols, late-night transport/escort service, controlled dormitory access.

Student services: health clinic, personal/psychological counseling.

COSTS & FINANCIAL AID

Costs (2018–19) *Comprehensive fee:* $56,550 includes full-time tuition ($42,355), mandatory fees ($1510), and room and board ($12,685). *Payment plan:* installment. *Waivers:* employees or children of employees.

Financial Aid Of all full-time matriculated undergraduates who enrolled in 2017, 1,203 applied for aid, 990 were judged to have need, 386 had their need fully met. In 2017, 444 non-need-based awards were made. *Average percent of need met:* 82. *Average financial aid package:* $36,140. *Average need-based loan:* $4410. *Average need-based gift aid:* $32,355. *Average non-need-based aid:* $17,161. *Average indebtedness upon graduation:* $32,043.

APPLYING

Standardized Tests *Required:* SAT or ACT (for admission).

Options: electronic application, early admission, early decision, early action, deferred entrance.

Application fee: $35.

Required: essay or personal statement, high school transcript. *Recommended:* 2 letters of recommendation, interview.

Application deadlines: 1/15 (freshmen), rolling (transfers), 11/15 (early action).

Early decision deadline: 11/1.

Notification: 3/1 (freshmen), continuous (transfers), 12/1 (early decision), 2/1 (early action).

CONTACT

Ms. Britt Shisler, Visit Coordinator, Wofford College, 429 N. Church Street, Spartanburg, SC 29303. *Phone:* 864-597-4132. *Fax:* 864-597-4147. *E-mail:* admission@wofford.edu.

SOUTH DAKOTA

Augustana University

Sioux Falls, South Dakota

http://www.augie.edu/

- **Independent** comprehensive, founded 1860, affiliated with Evangelical Lutheran Church in America
- **Urban** 100-acre campus
- **Endowment** $81.0 million
- **Coed** 1,749 undergraduate students, 96% full-time, 62% women, 38% men
- **Moderately difficult** entrance level, 68% of applicants were admitted

UNDERGRAD STUDENTS

1,679 full-time, 70 part-time. Students come from 33 states and territories; 32 other countries; 50% are from out of state; 2% Black or African American, non-Hispanic/Latino; 3% Hispanic/Latino; 1% Asian, non-Hispanic/Latino; 0.5% American Indian or Alaska Native, non-Hispanic/Latino; 1% Two or more races, non-Hispanic/Latino; 0.1% Race/ethnicity unknown; 8% international; 3% transferred in; 70% live on campus.

Freshmen:

Admission: 1,975 applied, 1,339 admitted, 481 enrolled. *Average high school GPA:* 3.7. *Test scores:* SAT evidence-based reading and writing scores over 500: 84%; SAT math scores over 500: 90%; ACT scores over 18: 99%; SAT evidence-based reading and writing scores over 600: 42%; SAT math scores over 600: 48%; ACT scores over 24: 68%; SAT evidence-based reading and writing scores over 700: 6%; SAT math scores over 700: 10%; ACT scores over 30: 20%.

Retention: 86% of full-time freshmen returned.

FACULTY

Total: 176, 74% full-time, 75% with terminal degrees.

Student/faculty ratio: 12:1.

ACADEMICS

Calendar: 4-1-4. *Degrees:* bachelor's and master's.

Special study options: academic remediation for entering students, accelerated degree program, advanced placement credit, distance learning, double majors, external degree program, honors programs, independent

study, internships, off-campus study, part-time degree program, services for LD students, student-designed majors, study abroad, summer session for credit. *ROTC:* Army (c), Air Force (c).

Unusual degree programs: 3-2 engineering with Columbia University, Washington University in St. Louis.

Computers: 295 computers/terminals are available on campus for general student use. Students can access the following: campus intranet, computer help desk, free student e-mail accounts, online (class) grades, online (class) registration, online (class) schedules. Campuswide network is available. 100% of college-owned or -operated housing units are wired for high-speed Internet access. Wireless service is available via entire campus.

Library: Mikkelsen Library. Students can reserve study rooms.

STUDENT LIFE

Housing options: on-campus residence required through sophomore year; coed, special housing for students with disabilities. Campus housing is university owned. Freshman campus housing is guaranteed.

Activities and organizations: drama/theater group, student-run newspaper, choral group, Augieholics (student athletics support organization), intramurals, Union Board of Governors (student union), Augie Green, Campus Ministries.

Athletics Member NCAA. All Division II. *Intercollegiate sports:* baseball M(s), basketball M(s)/W(s), cheerleading M/W, cross-country running M(s)/W(s), football M(s), golf M(s)/W(s), rugby W(c), soccer M(c)/W(s), softball W(s), swimming and diving W(s), tennis M(s)/W(s), track and field M(s)/W(s), ultimate Frisbee M(c)/W(c), volleyball W(s), wrestling M(s). *Intramural sports:* basketball M/W, bowling M/W, cross-country running M/W, football M/W, golf M/W, racquetball M/W, rock climbing M/W, skiing (cross-country) M/W, soccer M/W, softball M/W, swimming and diving M/W, table tennis M/W, tennis M/W, ultimate Frisbee M/W, volleyball M(c)/W(c), weight lifting M/W.

Campus security: 24-hour emergency response devices and patrols, late-night transport/escort service, controlled dormitory access, special "day lighting" night lights throughout the campus grounds.

Student services: health clinic, personal/psychological counseling.

COSTS & FINANCIAL AID

Costs (2018–19) *Comprehensive fee:* $41,266 includes full-time tuition ($32,488), mandatory fees ($530), and room and board ($8248). Full-time tuition and fees vary according to course load and degree level. Part-time tuition and fees vary according to course load and degree level. *College room only:* $3778. Room and board charges vary according to board plan and housing facility. *Payment plan:* installment. *Waivers:* employees or children of employees.

Financial Aid Of all full-time matriculated undergraduates who enrolled in 2017, 1,237 applied for aid, 1,073 were judged to have need, 162 had their need fully met. 372 Federal Work-Study jobs (averaging $1850). 107 state and other part-time jobs (averaging $940). In 2017, 585 non-need-based awards were made. *Average percent of need met:* 86. *Average financial aid package:* $26,851. *Average need-based loan:* $5158. *Average need-based gift aid:* $22,965. *Average non-need-based aid:* $16,217. *Average indebtedness upon graduation:* $36,950.

APPLYING

Standardized Tests *Required:* SAT or ACT (for admission).

Options: electronic application, deferred entrance.

Required: high school transcript, minimum 2.7 GPA, minimum ACT score of 20. *Recommended:* essay or personal statement, 1 letter of recommendation, interview.

Application deadlines: rolling (freshmen), rolling (transfers).

Notification: continuous until 10/1 (freshmen), continuous (transfers).

CONTACT

Nancy Davidson, Vice President for Enrollment, Augustana University, 2001 South Summit Avenue, Sioux Falls, SD 57197. *Phone:* 605-274-5516. *Toll-free phone:* 800-727-2844. *Fax:* 605-274-5518. *E-mail:* admission@augie.edu.

Black Hills State University

Spearfish, South Dakota

http://www.bhsu.edu/

- **State-supported** comprehensive, founded 1883, part of South Dakota Board of Regents
- **Small-town** 123-acre campus
- **Coed** 3,947 undergraduate students, 56% full-time, 63% women, 37% men

UNDERGRAD STUDENTS

2,195 full-time, 1,752 part-time. Students come from 45 states and territories; 36 other countries; 31% are from out of state; 2% Black or African American, non-Hispanic/Latino; 6% Hispanic/Latino; 0.8% Asian, non-Hispanic/Latino; 4% American Indian or Alaska Native, non-Hispanic/Latino; 5% Two or more races, non-Hispanic/Latino; 0.4% Race/ethnicity unknown; 1% international; 7% transferred in.

Freshmen:

Admission: 541 enrolled. *Average high school GPA:* 3.1.

Retention: 69% of full-time freshmen returned.

FACULTY

Total: 128, 70% with terminal degrees.

ACADEMICS

Calendar: semesters. *Degrees:* associate, bachelor's, master's, post-master's, and postbachelor's certificates.

Special study options: academic remediation for entering students, accelerated degree program, advanced placement credit, cooperative education, distance learning, double majors, English as a second language, honors programs, independent study, internships, off-campus study, part-time degree program, services for LD students, study abroad, summer session for credit. *ROTC:* Army (b).

Computers: Students can access the following: campus intranet, computer help desk, free student e-mail accounts, online (class) grades, online (class) registration, online (class) schedules. Campuswide network is available. 100% of college-owned or -operated housing units are wired for high-speed Internet access. Wireless service is available via classrooms, computer centers, computer labs, dorm rooms, learning centers, libraries, student centers.

Library: E. Y. Berry Library. Students can reserve study rooms.

STUDENT LIFE

Housing options: on-campus residence required through sophomore year; coed, men-only, women-only, special housing for students with disabilities. Campus housing is university owned. Freshman applicants given priority for college housing.

Activities and organizations: drama/theater group, student-run newspaper, radio and television station, choral group, Student Activities Committee, Student Government, national fraternities, national sororities.

Athletics Member NCAA. All Division II. *Intercollegiate sports:* basketball M(s)/W(s), cross-country running M(s)/W(s), football M(s), golf W, track and field M(s)/W(s), volleyball W(s). *Intramural sports:* archery M/W, badminton M/W, basketball M/W, bowling M/W, football M, golf M/W, racquetball M/W, skiing (cross-country) M/W, skiing (downhill) M/W, soccer M/W, softball M/W, tennis M/W, volleyball M/W, weight lifting M/W.

Campus security: 24-hour patrols, late-night transport/escort service, controlled dormitory access.

Student services: health clinic, personal/psychological counseling.

COSTS

Costs (2018–19) *Tuition:* state resident $7514 full-time, $287 per credit hour part-time; nonresident $10,514 full-time, $387 per credit hour part-time. Full-time tuition and fees vary according to course load, location, and reciprocity agreements. Part-time tuition and fees vary according to course load, location, and reciprocity agreements. *Required fees:* $1088 full-time. *Room and board:* $6820; room only: $3467. Room and board charges vary according to board plan and housing facility. *Payment plans:* installment, deferred payment. *Waivers:* children of alumni, senior citizens, and employees or children of employees.

APPLYING

Standardized Tests *Required:* SAT or ACT (for admission).

Required: high school transcript, minimum 2.0 high school GPA in core curriculum.

CONTACT

Mrs. Beth Oaks, Director of Admissions, Black Hills State University, 1200 University St, Unit 9502, Spearfish, SD 57799-9502. *Phone:* 605-642-6343. *Toll-free phone:* 800-255-2478. *Fax:* 605-642-6254. *E-mail:* admissions@bhsu.edu.

Dakota State University

Madison, South Dakota

http://www.dsu.edu/

- **State-supported** comprehensive, founded 1881, part of South Dakota Board of Regents
- **Rural** 62-acre campus with easy access to Sioux Falls
- **Endowment** $11.2 million
- **Coed** 2,962 undergraduate students, 47% full-time, 42% women, 58% men
- **Moderately difficult** entrance level, 84% of applicants were admitted

UNDERGRAD STUDENTS

1,397 full-time, 1,565 part-time. Students come from 50 states and territories; 19 other countries; 39% are from out of state; 4% Black or African American, non-Hispanic/Latino; 4% Hispanic/Latino; 2% Asian, non-Hispanic/Latino; 0.0% Native Hawaiian or other Pacific Islander, non-Hispanic/Latino; 0.8% American Indian or Alaska Native, non-Hispanic/Latino; 4% Two or more races, non-Hispanic/Latino; 0.8% Race/ethnicity unknown; 1% international; 10% transferred in.

Freshmen:

Admission: 972 applied, 820 admitted, 381 enrolled. *Average high school GPA:* 3.2. *Test scores:* SAT evidence-based reading and writing scores over 500: 74%; SAT math scores over 500: 70%; ACT scores over 18: 86%; SAT evidence-based reading and writing scores over 600: 39%; SAT math scores over 600: 35%; ACT scores over 24: 42%; ACT scores over 30: 6%.

Retention: 72% of full-time freshmen returned.

FACULTY

Total: 145, 66% full-time, 62% with terminal degrees.

ACADEMICS

Calendar: semesters. *Degrees:* certificates, associate, bachelor's, master's, doctoral, and postbachelor's certificates.

Special study options: academic remediation for entering students, advanced placement credit, cooperative education, distance learning, double majors, honors programs, independent study, internships, off-campus study, part-time degree program, services for LD students, study abroad, summer session for credit. *ROTC:* Army (c), Air Force (c).

Computers: 135 computers/terminals are available on campus for general student use. Students can access the following: campus intranet, computer help desk, free student e-mail accounts, online (class) grades, online (class) registration, online (class) schedules. Campuswide network is available. 100% of college-owned or -operated housing units are wired for high-speed Internet access. Wireless service is available via entire campus.

Library: Karl E. Mundt Library & Learning Commons plus 1 other. *Books:* 43,699 (physical), 162,866 (digital/electronic); *Serial titles:* 200 (physical); *Databases:* 121. Weekly public service hours: 85.

STUDENT LIFE

Housing options: on-campus residence required through sophomore year; coed, men-only. Campus housing is university owned and leased by the school. Freshman campus housing is guaranteed.

Activities and organizations: drama/theater group, student-run newspaper, radio station, choral group, Gaming Club, Computer Club, Student Senate, Fellowship of Christian Athletes, Campus Crusade for Christ (Cru).

Athletics Member NAIA. *Intercollegiate sports:* baseball M(s), basketball M(s)/W(s), cheerleading M/W, cross-country running M(s)/W(s), football M(s), softball W(s), track and field M(s)/W(s), volleyball W(s). *Intramural sports:* basketball M/W, soccer M(c)/W(c), softball M/W, table tennis M/W, tennis M/W, volleyball M/W, weight lifting M(c)/W(c).

Campus security: controlled dormitory access.

Student services: health clinic, personal/psychological counseling.

COSTS & FINANCIAL AID

Costs (2017–18) *Tuition:* state resident $7191 full-time, $240 per credit hour part-time; nonresident $10,121 full-time, $337 per credit hour part-time. Full-time tuition and fees vary according to location and reciprocity agreements. Part-time tuition and fees vary according to location and reciprocity agreements. *Required fees:* $1956 full-time, $39 per credit part-time. *Room and board:* $6720; room only: $3658. Room and board charges vary according to board plan and housing facility. *Payment plan:* installment. *Waivers:* senior citizens and employees or children of employees.

Financial Aid Of all full-time matriculated undergraduates who enrolled in 2016, 1,091 applied for aid, 895 were judged to have need, 89 had their need fully met. 133 Federal Work-Study jobs (averaging $2103). 22 state and other part-time jobs (averaging $6031). In 2016, 117 non-need-based awards were made. *Average percent of need met:* 74. *Average financial aid package:* $7954. *Average need-based loan:* $4167. *Average need-based gift aid:* $4333. *Average non-need-based aid:* $5095. *Average indebtedness upon graduation:* $29,962.

APPLYING

Standardized Tests *Required:* SAT or ACT (for admission).

Options: electronic application, deferred entrance.

Application fee: $20.

Required: high school transcript, minimum 2.6 GPA.

Application deadlines: rolling (freshmen), rolling (out-of-state freshmen), rolling (transfers).

Notification: continuous (freshmen), continuous (out-of-state freshmen), continuous (transfers).

CONTACT

Ms. Tory Bickett, Admissions Senior Secretary, Dakota State University, 820 North Washington, Madison, SD 57042-1799. *Phone:* 605-256-5139. *Toll-free phone:* 888-DSU-9988. *Fax:* 605-256-5020. *E-mail:* admissions@dsu.edu.

Dakota Wesleyan University

Mitchell, South Dakota

http://www.dwu.edu/

CONTACT

Mrs. Melissa Herr-Valburg, Director of Admissions, Dakota Wesleyan University, 1200 West University Avenue, Mitchell, SD 57301-4398. *Phone:* 605-995-2600 Ext. 2652. *Toll-free phone:* 800-333-8506. *Fax:* 605-995-2699. *E-mail:* admissions@dwu.edu.

Mount Marty College

Yankton, South Dakota

http://www.mtmc.edu/

- **Independent Roman Catholic** comprehensive, founded 1936
- **Small-town** 80-acre campus
- **Endowment** $26.5 million
- **Coed** 876 undergraduate students, 52% full-time, 58% women, 42% men
- **Minimally difficult** entrance level, 67% of applicants were admitted

UNDERGRAD STUDENTS

457 full-time, 419 part-time. Students come from 30 states and territories; 3 other countries; 47% are from out of state; 3% Black or African American, non-Hispanic/Latino; 6% Hispanic/Latino; 0.7% Asian, non-Hispanic/Latino; 0.2% Native Hawaiian or other Pacific Islander, non-Hispanic/Latino; 3% American Indian or Alaska Native, non-Hispanic/Latino; 0.8% Two or more races, non-Hispanic/Latino; 1% Race/ethnicity unknown; 5% transferred in; 72% live on campus.

Freshmen:
Admission: 466 applied, 310 admitted, 121 enrolled. *Average high school GPA:* 3.4.
Retention: 72% of full-time freshmen returned.

FACULTY

Total: 50, 82% full-time, 64% with terminal degrees.

Student/faculty ratio: 11:1.

ACADEMICS

Calendar: semesters. *Degrees:* certificates, associate, bachelor's, master's, doctoral, and post-master's certificates.

Special study options: academic remediation for entering students, accelerated degree program, adult/continuing education programs, advanced placement credit, cooperative education, distance learning, double majors, honors programs, independent study, internships, off-campus study, part-time degree program, services for LD students, student-designed majors, summer session for credit. *ROTC:* Army (c).

Computers: 12 computers/terminals are available on campus for general student use. Students can access the following: campus intranet, computer help desk, free student e-mail accounts, online (class) grades, online (class) registration, online (class) schedules. Campuswide network is available. 100% of college-owned or -operated housing units are wired for high-speed Internet access. Wireless service is available via entire campus.

Library: Mount Marty College Library. Study areas open 24 hours, 5–7 days a week; students can reserve study rooms.

STUDENT LIFE

Housing options: on-campus residence required through senior year; coed, men-only, women-only. Campus housing is university owned. Freshman campus housing is guaranteed.

Activities and organizations: drama/theater group, choral group, Campus Ministry, Student Government Association, Nursing Club, Education Club, Theater Club.

Athletics Member NAIA. *Intercollegiate sports:* archery M(c)/W(c), baseball M(s), basketball M(s)/W(s), cross-country running M(s)/W(s), golf M(s)/W(s), riflery M(c)/W(c), soccer M(s)/W(s), softball W(s), tennis W(s), track and field M(s)/W(s), volleyball W(s). *Intramural sports:* archery M/W, basketball M/W, soccer M/W, softball W, volleyball M/W.

Campus security: 24-hour emergency response devices and patrols, late-night transport/escort service.

Student services: health clinic, personal/psychological counseling.

COSTS & FINANCIAL AID

Costs (2017–18) *Comprehensive fee:* $34,156 includes full-time tuition ($24,160), mandatory fees ($2150), and room and board ($7846). Full-time tuition and fees vary according to degree level, location, and program. Part-time tuition: $530 per credit hour. Part-time tuition and fees vary according to course load, degree level, location, and program. *Required fees:* $45 per credit hour part-time. *Room and board:* Room and board charges vary according to board plan. *Payment plan:* installment. *Waivers:* employees or children of employees.

Financial Aid Of all full-time matriculated undergraduates who enrolled in 2017, 423 applied for aid, 372 were judged to have need, 166 had their need fully met. 127 Federal Work-Study jobs (averaging $1758). 55 state and other part-time jobs (averaging $1784). In 2017, 45 non-need-based awards were made. *Average percent of need met:* 86. *Average financial aid package:* $27,350. *Average need-based loan:* $5198. *Average need-based gift aid:* $16,832. *Average non-need-based aid:* $10,339. *Average indebtedness upon graduation:* $32,744.

APPLYING

Standardized Tests *Required:* SAT or ACT (for admission).

Options: electronic application, early admission, deferred entrance.

Application fee: $35.

Required: high school transcript, minimum 2.0 GPA. *Recommended:* interview.

Application deadlines: rolling (freshmen), rolling (transfers).

Notification: continuous (freshmen), continuous (transfers).

CONTACT

Stephanie Moser, Dean of Enrollment, Mount Marty College, 1105 W. 8th Street, Yankton, SD 57078. *Phone:* 605-668-1545. *Toll-free phone:* 800-658-4552. *E-mail:* stephanie.moser@mtmc.edu.

National American University

Ellsworth AFB, South Dakota

http://www.national.edu/

CONTACT

Admissions Office, National American University, 1000 Ellsworth Street, Rushmore Center, Suite 2400B, Ellsworth AFB, SD 57706.

National American University

Rapid City, South Dakota

http://www.national.edu/

CONTACT

Ms. Angela Beck, Director of Enrollment Management, National American University, 321 Kansas City Street, Rapid City, SD 57701. *Phone:* 605-394-4902. *Toll-free phone:* 800-209-0490. *Fax:* 605-394-4871. *E-mail:* abeck@national.edu.

National American University

Sioux Falls, South Dakota

http://www.national.edu/

CONTACT

Ms. Lisa Houtsma, Director of Admissions, National American University, 5801 South Corporate Place, Sioux Falls, SD 57108. *Phone:* 605-336-4600. *Toll-free phone:* 800-388-5430. *Fax:* 605-336-4605. *E-mail:* lhoutsma@national.edu.

Northern State University

Aberdeen, South Dakota

http://www.northern.edu/

- **State-supported** comprehensive, founded 1901, part of South Dakota Board of Regents
- **Small-town** 72-acre campus
- **Endowment** $28.0 million
- **Coed** 3,162 undergraduate students, 43% full-time, 57% women, 43% men
- **Minimally difficult** entrance level, 88% of applicants were admitted

UNDERGRAD STUDENTS

1,346 full-time, 1,816 part-time. Students come from 42 states and territories; 39 other countries; 29% are from out of state; 1% Black or African American, non-Hispanic/Latino; 3% Hispanic/Latino; 1% Asian, non-Hispanic/Latino; 0.1% Native Hawaiian or other Pacific Islander, non-Hispanic/Latino; 2% American Indian or Alaska Native, non-Hispanic/Latino; 3% Two or more races, non-Hispanic/Latino; 1% Race/ethnicity unknown; 5% international; 3% transferred in; 35% live on campus.

Freshmen:

Admission: 994 applied, 873 admitted, 324 enrolled. *Average high school GPA:* 3.3. *Test scores:* SAT evidence-based reading and writing scores over 500: 58%; SAT math scores over 500: 58%; ACT scores over 18: 89%; SAT evidence-based reading and writing scores over 600: 11%; SAT math scores over 600: 11%; ACT scores over 24: 32%; ACT scores over 30: 5%.

Retention: 77% of full-time freshmen returned.

FACULTY

Total: 148, 61% full-time, 59% with terminal degrees.

Student/faculty ratio: 19:1.

ACADEMICS

Calendar: semesters. *Degrees:* certificates, associate, bachelor's, master's, and postbachelor's certificates.

Special study options: academic remediation for entering students, accelerated degree program, adult/continuing education programs, advanced placement credit, cooperative education, distance learning, double majors, English as a second language, freshman honors college, honors programs, independent study, internships, off-campus study, part-time degree program, services for LD students, student-designed majors, study abroad, summer session for credit.

Computers: 130 computers/terminals and 20 ports are available on campus for general student use. Students can access the following: campus intranet, computer help desk, free student e-mail accounts, online (class) grades, online (class) registration, online (class) schedules. Campuswide network is available. 100% of college-owned or -operated housing units are wired for high-speed Internet access. Wireless service is available via entire campus.

Library: Beulah Williams Library. *Books:* 159,000 (physical), 15,000 (digital/electronic); *Serial titles:* 7,500 (physical), 250 (digital/electronic); *Databases:* 83. Weekly public service hours: 90; students can reserve study rooms.

STUDENT LIFE

Housing options: on-campus residence required through sophomore year; coed. Campus housing is university owned. Freshman campus housing is guaranteed.

Activities and organizations: drama/theater group, student-run newspaper, television station, choral group, marching band.

Athletics Member NCAA. All Division II. *Intercollegiate sports:* baseball M(s), basketball M(s)/W(s), cross-country running M(s)/W(s), football M(s), soccer W(s), softball W(s), swimming and diving W(s), track and field M(s)/W(s), volleyball W(s), wrestling M(s). *Intramural sports:* badminton M(c)/W(c), basketball M/W, football M/W, racquetball M/W, rugby M(c)/W(c), soccer M/W, softball M/W, table tennis M/W, ultimate Frisbee M/W, volleyball M/W.

Campus security: 24-hour emergency response devices, controlled dormitory access, evening patrols.

Student services: health clinic, personal/psychological counseling, legal services.

COSTS & FINANCIAL AID

Costs (2018–19) *Tuition:* state resident $7191 full-time, $240 per credit hour part-time; nonresident $10,120 full-time, $337 per credit hour part-time. Full-time tuition and fees vary according to course load, program, and reciprocity agreements. Part-time tuition and fees vary according to course load, program, and reciprocity agreements. *Required fees:* $1089 full-time, $36 per credit hour part-time. *Room and board:* $7844; room only: $3640. Room and board charges vary according to board plan and housing facility. *Payment plan:* installment. *Waivers:* senior citizens and employees or children of employees.

Financial Aid Of all full-time matriculated undergraduates who enrolled in 2016, 988 applied for aid, 749 were judged to have need, 232 had their need fully met. 334 Federal Work-Study jobs (averaging $2504). 369 state and other part-time jobs (averaging $1009). In 2016, 127 non-need-based awards were made. *Average percent of need met:* 77. *Average financial aid package:* $10,128. *Average need-based loan:* $5346. *Average need-based gift aid:* $4730. *Average non-need-based aid:* $1702. *Average indebtedness upon graduation:* $28,142.

APPLYING

Standardized Tests *Required:* SAT or ACT (for admission).

Options: electronic application, early admission, deferred entrance.

Application fee: $20.

Required: high school transcript, minimum 2.6 GPA.

Notification: continuous (freshmen), continuous (transfers).

CONTACT

Dr. Jeremy Reed, Vice President of Enrollment Management and Student Affairs, Northern State University, 1200 South Jay Street, Aberdeen, SD 57401. *Phone:* 605-626-2530. *Toll-free phone:* 800-678-5330. *Fax:* 605-626-2531. *E-mail:* admissions@northern.edu.

Oglala Lakota College

Kyle, South Dakota

http://www.olc.edu/

CONTACT

Director of Admissions, Oglala Lakota College, 490 Piya Wiconi Road, Kyle, SD 57752-0490. *Phone:* 605-455-2321 Ext. 236. *E-mail:* lmeseteth@olc.edu.

Presentation College
Aberdeen, South Dakota
http://www.presentation.edu/

CONTACT
Mr. Robert Schuchardt, Vice President for Student Services, Presentation College, 1500 North Main Street, Aberdeen, SD 57401. *Phone:* 605-229-8406. *Toll-free phone:* 800-437-6060. *Fax:* 605-229-8425. *E-mail:* admit@presentation.edu.

Sinte Gleska University
Mission, South Dakota
http://www.sintegleska.edu/

CONTACT
Mr. Jack Herman, Registrar and Director of Admissions, Sinte Gleska University, 101 Antelope Lake Circle, PO Box 105, Mission, SD 57555. *Phone:* 605-856-8100 Ext. 8479.

South Dakota School of Mines and Technology
Rapid City, South Dakota
http://www.sdsmt.edu/
- **State-supported** university, founded 1885, part of South Dakota Board of Regents
- **Suburban** 120-acre campus
- **Endowment** $53.7 million
- **Coed**
- **Moderately difficult** entrance level

FACULTY
Student/faculty ratio: 15:1.

ACADEMICS
Calendar: semesters. *Degrees:* certificates, associate, bachelor's, master's, doctoral, and postbachelor's certificates.
Library: Devereaux Library plus 1 other. *Books:* 130,971 (physical), 142,661 (digital/electronic); *Serial titles:* 1,663 (physical), 23,896 (digital/electronic); *Databases:* 200. Weekly public service hours: 32; students can reserve study rooms.

STUDENT LIFE
Housing options: on-campus residence required through sophomore year; coed, men-only, women-only, special housing for students with disabilities. Campus housing is university owned and leased by the school. Freshman campus housing is guaranteed.

Activities and organizations: drama/theater group, student-run newspaper, radio station, choral group, eSports 144, ASME (American Society of Mechanical Engineers), Skid Snowboard Club 115, AIChe 107, ASCE 105, national fraternities, national sororities.

Athletics Member NCAA. All Division II.

Campus security: 24-hour emergency response devices and patrols, student patrols, late-night transport/escort service, controlled dormitory access.

Student services: health clinic, personal/psychological counseling.

FINANCIAL AID
Financial Aid Of all full-time matriculated undergraduates who enrolled in 2015, 1,812 applied for aid, 1,095 were judged to have need, 334 had their need fully met. 148 Federal Work-Study jobs (averaging $1718). In 2015, 405 non-need-based awards were made. *Average percent of need met:* 71. *Average financial aid package:* $14,262. *Average need-based loan:* $4106. *Average need-based gift aid:* $4616. *Average non-need-based aid:* $3360. *Average indebtedness upon graduation:* $32,995.

APPLYING
Standardized Tests *Required:* SAT or ACT (for admission).
Options: electronic application.
Application fee: $20.

Required: high school transcript. *Recommended:* minimum 2.8 GPA.

CONTACT
Genene Sigler, Applications Processor, South Dakota School of Mines and Technology, 501 East Saint Joseph Street, Rapid City, SD 57701-3995. *Phone:* 605-394-2414 Ext. 5209. *Toll-free phone:* 800-544-8162. *Fax:* 605-394-1979. *E-mail:* admissions@sdsmt.edu.

South Dakota State University
Brookings, South Dakota
http://www.sdstate.edu/
- **State-supported** university, founded 1881, part of South Dakota Board of Regents
- **Small-town** 363-acre campus
- **Coed**
- **Minimally difficult** entrance level

FACULTY
Student/faculty ratio: 17:1.

ACADEMICS
Calendar: semesters. *Degrees:* certificates, associate, bachelor's, master's, doctoral, post-master's, and postbachelor's certificates.
Library: H. M. Briggs Library. *Books:* 778,376 (physical), 134,615 (digital/electronic); *Serial titles:* 19,899 (physical), 19,850 (digital/electronic); *Databases:* 108. Students can reserve study rooms.

STUDENT LIFE
Housing options: on-campus residence required through sophomore year; coed, special housing for students with disabilities. Campus housing is university owned. Freshman campus housing is guaranteed.

Activities and organizations: drama/theater group, student-run newspaper, radio station, choral group, marching band, national fraternities, national sororities.

Athletics Member NCAA. All Division I.

Campus security: 24-hour emergency response devices and patrols, student patrols, late-night transport/escort service, controlled dormitory access.

Student services: health clinic, personal/psychological counseling, legal services.

COSTS & FINANCIAL AID
Costs (2017–18) *Tuition:* state resident $7200 full-time, $240 per credit hour part-time; nonresident $10,440 full-time, $348 per credit hour part-time. Full-time tuition and fees vary according to course level, course load, degree level, location, program, and reciprocity agreements. Part-time tuition and fees vary according to course level, course load, degree level, location, program, and reciprocity agreements. *Required fees:* $1260 full-time, $42 per credit hour part-time. *Room and board:* $7110; room only: $3710. Room and board charges vary according to board plan and housing facility. *Payment plans:* installment, deferred payment.

Financial Aid Of all full-time matriculated undergraduates who enrolled in 2014, 7,135 applied for aid, 5,684 were judged to have need, 575 had their need fully met. In 2014, 1322 non-need-based awards were made. *Average percent of need met:* 44. *Average financial aid package:* $8636. *Average need-based loan:* $3709. *Average need-based gift aid:* $3755. *Average non-need-based aid:* $1949. *Average indebtedness upon graduation:* $28,769.

APPLYING
Standardized Tests *Required:* SAT or ACT (for admission).
Options: electronic application.
Application fee: $20.
Required: high school transcript, minimum 2.6 GPA.

CONTACT
Ms. Michelle Kuebler, Assistant Director of Admissions, South Dakota State University, PO Box 2201, Brookings, SD 57007. *Phone:* 605-688-4121. *Toll-free phone:* 800-952-3541. *Fax:* 605-688-6891. *E-mail:* sdsu.admissions@sdstate.edu.

University of Sioux Falls
Sioux Falls, South Dakota
http://www.usiouxfalls.edu/

- **Independent American Baptist Churches in the USA** comprehensive, founded 1883
- **Suburban** 140-acre campus
- **Endowment** $28.3 million
- **Coed** 1,215 undergraduate students, 85% full-time, 63% women, 37% men
- **Moderately difficult** entrance level, 92% of applicants were admitted

UNDERGRAD STUDENTS
1,036 full-time, 179 part-time. Students come from 32 states and territories; 10 other countries; 43% are from out of state; 4% Black or African American, non-Hispanic/Latino; 1% Hispanic/Latino; 1% Asian, non-Hispanic/Latino; 0.2% Native Hawaiian or other Pacific Islander, non-Hispanic/Latino; 0.7% American Indian or Alaska Native, non-Hispanic/Latino; 4% Two or more races, non-Hispanic/Latino; 2% Race/ethnicity unknown; 2% international; 6% transferred in; 55% live on campus.

Freshmen:
Admission: 1,602 applied, 1,474 admitted, 280 enrolled. *Average high school GPA:* 3.4. *Test scores:* SAT evidence-based reading and writing scores over 500: 75%; SAT math scores over 500: 76%; ACT scores over 18: 94%; SAT evidence-based reading and writing scores over 600: 42%; SAT math scores over 600: 26%; ACT scores over 24: 40%; ACT scores over 30: 4%.
Retention: 73% of full-time freshmen returned.

FACULTY
Total: 169, 36% full-time, 33% with terminal degrees.
Student/faculty ratio: 13:1.

ACADEMICS
Calendar: 4-1-4. *Degrees:* associate, bachelor's, master's, and post-master's certificates.

Special study options: academic remediation for entering students, accelerated degree program, adult/continuing education programs, advanced placement credit, distance learning, double majors, honors programs, independent study, internships, off-campus study, part-time degree program, services for LD students, student-designed majors, study abroad, summer session for credit. *ROTC:* Air Force (c).

Unusual degree programs: 3-2 business administration; divinity and youth ministry with North American Baptist Seminary.

Computers: 190 computers/terminals are available on campus for general student use. Students can access the following: campus intranet, computer help desk, free student e-mail accounts, online (class) grades, online (class) registration, online (class) schedules. Campuswide network is available. 100% of college-owned or -operated housing units are wired for high-speed Internet access. Wireless service is available via entire campus.

Library: Norman B. Mears Library. *Books:* 64,059 (physical), 138,760 (digital/electronic); *Serial titles:* 290 (physical), 30,000 (digital/electronic); *Databases:* 58. Weekly public service hours: 78.

STUDENT LIFE
Housing options: on-campus residence required through sophomore year; coed, women-only. Campus housing is university owned. Freshman campus housing is guaranteed.

Activities and organizations: drama/theater group, student-run newspaper, radio and television station, choral group, Campus Ministries, Student Senate, Fellowship of Christian Athletes, Association of Cougar Education Students (ACES), National Society for Leadership and Success (NCLS).

Athletics Member NCAA. All Division II. *Intercollegiate sports:* baseball M(s), basketball M(s)/W(s), cheerleading M(s)/W(s), cross-country running M(s)/W(s), football M(s), golf M(s)/W(s), soccer W(s), softball W(s), swimming and diving W(s), tennis W(s), track and field M(s)/W(s), volleyball W(s). *Intramural sports:* basketball M/W, football M/W, ice hockey M/W, soccer M/W, softball M/W, table tennis M/W, ultimate Frisbee M/W, volleyball M/W.

Campus security: 24-hour emergency response devices and patrols, student patrols, late-night transport/escort service, controlled dormitory access.

Student services: personal/psychological counseling.

COSTS & FINANCIAL AID
Costs (2018–19) *Comprehensive fee:* $25,630 includes full-time tuition ($17,980), mandatory fees ($300), and room and board ($7350). Full-time tuition and fees vary according to course load and program. Part-time tuition: $370 per semester hour. *College room only:* $3850. Room and board charges vary according to board plan and housing facility. *Payment plan:* installment. *Waivers:* employees or children of employees.

Financial Aid Of all full-time matriculated undergraduates who enrolled in 2016, 857 applied for aid, 739 were judged to have need, 181 had their need fully met. In 2016, 229 non-need-based awards were made. *Average percent of need met:* 84. *Average financial aid package:* $20,557. *Average need-based loan:* $5061. *Average need-based gift aid:* $15,303. *Average non-need-based aid:* $12,385. *Average indebtedness upon graduation:* $31,146.

APPLYING
Standardized Tests *Required:* SAT or ACT (for admission).
Options: electronic application, deferred entrance.
Application fee: $25.
Required: high school transcript. *Required for some:* essay or personal statement, 2 letters of recommendation, interview. *Recommended:* minimum 2.8 GPA.
Application deadlines: rolling (freshmen), rolling (transfers).
Notification: continuous (freshmen), continuous (transfers).

CONTACT
Mr. Ben Weins, Director of Enrollment Management, University of Sioux Falls, 1101 West 22nd Street, Sioux Falls, SD 57105. *Phone:* 605-331-6700. *Toll-free phone:* 800-888-1047. *Fax:* 605-331-6615. *E-mail:* admissions@usiouxfalls.edu.

University of South Dakota
Vermillion, South Dakota
http://www.usd.edu/

- **State-supported** university, founded 1862, part of South Dakota Board of Regents
- **Small-town** 275-acre campus
- **Endowment** $214.5 million
- **Coed** 7,648 undergraduate students, 64% full-time, 62% women, 38% men
- **Minimally difficult** entrance level, 87% of applicants were admitted

UNDERGRAD STUDENTS
4,908 full-time, 2,740 part-time. Students come from 50 states and territories; 77 other countries; 35% are from out of state; 3% Black or African American, non-Hispanic/Latino; 4% Hispanic/Latino; 1% Asian, non-Hispanic/Latino; 0.1% Native Hawaiian or other Pacific Islander, non-Hispanic/Latino; 2% American Indian or Alaska Native, non-Hispanic/Latino; 3% Two or more races, non-Hispanic/Latino; 1% Race/ethnicity unknown; 2% international; 8% transferred in; 29% live on campus.

Freshmen:
Admission: 3,865 applied, 3,359 admitted, 1,341 enrolled. *Average high school GPA:* 3.3. *Test scores:* SAT evidence-based reading and writing scores over 500: 81%; SAT math scores over 500: 76%; ACT scores over 18: 90%; SAT evidence-based reading and writing scores over 600: 24%; SAT math scores over 600: 35%; ACT scores over 24: 42%; SAT math scores over 700: 11%; ACT scores over 30: 5%.
Retention: 72% of full-time freshmen returned.

FACULTY
Total: 594, 73% full-time, 51% with terminal degrees.
Student/faculty ratio: 17:1.

ACADEMICS
Calendar: semesters. *Degrees:* certificates, associate, bachelor's, master's, doctoral, and postbachelor's certificates.

Special study options: academic remediation for entering students, accelerated degree program, adult/continuing education programs, advanced placement credit, distance learning, double majors, English as a second language, honors programs, independent study, internships, off-campus study, part-time degree program, services for LD students, student-designed majors, study abroad, summer session for credit. *ROTC:* Army (b).

Unusual degree programs: 3-2 business administration.

Computers: 975 computers/terminals are available on campus for general student use. Students can access the following: campus intranet, computer help desk, free student e-mail accounts, online (class) grades, online (class) registration, online (class) schedules. Campuswide network is available. 100% of college-owned or -operated housing units are wired for high-speed Internet access. Wireless service is available via entire campus.

Library: I. D. Weeks Library plus 2 others. *Books:* 530,277 (physical), 112,215 (digital/electronic); *Serial titles:* 5,139 (physical), 68,439 (digital/electronic); *Databases:* 302. Weekly public service hours: 119; students can reserve study rooms.

STUDENT LIFE
Housing options: on-campus residence required through sophomore year; coed, special housing for students with disabilities. Campus housing is university owned. Freshman campus housing is guaranteed.

Activities and organizations: drama/theater group, student-run newspaper, radio and television station, choral group, marching band, Dakotathon, International Club, SERVE, Campus Activities Board, national fraternities, national sororities.

Athletics Member NCAA. All Division I. *Intercollegiate sports:* basketball M(s)/W(s), cross-country running M(s)/W(s), football M(s), golf M/W(s), soccer W(s), softball W(s), swimming and diving M(s)/W(s), tennis W(s), track and field M(s)/W(s), volleyball W(s). *Intramural sports:* archery M(c)/W(c), baseball M(c)/W(c), basketball M/W, fencing M(c)/W(c), football M, rugby M(c)/W(c), soccer M(c)/W(c), tennis M(c)/W(c), ultimate Frisbee M(c)/W(c).

Campus security: 24-hour emergency response devices and patrols, student patrols, late-night transport/escort service, controlled dormitory access.

Student services: health clinic, personal/psychological counseling, legal services.

COSTS & FINANCIAL AID
Costs (2017–18) *Tuition:* state resident $7191 full-time, $240 per credit hour part-time; nonresident $10,439 full-time, $348 per credit hour part-time. Full-time tuition and fees vary according to course load, location, and reciprocity agreements. Part-time tuition and fees vary according to course load, location, and reciprocity agreements. *Required fees:* $1581 full-time, $53 per credit hour part-time. *Room and board:* $7672; room only: $4114. Room and board charges vary according to housing facility. *Payment plan:* deferred payment. *Waivers:* children of alumni, senior citizens, and employees or children of employees.

Financial Aid Of all full-time matriculated undergraduates who enrolled in 2016, 3,872 applied for aid, 2,888 were judged to have need, 421 had their need fully met. In 2016, 970 non-need-based awards were made. *Average percent of need met:* 57. *Average financial aid package:* $8631. *Average need-based loan:* $4434. *Average need-based gift aid:* $4482. *Average non-need-based aid:* $2202. *Average indebtedness upon graduation:* $29,686.

APPLYING
Standardized Tests *Required:* SAT or ACT (for admission).
Options: electronic application, early admission.
Application fee: $20.
Required: high school transcript. *Recommended:* minimum 2.0 GPA.
Application deadlines: rolling (freshmen), rolling (transfers).
Notification: continuous (freshmen), continuous (transfers).

CONTACT
Mr. Travis Vlasman, Senior Associate Director of Admissions, University of South Dakota, 414 East Clark Street, Vermillion, SD 57069-2390. *Phone:* 605-658-6200. *Toll-free phone:* 877-269-6837. *Fax:* 605-677-6323. *E-mail:* admissions@usd.edu.

TENNESSEE

American Baptist College
Nashville, Tennessee
http://www.abcnash.edu/
- Independent Baptist 4-year, founded 1924
- Urban 52-acre campus with easy access to Nashville
- Endowment $626,121
- Coed 152 undergraduate students, 75% full-time, 33% women, 67% men
- Noncompetitive entrance level, 82% of applicants were admitted

UNDERGRAD STUDENTS
114 full-time, 38 part-time. Students come from 12 states and territories; 1 other country; 8% transferred in; 30% live on campus.

Freshmen:
Admission: 45 applied, 37 admitted, 18 enrolled.
Retention: 6% of full-time freshmen returned.

FACULTY
Total: 18, 22% full-time, 22% with terminal degrees.
Student/faculty ratio: 12:1.

ACADEMICS
Calendar: semesters. *Degrees:* diplomas, associate, and bachelor's.

Special study options: academic remediation for entering students, adult/continuing education programs, double majors, off-campus study, part-time degree program, summer session for credit.

Computers: 22 computers/terminals and 32 ports are available on campus for general student use. Students can access the following: campus intranet, free student e-mail accounts, online (class) grades, online (class) registration, online (class) schedules, IT support person on campus during regular campus hours. Campuswide network is available. 100% of college-owned or -operated housing units are wired for high-speed Internet access. Wireless service is available via entire campus.

Library: T. L. Holcolm Library. *Books:* 14,290 (physical); *Serial titles:* 2 (physical); *Databases:* 2. Weekly public service hours: 2; students can reserve study rooms.

STUDENT LIFE
Housing options: coed, men-only, women-only. Campus housing is university owned.

Activities and organizations: choral group, Student Government Association, Vespers Service, Baptist Student Union, Choir, Greek Letter Fraternity and Hoi Adelphoi Fraternity, national fraternities.

Campus security: 24-hour emergency response devices and patrols, controlled dormitory access.

Student services: health clinic.

COSTS & FINANCIAL AID
Costs (2018–19) *Comprehensive fee:* $13,737 includes full-time tuition ($8760), mandatory fees ($657), and room and board ($4320). Full-time tuition and fees vary according to course load and program. Part-time tuition: $380 per credit hour. Part-time tuition and fees vary according to course load and program. *College room only:* $2120. Room and board charges vary according to board plan and housing facility. *Payment plan:* deferred payment.

Financial Aid Of all full-time matriculated undergraduates who enrolled in 2014, 128 applied for aid, 128 were judged to have need. 5 Federal Work-Study jobs (averaging $7452). *Average percent of need met:* 40. *Average financial aid package:* $10,412. *Average need-based loan:* $3823. *Average need-based gift aid:* $8263. *Average indebtedness upon graduation:* $9743. *Financial aid deadline:* 7/23.

APPLYING
Standardized Tests *Required:* (for admission).
Options: electronic application, deferred entrance.
Application fee: $30.
Required: essay or personal statement, high school transcript, minimum 2.0 GPA, 2 letters of recommendation, official transcript(s). *Required for some:* interview.
Application deadlines: rolling (freshmen), rolling (out-of-state freshmen), rolling (transfers).

Notification: continuous (freshmen), continuous (out-of-state freshmen), continuous (transfers).

CONTACT
American Baptist College, 1800 Baptist World Center Drive, Nashville, TN 37207.

Aquinas College
Nashville, Tennessee
http://www.aquinascollege.edu/

- **Independent Roman Catholic** comprehensive, founded 1961
- **Urban** 83-acre campus
- **Endowment** $16.5 million
- **Coed**
- **Minimally difficult** entrance level

FACULTY
Student/faculty ratio: 8:1.

ACADEMICS
Calendar: semesters. *Degrees:* associate, bachelor's, master's, and post-master's certificates.
Library: Aquinas College Library. *Books:* 55,934 (physical), 71,042 (digital/electronic); *Serial titles:* 381 (physical), 17,998 (digital/electronic); *Databases:* 95. Weekly public service hours: 64.

STUDENT LIFE
Housing options: on-campus residence required through sophomore year; men-only, women-only. Campus housing is leased by the school. Freshman applicants given priority for college housing.
Activities and organizations: choral group, Campus Ministry, Student Activities Board, Association for Supervision and Curriculum Development, Association of Student Nurses, Socratic Club.
Campus security: 24-hour patrols, late-night transport/escort service.
Student services: personal/psychological counseling.

APPLYING
Standardized Tests *Required:* SAT or ACT (for admission).
Options: electronic application, deferred entrance.
Required: high school transcript, minimum 2.4 GPA. *Required for some:* essay or personal statement.

CONTACT
Ms. Connie Hansom, Director of Admissions, Aquinas College, 4210 Harding Pike, Nashville, TN 37205-2005. *Phone:* 615-297-7545 Ext. 411. *Toll-free phone:* 800-649-9956. *Fax:* 615-279-3893. *E-mail:* hansomc@aquinascollege.edu.

Argosy University, Nashville
Nashville, Tennessee
http://www.argosy.edu/locations/nashville/

CONTACT
Argosy University, Nashville, 100 Centerview Drive, Suite 225, Nashville, TN 37214. *Phone:* 615-525-2800. *Toll-free phone:* 866-833-6598.

The Art Institute of Tennessee–Nashville, a branch of The Art Institute of Atlanta
Nashville, Tennessee
http://www.artinstitutes.edu/nashville/

CONTACT
The Art Institute of Tennessee–Nashville, a branch of The Art Institute of Atlanta, 100 Centerview Drive, Suite 250, Nashville, TN 37214. *Phone:* 615-874-1067. *Toll-free phone:* 866-747-5770.

Austin Peay State University
Clarksville, Tennessee
http://www.apsu.edu/

- **State-supported** comprehensive, founded 1927
- **Suburban** 169-acre campus with easy access to Nashville
- **Endowment** $9.3 million
- **Coed** 9,591 undergraduate students, 74% full-time, 59% women, 41% men
- **Moderately difficult** entrance level, 90% of applicants were admitted

UNDERGRAD STUDENTS
7,065 full-time, 2,526 part-time. Students come from 44 states and territories; 18 other countries; 10% are from out of state; 22% Black or African American, non-Hispanic/Latino; 7% Hispanic/Latino; 2% Asian, non-Hispanic/Latino; 0.3% Native Hawaiian or other Pacific Islander, non-Hispanic/Latino; 0.3% American Indian or Alaska Native, non-Hispanic/Latino; 6% Two or more races, non-Hispanic/Latino; 3% Race/ethnicity unknown; 0.5% international; 10% transferred in; 17% live on campus.

Freshmen:
Admission: 7,199 applied, 6,488 admitted, 1,988 enrolled. *Average high school GPA:* 3.3. *Test scores:* SAT evidence-based reading and writing scores over 500: 83%; SAT math scores over 500: 63%; ACT scores over 18: 87%; SAT evidence-based reading and writing scores over 600: 26%; SAT math scores over 600: 26%; ACT scores over 24: 25%; SAT evidence-based reading and writing scores over 700: 6%; SAT math scores over 700: 3%; ACT scores over 30: 3%.
Retention: 67% of full-time freshmen returned.

FACULTY
Total: 675, 55% full-time.
Student/faculty ratio: 18:1.

ACADEMICS
Calendar: semesters. *Degrees:* certificates, associate, bachelor's, master's, post-master's, and postbachelor's certificates.
Special study options: academic remediation for entering students, accelerated degree program, adult/continuing education programs, advanced placement credit, cooperative education, distance learning, double majors, English as a second language, honors programs, independent study, internships, part-time degree program, services for LD students, study abroad, summer session for credit. *ROTC:* Army (b), Air Force (c).
Computers: 1,400 computers/terminals are available on campus for general student use. Students can access the following: campus intranet, computer help desk, free student e-mail accounts, online (class) grades, online (class) registration, online (class) schedules. Campuswide network is available. Wireless service is available via entire campus.
Library: Felix G. Woodward Library. *Books:* 195,467 (physical), 317,822 (digital/electronic); *Serial titles:* 2,800 (physical), 54,971 (digital/electronic); *Databases:* 294. Weekly public service hours: 109.

STUDENT LIFE
Housing options: on-campus residence required for freshman year; coed, men-only, women-only, special housing for students with disabilities. Campus housing is university owned.
Activities and organizations: drama/theater group, student-run newspaper, radio and television station, choral group, marching band, national fraternities, national sororities.
Athletics Member NCAA. All Division I except football (Division I-AA). *Intercollegiate sports:* baseball M(s), basketball M(s)/W(s), cheerleading M(s)/W(s), cross-country running M(s)/W(s), golf M(s)/W(s), soccer W(s), softball W(s), tennis M(s)/W(s), track and field W(s), volleyball W(s). *Intramural sports:* badminton M/W, basketball M/W, football M/W, golf M/W, racquetball M/W, soccer M/W, softball M/W, table tennis M/W, ultimate Frisbee M/W, volleyball M/W.
Campus security: 24-hour emergency response devices and patrols, student patrols, late-night transport/escort service, controlled dormitory access.
Student services: health clinic, personal/psychological counseling.

COSTS & FINANCIAL AID

Costs (2018–19) *One-time required fee:* $75. *Tuition:* state resident $6696 full-time, $266 per credit hour part-time; nonresident $22,692 full-time, $901 per credit hour part-time. Full-time tuition and fees vary according to location and program. Part-time tuition and fees vary according to location and program. *Required fees:* $1529 full-time. *Room and board:* $9170; room only: $5520. Room and board charges vary according to board plan and housing facility. *Payment plan:* installment. *Waivers:* senior citizens and employees or children of employees.

Financial Aid Of all full-time matriculated undergraduates who enrolled in 2016, 6,425 applied for aid, 5,670 were judged to have need. 103 Federal Work-Study jobs (averaging $2402). 473 state and other part-time jobs (averaging $1741). In 2016, 589 non-need-based awards were made. *Average financial aid package:* $11,135. *Average need-based loan:* $3953. *Average need-based gift aid:* $7788. *Average non-need-based aid:* $5026. *Average indebtedness upon graduation:* $18,044.

APPLYING

Standardized Tests *Required for some:* SAT or ACT (for admission).

Options: electronic application, deferred entrance.

Application fee: $25.

Required: high school transcript. *Required for some:* minimum 2.8 GPA.

Application deadlines: 8/8 (freshmen), rolling (transfers).

Notification: continuous (freshmen), continuous (transfers).

CONTACT

Ms. Amy Corlew, Director of Admissions, Austin Peay State University, 601 College Street, Clarksville, TN 37044. *Phone:* 931-221-7661. *Toll-free phone:* 800-844-2778. *Fax:* 931-221-6168. *E-mail:* admissions@ apsu.edu.

Baptist College of Health Sciences

Memphis, Tennessee
http://www.bchs.edu/

- **Independent Southern Baptist** 4-year, founded 1994
- **Urban** 17-acre campus with easy access to Memphis, TN
- **Endowment** $35.5 million
- **Coed, primarily women** 1,076 undergraduate students, 43% full-time, 91% women, 9% men
- **Moderately difficult** entrance level, 54% of applicants were admitted

UNDERGRAD STUDENTS

466 full-time, 610 part-time. 34% are from out of state; 43% Black or African American, non-Hispanic/Latino; 2% Hispanic/Latino; 2% Asian, non-Hispanic/Latino; 0.3% American Indian or Alaska Native, non-Hispanic/Latino; 3% Race/ethnicity unknown; 11% live on campus.

Freshmen:
Admission: 376 applied, 202 admitted. *Average high school GPA:* 3.2. *Test scores:* ACT scores over 18: 100%; ACT scores over 24: 45%; ACT scores over 30: 10%.
Retention: 75% of full-time freshmen returned.

FACULTY
Total: 65.
Student/faculty ratio: 11:1.

ACADEMICS

Calendar: trimesters. *Degree:* bachelor's and doctoral.

Special study options: accelerated degree program, advanced placement credit, distance learning, double majors, honors programs, part-time degree program, services for LD students, summer session for credit.

Computers: 26 computers/terminals are available on campus for general student use. Students can access the following: campus intranet, computer help desk, free student e-mail accounts, online (class) grades, online (class) registration, online (class) schedules. Campuswide network is available. 100% of college-owned or -operated housing units are wired for high-speed Internet access. Wireless service is available via entire campus.

Library: Health Sciences Library. *Books:* 1,641 (physical), 4,426 (digital/electronic); *Serial titles:* 7 (physical), 115,248 (digital/electronic); *Databases:* 37. Students can reserve study rooms.

STUDENT LIFE

Housing options: coed. Campus housing is university owned.

Activities and organizations: Student Government Association, Student Nursing Association, Allied Health Organization.

Campus security: 24-hour emergency response devices, late-night transport/escort service, controlled dormitory access, trained security personnel.

Student services: health clinic, personal/psychological counseling.

COSTS

Costs (2018–19) *Tuition:* $10,152 full-time, $423 per credit hour part-time. Full-time tuition and fees vary according to program. Part-time tuition and fees vary according to program. *Required fees:* $1340 full-time, $50 per course part-time. *Room only:* $2900. *Payment plan:* installment.

APPLYING

Standardized Tests *Required:* SAT or ACT (for admission).

Options: electronic application.

Application fee: $25.

Required: high school transcript, minimum 2.8 GPA, immunizations, health physical. *Required for some:* interview.

Application deadlines: 5/1 (freshmen), 5/1 (transfers).

CONTACT

Baptist College of Health Sciences, 1003 Monroe Avenue, Memphis, TN 38104. *Phone:* 901-572-2441. *Toll-free phone:* 866-575-2247.

Belhaven University

Memphis, Tennessee
http://memphis.belhaven.edu/

CONTACT

Don Jones, Director of Admission, Belhaven University, 5100 Poplar Avenue, Suite 200, Memphis, TN 38137. *Phone:* 901-888-3343. *Fax:* 901-888-0771. *E-mail:* memphisadmission@belhaven.edu.

Belmont University

Nashville, Tennessee
http://www.belmont.edu/

- **Independent Christian** university, founded 1951
- **Urban** 77-acre campus
- **Endowment** $107.8 million
- **Coed** 6,497 undergraduate students, 95% full-time, 65% women, 35% men
- **Moderately difficult** entrance level, 81% of applicants were admitted

UNDERGRAD STUDENTS

6,161 full-time, 336 part-time. Students come from 51 states and territories; 28 other countries; 70% are from out of state; 5% Black or African American, non-Hispanic/Latino; 5% Hispanic/Latino; 2% Asian, non-Hispanic/Latino; 0.1% Native Hawaiian or other Pacific Islander, non-Hispanic/Latino; 0.3% American Indian or Alaska Native, non-Hispanic/Latino; 4% Two or more races, non-Hispanic/Latino; 2% Race/ethnicity unknown; 1% international; 6% transferred in; 52% live on campus.

Freshmen:
Admission: 7,737 applied, 6,282 admitted, 1,568 enrolled. *Average high school GPA:* 3.7. *Test scores:* SAT evidence-based reading and writing scores over 500: 98%; SAT math scores over 500: 94%; ACT scores over 18: 100%; SAT evidence-based reading and writing scores over 600: 70%; SAT math scores over 600: 47%; ACT scores over 24: 77%; SAT evidence-based reading and writing scores over 700: 12%; SAT math scores over 700: 10%; ACT scores over 30: 21%.
Retention: 85% of full-time freshmen returned.

FACULTY
Total: 853, 42% full-time, 55% with terminal degrees.
Student/faculty ratio: 14:1.

ACADEMICS

Calendar: semesters. *Degrees:* bachelor's, master's, doctoral, and post-master's certificates.

Special study options: accelerated degree program, adult/continuing education programs, advanced placement credit, cooperative education, distance learning, double majors, English as a second language, honors programs, independent study, internships, off-campus study, part-time degree program, services for LD students, student-designed majors, study abroad, summer session for credit. *ROTC:* Army (c), Navy (c), Air Force (c).

Unusual degree programs: 3-2 engineering with Auburn University, Georgia Institute of Technology, University of Tennessee.

Computers: 500 computers/terminals are available on campus for general student use. Students can access the following: campus intranet, free student e-mail accounts, online (class) grades, online (class) registration, online (class) schedules, individual student information via course management system. Campuswide network is available. 100% of college-owned or -operated housing units are wired for high-speed Internet access. Wireless service is available via entire campus.

Library: Lila D. Bunch Library plus 1 other. *Books:* 184,352 (physical), 224,292 (digital/electronic); *Serial titles:* 1,033 (physical), 94,560 (digital/electronic); *Databases:* 288. Weekly public service hours: 127; students can reserve study rooms.

STUDENT LIFE

Housing options: on-campus residence required through sophomore year; men-only, women-only. Campus housing is university owned. Freshman campus housing is guaranteed.

Activities and organizations: drama/theater group, student-run newspaper, radio and television station, choral group, marching band, Service Corp, Alpha Sigma Tau, Phi Mu, Phi Kappa Tau, MOB, national fraternities, national sororities.

Athletics Member NCAA. All Division I. *Intercollegiate sports:* baseball M(s), basketball M(s)/W(s), cross-country running M(s)/W(s), golf M(s)/W(s), soccer M(s)/W(s), softball W(s), tennis M(s)/W(s), track and field M(s)/W(s), volleyball W(s). *Intramural sports:* baseball M, basketball M/W, bowling M/W, cheerleading M/W, football M, golf M, ice hockey M/W, racquetball M/W, soccer M/W, softball M/W, table tennis M/W, tennis M/W, volleyball M/W.

Campus security: 24-hour emergency response devices and patrols, late-night transport/escort service, controlled dormitory access, bicycle patrol.

Student services: health clinic, personal/psychological counseling, women's center.

COSTS & FINANCIAL AID

Costs (2017–18) *Comprehensive fee:* $44,500 includes full-time tuition ($31,300), mandatory fees ($1520), and room and board ($11,680). Full-time tuition and fees vary according to course load. Part-time tuition: $1190 per credit hour. Part-time tuition and fees vary according to course load. *College room only:* $6440. Room and board charges vary according to board plan and housing facility. *Payment plans:* installment, deferred payment. *Waivers:* senior citizens and employees or children of employees.

Financial Aid Of all full-time matriculated undergraduates who enrolled in 2017, 4,160 applied for aid, 3,198 were judged to have need, 328 had their need fully met. 1,159 Federal Work-Study jobs (averaging $1952). In 2017, 1618 non-need-based awards were made. *Average percent of need met:* 56. *Average financial aid package:* $19,176. *Average need-based loan:* $4445. *Average need-based gift aid:* $15,526. *Average non-need-based aid:* $7714. *Average indebtedness upon graduation:* $29,207.

APPLYING

Standardized Tests *Required:* SAT or ACT (for admission).

Options: electronic application, early admission, deferred entrance.

Application fee: $50.

Required: essay or personal statement, high school transcript. *Required for some:* interview, resumé of activities.

Application deadlines: 8/1 (freshmen), 8/1 (transfers).

Notification: continuous (freshmen), continuous (transfers).

CONTACT

Mr. David Mee, Associate Provost and Dean of Enrollment, Belmont University, 1900 Belmont Boulevard, Nashville, TN 37212-3757. *Phone:* 615-460-5479. *Fax:* 615-460-5434. *E-mail:* david.mee@belmont.edu.

Bethel University
McKenzie, Tennessee
http://www.bethelu.edu/

- **Independent Cumberland Presbyterian** comprehensive, founded 1842
- **Small-town** 100-acre campus
- **Endowment** $2.9 million
- **Coed** 4,239 undergraduate students, 85% full-time, 56% women, 44% men
- **Minimally difficult** entrance level, 62% of applicants were admitted

UNDERGRAD STUDENTS

3,606 full-time, 633 part-time. Students come from 25 states and territories; 19 other countries; 9% are from out of state; 50% Black or African American, non-Hispanic/Latino; 2% Hispanic/Latino; 0.4% Asian, non-Hispanic/Latino; 0.2% Native Hawaiian or other Pacific Islander, non-Hispanic/Latino; 0.8% Two or more races, non-Hispanic/Latino; 12% Race/ethnicity unknown; 2% international; 1% transferred in; 29% live on campus.

Freshmen:
Admission: 1,573 applied, 969 admitted, 562 enrolled. *Average high school GPA:* 3.1.
Retention: 64% of full-time freshmen returned.

FACULTY
Total: 325, 57% full-time.
Student/faculty ratio: 14:1.

ACADEMICS

Calendar: semesters. *Degrees:* associate, bachelor's, and master's.

Special study options: academic remediation for entering students, accelerated degree program, adult/continuing education programs, advanced placement credit, cooperative education, distance learning, double majors, external degree program, honors programs, independent study, internships, off-campus study, part-time degree program, services for LD students, student-designed majors, summer session for credit.

Unusual degree programs: engineering with Tennessee Technological University; pharmacy with University of Tennessee, Memphis.

Computers: 12 computers/terminals and 30 ports are available on campus for general student use. Students can access the following: campus intranet, computer help desk, free student e-mail accounts, online (class) grades, online (class) registration, online (class) schedules. Campuswide network is available. 100% of college-owned or -operated housing units are wired for high-speed Internet access. Wireless service is available via entire campus.

Library: Burroughs Learning Center plus 1 other. *Books:* 24,618 (physical), 175,995 (digital/electronic); *Serial titles:* 26 (physical), 58,233 (digital/electronic); *Databases:* 92. Students can reserve study rooms.

STUDENT LIFE

Housing options: on-campus residence required through junior year; coed, men-only, women-only, special housing for students with disabilities. Campus housing is university owned and leased by the school. Freshman applicants given priority for college housing.

Activities and organizations: drama/theater group, choral group, marching band, Campus Crusade for Christ, STEA (Education), Student Government Association, Students in Free Enterprise (SIFE), Arete.

Athletics Member NAIA. *Intercollegiate sports:* baseball M(s), basketball M(s)/W(s), bowling M(s)/W(s), cheerleading M(s)/W(s), cross-country running M(s)/W(s), football M(s), golf M(s)/W(s), riflery M(s)/W(s), soccer M(s)/W(s), softball W(s), tennis M(s)/W(s), track and field M(s)/W(s), volleyball W(s). *Intramural sports:* basketball M/W, football M, golf M/W, soccer M/W, softball M/W, table tennis M/W, tennis M/W, volleyball M/W.

Campus security: night patrols by trained security personnel.

Student services: personal/psychological counseling.

COSTS

Costs (2018–19) *Comprehensive fee:* $25,750 includes full-time tuition ($15,292), mandatory fees ($1260), and room and board ($9198). Full-time tuition and fees vary according to course load and program. Part-time tuition: $462 per credit hour. Part-time tuition and fees vary according to course load and program. *Required fees:* $53 per credit hour part-time. *College room only:* $5814. Room and board charges vary according to board plan and housing facility. *Payment plan:* installment. *Waivers:* employees or children of employees.

APPLYING

Standardized Tests *Recommended:* SAT or ACT (for admission).

Options: electronic application, early admission, deferred entrance.

Application fee: $30.

Required: high school transcript, minimum 2.0 GPA. *Required for some:* essay or personal statement, interview.

Application deadlines: rolling (freshmen), rolling (transfers).

Notification: continuous (freshmen), continuous (transfers).

CONTACT

Tina Hodges, Admissions Coordinator, Bethel University, 325 Cherry Avenue, McKenzie, TN 38201. *Phone:* 731-352-4030. *Fax:* 731-352-4069. *E-mail:* hodgest@bethelu.edu.

Bryan College
Dayton, Tennessee
http://www.bryan.edu/

- **Independent interdenominational** comprehensive, founded 1930
- **Small-town** 130-acre campus
- **Coed** 1,401 undergraduate students, 57% full-time, 54% women, 46% men
- **Moderately difficult** entrance level, 54% of applicants were admitted

UNDERGRAD STUDENTS

802 full-time, 599 part-time. 68% are from out of state; 6% Black or African American, non-Hispanic/Latino; 5% Hispanic/Latino; 0.8% Asian, non-Hispanic/Latino; 0.6% American Indian or Alaska Native, non-Hispanic/Latino; 3% Two or more races, non-Hispanic/Latino; 0.3% Race/ethnicity unknown; 5% international; 3% transferred in; 72% live on campus.

Freshmen:
Admission: 679 applied, 369 admitted, 173 enrolled. *Average high school GPA:* 3.5. *Test scores:* SAT evidence-based reading and writing scores over 500: 81%; SAT math scores over 500: 70%; ACT scores over 18: 95%; SAT evidence-based reading and writing scores over 600: 39%; SAT math scores over 600: 19%; ACT scores over 24: 43%; SAT evidence-based reading and writing scores over 700: 4%; SAT math scores over 700: 4%; ACT scores over 30: 7%.
Retention: 67% of full-time freshmen returned.

FACULTY
Total: 120, 33% full-time, 53% with terminal degrees.
Student/faculty ratio: 15:1.

ACADEMICS
Calendar: semesters. *Degrees:* diplomas, associate, bachelor's, master's, and postbachelor's certificates.

Special study options: academic remediation for entering students, adult/continuing education programs, advanced placement credit, distance learning, double majors, honors programs, independent study, internships, off-campus study, part-time degree program, services for LD students, study abroad, summer session for credit.

Unusual degree programs: 3-2 nursing with Vanderbilt University; psychology with Richmont Graduate University.

Computers: Students can access the following: campus intranet, computer help desk, free student e-mail accounts, online (class) grades, online (class) registration, online (class) schedules. Campuswide network is available. Wireless service is available via entire campus.
Library: Bryan College Library.

STUDENT LIFE
Housing options: on-campus residence required through senior year; men-only, women-only, special housing for students with disabilities.

Campus housing is university owned. Freshman campus housing is guaranteed.

Activities and organizations: drama/theater group, student-run newspaper, choral group, Practical Christian Involvement (PCI), International Students Association, Rugby club, Nutella Club, Navigators.

Athletics Member NAIA. *Intercollegiate sports:* baseball M(s), basketball M(s)/W(s), cross-country running M(s)/W(s), golf M(s)/W(s), soccer M(s)/W(s), softball W(s), track and field M(s)/W(s), volleyball M(s)/W(s). *Intramural sports:* basketball M/W, cheerleading M(c)/W(c), football M, rugby M(c), soccer M/W, softball M/W, table tennis M/W, ultimate Frisbee M/W, volleyball M/W.

Campus security: controlled dormitory access, police patrols, night watch.

Student services: health clinic, personal/psychological counseling.

COSTS & FINANCIAL AID
Costs (2017–18) *Comprehensive fee:* $32,900 includes full-time tuition ($25,600) and room and board ($7300). Part-time tuition: $1100 per credit hour. *College room only:* $4550. Room and board charges vary according to housing facility. *Payment plan:* installment. *Waivers:* employees or children of employees.

Financial Aid Of all full-time matriculated undergraduates who enrolled in 2016, 603 applied for aid, 544 were judged to have need, 156 had their need fully met. *Average financial aid package:* $23,175. *Average need-based loan:* $4105. *Average need-based gift aid:* $12,382.

APPLYING
Standardized Tests *Required:* SAT or ACT (for admission).

Options: electronic application, early action, deferred entrance.

Application fee: $35.

Required: essay or personal statement, high school transcript, minimum 2.0 GPA, 3 letters of recommendation, minimum ACT score of 18 or RSAT of 940. *Required for some:* interview.

Application deadlines: rolling (freshmen), rolling (out-of-state freshmen), rolling (transfers), 5/1 (early action).

Notification: continuous (freshmen), continuous (out-of-state freshmen), rolling (early action).

CONTACT
Mr. Andrew Smith, Senior Enrollment Counselor, Bryan College, 721 Bryan Drive, Dayton, TN 37321-7000. *Phone:* 423-775-2041 Ext. 218. *Toll-free phone:* 800-277-9522. *Fax:* 423-775-7199. *E-mail:* admissions@bryan.edu.

Carson-Newman University
Jefferson City, Tennessee
http://www.cn.edu/

- **Independent Southern Baptist** comprehensive, founded 1851
- **Small-town** 90-acre campus with easy access to Knoxville
- **Endowment** $54.6 million
- **Coed** 1,690 undergraduate students, 95% full-time, 58% women, 42% men
- **Moderately difficult** entrance level, 67% of applicants were admitted

UNDERGRAD STUDENTS

1,608 full-time, 82 part-time. Students come from 34 states and territories; 19 other countries; 20% are from out of state; 8% Black or African American, non-Hispanic/Latino; 4% Hispanic/Latino; 0.7% Asian, non-Hispanic/Latino; 0.5% American Indian or Alaska Native, non-Hispanic/Latino; 3% Two or more races, non-Hispanic/Latino; 2% Race/ethnicity unknown; 4% international; 5% transferred in; 52% live on campus.

Freshmen:
Admission: 3,294 applied, 2,219 admitted, 395 enrolled. *Average high school GPA:* 3.4. *Test scores:* SAT evidence-based reading and writing scores over 500: 56%; SAT math scores over 500: 59%; ACT scores over 18: 91%; SAT evidence-based reading and writing scores over 600: 6%; SAT math scores over 600: 19%; ACT scores over 24: 41%; ACT scores over 30: 6%.

Retention: 70% of full-time freshmen returned.

FACULTY

Total: 254, 48% full-time, 55% with terminal degrees.

Student/faculty ratio: 13:1.

ACADEMICS

Calendar: semesters. *Degrees:* associate, bachelor's, master's, doctoral, and post-master's certificates.

Special study options: academic remediation for entering students, accelerated degree program, adult/continuing education programs, advanced placement credit, English as a second language, honors programs, internships, off-campus study, part-time degree program, services for LD students, student-designed majors, study abroad, summer session for credit. *ROTC:* Army (b).

Unusual degree programs: 3-2 engineering with Georgia Institute of Technology, University of Tennessee, Tennessee Technological University; pharmacy with Campbell University, Mercer University, University of Georgia.

Computers: 200 computers/terminals and 200 ports are available on campus for general student use. Students can access the following: campus intranet, computer help desk, free student e-mail accounts, online (class) grades, online (class) registration, online (class) schedules. Campuswide network is available. 100% of college-owned or -operated housing units are wired for high-speed Internet access. Wireless service is available via entire campus.

Library: Stephens-Burnett Library plus 3 others. Study areas open 24 hours, 5–7 days a week; students can reserve study rooms.

STUDENT LIFE

Housing options: on-campus residence required through junior year; men-only, women-only, special housing for students with disabilities. Campus housing is university owned. Freshman campus housing is guaranteed.

Activities and organizations: drama/theater group, student-run newspaper, choral group, marching band, Baptist Student Union, Fellowship of Christian Athletes, Student Government Association, Student Ambassadors Association, Columbians, national fraternities, national sororities.

Athletics Member NCAA. All Division II. *Intercollegiate sports:* baseball M(s), basketball M(s)/W(s), cross-country running M(s)/W(s), football M(s), golf M(s)/W, soccer M(s)/W(s), softball W(s), swimming and diving M(s)/W(s), tennis M(s)/W(s), track and field M(s)/W(s), volleyball W(s). *Intramural sports:* badminton M/W, baseball M/W, basketball M/W, football M/W, golf M/W, racquetball M/W, skiing (downhill) M/W, soccer M/W, softball M/W, swimming and diving M/W, table tennis M/W, tennis M/W, volleyball M/W.

Campus security: 24-hour emergency response devices and patrols, late-night transport/escort service, controlled dormitory access.

Student services: health clinic, personal/psychological counseling.

COSTS & FINANCIAL AID

Costs (2017–18) *Comprehensive fee:* $36,030 includes full-time tuition ($26,200), mandatory fees ($1200), and room and board ($8630). Full-time tuition and fees vary according to class time and course load. Part-time tuition: $1090 per credit hour. Part-time tuition and fees vary according to class time and course load. *Required fees:* $375 per term part-time. *College room only:* $3930. Room and board charges vary according to board plan, gender, and housing facility. *Payment plans:* installment, deferred payment. *Waivers:* senior citizens and employees or children of employees.

Financial Aid Of all full-time matriculated undergraduates who enrolled in 2015, 1,366 applied for aid, 1,366 were judged to have need, 323 had their need fully met. 188 Federal Work-Study jobs (averaging $1899). 5 state and other part-time jobs (averaging $1280). In 2015, 177 non-need-based awards were made. *Average percent of need met:* 79. *Average financial aid package:* $23,514. *Average need-based loan:* $3623. *Average need-based gift aid:* $17,873. *Average non-need-based aid:* $10,223. *Average indebtedness upon graduation:* $27,418.

APPLYING

Standardized Tests *Required:* SAT or ACT (for admission).

Options: electronic application, deferred entrance.

Required: high school transcript, minimum 2.3 GPA, medical history. *Required for some:* essay or personal statement, interview. *Recommended:* interview.

Application deadlines: 8/1 (freshmen), 8/1 (transfers).

Notification: continuous (freshmen), continuous (transfers).

CONTACT

Mr. Aaron Porter, Vice President for Enrollment Management, Carson-Newman University, 1646 Russell Avenue, PO Box 557, Jefferson City, TN 37760. *Phone:* 865-471-3223. *Toll-free phone:* 800-678-9061. *Fax:* 865-471-4817. *E-mail:* cnadmiss@cn.edu.

Christian Brothers University

Memphis, Tennessee

http://www.cbu.edu/

- **Independent Roman Catholic** comprehensive, founded 1871
- **Urban** 75-acre campus with easy access to Memphis
- **Endowment** $38.6 million
- **Coed** 1,526 undergraduate students, 92% full-time, 53% women, 47% men
- **Moderately difficult** entrance level, 53% of applicants were admitted

UNDERGRAD STUDENTS

1,402 full-time, 124 part-time. Students come from 29 states and territories; 29 other countries; 23% are from out of state; 27% Black or African American, non-Hispanic/Latino; 9% Hispanic/Latino; 5% Asian, non-Hispanic/Latino; 0.5% American Indian or Alaska Native, non-Hispanic/Latino; 3% Two or more races, non-Hispanic/Latino; 12% Race/ethnicity unknown; 3% international; 6% transferred in; 40% live on campus.

Freshmen:
Admission: 2,757 applied, 1,451 admitted, 385 enrolled. *Average high school GPA:* 3.7. *Test scores:* ACT scores over 18: 99%; ACT scores over 24: 52%; ACT scores over 30: 10%.

Retention: 80% of full-time freshmen returned.

FACULTY

Total: 193, 54% full-time, 76% with terminal degrees.

Student/faculty ratio: 13:1.

ACADEMICS

Calendar: semesters. *Degrees:* associate, bachelor's, and master's.

Special study options: accelerated degree program, adult/continuing education programs, advanced placement credit, cooperative education, distance learning, double majors, honors programs, independent study, internships, part-time degree program, services for LD students, student-designed majors, study abroad, summer session for credit. *ROTC:* Army (c), Navy (c), Air Force (c).

Unusual degree programs: 3-2 engineering with Rhodes College.

Computers: 310 computers/terminals are available on campus for general student use. Students can access the following: campus intranet, computer help desk, free student e-mail accounts, online (class) grades, online (class) registration, online (class) schedules. Campuswide network is available. 100% of college-owned or -operated housing units are wired for high-speed Internet access. Wireless service is available via entire campus.

Library: Plough Memorial Library and Media Center. *Books:* 69,148 (physical), 195,783 (digital/electronic); *Serial titles:* 120 (physical), 95 (digital/electronic); *Databases:* 26. Weekly public service hours: 70; students can reserve study rooms.

STUDENT LIFE

Housing options: on-campus residence required through sophomore year; coed, men-only, women-only. Campus housing is university owned. Freshman campus housing is guaranteed.

Activities and organizations: choral group, Black Student Association, Tri-Beta, Hola CBU, Delta Sigma Pi, national fraternities, national sororities.

Athletics Member NCAA. All Division II. *Intercollegiate sports:* baseball M(s), basketball M(s)/W(s), cross-country running M(s)/W(s), golf M(s)/W(s), soccer M(s)/W(s), softball W(s), tennis M(s)/W(s), track and field M(s)/W(s), volleyball W(s). *Intramural sports:* basketball M/W, soccer M/W, softball M/W, ultimate Frisbee M(c)/W(c), volleyball M/W.

Campus security: 24-hour emergency response devices and patrols, late-night transport/escort service, controlled dormitory access.

Student services: health clinic, personal/psychological counseling.

COSTS & FINANCIAL AID
Costs (2018–19) *Comprehensive fee:* $40,220 includes full-time tuition ($31,900), mandatory fees ($920), and room and board ($7400). Full-time tuition and fees vary according to class time, course load, and program. Part-time tuition: $1135 per credit hour. Part-time tuition and fees vary according to class time, course load, and program. *Required fees:* $215 per term part-time. *Room and board:* Room and board charges vary according to housing facility. *Payment plan:* installment. *Waivers:* employees or children of employees.

Financial Aid Of all full-time matriculated undergraduates who enrolled in 2017, 1,388 applied for aid, 964 were judged to have need, 276 had their need fully met. 126 Federal Work-Study jobs (averaging $696). 99 state and other part-time jobs (averaging $581). In 2017, 402 non-need-based awards were made. *Average percent of need met:* 74. *Average financial aid package:* $24,970. *Average need-based loan:* $4006. *Average need-based gift aid:* $21,001. *Average non-need-based aid:* $17,121. *Average indebtedness upon graduation:* $30,694.

APPLYING
Standardized Tests *Required:* SAT or ACT (for admission).
Options: electronic application, deferred entrance.
Application fee: $25.
Required: essay or personal statement, high school transcript, minimum 2.0 GPA. *Required for some:* 2 letters of recommendation. *Recommended:* interview.
Application deadlines: 8/1 (freshmen), 8/23 (transfers).
Notification: 12/1 (freshmen), continuous (transfers).

CONTACT
Ms. Kristi Forman, Director of Admissions, Christian Brothers University, 650 East Parkway South, Memphis, TN 38104. *Phone:* 901-321-3205. *Toll-free phone:* 877-321-4CBU. *Fax:* 901-321-3202. *E-mail:* admissions@cbu.edu.

Cumberland University
Lebanon, Tennessee
http://www.cumberland.edu/

CONTACT
Ms. Beatrice LaChance, Director of Enrollment Services, Cumberland University, One Cumberland Square, Lebanon, TN 37087. *Phone:* 615-547-1244. *Toll-free phone:* 800-467-0562. *Fax:* 615-444-2569. *E-mail:* admissions@cumberland.edu.

Daymar College
Clarksville, Tennessee
http://www.daymarcollege.edu/

CONTACT
Daymar College, 2691 Trenton Road, Clarksville, TN 37040. *Phone:* 931-552-7600 Ext. 204.

Daymar College
Murfreesboro, Tennessee
http://www.daymarcollege.edu/

CONTACT
Daymar College, 415 Golden Bear Court, Murfreesboro, TN 37128.

DeVry University–Nashville Campus
Nashville, Tennessee
http://www.devry.edu/

CONTACT
Admissions Office, DeVry University–Nashville Campus, 3343 Perimeter Hill Drive, Suite 200, Nashville, TN 37211-4147. *Phone:* 615-445-3456. *Toll-free phone:* 866-338-7934.

East Tennessee State University
Johnson City, Tennessee
http://www.etsu.edu/
- **State-supported** university, founded 1911, part of State University and Community College System of Tennessee
- **Small-town** 366-acre campus
- **Endowment** $113.3 million
- **Coed** 11,323 undergraduate students, 85% full-time, 56% women, 44% men
- **Moderately difficult** entrance level, 85% of applicants were admitted

UNDERGRAD STUDENTS
9,641 full-time, 1,682 part-time. Students come from 42 states and territories; 60 other countries; 20% are from out of state; 7% Black or African American, non-Hispanic/Latino; 3% Hispanic/Latino; 1% Asian, non-Hispanic/Latino; 0.1% Native Hawaiian or other Pacific Islander, non-Hispanic/Latino; 0.2% American Indian or Alaska Native, non-Hispanic/Latino; 3% Two or more races, non-Hispanic/Latino; 1% Race/ethnicity unknown; 4% international; 9% transferred in; 25% live on campus.

Freshmen:
Admission: 8,158 applied, 6,972 admitted, 2,050 enrolled. *Average high school GPA:* 3.4. *Test scores:* ACT scores over 18: 88%; ACT scores over 24: 40%; ACT scores over 30: 7%.
Retention: 76% of full-time freshmen returned.

FACULTY
Total: 1,144, 52% full-time.
Student/faculty ratio: 15:1.

ACADEMICS
Calendar: semesters. *Degrees:* certificates, bachelor's, master's, doctoral, post-master's, and postbachelor's certificates.

Special study options: adult/continuing education programs, advanced placement credit, cooperative education, distance learning, double majors, English as a second language, external degree program, freshman honors college, honors programs, independent study, internships, off-campus study, part-time degree program, services for LD students, student-designed majors, study abroad, summer session for credit. *ROTC:* Army (b).

Computers: 1,400 computers/terminals are available on campus for general student use. Students can access the following: computer help desk, free student e-mail accounts, online (class) grades, online (class) registration, online (class) schedules. Campuswide network is available. Wireless service is available via entire campus.
Library: Charles C. Sherrod Library plus 2 others. *Books:* 731,960 (physical), 98,312 (digital/electronic); *Databases:* 210. Study areas open 24 hours, 5–7 days a week; students can reserve study rooms.

STUDENT LIFE
Housing options: coed, men-only, women-only, special housing for students with disabilities. Campus housing is university owned.

Activities and organizations: drama/theater group, student-run newspaper, radio and television station, choral group, marching band, honor societies, Volunteer ETSU, religious groups, residence hall councils, national fraternities, national sororities.

Athletics Member NCAA. All Division I except football (Division I-AA). *Intercollegiate sports:* baseball M(s), basketball M(s)/W(s), cross-country running M(s)/W(s), golf M(s)/W(s), soccer M(s)/W(s), softball W(s), tennis M(s)/W(s), track and field M(s)/W(s), volleyball W(s). *Intramural sports:* basketball M/W, cross-country running M/W, football M/W, golf M/W, racquetball M/W, softball M/W, tennis M/W, volleyball W, weight lifting M.

Campus security: 24-hour emergency response devices and patrols, student patrols, late-night transport/escort service, controlled dormitory access.

Student services: health clinic, personal/psychological counseling, women's center.

COSTS & FINANCIAL AID
Costs (2017–18) *Tuition:* state resident $7224 full-time, $287 per credit hour part-time; nonresident $25,902 full-time, $1028 per credit hour part-time. Full-time tuition and fees vary according to course load and

program. Part-time tuition and fees vary according to course load and program. *Required fees:* $1791 full-time, $113 per credit hour part-time. *Room and board:* $8038; room only: $4602. Room and board charges vary according to board plan and housing facility. *Payment plans:* tuition prepayment, installment. *Waivers:* senior citizens and employees or children of employees.

Financial Aid Of all full-time matriculated undergraduates who enrolled in 2015, 8,121 applied for aid, 6,967 were judged to have need, 517 had their need fully met. 359 state and other part-time jobs (averaging $1156). In 2015, 1145 non-need-based awards were made. *Average percent of need met:* 54. *Average financial aid package:* $10,182. *Average need-based loan:* $4198. *Average need-based gift aid:* $6449. *Average non-need-based aid:* $9680. *Average indebtedness upon graduation:* $27,866.

APPLYING
Standardized Tests *Required:* SAT or ACT (for admission).
Options: electronic application, early admission.
Application fee: $25.
Required: high school transcript, minimum 2.3 GPA, 2.3 high school GPA or 19 ACT.
Application deadlines: rolling (freshmen), rolling (transfers).
Notification: continuous (freshmen), continuous (transfers).

CONTACT
Mr. Michelle Williams, Director of Admissions, East Tennessee State University, PO Box 70731, Johnson City, TN 37614-0734. *Phone:* 423-439-4213. *Toll-free phone:* 800-462-3878. *Fax:* 423-439-4630. *E-mail:* go2etsu@etsu.edu.

Fisk University
Nashville, Tennessee
http://www.fisk.edu/

CONTACT
Ms. Loretta McDonald, Dean of the Office of Recruitment and Admission, Fisk University, 1000 17th Avenue North, Nashville, TN 37208-3051. *Phone:* 615-329-8503. *Toll-free phone:* 888-702-0022. *Fax:* 615-329-8774. *E-mail:* lmcdonald@fisk.edu.

Fountainhead College of Technology
Knoxville, Tennessee
http://www.fountainheadcollege.edu/

CONTACT
Mr. Joel B. Southern, Director of Admissions, Fountainhead College of Technology, 10208 Technology Drive, Knoxville, TN 37932. *Phone:* 865-688-9422. *Toll-free phone:* 888-218-7335. *Fax:* 865-688-2419. *E-mail:* joel.southern@fountainheadcollege.edu.

Freed-Hardeman University
Henderson, Tennessee
http://www.fhu.edu/
- **Independent** comprehensive, founded 1869, affiliated with Church of Christ
- **Small-town** 120-acre campus
- **Coed**
- **Moderately difficult** entrance level

FACULTY
Student/faculty ratio: 13:1.

ACADEMICS
Calendar: semesters. *Degrees:* diplomas, bachelor's, master's, doctoral, post-master's, and postbachelor's certificates.
Library: Hope Barber Shull Academic Resource Center plus 1 other. Students can reserve study rooms.

STUDENT LIFE
Housing options: on-campus residence required through senior year; men-only, women-only, special housing for students with disabilities. Campus housing is university owned. Freshman campus housing is guaranteed.

Activities and organizations: drama/theater group, student-run newspaper, radio station, choral group.
Athletics Member NAIA.
Campus security: 24-hour patrols, controlled dormitory access.
Student services: health clinic, personal/psychological counseling.

COSTS & FINANCIAL AID
Costs (2017–18) *Comprehensive fee:* $29,900 includes full-time tuition ($21,950) and room and board ($7950). Full-time tuition and fees vary according to location. Part-time tuition: $725 per credit hour. Part-time tuition and fees vary according to location. *College room only:* $4320. Room and board charges vary according to board plan and housing facility.

Financial Aid Of all full-time matriculated undergraduates who enrolled in 2016, 1,128 applied for aid, 953 were judged to have need, 257 had their need fully met. In 2016, 237 non-need-based awards were made. *Average percent of need met:* 73. *Average financial aid package:* $18,818. *Average need-based loan:* $3829. *Average need-based gift aid:* $13,949. *Average non-need-based aid:* $11,094. *Average indebtedness upon graduation:* $32,899.

APPLYING
Standardized Tests *Required:* SAT or ACT (for admission).
Options: electronic application, deferred entrance.
Required: high school transcript, minimum 2.3 GPA. *Required for some:* interview.

CONTACT
Freed-Hardeman University, 158 East Main Street, Henderson, TN 38340-2399. *Phone:* 731-989-6557. *Toll-free phone:* 800-FHU-FHU-1.

Huntington College of Health Sciences
Knoxville, Tennessee
http://www.hchs.edu/
- **Proprietary** comprehensive, founded 1984
- **Suburban** campus
- **Coed**
- **Noncompetitive** entrance level, 52% of applicants were admitted

UNDERGRAD STUDENTS
Students come from 44 states and territories; 7 other countries; 99% are from out of state.

Freshmen:
Admission: 220 applied, 114 admitted.
Retention: 85% of full-time freshmen returned.

FACULTY
Total: 22, 14% full-time, 41% with terminal degrees.
Student/faculty ratio: 13:1.

ACADEMICS
Calendar: continuous. *Degrees:* certificates, diplomas, associate, bachelor's, master's, doctoral, and postbachelor's certificates (offers only external degree programs conducted through home study).
Special study options: academic remediation for entering students, accelerated degree program, adult/continuing education programs, distance learning, external degree program, independent study, part-time degree program, summer session for credit.
Library: HCHS Online Library.

STUDENT LIFE
Housing options: college housing not available.

COSTS
Costs (2018–19) *Tuition:* $5880 full-time, $245 per credit hour part-time. Full-time tuition and fees vary according to course load, degree level, and program. Part-time tuition and fees vary according to course load, degree level, and program. *Required fees:* $200 full-time. *Payment plan:* installment.

APPLYING
Options: deferred entrance.
Application fee: $75.

Required for some: high school transcript, interview. *Recommended:* minimum 2.0 GPA.

Application deadlines: rolling (freshmen), rolling (transfers).

Notification: continuous (freshmen), continuous (transfers).

CONTACT
Kimberly Marquis, Director of Admissions, Huntington College of Health Sciences, 117 Legacy View Way, Knoxville, TN 37918. *Phone:* 800-290-4226 Ext. 1. *Toll-free phone:* 800-290-4226. *Fax:* 865-524-8339. *E-mail:* admissions@hchs.edu.

Johnson University

Knoxville, Tennessee

http://www.johnsonu.edu/

- **Independent** comprehensive, founded 1893, affiliated with Christian Churches and Churches of Christ
- **Rural** 175-acre campus with easy access to Knoxville
- **Coed** 814 undergraduate students, 85% full-time, 47% women, 53% men
- **Moderately difficult** entrance level, 98% of applicants were admitted

UNDERGRAD STUDENTS
689 full-time, 125 part-time. 65% are from out of state; 3% Black or African American, non-Hispanic/Latino; 2% Hispanic/Latino; 0.2% American Indian or Alaska Native, non-Hispanic/Latino; 2% Two or more races, non-Hispanic/Latino; 4% Race/ethnicity unknown; 3% international; 7% transferred in; 16% live on campus.

Freshmen:
Admission: 247 applied, 242 admitted, 153 enrolled. *Average high school GPA:* 3.4. *Test scores:* SAT evidence-based reading and writing scores over 500: 79%; SAT math scores over 500: 70%; ACT scores over 18: 89%; SAT evidence-based reading and writing scores over 600: 38%; SAT math scores over 600: 30%; ACT scores over 24: 34%; SAT evidence-based reading and writing scores over 700: 8%; SAT math scores over 700: 4%; ACT scores over 30: 4%.

Retention: 78% of full-time freshmen returned.

FACULTY
Total: 165, 46% full-time, 58% with terminal degrees.
Student/faculty ratio: 20:1.

ACADEMICS
Calendar: semesters. *Degrees:* certificates, associate, bachelor's, master's, doctoral, and post-master's certificates.

Special study options: academic remediation for entering students, accelerated degree program, adult/continuing education programs, advanced placement credit, cooperative education, distance learning, double majors, English as a second language, honors programs, independent study, internships, part-time degree program, services for LD students, study abroad, summer session for credit.

Computers: Students can access the following: campus intranet, computer help desk, free student e-mail accounts, online (class) grades, online (class) registration, online (class) schedules. Campuswide network is available. 100% of college-owned or -operated housing units are wired for high-speed Internet access. Wireless service is available via entire campus.

Library: Glass Memorial Library plus 1 other. Weekly public service hours: 80.

STUDENT LIFE
Housing options: on-campus residence required through senior year; men-only, women-only. Campus housing is university owned.

Activities and organizations: drama/theater group, student-run newspaper, radio station, choral group, Student Government Association, International student Association, Harvesters (Missions), International Justice Mission, Students Promoting Social Unity.

Athletics Member NCCAA. *Intercollegiate sports:* baseball M, basketball M/W, cheerleading M/W, cross-country running M/W, soccer M/W, volleyball W. *Intramural sports:* basketball M, tennis M/W, ultimate Frisbee M/W, volleyball M/W.

Campus security: 24-hour emergency response devices and patrols, student patrols, controlled dormitory access.

Student services: health clinic, personal/psychological counseling.

COSTS & FINANCIAL AID
Costs (2018–19) *Comprehensive fee:* $22,760 includes full-time tuition ($14,880), mandatory fees ($1180), and room and board ($6700). Full-time tuition and fees vary according to class time, course load, degree level, location, and program. Part-time tuition: $470 per credit hour. Part-time tuition and fees vary according to class time, course load, degree level, location, and program. *College room only:* $3000. Room and board charges vary according to board plan, housing facility, and location. *Payment plan:* installment. *Waivers:* employees or children of employees.

Financial Aid Of all full-time matriculated undergraduates who enrolled in 2010, 649 applied for aid, 543 were judged to have need, 51 had their need fully met. 64 Federal Work-Study jobs (averaging $1602). 335 state and other part-time jobs (averaging $1611). *Average percent of need met:* 63. *Average financial aid package:* $11,642. *Average need-based loan:* $3414. *Average need-based gift aid:* $6471. *Average indebtedness upon graduation:* $18,494.

APPLYING
Standardized Tests *Required:* SAT or ACT (for admission).

Options: electronic application, early admission, deferred entrance.

Application fee: $35.

Required: essay or personal statement, high school transcript, minimum 2.5 GPA, 3 letters of recommendation. *Required for some:* interview.

Application deadlines: 7/1 (freshmen), 7/1 (transfers).

Notification: continuous (freshmen), continuous (transfers).

CONTACT
Ms. Julee Schultz, Director of Admissions, Johnson University, 7900 Johnson Drive, Knoxville, TN 37998. *Phone:* 865-251-2233. *Toll-free phone:* 800-827-2122. *Fax:* 865-251-2336. *E-mail:* jschultz@johnsonu.edu.

King University

Bristol, Tennessee

http://www.king.edu/

- **Independent** comprehensive, founded 1867, affiliated with Presbyterian Church (U.S.A.)
- **Suburban** 135-acre campus
- **Endowment** $33.4 million
- **Coed** 1,799 undergraduate students, 89% full-time, 61% women, 39% men
- **Moderately difficult** entrance level, 59% of applicants were admitted

UNDERGRAD STUDENTS
1,608 full-time, 191 part-time. Students come from 38 states and territories; 26 other countries; 40% are from out of state; 7% Black or African American, non-Hispanic/Latino; 4% Hispanic/Latino; 0.6% Asian, non-Hispanic/Latino; 0.1% Native Hawaiian or other Pacific Islander, non-Hispanic/Latino; 0.1% American Indian or Alaska Native, non-Hispanic/Latino; 2% Two or more races, non-Hispanic/Latino; 5% Race/ethnicity unknown; 3% international; 9% transferred in; 16% live on campus.

Freshmen:
Admission: 1,152 applied, 683 admitted, 170 enrolled. *Average high school GPA:* 3.5. *Test scores:* ACT scores over 18: 91%; ACT scores over 24: 40%; ACT scores over 30: 5%.

Retention: 69% of full-time freshmen returned.

FACULTY
Total: 272, 36% full-time, 48% with terminal degrees.
Student/faculty ratio: 13:1.

ACADEMICS
Calendar: semesters. *Degrees:* associate, bachelor's, master's, doctoral, and post-master's certificates.

Special study options: adult/continuing education programs, advanced placement credit, distance learning, double majors, honors programs, independent study, internships, off-campus study, part-time degree program, services for LD students, student-designed majors, study abroad, summer session for credit.

Unusual degree programs: 3-2 engineering with The University of Tennessee.

Computers: 90 computers/terminals and 500 ports are available on campus for general student use. Students can access the following: campus intranet, computer help desk, free student e-mail accounts, online (class) grades, online (class) registration, online (class) schedules, Student Portal. Campuswide network is available. 100% of college-owned or -operated housing units are wired for high-speed Internet access. Wireless service is available via entire campus.

Library: E. W. King Library plus 3 others. *Books:* 78,462 (physical), 179,775 (digital/electronic); *Serial titles:* 156 (physical); *Databases:* 97. Weekly public service hours: 91.

STUDENT LIFE
Housing options: on-campus residence required through junior year; men-only, women-only. Campus housing is university owned. Freshman campus housing is guaranteed.

Activities and organizations: drama/theater group, student-run newspaper, choral group, Student Government Association, Fellowship of Christian Athletes, King Security and Intelligence Studies Student Group, Enactus (formerly Students in Free Enterprise).

Athletics Member NCAA. All Division II. *Intercollegiate sports:* baseball M(s), basketball M(s)/W(s), cheerleading M(s)/W(s), cross-country running M(s)/W(s), golf M(s)/W(s), soccer M(s)/W(s), softball W(s), swimming and diving M(s)/W(s), tennis M(s)/W(s), track and field M(s)/W(s), volleyball M(s)/W(s), wrestling M(s)/W(s). *Intramural sports:* basketball M/W, soccer M/W, softball M/W, table tennis M/W, tennis M/W, ultimate Frisbee M/W, volleyball M/W.

Campus security: 24-hour emergency response devices and patrols, late-night transport/escort service, controlled dormitory access, Emergency Notification System.

Student services: personal/psychological counseling.

COSTS & FINANCIAL AID
Costs (2018–19) *One-time required fee:* $125. *Comprehensive fee:* $34,114 includes full-time tuition ($28,104), mandatory fees ($1610), and room and board ($4400). Full-time tuition and fees vary according to class time, course load, degree level, location, and program. Part-time tuition: $600 per semester hour. Part-time tuition and fees vary according to class time, course load, degree level, location, and program. *Required fees:* $120 per term part-time. *College room only:* $4362. Room and board charges vary according to board plan and housing facility. *Payment plan:* installment. *Waivers:* senior citizens and employees or children of employees.

Financial Aid Of all full-time matriculated undergraduates who enrolled in 2017, 1,442 applied for aid, 1,325 were judged to have need, 168 had their need fully met. 137 Federal Work-Study jobs (averaging $1036). 115 state and other part-time jobs (averaging $1236). In 2017, 103 non-need-based awards were made. *Average percent of need met:* 68. *Average financial aid package:* $16,036. *Average need-based loan:* $4676. *Average need-based gift aid:* $13,202. *Average non-need-based aid:* $10,261. *Average indebtedness upon graduation:* $24,370.

APPLYING
Options: electronic application, deferred entrance.

Required: high school transcript. *Required for some:* essay or personal statement. *Recommended:* minimum 3.0 GPA.

Application deadlines: rolling (freshmen), rolling (out-of-state freshmen), rolling (transfers).

Notification: continuous (freshmen), continuous (out-of-state freshmen), continuous (transfers).

CONTACT
Mr. Tom VerDow, Director of Undergraduate Recruitment, King University, 1350 King College Road, Bristol, TN 37620. *Phone:* 423-652-4149. *Toll-free phone:* 800-362-0014. *Fax:* 423-652-4727. *E-mail:* admissions@king.edu.

Lane College
Jackson, Tennessee
http://www.lanecollege.edu/

- **Independent** 4-year, founded 1882, affiliated with Christian Methodist Episcopal Church
- **Suburban** 55-acre campus with easy access to Memphis
- **Coed**
- **Minimally difficult** entrance level

FACULTY
Student/faculty ratio: 19:1.

ACADEMICS
Calendar: semesters. *Degree:* bachelor's.
Library: Chambers-McClure Academic Center.

STUDENT LIFE
Housing options: on-campus residence required for freshman year; coed, men-only, women-only. Campus housing is university owned. Freshman applicants given priority for college housing.

Activities and organizations: drama/theater group, choral group, marching band, Student Government Association, Pre-Law Club, Student Christian Association, Drama Club, Sociology Club, national fraternities, national sororities.

Athletics Member NCAA. All Division II.

Campus security: 24-hour emergency response devices and patrols, late-night transport/escort service, surveillance cameras, lighted parking areas.

Student services: health clinic, personal/psychological counseling, legal services.

COSTS & FINANCIAL AID
Costs (2017–18) *Comprehensive fee:* $18,050 includes full-time tuition ($9000), mandatory fees ($1690), and room and board ($7360). Full-time tuition and fees vary according to course load. Part-time tuition: $375 per credit hour. Part-time tuition and fees vary according to course load. *College room only:* $4570. *Payment plans:* installment, deferred payment.

Financial Aid Of all full-time matriculated undergraduates who enrolled in 2016, 1,365 applied for aid, 1,365 were judged to have need. In 2016, 2 non-need-based awards were made. *Average financial aid package:* $12,240. *Average need-based loan:* $3568. *Average need-based gift aid:* $13,527. *Average non-need-based aid:* $4761.

APPLYING
Standardized Tests *Required:* SAT or ACT (for admission).

Options: electronic application, deferred entrance.

Required: high school transcript, 2 letters of recommendation.

CONTACT
Dr. Monica C. Scott, Director of Enrollment Management, Lane College, 545 Lane Avenue, Jackson, TN 38301. *Phone:* 731-426-7533. *Toll-free phone:* 800-960-7533. *Fax:* 731-426-7559. *E-mail:* mclayborne@lanecollege.edu.

Lee University
Cleveland, Tennessee
http://www.leeuniversity.edu/

- **Independent** comprehensive, founded 1918, affiliated with Church of God
- **Small-town** 120-acre campus with easy access to Chattanooga, TN
- **Endowment** $20.6 million
- **Coed** 4,860 undergraduate students, 79% full-time, 62% women, 38% men

UNDERGRAD STUDENTS
3,854 full-time, 1,006 part-time. Students come from 51 states and territories; 51 other countries; 55% are from out of state; 5% Black or African American, non-Hispanic/Latino; 2% Hispanic/Latino; 0.9% Asian, non-Hispanic/Latino; 0.2% Native Hawaiian or other Pacific Islander, non-Hispanic/Latino; 0.5% American Indian or Alaska Native, non-Hispanic/Latino; 3% Two or more races, non-Hispanic/Latino; 9% Race/ethnicity unknown; 3% international; 5% transferred in; 48% live on campus.

Freshmen:
Admission: 901 enrolled. *Average high school GPA:* 3.6. *Test scores:* SAT evidence-based reading and writing scores over 500: 79%; SAT math scores over 500: 74%; ACT scores over 18: 93%; SAT evidence-based reading and writing scores over 600: 43%; SAT math scores over 600: 29%; ACT scores over 24: 61%; SAT evidence-based reading and writing scores over 700: 5%; SAT math scores over 700: 5%; ACT scores over 30: 15%.

Retention: 81% of full-time freshmen returned.

FACULTY
Total: 463, 40% full-time, 53% with terminal degrees.
Student/faculty ratio: 16:1.

ACADEMICS
Calendar: semesters. *Degrees:* bachelor's, master's, and post-master's certificates.

Special study options: academic remediation for entering students, adult/continuing education programs, advanced placement credit, cooperative education, distance learning, double majors, English as a second language, external degree program, honors programs, independent study, internships, off-campus study, part-time degree program, services for LD students, student-designed majors, study abroad, summer session for credit.

Computers: 348 computers/terminals and 650 ports are available on campus for general student use. Students can access the following: campus intranet, computer help desk, free student e-mail accounts, online (class) grades, online (class) registration, online (class) schedules. Campuswide network is available. 95% of college-owned or -operated housing units are wired for high-speed Internet access. Wireless service is available via entire campus.
Library: William G. Squires Library plus 2 others. *Books:* 159,161 (physical), 279,837 (digital/electronic); *Serial titles:* 244 (physical), 93,815 (digital/electronic); *Databases:* 137. Weekly public service hours: 91; students can reserve study rooms.

STUDENT LIFE
Housing options: on-campus residence required through sophomore year; men-only, women-only. Campus housing is university owned and leased by the school. Freshman campus housing is guaranteed.

Activities and organizations: drama/theater group, student-run newspaper, choral group, Student Leadership Council, CRU, Big Pal Little Pal, Delta Zeta Tau, Crossover.

Athletics Member NCAA, NCCAA. All NCAA Division II.
Intercollegiate sports: baseball M(s), basketball M(s)/W(s), cross-country running M(s)/W(s), golf M(s)/W(s), lacrosse W(s), soccer M(s)/W(s), softball W(s), tennis M(s)/W(s), track and field M(s)/W(s), volleyball W(s). *Intramural sports:* basketball M/W, bowling M/W, football M/W, golf M/W, racquetball M/W, rugby M(c)/W(c), sand volleyball M/W, soccer M/W, softball M/W, table tennis M/W, tennis M/W, ultimate Frisbee M(c)/W(c), volleyball M/W.

Campus security: 24-hour emergency response devices and patrols, late-night transport/escort service, controlled dormitory access.

Student services: health clinic, personal/psychological counseling.

COSTS & FINANCIAL AID
Costs (2018–19) *Comprehensive fee:* $25,990 includes full-time tuition ($17,040), mandatory fees ($650), and room and board ($8300). Full-time tuition and fees vary according to course load, location, and program. Part-time tuition: $710 per credit hour. Part-time tuition and fees vary according to course load, location, and program. *Required fees:* $35 per term part-time. *College room only:* $4530. Room and board charges vary according to board plan and housing facility. *Payment plan:* deferred payment. *Waivers:* senior citizens and employees or children of employees.

Financial Aid Of all full-time matriculated undergraduates who enrolled in 2017, 3,357 applied for aid, 2,781 were judged to have need, 496 had their need fully met. 235 Federal Work-Study jobs (averaging $1980). 675 state and other part-time jobs (averaging $1484). In 2017, 591 non-need-based awards were made. *Average percent of need met:* 55. *Average financial aid package:* $12,666. *Average need-based loan:* $4214. *Average need-based gift aid:* $9970. *Average non-need-based aid:* $7177. *Average indebtedness upon graduation:* $32,792.

APPLYING
Standardized Tests *Required:* SAT or ACT (for admission). *Recommended:* SAT (for admission), ACT (for admission).
Required: high school transcript, minimum 2.0 GPA, MMR immunization record. *Required for some:* 3 letters of recommendation.

CONTACT
Mr. Phillip Cook, Vice President for Enrollment, Lee University, 1120 N. Ocoee Street, Cleveland, TN 37311. *Phone:* 423-614-8500. *Toll-free phone:* 800-533-9930. *Fax:* 423-614-8533. *E-mail:* admissions@leeuniversity.edu.

LeMoyne-Owen College
Memphis, Tennessee
http://www.loc.edu/

CONTACT
LeMoyne-Owen College, 807 Walker Avenue, Memphis, TN 38126-6595. *Phone:* 901-435-1500. *Toll-free phone:* 800-737-7778.

Lincoln Memorial University
Harrogate, Tennessee
http://www.lmunet.edu/
- **Independent** comprehensive, founded 1897
- **Small-town** 1000-acre campus
- **Endowment** $40.8 million
- **Coed** 1,919 undergraduate students, 71% full-time, 70% women, 30% men
- **Moderately difficult** entrance level, 61% of applicants were admitted

UNDERGRAD STUDENTS
1,356 full-time, 563 part-time. Students come from 49 states and territories; 24 other countries; 36% are from out of state; 6% Black or African American, non-Hispanic/Latino; 0.3% Hispanic/Latino; 1% Asian, non-Hispanic/Latino; 1% American Indian or Alaska Native, non-Hispanic/Latino; 8% Race/ethnicity unknown; 13% transferred in; 37% live on campus.

Freshmen:
Admission: 1,676 applied, 1,029 admitted, 346 enrolled. *Average high school GPA:* 3.5. *Test scores:* SAT math scores over 500: 64%; SAT math scores over 600: 19%; SAT math scores over 700: 2%.
Retention: 73% of full-time freshmen returned.

FACULTY
Total: 343, 52% full-time, 71% with terminal degrees.
Student/faculty ratio: 14:1.

ACADEMICS
Calendar: semesters. *Degrees:* associate, bachelor's, master's, doctoral, and post-master's certificates.

Special study options: academic remediation for entering students, accelerated degree program, adult/continuing education programs, advanced placement credit, cooperative education, distance learning, double majors, English as a second language, honors programs, independent study, internships, part-time degree program, services for LD students, study abroad, summer session for credit. *ROTC:* Army (c).

Computers: 121 computers/terminals are available on campus for general student use. Students can access the following: campus intranet, computer help desk, free student e-mail accounts, online (class) grades, online (class) registration, online (class) schedules. Campuswide network is available. 100% of college-owned or -operated housing units are wired for high-speed Internet access. Wireless service is available via classrooms, computer centers, computer labs, dorm rooms, learning centers, libraries, student centers.
Library: Carnegie-Vincent Library. *Books:* 85,346 (physical), 355,314 (digital/electronic); *Serial titles:* 1,548 (physical), 32,592 (digital/electronic); *Databases:* 225. Weekly public service hours: 92; students can reserve study rooms.

STUDENT LIFE
Housing options: coed, men-only, women-only, special housing for students with disabilities. Campus housing is university owned and leased by the school.

A ★ *indicates that the school has detailed information with a Premium Profile on Petersons.com.*

Activities and organizations: drama/theater group, student-run radio and television station, choral group, Enactus, Pre-Vet Club, Pre-Med Club, Fishing Club, Earth Club, national fraternities, national sororities.

Athletics Member NCAA. All Division II. *Intercollegiate sports:* baseball M(s), basketball M(s)/W(s), bowling M(s)/W(s), cross-country running M(s)/W(s), golf M(s)/W(s), lacrosse M(s)/W(s), sand volleyball W(s), soccer M(s)/W(s), softball W(s), tennis M(s)/W(s), volleyball W(s). *Intramural sports:* basketball M/W, football M/W, soccer M/W, softball M/W, swimming and diving M/W, table tennis M/W, tennis M/W, ultimate Frisbee M/W, volleyball M/W.

Campus security: 24-hour emergency response devices and patrols, late-night transport/escort service.

Student services: health clinic, personal/psychological counseling.

COSTS & FINANCIAL AID

Costs (2018–19) *Room and board:* $10,196; room only: $5796. Room and board charges vary according to board plan and housing facility. *Payment plan:* installment. *Waivers:* employees or children of employees.

Financial Aid Of all full-time matriculated undergraduates who enrolled in 2016, 1,058 applied for aid, 946 were judged to have need, 307 had their need fully met. In 2016, 77 non-need-based awards were made. *Average percent of need met:* 83. *Average financial aid package:* $22,114. *Average need-based loan:* $6522. *Average need-based gift aid:* $14,876. *Average non-need-based aid:* $9788. *Average indebtedness upon graduation:* $18,038.

APPLYING

Standardized Tests *Required:* SAT or ACT (for admission).

Options: electronic application.

Required: high school transcript, immunization records, financial aid application. *Recommended:* minimum 3.0 GPA.

Application deadlines: rolling (freshmen), rolling (transfers).

Notification: continuous (freshmen), continuous (transfers).

CONTACT

Lincoln Memorial University, 6965 Cumberland Gap Parkway, Harrogate, TN 37752-1901. *Phone:* 423-869-6280. *Toll-free phone:* 800-325-0900.

Lipscomb University

Nashville, Tennessee

http://www.lipscomb.edu/

- **Independent** comprehensive, founded 1891, affiliated with Church of Christ
- **Suburban** 89-acre campus
- **Endowment** $79.1 million
- **Coed** 2,987 undergraduate students, 91% full-time, 61% women, 39% men
- **Moderately difficult** entrance level, 60% of applicants were admitted

UNDERGRAD STUDENTS

2,723 full-time, 264 part-time. Students come from 47 states and territories; 44 other countries; 34% are from out of state; 7% Black or African American, non-Hispanic/Latino; 7% Hispanic/Latino; 3% Asian, non-Hispanic/Latino; 0.1% Native Hawaiian or other Pacific Islander, non-Hispanic/Latino; 0.2% American Indian or Alaska Native, non-Hispanic/Latino; 3% Two or more races, non-Hispanic/Latino; 1% Race/ethnicity unknown; 3% international; 6% transferred in; 50% live on campus.

Freshmen:

Admission: 3,581 applied, 2,164 admitted, 641 enrolled. *Average high school GPA:* 3.6. *Test scores:* ACT scores over 18: 99%; ACT scores over 24: 65%; ACT scores over 30: 17%.

Retention: 79% of full-time freshmen returned.

FACULTY

Total: 561, 38% full-time, 58% with terminal degrees.
Student/faculty ratio: 14:1.

ACADEMICS

Calendar: semesters. *Degrees:* associate, bachelor's, master's, doctoral, and postbachelor's certificates.

Special study options: academic remediation for entering students, accelerated degree program, adult/continuing education programs, advanced placement credit, distance learning, double majors, English as a second language, honors programs, independent study, internships, part-time degree program, services for LD students, student-designed majors, study abroad, summer session for credit. *ROTC:* Army (c), Air Force (c).

Computers: 150 computers/terminals are available on campus for general student use. Students can access the following: campus intranet, computer help desk, free student e-mail accounts, online (class) grades, online (class) registration, online (class) schedules. Campuswide network is available. 100% of college-owned or -operated housing units are wired for high-speed Internet access. Wireless service is available via entire campus.

Library: Beaman Library plus 1 other. *Books:* 157,824 (physical), 167,520 (digital/electronic); *Serial titles:* 253 (physical), 489 (digital/electronic); *Databases:* 100. Students can reserve study rooms.

STUDENT LIFE

Housing options: on-campus residence required through junior year; men-only, women-only. Campus housing is university owned. Freshman applicants given priority for college housing.

Activities and organizations: drama/theater group, student-run newspaper, radio and television station, choral group, Sigma Pi Beta, business fraternities, Multicultural Association, Alpha Phi Chi men's service club, Pi Kappa Sigma women's service club.

Athletics Member NCAA. All Division I. *Intercollegiate sports:* baseball M(s), basketball M(s)/W(s), cross-country running M(s)/W(s), golf M(s)/W(s), ice hockey M(c), soccer M(s)/W(s), softball W(s), tennis M(s)/W(s), track and field M(s)/W(s), volleyball W(s). *Intramural sports:* basketball M/W, football M/W, golf M/W, racquetball M/W, sand volleyball M/W, soccer M/W, softball M/W, table tennis M/W, ultimate Frisbee M/W, volleyball M/W.

Campus security: 24-hour emergency response devices and patrols, late-night transport/escort service, controlled dormitory access.

Student services: health clinic, personal/psychological counseling.

COSTS & FINANCIAL AID

Costs (2018–19) *Comprehensive fee:* $44,796 includes full-time tuition ($29,676), mandatory fees ($2468), and room and board ($12,652). Full-time tuition and fees vary according to course load. Part-time tuition: $1240 per credit hour. Part-time tuition and fees vary according to course load. *College room only:* $7164. Room and board charges vary according to board plan and housing facility. *Payment plan:* installment. *Waivers:* employees or children of employees.

Financial Aid Of all full-time matriculated undergraduates who enrolled in 2017, 2,626 applied for aid, 1,742 were judged to have need, 386 had their need fully met. 195 Federal Work-Study jobs (averaging $2320). In 2017, 794 non-need-based awards were made. *Average percent of need met:* 64. *Average financial aid package:* $26,236. *Average need-based loan:* $5682. *Average need-based gift aid:* $23,054. *Average non-need-based aid:* $15,436. *Average indebtedness upon graduation:* $29,673.

APPLYING

Standardized Tests *Required:* SAT or ACT (for admission).

Options: electronic application, early admission, deferred entrance.

Application fee: $50.

Required: essay or personal statement, high school transcript, minimum 2.5 GPA, 1 letter of recommendation. *Recommended:* interview.

Application deadlines: rolling (freshmen), rolling (out-of-state freshmen), rolling (transfers).

Notification: continuous (freshmen), continuous (out-of-state freshmen), continuous (transfers).

CONTACT

Mr. Reggie Blair, Senior Director of Admissions, Lipscomb University, One University Park Drive, Nashville, TN 37204-3951. *Phone:* 615-966-1776. *Toll-free phone:* 877-582-4766. *Fax:* 615-966-1804. *E-mail:* admissions@lipscomb.edu.

Martin Methodist College

Pulaski, Tennessee

http://www.martinmethodist.edu/

CONTACT
Lisa Smith, Director of Admissions, Martin Methodist College, 433 West Madison Street, Pulaski, TN 38478-2716. *Phone:* 931-363-9868. *Toll-free phone:* 800-467-1273. *Fax:* 931-363-9818. *E-mail:* admit@ martinmethodist.edu.

Maryville College

Maryville, Tennessee

http://www.maryvillecollege.edu/

- **Independent Presbyterian** 4-year, founded 1819
- **Suburban** 263-acre campus
- **Endowment** $69.2 million
- **Coed** 1,181 undergraduate students, 98% full-time, 54% women, 46% men
- **Moderately difficult** entrance level, 49% of applicants were admitted

UNDERGRAD STUDENTS
1,158 full-time, 23 part-time. Students come from 35 states and territories; 23 other countries; 32% are from out of state; 13% Black or African American, non-Hispanic/Latino; 4% Hispanic/Latino; 0.9% Asian, non-Hispanic/Latino; 0.1% Native Hawaiian or other Pacific Islander, non-Hispanic/Latino; 0.6% American Indian or Alaska Native, non-Hispanic/Latino; 5% Two or more races, non-Hispanic/Latino; 0.4% Race/ethnicity unknown; 3% international; 6% transferred in; 74% live on campus.

Freshmen:
Admission: 2,778 applied, 1,371 admitted, 301 enrolled. *Average high school GPA:* 3.5. *Test scores:* SAT evidence-based reading and writing scores over 500: 61%; SAT math scores over 500: 63%; ACT scores over 18: 95%; SAT evidence-based reading and writing scores over 600: 20%; SAT math scores over 600: 19%; ACT scores over 24: 50%; SAT evidence-based reading and writing scores over 700: 3%; ACT scores over 30: 13%.
Retention: 72% of full-time freshmen returned.

FACULTY
Total: 117, 65% full-time, 74% with terminal degrees.
Student/faculty ratio: 13:1.

ACADEMICS
Calendar: 4-1-4. *Degree:* bachelor's.
Special study options: academic remediation for entering students, adult/continuing education programs, advanced placement credit, double majors, English as a second language, honors programs, independent study, internships, off-campus study, part-time degree program, services for LD students, student-designed majors, study abroad, summer session for credit.
Unusual degree programs: 3-2 engineering with Vanderbilt University, Washington University in St. Louis, Auburn University, Tennessee Technological University; nursing.
Computers: 290 computers/terminals are available on campus for general student use. Students can access the following: campus intranet, computer help desk, free student e-mail accounts, online (class) grades, online (class) registration, online (class) schedules. Campuswide network is available. 100% of college-owned or -operated housing units are wired for high-speed Internet access. Wireless service is available via entire campus.
Library: Lamar Memorial Library plus 1 other. *Books:* 123,369 (physical), 272,064 (digital/electronic); *Serial titles:* 181 (physical), 37,204 (digital/electronic); *Databases:* 112. Weekly public service hours: 93; students can reserve study rooms.

STUDENT LIFE
Housing options: on-campus residence required through senior year; coed, men-only, women-only, special housing for students with disabilities. Campus housing is university owned. Freshman campus housing is guaranteed.

Activities and organizations: drama/theater group, student-run newspaper, choral group, Voices of Praise, student government, Student Programming Board, Global Citizenship, Peer Mentors.
Athletics Member NCAA. All Division III. *Intercollegiate sports:* baseball M, basketball M/W, cheerleading M/W, cross-country running M/W, equestrian sports M(s)(c)/W(s)(c), football M, golf M/W, soccer M/W, softball W, tennis M/W, volleyball W. *Intramural sports:* archery M/W, badminton M/W, basketball M/W, bowling M/W, football M/W, racquetball M/W, rugby M/W, sand volleyball M/W, skiing (downhill) M/W, soccer M/W, softball M/W, table tennis M/W, tennis M/W, track and field M/W, ultimate Frisbee M/W, volleyball M/W.
Campus security: 24-hour emergency response devices and patrols, late-night transport/escort service, controlled dormitory access, campus-wide emergency alert system via cell phones, home phones, and email.
Student services: health clinic, personal/psychological counseling.

COSTS & FINANCIAL AID
Costs (2018–19) *Comprehensive fee:* $46,304 includes full-time tuition ($34,070), mandatory fees ($810), and room and board ($11,424). Part-time tuition: $876 per credit hour. Part-time tuition and fees vary according to course load. *Required fees:* $15 per credit hour part-time, $195 per term part-time. *College room only:* $5674. Room and board charges vary according to board plan and housing facility. *Payment plan:* installment. *Waivers:* employees or children of employees.
Financial Aid Of all full-time matriculated undergraduates who enrolled in 2017, 1,158 applied for aid, 987 were judged to have need, 217 had their need fully met. 643 Federal Work-Study jobs (averaging $1713). In 2017, 171 non-need-based awards were made. *Average percent of need met:* 80. *Average financial aid package:* $32,881. *Average need-based loan:* $4797. *Average need-based gift aid:* $26,451. *Average non-need-based aid:* $22,292. *Average indebtedness upon graduation:* $27,889.

APPLYING
Standardized Tests *Required:* SAT or ACT (for admission).
Options: electronic application, early admission, deferred entrance.
Required: high school transcript, minimum 2.5 GPA, letters of recommendation. *Required for some:* essay or personal statement, interview.
Application deadlines: 3/1 (freshmen), rolling (transfers).
Notification: continuous until 4/1 (freshmen).

CONTACT
Ms. Arielle Kilday, Associate Director of Admissions, Maryville College, 502 East Lamar Alexander Parkway, Maryville, TN 37804-5907. *Phone:* 865-981-8042. *Toll-free phone:* 800-597-2687. *Fax:* 865-981-8005. *E-mail:* admissions@maryvillecollege.edu.

Mid-America Baptist Theological Seminary

Cordova, Tennessee

http://www.mabts.edu/

- **Independent Southern Baptist** comprehensive, founded 1972
- **Suburban** campus with easy access to Memphis
- **Endowment** $3.6 million
- **Men only** 51 undergraduate students, 57% full-time
- **Noncompetitive** entrance level

UNDERGRAD STUDENTS
29 full-time, 22 part-time. Students come from 26 states and territories.

Freshmen:
Admission: 77 applied.

FACULTY
Total: 27, 100% full-time, 100% with terminal degrees.
Student/faculty ratio: 11:1.

ACADEMICS
Calendar: semesters. *Degrees:* associate, bachelor's, master's, and doctoral.
Special study options: distance learning, internships, part-time degree program, summer session for credit.

Computers: 10 computers/terminals are available on campus for general student use. Campuswide network is available. 100% of college-owned or -operated housing units are wired for high-speed Internet access. Wireless service is available via entire campus.

Library: Ora Byram Allison Memorial Library. Students can reserve study rooms.

STUDENT LIFE

Housing options: men-only, women-only, special housing for students with disabilities. Campus housing is university owned.

Campus security: 24-hour emergency response devices.

COSTS

Costs (2017–18) *Tuition:* $250 per credit hour part-time. Full-time tuition and fees vary according to course load, degree level, and location. Part-time tuition and fees vary according to course load and location. *Required fees:* $220 per term part-time. *Room only:* Room and board charges vary according to housing facility and location. *Payment plan:* installment. *Waivers:* minority students, children of alumni, and employees or children of employees.

APPLYING

Options: electronic application.

Application fee: $25.

Required: essay or personal statement, 2 letters of recommendation. *Required for some:* high school transcript.

CONTACT

Mid-America Baptist Theological Seminary, 2095 Appling Road, Cordova, TN 38016. *Toll-free phone:* 800-968-4508.

Middle Tennessee State University

Murfreesboro, Tennessee

http://www.mtsu.edu/

- **State-supported** university, founded 1911
- **Urban** 500-acre campus with easy access to Nashville
- **Coed** 19,523 undergraduate students, 81% full-time, 54% women, 46% men
- **Moderately difficult** entrance level, 59% of applicants were admitted

UNDERGRAD STUDENTS

15,812 full-time, 3,711 part-time. 21% Black or African American, non-Hispanic/Latino; 5% Hispanic/Latino; 3% Asian, non-Hispanic/Latino; 0.3% American Indian or Alaska Native, non-Hispanic/Latino; 3% Two or more races, non-Hispanic/Latino; 0.2% Race/ethnicity unknown; 4% international; 10% transferred in; 18% live on campus.

Freshmen:
Admission: 9,938 applied, 5,898 admitted, 3,016 enrolled. *Average high school GPA:* 3.5. *Test scores:* ACT scores over 18: 90%; ACT scores over 24: 39%; ACT scores over 30: 6%.

FACULTY

Total: 1,238, 75% full-time, 63% with terminal degrees.

Student/faculty ratio: 18:1.

ACADEMICS

Calendar: semesters. *Degrees:* certificates, bachelor's, master's, doctoral, post-master's, and postbachelor's certificates.

Special study options: adult/continuing education programs, external degree program, part-time degree program. *ROTC:* Army (b), Air Force (c).

Computers: Students can access the following: computer help desk, free student e-mail accounts, online (class) grades, online (class) registration, online (class) schedules. Campuswide network is available.

Library: James E. Walker Library.

STUDENT LIFE

Housing options: coed, men-only, women-only, special housing for students with disabilities. Campus housing is university owned.

Activities and organizations: drama/theater group, student-run newspaper, radio and television station, choral group, marching band, national fraternities, national sororities.

Athletics Member NCAA. All Division I except football (Division I-A). *Intercollegiate sports:* baseball M(s), basketball M(s)/W(s), cheerleading M(s)/W(s), cross-country running M(s)/W(s), equestrian sports M/W, golf M(s), soccer W(s), softball W(s), tennis M(s)/W(s), track and field M(s)/W(s), volleyball W(s). *Intramural sports:* badminton M/W, basketball M/W, bowling M(c)/W(c), fencing M(c)/W(c), field hockey M(c)/W(c), football M, ice hockey M(c)/W(c), lacrosse M(c)/W(c), racquetball M(c)/W(c), riflery M/W(c), rock climbing M(c)/W(c), rugby M(c)/W(c), soccer M(c)/W, softball M/W, swimming and diving M/W, tennis M/W, ultimate Frisbee M(c)/W(c), volleyball M(c)/W(c), wrestling M(c)/W(c).

Campus security: 24-hour emergency response devices and patrols, student patrols, late-night transport/escort service, controlled dormitory access.

Student services: health clinic, personal/psychological counseling, women's center, legal services.

COSTS & FINANCIAL AID

Costs (2017–18) *Tuition:* state resident $7176 full-time, $285 per credit hour part-time; nonresident $25,806 full-time, $1024 per credit hour part-time. Full-time tuition and fees vary according to course load. Part-time tuition and fees vary according to course load. *Required fees:* $1772 full-time, $74 per credit hour part-time. *Room and board:* $6408; room only: $5304. Room and board charges vary according to board plan and housing facility. *Payment plan:* installment. *Waivers:* employees or children of employees.

Financial Aid Of all full-time matriculated undergraduates who enrolled in 2017, 13,528 applied for aid, 10,789 were judged to have need, 1,123 had their need fully met. 336 Federal Work-Study jobs (averaging $2095). In 2017, 1928 non-need-based awards were made. *Average percent of need met:* 63. *Average financial aid package:* $10,111. *Average need-based loan:* $4001. *Average need-based gift aid:* $6170. *Average non-need-based aid:* $8161. *Average indebtedness upon graduation:* $25,717.

APPLYING

Standardized Tests *Required:* SAT or ACT (for admission).

Application fee: $25.

Required: high school transcript, minimum 3.0 GPA. *Required for some:* essay or personal statement.

CONTACT

Director of Admissions, Middle Tennessee State University, 1301 East Main Street, Murfreesboro, TN 37132. *Phone:* 615-898-2111. *Toll-free phone:* 800-331-MTSU. *Fax:* 615-898-5478. *E-mail:* admissions@ mtsu.edu.

Mid-South Christian College

Memphis, Tennessee

http://www.midsouthchristian.edu/

CONTACT

Mrs. Wendy Lambert, Student Recruiter, Mid-South Christian College, PO Box 181056, Memphis, TN 38181. *Phone:* 901-375-4400 Ext. 103. *Fax:* 901-375-4085. *E-mail:* wendylambert@midsouthcc.org.

Milligan College

Milligan College, Tennessee

http://www.milligan.edu/

- **Independent Christian** comprehensive, founded 1866
- **Suburban** 181-acre campus
- **Endowment** $42.9 million
- **Coed** 859 undergraduate students, 89% full-time, 57% women, 43% men
- **Moderately difficult** entrance level, 67% of applicants were admitted

UNDERGRAD STUDENTS

764 full-time, 95 part-time. Students come from 32 states and territories; 15 other countries; 38% are from out of state; 3% Black or African American, non-Hispanic/Latino; 4% Hispanic/Latino; 2% Asian, non-Hispanic/Latino; 0.1% Native Hawaiian or other Pacific Islander, non-Hispanic/Latino; 2% Two or more races, non-Hispanic/Latino; 5% international; 8% transferred in; 74% live on campus.

Freshmen:
Admission: 621 applied, 417 admitted, 204 enrolled. *Average high school GPA:* 3.7. *Test scores:* SAT evidence-based reading and writing scores over 500: 81%; SAT math scores over 500: 76%; ACT scores over 18: 98%; SAT evidence-based reading and writing scores over 600: 36%; SAT math scores over 600: 23%; ACT scores over 24: 66%; SAT evidence-based reading and writing scores over 700: 9%; SAT math scores over 700: 7%; ACT scores over 30: 14%.
Retention: 76% of full-time freshmen returned.

FACULTY
Total: 147, 57% full-time, 63% with terminal degrees.
Student/faculty ratio: 9:1.

ACADEMICS
Calendar: semesters. *Degrees:* bachelor's, master's, and doctoral.
Special study options: academic remediation for entering students, adult/continuing education programs, advanced placement credit, cooperative education, distance learning, double majors, honors programs, independent study, internships, off-campus study, part-time degree program, student-designed majors, study abroad, summer session for credit.
Unusual degree programs: 3-2 pharmacy with East Tennessee State University.
Computers: 97 computers/terminals are available on campus for general student use. Students can access the following: campus intranet, computer help desk, free student e-mail accounts, online (class) grades, online (class) registration, online (class) schedules. Campuswide network is available. 100% of college-owned or -operated housing units are wired for high-speed Internet access. Wireless service is available via classrooms, computer centers, computer labs, dorm rooms, libraries, student centers.
Library: P. H. Welshimer Memorial Library plus 1 other. *Books:* 170,942 (physical), 263,494 (digital/electronic); *Serial titles:* 982 (physical), 22,049 (digital/electronic); *Databases:* 83. Weekly public service hours: 89; students can reserve study rooms.

STUDENT LIFE
Housing options: on-campus residence required through senior year; men-only, women-only. Campus housing is university owned. Freshman campus housing is guaranteed.
Activities and organizations: drama/theater group, student-run newspaper, radio and television station, choral group, Student Government Association, Vespers-worship team, LINC-service organization, Campus Activities Board, Club Ultimate-frisbee.
Athletics Member NAIA. *Intercollegiate sports:* baseball M(s), basketball M(s)/W(s), cross-country running M(s)/W(s), golf M(s)/W(s), soccer M(s)/W(s), softball W(s), swimming and diving M(s)/W(s), tennis M(s)/W(s), track and field M(s)/W(s), volleyball M(s)/W(s). *Intramural sports:* basketball M/W, cheerleading W, football M/W, softball M/W, swimming and diving M/W, table tennis M/W, tennis M/W, ultimate Frisbee M/W, volleyball M/W, weight lifting M/W.
Campus security: 24-hour emergency response devices and patrols, late-night transport/escort service, controlled dormitory access.
Student services: health clinic, personal/psychological counseling.

COSTS & FINANCIAL AID
Costs (2018–19) *Comprehensive fee:* $40,800 includes full-time tuition ($32,500), mandatory fees ($1200), and room and board ($7100). Full-time tuition and fees vary according to course load and degree level. Part-time tuition and fees vary according to course load and degree level. *Required fees:* $905 per semester hour part-time, $375 per term part-time. *College room only:* $3550. Room and board charges vary according to housing facility. *Payment plan:* installment. *Waivers:* employees or children of employees.
Financial Aid Of all full-time matriculated undergraduates who enrolled in 2017, 713 applied for aid, 631 were judged to have need, 164 had their need fully met. 113 Federal Work-Study jobs (averaging $1200). 132 state and other part-time jobs (averaging $1504). In 2017, 114 non-need-based awards were made. *Average percent of need met:* 77. *Average financial aid package:* $24,449. *Average need-based loan:* $4760. *Average need-based gift aid:* $20,974. *Average non-need-based aid:* $11,258. *Average indebtedness upon graduation:* $29,277.

APPLYING
Standardized Tests *Required:* SAT or ACT (for admission).
Options: electronic application, deferred entrance.
Application fee: $30.
Required: essay or personal statement, high school transcript, minimum 2.0 GPA, 2 letters of recommendation. *Required for some:* interview. *Recommended:* minimum 3.0 GPA.
Application deadlines: 8/1 (freshmen), rolling (transfers).
Notification: continuous (freshmen), continuous (transfers).

CONTACT
Ms. Kristin Wright, Director of Enrollment Management, Milligan College, PO Box 210, Milligan College, TN 37682. *Phone:* 423-461-8730. *Toll-free phone:* 800-262-8337. *Fax:* 423-461-8982. *E-mail:* admissions@milligan.edu.

National College
Bristol, Tennessee
http://www.national-college.edu/

CONTACT
National College, 1328 Highway 11 West, Bristol, TN 37620. *Phone:* 423-878-4440. *Toll-free phone:* 888-9-JOBREADY.

Nossi College of Art
Nashville, Tennessee
http://www.nossi.edu/
- **Proprietary** 4-year, founded 1973
- **Urban** 10-acre campus with easy access to Nashville
- **Coed** 254 undergraduate students, 100% full-time, 62% women, 38% men

UNDERGRAD STUDENTS
254 full-time. Students come from 9 states and territories; 37% are from out of state; 20% Black or African American, non-Hispanic/Latino; 4% Hispanic/Latino; 0.8% Asian, non-Hispanic/Latino; 0.4% Native Hawaiian or other Pacific Islander, non-Hispanic/Latino; 0.8% American Indian or Alaska Native, non-Hispanic/Latino; 2% Two or more races, non-Hispanic/Latino; 0.8% Race/ethnicity unknown; 11% transferred in.

Freshmen:
Admission: 67 enrolled.
Retention: 88% of full-time freshmen returned.

FACULTY
Total: 38, 11% full-time.
Student/faculty ratio: 8:1.

ACADEMICS
Calendar: semesters. *Degrees:* associate and bachelor's.
Special study options: independent study, internships, off-campus study, part-time degree program.
Computers: 22 computers/terminals are available on campus for general student use. Students can access the following: campus intranet, free student e-mail accounts, online (class) grades, online (class) schedules. Wireless service is available via entire campus.
Library: Learning Resource Center.

STUDENT LIFE
Housing options: college housing not available.
Activities and organizations: Kappa Pi, CMA.EDU, Fashion Alliance, national fraternities, national sororities.
Campus security: gated entrance, ID badges for building accesss, doors are locked at all times.

COSTS
Costs (2018–19) *Tuition:* $17,700 full-time. No tuition increase for student's term of enrollment. *Required fees:* $100 full-time. *Payment plan:* installment.

APPLYING
Standardized Tests *Required for some:* ACT (for admission).
Options: electronic application, early admission.

Application fee: $100.

Required: essay or personal statement, high school transcript, interview, portfolio of work.

Notification: continuous (freshmen).

CONTACT
Ms. Mitzi Hatfield, Admissions Director, Nossi College of Art, 590 Cheron Road, Madison, TN 37115. *Phone:* 615-514-2787 (ARTS). *Toll-free phone:* 888-986-ARTS. *Fax:* 615-514-2788. *E-mail:* admissions@nossi.edu.

O'More College of Design
Franklin, Tennessee
http://www.omorecollege.edu/

- **Independent** 4-year, founded 1970
- **Small-town** 7-acre campus with easy access to Nashville
- **Coed** 148 undergraduate students, 89% full-time, 89% women, 11% men
- **Moderately difficult** entrance level, 31% of applicants were admitted

UNDERGRAD STUDENTS
131 full-time, 17 part-time. Students come from 20 states and territories; 1 other country; 22% are from out of state; 6% Black or African American, non-Hispanic/Latino; 4% Hispanic/Latino; 3% Asian, non-Hispanic/Latino; 0.7% Native Hawaiian or other Pacific Islander, non-Hispanic/Latino; 0.7% American Indian or Alaska Native, non-Hispanic/Latino; 3% Two or more races, non-Hispanic/Latino; 2% Race/ethnicity unknown; 1% international; 7% transferred in.

Freshmen:
Admission: 89 applied, 28 admitted, 16 enrolled. *Average high school GPA:* 3.3. *Test scores:* ACT scores over 18: 70%; ACT scores over 24: 10%; ACT scores over 30: 1%.
Retention: 83% of full-time freshmen returned.

FACULTY
Total: 44, 27% full-time, 50% with terminal degrees.
Student/faculty ratio: 7:1.

ACADEMICS
Calendar: semesters. *Degree:* bachelor's.
Special study options: advanced placement credit, cooperative education, independent study, internships, part-time degree program, services for LD students, summer session for credit.
Computers: 19 computers/terminals and 15 ports are available on campus for general student use. Students can access the following: campus intranet, computer help desk, free student e-mail accounts, online (class) grades, online (class) registration, online (class) schedules. Campuswide network is available. Wireless service is available via entire campus.
Library: McAfee Library. *Books:* 2,242 (physical); *Databases:* 30. Weekly public service hours: 40.

STUDENT LIFE
Housing options: college housing not available.
Activities and organizations: Student Activities Council, Magnolia Social, O'More Fashion Association, LeP (Interior Design Association), Graphic Designers Guild.
Campus security: on-campus security/contracted security until 10pm M-F, 24-hour studio key access.

COSTS & FINANCIAL AID
Costs (2017–18) *Tuition:* $29,880 full-time, $1245 per credit hour part-time. Full-time tuition and fees vary according to course load. *Payment plan:* installment. *Waivers:* employees or children of employees.
Financial Aid Of all full-time matriculated undergraduates who enrolled in 2015, 147 applied for aid, 130 were judged to have need, 18 had their need fully met. 13 Federal Work-Study jobs (averaging $1285). 17 state and other part-time jobs (averaging $2130). In 2015, 34 non-need-based awards were made. *Average percent of need met:* 76. *Average financial aid package:* $16,617. *Average need-based loan:* $4762. *Average need-based gift aid:* $13,756. *Average non-need-based aid:* $5934. *Average indebtedness upon graduation:* $31,773.

APPLYING
Standardized Tests *Required:* SAT or ACT (for admission).

Options: electronic application, early admission, deferred entrance.
Application fee: $50.
Required: high school transcript, interview, 3.0 GPA or minimum ACT score of 20. *Required for some:* essay or personal statement.
Application deadlines: 7/31 (freshmen), 7/31 (transfers).
Notification: continuous (freshmen), continuous (out-of-state freshmen), continuous (transfers).

CONTACT
Tori Bagsby, Admissions Manager, O'More College of Design, 423 South Margin Street, Franklin, TN 37064-2816. *Phone:* 615-794-4254 Ext. 230. *Toll-free phone:* 888-662-1970. *Fax:* 615-790-1662. *E-mail:* tbagsby@omorecollege.edu.

Remington College–Memphis Campus
Memphis, Tennessee
http://www.remingtoncollege.edu/

CONTACT
Randal Hayes, Director of Recruitment, Remington College–Memphis Campus, 2710 Nonconnah Boulevard, Memphis, TN 38132. *Phone:* 901-345-1000. *Toll-free phone:* 800-323-8122. *Fax:* 901-396-8310. *E-mail:* randal.hayes@remingtoncollege.edu.

Rhodes College
Memphis, Tennessee
http://www.rhodes.edu/

- **Independent** comprehensive, founded 1848
- **Urban** 100-acre campus with easy access to Memphis
- **Endowment** $342.3 million
- **Coed** 1,988 undergraduate students, 100% full-time, 56% women, 44% men
- **Very difficult** entrance level, 51% of applicants were admitted

UNDERGRAD STUDENTS
1,979 full-time, 9 part-time. Students come from 46 states and territories; 35 other countries; 72% are from out of state; 8% Black or African American, non-Hispanic/Latino; 5% Hispanic/Latino; 6% Asian, non-Hispanic/Latino; 0.1% Native Hawaiian or other Pacific Islander, non-Hispanic/Latino; 0.3% American Indian or Alaska Native, non-Hispanic/Latino; 4% Two or more races, non-Hispanic/Latino; 2% Race/ethnicity unknown; 4% international; 0.9% transferred in; 70% live on campus.

Freshmen:
Admission: 4,733 applied, 2,416 admitted, 512 enrolled. *Average high school GPA:* 3.9. *Test scores:* SAT evidence-based reading and writing scores over 500: 99%; SAT math scores over 500: 99%; ACT scores over 18: 100%; SAT evidence-based reading and writing scores over 600: 87%; SAT math scores over 600: 79%; ACT scores over 24: 96%; SAT evidence-based reading and writing scores over 700: 34%; SAT math scores over 700: 26%; ACT scores over 30: 48%.
Retention: 91% of full-time freshmen returned.

FACULTY
Total: 222, 81% full-time, 92% with terminal degrees.
Student/faculty ratio: 10:1.

ACADEMICS
Calendar: semesters. *Degrees:* bachelor's and master's (master's degree in accounting only).
Special study options: advanced placement credit, cooperative education, double majors, honors programs, independent study, internships, off-campus study, part-time degree program, services for LD students, student-designed majors, study abroad, summer session for credit. *ROTC:* Army (c), Navy (c), Air Force (c).
Unusual degree programs: 3-2 engineering with Washington University in St. Louis, Christian Brothers University, University of Memphis, The University of Tennessee.
Computers: 900 computers/terminals are available on campus for general student use. Students can access the following: campus intranet, computer

help desk, free student e-mail accounts, online (class) grades, online (class) registration, online (class) schedules. Campuswide network is available. 100% of college-owned or -operated housing units are wired for high-speed Internet access. Wireless service is available via entire campus.

Library: Paul Barret, Jr. Library. *Books:* 246,054 (physical); *Serial titles:* 94,665 (digital/electronic); *Databases:* 151. Weekly public service hours: 113.

STUDENT LIFE

Housing options: on-campus residence required through sophomore year; coed, men-only, women-only. Campus housing is university owned. Freshman campus housing is guaranteed.

Activities and organizations: drama/theater group, student-run newspaper, radio and television station, choral group, Rhodes Outdoors Club, South Asian Culture and Advocacy, Rhodes College Crew Team, Gender and Sexuality Alliance, Culture of Consent, national fraternities, national sororities.

Athletics Member NCAA. All Division III. *Intercollegiate sports:* badminton M(c)/W(c), baseball M, basketball M/W, crew M(c)/W(c), cross-country running M/W, equestrian sports M(c)/W(c), fencing M(c)/W(c), field hockey W, football M, golf M/W, ice hockey M(c), lacrosse M/W, rugby M(c), soccer M/W, softball W, swimming and diving M/W, tennis M/W, track and field M/W, ultimate Frisbee M(c)/W(c), volleyball W, wrestling M(c). *Intramural sports:* basketball M/W, racquetball M/W, soccer M/W, squash M(c), volleyball M/W.

Campus security: 24-hour emergency response devices and patrols, student patrols, late-night transport/escort service, 24-hour monitored security cameras in parking areas, fenced campus with monitored access at night.

Student services: health clinic, personal/psychological counseling, women's center.

COSTS & FINANCIAL AID

Costs (2018–19) *Comprehensive fee:* $57,794 includes full-time tuition ($46,194), mandatory fees ($310), and room and board ($11,290). Part-time tuition: $1930 per credit hour. Part-time tuition and fees vary according to course load. *College room only:* $5373. Room and board charges vary according to board plan and housing facility. *Payment plan:* installment. *Waivers:* employees or children of employees.

Financial Aid Of all full-time matriculated undergraduates who enrolled in 2017, 1,320 applied for aid, 968 were judged to have need, 426 had their need fully met. In 2017, 859 non-need-based awards were made. *Average percent of need met:* 90. *Average financial aid package:* $38,952. *Average need-based loan:* $3303. *Average need-based gift aid:* $31,751. *Average non-need-based aid:* $22,626. *Average indebtedness upon graduation:* $27,576. *Financial aid deadline:* 3/1.

APPLYING

Standardized Tests *Required:* SAT or ACT (for admission).

Options: electronic application, early admission, early decision, early action, deferred entrance.

Required: essay or personal statement, high school transcript, 2 letters of recommendation. *Recommended:* interview.

Application deadlines: 1/15 (freshmen), 1/15 (transfers), 11/15 (early action).

Early decision deadline: 11/1 (for plan 1), 1/1 (for plan 2).

Notification: 4/1 (freshmen), 4/1 (transfers), 12/1 (early decision plan 1), 2/1 (early decision plan 2), 1/15 (early action).

CONTACT

Mr. Carey Thompson, Vice President of Enrollment and Communications, Dean of Admissions, Rhodes College, 2000 N. Parkway, Memphis, TN 38112. *Phone:* 901-843-3700. *Toll-free phone:* 800-844-5969. *Fax:* 901-843-3631. *E-mail:* adminfo@rhodes.edu.

Sewanee: The University of the South
Sewanee, Tennessee
http://www.sewanee.edu/
- **Independent Episcopal** comprehensive, founded 1857
- **Small-town** 13,000-acre campus with easy access to Chattanooga
- **Endowment** $395.0 million
- **Coed** 1,702 undergraduate students, 99% full-time, 53% women, 47% men
- **Very difficult** entrance level, 47% of applicants were admitted

UNDERGRAD STUDENTS

1,687 full-time, 15 part-time. Students come from 44 states and territories; 27 other countries; 78% are from out of state; 5% Black or African American, non-Hispanic/Latino; 6% Hispanic/Latino; 1% Asian, non-Hispanic/Latino; 0.1% American Indian or Alaska Native, non-Hispanic/Latino; 3% Two or more races, non-Hispanic/Latino; 3% international; 0.9% transferred in; 98% live on campus.

Freshmen:
Admission: 4,218 applied, 1,971 admitted, 448 enrolled. *Average high school GPA:* 3.7. *Test scores:* SAT evidence-based reading and writing scores over 500: 100%; SAT math scores over 500: 100%; ACT scores over 18: 100%; SAT evidence-based reading and writing scores over 600: 86%; SAT math scores over 600: 68%; ACT scores over 24: 95%; SAT evidence-based reading and writing scores over 700: 25%; SAT math scores over 700: 20%; ACT scores over 30: 35%.
Retention: 88% of full-time freshmen returned.

FACULTY
Total: 242, 68% full-time, 86% with terminal degrees.
Student/faculty ratio: 10:1.

ACADEMICS
Calendar: semesters. *Degrees:* bachelor's, master's, doctoral, post-master's, and postbachelor's certificates.

Special study options: advanced placement credit, double majors, independent study, internships, off-campus study, services for LD students, student-designed majors, study abroad, summer session for credit.

Unusual degree programs: 3-2 engineering with Columbia University, Rensselaer Polytechnic Institute, Vanderbilt University, Washington University in St. Louis.

Computers: 150 computers/terminals and 3,000 ports are available on campus for general student use. Students can access the following: computer help desk, free student e-mail accounts, online (class) grades, online (class) registration, online (class) schedules. Campuswide network is available. 100% of college-owned or -operated housing units are wired for high-speed Internet access. Wireless service is available via entire campus.

Library: Jessie Ball duPont Library. *Books:* 508,288 (physical), 559,530 (digital/electronic); *Serial titles:* 3,975 (physical), 16,012 (digital/electronic); *Databases:* 377. Study areas open 24 hours, 5–7 days a week; students can reserve study rooms.

STUDENT LIFE
Housing options: on-campus residence required through senior year; coed, men-only, women-only. Campus housing is university owned. Freshman campus housing is guaranteed.

Activities and organizations: drama/theater group, student-run newspaper, radio station, choral group, Sewanee Outing Program, Sewanee Outreach, Organization for Cross Cultural Understanding, Alpha Phi Omega (APO) National Service Fraternity, African American Alliance, national fraternities, national sororities.

Athletics Member NCAA. All Division III. *Intercollegiate sports:* baseball M, basketball M/W, cheerleading W, crew M(c)/W(c), cross-country running M/W, equestrian sports M/W, fencing M(c)/W(c), field hockey W, football M, golf M/W, ice hockey M(c)/W(c), lacrosse M/W, rugby M(c)/W(c), soccer M/W, softball W, squash M(c)/W(c), swimming and diving M/W, tennis M/W, track and field M/W, volleyball W. *Intramural sports:* basketball M/W, football M/W, soccer M/W, table tennis M/W.

Campus security: 24-hour emergency response devices and patrols, late-night transport/escort service, controlled dormitory access, security lighting.

Student services: health clinic, personal/psychological counseling, women's center.

COSTS & FINANCIAL AID

Costs (2018–19) *Comprehensive fee:* $58,000 includes full-time tuition ($44,848), mandatory fees ($272), and room and board ($12,880). Part-time tuition: $1425 per credit hour. *College room only:* $6675. *Payment plan:* installment. *Waivers:* employees or children of employees.

Financial Aid Of all full-time matriculated undergraduates who enrolled in 2017, 1,013 applied for aid, 806 were judged to have need, 273 had their need fully met. 453 Federal Work-Study jobs (averaging $1634). 152 state and other part-time jobs (averaging $3153). In 2017, 641 non-need-based awards were made. *Average percent of need met:* 91. *Average financial aid package:* $34,591. *Average need-based loan:* $4287. *Average need-based gift aid:* $28,853. *Average non-need-based aid:* $14,019. *Average indebtedness upon graduation:* $26,772.

APPLYING

Standardized Tests *Required for some:* TOEFL for international students. *Recommended:* SAT or ACT (for admission).

Options: electronic application, early admission, early decision, early action, deferred entrance.

Required: essay or personal statement, high school transcript, 2 letters of recommendation. *Recommended:* interview.

Application deadlines: 2/1 (freshmen), 4/1 (transfers), 12/1 (early action).

Early decision deadline: 11/15 (for plan 1), 1/15 (for plan 2).

Notification: continuous (transfers), 12/15 (early decision plan 1), 2/15 (early decision plan 2).

CONTACT

Ms. Lisa Burns, Associate Dean of Admission, Sewanee: The University of the South, 735 University Avenue, Sewanee, TN 37383-1000. *Phone:* 931-598-1238. *Toll-free phone:* 800-522-2234. *Fax:* 931-598-3248. *E-mail:* admiss@sewanee.edu.

South College

Knoxville, Tennessee

http://www.southcollegetn.edu/

CONTACT

Mr. Walter Hosea, Director of Admissions, South College, 720 North Fifth Avenue, Knoxville, TN 37917. *Phone:* 865-524-3043 Ext. 1825. *E-mail:* whosea@southcollegetn.edu.

Southern Adventist University

Collegedale, Tennessee

http://www.southern.edu/

- **Independent Seventh-day Adventist** comprehensive, founded 1892
- **Small-town** 1000-acre campus with easy access to Chattanooga
- **Endowment** $38.1 million
- **Coed** 2,564 undergraduate students, 84% full-time, 58% women, 42% men
- **Moderately difficult** entrance level, 95% of applicants were admitted

UNDERGRAD STUDENTS

2,160 full-time, 404 part-time. Students come from 50 states and territories; 39 other countries; 10% Black or African American, non-Hispanic/Latino; 21% Hispanic/Latino; 9% Asian, non-Hispanic/Latino; 0.5% Native Hawaiian or other Pacific Islander, non-Hispanic/Latino; 0.1% American Indian or Alaska Native, non-Hispanic/Latino; 6% Two or more races, non-Hispanic/Latino; 9% international; 3% transferred in.

Freshmen:

Admission: 1,423 applied, 1,349 admitted, 567 enrolled. *Average high school GPA:* 3.5. *Test scores:* SAT evidence-based reading and writing scores over 500: 76%; SAT math scores over 500: 69%; ACT scores over 18: 91%; SAT evidence-based reading and writing scores over 600: 45%; SAT math scores over 600: 44%; ACT scores over 24: 43%; SAT evidence-based reading and writing scores over 700: 3%; SAT math scores over 700: 13%; ACT scores over 30: 11%.

Retention: 74% of full-time freshmen returned.

FACULTY

Total: 169, 98% full-time, 64% with terminal degrees.

Student/faculty ratio: 14:1.

ACADEMICS

Calendar: semesters. *Degrees:* certificates, associate, bachelor's, master's, doctoral, and post-master's certificates.

Special study options: advanced placement credit, distance learning, double majors, English as a second language, honors programs, independent study, internships, off-campus study, services for LD students, student-designed majors, study abroad, summer session for credit.

Computers: 300 computers/terminals are available on campus for general student use. Students can access the following: campus intranet, computer help desk, free student e-mail accounts, online (class) grades, online (class) registration, online (class) schedules. Campuswide network is available. 100% of college-owned or -operated housing units are wired for high-speed Internet access. Wireless service is available via entire campus.

Library: McKee Library plus 7 others. *Books:* 173,284 (physical), 107,663 (digital/electronic); *Serial titles:* 510 (physical), 170 (digital/electronic); *Databases:* 160. Weekly public service hours: 82; students can reserve study rooms.

STUDENT LIFE

Housing options: on-campus residence required through junior year; men-only, women-only. Campus housing is university owned. Freshman campus housing is guaranteed.

Activities and organizations: drama/theater group, student-run newspaper, radio and television station, choral group, Asian Club, Black Christian Union, Business Society, School of Nursing, Student Ministerial Association.

Athletics *Intramural sports:* basketball M/W, football M/W, soccer M/W, softball M/W, volleyball M/W.

Campus security: 24-hour emergency response devices and patrols, student patrols, late-night transport/escort service, controlled dormitory access.

Student services: health clinic, personal/psychological counseling.

COSTS & FINANCIAL AID

Costs (2018–19) *Comprehensive fee:* $28,890 includes full-time tuition ($21,100), mandatory fees ($850), and room and board ($6940). Full-time tuition and fees vary according to course load. Part-time tuition: $890 per credit hour. Part-time tuition and fees vary according to course load. *Required fees:* $850 per term part-time. *College room only:* $4400. Room and board charges vary according to board plan. *Payment plan:* installment. *Waivers:* senior citizens.

Financial Aid Of all full-time matriculated undergraduates who enrolled in 2017, 1,704 applied for aid, 1,464 were judged to have need, 24 had their need fully met. 801 Federal Work-Study jobs (averaging $2500). In 2017, 575 non-need-based awards were made. *Average percent of need met:* 68. *Average financial aid package:* $16,298. *Average need-based loan:* $4660. *Average need-based gift aid:* $10,702. *Average non-need-based aid:* $7645. *Average indebtedness upon graduation:* $33,445.

APPLYING

Standardized Tests *Required:* SAT or ACT (for admission).

Options: electronic application, deferred entrance.

Application fee: $25.

Required: high school transcript, minimum 2.5 GPA. *Required for some:* essay or personal statement, minimum 2.3 GPA.

Application deadlines: rolling (freshmen), rolling (transfers).

Notification: continuous (freshmen), continuous (transfers).

CONTACT

Jennifer Landivar, Applications Manager, Southern Adventist University, PO Box 370, Collegedale, TN 37315-0370. *Phone:* 423-236-2655. *Toll-free phone:* 800-768-8437. *Fax:* 423-236-1835. *E-mail:* jlandivar@ southern.edu.

Strayer University–Knoxville Campus

Knoxville, Tennessee
http://www.strayer.edu/tennessee/knoxville/

CONTACT
Strayer University–Knoxville Campus, 10118 Parkside Drive, Suite 200, Knoxville, TN 37922. *Toll-free phone:* 888-311-0355.

Strayer University–Nashville Campus

Nashville, Tennessee
http://www.strayer.edu/tennessee/nashville/

CONTACT
Strayer University–Nashville Campus, 1809 Dabbs Avenue, Nashville, TN 37210. *Toll-free phone:* 888-311-0355.

Strayer University–Shelby Campus

Memphis, Tennessee
http://www.strayer.edu/tennessee/shelby/

CONTACT
Strayer University–Shelby Campus, 7275 Appling Farms Parkway, Memphis, TN 38133. *Toll-free phone:* 888-311-0355.

Strayer University–Thousand Oaks Campus

Memphis, Tennessee
http://www.strayer.edu/tennessee/thousand-oaks/

CONTACT
Strayer University–Thousand Oaks Campus, 2620 Thousand Oaks Boulevard, Suite 1100, Memphis, TN 38118. *Toll-free phone:* 888-311-0355.

Tennessee State University

Nashville, Tennessee
http://www.tnstate.edu/

- **State-supported** comprehensive, founded 1912, part of Tennessee Board of Regents
- **Urban** 450-acre campus with easy access to Nashville
- **Coed**
- **Minimally difficult** entrance level

FACULTY
Student/faculty ratio: 14:1.

ACADEMICS
Calendar: semesters. *Degrees:* associate, bachelor's, master's, doctoral, and postbachelor's certificates.
Library: Martha M. Brown/Lois H. Daniel Library plus 1 other.

STUDENT LIFE
Housing options: coed, men-only, women-only. Campus housing is university owned. Freshman applicants given priority for college housing.
Activities and organizations: drama/theater group, student-run newspaper, radio and television station, choral group, marching band, national fraternities, national sororities.
Athletics Member NCAA. All Division I except football (Division I-AA).
Campus security: 24-hour patrols, controlled dormitory access.
Student services: health clinic, personal/psychological counseling, women's center.

COSTS & FINANCIAL AID
Costs (2017–18) *Tuition:* state resident $6408 full-time, $267 per hour part-time; nonresident $19,128 full-time, $797 per hour part-time.
Required fees: $1050 full-time, $66 per hour part-time.
Financial Aid Of all full-time matriculated undergraduates who enrolled in 2015, 5,534 applied for aid, 5,236 were judged to have need, 271 had their need fully met. In 2015, 232 non-need-based awards were made. *Average percent of need met:* 53. *Average financial aid package:* $10,539. *Average need-based loan:* $4060. *Average need-based gift aid:*

$5332. *Average non-need-based aid:* $14,290. *Average indebtedness upon graduation:* $35,214.

APPLYING
Standardized Tests *Required:* SAT or ACT (for admission).
Options: electronic application.
Application fee: $25.

CONTACT
Dr. John Cade, Associate Vice President/Interim Vice President, Tennessee State University, 3500 John A. Merritt Boulevard, Nashville, TN 37209. *Phone:* 615-963-5101. *E-mail:* jcade@tnstate.edu.

Tennessee Technological University

Cookeville, Tennessee
http://www.tntech.edu/

- **State-supported** university, founded 1915, part of Tennessee Board of Regents
- **Small-town** campus
- **Endowment** $65.9 million
- **Coed** 9,365 undergraduate students, 88% full-time, 45% women, 55% men
- **Moderately difficult** entrance level, 64% of applicants were admitted

UNDERGRAD STUDENTS
8,259 full-time, 1,106 part-time. Students come from 32 states and territories; 51 other countries; 3% are from out of state; 4% Black or African American, non-Hispanic/Latino; 3% Hispanic/Latino; 1% Asian, non-Hispanic/Latino; 0.1% American Indian or Alaska Native, non-Hispanic/Latino; 3% Two or more races, non-Hispanic/Latino; 0.6% Race/ethnicity unknown; 4% international; 8% transferred in; 30% live on campus.

Freshmen:
Admission: 7,143 applied, 4,600 admitted, 1,761 enrolled. *Average high school GPA:* 3.6. *Test scores:* SAT evidence-based reading and writing scores over 500: 57%; SAT math scores over 500: 56%; ACT scores over 18: 97%; SAT evidence-based reading and writing scores over 600: 21%; SAT math scores over 600: 21%; ACT scores over 24: 56%; SAT math scores over 700: 7%; ACT scores over 30: 13%.
Retention: 79% of full-time freshmen returned.

FACULTY
Total: 645, 66% full-time, 53% with terminal degrees.
Student/faculty ratio: 18:1.

ACADEMICS
Calendar: semesters. *Degrees:* bachelor's, master's, doctoral, postmaster's, and postbachelor's certificates.
Special study options: academic remediation for entering students, accelerated degree program, adult/continuing education programs, advanced placement credit, cooperative education, distance learning, double majors, English as a second language, external degree program, honors programs, independent study, internships, off-campus study, part-time degree program, services for LD students, student-designed majors, study abroad, summer session for credit. *ROTC:* Army (b), Air Force (c).
Computers: 227 computers/terminals are available on campus for general student use. Students can access the following: campus intranet, computer help desk, free student e-mail accounts, online (class) grades, online (class) registration, online (class) schedules, 590 additional computers are available for student use in individual departmental labs. Campuswide network is available. 100% of college-owned or -operated housing units are wired for high-speed Internet access. Wireless service is available via entire campus.
Library: Angelo and Jennette Volpe Library and Media Center. *Books:* 235,249 (physical), 267,168 (digital/electronic); *Serial titles:* 120,118 (physical); *Databases:* 193.

STUDENT LIFE
Housing options: on-campus residence required for freshman year; coed, men-only, women-only, special housing for students with disabilities. Campus housing is university owned. Freshman campus housing is guaranteed.
Activities and organizations: drama/theater group, student-run newspaper, choral group, marching band, Baptist Collegiate Center,

Fellowship of Christian Athletes, University Christian Student Center, Residence Hall Association, national fraternities, national sororities.

Athletics Member NCAA. All Division I except football (Division I-AA). *Intercollegiate sports:* baseball M(s), basketball M(s)/W(s), cheerleading M(s)/W(s), cross-country running M(s)/W(s), golf M(s)/W(s), soccer W(s), softball W(s), tennis M(s), track and field W(s), volleyball W(s). *Intramural sports:* basketball M/W, bowling M/W, fencing M(c)/W(c), football M/W, golf M/W, racquetball M/W, rugby M(c), soccer M/W, softball M/W, tennis M/W, ultimate Frisbee M/W, volleyball M/W, water polo M/W, wrestling M.

Campus security: 24-hour emergency response devices and patrols, late-night transport/escort service, controlled dormitory access, student safety organization, lighted pathways.

Student services: health clinic, personal/psychological counseling, women's center.

COSTS & FINANCIAL AID
Costs (2017–18) *Tuition:* state resident $8513 full-time, $379 per credit hour part-time; nonresident $24,337 full-time, $1040 per credit hour part-time. Full-time tuition and fees vary according to program. Part-time tuition and fees vary according to program. *Room and board:* $9274; room only: $4920. Room and board charges vary according to board plan and housing facility. *Payment plan:* deferred payment. *Waivers:* senior citizens and employees or children of employees.

Financial Aid Of all full-time matriculated undergraduates who enrolled in 2016, 7,301 applied for aid, 5,815 were judged to have need, 538 had their need fully met. 456 Federal Work-Study jobs (averaging $963). In 2016, 1620 non-need-based awards were made. *Average percent of need met:* 60. *Average financial aid package:* $10,151. *Average need-based loan:* $4029. *Average need-based gift aid:* $5694. *Average non-need-based aid:* $9264. *Average indebtedness upon graduation:* $22,018.

APPLYING
Standardized Tests *Required:* SAT or ACT (for admission). *Recommended:* ACT (for admission).

Options: electronic application, early admission, deferred entrance.

Application fee: $25.

Required: high school transcript, minimum 2.5 GPA. *Recommended:* interview.

Application deadlines: 8/1 (freshmen), 8/1 (transfers).

Notification: continuous (freshmen), continuous (transfers).

CONTACT
Tennessee Technological University, North Dixie Avenue, Cookeville, TN 38505. *Toll-free phone:* 800-255-8881.

Tennessee Wesleyan University
Athens, Tennessee
http://www.tnwesleyan.edu/

- **Independent United Methodist** comprehensive, founded 1857
- **Small-town** 40-acre campus with easy access to Knoxville, Chattanooga
- **Endowment** $9.4 million
- **Coed** 935 undergraduate students, 92% full-time, 63% women, 37% men
- **Minimally difficult** entrance level, 58% of applicants were admitted

UNDERGRAD STUDENTS
863 full-time, 72 part-time. Students come from 33 states and territories; 25 other countries; 14% are from out of state; 9% Black or African American, non-Hispanic/Latino; 5% Hispanic/Latino; 1% Asian, non-Hispanic/Latino; 0.1% American Indian or Alaska Native, non-Hispanic/Latino; 4% Two or more races, non-Hispanic/Latino; 1% Race/ethnicity unknown; 4% international; 13% transferred in; 30% live on campus.

Freshmen:
Admission: 988 applied, 570 admitted, 208 enrolled. *Average high school GPA:* 3.3. *Test scores:* SAT evidence-based reading and writing scores over 500: 33%; ACT scores over 18: 86%; ACT scores over 24: 26%; ACT scores over 30: 1%.

Retention: 68% of full-time freshmen returned.

FACULTY
Total: 113, 56% full-time, 52% with terminal degrees.
Student/faculty ratio: 12:1.

ACADEMICS
Calendar: semesters. *Degrees:* bachelor's and master's (profile includes information for both the main and branch campuses).

Special study options: academic remediation for entering students, accelerated degree program, adult/continuing education programs, advanced placement credit, distance learning, double majors, honors programs, independent study, internships, off-campus study, part-time degree program, services for LD students, student-designed majors, study abroad, summer session for credit.

Computers: 205 computers/terminals and 350 ports are available on campus for general student use. Students can access the following: campus intranet, computer help desk, free student e-mail accounts, online (class) grades, online (class) registration, online (class) schedules. Campuswide network is available. 100% of college-owned or -operated housing units are wired for high-speed Internet access. Wireless service is available via entire campus.

Library: Merner-Pfeiffer Library plus 1 other. *Books:* 52,465 (physical), 356,697 (digital/electronic); *Serial titles:* 82 (physical); *Databases:* 76. Weekly public service hours: 69.

STUDENT LIFE
Housing options: men-only, women-only. Campus housing is university owned. Freshman campus housing is guaranteed.

Activities and organizations: drama/theater group, student-run newspaper, choral group, Student Government Association, national sororities.

Athletics Member NAIA. *Intercollegiate sports:* baseball M(s), basketball M(s)/W(s), bowling M(s)/W(s), cheerleading M(s)/W(s), cross-country running M(s)/W(s), golf M(s)/W(s), lacrosse M(s)/W(s), soccer M(s)/W(s), softball W(s), tennis M(s)/W(s), track and field M(s)/W(s), volleyball W(s).

Campus security: 24-hour patrols, late-night transport/escort service, controlled dormitory access, night patrols by trained security personnel.

Student services: health clinic, personal/psychological counseling.

COSTS & FINANCIAL AID
Costs (2017–18) *Comprehensive fee:* $31,550 includes full-time tuition ($22,800), mandatory fees ($1000), and room and board ($7750). Full-time tuition and fees vary according to class time and degree level. Part-time tuition: $580 per credit hour. Part-time tuition and fees vary according to class time, course load, degree level, location, and program. *Required fees:* $10 per credit hour part-time. *College room only:* $2230. Room and board charges vary according to board plan and housing facility. *Payment plan:* installment. *Waivers:* employees or children of employees.

Financial Aid Of all full-time matriculated undergraduates who enrolled in 2016, 1,019 applied for aid, 922 were judged to have need, 185 had their need fully met. In 2016, 184 non-need-based awards were made. *Average percent of need met:* 67. *Average financial aid package:* $17,516. *Average need-based loan:* $3927. *Average need-based gift aid:* $15,404. *Average non-need-based aid:* $7756. *Average indebtedness upon graduation:* $18,540.

APPLYING
Standardized Tests *Required:* SAT or ACT (for admission).

Options: electronic application, deferred entrance.

Required: high school transcript, minimum 2.3 GPA, 1 letter of recommendation. *Required for some:* essay or personal statement, interview. *Recommended:* essay or personal statement.

Application deadlines: rolling (freshmen), rolling (transfers).

Notification: continuous (freshmen), continuous (transfers).

CONTACT
Ms. Joanne Landers, Vice President for Admissions, Tennessee Wesleyan University, 204 East College Street, Athens, TN 37303. *Phone:* 423-746-7504. *Toll-free phone:* 800-PICK-TWU. *Fax:* 423-745-9335. *E-mail:* admissions@twcnet.edu.

Trevecca Nazarene University

Nashville, Tennessee

http://www.trevecca.edu/

- **Independent Nazarene** comprehensive, founded 1901
- **Urban** 80-acre campus
- **Endowment** $28.9 million
- **Coed** 2,219 undergraduate students, 59% full-time, 62% women, 38% men
- **Moderately difficult** entrance level, 70% of applicants were admitted

UNDERGRAD STUDENTS

1,317 full-time, 902 part-time. Students come from 44 states and territories; 23 other countries; 33% are from out of state; 12% Black or African American, non-Hispanic/Latino; 9% Hispanic/Latino; 1% Asian, non-Hispanic/Latino; 0.1% Native Hawaiian or other Pacific Islander, non-Hispanic/Latino; 0.3% American Indian or Alaska Native, non-Hispanic/Latino; 3% Two or more races, non-Hispanic/Latino; 7% Race/ethnicity unknown; 5% international; 4% transferred in; 39% live on campus.

Freshmen:
Admission: 1,489 applied, 1,048 admitted, 421 enrolled. *Average high school GPA:* 3.5. *Test scores:* SAT evidence-based reading and writing scores over 500: 82%; SAT math scores over 500: 72%; ACT scores over 18: 93%; SAT evidence-based reading and writing scores over 600: 44%; SAT math scores over 600: 22%; ACT scores over 24: 38%; SAT evidence-based reading and writing scores over 700: 3%; SAT math scores over 700: 2%; ACT scores over 30: 11%.
Retention: 76% of full-time freshmen returned.

FACULTY

Total: 268, 34% full-time, 61% with terminal degrees.
Student/faculty ratio: 18:1.

ACADEMICS

Calendar: semesters. *Degrees:* certificates, associate, bachelor's, master's, doctoral, and post-master's certificates.

Special study options: academic remediation for entering students, adult/continuing education programs, advanced placement credit, distance learning, double majors, internships, services for LD students, study abroad, summer session for credit. *ROTC:* Army (c).

Computers: 200 computers/terminals and 1,460 ports are available on campus for general student use. Students can access the following: campus intranet, computer help desk, free student e-mail accounts, online (class) grades, online (class) registration, online (class) schedules, Non-traditional and graduate students are registered through Academic Records. Campuswide network is available. 100% of college-owned or -operated housing units are wired for high-speed Internet access. Wireless service is available via entire campus.
Library: Waggoner Library. *Books:* 85,560 (physical), 49,113 (digital/electronic); *Serial titles:* 299 (physical), 60,127 (digital/electronic); *Databases:* 44. Weekly public service hours: 91; students can reserve study rooms.

STUDENT LIFE

Housing options: on-campus residence required through senior year; men-only, women-only. Campus housing is university owned.

Activities and organizations: drama/theater group, student-run newspaper, choral group, marching band.

Athletics Member NCAA. All Division II. *Intercollegiate sports:* baseball M(s), basketball M(s)/W(s), cross-country running M(s)/W(s), golf M(s)/W(s), soccer M(s)/W(s), softball W(s), track and field M(s)/W(s), volleyball W(s). *Intramural sports:* basketball M/W, football M/W, soccer M/W, softball M/W, tennis M/W, ultimate Frisbee M/W, volleyball M/W.

Campus security: 24-hour patrols, late-night transport/escort service, weather alert warning system (phone, email, siren).

Student services: health clinic, personal/psychological counseling.

COSTS & FINANCIAL AID

Costs (2018–19) *Comprehensive fee:* $33,998 includes full-time tuition ($24,698), mandatory fees ($900), and room and board ($8400). Full-time tuition and fees vary according to course load and program. Part-time tuition: $955 per credit hour. Part-time tuition and fees vary according to course load and program. *College room only:* $4200. Room and board charges vary according to board plan. *Payment plans:* tuition prepayment, installment. *Waivers:* senior citizens and employees or children of employees.

Financial Aid *Average indebtedness upon graduation:* $29,487.

APPLYING

Standardized Tests *Required:* SAT or ACT (for admission).
Options: electronic application, early admission, deferred entrance.
Application fee: $25.
Required: high school transcript, minimum 2.5 GPA, minimum ACT composite score of 18, SAT Evidence-Based Reading and Writing and Math score of 940, medical history and immunization records.
Application deadlines: 8/1 (freshmen), rolling (transfers).
Notification: continuous (freshmen), continuous (transfers).

CONTACT

Ms. Melinda Miller, Director of Undergraduate Admissions, Trevecca Nazarene University, 333 Murfreesboro Road, Nashville, TN 37210. *Phone:* 615-248-1320. *Toll-free phone:* 888-210-4TNU. *Fax:* 615-248-7406. *E-mail:* admissions_und@trevecca.edu.

Tusculum College

Greeneville, Tennessee

http://www.tusculum.edu/

- **Independent Presbyterian** comprehensive, founded 1794
- **Small-town** 140-acre campus
- **Endowment** $21.1 million
- **Coed** 1,488 undergraduate students, 92% full-time, 51% women, 49% men
- **Moderately difficult** entrance level, 89% of applicants were admitted

UNDERGRAD STUDENTS

1,376 full-time, 112 part-time. 30% are from out of state; 17% Black or African American, non-Hispanic/Latino; 4% Hispanic/Latino; 0.3% Asian, non-Hispanic/Latino; 0.1% Native Hawaiian or other Pacific Islander, non-Hispanic/Latino; 0.5% American Indian or Alaska Native, non-Hispanic/Latino; 2% Two or more races, non-Hispanic/Latino; 2% Race/ethnicity unknown; 5% international; 5% transferred in.

Freshmen:
Admission: 2,139 applied, 1,896 admitted, 337 enrolled.
Retention: 65% of full-time freshmen returned.

FACULTY

Total: 147, 49% full-time.
Student/faculty ratio: 17:1.

ACADEMICS

Calendar: semesters. *Degrees:* associate, bachelor's, and master's.

Special study options: academic remediation for entering students, adult/continuing education programs, advanced placement credit, double majors, honors programs, independent study, internships, part-time degree program, services for LD students, student-designed majors, study abroad, summer session for credit.

Computers: Students can access the following: campus intranet, computer help desk, free student e-mail accounts, online (class) grades, online (class) registration, online (class) schedules. Campuswide network is available. 100% of college-owned or -operated housing units are wired for high-speed Internet access. Wireless service is available via entire campus.
Library: Thomas J. Garland Library plus 2 others. Students can reserve study rooms.

STUDENT LIFE

Housing options: coed, men-only, women-only, special housing for students with disabilities. Campus housing is university owned. Freshman campus housing is guaranteed.

Activities and organizations: drama/theater group, student-run newspaper, radio and television station, choral group, marching band.

Athletics Member NCAA. All Division II. *Intercollegiate sports:* baseball M(s), basketball M(s)/W(s), cheerleading M(s)/W(s), cross-country running M(s)/W(s), football M(s), golf M(s)/W, lacrosse

M(s)/W(s), sand volleyball W, soccer M(s)/W(s), softball W(s), tennis M(s)/W(s), track and field M(s)/W(s), volleyball W(s). *Intramural sports:* baseball M, basketball M/W, football M, softball M, tennis M/W, volleyball M/W.

Campus security: 24-hour emergency response devices and patrols, student patrols, late-night transport/escort service, controlled dormitory access, trained security personnel on duty.

Student services: health clinic, personal/psychological counseling, women's center.

COSTS & FINANCIAL AID

Costs (2018–19) *Comprehensive fee:* $34,050 includes full-time tuition ($24,860) and room and board ($9190). Part-time tuition: $768 per credit hour. *College room only:* $5600. *Payment plan:* installment. *Waivers:* employees or children of employees.

Financial Aid Of all full-time matriculated undergraduates who enrolled in 2016, 1,286 applied for aid, 1,196 were judged to have need, 103 had their need fully met. 293 Federal Work-Study jobs (averaging $963). In 2016, 72 non-need-based awards were made. *Average percent of need met:* 77. *Average financial aid package:* $17,079. *Average need-based loan:* $4098. *Average need-based gift aid:* $9629. *Average non-need-based aid:* $8329. *Average indebtedness upon graduation:* $33,916.

APPLYING

Standardized Tests *Required:* SAT or ACT (for admission).

Options: electronic application, early admission, early decision, deferred entrance.

Application deadlines: rolling (freshmen), rolling (transfers).

CONTACT

Tusculum College, PO Box 50627, Greeneville, TN 37743-9997. *Phone:* 423-636-7300 Ext. 5374. *Toll-free phone:* 800-729-0256. *E-mail:* admissions@tusculum.edu.

Union University

Jackson, Tennessee

http://www.uu.edu/

- **Independent Southern Baptist** comprehensive, founded 1823
- **Suburban** 360-acre campus with easy access to Memphis
- **Endowment** $39.1 million
- **Coed** 1,581 undergraduate students, 94% full-time, 62% women, 38% men
- **Moderately difficult** entrance level, 60% of applicants were admitted

UNDERGRAD STUDENTS

1,487 full-time, 94 part-time. Students come from 46 states and territories; 21 other countries; 25% are from out of state; 9% Black or African American, non-Hispanic/Latino; 3% Hispanic/Latino; 3% Asian, non-Hispanic/Latino; 0.1% Native Hawaiian or other Pacific Islander, non-Hispanic/Latino; 1% American Indian or Alaska Native, non-Hispanic/Latino; 1% Race/ethnicity unknown; 3% transferred in.

Freshmen:

Admission: 2,634 applied, 1,580 admitted, 344 enrolled. *Average high school GPA:* 3.8. *Test scores:* SAT evidence-based reading and writing scores over 500: 89%; SAT math scores over 500: 80%; ACT scores over 18: 99%; SAT evidence-based reading and writing scores over 600: 59%; SAT math scores over 600: 39%; ACT scores over 24: 72%; SAT evidence-based reading and writing scores over 700: 15%; SAT math scores over 700: 13%; ACT scores over 30: 24%.

Retention: 83% of full-time freshmen returned.

FACULTY

Total: 228, 98% full-time, 81% with terminal degrees.

Student/faculty ratio: 9:1.

ACADEMICS

Calendar: 4-1-4. *Degrees:* certificates, associate, bachelor's, master's, doctoral, post-master's, and postbachelor's certificates.

Special study options: academic remediation for entering students, accelerated degree program, adult/continuing education programs, advanced placement credit, cooperative education, distance learning, double majors, English as a second language, external degree program, honors programs, independent study, internships, off-campus study, part-time degree program, services for LD students, study abroad, summer session for credit. *ROTC:* Army (c).

Unusual degree programs: 3-2 pharmacy.

Computers: 202 computers/terminals are available on campus for general student use. Students can access the following: campus intranet, computer help desk, free student e-mail accounts, online (class) grades, online (class) registration, online (class) schedules. Campuswide network is available. 100% of college-owned or -operated housing units are wired for high-speed Internet access. Wireless service is available via entire campus.

Library: The Logos Library plus 1 other. *Books:* 136,991 (physical), 265,352 (digital/electronic); *Serial titles:* 2,362 (physical), 33,609 (digital/electronic); *Databases:* 135. Weekly public service hours: 93; students can reserve study rooms.

STUDENT LIFE

Housing options: on-campus residence required through junior year; men-only, women-only, special housing for students with disabilities. Campus housing is university owned. Freshman applicants given priority for college housing.

Activities and organizations: drama/theater group, student-run newspaper, choral group, Campus Ministries, Student Government Association, Student Activities Council, Students in Free Enterprise (SIFE), national fraternities, national sororities.

Athletics Member NCAA. All Division II. *Intercollegiate sports:* baseball M(s), basketball M(s)/W(s), cheerleading M/W(s), cross-country running M(s)/W(s), golf M(s)/W(s), soccer M(s)/W(s), softball W(s), ultimate Frisbee M(c)/W(c), volleyball W(s). *Intramural sports:* basketball M/W, cross-country running M/W, football M/W, golf M/W, racquetball M/W, sand volleyball M/W, soccer M/W, softball M/W, swimming and diving M/W, table tennis M/W, ultimate Frisbee M/W, volleyball M/W, weight lifting M/W.

Campus security: 24-hour emergency response devices and patrols, student patrols, late-night transport/escort service.

Student services: health clinic, personal/psychological counseling.

COSTS & FINANCIAL AID

Costs (2018–19) *Comprehensive fee:* $43,090 includes full-time tuition ($31,550), mandatory fees ($1340), and room and board ($10,200). Full-time tuition and fees vary according to class time, course load, degree level, location, and program. Part-time tuition: $1015 per credit hour. Part-time tuition and fees vary according to class time, course load, degree level, location, and program. *Required fees:* $45 per credit hour part-time. *College room only:* $7900. Room and board charges vary according to board plan and housing facility. *Payment plans:* installment, deferred payment. *Waivers:* children of alumni and employees or children of employees.

Financial Aid Of all full-time matriculated undergraduates who enrolled in 2017, 1,292 applied for aid, 1,135 were judged to have need, 209 had their need fully met. In 2017, 311 non-need-based awards were made. *Average percent of need met:* 70. *Average financial aid package:* $26,805. *Average need-based loan:* $4264. *Average need-based gift aid:* $6434. *Average non-need-based aid:* $14,733. *Average indebtedness upon graduation:* $39,022.

APPLYING

Standardized Tests *Required:* SAT or ACT (for admission).

Options: electronic application, early admission, deferred entrance.

Application fee: $35.

Required: high school transcript, minimum 2.5 GPA. *Required for some:* 3 letters of recommendation. *Recommended:* essay or personal statement, interview.

Application deadlines: rolling (freshmen), rolling (out-of-state freshmen), rolling (transfers).

Notification: continuous (freshmen), continuous (out-of-state freshmen), continuous (transfers).

CONTACT

Mr. Robbie Graves, Director of Enrollment Services, Union University, 1050 Union University Drive, Jackson, TN 38305-3697. *Phone:* 731-661-5590. *Toll-free phone:* 800-33-UNION. *Fax:* 731-661-5589. *E-mail:* rgraves@uu.edu.

University of Memphis

Memphis, Tennessee
http://www.memphis.edu/

- **State-supported** university, founded 1912
- **Urban** 1160-acre campus with easy access to Memphis
- **Endowment** $208.1 million
- **Coed** 17,394 undergraduate students, 71% full-time, 58% women, 42% men
- **Moderately difficult** entrance level, 85% of applicants were admitted

UNDERGRAD STUDENTS
12,400 full-time, 4,994 part-time. Students come from 44 states and territories; 44 other countries; 12% are from out of state; 37% Black or African American, non-Hispanic/Latino; 5% Hispanic/Latino; 3% Asian, non-Hispanic/Latino; 0.1% Native Hawaiian or other Pacific Islander, non-Hispanic/Latino; 0.3% American Indian or Alaska Native, non-Hispanic/Latino; 4% Two or more races, non-Hispanic/Latino; 0.9% Race/ethnicity unknown; 2% international; 8% transferred in; 14% live on campus.

Freshmen:
Admission: 13,727 applied, 11,647 admitted, 2,669 enrolled. *Average high school GPA:* 3.4. *Test scores:* SAT evidence-based reading and writing scores over 500: 79%; SAT math scores over 500: 74%; ACT scores over 18: 91%; SAT evidence-based reading and writing scores over 600: 34%; SAT math scores over 600: 25%; ACT scores over 24: 36%; SAT evidence-based reading and writing scores over 700: 5%; SAT math scores over 700: 5%; ACT scores over 30: 7%.
Retention: 76% of full-time freshmen returned.

FACULTY
Total: 1,482, 60% full-time, 60% with terminal degrees.
Student/faculty ratio: 16:1.

ACADEMICS
Calendar: semesters. *Degrees:* bachelor's, master's, doctoral, post-master's, and postbachelor's certificates.

Special study options: accelerated degree program, adult/continuing education programs, advanced placement credit, cooperative education, distance learning, double majors, English as a second language, external degree program, honors programs, independent study, internships, off-campus study, part-time degree program, services for LD students, student-designed majors, study abroad, summer session for credit. *ROTC:* Army (b), Navy (b), Air Force (b).

Computers: 1,255 computers/terminals and 35 ports are available on campus for general student use. Students can access the following: campus intranet, computer help desk, free student e-mail accounts, online (class) grades, online (class) registration, online (class) schedules. Campuswide network is available. 100% of college-owned or -operated housing units are wired for high-speed Internet access. Wireless service is available via entire campus.
Library: McWherter Library plus 4 others. *Books:* 2.3 million (physical), 333,541 (digital/electronic); *Serial titles:* 519 (physical); *Databases:* 646. Weekly public service hours: 91; students can reserve study rooms.

STUDENT LIFE
Housing options: coed, men-only, women-only, cooperative, special housing for students with disabilities. Campus housing is university owned.

Activities and organizations: drama/theater group, student-run newspaper, radio station, choral group, marching band, Student Activities Council, Fraternity and Sorority Life, Black Student Association, Student Government Association, Up 'til Dawn- St. Jude Philanthropy, national fraternities, national sororities.
Athletics Member NCAA. All Division I except football (Division I-A). *Intercollegiate sports:* baseball M(s), basketball M(s)/W(s), cheerleading M(s)/W(s), cross-country running M(s)/W(s), golf M(s)/W(s), riflery M(s)/W(s), soccer M(s)/W(s), softball W(s), tennis M(s)/W(s), track and field M(s)/W(s), volleyball W(s). *Intramural sports:* badminton M/W, basketball M/W, equestrian sports W(c), football M/W, golf M/W, ice hockey M(c), lacrosse M(c), racquetball M/W, rugby M(c), soccer M/W, softball M/W, table tennis M/W, ultimate Frisbee M/W, volleyball M/W, water polo M(c).

Campus security: 24-hour emergency response devices and patrols, student patrols, late-night transport/escort service, controlled dormitory access.
Student services: health clinic, personal/psychological counseling, women's center.

COSTS & FINANCIAL AID
Costs (2017–18) *Tuition:* state resident $8064 full-time, $320 per credit hour part-time; nonresident $21,413 full-time, $808 per credit hour part-time. Full-time tuition and fees vary according to course load, degree level, program, and reciprocity agreements. Part-time tuition and fees vary according to course load, degree level, and program. *Required fees:* $1637 full-time, $114 per credit hour part-time. *Room and board:* $9366; room only: $5460. Room and board charges vary according to board plan, housing facility, and location. *Payment plan:* installment. *Waivers:* senior citizens and employees or children of employees.

Financial Aid Of all full-time matriculated undergraduates who enrolled in 2017, 11,407 applied for aid, 9,484 were judged to have need, 512 had their need fully met. 179 Federal Work-Study jobs (averaging $2574). In 2017, 965 non-need-based awards were made. *Average percent of need met:* 74. *Average financial aid package:* $10,102. *Average need-based loan:* $3964. *Average need-based gift aid:* $6667. *Average non-need-based aid:* $4799. *Average indebtedness upon graduation:* $27,002.

APPLYING
Standardized Tests *Required:* SAT or ACT (for admission).
Options: electronic application, early admission.
Application fee: $25.
Required: high school transcript. *Required for some:* essay or personal statement, minimum 2.0 GPA, 2 letters of recommendation, interview.
Application deadlines: 7/1 (freshmen), 7/1 (transfers).
Notification: continuous (freshmen), continuous (transfers).

CONTACT
Drusilla Welch, Associate Director of Operations for Admissions, University of Memphis, Admissions Operations, 204A Wilder Tower, Memphis, TN 38152. *Phone:* 901-678-3007. *Toll-free phone:* 800-669-2678. *E-mail:* dwelch@memphis.edu.

The University of Tennessee

Knoxville, Tennessee
http://www.utk.edu/

- **State-supported** university, founded 1794, part of University of Tennessee System
- **Urban** 600-acre campus
- **Endowment** $492.8 million
- **Coed** 22,317 undergraduate students, 94% full-time, 50% women, 50% men
- **Moderately difficult** entrance level, 77% of applicants were admitted

UNDERGRAD STUDENTS
20,965 full-time, 1,352 part-time. Students come from 46 states and territories; 42 other countries; 13% are from out of state; 7% Black or African American, non-Hispanic/Latino; 4% Hispanic/Latino; 4% Asian, non-Hispanic/Latino; 0.2% American Indian or Alaska Native, non-Hispanic/Latino; 3% Two or more races, non-Hispanic/Latino; 3% Race/ethnicity unknown; 2% international; 6% transferred in; 33% live on campus.

Freshmen:
Admission: 18,872 applied, 14,526 admitted, 4,895 enrolled. *Average high school GPA:* 3.9. *Test scores:* SAT evidence-based reading and writing scores over 500: 97%; SAT math scores over 500: 96%; ACT scores over 18: 100%; SAT evidence-based reading and writing scores over 600: 62%; SAT math scores over 600: 54%; ACT scores over 24: 84%; SAT evidence-based reading and writing scores over 700: 12%; SAT math scores over 700: 13%; ACT scores over 30: 30%.
Retention: 86% of full-time freshmen returned.

FACULTY
Total: 1,752, 89% full-time, 84% with terminal degrees.
Student/faculty ratio: 17:1.

ACADEMICS

Calendar: semesters. *Degrees:* bachelor's, master's, doctoral, and postbachelor's certificates.

Special study options: accelerated degree program, advanced placement credit, cooperative education, distance learning, double majors, English as a second language, external degree program, freshman honors college, honors programs, independent study, internships, off-campus study, part-time degree program, services for LD students, student-designed majors, study abroad, summer session for credit. *ROTC:* Army (b), Air Force (b).

Computers: 1,298 computers/terminals are available on campus for general student use. Students can access the following: campus intranet, computer help desk, free student e-mail accounts, online (class) grades, online (class) registration, online (class) schedules, course management system. Campuswide network is available. 100% of college-owned or -operated housing units are wired for high-speed Internet access. Wireless service is available via entire campus.

Library: John C. Hodges Library plus 4 others. *Books:* 1.5 million (physical), 778,546 (digital/electronic); *Serial titles:* 51,623 (physical), 90,121 (digital/electronic); *Databases:* 713. Weekly public service hours: 160; study areas open 24 hours, 5–7 days a week; students can reserve study rooms.

STUDENT LIFE

Housing options: on-campus residence required for freshman year; coed, men-only, women-only, special housing for students with disabilities. Campus housing is university owned. Freshman campus housing is guaranteed.

Activities and organizations: drama/theater group, student-run newspaper, radio and television station, choral group, marching band, Fraternities/Sororities, Religious organizations, Campus Events Board, Black Cultural Programming Committee, Student Government Association, national fraternities, national sororities.

Athletics Member NCAA. All Division I. *Intercollegiate sports:* baseball M(s), basketball M(s)/W(s), crew W(s), cross-country running M/W, football M(s), golf M(s)/W(s), soccer W(s), softball W(s), swimming and diving M(s)/W(s), tennis M(s)/W(s), track and field M(s)/W(s), volleyball W(s). *Intramural sports:* badminton M/W, baseball M(c), basketball M/W, bowling M/W, crew M(c)/W(c), cross-country running M(c)/W(c), equestrian sports M(c)/W(c), fencing M(c)/W(c), field hockey M/W, golf M(c)/W(c), gymnastics M(c)/W(c), ice hockey M(c)/W(c), lacrosse M(c)/W(c), racquetball M/W, rock climbing M(c)/W(c), rowing M(c)/W(c), rugby M(c)/W(c), sailing M(c)/W(c), sand volleyball M/W, skiing (downhill) M(c)/W(c), soccer M/W, softball M/W, swimming and diving M(c)/W(c), table tennis M/W, tennis M/W, triathlon M(c)/W(c), ultimate Frisbee M/W, volleyball M/W, water polo M/W, weight lifting M/W, wrestling M(c)/W(c).

Campus security: 24-hour emergency response devices and patrols, late-night transport/escort service, controlled dormitory access, security cameras on all building entrances.

Student services: health clinic, personal/psychological counseling, women's center.

COSTS & FINANCIAL AID

Costs (2017–18) *Tuition:* state resident $11,110 full-time, $371 per credit hour part-time; nonresident $29,300 full-time, $1130 per credit hour part-time. Full-time tuition and fees vary according to course level, location, program, reciprocity agreements, and student level. Part-time tuition and fees vary according to course level, location, program, reciprocity agreements, and student level. *Required fees:* $1860 full-time. *Room and board:* $10,696. Room and board charges vary according to board plan and housing facility. *Payment plan:* installment. *Waivers:* senior citizens and employees or children of employees.

Financial Aid Of all full-time matriculated undergraduates who enrolled in 2017, 18,421 applied for aid, 12,244 were judged to have need, 2,383 had their need fully met. 539 Federal Work-Study jobs (averaging $2792). In 2017, 2968 non-need-based awards were made. *Average percent of need met:* 53. *Average financial aid package:* $13,351. *Average need-based loan:* $6814. *Average need-based gift aid:* $10,498. *Average non-need-based aid:* $5988. *Average indebtedness upon graduation:* $21,872.

APPLYING

Standardized Tests *Required:* SAT or ACT (for admission).

Options: electronic application.

Application fee: $50.

Required: essay or personal statement, high school transcript, high school prerequisite units. *Recommended:* letters of recommendation.

Application deadlines: rolling (freshmen), rolling (out-of-state freshmen), 7/1 (transfers).

Notification: continuous until 9/15 (freshmen), 9/15 (out-of-state freshmen), continuous (transfers).

CONTACT

Ms. Norma Harrington, Senior Associate Director, The University of Tennessee, 320 Student Services Building, Knoxville, TN 37996-0230. *Phone:* 865-974-2184. *E-mail:* admissions@utk.edu.

The University of Tennessee at Chattanooga
Chattanooga, Tennessee
http://www.utc.edu/

- **State-supported** comprehensive, founded 1886, part of University of Tennessee System
- **Urban** 425-acre campus
- **Coed** 10,176 undergraduate students, 88% full-time, 56% women, 44% men
- **Moderately difficult** entrance level, 83% of applicants were admitted

UNDERGRAD STUDENTS

8,962 full-time, 1,214 part-time. Students come from 36 states and territories; 28 other countries; 6% are from out of state; 10% Black or African American, non-Hispanic/Latino; 4% Hispanic/Latino; 2% Asian, non-Hispanic/Latino; 0.3% American Indian or Alaska Native, non-Hispanic/Latino; 4% Two or more races, non-Hispanic/Latino; 2% Race/ethnicity unknown; 1% international; 9% transferred in; 31% live on campus.

Freshmen:

Admission: 7,235 applied, 5,990 admitted, 2,147 enrolled. *Average high school GPA:* 3.5. *Test scores:* SAT evidence-based reading and writing scores over 500: 85%; SAT math scores over 500: 85%; ACT scores over 18: 98%; SAT evidence-based reading and writing scores over 600: 43%; SAT math scores over 600: 26%; ACT scores over 24: 46%; SAT evidence-based reading and writing scores over 700: 5%; SAT math scores over 700: 4%; ACT scores over 30: 7%.

Retention: 73% of full-time freshmen returned.

FACULTY

Total: 717, 65% full-time, 66% with terminal degrees.

Student/faculty ratio: 19:1.

ACADEMICS

Calendar: semesters. *Degrees:* certificates, bachelor's, master's, doctoral, post-master's, and postbachelor's certificates.

Special study options: accelerated degree program, advanced placement credit, cooperative education, distance learning, double majors, English as a second language, freshman honors college, honors programs, independent study, internships, off-campus study, part-time degree program, services for LD students, student-designed majors, study abroad, summer session for credit. *ROTC:* Army (b).

Computers: Students can access the following: campus intranet, computer help desk, free student e-mail accounts, online (class) grades, online (class) registration, online (class) schedules. Campuswide network is available. 100% of college-owned or -operated housing units are wired for high-speed Internet access. Wireless service is available via entire campus.

Library: UTC Library plus 1 other. *Books:* 743,490 (physical); *Databases:* 219. Study areas open 24 hours, 5–7 days a week; students can reserve study rooms.

STUDENT LIFE

Housing options: on-campus residence required for freshman year; coed, special housing for students with disabilities. Campus housing is university owned. Freshman applicants given priority for college housing.

Activities and organizations: drama/theater group, student-run newspaper, choral group, marching band, national fraternities, national sororities.

Athletics Member NCAA. All Division I except football (Division I-AA). *Intercollegiate sports:* basketball M(s)/W(s), cross-country running M(s)/W(s), golf M(s)/W(s), soccer W(s), softball W(s), tennis M(s)/W(s), track and field M(s)/W(s), volleyball W(s), wrestling M(s). *Intramural sports:* badminton M/W, baseball M(c), basketball M/W, crew M(c)/W(c), cross-country running M/W, fencing M(c)/W(c), golf M/W, racquetball M/W, soccer M/W, swimming and diving M/W, tennis M/W, ultimate Frisbee M(c)/W(c), volleyball W, wrestling M.

Campus security: 24-hour emergency response devices.

Student services: health clinic, personal/psychological counseling, women's center.

COSTS & FINANCIAL AID
Costs (2017–18) *Tuition:* state resident $6888 full-time, $287 per credit hour part-time; nonresident $23,006 full-time, $984 per credit hour part-time. Full-time tuition and fees vary according to degree level. Part-time tuition and fees vary according to degree level. *Required fees:* $1776 full-time, $264 per credit hour part-time. *Room and board:* $8676; room only: $5226. Room and board charges vary according to board plan, housing facility, and location. *Payment plan:* installment. *Waivers:* senior citizens and employees or children of employees.

Financial Aid Of all full-time matriculated undergraduates who enrolled in 2017, 7,928 applied for aid, 5,514 were judged to have need, 841 had their need fully met. In 2017, 957 non-need-based awards were made. *Average percent of need met:* 65. *Average financial aid package:* $10,084. *Average need-based loan:* $3935. *Average need-based gift aid:* $8116. *Average non-need-based aid:* $3258. *Average indebtedness upon graduation:* $22,293. *Financial aid deadline:* 5/1.

APPLYING
Standardized Tests *Required:* SAT or ACT (for admission).

Options: electronic application, early admission, deferred entrance.

Application fee: $30.

Required: high school transcript, 2.5 GPA with minimum ACT score of 21/SAT of 990 or minimum GPA of 2.85 with minimum ACT score of 18/SAT score of 870.

Application deadlines: 5/1 (freshmen), 7/1 (transfers).

CONTACT
Ms. Lee Pierce, Director of Admissions, The University of Tennessee at Chattanooga, 615 McCallie Ave, 101 University Center, Department 5105, Chattanooga, TN 37403. *Phone:* 423-425-4662. *Toll-free phone:* 800-882-6627. *Fax:* 423-425-4157. *E-mail:* admissions@utc.edu.

The University of Tennessee at Martin
Martin, Tennessee
http://www.utm.edu/

- **State-supported** comprehensive, founded 1900, part of University of Tennessee System
- **Small-town** 250-acre campus
- **Endowment** $33.6 million
- **Coed** 6,358 undergraduate students, 78% full-time, 59% women, 41% men
- **Moderately difficult** entrance level, 62% of applicants were admitted

UNDERGRAD STUDENTS
4,950 full-time, 1,408 part-time. Students come from 40 states and territories; 17 other countries; 8% are from out of state; 13% Black or African American, non-Hispanic/Latino; 3% Hispanic/Latino; 0.7% Asian, non-Hispanic/Latino; 0.2% American Indian or Alaska Native, non-Hispanic/Latino; 2% Two or more races, non-Hispanic/Latino; 2% international; 9% transferred in; 29% live on campus.

Freshmen
Admission: 4,884 applied, 3,004 admitted, 1,052 enrolled. *Average high school GPA:* 3.5. *Test scores:* ACT scores over 18: 98%; ACT scores over 24: 40%; ACT scores over 30: 5%.

Retention: 76% of full-time freshmen returned.

FACULTY
Total: 486, 59% full-time, 50% with terminal degrees.
Student/faculty ratio: 15:1.

ACADEMICS
Calendar: semesters. *Degrees:* bachelor's and master's.

Special study options: accelerated degree program, adult/continuing education programs, advanced placement credit, cooperative education, distance learning, double majors, English as a second language, honors programs, independent study, internships, off-campus study, part-time degree program, services for LD students, student-designed majors, study abroad, summer session for credit. *ROTC:* Army (b).

Unusual degree programs: veterinary medicine, dentistry, medicine, pharmacy.

Computers: 1,402 computers/terminals and 7,203 ports are available on campus for general student use. Students can access the following: campus intranet, computer help desk, free student e-mail accounts, online (class) grades, online (class) registration, online (class) schedules, online fee payments, degree progress, financial aid data, housing applications, transcripts. Campuswide network is available. 100% of college-owned or -operated housing units are wired for high-speed Internet access. Wireless service is available via entire campus.

Library: Paul Meek Library. *Books:* 309,179 (physical), 90,675 (digital/electronic); *Serial titles:* 2,377 (physical), 335,337 (digital/electronic); *Databases:* 215. Weekly public service hours: 92; study areas open 24 hours, 5–7 days a week.

STUDENT LIFE
Housing options: on-campus residence required for freshman year; men-only, women-only, special housing for students with disabilities. Campus housing is university owned. Freshman applicants given priority for college housing.

Activities and organizations: drama/theater group, student-run newspaper, radio and television station, choral group, marching band, Student Government Association, Black Student Association, National Society for Leadership and Success, Gamma Beta Phi, Student Tennessee Education Association, national fraternities, national sororities.

Athletics Member NCAA. All Division I except football (Division I-AA). *Intercollegiate sports:* baseball M(s), basketball M(s)/W(s), cheerleading W(s), cross-country running M(s)/W(s), equestrian sports W(s), golf M(s), riflery M(s)/W(s), sand volleyball W(s), soccer W(s), softball W(s), tennis W(s), volleyball W(s). *Intramural sports:* basketball M/W, football M/W, golf M/W, racquetball M/W, soccer M/W, softball M/W, tennis M/W, ultimate Frisbee M/W, volleyball M/W, water polo M/W.

Campus security: 24-hour emergency response devices and patrols, student patrols, controlled dormitory access.

Student services: health clinic, personal/psychological counseling, women's center.

COSTS & FINANCIAL AID
Costs (2017–18) *Tuition:* state resident $7818 full-time, $299 per credit hour part-time; nonresident $13,578 full-time, $539 per credit hour part-time. Full-time tuition and fees vary according to student level. Part-time tuition and fees vary according to course level and course load. *Required fees:* $1418 full-time, $59 per credit hour part-time. *Room and board:* $5976; room only: $2730. Room and board charges vary according to board plan and housing facility. *Payment plans:* installment, deferred payment. *Waivers:* senior citizens and employees or children of employees.

Financial Aid Of all full-time matriculated undergraduates who enrolled in 2017, 4,568 applied for aid, 3,726 were judged to have need, 783 had their need fully met. 308 Federal Work-Study jobs (averaging $2505). In 2017, 313 non-need-based awards were made. *Average percent of need met:* 45. *Average financial aid package:* $11,501. *Average need-based loan:* $4315. *Average need-based gift aid:* $6649. *Average non-need-based aid:* $2065. *Average indebtedness upon graduation:* $27,335.

APPLYING
Standardized Tests *Required:* SAT or ACT (for admission).

Options: electronic application, early admission, deferred entrance.

Application fee: $30.

Required: high school transcript, minimum 2.7 GPA.

Application deadlines: rolling (freshmen), rolling (transfers).

Notification: continuous until 8/1 (freshmen), continuous until 8/1 (transfers).

CONTACT
Ms. Destin Tucker, Director of Admission, The University of Tennessee at Martin, 200 Hall-Moody Administration Building, Martin, TN 38238. *Phone:* 731-881-7020. *Toll-free phone:* 800-829-8861. *Fax:* 731-881-7029. *E-mail:* dtucker@utm.edu.

Vanderbilt University
Nashville, Tennessee
http://www.vanderbilt.edu/

- **Independent** university, founded 1873
- **Urban** 330-acre campus with easy access to Nashville, TN
- **Endowment** $3.8 billion
- **Coed** 6,871 undergraduate students, 99% full-time, 51% women, 49% men
- **Most difficult** entrance level, 11% of applicants were admitted

UNDERGRAD STUDENTS
6,817 full-time, 54 part-time. Students come from 53 states and territories; 47 other countries; 90% are from out of state; 9% Black or African American, non-Hispanic/Latino; 9% Hispanic/Latino; 12% Asian, non-Hispanic/Latino; 0.2% Native Hawaiian or other Pacific Islander, non-Hispanic/Latino; 0.5% American Indian or Alaska Native, non-Hispanic/Latino; 5% Two or more races, non-Hispanic/Latino; 5% Race/ethnicity unknown; 7% international; 3% transferred in; 90% live on campus.

Freshmen:
Admission: 32,442 applied, 3,487 admitted, 1,601 enrolled. *Average high school GPA:* 3.8. *Test scores:* SAT evidence-based reading and writing scores over 500: 100%; SAT math scores over 500: 99%; ACT scores over 18: 100%; SAT evidence-based reading and writing scores over 600: 95%; SAT math scores over 600: 94%; ACT scores over 24: 98%; SAT evidence-based reading and writing scores over 700: 80%; SAT math scores over 700: 76%; ACT scores over 30: 91%.
Retention: 97% of full-time freshmen returned.

FACULTY
Total: 1,225, 78% full-time.
Student/faculty ratio: 8:1.

ACADEMICS
Calendar: semesters. *Degrees:* bachelor's, master's, and doctoral.
Special study options: accelerated degree program, advanced placement credit, cooperative education, double majors, English as a second language, honors programs, independent study, internships, off-campus study, services for LD students, student-designed majors, study abroad, summer session for credit. *ROTC:* Army (b), Navy (b), Air Force (c).
Unusual degree programs: 3-2 business administration; engineering; nursing; English, French, German, history, Latin American Studies, mathematics, philosophy, political science, psychology, and medicine, health and society.
Computers: Students can access the following: campus intranet, computer help desk, free student e-mail accounts, online (class) grades, online (class) registration, online (class) schedules, productivity and educational software. Campuswide network is available. Wireless service is available via entire campus.
Library: Jean and Alexander Heard Library plus 7 others. *Books:* 3.1 million (physical), 1.7 million (digital/electronic); *Databases:* 3,700.

STUDENT LIFE
Housing options: on-campus residence required for freshman year; coed, men-only, women-only, special housing for students with disabilities. Campus housing is university owned. Freshman campus housing is guaranteed.
Activities and organizations: drama/theater group, student-run newspaper, radio and television station, choral group, marching band, national fraternities, national sororities.
Athletics Member NCAA. All Division I except football (Division I-A). *Intercollegiate sports:* baseball M(s), basketball M(s)/W(s), bowling W(s), cross-country running M(s)/W(s), golf M(s)/W(s), lacrosse W(s), soccer W(s), swimming and diving M(s)/W(s), tennis M(s)/W(s), track and field W(s). *Intramural sports:* badminton M(c)/W(c), baseball M(c), basketball M(c)/W(c), bowling M(c)/W(c), crew M(c)/W(c), cross-

country running M(c)/W(c), equestrian sports M(c)/W(c), fencing M(c)/W(c), field hockey M(c)/W(c), golf M(c)/W(c), ice hockey M(c), lacrosse M(c)/W(c), racquetball M(c)/W(c), rowing M(c)/W(c), rugby M(c), sailing M(c)/W(c), sand volleyball M/W, soccer M(c)/W(c), softball M/W, squash M(c)/W(c), swimming and diving M(c)/W(c), table tennis M(c)/W(c), tennis M(c)/W(c), track and field M(c)/W(c), triathlon M(c)/W(c), ultimate Frisbee M/W, volleyball M(c)/W(c), water polo M(c)/W(c).
Campus security: 24-hour emergency response devices and patrols, student patrols, late-night transport/escort service, controlled dormitory access.
Student services: health clinic, personal/psychological counseling, women's center.

COSTS & FINANCIAL AID
Costs (2017–18) *One-time required fee:* $865. *Comprehensive fee:* $63,248 includes full-time tuition ($46,500), mandatory fees ($1164), and room and board ($15,584). Part-time tuition: $1938 per credit hour. *College room only:* $10,212. Room and board charges vary according to board plan. *Payment plans:* tuition prepayment, installment. *Waivers:* employees or children of employees.
Financial Aid Of all full-time matriculated undergraduates who enrolled in 2017, 3,878 applied for aid, 3,441 were judged to have need, 3,416 had their need fully met. 1,570 Federal Work-Study jobs (averaging $2386). In 2017, 695 non-need-based awards were made. *Average percent of need met:* 100. *Average financial aid package:* $49,242. *Average need-based loan:* $3534. *Average need-based gift aid:* $47,294. *Average non-need-based aid:* $24,444. *Average indebtedness upon graduation:* $23,973.

APPLYING
Standardized Tests *Required:* SAT or ACT (for admission).
Options: electronic application, early admission, early decision, deferred entrance.
Application fee: $50.
Required: essay or personal statement, high school transcript, 3 letters of recommendation, 3 letters of recommendation (2 from teachers in core subject areas and 1 from counselor).
Application deadlines: 1/1 (freshmen), 3/15 (transfers).
Early decision deadline: 11/1 (for plan 1), 1/1 (for plan 2).
Notification: 4/1 (freshmen), 4/15 (transfers), 12/15 (early decision plan 1), 2/15 (early decision plan 2).

CONTACT
Mr. John O. Gaines, Director of Undergraduate Admissions, Vanderbilt University, 2305 West End Avenue, Nashville, TN 37203. *Phone:* 615-936-2811. *Toll-free phone:* 800-288-0432. *Fax:* 615-343-8326. *E-mail:* admissions@vanderbilt.edu.

See page 1488 for the College Close-Up.

Visible Music College
Memphis, Tennessee
http://visible.edu/

CONTACT
Visible Music College, 200 Madison Avenue, Memphis, TN 38103.

Watkins College of Art, Design, & Film
Nashville, Tennessee
http://www.watkins.edu/

- **Independent** comprehensive, founded 1885
- **Urban** 13-acre campus
- **Endowment** $1.8 million
- **Coed**
- **Moderately difficult** entrance level

FACULTY
Student/faculty ratio: 13:1.

ACADEMICS
Calendar: semesters. *Degrees:* bachelor's and master's.
Library: The Watkins Library plus 1 other.

STUDENT LIFE

Housing options: on-campus residence required for freshman year; men-only, women-only, special housing for students with disabilities. Campus housing is university owned. Freshman applicants given priority for college housing.

Activities and organizations: Company Q (art society), Film club, sports club, Student Government.

Campus security: 24-hour emergency response devices and patrols, late-night transport/escort service, controlled dormitory access, monitored 24 hour camera security.

Student services: health clinic, personal/psychological counseling.

FINANCIAL AID

Financial Aid *Average indebtedness upon graduation:* $15,000.

APPLYING

Standardized Tests *Required:* SAT or ACT (for admission).

Options: electronic application, early admission, deferred entrance.

Application fee: $50.

Required: essay or personal statement, high school transcript, minimum 2.6 GPA, 1 letter of recommendation. *Required for some:* artistic exercises, optional portfolio. *Recommended:* interview.

CONTACT

Ms. Jaime Raybin, Recruiter, Watkins College of Art, Design, & Film, 2298 Rosa L. Parks Boulevard, Nashville, TN 37228. *Phone:* 615-383-4848 Ext. 5397. *Fax:* 615-383-4849. *E-mail:* admissions@watkins.edu.

Welch College

Gallatin, Tennessee

http://www.welch.edu/

- **Independent Free Will Baptist** comprehensive, founded 1942
- **Suburban** 120-acre campus with easy access to Nashville
- **Endowment** $2.5 million
- **Coed** 327 undergraduate students, 67% full-time, 47% women, 53% men
- **Noncompetitive** entrance level, 69% of applicants were admitted

UNDERGRAD STUDENTS

220 full-time, 107 part-time. Students come from 23 states and territories; 1 other country; 58% are from out of state; 9% Black or African American, non-Hispanic/Latino; 3% Hispanic/Latino; 1% Asian, non-Hispanic/Latino; 0.3% American Indian or Alaska Native, non-Hispanic/Latino; 1% Two or more races, non-Hispanic/Latino; 8% international; 6% transferred in.

Freshmen:

Admission: 115 applied, 79 admitted, 45 enrolled. *Average high school GPA:* 3.3.

Retention: 66% of full-time freshmen returned.

FACULTY

Total: 58, 28% full-time, 43% with terminal degrees.

Student/faculty ratio: 8:1.

ACADEMICS

Calendar: semesters. *Degrees:* associate, bachelor's, and master's.

Special study options: academic remediation for entering students, adult/continuing education programs, advanced placement credit, distance learning, double majors, external degree program, independent study, internships, part-time degree program, student-designed majors, summer session for credit. *ROTC:* Army (c), Air Force (c).

Unusual degree programs: nursing.

Computers: 15 computers/terminals are available on campus for general student use. Students can access the following: campus intranet, computer help desk, free student e-mail accounts, online (class) grades, online (class) schedules. Campuswide network is available. 100% of college-owned or -operated housing units are wired for high-speed Internet access. Wireless service is available via entire campus.

Library: Welch Library. *Books:* 64,478 (physical), 48,741 (digital/electronic); *Databases:* 56.

STUDENT LIFE

Housing options: on-campus residence required through senior year; men-only, women-only. Campus housing is university owned. Freshman campus housing is guaranteed.

Activities and organizations: drama/theater group, choral group, GMF-Global Missions Fellowship, Four Women's Societies, Four Men's Societies.

Athletics Member NCCAA. *Intercollegiate sports:* basketball M/W, cross-country running M/W, golf M/W, volleyball W. *Intramural sports:* basketball M/W, tennis M/W, ultimate Frisbee M/W, volleyball M/W.

Campus security: 24-hour emergency response devices, student patrols, late-night transport/escort service, controlled dormitory access.

Student services: personal/psychological counseling.

COSTS & FINANCIAL AID

Costs (2018–19) *Comprehensive fee:* $26,716 includes full-time tuition ($19,012) and room and board ($7704). Full-time tuition and fees vary according to location. Part-time tuition: $630 per credit hour. Part-time tuition and fees vary according to location. *College room only:* $2926. Room and board charges vary according to board plan. *Payment plans:* installment, deferred payment. *Waivers:* employees or children of employees.

Financial Aid Of all full-time matriculated undergraduates who enrolled in 2011, 178 applied for aid, 172 were judged to have need. 7 Federal Work-Study jobs (averaging $1871). 101 state and other part-time jobs (averaging $1960). *Average percent of need met:* 71. *Average financial aid package:* $5331. *Average need-based loan:* $2195. *Average need-based gift aid:* $4214. *Average indebtedness upon graduation:* $19,688.

APPLYING

Standardized Tests *Required:* SAT or ACT (for admission).

Options: electronic application, early admission, deferred entrance.

Application fee: $35.

Required: essay or personal statement, high school transcript, 3 letters of recommendation, medical history.

Application deadlines: rolling (freshmen), rolling (out-of-state freshmen), rolling (transfers).

Notification: continuous (freshmen), continuous (out-of-state freshmen), continuous (transfers).

CONTACT

Mr. Daniel Webster, Director of Enrollment Services, Welch College, 1045 Bison Trail, Gallatin, TN 37066. *Phone:* 615-675-5295. *Toll-free phone:* 800-763-9222. *Fax:* 615-296-0400. *E-mail:* daniel.webster@welch.edu.

Williamson College

Franklin, Tennessee

http://www.williamsoncc.edu/

- **Independent interdenominational** comprehensive, founded 1997
- **Suburban** 1-acre campus with easy access to Nashville
- **Coed**
- **Noncompetitive** entrance level

FACULTY

Student/faculty ratio: 7:1.

ACADEMICS

Calendar: semesters. *Degrees:* associate, bachelor's, and master's.

Library: John W. Neth, Jr. Library plus 1 other. *Books:* 4,836 (physical); *Serial titles:* 11,203 (digital/electronic); *Databases:* 70. Weekly public service hours: 40; students can reserve study rooms.

STUDENT LIFE

Housing options: college housing not available.

Activities and organizations: Student Government Association.

Campus security: 24-hour emergency response devices.

Student services: health clinic, personal/psychological counseling.

COSTS & FINANCIAL AID

Costs (2017–18) *One-time required fee:* $150. *Tuition:* $12,150 full-time, $425 per semester hour part-time. *Required fees:* $600 full-time.

COLLEGES AT-A-GLANCE

Financial Aid Of all full-time matriculated undergraduates who enrolled in 2003, 11 applied for aid, 10 were judged to have need, 1 had their need fully met. 2 Federal Work-Study jobs (averaging $2000). *Average percent of need met:* 50. *Average financial aid package:* $4858. *Average need-based gift aid:* $2556.

APPLYING
Standardized Tests *Required for some:* SAT or ACT (for admission).

Options: early admission, deferred entrance.

Application fee: $25.

Required: essay or personal statement, high school transcript, minimum 2.0 GPA, 1 letter of recommendation. *Required for some:* interview.

CONTACT
Ms. Laura Flowers, Admissions Coordinator, Williamson College, 274 Mallory Station Road, Franklin, TN 37067. *Phone:* 615-771-7821. *Fax:* 615-771-7810. *E-mail:* laura@williamsoncc.edu.

TEXAS

Abilene Christian University

Abilene, Texas
http://www.acu.edu/

- **Independent** university, founded 1906, affiliated with Church of Christ
- **Urban** 262-acre campus
- **Endowment** $384.6 million
- **Coed** 3,670 undergraduate students, 96% full-time, 58% women, 42% men
- **Moderately difficult** entrance level, 51% of applicants were admitted

UNDERGRAD STUDENTS
3,512 full-time, 158 part-time. Students come from 50 states and territories; 42 other countries; 11% are from out of state; 9% Black or African American, non-Hispanic/Latino; 17% Hispanic/Latino; 1% Asian, non-Hispanic/Latino; 0.1% Native Hawaiian or other Pacific Islander, non-Hispanic/Latino; 0.3% American Indian or Alaska Native, non-Hispanic/Latino; 5% Two or more races, non-Hispanic/Latino; 0.2% Race/ethnicity unknown; 4% international; 3% transferred in; 47% live on campus.

Freshmen:
Admission: 10,252 applied, 5,217 admitted, 972 enrolled. *Average high school GPA:* 3.6. *Test scores:* SAT evidence-based reading and writing scores over 500: 81%; SAT math scores over 500: 81%; ACT scores over 18: 96%; SAT evidence-based reading and writing scores over 600: 37%; SAT math scores over 600: 28%; ACT scores over 24: 51%; SAT evidence-based reading and writing scores over 700: 5%; SAT math scores over 700: 3%; ACT scores over 30: 8%.
Retention: 77% of full-time freshmen returned.

FACULTY
Total: 449, 59% full-time, 61% with terminal degrees.
Student/faculty ratio: 13:1.

ACADEMICS
Calendar: semesters. *Degrees:* certificates, associate, bachelor's, master's, doctoral, post-master's, and postbachelor's certificates.

Special study options: advanced placement credit, distance learning, double majors, English as a second language, honors programs, independent study, internships, off-campus study, part-time degree program, services for LD students, student-designed majors, study abroad, summer session for credit.

Unusual degree programs: 3-2 animal health professions.

Computers: 466 computers/terminals and 3,900 ports are available on campus for general student use. Students can access the following: campus intranet, computer help desk, free student e-mail accounts, online (class) grades, online (class) registration, online (class) schedules. Campuswide network is available. 100% of college-owned or -operated housing units are wired for high-speed Internet access. Wireless service is available via entire campus.

Library: Brown Library. *Books:* 406,890 (physical), 347,095 (digital/electronic); *Serial titles:* 20,683 (physical), 52,058 (digital/electronic); *Databases:* 109. Weekly public service hours: 97; students can reserve study rooms.

STUDENT LIFE
Housing options: on-campus residence required through sophomore year; men-only, women-only. Campus housing is university owned. Freshman campus housing is guaranteed.

Activities and organizations: drama/theater group, student-run newspaper, radio and television station, choral group, marching band, Student Association, Graduate Students Association, Spring Break Campaigns, International Students Association, LYNAY.

Athletics Member NCAA. All Division I. *Intercollegiate sports:* baseball M(s), basketball M(s)/W(s), cross-country running M(s)/W(s), football M(s), golf M(s), sand volleyball W, soccer W(s), softball W(s), tennis M(s)/W(s), track and field M(s)/W(s), volleyball W(s). *Intramural sports:* basketball M/W, football M/W, golf M(c)/W(c), lacrosse M(c), racquetball M/W, rugby M(c), soccer M(c)/W, softball M/W, table tennis M/W, tennis M/W, volleyball M/W.

Campus security: 24-hour emergency response devices and patrols, student patrols, late-night transport/escort service, controlled dormitory access.

Student services: health clinic, personal/psychological counseling.

COSTS & FINANCIAL AID
Costs (2017–18) *Comprehensive fee:* $43,708 includes full-time tuition ($33,280), mandatory fees ($50), and room and board ($10,378). Full-time tuition and fees vary according to course load. Part-time tuition: $1338 per credit hour. Part-time tuition and fees vary according to course load. *College room only:* $5186. Room and board charges vary according to board plan and housing facility. *Payment plans:* tuition prepayment, installment. *Waivers:* employees or children of employees.

Financial Aid Of all full-time matriculated undergraduates who enrolled in 2017, 2,877 applied for aid, 2,379 were judged to have need, 633 had their need fully met. In 2017, 1157 non-need-based awards were made. *Average percent of need met:* 67. *Average financial aid package:* $23,433. *Average need-based loan:* $4489. *Average need-based gift aid:* $20,532. *Average non-need-based aid:* $13,365.

APPLYING
Standardized Tests *Required:* SAT or ACT (for admission).

Options: electronic application, early admission, early action.

Application fee: $50.

Required: high school transcript. *Required for some:* essay or personal statement.

Application deadlines: 2/15 (freshmen), rolling (transfers).

Notification: 3/15 (freshmen), continuous until 9/1 (transfers).

CONTACT
Admissions, Abilene Christian University, ACU Box 29000, Abilene, TX 79699-9000. *Phone:* 325-674-2650. *Toll-free phone:* 800-460-6228. *Fax:* 325-674-2130. *E-mail:* info@admissions.acu.edu.

Amberton University

Garland, Texas
http://www.amberton.edu/

CONTACT
Academic Dean, Amberton University, 1700 Eastgate Drive, Garland, TX 75041-5595. *Phone:* 972-279-6511. *E-mail:* advisor@amberton.edu.

American InterContinental University Houston

Houston, Texas
http://www.aiuniv.edu/

CONTACT
American InterContinental University Houston, 9999 Richmond Avenue, Houston, TX 77042. *Phone:* 877-564-6248. *Toll-free phone:* 888-607-9888.

Angelo State University

San Angelo, Texas

http://www.angelo.edu/

- **State-supported** comprehensive, founded 1928, part of Texas Tech University System
- **Urban** 268-acre campus
- **Endowment** $158.8 million
- **Coed** 8,798 undergraduate students, 61% full-time, 56% women, 44% men
- **Moderately difficult** entrance level, 74% of applicants were admitted

UNDERGRAD STUDENTS

5,377 full-time, 3,421 part-time. Students come from 37 states and territories; 25 other countries; 3% are from out of state; 6% Black or African American, non-Hispanic/Latino; 35% Hispanic/Latino; 1% Asian, non-Hispanic/Latino; 0.1% Native Hawaiian or other Pacific Islander, non-Hispanic/Latino; 0.5% American Indian or Alaska Native, non-Hispanic/Latino; 3% Two or more races, non-Hispanic/Latino; 0.1% Race/ethnicity unknown; 2% international; 5% transferred in; 35% live on campus.

Freshmen:

Admission: 4,316 applied, 3,174 admitted, 1,431 enrolled. *Test scores:* ACT scores over 18: 70%; ACT scores over 24: 34%; ACT scores over 30: 2%.

Retention: 67% of full-time freshmen returned.

FACULTY

Total: 412, 72% full-time, 63% with terminal degrees.

Student/faculty ratio: 20:1.

ACADEMICS

Calendar: semesters. *Degrees:* certificates, bachelor's, master's, and doctoral.

Special study options: academic remediation for entering students, advanced placement credit, distance learning, double majors, English as a second language, honors programs, independent study, internships, part-time degree program, study abroad, summer session for credit. *ROTC:* Air Force (b).

Unusual degree programs: 3-2 business administration.

Computers: 750 computers/terminals and 3,900 ports are available on campus for general student use. Students can access the following: campus intranet, computer help desk, free student e-mail accounts, online (class) grades, online (class) registration, online (class) schedules, online courses, tuition payments, book purchase, parking permits, university calendar, discounted hardware and software. Campuswide network is available. 100% of college-owned or -operated housing units are wired for high-speed Internet access. Wireless service is available via entire campus.

Library: Porter Henderson Library. *Books:* 487,297 (physical), 85,488 (digital/electronic); *Serial titles:* 108 (physical), 77,153 (digital/electronic); *Databases:* 237. Weekly public service hours: 137; study areas open 24 hours, 5–7 days a week; students can reserve study rooms.

STUDENT LIFE

Housing options: on-campus residence required through sophomore year; coed, special housing for students with disabilities. Campus housing is university owned.

Activities and organizations: drama/theater group, student-run newspaper, radio and television station, choral group, marching band, Association of Mexican-American Students, Block and Bridle Club, Air force ROTC, University Center Program Council, Baptist Student Union, national fraternities, national sororities.

Athletics Member NCAA. All Division II. *Intercollegiate sports:* baseball M(s), basketball M(s)/W(s), cross-country running M(s)/W(s), football M(s), golf W(s), soccer W(s), softball W(s), tennis W, track and field M(s)/W(s), volleyball W(s). *Intramural sports:* badminton M/W, basketball M/W, bowling M/W, football M/W, golf M/W, racquetball M/W, soccer M/W, softball M/W, swimming and diving M/W, table tennis M/W, tennis M/W, ultimate Frisbee M/W, volleyball M/W, weight lifting M/W.

Campus security: 24-hour emergency response devices and patrols, student patrols, late-night transport/escort service, controlled dormitory access.

Student services: health clinic, personal/psychological counseling.

COSTS & FINANCIAL AID

Costs (2017–18) *Tuition:* state resident $5076 full-time, $169 per credit hour part-time; nonresident $17,526 full-time, $584 per credit hour part-time. Full-time tuition and fees vary according to course load. Part-time tuition and fees vary according to course load. No tuition increase for student's term of enrollment. *Required fees:* $3139 full-time. *Room and board:* $7666. Room and board charges vary according to board plan and housing facility. *Payment plan:* installment.

Financial Aid Of all full-time matriculated undergraduates who enrolled in 2016, 4,039 applied for aid, 3,371 were judged to have need, 522 had their need fully met. In 2016, 971 non-need-based awards were made. *Average percent of need met:* 84. *Average financial aid package:* $10,567. *Average need-based loan:* $3822. *Average need-based gift aid:* $2905. *Average non-need-based aid:* $3788. *Average indebtedness upon graduation:* $24,926.

APPLYING

Standardized Tests *Required:* SAT or ACT (for admission).

Options: electronic application, early admission, deferred entrance.

Application fee: $35.

Required: high school transcript, high school class rank.

Application deadlines: rolling (freshmen), rolling (transfers).

Notification: continuous (freshmen), continuous (transfers).

CONTACT

Ms. Sharla Adam, Director of Admissions, Angelo State University, 2601 West Avenue N., San Angelo, TX 76909. *Phone:* 325-942-2185. *Toll-free phone:* 800-946-8627. *Fax:* 325-942-2078. *E-mail:* admissions@ angelo.edu.

Argosy University, Dallas

Farmers Branch, Texas

http://www.argosy.edu/dallas-texas/default.aspx

CONTACT

Argosy University, Dallas, 5001 Lyndon B. Johnson Freeway, Heritage Square, Farmers Branch, TX 75244. *Phone:* 214-890-9900. *Toll-free phone:* 866-954-9900.

Arlington Baptist University

Arlington, Texas

http://www.abu.edu/

- **Independent Baptist** comprehensive, founded 1939
- **Urban** 32-acre campus with easy access to Dallas-Fort Worth
- **Endowment** $17,000
- **Coed** 164 undergraduate students, 88% full-time, 45% women, 55% men
- **Noncompetitive** entrance level, 59% of applicants were admitted

UNDERGRAD STUDENTS

145 full-time, 19 part-time. Students come from 5 states and territories; 1 other country; 6% are from out of state; 24% Black or African American, non-Hispanic/Latino; 17% Hispanic/Latino; 0.6% Asian, non-Hispanic/Latino; 0.6% Native Hawaiian or other Pacific Islander, non-Hispanic/Latino; 1% American Indian or Alaska Native, non-Hispanic/Latino; 1% Race/ethnicity unknown; 0.6% international; 35% live on campus.

Freshmen:

Admission: 126 applied, 74 admitted.

Retention: 35% of full-time freshmen returned.

FACULTY

Total: 32, 34% full-time, 25% with terminal degrees.

Student/faculty ratio: 9:1.

ACADEMICS

Calendar: semesters. *Degrees:* bachelor's and master's.

STUDENT LIFE

Housing options: on-campus residence required through junior year; coed, men-only, women-only, special housing for students with disabilities. Campus housing is university owned. Freshman campus housing is guaranteed.

Activities and organizations: drama/theater group, student-run newspaper, choral group, Inter-Varsity Christian Fellowship (IVCF), Campus Activity Board (CAB), Indian Cultural Association, Students Today Alumni Tomorrow (STAT), ACtivators.

Athletics Member NCAA. All Division III. *Intercollegiate sports:* baseball M, basketball M/W, cheerleading M(c)/W(c), cross-country running M/W, football M, soccer M/W, softball W, swimming and diving M/W, tennis M/W, volleyball W, water polo M(c)/W(c). *Intramural sports:* basketball M/W, football M/W, soccer M/W, softball W, ultimate Frisbee M/W, volleyball M/W.

Campus security: 24-hour emergency response devices and patrols, late-night transport/escort service, controlled dormitory access.

Student services: health clinic, personal/psychological counseling.

COSTS & FINANCIAL AID

Costs (2017–18) *One-time required fee:* $25. *Comprehensive fee:* $51,344 includes full-time tuition ($38,825), mandatory fees ($185), and room and board ($12,334). Full-time tuition and fees vary according to student level. Part-time tuition: $5495 per course. *Required fees:* $93 per term part-time. *College room only:* $5750. Room and board charges vary according to board plan and housing facility. *Payment plan:* installment. *Waivers:* employees or children of employees.

Financial Aid Of all full-time matriculated undergraduates who enrolled in 2016, 952 applied for aid, 834 were judged to have need, 354 had their need fully met. 345 Federal Work-Study jobs (averaging $1844). 119 state and other part-time jobs (averaging $1464). In 2016, 423 non-need-based awards were made. *Average percent of need met:* 94. *Average financial aid package:* $34,859. *Average need-based loan:* $4792. *Average need-based gift aid:* $29,091. *Average non-need-based aid:* $22,355.

APPLYING

Standardized Tests *Required:* SAT or ACT (for admission).

Options: electronic application, early admission, early decision, early action, deferred entrance.

Required: essay or personal statement, high school transcript, 2 letters of recommendation. *Recommended:* minimum 3.0 GPA, interview.

Application deadlines: 3/1 (freshmen), 8/1 (transfers), 12/1 (early action).

Early decision deadline: 11/1 (for plan 1), 1/15 (for plan 2).

Notification: 4/1 (freshmen), 12/4 (early decision plan 1), 3/1 (early decision plan 2), 1/15 (early action).

CONTACT

Mrs. Nan Davis, Vice President for Institutional Enrollment, Austin College, 900 North Grand Avenue, Suite 6N, Sherman, TX 75090-4400. *Phone:* 903-813-3000. *Toll-free phone:* 800-596-4276 (in-state); 800-526-4276 (out-of-state). *Fax:* 903-813-3198. *E-mail:* admission@austincollege.edu.

Austin Graduate School of Theology

Austin, Texas
http://www.austingrad.edu/

- **Independent** upper-level, founded 1917, affiliated with Church of Christ
- **Urban** 2-acre campus with easy access to Austin
- **Endowment** $4.6 million
- **Coed** 22 undergraduate students, 18% full-time, 23% women, 77% men
- **Minimally difficult** entrance level

UNDERGRAD STUDENTS

4 full-time, 18 part-time. Students come from 1 other state; 1 other country; 1% are from out of state; 41% Black or African American, non-Hispanic/Latino; 14% Hispanic/Latino; 14% Race/ethnicity unknown.

FACULTY

Total: 10, 40% full-time, 80% with terminal degrees.

Student/faculty ratio: 4:1.

ACADEMICS

Calendar: semesters. *Degrees:* bachelor's and master's.

Special study options: adult/continuing education programs, part-time degree program, summer session for credit.

Computers: 6 computers/terminals are available on campus for general student use. Campuswide network is available. Wireless service is available via entire campus.

Library: David Worley Library.

STUDENT LIFE

Housing options: college housing not available.

Activities and organizations: Student Association (government).

COSTS

Costs (2017–18) *Tuition:* $8400 full-time, $350 per credit hour part-time. *Required fees:* $350 full-time, $175 per term part-time. *Payment plan:* installment.

APPLYING

Options: electronic application, early admission, deferred entrance.

CONTACT

Dawn Bond, Director of Admissions, Austin Graduate School of Theology, 7640 Guadalupe Street, Austin, TX 78752. *Phone:* 512-476-2772. *Toll-free phone:* 866-AUS-GRAD. *Fax:* 512-476-3919. *E-mail:* registrar@austingrad.edu.

Baptist Health System School of Health Professions

San Antonio, Texas
http://www.bshp.edu/

CONTACT

Baptist Health System School of Health Professions, 8400 Datapoint Drive, San Antonio, TX 78229.

Baptist Missionary Association Theological Seminary

Jacksonville, Texas
http://www.bmats.edu/

CONTACT

Baptist Missionary Association Theological Seminary, 1530 East Pine Street, Jacksonville, TX 75766-5407. *Phone:* 903-586-2501 Ext. 229. *Toll-free phone:* 800-259-5673.

Baptist University of the Americas

San Antonio, Texas
http://www.bua.edu/

- **Independent Baptist** 4-year, founded 1947
- **Urban** 75-acre campus with easy access to San Antonio
- **Endowment** $2.1 million
- **Coed** 195 undergraduate students, 66% full-time, 48% women, 52% men

UNDERGRAD STUDENTS

128 full-time, 67 part-time. Students come from 3 states and territories; 14 other countries; 21% are from out of state; 2% Black or African American, non-Hispanic/Latino; 70% Hispanic/Latino; 1% Asian, non-Hispanic/Latino; 21% international; 9% transferred in; 40% live on campus.

Freshmen:

Admission: 30 enrolled.

Retention: 87% of full-time freshmen returned.

FACULTY

Total: 36, 22% full-time, 39% with terminal degrees.

Student/faculty ratio: 8:1.

ACADEMICS

Calendar: semesters May term is a two week intensive course. *Degrees:* certificates, diplomas, associate, and bachelor's (associate degree in Cross-Cultural Studies).

Special study options: academic remediation for entering students, advanced placement credit, distance learning, double majors, English as a second language, independent study, internships, off-campus study, part-time degree program, services for LD students.

Computers: 122 computers/terminals and 328 ports are available on campus for general student use. Students can access the following: campus intranet, computer help desk, free student e-mail accounts, online (class) grades, online (class) registration, online (class) schedules. Campuswide network is available. 100% of college-owned or -operated housing units are wired for high-speed Internet access. Wireless service is available via entire campus.

Library: Baptist University of the Americas Learning Resource Center. *Books:* 21,947 (physical), 362 (digital/electronic); *Serial titles:* 252 (physical), 252 (digital/electronic); *Databases:* 8. Weekly public service hours: 72; students can reserve study rooms.

STUDENT LIFE

Housing options: coed, men-only, women-only, special housing for students with disabilities. Campus housing is university owned.

Activities and organizations: choral group, Called Club, Spanish Club, Missions Society, Business Society, BUA Band.

Athletics *Intramural sports:* soccer M(c).

Campus security: 24-hour emergency response devices, student patrols, late-night transport/escort service, gate code required to enter the residence area.

Student services: personal/psychological counseling.

COSTS & FINANCIAL AID

Costs (2017–18) *Comprehensive fee:* $13,910 includes full-time tuition ($5520), mandatory fees ($720), and room and board ($7670). Part-time tuition: $230 per credit hour. *Required fees:* $30 per credit hour part-time. *College room only:* $2500. Room and board charges vary according to housing facility. *Payment plan:* installment. *Waivers:* employees or children of employees.

Financial Aid Of all full-time matriculated undergraduates who enrolled in 2016, 4 Federal Work-Study jobs (averaging $1312). 131 state and other part-time jobs (averaging $2257).

APPLYING

Standardized Tests *Required:* SAT and SAT Subject Tests or ACT (for admission), ACCUPLACER, THEA (Texas Higher Education Assessment), CPT (Computer Proficiency Test)and TSI (for admission). *Recommended:* SAT (for admission), ACT (for admission), SAT or ACT (for admission).

Required: essay or personal statement, high school transcript, minimum 2.0 GPA, 2 letters of recommendation, meningitis vaccination for students under 22 years. *Required for some:* minimum 2.0 GPA, 2 letters of recommendation, interview. *Recommended:* minimum 2.0 GPA, 2 letters of recommendation.

CONTACT

Admissions Counselor, Baptist University of the Americas, 8019 Pan Am Expressway, San Antonio, TX 78224. *Phone:* 210-924-4338 Ext. 229. *Toll-free phone:* 800-721-1396. *Fax:* 210-924-2701. *E-mail:* admissions@bua.edu.

Baylor University

Waco, Texas

http://www.baylor.edu/

- **Independent Baptist** university, founded 1845
- **Urban** 1000-acre campus with easy access to Dallas-Fort Worth
- **Endowment** $1.2 billion
- **Coed** 14,316 undergraduate students, 98% full-time, 59% women, 41% men
- **Moderately difficult** entrance level, 39% of applicants were admitted

UNDERGRAD STUDENTS

14,100 full-time, 216 part-time. Students come from 51 states and territories; 75 other countries; 30% are from out of state; 6% Black or African American, non-Hispanic/Latino; 15% Hispanic/Latino; 6% Asian, non-Hispanic/Latino; 0.4% American Indian or Alaska Native, non-Hispanic/Latino; 5% Two or more races, non-Hispanic/Latino; 0.3% Race/ethnicity unknown; 3% international; 3% transferred in; 35% live on campus.

Freshmen:

Admission: 37,083 applied, 14,442 admitted, 3,320 enrolled. *Test scores:* SAT evidence-based reading and writing scores over 500: 98%; SAT math scores over 500: 99%; ACT scores over 18: 99%; SAT evidence-based reading and writing scores over 600: 78%; SAT math scores over 600: 71%; ACT scores over 24: 93%; SAT evidence-based reading and writing scores over 700: 18%; SAT math scores over 700: 20%; ACT scores over 30: 37%.

Retention: 90% of full-time freshmen returned.

FACULTY

Total: 1,352, 78% full-time, 65% with terminal degrees.

Student/faculty ratio: 14:1.

ACADEMICS

Calendar: semesters. *Degrees:* bachelor's, master's, doctoral, and post-master's certificates.

Special study options: accelerated degree program, advanced placement credit, double majors, honors programs, internships, part-time degree program, services for LD students, student-designed majors, study abroad, summer session for credit. *ROTC:* Army (b), Air Force (b).

Unusual degree programs: 3-2 clinical laboratory science.

Computers: Students can access the following: campus intranet, computer help desk, free student e-mail accounts, online (class) grades, online (class) registration, online (class) schedules. Campuswide network is available. 99% of college-owned or -operated housing units are wired for high-speed Internet access. Wireless service is available via entire campus.

Library: Moody Memorial Library plus 8 others.

STUDENT LIFE

Housing options: on-campus residence required for freshman year; coed, men-only, women-only, cooperative, special housing for students with disabilities. Campus housing is university owned. Freshman campus housing is guaranteed.

Activities and organizations: drama/theater group, student-run newspaper, radio and television station, choral group, marching band, national fraternities, national sororities.

Athletics Member NCAA. All Division I except football (Division I-A). *Intercollegiate sports:* baseball M(s), basketball M(s)/W(s), cheerleading M(s)/W(s), cross-country running M(s)/W(s), equestrian sports W(s), golf M(s)/W(s), soccer W(s), softball W(s), tennis M(s)/W(s), track and field M(s)/W(s), volleyball W(s). *Intramural sports:* baseball M(c), basketball M/W, bowling M/W, crew M(c)/W(c), cross-country running M/W, fencing M(c)/W(c), football M/W, golf M(c), gymnastics M(c)/W(c), lacrosse M(c)/W(c), racquetball M/W, rock climbing M(c)/W(c), rowing M(c)/W(c), rugby M(c)/W(c), sailing (downhill) M(c)/W(c), skiing (downhill) M(c)/W(c), soccer M(c)/W(c), softball M/W, swimming and diving M(c)/W(c), table tennis M/W, tennis M(c)/W(c), track and field M/W, triathlon M(c)/W(c), ultimate Frisbee M(c)/W(c), volleyball M(c), water polo M(c)/W(c).

Campus security: 24-hour emergency response devices and patrols, late-night transport/escort service, controlled dormitory access, bicycle patrols.

Student services: health clinic, personal/psychological counseling, legal services.

COSTS & FINANCIAL AID

Costs (2018–19) *Comprehensive fee:* $58,137 includes full-time tuition ($41,194), mandatory fees ($4348), and room and board ($12,595). Part-time tuition: $1716 per semester hour. *Required fees:* $181 per semester hour part-time. *College room only:* $6920. Room and board charges vary according to board plan and housing facility. *Payment plan:* installment. *Waivers:* employees or children of employees.

Financial Aid Of all full-time matriculated undergraduates who enrolled in 2017, 9,305 applied for aid, 7,862 were judged to have need, 1,177 had their need fully met. 5,562 Federal Work-Study jobs (averaging $2937). In 2017, 5093 non-need-based awards were made. *Average percent of need met:* 67. *Average financial aid package:* $30,498. *Average need-based loan:* $3580. *Average need-based gift aid:* $24,420. *Average non-need-based aid:* $15,059. *Average indebtedness upon graduation:* $44,859.

APPLYING

Standardized Tests *Required:* SAT or ACT (for admission).

Options: electronic application, early admission, early action, deferred entrance.

Required: high school transcript. *Required for some:* essay or personal statement, minimum 2.5 GPA, 2 letters of recommendation.

Application deadlines: 2/1 (freshmen), rolling (transfers), 11/1 (early action).

Notification: 4/10 (freshmen), continuous (transfers), 1/15 (early action).

CONTACT
Ms. Jessica King Gereghty, Assistant Vice President of Undergraduate Admissions, Baylor University, PO Box 97056, Waco, TX 76798. *Phone:* 254-710-3435. *Toll-free phone:* 800-BAYLORU. *Fax:* 254-710-3436. *E-mail:* admissions@baylor.edu.

Brazosport College
Lake Jackson, Texas
http://www.brazosport.edu/

CONTACT
Brazosport College, 500 College Drive, Lake Jackson, TX 77566-3199. *Phone:* 979-230-3020.

Chamberlain College of Nursing
Houston, Texas
http://www.chamberlain.edu/

- **Proprietary** 4-year
- **Coed**
- **Moderately difficult** entrance level

FACULTY
Student/faculty ratio: 5:1.

ACADEMICS
Degree: bachelor's.

STUDENT LIFE
Housing options: college housing not available.

COSTS
Costs (2017–18) *Tuition:* $18,900 full-time. *Required fees:* $600 full-time.

APPLYING
Standardized Tests *Required:* SAT or ACT (for admission).

Options: deferred entrance.

Application fee: $95.

CONTACT
Director of Recruitment, Chamberlain College of Nursing, 11025 Equity Drive, Houston, TX 77041. *Phone:* 713-277-9800. *Toll-free phone:* 877-751-5783.

Chamberlain College of Nursing
Irving, Texas
http://www.chamberlain.edu/

CONTACT
Chamberlain College of Nursing, 4800 Regent Boulevard, Irving, TX 75063. *Toll-free phone:* 866-593-8669.

Chamberlain College of Nursing
Pearland, Texas
http://www.chamberlain.edu/

- **Proprietary** 4-year
- **Coed**

FACULTY
Student/faculty ratio: 9:1.

ACADEMICS
Degree: bachelor's.

STUDENT LIFE
Housing options: college housing not available.

COSTS
Costs (2017–18) *Tuition:* $18,900 full-time. *Required fees:* $600 full-time.

APPLYING
Standardized Tests *Required:* SAT or ACT (for admission).

Options: deferred entrance.

Application fee: $95.

CONTACT
Chamberlain College of Nursing, 12000 Shadow Creek Parkway, Pearland, TX 77584. *Toll-free phone:* 877-751-5783.

College of Biblical Studies–Houston
Houston, Texas
http://www.cbshouston.edu/

- **Independent nondenominational** 4-year, founded 1976
- **Urban** 14-acre campus with easy access to Houston
- **Endowment** $656,713
- **Coed** 428 undergraduate students, 15% full-time, 46% women, 54% men
- **Noncompetitive** entrance level

UNDERGRAD STUDENTS
66 full-time, 362 part-time. Students come from 2 states and territories; 42% Black or African American, non-Hispanic/Latino; 28% Hispanic/Latino; 1% Asian, non-Hispanic/Latino; 3% Two or more races, non-Hispanic/Latino; 1% Race/ethnicity unknown; 71% transferred in.

Freshmen:
Admission: 33 enrolled.
Retention: 50% of full-time freshmen returned.

FACULTY
Total: 48, 33% full-time, 38% with terminal degrees.
Student/faculty ratio: 10:1.

ACADEMICS
Calendar: semesters. *Degrees:* certificates, associate, and bachelor's.

Special study options: academic remediation for entering students, accelerated degree program, adult/continuing education programs, cooperative education, distance learning, double majors, English as a second language, independent study, off-campus study, part-time degree program, services for LD students, summer session for credit.

Computers: 50 computers/terminals and 24 ports are available on campus for general student use. Students can access the following: computer help desk, free student e-mail accounts, online (class) grades, online (class) registration, online (class) schedules. Campuswide network is available. Wireless service is available via entire campus.

Library: College of Biblical Studies Library. *Books:* 88,005 (physical), 161,601 (digital/electronic); *Serial titles:* 476 (physical), 5,325 (digital/electronic). Weekly public service hours: 53; students can reserve study rooms.

STUDENT LIFE
Housing options: college housing not available.

Activities and organizations: choral group, Student Ministries.

Campus security: 24-hour emergency response devices, late-night transport/escort service, hourly patrols by trained security guards and police.

Student services: personal/psychological counseling.

COSTS & FINANCIAL AID
Costs (2018–19) *Tuition:* $6576 full-time, $274 per credit hour part-time. Full-time tuition and fees vary according to program. Part-time tuition and fees vary according to program. *Required fees:* $370 full-time, $185 per term part-time. *Payment plans:* installment, deferred payment. *Waivers:* employees or children of employees.

Financial Aid *Financial aid deadline:* 8/5.

APPLYING
Options: electronic application.

Application fee: $40.

Required: essay or personal statement, high school transcript. *Required for some:* interview.

Application deadlines: rolling (freshmen), rolling (transfers).

CONTACT
Admissions Office, College of Biblical Studies–Houston, 7000 Regency Square Boulevard, Houston, TX 77036. *Phone:* 713-772-4253. *Toll-free phone:* 844-227-9673. *E-mail:* admissions@cbshouston.edu.

Concordia University Texas
Austin, Texas
http://www.concordia.edu/

CONTACT
Ms. Kristin Coulter, Director of Admissions, Concordia University Texas, 11400 Concordia University Drive, Austin, TX 78726. *Phone:* 800-865-4282. *Toll-free phone:* 800-865-4282. *Fax:* 512-313-3999. *E-mail:* admissions@concordia.edu.

Criswell College
Dallas, Texas
http://www.criswell.edu/

- **Independent** comprehensive, founded 1970, affiliated with Southern Baptist Convention
- **Urban** campus with easy access to Dallas-Fort Worth
- **Endowment** $15.0 million
- **Coed** 198 undergraduate students, 52% full-time, 33% women, 67% men
- **Minimally difficult** entrance level, 93% of applicants were admitted

UNDERGRAD STUDENTS
103 full-time, 95 part-time. 2% are from out of state; 14% Black or African American, non-Hispanic/Latino; 14% Hispanic/Latino; 1% Asian, non-Hispanic/Latino; 8% Two or more races, non-Hispanic/Latino; 9% Race/ethnicity unknown; 3% international; 12% transferred in.

Freshmen:
Admission: 27 applied, 25 admitted, 17 enrolled. *Average high school GPA:* 3.2. *Test scores:* SAT evidence-based reading and writing scores over 500: 50%; SAT math scores over 500: 38%; ACT scores over 18: 80%; SAT evidence-based reading and writing scores over 600: 38%; SAT math scores over 600: 25%; ACT scores over 24: 20%; SAT evidence-based reading and writing scores over 700: 13%; SAT math scores over 700: 13%.

Retention: 92% of full-time freshmen returned.

FACULTY
Total: 31, 52% full-time, 71% with terminal degrees.
Student/faculty ratio: 8:1.

ACADEMICS
Calendar: semesters. *Degrees:* associate, bachelor's, and master's.
Special study options: academic remediation for entering students, advanced placement credit, distance learning, double majors, independent study, part-time degree program, services for LD students, summer session for credit.
Computers: 21 computers/terminals are available on campus for general student use. Students can access the following: computer help desk, free student e-mail accounts, online (class) grades, online (class) schedules. Wireless service is available via entire campus.
Library: Wallace Library. *Books:* 45,906 (physical), 200,891 (digital/electronic); *Serial titles:* 8 (physical), 19,721 (digital/electronic); *Databases:* 71. Students can reserve study rooms.

STUDENT LIFE
Housing options: college housing not available.
Campus security: 24-hour emergency response devices, late-night transport/escort service, electronically-operated building entrances.
Student services: personal/psychological counseling.

COSTS & FINANCIAL AID
Costs (2018–19) *Tuition:* $9960 full-time, $415 per credit hour part-time. Full-time tuition and fees vary according to course load. Part-time tuition and fees vary according to course load. *Required fees:* $750 full-time, $750 per year part-time. *Payment plan:* installment. *Waivers:* employees or children of employees.

Financial Aid Of all full-time matriculated undergraduates who enrolled in 2016, 112 applied for aid, 86 were judged to have need, 3 had their need fully met. In 2016, 20 non-need-based awards were made. *Average percent of need met:* 33. *Average financial aid package:* $7082. *Average need-based loan:* $3776. *Average need-based gift aid:* $3921. *Average non-need-based aid:* $5529.

APPLYING
Standardized Tests *Required for some:* SAT or ACT (for admission).
Options: electronic application.
Application fee: $35.
Required: essay or personal statement, 1 letter of recommendation. *Required for some:* high school transcript.
Application deadlines: rolling (freshmen), rolling (out-of-state freshmen), rolling (transfers).
Notification: continuous (freshmen), continuous (out-of-state freshmen), continuous (transfers).

CONTACT
Sam Hagos, Enrollment Assistant, Criswell College, 4010 Gaston Ave, Dallas, TX 75246. *Phone:* 214-818-1391. *Toll-free phone:* 800-899-0012. *E-mail:* shagos@criswell.edu.

Dallas Baptist University
Dallas, Texas
http://www.dbu.edu/

- **Independent** comprehensive, founded 1965, affiliated with Baptist General Convention of Texas
- **Suburban** 292-acre campus with easy access to Dallas-Fort Worth
- **Endowment** $47.2 million
- **Coed** 3,161 undergraduate students, 77% full-time, 59% women, 41% men
- **Moderately difficult** entrance level, 39% of applicants were admitted

UNDERGRAD STUDENTS
2,423 full-time, 738 part-time. Students come from 40 states and territories; 43 other countries; 8% are from out of state; 13% Black or African American, non-Hispanic/Latino; 17% Hispanic/Latino; 2% Asian, non-Hispanic/Latino; 0.3% Native Hawaiian or other Pacific Islander, non-Hispanic/Latino; 0.9% American Indian or Alaska Native, non-Hispanic/Latino; 7% international; 8% transferred in; 62% live on campus.

Freshmen:
Admission: 3,770 applied, 1,486 admitted, 540 enrolled. *Average high school GPA:* 3.5. *Test scores:* SAT evidence-based reading and writing scores over 500: 91%; SAT math scores over 500: 91%; ACT scores over 18: 90%; SAT evidence-based reading and writing scores over 600: 53%; SAT math scores over 600: 36%; ACT scores over 24: 27%; SAT evidence-based reading and writing scores over 700: 9%; SAT math scores over 700: 3%; ACT scores over 30: 4%.

Retention: 70% of full-time freshmen returned.

FACULTY
Total: 660, 20% full-time, 51% with terminal degrees.
Student/faculty ratio: 13:1.

ACADEMICS
Calendar: 4-1-4. *Degrees:* certificates, associate, bachelor's, master's, doctoral, post-master's, and postbachelor's certificates.
Special study options: academic remediation for entering students, accelerated degree program, adult/continuing education programs, advanced placement credit, distance learning, double majors, English as a second language, honors programs, independent study, internships, off-campus study, part-time degree program, services for LD students, study abroad, summer session for credit. *ROTC:* Army (c), Air Force (c).
Unusual degree programs: 3-2 business administration.
Computers: 214 computers/terminals are available on campus for general student use. Students can access the following: computer help desk, free student e-mail accounts, online (class) grades, online (class) registration, online (class) schedules. Campuswide network is available. 100% of college-owned or -operated housing units are wired for high-speed Internet access. Wireless service is available via entire campus.

Library: Vance Memorial Library plus 3 others. *Books:* 237,744 (physical), 156,156 (digital/electronic); *Serial titles:* 567 (physical), 35,666 (digital/electronic); *Databases:* 194. Weekly public service hours: 108.

STUDENT LIFE

Housing options: men-only, women-only, special housing for students with disabilities. Campus housing is university owned and leased by the school. Freshman applicants given priority for college housing.

Activities and organizations: drama/theater group, choral group, Ministry Fellowship, Baptist Student Ministry, Student Government Association, Student Education Association, International Student Organization.

Athletics Member NCAA, NCCAA. All NCAA Division II except baseball (Division I). *Intercollegiate sports:* baseball M(s), basketball M(s), cheerleading W(c), cross-country running M/W(s), golf M/W(s), ice hockey M(c), lacrosse M(c), soccer M/W(s), tennis M/W(s), track and field M/W(s), volleyball W(s). *Intramural sports:* badminton M/W, basketball M/W, football M/W, golf M/W, soccer M/W, softball M/W, table tennis M/W, tennis M/W, ultimate Frisbee M/W, volleyball M/W.

Campus security: 24-hour emergency response devices and patrols, late-night transport/escort service, controlled dormitory access.

Student services: health clinic, personal/psychological counseling.

COSTS & FINANCIAL AID

Costs (2018–19) *Comprehensive fee:* $36,862 includes full-time tuition ($27,870), mandatory fees ($1000), and room and board ($7992). Full-time tuition and fees vary according to course load. Part-time tuition: $929 per credit hour. Part-time tuition and fees vary according to course load. *Required fees:* $500 per term part-time. *College room only:* $3915. Room and board charges vary according to board plan and housing facility. *Payment plans:* installment, deferred payment. *Waivers:* employees or children of employees.

Financial Aid Of all full-time matriculated undergraduates who enrolled in 2017, 1,973 applied for aid, 1,518 were judged to have need, 516 had their need fully met. 122 Federal Work-Study jobs (averaging $2304). 9 state and other part-time jobs (averaging $2566). In 2017, 490 non-need-based awards were made. *Average percent of need met:* 57. *Average financial aid package:* $16,211. *Average need-based loan:* $4209. *Average need-based gift aid:* $4095. *Average non-need-based aid:* $9490. *Average indebtedness upon graduation:* $24,805.

APPLYING

Standardized Tests *Required:* SAT or ACT (for admission).

Options: electronic application, early admission, deferred entrance.

Application fee: $25.

Required: essay or personal statement, high school transcript, minimum 2.5 GPA, rank in upper 50% of high school class. *Recommended:* interview.

Application deadlines: rolling (freshmen), rolling (transfers).

Notification: continuous (freshmen), continuous (transfers).

CONTACT

Mr. Bobby Soto, Director of Admissions, Dallas Baptist University, 3000 Mountain Creek Parkway, Dallas, TX 75211-9299. *Phone:* 214-333-5360. *Toll-free phone:* 800-460-1328. *Fax:* 214-333-5447. *E-mail:* admiss@dbu.edu.

Dallas Christian College

Dallas, Texas

http://www.dallas.edu/

- **Independent** 4-year, founded 1950, affiliated with Christian Churches and Churches of Christ
- **Suburban** 22-acre campus with easy access to Dallas-Fort Worth
- **Endowment** $169,907
- **Coed**
- **Moderately difficult** entrance level

FACULTY

Student/faculty ratio: 16:1.

ACADEMICS

Calendar: semesters. *Degrees:* associate, bachelor's, and postbachelor's certificates.

Library: The Crawford Library. *Books:* 35,000 (physical), 26,000 (digital/electronic); *Serial titles:* 100 (physical); *Databases:* 60.

STUDENT LIFE

Housing options: on-campus residence required through sophomore year; men-only, women-only. Campus housing is university owned.

Activities and organizations: drama/theater group, choral group.

Athletics Member NCCAA.

Campus security: controlled dormitory access.

Student services: personal/psychological counseling.

COSTS & FINANCIAL AID

Costs (2017–18) *Comprehensive fee:* $25,516 includes full-time tuition ($15,596), mandatory fees ($910), and room and board ($9010). Full-time tuition and fees vary according to program. Part-time tuition: $557 per credit hour. Part-time tuition and fees vary according to program. *Required fees:* $285 per term part-time.

Financial Aid Of all full-time matriculated undergraduates who enrolled in 2005, 189 applied for aid, 132 were judged to have need. 36 Federal Work-Study jobs (averaging $1404). In 2005, 26 non-need-based awards were made. *Average percent of need met:* 43. *Average financial aid package:* $3940. *Average need-based loan:* $3589. *Average need-based gift aid:* $1282. *Average non-need-based aid:* $3664. *Average indebtedness upon graduation:* $15,000.

APPLYING

Standardized Tests *Required:* SAT or ACT (for admission).

Options: electronic application, deferred entrance.

Application fee: $30.

Required: essay or personal statement, high school transcript, minimum 2.0 GPA, interview. *Required for some:* letters of recommendation.

CONTACT

Mr. Brian Condra, Admissions Counselor, Dallas Christian College, 2700 Christian Parkway, Dallas, TX 75234-7299. *Phone:* 972-241-3371 Ext. 104. *Toll-free phone:* 800-688-1029. *Fax:* 972-241-8021. *E-mail:* bcondra@dallas.edu.

Dallas Nursing Institute

Dallas, Texas

http://www.dni.edu/

CONTACT

Dallas Nursing Institute, 12170 N. Abrams Road, Suite 200, Dallas, TX 75243.

DeVry University–Irving Campus

Irving, Texas

http://www.devry.edu/

- **Proprietary** comprehensive, founded 1969, part of DeVry University
- **Suburban** campus
- **Coed**
- **Minimally difficult** entrance level

FACULTY

Student/faculty ratio: 20:1.

ACADEMICS

Calendar: semesters. *Degrees:* associate, bachelor's, master's, and postbachelor's certificates.

Library: Learning Resource Center.

STUDENT LIFE

Housing options: college housing not available.

COSTS

Costs (2017–18) *Tuition:* $14,560 full-time. *Required fees:* $500 full-time.

APPLYING

Options: deferred entrance.

Application fee: $30.

Required: high school transcript, interview.

CONTACT
DeVry University–Irving Campus, 4800 Regent Boulevard, Suite 200, Irving, TX 75063. *Phone:* 972-929-6777. *Toll-free phone:* 866-338-7934.

East Texas Baptist University

Marshall, Texas
http://www.etbu.edu/

- **Independent Baptist** comprehensive, founded 1912
- **Small-town** 250-acre campus
- **Endowment** $70.8 million
- **Coed** 1,421 undergraduate students, 86% full-time, 54% women, 46% men
- **Moderately difficult** entrance level, 54% of applicants were admitted

UNDERGRAD STUDENTS

1,216 full-time, 205 part-time. Students come from 24 states and territories; 7 other countries; 11% are from out of state; 16% Black or African American, non-Hispanic/Latino; 10% Hispanic/Latino; 0.2% Asian, non-Hispanic/Latino; 0.1% Native Hawaiian or other Pacific Islander, non-Hispanic/Latino; 0.2% American Indian or Alaska Native, non-Hispanic/Latino; 4% Two or more races, non-Hispanic/Latino; 0.2% Race/ethnicity unknown; 0.9% international; 8% transferred in; 82% live on campus.

Freshmen:
Admission: 1,839 applied, 999 admitted, 420 enrolled. *Average high school GPA:* 3.4. *Test scores:* SAT evidence-based reading and writing scores over 500: 69%; SAT math scores over 500: 65%; ACT scores over 18: 88%; SAT evidence-based reading and writing scores over 600: 18%; SAT math scores over 600: 12%; ACT scores over 24: 22%; SAT evidence-based reading and writing scores over 700: 2%; SAT math scores over 700: 1%; ACT scores over 30: 2%.

Retention: 55% of full-time freshmen returned.

FACULTY
Total: 141, 50% full-time, 57% with terminal degrees.
Student/faculty ratio: 15:1.

ACADEMICS
Calendar: semesters. *Degrees:* certificates, bachelor's, and master's.
Special study options: accelerated degree program, adult/continuing education programs, advanced placement credit, distance learning, double majors, English as a second language, honors programs, independent study, internships, off-campus study, part-time degree program, services for LD students, student-designed majors, study abroad, summer session for credit.
Computers: 301 computers/terminals and 800 ports are available on campus for general student use. Students can access the following: campus intranet, free student e-mail accounts, online (class) grades, online (class) registration, online (class) schedules. Campuswide network is available. 100% of college-owned or -operated housing units are wired for high-speed Internet access. Wireless service is available via entire campus.
Library: Mamye Jarrett Library. *Books:* 92,020 (physical), 3.7 million (digital/electronic); *Serial titles:* 695 (physical), 47,336 (digital/electronic); *Databases:* 217. Weekly public service hours: 88.

STUDENT LIFE
Housing options: on-campus residence required through senior year; men-only, women-only. Campus housing is university owned. Freshman campus housing is guaranteed.
Activities and organizations: drama/theater group, choral group, marching band, Baptist Student Ministry, Student Government Association (SGA), Student Foundation, Fellowship of Christian Athletes (FCA), Enactus.
Athletics Member NCAA. All Division III. *Intercollegiate sports:* baseball M, basketball M/W, cross-country running M/W, football M, soccer M/W, softball W, tennis M/W, track and field M/W, volleyball W. *Intramural sports:* basketball M/W, football M/W, sand volleyball M/W, soccer M/W, softball M/W, table tennis W, ultimate Frisbee M/W, volleyball M/W.
Campus security: 24-hour emergency response devices and patrols, student patrols, late-night transport/escort service, controlled dormitory access.

Student services: personal/psychological counseling.

COSTS & FINANCIAL AID
Costs (2017–18) *Comprehensive fee:* $34,385 includes full-time tuition ($24,420), mandatory fees ($1050), and room and board ($8915). Part-time tuition: $814 per credit hour. *Required fees:* $45 per credit hour part-time. *College room only:* $4576. Room and board charges vary according to board plan and housing facility. *Payment plan:* installment. *Waivers:* employees or children of employees.

Financial Aid Of all full-time matriculated undergraduates who enrolled in 2016, 1,101 applied for aid, 1,000 were judged to have need, 128 had their need fully met. 83 Federal Work-Study jobs (averaging $1512). 262 state and other part-time jobs (averaging $1480). In 2016, 177 non-need-based awards were made. *Average percent of need met:* 30. *Average financial aid package:* $19,276. *Average need-based loan:* $3884. *Average need-based gift aid:* $6424. *Average non-need-based aid:* $11,448. *Average indebtedness upon graduation:* $33,823.

APPLYING
Standardized Tests *Required:* SAT or ACT (for admission).
Options: electronic application.
Application fee: $25.
Required: high school transcript.
Application deadlines: 8/31 (freshmen), 8/31 (transfers).
Notification: continuous (freshmen), continuous (transfers).

CONTACT
Mrs. Meredith Palmer, Director of Admissions and Recruitment, East Texas Baptist University, One Tiger Drive, Marshall, TX 75670. *Phone:* 903-923-2000. *Toll-free phone:* 800-804-ETBU. *Fax:* 903-923-2001. *E-mail:* admissions@etbu.edu.

Grace School of Theology

Conroe, Texas
http://www.gsot.edu/

CONTACT
Grace School of Theology, 3705 College Park Drive Suite 140, Conroe, TX 77384-4894.

Hallmark University

San Antonio, Texas
http://www.hallmarkuniversity.edu/

- **Independent** comprehensive, founded 1969
- **Suburban** 2-acre campus with easy access to San Antonio
- **Coed** 872 undergraduate students, 100% full-time, 28% women, 72% men
- **Moderately difficult** entrance level

UNDERGRAD STUDENTS

872 full-time. Students come from 17 states and territories; 2% are from out of state; 12% Black or African American, non-Hispanic/Latino; 45% Hispanic/Latino; 2% Asian, non-Hispanic/Latino; 1% Native Hawaiian or other Pacific Islander, non-Hispanic/Latino; 2% American Indian or Alaska Native, non-Hispanic/Latino; 5% Two or more races, non-Hispanic/Latino; 3% Race/ethnicity unknown; 2% transferred in.

Freshmen:
Admission: 231 enrolled.
Retention: 47% of full-time freshmen returned.

FACULTY
Total: 65, 51% full-time, 14% with terminal degrees.
Student/faculty ratio: 20:1.

ACADEMICS
Calendar: continuous. *Degrees:* associate, bachelor's, and master's.
Special study options: academic remediation for entering students, accelerated degree program, advanced placement credit, distance learning, internships.
Computers: 250 computers/terminals and 250 ports are available on campus for general student use. Students can access the following: campus intranet, computer help desk, free student e-mail accounts, online

(class) grades, online (class) registration, online (class) schedules. Campuswide network is available. Wireless service is available via entire campus.

Library: Randall K. Williams Assessment Center/ Virtual Library plus 1 other. *Books:* 172,325 (digital/electronic); *Serial titles:* 26,880 (digital/electronic); *Databases:* 32. Weekly public service hours: 4.

STUDENT LIFE

Housing options: college housing not available.

Activities and organizations: Alpha Beta Kappa Honor Society, Student Veteran's Organization.

Campus security: 24-hour emergency response devices and patrols, security guard on duty during hours when students are on campus.

COSTS

Costs (2018–19) *One-time required fee:* $110. *Tuition:* $36,806 full-time. Full-time tuition and fees vary according to degree level, location, and program. *Required fees:* $900 full-time. *Payment plans:* tuition prepayment, installment. *Waivers:* children of alumni and employees or children of employees.

APPLYING

Standardized Tests *Required:* Wonderlic aptitude test for Main Campus, Aviation Assessment for Satellite Campus, SAT/ACT is used for some degree programs (for admission).

Options: electronic application, early admission.

Required: high school transcript, interview, hybrid readiness test (main campus only). *Required for some:* essay or personal statement, letters of recommendation.

Application deadlines: rolling (freshmen), rolling (transfers).

Notification: continuous (freshmen), continuous (transfers).

CONTACT

Ms. Jennifer Sanchez, Director of Admissions, Hallmark University, 10401 IH-10 West, San Antonio, TX 78230. *Phone:* 210-690-9000 Ext. 7540. *Toll-free phone:* 800-880-6600. *Fax:* 210-697-8225. *E-mail:* jsanchez@hallmarkuniversity.edu.

Hardin-Simmons University

Abilene, Texas

http://www.hsutx.edu/

- **Independent Baptist** comprehensive, founded 1891
- **Urban** 220-acre campus
- **Endowment** $161.3 million
- **Coed** 1,749 undergraduate students, 91% full-time, 52% women, 48% men
- **Moderately difficult** entrance level, 82% of applicants were admitted

UNDERGRAD STUDENTS

1,585 full-time, 164 part-time. Students come from 25 states and territories; 26 other countries; 3% are from out of state; 8% Black or African American, non-Hispanic/Latino; 19% Hispanic/Latino; 1% Asian, non-Hispanic/Latino; 0.1% Native Hawaiian or other Pacific Islander, non-Hispanic/Latino; 0.3% American Indian or Alaska Native, non-Hispanic/Latino; 5% Two or more races, non-Hispanic/Latino; 1% Race/ethnicity unknown; 2% international; 7% transferred in; 49% live on campus.

Freshmen:

Admission: 1,673 applied, 1,368 admitted, 457 enrolled. *Average high school GPA:* 3.6. *Test scores:* SAT evidence-based reading and writing scores over 500: 76%; SAT math scores over 500: 76%; ACT scores over 18: 86%; SAT evidence-based reading and writing scores over 600: 25%; SAT math scores over 600: 20%; ACT scores over 24: 27%; SAT evidence-based reading and writing scores over 700: 1%; SAT math scores over 700: 2%; ACT scores over 30: 3%.

Retention: 75% of full-time freshmen returned.

FACULTY

Total: 228, 59% full-time, 71% with terminal degrees.

Student/faculty ratio: 12:1.

ACADEMICS

Calendar: semesters. *Degrees:* bachelor's, master's, doctoral, post-master's, and postbachelor's certificates.

Special study options: academic remediation for entering students, accelerated degree program, adult/continuing education programs, advanced placement credit, distance learning, double majors, honors programs, independent study, internships, off-campus study, part-time degree program, services for LD students, study abroad, summer session for credit.

Computers: 115 computers/terminals are available on campus for general student use. Students can access the following: campus intranet, computer help desk, free student e-mail accounts, online (class) grades, online (class) registration, online (class) schedules. Campuswide network is available. 100% of college-owned or -operated housing units are wired for high-speed Internet access. Wireless service is available via entire campus.

Library: Richardson Library plus 1 other. *Books:* 254,854 (physical), 120,497 (digital/electronic); *Serial titles:* 212 (physical), 48,069 (digital/electronic); *Databases:* 141. Weekly public service hours: 89.

STUDENT LIFE

Housing options: on-campus residence required through sophomore year; men-only, women-only, special housing for students with disabilities. Campus housing is university owned. Freshman campus housing is guaranteed.

Activities and organizations: drama/theater group, student-run newspaper, choral group, marching band, Baptist Student Ministries, Student Government, Alpha Phi Omega, Student Activities Board, Fellowship of Christian Athletes.

Athletics Member NCAA. All Division III. *Intercollegiate sports:* baseball M, basketball M/W, cheerleading M(c)/W(c), cross-country running M/W, football M, golf M/W, soccer M/W, softball W, tennis M/W, track and field M/W, volleyball W. *Intramural sports:* badminton M/W, basketball M/W, bowling M/W, football M/W, golf M/W, racquetball M/W, rock climbing M(c)/W(c), soccer M/W, softball M/W, table tennis M(c)/W(c), tennis M(c)/W(c), ultimate Frisbee M/W, volleyball M/W.

Campus security: 24-hour emergency response devices and patrols, late-night transport/escort service, controlled dormitory access.

Student services: personal/psychological counseling.

COSTS & FINANCIAL AID

Costs (2018–19) *Comprehensive fee:* $37,070 includes full-time tuition ($27,290), mandatory fees ($1700), and room and board ($8080). Full-time tuition and fees vary according to program. Part-time tuition: $810 per credit hour. Part-time tuition and fees vary according to course load and program. No tuition increase for student's term of enrollment. *Required fees:* $400 per term part-time. *College room only:* $4080. Room and board charges vary according to board plan and housing facility. *Payment plan:* installment. *Waivers:* employees or children of employees.

Financial Aid Of all full-time matriculated undergraduates who enrolled in 2017, 1,564 applied for aid, 1,191 were judged to have need, 229 had their need fully met. In 2017, 374 non-need-based awards were made. *Average percent of need met:* 68. *Average financial aid package:* $24,855. *Average need-based loan:* $4142. *Average need-based gift aid:* $6018. *Average non-need-based aid:* $12,914. *Average indebtedness upon graduation:* $51,346.

APPLYING

Standardized Tests *Required:* SAT or ACT (for admission).

Options: electronic application, deferred entrance.

Required: high school transcript, minimum 2.0 GPA.

Application deadlines: rolling (freshmen), rolling (transfers).

Notification: continuous (freshmen), continuous (transfers).

CONTACT

Ms. Bobbie Turner, Campus Guest Coordinator, Hardin-Simmons University, Box 16050, Abilene, TX 79698-0001. *Phone:* 325-670-5890. *Toll-free phone:* 877-464-7889. *Fax:* 325-671-2115. *E-mail:* visit@ hsutx.edu.

Houston Baptist University

Houston, Texas
http://www.hbu.edu/

- **Independent Baptist** comprehensive, founded 1960
- **Suburban** 100-acre campus with easy access to Houston
- **Endowment** $102.8 million
- **Coed** 2,316 undergraduate students, 91% full-time, 64% women, 36% men
- **Moderately difficult** entrance level, 69% of applicants were admitted

UNDERGRAD STUDENTS
2,098 full-time, 218 part-time. Students come from 24 states and territories; 30 other countries; 3% are from out of state; 18% Black or African American, non-Hispanic/Latino; 35% Hispanic/Latino; 9% Asian, non-Hispanic/Latino; 0.3% Native Hawaiian or other Pacific Islander, non-Hispanic/Latino; 0.3% American Indian or Alaska Native, non-Hispanic/Latino; 4% Two or more races, non-Hispanic/Latino; 6% Race/ethnicity unknown; 3% international; 8% transferred in; 36% live on campus.

Freshmen:
Admission: 6,461 applied, 4,459 admitted, 519 enrolled. *Average high school GPA:* 3.4. *Test scores:* SAT evidence-based reading and writing scores over 500: 85%; SAT math scores over 500: 89%; ACT scores over 18: 96%; SAT evidence-based reading and writing scores over 600: 26%; SAT math scores over 600: 23%; ACT scores over 24: 43%; SAT evidence-based reading and writing scores over 700: 2%; SAT math scores over 700: 2%; ACT scores over 30: 5%.
Retention: 72% of full-time freshmen returned.

FACULTY
Total: 279, 54% full-time, 68% with terminal degrees.
Student/faculty ratio: 14:1.

ACADEMICS
Calendar: semesters. *Degrees:* bachelor's, master's, and doctoral.
Special study options: academic remediation for entering students, accelerated degree program, adult/continuing education programs, advanced placement credit, distance learning, double majors, freshman honors college, honors programs, independent study, internships, off-campus study, part-time degree program, services for LD students, summer session for credit. *ROTC:* Army (c), Navy (c), Air Force (c).
Unusual degree programs: 3-2 business administration.
Computers: 100 computers/terminals are available on campus for general student use. Students can access the following: campus intranet, computer help desk, free student e-mail accounts, online (class) grades, online (class) registration, online (class) schedules, office software for 5 devices for each student. Campuswide network is available. 100% of college-owned or -operated housing units are wired for high-speed Internet access. Wireless service is available via entire campus.
Library: Moody Library. *Books:* 109,715 (physical); *Serial titles:* 252 (physical), 57,209 (digital/electronic); *Databases:* 111. Students can reserve study rooms.

STUDENT LIFE
Housing options: on-campus residence required for freshman year; coed, men-only, women-only, special housing for students with disabilities. Campus housing is university owned. Freshman campus housing is guaranteed.
Activities and organizations: drama/theater group, student-run newspaper, choral group, marching band, Filipino Student Association, Baptist Student Ministry, Nursing Student Association, Phi Mu, Alpha Epsilon Delta, national fraternities, national sororities.
Athletics Member NCAA. All Division I. *Intercollegiate sports:* baseball M(s), basketball M(s)/W(s), cross-country running M(s)/W(s), football M(s), golf M(s)/W(s), soccer M(s)/W(s), softball W(s), track and field M(s)/W(s), volleyball W(s). *Intramural sports:* basketball M(c)/W(c), football M/W, soccer M(c)/W(c), ultimate Frisbee M(c)/W, volleyball M/W(c).
Campus security: 24-hour emergency response devices and patrols, late-night transport/escort service, controlled dormitory access.
Student services: health clinic, personal/psychological counseling.

COSTS & FINANCIAL AID
Costs (2018–19) *Comprehensive fee:* $41,344 includes full-time tuition ($30,480), mandatory fees ($2050), and room and board ($8814). Part-time tuition: $1270 per semester hour. Part-time tuition and fees vary according to course load. *Required fees:* $1025 per term part-time. *College room only:* $4800. Room and board charges vary according to board plan and housing facility. *Payment plan:* installment. *Waivers:* senior citizens and employees or children of employees.
Financial Aid Of all full-time matriculated undergraduates who enrolled in 2017, 1,619 applied for aid, 1,518 were judged to have need, 218 had their need fully met. 924 Federal Work-Study jobs (averaging $985). In 2017, 520 non-need-based awards were made. *Average percent of need met:* 69. *Average financial aid package:* $27,234. *Average need-based loan:* $4471. *Average need-based gift aid:* $20,468. *Average non-need-based aid:* $14,111. *Average indebtedness upon graduation:* $31,767.

APPLYING
Standardized Tests *Required:* SAT or ACT (for admission).
Options: electronic application, deferred entrance.
Required: high school transcript. *Required for some:* essay or personal statement.
Application deadlines: rolling (freshmen), rolling (transfers).
Notification: continuous (freshmen), continuous (transfers).

CONTACT
Mr. James Steen, Vice President for Enrollment Management, Houston Baptist University, 7502 Fondren Road, Houston, TX 77074-3298. *Phone:* 281-649-3752. *Toll-free phone:* 800-696-3210. *Fax:* 281-649-3217. *E-mail:* jsteen@hbu.edu.

Howard Payne University

Brownwood, Texas
http://www.hputx.edu/

- **Independent** comprehensive, founded 1889, affiliated with Baptist General Convention of Texas
- **Small-town** 80-acre campus
- **Endowment** $56.5 million
- **Coed** 990 undergraduate students, 87% full-time, 48% women, 52% men
- **Moderately difficult** entrance level, 59% of applicants were admitted

UNDERGRAD STUDENTS
866 full-time, 124 part-time. Students come from 10 states and territories; 2% are from out of state; 5% Black or African American, non-Hispanic/Latino; 12% Hispanic/Latino; 1% Asian, non-Hispanic/Latino; 0.7% Native Hawaiian or other Pacific Islander, non-Hispanic/Latino; 1% American Indian or Alaska Native, non-Hispanic/Latino; 2% Two or more races, non-Hispanic/Latino; 8% Race/ethnicity unknown; 9% transferred in; 59% live on campus.

Freshmen:
Admission: 1,305 applied, 768 admitted, 262 enrolled. *Average high school GPA:* 3.3.
Retention: 48% of full-time freshmen returned.

FACULTY
Total: 141, 59% full-time, 47% with terminal degrees.
Student/faculty ratio: 10:1.

ACADEMICS
Calendar: semesters. *Degrees:* certificates, bachelor's, and master's.
Special study options: academic remediation for entering students, accelerated degree program, advanced placement credit, distance learning, double majors, honors programs, independent study, internships, off-campus study, part-time degree program, services for LD students, study abroad, summer session for credit.
Computers: 260 computers/terminals and 200 ports are available on campus for general student use. Students can access the following: campus intranet, computer help desk, free student e-mail accounts, online (class) grades, online (class) schedules. Campuswide network is available. 100% of college-owned or -operated housing units are wired for high-speed Internet access. Wireless service is available via entire campus.
Library: Walker Memorial Library. *Books:* 125,784 (physical), 144,053 (digital/electronic); *Serial titles:* 27,347 (physical). Weekly public service hours: 84.

STUDENT LIFE

Housing options: on-campus residence required through sophomore year; men-only, women-only. Campus housing is university owned. Freshman campus housing is guaranteed.

Activities and organizations: drama/theater group, student-run newspaper, choral group, marching band, Baptist Student Ministry, Fellowship of Christian Athletes, Gaming Guild, Spanish Club, Social Work Club, national fraternities, national sororities.

Athletics Member NCAA. All Division III. *Intercollegiate sports:* baseball M, basketball M/W, football M, soccer M/W, softball W, tennis M/W, volleyball W. *Intramural sports:* basketball M/W, football M/W, soccer M/W, softball W, table tennis M/W, tennis M/W, ultimate Frisbee M/W, volleyball M/W.

Campus security: 24-hour emergency response devices and patrols, late-night transport/escort service, controlled dormitory access.

Student services: health clinic, personal/psychological counseling.

COSTS & FINANCIAL AID

Costs (2018–19) *Comprehensive fee:* $36,476 includes full-time tuition ($25,290), mandatory fees ($2800), and room and board ($8386). Full-time tuition and fees vary according to course load, location, and program. Part-time tuition: $845 per credit hour. Part-time tuition and fees vary according to location and program. *Room and board:* Room and board charges vary according to board plan and housing facility. *Payment plan:* installment. *Waivers:* employees or children of employees.

Financial Aid Of all full-time matriculated undergraduates who enrolled in 2016, 871 applied for aid, 811 were judged to have need, 158 had their need fully met. In 2016, 142 non-need-based awards were made. *Average percent of need met:* 78. *Average financial aid package:* $20,390. *Average need-based loan:* $5129. *Average need-based gift aid:* $16,195. *Average non-need-based aid:* $12,984. *Average indebtedness upon graduation:* $34,875.

APPLYING

Standardized Tests *Required:* SAT or ACT (for admission). *Required for some:* ACCUPLACER.

Options: electronic application, early admission.

Required: high school transcript. *Required for some:* 3 letters of recommendation, interview. *Recommended:* essay or personal statement, minimum 3.0 GPA.

Application deadlines: rolling (freshmen), rolling (transfers).

Notification: continuous (freshmen), continuous (transfers).

CONTACT

Mrs. P. J. Gramling, Director of Admission, Howard Payne University, 1000 Fisk Street, Brownwood, TX 76801. *Phone:* 325-649-8406. *Toll-free phone:* 800-880-4478. *Fax:* 325-649-8901. *E-mail:* enroll@hputx.edu.

Huston-Tillotson University

Austin, Texas
http://www.htu.edu/

- **Independent interdenominational** comprehensive, founded 1875
- **Urban** 23-acre campus
- **Coed** 1,053 undergraduate students, 95% full-time, 60% women, 40% men
- **Moderately difficult** entrance level, 30% of applicants were admitted

UNDERGRAD STUDENTS

1,003 full-time, 50 part-time. 62% Black or African American, non-Hispanic/Latino; 27% Hispanic/Latino; 0.1% Asian, non-Hispanic/Latino; 0.2% American Indian or Alaska Native, non-Hispanic/Latino; 0.7% Two or more races, non-Hispanic/Latino; 1% Race/ethnicity unknown; 3% international.

Freshmen:

Admission: 4,167 applied, 1,242 admitted, 183 enrolled.
Retention: 51% of full-time freshmen returned.

ACADEMICS

Calendar: semesters. *Degrees:* associate, bachelor's, and master's.

Special study options: academic remediation for entering students, advanced placement credit, cooperative education, distance learning, double majors, English as a second language, honors programs, independent study, internships, part-time degree program, services for LD students, study abroad, summer session for credit.

Unusual degree programs: 3-2 engineering with Prairie View A&M University.

Computers: Students can access the following: campus intranet, computer help desk, free student e-mail accounts, online (class) grades, online (class) registration, online (class) schedules. Campuswide network is available. Wireless service is available via entire campus.
Library: Downs-Jones Library.

STUDENT LIFE

Housing options: on-campus residence required for freshman yearCampus housing is university owned. Freshman campus housing is guaranteed.

Activities and organizations: drama/theater group, choral group, Campus Ministries, Zeta Phi Beta Sorority, Inc, Alpha Phi Alpha Fraternity, Inc, The Gentlemen's Club, Pre-Alumni Council, national fraternities, national sororities.

Athletics Member NAIA. *Intercollegiate sports:* baseball M(s), basketball M(s)/W(s), cross-country running M(s), soccer M(s)/W(s), softball W(s), track and field M(s)/W(s), volleyball W(s). *Intramural sports:* cheerleading W.

Campus security: 24-hour emergency response devices and patrols, late-night transport/escort service, controlled dormitory access.

Student services: health clinic, personal/psychological counseling.

COSTS

Costs (2017–18) *Comprehensive fee:* $21,914 includes full-time tuition ($12,262), mandatory fees ($2084), and room and board ($7568). Full-time tuition and fees vary according to course load. Part-time tuition: $410 per credit hour. Part-time tuition and fees vary according to course load. *College room only:* $3642. Room and board charges vary according to housing facility. *Payment plans:* installment, deferred payment. *Waivers:* employees or children of employees.

APPLYING

Standardized Tests *Required:* SAT or ACT (for admission). *Recommended:* SAT (for admission), ACT (for admission), SAT and SAT Subject Tests or ACT (for admission).

Options: electronic application, deferred entrance.

Application fee: $25.

Required: high school transcript, minimum 2.5 GPA. *Required for some:* interview.

CONTACT

Ms. Shakitha Stinson, Director of Admission, Huston-Tillotson University, 900 Chicon Street, Austin, TX 78702. *Phone:* 512-505-3029. *Fax:* 512-505-3192. *E-mail:* slstinson@htu.edu.

Jarvis Christian College

Hawkins, Texas
http://www.jarvis.edu/

CONTACT

Mr. Brandon Byrd, Director of Admissions and Enrollment, Jarvis Christian College, PO Box 1470, Hawkins, TX 75765-9989. *Phone:* 903-730-4890 Ext. 2201. *Fax:* 903-769-4842.

The King's University

Southlake, Texas
http://www.tku.edu/

CONTACT

Tyler Maxey, Director of Admissions, The King's University, 2121 E. Southlake Boulevard, Southlake, TX 76092. *Phone:* 817-552-7570. *Toll-free phone:* 888-779-8040. *E-mail:* tyler.maxey@tku.edu.

Lamar University

Beaumont, Texas
http://www.lamar.edu/

- **State-supported** university, founded 1923, part of Texas State University System
- **Suburban** 292-acre campus with easy access to Houston
- **Endowment** $105.9 million
- **Coed** 9,234 undergraduate students, 65% full-time, 58% women, 42% men
- **Minimally difficult** entrance level, 82% of applicants were admitted

UNDERGRAD STUDENTS
5,965 full-time, 3,269 part-time. Students come from 37 states and territories; 46 other countries; 3% are from out of state; 28% Black or African American, non-Hispanic/Latino; 17% Hispanic/Latino; 5% Asian, non-Hispanic/Latino; 0.1% Native Hawaiian or other Pacific Islander, non-Hispanic/Latino; 0.5% American Indian or Alaska Native, non-Hispanic/Latino; 1% Two or more races, non-Hispanic/Latino; 2% Race/ethnicity unknown; 1% international; 9% transferred in; 25% live on campus.

Freshmen:
Admission: 5,445 applied, 4,446 admitted, 1,447 enrolled. *Average high school GPA:* 3.3. *Test scores:* SAT evidence-based reading and writing scores over 500: 64%; SAT math scores over 500: 62%; ACT scores over 18: 81%; SAT evidence-based reading and writing scores over 600: 17%; SAT math scores over 600: 13%; ACT scores over 24: 23%; SAT evidence-based reading and writing scores over 700: 2%; SAT math scores over 700: 1%; ACT scores over 30: 3%.

Retention: 64% of full-time freshmen returned.

FACULTY
Total: 592, 81% full-time, 62% with terminal degrees.
Student/faculty ratio: 18:1.

ACADEMICS
Calendar: semesters. *Degrees:* bachelor's, master's, doctoral, post-master's, and postbachelor's certificates.

Special study options: academic remediation for entering students, accelerated degree program, advanced placement credit, cooperative education, distance learning, double majors, English as a second language, freshman honors college, honors programs, independent study, internships, off-campus study, part-time degree program, services for LD students, student-designed majors, study abroad, summer session for credit. *ROTC:* Air Force (c).

Computers: 1,104 computers/terminals are available on campus for general student use. Students can access the following: campus intranet, computer help desk, free student e-mail accounts, online (class) grades, online (class) registration, online (class) schedules. Campuswide network is available. 100% of college-owned or -operated housing units are wired for high-speed Internet access. Wireless service is available via entire campus.

Library: Mary and John Gray Library plus 1 other. *Books:* 496,121 (physical), 91,469 (digital/electronic); *Serial titles:* 42,694 (physical), 47,629 (digital/electronic); *Databases:* 142. Weekly public service hours: 87; students can reserve study rooms.

STUDENT LIFE
Housing options: on-campus residence required for freshman year; coed, special housing for students with disabilities. Campus housing is university owned. Freshman campus housing is guaranteed.

Activities and organizations: drama/theater group, student-run newspaper, television station, choral group, marching band, national fraternities, national sororities.

Athletics Member NCAA. All Division I except football (Division I-AA). *Intercollegiate sports:* baseball M(s), basketball M(s)/W(s), cheerleading M/W, cross-country running M(s)/W(s), golf M(s)/W(s), soccer W(s), softball W, tennis M(s)/W(s), track and field M(s)/W(s), volleyball W(s). *Intramural sports:* badminton M/W, basketball M/W, cross-country running M/W, football M, golf M/W, racquetball M/W, rugby M/W, sailing M/W, soccer M/W, softball M/W, swimming and diving M/W, table tennis M/W, tennis M/W, track and field M/W, volleyball M/W, weight lifting M/W.

Campus security: 24-hour emergency response devices and patrols, student patrols, late-night transport/escort service, controlled dormitory access.

Student services: health clinic, personal/psychological counseling.

COSTS & FINANCIAL AID
Costs (2017–18) *One-time required fee:* $10. *Tuition:* state resident $7290 full-time, $243 per credit hour part-time; nonresident $19,740 full-time, $658 per credit hour part-time. Full-time tuition and fees vary according to course load, location, and program. Part-time tuition and fees vary according to course load, location, and program. No tuition increase for student's term of enrollment. *Required fees:* $2821 full-time, $392 per credit hour part-time. *Room and board:* $8740; room only: $5540. Room and board charges vary according to board plan. *Payment plan:* installment. *Waivers:* senior citizens and employees or children of employees.

Financial Aid Of all full-time matriculated undergraduates who enrolled in 2016, 5,280 applied for aid, 4,434 were judged to have need, 490 had their need fully met. 274 Federal Work-Study jobs (averaging $2852). 101 state and other part-time jobs (averaging $1276). In 2016, 599 non-need-based awards were made. *Average percent of need met:* 23. *Average financial aid package:* $5125. *Average need-based loan:* $3909. *Average need-based gift aid:* $6660. *Average indebtedness upon graduation:* $4371.

APPLYING
Standardized Tests *Required:* SAT or ACT (for admission).
Options: electronic application, early admission.
Application fee: $25.
Required: high school transcript. *Required for some:* essay or personal statement.

CONTACT
Celeste Contreras, Director of Admissions, Lamar University, PO Box 10009, Beaumont, TX 77710. *Phone:* 409-880-8888. *Fax:* 409-880-8463. *E-mail:* admissions@lamar.edu.

LeTourneau University

Longview, Texas
http://www.letu.edu/

- **Independent nondenominational** comprehensive, founded 1946
- **Suburban** 162-acre campus
- **Coed** 2,611 undergraduate students, 50% full-time, 46% women, 54% men
- **Moderately difficult** entrance level, 47% of applicants were admitted

UNDERGRAD STUDENTS
1,302 full-time, 1,309 part-time. 35% are from out of state; 8% Black or African American, non-Hispanic/Latino; 5% Hispanic/Latino; 2% Asian, non-Hispanic/Latino; 0.1% Native Hawaiian or other Pacific Islander, non-Hispanic/Latino; 0.7% American Indian or Alaska Native, non-Hispanic/Latino; 5% Two or more races, non-Hispanic/Latino; 8% Race/ethnicity unknown; 3% international; 7% transferred in; 70% live on campus.

Freshmen:
Admission: 1,780 applied, 838 admitted, 303 enrolled. *Average high school GPA:* 3.6. *Test scores:* SAT evidence-based reading and writing scores over 500: 92%; SAT math scores over 500: 91%; ACT scores over 18: 100%; SAT evidence-based reading and writing scores over 600: 48%; SAT math scores over 600: 53%; ACT scores over 24: 58%; SAT evidence-based reading and writing scores over 700: 12%; SAT math scores over 700: 15%; ACT scores over 30: 20%.

Retention: 81% of full-time freshmen returned.

FACULTY
Total: 227, 37% full-time, 59% with terminal degrees.
Student/faculty ratio: 15:1.

ACADEMICS
Calendar: semesters. *Degrees:* associate, bachelor's, and master's.

Special study options: accelerated degree program, advanced placement credit, cooperative education, distance learning, double majors, English as a second language, freshman honors college, honors programs, independent study, internships, part-time degree program, services for LD students, study abroad, summer session for credit.

Computers: Students can access the following: campus intranet, computer help desk, free student e-mail accounts, online (class) grades, online (class) registration, online (class) schedules. Campuswide network is available. 100% of college-owned or -operated housing units are wired for high-speed Internet access. Wireless service is available via entire campus.

Library: Margaret Estes Library plus 1 other. *Books:* 36,383 (physical), 233,450 (digital/electronic); *Serial titles:* 200 (physical), 29,839 (digital/electronic); *Databases:* 98.

STUDENT LIFE

Housing options: on-campus residence required through junior year; men-only, women-only, special housing for students with disabilities. Campus housing is university owned. Freshman campus housing is guaranteed.

Activities and organizations: drama/theater group, choral group.

Athletics Member NCAA. All Division III. *Intercollegiate sports:* baseball M, basketball M/W, cross-country running M/W, golf M/W, rugby M(c)/W(c), soccer M/W, softball W, tennis M/W, track and field M/W, volleyball W. *Intramural sports:* basketball M/W, football M/W, sand volleyball M/W, soccer M/W, softball M/W, tennis M/W, ultimate Frisbee M/W, volleyball M/W.

Campus security: 24-hour emergency response devices and patrols, student patrols, late-night transport/escort service, controlled dormitory access, University police department.

Student services: personal/psychological counseling.

COSTS & FINANCIAL AID

Costs (2018–19) *Comprehensive fee:* $40,180 includes full-time tuition ($29,630), mandatory fees ($580), and room and board ($9970). Full-time tuition and fees vary according to course level, course load, location, and program. Part-time tuition and fees vary according to course level, course load, location, and program. *Room and board:* Room and board charges vary according to board plan and housing facility. *Payment plan:* installment. *Waivers:* employees or children of employees.

Financial Aid Of all full-time matriculated undergraduates who enrolled in 2017, 1,001 applied for aid, 904 were judged to have need, 124 had their need fully met. In 2017, 310 non-need-based awards were made. *Average percent of need met:* 70. *Average financial aid package:* $23,366. *Average need-based loan:* $5279. *Average need-based gift aid:* $17,806. *Average non-need-based aid:* $14,058. *Average indebtedness upon graduation:* $36,704. *Financial aid deadline:* 8/1.

APPLYING

Standardized Tests *Required for some:* SAT or ACT (for admission).

Options: electronic application, deferred entrance.

Application deadlines: rolling (freshmen), rolling (transfers).

Notification: continuous (freshmen), continuous (transfers).

CONTACT

LeTourneau University, TX. *Toll-free phone:* 800-759-8811.

Lubbock Christian University

Lubbock, Texas

http://www.lcu.edu/

- **Independent** comprehensive, founded 1957, affiliated with Church of Christ
- **Suburban** 120-acre campus
- **Endowment** $20.5 million
- **Coed** 1,484 undergraduate students, 86% full-time, 58% women, 42% men
- **Moderately difficult** entrance level, 94% of applicants were admitted

UNDERGRAD STUDENTS

1,276 full-time, 208 part-time. Students come from 32 states and territories; 17 other countries; 9% are from out of state; 5% Black or African American, non-Hispanic/Latino; 24% Hispanic/Latino; 0.8% Asian, non-Hispanic/Latino; 0.7% Native Hawaiian or other Pacific Islander, non-Hispanic/Latino; 0.9% American Indian or Alaska Native, non-Hispanic/Latino; 0.4% Race/ethnicity unknown; 1% international; 13% transferred in; 36% live on campus.

Freshmen:

Admission: 810 applied, 762 admitted, 310 enrolled. *Average high school GPA:* 3.5. *Test scores:* SAT evidence-based reading and writing scores over 500: 69%; SAT math scores over 500: 64%; ACT scores over 18: 90%; SAT evidence-based reading and writing scores over 600: 25%; SAT math scores over 600: 21%; ACT scores over 24: 40%; SAT evidence-based reading and writing scores over 700: 4%; SAT math scores over 700: 3%; ACT scores over 30: 8%.

Retention: 69% of full-time freshmen returned.

FACULTY

Total: 187, 50% full-time, 55% with terminal degrees.

Student/faculty ratio: 13:1.

ACADEMICS

Calendar: semesters. *Degrees:* bachelor's and master's.

Special study options: academic remediation for entering students, adult/continuing education programs, advanced placement credit, cooperative education, distance learning, double majors, honors programs, internships, part-time degree program, services for LD students, study abroad, summer session for credit. *ROTC:* Army (c), Air Force (c).

Unusual degree programs: engineering with Texas Tech University.

Computers: 169 computers/terminals are available on campus for general student use. Students can access the following: campus intranet, computer help desk, free student e-mail accounts, online (class) grades, online (class) registration, online (class) schedules. Campuswide network is available. 100% of college-owned or -operated housing units are wired for high-speed Internet access. Wireless service is available via entire campus.

Library: University Library. *Books:* 123,604 (physical), 159,649 (digital/electronic); *Serial titles:* 5 (digital/electronic); *Databases:* 84. Weekly public service hours: 93.

STUDENT LIFE

Housing options: on-campus residence required through sophomore year; men-only, women-only. Campus housing is university owned. Freshman campus housing is guaranteed.

Activities and organizations: drama/theater group, student-run newspaper, radio station, choral group, Student Senate, Enactus, Ag Club, Behavioral Science Society, International Student Association.

Athletics Member NCAA. All Division II. *Intercollegiate sports:* baseball M(s), basketball M(s)/W(s), cheerleading M/W, cross-country running M(s)/W(s), golf M(s)/W(s), soccer M(s)/W(s), softball W(s), track and field M/W, volleyball W(s). *Intramural sports:* badminton M/W, basketball M/W, cross-country running M/W, football M/W, golf M/W, racquetball M/W, rock climbing M/W, soccer M/W, softball M/W, table tennis M/W, tennis M/W, track and field M/W, ultimate Frisbee M/W, volleyball M/W.

Campus security: 24-hour patrols, late-night transport/escort service, controlled dormitory access.

Student services: health clinic, personal/psychological counseling.

COSTS & FINANCIAL AID

Costs (2017–18) *Comprehensive fee:* $29,272 includes full-time tuition ($21,794) and room and board ($7478). Full-time tuition and fees vary according to degree level and program. Part-time tuition: $705 per credit hour. Part-time tuition and fees vary according to course load, degree level, and program. *Required fees:* $60 per term part-time. *Room and board:* Room and board charges vary according to board plan and housing facility. *Payment plan:* installment. *Waivers:* employees or children of employees.

Financial Aid Of all full-time matriculated undergraduates who enrolled in 2017, 1,101 applied for aid, 954 were judged to have need, 96 had their need fully met. 630 Federal Work-Study jobs (averaging $1714). 15 state and other part-time jobs (averaging $776). In 2017, 201 non-need-based awards were made. *Average percent of need met:* 64. *Average financial aid package:* $15,700. *Average need-based loan:* $4469. *Average need-based gift aid:* $11,316. *Average non-need-based aid:* $6550. *Average indebtedness upon graduation:* $35,879.

APPLYING

Standardized Tests *Required:* SAT or ACT (for admission).

Options: electronic application, early decision, early action.

Application fee: $25.

Required: high school transcript.

Application deadlines: 8/1 (freshmen), rolling (transfers).

Early decision deadline: 10/31.

Notification: continuous (freshmen), continuous (transfers), 12/15 (early decision).

CONTACT

Mr. Chris Hayes, Director of Admissions, Lubbock Christian University, 5601 19th Street, Lubbock, TX 79407. *Phone:* 806-720-7156. *Toll-free phone:* 800-933-7601. *Fax:* 806-720-7162. *E-mail:* admissions@lcu.edu.

McMurry University

Abilene, Texas

http://www.mcm.edu/

- **Independent United Methodist** comprehensive, founded 1923
- **Suburban** 52-acre campus
- **Endowment** $81.5 million
- **Coed** 1,105 undergraduate students, 87% full-time, 48% women, 52% men
- **Moderately difficult** entrance level, 43% of applicants were admitted

UNDERGRAD STUDENTS

956 full-time, 149 part-time. Students come from 17 states and territories; 10 other countries; 5% are from out of state; 15% Black or African American, non-Hispanic/Latino; 26% Hispanic/Latino; 1% Asian, non-Hispanic/Latino; 0.1% Native Hawaiian or other Pacific Islander, non-Hispanic/Latino; 0.8% American Indian or Alaska Native, non-Hispanic/Latino; 3% Two or more races, non-Hispanic/Latino; 0.9% Race/ethnicity unknown; 6% international; 12% transferred in; 54% live on campus.

Freshmen:

Admission: 1,843 applied, 799 admitted, 246 enrolled. *Average high school GPA:* 3.5. *Test scores:* SAT evidence-based reading and writing scores over 500: 55%; SAT math scores over 500: 59%; ACT scores over 18: 69%; SAT evidence-based reading and writing scores over 600: 12%; SAT math scores over 600: 11%; ACT scores over 24: 15%; SAT evidence-based reading and writing scores over 700: 1%; ACT scores over 30: 2%.

Retention: 62% of full-time freshmen returned.

FACULTY

Total: 124, 63% full-time, 60% with terminal degrees.

Student/faculty ratio: 11:1.

ACADEMICS

Calendar: semesters plus May term. *Degrees:* bachelor's and master's.

Special study options: academic remediation for entering students, accelerated degree program, adult/continuing education programs, advanced placement credit, distance learning, double majors, English as a second language, honors programs, internships, off-campus study, part-time degree program, services for LD students, student-designed majors, study abroad, summer session for credit.

Computers: 50 computers/terminals and 705 ports are available on campus for general student use. Students can access the following: campus intranet, computer help desk, free student e-mail accounts, online (class) grades, online (class) registration, online (class) schedules, learning management system. Campuswide network is available. 100% of college-owned or -operated housing units are wired for high-speed Internet access. Wireless service is available via entire campus.

Library: Jay-Rollins Library. *Books:* 128,329 (physical), 193,689 (digital/electronic); *Serial titles:* 115 (physical), 377 (digital/electronic); *Databases:* 95. Weekly public service hours: 86.

STUDENT LIFE

Housing options: on-campus residence required through junior year; coed, men-only, women-only. Campus housing is university owned and is provided by a third party. Freshman campus housing is guaranteed.

Activities and organizations: drama/theater group, student-run newspaper, choral group, marching band, Alpha Phi Omega, Religious Life Council, McMurry Student Government, Campus Activity Board, Servant Leadership.

Athletics Member NCAA, NCCAA. All NCAA Division III.

Intercollegiate sports: baseball M, basketball M/W, cross-country running M/W, football M, golf M/W, soccer M/W, softball W, swimming and diving M/W, tennis M/W, track and field M/W, volleyball W. *Intramural sports:* basketball M/W, football M/W, soccer M/W, softball M/W, ultimate Frisbee M/W, volleyball M/W.

Campus security: 24-hour emergency response devices and patrols, late-night transport/escort service, controlled dormitory access.

Student services: health clinic, personal/psychological counseling.

COSTS & FINANCIAL AID

Costs (2017–18) *One-time required fee:* $175. *Comprehensive fee:* $35,036 includes full-time tuition ($26,622), mandatory fees ($90), and room and board ($8324). Full-time tuition and fees vary according to course load. Part-time tuition: $887 per credit hour. Part-time tuition and fees vary according to course load. *Required fees:* $3 per credit hour part-time. *College room only:* $4104. Room and board charges vary according to board plan and housing facility. *Payment plan:* installment. *Waivers:* employees or children of employees.

Financial Aid Of all full-time matriculated undergraduates who enrolled in 2016, 815 applied for aid, 773 were judged to have need, 89 had their need fully met. 164 Federal Work-Study jobs (averaging $1440). 58 state and other part-time jobs (averaging $1321). In 2016, 130 non-need-based awards were made. *Average percent of need met:* 71. *Average financial aid package:* $21,766. *Average need-based loan:* $4527. *Average need-based gift aid:* $16,294. *Average non-need-based aid:* $10,262. *Average indebtedness upon graduation:* $38,844.

APPLYING

Standardized Tests *Required:* SAT or ACT (for admission).

Options: electronic application, deferred entrance.

Application fee: $25.

Required: essay or personal statement, high school transcript, minimum 2.0 GPA. *Required for some:* 3 letters of recommendation, interview.

Application deadlines: 8/15 (freshmen), 8/15 (transfers).

Notification: continuous (freshmen), continuous (transfers).

CONTACT

Ms. Teresa Bridwell, Admission Counselor, McMurry University, 1 McMurry University, #278, Abilene, TX 79697. *Phone:* 325-793-4700. *Toll-free phone:* 800-460-2392. *Fax:* 325-793-4701. *E-mail:* admissions@mcm.edu.

Messenger College

Euless, Texas

http://www.messengercollege.edu/

- **Independent Pentecostal** 4-year, founded 1987
- **Suburban** 3-acre campus with easy access to Dallas-Fort Worth
- **Endowment** $542,452
- **Coed**
- **Moderately difficult** entrance level, 45% of applicants were admitted

Freshmen:

Admission: 22 applied, 10 admitted.

FACULTY

Total: 42, 5% full-time, 31% with terminal degrees.

ACADEMICS

Calendar: semesters. *Degrees:* associate and bachelor's.

Special study options: academic remediation for entering students, advanced placement credit, cooperative education, distance learning, double majors, external degree program, honors programs, independent study, internships, part-time degree program.

Computers: 5 computers/terminals are available on campus for general student use. Students can access the following: campus intranet, free student e-mail accounts, online (class) grades, online (class) registration, online (class) schedules. Campuswide network is available. Wireless service is available via entire campus.

Library: McDole-McDonald Library. *Books:* 12,617 (physical), 10,290 (digital/electronic); *Serial titles:* 12,705 (physical), 14,979 (digital/electronic); *Databases:* 15. Students can reserve study rooms.

STUDENT LIFE

Housing options: men-only, women-only. Campus housing is university owned.

Campus security: 24-hour emergency response devices, student patrols, controlled dormitory access.

COSTS & FINANCIAL AID

Costs (2018–19) *Comprehensive fee:* $17,160 includes full-time tuition ($9750), mandatory fees ($1260), and room and board ($6150). Full-time tuition and fees vary according to course load, location, program, and reciprocity agreements. Part-time tuition: $325 per credit hour. Part-time tuition and fees vary according to course load, location, program, and reciprocity agreements. *Required fees:* $630 per term part-time. *College room only:* $3350. Room and board charges vary according to location. *Payment plans:* installment, deferred payment. *Waivers:* employees or children of employees.

Financial Aid Of all full-time matriculated undergraduates who enrolled in 2010, 64 applied for aid, 64 were judged to have need. 16 Federal Work-Study jobs (averaging $460). *Average percent of need met:* 44. *Average financial aid package:* $8338. *Average need-based loan:* $3791. *Average need-based gift aid:* $5198. *Average indebtedness upon graduation:* $20,805.

APPLYING

Standardized Tests *Required for some:* SAT (for admission), ACT (for admission), SAT or ACT (for admission).

Options: electronic application, early admission.

Application fee: $35.

Required: essay or personal statement, high school transcript, minimum 2.0 GPA, 3 letters of recommendation, health form. *Required for some:* interview.

Application deadlines: 8/14 (freshmen), 8/14 (transfers).

Notification: 8/25 (freshmen), continuous until 8/25 (transfers).

CONTACT

Carrie Underwood, Director of Enrollment Services, Messenger College, 400 South Industrial Boulevard, Suite 300, Euless, TX 76040. *Phone:* 817-554-5950 Ext. 165. *Toll-free phone:* 800-385-8940. *Fax:* 817-391.4003. *E-mail:* enrollment@messengercollege.edu.

Midland College

Midland, Texas

http://www.midland.edu/

- **State and locally supported** 4-year, founded 1969
- **Suburban** 163-acre campus
- **Coed** 5,564 undergraduate students, 29% full-time, 56% women, 44% men
- **Noncompetitive** entrance level

UNDERGRAD STUDENTS

1,603 full-time, 3,961 part-time. 6% Black or African American, non-Hispanic/Latino; 49% Hispanic/Latino; 2% Asian, non-Hispanic/Latino; 0.2% Native Hawaiian or other Pacific Islander, non-Hispanic/Latino; 0.5% American Indian or Alaska Native, non-Hispanic/Latino; 2% Two or more races, non-Hispanic/Latino; 3% Race/ethnicity unknown; 7% transferred in.

Freshmen:

Admission: 780 enrolled.

FACULTY

Student/faculty ratio: 17:1.

ACADEMICS

Calendar: semesters. *Degrees:* certificates, associate, and bachelor's.

Special study options: academic remediation for entering students, advanced placement credit, cooperative education, distance learning, English as a second language, honors programs, off-campus study, services for LD students, summer session for credit.

Computers: 950 computers/terminals are available on campus for general student use. Students can access the following: computer help desk, free student e-mail accounts, online (class) grades, online (class) registration, online (class) schedules. Campuswide network is available. 100% of college-owned or -operated housing units are wired for high-speed Internet access. Wireless service is available via entire campus.

Library: Murray Fasken Learning Resource Center. Weekly public service hours: 84.

STUDENT LIFE

Housing options: coed, men-only, women-only. Campus housing is university owned.

Activities and organizations: drama/theater group, student-run newspaper, choral group, OIKOS, Midland College Latin American Student Society, Student Government Association, Student Nurses Association, Baptist Student Ministries.

Athletics Member NJCAA. *Intercollegiate sports:* baseball M(s), basketball M(s)/W(s), cheerleading M(s)/W(s), golf M(s), softball W(s), volleyball W(s). *Intramural sports:* basketball M/W, cheerleading M/W, volleyball M/W.

Campus security: 24-hour patrols, controlled dormitory access.

Student services: personal/psychological counseling.

COSTS

Costs (2017–18) *Tuition:* area resident $2670 full-time, $89 per credit hour part-time; state resident $4230 full-time, $141 per credit hour part-time; nonresident $5490 full-time, $183 per credit hour part-time. Full-time tuition and fees vary according to course level, course load, degree level, location, program, reciprocity agreements, and student level. Part-time tuition and fees vary according to course level, course load, degree level, location, program, reciprocity agreements, and student level. *Room and board:* $4900. *Payment plan:* installment. *Waivers:* senior citizens and employees or children of employees.

APPLYING

Options: electronic application.

Application deadlines: rolling (freshmen), rolling (transfers).

Notification: continuous (freshmen), continuous (transfers).

CONTACT

Ms. Amy Webb, Enrollment Services & Navigation Director, Midland College, 3600 North Garfield, Midland, TX 79705-6399. *Phone:* 432-685-4816. *E-mail:* amyw@midland.edu.

Midwestern State University

Wichita Falls, Texas

http://www.mwsu.edu/

CONTACT

Ms. Leah Vineyard, Interim Director of Admissions, Midwestern State University, 3410 Taft Boulevard, Wichita Falls, TX 76308. *Phone:* 940-397-4343. *Toll-free phone:* 800-842-1922. *Fax:* 940-397-4672. *E-mail:* leah.vineyard@mwsu.edu.

National American University

Austin, Texas

http://www.national.edu/

CONTACT

National American University, 13801 Burnet Road, Suite 300, Austin, TX 78727. *Toll-free phone:* 888-628-8392.

National American University

Georgetown, Texas

http://www.national.edu/

CONTACT

National American University, 1015 West University Avenue, Suite 700, Georgetown, TX 78628. *Toll-free phone:* 888-628-8392.

National American University

Houston, Texas

http://www.national.edu/

CONTACT

National American University, 11511 Katy Freeway, Suite 200, Houston, TX 77079. *Toll-free phone:* 855-455-8029.

National American University
Lewisville, Texas
http://www.national.edu/

CONTACT
National American University, 475 State Highway 121 Bypass, Suite 150, Lewisville, TX 75067. *Toll-free phone:* 800-548-0605.

National American University
Mesquite, Texas
http://www.national.edu/

CONTACT
National American University, 18600 LBJ Freeway, Mesquite, TX 75150. *Toll-free phone:* 800-548-0605.

National American University
Richardson, Texas
http://www.national.edu/

CONTACT
National American University, 300 North Coit Road, Suite 225, Richardson, TX 75080. *Toll-free phone:* 800-548-0605.

North American University
Stafford, Texas
http://www.na.edu/

- **Independent** comprehensive, founded 2010
- **Urban** 12-acre campus with easy access to Houston, TX
- **Coed** 340 undergraduate students, 92% full-time, 40% women, 60% men
- **Minimally difficult** entrance level, 57% of applicants were admitted

UNDERGRAD STUDENTS
313 full-time, 27 part-time. Students come from 21 states and territories; 52 other countries; 11% are from out of state; 11% Black or African American, non-Hispanic/Latino; 15% Hispanic/Latino; 5% Asian, non-Hispanic/Latino; 4% Two or more races, non-Hispanic/Latino; 0.3% Race/ethnicity unknown; 58% international; 6% transferred in.

Freshmen:
Admission: 215 applied, 123 admitted, 50 enrolled.
Retention: 46% of full-time freshmen returned.

FACULTY
Total: 42, 19% full-time, 62% with terminal degrees.
Student/faculty ratio: 19:1.

ACADEMICS
Calendar: semesters. *Degrees:* bachelor's and master's.
Special study options: academic remediation for entering students, advanced placement credit, distance learning, English as a second language, internships, part-time degree program, summer session for credit.
Computers: 150 computers/terminals are available on campus for general student use. Students can access the following: campus intranet, computer help desk, free student e-mail accounts, online (class) grades, online (class) registration, online (class) schedules. Campuswide network is available. 100% of college-owned or -operated housing units are wired for high-speed Internet access. Wireless service is available via entire campus.
Library: North American University Library. *Books:* 4,857 (physical), 168,629 (digital/electronic); *Serial titles:* 3 (physical), 2 (digital/electronic); *Databases:* 8. Weekly public service hours: 61; students can reserve study rooms.

STUDENT LIFE
Housing options: men-only, women-only. Campus housing is leased by the school.
Activities and organizations: Computer Science, Women's Computer Science, NAU Care Services, Student Athlete Association, Harmony Stallions Association.
Student services: personal/psychological counseling.

COSTS
Costs (2018–19) *One-time required fee:* $110. *Comprehensive fee:* $18,800 includes full-time tuition ($9450), mandatory fees ($450), and room and board ($8900). Full-time tuition and fees vary according to course load, degree level, and program. Part-time tuition: $475 per credit hour. Part-time tuition and fees vary according to course load, degree level, and program. No tuition increase for student's term of enrollment. *Required fees:* $225 per term part-time. *College room only:* $4500. Room and board charges vary according to board plan. *Payment plan:* installment. *Waivers:* employees or children of employees.

APPLYING
Standardized Tests *Recommended:* SAT or ACT (for admission).
Options: electronic application, early admission, deferred entrance.
Required: high school transcript, interview. *Required for some:* essay or personal statement, 1 letter of recommendation. *Recommended:* minimum 2.7 GPA.
Application deadlines: rolling (freshmen), rolling (out-of-state freshmen), rolling (transfers).
Early decision deadline: rolling (for plan 1), rolling (for plan 2).
Notification: continuous (freshmen), continuous (out-of-state freshmen), continuous (transfers).

CONTACT
Mr. Shawn Washington, Associate Director of Admissions, North American University, 11929 West Airport Boulevard, Stafford, TX 77477. *Phone:* 832-230-5555. *E-mail:* admissions@na.edu.

Our Lady of the Lake University
San Antonio, Texas
http://www.ollusa.edu/

- **Independent Roman Catholic** comprehensive, founded 1895
- **Urban** 75-acre campus with easy access to San Antonio, TX
- **Endowment** $27.7 million
- **Coed** 1,342 undergraduate students, 91% full-time, 69% women, 31% men

UNDERGRAD STUDENTS
1,221 full-time, 121 part-time. 2% are from out of state; 8% Black or African American, non-Hispanic/Latino; 76% Hispanic/Latino; 0.5% Asian, non-Hispanic/Latino; 0.1% Native Hawaiian or other Pacific Islander, non-Hispanic/Latino; 0.5% American Indian or Alaska Native, non-Hispanic/Latino; 2% Two or more races, non-Hispanic/Latino; 2% Race/ethnicity unknown; 2% international; 12% transferred in; 39% live on campus.

Freshmen:
Admission: 338 enrolled. *Average high school GPA:* 3.5. *Test scores:* SAT evidence-based reading and writing scores over 500: 57%; SAT math scores over 500: 53%; ACT scores over 18: 73%; SAT evidence-based reading and writing scores over 600: 10%; SAT math scores over 600: 5%; ACT scores over 24: 13%; SAT evidence-based reading and writing scores over 700: 2%; ACT scores over 30: 1%.
Retention: 61% of full-time freshmen returned.

FACULTY
Total: 315, 32% full-time, 56% with terminal degrees.
Student/faculty ratio: 14:1.

ACADEMICS
Calendar: semesters plus summer sessions. *Degrees:* bachelor's, master's, and doctoral.
Special study options: accelerated degree program, adult/continuing education programs, advanced placement credit, cooperative education, distance learning, double majors, honors programs, independent study, internships, off-campus study, part-time degree program, services for LD students, study abroad, summer session for credit. *ROTC:* Army (c).
Computers: 236 computers/terminals are available on campus for general student use. Students can access the following: computer help desk, free student e-mail accounts, online (class) grades, online (class) registration, online (class) schedules. Campuswide network is available. 100% of college-owned or -operated housing units are wired for high-speed Internet access. Wireless service is available via entire campus.

Library: The Sueltenfuss Library. *Books:* 82,924 (physical), 51,160 (digital/electronic); *Serial titles:* 16,651 (physical), 167,665 (digital/electronic); *Databases:* 96. Weekly public service hours: 95; study areas open 24 hours, 5–7 days a week.

STUDENT LIFE
Housing options: coed, women-only, special housing for students with disabilities. Campus housing is university owned.

Activities and organizations: drama/theater group, student-run newspaper, television station, choral group, First Year Connection, Kappa Delta Chi, Epsilon Sigma Alpha, Social Justice Organization, Higher Achievement Through Leadership Opportunities, national sororities.

Athletics Member NAIA. *Intercollegiate sports:* baseball M(s), basketball M(s)/W(s), cross-country running M(s)/W(s), golf M(s), soccer M(s)/W(s), softball W(s), tennis M(s)/W(s), track and field M(s)/W(s), volleyball W(s). *Intramural sports:* cheerleading W, football M/W, volleyball M.

Campus security: 24-hour emergency response devices and patrols, late-night transport/escort service, controlled dormitory access.

Student services: health clinic, personal/psychological counseling, women's center.

COSTS & FINANCIAL AID
Costs (2018–19) *Comprehensive fee:* $38,342 includes full-time tuition ($27,912), mandatory fees ($828), and room and board ($9602). Full-time tuition and fees vary according to course load and location. Part-time tuition: $895 per credit hour. Part-time tuition and fees vary according to course load and location. *Required fees:* $414 per term part-time. *College room only:* $5814. Room and board charges vary according to board plan and housing facility. *Payment plans:* installment, deferred payment. *Waivers:* employees or children of employees.

Financial Aid Of all full-time matriculated undergraduates who enrolled in 2016, 1,084 applied for aid, 1,016 were judged to have need, 418 had their need fully met. In 2016, 108 non-need-based awards were made. *Average percent of need met:* 84. *Average financial aid package:* $22,549. *Average need-based loan:* $4785. *Average need-based gift aid:* $15,648. *Average non-need-based aid:* $8806. *Average indebtedness upon graduation:* $34,224.

APPLYING
Standardized Tests *Required:* SAT or ACT (for admission).

Required: high school transcript, minimum 2.0 GPA.

CONTACT
Shannon Tijerina, Assistant Director of Traditional Admissions, Our Lady of the Lake University, 411 Southwest 24th Street, San Antonio, TX 78207-4689. *Phone:* 210-434-6711 Ext. 4133. *Toll-free phone:* 800-436-6558. *Fax:* 210-431-4036. *E-mail:* sytijeria@lake.ollusa.edu.

Paul Quinn College
Dallas, Texas
http://www.pqc.edu/

CONTACT
Paul Quinn College, 3837 Simpson-Stuart Road, Dallas, TX 75241-4331. *Phone:* 214-379-5494. *Toll-free phone:* 877-346-1063.

Prairie View A&M University
Prairie View, Texas
http://www.pvamu.edu/
- **State-supported** university, founded 1878, part of Texas A&M University System
- **Small-town** 1502-acre campus with easy access to Houston
- **Endowment** $71.2 million
- **Coed** 8,026 undergraduate students, 91% full-time, 61% women, 39% men
- **Moderately difficult** entrance level, 79% of applicants were admitted

UNDERGRAD STUDENTS
7,341 full-time, 685 part-time. Students come from 39 states and territories; 28 other countries; 7% are from out of state; 83% Black or African American, non-Hispanic/Latino; 9% Hispanic/Latino; 2% Asian, non-Hispanic/Latino; 0.1% Native Hawaiian or other Pacific Islander,

non-Hispanic/Latino; 0.3% American Indian or Alaska Native, non-Hispanic/Latino; 1% Two or more races, non-Hispanic/Latino; 0.2% Race/ethnicity unknown; 1% international; 5% transferred in; 53% live on campus.

Freshmen:
Admission: 6,422 applied, 5,069 admitted, 2,051 enrolled. *Average high school GPA:* 3.1. *Test scores:* SAT evidence-based reading and writing scores over 500: 40%; SAT math scores over 500: 39%; ACT scores over 18: 49%; SAT evidence-based reading and writing scores over 600: 8%; SAT math scores over 600: 4%; ACT scores over 24: 8%; SAT evidence-based reading and writing scores over 700: 1%.
Retention: 69% of full-time freshmen returned.

FACULTY
Total: 481, 81% full-time, 57% with terminal degrees.
Student/faculty ratio: 18:1.

ACADEMICS
Calendar: semesters. *Degrees:* bachelor's, master's, doctoral, post-master's, and postbachelor's certificates.

Special study options: academic remediation for entering students, accelerated degree program, advanced placement credit, cooperative education, distance learning, double majors, honors programs, independent study, internships, off-campus study, part-time degree program, services for LD students, study abroad, summer session for credit. *ROTC:* Army (b), Navy (b), Air Force (c).

Computers: 2,500 computers/terminals are available on campus for general student use. Students can access the following: campus intranet, computer help desk, free student e-mail accounts, online (class) grades, online (class) registration, online (class) schedules. Campuswide network is available. 100% of college-owned or -operated housing units are wired for high-speed Internet access. Wireless service is available via entire campus.

Library: John B. Coleman Library plus 3 others. *Books:* 257,702 (physical), 16,626 (digital/electronic); *Serial titles:* 199 (physical); *Databases:* 23. Weekly public service hours: 97; students can reserve study rooms.

STUDENT LIFE
Housing options: men-only, women-only, special housing for students with disabilities. Campus housing is provided by a third party. Freshman applicants given priority for college housing.

Activities and organizations: drama/theater group, student-run newspaper, radio and television station, choral group, marching band, Student Government Association, Campus Activities Board, National Association for the Advancement of Colored People, National Society of Black Engineers, Peer Advisors to Leadership Students, national fraternities, national sororities.

Athletics Member NCAA, NAIA. All NCAA Division I except football (Division I-AA). *Intercollegiate sports:* baseball M(s), basketball M(s)/W(s), bowling W(s), cheerleading M(s)/W(s), cross-country running M(s)/W(s), golf M(s)/W(s), soccer W(s), softball W(s), tennis M(s)/W(s), track and field M(s)/W(s), volleyball W(s). *Intramural sports:* basketball M/W, football M/W, rugby M/W, soccer M, swimming and diving M/W, tennis M/W, volleyball W, weight lifting M/W.

Campus security: 24-hour emergency response devices and patrols, late-night transport/escort service, controlled dormitory access.

Student services: health clinic, personal/psychological counseling, women's center.

COSTS & FINANCIAL AID
Costs (2018–19) *One-time required fee:* $40. *Tuition:* state resident $6790 full-time; nonresident $21,100 full-time. Full-time tuition and fees vary according to course load, degree level, program, and reciprocity agreements. Part-time tuition and fees vary according to course load, degree level, program, and reciprocity agreements. No tuition increase for student's term of enrollment. *Required fees:* $3743 full-time. *Room and board:* $8743; room only: $5774. Room and board charges vary according to board plan, housing facility, and student level. *Payment plan:* installment. *Waivers:* senior citizens and employees or children of employees.

Financial Aid Of all full-time matriculated undergraduates who enrolled in 2016, 6,351 applied for aid, 5,891 were judged to have need, 630 had their need fully met. 420 Federal Work-Study jobs (averaging $2754). 32

state and other part-time jobs (averaging $2216). In 2016, 187 non-need-based awards were made. *Average percent of need met:* 73. *Average financial aid package:* $15,507. *Average need-based loan:* $7575. *Average need-based gift aid:* $7745. *Average non-need-based aid:* $5773. *Average indebtedness upon graduation:* $37,209. *Financial aid deadline:* 3/15.

APPLYING

Standardized Tests *Required:* SAT or ACT (for admission).

Options: electronic application, early admission, deferred entrance.

Application fee: $40.

Required: high school transcript, minimum 2.8 GPA.

Application deadlines: 6/1 (freshmen), 6/1 (transfers).

Notification: 8/15 (freshmen), 8/15 (transfers).

CONTACT

Ms. Nicole Woods, Administrative Assistant, Prairie View A&M University, PO Box 519, MS #1009, Prairie View, TX 77446-0188. *Phone:* 936-261-1000. *E-mail:* admissions@pvamu.edu.

Rice University

Houston, Texas

http://www.rice.edu/

- **Independent** university, founded 1912
- **Urban** 300-acre campus with easy access to Houston
- **Endowment** $5.8 billion
- **Coed** 4,001 undergraduate students, 98% full-time, 47% women, 53% men
- **Most difficult** entrance level, 16% of applicants were admitted

UNDERGRAD STUDENTS

3,916 full-time, 85 part-time. Students come from 53 states and territories; 42 other countries; 52% are from out of state; 7% Black or African American, non-Hispanic/Latino; 15% Hispanic/Latino; 26% Asian, non-Hispanic/Latino; 0.1% Native Hawaiian or other Pacific Islander, non-Hispanic/Latino; 0.1% American Indian or Alaska Native, non-Hispanic/Latino; 4% Two or more races, non-Hispanic/Latino; 2% Race/ethnicity unknown; 12% international; 0.7% transferred in; 72% live on campus.

Freshmen:

Admission: 18,063 applied, 2,864 admitted, 1,046 enrolled. *Test scores:* SAT evidence-based reading and writing scores over 500: 99%; SAT math scores over 500: 100%; ACT scores over 18: 100%; SAT evidence-based reading and writing scores over 600: 95%; SAT math scores over 600: 96%; ACT scores over 24: 99%; SAT evidence-based reading and writing scores over 700: 83%; SAT math scores over 700: 84%; ACT scores over 30: 94%.

Retention: 97% of full-time freshmen returned.

FACULTY

Total: 870, 78% full-time, 92% with terminal degrees.

Student/faculty ratio: 6:1.

ACADEMICS

Calendar: semesters. *Degrees:* bachelor's, master's, and doctoral.

Special study options: accelerated degree program, advanced placement credit, double majors, English as a second language, honors programs, independent study, internships, off-campus study, services for LD students, student-designed majors, study abroad, summer session for credit. *ROTC:* Army (c), Navy (b), Air Force (c).

Computers: 258 computers/terminals are available on campus for general student use. Students can access the following: campus intranet, computer help desk, free student e-mail accounts, online (class) grades, online (class) registration, online (class) schedules. Campuswide network is available. 100% of college-owned or -operated housing units are wired for high-speed Internet access. Wireless service is available via entire campus.

Library: Fondren Library. *Books:* 3.0 million (physical), 50,625 (digital/electronic); *Serial titles:* 160,917 (digital/electronic).

STUDENT LIFE

Housing options: coed. Campus housing is university owned. Freshman applicants given priority for college housing.

Activities and organizations: drama/theater group, student-run newspaper, radio and television station, choral group, marching band, Drama Club, Community service/volunteer program, intramural sports, College government, Marching Owl Band.

Athletics Member NCAA. All Division I except football (Division I-A). *Intercollegiate sports:* badminton M(c)/W(c), baseball M(s), basketball M(s)/W(s), cheerleading M(c)/W(c), crew M(c)/W(c), cross-country running M(s)/W(s), equestrian sports M(c)/W(c), fencing M(c)/W(c), field hockey W(c), golf M(s), lacrosse M(c)/W(c), riflery M(c)/W(c), rugby M(c)/W(c), sailing M(c)/W(c), soccer M(c)/W(s), softball W(c), swimming and diving W(s), tennis M(s)/W(s), track and field M(s)/W(s), ultimate Frisbee M(c)/W(c), volleyball M(c)/W(c), water polo M(c)/W(c). *Intramural sports:* badminton M/W, basketball M/W, cross-country running M/W, football M/W, racquetball M/W, soccer M/W, softball M/W, swimming and diving M/W, table tennis M/W, tennis M/W, track and field M/W, ultimate Frisbee M/W, volleyball M/W.

Campus security: 24-hour emergency response devices and patrols, late-night transport/escort service, controlled dormitory access.

Student services: health clinic, personal/psychological counseling, women's center.

COSTS & FINANCIAL AID

Costs (2017–18) *One-time required fee:* $625. *Comprehensive fee:* $59,458 includes full-time tuition ($44,900), mandatory fees ($708), and room and board ($13,850). Part-time tuition: $1871 per credit hour. *College room only:* $9490. Room and board charges vary according to board plan. *Payment plan:* installment. *Waivers:* employees or children of employees.

Financial Aid Of all full-time matriculated undergraduates who enrolled in 2016, 2,701 applied for aid, 1,493 were judged to have need, 1,483 had their need fully met. In 2016, 404 non-need-based awards were made. *Average percent of need met:* 100. *Average financial aid package:* $41,888. *Average need-based loan:* $3643. *Average need-based gift aid:* $36,772. *Average non-need-based aid:* $19,019. *Average indebtedness upon graduation:* $22,497. *Financial aid deadline:* 4/15.

APPLYING

Standardized Tests *Required:* SAT or ACT (for admission). *Recommended:* SAT Subject Tests (for admission).

Options: electronic application, early decision, deferred entrance.

Application fee: $75.

Required: essay or personal statement, high school transcript, 2 letters of recommendation. *Required for some:* portfolio for architecture, audition for music. *Recommended:* interview.

Application deadlines: 1/1 (freshmen), 3/15 (transfers).

Early decision deadline: 11/1.

Notification: 4/1 (freshmen), continuous until 5/15 (transfers), 12/15 (early decision).

CONTACT

Office of Admission, Rice University, Office of Admission, PO Box 1892, MS 17, Houston, TX 77251-1892. *Phone:* 713-348-RICE. *E-mail:* admi@rice.edu.

Rio Grande Bible Institute

Edinburg, Texas

http://www.riogrande.edu/

CONTACT

David Loyola, Director of Admissions, Rio Grande Bible Institute, 4300 S US Hwy 281, Edinburg, TX 78539. *Phone:* 956-380-8100. *Fax:* 956-380-8256. *E-mail:* admisiones@riogrande.edu.

St. Edward's University

Austin, Texas

http://www.stedwards.edu/

- **Independent Roman Catholic** comprehensive, founded 1885
- **Urban** 160-acre campus with easy access to Austin
- **Endowment** $94.9 million
- **Coed**
- **Moderately difficult** entrance level

FACULTY
Student/faculty ratio: 14:1.

ACADEMICS
Calendar: semesters. *Degrees:* bachelor's, master's, and postbachelor's certificates.
Library: Munday Library. *Books:* 71,983 (physical), 273,440 (digital/electronic); *Serial titles:* 202 (physical), 121,477 (digital/electronic); *Databases:* 230. Weekly public service hours: 103; students can reserve study rooms.

STUDENT LIFE
Housing options: on-campus residence required for freshman year; coed, special housing for students with disabilities. Campus housing is university owned. Freshman campus housing is guaranteed.
Activities and organizations: drama/theater group, student-run newspaper, radio and television station, choral group, American Medical Student Association, Students for Sustainability, Academy of Science, PRIDE, Asian Student Association.
Athletics Member NCAA. All Division II.
Campus security: 24-hour emergency response devices and patrols, late-night transport/escort service, controlled dormitory access, self-defense education, informal discussions, pamphlets, posters, alcohol awareness meetings, lighted pathways and sidewalks.
Student services: health clinic, personal/psychological counseling.

COSTS & FINANCIAL AID
Costs (2017–18) *One-time required fee:* $250. *Comprehensive fee:* $55,990 includes full-time tuition ($42,550), mandatory fees ($500), and room and board ($12,940). Full-time tuition and fees vary according to degree level. Part-time tuition: $1419 per credit hour. Part-time tuition and fees vary according to course load and degree level. *Required fees:* $150 per year part-time. *Room and board:* Room and board charges vary according to board plan and housing facility.
Financial Aid Of all full-time matriculated undergraduates who enrolled in 2016, 2,714 applied for aid, 2,473 were judged to have need, 258 had their need fully met. 233 Federal Work-Study jobs (averaging $1974). 18 state and other part-time jobs (averaging $2000). In 2016, 161 non-need-based awards were made. *Average percent of need met:* 68. *Average financial aid package:* $32,523. *Average need-based loan:* $4517. *Average need-based gift aid:* $20,681. *Average non-need-based aid:* $16,563. *Average indebtedness upon graduation:* $37,377.

APPLYING
Standardized Tests *Required:* SAT or ACT (for admission).
Options: electronic application, deferred entrance.
Application fee: $50.
Required: essay or personal statement, high school transcript, 1 letter of recommendation. *Recommended:* interview.

CONTACT
Ms. Kelsey McClure, Administrative Coordinator, St. Edward's University, 3001 South Congress Avenue, Austin, TX 78704. *Phone:* 512-448-8500. *Toll-free phone:* 800-555-0164. *Fax:* 512-464-8877. *E-mail:* seu.admit@stedwards.edu.

St. Mary's University

San Antonio, Texas
http://www.stmarytx.edu/

- **Independent Roman Catholic** comprehensive, founded 1852
- **Urban** 135-acre campus with easy access to San Antonio
- **Endowment** $183.0 million
- **Coed** 2,327 undergraduate students, 96% full-time, 54% women, 46% men
- **Moderately difficult** entrance level, 80% of applicants were admitted

UNDERGRAD STUDENTS
2,228 full-time, 99 part-time. Students come from 26 states and territories; 32 other countries; 8% are from out of state; 3% Black or African American, non-Hispanic/Latino; 67% Hispanic/Latino; 2% Asian, non-Hispanic/Latino; 0.3% American Indian or Alaska Native, non-Hispanic/Latino; 1% Two or more races, non-Hispanic/Latino; 2% Race/ethnicity unknown; 9% international; 5% transferred in; 56% live on campus.

Freshmen:
Admission: 4,468 applied, 3,570 admitted, 643 enrolled. *Average high school GPA:* 3.6. *Test scores:* ACT scores over 18: 95%; ACT scores over 24: 33%; ACT scores over 30: 4%.
Retention: 73% of full-time freshmen returned.

FACULTY
Total: 385, 57% full-time, 76% with terminal degrees.
Student/faculty ratio: 11:1.

ACADEMICS
Calendar: semesters. *Degrees:* bachelor's, master's, and doctoral.
Special study options: academic remediation for entering students, adult/continuing education programs, advanced placement credit, cooperative education, distance learning, double majors, English as a second language, honors programs, independent study, internships, off-campus study, part-time degree program, services for LD students, study abroad, summer session for credit. *ROTC:* Army (b), Air Force (c).
Computers: 200 computers/terminals and 125 ports are available on campus for general student use. Students can access the following: campus intranet, computer help desk, free student e-mail accounts, online (class) grades, online (class) registration, online (class) schedules. Campuswide network is available. 100% of college-owned or -operated housing units are wired for high-speed Internet access. Wireless service is available via entire campus.
Library: Louis J. Blume Library plus 1 other. *Books:* 265,910 (physical), 194,058 (digital/electronic); *Serial titles:* 486 (physical), 76,976 (digital/electronic); *Databases:* 97. Weekly public service hours: 100.

STUDENT LIFE
Housing options: on-campus residence required for freshman year; coed, special housing for students with disabilities. Campus housing is university owned. Freshman applicants given priority for college housing.
Activities and organizations: drama/theater group, student-run newspaper, choral group, Alpha Phi Omega (Professional Service Fraternity), Beta Beta Beta Biological Honor Society, Delta Sigma Pi (Professional Business Fraternity), Society of Hispanic Engineers, Pre-Medical Society, national fraternities, national sororities.
Athletics Member NCAA. All Division II. *Intercollegiate sports:* baseball M(s), basketball M(s)/W(s), cheerleading M/W, golf M(s)/W(s), soccer M(s)/W(s), softball W, tennis M(s)/W(s), volleyball W(s). *Intramural sports:* badminton M/W, basketball M/W, football M/W, racquetball M/W, rock climbing M/W, sand volleyball M/W, soccer M/W, softball M/W, swimming and diving M/W, table tennis M/W, tennis M/W, ultimate Frisbee M(c)/W(c), volleyball M/W.
Campus security: 24-hour emergency response devices and patrols, late-night transport/escort service, controlled dormitory access.
Student services: health clinic, personal/psychological counseling.

COSTS & FINANCIAL AID
Costs (2018–19) *Comprehensive fee:* $41,390 includes full-time tuition ($29,710), mandatory fees ($890), and room and board ($10,790). Full-time tuition and fees vary according to course level, course load, degree level, and program. Part-time tuition: $925 per credit hour. Part-time tuition and fees vary according to course level, course load, degree level, and program. *Required fees:* $260 per term part-time. *College room only:* $6800. Room and board charges vary according to board plan, housing facility, and student level. *Payment plan:* installment. *Waivers:* employees or children of employees.
Financial Aid Of all full-time matriculated undergraduates who enrolled in 2016, 1,658 applied for aid, 1,560 were judged to have need, 174 had their need fully met. 426 Federal Work-Study jobs (averaging $2131). 81 state and other part-time jobs (averaging $2193). In 2016, 430 non-need-based awards were made. *Average percent of need met:* 71. *Average financial aid package:* $25,624. *Average need-based loan:* $4378. *Average need-based gift aid:* $19,727. *Average non-need-based aid:* $18,516. *Average indebtedness upon graduation:* $37,866. *Financial aid deadline:* 6/1.

APPLYING
Standardized Tests *Required:* SAT or ACT (for admission).
Options: electronic application, deferred entrance.
Required: essay or personal statement, high school transcript, minimum 2.5 GPA, 1 letter of recommendation. *Required for some:* interview.

Application deadlines: rolling (freshmen), rolling (transfers).
Notification: continuous (freshmen), continuous (transfers).

CONTACT
Ms. Melissa Romero, Associate Director, Freshman Admission, St. Mary's University, One Camino Santa Maria, Box #3, San Antonio, TX 78228. *Phone:* 210-436-3126. *Toll-free phone:* 800-367-7868. *Fax:* 210-431-6742. *E-mail:* uadm@stmarytx.edu.

Sam Houston State University

Huntsville, Texas
http://www.shsu.edu/

- **State-supported** university, founded 1879, part of Texas State University System
- **Small-town** campus with easy access to Houston
- **Endowment** $96.5 million
- **Coed** 18,416 undergraduate students, 80% full-time, 62% women, 38% men
- **Moderately difficult** entrance level, 75% of applicants were admitted

UNDERGRAD STUDENTS
14,808 full-time, 3,608 part-time. 1% are from out of state; 18% Black or African American, non-Hispanic/Latino; 23% Hispanic/Latino; 2% Asian, non-Hispanic/Latino; 0.2% Native Hawaiian or other Pacific Islander, non-Hispanic/Latino; 0.6% American Indian or Alaska Native, non-Hispanic/Latino; 3% Two or more races, non-Hispanic/Latino; 2% Race/ethnicity unknown; 1% international; 14% transferred in; 21% live on campus.

Freshmen:
Admission: 12,365 applied, 9,212 admitted, 2,873 enrolled. *Test scores:* SAT evidence-based reading and writing scores over 500: 77%; SAT math scores over 500: 75%; ACT scores over 18: 92%; SAT evidence-based reading and writing scores over 600: 19%; SAT math scores over 600: 10%; ACT scores over 24: 24%; SAT evidence-based reading and writing scores over 700: 1%; SAT math scores over 700: 1%; ACT scores over 30: 2%.

Retention: 77% of full-time freshmen returned.

FACULTY
Total: 955, 66% full-time, 74% with terminal degrees.
Student/faculty ratio: 23:1.

ACADEMICS
Calendar: semesters. *Degrees:* bachelor's, master's, doctoral, and postbachelor's certificates.
Special study options: academic remediation for entering students, advanced placement credit, distance learning, double majors, English as a second language, honors programs, independent study, internships, off-campus study, part-time degree program, services for LD students, study abroad, summer session for credit. *ROTC:* Army (b).
Computers: 1,600 computers/terminals and 5,544 ports are available on campus for general student use. Students can access the following: computer help desk, free student e-mail accounts, online (class) grades, online (class) registration, online (class) schedules. Campuswide network is available. 100% of college-owned or -operated housing units are wired for high-speed Internet access. Wireless service is available via entire campus.
Library: Newton Gresham Library. Students can reserve study rooms.

STUDENT LIFE
Housing options: on-campus residence required for freshman year; coed, women-only, special housing for students with disabilities. Campus housing is university owned and is provided by a third party. Freshman campus housing is guaranteed.
Activities and organizations: drama/theater group, student-run newspaper, radio and television station, choral group, marching band, national fraternities, national sororities.
Athletics Member NCAA. All Division I except football (Division I-AA). *Intercollegiate sports:* baseball M(s), basketball M(s)/W(s), bowling W(s), cheerleading M(s)/W(s), cross-country running M(s)/W(s), equestrian sports M/W, golf M(s)/W(s), lacrosse M(c)/W(c), soccer W(s), softball W(s), tennis W(s), track and field M(s)/W(s), ultimate Frisbee M(c)/W(c), volleyball W(s). *Intramural sports:* basketball M/W, football M/W, racquetball M/W, riflery M(c), rugby M(c)/W(c), soccer M/W, softball M/W, tennis M(c)/W(c), volleyball M/W.
Campus security: 24-hour emergency response devices and patrols, student patrols, late-night transport/escort service, controlled dormitory access.
Student services: health clinic, personal/psychological counseling, legal services.

COSTS & FINANCIAL AID
Costs (2017–18) *Tuition:* state resident $6840 full-time, $228 per credit hour part-time; nonresident $19,290 full-time, $643 per credit hour part-time. Full-time tuition and fees vary according to course load and location. Part-time tuition and fees vary according to course load and location. No tuition increase for student's term of enrollment. *Required fees:* $3051 full-time. *Room and board:* $9180; room only: $5238. Room and board charges vary according to board plan and housing facility. *Payment plan:* installment. *Waivers:* employees or children of employees.
Financial Aid Of all full-time matriculated undergraduates who enrolled in 2016, 11,217 applied for aid, 9,556 were judged to have need, 895 had their need fully met. In 2016, 476 non-need-based awards were made. *Average percent of need met:* 56. *Average financial aid package:* $11,263. *Average need-based loan:* $7582. *Average need-based gift aid:* $7560. *Average non-need-based aid:* $2624. *Average indebtedness upon graduation:* $27,920.

APPLYING
Standardized Tests *Required:* SAT or ACT (for admission).
Options: electronic application, early admission.
Application fee: $45.
Required: high school transcript.
Application deadlines: 8/1 (freshmen), 8/1 (transfers).

CONTACT
Ms. Angie Taylor, Director of Admissions, Sam Houston State University, Box 2418, Huntsville, TX 77341. *Phone:* 936-294-1845. *Toll-free phone:* 866-232-7528 Ext. 1828. *Fax:* 936-294-3758. *E-mail:* agb003@shsu.edu.

Schreiner University

Kerrville, Texas
http://www.schreiner.edu/

- **Independent Presbyterian** comprehensive, founded 1923
- **Small-town** 211-acre campus with easy access to San Antonio, Austin
- **Endowment** $69.2 million
- **Coed** 1,237 undergraduate students, 87% full-time, 58% women, 42% men
- **Moderately difficult** entrance level, 91% of applicants were admitted

UNDERGRAD STUDENTS
1,075 full-time, 162 part-time. Students come from 15 states and territories; 14 other countries; 3% are from out of state; 3% Black or African American, non-Hispanic/Latino; 37% Hispanic/Latino; 1% Asian, non-Hispanic/Latino; 0.3% American Indian or Alaska Native, non-Hispanic/Latino; 2% Two or more races, non-Hispanic/Latino; 7% Race/ethnicity unknown; 0.8% international; 5% transferred in; 61% live on campus.

Freshmen:
Admission: 998 applied, 906 admitted, 302 enrolled. *Average high school GPA:* 3.6. *Test scores:* ACT scores over 18: 90%; ACT scores over 24: 25%; ACT scores over 30: 3%.

Retention: 69% of full-time freshmen returned.

FACULTY
Total: 125, 50% full-time, 38% with terminal degrees.
Student/faculty ratio: 13:1.

ACADEMICS
Calendar: semesters. *Degrees:* certificates, associate, bachelor's, and master's.
Special study options: academic remediation for entering students, accelerated degree program, advanced placement credit, cooperative education, distance learning, double majors, honors programs, independent study, internships, part-time degree program, services for LD

students, student-designed majors, study abroad, summer session for credit.

Unusual degree programs: 3-2 engineering with University of Texas at Austin, Texas A&M University, University of North Dakota.

Computers: 120 computers/terminals are available on campus for general student use. Students can access the following: campus intranet, computer help desk, free student e-mail accounts, online (class) grades, online (class) registration, online (class) schedules. Campuswide network is available. 100% of college-owned or -operated housing units are wired for high-speed Internet access. Wireless service is available via entire campus.

Library: W. M. Logan Library. *Books:* 80,478 (physical); *Serial titles:* 404 (physical). Weekly public service hours: 30; students can reserve study rooms.

STUDENT LIFE

Housing options: on-campus residence required through junior year; coed, special housing for students with disabilities. Campus housing is university owned. Freshman campus housing is guaranteed.

Activities and organizations: drama/theater group, student-run newspaper, choral group, Student Senate, Greek Life, Campus Ministry, honor societies, Hall Councils, national fraternities, national sororities.

Athletics Member NCAA. All Division III. *Intercollegiate sports:* baseball M, basketball M/W, cross-country running M/W, golf M/W, soccer M/W, softball W, tennis M/W, volleyball W. *Intramural sports:* cheerleading W, riflery M/W.

Campus security: 24-hour emergency response devices and patrols, student patrols, late-night transport/escort service, controlled dormitory access.

Student services: health clinic, personal/psychological counseling.

COSTS & FINANCIAL AID

Costs (2017–18) *Comprehensive fee:* $37,052 includes full-time tuition ($24,990), mandatory fees ($1910), and room and board ($10,152). Full-time tuition and fees vary according to course load, location, and program. Part-time tuition: $1069 per credit hour. Part-time tuition and fees vary according to course load and program. *Required fees:* $1155 per year part-time. *College room only:* $4980. Room and board charges vary according to board plan and housing facility. *Payment plan:* installment. *Waivers:* employees or children of employees.

Financial Aid Of all full-time matriculated undergraduates who enrolled in 2017, 928 applied for aid, 819 were judged to have need, 98 had their need fully met. In 2017, 234 non-need-based awards were made. *Average percent of need met:* 68. *Average financial aid package:* $19,518. *Average need-based loan:* $3761. *Average need-based gift aid:* $16,266. *Average non-need-based aid:* $10,118. *Average indebtedness upon graduation:* $29,746. *Financial aid deadline:* 5/15.

APPLYING

Standardized Tests *Required:* SAT or ACT (for admission).

Options: electronic application, deferred entrance.

Application fee: $25.

Required: high school transcript.

Application deadlines: 5/1 (freshmen), 5/1 (transfers).

Notification: continuous (freshmen), continuous (transfers).

CONTACT

Caroline Randall, Director of Admissions, Schreiner University, 2100 Memorial Boulevard, Kerrville, TX 78028. *Phone:* 800-343-4919. *Toll-free phone:* 800-343-4919. *E-mail:* carandall@schreiner.edu.

★ Southern Methodist University
Dallas, Texas
http://www.smu.edu/

- **Independent** university, founded 1911, affiliated with United Methodist Church
- **Urban** 234-acre campus with easy access to Dallas-Fort Worth
- **Endowment** $1.5 billion
- **Coed** 6,452 undergraduate students, 97% full-time, 50% women, 50% men
- **Moderately difficult** entrance level, 49% of applicants were admitted

UNDERGRAD STUDENTS

6,240 full-time, 212 part-time. Students come from 47 states and territories; 62 other countries; 55% are from out of state; 5% Black or

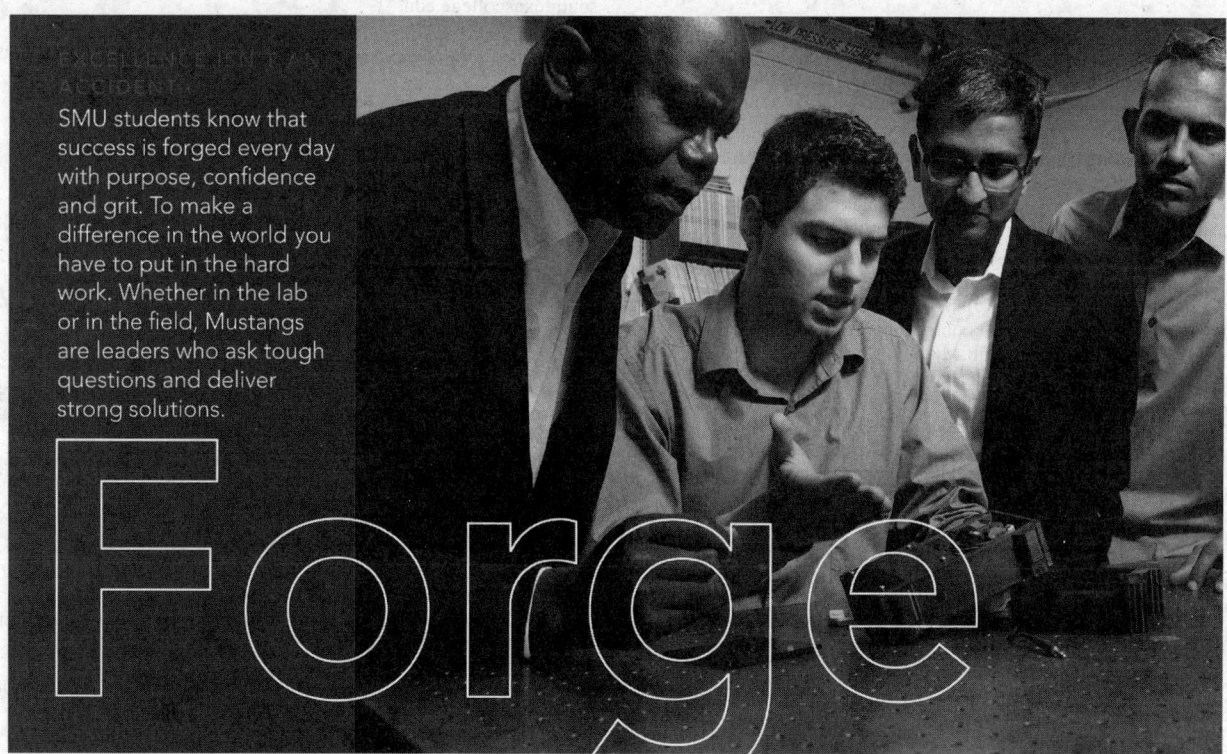

SMU students know that success is forged every day with purpose, confidence and grit. To make a difference in the world you have to put in the hard work. Whether in the lab or in the field, Mustangs are leaders who ask tough questions and deliver strong solutions.

World Changers Shaped Here SMU.

African American, non-Hispanic/Latino; 11% Hispanic/Latino; 6% Asian, non-Hispanic/Latino; 0.1% Native Hawaiian or other Pacific Islander, non-Hispanic/Latino; 0.3% American Indian or Alaska Native, non-Hispanic/Latino; 4% Two or more races, non-Hispanic/Latino; 9% international; 4% transferred in; 54% live on campus.

Freshmen:
Admission: 13,128 applied, 6,402 admitted, 1,423 enrolled. *Average high school GPA:* 3.6. *Test scores:* ACT scores over 18: 100%; ACT scores over 24: 98%; ACT scores over 30: 62%.

Retention: 91% of full-time freshmen returned.

FACULTY
Total: 1,156, 66% full-time, 64% with terminal degrees.
Student/faculty ratio: 11:1.

ACADEMICS
Calendar: semesters. *Degrees:* bachelor's, master's, doctoral, post-master's, and postbachelor's certificates.
Special study options: academic remediation for entering students, accelerated degree program, adult/continuing education programs, advanced placement credit, cooperative education, distance learning, double majors, English as a second language, honors programs, independent study, internships, part-time degree program, services for LD students, student-designed majors, study abroad, summer session for credit. *ROTC:* Army (b), Air Force (c).
Computers: 758 computers/terminals and 758 ports are available on campus for general student use. Students can access the following: campus intranet, computer help desk, free student e-mail accounts, online (class) grades, online (class) registration, online (class) schedules, online billing/payment processing. Campuswide network is available. 100% of college-owned or -operated housing units are wired for high-speed Internet access. Wireless service is available via classrooms, computer centers, computer labs, dorm rooms, learning centers, libraries, student centers.
Library: Fondren Library plus 7 others. *Books:* 3.0 million (physical), 1.2 million (digital/electronic); *Serial titles:* 16,580 (physical), 139,891 (digital/electronic); *Databases:* 667. Weekly public service hours: 150; study areas open 24 hours, 5–7 days a week; students can reserve study rooms.

STUDENT LIFE
Housing options: on-campus residence required through sophomore year; coed, special housing for students with disabilities. Campus housing is university owned, leased by the school and is provided by a third party. Freshman campus housing is guaranteed.
Activities and organizations: drama/theater group, student-run newspaper, radio and television station, choral group, marching band, Program Council, Student Foundation, Student Senate, Student Foundation, Residence Hall Association, SPARC (Students Promoting Awareness, Responsibility, and Citizenship), national fraternities, national sororities.
Athletics Member NCAA. All Division I except football (Division I-A). *Intercollegiate sports:* baseball M(c), basketball M(s)/W(s), cheerleading M(s)(c)/W(s)(c), crew W(s), cross-country running W(s), equestrian sports W(s), fencing M(c)/W(c), golf M(s)/W(s), ice hockey M(c), lacrosse M(c), rugby M(c)/W(c), soccer M(s)/W(s), swimming and diving M(s)/W(s), tennis M(s)/W(s), track and field W, volleyball W(s), wrestling M(c). *Intramural sports:* basketball M/W, bowling M/W, football M, golf M/W, racquetball M/W, rock climbing M(c)/W(c), soccer M/W, softball M/W, swimming and diving M/W, table tennis M(c)/W(c), tennis M/W, ultimate Frisbee M/W, volleyball M/W, water polo M/W, weight lifting M(c)/W(c).
Campus security: 24-hour emergency response devices and patrols, late-night transport/escort service, controlled dormitory access.
Student services: health clinic, personal/psychological counseling, women's center.

COSTS & FINANCIAL AID
Costs (2018–19) *Comprehensive fee:* $71,338 includes full-time tuition ($48,365), mandatory fees ($6128), and room and board ($16,845). Part-time tuition: $2020 per credit hour. Part-time tuition and fees vary according to course load. *Room and board:* Room and board charges vary according to board plan and housing facility. *Payment plans:* tuition prepayment, installment. *Waivers:* employees or children of employees.

Financial Aid Of all full-time matriculated undergraduates who enrolled in 2017, 2,442 applied for aid, 1,981 were judged to have need, 735 had their need fully met. In 2017, 2319 non-need-based awards were made. *Average percent of need met:* 87. *Average financial aid package:* $44,049. *Average need-based loan:* $4343. *Average need-based gift aid:* $22,487. *Average non-need-based aid:* $25,304. *Average indebtedness upon graduation:* $32,468.

APPLYING
Standardized Tests *Required:* SAT or ACT (for admission). *Required for some:* SAT Subject Tests (for admission).
Options: electronic application, early decision, early action, deferred entrance.
Application fee: $60.
Required: high school transcript, minimum 2.0 GPA, 1 letter of recommendation, statement of good standing from prior institution(s). *Recommended:* essay or personal statement, minimum 2.7 GPA.
Application deadlines: 1/15 (freshmen), 4/1 (transfers), 11/1 (early action).
Early decision deadline: 11/1 (for plan 1), 1/15 (for plan 2).
Notification: continuous (freshmen), 12/31 (early decision plan 1), 4/1 (early decision plan 2), 12/31 (early action).
CONTACT
Ms. Elena Hicks, Dean of Undergraduate Admission, Southern Methodist University, PO Box 750181, Dallas, TX 75275-0181. *Phone:* 214-768-3417. *Toll-free phone:* 800-323-0672. *Fax:* 214-768-1083. *E-mail:* ugadmission@smu.edu.

See previous page for display ad and page 1430 for the College Close-Up.

South Texas College
McAllen, Texas
http://www.southtexascollege.edu/

CONTACT
Mr. Matthew Hebbard, Director of Enrollment Services and Registrar, South Texas College, 3201 West Pecan, McAllen, TX 78501. *Phone:* 956-872-2147. *Toll-free phone:* 800-742-7822. *E-mail:* mshebbar@southtexascollege.edu.

South University
Round Rock, Texas
http://www.southuniversity.edu/austin.aspx

CONTACT
Director of Admissions, South University, 1220 West Louis Henna Boulevard, Round Rock, TX 78681. *Phone:* 512-516-8800. *Toll-free phone:* 877-659-5706. *Fax:* 512-516-8680.

Southwestern Adventist University
Keene, Texas
http://www.swau.edu/
- **Independent Seventh-day Adventist** comprehensive, founded 1894
- **Small-town** 150-acre campus with easy access to Dallas-Fort Worth
- **Endowment** $11.4 million
- **Coed** 799 undergraduate students, 82% full-time, 57% women, 43% men
- **Minimally difficult** entrance level, 60% of applicants were admitted

UNDERGRAD STUDENTS
653 full-time, 146 part-time. Students come from 35 states and territories; 18 other countries; 31% are from out of state; 14% Black or African American, non-Hispanic/Latino; 44% Hispanic/Latino; 4% Asian, non-Hispanic/Latino; 2% Native Hawaiian or other Pacific Islander, non-Hispanic/Latino; 0.3% American Indian or Alaska Native, non-Hispanic/Latino; 4% Two or more races, non-Hispanic/Latino; 2% Race/ethnicity unknown; 8% international; 7% transferred in; 47% live on campus.

Freshmen:
Admission: 1,400 applied, 842 admitted, 129 enrolled. *Average high school GPA:* 3.3. *Test scores:* SAT evidence-based reading and writing scores over 500: 56%; SAT math scores over 500: 49%; SAT evidence-

based reading and writing scores over 600: 28%; SAT math scores over 600: 11%; SAT evidence-based reading and writing scores over 700: 3%; SAT math scores over 700: 3%.

Retention: 81% of full-time freshmen returned.

FACULTY
Total: 81, 60% full-time, 51% with terminal degrees.
Student/faculty ratio: 12:1.

ACADEMICS
Calendar: semesters. *Degrees:* certificates, associate, bachelor's, and master's.

Special study options: academic remediation for entering students, accelerated degree program, adult/continuing education programs, advanced placement credit, distance learning, double majors, English as a second language, external degree program, honors programs, independent study, internships, off-campus study, part-time degree program, services for LD students, student-designed majors, study abroad, summer session for credit.

Computers: 275 computers/terminals and 1,600 ports are available on campus for general student use. Students can access the following: campus intranet, computer help desk, free student e-mail accounts, online (class) grades, online (class) registration, online (class) schedules. Campuswide network is available. 100% of college-owned or -operated housing units are wired for high-speed Internet access. Wireless service is available via entire campus.

Library: Chan Shun Centennial Library. *Books:* 90,431 (physical), 29,515 (digital/electronic); *Serial titles:* 5,000 (digital/electronic); *Databases:* 85. Weekly public service hours: 60; students can reserve study rooms.

STUDENT LIFE
Housing options: men-only, women-only, cooperative. Campus housing is university owned. Freshman campus housing is guaranteed.

Activities and organizations: drama/theater group, student-run newspaper, radio and television station, choral group, Student Association, Enactus (to enable progress through entrepreneurial action), Education/Psychology Club, Theology Club, Nursing Club.

Athletics Member USCAA. *Intercollegiate sports:* basketball M/W, soccer M/W, volleyball W. *Intramural sports:* badminton M/W, basketball M/W, football M/W, racquetball M/W, soccer M/W, softball M/W, table tennis M/W, tennis M/W, volleyball M/W(c).

Campus security: 24-hour emergency response devices, student patrols, controlled dormitory access.

Student services: health clinic, personal/psychological counseling.

COSTS
Costs (2017–18) *Comprehensive fee:* $28,232 includes full-time tuition ($20,112), mandatory fees ($620), and room and board ($7500). Full-time tuition and fees vary according to program. Part-time tuition: $838 per semester hour. Part-time tuition and fees vary according to program. *Required fees:* $620 per term part-time. *Room and board:* Room and board charges vary according to board plan. *Payment plan:* installment. *Waivers:* senior citizens and employees or children of employees.

APPLYING
Standardized Tests *Required:* SAT or ACT (for admission).
Options: electronic application, early admission, deferred entrance.
Application fee: $25.
Required: high school transcript, minimum 2.5 GPA. *Required for some:* essay or personal statement, 1 letter of recommendation, interview.
Application deadlines: 8/1 (freshmen), 8/7 (transfers).
Notification: continuous (freshmen), continuous until 9/1 (transfers).

CONTACT
Ms. Rahneeka Hazelton, Director of Admissions, Southwestern Adventist University, 100 West Hillcrest, Keene, TX 76059. *Phone:* 817-202-6733. *Toll-free phone:* 800-433-2240. *E-mail:* rahneeka@swau.edu.

Southwestern Assemblies of God University
Waxahachie, Texas
http://www.sagu.edu/

- **Independent** comprehensive, founded 1927, affiliated with Assemblies of God
- **Small-town** 70-acre campus with easy access to Dallas-Fort Worth
- **Endowment** $10.3 million
- **Coed** 1,790 undergraduate students, 83% full-time, 52% women, 48% men
- **Noncompetitive** entrance level, 97% of applicants were admitted

UNDERGRAD STUDENTS
1,492 full-time, 298 part-time. 13% Black or African American, non-Hispanic/Latino; 17% Hispanic/Latino; 0.7% Asian, non-Hispanic/Latino; 0.6% Native Hawaiian or other Pacific Islander, non-Hispanic/Latino; 3% American Indian or Alaska Native, non-Hispanic/Latino; 4% Two or more races, non-Hispanic/Latino; 0.3% Race/ethnicity unknown; 0.6% international.

Freshmen:
Admission: 515 applied, 502 admitted, 332 enrolled.
Retention: 72% of full-time freshmen returned.

FACULTY
Total: 148, 49% full-time, 38% with terminal degrees.
Student/faculty ratio: 16:1.

ACADEMICS
Calendar: semesters. *Degrees:* associate, bachelor's, and master's.

Special study options: academic remediation for entering students, adult/continuing education programs, advanced placement credit, distance learning, double majors, external degree program, internships, part-time degree program, services for LD students, summer session for credit.

Computers: 80 computers/terminals and 1,000 ports are available on campus for general student use. Students can access the following: computer help desk, free student e-mail accounts, online (class) grades, online (class) registration, online (class) schedules. Campuswide network is available. 95% of college-owned or -operated housing units are wired for high-speed Internet access. Wireless service is available via entire campus.

Library: P. C. Nelson Memorial Library plus 1 other. *Books:* 100,582 (physical), 256 (digital/electronic); *Serial titles:* 414 (physical), 13,284 (digital/electronic); *Databases:* 70. Weekly public service hours: 90; students can reserve study rooms.

STUDENT LIFE
Housing options: on-campus residence required through senior year; coed, women-only. Campus housing is university owned. Freshman campus housing is guaranteed.

Activities and organizations: drama/theater group, student-run newspaper, choral group, Student Congress, Southwestern Missions Association, Street Hope, Gold Jackets, Women in Ministry.

Athletics Member NAIA, NCCAA. *Intercollegiate sports:* baseball M(s), basketball M(s)/W(s), cross-country running M(s)/W(s), football M(s), soccer M(s)/W(s), softball W(s), track and field M(s)/W(s), volleyball W(s). *Intramural sports:* basketball M/W, cheerleading W, football M/W, soccer M(c)/W, softball M/W, table tennis M/W, tennis M/W, ultimate Frisbee M/W, volleyball M/W.

Campus security: 24-hour patrols, late-night transport/escort service, controlled dormitory access, electronic and key access in dorms, camera surveillance, 24-hour dispatch monitored fire alarm systems (offsite).

Student services: health clinic, personal/psychological counseling.

COSTS & FINANCIAL AID
Costs (2018–19) *Comprehensive fee:* $28,452 includes full-time tuition ($19,992), mandatory fees ($960), and room and board ($7500). Full-time tuition and fees vary according to course load, degree level, and location. Part-time tuition and fees vary according to course load, degree level, and location. *Room and board:* Room and board charges vary according to board plan, housing facility, and location. *Payment plan:* deferred payment. *Waivers:* employees or children of employees.

Financial Aid Of all full-time matriculated undergraduates who enrolled in 2000, 1,116 applied for aid, 1,002 were judged to have need, 110 had their need fully met. 178 Federal Work-Study jobs, 7 state and other part-time jobs (averaging $890). In 2000, 316 non-need-based awards were made. *Average percent of need met:* 64. *Average financial aid package:* $6728. *Average need-based loan:* $3177. *Average need-based gift aid:* $3511. *Average indebtedness upon graduation:* $13,938. *Financial aid deadline:* 7/1.

APPLYING
Standardized Tests *Required:* SAT or ACT (for admission). *Recommended:* ACT (for admission).

Options: electronic application.

Application fee: $35.

Required: essay or personal statement, high school transcript, minimum 2.0 GPA, 1 letter of recommendation.

Application deadlines: 8/1 (freshmen), rolling (transfers).

Notification: continuous (freshmen), continuous (transfers).

CONTACT
Mr. Joshua Martin, Assistant Dean of Admissions, Southwestern Assemblies of God University, 1200 Sycamore Street, Waxahachie, TX 75165. *Phone:* 972-825-4821. *Toll-free phone:* 888-937-7248. *E-mail:* jmartin@sagu.edu.

Southwestern Christian College

Terrell, Texas
http://www.swcc.edu/

CONTACT
Admissions Department, Southwestern Christian College, Box 10, 200 Bowser Street, Terrell, TX 75160. *Phone:* 214-524-3341.

Southwestern University

Georgetown, Texas
http://www.southwestern.edu/

- **Independent Methodist** 4-year, founded 1840
- **Suburban** 700-acre campus with easy access to Austin
- **Endowment** $255.5 million
- **Coed** 1,387 undergraduate students, 99% full-time, 57% women, 43% men
- **Very difficult** entrance level, 43% of applicants were admitted

UNDERGRAD STUDENTS
1,367 full-time, 20 part-time. Students come from 34 states and territories; 12 other countries; 10% are from out of state; 5% Black or African American, non-Hispanic/Latino; 24% Hispanic/Latino; 3% Asian, non-Hispanic/Latino; 0.1% Native Hawaiian or other Pacific Islander, non-Hispanic/Latino; 0.3% American Indian or Alaska Native, non-Hispanic/Latino; 5% Two or more races, non-Hispanic/Latino; 1% Race/ethnicity unknown; 1% international; 3% transferred in; 77% live on campus.

Freshmen:
Admission: 4,133 applied, 1,783 admitted, 362 enrolled. *Test scores:* SAT evidence-based reading and writing scores over 500: 97%; SAT math scores over 500: 96%; ACT scores over 18: 99%; SAT evidence-based reading and writing scores over 600: 56%; SAT math scores over 600: 50%; ACT scores over 24: 72%; SAT evidence-based reading and writing scores over 700: 13%; SAT math scores over 700: 7%; ACT scores over 30: 21%.
Retention: 86% of full-time freshmen returned.

FACULTY
Total: 146, 77% full-time, 91% with terminal degrees.
Student/faculty ratio: 11:1.

ACADEMICS
Calendar: semesters. *Degree:* bachelor's.
Special study options: advanced placement credit, double majors, honors programs, independent study, internships, off-campus study, services for LD students, student-designed majors, study abroad, summer session for credit. *ROTC:* Air Force (c).

Unusual degree programs: 3-2 engineering.

Computers: 410 computers/terminals are available on campus for general student use. Students can access the following: campus intranet, computer help desk, free student e-mail accounts, online (class) grades, online (class) registration, online (class) schedules, transcripts. Campuswide network is available. 100% of college-owned or -operated housing units are wired for high-speed Internet access. Wireless service is available via entire campus.

Library: A. Frank Smith, Jr. Library Center. *Books:* 268,906 (physical), 514,199 (digital/electronic); *Serial titles:* 284 (physical), 140,590 (digital/electronic); *Databases:* 151. Weekly public service hours: 90; study areas open 24 hours, 5–7 days a week.

STUDENT LIFE
Housing options: on-campus residence required through sophomore year; coed, men-only, women-only, special housing for students with disabilities. Campus housing is university owned. Freshman campus housing is guaranteed.

Activities and organizations: drama/theater group, student-run newspaper, radio station, choral group, Students for Environmental Activism and Knowledge (SEAK), Alpha Phi Omega, Women's Panhellenic, Men's IFC, national fraternities, national sororities.

Athletics Member NCAA. All Division III. *Intercollegiate sports:* baseball M, basketball M/W, cross-country running M/W, football M, golf M/W, lacrosse M/W, soccer M/W, softball W, swimming and diving M/W, tennis M/W, track and field M/W, volleyball W. *Intramural sports:* basketball M/W, cheerleading M(c)/W(c), fencing M(c)/W(c), football M/W, racquetball M/W, sand volleyball M/W, soccer M/W, table tennis M/W, ultimate Frisbee M(c)/W(c), volleyball M/W.

Campus security: 24-hour emergency response devices and patrols, late-night transport/escort service, controlled dormitory access.

Student services: health clinic, personal/psychological counseling, women's center.

COSTS & FINANCIAL AID
Costs (2018–19) *Comprehensive fee:* $54,000 includes full-time tuition ($42,000) and room and board ($12,000). Part-time tuition: $1750 per credit hour. Part-time tuition and fees vary according to course load. *College room only:* $6480. Room and board charges vary according to board plan and housing facility. *Payment plan:* installment. *Waivers:* employees or children of employees.

Financial Aid Of all full-time matriculated undergraduates who enrolled in 2017, 1,016 applied for aid, 880 were judged to have need, 205 had their need fully met. 227 Federal Work-Study jobs (averaging $2097). 469 state and other part-time jobs (averaging $2475). In 2017, 466 non-need-based awards were made. *Average percent of need met:* 86. *Average financial aid package:* $36,217. *Average need-based loan:* $5005. *Average need-based gift aid:* $30,483. *Average non-need-based aid:* $21,445. *Average indebtedness upon graduation:* $34,788.

APPLYING
Standardized Tests *Required:* SAT or ACT (for admission).

Options: electronic application, early admission, early decision, early action, deferred entrance.

Required: essay or personal statement, high school transcript, 1 letter of recommendation, counselor recommendation. *Required for some:* interview. *Recommended:* interview.

Application deadlines: 2/1 (freshmen), 4/1 (transfers), 12/1 (early action).

Early decision deadline: 11/1.

Notification: 4/1 (freshmen), 7/1 (transfers), 12/1 (early decision), 3/1 (early action).

CONTACT
Mr. Bob Baldwin, Director of Admission, Southwestern University, 1001 East University Avenue, Georgetown, TX 78626. *Phone:* 512-863-1200. *Toll-free phone:* 800-252-3166. *Fax:* 512-863-9601. *E-mail:* admission@southwestern.edu.

Southwest University at El Paso
El Paso, Texas
http://southwestuniversity.edu/

CONTACT
Southwest University at El Paso, 1414 Geronimo Drive, El Paso, TX 79925.

Stephen F. Austin State University
Nacogdoches, Texas
http://www.sfasu.edu/
- **State-supported** comprehensive, founded 1923
- **Small-town** 419-acre campus
- **Endowment** $81.7 million
- **Coed** 10,985 undergraduate students, 87% full-time, 63% women, 37% men
- **Moderately difficult** entrance level, 65% of applicants were admitted

UNDERGRAD STUDENTS
9,567 full-time, 1,418 part-time. Students come from 37 states and territories; 40 other countries; 2% are from out of state; 17% Black or African American, non-Hispanic/Latino; 19% Hispanic/Latino; 1% Asian, non-Hispanic/Latino; 0.1% Native Hawaiian or other Pacific Islander, non-Hispanic/Latino; 0.5% American Indian or Alaska Native, non-Hispanic/Latino; 4% Two or more races, non-Hispanic/Latino; 0.8% Race/ethnicity unknown; 0.6% international; 8% transferred in; 44% live on campus.

Freshmen:
Admission: 11,081 applied, 7,250 admitted, 2,150 enrolled. *Test scores:* SAT evidence-based reading and writing scores over 500: 78%; SAT math scores over 500: 73%; ACT scores over 18: 87%; SAT evidence-based reading and writing scores over 600: 24%; SAT math scores over 600: 15%; ACT scores over 24: 27%; SAT evidence-based reading and writing scores over 700: 1%; SAT math scores over 700: 1%; ACT scores over 30: 2%.
Retention: 72% of full-time freshmen returned.

FACULTY
Total: 718, 71% full-time, 67% with terminal degrees.
Student/faculty ratio: 19:1.

ACADEMICS
Calendar: semesters. *Degrees:* bachelor's, master's, and doctoral.
Special study options: academic remediation for entering students, accelerated degree program, adult/continuing education programs, advanced placement credit, cooperative education, distance learning, double majors, freshman honors college, honors programs, independent study, internships, off-campus study, part-time degree program, services for LD students, student-designed majors, study abroad, summer session for credit. *ROTC:* Army (b).
Unusual degree programs: 3-2 professional accountancy.
Computers: 1,000 computers/terminals are available on campus for general student use. Students can access the following: campus intranet, computer help desk, free student e-mail accounts, online (class) grades, online (class) registration, online (class) schedules. Campuswide network is available. 100% of college-owned or -operated housing units are wired for high-speed Internet access. Wireless service is available via classrooms, computer centers, computer labs, dorm rooms, learning centers, libraries, student centers.
Library: Ralph W. Steen Library. *Books:* 685,436 (physical), 341,357 (digital/electronic); *Serial titles:* 5,582 (physical), 119,163 (digital/electronic); *Databases:* 265. Weekly public service hours: 99; students can reserve study rooms.

STUDENT LIFE
Housing options: on-campus residence required through sophomore year; coed, men-only, women-only, special housing for students with disabilities. Campus housing is university owned and is provided by a third party. Freshman campus housing is guaranteed.
Activities and organizations: drama/theater group, student-run newspaper, radio and television station, choral group, marching band, Residence Hall Association, Baptist Student Ministries, Greek Life, Student Activities Association, Student Government Association, national fraternities, national sororities.
Athletics Member NCAA. All Division I except football (Division I-AA). *Intercollegiate sports:* baseball M(s), basketball M(s)/W(s), bowling W(s), cheerleading M(s)/W(s), cross-country running M(s)/W(s), golf M(s)/W(s), lacrosse M(c), rugby M(c)/W, soccer M(c)/W(s), softball W(s), tennis M(c)/W(s), track and field M(s)/W(s), volleyball W(s). *Intramural sports:* baseball M(c), basketball M(c)/W(c), football M/W, golf M/W, racquetball M/W, rock climbing M/W, soccer M/W, softball M/W, swimming and diving M(c)/W(c), table tennis M/W, tennis M/W, ultimate Frisbee M/W, volleyball M/W, water polo M/W.
Campus security: 24-hour emergency response devices and patrols, student patrols, late-night transport/escort service, controlled dormitory access.
Student services: health clinic, personal/psychological counseling.

COSTS & FINANCIAL AID
Costs (2017–18) *Tuition:* state resident $7260 full-time, $242 per credit hour part-time; nonresident $19,710 full-time, $657 per credit hour part-time. Full-time tuition and fees vary according to course load, degree level, and location. Part-time tuition and fees vary according to course load, degree level, and location. No tuition increase for student's term of enrollment. *Required fees:* $2277 full-time, $158 per credit hour part-time. *Room and board:* $8868. Room and board charges vary according to board plan and housing facility. *Payment plan:* installment. *Waivers:* senior citizens and employees or children of employees.
Financial Aid Of all full-time matriculated undergraduates who enrolled in 2016, 8,179 applied for aid, 6,630 were judged to have need, 1,111 had their need fully met. In 2016, 867 non-need-based awards were made. *Average percent of need met:* 61. *Average financial aid package:* $12,338. *Average need-based loan:* $4704. *Average need-based gift aid:* $7504. *Average non-need-based aid:* $2911. *Average indebtedness upon graduation:* $30,101.

APPLYING
Standardized Tests *Required:* SAT or ACT (for admission).
Options: electronic application.
Application fee: $45.
Required: high school transcript.
Application deadlines: rolling (freshmen), rolling (transfers).
Notification: continuous (freshmen), continuous (transfers).

CONTACT
Mr. Kevin Davis, Associate Director of Admissions, Stephen F. Austin State University, PO Box 13051, SFA Station, Nacogdoches, TX 75962. *Phone:* 936-468-2504. *Toll-free phone:* 800-731-2902. *Fax:* 936-468-3849. *E-mail:* admissions@sfasu.edu.

Strayer University–Cedar Hill Campus
Cedar Hill, Texas
http://www.strayer.edu/texas/cedar-hill/

CONTACT
Strayer University–Cedar Hill Campus, 610 Uptown Boulevard, Suite 3500, Cedar Hill, TX 75104. *Toll-free phone:* 888-311-0355.

Strayer University–Irving Campus
Irving, Texas
http://www.strayer.edu/texas/irving/

CONTACT
Strayer University–Irving Campus, 7701 Las Colinas Ridge, Suite 450, Irving, TX 75063. *Toll-free phone:* 888-311-0355.

Strayer University–Katy Campus
Houston, Texas
http://www.strayer.edu/texas/katy/

CONTACT
Strayer University–Katy Campus, 14511 Old Katy Road, Suite 200, Houston, TX 77079. *Toll-free phone:* 888-311-0355.

Strayer University–North Austin Campus

Austin, Texas

http://www.strayer.edu/texas/north-austin/

CONTACT
Strayer University–North Austin Campus, 8501 North Mopac Expressway, Suite 100, Austin, TX 78759. *Toll-free phone:* 888-311-0355.

Strayer University–North Dallas Campus

Dallas, Texas

http://www.strayer.edu/texas/north-dallas

CONTACT
Strayer University–North Dallas Campus, 8111 LBJ Freeway, Suite 1100, Dallas, TX 75251.

Strayer University–Northwest Houston Campus

Houston, Texas

http://www.strayer.edu/texas/northwest-houston/

CONTACT
Strayer University–Northwest Houston Campus, 10940 West Sam Houston Parkway North, Suite 200, Houston, TX 77064. *Toll-free phone:* 888-311-0355.

Strayer University–San Antonio Campus

San Antonio, Texas

http://www.strayer.edu/texas/san-antonio

CONTACT
Strayer University–San Antonio Campus, 40 NE Loop 410, Suite 500, San Antonio, TX 78216.

Strayer University–Stafford Campus

Stafford, Texas

http://www.strayer.edu/texas/stafford

CONTACT
Strayer University–Stafford Campus, 12603 Southwest Freeway, Suite 400, Stafford, TX 77477.

Sul Ross State University

Alpine, Texas

http://www.sulross.edu/

CONTACT
Sul Ross State University, PO Box C - 114, Alpine, TX 79832. *Phone:* 432-837-8050. *Toll-free phone:* 888-722-7778.

Tarleton State University

Stephenville, Texas

http://www.tarleton.edu/

- **State-supported** comprehensive, founded 1899, part of Texas A&M University System
- **Small-town** 175-acre campus with easy access to Fort Worth
- **Endowment** $29.8 million
- **Coed** 11,288 undergraduate students, 75% full-time, 61% women, 39% men
- **Moderately difficult** entrance level, 74% of applicants were admitted

UNDERGRAD STUDENTS
8,428 full-time, 2,860 part-time. 2% are from out of state; 8% Black or African American, non-Hispanic/Latino; 20% Hispanic/Latino; 1% Asian, non-Hispanic/Latino; 0.2% Native Hawaiian or other Pacific Islander, non-Hispanic/Latino; 0.5% American Indian or Alaska Native, non-Hispanic/Latino; 3% Two or more races, non-Hispanic/Latino; 0.8% Race/ethnicity unknown; 0.3% international; 13% transferred in; 25% live on campus.

Freshmen:
Admission: 7,158 applied, 5,324 admitted, 1,754 enrolled. *Test scores:* SAT evidence-based reading and writing scores over 500: 68%; SAT math scores over 500: 66%; ACT scores over 18: 80%; SAT evidence-based reading and writing scores over 600: 15%; SAT math scores over 600: 12%; ACT scores over 24: 21%; SAT evidence-based reading and writing scores over 700: 1%; SAT math scores over 700: 1%; ACT scores over 30: 1%.
Retention: 67% of full-time freshmen returned.

FACULTY
Total: 766, 51% full-time.
Student/faculty ratio: 17:1.

ACADEMICS
Calendar: semesters. *Degrees:* certificates, associate, bachelor's, master's, and doctoral.

Special study options: academic remediation for entering students, accelerated degree program, adult/continuing education programs, advanced placement credit, cooperative education, distance learning, double majors, freshman honors college, honors programs, independent study, internships, off-campus study, part-time degree program, services for LD students, study abroad, summer session for credit. *ROTC:* Army (b), Air Force (c).

Computers: 1,200 computers/terminals are available on campus for general student use. Students can access the following: campus intranet, computer help desk, free student e-mail accounts, online (class) grades, online (class) registration, online (class) schedules. Campuswide network is available. 100% of college-owned or -operated housing units are wired for high-speed Internet access. Wireless service is available via entire campus.
Library: Dick Smith Library plus 1 other. Students can reserve study rooms.

STUDENT LIFE
Housing options: on-campus residence required through sophomore year; coed, men-only, women-only, cooperative. Campus housing is university owned and leased by the school. Freshman campus housing is guaranteed.

Activities and organizations: drama/theater group, student-run newspaper, radio station, choral group, marching band, Student Government Association, Student Programming Association, Kappa Delta Rho, Delta Zeta, Chi Alpha, national fraternities, national sororities.

Athletics Member NCAA. All Division II. *Intercollegiate sports:* baseball M(s), basketball M(s)/W(s), cheerleading M(s)/W(s), cross-country running M(s)/W(s), football M(s), golf W(s), softball W(s), tennis W(s), track and field M(s)/W(s), volleyball W(s). *Intramural sports:* archery M/W, basketball M/W, football M/W, golf M/W, racquetball M/W, soccer M/W, softball M/W, table tennis M/W, tennis M/W, volleyball M/W.

Campus security: 24-hour emergency response devices and patrols, student patrols, late-night transport/escort service, controlled dormitory access.

Student services: health clinic, personal/psychological counseling, legal services.

COSTS & FINANCIAL AID
Costs (2018–19) *Tuition:* state resident $5012 full-time, $167 per credit hour part-time; nonresident $17,200 full-time, $573 per credit hour part-time. Full-time tuition and fees vary according to course load, degree level, program, and student level. Part-time tuition and fees vary according to course load, degree level, program, and student level. No tuition increase for student's term of enrollment. *Required fees:* $4066 full-time. *Room and board:* $9872; room only: $6220. Room and board charges vary according to board plan and housing facility. *Payment plan:* installment.

Financial Aid Of all full-time matriculated undergraduates who enrolled in 2017, 6,688 applied for aid, 5,458 were judged to have need, 175 had their need fully met. *Average percent of need met:* 54. *Average financial aid package:* $9445. *Average need-based loan:* $4040. *Average need-based gift aid:* $7256. *Average indebtedness upon graduation:* $24,695. *Financial aid deadline:* 11/1.

APPLYING

Standardized Tests *Required:* SAT or ACT (for admission).

Options: electronic application, early action.

Application fee: $45.

Required: high school transcript.

Application deadlines: 8/20 (freshmen), 8/20 (transfers), 3/1 (early action).

CONTACT

Ms. Cindy Hess, Director of Undergraduate Admissions, Tarleton State University, Box T-0030, Tarleton Station, Stephenville, TX 76402. *Phone:* 254-968-9123. *Toll-free phone:* 800-687-8236. *Fax:* 254-968-9951. *E-mail:* uadm@tarleton.edu.

Texas A&M International University

Laredo, Texas

http://www.tamiu.edu/

- **State-supported** comprehensive, founded 1969, part of Texas A&M University System
- **Urban** 300-acre campus
- **Endowment** $49.9 million
- **Coed** 6,799 undergraduate students, 76% full-time, 60% women, 40% men
- **Moderately difficult** entrance level, 50% of applicants were admitted

UNDERGRAD STUDENTS

5,191 full-time, 1,608 part-time. Students come from 24 states and territories; 26 other countries; 0.9% are from out of state; 0.4% Black or African American, non-Hispanic/Latino; 95% Hispanic/Latino; 0.3% Asian, non-Hispanic/Latino; 0.3% Two or more races, non-Hispanic/Latino; 0.3% Race/ethnicity unknown; 2% international; 8% transferred in; 8% live on campus.

Freshmen:

Admission: 7,762 applied, 3,854 admitted, 1,148 enrolled. *Average high school GPA:* 3.6. *Test scores:* SAT evidence-based reading and writing scores over 500: 59%; SAT math scores over 500: 55%; ACT scores over 18: 58%; SAT evidence-based reading and writing scores over 600: 12%; SAT math scores over 600: 11%; ACT scores over 24: 11%; SAT evidence-based reading and writing scores over 700: 1%; SAT math scores over 700: 1%; ACT scores over 30: 1%.

Retention: 76% of full-time freshmen returned.

FACULTY

Total: 370, 62% full-time, 54% with terminal degrees.

Student/faculty ratio: 21:1.

ACADEMICS

Calendar: semesters. *Degrees:* bachelor's, master's, and doctoral.

Special study options: academic remediation for entering students, advanced placement credit, distance learning, double majors, English as a second language, honors programs, independent study, internships, part-time degree program, services for LD students, study abroad, summer session for credit. *ROTC:* Army (b).

Computers: 970 computers/terminals are available on campus for general student use. Students can access the following: free student e-mail accounts, online (class) grades, online (class) registration, online (class) schedules. Campuswide network is available. 100% of college-owned or -operated housing units are wired for high-speed Internet access. Wireless service is available via entire campus.

Library: Sue and Radcliff Killam Library. *Books:* 251,959 (physical), 635,542 (digital/electronic); *Serial titles:* 299 (physical), 72,439 (digital/electronic); *Databases:* 289. Weekly public service hours: 96; students can reserve study rooms.

STUDENT LIFE

Housing options: coed. Campus housing is university owned and is provided by a third party.

Activities and organizations: student-run newspaper, choral group, Tri-Beta Biological Honor Society, Global Medical Brigades, Campus Activities Board, Philosophy Society, Fellowship of Christian Athletes, national fraternities, national sororities.

Athletics *Intercollegiate sports:* baseball M(s), basketball M(s)/W(s), cross-country running M(s)/W(s), golf M(s)/W(s), soccer M(s)/W(s), softball W(s), volleyball W(s). *Intramural sports:* badminton M/W, basketball M/W, soccer M/W, softball M/W, table tennis M/W, ultimate Frisbee M/W, volleyball M/W.

Campus security: 24-hour emergency response devices and patrols, late-night transport/escort service, controlled dormitory access, active shooter response training for faculty, staff, and new students; timely on-going threat information dissemination.

Student services: health clinic, personal/psychological counseling.

COSTS & FINANCIAL AID

Costs (2017–18) *Tuition:* state resident $4773 full-time; nonresident $17,223 full-time. Full-time tuition and fees vary according to course load. Part-time tuition and fees vary according to course load and reciprocity agreements. No tuition increase for student's term of enrollment. *Required fees:* $3547 full-time. *Room and board:* $8160; room only: $5340. Room and board charges vary according to board plan and housing facility. *Payment plan:* installment. *Waivers:* senior citizens.

Financial Aid Of all full-time matriculated undergraduates who enrolled in 2017, 5,016 applied for aid, 4,342 were judged to have need, 19 had their need fully met. 104 Federal Work-Study jobs (averaging $1951). 26 state and other part-time jobs (averaging $1757). In 2017, 329 non-need-based awards were made. *Average percent of need met:* 67. *Average financial aid package:* $9553. *Average need-based loan:* $2845. *Average need-based gift aid:* $6936. *Average non-need-based aid:* $3924. *Average indebtedness upon graduation:* $17,394. *Financial aid deadline:* 7/30.

APPLYING

Standardized Tests *Required:* SAT or ACT (for admission).

Options: electronic application, deferred entrance.

Required: high school transcript.

Notification: continuous (freshmen), continuous (transfers).

CONTACT

Ms. Rosie A Dickinson, Admissions Director, Office of Admissions, Texas A&M International University, 5201 University Boulevard, Laredo, TX 78041-1900. *Phone:* 956-326-2202. *Toll-free phone:* 888-489-2648. *E-mail:* adms@tamiu.edu.

Texas A&M University

College Station, Texas

http://www.tamu.edu/

- **State-supported** university, founded 1876, part of Texas A&M University System
- **Suburban** campus with easy access to Houston
- **Endowment** $11.6 billion
- **Coed** 53,065 undergraduate students, 88% full-time, 48% women, 52% men
- **Moderately difficult** entrance level, 70% of applicants were admitted

UNDERGRAD STUDENTS

46,724 full-time, 6,341 part-time. Students come from 53 states and territories; 96 other countries; 4% are from out of state; 3% Black or African American, non-Hispanic/Latino; 23% Hispanic/Latino; 7% Asian, non-Hispanic/Latino; 0.1% Native Hawaiian or other Pacific Islander, non-Hispanic/Latino; 0.3% American Indian or Alaska Native, non-Hispanic/Latino; 3% Two or more races, non-Hispanic/Latino; 0.2% Race/ethnicity unknown; 1% international; 5% transferred in; 23% live on campus.

Freshmen:

Admission: 37,191 applied, 26,064 admitted, 11,639 enrolled. *Test scores:* SAT evidence-based reading and writing scores over 500: 95%; SAT math scores over 500: 97%; ACT scores over 18: 100%; SAT evidence-based reading and writing scores over 600: 63%; SAT math scores over 600: 66%; ACT scores over 24: 84%; SAT evidence-based reading and writing scores over 700: 14%; SAT math scores over 700: 21%; ACT scores over 30: 34%.

Retention: 92% of full-time freshmen returned.

FACULTY
Total: 3,585, 78% full-time, 85% with terminal degrees.
Student/faculty ratio: 20:1.

ACADEMICS
Calendar: semesters. *Degrees:* bachelor's, master's, doctoral, post-master's, and postbachelor's certificates.

Special study options: academic remediation for entering students, accelerated degree program, advanced placement credit, cooperative education, distance learning, double majors, English as a second language, honors programs, independent study, internships, off-campus study, part-time degree program, services for LD students, study abroad, summer session for credit. *ROTC:* Army (b), Navy (b), Air Force (b).

Computers: 2,776 computers/terminals and 500 ports are available on campus for general student use. Students can access the following: campus intranet, computer help desk, free student e-mail accounts, online (class) grades, online (class) registration, online (class) schedules. Campuswide network is available. 100% of college-owned or -operated housing units are wired for high-speed Internet access. Wireless service is available via entire campus.

Library: Sterling C. Evans Library plus 9 others. *Books:* 4.3 million (physical), 1.9 million (digital/electronic); *Serial titles:* 10,083 (physical), 199,378 (digital/electronic); *Databases:* 1,162. Weekly public service hours: 144; study areas open 24 hours, 5–7 days a week; students can reserve study rooms.

STUDENT LIFE
Housing options: coed, men-only, women-only, special housing for students with disabilities. Campus housing is university owned, leased by the school and is provided by a third party.

Activities and organizations: drama/theater group, student-run newspaper, radio and television station, choral group, marching band, Memorial Student Center, Corps of Cadets, Fish Camp, Student Government, national fraternities, national sororities.

Athletics Member NCAA. All Division I except football (Division I-A). *Intercollegiate sports:* baseball M(s), basketball M(s)/W(s), cross-country running M/W, equestrian sports W(s), golf M(s)/W(s), soccer W(s), softball W(s), swimming and diving M(s)/W(s), tennis M(s)/W(s), track and field M(s)/W(s), volleyball W(s). *Intramural sports:* archery M(c)/W(c), baseball M(c), basketball M/W, bowling M(c)/W(c), equestrian sports M(c)/W(c), fencing M(c)/W(c), football M/W, golf M/W, lacrosse M(c)/W(c), racquetball M(c)/W(c), riflery M(c)/W(c), rowing M(c)/W(c), rugby M(c)/W(c), sailing M(c)/W(c), soccer M/W, softball M/W, table tennis M/W, tennis M/W, triathlon M(c)/W(c), ultimate Frisbee M(c), volleyball M(c)/W(c), water polo M(c)/W(c), weight lifting M(c)/W(c), wrestling M(c)/W(c).

Campus security: 24-hour emergency response devices and patrols, late-night transport/escort service, controlled dormitory access, student escorts.

Student services: health clinic, personal/psychological counseling, women's center, legal services.

COSTS & FINANCIAL AID
Costs (2018–19) *Tuition:* state resident $7052 full-time, $235 per credit hour part-time; nonresident $33,803 full-time, $1127 per credit hour part-time. Full-time tuition and fees vary according to program. Part-time tuition and fees vary according to program. No tuition increase for student's term of enrollment. *Required fees:* $3351 full-time. *Room and board:* $12,250. Room and board charges vary according to board plan, housing facility, and location. *Payment plan:* installment.

Financial Aid Of all full-time matriculated undergraduates who enrolled in 2016, 27,389 applied for aid, 20,193 were judged to have need, 4,363 had their need fully met. 755 Federal Work-Study jobs (averaging $2807). 74 state and other part-time jobs (averaging $2790). In 2016, 5470 non-need-based awards were made. *Average percent of need met:* 72. *Average financial aid package:* $16,491. *Average need-based loan:* $8101. *Average need-based gift aid:* $10,237. *Average non-need-based aid:* $4134. *Average indebtedness upon graduation:* $24,072.

APPLYING
Standardized Tests *Required:* SAT or ACT (for admission).
Options: electronic application.
Application fee: $75.
Required: essay or personal statement, high school transcript. *Required for some:* Apply Texas application, minimum SAT math score of 550 or ACT math score of 24 for the College of Engineering.
Application deadlines: 12/1 (freshmen), 3/15 (transfers).
Notification: continuous (freshmen), continuous (transfers).

CONTACT
Office of Admissions, Texas A&M University, Freshman Admissions, PO Box 30014, College Station, TX 77842-3014. *Phone:* 979-845-1060. *Fax:* 979-845-1808.

Texas A&M University–Central Texas
Killeen, Texas
http://www.tamuct.edu/

- **State-supported** upper-level, founded 2009, part of Texas A&M University System
- **Rural** 662-acre campus
- **Coed** 2,021 undergraduate students, 31% full-time, 60% women, 40% men

UNDERGRAD STUDENTS
633 full-time, 1,388 part-time. Students come from 30 states and territories; 3 other countries; 3% are from out of state; 99% transferred in.

FACULTY
Total: 190, 33% full-time, 49% with terminal degrees.
Student/faculty ratio: 20:1.

ACADEMICS
Calendar: semesters. *Degrees:* certificates, bachelor's, master's, and post-master's certificates.

Special study options: accelerated degree program, advanced placement credit, cooperative education, distance learning, double majors, independent study, internships, off-campus study, part-time degree program, services for LD students, study abroad, summer session for credit. *ROTC:* Army (b).

Computers: 48 computers/terminals are available on campus for general student use. Students can access the following: computer help desk, free student e-mail accounts, online (class) grades, online (class) registration, online (class) schedules. Campuswide network is available. Wireless service is available via entire campus.

Library: University Library. *Books:* 79,788 (physical), 440,601 (digital/electronic); *Serial titles:* 155 (physical), 116,827 (digital/electronic); *Databases:* 175. Weekly public service hours: 81; students can reserve study rooms.

STUDENT LIFE
Housing options: college housing not available.
Activities and organizations: student-run newspaper.
Athletics *Intramural sports:* rugby M(c)/W(c).
Campus security: 24-hour emergency response devices and patrols.
Student services: personal/psychological counseling.

COSTS
Costs (2017–18) *Tuition:* state resident $21,631 full-time, $179 per credit hour part-time; nonresident $33,079 full-time, $645 per credit hour part-time. Full-time tuition and fees vary according to course load. Part-time tuition and fees vary according to course load. No tuition increase for student's term of enrollment. *Required fees:* $2085 full-time, $261 per credit hour part-time. *Payment plan:* installment.

APPLYING
Options: electronic application, deferred entrance.
Notification: continuous (transfers).

CONTACT
Texas A&M University–Central Texas, 1001 Leadership Place, Killeen, TX 76549. *Phone:* 254-519-5438.

Texas A&M University–Commerce

Commerce, Texas

http://www.tamuc.edu/

- **State-supported** university, founded 1889, part of Texas A&M University System
- **Small-town** 1883-acre campus with easy access to Dallas-Fort Worth
- **Coed** 8,031 undergraduate students, 70% full-time, 60% women, 40% men
- **Moderately difficult** entrance level, 34% of applicants were admitted

UNDERGRAD STUDENTS

5,650 full-time, 2,381 part-time. 3% are from out of state; 22% Black or African American, non-Hispanic/Latino; 21% Hispanic/Latino; 2% Asian, non-Hispanic/Latino; 0.2% Native Hawaiian or other Pacific Islander, non-Hispanic/Latino; 0.6% American Indian or Alaska Native, non-Hispanic/Latino; 7% Two or more races, non-Hispanic/Latino; 0.8% Race/ethnicity unknown; 2% international; 17% transferred in; 31% live on campus.

Freshmen:

Admission: 9,730 applied, 3,335 admitted, 940 enrolled. *Average high school GPA:* 3.4. *Test scores:* SAT evidence-based reading and writing scores over 500: 69%; SAT math scores over 500: 67%; ACT scores over 18: 71%; SAT evidence-based reading and writing scores over 600: 19%; SAT math scores over 600: 17%; ACT scores over 24: 25%; SAT evidence-based reading and writing scores over 700: 1%; SAT math scores over 700: 1%; ACT scores over 30: 2%.
Retention: 68% of full-time freshmen returned.

FACULTY

Total: 674, 58% full-time, 63% with terminal degrees.
Student/faculty ratio: 18:1.

ACADEMICS

Calendar: semesters. *Degrees:* bachelor's, master's, doctoral, and postbachelor's certificates.

Special study options: academic remediation for entering students, accelerated degree program, adult/continuing education programs, advanced placement credit, cooperative education, distance learning, double majors, English as a second language, freshman honors college, honors programs, independent study, internships, off-campus study, part-time degree program, services for LD students, student-designed majors, study abroad, summer session for credit. *ROTC:* Air Force (c).

Computers: Students can access the following: campus intranet, computer help desk, free student e-mail accounts, online (class) grades, online (class) registration, online (class) schedules. Campuswide network is available. 100% of college-owned or -operated housing units are wired for high-speed Internet access. Wireless service is available via entire campus.
Library: Gee Library.

STUDENT LIFE

Housing options: on-campus residence required for freshman year; coed, women-only, special housing for students with disabilities. Campus housing is university owned. Freshman campus housing is guaranteed.

Activities and organizations: drama/theater group, student-run newspaper, radio and television station, choral group, marching band, National Society for Leadership and Success, Residence Hall Association, Indian Students Association, The Pride Alliance, National Association of Colored Women's Club, Inc., national fraternities, national sororities.

Athletics Member NCAA. All Division II. *Intercollegiate sports:* basketball M(s)/W(s), cheerleading M(s)/W(s), cross-country running M(s)/W(s), football M(s), golf M(s)/W(s), soccer W(s), softball W, track and field M(s)/W(s), volleyball W(s). *Intramural sports:* archery M/W, badminton M/W, basketball M/W, bowling M/W, cross-country running M/W, equestrian sports M/W, football M/W, golf M/W, racquetball M/W, soccer M, softball M/W, swimming and diving M/W, table tennis M/W, tennis M/W, track and field M/W, volleyball W.

Campus security: 24-hour emergency response devices and patrols, controlled dormitory access.

Student services: health clinic, personal/psychological counseling, legal services.

COSTS & FINANCIAL AID

Costs (2018–19) *Tuition:* state resident $4790 full-time, $160 per credit hour part-time; nonresident $17,240 full-time, $575 per credit hour part-time. Full-time tuition and fees vary according to course load, degree level, location, program, and reciprocity agreements. Part-time tuition and fees vary according to course load, degree level, location, program, and reciprocity agreements. *Required fees:* $3958 full-time. *Room and board:* $8326; room only: $4426. Room and board charges vary according to board plan and housing facility. *Payment plan:* installment. *Waivers:* senior citizens and employees or children of employees.

Financial Aid Of all full-time matriculated undergraduates who enrolled in 2017, 5,041 applied for aid, 4,476 were judged to have need, 273 had their need fully met. 146 Federal Work-Study jobs (averaging $2458). 27 state and other part-time jobs (averaging $3011). In 2017, 66 non-need-based awards were made. *Average percent of need met:* 55. *Average financial aid package:* $9974. *Average need-based loan:* $3682. *Average need-based gift aid:* $8496. *Average non-need-based aid:* $2398. *Average indebtedness upon graduation:* $27,961.

APPLYING

Standardized Tests *Required:* SAT or ACT (for admission).

Options: electronic application, deferred entrance.

Required: high school transcript. *Required for some:* interview for honors college.

Application deadlines: 8/1 (freshmen), 8/1 (transfers).

CONTACT

Mr. Jody Todhunter, Director of Admissions, Texas A&M University–Commerce, PO Box 3011, Commerce, TX 75429. *Phone:* 903-886-5072. *Toll-free phone:* 888-868-2682. *Fax:* 903-468-8698. *E-mail:* admissions@tamu-commerce.edu.

Texas A&M University–Corpus Christi

Corpus Christi, Texas

http://www.tamucc.edu/

- **State-supported** university, founded 1947, part of Texas A&M University System
- **Suburban** 317-acre campus
- **Endowment** $12.4 million
- **Coed** 10,174 undergraduate students, 82% full-time, 58% women, 42% men
- **Moderately difficult** entrance level, 86% of applicants were admitted

UNDERGRAD STUDENTS

8,357 full-time, 1,817 part-time. Students come from 43 states and territories; 41 other countries; 3% are from out of state; 6% Black or African American, non-Hispanic/Latino; 50% Hispanic/Latino; 3% Asian, non-Hispanic/Latino; 0.2% American Indian or Alaska Native, non-Hispanic/Latino; 0.9% Two or more races, non-Hispanic/Latino; 2% Race/ethnicity unknown; 2% international; 8% transferred in; 51% live on campus.

Freshmen:

Admission: 9,002 applied, 7,773 admitted, 2,074 enrolled. *Average high school GPA:* 3.3. *Test scores:* SAT evidence-based reading and writing scores over 500: 67%; SAT math scores over 500: 65%; ACT scores over 18: 76%; SAT evidence-based reading and writing scores over 600: 19%; SAT math scores over 600: 13%; ACT scores over 24: 21%; SAT evidence-based reading and writing scores over 700: 1%; SAT math scores over 700: 1%; ACT scores over 30: 1%.
Retention: 55% of full-time freshmen returned.

FACULTY

Total: 723, 67% full-time, 60% with terminal degrees.
Student/faculty ratio: 18:1.

ACADEMICS

Calendar: semesters. *Degrees:* bachelor's, master's, and doctoral.

Special study options: academic remediation for entering students, advanced placement credit, cooperative education, distance learning, double majors, English as a second language, honors programs, independent study, internships, off-campus study, part-time degree program, services for LD students, study abroad, summer session for credit. *ROTC:* Army (b).

Unusual degree programs: 3-2 business administration; engineering; nursing.

Computers: 1,236 computers/terminals are available on campus for general student use. Students can access the following: campus intranet, computer help desk, free student e-mail accounts, online (class) grades, online (class) registration, online (class) schedules. Campuswide network is available. 100% of college-owned or -operated housing units are wired for high-speed Internet access. Wireless service is available via entire campus.

Library: Mary and Jeff Bell Library. *Books:* 329,340 (physical), 145,756 (digital/electronic); *Serial titles:* 10,348 (physical), 80,843 (digital/electronic); *Databases:* 271. Weekly public service hours: 106; students can reserve study rooms.

STUDENT LIFE

Housing options: coed. Campus housing is provided by a third party.

Activities and organizations: drama/theater group, student-run newspaper, choral group, Student Accounting Society: Alpha Epsilon Delta, Student Art Association: Golden Key, Islander Cultural Alliance: Kinesiology Club, Graduate Student Association: Sea Turtle Club, Student Nurses Association, national fraternities, national sororities.

Athletics Member NCAA. All Division I. *Intercollegiate sports:* baseball M(s), basketball M(s)/W(s), cheerleading M/W, cross-country running M(s)/W(s), golf W(s), sand volleyball W, soccer W(s), softball W(s), tennis M(s)/W(s), track and field M(s)/W(s), volleyball W(s). *Intramural sports:* badminton M/W, basketball M/W, fencing M/W, football M/W, lacrosse M/W, riflery M/W, rock climbing M/W, rugby M/W, sailing M/W, sand volleyball M/W, soccer M/W, softball M/W, swimming and diving M/W, table tennis M/W, tennis M/W, track and field M/W, ultimate Frisbee M/W, volleyball M/W, weight lifting M/W.

Campus security: 24-hour emergency response devices and patrols, late-night transport/escort service, controlled dormitory access.

Student services: health clinic, personal/psychological counseling.

COSTS & FINANCIAL AID

Costs (2017–18) *Tuition:* state resident $4994 full-time; nonresident $8658 full-time. Full-time tuition and fees vary according to course load, degree level, location, program, and student level. Part-time tuition and fees vary according to course load, degree level, location, program, and student level. No tuition increase for student's term of enrollment. *Required fees:* $3975 full-time, $1061 per term part-time. *Room and board:* $10,410; room only: $6890. Room and board charges vary according to board plan and housing facility. *Payment plan:* installment. *Waivers:* senior citizens.

Financial Aid Of all full-time matriculated undergraduates who enrolled in 2017, 6,439 applied for aid, 5,359 were judged to have need, 120 had their need fully met. 148 Federal Work-Study jobs (averaging $3254). 256 state and other part-time jobs (averaging $3515). In 2017, 323 non-need-based awards were made. *Average percent of need met:* 1. *Average financial aid package:* $9651. *Average need-based loan:* $4091. *Average need-based gift aid:* $7167. *Average non-need-based aid:* $2787. *Average indebtedness upon graduation:* $16,998.

APPLYING

Standardized Tests *Required:* SAT or ACT (for admission).

Options: electronic application.

Application fee: $50.

Required: high school transcript, minimum 2.0 GPA.

Application deadlines: 7/1 (freshmen), 7/1 (transfers).

Notification: continuous (freshmen), continuous (out-of-state freshmen), continuous (transfers).

CONTACT

Mrs. Monica Martinez, Assistant Director of Admissions, Texas A&M University–Corpus Christi, SSC 107, 6300 Ocean Drive, Unit 5774, Corpus Christi, TX 78412-5774. *Phone:* 361-825-2624. *Toll-free phone:* 800-482-6822. *Fax:* 361-825-5887. *E-mail:* monica.martinez@tamucc.edu.

Texas A&M University–Kingsville
Kingsville, Texas
http://www.tamuk.edu/

- **State-supported** university, founded 1925, part of Texas A&M University System
- **Small-town** 250-acre campus
- **Coed** 6,775 undergraduate students, 74% full-time, 49% women, 51% men
- **Moderately difficult** entrance level, 84% of applicants were admitted

UNDERGRAD STUDENTS

5,020 full-time, 1,755 part-time. 6% Black or African American, non-Hispanic/Latino; 71% Hispanic/Latino; 0.8% Asian, non-Hispanic/Latino; 0.2% Native Hawaiian or other Pacific Islander, non-Hispanic/Latino; 0.2% American Indian or Alaska Native, non-Hispanic/Latino; 0.5% Two or more races, non-Hispanic/Latino; 0.3% Race/ethnicity unknown; 4% international; 7% transferred in; 27% live on campus.

Freshmen:
Admission: 6,717 applied, 5,651 admitted, 1,114 enrolled. *Test scores:* SAT evidence-based reading and writing scores over 500: 60%; SAT math scores over 500: 60%; ACT scores over 18: 71%; SAT evidence-based reading and writing scores over 600: 15%; SAT math scores over 600: 14%; ACT scores over 24: 14%; SAT evidence-based reading and writing scores over 700: 1%; SAT math scores over 700: 2%; ACT scores over 30: 1%.

ACADEMICS

Calendar: semesters. *Degrees:* bachelor's, master's, doctoral, post-master's, and postbachelor's certificates.

Special study options: academic remediation for entering students, adult/continuing education programs, advanced placement credit, distance learning, double majors, English as a second language, honors programs, independent study, internships, off-campus study, part-time degree program, services for LD students, study abroad, summer session for credit. *ROTC:* Army (b).

Computers: Students can access the following: campus intranet, computer help desk, free student e-mail accounts, online (class) grades, online (class) registration, online (class) schedules. Campuswide network is available.

Library: James C. Jernigan Library. Students can reserve study rooms.

STUDENT LIFE

Housing options: on-campus residence required for freshman year; coed, men-only, women-only. Campus housing is university owned. Freshman campus housing is guaranteed.

Activities and organizations: drama/theater group, student-run newspaper, radio and television station, choral group, marching band, national fraternities, national sororities.

Athletics Member NCAA. All Division II. *Intercollegiate sports:* baseball M, basketball M/W, cross-country running M/W, football M, golf W, softball W, tennis W, track and field M/W, volleyball W. *Intramural sports:* badminton M/W, basketball M/W, racquetball M/W, soccer M/W, softball M/W, tennis M/W, ultimate Frisbee M/W, volleyball W.

Campus security: controlled dormitory access.

Student services: health clinic, personal/psychological counseling.

COSTS & FINANCIAL AID

Costs (2017–18) *Tuition:* state resident $8462 full-time, $120 per credit hour part-time; nonresident $22,034 full-time, $465 per credit hour part-time. Full-time tuition and fees vary according to course load and degree level. Part-time tuition and fees vary according to course load and degree level. No tuition increase for student's term of enrollment. *Room and board:* $8760. Room and board charges vary according to board plan and housing facility. *Payment plan:* installment. *Waivers:* senior citizens and employees or children of employees.

Financial Aid Of all full-time matriculated undergraduates who enrolled in 2015, 5,306 applied for aid, 4,864 were judged to have need, 4,706 had their need fully met. In 2015, 42 non-need-based awards were made. *Average percent of need met:* 65. *Average financial aid package:* $10,871. *Average need-based loan:* $4064. *Average need-based gift aid:* $6503. *Average non-need-based aid:* $1897. *Average indebtedness upon graduation:* $29,307.

APPLYING

Standardized Tests *Required:* SAT or ACT (for admission).

Options: electronic application.

Application fee: $25.

Required for some: essay or personal statement, high school transcript, minimum 2.0 GPA, 2 letters of recommendation, written statement and two letters of recommendation for alternate admissions process.

Application deadlines: rolling (freshmen), rolling (out-of-state freshmen), rolling (transfers).

CONTACT

Laura Knippers, Associate Director of Admissions, Texas A&M University–Kingsville, MSC 128, 700 University Boulevard, Kingsville, TX 78363. *Phone:* 361-593-2311. *Toll-free phone:* 800-687-6000. *E-mail:* laura.knippers@tamuk.edu.

Texas A&M University–San Antonio

San Antonio, Texas

http://www.tamusa.edu/

CONTACT

Ms. Jennifer Zamarripa, Director of Admissions and Registrar, Texas A&M University–San Antonio, One University Way, San Antonio, TX 78224. *Phone:* 210-932-6201. *E-mail:* jennifer.zamarripa@tamusa.tamus.edu.

Texas A&M University–Texarkana

Texarkana, Texas

http://www.tamut.edu/

- **State-supported** upper-level, founded 1971, part of Texas A&M University System
- **Small-town** 1-acre campus
- **Endowment** $6.8 million
- **Coed** 1,644 undergraduate students, 72% full-time, 61% women, 39% men
- **Noncompetitive** entrance level, 65% of applicants were admitted

UNDERGRAD STUDENTS

1,191 full-time, 453 part-time. 20% are from out of state; 14% Black or African American, non-Hispanic/Latino; 15% Hispanic/Latino; 1% Asian, non-Hispanic/Latino; 0.2% Native Hawaiian or other Pacific Islander, non-Hispanic/Latino; 0.8% American Indian or Alaska Native, non-Hispanic/Latino; 4% Two or more races, non-Hispanic/Latino; 2% Race/ethnicity unknown; 2% international; 17% transferred in; 15% live on campus.

Freshmen:

Admission: 3,766 applied, 2,436 admitted.

FACULTY

Student/faculty ratio: 15:1.

ACADEMICS

Calendar: semesters. *Degrees:* bachelor's, master's, and doctoral.

Special study options: advanced placement credit, distance learning, independent study, internships, part-time degree program, services for LD students, student-designed majors, summer session for credit.

Computers: Students can access the following: computer help desk, free student e-mail accounts, online (class) grades, online (class) registration, online (class) schedules. Campuswide network is available. Wireless service is available via entire campus.

Library: John F. Moss Library plus 1 other. *Books:* 128,838 (physical), 583,387 (digital/electronic); *Serial titles:* 1,184 (physical), 72,678 (digital/electronic); *Databases:* 299. Weekly public service hours: 84; students can reserve study rooms.

STUDENT LIFE

Housing options: coed. Campus housing is university owned.

Activities and organizations: student-run newspaper, Campus Activities Board, Student Government Association, Alpha Sigma Alpha, Omega Delta Chi, Phi Lambda Chi.

Athletics Member NAIA. *Intercollegiate sports:* baseball M(s)/W(s), soccer M(s)/W(s), softball M(s)/W(s), tennis M(s)/W(s).

Campus security: 24-hour patrols, late-night transport/escort service.

Student services: personal/psychological counseling.

COSTS & FINANCIAL AID

Costs (2017–18) *One-time required fee:* $30. *Tuition:* state resident $5569 full-time, $218 per credit hour part-time; nonresident $19,835 full-time, $694 per credit hour part-time. Full-time tuition and fees vary according to course load, degree level, location, reciprocity agreements, and student level. Part-time tuition and fees vary according to course load, degree level, location, reciprocity agreements, and student level. No tuition increase for student's term of enrollment. *Required fees:* $2065 full-time, $110 per credit hour part-time, $150 per term part-time. *Room and board:* $7462; room only: $4400. Room and board charges vary according to board plan. *Payment plan:* installment. *Waivers:* senior citizens and employees or children of employees.

Financial Aid Of all full-time matriculated undergraduates who enrolled in 2016, 879 applied for aid, 776 were judged to have need, 50 had their need fully met. 22 Federal Work-Study jobs (averaging $2076). In 2016, 103 non-need-based awards were made. *Average percent of need met:* 69. *Average financial aid package:* $10,222. *Average need-based loan:* $3698. *Average need-based gift aid:* $8154. *Average non-need-based aid:* $2321. *Average indebtedness upon graduation:* $19,410.

APPLYING

Standardized Tests *Required:* SAT or ACT (for admission).

Options: electronic application.

Application fee: $30.

Notification: continuous (transfers).

CONTACT

Ms. Chrissy Gonzalez, Assistant Director of Admissions, Texas A&M University–Texarkana, Texarkana, TX 75505-5518. *Phone:* 903-223-3180. *E-mail:* admissions@tamut.edu.

Texas Christian University

Fort Worth, Texas

http://www.tcu.edu/

- **Independent** university, founded 1873, affiliated with Christian Church (Disciples of Christ)
- **Suburban** 290-acre campus with easy access to Dallas-Fort Worth
- **Endowment** $1.5 billion
- **Coed** 9,011 undergraduate students, 97% full-time, 59% women, 41% men
- **Very difficult** entrance level, 41% of applicants were admitted

UNDERGRAD STUDENTS

8,738 full-time, 273 part-time. Students come from 51 states and territories; 69 other countries; 46% are from out of state; 5% Black or African American, non-Hispanic/Latino; 13% Hispanic/Latino; 3% Asian, non-Hispanic/Latino; 0.2% Native Hawaiian or other Pacific Islander, non-Hispanic/Latino; 0.8% American Indian or Alaska Native, non-Hispanic/Latino; 0.4% Two or more races, non-Hispanic/Latino; 1% Race/ethnicity unknown; 5% international; 6% transferred in; 48% live on campus.

Freshmen:

Admission: 19,740 applied, 8,110 admitted, 1,955 enrolled.

Retention: 91% of full-time freshmen returned.

FACULTY

Total: 1,020, 66% full-time, 70% with terminal degrees.

Student/faculty ratio: 13:1.

ACADEMICS

Calendar: semesters. *Degrees:* certificates, diplomas, bachelor's, master's, doctoral, post-master's, and postbachelor's certificates.

Special study options: accelerated degree program, advanced placement credit, distance learning, double majors, English as a second language, honors programs, independent study, internships, part-time degree program, services for LD students, student-designed majors, study abroad, summer session for credit. *ROTC:* Army (b), Air Force (b).

Computers: 1,400 computers/terminals and 10,000 ports are available on campus for general student use. Students can access the following: campus intranet, computer help desk, free student e-mail accounts, online

COLLEGES AT-A-GLANCE

(class) grades, online (class) registration, online (class) schedules. Campuswide network is available. 100% of college-owned or -operated housing units are wired for high-speed Internet access. Wireless service is available via entire campus.

Library: Mary Couts Burnett Library. *Books:* 1.4 million (physical), 1.2 million (digital/electronic); *Serial titles:* 10,520 (physical), 129,287 (digital/electronic); *Databases:* 523. Study areas open 24 hours, 5–7 days a week; students can reserve study rooms.

STUDENT LIFE

Housing options: on-campus residence required through sophomore year; coed, men-only, women-only, special housing for students with disabilities. Campus housing is university owned and leased by the school. Freshman campus housing is guaranteed.

Activities and organizations: drama/theater group, student-run newspaper, radio and television station, choral group, marching band, the Crew, Catholic Community, Ignite, LEAPS, Business School organizations, national fraternities, national sororities.

Athletics Member NCAA. All Division I. *Intercollegiate sports:* baseball M(s), basketball M(s)/W(s), cross-country running M(s)/W(s), equestrian sports W(s), football M(s), golf M(s)/W(s), gymnastics M(c)/W(c), ice hockey M(c), lacrosse M(c)/W(c), riflery W(s), rock climbing M(c)/W(c), rowing M(c)/W(c), rugby M(c)/W(c), sand volleyball W(s), soccer M(c)/W(s), swimming and diving M(s)/W(s), tennis M(s)/W(s), track and field M(s)/W(s), triathlon M(c)/W(c), ultimate Frisbee M(c)/W(c), volleyball M(c)/W(s), water polo M(c)/W(c). *Intramural sports:* baseball M(c), basketball M/W, bowling M/W, football M/W, golf M(c)/W(c), racquetball M/W, sand volleyball M/W, soccer M/W(c), table tennis M/W, tennis M(c)/W(c), ultimate Frisbee M/W, volleyball M/W(c).

Campus security: 24-hour emergency response devices and patrols, late-night transport/escort service, controlled dormitory access, emergency call boxes, video surveillance in parking lots, self-defense education, lighted sidewalks, Emergency Mass Notification System.

Student services: health clinic, personal/psychological counseling, women's center.

COSTS & FINANCIAL AID

Costs (2017–18) *Comprehensive fee:* $57,120 includes full-time tuition ($44,670), mandatory fees ($90), and room and board ($12,360). Part-time tuition: $1890 per credit hour. Part-time tuition and fees vary according to course load. *Required fees:* $45 per term part-time. *College room only:* $7520. Room and board charges vary according to board plan and housing facility. *Payment plan:* installment. *Waivers:* employees or children of employees.

Financial Aid Of all full-time matriculated undergraduates who enrolled in 2017, 4,360 applied for aid, 3,404 were judged to have need, 890 had their need fully met. 1,325 Federal Work-Study jobs (averaging $2065). In 2017, 2474 non-need-based awards were made. *Average percent of need met:* 65. *Average financial aid package:* $30,763. *Average need-based loan:* $4511. *Average need-based gift aid:* $27,790. *Average non-need-based aid:* $17,963. *Average indebtedness upon graduation:* $42,212. *Financial aid deadline:* 5/1.

APPLYING

Standardized Tests *Required:* SAT or ACT (for admission).

Options: electronic application, early decision, early action, deferred entrance.

Application fee: $50.

Required: essay or personal statement, high school transcript, 2 letters of recommendation.

Application deadlines: 2/1 (freshmen), 8/1 (transfers), 11/1 (early action).

Early decision deadline: 11/1.

Notification: 4/1 (freshmen), continuous (transfers), 12/5 (early decision), 12/15 (early action).

CONTACT

Mr. Mike Mooneyham, Director of Freshman Admission, Texas Christian University, Office of Admission, Box 297013, Fort Worth, TX 76129. *Phone:* 817-257-7490. *Toll-free phone:* 800-828-3764. *Fax:* 817-257-7268. *E-mail:* frogmail@tcu.edu.

Texas College
Tyler, Texas
http://www.texascollege.edu/

- **Independent** 4-year, founded 1894, affiliated with Christian Methodist Episcopal Church
- **Urban** 25-acre campus
- **Endowment** $1.3 million
- **Coed**
- 32% of applicants were admitted

FACULTY
Student/faculty ratio: 20:1.

ACADEMICS
Calendar: semesters. *Degrees:* associate and bachelor's.
Library: D. R. Glass Library. *Books:* 40,000 (physical), 155,000 (digital/electronic); *Serial titles:* 500 (physical); *Databases:* 73. Weekly public service hours: 69; students can reserve study rooms.

STUDENT LIFE
Housing options: men-only, women-only, special housing for students with disabilities. Campus housing is university owned.

Activities and organizations: choral group, marching band, national fraternities, national sororities.

Athletics Member NAIA.

Campus security: 24-hour emergency response devices and patrols.

Student services: health clinic.

COSTS & FINANCIAL AID
Costs (2017–18) *Comprehensive fee:* $13,604 includes full-time tuition ($8204), mandatory fees ($1800), and room and board ($3600).

Financial Aid Of all full-time matriculated undergraduates who enrolled in 2011, 928 applied for aid, 906 were judged to have need, 26 had their need fully met. 160 Federal Work-Study jobs (averaging $1320). 17 state and other part-time jobs (averaging $1010). In 2011, 16 non-need-based awards were made. *Average percent of need met:* 53. *Average financial aid package:* $9329. *Average need-based loan:* $3288. *Average need-based gift aid:* $6285. *Average non-need-based aid:* $2433. *Average indebtedness upon graduation:* $21,147.

APPLYING
Options: electronic application, early admission.

Application fee: $20.

Required: high school transcript, minimum 2.0 GPA.

CONTACT
Mr. Ronald MsDowell, Director of Financial Aid, Texas College, 2404 North Grand Avenue, Tyler, TX 75702. *Phone:* 903-593-8311 Ext. 2297. *Toll-free phone:* 800-306-6299. *Fax:* 903-593-6551. *E-mail:* rmcdowell@texascollege.edu.

Texas Lutheran University
Seguin, Texas
http://www.tlu.edu/

- **Independent** comprehensive, founded 1891, affiliated with Evangelical Lutheran Church
- **Suburban** 196-acre campus with easy access to San Antonio, Austin
- **Endowment** $94.0 million
- **Coed** 1,359 undergraduate students, 96% full-time, 52% women, 48% men

UNDERGRAD STUDENTS
1,305 full-time, 54 part-time. Students come from 14 states and territories; 11 other countries; 1% are from out of state; 10% Black or African American, non-Hispanic/Latino; 34% Hispanic/Latino; 0.7% Asian, non-Hispanic/Latino; 0.1% Native Hawaiian or other Pacific Islander, non-Hispanic/Latino; 0.2% American Indian or Alaska Native, non-Hispanic/Latino; 0.5% Two or more races, non-Hispanic/Latino; 3% Race/ethnicity unknown; 0.4% international; 4% transferred in; 60% live on campus.

Freshmen:
Admission: 417 enrolled. *Average high school GPA:* 3.6. *Test scores:* SAT evidence-based reading and writing scores over 500: 67%; SAT math

scores over 500: 69%; ACT scores over 18: 85%; SAT evidence-based reading and writing scores over 600: 20%; SAT math scores over 600: 17%; ACT scores over 24: 26%; SAT evidence-based reading and writing scores over 700: 3%; SAT math scores over 700: 3%; ACT scores over 30: 4%.

Retention: 72% of full-time freshmen returned.

FACULTY
Total: 127, 65% full-time, 65% with terminal degrees.
Student/faculty ratio: 14:1.

ACADEMICS
Calendar: semesters. *Degrees:* bachelor's and master's.

Special study options: advanced placement credit, double majors, external degree program, honors programs, independent study, internships, part-time degree program, services for LD students, study abroad, summer session for credit. *ROTC:* Army (c), Air Force (c).

Unusual degree programs: 3-2 engineering with Texas A&M University, Texas Tech University, Texas State University.

Computers: 264 computers/terminals and 57 ports are available on campus for general student use. Students can access the following: campus intranet, computer help desk, free student e-mail accounts, online (class) grades, online (class) registration, online (class) schedules, free printing. Campuswide network is available. 100% of college-owned or -operated housing units are wired for high-speed Internet access. Wireless service is available via entire campus.

Library: Blumberg Memorial Library plus 1 other. *Books:* 108,091 (physical), 277,673 (digital/electronic); *Serial titles:* 1,222 (physical), 50,752 (digital/electronic); *Databases:* 56. Weekly public service hours: 86; students can reserve study rooms.

STUDENT LIFE
Housing options: coed, special housing for students with disabilities. Campus housing is university owned. Freshman campus housing is guaranteed.

Activities and organizations: drama/theater group, student-run newspaper, choral group, Alpha Lambda Delta, Pre Health Professions Club, Xi Tau, Sigma Phi Theta, Mexican American Student Association.

Athletics Member NCAA. All Division III. *Intercollegiate sports:* baseball M, basketball M/W, cross-country running M/W, football M, golf M/W, soccer M/W, softball W, tennis M/W, track and field M/W, volleyball W. *Intramural sports:* basketball M/W, bowling M/W, football M, racquetball M/W, softball M/W, tennis M/W, volleyball M/W.

Campus security: 24-hour emergency response devices and patrols, late-night transport/escort service, controlled dormitory access.

Student services: health clinic, personal/psychological counseling, women's center.

COSTS & FINANCIAL AID
Costs (2018–19) *One-time required fee:* $300. *Comprehensive fee:* $40,110 includes full-time tuition ($29,650), mandatory fees ($310), and room and board ($10,150). Full-time tuition and fees vary according to course load. Part-time tuition: $980 per semester hour. *Required fees:* $155 per term part-time. *College room only:* $5750. Room and board charges vary according to board plan and housing facility. *Payment plan:* installment. *Waivers:* children of alumni and employees or children of employees.

Financial Aid Of all full-time matriculated undergraduates who enrolled in 2017, 1,193 applied for aid, 1,071 were judged to have need, 210 had their need fully met. 137 Federal Work-Study jobs (averaging $2317). 4 state and other part-time jobs (averaging $2318). In 2017, 239 non-need-based awards were made. *Average percent of need met:* 83. *Average financial aid package:* $25,526. *Average need-based loan:* $4286. *Average need-based gift aid:* $21,262. *Average non-need-based aid:* $15,918. *Average indebtedness upon graduation:* $32,437.

APPLYING
Standardized Tests *Required:* SAT or ACT (for admission).
Required: high school transcript. *Recommended:* essay or personal statement, letters of recommendation, interview.

CONTACT
Mrs. Alecia McCain, Director for Admissions Recruiting, Texas Lutheran University, 1000 West Court Street, Seguin, TX 78155-5999. *Phone:* 830-372-6078. *Toll-free phone:* 800-771-8521. *Fax:* 830-372-8096. *E-mail:* almccain@tlu.edu.

Texas Southern University
Houston, Texas
http://www.tsu.edu/

CONTACT
Enrollment Services Customer Service Center, Texas Southern University, 3100 Cleburne Street, Houston, TX 77004-4598. *Phone:* 713-313-7071. *Fax:* 713-313-7851. *E-mail:* eservices@em.tsu.edu.

Texas State University
San Marcos, Texas
http://www.txstate.edu/.

- **State-supported** university, founded 1899, part of Texas State University System
- **Suburban** 491-acre campus with easy access to San Antonio, Austin
- **Endowment** $186.7 million
- **Coed** 34,180 undergraduate students, 82% full-time, 57% women, 43% men
- **Moderately difficult** entrance level, 73% of applicants were admitted

UNDERGRAD STUDENTS
28,019 full-time, 6,161 part-time. Students come from 50 states and territories; 49 other countries; 2% are from out of state; 10% Black or African American, non-Hispanic/Latino; 37% Hispanic/Latino; 2% Asian, non-Hispanic/Latino; 0.2% Native Hawaiian or other Pacific Islander, non-Hispanic/Latino; 0.3% American Indian or Alaska Native, non-Hispanic/Latino; 4% Two or more races, non-Hispanic/Latino; 0.3% Race/ethnicity unknown; 0.5% international; 11% transferred in; 20% live on campus.

Freshmen:
Admission: 24,277 applied, 17,717 admitted, 5,874 enrolled. *Test scores:* SAT evidence-based reading and writing scores over 500: 85%; SAT math scores over 500: 81%; ACT scores over 18: 96%; SAT evidence-based reading and writing scores over 600: 30%; SAT math scores over 600: 20%; ACT scores over 24: 42%; SAT evidence-based reading and writing scores over 700: 3%; SAT math scores over 700: 2%; ACT scores over 30: 5%.

Retention: 78% of full-time freshmen returned.

FACULTY
Total: 2,013, 70% full-time, 68% with terminal degrees.
Student/faculty ratio: 21:1.

ACADEMICS
Calendar: semesters. *Degrees:* bachelor's, master's, doctoral, and postbachelor's certificates.

Special study options: academic remediation for entering students, accelerated degree program, adult/continuing education programs, advanced placement credit, distance learning, double majors, English as a second language, freshman honors college, honors programs, independent study, internships, off-campus study, part-time degree program, services for LD students, study abroad, summer session for credit. *ROTC:* Army (b), Air Force (b).

Unusual degree programs: 3-2 business administration; engineering with University of Texas at Austin, Texas A&M University, Texas Tech University, University of Texas at San Antonio.

Computers: 3,233 computers/terminals are available on campus for general student use. Students can access the following: computer help desk, free student e-mail accounts, online (class) grades, online (class) registration, online (class) schedules. Campuswide network is available. 100% of college-owned or -operated housing units are wired for high-speed Internet access. Wireless service is available via entire campus.

Library: Alkek Library plus 1 other. *Books:* 1.5 million (physical), 664,569 (digital/electronic); *Serial titles:* 32,501 (physical), 129,479 (digital/electronic); *Databases:* 503. Weekly public service hours: 103; students can reserve study rooms.

STUDENT LIFE

Housing options: on-campus residence required for freshman year; coed, men-only, women-only. Campus housing is university owned. Freshman campus housing is guaranteed.

Activities and organizations: drama/theater group, student-run newspaper, radio station, choral group, marching band, Veterans Alliance of Texas State, Texas State Strutters (Dance performance group), Student Foundation, Sport Clubs Alliance, Student Association for Campus Activities, national fraternities, national sororities.

Athletics Member NCAA. All Division I. *Intercollegiate sports:* baseball M(s), basketball M(s)/W(s), cheerleading M/W, cross-country running M(s)/W(s), equestrian sports M(c)/W(c), fencing M(c)/W(c), football M(s), golf M(s)/W(s), gymnastics M(c)/W(c), ice hockey M(c), lacrosse M(c)/W(c), rugby M(c)/W(c), soccer M(c)/W(s), softball M(c)/W(s), tennis M(c)/W(s), track and field M(s)/W(s), ultimate Frisbee M(c)/W(c), volleyball W(s), water polo M(c)/W(c), weight lifting M(c)/W(c), wrestling M(c)/W(c). *Intramural sports:* basketball M/W, bowling M/W, cross-country running M/W, football M/W, golf M/W, racquetball M/W, rock climbing M/W, soccer M/W, softball M/W, tennis M/W, ultimate Frisbee M/W, volleyball M/W.

Campus security: 24-hour emergency response devices and patrols, late-night transport/escort service, controlled dormitory access, Emergency Notification System (electronic signs) within classrooms and offices.

Student services: health clinic, personal/psychological counseling, legal services.

COSTS & FINANCIAL AID

Costs (2017–18) *Tuition:* state resident $8087 full-time, $270 per credit hour part-time; nonresident $20,537 full-time, $685 per credit hour part-time. Full-time tuition and fees vary according to course load and degree level. Part-time tuition and fees vary according to course load and degree level. No tuition increase for student's term of enrollment. *Required fees:* $2534 full-time, $59 per credit hour part-time, $446 per term part-time. *Room and board:* $8100; room only: $5390. Room and board charges vary according to board plan and housing facility. *Payment plans:* tuition prepayment, installment. *Waivers:* employees or children of employees.

Financial Aid Of all full-time matriculated undergraduates who enrolled in 2017, 23,924 applied for aid, 16,852 were judged to have need, 3,235 had their need fully met. 1,783 Federal Work-Study jobs (averaging $3322). 153 state and other part-time jobs (averaging $3290). In 2017, 713 non-need-based awards were made. *Average percent of need met:* 65. *Average financial aid package:* $11,616. *Average need-based loan:* $3965. *Average need-based gift aid:* $7404. *Average non-need-based aid:* $4056. *Average indebtedness upon graduation:* $26,568.

APPLYING

Standardized Tests *Required:* SAT or ACT (for admission). *Required for some:* TOEFL for international students. *Recommended:* SAT (for admission), ACT (for admission).

Options: electronic application, early admission, deferred entrance.

Application fee: $75.

Required: essay or personal statement, high school transcript.

Application deadlines: 3/1 (freshmen), 7/1 (transfers).

Notification: continuous (freshmen), continuous (transfers).

CONTACT

Texas State University, 429 N. Guadalupe Street, San Marcos, TX 78666. *Phone:* 512-245-2364. *Fax:* 512-245-8100. *E-mail:* admissions@ txstate.edu.

Texas Tech University

Lubbock, Texas

http://www.ttu.edu/

- **State-supported** university, founded 1923, part of Texas Tech University System
- **Urban** 1839-acre campus
- **Endowment** $715.7 million
- **Coed** 30,737 undergraduate students, 89% full-time, 46% women, 54% men
- **Moderately difficult** entrance level, 69% of applicants were admitted

UNDERGRAD STUDENTS

27,318 full-time, 3,419 part-time. Students come from 53 states and territories; 90 other countries; 6% are from out of state; 6% Black or African American, non-Hispanic/Latino; 28% Hispanic/Latino; 2% Asian, non-Hispanic/Latino; 0.1% Native Hawaiian or other Pacific Islander, non-Hispanic/Latino; 0.3% American Indian or Alaska Native, non-Hispanic/Latino; 2% Two or more races, non-Hispanic/Latino; 0.5% Race/ethnicity unknown; 5% international; 9% transferred in; 26% live on campus.

Freshmen:

Admission: 25,207 applied, 17,438 admitted, 5,883 enrolled. *Average high school GPA:* 3.8. *Test scores:* SAT evidence-based reading and writing scores over 500: 93%; SAT math scores over 500: 93%; ACT scores over 18: 99%; SAT evidence-based reading and writing scores over 600: 38%; SAT math scores over 600: 37%; ACT scores over 24: 54%; SAT evidence-based reading and writing scores over 700: 4%; SAT math scores over 700: 5%; ACT scores over 30: 8%.

Retention: 84% of full-time freshmen returned.

FACULTY

Total: 1,790, 88% full-time.

Student/faculty ratio: 20:1.

ACADEMICS

Calendar: semesters. *Degrees:* bachelor's, master's, doctoral, and postbachelor's certificates.

Special study options: academic remediation for entering students, accelerated degree program, advanced placement credit, cooperative education, distance learning, double majors, English as a second language, external degree program, freshman honors college, honors programs, independent study, internships, off-campus study, part-time degree program, services for LD students, student-designed majors, study abroad, summer session for credit. *ROTC:* Army (b), Air Force (b).

Unusual degree programs: 3-2 business administration; engineering; architecture, environmental design, hospitality & retail management, music education, personal and financial planning.

Computers: 2,597 computers/terminals and 3,250 ports are available on campus for general student use. Students can access the following: campus intranet, computer help desk, free student e-mail accounts, online (class) grades, online (class) registration, online (class) schedules, online degree plans, accounts, transcripts, financial aid, course and instructor evaluations, scholarship applications and submissions. Campuswide network is available. 100% of college-owned or -operated housing units are wired for high-speed Internet access. Wireless service is available via classrooms, computer centers, computer labs, dorm rooms, learning centers, libraries, student centers.

Library: Texas Tech Library plus 3 others. *Books:* 2.9 million (physical), 158,677 (digital/electronic); *Serial titles:* 3,323 (physical), 155,124 (digital/electronic); *Databases:* 399. Weekly public service hours: 146; study areas open 24 hours, 5–7 days a week; students can reserve study rooms.

STUDENT LIFE

Housing options: on-campus residence required for freshman year; coed, men-only, women-only, special housing for students with disabilities. Campus housing is university owned. Freshman campus housing is guaranteed.

Activities and organizations: drama/theater group, student-run newspaper, radio station, choral group, marching band, Society of Petroleum Engineers, Hispanic Student Society, Pre-Nursing Association, Alpha Lambda Delta & PES, Catholic Student Association, national fraternities, national sororities.

Athletics Member NCAA. All Division I except football (Division I-A). *Intercollegiate sports:* baseball M(s), basketball M(s)/W(s), cross-country running M(s)/W(s), golf M(s)/W(s), soccer W(s), softball W(s), tennis M(s)/W(s), track and field M(s)/W(s), volleyball W(s). *Intramural sports:* archery M(c)/W(c), badminton M(c)/W(c), baseball M(c), basketball M/W, bowling M/W, equestrian sports M(c)/W(c), fencing M(c)/W(c), golf M/W, gymnastics M(c)/W(c), ice hockey M(c), lacrosse M(c)/W(c), racquetball M/W, rock climbing M(c)/W(c), rugby M(c)/W(c), sand volleyball M/W, soccer M/W, softball M/W, swimming and diving M(c)/W(c), table tennis M/W, tennis M/W, triathlon M(c)/W(c), ultimate Frisbee M(c)/W(c), volleyball M/W, water polo M(c)/W(c), weight lifting M, wrestling M(c)/W(c).

Campus security: 24-hour emergency response devices and patrols, late-night transport/escort service, controlled dormitory access, TechAlert system, bike registration, crime prevention programs.

Student services: health clinic, personal/psychological counseling, legal services.

COSTS & FINANCIAL AID

Costs (2017–18) *Tuition:* state resident $8040 full-time, $268 per credit hour part-time; nonresident $20,280 full-time, $676 per credit hour part-time. Full-time tuition and fees vary according to course load, location, program, and reciprocity agreements. Part-time tuition and fees vary according to course load, location, program, and reciprocity agreements. *Required fees:* $2732 full-time, $51 per credit hour part-time, $608 per term part-time. *Room and board:* $5956; room only: $3428. Room and board charges vary according to board plan and housing facility. *Payment plan:* installment. *Waivers:* senior citizens and employees or children of employees.

Financial Aid Of all full-time matriculated undergraduates who enrolled in 2016, 16,239 applied for aid, 13,251 were judged to have need, 1,075 had their need fully met. 360 Federal Work-Study jobs (averaging $2520). 6 state and other part-time jobs (averaging $1296). In 2016, 3132 non-need-based awards were made. *Average percent of need met:* 67. *Average financial aid package:* $15,085. *Average need-based loan:* $5307. *Average need-based gift aid:* $7786. *Average non-need-based aid:* $3564. *Average indebtedness upon graduation:* $29,540.

APPLYING

Standardized Tests *Required:* SAT or ACT (for admission).

Options: electronic application.

Application fee: $75.

Required: high school transcript. *Recommended:* essay or personal statement, letters of recommendation.

Application deadlines: 8/1 (freshmen), rolling (transfers).

Notification: 9/1 (freshmen), continuous (transfers).

CONTACT
Texas Tech University, 2500 Broadway, Lubbock, TX 79409. *Phone:* 806-742-1480.

Texas Wesleyan University
Fort Worth, Texas
http://www.txwes.edu/

- **Independent United Methodist** university, founded 1890
- **Urban** 74-acre campus with easy access to Dallas-Fort Worth
- **Endowment** $59.7 million
- **Coed**
- **Moderately difficult** entrance level

FACULTY
Student/faculty ratio: 13:1.

ACADEMICS
Calendar: semesters. *Degrees:* bachelor's, master's, and doctoral.
Library: Eunice and James L. West Library plus 1 other. *Books:* 185,461 (physical), 171,492 (digital/electronic); *Serial titles:* 1,500 (physical), 150,836 (digital/electronic); *Databases:* 104. Weekly public service hours: 101.

STUDENT LIFE
Housing options: on-campus residence required for freshman year; coed, special housing for students with disabilities. Campus housing is university owned.

Activities and organizations: drama/theater group, student-run newspaper, radio and television station, choral group, Mortar Board, Delta Sigma Phi, Alpha Xi Delta, Bilingual Education Student Organization, Alpha Lambda Delta, national fraternities, national sororities.

Athletics Member NAIA.

Campus security: 24-hour emergency response devices and patrols, student patrols, late-night transport/escort service, controlled dormitory access.

Student services: health clinic, personal/psychological counseling.

COSTS & FINANCIAL AID
Costs (2017–18) *Comprehensive fee:* $37,338 includes full-time tuition ($24,178), mandatory fees ($3622), and room and board ($9538). Full-time tuition and fees vary according to course level, course load, degree level, and program. Part-time tuition: $828 per credit hour. Part-time tuition and fees vary according to course level, course load, degree level, and program. *College room only:* $5592. Room and board charges vary according to housing facility. *Payment plans:* installment, deferred payment.

Financial Aid Of all full-time matriculated undergraduates who enrolled in 2016, 1,192 applied for aid, 1,098 were judged to have need, 122 had their need fully met. 87 Federal Work-Study jobs (averaging $4000). 4 state and other part-time jobs (averaging $4000). In 2016, 262 non-need-based awards were made. *Average percent of need met:* 66. *Average financial aid package:* $23,340. *Average need-based loan:* $3966. *Average need-based gift aid:* $17,945. *Average non-need-based aid:* $11,241. *Average indebtedness upon graduation:* $12,360.

APPLYING
Standardized Tests *Required:* SAT or ACT (for admission).

Options: electronic application, deferred entrance.

Required: minimum 2.5 GPA, minimum ACT score of 19 or SAT of 920. *Required for some:* essay or personal statement, high school transcript.

CONTACT
Mrs. Djuana Young, Associate Vice President for Enrollment, Admissions, Texas Wesleyan University, 1201 Wesleyan Street, Fort Worth, TX 76105-1536. *Phone:* 817-531-4422. *Toll-free phone:* 800-580-8980. *Fax:* 817-531-7515. *E-mail:* admissions@txwes.edu.

Texas Woman's University
Denton, Texas
http://www.twu.edu/

- **State-supported** university, founded 1901
- **Suburban** 270-acre campus with easy access to Dallas-Fort Worth
- **Endowment** $65.9 million
- **Coed, primarily women** 10,309 undergraduate students, 68% full-time, 88% women, 12% men
- **Minimally difficult** entrance level, 86% of applicants were admitted

UNDERGRAD STUDENTS
6,968 full-time, 3,341 part-time. Students come from 31 states and territories; 29 other countries; 1% are from out of state; 17% Black or African American, non-Hispanic/Latino; 30% Hispanic/Latino; 8% Asian, non-Hispanic/Latino; 0.1% Native Hawaiian or other Pacific Islander, non-Hispanic/Latino; 0.3% American Indian or Alaska Native, non-Hispanic/Latino; 4% Two or more races, non-Hispanic/Latino; 0.9% Race/ethnicity unknown; 0.7% international; 14% transferred in; 13% live on campus.

Freshmen:
Admission: 5,502 applied, 4,716 admitted, 1,272 enrolled. *Average high school GPA:* 3.1. *Test scores:* SAT evidence-based reading and writing scores over 500: 56%; SAT math scores over 500: 48%; ACT scores over 18: 68%; SAT evidence-based reading and writing scores over 600: 9%; SAT math scores over 600: 10%; ACT scores over 24: 22%; SAT evidence-based reading and writing scores over 700: 1%; ACT scores over 30: 3%.

Retention: 78% of full-time freshmen returned.

FACULTY
Total: 937, 53% full-time, 57% with terminal degrees.
Student/faculty ratio: 18:1.

ACADEMICS
Calendar: semesters. *Degrees:* bachelor's, master's, doctoral, post-master's, and postbachelor's certificates.

Special study options: academic remediation for entering students, accelerated degree program, adult/continuing education programs, advanced placement credit, cooperative education, distance learning, double majors, honors programs, independent study, internships, off-campus study, part-time degree program, services for LD students, study abroad, summer session for credit. *ROTC:* Army (c), Navy (c), Air Force (c).

Computers: 285 computers/terminals and 570 ports are available on campus for general student use. Students can access the following: campus intranet, computer help desk, free student e-mail accounts, online (class) grades, online (class) registration, online (class) schedules. Campuswide network is available. 100% of college-owned or -operated housing units are wired for high-speed Internet access. Wireless service is available via entire campus.

Library: Blagg-Huey Library. *Books:* 383,183 (physical), 407,446 (digital/electronic); *Serial titles:* 155,452 (physical), 595,316 (digital/electronic); *Databases:* 227. Weekly public service hours: 116; students can reserve study rooms.

STUDENT LIFE

Housing options: on-campus residence required through sophomore year; coed, men-only, women-only, special housing for students with disabilities. Campus housing is university owned, leased by the school and is provided by a third party. Freshman campus housing is guaranteed.

Activities and organizations: drama/theater group, student-run newspaper, choral group, Athenian Honors Society, Phi Kappa Phi, Epsilon Omega Epsilon Honor Society, Alpha Sigma Lambda Honor Society, Touchstone Honors Student, national fraternities, national sororities.

Athletics Member NCAA. All Division II. *Intercollegiate sports:* basketball W(s), gymnastics W(s), soccer W(s), softball W(s), volleyball W(s). *Intramural sports:* badminton M/W, basketball M(c)/W(c), football M/W, golf M(c)/W(c), soccer M(c)/W(c), softball M(c)/W(c), tennis M/W, track and field M(c)/W(c), volleyball M/W, weight lifting M(c)/W(c), wrestling M(c)/W(c).

Campus security: 24-hour emergency response devices and patrols, late-night transport/escort service, controlled dormitory access.

Student services: health clinic, personal/psychological counseling, women's center, legal services.

COSTS & FINANCIAL AID

Costs (2018–19) *Tuition:* state resident $6450 full-time, $215 per credit hour part-time; nonresident $18,630 full-time, $621 per credit hour part-time. Full-time tuition and fees vary according to course level, course load, program, and reciprocity agreements. Part-time tuition and fees vary according to course level, course load, program, and reciprocity agreements. No tuition increase for student's term of enrollment. *Required fees:* $2910 full-time, $87 per credit hour part-time, $290 per term part-time. *Room and board:* $8181; room only: $4470. Room and board charges vary according to board plan and housing facility. *Payment plan:* installment. *Waivers:* senior citizens.

Financial Aid Of all full-time matriculated undergraduates who enrolled in 2017, 5,396 applied for aid, 4,686 were judged to have need, 1,387 had their need fully met. In 2017, 406 non-need-based awards were made. *Average percent of need met:* 84. *Average financial aid package:* $13,486. *Average need-based loan:* $6825. *Average need-based gift aid:* $7381. *Average non-need-based aid:* $4526. *Average indebtedness upon graduation:* $23,983. *Financial aid deadline:* 3/15.

APPLYING

Standardized Tests *Required for some:* SAT or ACT (for admission).

Options: electronic application, early admission, deferred entrance.

Application fee: $50.

Required: minimum 2.0 GPA. *Required for some:* high school transcript.

Application deadlines: 8/25 (freshmen), 8/25 (transfers).

Notification: continuous (freshmen), continuous (transfers).

CONTACT

Ms. Erma Nieto-Brecht, Director of Admissions, Texas Woman's University, 304 Administration Drive, Denton, TX 76201. *Phone:* 940-898-3188. *Toll-free phone:* 866-809-6130. *Fax:* 940-898-3081. *E-mail:* admissions@twu.edu.

Trinity University
San Antonio, Texas
http://www.trinity.edu/

- **Independent** comprehensive, founded 1869, affiliated with Presbyterian Church
- **Urban** 117-acre campus with easy access to San Antonio
- **Endowment** $1.2 billion
- **Coed** 2,428 undergraduate students, 98% full-time, 53% women, 47% men
- **Very difficult** entrance level, 38% of applicants were admitted

UNDERGRAD STUDENTS

2,383 full-time, 45 part-time. Students come from 48 states and territories; 62 other countries; 22% are from out of state; 4% Black or African American, non-Hispanic/Latino; 21% Hispanic/Latino; 7% Asian, non-Hispanic/Latino; 0.3% American Indian or Alaska Native, non-Hispanic/Latino; 5% Two or more races, non-Hispanic/Latino; 2% Race/ethnicity unknown; 6% international; 1% transferred in; 80% live on campus.

Freshmen:
Admission: 7,663 applied, 2,946 admitted, 642 enrolled. *Average high school GPA:* 3.6. *Test scores:* SAT evidence-based reading and writing scores over 500: 100%; SAT math scores over 500: 100%; ACT scores over 18: 100%; SAT evidence-based reading and writing scores over 600: 88%; SAT math scores over 600: 84%; ACT scores over 24: 99%; SAT evidence-based reading and writing scores over 700: 33%; SAT math scores over 700: 31%; ACT scores over 30: 55%.
Retention: 89% of full-time freshmen returned.

FACULTY
Total: 322, 73% full-time, 80% with terminal degrees.

Student/faculty ratio: 9:1.

ACADEMICS
Calendar: semesters. *Degrees:* bachelor's and master's.

Special study options: accelerated degree program, advanced placement credit, double majors, honors programs, independent study, internships, off-campus study, part-time degree program, services for LD students, student-designed majors, study abroad, summer session for credit. *ROTC:* Army (c), Air Force (c).

Computers: 500 computers/terminals and 2,000 ports are available on campus for general student use. Students can access the following: campus intranet, computer help desk, free student e-mail accounts, online (class) grades, online (class) registration, online (class) schedules. Campuswide network is available. 100% of college-owned or -operated housing units are wired for high-speed Internet access. Wireless service is available via entire campus.

Library: Elizabeth Huth Coates Library plus 1 other. *Books:* 716,500 (physical); *Serial titles:* 1,907 (physical), 95,000 (digital/electronic); *Databases:* 297. Weekly public service hours: 96; students can reserve study rooms.

STUDENT LIFE

Housing options: on-campus residence required through junior year; coed. Campus housing is university owned. Freshman campus housing is guaranteed.

Activities and organizations: drama/theater group, student-run newspaper, radio and television station, choral group, Tiger Stand Band, Alpha Phi Omega, Association of Student Representatives, Acabellas/Trinitones, Multicultural Network.

Athletics Member NCAA. All Division III. *Intercollegiate sports:* baseball M, basketball M/W, cross-country running M/W, fencing M(c)/W(c), football M, golf M/W, lacrosse M(c)/W(c), soccer M/W, softball W, swimming and diving M/W, tennis M/W, track and field M/W, volleyball W. *Intramural sports:* basketball M/W, cross-country running M/W, equestrian sports M(c)/W(c), football M, racquetball M/W, soccer M/W, softball M/W, swimming and diving M/W, table tennis M/W, tennis M/W, ultimate Frisbee M/W, volleyball M/W.

Campus security: 24-hour emergency response devices and patrols, late-night transport/escort service, controlled dormitory access.

Student services: health clinic, personal/psychological counseling.

COSTS & FINANCIAL AID

Costs (2018–19) *Comprehensive fee:* $56,440 includes full-time tuition ($42,360), mandatory fees ($616), and room and board ($13,464). Full-time tuition and fees vary according to course load. Part-time tuition: $1765 per credit hour. Part-time tuition and fees vary according to course load. *Required fees:* $13 per credit hour part-time. *College room only:* $8690. Room and board charges vary according to board plan. *Payment plan:* installment. *Waivers:* employees or children of employees.

Financial Aid Of all full-time matriculated undergraduates who enrolled in 2016, 1,395 applied for aid, 1,090 were judged to have need, 488 had their need fully met. In 2016, 1167 non-need-based awards were made. *Average percent of need met:* 93. *Average financial aid package:* $38,968. *Average need-based loan:* $4828. *Average need-based gift aid:* $31,374. *Average non-need-based aid:* $20,549. *Average indebtedness upon graduation:* $40,800.

APPLYING

Standardized Tests *Required:* SAT or ACT (for admission).

Options: electronic application, early decision, early action, deferred entrance.

Required: essay or personal statement, high school transcript, 2 letters of recommendation. *Recommended:* interview.

Application deadlines: 2/1 (freshmen), 4/1 (transfers), 11/1 (early action).

Early decision deadline: 11/1 (for plan 1), 1/1 (for plan 2).

Notification: 4/1 (freshmen), 5/1 (transfers), 12/1 (early decision plan 1), 2/1 (early decision plan 2), 12/1 (early action).

CONTACT

Office of Admissions, Trinity University, One Trinity Place, Northrup Hall 140, San Antonio, TX 78212-7200. *Phone:* 210-999-7207. *Toll-free phone:* 800-TRINITY. *Fax:* 210-999-8164. *E-mail:* admissions@ trinity.edu.

Tyler Junior College

Tyler, Texas

http://www.tjc.edu/

- **State and locally supported** primarily 2-year, founded 1926
- **Suburban** 137-acre campus
- **Endowment** $42.2 million
- **Coed** 11,478 undergraduate students, 51% full-time, 58% women, 42% men
- **Noncompetitive** entrance level, 100% of applicants were admitted

UNDERGRAD STUDENTS

5,904 full-time, 5,574 part-time. Students come from 27 states and territories; 31 other countries; 3% are from out of state; 20% Black or African American, non-Hispanic/Latino; 20% Hispanic/Latino; 1% Asian, non-Hispanic/Latino; 0.2% Native Hawaiian or other Pacific Islander, non-Hispanic/Latino; 0.5% American Indian or Alaska Native, non-Hispanic/Latino; 3% Two or more races, non-Hispanic/Latino; 1% Race/ethnicity unknown; 0.8% international; 5% transferred in; 11% live on campus.

Freshmen:

Admission: 10,778 applied, 10,778 admitted, 2,995 enrolled. *Retention:* 54% of full-time freshmen returned.

FACULTY

Total: 559, 56% full-time, 9% with terminal degrees. **Student/faculty ratio:** 20:1.

ACADEMICS

Calendar: semesters. *Degrees:* certificates, diplomas, associate, and bachelor's.

Special study options: academic remediation for entering students, accelerated degree program, adult/continuing education programs, advanced placement credit, distance learning, freshman honors college, honors programs, part-time degree program, services for LD students, study abroad, summer session for credit.

Computers: Students can access the following: campus intranet, computer help desk, free student e-mail accounts, online (class) grades, online (class) registration, online (class) schedules. Campuswide network

is available. 100% of college-owned or -operated housing units are wired for high-speed Internet access. Wireless service is available via entire campus.

Library: Vaughn Library and Learning Resource Center. *Books:* 85,418 (physical), 135,816 (digital/electronic); *Databases:* 100. Weekly public service hours: 74.

STUDENT LIFE

Housing options: coed, men-only, women-only. Campus housing is university owned and is provided by a third party.

Activities and organizations: drama/theater group, student-run newspaper, choral group, marching band, Student Government, Religious Affiliation Clubs, Phi Theta Kappa, national sororities.

Athletics Member NJCAA. *Intercollegiate sports:* baseball M, basketball M(s)/W(s), cheerleading W(s), football M(s), golf M/W, soccer M(s)/W(s), softball W(s), tennis M(s)/W(s), volleyball W(s). *Intramural sports:* basketball M/W, cheerleading W, racquetball M/W, volleyball M/W, weight lifting M/W.

Campus security: 24-hour emergency response devices and patrols, controlled dormitory access.

Student services: health clinic, personal/psychological counseling.

COSTS & FINANCIAL AID

Costs (2017–18) *Tuition:* area resident $960 full-time, $32 per credit hour part-time; state resident $2700 full-time, $92 per credit hour part-time; nonresident $3420 full-time, $116 per credit hour part-time. *Required fees:* $10 per credit hour part-time, $132 per term part-time. *Room and board:* $8538; room only: $5940. Room and board charges vary according to housing facility. *Payment plan:* installment. *Waivers:* senior citizens and employees or children of employees.

Financial Aid Of all full-time matriculated undergraduates who enrolled in 2015, 4,408 applied for aid, 3,832 were judged to have need, 59 had their need fully met. 41 Federal Work-Study jobs (averaging $1707). 33 state and other part-time jobs (averaging $1869). In 2015, 687 non-need-based awards were made. *Average percent of need met:* 59. *Average financial aid package:* $6573. *Average need-based loan:* $3346. *Average need-based gift aid:* $4481. *Average non-need-based aid:* $1061. *Average indebtedness upon graduation:* $14,743. *Financial aid deadline:* 6/1.

APPLYING

Options: electronic application, early admission.

Required: high school transcript.

Application deadlines: rolling (freshmen), rolling (transfers).

Notification: continuous (freshmen), continuous (transfers).

CONTACT

Ms. Janna Chancey, Director of Enrollment Management, Tyler Junior College, PO Box 9020, Tyler, TX 75711-9020. *Phone:* 903-510-3325. *Toll-free phone:* 800-687-5680. *E-mail:* jcha@tjc.edu.

University of Dallas

Irving, Texas

http://www.udallas.edu/

- **Independent Roman Catholic** university, founded 1955
- **Suburban** 215-acre campus with easy access to Dallas-Fort Worth
- **Endowment** $54.9 million
- **Coed** 1,450 undergraduate students, 98% full-time, 54% women, 46% men
- **Moderately difficult** entrance level, 47% of applicants were admitted

UNDERGRAD STUDENTS

1,421 full-time, 29 part-time. Students come from 48 states and territories; 40 other countries; 52% are from out of state; 2% Black or African American, non-Hispanic/Latino; 23% Hispanic/Latino; 6% Asian, non-Hispanic/Latino; 0.1% Native Hawaiian or other Pacific Islander, non-Hispanic/Latino; 0.6% American Indian or Alaska Native, non-Hispanic/Latino; 3% Two or more races, non-Hispanic/Latino; 2% Race/ethnicity unknown; 4% international; 2% transferred in; 68% live on campus.

Freshmen:

Admission: 3,857 applied, 1,830 admitted, 419 enrolled. *Average high school GPA:* 3.9. *Test scores:* SAT evidence-based reading and writing

scores over 500: 99%; SAT math scores over 500: 97%; ACT scores over 18: 100%; SAT evidence-based reading and writing scores over 600: 73%; SAT math scores over 600: 51%; ACT scores over 24: 82%; SAT evidence-based reading and writing scores over 700: 29%; SAT math scores over 700: 13%; ACT scores over 30: 33%.

Retention: 85% of full-time freshmen returned.

FACULTY
Total: 211, 73% full-time, 60% with terminal degrees.
Student/faculty ratio: 10:1.

ACADEMICS
Calendar: semesters. *Degrees:* bachelor's, master's, doctoral, post-master's, and postbachelor's certificates.

Special study options: advanced placement credit, double majors, independent study, internships, off-campus study, part-time degree program, services for LD students, student-designed majors, study abroad, summer session for credit. *ROTC:* Army (c), Air Force (c).

Unusual degree programs: 3-2 engineering with University of Texas at Arlington; nursing with Texas Woman's University.

Computers: 125 computers/terminals are available on campus for general student use. Students can access the following: campus intranet, computer help desk, free student e-mail accounts, online (class) grades, online (class) registration, online (class) schedules. Campuswide network is available. 100% of college-owned or -operated housing units are wired for high-speed Internet access. Wireless service is available via entire campus.
Library: William A. Blakley Library.

STUDENT LIFE
Housing options: on-campus residence required through junior year; men-only, women-only. Campus housing is university owned. Freshman campus housing is guaranteed.

Activities and organizations: drama/theater group, student-run newspaper, choral group, SPUD (Programming Board), Residence Hall Association, Student Government, Best Buddies, Alpha Phi Omega.

Athletics Member NCAA. All Division III. *Intercollegiate sports:* baseball M, basketball M/W, cross-country running M/W, golf M, lacrosse M/W, soccer M/W, softball W, track and field M/W, volleyball W. *Intramural sports:* basketball M, equestrian sports M(c)/W(c), football M/W, rugby M(c)/W(c), sailing M(c)/W(c), soccer M/W, softball M/W, tennis M(c)/W(c), ultimate Frisbee M(c)/W(c), volleyball M/W.

Campus security: 24-hour emergency response devices and patrols, late-night transport/escort service, controlled dormitory access.

Student services: health clinic, personal/psychological counseling.

COSTS & FINANCIAL AID
Costs (2017–18) *Comprehensive fee:* $50,676 includes full-time tuition ($36,000), mandatory fees ($2716), and room and board ($11,960). Full-time tuition and fees vary according to course load. Part-time tuition: $1485 per credit hour. Part-time tuition and fees vary according to course load. *Required fees:* $2716 per year part-time. *College room only:* $6580. Room and board charges vary according to board plan and housing facility. *Payment plan:* installment. *Waivers:* employees or children of employees.

Financial Aid Of all full-time matriculated undergraduates who enrolled in 2017, 998 applied for aid, 904 were judged to have need, 185 had their need fully met. 253 Federal Work-Study jobs (averaging $1550). 6 state and other part-time jobs (averaging $1550). In 2017, 488 non-need-based awards were made. *Average percent of need met:* 79. *Average financial aid package:* $32,804. *Average need-based loan:* $5403. *Average need-based gift aid:* $28,420. *Average non-need-based aid:* $20,613. *Average indebtedness upon graduation:* $35,161.

APPLYING
Standardized Tests *Required:* SAT or ACT (for admission).

Options: electronic application, early action, deferred entrance.

Application fee: $50.

Required: essay or personal statement, high school transcript, 2 letters of recommendation. *Required for some:* interview.

Application deadlines: 3/1 (freshmen), 8/1 (transfers), 12/1 (early action).

Notification: continuous (freshmen), continuous (transfers), 1/15 (early action).

CONTACT
Elizabeth Griffin-Smith, Director of Admissions, University of Dallas, 1845 East Northgate Drive, Irving, TX 75062-4736. *Phone:* 800-628-6999. *Toll-free phone:* 800-628-6999. *Fax:* 972-721-5017. *E-mail:* ugadmis@udallas.edu.

University of Houston
Houston, Texas
http://www.uh.edu/
- **State-supported** university, founded 1927, part of University of Houston System
- **Urban** 594-acre campus with easy access to Houston
- **Endowment** $744.6 million
- **Coed** 37,215 undergraduate students, 73% full-time, 50% women, 50% men
- **Moderately difficult** entrance level, 61% of applicants were admitted

UNDERGRAD STUDENTS
27,159 full-time, 10,056 part-time. Students come from 48 states and territories; 107 other countries; 1% are from out of state; 10% Black or African American, non-Hispanic/Latino; 34% Hispanic/Latino; 22% Asian, non-Hispanic/Latino; 0.2% Native Hawaiian or other Pacific Islander, non-Hispanic/Latino; 0.1% American Indian or Alaska Native, non-Hispanic/Latino; 3% Two or more races, non-Hispanic/Latino; 2% Race/ethnicity unknown; 4% international; 14% transferred in; 17% live on campus.

Freshmen:
Admission: 20,768 applied, 12,691 admitted, 4,959 enrolled. *Test scores:* SAT evidence-based reading and writing scores over 500: 94%; SAT math scores over 500: 96%; ACT scores over 18: 98%; SAT evidence-based reading and writing scores over 600: 51%; SAT math scores over 600: 50%; ACT scores over 24: 64%; SAT evidence-based reading and writing scores over 700: 4%; SAT math scores over 700: 5%; ACT scores over 30: 14%.

Retention: 85% of full-time freshmen returned.

FACULTY
Total: 2,428, 64% full-time, 76% with terminal degrees.
Student/faculty ratio: 22:1.

ACADEMICS
Calendar: semesters. *Degrees:* bachelor's, master's, and doctoral.

Special study options: academic remediation for entering students, adult/continuing education programs, advanced placement credit, cooperative education, distance learning, double majors, freshman honors college, honors programs, independent study, internships, off-campus study, part-time degree program, services for LD students, study abroad, summer session for credit. *ROTC:* Army (b), Navy (c), Air Force (b).

Unusual degree programs: 3-2 business administration.

Computers: 1,006 computers/terminals and 80,482 ports are available on campus for general student use. Students can access the following: campus intranet, computer help desk, free student e-mail accounts, online (class) grades, online (class) registration, online (class) schedules, online Bus Loop schedule. Campuswide network is available. 100% of college-owned or -operated housing units are wired for high-speed Internet access. Wireless service is available via entire campus.
Library: M. D. Anderson Library plus 4 others. *Books:* 1.8 million (physical), 672,679 (digital/electronic); *Serial titles:* 45,924 (physical), 88,370 (digital/electronic); *Databases:* 466. Weekly public service hours: 122; study areas open 24 hours, 5–7 days a week; students can reserve study rooms.

STUDENT LIFE
Housing options: coed, special housing for students with disabilities. Campus housing is university owned and is provided by a third party.

Activities and organizations: drama/theater group, student-run newspaper, radio and television station, choral group, marching band, Metropolitan Volunteer Program, Interfraternity Council, Delta Omega Chi Medical Service Society, Health Occupation Students of America, Pre-Pharmacy Association, national fraternities, national sororities.

Athletics Member NCAA. All Division I except football (Division I-A). *Intercollegiate sports:* baseball M(s), basketball M(s)/W(s), cross-country running M(s)/W(s), golf M(s)/W(s), soccer W(s), softball W(s), swimming and diving W(s), tennis W(s), track and field M(s)/W(s), volleyball W(s). *Intramural sports:* badminton M/W, basketball M/W, bowling M(c)/W, fencing M(c)/W(c), golf M/W, racquetball M/W, rock climbing M/W, soccer M/W, softball M/W, swimming and diving M/W, table tennis M/W, tennis M/W, track and field M/W, ultimate Frisbee M(c)/W(c), volleyball M/W(c), water polo M(c)/W(c), weight lifting M/W.

Campus security: 24-hour emergency response devices and patrols, student patrols, late-night transport/escort service, controlled dormitory access, vehicle assistance.

Student services: health clinic, personal/psychological counseling, women's center, legal services.

COSTS & FINANCIAL AID

Costs (2017–18) *Tuition:* state resident $10,905 full-time, $364 per credit hour part-time; nonresident $26,355 full-time, $879 per credit hour part-time. Full-time tuition and fees vary according to course level, course load, degree level, program, and student level. Part-time tuition and fees vary according to course level, course load, degree level, program, and student level. No tuition increase for student's term of enrollment. *Required fees:* $982 full-time. *Room and board:* $9984. Room and board charges vary according to board plan and housing facility. *Payment plans:* installment, deferred payment.

Financial Aid Of all full-time matriculated undergraduates who enrolled in 2016, 17,691 applied for aid, 15,649 were judged to have need, 2,007 had their need fully met. 858 Federal Work-Study jobs (averaging $3909). In 2016, 758 non-need-based awards were made. *Average percent of need met:* 58. *Average financial aid package:* $12,167. *Average need-based loan:* $7389. *Average need-based gift aid:* $8121. *Average non-need-based aid:* $5233. *Average indebtedness upon graduation:* $23,665.

APPLYING

Standardized Tests *Required:* SAT or ACT (for admission).

Options: electronic application.

Application fee: $75.

Required: high school transcript.

Application deadlines: 6/15 (freshmen), 6/30 (transfers).

Notification: continuous (freshmen), continuous (transfers).

CONTACT

Mardell Maxwell, Exec Director, Admissions, University of Houston, Welcome Center, 4400 University Boulevard, Houston, TX 77204-2023. *Phone:* 713-743-1010. *Fax:* 713-743-9633. *E-mail:* mrmaxwe2@central.uh.edu.

University of Houston–Clear Lake

Houston, Texas

http://www.uhcl.edu/

- **State-supported** comprehensive, founded 1971, part of University of Houston System
- **Suburban** 524-acre campus with easy access to Houston
- **Endowment** $27.7 million
- **Coed** 5,798 undergraduate students, 51% full-time, 64% women, 36% men
- **Minimally difficult** entrance level, 73% of applicants were admitted

UNDERGRAD STUDENTS

2,946 full-time, 2,852 part-time. Students come from 19 other countries; 0.2% are from out of state; 8% Black or African American, non-Hispanic/Latino; 39% Hispanic/Latino; 6% Asian, non-Hispanic/Latino; 0.1% Native Hawaiian or other Pacific Islander, non-Hispanic/Latino; 0.3% American Indian or Alaska Native, non-Hispanic/Latino; 3% Two or more races, non-Hispanic/Latino; 1% Race/ethnicity unknown; 2% international; 23% transferred in; 3% live on campus.

Freshmen:

Admission: 1,037 applied, 752 admitted, 218 enrolled. *Average high school GPA:* 3.4. *Test scores:* SAT evidence-based reading and writing

scores over 500: 85%; SAT math scores over 500: 84%; ACT scores over 18: 98%; SAT evidence-based reading and writing scores over 600: 28%; SAT math scores over 600: 21%; ACT scores over 24: 36%; SAT evidence-based reading and writing scores over 700: 4%; SAT math scores over 700: 2%; ACT scores over 30: 1%.

Retention: 74% of full-time freshmen returned.

FACULTY

Total: 510, 59% full-time.

Student/faculty ratio: 15:1.

ACADEMICS

Calendar: semesters. *Degrees:* bachelor's, master's, doctoral, post-master's, and postbachelor's certificates.

Special study options: academic remediation for entering students, advanced placement credit, distance learning, double majors, English as a second language, independent study, internships, off-campus study, part-time degree program, services for LD students, study abroad, summer session for credit.

Computers: 723 computers/terminals are available on campus for general student use. Students can access the following: campus intranet, computer help desk, free student e-mail accounts, online (class) grades, online (class) registration, online (class) schedules. Campuswide network is available. Wireless service is available via entire campus.

Library: Alfred R. Neuman Library. *Books:* 445,986 (physical), 490,261 (digital/electronic); *Serial titles:* 5,480 (physical), 85,734 (digital/electronic); *Databases:* 233. Weekly public service hours: 89; students can reserve study rooms.

STUDENT LIFE

Housing options: special housing for students with disabilities. Campus housing is provided by a third party. Freshman applicants given priority for college housing.

Activities and organizations: drama/theater group, student-run newspaper.

Athletics *Intramural sports:* football M/W, golf M/W, soccer M(c), tennis M/W, volleyball M/W.

Campus security: 24-hour emergency response devices and patrols, student patrols, late-night transport/escort service.

Student services: health clinic, personal/psychological counseling, women's center.

COSTS & FINANCIAL AID

Costs (2017–18) *Tuition:* state resident $6240 full-time, $215 per credit hour part-time; nonresident $18,630 full-time, $738 per credit hour part-time. Full-time tuition and fees vary according to course load, degree level, and program. Part-time tuition and fees vary according to course load, degree level, and program. *Required fees:* $633 full-time, $602 per term part-time. *Room only:* $4852. Room and board charges vary according to housing facility. *Payment plans:* installment, deferred payment. *Waivers:* senior citizens.

Financial Aid Of all full-time matriculated undergraduates who enrolled in 2015, 1,928 applied for aid, 1,799 were judged to have need, 64 had their need fully met. In 2015, 253 non-need-based awards were made. *Average percent of need met:* 44. *Average financial aid package:* $8122. *Average need-based loan:* $4317. *Average need-based gift aid:* $6097. *Average non-need-based aid:* $1229.

APPLYING

Standardized Tests *Required:* SAT or ACT (for admission).

Options: electronic application, early admission, deferred entrance.

Application fee: $45.

Required: high school transcript, State of Texas Uniform Admission Policy criteria. *Required for some:* essay or personal statement, 2 letters of recommendation.

Application deadlines: 6/1 (freshmen), rolling (transfers).

Notification: continuous (transfers).

CONTACT

University of Houston–Clear Lake, 2700 Bay Area Boulevard, Houston, TX 77058-1002.

University of Houston–Downtown
Houston, Texas
http://www.uhd.edu/

- **State-supported** comprehensive, founded 1974, part of University of Houston System
- **Urban** 24-acre campus
- **Endowment** $41.4 million
- **Coed** 12,407 undergraduate students, 51% full-time, 61% women, 39% men
- **Noncompetitive** entrance level, 84% of applicants were admitted

UNDERGRAD STUDENTS
6,320 full-time, 6,087 part-time. Students come from 26 states and territories; 59 other countries; 1% are from out of state; 20% Black or African American, non-Hispanic/Latino; 48% Hispanic/Latino; 9% Asian, non-Hispanic/Latino; 0.2% Native Hawaiian or other Pacific Islander, non-Hispanic/Latino; 0.3% American Indian or Alaska Native, non-Hispanic/Latino; 1% Two or more races, non-Hispanic/Latino; 1% Race/ethnicity unknown; 5% international; 15% transferred in.

Freshmen:
Admission: 3,931 applied, 3,305 admitted, 967 enrolled. *Test scores:* SAT evidence-based reading and writing scores over 500: 51%; SAT math scores over 500: 59%; ACT scores over 18: 68%; SAT evidence-based reading and writing scores over 600: 5%; SAT math scores over 600: 5%; ACT scores over 24: 3%; ACT scores over 30: 1%.

Retention: 72% of full-time freshmen returned.

FACULTY
Total: 748, 50% full-time, 63% with terminal degrees.
Student/faculty ratio: 19:1.

ACADEMICS
Calendar: semesters. *Degrees:* bachelor's, master's, and postbachelor's certificates.

Special study options: academic remediation for entering students, advanced placement credit, distance learning, double majors, English as a second language, honors programs, independent study, internships, off-campus study, part-time degree program, services for LD students, study abroad, summer session for credit. *ROTC:* Army (c), Air Force (c).

Computers: 613 computers/terminals are available on campus for general student use. Students can access the following: computer help desk, free student e-mail accounts, online (class) grades, online (class) registration, online (class) schedules, electronic classrooms and labs - 2,229. Campuswide network is available. Wireless service is available via entire campus.

Library: W. I. Dykes Library. *Books:* 188,649 (physical), 531,458 (digital/electronic); *Serial titles:* 88,715 (digital/electronic). Weekly public service hours: 85; study areas open 24 hours, 5–7 days a week; students can reserve study rooms.

STUDENT LIFE
Housing options: college housing not available.

Activities and organizations: drama/theater group, student-run newspaper, radio station, Student Government Association, Campus Activities Board, Professional Accounting Society, American Marketing Association, Bilingual Education Student Organization, national fraternities, national sororities.

Athletics *Intramural sports:* badminton M/W, baseball M(c), basketball M(c)/W(c), bowling M/W, cheerleading M(c)/W(c), soccer M(c)/W(c), tennis M/W, volleyball M(c)/W(c), weight lifting M(c)/W(c).

Campus security: 24-hour emergency response devices and patrols, late-night transport/escort service.

Student services: health clinic, personal/psychological counseling, legal services.

COSTS & FINANCIAL AID
Costs (2018–19) *Tuition:* state resident $6660 full-time, $222 per credit hour part-time; nonresident $19,110 full-time, $637 per credit hour part-time. Full-time tuition and fees vary according to course load and program. Part-time tuition and fees vary according to course load and program. *Required fees:* $1172 full-time. *Payment plan:* installment. *Waivers:* senior citizens.

Financial Aid Of all full-time matriculated undergraduates who enrolled in 2017, 5,116 applied for aid, 4,684 were judged to have need, 1,785 had their need fully met. In 2017, 286 non-need-based awards were made. *Average percent of need met:* 58. *Average financial aid package:* $9634. *Average need-based loan:* $8160. *Average need-based gift aid:* $4453. *Average non-need-based aid:* $2300. *Average indebtedness upon graduation:* $25,747.

APPLYING
Standardized Tests *Required:* SAT or ACT (for admission).
Options: electronic application.
Application fee: $50.
Required: high school transcript.

CONTACT
Mr. Jordan Green, Assistant Director, Customer Service, University of Houston–Downtown, One Main Street, Suite GSB308, Houston, TX 77002. *Phone:* 713-221-8021. *Fax:* 713-221-8157. *E-mail:* uhdadmit@uhd.edu.

University of Houston–Victoria
Victoria, Texas
http://www.uhv.edu/

CONTACT
Mrs. Trudy Wortham, Registrar, University of Houston–Victoria, 3007 North Ben Wilson, Victoria, TX 77901. *Phone:* 361-485-4521 Ext. 4184. *Toll-free phone:* 877-970-4848 Ext. 110. *E-mail:* worthamt@uhv.edu.

University of Mary Hardin-Baylor
Belton, Texas
http://www.umhb.edu/

- **Independent Southern Baptist** comprehensive, founded 1845
- **Small-town** 340-acre campus with easy access to Austin
- **Endowment** $82.1 million
- **Coed** 3,333 undergraduate students, 91% full-time, 64% women, 36% men
- **Moderately difficult** entrance level, 79% of applicants were admitted

UNDERGRAD STUDENTS
3,045 full-time, 288 part-time. Students come from 35 states and territories; 22 other countries; 3% are from out of state; 15% Black or African American, non-Hispanic/Latino; 21% Hispanic/Latino; 2% Asian, non-Hispanic/Latino; 0.3% Native Hawaiian or other Pacific Islander, non-Hispanic/Latino; 0.8% American Indian or Alaska Native, non-Hispanic/Latino; 3% Two or more races, non-Hispanic/Latino; 2% Race/ethnicity unknown; 0.8% international; 8% transferred in; 56% live on campus.

Freshmen:
Admission: 8,289 applied, 6,535 admitted, 754 enrolled. *Average high school GPA:* 3.5. *Test scores:* SAT evidence-based reading and writing scores over 500: 83%; SAT math scores over 500: 81%; ACT scores over 18: 88%; SAT evidence-based reading and writing scores over 600: 32%; SAT math scores over 600: 21%; ACT scores over 24: 37%; SAT evidence-based reading and writing scores over 700: 3%; SAT math scores over 700: 1%; ACT scores over 30: 5%.

Retention: 73% of full-time freshmen returned.

FACULTY
Total: 281, 56% full-time, 64% with terminal degrees.
Student/faculty ratio: 18:1.

ACADEMICS
Calendar: semesters. *Degrees:* bachelor's, master's, doctoral, and post-master's certificates.

Special study options: academic remediation for entering students, adult/continuing education programs, advanced placement credit, distance learning, double majors, English as a second language, honors programs, independent study, internships, off-campus study, part-time degree program, services for LD students, study abroad, summer session for credit. *ROTC:* Army (b), Air Force (c).

Unusual degree programs: 3-2 business administration.

Computers: 275 computers/terminals and 1,000 ports are available on campus for general student use. Students can access the following: campus intranet, computer help desk, free student e-mail accounts, online (class) grades, online (class) registration, online (class) schedules. Campuswide network is available. 100% of college-owned or -operated housing units are wired for high-speed Internet access. Wireless service is available via entire campus.

Library: Townsend Memorial Library. *Books:* 183,109 (physical), 28,162 (digital/electronic); *Serial titles:* 507 (physical), 144,900 (digital/electronic); *Databases:* 128. Weekly public service hours: 99; students can reserve study rooms.

STUDENT LIFE

Housing options: men-only, women-only, special housing for students with disabilities. Campus housing is university owned. Freshman applicants given priority for college housing.

Activities and organizations: drama/theater group, student-run newspaper, choral group, Baptist Student Ministry, Student Government Association, Nursing Student Association, Campus Activities Board, Search Cru.

Athletics Member NCAA. All Division III. *Intercollegiate sports:* baseball M, basketball M/W, football M, golf M/W, soccer M/W, softball W, tennis M/W, volleyball W. *Intramural sports:* basketball M/W, football M/W, golf M/W, soccer M/W, softball M/W, table tennis M/W, tennis M/W, ultimate Frisbee M/W, volleyball M/W.

Campus security: 24-hour emergency response devices and patrols, late-night transport/escort service, controlled dormitory access, campus police force, lighted pathways and sidewalks.

Student services: health clinic, personal/psychological counseling.

COSTS & FINANCIAL AID

Costs (2018–19) *Comprehensive fee:* $35,336 includes full-time tuition ($24,640), mandatory fees ($2250), and room and board ($8446). Full-time tuition and fees vary according to course load and degree level. Part-time tuition: $880 per credit hour. Part-time tuition and fees vary according to course load and degree level. *Room and board:* Room and board charges vary according to board plan and housing facility. *Payment plan:* installment. *Waivers:* employees or children of employees.

Financial Aid Of all full-time matriculated undergraduates who enrolled in 2017, 2,682 applied for aid, 2,425 were judged to have need, 181 had their need fully met. In 2017, 380 non-need-based awards were made. *Average percent of need met:* 57. *Average financial aid package:* $17,854. *Average need-based loan:* $4385. *Average need-based gift aid:* $13,995. *Average non-need-based aid:* $7698. *Average indebtedness upon graduation:* $43,344.

APPLYING

Standardized Tests *Required:* SAT or ACT (for admission).

Options: electronic application, early admission, deferred entrance.

Application fee: $35.

Required: high school transcript. *Required for some:* essay or personal statement, interview.

Application deadlines: rolling (freshmen), rolling (transfers).

Notification: continuous (freshmen), continuous (transfers).

CONTACT

University of Mary Hardin-Baylor, 900 College Street, Belton, TX 76513. *Toll-free phone:* 800-727-8642.

University of North Texas

Denton, Texas

http://www.unt.edu/

- **State-supported** university, founded 1890, part of University of North Texas System
- **Suburban** 875-acre campus with easy access to Dallas-Fort Worth
- **Endowment** $166.4 million
- **Coed** 31,405 undergraduate students, 82% full-time, 52% women, 48% men
- **Moderately difficult** entrance level, 72% of applicants were admitted

UNDERGRAD STUDENTS

25,618 full-time, 5,787 part-time. Students come from 54 states and territories; 139 other countries; 3% are from out of state; 14% Black or African American, non-Hispanic/Latino; 25% Hispanic/Latino; 6% Asian, non-Hispanic/Latino; 0.1% Native Hawaiian or other Pacific Islander, non-Hispanic/Latino; 0.3% American Indian or Alaska Native, non-Hispanic/Latino; 4% Two or more races, non-Hispanic/Latino; 0.7% Race/ethnicity unknown; 3% international; 13% transferred in; 19% live on campus.

Freshmen:

Admission: 16,826 applied, 12,046 admitted, 4,905 enrolled. *Test scores:* SAT evidence-based reading and writing scores over 500: 91%; SAT math scores over 500: 89%; SAT evidence-based reading and writing scores over 600: 45%; SAT math scores over 600: 34%; SAT evidence-based reading and writing scores over 700: 7%; SAT math scores over 700: 7%.

Retention: 78% of full-time freshmen returned.

FACULTY

Total: 1,683, 66% full-time, 59% with terminal degrees.

Student/faculty ratio: 24:1.

ACADEMICS

Calendar: semesters. *Degrees:* bachelor's, master's, doctoral, and postbachelor's certificates.

Special study options: academic remediation for entering students, accelerated degree program, advanced placement credit, cooperative education, distance learning, double majors, English as a second language, freshman honors college, honors programs, independent study, internships, off-campus study, part-time degree program, services for LD students, study abroad, summer session for credit. *ROTC:* Army (b), Air Force (b).

Unusual degree programs: accounting.

Computers: 925 computers/terminals are available on campus for general student use. Students can access the following: campus intranet, computer help desk, free student e-mail accounts, online (class) grades, online (class) registration, online (class) schedules. Campuswide network is available. 100% of college-owned or -operated housing units are wired for high-speed Internet access. Wireless service is available via entire campus.

Library: Willis Library plus 5 others. *Books:* 2.1 million (physical), 1.0 million (digital/electronic); *Serial titles:* 19,763 (physical), 166,076 (digital/electronic); *Databases:* 391. Weekly public service hours: 168; study areas open 24 hours, 5–7 days a week; students can reserve study rooms.

STUDENT LIFE

Housing options: on-campus residence required for freshman year; coed, special housing for students with disabilities. Campus housing is university owned. Freshman applicants given priority for college housing.

Activities and organizations: drama/theater group, student-run newspaper, radio and television station, choral group, marching band, Student Government Association, Residence Hall Association, Panhellenic Association, Interfraternity Council, Black Student Union, national fraternities, national sororities.

Athletics Member NCAA. All Division I except football (Division I-A). *Intercollegiate sports:* archery M(c)/W(c), badminton M(c)/W(c), baseball M(c), basketball M(s)/W(s), bowling M(c)/W(c), cross-country running M(s)/W(s), equestrian sports M(c)/W(c), fencing M(c)/W(c), golf M(s)/W(s), ice hockey M(c)/W(c), lacrosse M(c)/W(c), racquetball M(c)/W(c), rugby M(c), sailing M(c)/W(c), soccer M(c)/W(s), softball M/W(s), swimming and diving W(s), table tennis M(c)/W(c), tennis M(c)/W, track and field M(s)/W(s), ultimate Frisbee M(c)/W(c), volleyball M(c)/W(s), wrestling M(c)/W(c). *Intramural sports:* basketball M/W, football M, racquetball M/W, soccer M/W, softball M/W, table tennis M/W, tennis M/W, ultimate Frisbee M/W, volleyball M/W.

Campus security: 24-hour emergency response devices and patrols, late-night transport/escort service, controlled dormitory access.

Student services: health clinic, personal/psychological counseling, legal services.

COSTS & FINANCIAL AID

Costs (2018–19) *Tuition:* state resident $8404 full-time; nonresident $21,214 full-time. Full-time tuition and fees vary according to course load. Part-time tuition and fees vary according to course load. No tuition increase for student's term of enrollment. *Required fees:* $3110 full-time. *Room and board:* $9610. Room and board charges vary according to board plan and housing facility. *Payment plan:* installment. *Waivers:* senior citizens and employees or children of employees.

Financial Aid Of all full-time matriculated undergraduates who enrolled in 2017, 18,991 applied for aid, 15,866 were judged to have need, 1,305 had their need fully met. In 2017, 3150 non-need-based awards were made. *Average percent of need met:* 53. *Average financial aid package:* $10,975. *Average need-based loan:* $4087. *Average need-based gift aid:* $8311. *Average non-need-based aid:* $6712. *Average indebtedness upon graduation:* $25,203.

APPLYING

Standardized Tests *Required:* SAT or ACT (for admission).

Options: electronic application, early admission, deferred entrance.

Application fee: $75.

Required: high school transcript. *Required for some:* essay or personal statement.

Application deadlines: 8/1 (freshmen), rolling (transfers).

Notification: continuous (freshmen), continuous (transfers).

CONTACT
Mr. Randall Nunn, Associate Director of Admissions, University of North Texas, Denton, TX 76203. *Phone:* 940-565-3920. *Toll-free phone:* 800-868-8211. *E-mail:* randall.nunn@unt.edu.

University of North Texas at Dallas
Dallas, Texas
http://untdallas.edu/

- **State-supported** comprehensive, founded 2001, part of University of North Texas System
- **Urban** 264-acre campus with easy access to Dallas-Fort Worth
- **Endowment** $823,724
- **Coed** 2,727 undergraduate students, 63% full-time, 68% women, 32% men
- 74% of applicants were admitted

UNDERGRAD STUDENTS
1,705 full-time, 1,022 part-time. Students come from 11 states and territories; 17 other countries; 1% are from out of state; 31% Black or African American, non-Hispanic/Latino; 52% Hispanic/Latino; 2% Asian, non-Hispanic/Latino; 0.1% Native Hawaiian or other Pacific Islander, non-Hispanic/Latino; 0.1% American Indian or Alaska Native, non-Hispanic/Latino; 2% Two or more races, non-Hispanic/Latino; 0.9% Race/ethnicity unknown; 1% international; 20% transferred in.

Freshmen:
Admission: 1,483 applied, 1,097 admitted, 316 enrolled. *Test scores:* ACT scores over 18: 57%; ACT scores over 24: 10%; ACT scores over 30: 1%.
Retention: 66% of full-time freshmen returned.

FACULTY
Total: 167, 56% full-time.
Student/faculty ratio: 15:1.

ACADEMICS
Degrees: bachelor's, master's, and doctoral.
Special study options: accelerated degree program, advanced placement credit, cooperative education, distance learning, independent study, internships, off-campus study, part-time degree program, services for LD students, summer session for credit.
Computers: Students can access the following: computer help desk, free student e-mail accounts, online (class) grades. Campuswide network is available.
Library: UNTD Library. *Books:* 3,980 (physical), 44,401 (digital/electronic); *Serial titles:* 330 (physical), 10,899 (digital/electronic); *Databases:* 281.

STUDENT LIFE
Activities and organizations: national fraternities, national sororities.
Athletics *Intramural sports:* basketball M/W, soccer M/W, volleyball M/W.
Campus security: 24-hour emergency response devices, late-night transport/escort service.

Student services: personal/psychological counseling.

COSTS & FINANCIAL AID
Costs (2018–19) *Tuition:* state resident $7548 full-time, $252 per credit hour part-time; nonresident $19,788 full-time, $660 per credit hour part-time. Full-time tuition and fees vary according to degree level. Part-time tuition and fees vary according to degree level. No tuition increase for student's term of enrollment. *Required fees:* $300 full-time, $10 per credit hour part-time. *Room and board:* $8948. Room and board charges vary according to board plan and housing facility. *Waivers:* senior citizens and employees or children of employees.

Financial Aid Of all full-time matriculated undergraduates who enrolled in 2016, 1,168 applied for aid, 1,111 were judged to have need, 65 had their need fully met. In 2016, 107 non-need-based awards were made. *Average percent of need met:* 46. *Average financial aid package:* $9152. *Average need-based loan:* $4186. *Average need-based gift aid:* $6263. *Average non-need-based aid:* $5108. *Average indebtedness upon graduation:* $6927.

APPLYING

Standardized Tests *Required:* SAT or ACT (for admission).

Options: electronic application.

Application fee: $50.

Required: high school transcript.

CONTACT
Mr. Jason Faulk, Director of Undergraduate Admission, University of North Texas at Dallas, 7300 University Hill Drive, Admin (B1)105, Dallas 76039. *Phone:* 972-780-3642. *E-mail:* admissions@untdallas.edu.

University of Phoenix–Dallas Campus
Dallas, Texas
http://www.phoenix.edu/

CONTACT
Marc Booker, Sr. Director, Office of Admissions and Evaluation, University of Phoenix–Dallas Campus, 4035 South Riverpoint Parkway, Mail Stop CF-L101, Phoenix, AZ 85040. *Phone:* 602-557-4609. *Toll-free phone:* 866-766-0766. *Fax:* 480-643-1156.

University of Phoenix–Houston Campus
Houston, Texas
http://www.phoenix.edu/

CONTACT
Marc Booker, Sr. Director, Office of Admissions and Evaluation, University of Phoenix–Houston Campus, 4305 South Riverpoint Parkway, Mail Stop CF-L101, Phoenix, AZ 85040. *Phone:* 602-557-4609. *Toll-free phone:* 866-766-0766. *Fax:* 480-643-1156.

University of Phoenix–San Antonio Campus
San Antonio, Texas
http://www.phoenix.edu/

CONTACT
University of Phoenix–San Antonio Campus, 8200 IH-10 West, San Antonio, TX 78230. *Toll-free phone:* 866-766-0766.

University of St. Thomas
Houston, Texas
http://www.stthom.edu/

- **Independent Roman Catholic** comprehensive, founded 1947
- **Urban** 23-acre campus with easy access to Houston, TX
- **Endowment** $98.5 million
- **Coed** 1,814 undergraduate students, 77% full-time, 60% women, 40% men
- **Moderately difficult** entrance level, 77% of applicants were admitted

UNDERGRAD STUDENTS

1,391 full-time, 423 part-time. Students come from 24 states and territories; 38 other countries; 3% are from out of state; 7% Black or African American, non-Hispanic/Latino; 43% Hispanic/Latino; 11% Asian, non-Hispanic/Latino; 0.2% Native Hawaiian or other Pacific Islander, non-Hispanic/Latino; 0.2% American Indian or Alaska Native, non-Hispanic/Latino; 3% Two or more races, non-Hispanic/Latino; 2% Race/ethnicity unknown; 9% international; 10% transferred in; 22% live on campus.

Freshmen:

Admission: 942 applied, 729 admitted, 277 enrolled. *Average high school GPA:* 3.6. *Test scores:* ACT scores over 18: 98%; ACT scores over 24: 55%; ACT scores over 30: 10%.

Retention: 82% of full-time freshmen returned.

FACULTY

Total: 350, 51% full-time, 62% with terminal degrees.
Student/faculty ratio: 10:1.

ACADEMICS

Calendar: semesters. *Degrees:* diplomas, bachelor's, master's, doctoral, and postbachelor's certificates.

Special study options: accelerated degree program, adult/continuing education programs, advanced placement credit, distance learning, double majors, honors programs, independent study, internships, off-campus study, part-time degree program, services for LD students, student-designed majors, study abroad, summer session for credit. *ROTC:* Army (c), Air Force (c).

Unusual degree programs: 3-2 business administration; engineering with University of Notre Dame, University of Houston, Texas A&M University, The Catholic University of America.

Computers: 441 computers/terminals and 800 ports are available on campus for general student use. Students can access the following: campus intranet, computer help desk, free student e-mail accounts, online (class) grades, online (class) registration, online (class) schedules. Campuswide network is available. 100% of college-owned or -operated housing units are wired for high-speed Internet access. Wireless service is available via entire campus.

Library: Doherty Library. *Books:* 262,245 (physical), 2,496 (digital/electronic); *Serial titles:* 74,347 (physical), 74,347 (digital/electronic); *Databases:* 274. Weekly public service hours: 100.

STUDENT LIFE

Housing options: coed, men-only, women-only, special housing for students with disabilities. Campus housing is university owned. Freshman applicants given priority for college housing.

Activities and organizations: drama/theater group, choral group, Health Occupations Students of America (HOSA), Filipino Student Association (FSA), Tri-Beta, American Chemical Society, Ultimate Frisbee.

Athletics Member NAIA. *Intercollegiate sports:* basketball M(s)/W(s), cross-country running M(s)/W(s), golf M(s)/W(s), soccer M(s)/W(s), volleyball W(s). *Intramural sports:* badminton M/W, basketball M/W, cheerleading M(c)/W(c), fencing M(c)/W(c), football M(c)/W(c), soccer M(c)/W(c), table tennis M(c)/W(c), tennis M(c)/W(c), ultimate Frisbee M(c)/W(c), volleyball M(c)/W(c).

Campus security: 24-hour emergency response devices and patrols, late-night transport/escort service, controlled dormitory access.

Student services: personal/psychological counseling.

COSTS & FINANCIAL AID

Costs (2018–19) *Tuition:* $33,000 full-time, $2200 per credit hour part-time. Full-time tuition and fees vary according to course load. Part-time tuition and fees vary according to course load. *Required fees:* $580 full-time. *Room only:* Room and board charges vary according to board plan and housing facility. *Payment plans:* installment, deferred payment. *Waivers:* senior citizens and employees or children of employees.

Financial Aid Of all full-time matriculated undergraduates who enrolled in 2017, 1,030 applied for aid, 987 were judged to have need, 84 had their need fully met. 92 Federal Work-Study jobs (averaging $3870). 3 state and other part-time jobs (averaging $3333). In 2017, 326 non-need-based awards were made. *Average percent of need met:* 65. *Average financial aid package:* $24,587. *Average need-based loan:* $4604. *Average need-*

based gift aid: $21,750. *Average non-need-based aid:* $12,308. *Average indebtedness upon graduation:* $29,857.

APPLYING

Standardized Tests *Required:* SAT or ACT (for admission).

Options: electronic application, early action, deferred entrance.

Required: essay or personal statement, high school transcript, minimum 2.8 GPA. *Required for some:* letters of recommendation.

Application deadlines: 8/1 (freshmen), rolling (transfers), 12/1 (early action).

Notification: continuous until 11/1 (freshmen), continuous until 11/1 (out-of-state freshmen), continuous (transfers), 12/15 (early action).

CONTACT

Mr. Arthur Ortiz, Vice President of Enrollment Management, University of St. Thomas, 3800 Montrose Boulevard, Houston, TX 77006-4696. *Phone:* 713-525-3848. *Toll-free phone:* 800-856-8565. *Fax:* 713-525-3558. *E-mail:* admissions@stthom.edu.

The University of Texas at Arlington

Arlington, Texas

http://www.uta.edu/

CONTACT

Dr. Hans Gatterdam, Executive Director of Admissions, Records and Registration, The University of Texas at Arlington, UTA Box 19088, 701 South Nedderman Drive, Arlington, TX 76019-0088. *Phone:* 817-272-3275. *Fax:* 817-272-5114.

The University of Texas at Austin

Austin, Texas

http://www.utexas.edu/

- **State-supported** university, founded 1883, part of University of Texas System
- **Urban** 437-acre campus with easy access to Austin
- **Endowment** $3.7 billion
- **Coed** 40,492 undergraduate students, 93% full-time, 53% women, 47% men
- **Moderately difficult** entrance level, 36% of applicants were admitted

UNDERGRAD STUDENTS

37,740 full-time, 2,752 part-time. Students come from 54 states and territories; 123 other countries; 6% are from out of state; 4% Black or African American, non-Hispanic/Latino; 23% Hispanic/Latino; 21% Asian, non-Hispanic/Latino; 0.1% Native Hawaiian or other Pacific Islander, non-Hispanic/Latino; 0.2% American Indian or Alaska Native, non-Hispanic/Latino; 4% Two or more races, non-Hispanic/Latino; 0.9% Race/ethnicity unknown; 5% international; 6% transferred in; 18% live on campus.

Freshmen:

Admission: 51,033 applied, 18,620 admitted, 8,381 enrolled. *Test scores:* SAT evidence-based reading and writing scores over 500: 95%; SAT math scores over 500: 95%; ACT scores over 18: 99%; SAT evidence-based reading and writing scores over 600: 60%; SAT math scores over 600: 72%; ACT scores over 24: 89%; SAT evidence-based reading and writing scores over 700: 26%; SAT math scores over 700: 30%; ACT scores over 30: 54%.

Retention: 95% of full-time freshmen returned.

FACULTY

Total: 3,133, 84% full-time, 86% with terminal degrees.
Student/faculty ratio: 18:1.

ACADEMICS

Calendar: semesters. *Degrees:* certificates, bachelor's, master's, doctoral, and postbachelor's certificates.

Special study options: academic remediation for entering students, accelerated degree program, advanced placement credit, cooperative education, distance learning, double majors, English as a second language, honors programs, independent study, internships, off-campus study, part-time degree program, services for LD students, student-designed majors, study abroad, summer session for credit. *ROTC:* Army (b), Navy (b), Air Force (b).

Unusual degree programs: 3-2 business administration; engineering; nursing; social work; computer science.

Computers: 550 computers/terminals and 1,650 ports are available on campus for general student use. Students can access the following: campus intranet, computer help desk, free student e-mail accounts, online (class) grades, online (class) registration, online (class) schedules. Campuswide network is available. 100% of college-owned or -operated housing units are wired for high-speed Internet access. Wireless service is available via entire campus.

Library: PCL (Perry Castaneda Library) plus 23 others. *Books:* 11.5 million (physical), 1.4 million (digital/electronic); *Serial titles:* 3,554 (physical), 224,040 (digital/electronic); *Databases:* 1,570. Weekly public service hours: 94; study areas open 24 hours, 5–7 days a week; students can reserve study rooms.

STUDENT LIFE

Housing options: coed, men-only, women-only, special housing for students with disabilities. Campus housing is university owned. Freshman applicants given priority for college housing.

Activities and organizations: drama/theater group, student-run newspaper, radio and television station, choral group, marching band, Alpha Phi Omega, University Panhellenic Council, Asian Business Students Association, Longhorn Band Student Organization, Campus Events + Entertainment, national fraternities, national sororities.

Athletics Member NCAA. All Division I except football (Division I-A). *Intercollegiate sports:* archery M(c)/W(c), badminton M(c)/W(c), baseball M(s)/W(c), basketball M(s)/W(s), crew M(c)/W(s), cross-country running M(s)/W(s), fencing M(c)/W(c), golf M(s)/W(s), gymnastics M(c)/W(c), ice hockey M(c)/W(c), lacrosse M(c)/W(c), racquetball M(c)/W(c), rock climbing M(c)/W(c), rugby M(c)/W(c), sailing M(c)/W(c), soccer M(c)/W(s), softball W(s), swimming and diving M(s)/W(s), table tennis M(c)/W(c), tennis M(s)/W(s), track and field M(s)/W(s), ultimate Frisbee M(c)/W(c), volleyball M(c)/W(s), water polo M(c)/W(c), weight lifting M(c)/W(c), wrestling M(c)/W(c). *Intramural sports:* basketball M/W, football M/W, golf M/W, racquetball M/W, rock climbing M/W, soccer M/W, softball M/W, swimming and diving M/W, table tennis M/W, tennis M/W, track and field M/W, ultimate Frisbee M/W, volleyball M/W.

Campus security: 24-hour emergency response devices and patrols, late-night transport/escort service, controlled dormitory access.

Student services: health clinic, personal/psychological counseling, women's center, legal services.

COSTS & FINANCIAL AID

Costs (2017–18) *Tuition:* state resident $10,398 full-time; nonresident $36,744 full-time. Full-time tuition and fees vary according to course load and program. Part-time tuition and fees vary according to course load and program. No tuition increase for student's term of enrollment. *Room and board:* $10,070. Room and board charges vary according to housing facility. *Payment plan:* installment. *Waivers:* senior citizens and employees or children of employees.

Financial Aid Of all full-time matriculated undergraduates who enrolled in 2016, 22,096 applied for aid, 14,955 were judged to have need, 3,355 had their need fully met. In 2016, 189 non-need-based awards were made. *Average percent of need met:* 71. *Average financial aid package:* $12,313. *Average need-based loan:* $4725. *Average need-based gift aid:* $9457. *Average non-need-based aid:* $2444. *Average indebtedness upon graduation:* $24,883.

APPLYING

Standardized Tests *Required:* SAT or ACT (for admission).

Options: electronic application.

Application fee: $75.

Required: essay or personal statement, high school transcript. *Recommended:* letters of recommendation.

Application deadlines: 12/1 (freshmen), 3/1 (transfers).

Notification: continuous (freshmen), continuous (transfers).

CONTACT

Susan Kearns, Director of Admissions, The University of Texas at Austin, Office of Admissions, Freshman Admissions Center, PO Box 8058, Austin, TX 78713-8058. *Phone:* 512-475-7368. *Fax:* 512-232-4241. *E-mail:* susan.kearns@austin.utexas.edu.

The University of Texas at Dallas
Richardson, Texas
http://www.utdallas.edu/

- **State-supported** university, founded 1969, part of University of Texas System
- **Suburban** 500-acre campus with easy access to Dallas-Fort Worth
- **Endowment** $482.8 million
- **Coed** 18,388 undergraduate students, 83% full-time, 43% women, 57% men
- **Very difficult** entrance level, 76% of applicants were admitted

UNDERGRAD STUDENTS

15,294 full-time, 3,094 part-time. Students come from 48 states and territories; 78 other countries; 4% are from out of state; 6% Black or African American, non-Hispanic/Latino; 18% Hispanic/Latino; 31% Asian, non-Hispanic/Latino; 0.2% Native Hawaiian or other Pacific Islander, non-Hispanic/Latino; 0.2% American Indian or Alaska Native, non-Hispanic/Latino; 4% Two or more races, non-Hispanic/Latino; 2% Race/ethnicity unknown; 4% international; 11% transferred in; 26% live on campus.

Freshmen:

Admission: 11,791 applied, 8,965 admitted, 3,177 enrolled. *Test scores:* SAT evidence-based reading and writing scores over 500: 98%; SAT math scores over 500: 99%; ACT scores over 18: 100%; SAT evidence-based reading and writing scores over 600: 77%; SAT math scores over 600: 83%; ACT scores over 24: 95%; SAT evidence-based reading and writing scores over 700: 27%; SAT math scores over 700: 39%; ACT scores over 30: 48%.

Retention: 87% of full-time freshmen returned.

FACULTY

Total: 1,319, 68% full-time, 73% with terminal degrees.

Student/faculty ratio: 23:1.

ACADEMICS

Calendar: semesters. *Degrees:* bachelor's, master's, doctoral, and postbachelor's certificates.

Special study options: academic remediation for entering students, accelerated degree program, adult/continuing education programs, advanced placement credit, cooperative education, distance learning, double majors, freshman honors college, honors programs, independent study, internships, part-time degree program, services for LD students, student-designed majors, study abroad, summer session for credit. *ROTC:* Army (c), Air Force (c).

Unusual degree programs: 3-2 engineering with Abilene Christian University, Austin College, Paul Quinn College, Texas Woman's University.

Computers: 170 computers/terminals are available on campus for general student use. Students can access the following: computer help desk, free student e-mail accounts, online (class) grades, online (class) registration, online (class) schedules. Campuswide network is available. 100% of college-owned or -operated housing units are wired for high-speed Internet access. Wireless service is available via classrooms, computer centers, dorm rooms, libraries, student centers.

Library: Eugene McDermott Library plus 1 other. *Books:* 652,018 (physical), 1.5 million (digital/electronic); *Serial titles:* 135,287 (physical), 149,406 (digital/electronic); *Databases:* 530. Weekly public service hours: 152; study areas open 24 hours, 5–7 days a week; students can reserve study rooms.

STUDENT LIFE

Housing options: coed. Campus housing is university owned. Freshman applicants given priority for college housing.

Activities and organizations: drama/theater group, student-run newspaper, radio and television station, choral group, Student Government Association, Golden Key National Honor Society, Muslim Students Association, Indian Student Association, Friendship Association of Chinese Students and Scholars, national fraternities, national sororities.

Athletics Member NCAA. All Division III. *Intercollegiate sports:* baseball M, basketball M/W, cross-country running M/W, golf M/W, soccer M/W, softball W, tennis M/W, volleyball W. *Intramural sports:* archery M(c)/W(c), badminton M(c)/W(c), basketball M/W, cheerleading M/W, cross-country running M(c)/W(c), fencing M(c)/W(c), gymnastics M(c)/W(c), lacrosse M(c), racquetball M(c)/W(c), rock climbing M(c)/W(c), rugby M(c)/W(c), soccer M(c)/W(c), swimming and diving M(c)/W(c), table tennis M(c)/W(c), tennis M(c)/W(c), ultimate Frisbee M(c)/W(c), volleyball M(c)/W(c), weight lifting M(c)/W(c).

Campus security: 24-hour emergency response devices and patrols, student patrols, late-night transport/escort service, controlled dormitory access.

Student services: health clinic, personal/psychological counseling, women's center, legal services.

COSTS & FINANCIAL AID
Costs (2017–18) *Tuition:* state resident $12,528 full-time, $418 per credit hour part-time; nonresident $34,644 full-time, $1155 per credit hour part-time. Full-time tuition and fees vary according to course load and degree level. Part-time tuition and fees vary according to course load and degree level. No tuition increase for student's term of enrollment. *Room and board:* $11,112. Room and board charges vary according to board plan and housing facility. *Payment plan:* installment. *Waivers:* senior citizens and employees or children of employees.

Financial Aid Of all full-time matriculated undergraduates who enrolled in 2016, 8,877 applied for aid, 7,447 were judged to have need, 1,203 had their need fully met. In 2016, 2951 non-need-based awards were made. *Average percent of need met:* 65. *Average financial aid package:* $13,220. *Average need-based loan:* $4414. *Average need-based gift aid:* $9183. *Average non-need-based aid:* $11,953. *Average indebtedness upon graduation:* $23,565.

APPLYING
Standardized Tests *Required:* SAT or ACT (for admission). *Required for some:* THEA.

Options: electronic application, deferred entrance.

Application fee: $50.

Required: essay or personal statement, high school transcript. *Required for some:* interview. *Recommended:* 3 letters of recommendation.

Notification: continuous (freshmen), continuous (transfers).

CONTACT
Enrollment Services, The University of Texas at Dallas, 800 West Campbell Road, Mail Station ROC12, Richardson, TX 75083-0688. *Phone:* 972-883-2270. *Toll-free phone:* 800-889-2443. *Fax:* 972-883-2599. *E-mail:* interest@utdallas.edu.

The University of Texas at El Paso
El Paso, Texas
http://www.utep.edu/
- **State-supported** university, founded 1913, part of University of Texas System
- **Urban** 360-acre campus
- **Coed** 21,341 undergraduate students, 66% full-time, 53% women, 47% men
- **Minimally difficult** entrance level, 100% of applicants were admitted

UNDERGRAD STUDENTS
14,025 full-time, 7,316 part-time. 4% are from out of state; 2% Black or African American, non-Hispanic/Latino; 83% Hispanic/Latino; 0.7% Asian, non-Hispanic/Latino; 0.1% Native Hawaiian or other Pacific Islander, non-Hispanic/Latino; 0.1% American Indian or Alaska Native, non-Hispanic/Latino; 0.9% Two or more races, non-Hispanic/Latino; 0.4% Race/ethnicity unknown; 6% international; 9% transferred in.

Freshmen:
Admission: 9,382 applied, 9,382 admitted, 3,066 enrolled. *Average high school GPA:* 3.3. *Test scores:* SAT evidence-based reading and writing scores over 500: 59%; SAT math scores over 500: 61%; SAT evidence-based reading and writing scores over 600: 14%; SAT math scores over 600: 12%; SAT evidence-based reading and writing scores over 700: 1%; SAT math scores over 700: 1%.

Retention: 74% of full-time freshmen returned.

FACULTY
Total: 1,327, 59% full-time.

Student/faculty ratio: 21:1.

ACADEMICS
Calendar: semesters. *Degrees:* certificates, diplomas, bachelor's, master's, and doctoral.

Special study options: distance learning, double majors, honors programs, independent study, study abroad. *ROTC:* Army (b).

Computers: Students can access the following: computer help desk, free student e-mail accounts, online (class) grades, online (class) registration, online (class) schedules. Campuswide network is available. 100% of college-owned or -operated housing units are wired for high-speed Internet access. Wireless service is available via entire campus.
Library: University Library.

STUDENT LIFE
Housing options: coed. Campus housing is university owned.

Activities and organizations: drama/theater group, student-run newspaper, radio station, choral group, marching band, national fraternities, national sororities.

Athletics Member NCAA. All Division I except football (Division I-A). *Intercollegiate sports:* basketball M(s)/W(s), cross-country running M(s)/W(s), golf M(s), riflery M/W, tennis W(s), track and field M(s)/W(s), volleyball W(s). *Intramural sports:* archery M/W, badminton M/W, basketball M/W, bowling M/W, fencing M/W, field hockey M, golf M/W, gymnastics M/W, racquetball M/W, skiing (downhill) M, soccer M/W, squash M/W, swimming and diving M/W, tennis M/W, track and field M/W, volleyball M/W, water polo M/W, weight lifting M, wrestling M/W.

Campus security: 24-hour emergency response devices and patrols, late-night transport/escort service.

Student services: health clinic, personal/psychological counseling, women's center, legal services.

COSTS & FINANCIAL AID
Costs (2017–18) *Tuition:* state resident $5931 full-time, $193 per credit hour part-time; nonresident $19,676 full-time, $656 per credit hour part-time. No tuition increase for student's term of enrollment. *Required fees:* $1720 full-time, $52 per credit hour part-time, $126 per term part-time. *Room and board:* $9495; room only: $4914. *Payment plan:* installment.

Financial Aid Of all full-time matriculated undergraduates who enrolled in 2017, 12,305 applied for aid, 10,363 were judged to have need, 1,622 had their need fully met. In 2017, 655 non-need-based awards were made. *Average percent of need met:* 55. *Average financial aid package:* $11,820. *Average need-based loan:* $6172. *Average need-based gift aid:* $7873. *Average non-need-based aid:* $4229. *Average indebtedness upon graduation:* $22,938.

APPLYING
Standardized Tests *Required:* SAT or ACT (for admission).

Options: deferred entrance.

Required: high school transcript.

CONTACT
Mr. Michael J. Talamantes, Director of Admissions and Recruitment, The University of Texas at El Paso, Academic Services Building, Room 102, El Paso, TX 779968. *Phone:* 915-747-5890. *Toll-free phone:* 877-74MINER. *Fax:* 915-747-5890. *E-mail:* futureminer@utep.edu.

The University of Texas at San Antonio
San Antonio, Texas
http://www.utsa.edu/
- **State-supported** university, founded 1969, part of University of Texas System
- **Suburban** 725-acre campus with easy access to San Antonio
- **Endowment** $134.5 million
- **Coed** 26,444 undergraduate students, 81% full-time, 50% women, 50% men
- **Moderately difficult** entrance level, 79% of applicants were admitted

UNDERGRAD STUDENTS
21,510 full-time, 4,934 part-time. Students come from 51 states and territories; 75 other countries; 2% are from out of state; 9% Black or

A ★ indicates that the school has detailed information with a Premium Profile on Petersons.com.

www.petersons.com 1063

African American, non-Hispanic/Latino; 55% Hispanic/Latino; 6% Asian, non-Hispanic/Latino; 0.2% Native Hawaiian or other Pacific Islander, non-Hispanic/Latino; 0.2% American Indian or Alaska Native, non-Hispanic/Latino; 3% Two or more races, non-Hispanic/Latino; 0.7% Race/ethnicity unknown; 2% international; 10% transferred in; 12% live on campus.

Freshmen:
Admission: 15,973 applied, 12,692 admitted, 5,029 enrolled. *Test scores:* SAT evidence-based reading and writing scores over 500: 85%; SAT math scores over 500: 84%; ACT scores over 18: 91%; SAT evidence-based reading and writing scores over 600: 31%; SAT math scores over 600: 27%; ACT scores over 24: 35%; SAT evidence-based reading and writing scores over 700: 3%; SAT math scores over 700: 3%; ACT scores over 30: 5%.
Retention: 74% of full-time freshmen returned.

FACULTY
Total: 1,276, 69% full-time, 75% with terminal degrees.
Student/faculty ratio: 25:1.

ACADEMICS
Calendar: semesters. *Degrees:* certificates, bachelor's, master's, doctoral, and postbachelor's certificates.

Special study options: academic remediation for entering students, adult/continuing education programs, advanced placement credit, cooperative education, distance learning, double majors, English as a second language, honors programs, independent study, internships, off-campus study, part-time degree program, services for LD students, student-designed majors, study abroad, summer session for credit. *ROTC:* Army (b), Air Force (b).

Computers: 510 computers/terminals and 104 ports are available on campus for general student use. Students can access the following: campus intranet, computer help desk, free student e-mail accounts, online (class) grades, online (class) registration, online (class) schedules. Campuswide network is available. 100% of college-owned or -operated housing units are wired for high-speed Internet access. Wireless service is available via entire campus.
Library: John Peace Library plus 3 others. Students can reserve study rooms.

STUDENT LIFE
Housing options: coed. Campus housing is university owned and is provided by a third party.

Activities and organizations: student-run newspaper, radio and television station, choral group, marching band, Student Government, VOICES, Chi Alpha Christian Fellowship, Hispanic Student Association, Panhellenic Council, national fraternities, national sororities.

Athletics Member NCAA. All Division I. *Intercollegiate sports:* badminton M(c)/W(c), baseball M(s), basketball M(s)/W(s), cross-country running M(s)/W(s), fencing M(c)/W(c), football M(s), golf M(s)/W(s), ice hockey M(c), lacrosse M(c)/W(c), racquetball M(c)/W(c), rock climbing M(c)/W(c), rugby M(c)/W(c), soccer M(c)/W(s), softball W(s), swimming and diving M(c)/W(c), table tennis M(c)/W(c), tennis M(s)/W(s), track and field M(s)/W(s), ultimate Frisbee M(c)/W(c), volleyball M(c)/W(s), weight lifting M(c)/W(c), wrestling M(c). *Intramural sports:* badminton M/W, baseball M(c), basketball M/W, cross-country running M/W, football M, golf M/W, racquetball M/W, soccer M/W, softball M/W, table tennis M/W, tennis M/W, track and field M/W, ultimate Frisbee M/W, volleyball M/W.

Campus security: 24-hour emergency response devices and patrols, late-night transport/escort service, controlled dormitory access, close to 1000 security cameras, Reverse 911 emergency telephone notification system, warning speaker arrays.

Student services: health clinic, personal/psychological counseling, women's center.

COSTS & FINANCIAL AID
Costs (2017–18) *Tuition:* state resident $6635 full-time, $221 per credit hour part-time; nonresident $20,634 full-time, $688 per credit hour part-time. Full-time tuition and fees vary according to course load and degree level. Part-time tuition and fees vary according to course load and degree level. No tuition increase for student's term of enrollment. *Required fees:* $2745 full-time. *Room and board:* $7190; room only: $4490. Room and board charges vary according to board plan and housing facility. *Payment*

plans: installment, deferred payment. *Waivers:* employees or children of employees.

Financial Aid Of all full-time matriculated undergraduates who enrolled in 2015, 15,632 applied for aid, 13,304 were judged to have need, 609 had their need fully met. 366 Federal Work-Study jobs (averaging $2877). 900 state and other part-time jobs (averaging $2133). In 2015, 707 non-need-based awards were made. *Average percent of need met:* 53. *Average financial aid package:* $9751. *Average need-based loan:* $4109. *Average need-based gift aid:* $7147. *Average non-need-based aid:* $3418. *Average indebtedness upon graduation:* $26,763.

APPLYING
Standardized Tests *Required:* SAT or ACT (for admission).
Options: electronic application.
Application fee: $60.
Required: high school transcript. *Required for some:* transfer applicants with less than 30 hours must meet freshman requirements and have a 2.25 GPA on a 4.0 scale and submit all college transcripts; transfer applicants with 30 or more completed hours must have a 2.25 GPA on a 4.0 scale and submit all college transcripts. *Recommended:* essay or personal statement, 1 letter of recommendation.
Application deadlines: 6/1 (freshmen), 6/1 (transfers).
Notification: continuous (freshmen), continuous (out-of-state freshmen), continuous (transfers).

CONTACT
Mrs. Beverly Woodson Day, Director of Admissions, The University of Texas at San Antonio, One UTSA Circle, San Antonio, TX 78249. *Phone:* 210-458-4536. *Toll-free phone:* 800-669-0919. *Fax:* 210-458-2001. *E-mail:* prospects@utsa.edu.

The University of Texas at Tyler
Tyler, Texas
http://www.uttyler.edu/

CONTACT
Ms. Sarah Bowdin, Interim Assistant Vice President for Enrollment Management, The University of Texas at Tyler, 3900 University Boulevard, Tyler, TX 75799-0001. *Phone:* 903-566-7057. *Toll-free phone:* 800-UTTYLER. *Fax:* 903-566-7068. *E-mail:* admissions@ uttyler.edu.

The University of Texas Health Science Center at Houston
Houston, Texas
http://www.uthouston.edu/

CONTACT
The University of Texas Health Science Center at Houston, PO Box 20036, Houston, TX 77225-0036. *Phone:* 713-500-3388.

The University of Texas Health Science Center at San Antonio
San Antonio, Texas
http://www.uthscsa.edu/

CONTACT
The University of Texas Health Science Center at San Antonio, 7703 Floyd Curl Drive, San Antonio, TX 78229-3900. *Phone:* 210-567-2659.

The University of Texas MD Anderson Cancer Center
Houston, Texas
http://www.mdanderson.org/education-and-research/

CONTACT
The University of Texas MD Anderson Cancer Center, 1515 Holcombe Boulevard, Houston, TX 77030.

The University of Texas Medical Branch

Galveston, Texas
http://www.utmb.edu/

CONTACT
The University of Texas Medical Branch, 301 University Boulevard, Galveston, TX 77555. *Phone:* 409-772-1215.

The University of Texas of the Permian Basin

Odessa, Texas
http://www.utpb.edu/

- **State-supported** comprehensive, founded 1969, part of The University of Texas System
- **Urban** 600-acre campus
- **Endowment** $42.2 million
- **Coed** 6,065 undergraduate students, 36% full-time, 57% women, 43% men
- **Moderately difficult** entrance level, 82% of applicants were admitted

UNDERGRAD STUDENTS
2,192 full-time, 3,873 part-time. Students come from 42 states and territories; 36 other countries; 3% are from out of state; 5% Black or African American, non-Hispanic/Latino; 47% Hispanic/Latino; 3% Asian, non-Hispanic/Latino; 0.2% Native Hawaiian or other Pacific Islander, non-Hispanic/Latino; 0.4% American Indian or Alaska Native, non-Hispanic/Latino; 2% Two or more races, non-Hispanic/Latino; 3% Race/ethnicity unknown; 2% international; 7% transferred in; 19% live on campus.

Freshmen:
Admission: 940 applied, 768 admitted, 396 enrolled. *Test scores:* SAT math scores over 500: 65%; ACT scores over 18: 75%; SAT math scores over 600: 19%; ACT scores over 24: 17%; SAT math scores over 700: 1%; ACT scores over 30: 1%.
Retention: 66% of full-time freshmen returned.

FACULTY
Total: 290, 40% full-time, 47% with terminal degrees.
Student/faculty ratio: 27:1.

ACADEMICS
Calendar: semesters. *Degrees:* bachelor's, master's, and postbachelor's certificates.
Special study options: academic remediation for entering students, accelerated degree program, advanced placement credit, cooperative education, distance learning, double majors, English as a second language, honors programs, independent study, internships, part-time degree program, services for LD students, study abroad, summer session for credit.
Unusual degree programs: 3-2 business administration.
Computers: 511 computers/terminals are available on campus for general student use. Students can access the following: campus intranet, computer help desk, free student e-mail accounts, online (class) grades, online (class) registration, online (class) schedules. Campuswide network is available. 100% of college-owned or -operated housing units are wired for high-speed Internet access. Wireless service is available via entire campus.
Library: J. Conrad Dunagan Library. *Books:* 294,556 (physical), 1.0 million (digital/electronic); *Serial titles:* 358 (physical), 86,390 (digital/electronic); *Databases:* 226. Weekly public service hours: 86; students can reserve study rooms.

STUDENT LIFE
Housing options: coed. Campus housing is university owned.
Activities and organizations: drama/theater group, student-run newspaper, choral group, marching band, The American Society for Mechanical Engineers, The Student Veteran Association, Marketing Experiences, The National Society for Leadership and Success, Students in Free Enterprise, national fraternities.

Athletics Member NCAA. All Division II. *Intercollegiate sports:* baseball M(s), basketball M(s)/W(s), cheerleading M(s)/W(s), cross-country running M(s)/W(s), football M(s), golf M(s)/W(s), soccer M(s)/W(s), softball W(s), swimming and diving M(s)/W(s), tennis M(s)/W(s), volleyball W(s). *Intramural sports:* basketball M/W, bowling M/W, cross-country running M/W, golf M/W, soccer M/W, softball W, swimming and diving M/W, tennis M/W, volleyball M/W.

Campus security: 24-hour emergency response devices and patrols, late-night transport/escort service, controlled dormitory access.

Student services: health clinic, personal/psychological counseling.

COSTS & FINANCIAL AID
Costs (2018–19) *Tuition:* state resident $5662 full-time, $189 per credit hour part-time; nonresident $6812 full-time, $454 per credit hour part-time. Full-time tuition and fees vary according to course load, degree level, and location. Part-time tuition and fees vary according to course load, degree level, and location. No tuition increase for student's term of enrollment. *Required fees:* $1462 full-time, $70 per credit hour part-time. *Room and board:* $10,944; room only: $7200. Room and board charges vary according to board plan and housing facility. *Payment plan:* installment.
Financial Aid Of all full-time matriculated undergraduates who enrolled in 2015, 1,946 applied for aid, 1,646 were judged to have need, 1,170 had their need fully met. In 2015, 906 non-need-based awards were made. *Average percent of need met:* 65. *Average financial aid package:* $10,560. *Average need-based loan:* $3750. *Average need-based gift aid:* $7926. *Average non-need-based aid:* $2447. *Average indebtedness upon graduation:* $17,578.

APPLYING
Standardized Tests *Required:* SAT or ACT (for admission).
Options: electronic application.
Application fee: $40.
Required: high school transcript.
Application deadlines: 8/26 (freshmen), 8/26 (transfers).
Notification: continuous (freshmen), continuous (transfers).

CONTACT
The University of Texas of the Permian Basin, 4901 East University Boulevard, Odessa, TX 79762-0001. *Phone:* 432-552-2605. *Toll-free phone:* 866-552-UTPB.

The University of Texas Rio Grande Valley

Edinburg, Texas
http://www.utrgv.edu/

- **State-supported** university, founded 1927, part of University of Texas System
- **Small-town** 414-acre campus with easy access to McAllen, Edinburg, Mission
- **Coed** 24,634 undergraduate students, 76% full-time, 56% women, 44% men
- **Noncompetitive** entrance level, 80% of applicants were admitted

UNDERGRAD STUDENTS
18,754 full-time, 5,880 part-time. 0.5% Black or African American, non-Hispanic/Latino; 91% Hispanic/Latino; 1% Asian, non-Hispanic/Latino; 0.3% Two or more races, non-Hispanic/Latino; 2% Race/ethnicity unknown; 2% international; 7% transferred in; 4% live on campus.

Freshmen:
Admission: 10,540 applied, 8,483 admitted, 4,504 enrolled. *Test scores:* SAT evidence-based reading and writing scores over 500: 66%; SAT math scores over 500: 61%; ACT scores over 18: 74%; SAT evidence-based reading and writing scores over 600: 15%; SAT math scores over 600: 11%; ACT scores over 24: 11%; SAT evidence-based reading and writing scores over 700: 1%; SAT math scores over 700: 1%; ACT scores over 30: 1%.

ACADEMICS
Calendar: semesters. *Degrees:* bachelor's, master's, doctoral, and post-master's certificates.

Special study options: academic remediation for entering students, accelerated degree program, adult/continuing education programs, advanced placement credit, cooperative education, distance learning, double majors, English as a second language, honors programs, independent study, internships, off-campus study, part-time degree program, services for LD students, study abroad, summer session for credit. *ROTC:* Army (b).

Unusual degree programs: 3-2 business administration.

Computers: Students can access the following: campus intranet, computer help desk, free student e-mail accounts, online (class) grades, online (class) registration, online (class) schedules. Campuswide network is available. 66% of college-owned or -operated housing units are wired for high-speed Internet access. Wireless service is available via entire campus.

Library: University Library. Students can reserve study rooms.

STUDENT LIFE
Housing options: men-only, women-only, special housing for students with disabilities. Campus housing is university owned.

Activities and organizations: drama/theater group, student-run newspaper, radio and television station, choral group, Alpha Lambda Delta National Honor Society for First-Year Students, The National Society of Collegiate Scholars, Golden Key International Honor Society, Pre-Medical Bio-Medical Society, Environmental Awareness Club, national fraternities, national sororities.

Athletics Member NCAA. All Division I. *Intercollegiate sports:* baseball M, basketball M/W, cross-country running M/W, golf M/W, soccer M/W, tennis M/W, track and field M/W, volleyball W.

Campus security: 24-hour emergency response devices and patrols, late-night transport/escort service.

Student services: health clinic, personal/psychological counseling.

COSTS & FINANCIAL AID
Costs (2017–18) *Tuition:* state resident $7588 full-time, $367 per credit hour part-time; nonresident $17,548 full-time, $782 per credit hour part-time. Full-time tuition and fees vary according to course load, degree level, program, and student level. Part-time tuition and fees vary according to course load, degree level, program, and student level. No tuition increase for student's term of enrollment. *Required fees:* $1467 full-time, $185 per semester hour part-time. *Room and board:* $7986. Room and board charges vary according to board plan, housing facility, and location. *Payment plan:* installment.

Financial Aid Of all full-time matriculated undergraduates who enrolled in 2016, 12,806 applied for aid, 12,179 were judged to have need, 569 had their need fully met. 785 Federal Work-Study jobs (averaging $2732). 426 state and other part-time jobs (averaging $1908). In 2016, 434 non-need-based awards were made. *Average percent of need met:* 79. *Average financial aid package:* $9987. *Average need-based loan:* $4392. *Average need-based gift aid:* $10,455. *Average non-need-based aid:* $3174. *Average indebtedness upon graduation:* $14,291.

APPLYING
Standardized Tests *Required:* SAT or ACT (for admission).

Options: electronic application.

Required: high school transcript, minimum 2.0 GPA. *Required for some:* interview.

Application deadlines: 7/1 (freshmen), 7/1 (transfers).

Notification: continuous (freshmen), continuous (transfers).

CONTACT
Dr. Debbie Gilchrist, Interim Registrar, The University of Texas Rio Grande Valley, Office of Enrollment Services, 1201 West University Drive, Edinburg, TX 78539. *Phone:* 956-665-2926. *Toll-free phone:* 888-882-4026. *Fax:* 956-665-2212. *E-mail:* debbie.gilchrist@utrgv.edu.

University of the Incarnate Word
San Antonio, Texas
http://www.uiw.edu/
- **Independent Roman Catholic** comprehensive, founded 1881
- **Urban** 200-acre campus with easy access to San Antonio
- **Coed** 5,994 undergraduate students, 74% full-time, 60% women, 40% men
- **Minimally difficult** entrance level, 94% of applicants were admitted

UNDERGRAD STUDENTS
4,461 full-time, 1,533 part-time. 8% are from out of state; 7% Black or African American, non-Hispanic/Latino; 56% Hispanic/Latino; 2% Asian, non-Hispanic/Latino; 0.4% Native Hawaiian or other Pacific Islander, non-Hispanic/Latino; 0.3% American Indian or Alaska Native, non-Hispanic/Latino; 2% Two or more races, non-Hispanic/Latino; 7% Race/ethnicity unknown; 6% international; 9% transferred in; 17% live on campus.

Freshmen:
Admission: 4,149 applied, 3,894 admitted, 758 enrolled. *Average high school GPA:* 3.5. *Test scores:* SAT evidence-based reading and writing scores over 500: 64%; SAT math scores over 500: 58%; ACT scores over 18: 74%; SAT evidence-based reading and writing scores over 600: 13%; SAT math scores over 600: 10%; ACT scores over 24: 22%; ACT scores over 30: 2%.

Retention: 76% of full-time freshmen returned.

FACULTY
Total: 711, 47% full-time, 30% with terminal degrees.

Student/faculty ratio: 15:1.

ACADEMICS
Calendar: semesters. *Degrees:* diplomas, associate, bachelor's, master's, and doctoral.

Special study options: academic remediation for entering students, accelerated degree program, adult/continuing education programs, advanced placement credit, cooperative education, distance learning, double majors, English as a second language, freshman honors college, honors programs, independent study, internships, off-campus study, part-time degree program, services for LD students, study abroad, summer session for credit. *ROTC:* Army (c).

Unusual degree programs: 3-2 business administration.

Computers: 185 computers/terminals are available on campus for general student use. Students can access the following: computer help desk, free student e-mail accounts, online (class) grades, online (class) registration, online (class) schedules. Campuswide network is available. 100% of college-owned or -operated housing units are wired for high-speed Internet access. Wireless service is available via entire campus.

Library: J. E. and M. E. Mabee Library plus 1 other. *Books:* 214,768 (physical), 42,478 (digital/electronic); *Serial titles:* 1,867 (physical), 75,557 (digital/electronic); *Databases:* 201. Weekly public service hours: 105.

STUDENT LIFE
Housing options: coed, men-only, women-only, special housing for students with disabilities. Campus housing is university owned.

Activities and organizations: drama/theater group, student-run newspaper, radio and television station, choral group, marching band, Business Club, Biology Club, Student Government Association, International Students Association, Multicultural Greek Council, national fraternities, national sororities.

Athletics Member NCAA. All Division I except football (Division I-AA), softball (Division II). *Intercollegiate sports:* baseball M(s), basketball M(s)/W(s), cross-country running M(s)/W(s), golf M(s)/W(s), soccer M(s)/W(s), softball W(s), swimming and diving M(s)/W(s), tennis M(s)/W(s), track and field M(s)/W(s), volleyball W(s). *Intramural sports:* basketball M/W, cheerleading M/W, football M/W, racquetball M/W, soccer M/W, softball M/W, tennis M/W, ultimate Frisbee M/W, volleyball M/W, water polo M/W.

Campus security: 24-hour emergency response devices and patrols, late-night transport/escort service, controlled dormitory access.

Student services: health clinic, personal/psychological counseling.

COSTS & FINANCIAL AID
Costs (2017–18) *Comprehensive fee:* $42,426 includes full-time tuition ($27,900), mandatory fees ($2090), and room and board ($12,436). Full-time tuition and fees vary according to course load, degree level, location, program, and reciprocity agreements. Part-time tuition: $915 per credit hour. Part-time tuition and fees vary according to course load, degree level, location, program, and reciprocity agreements. *Room and board:* Room and board charges vary according to board plan and housing facility. *Payment plan:* installment. *Waivers:* senior citizens and employees or children of employees.

Financial Aid Of all full-time matriculated undergraduates who enrolled in 2016, 3,613 applied for aid, 3,372 were judged to have need, 269 had their need fully met. *Average percent of need met:* 59. *Average financial aid package:* $20,142. *Average need-based loan:* $3960. *Average need-based gift aid:* $15,340. *Average indebtedness upon graduation:* $6271.

APPLYING
Standardized Tests *Required:* SAT or ACT (for admission).
Options: electronic application, deferred entrance.
Application fee: $20.
Required: high school transcript. *Required for some:* essay or personal statement, interview. *Recommended:* minimum 2.0 GPA, interview.
Application deadlines: rolling (freshmen), rolling (transfers).
Notification: continuous (freshmen), continuous (transfers).

CONTACT
Mr. Javier Lara, Director of Undergraduate Admissions, University of the Incarnate Word, 4301 Broadway Avenue, San Antonio, TX 78209. *Phone:* 210-829-6005. *Toll-free phone:* 800-749-WORD. *Fax:* 210-829-3921. *E-mail:* jdlara@uiwtx.edu.

Wade College
Dallas, Texas
http://www.wadecollege.edu/
- **Proprietary** primarily 2-year, founded 1965
- **Urban** 175-acre campus with easy access to Dallas Fort Worth
- **Coed, primarily women** 238 undergraduate students
- **Minimally difficult** entrance level

UNDERGRAD STUDENTS
Students come from 4 other countries; 10% are from out of state.

FACULTY
Total: 18, 50% full-time, 33% with terminal degrees.
Student/faculty ratio: 12:1.

ACADEMICS
Calendar: trimesters. *Degrees:* associate and bachelor's.
Special study options: academic remediation for entering students, advanced placement credit, internships, part-time degree program, services for LD students, summer session for credit.
Computers: 75 computers/terminals are available on campus for general student use. Students can access the following: campus intranet, free student e-mail accounts, online (class) grades, online (class) schedules. Campuswide network is available. Wireless service is available via entire campus.
Library: College Library. *Books:* 8,500 (physical), 45,000 (digital/electronic); *Databases:* 10.

STUDENT LIFE
Activities and organizations: student-run newspaper, Wade College Student Association.
Campus security: 24-hour emergency response devices and patrols, late-night transport/escort service, controlled dormitory access.

APPLYING
Options: electronic application.
Required: high school transcript, interview.
Application deadlines: 9/26 (freshmen), 9/26 (transfers).
Notification: continuous (freshmen), continuous (transfers).

CONTACT
Wade College, INFOMart, 1950 Stemmons Freeway, Suite 4080, LB 562, Dallas, TX 75207. *Phone:* 214-637-3530. *Toll-free phone:* 800-624-4850.

Wayland Baptist University
Plainview, Texas
http://www.wbu.edu/
- **Independent Baptist** comprehensive, founded 1908
- **Small-town** 80-acre campus
- **Endowment** $82.8 million
- **Coed** 3,543 undergraduate students, 28% full-time, 50% women, 50% men
- **Minimally difficult** entrance level, 98% of applicants were admitted

UNDERGRAD STUDENTS
978 full-time, 2,565 part-time. Students come from 44 states and territories; 26 other countries; 30% are from out of state; 18% Black or African American, non-Hispanic/Latino; 32% Hispanic/Latino; 2% Asian, non-Hispanic/Latino; 0.9% Native Hawaiian or other Pacific Islander, non-Hispanic/Latino; 0.8% American Indian or Alaska Native, non-Hispanic/Latino; 4% Two or more races, non-Hispanic/Latino; 4% Race/ethnicity unknown; 1% international; 10% transferred in; 52% live on campus.

Freshmen:
Admission: 652 applied, 642 admitted, 297 enrolled. *Average high school GPA:* 3.3. *Test scores:* SAT evidence-based reading and writing scores over 500: 40%; SAT math scores over 500: 53%; ACT scores over 18: 67%; SAT evidence-based reading and writing scores over 600: 10%; SAT math scores over 600: 10%; ACT scores over 24: 24%; SAT evidence-based reading and writing scores over 700: 1%; SAT math scores over 700: 1%; ACT scores over 30: 3%.
Retention: 42% of full-time freshmen returned.

FACULTY
Total: 554, 25% full-time.
Student/faculty ratio: 8:1.

ACADEMICS
Calendar: semesters. *Degrees:* associate, bachelor's, master's, and doctoral (branch locations in Anchorage, AK; Amarillo, TX; Luke Air Force Base, AZ; Glorieta, NM; Aiea, HI; Lubbock, TX; San Antonio, TX; Wichita Falls, TX).
Special study options: academic remediation for entering students, accelerated degree program, adult/continuing education programs, advanced placement credit, distance learning, double majors, external degree program, honors programs, part-time degree program, services for LD students, study abroad, summer session for credit. *ROTC:* Army (c), Air Force (c).
Unusual degree programs: 3-2 engineering with Texas Tech University.
Computers: 840 computers/terminals are available on campus for general student use. Students can access the following: computer help desk, free student e-mail accounts, online (class) grades, online (class) registration, online (class) schedules. Campuswide network is available. 100% of college-owned or -operated housing units are wired for high-speed Internet access. Wireless service is available via classrooms, computer labs, dorm rooms, libraries, student centers.
Library: J.E. and L.E. Mabee Learning Resource Center. *Books:* 130,903 (physical), 49,479 (digital/electronic); *Serial titles:* 555,663 (digital/electronic); *Databases:* 104.

STUDENT LIFE
Housing options: on-campus residence required through junior year; men-only, women-only. Campus housing is university owned. Freshman campus housing is guaranteed.
Activities and organizations: drama/theater group, student-run newspaper, radio and television station, choral group, marching band, Student Government, Wayland Singers, Baptist Student Ministries, International Choir, President's Ambassadors, national fraternities, national sororities.
Athletics Member NAIA. *Intercollegiate sports:* baseball M(s), basketball M(s)/W(s), cheerleading M(s)/W(s), cross-country running M(s)/W(s), football M(s), golf M(s)/W(s), soccer M(s)/W(s), track and field M(s)/W(s), volleyball W(s), wrestling M(s)/W(s). *Intramural sports:* basketball M/W, football M, soccer M/W, volleyball M/W.
Campus security: 24-hour emergency response devices and patrols, security lighting, campus police department.

Student services: health clinic, personal/psychological counseling.

COSTS & FINANCIAL AID

Costs (2017–18) *Comprehensive fee:* $26,964 includes full-time tuition ($18,150), mandatory fees ($1280), and room and board ($7534). Full-time tuition and fees vary according to course load and location. Part-time tuition: $605 per credit hour. Part-time tuition and fees vary according to course load and location. *College room only:* $3044. Room and board charges vary according to board plan and housing facility. *Payment plan:* installment.

Financial Aid Of all full-time matriculated undergraduates who enrolled in 2016, 879 applied for aid, 813 were judged to have need, 78 had their need fully met. 130 Federal Work-Study jobs (averaging $1650). 351 state and other part-time jobs (averaging $1368). In 2016, 95 non-need-based awards were made. *Average percent of need met:* 58. *Average financial aid package:* $13,894. *Average need-based loan:* $4245. *Average need-based gift aid:* $10,622. *Average non-need-based aid:* $5344. *Average indebtedness upon graduation:* $23,764.

APPLYING

Standardized Tests *Required:* SAT or ACT (for admission).

Options: electronic application.

Application fee: $35.

Required: high school transcript. *Required for some:* interview.

Application deadlines: 8/1 (freshmen), rolling (transfers).

Notification: continuous (freshmen), continuous (transfers).

CONTACT

Ms. Debbie Stennett, Director of Student Admissions, Wayland Baptist University, 1900 West 7th Street, CMB 1294, Plainview, TX 79072. *Phone:* 806-291-3500. *Toll-free phone:* 800-588-1928. *Fax:* 806-291-1973. *E-mail:* admityou@wbu.edu.

West Coast University

Dallas, Texas

http://www.westcoastuniversity.edu/

CONTACT

West Coast University, 8435 N. Stemmons Freeway, Dallas, TX 75247. *Toll-free phone:* 866-508-2684.

West Texas A&M University

Canyon, Texas

http://www.wtamu.edu/

- **State-supported** comprehensive, founded 1909, part of Texas A&M University System
- **Small-town** 128-acre campus
- **Endowment** $80.4 million
- **Coed** 7,394 undergraduate students, 76% full-time, 57% women, 43% men
- **Moderately difficult** entrance level, 61% of applicants were admitted

UNDERGRAD STUDENTS

5,615 full-time, 1,779 part-time. Students come from 53 states and territories; 65 other countries; 14% are from out of state; 5% Black or African American, non-Hispanic/Latino; 28% Hispanic/Latino; 2% Asian, non-Hispanic/Latino; 0.1% Native Hawaiian or other Pacific Islander, non-Hispanic/Latino; 0.4% American Indian or Alaska Native, non-Hispanic/Latino; 3% Two or more races, non-Hispanic/Latino; 2% Race/ethnicity unknown; 2% international; 14% transferred in; 26% live on campus.

Freshmen

Admission: 6,116 applied, 3,753 admitted, 1,245 enrolled. *Test scores:* SAT evidence-based reading and writing scores over 500: 74%; SAT math scores over 500: 71%; ACT scores over 18: 85%; SAT evidence-based reading and writing scores over 600: 21%; SAT math scores over 600: 20%; ACT scores over 24: 22%; SAT evidence-based reading and writing scores over 700: 2%; SAT math scores over 700: 2%; ACT scores over 30: 2%.

Retention: 64% of full-time freshmen returned.

FACULTY

Total: 444, 77% full-time, 51% with terminal degrees.

Student/faculty ratio: 20:1.

ACADEMICS

Calendar: semesters. *Degrees:* bachelor's, master's, and doctoral.

Special study options: academic remediation for entering students, adult/continuing education programs, advanced placement credit, cooperative education, distance learning, double majors, English as a second language, honors programs, independent study, internships, part-time degree program, services for LD students, study abroad, summer session for credit.

Computers: 1,200 computers/terminals and 1,200 ports are available on campus for general student use. Students can access the following: campus intranet, computer help desk, free student e-mail accounts, online (class) grades, online (class) registration, online (class) schedules. Campuswide network is available. 100% of college-owned or -operated housing units are wired for high-speed Internet access. Wireless service is available via entire campus.

Library: Cornette Library plus 3 others. *Books:* 305,487 (physical), 516,531 (digital/electronic); *Serial titles:* 12,207 (physical), 12,592 (digital/electronic); *Databases:* 181. Weekly public service hours: 91; students can reserve study rooms.

STUDENT LIFE

Housing options: on-campus residence required through sophomore year; coed, men-only, women-only, special housing for students with disabilities. Campus housing is university owned. Freshman campus housing is guaranteed.

Activities and organizations: drama/theater group, student-run newspaper, radio station, choral group, marching band, Residence Hall Association, Wesley, Student Government, SAGE, Baptist Student Ministries, national fraternities, national sororities.

Athletics Member NCAA. All Division II. *Intercollegiate sports:* baseball M(s), basketball M(s)/W(s), bowling M(s)(c)/W(s)(c), cross-country running M(s)/W(s), equestrian sports M(c)/W(s), football M(s), golf M(s)/W(s), soccer M(s)/W(s), softball W(s), track and field M(s)/W(s), volleyball W(s). *Intramural sports:* badminton M/W, basketball M/W, bowling M/W, football M/W, golf M/W, racquetball M/W, soccer M/W, softball M/W, swimming and diving M/W, table tennis M/W, tennis M/W, volleyball M/W, wrestling M.

Campus security: 24-hour emergency response devices and patrols, late-night transport/escort service, controlled dormitory access.

Student services: health clinic, personal/psychological counseling.

COSTS & FINANCIAL AID

Costs (2017–18) *Tuition:* state resident $5414 full-time, $50 per credit hour part-time; nonresident $7047 full-time, $80 per credit hour part-time. Full-time tuition and fees vary according to course load, degree level, program, and student level. Part-time tuition and fees vary according to course load, degree level, program, and student level. No tuition increase for student's term of enrollment. *Required fees:* $2471 full-time, $224 per credit hour part-time. *Room and board:* $7196. Room and board charges vary according to board plan and housing facility. *Payment plan:* installment. *Waivers:* employees or children of employees.

Financial Aid Of all full-time matriculated undergraduates who enrolled in 2017, 4,354 applied for aid, 3,506 were judged to have need, 298 had their need fully met. 212 Federal Work-Study jobs (averaging $2749). 13 state and other part-time jobs (averaging $2941). In 2017, 668 non-need-based awards were made. *Average percent of need met:* 58. *Average financial aid package:* $8975. *Average need-based loan:* $3893. *Average need-based gift aid:* $6088. *Average non-need-based aid:* $2286. *Average indebtedness upon graduation:* $22,569.

APPLYING

Standardized Tests *Required:* SAT or ACT (for admission).

Options: electronic application, deferred entrance.

Application fee: $40.

Required: high school transcript, class rank and Texas high school curriculum or equivalent.

Application deadlines: rolling (freshmen), rolling (transfers).

Notification: continuous (freshmen), continuous (transfers).

CONTACT

Mrs. Tana Miller, Assistant Vice President for SEES/Registrar, West Texas A&M University, WTAMU Box 60907, Canyon, TX 79016-0001. *Phone:* 806-651-4911. *Toll-free phone:* 800-99-WTAMU. *Fax:* 806-651-5285. *E-mail:* tmiller@wtamu.edu.

Wiley College

Marshall, Texas

http://www.wileyc.edu/

CONTACT

Ms. Alvena Jones, Interim Director of Admissions/Recruitment, Wiley College, 711 Wiley Avenue, Marshall, TX 75670-5199. *Phone:* 903-927-3222. *Toll-free phone:* 800-658-6889. *Fax:* 903-923-8878. *E-mail:* ajones@wileyc.edu.

UTAH

Ameritech College of Healthcare

Draper, Utah

http://www.ameritech.edu/

CONTACT

Ameritech College of Healthcare, 12257 South Business Park Drive, Suite 108, Draper, UT 84020-6545.

Argosy University, Salt Lake City

Draper, Utah

http://www.argosy.edu/locations/salt-lake-city/

CONTACT

Argosy University, Salt Lake City, 121 Election Road, Suite 300, Draper, UT 84020. *Phone:* 801-601-5000. *Toll-free phone:* 888-639-4756.

Brigham Young University

Provo, Utah

http://www.byu.edu/

- **Independent** university, founded 1875, affiliated with The Church of Jesus Christ of Latter-day Saints, part of Church Education System (CES) of The Church of Jesus Christ of Latter-day Saints
- **Suburban** 557-acre campus with easy access to Salt Lake City
- **Coed** 31,233 undergraduate students, 90% full-time, 49% women, 51% men
- **Moderately difficult** entrance level, 52% of applicants were admitted

UNDERGRAD STUDENTS

28,156 full-time, 3,077 part-time. 64% are from out of state; 0.5% Black or African American, non-Hispanic/Latino; 6% Hispanic/Latino; 2% Asian, non-Hispanic/Latino; 0.7% Native Hawaiian or other Pacific Islander, non-Hispanic/Latino; 0.3% American Indian or Alaska Native, non-Hispanic/Latino; 4% Two or more races, non-Hispanic/Latino; 1% Race/ethnicity unknown; 3% international; 2% transferred in; 19% live on campus.

Freshmen:

Admission: 12,858 applied, 6,738 admitted, 5,340 enrolled. *Average high school GPA:* 3.8. *Test scores:* SAT evidence-based reading and writing scores over 500: 98%; SAT math scores over 500: 98%; ACT scores over 18: 100%; SAT evidence-based reading and writing scores over 600: 82%; SAT math scores over 600: 78%; ACT scores over 24: 94%; SAT evidence-based reading and writing scores over 700: 31%; SAT math scores over 700: 25%; ACT scores over 30: 48%.

Retention: 90% of full-time freshmen returned.

FACULTY

Total: 1,840, 68% full-time, 72% with terminal degrees.

Student/faculty ratio: 20:1.

ACADEMICS

Calendar: semesters. *Degrees:* bachelor's, master's, doctoral, post-master's, and postbachelor's certificates.

Special study options: adult/continuing education programs, external degree program, off-campus study, part-time degree program. *ROTC:* Army (b), Air Force (b).

Computers: Students can access the following: campus intranet, computer help desk, online (class) grades, online (class) registration, online (class) schedules. Campuswide network is available.

Library: Harold B. Lee Library plus 2 others.

STUDENT LIFE

Housing options: men-only, women-only, special housing for students with disabilities. Campus housing is university owned.

Athletics Member NCAA. All Division I except football (Division I-A). *Intercollegiate sports:* baseball M(s), basketball M(s)/W(s), cheerleading M(s)/W(s), cross-country running M(s)/W(s), golf M(s)/W(s), gymnastics W(s), lacrosse M(c), racquetball M/W, rugby M(c), soccer M(c)/W(s), softball W(s), swimming and diving M(s)/W(s), tennis M(s)/W(s), track and field M(s)/W(s), volleyball M(s)/W(s). *Intramural sports:* badminton W, basketball M/W, field hockey M, football M/W, golf M/W, racquetball M/W, soccer M/W, softball M/W, table tennis M/W, tennis M/W, ultimate Frisbee M/W, volleyball M/W, water polo M/W, wrestling M.

Campus security: 24-hour emergency response devices and patrols, late-night transport/escort service, controlled dormitory access.

COSTS & FINANCIAL AID

Costs (2018–19) *Comprehensive fee:* $13,248 includes full-time tuition ($5620) and room and board ($7628). Part-time tuition: $294 per credit hour. Part-time tuition and fees vary according to course load. *Room and board:* Room and board charges vary according to board plan, housing facility, and location. *Waivers:* employees or children of employees.

Financial Aid Of all full-time matriculated undergraduates who enrolled in 2016, 16,073 applied for aid, 13,636 were judged to have need, 319 had their need fully met. In 2016, 7558 non-need-based awards were made. *Average percent of need met:* 33. *Average financial aid package:* $7637. *Average need-based loan:* $4060. *Average need-based gift aid:* $5017. *Average non-need-based aid:* $4398. *Average indebtedness upon graduation:* $14,998.

APPLYING

Standardized Tests *Required:* SAT or ACT (for admission).

Options: electronic application, early admission, deferred entrance.

Application fee: $35.

Required: essay or personal statement, high school transcript, 1 letter of recommendation, interview.

CONTACT

Dean of Admissions, Brigham Young University, A-153 Abraham Smoot Building, Provo, UT 84602. *Phone:* 801-422-2507. *Fax:* 801-422-0005. *E-mail:* admissions@byu.edu.

Broadview Entertainment Arts University

Salt Lake City, Utah

http://www.broadviewuniversity.edu/

CONTACT

Broadview Entertainment Arts University, 240 East Morris Avenue, Salt Lake City, UT 84115. *Toll-free phone:* 877-801-8889.

Broadview University–West Jordan

West Jordan, Utah

http://www.broadviewuniversity.edu/

CONTACT

Broadview University–West Jordan, 1902 West 7800 South, West Jordan, UT 84088. *Toll-free phone:* 866-304-4224.

Careers Unlimited

Orem, Utah

http://www.ucdh.edu/

CONTACT
Careers Unlimited, 1176 South 1480 West, Orem, UT 84058.

Dixie State University

St. George, Utah

http://www.dixie.edu/

- **State-supported** 4-year, founded 1911, part of Utah System of Higher Education
- **Small-town** 117-acre campus
- **Endowment** $14.4 million
- **Coed**
- **Noncompetitive** entrance level

FACULTY
Student/faculty ratio: 20:1.

ACADEMICS
Calendar: semesters. *Degrees:* certificates, diplomas, associate, and bachelor's.
Library: Val A. Browning Library. *Books:* 92,371 (physical), 133,819 (digital/electronic); *Serial titles:* 265 (physical), 41,536 (digital/electronic); *Databases:* 126. Weekly public service hours: 96.

STUDENT LIFE
Housing options: coed, men-only. Campus housing is university owned.

Activities and organizations: drama/theater group, student-run newspaper, radio and television station, choral group, marching band, Dixie Spirit, Outdoor Club, Association of Women Students, intramurals, Futbol Club.

Athletics Member NCAA. All Division II.

Campus security: 24-hour emergency response devices and patrols.

Student services: health clinic, personal/psychological counseling, women's center.

COSTS & FINANCIAL AID
Costs (2017–18) *Tuition:* state resident $4308 full-time, $180 per credit hour part-time; nonresident $13,776 full-time, $574 per credit hour part-time. Full-time tuition and fees vary according to course load. Part-time tuition and fees vary according to course load. *Required fees:* $772 full-time, $32 per credit hour part-time. *Room and board:* $6328. Room and board charges vary according to board plan, housing facility, and location.

Financial Aid Of all full-time matriculated undergraduates who enrolled in 2016, 3,994 applied for aid, 3,624 were judged to have need, 364 had their need fully met. 132 Federal Work-Study jobs (averaging $3678). 42 state and other part-time jobs (averaging $3702). In 2016, 93 non-need-based awards were made. *Average percent of need met:* 60. *Average financial aid package:* $10,256. *Average need-based loan:* $4261. *Average need-based gift aid:* $6657. *Average non-need-based aid:* $2348. *Average indebtedness upon graduation:* $15,882. *Financial aid deadline:* 6/30.

APPLYING
Options: electronic application, early admission, deferred entrance.

Required: high school transcript.

CONTACT
Dixie State University, 225 South 700 East, St. George, UT 84770-3876. *Phone:* 435-652-7698.

Eagle Gate College

Layton, Utah

http://eaglegatecollege.edu/

CONTACT
Eagle Gate College, 915 North 400 West, Layton, UT 84041. *Phone:* 801-546-7500. *Toll-free phone:* 866-29-EAGLE.

Eagle Gate College

Murray, Utah

http://eaglegatecollege.edu/

CONTACT
Eagle Gate College, 5588 South Green Street, Murray, UT 84123. *Phone:* 801-333-8100. *Toll-free phone:* 866-29-EAGLE.

Independence University

Salt Lake City, Utah

http://www.independence.edu/

CONTACT
Ms. Deborah Hopkins, Enrollment Manager, Independence University, 4021 South 700 East, Suite 400, Salt Lake City, UT 84107. *Toll-free phone:* 800-917-6391.

Midwives College of Utah

Salt Lake City, Utah

http://www.midwifery.edu/

- **Independent** comprehensive, founded 1980
- **Urban** campus with easy access to Salt Lake City
- **Women only** 235 undergraduate students, 100% full-time

UNDERGRAD STUDENTS
235 full-time. Students come from 12 other countries; 196% are from out of state; 5% Black or African American, non-Hispanic/Latino; 9% Hispanic/Latino; 1% American Indian or Alaska Native, non-Hispanic/Latino; 5% Race/ethnicity unknown; 11% transferred in.

Freshmen:
Admission: 2 enrolled.

FACULTY
Total: 22, 5% with terminal degrees.

ACADEMICS
Calendar: semesters. *Degrees:* bachelor's and master's.

Special study options: adult/continuing education programs, distance learning, independent study, internships, off-campus study, part-time degree program, services for LD students.

Computers: Students can access the following: free student e-mail accounts, online (class) grades, online (class) schedules.
Library: MCU Library. *Books:* 644 (physical); *Serial titles:* 5 (digital/electronic). Weekly public service hours: 35.

STUDENT LIFE
Housing options: college housing not available.

Athletics *Intercollegiate sports:* ultimate Frisbee M(s)/W(s), volleyball M(s)/W(s). *Intramural sports:* ultimate Frisbee M/W, volleyball M/W.

Student services: personal/psychological counseling.

COSTS
Costs (2018–19) *One-time required fee:* $235. *Tuition:* $4400 full-time, $2200 per year part-time. *Required fees:* $345 full-time, $345 per year part-time. *Payment plan:* installment. *Waivers:* minority students, adult students, and employees or children of employees.

APPLYING
Options: electronic application, deferred entrance.

Application fee: $50.

Required: essay or personal statement, 2 letters of recommendation. *Required for some:* high school transcript, interview, transcripts from previous college.

Notification: 4/16 (freshmen).

CONTACT
Mel Smith-Tourville, Admissions Director, Midwives College of Utah, 1174 East Graystone Way, Suite 2, Suite 2, Salt Lake City, UT 84106. *Phone:* 801-649-5230. *Toll-free phone:* 866-680-2756. *Fax:* 866-207-2024. *E-mail:* admission@midwifery.edu.

★ Neumont College of Computer Science

Salt Lake City, Utah

http://www.neumont.edu/

- **Proprietary** 4-year, founded 2002
- **Urban** campus with easy access to Salt Lake City
- **Coed** 431 undergraduate students, 100% full-time, 11% women, 89% men
- **Moderately difficult** entrance level, 84% of applicants were admitted

UNDERGRAD STUDENTS

431 full-time. 81% are from out of state; 5% Black or African American, non-Hispanic/Latino; 13% Hispanic/Latino; 3% Asian, non-Hispanic/Latino; 0.7% Native Hawaiian or other Pacific Islander, non-Hispanic/Latino; 0.7% American Indian or Alaska Native, non-Hispanic/Latino; 0.5% Two or more races, non-Hispanic/Latino; 10% Race/ethnicity unknown; 41% transferred in.

Freshmen:

Admission: 833 applied, 698 admitted, 178 enrolled. *Average high school GPA:* 3.1.

FACULTY

Total: 46, 35% full-time, 4% with terminal degrees.
Student/faculty ratio: 29:1.

ACADEMICS

Calendar: quarters. *Degree:* bachelor's.

Special study options: accelerated degree program, internships, services for LD students.

Computers: Students can access the following: campus intranet, computer help desk, free student e-mail accounts, online (class) grades, online (class) registration, online (class) schedules. Campuswide network is available. 100% of college-owned or -operated housing units are wired for high-speed Internet access. Wireless service is available via entire campus.

STUDENT LIFE

Housing options: on-campus residence required for freshman year; coed, special housing for students with disabilities. Campus housing is university owned and leased by the school. Freshman campus housing is guaranteed.

Activities and organizations: Unified Student Government, Society of Women Engineers, Pathfinder- (RPG group), Game Gurus, Soccer Club.

Athletics *Intramural sports:* basketball M(c), soccer M(c), table tennis M(c)/W(c).

Campus security: 24-hour emergency response devices and patrols.

Student services: health clinic, personal/psychological counseling.

COSTS & FINANCIAL AID

Costs (2018–19) *One-time required fee:* $2500. *Tuition:* $22,950 full-time. Full-time tuition and fees vary according to course load, degree level, and program. Part-time tuition and fees vary according to course load, degree level, and program. *Required fees:* $1800 full-time. *Room only:* $5970. Room and board charges vary according to housing facility. *Payment plan:* installment. *Waivers:* employees or children of employees.

Financial Aid *Average indebtedness upon graduation:* $39,623. *Financial aid deadline:* 7/30.

APPLYING

Standardized Tests *Required:* SAT or ACT (for admission).

Options: electronic application.

Application fee: $35.

Required: essay or personal statement, high school transcript. *Recommended:* 2 letters of recommendation, interview.

Application deadlines: rolling (freshmen), rolling (transfers).

CONTACT

Neumont College of Computer Science, 143 South Main Street, Salt Lake City, UT 84111. *Toll-free phone:* 888-NEUMONT.

See below for display ad and page 1360 for the College Close-Up.

New Charter University
Salt Lake City, Utah
http://www.new.edu/

CONTACT
Ms. Tammy J. Kassner, Director of Admissions, New Charter University, 2919 John Hawkins Parkway, Birmingham, AL 35244. *Phone:* 205-871-9288 Ext. 107. *Toll-free phone:* 888-639-1388. *Fax:* 800-871-9294. *E-mail:* admissions@aju.edu.

Nightingale College
Ogden, Utah
http://www.nightingale.edu/

CONTACT
Nightingale College, 4155 Harrison Boulevard #100, Ogden, UT 84403.

Southern Utah University
Cedar City, Utah
http://www.suu.edu/

- **State-supported** comprehensive, founded 1897, part of Utah System of Higher Education
- **Small-town** 130-acre campus
- **Endowment** $273.2 million
- **Coed** 8,550 undergraduate students, 73% full-time, 56% women, 44% men
- **Moderately difficult** entrance level, 76% of applicants were admitted

UNDERGRAD STUDENTS
6,279 full-time, 2,271 part-time. Students come from 51 states and territories; 46 other countries; 17% are from out of state; 2% Black or African American, non-Hispanic/Latino; 6% Hispanic/Latino; 1% Asian, non-Hispanic/Latino; 1% Native Hawaiian or other Pacific Islander, non-Hispanic/Latino; 1% American Indian or Alaska Native, non-Hispanic/Latino; 0.3% Two or more races, non-Hispanic/Latino; 6% Race/ethnicity unknown; 6% international; 4% transferred in; 8% live on campus.

Freshmen:
Admission: 11,693 applied, 8,863 admitted, 1,899 enrolled. *Average high school GPA:* 3.5. *Test scores:* SAT evidence-based reading and writing scores over 500: 83%; SAT math scores over 500: 76%; ACT scores over 18: 91%; SAT evidence-based reading and writing scores over 600: 35%; SAT math scores over 600: 27%; ACT scores over 24: 50%; SAT evidence-based reading and writing scores over 700: 6%; SAT math scores over 700: 4%; ACT scores over 30: 9%.
Retention: 71% of full-time freshmen returned.

FACULTY
Total: 581, 52% full-time, 41% with terminal degrees.
Student/faculty ratio: 19:1.

ACADEMICS
Calendar: semesters. *Degrees:* certificates, diplomas, associate, bachelor's, and master's.
Special study options: academic remediation for entering students, adult/continuing education programs, advanced placement credit, cooperative education, distance learning, double majors, English as a second language, honors programs, independent study, internships, part-time degree program, services for LD students, study abroad, summer session for credit. *ROTC:* Army (b).
Computers: Students can access the following: campus intranet, computer help desk, free student e-mail accounts, online (class) grades, online (class) registration, online (class) schedules. Campuswide network is available. 100% of college-owned or -operated housing units are wired for high-speed Internet access. Wireless service is available via entire campus.
Library: Gerald R Sherratt Library. *Books:* 241,434 (physical), 441,219 (digital/electronic); *Serial titles:* 676 (physical), 22,603 (digital/electronic); *Databases:* 218. Students can reserve study rooms.

STUDENT LIFE
Housing options: coed, special housing for students with disabilities. Campus housing is university owned.
Activities and organizations: drama/theater group, student-run newspaper, radio and television station, choral group, national fraternities, national sororities.
Athletics Member NCAA. All Division I. *Intercollegiate sports:* basketball M(s)/W(s), cross-country running M(s)/W(s), football M(s), golf M(s)/W(s), gymnastics W(s), soccer W(s), softball W(s), tennis M(s)/W(s), track and field M(s)/W(s), volleyball W(s). *Intramural sports:* basketball M/W, cheerleading M(c)/W(c), golf M/W, soccer M/W, tennis M/W, volleyball M/W.
Campus security: 24-hour emergency response devices, student patrols, late-night transport/escort service, controlled dormitory access.
Student services: health clinic, personal/psychological counseling, women's center.

COSTS & FINANCIAL AID
Costs (2017–18) *Tuition:* state resident $5918 full-time, $278 per credit part-time; nonresident $19,530 full-time, $919 per credit part-time. Full-time tuition and fees vary according to program. Part-time tuition and fees vary according to course load and program. *Required fees:* $758 full-time, $379 per term part-time. *Room and board:* $7067; room only: $3167. Room and board charges vary according to board plan and housing facility. *Payment plan:* installment. *Waivers:* children of alumni, senior citizens, and employees or children of employees.
Financial Aid Of all full-time matriculated undergraduates who enrolled in 2016, 4,132 applied for aid, 3,599 were judged to have need, 394 had their need fully met. In 2016, 1401 non-need-based awards were made. *Average percent of need met:* 59. *Average financial aid package:* $9187. *Average need-based loan:* $3659. *Average need-based gift aid:* $4397. *Average non-need-based aid:* $6517. *Average indebtedness upon graduation:* $16,824.

APPLYING
Standardized Tests *Required:* SAT or ACT (for admission).
Options: electronic application, deferred entrance.
Application fee: $50.
Required: high school transcript.
Notification: continuous (freshmen), continuous (out-of-state freshmen).

CONTACT
Southern Utah University, 351 West University Boulevard, Cedar City, UT 84720-2498. *Phone:* 435-586-7740.

Stevens-Henager College
Logan, Utah
http://www.stevenshenager.edu/

CONTACT
Stevens-Henager College, 755 South Main Street, Logan, UT 84321. *Toll-free phone:* 800-622-2640.

Stevens-Henager College
Orem, Utah
http://www.stevenshenager.edu/

CONTACT
Stevens-Henager College, 1476 South Sandhill Road, Orem, UT 84058. *Toll-free phone:* 800-622-2640.

Stevens-Henager College
St. George, Utah
http://www.stevenshenager.edu/

CONTACT
Stevens-Henager College, 720 South River Road, Suite C-130, St. George, UT 84790. *Toll-free phone:* 800-622-2640.

Stevens-Henager College

Salt Lake City, Utah

http://www.stevenshenager.edu/

CONTACT
Stevens-Henager College, 383 West Vine Street, Salt Lake City, UT 84123. *Toll-free phone:* 800-622-2640.

Stevens-Henager College

West Haven, Utah

http://www.stevenshenager.edu/

CONTACT
Admissions Office, Stevens-Henager College, 1890 South 1350 West, West Haven, UT 84401. *Phone:* 801-394-7791. *Toll-free phone:* 800-622-2640.

University of Utah

Salt Lake City, Utah

http://www.utah.edu/

- **State-supported** university, founded 1850, part of Utah System of Higher Education
- **Urban** 1535-acre campus with easy access to Salt Lake City
- **Endowment** $958.0 million
- **Coed** 24,635 undergraduate students, 73% full-time, 47% women, 53% men
- **Moderately difficult** entrance level, 66% of applicants were admitted

UNDERGRAD STUDENTS
18,066 full-time, 6,569 part-time. Students come from 52 states and territories; 105 other countries; 20% are from out of state; 1% Black or African American, non-Hispanic/Latino; 12% Hispanic/Latino; 6% Asian, non-Hispanic/Latino; 0.5% Native Hawaiian or other Pacific Islander, non-Hispanic/Latino; 0.4% American Indian or Alaska Native, non-Hispanic/Latino; 5% Two or more races, non-Hispanic/Latino; 2% Race/ethnicity unknown; 5% international; 8% transferred in; 14% live on campus.

Freshmen:
Admission: 22,400 applied, 14,818 admitted, 4,119 enrolled. *Average high school GPA:* 3.6. *Test scores:* SAT evidence-based reading and writing scores over 500: 94%; SAT math scores over 500: 93%; ACT scores over 18: 96%; SAT evidence-based reading and writing scores over 600: 59%; SAT math scores over 600: 58%; ACT scores over 24: 62%; SAT evidence-based reading and writing scores over 700: 14%; SAT math scores over 700: 16%; ACT scores over 30: 20%.
Retention: 91% of full-time freshmen returned.

FACULTY
Total: 2,196, 69% full-time, 67% with terminal degrees.
Student/faculty ratio: 16:1.

ACADEMICS
Calendar: semesters. *Degrees:* bachelor's, master's, doctoral, post-master's, and postbachelor's certificates.

Special study options: academic remediation for entering students, accelerated degree program, advanced placement credit, cooperative education, distance learning, double majors, English as a second language, freshman honors college, honors programs, independent study, internships, off-campus study, part-time degree program, services for LD students, student-designed majors, study abroad, summer session for credit. *ROTC:* Army (b), Navy (b), Air Force (b).

Unusual degree programs: 3-2 engineering; nursing; computer science, chemistry, math, public policy.

Computers: 1,099 computers/terminals are available on campus for general student use. Students can access the following: campus intranet, computer help desk, free student e-mail accounts, online (class) grades, online (class) registration, online (class) schedules, online classes. Campuswide network is available. 100% of college-owned or -operated housing units are wired for high-speed Internet access. Wireless service is available via entire campus.

Library: J. Willard Marriott Library plus 3 others. *Books:* 3.2 million (physical), 460,000 (digital/electronic); *Serial titles:* 500 (physical), 11,500 (digital/electronic); *Databases:* 325. Weekly public service hours: 111; students can reserve study rooms.

STUDENT LIFE
Housing options: coed, men-only, women-only, special housing for students with disabilities. Campus housing is university owned.

Activities and organizations: drama/theater group, student-run newspaper, radio station, choral group, marching band, TEK Club, International Business Club, Golden Key International Honours Society, Tennis Club, Thai Student Association, national fraternities, national sororities.

Athletics Member NCAA. All Division I. *Intercollegiate sports:* baseball M(s), basketball M(s)/W(s), cheerleading M(s)/W(s), cross-country running W(s), fencing M(c)/W(c), football M(s), golf M(s), gymnastics W(s), ice hockey M(c), lacrosse M(c)/W(c), racquetball M(c)/W(c), riflery M(c)/W(c), rugby M(c), skiing (cross-country) M(s)/W(s), skiing (downhill) M(s)/W(s), soccer M(c)/W(s), softball W(s), swimming and diving M(s)/W(s), table tennis M(c)/W(c), tennis M(s)/W(s), track and field W(s), ultimate Frisbee M(c)/W(c), volleyball M(c)/W(s), water polo M(c)/W(c), weight lifting M(c)/W(c), wrestling M(c). *Intramural sports:* basketball M/W, fencing M/W, football M, racquetball M/W, soccer M/W, softball M/W, tennis M/W, ultimate Frisbee M/W, volleyball M/W, water polo M/W, weight lifting M/W.

Campus security: 24-hour emergency response devices and patrols, student patrols, late-night transport/escort service, controlled dormitory access.

Student services: health clinic, personal/psychological counseling, women's center.

COSTS & FINANCIAL AID
Costs (2017–18) *Tuition:* state resident $7697 full-time, $216 per credit hour part-time; nonresident $26,940 full-time, $743 per credit hour part-time. Full-time tuition and fees vary according to course level, course load, degree level, location, program, and student level. Part-time tuition and fees vary according to course level, course load, degree level, location, program, and student level. *Required fees:* $1127 full-time, $464 per term part-time. *Room and board:* $9867; room only: $5118. Room and board charges vary according to board plan, housing facility, and location. *Payment plans:* installment, deferred payment. *Waivers:* senior citizens and employees or children of employees.

Financial Aid Of all full-time matriculated undergraduates who enrolled in 2017, 10,810 applied for aid, 8,628 were judged to have need, 1,247 had their need fully met. 350 Federal Work-Study jobs (averaging $3999). In 2017, 5233 non-need-based awards were made. *Average percent of need met:* 65. *Average financial aid package:* $21,290. *Average need-based loan:* $4184. *Average need-based gift aid:* $7178. *Average non-need-based aid:* $6410. *Average indebtedness upon graduation:* $21,188.

APPLYING
Standardized Tests *Required:* SAT or ACT (for admission).

Options: electronic application, early admission, early action, deferred entrance.

Application fee: $55.

Required: high school transcript.

Application deadlines: 4/1 (freshmen), 4/1 (transfers), 12/1 (early action).

Notification: continuous (freshmen), continuous (out-of-state freshmen), continuous (transfers).

CONTACT
Mateo Remsburg, Associate Director, Office of Admissions, University of Utah, 201 S. 1460 E., Room 250 S., Salt Lake City, UT 84112. *Phone:* 801-581-8761. *Toll-free phone:* 800-685-8856. *Fax:* 801-585-3257. *E-mail:* mremsburg@sa.utah.edu.

Utah State University
Logan, Utah
http://www.usu.edu/

- **State-supported** university, founded 1888, part of Utah System of Higher Education
- **Urban** 456-acre campus
- **Endowment** $360.2 million
- **Coed** 24,618 undergraduate students, 70% full-time, 53% women, 47% men
- **Moderately difficult** entrance level, 89% of applicants were admitted

UNDERGRAD STUDENTS
17,188 full-time, 7,430 part-time. Students come from 53 states and territories; 61 other countries; 27% are from out of state; 0.8% Black or African American, non-Hispanic/Latino; 6% Hispanic/Latino; 1% Asian, non-Hispanic/Latino; 0.4% Native Hawaiian or other Pacific Islander, non-Hispanic/Latino; 2% American Indian or Alaska Native, non-Hispanic/Latino; 2% Two or more races, non-Hispanic/Latino; 4% Race/ethnicity unknown; 1% international; 6% transferred in.

Freshmen:
Admission: 15,555 applied, 13,857 admitted, 4,242 enrolled. *Average high school GPA:* 3.5. *Test scores:* SAT evidence-based reading and writing scores over 500: 74%; SAT math scores over 500: 82%; ACT scores over 18: 91%; SAT evidence-based reading and writing scores over 600: 28%; SAT math scores over 600: 40%; ACT scores over 24: 53%; SAT evidence-based reading and writing scores over 700: 13%; SAT math scores over 700: 7%; ACT scores over 30: 14%.

Retention: 69% of full-time freshmen returned.

FACULTY
Total: 1,231, 79% full-time, 68% with terminal degrees.

Student/faculty ratio: 20:1.

ACADEMICS
Calendar: semesters. *Degrees:* certificates, associate, bachelor's, master's, doctoral, and postbachelor's certificates.

Special study options: academic remediation for entering students, accelerated degree program, adult/continuing education programs, advanced placement credit, cooperative education, distance learning, double majors, English as a second language, freshman honors college, honors programs, independent study, internships, off-campus study, part-time degree program, services for LD students, student-designed majors, study abroad, summer session for credit. *ROTC:* Army (b), Air Force (b).

Computers: 1,000 computers/terminals are available on campus for general student use. Students can access the following: computer help desk, free student e-mail accounts, online (class) grades, online (class) registration, online (class) schedules. Campuswide network is available. 100% of college-owned or -operated housing units are wired for high-speed Internet access. Wireless service is available via classrooms, computer centers, computer labs, dorm rooms, learning centers, libraries, student centers.

Library: Merrill-Cazier Library plus 4 others. *Books:* 1.9 million (physical), 700,222 (digital/electronic); *Serial titles:* 44,565 (physical), 74,377 (digital/electronic); *Databases:* 4,418. Weekly public service hours: 101; students can reserve study rooms.

STUDENT LIFE
Housing options: coed, men-only, women-only, special housing for students with disabilities. Campus housing is university owned.

Activities and organizations: drama/theater group, student-run newspaper, radio station, choral group, marching band, Latter-Day Saints Student Association, multicultural clubs, volunteer groups, college councils, national fraternities, national sororities.

Athletics Member NCAA. All Division I except football (Division I-A). *Intercollegiate sports:* baseball M(c), basketball M(s)/W(s), cross-country running M(s)/W(s), equestrian sports M(c)/W(c), golf M(s), gymnastics W(s), ice hockey M(c), racquetball M(c)/W(c), rugby M(c)/W(c), soccer M(c)/W(s), softball W(s), tennis M(s)/W(s), track and field M(s)/W(s), ultimate Frisbee M(c)/W(c), volleyball M(c)/W(s). *Intramural sports:* basketball M/W, football M/W, lacrosse M(c)/W(c), soccer M/W, softball M/W, swimming and diving M(c)/W(c), table tennis M/W, tennis M/W, ultimate Frisbee M/W, volleyball M/W, wrestling M(c).

Campus security: 24-hour emergency response devices and patrols, student patrols, late-night transport/escort service, video monitors in pedestrian tunnels.

Student services: health clinic, personal/psychological counseling, women's center, legal services.

COSTS & FINANCIAL AID
Costs (2017–18) *Tuition:* state resident $6105 full-time; nonresident $19,657 full-time. Full-time tuition and fees vary according to course level, course load, program, and reciprocity agreements. Part-time tuition and fees vary according to course level, course load, program, and reciprocity agreements. *Required fees:* $1070 full-time. *Room and board:* $6060; room only: $2160. Room and board charges vary according to board plan and housing facility. *Payment plan:* deferred payment. *Waivers:* minority students, children of alumni, adult students, senior citizens, and employees or children of employees.

Financial Aid Of all full-time matriculated undergraduates who enrolled in 2016, 10,972 applied for aid, 9,298 were judged to have need, 818 had their need fully met. 465 Federal Work-Study jobs (averaging $3567). In 2016, 2145 non-need-based awards were made. *Average percent of need met:* 57. *Average financial aid package:* $9705. *Average need-based loan:* $4282. *Average need-based gift aid:* $4553. *Average non-need-based aid:* $3252. *Average indebtedness upon graduation:* $23,000.

APPLYING
Standardized Tests *Required:* SAT or ACT (for admission).

Options: electronic application, deferred entrance.

Application fee: $50.

Required: high school transcript. *Recommended:* minimum 2.8 GPA.

Application deadlines: rolling (freshmen), rolling (transfers).

Notification: continuous (freshmen), continuous (transfers).

CONTACT
Mr. Jeff Sorenson, Assistant Director, Admissions Office, Utah State University, 0160 Old Main Hill, Logan, UT 84322-0160. *Phone:* 435-797-1079. *Toll-free phone:* 800-488-8108. *Fax:* 435-797-3708. *E-mail:* admit@usu.edu.

Utah Valley University
Orem, Utah
http://www.uvu.edu/

- **State-supported** comprehensive, founded 1941, affiliated with Advent Christian Church, part of Utah System of Higher Education
- **Suburban** 524-acre campus with easy access to Salt Lake City
- **Coed** 36,868 undergraduate students, 50% full-time, 47% women, 53% men
- **Noncompetitive** entrance level, 88% of applicants were admitted

UNDERGRAD STUDENTS
18,404 full-time, 18,464 part-time. Students come from 50 states and territories; 82 other countries; 13% are from out of state; 0.8% Black or African American, non-Hispanic/Latino; 11% Hispanic/Latino; 1% Asian, non-Hispanic/Latino; 0.8% Native Hawaiian or other Pacific Islander, non-Hispanic/Latino; 0.6% American Indian or Alaska Native, non-Hispanic/Latino; 1% Two or more races, non-Hispanic/Latino; 3% Race/ethnicity unknown; 2% international; 5% transferred in.

Freshmen:
Admission: 11,735 applied, 10,376 admitted, 4,176 enrolled. *Average high school GPA:* 3.3.

Retention: 66% of full-time freshmen returned.

FACULTY
Total: 1,982, 35% full-time, 30% with terminal degrees.

Student/faculty ratio: 25:1.

ACADEMICS
Calendar: semesters. *Degrees:* certificates, diplomas, associate, bachelor's, master's, and postbachelor's certificates.

Special study options: academic remediation for entering students, advanced placement credit, cooperative education, distance learning, double majors, English as a second language, honors programs, independent study, internships, off-campus study, part-time degree program, services for LD students, student-designed majors, study abroad, summer session for credit. *ROTC:* Army (b), Air Force (c).

Computers: 1,000 computers/terminals are available on campus for general student use. Students can access the following: campus intranet, computer help desk, free student e-mail accounts, online (class) grades, online (class) registration, online (class) schedules. Campuswide network is available. Wireless service is available via entire campus.

Library: Utah Valley University Library plus 1 other. Students can reserve study rooms.

STUDENT LIFE

Housing options: college housing not available.

Activities and organizations: drama/theater group, student-run newspaper, television station, choral group, LDSSA Orem Institute, Center for the Advancement of Leadership, national fraternities, national sororities.

Athletics Member NCAA. All Division I. *Intercollegiate sports:* baseball M(s), basketball M(s)/W(s), cross-country running M(s)/W(s), golf M(s)/W(s), soccer W(s), softball W(s), track and field M(s)/W(s), volleyball W(s), wrestling M(s).

Campus security: 24-hour patrols.

Student services: health clinic, personal/psychological counseling, women's center, legal services.

COSTS & FINANCIAL AID

Costs (2017–18) *Tuition:* state resident $4962 full-time, $216 per credit part-time; nonresident $15,376 full-time, $671 per credit part-time. Full-time tuition and fees vary according to course load and program. Part-time tuition and fees vary according to course load. *Required fees:* $690 full-time, $345 per term part-time. *Payment plan:* deferred payment. *Waivers:* employees or children of employees.

Financial Aid Of all full-time matriculated undergraduates who enrolled in 2017, 11,792 applied for aid, 10,192 were judged to have need, 946 had their need fully met. In 2017, 136 non-need-based awards were made. *Average percent of need met:* 64. *Average financial aid package:* $8129. *Average need-based loan:* $2863. *Average need-based gift aid:* $5187. *Average non-need-based aid:* $1509. *Average indebtedness upon graduation:* $20,832.

APPLYING

Options: electronic application, deferred entrance.

Application fee: $35.

Required: high school transcript.

Application deadlines: 8/1 (freshmen), 8/1 (transfers).

Notification: continuous (freshmen), continuous (out-of-state freshmen), continuous (transfers).

CONTACT

Mr. Kristopher Coles, Director of Admissions, Utah Valley University, 800 West University Parkway, Orem, UT 84058-5999. *Phone:* 801-863-6368. *Fax:* 801-863-7229. *E-mail:* coleskr@uvu.edu.

Weber State University

Ogden, Utah

http://www.weber.edu/

- **State-supported** comprehensive, founded 1889, part of Utah System of Higher Education
- **Urban** 504-acre campus with easy access to Salt Lake City
- **Endowment** $124.3 million
- **Coed** 27,111 undergraduate students, 42% full-time, 54% women, 46% men
- **Noncompetitive** entrance level, 100% of applicants were admitted

UNDERGRAD STUDENTS

11,311 full-time, 15,800 part-time. Students come from 54 states and territories; 61 other countries; 8% are from out of state; 1% Black or African American, non-Hispanic/Latino; 11% Hispanic/Latino; 2% Asian, non-Hispanic/Latino; 0.5% Native Hawaiian or other Pacific Islander, non-Hispanic/Latino; 0.4% American Indian or Alaska Native, non-Hispanic/Latino; 3% Two or more races, non-Hispanic/Latino; 5% Race/ethnicity unknown; 1% international; 5% transferred in; 4% live on campus.

Freshmen:

Admission: 6,255 applied, 6,255 admitted, 3,118 enrolled. *Average high school GPA:* 3.3. *Test scores:* ACT scores over 18: 76%; ACT scores over 24: 27%; ACT scores over 30: 4%.

Retention: 63% of full-time freshmen returned.

FACULTY

Total: 1,404, 37% full-time, 33% with terminal degrees.

Student/faculty ratio: 21:1.

ACADEMICS

Calendar: semesters. *Degrees:* certificates, associate, bachelor's, master's, post-master's, and postbachelor's certificates.

Special study options: academic remediation for entering students, accelerated degree program, adult/continuing education programs, advanced placement credit, cooperative education, distance learning, double majors, English as a second language, external degree program, freshman honors college, honors programs, independent study, internships, off-campus study, part-time degree program, services for LD students, student-designed majors, study abroad, summer session for credit. *ROTC:* Army (b), Navy (c), Air Force (c).

Computers: 650 computers/terminals are available on campus for general student use. Students can access the following: campus intranet, computer help desk, free student e-mail accounts, online (class) grades, online (class) registration, online (class) schedules. Campuswide network is available. 100% of college-owned or -operated housing units are wired for high-speed Internet access. Wireless service is available via entire campus.

Library: Stewart Library. *Books:* 498,531 (physical); *Serial titles:* 425 (physical); *Databases:* 223,410.

STUDENT LIFE

Housing options: men-only, women-only, cooperative, special housing for students with disabilities. Campus housing is university owned and is provided by a third party.

Activities and organizations: drama/theater group, student-run newspaper, radio and television station, choral group, marching band, LDSSA (Latter-day Saint Student Association), SAA (Student Alumni Association), GSA (Gay-Straight Alliance), Chinese Club, Golden Key Honor Society, national fraternities, national sororities.

Athletics Member NCAA. All Division I. *Intercollegiate sports:* archery M(c)/W(c), baseball M(c), basketball M(s)/W(s), bowling M(c)/W(c), cheerleading M(s)/W(s), cross-country running M(s)/W(s), football M(s), golf M(s)/W(s), ice hockey M(c), lacrosse M(c), racquetball M/W, rugby M(c), skiing (downhill) W(c), soccer M(c)/W(s), softball W(s), swimming and diving M(c)/W(c), tennis M(s)(c)/W(s)(c), track and field M(s)/W(s), volleyball M(c)/W(s), weight lifting M(c)/W(c), wrestling M(c). *Intramural sports:* racquetball M(c)/W(c), rock climbing M/W, tennis M(c)/W(c), ultimate Frisbee M(c)/W(c), volleyball M(c)/W(c).

Campus security: 24-hour emergency response devices and patrols, student patrols, late-night transport/escort service, controlled dormitory access.

Student services: health clinic, personal/psychological counseling, women's center, legal services.

COSTS & FINANCIAL AID

Costs (2017–18) *Tuition:* state resident $4773 full-time, $2816 per year part-time; nonresident $14,321 full-time, $8450 per year part-time. Full-time tuition and fees vary according to course level, course load, degree level, and program. Part-time tuition and fees vary according to course level, course load, degree level, and program. *Required fees:* $939 full-time, $575 per year part-time. *Room and board:* $8400. Room and board charges vary according to board plan and housing facility. *Payment plan:* installment. *Waivers:* senior citizens and employees or children of employees.

Financial Aid Of all full-time matriculated undergraduates who enrolled in 2016, 7,423 applied for aid, 6,467 were judged to have need, 4,243 had their need fully met. In 2016, 2196 non-need-based awards were made. *Average financial aid package:* $6004. *Average need-based loan:* $3684. *Average need-based gift aid:* $4232. *Average non-need-based aid:* $3732. *Average indebtedness upon graduation:* $22,657.

APPLYING

Standardized Tests *Required for some:* ACCUPLACER. *Recommended:* SAT or ACT (for admission).

Options: electronic application, early admission, deferred entrance.

Application fee: $30.

Required: high school transcript.

Application deadlines: 8/31 (freshmen), rolling (transfers).

Notification: continuous (freshmen), continuous (out-of-state freshmen), continuous (transfers).

CONTACT
Brant Brown, Associate Director of Admissions, Weber State University, 1137 University Circle, Ogden, UT 84408-1137. *Phone:* 801-626-6050. *Toll-free phone:* 800-848-7700 (in-state); 800-848-7770 (out-of-state). *Fax:* 801-626-6747. *E-mail:* admissions@weber.edu.

Western Governors University

Salt Lake City, Utah

http://www.wgu.edu/

CONTACT
Western Governors University, 4001 South 700 East, Suite 700, Salt Lake City, UT 84107. *Phone:* 801-274-3280 Ext. 336. *Toll-free phone:* 866-225-5948.

Westminster College

Salt Lake City, Utah

http://www.westminstercollege.edu/

- **Independent** comprehensive, founded 1875
- **Suburban** 27-acre campus
- **Endowment** $77.4 million
- **Coed** 2,030 undergraduate students, 94% full-time, 59% women, 41% men
- **Moderately difficult** entrance level, 93% of applicants were admitted

UNDERGRAD STUDENTS
1,906 full-time, 124 part-time. 39% are from out of state; 2% Black or African American, non-Hispanic/Latino; 11% Hispanic/Latino; 3% Asian, non-Hispanic/Latino; 0.3% Native Hawaiian or other Pacific Islander, non-Hispanic/Latino; 0.6% American Indian or Alaska Native, non-Hispanic/Latino; 5% Two or more races, non-Hispanic/Latino; 3% Race/ethnicity unknown; 5% international; 7% transferred in; 30% live on campus.

Freshmen:
Admission: 1,702 applied, 1,578 admitted, 369 enrolled. *Average high school GPA:* 3.6. *Test scores:* SAT evidence-based reading and writing scores over 500: 86%; SAT math scores over 500: 90%; ACT scores over 18: 97%; SAT evidence-based reading and writing scores over 600: 53%; SAT math scores over 600: 39%; ACT scores over 24: 50%; SAT evidence-based reading and writing scores over 700: 9%; SAT math scores over 700: 6%; ACT scores over 30: 13%.
Retention: 80% of full-time freshmen returned.

FACULTY
Total: 382, 40% full-time, 36% with terminal degrees.
Student/faculty ratio: 9:1.

ACADEMICS
Calendar: semesters. *Degrees:* bachelor's, master's, and postbachelor's certificates.

Special study options: academic remediation for entering students, accelerated degree program, adult/continuing education programs, advanced placement credit, cooperative education, distance learning, double majors, English as a second language, external degree program, freshman honors college, honors programs, independent study, internships, off-campus study, part-time degree program, services for LD students, student-designed majors, study abroad, summer session for credit. *ROTC:* Army (c), Navy (c), Air Force (c).

Unusual degree programs: 3-2 engineering with University of Southern California, Washington University in St. Louis.

Computers: 200 computers/terminals are available on campus for general student use. Students can access the following: campus intranet, computer help desk, free student e-mail accounts, online (class) grades, online (class) registration, online (class) schedules. Campuswide network is

available. 100% of college-owned or -operated housing units are wired for high-speed Internet access. Wireless service is available via entire campus.
Library: Giovale Library plus 1 other. *Books:* 95,039 (physical), 364,687 (digital/electronic); *Databases:* 56. Students can reserve study rooms.

STUDENT LIFE
Housing options: on-campus residence required through sophomore year; coed, special housing for students with disabilities. Campus housing is university owned and leased by the school. Freshman campus housing is guaranteed.

Activities and organizations: drama/theater group, student-run newspaper, choral group, Westminster Ski and Snowboard Club (WSSC), Residence Hall Association (Residential Government), Feminist Club, Latin X, Theatre Society.

Athletics Member NCAA. All Division II. *Intercollegiate sports:* basketball M(s)/W(s), cross-country running M(s)/W(s), golf M(s)/W(s), lacrosse M(s)/W(s), skiing (downhill) M(s)/W(s), soccer M(s)/W(s), track and field M(s)/W(s), volleyball W(s). *Intramural sports:* badminton M/W, basketball M/W, football M/W, rock climbing M/W, skiing (cross-country) M/W, soccer M/W, volleyball M/W.

Campus security: 24-hour emergency response devices and patrols, student patrols, late-night transport/escort service, controlled dormitory access.

Student services: health clinic, personal/psychological counseling.

COSTS & FINANCIAL AID
Costs (2018–19) *One-time required fee:* $300. *Comprehensive fee:* $44,285 includes full-time tuition ($33,480), mandatory fees ($560), and room and board ($10,245). Full-time tuition and fees vary according to course load and program. Part-time tuition: $1395 per credit hour. Part-time tuition and fees vary according to course load and program. *Required fees:* $154 per credit hour part-time. *College room only:* $5526. Room and board charges vary according to board plan. *Payment plans:* installment, deferred payment. *Waivers:* employees or children of employees.

Financial Aid Of all full-time matriculated undergraduates who enrolled in 2017, 1,346 applied for aid, 1,156 were judged to have need, 264 had their need fully met. In 2017, 468 non-need-based awards were made. *Average percent of need met:* 77. *Average financial aid package:* $25,833. *Average need-based loan:* $4762. *Average need-based gift aid:* $20,809. *Average non-need-based aid:* $15,120. *Average indebtedness upon graduation:* $28,774.

APPLYING
Standardized Tests *Required:* SAT or ACT (for admission).

Options: electronic application, deferred entrance.

Application fee: $50.

Required: essay or personal statement, high school transcript, minimum 2.5 GPA, 1 letter of recommendation. *Recommended:* interview.

Application deadlines: rolling (freshmen), rolling (transfers).

Notification: continuous (freshmen), continuous (transfers).

CONTACT
Jen Dahl, Director of Admissions, Westminster College, 1840 South 1300 East, Salt Lake City, UT 84105-3697. *Phone:* 801-832-2200. *Toll-free phone:* 800-748-4753. *Fax:* 801-832-3101. *E-mail:* admission@westminstercollege.edu.

VERMONT

Bennington College

Bennington, Vermont

http://www.bennington.edu/

- **Independent** comprehensive, founded 1932
- **Small-town** 440-acre campus with easy access to Albany, NY
- **Endowment** $19.2 million
- **Coed** 775 undergraduate students, 93% full-time, 65% women, 35% men
- **Very difficult** entrance level, 57% of applicants were admitted

UNDERGRAD STUDENTS

724 full-time, 51 part-time. Students come from 45 states and territories; 56 other countries; 98% are from out of state; 4% Black or African American, non-Hispanic/Latino; 10% Hispanic/Latino; 2% Asian, non-Hispanic/Latino; 0.1% Native Hawaiian or other Pacific Islander, non-Hispanic/Latino; 0.4% American Indian or Alaska Native, non-Hispanic/Latino; 4% Two or more races, non-Hispanic/Latino; 4% Race/ethnicity unknown; 17% international; 1% transferred in; 98% live on campus.

Freshmen:

Admission: 1,465 applied, 829 admitted, 225 enrolled. *Test scores:* ACT scores over 18: 100%; ACT scores over 24: 82%; ACT scores over 30: 41%.

Retention: 78% of full-time freshmen returned.

FACULTY

Total: 125, 48% full-time, 54% with terminal degrees.

Student/faculty ratio: 10:1.

ACADEMICS

Calendar: semesters plus winter work term in January and February. *Degrees:* bachelor's and master's.

Special study options: advanced placement credit, double majors, English as a second language, independent study, internships, off-campus study, services for LD students, student-designed majors, study abroad.

Computers: 40 computers/terminals are available on campus for general student use. Students can access the following: campus intranet, computer help desk, free student e-mail accounts, online (class) grades, online (class) registration, online (class) schedules. Campuswide network is available. 100% of college-owned or -operated housing units are wired for high-speed Internet access. Wireless service is available via entire campus.

Library: Crossett Library plus 1 other. *Books:* 89,000 (physical), 162,000 (digital/electronic); *Serial titles:* 200 (physical), 48,000 (digital/electronic); *Databases:* 56. Weekly public service hours: 111; students can reserve study rooms.

STUDENT LIFE

Housing options: on-campus residence required through senior year; coed. Campus housing is university owned and leased by the school. Freshman campus housing is guaranteed.

Activities and organizations: drama/theater group, student-run newspaper, radio station, choral group, Program Activity Council, Bennington Free Press, Student Endowment for the Arts, SILO: Student Journal of Arts and Letters, The Purple Carrot Farm.

Athletics *Intercollegiate sports:* basketball M(c)/W(c), soccer M(c)/W(c), ultimate Frisbee M(c)/W(c). *Intramural sports:* archery M/W, badminton M/W, basketball M/W, bowling M/W, cross-country running M/W, equestrian sports M/W, golf M/W, skiing (cross-country) M/W, skiing (downhill) M/W, softball M/W, table tennis M/W, tennis M/W, volleyball M/W.

Campus security: 24-hour emergency response devices and patrols, late-night transport/escort service, controlled dormitory access, prevention/awareness program.

Student services: health clinic, personal/psychological counseling.

COSTS & FINANCIAL AID

Costs (2018–19) *One-time required fee:* $650. *Comprehensive fee:* $69,470 includes full-time tuition ($53,160), mandatory fees ($700), and room and board ($15,610). Full-time tuition and fees vary according to degree level. Part-time tuition: $2215 per credit hour. *College room only:* $8460. Room and board charges vary according to board plan. *Payment plan:* installment. *Waivers:* employees or children of employees.

Financial Aid Of all full-time matriculated undergraduates who enrolled in 2016, 446 applied for aid, 418 were judged to have need, 48 had their need fully met. 349 Federal Work-Study jobs (averaging $2128). 96 state and other part-time jobs (averaging $2134). In 2016, 201 non-need-based awards were made. *Average percent of need met:* 82. *Average financial aid package:* $41,595. *Average need-based loan:* $3558. *Average need-based gift aid:* $36,862. *Average non-need-based aid:* $25,589. *Average indebtedness upon graduation:* $27,470. *Financial aid deadline:* 1/3.

APPLYING

Options: electronic application, early admission, early decision, early action, deferred entrance.

Required: essay or personal statement, high school transcript, 2 letters of recommendation, graded analytic paper. *Recommended:* interview.

Application deadlines: 1/15 (freshmen), 3/15 (transfers), 12/1 (early action).

Early decision deadline: 11/15 (for plan 1), 1/15 (for plan 2).

Notification: 3/22 (freshmen), 5/1 (transfers), 12/14 (early decision plan 1), 2/8 (early decision plan 2), 2/1 (early action).

CONTACT

Mr. Fumio Sugihara, Director of Admissions, Bennington College, One College Drive, Bennington, VT 05201-6003. *Phone:* 802-440-4316. *Toll-free phone:* 800-833-6845. *Fax:* 802-440-4320. *E-mail:* admissions@bennington.edu.

Castleton University

Castleton, Vermont

http://www.castleton.edu/

CONTACT

Mr. Maurice Ouimet Jr., Dean of Enrollment, Castleton University, 62 Alumni Drive, Woodruff Hall, Castleton, VT 05735. *Phone:* 802-468-1213. *Toll-free phone:* 800-639-8521. *Fax:* 802-468-1476. *E-mail:* info@castleton.edu.

See next page for display ad and page 1256 for the College Close-Up.

Champlain College

Burlington, Vermont

http://www.champlain.edu/

- **Independent** comprehensive, founded 1878
- **Suburban** 22-acre campus with easy access to Montreal
- **Coed** 2,222 undergraduate students, 98% full-time, 38% women, 62% men
- **Moderately difficult** entrance level, 75% of applicants were admitted

UNDERGRAD STUDENTS

2,170 full-time, 52 part-time. Students come from 44 states and territories; 79% are from out of state; 2% Black or African American, non-Hispanic/Latino; 6% Hispanic/Latino; 3% Asian, non-Hispanic/Latino; 0.3% American Indian or Alaska Native, non-Hispanic/Latino; 3% Two or more races, non-Hispanic/Latino; 10% Race/ethnicity unknown; 0.8% international; 3% transferred in; 68% live on campus.

Freshmen:

Admission: 5,197 applied, 3,900 admitted, 587 enrolled. *Average high school GPA:* 3.2. *Test scores:* SAT evidence-based reading and writing scores over 500: 92%; SAT math scores over 500: 88%; ACT scores over 18: 90%; SAT evidence-based reading and writing scores over 600: 56%; SAT math scores over 600: 42%; ACT scores over 24: 62%; SAT evidence-based reading and writing scores over 700: 11%; SAT math scores over 700: 7%; ACT scores over 30: 21%.

Retention: 79% of full-time freshmen returned.

FACULTY

Total: 467, 26% full-time, 39% with terminal degrees.

Student/faculty ratio: 14:1.

ACADEMICS

Calendar: semesters. *Degrees:* certificates, associate, bachelor's, master's, and postbachelor's certificates.

Special study options: adult/continuing education programs, advanced placement credit, cooperative education, distance learning, double majors, independent study, internships, off-campus study, part-time degree program, services for LD students, study abroad, summer session for credit. *ROTC:* Army (c).

Computers: 640 computers/terminals are available on campus for general student use. Students can access the following: campus intranet, computer help desk, free student e-mail accounts, online (class) grades, online (class) registration, online (class) schedules. Campuswide network is available. 100% of college-owned or -operated housing units are wired for

high-speed Internet access. Wireless service is available via entire campus.

Library: Miller Information Commons. *Books:* 49,324 (physical), 208,755 (digital/electronic); *Serial titles:* 150 (physical), 66,446 (digital/electronic); *Databases:* 148. Weekly public service hours: 105; students can reserve study rooms.

STUDENT LIFE

Housing options: coed, women-only, special housing for students with disabilities. Campus housing is university owned and leased by the school. Freshman campus housing is guaranteed.

Activities and organizations: drama/theater group, student-run newspaper, radio station, choral group, Diversity Champlain, International Club, community service organization, Champlain Players (theater group), Outing Club/Skiing Snowboarding Club.

Athletics *Intramural sports:* basketball M/W, cross-country running M(c)/W(c), equestrian sports M(c)/W(c), field hockey W, football M/W, ice hockey M, lacrosse M, rock climbing M/W, rugby M(c)/W(c), skiing (cross-country) M/W, skiing (downhill) M(c)/W(c), soccer M/W, table tennis M/W, tennis M/W, ultimate Frisbee M/W, volleyball M/W.

Campus security: 24-hour emergency response devices and patrols, late-night transport/escort service, controlled dormitory access.

Student services: health clinic, personal/psychological counseling, women's center.

COSTS & FINANCIAL AID

Costs (2017–18) *Comprehensive fee:* $54,724 includes full-time tuition ($39,718), mandatory fees ($100), and room and board ($14,906). Part-time tuition: $1658 per credit hour. *Room and board:* Room and board charges vary according to housing facility. *Payment plans:* tuition prepayment, installment. *Waivers:* employees or children of employees.

Financial Aid Of all full-time matriculated undergraduates who enrolled in 2017, 1,970 applied for aid, 1,727 were judged to have need, 257 had their need fully met. In 2017, 208 non-need-based awards were made. *Average percent of need met:* 65. *Average financial aid package:* $25,094. *Average need-based loan:* $4028. *Average need-based gift aid:* $19,527. *Average non-need-based aid:* $10,660. *Average indebtedness upon graduation:* $38,818. *Financial aid deadline:* 1/15.

APPLYING

Standardized Tests *Required:* SAT or ACT (for admission).

Options: electronic application, early admission, early decision, deferred entrance.

Required: essay or personal statement, high school transcript. *Required for some:* portfolio for creative media, filmmaking, game art and animation, game design, and graphic design and digital media majors. *Recommended:* 2 letters of recommendation.

Application deadlines: 1/15 (freshmen), rolling (transfers).

Early decision deadline: 11/15.

Notification: 3/15 (freshmen), continuous (transfers), 12/15 (early decision).

CONTACT

Chris Perlongo, Director of Undergraduate Admissions, Champlain College, PO Box 670, Burlington, VT 05401. *Phone:* 802-860-5740. *Toll-free phone:* 800-570-5858. *Fax:* 802-860-2767. *E-mail:* admission@champlain.edu.

College of St. Joseph
Rutland, Vermont
http://www.csj.edu/

CONTACT

Mr. Alan Young, Dean of Admissions, College of St. Joseph, 71 Clement Road, Rutland, VT 05701-3899. *Phone:* 802-773-5227. *Toll-free phone:* 877-270-9998. *Fax:* 802-776-5310. *E-mail:* admissions@csj.edu.

★ Goddard College
Plainfield, Vermont
http://www.goddard.edu/

- **Independent** comprehensive, founded 1938
- **Rural** 200-acre campus
- **Coed**
- **Minimally difficult** entrance level

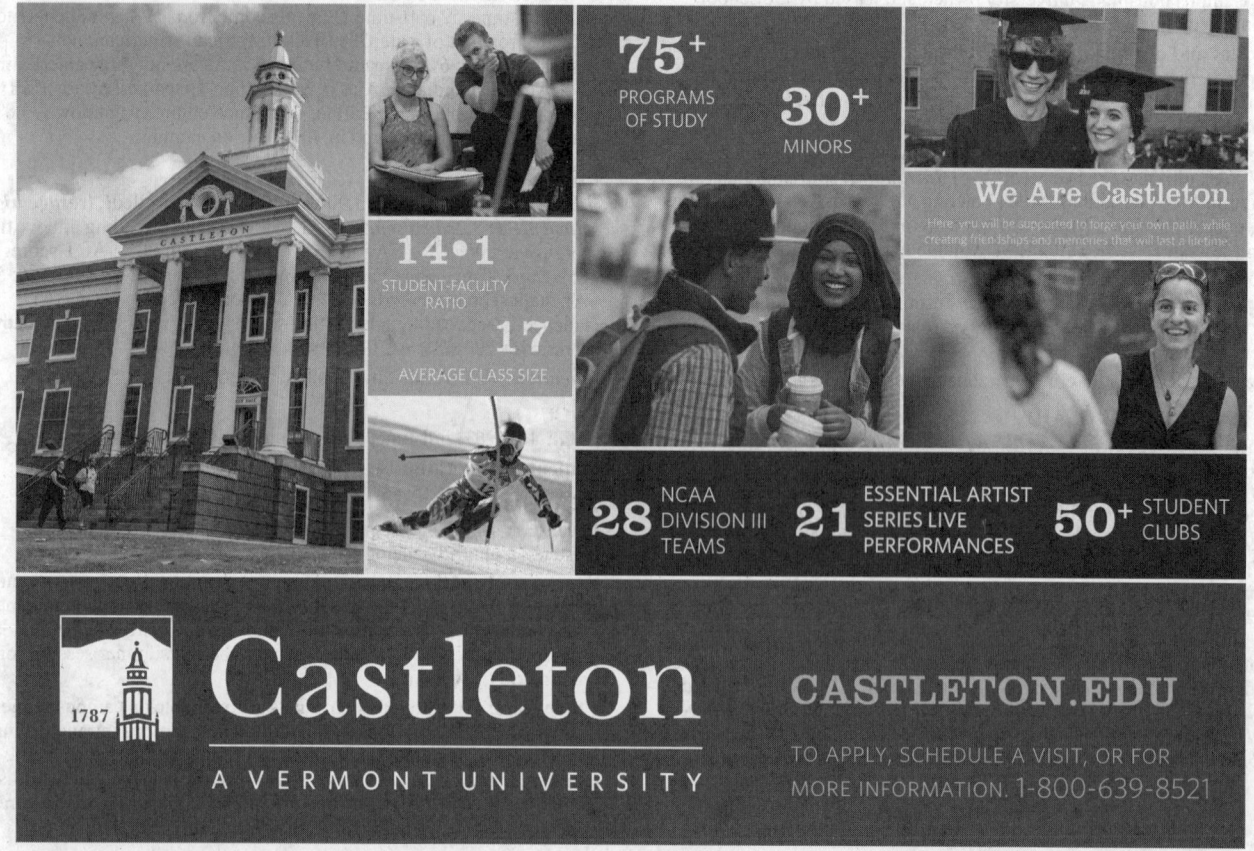

ACADEMICS
Calendar: semesters. *Degrees:* bachelor's and master's.
Library: Eliot Pratt Center. *Books:* 34,000 (physical), 151,000 (digital/electronic); *Databases:* 21.

STUDENT LIFE
Housing options: coed, women-only, special housing for students with disabilities. Campus housing is university owned.

Activities and organizations: student-run radio station.

Campus security: 24-hour patrols, patrols by trained security personnel 9 pm to 6 am.

Student services: personal/psychological counseling.

FINANCIAL AID
Financial Aid Of all full-time matriculated undergraduates who enrolled in 2015, 147 applied for aid, 141 were judged to have need, 1 had their need fully met. In 2015, 4 non-need-based awards were made. *Average percent of need met:* 35. *Average financial aid package:* $8211. *Average need-based loan:* $4379. *Average need-based gift aid:* $4622. *Average non-need-based aid:* $1062.

APPLYING
Options: electronic application, deferred entrance.

Application fee: $65.

Required: essay or personal statement, 2 letters of recommendation, interview. *Required for some:* high school transcript, 3 letters of recommendation. *Recommended:* 4 years of English, mathematics, social studies, natural sciences; 3 years of lab science; 2 years of a foreign language; creative portfolio for arts.

CONTACT
Admissions Office, Goddard College, 123 Pitkin Road, Plainfield, VT 05667-9432. *Phone:* 800-906-8312. *Toll-free phone:* 800-906-8312. *Fax:* 802-454-1029. *E-mail:* admissions@goddard.edu.

Green Mountain College
Poultney, Vermont
http://www.greenmtn.edu/
- **Independent** comprehensive, founded 1834
- **Small-town** 155-acre campus
- **Endowment** $3.1 million
- **Coed** 468 undergraduate students, 96% full-time, 57% women, 43% men
- **Moderately difficult** entrance level, 82% of applicants were admitted

UNDERGRAD STUDENTS
447 full-time, 21 part-time. Students come from 38 states and territories; 7 other countries; 83% are from out of state; 6% Black or African American, non-Hispanic/Latino; 3% Hispanic/Latino; 1% Asian, non-Hispanic/Latino; 1% American Indian or Alaska Native, non-Hispanic/Latino; 2% Two or more races, non-Hispanic/Latino; 19% Race/ethnicity unknown; 1% international; 8% transferred in; 82% live on campus.

Freshmen:
Admission: 677 applied, 554 admitted, 111 enrolled. *Average high school GPA:* 3.1.
Retention: 74% of full-time freshmen returned.

FACULTY
Total: 63, 63% full-time, 70% with terminal degrees.
Student/faculty ratio: 14:1.

ACADEMICS
Calendar: semesters. *Degrees:* certificates, bachelor's, and master's.
Special study options: accelerated degree program, advanced placement credit, cooperative education, distance learning, double majors, honors programs, independent study, internships, off-campus study, part-time degree program, services for LD students, student-designed majors, study abroad, summer session for credit.
Unusual degree programs: 3-2 environmental law and policy, energy regulation and law with Vermont Law School.

Computers: 102 computers/terminals are available on campus for general student use. Students can access the following: campus intranet, computer help desk, free student e-mail accounts, online (class) grades, online (class) registration, online (class) schedules, personal network folders, electronic course folders. Campuswide network is available. 100% of college-owned or -operated housing units are wired for high-speed Internet access. Wireless service is available via entire campus.
Library: Griswold Library. *Books:* 69,000 (physical), 146,000 (digital/electronic); *Serial titles:* 112 (physical), 38,000 (digital/electronic); *Databases:* 36. Weekly public service hours: 97; study areas open 24 hours, 5–7 days a week.

STUDENT LIFE
Housing options: on-campus residence required through senior year; coed. Campus housing is university owned. Freshman campus housing is guaranteed.

Activities and organizations: drama/theater group, student-run newspaper, choral group, Student Government Association, Green Mountain College Ultimate Frisbee, Diversity, College Programming Board, International Awareness Club.

Athletics Member NCAA. All Division III. *Intercollegiate sports:* basketball M/W, cross-country running M/W, golf M/W, lacrosse M, soccer M/W, tennis W, volleyball W. *Intramural sports:* rugby M(c)/W(c), ultimate Frisbee M(c)/W(c).

Campus security: 24-hour emergency response devices and patrols, late-night transport/escort service.

Student services: personal/psychological counseling.

COSTS & FINANCIAL AID
Costs (2018–19) *One-time required fee:* $250. *Comprehensive fee:* $48,724 includes full-time tuition ($35,560), mandatory fees ($1442), and room and board ($11,722). Full-time tuition and fees vary according to degree level, location, and program. Part-time tuition: $1185 per credit hour. Part-time tuition and fees vary according to degree level and location. No tuition increase for student's term of enrollment. *Required fees:* $30 per course part-time, $741 per term part-time. *Room and board:* Room and board charges vary according to location. *Payment plan:* installment. *Waivers:* employees or children of employees.

Financial Aid Of all full-time matriculated undergraduates who enrolled in 2012, 520 applied for aid, 486 were judged to have need, 52 had their need fully met. 188 Federal Work-Study jobs (averaging $1700). 122 state and other part-time jobs (averaging $1700). In 2012, 110 non-need-based awards were made. *Average percent of need met:* 67. *Average financial aid package:* $23,458. *Average need-based loan:* $3753. *Average need-based gift aid:* $19,712. *Average non-need-based aid:* $13,191. *Average indebtedness upon graduation:* $42,269.

APPLYING
Options: electronic application, early action, deferred entrance.

Required: essay or personal statement, high school transcript, 1 letter of recommendation. *Required for some:* interview. *Recommended:* minimum 2.5 GPA, interview.

Application deadlines: rolling (freshmen), rolling (transfers), rolling (early action).

Notification: continuous until 9/1 (freshmen), continuous until 9/1 (transfers), 12/14 (early action).

CONTACT
Green Mountain College, One Brennan Circle, Poultney, VT 05764. *Phone:* 802-287-2150. *Toll-free phone:* 800-776-6675.

Landmark College
Putney, Vermont
http://www.landmark.edu/

CONTACT
Admissions Main Desk, Landmark College, Admissions Office, River Road South, Putney, VT 05346. *Phone:* 802-387-6718. *Fax:* 802-387-6868. *E-mail:* admissions@landmark.edu.

★ Marlboro College

Marlboro, Vermont
http://www.marlboro.edu/

- **Independent** comprehensive, founded 1946
- **Rural** 350-acre campus
- **Endowment** $37.3 million
- **Coed** 183 undergraduate students, 97% full-time, 54% women, 46% men
- **Moderately difficult** entrance level, 97% of applicants were admitted

UNDERGRAD STUDENTS

177 full-time, 6 part-time. Students come from 34 states and territories; 4 other countries; 93% are from out of state; 4% Black or African American, non-Hispanic/Latino; 3% Hispanic/Latino; 1% Asian, non-Hispanic/Latino; 0.5% American Indian or Alaska Native, non-Hispanic/Latino; 4% Two or more races, non-Hispanic/Latino; 11% Race/ethnicity unknown; 2% international; 13% transferred in; 78% live on campus.

Freshmen:
Admission: 120 applied, 116 admitted, 28 enrolled. *Average high school GPA:* 3.1. *Test scores:* ACT scores over 18: 100%; ACT scores over 24: 79%; ACT scores over 30: 29%.

Retention: 85% of full-time freshmen returned.

FACULTY

Total: 42, 76% full-time, 74% with terminal degrees.
Student/faculty ratio: 5:1.

ACADEMICS

Calendar: semesters. *Degrees:* bachelor's and master's.

Special study options: accelerated degree program, advanced placement credit, double majors, English as a second language, independent study, internships, off-campus study, services for LD students, student-designed majors, study abroad.

Computers: 47 computers/terminals are available on campus for general student use. Students can access the following: campus intranet, computer help desk, free student e-mail accounts, online (class) grades, online (class) registration, online (class) schedules. Campuswide network is

available. 100% of college-owned or -operated housing units are wired for high-speed Internet access. Wireless service is available via entire campus.

Library: Rice-Aron Library. *Books:* 88,500 (physical), 137,548 (digital/electronic); *Serial titles:* 5,400 (physical), 150 (digital/electronic); *Databases:* 75. Study areas open 24 hours, 5–7 days a week.

STUDENT LIFE

Housing options: on-campus residence required for freshman year; coed, women-only, cooperative, special housing for students with disabilities. Campus housing is university owned. Freshman campus housing is guaranteed.

Activities and organizations: drama/theater group, student-run newspaper, radio station, choral group, outdoor program, theater, farm program, Gay/Lesbian/Bisexual Alliance, madrigal and a cappella groups.

Athletics *Intercollegiate sports:* soccer M/W. *Intramural sports:* basketball M/W, fencing M/W, rock climbing M/W, skiing (cross-country) M/W, skiing (downhill) M/W, soccer M/W, softball M/W, table tennis M/W, ultimate Frisbee M/W.

Campus security: 24-hour emergency response devices and patrols.

Student services: health clinic, personal/psychological counseling, women's center.

COSTS & FINANCIAL AID

Costs (2018–19) *Comprehensive fee:* $53,225 includes full-time tuition ($39,870), mandatory fees ($970), and room and board ($12,385). Full-time tuition and fees vary according to reciprocity agreements. Part-time tuition: $1329 per credit hour. Part-time tuition and fees vary according to course load. *Required fees:* $105 per term part-time. *College room only:* $7142. Room and board charges vary according to board plan. *Payment plan:* installment. *Waivers:* employees or children of employees.

Financial Aid Of all full-time matriculated undergraduates who enrolled in 2017, 147 applied for aid, 140 were judged to have need, 48 had their need fully met. In 2017, 28 non-need-based awards were made. *Average percent of need met:* 74. *Average financial aid package:* $39,880. *Average need-based loan:* $4411. *Average need-based gift aid:* $32,707. *Average non-need-based aid:* $22,756. *Average indebtedness upon graduation:* $31,747. *Financial aid deadline:* 3/1.

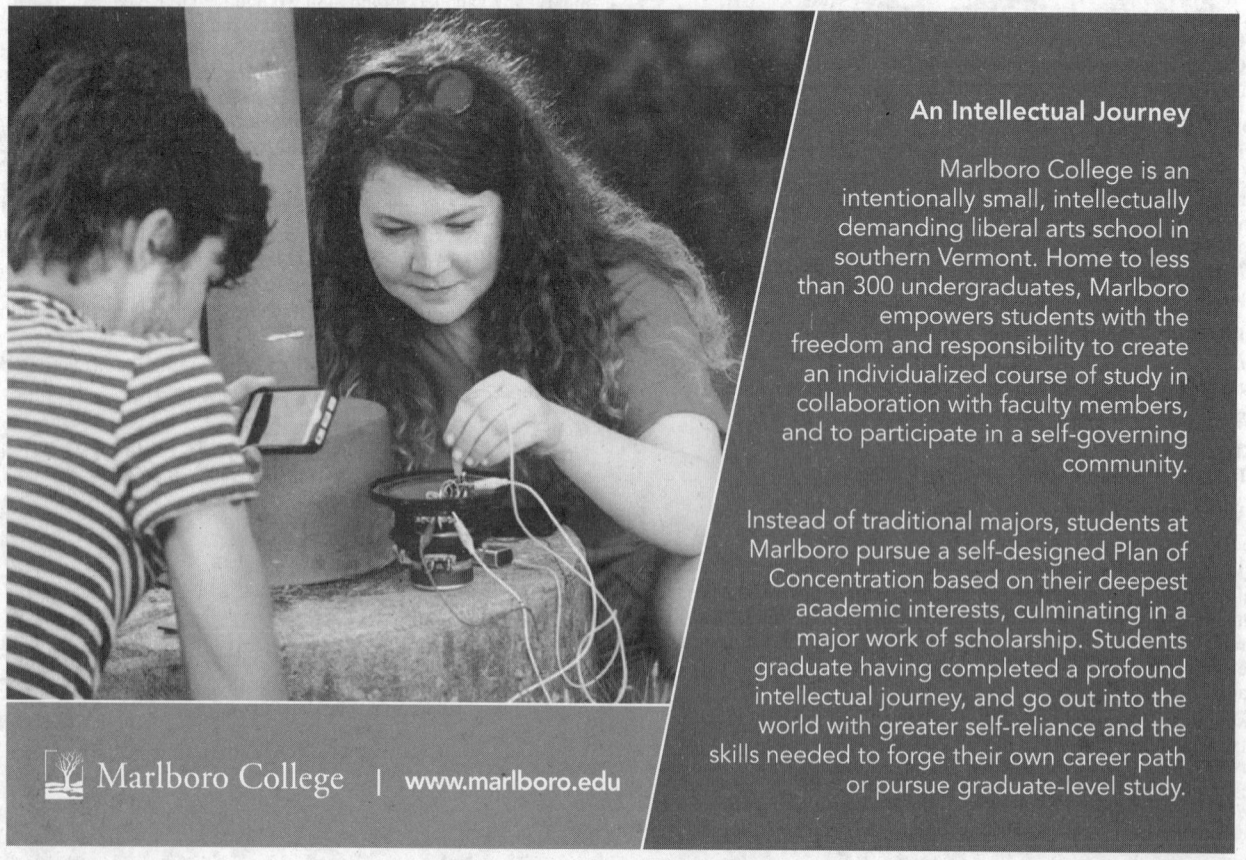

An Intellectual Journey

Marlboro College is an intentionally small, intellectually demanding liberal arts school in southern Vermont. Home to less than 300 undergraduates, Marlboro empowers students with the freedom and responsibility to create an individualized course of study in collaboration with faculty members, and to participate in a self-governing community.

Instead of traditional majors, students at Marlboro pursue a self-designed Plan of Concentration based on their deepest academic interests, culminating in a major work of scholarship. Students graduate having completed a profound intellectual journey, and go out into the world with greater self-reliance and the skills needed to forge their own career path or pursue graduate-level study.

Marlboro College | www.marlboro.edu

APPLYING

Standardized Tests *Recommended:* SAT or ACT (for admission).

Options: electronic application, early admission, early decision, early action, deferred entrance.

Application fee: $50.

Required: essay or personal statement, high school transcript, 2 letters of recommendation, analytical essay. *Required for some:* interview. *Recommended:* interview.

Application deadlines: 3/1 (freshmen), 4/1 (transfers), 1/15 (early action).

Early decision deadline: 11/15.

Notification: continuous until 3/15 (freshmen), continuous until 4/15 (transfers), 12/1 (early decision), 2/1 (early action).

CONTACT

Marlboro College, PO Box A, South Road, Marlboro, VT 05344. *Toll-free phone:* 800-343-0049.

See previous page for display ad and page 1338 for the College Close-Up.

Middlebury College

Middlebury, Vermont

http://www.middlebury.edu/

- **Independent** comprehensive, founded 1800
- **Small-town** 350-acre campus
- **Coed** 2,561 undergraduate students, 99% full-time, 52% women, 48% men
- **Most difficult** entrance level, 17% of applicants were admitted

UNDERGRAD STUDENTS

2,531 full-time, 30 part-time. Students come from 52 states and territories; 68 other countries; 94% are from out of state; 4% Black or African American, non-Hispanic/Latino; 10% Hispanic/Latino; 6% Asian, non-Hispanic/Latino; 5% Two or more races, non-Hispanic/Latino; 2% Race/ethnicity unknown; 10% international; 0.4% transferred in; 95% live on campus.

Freshmen:

Admission: 8,909 applied, 1,523 admitted, 635 enrolled. *Test scores:* SAT evidence-based reading and writing scores over 500: 100%; SAT math scores over 500: 100%; ACT scores over 18: 100%; SAT evidence-based reading and writing scores over 600: 95%; SAT math scores over 600: 94%; ACT scores over 24: 98%; SAT evidence-based reading and writing scores over 700: 57%; SAT math scores over 700: 57%; ACT scores over 30: 81%.

Retention: 96% of full-time freshmen returned.

FACULTY

Total: 343, 85% full-time, 93% with terminal degrees.

Student/faculty ratio: 8:1.

ACADEMICS

Calendar: 4-1-4. *Degrees:* bachelor's, master's, and doctoral.

Special study options: accelerated degree program, advanced placement credit, double majors, honors programs, independent study, internships, off-campus study, services for LD students, student-designed majors, study abroad, summer session for credit. *ROTC:* Army (c).

Unusual degree programs: 3-2 engineering with Columbia University, Dartmouth College.

Computers: 250 computers/terminals are available on campus for general student use. Students can access the following: campus intranet, computer help desk, free student e-mail accounts, online (class) grades, online (class) registration, online (class) schedules, personal Web pages, file servers. Campuswide network is available. Wireless service is available via entire campus.

Library: Davis Family Library plus 2 others. *Books:* 764,667 (physical), 644,056 (digital/electronic); *Databases:* 695. Weekly public service hours: 112; students can reserve study rooms.

STUDENT LIFE

Housing options: on-campus residence required through junior year; coed, special housing for students with disabilities. Campus housing is university owned. Freshman campus housing is guaranteed.

Activities and organizations: drama/theater group, student-run newspaper, radio station, choral group, Middlebury College Activities Board, Middlebury Mountain Club, Student Government Association, International Students Organization, WRMC.

Athletics Member NCAA. All Division III except men's and women's skiing (cross-country) (Division I), men's and women's skiing (downhill) (Division I). *Intercollegiate sports:* baseball M, basketball M/W, cross-country running M/W, field hockey W, football M, golf M/W, ice hockey M/W, lacrosse M/W, skiing (cross-country) M/W, skiing (downhill) M/W, soccer M/W, softball W, squash M/W, swimming and diving M/W, tennis M/W, track and field M/W, volleyball W. *Intramural sports:* badminton M(c)/W(c), basketball M/W, crew M(c)/W(c), equestrian sports M(c)/W(c), fencing M(c)/W(c), football M/W, golf M/W, ice hockey M/W, rugby M(c)/W(c), sailing M(c)/W(c), soccer M/W, softball M/W, squash M/W, tennis M/W, ultimate Frisbee M(c)/W(c), volleyball M(c)/W(c), water polo M(c)/W(c).

Campus security: 24-hour emergency response devices and patrols, student patrols, late-night transport/escort service, controlled dormitory access.

Student services: health clinic, personal/psychological counseling, women's center.

COSTS & FINANCIAL AID

Costs (2017–18) *Comprehensive fee:* $67,464 includes full-time tuition ($52,080), mandatory fees ($416), and room and board ($14,968). *Payment plan:* tuition prepayment. *Waivers:* employees or children of employees.

Financial Aid Of all full-time matriculated undergraduates who enrolled in 2017, 1,344 applied for aid, 1,138 were judged to have need, 1,138 had their need fully met. In 2017, 5 non-need-based awards were made. *Average percent of need met:* 100. *Average financial aid package:* $50,792. *Average need-based loan:* $3637. *Average need-based gift aid:* $47,439. *Average non-need-based aid:* $5000. *Average indebtedness upon graduation:* $19,382. *Financial aid deadline:* 2/1.

APPLYING

Standardized Tests *Required:* SAT and SAT Subject Tests or ACT (for admission).

Options: electronic application, early admission, early decision, deferred entrance.

Application fee: $65.

Required: essay or personal statement, high school transcript, 2 letters of recommendation. *Recommended:* interview.

Application deadlines: 1/1 (freshmen), 3/1 (transfers).

Early decision deadline: 11/1 (for plan 1), 1/1 (for plan 2).

Notification: 3/31 (freshmen), 4/10 (transfers), 12/15 (early decision plan 1), 2/15 (early decision plan 2).

CONTACT

Mr. Greg Buckles, Dean of Admissions, Middlebury College, Emma Willard House, Middlebury, VT 05753-6002. *Phone:* 802-443-3000. *Fax:* 802-443-2056. *E-mail:* admissions@middlebury.edu.

New England Culinary Institute

Montpelier, Vermont

http://www.neci.edu/

- **Proprietary** primarily 2-year, founded 1980
- **Small-town** campus
- **Coed**
- **Moderately difficult** entrance level

FACULTY

Student/faculty ratio: 15:1.

ACADEMICS

Calendar: quarters. *Degrees:* certificates, associate, and bachelor's.

Library: New England Culinary Institute Library.

STUDENT LIFE

Housing options: on-campus residence required for freshman year; coed, men-only, women-only. Campus housing is leased by the school. Freshman applicants given priority for college housing.

COLLEGES AT-A-GLANCE

Activities and organizations: American Culinary Federation, Slow Food, Student Council, Special Guest Lecture Series, Student Ambassadors (leadership program).

Campus security: 24-hour emergency response devices, student patrols.

COSTS & FINANCIAL AID

Costs (2017–18) *Comprehensive fee:* $33,419 includes full-time tuition ($16,800), mandatory fees ($2420), and room and board ($14,199). Full-time tuition and fees vary according to course load. Part-time tuition: $700 per credit hour. Part-time tuition and fees vary according to course load.

Financial Aid Of all full-time matriculated undergraduates who enrolled in 2016, 320 Federal Work-Study jobs (averaging $1000).

APPLYING

Standardized Tests *Recommended:* SAT or ACT (for admission).

Options: electronic application, early admission, deferred entrance.

Application fee: $35.

Required: essay or personal statement, high school transcript, 1 letter of recommendation, interview. *Recommended:* culinary experience.

CONTACT

Adonica Williams, New England Culinary Institute, 7 School Street, Montpelier, VT 05602-3115. *Phone:* 802-225-3210. *Toll-free phone:* 877-223-6324. *Fax:* 802-225-3280. *E-mail:* admissions@neci.edu.

Northern Vermont University–Johnson

Johnson, Vermont

http://www.northernvermont.edu/

CONTACT

Bethany Harrington, Admissions Specialist, Northern Vermont University–Johnson, 337 College Hill, Johnson, VT 05656. *Phone:* 802-635-1219. *Toll-free phone:* 800-635-2356. *Fax:* 802-635-1230. *E-mail:* admissions@jsc.edu.

 ## Northern Vermont University–Lyndon

Lyndonville, Vermont

http://www.northernvermont.edu/

- **State-supported** comprehensive, founded 2018, part of Vermont State Colleges System
- **Rural** 175-acre campus
- **Coed**
- **Moderately difficult** entrance level

UNDERGRAD STUDENTS

Students come from 19 states and territories; 11 other countries; 39% are from out of state.

FACULTY

Total: 257, 37% full-time, 36% with terminal degrees.

Student/faculty ratio: 15:1.

ACADEMICS

Calendar: semesters. *Degrees:* certificates, diplomas, associate, bachelor's, master's, and post-master's certificates.

Special study options: academic remediation for entering students, accelerated degree program, adult/continuing education programs, advanced placement credit, cooperative education, distance learning, double majors, external degree program, honors programs, independent study, internships, off-campus study, part-time degree program, services for LD students, student-designed majors, study abroad, summer session for credit. *ROTC:* Army (c), Air Force (c).

Computers: Students can access the following: campus intranet, computer help desk, free student e-mail accounts, online (class) grades, online (class) registration, online (class) schedules. Campuswide network is available. 100% of college-owned or -operated housing units are wired for high-speed Internet access. Wireless service is available via entire campus.

Library: Samuel Read Hall Library (NVU-Lyndon) and Willey Library (NVU-Johnson). Weekly public service hours: 38.

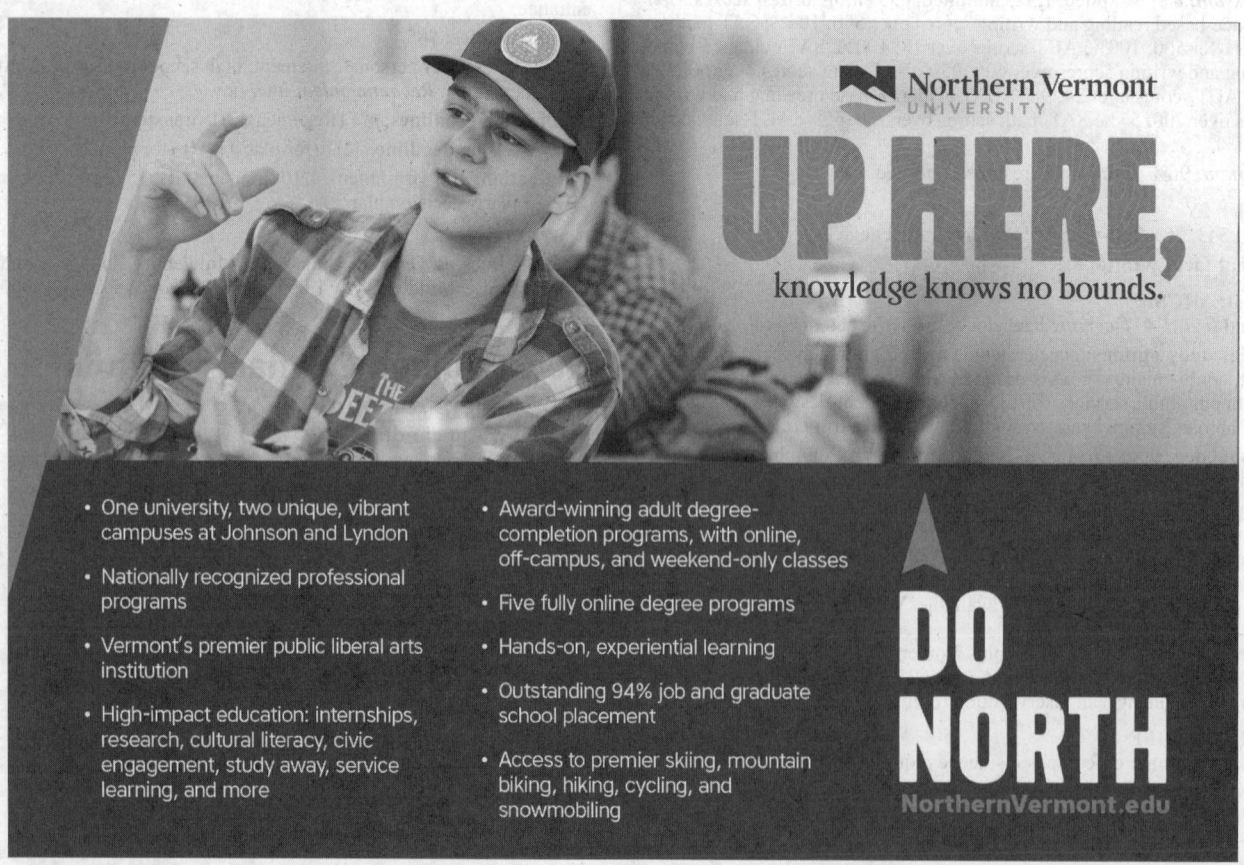

STUDENT LIFE

Housing options: on-campus residence required through sophomore year; coed, women-only, cooperative, special housing for students with disabilities. Campus housing is university owned and leased by the school. Freshman campus housing is guaranteed.

Activities and organizations: drama/theater group, student-run newspaper, radio and television station, choral group, American Meteorological Society, ASSIST and SERVE, Student Government, Campus Activities, Outing Club, Dance Club.

Athletics Member NCAA. All Division III. *Intercollegiate sports:* baseball M, basketball M/W, cross-country running M/W, golf M, lacrosse M/W, soccer M/W, softball W, tennis M/W, track and field M/W, triathlon M/W, volleyball M/W. *Intramural sports:* badminton M/W, basketball M/W, bowling M(c)/W(c), cross-country running M/W, ice hockey M(c)/W(c), racquetball M/W, rock climbing M/W, rugby M(c)/W(c), swimming and diving M/W, table tennis M/W, tennis M/W, ultimate Frisbee M(c)/W(c), volleyball M/W, water polo M/W.

Campus security: 24-hour emergency response devices, student patrols, late-night transport/escort service, controlled dormitory access.

Student services: health clinic, personal/psychological counseling.

APPLYING

Options: electronic application, early admission, deferred entrance.

Application fee: $36.

Required: high school transcript, minimum 2.0 GPA, 1 letter of recommendation. *Required for some:* essay or personal statement, minimum 3.0 GPA. *Recommended:* minimum 3.0 GPA, interview.

Application deadlines: rolling (freshmen), rolling (transfers).

Notification: continuous (freshmen), continuous (transfers).

CONTACT

Ms. Cheri Goldrick, Admissions Assistant, Northern Vermont University–Lyndon, 1001 College Road, PO Box 919, Lyndonville, VT 05851. *Phone:* 802-626-6451. *Toll-free phone:* 800-225-1998. *Fax:* 802-626-6335. *E-mail:* admissions@lyndonstate.edu.

See previous page for display ad and page 1372 for the College Close-Up.

Norwich University

Northfield, Vermont
http://www.norwich.edu/

CONTACT
Norwich University, 158 Harmon Drive, Northfield, VT 05663. *Phone:* 802-485-2658. *Toll-free phone:* 800-468-6679.

Saint Michael's College

Colchester, Vermont
http://www.smcvt.edu/

- **Independent Roman Catholic** comprehensive, founded 1904
- **Suburban** 440-acre campus with easy access to Montreal
- **Endowment** $87.5 million
- **Coed** 1,792 undergraduate students, 99% full-time, 56% women, 44% men
- **Moderately difficult** entrance level, 85% of applicants were admitted

UNDERGRAD STUDENTS
1,766 full-time, 26 part-time. Students come from 36 states and territories; 24 other countries; 85% are from out of state; 2% Black or African American, non-Hispanic/Latino; 5% Hispanic/Latino; 1% Asian, non-Hispanic/Latino; 0.1% Native Hawaiian or other Pacific Islander, non-Hispanic/Latino; 0.1% American Indian or Alaska Native, non-Hispanic/Latino; 2% Two or more races, non-Hispanic/Latino; 2% Race/ethnicity unknown; 4% international; 2% transferred in; 96% live on campus.

Freshmen:
Admission: 3,094 applied, 2,633 admitted, 409 enrolled. *Test scores:* SAT evidence-based reading and writing scores over 500: 99%; SAT math scores over 500: 96%; ACT scores over 18: 100%; SAT evidence-based reading and writing scores over 600: 67%; SAT math scores over 600: 55%; ACT scores over 24: 90%; SAT evidence-based reading and writing

scores over 700: 10%; SAT math scores over 700: 7%; ACT scores over 30: 18%.

Retention: 83% of full-time freshmen returned.

FACULTY
Total: 170, 81% full-time.

Student/faculty ratio: 13:1.

ACADEMICS
Calendar: semesters. *Degrees:* bachelor's, master's, post-master's, and postbachelor's certificates.

Special study options: accelerated degree program, advanced placement credit, cooperative education, distance learning, double majors, English as a second language, honors programs, independent study, internships, off-campus study, part-time degree program, services for LD students, student-designed majors, study abroad, summer session for credit. *ROTC:* Army (c), Air Force (c).

Unusual degree programs: 3-2 business administration with Clarkson University, Syracuse University, Northeastern University, Boston College; engineering with University of Vermont, Clarkson University; pharmacy with Albany College of Pharmacy and Health Sciences, law/environmental law and policy with Vermont Law School.

Computers: 97 computers/terminals and 5,000 ports are available on campus for general student use. Students can access the following: campus intranet, computer help desk, free student e-mail accounts, online (class) grades, online (class) registration, online (class) schedules. Campuswide network is available. 100% of college-owned or -operated housing units are wired for high-speed Internet access. Wireless service is available via entire campus.

Library: Durick Library. *Books:* 231,418 (physical), 231,171 (digital/electronic); *Serial titles:* 1,653 (physical), 128,515 (digital/electronic); *Databases:* 142. Weekly public service hours: 102.

STUDENT LIFE
Housing options: on-campus residence required through senior year; coed, men-only, women-only, special housing for students with disabilities. Campus housing is university owned. Freshman campus housing is guaranteed.

Activities and organizations: drama/theater group, student-run newspaper, radio station, choral group, Student Association (governing board), Mobilization of Volunteer Efforts (MOVE), Wilderness Program, Martin Luther King Society, ShredMC.

Athletics Member NCAA. All Division II. *Intercollegiate sports:* baseball M, basketball M(s)/W(s), cross-country running M/W, field hockey W, golf M, ice hockey M/W, lacrosse M/W, skiing (cross-country) M/W, skiing (downhill) M/W, soccer M/W, softball W, swimming and diving M/W, tennis M/W, volleyball W. *Intramural sports:* basketball M/W, ice hockey M/W, racquetball M/W, rock climbing M/W, rugby M(c)/W(c), skiing (cross-country) M/W, skiing (downhill) M/W, soccer M/W, track and field M(c)/W(c), ultimate Frisbee M(c)/W(c), water polo M(c)/W(c).

Campus security: 24-hour emergency response devices and patrols, student patrols, late-night transport/escort service, controlled dormitory access, bicycle patrols, fire and rescue squad with professionals and trained student volunteers.

Student services: health clinic, personal/psychological counseling, women's center.

COSTS & FINANCIAL AID
Costs (2018–19) *Comprehensive fee:* $57,595 includes full-time tuition ($45,050), mandatory fees ($325), and room and board ($12,220). Full-time tuition and fees vary according to course load. Part-time tuition: $1445 per credit hour. Part-time tuition and fees vary according to course load. *Room and board:* Room and board charges vary according to board plan and housing facility. *Payment plan:* installment. *Waivers:* senior citizens and employees or children of employees.

Financial Aid Of all full-time matriculated undergraduates who enrolled in 2017, 1,269 applied for aid, 1,131 were judged to have need, 289 had their need fully met. 250 Federal Work-Study jobs (averaging $1750). 280 state and other part-time jobs (averaging $1750). In 2017, 576 non-need-based awards were made. *Average percent of need met:* 78. *Average financial aid package:* $32,102. *Average need-based loan:* $5529. *Average need-based gift aid:* $25,274. *Average non-need-based aid:* $17,739. *Average indebtedness upon graduation:* $40,009.

APPLYING

Options: electronic application, early action, deferred entrance.

Application fee: $50.

Required: essay or personal statement, high school transcript, 1 letter of recommendation. *Recommended:* minimum 3.0 GPA, 3 letters of recommendation, interview.

Application deadlines: 2/1 (freshmen), 3/15 (transfers), 11/1 (early action).

Notification: 4/1 (freshmen), 4/15 (transfers), 12/21 (early action).

CONTACT

Mr. Michael Stefanowicz, Director of Admission, Saint Michael's College, One Winooski Park, Colchester, VT 05439. *Phone:* 802-654-2108. *Toll-free phone:* 800-762-8000. *Fax:* 802-654-2906. *E-mail:* admission@smcvt.edu.

Southern Vermont College

Bennington, Vermont

http://www.svc.edu/

- **Independent** 4-year, founded 1926
- **Small-town** 371-acre campus with easy access to Albany, NY
- **Endowment** $3.5 million
- **Coed** 361 undergraduate students, 94% full-time, 57% women, 43% men
- **Noncompetitive** entrance level, 91% of applicants were admitted

UNDERGRAD STUDENTS

339 full-time, 22 part-time. Students come from 19 states and territories; 1 other country; 75% are from out of state; 9% Black or African American, non-Hispanic/Latino; 8% Hispanic/Latino; 1% Asian, non-Hispanic/Latino; 0.3% American Indian or Alaska Native, non-Hispanic/Latino; 3% Two or more races, non-Hispanic/Latino; 23% Race/ethnicity unknown; 0.3% international; 10% transferred in; 67% live on campus.

Freshmen:

Admission: 353 applied, 320 admitted, 84 enrolled. *Average high school GPA:* 2.4. *Test scores:* ACT scores over 18: 56%; ACT scores over 24: 12%.

Retention: 64% of full-time freshmen returned.

FACULTY

Total: 50, 44% full-time.

Student/faculty ratio: 14:1.

ACADEMICS

Calendar: semesters. *Degrees:* certificates, associate, and bachelor's.

Special study options: academic remediation for entering students, advanced placement credit, cooperative education, distance learning, double majors, independent study, internships, off-campus study, part-time degree program, services for LD students, student-designed majors, study abroad, summer session for credit.

Computers: 50 computers/terminals are available on campus for general student use. Students can access the following: campus intranet, computer help desk, free student e-mail accounts, online (class) grades, online (class) registration, online (class) schedules. Campuswide network is available. 100% of college-owned or -operated housing units are wired for high-speed Internet access. Wireless service is available via entire campus.

Library: Southern Vermont College Library. *Books:* 10,025 (physical), 8,818 (digital/electronic); *Serial titles:* 792 (physical); *Databases:* 70. Students can reserve study rooms.

STUDENT LIFE

Housing options: on-campus residence required through junior year; coed. Campus housing is university owned. Freshman campus housing is guaranteed.

Activities and organizations: drama/theater group, Student Government Association, Mountaineer Event Board, Japanese Culture and Anime Club, Big Brothers Big Sisters, Moosecorps.

Athletics Member NCAA. All Division III. *Intercollegiate sports:* baseball M, basketball M/W, cross-country running M/W, lacrosse W, soccer M/W, softball W, track and field M/W, volleyball M/W.

Campus security: 24-hour patrols, late-night transport/escort service, controlled dormitory access.

Student services: health clinic, personal/psychological counseling.

COSTS & FINANCIAL AID

Costs (2018–19) *One-time required fee:* $100. *Comprehensive fee:* $36,511 includes full-time tuition ($25,236), mandatory fees ($275), and room and board ($11,000). Part-time tuition: $1052 per credit hour. Part-time tuition and fees vary according to course load. *Room and board:* Room and board charges vary according to board plan and housing facility. *Payment plan:* installment. *Waivers:* senior citizens and employees or children of employees.

Financial Aid Of all full-time matriculated undergraduates who enrolled in 2017, 307 applied for aid, 307 were judged to have need. 99 Federal Work-Study jobs (averaging $1500). 6 state and other part-time jobs (averaging $1500). In 2017, 34 non-need-based awards were made. *Average percent of need met:* 42. *Average financial aid package:* $16,000. *Average need-based loan:* $4500. *Average need-based gift aid:* $16,000. *Average non-need-based aid:* $12,000. *Average indebtedness upon graduation:* $35,728.

APPLYING

Standardized Tests *Required:* SAT or ACT (for admission).

Options: electronic application, early admission, deferred entrance.

Application fee: $30.

Required: high school transcript. *Required for some:* college transcripts for transfer students. *Recommended:* essay or personal statement, minimum 2.0 GPA.

Application deadlines: rolling (freshmen), rolling (out-of-state freshmen), rolling (transfers).

Notification: continuous (freshmen), continuous (out-of-state freshmen), continuous (transfers).

CONTACT

Southern Vermont College, 897 Monument Avenue, Bennington, VT 05201. *Phone:* 802-447-6300. *Fax:* 802-681-2868. *E-mail:* admissions@svc.edu.

Sterling College

Craftsbury Common, Vermont

http://www.sterlingcollege.edu/

CONTACT

Tim Patterson, Director of Admission and Financial Aid, Sterling College, PO Box 72, Craftsbury Common, VT 05827. *Phone:* 802-586-7711 Ext. 135. *Toll-free phone:* 800-648-3591 Ext. 100. *Fax:* 802-586-2596. *E-mail:* tpatterson@sterlingcollege.edu.

See next page for display ad and page 1440 for the College Close-Up.

University of Vermont

Burlington, Vermont

http://www.uvm.edu/

- **State-supported** university, founded 1791
- **Suburban** 459-acre campus
- **Endowment** $453.3 million
- **Coed** 11,339 undergraduate students, 92% full-time, 58% women, 42% men
- **Moderately difficult** entrance level, 67% of applicants were admitted

UNDERGRAD STUDENTS

10,395 full-time, 944 part-time. Students come from 48 states and territories; 51 other countries; 71% are from out of state; 1% Black or African American, non-Hispanic/Latino; 4% Hispanic/Latino; 3% Asian, non-Hispanic/Latino; 0.1% American Indian or Alaska Native, non-Hispanic/Latino; 3% Two or more races, non-Hispanic/Latino; 2% Race/ethnicity unknown; 6% international; 4% transferred in; 51% live on campus.

Freshmen:

Admission: 21,991 applied, 14,777 admitted, 2,642 enrolled. *Average high school GPA:* 3.7. *Test scores:* SAT evidence-based reading and writing scores over 500: 98%; SAT math scores over 500: 98%; ACT scores over 18: 100%; SAT evidence-based reading and writing scores over 600: 75%; SAT math scores over 600: 66%; ACT scores over 24: 89%; SAT evidence-based reading and writing scores over 700: 17%; SAT math scores over 700: 13%; ACT scores over 30: 34%.

Retention: 86% of full-time freshmen returned.

FACULTY
Total: 826, 76% full-time, 72% with terminal degrees.
Student/faculty ratio: 17:1.

ACADEMICS
Calendar: semesters. *Degrees:* bachelor's, master's, doctoral, post-master's, and postbachelor's certificates.

Special study options: adult/continuing education programs, advanced placement credit, cooperative education, distance learning, double majors, freshman honors college, honors programs, independent study, internships, off-campus study, part-time degree program, services for LD students, student-designed majors, study abroad, summer session for credit. *ROTC:* Army (b).

Unusual degree programs: 3-2 computer science, law with Vermont Law School.

Computers: 530 computers/terminals and 300 ports are available on campus for general student use. Students can access the following: campus intranet, computer help desk, free student e-mail accounts, online (class) grades, online (class) registration, online (class) schedules, Web pages, online course support, learning management system. Campuswide network is available. 100% of college-owned or -operated housing units are wired for high-speed Internet access. Wireless service is available via entire campus.

Library: Bailey-Howe Library plus 2 others. *Books:* 1.1 million (physical), 339,186 (digital/electronic); *Serial titles:* 43,466 (physical), 96,209 (digital/electronic); *Databases:* 359. Weekly public service hours: 107; study areas open 24 hours, 5–7 days a week; students can reserve study rooms.

STUDENT LIFE
Housing options: on-campus residence required through sophomore year; coed. Campus housing is university owned. Freshman campus housing is guaranteed.

Activities and organizations: drama/theater group, student-run newspaper, radio and television station, choral group, Outing Club, Ski and Snowboard Club, national fraternities, national sororities.

Athletics Member NCAA. All Division I. *Intercollegiate sports:* badminton M(c)/W(c), baseball M(c)/W(c), basketball M(s)/W(s), cheerleading M(c)/W(c), crew M(c)/W(c), cross-country running M(s)/W(s), equestrian sports M(c)/W(c), fencing M(c)/W(c), field hockey W(s), football M(c)/W(c), golf M(c)/W(c), gymnastics M(c)/W(c), ice hockey M(s)/W(s), lacrosse M(s)/W(s), riflery M(c)/W(c), rock climbing M(c)/W(c), rugby M(c)/W(c), sailing M(c)/W(c), skiing (cross-country) M(s)/W(s), skiing (downhill) M(s)/W(s), soccer M(s)/W(s), squash M(c)/W(c), swimming and diving W(s), table tennis M(c)/W(c), tennis M(c)/W(c), track and field M(s)/W(s), triathlon M(c)/W(c), ultimate Frisbee M(c)/W(c), volleyball M(c)/W(c), water polo M(c)/W(c), wrestling M(c)/W(c). *Intramural sports:* badminton M/W, basketball M/W, football M/W, ice hockey M/W, lacrosse M/W, soccer M/W, tennis M/W, track and field M/W, ultimate Frisbee M/W, volleyball M/W.

Campus security: 24-hour emergency response devices and patrols, late-night transport/escort service, controlled dormitory access, campus alert system (via phone, email, text).

Student services: health clinic, personal/psychological counseling, women's center, legal services.

COSTS & FINANCIAL AID
Costs (2017–18) *Tuition:* state resident $15,504 full-time, $646 per credit hour part-time; nonresident $39,120 full-time, $1630 per credit hour part-time. Full-time tuition and fees vary according to reciprocity agreements. Part-time tuition and fees vary according to course load and reciprocity agreements. *Required fees:* $2236 full-time. *Room and board:* $12,022; room only: $7900. Room and board charges vary according to board plan and housing facility. *Payment plan:* installment. *Waivers:* employees or children of employees.

Financial Aid Of all full-time matriculated undergraduates who enrolled in 2016, 6,734 applied for aid, 5,369 were judged to have need, 832 had their need fully met. 1,412 Federal Work-Study jobs (averaging $1600). In 2016, 3097 non-need-based awards were made. *Average percent of need met:* 66. *Average financial aid package:* $25,251. *Average need-based*

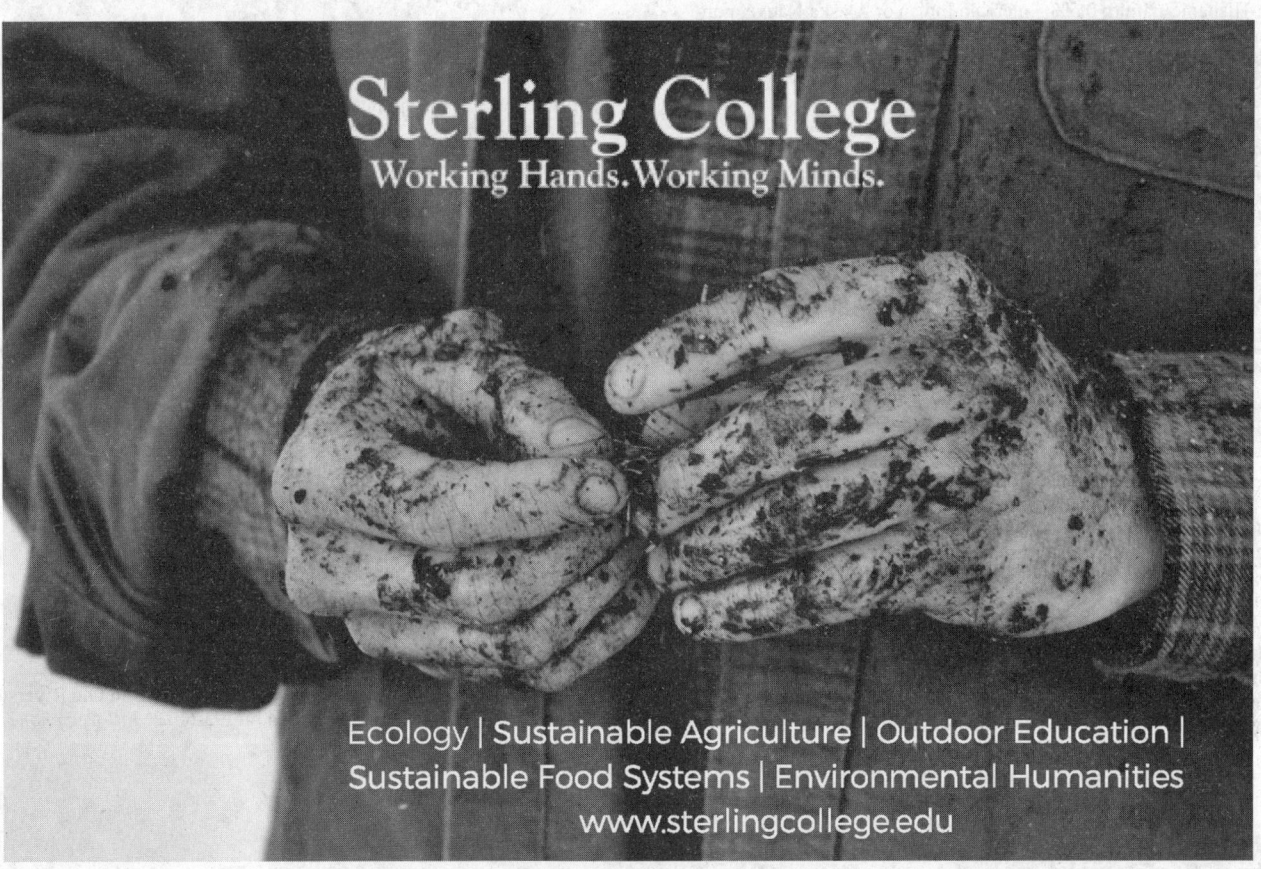

loan: $4562. *Average need-based gift aid:* $16,278. *Average non-need-based aid:* $12,751. *Average indebtedness upon graduation:* $28,894.

APPLYING

Standardized Tests *Required:* SAT or ACT (for admission).

Options: electronic application, early admission, early action, deferred entrance.

Application fee: $55.

Required: essay or personal statement, high school transcript, 1 letter of recommendation. *Required for some:* audition for music or music education.

Application deadlines: 1/15 (freshmen), 4/15 (transfers), 11/1 (early action).

Notification: 2/23 (freshmen), continuous (transfers), 12/14 (early action).

CONTACT

Mr. Ryan Hargraves, Director of Admissions, University of Vermont, Office of Admissions, 194 South Prospect Street, Burlington, VT 05401. *Phone:* 802-656-3370. *Fax:* 802-656-8611. *E-mail:* admissions@ uvm.edu.

Vermont Technical College

Randolph Center, Vermont

http://www.vtc.edu/

- **State-supported** comprehensive, founded 1866, part of Vermont State Colleges System
- **Rural** 544-acre campus
- **Endowment** $5.5 million
- **Coed** 1,615 undergraduate students, 65% full-time, 48% women, 52% men
- **Moderately difficult** entrance level, 63% of applicants were admitted

UNDERGRAD STUDENTS

1,052 full-time, 563 part-time. Students come from 23 states and territories; 6 other countries; 19% are from out of state; 1% Black or African American, non-Hispanic/Latino; 3% Hispanic/Latino; 2% Asian, non-Hispanic/Latino; 0.1% Native Hawaiian or other Pacific Islander, non-Hispanic/Latino; 0.5% American Indian or Alaska Native, non-Hispanic/Latino; 4% Two or more races, non-Hispanic/Latino; 3% Race/ethnicity unknown; 2% international; 19% transferred in; 26% live on campus.

Freshmen:

Admission: 684 applied, 433 admitted, 219 enrolled. *Test scores:* SAT evidence-based reading and writing scores over 500: 61%; SAT math scores over 500: 61%; ACT scores over 18: 85%; SAT evidence-based reading and writing scores over 600: 17%; SAT math scores over 600: 28%; ACT scores over 24: 23%.

Retention: 70% of full-time freshmen returned.

FACULTY

Total: 172, 47% full-time, 19% with terminal degrees.

Student/faculty ratio: 12:1.

ACADEMICS

Calendar: semesters. *Degrees:* certificates, associate, bachelor's, and master's.

Special study options: academic remediation for entering students, accelerated degree program, advanced placement credit, cooperative education, distance learning, double majors, English as a second language, honors programs, independent study, internships, part-time degree program, services for LD students, summer session for credit. *ROTC:* Army (c).

Computers: 480 computers/terminals and 600 ports are available on campus for general student use. Students can access the following: campus intranet, computer help desk, free student e-mail accounts, online (class) grades, online (class) registration, online (class) schedules, online (network) file storage. Campuswide network is available. 98% of college-

owned or -operated housing units are wired for high-speed Internet access. Wireless service is available via entire campus. **Library:** Hartness Library. *Books:* 59,000 (physical).

STUDENT LIFE

Housing options: on-campus residence required through sophomore year; coed. Campus housing is university owned.

Activities and organizations: student-run radio and television station, choral group, Student Council (student government), Adventurer's Guild (board and video gaming), WVTC (student radio station), Outing Club, Veterinary Technology Club.

Athletics Member USCAA. *Intercollegiate sports:* baseball M, basketball M/W, soccer M/W, softball W. *Intramural sports:* basketball M/W, bowling M(c)/W(c), cross-country running M/W, fencing M(c)/W(c), football M/W, golf M(c)/W(c), ice hockey M(c)/W(c), racquetball M/W, riflery M(c)/W(c), rock climbing M(c)/W(c), rugby M(c), skiing (cross-country) M(c)/W(c), skiing (downhill) M(c)/W(c), soccer M/W, softball M/W, swimming and diving M/W, table tennis M/W, tennis M/W, volleyball M/W, water polo M/W, weight lifting M(c)/W(c).

Campus security: 24-hour emergency response devices and patrols, late-night transport/escort service, controlled dormitory access.

Student services: health clinic.

COSTS & FINANCIAL AID

Costs (2018–19) *Tuition:* state resident $13,896 full-time, $579 per credit hour part-time; nonresident $26,568 full-time, $1107 per credit hour part-time. Full-time tuition and fees vary according to course load and program. Part-time tuition and fees vary according to program. *Required fees:* $1614 full-time, $48 per credit hour part-time. *Room and board:* $10,598; room only: $6312. Room and board charges vary according to board plan. *Payment plan:* installment. *Waivers:* senior citizens and employees or children of employees.

Financial Aid Of all full-time matriculated undergraduates who enrolled in 2016, 902 applied for aid, 816 were judged to have need, 71 had their need fully met. 177 Federal Work-Study jobs (averaging $1260). In 2016, 66 non-need-based awards were made. *Average percent of need met:* 61. *Average financial aid package:* $14,736. *Average need-based loan:* $3920. *Average need-based gift aid:* $5648. *Average non-need-based aid:* $4740. *Average indebtedness upon graduation:* $29,988.

APPLYING

Standardized Tests *Required for some:* SAT (for admission), SAT or ACT (for admission).

Options: electronic application.

Application fee: $47.

Required: high school transcript. *Required for some:* essay or personal statement, 2 letters of recommendation, interview. *Recommended:* minimum 3.0 GPA, 2 letters of recommendation, interview.

Application deadlines: rolling (freshmen), rolling (transfers).

Notification: continuous (freshmen), continuous (transfers).

CONTACT

Jessica Van Deren, Director of Admissions, Vermont Technical College, PO Box 500, Randolph Center, VT 05061. *Phone:* 802-728-1244. *Toll-free phone:* 800-442-VTC1. *Fax:* 802-728-1390. *E-mail:* admissions@ vtc.edu.

VIRGINIA

American National University

Danville, Virginia

http://www.an.edu/

CONTACT

Admissions Office, American National University, 336 Old Riverside Drive, Danville, VA 24541. *Phone:* 434-793-6822. *Toll-free phone:* 888-9-JOBREADY.

American National University
Harrisonburg, Virginia
http://www.an.edu/

CONTACT
Jack Evey, Campus Director, American National University, 1515 Country Club Road, Harrisonburg, VA 22802. *Phone:* 540-432-0943. *Toll-free phone:* 888-9-JOBREADY.

American National University
Lynchburg, Virginia
http://www.an.edu/

CONTACT
Admissions Representative, American National University, 104 Candlewood Court, Lynchburg, VA 24502. *Phone:* 804-239-3500. *Toll-free phone:* 888-9-JOBREADY.

American National University
Salem, Virginia
http://www.an.edu/

CONTACT
Director of Admissions, American National University, 1813 East Main Street, Salem, VA 24153. *Phone:* 540-986-1800. *Toll-free phone:* 888-9-JOBREADY. *Fax:* 540-444-4198.

Argosy University, Northern Virginia
Arlington, Virginia
http://www.argosy.edu/locations/northern-virginia/

CONTACT
Argosy University, Northern Virginia, 1550 Wilson Boulevard, Suite 600, Arlington, VA 22209. *Phone:* 703-526-5800. *Toll-free phone:* 866-703-2777.

The Art Institute of Virginia Beach, a branch of The Art Institute of Atlanta
Virginia Beach, Virginia
http://www.artinstitutes.edu/virginia-beach/

CONTACT
The Art Institute of Virginia Beach, a branch of The Art Institute of Atlanta, Two Columbus Center, 4500 Main Street, Suite 100, Virginia Beach, VA 23462. *Phone:* 757-493-6700. *Toll-free phone:* 877-437-4428.

The Art Institute of Washington, a branch of The Art Institute of Atlanta
Arlington, Virginia
http://www.artinstitutes.edu/arlington/

CONTACT
The Art Institute of Washington, a branch of The Art Institute of Atlanta, 1820 North Fort Meyer Drive, Arlington, VA 22209. *Phone:* 703-358-9550. *Toll-free phone:* 877-303-3771.

Averett University
Danville, Virginia
http://www.averett.edu/

- **Independent** comprehensive, founded 1859, affiliated with Baptist General Association of Virginia
- **Small-town** 185-acre campus with easy access to Greensboro, NC
- **Endowment** $26.8 million
- **Coed** 929 undergraduate students, 96% full-time, 45% women, 55% men
- **Moderately difficult** entrance level, 62% of applicants were admitted

UNDERGRAD STUDENTS
892 full-time, 37 part-time. Students come from 20 states and territories; 21 other countries; 39% are from out of state; 29% Black or African American, non-Hispanic/Latino; 5% Hispanic/Latino; 0.5% Asian, non-Hispanic/Latino; 0.3% Native Hawaiian or other Pacific Islander, non-Hispanic/Latino; 0.4% American Indian or Alaska Native, non-Hispanic/Latino; 2% Two or more races, non-Hispanic/Latino; 0.5% Race/ethnicity unknown; 6% international; 8% transferred in; 57% live on campus.

Freshmen:
Admission: 2,721 applied, 1,684 admitted, 281 enrolled. *Average high school GPA:* 3.2. *Test scores:* SAT evidence-based reading and writing scores over 500: 42%; SAT math scores over 500: 29%; ACT scores over 18: 68%; SAT evidence-based reading and writing scores over 600: 7%; SAT math scores over 600: 3%; ACT scores over 24: 17%; SAT evidence-based reading and writing scores over 700: 1%.
Retention: 62% of full-time freshmen returned.

FACULTY
Total: 115, 50% full-time, 44% with terminal degrees.
Student/faculty ratio: 12:1.

ACADEMICS
Calendar: semesters. *Degree:* bachelor's.

Special study options: academic remediation for entering students, accelerated degree program, adult/continuing education programs, advanced placement credit, cooperative education, distance learning, double majors, external degree program, honors programs, independent study, internships, off-campus study, part-time degree program, services for LD students, student-designed majors, study abroad, summer session for credit.

Computers: 150 computers/terminals and 25 ports are available on campus for general student use. Students can access the following: computer help desk, free student e-mail accounts, online (class) grades, online (class) registration, online (class) schedules. Campuswide network is available. 100% of college-owned or -operated housing units are wired for high-speed Internet access. Wireless service is available via entire campus.
Library: Mary B. Blount Library. *Books:* 88,079 (physical), 307,115 (digital/electronic); *Serial titles:* 2,490 (physical), 32,577 (digital/electronic); *Databases:* 93. Weekly public service hours: 81; students can reserve study rooms.

STUDENT LIFE
Housing options: on-campus residence required through junior year; coed, men-only, women-only. Campus housing is university owned. Freshman campus housing is guaranteed.

Activities and organizations: drama/theater group, student-run newspaper, choral group, Cougar Activities Board (CAB), Student Athletic Advisory Committee (SAAC), Student Government Association (SGA), IMPACT, Christian Student Union, national fraternities.

Athletics Member NCAA. All Division III. *Intercollegiate sports:* baseball M, basketball M/W, cheerleading M(c)/W(c), cross-country running M/W, equestrian sports M(c)/W(c), football M, golf M, lacrosse M/W, soccer M/W, softball W, tennis M/W, volleyball W, wrestling M. *Intramural sports:* soccer M/W, volleyball M/W.

Campus security: 24-hour emergency response devices and patrols, late-night transport/escort service, controlled dormitory access.
Student services: health clinic, personal/psychological counseling.

COSTS & FINANCIAL AID
Costs (2017–18) *Comprehensive fee:* $43,034 includes full-time tuition ($33,350) and room and board ($9684). Full-time tuition and fees vary according to class time, course load, degree level, location, and program. Part-time tuition: $1045 per credit. Part-time tuition and fees vary according to class time, course load, degree level, location, and program. *College room only:* $6184. Room and board charges vary according to board plan and housing facility. *Payment plan:* installment. *Waivers:* senior citizens and employees or children of employees.

Financial Aid Of all full-time matriculated undergraduates who enrolled in 2017, 805 applied for aid, 768 were judged to have need, 86 had their need fully met. 244 Federal Work-Study jobs (averaging $615). In 2017, 120 non-need-based awards were made. *Average percent of need met:* 72. *Average financial aid package:* $26,742. *Average need-based loan:*

$4503. *Average need-based gift aid:* $22,850. *Average non-need-based aid:* $15,702. *Average indebtedness upon graduation:* $35,373.

APPLYING

Standardized Tests *Required:* TOEFL for international students (for admission). *Required for some:* SAT or ACT (for admission).

Options: electronic application, deferred entrance.

Required: high school transcript, minimum 2.5 GPA. *Recommended:* essay or personal statement, 1 letter of recommendation, interview.

Application deadlines: 9/1 (freshmen), 8/15 (transfers).

Notification: continuous (freshmen), continuous (transfers).

CONTACT

Mr. Joel Nester, Director of Admissions and International Counselor, Averett University, 420 West Main Street, English Hall, Danville, VA 24541. *Phone:* 434-791-5663. *Toll-free phone:* 800-AVERETT. *E-mail:* joel.nester@averett.edu.

Bethel College

Hampton, Virginia

http://www.bcva.edu/

CONTACT

Ms. Nanette Bartholomew, Student Affairs, Bethel College, 1705 Todds Lane, Hampton, VA 23666. *Phone:* 757-826-1883 Ext. 215.

Bluefield College

Bluefield, Virginia

http://www.bluefield.edu/

- **Independent Southern Baptist** comprehensive, founded 1922
- **Small-town** 82-acre campus
- **Endowment** $6.7 million
- **Coed** 951 undergraduate students, 88% full-time, 53% women, 47% men

UNDERGRAD STUDENTS

833 full-time, 118 part-time. Students come from 33 states and territories; 28 other countries; 26% are from out of state; 23% Black or African American, non-Hispanic/Latino; 5% Hispanic/Latino; 0.2% Asian, non-Hispanic/Latino; 0.2% Native Hawaiian or other Pacific Islander, non-Hispanic/Latino; 5% Two or more races, non-Hispanic/Latino; 2% Race/ethnicity unknown; 4% international; 61% live on campus.

Freshmen:

Average high school GPA: 3.1. *Test scores:* SAT evidence-based reading and writing scores over 500: 31%; SAT math scores over 500: 35%; ACT scores over 18: 70%; SAT evidence-based reading and writing scores over 600: 8%; SAT math scores over 600: 8%; ACT scores over 24: 14%; ACT scores over 30: 2%.

Retention: 53% of full-time freshmen returned.

FACULTY

Total: 110, 39% full-time, 46% with terminal degrees.

Student/faculty ratio: 14:1.

ACADEMICS

Calendar: semesters. *Degrees:* bachelor's and master's.

Special study options: academic remediation for entering students, adult/continuing education programs, advanced placement credit, cooperative education, distance learning, double majors, honors programs, independent study, internships, off-campus study, part-time degree program, services for LD students, study abroad, summer session for credit.

Computers: 110 computers/terminals are available on campus for general student use. Students can access the following: campus intranet, free student e-mail accounts, online (class) grades, online (class) registration, online (class) schedules. Campuswide network is available. 100% of college-owned or -operated housing units are wired for high-speed Internet access. Wireless service is available via entire campus.

Library: Easley Library. *Books:* 44,352 (physical), 165,829 (digital/electronic); *Serial titles:* 7,976 (physical), 334 (digital/electronic); *Databases:* 72. Students can reserve study rooms.

STUDENT LIFE

Housing options: on-campus residence required through junior year; men-only, women-only. Campus housing is university owned. Freshman applicants given priority for college housing.

Activities and organizations: drama/theater group, student-run newspaper, choral group, Baptist Collegiate Ministries, Fellowship of Christian Athletes, Student Union Board, Student Government Association, Arts Club.

Athletics Member NAIA, NCCAA. *Intercollegiate sports:* baseball M(s), basketball M(s)/W(s), cheerleading M(s)/W(s), cross-country running M(s)/W(s), football M(s), golf M(s), skiing (cross-country) M(s)/W(s), soccer M(s)/W(s), softball W(s), tennis M(s)/W(s), volleyball M(s)/W(s), wrestling M(s). *Intramural sports:* baseball M, basketball M/W, football M/W, softball M/W, table tennis M/W, tennis M/W, volleyball M/W.

Campus security: controlled dormitory access, night security patrols.

Student services: personal/psychological counseling.

COSTS & FINANCIAL AID

Costs (2018–19) *Comprehensive fee:* $34,314 includes full-time tuition ($24,520), mandatory fees ($770), and room and board ($9024). Full-time tuition and fees vary according to course load and program. Part-time tuition: $970 per credit hour. Part-time tuition and fees vary according to course load and program. *Required fees:* $28 per credit hour part-time. *College room only:* $3770. Room and board charges vary according to housing facility. *Payment plan:* installment. *Waivers:* senior citizens and employees or children of employees.

Financial Aid Of all full-time matriculated undergraduates who enrolled in 2017, 748 applied for aid, 707 were judged to have need, 75 had their need fully met. 74 Federal Work-Study jobs (averaging $1038). 12 state and other part-time jobs (averaging $375). In 2017, 84 non-need-based awards were made. *Average percent of need met:* 66. *Average financial aid package:* $16,862. *Average need-based loan:* $4176. *Average need-based gift aid:* $13,152. *Average non-need-based aid:* $6244. *Average indebtedness upon graduation:* $33,772.

APPLYING

Standardized Tests *Required:* SAT or ACT (for admission).

Required: high school transcript, minimum 2.0 GPA. *Required for some:* essay or personal statement.

CONTACT

Mr. Matthew Hamilton, Director of Traditional Admissions, Bluefield College, 3000 College Avenue, Bluefield, VA 24605-1799. *Phone:* 276-326-4602. *Toll-free phone:* 800-872-0175. *Fax:* 276-326-4395. *E-mail:* mrh263676@bluefield.edu.

Bon Secours Memorial College of Nursing

Richmond, Virginia

http://www.bsmcon.edu/

CONTACT

Bon Secours Memorial College of Nursing, 8550 Magellan Parkway, Suite 1100, Richmond, VA 23227-1149. *Toll-free phone:* 866-238-7414.

Bridgewater College

Bridgewater, Virginia

http://www.bridgewater.edu/

- **Independent** comprehensive, founded 1880, affiliated with Church of the Brethren
- **Small-town** 300-acre campus
- **Endowment** $92.2 million
- **Coed** 1,882 undergraduate students, 100% full-time, 54% women, 46% men
- **Moderately difficult** entrance level, 52% of applicants were admitted

UNDERGRAD STUDENTS

1,876 full-time, 6 part-time. Students come from 29 states and territories; 20 other countries; 26% are from out of state; 16% Black or African American, non-Hispanic/Latino; 7% Hispanic/Latino; 1% Asian, non-Hispanic/Latino; 0.1% Native Hawaiian or other Pacific Islander, non-Hispanic/Latino; 0.3% American Indian or Alaska Native, non-

Hispanic/Latino; 5% Two or more races, non-Hispanic/Latino; 4% Race/ethnicity unknown; 1% international; 3% transferred in; 81% live on campus.

Freshmen:
Admission: 7,241 applied, 3,764 admitted, 534 enrolled. *Average high school GPA:* 3.4. *Test scores:* SAT evidence-based reading and writing scores over 500: 77%; SAT math scores over 500: 66%; ACT scores over 18: 84%; SAT evidence-based reading and writing scores over 600: 27%; SAT math scores over 600: 15%; ACT scores over 24: 36%; SAT evidence-based reading and writing scores over 700: 3%; SAT math scores over 700: 2%; ACT scores over 30: 7%.
Retention: 75% of full-time freshmen returned.

FACULTY
Total: 167, 72% full-time, 72% with terminal degrees.
Student/faculty ratio: 14:1.

ACADEMICS
Calendar: semesters. *Degrees:* bachelor's and master's.
Special study options: adult/continuing education programs, advanced placement credit, distance learning, double majors, honors programs, independent study, internships, off-campus study, part-time degree program, services for LD students, study abroad, summer session for credit.
Unusual degree programs: 3-2 engineering with Virginia Polytechnic Institute and State University; athletic training.
Computers: 158 computers/terminals and 700 ports are available on campus for general student use. Students can access the following: campus intranet, computer help desk, free student e-mail accounts, online (class) grades, online (class) registration, online (class) schedules, course management system, campus bulletin board system. Campuswide network is available. 100% of college-owned or -operated housing units are wired for high-speed Internet access. Wireless service is available via entire campus.
Library: Alexander Mack Memorial Library. *Books:* 92,369 (physical), 23,752 (digital/electronic); *Serial titles:* 15,720 (physical); *Databases:* 111.

STUDENT LIFE
Housing options: on-campus residence required through junior year; coed, men-only, women-only, special housing for students with disabilities. Campus housing is university owned.
Activities and organizations: drama/theater group, student-run newspaper, radio station, choral group, Eagle Productions (program board), Physics Club, Active Minds, BC Allies.
Athletics Member NCAA. All Division III. *Intercollegiate sports:* baseball M, basketball M/W, cheerleading M(c)/W(c), cross-country running M/W, equestrian sports M(c)/W(c), field hockey W, football M, golf M/W, lacrosse M/W, soccer M/W, softball W, swimming and diving M/W, tennis M/W, track and field M/W, volleyball W, wrestling M(c). *Intramural sports:* badminton M/W, basketball M/W, bowling M/W, football M/W, golf M/W, racquetball M/W, sand volleyball M/W, soccer M/W, softball M/W, table tennis M/W, tennis M/W, ultimate Frisbee M/W, volleyball M/W.
Campus security: 24-hour emergency response devices and patrols, controlled dormitory access, emergency alert system.
Student services: health clinic, personal/psychological counseling.

COSTS & FINANCIAL AID
Costs (2018–19) *Comprehensive fee:* $47,880 includes full-time tuition ($34,300), mandatory fees ($860), and room and board ($12,720). Part-time tuition: $1190 per credit hour. *Required fees:* $40 per term part-time.
Room and board: Room and board charges vary according to housing facility. *Payment plan:* installment. *Waivers:* employees or children of employees.
Financial Aid Of all full-time matriculated undergraduates who enrolled in 2017, 1,665 applied for aid, 1,533 were judged to have need, 412 had their need fully met. 405 Federal Work-Study jobs (averaging $1440). 100 state and other part-time jobs (averaging $1245). In 2017, 337 non-need-based awards were made. *Average percent of need met:* 85. *Average financial aid package:* $31,101. *Average need-based loan:* $4694. *Average need-based gift aid:* $27,289. *Average non-need-based aid:* $20,900. *Average indebtedness upon graduation:* $33,567.

APPLYING
Standardized Tests *Required:* SAT or ACT (for admission).
Options: electronic application, deferred entrance.
Required: high school transcript. *Recommended:* minimum 3.0 GPA.
Application deadlines: 5/1 (freshmen), 5/1 (transfers).
Notification: continuous (freshmen), continuous (transfers).
CONTACT
Mr. Jarret L. Smith, Director of Admissions, Bridgewater College, 402 East College Street, Bridgewater, VA 22812. *Phone:* 540-828-5469. *Toll-free phone:* 800-759-8328. *Fax:* 540-828-5481. *E-mail:* admissions@bridgewater.edu.

Bryant & Stratton College–Hampton Campus
Hampton, Virginia
http://www.bryantstratton.edu/

CONTACT
Bryant & Stratton College–Hampton Campus, 4410 East Claiborne Square, Suite 233, Hampton, VA 23666.

Bryant & Stratton College–Richmond Campus
Richmond, Virginia
http://www.bryantstratton.edu/

CONTACT
Mr. David K. Mayle, Director of Admissions, Bryant & Stratton College–Richmond Campus, 8141 Hull Street Road, Richmond, VA 23235-6411. *Phone:* 804-745-2444. *Fax:* 804-745-6884. *E-mail:* tlawson@bryanstratton.edu.

Bryant & Stratton College–Virginia Beach Campus
Virginia Beach, Virginia
http://www.bryantstratton.edu/

CONTACT
Bryant & Stratton College–Virginia Beach Campus, 301 Centre Pointe Drive, Virginia Beach, VA 23462. *Phone:* 757-499-7900 Ext. 173.

Centura College
Virginia Beach, Virginia
http://www.centuracollege.edu/

CONTACT
Admissions Office, Centura College, 2697 Dean Drive, Suite 100, Virginia Beach, VA 23452. *Phone:* 757-340-2121. *Toll-free phone:* 877-575-5627. *Fax:* 757-340-9704.

Chamberlain College of Nursing
Arlington, Virginia
http://www.chamberlain.edu/
- Proprietary 4-year
- Coed

FACULTY
Student/faculty ratio: 11:1.

ACADEMICS
Calendar: semesters. *Degree:* bachelor's.

STUDENT LIFE
Housing options: college housing not available.

COSTS
Costs (2017–18) *Tuition:* $18,900 full-time. *Required fees:* $600 full-time.

APPLYING
Standardized Tests *Required:* SAT or ACT (for admission).

Options: deferred entrance.

Application fee: $95.

CONTACT
Admissions, Chamberlain College of Nursing, 2450 Crystal Drive, Suite 319, Arlington, VA 22202. *Phone:* 703-416-7300. *Toll-free phone:* 877-751-5783.

Christendom College
Front Royal, Virginia
http://www.christendom.edu/
- **Independent Roman Catholic** comprehensive, founded 1977
- **Rural** 200-acre campus with easy access to Washington, DC
- **Endowment** $15.8 million
- **Coed** 493 undergraduate students, 99% full-time, 57% women, 43% men
- **Moderately difficult** entrance level, 89% of applicants were admitted

UNDERGRAD STUDENTS
489 full-time, 4 part-time. Students come from 45 states and territories; 4 other countries; 75% are from out of state; 0.2% Black or African American, non-Hispanic/Latino; 4% Hispanic/Latino; 2% Asian, non-Hispanic/Latino; 90% Race/ethnicity unknown; 3% international; 3% transferred in; 90% live on campus.

Freshmen:
Admission: 322 applied, 286 admitted, 133 enrolled. *Average high school GPA:* 3.6. *Test scores:* SAT evidence-based reading and writing scores over 500: 93%; SAT math scores over 500: 90%; ACT scores over 18: 98%; SAT evidence-based reading and writing scores over 600: 78%; SAT math scores over 600: 51%; ACT scores over 24: 66%; SAT evidence-based reading and writing scores over 700: 37%; SAT math scores over 700: 15%; ACT scores over 30: 28%.

Retention: 85% of full-time freshmen returned.

FACULTY
Total: 50, 50% full-time, 74% with terminal degrees.

Student/faculty ratio: 15:1.

ACADEMICS
Calendar: semesters. *Degrees:* associate, bachelor's, and master's.

Special study options: academic remediation for entering students, accelerated degree program, advanced placement credit, cooperative education, double majors, independent study, internships, services for LD students, study abroad, summer session for credit.

Computers: Students can access the following: campus intranet, computer help desk, free student e-mail accounts. Campuswide network is available. Wireless service is available via classrooms, computer centers, computer labs, learning centers, libraries, student centers.

Library: St. John the Evangelist Library. *Books:* 100,000 (physical), 1,000 (digital/electronic); *Serial titles:* 250 (physical), 1,000 (digital/electronic); *Databases:* 45. Weekly public service hours: 97.

STUDENT LIFE
Housing options: on-campus residence required through senior year; men-only, women-only. Campus housing is university owned. Freshman campus housing is guaranteed.

Activities and organizations: drama/theater group, student-run newspaper, choral group, drama, choir, Chester-Belloc Debate Society, Swing Dance Club, Shields of Rose Pro-life group.

Athletics Member USCAA. *Intercollegiate sports:* baseball M, basketball M/W, cross-country running M/W, rugby M, soccer M/W, softball W, volleyball W. *Intramural sports:* basketball M/W, equestrian sports M/W, football M/W, racquetball M/W, soccer M/W, swimming and diving M/W, table tennis M/W, tennis M/W, ultimate Frisbee M/W, volleyball M/W.

Campus security: 24-hour emergency response devices, late-night transport/escort service, night patrols by trained security personnel.

Student services: health clinic, personal/psychological counseling.

COSTS & FINANCIAL AID
Costs (2018–19) *Comprehensive fee:* $36,640 includes full-time tuition ($25,460), mandatory fees ($900), and room and board ($10,280).

Payment plan: installment. *Waivers:* children of alumni and employees or children of employees.

Financial Aid Of all full-time matriculated undergraduates who enrolled in 2016, 287 applied for aid, 258 were judged to have need. 150 state and other part-time jobs (averaging $2168). In 2016, 92 non-need-based awards were made. *Average percent of need met:* 75. *Average financial aid package:* $19,472. *Average need-based loan:* $7343. *Average need-based gift aid:* $12,511. *Average non-need-based aid:* $10,452. *Average indebtedness upon graduation:* $27,005.

APPLYING
Standardized Tests *Required:* SAT or ACT (for admission).

Options: electronic application, early admission, early action.

Required: essay or personal statement, high school transcript, 1 letter of recommendation. *Required for some:* 2 letters of recommendation, two writing samples for those with SAT scores lower than 1000 or ACT scores lower than 21. *Recommended:* minimum 2.0 GPA, interview.

Application deadlines: 3/1 (freshmen), 3/1 (transfers), 12/1 (early action).

Notification: 4/1 (freshmen), continuous until 4/1 (transfers), 12/15 (early action).

CONTACT
Mr. Sam Phillips, Director of Admissions, Christendom College, 134 Christendom Drive, Front Royal, VA 22630. *Phone:* 800-877-5456 Ext. 1290. *Toll-free phone:* 800-877-5456. *E-mail:* sam.phillips@christendom.edu.

Christopher Newport University
Newport News, Virginia
http://www.cnu.edu/
- **State-supported** comprehensive, founded 1960
- **Suburban** 260-acre campus with easy access to Virginia Beach
- **Endowment** $28.6 million
- **Coed** 4,954 undergraduate students, 98% full-time, 56% women, 44% men
- **Moderately difficult** entrance level, 72% of applicants were admitted

UNDERGRAD STUDENTS
4,867 full-time, 87 part-time. Students come from 33 states and territories; 34 other countries; 8% are from out of state; 7% Black or African American, non-Hispanic/Latino; 5% Hispanic/Latino; 3% Asian, non-Hispanic/Latino; 0.1% Native Hawaiian or other Pacific Islander, non-Hispanic/Latino; 0.2% American Indian or Alaska Native, non-Hispanic/Latino; 5% Two or more races, non-Hispanic/Latino; 4% Race/ethnicity unknown; 0.3% international; 3% transferred in; 78% live on campus.

Freshmen:
Admission: 6,948 applied, 5,030 admitted, 1,293 enrolled. *Average high school GPA:* 3.8. *Test scores:* SAT evidence-based reading and writing scores over 500: 99%; SAT math scores over 500: 96%; ACT scores over 18: 99%; SAT evidence-based reading and writing scores over 600: 67%; SAT math scores over 600: 49%; ACT scores over 24: 75%; SAT evidence-based reading and writing scores over 700: 11%; SAT math scores over 700: 5%; ACT scores over 30: 15%.

Retention: 88% of full-time freshmen returned.

FACULTY
Total: 459, 61% full-time, 66% with terminal degrees.

Student/faculty ratio: 15:1.

ACADEMICS
Calendar: semesters. *Degrees:* bachelor's and master's.

Special study options: advanced placement credit, double majors, honors programs, independent study, internships, off-campus study, student-designed majors, study abroad, summer session for credit. *ROTC:* Army (b).

Computers: 540 computers/terminals and 1,000 ports are available on campus for general student use. Students can access the following: campus intranet, computer help desk, free student e-mail accounts, online (class) grades, online (class) registration, online (class) schedules. Campuswide network is available. 100% of college-owned or -operated

housing units are wired for high-speed Internet access. Wireless service is available via entire campus.

Library: Paul and Rosemary Trible Library. *Books:* 229,577 (physical), 578,114 (digital/electronic); *Serial titles:* 745 (physical), 65,202 (digital/electronic); *Databases:* 282. Weekly public service hours: 101; study areas open 24 hours, 5–7 days a week; students can reserve study rooms.

STUDENT LIFE

Housing options: on-campus residence required through junior year; coed. Campus housing is university owned. Freshman campus housing is guaranteed.

Activities and organizations: drama/theater group, student-run newspaper, radio and television station, choral group, marching band, Intervarsity Christian Fellowship, Alpha Delta Pi, Delta Gamma, Gamma Phi Beta, Alpha Phi, national fraternities, national sororities.

Athletics Member NCAA. All Division III. *Intercollegiate sports:* baseball M, basketball M/W, cheerleading M(c)/W(c), crew M(c)/W(c), cross-country running M/W, equestrian sports M(c)/W(c), field hockey W, football M, golf M/W, gymnastics M(c)/W(c), ice hockey M(c), lacrosse M/W, rowing M(c)/W(c), rugby M(c), sailing M(c)/W(c), skiing (cross-country) M(c)/W(c), skiing (downhill) M(c)/W(c), soccer M/W, softball W, swimming and diving M(c)/W(c), table tennis M(c)/W(c), tennis M/W, track and field M/W, ultimate Frisbee M(c)/W(c), volleyball M(c)/W. *Intramural sports:* basketball M/W, football M/W, sand volleyball M/W, soccer M/W, softball M/W, ultimate Frisbee M/W, volleyball M/W.

Campus security: 24-hour emergency response devices and patrols, late-night transport/escort service, controlled dormitory access, campus-based university police, Emergency Notification System, crime prevention programs.

Student services: health clinic, personal/psychological counseling.

COSTS & FINANCIAL AID

Costs (2017–18) *Tuition:* state resident $8236 full-time, $343 per credit hour part-time; nonresident $20,032 full-time, $834 per credit hour part-time. Full-time tuition and fees vary according to course load. Part-time tuition and fees vary according to course load. *Required fees:* $5418 full-time, $225 per credit hour part-time. *Room and board:* $11,224; room only: $6904. Room and board charges vary according to board plan and housing facility. *Payment plan:* installment. *Waivers:* senior citizens and employees or children of employees.

Financial Aid Of all full-time matriculated undergraduates who enrolled in 2017, 3,208 applied for aid, 2,144 were judged to have need, 423 had their need fully met. 82 Federal Work-Study jobs (averaging $1372). 1,576 state and other part-time jobs (averaging $1867). In 2017, 733 non-need-based awards were made. *Average percent of need met:* 65. *Average financial aid package:* $9690. *Average need-based loan:* $4335. *Average need-based gift aid:* $6982. *Average non-need-based aid:* $2979. *Average indebtedness upon graduation:* $32,994.

APPLYING

Standardized Tests *Required for some:* SAT or ACT (for admission).

Options: electronic application, early admission, early decision, early action, deferred entrance.

Application fee: $65.

Required: essay or personal statement, high school transcript. *Required for some:* interview. *Recommended:* minimum 3.5 GPA, 2 letters of recommendation.

Application deadlines: 2/1 (freshmen), 3/1 (transfers), 12/1 (early action).

Early decision deadline: 11/15.

Notification: 3/15 (freshmen), 4/15 (transfers), 12/15 (early decision), 1/15 (early action).

CONTACT

Mr. Rob J. Lange III, Dean of Admission, Christopher Newport University, Office of Admission, 1 Avenue of the Arts, Newport News, VA 23606-3072. *Phone:* 757-594-7015. *Toll-free phone:* 800-333-4268. *Fax:* 757-594-7333. *E-mail:* admit@cnu.edu.

The College of William and Mary
Williamsburg, Virginia
http://www.wm.edu/

- **State-supported** university, founded 1693
- **Small-town** 1200-acre campus with easy access to Richmond
- **Endowment** $874.1 million
- **Coed** 6,285 undergraduate students, 99% full-time, 58% women, 42% men
- **Most difficult** entrance level, 36% of applicants were admitted

UNDERGRAD STUDENTS

6,199 full-time, 86 part-time. Students come from 54 states and territories; 81 other countries; 30% are from out of state; 7% Black or African American, non-Hispanic/Latino; 9% Hispanic/Latino; 8% Asian, non-Hispanic/Latino; 0.2% American Indian or Alaska Native, non-Hispanic/Latino; 5% Two or more races, non-Hispanic/Latino; 5% Race/ethnicity unknown; 6% international; 3% transferred in; 72% live on campus.

Freshmen:
Admission: 14,921 applied, 5,359 admitted, 1,531 enrolled. *Average high school GPA:* 4.2. *Test scores:* SAT evidence-based reading and writing scores over 500: 100%; SAT math scores over 500: 100%; ACT scores over 18: 100%; SAT evidence-based reading and writing scores over 600: 93%; SAT math scores over 600: 87%; ACT scores over 24: 97%; SAT evidence-based reading and writing scores over 700: 55%; SAT math scores over 700: 47%; ACT scores over 30: 74%.

Retention: 95% of full-time freshmen returned.

ACADEMICS

Calendar: semesters. *Degrees:* certificates, bachelor's, master's, doctoral, post-master's, and postbachelor's certificates.

Special study options: accelerated degree program, advanced placement credit, distance learning, double majors, English as a second language, honors programs, independent study, internships, off-campus study, part-time degree program, services for LD students, student-designed majors, study abroad, summer session for credit. *ROTC:* Army (b).

Unusual degree programs: 3-2 elementary education, secondary education, special education, chemistry.

Computers: 400 computers/terminals and 8,000 ports are available on campus for general student use. Students can access the following: campus intranet, computer help desk, free student e-mail accounts, online (class) grades, online (class) registration, online (class) schedules. Campuswide network is available. 100% of college-owned or -operated housing units are wired for high-speed Internet access. Wireless service is available via entire campus.

Library: Earl Gregg Swem Library plus 7 others. *Books:* 1.3 million (physical), 2.5 million (digital/electronic); *Serial titles:* 40,439 (physical), 132,861 (digital/electronic); *Databases:* 533. Weekly public service hours: 110; study areas open 24 hours, 5–7 days a week; students can reserve study rooms.

STUDENT LIFE

Housing options: on-campus residence required for freshman year; coed, special housing for students with disabilities. Campus housing is university owned and leased by the school. Freshman campus housing is guaranteed.

Activities and organizations: drama/theater group, student-run newspaper, radio and television station, choral group, Alma Mater Productions, Student Assembly, Residence Hall Association, Alpha Phi Omega, International Relations Club, national fraternities, national sororities.

Athletics Member NCAA. All Division I except football (Division I-AA). *Intercollegiate sports:* baseball M(s), basketball M(s)/W(s), cross-country running M(s)/W(s), field hockey W(s), golf M(s)/W(s), gymnastics M(s)/W(s), lacrosse W(s), soccer M(s)/W(s), swimming and diving M/W, tennis M(s)/W(s), track and field M(s)/W(s), volleyball W(s). *Intramural sports:* badminton M(c)/W(c), baseball M(c), basketball M/W, bowling M/W, cheerleading M(c)/W(c), crew M(c)/W(c), cross-country running M(c)/W(c), equestrian sports M(c)/W(c), fencing M(c)/W(c), field hockey M(c)/W(c), football M/W, golf M(c)/W(c), gymnastics M(c)/W(c), ice hockey M(c), lacrosse M(c)/W(c), racquetball M(c)/W(c), rock climbing M(c)/W(c), rugby M(c)/W(c), sailing M(c)/W(c), soccer M/W, softball M/W, swimming and diving M(c)/W(c), table tennis M(c)/W(c), tennis

M(c)/W(c), ultimate Frisbee M(c)/W(c), volleyball M/W, water polo M(c)/W(c), weight lifting M/W, wrestling M(c).

Campus security: 24-hour emergency response devices and patrols, late-night transport/escort service, controlled dormitory access, state-certified law enforcement officers.

Student services: health clinic, personal/psychological counseling, legal services.

COSTS & FINANCIAL AID
Costs (2017–18) *Tuition:* state resident $16,370 full-time, $420 per credit hour part-time; nonresident $37,425 full-time, $1195 per credit hour part-time. *Required fees:* $5674 full-time. *Room and board:* $11,799; room only: $7183. Room and board charges vary according to board plan and housing facility. *Payment plan:* installment. *Waivers:* senior citizens and employees or children of employees.

Financial Aid Of all full-time matriculated undergraduates who enrolled in 2016, 3,098 applied for aid, 2,172 were judged to have need, 500 had their need fully met. 385 Federal Work-Study jobs (averaging $1027). In 2016, 401 non-need-based awards were made. *Average percent of need met:* 80. *Average financial aid package:* $22,087. *Average need-based loan:* $3838. *Average need-based gift aid:* $16,295. *Average non-need-based aid:* $6127. *Average indebtedness upon graduation:* $24,072.

APPLYING
Standardized Tests *Required:* SAT or ACT (for admission).
Options: electronic application, early admission, early decision, deferred entrance.
Application fee: $75.
Required: essay or personal statement, high school transcript, 1 letter of recommendation. *Recommended:* 2 letters of recommendation.
Application deadlines: 1/1 (freshmen), 3/1 (transfers).
Early decision deadline: 11/1.
Notification: 4/1 (freshmen), 5/1 (transfers), 12/1 (early decision).

CONTACT
Ms. David Trott, Associate Dean of Admission, The College of William and Mary, PO Box 8795, Williamsburg, VA 23187-8795. *Phone:* 757-221-3059. *Fax:* 757-221-1242. *E-mail:* admission@wm.edu.

Culinary Institute of Virginia
Norfolk, Virginia
http://www.chefva.com/

CONTACT
Director of Admissions, Culinary Institute of Virginia, 2428 Almeda Avenue, Suite 316, Norfolk, VA 23513. *Phone:* 757-858-2433. *Toll-free phone:* 866-619-CHEF. *E-mail:* hsadmissions@chefva.com.

DeVry University–Arlington Campus
Arlington, Virginia
http://www.devry.edu/

- **Proprietary** comprehensive, founded 2001, part of DeVry University
- **Coed**
- **Minimally difficult** entrance level

FACULTY
Student/faculty ratio: 17:1.

ACADEMICS
Calendar: semesters. *Degrees:* associate, bachelor's, master's, and postbachelor's certificates.
Library: Learning Resource Center.

STUDENT LIFE
Housing options: college housing not available.

COSTS & FINANCIAL AID
Costs (2017–18) *Tuition:* $14,588 full-time. *Required fees:* $500 full-time.

Financial Aid Of all full-time matriculated undergraduates who enrolled in 2007, 175 applied for aid, 164 were judged to have need, 9 had their need fully met. In 2007, 21 non-need-based awards were made. *Average percent of need met:* 38. *Average financial aid package:* $11,581.

Average need-based loan: $7979. *Average need-based gift aid:* $5610. *Average non-need-based aid:* $18,172. *Average indebtedness upon graduation:* $12,479.

APPLYING
Options: deferred entrance.
Application fee: $30.
Required: high school transcript, interview.

CONTACT
DeVry University–Arlington Campus, 2450 Crystal Drive, Arlington, VA 22202. *Phone:* 703-414-4000. *Toll-free phone:* 866-338-7934.

DeVry University–Chesapeake Campus
Chesapeake, Virginia
http://www.devry.edu/

CONTACT
Admissions Office, DeVry University–Chesapeake Campus, 1317 Executive Boulevard, Suite 100, Chesapeake, VA 23320-3671. *Phone:* 757-382-5680. *Toll-free phone:* 866-338-7934.

Eastern Mennonite University
Harrisonburg, Virginia
http://www.emu.edu/

- **Independent Mennonite** comprehensive, founded 1917
- **Small-town** 93-acre campus
- **Endowment** $24.6 million
- **Coed** 1,098 undergraduate students, 86% full-time, 63% women, 37% men
- **Moderately difficult** entrance level, 54% of applicants were admitted

UNDERGRAD STUDENTS
942 full-time, 156 part-time. Students come from 28 states and territories; 33 other countries; 34% are from out of state; 9% Black or African American, non-Hispanic/Latino; 7% Hispanic/Latino; 2% Asian, non-Hispanic/Latino; 0.1% Native Hawaiian or other Pacific Islander, non-Hispanic/Latino; 0.5% American Indian or Alaska Native, non-Hispanic/Latino; 3% Two or more races, non-Hispanic/Latino; 4% Race/ethnicity unknown; 4% international; 9% transferred in; 59% live on campus.

Freshmen:
Admission: 1,232 applied, 662 admitted, 189 enrolled. *Average high school GPA:* 3.5. *Test scores:* SAT evidence-based reading and writing scores over 500: 76%; SAT math scores over 500: 72%; ACT scores over 18: 91%; SAT evidence-based reading and writing scores over 600: 25%; SAT math scores over 600: 22%; ACT scores over 24: 51%; SAT evidence-based reading and writing scores over 700: 5%; SAT math scores over 700: 5%; ACT scores over 30: 17%.
Retention: 79% of full-time freshmen returned.

FACULTY
Total: 190, 60% full-time.
Student/faculty ratio: 9:1.

ACADEMICS
Calendar: semesters. *Degrees:* certificates, associate, bachelor's, master's, and postbachelor's certificates.

Special study options: adult/continuing education programs, advanced placement credit, distance learning, double majors, English as a second language, honors programs, independent study, internships, off-campus study, part-time degree program, services for LD students, study abroad, summer session for credit.

Unusual degree programs: 3-2 engineering with The Catholic University of America.

Computers: 154 computers/terminals are available on campus for general student use. Students can access the following: campus intranet, computer help desk, free student e-mail accounts, online (class) grades, online (class) registration, online (class) schedules. Campuswide network is available. 98% of college-owned or -operated housing units are wired for

high-speed Internet access. Wireless service is available via classrooms, dorm rooms, learning centers, libraries, student centers.
Library: Sadie Hartzler Library. *Books:* 166,455 (physical), 179,434 (digital/electronic); *Serial titles:* 69,668 (physical), 34,489 (digital/electronic); *Databases:* 94. Weekly public service hours: 92.

STUDENT LIFE
Housing options: on-campus residence required through junior year; coed, cooperative, special housing for students with disabilities. Campus housing is university owned. Freshman campus housing is guaranteed.

Activities and organizations: drama/theater group, student-run newspaper, choral group, Young People's Christian Association, Student Government Association, Student Education Association, Creation Care Council, Black Student Union.

Athletics Member NCAA. All Division III. *Intercollegiate sports:* baseball M, basketball M/W, cross-country running M/W, field hockey W, golf M/W, soccer M/W, softball W, track and field M/W, volleyball M/W. *Intramural sports:* basketball M/W, football M/W, golf M/W, lacrosse M(c), rock climbing M/W, soccer M/W, softball M/W, table tennis M/W, tennis M/W, volleyball M/W.

Campus security: 24-hour emergency response devices, controlled dormitory access, night watchman.

Student services: health clinic, personal/psychological counseling.

COSTS & FINANCIAL AID
Costs (2018–19) *Comprehensive fee:* $48,260 includes full-time tuition ($36,760), mandatory fees ($340), and room and board ($11,160). Part-time tuition: $1400 per credit hour. Part-time tuition and fees vary according to course load. *Room and board:* Room and board charges vary according to board plan and housing facility. *Payment plan:* installment. *Waivers:* employees or children of employees.

Financial Aid Of all full-time matriculated undergraduates who enrolled in 2016, 840 applied for aid, 772 were judged to have need, 133 had their need fully met. 316 Federal Work-Study jobs (averaging $1266). 49 state and other part-time jobs (averaging $1453). In 2016, 168 non-need-based awards were made. *Average percent of need met:* 75. *Average financial aid package:* $31,315. *Average need-based loan:* $8346. *Average need-based gift aid:* $19,417. *Average non-need-based aid:* $15,317. *Average indebtedness upon graduation:* $39,845.

APPLYING
Standardized Tests *Required:* SAT or ACT (for admission).

Options: electronic application, deferred entrance.

Application fee: $25.

Required: high school transcript, minimum 2.2 GPA, Community Lifestyle Commitment. *Required for some:* 2 letters of recommendation. *Recommended:* interview.

Application deadlines: rolling (freshmen), rolling (transfers).

Notification: continuous (freshmen), continuous (transfers).

CONTACT
Matthew Ruth, Director of Admissions, Eastern Mennonite University, 1200 Park Road, Harrisonburg, VA 22802. *Phone:* 540-432-4118. *Toll-free phone:* 800-368-2665. *Fax:* 540-432-4444. *E-mail:* admiss@emu.edu.

ECPI University
Virginia Beach, Virginia
http://www.ecpi.edu/

- **Proprietary** comprehensive, founded 1966
- **Suburban** 8-acre campus
- **Coed** 11,745 undergraduate students, 98% full-time, 56% women, 44% men
- **Moderately difficult** entrance level, 84% of applicants were admitted

UNDERGRAD STUDENTS
11,512 full-time, 233 part-time. Students come from 52 states and territories; 4 other countries; 8% are from out of state; 42% Black or African American, non-Hispanic/Latino; 9% Hispanic/Latino; 3% Asian, non-Hispanic/Latino; 0.6% Native Hawaiian or other Pacific Islander, non-Hispanic/Latino; 1% American Indian or Alaska Native, non-Hispanic/Latino; 3% Two or more races, non-Hispanic/Latino; 0.6% Race/ethnicity unknown; 17% transferred in.

Freshmen:
Admission: 4,176 applied, 3,510 admitted, 1,309 enrolled.
Retention: 53% of full-time freshmen returned.

FACULTY
Total: 1,109, 39% full-time, 11% with terminal degrees.
Student/faculty ratio: 16:1.

ACADEMICS
Calendar: continuous. *Degrees:* certificates, diplomas, associate, bachelor's, and master's.

Special study options: academic remediation for entering students, accelerated degree program, adult/continuing education programs, advanced placement credit, cooperative education, distance learning, double majors, independent study, internships, off-campus study, part-time degree program, services for LD students, study abroad, summer session for credit.

Computers: 6,500 computers/terminals are available on campus for general student use. Students can access the following: campus intranet, computer help desk, free student e-mail accounts, online (class) grades, online (class) registration, online (class) schedules. Campuswide network is available. Wireless service is available via entire campus.
Library: ECPI-Virginia Beach Campus Library plus 14 others. *Books:* 25,945 (physical), 189,050 (digital/electronic); *Serial titles:* 118 (physical); *Databases:* 83. Weekly public service hours: 62; students can reserve study rooms.

STUDENT LIFE
Housing options: college housing not availableCampus housing is provided by a third party.

Activities and organizations: Student Electronic Technicians Association (SETA), Institute of Electrical and Electronic Engineers (IEEE), Phi Theta Kappa Honor Society, Information Technology Exchange (ITE), Medical Student Association, national fraternities, national sororities.

Campus security: building and parking lot security.

Student services: personal/psychological counseling.

COSTS & FINANCIAL AID
Costs (2018–19) *Tuition:* $14,996 full-time. Full-time tuition and fees vary according to course load, degree level, location, and program. No tuition increase for student's term of enrollment. *Required fees:* $445 full-time. *Payment plan:* installment. *Waivers:* employees or children of employees.

Financial Aid Of all full-time matriculated undergraduates who enrolled in 2015, 8,400 applied for aid.

APPLYING
Options: electronic application, deferred entrance.

Application fee: $45.

Required: high school transcript, interview, Entrance Exam. *Required for some:* minimum 2.5 GPA.

Notification: continuous (freshmen), continuous (transfers).

CONTACT
Mr. Chad Samuelson, University Director of Student Recruitment, ECPI University, 5555 Greenwich Road, Virginia Beach, VA 23462. *Phone:* 757-671-7171 Ext. 55839. *Toll-free phone:* 844-611-0766. *E-mail:* csamuelson@ecpi.edu.

Emory & Henry College
Emory, Virginia
http://www.ehc.edu/

- **Independent United Methodist** comprehensive, founded 1836
- **Rural** 330-acre campus
- **Endowment** $81.8 million
- **Coed** 1,000 undergraduate students, 97% full-time, 51% women, 49% men
- 72% of applicants were admitted

UNDERGRAD STUDENTS
966 full-time, 34 part-time. 58% are from out of state; 8% Black or African American, non-Hispanic/Latino; 4% Hispanic/Latino; 1% Asian, non-Hispanic/Latino; 0.2% Native Hawaiian or other Pacific Islander,

COLLEGES AT-A-GLANCE

non-Hispanic/Latino; 0.4% American Indian or Alaska Native, non-Hispanic/Latino; 2% Two or more races, non-Hispanic/Latino; 5% Race/ethnicity unknown; 0.4% international; 6% transferred in; 78% live on campus.

Freshmen:
Admission: 1,426 applied, 1,030 admitted, 253 enrolled. *Average high school GPA:* 3.6. *Test scores:* SAT evidence-based reading and writing scores over 500: 75%; SAT math scores over 500: 72%; ACT scores over 18: 88%; SAT evidence-based reading and writing scores over 600: 24%; SAT math scores over 600: 18%; ACT scores over 24: 35%; SAT evidence-based reading and writing scores over 700: 4%; SAT math scores over 700: 1%; ACT scores over 30: 7%.
Retention: 76% of full-time freshmen returned.

FACULTY
Total: 147, 65% full-time, 65% with terminal degrees.
Student/faculty ratio: 11:1.

ACADEMICS
Calendar: semesters. *Degrees:* bachelor's, master's, and doctoral.
Special study options: academic remediation for entering students, advanced placement credit, cooperative education, double majors, honors programs, independent study, internships, part-time degree program, services for LD students, student-designed majors, study abroad, summer session for credit.
Computers: 200 computers/terminals are available on campus for general student use. Students can access the following: campus intranet, computer help desk, free student e-mail accounts, online (class) grades, online (class) registration, online (class) schedules. Campuswide network is available. 100% of college-owned or -operated housing units are wired for high-speed Internet access. Wireless service is available via entire campus.
Library: Kelly Library plus 1 other. *Books:* 225,739 (physical), 126,654 (digital/electronic); *Serial titles:* 728 (physical), 113,345 (digital/electronic); *Databases:* 105. Weekly public service hours: 90; students can reserve study rooms.

STUDENT LIFE
Housing options: on-campus residence required through junior year; coed, men-only, women-only, special housing for students with disabilities. Campus housing is university owned. Freshman campus housing is guaranteed.
Activities and organizations: drama/theater group, student-run newspaper, radio and television station, choral group, marching band, E&H Outdoor Program, Alpha Psi Omega Honors Fraternity, Alpha Phi Omega Honors Fraternity, Blue Key/ Cardinal Key Honors Society, The Emory Activities Board.
Athletics Member NCAA. All Division III. *Intercollegiate sports:* baseball M, basketball M/W, cheerleading M(c)/W(c), cross-country running M/W, equestrian sports M/W, football M, golf M/W, soccer M/W, softball W, swimming and diving W, tennis M/W, volleyball W. *Intramural sports:* basketball M/W, football M/W, racquetball M/W, rugby M(c)/W(c), sand volleyball M/W, soccer M/W, table tennis M/W, tennis M/W, ultimate Frisbee M/W, volleyball M/W.
Campus security: 24-hour emergency response devices and patrols, late-night transport/escort service, controlled dormitory access.
Student services: health clinic, personal/psychological counseling.

COSTS & FINANCIAL AID
Costs (2017–18) *Comprehensive fee:* $46,870 includes full-time tuition ($34,500), mandatory fees ($550), and room and board ($11,820). Full-time tuition and fees vary according to degree level, location, and student level. Part-time tuition: $1300 per credit hour. Part-time tuition and fees vary according to course load, degree level, location, and student level. No tuition increase for student's term of enrollment. *Required fees:* $50 per term part-time. *College room only:* $6200. Room and board charges vary according to board plan and housing facility. *Payment plan:* installment. *Waivers:* employees or children of employees.
Financial Aid Of all full-time matriculated undergraduates who enrolled in 2017, 883 applied for aid, 821 were judged to have need, 201 had their need fully met. 367 Federal Work-Study jobs (averaging $1798). In 2017, 139 non-need-based awards were made. *Average percent of need met:* 82. *Average financial aid package:* $32,567. *Average need-based loan:*

$4659. *Average need-based gift aid:* $27,203. *Average non-need-based aid:* $17,579. *Average indebtedness upon graduation:* $27,825.

APPLYING
Standardized Tests *Required:* SAT or ACT (for admission).
Options: electronic application, early decision.
Required: high school transcript. *Recommended:* essay or personal statement, interview.
Application deadlines: rolling (freshmen), rolling (transfers).
Early decision deadline: 11/15 (for plan 1), 1/15 (for plan 2).
Notification: continuous (freshmen), continuous (transfers), 12/15 (early decision).

CONTACT
Mr. Matt Crisman, Director of Admissions, Emory & Henry College, PO Box 947, Emory, VA 24327-0947. *Phone:* 276-944-6491. *Toll-free phone:* 800-848-5493. *E-mail:* mcrisman@ehc.edu.

Ferrum College
Ferrum, Virginia
http://www.ferrum.edu/
CONTACT
Ms. Gilda Q. Woods, Associate Vice President for Enrollment Management and Dean of Admissions, Ferrum College, Spilman-Daniel House, PO Box 1000, Ferrum, VA 24088-9001. *Phone:* 540-365-4290. *Toll-free phone:* 800-868-9797. *Fax:* 540-365-4266. *E-mail:* admissions@ferrum.edu.

George Mason University
Fairfax, Virginia
http://www.gmu.edu/
- **State-supported** university, founded 1972
- **Suburban** 817-acre campus with easy access to Washington, DC
- **Endowment** $77.7 million
- **Coed** 24,987 undergraduate students, 81% full-time, 50% women, 50% men

UNDERGRAD STUDENTS
20,199 full-time, 4,788 part-time. Students come from 49 states and territories; 106 other countries; 10% are from out of state; 11% Black or African American, non-Hispanic/Latino; 14% Hispanic/Latino; 20% Asian, non-Hispanic/Latino; 0.3% Native Hawaiian or other Pacific Islander, non-Hispanic/Latino; 0.1% American Indian or Alaska Native, non-Hispanic/Latino; 5% Two or more races, non-Hispanic/Latino; 3% Race/ethnicity unknown; 5% international; 12% transferred in; 24% live on campus.

Freshmen:
Admission: 3,489 enrolled. *Average high school GPA:* 3.7. *Test scores:* SAT evidence-based reading and writing scores over 500: 96%; SAT math scores over 500: 93%; ACT scores over 18: 97%; SAT evidence-based reading and writing scores over 600: 54%; SAT math scores over 600: 45%; ACT scores over 24: 74%; SAT evidence-based reading and writing scores over 700: 10%; SAT math scores over 700: 9%; ACT scores over 30: 18%.
Retention: 88% of full-time freshmen returned.

FACULTY
Total: 2,692, 48% full-time.
Student/faculty ratio: 17:1.

ACADEMICS
Calendar: semesters. *Degrees:* bachelor's, master's, doctoral, post-master's, and postbachelor's certificates.
Special study options: accelerated degree program, adult/continuing education programs, advanced placement credit, cooperative education, distance learning, double majors, English as a second language, freshman honors college, honors programs, independent study, internships, off-campus study, part-time degree program, services for LD students, student-designed majors, study abroad, summer session for credit. *ROTC:* Army (b), Air Force (c).

Computers: 622 computers/terminals and 45,871 ports are available on campus for general student use. Students can access the following: campus intranet, computer help desk, free student e-mail accounts, online (class) grades, online (class) registration, online (class) schedules. Campuswide network is available. 100% of college-owned or -operated housing units are wired for high-speed Internet access. Wireless service is available via entire campus.

Library: Fenwick Library plus 3 others. *Books:* 1.4 million (physical), 1.8 million (digital/electronic); *Serial titles:* 1,177 (physical), 189,776 (digital/electronic); *Databases:* 775. Weekly public service hours: 87; study areas open 24 hours, 5–7 days a week; students can reserve study rooms.

STUDENT LIFE
Housing options: coed, special housing for students with disabilities. Campus housing is university owned and leased by the school. Freshman campus housing is guaranteed.

Activities and organizations: drama/theater group, student-run newspaper, radio and television station, choral group, Catholic Campus Ministry, Indian Student Association, Black Student Alliance, Hispanic Student Association, CRU (Campus Crusade for Christ), national fraternities, national sororities.

Athletics Member NCAA. All Division I. *Intercollegiate sports:* baseball M(s), basketball M(s)/W(s), crew W(s), cross-country running M(s)/W(s), golf M(s), lacrosse W(s), soccer M(s)/W(s), softball W(s), swimming and diving M(s)/W(s), tennis M(s)/W(s), track and field M(s)/W(s), volleyball M(s)/W(s), wrestling M(s). *Intramural sports:* badminton M(c)/W(c), baseball M(c), basketball M/W, bowling M(c)/W(c), crew M(c)/W(c), cross-country running M(c)/W(c), equestrian sports M(c)/W(c), fencing M(c)/W(c), field hockey M(c)/W(c), football M(c), golf M/W, ice hockey M(c), lacrosse M(c)/W(c), rugby M(c)/W(c), soccer M(c)/W(c), softball M/W(c), swimming and diving M/W, tennis M(c)/W(c), track and field M(c)/W(c), ultimate Frisbee M(c)/W(c), volleyball M(c)/W(c), water polo M/W, wrestling M(c).

Campus security: 24-hour emergency response devices and patrols, student patrols, late-night transport/escort service, controlled dormitory access.

Student services: health clinic, personal/psychological counseling, women's center.

COSTS & FINANCIAL AID
Costs (2017–18) *Tuition:* state resident $11,724 full-time, $489 per credit hour part-time; nonresident $35,323 full-time, $1424 per credit hour part-time. Full-time tuition and fees vary according to course load. Part-time tuition and fees vary according to course load. *Room and board:* Room and board charges vary according to board plan and housing facility. *Payment plans:* installment, deferred payment. *Waivers:* senior citizens and employees or children of employees.

Financial Aid Of all full-time matriculated undergraduates who enrolled in 2016, 13,244 applied for aid, 10,862 were judged to have need, 175 had their need fully met. 591 Federal Work-Study jobs (averaging $2129). In 2016, 1485 non-need-based awards were made. *Average percent of need met:* 54. *Average financial aid package:* $12,989. *Average need-based loan:* $4453. *Average need-based gift aid:* $6408. *Average non-need-based aid:* $3968. *Average indebtedness upon graduation:* $30,755.

APPLYING
Standardized Tests *Required for some:* SAT or ACT (for admission).

Required: high school transcript. *Required for some:* audition for dance and music, portfolio for art and visual technology and computer game design, interview and audition or portfolio for theater. *Recommended:* essay or personal statement, 3 letters of recommendation.

CONTACT
Melissa Bevacqua, Director, Undergraduate Admissions, George Mason University, 4400 University Drive, MSN 3A4, Fairfax, VA 22030-4444. *Phone:* 703-993-2291. *Toll-free phone:* 888-627-6612. *Fax:* 703-993-2392. *E-mail:* mbevacqu@gmu.edu.

Hampden-Sydney College
Hampden-Sydney, Virginia
http://www.hsc.edu/
- **Independent** 4-year, founded 1776, affiliated with Presbyterian Church (U.S.A.)
- **Rural** 1343-acre campus with easy access to Richmond, Lynchburg, Charlottesville
- **Endowment** $145.4 million
- **Men only** 1,046 undergraduate students, 100% full-time
- **Moderately difficult** entrance level, 55% of applicants were admitted

UNDERGRAD STUDENTS
1,046 full-time. Students come from 26 states and territories; 6 other countries; 31% are from out of state; 4% Black or African American, non-Hispanic/Latino; 4% Hispanic/Latino; 0.5% Asian, non-Hispanic/Latino; 0.1% Native Hawaiian or other Pacific Islander, non-Hispanic/Latino; 0.6% American Indian or Alaska Native, non-Hispanic/Latino; 3% Two or more races, non-Hispanic/Latino; 1% Race/ethnicity unknown; 0.3% international; 1% transferred in; 98% live on campus.

Freshmen:
Admission: 3,573 applied, 1,967 admitted, 312 enrolled. *Average high school GPA:* 3.4. *Test scores:* SAT evidence-based reading and writing scores over 500: 86%; SAT math scores over 500: 84%; SAT evidence-based reading and writing scores over 600: 44%; SAT math scores over 600: 37%; SAT evidence-based reading and writing scores over 700: 9%; SAT math scores over 700: 5%.

Retention: 84% of full-time freshmen returned.

FACULTY
Total: 110, 86% full-time, 90% with terminal degrees.
Student/faculty ratio: 10:1.

ACADEMICS
Calendar: semesters. *Degree:* bachelor's.

Special study options: academic remediation for entering students, advanced placement credit, cooperative education, double majors, honors programs, independent study, internships, off-campus study, study abroad, summer session for credit. *ROTC:* Army (c).

Unusual degree programs: 3-2 engineering with University of Virginia, Old Dominion University.

Computers: 200 computers/terminals are available on campus for general student use. Students can access the following: campus intranet, computer help desk, free student e-mail accounts, online (class) grades, online (class) registration, online (class) schedules. Campuswide network is available. 100% of college-owned or -operated housing units are wired for high-speed Internet access. Wireless service is available via entire campus.

Library: Walter M. Bortz III Library. *Books:* 232,898 (physical), 114,108 (digital/electronic); *Serial titles:* 53 (physical), 114,895 (digital/electronic); *Databases:* 98. Weekly public service hours: 99; students can reserve study rooms.

STUDENT LIFE
Housing options: on-campus residence required through senior year; men-only, special housing for students with disabilities. Campus housing is university owned. Freshman campus housing is guaranteed.

Activities and organizations: drama/theater group, student-run newspaper, radio station, choral group, Republican Society, Pre-Health Society, Outdoors Club, Tiger Athletic Club, Pre-Law Society, national fraternities.

Athletics Member NCAA. All Division III. *Intercollegiate sports:* baseball M, basketball M, crew M(c), cross-country running M, fencing M(c), football M, golf M, lacrosse M, riflery M(c), rugby M(c), soccer M, swimming and diving M, tennis M, ultimate Frisbee M(c), wrestling M. *Intramural sports:* archery M(c), basketball M, fencing M(c), football M, lacrosse M(c), racquetball M(c), riflery M(c), soccer M, softball M, swimming and diving M(c), volleyball M, water polo M(c), wrestling M(c).

Campus security: 24-hour emergency response devices and patrols.

Student services: health clinic, personal/psychological counseling.

COSTS & FINANCIAL AID

Costs (2018–19) *Comprehensive fee:* $59,410 includes full-time tuition ($43,446), mandatory fees ($2406), and room and board ($13,558). Full-time tuition and fees vary according to course load and student level. Part-time tuition: $1360 per credit hour. Part-time tuition and fees vary according to course load and student level. *College room only:* $6150. Room and board charges vary according to board plan and housing facility. *Payment plan:* installment. *Waivers:* employees or children of employees.

Financial Aid Of all full-time matriculated undergraduates who enrolled in 2017, 792 applied for aid, 687 were judged to have need, 161 had their need fully met. 175 Federal Work-Study jobs (averaging $1395). In 2017, 341 non-need-based awards were made. *Average percent of need met:* 79. *Average financial aid package:* $33,875. *Average need-based loan:* $4698. *Average need-based gift aid:* $29,908. *Average non-need-based aid:* $17,872. *Average indebtedness upon graduation:* $35,921.

APPLYING

Standardized Tests *Required:* SAT or ACT (for admission). *Recommended:* SAT and SAT Subject Tests or ACT (for admission).

Options: electronic application, early admission, early decision, early action.

Application fee: $30.

Required: essay or personal statement, high school transcript, 2 letters of recommendation. *Recommended:* interview.

Application deadlines: 3/1 (freshmen), 7/1 (transfers), 1/15 (early action).

Early decision deadline: 11/1.

Notification: 4/15 (freshmen), 7/31 (transfers), 12/1 (early decision), 2/15 (early action).

CONTACT

Dean Anita Garland, Dean of Admissions, Hampden-Sydney College, PO Box 667, Hampden-Sydney, VA 23943-0667. *Phone:* 434-223-6120. *Toll-free phone:* 800-755-0733. *Fax:* 434-223-6346. *E-mail:* hsapp@hsc.edu.

Hampton University

Hampton, Virginia

http://www.hamptonu.edu/

- **Independent** comprehensive, founded 1868
- **Urban** 314-acre campus with easy access to Norfolk
- **Coed** 3,799 undergraduate students, 96% full-time, 67% women, 33% men
- **Moderately difficult** entrance level, 36% of applicants were admitted

UNDERGRAD STUDENTS

3,651 full-time, 148 part-time. Students come from 44 states and territories; 22 other countries; 73% are from out of state; 96% Black or African American, non-Hispanic/Latino; 1% Hispanic/Latino; 0.3% Asian, non-Hispanic/Latino; 0.1% Native Hawaiian or other Pacific Islander, non-Hispanic/Latino; 0.4% American Indian or Alaska Native, non-Hispanic/Latino; 0.4% Race/ethnicity unknown; 0.7% international; 2% transferred in; 64% live on campus.

Freshmen:

Admission: 12,130 applied, 4,391 admitted, 1,018 enrolled. *Average high school GPA:* 3.7. *Test scores:* SAT evidence-based reading and writing scores over 500: 69%; SAT math scores over 500: 67%; ACT scores over 18: 100%; SAT evidence-based reading and writing scores over 600: 15%; SAT math scores over 600: 10%; ACT scores over 24: 32%; SAT evidence-based reading and writing scores over 700: 1%; SAT math scores over 700: 1%; ACT scores over 30: 4%.
Retention: 77% of full-time freshmen returned.

FACULTY

Total: 367, 78% full-time, 74% with terminal degrees.

Student/faculty ratio: 13:1.

ACADEMICS

Calendar: semesters. *Degrees:* certificates, associate, bachelor's, master's, doctoral, and post-master's certificates.

Special study options: academic remediation for entering students, accelerated degree program, adult/continuing education programs, advanced placement credit, cooperative education, distance learning, double majors, English as a second language, honors programs, independent study, internships, off-campus study, part-time degree program, services for LD students, study abroad, summer session for credit. *ROTC:* Army (b), Navy (b).

Computers: 1,500 computers/terminals are available on campus for general student use. Students can access the following: campus intranet, computer help desk, free student e-mail accounts, online (class) grades, online (class) registration, online (class) schedules, learning management system. Campuswide network is available. 100% of college-owned or -operated housing units are wired for high-speed Internet access. Wireless service is available via entire campus.

Library: William R. and Norma B. Harvey Library plus 4 others. *Books:* 307,143 (physical), 91,991 (digital/electronic); *Serial titles:* 8,240 (physical); *Databases:* 115. Study areas open 24 hours, 5–7 days a week; students can reserve study rooms.

STUDENT LIFE

Housing options: on-campus residence required for freshman year; coed, men-only, women-only, special housing for students with disabilities. Campus housing is university owned. Freshman applicants given priority for college housing.

Activities and organizations: drama/theater group, student-run newspaper, radio station, choral group, marching band, Student Government, student leaders, Student Union Board, student recruitment team, resident assistants, national fraternities, national sororities.

Athletics Member NCAA. All Division I. *Intercollegiate sports:* basketball M(s)/W(s), bowling W(s), cheerleading W, cross-country running M(s)/W(s), football M(s), golf M(s)/W(s), lacrosse M(s), sailing M(s)/W(s), soccer W, softball W(s), tennis M(s)/W(s), track and field M(s)/W(s), volleyball W(s). *Intramural sports:* badminton M/W, basketball M/W, bowling W, football M, lacrosse M/W, soccer M, softball W, swimming and diving M/W, table tennis M/W, volleyball W.

Campus security: 24-hour emergency response devices and patrols.

Student services: health clinic, personal/psychological counseling, women's center.

COSTS & FINANCIAL AID

Costs (2017–18) *Comprehensive fee:* $36,660 includes full-time tuition ($22,630), mandatory fees ($2812), and room and board ($11,218). Full-time tuition and fees vary according to course load, degree level, location, program, and reciprocity agreements. Part-time tuition: $575 per credit hour. Part-time tuition and fees vary according to class time, course load, location, and reciprocity agreements. *College room only:* $5834. Room and board charges vary according to board plan, housing facility, and location. *Payment plans:* installment, deferred payment. *Waivers:* employees or children of employees.

Financial Aid Of all full-time matriculated undergraduates who enrolled in 2016, 2,356 applied for aid, 1,825 were judged to have need, 769 had their need fully met. 264 Federal Work-Study jobs (averaging $1249). In 2016, 765 non-need-based awards were made. *Average percent of need met:* 44. *Average financial aid package:* $5803. *Average need-based loan:* $5575. *Average need-based gift aid:* $5322. *Average non-need-based aid:* $9947. *Average indebtedness upon graduation:* $34,131. *Financial aid deadline:* 4/15.

APPLYING

Standardized Tests *Required for some:* SAT or ACT (for admission).

Options: electronic application, early admission, early action, deferred entrance.

Application fee: $35.

Required: essay or personal statement, high school transcript, minimum 2.5 GPA, 1 letter of recommendation. *Required for some:* interview, audition for music.

Application deadlines: 3/1 (freshmen), 11/1 (early action).

Notification: 12/15 (early action).

CONTACT

Ms. Patra Johnson, Director, Freshman Studies, Hampton University, 204 Student Center, Hampton University, Hampton, VA 23668. *Phone:* 757-727-5901. *Toll-free phone:* 800-624-3328. *Fax:* 757-727-5095. *E-mail:* patra.johnson@hamptonu.edu.

Hollins University

Roanoke, Virginia
http://www.hollins.edu/

- **Independent** comprehensive, founded 1842
- **Suburban** 475-acre campus
- **Endowment** $182.2 million
- **Undergraduate: women only; graduate: coed** 654 undergraduate students, 97% full-time, 99% women, 1% men
- **Moderately difficult** entrance level, 48% of applicants were admitted

UNDERGRAD STUDENTS
632 full-time, 22 part-time. Students come from 43 states and territories; 14 other countries; 53% are from out of state; 11% Black or African American, non-Hispanic/Latino; 5% Hispanic/Latino; 2% Asian, non-Hispanic/Latino; 0.2% Native Hawaiian or other Pacific Islander, non-Hispanic/Latino; 0.9% American Indian or Alaska Native, non-Hispanic/Latino; 5% Two or more races, non-Hispanic/Latino; 3% Race/ethnicity unknown; 5% international; 2% transferred in; 87% live on campus.

Freshmen:
Admission: 2,842 applied, 1,375 admitted, 155 enrolled. *Average high school GPA:* 3.8. *Test scores:* SAT evidence-based reading and writing scores over 500: 98%; SAT math scores over 500: 92%; ACT scores over 18: 97%; SAT evidence-based reading and writing scores over 600: 70%; SAT math scores over 600: 31%; ACT scores over 24: 66%; SAT evidence-based reading and writing scores over 700: 16%; SAT math scores over 700: 4%; ACT scores over 30: 16%.

Retention: 78% of full-time freshmen returned.

FACULTY
Total: 98, 71% full-time, 86% with terminal degrees.
Student/faculty ratio: 10:1.

ACADEMICS
Calendar: 4-1-4. *Degrees:* bachelor's, master's, and post-master's certificates.
Special study options: accelerated degree program, adult/continuing education programs, advanced placement credit, cooperative education, double majors, honors programs, independent study, internships, off-campus study, part-time degree program, services for LD students, student-designed majors, study abroad.
Computers: 102 computers/terminals and 1,000 ports are available on campus for general student use. Students can access the following: campus intranet, computer help desk, free student e-mail accounts, online (class) grades, online (class) registration, online (class) schedules. Campuswide network is available. 100% of college-owned or -operated housing units are wired for high-speed Internet access. Wireless service is available via entire campus.
Library: Wyndham Robertson Library plus 1 other. *Books:* 246,065 (physical), 122,121 (digital/electronic); *Serial titles:* 1,160 (physical), 51,262 (digital/electronic); *Databases:* 130. Weekly public service hours: 94.

STUDENT LIFE
Housing options: on-campus residence required through senior year; women-only, special housing for students with disabilities. Campus housing is university owned. Freshman campus housing is guaranteed.
Activities and organizations: drama/theater group, choral group, Hollins Activity Board, Black Student Alliance, Hollins Repertory Dance Club, Arts Association, Voices for Unity.
Athletics Member NCAA. All Division III. *Intercollegiate sports:* basketball W, cross-country running W, equestrian sports W, golf W, lacrosse W, soccer W, swimming and diving W, tennis W, volleyball W.
Campus security: 24-hour emergency response devices and patrols, late-night transport/escort service, controlled dormitory access, emergency call boxes.
Student services: health clinic, personal/psychological counseling, women's center.

COSTS & FINANCIAL AID
Costs (2018–19) *Comprehensive fee:* $52,555 includes full-time tuition ($38,400), mandatory fees ($635), and room and board ($13,520). Part-time tuition and fees vary according to course load. *Room and board:* Room and board charges vary according to housing facility. *Payment plans:* tuition prepayment, installment. *Waivers:* employees or children of employees.
Financial Aid Of all full-time matriculated undergraduates who enrolled in 2017, 536 applied for aid, 497 were judged to have need, 118 had their need fully met. 105 Federal Work-Study jobs (averaging $1500). 186 state and other part-time jobs (averaging $1500). In 2017, 120 non-need-based awards were made. *Average percent of need met:* 84. *Average financial aid package:* $36,843. *Average need-based loan:* $4982. *Average need-based gift aid:* $32,377. *Average non-need-based aid:* $29,506. *Average indebtedness upon graduation:* $31,211.

APPLYING
Standardized Tests *Required:* SAT or ACT (for admission).
Options: electronic application, early admission, early decision, early action, deferred entrance.
Required: essay or personal statement, high school transcript, 1 letter of recommendation. *Recommended:* interview.
Application deadlines: rolling (freshmen), 11/15 (early action).
Early decision deadline: 11/1.
Notification: continuous (freshmen), 11/15 (early decision), 12/1 (early action).

CONTACT
Ms. Madeline Aliff, Director of Recruitment, Hollins University, Hollins University, 7916 Williamson Road, Box 9707, Roanoke, VA 24020. *Phone:* 540-362-6401. *Toll-free phone:* 800-456-9595. *Fax:* 540-362-6218. *E-mail:* huadm@hollins.edu.

IGlobal University

Vienna, Virginia
http://www.igu.edu/

CONTACT
IGlobal University, 8133 Leesburg Pike, #230, Vienna, VA 22182.

James Madison University

Harrisonburg, Virginia
http://www.jmu.edu/

- **State-supported** comprehensive, founded 1908
- **Small-town** 721-acre campus
- **Coed** 19,975 undergraduate students, 95% full-time, 59% women, 41% men
- **Very difficult** entrance level, 75% of applicants were admitted

UNDERGRAD STUDENTS
18,905 full-time, 1,070 part-time. 23% are from out of state; 5% Black or African American, non-Hispanic/Latino; 7% Hispanic/Latino; 5% Asian, non-Hispanic/Latino; 0.1% Native Hawaiian or other Pacific Islander, non-Hispanic/Latino; 0.1% American Indian or Alaska Native, non-Hispanic/Latino; 4% Two or more races, non-Hispanic/Latino; 3% Race/ethnicity unknown; 2% international; 4% transferred in; 30% live on campus.

Freshmen:
Admission: 21,099 applied, 15,866 admitted, 4,668 enrolled. *Test scores:* SAT evidence-based reading and writing scores over 500: 96%; SAT math scores over 500: 94%; ACT scores over 18: 99%; SAT evidence-based reading and writing scores over 600: 52%; SAT math scores over 600: 40%; ACT scores over 24: 67%; SAT evidence-based reading and writing scores over 700: 5%; SAT math scores over 700: 4%; ACT scores over 30: 11%.

Retention: 90% of full-time freshmen returned.

FACULTY
Total: 1,541, 68% full-time, 61% with terminal degrees.
Student/faculty ratio: 16:1.

ACADEMICS
Calendar: semesters. *Degrees:* bachelor's, master's, and doctoral (also offers specialist in education degree).
Special study options: accelerated degree program, adult/continuing education programs, advanced placement credit, distance learning, double

majors, English as a second language, freshman honors college, honors programs, independent study, internships, off-campus study, part-time degree program, services for LD students, student-designed majors, study abroad, summer session for credit. *ROTC:* Army (b), Air Force (c).

Unusual degree programs: 3-2 forestry with Virginia Polytechnic Institute and State University.

Computers: Students can access the following: campus intranet, computer help desk, free student e-mail accounts, online (class) grades, online (class) registration, online (class) schedules. Campuswide network is available. Wireless service is available via entire campus.

Library: Carrier Library plus 2 others. Students can reserve study rooms.

STUDENT LIFE

Housing options: on-campus residence required for freshman year; coed, special housing for students with disabilities. Campus housing is university owned and leased by the school. Freshman campus housing is guaranteed.

Activities and organizations: drama/theater group, student-run newspaper, radio station, choral group, marching band, national fraternities, national sororities.

Athletics Member NCAA. All Division I except football (Division I-AA). *Intercollegiate sports:* baseball M(s), basketball M(s)/W(s), cheerleading M/W, cross-country running W(s), field hockey W(s), golf M(s)/W(s), lacrosse W(s), soccer M(s)/W(s), softball W(s), swimming and diving W(s), tennis M(s)/W(s), track and field W(s), volleyball W(s). *Intramural sports:* archery M(c)/W(c), baseball M(c), basketball M/W, bowling M/W, cheerleading W(c), crew M(c)/W(c), cross-country running M(c)/W(c), equestrian sports M(c)/W(c), fencing M(c)/W(c), field hockey W(c), football M/W, golf M/W, gymnastics M(c)/W(c), ice hockey M(c)/W(c), lacrosse M(c)/W(c), racquetball M/W, rugby M(c)/W(c), skiing (downhill) M(c)/W(c), soccer M/W, softball M/W, squash M(c)/W(c), swimming and diving M(c)/W(c), table tennis M/W, tennis M/W, track and field M(c)/W(c), ultimate Frisbee M(c)/W(c), volleyball M/W, water polo M(c)/W(c), wrestling M(c).

Campus security: 24-hour emergency response devices and patrols, student patrols, late-night transport/escort service, controlled dormitory access, lighted pathways.

Student services: health clinic, personal/psychological counseling, women's center.

COSTS & FINANCIAL AID

Costs (2017–18) *Tuition:* state resident $6250 full-time, $208 per credit hour part-time; nonresident $22,614 full-time, $735 per credit hour part-time. *Required fees:* $4580 full-time. *Room and board:* $9822; room only: $5114. Room and board charges vary according to board plan. *Waivers:* employees or children of employees.

Financial Aid Of all full-time matriculated undergraduates who enrolled in 2017, 11,329 applied for aid, 7,884 were judged to have need, 5,198 had their need fully met. In 2017, 205 non-need-based awards were made. *Average percent of need met:* 41. *Average financial aid package:* $8945. *Average need-based loan:* $4320. *Average need-based gift aid:* $7487. *Average non-need-based aid:* $5219. *Average indebtedness upon graduation:* $27,656.

APPLYING

Options: electronic application, early action, deferred entrance.

Application fee: $70.

Required: high school transcript. *Recommended:* minimum 3.0 GPA.

Notification: 4/1 (freshmen).

CONTACT

James Madison University, 800 South Main Street, Harrisonburg, VA 22807. *Phone:* 540-568-5681.

Jefferson College of Health Sciences
Roanoke, Virginia
http://www.jchs.edu/

- **Independent** comprehensive, founded 1982
- **Urban** 1-acre campus
- **Endowment** $2.4 million
- **Coed** 800 undergraduate students, 83% full-time, 81% women, 19% men
- **Moderately difficult** entrance level

UNDERGRAD STUDENTS

666 full-time, 134 part-time. Students come from 22 states and territories; 7% are from out of state; 10% Black or African American, non-Hispanic/Latino; 5% Hispanic/Latino; 2% Asian, non-Hispanic/Latino; 2% Two or more races, non-Hispanic/Latino; 4% Race/ethnicity unknown; 0.3% international; 22% transferred in; 16% live on campus.

Freshmen:
Admission: 510 applied, 133 enrolled. *Average high school GPA:* 3.3.
Retention: 66% of full-time freshmen returned.

ACADEMICS

Calendar: semesters. *Degrees:* certificates, associate, bachelor's, master's, and doctoral.

Special study options: accelerated degree program, adult/continuing education programs, advanced placement credit, cooperative education, distance learning, double majors, English as a second language, independent study, internships, off-campus study, part-time degree program, services for LD students, summer session for credit.

Computers: 72 computers/terminals are available on campus for general student use. Students can access the following: free student e-mail accounts, online (class) grades, online (class) registration, online (class) schedules. Campuswide network is available. 100% of college-owned or -operated housing units are wired for high-speed Internet access. Wireless service is available via classrooms, computer labs, learning centers, libraries.

Library: JCHS Library. *Books:* 4,971 (physical), 41,000 (digital/electronic); *Serial titles:* 99 (physical), 65 (digital/electronic); *Databases:* 29.

STUDENT LIFE

Housing options: coed. Campus housing is university owned.

Activities and organizations: student-run newspaper, choral group, Jefferson Activities Group (JAG), Student Ambassadors, Hands of Healing, American Medical Students Association (AMSA), Student Nurses Association.

Athletics *Intercollegiate sports:* basketball M(c), cross-country running M(c)/W(c), softball M(c)/W(c), tennis M(c)/W(c), volleyball M(c)/W(c). *Intramural sports:* table tennis M(c)/W(c).

Campus security: 24-hour emergency response devices and patrols, late-night transport/escort service, controlled dormitory access.

Student services: personal/psychological counseling.

COSTS & FINANCIAL AID

Costs (2018–19) *Comprehensive fee:* $36,380 includes full-time tuition ($26,416), mandatory fees ($450), and room and board ($9514). Full-time tuition and fees vary according to course load. Part-time tuition: $765 per credit hour. Part-time tuition and fees vary according to course load. *Required fees:* $150 per year part-time. *Room and board:* Room and board charges vary according to location. *Waivers:* employees or children of employees.

Financial Aid Of all full-time matriculated undergraduates who enrolled in 2016, 582 applied for aid, 559 were judged to have need.

APPLYING

Standardized Tests *Required:* SAT or ACT (for admission). *Recommended:* SAT (for admission).

Options: electronic application, early action, deferred entrance.

Application fee: $35.

Required: high school transcript, minimum 2.5 GPA. *Required for some:* interview.

Application deadlines: rolling (freshmen), rolling (transfers).

Notification: continuous (freshmen), continuous (transfers).

CONTACT

Jefferson College of Health Sciences, 101 Elm Avenue SE, Roanoke, VA 24013. *Phone:* 540-985-8309. *Toll-free phone:* 888-985-8483.

Liberty University

Lynchburg, Virginia

http://www.liberty.edu/

- **Independent nondenominational** comprehensive, founded 1971
- **Suburban** 6500-acre campus
- **Coed** 13,785 undergraduate students, 96% full-time, 54% women, 46% men
- **Minimally difficult** entrance level, 39% of applicants were admitted

UNDERGRAD STUDENTS

13,255 full-time, 530 part-time. Students come from 52 states and territories; 84 other countries; 61% are from out of state; 4% Black or African American, non-Hispanic/Latino; 5% Hispanic/Latino; 2% Asian, non-Hispanic/Latino; 0.1% Native Hawaiian or other Pacific Islander, non-Hispanic/Latino; 0.4% American Indian or Alaska Native, non-Hispanic/Latino; 2% Two or more races, non-Hispanic/Latino; 14% Race/ethnicity unknown; 5% international; 11% transferred in; 58% live on campus.

Freshmen:

Admission: 14,567 applied, 5,741 admitted, 2,816 enrolled. *Average high school GPA:* 3.5. *Test scores:* SAT evidence-based reading and writing scores over 500: 85%; SAT math scores over 500: 79%; ACT scores over 18: 95%; SAT evidence-based reading and writing scores over 600: 43%; SAT math scores over 600: 29%; ACT scores over 24: 52%; SAT evidence-based reading and writing scores over 700: 10%; SAT math scores over 700: 7%; ACT scores over 30: 14%.

Retention: 86% of full-time freshmen returned.

ACADEMICS

Calendar: semesters. *Degrees:* certificates, associate, bachelor's, master's, doctoral, post-master's, and postbachelor's certificates (also offers external degree program with significant enrollment not reflected in profile).

Special study options: academic remediation for entering students, accelerated degree program, advanced placement credit, cooperative education, distance learning, double majors, English as a second language, external degree program, honors programs, independent study, internships, off-campus study, part-time degree program, services for LD students, student-designed majors, study abroad, summer session for credit. *ROTC:* Army (b), Air Force (c).

Computers: 1,640 computers/terminals are available on campus for general student use. Students can access the following: computer help desk, free student e-mail accounts, online (class) grades, online (class) registration, online (class) schedules. Campuswide network is available. 100% of college-owned or -operated housing units are wired for high-speed Internet access. Wireless service is available via entire campus. **Library:** Jerry Falwell Library plus 1 other. *Books:* 313,657 (physical), 377,967 (digital/electronic); *Serial titles:* 4,323 (physical), 118,877 (digital/electronic); *Databases:* 512. Students can reserve study rooms.

STUDENT LIFE

Housing options: on-campus residence required through senior year; men-only, women-only, special housing for students with disabilities. Campus housing is university owned. Freshman campus housing is guaranteed.

Activities and organizations: drama/theater group, student-run newspaper, radio station, choral group, marching band, Campus Serve.

Athletics Member NCAA. All Division I except football (Division I-AA). *Intercollegiate sports:* baseball M(s), basketball M(s)/W(s), cheerleading M(s)/W(s), crew M(c)/W(c), cross-country running M(s)/W(s), equestrian sports W(c), field hockey W(s), golf M(s), ice hockey M(c)/W(c), lacrosse W(s), soccer M(s)/W(s), softball W(s), swimming and diving W(s), tennis M(s)/W(s), track and field M(s)/W(s), volleyball M(c)/W(s). *Intramural sports:* archery M(c)/W(c), basketball M/W, football M/W, gymnastics M(c)/W(c), lacrosse M(c), racquetball M(c)/W(c), skiing (downhill) M(c)/W(c), soccer M/W, softball M/W, table tennis M/W, tennis M/W, ultimate Frisbee M(c)/W(c), wrestling M(c).

Campus security: 24-hour patrols, late-night transport/escort service, 24-hour emergency dispatch.

Student services: health clinic, personal/psychological counseling.

COSTS & FINANCIAL AID

Costs (2017–18) *Comprehensive fee:* $33,790 includes full-time tuition ($22,880), mandatory fees ($1060), and room and board ($9850). Full-time tuition and fees vary according to course load. Part-time tuition: $780 per credit hour. Part-time tuition and fees vary according to course load. *College room only:* $6210. Room and board charges vary according to housing facility. *Payment plan:* installment. *Waivers:* employees or children of employees.

Financial Aid Of all full-time matriculated undergraduates who enrolled in 2017, 12,158 applied for aid, 9,848 were judged to have need, 1,068 had their need fully met. In 2017, 2219 non-need-based awards were made. *Average percent of need met:* 56. *Average financial aid package:* $15,024. *Average need-based loan:* $4331. *Average need-based gift aid:* $10,905. *Average non-need-based aid:* $7540. *Average indebtedness upon graduation:* $21,875. *Financial aid deadline:* 3/1.

APPLYING

Standardized Tests *Required:* SAT or ACT (for admission).

Options: electronic application.

Application fee: $50.

Required: essay or personal statement, high school transcript, minimum 2.0 GPA. *Recommended:* minimum 2.0 GPA.

Application deadlines: rolling (freshmen), rolling (transfers).

Notification: continuous (freshmen), continuous (transfers).

CONTACT

Dr. Terry Elam, Director of Admissions, Liberty University, 1971 University Boulevard, Lynchburg, VA 24515. *Phone:* 434-592-3966. *Toll-free phone:* 800-543-5317. *Fax:* 800-542-2311. *E-mail:* admissions@liberty.edu.

Longwood University

Farmville, Virginia

http://www.longwood.edu/

- **State-supported** comprehensive, founded 1839
- **Small-town** 60-acre campus with easy access to Richmond
- **Endowment** $59.1 million
- **Coed** 4,386 undergraduate students, 90% full-time, 67% women, 33% men
- **Moderately difficult** entrance level, 92% of applicants were admitted

UNDERGRAD STUDENTS

3,952 full-time, 434 part-time. Students come from 31 states and territories; 26 other countries; 4% are from out of state; 10% Black or African American, non-Hispanic/Latino; 5% Hispanic/Latino; 1% Asian, non-Hispanic/Latino; 0.2% Native Hawaiian or other Pacific Islander, non-Hispanic/Latino; 0.3% American Indian or Alaska Native, non-Hispanic/Latino; 4% Two or more races, non-Hispanic/Latino; 4% Race/ethnicity unknown; 2% international; 5% transferred in; 66% live on campus.

Freshmen:

Admission: 4,873 applied, 4,475 admitted, 929 enrolled. *Average high school GPA:* 3.4. *Test scores:* SAT evidence-based reading and writing scores over 500: 75%; SAT math scores over 500: 63%; ACT scores over 18: 83%; SAT evidence-based reading and writing scores over 600: 21%; SAT math scores over 600: 8%; ACT scores over 24: 22%; SAT evidence-based reading and writing scores over 700: 2%; ACT scores over 30: 1%.

Retention: 80% of full-time freshmen returned.

FACULTY

Total: 340, 73% full-time, 76% with terminal degrees.

Student/faculty ratio: 14:1.

ACADEMICS

Calendar: semesters. *Degrees:* bachelor's, master's, post-master's, and postbachelor's certificates.

Special study options: accelerated degree program, distance learning, double majors, English as a second language, honors programs, independent study, internships, off-campus study, services for LD students, study abroad, summer session for credit. *ROTC:* Army (b).

Unusual degree programs: 3-2 engineering with University of Virginia, Old Dominion University, Virginia Polytechnic Institute and State University.

Computers: 291 computers/terminals and 701 ports are available on campus for general student use. Students can access the following: campus intranet, computer help desk, free student e-mail accounts, online (class) grades, online (class) schedules. Campuswide network is available. 100% of college-owned or -operated housing units are wired for high-speed Internet access. Wireless service is available via entire campus.

Library: The Janet D. Greenwood Library. *Books:* 216,525 (physical), 333,909 (digital/electronic); *Serial titles:* 2,667 (physical), 403 (digital/electronic); *Databases:* 295. Weekly public service hours: 93.

STUDENT LIFE

Housing options: on-campus residence required through sophomore year; coed, women-only, special housing for students with disabilities. Campus housing is university owned. Freshman campus housing is guaranteed.

Activities and organizations: drama/theater group, student-run newspaper, radio station, choral group, Alpha Lambda Delta, Student Nursing Association, Longwood University, Bare Naked Ladies, Chi Alpha, Sigma Alpha Pi, national fraternities, national sororities.

Athletics Member NCAA. All Division I. *Intercollegiate sports:* baseball M(s), basketball M(s)/W(s), cross-country running M(s)/W(s), field hockey W(s), football M(c), golf M(s)/W(s), lacrosse W(s), soccer M(s)/W(s), softball W(s), tennis M(s)/W(s). *Intramural sports:* baseball M(c), basketball M(c)/W(c), cheerleading M/W, equestrian sports M(c)/W(c), field hockey M(c)/W(c), football M/W, golf M/W, lacrosse M(c)/W(c), racquetball M/W, rock climbing M/W, rugby W(c), sand volleyball M/W, soccer M(c)/W(c), softball M/W(c), swimming and diving M(c)/W(c), table tennis M/W, tennis M/W, ultimate Frisbee M/W, volleyball M/W, weight lifting M/W, wrestling M(c).

Campus security: 24-hour emergency response devices and patrols, late-night transport/escort service, controlled dormitory access.

Student services: health clinic, personal/psychological counseling.

COSTS & FINANCIAL AID

Costs (2018–19) *Tuition:* state resident $8280 full-time, $276 per credit hour part-time; nonresident $22,800 full-time, $760 per credit hour part-time. Full-time tuition and fees vary according to course load and program. Part-time tuition and fees vary according to course load and program. *Required fees:* $4800 full-time. *Room and board:* $10,732; room only: $7336. Room and board charges vary according to board plan, housing facility, and location. *Payment plan:* installment. *Waivers:* senior citizens and employees or children of employees.

Financial Aid Of all full-time matriculated undergraduates who enrolled in 2015, 3,102 applied for aid, 2,350 were judged to have need, 1,005 had their need fully met. 384 Federal Work-Study jobs (averaging $1896). In 2015, 234 non-need-based awards were made. *Average percent of need met:* 80. *Average financial aid package:* $14,059. *Average need-based loan:* $4380. *Average need-based gift aid:* $7045. *Average non-need-based aid:* $4283. *Average indebtedness upon graduation:* $28,047.

APPLYING

Standardized Tests *Required:* SAT or ACT (for admission).

Options: electronic application, early admission, early action, deferred entrance.

Application fee: $50.

Required: essay or personal statement, high school transcript. *Recommended:* 3 letters of recommendation.

Application deadlines: 3/1 (freshmen), 3/1 (transfers), 12/1 (early action).

Notification: 6/1 (freshmen), continuous until 6/1 (transfers), 1/15 (early action).

CONTACT

Mr. Jason Faulk, Dean of Admissions, Longwood University, 201 High Street, Farmville, VA 23909. *Phone:* 434-395-2809. *Toll-free phone:* 800-281-4677. *Fax:* 434-395-2332. *E-mail:* faulkjc@longwood.edu.

Lynchburg College

Lynchburg, Virginia

http://www.lynchburg.edu/

- **Independent** comprehensive, founded 1903, affiliated with Christian Church (Disciples of Christ)
- **Suburban** 264-acre campus
- **Endowment** $104.4 million
- **Coed** 2,048 undergraduate students, 94% full-time, 61% women, 39% men
- **Moderately difficult** entrance level, 75% of applicants were admitted

UNDERGRAD STUDENTS

1,928 full-time, 120 part-time. Students come from 33 states and territories; 11 other countries; 49% are from out of state; 10% Black or African American, non-Hispanic/Latino; 4% Hispanic/Latino; 1% Asian, non-Hispanic/Latino; 0.4% American Indian or Alaska Native, non-Hispanic/Latino; 4% Two or more races, non-Hispanic/Latino; 4% Race/ethnicity unknown; 2% international; 3% transferred in; 72% live on campus.

Freshmen:

Admission: 4,880 applied, 3,638 admitted, 544 enrolled. *Average high school GPA:* 3.4. *Test scores:* SAT evidence-based reading and writing scores over 500: 79%; SAT math scores over 500: 71%; ACT scores over 18: 90%; SAT evidence-based reading and writing scores over 600: 28%; SAT math scores over 600: 20%; ACT scores over 24: 29%; SAT evidence-based reading and writing scores over 700: 4%; SAT math scores over 700: 2%; ACT scores over 30: 3%.

Retention: 75% of full-time freshmen returned.

FACULTY

Total: 270, 60% full-time, 66% with terminal degrees.

Student/faculty ratio: 11:1.

ACADEMICS

Calendar: semesters. *Degrees:* bachelor's, master's, doctoral, post-master's, and postbachelor's certificates.

Special study options: accelerated degree program, adult/continuing education programs, advanced placement credit, distance learning, double majors, English as a second language, honors programs, independent study, internships, off-campus study, part-time degree program, services for LD students, student-designed majors, study abroad, summer session for credit.

Unusual degree programs: 3-2 engineering with Old Dominion University, University of Virginia.

Computers: 300 computers/terminals are available on campus for general student use. Students can access the following: campus intranet, computer help desk, free student e-mail accounts, online (class) grades, online (class) registration, online (class) schedules. Campuswide network is available. 100% of college-owned or -operated housing units are wired for high-speed Internet access. Wireless service is available via entire campus.

Library: Knight-Capron Library. *Books:* 109,236 (physical), 323,591 (digital/electronic); *Serial titles:* 109 (physical), 58,732 (digital/electronic); *Databases:* 98. Study areas open 24 hours, 5–7 days a week; students can reserve study rooms.

STUDENT LIFE

Housing options: on-campus residence required through junior year; coed, special housing for students with disabilities. Campus housing is university owned. Freshman campus housing is guaranteed.

Activities and organizations: drama/theater group, student-run newspaper, choral group, Student Government Association, Student Activities Board, Enrollment Student Ambassadors, Emergency Services, Greek Life, national fraternities, national sororities.

Athletics Member NCAA. All Division III. *Intercollegiate sports:* baseball M, basketball M/W, cheerleading M/W, cross-country running M/W, equestrian sports M/W, field hockey W, golf M, lacrosse M/W, soccer M/W, softball W, tennis M/W, track and field M/W, volleyball W. *Intramural sports:* basketball M(c)/W(c), golf M(c)/W(c), lacrosse M(c)/W(c), rugby M/W, soccer M(c)/W(c), tennis M(c)/W(c), volleyball M/W, wrestling M(c).

Campus security: 24-hour emergency response devices and patrols, late-night transport/escort service, controlled dormitory access.

Student services: health clinic, personal/psychological counseling.

COSTS & FINANCIAL AID

Costs (2018–19) *Comprehensive fee:* $48,370 includes full-time tuition ($36,720), mandatory fees ($970), and room and board ($10,680). Part-time tuition: $510 per credit hour. Part-time tuition and fees vary according to course load. *College room only:* $5470. Room and board charges vary according to board plan and housing facility. *Payment plans:* tuition prepayment, installment. *Waivers:* adult students, senior citizens, and employees or children of employees.

Financial Aid Of all full-time matriculated undergraduates who enrolled in 2017, 1,646 applied for aid, 1,497 were judged to have need, 329 had their need fully met. 187 Federal Work-Study jobs (averaging $1347). 513 state and other part-time jobs (averaging $1300). In 2017, 424 non-need-based awards were made. *Average percent of need met:* 78. *Average financial aid package:* $28,781. *Average need-based loan:* $3587. *Average need-based gift aid:* $25,227. *Average non-need-based aid:* $18,983. *Average indebtedness upon graduation:* $35,290.

APPLYING

Standardized Tests *Required:* SAT or ACT (for admission).

Options: electronic application, early admission, early decision, deferred entrance.

Application fee: $30.

Required: high school transcript. *Recommended:* essay or personal statement, 2 letters of recommendation, interview.

Application deadlines: rolling (freshmen), rolling (transfers).

Early decision deadline: 11/15.

Notification: continuous (freshmen), continuous (transfers), 12/15 (early decision).

CONTACT

Lynchburg College, 1501 Lakeside Drive, Lynchburg, VA 24501-3199. *Phone:* 434-544-8300. *Toll-free phone:* 800-426-8101.

See below for display ad and page 1334 for the College Close-Up.

Mary Baldwin University
Staunton, Virginia
http://www.marybaldwin.edu/

- **Independent** comprehensive, founded 1842
- **Small-town** 59-acre campus
- **Endowment** $35.1 million
- **Coed, primarily women** 1,137 undergraduate students, 63% full-time, 93% women, 7% men
- **Moderately difficult** entrance level, 95% of applicants were admitted

UNDERGRAD STUDENTS

720 full-time, 417 part-time. Students come from 39 states and territories; 13 other countries; 23% are from out of state; 20% Black or African American, non-Hispanic/Latino; 7% Hispanic/Latino; 2% Asian, non-Hispanic/Latino; 0.1% Native Hawaiian or other Pacific Islander, non-Hispanic/Latino; 0.9% American Indian or Alaska Native, non-Hispanic/Latino; 4% Two or more races, non-Hispanic/Latino; 5% Race/ethnicity unknown; 2% international; 11% transferred in; 85% live on campus.

Freshmen:

Admission: 1,397 applied, 1,323 admitted, 109 enrolled. *Average high school GPA:* 3.6. *Test scores:* SAT evidence-based reading and writing scores over 500: 74%; SAT math scores over 500: 59%; ACT scores over 18: 88%; SAT evidence-based reading and writing scores over 600: 36%; SAT math scores over 600: 18%; ACT scores over 24: 39%; SAT evidence-based reading and writing scores over 700: 8%; SAT math scores over 700: 5%; ACT scores over 30: 10%.

Retention: 65% of full-time freshmen returned.

FACULTY

Total: 235, 41% full-time, 79% with terminal degrees.

Student/faculty ratio: 9:1.

ACADEMICS

Calendar: 4-1-4. *Degrees:* certificates, bachelor's, master's, doctoral, and postbachelor's certificates.

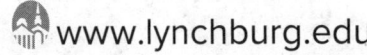

Special study options: academic remediation for entering students, accelerated degree program, adult/continuing education programs, advanced placement credit, distance learning, double majors, English as a second language, external degree program, freshman honors college, honors programs, independent study, internships, off-campus study, part-time degree program, services for LD students, student-designed majors, study abroad, summer session for credit. *ROTC:* Army (c), Navy (c), Air Force (c).

Unusual degree programs: 3-2 engineering with University of Virginia; nursing with Vanderbilt University, Jefferson College of Health Sciences; osteopathy with Edward Via College of Osteopathic Medicine.

Computers: 247 computers/terminals are available on campus for general student use. Students can access the following: computer help desk, free student e-mail accounts, online (class) grades, online (class) registration, online (class) schedules. Campuswide network is available. 100% of college-owned or -operated housing units are wired for high-speed Internet access. Wireless service is available via entire campus.
Library: Grafton Library. *Books:* 104,405 (physical), 367,524 (digital/electronic); *Serial titles:* 348 (physical), 31,879 (digital/electronic); *Databases:* 76. Weekly public service hours: 92; students can reserve study rooms.

STUDENT LIFE

Housing options: on-campus residence required through senior year; coed, women-only. Campus housing is university owned. Freshman campus housing is guaranteed.

Activities and organizations: drama/theater group, choral group, marching band, Minority Clubs United, Greater Things Dance Ministry, MBU Cheer, Ladies of Elegance, Math Club.

Athletics Member NCAA. All Division III. *Intercollegiate sports:* basketball W, cross-country running W, softball W, tennis W, track and field W, volleyball W. *Intramural sports:* equestrian sports W(c).

Campus security: 24-hour emergency response devices and patrols, late-night transport/escort service, controlled dormitory access.

Student services: health clinic, personal/psychological counseling.

COSTS & FINANCIAL AID

Costs (2018–19) Comprehensive fee: $40,495 includes full-time tuition ($30,690), mandatory fees ($395), and room and board ($9410). Part-time tuition: $460 per semester hour. *Required fees:* $60 per term part-time. *Room and board:* Room and board charges vary according to housing facility and student level. *Payment plan:* installment. *Waivers:* employees or children of employees.

Financial Aid Of all full-time matriculated undergraduates who enrolled in 2017, 670 applied for aid, 643 were judged to have need, 75 had their need fully met. 188 Federal Work-Study jobs (averaging $1608). 97 state and other part-time jobs (averaging $1870). In 2017, 22 non-need-based awards were made. *Average percent of need met:* 74. *Average financial aid package:* $26,009. *Average need-based loan:* $4475. *Average need-based gift aid:* $22,046. *Average non-need-based aid:* $15,189. *Average indebtedness upon graduation:* $32,679.

APPLYING

Standardized Tests *Required:* SAT or ACT (for admission).

Options: electronic application, early admission, deferred entrance.

Required: high school transcript. *Required for some:* essay or personal statement, 1 letter of recommendation, interview. *Recommended:* 1 letter of recommendation.

Application deadlines: rolling (freshmen), rolling (transfers).

Notification: continuous until 9/15 (freshmen), continuous until 9/15 (transfers).

CONTACT

Mr. Matthew Munsey, Director of Admissions, Mary Baldwin University, Frederick and New Streets, Staunton, VA 24401. *Phone:* 540-887-7211. *Toll-free phone:* 800-468-2262. *Fax:* 540-887-7292. *E-mail:* mmunsey@marybaldwin.edu.

Marymount University
Arlington, Virginia
http://www.marymount.edu/

- **Independent** comprehensive, founded 1950, affiliated with Roman Catholic Church
- **Suburban** 21-acre campus with easy access to Washington, DC
- **Endowment** $43.0 million
- **Coed** 2,305 undergraduate students, 90% full-time, 65% women, 35% men
- **Moderately difficult** entrance level, 92% of applicants were admitted

UNDERGRAD STUDENTS

2,069 full-time, 236 part-time. Students come from 38 states and territories; 66 other countries; 40% are from out of state; 14% Black or African American, non-Hispanic/Latino; 17% Hispanic/Latino; 7% Asian, non-Hispanic/Latino; 0.3% Native Hawaiian or other Pacific Islander, non-Hispanic/Latino; 0.4% American Indian or Alaska Native, non-Hispanic/Latino; 4% Two or more races, non-Hispanic/Latino; 5% Race/ethnicity unknown; 17% international; 11% transferred in; 31% live on campus.

Freshmen:
Admission: 2,416 applied, 2,229 admitted, 405 enrolled. *Average high school GPA:* 3.3. *Test scores:* SAT evidence-based reading and writing scores over 500: 70%; SAT math scores over 500: 55%; ACT scores over 18: 87%; SAT evidence-based reading and writing scores over 600: 21%; SAT math scores over 600: 14%; ACT scores over 24: 35%; SAT evidence-based reading and writing scores over 700: 2%; SAT math scores over 700: 1%; ACT scores over 30: 10%.
Retention: 78% of full-time freshmen returned.

FACULTY

Total: 363, 45% full-time, 64% with terminal degrees.
Student/faculty ratio: 13:1.

ACADEMICS

Calendar: semesters plus 2 summer terms. *Degrees:* certificates, bachelor's, master's, doctoral, post-master's, and postbachelor's certificates.

Special study options: academic remediation for entering students, accelerated degree program, advanced placement credit, distance learning, double majors, honors programs, independent study, internships, off-campus study, part-time degree program, services for LD students, student-designed majors, study abroad, summer session for credit. *ROTC:* Army (c), Air Force (c).

Unusual degree programs: 3-2 business administration; information technology, health sciences.

Computers: 250 computers/terminals are available on campus for general student use. Students can access the following: campus intranet, computer help desk, free student e-mail accounts, online (class) grades, online (class) registration, online (class) schedules, Online drive space. Campuswide network is available. 100% of college-owned or -operated housing units are wired for high-speed Internet access. Wireless service is available via entire campus.
Library: Emerson C. Reinsch Library plus 1 other. Weekly public service hours: 104; students can reserve study rooms.

STUDENT LIFE

Housing options: on-campus residence required through sophomore year; coed, men-only, special housing for students with disabilities. Campus housing is university owned and leased by the school. Freshman applicants given priority for college housing.

Activities and organizations: drama/theater group, student-run newspaper, choral group, Fashion Club, Student Nurses Association, International Club, Association for Campus Events, Blue Harmony (show choir).

Athletics Member NCAA. All Division III. *Intercollegiate sports:* baseball M, basketball M/W, cheerleading W(c), cross-country running M/W, golf M/W, ice hockey M(c), lacrosse M/W, soccer M/W, swimming and diving M/W, triathlon M(c)/W(c), volleyball M/W. *Intramural sports:* basketball M/W, soccer M, ultimate Frisbee M/W, volleyball M, water polo M/W.

Campus security: 24-hour emergency response devices and patrols, student patrols, late-night transport/escort service, controlled dormitory access.

Student services: health clinic, personal/psychological counseling.

COSTS & FINANCIAL AID

Costs (2017–18) *One-time required fee:* $450. *Comprehensive fee:* $43,230 includes full-time tuition ($29,950), mandatory fees ($475), and room and board ($12,805). Part-time tuition: $975 per credit hour. *Required fees:* $11 per credit hour part-time. *Room and board:* Room and board charges vary according to housing facility. *Payment plan:* installment. *Waivers:* senior citizens and employees or children of employees.

Financial Aid Of all full-time matriculated undergraduates who enrolled in 2017, 1,382 applied for aid, 1,255 were judged to have need, 158 had their need fully met. 668 Federal Work-Study jobs (averaging $2044). In 2017, 440 non-need-based awards were made. *Average percent of need met:* 60. *Average financial aid package:* $20,543. *Average need-based loan:* $4468. *Average need-based gift aid:* $6828. *Average non-need-based aid:* $13,216. *Average indebtedness upon graduation:* $34,051.

APPLYING

Standardized Tests *Required for some:* SAT or ACT (for admission).

Options: electronic application, deferred entrance.

Application fee: $40.

Required: essay or personal statement, high school transcript, minimum 2.6 GPA, 1 letter of recommendation. *Required for some:* interview. *Recommended:* interview.

Application deadlines: rolling (freshmen), rolling (transfers).

Notification: continuous (freshmen), continuous (transfers).

CONTACT

Ms. Dana Matassino, Director of Undergraduate Admissions, Marymount University, 2807 North Glebe Road, Arlington, VA 22207-4299. *Phone:* 703-284-1500. *Toll-free phone:* 800-548-7638. *Fax:* 703-522-0349. *E-mail:* admissions@marymount.edu.

Norfolk State University

Norfolk, Virginia

http://www.nsu.edu/

CONTACT

Mr. Kevin M. Holmes, Director of Recruitment and Admissions, Norfolk State University, 700 Park Avenue, Norfolk, VA 23504. *Phone:* 757-823-9222. *Toll-free phone:* 800-274-1821. *Fax:* 757-823-2078. *E-mail:* admissions@nsu.edu.

Old Dominion University

Norfolk, Virginia

http://www.odu.edu/

- **State-supported** university, founded 1930
- **Urban** 251-acre campus with easy access to Virginia Beach
- **Endowment** $223.1 million
- **Coed** 19,540 undergraduate students, 77% full-time, 55% women, 45% men
- **Moderately difficult** entrance level, 86% of applicants were admitted

UNDERGRAD STUDENTS

15,036 full-time, 4,504 part-time. Students come from 50 states and territories; 88 other countries; 8% are from out of state; 31% Black or African American, non-Hispanic/Latino; 9% Hispanic/Latino; 5% Asian, non-Hispanic/Latino; 0.3% Native Hawaiian or other Pacific Islander, non-Hispanic/Latino; 0.3% American Indian or Alaska Native, non-Hispanic/Latino; 7% Two or more races, non-Hispanic/Latino; 3% Race/ethnicity unknown; 2% international; 10% transferred in; 24% live on campus.

Freshmen:

Admission: 11,159 applied, 9,566 admitted, 2,938 enrolled. *Average high school GPA:* 3.3. *Test scores:* SAT evidence-based reading and writing scores over 500: 79%; SAT math scores over 500: 70%; ACT scores over 18: 83%; SAT evidence-based reading and writing scores over 600: 31%; SAT math scores over 600: 21%; ACT scores over 24: 34%; SAT

evidence-based reading and writing scores over 700: 3%; SAT math scores over 700: 2%; ACT scores over 30: 4%.

Retention: 80% of full-time freshmen returned.

FACULTY

Total: 1,500, 56% full-time, 65% with terminal degrees.

Student/faculty ratio: 18:1.

ACADEMICS

Calendar: semesters. *Degrees:* certificates, bachelor's, master's, doctoral, post-master's, and postbachelor's certificates.

Special study options: accelerated degree program, adult/continuing education programs, advanced placement credit, cooperative education, distance learning, double majors, English as a second language, freshman honors college, honors programs, independent study, internships, off-campus study, part-time degree program, services for LD students, student-designed majors, study abroad, summer session for credit. *ROTC:* Army (b), Navy (b).

Unusual degree programs: 3-2 business administration; engineering; nursing; international studies, dental hygiene, communications/humanities, English, English/applied linguistics, history, interdisciplinary studies/humanities, computer science, women's studies/humanities, philosophy/humanities, health science/public health, environmental health/public health.

Computers: 2,028 computers/terminals and 12,122 ports are available on campus for general student use. Students can access the following: campus intranet, computer help desk, free student e-mail accounts, online (class) grades, online (class) registration, online (class) schedules, online courses. Campuswide network is available. 100% of college-owned or -operated housing units are wired for high-speed Internet access. Wireless service is available via entire campus.

Library: Patricia W. and Douglas Perry Library plus 3 others. *Books:* 1.1 million (physical), 1.6 million (digital/electronic); *Serial titles:* 14,465 (physical), 87,579 (digital/electronic); *Databases:* 449. Weekly public service hours: 146; study areas open 24 hours, 5–7 days a week; students can reserve study rooms.

STUDENT LIFE

Housing options: coed, women-only, special housing for students with disabilities. Campus housing is university owned and leased by the school. Freshman campus housing is guaranteed.

Activities and organizations: drama/theater group, student-run newspaper, radio station, choral group, marching band, Asian Pacific American Student Union, Student Government Association, Student Veterans Association, Colleges Against Cancer, Student Activities Council, national fraternities, national sororities.

Athletics Member NCAA. All Division I. *Intercollegiate sports:* baseball M(s), basketball M(s)/W(s), cheerleading M(s)/W(s), crew M(c)/W(s), equestrian sports M(c)/W(c), field hockey W(s), football M(s), golf M(s)/W(s), ice hockey M(c)/W(c), lacrosse M(c)/W(s), rugby M(c)/W(c), sailing M/W, soccer M(s)/W(s), softball W(c), swimming and diving M(s)/W(s), tennis M(s)/W(s), ultimate Frisbee M(c)/W(c), volleyball M(c)/W(c), wrestling M(s). *Intramural sports:* badminton M/W, basketball M/W, golf M/W, racquetball M/W, soccer M/W, softball M/W, table tennis M/W, ultimate Frisbee M/W, volleyball M/W.

Campus security: 24-hour emergency response devices and patrols, student patrols, late-night transport/escort service, controlled dormitory access, lighted pathways, video cameras, on-campus EMTs, emergency notification system.

Student services: health clinic, personal/psychological counseling, women's center.

COSTS & FINANCIAL AID

Costs (2017–18) *Tuition:* state resident $10,050 full-time, $335 per credit hour part-time; nonresident $27,900 full-time, $930 per credit hour part-time. *Required fees:* $300 full-time, $66 per term part-time. *Room and board:* $11,268; room only: $6278. Room and board charges vary according to board plan, housing facility, location, and student level. *Payment plans:* installment, deferred payment. *Waivers:* senior citizens and employees or children of employees.

Financial Aid Of all full-time matriculated undergraduates who enrolled in 2017, 12,100 applied for aid, 10,404 were judged to have need, 1,484 had their need fully met. 200 Federal Work-Study jobs (averaging $2400). In 2017, 912 non-need-based awards were made. *Average percent of need*

met: 47. *Average financial aid package:* $11,059. *Average need-based loan:* $4361. *Average need-based gift aid:* $7369. *Average non-need-based aid:* $5170. *Average indebtedness upon graduation:* $32,092.

APPLYING
Standardized Tests *Required for some:* SAT or ACT (for admission).

Options: electronic application, early admission, early action, deferred entrance.

Application fee: $50.

Required: high school transcript, minimum 2.7 GPA. *Recommended:* essay or personal statement, 1 letter of recommendation.

Application deadlines: 2/1 (freshmen), 5/1 (transfers), 12/1 (early action).

Notification: continuous (freshmen), continuous (out-of-state freshmen), continuous (transfers), 1/15 (early action).

CONTACT
Ms. Shereen Williams, Customer Service Manager, Admissions Office, Old Dominion University, 108 Rollins Hall, 5215 Hampton Boulevard, Norfolk, VA 23529. *Phone:* 757-683-3648. *Toll-free phone:* 800-348-7926. *Fax:* 757-683-3255. *E-mail:* admissions@odu.edu.

Patrick Henry College
Purcellville, Virginia
http://www.phc.edu/
- **Independent nondenominational** 4-year, founded 2000
- **Small-town** 119-acre campus with easy access to Washington, DC
- **Endowment** $1.2 million
- **Coed**
- **Moderately difficult** entrance level

FACULTY
Student/faculty ratio: 10:1.

ACADEMICS
Calendar: semesters. *Degree:* bachelor's.
Library: Patrick Henry College Library. *Books:* 38,995 (physical), 387,798 (digital/electronic); *Serial titles:* 240 (physical), 42,361 (digital/electronic); *Databases:* 33. Weekly public service hours: 80; students can reserve study rooms.

STUDENT LIFE
Housing options: on-campus residence required through sophomore year; men-only, women-only. Campus housing is university owned. Freshman applicants given priority for college housing.

Activities and organizations: drama/theater group, student-run newspaper, choral group, Drama Club, Eden Troupe, Student Government, Chorale, College Republicans, Debate/Moot Court.

Athletics Member USCAA.

Campus security: 24-hour emergency response devices and patrols, student patrols, late-night transport/escort service, controlled dormitory access, after hours patrols by trained security personnel.

Student services: health clinic, personal/psychological counseling.

COSTS & FINANCIAL AID
Costs (2017–18) *Comprehensive fee:* $38,900 includes full-time tuition ($27,922), mandatory fees ($250), and room and board ($10,728). Full-time tuition and fees vary according to course load. Part-time tuition: $1163 per credit hour. Part-time tuition and fees vary according to course level and course load. *Room and board:* Room and board charges vary according to board plan and housing facility. *Payment plans:* installment, deferred payment.

Financial Aid Of all full-time matriculated undergraduates who enrolled in 2016, 94 applied for aid, 70 were judged to have need. In 2016, 140 non-need-based awards were made. *Average percent of need met:* 35. *Average financial aid package:* $14,600. *Average need-based gift aid:* $7000. *Average non-need-based aid:* $9100. *Average indebtedness upon graduation:* $44,000. *Financial aid deadline:* 6/15.

APPLYING
Standardized Tests *Required:* SAT or ACT (for admission).

Options: electronic application, early action, deferred entrance.

Application fee: $20.

Required: essay or personal statement, high school transcript, 2 letters of recommendation, interview, official transcripts from all colleges attended, reading list.

CONTACT
Mr. Stephen C. Allen, Director of Admissions and Communications, Patrick Henry College, 10 Patrick Henry Circle, Purcellville, VA 20132. *Phone:* 540-338-1776. *Toll-free phone:* 888-338-1776. *Fax:* 540-441-8119. *E-mail:* admissions@phc.edu.

Radford University
Radford, Virginia
http://www.radford.edu/
- **State-supported** university, founded 1910
- **Small-town** 204-acre campus
- **Endowment** $50.3 million
- **Coed** 8,418 undergraduate students, 96% full-time, 57% women, 43% men
- **Minimally difficult** entrance level, 74% of applicants were admitted

UNDERGRAD STUDENTS
8,049 full-time, 369 part-time. Students come from 41 states and territories; 63 other countries; 6% are from out of state; 17% Black or African American, non-Hispanic/Latino; 7% Hispanic/Latino; 1% Asian, non-Hispanic/Latino; 0.1% Native Hawaiian or other Pacific Islander, non-Hispanic/Latino; 0.2% American Indian or Alaska Native, non-Hispanic/Latino; 5% Two or more races, non-Hispanic/Latino; 2% Race/ethnicity unknown; 1% international; 8% transferred in; 41% live on campus.

Freshmen:
Admission: 14,620 applied, 10,866 admitted, 1,848 enrolled. *Average high school GPA:* 3.2. *Test scores:* SAT evidence-based reading and writing scores over 500: 68%; SAT math scores over 500: 57%; ACT scores over 18: 75%; SAT evidence-based reading and writing scores over 600: 17%; SAT math scores over 600: 8%; ACT scores over 24: 21%; SAT evidence-based reading and writing scores over 700: 1%; ACT scores over 30: 2%.

Retention: 76% of full-time freshmen returned.

FACULTY
Total: 739, 62% full-time, 60% with terminal degrees.
Student/faculty ratio: 16:1.

ACADEMICS
Calendar: semesters. *Degrees:* certificates, bachelor's, master's, doctoral, post-master's, and postbachelor's certificates.

Special study options: accelerated degree program, advanced placement credit, distance learning, double majors, English as a second language, honors programs, independent study, internships, off-campus study, part-time degree program, services for LD students, student-designed majors, study abroad, summer session for credit. *ROTC:* Army (b).

Computers: 900 computers/terminals are available on campus for general student use. Students can access the following: campus intranet, computer help desk, free student e-mail accounts, online (class) grades, online (class) registration, online (class) schedules, online financial aid status and student accounts payable. Campuswide network is available. 100% of college-owned or -operated housing units are wired for high-speed Internet access. Wireless service is available via entire campus.
Library: McConnell Library. *Books:* 271,383 (physical), 332,165 (digital/electronic); *Serial titles:* 558 (physical), 28,298 (digital/electronic); *Databases:* 535. Students can reserve study rooms.

STUDENT LIFE
Housing options: on-campus residence required through sophomore year; coed, special housing for students with disabilities. Campus housing is university owned and leased by the school. Freshman campus housing is guaranteed.

Activities and organizations: drama/theater group, student-run newspaper, radio station, choral group, Radford Crafty, American Sign Language Club, Radford Student Programming and Campus Events (R-SPaCE), National Society for Collegiate Scholars, Scholar-Citizen Initiative Student Organization, national fraternities, national sororities.

Athletics Member NCAA. All Division I. *Intercollegiate sports:* baseball M(s), basketball M(s)/W(s), cross-country running M(s)/W(s), golf M(s)/W(s), lacrosse W(s), soccer M(s)/W(s), softball W(s), tennis M(s)/W(s), track and field W(s), volleyball W(s). *Intramural sports:* basketball M/W, bowling M(c)/W(c), cheerleading M(c)/W(c), cross-country running M/W, equestrian sports M(c)/W(c), field hockey W(c), football M/W, ice hockey M(c)/W(c), lacrosse M(c)/W(c), riflery M(c)/W(c), rugby M(c)/W(c), skiing (downhill) M(c)/W(c), soccer M(c)/W(c), softball M/W, swimming and diving M(c)/W(c), table tennis M/W, tennis M/W, ultimate Frisbee M/W, volleyball M/W, wrestling M(c)/W(c).

Campus security: 24-hour emergency response devices and patrols, late-night transport/escort service, controlled dormitory access.

Student services: health clinic, personal/psychological counseling.

COSTS & FINANCIAL AID
Costs (2017–18) *Tuition:* state resident $7407 full-time, $308 per credit hour part-time; nonresident $19,042 full-time, $793 per credit hour part-time. Full-time tuition and fees vary according to course load. Part-time tuition and fees vary according to course load. *Required fees:* $3220 full-time, $135 per credit hour part-time. *Room and board:* $9131; room only: $5026. Room and board charges vary according to board plan and housing facility. *Payment plan:* installment. *Waivers:* senior citizens and employees or children of employees.

Financial Aid Of all full-time matriculated undergraduates who enrolled in 2017, 6,378 applied for aid, 5,140 were judged to have need, 1,107 had their need fully met. 272 Federal Work-Study jobs (averaging $2458). 329 state and other part-time jobs (averaging $2442). In 2017, 302 non-need-based awards were made. *Average percent of need met:* 77. *Average financial aid package:* $10,054. *Average need-based loan:* $4084. *Average need-based gift aid:* $7452. *Average non-need-based aid:* $4056. *Average indebtedness upon graduation:* $31,463.

APPLYING
Standardized Tests *Recommended:* SAT or ACT (for admission).

Options: electronic application, early admission, early action, deferred entrance.

Required: high school transcript. *Recommended:* essay or personal statement, letters of recommendation.

Application deadlines: 2/1 (freshmen), 6/1 (transfers), 12/1 (early action).

Notification: 4/1 (freshmen), continuous (transfers), 1/15 (early action).

CONTACT
Ms. Mildred Johnson, Dean of Admissions, Radford University, PO Box 6903, Radford University, Radford, VA 24142. *Phone:* 540-831-5371. *Fax:* 540-831-5038. *E-mail:* admissions@radford.edu.

Randolph College
Lynchburg, Virginia
http://www.randolphcollege.edu/
- **Independent Methodist** comprehensive, founded 1891
- **Suburban** 100-acre campus
- **Coed** 663 undergraduate students, 97% full-time, 63% women, 37% men
- **Moderately difficult** entrance level, 86% of applicants were admitted

UNDERGRAD STUDENTS
645 full-time, 18 part-time. 29% are from out of state; 15% Black or African American, non-Hispanic/Latino; 6% Hispanic/Latino; 3% Asian, non-Hispanic/Latino; 0.2% Native Hawaiian or other Pacific Islander, non-Hispanic/Latino; 6% Two or more races, non-Hispanic/Latino; 0.3% Race/ethnicity unknown; 4% international; 5% transferred in; 76% live on campus.

Freshmen:
Admission: 1,696 applied, 1,466 admitted, 202 enrolled. *Average high school GPA:* 3.4. *Test scores:* SAT evidence-based reading and writing scores over 500: 72%; SAT math scores over 500: 62%; ACT scores over 18: 86%; SAT evidence-based reading and writing scores over 600: 35%; SAT math scores over 600: 19%; ACT scores over 24: 30%; SAT evidence-based reading and writing scores over 700: 2%; SAT math scores over 700: 2%; ACT scores over 30: 7%.

Retention: 67% of full-time freshmen returned.

FACULTY
Total: 83, 86% full-time, 82% with terminal degrees.
Student/faculty ratio: 9:1.

ACADEMICS
Calendar: semesters. *Degrees:* bachelor's and master's.

Special study options: adult/continuing education programs, part-time degree program.

Computers: Students can access the following: campus intranet, computer help desk, free student e-mail accounts, online (class) grades, online (class) registration, online (class) schedules. Campuswide network is available. Wireless service is available via entire campus.
Library: Lipscomb Library.

STUDENT LIFE
Housing options: on-campus residence required through senior year; coed. Campus housing is university owned. Freshman campus housing is guaranteed.

Athletics Member NCAA. All Division III. *Intercollegiate sports:* basketball M/W, cross-country running M/W, equestrian sports M/W, lacrosse M/W, soccer M/W, softball W, tennis M/W, volleyball W.

Campus security: 24-hour emergency response devices and patrols, late-night transport/escort service.

COSTS & FINANCIAL AID
Costs (2018–19) *Comprehensive fee:* $53,275 includes full-time tuition ($39,000), mandatory fees ($695), and room and board ($13,580). Part-time tuition: $1565 per credit hour. Part-time tuition and fees vary according to course load. *Payment plan:* installment. *Waivers:* adult students and employees or children of employees.

Financial Aid Of all full-time matriculated undergraduates who enrolled in 2017, 556 applied for aid, 510 were judged to have need, 93 had their need fully met. In 2017, 129 non-need-based awards were made. *Average percent of need met:* 76. *Average financial aid package:* $32,962. *Average need-based loan:* $4742. *Average need-based gift aid:* $28,380. *Average non-need-based aid:* $23,376. *Average indebtedness upon graduation:* $33,830.

APPLYING
Standardized Tests *Required:* SAT or ACT (for admission).

Options: electronic application, early admission, early action, deferred entrance.

Required: essay or personal statement, high school transcript, 2 letters of recommendation. *Recommended:* interview.

CONTACT
Ms. Margaret Blount, Director of Admissions, Randolph College, 2500 Rivermont Avenue, Lynchburg, VA 24503-1555. *Phone:* 434-947-8100. *Toll-free phone:* 800-745-7692. *Fax:* 434-947-8996. *E-mail:* admissions@randolphcollege.edu.

Randolph-Macon College
Ashland, Virginia
http://www.rmc.edu/
- **Independent United Methodist** 4-year, founded 1830
- **Suburban** 116-acre campus with easy access to Richmond
- **Endowment** $152.1 million
- **Coed** 1,453 undergraduate students, 98% full-time, 54% women, 46% men
- **Moderately difficult** entrance level, 62% of applicants were admitted

UNDERGRAD STUDENTS
1,428 full-time, 25 part-time. Students come from 24 states and territories; 19 other countries; 25% are from out of state; 9% Black or African American, non-Hispanic/Latino; 4% Hispanic/Latino; 2% Asian, non-Hispanic/Latino; 0.1% Native Hawaiian or other Pacific Islander, non-Hispanic/Latino; 0.6% American Indian or Alaska Native, non-Hispanic/Latino; 4% Two or more races, non-Hispanic/Latino; 1% Race/ethnicity unknown; 1% international; 3% transferred in; 85% live on campus.

Freshmen:
Admission: 2,820 applied, 1,755 admitted, 374 enrolled. *Average high school GPA:* 3.7. *Test scores:* SAT evidence-based reading and writing

scores over 500: 95%; SAT math scores over 500: 84%; ACT scores over 18: 98%; SAT evidence-based reading and writing scores over 600: 54%; SAT math scores over 600: 29%; ACT scores over 24: 59%; SAT evidence-based reading and writing scores over 700: 9%; SAT math scores over 700: 4%; ACT scores over 30: 13%.

Retention: 84% of full-time freshmen returned.

FACULTY

Total: 171, 64% full-time, 80% with terminal degrees.

Student/faculty ratio: 11:1.

ACADEMICS

Calendar: 4-1-4. *Degree:* bachelor's.

Special study options: academic remediation for entering students, accelerated degree program, advanced placement credit, double majors, honors programs, independent study, internships, off-campus study, part-time degree program, services for LD students, study abroad, summer session for credit. *ROTC:* Army (c).

Unusual degree programs: 3-2 business administration with Virginia Commonwealth University; engineering with Columbia University, University of Virginia; forestry with Duke University.

Computers: 345 computers/terminals and 1,500 ports are available on campus for general student use. Students can access the following: campus intranet, computer help desk, free student e-mail accounts, online (class) registration, online (class) schedules. Campuswide network is available. 100% of college-owned or -operated housing units are wired for high-speed Internet access. Wireless service is available via classrooms, computer centers, computer labs, dorm rooms, learning centers, libraries, student centers.

Library: McGraw-Page Library. *Books:* 138,901 (physical), 408,846 (digital/electronic); *Serial titles:* 722 (physical), 101,405 (digital/electronic); *Databases:* 130. Study areas open 24 hours, 5–7 days a week; students can reserve study rooms.

STUDENT LIFE

Housing options: on-campus residence required through junior year; coed, men-only, women-only, special housing for students with disabilities. Campus housing is university owned. Freshman campus housing is guaranteed.

Activities and organizations: drama/theater group, student-run newspaper, radio and television station, choral group, marching band, Habitat for Humanity, Macon Outdoors, Relay for Life, College Panhellenic Council, R-MC Angler's Club, national fraternities, national sororities.

Athletics Member NCAA. All Division III. *Intercollegiate sports:* baseball M, basketball M/W, cheerleading W(c), equestrian sports M(c)/W(c), field hockey W, football M, golf M/W, lacrosse M/W, soccer M/W, softball W, swimming and diving M/W, tennis M/W, volleyball M/W. *Intramural sports:* badminton M/W, basketball M/W, cheerleading M(c)/W(c), cross-country running M(c)/W(c), football M/W, lacrosse M/W, racquetball M/W, rugby M/W, sand volleyball M(c)/W, soccer M/W, softball M/W, table tennis M/W, tennis M/W, ultimate Frisbee M/W, volleyball M/W, water polo M/W.

Campus security: 24-hour emergency response devices and patrols, late-night transport/escort service, controlled dormitory access.

Student services: health clinic, personal/psychological counseling, women's center.

COSTS & FINANCIAL AID

Costs (2018–19) *One-time required fee:* $100. *Comprehensive fee:* $53,160 includes full-time tuition ($40,000), mandatory fees ($1300), and room and board ($11,860). Full-time tuition and fees vary according to reciprocity agreements. *College room only:* $6600. Room and board charges vary according to board plan and housing facility. *Payment plan:* installment. *Waivers:* employees or children of employees.

Financial Aid Of all full-time matriculated undergraduates who enrolled in 2016, 1,234 applied for aid, 1,037 were judged to have need, 318 had their need fully met. In 2016, 370 non-need-based awards were made. *Average percent of need met:* 82. *Average financial aid package:* $28,588. *Average need-based loan:* $5271. *Average need-based gift aid:* $24,444. *Average non-need-based aid:* $17,939. *Average indebtedness upon graduation:* $33,015.

APPLYING

Standardized Tests *Required:* SAT or ACT (for admission). *Recommended:* SAT Subject Tests (for admission).

Options: electronic application, early admission, early action, deferred entrance.

Application fee: $30.

Required: essay or personal statement, high school transcript, minimum 2.0 GPA, 1 letter of recommendation. *Recommended:* interview.

Application deadlines: 3/1 (freshmen), 4/1 (transfers), 11/15 (early action).

Notification: 4/1 (freshmen), 5/1 (transfers), 1/1 (early action).

CONTACT

Erin Slater, Director of Admissions, Randolph-Macon College, PO Box 5005, Ashland, VA 23005-5505. *Phone:* 804-752-7305. *Toll-free phone:* 800-888-1762. *Fax:* 804-752-4707. *E-mail:* admissions@rmc.edu.

Regent University

Virginia Beach, Virginia

http://www.regent.edu/

- **Independent Christian** comprehensive, founded 1977
- **Suburban** 70-acre campus
- **Endowment** $101.1 million
- **Coed** 4,660 undergraduate students, 51% full-time, 63% women, 37% men
- **Minimally difficult** entrance level, 81% of applicants were admitted

UNDERGRAD STUDENTS

2,364 full-time, 2,296 part-time. Students come from 50 states and territories; 19 other countries; 57% are from out of state; 29% Black or African American, non-Hispanic/Latino; 9% Hispanic/Latino; 1% Asian, non-Hispanic/Latino; 0.3% Native Hawaiian or other Pacific Islander, non-Hispanic/Latino; 0.6% American Indian or Alaska Native, non-Hispanic/Latino; 5% Two or more races, non-Hispanic/Latino; 2% Race/ethnicity unknown; 0.6% international; 30% transferred in; 14% live on campus.

Freshmen:
Admission: 1,887 applied, 1,530 admitted, 487 enrolled. *Average high school GPA:* 3.3. *Test scores:* SAT evidence-based reading and writing scores over 500: 78%; SAT math scores over 500: 63%; ACT scores over 18: 88%; SAT evidence-based reading and writing scores over 600: 27%; SAT math scores over 600: 19%; ACT scores over 24: 42%; SAT evidence-based reading and writing scores over 700: 3%; SAT math scores over 700: 3%; ACT scores over 30: 7%.

Retention: 78% of full-time freshmen returned.

FACULTY

Total: 837, 18% full-time, 68% with terminal degrees.

Student/faculty ratio: 21:1.

ACADEMICS

Calendar: trimesters. *Degrees:* certificates, associate, bachelor's, master's, doctoral, post-master's, and postbachelor's certificates.

Special study options: academic remediation for entering students, adult/continuing education programs, advanced placement credit, distance learning, double majors, external degree program, freshman honors college, honors programs, internships, off-campus study, part-time degree program, services for LD students, study abroad, summer session for credit. *ROTC:* Army (c), Navy (c).

Unusual degree programs: 3-2 business administration with Regent University.

Computers: 70 computers/terminals and 75 ports are available on campus for general student use. Students can access the following: campus intranet, computer help desk, free student e-mail accounts, online (class) grades, online (class) registration, online (class) schedules. Campuswide network is available. 100% of college-owned or -operated housing units are wired for high-speed Internet access. Wireless service is available via entire campus.

Library: Regent University Library plus 1 other. *Books:* 321,395 (physical), 470,995 (digital/electronic); *Serial titles:* 106 (physical), 84,710 (digital/electronic); *Databases:* 155. Weekly public service hours: 98; students can reserve study rooms.

STUDENT LIFE

Housing options: on-campus residence required for freshman year; men-only, women-only, special housing for students with disabilities. Campus housing is university owned. Freshman applicants given priority for college housing.

Activities and organizations: drama/theater group, student-run newspaper, choral group, College Student Leadership Board, Student Activities Board, Psychology Club, Student Alumni Ambassadors (SAA), Undergraduate Debate Association, national fraternities, national sororities.

Athletics Member NCCAA. *Intercollegiate sports:* cross-country running M/W, soccer M/W, track and field M/W, volleyball W. *Intramural sports:* basketball M/W, soccer M/W, ultimate Frisbee M/W, volleyball M/W.

Campus security: 24-hour emergency response devices and patrols, student patrols, late-night transport/escort service, controlled dormitory access.

Student services: personal/psychological counseling.

COSTS & FINANCIAL AID

Costs (2017–18) *Comprehensive fee:* $25,728 includes full-time tuition ($16,650), mandatory fees ($828), and room and board ($8250). Full-time tuition and fees vary according to course load. Part-time tuition: $555 per credit hour. Part-time tuition and fees vary according to course load. *Required fees:* $564 per term part-time. *College room only:* $5730. Room and board charges vary according to board plan and housing facility. *Payment plan:* installment. *Waivers:* employees or children of employees.

Financial Aid Of all full-time matriculated undergraduates who enrolled in 2017, 2,030 applied for aid, 1,859 were judged to have need, 170 had their need fully met. In 2017, 296 non-need-based awards were made. *Average percent of need met:* 60. *Average financial aid package:* $10,819. *Average need-based loan:* $3703. *Average need-based gift aid:* $8566. *Average non-need-based aid:* $7253. *Average indebtedness upon graduation:* $28,035.

APPLYING

Standardized Tests *Required for some:* SAT or ACT (for admission).

Options: electronic application, deferred entrance.

Application fee: $50.

Required: high school transcript. *Required for some:* essay or personal statement, minimum 3.0 GPA.

Application deadlines: 8/1 (freshmen), 8/1 (transfers).

Notification: continuous (freshmen), continuous (transfers).

CONTACT

Mrs. Heidi Cece, Associate Vice President, Enrollment Management, Regent University, 1000 Regent University Drive, Virginia Beach, VA 23464. *Phone:* 800-373-5504. *Toll-free phone:* 800-373-5504. *Fax:* 757-352-4839. *E-mail:* admissions@regent.edu.

Roanoke College
Salem, Virginia
http://www.roanoke.edu/

- **Independent** 4-year, founded 1842, affiliated with Evangelical Lutheran Church in America
- **Suburban** 80-acre campus
- **Endowment** $129.7 million
- **Coed** 2,037 undergraduate students, 97% full-time, 58% women, 42% men
- **Moderately difficult** entrance level, 67% of applicants were admitted

UNDERGRAD STUDENTS

1,973 full-time, 64 part-time. Students come from 42 states and territories; 32 other countries; 48% are from out of state; 6% Black or African American, non-Hispanic/Latino; 5% Hispanic/Latino; 1% Asian, non-Hispanic/Latino; 0.1% Native Hawaiian or other Pacific Islander, non-Hispanic/Latino; 0.1% American Indian or Alaska Native, non-Hispanic/Latino; 5% Two or more races, non-Hispanic/Latino; 3% international; 3% transferred in; 76% live on campus.

Freshmen:

Admission: 5,117 applied, 3,438 admitted, 557 enrolled. *Average high school GPA:* 3.5. *Test scores:* SAT evidence-based reading and writing scores over 500: 90%; SAT math scores over 500: 84%; ACT scores over

18: 96%; SAT evidence-based reading and writing scores over 600: 43%; SAT math scores over 600: 29%; ACT scores over 24: 59%; SAT evidence-based reading and writing scores over 700: 5%; SAT math scores over 700: 4%; ACT scores over 30: 9%.

Retention: 84% of full-time freshmen returned.

FACULTY

Total: 221, 75% full-time, 74% with terminal degrees.

Student/faculty ratio: 11:1.

ACADEMICS

Calendar: semesters. *Degree:* bachelor's.

Special study options: accelerated degree program, adult/continuing education programs, advanced placement credit, distance learning, double majors, English as a second language, honors programs, independent study, internships, off-campus study, part-time degree program, services for LD students, study abroad, summer session for credit.

Unusual degree programs: 3-2 engineering with Virginia Polytechnic Institute and State University.

Computers: 270 computers/terminals and 1,600 ports are available on campus for general student use. Students can access the following: campus intranet, computer help desk, free student e-mail accounts, online (class) grades, online (class) registration, online (class) schedules, discounts on computer hardware and software purchases, free office software, free security software. Campuswide network is available. 100% of college-owned or -operated housing units are wired for high-speed Internet access. Wireless service is available via entire campus.

Library: Fintel Library. *Books:* 184,114 (physical), 195,325 (digital/electronic); *Serial titles:* 266 (physical), 75,297 (digital/electronic); *Databases:* 222. Weekly public service hours: 93; study areas open 24 hours, 5–7 days a week; students can reserve study rooms.

STUDENT LIFE

Housing options: on-campus residence required through senior year; coed, women-only, special housing for students with disabilities. Campus housing is university owned. Freshman campus housing is guaranteed.

Activities and organizations: drama/theater group, student-run newspaper, radio station, choral group, Catholic Campus Ministry, Roanoke College Lutherans, International Club, Colleges Against Cancer, College Republicans, national fraternities, national sororities.

Athletics Member NCAA. All Division III. *Intercollegiate sports:* baseball M, basketball M/W, cross-country running M/W, field hockey W, golf M, lacrosse M/W, soccer M/W, softball W, swimming and diving M/W, tennis M/W, track and field M/W, volleyball W. *Intramural sports:* badminton M(c)/W(c), baseball M(c), basketball M(c)/W, cheerleading M(c)/W(c), equestrian sports W(c), football M/W, ice hockey M(c), rock climbing M(c)/W(c), rugby M(c), soccer M/W(c), ultimate Frisbee M(c)/W(c), volleyball M/W, weight lifting M(c)/W(c).

Campus security: 24-hour emergency response devices and patrols, late-night transport/escort service, controlled dormitory access, campus emergency phones, Maroon Alert system.

Student services: health clinic, personal/psychological counseling.

COSTS & FINANCIAL AID

Costs (2018–19) *One-time required fee:* $125. *Comprehensive fee:* $57,720 includes full-time tuition ($42,446), mandatory fees ($1584), and room and board ($13,690). Part-time tuition: $2028 per course. Part-time tuition and fees vary according to course load and reciprocity agreements. *Required fees:* $60 per term part-time. *College room only:* $6356. Room and board charges vary according to board plan and housing facility. *Payment plan:* installment. *Waivers:* adult students, senior citizens, and employees or children of employees.

Financial Aid Of all full-time matriculated undergraduates who enrolled in 2017, 1,639 applied for aid, 1,472 were judged to have need, 229 had their need fully met. In 2017, 502 non-need-based awards were made. *Average percent of need met:* 81. *Average financial aid package:* $34,319. *Average need-based loan:* $4877. *Average need-based gift aid:* $28,109. *Average non-need-based aid:* $20,257. *Average indebtedness upon graduation:* $41,187.

APPLYING

Standardized Tests *Required:* SAT or ACT (for admission).

VirginiaCOLLEGES AT-A-GLANCE

Options: electronic application, early admission, early decision, deferred entrance.

Application fee: $30.

Required: high school transcript. *Recommended:* essay or personal statement, 1 letter of recommendation, interview.

Application deadlines: 3/15 (freshmen), 8/1 (transfers).

Early decision deadline: 11/15.

Notification: continuous until 4/1 (freshmen), continuous until 8/15 (transfers), 12/15 (early decision).

CONTACT
Admissions Office, Roanoke College, 221 College Lane, Salem, VA 24153. *Phone:* 540-375-2270. *Toll-free phone:* 800-388-2276. *Fax:* 540-375-2267. *E-mail:* admissions@roanoke.edu.

Sentara College of Health Sciences
Chesapeake, Virginia
http://www.sentara.edu/
- **Independent** 4-year, founded 1892
- **Urban** campus with easy access to Virginia Beach
- **Coed** 440 undergraduate students, 53% full-time, 92% women, 8% men

UNDERGRAD STUDENTS
231 full-time, 209 part-time. Students come from 4 states and territories; 10% Black or African American, non-Hispanic/Latino; 4% Hispanic/Latino; 8% Asian, non-Hispanic/Latino; 0.9% Native Hawaiian or other Pacific Islander, non-Hispanic/Latino; 0.2% American Indian or Alaska Native, non-Hispanic/Latino; 5% Two or more races, non-Hispanic/Latino; 2% Race/ethnicity unknown.

FACULTY
Total: 63, 44% full-time.

ACADEMICS
Calendar: semesters. *Degrees:* associate and bachelor's.

Special study options: academic remediation for entering students, adult/continuing education programs, advanced placement credit, distance learning, part-time degree program, services for LD students, summer session for credit.

Computers: 13 computers/terminals are available on campus for general student use. Students can access the following: free student e-mail accounts, online (class) grades. Campuswide network is available. Wireless service is available via entire campus.
Library: Sentara Healthcare Library. *Books:* 1,790 (physical); *Serial titles:* 65 (physical); *Databases:* 29.

STUDENT LIFE
Housing options: college housing not available.

Activities and organizations: Sentara Nursing Student Association (SNSA), Alpha Eta National Honor Society for Allied Health Professionals, Sigma Theta Tau International Nursing Honor Society, Chi Kappa Chapter (STTI), Student Community Outreach Program of Excellence (SCOPE).

Campus security: 24-hour emergency response devices.

Student services: personal/psychological counseling.

COSTS
Costs (2017–18) *One-time required fee:* $85. *Tuition:* $9800 full-time, $350 per credit hour part-time. Full-time tuition and fees vary according to course level, course load, degree level, and program. Part-time tuition and fees vary according to course level, course load, degree level, and program. *Required fees:* $1950 full-time, $1950 per year part-time.

APPLYING
Standardized Tests *Required:* ATI Teas (BSN, CVT, ST) (for admission).
Required for some: high school transcript, minimum 3.5 GPA.

CONTACT
Sentara College of Health Sciences, 1441 Crossways Boulevard, Crossways I, Suite 105, Chesapeake, VA 23320. *Phone:* 757-388-2604.

Shenandoah University
Winchester, Virginia
http://www.su.edu/
- **Independent United Methodist** university, founded 1875
- **Suburban** 359-acre campus with easy access to Washington, D.C.
- **Endowment** $63.4 million
- **Coed** 2,066 undergraduate students, 96% full-time, 60% women, 40% men

UNDERGRAD STUDENTS
1,991 full-time, 75 part-time. Students come from 39 states and territories; 17 other countries; 40% are from out of state; 11% Black or African American, non-Hispanic/Latino; 7% Hispanic/Latino; 3% Asian, non-Hispanic/Latino; 0.2% Native Hawaiian or other Pacific Islander, non-Hispanic/Latino; 0.7% American Indian or Alaska Native, non-Hispanic/Latino; 2% Two or more races, non-Hispanic/Latino; 16% Race/ethnicity unknown; 3% international; 8% transferred in; 48% live on campus.

Freshmen:
Admission: 438 enrolled. *Average high school GPA:* 3.5. *Test scores:* SAT evidence-based reading and writing scores over 500: 81%; SAT math scores over 500: 76%; ACT scores over 18: 94%; SAT evidence-based reading and writing scores over 600: 33%; SAT math scores over 600: 22%; ACT scores over 24: 44%; SAT evidence-based reading and writing scores over 700: 4%; SAT math scores over 700: 2%; ACT scores over 30: 10%.
Retention: 80% of full-time freshmen returned.

FACULTY
Total: 460, 55% full-time, 57% with terminal degrees.
Student/faculty ratio: 10:1.

ACADEMICS
Calendar: semesters. *Degrees:* certificates, bachelor's, master's, doctoral, post-master's, and postbachelor's certificates.

Special study options: accelerated degree program, adult/continuing education programs, advanced placement credit, distance learning, double majors, English as a second language, independent study, internships, off-campus study, part-time degree program, services for LD students, student-designed majors, study abroad, summer session for credit.

Unusual degree programs: 3-2 occupational therapy, athletic training, public health.

Computers: 32 computers/terminals and 218 ports are available on campus for general student use. Students can access the following: campus intranet, computer help desk, free student e-mail accounts, online (class) grades, online (class) registration, online (class) schedules, online student account information. Campuswide network is available. 100% of college-owned or -operated housing units are wired for high-speed Internet access. Wireless service is available via entire campus.
Library: Alson H. Smith, Jr. Library plus 1 other. *Books:* 122,422 (physical), 217,000 (digital/electronic); *Serial titles:* 700 (physical), 86,500 (digital/electronic); *Databases:* 135. Weekly public service hours: 96; students can reserve study rooms.

STUDENT LIFE
Housing options: on-campus residence required through sophomore year; coed, special housing for students with disabilities. Campus housing is university owned and leased by the school. Freshman campus housing is guaranteed.

Activities and organizations: drama/theater group, student-run newspaper, radio station, choral group, Student Government Association, Graduate Student Assembly, Campus Activities Network, Athletic Training Club, Variety of Groups for Professional Fraternities.

Athletics Member NCAA. All Division III. *Intercollegiate sports:* baseball M, basketball M/W, cross-country running M/W, field hockey W, football M, golf M/W, lacrosse M/W, soccer M/W, softball W, tennis M/W, track and field M/W, volleyball W. *Intramural sports:* basketball M/W, cheerleading M(c)/W(c), football M/W, sand volleyball M/W, soccer M/W, softball M/W, table tennis M/W, ultimate Frisbee M/W, volleyball M/W.

Campus security: 24-hour emergency response devices and patrols, late-night transport/escort service, controlled dormitory access, LiveSafe

1108 Peterson's® Four-Year Colleges 2019

mobile app, anonymous reporting, side-door alarms, campus shuttle, Safe in Sixty Seconds Program, Safe Walk/Safe Ride Program.
Student services: health clinic, personal/psychological counseling, women's center.

COSTS & FINANCIAL AID
Costs (2018–19) *Comprehensive fee:* $42,900 includes full-time tuition ($31,280), mandatory fees ($1250), and room and board ($10,370). Full-time tuition and fees vary according to course load and program. Part-time tuition: $910 per credit hour. Part-time tuition and fees vary according to course load and program. *Required fees:* $90 per term part-time. *Room and board:* Room and board charges vary according to board plan and housing facility. *Payment plan:* installment. *Waivers:* employees or children of employees.

Financial Aid Of all full-time matriculated undergraduates who enrolled in 2016, 1,882 applied for aid, 1,680 were judged to have need, 183 had their need fully met. 640 Federal Work-Study jobs (averaging $2300). 483 state and other part-time jobs (averaging $2300). In 2016, 419 non-need-based awards were made. *Average percent of need met:* 59. *Average financial aid package:* $18,768. *Average need-based loan:* $4329. *Average need-based gift aid:* $6265. *Average non-need-based aid:* $10,168. *Average indebtedness upon graduation:* $34,121.

APPLYING
Standardized Tests *Required:* SAT or ACT (for admission).

Required: high school transcript. *Required for some:* essay or personal statement, interview, audition for conservatory applicants, interview for some Conservatory programs and for Guaranteed Admission for Health Professions programs.

CONTACT
Mr. Thomas McKenna, Associate Director of Admissions, Shenandoah University, 1460 University Drive, Wilkins Building, Admissions Office, Winchester, VA 22601-5195. *Phone:* 540-545-7327. *Toll-free phone:* 800-432-2266. *Fax:* 540-665.4627. *E-mail:* admit@su.edu.

Southern Virginia University
Buena Vista, Virginia
http://www.svu.edu/

CONTACT
Mr. Tony Caputo, Dean of Admissions, Southern Virginia University, One University Hill Drive, Buena Vista, VA 24416. *Phone:* 540-261-2756. *Toll-free phone:* 800-229-8420. *Fax:* 540-261-8559. *E-mail:* admissions@southernvirginia.edu.

South University
Glen Allen, Virginia
http://www.southuniversity.edu/richmond

CONTACT
South University, 2151 Old Brick Road, Glen Allen, VA 23060. *Phone:* 804-727-6800. *Toll-free phone:* 888-422-5076.

South University
Virginia Beach, Virginia
http://www.southuniversity.edu/virginia-beach

CONTACT
South University, 301 Bendix Road, Suite 100, Virginia Beach, VA 23452. *Phone:* 757-493-6900. *Toll-free phone:* 877-206-1845.

Stratford University
Alexandria, Virginia
http://www.stratford.edu/
- **Proprietary** comprehensive, founded 1976
- **Urban** campus with easy access to Washington DC
- **Coed**

ACADEMICS
Calendar: quarters. *Degrees:* associate, bachelor's, and master's.
Library: Learning Resource Center.

STUDENT LIFE
Housing options: college housing not available.

COSTS
Costs (2017–18) *One-time required fee:* $100. *Tuition:* $24,975 full-time, $1665 per course part-time. Full-time tuition and fees vary according to course level, course load, degree level, and program. Part-time tuition and fees vary according to course level, course load, degree level, and program.

APPLYING
Options: electronic application.

Application fee: $50.

Required: high school transcript, interview. *Recommended:* essay or personal statement.

CONTACT
Admissions, Stratford University, 2900 Eisenhower Avenue, Alexandria, VA 22314. *Phone:* 571-699-3200. *Toll-free phone:* 800-444-0804. *E-mail:* alexandriaadmissions@stratford.edu.

Stratford University
Falls Church, Virginia
http://www.stratford.edu/
- **Proprietary** comprehensive, founded 1976
- **Urban** campus with easy access to Washington, DC
- **Coed**
- **Noncompetitive** entrance level

ACADEMICS
Calendar: quarters. *Degrees:* diplomas, associate, bachelor's, master's, and doctoral.
Library: Learning Resource Center.

STUDENT LIFE
Housing options: college housing not available.

COSTS
Costs (2017–18) *One-time required fee:* $100. *Tuition:* $24,975 full-time, $1665 per course part-time. Full-time tuition and fees vary according to course level, course load, degree level, and program. Part-time tuition and fees vary according to course level, course load, degree level, and program.

APPLYING
Options: electronic application.

Application fee: $50.

Required: high school transcript, interview. *Recommended:* essay or personal statement.

CONTACT
Admissions, Stratford University, 7777 Leesburg Pike, Falls Church, VA 22043. *Phone:* 703-821-8570. *Toll-free phone:* 800-444-0804. *E-mail:* fcadmissions@stratford.edu.

Stratford University
Glen Allen, Virginia
http://www.stratford.edu/
- **Proprietary** comprehensive, founded 1976
- **Suburban** campus with easy access to Richmond, VA
- **Coed**

ACADEMICS
Calendar: quarters. *Degrees:* associate, bachelor's, and master's.
Library: Learning Resource Center.

STUDENT LIFE
Housing options: college housing not available.

COSTS
Costs (2017–18) *One-time required fee:* $100. *Tuition:* $24,975 full-time, $1665 per course part-time. Full-time tuition and fees vary according to course level, course load, degree level, and program. Part-time tuition and fees vary according to course level, course load, degree level, and program.

APPLYING

Required: high school transcript, interview. *Recommended:* essay or personal statement.

CONTACT
Admissions, Stratford University, 11104 West Broad Street, Glen Allen, VA 23060. *Phone:* 804-290-4231. *Toll-free phone:* 877-373-5173. *E-mail:* gaadmissions@stratford.edu.

Stratford University
Newport News, Virginia
http://www.stratford.edu/

- **Proprietary** comprehensive, founded 1976
- **Urban** campus with easy access to Richmond
- **Coed**

ACADEMICS
Calendar: quarters. *Degrees:* associate, bachelor's, and master's.
Library: Learning Resource Center.

STUDENT LIFE
Housing options: college housing not available.

COSTS
Costs (2017–18) *One-time required fee:* $100. *Tuition:* $24,975 full-time, $1665 per course part-time. Full-time tuition and fees vary according to course level, course load, degree level, and program. Part-time tuition and fees vary according to course level, course load, degree level, and program.

APPLYING
Required: high school transcript, interview. *Recommended:* essay or personal statement.

CONTACT
Admissions, Stratford University, 836 J. Clyde Morris Boulevard, Newport News, VA 23601. *Phone:* 757-873-4235. *Toll-free phone:* 855-873-4235. *E-mail:* newportnewsadmissions@stratford.edu.

Stratford University
Virginia Beach, Virginia
http://www.stratford.edu/

- **Proprietary** comprehensive, founded 1976
- **Urban** campus
- **Coed**

ACADEMICS
Calendar: quarters. *Degrees:* associate, bachelor's, and master's.
Library: Learning Resource Center.

STUDENT LIFE
Housing options: college housing not available.

COSTS
Costs (2017–18) *One-time required fee:* $100. *Tuition:* $24,975 full-time, $1665 per course part-time. Full-time tuition and fees vary according to course level, course load, degree level, and program. Part-time tuition and fees vary according to course level, course load, degree level, and program.

APPLYING
Options: electronic application.
Application fee: $50.
Required: high school transcript, interview. *Recommended:* essay or personal statement.

CONTACT
Admissions, Stratford University, 555 South Independence Boulevard, Virginia Beach, VA 23452. *Phone:* 757-497-4466. *Toll-free phone:* 866-528-8363. *E-mail:* virginiabeachadmissions@stratford.edu.

Stratford University
Woodbridge, Virginia
http://www.stratford.edu/

- **Proprietary** comprehensive, founded 1976
- **Suburban** campus with easy access to Washington DC
- **Coed**

ACADEMICS
Calendar: quarters. *Degrees:* diplomas, associate, bachelor's, and master's.
Library: Learning Resource Center.

STUDENT LIFE
Housing options: college housing not available.

COSTS
Costs (2017–18) *One-time required fee:* $100. *Tuition:* $24,975 full-time, $1665 per course part-time. Full-time tuition and fees vary according to course level, course load, degree level, and program. Part-time tuition and fees vary according to course level, course load, degree level, and program.

APPLYING
Options: electronic application.
Application fee: $50.
Required: high school transcript, interview. *Required for some:* letters of recommendation. *Recommended:* essay or personal statement.

CONTACT
Admissions, Stratford University, 14349 Gideon Drive, Woodbridge, VA 22192. *Phone:* 703-897-1982. *Toll-free phone:* 888-546-1250. *E-mail:* woodbridgeadmissions@stratford.edu.

Strayer University–Alexandria Campus
Alexandria, Virginia
http://www.strayer.edu/virginia/alexandria/

CONTACT
Strayer University–Alexandria Campus, 2730 Eisenhower Avenue, Alexandria, VA 22314. *Toll-free phone:* 888-311-0355.

Strayer University–Arlington Campus
Arlington, Virginia
http://www.strayer.edu/virginia/arlington/

CONTACT
Strayer University–Arlington Campus, 2121 15th Street North, Arlington, VA 22201. *Toll-free phone:* 888-311-0355.

Strayer University–Chesapeake Campus
Chesapeake, Virginia
http://www.strayer.edu/virginia/chesapeake/

CONTACT
Strayer University–Chesapeake Campus, 676 Independence Parkway, Suite 300, Chesapeake, VA 23320. *Toll-free phone:* 888-311-0355.

Strayer University–Chesterfield Campus
Midlothian, Virginia
http://www.strayer.edu/virginia/chesterfield/

CONTACT
Strayer University–Chesterfield Campus, 15521 Midlothian Turnpike, Suite 401, Midlothian, VA 23113. *Toll-free phone:* 888-311-0355.

Strayer University–Fredericksburg Campus

Fredericksburg, Virginia
http://www.strayer.edu/virginia/fredericksburg/

CONTACT
Strayer University–Fredericksburg Campus, 150 Riverside Parkway, Suite 100, Fredericksburg, VA 22406. *Toll-free phone:* 888-311-0355.

Strayer University–Henrico Campus

Glen Allen, Virginia
http://www.strayer.edu/virginia/henrico/

CONTACT
Strayer University–Henrico Campus, 11501 Nuckols Road, Glen Allen, VA 23059. *Toll-free phone:* 888-311-0355.

Strayer University–Loudoun Campus

Ashburn, Virginia
http://www.strayer.edu/virginia/loudoun/

CONTACT
Strayer University–Loudoun Campus, 45150 Russell Branch Parkway, Suite 200, Ashburn, VA 20147. *Toll-free phone:* 888-311-0355.

Strayer University–Manassas Campus

Manassas, Virginia
http://www.strayer.edu/virginia/manassas/

CONTACT
Strayer University–Manassas Campus, 9990 Battleview Parkway, Manassas, VA 20109. *Toll-free phone:* 888-311-0355.

Strayer University–Newport News Campus

Newport News, Virginia
http://www.strayer.edu/virginia/newport-news/

CONTACT
Strayer University–Newport News Campus, 99 Old Oyster Point Road, Unit 1, Newport News, VA 23602. *Toll-free phone:* 888-311-0355.

Strayer University–Virginia Beach Campus

Virginia Beach, Virginia
http://www.strayer.edu/virginia/virginia-beach/

CONTACT
Strayer University–Virginia Beach Campus, 249 Central Park Avenue, Suite 350, Virginia Beach, VA 23462. *Toll-free phone:* 888-311-0355.

Strayer University–Woodbridge Campus

Woodbridge, Virginia
http://www.strayer.edu/virginia/woodbridge/

CONTACT
Strayer University–Woodbridge Campus, 13385 Minnieville Road, Woodbridge, VA 22192. *Toll-free phone:* 888-311-0355.

Sweet Briar College

Sweet Briar, Virginia
http://www.sbc.edu/
- **Independent** comprehensive, founded 1901
- **Rural** 3250-acre campus
- **Endowment** $76.9 million
- **Women only** 319 undergraduate students, 98% full-time
- **Minimally difficult** entrance level, 93% of applicants were admitted

UNDERGRAD STUDENTS
314 full-time, 5 part-time. 47% are from out of state; 9% Black or African American, non-Hispanic/Latino; 10% Hispanic/Latino; 2% Asian, non-Hispanic/Latino; 0.4% Native Hawaiian or other Pacific Islander, non-Hispanic/Latino; 4% Two or more races, non-Hispanic/Latino; 1% Race/ethnicity unknown; 0.4% international; 4% transferred in; 93% live on campus.

Freshmen:
Admission: 361 applied, 335 admitted, 79 enrolled. *Average high school GPA:* 3.3.
Retention: 72% of full-time freshmen returned.

FACULTY
Total: 71, 83% full-time, 80% with terminal degrees.
Student/faculty ratio: 5:1.

ACADEMICS
Calendar: semesters. *Degrees:* bachelor's and master's.
Special study options: adult/continuing education programs, advanced placement credit, double majors, honors programs, independent study, internships, off-campus study, part-time degree program, services for LD students, student-designed majors, study abroad, summer session for credit.
Unusual degree programs: 3-2 engineering with Virginia Polytechnic Institute and State University, University of Virginia, Columbia University, Washington University in St. Louis.
Computers: Students can access the following: campus intranet, computer help desk, free student e-mail accounts, online (class) grades, online (class) registration, online (class) schedules. Campuswide network is available. 100% of college-owned or -operated housing units are wired for high-speed Internet access. Wireless service is available via entire campus.
Library: Mary Helen Cochran Library plus 1 other. Study areas open 24 hours, 5–7 days a week.

STUDENT LIFE
Housing options: on-campus residence required through senior year; women-only. Campus housing is university owned. Freshman campus housing is guaranteed.
Activities and organizations: drama/theater group, student-run newspaper, radio station, choral group.
Athletics Member NCAA. All Division III. *Intercollegiate sports:* cross-country running W, equestrian sports W, field hockey W, golf W, lacrosse W, soccer W, softball W, swimming and diving W, tennis W.
Campus security: 24-hour emergency response devices and patrols, student patrols, late-night transport/escort service, controlled dormitory access, front gate security.
Student services: health clinic, personal/psychological counseling, women's center.

COSTS & FINANCIAL AID
Costs (2018–19) *Comprehensive fee:* $34,000 includes full-time tuition ($21,000) and room and board ($13,000). Part-time tuition: $875 per credit hour. *Room and board:* Room and board charges vary according to board plan. *Payment plan:* installment. *Waivers:* adult students, senior citizens, and employees or children of employees.
Financial Aid Of all full-time matriculated undergraduates who enrolled in 2015, 199 applied for aid, 180 were judged to have need, 44 had their need fully met. In 2015, 51 non-need-based awards were made. *Average percent of need met:* 83. *Average financial aid package:* $33,548. *Average need-based loan:* $4973. *Average need-based gift aid:* $28,394. *Average non-need-based aid:* $20,074. *Average indebtedness upon graduation:* $33,026.

APPLYING

Standardized Tests *Required:* SAT or ACT (for admission).

Options: electronic application, deferred entrance.

Required: essay or personal statement, high school transcript, 2 letters of recommendation.

Notification: continuous (freshmen).

CONTACT

Sweet Briar College, PO Box 1052, Sweet Briar, VA 24595. *Phone:* 434-381-6142. *Toll-free phone:* 800-381-6142. *E-mail:* admissions@sbc.edu.

University of Management and Technology

Arlington, Virginia

http://www.umtweb.edu/

- **Proprietary** comprehensive, founded 1998
- **Urban** campus with easy access to Washington, DC
- **Coed** 1,029 undergraduate students, 46% full-time, 26% women, 74% men

UNDERGRAD STUDENTS

476 full-time, 553 part-time.

FACULTY

Student/faculty ratio: 25:1.

ACADEMICS

Calendar: continuous. *Degrees:* certificates, associate, bachelor's, master's, doctoral, post-master's, and postbachelor's certificates.

Special study options: adult/continuing education programs, part-time degree program.

Computers: Students can access the following: campus intranet, online (class) grades, online (class) registration, online (class) schedules. Campuswide network is available. Wireless service is available via entire campus.

Library:*Books:* 9,149 (physical), 35 (digital/electronic).

FINANCIAL AID

Financial Aid Of all full-time matriculated undergraduates who enrolled in 2014, 71 applied for aid, 67 were judged to have need, 67 had their need fully met. *Average percent of need met:* 100. *Average financial aid package:* $16,980. *Average need-based loan:* $3414. *Average need-based gift aid:* $3989. *Average indebtedness upon graduation:* $15,415.

APPLYING

Application fee: $30.

CONTACT

University of Management and Technology, 1901 Fort Myer Drive, Arlington, VA 22209-1609. *Toll-free phone:* 800-924-4883.

University of Mary Washington

Fredericksburg, Virginia

http://www.umw.edu/

- **State-supported** comprehensive, founded 1908
- **Small-town** 234-acre campus with easy access to Richmond; Washington, D.C.
- **Endowment** $50.0 million
- **Coed** 4,398 undergraduate students, 89% full-time, 64% women, 36% men
- **Very difficult** entrance level, 73% of applicants were admitted

UNDERGRAD STUDENTS

3,905 full-time, 493 part-time. Students come from 34 states and territories; 20 other countries; 8% are from out of state; 8% Black or African American, non-Hispanic/Latino; 9% Hispanic/Latino; 4% Asian, non-Hispanic/Latino; 0.1% Native Hawaiian or other Pacific Islander, non-Hispanic/Latino; 0.3% American Indian or Alaska Native, non-Hispanic/Latino; 6% Two or more races, non-Hispanic/Latino; 3% Race/ethnicity unknown; 1% international; 9% transferred in; 57% live on campus.

Freshmen:
Admission: 5,977 applied, 4,393 admitted, 950 enrolled. *Average high school GPA:* 3.6. *Test scores:* SAT evidence-based reading and writing scores over 500: 94%; SAT math scores over 500: 89%; ACT scores over 18: 95%; SAT evidence-based reading and writing scores over 600: 53%; SAT math scores over 600: 32%; ACT scores over 24: 58%; SAT evidence-based reading and writing scores over 700: 10%; SAT math scores over 700: 5%; ACT scores over 30: 12%.

Retention: 84% of full-time freshmen returned.

FACULTY

Total: 402, 62% full-time, 43% with terminal degrees.

Student/faculty ratio: 14:1.

ACADEMICS

Calendar: semesters. *Degrees:* certificates, bachelor's, master's, and postbachelor's certificates.

Special study options: accelerated degree program, adult/continuing education programs, advanced placement credit, distance learning, double majors, honors programs, independent study, internships, part-time degree program, services for LD students, student-designed majors, study abroad, summer session for credit. *ROTC:* Army (c).

Computers: 579 computers/terminals are available on campus for general student use. Students can access the following: campus intranet, computer help desk, free student e-mail accounts, online (class) grades, online (class) registration, online (class) schedules, student Web hosting. Campuswide network is available. 100% of college-owned or -operated housing units are wired for high-speed Internet access. Wireless service is available via entire campus.

Library: Simpson Library plus 2 others. *Books:* 373,290 (physical), 243,338 (digital/electronic); *Serial titles:* 3,164 (physical), 76,994 (digital/electronic); *Databases:* 210. Weekly public service hours: 90; students can reserve study rooms.

STUDENT LIFE

Housing options: on-campus residence required through sophomore year; coed, women-only, special housing for students with disabilities. Campus housing is university owned. Freshman campus housing is guaranteed.

Activities and organizations: drama/theater group, student-run newspaper, radio station, choral group, Class Council, Campus Programming Board, Community Outreach and Participation, Association of Residence Halls, Student Government Association.

Athletics Member NCAA. All Division III. *Intercollegiate sports:* baseball M, basketball M/W, crew M(c)/W(c), cross-country running M/W, equestrian sports M/W, field hockey W, golf M/W, lacrosse M/W, rugby M(c)/W(c), soccer M/W, softball W, swimming and diving M/W, tennis M/W, track and field M/W, volleyball W. *Intramural sports:* badminton M/W, baseball M(c), basketball M/W, cheerleading M(c)/W(c), fencing M(c)/W(c), field hockey W(c), football M/W, lacrosse M(c)/W(c), sand volleyball M/W, soccer M(c)/W(c), softball W, swimming and diving M(c)/W(c), tennis M(c)/W(c), ultimate Frisbee M(c)/W(c), volleyball M(c)/W(c).

Campus security: 24-hour emergency response devices and patrols, student patrols, late-night transport/escort service, controlled dormitory access, self-defense and safety classes. Guardian App.

Student services: health clinic, personal/psychological counseling.

COSTS & FINANCIAL AID

Costs (2018–19) *Tuition:* state resident $5772 full-time; nonresident $20,362 full-time. Full-time tuition and fees vary according to course load, degree level, and location. Part-time tuition and fees vary according to course load, degree level, and location. *Required fees:* $5858 full-time. *Room and board:* $11,118; room only: $7326. Room and board charges vary according to board plan and housing facility. *Payment plan:* installment. *Waivers:* senior citizens.

Financial Aid Of all full-time matriculated undergraduates who enrolled in 2015, 2,449 applied for aid, 1,652 were judged to have need, 217 had their need fully met. In 2015, 769 non-need-based awards were made. *Average percent of need met:* 49. *Average financial aid package:* $9283. *Average need-based loan:* $4145. *Average need-based gift aid:* $3352. *Average non-need-based aid:* $2825. *Average indebtedness upon graduation:* $19,444. *Financial aid deadline:* 7/1.

APPLYING

Standardized Tests *Required for some:* SAT or ACT (for admission).

Options: electronic application, early admission, early decision, early action, deferred entrance.

Application fee: $50.

Required: essay or personal statement, high school transcript.

Application deadlines: 2/1 (freshmen), 4/1 (transfers), 11/15 (early action).

Early decision deadline: 11/1.

Notification: 4/1 (freshmen), 5/15 (transfers), 1/31 (early decision), 1/31 (early action).

CONTACT
Ms. Melissa Yakabouski, Director of Undergraduate Admissions, University of Mary Washington, 1301 College Avenue, Fredericksburg, VA 22401-5358. *Phone:* 540-654-1669. *Toll-free phone:* 800-468-5614. *Fax:* 540-654-1857. *E-mail:* myak@umw.edu.

University of Richmond
Richmond, Virginia
http://www.richmond.edu/
- **Independent** comprehensive, founded 1830
- **Suburban** 350-acre campus
- **Endowment** $2.4 billion
- **Coed** 2,999 undergraduate students, 99% full-time, 52% women, 48% men
- **Very difficult** entrance level, 33% of applicants were admitted

UNDERGRAD STUDENTS
2,959 full-time, 40 part-time. Students come from 48 states and territories; 71 other countries; 80% are from out of state; 7% Black or African American, non-Hispanic/Latino; 9% Hispanic/Latino; 9% Asian, non-Hispanic/Latino; 0.1% American Indian or Alaska Native, non-Hispanic/Latino; 4% Two or more races, non-Hispanic/Latino; 4% Race/ethnicity unknown; 9% international; 2% transferred in; 91% live on campus.

Freshmen:
Admission: 10,013 applied, 3,301 admitted, 801 enrolled. *Test scores:* SAT evidence-based reading and writing scores over 500: 100%; SAT math scores over 500: 100%; ACT scores over 18: 100%; SAT evidence-based reading and writing scores over 600: 90%; SAT math scores over 600: 86%; ACT scores over 24: 98%; SAT evidence-based reading and writing scores over 700: 38%; SAT math scores over 700: 46%; ACT scores over 30: 70%.

Retention: 93% of full-time freshmen returned.

FACULTY
Total: 438, 78% full-time, 86% with terminal degrees.
Student/faculty ratio: 8:1.

ACADEMICS
Calendar: semesters. *Degrees:* certificates, bachelor's, master's, and doctoral.

Special study options: advanced placement credit, double majors, English as a second language, honors programs, independent study, internships, off-campus study, part-time degree program, services for LD students, student-designed majors, study abroad, summer session for credit. *ROTC:* Army (b).

Unusual degree programs: 3-2 engineering with Columbia University; Duke University Environmental Studies, Virginia Commonwealth University Environmental Studies.

Computers: 1,100 computers/terminals and 4,620 ports are available on campus for general student use. Students can access the following: campus intranet, computer help desk, free student e-mail accounts, online (class) grades, online (class) registration, online (class) schedules. Campuswide network is available. 100% of college-owned or -operated housing units are wired for high-speed Internet access. Wireless service is available via entire campus.

Library: Boatwright Memorial Library plus 2 others. *Books:* 510,145 (physical), 427,241 (digital/electronic); *Serial titles:* 526 (physical), 149,575 (digital/electronic); *Databases:* 444. Weekly public service hours: 100; study areas open 24 hours, 5–7 days a week; students can reserve study rooms.

STUDENT LIFE
Housing options: coed, men-only, women-only, special housing for students with disabilities. Campus housing is university owned. Freshman campus housing is guaranteed.

Activities and organizations: drama/theater group, student-run newspaper, radio station, choral group, Greek Life, Sport Clubs, SpiderBoard, InterVarsity Christian Fellowship, Alpha Phi Omega Service Fraternity, national fraternities, national sororities.

Athletics Member NCAA. All Division I except football (Division I-AA). *Intercollegiate sports:* baseball M(s), basketball M(s)/W(s), cross-country running M/W(s), field hockey W(s), golf M(s)/W(s), lacrosse M(s)/W(s), soccer W(s), swimming and diving W(s), tennis M(s)/W(s), track and field W(s). *Intramural sports:* archery M(c)/W(c), badminton M(c)/W(c), baseball M(c), basketball M(c)/W(c), crew M(c)/W(c), equestrian sports M(c)/W(c), field hockey M(c)/W(c), golf M(c)/W(c), ice hockey M(c), lacrosse M(c)/W(c), racquetball M/W, rugby M(c)/W(c), soccer M(c)/W(c), softball M/W, squash M(c)/W(c), table tennis M/W, tennis M(c)/W(c), track and field M(c)/W(c), ultimate Frisbee M(c)/W(c), volleyball M(c)/W(c), water polo M(c).

Campus security: 24-hour emergency response devices and patrols, late-night transport/escort service, controlled dormitory access, campus police.

Student services: health clinic, personal/psychological counseling, women's center.

COSTS & FINANCIAL AID
Costs (2018–19) *Comprehensive fee:* $64,860 includes full-time tuition ($52,610) and room and board ($12,250). Full-time tuition and fees vary according to course load. Part-time tuition: $2631 per credit hour. Part-time tuition and fees vary according to course load. *College room only:* $5620. Room and board charges vary according to board plan and housing facility. *Payment plan:* installment. *Waivers:* employees or children of employees.

Financial Aid Of all full-time matriculated undergraduates who enrolled in 2017, 1,643 applied for aid, 1,340 were judged to have need, 1,069 had their need fully met. 638 Federal Work-Study jobs (averaging $1375). In 2017, 588 non-need-based awards were made. *Average percent of need met:* 100. *Average financial aid package:* $47,968. *Average need-based loan:* $3858. *Average need-based gift aid:* $41,831. *Average non-need-based aid:* $23,009. *Average indebtedness upon graduation:* $27,125. *Financial aid deadline:* 2/1.

APPLYING
Standardized Tests *Required:* SAT or ACT (for admission).

Options: electronic application, early decision, early action, deferred entrance.

Application fee: $50.

Required: essay or personal statement, high school transcript, 1 letter of recommendation.

Application deadlines: 1/15 (freshmen), 2/15 (transfers), 11/1 (early action).

Early decision deadline: 11/1 (for plan 1), 1/15 (for plan 2).

Notification: 4/1 (freshmen), 4/15 (transfers), 12/15 (early decision plan 1), 2/15 (early decision plan 2), 1/20 (early action).

CONTACT
Mr. Gil Villanueva, Dean of Admission, University of Richmond, Brunet Memorial Hall, 28 Westhampton Way, University of Richmond, VA 23173. *Phone:* 804-289-8640. *Toll-free phone:* 800-700-1662. *Fax:* 804-287-6003. *E-mail:* admissions@richmond.edu.

University of Valley Forge Virginia Campus
Woodbridge, Virginia
http://www.valleyforge.edu/

CONTACT
Admissions Coordinator, University of Valley Forge Virginia Campus, 13909 Smoketown Road, Woodbridge, VA 22192. *Phone:* 703-580-4810 Ext. 210. *Toll-free phone:* 800-432-8322.

University of Virginia
Charlottesville, Virginia
http://www.virginia.edu/

- **State-supported** university, founded 1819
- **Suburban** 1167-acre campus with easy access to Richmond
- **Endowment** $5.9 billion
- **Coed** 16,655 undergraduate students, 95% full-time, 55% women, 45% men
- **Very difficult** entrance level, 27% of applicants were admitted

UNDERGRAD STUDENTS

15,774 full-time, 881 part-time. Students come from 54 states and territories; 125 other countries; 27% are from out of state; 7% Black or African American, non-Hispanic/Latino; 7% Hispanic/Latino; 14% Asian, non-Hispanic/Latino; 0.1% Native Hawaiian or other Pacific Islander, non-Hispanic/Latino; 0.1% American Indian or Alaska Native, non-Hispanic/Latino; 4% Two or more races, non-Hispanic/Latino; 6% Race/ethnicity unknown; 4% international; 4% transferred in; 39% live on campus.

Freshmen:

Admission: 36,779 applied, 10,058 admitted, 3,788 enrolled. *Average high school GPA:* 4.3. *Test scores:* SAT evidence-based reading and writing scores over 500: 99%; SAT math scores over 500: 99%; ACT scores over 18: 100%; SAT evidence-based reading and writing scores over 600: 93%; SAT math scores over 600: 89%; ACT scores over 24: 96%; SAT evidence-based reading and writing scores over 700: 47%; SAT math scores over 700: 45%; ACT scores over 30: 75%.

Retention: 97% of full-time freshmen returned.

FACULTY

Total: 1,575, 94% full-time, 89% with terminal degrees.

Student/faculty ratio: 15:1.

ACADEMICS

Calendar: semesters. *Degrees:* certificates, bachelor's, master's, doctoral, post-master's, and postbachelor's certificates.

Special study options: accelerated degree program, adult/continuing education programs, advanced placement credit, cooperative education, distance learning, double majors, English as a second language, honors programs, independent study, internships, part-time degree program, services for LD students, student-designed majors, study abroad, summer session for credit. *ROTC:* Army (b), Navy (b), Air Force (b).

Unusual degree programs: 3-2 education.

Computers: 250 computers/terminals are available on campus for general student use. Students can access the following: campus intranet, computer help desk, free student e-mail accounts, online (class) grades, online (class) registration, online (class) schedules, online course management tool. Campuswide network is available. 100% of college-owned or -operated housing units are wired for high-speed Internet access. Wireless service is available via classrooms, computer centers, computer labs, dorm rooms, learning centers, libraries, student centers.

Library: Alderman Library plus 14 others. *Books:* 5.1 million (physical), 749,287 (digital/electronic); *Serial titles:* 7,910 (physical), 189,860 (digital/electronic); *Databases:* 1,340. Weekly public service hours: 149; study areas open 24 hours, 5–7 days a week; students can reserve study rooms.

STUDENT LIFE

Housing options: on-campus residence required for freshman year; coed. Campus housing is university owned. Freshman campus housing is guaranteed.

Activities and organizations: drama/theater group, student-run newspaper, radio and television station, choral group, marching band, Madison House, student government, university guides, University Union, The Cavalier Daily, national fraternities, national sororities.

Athletics Member NCAA. All Division I except football (Division I-A). *Intercollegiate sports:* baseball M(s), basketball M(s)/W(s), crew W(s), cross-country running M(s)/W(s), field hockey W(s), golf M(s)/W(s), lacrosse M(s)/W(s), soccer M(s)/W(s), softball W(s), squash M(s)/W(s), swimming and diving M(s)/W(s), tennis M(s)/W(s), track and field M(s)/W(s), volleyball W(s), wrestling M(s). *Intramural sports:* archery M(c)/W(c), badminton M(c)/W(c), baseball M(c), basketball M(c)/W(c), cheerleading M(c)/W(c), crew M(c)/W, cross-country running M(c)/W(c),

equestrian sports M(c)/W(c), fencing M(c)/W(c), field hockey W(c), football M, golf M(c)/W(c), gymnastics M(c)/W(c), ice hockey M(c), lacrosse W(c), racquetball M(c)/W(c), riflery M(c)/W(c), rock climbing M(c)/W(c), rugby M(c)/W(c), sailing M(c)/W(c), skiing (downhill) M(c)/W(c), soccer M(c)/W(c), softball W(c), squash M(c)/W(c), swimming and diving M(c)/W(c), tennis M(c)/W(c), track and field M(c)/W(c), ultimate Frisbee M(c)/W(c), volleyball M(c)/W(c), water polo M(c)/W(c), wrestling M(c)/W(c).

Campus security: 24-hour emergency response devices and patrols, student patrols, late-night transport/escort service, controlled dormitory access.

Student services: health clinic, personal/psychological counseling, women's center, legal services.

COSTS & FINANCIAL AID

Costs (2017–18) *Tuition:* state resident $13,412 full-time, $445 per credit hour part-time; nonresident $44,241 full-time, $1440 per credit hour part-time. Full-time tuition and fees vary according to location, program, and student level. Part-time tuition and fees vary according to location, program, and student level. *Required fees:* $2734 full-time, $2720 per year part-time. *Room and board:* $11,220; room only: $6270. Room and board charges vary according to board plan and housing facility. *Payment plan:* installment. *Waivers:* senior citizens and employees or children of employees.

Financial Aid Of all full-time matriculated undergraduates who enrolled in 2017, 9,414 applied for aid, 5,309 were judged to have need, 5,309 had their need fully met. In 2017, 656 non-need-based awards were made. *Average percent of need met:* 100. *Average financial aid package:* $27,936. *Average need-based loan:* $5695. *Average need-based gift aid:* $22,284. *Average non-need-based aid:* $4185. *Average indebtedness upon graduation:* $24,501.

APPLYING

Standardized Tests *Required:* SAT or ACT (for admission).

Options: electronic application, early action, deferred entrance.

Application fee: $60.

Required: essay or personal statement, high school transcript, 2 letters of recommendation.

Application deadlines: 1/1 (freshmen), 3/1 (transfers), 11/1 (early action).

Notification: 4/1 (freshmen), 5/1 (transfers), 1/31 (early action).

CONTACT

Mr. Gregory W. Roberts, Dean of Admission, University of Virginia, PO Box 400160, Charlottesville, VA 22904-4727. *Phone:* 434-982-3200. *Fax:* 434-924-3587. *E-mail:* undergrad-admission@virginia.edu.

The University of Virginia's College at Wise
Wise, Virginia
http://www.uvawise.edu/

- **State-supported** 4-year, founded 1954, part of University of Virginia
- **Small-town** 396-acre campus
- **Endowment** $6.5 billion
- **Coed** 2,095 undergraduate students, 58% full-time, 61% women, 39% men
- **Moderately difficult** entrance level, 78% of applicants were admitted

UNDERGRAD STUDENTS

1,210 full-time, 885 part-time. Students come from 18 states and territories; 11 other countries; 6% are from out of state; 12% Black or African American, non-Hispanic/Latino; 1% Hispanic/Latino; 1% Asian, non-Hispanic/Latino; 0.2% American Indian or Alaska Native, non-Hispanic/Latino; 0.2% Two or more races, non-Hispanic/Latino; 10% Race/ethnicity unknown; 5% transferred in; 23% live on campus.

Freshmen:

Admission: 845 applied, 655 admitted, 261 enrolled. *Average high school GPA:* 3.4. *Test scores:* SAT evidence-based reading and writing scores over 500: 69%; SAT math scores over 500: 58%; ACT scores over 18: 69%; SAT evidence-based reading and writing scores over 600: 16%; SAT math scores over 600: 10%; ACT scores over 24: 16%; ACT scores over 30: 2%.

Retention: 68% of full-time freshmen returned.

FACULTY
Total: 162, 63% full-time.
Student/faculty ratio: 12:1.

ACADEMICS
Calendar: semesters. *Degree:* bachelor's.

Special study options: academic remediation for entering students, accelerated degree program, adult/continuing education programs, advanced placement credit, cooperative education, distance learning, double majors, honors programs, independent study, internships, part-time degree program, services for LD students, student-designed majors, summer session for credit. *ROTC:* Army (b).

Computers: 330 computers/terminals are available on campus for general student use. Students can access the following: campus intranet, computer help desk, free student e-mail accounts, online (class) grades, online (class) registration, online (class) schedules. Campuswide network is available. 100% of college-owned or -operated housing units are wired for high-speed Internet access. Wireless service is available via learning centers, libraries, student centers.

Library: University of Virginia's College at Wise Library. *Books:* 148,612 (physical), 179,697 (digital/electronic); *Serial titles:* 719 (physical), 3,284 (digital/electronic); *Databases:* 124. Weekly public service hours: 78; study areas open 24 hours, 5–7 days a week; students can reserve study rooms.

STUDENT LIFE
Housing options: on-campus residence required for freshman year; coed, men-only, women-only, special housing for students with disabilities. Campus housing is university owned.

Activities and organizations: drama/theater group, student-run newspaper, radio and television station, choral group, marching band, Student Government, Student Activities Board, Multicultural Association, Residence Hall Association, intramurals, national fraternities, national sororities.

Athletics Member NCAA. All Division II. *Intercollegiate sports:* baseball M(s), basketball M(s)/W(s), cross-country running M(s)/W(s), football M(s), golf M/W, lacrosse W(s), softball W(s), tennis M(s)/W(s), track and field M/W, volleyball W(s). *Intramural sports:* badminton M/W, basketball M/W, football M/W, golf M/W, racquetball M/W, soccer M/W, softball M/W, table tennis M/W, tennis M/W, ultimate Frisbee M/W, volleyball M/W, water polo M/W.

Campus security: 24-hour emergency response devices and patrols, student patrols, late-night transport/escort service, self-defense, informal discussions, pamphlets/posters/films, and crime prevention office.

Student services: health clinic, personal/psychological counseling.

COSTS & FINANCIAL AID
Costs (2017–18) *Tuition:* state resident $5366 full-time, $229 per credit hour part-time; nonresident $21,926 full-time, $927 per credit hour part-time. Part-time tuition and fees vary according to course load. *Required fees:* $4459 full-time, $144 per credit hour part-time, $36 per term part-time. *Room and board:* $10,314. Room and board charges vary according to board plan and housing facility. *Payment plans:* installment, deferred payment. *Waivers:* senior citizens and employees or children of employees.

Financial Aid Of all full-time matriculated undergraduates who enrolled in 2017, 1,072 applied for aid, 939 were judged to have need, 141 had their need fully met. In 2017, 130 non-need-based awards were made. *Average percent of need met:* 73. *Average financial aid package:* $13,971. *Average need-based loan:* $3455. *Average need-based gift aid:* $7767. *Average non-need-based aid:* $6509. *Average indebtedness upon graduation:* $21,389.

APPLYING
Standardized Tests *Required:* SAT or ACT (for admission).
Options: early admission, early action.
Application fee: $25.
Required: high school transcript, minimum 2.3 GPA. *Recommended:* 2 letters of recommendation.
Application deadlines: 8/1 (freshmen), 8/15 (transfers), 12/1 (early action).

Notification: 8/20 (freshmen), continuous until 8/20 (transfers), 12/15 (early action).

CONTACT
Mr. Russell D. Necessary, Vice Chancellor for Enrollment Management and Student Life, The University of Virginia's College at Wise, 1 College Avenue, Wise, VA 24293. *Phone:* 276-328-0322. *Toll-free phone:* 888-282-9324. *Fax:* 276-328-0251. *E-mail:* admissions@uvawise.edu.

Virginia Baptist College
Fredericksburg, Virginia
http://www.vbc.edu/
CONTACT
Virginia Baptist College, 4111 Plank Road, Fredericksburg, VA 22407.

Virginia Commonwealth University
Richmond, Virginia
http://www.vcu.edu/
- **State-supported** university, founded 1838
- **Urban** 172-acre campus
- **Endowment** $49.7 million
- **Coed** 24,010 undergraduate students, 85% full-time, 59% women, 41% men
- 77% of applicants were admitted

UNDERGRAD STUDENTS
20,338 full-time, 3,672 part-time. Students come from 43 states and territories; 77 other countries; 7% are from out of state; 19% Black or African American, non-Hispanic/Latino; 9% Hispanic/Latino; 13% Asian, non-Hispanic/Latino; 0.1% Native Hawaiian or other Pacific Islander, non-Hispanic/Latino; 0.2% American Indian or Alaska Native, non-Hispanic/Latino; 6% Two or more races, non-Hispanic/Latino; 3% Race/ethnicity unknown; 3% international; 8% transferred in; 16% live on campus.

Freshmen:
Admission: 16,847 applied, 12,901 admitted, 4,201 enrolled. *Average high school GPA:* 3.6. *Test scores:* SAT evidence-based reading and writing scores over 500: 94%; SAT math scores over 500: 88%; ACT scores over 18: 96%; SAT evidence-based reading and writing scores over 600: 49%; SAT math scores over 600: 34%; ACT scores over 24: 54%; SAT evidence-based reading and writing scores over 700: 9%; SAT math scores over 700: 7%; ACT scores over 30: 15%.
Retention: 83% of full-time freshmen returned.

FACULTY
Total: 2,152, 58% full-time.
Student/faculty ratio: 18:1.

ACADEMICS
Calendar: semesters. *Degrees:* certificates, bachelor's, master's, doctoral, post-master's, and postbachelor's certificates.

Special study options: academic remediation for entering students, accelerated degree program, adult/continuing education programs, advanced placement credit, cooperative education, distance learning, double majors, English as a second language, freshman honors college, honors programs, independent study, internships, off-campus study, part-time degree program, services for LD students, student-designed majors, study abroad, summer session for credit. *ROTC:* Army (c).

Computers: 2,500 computers/terminals and 90,000 ports are available on campus for general student use. Students can access the following: campus intranet, computer help desk, free student e-mail accounts, online (class) grades, online (class) registration, online (class) schedules. Campuswide network is available. 100% of college-owned or -operated housing units are wired for high-speed Internet access. Wireless service is available via entire campus.

Library: Cabell Library and Thompkins McCaw Library plus 3 others. *Books:* 1.9 million (physical), 1.1 million (digital/electronic); *Serial titles:* 262,828 (physical), 123,017 (digital/electronic); *Databases:* 487. Weekly public service hours: 146; study areas open 24 hours, 5–7 days a week; students can reserve study rooms.

STUDENT LIFE

Housing options: coed. Campus housing is university owned. Freshman applicants given priority for college housing.

Activities and organizations: drama/theater group, student-run newspaper, radio and television station, choral group, national fraternities, national sororities.

Athletics Member NCAA. All Division I. *Intercollegiate sports:* baseball M(s), basketball M(s)/W(s), cross-country running M(s)/W(s), field hockey W(s), golf M(s), lacrosse W(s), soccer M(s)/W(s), tennis M(s)/W(s), track and field M(s)/W(s), volleyball W(s). *Intramural sports:* badminton M(c)/W(c), baseball M(c), basketball M(c)/W(c), bowling M(c)/W(c), equestrian sports M(c)/W(c), field hockey M(c)/W(c), ice hockey M(c), lacrosse M(c)/W(c), rowing M(c)/W(c), rugby M(c)/W(c), soccer M(c)/W(c), softball W(c), swimming and diving M(c)/W(c), table tennis M(c)/W(c), tennis M(c)/W(c), triathlon M(c)/W(c), ultimate Frisbee M(c)/W(c), volleyball M(c)/W(c).

Campus security: 24-hour emergency response devices and patrols, student patrols, late-night transport/escort service, controlled dormitory access, security personnel in residence halls, RAD classes/special event coverage, more than 90 sworn officers and 200 security personnel.

Student services: health clinic, personal/psychological counseling, women's center.

COSTS & FINANCIAL AID

Costs (2017–18) *Tuition:* state resident $11,340 full-time, $391 per credit hour part-time; nonresident $30,712 full-time, $1059 per credit hour part-time. *Required fees:* $2230 full-time. *Room and board:* $10,187. Room and board charges vary according to board plan and housing facility. *Payment plan:* installment. *Waivers:* employees or children of employees.

Financial Aid Of all full-time matriculated undergraduates who enrolled in 2016, 14,387 applied for aid, 12,053 were judged to have need, 728 had their need fully met. 759 Federal Work-Study jobs (averaging $2397). 7 state and other part-time jobs (averaging $161). In 2016, 1339 non-need-based awards were made. *Average percent of need met:* 53. *Average financial aid package:* $11,623. *Average need-based loan:* $4413. *Average need-based gift aid:* $8758. *Average non-need-based aid:* $7245. *Average indebtedness upon graduation:* $31,919.

APPLYING

Standardized Tests *Required for some:* SAT or ACT (for admission).

Options: electronic application, early admission, deferred entrance.

Application fee: $65.

Required: high school transcript.

Notification: 11/1 (freshmen).

CONTACT

Office of Admissions, Virginia Commonwealth University, 821 West Franklin Street, Richmond, VA 23284-2526. *Phone:* 800-841-3638. *Toll-free phone:* 800-841-3638. *Fax:* 804-828-1899. *E-mail:* ugrad@vcu.edu.

Virginia International University

Fairfax, Virginia

http://www.viu.edu/

CONTACT

Admissions Department, Virginia International University, 4401 Village Drive, Fairfax, VA 22030. *Phone:* 703-591-7042 Ext. 313. *Toll-free phone:* 800-514-6848. *Fax:* 703-591-7048. *E-mail:* admissions@viu.edu.

★ Virginia Military Institute

Lexington, Virginia

http://www.vmi.edu/

- **State-supported** 4-year, founded 1839
- **Small-town** 134-acre campus
- **Endowment** $381.9 million
- **Coed** 1,722 undergraduate students, 100% full-time, 12% women, 88% men
- **Moderately difficult** entrance level, 53% of applicants were admitted

UNDERGRAD STUDENTS

1,722 full-time. Students come from 46 states and territories; 6 other countries; 36% are from out of state; 6% Black or African American, non-Hispanic/Latino; 7% Hispanic/Latino; 4% Asian, non-Hispanic/Latino; 0.3% Native Hawaiian or other Pacific Islander, non-Hispanic/Latino; 0.5% American Indian or Alaska Native, non-Hispanic/Latino; 1% Two or more races, non-Hispanic/Latino; 0.1% Race/ethnicity unknown; 2% international; 3% transferred in; 100% live on campus.

Freshmen:

Admission: 1,718 applied, 913 admitted, 424 enrolled. *Average high school GPA:* 3.7. *Test scores:* SAT evidence-based reading and writing scores over 500: 98%; SAT math scores over 500: 96%; ACT scores over 18: 100%; SAT evidence-based reading and writing scores over 600: 53%; SAT math scores over 600: 44%; ACT scores over 24: 73%; SAT evidence-based reading and writing scores over 700: 6%; SAT math scores over 700: 7%; ACT scores over 30: 12%.

Retention: 87% of full-time freshmen returned.

FACULTY

Total: 207, 66% full-time, 78% with terminal degrees.

Student/faculty ratio: 11:1.

ACADEMICS

Calendar: semesters. *Degree:* bachelor's.

Special study options: advanced placement credit, double majors, honors programs, independent study, internships, services for LD students, study abroad, summer session for credit. *ROTC:* Army (b), Navy (b), Air Force (b).

Computers: 200 computers/terminals are available on campus for general student use. Students can access the following: campus intranet, computer help desk, free student e-mail accounts, online (class) registration, online (class) schedules. Campuswide network is available. 100% of college-owned or -operated housing units are wired for high-speed Internet access. Wireless service is available via classrooms, computer labs, dorm rooms, libraries, student centers.

Library: Preston Library. *Books:* 280,000 (physical), 240,000 (digital/electronic); *Databases:* 150. Weekly public service hours: 113.

STUDENT LIFE

Housing options: on-campus residence required through senior year; coed. Campus housing is university owned. Freshman campus housing is guaranteed.

Activities and organizations: drama/theater group, student-run newspaper, choral group, marching band, Newman Club, Officers Christian Fellowship, strength and fitness organizations, Promaji, Pre-Law Society.

Athletics Member NCAA. All Division I. *Intercollegiate sports:* baseball M(s), basketball M(s), cross-country running M(s)/W(s), football M(s), lacrosse M(s), riflery M(s)/W(s), soccer M(s)/W, swimming and diving M(s)/W, track and field M(s)/W(s), water polo W, wrestling M(s).

Campus security: 24-hour emergency response devices and patrols, student patrols.

Student services: health clinic, personal/psychological counseling.

COSTS & FINANCIAL AID

Costs (2017–18) *Tuition:* state resident $8884 full-time, $336 per credit hour part-time; nonresident $34,572 full-time, $1155 per credit hour part-time. *Required fees:* $9330 full-time, $71 per term part-time. *Room and board:* $9236. *Payment plan:* installment.

Financial Aid Of all full-time matriculated undergraduates who enrolled in 2016, 1,145 applied for aid, 906 were judged to have need, 355 had their need fully met. In 2016, 52 non-need-based awards were made. *Average percent of need met:* 85. *Average financial aid package:* $24,778. *Average need-based loan:* $4113. *Average need-based gift aid:* $12,449. *Average non-need-based aid:* $4284. *Average indebtedness upon graduation:* $30,367. *Financial aid deadline:* 3/1.

APPLYING

Standardized Tests *Required:* SAT or ACT (for admission).

Options: electronic application, early decision.

Application fee: $40.

Required: high school transcript. *Recommended:* essay or personal statement, 2 letters of recommendation, interview, statement of good standing from prior institution.

Application deadlines: 2/1 (freshmen), 2/1 (transfers).

Early decision deadline: 11/15.

Notification: continuous (freshmen), continuous (transfers), 12/15 (early decision).

CONTACT
Office of Admissions, Virginia Military Institute, Lexington, VA 24450. *Phone:* 800-767-4207. *Toll-free phone:* 800-767-4207. *Fax:* 540-464-7746. *E-mail:* admissions@vmi.edu.

Virginia Polytechnic Institute and State University
Blacksburg, Virginia
http://www.vt.edu/

- **State-supported** university, founded 1872
- **Small-town** 2600-acre campus
- **Endowment** $995.8 million
- **Coed** 27,193 undergraduate students, 98% full-time, 43% women, 57% men
- **Moderately difficult** entrance level, 70% of applicants were admitted

UNDERGRAD STUDENTS
26,603 full-time, 590 part-time. Students come from 48 states and territories; 86 other countries; 24% are from out of state; 4% Black or African American, non-Hispanic/Latino; 6% Hispanic/Latino; 10% Asian, non-Hispanic/Latino; 0.1% Native Hawaiian or other Pacific Islander, non-Hispanic/Latino; 0.1% American Indian or Alaska Native, non-Hispanic/Latino; 4% Two or more races, non-Hispanic/Latino; 3% Race/ethnicity unknown; 6% international; 4% transferred in; 35% live on campus.

Freshmen:
Admission: 27,423 applied, 19,212 admitted, 6,836 enrolled. *Average high school GPA:* 4.0. *Test scores:* SAT evidence-based reading and writing scores over 500: 98%; SAT math scores over 500: 98%; ACT scores over 18: 100%; SAT evidence-based reading and writing scores over 600: 72%; SAT math scores over 600: 71%; ACT scores over 24: 85%; SAT evidence-based reading and writing scores over 700: 15%; SAT math scores over 700: 23%; ACT scores over 30: 31%.
Retention: 93% of full-time freshmen returned.

FACULTY
Total: 2,032, 89% full-time, 85% with terminal degrees.
Student/faculty ratio: 14:1.

ACADEMICS
Calendar: semesters. *Degrees:* bachelor's, master's, doctoral, postmaster's, and postbachelor's certificates.
Special study options: accelerated degree program, adult/continuing education programs, advanced placement credit, cooperative education, distance learning, double majors, English as a second language, honors programs, independent study, internships, part-time degree program, services for LD students, study abroad, summer session for credit. *ROTC:* Army (b), Navy (b), Air Force (b).
Computers: Students can access the following: campus intranet, computer help desk, free student e-mail accounts, online (class) grades, online (class) registration, online (class) schedules. Campuswide network is available. Wireless service is available via entire campus.
Library: Newman Library plus 2 others. Study areas open 24 hours, 5–7 days a week.

STUDENT LIFE
Housing options: on-campus residence required for freshman year; coed, men-only, women-only, special housing for students with disabilities. Campus housing is university owned. Freshman campus housing is guaranteed.
Activities and organizations: drama/theater group, student-run newspaper, radio and television station, choral group, marching band, Virginia Tech Union, Student Government Association, International student organizations, national fraternities, national sororities.
Athletics Member NCAA. All Division I except football (Division I-A). *Intercollegiate sports:* baseball M, basketball M, cross-country running M/W, golf M(s), lacrosse W(s), soccer M(s)/W(s), swimming and diving M(s)/W(s), tennis M(s)/W(s), track and field M(s)/W(s), ultimate Frisbee M/W, volleyball W. *Intramural sports:* baseball M(c), basketball M, bowling M/W, crew M(c)/W(c), cross-country running M/W, equestrian

sports M(c)/W(c), fencing M(c)/W(c), field hockey M(c)/W(c), football M/W, golf M/W, gymnastics M(c)/W(c), ice hockey M/W, lacrosse M(c)/W(c), racquetball M/W, riflery M(c)/W(c), rugby M(c)/W(c), soccer M/W, softball M/W, swimming and diving M/W, table tennis M/W, tennis M/W, volleyball M/W, water polo M/W.
Campus security: 24-hour emergency response devices and patrols, student patrols, late-night transport/escort service, controlled dormitory access.
Student services: health clinic, personal/psychological counseling, women's center, legal services.

COSTS & FINANCIAL AID
Costs (2017–18) *Tuition:* state resident $11,093 full-time, $462 per hour part-time; nonresident $28,272 full-time, $1178 per hour part-time. *Required fees:* $2137 full-time, $351 per term part-time. *Room and board:* $8690. Room and board charges vary according to board plan and housing facility. *Payment plan:* installment. *Waivers:* senior citizens.
Financial Aid Of all full-time matriculated undergraduates who enrolled in 2016, 16,298 applied for aid, 10,922 were judged to have need, 1,757 had their need fully met. In 2016, 2232 non-need-based awards were made. *Average percent of need met:* 64. *Average financial aid package:* $17,772. *Average need-based loan:* $4528. *Average need-based gift aid:* $7097. *Average non-need-based aid:* $4064. *Average indebtedness upon graduation:* $30,221. *Financial aid deadline:* 1/15.

APPLYING
Standardized Tests *Required:* SAT or ACT (for admission).
Options: electronic application, early admission, early decision, deferred entrance.
Application fee: $60.
Required: high school transcript. *Recommended:* essay or personal statement.
Application deadlines: 1/15 (freshmen), 2/15 (transfers).
Early decision deadline: 11/1.
Notification: 4/1 (freshmen), 5/1 (transfers), 12/15 (early decision).

CONTACT
Virginia Polytechnic Institute and State University, Blacksburg, VA 24061. *Phone:* 540-231-6267.

Virginia State University
Petersburg, Virginia
http://www.vsu.edu/

- **State-supported** comprehensive, founded 1882, part of State Council of Higher Education for Virginia
- **Suburban** 236-acre campus with easy access to Richmond
- **Endowment** $32.5 million
- **Coed**
- **Minimally difficult** entrance level

FACULTY
Student/faculty ratio: 13:1.

ACADEMICS
Calendar: semesters. *Degrees:* bachelor's, master's, doctoral, and postbachelor's certificates.
Library: Johnston Memorial Library. *Books:* 434,496 (physical); *Serial titles:* 5,805 (physical); *Databases:* 245. Weekly public service hours: 82.

STUDENT LIFE
Housing options: on-campus residence required for freshman year; coed, men-only, women-only. Campus housing is university owned. Freshman applicants given priority for college housing.
Activities and organizations: drama/theater group, student-run newspaper, choral group, marching band, AbstraKt Entertainment, Golden Key Honor Society, The Betterment of Brothers and Sisters, Diversified Virtue Entertainment, Sankofa, national fraternities, national sororities.
Athletics Member NCAA. All Division II.
Campus security: 24-hour emergency response devices and patrols, late-night transport/escort service, controlled dormitory access.
Student services: health clinic, personal/psychological counseling.

COSTS & FINANCIAL AID

Costs (2017–18) *Tuition:* state resident $5327 full-time, $380 per credit hour part-time; nonresident $15,442 full-time, $842 per credit hour part-time. Full-time tuition and fees vary according to course load. Part-time tuition and fees vary according to course load. *Required fees:* $3399 full-time, $10 per credit hour part-time. *Room and board:* $10,880; room only: $6356. Room and board charges vary according to board plan and housing facility.

Financial Aid Of all full-time matriculated undergraduates who enrolled in 2016, 3,828 applied for aid, 3,828 were judged to have need, 602 had their need fully met. 300 Federal Work-Study jobs (averaging $2000). 150 state and other part-time jobs (averaging $3000). In 2016, 428 non-need-based awards were made. *Average percent of need met:* 60. *Average financial aid package:* $11,600. *Average need-based loan:* $5500. *Average need-based gift aid:* $6948. *Average non-need-based aid:* $1000. *Average indebtedness upon graduation:* $28,250.

APPLYING

Standardized Tests *Required:* SAT or ACT (for admission).

Options: electronic application.

Application fee: $25.

Required: high school transcript, minimum 2.2 GPA, 2 letters of recommendation. *Recommended:* essay or personal statement.

CONTACT

Mr. Rodney Hall, Director of Enrollment Services, Virginia State University, Office of Admissions, Petersburg, VA 23806. *Phone:* 804-524-2954. *Toll-free phone:* 800-871-7611. *Fax:* 804-524-5055. *E-mail:* rhall@vsu.edu.

Virginia Union University
Richmond, Virginia
http://www.vuu.edu/

- **Independent Baptist** comprehensive, founded 1865
- **Urban** 100-acre campus
- **Coed**
- **Moderately difficult** entrance level

FACULTY
Student/faculty ratio: 15:1.

ACADEMICS
Calendar: semesters. *Degrees:* bachelor's, master's, and doctoral.
Library: L. Douglas Wilder Learning Resource Center and Library plus 1 other. *Books:* 123,475 (physical), 66,271 (digital/electronic); *Databases:* 100. Weekly public service hours: 41; students can reserve study rooms.

STUDENT LIFE
Housing options: coed, men-only, women-only. Campus housing is university owned and leased by the school. Freshman applicants given priority for college housing.

Activities and organizations: drama/theater group, student-run newspaper, choral group, marching band, Student Government Association, Panther PALS (Peer Advisory Leadership Students), Men About Positive Purpose, NAACP, Student Athlete Advisory Committee, national fraternities, national sororities.

Athletics Member NCAA. All Division II.

Campus security: 24-hour emergency response devices and patrols, controlled dormitory access.

Student services: health clinic, personal/psychological counseling.

COSTS & FINANCIAL AID
Costs (2017–18) *One-time required fee:* $200. *Comprehensive fee:* $25,960 includes full-time tuition ($15,530), mandatory fees ($1918), and room and board ($8512). Full-time tuition and fees vary according to course level, course load, and reciprocity agreements. Part-time tuition: $482 per credit hour. Part-time tuition and fees vary according to course level, course load, and reciprocity agreements. *Required fees:* $43 per credit hour part-time, $250 per credit hour part-time. *College room only:* $3976. Room and board charges vary according to housing facility.
Payment plans: installment, deferred payment.

Financial Aid Of all full-time matriculated undergraduates who enrolled in 2016, 1,265 applied for aid, 1,220 were judged to have need, 73 had their need fully met. In 2016, 34 non-need-based awards were made.

Average percent of need met: 48. *Average financial aid package:* $12,908. *Average need-based loan:* $3738. *Average need-based gift aid:* $9453. *Average non-need-based aid:* $6248. *Average indebtedness upon graduation:* $35,789.

APPLYING
Standardized Tests *Required:* SAT or ACT (for admission).

Options: electronic application, deferred entrance.

Application fee: $25.

Required: high school transcript. *Required for some:* interview. *Recommended:* essay or personal statement.

CONTACT
Ms. Danitra Morrison, Assistant Director of Admissions, Virginia Union University, 1500 North Lombardy Street, Richmond, VA 23220-1170. *Phone:* 804-257-5853. *Toll-free phone:* 800-368-3227. *Fax:* 804-342-3511. *E-mail:* dvmorrison@vuu.edu.

Virginia University of Lynchburg
Lynchburg, Virginia
http://www.vul.edu/

CONTACT
Ms. Cheryl Glass, Director of Admissions, Virginia University of Lynchburg, 2058 Garfield Avenue, Lynchburg, VA 24501. *Phone:* 434-528-5276 Ext. 106. *Fax:* 434-528-4275. *E-mail:* cglass@vul.edu.

Virginia Wesleyan University
Virginia Beach, Virginia
http://www.vwu.edu/

- **Independent United Methodist** comprehensive, founded 1961
- **Urban** 284-acre campus with easy access to Hampton Roads
- **Endowment** $56.6 million
- **Coed** 1,436 undergraduate students, 94% full-time, 60% women, 40% men
- **Moderately difficult** entrance level, 71% of applicants were admitted

UNDERGRAD STUDENTS
1,354 full-time, 82 part-time. Students come from 34 states and territories; 11 other countries; 24% are from out of state; 27% Black or African American, non-Hispanic/Latino; 9% Hispanic/Latino; 1% Asian, non-Hispanic/Latino; 0.1% Native Hawaiian or other Pacific Islander, non-Hispanic/Latino; 1% American Indian or Alaska Native, non-Hispanic/Latino; 7% Two or more races, non-Hispanic/Latino; 5% Race/ethnicity unknown; 3% international; 7% transferred in; 64% live on campus.

Freshmen:
Admission: 2,200 applied, 1,559 admitted, 423 enrolled. *Average high school GPA:* 3.2. *Test scores:* SAT evidence-based reading and writing scores over 500: 71%; SAT math scores over 500: 63%; ACT scores over 18: 83%; SAT evidence-based reading and writing scores over 600: 25%; SAT math scores over 600: 17%; ACT scores over 24: 45%; SAT evidence-based reading and writing scores over 700: 4%; SAT math scores over 700: 2%; ACT scores over 30: 7%.

Retention: 63% of full-time freshmen returned.

FACULTY
Total: 128, 71% full-time, 77% with terminal degrees.
Student/faculty ratio: 12:1.

ACADEMICS
Calendar: 4-1-4. *Degrees:* certificates, bachelor's, and master's.

Special study options: academic remediation for entering students, adult/continuing education programs, advanced placement credit, double majors, external degree program, freshman honors college, honors programs, independent study, internships, off-campus study, part-time degree program, services for LD students, student-designed majors, study abroad, summer session for credit. *ROTC:* Army (c).

Unusual degree programs: 3-2 engineering with Old Dominion University; forestry with Duke University; medicine with Eastern Virginia Medical School, law with Regent University, pharmacy with Shenandoah University, occupational therapy with Washington University in St. Louis.

Computers: 137 computers/terminals are available on campus for general student use. Students can access the following: campus intranet, computer help desk, free student e-mail accounts, online (class) grades, online (class) registration, online (class) schedules. Campuswide network is available. 100% of college-owned or -operated housing units are wired for high-speed Internet access. Wireless service is available via entire campus.

Library: H. C. Hofheimer II Library plus 1 other. *Books:* 118,216 (physical), 256,770 (digital/electronic); *Serial titles:* 111 (physical), 71,260 (digital/electronic); *Databases:* 73. Weekly public service hours: 93; study areas open 24 hours, 5–7 days a week; students can reserve study rooms.

STUDENT LIFE

Housing options: on-campus residence required through senior year; coed, women-only, special housing for students with disabilities. Campus housing is university owned. Freshman campus housing is guaranteed.

Activities and organizations: drama/theater group, student-run newspaper, radio station, choral group, Wesleyan Activities Council, community service, Student Government Association, student newspaper, Black Student Union, national fraternities, national sororities.

Athletics Member NCAA. All Division III. *Intercollegiate sports:* baseball M, basketball M/W, cheerleading W, cross-country running M/W, field hockey W, golf M/W, lacrosse M/W, soccer M/W, softball W, swimming and diving M/W, tennis M/W, track and field M/W, volleyball W. *Intramural sports:* basketball M/W, crew M(c)/W(c), fencing M(c)/W(c), field hockey W, football M/W, racquetball M/W, soccer M/W, softball M/W, table tennis M/W, ultimate Frisbee M/W, volleyball M/W.

Campus security: 24-hour emergency response devices and patrols, late-night transport/escort service, controlled dormitory access, well-lit pathways.

Student services: health clinic, personal/psychological counseling, women's center.

COSTS & FINANCIAL AID

Costs (2018–19) *One-time required fee:* $1520. *Comprehensive fee:* $45,916 includes full-time tuition ($36,010), mandatory fees ($650), and room and board ($9256). Full-time tuition and fees vary according to course load. Part-time tuition: $1500 per credit hour. Part-time tuition and fees vary according to course load. *Room and board:* Room and board charges vary according to board plan and housing facility. *Payment plan:* installment. *Waivers:* adult students, senior citizens, and employees or children of employees.

Financial Aid Of all full-time matriculated undergraduates who enrolled in 2016, 1,315 applied for aid, 1,119 were judged to have need, 149 had their need fully met. 196 Federal Work-Study jobs (averaging $1243). In 2016, 183 non-need-based awards were made. *Average percent of need met:* 65. *Average financial aid package:* $24,597. *Average need-based loan:* $7866. *Average need-based gift aid:* $20,792. *Average non-need-based aid:* $17,682. *Average indebtedness upon graduation:* $34,212.

APPLYING

Standardized Tests *Required:* SAT or ACT (for admission).

Options: electronic application.

Required: high school transcript. *Required for some:* interview. *Recommended:* letters of recommendation.

Application deadlines: rolling (freshmen), rolling (out-of-state freshmen), rolling (transfers).

Notification: continuous (freshmen), continuous (out-of-state freshmen), continuous (transfers).

CONTACT

Ms. Elizabeth Clarke, Assistant Vice President for Enrollment, Virginia Wesleyan University, 5817 Wesleyan Drive, Virginia Beach, VA 23455. *Phone:* 757-455-3208. *Toll-free phone:* 800-737-8684. *Fax:* 757-461-5238. *E-mail:* admissions@vwu.edu.

Washington and Lee University
Lexington, Virginia
http://www.wlu.edu/

- **Independent** comprehensive, founded 1749
- **Small-town** 415-acre campus
- **Endowment** $1.5 billion
- **Coed** 1,827 undergraduate students, 100% full-time, 48% women, 52% men
- **Most difficult** entrance level, 22% of applicants were admitted

UNDERGRAD STUDENTS

1,823 full-time, 4 part-time. Students come from 50 states and territories; 33 other countries; 84% are from out of state; 2% Black or African American, non-Hispanic/Latino; 5% Hispanic/Latino; 3% Asian, non-Hispanic/Latino; 3% Two or more races, non-Hispanic/Latino; 0.7% Race/ethnicity unknown; 4% international; 0.2% transferred in; 75% live on campus.

Freshmen:
Admission: 5,455 applied, 1,200 admitted, 471 enrolled. *Test scores:* SAT evidence-based reading and writing scores over 500: 100%; ACT scores over 18: 100%; SAT evidence-based reading and writing scores over 600: 99%; ACT scores over 24: 100%; SAT evidence-based reading and writing scores over 700: 55%; ACT scores over 30: 90%.
Retention: 96% of full-time freshmen returned.

FACULTY
Total: 234, 87% full-time, 87% with terminal degrees.
Student/faculty ratio: 8:1.

ACADEMICS
Calendar: 4-4-2. *Degree:* bachelor's and doctoral.

Special study options: advanced placement credit, double majors, honors programs, independent study, internships, off-campus study, services for LD students, student-designed majors, study abroad. *ROTC:* Army (c).

Computers: 176 computers/terminals and 1,200 ports are available on campus for general student use. Students can access the following: campus intranet, computer help desk, free student e-mail accounts, online (class) grades, online (class) registration, online (class) schedules. Campuswide network is available. 100% of college-owned or -operated housing units are wired for high-speed Internet access. Wireless service is available via entire campus.

Library: James G. Leyburn Library plus 2 others. *Books:* 1.0 million (physical), 321,493 (digital/electronic); *Serial titles:* 66,967 (digital/electronic); *Databases:* 441. Study areas open 24 hours, 5–7 days a week; students can reserve study rooms.

STUDENT LIFE

Housing options: on-campus residence required through junior year; coed, men-only, women-only, special housing for students with disabilities. Campus housing is university owned. Freshman campus housing is guaranteed.

Activities and organizations: drama/theater group, student-run newspaper, radio and television station, choral group, Mock Convention, General Activities Board, Nabors Service League, Outing Club, Sports Clubs, national fraternities, national sororities.

Athletics Member NCAA. All Division III. *Intercollegiate sports:* baseball M, basketball M/W, cross-country running M/W, equestrian sports M/W, field hockey W, football M, golf M/W, lacrosse M/W, rugby M(c), soccer M/W, swimming and diving M/W, tennis M/W, track and field M/W, volleyball W, wrestling M. *Intramural sports:* badminton M/W, baseball M(c), cheerleading M/W, equestrian sports W(c), golf M/W, ice hockey M(c), rock climbing M(c)/W(c), table tennis M/W, tennis M/W, track and field M/W, ultimate Frisbee M/W, volleyball W.

Campus security: 24-hour emergency response devices and patrols, late-night transport/escort service, controlled dormitory access, Emergency Alert System.

Student services: health clinic, personal/psychological counseling.

COSTS & FINANCIAL AID
Costs (2017–18) *Comprehensive fee:* $61,900 includes full-time tuition ($49,170), mandatory fees ($1000), and room and board ($11,730). Full-time tuition and fees vary according to degree level. Part-time tuition: $1756 per credit hour. Part-time tuition and fees vary according to course

load and degree level. *College room only:* $5600. Room and board charges vary according to board plan and housing facility. *Waivers:* employees or children of employees.

Financial Aid Of all full-time matriculated undergraduates who enrolled in 2017, 844 applied for aid, 779 were judged to have need, 779 had their need fully met. 220 Federal Work-Study jobs (averaging $2000). 296 state and other part-time jobs (averaging $2000). In 2017, 141 non-need-based awards were made. *Average percent of need met:* 100. *Average financial aid package:* $50,827. *Average need-based loan:* $804. *Average need-based gift aid:* $43,766. *Average non-need-based aid:* $39,088. *Average indebtedness upon graduation:* $22,651. *Financial aid deadline:* 2/15.

APPLYING
Standardized Tests *Required:* SAT or ACT (for admission).
Options: electronic application, early decision, deferred entrance.
Application fee: $60.
Required: high school transcript, 3 letters of recommendation. *Recommended:* essay or personal statement, interview.
Application deadlines: 1/1 (freshmen), 4/1 (transfers).
Early decision deadline: 11/1 (for plan 1), 1/1 (for plan 2).
Notification: 4/1 (freshmen), continuous (transfers), 12/22 (early decision plan 1), 2/1 (early decision plan 2).

CONTACT
Sally S. Richmond, Vice President for Admissions and Financial Aid, Washington and Lee University, 204 West Washington Street, Lexington, VA 24450-2116. *Phone:* 540-458-8710. *Fax:* 540-458-8062. *E-mail:* admissions@wlu.edu.

WASHINGTON

Antioch University Seattle
Seattle, Washington
http://www.antioch.edu/seattle/
- **Independent** university, founded 1975, part of Antioch University
- **Urban** campus
- **Coed**
- **Noncompetitive** entrance level

ACADEMICS
Calendar: quarters. *Degrees:* certificates, bachelor's, master's, and doctoral.
Library: Antioch Seattle Library. *Books:* 8,425 (physical), 264,631 (digital/electronic); *Serial titles:* 40,950 (digital/electronic); *Databases:* 222.

STUDENT LIFE
Housing options: college housing not available.

COSTS & FINANCIAL AID
Costs (2017–18) *Tuition:* $600 per credit hour part-time. Full-time tuition and fees vary according to course load, degree level, location, and program. Part-time tuition and fees vary according to course load, degree level, location, and program. *Required fees:* $435 full-time, $600 per credit hour part-time, $145 per term part-time.

Financial Aid Of all full-time matriculated undergraduates who enrolled in 2006, 259 applied for aid, 150 had their need fully met. 18 Federal Work-Study jobs (averaging $6000). 2 state and other part-time jobs (averaging $5000). *Average percent of need met:* 75. *Average financial aid package:* $6701. *Average need-based loan:* $5500. *Average need-based gift aid:* $4000. *Average indebtedness upon graduation:* $15,999.

APPLYING
Options: electronic application, deferred entrance.
Application fee: $75.

CONTACT
Admissions Office, Antioch University Seattle, 2400 3rd Avenue, Suite 200, Seattle, WA 98121. *Phone:* 206-268-4202. *Toll-free phone:* 888-268-4477. *E-mail:* admissions@antiochseattle.edu.

Argosy University, Seattle
Seattle, Washington
http://www.argosy.edu/locations/seattle/
CONTACT
Argosy University, Seattle, 2601-A Elliott Avenue, Seattle, WA 98121. *Phone:* 206-283-4500. *Toll-free phone:* 866-283-2777.

The Art Institute of Seattle
Seattle, Washington
http://www.artinstitutes.edu/seattle/
CONTACT
The Art Institute of Seattle, 2323 Elliott Avenue, Seattle, WA 98121-1642. *Phone:* 206-448-6600. *Toll-free phone:* 800-275-2471.

Bastyr University
Kenmore, Washington
http://www.bastyr.edu/
CONTACT
Ms. Lauren Marani, Assistant Director of Admissions, Bastyr University, 14500 Juanita Drive NE, Kenmore, WA 98028-4966. *Phone:* 425-602-1300. *Fax:* 425-602-3090. *E-mail:* admissions@bastyr.edu.

Bellevue College
Bellevue, Washington
http://www.bcc.ctc.edu/
CONTACT
Morenika Jacobs, Associate Dean of Enrollment Services, Bellevue College, 3000 Landerholm Circle, SE, Bellevue, WA 98007-6484. *Phone:* 425-564-2205. *Fax:* 425-564-4065.

Cascadia College
Bothell, Washington
http://www.cascadia.edu/
CONTACT
Ms. Erin Blakeney, Dean for Student Success, Cascadia College, 18345 Campus Way, NE, Bothell, WA 98011. *Phone:* 425-352-8000. *Fax:* 425-352-8137. *E-mail:* admissions@cascadia.edu.

Central Washington University
Ellensburg, Washington
http://www.cwu.edu/
- **State-supported** comprehensive, founded 1891
- **Small-town** 380-acre campus with easy access to Seattle
- **Endowment** $5.7 million
- **Coed**
- **Moderately difficult** entrance level

FACULTY
Student/faculty ratio: 18:1.

ACADEMICS
Calendar: quarters. *Degrees:* certificates, bachelor's, master's, post-master's, and postbachelor's certificates.
Library: James E. Brooks Library plus 2 others. *Books:* 900,981 (physical), 251,073 (digital/electronic); *Serial titles:* 327 (physical), 72,453 (digital/electronic); *Databases:* 112. Weekly public service hours: 101; students can reserve study rooms.

STUDENT LIFE
Housing options: on-campus residence required for freshman year; coed, cooperative, special housing for students with disabilities. Campus housing is university owned. Freshman campus housing is guaranteed.

Activities and organizations: drama/theater group, student-run newspaper, radio and television station, choral group, marching band, SISTERS, Brother 2 Brother, Cosplay, Alpha Kappa Si, Society of Human Resource Management.

Athletics Member NCAA. All Division II.

Campus security: 24-hour emergency response devices and patrols, late-night transport/escort service, controlled dormitory access, alert update system: emergency notification across digital platforms, Rape Aggression Defense System: realistic self-defense for women.

Student services: health clinic, personal/psychological counseling.

COSTS & FINANCIAL AID

Costs (2017–18) *Tuition:* state resident $6037 full-time, $225 per credit part-time; nonresident $20,144 full-time, $695 per credit part-time. Full-time tuition and fees vary according to course load, degree level, location, and reciprocity agreements. Part-time tuition and fees vary according to course load, degree level, location, and reciprocity agreements. *Required fees:* $1812 full-time. *Room and board:* $10,684. Room and board charges vary according to board plan, housing facility, and location.

Financial Aid Of all full-time matriculated undergraduates who enrolled in 2015, 7,422 applied for aid, 5,859 were judged to have need, 1,674 had their need fully met. In 2015, 14 non-need-based awards were made. *Average percent of need met:* 80. *Average financial aid package:* $11,434. *Average need-based loan:* $4376. *Average need-based gift aid:* $8841. *Average non-need-based aid:* $821. *Average indebtedness upon graduation:* $22,827.

APPLYING

Standardized Tests *Required:* SAT or ACT (for admission).

Options: electronic application.

Application fee: $50.

Required: high school transcript, minimum 2.0 GPA. *Required for some:* essay or personal statement, interview.

CONTACT

Ms. Kathy Gaer-Carlton, Director of Admissions, Central Washington University, 400 East University Way, Ellensburg, WA 98926-7463. *Phone:* 509-963-1211. *Fax:* 509-963-3065. *E-mail:* admissions@cwu.edu.

Charter College
Vancouver, Washington
http://www.chartercollege.edu/

CONTACT
Charter College, 17720 SE Mill Plain Boulevard, Suite 170, Vancouver, WA 98683.

City University of Seattle
Seattle, Washington
http://www.cityu.edu/

CONTACT
Student Services Center, City University of Seattle, 11900 NE First Street, Bellevue, WA 98005. *Phone:* 888-422-4898. *Toll-free phone:* 800-426-5596. *E-mail:* info@cityu.edu.

Clark College
Vancouver, Washington
http://www.clark.edu/

CONTACT
Ms. Sheryl Anderson, Director of Admissions, Clark College, Vancouver, WA 98663. *Phone:* 360-992-2308. *Fax:* 360-992-2867. *E-mail:* admissions@clark.edu.

Cornish College of the Arts
Seattle, Washington
http://www.cornish.edu/
- **Independent** 4-year, founded 1914
- **Urban** 4-acre campus with easy access to Seattle
- **Coed** 654 undergraduate students, 100% full-time, 66% women, 34% men
- **Moderately difficult** entrance level, 63% of applicants were admitted

UNDERGRAD STUDENTS
652 full-time, 2 part-time. Students come from 40 states and territories; 5 other countries; 51% are from out of state; 3% Black or African American, non-Hispanic/Latino; 14% Hispanic/Latino; 4% Asian, non-Hispanic/Latino; 0.6% Native Hawaiian or other Pacific Islander, non-Hispanic/Latino; 0.8% American Indian or Alaska Native, non-Hispanic/Latino; 10% Two or more races, non-Hispanic/Latino; 4% Race/ethnicity unknown; 1% international; 7% transferred in.

Freshmen:
Admission: 1,023 applied, 642 admitted, 213 enrolled.
Retention: 126% of full-time freshmen returned.

FACULTY
Total: 203, 27% full-time.
Student/faculty ratio: 6:1.

ACADEMICS
Calendar: semesters. *Degrees:* bachelor's and postbachelor's certificates.

Special study options: accelerated degree program, advanced placement credit, cooperative education, independent study, internships, services for LD students, study abroad, summer session for credit.

Computers: Students can access the following: campus intranet, computer help desk, free student e-mail accounts, online (class) grades, online (class) registration, online (class) schedules. Campuswide network is available. 100% of college-owned or -operated housing units are wired for high-speed Internet access. Wireless service is available via entire campus.

Library: Cornish Library. *Books:* 30,000 (physical), 130,000 (digital/electronic).

STUDENT LIFE
Housing options: on-campus residence required for freshman year; coed. Campus housing is university owned. Freshman campus housing is guaranteed.

Activities and organizations: drama/theater group, choral group, Student Leadership Council, Black Student Alliance, Sigma Alpha Phi, AIGA, Cheese Tasting.

Campus security: 24-hour emergency response devices and patrols, late-night transport/escort service, controlled dormitory access.

Student services: personal/psychological counseling.

COSTS & FINANCIAL AID
Costs (2018–19) *Comprehensive fee:* $53,142 includes full-time tuition ($40,442), mandatory fees ($1200), and room and board ($11,500). Full-time tuition and fees vary according to course load and program. Part-time tuition: $1686 per credit hour. Part-time tuition and fees vary according to course load. *Required fees:* $600 per term part-time. *College room only:* $8400. Room and board charges vary according to board plan and housing facility. *Payment plan:* installment. *Waivers:* employees or children of employees.

Financial Aid Of all full-time matriculated undergraduates who enrolled in 2015, 629 applied for aid, 559 were judged to have need, 45 had their need fully met. In 2015, 142 non-need-based awards were made. *Average percent of need met:* 59. *Average financial aid package:* $24,566. *Average need-based loan:* $4930. *Average need-based gift aid:* $18,098. *Average non-need-based aid:* $9626. *Average indebtedness upon graduation:* $37,686.

APPLYING
Standardized Tests *Recommended:* SAT or ACT (for admission).

Options: electronic application, early action, deferred entrance.

Application fee: $60.

Required: essay or personal statement, high school transcript, minimum 2.5 GPA, portfolio or audition. *Required for some:* 2 letters of recommendation. *Recommended:* 2 letters of recommendation, interview.

Application deadlines: rolling (freshmen), rolling (out-of-state freshmen), rolling (transfers), 12/1 (early action).

Notification: continuous (freshmen), continuous (out-of-state freshmen).

CONTACT
Ms. Sharron Starling, Director of Admissions, Cornish College of the Arts, 1000 Lenora Street, Seattle, WA 98121. *Phone:* 206-726-5017. *Toll-free phone:* 800-726-ARTS. *Fax:* 206-720-1011. *E-mail:* admissions@cornish.edu.

DigiPen Institute of Technology
Redmond, Washington
http://www.digipen.edu/
- **Proprietary** comprehensive, founded 1988
- **Suburban** 3-acre campus with easy access to Seattle
- **Coed** 1,028 undergraduate students
- **Minimally difficult** entrance level, 53% of applicants were admitted

UNDERGRAD STUDENTS
50% are from out of state; 1% Black or African American, non-Hispanic/Latino; 6% Hispanic/Latino; 9% Asian, non-Hispanic/Latino; 0.2% Native Hawaiian or other Pacific Islander, non-Hispanic/Latino; 0.3% American Indian or Alaska Native, non-Hispanic/Latino; 5% Two or more races, non-Hispanic/Latino; 27% Race/ethnicity unknown; 5% international; 66% live on campus.

Freshmen:
Admission: 742 applied, 396 admitted.
Retention: 81% of full-time freshmen returned.

FACULTY
Total: 179, 43% full-time, 28% with terminal degrees.
Student/faculty ratio: 11:1.

ACADEMICS
Calendar: semesters. *Degrees:* bachelor's and master's.

Special study options: academic remediation for entering students, accelerated degree program, advanced placement credit, cooperative education, English as a second language, independent study, internships, services for LD students, summer session for credit.

Computers: 794 computers/terminals are available on campus for general student use. Students can access the following: campus intranet, computer help desk, free student e-mail accounts, online (class) grades, online (class) registration, online (class) schedules. Campuswide network is available. 100% of college-owned or -operated housing units are wired for high-speed Internet access. Wireless service is available via entire campus.

Library: DigiPen Library plus 1 other. *Books:* 4,484 (physical), 186,538 (digital/electronic); *Serial titles:* 1,235 (physical), 5,028 (digital/electronic); *Databases:* 11. Weekly public service hours: 72.

STUDENT LIFE
Housing options: coed, men-only, women-only, special housing for students with disabilities. Campus housing is leased by the school and is provided by a third party. Freshman applicants given priority for college housing.

Activities and organizations: choral group, Dungeons and Dragons Club, Counterstrike Club, Ping Pong Club, Outbreak Club, Wellness Club.

Campus security: 24-hour patrols, late-night transport/escort service, controlled dormitory access, on-site security during campus hours.

Student services: personal/psychological counseling.

COSTS & FINANCIAL AID
Costs (2018–19) *One-time required fee:* $150. *Tuition:* $31,140 full-time, $1005 per credit part-time. Full-time tuition and fees vary according to course load, degree level, and program. Part-time tuition and fees vary according to course load, degree level, and program. *Required fees:* $200 full-time. *Room only:* Room and board charges vary according to board plan and housing facility. *Payment plan:* installment. *Waivers:* employees or children of employees.

Financial Aid Of all full-time matriculated undergraduates who enrolled in 2016, 652 applied for aid, 548 were judged to have need, 30 had their need fully met. In 2016, 61 non-need-based awards were made. *Average percent of need met:* 33. *Average financial aid package:* $11,022. *Average need-based loan:* $4179. *Average need-based gift aid:* $9352. *Average non-need-based aid:* $8987. *Average indebtedness upon graduation:* $28,539.

APPLYING
Standardized Tests *Required for some:* SAT or ACT (for admission).
Options: electronic application, deferred entrance.
Application fee: $60.

Required: essay or personal statement, high school transcript, minimum 2.5 GPA. *Required for some:* pre-calculus for Bachelor of Science, art portfolio for BFA in Digital Art and Animation, performance portfolio for BA in Music and Sound Design, design portfolio for Bachelor of Art in Game Design. *Recommended:* 2 letters of recommendation.

Application deadlines: rolling (freshmen), rolling (transfers).
Notification: continuous (freshmen), continuous (transfers).

CONTACT
Ms. Danial Powers, Director of Admissions, DigiPen Institute of Technology, 9931 Willows Road NE, Redmond, WA 98052. *Phone:* 425-629-5071. *Toll-free phone:* 866-478-5236. *Fax:* 425-558-0378. *E-mail:* admissions@digipen.edu.

Eastern Washington University
Cheney, Washington
http://www.ewu.edu/
- **State-supported** comprehensive, founded 1882
- **Suburban** 335-acre campus with easy access to Spokane
- **Coed** 11,473 undergraduate students, 88% full-time, 54% women, 46% men

UNDERGRAD STUDENTS
10,060 full-time, 1,413 part-time. 5% are from out of state; 3% Black or African American, non-Hispanic/Latino; 16% Hispanic/Latino; 3% Asian, non-Hispanic/Latino; 0.3% Native Hawaiian or other Pacific Islander, non-Hispanic/Latino; 1% American Indian or Alaska Native, non-Hispanic/Latino; 7% Two or more races, non-Hispanic/Latino; 2% Race/ethnicity unknown; 5% international; 11% transferred in; 16% live on campus.

Freshmen:
Admission: 1,634 enrolled. *Average high school GPA:* 3.2. *Test scores:* SAT evidence-based reading and writing scores over 500: 52%; SAT math scores over 500: 50%; ACT scores over 18: 74%; SAT evidence-based reading and writing scores over 600: 7%; SAT math scores over 600: 12%; ACT scores over 24: 26%; SAT evidence-based reading and writing scores over 700: 1%; ACT scores over 30: 2%.
Retention: 76% of full-time freshmen returned.

FACULTY
Total: 676, 71% full-time, 55% with terminal degrees.
Student/faculty ratio: 21:1.

ACADEMICS
Calendar: quarters. *Degrees:* certificates, bachelor's, master's, doctoral, and postbachelor's certificates.

Special study options: academic remediation for entering students, accelerated degree program, adult/continuing education programs, advanced placement credit, cooperative education, distance learning, double majors, English as a second language, honors programs, independent study, internships, off-campus study, part-time degree program, services for LD students, student-designed majors, study abroad, summer session for credit. *ROTC:* Army (b).

Unusual degree programs: 3-2 exercise science/occupational therapy, therapeutic recreation, interdisciplinary studies.

Computers: Students can access the following: campus intranet, computer help desk, free student e-mail accounts, online (class) grades, online (class) registration, online (class) schedules, network disk storage; discounted software; laptops, still and video cameras, projectors for checkout; print credit; black white laser, color laser, and color photo options, large format print service. Campuswide network is available. 100% of college-owned or -operated housing units are wired for high-speed Internet access. Wireless service is available via entire campus.

Library: John F. Kennedy Library. Students can reserve study rooms.

STUDENT LIFE
Housing options: on-campus residence required for freshman year; coed, special housing for students with disabilities. Campus housing is university owned. Freshman campus housing is guaranteed.

Activities and organizations: drama/theater group, student-run newspaper, radio station, choral group, marching band, national fraternities, national sororities.

Athletics Member NCAA. All Division I except football (Division I-AA). *Intercollegiate sports:* archery M(c)/W(c), baseball M(c), basketball M(s)/W(s), cheerleading W(c), cross-country running M(s)/W(s), equestrian sports M(c)/W(c), fencing M(c)/W(c), golf W(s), ice hockey M(c)/W(c), rugby M(c)/W(c), soccer M(c)/W(s), softball W(c), tennis M(s)/W(s), track and field M(s)/W(s), volleyball W(s). *Intramural sports:* baseball M/W, basketball M/W, bowling M/W, cross-country running M/W, football M/W, golf W, racquetball M/W, soccer M/W, softball M/W, tennis M/W, track and field M/W, ultimate Frisbee M(c)/W(c), volleyball M/W, wrestling M(c)/W(c).

Campus security: 24-hour emergency response devices and patrols, student patrols, late-night transport/escort service, controlled dormitory access, emergency call boxes.

Student services: health clinic, personal/psychological counseling, women's center.

COSTS & FINANCIAL AID

Costs (2017–18) *Tuition:* state resident $6242 full-time, $208 per credit hour part-time; nonresident $22,995 full-time, $767 per credit hour part-time. Full-time tuition and fees vary according to course load, degree level, location, and program. Part-time tuition and fees vary according to course load, degree level, location, and program. *Required fees:* $867 full-time. *Room and board:* $11,493; room only: $6528. Room and board charges vary according to board plan and housing facility. *Waivers:* employees or children of employees.

Financial Aid Of all full-time matriculated undergraduates who enrolled in 2016, 7,553 applied for aid, 6,210 were judged to have need, 456 had their need fully met. 205 Federal Work-Study jobs (averaging $2723). 172 state and other part-time jobs (averaging $2620). In 2016, 529 non-need-based awards were made. *Average percent of need met:* 59. *Average financial aid package:* $13,055. *Average need-based loan:* $4138. *Average need-based gift aid:* $8019. *Average non-need-based aid:* $3710. *Average indebtedness upon graduation:* $27,961.

APPLYING

Standardized Tests *Required:* SAT or ACT (for admission).

Required: high school transcript, minimum 2.0 GPA. *Required for some:* essay or personal statement. *Recommended:* minimum 3.0 GPA.

CONTACT
Jana Jaraysi, Director of Recruitment, Eastern Washington University, 304 Sutton Hall, Cheney, WA 99004-2447. *Phone:* 509-359-2450. *Fax:* 509-359-6692. *E-mail:* admissions@ewu.edu.

★ The Evergreen State College
Olympia, Washington
http://www.evergreen.edu/

- **State-supported** comprehensive, founded 1967, part of Washington State Public Baccalaureate Institution
- **Rural** 1000-acre campus with easy access to Seattle
- **Endowment** $13.4 million
- **Coed** 3,610 undergraduate students, 92% full-time, 58% women, 42% men
- **Moderately difficult** entrance level, 96% of applicants were admitted

UNDERGRAD STUDENTS
3,330 full-time, 280 part-time. Students come from 48 states and territories; 18 other countries; 20% are from out of state; 5% Black or African American, non-Hispanic/Latino; 11% Hispanic/Latino; 3% Asian, non-Hispanic/Latino; 0.4% Native Hawaiian or other Pacific Islander, non-Hispanic/Latino; 2% American Indian or Alaska Native, non-Hispanic/Latino; 8% Two or more races, non-Hispanic/Latino; 4% Race/ethnicity unknown; 0.6% international; 16% transferred in; 24% live on campus.

Freshmen:
Admission: 1,772 applied, 1,706 admitted, 521 enrolled. *Average high school GPA:* 3.0. *Test scores:* ACT scores over 18: 85%; ACT scores over 24: 49%; ACT scores over 30: 12%.

Retention: 61% of full-time freshmen returned.

FACULTY
Total: 223, 70% full-time, 79% with terminal degrees.
Student/faculty ratio: 21:1.

ACADEMICS
Calendar: quarters. *Degrees:* bachelor's and master's.

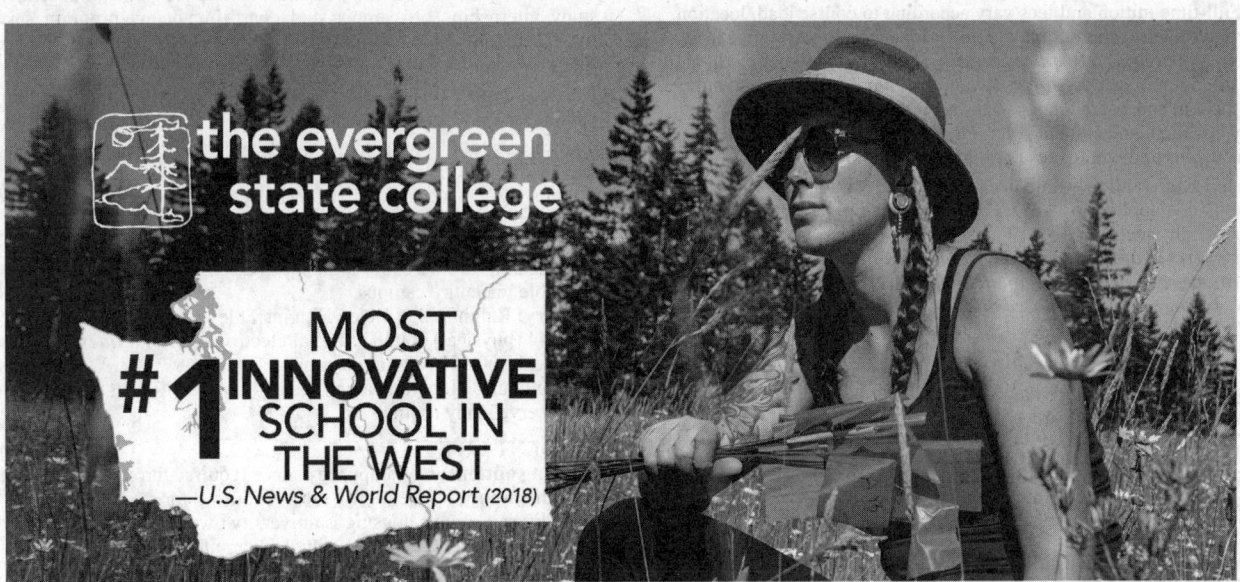

Special study options: accelerated degree program, advanced placement credit, double majors, independent study, internships, off-campus study, part-time degree program, services for LD students, student-designed majors, study abroad, summer session for credit.

Computers: 556 computers/terminals are available on campus for general student use. Students can access the following: campus intranet, computer help desk, free student e-mail accounts, online (class) grades, online (class) registration, online (class) schedules, online payment, student accounts history, financial aid records, academic history, housing application, evaluations. Campuswide network is available. 100% of college-owned or -operated housing units are wired for high-speed Internet access. Wireless service is available via entire campus.

Library: Daniel J. Evans Library. *Books:* 326,129 (physical), 160,427 (digital/electronic); *Serial titles:* 69 (physical), 65,977 (digital/electronic); *Databases:* 64. Weekly public service hours: 83; students can reserve study rooms.

STUDENT LIFE

Housing options: coed, special housing for students with disabilities. Campus housing is university owned. Freshman campus housing is guaranteed.

Activities and organizations: drama/theater group, student-run newspaper, radio and television station, choral group, Black Cottonwood Collective, Zombies at Evergreen, Student Veteran Organization, Chemistry and Other Sciences, Common Bread.

Athletics Member NAIA. *Intercollegiate sports:* basketball M(s)/W(s), soccer M(s)/W(s), track and field M/W, volleyball W(s). *Intramural sports:* archery M(c)/W(c), badminton M/W, basketball M/W, crew M(c)/W(c), fencing M(c)/W(c), rowing M(c)/W(c), sailing M(c)/W(c), soccer M/W, volleyball M/W.

Campus security: 24-hour emergency response devices and patrols, student patrols, late-night transport/escort service, controlled dormitory access, car lockouts, jump-starts.

Student services: health clinic, personal/psychological counseling, women's center.

COSTS & FINANCIAL AID

Costs (2017–18) *Tuition:* state resident $6678 full-time, $227 per credit hour part-time; nonresident $24,138 full-time, $805 per credit hour part-time. Full-time tuition and fees vary according to course load, location, and program. Part-time tuition and fees vary according to course load, location, and program. *Required fees:* $738 full-time, $9 per credit hour part-time, $5 per term part-time. *Room and board:* $9681; room only: $6471. Room and board charges vary according to board plan, housing facility, location, and student level. *Payment plan:* installment. *Waivers:* senior citizens and employees or children of employees.

Financial Aid Of all full-time matriculated undergraduates who enrolled in 2016, 2,664 applied for aid, 2,320 were judged to have need, 163 had their need fully met. In 2016, 19 non-need-based awards were made. *Average percent of need met:* 62. *Average financial aid package:* $12,210. *Average need-based loan:* $4148. *Average need-based gift aid:* $9456. *Average non-need-based aid:* $2504. *Average indebtedness upon graduation:* $21,147.

APPLYING

Standardized Tests *Required:* SAT or ACT (for admission).

Options: electronic application, deferred entrance.

Application fee: $50.

Required: high school transcript, minimum 2.0 GPA. *Required for some:* essay or personal statement. *Recommended:* essay or personal statement.

Application deadlines: 2/1 (freshmen), 2/1 (transfers).

Notification: continuous until 11/1 (freshmen), continuous until 11/1 (transfers).

CONTACT

The Evergreen State College, 2700 Evergreen Parkway, NW, Olympia, WA 98505. *Phone:* 360-867-6170.

See previous page for display ad and page 1290 for the College Close-Up.

Gonzaga University
Spokane, Washington
http://www.gonzaga.edu/

- **Independent Roman Catholic** university, founded 1887
- **Urban** 152-acre campus
- **Endowment** $262.8 million
- **Coed** 5,209 undergraduate students, 98% full-time, 52% women, 48% men
- **Moderately difficult** entrance level, 65% of applicants were admitted

UNDERGRAD STUDENTS

5,110 full-time, 99 part-time. Students come from 43 states and territories; 28 other countries; 51% are from out of state; 1% Black or African American, non-Hispanic/Latino; 11% Hispanic/Latino; 5% Asian, non-Hispanic/Latino; 0.4% Native Hawaiian or other Pacific Islander, non-Hispanic/Latino; 0.6% American Indian or Alaska Native, non-Hispanic/Latino; 6% Two or more races, non-Hispanic/Latino; 3% Race/ethnicity unknown; 1% international; 2% transferred in; 55% live on campus.

Freshmen:

Admission: 7,613 applied, 4,937 admitted, 1,257 enrolled. *Average high school GPA:* 3.8. *Test scores:* SAT evidence-based reading and writing scores over 500: 99%; SAT math scores over 500: 99%; ACT scores over 18: 100%; SAT evidence-based reading and writing scores over 600: 74%; SAT math scores over 600: 70%; ACT scores over 24: 93%; SAT evidence-based reading and writing scores over 700: 12%; SAT math scores over 700: 15%; ACT scores over 30: 34%.

Retention: 94% of full-time freshmen returned.

FACULTY

Total: 770, 57% full-time, 49% with terminal degrees.

Student/faculty ratio: 12:1.

ACADEMICS

Calendar: semesters. *Degrees:* bachelor's, master's, and doctoral.

Special study options: accelerated degree program, adult/continuing education programs, advanced placement credit, distance learning, double majors, English as a second language, honors programs, independent study, internships, off-campus study, part-time degree program, services for LD students, study abroad, summer session for credit. *ROTC:* Army (b).

Unusual degree programs: 3-2 business administration; engineering; nursing.

Computers: 500 computers/terminals and 900 ports are available on campus for general student use. Students can access the following: campus intranet, computer help desk, free student e-mail accounts, online (class) grades, online (class) registration, online (class) schedules. Campuswide network is available. 100% of college-owned or -operated housing units are wired for high-speed Internet access. Wireless service is available via entire campus.

Library: Ralph E. and Helen Higgins Foley Center plus 1 other. *Books:* 266,244 (physical), 33,682 (digital/electronic); *Serial titles:* 6,301 (physical), 60,559 (digital/electronic); *Databases:* 328. Weekly public service hours: 112; study areas open 24 hours, 5–7 days a week; students can reserve study rooms.

STUDENT LIFE

Housing options: on-campus residence required through sophomore year; coed, men-only, women-only, special housing for students with disabilities. Campus housing is university owned and leased by the school. Freshman campus housing is guaranteed.

Activities and organizations: drama/theater group, student-run newspaper, radio and television station, choral group, Student Body Association, Kennel Club, Search, Circle K, Encore.

Athletics Member NCAA. All Division I. *Intercollegiate sports:* baseball M(s), basketball M(s)/W(s), cross-country running M(s)/W(s), golf M(s)/W(s), rowing M/W(s), soccer M(s)/W(s), tennis M(s)/W(s), track and field M(s)/W(s), volleyball W(s). *Intramural sports:* badminton M/W, basketball M/W, cheerleading M(c)/W(c), football M/W, golf M(c)/W(c), ice hockey M(c)/W(c), lacrosse M(c)/W(c), racquetball M/W, riflery M(c)/W(c), rugby M(c)/W(c), skiing (downhill) M(c)/W(c), soccer M(c)/W(c), softball M/W, swimming and diving M(c)/W(c), tennis M/W, track and field M(c)/W(c), triathlon M(c)/W(c), ultimate Frisbee M(c)/W(c), water polo M(c)/W(c), weight lifting M(c)/W(c), wrestling M.

Campus security: 24-hour emergency response devices and patrols, late-night transport/escort service, controlled dormitory access.

Student services: health clinic, personal/psychological counseling.

COSTS & FINANCIAL AID

Costs (2017–18) *Comprehensive fee:* $52,880 includes full-time tuition ($40,540), mandatory fees ($790), and room and board ($11,550). Full-time tuition and fees vary according to course load, location, program, reciprocity agreements, and student level. Part-time tuition: $1110 per credit. Part-time tuition and fees vary according to course load, location, program, reciprocity agreements, and student level. *Required fees:* $180 per term part-time. *College room only:* $5900. Room and board charges vary according to board plan, housing facility, and location. *Payment plans:* installment, deferred payment. *Waivers:* senior citizens and employees or children of employees.

Financial Aid Of all full-time matriculated undergraduates who enrolled in 2016, 3,404 applied for aid, 2,687 were judged to have need, 742 had their need fully met. 346 Federal Work-Study jobs (averaging $2457). 188 state and other part-time jobs (averaging $2879). In 2016, 2174 non-need-based awards were made. *Average percent of need met:* 80. *Average financial aid package:* $30,040. *Average need-based loan:* $5578. *Average need-based gift aid:* $22,206. *Average non-need-based aid:* $15,837. *Average indebtedness upon graduation:* $29,692.

APPLYING

Standardized Tests *Required:* SAT or ACT (for admission).

Options: electronic application, early action, deferred entrance.

Application fee: $50.

Required: essay or personal statement, high school transcript, minimum 3.2 GPA, 1 letter of recommendation. *Recommended:* interview.

Application deadlines: 2/1 (freshmen), 6/1 (transfers), 11/15 (early action).

Notification: 3/15 (freshmen), continuous (transfers), 1/15 (early action).

CONTACT

Ms. Julie McCulloh, Dean of Admission, Gonzaga University, 502 East Boone Avenue, Spokane, WA 99258-0102. *Phone:* 800-322-2584. *Toll-free phone:* 800-322-2584 Ext. 6572. *Fax:* 509-313-6572. *E-mail:* admissions@gonzaga.edu.

Heritage University
Toppenish, Washington
http://www.heritage.edu/

CONTACT

Olivia Gutierrez, Director of Admissions, Heritage University, 3240 Fort Road, Toppenish, WA 98948-9599. *Phone:* 509-865-8697. *Toll-free phone:* 888-272-6190. *Fax:* 509-865-4469. *E-mail:* admissions@heritage.edu.

Northwest College of Art & Design
Tacoma, Washington
http://www.ncad.edu/
- **Proprietary** 4-year, founded 1982
- **Small-town** 26-acre campus with easy access to Seattle
- **Coed**

FACULTY
Student/faculty ratio: 5:1.

ACADEMICS
Calendar: semesters. *Degree:* bachelor's.
Library: Northwest College of Art & Design Library. *Books:* 600 (physical); *Serial titles:* 500 (physical). Weekly public service hours: 48.

COSTS & FINANCIAL AID
Costs (2017–18) *Tuition:* $20,500 full-time, $870 per credit hour part-time. Full-time tuition and fees vary according to degree level. Part-time tuition and fees vary according to course load. *Required fees:* $100 full-time, $100 per year part-time.

Financial Aid Of all full-time matriculated undergraduates who enrolled in 2015, 75 applied for aid, 75 were judged to have need, 60 had their need fully met. In 2015, 1 non-need-based awards were made. *Average percent of need met:* 55. *Average financial aid package:* $11,429. *Average need-based gift aid:* $9892. *Average non-need-based aid:* $1111. *Average indebtedness upon graduation:* $20,426.

APPLYING
Required: essay or personal statement, high school transcript, interview, 5 piece portfolio.

CONTACT
Mrs. Ashley Miller, Admissions Representative, Northwest College of Art & Design, 16301 Creative Drive NE, Poulsbo, WA 98370. *Phone:* 360-779-9993. *Toll-free phone:* 800-769-ARTS. *Fax:* 360-7799933. *E-mail:* amiller@ncad.edu.

Northwest Indian College
Bellingham, Washington
http://www.nwic.edu/

CONTACT
Office of Admissions, Northwest Indian College, 2522 Kwina Road, Bellingham, WA 98226. *Phone:* 360-676-2772. *Toll-free phone:* 866-676-2772. *Fax:* 360-392-4333. *E-mail:* admissions@nwic.edu.

Northwest University
Kirkland, Washington
http://www.northwestu.edu/
- **Independent** comprehensive, founded 1934, affiliated with Assemblies of God
- **Suburban** 56-acre campus with easy access to Seattle
- **Endowment** $6.8 million
- **Coed** 1,871 undergraduate students, 74% full-time, 60% women, 40% men
- **Moderately difficult** entrance level, 100% of applicants were admitted

UNDERGRAD STUDENTS
1,377 full-time, 494 part-time. Students come from 34 states and territories; 24 other countries; 26% are from out of state; 6% Black or African American, non-Hispanic/Latino; 10% Hispanic/Latino; 6% Asian, non-Hispanic/Latino; 2% Native Hawaiian or other Pacific Islander, non-Hispanic/Latino; 2% American Indian or Alaska Native, non-Hispanic/Latino; 5% Two or more races, non-Hispanic/Latino; 8% Race/ethnicity unknown; 0.8% international; 13% transferred in; 55% live on campus.

Freshmen:
Admission: 493 applied, 491 admitted, 215 enrolled. *Average high school GPA:* 3.4. *Test scores:* SAT evidence-based reading and writing scores over 500: 75%; SAT math scores over 500: 73%; ACT scores over 18: 77%; SAT evidence-based reading and writing scores over 600: 33%; SAT math scores over 600: 23%; ACT scores over 24: 32%; SAT evidence-based reading and writing scores over 700: 5%; SAT math scores over 700: 3%; ACT scores over 30: 6%.
Retention: 80% of full-time freshmen returned.

FACULTY
Total: 252, 33% full-time, 15% with terminal degrees.
Student/faculty ratio: 14:1.

ACADEMICS
Calendar: semesters. *Degrees:* certificates, diplomas, associate, bachelor's, master's, and doctoral.

Special study options: academic remediation for entering students, accelerated degree program, adult/continuing education programs, advanced placement credit, cooperative education, double majors, English as a second language, independent study, internships, part-time degree program, study abroad, summer session for credit. *ROTC:* Army (c), Air Force (c).

Computers: 134 computers/terminals are available on campus for general student use. Students can access the following: campus intranet, computer help desk, free student e-mail accounts, online (class) grades, online (class) registration, online (class) schedules, online classes. Campuswide network is available. 100% of college-owned or -operated housing units are wired for high-speed Internet access. Wireless service is available via entire campus.

Library: Hurst Library. *Books:* 170,000 (physical); *Serial titles:* 7,000 (physical); *Databases:* 81. Weekly public service hours: 91; study areas open 24 hours, 5–7 days a week; students can reserve study rooms.

STUDENT LIFE

Housing options: on-campus residence required through sophomore year; men-only, women-only. Campus housing is university owned. Freshman campus housing is guaranteed.

Activities and organizations: drama/theater group, student-run newspaper, choral group, Student Ministries, Pursuit (worship service), Northwest University Business Club, Environmental Stewardship Club.

Athletics Member NAIA. *Intercollegiate sports:* basketball M(s)/W(s), cross-country running M(s)/W(s), soccer M(s)/W(s), softball W(s), track and field M(s)/W(s), volleyball W(s).

Campus security: 24-hour emergency response devices and patrols, late-night transport/escort service, controlled dormitory access.

Student services: health clinic, personal/psychological counseling.

COSTS & FINANCIAL AID

Costs (2018–19) *Comprehensive fee:* $40,170 includes full-time tuition ($31,100), mandatory fees ($440), and room and board ($8630). Full-time tuition and fees vary according to class time, course load, location, program, and reciprocity agreements. Part-time tuition: $1250 per credit hour. Part-time tuition and fees vary according to class time, course load, and location. *Required fees:* $120 per term part-time. *College room only:* $4315. Room and board charges vary according to housing facility and location. *Payment plan:* installment. *Waivers:* employees or children of employees.

Financial Aid Of all full-time matriculated undergraduates who enrolled in 2016, 1,107 applied for aid, 974 were judged to have need, 140 had their need fully met. 9 Federal Work-Study jobs (averaging $3551). 5 state and other part-time jobs (averaging $2642). In 2016, 170 non-need-based awards were made. *Average percent of need met:* 71. *Average financial aid package:* $17,638. *Average need-based loan:* $3866. *Average need-based gift aid:* $15,035. *Average non-need-based aid:* $10,384. *Average indebtedness upon graduation:* $24,930.

APPLYING

Standardized Tests *Required:* SAT or ACT (for admission).

Options: electronic application, early action, deferred entrance.

Application fee: $30.

Required: essay or personal statement, high school transcript, minimum 2.3 GPA, 2 letters of recommendation. *Required for some:* interview.

Application deadlines: 8/1 (freshmen), 8/1 (transfers), 1/15 (early action).

Notification: continuous (freshmen), continuous (transfers), 2/15 (early action).

CONTACT

Andy Hall, Northwest University, 5520 108th Avenue NE, PO Box 579, Kirkland, WA 98083-0579. *Phone:* 425-889-5212. *Toll-free phone:* 800-669-3781. *Fax:* 425-889-5224. *E-mail:* admissions@northwestu.edu.

Olympic College

Bremerton, Washington

http://www.olympic.edu/

- **State-supported** primarily 2-year, founded 1946, part of Washington State Board for Community and Technical Colleges
- **Suburban** 33-acre campus with easy access to Seattle, Tacoma
- **Coed**
- **Noncompetitive** entrance level

ACADEMICS

Calendar: quarters. *Degrees:* certificates, diplomas, associate, and bachelor's.

Library: Haselwood Library plus 1 other. Students can reserve study rooms.

STUDENT LIFE

Housing options: coed. Campus housing is university owned.

Activities and organizations: drama/theater group, student-run newspaper, choral group, International Club, Armed Forces Club, Gay/Straight Alliance, Engineering Club, Clay Club.

Campus security: 24-hour emergency response devices and patrols, student patrols, late-night transport/escort service.

Student services: personal/psychological counseling.

FINANCIAL AID

Financial Aid Of all full-time matriculated undergraduates who enrolled in 2016, 105 Federal Work-Study jobs (averaging $2380). 31 state and other part-time jobs (averaging $2880).

APPLYING

Options: electronic application.

Required for some: essay or personal statement, high school transcript, 2 letters of recommendation.

CONTACT

Ms. Nora Downard, Program Manager, Olympic College, 1600 Chester Avenue, Bremerton, WA 98337-1699. *Phone:* 360-475-7445. *Toll-free phone:* 800-259-6718. *Fax:* 360-475-7202. *E-mail:* ndownard@olympic.edu.

Pacific Lutheran University

Tacoma, Washington

http://www.plu.edu/

- **Independent** comprehensive, founded 1890, affiliated with Evangelical Lutheran Church in America
- **Suburban** 156-acre campus with easy access to Seattle
- **Endowment** $95.2 million
- **Coed** 2,709 undergraduate students, 97% full-time, 63% women, 37% men
- **Moderately difficult** entrance level, 75% of applicants were admitted

UNDERGRAD STUDENTS

2,638 full-time, 71 part-time. Students come from 43 states and territories; 19 other countries; 22% are from out of state; 3% Black or African American, non-Hispanic/Latino; 9% Hispanic/Latino; 10% Asian, non-Hispanic/Latino; 1% Native Hawaiian or other Pacific Islander, non-Hispanic/Latino; 0.5% American Indian or Alaska Native, non-Hispanic/Latino; 9% Two or more races, non-Hispanic/Latino; 0.8% Race/ethnicity unknown; 3% international; 6% transferred in; 49% live on campus.

Freshmen:

Admission: 3,629 applied, 2,736 admitted, 535 enrolled. *Average high school GPA:* 3.7. *Test scores:* SAT evidence-based reading and writing scores over 500: 87%; SAT math scores over 500: 85%; ACT scores over 18: 94%; SAT evidence-based reading and writing scores over 600: 48%; SAT math scores over 600: 37%; ACT scores over 24: 58%; SAT evidence-based reading and writing scores over 700: 8%; SAT math scores over 700: 6%; ACT scores over 30: 11%.

Retention: 83% of full-time freshmen returned.

FACULTY

Total: 221, 83% full-time, 84% with terminal degrees.

Student/faculty ratio: 15:1.

ACADEMICS

Calendar: 4-1-4. *Degrees:* certificates, bachelor's, master's, doctoral, and post-master's certificates.

Special study options: advanced placement credit, cooperative education, distance learning, double majors, English as a second language, honors programs, independent study, internships, part-time degree program, services for LD students, student-designed majors, study abroad, summer session for credit. *ROTC:* Army (b).

Unusual degree programs: 3-2 engineering with Columbia University (New York), Washington University in St. Louis.

Computers: 810 computers/terminals and 3,500 ports are available on campus for general student use. Students can access the following: campus intranet, computer help desk, free student e-mail accounts, online (class) grades, online (class) registration, online (class) schedules. Campuswide network is available. 100% of college-owned or -operated

housing units are wired for high-speed Internet access. Wireless service is available via entire campus.
Library: Robert A. L. Mortvedt Library. *Books:* 256,165 (physical), 43,611 (digital/electronic); *Databases:* 118. Weekly public service hours: 80; students can reserve study rooms.

STUDENT LIFE
Housing options: on-campus residence required through sophomore year; coed, women-only, special housing for students with disabilities. Campus housing is university owned. Freshman campus housing is guaranteed.

Activities and organizations: drama/theater group, student-run newspaper, radio and television station, choral group, Delta Iota Chi, Swing Club, Club Keithly, Young Life College Club, ROTC Cadet Activities Council.

Athletics Member NCAA. All Division III. *Intercollegiate sports:* baseball M, basketball M/W, cheerleading M(c)/W(c), crew M(c)/W, cross-country running M/W, football M, golf M/W, lacrosse M(c)/W(c), rowing M(c)/W, soccer M/W, softball W, swimming and diving M/W, tennis M/W, track and field M/W, ultimate Frisbee M(c)/W(c), volleyball W. *Intramural sports:* badminton M/W, basketball M/W, bowling M/W, cross-country running M/W, football M/W, soccer M/W, softball M/W, swimming and diving M/W, table tennis M/W, tennis M/W, ultimate Frisbee M/W, volleyball M/W, water polo M/W, wrestling M/W.

Campus security: 24-hour emergency response devices and patrols, student patrols, late-night transport/escort service, controlled dormitory access, over 60 surveillance camera monitoring stations. Emergency notification system with indoor/outdoor speakers and text/phone/email alerts.

Student services: health clinic, personal/psychological counseling, women's center.

COSTS & FINANCIAL AID
Costs (2017–18) *Comprehensive fee:* $51,242 includes full-time tuition ($40,352), mandatory fees ($370), and room and board ($10,520). Full-time tuition and fees vary according to course load and degree level. Part-time tuition: $1261 per semester hour. Part-time tuition and fees vary according to course load and degree level. *Required fees:* $370 per year part-time. *College room only:* $4940. Room and board charges vary according to board plan and housing facility. *Payment plan:* installment. *Waivers:* children of alumni and employees or children of employees.

Financial Aid Of all full-time matriculated undergraduates who enrolled in 2015, 2,269 applied for aid, 2,048 were judged to have need, 406 had their need fully met. 675 Federal Work-Study jobs (averaging $3189). 477 state and other part-time jobs (averaging $3808). In 2015, 640 non-need-based awards were made. *Average percent of need met:* 84. *Average financial aid package:* $35,634. *Average need-based loan:* $9177. *Average need-based gift aid:* $23,228. *Average non-need-based aid:* $16,755. *Average indebtedness upon graduation:* $29,866.

APPLYING
Standardized Tests *Required:* SAT or ACT (for admission).
Options: electronic application, deferred entrance.
Application fee: $40.
Required: essay or personal statement, high school transcript, 1 letter of recommendation. *Required for some:* interview. *Recommended:* minimum 2.5 GPA.
Application deadlines: rolling (freshmen), rolling (out-of-state freshmen), rolling (transfers).
Notification: continuous (freshmen), continuous (out-of-state freshmen), continuous (transfers).

CONTACT
Melody A. Ferguson, Director of Admission, Pacific Lutheran University, 12180 Park Avenue S., Tacoma, WA 98447. *Phone:* 253-535-7151. *Toll-free phone:* 800-274-6758. *Fax:* 253-536-5136. *E-mail:* admission@plu.edu.

Peninsula College
Port Angeles, Washington
http://www.pc.ctc.edu/

CONTACT
Ms. Pauline Marvin, Peninsula College, 1502 East Lauridsen Boulevard, Port Angeles, WA 98362. *Phone:* 360-417-6596. *Toll-free phone:* 877-452-9277. *Fax:* 360-457-8100. *E-mail:* admissions@pencol.edu.

Pima Medical Institute
Seattle, Washington
http://www.pmi.edu/

CONTACT
Admissions Office, Pima Medical Institute, 9709 Third Avenue NE, Suite 400, Seattle, WA 98115. *Phone:* 206-322-6100. *Toll-free phone:* 800-477-PIMA.

Renton Technical College
Renton, Washington
http://www.rtc.edu/
- **State-supported** primarily 2-year, founded 1942, part of Washington State Board for Community and Technical Colleges
- **Suburban** 30-acre campus with easy access to Seattle
- **Endowment** $837,103
- **Coed** 3,763 undergraduate students, 38% full-time, 31% women, 69% men
- **Noncompetitive** entrance level

UNDERGRAD STUDENTS
1,420 full-time, 2,343 part-time. Students come from 22 states and territories; 0.1% are from out of state; 14% Black or African American, non-Hispanic/Latino; 12% Hispanic/Latino; 21% Asian, non-Hispanic/Latino; 0.9% Native Hawaiian or other Pacific Islander, non-Hispanic/Latino; 0.3% American Indian or Alaska Native, non-Hispanic/Latino; 6% Two or more races, non-Hispanic/Latino; 7% Race/ethnicity unknown; 0.5% international; 16% transferred in.

Freshmen:
Admission: 174 enrolled.

FACULTY
Total: 242, 29% full-time.
Student/faculty ratio: 16:1.

ACADEMICS
Calendar: quarters. *Degrees:* certificates, diplomas, associate, and bachelor's.

Special study options: academic remediation for entering students, adult/continuing education programs, advanced placement credit, cooperative education, distance learning, English as a second language, internships, off-campus study, part-time degree program, services for LD students, summer session for credit.

Computers: 96 computers/terminals are available on campus for general student use. Campuswide network is available.
Library: Renton Technical College Library.

STUDENT LIFE
Housing options: college housing not available.
Campus security: patrols by security, security system.
Student services: personal/psychological counseling.

COSTS
Costs (2018–19) *Tuition:* state resident $4836 full-time. Full-time tuition and fees vary according to course load, degree level, and program. Part-time tuition and fees vary according to course load, degree level, and program. *Payment plan:* installment. *Waivers:* employees or children of employees.

APPLYING
Standardized Tests *Required for some:* ACT ASSET, CLEP, ACCUPLACER, DSP.
Options: electronic application, early admission.

Application fee: $30.

Required for some: essay or personal statement, high school transcript, interview.

Application deadlines: rolling (freshmen), rolling (transfers).

Notification: continuous (freshmen), continuous (transfers).

CONTACT
Renton Technical College, 3000 NE Fourth Street, Renton, WA 98056.

Saint Martin's University
Lacey, Washington
http://www.stmartin.edu/
- **Independent Roman Catholic** comprehensive, founded 1895
- **Suburban** 300-acre campus with easy access to Seattle
- **Endowment** $20.6 million
- **Coed** 1,310 undergraduate students, 85% full-time, 48% women, 52% men
- **Moderately difficult** entrance level, 99% of applicants were admitted

UNDERGRAD STUDENTS
1,119 full-time, 191 part-time. Students come from 34 states and territories; 6 other countries; 28% are from out of state; 6% Black or African American, non-Hispanic/Latino; 14% Hispanic/Latino; 9% Asian, non-Hispanic/Latino; 5% Native Hawaiian or other Pacific Islander, non-Hispanic/Latino; 1% American Indian or Alaska Native, non-Hispanic/Latino; 7% Two or more races, non-Hispanic/Latino; 4% Race/ethnicity unknown; 6% international; 11% transferred in; 41% live on campus.

Freshmen:
Admission: 1,367 applied, 1,353 admitted, 278 enrolled. *Average high school GPA:* 3.4. *Test scores:* SAT evidence-based reading and writing scores over 500: 71%; SAT math scores over 500: 68%; ACT scores over 18: 80%; SAT evidence-based reading and writing scores over 600: 26%; SAT math scores over 600: 22%; ACT scores over 24: 27%; SAT evidence-based reading and writing scores over 700: 3%; SAT math scores over 700: 2%; ACT scores over 30: 6%.
Retention: 76% of full-time freshmen returned.

FACULTY
Total: 196, 43% full-time, 58% with terminal degrees.
Student/faculty ratio: 11:1.

ACADEMICS
Calendar: semesters. *Degrees:* certificates, bachelor's, master's, post-master's, and postbachelor's certificates.

Special study options: academic remediation for entering students, adult/continuing education programs, advanced placement credit, cooperative education, distance learning, double majors, English as a second language, honors programs, independent study, internships, off-campus study, part-time degree program, services for LD students, study abroad, summer session for credit. *ROTC:* Army (c), Air Force (c).

Unusual degree programs: 3-2 business administration; engineering.

Computers: 80 computers/terminals and 130 ports are available on campus for general student use. Students can access the following: campus intranet, computer help desk, free student e-mail accounts, online (class) grades, online (class) registration, online (class) schedules. Campuswide network is available. 100% of college-owned or -operated housing units are wired for high-speed Internet access. Wireless service is available via entire campus.

Library: O'Grady Library. *Books:* 86,191 (physical), 199,723 (digital/electronic); *Serial titles:* 94 (physical), 47,915 (digital/electronic); *Databases:* 115. Weekly public service hours: 88; students can reserve study rooms.

STUDENT LIFE
Housing options: on-campus residence required through sophomore year; coed. Campus housing is university owned. Freshman campus housing is guaranteed.

Activities and organizations: drama/theater group, student-run newspaper, choral group.

Athletics Member NCAA. All Division II. *Intercollegiate sports:* baseball M(s), basketball M(s)/W(s), cross-country running M(s)/W(s),

golf M(s)/W(s), soccer M/W(s), softball W(s), track and field M(s)/W(s), volleyball W(s). *Intramural sports:* basketball M/W, bowling M/W, golf M/W, soccer M/W, softball M/W, table tennis M/W, tennis M/W, ultimate Frisbee M/W, volleyball M/W.

Campus security: 24-hour emergency response devices and patrols, student patrols, late-night transport/escort service, controlled dormitory access, close-circuit TV cameras throughout campus, emergency text messaging/notification.

Student services: health clinic, personal/psychological counseling.

COSTS & FINANCIAL AID
Costs (2018–19) *Comprehensive fee:* $48,801 includes full-time tuition ($36,950), mandatory fees ($406), and room and board ($11,445). Full-time tuition and fees vary according to degree level, location, and program. Part-time tuition: $1240 per credit. Part-time tuition and fees vary according to course load, degree level, location, and program. *College room only:* $5550. Room and board charges vary according to board plan and housing facility. *Payment plan:* installment. *Waivers:* children of alumni and employees or children of employees.

Financial Aid Of all full-time matriculated undergraduates who enrolled in 2016, 869 applied for aid, 800 were judged to have need, 176 had their need fully met. 132 Federal Work-Study jobs (averaging $1647). 22 state and other part-time jobs (averaging $7506). In 2016, 129 non-need-based awards were made. *Average percent of need met:* 76. *Average financial aid package:* $27,128. *Average need-based loan:* $4022. *Average need-based gift aid:* $24,061. *Average non-need-based aid:* $13,883. *Average indebtedness upon graduation:* $30,744.

APPLYING
Standardized Tests *Required:* SAT or ACT (for admission).
Options: electronic application, deferred entrance.
Required: essay or personal statement, high school transcript, 1 letter of recommendation.
Application deadlines: 7/31 (freshmen), 8/1 (transfers).
Notification: continuous (freshmen), continuous (out-of-state freshmen), continuous (transfers).

CONTACT
Saint Martin's University, 5000 Abbey Way SE, Lacey, WA 98503-7500. *Phone:* 360-688-2104. *Toll-free phone:* 800-368-8803. *Fax:* 360-412-6189. *E-mail:* admissions@stmartin.edu.

Seattle Pacific University
Seattle, Washington
http://www.spu.edu/
- **Independent Free Methodist** comprehensive, founded 1891
- **Urban** 40-acre campus
- **Coed** 2,911 undergraduate students, 96% full-time, 67% women, 33% men
- **Moderately difficult** entrance level, 91% of applicants were admitted

UNDERGRAD STUDENTS
2,783 full-time, 128 part-time. 37% are from out of state; 4% Black or African American, non-Hispanic/Latino; 12% Hispanic/Latino; 12% Asian, non-Hispanic/Latino; 0.9% Native Hawaiian or other Pacific Islander, non-Hispanic/Latino; 0.3% American Indian or Alaska Native, non-Hispanic/Latino; 9% Two or more races, non-Hispanic/Latino; 2% Race/ethnicity unknown; 5% international; 7% transferred in; 52% live on campus.

Freshmen:
Admission: 3,692 applied, 3,355 admitted, 647 enrolled. *Average high school GPA:* 3.5. *Test scores:* ACT scores over 18: 98%; ACT scores over 24: 68%; ACT scores over 30: 16%.
Retention: 79% of full-time freshmen returned.

FACULTY
Total: 395, 53% full-time, 47% with terminal degrees.
Student/faculty ratio: 13:1.

ACADEMICS
Calendar: quarters. *Degrees:* bachelor's, master's, doctoral, and post-master's certificates.

Special study options: academic remediation for entering students, adult/continuing education programs, advanced placement credit, distance learning, double majors, external degree program, honors programs, independent study, internships, off-campus study, part-time degree program, services for LD students, student-designed majors, study abroad, summer session for credit. *ROTC:* Army (c), Navy (c), Air Force (c).

Computers: 150 computers/terminals are available on campus for general student use. Students can access the following: campus intranet, computer help desk, free student e-mail accounts, online (class) grades, online (class) registration, online (class) schedules. Campuswide network is available. Wireless service is available via entire campus.

Library: University Library.

STUDENT LIFE

Housing options: on-campus residence required through sophomore year; coed, special housing for students with disabilities. Campus housing is university owned. Freshman campus housing is guaranteed.

Activities and organizations: drama/theater group, student-run newspaper, radio station, choral group, Centurions, Falconettes, forensics organization, Amnesty International, University Players.

Athletics Member NCAA. All Division II. *Intercollegiate sports:* basketball M(s)/W(s), crew M/W(s), cross-country running M(s)/W(s), gymnastics W(s), soccer M(s)/W(s), track and field M(s)/W(s), volleyball W(s). *Intramural sports:* archery M/W, basketball M/W, bowling M/W, cross-country running M/W, football M/W, soccer M/W(c), softball M/W, tennis M/W, volleyball M(c)/W(c), weight lifting M/W.

Campus security: 24-hour emergency response devices and patrols, student patrols, late-night transport/escort service, closed-circuit TV monitors.

Student services: health clinic, personal/psychological counseling.

COSTS & FINANCIAL AID

Costs (2017–18) *Comprehensive fee:* $52,080 includes full-time tuition ($40,464), mandatory fees ($438), and room and board ($11,178). Part-time tuition: $1124 per credit hour. Part-time tuition and fees vary according to course load. *College room only:* $6093. Room and board charges vary according to board plan and housing facility. *Payment plans:* installment, deferred payment. *Waivers:* senior citizens and employees or children of employees.

Financial Aid Of all full-time matriculated undergraduates who enrolled in 2017, 2,199 applied for aid, 1,915 were judged to have need, 127 had their need fully met. 436 Federal Work-Study jobs (averaging $2392). 109 state and other part-time jobs (averaging $2931). In 2017, 668 non-need-based awards were made. *Average percent of need met:* 78. *Average financial aid package:* $34,345. *Average need-based loan:* $5157. *Average need-based gift aid:* $33,723. *Average non-need-based aid:* $23,152. *Average indebtedness upon graduation:* $28,646.

APPLYING

Standardized Tests *Required:* SAT or ACT (for admission). *Required for some:* SAT and SAT Subject Tests or ACT (for admission), SAT Subject Tests (for admission).

Options: electronic application, early admission, early action.

Application fee: $50.

Required: essay or personal statement, high school transcript, minimum 2.5 GPA, 2 letters of recommendation. *Recommended:* interview.

Application deadlines: 2/1 (freshmen), 8/1 (transfers), 11/15 (early action).

Notification: 3/1 (freshmen), continuous (transfers), 1/5 (early action).

CONTACT

Ineliz Soto-Fuller, Director of Undergraduate Admissions, Seattle Pacific University, 3307 3rd Avenue, West, Seattle, WA 98119-1997. *Phone:* 206-281-2021. *Toll-free phone:* 800-366-3344. *Fax:* 206-281-2544. *E-mail:* admissions@spu.edu.

Seattle University
Seattle, Washington
http://www.seattleu.edu/

- **Independent Roman Catholic** comprehensive, founded 1891
- **Urban** 50-acre campus with easy access to Seattle
- **Coed** 4,647 undergraduate students, 94% full-time, 62% women, 38% men
- **Moderately difficult** entrance level, 74% of applicants were admitted

UNDERGRAD STUDENTS

4,383 full-time, 264 part-time. Students come from 50 states and territories; 101 other countries; 59% are from out of state; 3% Black or African American, non-Hispanic/Latino; 12% Hispanic/Latino; 16% Asian, non-Hispanic/Latino; 0.9% Native Hawaiian or other Pacific Islander, non-Hispanic/Latino; 0.3% American Indian or Alaska Native, non-Hispanic/Latino; 8% Two or more races, non-Hispanic/Latino; 5% Race/ethnicity unknown; 10% international; 9% transferred in; 45% live on campus.

Freshmen:
Admission: 8,576 applied, 6,329 admitted, 957 enrolled. *Average high school GPA:* ####. *Test scores:* SAT evidence-based reading and writing scores over 500: 97%; SAT math scores over 500: 95%; ACT scores over 18: 100%; SAT evidence-based reading and writing scores over 600: 62%; SAT math scores over 600: 53%; ACT scores over 24: 79%; SAT evidence-based reading and writing scores over 700: 13%; SAT math scores over 700: 13%; ACT scores over 30: 24%.

Retention: 84% of full-time freshmen returned.

FACULTY
Total: 736, 71% full-time, 78% with terminal degrees.

Student/faculty ratio: 11:1.

ACADEMICS

Calendar: quarters. *Degrees:* bachelor's, master's, doctoral, post-master's, and postbachelor's certificates.

Special study options: accelerated degree program, adult/continuing education programs, advanced placement credit, double majors, English as a second language, freshman honors college, honors programs, independent study, internships, off-campus study, part-time degree program, services for LD students, student-designed majors, study abroad, summer session for credit. *ROTC:* Army (b), Navy (c), Air Force (c).

Computers: 467 computers/terminals are available on campus for general student use. Students can access the following: campus intranet, computer help desk, free student e-mail accounts, online (class) grades, online (class) registration, online (class) schedules. Campuswide network is available. 99% of college-owned or -operated housing units are wired for high-speed Internet access. Wireless service is available via entire campus.

Library: Lemieux Library & McGoldrick Learning Commons plus 1 other. *Books:* 472,572 (physical), 257,641 (digital/electronic); *Serial titles:* 118,353 (physical), 8,597 (digital/electronic); *Databases:* 235. Students can reserve study rooms.

STUDENT LIFE

Housing options: on-campus residence required through sophomore year; coed, special housing for students with disabilities. Campus housing is university owned and leased by the school. Freshman campus housing is guaranteed.

Activities and organizations: drama/theater group, student-run newspaper, radio station, choral group, Student Government of Seattle University (SGSU), Student Events and Activities Council (SEAC), Redzone, Dance Marathon, Hui 'O Nani Hawaii Club.

Athletics Member NCAA. All Division I. *Intercollegiate sports:* baseball M, basketball M(s)/W(s), cheerleading M(c)/W(c), crew W(c), cross-country running M(s)/W(s), golf M(s)/W(s), soccer M(s)/W(s), softball W(s), swimming and diving M(s)/W(s), tennis M/W, track and field M(s)/W(s), volleyball W(s). *Intramural sports:* archery M(c)/W(c), basketball M/W, crew M(c)/W(c), field hockey M/W, football M/W, riflery M(c)/W(c), rock climbing M/W, skiing (downhill) M(c)/W(c), soccer M/W, softball M/W, tennis M/W, ultimate Frisbee M/W, volleyball M/W, water polo M/W.

Campus security: 24-hour emergency response devices and patrols, late-night transport/escort service, controlled dormitory access, bicycle patrols.

Student services: health clinic, personal/psychological counseling, women's center.

COSTS & FINANCIAL AID

Costs (2017–18) *Comprehensive fee:* $54,957 includes full-time tuition ($42,120), mandatory fees ($765), and room and board ($12,072). Full-time tuition and fees vary according to course load. Part-time tuition: $936 per credit hour. Part-time tuition and fees vary according to course load. *College room only:* $7272. Room and board charges vary according to board plan and housing facility. *Payment plans:* installment, deferred payment. *Waivers:* employees or children of employees.

Financial Aid Of all full-time matriculated undergraduates who enrolled in 2017, 3,066 applied for aid, 2,517 were judged to have need, 321 had their need fully met. 506 Federal Work-Study jobs (averaging $3657). 531 state and other part-time jobs (averaging $4742). In 2017, 175 non-need-based awards were made. *Average percent of need met:* 65. *Average financial aid package:* $36,167. *Average need-based loan:* $6746. *Average need-based gift aid:* $25,021. *Average non-need-based aid:* $14,628. *Average indebtedness upon graduation:* $28,848.

APPLYING

Standardized Tests *Required:* SAT or ACT (for admission).

Options: electronic application, early action, deferred entrance.

Application fee: $55.

Required: essay or personal statement, high school transcript, minimum 2.5 GPA, 2 letters of recommendation.

Application deadlines: rolling (freshmen), 3/1 (transfers), 11/15 (early action).

Notification: continuous until 3/1 (freshmen), continuous (transfers), 12/23 (early action).

CONTACT

Seattle University, 902 12th Avenue, PO Box 222000, Seattle, WA 98122-1090. *Toll-free phone:* 800-542-0833 (in-state); 800-426-7123 (out-of-state).

University of Puget Sound
Tacoma, Washington
http://www.pugetsound.edu/

- **Independent** comprehensive, founded 1888
- **Urban** 97-acre campus with easy access to Seattle
- **Endowment** $344.6 million
- **Coed** 2,413 undergraduate students, 99% full-time, 60% women, 40% men
- **Moderately difficult** entrance level, 84% of applicants were admitted

UNDERGRAD STUDENTS

2,390 full-time, 23 part-time. Students come from 46 states and territories; 10 other countries; 79% are from out of state; 1% Black or African American, non-Hispanic/Latino; 8% Hispanic/Latino; 6% Asian, non-Hispanic/Latino; 0.3% Native Hawaiian or other Pacific Islander, non-Hispanic/Latino; 0.1% American Indian or Alaska Native, non-Hispanic/Latino; 9% Two or more races, non-Hispanic/Latino; 4% Race/ethnicity unknown; 0.6% international; 2% transferred in; 65% live on campus.

Freshmen:

Admission: 5,958 applied, 4,997 admitted, 593 enrolled. *Average high school GPA:* 3.5. *Test scores:* SAT evidence-based reading and writing scores over 500: 96%; SAT math scores over 500: 95%; ACT scores over 18: 99%; SAT evidence-based reading and writing scores over 600: 72%; SAT math scores over 600: 59%; ACT scores over 24: 86%; SAT evidence-based reading and writing scores over 700: 23%; SAT math scores over 700: 17%; ACT scores over 30: 33%.

Retention: 86% of full-time freshmen returned.

FACULTY

Total: 288, 81% full-time.

Student/faculty ratio: 11:1.

ACADEMICS

Calendar: semesters. *Degrees:* bachelor's, master's, and doctoral.

Special study options: advanced placement credit, cooperative education, double majors, honors programs, independent study, internships, part-time degree program, services for LD students, student-designed majors, study abroad, summer session for credit. *ROTC:* Army (c).

Unusual degree programs: 3-2 engineering with Washington University in St. Louis, Columbia University, University of Southern California.

Computers: 329 computers/terminals are available on campus for general student use. Students can access the following: campus intranet, computer help desk, free student e-mail accounts, online (class) grades, online (class) registration, online (class) schedules, financial aid, admission, student employment. Campuswide network is available. 100% of college-owned or -operated housing units are wired for high-speed Internet access. Wireless service is available via entire campus.

Library: Collins Memorial Library. *Books:* 424,267 (physical), 373,552 (digital/electronic); *Serial titles:* 17,063 (physical), 49,059 (digital/electronic); *Databases:* 243. Weekly public service hours: 117.

STUDENT LIFE

Housing options: on-campus residence required through sophomore year; coed, special housing for students with disabilities. Campus housing is university owned. Freshman campus housing is guaranteed.

Activities and organizations: drama/theater group, student-run newspaper, radio station, choral group, Puget Sound Outdoors, Repertory Dance Group, Ka Ohana me ke Aloha, Student Theatre Productions, Relay for Life, national fraternities, national sororities.

Athletics Member NCAA. All Division III. *Intercollegiate sports:* baseball M, basketball M/W, cheerleading M/W, crew M/W, cross-country running M/W, fencing M(c)/W(c), football M/W, golf M/W, ice hockey M(c)/W(c), lacrosse M(c)/W, rugby M(c)/W(c), sailing M(c)/W(c), skiing (downhill) M(c)/W(c), soccer M/W, softball W, swimming and diving M/W, tennis M/W, track and field M/W, ultimate Frisbee M(c)/W(c), volleyball W. *Intramural sports:* basketball M/W, football M(c)/W, soccer M/W, softball M/W, volleyball M/W.

Campus security: 24-hour emergency response devices and patrols, student patrols, late-night transport/escort service, controlled dormitory access, 24-hour locked residence hall entrances, surveillance cameras, and emergency telephone towers.

Student services: health clinic, personal/psychological counseling.

COSTS & FINANCIAL AID

Costs (2018–19) *Comprehensive fee:* $62,316 includes full-time tuition ($49,510), mandatory fees ($266), and room and board ($12,540). Full-time tuition and fees vary according to course load. Part-time tuition: $1563 per unit. Part-time tuition and fees vary according to course load. *College room only:* $6820. Room and board charges vary according to board plan and housing facility. *Payment plans:* installment, deferred payment. *Waivers:* employees or children of employees.

Financial Aid Of all full-time matriculated undergraduates who enrolled in 2017, 1,512 applied for aid, 1,251 were judged to have need, 220 had their need fully met. 505 Federal Work-Study jobs (averaging $3070). 894 state and other part-time jobs (averaging $2624). In 2017, 1119 non-need-based awards were made. *Average percent of need met:* 77. *Average financial aid package:* $34,720. *Average need-based loan:* $6961. *Average need-based gift aid:* $27,487. *Average non-need-based aid:* $16,352. *Average indebtedness upon graduation:* $34,791.

APPLYING

Options: electronic application, early admission, early decision, early action, deferred entrance.

Application fee: $60.

Required: essay or personal statement, high school transcript, 2 letters of recommendation. *Recommended:* minimum 3.0 GPA, interview.

CONTACT

Laura Martin-Fedich, Vice President for Enrollment, University of Puget Sound, 1500 North Warner Street, CMB 1062, Tacoma, WA 98416. *Phone:* 253-879-3211. *Toll-free phone:* 800-396-7191. *Fax:* 253-879-3993. *E-mail:* admission@pugetsound.edu.

University of Washington

Seattle, Washington

http://www.washington.edu/

- **State-supported** university, founded 1861, part of University of Washington
- **Urban** 634-acre campus with easy access to Seattle, WA
- **Endowment** $3.1 billion
- **Coed** 31,331 undergraduate students, 92% full-time, 53% women, 47% men
- **Very difficult** entrance level, 46% of applicants were admitted

UNDERGRAD STUDENTS

28,759 full-time, 2,572 part-time. Students come from 50 states and territories; 84 other countries; 18% are from out of state; 3% Black or African American, non-Hispanic/Latino; 8% Hispanic/Latino; 24% Asian, non-Hispanic/Latino; 0.5% Native Hawaiian or other Pacific Islander, non-Hispanic/Latino; 0.4% American Indian or Alaska Native, non-Hispanic/Latino; 7% Two or more races, non-Hispanic/Latino; 2% Race/ethnicity unknown; 15% international; 5% transferred in; 27% live on campus.

Freshmen:

Admission: 44,877 applied, 20,833 admitted, 6,793 enrolled. *Average high school GPA:* 3.8. *Test scores:* SAT evidence-based reading and writing scores over 500: 95%; SAT math scores over 500: 97%; ACT scores over 18: 98%; SAT evidence-based reading and writing scores over 600: 73%; SAT math scores over 600: 78%; ACT scores over 24: 89%; SAT evidence-based reading and writing scores over 700: 23%; SAT math scores over 700: 38%; ACT scores over 30: 49%.

Retention: 94% of full-time freshmen returned.

FACULTY

Total: 2,636, 78% full-time, 72% with terminal degrees.

Student/faculty ratio: 19:1.

ACADEMICS

Calendar: quarters. *Degrees:* bachelor's, master's, doctoral, and post-master's certificates.

Special study options: adult/continuing education programs, advanced placement credit, cooperative education, distance learning, double majors, English as a second language, external degree program, honors programs, independent study, internships, off-campus study, part-time degree program, services for LD students, student-designed majors, study abroad, summer session for credit. *ROTC:* Army (b), Navy (b), Air Force (b).

Computers: 919 computers/terminals are available on campus for general student use. Students can access the following: computer help desk, free student e-mail accounts, online (class) grades, online (class) registration, online (class) schedules. Campuswide network is available. 100% of college-owned or -operated housing units are wired for high-speed Internet access. Wireless service is available via entire campus.

Library: Odegaard Undergraduate Library plus 12 others. *Books:* 8.7 million (physical), 833,635 (digital/electronic); *Serial titles:* 25,000 (physical), 100,000 (digital/electronic); *Databases:* 500. Weekly public service hours: 124; study areas open 24 hours, 5–7 days a week; students can reserve study rooms.

STUDENT LIFE

Housing options: coed, special housing for students with disabilities. Campus housing is university owned, leased by the school and is provided by a third party.

Activities and organizations: drama/theater group, student-run newspaper, radio and television station, choral group, marching band, Interfraternity Council/Pan-Hellenic Council, Taiwanese Student Association, Chinese Student Association, Yacht Club, Asian American Intervarsity Christian Fellowship/Muslim Students Association, national fraternities, national sororities.

Athletics Member NCAA, NAIA. All NCAA Division I except football (Division I-A). *Intercollegiate sports:* baseball M(s), basketball M(s)/W(s), cheerleading M(s)/W(s), crew M(s)/W(s), cross-country running M(s)/W(s), golf M(s)/W(s), gymnastics W(s), rowing M(s)/W(s), soccer M(s)/W(s), softball W(s), tennis M(s)/W(s), track and field M(s)/W(s), volleyball W(s). *Intramural sports:* archery M(c)/W(c), badminton M/W, baseball M(c)/W(c), basketball M/W, bowling M/W(c), crew M(c)/W(c), equestrian sports M(c)/W(c), football M/W, ice hockey M(c)/W(c), lacrosse M(c)/W(c), racquetball M/W, rock climbing M/W, rowing M/W, rugby M(c)/W(c), sailing M(c)/W(c), skiing (cross-country) M(c)/W(c), skiing (downhill) M(c)/W(c), soccer M/W, softball M/W, squash M(c)/W(c), swimming and diving M/W, table tennis M(c)/W(c), tennis M/W, triathlon M(c)/W(c), ultimate Frisbee M/W, volleyball M/W, water polo M(c)/W(c), wrestling M(c)/W(c).

Campus security: 24-hour emergency response devices and patrols, late-night transport/escort service, controlled dormitory access.

Student services: health clinic, personal/psychological counseling, women's center, legal services.

COSTS & FINANCIAL AID

Costs (2017–18) *Tuition:* state resident $9694 full-time, $323 per credit part-time; nonresident $33,732 full-time, $1124 per credit part-time. Full-time tuition and fees vary according to course load and location. Part-time tuition and fees vary according to course load and location. *Required fees:* $1059 full-time, $27 per credit part-time, $84 per term part-time. *Room and board:* $11,691. Room and board charges vary according to board plan and housing facility. *Payment plan:* tuition prepayment. *Waivers:* senior citizens and employees or children of employees.

Financial Aid Of all full-time matriculated undergraduates who enrolled in 2017, 16,288 applied for aid, 12,270 were judged to have need, 3,007 had their need fully met. 561 Federal Work-Study jobs (averaging $4000). 59 state and other part-time jobs (averaging $4618). In 2017, 2351 non-need-based awards were made. *Average percent of need met:* 77. *Average financial aid package:* $17,380. *Average need-based loan:* $4620. *Average need-based gift aid:* $15,550. *Average non-need-based aid:* $5000. *Average indebtedness upon graduation:* $19,880.

APPLYING

Standardized Tests *Required:* SAT or ACT (for admission).

Options: electronic application, early admission.

Application fee: $70.

Required: essay or personal statement. *Required for some:* high school transcript.

Application deadlines: 11/15 (freshmen), 2/15 (transfers).

Notification: 3/15 (freshmen), 6/30 (transfers).

CONTACT

Office of Admissions, University of Washington, 1410 NE Campus Parkway, Seattle, WA 98195. *Phone:* 206-543-9686. *Fax:* 206-685-3655.

University of Washington, Bothell

Bothell, Washington

http://www.uwb.edu/

- **State-supported** comprehensive, founded 1990, part of University of Washington
- **Suburban** 127-acre campus with easy access to Seattle
- **Endowment** $4.1 million
- **Coed** 5,365 undergraduate students, 87% full-time, 49% women, 51% men
- **Moderately difficult** entrance level, 80% of applicants were admitted

UNDERGRAD STUDENTS

4,641 full-time, 724 part-time. Students come from 27 states and territories; 26 other countries; 6% Black or African American, non-Hispanic/Latino; 10% Hispanic/Latino; 27% Asian, non-Hispanic/Latino; 0.6% Native Hawaiian or other Pacific Islander, non-Hispanic/Latino; 0.3% American Indian or Alaska Native, non-Hispanic/Latino; 6% Two or more races, non-Hispanic/Latino; 2% Race/ethnicity unknown; 9% international; 15% transferred in; 5% live on campus.

Freshmen:

Admission: 3,148 applied, 2,522 admitted, 800 enrolled. *Average high school GPA:* 3.4. *Test scores:* SAT evidence-based reading and writing scores over 500: 81%; SAT math scores over 500: 84%; ACT scores over 18: 86%; SAT evidence-based reading and writing scores over 600: 34%; SAT math scores over 600: 36%; ACT scores over 24: 41%; SAT evidence-based reading and writing scores over 700: 5%; SAT math scores over 700: 7%; ACT scores over 30: 11%.

Retention: 88% of full-time freshmen returned.

FACULTY

Total: 347, 63% full-time, 57% with terminal degrees.

Student/faculty ratio: 20:1.

ACADEMICS

Calendar: quarters. *Degrees:* bachelor's and master's.

Special study options: adult/continuing education programs, advanced placement credit, cooperative education, distance learning, double majors, English as a second language, honors programs, independent study, internships, off-campus study, part-time degree program, services for LD students, student-designed majors, study abroad, summer session for credit. *ROTC:* Army (c), Navy (c), Air Force (c).

Computers: 538 computers/terminals are available on campus for general student use. Students can access the following: campus intranet, computer help desk, free student e-mail accounts, online (class) grades, online (class) registration, online (class) schedules. Campuswide network is available. 100% of college-owned or -operated housing units are wired for high-speed Internet access. Wireless service is available via classrooms, computer centers, computer labs, learning centers, libraries, student centers.

Library: Campus Library. *Books:* 118,611 (physical), 833,635 (digital/electronic); *Serial titles:* 100,000 (digital/electronic); *Databases:* 500. Weekly public service hours: 86; students can reserve study rooms.

STUDENT LIFE

Housing options: coed, men-only, women-only, special housing for students with disabilities. Campus housing is university owned and leased by the school. Freshman applicants given priority for college housing.

Activities and organizations: student-run newspaper, radio station, Campus Events Board, Social Justice Organizers, Associated Students of University of Washington Bothell (ASUWB), Recreation and Intramurals Program, Club Council.

Athletics *Intramural sports:* basketball M/W, football M/W, soccer M/W, softball M/W, tennis M/W, ultimate Frisbee M(c)/W(c), volleyball M/W.

Campus security: 24-hour emergency response devices and patrols, late-night transport/escort service.

Student services: personal/psychological counseling.

COSTS & FINANCIAL AID

Costs (2017–18) *Tuition:* state resident $9694 full-time, $323 per credit part-time; nonresident $33,732 full-time, $1124 per credit part-time. Full-time tuition and fees vary according to course load. Part-time tuition and fees vary according to course load. *Required fees:* $996 full-time, $33 per credit part-time. *Room and board:* $10,833. Room and board charges vary according to board plan, housing facility, and location. *Payment plans:* tuition prepayment, installment. *Waivers:* senior citizens and employees or children of employees.

Financial Aid Of all full-time matriculated undergraduates who enrolled in 2017, 3,208 applied for aid, 2,607 were judged to have need, 375 had their need fully met. 44 Federal Work-Study jobs (averaging $3750). 14 state and other part-time jobs (averaging $4014). In 2017, 38 non-need-based awards were made. *Average percent of need met:* 74. *Average financial aid package:* $15,500. *Average need-based loan:* $4550. *Average need-based gift aid:* $14,220. *Average non-need-based aid:* $7200. *Average indebtedness upon graduation:* $18,850.

APPLYING

Standardized Tests *Required:* SAT or ACT (for admission).

Options: electronic application.

Application fee: $60.

Required: essay or personal statement, high school transcript, minimum 2.0 GPA. *Required for some:* 1 letter of recommendation.

Application deadlines: 1/15 (freshmen), 1/15 (transfers).

Notification: continuous (freshmen), continuous (transfers).

CONTACT

Office of Admissions, University of Washington, Bothell, 18115 Campus Way NE, Box 358500, Bothell, WA 8011-8246. *Phone:* 425-352-5000. *Fax:* 425-352-5455. *E-mail:* uwbinfo@uw.edu.

University of Washington, Tacoma
Tacoma, Washington
http://www.tacoma.uw.edu/

- **State-supported** comprehensive, founded 1990, part of University of Washington
- **Urban** 31-acre campus with easy access to Seattle
- **Endowment** $40.5 million
- **Coed** 4,436 undergraduate students, 89% full-time, 52% women, 48% men
- **Moderately difficult** entrance level, 84% of applicants were admitted

UNDERGRAD STUDENTS

3,945 full-time, 491 part-time. Students come from 31 states and territories; 21 other countries; 1% are from out of state; 9% Black or African American, non-Hispanic/Latino; 15% Hispanic/Latino; 20% Asian, non-Hispanic/Latino; 1% Native Hawaiian or other Pacific Islander, non-Hispanic/Latino; 0.8% American Indian or Alaska Native, non-Hispanic/Latino; 9% Two or more races, non-Hispanic/Latino; 2% Race/ethnicity unknown; 4% international; 20% transferred in; 6% live on campus.

Freshmen:
Admission: 1,982 applied, 1,662 admitted, 588 enrolled. *Average high school GPA:* 3.3. *Test scores:* SAT evidence-based reading and writing scores over 500: 73%; SAT math scores over 500: 72%; ACT scores over 18: 81%; SAT evidence-based reading and writing scores over 600: 28%; SAT math scores over 600: 23%; ACT scores over 24: 31%; SAT evidence-based reading and writing scores over 700: 3%; SAT math scores over 700: 3%; ACT scores over 30: 3%.
Retention: 76% of full-time freshmen returned.

FACULTY
Total: 345, 74% full-time, 59% with terminal degrees.
Student/faculty ratio: 16:1.

ACADEMICS
Calendar: quarters. *Degrees:* bachelor's, master's, doctoral, and postbachelor's certificates.

Special study options: academic remediation for entering students, advanced placement credit, distance learning, double majors, external degree program, honors programs, independent study, internships, off-campus study, part-time degree program, services for LD students, student-designed majors, study abroad, summer session for credit. *ROTC:* Army (c), Navy (c), Air Force (c).

Computers: 166 computers/terminals are available on campus for general student use. Students can access the following: campus intranet, computer help desk, free student e-mail accounts, online (class) grades, online (class) registration, online (class) schedules, learning management system, course management system. Campuswide network is available. 100% of college-owned or -operated housing units are wired for high-speed Internet access. Wireless service is available via entire campus.

Library: University of Washington Tacoma Library. *Books:* 123,187 (physical), 833,635 (digital/electronic); *Serial titles:* 100,000 (digital/electronic); *Databases:* 500. Weekly public service hours: 84; students can reserve study rooms.

STUDENT LIFE
Housing options: men-only, women-only. Campus housing is leased by the school. Freshman applicants given priority for college housing.

Activities and organizations: drama/theater group, student-run newspaper, choral group, Accounting Student Association, International Student Association, Partners in Action to Transform Healthcare (PATH), Asian Pacific Islander Student Union (APISU).

Athletics *Intramural sports:* badminton M/W, basketball M/W, soccer M(c)/W(c), volleyball M(c)/W(c), wrestling M(c)/W(c).

Campus security: 24-hour emergency response devices and patrols, late-night transport/escort service, key card access to buildings after hours.

Student services: health clinic, personal/psychological counseling.

COSTS & FINANCIAL AID
Costs (2017–18) *Tuition:* state resident $9694 full-time, $323 per credit part-time; nonresident $33,732 full-time, $1124 per credit part-time. Full-time tuition and fees vary according to course load. Part-time tuition and fees vary according to course load. *Required fees:* $1137 full-time, $38

per credit part-time. *Room and board:* $10,230. Room and board charges vary according to housing facility and location. *Payment plans:* tuition prepayment, installment. *Waivers:* senior citizens and employees or children of employees.

Financial Aid Of all full-time matriculated undergraduates who enrolled in 2017, 3,208 applied for aid, 2,884 were judged to have need, 350 had their need fully met. 44 Federal Work-Study jobs (averaging $4500). 26 state and other part-time jobs (averaging $3912). In 2017, 166 non-need-based awards were made. *Average percent of need met:* 73. *Average financial aid package:* $15,770. *Average need-based loan:* $4820. *Average need-based gift aid:* $14,120. *Average non-need-based aid:* $3600. *Average indebtedness upon graduation:* $17,480.

APPLYING
Standardized Tests *Required:* SAT or ACT (for admission).
Options: electronic application, deferred entrance.
Application fee: $60.
Required: essay or personal statement. *Required for some:* high school transcript, 3 letters of recommendation.
Application deadlines: 6/30 (freshmen), 3/15 (transfers).
Notification: continuous (freshmen), continuous (transfers).

CONTACT
Ms. Megan Beresford, Associate Director of University Recruitment, University of Washington, Tacoma, 1900 Commerce Street, Tacoma, WA 98402-3100. *Phone:* 253-692-4738. *Toll-free phone:* 800-736-7750. *Fax:* 253-692-4414. *E-mail:* megan61@uw.edu.

Walla Walla University
College Place, Washington
http://www.wallawalla.edu/
- **Independent Seventh-day Adventist** comprehensive, founded 1892
- **Small-town** 77-acre campus
- **Coed**
- **Moderately difficult** entrance level

FACULTY
Student/faculty ratio: 15:1.

ACADEMICS
Calendar: quarters. *Degrees:* associate, bachelor's, and master's.
Library: Peterson Memorial Library plus 3 others.

STUDENT LIFE
Housing options: on-campus residence required through junior year; men-only, women-only, special housing for students with disabilities. Campus housing is university owned and leased by the school. Freshman campus housing is guaranteed.
Activities and organizations: drama/theater group, student-run newspaper, choral group, Associated Students of Walla Walla University, Campus Ministries, Village Club, OPS Club (Men's residence hall club), AGA Club (women's residence hall club).
Athletics Member NAIA.
Campus security: 24-hour emergency response devices and patrols, student patrols, late-night transport/escort service, controlled dormitory access.
Student services: health clinic, personal/psychological counseling.

COSTS & FINANCIAL AID
Costs (2017–18) *Comprehensive fee:* $34,845 includes full-time tuition ($26,595), mandatory fees ($900), and room and board ($7350). Part-time tuition: $738 per quarter hour. *College room only:* $4185.
Financial Aid Of all full-time matriculated undergraduates who enrolled in 2015, 1,138 applied for aid, 962 were judged to have need, 378 had their need fully met. In 2015, 437 non-need-based awards were made. *Average percent of need met:* 92. *Average financial aid package:* $22,193. *Average need-based loan:* $4160. *Average need-based gift aid:* $6334. *Average non-need-based aid:* $8677. *Average indebtedness upon graduation:* $33,018.

APPLYING
Standardized Tests *Required:* SAT or ACT (for admission).
Options: electronic application.

Application fee: $40.
Required: high school transcript, minimum 2.5 GPA.

CONTACT
Mr. Dallas Weis, Director of Admissions, Walla Walla University, Marketing and Enrollment Services, 204 S. College Avenue, College Place, WA 99324. *Phone:* 509-527-2327. *Toll-free phone:* 800-541-8900. *Fax:* 509-527-2397.

Washington State University
Pullman, Washington
http://www.wsu.edu/
- **State-supported** university, founded 1890
- **Small-town** 620-acre campus with easy access to Spokane
- **Endowment** $975.2 million
- **Coed** 17,868 undergraduate students, 95% full-time, 49% women, 51% men
- **Moderately difficult** entrance level, 74% of applicants were admitted

UNDERGRAD STUDENTS
17,011 full-time, 857 part-time. Students come from 48 states and territories; 69 other countries; 14% are from out of state; 4% Black or African American, non-Hispanic/Latino; 14% Hispanic/Latino; 6% Asian, non-Hispanic/Latino; 0.4% Native Hawaiian or other Pacific Islander, non-Hispanic/Latino; 0.7% American Indian or Alaska Native, non-Hispanic/Latino; 7% Two or more races, non-Hispanic/Latino; 2% Race/ethnicity unknown; 6% international; 7% transferred in; 24% live on campus.

Freshmen:
Admission: 20,591 applied, 15,222 admitted, 3,938 enrolled. *Average high school GPA:* 3.4. *Test scores:* SAT evidence-based reading and writing scores over 500: 83%; SAT math scores over 500: 83%; ACT scores over 18: 92%; SAT evidence-based reading and writing scores over 600: 34%; SAT math scores over 600: 32%; ACT scores over 24: 47%; SAT evidence-based reading and writing scores over 700: 4%; SAT math scores over 700: 4%; ACT scores over 30: 9%.
Retention: 82% of full-time freshmen returned.

FACULTY
Total: 1,854, 74% full-time, 77% with terminal degrees.
Student/faculty ratio: 15:1.

ACADEMICS
Calendar: semesters. *Degrees:* certificates, bachelor's, master's, doctoral, post-master's, and postbachelor's certificates.
Special study options: academic remediation for entering students, accelerated degree program, adult/continuing education programs, advanced placement credit, cooperative education, distance learning, double majors, English as a second language, external degree program, freshman honors college, honors programs, independent study, internships, off-campus study, part-time degree program, services for LD students, student-designed majors, study abroad, summer session for credit. *ROTC:* Army (b), Navy (c), Air Force (b).
Computers: 2,500 computers/terminals and 2,500 ports are available on campus for general student use. Students can access the following: campus intranet, computer help desk, free student e-mail accounts, online (class) grades, online (class) registration, online (class) schedules. Campuswide network is available. 100% of college-owned or -operated housing units are wired for high-speed Internet access. Wireless service is available via classrooms, computer centers, computer labs, dorm rooms, learning centers, libraries, student centers.
Library: Holland and Terrell Libraries plus 3 others. *Books:* 3.1 million (physical), 677,302 (digital/electronic); *Serial titles:* 98,278 (physical), 58,249 (digital/electronic); *Databases:* 216. Weekly public service hours: 140; students can reserve study rooms.

STUDENT LIFE
Housing options: on-campus residence required for freshman year; coed, men-only, women-only, cooperative, special housing for students with disabilities. Campus housing is university owned. Freshman campus housing is guaranteed.
Activities and organizations: drama/theater group, student-run newspaper, radio and television station, choral group, marching band,

Panhellenic Association - Sororities, Interfraternity Council - Fraternities, Student Entertainment Board, International Students Council, ChiLaStAl (Chicana/o Latina/o Student Alliance), national fraternities, national sororities.

Athletics Member NCAA. All Division I except football (Division I-A). *Intercollegiate sports:* baseball M(s), basketball M(s)/W(s), bowling M(c)/W(c), cheerleading M/W, crew M(c)/W(s), cross-country running M(s)/W(s), equestrian sports W(c), fencing M(c)/W(c), golf M(s)/W(s), ice hockey M(c)/W(c), lacrosse M(c)/W(c), rowing M(c)/W, rugby M(c)/W(c), skiing (cross-country) M(c)/W(c), skiing (downhill) M(c)/W(c), soccer M(c)/W(s), softball W(c), swimming and diving W(s), tennis M(c)/W(s), track and field M(s)/W(s), triathlon M(c)/W(c), ultimate Frisbee M(c)/W(c), volleyball M(c)/W(s), water polo W(c), weight lifting M(c)/W(c), wrestling M(c). *Intramural sports:* badminton M/W, basketball M/W, football M/W, golf M/W, racquetball M/W, rock climbing M/W, soccer M/W, softball M/W, table tennis M/W, tennis M/W, triathlon M/W, ultimate Frisbee M/W, volleyball M/W.

Campus security: 24-hour emergency response devices and patrols, student patrols, late-night transport/escort service, controlled dormitory access.

Student services: health clinic, personal/psychological counseling, women's center, legal services.

COSTS & FINANCIAL AID
Costs (2017–18) *Tuition:* state resident $9530 full-time, $494 per credit part-time; nonresident $23,956 full-time, $1226 per credit part-time. Full-time tuition and fees vary according to course load, location, and reciprocity agreements. Part-time tuition and fees vary according to course load, location, and reciprocity agreements. *Required fees:* $1861 full-time. *Room and board:* $11,356; room only: $6858. Room and board charges vary according to board plan, housing facility, and location. *Waivers:* senior citizens and employees or children of employees.

Financial Aid Of all full-time matriculated undergraduates who enrolled in 2016, 15,952 applied for aid, 12,691 were judged to have need, 1,445 had their need fully met. In 2016, 3927 non-need-based awards were made. *Average percent of need met:* 63. *Average financial aid package:* $12,694. *Average need-based loan:* $4219. *Average need-based gift aid:* $10,650. *Average non-need-based aid:* $3922. *Average indebtedness upon graduation:* $26,807. *Financial aid deadline:* 1/31.

APPLYING
Standardized Tests *Required:* SAT or ACT (for admission).

Options: electronic application.

Application fee: $50.

Required: high school transcript, minimum 2.0 GPA. *Recommended:* essay or personal statement.

Application deadlines: 1/31 (freshmen), rolling (out-of-state freshmen), 1/31 (transfers).

Notification: continuous until 11/1 (freshmen), continuous until 11/1 (out-of-state freshmen), continuous until 11/1 (transfers).

CONTACT
Ms. Wendy Peterson, Director of Admissions, Washington State University, PO Box 641067, Pullman, WA 99164-1067. *Phone:* 888-468-6978. *Toll-free phone:* 888-468-6978. *Fax:* 509-335-4902. *E-mail:* admissions@wsu.edu.

Washington State University–Global Campus
Pullman, Washington
http://www.globalcampus.wsu.edu/
- **State-supported** comprehensive
- **Coed** 2,005 undergraduate students, 44% full-time, 69% women, 31% men
- **Moderately difficult** entrance level, 48% of applicants were admitted

UNDERGRAD STUDENTS
876 full-time, 1,129 part-time. Students come from 40 states and territories; 30 other countries; 17% are from out of state; 3% Black or African American, non-Hispanic/Latino; 11% Hispanic/Latino; 5% Asian, non-Hispanic/Latino; 0.5% Native Hawaiian or other Pacific Islander, non-Hispanic/Latino; 1% American Indian or Alaska Native, non-Hispanic/Latino; 5% Two or more races, non-Hispanic/Latino; 4% Race/ethnicity unknown; 6% international; 24% transferred in.

Freshmen:
Admission: 127 applied, 61 admitted, 36 enrolled. *Average high school GPA:* 3.3. *Test scores:* SAT evidence-based reading and writing scores over 500: 88%; SAT math scores over 500: 75%; ACT scores over 18: 64%; SAT evidence-based reading and writing scores over 600: 31%; SAT math scores over 600: 25%; ACT scores over 24: 27%; SAT evidence-based reading and writing scores over 700: 6%; ACT scores over 30: 9%.

ACADEMICS
Calendar: semesters. *Degrees:* certificates, bachelor's, master's, post-master's, and postbachelor's certificates.

Special study options: adult/continuing education programs, distance learning, part-time degree program.

COSTS
Costs (2017–18) *Tuition:* state resident $9991 full-time, $494 per credit part-time; nonresident $11,335 full-time, $569 per credit part-time. Full-time tuition and fees vary according to course load, location, and reciprocity agreements. Part-time tuition and fees vary according to course load, location, and reciprocity agreements. *Waivers:* employees or children of employees.

APPLYING
Standardized Tests *Required:* SAT or ACT (for admission).

Options: electronic application.

Application fee: $50.

Required: high school transcript, minimum 2.0 GPA. *Recommended:* essay or personal statement.

Application deadlines: 7/24 (freshmen), 7/24 (transfers).

CONTACT
Ms. Wendy Peterson, Director of Admissions, Washington State University–Global Campus, 370 Lighty Student Services Building, PO Box 641067, Pullman, WA 99164-1067. *Phone:* 509-335-5586. *Toll-free phone:* 800-222-4978. *Fax:* 509-335-4902. *E-mail:* admissions@wsu.edu.

Washington State University–Spokane
Spokane, Washington
http://www.spokane.wsu.edu/
- **State-supported** upper-level, founded 1989
- **Urban** 48-acre campus
- **Coed** 594 undergraduate students, 91% full-time, 87% women, 13% men
- **Moderately difficult** entrance level, 40% of applicants were admitted

UNDERGRAD STUDENTS
539 full-time, 55 part-time. Students come from 9 states and territories; 5 other countries; 8% are from out of state; 3% Black or African American, non-Hispanic/Latino; 10% Hispanic/Latino; 5% Asian, non-Hispanic/Latino; 0.3% American Indian or Alaska Native, non-Hispanic/Latino; 6% Two or more races, non-Hispanic/Latino; 5% Race/ethnicity unknown; 0.7% international; 15% transferred in.

Freshmen:
Admission: 5 applied, 2 admitted.

ACADEMICS
Calendar: semesters. *Degrees:* bachelor's, master's, and doctoral.

Special study options: accelerated degree program, adult/continuing education programs, advanced placement credit, cooperative education, distance learning, double majors, English as a second language, external degree program, freshman honors college, honors programs, independent study, internships, off-campus study, part-time degree program, services for LD students, student-designed majors, study abroad, summer session for credit.

Computers: Campuswide network is available. Wireless service is available via entire campus.

STUDENT LIFE
Housing options: college housing not available.

Activities and organizations: ASWSU Spokane, Simulation Club, Multicultural Club, IHI Open School (Interprofessional Club), Diversity Club.

Campus security: 24-hour emergency response devices and patrols.

Student services: personal/psychological counseling.

COSTS

Costs (2017–18) *Tuition:* state resident $9530 full-time, $494 per credit part-time; nonresident $23,956 full-time, $1226 per credit part-time. Full-time tuition and fees vary according to course load, location, and reciprocity agreements. Part-time tuition and fees vary according to course load, location, and reciprocity agreements. *Required fees:* $755 full-time. *Waivers:* senior citizens and employees or children of employees.

APPLYING

Standardized Tests *Required:* SAT or ACT (for admission).

Options: electronic application.

Application fee: $50.

Notification: continuous until 11/1 (transfers).

CONTACT

Washington State University–Spokane, 412 East Spokane Falls Boulevard, PO Box 1495, Spokane, WA 99210-1495. *Phone:* 509-335-5586.

Washington State University–Tri-Cities

Richland, Washington

http://www.tricities.wsu.edu/

- **State-supported** comprehensive, founded 1989
- **Urban** 84-acre campus
- **Coed** 1,719 undergraduate students, 75% full-time, 58% women, 42% men
- **Moderately difficult** entrance level, 67% of applicants were admitted

UNDERGRAD STUDENTS

1,294 full-time, 425 part-time. Students come from 13 states and territories; 5 other countries; 2% are from out of state; 1% Black or African American, non-Hispanic/Latino; 32% Hispanic/Latino; 3% Asian, non-Hispanic/Latino; 0.1% Native Hawaiian or other Pacific Islander, non-Hispanic/Latino; 0.2% American Indian or Alaska Native, non-Hispanic/Latino; 4% Two or more races, non-Hispanic/Latino; 9% Race/ethnicity unknown; 0.8% international; 16% transferred in.

Freshmen:

Admission: 630 applied, 424 admitted, 253 enrolled. *Average high school GPA:* 3.4. *Test scores:* SAT evidence-based reading and writing scores over 500: 69%; SAT math scores over 500: 75%; ACT scores over 18: 72%; SAT evidence-based reading and writing scores over 600: 23%; SAT math scores over 600: 23%; ACT scores over 24: 32%; SAT evidence-based reading and writing scores over 700: 1%; SAT math scores over 700: 2%; ACT scores over 30: 6%.

Retention: 71% of full-time freshmen returned.

ACADEMICS

Calendar: semesters. *Degrees:* certificates, bachelor's, master's, doctoral, and postbachelor's certificates.

Special study options: accelerated degree program, adult/continuing education programs, advanced placement credit, cooperative education, distance learning, double majors, English as a second language, external degree program, independent study, internships, part-time degree program, services for LD students, study abroad, summer session for credit.

Computers: Students can access the following: campus intranet, computer help desk, free student e-mail accounts, online (class) grades, online (class) registration. Campuswide network is available. Wireless service is available via entire campus.

Library: Max E. Benitz Memorial Library plus 2 others.

STUDENT LIFE

Housing options: Campus housing is provided by a third party.

Activities and organizations: American Society of Civil Engineers, Environmental Club, Gaming Club, Pre-Health Club, Robotics Club.

Athletics *Intercollegiate sports:* rugby M(c), soccer M(c)/W(c), volleyball W(c).

Campus security: 24-hour emergency response devices.

Student services: personal/psychological counseling.

COSTS

Costs (2017–18) *Tuition:* state resident $9530 full-time, $492 per credit part-time; nonresident $23,956 full-time, $1123 per credit part-time. Full-time tuition and fees vary according to course load, location, and reciprocity agreements. Part-time tuition and fees vary according to course load, location, and reciprocity agreements. *Required fees:* $812 full-time. *Room and board:* Room and board charges vary according to housing facility and location. *Waivers:* senior citizens and employees or children of employees.

APPLYING

Standardized Tests *Required:* SAT or ACT (for admission).

Options: electronic application.

Application fee: $50.

Required: high school transcript, minimum 2.0 GPA. *Recommended:* essay or personal statement.

Application deadlines: 1/31 (freshmen), 1/7 (out-of-state freshmen), 1/31 (transfers).

Notification: continuous until 11/1 (freshmen), continuous until 11/1 (out-of-state freshmen), continuous until 11/1 (transfers).

CONTACT

Ms. Mika McAskill, Director of Admissions, Washington State University–Tri-Cities, 2710 Crimson Way, Richland, WA 99354. *Phone:* 509-372-7250. *E-mail:* admissions@tricity.wsu.edu.

Washington State University–Vancouver

Vancouver, Washington

http://www.vancouver.wsu.edu/

- **State-supported** comprehensive, founded 1989
- **Suburban** 351-acre campus with easy access to Portland, OR
- **Coed** 3,091 undergraduate students, 79% full-time, 52% women, 48% men
- **Moderately difficult** entrance level, 64% of applicants were admitted

UNDERGRAD STUDENTS

2,446 full-time, 645 part-time. Students come from 25 states and territories; 9 other countries; 4% are from out of state; 1% Black or African American, non-Hispanic/Latino; 13% Hispanic/Latino; 6% Asian, non-Hispanic/Latino; 0.5% Native Hawaiian or other Pacific Islander, non-Hispanic/Latino; 0.6% American Indian or Alaska Native, non-Hispanic/Latino; 6% Two or more races, non-Hispanic/Latino; 4% Race/ethnicity unknown; 1% international; 22% transferred in.

Freshmen:

Admission: 1,212 applied, 778 admitted, 384 enrolled. *Average high school GPA:* 3.4. *Test scores:* SAT evidence-based reading and writing scores over 500: 75%; SAT math scores over 500: 77%; ACT scores over 18: 81%; SAT evidence-based reading and writing scores over 600: 35%; SAT math scores over 600: 25%; ACT scores over 24: 43%; SAT evidence-based reading and writing scores over 700: 3%; SAT math scores over 700: 4%; ACT scores over 30: 5%.

Retention: 77% of full-time freshmen returned.

ACADEMICS

Calendar: semesters. *Degrees:* certificates, bachelor's, master's, and doctoral.

Special study options: accelerated degree program, adult/continuing education programs, advanced placement credit, cooperative education, distance learning, double majors, English as a second language, external degree program, honors programs, independent study, internships, off-campus study, part-time degree program, services for LD students, student-designed majors, study abroad, summer session for credit. *ROTC:* Army (c), Air Force (c).

Computers: Students can access the following: free student e-mail accounts, online (class) grades, online (class) registration, online (class) schedules. Campuswide network is available. Wireless service is available via classrooms, computer centers, computer labs, learning centers, libraries, student centers.

Library: WSU Vancouver Library plus 1 other. Students can reserve study rooms.

STUDENT LIFE

Housing options: college housing not available.

Activities and organizations: student-run newspaper, radio station.

Athletics *Intramural sports:* basketball M/W, soccer M/W, volleyball M/W.

Campus security: 24-hour emergency response devices and patrols, student patrols.

Student services: personal/psychological counseling.

COSTS

Costs (2017–18) *Tuition:* state resident $9530 full-time, $494 per credit part-time; nonresident $23,956 full-time, $1224 per credit part-time. Full-time tuition and fees vary according to course load, location, and reciprocity agreements. Part-time tuition and fees vary according to course load, location, and reciprocity agreements. *Required fees:* $599 full-time. *Waivers:* senior citizens and employees or children of employees.

APPLYING

Standardized Tests *Required:* SAT or ACT (for admission).

Options: electronic application.

Application fee: $50.

Required: high school transcript, minimum 2.0 GPA. *Recommended:* essay or personal statement.

Application deadlines: 1/31 (freshmen), 1/7 (out-of-state freshmen), 1/31 (transfers).

Notification: continuous until 11/1 (freshmen), continuous until 11/1 (out-of-state freshmen), continuous until 11/1 (transfers).

CONTACT

Ms. Kim Hiatt, Associate Director of Admissions, Washington State University–Vancouver, 14204 NE Salmon Creek Avenue, Vancouver, WA 98686. *Phone:* 360-546-9779. *Fax:* 360-546-9032. *E-mail:* van.admissions@wsu.edu.

Western Washington University

Bellingham, Washington

http://www.wwu.edu/

- **State-supported** comprehensive, founded 1893
- **Small-town** 223-acre campus with easy access to Seattle, WA and Vancouver, BC Canada
- **Endowment** $79.1 million
- **Coed** 14,968 undergraduate students, 92% full-time, 56% women, 44% men
- **Moderately difficult** entrance level, 85% of applicants were admitted

UNDERGRAD STUDENTS

13,728 full-time, 1,240 part-time. Students come from 48 states and territories; 43 other countries; 11% are from out of state; 2% Black or African American, non-Hispanic/Latino; 9% Hispanic/Latino; 6% Asian, non-Hispanic/Latino; 0.2% Native Hawaiian or other Pacific Islander, non-Hispanic/Latino; 0.4% American Indian or Alaska Native, non-Hispanic/Latino; 8% Two or more races, non-Hispanic/Latino; 1% Race/ethnicity unknown; 1% international; 8% transferred in; 27% live on campus.

Freshmen:

Admission: 11,244 applied, 9,534 admitted, 3,114 enrolled. *Average high school GPA:* 3.4. *Test scores:* ACT scores over 18: 97%; ACT scores over 24: 66%; ACT scores over 30: 14%.

Retention: 81% of full-time freshmen returned.

FACULTY

Total: 953, 67% full-time, 73% with terminal degrees.

Student/faculty ratio: 18:1.

ACADEMICS

Calendar: quarters. *Degrees:* certificates, bachelor's, master's, and post-master's certificates.

Special study options: accelerated degree program, advanced placement credit, cooperative education, distance learning, double majors, English as a second language, external degree program, honors programs, independent study, internships, off-campus study, part-time degree program, services for LD students, student-designed majors, study abroad, summer session for credit.

Computers: 2,268 computers/terminals are available on campus for general student use. Students can access the following: computer help desk, free student e-mail accounts, online (class) grades, online (class) registration, online (class) schedules. Campuswide network is available. 99% of college-owned or -operated housing units are wired for high-speed Internet access. Wireless service is available via entire campus.

Library: Wilson Library plus 2 others. *Books:* 631,958 (physical), 363,547 (digital/electronic); *Serial titles:* 21,547 (physical), 101,542 (digital/electronic); *Databases:* 95. Weekly public service hours: 97; students can reserve study rooms.

STUDENT LIFE

Housing options: coed, special housing for students with disabilities. Campus housing is university owned. Freshman campus housing is guaranteed.

Activities and organizations: drama/theater group, student-run newspaper, radio and television station, choral group, Intramurals, Residence Hall Association, Associated Students, Outdoor Center, Ethnic Student Center.

Athletics Member NCAA. All Division II. *Intercollegiate sports:* basketball M(s)/W(s), crew W(s), cross-country running M(s)/W(s), golf M(s)/W(s), soccer M(s)/W(s), softball M/W(s), track and field M(s)/W(s), volleyball W(s). *Intramural sports:* baseball M(c), basketball M/W, crew M(c)/W(c), equestrian sports M(c)/W(c), fencing M(c)/W(c), football M/W, golf M/W, ice hockey M(c), lacrosse M(c)/W(c), racquetball M/W, rock climbing M/W, rugby M(c)/W(c), sailing M(c)/W(c), skiing (downhill) M(c)/W(c), soccer M/W, softball M, swimming and diving M(c)/W(c), table tennis M/W, tennis M/W, ultimate Frisbee M(c)/W(c), volleyball M(c)/W(c), water polo M(c)/W(c), wrestling M(c)/W(c).

Campus security: 24-hour emergency response devices and patrols, student patrols, late-night transport/escort service, controlled dormitory access.

Student services: health clinic, personal/psychological counseling, women's center, legal services.

COSTS & FINANCIAL AID

Costs (2017–18) *One-time required fee:* $250. *Tuition:* state resident $6879 full-time; nonresident $21,391 full-time. Full-time tuition and fees vary according to course load, location, and reciprocity agreements. Part-time tuition and fees vary according to course load, location, and reciprocity agreements. *Required fees:* $1054 full-time, $208 per credit hour part-time. *Room and board:* $11,400; room only: $7187. Room and board charges vary according to board plan, housing facility, and location. *Payment plan:* installment. *Waivers:* minority students, senior citizens, and employees or children of employees.

Financial Aid Of all full-time matriculated undergraduates who enrolled in 2017, 9,503 applied for aid, 6,847 were judged to have need, 1,019 had their need fully met. 219 Federal Work-Study jobs (averaging $4438). 395 state and other part-time jobs (averaging $4304). In 2017, 312 non-need-based awards were made. *Average percent of need met:* 91. *Average financial aid package:* $15,563. *Average need-based loan:* $4486. *Average need-based gift aid:* $9138. *Average non-need-based aid:* $1194. *Average indebtedness upon graduation:* $15,663.

APPLYING

Standardized Tests *Required:* SAT or ACT (for admission).

Options: electronic application, early action, deferred entrance.

Application fee: $60.

Required: high school transcript. *Recommended:* essay or personal statement.

Application deadlines: 1/31 (freshmen), 3/1 (transfers).

Notification: continuous until 11/1 (freshmen), continuous until 5/1 (transfers).

CONTACT
Western Washington University, 516 High Street, Bellingham, WA 98225-5996.

Whitman College
Walla Walla, Washington
http://www.whitman.edu/

- **Independent** 4-year, founded 1859
- **Small-town** 117-acre campus
- **Endowment** $518.3 million
- **Coed** 1,510 undergraduate students, 96% full-time, 57% women, 43% men
- **Very difficult** entrance level, 52% of applicants were admitted

UNDERGRAD STUDENTS
1,455 full-time, 55 part-time. 66% are from out of state; 2% Black or African American, non-Hispanic/Latino; 7% Hispanic/Latino; 5% Asian, non-Hispanic/Latino; 0.5% Native Hawaiian or other Pacific Islander, non-Hispanic/Latino; 0.5% American Indian or Alaska Native, non-Hispanic/Latino; 7% Two or more races, non-Hispanic/Latino; 2% Race/ethnicity unknown; 7% international; 1% transferred in; 64% live on campus.

Freshmen:
Admission: 4,081 applied, 2,111 admitted, 389 enrolled. *Average high school GPA:* 3.8. *Test scores:* SAT evidence-based reading and writing scores over 500: 99%; SAT math scores over 500: 98%; ACT scores over 18: 100%; SAT evidence-based reading and writing scores over 600: 86%; SAT math scores over 600: 81%; ACT scores over 24: 95%; SAT evidence-based reading and writing scores over 700: 43%; SAT math scores over 700: 41%; ACT scores over 30: 60%.

Retention: 94% of full-time freshmen returned.

FACULTY
Total: 222, 74% full-time, 83% with terminal degrees.
Student/faculty ratio: 9:1.

ACADEMICS
Calendar: semesters. *Degree:* bachelor's.

Special study options: advanced placement credit, cooperative education, double majors, honors programs, independent study, internships, off-campus study, services for LD students, student-designed majors, study abroad.

Computers: 397 computers/terminals are available on campus for general student use. Students can access the following: computer help desk, free student e-mail accounts, online (class) grades, online (class) registration, online (class) schedules. Campuswide network is available. 100% of college-owned or -operated housing units are wired for high-speed Internet access. Wireless service is available via entire campus.
Library: Penrose Library plus 1 other. *Books:* 406,675 (physical), 305,206 (digital/electronic); *Serial titles:* 5,082 (physical), 98,012 (digital/electronic); *Databases:* 206. Weekly public service hours: 84; study areas open 24 hours, 5–7 days a week; students can reserve study rooms.

STUDENT LIFE
Housing options: on-campus residence required through sophomore year; coed, women-only. Campus housing is university owned. Freshman campus housing is guaranteed.

Activities and organizations: drama/theater group, student-run newspaper, radio station, choral group, national fraternities, national sororities.

Athletics Member NCAA. All Division III. *Intercollegiate sports:* baseball M, basketball M/W, cross-country running M/W, golf M/W, lacrosse M(c)/W, rugby M(c)/W(c), skiing (cross-country) M(c)/W(c), skiing (downhill) M(c)/W(c), soccer M/W, swimming and diving M/W, tennis M/W, track and field M(c)/W(c), ultimate Frisbee M(c)/W(c), volleyball M(c)/W, water polo M(c)/W(c). *Intramural sports:* archery M(c)/W(c), badminton M(c)/W(c), basketball M/W, fencing M(c)/W(c), football M/W, racquetball M(c)/W(c), rock climbing M(c)/W(c), soccer M/W, softball M/W, table tennis M/W, tennis M/W, ultimate Frisbee M/W, volleyball M/W.

Campus security: 24-hour emergency response devices and patrols, student patrols, late-night transport/escort service, controlled dormitory access.

Student services: health clinic, personal/psychological counseling, women's center.

COSTS & FINANCIAL AID
Costs (2018–19) *Comprehensive fee:* $64,920 includes full-time tuition ($51,370), mandatory fees ($376), and room and board ($13,174). Part-time tuition and fees vary according to course load. *College room only:* $5844.

Financial Aid Of all full-time matriculated undergraduates who enrolled in 2017, 738 applied for aid, 625 were judged to have need, 224 had their need fully met. In 2017, 454 non-need-based awards were made. *Average percent of need met:* 93. *Average financial aid package:* $41,281. *Average need-based loan:* $4485. *Average need-based gift aid:* $36,371. *Average non-need-based aid:* $11,279. *Average indebtedness upon graduation:* $23,254. *Financial aid deadline:* 2/1.

APPLYING
Standardized Tests *Required for some:* SAT or ACT (for admission).

Options: electronic application, early decision, deferred entrance.

Application fee: $50.

Required: high school transcript. *Required for some:* statement of good standing from prior institutions. *Recommended:* essay or personal statement, interview.

Application deadlines: 1/15 (freshmen), 3/1 (transfers).

Early decision deadline: 11/15.

Notification: 4/1 (freshmen), 4/20 (transfers), 12/20 (early decision).

CONTACT
Whitman College, Penrose House, 345 Boyer Ave, Walla Walla, WA 99362. *Phone:* 509-527-5176. *Toll-free phone:* 877-462-9448. *E-mail:* admission@whitman.edu.

Whitworth University
Spokane, Washington
http://www.whitworth.edu/

- **Independent Presbyterian** comprehensive, founded 1890
- **Suburban** 200-acre campus
- **Endowment** $141.9 million
- **Coed** 2,251 undergraduate students, 98% full-time, 60% women, 40% men
- **Moderately difficult** entrance level, 89% of applicants were admitted

UNDERGRAD STUDENTS
2,211 full-time, 40 part-time. Students come from 26 states and territories; 42 other countries; 33% are from out of state; 2% Black or African American, non-Hispanic/Latino; 9% Hispanic/Latino; 5% Asian, non-Hispanic/Latino; 0.5% Native Hawaiian or other Pacific Islander, non-Hispanic/Latino; 0.8% American Indian or Alaska Native, non-Hispanic/Latino; 7% Two or more races, non-Hispanic/Latino; 1% Race/ethnicity unknown; 4% international; 4% transferred in; 51% live on campus.

Freshmen:
Admission: 3,166 applied, 2,818 admitted, 505 enrolled. *Average high school GPA:* 3.8. *Test scores:* SAT evidence-based reading and writing scores over 500: 92%; SAT math scores over 500: 89%; ACT scores over 18: 94%; SAT evidence-based reading and writing scores over 600: 57%; SAT math scores over 600: 48%; ACT scores over 24: 68%; SAT evidence-based reading and writing scores over 700: 12%; SAT math scores over 700: 9%; ACT scores over 30: 23%.

Retention: 85% of full-time freshmen returned.

FACULTY
Total: 361, 51% full-time, 39% with terminal degrees.
Student/faculty ratio: 11:1.

ACADEMICS
Calendar: 4-1-4. *Degrees:* bachelor's, master's, post-master's, and postbachelor's certificates.

Special study options: adult/continuing education programs, advanced placement credit, double majors, honors programs, independent study, internships, off-campus study, part-time degree program, services for LD students, student-designed majors, study abroad, summer session for credit. *ROTC:* Army (c).

Unusual degree programs: 3-2 engineering with Seattle Pacific University, University of Southern California, Washington University in St. Louis, Columbia University, Washington State University; nursing with Washington State University; athletic training at Whitworth University.

Computers: 280 computers/terminals and 1,355 ports are available on campus for general student use. Students can access the following: campus intranet, computer help desk, free student e-mail accounts, online (class) grades, online (class) registration, online (class) schedules, learning management system. Campuswide network is available. 100% of college-owned or -operated housing units are wired for high-speed Internet access. Wireless service is available via entire campus.

Library: Harriet Cheney Cowles Library. *Books:* 210,113 (physical), 160,000 (digital/electronic); *Serial titles:* 278 (physical), 36,239 (digital/electronic); *Databases:* 153. Weekly public service hours: 97; students can reserve study rooms.

STUDENT LIFE

Housing options: on-campus residence required through sophomore year; coed, men-only, women-only. Campus housing is university owned. Freshman campus housing is guaranteed.

Activities and organizations: drama/theater group, student-run newspaper, radio station, choral group, International Club, Whitworth Student Investment Group, En Christo, Hawaiian Club, Swing and Ballroom Dance Club.

Athletics Member NCAA. All Division III. *Intercollegiate sports:* baseball M, basketball M/W, cross-country running M/W, football M, golf M/W, soccer M/W, softball W, swimming and diving M/W, tennis M/W, track and field M/W, volleyball W. *Intramural sports:* badminton M/W, basketball M(c)/W, football M/W, soccer M/W, softball M/W, table tennis M/W, tennis M/W, ultimate Frisbee M(c)/W(c), volleyball M/W.

Campus security: 24-hour emergency response devices and patrols, late-night transport/escort service, controlled dormitory access.

Student services: health clinic, personal/psychological counseling.

COSTS & FINANCIAL AID

Costs (2018–19) *Comprehensive fee:* $55,136 includes full-time tuition ($42,540), mandatory fees ($1100), and room and board ($11,496). Part-time tuition: $1773 per credit hour. Part-time tuition and fees vary according to course load. *Required fees:* $490 per term part-time. *College room only:* $6250. Room and board charges vary according to board plan and housing facility. *Payment plan:* installment. *Waivers:* senior citizens and employees or children of employees.

Financial Aid Of all full-time matriculated undergraduates who enrolled in 2017, 1,699 applied for aid, 1,521 were judged to have need, 232 had their need fully met. 806 Federal Work-Study jobs (averaging $2810). 92 state and other part-time jobs (averaging $3507). In 2017, 592 non-need-based awards were made. *Average percent of need met:* 79. *Average financial aid package:* $36,320. *Average need-based loan:* $5184. *Average need-based gift aid:* $27,827. *Average non-need-based aid:* $20,509. *Average indebtedness upon graduation:* $26,940.

APPLYING

Standardized Tests *Required for some:* SAT or ACT (for admission).

Options: electronic application, early admission, early action, deferred entrance.

Required: essay or personal statement, high school transcript, 1 letter of recommendation. *Required for some:* minimum 3.0 GPA, 2 letters of recommendation, interview.

Application deadlines: 8/1 (freshmen), 8/1 (transfers), 11/15 (early action).

Notification: continuous (freshmen), continuous (transfers), rolling (early action).

CONTACT

Ms. Lara Ramsay, Director of Admission, Whitworth University, 300 West, Hawthorne Road, Spokane, WA 99251. *Phone:* 509-777-4347. *Toll-free phone:* 800-533-4668. *Fax:* 509-777-3758. *E-mail:* admission@whitworth.edu.

WEST VIRGINIA

Alderson Broaddus University

Philippi, West Virginia

http://www.ab.edu/

- **Independent** comprehensive, founded 1871, affiliated with American Baptist Churches in the U.S.A.
- **Rural** 170-acre campus
- **Endowment** $17.6 million
- **Coed**
- **Moderately difficult** entrance level

FACULTY

Student/faculty ratio: 17:1.

ACADEMICS

Calendar: semesters. *Degrees:* associate, bachelor's, and master's.

Library: Pickett Library. *Books:* 40,000 (physical), 160,000 (digital/electronic); *Serial titles:* 8 (physical), 11,000 (digital/electronic); *Databases:* 31. Weekly public service hours: 78; study areas open 24 hours, 5–7 days a week; students can reserve study rooms.

STUDENT LIFE

Housing options: on-campus residence required through senior year; coed, special housing for students with disabilities. Campus housing is university owned. Freshman campus housing is guaranteed.

Activities and organizations: drama/theater group, student-run newspaper, radio and television station, choral group, marching band, AAPA/Hu C. Myers Society, Alpha Beta Nu, Student Athletic Advisory Committee, Sigma Alpha Iota, Kappa Xi Omega.

Athletics Member NCAA. All Division II.

Campus security: 24-hour patrols, controlled dormitory access, emergency notification system, lighted pathways and sidewalks.

Student services: health clinic, personal/psychological counseling.

COSTS & FINANCIAL AID

Costs (2017–18) *Comprehensive fee:* $35,000 includes full-time tuition ($26,400), mandatory fees ($210), and room and board ($8390). Part-time tuition: $880 per credit hour. *Required fees:* $53 per term part-time. *Room and board:* Room and board charges vary according to housing facility.

Financial Aid Of all full-time matriculated undergraduates who enrolled in 2016, 887 applied for aid, 787 were judged to have need, 260 had their need fully met. 430 Federal Work-Study jobs (averaging $1435). 95 state and other part-time jobs (averaging $2410). In 2016, 126 non-need-based awards were made. *Average percent of need met:* 90. *Average financial aid package:* $22,284. *Average need-based loan:* $4047. *Average need-based gift aid:* $20,274. *Average non-need-based aid:* $9505. *Average indebtedness upon graduation:* $24,079.

APPLYING

Standardized Tests *Required:* SAT and SAT Subject Tests or ACT (for admission).

Options: electronic application, deferred entrance.

Required: high school transcript, minimum 2.0 GPA. *Required for some:* 3 letters of recommendation, interview.

CONTACT

Mr. Erika L. Thon, Director of Admissions, Alderson Broaddus University, 101 College Hill Drive, Campus Box 2003, Philippi, WV 26416. *Phone:* 304-457-6256. *Toll-free phone:* 800-263-1549. *Fax:* 304-457-6239. *E-mail:* thonel@ab.edu.

American Public University System

Charles Town, West Virginia

http://www.apus.edu/

- **Proprietary** comprehensive, founded 1991
- **Rural** campus with easy access to Washington, DC
- **Coed** 37,910 undergraduate students, 8% full-time, 36% women, 64% men
- **Noncompetitive** entrance level

UNDERGRAD STUDENTS

2,914 full-time, 34,996 part-time. 16% Black or African American, non-Hispanic/Latino; 12% Hispanic/Latino; 2% Asian, non-Hispanic/Latino; 1% Native Hawaiian or other Pacific Islander, non-Hispanic/Latino; 0.6% American Indian or Alaska Native, non-Hispanic/Latino; 4% Two or more races, non-Hispanic/Latino; 7% Race/ethnicity unknown; 0.7% international; 13% transferred in.

Freshmen:

Admission: 1,243 enrolled.

Retention: 92% of full-time freshmen returned.

FACULTY

Total: 1,863, 20% full-time, 57% with terminal degrees.

Student/faculty ratio: 20:1.

ACADEMICS

Calendar: courses start on the first Monday of each month. *Degrees:* certificates, associate, bachelor's, master's, doctoral, and postbachelor's certificates (profile includes American Public University, American Military University and American Community College).

Special study options: advanced placement credit, distance learning, external degree program, independent study, internships, part-time degree program, services for LD students, summer session for credit.

Computers: Students can access the following: free student e-mail accounts, online (class) grades, online (class) registration, online (class) schedules.

Library: APUS Online Library.

STUDENT LIFE

Housing options: college housing not available.

APPLYING

Options: electronic application, deferred entrance.

Required: high school transcript.

CONTACT

Mr. Greg Hill, Assistant Vice President, Prospect Management and Undergraduate Admissions, American Public University System, 111 West Congress Street, Charles Town, WV 25414. *Phone:* 877-468-6268. *Toll-free phone:* 877-755-2787. *Fax:* 304-724-3788. *E-mail:* info@apus.edu.

Appalachian Bible College

Mount Hope, West Virginia

http://www.abc.edu/

- **Independent nondenominational** comprehensive, founded 1950
- **Small-town** 110-acre campus
- **Endowment** $316,677
- **Coed** 259 undergraduate students, 57% full-time, 39% women, 61% men
- **Noncompetitive** entrance level, 56% of applicants were admitted

UNDERGRAD STUDENTS

148 full-time, 111 part-time. Students come from 23 states and territories; 9 other countries; 61% are from out of state; 1% Black or African American, non-Hispanic/Latino; 0.7% Hispanic/Latino; 1% Asian, non-Hispanic/Latino; 4% international; 7% transferred in; 95% live on campus.

Freshmen:

Admission: 133 applied, 74 admitted, 41 enrolled. *Test scores:* SAT evidence-based reading and writing scores over 500: 81%; SAT math scores over 500: 73%; ACT scores over 18: 84%; SAT evidence-based reading and writing scores over 600: 36%; SAT math scores over 600: 14%; ACT scores over 24: 27%; SAT evidence-based reading and writing scores over 700: 4%; ACT scores over 30: 4%.

Retention: 74% of full-time freshmen returned.

FACULTY

Total: 35, 66% full-time, 17% with terminal degrees.

Student/faculty ratio: 8:1.

ACADEMICS

Calendar: semesters. *Degrees:* certificates, diplomas, associate, bachelor's, master's, and postbachelor's certificates.

Special study options: academic remediation for entering students, adult/continuing education programs, advanced placement credit, distance learning, double majors, honors programs, independent study, internships, part-time degree program, student-designed majors.

Computers: 15 computers/terminals and 15 ports are available on campus for general student use. Students can access the following: campus intranet, computer help desk, free student e-mail accounts. Campuswide network is available. 100% of college-owned or -operated housing units are wired for high-speed Internet access. Wireless service is available via entire campus.

Library: John Van Pufflen Library.

STUDENT LIFE

Housing options: on-campus residence required for freshman year; men-only, women-only. Campus housing is university owned. Freshman campus housing is guaranteed.

Activities and organizations: drama/theater group, choral group.

Athletics Member NCCAA. *Intercollegiate sports:* basketball M/W, soccer M, volleyball W.

Campus security: 24-hour emergency response devices, controlled dormitory access, patrols by trained security personnel.

Student services: health clinic, personal/psychological counseling.

COSTS & FINANCIAL AID

Costs (2018–19) *Comprehensive fee:* $21,880 includes full-time tuition ($13,010), mandatory fees ($910), and room and board ($7960). Full-time tuition and fees vary according to course load. Part-time tuition: $395 per credit hour. Part-time tuition and fees vary according to course load. *Required fees:* $42 per credit hour part-time, $160 per term part-time. *Room and board:* Room and board charges vary according to housing facility. *Payment plans:* installment, deferred payment. *Waivers:* minority students, children of alumni, senior citizens, and employees or children of employees.

Financial Aid Of all full-time matriculated undergraduates who enrolled in 2017, 143 applied for aid, 105 were judged to have need, 1 had their need fully met. 23 Federal Work-Study jobs (averaging $721). In 2017, 7 non-need-based awards were made. *Average percent of need met:* 64. *Average financial aid package:* $13,511. *Average need-based loan:* $3807. *Average need-based gift aid:* $5243. *Average indebtedness upon graduation:* $15,421.

APPLYING

Standardized Tests *Required:* SAT or ACT (for admission).

Options: electronic application, early admission, deferred entrance.

Application fee: $35.

Required: essay or personal statement, high school transcript, 2 letters of recommendation. *Required for some:* interview. *Recommended:* minimum 2.3 GPA.

Application deadlines: rolling (freshmen), rolling (transfers).

CONTACT

Miss Megan Mullens, Admissions Assistant, Appalachian Bible College, 161 College Drive, Mount Hope, WV 25880. *Phone:* 304-877-6428 Ext. 313. *Toll-free phone:* 800-678-9ABC. *Fax:* 304-877-5082. *E-mail:* admissions@abc.edu.

Bethany College

Bethany, West Virginia

http://www.bethanywv.edu/

CONTACT

Ms. Mollie Cecere, Director of Enrollment, Bethany College, Bethany College Center for Enrollment and Financial Aid, 31 E Campus Drive #4, Bethany, WV 26032. *Phone:* 304-829-7611. *Toll-free phone:* 800-922-7611. *Fax:* 304-829-7142. *E-mail:* enrollment@bethanywv.edu.

Bluefield State College

Bluefield, West Virginia
http://www.bluefieldstate.edu/

- **State-supported** 4-year, founded 1895, part of West Virginia Higher Education Policy Commission
- **Small-town** 45-acre campus
- **Coed**
- **Noncompetitive** entrance level

FACULTY
Student/faculty ratio: 13:1.

ACADEMICS
Calendar: semesters. *Degrees:* associate and bachelor's.
Library: Hardway Library.

STUDENT LIFE
Housing options: college housing not available.

Activities and organizations: drama/theater group, student-run newspaper, radio station, choral group, national fraternities, national sororities.

Athletics Member NCAA. All Division II.

Campus security: 24-hour emergency response devices and patrols, student patrols.

Student services: health clinic, personal/psychological counseling.

COSTS & FINANCIAL AID
Costs (2017–18) *Tuition:* state resident $6728 full-time, $279 per credit hour part-time; nonresident $13,032 full-time, $541 per credit hour part-time.

Financial Aid Of all full-time matriculated undergraduates who enrolled in 2017, 1,380 applied for aid, 1,150 were judged to have need, 140 had their need fully met. 55 Federal Work-Study jobs (averaging $3000). In 2017, 10 non-need-based awards were made. *Average percent of need met:* 67. *Average financial aid package:* $3500. *Average need-based loan:* $4250. *Average need-based gift aid:* $3700. *Average non-need-based aid:* $850. *Average indebtedness upon graduation:* $29,000.

APPLYING
Standardized Tests *Required:* SAT or ACT (for admission).
Options: early admission, deferred entrance.
Required: high school transcript, minimum 2.0 GPA.

CONTACT
Bluefield State College, 219 Rock Street, Bluefield, WV 24701-2198. *Phone:* 304-327-4067. *Toll-free phone:* 800-344-8892 Ext. 4065 (in-state); 800-654-7798 Ext. 4065 (out-of-state).

Concord University

Athens, West Virginia
http://www.concord.edu/

- **State-supported** comprehensive, founded 1872, part of State College System of West Virginia
- **Rural** 100-acre campus
- **Endowment** $24.5 million
- **Coed** 1,853 undergraduate students, 92% full-time, 58% women, 42% men
- **Minimally difficult** entrance level, 90% of applicants were admitted

UNDERGRAD STUDENTS
1,696 full-time, 157 part-time. Students come from 24 states and territories; 26 other countries; 14% are from out of state; 6% Black or African American, non-Hispanic/Latino; 1% Hispanic/Latino; 0.9% Asian, non-Hispanic/Latino; 0.2% Native Hawaiian or other Pacific Islander, non-Hispanic/Latino; 0.3% American Indian or Alaska Native, non-Hispanic/Latino; 2% Two or more races, non-Hispanic/Latino; 0.6% Race/ethnicity unknown; 6% international; 5% transferred in; 40% live on campus.

Freshmen:
Admission: 2,507 applied, 2,261 admitted, 434 enrolled. *Average high school GPA:* 3.4. *Test scores:* ACT scores over 18: 63%; ACT scores over 24: 14%.

Retention: 64% of full-time freshmen returned.

FACULTY
Total: 172, 67% full-time, 55% with terminal degrees.
Student/faculty ratio: 15:1.

ACADEMICS
Calendar: semesters. *Degrees:* bachelor's, master's, and post-master's certificates.

Special study options: academic remediation for entering students, accelerated degree program, adult/continuing education programs, advanced placement credit, cooperative education, distance learning, double majors, English as a second language, external degree program, honors programs, independent study, internships, off-campus study, part-time degree program, services for LD students, student-designed majors, study abroad, summer session for credit.

Computers: 350 computers/terminals and 1,100 ports are available on campus for general student use. Students can access the following: campus intranet, computer help desk, free student e-mail accounts, online (class) grades, online (class) registration, online (class) schedules. Campuswide network is available. 100% of college-owned or -operated housing units are wired for high-speed Internet access. Wireless service is available via entire campus.

Library: J. Frank Marsh Library. *Books:* 162,020 (physical), 34,329 (digital/electronic); *Serial titles:* 68 (physical), 110 (digital/electronic); *Databases:* 14. Weekly public service hours: 77; study areas open 24 hours, 5–7 days a week; students can reserve study rooms.

STUDENT LIFE
Housing options: coed, men-only, women-only. Campus housing is university owned. Freshman campus housing is guaranteed.

Activities and organizations: drama/theater group, student-run newspaper, radio and television station, choral group, marching band, Service Groups, student government, student-run publications, intramurals, Student Activities Committee, national fraternities, national sororities.

Athletics Member NCAA. All Division II. *Intercollegiate sports:* baseball M(s), basketball M(s)/W(s), cheerleading M/W, cross-country running M(s)/W(s), football M(s), golf M(s)/W(s), soccer M(s)/W(s), softball W(s), tennis M(s)/W(s), track and field M(s)/W(s), volleyball W(s). *Intramural sports:* basketball M/W, football M, soccer M/W, tennis M/W, volleyball M/W.

Campus security: 24-hour emergency response devices and patrols, student patrols, late-night transport/escort service, controlled dormitory access.

Student services: health clinic, personal/psychological counseling.

COSTS & FINANCIAL AID
Costs (2017–18) *Tuition:* state resident $7574 full-time, $316 per credit hour part-time; nonresident $16,654 full-time, $694 per credit hour part-time. Full-time tuition and fees vary according to course load and program. Part-time tuition and fees vary according to course load and program. *Required fees:* $158 full-time. *Room and board:* $8642. Room and board charges vary according to board plan. *Payment plan:* installment. *Waivers:* employees or children of employees.

Financial Aid Of all full-time matriculated undergraduates who enrolled in 2017, 1,520 applied for aid, 1,299 were judged to have need, 601 had their need fully met. 184 Federal Work-Study jobs (averaging $1765). In 2017, 212 non-need-based awards were made. *Average percent of need met:* 86. *Average financial aid package:* $8471. *Average need-based loan:* $3179. *Average need-based gift aid:* $5843. *Average non-need-based aid:* $3578. *Average indebtedness upon graduation:* $21,176. *Financial aid deadline:* 4/15.

APPLYING
Standardized Tests *Required:* SAT or ACT (for admission).
Options: electronic application, early admission.
Required: high school transcript, minimum 2.0 GPA. *Required for some:* essay or personal statement, interview. *Recommended:* interview.
Application deadlines: rolling (freshmen), rolling (transfers).
Notification: continuous (freshmen), continuous (transfers).

CONTACT
Mr. Jamie Ealy, Vice President of Enrollment Management, Concord University, 1000 Vermillion Street, Athens, WV 24712. *Phone:* 304-384-

6305. *Toll-free phone:* 888-384-5249. *Fax:* 304-384-9044. *E-mail:* admissions@concord.edu.

Davis & Elkins College

Elkins, West Virginia
http://www.dewv.edu/

CONTACT
Ms. ReneÃ© Heckel, Director of Enrollment Management, Davis & Elkins College, 100 Campus Drive, Elkins, WV 26241. *Phone:* 304-637-1974. *Toll-free phone:* 800-624-3157. *Fax:* 304-637-1800. *E-mail:* admiss@davisandelkins.edu.

Fairmont State University

Fairmont, West Virginia
http://www.fairmontstate.edu/

CONTACT
Mrs. Amie Fazalare, Director of Recruiting, Fairmont State University, 1201 Locust Avenue, Fairmont, WV 26554. *Phone:* 304-367-4892. *Toll-free phone:* 800-641-5678. *Fax:* 304-367-4789. *E-mail:* admit@fairmontstate.edu.

Glenville State College

Glenville, West Virginia
http://www.glenville.edu/

CONTACT
Ms. Ashley Weir, Admission Counselor, Glenville State College, 200 High Street, Glenville, WV 26351-1200. *Phone:* 304-462-4128 Ext. 6133. *Toll-free phone:* 800-924-2010. *Fax:* 304-462-8619. *E-mail:* ashley.weir@glenville.edu.

Marshall University

Huntington, West Virginia
http://www.marshall.edu/

- **State-supported** university, founded 1837, part of University System of West Virginia
- **Urban** 114-acre campus
- **Coed** 9,489 undergraduate students, 83% full-time, 58% women, 42% men
- **Moderately difficult** entrance level, 89% of applicants were admitted

UNDERGRAD STUDENTS
7,846 full-time, 1,643 part-time. Students come from 43 states and territories; 47 other countries; 20% are from out of state; 6% Black or African American, non-Hispanic/Latino; 2% Hispanic/Latino; 0.7% Asian, non-Hispanic/Latino; 0.1% Native Hawaiian or other Pacific Islander, non-Hispanic/Latino; 0.3% American Indian or Alaska Native, non-Hispanic/Latino; 3% Two or more races, non-Hispanic/Latino; 5% Race/ethnicity unknown; 2% international; 5% transferred in.

Freshmen:
Admission: 4,891 applied, 4,374 admitted, 1,801 enrolled. *Average high school GPA:* 3.5. *Test scores:* SAT evidence-based reading and writing scores over 500: 61%; SAT math scores over 500: 61%; ACT scores over 18: 90%; SAT evidence-based reading and writing scores over 600: 16%; SAT math scores over 600: 12%; ACT scores over 24: 35%; SAT evidence-based reading and writing scores over 700: 4%; SAT math scores over 700: 1%; ACT scores over 30: 5%.
Retention: 72% of full-time freshmen returned.

FACULTY
Total: 688, 71% full-time, 62% with terminal degrees.
Student/faculty ratio: 19:1.

ACADEMICS
Calendar: semesters. *Degrees:* certificates, associate, bachelor's, master's, doctoral, post-master's, and postbachelor's certificates.
Special study options: academic remediation for entering students, accelerated degree program, adult/continuing education programs, advanced placement credit, cooperative education, distance learning,

double majors, English as a second language, honors programs, independent study, internships, off-campus study, part-time degree program, services for LD students, study abroad, summer session for credit. *ROTC:* Army (b).

Unusual degree programs: 3-2 forestry with Duke University.
Computers: 1,200 computers/terminals and 500 ports are available on campus for general student use. Students can access the following: campus intranet, computer help desk, free student e-mail accounts, online (class) grades, online (class) registration, online (class) schedules, virtual computer lab: remote and Web conferencing. Campuswide network is available. 100% of college-owned or -operated housing units are wired for high-speed Internet access. Wireless service is available via classrooms, computer centers, computer labs, dorm rooms, learning centers, libraries, student centers.
Library: John Deaver Drinko Library plus 1 other. *Books:* 399,125 (physical), 128,967 (digital/electronic); *Serial titles:* 2,014 (physical), 51,061 (digital/electronic); *Databases:* 256. Weekly public service hours: 133; study areas open 24 hours, 5–7 days a week; students can reserve study rooms.

STUDENT LIFE
Housing options: on-campus residence required through sophomore year; coed, women-only, special housing for students with disabilities. Campus housing is university owned and is provided by a third party. Freshman campus housing is guaranteed.

Activities and organizations: drama/theater group, student-run newspaper, radio and television station, choral group, marching band, Campus Crusade for Christ, Gamma Beta Phi, The International Students'; Organization, Newman Association, Phi Alpha Theta, national fraternities, national sororities.

Athletics Member NCAA. All Division I except football (Division I-A). *Intercollegiate sports:* baseball M(s), basketball M(s)/W(s), cross-country running M(s)/W(s), golf M(s)/W(s), lacrosse M(c), rugby M(c)/W(c), soccer M(s)/W(s), softball W(s), swimming and diving W(s), tennis W(s), track and field M(s)/W(s), volleyball W(s). *Intramural sports:* basketball M/W, bowling M/W, football M/W, golf M/W, racquetball M/W, soccer M/W, softball M/W, swimming and diving M/W, tennis M/W, track and field M/W, volleyball M/W.

Campus security: 24-hour emergency response devices and patrols, student patrols, late-night transport/escort service, controlled dormitory access.

Student services: health clinic, personal/psychological counseling, women's center, legal services.

COSTS & FINANCIAL AID
Costs (2017–18) *Tuition:* state resident $6676 full-time, $278 per credit hour part-time; nonresident $16,734 full-time, $698 per credit hour part-time. Full-time tuition and fees vary according to degree level, location, program, and reciprocity agreements. Part-time tuition and fees vary according to course load, degree level, location, program, and reciprocity agreements. *Required fees:* $1122 full-time, $47 per credit hour part-time. *Room and board:* $10,126; room only: $6266. Room and board charges vary according to board plan and housing facility. *Payment plan:* installment. *Waivers:* children of alumni, senior citizens, and employees or children of employees.

Financial Aid Of all full-time matriculated undergraduates who enrolled in 2017, 6,913 applied for aid, 5,624 were judged to have need, 1,128 had their need fully met. In 2017, 1032 non-need-based awards were made. *Average percent of need met:* 48. *Average financial aid package:* $11,101. *Average need-based loan:* $6896. *Average need-based gift aid:* $6459. *Average non-need-based aid:* $2707. *Average indebtedness upon graduation:* $28,095.

APPLYING
Standardized Tests *Required:* SAT or ACT (for admission).
Options: electronic application, deferred entrance.
Application fee: $30.
Required for some: high school transcript.
Application deadlines: rolling (freshmen), rolling (transfers).
Notification: continuous (freshmen), continuous (transfers).

CONTACT
Dr. Tammy Johnson, Director of Admissions, Marshall University, 1 John Marshall Drive, Huntington, WV 25755. *Phone:* 800-642-3499. *Toll-free*

phone: 800-642-3499. *Fax:* 304-696-3135. *E-mail:* admissions@ marshall.edu.

Ohio Valley University
Vienna, West Virginia
http://www.ovu.edu/

- **Independent** comprehensive, founded 1960, affiliated with Church of Christ
- **Small-town** 299-acre campus
- **Coed**
- **Minimally difficult** entrance level

FACULTY
Student/faculty ratio: 10:1.

ACADEMICS
Calendar: semesters. *Degrees:* associate, bachelor's, master's, and postbachelor's certificates.
Library: Icy Belle Library.

STUDENT LIFE
Housing options: on-campus residence required through sophomore year; men-only, women-only, special housing for students with disabilities. Campus housing is university owned. Freshman campus housing is guaranteed.

Activities and organizations: drama/theater group, student-run newspaper, choral group, Social Clubs, intramural sports, Theatre Production, A cappella Choir, Ambassadors.

Athletics Member NCAA. All Division II.

Campus security: 24-hour emergency response devices and patrols, controlled dormitory access.

COSTS & FINANCIAL AID
Costs (2017–18) *Comprehensive fee:* $28,800 includes full-time tuition ($21,100) and room and board ($7700). Full-time tuition and fees vary according to course load. Part-time tuition: $825 per credit hour. Part-time tuition and fees vary according to course load. *College room only:* $3850. Room and board charges vary according to board plan, housing facility, and location.

Financial Aid Of all full-time matriculated undergraduates who enrolled in 2015, 337 applied for aid, 313 were judged to have need, 60 had their need fully met. In 2015, 60 non-need-based awards were made. *Average percent of need met:* 65. *Average financial aid package:* $14,912. *Average need-based loan:* $3471. *Average need-based gift aid:* $12,093. *Average non-need-based aid:* $5588. *Average indebtedness upon graduation:* $23,841.

APPLYING
Standardized Tests *Required for some:* SAT or ACT (for admission).
Options: electronic application.
Required: high school transcript. *Required for some:* essay or personal statement, interview.

CONTACT
Mrs. Valerie Wright, Admissions Office Manager, Ohio Valley University, 1 Campus View Drive, Vienna, WV 26105. *Phone:* 304-865-6200. *Toll-free phone:* 877-446-8668. *Fax:* 304-865-6001. *E-mail:* admissions@ ovu.edu.

Potomac State College of West Virginia University
Keyser, West Virginia
http://www.potomacstatecollege.edu/

- **State-supported** primarily 2-year, founded 1901, part of West Virginia Higher Education Policy Commission
- **Small-town** 18-acre campus
- **Coed** 1,475 undergraduate students, 78% full-time, 54% women, 46% men
- **Noncompetitive** entrance level, 48% of applicants were admitted

UNDERGRAD STUDENTS
1,156 full-time, 319 part-time. Students come from 24 states and territories; 2 other countries; 37% are from out of state; 21% Black or African American, non-Hispanic/Latino; 3% Hispanic/Latino; 0.2% Asian, non-Hispanic/Latino; 0.2% Native Hawaiian or other Pacific Islander, non-Hispanic/Latino; 0.5% American Indian or Alaska Native, non-Hispanic/Latino; 4% Two or more races, non-Hispanic/Latino; 1% Race/ethnicity unknown; 0.6% international; 3% transferred in; 52% live on campus.

Freshmen:
Admission: 2,582 applied, 1,241 admitted, 588 enrolled. *Average high school GPA:* 2.9. *Test scores:* ACT scores over 18: 60%; ACT scores over 24: 19%; ACT scores over 30: 1%.
Retention: 44% of full-time freshmen returned.

FACULTY
Total: 85, 53% full-time, 16% with terminal degrees.
Student/faculty ratio: 22:1.

ACADEMICS
Calendar: semesters. *Degrees:* associate and bachelor's.

Special study options: academic remediation for entering students, adult/continuing education programs, advanced placement credit, cooperative education, distance learning, double majors, honors programs, independent study, internships, part-time degree program, services for LD students, study abroad, summer session for credit.

Computers: 69 computers/terminals are available on campus for general student use. Students can access the following: computer help desk, free student e-mail accounts, online (class) grades, online (class) registration, online (class) schedules. 100% of college-owned or -operated housing units are wired for high-speed Internet access. Wireless service is available via classrooms, computer labs, libraries, student centers.
Library: Mary F. Shipper Library.

STUDENT LIFE
Housing options: on-campus residence required through sophomore year; coed. Campus housing is university owned. Freshman applicants given priority for college housing.

Activities and organizations: drama/theater group, student-run newspaper, choral group, Agriculture and Forestry Club, Black Student Alliance, Gamers and Geeks Club, Campus and Community Ministries.

Athletics Member NJCAA. *Intercollegiate sports:* baseball M(s), basketball M(s)/W(s), cross-country running M(s)/W(s), lacrosse M(s)/W(s), soccer M/W, softball W(s), volleyball W(s). *Intramural sports:* basketball M/W, football M/W, soccer M/W, softball M/W, table tennis M/W, ultimate Frisbee M/W, volleyball M/W.

Campus security: 24-hour patrols, late-night transport/escort service, controlled dormitory access.

Student services: health clinic, personal/psychological counseling.

FINANCIAL AID
Financial Aid Of all full-time matriculated undergraduates who enrolled in 2016, 949 applied for aid, 779 were judged to have need, 76 had their need fully met. In 2016, 49 non-need-based awards were made. *Average financial aid package:* $7048. *Average need-based loan:* $4663. *Average need-based gift aid:* $5295. *Average non-need-based aid:* $1456. *Average indebtedness upon graduation:* $19,002.

APPLYING
Standardized Tests *Recommended:* SAT or ACT (for admission).
Options: electronic application.
Required: high school transcript.
Application deadlines: rolling (freshmen), rolling (transfers).

CONTACT
Ms. Beth Little, Director of Enrollment Services, Potomac State College of West Virginia University, 75 Arnold Street, Keyser, WV 26726. *Phone:* 304-788-6820. *Toll-free phone:* 800-262-7332 Ext. 6820. *Fax:* 304-788-6939. *E-mail:* go2psc@mail.wvu.edu.

Salem International University

Salem, West Virginia
http://www.salemu.edu/

CONTACT
Mrs. Brenda Davis, Admissions Representative, Salem International University, PO Box 500, Salem, WV 26426-0500. *Phone:* 304-326-1359. *Toll-free phone:* 888-235-5024. *Fax:* 304-326-1592. *E-mail:* admissions@salemiu.edu.

Shepherd University

Shepherdstown, West Virginia
http://www.shepherd.edu/

- **State-supported** comprehensive, founded 1871, part of West Virginia Higher Education Policy Commission
- **Small-town** 325-acre campus with easy access to Washington, D.C.
- **Endowment** $25.9 million
- **Coed** 3,421 undergraduate students, 76% full-time, 57% women, 43% men
- **Moderately difficult** entrance level, 89% of applicants were admitted

UNDERGRAD STUDENTS
2,613 full-time, 807 part-time. Students come from 50 states and territories; 11 other countries; 33% are from out of state; 8% Black or African American, non-Hispanic/Latino; 4% Hispanic/Latino; 2% Asian, non-Hispanic/Latino; 0.1% Native Hawaiian or other Pacific Islander, non-Hispanic/Latino; 0.5% American Indian or Alaska Native, non-Hispanic/Latino; 3% Two or more races, non-Hispanic/Latino; 2% Race/ethnicity unknown; 0.7% international; 10% transferred in; 34% live on campus.

Freshmen:
Admission: 1,573 applied, 1,402 admitted, 598 enrolled. *Average high school GPA:* 3.4. *Test scores:* ACT scores over 18: 86%; ACT scores over 24: 27%; ACT scores over 30: 2%.
Retention: 65% of full-time freshmen returned.

FACULTY
Total: 347, 39% full-time, 52% with terminal degrees.
Student/faculty ratio: 15:1.

ACADEMICS
Calendar: semesters. *Degrees:* bachelor's, master's, and doctoral.
Special study options: academic remediation for entering students, adult/continuing education programs, advanced placement credit, cooperative education, distance learning, double majors, English as a second language, honors programs, independent study, internships, part-time degree program, services for LD students, study abroad, summer session for credit. *ROTC:* Air Force (c).
Unusual degree programs: 3-2 business administration; biochemistry (biopharmaceutical science) with West Virginia University.
Computers: 567 computers/terminals and 25 ports are available on campus for general student use. Students can access the following: computer help desk, free student e-mail accounts, online (class) grades, online (class) registration, online (class) schedules, virtual labs. Campuswide network is available. 100% of college-owned or -operated housing units are wired for high-speed Internet access. Wireless service is available via entire campus.
Library: Scarborough Library. *Books:* 143,245 (physical), 6,727 (digital/electronic); *Serial titles:* 373 (physical), 69,441 (digital/electronic); *Databases:* 71. Weekly public service hours: 87; study areas open 24 hours, 5–7 days a week; students can reserve study rooms.

STUDENT LIFE
Housing options: on-campus residence required through senior year; coed, special housing for students with disabilities. Campus housing is university owned. Freshman campus housing is guaranteed.
Activities and organizations: drama/theater group, student-run newspaper, radio station, choral group, marching band, Relay for Life, Student Government Association, Ram Marching Band, Sigma Sigma Sigma, Alpha Phi Omega, national fraternities, national sororities.
Athletics Member NCAA. All Division II. *Intercollegiate sports:* baseball M(s), basketball M(s)/W(s), football M(s), golf M(s), lacrosse W(s), soccer M(s)/W(s), softball W(s), tennis M(s)/W(s), volleyball W(s). *Intramural sports:* basketball M/W, football M/W, racquetball M/W, sand volleyball M/W, soccer M/W, volleyball M/W.
Campus security: 24-hour emergency response devices and patrols, late-night transport/escort service, controlled dormitory access, student security in academic buildings, RAVE emergency alert system.
Student services: health clinic, personal/psychological counseling.

COSTS & FINANCIAL AID
Costs (2018–19) *Tuition:* state resident $7548 full-time, $315 per credit hour part-time; nonresident $18,052 full-time, $752 per credit hour part-time. Full-time tuition and fees vary according to program and reciprocity agreements. Part-time tuition and fees vary according to program. *Room and board:* $10,500. Room and board charges vary according to board plan and housing facility. *Payment plan:* installment. *Waivers:* minority students, senior citizens, and employees or children of employees.
Financial Aid Of all full-time matriculated undergraduates who enrolled in 2017, 2,511 applied for aid, 1,756 were judged to have need, 536 had their need fully met. 116 Federal Work-Study jobs (averaging $1130). 428 state and other part-time jobs (averaging $1514). In 2017, 583 non-need-based awards were made. *Average percent of need met:* 76. *Average financial aid package:* $12,802. *Average need-based loan:* $4048. *Average need-based gift aid:* $5611. *Average non-need-based aid:* $10,904. *Average indebtedness upon graduation:* $27,686.

APPLYING
Standardized Tests *Required:* SAT or ACT (for admission).
Options: electronic application, early admission, early action, deferred entrance.
Application fee: $45.
Required: high school transcript, minimum 2.0 GPA. *Recommended:* essay or personal statement, minimum 3.0 GPA, 2 letters of recommendation.
Application deadlines: rolling (freshmen), rolling (transfers), 11/15 (early action).
Notification: continuous until 8/15 (freshmen), continuous until 8/15 (transfers), 12/15 (early action).

CONTACT
Ms. Kristen Lorenz, Director of Admissions, Shepherd University, PO Box 5000, Shepherdstown, WV 25443-5000. *Phone:* 304-876-5212. *Toll-free phone:* 800-344-5231. *Fax:* 304-876-5165. *E-mail:* admission@shepherd.edu.

Strayer University–Teays Valley Campus

Scott Depot, West Virginia
http://www.strayer.edu/west-virginia/teays-valley/

CONTACT
Strayer University–Teays Valley Campus, 3 Corporate Center Drive, Scott Depot, WV 25560. *Toll-free phone:* 888-311-0355.

University of Charleston

Charleston, West Virginia
http://www.ucwv.edu/

- **Independent** comprehensive, founded 1888
- **Small-town** 40-acre campus
- **Coed** 1,831 undergraduate students, 67% full-time, 45% women, 55% men
- **Moderately difficult** entrance level, 64% of applicants were admitted

UNDERGRAD STUDENTS
1,220 full-time, 611 part-time. Students come from 49 states and territories; 42 other countries; 48% are from out of state; 8% Black or African American, non-Hispanic/Latino; 2% Hispanic/Latino; 1% Asian, non-Hispanic/Latino; 0.4% Native Hawaiian or other Pacific Islander, non-Hispanic/Latino; 1% American Indian or Alaska Native, non-Hispanic/Latino; 31% Race/ethnicity unknown; 7% international; 10% transferred in.

Freshmen:
Admission: 2,737 applied, 1,765 admitted, 343 enrolled. *Average high school GPA:* 3.4.
Retention: 61% of full-time freshmen returned.

ACADEMICS
Calendar: semesters. *Degrees:* associate, bachelor's, master's, and doctoral.

Special study options: academic remediation for entering students, accelerated degree program, adult/continuing education programs, advanced placement credit, cooperative education, distance learning, double majors, English as a second language, freshman honors college, honors programs, independent study, internships, off-campus study, part-time degree program, services for LD students, student-designed majors, study abroad, summer session for credit. *ROTC:* Army (b).

Computers: 200 computers/terminals are available on campus for general student use. Students can access the following: campus intranet, computer help desk, free student e-mail accounts, online (class) grades, online (class) registration, online (class) schedules. Campuswide network is available. Wireless service is available via entire campus.
Library: Schoenbaum Library plus 1 other. *Books:* 189,000 (physical), 210,000 (digital/electronic); *Databases:* 56. Students can reserve study rooms.

STUDENT LIFE
Housing options: on-campus residence required through sophomore year; coed, special housing for students with disabilities. Campus housing is university owned. Freshman campus housing is guaranteed.

Activities and organizations: student-run newspaper, choral group, marching band, Student Activities Board, American Society of Interior Designers, Student Government Association, Capito Association of Nursing Students, International Student Organization, national fraternities, national sororities.

Athletics Member NCAA. All Division II. *Intercollegiate sports:* baseball M(s), basketball M(s)/W(s), cheerleading M(s)/W(s), cross-country running M(s)/W(s), football M(s), golf M(s)/W(s), lacrosse W(s), soccer M(s)/W(s), softball W(s), tennis M(s)/W(s), track and field M(s)/W(s), volleyball M(s)/W(s). *Intramural sports:* basketball M/W, bowling M/W, football M/W, tennis M/W, volleyball M/W, water polo M/W.

Campus security: 24-hour emergency response devices and patrols, student patrols, late-night transport/escort service, controlled dormitory access, radio connection to city police and ambulance.

Student services: health clinic, personal/psychological counseling.

COSTS & FINANCIAL AID
Costs (2018–19) *Comprehensive fee:* $40,080 includes full-time tuition ($29,900), mandatory fees ($1000), and room and board ($9180). Full-time tuition and fees vary according to location and program. Part-time tuition: $380 per credit hour. Part-time tuition and fees vary according to course load, location, and program. *College room only:* $5000. Room and board charges vary according to board plan, housing facility, and location. *Payment plan:* installment. *Waivers:* children of alumni, senior citizens, and employees or children of employees.

Financial Aid Of all full-time matriculated undergraduates who enrolled in 2015, 1,162 applied for aid, 1,083 were judged to have need, 197 had their need fully met. In 2015, 85 non-need-based awards were made. *Average percent of need met:* 52. *Average financial aid package:* $19,719. *Average need-based loan:* $5500. *Average need-based gift aid:* $5025. *Average non-need-based aid:* $10,250. *Financial aid deadline:* 8/15.

APPLYING
Options: electronic application, early admission, deferred entrance.
Application fee: $25.
Required: high school transcript, minimum 2.3 GPA. *Required for some:* interview. *Recommended:* essay or personal statement.
Application deadlines: rolling (freshmen), rolling (transfers).
Notification: continuous (freshmen), continuous (transfers).

CONTACT
Sandy Dolin, Application Coordinator, University of Charleston, 2300 MacCorkle Avenue, SE, Charleston, WV 25304. *Phone:* 304-357-4752. *Toll-free phone:* 800-995-GOUC. *E-mail:* admissions@ucwv.edu.

West Liberty University
West Liberty, West Virginia
http://www.westliberty.edu/
CONTACT
Ms. Stephanie North, Admissions Counselor, West Liberty University, 208 University Drive, West Liberty, WV 26074. *Phone:* 304-336-8078. *Toll-free phone:* 800-732-6204 (in-state); 866-WESTLIB (out-of-state). *Fax:* 304-336-8403. *E-mail:* wladmsn1@westliberty.edu.

West Virginia State University
Institute, West Virginia
http://www.wvstateu.edu/
- **State-supported** comprehensive, founded 1891, part of West Virginia four-year public higher education system
- **Small-town** 98-acre campus
- **Endowment** $7.0 million
- **Coed** 3,755 undergraduate students, 48% full-time, 58% women, 42% men
- **Minimally difficult** entrance level, 98% of applicants were admitted

UNDERGRAD STUDENTS
1,786 full-time, 1,969 part-time. Students come from 25 states and territories; 13 other countries; 15% are from out of state; 16% Black or African American, non-Hispanic/Latino; 2% Hispanic/Latino; 0.3% Asian, non-Hispanic/Latino; 0.1% Native Hawaiian or other Pacific Islander, non-Hispanic/Latino; 6% American Indian or Alaska Native, non-Hispanic/Latino; 11% Two or more races, non-Hispanic/Latino; 4% Race/ethnicity unknown; 1% international; 6% transferred in; 17% live on campus.

Freshmen:
Admission: 3,182 applied, 3,105 admitted, 394 enrolled. *Average high school GPA:* 3.1. *Test scores:* ACT scores over 18: 70%; ACT scores over 24: 14%; ACT scores over 30: 1%.
Retention: 59% of full-time freshmen returned.

FACULTY
Total: 193, 55% full-time, 48% with terminal degrees.
Student/faculty ratio: 13:1.

ACADEMICS
Calendar: semesters. *Degrees:* bachelor's, master's, and postbachelor's certificates.

Special study options: academic remediation for entering students, accelerated degree program, adult/continuing education programs, advanced placement credit, cooperative education, double majors, external degree program, honors programs, internships, part-time degree program, services for LD students, summer session for credit. *ROTC:* Army (b).

Computers: 625 computers/terminals and 5,500 ports are available on campus for general student use. Students can access the following: campus intranet, computer help desk, free student e-mail accounts, online (class) grades, online (class) registration, online (class) schedules. Campuswide network is available. 100% of college-owned or -operated housing units are wired for high-speed Internet access. Wireless service is available via entire campus.
Library: Drain-Jordan Library. *Books:* 135,848 (physical), 25,361 (digital/electronic); *Serial titles:* 1,454 (physical), 33,375 (digital/electronic); *Databases:* 28. Weekly public service hours: 82.

STUDENT LIFE
Housing options: on-campus residence required through sophomore year; coed, special housing for students with disabilities. Campus housing is university owned.

Activities and organizations: student-run newspaper, radio station, choral group, marching band, Student Social Work Organization 20, WVSU College Chapter - NAACP 17, CHOICES Peer Educators 13, WVSU International Student Services 13, C.E. Jones Historical Society 12, national fraternities, national sororities.

Athletics Member NCAA. All Division II. *Intercollegiate sports:* baseball M(s), basketball M(s)/W(s), cross-country running W(s), football M(s), golf M(s), softball W(s), tennis M(s)/W(s), volleyball W(s).

Intramural sports: baseball M, basketball M/W, cheerleading W, cross-country running W, football M, golf M, softball W, tennis M/W, volleyball W.

Campus security: 24-hour emergency response devices and patrols, student patrols, controlled dormitory access.

Student services: health clinic, personal/psychological counseling.

COSTS & FINANCIAL AID
Costs (2018–19) *Tuition:* state resident $7667 full-time; nonresident $15,572 full-time. Full-time tuition and fees vary according to course load, program, and reciprocity agreements. Part-time tuition and fees vary according to course load, program, and reciprocity agreements. *Required fees:* $500 full-time. *Room and board:* $11,892. Room and board charges vary according to board plan and housing facility. *Payment plan:* installment.

Financial Aid *Financial aid deadline:* 6/15.

APPLYING
Standardized Tests *Required:* SAT or ACT (for admission).

Options: electronic application.

Application fee: $20.

Required: high school transcript, minimum 2.0 GPA, minimum ACT composite score of 18 (870 SAT).

Application deadlines: 8/17 (freshmen), 8/10 (transfers).

Notification: continuous (freshmen), continuous (out-of-state freshmen), continuous (transfers).

CONTACT
Jameelah Means, Interim Director of Admissions, West Virginia State University, PO Box 1000, Ferrell Hall, Room 106, Institute, WV 25112-1000. *Phone:* 304-204-4340. *Toll-free phone:* 800-987-2112. *Fax:* 304-766-5182. *E-mail:* jmeans9@wvstateu.edu.

West Virginia University
Morgantown, West Virginia
http://www.wvu.edu/

- **State-supported** university, founded 1867, part of West Virginia Higher Education Policy Commission
- **Small-town** 1892-acre campus with easy access to Pittsburgh
- **Endowment** $574.9 million
- **Coed** 22,504 undergraduate students, 92% full-time, 47% women, 53% men
- **Moderately difficult** entrance level, 72% of applicants were admitted

UNDERGRAD STUDENTS
20,713 full-time, 1,791 part-time. Students come from 52 states and territories; 84 other countries; 43% are from out of state; 4% Black or African American, non-Hispanic/Latino; 4% Hispanic/Latino; 2% Asian, non-Hispanic/Latino; 0.1% Native Hawaiian or other Pacific Islander, non-Hispanic/Latino; 0.1% American Indian or Alaska Native, non-Hispanic/Latino; 4% Two or more races, non-Hispanic/Latino; 0.3% Race/ethnicity unknown; 7% international; 4% transferred in; 15% live on campus.

Freshmen:
Admission: 20,594 applied, 14,807 admitted, 5,225 enrolled. *Average high school GPA:* 3.5. *Test scores:* ACT scores over 18: 92%; ACT scores over 24: 43%; ACT scores over 30: 7%.

Retention: 80% of full-time freshmen returned.

FACULTY
Total: 1,486, 77% full-time, 67% with terminal degrees.
Student/faculty ratio: 20:1.

ACADEMICS
Calendar: semesters. *Degrees:* bachelor's, master's, and doctoral.

Special study options: academic remediation for entering students, accelerated degree program, adult/continuing education programs, advanced placement credit, distance learning, double majors, English as a second language, external degree program, honors programs, independent study, internships, off-campus study, part-time degree program, services for LD students, student-designed majors, study abroad, summer session for credit. *ROTC:* Army (b), Air Force (b).

Unusual degree programs: 3-2 education, business/foreign language, occupational therapy, physical therapy, social work.

Computers: 1,800 computers/terminals and 900 ports are available on campus for general student use. Students can access the following: campus intranet, computer help desk, free student e-mail accounts, online (class) grades, online (class) registration, online (class) schedules. Campuswide network is available. 100% of college-owned or -operated housing units are wired for high-speed Internet access. Wireless service is available via entire campus.

Library: Downtown Library Complex plus 5 others. *Books:* 1.1 million (physical), 621,166 (digital/electronic); *Serial titles:* 56,340 (physical), 96,553 (digital/electronic); *Databases:* 975. Study areas open 24 hours, 5–7 days a week; students can reserve study rooms.

STUDENT LIFE
Housing options: on-campus residence required for freshman year; coed, men-only, women-only, cooperative, special housing for students with disabilities. Campus housing is university owned and leased by the school. Freshman campus housing is guaranteed.

Activities and organizations: drama/theater group, student-run newspaper, radio station, choral group, marching band, Residential Hall Association, Alpha Phi Omega, WVU Greek System, Mountaineer Maniacs, Campus Crusade for Christ, national fraternities, national sororities.

Athletics Member NCAA. All Division I except football (Division I-A). *Intercollegiate sports:* baseball M(s), basketball M(s)/W(s), crew W(s), cross-country running W(s), golf M(s), gymnastics W(s), riflery M(s)/W(s), soccer M(s)/W(s), swimming and diving M(s)/W(s), tennis W(s), track and field W(s), volleyball W(s), wrestling M(s). *Intramural sports:* archery M(c)/W(c), baseball M(c), basketball M(c)/W(c), bowling M(c)/W(c), cheerleading M(c)/W(c), crew M(c)/W(c), cross-country running M(c)/W(c), equestrian sports M(c)/W(c), fencing M(c)/W(c), field hockey M(c)/W(c), football M, golf M(c), ice hockey M(c), lacrosse M(c)/W(c), racquetball M(c)/W(c), riflery M(c)/W(c), rock climbing M(c)/W(c), rugby M(c)/W(c), skiing (cross-country) M(c)/W(c), skiing (downhill) M(c)/W(c), soccer M(c)/W(c), softball M(c)/W(c), swimming and diving M(c)/W(c), table tennis M(c)/W(c), tennis M(c)/W(c), track and field M(c)/W(c), ultimate Frisbee M(c)/W(c), volleyball M(c)/W(c), weight lifting M(c), wrestling M(c).

Campus security: 24-hour emergency response devices and patrols, student patrols, late-night transport/escort service, controlled dormitory access, patrol officers just for housing.

Student services: health clinic, personal/psychological counseling, women's center, legal services.

COSTS & FINANCIAL AID
Costs (2017–18) *Tuition:* state resident $8376 full-time, $349 per credit hour part-time; nonresident $23,616 full-time, $984 per credit hour part-time. Full-time tuition and fees vary according to location, program, and reciprocity agreements. Part-time tuition and fees vary according to course load, location, program, and reciprocity agreements. *Room and board:* $10,576. Room and board charges vary according to board plan, housing facility, and location. *Payment plan:* installment. *Waivers:* senior citizens and employees or children of employees.

Financial Aid Of all full-time matriculated undergraduates who enrolled in 2016, 16,234 applied for aid, 10,513 were judged to have need, 605 had their need fully met. In 2016, 2582 non-need-based awards were made. *Average financial aid package:* $7292. *Average need-based loan:* $4290. *Average need-based gift aid:* $5212. *Average non-need-based aid:* $3127. *Average indebtedness upon graduation:* $29,358. *Financial aid deadline:* 3/1.

APPLYING
Standardized Tests *Required:* SAT or ACT (for admission).

Options: electronic application.

Application fee: $45.

Required: high school transcript, minimum 2.0 GPA. *Required for some:* essay or personal statement, minimum 2.3 GPA.

Application deadlines: 8/1 (freshmen), 8/1 (transfers).

Notification: continuous (transfers).

CONTACT
Ms. Marilyn Potts, Director of Admissions, West Virginia University, PO Box 6009, Morgantown, WV 26506-6009. *Phone:* 304-293-2121. *Toll-*

A ⭐ *indicates that the school has detailed information with a Premium Profile on Petersons.com.*

free phone: 800-344-9881. *Fax:* 304-293-3080. *E-mail:* marilyn.potts@
mail.wvu.edu.

West Virginia University at Parkersburg

Parkersburg, West Virginia
http://www.wvup.edu/

CONTACT
Christine Post, Associate Dean of Enrollment Management, West Virginia
University at Parkersburg, 300 Campus Drive, Parkersburg, WV 26104.
Phone: 304-424-8223 Ext. 223. *Toll-free phone:* 800-WVA-WVUP. *Fax:*
304-424-8332. *E-mail:* christine.post@mail.wvu.edu.

West Virginia University Institute of Technology

Beckley, West Virginia
http://www.wvutech.edu/

- **State-supported** 4-year, founded 1895
- **Small-town** 114-acre campus
- **Endowment** $532.6 million
- **Coed** 1,623 undergraduate students, 68% full-time, 44% women, 56%
  men
- **Minimally difficult** entrance level, 53% of applicants were admitted

UNDERGRAD STUDENTS
1,111 full-time, 512 part-time. Students come from 33 states and
territories; 30 other countries; 12% are from out of state; 6% Black or
African American, non-Hispanic/Latino; 3% Hispanic/Latino; 1% Asian,
non-Hispanic/Latino; 0.2% American Indian or Alaska Native, non-
Hispanic/Latino; 4% Two or more races, non-Hispanic/Latino; 3%
Race/ethnicity unknown; 6% international; 9% transferred in; 35% live on
campus.

Freshmen:
Admission: 1,597 applied, 845 admitted, 351 enrolled. *Average high
school GPA:* 3.4. *Test scores:* ACT scores over 18: 71%; ACT scores over
24: 19%; ACT scores over 30: 1%.
Retention: 63% of full-time freshmen returned.

FACULTY
Total: 117, 78% full-time, 56% with terminal degrees.
Student/faculty ratio: 13:1.

ACADEMICS
Calendar: semesters. *Degrees:* bachelor's and postbachelor's certificates.
Special study options: academic remediation for entering students,
advanced placement credit, cooperative education, distance learning,
double majors, independent study, internships, part-time degree program,
services for LD students, student-designed majors, study abroad, summer
session for credit. *ROTC:* Army (b).
Unusual degree programs: 3-2 teacher education with West Virginia
University.
Computers: 200 computers/terminals are available on campus for general
student use. Students can access the following: computer help desk, free
student e-mail accounts, online (class) grades, online (class) registration,
online (class) schedules, electronic course materials. Campuswide
network is available. 100% of college-owned or -operated housing units
are wired for high-speed Internet access. Wireless service is available via
classrooms, computer centers, computer labs, dorm rooms, learning
centers, libraries, student centers.
Library: Vining Library plus 1 other. *Books:* 147,685 (physical), 11
(digital/electronic); *Serial titles:* 16,253 (physical). Students can reserve
study rooms.

STUDENT LIFE
Housing options: on-campus residence required through sophomore year;
coed. Campus housing is university owned. Freshman campus housing is
guaranteed.
Activities and organizations: drama/theater group, student-run
newspaper, Christian Student Union, Student Activities Board, Alpha Phi

Omega, Student Government Association, American Society of
Mechanical Engineers, national fraternities, national sororities.
Athletics Member NAIA, USCAA. *Intercollegiate sports:* baseball M(s),
basketball M(s)/W(s), cross-country running M(s)/W(s), golf M(s), soccer
M(s)/W(s), softball W(s), swimming and diving M(s)/W(s), volleyball
W(s), wrestling M(s). *Intramural sports:* badminton M(c)/W(c),
basketball M(c)/W(c), cheerleading M(c)/W(c), soccer M(c)/W(c),
ultimate Frisbee M(c)/W(c), volleyball M(c)/W(c).
Campus security: 24-hour emergency response devices and patrols.
Student services: health clinic, personal/psychological counseling.

COSTS & FINANCIAL AID
Costs (2017–18) *Tuition:* state resident $6960 full-time, $290 per credit
hour part-time; nonresident $17,544 full-time, $731 per credit hour part-
time. Full-time tuition and fees vary according to program. Part-time
tuition and fees vary according to course load and program. *Room and
board:* $11,304. Room and board charges vary according to board plan
and housing facility. *Payment plan:* installment. *Waivers:* senior citizens.
Financial Aid Of all full-time matriculated undergraduates who enrolled
in 2016, 820 applied for aid, 619 were judged to have need, 46 had their
need fully met. In 2016, 73 non-need-based awards were made. *Average
financial aid package:* $8238. *Average need-based loan:* $5848. *Average
need-based gift aid:* $5793. *Average non-need-based aid:* $3454.
Average indebtedness upon graduation: $25,155.

APPLYING
Standardized Tests *Required:* SAT or ACT (for admission). *Required for
some:* TOEFL or IELTS.
Options: electronic application, early admission.
Required: high school transcript, minimum 2.0 GPA, minimum ACT
composite score of 18 or 870 SAT math and verbal or minimum 3.0 high
school GPA.
Application deadlines: rolling (freshmen), rolling (out-of-state
freshmen), rolling (transfers).
Notification: continuous until 8/15 (freshmen), continuous (out-of-state
freshmen), continuous until 8/15 (transfers).

CONTACT
William Allen Jr., Dean of Enrollment Services, West Virginia University
Institute of Technology, Old Main Box 80, 405 Fayette Pike,
Montgomery, WV 25136. *Phone:* 304-442-3146. *Toll-free phone:* 888-
554-8324. *Fax:* 304-442-3067. *E-mail:* tech-admissions@mail.wvu.edu.

West Virginia Wesleyan College

Buckhannon, West Virginia
http://www.wvwc.edu/

- **Independent** comprehensive, founded 1890, affiliated with United
  Methodist Church
- **Small-town** 180-acre campus
- **Endowment** $47.4 million
- **Coed** 1,320 undergraduate students, 98% full-time, 56% women, 44%
  men
- **Moderately difficult** entrance level, 71% of applicants were admitted

UNDERGRAD STUDENTS
1,289 full-time, 31 part-time. Students come from 37 states and territories;
27 other countries; 38% are from out of state; 9% Black or African
American, non-Hispanic/Latino; 3% Hispanic/Latino; 0.2% Asian, non-
Hispanic/Latino; 0.1% Native Hawaiian or other Pacific Islander, non-
Hispanic/Latino; 0.4% American Indian or Alaska Native, non-
Hispanic/Latino; 4% Two or more races, non-Hispanic/Latino; 0.5%
Race/ethnicity unknown; 6% international; 3% transferred in; 76% live on
campus.

Freshmen:
Admission: 2,278 applied, 1,607 admitted, 366 enrolled. *Average high
school GPA:* 3.5. *Test scores:* SAT evidence-based reading and writing
scores over 500: 62%; SAT math scores over 500: 74%; ACT scores over
18: 86%; SAT evidence-based reading and writing scores over 600: 22%;
SAT math scores over 600: 16%; ACT scores over 24: 38%; SAT
evidence-based reading and writing scores over 700: 1%; SAT math
scores over 700: 2%; ACT scores over 30: 6%.
Retention: 74% of full-time freshmen returned.

FACULTY
Total: 150, 55% full-time, 48% with terminal degrees.
Student/faculty ratio: 13:1.

ACADEMICS
Calendar: semesters. *Degrees:* bachelor's, master's, post-master's, and postbachelor's certificates.

Special study options: academic remediation for entering students, advanced placement credit, distance learning, double majors, English as a second language, honors programs, independent study, internships, off-campus study, part-time degree program, services for LD students, student-designed majors, study abroad, summer session for credit.

Unusual degree programs: 3-2 engineering with University of Virginia, West Virginia University, Virginia Polytechnic Institute and State University.

Computers: Students can access the following: campus intranet, computer help desk, free student e-mail accounts, online (class) grades, online (class) registration, online (class) schedules. Campuswide network is available. 100% of college-owned or -operated housing units are wired for high-speed Internet access. Wireless service is available via entire campus.

Library: Annie Merner Pfeifer Library plus 1 other. *Books:* 122,495 (physical), 271,641 (digital/electronic); *Serial titles:* 11,057 (physical), 112,139 (digital/electronic); *Databases:* 110. Students can reserve study rooms.

STUDENT LIFE
Housing options: on-campus residence required through senior year; coed, men-only, women-only, special housing for students with disabilities. Campus housing is university owned. Freshman campus housing is guaranteed.

Activities and organizations: drama/theater group, student-run newspaper, radio station, choral group, marching band, Campus Activities Board, Green Club, WE LEAD, Wesleyan Ambassadors, Enactus, national fraternities, national sororities.

Athletics Member NCAA. All Division II. *Intercollegiate sports:* baseball M(s), basketball M(s)/W(s), cheerleading M/W, cross-country running M(s)/W(s), football M(s), golf M(s)/W(s), lacrosse M(c)/W(s), skiing (downhill) M(c)/W(c), soccer M(s)/W(s), softball W(s), swimming and diving M(s)/W(s), tennis M(s)/W(s), track and field M(s)/W(s), volleyball W(s). *Intramural sports:* basketball M/W, bowling M/W, football M/W, golf M/W, racquetball M/W, soccer M/W, softball M/W, table tennis M/W, volleyball M/W, water polo M/W.

Campus security: 24-hour emergency response devices and patrols, student patrols, late-night transport/escort service, controlled dormitory access.

Student services: health clinic, personal/psychological counseling.

COSTS & FINANCIAL AID
Costs (2018–19) *Comprehensive fee:* $40,496 includes full-time tuition ($30,462), mandatory fees ($1178), and room and board ($8856). Full-time tuition and fees vary according to course load and student level. Part-time tuition and fees vary according to course load. *College room only:* $4326. Room and board charges vary according to housing facility. *Payment plan:* installment. *Waivers:* employees or children of employees.

Financial Aid Of all full-time matriculated undergraduates who enrolled in 2017, 1,141 applied for aid, 1,031 were judged to have need, 250 had their need fully met. In 2017, 258 non-need-based awards were made. *Average percent of need met:* 80. *Average financial aid package:* $25,260. *Average need-based loan:* $4225. *Average need-based gift aid:* $28,139. *Average non-need-based aid:* $17,879. *Average indebtedness upon graduation:* $31,996.

APPLYING
Standardized Tests *Required:* SAT or ACT (for admission). *Required for some:* SAT Subject Tests (for admission).

Options: electronic application, deferred entrance.

Application fee: $35.

Required: high school transcript. *Required for some:* letters of recommendation. *Recommended:* essay or personal statement, interview.

Notification: continuous (freshmen), continuous (transfers).

CONTACT
John Waltz, Vice President for Enrollment Management, West Virginia Wesleyan College, 59 College Avenue, Buckhannon, WV 26201. *Phone:* 304-473-8510. *Toll-free phone:* 800-722-9933. *Fax:* 304-473-8108. *E-mail:* admission@wvwc.edu.

See below for display ad and page 1500 for the College Close-Up.

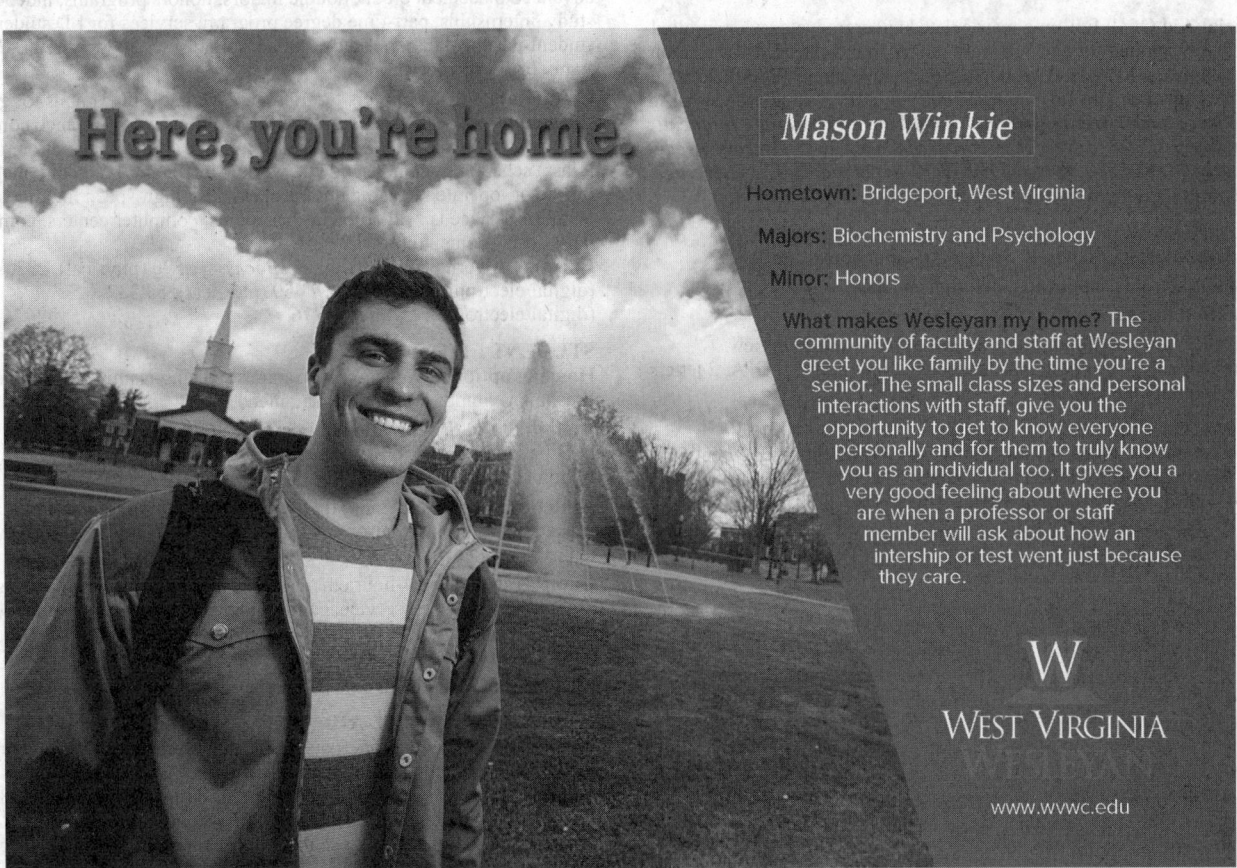

Here, you're home.

Mason Winkie

Hometown: Bridgeport, West Virginia

Majors: Biochemistry and Psychology

Minor: Honors

What makes Wesleyan my home? The community of faculty and staff at Wesleyan greet you like family by the time you're a senior. The small class sizes and personal interactions with staff, give you the opportunity to get to know everyone personally and for them to truly know you as an individual too. It gives you a very good feeling about where you are when a professor or staff member will ask about how an intership or test went just because they care.

W
WEST VIRGINIA
www.wvwc.edu

Wheeling Jesuit University

Wheeling, West Virginia
http://www.wju.edu/

- **Independent Roman Catholic (Jesuit)** comprehensive, founded 1954
- **Suburban** 65-acre campus with easy access to Pittsburgh
- **Endowment** $12.5 million
- **Coed**
- **Moderately difficult** entrance level

FACULTY
Student/faculty ratio: 10:1.

ACADEMICS
Calendar: semesters. *Degrees:* bachelor's, master's, doctoral, post-master's, and postbachelor's certificates.
Library: Bishop Hodges Library. *Books:* 134,540 (physical), 165,927 (digital/electronic); *Serial titles:* 107 (physical), 42 (digital/electronic); *Databases:* 69. Weekly public service hours: 85; students can reserve study rooms.

STUDENT LIFE
Housing options: on-campus residence required through sophomore year; coed, women-only, special housing for students with disabilities. Campus housing is university owned and is provided by a third party. Freshman campus housing is guaranteed.

Activities and organizations: drama/theater group, student-run newspaper, choral group, Campus Activity Board (CAB), Theater Guild, Student Senate, International Student Club, Campus Ministry.

Athletics Member NCAA. All Division II except rugby (Division I).

Campus security: 24-hour patrols, late-night transport/escort service, controlled dormitory access, cameras at residence hall entrances.

Student services: health clinic, personal/psychological counseling.

COSTS & FINANCIAL AID
Costs (2017–18) *Comprehensive fee:* $37,106 includes full-time tuition ($27,000), mandatory fees ($1110), and room and board ($8996). Part-time tuition: $735 per credit hour. *College room only:* $5006. Room and board charges vary according to board plan, housing facility, and student level.

Financial Aid Of all full-time matriculated undergraduates who enrolled in 2017, 589 applied for aid, 518 were judged to have need, 148 had their need fully met. 140 Federal Work-Study jobs (averaging $2800). 25 state and other part-time jobs (averaging $2800). In 2017, 143 non-need-based awards were made. *Average percent of need met:* 85. *Average financial aid package:* $27,281. *Average need-based loan:* $4645. *Average need-based gift aid:* $10,589. *Average non-need-based aid:* $12,711. *Average indebtedness upon graduation:* $32,428. *Financial aid deadline:* 8/1.

APPLYING
Standardized Tests *Required:* SAT or ACT (for admission).

Options: electronic application, deferred entrance.

Application fee: $25.

Required: high school transcript. *Required for some:* interview.
Recommended: essay or personal statement, minimum 3.0 GPA, 2 letters of recommendation, interview.

CONTACT
Mr. Christopher Rouhier, Senior Admissions Representative, Wheeling Jesuit University, 316 Washington Avenue, Wheeling, WV 26003. *Phone:* 304-243-2106. *Toll-free phone:* 800-624-6992 Ext. 2359. *Fax:* 304-243-2397. *E-mail:* crouhier@wju.edu.

WISCONSIN

Alverno College

Milwaukee, Wisconsin
http://www.alverno.edu/

- **Independent Roman Catholic** comprehensive, founded 1887
- **Urban** 46-acre campus
- **Endowment** $27.7 million
- **Undergraduate: women only; graduate: coed** 1,312 undergraduate students, 79% full-time, 100% women, 0% men
- **Moderately difficult** entrance level, 78% of applicants were admitted

UNDERGRAD STUDENTS
1,036 full-time, 276 part-time. Students come from 17 states and territories; 5 other countries; 7% are from out of state; 13% Black or African American, non-Hispanic/Latino; 27% Hispanic/Latino; 6% Asian, non-Hispanic/Latino; 0.1% Native Hawaiian or other Pacific Islander, non-Hispanic/Latino; 0.5% American Indian or Alaska Native, non-Hispanic/Latino; 4% Two or more races, non-Hispanic/Latino; 0.5% international; 10% transferred in; 16% live on campus.

Freshmen:
Admission: 610 applied, 475 admitted, 198 enrolled. *Average high school GPA:* 3.0. *Test scores:* ACT scores over 18: 71%; ACT scores over 24: 9%; ACT scores over 30: 2%.
Retention: 71% of full-time freshmen returned.

FACULTY
Total: 211, 41% full-time, 47% with terminal degrees.
Student/faculty ratio: 10:1.

ACADEMICS
Calendar: semesters. *Degrees:* associate, bachelor's, master's, doctoral, post-master's, and postbachelor's certificates (also offers weekend program with significant enrollment not reflected in profile).

Special study options: academic remediation for entering students, accelerated degree program, adult/continuing education programs, advanced placement credit, double majors, honors programs, independent study, internships, part-time degree program, services for LD students, student-designed majors, study abroad, summer session for credit. *ROTC:* Army (c), Air Force (c).

Computers: 706 computers/terminals are available on campus for general student use. Students can access the following: campus intranet, computer help desk, free student e-mail accounts, online (class) registration, online (class) schedules. Campuswide network is available. 100% of college-owned or -operated housing units are wired for high-speed Internet access. Wireless service is available via classrooms, computer centers, computer labs, dorm rooms, libraries.
Library: Alverno College Library. *Books:* 61,590 (physical), 233,437 (digital/electronic); *Serial titles:* 459 (physical), 53,337 (digital/electronic); *Databases:* 76.

STUDENT LIFE
Housing options: women-only. Campus housing is university owned. Freshman campus housing is guaranteed.

Activities and organizations: drama/theater group, student-run newspaper, radio station, choral group, Alverno Cru, CHICA, Love Your Melon Crew, Circle K, Gay-Straight Alliance.

Athletics Member NCAA. All Division III. *Intercollegiate sports:* basketball W, cross-country running W, golf W, soccer W, softball W, tennis W, volleyball W.

Campus security: 24-hour emergency response devices and patrols, late-night transport/escort service, controlled dormitory access, well-lit parking lots and pathways, emergency first-aid and CPR, crisis intervention team and plan in place.

Student services: health clinic, personal/psychological counseling.

COSTS & FINANCIAL AID
Costs (2017–18) *Comprehensive fee:* $36,573 includes full-time tuition ($27,552), mandatory fees ($725), and room and board ($8296). Full-time tuition and fees vary according to program. Part-time tuition: $1148 per credit hour. Part-time tuition and fees vary according to program. *Room and board:* Room and board charges vary according to board plan and

housing facility. *Payment plans:* installment, deferred payment. *Waivers:* employees or children of employees.

Financial Aid Of all full-time matriculated undergraduates who enrolled in 2017, 973 applied for aid, 930 were judged to have need. 263 Federal Work-Study jobs (averaging $2012). In 2017, 86 non-need-based awards were made. *Average financial aid package:* $21,312. *Average need-based loan:* $3847. *Average need-based gift aid:* $12,685. *Average non-need-based aid:* $11,782. *Average indebtedness upon graduation:* $36,659.

APPLYING
Standardized Tests *Required:* SAT or ACT (for admission).
Options: electronic application, deferred entrance.
Required: essay or personal statement, high school transcript, minimum 2.0 college GPA. *Recommended:* minimum 2.0 GPA, interview.
Application deadlines: rolling (freshmen), rolling (transfers).
Notification: continuous (freshmen), continuous (transfers).

CONTACT
Ms. Becky Kurter, Director of Undergraduate Admissions, Alverno College, 3400 South 43 Street, PO Box 343922, Milwaukee, WI 53234-3922. *Phone:* 414-382-6110. *Toll-free phone:* 800-933-3401. *Fax:* 414-382-6055. *E-mail:* admissions@alverno.edu.

Bellin College

Green Bay, Wisconsin
http://www.bellincollege.edu/
- **Independent** comprehensive, founded 1909
- **Small-town** 25-acre campus
- **Coed, primarily women**
- **Moderately difficult** entrance level

FACULTY
Student/faculty ratio: 11:1.

ACADEMICS
Calendar: semesters. *Degrees:* bachelor's and master's.
Library: Phil and Betsy Hendrickson Library. Weekly public service hours: 63; students can reserve study rooms.

STUDENT LIFE
Housing options: college housing not available.
Activities and organizations: Bellin Student Nurses Association, Institute for Healthcare Improvement, American Assembly for Men in Nursing, Student Senate, Bellin College Love Your Melon Campus Crew.
Campus security: 24-hour emergency response devices and patrols, late-night transport/escort service, electronically operated building access after hours.
Student services: health clinic, personal/psychological counseling, legal services.

COSTS & FINANCIAL AID
Costs (2017–18) *Tuition:* $998 per credit hour part-time.
Financial Aid Of all full-time matriculated undergraduates who enrolled in 2012, 122 applied for aid, 117 were judged to have need, 2 had their need fully met. In 2012, 1 non-need-based award were made. *Average percent of need met:* 67. *Average financial aid package:* $21,230. *Average need-based loan:* $4979. *Average need-based gift aid:* $5448. *Average non-need-based aid:* $857. *Average indebtedness upon graduation:* $33,961.

APPLYING
Standardized Tests *Required:* SAT or ACT (for admission).
Options: electronic application.
Required: essay or personal statement, high school transcript, minimum 3.3 GPA, 3 letters of recommendation, interview. *Recommended:* minimum 3.3 GPA.

CONTACT
Kathryn Wall, Director of Enrollment Management, Bellin College, 3201 Eaton Road, Green Bay, WI 54311. *Phone:* 920-433-6651. *Toll-free phone:* 800-236-8707. *E-mail:* admissions@bellincollege.edu.

Beloit College

Beloit, Wisconsin
http://www.beloit.edu/
- **Independent** 4-year, founded 1846
- **Small-town** 84-acre campus with easy access to Chicago, Milwaukee
- **Endowment** $145.3 million
- **Coed** 1,402 undergraduate students, 96% full-time, 53% women, 47% men

UNDERGRAD STUDENTS
1,346 full-time, 56 part-time. Students come from 46 states and territories; 39 other countries; 85% are from out of state; 7% Black or African American, non-Hispanic/Latino; 10% Hispanic/Latino; 3% Asian, non-Hispanic/Latino; 0.3% Native Hawaiian or other Pacific Islander, non-Hispanic/Latino; 0.2% American Indian or Alaska Native, non-Hispanic/Latino; 4% Two or more races, non-Hispanic/Latino; 4% Race/ethnicity unknown; 15% international; 2% transferred in; 88% live on campus.

Freshmen:
Admission: 323 enrolled. *Average high school GPA:* 3.3. *Test scores:* SAT evidence-based reading and writing scores over 500: 79%; SAT math scores over 500: 79%; ACT scores over 18: 99%; SAT evidence-based reading and writing scores over 600: 57%; SAT math scores over 600: 50%; ACT scores over 24: 78%; SAT evidence-based reading and writing scores over 700: 14%; SAT math scores over 700: 7%; ACT scores over 30: 27%.
Retention: 85% of full-time freshmen returned.

FACULTY
Total: 141, 82% full-time, 89% with terminal degrees.
Student/faculty ratio: 11:1.

ACADEMICS
Calendar: semesters. *Degree:* bachelor's.
Special study options: adult/continuing education programs, advanced placement credit, double majors, English as a second language, independent study, internships, off-campus study, services for LD students, student-designed majors, study abroad, summer session for credit.
Unusual degree programs: 3-2 engineering with Columbia University, Rensselaer Polytechnic Institute, Washington University in St. Louis; forestry with Duke University.
Computers: 300 computers/terminals are available on campus for general student use. Students can access the following: campus intranet, computer help desk, free student e-mail accounts, online (class) grades, online (class) registration, online (class) schedules. Campuswide network is available. 100% of college-owned or -operated housing units are wired for high-speed Internet access. Wireless service is available via entire campus.
Library: Morse Library and Black Information Center. *Books:* 207,000 (physical), 210,000 (digital/electronic); *Serial titles:* 11,700 (physical), 76,000 (digital/electronic); *Databases:* 151. Weekly public service hours: 109; students can reserve study rooms.

STUDENT LIFE
Housing options: on-campus residence required through junior year; coed, women-only, cooperative. Campus housing is university owned. Freshman campus housing is guaranteed.
Activities and organizations: drama/theater group, student-run newspaper, radio and television station, choral group, BSFFA - Beloit Science Fiction and Fantasy Association, Ceramics Club, Anthropology Club, Yoga Club, Outdoor Environmental Club, national fraternities, national sororities.
Athletics Member NCAA. All Division III. *Intercollegiate sports:* baseball M, basketball M/W, cross-country running M/W, football M, ice hockey M(c)/W(c), lacrosse M/W, soccer M/W, softball W, swimming and diving M/W, tennis W, track and field M/W, volleyball W. *Intramural sports:* archery M(c)/W(c), badminton M/W, basketball M/W, fencing M(c)/W(c), football M, golf M(c)/W(c), racquetball M/W, sailing M(c)/W(c), skiing (downhill) M(c)/W(c), soccer M/W, ultimate Frisbee M/W, volleyball M/W.
Campus security: 24-hour emergency response devices and patrols, late-night transport/escort service, controlled dormitory access.

Student services: health clinic, personal/psychological counseling, women's center.

COSTS & FINANCIAL AID

Costs (2018–19) *Comprehensive fee:* $58,870 includes full-time tuition ($49,564), mandatory fees ($476), and room and board ($8830). Part-time tuition: $1549 per credit hour. *College room only:* $5030. Room and board charges vary according to board plan. *Payment plan:* installment. *Waivers:* employees or children of employees.

Financial Aid Of all full-time matriculated undergraduates who enrolled in 2016, 925 applied for aid, 830 were judged to have need, 280 had their need fully met. In 2016, 450 non-need-based awards were made. *Average percent of need met:* 94. *Average financial aid package:* $39,976. *Average need-based loan:* $6497. *Average need-based gift aid:* $30,133. *Average non-need-based aid:* $22,962. *Average indebtedness upon graduation:* $31,308. *Financial aid deadline:* 3/1.

APPLYING

Standardized Tests *Required for some:* SAT or ACT (for admission).

Required: essay or personal statement, high school transcript, 1 letter of recommendation. *Recommended:* interview.

CONTACT

Mr. William Mortimer, Director of Enrollment, Beloit College, 700 College Street, Beloit, WI 53511-5596. *Phone:* 608-561-9724. *Toll-free phone:* 800-9-BELOIT. *Fax:* 608-363-2179. *E-mail:* mortimerwr@beloit.edu.

Broadview University–Madison

Madison, Wisconsin

http://www.broadviewuniversity.edu/

CONTACT

Broadview University–Madison, 4901 Eastpark Boulevard, Madison, WI 53718.

Bryant & Stratton College–Bayshore Campus

Glendale, Wisconsin

http://www.bryantstratton.edu/

CONTACT

Bryant & Stratton College–Bayshore Campus, 500 West Silver Spring Drive, Bayshore Town Center, Suite K340, Glendale, WI 53217.

Bryant & Stratton College–Milwaukee Campus

Milwaukee, Wisconsin

http://www.bryantstratton.edu/

CONTACT

Mr. Dan Basile, Director of Admissions, Bryant & Stratton College–Milwaukee Campus, 310 West Wisconsin Avenue, Suite 500 East, Milwaukee, WI 53203-2214. *Phone:* 414-276-5200.

Bryant & Stratton College–Wauwatosa Campus

Wauwatosa, Wisconsin

http://www.bryantstratton.edu/

CONTACT

Bryant & Stratton College–Wauwatosa Campus, 10950 West Potter Road, Wauwatosa, WI 53226. *Phone:* 414-302-7000 Ext. 502.

Cardinal Stritch University

Milwaukee, Wisconsin

http://www.stritch.edu/

- **Independent Roman Catholic** university, founded 1937
- **Suburban** 40-acre campus with easy access to Milwaukee
- **Endowment** $19.4 million
- **Coed** 1,543 undergraduate students, 58% full-time, 68% women, 32% men
- **Moderately difficult** entrance level, 78% of applicants were admitted

UNDERGRAD STUDENTS

901 full-time, 642 part-time. Students come from 27 states and territories; 39 other countries; 13% are from out of state; 16% Black or African American, non-Hispanic/Latino; 16% Hispanic/Latino; 2% Asian, non-Hispanic/Latino; 0.1% Native Hawaiian or other Pacific Islander, non-Hispanic/Latino; 0.5% American Indian or Alaska Native, non-Hispanic/Latino; 2% Two or more races, non-Hispanic/Latino; 16% Race/ethnicity unknown; 11% international; 12% transferred in; 10% live on campus.

Freshmen:
Admission: 642 applied, 503 admitted, 141 enrolled. *Average high school GPA:* 3.2. *Test scores:* SAT evidence-based reading and writing scores over 500: 44%; SAT math scores over 500: 56%; ACT scores over 18: 87%; SAT evidence-based reading and writing scores over 600: 13%; SAT math scores over 600: 25%; ACT scores over 24: 17%; ACT scores over 30: 1%.

Retention: 77% of full-time freshmen returned.

FACULTY

Total: 311, 27% full-time.

Student/faculty ratio: 10:1.

ACADEMICS

Calendar: semesters. *Degrees:* certificates, associate, bachelor's, master's, doctoral, post-master's, and postbachelor's certificates.

Special study options: academic remediation for entering students, accelerated degree program, adult/continuing education programs, advanced placement credit, cooperative education, distance learning, double majors, independent study, internships, off-campus study, part-time degree program, services for LD students, study abroad, summer session for credit.

Computers: 458 computers/terminals and 1,283 ports are available on campus for general student use. Students can access the following: computer help desk, free student e-mail accounts, online (class) grades, online (class) registration, online (class) schedules. Campuswide network is available. 100% of college-owned or -operated housing units are wired for high-speed Internet access. Wireless service is available via entire campus.

Library: Cardinal Stritch University Library. *Books:* 122,184 (physical), 146,127 (digital/electronic); *Serial titles:* 66 (physical), 68 (digital/electronic); *Databases:* 71. Weekly public service hours: 90.

STUDENT LIFE

Housing options: on-campus residence required for freshman year; coed. Campus housing is university owned and leased by the school. Freshman campus housing is guaranteed.

Activities and organizations: drama/theater group, choral group, Student Government, Student Programming Board, Hispanic Club, University Ministry, Circle K International, national fraternities.

Athletics Member NAIA. *Intercollegiate sports:* basketball M(s)/W(s), cross-country running M(s)/W(s), golf M(s)/W(s), soccer M(s)/W(s), softball W(s), tennis M(s)/W(s), track and field M(s)/W(s), volleyball M(s)/W(s).

Campus security: 24-hour emergency response devices and patrols, controlled dormitory access.

Student services: health clinic, personal/psychological counseling.

COSTS & FINANCIAL AID

Costs (2017–18) *Comprehensive fee:* $36,962 includes full-time tuition ($28,844) and room and board ($8118). Full-time tuition and fees vary according to degree level, program, and reciprocity agreements. Part-time tuition: $900 per credit hour. Part-time tuition and fees vary according to course load, degree level, program, and reciprocity agreements. *Room* *and board:* Room and board charges vary according to board plan and housing facility. *Payment plan:* installment. *Waivers:* employees or children of employees.

Financial Aid Of all full-time matriculated undergraduates who enrolled in 2017, 693 applied for aid, 623 were judged to have need, 63 had their need fully met. 397 Federal Work-Study jobs (averaging $2093). In 2017, 241 non-need-based awards were made. *Average percent of need met:* 70. *Average financial aid package:* $23,056. *Average need-based loan:* $4046. *Average need-based gift aid:* $18,528. *Average non-need-based aid:* $18,306. *Average indebtedness upon graduation:* $31,526.

APPLYING
Standardized Tests *Required for some:* SAT or ACT (for admission), TOEFL for international students.

Options: electronic application, deferred entrance.

Required for some: high school transcript, minimum 2.0 GPA.

Application deadlines: rolling (freshmen), rolling (transfers).

Notification: continuous (freshmen), continuous (transfers).

CONTACT
Mary-Grace Linse, Associate Director of Undergraduate Admissions, Cardinal Stritch University, 6801 N. Yates Road, Milwaukee, WI 53217. *Phone:* 414-410-4052. *Toll-free phone:* 800-347-8822 Ext. 4040. *Fax:* 414-410-4058. *E-mail:* admissions@stritch.edu.

Carroll University
Waukesha, Wisconsin
http://www.carrollu.edu/

- **Independent Presbyterian** comprehensive, founded 1846
- **Suburban** 136-acre campus with easy access to Milwaukee
- **Endowment** $57.5 million
- **Coed** 2,981 undergraduate students, 92% full-time, 64% women, 36% men
- **Moderately difficult** entrance level, 71% of applicants were admitted

UNDERGRAD STUDENTS
2,736 full-time, 245 part-time. Students come from 30 states and territories; 38 other countries; 31% are from out of state; 2% Black or African American, non-Hispanic/Latino; 8% Hispanic/Latino; 4% Asian, non-Hispanic/Latino; 0.1% Native Hawaiian or other Pacific Islander, non-Hispanic/Latino; 0.3% American Indian or Alaska Native, non-Hispanic/Latino; 3% Two or more races, non-Hispanic/Latino; 2% Race/ethnicity unknown; 3% international; 3% transferred in; 59% live on campus.

Freshmen:
Admission: 3,688 applied, 2,612 admitted, 724 enrolled. *Test scores:* ACT scores over 18: 98%; ACT scores over 24: 51%; ACT scores over 30: 7%.

Retention: 79% of full-time freshmen returned.

FACULTY
Total: 401, 34% full-time.

Student/faculty ratio: 16:1.

ACADEMICS
Calendar: semesters. *Degrees:* bachelor's, master's, doctoral, and postbachelor's certificates.

Special study options: academic remediation for entering students, adult/continuing education programs, advanced placement credit, distance learning, double majors, English as a second language, honors programs, independent study, internships, part-time degree program, services for LD students, student-designed majors, study abroad, summer session for credit. *ROTC:* Army (c), Air Force (c).

Unusual degree programs: 3-2 engineering with University of Wisconsin–Platteville, University of Wisconsin–Milwaukee; pharmacy with Rosalind Franklin University of Medicine and Science.

Computers: 400 computers/terminals and 100 ports are available on campus for general student use. Students can access the following: campus intranet, computer help desk, free student e-mail accounts, online (class) grades, online (class) registration, online (class) schedules. Campuswide network is available. 100% of college-owned or -operated

housing units are wired for high-speed Internet access. Wireless service is available via entire campus.

Library: Todd Wehr Memorial Library.

STUDENT LIFE
Housing options: on-campus residence required through sophomore year; coed, women-only, special housing for students with disabilities. Campus housing is university owned. Freshman campus housing is guaranteed.

Activities and organizations: drama/theater group, student-run newspaper, radio station, choral group, College Activities Board, Student Senate, Black Student Union, Intervarsity Christian Fellowship, Latin American Student Organization, national sororities.

Athletics Member NCAA. All Division III. *Intercollegiate sports:* baseball M, basketball M/W, cross-country running M/W, football M, golf M/W, soccer M/W, swimming and diving M/W, tennis M/W, track and field M/W, volleyball W. *Intramural sports:* basketball M/W, bowling M/W, cheerleading M/W, football M/W, soccer M/W, tennis M/W, ultimate Frisbee M/W, volleyball M/W.

Campus security: 24-hour emergency response devices and patrols, student patrols, late-night transport/escort service, controlled dormitory access.

Student services: health clinic, personal/psychological counseling.

COSTS & FINANCIAL AID
Costs (2018–19) *Comprehensive fee:* $41,814 includes full-time tuition ($31,162), mandatory fees ($756), and room and board ($9896). Full-time tuition and fees vary according to program. Part-time tuition: $400 per credit hour. Part-time tuition and fees vary according to course load and program. *College room only:* $5180. Room and board charges vary according to board plan and housing facility. *Payment plans:* installment, deferred payment. *Waivers:* employees or children of employees.

Financial Aid Of all full-time matriculated undergraduates who enrolled in 2017, 2,485 applied for aid, 2,154 were judged to have need, 716 had their need fully met. 475 Federal Work-Study jobs (averaging $2247). 1,618 state and other part-time jobs (averaging $2298). In 2017, 589 non-need-based awards were made. *Average percent of need met:* 87. *Average financial aid package:* $24,794. *Average need-based loan:* $4542. *Average need-based gift aid:* $19,049. *Average non-need-based aid:* $15,362. *Average indebtedness upon graduation:* $35,802.

APPLYING
Standardized Tests *Required:* SAT or ACT (for admission). *Recommended:* ACT (for admission).

Options: electronic application, deferred entrance.

Required: high school transcript, minimum 2.0 GPA, 1 letter of recommendation. *Required for some:* essay or personal statement. *Recommended:* interview.

Application deadlines: rolling (freshmen), rolling (transfers).

Notification: 8/20 (freshmen), continuous until 8/20 (transfers).

CONTACT
Mr. James Wiseman, Vice President of Enrollment, Carroll University, 100 North East Avenue, Waukesha, WI 53186-5593. *Phone:* 262-524-7221. *Toll-free phone:* 800-CARROLL. *Fax:* 262-524-7139. *E-mail:* info@carrollu.edu.

Carthage College
Kenosha, Wisconsin
http://www.carthage.edu/

- **Independent** comprehensive, founded 1847, affiliated with Evangelical Lutheran Church in America
- **Suburban** 72-acre campus with easy access to Chicago, Milwaukee
- **Coed** 2,748 undergraduate students, 94% full-time, 56% women, 44% men
- **Moderately difficult** entrance level, 68% of applicants were admitted

UNDERGRAD STUDENTS
2,596 full-time, 152 part-time. Students come from 34 states and territories; 8 other countries; 65% are from out of state; 6% Black or African American, non-Hispanic/Latino; 8% Hispanic/Latino; 2% Asian, non-Hispanic/Latino; 0.3% Native Hawaiian or other Pacific Islander, non-Hispanic/Latino; 0.5% American Indian or Alaska Native, non-Hispanic/Latino; 4% Two or more races, non-Hispanic/Latino; 5%

Race/ethnicity unknown; 1% international; 3% transferred in; 66% live on campus.

Freshmen:
Admission: 7,649 applied, 5,186 admitted, 711 enrolled. *Average high school GPA:* 3.3. *Test scores:* ACT scores over 18: 99%; ACT scores over 24: 53%; ACT scores over 30: 10%.
Retention: 78% of full-time freshmen returned.

FACULTY
Total: 348, 47% full-time, 62% with terminal degrees.
Student/faculty ratio: 12:1.

ACADEMICS
Calendar: 4-1-4. *Degrees:* bachelor's and master's.

Special study options: accelerated degree program, adult/continuing education programs, advanced placement credit, double majors, honors programs, internships, off-campus study, part-time degree program, services for LD students, student-designed majors, study abroad, summer session for credit.

Unusual degree programs: 3-2 engineering with Case Western Reserve University; occupational therapy with Washington University in St. Louis.

Computers: 275 computers/terminals are available on campus for general student use. Students can access the following: campus intranet, computer help desk, free student e-mail accounts, online (class) grades, online (class) registration, online (class) schedules. Campuswide network is available. 96% of college-owned or -operated housing units are wired for high-speed Internet access. Wireless service is available via entire campus.

Library: Hedberg Library. *Books:* 107,321 (physical), 282,334 (digital/electronic); *Serial titles:* 4,768 (physical), 425,122 (digital/electronic); *Databases:* 208. Students can reserve study rooms.

STUDENT LIFE
Housing options: on-campus residence required through junior year; coed, men-only, women-only. Campus housing is university owned and leased by the school. Freshman campus housing is guaranteed.

Activities and organizations: drama/theater group, student-run newspaper, radio station, choral group, national fraternities, national sororities.

Athletics Member NCAA. All Division III. *Intercollegiate sports:* baseball M, basketball M/W, bowling M(c)/W(c), cross-country running M/W, football M, golf M/W, ice hockey M(c)/W(c), lacrosse M/W, soccer M/W, softball W, swimming and diving M/W, tennis M/W, track and field M/W, volleyball M/W, water polo W. *Intramural sports:* basketball M/W, football M/W, racquetball M/W, rock climbing M/W, soccer M/W, softball M/W, volleyball M/W.

Campus security: 24-hour emergency response devices and patrols, student patrols, late-night transport/escort service, controlled dormitory access.

Student services: health clinic, personal/psychological counseling.

COSTS & FINANCIAL AID
Costs (2018–19) *Comprehensive fee:* $55,540 includes full-time tuition ($43,550) and room and board ($11,990). Full-time tuition and fees vary according to course load. Part-time tuition: $575 per credit hour. Part-time tuition and fees vary according to course load. *Room and board:* Room and board charges vary according to board plan, housing facility, and location. *Payment plan:* installment. *Waivers:* employees or children of employees.

Financial Aid Of all full-time matriculated undergraduates who enrolled in 2009, 2,172 applied for aid, 1,855 were judged to have need, 264 had their need fully met. 843 Federal Work-Study jobs (averaging $4000). In 2009, 571 non-need-based awards were made. *Average percent of need met:* 65. *Average financial aid package:* $18,268. *Average need-based loan:* $4266. *Average need-based gift aid:* $13,416. *Average non-need-based aid:* $9564. *Average indebtedness upon graduation:* $29,075.

APPLYING
Standardized Tests *Recommended:* SAT and SAT Subject Tests or ACT (for admission).
Options: electronic application, deferred entrance.
Application fee: $35.

Required: high school transcript. *Required for some:* minimum 2.3 GPA, 2 letters of recommendation, statement of good standing from prior institution(s). *Recommended:* essay or personal statement, interview.
Application deadlines: rolling (freshmen), rolling (transfers).
Notification: continuous (freshmen), continuous (transfers).

CONTACT
Carthage College, 2001 Alford Park Drive, Kenosha, WI 53140. *Phone:* 262-551-6000. *Toll-free phone:* 800-351-4058.

Columbia College of Nursing
Glendale, Wisconsin
http://www.ccon.edu/

CONTACT
Columbia College of Nursing, 4425 North Port Washington Road, Glendale, WI 53212. *Phone:* 414-326-2336.

Concordia University Wisconsin
Mequon, Wisconsin
http://www.cuw.edu/
- **Independent** comprehensive, founded 1881, affiliated with Lutheran Church–Missouri Synod, part of Concordia University System
- **Suburban** 192-acre campus with easy access to Milwaukee
- **Coed** 3,709 undergraduate students, 71% full-time, 66% women, 34% men
- **Moderately difficult** entrance level, 63% of applicants were admitted

UNDERGRAD STUDENTS
2,616 full-time, 1,093 part-time. 25% are from out of state; 12% Black or African American, non-Hispanic/Latino; 1% Hispanic/Latino; 2% Asian, non-Hispanic/Latino; 0.1% Native Hawaiian or other Pacific Islander, non-Hispanic/Latino; 0.9% American Indian or Alaska Native, non-Hispanic/Latino; 4% Two or more races, non-Hispanic/Latino; 4% Race/ethnicity unknown; 3% international; 2% transferred in; 46% live on campus.

Freshmen:
Admission: 3,612 applied, 2,288 admitted, 558 enrolled. *Average high school GPA:* 3.5. *Test scores:* ACT scores over 18: 95%; ACT scores over 24: 44%; ACT scores over 30: 7%.
Retention: 82% of full-time freshmen returned.

FACULTY
Total: 508, 41% full-time, 45% with terminal degrees.
Student/faculty ratio: 11:1.

ACADEMICS
Calendar: 4-1-4. *Degrees:* certificates, associate, bachelor's, master's, doctoral, and post-master's certificates.

Special study options: academic remediation for entering students, accelerated degree program, adult/continuing education programs, advanced placement credit, distance learning, double majors, English as a second language, independent study, internships, off-campus study, part-time degree program, services for LD students, student-designed majors, study abroad, summer session for credit.

Computers: Students can access the following: computer help desk, free student e-mail accounts. Campuswide network is available.
Library: Rinker Memorial Library.

STUDENT LIFE
Housing options: men-only, women-only. Campus housing is university owned. Freshman applicants given priority for college housing.

Activities and organizations: drama/theater group, student-run newspaper, radio station, choral group.

Athletics Member NCAA. All Division III. *Intercollegiate sports:* baseball M, basketball M/W, cross-country running M/W, football M, golf M/W, ice hockey M/W, soccer M/W, softball W, tennis M/W, track and field M/W, volleyball W, wrestling M. *Intramural sports:* basketball M/W, softball M/W, volleyball M/W.

Campus security: 24-hour patrols, student patrols, late-night transport/escort service, controlled dormitory access.

Student services: health clinic, personal/psychological counseling.

COSTS & FINANCIAL AID

Costs (2017–18) *Comprehensive fee:* $39,130 includes full-time tuition ($28,330), mandatory fees ($270), and room and board ($10,530). Full-time tuition and fees vary according to program. Part-time tuition and fees vary according to program. *College room only:* $7970. Room and board charges vary according to board plan.

Financial Aid Of all full-time matriculated undergraduates who enrolled in 2016, 2,287 applied for aid, 2,009 were judged to have need, 509 had their need fully met. In 2016, 397 non-need-based awards were made. *Average percent of need met:* 71. *Average financial aid package:* $21,208. *Average need-based loan:* $7753. *Average need-based gift aid:* $13,500. *Average non-need-based aid:* $11,364. *Average indebtedness upon graduation:* $33,298. *Financial aid deadline:* 4/15.

APPLYING

Standardized Tests *Required:* SAT or ACT (for admission).

Required: high school transcript, minimum 2.0 GPA. *Required for some:* essay or personal statement, minimum 3.0 GPA, 3 letters of recommendation. *Recommended:* interview.

Notification: continuous (freshmen).

CONTACT

Ms. Julie Schroeder, Concordia University Wisconsin, Admissions Office, 12800 North Lake Drive, Mequon, WI 53097. *Phone:* 262-243-4305 Ext. 4305. *Toll-free phone:* 888-628-9472. *E-mail:* admission@cuw.edu.

Edgewood College

Madison, Wisconsin

http://www.edgewood.edu/

- **Independent Roman Catholic** comprehensive, founded 1927
- **Urban** 55-acre campus
- **Endowment** $37.8 million
- **Coed** 1,564 undergraduate students, 87% full-time, 73% women, 27% men
- **Moderately difficult** entrance level, 71% of applicants were admitted

UNDERGRAD STUDENTS

1,361 full-time, 203 part-time. Students come from 19 states and territories; 20 other countries; 8% are from out of state; 3% Black or African American, non-Hispanic/Latino; 6% Hispanic/Latino; 3% Asian, non-Hispanic/Latino; 0.2% Native Hawaiian or other Pacific Islander, non-Hispanic/Latino; 0.3% American Indian or Alaska Native, non-Hispanic/Latino; 3% Two or more races, non-Hispanic/Latino; 3% Race/ethnicity unknown; 3% international; 6% transferred in; 35% live on campus.

Freshmen:
Admission: 1,447 applied, 1,029 admitted, 284 enrolled. *Average high school GPA:* 3.5. *Test scores:* SAT evidence-based reading and writing scores over 500: 86%; SAT math scores over 500: 86%; ACT scores over 18: 93%; SAT evidence-based reading and writing scores over 600: 14%; SAT math scores over 600: 43%; ACT scores over 24: 41%; ACT scores over 30: 6%.
Retention: 78% of full-time freshmen returned.

FACULTY

Total: 284, 54% full-time, 51% with terminal degrees.

Student/faculty ratio: 9:1.

ACADEMICS

Calendar: semesters. *Degrees:* certificates, bachelor's, master's, doctoral, and postbachelor's certificates.

Special study options: academic remediation for entering students, accelerated degree program, adult/continuing education programs, advanced placement credit, cooperative education, distance learning, double majors, honors programs, independent study, internships, off-campus study, part-time degree program, services for LD students, student-designed majors, study abroad, summer session for credit. *ROTC:* Army (c), Navy (c), Air Force (c).

Computers: 180 computers/terminals and 200 ports are available on campus for general student use. Students can access the following: campus intranet, computer help desk, free student e-mail accounts, online (class) grades, online (class) registration, online (class) schedules. Campuswide network is available. 100% of college-owned or -operated housing units are wired for high-speed Internet access. Wireless service is available via entire campus.

Library: Oscar Rennebohm Library. *Books:* 82,008 (physical), 140,319 (digital/electronic); *Serial titles:* 219 (physical), 38,116 (digital/electronic); *Databases:* 90. Weekly public service hours: 98; students can reserve study rooms.

STUDENT LIFE

Housing options: on-campus residence required through sophomore year; coed, cooperative, special housing for students with disabilities. Campus housing is university owned. Freshman campus housing is guaranteed.

Activities and organizations: drama/theater group, student-run newspaper, choral group, Circle K, Student Education Association, Student Government Association, Rotaract, Ambassadors.

Athletics Member NCAA. All Division III. *Intercollegiate sports:* baseball M, basketball M/W, cross-country running M/W, golf M/W, soccer M/W, softball W, tennis M/W, track and field M/W, volleyball W. *Intramural sports:* basketball M/W, soccer M/W, swimming and diving M/W, volleyball M/W.

Campus security: 24-hour emergency response devices and patrols, student patrols, late-night transport/escort service, controlled dormitory access, lighted pathways/sidewalks, Eagle Alert System, Public Address System, Safe Ride Shuttle, extensive video surveillance system.

Student services: health clinic, personal/psychological counseling.

COSTS & FINANCIAL AID

Costs (2018–19) *Comprehensive fee:* $40,520 includes full-time tuition ($29,500) and room and board ($11,020). Full-time tuition and fees vary according to degree level. Part-time tuition: $927 per credit. Part-time tuition and fees vary according to course load and degree level. *Room and board:* Room and board charges vary according to housing facility. *Payment plan:* installment. *Waivers:* employees or children of employees.

Financial Aid Of all full-time matriculated undergraduates who enrolled in 2016, 1,197 applied for aid, 1,061 were judged to have need, 135 had their need fully met. 567 Federal Work-Study jobs (averaging $1972). 466 state and other part-time jobs (averaging $2022). In 2016, 255 non-need-based awards were made. *Average percent of need met:* 75. *Average financial aid package:* $19,031. *Average need-based loan:* $5582. *Average need-based gift aid:* $13,323. *Average non-need-based aid:* $6399. *Average indebtedness upon graduation:* $35,300.

APPLYING

Standardized Tests *Required:* SAT or ACT (for admission).

Options: electronic application, deferred entrance.

Application fee: $30.

Required: high school transcript, minimum 2.5 GPA, two of the following: cumulative high school GPA of 2.5 on a 4.0 scale, a rank in the top 50% of their high school graduating class and/or a composite score of 18 on the ACT or an equivalent SAT score. *Required for some:* essay or personal statement, 2 letters of recommendation, interview.

Application deadlines: 8/1 (freshmen), 8/1 (transfers).

Notification: continuous until 8/15 (freshmen), continuous until 8/15 (transfers).

CONTACT

Ms. Christine Benedict, Vice President for Enrollment Management, Edgewood College, 1000 Edgewood College Drive, Madison, WI 53711-1997. *Phone:* 608-663-2294. *Toll-free phone:* 800-444-4861 Ext. 2294. *Fax:* 608-663-2214. *E-mail:* admissions@edgewood.edu.

Herzing University

Brookfield, Wisconsin

http://www.herzing.edu/brookfield

CONTACT

Herzing University, 555 South Executive Drive, Brookfield, WI 53005. *Toll-free phone:* 800-596-0724.

A ★ *indicates that the school has detailed information with a Premium Profile on Petersons.com.*

Herzing University

Kenosha, Wisconsin

http://www.herzing.edu/kenosha

CONTACT

Herzing University, 4006 Washington Road, Kenosha, WI 53144. *Toll-free phone:* 800-596-0724.

Herzing University

Madison, Wisconsin

http://www.herzing.edu/madison/

CONTACT

Herzing University, 5218 East Terrace Drive, Madison, WI 53718. *Toll-free phone:* 800-596-0724.

Herzing University Online

Menomonee Falls, Wisconsin

http://www.herzingonline.edu/

CONTACT

Herzing University Online, W140N8917 Lilly Road, Menomonee Falls, WI 53051. *Toll-free phone:* 866-508-0748.

Lakeland University

Plymouth, Wisconsin

http://www.lakeland.edu/

CONTACT

Mr. Nick Spaeth, Director of Admissions, Lakeland University, PO Box 359, Nash Visitors Center, Sheboygan, WI 53082-0359. *Phone:* 920-565-1007. *Toll-free phone:* 800-569-2166. *Fax:* 920-565-1215. *E-mail:* admissions@lakeland.edu.

★ Lawrence University

Appleton, Wisconsin

http://www.lawrence.edu/

- **Independent** 4-year, founded 1847
- **Small-town** 88-acre campus
- **Endowment** $318.2 million
- **Coed** 1,473 undergraduate students, 97% full-time, 53% women, 47% men
- **Very difficult** entrance level, 61% of applicants were admitted

UNDERGRAD STUDENTS

1,434 full-time, 39 part-time. Students come from 47 states and territories; 37 other countries; 71% are from out of state; 5% Black or African American, non-Hispanic/Latino; 9% Hispanic/Latino; 5% Asian, non-Hispanic/Latino; 0.1% Native Hawaiian or other Pacific Islander, non-Hispanic/Latino; 0.2% American Indian or Alaska Native, non-Hispanic/Latino; 4% Two or more races, non-Hispanic/Latino; 0.7% Race/ethnicity unknown; 12% international; 1% transferred in; 94% live on campus.

Freshmen:

Admission: 3,612 applied, 2,216 admitted, 353 enrolled. *Average high school GPA:* 3.5. *Test scores:* SAT evidence-based reading and writing scores over 500: 98%; SAT math scores over 500: 98%; ACT scores over 18: 100%; SAT evidence-based reading and writing scores over 600: 86%; SAT math scores over 600: 76%; ACT scores over 24: 88%; SAT evidence-based reading and writing scores over 700: 41%; SAT math scores over 700: 37%; ACT scores over 30: 47%.

Retention: 88% of full-time freshmen returned.

FACULTY

Total: 214, 81% full-time, 85% with terminal degrees.

Student/faculty ratio: 8:1.

ACADEMICS

Calendar: trimesters. *Degree:* bachelor's.

Special study options: advanced placement credit, double majors, independent study, internships, off-campus study, part-time degree program, services for LD students, student-designed majors, study abroad.

Unusual degree programs: 3-2 engineering with Columbia University, Rensselaer Polytechnic Institute, Washington University in St. Louis; forestry with Duke University; occupational therapy with Washington University in St. Louis.

Computers: 250 computers/terminals and 400 ports are available on campus for general student use. Students can access the following: campus intranet, computer help desk, free student e-mail accounts, online (class) grades, online (class) registration, online (class) schedules, online transcripts, financial aid, financial account information. Campuswide network is available. 100% of college-owned or -operated housing units are wired for high-speed Internet access. Wireless service is available via classrooms, computer centers, computer labs, dorm rooms, learning centers, libraries, student centers.

Library: Seeley G. Mudd Library. *Books:* 551,687 (physical), 220,704 (digital/electronic); *Serial titles:* 592 (physical), 364,146 (digital/electronic); *Databases:* 171. Weekly public service hours: 110; students can reserve study rooms.

STUDENT LIFE

Housing options: on-campus residence required through senior year; coed, men-only, women-only, cooperative, special housing for students with disabilities. Campus housing is university owned. Freshman campus housing is guaranteed.

Activities and organizations: drama/theater group, student-run newspaper, radio station, choral group, Gaming, Dance, Lawrence International, Outdoor Recreation Club, Sustainable Lawrence University Gardens (SLUG), national fraternities, national sororities.

Athletics Member NCAA. All Division III. *Intercollegiate sports:* baseball M, basketball M/W, crew M(c)/W(c), cross-country running M/W, fencing M/W, football M, ice hockey M/W(c), soccer M/W, softball W, swimming and diving M/W, tennis M/W, track and field M/W, ultimate Frisbee M(c)/W(c), volleyball M(c)/W. *Intramural sports:* badminton M/W, basketball M/W, fencing M/W, racquetball M/W, skiing (downhill) M/W, soccer M/W, softball M/W, table tennis M/W, tennis M/W, volleyball M/W, water polo M/W.

Campus security: 24-hour emergency response devices and patrols, student patrols, late-night transport/escort service, controlled dormitory access, evening patrols by trained security personnel.

Student services: health clinic, personal/psychological counseling.

COSTS & FINANCIAL AID

Costs (2017–18) *Comprehensive fee:* $56,133 includes full-time tuition ($45,801), mandatory fees ($300), and room and board ($10,032). *College room only:* $4989. *Payment plan:* installment. *Waivers:* employees or children of employees.

Financial Aid Of all full-time matriculated undergraduates who enrolled in 2017, 1,016 applied for aid, 873 were judged to have need, 408 had their need fully met. 545 Federal Work-Study jobs (averaging $2100). 415 state and other part-time jobs (averaging $2000). In 2017, 515 non-need-based awards were made. *Average percent of need met:* 94. *Average financial aid package:* $39,869. *Average need-based loan:* $5657. *Average need-based gift aid:* $33,921. *Average non-need-based aid:* $22,044. *Average indebtedness upon graduation:* $32,488.

APPLYING

Standardized Tests *Required for some:* English Language Proficiency Exam (SAT/TOEFL/IELTS/ACT).

Options: electronic application, early decision, early action, deferred entrance.

Required: essay or personal statement, high school transcript, 1 letter of recommendation. *Required for some:* audition for music majors. *Recommended:* minimum 3.0 GPA, interview.

Application deadlines: 1/15 (freshmen), 7/1 (transfers), 12/1 (early action).

Early decision deadline: 10/31.

Notification: continuous until 4/1 (freshmen), continuous until 7/15 (transfers), 12/1 (early decision), 1/25 (early action).

CONTACT

Mr. Ken Anselment, Dean of Admissions and Financial Aid, Lawrence University, 711 East Boldt Way, Admissions Office, Appleton, WI 54911.

Phone: 920-832-6506. *Toll-free phone:* 800-227-0982. *Fax:* 920-832-6782. *E-mail:* ken.anselment@lawrence.edu.

Maranatha Baptist University

Watertown, Wisconsin
http://www.mbu.edu/

- **Independent Baptist** comprehensive, founded 1968
- **Small-town** 60-acre campus with easy access to Milwaukee
- **Coed** 926 undergraduate students, 64% full-time, 56% women, 44% men
- **Noncompetitive** entrance level, 73% of applicants were admitted

UNDERGRAD STUDENTS
591 full-time, 335 part-time. 75% are from out of state; 2% Black or African American, non-Hispanic/Latino; 3% Hispanic/Latino; 1% Asian, non-Hispanic/Latino; 0.1% Native Hawaiian or other Pacific Islander, non-Hispanic/Latino; 0.1% American Indian or Alaska Native, non-Hispanic/Latino; 3% Two or more races, non-Hispanic/Latino; 10% Race/ethnicity unknown; 0.6% international; 4% transferred in; 72% live on campus.

Freshmen:
Admission: 279 applied, 204 admitted, 146 enrolled. *Average high school GPA:* 3.5. *Test scores:* ACT scores over 18: 92%; ACT scores over 24: 42%; ACT scores over 30: 6%.
Retention: 67% of full-time freshmen returned.

FACULTY
Total: 138, 31% full-time, 30% with terminal degrees.
Student/faculty ratio: 11:1.

ACADEMICS
Calendar: semesters. *Degrees:* certificates, associate, bachelor's, master's, and doctoral.

Special study options: academic remediation for entering students, adult/continuing education programs, advanced placement credit, distance learning, double majors, independent study, internships, off-campus study, part-time degree program, study abroad, summer session for credit. *ROTC:* Army (b), Air Force (c).

Computers: Students can access the following: campus intranet, computer help desk, free student e-mail accounts, online (class) grades, online (class) registration, online (class) schedules. Campuswide network is available. 100% of college-owned or -operated housing units are wired for high-speed Internet access. Wireless service is available via entire campus.
Library: Cedarholm Library and Resource Center. Students can reserve study rooms.

STUDENT LIFE
Housing options: on-campus residence required through senior year; men-only, women-only. Campus housing is university owned. Freshman campus housing is guaranteed.
Activities and organizations: drama/theater group, choral group.
Athletics Member NCAA, NCCAA. All NCAA Division III.
Intercollegiate sports: baseball M, basketball M/W, cross-country running M/W, soccer M/W, softball W, volleyball M/W. *Intramural sports:* basketball M/W.
Campus security: student patrols, late-night transport/escort service, controlled dormitory access.
Student services: health clinic, personal/psychological counseling.

COSTS & FINANCIAL AID
Costs (2018–19) *Comprehensive fee:* $22,510 includes full-time tuition ($14,250), mandatory fees ($1160), and room and board ($7100). Full-time tuition and fees vary according to location and program. Part-time tuition: $594 per semester hour. Part-time tuition and fees vary according to course load. *Required fees:* $48 per semester hour part-time. *Payment plan:* installment. *Waivers:* employees or children of employees.
Financial Aid Of all full-time matriculated undergraduates who enrolled in 2015, 523 applied for aid, 478 were judged to have need, 53 had their need fully met. In 2015, 55 non-need-based awards were made. *Average percent of need met:* 52. *Average financial aid package:* $10,139. *Average need-based loan:* $4129. *Average need-based gift aid:* $6718. *Average non-need-based aid:* $3962. *Average indebtedness upon graduation:* $20,965.

APPLYING
Standardized Tests *Required:* SAT or ACT (for admission).
Options: electronic application.
Application fee: $50.
Required: essay or personal statement, high school transcript, 4 letters of recommendation.

CONTACT
Jonathan Sheeley, Director of Admissions, Maranatha Baptist University, 745 West Main Street, Watertown, WI 53094. *Phone:* 920-206-2327. *Toll-free phone:* 800-622-2947. *Fax:* 920-261-9109. *E-mail:* admissions@mbu.edu.

Marian University

Fond du Lac, Wisconsin
http://www.marianuniversity.edu/

- **Independent Roman Catholic** comprehensive, founded 1936
- **Small-town** 78-acre campus with easy access to Milwaukee
- **Endowment** $11.7 million
- **Coed** 1,462 undergraduate students, 85% full-time, 68% women, 32% men
- **Moderately difficult** entrance level, 77% of applicants were admitted

UNDERGRAD STUDENTS
1,250 full-time, 212 part-time. Students come from 23 states and territories; 12 other countries; 16% are from out of state; 6% Black or African American, non-Hispanic/Latino; 6% Hispanic/Latino; 2% Asian, non-Hispanic/Latino; 0.3% Native Hawaiian or other Pacific Islander, non-Hispanic/Latino; 1% American Indian or Alaska Native, non-Hispanic/Latino; 2% Race/ethnicity unknown; 1% international; 6% transferred in.

Freshmen:
Admission: 1,245 applied, 961 admitted, 351 enrolled. *Test scores:* ACT scores over 18: 74%; ACT scores over 24: 23%; ACT scores over 30: 1%.
Retention: 68% of full-time freshmen returned.

FACULTY
Total: 233, 41% full-time, 36% with terminal degrees.
Student/faculty ratio: 9:1.

ACADEMICS
Calendar: semesters. *Degrees:* certificates, bachelor's, master's, doctoral, post-master's, and postbachelor's certificates.

Special study options: academic remediation for entering students, accelerated degree program, advanced placement credit, cooperative education, distance learning, double majors, honors programs, independent study, internships, part-time degree program, services for LD students, student-designed majors, study abroad, summer session for credit. *ROTC:* Army (c).

Computers: 500 computers/terminals are available on campus for general student use. Students can access the following: campus intranet, computer help desk, free student e-mail accounts, online (class) grades, online (class) registration, online (class) schedules. Campuswide network is available. 100% of college-owned or -operated housing units are wired for high-speed Internet access. Wireless service is available via entire campus.
Library: Cardinal Meyer Library plus 1 other. *Books:* 210,079 (physical), 147,236 (digital/electronic); *Databases:* 1,805.

STUDENT LIFE
Housing options: on-campus residence required through sophomore year; coed, special housing for students with disabilities. Campus housing is university owned. Freshman campus housing is guaranteed.
Activities and organizations: student-run newspaper, choral group, Student Senate, Student Nurses Association, Student Education Association, Science and Math Association, Business Club, national sororities.
Athletics Member NCAA. All Division III. *Intercollegiate sports:* baseball M, basketball M/W, cross-country running M/W, golf M/W, ice hockey M/W, lacrosse M, soccer M/W, softball W, tennis M/W, track and field M/W, volleyball M/W. *Intramural sports:* badminton M/W, basketball M/W, bowling M/W, football M, skiing (downhill) M/W, softball M, tennis M/W, volleyball M/W.

Campus security: 24-hour emergency response devices and patrols, student patrols, late-night transport/escort service, controlled dormitory access.

Student services: health clinic, personal/psychological counseling.

COSTS & FINANCIAL AID
Costs (2017–18) *One-time required fee:* $100. *Comprehensive fee:* $34,592 includes full-time tuition ($26,950), mandatory fees ($420), and room and board ($7222). Full-time tuition and fees vary according to course load and program. Part-time tuition: $450 per credit hour. Part-time tuition and fees vary according to course load and program. *College room only:* $4352. Room and board charges vary according to board plan. *Payment plan:* installment. *Waivers:* senior citizens and employees or children of employees.

Financial Aid Of all full-time matriculated undergraduates who enrolled in 2015, 1,271 applied for aid, 1,176 were judged to have need, 66 had their need fully met. 146 Federal Work-Study jobs (averaging $443). 342 state and other part-time jobs (averaging $1465). In 2015, 87 non-need-based awards were made. *Average percent of need met:* 60. *Average financial aid package:* $16,769. *Average need-based loan:* $3444. *Average need-based gift aid:* $12,996. *Average non-need-based aid:* $6038. *Average indebtedness upon graduation:* $30,565.

APPLYING
Standardized Tests *Required:* SAT or ACT (for admission). *Recommended:* ACT (for admission).

Options: electronic application, deferred entrance.

Application fee: $20.

Required: high school transcript. *Required for some:* interview. *Recommended:* interview.

Application deadlines: rolling (freshmen), rolling (transfers).

Notification: 8/15 (freshmen), continuous until 8/15 (transfers).

CONTACT
Shannon LaLuzerne, Dean of Admission, Marian University, 45 S. National Avenue, Fond du Lac, WI 54935-4699. *Phone:* 920-923-7650. *Toll-free phone:* 800-2-MARIAN. *E-mail:* admission@ marianuniversity.edu.

Marquette University
Milwaukee, Wisconsin
http://www.marquette.edu/
- **Independent Roman Catholic (Jesuit)** university, founded 1881
- **Urban** 107-acre campus with easy access to Milwaukee
- **Coed** 8,335 undergraduate students, 96% full-time, 53% women, 47% men
- **Moderately difficult** entrance level, 89% of applicants were admitted

UNDERGRAD STUDENTS
8,026 full-time, 309 part-time. 69% are from out of state; 4% Black or African American, non-Hispanic/Latino; 12% Hispanic/Latino; 7% Asian, non-Hispanic/Latino; 0.0% Native Hawaiian or other Pacific Islander, non-Hispanic/Latino; 0.1% American Indian or Alaska Native, non-Hispanic/Latino; 4% Two or more races, non-Hispanic/Latino; 0.3% Race/ethnicity unknown; 3% international; 2% transferred in; 54% live on campus.

Freshmen:
Admission: 12,957 applied, 11,574 admitted, 2,023 enrolled. *Test scores:* SAT evidence-based reading and writing scores over 500: 96%; SAT math scores over 500: 94%; ACT scores over 18: 100%; SAT evidence-based reading and writing scores over 600: 62%; SAT math scores over 600: 54%; ACT scores over 24: 83%; SAT evidence-based reading and writing scores over 700: 9%; SAT math scores over 700: 9%; ACT scores over 30: 25%.

Retention: 89% of full-time freshmen returned.

FACULTY
Total: 1,164, 55% full-time, 74% with terminal degrees.
Student/faculty ratio: 14:1.

ACADEMICS
Calendar: semesters. *Degrees:* bachelor's, master's, doctoral, post-master's, and postbachelor's certificates.

Special study options: accelerated degree program, adult/continuing education programs, advanced placement credit, cooperative education, distance learning, double majors, English as a second language, honors programs, independent study, internships, off-campus study, part-time degree program, services for LD students, student-designed majors, study abroad, summer session for credit. *ROTC:* Army (b), Navy (b), Air Force (b).

Unusual degree programs: 3-2 business administration; engineering; exercise science/clinical and translational rehabilitation health sciences, speech and language pathology, international affairs, physical therapy.

Computers: Students can access the following: campus intranet, computer help desk, free student e-mail accounts, online (class) grades, online (class) registration, online (class) schedules, AV Software, MATLAB, Printwise. Campuswide network is available. 100% of college-owned or -operated housing units are wired for high-speed Internet access. Wireless service is available via classrooms, computer centers, computer labs, dorm rooms, learning centers, libraries, student centers.

Library: Raynor Memorial Libraries plus 1 other. Study areas open 24 hours, 5–7 days a week; students can reserve study rooms.

STUDENT LIFE
Housing options: on-campus residence required through sophomore year; coed, men-only, women-only, cooperative, special housing for students with disabilities. Campus housing is university owned. Freshman campus housing is guaranteed.

Activities and organizations: drama/theater group, student-run newspaper, radio and television station, choral group, Student Government, club sports, community service organizations, band/jazz/orchestra, Residence Hall Association, national fraternities, national sororities.

Athletics Member NCAA. All Division I. *Intercollegiate sports:* basketball M(s)/W(s), cheerleading M/W, cross-country running M(s)/W(s), golf M(s), lacrosse M(s)/W(s), soccer M(s)/W(s), tennis M(s)/W(s), track and field M(s)/W(s), volleyball W(s). *Intramural sports:* badminton M/W, baseball M(c), basketball M(c)/W(c), crew M(c)/W(c), cross-country running M(c)/W(c), equestrian sports M(c)/W(c), fencing M(c)/W(c), football M/W, golf M(c)/W(c), ice hockey M(c), lacrosse M(c)/W(c), rowing M(c)/W(c), rugby M(c)/W(c), sailing M(c)/W(c), sand volleyball M/W, skiing (downhill) M(c)/W(c), soccer M(c)/W(c), softball M/W(c), swimming and diving M(c)/W(c), table tennis M(c)/W(c), tennis M(c)/W(c), ultimate Frisbee M(c)/W(c), volleyball M(c)/W(c), water polo M(c)/W(c), weight lifting M/W.

Campus security: 24-hour emergency response devices and patrols, student patrols, late-night transport/escort service, 24-hour desk attendants in residence halls.

Student services: health clinic, personal/psychological counseling.

COSTS & FINANCIAL AID
Costs (2017–18) *Comprehensive fee:* $51,790 includes full-time tuition ($39,330), mandatory fees ($570), and room and board ($11,890). Full-time tuition and fees vary according to course load and program. Part-time tuition: $1025 per credit hour. Part-time tuition and fees vary according to program. *College room only:* $4180. Room and board charges vary according to housing facility. *Payment plan:* installment. *Waivers:* senior citizens and employees or children of employees.

Financial Aid Of all full-time matriculated undergraduates who enrolled in 2017, 5,721 applied for aid, 4,651 were judged to have need, 1,127 had their need fully met. In 2017, 3060 non-need-based awards were made. *Average percent of need met:* 79. *Average financial aid package:* $29,472. *Average need-based loan:* $6920. *Average need-based gift aid:* $22,290. *Average non-need-based aid:* $13,065. *Average indebtedness upon graduation:* $37,713.

APPLYING
Standardized Tests *Required:* SAT or ACT (for admission).

Options: electronic application, deferred entrance.

Required: essay or personal statement, high school transcript, minimum 2.5 GPA. *Recommended:* minimum 3.4 GPA.

Application deadlines: 12/1 (freshmen), 6/1 (transfers).

Notification: 12/23 (freshmen), continuous (transfers).

CONTACT
Mr. Brian Troyer, Dean of Undergraduate Admissions, Marquette University, PO Box 1881, Milwaukee, WI 53201-1881. *Phone:* 414-288-

7004. *Toll-free phone:* 800-222-6544. *Fax:* 414-288-3764. *E-mail:* admissions@marquette.edu.

Milwaukee Institute of Art and Design
Milwaukee, Wisconsin
http://www.miad.edu/

- **Independent** 4-year, founded 1974
- **Urban** campus with easy access to Milwaukee
- **Coed**
- **Moderately difficult** entrance level

FACULTY
Student/faculty ratio: 15:1.

ACADEMICS
Calendar: semesters. *Degree:* bachelor's.

STUDENT LIFE
Housing options: on-campus residence required through sophomore year; coed. Campus housing is provided by a third party. Freshman applicants given priority for college housing.

Activities and organizations: drama/theater group.

Campus security: 24-hour emergency response devices, late-night transport/escort service.

Student services: health clinic, personal/psychological counseling.

COSTS & FINANCIAL AID
Costs (2017–18) *Tuition:* $34,820 full-time. *Required fees:* $1700 full-time. *Room only:* $7730.

Financial Aid Of all full-time matriculated undergraduates who enrolled in 2008, 566 applied for aid, 530 were judged to have need, 58 had their need fully met. In 2008, 81 non-need-based awards were made. *Average percent of need met:* 68. *Average financial aid package:* $19,455. *Average need-based loan:* $6236. *Average need-based gift aid:* $12,888. *Average non-need-based aid:* $9611. *Average indebtedness upon graduation:* $24,162. *Financial aid deadline:* 2/15.

APPLYING
Options: electronic application, deferred entrance.

Required: high school transcript, portfolio. *Recommended:* essay or personal statement, minimum 2.0 GPA, interview.

CONTACT
David Sigman, Director of Admissions, Milwaukee Institute of Art and Design, 273 East Erie Street, Milwaukee, WI 53202. *Phone:* 414-847-3200. *Toll-free phone:* 888-749-MIAD. *Fax:* 414-291-8077. *E-mail:* admissions@miad.edu.

Milwaukee School of Engineering
Milwaukee, Wisconsin
http://www.msoe.edu/

- **Independent** comprehensive, founded 1903
- **Urban** 22-acre campus
- **Endowment** $65.0 million
- **Coed, primarily men** 2,610 undergraduate students, 96% full-time, 27% women, 73% men
- **Moderately difficult** entrance level, 63% of applicants were admitted

UNDERGRAD STUDENTS
2,508 full-time, 102 part-time. Students come from 42 states and territories; 26 other countries; 34% are from out of state; 2% Black or African American, non-Hispanic/Latino; 6% Hispanic/Latino; 4% Asian, non-Hispanic/Latino; 0.2% American Indian or Alaska Native, non-Hispanic/Latino; 3% Two or more races, non-Hispanic/Latino; 8% Race/ethnicity unknown; 10% international; 7% transferred in; 30% live on campus.

Freshmen:
Admission: 2,893 applied, 1,818 admitted, 513 enrolled. *Average high school GPA:* 3.7. *Test scores:* SAT evidence-based reading and writing scores over 500: 88%; SAT math scores over 500: 100%; ACT scores over 18: 100%; SAT evidence-based reading and writing scores over 600: 53%; SAT math scores over 600: 76%; ACT scores over 24: 88%; SAT

evidence-based reading and writing scores over 700: 15%; SAT math scores over 700: 32%; ACT scores over 30: 26%.
Retention: 85% of full-time freshmen returned.

FACULTY
Total: 252, 55% full-time, 63% with terminal degrees.
Student/faculty ratio: 16:1.

ACADEMICS
Calendar: quarters. *Degrees:* bachelor's and master's.

Special study options: academic remediation for entering students, adult/continuing education programs, advanced placement credit, double majors, English as a second language, honors programs, independent study, internships, part-time degree program, services for LD students, study abroad, summer session for credit. *ROTC:* Army (c), Navy (c), Air Force (c).

Computers: 50 computers/terminals are available on campus for general student use. Students can access the following: campus intranet, computer help desk, free student e-mail accounts, online (class) grades, online (class) registration, online (class) schedules. Campuswide network is available. 100% of college-owned or -operated housing units are wired for high-speed Internet access. Wireless service is available via entire campus.
Library: Walter Schroeder. *Books:* 51,408 (physical), 370,802 (digital/electronic); *Serial titles:* 345 (physical), 114,238 (digital/electronic); *Databases:* 124. Weekly public service hours: 96; students can reserve study rooms.

STUDENT LIFE
Housing options: on-campus residence required through sophomore year; coed, special housing for students with disabilities. Campus housing is university owned. Freshman campus housing is guaranteed.

Activities and organizations: drama/theater group, student-run radio station, choral group, Student Union Board, Greek Council, Student Government Association, Residence Hall Association, Intervarsity Christian Fellowship, national fraternities, national sororities.

Athletics Member NCAA. All Division III. *Intercollegiate sports:* baseball M, basketball M/W, cheerleading M/W, crew M/W, cross-country running M/W, golf M, ice hockey M, lacrosse M, soccer M/W, softball W, tennis M/W, track and field M/W, volleyball M/W, wrestling M. *Intramural sports:* badminton M(c)/W(c), basketball M/W, bowling M(c)/W(c), fencing M(c)/W(c), football M/W, rugby M(c), soccer M/W, softball M/W, ultimate Frisbee M(c)/W(c), volleyball M/W, weight lifting M(c)/W(c).

Campus security: 24-hour emergency response devices and patrols, late-night transport/escort service, controlled dormitory access.

Student services: health clinic, personal/psychological counseling, women's center.

COSTS & FINANCIAL AID
Costs (2018–19) *Comprehensive fee:* $50,157 includes full-time tuition ($39,039), mandatory fees ($1710), and room and board ($9408). Full-time tuition and fees vary according to course load. Part-time tuition: $678 per credit hour. Part-time tuition and fees vary according to course load. *Required fees:* $13 per credit hour part-time. *College room only:* $5889. Room and board charges vary according to board plan and housing facility. *Payment plan:* installment. *Waivers:* employees or children of employees.

Financial Aid Of all full-time matriculated undergraduates who enrolled in 2016, 2,184 applied for aid, 1,983 were judged to have need, 435 had their need fully met. 269 Federal Work-Study jobs (averaging $1248). In 2016, 422 non-need-based awards were made. *Average percent of need met:* 77. *Average financial aid package:* $28,577. *Average need-based loan:* $4267. *Average need-based gift aid:* $24,940. *Average non-need-based aid:* $13,893. *Average indebtedness upon graduation:* $38,421.

APPLYING
Standardized Tests *Required:* SAT or ACT (for admission).

Options: electronic application, deferred entrance.

Required: high school transcript, minimum 3.0 GPA. *Required for some:* essay or personal statement, interview.

Application deadlines: 1/1 (freshmen), rolling (out-of-state freshmen), 1/1 (transfers).

Notification: continuous until 10/1 (freshmen), continuous (out-of-state freshmen), continuous until 10/1 (transfers).

CONTACT
Seandra Mitchell, Director, Undergraduate Admission, Milwaukee School of Engineering, 1025 N. Broadway, Milwaukee, WI 53202. *Phone:* 414-277-6762. *Toll-free phone:* 800-332-6763. *E-mail:* mitchell@msoe.edu.

Mount Mary University
Milwaukee, Wisconsin
http://www.mtmary.edu/

- **Independent Roman Catholic** comprehensive, founded 1913
- **Urban** 80-acre campus with easy access to Milwaukee
- **Endowment** $17.0 million
- **Undergraduate: women only; graduate: coed** 735 undergraduate students, 89% full-time, 100% women, 0% men
- **Moderately difficult** entrance level, 56% of applicants were admitted

UNDERGRAD STUDENTS
652 full-time, 83 part-time. Students come from 6 states and territories; 14 other countries; 2% are from out of state; 17% Black or African American, non-Hispanic/Latino; 20% Hispanic/Latino; 8% Asian, non-Hispanic/Latino; 0.3% Native Hawaiian or other Pacific Islander, non-Hispanic/Latino; 0.1% American Indian or Alaska Native, non-Hispanic/Latino; 4% Two or more races, non-Hispanic/Latino; 0.4% Race/ethnicity unknown; 1% international; 6% transferred in; 31% live on campus.

Freshmen:
Admission: 709 applied, 397 admitted, 123 enrolled. *Average high school GPA:* 3.1. *Test scores:* ACT scores over 18: 66%; ACT scores over 24: 13%; ACT scores over 30: 3%.
Retention: 79% of full-time freshmen returned.

FACULTY
Total: 194, 31% full-time, 47% with terminal degrees.
Student/faculty ratio: 11:1.

ACADEMICS
Calendar: semesters. *Degrees:* bachelor's, master's, doctoral, postmaster's, and postbachelor's certificates.
Special study options: academic remediation for entering students, accelerated degree program, advanced placement credit, double majors, honors programs, independent study, internships, part-time degree program, services for LD students, student-designed majors, study abroad, summer session for credit.
Unusual degree programs: 3-2 occupational therapy, public health.
Computers: 177 computers/terminals and 10 ports are available on campus for general student use. Students can access the following: campus intranet, computer help desk, free student e-mail accounts, online (class) grades, online (class) registration, online (class) schedules. Campuswide network is available. 100% of college-owned or -operated housing units are wired for high-speed Internet access. Wireless service is available via entire campus.
Library: The Patrick and Beatrice Haggerty Library. *Books:* 77,098 (physical), 142,434 (digital/electronic); *Serial titles:* 5,268 (physical), 155,028 (digital/electronic); *Databases:* 92. Students can reserve study rooms.

STUDENT LIFE
Housing options: on-campus residence required for freshman year; women-only. Campus housing is university owned. Freshman applicants given priority for college housing.
Activities and organizations: student-run newspaper, choral group, Programming and Activities Council, Student Government Association, International Club, Caroline Hall Council, Department Affiliated Clubs.
Athletics Member NCAA. All Division III. *Intercollegiate sports:* basketball W, cross-country running W, golf W, soccer W, softball W, tennis W, volleyball W.
Campus security: 24-hour emergency response devices and patrols, late-night transport/escort service, controlled dormitory access.
Student services: personal/psychological counseling.

COSTS & FINANCIAL AID
Costs (2018–19) *Comprehensive fee:* $38,700 includes full-time tuition ($29,510), mandatory fees ($590), and room and board ($8600). Full-time tuition and fees vary according to degree level and program. Part-time tuition: $895 per credit hour. Part-time tuition and fees vary according to course load, degree level, and program. *Required fees:* $370 per year part-time. *Room and board:* Room and board charges vary according to board plan. *Payment plan:* installment. *Waivers:* senior citizens and employees or children of employees.
Financial Aid Of all full-time matriculated undergraduates who enrolled in 2017, 602 applied for aid, 581 were judged to have need, 55 had their need fully met. 90 Federal Work-Study jobs (averaging $1444). 100 state and other part-time jobs (averaging $1700). In 2017, 40 non-need-based awards were made. *Average percent of need met:* 72. *Average financial aid package:* $25,609. *Average need-based loan:* $4647. *Average need-based gift aid:* $20,645. *Average non-need-based aid:* $13,909. *Average indebtedness upon graduation:* $27,308.

APPLYING
Standardized Tests *Required:* SAT or ACT (for admission).
Options: electronic application, deferred entrance.
Required: high school transcript. *Required for some:* essay or personal statement, 1 letter of recommendation. *Recommended:* minimum 2.5 GPA.
Application deadlines: rolling (freshmen), rolling (transfers).
Notification: continuous (freshmen), continuous (transfers).

CONTACT
Liz Saffold, Admission Counselor Assistant/Receptionist, Mount Mary University, 2900 North Menomonee River Parkway, Milwaukee, WI 53222. *Phone:* 414-930-3000 Ext. 219. *Toll-free phone:* 800-321-6265. *Fax:* 414-256-0180. *E-mail:* mmu-admiss@mtmary.edu.

Northland College
Ashland, Wisconsin
http://www.northland.edu/

- **Independent** 4-year, founded 1892, affiliated with United Church of Christ
- **Small-town** 130-acre campus
- **Endowment** $22.6 million
- **Coed** 635 undergraduate students, 94% full-time, 54% women, 46% men
- **Moderately difficult** entrance level, 61% of applicants were admitted

UNDERGRAD STUDENTS
594 full-time, 41 part-time. Students come from 37 states and territories; 4 other countries; 50% are from out of state; 3% Black or African American, non-Hispanic/Latino; 5% Hispanic/Latino; 1% Asian, non-Hispanic/Latino; 2% American Indian or Alaska Native, non-Hispanic/Latino; 3% Two or more races, non-Hispanic/Latino; 2% Race/ethnicity unknown; 4% international; 6% transferred in; 74% live on campus.

Freshmen:
Admission: 1,625 applied, 994 admitted, 189 enrolled. *Average high school GPA:* 3.3. *Test scores:* ACT scores over 18: 94%; ACT scores over 24: 49%; ACT scores over 30: 9%.
Retention: 73% of full-time freshmen returned.

FACULTY
Total: 69, 72% full-time, 67% with terminal degrees.
Student/faculty ratio: 11:1.

ACADEMICS
Calendar: 4-4-1. *Degree:* bachelor's.
Special study options: advanced placement credit, double majors, honors programs, independent study, internships, off-campus study, part-time degree program, services for LD students, student-designed majors, study abroad, summer session for credit.
Unusual degree programs: 3-2 engineering with Washington University in St. Louis.
Computers: 125 computers/terminals are available on campus for general student use. Students can access the following: campus intranet, computer help desk, free student e-mail accounts, online (class) grades, online

(class) registration, online (class) schedules. Campuswide network is available. 100% of college-owned or -operated housing units are wired for high-speed Internet access. Wireless service is available via entire campus.

Library: Dexter Library. *Books:* 74,451 (physical); *Serial titles:* 82 (physical), 50 (digital/electronic); *Databases:* 38. Weekly public service hours: 88; students can reserve study rooms.

STUDENT LIFE
Housing options: on-campus residence required through junior year; coed, women-only, special housing for students with disabilities. Campus housing is university owned. Freshman campus housing is guaranteed.

Activities and organizations: drama/theater group, student-run newspaper, choral group, Northland Volunteer Program, Northland College Student Association, Native American Student Association, Environmental Council, SAAC (Student Athlete Organization).

Athletics Member NCAA. All Division III. *Intercollegiate sports:* baseball M, basketball M/W, cross-country running M/W, golf M/W, ice hockey M/W, lacrosse M/W, soccer M/W, softball W, volleyball W.

Campus security: 24-hour emergency response devices and patrols, late-night transport/escort service, controlled dormitory access.

Student services: health clinic, personal/psychological counseling.

COSTS & FINANCIAL AID
Costs (2018–19) *Comprehensive fee:* $45,359 includes full-time tuition ($34,666), mandatory fees ($1517), and room and board ($9176). Full-time tuition and fees vary according to course load. Part-time tuition: $670 per credit. Part-time tuition and fees vary according to course load. *College room only:* $4234. Room and board charges vary according to board plan and housing facility. *Payment plan:* installment. *Waivers:* employees or children of employees.

Financial Aid Of all full-time matriculated undergraduates who enrolled in 2017, 565 applied for aid, 512 were judged to have need, 100 had their need fully met. 313 Federal Work-Study jobs (averaging $1741). 231 state and other part-time jobs (averaging $1572). In 2017, 79 non-need-based awards were made. *Average percent of need met:* 84. *Average financial aid package:* $30,526. *Average need-based loan:* $4801. *Average need-based gift aid:* $25,259. *Average non-need-based aid:* $19,101. *Average indebtedness upon graduation:* $28,731.

APPLYING
Standardized Tests *Required for some:* SAT (for admission), ACT (for admission), SAT or ACT (for admission).

Options: electronic application, deferred entrance.

Required: high school transcript.

Application deadlines: rolling (freshmen), rolling (transfers).

Notification: continuous (freshmen), continuous (transfers).

CONTACT
Teege Mettille, Executive Director of Admissions, Northland College, 1411 Ellis Avenue, Ashland, WI 54806. *Phone:* 715-682-1224. *Toll-free phone:* 800-753-1840 (in-state); 800-753-1040 (out-of-state). *Fax:* 715-682-1258. *E-mail:* admit@northland.edu.

Rasmussen College Green Bay
Green Bay, Wisconsin
http://www.rasmussen.edu/
- Proprietary 4-year, part of Rasmussen College System
- Suburban campus
- Coed
- Minimally difficult entrance level

FACULTY
Student/faculty ratio: 22:1.

ACADEMICS
Calendar: quarters. *Degrees:* certificates, diplomas, associate, and bachelor's.
Library: Rasmussen College Library - Green Bay.

STUDENT LIFE
Housing options: college housing not available.

COSTS
Costs (2017–18) *Tuition:* $11,055 full-time, $290 per credit hour part-time. Full-time tuition and fees vary according to course level, course load, degree level, location, and program. Part-time tuition and fees vary according to course level, course load, degree level, location, and program. No tuition increase for student's term of enrollment. *Required fees:* $1695 full-time, $44 per credit hour part-time. *Payment plans:* installment, deferred payment.

APPLYING
Standardized Tests *Required:* institutional exam (for admission).

Options: electronic application, early admission, deferred entrance.

Required: high school transcript, minimum 2.0 GPA. *Required for some:* interview.

CONTACT
Ms. Susan Hammerstrom, Director of Admissions, Rasmussen College Green Bay, 904 South Taylor Street, Suite 100, Green Bay, WI 54303. *Phone:* 920-593-8400. *Toll-free phone:* 888-549-6755. *E-mail:* susan.hammerstrom@rasmussen.edu.

Rasmussen College Wausau
Wausau, Wisconsin
http://www.rasmussen.edu/
- Proprietary 4-year, part of Rasmussen College System
- Suburban campus
- Coed
- Minimally difficult entrance level

FACULTY
Student/faculty ratio: 22:1.

ACADEMICS
Calendar: quarters. *Degrees:* certificates, diplomas, associate, and bachelor's.
Library: Rasmussen College Library - Wausau.

STUDENT LIFE
Housing options: college housing not available.

COSTS
Costs (2017–18) *Tuition:* $11,055 full-time, $290 per credit hour part-time. Full-time tuition and fees vary according to course level, course load, degree level, location, and program. Part-time tuition and fees vary according to course level, course load, degree level, location, and program. No tuition increase for student's term of enrollment. *Required fees:* $1695 full-time, $44 per credit hour part-time. *Payment plans:* installment, deferred payment.

APPLYING
Standardized Tests *Required:* institutional exam (for admission).

Options: electronic application, early admission, deferred entrance.

Required: high school transcript, minimum 2.0 GPA. *Required for some:* interview.

CONTACT
Ms. Susan Hammerstrom, Director of Admissions, Rasmussen College Wausau, 1101 Westwood Drive, Wausau, WI 54401. *Phone:* 715-841-8000. *Toll-free phone:* 888-549-6755. *E-mail:* susan.hammerstrom@rasmussen.edu.

Ripon College
Ripon, Wisconsin
http://www.ripon.edu/
- Independent 4-year, founded 1851
- Small-town 250-acre campus with easy access to Milwaukee
- Endowment $84.5 million
- Coed 756 undergraduate students, 98% full-time, 54% women, 46% men
- Moderately difficult entrance level, 65% of applicants were admitted

UNDERGRAD STUDENTS
739 full-time, 17 part-time. Students come from 30 states and territories; 7 other countries; 30% are from out of state; 4% Black or African American, non-Hispanic/Latino; 9% Hispanic/Latino; 0.9% Asian, non-Hispanic/Latino; 0.3% American Indian or Alaska Native, non-

Hispanic/Latino; 3% Two or more races, non-Hispanic/Latino; 0.3% Race/ethnicity unknown; 4% international; 2% transferred in; 93% live on campus.

Freshmen:
Admission: 2,553 applied, 1,666 admitted, 234 enrolled. *Average high school GPA:* 3.4. *Test scores:* ACT scores over 18: 97%; ACT scores over 24: 47%; ACT scores over 30: 13%.
Retention: 71% of full-time freshmen returned.

FACULTY
Total: 78, 79% full-time, 85% with terminal degrees.
Student/faculty ratio: 12:1.

ACADEMICS
Calendar: semesters. *Degree:* bachelor's.
Special study options: accelerated degree program, advanced placement credit, double majors, internships, off-campus study, part-time degree program, services for LD students, student-designed majors, study abroad. *ROTC:* Army (b).
Unusual degree programs: 3-2 engineering with Rensselaer Polytechnic Institute, Washington University in St. Louis, University of Wisconsin–Madison; forestry with Duke University; nursing with Rush University; environmental studies with Duke University.
Computers: 150 computers/terminals are available on campus for general student use. Students can access the following: campus intranet, computer help desk, free student e-mail accounts, online (class) grades, online (class) schedules. Campuswide network is available. 100% of college-owned or -operated housing units are wired for high-speed Internet access. Wireless service is available via entire campus.
Library: Lane Library. *Books:* 160,664 (physical), 142,427 (digital/electronic); *Serial titles:* 86 (physical), 61,132 (digital/electronic); *Databases:* 26. Weekly public service hours: 52; students can reserve study rooms.

STUDENT LIFE
Housing options: on-campus residence required through senior year; coed, men-only, women-only. Campus housing is university owned. Freshman campus housing is guaranteed.

Activities and organizations: drama/theater group, student-run newspaper, radio station, choral group, Environmental Group, Student Senate, Community Service Coalition, SMAC (Student Media and Activities Committee), national fraternities, national sororities.
Athletics Member NCAA. All Division III. *Intercollegiate sports:* baseball M, basketball M/W, cheerleading M(c)/W, cross-country running M/W, football M, rugby M(c)/W(c), soccer M/W, softball W, swimming and diving M/W, tennis M/W, track and field M/W, volleyball W. *Intramural sports:* basketball M/W, bowling M/W, equestrian sports M(c)/W(c), fencing M/W, football M/W, racquetball M/W, soccer M/W, softball M/W, table tennis M/W, tennis M/W, ultimate Frisbee M/W, volleyball M/W.
Campus security: 24-hour emergency response devices and patrols, student patrols, late-night transport/escort service, controlled dormitory access.
Student services: health clinic, personal/psychological counseling.

COSTS & FINANCIAL AID
Costs (2018–19) *Comprehensive fee:* $52,208 includes full-time tuition ($43,508), mandatory fees ($300), and room and board ($8400). Part-time tuition: $1500 per credit. *Payment plan:* installment. *Waivers:* employees or children of employees.
Financial Aid Of all full-time matriculated undergraduates who enrolled in 2012, 840 applied for aid, 760 were judged to have need, 135 had their need fully met. 437 Federal Work-Study jobs (averaging $1777). 326 state and other part-time jobs (averaging $1727). In 2012, 124 non-need-based awards were made. *Average percent of need met:* 84. *Average financial aid package:* $25,418. *Average need-based loan:* $5329. *Average need-based gift aid:* $19,763. *Average non-need-based aid:* $10,803. *Average indebtedness upon graduation:* $31,216.

APPLYING
Options: electronic application, deferred entrance.
Application fee: $30.
Required: high school transcript, minimum 2.0 GPA, 1 letter of recommendation. *Required for some:* essay or personal statement, interview. *Recommended:* essay or personal statement, interview.
Application deadlines: rolling (freshmen), rolling (transfers).

Notification: continuous (freshmen), continuous (transfers).

CONTACT
Office of Admission, Ripon College, 300 Seward Street, PO Box 248, Ripon, WI 54971. *Phone:* 920-748-8337. *Toll-free phone:* 800-947-4766. *Fax:* 920-748-8335. *E-mail:* adminfo@ripon.edu.

See previous page for display ad and page 1398 for the College Close-Up.

St. Norbert College

De Pere, Wisconsin
http://www.snc.edu/

- **Independent Roman Catholic** comprehensive, founded 1898
- **Suburban** 113-acre campus
- **Endowment** $109.2 million
- **Coed** 2,067 undergraduate students, 98% full-time, 57% women, 43% men
- **Moderately difficult** entrance level, 79% of applicants were admitted

UNDERGRAD STUDENTS
2,021 full-time, 46 part-time. Students come from 28 states and territories; 26 other countries; 22% are from out of state; 1% Black or African American, non-Hispanic/Latino; 4% Hispanic/Latino; 2% Asian, non-Hispanic/Latino; 1% American Indian or Alaska Native, non-Hispanic/Latino; 1% Two or more races, non-Hispanic/Latino; 0.5% Race/ethnicity unknown; 3% international; 2% transferred in; 85% live on campus.

Freshmen:
Admission: 3,860 applied, 3,058 admitted, 526 enrolled. *Average high school GPA:* 3.5. *Test scores:* ACT scores over 18: 99%; ACT scores over 24: 56%; ACT scores over 30: 9%.
Retention: 83% of full-time freshmen returned.

FACULTY
Total: 209, 67% full-time, 75% with terminal degrees.
Student/faculty ratio: 13:1.

ACADEMICS
Calendar: semesters. *Degrees:* bachelor's and master's.

Special study options: academic remediation for entering students, advanced placement credit, distance learning, double majors, English as a second language, honors programs, independent study, internships, off-campus study, part-time degree program, services for LD students, student-designed majors, study abroad, summer session for credit. *ROTC:* Army (b).

Computers: 174 computers/terminals are available on campus for general student use. Students can access the following: campus intranet, computer help desk, free student e-mail accounts, online (class) grades, online (class) registration, online (class) schedules. Campuswide network is available. 100% of college-owned or -operated housing units are wired for high-speed Internet access. Wireless service is available via classrooms, computer centers, computer labs, dorm rooms, learning centers, libraries, student centers.

Library: Miriam B. and James J. Mulva Library plus 1 other. *Books:* 249,694 (physical), 89,890 (digital/electronic); *Serial titles:* 100,960 (physical), 100,893 (digital/electronic). Weekly public service hours: 116; students can reserve study rooms.

STUDENT LIFE
Housing options: on-campus residence required through senior year; coed, women-only, special housing for students with disabilities. Campus housing is university owned. Freshman campus housing is guaranteed.

Activities and organizations: drama/theater group, student-run newspaper, radio and television station, choral group, Pen Pals, Aspiring Educators, CC Hams, Investment Club, CRU, national fraternities, national sororities.

Athletics Member NCAA. All Division III. *Intercollegiate sports:* baseball M, basketball M/W, cross-country running M/W, football M, golf M/W, ice hockey M/W, soccer M/W, softball W, swimming and diving M/W, tennis M/W, track and field M/W, volleyball W. *Intramural sports:* basketball M/W, cheerleading W, crew M(c)/W(c), football M/W, riflery M(c)/W(c), skiing (downhill) M(c)/W(c), soccer M/W, triathlon M(c)/W(c), ultimate Frisbee M(c)/W(c), volleyball M/W.

Campus security: 24-hour emergency response devices and patrols, student patrols, late-night transport/escort service, controlled dormitory

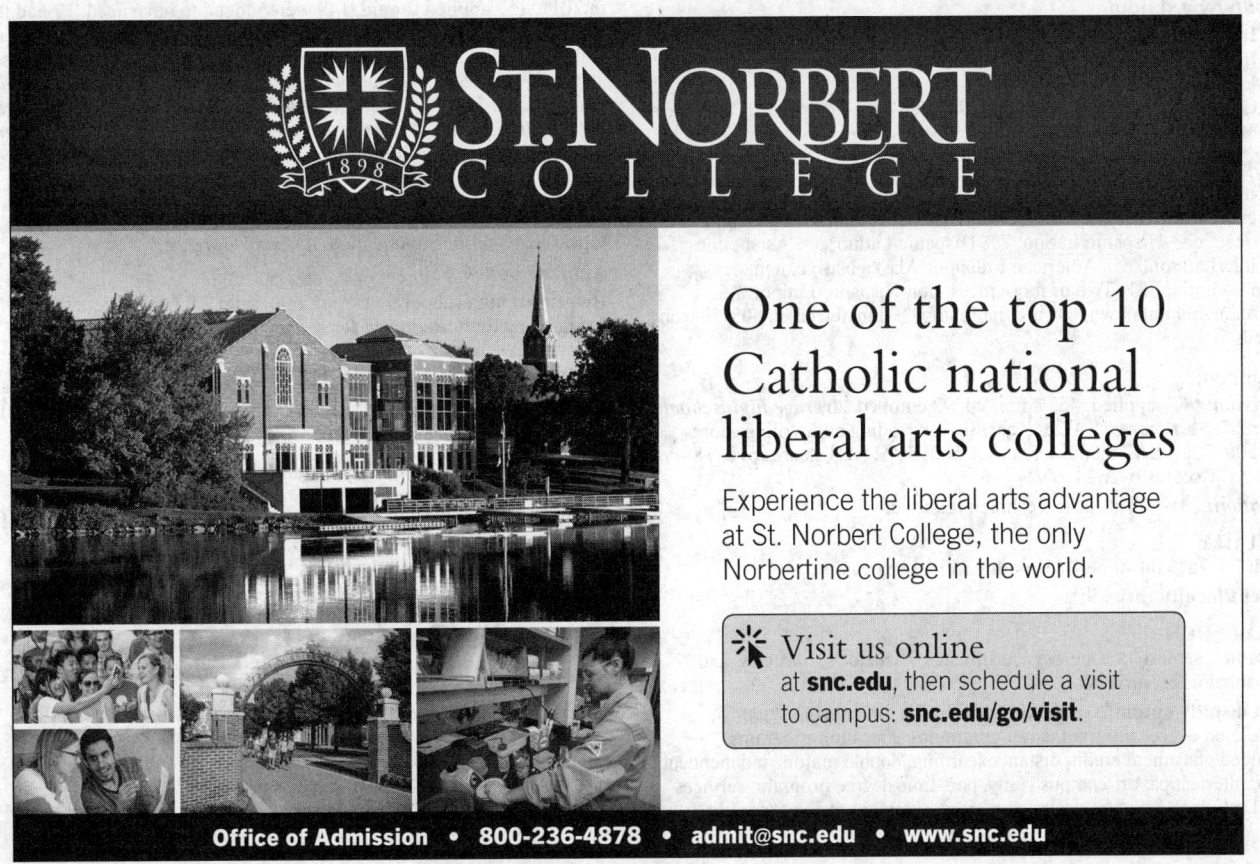

A ★ *indicates that the school has detailed information with a Premium Profile on Petersons.com.*

access, ConnectED emergency information system, crime prevention programs.

Student services: health clinic, personal/psychological counseling, women's center.

COSTS & FINANCIAL AID

Costs (2018–19) *Comprehensive fee:* $48,083 includes full-time tuition ($37,314), mandatory fees ($815), and room and board ($9954). Full-time tuition and fees vary according to course load. Part-time tuition: $1166 per credit hour. Part-time tuition and fees vary according to course load. *College room only:* $5536. Room and board charges vary according to board plan and housing facility. *Payment plans:* installment, deferred payment. *Waivers:* employees or children of employees.

Financial Aid Of all full-time matriculated undergraduates who enrolled in 2016, 1,733 applied for aid, 1,510 were judged to have need, 395 had their need fully met. 373 Federal Work-Study jobs (averaging $1238). In 2016, 507 non-need-based awards were made. *Average percent of need met:* 82. *Average financial aid package:* $26,100. *Average need-based loan:* $4737. *Average need-based gift aid:* $20,136. *Average non-need-based aid:* $12,873. *Average indebtedness upon graduation:* $33,794.

APPLYING

Standardized Tests *Required:* SAT or ACT (for admission).

Options: electronic application, deferred entrance.

Required: high school transcript. *Required for some:* interview. *Recommended:* essay or personal statement, letters of recommendation.

Application deadlines: rolling (freshmen), rolling (transfers).

Notification: continuous (freshmen), continuous (transfers).

CONTACT

Mr. Mark Selin, Executive Director of Enrollment and Marketing, St. Norbert College, 100 Grant Street, De Pere, WI 54115-2099. *Phone:* 920-403-3005. *Toll-free phone:* 800-236-4878. *Fax:* 920-403-4072. *E-mail:* admit@snc.edu.

See previous page for display ad and page 1416 for the College Close-Up.

Silver Lake College of the Holy Family

Manitowoc, Wisconsin

http://www.sl.edu/

- **Independent Roman Catholic** comprehensive, founded 1869
- **Rural** 30-acre campus with easy access to Milwaukee
- **Endowment** $7.2 million
- **Coed** 392 undergraduate students, 68% full-time, 66% women, 34% men
- **Minimally difficult** entrance level, 52% of applicants were admitted

UNDERGRAD STUDENTS

267 full-time, 125 part-time. Students come from 10 states and territories; 9 other countries; 15% are from out of state; 18% Black or African American, non-Hispanic/Latino; 7% Hispanic/Latino; 5% Asian, non-Hispanic/Latino; 0.5% American Indian or Alaska Native, non-Hispanic/Latino; 2% Two or more races, non-Hispanic/Latino; 7% Race/ethnicity unknown; 4% international; 9% transferred in; 50% live on campus.

Freshmen:

Admission: 877 applied, 452 admitted, 92 enrolled. *Average high school GPA:* 2.7. *Test scores:* SAT evidence-based reading and writing scores over 500: 25%; SAT math scores over 500: 50%; ACT scores over 18: 32%; ACT scores over 24: 5%.

Retention: 73% of full-time freshmen returned.

FACULTY

Total: 73, 38% full-time, 16% with terminal degrees.
Student/faculty ratio: 9:1.

ACADEMICS

Calendar: semesters. *Degrees:* certificates, bachelor's, master's, and postbachelor's certificates.

Special study options: academic remediation for entering students, accelerated degree program, adult/continuing education programs, advanced placement credit, distance learning, double majors, independent study, internships, off-campus study, part-time degree program, services for LD students, student-designed majors, summer session for credit.

Computers: 120 computers/terminals are available on campus for general student use. Students can access the following: campus intranet, computer help desk, free student e-mail accounts, online (class) grades, online (class) registration, online (class) schedules. Campuswide network is available. 100% of college-owned or -operated housing units are wired for high-speed Internet access. Wireless service is available via entire campus.

Library: The Erma M. and Theodore M. Zigmunt Library. *Books:* 53,862 (physical), 93 (digital/electronic); *Serial titles:* 488 (physical); *Databases:* 32. Weekly public service hours: 80; study areas open 24 hours, 5–7 days a week; students can reserve study rooms.

STUDENT LIFE

Housing options: on-campus residence required through junior year; coed, men-only, women-only, special housing for students with disabilities. Campus housing is university owned. Freshman campus housing is guaranteed.

Activities and organizations: choral group, Wellness Club, Card and Game Club, Student For Life, Campus Activity Board, Silver Lake Serves.

Athletics Member NAIA, USCAA. *Intercollegiate sports:* basketball M(s)/W(s), cross-country running M(s)/W(s), soccer M(s), softball W(s), volleyball W(s). *Intramural sports:* table tennis M/W.

Campus security: 24-hour emergency response devices and patrols, student patrols, late-night transport/escort service, controlled dormitory access.

Student services: health clinic, personal/psychological counseling.

COSTS & FINANCIAL AID

Costs (2017–18) *One-time required fee:* $280. *Comprehensive fee:* $34,560 includes full-time tuition ($26,800), mandatory fees ($560), and room and board ($7200). Full-time tuition and fees vary according to course load and degree level. Part-time tuition: $540 per credit hour. Part-time tuition and fees vary according to course load and degree level. *Required fees:* $270 per year part-time. *College room only:* $3500. Room and board charges vary according to board plan and housing facility. *Payment plan:* installment. *Waivers:* senior citizens and employees or children of employees.

Financial Aid Of all full-time matriculated undergraduates who enrolled in 2011, 157 applied for aid, 149 were judged to have need, 17 had their need fully met. 97 Federal Work-Study jobs (averaging $1429). 3 state and other part-time jobs (averaging $2450). In 2011, 7 non-need-based awards were made. *Average percent of need met:* 77. *Average financial aid package:* $18,970. *Average need-based loan:* $4210. *Average need-based gift aid:* $14,197. *Average non-need-based aid:* $10,140. *Average indebtedness upon graduation:* $35,164.

APPLYING

Standardized Tests *Recommended:* SAT or ACT (for admission).

Options: electronic application, deferred entrance.

Application fee: $50.

Required: high school transcript, minimum 2.0 GPA, 1 letter of recommendation. *Required for some:* essay or personal statement, interview.

Application deadlines: rolling (freshmen), 9/1 (transfers).

Notification: continuous until 9/1 (freshmen), continuous (transfers).

CONTACT

Daniel Connolly, Director of Enrollment Management, Silver Lake College of the Holy Family, 2406 South Alverno Road, Manitowoc, WI 54220-9319. *Phone:* 920-686-6175. *Toll-free phone:* 800-236-4752 Ext. 175. *Fax:* 920-686-6322. *E-mail:* Dan.Connolly@sl.edu.

University of Wisconsin–Baraboo/Sauk County

Baraboo, Wisconsin

http://www.baraboo.uwc.edu/

- **State-supported** primarily 2-year, founded 1968, part of University of Wisconsin System
- **Small-town** 68-acre campus with easy access to Madison
- **Coed** 512 undergraduate students

FACULTY
Student/faculty ratio: 16:1.

ACADEMICS
Calendar: semesters. *Degrees:* certificates, associate, and bachelor's.

Special study options: academic remediation for entering students, advanced placement credit, distance learning, external degree program, honors programs, independent study, internships, off-campus study, part-time degree program, services for LD students, student-designed majors, study abroad, summer session for credit.

Computers: Students can access the following: computer help desk, free student e-mail accounts, online (class) grades, online (class) registration, online (class) schedules, financial aid application. Campuswide network is available.

Library: T. N. Savides Library plus 1 other.

STUDENT LIFE
Housing options: college housing not available.

Activities and organizations: drama/theater group, student-run newspaper, choral group.

Athletics Member NJCAA. *Intercollegiate sports:* basketball M(s), soccer M/W, tennis M/W, volleyball W. *Intramural sports:* softball M/W.

Student services: personal/psychological counseling.

COSTS
Costs (2017–18) *One-time required fee:* $180. *Tuition:* state resident $4750 full-time, $198 per credit hour part-time; nonresident $12,321 full-time, $513 per credit hour part-time. Full-time tuition and fees vary according to reciprocity agreements. Part-time tuition and fees vary according to course load. *Required fees:* $487 full-time, $41 per year part-time. *Room and board:* Room and board charges vary according to location. *Payment plan:* installment.

APPLYING
Standardized Tests *Required:* ACT (for admission).

Options: electronic application.

Application fee: $50.

Required: high school transcript.

Application deadlines: 8/30 (freshmen), rolling (out-of-state freshmen), 8/30 (transfers).

CONTACT
University of Wisconsin–Baraboo/Sauk County, 1006 Connie Road, Baraboo, WI 53913-1015.

University of Wisconsin–Barron County
Rice Lake, Wisconsin
http://www.barron.uwc.edu/
- **State-supported** primarily 2-year, founded 1966, part of University of Wisconsin System
- **Small-town** 110-acre campus
- **Coed** 505 undergraduate students

FACULTY
Student/faculty ratio: 12:1.

ACADEMICS
Calendar: semesters. *Degrees:* associate and bachelor's.

Special study options: academic remediation for entering students, adult/continuing education programs, advanced placement credit, distance learning, independent study, internships, off-campus study, part-time degree program, services for LD students, study abroad, summer session for credit.

Computers: Students can access the following: computer help desk, free student e-mail accounts, online (class) grades, online (class) registration, online (class) schedules, financial aid application. Campuswide network is available.

Library: UW-Barron County Library plus 1 other.

STUDENT LIFE
Housing options: college housing not available.

Athletics *Intercollegiate sports:* baseball M(c), basketball M, cross-country running M(c)/W(c), golf M(c)/W(c), volleyball W.

COSTS
Costs (2017–18) *One-time required fee:* $180. *Tuition:* state resident $4750 full-time, $198 per credit hour part-time; nonresident $12,321 full-time, $513 per credit hour part-time. Full-time tuition and fees vary according to reciprocity agreements. Part-time tuition and fees vary according to course load. *Required fees:* $472 full-time, $39 per year part-time. *Room and board:* Room and board charges vary according to location. *Payment plan:* installment.

APPLYING
Standardized Tests *Required:* ACT (for admission).

Options: electronic application, deferred entrance.

Application fee: $50.

Required: high school transcript.

Application deadlines: 8/30 (freshmen), 8/30 (transfers).

CONTACT
University of Wisconsin–Barron County, 1800 College Drive, Rice Lake, WI 54868-2497.

University of Wisconsin–Eau Claire
Eau Claire, Wisconsin
http://www.uwec.edu/
- **State-supported** comprehensive, founded 1916, part of University of Wisconsin System
- **Small-town** 337-acre campus with easy access to Minneapolis-St. Paul
- **Endowment** $71.5 million
- **Coed** 10,022 undergraduate students, 93% full-time, 61% women, 39% men
- **Moderately difficult** entrance level, 86% of applicants were admitted

UNDERGRAD STUDENTS
9,347 full-time, 675 part-time. Students come from 39 states and territories; 32 other countries; 30% are from out of state; 1% Black or African American, non-Hispanic/Latino; 3% Hispanic/Latino; 3% Asian, non-Hispanic/Latino; 0.3% American Indian or Alaska Native, non-Hispanic/Latino; 2% Two or more races, non-Hispanic/Latino; 0.1% Race/ethnicity unknown; 2% international; 5% transferred in; 38% live on campus.

Freshmen:
Admission: 5,990 applied, 5,133 admitted, 2,337 enrolled. *Test scores:* SAT evidence-based reading and writing scores over 500: 96%; SAT math scores over 500: 84%; ACT scores over 18: 98%; SAT evidence-based reading and writing scores over 600: 40%; SAT math scores over 600: 60%; ACT scores over 24: 50%; SAT evidence-based reading and writing scores over 700: 20%; SAT math scores over 700: 16%; ACT scores over 30: 6%.

Retention: 82% of full-time freshmen returned.

FACULTY
Total: 570, 68% full-time, 63% with terminal degrees.

Student/faculty ratio: 22:1.

ACADEMICS
Calendar: semesters. *Degrees:* certificates, associate, bachelor's, master's, doctoral, post-master's, and postbachelor's certificates.

Special study options: academic remediation for entering students, accelerated degree program, advanced placement credit, cooperative education, distance learning, double majors, English as a second language, external degree program, honors programs, independent study, internships, off-campus study, part-time degree program, services for LD students, student-designed majors, study abroad, summer session for credit. *ROTC:* Army (b).

Computers: 900 computers/terminals are available on campus for general student use. Students can access the following: campus intranet, computer help desk, free student e-mail accounts, online (class) grades, online (class) registration, online (class) schedules, course management system, online library databases and card catalog, other online library services (e.g. Interlibrary loan), library reference staff online chat, ability to check where there are open seats in the general access computer labs, laptop check. Campuswide network is available. 100% of college-owned or - operated housing units are wired for high-speed Internet access. Wireless service is available via entire campus.

Library: William D. McIntyre Library. *Books:* 381,168 (physical), 231,381 (digital/electronic); *Serial titles:* 141 (physical), 216,577 (digital/electronic); *Databases:* 207. Weekly public service hours: 112; study areas open 24 hours, 5–7 days a week; students can reserve study rooms.

STUDENT LIFE
Housing options: on-campus residence required through sophomore year; coed. Campus housing is university owned and leased by the school. Freshman campus housing is guaranteed.

Activities and organizations: drama/theater group, student-run newspaper, radio and television station, choral group, marching band, Student Wisconsin Education Association, Pre- Professional Health Club, Kinesiology Club, RHA (Residence Hall Association), Blugold Beginnings, national fraternities, national sororities.

Athletics Member NCAA. All Division III. *Intercollegiate sports:* basketball M/W, cross-country running M/W, football M, golf M/W, gymnastics W, ice hockey M/W, soccer W, softball W, swimming and diving M/W, tennis M/W, track and field M/W, volleyball W, wrestling M. *Intramural sports:* baseball M(c)/W(c), basketball M/W, bowling M(c)/W(c), cheerleading M(c)/W(c), equestrian sports M(c)/W(c), football M/W, ice hockey M(c), lacrosse M(c)/W(c), rugby M(c)/W(c), sand volleyball M/W, skiing (cross-country) M(c)/W(c), soccer M/W, softball M/W, table tennis M(c)/W(c), tennis M/W, triathlon M(c)/W(c), ultimate Frisbee M/W, volleyball M/W.

Campus security: 24-hour emergency response devices and patrols, student patrols, late-night transport/escort service, controlled dormitory access.

Student services: health clinic, personal/psychological counseling, women's center, legal services.

COSTS & FINANCIAL AID
Costs (2017–18) *Tuition:* state resident $7361 full-time, $307 per credit part-time; nonresident $15,281 full-time, $637 per credit part-time. Full-time tuition and fees vary according to program and reciprocity agreements. Part-time tuition and fees vary according to program and reciprocity agreements. *Required fees:* $1455 full-time, $61 per credit part-time. *Room and board:* $7538; room only: $4436. Room and board charges vary according to board plan and housing facility. *Payment plan:* installment.

Financial Aid Of all full-time matriculated undergraduates who enrolled in 2016, 7,013 applied for aid, 4,816 were judged to have need, 1,009 had their need fully met. 4,020 Federal Work-Study jobs (averaging $1142). In 2016, 457 non-need-based awards were made. *Average percent of need met:* 84. *Average financial aid package:* $9479. *Average need-based loan:* $4405. *Average need-based gift aid:* $6043. *Average non-need-based aid:* $2135. *Average indebtedness upon graduation:* $26,244.

APPLYING
Standardized Tests *Required:* SAT or ACT (for admission).

Options: electronic application, early admission.

Application fee: $50.

Required: essay or personal statement, high school transcript.

Application deadlines: 8/20 (freshmen), 8/20 (transfers).

Notification: continuous (freshmen), continuous (transfers).

CONTACT
Heather Kretz, Director of Admissions, University of Wisconsin–Eau Claire, PO Box 4004, Eau Claire, WI 54702-4004. *Phone:* 715-836-5188. *Fax:* 715-831-4799. *E-mail:* admissions@uwec.edu.

University of Wisconsin–Green Bay
Green Bay, Wisconsin
http://www.uwgb.edu/
- **State-supported** comprehensive, founded 1968, part of University of Wisconsin System
- **Suburban** 700-acre campus with easy access to Milwaukee
- **Endowment** $28.0 million
- **Coed**
- **Moderately difficult** entrance level

FACULTY
Student/faculty ratio: 22:1.

ACADEMICS
Calendar: semesters. *Degrees:* associate, bachelor's, and master's.
Library: Cofrin Library. *Books:* 353,331 (physical); *Serial titles:* 7,592 (physical); *Databases:* 179. Weekly public service hours: 100; students can reserve study rooms.

STUDENT LIFE
Housing options: coed. Campus housing is university owned and is provided by a third party. Freshman applicants given priority for college housing.

Activities and organizations: drama/theater group, student-run newspaper, radio station, choral group, Good Times, Psychology and Human Development Club, Student Ambassadors, Residence Hall Apartment Association, Student Government Association.

Athletics Member NCAA. All Division I.

Campus security: 24-hour emergency response devices and patrols, late-night transport/escort service, controlled dormitory access.

Student services: health clinic, personal/psychological counseling.

COSTS & FINANCIAL AID
Costs (2017–18) *One-time required fee:* $212. *Tuition:* state resident $6298 full-time, $262 per credit hour part-time; nonresident $14,148 full-time, $589 per credit hour part-time. Full-time tuition and fees vary according to course load and reciprocity agreements. Part-time tuition and fees vary according to reciprocity agreements. *Required fees:* $1580 full-time, $66 per credit hour part-time. *Room and board:* $7306; room only: $4380. Room and board charges vary according to board plan and housing facility.

Financial Aid Of all full-time matriculated undergraduates who enrolled in 2016, 3,282 applied for aid, 2,678 were judged to have need, 922 had their need fully met. 289 Federal Work-Study jobs (averaging $1893). In 2016, 173 non-need-based awards were made. *Average percent of need met:* 76. *Average financial aid package:* $10,328. *Average need-based loan:* $6565. *Average need-based gift aid:* $5976. *Average non-need-based aid:* $1226. *Average indebtedness upon graduation:* $28,940.

APPLYING
Standardized Tests *Required:* SAT or ACT (for admission).

Options: electronic application, deferred entrance.

Application fee: $50.

Required: essay or personal statement, high school transcript. *Required for some:* interview.

CONTACT
Ms. Jen Jones, Director of Admissions, University of Wisconsin–Green Bay, 2420 Nicolet Drive, Green Bay, WI 54311-7001. *Phone:* 920-465-2111. *Fax:* 920-465-5754. *E-mail:* uwgb@uwgb.edu.

University of Wisconsin–La Crosse
La Crosse, Wisconsin
http://www.uwlax.edu/
- **State-supported** comprehensive, founded 1909, part of University of Wisconsin System
- **Suburban** 128-acre campus
- **Endowment** $23.0 million
- **Coed** 9,655 undergraduate students, 94% full-time, 56% women, 44% men
- **Moderately difficult** entrance level, 82% of applicants were admitted

UNDERGRAD STUDENTS
9,064 full-time, 591 part-time. Students come from 29 states and territories; 20 other countries; 18% are from out of state; 0.8% Black or African American, non-Hispanic/Latino; 3% Hispanic/Latino; 2% Asian, non-Hispanic/Latino; 0.2% American Indian or Alaska Native, non-Hispanic/Latino; 3% Two or more races, non-Hispanic/Latino; 0.8% international; 5% transferred in; 36% live on campus.

Freshmen:
Admission: 5,801 applied, 4,782 admitted, 2,106 enrolled. *Test scores:* SAT evidence-based reading and writing scores over 500: 96%; SAT math scores over 500: 100%; ACT scores over 18: 100%; SAT evidence-based

reading and writing scores over 600: 57%; SAT math scores over 600: 52%; ACT scores over 24: 61%; SAT evidence-based reading and writing scores over 700: 9%; SAT math scores over 700: 9%; ACT scores over 30: 7%.

Retention: 83% of full-time freshmen returned.

FACULTY
Total: 632, 74% full-time, 69% with terminal degrees.
Student/faculty ratio: 19:1.

ACADEMICS
Calendar: semesters. *Degrees:* associate, bachelor's, master's, doctoral, post-master's, and postbachelor's certificates.

Special study options: academic remediation for entering students, advanced placement credit, distance learning, double majors, English as a second language, honors programs, independent study, internships, off-campus study, part-time degree program, services for LD students, study abroad, summer session for credit. *ROTC:* Army (b).

Unusual degree programs: 3-2 engineering with University of Wisconsin-Madison; University of Wisconsin-Milwaukee; University of Wisconsin-Platteville; University of Minnesota-Duluth; Winona State University; physical therapy and physics; physical therapy and biology.

Computers: 200 computers/terminals are available on campus for general student use. Students can access the following: campus intranet, computer help desk, free student e-mail accounts, online (class) grades, online (class) registration, online (class) schedules. Campuswide network is available. 100% of college-owned or -operated housing units are wired for high-speed Internet access. Wireless service is available via entire campus.

Library: Murphy Library plus 6 others. *Books:* 427,203 (physical), 415,020 (digital/electronic); *Serial titles:* 8,561 (physical), 556,900 (digital/electronic); *Databases:* 255. Weekly public service hours: 55; students can reserve study rooms.

STUDENT LIFE
Housing options: on-campus residence required for freshman year; coed, special housing for students with disabilities. Campus housing is university owned. Freshman applicants given priority for college housing.

Activities and organizations: drama/theater group, student-run newspaper, radio and television station, choral group, marching band, Sports and Activities Club, Residential Hall Council, Religious/Spiritual Organizations, Human Diversity Organizations, Departmental/Professional, national fraternities, national sororities.

Athletics Member NCAA, NAIA. All NCAA Division III. *Intercollegiate sports:* baseball M, basketball M/W, cross-country running M/W, football M, gymnastics W, soccer W, softball W, swimming and diving M/W, tennis M/W, track and field M/W, volleyball W, wrestling M. *Intramural sports:* archery M(c)/W(c), badminton M/W, basketball M/W, cheerleading M/W, equestrian sports M(c)/W(c), football M/W, ice hockey M(c)/W(c), lacrosse M(c)/W(c), racquetball M/W, rugby M(c)/W(c), sand volleyball M/W, skiing (cross-country) M(c)/W(c), skiing (downhill) M(c)/W(c), soccer M(c)/W(c), softball M/W, table tennis M/W, tennis M/W, ultimate Frisbee M(c)/W(c), volleyball M(c)/W(c), weight lifting M(c)/W(c), wrestling M/W.

Campus security: 24-hour emergency response devices and patrols, late-night transport/escort service, controlled dormitory access.

Student services: health clinic, personal/psychological counseling, legal services.

COSTS & FINANCIAL AID
Costs (2017–18) *Tuition:* state resident $7585 full-time, $370 per credit part-time; nonresident $16,254 full-time, $725 per credit part-time. Full-time tuition and fees vary according to reciprocity agreements. Part-time tuition and fees vary according to course load and reciprocity agreements. *Required fees:* $1337 full-time. *Room and board:* $6206; room only: $3750. Room and board charges vary according to board plan and housing facility. *Payment plan:* installment.

Financial Aid Of all full-time matriculated undergraduates who enrolled in 2016, 7,341 applied for aid, 4,778 were judged to have need, 1,213 had their need fully met. In 2016, 312 non-need-based awards were made. *Average percent of need met:* 69. *Average financial aid package:* $8016. *Average need-based loan:* $5452. *Average need-based gift aid:* $4672. *Average non-need-based aid:* $1300. *Average indebtedness upon graduation:* $26,768.

APPLYING
Standardized Tests *Required:* SAT or ACT (for admission).
Options: electronic application.
Application fee: $50.
Required: essay or personal statement, high school transcript.
Application deadlines: rolling (freshmen), rolling (transfers).
Notification: continuous (freshmen), continuous (transfers).

CONTACT
Mr. Corey Sjoquist, Director of Admissions, University of Wisconsin-La Crosse, 1725 State Street, La Crosse, WI 54601. *Phone:* 608-785-8939. *Fax:* 608-785-8940. *E-mail:* admissions@uwlax.edu.

University of Wisconsin–Madison
Madison, Wisconsin
http://www.wisc.edu/

- **State-supported** university, founded 1848, part of University of Wisconsin System
- **Urban** 936-acre campus with easy access to Milwaukee
- **Endowment** $2.5 billion
- **Coed** 32,198 undergraduate students, 90% full-time, 51% women, 49% men
- **Very difficult** entrance level, 54% of applicants were admitted

UNDERGRAD STUDENTS
29,016 full-time, 3,182 part-time. Students come from 52 states and territories; 79 other countries; 34% are from out of state; 2% Black or African American, non-Hispanic/Latino; 5% Hispanic/Latino; 6% Asian, non-Hispanic/Latino; 0.1% Native Hawaiian or other Pacific Islander, non-Hispanic/Latino; 0.2% American Indian or Alaska Native, non-Hispanic/Latino; 3% Two or more races, non-Hispanic/Latino; 0.8% Race/ethnicity unknown; 9% international; 4% transferred in; 25% live on campus.

Freshmen:
Admission: 35,615 applied, 19,150 admitted, 6,612 enrolled. *Average high school GPA:* 3.8. *Test scores:* SAT math scores over 500: 100%; ACT scores over 18: 100%; SAT math scores over 600: 92%; ACT scores over 24: 95%; SAT math scores over 700: 58%; ACT scores over 30: 43%.

Retention: 95% of full-time freshmen returned.

FACULTY
Total: 2,858, 84% full-time, 85% with terminal degrees.
Student/faculty ratio: 18:1.

ACADEMICS
Calendar: semesters. *Degrees:* bachelor's, master's, doctoral, and postbachelor's certificates.

Special study options: accelerated degree program, adult/continuing education programs, advanced placement credit, cooperative education, distance learning, double majors, English as a second language, honors programs, independent study, internships, part-time degree program, services for LD students, student-designed majors, study abroad, summer session for credit. *ROTC:* Army (b), Navy (b), Air Force (b).

Unusual degree programs: 3-2 business administration.

Computers: 1,000 computers/terminals are available on campus for general student use. Students can access the following: computer help desk, free student e-mail accounts, online (class) grades, online (class) registration, online (class) schedules. Campuswide network is available. 100% of college-owned or -operated housing units are wired for high-speed Internet access. Wireless service is available via entire campus.

Library: Memorial Library plus 40 others. Study areas open 24 hours, 5–7 days a week; students can reserve study rooms.

STUDENT LIFE
Housing options: coed, men-only, women-only, cooperative. Campus housing is university owned. Freshman applicants given priority for college housing.

Activities and organizations: drama/theater group, student-run newspaper, radio station, choral group, marching band, national fraternities, national sororities.

Athletics Member NCAA. All Division I except football (Division I-A). *Intercollegiate sports:* basketball M(s)/W(s), cheerleading M/W, crew M/W, cross-country running M(s)/W(s), fencing M(c)/W(c), golf M(s)/W(s), ice hockey M(s)/W(s), lacrosse M(c)/W(c), racquetball M(c)/W(c), rugby M(c)/W(c), sailing M(c)/W(c), soccer M(s)/W(s), softball W(s), swimming and diving M(s)/W(s), tennis M(s)/W(s), track and field M(s)/W(s), ultimate Frisbee M(c)/W(c), volleyball M(c)/W(s), water polo M(c)/W(c), wrestling M(s). *Intramural sports:* archery M(c)/W(c), badminton M(c)/W(c), baseball M(c), basketball M/W, cheerleading M(c)/W(c), fencing M(c)/W(c), field hockey M(c)/W(c), golf M(c)/W(c), gymnastics M(c)/W(c), ice hockey M(c)/W(c), lacrosse M(c)/W(c), racquetball M(c)/W(c), rugby M(c)/W(c), soccer M(c)/W(c), softball W, swimming and diving M(c)/W(c), table tennis M(c)/W(c), tennis M(c)/W(c), track and field M(c)/W(c), ultimate Frisbee M(c)/W(c), volleyball M(c)/W(c), water polo M(c)/W(c), wrestling M(c)/W(c).

Campus security: 24-hour emergency response devices and patrols, late-night transport/escort service, controlled dormitory access.

Student services: health clinic, personal/psychological counseling, women's center.

COSTS & FINANCIAL AID

Costs (2017–18) *Tuition:* state resident $9273 full-time, $386 per credit hour part-time; nonresident $33,523 full-time, $1397 per credit hour part-time. Full-time tuition and fees vary according to program and reciprocity agreements. Part-time tuition and fees vary according to course load, program, and reciprocity agreements. *Required fees:* $1260 full-time, $99 per credit hour part-time. *Room and board:* $10,842. Room and board charges vary according to board plan and housing facility. *Payment plan:* installment.

Financial Aid Of all full-time matriculated undergraduates who enrolled in 2017, 15,904 applied for aid, 10,902 were judged to have need, 4,346 had their need fully met. In 2017, 2098 non-need-based awards were made. *Average percent of need met:* 80. *Average financial aid package:* $16,308. *Average need-based loan:* $6458. *Average need-based gift aid:* $11,806. *Average non-need-based aid:* $5265. *Average indebtedness upon graduation:* $27,979.

APPLYING

Standardized Tests *Required:* SAT or ACT (for admission).

Options: electronic application, early action, deferred entrance.

Application fee: $60.

Required: essay or personal statement, high school transcript. *Recommended:* 2 letters of recommendation.

Application deadlines: 2/1 (freshmen), 3/1 (transfers), 11/1 (early action).

Notification: 3/31 (freshmen), 4/30 (transfers), 1/31 (early action).

CONTACT

Office of Admissions and Recruitment, University of Wisconsin–Madison, 702 West Johnson Street, Suite 101, Madison, WI 53706-1481. *Phone:* 608-262-3961. *Fax:* 608-262-7706. *E-mail:* onwisconsin@admissions.wisc.edu.

University of Wisconsin–Marshfield/Wood County

Marshfield, Wisconsin

http://marshfield.uwc.edu/

- **State-supported** primarily 2-year, founded 1964, part of University of Wisconsin System
- **Small-town** 114-acre campus
- **Coed** 535 undergraduate students

FACULTY

Student/faculty ratio: 15:1.

ACADEMICS

Calendar: semesters. *Degrees:* certificates, associate, and bachelor's.

Special study options: academic remediation for entering students, accelerated degree program, advanced placement credit, distance learning, external degree program, independent study, off-campus study, part-time degree program, services for LD students, study abroad, summer session for credit. *ROTC:* Army (c).

Computers: Students can access the following: computer help desk, free student e-mail accounts, online (class) grades, online (class) registration, online (class) schedules, financial aid application. Campuswide network is available.

Library: Hamilton Roddis Memorial Library plus 1 other.

STUDENT LIFE

Activities and organizations: drama/theater group, student-run newspaper, choral group.

Athletics *Intercollegiate sports:* basketball M/W, golf M, tennis M/W, volleyball W.

Campus security: 24-hour patrols, patrols by city police.

COSTS

Costs (2017–18) *One-time required fee:* $180. *Tuition:* state resident $4750 full-time, $198 per credit hour part-time; nonresident $12,321 full-time, $513 per credit hour part-time. Full-time tuition and fees vary according to reciprocity agreements. Part-time tuition and fees vary according to course load. *Required fees:* $386 full-time, $32 per year part-time. *Room and board:* Room and board charges vary according to location. *Payment plan:* installment.

APPLYING

Standardized Tests *Required:* ACT (for admission).

Options: electronic application, early admission, deferred entrance.

Application fee: $50.

Required: high school transcript.

Application deadlines: 8/30 (freshmen), 8/30 (transfers).

CONTACT

University of Wisconsin–Marshfield/Wood County, 2000 West 5th Street, Marshfield, WI 54449.

University of Wisconsin–Milwaukee

Milwaukee, Wisconsin

http://www.uwm.edu/

- **State-supported** university, founded 1956, part of University of Wisconsin System
- **Urban** 104-acre campus with easy access to Milwaukee
- **Coed** 20,750 undergraduate students, 82% full-time, 52% women, 48% men
- **Moderately difficult** entrance level, 72% of applicants were admitted

UNDERGRAD STUDENTS

17,055 full-time, 3,695 part-time. Students come from 52 states and territories; 91 other countries; 11% are from out of state; 7% Black or African American, non-Hispanic/Latino; 11% Hispanic/Latino; 7% Asian, non-Hispanic/Latino; 0.1% Native Hawaiian or other Pacific Islander, non-Hispanic/Latino; 0.4% American Indian or Alaska Native, non-Hispanic/Latino; 4% Two or more races, non-Hispanic/Latino; 0.5% Race/ethnicity unknown; 4% international; 7% transferred in; 19% live on campus.

Freshmen:
Admission: 10,000 applied, 7,227 admitted, 3,230 enrolled. *Average high school GPA:* 3.1. *Test scores:* ACT scores over 18: 92%; ACT scores over 24: 36%; ACT scores over 30: 4%.

Retention: 74% of full-time freshmen returned.

FACULTY

Total: 1,519, 65% full-time, 52% with terminal degrees.

Student/faculty ratio: 19:1.

ACADEMICS

Calendar: semesters. *Degrees:* certificates, bachelor's, master's, doctoral, post-master's, and postbachelor's certificates.

Special study options: academic remediation for entering students, accelerated degree program, adult/continuing education programs, advanced placement credit, cooperative education, distance learning, double majors, English as a second language, external degree program, freshman honors college, honors programs, independent study, internships, off-campus study, part-time degree program, services for LD students, student-designed majors, study abroad, summer session for credit. *ROTC:* Army (c), Navy (c), Air Force (c).

Computers: 500 computers/terminals are available on campus for general student use. Students can access the following: campus intranet, computer help desk, free student e-mail accounts, online (class) grades, online (class) registration, online (class) schedules. Campuswide network is available. 100% of college-owned or -operated housing units are wired for high-speed Internet access. Wireless service is available via classrooms, computer centers, computer labs, dorm rooms, learning centers, libraries, student centers.

Library: Golda Meir Library. *Books:* 2.5 million (physical), 178,268 (digital/electronic); *Serial titles:* 112,752 (physical). Students can reserve study rooms.

STUDENT LIFE

Housing options: on-campus residence required for freshman year; coed, special housing for students with disabilities. Campus housing is university owned. Freshman applicants given priority for college housing.

Activities and organizations: drama/theater group, student-run newspaper, choral group, national fraternities, national sororities.

Athletics Member NCAA. All Division I. *Intercollegiate sports:* baseball M(s), basketball M(s)/W(s), bowling M(c)/W(c), cross-country running M(s)/W(s), equestrian sports M(c)/W(c), football M(c)/W(c), ice hockey M(c)/W(c), lacrosse M(c)/W(c), rugby M(c)/W(c), sailing M(c)/W(c), soccer M(s)/W(s), swimming and diving M(s)/W(s), tennis W(s), track and field M(s)/W(s), ultimate Frisbee M(c)/W(c), volleyball M(c)/W(s). *Intramural sports:* badminton M/W, baseball M(c)/W(c), basketball M/W, cross-country running M/W, football M/W, racquetball M/W, skiing (downhill) M(c)/W(c), soccer M/W, swimming and diving M/W, tennis M(c)/W(c), track and field M(c)/W(c), volleyball M/W.

Campus security: 24-hour emergency response devices and patrols, student patrols, late-night transport/escort service, controlled dormitory access.

Student services: health clinic, personal/psychological counseling, women's center, legal services.

COSTS & FINANCIAL AID

Costs (2018–19) *Tuition:* state resident $9566 full-time, $398 per credit hour part-time; nonresident $20,844 full-time, $868 per credit hour part-time. Full-time tuition and fees vary according to course load, degree level, location, program, and reciprocity agreements. Part-time tuition and fees vary according to course load, degree level, location, program, and reciprocity agreements. *Required fees:* $1444 full-time. *Room and board:* $10,728; room only: $6602. Room and board charges vary according to board plan, housing facility, and location. *Payment plan:* installment. *Waivers:* senior citizens.

Financial Aid Of all full-time matriculated undergraduates who enrolled in 2016, 15,406 applied for aid, 13,200 were judged to have need, 2,743 had their need fully met. In 2016, 117 non-need-based awards were made. *Average percent of need met:* 46. *Average financial aid package:* $7858. *Average need-based loan:* $4343. *Average need-based gift aid:* $6117. *Average non-need-based aid:* $2086. *Average indebtedness upon graduation:* $37,131.

APPLYING

Standardized Tests *Required:* SAT or ACT (for admission). *Required for some:* TOEFL for students whose native language is not English and who were not educated in an entirely English-speaking country.

Options: electronic application, deferred entrance.

Application fee: $50.

Required: high school transcript. *Recommended:* essay or personal statement.

Application deadlines: rolling (freshmen), 8/10 (transfers).

Notification: continuous (freshmen), continuous (transfers).

CONTACT

Katie Miota, Director, Undergraduate Admissions, University of Wisconsin–Milwaukee, PO Box 413, Milwaukee, WI 53201-0413. *Phone:* 414-229-4445. *E-mail:* uwmlook@uwm.edu.

University of Wisconsin–Oshkosh
Oshkosh, Wisconsin
http://www.uwosh.edu/

CONTACT
Associate Director of Admissions, University of Wisconsin–Oshkosh, 800 Algoma Boulevard, Oshkosh, WI 54901. *Phone:* 920-424-0202. *E-mail:* oshadmuw@uwosh.edu.

University of Wisconsin–Parkside
Kenosha, Wisconsin
http://www.uwp.edu/

- **State-supported** comprehensive, founded 1968, part of University of Wisconsin System
- **Suburban** 700-acre campus with easy access to Chicago, Milwaukee
- **Coed** 4,168 undergraduate students, 79% full-time, 53% women, 47% men
- **Moderately difficult** entrance level, 80% of applicants were admitted

UNDERGRAD STUDENTS
3,275 full-time, 893 part-time. Students come from 33 states and territories; 29 other countries; 18% are from out of state; 9% Black or African American, non-Hispanic/Latino; 16% Hispanic/Latino; 4% Asian, non-Hispanic/Latino; 0.1% Native Hawaiian or other Pacific Islander, non-Hispanic/Latino; 0.1% American Indian or Alaska Native, non-Hispanic/Latino; 4% Two or more races, non-Hispanic/Latino; 2% international; 8% transferred in; 19% live on campus.

Freshmen:
Admission: 1,743 applied, 1,399 admitted, 712 enrolled. *Average high school GPA:* 3.1. *Test scores:* ACT scores over 18: 84%; ACT scores over 24: 22%; ACT scores over 30: 1%.
Retention: 73% of full-time freshmen returned.

FACULTY
Total: 261, 62% full-time, 58% with terminal degrees.
Student/faculty ratio: 19:1.

ACADEMICS
Calendar: semesters. *Degrees:* certificates, associate, bachelor's, and master's.

Special study options: academic remediation for entering students, adult/continuing education programs, advanced placement credit, cooperative education, distance learning, double majors, external degree program, honors programs, independent study, internships, off-campus study, part-time degree program, services for LD students, study abroad, summer session for credit. *ROTC:* Army (b), Air Force (c).

Unusual degree programs: 3-2 molecular biology; pharmacy with Rosalind-Franklin University.

Computers: Students can access the following: campus intranet, computer help desk, free student e-mail accounts, online (class) grades, online (class) registration, online (class) schedules. Campuswide network is available. 100% of college-owned or -operated housing units are wired for high-speed Internet access. Wireless service is available via entire campus.

Library: UWP Library. Students can reserve study rooms.

STUDENT LIFE
Housing options: on-campus residence required through sophomore year; coed, special housing for students with disabilities. Campus housing is university owned.

Activities and organizations: drama/theater group, student-run newspaper, radio station, choral group, Habitat for Humanity, Criminal Justice Association, Next Level Gaming, Parkside Asian Organization, Active Minds, national fraternities, national sororities.

Athletics Member NCAA. All Division II. *Intercollegiate sports:* baseball M(s), basketball M(s)/W(s), cross-country running M(s)/W(s), golf M(s), soccer M(s)/W(s), softball W(s), track and field M(s)/W(s), volleyball W(s), wrestling M(s). *Intramural sports:* badminton M/W, basketball M/W, football M/W, racquetball M/W, rugby M(c), soccer M/W, softball M/W, table tennis M/W, tennis M/W, volleyball M/W.

Campus security: 24-hour emergency response devices and patrols, late-night transport/escort service, controlled dormitory access.

Student services: health clinic, personal/psychological counseling, women's center.

COSTS & FINANCIAL AID

Costs (2018–19) *One-time required fee:* $260. *Tuition:* state resident $6298 full-time, $262 per credit hour part-time; nonresident $14,287 full-time, $595 per credit hour part-time. Full-time tuition and fees vary according to course load, program, and reciprocity agreements. Part-time tuition and fees vary according to course load, program, and reciprocity agreements. *Required fees:* $1351 full-time, $45 per credit hour part-time. *Room and board:* $7924; room only: $4494. Room and board charges vary according to board plan and housing facility. *Payment plan:* installment. *Waivers:* senior citizens.

Financial Aid Of all full-time matriculated undergraduates who enrolled in 2016, 2,537 applied for aid, 2,080 were judged to have need, 281 had their need fully met. 117 Federal Work-Study jobs (averaging $1564). In 2016, 87 non-need-based awards were made. *Average percent of need met:* 66. *Average financial aid package:* $9703. *Average need-based loan:* $4494. *Average need-based gift aid:* $6311. *Average non-need-based aid:* $2149. *Average indebtedness upon graduation:* $28,504.

APPLYING

Standardized Tests *Required for some:* SAT or ACT (for admission).

Options: electronic application.

Application fee: $50.

Required: high school transcript, minimum of 17 high school units distribution.

Application deadlines: rolling (freshmen), rolling (transfers).

Notification: continuous (freshmen), continuous (transfers).

CONTACT

Troy Moldenhauer, Director, Admissions and Recruitment, University of Wisconsin–Parkside, PO Box 2000, 900 Wood Road, Kenosha, WI 53141-2000. *Phone:* 262-595-2355. *Fax:* 262-595-2006. *E-mail:* moldenht@uwp.edu.

University of Wisconsin–Platteville

Platteville, Wisconsin

http://www.uwplatt.edu/

- **State-supported** comprehensive, founded 1866, part of University of Wisconsin System
- **Small-town** 821-acre campus
- **Endowment** $28.6 million
- **Coed** 7,520 undergraduate students, 90% full-time, 34% women, 66% men

UNDERGRAD STUDENTS

6,751 full-time, 769 part-time. Students come from 26 other countries; 24% are from out of state; 1% Black or African American, non-Hispanic/Latino; 3% Hispanic/Latino; 1% Asian, non-Hispanic/Latino; 0.1% Native Hawaiian or other Pacific Islander, non-Hispanic/Latino; 3% Two or more races, non-Hispanic/Latino; 0.9% Race/ethnicity unknown; 1% international; 6% transferred in; 17% live on campus.

Freshmen:

Admission: 1,407 enrolled. *Test scores:* SAT evidence-based reading and writing scores over 500: 50%; SAT math scores over 500: 100%; ACT scores over 18: 94%; SAT evidence-based reading and writing scores over 600: 50%; SAT math scores over 600: 50%; ACT scores over 24: 43%; SAT evidence-based reading and writing scores over 700: 50%; ACT scores over 30: 5%.

Retention: 79% of full-time freshmen returned.

FACULTY

Total: 441, 72% full-time, 61% with terminal degrees.

Student/faculty ratio: 21:1.

ACADEMICS

Calendar: semesters. *Degrees:* certificates, associate, bachelor's, master's, and postbachelor's certificates.

Special study options: academic remediation for entering students, adult/continuing education programs, advanced placement credit, cooperative education, distance learning, double majors, English as a second language, external degree program, independent study, internships, off-campus study, part-time degree program, services for LD students, student-designed majors, study abroad, summer session for credit. *ROTC:* Army (c).

Computers: 200 computers/terminals and 50 ports are available on campus for general student use. Students can access the following: campus intranet, computer help desk, free student e-mail accounts, online (class) grades, online (class) registration, online (class) schedules. Campuswide network is available. 100% of college-owned or -operated housing units are wired for high-speed Internet access. Wireless service is available via entire campus.

Library: Karrmann Library plus 1 other. *Books:* 167,304 (physical), 59,292 (digital/electronic); *Serial titles:* 1,151 (physical), 44,687 (digital/electronic); *Databases:* 123. Weekly public service hours: 87.

STUDENT LIFE

Housing options: on-campus residence required through sophomore year; coed, men-only, women-only, cooperative, special housing for students with disabilities. Campus housing is university owned. Freshman campus housing is guaranteed.

Activities and organizations: drama/theater group, student-run newspaper, radio and television station, choral group, marching band, Criminal Justice Association, Platteville Gaming Association, Dodgeball, American Society of Mechanical Engineers, Outdoor Adventure Club, national fraternities, national sororities.

Athletics Member NCAA. All Division III. *Intercollegiate sports:* baseball M, basketball M/W, bowling M(c)/W(c), cross-country running M/W, football M, golf W, ice hockey M(c)/W(c), lacrosse M(c)/W(c), rugby M(c)/W(c), soccer M/W, softball W, track and field M/W, ultimate Frisbee M(c)/W(c), volleyball M(c)/W, wrestling M. *Intramural sports:* badminton M/W, basketball M/W, bowling M(c)/W(c), cheerleading M(c)/W(c), football M/W, racquetball M/W, soccer M/W, softball M/W, tennis M/W, ultimate Frisbee M/W, volleyball M/W, water polo M/W.

Campus security: 24-hour emergency response devices and patrols, student patrols, late-night transport/escort service, controlled dormitory access.

Student services: health clinic, personal/psychological counseling, women's center.

COSTS & FINANCIAL AID

Costs (2017–18) *Tuition:* state resident $6298 full-time, $262 per credit hour part-time; nonresident $14,149 full-time, $590 per credit hour part-time. Full-time tuition and fees vary according to course load, degree level, and reciprocity agreements. Part-time tuition and fees vary according to course load, degree level, and reciprocity agreements. *Required fees:* $1245 full-time, $52 per credit hour part-time. *Room and board:* $7526; room only: $4380. Room and board charges vary according to board plan and housing facility. *Payment plan:* installment. *Waivers:* senior citizens.

Financial Aid Of all full-time matriculated undergraduates who enrolled in 2002, 3,289 applied for aid, 2,468 were judged to have need. 382 Federal Work-Study jobs (averaging $1392). In 2002, 652 non-need-based awards were made. *Average financial aid package:* $6161. *Average need-based loan:* $3499. *Average need-based gift aid:* $3599. *Average non-need-based aid:* $1427. *Average indebtedness upon graduation:* $15,785.

APPLYING

Standardized Tests *Required:* SAT or ACT (for admission).

Required: high school transcript. *Recommended:* essay or personal statement.

CONTACT

Ms. Heidi Tuescher-Gille, Director of Admission and Enrollment Services, University of Wisconsin–Platteville, 1 University Plaza, 1300 Ullsvik Hall, Platteville, WI 53818-3099. *Phone:* 608-342-1125. *Toll-free phone:* 877-897-5288. *Fax:* 608-342-1122. *E-mail:* tuescheh@uwplatt.edu.

University of Wisconsin–Richland

Richland Center, Wisconsin

http://richland.uwc.edu/

- **State-supported** primarily 2-year, founded 1967, part of University of Wisconsin System
- **Small-town** 135-acre campus
- **Coed** 259 undergraduate students

FACULTY
Student/faculty ratio: 8:1.

ACADEMICS
Calendar: semesters. *Degrees:* certificates, associate, and bachelor's.

Special study options: academic remediation for entering students, advanced placement credit, distance learning, external degree program, independent study, off-campus study, part-time degree program, services for LD students, study abroad, summer session for credit.

Computers: Students can access the following: computer help desk, free student e-mail accounts, online (class) grades, online (class) registration, online (class) schedules, financial aid application. Campuswide network is available. Wireless service is available via entire campus.
Library: Miller Memorial Library plus 1 other.

STUDENT LIFE
Housing options: coed. Campus housing is provided by a third party.
Activities and organizations: drama/theater group, choral group.
Athletics *Intercollegiate sports:* basketball M/W. *Intramural sports:* softball M/W, volleyball M/W.
Student services: personal/psychological counseling.

COSTS
Costs (2017–18) *One-time required fee:* $180. *Tuition:* state resident $4750 full-time, $198 per credit hour part-time; nonresident $12,321 full-time, $513 per credit hour part-time. Full-time tuition and fees vary according to reciprocity agreements. Part-time tuition and fees vary according to course load. *Required fees:* $597 full-time, $50 per year part-time. *Room only:* $3600. Room and board charges vary according to location. *Payment plan:* installment.

APPLYING
Standardized Tests *Required:* ACT (for admission).
Options: electronic application.
Application fee: $50.
Required: high school transcript.
Application deadlines: 8/30 (freshmen), 8/30 (transfers).

CONTACT
University of Wisconsin–Richland, 1200 Highway 14 West, Richland Center, WI 53581.

University of Wisconsin–River Falls

River Falls, Wisconsin

http://www.uwrf.edu/

- **State-supported** comprehensive, founded 1874, part of University of Wisconsin System
- **Suburban** 303-acre campus with easy access to Minneapolis-St. Paul
- **Endowment** $14.1 million
- **Coed** 5,678 undergraduate students, 88% full-time, 61% women, 39% men
- **Moderately difficult** entrance level, 75% of applicants were admitted

UNDERGRAD STUDENTS
4,988 full-time, 690 part-time. Students come from 33 states and territories; 15 other countries; 49% are from out of state; 2% Black or African American, non-Hispanic/Latino; 4% Hispanic/Latino; 3% Asian, non-Hispanic/Latino; 0.1% Native Hawaiian or other Pacific Islander, non-Hispanic/Latino; 0.2% American Indian or Alaska Native, non-Hispanic/Latino; 2% Two or more races, non-Hispanic/Latino; 0.2% Race/ethnicity unknown; 1% international; 8% transferred in; 41% live on campus.

Freshmen:
Admission: 3,450 applied, 2,571 admitted, 1,325 enrolled. *Average high school GPA:* 3.4. *Test scores:* ACT scores over 18: 95%; ACT scores over 24: 35%; ACT scores over 30: 3%.
Retention: 75% of full-time freshmen returned.

FACULTY
Total: 374, 70% full-time.
Student/faculty ratio: 18:1.

ACADEMICS
Calendar: semesters. *Degrees:* certificates, bachelor's, master's, post-master's, and postbachelor's certificates.

Special study options: academic remediation for entering students, adult/continuing education programs, advanced placement credit, distance learning, double majors, English as a second language, external degree program, honors programs, independent study, internships, off-campus study, part-time degree program, services for LD students, study abroad, summer session for credit. *ROTC:* Army (b).

Unusual degree programs: 3-2 engineering with University of Wisconsin–Madison; University of Minnesota, Twin Cities Campus.

Computers: 700 computers/terminals are available on campus for general student use. Students can access the following: computer help desk, free student e-mail accounts, online (class) grades, online (class) registration, online (class) schedules. Campuswide network is available. 100% of college-owned or -operated housing units are wired for high-speed Internet access. Wireless service is available via entire campus.
Library: Chalmer Davee Library plus 1 other. *Books:* 301,138 (physical), 159,542 (digital/electronic); *Serial titles:* 149 (physical), 8,350 (digital/electronic); *Databases:* 162. Weekly public service hours: 89; study areas open 24 hours, 5–7 days a week; students can reserve study rooms.

STUDENT LIFE
Housing options: on-campus residence required through sophomore year; coed, women-only, special housing for students with disabilities. Campus housing is university owned. Freshman campus housing is guaranteed.

Activities and organizations: drama/theater group, student-run newspaper, radio and television station, choral group, Pre-Vet Society, Dairy Club, Tomorrow's Educators, Block and Bridle, Agriculture Education Society, national fraternities, national sororities.

Athletics Member NCAA. All Division III. *Intercollegiate sports:* badminton M(c)/W(c), baseball M(c)/W(c), basketball M/W, cross-country running M/W, equestrian sports M(c)/W(c), football M, golf W, ice hockey M/W, lacrosse M(c)/W, racquetball M(c)/W(c), rock climbing M(c)/W(c), rugby M(c)/W(c), skiing (cross-country) M(c)/W(c), soccer W, softball W, tennis W, track and field M/W, volleyball M(c)/W. *Intramural sports:* basketball M/W, cross-country running M(c)/W(c), football M/W, lacrosse W(c), sand volleyball M(c)/W(c), soccer M/W, softball M/W, tennis M/W, ultimate Frisbee M/W, volleyball M/W.

Campus security: 24-hour emergency response devices and patrols, student patrols, late-night transport/escort service, controlled dormitory access.

Student services: health clinic, personal/psychological counseling.

COSTS & FINANCIAL AID
Costs (2017–18) *Tuition:* state resident $6428 full-time, $268 per credit hour part-time; nonresident $14,001 full-time, $583 per credit hour part-time. Full-time tuition and fees vary according to course load, degree level, program, and reciprocity agreements. Part-time tuition and fees vary according to course load, degree level, program, and reciprocity agreements. *Required fees:* $1585 full-time, $166 per credit hour part-time. *Room and board:* $6576; room only: $4136. Room and board charges vary according to board plan and housing facility.

Financial Aid Of all full-time matriculated undergraduates who enrolled in 2016, 3,984 applied for aid, 2,999 were judged to have need, 65 had their need fully met. In 2016, 281 non-need-based awards were made. *Average percent of need met:* 52. *Average financial aid package:* $6820. *Average need-based loan:* $4187. *Average need-based gift aid:* $4882. *Average non-need-based aid:* $1752. *Average indebtedness upon graduation:* $27,428.

APPLYING

Standardized Tests *Required:* SAT or ACT (for admission). *Recommended:* ACT (for admission).

Options: electronic application, deferred entrance.

Application fee: $44.

Required: essay or personal statement, high school transcript. *Recommended:* rank in upper 40% of high school class.

Notification: continuous (freshmen), continuous (transfers).

CONTACT

Sarah Egerstrom, Director of Admissions, University of Wisconsin–River Falls, 410 South Third Street, River Falls, WI 54022. *Phone:* 715-425-3500. *Fax:* 715-425-0676. *E-mail:* admit@uwrf.edu.

University of Wisconsin–Rock County

Janesville, Wisconsin

http://rock.uwc.edu/

- **State-supported** primarily 2-year, founded 1966, part of University of Wisconsin System
- **Small-town** 50-acre campus with easy access to Milwaukee
- **Coed** 970 undergraduate students

FACULTY

Student/faculty ratio: 16:1.

ACADEMICS

Calendar: semesters. *Degrees:* certificates, associate, and bachelor's.

Special study options: academic remediation for entering students, advanced placement credit, distance learning, external degree program, off-campus study, part-time degree program, services for LD students, summer session for credit.

Computers: Students can access the following: computer help desk, free student e-mail accounts, online (class) grades, online (class) registration, online (class) schedules, financial aid application. Campuswide network is available.

Library: Gary J. Lenox Library plus 1 other.

STUDENT LIFE

Housing options: college housing not available.

Athletics *Intercollegiate sports:* basketball M/W, tennis M/W, volleyball W.

COSTS

Costs (2017–18) *One-time required fee:* $180. *Tuition:* state resident $4750 full-time, $198 per credit hour part-time; nonresident $12,321 full-time, $513 per credit hour part-time. Full-time tuition and fees vary according to reciprocity agreements. Part-time tuition and fees vary according to course load. *Required fees:* $382 full-time, $32 per year part-time. *Room and board:* Room and board charges vary according to location. *Payment plan:* installment.

APPLYING

Standardized Tests *Required:* ACT (for admission).

Options: electronic application, deferred entrance.

Application fee: $50.

Required: high school transcript.

Application deadlines: 8/30 (freshmen), 8/30 (transfers).

CONTACT

University of Wisconsin–Rock County, 2909 Kellogg Avenue, Janesville, WI 53546-5699. *Toll-free phone:* 888-INFO-UWC.

University of Wisconsin–Stevens Point

Stevens Point, Wisconsin

http://www.uwsp.edu/

- **State-supported** comprehensive, founded 1894, part of University of Wisconsin System
- **Small-town** 400-acre campus
- **Endowment** $28.6 million
- **Coed** 7,788 undergraduate students, 92% full-time, 53% women, 47% men
- **Moderately difficult** entrance level, 81% of applicants were admitted

UNDERGRAD STUDENTS

7,158 full-time, 630 part-time. Students come from 41 states and territories; 29 other countries; 11% are from out of state; 2% Black or African American, non-Hispanic/Latino; 4% Hispanic/Latino; 3% Asian, non-Hispanic/Latino; 0.1% Native Hawaiian or other Pacific Islander, non-Hispanic/Latino; 0.4% American Indian or Alaska Native, non-Hispanic/Latino; 2% Two or more races, non-Hispanic/Latino; 0.3% Race/ethnicity unknown; 2% international; 37% live on campus.

Freshmen:

Admission: 6,857 applied, 5,568 admitted. *Average high school GPA:* 3.3. *Test scores:* SAT evidence-based reading and writing scores over 500: 63%; SAT math scores over 500: 73%; ACT scores over 18: 89%; SAT evidence-based reading and writing scores over 600: 33%; SAT math scores over 600: 36%; ACT scores over 24: 32%; SAT evidence-based reading and writing scores over 700: 3%; SAT math scores over 700: 9%; ACT scores over 30: 3%.

Retention: 73% of full-time freshmen returned.

FACULTY

Total: 476, 77% full-time, 61% with terminal degrees.

Student/faculty ratio: 17:1.

ACADEMICS

Calendar: semesters. *Degrees:* associate, bachelor's, master's, and doctoral.

Special study options: academic remediation for entering students, accelerated degree program, advanced placement credit, cooperative education, distance learning, double majors, English as a second language, independent study, internships, off-campus study, part-time degree program, services for LD students, student-designed majors, study abroad, summer session for credit. *ROTC:* Army (b).

Computers: 1,233 computers/terminals and 3,963 ports are available on campus for general student use. Students can access the following: computer help desk, free student e-mail accounts, online (class) grades, online (class) registration, online (class) schedules. Campuswide network is available. 100% of college-owned or -operated housing units are wired for high-speed Internet access. Wireless service is available via entire campus.

Library: Learning Resources Center plus 1 other. *Books:* 420,414 (physical), 247,207 (digital/electronic); *Serial titles:* 7,192 (physical), 133,235 (digital/electronic); *Databases:* 204. Study areas open 24 hours, 5–7 days a week; students can reserve study rooms.

STUDENT LIFE

Housing options: on-campus residence required through sophomore year; coed, men-only, women-only. Campus housing is university owned. Freshman applicants given priority for college housing.

Activities and organizations: drama/theater group, student-run newspaper, radio and television station, choral group, The Wildlife Society, Student Impact, WWSP 90-FM radio station, Gender and Sexuality Alliance, Student Wisconsin Education Association, national fraternities, national sororities.

Athletics Member NCAA. All Division III. *Intercollegiate sports:* baseball M, basketball M/W, cheerleading M/W, cross-country running M/W, football M, golf W, ice hockey M/W, soccer W, softball W, swimming and diving M/W, tennis W, track and field M/W, volleyball W, wrestling M. *Intramural sports:* archery M(c)/W(c), badminton M/W, basketball M/W, football M, golf M/W, ice hockey M/W, lacrosse M(c), racquetball M/W, rock climbing M/W, rugby M(c)/W(c), skiing (downhill) M(c)/W(c), soccer M/W, softball M/W, table tennis M/W, tennis M/W, ultimate Frisbee M/W, volleyball M/W.

Campus security: 24-hour emergency response devices and patrols, student patrols, late-night transport/escort service, controlled dormitory access.

Student services: health clinic, personal/psychological counseling, women's center.

COSTS & FINANCIAL AID
Costs (2018–19) *Tuition:* state resident $8308 full-time, $407 per credit part-time; nonresident $16,576 full-time, $752 per credit part-time. Full-time tuition and fees vary according to course load, location, program, reciprocity agreements, and student level. Part-time tuition and fees vary according to course load, location, program, reciprocity agreements, and student level. *Required fees:* $1426 full-time. *Room and board:* $7290; room only: $4420. Room and board charges vary according to board plan and housing facility. *Payment plans:* installment, deferred payment. *Waivers:* senior citizens.

Financial Aid Of all full-time matriculated undergraduates who enrolled in 2016, 6,468 applied for aid, 4,619 were judged to have need, 410 had their need fully met. In 2016, 674 non-need-based awards were made. *Average percent of need met:* 73. *Average financial aid package:* $9543. *Average need-based loan:* $5416. *Average need-based gift aid:* $5678. *Average non-need-based aid:* $1520. *Average indebtedness upon graduation:* $25,918. *Financial aid deadline:* 5/1.

APPLYING
Standardized Tests *Required:* SAT or ACT (for admission).

Options: electronic application, deferred entrance.

Application fee: $50.

Required: high school transcript. *Recommended:* essay or personal statement, 3 letters of recommendation.

Application deadlines: rolling (freshmen), rolling (transfers).

Notification: continuous (freshmen), continuous (transfers).

CONTACT
Mr. William Jordan, Director of Admissions, University of Wisconsin–Stevens Point, 102 Student Services Center, Stevens Point, WI 54481. *Phone:* 715-346-4021. *Fax:* 715-346-3296. *E-mail:* bjordan@uwsp.edu.

University of Wisconsin–Stout
Menomonie, Wisconsin
http://www.uwstout.edu/

- **State-supported** comprehensive, founded 1891, part of University of Wisconsin System
- **Small-town** 120-acre campus with easy access to Minneapolis-St. Paul
- **Coed** 8,116 undergraduate students, 81% full-time, 44% women, 56% men
- **Moderately difficult** entrance level, 86% of applicants were admitted

UNDERGRAD STUDENTS
6,585 full-time, 1,531 part-time. 33% are from out of state; 2% Black or African American, non-Hispanic/Latino; 0.6% Hispanic/Latino; 0.2% Asian, non-Hispanic/Latino; 87% Native Hawaiian or other Pacific Islander, non-Hispanic/Latino; 3% American Indian or Alaska Native, non-Hispanic/Latino; 4% Two or more races, non-Hispanic/Latino; 0.1% Race/ethnicity unknown; 2% international; 8% transferred in; 40% live on campus.

Freshmen:
Admission: 3,267 applied, 2,809 admitted, 1,528 enrolled. *Average high school GPA:* 3.2. *Test scores:* ACT scores over 18: 88%; ACT scores over 24: 33%; ACT scores over 30: 5%.
Retention: 69% of full-time freshmen returned.

FACULTY
Total: 483, 81% full-time, 69% with terminal degrees.
Student/faculty ratio: 20:1.

ACADEMICS
Calendar: 4-1-4. *Degrees:* certificates, bachelor's, master's, doctoral, post-master's, and postbachelor's certificates.

Special study options: accelerated degree program, adult/continuing education programs, cooperative education, distance learning, double majors, English as a second language, external degree program, honors programs, independent study, internships, off-campus study, part-time degree program, services for LD students, study abroad, summer session for credit. *ROTC:* Army (b), Air Force (c).

Computers: Students can access the following: computer help desk, free student e-mail accounts, online (class) grades, online (class) registration, online (class) schedules. Campuswide network is available. 100% of college-owned or -operated housing units are wired for high-speed Internet access. Wireless service is available via entire campus.
Library: Library Learning Center.

STUDENT LIFE
Housing options: on-campus residence required through sophomore year; coed, special housing for students with disabilities. Campus housing is university owned. Freshman campus housing is guaranteed.

Activities and organizations: drama/theater group, student-run newspaper, radio station, choral group, marching band, national fraternities, national sororities.

Athletics Member NCAA. All Division III. *Intercollegiate sports:* baseball M, basketball M/W, cross-country running M/W, football M, gymnastics W, ice hockey M/W(c), soccer M(c)/W, softball W, tennis W, track and field M/W, volleyball M(c)/W. *Intramural sports:* baseball M, basketball M/W, bowling M(c)/W(c), football M/W, golf M/W, ice hockey M/W, racquetball M/W, rugby M(c)/W(c), skiing (cross-country) M(c)/W(c), skiing (downhill) M(c)/W(c), softball M/W, ultimate Frisbee M/W, volleyball M/W.

Campus security: 24-hour emergency response devices and patrols, student patrols, controlled dormitory access.

Student services: health clinic, personal/psychological counseling, legal services.

COSTS & FINANCIAL AID
Costs (2017–18) *Tuition:* state resident $7014 full-time, $234 per credit hour part-time; nonresident $14,981 full-time, $499 per credit hour part-time. Full-time tuition and fees vary according to degree level and reciprocity agreements. Part-time tuition and fees vary according to degree level and reciprocity agreements. *Required fees:* $2442 full-time. *Room and board:* $6744; room only: $4140. Room and board charges vary according to board plan and housing facility.

Financial Aid Of all full-time matriculated undergraduates who enrolled in 2017, 5,154 applied for aid, 3,714 were judged to have need, 591 had their need fully met. 1,726 Federal Work-Study jobs (averaging $1627). In 2017, 182 non-need-based awards were made. *Average percent of need met:* 85. *Average financial aid package:* $11,237. *Average need-based loan:* $4729. *Average need-based gift aid:* $6033. *Average non-need-based aid:* $1865. *Average indebtedness upon graduation:* $30,409.

APPLYING
Standardized Tests *Required:* SAT or ACT (for admission).

Options: electronic application.

Application fee: $50.

Required: high school transcript. *Required for some:* minimum 2.8 GPA. *Recommended:* minimum 2.5 GPA.

Application deadlines: rolling (freshmen), rolling (out-of-state freshmen), rolling (transfers).

Notification: continuous until 9/1 (freshmen), continuous (out-of-state freshmen), continuous (transfers).

CONTACT
Dr. Pamela Holsinger-Fuchs, Executive Director of Enrollment Services, University of Wisconsin–Stout, Admissions, Bowman Hall, Menomonie, WI 54751. *Phone:* 715-232-2639. *Toll-free phone:* 800-HI-STOUT. *Fax:* 715-232-1667. *E-mail:* admissions@uwstout.edu.

University of Wisconsin–Superior
Superior, Wisconsin
http://www.uwsuper.edu/

- **State-supported** comprehensive, founded 1893, part of University of Wisconsin System
- **Suburban** 230-acre campus
- **Coed** 2,368 undergraduate students, 77% full-time, 62% women, 38% men
- **Minimally difficult** entrance level, 72% of applicants were admitted

UNDERGRAD STUDENTS

1,828 full-time, 540 part-time. Students come from 50 other countries; 49% are from out of state; 2% Black or African American, non-Hispanic/Latino; 3% Hispanic/Latino; 1% Asian, non-Hispanic/Latino; 2% American Indian or Alaska Native, non-Hispanic/Latino; 3% Two or more races, non-Hispanic/Latino; 0.5% Race/ethnicity unknown; 9% international; 11% transferred in; 32% live on campus.

Freshmen:

Admission: 1,002 applied, 718 admitted, 345 enrolled. *Average high school GPA:* 3.2. *Test scores:* SAT evidence-based reading and writing scores over 500: 22%; SAT math scores over 500: 13%; ACT scores over 18: 85%; ACT scores over 24: 22%; ACT scores over 30: 2%.

Retention: 72% of full-time freshmen returned.

FACULTY

Total: 224, 51% full-time, 40% with terminal degrees.
Student/faculty ratio: 14:1.

ACADEMICS

Calendar: semesters. *Degrees:* certificates, associate, bachelor's, master's, post-master's, and postbachelor's certificates.

Special study options: academic remediation for entering students, accelerated degree program, adult/continuing education programs, advanced placement credit, cooperative education, distance learning, double majors, English as a second language, external degree program, independent study, internships, off-campus study, part-time degree program, services for LD students, student-designed majors, study abroad, summer session for credit. *ROTC:* Air Force (c).

Unusual degree programs: 3-2 engineering with Michigan Technological University, University of Wisconsin–Madison; forestry with Michigan Technological University.

Computers: 375 computers/terminals are available on campus for general student use. Students can access the following: campus intranet, computer help desk, free student e-mail accounts, online (class) grades, online (class) registration, online (class) schedules. Campuswide network is available. 100% of college-owned or -operated housing units are wired for high-speed Internet access. Wireless service is available via entire campus.

Library: Jim Dan Hill Library.

STUDENT LIFE

Housing options: on-campus residence required through sophomore year; coed, women-only, special housing for students with disabilities. Campus housing is university owned. Freshman campus housing is guaranteed.

Activities and organizations: drama/theater group, student-run newspaper, radio station, choral group.

Athletics Member NCAA. All Division III. *Intercollegiate sports:* baseball M, basketball M/W, cross-country running M/W, ice hockey M/W, soccer M/W, softball W, tennis M/W, track and field M/W, volleyball W. *Intramural sports:* badminton M/W, baseball M(c), basketball M/W, bowling M/W, football M/W, ice hockey M(c)/W(c), racquetball M/W, riflery M/W, rock climbing M/W, soccer M/W, softball M/W, swimming and diving M/W, table tennis M/W, tennis M(c)/W(c), ultimate Frisbee M(c)/W(c), volleyball M(c)/W(c).

Campus security: 24-hour emergency response devices and patrols, student patrols, late-night transport/escort service, controlled dormitory access.

Student services: health clinic, personal/psychological counseling, women's center.

COSTS & FINANCIAL AID

Costs (2018–19) *Tuition:* state resident $6535 full-time; nonresident $14,108 full-time. Full-time tuition and fees vary according to course load and reciprocity agreements. Part-time tuition and fees vary according to course load and reciprocity agreements. *Required fees:* $1574 full-time. *Room and board:* $6730; room only: $3600. Room and board charges vary according to board plan and housing facility. *Payment plan:* installment.

Financial Aid Of all full-time matriculated undergraduates who enrolled in 2017, 1,416 applied for aid, 1,170 were judged to have need, 174 had their need fully met. In 2017, 48 non-need-based awards were made. *Average percent of need met:* 82. *Average financial aid package:*

$11,252. *Average need-based loan:* $4494. *Average need-based gift aid:* $5693. *Average non-need-based aid:* $1699. *Average indebtedness upon graduation:* $30,285.

APPLYING

Standardized Tests *Required:* SAT or ACT (for admission).

Options: electronic application, deferred entrance.

Application fee: $44.

Required: high school transcript. *Required for some:* interview. *Recommended:* essay or personal statement.

Application deadlines: 8/1 (freshmen), rolling (transfers).

Notification: continuous until 9/16 (freshmen), continuous (transfers).

CONTACT

University of Wisconsin–Superior, Belknap and Catlin, PO Box 2000, Superior, WI 54880-4500. *Phone:* 715-394-8230. *Fax:* 715-394-8407. *E-mail:* admissions@uwsuper.edu.

University of Wisconsin–Waukesha
Waukesha, Wisconsin
http://www.waukesha.uwc.edu/

- **State-supported** primarily 2-year, founded 1966, part of University of Wisconsin System
- **Small-town** 86-acre campus with easy access to Milwaukee
- **Coed** 1,782 undergraduate students

FACULTY
Student/faculty ratio: 17:1.

ACADEMICS
Calendar: semesters. *Degrees:* associate and bachelor's.

Special study options: academic remediation for entering students, accelerated degree program, advanced placement credit, distance learning, external degree program, honors programs, internships, off-campus study, part-time degree program, services for LD students, study abroad, summer session for credit.

Computers: Students can access the following: computer help desk, free student e-mail accounts, online (class) grades, online (class) registration, online (class) schedules, financial aid application. Campuswide network is available. Wireless service is available via entire campus.

Library: University of Wisconsin-Waukesha Library plus 1 other.

STUDENT LIFE
Housing options: college housing not available.

Activities and organizations: drama/theater group, student-run newspaper, choral group.

Athletics Member NJCAA. *Intercollegiate sports:* basketball M/W, golf M/W, soccer M/W, tennis M/W, volleyball W.

Campus security: late-night transport/escort service, part-time patrols by trained security personnel.

Student services: personal/psychological counseling.

COSTS
Costs (2017–18) *One-time required fee:* $230. *Tuition:* state resident $4750 full-time, $198 per credit hour part-time; nonresident $12,321 full-time, $513 per credit hour part-time. Full-time tuition and fees vary according to reciprocity agreements. Part-time tuition and fees vary according to course load. *Required fees:* $398 full-time, $33 per year part-time. *Room and board:* Room and board charges vary according to location. *Payment plan:* installment.

APPLYING
Standardized Tests *Required:* ACT (for admission).

Options: electronic application, early admission, deferred entrance.

Application fee: $50.

Required: high school transcript.

Application deadlines: 8/30 (freshmen), 8/30 (transfers).

CONTACT
University of Wisconsin–Waukesha, 1500 North University Drive, Waukesha, WI 53188-2799.

University of Wisconsin–Whitewater

Whitewater, Wisconsin

http://www.uww.edu/

- **State-supported** comprehensive, founded 1868, part of University of Wisconsin System
- **Small-town** 400-acre campus with easy access to Milwaukee
- **Coed** 11,128 undergraduate students, 88% full-time, 49% women, 51% men
- **Moderately difficult** entrance level, 83% of applicants were admitted

UNDERGRAD STUDENTS

9,806 full-time, 1,322 part-time. 20% are from out of state; 4% Black or African American, non-Hispanic/Latino; 6% Hispanic/Latino; 1% Asian, non-Hispanic/Latino; 0.2% American Indian or Alaska Native, non-Hispanic/Latino; 5% Two or more races, non-Hispanic/Latino; 0.1% Race/ethnicity unknown; 0.8% international; 6% transferred in; 40% live on campus.

Freshmen:

Admission: 5,706 applied, 4,745 admitted, 1,972 enrolled. *Average high school GPA:* 3.3. *Test scores:* SAT math scores over 500: 100%; ACT scores over 18: 91%; ACT scores over 24: 33%; ACT scores over 30: 3%.

FACULTY

Total: 636, 79% full-time.

Student/faculty ratio: 20:1.

ACADEMICS

Calendar: semesters. *Degrees:* associate, bachelor's, master's, and doctoral.

Special study options: academic remediation for entering students, accelerated degree program, adult/continuing education programs, advanced placement credit, cooperative education, distance learning, double majors, English as a second language, external degree program, honors programs, independent study, internships, part-time degree program, services for LD students, student-designed majors, study abroad, summer session for credit. *ROTC:* Army (b), Air Force (b).

Unusual degree programs: 3-2 engineering with University of Wisconsin–Madison, University of Wisconsin–Milwaukee.

Computers: Students can access the following: campus intranet, computer help desk, free student e-mail accounts, online (class) grades, online (class) registration, online (class) schedules. Campuswide network is available. 100% of college-owned or -operated housing units are wired for high-speed Internet access. Wireless service is available via entire campus.

Library: Andersen Library. Students can reserve study rooms.

STUDENT LIFE

Housing options: on-campus residence required through sophomore year; coed, special housing for students with disabilities. Campus housing is university owned. Freshman campus housing is guaranteed.

Activities and organizations: drama/theater group, student-run newspaper, radio and television station, choral group, marching band, Adult Student Connection, Pan Hellenic Council, Sigma Alpha Lambda (Academic Honors), Cru (Faith-Related Organization), National Society of Leadership and Success, national fraternities, national sororities.

Athletics Member NCAA. All Division III. *Intercollegiate sports:* baseball M, basketball M/W, bowling M(c)/W, cheerleading M(c)/W(c), cross-country running M/W, football M, golf W, gymnastics W, soccer M/W, softball W, swimming and diving M/W, tennis M/W, track and field M/W, volleyball M(c)/W, weight lifting M(c), wrestling M. *Intramural sports:* badminton M/W, baseball M(c), basketball M/W, bowling M/W, fencing M(c)/W(c), football M/W, golf M/W, lacrosse M(c)/W(c), racquetball M/W, rock climbing M(c)/W(c), rugby M(c)/W(c), skiing (downhill) M(c)/W(c), soccer M/W, softball M/W, table tennis M/W, tennis M/W, ultimate Frisbee M(c)/W(c), volleyball M/W, wrestling M/W.

Campus security: 24-hour emergency response devices and patrols, student patrols, late-night transport/escort service, controlled dormitory access.

Student services: health clinic, personal/psychological counseling, women's center, legal services.

COSTS & FINANCIAL AID

Costs (2017–18) *Tuition:* state resident $6519 full-time, $272 per credit hour part-time; nonresident $15,092 full-time, $629 per credit hour part-time. Full-time tuition and fees vary according to course load, degree level, and reciprocity agreements. *Required fees:* $1143 full-time. *Room and board:* $6492; room only: $3992. Room and board charges vary according to board plan and housing facility. *Payment plans:* installment, deferred payment. *Waivers:* senior citizens.

Financial Aid Of all full-time matriculated undergraduates who enrolled in 2017, 7,790 applied for aid, 5,654 were judged to have need, 2,284 had their need fully met. 545 Federal Work-Study jobs (averaging $1309). 2,365 state and other part-time jobs (averaging $1903). In 2017, 564 non-need-based awards were made. *Average percent of need met:* 62. *Average financial aid package:* $8582. *Average need-based loan:* $4350. *Average need-based gift aid:* $5874. *Average non-need-based aid:* $2154. *Average indebtedness upon graduation:* $24,704.

APPLYING

Standardized Tests *Required:* SAT or ACT (for admission).

Options: electronic application, deferred entrance.

Application fee: $50.

Required: high school transcript. *Recommended:* essay or personal statement.

Application deadlines: rolling (freshmen), rolling (transfers).

Notification: continuous (freshmen), continuous (transfers).

CONTACT

Mr. Jeremy Reed, Director of Admissions, University of Wisconsin–Whitewater, 800 West Main Street, Whitewater, WI 53190-1790. *Phone:* 262-472-1440. *E-mail:* uwwadmit@uww.edu.

Viterbo University

La Crosse, Wisconsin

http://www.viterbo.edu/

- **Independent Roman Catholic** comprehensive, founded 1890
- **Suburban** 72-acre campus
- **Coed**
- **Moderately difficult** entrance level

FACULTY

Student/faculty ratio: 11:1.

ACADEMICS

Calendar: semesters. *Degrees:* certificates, associate, bachelor's, master's, doctoral, post-master's, and postbachelor's certificates.

Library: Todd Wehr Memorial Library. *Books:* 69,288 (physical), 236 (digital/electronic); *Serial titles:* 105 (physical), 75 (digital/electronic); *Databases:* 36. Weekly public service hours: 97; study areas open 24 hours, 5–7 days a week; students can reserve study rooms.

STUDENT LIFE

Housing options: on-campus residence required for freshman year; coed. Campus housing is university owned. Freshman campus housing is guaranteed.

Activities and organizations: drama/theater group, student-run newspaper, choral group, Student Activities Board (SAB), Viterbo Student Nurses Association (VSNA), Education Club, Colleges Against Cancer (CAL), Residence Hall Association.

Athletics Member NAIA.

Campus security: 24-hour emergency response devices and patrols, late-night transport/escort service, controlled dormitory access, lighted pathways, emergency evacuation plan, self-defense education programs, security cameras.

Student services: health clinic, personal/psychological counseling.

COSTS

Costs (2017–18) *Comprehensive fee:* $35,680 includes full-time tuition ($26,230), mandatory fees ($690), and room and board ($8760). Full-time tuition and fees vary according to program. Part-time tuition and fees vary according to program. *College room only:* $3870. Room and board charges vary according to board plan and housing facility.

APPLYING

Standardized Tests *Required:* SAT or ACT (for admission).

Options: electronic application, deferred entrance.

Required: high school transcript, minimum 2.0 GPA. *Required for some:* essay or personal statement, interview, audition for theater and music, portfolio for art.

CONTACT
Mr. Eric Schmidt, Freshman Admission Counselor/Associate Director for Admission, Viterbo University, 900 Viterbo Drive, La Crosse, WI 54601. *Phone:* 608-796-3017. *Toll-free phone:* 800-VITERBO. *E-mail:* admission@viterbo.edu.

Wisconsin Lutheran College
Milwaukee, Wisconsin
http://www.wlc.edu/

- **Independent** comprehensive, founded 1973, affiliated with Wisconsin Evangelical Lutheran Synod
- **Suburban** 54-acre campus
- **Endowment** $32.9 million
- **Coed** 992 undergraduate students, 93% full-time, 55% women, 45% men
- **Moderately difficult** entrance level, 90% of applicants were admitted

UNDERGRAD STUDENTS
921 full-time, 71 part-time. Students come from 32 states and territories; 7 other countries; 24% are from out of state; 5% Black or African American, non-Hispanic/Latino; 6% Hispanic/Latino; 2% Asian, non-Hispanic/Latino; 0.7% American Indian or Alaska Native, non-Hispanic/Latino; 3% Two or more races, non-Hispanic/Latino; 0.5% Race/ethnicity unknown; 1% international; 5% transferred in; 63% live on campus.

Freshmen:
Admission: 708 applied, 639 admitted, 232 enrolled. *Average high school GPA:* 3.4. *Test scores:* SAT evidence-based reading and writing scores over 500: 88%; SAT math scores over 500: 66%; ACT scores over 18: 94%; SAT evidence-based reading and writing scores over 600: 42%; SAT math scores over 600: 37%; ACT scores over 24: 44%; SAT evidence-based reading and writing scores over 700: 4%; SAT math scores over 700: 8%; ACT scores over 30: 9%.
Retention: 79% of full-time freshmen returned.

FACULTY
Total: 164, 39% full-time, 35% with terminal degrees.
Student/faculty ratio: 10:1.

ACADEMICS
Calendar: semesters. *Degrees:* bachelor's and master's.
Special study options: accelerated degree program, adult/continuing education programs, advanced placement credit, distance learning, double majors, honors programs, independent study, internships, part-time degree program, services for LD students, student-designed majors, study abroad, summer session for credit. *ROTC:* Air Force (c).
Computers: 50 computers/terminals are available on campus for general student use. Students can access the following: campus intranet, computer help desk, free student e-mail accounts, online (class) grades, online (class) registration, online (class) schedules. Campuswide network is available. 100% of college-owned or -operated housing units are wired for high-speed Internet access. Wireless service is available via entire campus.
Library: Marvin M. Schwan Library. *Books:* 64,947 (physical), 3,778 (digital/electronic); *Serial titles:* 19 (physical), 37,529 (digital/electronic); *Databases:* 28.

STUDENT LIFE
Housing options: on-campus residence required through junior year; men-only, women-only. Campus housing is university owned. Freshman campus housing is guaranteed.
Activities and organizations: student-run newspaper, choral group.
Athletics Member NCAA. All Division III. *Intercollegiate sports:* baseball M, basketball M/W, cross-country running M/W, football M, golf M/W, soccer M/W, softball W, tennis M/W, track and field M/W, volleyball W. *Intramural sports:* cheerleading W(c).
Campus security: 24-hour emergency response devices and patrols, late-night transport/escort service, controlled dormitory access, closed-circuit TV monitors.

Student services: health clinic, personal/psychological counseling.

COSTS & FINANCIAL AID
Costs (2018–19) *Comprehensive fee:* $39,915 includes full-time tuition ($29,410), mandatory fees ($315), and room and board ($10,190). Part-time tuition: $765 per credit hour. *Room and board:* Room and board charges vary according to board plan and housing facility. *Payment plan:* installment. *Waivers:* employees or children of employees.

Financial Aid Of all full-time matriculated undergraduates who enrolled in 2017, 829 applied for aid, 756 were judged to have need, 134 had their need fully met. 76 Federal Work-Study jobs (averaging $2239). 341 state and other part-time jobs (averaging $2133). In 2017, 147 non-need-based awards were made. *Average percent of need met:* 80. *Average financial aid package:* $22,824. *Average need-based loan:* $4135. *Average need-based gift aid:* $18,668. *Average non-need-based aid:* $11,730. *Average indebtedness upon graduation:* $32,549.

APPLYING
Standardized Tests *Required:* SAT or ACT (for admission).
Options: electronic application, deferred entrance.
Required: high school transcript. *Required for some:* interview.
Application deadlines: rolling (freshmen), rolling (out-of-state freshmen), rolling (transfers).
Notification: continuous (freshmen), continuous (out-of-state freshmen), continuous (transfers).

CONTACT
Wisconsin Lutheran College, 8800 West Bluemound Road, Milwaukee, WI 53226-9942.

WYOMING

University of Wyoming
Laramie, Wyoming
http://www.uwyo.edu/

- **State-supported** university, founded 1886
- **Small-town** 835-acre campus
- **Endowment** $476.3 million
- **Coed** 9,791 undergraduate students, 85% full-time, 50% women, 50% men
- **Moderately difficult** entrance level, 97% of applicants were admitted

UNDERGRAD STUDENTS
8,281 full-time, 1,510 part-time. Students come from 51 states and territories; 64 other countries; 33% are from out of state; 1% Black or African American, non-Hispanic/Latino; 7% Hispanic/Latino; 1% Asian, non-Hispanic/Latino; 0.2% Native Hawaiian or other Pacific Islander, non-Hispanic/Latino; 0.5% American Indian or Alaska Native, non-Hispanic/Latino; 4% Two or more races, non-Hispanic/Latino; 11% Race/ethnicity unknown; 4% international; 11% transferred in; 24% live on campus.

Freshmen:
Admission: 4,306 applied, 4,169 admitted, 1,696 enrolled. *Average high school GPA:* 3.5. *Test scores:* SAT evidence-based reading and writing scores over 500: 85%; SAT math scores over 500: 86%; ACT scores over 18: 97%; SAT evidence-based reading and writing scores over 600: 47%; SAT math scores over 600: 44%; ACT scores over 24: 59%; SAT evidence-based reading and writing scores over 700: 11%; SAT math scores over 700: 7%; ACT scores over 30: 13%.
Retention: 78% of full-time freshmen returned.

FACULTY
Total: 732, 99% full-time, 78% with terminal degrees.
Student/faculty ratio: 15:1.

ACADEMICS
Calendar: semesters. *Degrees:* certificates, bachelor's, master's, doctoral, and postbachelor's certificates.
Special study options: accelerated degree program, advanced placement credit, cooperative education, distance learning, double majors, external degree program, honors programs, independent study, internships, off-

campus study, part-time degree program, services for LD students, student-designed majors, study abroad, summer session for credit. *ROTC:* Army (b), Air Force (b).

Computers: 1,683 computers/terminals and 10 ports are available on campus for general student use. Students can access the following: campus intranet, computer help desk, free student e-mail accounts, online (class) grades, online (class) registration, online (class) schedules. Campuswide network is available. 100% of college-owned or -operated housing units are wired for high-speed Internet access. Wireless service is available via classrooms, computer centers, computer labs, dorm rooms, learning centers, libraries, student centers.

Library: William Robertson Coe Library plus 4 others. *Books:* 1.8 million (physical), 943,656 (digital/electronic); *Serial titles:* 14,085 (physical), 96,240 (digital/electronic); *Databases:* 1,043. Study areas open 24 hours, 5–7 days a week; students can reserve study rooms.

STUDENT LIFE

Housing options: on-campus residence required for freshman year; coed, men-only, women-only, special housing for students with disabilities. Campus housing is university owned. Freshman campus housing is guaranteed.

Activities and organizations: drama/theater group, student-run newspaper, radio and television station, choral group, marching band, national fraternities, national sororities.

Athletics Member NCAA. All Division I except football (Division I-A). *Intercollegiate sports:* baseball M(c), basketball M(s)/W(s), cross-country running M(s)/W(s), equestrian sports M(c)/W(c), fencing M(c)/W(c), golf M(s)/W(s), ice hockey M(c)/W(c), lacrosse M(c)/W(c), racquetball M(c)/W(c), riflery M(c)/W(c), rugby M(c)/W(c), skiing (cross-country) M(c)/W(c), skiing (downhill) M(c)/W(c), soccer M(c)/W(s), softball W(c), swimming and diving M(s)/W(s), tennis M(c)/W(s), track and field M(s)/W(s), volleyball W(s), water polo M(c), wrestling M(s). *Intramural sports:* badminton M/W, basketball M/W, bowling M/W, football M/W, golf M/W, racquetball M(c)/W(c), soccer M/W, softball M/W, swimming and diving M/W, table tennis M/W, tennis M/W, track and field M/W, ultimate Frisbee M/W, volleyball M/W, water polo M/W, wrestling M/W.

Campus security: 24-hour emergency response devices and patrols, student patrols, late-night transport/escort service, controlled dormitory access, 24-hour front desk coverage at campus housing and at campus police.

Student services: health clinic, personal/psychological counseling, women's center, legal services.

COSTS & FINANCIAL AID

Costs (2018–19) *One-time required fee:* $40. *Tuition:* state resident $3870 full-time, $129 per credit hour part-time; nonresident $15,480 full-time, $516 per credit hour part-time. Full-time tuition and fees vary according to course load, location, and reciprocity agreements. Part-time tuition and fees vary according to course load, location, and reciprocity agreements. *Required fees:* $1347 full-time. *Room and board:* $10,320; room only: $4493. Room and board charges vary according to board plan and housing facility. *Payment plan:* installment. *Waivers:* children of alumni, senior citizens, and employees or children of employees.

Financial Aid Of all full-time matriculated undergraduates who enrolled in 2016, 5,116 applied for aid, 3,664 were judged to have need, 608 had their need fully met. 287 Federal Work-Study jobs (averaging $2045). In 2016, 1679 non-need-based awards were made. *Average percent of need met:* 60. *Average financial aid package:* $9904. *Average need-based loan:* $4060. *Average need-based gift aid:* $5158. *Average non-need-based aid:* $4182. *Average indebtedness upon graduation:* $22,524.

APPLYING

Standardized Tests *Required:* SAT or ACT (for admission).

Options: electronic application, deferred entrance.

Application fee: $40.

Required: high school transcript, minimum 3.0 GPA, pre-college curriculum, minimum ACT composite score of 21 or SAT of 980.

Application deadlines: 8/10 (freshmen), 8/10 (transfers).

Notification: continuous (freshmen), continuous (transfers).

CONTACT

Katie Watson, Assistant Director of Admissions, University of Wyoming, 1000 E. University Avenue, Dept 3435, Laramie, WY 82071. *Phone:* 307-766-4261. *Toll-free phone:* 800-342-5996. *Fax:* 307-766-4042. *E-mail:* admissions@uwyo.edu.

AMERICAN SAMOA

American Samoa Community College
Pago Pago, American Samoa
http://www.amsamoa.edu/

- **Territory-supported** primarily 2-year, founded 1969
- **Rural** 20-acre campus
- **Endowment** $3.1 million
- **Coed** 1,095 undergraduate students, 56% full-time, 66% women, 34% men
- **Noncompetitive** entrance level, 100% of applicants were admitted

UNDERGRAD STUDENTS
615 full-time, 480 part-time. Students come from 3 other countries; 0.8% Asian, non-Hispanic/Latino; 90% Native Hawaiian or other Pacific Islander, non-Hispanic/Latino; 9% international; 0.5% transferred in.

Freshmen:
Admission: 407 applied, 407 admitted, 382 enrolled.
Retention: 100% of full-time freshmen returned.

FACULTY
Total: 88, 69% full-time, 8% with terminal degrees.
Student/faculty ratio: 20:1.

ACADEMICS
Calendar: semesters. *Degrees:* certificates, associate, and bachelor's.

Special study options: academic remediation for entering students, adult/continuing education programs, cooperative education, double majors, independent study, internships, part-time degree program, services for LD students, summer session for credit. *ROTC:* Army (b).

Computers: 275 computers/terminals and 275 ports are available on campus for general student use. Students can access the following: campus intranet, computer help desk, online (class) grades, online (class) registration, online (class) schedules. Campuswide network is available. 98% of college-owned or -operated housing units are wired for high-speed Internet access. Wireless service is available via entire campus.

Library: ASCC Learning Resource Center/Library plus 1 other. *Books:* 33,000 (physical); *Serial titles:* 330 (physical). Weekly public service hours: 43.

STUDENT LIFE
Housing options: college housing not available.

Activities and organizations: student-run newspaper, Student Government Association, Phi Theta Kappa, ASCC Research Foundation Student Club, Fa'aSamoa (Samoan culture) Club, Journalism Club.

Athletics *Intramural sports:* basketball M/W, football M/W, golf M/W, rugby M, soccer M, tennis M/W, track and field M/W, volleyball M/W.

Campus security: 24-hour emergency response devices and patrols.

Student services: health clinic, personal/psychological counseling, legal services.

COSTS & FINANCIAL AID
Costs (2018–19) *Tuition:* territory resident $3300 full-time, $110 per credit part-time; nonresident $3600 full-time, $120 per credit part-time. Full-time tuition and fees vary according to course level, course load, and degree level. Part-time tuition and fees vary according to course level, course load, and degree level. *Required fees:* $650 full-time, $150 per term part-time. *Payment plan:* installment. *Waivers:* employees or children of employees.

Financial Aid Of all full-time matriculated undergraduates who enrolled in 2015, 588 applied for aid, 588 were judged to have need.

APPLYING
Standardized Tests *Recommended:* SAT (for admission), ACT (for admission), SAT or ACT (for admission), SAT and SAT Subject Tests or ACT (for admission).

Options: electronic application, early admission, deferred entrance.

Notification: continuous (freshmen).

CONTACT
Elizabeth Leuma, Admissions Officer, American Samoa Community College, PO Box 2609, Pago Pago 96799, American Samoa. *Phone:* 684-699-9155 Ext. 411. *Fax:* 684-699-1083.

GUAM

Pacific Islands University
Mangilao, Guam
http://www.piu.edu/

CONTACT
Ethel Laco, Admissions Office, Pacific Islands University, 172 Kinney's Road, Mangilao, GU 96913. *Phone:* 671-734-1812. *Fax:* 671-734-1813. *E-mail:* guamcampus@pibc.edu.

University of Guam
Mangilao, Guam
http://www.uog.edu/

- **Territory-supported** comprehensive, founded 1952
- **Suburban** 100-acre campus
- **Coed** 3,581 undergraduate students, 78% full-time, 57% women, 43% men
- **Noncompetitive** entrance level

UNDERGRAD STUDENTS
2,785 full-time, 796 part-time. Students come from 31 states and territories; 14 other countries; 0.7% are from out of state; 0.7% Black or African American, non-Hispanic/Latino; 0.5% Hispanic/Latino; 46% Asian, non-Hispanic/Latino; 47% Native Hawaiian or other Pacific Islander, non-Hispanic/Latino; 0.1% American Indian or Alaska Native, non-Hispanic/Latino; 3% Race/ethnicity unknown; 0.8% international; 4% transferred in; 4% live on campus.

Freshmen:
Admission: 530 applied, 481 enrolled. *Average high school GPA:* 3.5.
Retention: 72% of full-time freshmen returned.

ACADEMICS
Calendar: semesters. *Degrees:* certificates, bachelor's, master's, and postbachelor's certificates.

Special study options: academic remediation for entering students, accelerated degree program, advanced placement credit, cooperative education, distance learning, double majors, English as a second language, honors programs, independent study, internships, off-campus study, part-time degree program, services for LD students, study abroad, summer session for credit. *ROTC:* Army (b).

Computers: 262 computers/terminals and 262 ports are available on campus for general student use. Students can access the following: campus intranet, computer help desk, free student e-mail accounts, online (class) grades, online (class) registration, online (class) schedules. Campuswide network is available. 100% of college-owned or -operated housing units are wired for high-speed Internet access. Wireless service is available via entire campus.
Library: University of Guam Robert F. Kennedy Memorial Library. *Books:* 201,195 (physical), 153,000 (digital/electronic). Weekly public service hours: 56; study areas open 24 hours, 5–7 days a week; students can reserve study rooms.

STUDENT LIFE
Housing options: coed. Campus housing is university owned.
Activities and organizations: drama/theater group, student-run newspaper, choral group, American Marketing Association, Student Nurses Association of Guam, Social Work Student Alliance, Association of Early Childhood Education International CNMI, Public Administration and Legal Studies.
Athletics *Intramural sports:* basketball M/W, crew M(c)/W(c), football M, soccer M/W, softball M/W, table tennis M/W, volleyball M/W.

Campus security: 24-hour emergency response devices and patrols, late-night transport/escort service, Sexual Harassment Training Requirement for all Students, Faculty, Staff, and Administrators.
Student services: health clinic, personal/psychological counseling, women's center.

COSTS
Costs (2017–18) *Tuition:* territory resident $5040 full-time, $210 per credit part-time; nonresident $12,096 full-time, $504 per credit part-time. Part-time tuition and fees vary according to course load. *Required fees:* $538 full-time, $269 per term part-time. *Room and board:* $3850. Room and board charges vary according to housing facility. *Payment plan:* installment. *Waivers:* senior citizens and employees or children of employees.

APPLYING
Options: electronic application, deferred entrance.
Application fee: $52.
Required: high school transcript.
Application deadlines: 6/1 (freshmen), 6/1 (transfers).
Notification: continuous (freshmen), continuous (transfers).

CONTACT
Ms. Angelica Anthonio, Admissions Supervisor, University of Guam, Admissions and Records Office, UOG Station, Mangilao, GU 96923. *Phone:* 671-735-2201. *Fax:* 671-735-2203. *E-mail:* admitme@ triton.uog.edu.

NORTHERN MARIANA ISLANDS

Northern Marianas College
Saipan, Northern Mariana Islands
http://www.marianas.edu/

CONTACT
Ms. Leilani M. Basa-Alam, Admission Specialist, Northern Marianas College, PO Box 501250, Saipan, MP 96950-1250. *Phone:* 670-234-3690 Ext. 1539. *Fax:* 670-235-4967. *E-mail:* leilanib@nmcnet.edu.

PUERTO RICO

American University of Puerto Rico
Bayamon, Puerto Rico
http://www.aupr.edu/

CONTACT
Ms. Keren Llanos Figueroa, Director of Admissions, American University of Puerto Rico, PO Box 2037, Bayamon, PR 00960-2037. *Phone:* 787-620-2040 Ext. 2020. *Fax:* 787-785-7377. *E-mail:* kllanos@aupr.edu.

American University of Puerto Rico
Manati, Puerto Rico
http://www.aupr.edu/

CONTACT
American University of Puerto Rico, Carretera Estatal #2 Km. 48.7, PO Box 1082, Manati, PR 00674-1082.

Atenas College
Manati, Puerto Rico
http://www.atenascollege.edu/

CONTACT
Atenas College, Paseo de La Atenas #101 Altos, Manati, PR 00674.

Atlantic University College

Guaynabo, Puerto Rico

http://www.atlanticu.edu/

CONTACT
Ms. Zaida Perez, Admission's Officer, Atlantic University College, PO
Box 3918, Guaynabo, PR 00970. *Phone:* 787-720-1022 Ext. 13. *E-mail:*
admisiones@atlanticcollege.edu.

Bayamón Central University

Bayamón, Puerto Rico

http://www.ucb.edu.pr/
- **Independent Roman Catholic** comprehensive, founded 1970
- **Urban** 55-acre campus with easy access to San Juan
- **Endowment** $439,784
- **Coed**
- **45% of applicants were admitted**

FACULTY
Student/faculty ratio: 23:1.

ACADEMICS
Calendar: semesters for undergraduate programs, trimesters for graduate
programs. *Degrees:* certificates, associate, bachelor's, master's, post-
master's, and postbachelor's certificates.
Library: Bliblioteca Dra. Margot Arce de Vazquez plus 1 other. Weekly
public service hours: 50; students can reserve study rooms.

STUDENT LIFE
Housing options: college housing not available.
Campus security: 24-hour patrols.
Student services: health clinic, personal/psychological counseling.

COSTS
Costs (2017–18) *Tuition:* $6568 full-time, $185 per credit part-time.
Required fees: $950 full-time. *Payment plans:* installment, deferred
payment.

APPLYING
Standardized Tests *Required:* CEEB (for admission).
Options: electronic application.
Application fee: $25.
Required: high school transcript. *Recommended:* minimum 2.0 GPA.

CONTACT
Bayamón Central University, PO Box 1725, Bayamón, PR 00960-1725.
Phone: 787-786-3030 Ext. 2102.

Caribbean University

Bayamón, Puerto Rico

http://www.caribbean.edu/
- **Independent** comprehensive, founded 1969
- **Urban** 16-acre campus with easy access to San Juan
- **Coed** 2,920 undergraduate students, 72% full-time, 56% women, 44%
  men
- **Minimally difficult** entrance level, 57% of applicants were admitted

UNDERGRAD STUDENTS
2,099 full-time, 821 part-time. 100% Hispanic/Latino.

Freshmen:
Admission: 1,020 applied, 581 admitted, 293 enrolled. *Average high
school GPA:* 2.6.
Retention: 72% of full-time freshmen returned.

FACULTY
Total: 361, 24% full-time, 19% with terminal degrees.
Student/faculty ratio: 14:1.

ACADEMICS
Calendar: semesters. *Degrees:* certificates, associate, bachelor's,
master's, and doctoral.
Special study options: academic remediation for entering students,
accelerated degree program, adult/continuing education programs,
English as a second language, part-time degree program, services for LD
students, summer session for credit. **ROTC:** Army (c).
Computers: 378 computers/terminals are available on campus for general
student use. Students can access the following: campus intranet, computer
help desk, free student e-mail accounts, online (class) grades, online
(class) registration, online (class) schedules. Campuswide network is
available. Wireless service is available via entire campus.
Library: Biblioteca Virgilio Davila, Recinto de Bayamon plus 4 others.
Books: 76,606 (physical), 139,981 (digital/electronic); *Databases:* 2,346.

STUDENT LIFE
Housing options: college housing not available.
Activities and organizations: drama/theater group, choral group,
Engineering Student Association, Nursing, Social Work, Speech Therapy,
Criminal Justices.
Athletics *Intercollegiate sports:* baseball M, basketball M/W,
cheerleading M/W, cross-country running M/W, soccer M/W, softball W,
table tennis M, track and field M/W, volleyball M/W, wrestling M/W.
Intramural sports: basketball M/W, volleyball M/W.
Campus security: 24-hour patrols.
Student services: health clinic, personal/psychological counseling.

COSTS
Costs (2017–18) *Tuition:* $4464 full-time. Full-time tuition and fees vary
according to class time, degree level, location, and program. Part-time
tuition and fees vary according to class time, degree level, location, and
program. *Required fees:* $800 full-time. *Payment plan:* installment.
Waivers: employees or children of employees.

APPLYING
Standardized Tests *Required for some:* College Board math/verbal test
for engineering.
Options: deferred entrance.
Application fee: $30.
Required: high school transcript. *Required for some:* minimum 2.0 GPA,
1 letter of recommendation, interview.

CONTACT
Caribbean University, Box 493, Bayamón, PR 00960-0493. *Phone:* 787-
780-0070 Ext. 1129.

Caribbean University–Carolina

Carolina, Puerto Rico

http://www.caribbean.edu/

CONTACT
Caribbean University–Carolina, Calle Ignacio Arzuaga #208, Carolina,
PR 00985.

Caribbean University–Ponce

Ponce, Puerto Rico

http://www.caribbean.edu/

CONTACT
Caribbean University–Ponce, Ave. Ednita Nazario #1015, Ponce, PR
00716-7733.

Caribbean University–Vega Baja

Vega Baja, Puerto Rico

http://www.caribbean.edu/

CONTACT
Caribbean University–Vega Baja, Carr 671 K.M. 5, Sector El Criollo, Bo.
Algarrobo, Vega Baja, PR 00964.

Carlos Albizu University
San Juan, Puerto Rico
http://www.albizu.edu/

- **Independent** university, founded 1966
- **Urban** campus
- **Endowment** $732,270
- **Coed** 142 undergraduate students, 55% full-time, 89% women, 11% men
- **Noncompetitive** entrance level, 84% of applicants were admitted

UNDERGRAD STUDENTS
78 full-time, 64 part-time. 1% are from out of state; 95% Hispanic/Latino; 4% Race/ethnicity unknown; 74% transferred in.

Freshmen:
Admission: 63 applied, 53 admitted.

FACULTY
Total: 14, 7% full-time, 29% with terminal degrees.
Student/faculty ratio: 10:1.

ACADEMICS
Calendar: semesters. *Degrees:* bachelor's, master's, and doctoral.

Special study options: cooperative education, independent study, part-time degree program.

Computers: 68 computers/terminals are available on campus for general student use. Students can access the following: campus intranet, computer help desk, free student e-mail accounts, online (class) grades, online (class) registration, online (class) schedules. Campuswide network is available. Wireless service is available via entire campus.
Library: Carlos Albizu Miranda plus 2 others.

STUDENT LIFE
Housing options: college housing not available.
Activities and organizations: student-run newspaper, Student Council, Community Services, Gender and Sexual Diversity Organization, OASIS, Speech/Language Pathology Students Organization.
Campus security: 24-hour emergency response devices, late-night transport/escort service, security cameras.

FINANCIAL AID
Financial Aid Of all full-time matriculated undergraduates who enrolled in 2017, 147 applied for aid, 147 were judged to have need. *Average percent of need met:* 100. *Average financial aid package:* $4925. *Average need-based loan:* $3000. *Average need-based gift aid:* $4925.

APPLYING
Standardized Tests *Required:* CEEB or SAT (for admission).
Options: early admission, deferred entrance.
Application fee: $75.
Required: minimum 2.0 GPA, 2 letters of recommendation. *Required for some:* health certificate, Good Conduct Crete, official university transcript.
Application deadlines: 7/16 (freshmen), 7/17 (transfers).
Notification: continuous (freshmen), continuous (transfers).

CONTACT
Carlos Albizu University, 151 Tanca Street, San Juan, PR 00901.

Centro de Estudios Multidisciplinarios
Bayamon, Puerto Rico
http://www.cempr.edu/

CONTACT
Centro de Estudios Multidisciplinarios, Calle Degetau #25, Bayamon, PR 00961.

Centro de Estudios Multidisciplinarios
Humacao, Puerto Rico
http://www.cempr.edu/

CONTACT
Centro de Estudios Multidisciplinarios, Calle Dr. Vidal #8 y #53, Humacao, PR 00791. *Phone:* 787-850-8333.

Centro de Estudios Multidisciplinarios
Mayaguez, Puerto Rico
http://www.cempr.edu/

CONTACT
Centro de Estudios Multidisciplinarios, Calle Cristy #56, Mayaguez, PR 00680.

Centro de Estudios Multidisciplinarios
Rio Piedras, Puerto Rico
http://www.cempr.edu/

CONTACT
Admissions Department, Centro de Estudios Multidisciplinarios, Calle 13 #1206, Ext. San Agustin, Rio Piedras, PR 00926. *Phone:* 787-765-4210 Ext. 115. *Toll-free phone:* 877-779-CDEM.

Colegio Universitario de San Juan
San Juan, Puerto Rico
http://www.cunisanjuan.edu/

- **City-supported** 4-year, founded 1971
- **Urban** 5-acre campus
- **Coed** 1,480 undergraduate students, 83% full-time, 59% women, 41% men
- **Noncompetitive** entrance level, 88% of applicants were admitted

UNDERGRAD STUDENTS
1,234 full-time, 246 part-time. 15% transferred in.

Freshmen:
Admission: 306 applied, 270 admitted, 241 enrolled. *Average high school GPA:* 2.8.
Retention: 57% of full-time freshmen returned.

FACULTY
Total: 145, 13% full-time, 2% with terminal degrees.
Student/faculty ratio: 22:1.

ACADEMICS
Calendar: semesters. *Degrees:* certificates, diplomas, associate, and bachelor's.

Special study options: academic remediation for entering students, cooperative education, English as a second language, independent study, internships, off-campus study, part-time degree program, services for LD students, summer session for credit.
Computers: Students can access the following: free student e-mail accounts. Campuswide network is available. Wireless service is available via entire campus.
Library: Access to Information Center. *Books:* 17,569 (physical), 228,547 (digital/electronic); *Serial titles:* 82,010 (digital/electronic); *Databases:* 69. Weekly public service hours: 81; students can reserve study rooms.

STUDENT LIFE
Housing options: college housing not available.
Athletics *Intramural sports:* basketball M/W, volleyball M/W.
Campus security: 24-hour emergency response devices and patrols.
Student services: personal/psychological counseling.

COSTS

Costs (2018–19) *Tuition:* commonwealth resident $2040 full-time; nonresident $2040 full-time. *Required fees:* $330 full-time. *Payment plan:* deferred payment. *Waivers:* employees or children of employees.

APPLYING

Options: electronic application.

Application fee: $15.

Required: high school transcript, minimum 2.0 GPA, medical history. *Required for some:* interview.

Notification: continuous (freshmen), continuous (transfers).

CONTACT

Colegio Universitario de San Juan, Jose R. Oliver Street, Hato Rey, PR 00918. *Phone:* 787-250-7111 Ext. 2227.

Columbia Central University

Caguas, Puerto Rico

http://www.columbiacentral.edu/

- **Proprietary** comprehensive, founded 1966
- **Urban** 6-acre campus with easy access to San Juan
- **Coed** 1,270 undergraduate students, 47% full-time, 61% women, 39% men
- **Noncompetitive** entrance level

UNDERGRAD STUDENTS

591 full-time, 679 part-time. 100% Hispanic/Latino; 12% transferred in.

Freshmen:

Admission: 297 applied, 180 enrolled. *Average high school GPA:* 2.0.

Retention: 50% of full-time freshmen returned.

FACULTY

Total: 120, 24% full-time, 30% with terminal degrees.

Student/faculty ratio: 17:1.

ACADEMICS

Calendar: semesters. *Degrees:* certificates, associate, bachelor's, and master's.

Special study options: accelerated degree program, part-time degree program.

Computers: 179 computers/terminals are available on campus for general student use. Students can access the following: free student e-mail accounts, online (class) grades, online (class) registration, online (class) schedules, online courses / technical support / Microsoft office 365 products / Microsoft Imagine &; / Virtual library services / Moodle E-learning platform. Campuswide network is available. Wireless service is available via entire campus.

Library: Efrain Sola Bezares Library plus 1 other. *Books:* 14,877 (physical), 364 (digital/electronic); *Serial titles:* 21 (physical), 277,537 (digital/electronic); *Databases:* 13. Weekly public service hours: 85; students can reserve study rooms.

STUDENT LIFE

Housing options: college housing not available.

Campus security: 24-hour patrols.

Student services: personal/psychological counseling.

COSTS & FINANCIAL AID

Costs (2018–19) *Tuition:* $9630 full-time. Full-time tuition and fees vary according to class time, degree level, and program. Part-time tuition and fees vary according to class time, degree level, and program. *Required fees:* $120 full-time. *Payment plan:* installment. *Waivers:* employees or children of employees.

Financial Aid Of all full-time matriculated undergraduates who enrolled in 2008, 974 applied for aid, 818 were judged to have need. 61 Federal Work-Study jobs (averaging $982). *Average percent of need met:* 11. *Average financial aid package:* $4035.

APPLYING

Options: electronic application.

Application fee: $50.

Required: high school transcript, minimum 2.0 GPA. *Required for some:* essay or personal statement, 3 letters of recommendation, interview, Immunization Certificate for candidates who are under 21.

Notification: continuous (freshmen).

CONTACT

Mr. Pablo Soto, VicePresident Senior of Marketing and Admision, Columbia Central University, PO Box 8517, Caguas, PR 00726. *Phone:* 787-743-4041 Ext. 239. *Fax:* 787-744-7031. *E-mail:* psoto@ columbiacentral.edu.

Columbia Central University

Yauco, Puerto Rico

http://www.columbiacentral.edu/

- **Proprietary** 4-year, founded 1966
- **Urban** campus with easy access to Ponce, Mayaguez
- **Coed** 345 undergraduate students, 52% full-time, 72% women, 28% men
- **Minimally difficult** entrance level, 62% of applicants were admitted

UNDERGRAD STUDENTS

181 full-time, 164 part-time. Students come from 1 other state.

Freshmen:

Admission: 209 applied, 130 admitted, 76 enrolled. *Average high school GPA:* 3.0.

FACULTY

Total: 29, 28% full-time, 14% with terminal degrees.

Student/faculty ratio: 10:1.

ACADEMICS

Calendar: trimesters. *Degrees:* certificates, associate, and bachelor's.

Special study options: adult/continuing education programs, cooperative education, distance learning, internships, part-time degree program, services for LD students.

Computers: 14 computers/terminals and 20 ports are available on campus for general student use. Students can access the following: campus intranet, computer help desk, free student e-mail accounts, online (class) grades, online (class) registration, online (class) schedules. Campuswide network is available. Wireless service is available via entire campus.

Library: Centro de Informacion y Recursos Integrados (CIRI). *Books:* 2,845 (physical), 759 (digital/electronic); *Serial titles:* 533 (physical), 231,831 (digital/electronic); *Databases:* 25. Weekly public service hours: 66; students can reserve study rooms.

STUDENT LIFE

Housing options: college housing not available.

Activities and organizations: Student Association Pharmacy Technicians, Student Association Graphic Design, Student Council.

Campus security: trained security personnel during hours of operation.

Student services: personal/psychological counseling.

COSTS

Costs (2018–19) *Tuition:* $9630 full-time, $1605 per semester hour part-time. *Required fees:* $120 full-time, $230 per semester hour part-time. *Waivers:* employees or children of employees.

APPLYING

Options: electronic application, deferred entrance.

Application fee: $10.

Required: high school transcript, minimum 2.0 GPA.

Notification: continuous (freshmen).

CONTACT

Mrs. Carmen Ivette Pabon MSC, Admissions Coordinator, Columbia Central University, PO Box 3062, Yauco, PR 00698. *Phone:* 787-856-0845 Ext. 117. *Fax:* 787-267-0994. *E-mail:* cipabon@ columbiacentral.edu.

Conservatorio de Musica de Puerto Rico

San Juan, Puerto Rico

http://www.cmpr.edu/

- **Commonwealth-supported** comprehensive
- **Urban** 4-acre campus with easy access to Old San Juan
- **Endowment** $1.0 million
- **Coed** 432 undergraduate students, 68% full-time, 29% women, 71% men
- **Moderately difficult** entrance level, 66% of applicants were admitted

UNDERGRAD STUDENTS

292 full-time, 140 part-time. Students come from 3 states and territories; 5 other countries; 0.2% Black or African American, non-Hispanic/Latino; 96% Hispanic/Latino; 3% international; 6% transferred in.

Freshmen:

Admission: 102 applied, 67 admitted, 67 enrolled. *Average high school GPA:* 3.2.

Retention: 96% of full-time freshmen returned.

FACULTY

Total: 81, 59% full-time, 11% with terminal degrees.

Student/faculty ratio: 6:1.

ACADEMICS

Calendar: semesters. *Degrees:* bachelor's, master's, and postbachelor's certificates.

Special study options: academic remediation for entering students, advanced placement credit, cooperative education, English as a second language, honors programs, off-campus study, part-time degree program, services for LD students, summer session for credit.

Computers: 43 computers/terminals are available on campus for general student use. Students can access the following: campus intranet, free student e-mail accounts, online (class) registration. Campuswide network is available. Wireless service is available via classrooms, computer centers, computer labs, learning centers, libraries.

Library: Biblioteca Amaury Veray plus 1 other. *Books:* 29,276 (physical), 80,545 (digital/electronic); *Serial titles:* 197 (physical), 80,942 (digital/electronic); *Databases:* 108.

STUDENT LIFE

Housing options: college housing not available.

Activities and organizations: choral group.

Campus security: 24-hour patrols.

COSTS

Costs (2018–19) *One-time required fee:* $225. *Tuition:* commonwealth resident $2520 full-time; nonresident $2520 full-time. *Required fees:* $425 full-time. *Payment plan:* deferred payment. *Waivers:* employees or children of employees.

APPLYING

Application fee: $75.

Required: high school transcript, minimum 2.0 GPA, instrument audition, ear training test. *Required for some:* essay or personal statement, minimum 3.0 GPA. *Recommended:* interview.

Application deadlines: 12/15 (freshmen), 12/15 (transfers).

Notification: 3/1 (freshmen), 3/1 (transfers).

CONTACT

Mrs. Ana Marta Arraiza, Admission Coordinator, Conservatorio de Musica de Puerto Rico, 951 Ponce de Leon Avenue, San Juan, PR 00907-3373. *Phone:* 787-751-0160 Ext. 275. *Fax:* 787-7589511. *E-mail:* aarraiza2@cmpr.gobierno.pr.

Dewey University–Carolina

Carolina, Puerto Rico

http://www.dewey.edu/

CONTACT

Dewey University–Carolina, Carr. #3, Km. 11, Parque Industrial de Carolina, Lote 7, Carolina, PR 00986.

Dewey University–Hato Rey

Hato Rey, Puerto Rico

http://www.dewey.edu/

CONTACT

Dewey University–Hato Rey, 427 Avenida Barbosa, Hato Rey, PR 00923.

Dewey University–Manati

Manati, Puerto Rico

http://www.dewey.edu/

CONTACT

Dewey University–Manati, Carr. 604, Km. 49.1 Barrio Tierras Nuevas, Salientes, Manati, PR 00674. *Toll-free phone:* 866-773-3939.

EDIC College

Caguas, Puerto Rico

http://www.ediccollege.edu/

CONTACT

EDIC College, Ave. Rafael Cordero Calle GÃ©nova Urb. Caguas Norte, Caguas, PR 00726.

EDP University of Puerto Rico

Hato Rey, Puerto Rico

http://www.edpuniversity.edu/

- **Independent** comprehensive, founded 1968
- **Urban** 1-acre campus with easy access to San Juan
- **Coed** 1,666 undergraduate students, 56% full-time, 66% women, 34% men
- **Noncompetitive** entrance level, 84% of applicants were admitted

UNDERGRAD STUDENTS

937 full-time, 729 part-time. Students come from 23 states and territories; 31% are from out of state; 19% transferred in.

Freshmen:

Admission: 545 applied, 456 admitted, 109 enrolled. *Average high school GPA:* 3.0.

Retention: 33% of full-time freshmen returned.

FACULTY

Total: 198, 25% full-time, 17% with terminal degrees.

Student/faculty ratio: 12:1.

ACADEMICS

Calendar: semesters. *Degrees:* associate, bachelor's, master's, and postbachelor's certificates.

Special study options: academic remediation for entering students, accelerated degree program, adult/continuing education programs, advanced placement credit, cooperative education, distance learning, English as a second language, independent study, internships, part-time degree program, services for LD students, summer session for credit.

Computers: 207 computers/terminals and 230 ports are available on campus for general student use. Students can access the following: campus intranet, computer help desk, free student e-mail accounts, online (class) grades, online (class) registration, online (class) schedules. Campuswide network is available. Wireless service is available via classrooms, computer centers, computer labs, learning centers, libraries, student centers.

Library: Centro de Recursos para la Informacion plus 2 others. *Books:* 16,163 (physical), 50 (digital/electronic); *Serial titles:* 48 (physical), 13,800 (digital/electronic); *Databases:* 30. Weekly public service hours: 82; students can reserve study rooms.

STUDENT LIFE

Housing options: college housing not available.

Activities and organizations: choral group, Student Council, Graduate Student Association, Dance Group.

Campus security: 24-hour emergency response devices, student patrols, late-night transport/escort service, security and emergency telephones during working hours.

Student services: personal/psychological counseling.

COSTS & FINANCIAL AID
Costs (2018–19) *Tuition:* $5280 full-time, $176 per credit hour part-time. Full-time tuition and fees vary according to course load and program. Part-time tuition and fees vary according to course load and program. *Required fees:* $920 full-time, $460 per credit hour part-time. *Payment plan:* installment. *Waivers:* employees or children of employees.

Financial Aid Of all full-time matriculated undergraduates who enrolled in 2011, 1,028 applied for aid, 1,028 were judged to have need. 35 Federal Work-Study jobs (averaging $1972). *Average percent of need met:* 90. *Average financial aid package:* $5587. *Average need-based loan:* $3137. *Average need-based gift aid:* $5416. *Average indebtedness upon graduation:* $4256.

APPLYING
Standardized Tests *Required:* CEEB, institutional admission exam (for admission).

Options: electronic application, early admission, early decision, deferred entrance.

Application fee: $15.

Required: high school transcript, minimum 1.6 GPA. *Required for some:* essay or personal statement, minimum 2.5 GPA, 3 letters of recommendation, interview. *Recommended:* minimum 2.0 GPA.

Application deadlines: rolling (freshmen), rolling (transfers).

CONTACT
Mr. Oscar Morales, Dean of Student Affairs, EDP University of Puerto Rico, Avenue Ponce de Leon, #560, Hato Rey, PR 00918, Puerto Rico. *Phone:* 787-765-3560 Ext. 2272. *Fax:* 787-777-0024. *E-mail:* oscarmorales@edpuniversity.edu.

EDP University of Puerto Rico–San Sebastian
San Sebastian, Puerto Rico
http://www.edpuniversity.edu/
- **Independent** comprehensive, founded 1976
- **Rural** campus
- **Coed** 1,049 undergraduate students, 66% full-time, 64% women, 36% men
- **Minimally difficult** entrance level, 97% of applicants were admitted

UNDERGRAD STUDENTS
694 full-time, 355 part-time. Students come from 19 states and territories; 23 other countries; 15% are from out of state; 100% Hispanic/Latino; 0.1% international; 11% transferred in.

Freshmen:
Admission: 186 applied, 180 admitted, 144 enrolled. *Average high school GPA:* 3.0.

FACULTY
Total: 90, 33% full-time, 9% with terminal degrees.
Student/faculty ratio: 20:1.

ACADEMICS
Calendar: semesters. *Degrees:* associate, bachelor's, and master's.

Special study options: academic remediation for entering students, accelerated degree program, adult/continuing education programs, cooperative education, distance learning, external degree program, independent study, internships, services for LD students, summer session for credit.

Computers: 168 computers/terminals are available on campus for general student use. Students can access the following: computer help desk, free student e-mail accounts, online (class) grades, online (class) registration, online (class) schedules. Campuswide network is available. Wireless service is available via entire campus.
Library: Juan S. Robles Library. *Books:* 11,683 (physical), 222,135 (digital/electronic); *Serial titles:* 11 (physical), 25,540 (digital/electronic); *Databases:* 12. Weekly public service hours: 85; students can reserve study rooms.

STUDENT LIFE
Housing options: college housing not available.

Activities and organizations: student-run radio station, Nursing, Physical Therapy, Information Systems (SITA), Pharmacy, Digital Fashion Design.

Campus security: private security.

Student services: personal/psychological counseling.

COSTS & FINANCIAL AID
Costs (2018–19) *Tuition:* $5280 full-time, $176 per credit hour part-time. Full-time tuition and fees vary according to course load and program. Part-time tuition and fees vary according to course load and program. *Required fees:* $920 full-time, $460 per term part-time. *Payment plan:* installment. *Waivers:* employees or children of employees.

Financial Aid Of all full-time matriculated undergraduates who enrolled in 2012, 1,098 applied for aid, 1,097 were judged to have need. 32 Federal Work-Study jobs (averaging $1714). *Average percent of need met:* 92. *Average financial aid package:* $5000. *Average need-based loan:* $2601. *Average need-based gift aid:* $4545.

APPLYING
Standardized Tests *Required:* College Board exam or institutional entrance test (for admission).

Application fee: $15.

Required: high school transcript, minimum 1.6 GPA. *Required for some:* essay or personal statement, minimum 2.5 GPA, interview.

Application deadlines: rolling (freshmen), rolling (transfers).

CONTACT
Dra. Pilar Cordero de Vidal, Student Affairs Dean, EDP University of Puerto Rico–San Sebastian, Avenue Betances #49, San Sebastian, PR 00685. *Phone:* 787-896-2252 Ext. 3313. *Fax:* 787-896-5960. *E-mail:* pcordero@edpuniversity.edu.

Escuela de Artes Plasticas y Diseño de Puerto Rico
San Juan, Puerto Rico
http://www.eap.edu/
- **Commonwealth-supported** 4-year, founded 1966
- **Urban** campus
- **Endowment** $2.4 million
- **Coed** 497 undergraduate students, 71% full-time, 67% women, 33% men
- **Moderately difficult** entrance level, 85% of applicants were admitted

UNDERGRAD STUDENTS
354 full-time, 143 part-time. Students come from 1 other state; 2 other countries; 0.2% Black or African American, non-Hispanic/Latino; 99% Hispanic/Latino; 0.4% international; 29% transferred in.

Freshmen:
Admission: 81 applied, 69 admitted, 69 enrolled. *Average high school GPA:* 3.4.
Retention: 90% of full-time freshmen returned.

FACULTY
Total: 66, 27% full-time, 76% with terminal degrees.
Student/faculty ratio: 12:1.

ACADEMICS
Calendar: semesters 3 semesters each calendar year; participant in Year Round Pell. *Degree:* bachelor's.

Special study options: academic remediation for entering students, adult/continuing education programs, advanced placement credit, independent study, internships, part-time degree program, services for LD students, study abroad, summer session for credit.

Computers: 110 computers/terminals and 110 ports are available on campus for general student use. Students can access the following: computer help desk, free student e-mail accounts, library online catalog, wireless access. Wireless service is available via entire campus.
Library: Francisco Oller Library. *Books:* 23,366 (physical); *Serial titles:* 449 (digital/electronic); *Databases:* 3. Weekly public service hours: 59.

STUDENT LIFE
Housing options: college housing not available.

Activities and organizations: Student government, CINEAP, Arte-Sanacion.

Campus security: 24-hour emergency response devices and patrols, security cameras.

Student services: personal/psychological counseling.

COSTS & FINANCIAL AID

Costs (2018–19) *Tuition:* commonwealth resident $2860 full-time; nonresident $5020 full-time. *Required fees:* $602 full-time. *Payment plan:* installment. *Waivers:* employees or children of employees.

Financial Aid Of all full-time matriculated undergraduates who enrolled in 2007, 276 applied for aid, 276 were judged to have need. 10 Federal Work-Study jobs (averaging $1850). *Average percent of need met:* 82. *Financial aid deadline:* 5/25.

APPLYING

Standardized Tests *Recommended:* SAT (for admission).

Application fee: $25.

Required: high school transcript, minimum 2.0 GPA, portfolio or seminar.

Application deadlines: 4/25 (freshmen), 5/25 (transfers).

Notification: 5/18 (freshmen), 5/18 (transfers).

CONTACT

Andrea Acevedo, Officer of Admissions, Escuela de Artes Plasticas y Diseño de Puerto Rico, PO Box 902112, San Juan, PR 00902-1112. *Phone:* 787-725-8120 Ext. 319. *E-mail:* aacevedo@eap.edu.

Humacao Community College

Humacao, Puerto Rico

http://www.hccpr.edu/

- **Independent** primarily 2-year
- **Urban** campus
- **Endowment** $865,348
- **Coed**
- **Noncompetitive** entrance level

FACULTY

Student/faculty ratio: 30:1.

ACADEMICS

Calendar: trimesters. *Degrees:* certificates, diplomas, associate, and bachelor's.

Library: Santiago N. Manuez Educational Resources Center plus 1 other. *Books:* 5,320 (physical); *Serial titles:* 43 (physical), 2 (digital/electronic); *Databases:* 5. Weekly public service hours: 56.

STUDENT LIFE

Housing options: college housing not available.

Activities and organizations: Enactus Humacao Community College, Students Council.

Campus security: 24-hour emergency response devices and patrols.

Student services: personal/psychological counseling.

COSTS & FINANCIAL AID

Costs (2017–18) *One-time required fee:* $140. *Tuition:* $4932 full-time, $2466 per year part-time. Full-time tuition and fees vary according to course load and degree level. Part-time tuition and fees vary according to course load and degree level. *Required fees:* $450 full-time, $450 per year part-time.

Financial Aid Of all full-time matriculated undergraduates who enrolled in 2016, 64 Federal Work-Study jobs (averaging $546).

APPLYING

Application fee: $15.

Required: high school transcript, interview. *Required for some:* certificate of Immunization for students under 21 years.

CONTACT

Mrs. Adela Aponte, Director of Admissions, Humacao Community College, PO Box 9139, Humacao, PR 00792, Puerto Rico. *Phone:* 787-852-1430 Ext. 225. *Fax:* 787-850-1577. *E-mail:* adela.aponte@hccpr.edu.

Inter American University of Puerto Rico, Aguadilla Campus

Aguadilla, Puerto Rico

http://www.aguadilla.inter.edu/

- **Independent** comprehensive, founded 1957, part of Inter American University of Puerto Rico
- **Small-town** 50-acre campus
- **Endowment** $1.7 million
- **Coed** 3,974 undergraduate students, 85% full-time, 56% women, 44% men
- **Moderately difficult** entrance level

UNDERGRAD STUDENTS

3,376 full-time, 598 part-time. Students come from 23 states and territories; 1 other country; 2% are from out of state; 100% Hispanic/Latino; 0.2% American Indian or Alaska Native, non-Hispanic/Latino; 4% transferred in.

Freshmen:
Admission: 1,728 applied, 820 enrolled. *Average high school GPA:* 3.7.

FACULTY

Total: 263, 30% full-time, 100% with terminal degrees.

Student/faculty ratio: 30:1.

ACADEMICS

Calendar: semesters. *Degrees:* certificates, associate, bachelor's, master's, and postbachelor's certificates.

Special study options: academic remediation for entering students, accelerated degree program, adult/continuing education programs, advanced placement credit, cooperative education, distance learning, double majors, English as a second language, external degree program, honors programs, independent study, internships, part-time degree program, services for LD students, study abroad, summer session for credit. *ROTC:* Army (b), Air Force (b).

Computers: 861 computers/terminals are available on campus for general student use. Students can access the following: campus intranet, free student e-mail accounts, online (class) grades, online (class) registration, online (class) schedules. Campuswide network is available. Wireless service is available via entire campus.

Library: Manuel Mendez Ballester Information Access Center. *Books:* 63,309 (physical), 247,701 (digital/electronic); *Serial titles:* 194 (physical); *Databases:* 79. Weekly public service hours: 80; students can reserve study rooms.

STUDENT LIFE

Housing options: college housing not available.

Activities and organizations: drama/theater group, student-run newspaper, choral group, Criminal Justice Association, Microbiot Science Association, Social Workers Association, Nursing Association, Psychology Association.

Athletics *Intercollegiate sports:* baseball M(s), basketball M(s)/W(s), cheerleading M(s)/W(s), cross-country running M(s)/W(s), soccer M(s)/W(s), softball M(s)/W(s), swimming and diving M(s)/W(s), table tennis M(s)/W(s), tennis M(s)/W(s), track and field M(s)/W(s), volleyball M(s)/W(s), weight lifting M(s)/W(s), wrestling M(s). *Intramural sports:* basketball M/W, cross-country running M/W, soccer M/W, softball M/W, table tennis M/W, tennis M/W, track and field M/W, volleyball M/W, weight lifting M/W.

Campus security: 24-hour emergency response devices and patrols.

Student services: personal/psychological counseling.

COSTS

Costs (2018–19) *Tuition:* $4488 full-time, $187 per semester hour part-time. Full-time tuition and fees vary according to course load and program. Part-time tuition and fees vary according to course load and program. *Required fees:* $1410 full-time, $1012 per semester part-time. *Payment plan:* deferred payment.

APPLYING

Standardized Tests *Required:* SAT or ACT (for admission), PAA (for admission).

Options: electronic application.

Required: high school transcript, minimum 2.0 GPA.

Application deadlines: rolling (freshmen), rolling (transfers).

CONTACT
Mrs. Daisy Irizarry, Administrative Assistant, Inter American University of Puerto Rico, Aguadilla Campus, PO Box 20,000, Road 459 Intersection 463, Aguadilla, PR 00605. *Phone:* 787-891-0925 Ext. 2181. *Fax:* 787-882-3020.

Inter American University of Puerto Rico, Arecibo Campus

Arecibo, Puerto Rico
http://www.arecibo.inter.edu/

CONTACT
Ms. Provi Montalvo, Admission Director, Inter American University of Puerto Rico, Arecibo Campus, PO Box 4050, Arecibo, PR 00614-4050. *Phone:* 787-878-5475. *Fax:* 787-880-1624. *E-mail:* pmontalvo@ arecibo.inter.edu.

Inter American University of Puerto Rico, Barranquitas Campus

Barranquitas, Puerto Rico
http://www.br.inter.edu/

- **Independent** comprehensive, founded 1957, part of Inter American University of Puerto Rico
- **Small-town** campus with easy access to 35 miles from San Juan
- **Endowment** $1.0 million
- **Coed** 1,789 undergraduate students, 90% full-time, 63% women, 37% men

UNDERGRAD STUDENTS
1,605 full-time, 184 part-time. Students come from 3 states and territories; 0.2% are from out of state; 100% Hispanic/Latino; 0.1% American Indian or Alaska Native, non-Hispanic/Latino; 4% transferred in.

Freshmen:
Admission: 435 enrolled. *Average high school GPA:* 3.1.
Retention: 74% of full-time freshmen returned.

FACULTY
Total: 150, 21% full-time, 25% with terminal degrees.
Student/faculty ratio: 21:1.

ACADEMICS
Calendar: semesters. *Degrees:* certificates, associate, bachelor's, and master's.
Special study options: adult/continuing education programs, cooperative education, distance learning, English as a second language, external degree program, honors programs, off-campus study, part-time degree program, services for LD students, summer session for credit. *ROTC:* Army (c).
Computers: 403 computers/terminals and 403 ports are available on campus for general student use. Students can access the following: campus intranet, computer help desk, free student e-mail accounts, online (class) grades, online (class) registration, online (class) schedules. Campuswide network is available. Wireless service is available via entire campus.
Library: Centro de Accoso a la Informacio, Recinto de Barranquitas. *Books:* 34,547 (physical), 266,052 (digital/electronic); *Serial titles:* 187 (physical), 60,000 (digital/electronic); *Databases:* 84. Weekly public service hours: 71; students can reserve study rooms.

STUDENT LIFE
Activities and organizations: Alumni Student Chapter.
Athletics *Intercollegiate sports:* baseball M(s), basketball M(s), cross-country running M/W, softball M/W, table tennis M/W, tennis M/W, track and field M/W, volleyball M/W, weight lifting M/W. *Intramural sports:* basketball M, cross-country running M/W, softball M/W, table tennis M/W, track and field M/W, volleyball M/W.
Campus security: 24-hour patrols.
Student services: health clinic, personal/psychological counseling.

COSTS
Costs (2018–19) *One-time required fee:* $100. *Tuition:* $5610 full-time, $3020 per year part-time. Full-time tuition and fees vary according to course load, degree level, and program. Part-time tuition and fees vary according to course load, degree level, and program. *Required fees:* $652 full-time, $524 per year part-time, $262 per term part-time. *Payment plan:* deferred payment. *Waivers:* minority students and employees or children of employees.

APPLYING
Standardized Tests *Required:* CEEB (for admission). *Required for some:* SAT or ACT (for admission). *Recommended:* SAT (for admission), SAT Subject Tests (for admission).
Required: high school transcript. *Recommended:* letters of recommendation, interview.

CONTACT
Mrs. Aramilda Cartagena, Decana de Estudiantes, Inter American University of Puerto Rico, Barranquitas Campus, PO Box 517, Barranquitas, PR 00794. *Phone:* 787-857-3600 Ext. 2009. *Fax:* 787-857-2125. *E-mail:* aramildacartagena@br.inter.edu.

Inter American University of Puerto Rico, Bayamón Campus

Bayamón, Puerto Rico
http://bayamon.inter.edu/

- **Independent** comprehensive, founded 1912, part of Inter American University of Puerto Rico
- **Suburban** 51-acre campus with easy access to San Juan
- **Endowment** $224.1 million
- **Coed** 4,507 undergraduate students, 87% full-time, 44% women, 56% men
- 63% of applicants were admitted

UNDERGRAD STUDENTS
3,919 full-time, 588 part-time. Students come from 13 states and territories; 0.5% are from out of state; 0.3% Black or African American, non-Hispanic/Latino; 98% Hispanic/Latino; 0.1% Native Hawaiian or other Pacific Islander, non-Hispanic/Latino; 0.7% American Indian or Alaska Native, non-Hispanic/Latino; 4% transferred in.

Freshmen:
Admission: 1,697 applied, 1,062 admitted, 1,044 enrolled. *Average high school GPA:* 3.2.
Retention: 76% of full-time freshmen returned.

FACULTY
Total: 272, 35% full-time, 31% with terminal degrees.
Student/faculty ratio: 25:1.

ACADEMICS
Calendar: semesters. *Degrees:* certificates, associate, bachelor's, and master's.
Special study options: accelerated degree program, adult/continuing education programs, advanced placement credit, cooperative education, distance learning, external degree program, honors programs, independent study, internships, part-time degree program, services for LD students, summer session for credit. *ROTC:* Army (c).
Computers: 730 computers/terminals are available on campus for general student use. Students can access the following: computer help desk, free student e-mail accounts, online (class) grades, online (class) registration. Campuswide network is available. Wireless service is available via entire campus.
Library: Centro de Acceso a la Informacion plus 1 other. *Books:* 28,990 (physical), 242,686 (digital/electronic); *Serial titles:* 148 (physical); *Databases:* 75. Weekly public service hours: 75; students can reserve study rooms.

STUDENT LIFE
Housing options: men-only, women-only. Campus housing is university owned.
Activities and organizations: drama/theater group, student-run radio station, choral group, Consejo de Estudiantes, Asociacion Estudiantes de

Ingenieria, Asociacion Estudiantes de Aviacion, Estudiantes Unidos por la Ciencia, Asociacion de Estudiantes de Administracion de Empresas.

Athletics *Intercollegiate sports:* baseball M(s), basketball M(s)/W(s), cross-country running M(s)/W(s), softball M(s)/W(s), swimming and diving M(s)/W(s), table tennis M(s)/W(s), track and field M(s)/W(s), volleyball M(s)/W(s), weight lifting M(s). *Intramural sports:* basketball M/W, cross-country running M/W, softball M/W, swimming and diving M/W, table tennis M/W, tennis M/W, track and field M/W, volleyball M/W, weight lifting M.

Campus security: 24-hour patrols.

Student services: health clinic, personal/psychological counseling.

COSTS & FINANCIAL AID

Costs (2018–19) *Comprehensive fee:* $11,292 includes full-time tuition ($4488), mandatory fees ($690), and room and board ($6114). Full-time tuition and fees vary according to course load and program. Part-time tuition: $1122 per credit hour. Part-time tuition and fees vary according to course load and program. *Required fees:* $187 per credit hour part-time, $305 per semester part-time. *College room only:* $3113. *Payment plan:* deferred payment.

Financial Aid Of all full-time matriculated undergraduates who enrolled in 2017, 2,554 applied for aid, 2,530 were judged to have need, 4 had their need fully met. *Average percent of need met:* 30. *Average financial aid package:* $3615. *Average need-based loan:* $2844. *Average need-based gift aid:* $3110.

APPLYING

Standardized Tests *Required:* CEEB (for admission). *Required for some:* SAT (for admission).

Options: electronic application.

Required: high school transcript, minimum 2.0 GPA. *Required for some:* 2.5 GPA for engineering.

Notification: continuous (freshmen), continuous (transfers).

CONTACT

Inter American University of Puerto Rico, Bayamón Campus, 500 Dr. John Will Harris Road, Bayamón, PR 00957. *Phone:* 787-279-1912 Ext. 2017.

Inter American University of Puerto Rico, Fajardo Campus

Fajardo, Puerto Rico

http://www.fajardo.inter.edu/

- **Independent** comprehensive, founded 1965, part of Inter American University of Puerto Rico
- **Small-town** 11-acre campus with easy access to San Juan
- **Endowment** $4.3 million
- **Coed** 1,988 undergraduate students, 86% full-time, 58% women, 42% men
- **Moderately difficult** entrance level, 88% of applicants were admitted

UNDERGRAD STUDENTS

1,708 full-time, 280 part-time. Students come from 3 states and territories; 100% Hispanic/Latino.

Freshmen:

Admission: 708 applied, 626 admitted, 528 enrolled. *Average high school GPA:* 2.0.

Retention: 74% of full-time freshmen returned.

FACULTY

Total: 137, 31% full-time, 27% with terminal degrees.

Student/faculty ratio: 11:1.

ACADEMICS

Calendar: semesters. *Degrees:* certificates, associate, bachelor's, and master's.

Special study options: academic remediation for entering students, adult/continuing education programs, advanced placement credit, cooperative education, distance learning, English as a second language, external degree program, honors programs, independent study, internships, off-campus study, part-time degree program, services for LD students, summer session for credit. *ROTC:* Army (c).

Computers: 280 computers/terminals are available on campus for general student use. Students can access the following: free student e-mail accounts, online (class) grades, online (class) registration, online (class) schedules. Campuswide network is available. Wireless service is available via entire campus.

Library: Antonio S. Belaval Library plus 1 other. *Books:* 46,756 (physical), 185,479 (digital/electronic); *Serial titles:* 22,085 (physical), 49,284 (digital/electronic); *Databases:* 26. Weekly public service hours: 79; students can reserve study rooms.

STUDENT LIFE

Housing options: college housing not available.

Activities and organizations: choral group, Future Teachers Association, Criminal Justice Student Association, Honor Program Association, Computer Science Association, Social Work Association.

Athletics *Intercollegiate sports:* baseball M, basketball M(s)/W, cheerleading W, softball W, track and field M(s)/W(s), volleyball M/W.

Campus security: 24-hour patrols.

Student services: personal/psychological counseling.

COSTS

Costs (2018–19) *Tuition:* $4488 full-time, $187 per credit hour part-time. Full-time tuition and fees vary according to course level, course load, degree level, location, and program. Part-time tuition and fees vary according to course level, course load, degree level, location, and program. *Required fees:* $1410 full-time. *Payment plans:* installment, deferred payment. *Waivers:* employees or children of employees.

APPLYING

Standardized Tests *Required:* College Board exam (for admission).

Options: electronic application, early admission, deferred entrance.

Required: high school transcript. *Required for some:* interview.

Application deadlines: 5/15 (freshmen), rolling (transfers).

CONTACT

Ms. Ghisita M. Garcia, Administrative Assistant II, Inter American University of Puerto Rico, Fajardo Campus, Call Box 70003, Fajardo, PR 00738-7003. *Phone:* 787-863-2390 Ext. 2210. *Fax:* 787-860-3470. *E-mail:* ghisita.garcia@fajardo.inter.edu.

Inter American University of Puerto Rico, Guayama Campus

Guayama, Puerto Rico

http://www.guayama.inter.edu/

- **Independent** comprehensive, founded 1958, part of Inter American University of Puerto Rico
- **Small-town** 50-acre campus with easy access to San Juan
- **Coed**
- **Moderately difficult** entrance level

FACULTY

Student/faculty ratio: 12:1.

ACADEMICS

Calendar: semesters. *Degrees:* certificates, associate, bachelor's, and master's.

Library: Information Access Center. Weekly public service hours: 60.

STUDENT LIFE

Housing options: college housing not available.

Activities and organizations: student-run radio station, Natural Science and Technology, Nursing Student Association, Office Professionals, Medical Billers Organization, Pharmacy Technicians.

Campus security: 24-hour patrols.

Student services: health clinic, personal/psychological counseling.

COSTS & FINANCIAL AID

Costs (2017–18) *One-time required fee:* $55. *Tuition:* $5610 full-time. *Required fees:* $815 full-time.

Financial Aid Of all full-time matriculated undergraduates who enrolled in 2015, 1,039 applied for aid, 1,036 were judged to have need, 1 had their need fully met. *Average percent of need met:* 29. *Average financial aid package:* $4163. *Average need-based loan:* $2279. *Average need-based gift aid:* $3301.

APPLYING
Standardized Tests *Required:* PAA (for admission). *Recommended:* SAT (for admission).

Options: electronic application.

Required: high school transcript, minimum 2.0 GPA. *Required for some:* interview.

CONTACT
Mrs. Laura E. Ferrer, Director of Admissions, Inter American University of Puerto Rico, Guayama Campus, Call Box 10004, Guayama, PR 00785. *Phone:* 787-864-2222 Ext. 2220. *Fax:* 787-864-8232. *E-mail:* laura.ferrer@guayama.inter.edu.

Inter American University of Puerto Rico, Metropolitan Campus
San Juan, Puerto Rico
http://metro.inter.edu/

- **Independent** comprehensive, founded 1960, part of Inter American University of Puerto Rico
- **Urban** campus with easy access to San Juan
- **Endowment** $224.1 million
- **Coed** 6,168 undergraduate students, 78% full-time, 56% women, 44% men
- **Moderately difficult** entrance level, 57% of applicants were admitted

UNDERGRAD STUDENTS
4,820 full-time, 1,348 part-time. 0.7% Black or African American, non-Hispanic/Latino; 98% Hispanic/Latino; 0.2% Asian, non-Hispanic/Latino; 0.1% Native Hawaiian or other Pacific Islander, non-Hispanic/Latino; 0.3% American Indian or Alaska Native, non-Hispanic/Latino; 14% transferred in.

Freshmen:
Admission: 1,387 applied, 787 admitted, 737 enrolled. *Average high school GPA:* 3.2.

Retention: 71% of full-time freshmen returned.

FACULTY
Total: 606, 32% full-time, 46% with terminal degrees.

ACADEMICS
Calendar: trimesters. *Degrees:* certificates, associate, bachelor's, master's, doctoral, post-master's, and postbachelor's certificates.

Special study options: accelerated degree program, adult/continuing education programs, cooperative education, distance learning, English as a second language, external degree program, honors programs, independent study, internships, part-time degree program, services for LD students, study abroad, summer session for credit. *ROTC:* Army (c), Navy (c), Air Force (c).

Computers: 637 computers/terminals are available on campus for general student use. Students can access the following: campus intranet, computer help desk, free student e-mail accounts, online (class) grades, online (class) registration, online (class) schedules. Campuswide network is available. Wireless service is available via classrooms, computer centers, computer labs, learning centers, libraries, student centers.

Library: Centro de Acceso a la Informacion plus 1 other. *Books:* 121,223 (physical); *Serial titles:* 311 (physical); *Databases:* 24. Students can reserve study rooms.

STUDENT LIFE
Housing options: college housing not available.

Activities and organizations: drama/theater group, student-run newspaper, choral group, Intercultural Student Association, Club Rotaract, Roots and Shoots Inter Metro, Chemical Students Association, Social Work Students Association.

Athletics *Intercollegiate sports:* basketball M, soccer M, table tennis M/W, tennis M/W, volleyball M/W.

Campus security: 24-hour emergency response devices and patrols, Video Security System.

Student services: personal/psychological counseling, women's center.

FINANCIAL AID
Financial Aid Of all full-time matriculated undergraduates who enrolled in 1999, 4,328 applied for aid, 3,935 were judged to have need, 29 had their need fully met. *Average percent of need met:* 11. *Average financial aid package:* $2144. *Average need-based loan:* $1149. *Average need-based gift aid:* $1617. *Financial aid deadline:* 4/30.

APPLYING
Standardized Tests *Required:* CEEB (for admission). *Required for some:* SAT or ACT (for admission).

Options: electronic application.

Required: high school transcript, minimum 2.0 GPA.

Application deadlines: 5/15 (freshmen), 5/15 (transfers).

CONTACT
Inter American University of Puerto Rico, Metropolitan Campus, PO Box 191293, San Juan, PR 00919-1293. *Phone:* 787-250-1912 Ext. 2204.

Inter American University of Puerto Rico, Ponce Campus
Mercedita, Puerto Rico
http://www.ponce.inter.edu/

- **Independent** comprehensive, founded 1962, part of Inter American University of Puerto Rico
- **Urban** 50-acre campus with easy access to San Juan
- **Endowment** $14.5 million
- **Coed**
- **Moderately difficult** entrance level

FACULTY
Student/faculty ratio: 30:1.

ACADEMICS
Calendar: semesters. *Degrees:* certificates, associate, bachelor's, master's, and doctoral.

Library: Centro de Acceso a la Informacion plus 1 other. *Books:* 54,043 (physical), 243,183 (digital/electronic); *Serial titles:* 109 (physical); *Databases:* 130. Weekly public service hours: 56; students can reserve study rooms.

STUDENT LIFE
Housing options: college housing not available.

Activities and organizations: drama/theater group, choral group, Association of Future Teachers of Special Education, Hotel Management Association, American Chemical Society (ACS), Criminal Justice Association, Students Board of Honor Program, national fraternities.

Campus security: 24-hour emergency response devices and patrols.

Student services: health clinic, personal/psychological counseling.

FINANCIAL AID
Financial Aid Of all full-time matriculated undergraduates who enrolled in 2016, 11,837 applied for aid, 11,775 were judged to have need. *Average percent of need met:* 10. *Average need-based gift aid:* $3852.

APPLYING
Standardized Tests *Required:* CEEB (for admission). *Required for some:* SAT (for admission).

Options: deferred entrance.

Required: high school transcript, minimum 2.0 GPA.

CONTACT
Mr. Franco Diaz, Admissions Officer, Inter American University of Puerto Rico, Ponce Campus, 104 Turpo Industrial Park, Road #1, Mercedita, PR 00715-1602. *Phone:* 787-284-1912 Ext. 2025. *Fax:* 787-841-0103. *E-mail:* fidiaz@ponce.inter.edu.

Inter American University of Puerto Rico, San Germán Campus

San Germán, Puerto Rico

http://www.sg.inter.edu/

- **Independent** university, founded 1912, part of Inter American University of Puerto Rico
- **Small-town** 274-acre campus with easy access to Ponce, Aguadilla, Mayaguez
- **Endowment** $224.1 million
- **Coed** 4,115 undergraduate students, 90% full-time, 53% women, 47% men
- **Moderately difficult** entrance level, 69% of applicants were admitted

UNDERGRAD STUDENTS

3,693 full-time, 422 part-time. Students come from 9 states and territories; 2 other countries; 0.3% are from out of state; 0.2% Black or African American, non-Hispanic/Latino; 99% Hispanic/Latino; 0.2% American Indian or Alaska Native, non-Hispanic/Latino; 4% transferred in; 7% live on campus.

Freshmen:
Admission: 1,509 applied, 1,041 admitted, 980 enrolled. *Average high school GPA:* 3.0.
Retention: 559% of full-time freshmen returned.

FACULTY

Total: 330, 32% full-time, 37% with terminal degrees.
Student/faculty ratio: 13:1.

ACADEMICS

Calendar: semesters. *Degrees:* certificates, associate, bachelor's, master's, doctoral, and postbachelor's certificates.

Special study options: academic remediation for entering students, accelerated degree program, adult/continuing education programs, advanced placement credit, cooperative education, distance learning, double majors, English as a second language, external degree program, honors programs, independent study, internships, off-campus study, part-time degree program, services for LD students, summer session for credit. *ROTC:* Army (c), Navy (c), Air Force (c).

Computers: 950 computers/terminals are available on campus for general student use. Students can access the following: campus intranet, computer help desk, free student e-mail accounts, online (class) grades, online (class) registration, online (class) schedules. Campuswide network is available. Wireless service is available via entire campus.
Library: Juan Cancio Ortiz Library. *Books:* 125,059 (physical), 3,850 (digital/electronic); *Serial titles:* 240 (physical), 594,924 (digital/electronic); *Databases:* 96. Weekly public service hours: 69.

STUDENT LIFE

Housing options: men-only, women-only. Campus housing is university owned.

Activities and organizations: choral group, Asociacion de Pre-Medica-Caduceus, Business Professionals of America, Sociedad de Honor en Biologia Beta Beta Beta (TriBeta), Asociacion Estudiantes de EnfermerÃ-a, Asociacion de Estudiantes del Programa de Honor, national fraternities.

Athletics *Intercollegiate sports:* baseball M(s), basketball M(s)/W(s), cross-country running M(s)/W(s), sand volleyball M/W, soccer M/W, softball W, swimming and diving M/W, table tennis M(s)/W(s), tennis M(s)/W(s), track and field M(s)/W(s), volleyball M(s)/W(s), weight lifting M(s)/W(s), wrestling M. *Intramural sports:* baseball M, basketball M/W, cheerleading M/W, cross-country running M/W, softball M/W, table tennis M/W, tennis M/W, track and field M/W, volleyball M/W, weight lifting M/W.

Campus security: 24-hour patrols, electronic vigilance systems with nonstop digital video cameras, access control permits, periodic surveillance.

Student services: health clinic, personal/psychological counseling.

COSTS & FINANCIAL AID

Costs (2017–18) *Comprehensive fee:* $9000 includes full-time tuition ($5610), mandatory fees ($690), and room and board ($2700). Full-time tuition and fees vary according to degree level. Part-time tuition: $187 per credit hour. Part-time tuition and fees vary according to degree level. *Required fees:* $187 per credit hour part-time, $690 per year part-time. *College room only:* $1200. Room and board charges vary according to board plan and housing facility. *Payment plan:* installment. *Waivers:* employees or children of employees.

Financial Aid Of all full-time matriculated undergraduates who enrolled in 2009, 2,797 applied for aid, 2,755 were judged to have need, 4 had their need fully met. *Average percent of need met:* 12. *Average financial aid package:* $2009. *Average need-based loan:* $3080. *Average need-based gift aid:* $642.

APPLYING

Standardized Tests *Required:* CEEB (for admission). *Required for some:* SAT or ACT (for admission).

Options: electronic application, early admission.

Required: high school transcript, medical history, vaccination. *Required for some:* 1 letter of recommendation, interview. *Recommended:* essay or personal statement, minimum 2.0 GPA.

Application deadlines: 5/15 (freshmen), 5/15 (transfers).
Notification: continuous (freshmen), continuous (transfers).

CONTACT

Prof. Mildred Camacho, Director of Admissions, Inter American University of Puerto Rico, San Germán Campus, PO Box 5100, San German, PR 00683-5008. *Phone:* 787-264-1912 Ext. 7283. *Toll-free phone:* 800-981-8075. *Fax:* 787-892-7020. *E-mail:* milcama@intersg.edu.

National University College

Arecibo, Puerto Rico

http://www.nuc.edu/

CONTACT
National University College, Calle Manuel PÃ©rez AvilÃ©s, Avenida VÃctor Rojas, Arecibo, PR 00612.

National University College

Bayamón, Puerto Rico

http://www.nuc.edu/

CONTACT
Admissions, National University College, PO Box 2036, National College Plaza Building, Bayamón, PR 00960. *Toll-free phone:* 800-780-5134.

National University College

Caguas, Puerto Rico

http://www.nuc.edu/

CONTACT
National University College, 190 Avenida Gautier Benitez Esquina Avenida Federico Degetau, Caguas, PR 00725. *Toll-free phone:* 800-780-5134.

National University College

Ponce, Puerto Rico

http://www.nuc.edu/

CONTACT
National University College, PO Box 801243, Ponce, PR 00716.

National University College

Rio Grande, Puerto Rico

http://www.nuc.edu/

CONTACT
National University College, Carretera #3 Km. 22.1, Bo. CiÃ©naga Baja, Rio Grande, PR 00745. *Toll-free phone:* 800-981-0812.

Polytechnic University of Puerto Rico

Hato Rey, Puerto Rico
http://www.pupr.edu/

- **Independent** comprehensive, founded 1966
- **Urban** 10-acre campus with easy access to San Juan
- **Endowment** $14.3 million
- **Coed** 3,494 undergraduate students
- **Minimally difficult** entrance level, 72% of applicants were admitted

UNDERGRAD STUDENTS
Students come from 8 states and territories; 4 other countries; 0.1% Black or African American, non-Hispanic/Latino; 100% Hispanic/Latino.

Freshmen:
Admission: 746 applied, 536 admitted. *Average high school GPA:* 3.3. *Retention:* 77% of full-time freshmen returned.

FACULTY
Total: 211, 63% full-time, 34% with terminal degrees.
Student/faculty ratio: 14:1.

ACADEMICS
Calendar: trimesters. *Degrees:* associate, bachelor's, master's, and doctoral.

Special study options: academic remediation for entering students, advanced placement credit, distance learning, English as a second language, honors programs, independent study, internships, student-designed majors, summer session for credit. *ROTC:* Army (c).

Computers: 800 computers/terminals and 800 ports are available on campus for general student use. Students can access the following: campus intranet, computer help desk, free student e-mail accounts, online (class) grades, online (class) registration, online (class) schedules. Campuswide network is available. 100% of college-owned or -operated housing units are wired for high-speed Internet access. Wireless service is available via entire campus.
Library: Biblioteca de la Unidersidad Politecnica de Puerto Rico. *Books:* 66,518 (physical), 61,939 (digital/electronic); *Serial titles:* 1,794 (physical), 15,595 (digital/electronic); *Databases:* 46. Weekly public service hours: 82; study areas open 24 hours, 5–7 days a week; students can reserve study rooms.

STUDENT LIFE
Housing options: coed. Campus housing is university owned.

Activities and organizations: choral group, ASCE (American Society of Civil Engineering), PRWEA (Puerto Rico Water and Environment Association), ACI (American Concrete Institute), SAE PUPR AERO DESIGN TEAM, SHPE (Society of Hispanic Professional Engineers).

Athletics *Intercollegiate sports:* track and field M(s)/W(s), volleyball M(s)/W(s), weight lifting M(s)/W(s).

Campus security: 24-hour emergency response devices and patrols, late-night transport/escort service, controlled dormitory access, over 350 security cameras on campus.

Student services: health clinic, personal/psychological counseling.

COSTS & FINANCIAL AID
Costs (2018–19) *Comprehensive fee:* $20,186 includes full-time tuition ($7488), mandatory fees ($840), and room and board ($11,858). Full-time tuition and fees vary according to course level, degree level, and program. Part-time tuition: $208 per credit hour. Part-time tuition and fees vary according to course level, degree level, and program. *Required fees:* $280 per term part-time. *College room only:* $4950. *Payment plan:* deferred payment. *Waivers:* employees or children of employees.

Financial Aid Of all full-time matriculated undergraduates who enrolled in 2015, 1,918 applied for aid, 1,865 were judged to have need, 8 had their need fully met. *Average percent of need met:* 45. *Average financial aid package:* $7698. *Average need-based loan:* $2665. *Average need-based gift aid:* $2535. *Average non-need-based aid:* $245.

APPLYING
Standardized Tests *Recommended:* CEEB or PEAU.
Options: electronic application.
Application fee: $30.
Required: high school transcript, minimum 2.0 GPA.

CONTACT
Ms. Teresa Cardona, Director of Admissions, Polytechnic University of Puerto Rico, PO Box 192017, San Juan, PR 00919-2017. *Phone:* 787-622-8000 Ext. 240. *Fax:* 787-764-8712. *E-mail:* tcardona@pupr.edu.

Pontifical Catholic University of Puerto Rico

Ponce, Puerto Rico
http://www.pucpr.edu/

CONTACT
Sra. Ana O. Bonilla, Director of Admissions, Pontifical Catholic University of Puerto Rico, 2250 Avenida Las Americas Avenue, Suite 584, Ponce, PR 00717-9777. *Phone:* 787-841-2000 Ext. 1004. *Toll-free phone:* 800-961-7696. *Fax:* 787-840-4295. *E-mail:* admissions@email.pucpr.edu.

Pontifical Catholic University of Puerto Rico–Arecibo Campus

Arecibo, Puerto Rico
http://www.pucpr.edu/arecibo/

CONTACT
Pontifical Catholic University of Puerto Rico–Arecibo Campus, PO Box 144045, Arecibo, PR 00614-4045.

Pontifical Catholic University of Puerto Rico–Mayaguez Campus

Mayaguez, Puerto Rico
http://www.pucpr.edu/mayaguez/

CONTACT
Pontifical Catholic University of Puerto Rico–Mayaguez Campus, 482 Sur Calle Ramon Emerito Betances, Mayaguez, PR 00680.

Theological University of the Caribbean

Saint Just, Puerto Rico
http://www.utcpr.edu/

- **Independent Pentecostal** comprehensive, founded 1956
- **Suburban** 4-acre campus with easy access to San Juan
- **Endowment** $1.0 million
- **Coed** 279 undergraduate students, 67% full-time, 44% women, 56% men
- 100% of applicants were admitted

UNDERGRAD STUDENTS
187 full-time, 92 part-time. Students come from 1 other state; 100% Hispanic/Latino.

Freshmen:
Admission: 49 applied, 49 admitted, 49 enrolled.
Retention: 47% of full-time freshmen returned.

FACULTY
Total: 54, 15% full-time, 43% with terminal degrees.
Student/faculty ratio: 23:1.

ACADEMICS
Calendar: semesters. *Degrees:* certificates, diplomas, associate, bachelor's, and master's.

Special study options: distance learning, honors programs, independent study, internships, off-campus study, part-time degree program, services for LD students, summer session for credit.

Computers: 3 computers/terminals and 3 ports are available on campus for general student use. Students can access the following: campus intranet, computer help desk, free student e-mail accounts, online (class) grades, online (class) registration, online (class) schedules. Campuswide network is available. 90% of college-owned or -operated housing units are wired for high-speed Internet access. Wireless service is available via entire campus.

Library: Juan L. Lugo Library plus 1 other. *Books:* 17,220 (physical); *Serial titles:* 45 (physical). Weekly public service hours: 61.

STUDENT LIFE

Housing options: coed. Campus housing is university owned.

Activities and organizations: Student Council, Missionary Evangelistic Association, Ministerial Association, FESI, Free Night.

Campus security: patrols by security personnel at night from 6:00 pm-midnight.

Student services: personal/psychological counseling.

COSTS & FINANCIAL AID

Costs (2018–19) *Comprehensive fee:* $7842 includes full-time tuition ($4442), mandatory fees ($1000), and room and board ($2400). Full-time tuition and fees vary according to course load. Part-time tuition: $20 per credit hour. Part-time tuition and fees vary according to course load. *Required fees:* $148 per credit hour part-time, $3552 per term part-time. *College room only:* $1200. Room and board charges vary according to board plan. *Payment plan:* deferred payment. *Waivers:* employees or children of employees.

Financial Aid Of all full-time matriculated undergraduates who enrolled in 2016, 269 applied for aid, 269 were judged to have need. *Average financial aid package:* $2356. *Average need-based loan:* $2195. *Average need-based gift aid:* $2356. *Average indebtedness upon graduation:* $8906. *Financial aid deadline:* 6/30.

APPLYING

Options: early admission.

Application fee: $45.

Required: high school transcript, medical certificate, certificate of immunization, 1 2x2 photo, Bible content exam.

Notification: continuous (freshmen).

CONTACT

Avianny Paulino, Recruitment Officer, Theological University of the Caribbean, PO Box 901, Saint Just, PR 00978-901. *Phone:* 787-761-0640 Ext. 1246. *Fax:* 787-748-9220. *E-mail:* promociones@utcpr.edu.

Universidad Adventista de las Antillas

Mayagüez, Puerto Rico

http://www.uaa.edu/

- **Independent Seventh-day Adventist** comprehensive, founded 1957
- **Rural** 284-acre campus
- **Endowment** $134,104
- **Coed**
- **Minimally difficult** entrance level

FACULTY

Student/faculty ratio: 20:1.

ACADEMICS

Calendar: semesters. *Degrees:* associate, bachelor's, and master's.

Library: Dennis Soto Library. *Books:* 67,322 (physical); *Databases:* 42. Weekly public service hours: 67; students can reserve study rooms.

STUDENT LIFE

Housing options: on-campus residence required for freshman year; men-only, women-only. Campus housing is university owned. Freshman applicants given priority for college housing.

Activities and organizations: student-run newspaper, choral group, Score Group, Gymnastic Club, Student Council, Green Movement, 3AM.

Campus security: 24-hour emergency response devices and patrols, student patrols, controlled dormitory access.

Student services: health clinic, personal/psychological counseling.

COSTS & FINANCIAL AID

Costs (2017–18) *One-time required fee:* $20. *Comprehensive fee:* $11,770 includes full-time tuition ($5370), mandatory fees ($1100), and room and board ($5300). Full-time tuition and fees vary according to course load and program. Part-time tuition: $179 per credit hour. Part-time

tuition and fees vary according to course load and program. *Required fees:* $1100 per term part-time. *College room only:* $1800. Room and board charges vary according to board plan and housing facility.

Financial Aid Of all full-time matriculated undergraduates who enrolled in 2013, 1,249 applied for aid, 1,124 were judged to have need. 179 Federal Work-Study jobs (averaging $756). 278 state and other part-time jobs (averaging $961). *Average percent of need met:* 78. *Average financial aid package:* $2422. *Average need-based loan:* $1900. *Average need-based gift aid:* $2422. *Average indebtedness upon graduation:* $4801.

APPLYING

Standardized Tests *Recommended:* SAT or ACT (for admission), CEEB.

Options: electronic application, early admission.

Application fee: $20.

Required: high school transcript, minimum 2.0 GPA, 1 letter of recommendation. *Required for some:* essay or personal statement, interview.

CONTACT

Mrs. Yolanda Ferrer, Director of Admissions, Universidad Adventista de las Antillas, Oficina de Admisiones, PO Box 118, Mayaguez, PR 00681-0118. *Phone:* 787-834-9595 Ext. 2208. *Fax:* 787-834-9597. *E-mail:* admissions@uaa.edu.

Universidad Central del Caribe

Bayamón, Puerto Rico

http://www.uccaribe.edu/

CONTACT

Admissions Department, Universidad Central del Caribe, PO Box 60-327, Bayamón, PR 00960-6032. *Phone:* 787-740-1611.

Universidad del Este

Carolina, Puerto Rico

http://www.suagm.edu/une/

CONTACT

Universidad del Este, PO Box 2010, Carolina, PR 00984. *Phone:* 787-257-7373 Ext. 3401.

Universidad del Turabo

Gurabo, Puerto Rico

http://www.suagm.edu/ut/

CONTACT

Universidad del Turabo, PO Box 3030, Gurabo, PR 00778-3030. *Phone:* 787-743-7979 Ext. 4351.

Universidad Metropolitana

San Juan, Puerto Rico

http://www.suagm.edu/umet/

CONTACT

Mrs. Yadira Rivera Lugo, Director of Admissions, Universidad Metropolitana, Box 21150, San Juan, PR 00928-1150. *Phone:* 787-766-1717 Ext. 6683. *Toll-free phone:* 800-747-8362. *E-mail:* yrivera@suagm.edu.

Universidad Pentecostal Mizpa

San Juan, Puerto Rico

http://www.mizpa.edu/

CONTACT

Omar Alicea, Recruitment, Universidad Pentecostal Mizpa, Bo Caimito Road 199, Apartado 20966, San Juan, PR 00928-0966. *Phone:* 787-720-4476. *Fax:* 787-720-2012.

University of Puerto Rico–Aguadilla

Aguadilla, Puerto Rico
http://www.uprag.edu/

CONTACT
Ms. Melba Serrano Lugo, Admissions Officer, University of Puerto Rico–Aguadilla, PO Box 6150, Aguadilla, PR 00604. *Phone:* 787-890-2681 Ext. 280.

University of Puerto Rico–Arecibo

Arecibo, Puerto Rico
http://www.upra.edu/

CONTACT
University of Puerto Rico–Arecibo, Carretera 653 Km. 0.8, Sector Las Dunas, PO Box 4010, Arecibo, PR 00614. *Phone:* 787-878-2830 Ext. 4101.

University of Puerto Rico–Bayamón

Bayamón, Puerto Rico
http://www.uprb.edu/

- **Commonwealth-supported** 4-year, founded 1971, part of University of Puerto Rico System
- **Urban** 78-acre campus with easy access to San Juan
- **Coed**
- **Very difficult** entrance level

FACULTY
Student/faculty ratio: 20:1.

ACADEMICS
Calendar: semesters. *Degrees:* associate and bachelor's.
Library: Centro Recursos para el Aprendizaje. *Books:* 162,227 (physical), 3,399 (digital/electronic); *Serial titles:* 386 (physical), 2,947 (digital/electronic); *Databases:* 111. Weekly public service hours: 78; students can reserve study rooms.

STUDENT LIFE
Housing options: college housing not available.

Activities and organizations: drama/theater group, choral group, The National Society of Collegiate Scholars at UPRB (NSCS), American Medical Student Association (AMSA), Med Life Capitulo Vaquero, Asociacion de Estudiantes de Computadoras (AECC), Asociacion de Estudiantes de Contabilidad (ASEC).

Athletics Member NCAA. All Division II.

Campus security: 24-hour patrols.

Student services: health clinic, personal/psychological counseling.

COSTS & FINANCIAL AID
Costs (2017–18) *Tuition:* commonwealth resident $1938 full-time, $57 per credit part-time; nonresident $3960 full-time, $115 per credit part-time. Full-time tuition and fees vary according to class time, course load, and program. Part-time tuition and fees vary according to class time, course load, and program. No tuition increase for student's term of enrollment. *Required fees:* $144 full-time.

Financial Aid Of all full-time matriculated undergraduates who enrolled in 2016, 315 Federal Work-Study jobs (averaging $1111).

APPLYING
Standardized Tests *Required:* College Board exam (for admission).
Options: electronic application.
Application fee: $30.
Required: high school transcript.

CONTACT
Ms. Carmen I. Montes Burgos, Director, Office of Admissions, University of Puerto Rico–Bayamón, OPEI Office, Street 174 #170 Minillas Industrial Park, Bayamon, PR 00959-1919, Puerto Rico. *Phone:* 787-993-8952 Ext. 4016. *Fax:* 787-993-8929. *E-mail:* carmen.montes1@upr.edu.

University of Puerto Rico–Carolina

Carolina, Puerto Rico
http://www.uprc.edu/

CONTACT
Ms. Celia Mendez, Admissions Officer, University of Puerto Rico–Carolina, PO Box 4800, Carolina, PR 00984-4800. *Phone:* 787-757-1485.

University of Puerto Rico–Cayey

Cayey, Puerto Rico
http://www.cayey.upr.edu/

CONTACT
University of Puerto Rico–Cayey, 205 Avenue Antonio R. Barcelo, Cayey, PR 00736. *Phone:* 787-738-2161 Ext. 2233.

University of Puerto Rico–Humacao

Humacao, Puerto Rico
http://www.uprh.edu/

- **Commonwealth-supported** 4-year, founded 1962, part of University of Puerto Rico System
- **Suburban** 62-acre campus with easy access to San Juan
- **Coed** 3,723 undergraduate students, 90% full-time, 63% women, 37% men
- **Moderately difficult** entrance level, 40% of applicants were admitted

UNDERGRAD STUDENTS
3,356 full-time, 367 part-time. Students come from 2 states and territories; 1 other country; 2% Black or African American, non-Hispanic/Latino; 90% Hispanic/Latino; 0.2% Native Hawaiian or other Pacific Islander, non-Hispanic/Latino; 0.5% Two or more races, non-Hispanic/Latino; 6% Race/ethnicity unknown; 1% transferred in.

Freshmen:
Admission: 1,913 applied, 766 admitted, 672 enrolled. *Average high school GPA:* 3.7.
Retention: 80% of full-time freshmen returned.

FACULTY
Total: 254, 60% full-time, 52% with terminal degrees.
Student/faculty ratio: 17:1.

ACADEMICS
Calendar: semesters. *Degrees:* associate and bachelor's.

Special study options: academic remediation for entering students, advanced placement credit, English as a second language, honors programs, internships, part-time degree program, services for LD students, summer session for credit.

Computers: Students can access the following: free student e-mail accounts, online (class) grades, online (class) registration, online (class) schedules. Campuswide network is available. Wireless service is available via entire campus.
Library: Aguedo Mojica Marrero. *Books:* 101,475 (physical), 200 (digital/electronic); *Serial titles:* 15 (physical), 43,942 (digital/electronic); *Databases:* 7. Weekly public service hours: 92; study areas open 24 hours, 5–7 days a week; students can reserve study rooms.

STUDENT LIFE
Housing options: college housing not available.

Activities and organizations: drama/theater group, student-run newspaper, radio and television station, choral group, marching band, Accounting Students Association, Management Students Association, Microbiology Students Association, Human Resources Students Association, Biology Students Association.

Athletics *Intercollegiate sports:* baseball M(s), basketball M(s)/W(s), cheerleading M(s)/W(s), cross-country running M(s)/W(s), softball W(s), swimming and diving M, table tennis M(s)/W(s), track and field M(s)/W(s), volleyball M(s)/W(s), weight lifting M(s)/W(s), wrestling M(s). *Intramural sports:* basketball M/W, softball W, volleyball M/W.

Campus security: 24-hour emergency response devices and patrols, late-night transport/escort service, 24-hour gate security.

Student services: personal/psychological counseling, women's center.

COSTS & FINANCIAL AID

Costs (2017–18) *One-time required fee:* $30. *Tuition:* commonwealth resident $1938 full-time, $56 per credit part-time; nonresident $3959 full-time, $115 per credit part-time. Full-time tuition and fees vary according to class time, course load, and student level. Part-time tuition and fees vary according to class time, course load, and student level. No tuition increase for student's term of enrollment. *Required fees:* $179 full-time. *Room and board:* $11,161; room only: $3655. Room and board charges vary according to housing facility. *Payment plans:* tuition prepayment, deferred payment. *Waivers:* employees or children of employees.

Financial Aid Of all full-time matriculated undergraduates who enrolled in 2001, 3,515 applied for aid, 2,883 were judged to have need, 7 had their need fully met. 278 Federal Work-Study jobs (averaging $1318). *Average percent of need met:* 50. *Average financial aid package:* $3929. *Average need-based loan:* $3295. *Average need-based gift aid:* $3664. *Average indebtedness upon graduation:* $2749. *Financial aid deadline:* 6/30.

APPLYING

Standardized Tests *Required:* Pruebas de Evaluacion y Admision Universitaria (PEAU) (for admission).

Options: electronic application, deferred entrance.

Required: high school transcript. *Required for some:* interview.

Application deadlines: 2/15 (freshmen), 3/16 (transfers).

Notification: 4/19 (freshmen), continuous until 5/15 (transfers).

CONTACT

Mrs. Debbie GarcÃ-a, Admissions Officer, University of Puerto Rico–Humacao, Call Box 860, Humacao, PR 00792. *Phone:* 787-850-9301. *Fax:* 787-850-9428. *E-mail:* debbie.garcia@upr.edu.

University of Puerto Rico–Mayagüez

Mayagüez, Puerto Rico

http://www.uprm.edu/

CONTACT

Ms. Sheila Marty-Rodriquez, Director, Admissions Office, University of Puerto Rico–Mayagüez, PO Box 9000, Mayagüez, PR 00681-9000. *Phone:* 787-265-5465. *Fax:* 787-265-5465. *E-mail:* smarty@uprm.edu.

University of Puerto Rico–Medical Sciences Campus

San Juan, Puerto Rico

http://www.rcm.upr.edu/

CONTACT

University of Puerto Rico–Medical Sciences Campus, PO Box 365067, San Juan, PR 00936-5067. *Phone:* 787-758-2525 Ext. 5214.

University of Puerto Rico–Ponce

Ponce, Puerto Rico

http://www.uprp.edu/

CONTACT

University of Puerto Rico–Ponce, PO Box 7186, Ponce, PR 00732-7186. *Phone:* 787-844-8181 Ext. 2533.

University of Puerto Rico–Río Piedras

San Juan, Puerto Rico

http://www.uprrp.edu/

CONTACT

Mrs. Cruz B. Valentin, Director of Admissions, University of Puerto Rico–Río Piedras, PO Box 23300, San Juan, PR 00931-3300. *Phone:* 787-764-0000 Ext. 85700.

University of Puerto Rico–Utuado

Utuado, Puerto Rico

http://www.uprutuado.edu/

CONTACT

Mrs. Maria Robles Serrano, Admissions Officer, University of Puerto Rico–Utuado, PO Box 2500, Utuado, PR 00641-2500. *Phone:* 787-894-2828 Ext. 2240.

University of the Sacred Heart

San Juan, Puerto Rico

http://www.sagrado.edu/

CONTACT

Mr. Luis Heviquez, Director of Admissions, University of the Sacred Heart, PO Box 12383, San Juan, PR 00914-0383. *Phone:* 787-728-1515 Ext. 3237.

VIRGIN ISLANDS

University of the Virgin Islands

St. Thomas, Virgin Islands

http://www.uvi.edu/

- **Territory-supported** comprehensive, founded 1962
- **Small-town** 518-acre campus
- **Coed** 1,898 undergraduate students, 67% full-time, 66% women, 34% men
- **Noncompetitive** entrance level, 98% of applicants were admitted

UNDERGRAD STUDENTS

1,275 full-time, 623 part-time. Students come from 32 states and territories; 13 other countries; 5% are from out of state; 71% Black or African American, non-Hispanic/Latino; 9% Hispanic/Latino; 0.7% Asian, non-Hispanic/Latino; 0.3% American Indian or Alaska Native, non-Hispanic/Latino; 0.7% Two or more races, non-Hispanic/Latino; 7% Race/ethnicity unknown; 6% international; 5% transferred in.

Freshmen:
Admission: 899 applied, 885 admitted, 308 enrolled. *Average high school GPA:* 3.2.
Retention: 67% of full-time freshmen returned.

FACULTY

Total: 216, 45% full-time.
Student/faculty ratio: 12:1.

ACADEMICS

Calendar: semesters. *Degrees:* associate, bachelor's, master's, doctoral, and post-master's certificates.

Special study options: academic remediation for entering students, adult/continuing education programs, advanced placement credit, cooperative education, distance learning, double majors, English as a second language, external degree program, honors programs, independent study, internships, off-campus study, part-time degree program, services for LD students, study abroad, summer session for credit. *ROTC:* Army (b).

Unusual degree programs: 3-2 engineering with Columbia University, University of Florida, University of South Carolina.

Computers: 500 computers/terminals are available on campus for general student use. Students can access the following: campus intranet, computer help desk, free student e-mail accounts, online (class) grades, online (class) registration, online (class) schedules. Campuswide network is available. 100% of college-owned or -operated housing units are wired for high-speed Internet access. Wireless service is available via entire campus.

Library: Ralph M. Paiewonsky Library. Students can reserve study rooms.

STUDENT LIFE

Housing options: coed, men-only, women-only. Campus housing is university owned.

Activities and organizations: drama/theater group, student-run newspaper, radio station, choral group, Student Government Association, Golden Key Honor Society, Student Nurses Association, National Student Exchange Club, St. Kitts and Nevis, national sororities.

Athletics Member NAIA. *Intercollegiate sports:* basketball M(s)/W(s)(c), cross-country running M(c)/W(c), soccer M(s)(c), track and field M(c)/W(c), volleyball M(c)/W(c).

Campus security: 24-hour emergency response devices and patrols.

Student services: health clinic, personal/psychological counseling.

COSTS & FINANCIAL AID

Costs (2018–19) *Tuition:* territory resident $4631 full-time, $154 per credit part-time; nonresident $13,892 full-time, $463 per credit part-time. Full-time tuition and fees vary according to reciprocity agreements. Part-time tuition and fees vary according to course load and reciprocity agreements. *Required fees:* $604 full-time, $254 per term part-time. *Room and board:* $9900; room only: $4120. Room and board charges vary according to board plan and housing facility. *Payment plan:* installment. *Waivers:* senior citizens and employees or children of employees.

Financial Aid Of all full-time matriculated undergraduates who enrolled in 2007, 1,202 applied for aid, 1,118 were judged to have need, 10 had their need fully met. 39 Federal Work-Study jobs (averaging $2130). 28 state and other part-time jobs (averaging $1900). In 2007, 5 non-need-based awards were made. *Average financial aid package:* $4450. *Average need-based loan:* $3240. *Average need-based gift aid:* $3440. *Average non-need-based aid:* $8500. *Average indebtedness upon graduation:* $9480.

APPLYING

Options: electronic application, early admission, deferred entrance.

Application fee: $25.

Recommended: high school transcript, minimum 2.0 GPA.

Application deadlines: 4/30 (freshmen), 4/30 (transfers).

Notification: continuous until 10/1 (freshmen).

CONTACT

University of the Virgin Islands, 2 John Brewers Bay, St. Thomas, VI 00802. *Toll-free phone:* 877-468-6884.

CANADA

CANADA

Acadia University

Wolfville, Nova Scotia, Canada

http://www.acadiau.ca/

- **Province-supported** comprehensive, founded 1838
- **Small-town** 250-acre campus with easy access to Halifax, Nova Scotia
- **Coed** 3,434 undergraduate students, 96% full-time, 58% women, 42% men
- **Moderately difficult** entrance level, 29% of applicants were admitted

UNDERGRAD STUDENTS

3,287 full-time, 147 part-time. Students come from 13 provinces and territories; 64 other countries; 48% are from out of state; 8% transferred in.

Freshmen:
Admission: 4,407 applied, 1,263 admitted, 738 enrolled.
Retention: 79% of full-time freshmen returned.

FACULTY

Total: 246, 82% with terminal degrees.
Student/faculty ratio: 15:1.

ACADEMICS

Calendar: Canadian standard year. *Degrees:* bachelor's, master's, and doctoral.

Special study options: academic remediation for entering students, advanced placement credit, cooperative education, distance learning, double majors, English as a second language, honors programs, internships, off-campus study, part-time degree program, services for LD students, study abroad, summer session for credit.

Computers: 7,000 ports are available on campus for general student use. Students can access the following: campus intranet, computer help desk, free student e-mail accounts, online (class) grades, online (class) registration, online (class) schedules. Campuswide network is available. 100% of college-owned or -operated housing units are wired for high-speed Internet access. Wireless service is available via classrooms, dorm rooms, learning centers, libraries, student centers.

Library: Vaughan Memorial Library.

STUDENT LIFE

Housing options: coed, women-only. Campus housing is university owned. Freshman campus housing is guaranteed.

Activities and organizations: drama/theater group, student-run newspaper, radio station, choral group, Dance Acadia, Power Cheerleading, Water Watch Canada, LINC, Biology.

Athletics Member CIS. *Intercollegiate sports:* basketball M(s)/W(s), cross-country running W, football M(s), ice hockey M(s), rugby W(s), soccer M(s)/W(s), swimming and diving M(s)/W(s), track and field W, volleyball W. *Intramural sports:* basketball M/W, cheerleading M/W, equestrian sports M(c)/W(c), field hockey W(c), ice hockey M/W(c), lacrosse M(c), rugby M(c), soccer M/W, ultimate Frisbee M/W, volleyball M/W.

Campus security: 24-hour emergency response devices and patrols, student patrols, late-night transport/escort service, controlled dormitory access, video surveillance, emergency response, emergency notification, emergency management planning.

Student services: health clinic, personal/psychological counseling, women's center, legal services.

COSTS

Costs (2017–18) *One-time required fee:* $436. *Tuition:* province resident $7714 full-time, $967 per course part-time; nonresident $8997 full-time, $1095 per course part-time; International tuition $17,195 full-time. Full-time tuition and fees vary according to course level, course load, degree level, and program. Part-time tuition and fees vary according to course level, course load, degree level, and program. *Required fees:* $306 full-time, $10 per course part-time. *Room and board:* $10,215; room only: $5725. Room and board charges vary according to board plan and housing facility. *Payment plan:* installment. *Waivers:* senior citizens and employees or children of employees.

APPLYING

Options: electronic application, deferred entrance.

Application fee: $40 Canadian dollars.

Required: high school transcript, minimum 2.5 GPA. *Required for some:* essay or personal statement, 1 letter of recommendation, interview.

Application deadlines: 7/1 (freshmen), 7/1 (transfers).

Notification: continuous (freshmen), continuous (out-of-state freshmen), continuous (transfers).

CONTACT

Ms. Anne Scott, Manager of Admissions, Acadia University, 15 University Avenue, Wolfville, NS B4P 2R6, Canada. *Phone:* 902-585-1016. *Toll-free phone:* 877-585-1121. *Fax:* 902-585-1092. *E-mail:* admissions@acadiau.ca.

Alberta College of Art & Design

Calgary, Alberta, Canada
http://www.acad.ca/

- **Province-supported** 4-year, founded 1926
- **Urban** 1-acre campus with easy access to Calgary
- **Endowment** $4,4 million
- **Coed** 1,150 undergraduate students, 91% full-time, 73% women, 27% men
- **Moderately difficult** entrance level, 37% of applicants were admitted

UNDERGRAD STUDENTS

1,043 full-time, 107 part-time. Students come from 11 provinces and territories; 22 other countries; 12% are from out of state; 5% American Indian or Alaska Native, non-Hispanic/Latino; 90% Race/ethnicity unknown; 5% international; 7% transferred in; 9% live on campus.

Freshmen:
Admission: 561 applied, 208 admitted, 208 enrolled.
Retention: 67% of full-time freshmen returned.

FACULTY

Total: 122, 33% full-time, 22% with terminal degrees.
Student/faculty ratio: 16:1.

ACADEMICS

Calendar: semesters. *Degree:* bachelor's.

Special study options: academic remediation for entering students, adult/continuing education programs, advanced placement credit, independent study, internships, part-time degree program, services for LD students, study abroad, summer session for credit.

Computers: 77 computers/terminals and 20 ports are available on campus for general student use. Students can access the following: campus intranet, computer help desk, free student e-mail accounts, online (class) grades, online (class) registration, online (class) schedules, Network Storage, Self Serve Printing + Copying. Campuswide network is available. 100% of college-owned or -operated housing units are wired for high-speed Internet access. Wireless service is available via entire campus.
Library: Luke Lindoe Library.

STUDENT LIFE

Housing options: coed, special housing for students with disabilities. Campus housing is provided by a third party.

Activities and organizations: The Rendez-Vous Collective, Conceptual Arts Club, Arts Mob, Anime and Gaming Club, ACAD Glass.

Campus security: 24-hour emergency response devices and patrols, late-night transport/escort service, controlled dormitory access.

Student services: health clinic, personal/psychological counseling.

COSTS

Costs (2017–18) *Tuition:* province resident $4480 full-time, $149 per credit hour part-time; nonresident $4480 full-time, $149 per credit hour part-time; International tuition $14,500 full-time. Full-time tuition and fees vary according to course load, degree level, program, and student level. Part-time tuition and fees vary according to course load, degree level, program, and student level. *Required fees:* $1091 full-time, $15 per credit hour part-time, $677 per term part-time. *Waivers:* senior citizens.

APPLYING

Options: electronic application, early decision.

Application fee: $85 Canadian dollars.

Required: essay or personal statement, high school transcript, minimum 2.0 GPA, portfolio of artwork.

Application deadlines: 2/1 (freshmen), 4/1 (transfers).

Notification: 3/15 (freshmen), 3/15 (out-of-state freshmen), 5/30 (transfers).

CONTACT

Alberta College of Art & Design, 1407 14 Avenue NW, Calgary, AB T2N 4R3, Canada. *Toll-free phone:* 800-251-8290.

Ambrose University

Calgary, Alberta, Canada
http://www.ambrose.edu/

- **Independent** comprehensive, founded 1941, affiliated with The Christian and Missionary Alliance
- **Urban** 37-acre campus
- **Endowment** $6.0 million
- **Coed** 732 undergraduate students, 93% full-time, 60% women, 40% men

UNDERGRAD STUDENTS

682 full-time, 50 part-time. Students come from 10 provinces and territories; 26 other countries; 9% are from out of state; 3% Black or African American, non-Hispanic/Latino; 2% Hispanic/Latino; 13% Asian, non-Hispanic/Latino; 2% American Indian or Alaska Native, non-Hispanic/Latino; 15% Race/ethnicity unknown; 5% transferred in; 18% live on campus.

Freshmen:
Admission: 216 enrolled.
Retention: 70% of full-time freshmen returned.

FACULTY

Total: 84, 52% full-time, 44% with terminal degrees.
Student/faculty ratio: 13:1.

ACADEMICS

Calendar: semesters. *Degrees:* certificates, diplomas, bachelor's, and master's (graduate and professional degrees are offered by Canadian Theological Seminary).

Special study options: academic remediation for entering students, adult/continuing education programs, advanced placement credit, distance learning, double majors, independent study, internships, off-campus study, part-time degree program, services for LD students, study abroad, summer session for credit.

Unusual degree programs: 3-2 elementary education.

Computers: 20 computers/terminals are available on campus for general student use. Students can access the following: campus intranet, computer help desk, free student e-mail accounts, online (class) grades, online (class) registration, online (class) schedules. Campuswide network is available. 50% of college-owned or -operated housing units are wired for high-speed Internet access. Wireless service is available via entire campus.

Library: Archibald Foundation Library. *Books:* 127,484 (physical), 150,000 (digital/electronic); *Serial titles:* 152 (physical), 60,338 (digital/electronic); *Databases:* 42. Weekly public service hours: 81; students can reserve study rooms.

STUDENT LIFE

Housing options: on-campus residence required for freshman year; men-only, women-only. Campus housing is university owned. Freshman applicants given priority for college housing.

Activities and organizations: drama/theater group, student-run newspaper, choral group, Coffee Club, Business Society, Hockey Club, Biology Club, Outdoors Club.

Athletics *Intercollegiate sports:* basketball M(s)/W(s), soccer M(s)/W(s), volleyball M(s)/W(s). *Intramural sports:* basketball M/W, cross-country running M(c)/W(c), ice hockey M(c)/W(c), soccer M/W, volleyball M/W.

Campus security: 24-hour emergency response devices, student patrols, late-night transport/escort service, controlled dormitory access.

Student services: personal/psychological counseling.

COSTS & FINANCIAL AID

Costs (2018–19) *Comprehensive fee:* $19,008 includes full-time tuition ($11,400), mandatory fees ($908), and room and board ($6700). Full-time tuition and fees vary according to course load, degree level, and program. Part-time tuition: $380 per credit hour. Part-time tuition and fees vary according to course load, degree level, and program. *Required fees:* $30 per credit hour part-time. *College room only:* $3600. Room and board charges vary according to board plan and housing facility. *Payment plans:* installment, deferred payment. *Waivers:* employees or children of employees.

Financial Aid Of all full-time matriculated undergraduates who enrolled in 2016, 236 applied for aid. *Average financial aid package:* $1700.
Financial aid deadline: 6/1.

APPLYING

Standardized Tests *Required for some:* SAT or ACT (for admission).

Required: high school transcript. ***Required for some:*** essay or personal statement, 3 letters of recommendation, interview, minimum 60% overall average on 5 grade-12 level courses, program-specific requirements.

CONTACT

Kalie Eeles, Enrolment Coordinator, Ambrose University, 150 Ambrose Circle SW, Calgary, AB T3H 0L5, Canada. *Phone:* 403-410-2000 Ext. 2954. *Toll-free phone:* 800-461-1222. *Fax:* 403-571-6556. *E-mail:* enrolment@ambrose.edu.

Athabasca University

Athabasca, Alberta, Canada

http://www.athabascau.ca/

- **Province-supported** comprehensive, founded 1970
- **Small-town** 480-acre campus
- **Endowment** $1.0 million
- **Coed** 35,898 undergraduate students, 66% women, 34% men
- **Noncompetitive** entrance level

UNDERGRAD STUDENTS

35,898 part-time. Students come from 42 provinces and territories; 87 other countries.

FACULTY

Total: 384.

ACADEMICS

Calendar: continuous. *Degrees:* certificates, diplomas, bachelor's, master's, doctoral, post-master's, and postbachelor's certificates (offers only external degree programs).

Special study options: academic remediation for entering students, accelerated degree program, adult/continuing education programs, advanced placement credit, distance learning, double majors, English as a second language, external degree program, independent study, off-campus study, part-time degree program, services for LD students, student-designed majors, study abroad, summer session for credit.

Computers: 28 computers/terminals are available on campus for general student use. Students can access the following: online (class) registration. Campuswide network is available.

Library: Athabasca University Library.

STUDENT LIFE

Housing options: college housing not available.

Activities and organizations: student-run newspaper.

Campus security: 24-hour emergency response devices.

APPLYING

Options: electronic application.

Application fee: $60 Canadian dollars.

Application deadlines: rolling (freshmen), rolling (transfers).

Notification: continuous (freshmen), continuous (transfers).

CONTACT

Information Centre, Athabasca University, 1 University Drive, Athabasca, AB T9S 3A3, Canada. *Phone:* 800-788-9041. *Toll-free phone:* 800-788-9041. *Fax:* 780-675-6437.

Bishop's University

Sherbrooke, Quebec, Canada

http://www.ubishops.ca/

- **Province-supported** comprehensive, founded 1843, part of Association of Universities and Colleges of Canada (AUCC)
- **Small-town** 550-acre campus with easy access to Montreal
- **Coed**
- **Moderately difficult** entrance level

FACULTY

Student/faculty ratio: 16:1.

ACADEMICS

Calendar: semesters most students study from September to late April. Spring semester is May-June. *Degrees:* certificates, bachelor's, master's, and postbachelor's certificates.

Library: John Bassett Memorial Library plus 1 other. Students can reserve study rooms.

STUDENT LIFE

Housing options: coed, special housing for students with disabilities. Campus housing is university owned. Freshman campus housing is guaranteed.

Activities and organizations: drama/theater group, student-run newspaper, radio station, choral group, Ski and Snowboard Club, Bishop's University Commerce Society, BU Model UN, Big Buddies, Bishop's Psychology Club, national sororities.

Athletics Member CIS.

Campus security: 24-hour emergency response devices and patrols, student patrols, late-night transport/escort service, controlled dormitory access.

Student services: health clinic, personal/psychological counseling.

COSTS

Costs (2017–18) *Tuition:* province resident $2328 Canadian dollars full-time, $78 Canadian dollars per credit part-time; nonresident $7227 Canadian dollars full-time, $241 Canadian dollars per credit part-time; International tuition $17,807 Canadian dollars full-time. Full-time tuition and fees vary according to course load, program, and reciprocity agreements. Part-time tuition and fees vary according to course load and program. No tuition increase for student's term of enrollment. *Required fees:* $1385 Canadian dollars full-time, $1385 Canadian dollars per year part-time. *Room and board:* $9000 Canadian dollars; room only: $4500 Canadian dollars. Room and board charges vary according to board plan and housing facility.

APPLYING

Options: electronic application, early admission, deferred entrance.

Application fee: $85 Canadian dollars.

Required: high school transcript, minimum 3.4 GPA, birth certificate, copy of student visa. *Required for some:* essay or personal statement, 2 letters of recommendation.

CONTACT

Mr. Doug McCooeye, Manager Student Recruitment, Admissions and Student Exchange, Bishop's University, 2600 College Street, Sherbrooke, QC J1M 1Z7, Canada. *Phone:* 819-822-9600 Ext. 2206. *Toll-free phone:* 877-822-8200. *E-mail:* admissions@ubishops.ca.

Booth University College

Winnipeg, Manitoba, Canada

http://www.boothuc.ca/

CONTACT

Chantel Burt, Director of Admission, Booth University College, 447 Webb Place, Winnipeg, MB R3B 2P2, Canada. *Phone:* 204-924-4867. *Toll-free phone:* 877-942-6684. *E-mail:* cburt@boothcollege.ca.

Brandon University

Brandon, Manitoba, Canada

http://www.brandonu.ca/

- **Province-supported** comprehensive, founded 1899
- **Small-town** 30-acre campus
- **Endowment** $24.0 million
- **Coed** 3,155 undergraduate students
- **Noncompetitive** entrance level, 66% of applicants were admitted

UNDERGRAD STUDENTS

Students come from 13 provinces and territories; 88 other countries; 9% are from out of state; 9% live on campus.

Freshmen:

Admission: 2,562 applied, 1,694 admitted.

Retention: 73% of full-time freshmen returned.

FACULTY

Total: 239, 95% full-time.

Student/faculty ratio: 11:1.

ACADEMICS

Calendar: Canadian standard year. *Degrees:* certificates, bachelor's, and master's.

Special study options: academic remediation for entering students, accelerated degree program, cooperative education, distance learning, double majors, English as a second language, honors programs, off-campus study, part-time degree program, services for LD students, student-designed majors, study abroad, summer session for credit.

Unusual degree programs: 3-2 education.

Computers: 160 computers/terminals are available on campus for general student use. Students can access the following: computer help desk, free student e-mail accounts, online (class) grades, online (class) registration, online (class) schedules. Campuswide network is available. Wireless service is available via entire campus.

Library: John E. Robbins Library.

STUDENT LIFE

Housing options: coed, men-only, women-only. Campus housing is university owned. Freshman campus housing is guaranteed.

Activities and organizations: drama/theater group, student-run newspaper, radio station, choral group, Psychology Club, zoology club, Inter-Varsity Christian Fellowship, International Students Club, Business Administration Club.

Athletics Member CIS. *Intercollegiate sports:* basketball M(s)/W(s), soccer M(s)/W(s), volleyball M(s)/W(s). *Intramural sports:* badminton M/W, baseball M/W, bowling M/W, cheerleading M/W, soccer M/W, volleyball M/W, weight lifting M/W.

Campus security: 24-hour emergency response devices, controlled dormitory access, night residence hall security personnel.

Student services: personal/psychological counseling.

COSTS

Costs (2017–18) *Tuition:* area resident $3738 full-time, $125 per credit hour part-time; nonresident $226 per course part-time; International tuition $7475 full-time. Full-time tuition and fees vary according to class time, course level, course load, degree level, location, program, reciprocity agreements, and student level. Part-time tuition and fees vary according to class time, course level, course load, degree level, location, program, reciprocity agreements, and student level. *Required fees:* $919 full-time, $17 per credit hour part-time, $107 per term part-time. *Room and board:* $8409; room only: $5457. Room and board charges vary according to board plan, gender, and location. *Payment plan:* installment. *Waivers:* senior citizens and employees or children of employees.

APPLYING

Options: electronic application, deferred entrance.

Application fee: $68 Canadian dollars.

Required: high school transcript. *Required for some:* criminal and child abuse registry checks.

Application deadlines: rolling (freshmen), rolling (transfers).

Notification: continuous until 9/30 (freshmen), continuous until 9/30 (transfers).

CONTACT

Murray Kerr, Director of Admissions, Brandon University, 270 18th Street, Brandon, MB R7A 6A9, Canada. *Phone:* 204-727-7352. *Toll-free phone:* 800-644-7644. *Fax:* 204-728-3221. *E-mail:* kerr@brandonu.ca.

Briercrest College
Caronport, Saskatchewan, Canada
http://www.briercrest.ca/

CONTACT

Mr. Ralph Troshke, Director of Enrolment, Briercrest College, 510 College Drive, Caronport, SK S0H 0S0, Canada. *Phone:* 306-756-3200. *Toll-free phone:* 800-667-5199. *Fax:* 800-667.5199. *E-mail:* admissions@briercrest.ca.

British Columbia Institute of Technology
Burnaby, British Columbia, Canada
http://www.bcit.ca/

CONTACT

Ms. Anna Dosen, Supervisor of Admissions, British Columbia Institute of Technology, 3700 Willingdon Avenue, Burnaby, BC V5G 3H2, Canada. *Phone:* 604-432-8496. *Toll-free phone:* 866-434-1610. *Fax:* 604-431-6917.

Brock University
St. Catharines, Ontario, Canada
http://www.brocku.ca/

- **Province-supported** university, founded 1964
- **Urban** 540-acre campus with easy access to Toronto, ON and Buffalo, NY
- **Coed** 17,014 undergraduate students, 102% full-time, 58% women, 44% men

UNDERGRAD STUDENTS

17,336 full-time. Students come from 94 other countries; 14% live on campus.

Freshmen:

Admission: 19,885 applied. *Average high school GPA:* 3.0.

Retention: 86% of full-time freshmen returned.

FACULTY

Total: 559, 100% full-time.

Student/faculty ratio: 30:1.

ACADEMICS

Calendar: Canadian standard year. *Degrees:* certificates, bachelor's, master's, and doctoral.

Special study options: academic remediation for entering students, accelerated degree program, adult/continuing education programs, advanced placement credit, cooperative education, double majors, English as a second language, honors programs, internships, part-time degree program, services for LD students, student-designed majors, study abroad, summer session for credit.

Computers: 429 computers/terminals are available on campus for general student use. Students can access the following: computer help desk, free student e-mail accounts, online (class) grades, online (class) registration, online (class) schedules. Campuswide network is available. 100% of college-owned or -operated housing units are wired for high-speed Internet access. Wireless service is available via entire campus.

Library: James A. Gibson Library plus 1 other. *Books:* 492,672 (physical). Students can reserve study rooms.

STUDENT LIFE

Housing options: coed, special housing for students with disabilities. Campus housing is university owned and leased by the school. Freshman campus housing is guaranteed.

Activities and organizations: drama/theater group, student-run newspaper, radio and television station, choral group, International Students Association, Brock University Student Association, Business Administration Association, Brock Christian Fellowship, Ace Brock.

Athletics Member CIS. *Intercollegiate sports:* baseball M, basketball M(s)/W(s), cheerleading W, crew M(s)/W(s), cross-country running M/W, fencing M/W, field hockey W(c), golf M/W, ice hockey M(s)/W(s), lacrosse M/W, rowing M/W, rugby M/W, soccer M(s)/W(s), softball W, squash M/W, swimming and diving M/W, tennis M/W, track and field M/W, volleyball W, weight lifting M/W, wrestling M(s)/W(s). *Intramural sports:* badminton M/W, basketball M/W, ice hockey M/W, skiing (downhill) M/W, soccer M/W, softball M/W, swimming and diving M/W, ultimate Frisbee M/W, volleyball M/W, water polo M/W.

Campus security: 24-hour emergency response devices and patrols, student patrols, late-night transport/escort service, controlled dormitory access.

Student services: health clinic, personal/psychological counseling, women's center.

COSTS

Costs (2018–19) *Tuition:* province resident $7149 full-time; nonresident $7149 full-time; International tuition $24,386 full-time. Full-time tuition and fees vary according to course load, degree level, program, and student level. Part-time tuition and fees vary according to course load, program, and student level. *Room and board:* $6954. Room and board charges vary according to board plan and housing facility. *Waivers:* senior citizens and employees or children of employees.

APPLYING

Standardized Tests *Required:* SAT or ACT (for admission).

Options: electronic application.

Required: high school transcript. *Required for some:* essay or personal statement, interview, audition for Dramatic Arts and Music programs, profile questionnaire for Concurrent Education programs. *Recommended:* minimum 3.0 GPA.

CONTACT

Mrs. Lynn Thompson-Dovi, Admissions Officer, International Undergraduate, Brock University, 1812 Sir Isaac Brock Way, L2S 3A1, Canada. *Phone:* 905-688-5550 Ext. 3431. *E-mail:* central@brocku.ca.

Cape Breton University
Sydney, Nova Scotia, Canada
http://www.cbu.ca/

- **Province-supported** comprehensive, founded 1974
- **Urban** campus
- **Coed**
- **Moderately difficult** entrance level

ACADEMICS

Calendar: semesters. *Degrees:* certificates, diplomas, bachelor's, master's, and postbachelor's certificates.
Library: Cape Breton University Library plus 1 other. Students can reserve study rooms.

STUDENT LIFE

Housing options: coed. Campus housing is university owned. Freshman applicants given priority for college housing.

Activities and organizations: drama/theater group, student-run newspaper, radio station, choral group.

Athletics Member CIS.

Campus security: 24-hour emergency response devices and patrols, student patrols, late-night transport/escort service, controlled dormitory access.

Student services: health clinic, personal/psychological counseling, women's center, legal services.

COSTS & FINANCIAL AID

Costs (2017–18) *Tuition:* province resident $6087 Canadian dollars full-time, $609 Canadian dollars per course part-time; nonresident $7370 Canadian dollars full-time, $737 Canadian dollars per course part-time; International tuition $14,740 Canadian dollars full-time. Full-time tuition and fees vary according to program. Part-time tuition and fees vary according to program. *Required fees:* $619 Canadian dollars full-time, $55 Canadian dollars per course part-time, $66 Canadian dollars per year part-time. *Room and board:* $8760 Canadian dollars; room only: $4120 Canadian dollars.

Financial Aid Of all full-time matriculated undergraduates who enrolled in 2013, 2 applied for aid, 2 were judged to have need, 2 had their need fully met. *Average percent of need met:* 100. *Average financial aid package:* $5000. *Average need-based loan:* $5000.

APPLYING

Options: electronic application, early admission, deferred entrance.
Application fee: $36 Canadian dollars.

Required: high school transcript. *Required for some:* essay or personal statement, 2 letters of recommendation, interview, overall average of 65%.

CONTACT

Cape Breton University, Box 5300, 1250 Grand Lake Road, Sydney, NS B1P 6L2, Canada. *Phone:* 902-563-1117. *Toll-free phone:* 888-959-9995.

Capilano University
North Vancouver, British Columbia, Canada
http://www.capilanou.ca/

- **Public** 4-year, founded 1967, part of British Columbia's Advanced Education system
- **Suburban** 44-hectare campus with easy access to Vancouver
- **Endowment** $7.4 million
- **Coed** 6,766 undergraduate students, 72% full-time, 60% women, 40% men
- **Noncompetitive** entrance level

UNDERGRAD STUDENTS

4,879 full-time, 1,887 part-time. Students come from 15 provinces and territories; 64 other countries; 3% are from out of state; 1% live on campus.

Freshmen:
Admission: 2,200 applied, 573 enrolled.
Retention: 68% of full-time freshmen returned.

FACULTY

Total: 639, 26% full-time, 18% with terminal degrees.
Student/faculty ratio: 17:1.

ACADEMICS

Calendar: semesters. *Degrees:* certificates, diplomas, associate, bachelor's, and postbachelor's certificates.

Special study options: academic remediation for entering students, advanced placement credit, cooperative education, distance learning, English as a second language, independent study, internships, off-campus study, part-time degree program, services for LD students, study abroad, summer session for credit.

Computers: 400 computers/terminals are available on campus for general student use. Students can access the following: computer help desk, free student e-mail accounts, online (class) grades, online (class) registration, online (class) schedules, Moodle, student information web services. 100% of college-owned or -operated housing units are wired for high-speed Internet access. Wireless service is available via entire campus.
Library: Capilano University Library. *Books:* 77,491 (physical), 178,221 (digital/electronic); *Serial titles:* 125 (physical), 56,088 (digital/electronic); *Databases:* 55. Weekly public service hours: 73; students can reserve study rooms.

STUDENT LIFE

Housing options: coed, men-only, women-only, special housing for students with disabilities. Campus housing is leased by the school. Freshman applicants given priority for college housing.

Activities and organizations: student-run newspaper, radio station, choral group, Capilano Yoga Club, Climbing Club, 3D Printing Club, Tabletop Roleplaying Club, Young Women in Business.

Athletics *Intercollegiate sports:* basketball M(s)/W(s), soccer M(s)/W(s), volleyball M(s)/W(s). *Intramural sports:* badminton M/W, basketball M/W, rock climbing M(c)/W(c), soccer M/W, table tennis M/W, ultimate Frisbee M(c)/W(c), volleyball M/W.

Campus security: 24-hour emergency response devices and patrols, late-night transport/escort service.

Student services: health clinic, personal/psychological counseling, women's center, legal services.

COSTS

Costs (2018–19) *Tuition:* province resident $3908 full-time, $130 per credit part-time; nonresident $3908 full-time, $130 per credit part-time. Full-time tuition and fees vary according to course level, degree level, and program. Part-time tuition and fees vary according to course level, degree level, and program. *Required fees:* $13 per credit part-time, $29 per term part-time. *Room and board:* Room and board charges vary according to housing facility. *Payment plan:* deferred payment. *Waivers:* senior citizens and employees or children of employees.

APPLYING

Options: electronic application, early admission.

Required: high school transcript. *Required for some:* essay or personal statement, letters of recommendation, interview.

Application deadlines: 3/31 (freshmen), 3/31 (transfers).

CONTACT
Capilano University, 2055 Purcell Way, North Vancouver, BC V7J 3H5, Canada.

Carleton University
Ottawa, Ontario, Canada
http://www.carleton.ca/

CONTACT
Ms. Jean Mullan, Director, Undergraduate Recruitment Office, Carleton University, 1125 Colonel By Drive, Ottawa, ON K1S 5B6, Canada. *Phone:* 613-520-3663. *Toll-free phone:* 888-354-4414. *E-mail:* liaison@admissions.carleton.ca.

Centennial College
Scarborough, Ontario, Canada
http://www.centennialcollege.ca/
- **Province-supported** 4-year, part of Ontario College Application System
- **Urban** campus with easy access to Greater Toronto Area
- **Coed** 19,559 undergraduate students, 92% full-time, 47% women, 53% men

UNDERGRAD STUDENTS
17,902 full-time, 1,657 part-time.

ACADEMICS
Calendar: semesters. *Degrees:* certificates, diplomas, bachelor's, and postbachelor's certificates.

Special study options: advanced placement credit, cooperative education, distance learning, English as a second language, internships, services for LD students, study abroad, summer session for credit.

Computers: Students can access the following: campus intranet, computer help desk, free student e-mail accounts, online (class) grades, online (class) registration, online (class) schedules. Campuswide network is available. Wireless service is available via entire campus.

Library: Centennial College Libraries. Study areas open 24 hours, 5–7 days a week; students can reserve study rooms.

STUDENT LIFE
Housing options: Campus housing is university owned. Freshman applicants given priority for college housing.

Activities and organizations: choral group.

Athletics Member CIS. *Intercollegiate sports:* badminton M/W, basketball M/W, soccer M/W, volleyball M/W. *Intramural sports:* badminton M/W(c), basketball M/W, football M/W, volleyball M/W.

Campus security: 24-hour emergency response devices and patrols, late-night transport/escort service.

Student services: personal/psychological counseling.

COSTS
Costs (2017–18) *One-time required fee:* $525. *Tuition:* area resident $7710 full-time, $12 per contact hour part-time; nonresident $34 per contact hour part-time; International tuition $17,327 full-time. Full-time tuition and fees vary according to class time, course level, course load, degree level, program, and student level. Part-time tuition and fees vary according to class time, course level, course load, degree level, reciprocity agreements, and student level. *Required fees:* $1424 full-time, $1 per contact hour part-time, $17 per course part-time. *Room only:* $7360. Room and board charges vary according to housing facility. *Payment plan:* installment. *Waivers:* employees or children of employees.

APPLYING
Options: electronic application.

Application fee: $95 Canadian dollars.

Required: high school transcript.

CONTACT
Centennial College, PO Box 631, Station 'A', Scarborough, ON M1K 5E9, Canada. *Toll-free phone:* 800-268-4419.

Columbia Bible College
Abbotsford, British Columbia, Canada
http://www.columbiabc.edu/

CONTACT
Nathan Martin, Admissions Coordinator, Columbia Bible College, 2940 Clearbrook Road, Abbotsford, BC V2T 2Z8, Canada. *Phone:* 604-853-3358 Ext. 309. *Toll-free phone:* 800-283-0881. *Fax:* 604-853-3063. *E-mail:* nathan.martin@columbiabc.edu.

Concordia University
Montréal, Quebec, Canada
http://www.concordia.ca/
- **Province-supported** university, founded 1974, part of Quebec University Network
- **Urban** 52-acre campus with easy access to Montreal
- **Coed** 32,098 undergraduate students, 67% full-time, 52% women, 48% men
- **Moderately difficult** entrance level, 73% of applicants were admitted

UNDERGRAD STUDENTS
21,581 full-time, 10,517 part-time. Students come from 12 provinces and territories; 159 other countries; 8% are from out of state; 2% live on campus.

Freshmen:
Admission: 15,274 applied, 11,091 admitted, 5,858 enrolled.
Retention: 85% of full-time freshmen returned.

FACULTY
Total: 1,643, 62% full-time.
Student/faculty ratio: 25:1.

ACADEMICS
Calendar: semesters. *Degrees:* certificates, diplomas, bachelor's, master's, doctoral, and postbachelor's certificates.

Special study options: academic remediation for entering students, accelerated degree program, adult/continuing education programs, advanced placement credit, cooperative education, distance learning, double majors, English as a second language, honors programs, independent study, internships, off-campus study, part-time degree program, services for LD students, student-designed majors, study abroad, summer session for credit.

Computers: 350 computers/terminals are available on campus for general student use. Students can access the following: campus intranet, computer help desk, free student e-mail accounts, online (class) grades, online (class) registration, online (class) schedules, specialized software applications. Campuswide network is available. 100% of college-owned or -operated housing units are wired for high-speed Internet access. Wireless service is available via entire campus.

Library: Webster Library plus 1 other. *Books:* 994,394 (physical), 556,907 (digital/electronic); *Serial titles:* 18,752 (physical), 140,024 (digital/electronic); *Databases:* 1,000. Weekly public service hours: 70; study areas open 24 hours, 5–7 days a week; students can reserve study rooms.

STUDENT LIFE
Housing options: coed, special housing for students with disabilities. Campus housing is university owned. Freshman applicants given priority for college housing.

Activities and organizations: drama/theater group, student-run newspaper, radio and television station, choral group, Undergraduate Student Union, departmental clubs, religious clubs, ethnic clubs, social action groups, national fraternities, national sororities.

Athletics Member CIS. *Intercollegiate sports:* baseball M(s), basketball M(s)/W(s), cross-country running M(c)/W(c), football M(s), golf M(c)/W(c), ice hockey M(s)/W(s), rugby M(s)/W(s), skiing (downhill) M(c)/W(c), soccer M(s)/W(s), wrestling M(s)/W(s). *Intramural sports:* basketball M/W, cross-country running M/W, ice hockey M/W, lacrosse M, soccer M/W, ultimate Frisbee M/W, volleyball M/W, wrestling M/W.

Campus security: 24-hour emergency response devices and patrols, student patrols, late-night transport/escort service, controlled dormitory access.

Student services: health clinic, personal/psychological counseling, women's center.

COSTS & FINANCIAL AID
Costs (2018–19) *Tuition:* province resident $2391 full-time, $80 per credit part-time; nonresident $7403 full-time, $247 per credit part-time; International tuition $18,289 full-time. Full-time tuition and fees vary according to course load. Part-time tuition and fees vary according to course load. *Required fees:* $1424 full-time, $40 per credit part-time, $29 per term part-time. *Room and board:* $10,300; room only: $6000. Room and board charges vary according to housing facility and location. *Payment plan:* installment. *Waivers:* senior citizens and employees or children of employees.

Financial Aid Of all full-time matriculated undergraduates who enrolled in 2016, 349 state and other part-time jobs (averaging $1286). *Financial aid deadline:* 3/31.

APPLYING
Options: electronic application, deferred entrance.

Application fee: $100 Canadian dollars.

Required: high school transcript, minimum 2.5 GPA. *Required for some:* essay or personal statement, minimum 3.7 GPA, 2 letters of recommendation, interview, portfolio and/or auditions are for performing and visual arts, interview/essay/portfolio for communications, letter of intent and interview for some education programs.

Application deadlines: 3/1 (freshmen), 3/1 (transfers).

Notification: continuous (freshmen), continuous (transfers).

CONTACT
Dr. Matthew Stiegemeyer, Director, Student Recruitment (Enrolment and Student Services), Concordia University, 1455 de Maisonneuve Boulevard West, Building LB-718, Montreal, QC H3G 1M8, Canada. *Phone:* 514-848-2424 Ext. 4781. *Fax:* 514-848-2837. *E-mail:* matthew.stiegemeyer@concordia.ca.

Concordia University of Edmonton
Edmonton, Alberta, Canada
http://www.concordia.ab.ca/
- **Independent Lutheran** comprehensive, founded 1921
- **Urban** 15-acre campus
- **Coed** 1,775 undergraduate students
- **Moderately difficult** entrance level, 55% of applicants were admitted

UNDERGRAD STUDENTS
Students come from 11 provinces and territories; 26 other countries; 3% live on campus.

Freshmen:
Admission: 1,799 applied, 996 admitted.

FACULTY
Total: 153, 39% full-time.
Student/faculty ratio: 18:1.

ACADEMICS
Calendar: semesters. *Degrees:* certificates, diplomas, bachelor's, master's, and postbachelor's certificates.

Special study options: advanced placement credit, double majors, external degree program, honors programs, independent study, internships, part-time degree program, services for LD students, study abroad, summer session for credit.

Unusual degree programs: 3-2 elementary education, environmental health.

Computers: 250 computers/terminals are available on campus for general student use. Campuswide network is available. 100% of college-owned or -operated housing units are wired for high-speed Internet access. Wireless service is available via entire campus.

Library: Arnold Guebert Memorial Library plus 1 other.

STUDENT LIFE
Housing options: men-only, women-only. Campus housing is university owned.

Activities and organizations: drama/theater group, student-run newspaper, choral group, concert choir, Concordia Business Association,

Science Club, Education Undergraduate Society, Psychology Students' Association.

Athletics Member CIS. *Intercollegiate sports:* badminton M(s)/W(s), basketball M(s)/W(s), cross-country running M(s)/W(s), golf M(s)/W(s), ice hockey M(s), soccer M(s)/W(s), swimming and diving M(s)/W(s). *Intramural sports:* skiing (cross-country) M/W, volleyball M/W, weight lifting M/W.

Campus security: 24-hour patrols, late-night transport/escort service.

Student services: personal/psychological counseling.

FINANCIAL AID
Financial Aid In 2017, 321 non-need-based awards were made. *Financial aid deadline:* 10/15.

APPLYING
Options: electronic application, early admission.

Required: high school transcript, minimum 2.0 GPA. *Required for some:* essay or personal statement, 2 letters of recommendation, interview.

Application deadlines: 6/30 (freshmen), 5/1 (out-of-state freshmen).

Notification: 10/1 (freshmen), 10/1 (out-of-state freshmen).

CONTACT
Student and Enrollment Services, Concordia University of Edmonton, 7128 Ada Boulevard, Edmonton, AB T5B 4E4, Canada. *Phone:* 780-479-9220. *Toll-free phone:* 866-479-5200. *Fax:* 780-378-8460. *E-mail:* admits@concordia.ab.ca.

Crandall University
Moncton, New Brunswick, Canada
http://www.crandallu.ca/
- **Independent Baptist** comprehensive, founded 1949
- **Urban** 220-acre campus
- **Coed**
- **Minimally difficult** entrance level

FACULTY
Student/faculty ratio: 13:1.

ACADEMICS
Calendar: trimesters. *Degrees:* certificates, bachelor's, and master's.
Library: George A. Rawlyk Library.

STUDENT LIFE
Housing options: men-only, women-only, special housing for students with disabilities. Campus housing is university owned.

Activities and organizations: student-run newspaper, choral group, Crandall Student Association, Worship Ministry Teams, Community Service Teams, Student Newspaper, Student Ambassadors.

Campus security: student patrols, controlled dormitory access, trained security personnel on campus for specific times.

Student services: health clinic, personal/psychological counseling.

COSTS & FINANCIAL AID
Costs (2017–18) *One-time required fee:* $50 Canadian dollars. *Comprehensive fee:* $18,440 Canadian dollars includes full-time tuition ($8420 Canadian dollars), mandatory fees ($1200 Canadian dollars), and room and board ($8820 Canadian dollars). Full-time tuition and fees vary according to course load, degree level, and program. Part-time tuition: $845 Canadian dollars per course. Part-time tuition and fees vary according to course load, degree level, and program. *Required fees:* $120 Canadian dollars per course part-time. *Room and board:* Room and board charges vary according to board plan and housing facility.

Financial Aid *Financial aid deadline:* 5/15.

APPLYING
Options: electronic application, early admission, early decision, deferred entrance.

Application fee: $35 Canadian dollars.

Required: high school transcript, minimum 2.7 GPA. *Required for some:* essay or personal statement, minimum 3.0 GPA, 3 letters of recommendation, interview.

CONTACT
Mrs. Lorrie Weir, Admissions Administrative Assistant, Crandall University, Box 6004, Moncton, NB E1C 9L7, Canada. *Phone:* 506-858-

8970 Ext. 434. *Toll-free phone:* 888-968-6228. *Fax:* 506-863-6460. *E-mail:* admissions@crandallu.ca.

Dalhousie University
Halifax, Nova Scotia, Canada
http://www.dal.ca/
- **Province-supported** university, founded 1818
- **Urban** 80-acre campus
- **Endowment** $537.8 million
- **Coed**
- **Moderately difficult** entrance level

FACULTY
Student/faculty ratio: 14:1.

ACADEMICS
Calendar: semesters. *Degrees:* certificates, diplomas, bachelor's, master's, doctoral, and postbachelor's certificates.
Library: The Killam Library plus 5 others.

STUDENT LIFE
Housing options: coed, women-only, special housing for students with disabilities. Campus housing is university owned. Freshman applicants given priority for college housing.
Activities and organizations: drama/theater group, student-run newspaper, radio station, choral group, International Students Association, Arts Society, Science Society, Commerce Society, Dalhousie Outdoors Club, national fraternities, national sororities.
Athletics Member CIS.
Campus security: 24-hour emergency response devices and patrols, student patrols, late-night transport/escort service, controlled dormitory access.
Student services: health clinic, personal/psychological counseling, women's center, legal services.

COSTS
Costs (2017–18) *Tuition:* province resident $8265 Canadian dollars full-time; nonresident $8265 Canadian dollars full-time; International tuition $17,730 Canadian dollars full-time. Full-time tuition and fees vary according to course load, degree level, location, and program. Part-time tuition and fees vary according to course load, degree level, location, and program. *Required fees:* $1066 Canadian dollars full-time. *Room and board:* $10,880 Canadian dollars; room only: $7325 Canadian dollars. Room and board charges vary according to board plan, housing facility, and location.

APPLYING
Standardized Tests *Required:* SAT or ACT (for admission).
Options: electronic application, early admission, deferred entrance.
Application fee: $70 Canadian dollars.
Required: high school transcript, minimum 3.0 GPA. *Required for some:* essay or personal statement, 1 letter of recommendation, interview.

CONTACT
Ashley Jordan, Assistant Registrar, Associate Director Admissions, Dalhousie University, Office of the Registrar, Halifax, NS B3H 4H6, Canada. *Phone:* 902-494-1833. *Fax:* 902-494-1630. *E-mail:* admissions@dal.ca.

École Polytechnique de Montréal
Montréal, Quebec, Canada
http://www.polymtl.ca/

CONTACT
École Polytechnique de Montréal, CP 6079, Succursale Centre-Ville, Montréal, QC H3C 3A7, Canada.

Emily Carr University of Art + Design
Vancouver, British Columbia, Canada
http://www.ecuad.ca/
- **Province-supported** comprehensive, founded 1925
- **Urban** campus
- **Coed**
- **Moderately difficult** entrance level

FACULTY
Student/faculty ratio: 18:1.

ACADEMICS
Degrees: bachelor's and master's.

STUDENT LIFE
Housing options: college housing not available.
Activities and organizations: student-run newspaper, radio station.
Campus security: 24-hour emergency response devices and patrols.
Student services: personal/psychological counseling.

APPLYING
Options: electronic application.
Application fee: $70 Canadian dollars.
Required: essay or personal statement, high school transcript, minimum 2.7 GPA, portfolio and questionnaire.

CONTACT
Sara Liao, Admissions, Emily Carr University of Art + Design, 1399 Johnston Street, Vancouver, BC V6H 3R9, Canada. *Phone:* 604-844-3800. *Toll-free phone:* 800-832-7788. *Fax:* 604-844-3801. *E-mail:* admissions@ecuad.ca.

Emmanuel Bible College
Kitchener, Ontario, Canada
http://www.emmanuelbiblecollege.ca/

CONTACT
Emmanuel Bible College, 100 Fergus Avenue, Kitchener, ON N2A 2H2, Canada. *Phone:* 519-894-8900 Ext. 224.

Eston College
Eston, Saskatchewan, Canada
http://www.estoncollege.ca/

CONTACT
Admissions, Eston College, 730 1st Street E., Box 579, Eston, SK S0L 1A0, Canada. *Phone:* 306-962-3621. *Toll-free phone:* 888-440-3424. *Fax:* 306-962-3810. *E-mail:* admissions@estoncollege.ca.

HEC Montreal
Montréal, Quebec, Canada
http://www.hec.ca/
- **Province-supported** comprehensive, founded 1910, part of Universite de Montreal
- **Urban** 9-acre campus with easy access to Montreal, QC
- **Coed** 10,484 undergraduate students, 48% full-time, 52% women, 48% men
- **Moderately difficult** entrance level, 70% of applicants were admitted

UNDERGRAD STUDENTS
5,047 full-time, 5,437 part-time. Students come from 5 provinces and territories; 64 other countries; 0.3% are from out of state.

Freshmen:
Admission: 2,649 applied, 1,864 admitted, 956 enrolled.

FACULTY
Total: 641, 46% full-time, 41% with terminal degrees.
Student/faculty ratio: 23:1.

ACADEMICS
Calendar: trimesters. *Degrees:* certificates, bachelor's, master's, doctoral, and postbachelor's certificates.

Special study options: academic remediation for entering students, adult/continuing education programs, distance learning, English as a second language, honors programs, independent study, off-campus study, part-time degree program, student-designed majors, study abroad, summer session for credit.

Computers: 159 computers/terminals and 9,000 ports are available on campus for general student use. Students can access the following: computer help desk, free student e-mail accounts, online (class) grades, online (class) registration, online (class) schedules, learning management system, corporate calendar and Web sites for resources available for classes. Campuswide network is available. 100% of college-owned or -operated housing units are wired for high-speed Internet access. Wireless service is available via entire campus.

Library: HEC Montreal Library plus 1 other. *Books:* 116,690 (physical), 206,337 (digital/electronic); *Serial titles:* 952 (physical), 111,941 (digital/electronic); *Databases:* 161. Weekly public service hours: 100; students can reserve study rooms.

STUDENT LIFE

Housing options: coed. Campus housing is university owned. Freshman applicants given priority for college housing.

Activities and organizations: student-run newspaper, AEMBA (MBA Students' Association), AEHEC (BBA Students'; Association), AEPC (Certificate Students'; Association), AECS (Graduate Students'; Association).

Campus security: 24-hour emergency response devices and patrols.

Student services: health clinic, personal/psychological counseling.

COSTS & FINANCIAL AID

Costs (2017–18) *Tuition:* province resident $2391 full-time, $80 per credit part-time; nonresident $7403 full-time, $238 per credit part-time; International tuition $24,000 full-time. Full-time tuition and fees vary according to program. Part-time tuition and fees vary according to program. *Required fees:* $1489 full-time, $46 per credit part-time, $83 per credit part-time. *Room and board:* $3890. Room and board charges vary according to board plan and housing facility. *Waivers:* employees or children of employees.

Financial Aid Of all full-time matriculated undergraduates who enrolled in 2016, 2,400 applied for aid, 2,400 were judged to have need. 15 state and other part-time jobs (averaging $2600). *Average financial aid package:* $7900. *Average need-based loan:* $3200. *Average need-based gift aid:* $6200. *Average indebtedness upon graduation:* $3200.

APPLYING

Options: electronic application, deferred entrance.

Application fee: $88 Canadian dollars.

Required: high school transcript. *Required for some:* R score, collegial/college performance rating.

Application deadlines: 3/1 (freshmen), 2/15 (out-of-state freshmen).

CONTACT

Mrs. Virginie Lefebvre, Assistant Registrar, HEC Montreal, 3000 Chemin de la Cote-Sainte-Catherine, Montreal, QC H3T 2A7, Canada. *Phone:* 514-340-6151. *Fax:* 514-340-5640.

Heritage College and Seminary
Cambridge, Ontario, Canada
http://www.heritagecambridge.com/

CONTACT

Mr. Mark Walther, Assistant Dean of Students, Heritage College and Seminary, New York, NY 10023-6588. *Phone:* 519-651-2869 Ext. 251. *Toll-free phone:* 800-465-1961. *Fax:* 519-651-2870. *E-mail:* mwalther@heritagecollege.net.

Horizon College & Seminary
Saskatoon, Saskatchewan, Canada
http://www.horizon.edu/

CONTACT

Mrs. Jenn Lundy, Assistant Registrar, Horizon College & Seminary, 1303 Jackson Avenue, Saskatoon, SK S7H 2M9, Canada. *Phone:* 306-374-6655

Ext. 225. *Toll-free phone:* 877-374-6655. *Fax:* 306-373-6968. *E-mail:* admissions@horizon.edu.

The King's University
Edmonton, Alberta, Canada
http://www.kingsu.ca/
- **Independent interdenominational** 4-year, founded 1979
- **Suburban** 20-acre campus
- **Endowment** $3.1 million
- **Coed**
- **Moderately difficult** entrance level

FACULTY
Student/faculty ratio: 11:1.

ACADEMICS

Calendar: Canadian standard year. *Degrees:* certificates, diplomas, bachelor's, and postbachelor's certificates.

Library: Simona Maaskant. *Books:* 80,000 (physical), 301,000 (digital/electronic); *Serial titles:* 166 (physical), 130,000 (digital/electronic); *Databases:* 50. Weekly public service hours: 63.

STUDENT LIFE

Housing options: coed, women-only. Campus housing is university owned. Freshman applicants given priority for college housing.

Activities and organizations: drama/theater group, student-run newspaper, choral group, Micah Action and Awareness Students' Society, King's Eagles Hockey Club, King's Rugby Club, King's Science Society, The King's Commerce Association.

Campus security: 24-hour emergency response devices, student patrols, controlled dormitory access.

Student services: personal/psychological counseling.

COSTS & FINANCIAL AID

Costs (2017–18) *Comprehensive fee:* $19,887 Canadian dollars includes full-time tuition ($12,245 Canadian dollars), mandatory fees ($852 Canadian dollars), and room and board ($6790 Canadian dollars). Full-time tuition and fees vary according to course load. Part-time tuition: $395 Canadian dollars per credit hour. Part-time tuition and fees vary according to course load. *Required fees:* $163 Canadian dollars per term part-time. *College room only:* $3700 Canadian dollars. Room and board charges vary according to board plan and housing facility.

Financial Aid *Financial aid deadline:* 3/31.

APPLYING

Options: electronic application.

Application fee: $70 Canadian dollars.

Required: high school transcript, minimum 2.0 GPA, 1 letter of recommendation. *Required for some:* essay or personal statement, interview.

CONTACT

Ms. Hilda Buisman, Director of Admissions, The King's University, 9125-50 Street, Edmonton, AB T6B 2H3, Canada. *Phone:* 780-465-3500 Ext. 8031. *Toll-free phone:* 800-661-8582. *Fax:* 780-465-3534. *E-mail:* admissions@kingsu.ca.

Kingswood University
Sussex, New Brunswick, Canada
http://www.kingswood.edu/

CONTACT

Mrs. Shelley Vail, Associate Director for Admissions and Financial Aid, Kingswood University, PO Box 5125, Sussex, NB E4E 5L2, Canada. *Phone:* 506-432-4422. *Toll-free phone:* 888-432-4422. *Fax:* 506-432.4442. *E-mail:* vails@kingswood.edu.

Lakehead University
Thunder Bay, Ontario, Canada
http://www.lakeheadu.ca/

CONTACT
Mr. Nicholas Chamut, Manager of Undergraduate Admissions, Lakehead University, 955 Oliver Road, Thunder Bay, ON P7B 5E1, Canada. *Phone:* 807-343-8676. *Toll-free phone:* 800-465-3959. *Fax:* 807-766-7209. *E-mail:* admissions@lakeheadu.ca.

Laurentian University
Sudbury, Ontario, Canada
http://www.laurentian.ca/

CONTACT
Laurentian University, 935 Ramsey Lake Road, P3E 2C6, Canada. *Phone:* 800-263-4188. *Toll-free phone:* 800-263-4188. *E-mail:* explore@laurentian.ca.

Master's College and Seminary
Peterborough, Ontario, Canada
http://www.mcs.edu/

- **Independent Pentecostal** 4-year, founded 1939
- **Suburban** campus with easy access to Toronto
- **Endowment** $970,384
- **Coed** 227 undergraduate students
- **Noncompetitive** entrance level, 92% of applicants were admitted

UNDERGRAD STUDENTS
Students come from 7 provinces and territories; 1 other country; 21% are from out of state; 65% live on campus.

Freshmen:
Admission: 73 applied, 67 admitted.
Retention: 90% of full-time freshmen returned.

FACULTY
Total: 27, 15% full-time, 30% with terminal degrees.
Student/faculty ratio: 16:1.

ACADEMICS
Calendar: semesters. *Degree:* certificates, diplomas, and bachelor's.
Special study options: academic remediation for entering students, distance learning, independent study, internships, off-campus study, part-time degree program, services for LD students, summer session for credit.
Computers: 6 computers/terminals are available on campus for general student use. Students can access the following: computer help desk, free student e-mail accounts, online (class) grades, online (class) registration, online (class) schedules. Campuswide network is available. 100% of college-owned or -operated housing units are wired for high-speed Internet access. Wireless service is available via entire campus.
Library: Robert and Shirley Taitinger Learning Commons. *Books:* 35,418 (physical), 5,422 (digital/electronic); *Serial titles:* 542 (physical). Weekly public service hours: 71.

STUDENT LIFE
Housing options: on-campus residence required for freshman year; men-only, women-only. Campus housing is leased by the school. Freshman campus housing is guaranteed.
Campus security: 24-hour emergency response devices, controlled dormitory access.

COSTS
Costs (2018–19) *One-time required fee:* $535. *Comprehensive fee:* $15,682 includes full-time tuition ($6848), mandatory fees ($1414), and room and board ($7420). Full-time tuition and fees vary according to course load, location, and program. Part-time tuition: $214 per credit hour. Part-time tuition and fees vary according to course load, location, and program. *Required fees:* $29 per credit hour part-time. *Room and board:* Room and board charges vary according to board plan. *Payment plan:* deferred payment. *Waivers:* senior citizens and employees or children of employees.

APPLYING
Options: electronic application, deferred entrance.
Application fee: $75 Canadian dollars.
Required: essay or personal statement, high school transcript, 3 letters of recommendation, Christian commitment. *Required for some:* interview. *Recommended:* minimum 2.0 GPA.
Application deadlines: 8/1 (freshmen), 8/1 (transfers).
Notification: continuous (freshmen), continuous (transfers).

CONTACT
Ms. Flora Anthony, Admissions Counsellor, Master's College and Seminary, 780 Argyle Street, Peterborough, ON K9H 5T2, Canada. *Phone:* 800-295-6368 Ext. 237. *Toll-free phone:* 800-295-6368. *Fax:* 705-749-0417. *E-mail:* flora.anthony@mcs.edu.

McGill University
Montréal, Quebec, Canada
http://www.mcgill.ca/

CONTACT
Enrollment Services, McGill University, 845 Sherbrooke Street West, James Administration Building, Room 205, Montreal, QC H3A 2T5, Canada. *Phone:* 514-398-3910. *Fax:* 514-398-4193. *E-mail:* admissions@mcgill.ca.

McMaster University
Hamilton, Ontario, Canada
http://www.mcmaster.ca/

- **Province-supported** university, founded 1887
- **Suburban** 300-acre campus with easy access to Toronto
- **Endowment** $631.7 million
- **Coed**
- **Very difficult** entrance level

FACULTY
Student/faculty ratio: 25:1.

ACADEMICS
Calendar: Canadian standard year. *Degrees:* certificates, diplomas, bachelor's, master's, and doctoral.
Library: Mills Memorial Library plus 4 others.

STUDENT LIFE
Housing options: coed, women-only, special housing for students with disabilities. Campus housing is university owned. Freshman applicants given priority for college housing.
Activities and organizations: drama/theater group, student-run newspaper, radio station, choral group, Inter-Varsity Christian Fellowship, African-Caribbean Student Association, Chinese Students' Association, AIESEC (international leadership organization), Southeast Asian-American Society.
Athletics Member CIS.
Campus security: 24-hour emergency response devices and patrols, student patrols, late-night transport/escort service, controlled dormitory access.
Student services: health clinic, personal/psychological counseling, women's center, legal services.

APPLYING
Standardized Tests *Required:* SAT or ACT (for admission).
Options: electronic application, deferred entrance.
Required: high school transcript. *Required for some:* essay or personal statement, interview.

CONTACT
Olivia Demerling, Admissions Officer, McMaster University, 1280 Main Street West, Hamilton, ON L8S 4M2, Canada. *Phone:* 905-525-4600. *Fax:* 905-527-1105. *E-mail:* admitmac@mcmaster.ca.

Memorial University of Newfoundland

St. John's, Newfoundland and Labrador, Canada

http://www.mun.ca/

CONTACT
Ms. Marian Abbott, Admissions Office, Memorial University of Newfoundland, Elizabeth Avenue, St. John's, NL A1C 5S7, Canada. *Phone:* 709-737-3705. *E-mail:* sturecru@morgan.ucs.mun.ca.

Mount Allison University

Sackville, New Brunswick, Canada

http://www.mta.ca/

- **Province-supported** comprehensive, founded 1839
- **Small-town** 50-acre campus
- **Endowment** $65.0 million
- **Coed**
- **Moderately difficult** entrance level

FACULTY
Student/faculty ratio: 16:1.

ACADEMICS
Calendar: Canadian standard year. *Degrees:* certificates, bachelor's, and master's.
Library: Ralph Pickard Bell Library plus 3 others. Students can reserve study rooms.

STUDENT LIFE
Housing options: coed, women-only, cooperative. Campus housing is university owned. Freshman campus housing is guaranteed.

Activities and organizations: drama/theater group, student-run newspaper, radio station, choral group, Commerce Society, Windsor Theatre, President's Leadership Development Certificate, Leadership Mount Allison, Garnet and Gold Society.

Athletics Member CIS.

Campus security: 24-hour emergency response devices, late-night transport/escort service.

Student services: health clinic, personal/psychological counseling.

APPLYING
Options: electronic application, deferred entrance.
Application fee: $50 Canadian dollars.
Required: high school transcript, minimum 2.5 GPA. *Required for some:* essay or personal statement, interview. *Recommended:* 2 letters of recommendation.

CONTACT
Mr. Curtis Michaelis, Manager of Admissions, Mount Allison University, 65 York Street, Sackville, NB E4L 1E4, Canada. *Phone:* 506-364-3294. *Fax:* 506-364-2272. *E-mail:* admissions@mta.ca.

Mount Royal University

Calgary, Alberta, Canada

http://www.mtroyal.ca/

CONTACT
Admissions Office, Mount Royal University, 4825 Mount Royal Gate SW, Calgary, AB T3E 6K6, Canada. *Phone:* 403-440-5000. *Toll-free phone:* 877-440-5001.

Mount Saint Vincent University

Halifax, Nova Scotia, Canada

http://www.msvu.ca/

CONTACT
Ms. Heidi Tattrie, Assistant Registrar/Admissions, Mount Saint Vincent University, 166 Bedford Highway, Halifax, NS B3M2J6, Canada. *Phone:* 902-457-6117. *Toll-free phone:* 877-733-6788. *Fax:* 902-457-6498. *E-mail:* admissions@msvu.ca.

Ner Israel Yeshiva College of Toronto

Thornhill, Ontario, Canada

http://www.neryisroel.info/

CONTACT
Rabbi Y. Kravetz, Director of Admissions, Ner Israel Yeshiva College of Toronto, 8950 Bathurst Street, Thornhill, ON L4J 8A7, Canada. *Phone:* 905-731-1224.

Nipissing University

North Bay, Ontario, Canada

http://www.nipissingu.ca/

CONTACT
Ms. Lori-Ann Beckford, Assistant Registrar, Liaison, Nipissing University, 100 College Drive, Box 5002, North Bay, ON P1B 8L7, Canada. *Phone:* 705-474-3461 Ext. 4518. *Fax:* 705-474-1947. *E-mail:* liaison@nipissingu.ca.

NSCAD University

Halifax, Nova Scotia, Canada

http://www.nscad.ca/

CONTACT
Mr. Terry Bailey, Director of Admissions and Enrollment Services, NSCAD University, 5163 Duke Street, Halifax, NS B3J 3J6, Canada. *Phone:* 902-494-8129. *Toll-free phone:* 888-444-5989. *Fax:* 902-425-2987. *E-mail:* admissions@nscad.ca.

Okanagan College

Kelowna, British Columbia, Canada

http://www.okanagan.bc.ca/

CONTACT
Mr. Allan Hickey, Associate Registrar Systems, Okanagan College, 1000 K.L.O. Road, Kelowna, BC V1Y 4X8, Canada. *Phone:* 250-762-5445 Ext. 4332. *Toll-free phone:* 877-755-2266. *E-mail:* ahickey@okanagan.bc.ca.

Prairie Bible Institute

Three Hills, Alberta, Canada

http://www.prairie.edu/

CONTACT
Mr. Kevin Kirk, Vice President, Marketing and Enrollment Management, Prairie Bible Institute, 350 5th Avenue, NE, Box 4000, Three Hills, AB T0M 2N0, Canada. *Phone:* 403-443-5511 Ext. 3007. *Toll-free phone:* 800-661-2425. *E-mail:* admissions@prairie.edu.

Providence University College & Theological Seminary

Otterburne, Manitoba, Canada

http://www.providenceuc.ca/

CONTACT
Mr. Adrian Enns, Director of College Enrollment, Providence University College & Theological Seminary, 10 College Crescent, Otterburne, MB R0A 1G0, Canada. *Phone:* 204-433-7488. *Toll-free phone:* 800-668-7768. *Fax:* 204-433-7158. *E-mail:* info@prov.ca.

Queen's University at Kingston

Kingston, Ontario, Canada

http://www.queensu.ca/

CONTACT
Ms. Iveta Reinikovaite, Admission Coordinator, Queen's University at Kingston, Undergraduate Admissions, Gordon Hall, 74 Union Street, Kingston, ON K7L 3N6, Canada. *Phone:* 613-533-2218. *Fax:* 613-533-6810. *E-mail:* admission@queensu.ca.

Redeemer University College

Ancaster, Ontario, Canada
http://www.redeemer.ca/

- **Independent interdenominational** 4-year, founded 1980
- **Small-town** 86-acre campus with easy access to Toronto
- **Endowment** $3.9 million
- **Coed** 647 undergraduate students
- **94%** of applicants were admitted

UNDERGRAD STUDENTS

Students come from 8 provinces and territories; 20 other countries; 4% are from out of state.

Freshmen:

Admission: 210 applied, 198 admitted.
Retention: 84% of full-time freshmen returned.

FACULTY

Total: 91, 49% full-time, 54% with terminal degrees.
Student/faculty ratio: 11:1.

ACADEMICS

Calendar: semesters. *Degree:* certificates and bachelor's.

Special study options: academic remediation for entering students, cooperative education, double majors, honors programs, independent study, internships, off-campus study, part-time degree program, services for LD students, study abroad, summer session for credit.

Computers: 81 computers/terminals are available on campus for general student use. Students can access the following: campus intranet, computer help desk, free student e-mail accounts, online (class) grades, online (class) schedules. Campuswide network is available. 100% of college-owned or -operated housing units are wired for high-speed Internet access. Wireless service is available via entire campus.

Library: Peter Turkstra Library. *Books:* 92,733 (physical); *Serial titles:* 93 (physical), 9,387 (digital/electronic); *Databases:* 21. Students can reserve study rooms.

STUDENT LIFE

Housing options: on-campus residence required through sophomore year; men-only, women-only. Campus housing is university owned. Freshman campus housing is guaranteed.

Activities and organizations: drama/theater group, student-run newspaper, choral group, Church in the Box, Service Learning Trips, Deedz, Athletics and Recreation, Concert Choir.

Athletics *Intercollegiate sports:* badminton M/W, basketball M(s)/W(s), cross-country running M/W, soccer M/W, volleyball M/W. *Intramural sports:* basketball M/W, ice hockey M, soccer M/W, squash M/W, tennis M/W, ultimate Frisbee M/W, volleyball M/W.

Campus security: 24-hour emergency response devices, student patrols, late-night transport/escort service, controlled dormitory access, path lighting.

Student services: personal/psychological counseling.

COSTS & FINANCIAL AID

Costs (2017–18) *Comprehensive fee:* $24,307 includes full-time tuition ($16,382), mandatory fees ($555), and room and board ($7370). Full-time tuition and fees vary according to course load. Part-time tuition: $1638 per course. Part-time tuition and fees vary according to course load. *Required fees:* $39 per course part-time. *College room only:* $5092. Room and board charges vary according to board plan and housing facility. *Payment plan:* installment. *Waivers:* senior citizens and employees or children of employees.

Financial Aid Of all full-time matriculated undergraduates who enrolled in 2010, 640 applied for aid, 607 were judged to have need, 200 had their need fully met. 385 state and other part-time jobs (averaging $1238). In 2010, 99 non-need-based awards were made. *Average percent of need met:* 82. *Average financial aid package:* $12,582. *Average need-based loan:* $7464. *Average need-based gift aid:* $4587. *Average non-need-based aid:* $3061. *Average indebtedness upon graduation:* $23,598. *Financial aid deadline:* 3/31.

APPLYING

Standardized Tests *Required for some:* SAT or ACT (for admission).

Options: electronic application, deferred entrance.

Application fee: $40 Canadian dollars.

Required: essay or personal statement, high school transcript, minimum 2.0 GPA, 1 letter of recommendation. *Required for some:* interview.

Application deadlines: rolling (freshmen), rolling (transfers).

Notification: continuous (freshmen), continuous (transfers).

CONTACT

Recruitment, Redeemer University College, 777 Garner Road East, Ancaster, ON L9K 1J4, Canada. *Phone:* 905-648-2131 Ext. 4280. *Toll-free phone:* 800-263-6467. *Fax:* 905-648-9545. *E-mail:* recruitment@redeemer.ca.

Rocky Mountain College

Calgary, Alberta, Canada
http://www.rockymountaincollege.ca/

CONTACT

Rocky Mountain College, 4039 Brentwood Road, NW, Calgary, AB T2L 1L1, Canada. *Phone:* 403-284-5100 Ext. 222. *Toll-free phone:* 877-YOUnRMC.

Royal Military College of Canada

Kingston, Ontario, Canada
http://www.rmc.ca/

- **Federally supported** university, founded 1876, part of Council of Ontario Universities
- **Urban** 90-acre campus
- **Coed**

FACULTY

Student/faculty ratio: 5:1.

ACADEMICS

Calendar: trimesters. *Degrees:* certificates, diplomas, bachelor's, master's, and doctoral.

Library: Massey Library plus 1 other. Study areas open 24 hours, 5–7 days a week.

STUDENT LIFE

Housing options: on-campus residence required through senior year; coed. Campus housing is provided by a third party. Freshman campus housing is guaranteed.

Activities and organizations: drama/theater group, student-run newspaper, choral group, marching band.

Athletics Member CIS.

Campus security: 24-hour emergency response devices and patrols, late-night transport/escort service, controlled dormitory access.

Student services: health clinic, personal/psychological counseling, legal services.

COSTS

Costs (2017–18) *Tuition:* province resident $700 Canadian dollars per course part-time; nonresident $700 Canadian dollars per course part-time. *Required fees:* $75 Canadian dollars per degree program part-time.

APPLYING

Required: essay or personal statement, high school transcript, interview, medical, aptitude test, security screening.

CONTACT

Royal Military College of Canada, PO Box 17000, Station Forces, Kingston, ON K7K 7B4, Canada. *Phone:* 613-541-6000 Ext. 6579.

Royal Roads University

Victoria, British Columbia, Canada
http://www.royalroads.ca/

- **Province-supported** upper-level, founded 1995
- **Suburban** 565-acre campus
- **Coed**
- **Moderately difficult** entrance level

FACULTY

Student/faculty ratio: 12:1.

ACADEMICS
Calendar: continuous. *Degrees:* certificates, diplomas, bachelor's, master's, and doctoral.
Library: Coronel Memorial Library.

STUDENT LIFE
Housing options: college housing not available.
Campus security: 24-hour emergency response devices and patrols, late-night transport/escort service.

APPLYING
Options: electronic application.
Application fee: $110 Canadian dollars.

CONTACT
Royal Roads University, 2005 Sooke Road, Victoria, BC V9B 5Y2, Canada. *Phone:* 250-391-2511. *Toll-free phone:* 800-788-8028.

Ryerson University
Toronto, Ontario, Canada
http://www.ryerson.ca/

CONTACT
Michelle Beaton, Manager of International Student Recruitment, Ryerson University, 350 Victoria Street, Toronto, ON M5B 2K3, Canada. *Phone:* 416-979-5080. *Fax:* 416-979-5067. *E-mail:* inquire@ryerson.ca.

St. Francis Xavier University
Antigonish, Nova Scotia, Canada
http://www.stfx.ca/

CONTACT
Ms. Sarah Murray, Admissions Officer, St. Francis Xavier University, PO Box 5000, Antigonish, NS B2G 2W5, Canada. *Phone:* 902-867-2219. *Toll-free phone:* 877-867-7839 (in-state); 877-867-STFX (out-of-state). *Fax:* 902-867-2329. *E-mail:* mbarry@stfx.ca.

Saint Mary's University
Halifax, Nova Scotia, Canada
http://www.smu.ca/

CONTACT
Mr. Greg Ferguson, Director of Admissions, Saint Mary's University, Halifax, NS B3H 3C3, Canada. *Phone:* 902-420-5415. *Fax:* 902-496-8100. *E-mail:* greg.ferguson@smu.ca.

Saint Paul University
Ottawa, Ontario, Canada
http://www.ustpaul.ca/

CONTACT
Admission and Recruitment Office, Saint Paul University, 223 Main Street, Ottawa, ON K1S 1C4, Canada. *Phone:* 613-236-1393 Ext. 8990. *Toll-free phone:* 800-637-6859. *Fax:* 613-782-3014. *E-mail:* admission@ustpaul.ca.

St. Thomas University
Fredericton, New Brunswick, Canada
http://www.stu.ca/
- **Independent Roman Catholic** 4-year, founded 1910
- **Small-town** 16-acre campus
- **Endowment** $17.9 million
- **Coed** 1,796 undergraduate students, 95% full-time, 71% women, 29% men
- **Moderately difficult** entrance level, 89% of applicants were admitted

UNDERGRAD STUDENTS
1,713 full-time, 83 part-time. Students come from 10 provinces and territories; 38 other countries; 20% are from out of state; 92% Race/ethnicity unknown; 8% international; 6% transferred in; 28% live on campus.

Freshmen:
Admission: 939 applied, 839 admitted, 563 enrolled. *Average high school GPA:* 3.4.
Retention: 70% of full-time freshmen returned.

FACULTY
Total: 185, 54% full-time, 76% with terminal degrees.
Student/faculty ratio: 16:1.

ACADEMICS
Calendar: semesters. *Degrees:* certificates, bachelor's, and postbachelor's certificates.

Special study options: academic remediation for entering students, accelerated degree program, advanced placement credit, double majors, English as a second language, honors programs, independent study, internships, off-campus study, part-time degree program, services for LD students, student-designed majors, study abroad, summer session for credit.

Computers: 88 computers/terminals are available on campus for general student use. Students can access the following: computer help desk, free student e-mail accounts, online (class) grades, online (class) registration, online (class) schedules, learning management system. Campuswide network is available. 100% of college-owned or -operated housing units are wired for high-speed Internet access. Wireless service is available via entire campus.

Library: Harriet Irving Library plus 2 others. *Books:* 976,313 (physical), 532,787 (digital/electronic); *Serial titles:* 2,449 (physical), 44,800 (digital/electronic). Weekly public service hours: 113; students can reserve study rooms.

STUDENT LIFE
Housing options: coed, women-only, special housing for students with disabilities. Campus housing is university owned. Freshman campus housing is guaranteed.

Activities and organizations: drama/theater group, student-run newspaper, radio station, choral group, Theatre St. Thomas, St. Thomas Student Union, Criminology Society, Model UN, International Students' Association.

Athletics Member CIS. *Intercollegiate sports:* basketball M/W, cross-country running M/W, golf M/W, ice hockey W, soccer M/W, track and field M/W, volleyball M/W. *Intramural sports:* badminton M/W, basketball M/W, cross-country running M/W, fencing M/W, football M, ice hockey M/W, rock climbing M/W, soccer M/W, softball M/W, squash M/W, swimming and diving M/W, table tennis M/W, track and field M/W, ultimate Frisbee M/W, volleyball M/W, water polo M/W.

Campus security: 24-hour emergency response devices and patrols, student patrols, late-night transport/escort service, controlled dormitory access.

Student services: health clinic, personal/psychological counseling, women's center.

COSTS & FINANCIAL AID
Costs (2017–18) *Comprehensive fee:* $16,182 includes full-time tuition ($6643), mandatory fees ($738), and room and board ($8801). Full-time tuition and fees vary according to course load, degree level, and program. Part-time tuition: $669 per course. Part-time tuition and fees vary according to course load. *Required fees:* $633 per course part-time. *Room and board:* Room and board charges vary according to board plan, housing facility, and location. *Payment plans:* installment, deferred payment. *Waivers:* senior citizens and employees or children of employees.

Financial Aid *Financial aid deadline:* 3/1.

APPLYING
Standardized Tests *Recommended:* SAT (for admission).
Options: electronic application, early action.
Application fee: $55 Canadian dollars.
Required: essay or personal statement, high school transcript, minimum 3.0 GPA. *Required for some:* interview.
Application deadlines: 8/31 (freshmen), 8/31 (transfers), 12/7 (early action).
Notification: continuous (freshmen), continuous (transfers).

CONTACT

Ms. Kathryn Monti, Director of Admissions, St. Thomas University, Duffie Hall, Fredericton, NB E3B 5G3, Canada. *Phone:* 506-452-0532. *Fax:* 506-452-0617. *E-mail:* admissions@stu.ca.

Simon Fraser University
Burnaby, British Columbia, Canada
http://www.sfu.ca/

- **Province-supported** university, founded 1965
- **Suburban** 174-hectare campus with easy access to Vancouver
- **Coed** 25,343 undergraduate students, 51% full-time, 54% women, 46% men
- **Moderately difficult** entrance level, 56% of applicants were admitted

UNDERGRAD STUDENTS

12,944 full-time, 12,399 part-time. 7% are from out of state; 3% transferred in.

Freshmen:
Admission: 16,515 applied, 9,255 admitted, 3,232 enrolled.
Retention: 85% of full-time freshmen returned.

FACULTY

Total: 975, 99% full-time, 89% with terminal degrees.
Student/faculty ratio: 22:1.

ACADEMICS

Calendar: trimesters. *Degrees:* certificates, diplomas, bachelor's, master's, doctoral, post-master's, and postbachelor's certificates.

Special study options: academic remediation for entering students, adult/continuing education programs, advanced placement credit, cooperative education, distance learning, double majors, English as a second language, honors programs, independent study, internships, off-campus study, part-time degree program, services for LD students, study abroad, summer session for credit.

Computers: 200 computers/terminals and 30 ports are available on campus for general student use. Students can access the following: computer help desk, free student e-mail accounts, online (class) grades, online (class) registration, online (class) schedules. Campuswide network is available. 100% of college-owned or -operated housing units are wired for high-speed Internet access. Wireless service is available via entire campus.

Library: Bennett Library plus 2 others. *Books:* 1.5 million (physical), 1.1 million (digital/electronic); *Serial titles:* 2,500 (physical), 98,000 (digital/electronic). Weekly public service hours: 103; students can reserve study rooms.

STUDENT LIFE

Housing options: coed, special housing for students with disabilities. Campus housing is university owned. Freshman applicants given priority for college housing.

Activities and organizations: student-run newspaper, radio station, The Peak Newspaper, orientation/peer leaders, Crisis line, Women's Centre, Simon Fraser Public Interest Research Group.

Athletics Member NCAA. All Division II. *Intercollegiate sports:* basketball M(s)/W(s), cross-country running M(s)/W(s), football M(s), golf M(s)/W, gymnastics M, soccer M(s)/W(s), softball W(s), swimming and diving M(s)/W(s), track and field M(s)/W(s), volleyball W(s), wrestling M(s)/W(s). *Intramural sports:* archery M(c)/W(c), badminton M(c)/W(c), basketball M/W, cheerleading M(c)/W(c), crew M(c)/W(c), fencing M(c)/W(c), field hockey W(c), football M/W, golf W(c), gymnastics W(c), ice hockey M(c)/W(c), lacrosse M(c), rugby M(c)/W(c), soccer M/W, softball M/W, squash M(c)/W(c), table tennis M(c)/W(c), tennis M/W, ultimate Frisbee M(c)/W(c), volleyball M(c)/W(c), water polo M(c)/W(c).

Campus security: 24-hour emergency response devices and patrols, student patrols, late-night transport/escort service, controlled dormitory access, safe-walk stations, 24-hour safe study area.

Student services: health clinic, personal/psychological counseling, women's center.

COSTS & FINANCIAL AID

Costs (2017–18) *Tuition:* province resident $5540 full-time, $185 per unit part-time; nonresident $5540 full-time, $185 per unit part-time; International tuition $24,250 full-time. Full-time tuition and fees vary according to course level and program. Part-time tuition and fees vary according to course level and program. *Required fees:* $810 full-time, $405 per term part-time. *Room and board:* $10,572; room only: $6672. Room and board charges vary according to board plan and housing facility. *Waivers:* employees or children of employees.

Financial Aid *Financial aid deadline:* 11/15.

APPLYING

Standardized Tests *Required for some:* SAT or ACT (for admission).

Options: electronic application, early admission, early action, deferred entrance.

Application fee: $78 Canadian dollars.

Required: high school transcript, minimum 3.0 GPA. *Required for some:* essay or personal statement, interview.

Application deadlines: 2/28 (freshmen), 2/28 (transfers).

Notification: continuous until 6/30 (freshmen), continuous until 5/30 (transfers).

CONTACT

Louise Legris, Director of Admissions, Simon Fraser University, 8888 University Drive, MBC 3200, Burnaby, BC V5A 1S6, Canada. *Phone:* 778-782-3498. *Fax:* 778-782-4969.

Southern Alberta Institute of Technology
Calgary, Alberta, Canada
http://www.sait.ca/

CONTACT

Southern Alberta Institute of Technology, 1301 16th Avenue NW, Calgary, AB T2M 0L4, Canada. *Phone:* 403-284-8857. *Toll-free phone:* 877-284-SAIT.

Steinbach Bible College
Steinbach, Manitoba, Canada
http://www.sbcollege.ca/

CONTACT

Mrs. Kaylene Buhler, Admissions Counselor, Steinbach Bible College, 50 PTH 12 North, Steinbach, MB R5G 1T4, Canada. *Phone:* 204-326-6451 Ext. 232. *Toll-free phone:* 800-230-8478. *Fax:* 204-326-6908. *E-mail:* info@sbcollege.ca.

Summit Pacific College
Abbotsford, British Columbia, Canada
http://www.summitpacific.ca/

CONTACT

Ms. Melody Deeley, Admissions and Registration, Summit Pacific College, Box 1700, Abbotsford, BC V2S 7E7, Canada. *Phone:* 604-851-7225. *Toll-free phone:* 800-976-8388. *E-mail:* registrar@summitpacific.ca.

Télé-université
Québec, Quebec, Canada
http://www.teluq.uquebec.ca/

CONTACT

Ms. Louise Bertrand, Registraire, Télé-université, 455, rue de l'Église, C.P. 4800, succ. Terminus, Québec, QC G1K 9H5, Canada. *Phone:* 418-657-2262 Ext. 5307. *Toll-free phone:* 888-843-4333.

Thompson Rivers University

Kamloops, British Columbia, Canada

http://www.tru.ca/

CONTACT

Mr. Josh Keller, Director, Student Recruitment and Liaison, Thompson Rivers University, 900 McGill Road, Kamloops, BC V2C 0C8, Canada. *Phone:* 250-828-5008. *Fax:* 250-828-5159. *E-mail:* jkeller@tru.ca.

Trent University

Peterborough, Ontario, Canada

http://www.trentu.ca/

- **Province-supported** university, founded 1963
- **Suburban** 1400-acre campus with easy access to Toronto
- **Coed** 8,949 undergraduate students, 86% full-time, 67% women, 33% men
- **Moderately difficult** entrance level

UNDERGRAD STUDENTS

7,672 full-time, 1,277 part-time. Students come from 13 provinces and territories; 82 other countries; 2% are from out of state; 11% transferred in; 18% live on campus.

Freshmen:

Admission: 2,034 enrolled.

Retention: 84% of full-time freshmen returned.

FACULTY

Total: 207.

ACADEMICS

Calendar: Canadian standard year. *Degrees:* certificates, diplomas, bachelor's, master's, and doctoral.

Special study options: academic remediation for entering students, accelerated degree program, advanced placement credit, cooperative education, distance learning, double majors, English as a second language, honors programs, independent study, internships, off-campus study, part-time degree program, services for LD students, student-designed majors, study abroad, summer session for credit.

Computers: Students can access the following: campus intranet, computer help desk, free student e-mail accounts, online (class) grades, online (class) registration, online (class) schedules, online tuition payment. Campuswide network is available. 100% of college-owned or -operated housing units are wired for high-speed Internet access. Wireless service is available via entire campus.

Library: Thomas J. Bata Library plus 1 other. Students can reserve study rooms.

STUDENT LIFE

Housing options: coed, women-only. Campus housing is university owned. Freshman campus housing is guaranteed.

Activities and organizations: drama/theater group, student-run newspaper, radio station, choral group, Trent Radio, Trent International Program, Trent Central Student Association, Arthur (student newspaper), Excalibur (yearbook).

Athletics Member CIS. *Intercollegiate sports:* crew M/W, cross-country running M/W, golf M, lacrosse M/W, rugby M/W, soccer M/W, track and field M/W, volleyball M/W. *Intramural sports:* badminton M/W, baseball M/W, basketball M/W, cross-country running M/W, football M/W, ice hockey M/W, soccer M/W, softball M/W, squash M/W, swimming and diving M/W, tennis M/W, track and field M/W, ultimate Frisbee M/W, volleyball M/W, water polo M/W.

Campus security: 24-hour emergency response devices and patrols, student patrols, late-night transport/escort service, controlled dormitory access.

Student services: health clinic, personal/psychological counseling, women's center.

COSTS

Costs (2017–18) *Tuition:* province resident $6600 full-time, $1320 per credit part-time; nonresident $3879 per credit part-time; International tuition $19,397 full-time. Full-time tuition and fees vary according to course load, degree level, and program. Part-time tuition and fees vary according to course load, degree level, and program. *Required fees:* $1625 full-time, $143 per credit part-time. *Room and board:* $9724. Room and board charges vary according to board plan, housing facility, and location. *Payment plans:* installment, deferred payment. *Waivers:* employees or children of employees.

APPLYING

Options: electronic application, deferred entrance.

Application fee: $150 Canadian dollars.

Required: high school transcript, minimum 2.8 GPA. *Required for some:* essay or personal statement, interview.

Application deadlines: 6/1 (freshmen), 9/1 (transfers).

Notification: continuous (freshmen), continuous (transfers).

CONTACT

Mr. Kevin Whitmore, Director, Recruitment & Admissions, Trent University, 1600 West Bank Drive, Peterborough, ON K9J 7B8, Canada. *Phone:* 705-748-1011 Ext. 7748. *Fax:* 705-748-1629. *E-mail:* admissions@trentu.ca.

Trinity Western University

Langley, British Columbia, Canada

http://www.twu.ca/

CONTACT

Trinity Western University, 7600 Glover Road, Langley, BC V2Y 1Y1, Canada. *Toll-free phone:* 888-468-6898.

Tyndale University College & Seminary

Toronto, Ontario, Canada

http://www.tyndale.ca/

CONTACT

Tricia McKenley, Admissions Office Coordinator, Tyndale University College & Seminary, 3377 Bayview Avenue, Toronto, ON M2M 3S4, Canada. *Phone:* 416-218-6757 Ext. 6738. *Toll-free phone:* 877-896-3253. *E-mail:* admissions@tydale.ca.

Université de Moncton

Moncton, New Brunswick, Canada

http://www.umoncton.ca/

CONTACT

Miss Nicole Savois, Chief Admission Officer, Université de Moncton, Moncton, NB E1A 3E9, Canada. *Phone:* 506-858-4115. *Toll-free phone:* 800-363-8336. *E-mail:* gallanrm@umoncton.ca.

Université de Montréal

Montréal, Quebec, Canada

http://www.umontreal.ca/

- **Province-supported** university, founded 1920
- **Urban** 160-acre campus with easy access to Montreal
- **Endowment** $300.1 million
- **Coed**
- **Moderately difficult** entrance level

ACADEMICS

Calendar: trimesters. *Degrees:* certificates, diplomas, bachelor's, master's, doctoral, post-master's, and postbachelor's certificates.

Library: Bibliotheque des lettres et sciences humaines plus 18 others. *Books:* 1.5 million (physical), 366,149 (digital/electronic); *Serial titles:* 42,537 (physical), 88,591 (digital/electronic); *Databases:* 245. Weekly public service hours: 93; study areas open 24 hours, 5–7 days a week; students can reserve study rooms.

STUDENT LIFE

Housing options: coed, women-only, special housing for students with disabilities. Campus housing is university owned.

Activities and organizations: drama/theater group, student-run newspaper, radio station, choral group, Federation des Associations Etudiantes du Campus (FAECUM), Amnistie Internationale UdeM,

Action humanitaire et communautaire (AHC), Groupe de recherche et d'interet en developpement durable et en agriculture urbaine (GRIDDAU), Association generale des Etudiants de la Faculte de l'education permanente (AGEEFEP), national sororities.

Athletics Member CIS.

Campus security: 24-hour emergency response devices and patrols, student patrols, late-night transport/escort service, controlled dormitory access, cameras, alarm systems, access control system, crime prevention programs.

Student services: health clinic, personal/psychological counseling, legal services.

COSTS & FINANCIAL AID
Costs (2017–18) *One-time required fee:* $55 Canadian dollars. *Tuition:* province resident $3293 Canadian dollars full-time, $166 Canadian dollars per credit part-time; nonresident $8305 Canadian dollars full-time, $333 Canadian dollars per credit part-time; International tuition $22,494 Canadian dollars full-time. Full-time tuition and fees vary according to course load, location, and program. Part-time tuition and fees vary according to course load, location, and program. *Required fees:* $345 Canadian dollars full-time, $345 Canadian dollars per year part-time.

Financial Aid Of all full-time matriculated undergraduates who enrolled in 2006, 400 state and other part-time jobs.

APPLYING
Options: electronic application.

Application fee: $94.

Required: Diploma of Collegiate Studies (and transcript) or equivalent. *Required for some:* interview.

CONTACT
Mme. Marie-Claude Binette, Registrar, Université de Montréal, Bureau du registraire, CP 6128, Succursale Centre-Ville, Montreal, QC H3C 3J7, Canada. *Phone:* 514-343-2214. *Toll-free phone:* 866-977-7076 (in-state); 800-977-0761 (out-of-state). *Fax:* 514-343-2097. *E-mail:* marie-claude.binette@umontreal.ca.

Université de Saint-Boniface
Saint-Boniface, Manitoba, Canada
http://www.ustboniface.mb.ca/

CONTACT
Université de Saint-Boniface, 200 avenue de la Cathèdrale, Saint-Boniface, MB R2H 0H7, Canada.

Université de Sherbrooke
Sherbrooke, Quebec, Canada
http://www.usherbrooke.ca/

- **Independent** university, founded 1954
- **Urban** 800-acre campus with easy access to Montreal
- **Coed** 14,754 undergraduate students, 81% full-time, 54% women, 46% men
- **Moderately difficult** entrance level, 57% of applicants were admitted

UNDERGRAD STUDENTS
11,910 full-time, 2,844 part-time. Students come from 8 provinces and territories; 71 other countries; 1% are from out of state.

Freshmen:
Admission: 17,650 applied, 10,072 admitted, 3,168 enrolled.

FACULTY
Total: 3,126, 37% full-time.

ACADEMICS
Calendar: Canadian standard year. *Degrees:* certificates, diplomas, bachelor's, master's, and doctoral.

Special study options: accelerated degree program, adult/continuing education programs, cooperative education, English as a second language, internships, off-campus study, part-time degree program, services for LD students, study abroad, summer session for credit.

Computers: 300 computers/terminals are available on campus for general student use. Students can access the following: campus intranet, computer help desk, free student e-mail accounts, online (class) registration, online (class) schedules. Campuswide network is available. 100% of college-owned or -operated housing units are wired for high-speed Internet access. Wireless service is available via entire campus.

Library: Bibliotheque Roger-Maltais plus 5 others. Weekly public service hours: 73; students can reserve study rooms.

STUDENT LIFE
Housing options: coed, cooperative. Campus housing is university owned and is provided by a third party.

Activities and organizations: drama/theater group, student-run newspaper, radio station, choral group.

Athletics Member CIS. *Intercollegiate sports:* badminton M/W, cheerleading M/W, golf M/W, rugby M/W. *Intramural sports:* badminton M/W, basketball M/W, field hockey M/W, ice hockey M, racquetball M/W, soccer M/W, squash M/W, track and field M/W, ultimate Frisbee M/W, volleyball M/W, water polo M/W.

Campus security: 24-hour emergency response devices and patrols, late-night transport/escort service.

Student services: health clinic, personal/psychological counseling.

FINANCIAL AID
Financial Aid *Financial aid deadline:* 3/31.

APPLYING
Options: electronic application.

Application fee: $70 Canadian dollars.

Required: high school transcript. *Required for some:* interview, Test of French level, Casper test.

Notification: continuous until 4/15 (freshmen).

CONTACT
Mme. Lisa BEDARD, Admissions Officer, Université de Sherbrooke, 2500 boulevard de l'Universite, Sherbrooke, QC J1K 2R1, Canada. *Phone:* 819-821-7687. *Toll-free phone:* 800-267-UDES.

Université du Québec à Chicoutimi
Chicoutimi, Quebec, Canada
http://www.uqac.ca/

CONTACT
Jean Wauthier, Admissions Officer, Université du Québec à Chicoutimi, 555, boulevard de L'Université, Chicoutimi, QC G7H 2B1, Canada. *Phone:* 418-545-5005. *E-mail:* czoccast@uqac.uquebec.ca.

Université du Québec à Montréal
Montréal, Quebec, Canada
http://www.uqam.ca/

CONTACT
Ms. Lucille Boisselle-Roy, Admissions Officer, Université du Québec à Montréal, CP 8888, Succursale Centreville, Montréal, QC H2L 4S8, Canada. *Phone:* 514-987-3132. *E-mail:* admission@uqam.ca.

Université du Québec à Rimouski
Rimouski, Quebec, Canada
http://www.uqar.ca/

CONTACT
Ms. Marie Saint-Laurent, Admissions Officer, Université du Québec à Rimouski, 300 Allee des Ursulines, CP3300, Rimouski QC G5L 3A1, Canada. *Phone:* 418-724-1433. *E-mail:* philippe_horth@uqar.uquebec.ca.

Université du Québec à Trois-Rivières
Trois-Rivières, Quebec, Canada
http://www.uqtr.ca/

CONTACT
Ms. Jean Bois, Admissions Officer, Université du Québec à Trois-Rivières, 3351 blvd des Forges, Case post 500, Trois-Rivières, QC G9A 5H7, Canada. *Phone:* 819-376-5011. *Toll-free phone:* 800-365-0922. *Fax:* 819-376-5232. *E-mail:* registraire@uqtr.ca.

Université du Québec, École de technologie supérieure
Montréal, Quebec, Canada
http://www.etsmtl.ca/

CONTACT
Mme. Francine Gamache, Registraire, Université du Québec, École de technologie supérieure, 1100, rue Notre Dame Ouest, Montréal, QC H3C 1K3, Canada. *Phone:* 514-396-8885. *E-mail:* admission@ets.mtl.ca.

Université du Québec en Abitibi-Témiscamingue
Rouyn-Noranda, Quebec, Canada
http://www.uqat.ca/

CONTACT
Mrs. Monique Fay, Admissions Officer, Université du Québec en Abitibi-Témiscamingue, 445 boulevard de l'Université, Rouyn-Noranda, QC J9X 5E4, Canada. *Phone:* 819-762-0971. *E-mail:* micheline.chevalier@uqat.uquebec.ca.

Université du Québec en Outaouais
Gatineau, Quebec, Canada
http://www.uqo.ca/

CONTACT
Registrar's Office, Université du Québec en Outaouais, CP 1250, Succursale Hull, 101 Saint-Jean-Bosco, 101 rue Saint-Jean-Bosco, Gatineau, QC J8X 3X7, Canada. *Phone:* 819-595-3900 Ext. 1850. *Toll-free phone:* 800-567-1283. *Fax:* 819-773-1835. *E-mail:* registraire@uqo.ca.

Université Laval
Québec, Quebec, Canada
http://www.ulaval.ca/

CONTACT
Promotion and Recruitment Division, Université Laval, Quebec, QC G1K 7P4, Canada. *Phone:* 418-656-2764. *Toll-free phone:* 877-785-2825. *Fax:* 418-656-5216. *E-mail:* info@dap.ulaval.ca.

Université Sainte-Anne
Church Point, Nova Scotia, Canada
http://www.usainteanne.ca/

- **Province-supported** comprehensive, founded 1890
- **Rural** 115-acre campus
- **Endowment** $1.7 million
- **Coed** 304 undergraduate students, 97% full-time, 64% women, 36% men

UNDERGRAD STUDENTS
296 full-time, 8 part-time. Students come from 1 other province; 4 other countries; 9% are from out of state; 100% international; 60% live on campus.

FACULTY
Total: 65, 51% full-time.

ACADEMICS
Calendar: semesters. *Degrees:* certificates, diplomas, bachelor's, and master's.
Special study options: academic remediation for entering students, adult/continuing education programs, cooperative education, distance learning, double majors, English as a second language, off-campus study, part-time degree program, services for LD students, study abroad.
Unusual degree programs: 3-2 education.
Computers: 30 computers/terminals are available on campus for general student use. Students can access the following: campus intranet, free student e-mail accounts, online (class) grades, online (class) registration, online (class) schedules. Campuswide network is available. 100% of

college-owned or -operated housing units are wired for high-speed Internet access. Wireless service is available via entire campus.
Library: Louis R. Comea f. Number of weekly public service hours: g.u Library plus 1 other.

STUDENT LIFE
Housing options: coed. Campus housing is university owned and is provided by a third party.
Activities and organizations: drama/theater group, Student Organization, Amnesty International, Club de Plein Air, Education Committee, Commerce Committee.
Athletics Member CIS. *Intercollegiate sports:* badminton M/W, volleyball M(c)/W(c). *Intramural sports:* badminton M/W, cross-country running M/W, ice hockey M/W, rugby W, soccer M, swimming and diving M/W, table tennis M/W, tennis M/W, volleyball M/W, weight lifting M/W.
Campus security: student patrols, late-night transport/escort service, controlled dormitory access, 14-hour patrols by trained security personnel.
Student services: health clinic, personal/psychological counseling.

FINANCIAL AID
Financial Aid Of all full-time matriculated undergraduates who enrolled in 2013, 3 were judged to have need. *Financial aid deadline:* 11/15.

APPLYING
Required: high school transcript. *Required for some:* essay or personal statement, 3 letters of recommendation, criminal background ground check.

CONTACT
Université Sainte-Anne, Church Point, NS B0W 1M0, Canada.

University of Alberta
Edmonton, Alberta, Canada
http://www.ualberta.ca/

CONTACT
Melissa Padfield, Deputy Registrar, University of Alberta, Administration Building, Edmonton, AB T6G 2M7, Canada. *Phone:* 780-492-3113. *Toll-free phone:* 855-492-3113. *Fax:* 780-492-7172.

The University of British Columbia
Vancouver, British Columbia, Canada
http://www.ubc.ca/

CONTACT
The University of British Columbia, 2075 Wesbrook Mall, Vancouver, BC V6T 1Z1, Canada. *Phone:* 604-822-3014.

The University of British Columbia–Okanagan Campus
Kelowna, British Columbia, Canada
http://www.ubc.ca/okanagan/welcome.html

CONTACT
International Student Recruitment, The University of British Columbia–Okanagan Campus, UC222 University Centre, 3333 University Way, Kelowna, BC V1V 1V7, Canada. *Phone:* 250-807-9447. *Fax:* 250-807-8552.

★ University of Calgary
Calgary, Alberta, Canada
http://www.ucalgary.ca/

- **Province-supported** university, founded 1966, part of Campus Alberta
- **Urban** 213-hectare campus with easy access to Calgary
- **Endowment** $790.6 million
- **Coed**
- **Moderately difficult** entrance level

FACULTY
Student/faculty ratio: 23:1.

Canada

ACADEMICS
Calendar: semesters. _Degrees:_ diplomas, bachelor's, master's, doctoral, post-master's, and postbachelor's certificates.
Library: Taylor Family Digital Library plus 8 others. _Books:_ 3.2 million (physical), 975,202 (digital/electronic); _Databases:_ 92,645. Weekly public service hours: 101; students can reserve study rooms.

STUDENT LIFE
Housing options: coed, special housing for students with disabilities. Campus housing is university owned. Freshman applicants given priority for college housing.

Activities and organizations: drama/theater group, student-run newspaper, radio and television station, choral group, Muslim Students' Association, Snowboard Club, Ski Club, Video Game Club, Student Dance Club, national fraternities, national sororities.

Athletics Member CIS.

Campus security: 24-hour emergency response devices and patrols, late-night transport/escort service, controlled dormitory access.

Student services: health clinic, personal/psychological counseling, women's center, legal services.

COSTS & FINANCIAL AID
Costs (2017–18) _Tuition:_ province resident $5386 Canadian dollars full-time, $539 Canadian dollars per course part-time; nonresident $5386 Canadian dollars full-time, $539 Canadian dollars per course part-time; International tuition $18,338 Canadian dollars full-time. Full-time tuition and fees vary according to course load and program. Part-time tuition and fees vary according to course load and program. _Required fees:_ $1224 Canadian dollars full-time, $199 Canadian dollars per term part-time. _Room and board:_ $7771 Canadian dollars. Room and board charges vary according to board plan and housing facility.

Financial Aid _Financial aid deadline:_ 6/15.

APPLYING
Standardized Tests _Required for some:_ SAT or ACT (for admission).
Options: electronic application, early admission, deferred entrance.
Application fee: $145 Canadian dollars.

Required: high school transcript. _Required for some:_ essay or personal statement, minimum 3.7 GPA, 3 letters of recommendation.

CONTACT
Mr. Kaili Xu, Associate Registrar, Undergraduate Admissions, University of Calgary, 2500 University Drive NW, Calgary, AB T2N 1N4, Canada. _Phone:_ 403-210-7625. _E-mail:_ future.students@ucalgary.ca.

See below for display ad and page 1454 for the College Close-Up.

University of Guelph
Guelph, Ontario, Canada
http://www.uoguelph.ca/
- **Province-supported** university, founded 1964
- **Suburban** 1017-acre campus with easy access to Toronto
- **Endowment** $419.1 million
- **Coed** 21,179 undergraduate students
- **Moderately difficult** entrance level, 66% of applicants were admitted

UNDERGRAD STUDENTS
Students come from 13 provinces and territories; 100 other countries; 100% international; 28% live on campus.

Freshmen:
Admission: 23,750 applied, 15,564 admitted. _Average high school GPA:_ 3.5.
Retention: 91% of full-time freshmen returned.

FACULTY
Total: 756, 99% with terminal degrees.
Student/faculty ratio: 23:1.

ACADEMICS
Calendar: trimesters. _Degrees:_ certificates, diplomas, associate, bachelor's, master's, and doctoral.

Special study options: academic remediation for entering students, accelerated degree program, advanced placement credit, cooperative education, distance learning, double majors, English as a second language, honors programs, independent study, internships, off-campus study, part-

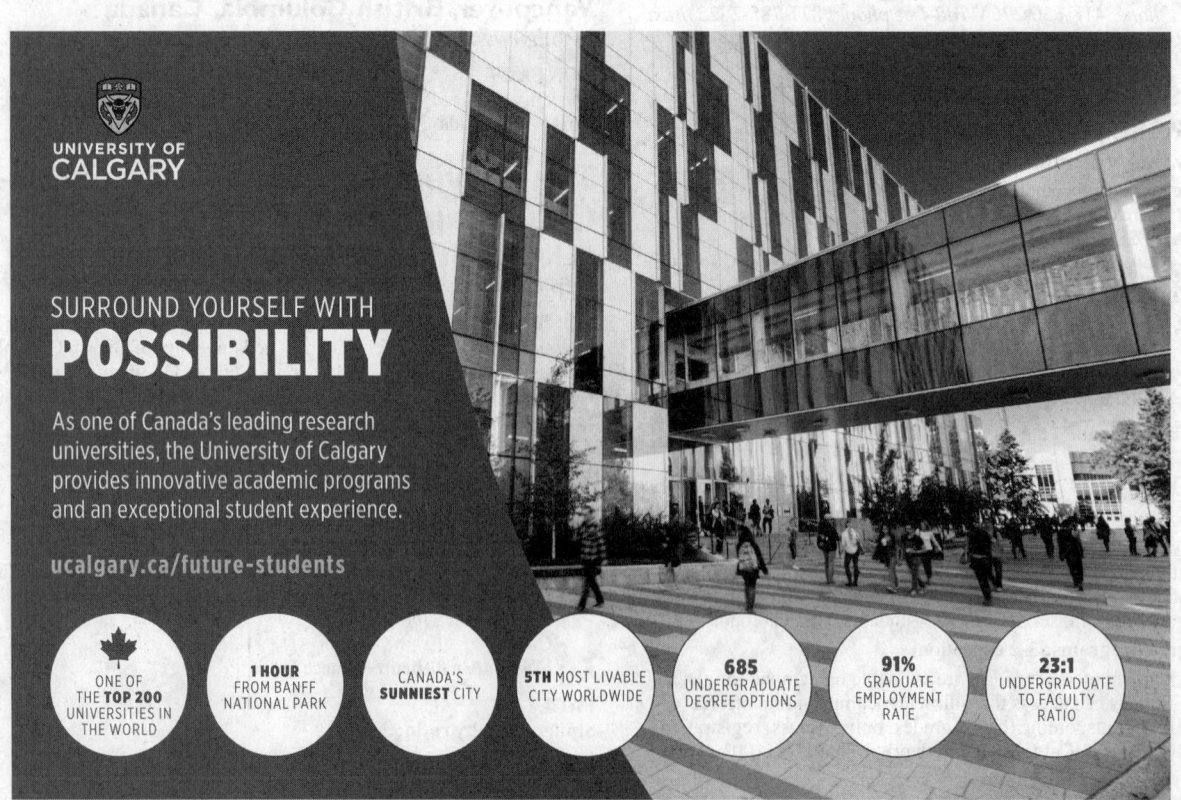

time degree program, services for LD students, student-designed majors, study abroad, summer session for credit.

Computers: 8,000 computers/terminals and 24,000 ports are available on campus for general student use. Students can access the following: campus intranet, computer help desk, free student e-mail accounts, online (class) grades, online (class) registration, online (class) schedules. Campuswide network is available. 100% of college-owned or -operated housing units are wired for high-speed Internet access. Wireless service is available via entire campus.

Library: University of Guelph Library plus 1 other. *Books:* 1.3 million (physical), 35,000 (digital/electronic); *Serial titles:* 1,617 (physical), 21,287 (digital/electronic); *Databases:* 280. Students can reserve study rooms.

STUDENT LIFE

Housing options: coed, women-only, cooperative, special housing for students with disabilities. Campus housing is university owned and is provided by a third party. Freshman campus housing is guaranteed.

Activities and organizations: drama/theater group, student-run newspaper, radio station, choral group, Guelph Gryphon Athletics, Habitat for Humanity, Curtain Call Productions, West Indian Students Association, OXFAM-Guelph Chapter.

Athletics Member CIS. *Intercollegiate sports:* baseball M, basketball M(s)/W(s), crew M/W, cross-country running M(s)/W(s), field hockey W(s), football M, golf M/W, ice hockey M(s)/W(s), lacrosse M/W, rowing M/W, rugby M(s)/W(s), skiing (cross-country) M/W, skiing (downhill) M/W, soccer M(s)/W(s), swimming and diving M(s)/W(s), track and field M(s)/W(s), volleyball M(s)/W(s), wrestling M(s)/W(s). *Intramural sports:* badminton M/W, basketball M/W, cheerleading M(c)/W(c), equestrian sports M(c)/W(c), fencing M(c)/W(c), football M/W, ice hockey M/W, rock climbing M(c)/W(c), sand volleyball M/W, soccer M/W, softball M/W(c), squash M(c)/W(c), table tennis M(c)/W(c), ultimate Frisbee M/W, volleyball M/W, water polo M(c)/W(c).

Campus security: 24-hour emergency response devices and patrols, student patrols, late-night transport/escort service, controlled dormitory access, video camera surveillance in parking lots, alarms in women's locker room.

Student services: health clinic, personal/psychological counseling, women's center, legal services.

COSTS

Costs (2018–19) *Tuition:* province resident $6571 full-time, $1313 per credit part-time; nonresident $6571 full-time; International tuition $20,840 full-time. Full-time tuition and fees vary according to degree level and program. Part-time tuition and fees vary according to course load, degree level, and program. No tuition increase for student's term of enrollment. *Required fees:* $22,501 full-time, $514 per credit part-time. *Room and board:* $11,132; room only: $6082. Room and board charges vary according to board plan and housing facility. *Payment plan:* installment. *Waivers:* senior citizens and employees or children of employees.

APPLYING

Standardized Tests *Required:* SAT or ACT (for admission).

Options: electronic application, early admission, deferred entrance.

Application fee: $150 Canadian dollars.

Required: high school transcript, minimum 3.0 GPA. *Required for some:* essay or personal statement.

Application deadlines: 3/1 (freshmen), 5/1 (transfers).

Notification: continuous until 5/27 (freshmen), continuous (transfers).

CONTACT

Ms. Janette Hogan, Assistant Registrar, Admissions, University of Guelph, L-3 University Centre, Guelph, ON N1G 2W1, Canada. *Phone:* 519-824-4120 Ext. 58529. *Fax:* 519-766-9481. *E-mail:* jhogan@uoguelph.ca.

University of King's College
Halifax, Nova Scotia, Canada
http://www.ukings.ca/
- **Province-supported** comprehensive, founded 1789
- **Urban** 4-acre campus
- **Endowment** $38.0 million
- **Coed** 827 undergraduate students
- **Moderately difficult** entrance level, 86% of applicants were admitted

UNDERGRAD STUDENTS
Students come from 12 provinces and territories; 15 other countries; 60% are from out of state; 23% live on campus.

Freshmen:
Admission: 566 applied, 488 admitted.

FACULTY
Total: 45, 100% full-time, 87% with terminal degrees.
Student/faculty ratio: 21:1.

ACADEMICS
Calendar: Canadian standard year. *Degrees:* bachelor's and master's.

Special study options: accelerated degree program, advanced placement credit, cooperative education, double majors, honors programs, independent study, internships, off-campus study, services for LD students, student-designed majors, study abroad, summer session for credit.

Computers: Students can access the following: online (class) grades, online (class) registration, online (class) schedules. Campuswide network is available. Wireless service is available via libraries, student centers.
Library: University of King's College Library. Students can reserve study rooms.

STUDENT LIFE
Housing options: coed, women-only. Campus housing is university owned. Freshman applicants given priority for college housing.

Activities and organizations: drama/theater group, student-run newspaper, radio station, choral group, King's Theatrical Society, student newspaper, King's College Dance Collective, St. Andrew's Missionary Society, King's Independent Film-Makers Society.

Athletics *Intercollegiate sports:* badminton M/W, basketball M/W, rugby M/W, soccer M/W, volleyball M/W. *Intramural sports:* badminton M/W, basketball M/W, soccer M/W, softball M/W, tennis M/W, ultimate Frisbee M/W, volleyball M/W, water polo M/W.

Campus security: student patrols, late-night transport/escort service, controlled dormitory access.

Student services: health clinic, personal/psychological counseling, women's center, legal services.

APPLYING
Standardized Tests *Required for some:* SAT or ACT (for admission).

Options: electronic application, early admission, early decision, deferred entrance.

Application fee: $65 Canadian dollars.

Required: high school transcript, minimum 3.0 GPA. *Required for some:* essay or personal statement, writing sample.

Application deadlines: 3/1 (freshmen), 6/1 (transfers).

Notification: continuous until 4/15 (freshmen), continuous (transfers).

CONTACT
Ms. Tara Wigglesworth-Hines, Assistant Registrar/Admissions, University of King's College, Registrar's Office, Halifax, NS B3H 3A1, Canada. *Phone:* 902-422-1271. *Fax:* 902-425-8183. *E-mail:* admissions@ukings.ns.ca.

University of Lethbridge
Lethbridge, Alberta, Canada
http://www.uleth.ca/
- **Province-supported** university, founded 1967
- **Urban** 576-acre campus
- **Coed**
- **Moderately difficult** entrance level

ACADEMICS

Calendar: semesters. *Degrees:* certificates, diplomas, bachelor's, master's, doctoral, post-master's, and postbachelor's certificates.
Library: The University of Lethbridge Library. Students can reserve study rooms.

STUDENT LIFE

Housing options: coed. Campus housing is university owned.
Activities and organizations: drama/theater group, student-run newspaper, radio station, choral group, national fraternities.
Athletics Member CIS.
Campus security: 24-hour emergency response devices and patrols, student patrols, late-night transport/escort service, controlled dormitory access, video camera monitored entrances, hallways.
Student services: health clinic, personal/psychological counseling, women's center.

COSTS

Costs (2017–18) *Tuition:* province resident $4974 Canadian dollars full-time; nonresident $4974 Canadian dollars full-time; International tuition $15,976 Canadian dollars full-time. Full-time tuition and fees vary according to course load. Part-time tuition and fees vary according to course load. *Required fees:* $1056 Canadian dollars full-time. *Room and board:* $6752 Canadian dollars; room only: $2792 Canadian dollars. Room and board charges vary according to board plan and housing facility.

APPLYING

Options: electronic application, deferred entrance.
Application fee: $100 Canadian dollars.
Required: high school transcript, minimum 2.0 GPA. *Required for some:* minimum 3.0 GPA, interview.

CONTACT

Registrar's Office, University of Lethbridge, 4401 University Drive, Lethbridge, AB T1K 3M4, Canada. *Phone:* 403-320-5700. *Fax:* 403-329-5159. *E-mail:* regoffice@uleth.ca.

University of Manitoba

Winnipeg, Manitoba, Canada
http://www.umanitoba.ca/

CONTACT

Mr. Peter Dueck, Director of Enrollment Services, University of Manitoba, Winnipeg, MB R3T 2N2, Canada. *Phone:* 204-474-6382.

University of New Brunswick Fredericton

Fredericton, New Brunswick, Canada
http://www.unb.ca/

CONTACT

University of New Brunswick Fredericton, PO Box 4400, Fredericton, NB E3B 5A3, Canada. *Phone:* 506-453-4865.

University of New Brunswick Saint John

Saint John, New Brunswick, Canada
http://www.unb.ca/

CONTACT

University of New Brunswick Saint John, PO Box 5050, Saint John, NB E2L 4L5, Canada.

University of Northern British Columbia

Prince George, British Columbia, Canada
http://www.unbc.ca/

CONTACT

Pamela Flagel, Associate Registrar Enrollment, University of Northern British Columbia, Office of the Registrar, 3333 University Way, Prince George, BC V2N 4Z9, Canada. *Phone:* 250-960-6300. *Fax:* 250-960-6330. *E-mail:* registrar-info@unbc.ca.

University of Ottawa

Ottawa, Ontario, Canada
http://www.uottawa.ca/

CONTACT

University of Ottawa, 550 Cumberland Street, Ottawa, ON K1N 6N5, Canada. *Phone:* 613-562-5800 Ext. 1594.

University of Prince Edward Island

Charlottetown, Prince Edward Island, Canada
http://home.upei.ca/

CONTACT

University of Prince Edward Island, 550 University Avenue, Charlottetown, PE C1A 4P3, Canada. *Phone:* 902-566-0634.

University of Regina

Regina, Saskatchewan, Canada
http://www.uregina.ca/

- **Province-supported** university, founded 1974, part of intentionally left blank
- **Urban** 76-hectare campus
- **Endowment** $46.8 million
- **Coed** 13,374 undergraduate students, 82% full-time, 61% women, 39% men
- 58% of applicants were admitted

UNDERGRAD STUDENTS

11,030 full-time, 2,344 part-time. Students come from 12 provinces and territories; 109 other countries; 16% are from out of state; 4% transferred in; 10% live on campus.

Freshmen:
Admission: 5,695 applied, 3,331 admitted, 2,096 enrolled. *Average high school GPA:* 3.7.
Retention: 83% of full-time freshmen returned.

FACULTY

Total: 417, 104% full-time, 75% with terminal degrees.
Student/faculty ratio: 23:1.

ACADEMICS

Calendar: semesters. *Degrees:* certificates, diplomas, bachelor's, master's, doctoral, and postbachelor's certificates.
Special study options: academic remediation for entering students, adult/continuing education programs, advanced placement credit, cooperative education, distance learning, double majors, English as a second language, honors programs, independent study, internships, off-campus study, part-time degree program, services for LD students, student-designed majors, study abroad, summer session for credit.
Computers: 412 computers/terminals are available on campus for general student use. Students can access the following: computer help desk, free student e-mail accounts, online (class) grades, online (class) registration, online (class) schedules. Campuswide network is available. 100% of college-owned or -operated housing units are wired for high-speed Internet access. Wireless service is available via entire campus.
Library: Dr. John Archer Library plus 5 others. *Books:* 832,203 (physical), 571,698 (digital/electronic); *Serial titles:* 133,988 (physical), 123,622 (digital/electronic); *Databases:* 517. Weekly public service hours: 105; students can reserve study rooms.

STUDENT LIFE

Housing options: special housing for students with disabilities. Campus housing is university owned. Freshman campus housing is guaranteed.

Activities and organizations: drama/theater group, student-run newspaper, University of Regina Students' Union, Biology Undergraduate and Graduate Society, Institute of Electrical and Electronics Engineers (IEEE) U of R Students Branch, UR Toastmasters, Inter-Varsity Christian Fellowship.

Athletics Member CIS. *Intercollegiate sports:* basketball M(s)/W(s), cross-country running M(s)/W(s), football M(s), ice hockey M(s)/W(s), soccer W(s), swimming and diving M(s)/W(s), track and field M(s)/W(s), volleyball M(s)/W(s), wrestling M(s)/W(s). *Intramural sports:* badminton M/W, basketball M/W, bowling M/W, cheerleading M(c)/W(c), fencing M(c)/W(c), football M/W, golf M(c)/W(c), rowing M(c)/W(c), rugby M(c)/W(c), soccer M/W, softball M/W(c), tennis M/W, ultimate Frisbee M/W, volleyball M/W.

Campus security: 24-hour emergency response devices and patrols, controlled dormitory access, CCTV, card access and some alarm monitoring.

Student services: health clinic, personal/psychological counseling, women's center.

COSTS

Costs (2017–18) *Tuition:* province resident $6353 full-time, $216 per credit hour part-time; International tuition $19,058 full-time. Full-time tuition and fees vary according to course load and program. Part-time tuition and fees vary according to course load and program. *Required fees:* $778 full-time. *Room and board:* $7320; room only: $6664. Room and board charges vary according to board plan and housing facility. *Waivers:* senior citizens and employees or children of employees.

APPLYING

Standardized Tests *Required for some:* SAT or ACT (for admission).

Options: electronic application, early admission, early action, deferred entrance.

Application fee: $100 Canadian dollars.

Required: high school transcript, minimum 2.3 GPA. *Required for some:* essay or personal statement, interview, portfolio, audition, 2.3 minimum GPA.

Application deadlines: 8/15 (freshmen), 8/15 (transfers), 6/15 (early action).

CONTACT

University of Regina, 3737 Wascana Parkway, Regina, SK S4S 0A2, Canada. *Phone:* 306-585-5345. *Toll-free phone:* 800-644-4756.

University of Saskatchewan
Saskatoon, Saskatchewan, Canada
http://www.usask.ca/

- **Province-supported** university, founded 1907
- **Urban** 1865-acre campus
- **Coed** 18,645 undergraduate students, 90% full-time, 57% women, 43% men
- 65% of applicants were admitted

UNDERGRAD STUDENTS

16,858 full-time, 1,787 part-time. 23% are from out of state; 12% live on campus.

Freshmen:

Admission: 11,061 applied, 7,209 admitted, 2,955 enrolled.

Retention: 82% of full-time freshmen returned.

FACULTY

Total: 1,001.

Student/faculty ratio: 20:1.

ACADEMICS

Calendar: Canadian standard year. *Degrees:* certificates, diplomas, bachelor's, master's, doctoral, and postbachelor's certificates.

Special study options: accelerated degree program, advanced placement credit, cooperative education, distance learning, double majors, English as a second language, honors programs, independent study, internships, off-

campus study, part-time degree program, services for LD students, study abroad, summer session for credit.

Computers: Students can access the following: computer help desk, free student e-mail accounts, online (class) grades, online (class) registration, online (class) schedules, student portal. 100% of college-owned or -operated housing units are wired for high-speed Internet access. Wireless service is available via entire campus.

Library: University of Saskatchewan Main Library plus 7 others.

STUDENT LIFE

Housing options: coed. Campus housing is university owned.

Activities and organizations: drama/theater group, student-run newspaper, choral group.

Athletics Member CIS. *Intercollegiate sports:* basketball M/W, cross-country running M/W, football M, ice hockey M/W, soccer M/W, track and field M/W, volleyball M/W, wrestling M/W. *Intramural sports:* badminton M/W, basketball M/W, football M/W, ice hockey M/W, soccer M/W, ultimate Frisbee M/W, volleyball M/W.

Campus security: 24-hour emergency response devices and patrols, student patrols, late-night transport/escort service, controlled dormitory access.

Student services: health clinic, personal/psychological counseling, women's center, legal services.

COSTS & FINANCIAL AID

Costs (2017–18) *Tuition:* province resident $5954 full-time; nonresident $5954 full-time; International tuition $15,480 full-time. Full-time tuition and fees vary according to course load and program. *Required fees:* $423 full-time. *Room and board:* $8050; room only: $2833. Room and board charges vary according to board plan, housing facility, and location. *Payment plan:* installment. *Waivers:* senior citizens and employees or children of employees.

Financial Aid *Financial aid deadline:* 3/15.

APPLYING

Options: electronic application, early admission.

Application fee: $90 Canadian dollars.

Required: high school transcript. *Required for some:* essay or personal statement, interview.

Notification: continuous (freshmen), continuous (transfers).

CONTACT

University of Saskatchewan, 105 Administration Place, Saskatoon, SK S7N 5A2, Canada. *Phone:* 306-966-5788.

University of the Fraser Valley
Abbotsford, British Columbia, Canada
http://www.ufv.ca/

- **Province-supported** comprehensive, founded 1974
- **Urban** 64-hectare campus with easy access to Vancouver
- **Endowment** $11.0 million
- **Coed** 8,763 undergraduate students, 44% full-time, 58% women, 42% men

UNDERGRAD STUDENTS

3,885 full-time, 4,878 part-time. Students come from 10 provinces and territories; 62 other countries; 4% American Indian or Alaska Native, non-Hispanic/Latino; 82% Race/ethnicity unknown; 14% international.

Freshmen:

Admission: 1,534 enrolled.

Retention: 80% of full-time freshmen returned.

FACULTY

Total: 688, 47% full-time, 29% with terminal degrees.

ACADEMICS

Calendar: semesters. *Degrees:* certificates, diplomas, associate, bachelor's, master's, and postbachelor's certificates.

Special study options: academic remediation for entering students, adult/continuing education programs, advanced placement credit, cooperative education, distance learning, double majors, English as a second language, honors programs, independent study, internships, off-campus study, part-time degree program, services for LD students, student-designed majors, study abroad, summer session for credit.

Computers: Students can access the following: computer help desk, free student e-mail accounts, online (class) grades, online (class) registration, online (class) schedules. Wireless service is available via entire campus.

Library: Peter Jones Library plus 3 others. *Books:* 181,000 (physical), 37,000 (digital/electronic). Students can reserve study rooms.

STUDENT LIFE

Housing options: coed. Campus housing is university owned. Freshman applicants given priority for college housing.

Activities and organizations: drama/theater group, student-run newspaper, radio station.

Athletics Member CIS. *Intercollegiate sports:* basketball M(s)/W(s), soccer M(s)/W(s), wrestling M(c)/W(c). *Intramural sports:* badminton M/W, basketball M/W, cross-country running M(c)/W(c), golf M/W, rowing M/W, soccer M/W, volleyball M/W, wrestling M(c)/W(c).

Campus security: 24-hour emergency response devices and patrols, late-night transport/escort service, controlled dormitory access.

Student services: personal/psychological counseling.

COSTS

Costs (2018–19) *Tuition:* province resident $4873 full-time, $162 per credit hour part-time; nonresident $4873 full-time, $162 per credit hour part-time; International tuition $17,150 full-time. Full-time tuition and fees vary according to course load. Part-time tuition and fees vary according to course load. *Required fees:* $526 full-time, $158 per term part-time. *Room and board:* $7941; room only: $5941. Room and board charges vary according to board plan. *Waivers:* senior citizens and employees or children of employees.

APPLYING

Options: electronic application, early admission, deferred entrance.

Application fee: $45 Canadian dollars.

Required: high school transcript. *Required for some:* essay or personal statement, 2 letters of recommendation, interview, minimum GPA of 2.0 to 2.67.

Notification: continuous (freshmen), continuous (transfers).

CONTACT

Mr. Daniel Goertz, Recruitment Coordinator, University of the Fraser Valley, 33844 King Road, Abbotsford, BC V2S 7M8, Canada. *Phone:* 604-504-7441 Ext. 4693. *Toll-free phone:* 888-504-7441. *E-mail:* daniel.goertz@ufv.ca.

University of Toronto
Toronto, Ontario, Canada
http://www.utoronto.ca/

- **Province-supported** university, founded 1827
- **Urban** 714-hectare campus with easy access to Greater Toronto Area
- **Endowment** $2.4 billion
- **Coed** 70,728 undergraduate students, 100% full-time, 52% women, 48% men
- **Very difficult** entrance level

UNDERGRAD STUDENTS

70,728 full-time. Students come from 12 provinces and territories; 168 other countries; 6% are from out of state; 14% live on campus.

FACULTY

Total: 14,420.

Student/faculty ratio: 24:1.

ACADEMICS

Calendar: fall/winter terms and a summer session. *Degrees:* certificates, diplomas, bachelor's, master's, and doctoral.

Special study options: adult/continuing education programs, cooperative education, double majors, English as a second language, independent study, internships, off-campus study, part-time degree program, services for LD students, study abroad, summer session for credit.

Computers: 2,000 computers/terminals are available on campus for general student use. Students can access the following: campus intranet, computer help desk, free student e-mail accounts, online (class) grades,

online (class) registration, online (class) schedules. Campuswide network is available. Wireless service is available via entire campus.

Library: Robarts Library plus 43 others. *Books:* 19.4 million (physical), 6.0 million (digital/electronic). Students can reserve study rooms.

STUDENT LIFE

Housing options: coed, women-only. Campus housing is university owned and leased by the school. Freshman campus housing is guaranteed.

Activities and organizations: drama/theater group, student-run newspaper, radio station, choral group, national fraternities, national sororities.

Athletics Member CIS. *Intercollegiate sports:* archery M/W, badminton M/W, basketball M/W, crew M, cross-country running M/W, fencing M/W, field hockey W, football M, golf M, gymnastics M/W, ice hockey M/W, rugby M, skiing (cross-country) M/W, skiing (downhill) M/W, soccer M/W, squash M/W, swimming and diving M/W, tennis M/W, track and field M/W, volleyball M/W, wrestling M. *Intramural sports:* archery M/W, badminton M/W, basketball M/W, crew M, fencing M/W, field hockey W, football M/W, gymnastics M/W, ice hockey M/W, lacrosse M/W, racquetball M, rugby M, skiing (downhill) M/W, soccer M/W, squash M/W, swimming and diving M/W, tennis M/W, track and field M/W, volleyball M/W, water polo M/W.

Campus security: 24-hour emergency response devices and patrols, student patrols, late-night transport/escort service.

Student services: health clinic, personal/psychological counseling, women's center, legal services.

COSTS & FINANCIAL AID

Costs (2017–18) *Tuition:* province resident $4883 Canadian dollars full-time; nonresident $4883 Canadian dollars full-time. Full-time tuition and fees vary according to course level, course load, program, and student level. Part-time tuition and fees vary according to course load, program, and student level. *Required fees:* $1000 Canadian dollars full-time. *Room and board:* Room and board charges vary according to board plan, housing facility, location, and student level. *Payment plan:* installment. *Waivers:* senior citizens and employees or children of employees.

Financial Aid Of all full-time matriculated undergraduates who enrolled in 2017, 3,500 state and other part-time jobs.

APPLYING

Standardized Tests *Required:* SAT and SAT Subject Tests or ACT (for admission).

Options: electronic application, deferred entrance.

Application fee: $255 Canadian dollars.

Required: high school transcript. *Required for some:* essay or personal statement, interview.

Application deadlines: 1/19 (freshmen), 7/1 (transfers).

Notification: continuous (freshmen), continuous (transfers).

CONTACT

University of Toronto, 27 King's College Circle, Toronto, ON M5S 1A1, Canada. *Phone:* 416-978-2190. *Fax:* 416-978-7022.

University of Victoria
Victoria, British Columbia, Canada
http://www.uvic.ca/

CONTACT

Mr. Bruno Rocca, Student Recruitment Director, University of Victoria, PO Box 1700, STN CSC, Victoria, BC V8W 2Y2, Canada. *Phone:* 250-721-8121 Ext. 8109. *Fax:* 250-721-6225. *E-mail:* admit@uvic.ca.

University of Waterloo
Waterloo, Ontario, Canada
http://www.uwaterloo.ca/

- **Province-supported** university, founded 1957
- **Suburban** 1112-acre campus with easy access to Toronto
- **Endowment** $294.5 million
- **Coed** 33,197 undergraduate students, 96% full-time, 47% women, 53% men
- **Moderately difficult** entrance level

UNDERGRAD STUDENTS
31,886 full-time, 1,311 part-time.

Freshmen:
Admission: 8,119 enrolled.

FACULTY
Total: 1,211.
Student/faculty ratio: 26:1.

ACADEMICS
Calendar: trimesters. *Degrees:* bachelor's, master's, and doctoral.

Special study options: cooperative education, distance learning, double majors, English as a second language, honors programs, internships, off-campus study, part-time degree program, services for LD students, study abroad.

Computers: 6,000 computers/terminals are available on campus for general student use. Students can access the following: campus intranet, computer help desk, free student e-mail accounts, online (class) grades, online (class) registration, online (class) schedules. Campuswide network is available. Wireless service is available via entire campus.
Library: Dana Porter Library plus 11 others. Students can reserve study rooms.

STUDENT LIFE
Housing options: coed. Campus housing is university owned. Freshman campus housing is guaranteed.

Activities and organizations: drama/theater group, student-run newspaper, choral group, marching band, national fraternities, national sororities.

Athletics *Intercollegiate sports:* badminton M/W, baseball M, basketball M/W, cheerleading M/W, cross-country running M/W, field hockey W, football M, golf M/W, ice hockey M/W, rugby M/W, skiing (cross-country) M/W, soccer M/W, squash M/W, swimming and diving M/W, tennis M/W, track and field M/W, volleyball M/W. *Intramural sports:* archery M(c)/W(c), badminton M(c)/W(c), baseball M/W, basketball M/W, bowling M/W, crew M(c)/W(c), cross-country running M(c)/W(c), equestrian sports M(c)/W(c), fencing M(c)/W(c), football M/W, golf M(c)/W(c), ice hockey M/W, racquetball M(c)/W(c), rock climbing M(c)/W(c), sailing M(c)/W(c), skiing (cross-country) M(c)/W(c), skiing (downhill) M(c)/W(c), soccer M(c)/W(c), softball M/W, squash M(c)/W(c), swimming and diving M(c)/W(c), table tennis M(c)/W(c), tennis M/W, ultimate Frisbee M(c)/W(c), volleyball M/W, water polo M(c)/W(c), weight lifting M(c)/W(c).

Campus security: 24-hour emergency response devices and patrols, student patrols, late-night transport/escort service, controlled dormitory access.

Student services: health clinic, personal/psychological counseling, women's center, legal services.

COSTS
Costs (2017–18) *Tuition:* province resident $10,400 full-time, $737 per course part-time; International tuition $28,000 full-time. Full-time tuition and fees vary according to course load, degree level, program, and student level. Part-time tuition and fees vary according to course load, degree level, program, and student level. *Required fees:* $800 full-time, $65 per term part-time. *Room and board:* $10,734; room only: $5534. Room and board charges vary according to board plan, housing facility, and location. *Payment plan:* deferred payment. *Waivers:* senior citizens and employees or children of employees.

APPLYING
Options: electronic application, early admission, deferred entrance.
Application fee: $140 Canadian dollars.
Required: high school transcript. *Required for some:* essay or personal statement, interview. *Recommended:* essay or personal statement.
Notification: 5/26 (freshmen).

CONTACT
University of Waterloo, 200 University Avenue West, Waterloo, ON N2L 3G1, Canada. *Phone:* 519-888-4567. *E-mail:* myapplication@uwaterloo.ca.

The University of Western Ontario
London, Ontario, Canada
http://www.uwo.ca/

CONTACT
Undergraduate Recruitment and Admissions, The University of Western Ontario, Western University, London, ON N6A 3K7, Canada. *Phone:* 519-661-2100. *Fax:* 519-661-3710. *E-mail:* reg-admissions@uwo.ca.

University of Windsor
Windsor, Ontario, Canada
http://www.uwindsor.ca/

- **Province-supported** university, founded 1857
- **Urban** 125-acre campus with easy access to Detroit
- **Endowment** $84.3 million
- **Coed**

FACULTY
Student/faculty ratio: 23:1.

ACADEMICS
Calendar: semesters. *Degrees:* certificates, bachelor's, master's, doctoral, and postbachelor's certificates.
Library: Leddy Library plus 2 others. *Books:* 886,201 (physical), 673,676 (digital/electronic); *Serial titles:* 33,354 (physical), 85,907 (digital/electronic). Weekly public service hours: 108; students can reserve study rooms.

STUDENT LIFE
Housing options: coed, men-only, women-only, special housing for students with disabilities. Campus housing is university owned. Freshman campus housing is guaranteed.

Activities and organizations: drama/theater group, student-run newspaper, radio station, choral group, University of Windsor Student Alliance, Environmental Awareness Association, Social Science Society, Commerce Society, Science Society, national fraternities.

Athletics Member CIS.

Campus security: 24-hour emergency response devices and patrols, student patrols, late-night transport/escort service, controlled dormitory access.

Student services: health clinic, personal/psychological counseling, women's center, legal services.

COSTS & FINANCIAL AID
Costs (2017–18) *Tuition:* province resident $8000 Canadian dollars full-time, $800 Canadian dollars per course part-time; nonresident $8000 Canadian dollars full-time, $2500 Canadian dollars per course part-time; International tuition $24,000 Canadian dollars full-time. Full-time tuition and fees vary according to course level, course load, degree level, program, and student level. Part-time tuition and fees vary according to course level, course load, degree level, program, and student level. *Required fees:* $600 Canadian dollars per year part-time. *Room and board:* $11,000 Canadian dollars; room only: $6400 Canadian dollars. Room and board charges vary according to board plan, housing facility, and location.

Financial Aid *Financial aid deadline:* 6/15.

APPLYING
Standardized Tests *Required for some:* SAT or ACT (for admission), SAT and SAT Subject Tests or ACT (for admission), SAT Subject Tests (for admission).
Options: electronic application.
Required: high school transcript, minimum 3.0 GPA. *Required for some:* essay or personal statement, minimum 3.3 GPA, 1 letter of recommendation, interview.

CONTACT
Ms. Charlene Yates, Associate Registrar, University of Windsor, Office of the Registrar, 401 Sunset Avenue, Windsor, ON N9B 3P4, Canada. *Phone:* 519-253-3000 Ext. 3332. *Toll-free phone:* 800-864-2860. *Fax:* 519-971-3653. *E-mail:* registrar@uwindsor.ca.

The University of Winnipeg
Winnipeg, Manitoba, Canada
http://www.uwinnipeg.ca/

CONTACT
Mr. Colin Russell, Registrar, The University of Winnipeg, 515 Portage Avenue, Winnipeg, MB R3B 2E9, Canada. *Phone:* 204-786-9776. *Fax:* 204-786-8656. *E-mail:* admissions@uwinnipeg.ca.

Vancouver Island University
Nanaimo, British Columbia, Canada
http://www.viu.ca/

CONTACT
Mr. Andrew Amour, Associate Registrar, Admissions and Registration, Vancouver Island University, 900 Fifth Street, Nanaimo, BC V9R 5S5, Canada. *Phone:* 250-740-6355. *Fax:* 250-740-6479.

Vanguard College
Edmonton, Alberta, Canada
http://www.vanguardcollege.com/

CONTACT
Vanguard College, 12140 103rd Street, Edmonton, AB T5G 2J9, Canada. *Phone:* 780-452-0808 Ext. 231. *Toll-free phone:* 866-222-0808. *E-mail:* admissions@vanguardcollege.com.

Wilfrid Laurier University
Waterloo, Ontario, Canada
http://www.wlu.ca/

CONTACT
Wilfrid Laurier University, 75 University Avenue West, Waterloo, ON N2L 3C5, Canada. *Phone:* 519-884-0710 Ext. 6099.

York University
Toronto, Ontario, Canada
http://www.yorku.ca/

CONTACT
International Recruitment, York University, N301 Bennett Centre for Student Services, 4700 Keele Street, Toronto, ON M3J 1P3, Canada. *Phone:* 416-736-5825. *Fax:* 416-736-5741. *E-mail:* intlenq@yorku.ca.

INTERNATIONAL

BULGARIA

American University in Bulgaria
Blagoevgrad, Bulgaria
http://www.aubg.edu/

- **Independent** comprehensive, founded 1991
- **Small-town** 12-acre campus with easy access to Sofia, Bulgaria
- **Endowment** $26.2 million
- **Coed** 857 undergraduate students, 100% full-time, 51% women, 49% men
- **Very difficult** entrance level, 82% of applicants were admitted

UNDERGRAD STUDENTS
857 full-time. Students come from 40 other countries; 100% Race/ethnicity unknown; 0.6% transferred in; 83% live on campus.

Freshmen:
Admission: 491 applied, 405 admitted, 183 enrolled. *Average high school GPA:* 3.8. *Test scores:* SAT evidence-based reading and writing scores over 500: 100%; SAT math scores over 500: 100%; ACT scores over 18: 100%; SAT evidence-based reading and writing scores over 600: 55%; SAT math scores over 600: 73%; ACT scores over 24: 100%; SAT math scores over 700: 41%.
Retention: 95% of full-time freshmen returned.

FACULTY
Total: 74, 59% full-time, 74% with terminal degrees.
Student/faculty ratio: 16:1.

ACADEMICS
Calendar: semesters. *Degrees:* bachelor's and master's.
Special study options: advanced placement credit, double majors, honors programs, independent study, internships, services for LD students, student-designed majors, study abroad.
Computers: 372 computers/terminals and 8 ports are available on campus for general student use. Students can access the following: campus intranet, computer help desk, free student e-mail accounts, online (class) grades, online (class) registration, online (class) schedules. Campuswide network is available. 100% of college-owned or -operated housing units

are wired for high-speed Internet access. Wireless service is available via entire campus.
Library: Panitza Library. *Books:* 129,703 (physical), 297,300 (digital/electronic); *Serial titles:* 684 (physical), 35,918 (digital/electronic); *Databases:* 33. Weekly public service hours: 56; study areas open 24 hours, 5–7 days a week; students can reserve study rooms.

STUDENT LIFE
Housing options: on-campus residence required through senior year; coed, special housing for students with disabilities. Campus housing is university owned. Freshman campus housing is guaranteed.

Activities and organizations: drama/theater group, student-run newspaper, radio station, choral group, Computer Science Student Union, AUBG Political Science Club, Better Community Club, AUBG Broadway Performance Club, Business Club.

Athletics *Intramural sports:* basketball M/W, cheerleading W(c), equestrian sports M(c)/W(c), football M(c), gymnastics W, soccer M(c), softball M/W, volleyball M/W.

Campus security: 24-hour emergency response devices and patrols, controlled dormitory access.

Student services: health clinic, personal/psychological counseling.

COSTS
Costs (2018–19) *Comprehensive fee:* $13,890 includes full-time tuition ($11,700), mandatory fees ($580), and room and board ($1610). Full-time tuition and fees vary according to course load and location. Part-time tuition: $975 per credit hour. Part-time tuition and fees vary according to course load and location. *College room only:* $1410. Room and board charges vary according to housing facility. *Payment plan:* installment. *Waivers:* employees or children of employees.

APPLYING
Standardized Tests *Required for some:* TOEFL, IELTS, or ESOL for students whose primary language is not English. *Recommended:* SAT (for admission), SAT or ACT (for admission).

Options: electronic application, early admission, deferred entrance.

Required: essay or personal statement, high school transcript, minimum 3.0 GPA, 2 letters of recommendation.

Application deadlines: 6/1 (freshmen), 6/1 (transfers).

CONTACT
Ms. Boriana Shalyavska, Director of Admissions, American University in Bulgaria, 1 Izmirliev Square, 1st Floor, Blagoevgrad 2700, Bulgaria. *Phone:* 359-73 888 218. *Fax:* 359-73 883 227. *E-mail:* admissions@aubg.edu.

EGYPT

The American University in Cairo
Cairo, Egypt
http://www.aucegypt.edu/
- **Independent** comprehensive, founded 1919
- **Suburban** 260-acre campus with easy access to Cairo
- **Endowment** $519
- **Coed** 5,545 undergraduate students, 89% full-time, 54% women, 46% men
- **Very difficult** entrance level, 54% of applicants were admitted

UNDERGRAD STUDENTS
4,916 full-time, 629 part-time. Students come from 26 other countries; 0.6% transferred in; 9% live on campus.

Freshmen:
Admission: 2,387 applied, 1,286 admitted, 921 enrolled. *Test scores:* SAT evidence-based reading and writing scores over 500: 82%; SAT math scores over 500: 92%; SAT evidence-based reading and writing scores over 600: 21%; SAT math scores over 600: 45%; SAT evidence-based reading and writing scores over 700: 1%; SAT math scores over 700: 8%.
Retention: 91% of full-time freshmen returned.

FACULTY
Total: 717, 58% full-time, 70% with terminal degrees.
Student/faculty ratio: 11:1.

ACADEMICS
Calendar: semesters. *Degrees:* diplomas, bachelor's, master's, and doctoral (majority of students are Egyptians; enrollment open to all nationalities).

Special study options: academic remediation for entering students, cooperative education, double majors, English as a second language, honors programs, independent study, internships, services for LD students, study abroad, summer session for credit.

Computers: 120 computers/terminals are available on campus for general student use. Students can access the following: campus intranet, computer help desk, free student e-mail accounts, online (class) grades, online (class) registration, online (class) schedules, learning management system, unofficial transcripts, ID creation. Campuswide network is available. 100% of college-owned or -operated housing units are wired for high-speed Internet access. Wireless service is available via entire campus.

Library: American University in Cairo Library plus 1 other. *Books:* 546,020 (physical), 311,887 (digital/electronic); *Databases:* 123. Weekly public service hours: 80; students can reserve study rooms.

STUDENT LIFE
Housing options: men-only, women-only, special housing for students with disabilities. Campus housing is university owned and leased by the school. Freshman applicants given priority for college housing.

Activities and organizations: drama/theater group, student-run newspaper, choral group, AIESEC, Theater and Film Club, VIA, ACT, Mashrou3 Kheir.

Athletics *Intercollegiate sports:* archery M, badminton M/W, basketball M/W, crew M/W, fencing M/W, gymnastics M/W, soccer M/W, squash M/W, swimming and diving M/W, table tennis M/W, tennis M/W, track and field M/W, volleyball M/W, water polo M. *Intramural sports:* basketball M/W, soccer M/W, squash M/W, table tennis M/W, tennis M/W, volleyball M/W, weight lifting M.

Campus security: 24-hour emergency response devices and patrols, controlled dormitory access.

Student services: health clinic, personal/psychological counseling.

FINANCIAL AID
Financial Aid *Average financial aid package:* $3711. *Average need-based gift aid:* $2991. *Financial aid deadline:* 3/14.

APPLYING
Standardized Tests *Required for some:* SAT (for admission), SAT or ACT (for admission), SAT Subject Tests (for admission).

Options: electronic application, early admission, early action, deferred entrance.

Application fee: $85.

Required: essay or personal statement, high school transcript, minimum 2.0 GPA.

Application deadlines: 3/1 (freshmen), 3/1 (transfers), 3/1 (early action).

Notification: continuous (freshmen), continuous (transfers).

CONTACT
Ms. Randa Kamel, Chief Enrollment Officer, The American University in Cairo, AUC Avenue, PO Box 74 New Cairo 11835, Cairo, Egypt. *Phone:* 202-26154601. *E-mail:* randakamel@aucegypt.edu.

FRANCE

The American University of Paris
Paris, France
http://www.aup.edu/
- **Independent** comprehensive, founded 1962
- **Urban** campus with easy access to Paris, France
- **Endowment** $852,072
- **Coed** 992 undergraduate students, 93% full-time, 69% women, 31% men
- **Moderately difficult** entrance level, 76% of applicants were admitted

UNDERGRAD STUDENTS
924 full-time, 68 part-time. Students come from 47 states and territories; 100 other countries; 6% transferred in.

Freshmen:
Admission: 1,293 applied, 981 admitted, 188 enrolled.
Retention: 71% of full-time freshmen returned.

FACULTY
Total: 117, 54% full-time, 60% with terminal degrees.
Student/faculty ratio: 9:1.

ACADEMICS
Calendar: semesters. *Degrees:* bachelor's and master's.

Special study options: advanced placement credit, double majors, English as a second language, honors programs, independent study, internships, off-campus study, part-time degree program, student-designed majors, study abroad, summer session for credit.

Computers: 155 computers/terminals are available on campus for general student use. Students can access the following: campus intranet, computer help desk, free student e-mail accounts, online (class) grades, online (class) registration, online (class) schedules, free office software. Campuswide network is available. Wireless service is available via entire campus.

Library: AUP Library. *Books:* 41,927 (physical), 545,019 (digital/electronic); *Serial titles:* 28 (physical), 44,960 (digital/electronic); *Databases:* 48. Students can reserve study rooms.

STUDENT LIFE
Housing options: on-campus residence required for freshman yearCampus housing is provided by a third party.

Activities and organizations: drama/theater group, student-run newspaper, television station, choral group, AUP Student Media (ASM) - Print, Video, Audio, Student Government Association (SGA), Sports Association, BVSyria (Refugee Assistance), Environmental and Community Services Committee.

Athletics *Intercollegiate sports:* basketball M, equestrian sports M/W, volleyball W. *Intramural sports:* badminton M(c)/W(c), basketball M, cheerleading M(c)/W(c), equestrian sports M/W, volleyball W.

Campus security: 24-hour emergency response devices, valid student ID required for all building entries.

Student services: personal/psychological counseling.

COSTS & FINANCIAL AID
Costs (2018–19) *Tuition:* $29,320 full-time, $940 per credit part-time. Full-time tuition and fees vary according to degree level. Part-time tuition and fees vary according to course load and degree level. *Required fees:* $1303 full-time. *Room only:* Room and board charges vary according to housing facility. *Payment plan:* installment. *Waivers:* children of alumni and employees or children of employees.

Financial Aid Of all full-time matriculated undergraduates who enrolled in 2016, 281 applied for aid, 143 were judged to have need, 6 had their need fully met. In 2016, 17 non-need-based awards were made. *Average percent of need met:* 22. *Average financial aid package:* $11,670. *Average need-based loan:* $4730. *Average need-based gift aid:* $9699. *Average non-need-based aid:* $4013. *Average indebtedness upon graduation:* $20,152.

APPLYING
Standardized Tests *Required for some:* TOEFL, TOEIC or IELTS for students whose primary language is not English. *Recommended:* SAT or ACT (for admission).

Options: electronic application, deferred entrance.

Application fee: $70.

Required: essay or personal statement, high school transcript, 2 letters of recommendation. *Recommended:* minimum 3.0 GPA, interview.

Application deadlines: 3/15 (freshmen), 3/15 (transfers).

Notification: continuous (freshmen), continuous (transfers).

CONTACT
International Admissions Office Counselors, The American University of Paris, 5 boulevard de la Tour Maubourg, Paris 75007, France. *Phone:* +33 1 40 62 07 20. *Fax:* +33 1 47 05 34 32. *E-mail:* admissions@aup.edu.

The New School–Parsons Paris
Paris, France
http://www.newschool.edu/parsons-paris/
- **Independent** comprehensive, founded 2013, part of The New School
- **Urban** campus with easy access to Paris
- **Endowment** $322.3 million
- **Coed** 156 undergraduate students, 98% full-time, 83% women, 17% men
- **Moderately difficult** entrance level

UNDERGRAD STUDENTS
153 full-time, 3 part-time. 4% Black or African American, non-Hispanic/Latino; 6% Hispanic/Latino; 9% Asian, non-Hispanic/Latino; 2% Race/ethnicity unknown; 60% international; 9% transferred in; 20% live on campus.

Freshmen:
Admission: 62 enrolled.
Retention: 90% of full-time freshmen returned.

FACULTY
Total: 54, 9% full-time, 31% with terminal degrees.
Student/faculty ratio: 8:1.

ACADEMICS
Calendar: semesters. *Degrees:* bachelor's and master's.

Special study options: advanced placement credit, cooperative education, distance learning, English as a second language, independent study, internships, off-campus study, part-time degree program, services for LD students, student-designed majors, study abroad, summer session for credit.

Computers: Students can access the following: campus intranet, computer help desk, free student e-mail accounts, online (class) grades, online (class) registration, online (class) schedules. Campuswide network is available. 100% of college-owned or -operated housing units are wired for high-speed Internet access.

Library: *Books:* 840,933 (digital/electronic); *Serial titles:* 113,452 (digital/electronic); *Databases:* 376.

STUDENT LIFE
Housing options: coed. Campus housing is provided by a third party. Freshman applicants given priority for college housing.

Activities and organizations: drama/theater group, student-run newspaper, choral group.

Campus security: 24-hour emergency response devices.

Student services: health clinic, personal/psychological counseling, legal services.

COSTS & FINANCIAL AID
Costs (2017–18) *Comprehensive fee:* $44,980 includes full-time tuition ($32,000), mandatory fees ($1100), and room and board ($11,880). Part-time tuition: $1090 per credit hour. Part-time tuition and fees vary according to course load. *Required fees:* $550 per term part-time. *College room only:* $11,880. Room and board charges vary according to location. *Payment plan:* installment. *Waivers:* employees or children of employees.

Financial Aid Of all full-time matriculated undergraduates who enrolled in 2016, 20 applied for aid, 17 were judged to have need, 6 had their need fully met. In 2016, 45 non-need-based awards were made. *Average percent of need met:* 60. *Average financial aid package:* $21,908. *Average need-based loan:* $4500. *Average need-based gift aid:* $14,924. *Average non-need-based aid:* $7616.

APPLYING
Options: electronic application, early action, deferred entrance.

Application fee: $50.

Required: essay or personal statement, high school transcript, 2 letters of recommendation.

Application deadlines: 1/15 (freshmen), 4/1 (transfers), 11/1 (early action).

Notification: continuous until 3/15 (freshmen), continuous until 12/20 (transfers), 3/15 (early action).

CONTACT
Mr. Mike Fakih, Director of Admissions, The New School–Parsons Paris, 79 Fifth Avenue, 5th floor, New York, NY 10011. *Phone:* 212-229-5150. *Toll-free phone:* 800-292-3040. *E-mail:* fakihm@newschool.edu.

Paris College of Art
Paris, France
http://www.paris.edu/
- **Independent** comprehensive
- **Urban** campus
- **Coed**

ACADEMICS
Calendar: semesters. *Degrees:* certificates, bachelor's, and master's.

Special study options: academic remediation for entering students, accelerated degree program, adult/continuing education programs, cooperative education, English as a second language, independent study, internships, off-campus study, part-time degree program, services for LD students, study abroad, summer session for credit.

Computers: Students can access the following: campus intranet, computer help desk, free student e-mail accounts, online (class) grades, online (class) schedules. Campuswide network is available. Wireless service is available via entire campus.

STUDENT LIFE
Housing options: college housing not available.
Student services: personal/psychological counseling.

COSTS & FINANCIAL AID
Costs (2018–19) *Tuition:* $28,900 full-time. Full-time tuition and fees vary according to program. Part-time tuition and fees vary according to course load. *Payment plan:* installment.

Financial Aid Of all full-time matriculated undergraduates who enrolled in 2010, 46 applied for aid, 41 were judged to have need. 40 state and other part-time jobs (averaging $2300). In 2010, 14 non-need-based awards were made. *Average percent of need met:* 75. *Average financial aid package:* $11,500. *Average need-based gift aid:* $8600. *Average non-need-based aid:* $4200. *Financial aid deadline:* 8/1.

APPLYING
Standardized Tests *Required for some:* SAT or ACT (for admission).

Required: essay or personal statement, high school transcript, interview. *Required for some:* letters of recommendation.

CONTACT
Paris College of Art, 15 rue Fénelon, 75010 Paris, France.

Schiller International University

Paris, France
http://www.schiller.edu/

CONTACT
Schiller International University, 9 rue d'Yvart, F-75015 Paris, France. *Toll-free phone:* 800-261-9571 (in-state); 800-261-9751 (out-of-state).

GERMANY

Schiller International University

Heidelberg, Germany
http://www.schiller.edu/

CONTACT
Ms. Kamala Dontamsetti, Associate Director of Admissions, Schiller International University, 300 East Bay Drive, Largo, FL 33770. *Phone:* 727-736-5082 Ext. 234. *Toll-free phone:* 800-261-9571 (in-state); 800-261-9751 (out-of-state). *Fax:* 727-734-0359. *E-mail:* kamala_dontamsetti@schiller.edu.

GREECE

American College of Thessaloniki

Pylea, Greece
http://www.act.edu/

- **Independent** comprehensive, founded 1886
- **Suburban** 40-acre campus with easy access to Thessaloniki
- **Endowment** $5.6 million
- **Coed** 636 undergraduate students, 86% full-time, 52% women, 48% men
- **Minimally difficult** entrance level, 90% of applicants were admitted

UNDERGRAD STUDENTS
545 full-time, 91 part-time. Students come from 20 other countries; 0.5% transferred in.

Freshmen:
Admission: 92 applied, 83 admitted, 57 enrolled. *Average high school GPA:* 3.3.

Retention: 56% of full-time freshmen returned.

FACULTY
Total: 69, 28% full-time, 48% with terminal degrees.
Student/faculty ratio: 18:1.

ACADEMICS
Calendar: semesters. *Degrees:* certificates, bachelor's, and master's.

Special study options: academic remediation for entering students, accelerated degree program, advanced placement credit, double majors, English as a second language, honors programs, independent study, internships, part-time degree program, services for LD students, study abroad, summer session for credit.

Computers: 165 computers/terminals and 30 ports are available on campus for general student use. Students can access the following: campus intranet, computer help desk, free student e-mail accounts, online (class) grades, online (class) schedules. Campuswide network is available. 100% of college-owned or -operated housing units are wired for high-speed Internet access. Wireless service is available via entire campus.
Library: Bissell Library plus 1 other. *Books:* 25,344 (physical), 165,086 (digital/electronic); *Serial titles:* 18 (physical), 40,122 (digital/electronic); *Databases:* 26. Weekly public service hours: 57; students can reserve study rooms.

STUDENT LIFE
Housing options: coed. Campus housing is university owned, leased by the school and is provided by a third party. Freshman applicants given priority for college housing.

Activities and organizations: drama/theater group, student-run newspaper, radio station, ACT Radio Station, Tennis Club, The Geopolitical Circle, Painting Club, Drama Club.

Athletics *Intercollegiate sports:* basketball M, soccer M, table tennis M/W, tennis M/W, volleyball M/W. *Intramural sports:* basketball M, lacrosse M/W, sailing M/W, sand volleyball M/W, soccer M/W, table tennis M/W, tennis M/W, volleyball M/W.

Campus security: 24-hour emergency response devices and patrols, controlled dormitory access.

Student services: health clinic, personal/psychological counseling.

COSTS
Costs (2018–19) *One-time required fee:* $70. *Tuition:* $8550 full-time, $285 per credit part-time. Part-time tuition and fees vary according to course load. *Required fees:* $50 full-time. *Room only:* Room and board charges vary according to housing facility. *Payment plan:* installment. *Waivers:* employees or children of employees.

APPLYING
Options: electronic application, deferred entrance.

Application fee: 75 euros.

Required: high school transcript, CV. *Required for some:* essay or personal statement, interview. *Recommended:* minimum 2.0 GPA.

Application deadlines: rolling (freshmen), rolling (transfers).

Notification: continuous (freshmen), continuous (transfers).

CONTACT
Mrs. Roula Lebetli, Director of Admissions, American College of Thessaloniki, PO Box 21021, Pylea, Thessaloniki 55510, Greece. *Phone:* +30-2310-398239. *Fax:* +30-2310-398389. *E-mail:* admissions@act.edu.

DEREE - The American College of Greece

Athens, Greece
http://www.acg.edu/

- **Independent** comprehensive, founded 1875
- **Suburban** 64-acre campus with easy access to Athens
- **Coed** 3,114 undergraduate students, 39% full-time, 52% women, 48% men
- **Moderately difficult** entrance level, 83% of applicants were admitted

UNDERGRAD STUDENTS
1,214 full-time, 1,900 part-time. Students come from 58 other countries; 3% transferred in; 4% live on campus.

Freshmen:
Admission: 609 applied, 503 admitted, 423 enrolled. *Average high school GPA:* 3.3.

Retention: 85% of full-time freshmen returned.

FACULTY
Total: 255, 39% full-time, 61% with terminal degrees.
Student/faculty ratio: 11:1.

ACADEMICS
Calendar: semesters 2 summer sessions. *Degrees:* bachelor's, master's, and postbachelor's certificates.

Special study options: academic remediation for entering students, accelerated degree program, adult/continuing education programs, advanced placement credit, double majors, English as a second language, honors programs, independent study, internships, part-time degree program, services for LD students, student-designed majors, study abroad, summer session for credit.

Computers: 306 computers/terminals are available on campus for general student use. Students can access the following: computer help desk, free student e-mail accounts, online (class) grades, online (class) registration, online (class) schedules, learning management system. Campuswide network is available. 100% of college-owned or -operated housing units are wired for high-speed Internet access. Wireless service is available via computer centers, computer labs, dorm rooms, learning centers, libraries. **Library:** John S. Bailey Library plus 1 other. *Books:* 129,000 (physical), 308,000 (digital/electronic); *Serial titles:* 60 (physical), 13,000 (digital/electronic); *Databases:* 45. Weekly public service hours: 72; students can reserve study rooms.

STUDENT LIFE

Housing options: coed, special housing for students with disabilities. Campus housing is university owned. Freshman applicants given priority for college housing.

Activities and organizations: drama/theater group, student-run newspaper, choral group, DEREE Ambassadors, DEREE Orientation Leaders, Debate Club, DEREE SAB (Student Activities Board), Innovation and Entrepreneurship Clib.

Athletics *Intercollegiate sports:* basketball M(s)/W(s), rugby M, soccer M(s)/W, swimming and diving M/W, volleyball M/W(s), water polo M. *Intramural sports:* archery M/W, basketball M/W, rock climbing M/W, soccer M/W, swimming and diving M/W, table tennis M/W, tennis M/W, track and field M/W, volleyball M/W.

Campus security: 24-hour emergency response devices and patrols, controlled dormitory access.

Student services: health clinic, personal/psychological counseling.

COSTS & FINANCIAL AID

Costs (2018–19) *Tuition:* $335 per credit part-time. Full-time tuition and fees vary according to course load. Part-time tuition and fees vary according to course load. No tuition increase for student's term of enrollment. *Room only:* Room and board charges vary according to housing facility. *Payment plan:* installment. *Waivers:* employees or children of employees.

Financial Aid *Financial aid deadline:* 9/1.

APPLYING

Options: electronic application, deferred entrance.

Required: essay or personal statement, high school transcript, minimum 2.1 GPA, 1 letter of recommendation, interview.

Application deadlines: rolling (freshmen), rolling (transfers).

Notification: continuous until 6/15 (freshmen), 6/15 (transfers).

CONTACT

Ms. Loukia Kanatsouli, Dean of Enrollment and International Students, DEREE - The American College of Greece, 6 Gravias Street, Aghia Paraskevi, Athens 15342, Greece. *Phone:* +30-210-600-9800 Ext. 1474. *Fax:* +30-210-608-2344. *E-mail:* lkanatsouli@acg.edu.

IRELAND

American College Dublin

Dublin, Ireland

http://www.amcd.ie/

CONTACT

American College Dublin, 2 Merrion Square, Dublin 2, Ireland.

Institute of Public Administration

Dublin, Ireland

http://www.ipa.ie/

CONTACT

Dr. Denis O'Brien, Registrar, Institute of Public Administration, 57-61 Lansdowne Road, Dublin 4, Ireland. *Phone:* 353-1-240-3600. *Fax:* 353-1-668-9135. *E-mail:* undergrad@ipa.ie.

ITALY

The American University of Rome

Rome, Italy

http://www.aur.edu/

- **Independent** comprehensive, founded 1969
- **Urban** 1-acre campus
- **Coed**
- **Moderately difficult** entrance level

FACULTY

Student/faculty ratio: 14:1.

ACADEMICS

Calendar: semesters. *Degrees:* associate, bachelor's, and master's. **Library:** The American University of Rome Library. *Books:* 13,489 (physical), 150,720 (digital/electronic). Weekly public service hours: 55; students can reserve study rooms.

STUDENT LIFE

Housing options: men-only, women-only. Campus housing is provided by a third party. Freshman applicants given priority for college housing.

Activities and organizations: drama/theater group, student-run newspaper, choral group, Student Government, Community Services, Men and Female soccer teams, Business Club, International Relations Club.

Campus security: 24-hour emergency response devices, security guards during hours of operation, 24-hour surveillance cameras.

Student services: health clinic, personal/psychological counseling.

COSTS

Costs (2017–18) *One-time required fee:* $230. *Comprehensive fee:* $28,712 includes full-time tuition ($23,000), mandatory fees ($382), and room and board ($5330). Full-time tuition and fees vary according to course load and degree level. Part-time tuition: $2875 per course. Part-time tuition and fees vary according to course load and degree level. *College room only:* $4550.

APPLYING

Standardized Tests *Required for some:* TOEFL or IELTS for non-English high school students. *Recommended:* SAT or ACT (for admission).

Options: electronic application, deferred entrance.

Application fee: $75.

Required: essay or personal statement, high school transcript, minimum 2.5 GPA, 1 letter of recommendation, interview.

CONTACT

Ms. Jessica York, Admissions Counselor, The American University of Rome, Via Pietro Roselli 4, Rome 00153, Italy. *Phone:* -+39 0658330919. *Toll-free phone:* 877-592-1287. *Fax:* +39 0658330992. *E-mail:* admissions@aur.edu.

★ John Cabot University

Rome, Italy

http://www.johncabot.edu/

- **Independent** comprehensive, founded 1972
- **Urban** campus with easy access to Rome
- **Coed** 1,316 undergraduate students

UNDERGRAD STUDENTS

Students come from 40 states and territories; 70 other countries; 46% live on campus.

Freshmen:

Average high school GPA: 3.1.

Retention: 98% of full-time freshmen returned.

FACULTY

Total: 139.

Student/faculty ratio: 9:1.

ACADEMICS

Calendar: semesters. *Degrees:* associate, bachelor's, and master's.

Special study options: adult/continuing education programs, advanced placement credit, double majors, English as a second language, freshman honors college, honors programs, independent study, internships, part-time degree program, services for LD students, study abroad, summer session for credit.

Computers: 153 computers/terminals are available on campus for general student use. Students can access the following: campus intranet, computer help desk, free student e-mail accounts, online (class) grades, online (class) registration, online (class) schedules. Campuswide network is available. 100% of college-owned or -operated housing units are wired for high-speed Internet access. Wireless service is available via entire campus.

Library: Frohring Library plus 1 other. *Books:* 34,218 (physical); *Databases:* 39. Weekly public service hours: 86; students can reserve study rooms.

STUDENT LIFE

Housing options: coed, men-only, women-only. Campus housing is leased by the school and is provided by a third party. Freshman campus housing is guaranteed.

Activities and organizations: drama/theater group, student-run newspaper, Business Club, Model United Nations, Student Government, Performing Arts Society, Student Newspaper.

Athletics *Intercollegiate sports:* basketball M/W, soccer M/W, volleyball M/W. *Intramural sports:* basketball M/W, cheerleading M/W, cross-country running M/W, sailing M/W, skiing (downhill) M/W, soccer M/W, swimming and diving M/W, tennis M/W, volleyball M/W, weight lifting M/W.

Campus security: 24-hour emergency response devices and patrols, controlled dormitory access.

Student services: health clinic, personal/psychological counseling.

APPLYING

Standardized Tests *Required for some:* SAT or ACT (for admission).

Required: essay or personal statement, high school transcript, 2 letters of recommendation, interview. *Recommended:* minimum 2.7 GPA.

CONTACT

Ms. Stefania Corrado, John Cabot University, Roma 00165, Italy. *Phone:* 855-528-7662. *Toll-free phone:* 855-528-7662. *E-mail:* admissions@johncabot.edu.

See below for display ad and page 1314 for the College Close-Up.

KENYA

United States International University–Africa

Nairobi, Kenya

http://www.usiu.ac.ke/

- **Independent** comprehensive, founded 1977, part of Alliant International University
- **Urban** 120-acre campus
- **Coed**
- **Moderately difficult** entrance level

FACULTY

Student/faculty ratio: 30:1.

ACADEMICS

Calendar: trimesters. *Degrees:* bachelor's and master's.

Library: Library and Information Center.

STUDENT LIFE

Housing options: coed. Campus housing is university owned and is provided by a third party.

Activities and organizations: drama/theater group, student-run newspaper, radio station, choral group, Business club, Aiesec, Basket Ball, Hockey, Drama club.

Campus security: 24-hour emergency response devices and patrols, 24-hour Hostel reception security desk.

Student services: health clinic, personal/psychological counseling.

COSTS

Costs (2017–18) *One-time required fee:* 7000 Kenyan shillings. *Comprehensive fee:* 530,580 Kenyan shillings includes full-time tuition (279,000 Kenyan shillings), mandatory fees (23,400 Kenyan shillings), and room and board (228,180 Kenyan shillings). Full-time tuition and fees vary according to course load, degree level, program, and reciprocity agreements. Part-time tuition: 7750 Kenyan shillings per unit. Part-time tuition and fees vary according to course load, degree level, program, and reciprocity agreements. *Required fees:* 7800 Kenyan shillings per term part-time. *College room only:* 90,000 Kenyan shillings. Room and board charges vary according to board plan.

APPLYING

Options: deferred entrance.

Application fee: 50 Kenyan shillings.

Required: high school transcript, minimum 2.5 GPA. *Required for some:* interview.

CONTACT

United States International University–Africa, PO Box 14634, Thika Road Kasarani, Nairobi 00800, Kenya. *Phone:* 254-02-3606563.

LEBANON

American University of Beirut

Beirut, Lebanon

http://www.aub.edu.lb/

- **Independent** university, founded 1866
- **Urban** 61-acre campus with easy access to Beirut
- **Endowment** $605.7 million
- **Coed** 7,225 undergraduate students, 95% full-time, 49% women, 51% men
- **69%** of applicants were admitted

UNDERGRAD STUDENTS

6,865 full-time, 360 part-time. Students come from 79 other countries; 0.5% transferred in; 15% live on campus.

Freshmen:

Admission: 5,241 applied, 3,599 admitted, 1,872 enrolled. *Test scores:* SAT evidence-based reading and writing scores over 500: 82%; SAT math scores over 500: 97%; SAT evidence-based reading and writing scores over 600: 27%; SAT math scores over 600: 70%; SAT evidence-based reading and writing scores over 700: 2%; SAT math scores over 700: 24%. *Retention:* 92% of full-time freshmen returned.

FACULTY

Total: 1,196, 76% full-time, 73% with terminal degrees.

Student/faculty ratio: 11:1.

ACADEMICS

Calendar: semesters. *Degrees:* certificates, diplomas, bachelor's, master's, doctoral, and postbachelor's certificates.

Special study options: academic remediation for entering students, advanced placement credit, double majors, English as a second language, honors programs, independent study, internships, services for LD students, study abroad, summer session for credit.

Computers: 1,600 computers/terminals and 1,320 ports are available on campus for general student use. Students can access the following: campus intranet, computer help desk, free student e-mail accounts, online (class) grades, online (class) registration, online (class) schedules. Campuswide network is available. 100% of college-owned or -operated housing units are wired for high-speed Internet access. Wireless service is available via entire campus.

Library: Jafet Library plus 3 others. *Books:* 400,000 (physical), 1.6 million (digital/electronic); *Serial titles:* 190,000 (digital/electronic); *Databases:* 350. Weekly public service hours: 107; study areas open 24 hours, 5–7 days a week; students can reserve study rooms.

STUDENT LIFE

Housing options: on-campus residence required for freshman year; men-only, women-only. Campus housing is university owned. Freshman campus housing is guaranteed.

Activities and organizations: drama/theater group, student-run newspaper, choral group, Red Cross Club, Biology Society, Business Society, Music Club, Palestinian Cultural Club.

Athletics *Intercollegiate sports:* badminton M/W, basketball M/W, cheerleading W, cross-country running M/W, football M, rugby M/W, skiing (downhill) M/W, soccer M/W, squash M/W, swimming and diving M/W, table tennis M/W, tennis M/W, track and field M/W, triathlon M/W, ultimate Frisbee M/W, volleyball M/W, water polo M. *Intramural sports:* archery M/W, basketball M/W, cross-country running M/W, football M, rugby M/W, soccer M/W, squash M/W, swimming and diving M/W, table tennis M/W, tennis M/W, track and field M/W, ultimate Frisbee M/W, volleyball M/W, water polo M, weight lifting M/W.

Campus security: 24-hour emergency response devices and patrols, late-night transport/escort service, controlled dormitory access, staff monitors entrance 24/7.

Student services: health clinic, personal/psychological counseling, legal services.

COSTS & FINANCIAL AID

Costs (2017–18) *Tuition:* $21,900 full-time, $730 per credit part-time. Full-time tuition and fees vary according to course load, degree level, program, and student level. Part-time tuition and fees vary according to course load, degree level, program, and student level. *Required fees:* $740 full-time. *Room only:* $2900. Room and board charges vary according to housing facility and location. *Payment plan:* deferred payment. *Waivers:* employees or children of employees.

Financial Aid Of all full-time matriculated undergraduates who enrolled in 2016, 4,229 applied for aid, 3,239 were judged to have need. 24 state and other part-time jobs (averaging $1350). In 2016, 33 non-need-based awards were made. *Average financial aid package:* $9378. *Average need-based loan:* $6097. *Average need-based gift aid:* $9474. *Average non-need-based aid:* $24,114. *Average indebtedness upon graduation:* $16,972. *Financial aid deadline:* 12/18.

APPLYING

Standardized Tests *Required:* SAT (for admission). *Required for some:* SAT Subject Tests (for admission), TOEFL, IELTS.

Options: electronic application, early admission, early decision, deferred entrance.

Application fee: $80.

Required: high school transcript. *Required for some:* essay or personal statement, 2 letters of recommendation, interview.

Application deadlines: 12/20 (freshmen), 4/30 (transfers).

Notification: 3/30 (freshmen), continuous until 6/30 (transfers).

CONTACT

Dr. Salim Kanaan, Director of Admissions Office, American University of Beirut, PO Box 11-0236, Riad El-Solh, 1107 2020, Lebanon. *Phone:* 961-1374374 Ext. 2592. *Fax:* 961-1750775. *E-mail:* admissions@aub.edu.lb.

Lebanese American University

Beirut, Lebanon

http://www.lau.edu.lb/

- **Private** comprehensive, founded 1835
- **Urban** 50-acre campus with easy access to Beirut, Byblos, Tripoli
- **Endowment** $477.2 million
- **Coed** 7,558 undergraduate students, 94% full-time, 50% women, 50% men
- **Moderately difficult** entrance level, 88% of applicants were admitted

UNDERGRAD STUDENTS

7,094 full-time, 464 part-time. Students come from 78 other countries; 19% are from out of state; 1% transferred in; 6% live on campus.

Freshmen:

Admission: 5,053 applied, 4,452 admitted, 1,716 enrolled. *Average high school GPA:* 2.8. *Test scores:* SAT evidence-based reading and writing scores over 500: 55%; SAT math scores over 500: 87%; SAT evidence-based reading and writing scores over 600: 12%; SAT math scores over

600: 45%; SAT evidence-based reading and writing scores over 700: 1%; SAT math scores over 700: 9%.

Retention: 89% of full-time freshmen returned.

FACULTY
Total: 828, 36% full-time, 47% with terminal degrees.
Student/faculty ratio: 16:1.

ACADEMICS
Calendar: semesters. *Degrees:* bachelor's, master's, doctoral, and postbachelor's certificates.

Special study options: academic remediation for entering students, advanced placement credit, double majors, honors programs, internships, part-time degree program, services for LD students, study abroad, summer session for credit.

Computers: 1,359 computers/terminals and 2,200 ports are available on campus for general student use. Students can access the following: campus intranet, computer help desk, free student e-mail accounts, online (class) grades, online (class) registration, online (class) schedules, online forms requests, online and mobile course management system. Campuswide network is available. 100% of college-owned or -operated housing units are wired for high-speed Internet access. Wireless service is available via entire campus.
Library: Riyad Nassar Library plus 3 others. *Books:* 509,382 (physical), 473,485 (digital/electronic); *Serial titles:* 604 (physical), 82,981 (digital/electronic); *Databases:* 178. Weekly public service hours: 98; students can reserve study rooms.

STUDENT LIFE
Housing options: coed, men-only, women-only, special housing for students with disabilities. Campus housing is university owned, leased by the school and is provided by a third party.

Activities and organizations: drama/theater group, student-run newspaper, choral group, Event Organization Club, Debate Club, Human Rights Club, International Affairs Club, Red Cross Club.

Athletics *Intercollegiate sports:* badminton M/W, basketball M(s)/W(s), cheerleading M/W, cross-country running M/W, rugby M(s)/W, skiing (downhill) M/W, soccer M(s)/W(s), swimming and diving M(s)/W(s), table tennis M(s)/W(s), tennis M(s)/W(s), track and field M(s)/W(s), triathlon M(s), volleyball M(s)/W(s), water polo M(s). *Intramural sports:* basketball M/W, soccer M/W, swimming and diving M/W, table tennis M/W, tennis M/W, volleyball M/W.

Campus security: 24-hour emergency response devices and patrols, 24/7 security at residence halls.

Student services: health clinic, personal/psychological counseling, women's center.

COSTS
Costs (2017–18) *Tuition:* $16,977 full-time, $709 per credit part-time. Full-time tuition and fees vary according to course load, degree level, and program. Part-time tuition and fees vary according to course load, degree level, and program. *Required fees:* $528 full-time, $528 per year part-time. *Room only:* Room and board charges vary according to housing facility and location. *Payment plans:* installment, deferred payment. *Waivers:* employees or children of employees.

APPLYING
Standardized Tests *Required:* SAT or ACT (for admission). *Required for some:* SAT and SAT Subject Tests or ACT (for admission), SAT Subject Tests (for admission), Institutional English Test (English Entrance Exam EEE) or International TOFEL.

Options: electronic application, deferred entrance.
Application fee: $85.
Required: high school transcript, minimum 2.0 GPA.
Application deadlines: 7/15 (freshmen), 7/15 (transfers).
Notification: continuous until 3/1 (freshmen), continuous until 3/1 (transfers).

CONTACT
Miss Nada Hajj, University Director of Admissions, Lebanese American University, PO Box 13-5053 Chouran Beirut 1102 2801, Lebanon, Beirut, Lebanon. *Phone:* 961-1786456 Ext. 1111. *Fax:* 961-1786456. *E-mail:* nhajj@lau.edu.lb.

MEXICO

Instituto Tecnológico y de Estudios Superiores de Monterrey, Campus Central de Veracruz
Córdoba, Mexico
http://www.ver.itesm.mx/

CONTACT
Ing. Luis Pablo Villareal, Registrar, Instituto Tecnológico y de Estudios Superiores de Monterrey, Campus Central de Veracruz, Avenida Eugenio Garza Sada 1, Apartado Postal 314, 94500 Córdoba, Veracruz, Mexico. *Phone:* -27-13-23-40 Ext. 123.

Instituto Tecnológico y de Estudios Superiores de Monterrey, Campus Chiapas
Tuxtla Gutiérrez, Mexico
http://www.chs.itesm.mx/

CONTACT
Lic. Luis Enrique Cancino, Registrar, Instituto Tecnológico y de Estudios Superiores de Monterrey, Campus Chiapas, Carretera a Tapanatepec Km 149&746, Apartado Postal 312, 29000 Tuxtla Gutiérrez, Chiapas, Mexico. *Phone:* -96-15-1723.

Instituto Tecnológico y de Estudios Superiores de Monterrey, Campus Chihuahua
Chihuahua, Mexico
http://www.chi.itesm.mx/

CONTACT
Ing. Juan Manuel Fernandez, Registrar, Instituto Tecnológico y de Estudios Superiores de Monterrey, Campus Chihuahua, Colegio Militar 4700, Colonia Nombre de Dios, Apartado Postal 728, 31300 Chihuahua, Chihuahua, Mexico. *Phone:* -14-17-48-58 Ext. 117.

Instituto Tecnológico y de Estudios Superiores de Monterrey, Campus Ciudad de México
Ciudad de Mexico, Mexico
http://www.ccm.itesm.mx/

CONTACT
Admissions Office, Instituto Tecnológico y de Estudios Superiores de Monterrey, Campus Ciudad de México, Calle del Puente #222 esquina con Periférico, 14380 Colonia Huipulco, Tlalpan, MDF, Mexico. *Phone:* -5-673-6488.

Instituto Tecnológico y de Estudios Superiores de Monterrey, Campus Ciudad Juárez
Ciudad Juárez, Mexico
http://www.cdj.itesm.mx/

CONTACT
Lic. Alberto Trejo, Registrar, Instituto Tecnológico y de Estudios Superiores de Monterrey, Campus Ciudad Juárez, Boulevard Tomas Fernandez y Avenida A J Bermudez, Apartado Postal 3105-J, 32320 Ciudad Juárez, Chihuahua, Mexico. *Phone:* -16-17-88-07 Ext. 113.

Instituto Tecnológico y de Estudios Superiores de Monterrey, Campus Ciudad Obregón

Ciudad Obregón, Mexico
http://www.cob.itesm.mx/

CONTACT
Lic. Judith Almeida, Registrar, Instituto Tecnológico y de Estudios Superiores de Monterrey, Campus Ciudad Obregón, Dr Norman E Borlaug Km 14, Apartado Postal 662, 85000 Ciudad Obregón, Sonora, Mexico. *Phone:* -64-15-03-12.

Instituto Tecnológico y de Estudios Superiores de Monterrey, Campus Colima

Colima, Mexico
http://www.itesm.edu/wps/wcm/connect/Campus/COL/colima/

CONTACT
Lic. Manuel Perez Rivera, Registrar, Instituto Tecnológico y de Estudios Superiores de Monterrey, Campus Colima, Prolongacion Ignacio Sandoval s/n, Fraccionamiento Jardines de Vista Hermosa, Apartado Postal 190, 28010 Colima, Colima, Mexico. *Phone:* -33-12-53-39.

Instituto Tecnológico y de Estudios Superiores de Monterrey, Campus Cuernavaca

Temixco, Mexico
http://www.cva.itesm.mx/

CONTACT
Lic. Miguel Angel Machua, Registrar, Instituto Tecnológico y de Estudios Superiores de Monterrey, Campus Cuernavaca, Paseo de la Reforma 182-A, Colonia Lomas de Cuernavaca, 62000 Temixco, Morelos, Mexico. *Phone:* -73 18-49-57.

Instituto Tecnológico y de Estudios Superiores de Monterrey, Campus Estado de México

Estado de Mexico, Mexico
http://www.cem.itesm.mx/

CONTACT
Prof. Jose de Jesus Molina, Registrar, Instituto Tecnológico y de Estudios Superiores de Monterrey, Campus Estado de México, Carretera Lago de Guadalupe Km. 3.5, Atizapan de Zaragoza, Estado de Mexico 52926, Mexico. *Phone:* -5-873-3600.

Instituto Tecnológico y de Estudios Superiores de Monterrey, Campus Guadalajara

Zapopan, Mexico
http://www.gda.itesm.mx/

CONTACT
Ms. Janet Martell Sotomayor, Registration Director, Instituto Tecnológico y de Estudios Superiores de Monterrey, Campus Guadalajara, Avenida General Ramón Corona 2514, Colonia Nuevo Mexico, 45140 Zapopan, Jalisco, Mexico. *Phone:* -3-669-3006.

Instituto Tecnológico y de Estudios Superiores de Monterrey, Campus Hidalgo

Pachuca, Mexico
http://www.hgo.itesm.mx/

CONTACT
Lic. Lizbet Melo, Registrar, Instituto Tecnológico y de Estudios Superiores de Monterrey, Campus Hidalgo, Boulevard Felipe Angeles s/n al lado de la Unidad Deportiva, Apartado Postal 337, 42090 Pachuca, Hidalgo, Mexico. *Phone:* -714-25-00 Ext. 128.

Instituto Tecnológico y de Estudios Superiores de Monterrey, Campus Irapuato

Irapuato, Mexico
http://www.ira.itesm.mx/

CONTACT
Ing. Marcela Beltrán, Registrar, Instituto Tecnológico y de Estudios Superiores de Monterrey, Campus Irapuato, Paseo Mirador del Valle No. 445, Col. Villas de Irapuato, Apartado Postal 568, 36660 Irapuato, Guanajuato, Mexico. *Phone:* -46-230342.

Instituto Tecnológico y de Estudios Superiores de Monterrey, Campus Laguna

Torreón, Mexico
http://www.lag.itesm.mx/

CONTACT
Ing. Aroldo Camargo Soto, Registrar, Instituto Tecnológico y de Estudios Superiores de Monterrey, Campus Laguna, Paseo del Tecnologico s/n Ampliacion La Rosita, Apartado Postal 506, 27250 Torreón, Coahuila, Mexico. *Phone:* -17-20-66-61 Ext. 23.

Instituto Tecnológico y de Estudios Superiores de Monterrey, Campus León

León, Mexico
http://www.leo.itesm.mx/

CONTACT
Lic. Eddie Villegas, Registrar, Instituto Tecnológico y de Estudios Superiores de Monterrey, Campus León, Avenida Eugenio Garza Sada s/n Colonia Cerro Gordo, Apartado Postal 872, 37120 León, Guanajuato, Mexico. *Phone:* -47-17-10-00 Ext. 131.

Instituto Tecnológico y de Estudios Superiores de Monterrey, Campus Monterrey

Monterrey, Mexico
http://www.mty.itesm.mx/

CONTACT
Lic. Carlos Ordoñez, International Student Advisor, Instituto Tecnológico y de Estudios Superiores de Monterrey, Campus Monterrey, Avenida Eugenio Garza Sada 2501 Sur Colonia Tecnnologico, Sucursal de Correos J, 64849 Monterrey, Nuevo León, Mexico. *Phone:* -52 81 8328 4065 Ext. 3942.

Instituto Tecnológico y de Estudios Superiores de Monterrey, Campus Querétaro

Santiago de Querétaro, Mexico
http://www.qro.itesm.mx/

CONTACT
Lic. Marco Vinicio Lopez, Registrar, Instituto Tecnológico y de Estudios Superiores de Monterrey, Campus Querétaro, Avenida Epigmenio González #500, Apartado Postal 37, 76130 Querétaro, Querétaro, Mexico. *Phone:* -42-17-38-25 Ext. 156.

Instituto Tecnológico y de Estudios Superiores de Monterrey, Campus Saltillo

Saltillo, Mexico
http://www.sal.itesm.mx/

CONTACT
Lic. Esteban Ramos, Registrar, Instituto Tecnológico y de Estudios Superiores de Monterrey, Campus Saltillo, Prolongacion Juan de la Barrera 1241 Ote, Apartado Postal 539, 25270 Saltillo, Coahuila, Mexico. *Phone:* -84-15-06-90 Ext. 12.

Instituto Tecnológico y de Estudios Superiores de Monterrey, Campus San Luis Potosí

San Luis Potosí, Mexico
http://www.slp.itesm.mx/

CONTACT
Ing. Consuelo Gonzalez, Registrar, Instituto Tecnológico y de Estudios Superiores de Monterrey, Campus San Luis Potosí, Avenida Robles 600, Colonia Jacarandas, Apartado Postal 1473 Suc E, 78140 San Luis Potosí, SLP, Mexico. *Phone:* -48 13-3441 Ext. 14.

Instituto Tecnológico y de Estudios Superiores de Monterrey, Campus Sinaloa

Culiacán, Mexico
http://www.sin.itesm.mx/

CONTACT
Lic. Hugo Guerrero, Registrar, Instituto Tecnológico y de Estudios Superiores de Monterrey, Campus Sinaloa, Boulevard Culiacán 3773, Apartado Postal 69-F, 80800 Culiacán, Sinaloa, Mexico. *Phone:* -67-14-03-69.

Instituto Tecnológico y de Estudios Superiores de Monterrey, Campus Sonora Norte

Hermosillo, Mexico
http://www.her.itesm.mx/

CONTACT
Ing. Victor Eduardo Perez Orozco, Library and Admissions/Registration Director, Instituto Tecnológico y de Estudios Superiores de Monterrey, Campus Sonora Norte, Carretera Hermosillo-Nogales Km 9, Apartado Postal 216, 83000 Hermosillo, Sonora, Mexico. *Phone:* -62-15-52-05 Ext. 131.

Instituto Tecnológico y de Estudios Superiores de Monterrey, Campus Tampico

Altimira, Mexico
http://www.itesm.edu/wps/portal?WCM_GLOBAL_CONTE XT=/migration/TAM2/Tampico

CONTACT
Ing. Javier Ponce, Registrar, Instituto Tecnológico y de Estudios Superiores de Monterrey, Campus Tampico, Boulevard Petrocel Km 1.3, Corredor Industrial, Carretera Tampico-Mante, 89120 Altimira, Tamaulipas, Mexico. *Phone:* -126-4-19-79.

Instituto Tecnológico y de Estudios Superiores de Monterrey, Campus Toluca

Toluca, Mexico
http://www.tol.itesm.mx/

CONTACT
Ing. Victor M. Martinez Orta, Registrar, Instituto Tecnológico y de Estudios Superiores de Monterrey, Campus Toluca, Ex-hacienda La Pila, 100 metros al norte de San Antonio Buenavista, 50252 Toluca, Estado de Mexico, Mexico. *Phone:* -72-74-11-92.

Instituto Tecnológico y de Estudios Superiores de Monterrey, Campus Zacatecas

Zacatecas, Mexico
http://www.zac.itesm.mx/

CONTACT
Lic. de Lourdes Zorrilla, Business Affairs Director and Registrar, Instituto Tecnológico y de Estudios Superiores de Monterrey, Campus Zacatecas, Calzada Pedro Coronel #16, Frente al Club Bernades, Municipio de Guadalupe, 98000 Zacatecas, Zacatecas, Mexico. *Phone:* -49 23-00-40.

Universidad de las Americas, A.C.

Mexico City, Mexico
http://www.udladf.mx/

CONTACT
Universidad de las Americas, A.C., Calle de Puebla 223, Col. Roma, 06700 Mexico City, Mexico.

Universidad de las Américas Puebla

Puebla, Mexico
http://www.udlap.mx/

CONTACT
Miss Madet Ruisenor-Quintero, Director of Student Enrollment Office, Universidad de las Américas Puebla, Ex-Hacienda Santa Catarina Martir, Cholula, Puebla 72820, Mexico. *Phone:* -52 229-2024.

Universidad de Monterrey

San Pedro Garza Garcia, Mexico
http://www.udem.edu.mx/

CONTACT
Universidad de Monterrey, Av. Ignacio Morones Prieto 4500 Pte, 66238 San Pedro Garza Garcia, NL, Mexico. *Toll-free phone:* 800-801-UDEM.

A ★ *indicates that the school has detailed information with a Premium Profile on Petersons.com.*

MONACO

The International University of Monaco
Monte Carlo, Monaco
http://www.monaco.edu/

CONTACT
Dr. Gisele Dudognon, Director of Admissions, The International University of Monaco, 2, Avenue Albert II, MC-98000 Principality of Monaco, Monaco. *Phone:* -377 97986 994. *Fax:* 377 92052 830. *E-mail:* gdudognon@monaco.edu.

SOUTH AFRICA

University of South Africa
Pretoria, South Africa
http://www.unisa.ac.za/

CONTACT
Contact Centre, University of South Africa, PO Box 392, Pretoria 0003, South Africa. *Phone:* 27-11 670-9000. *Fax:* 012 429 4150. *E-mail:* study-info@unisa.ac.za.

SPAIN

Saint Louis University–Madrid Campus
Madrid, Spain
http://www.slu.edu/madrid

- **Independent Roman Catholic (Jesuit)** comprehensive, founded 1967
- **Urban** 1-acre campus with easy access to Madrid, Spain
- **Coed** 751 undergraduate students, 97% full-time, 60% women, 40% men
- **Moderately difficult** entrance level, 48% of applicants were admitted

UNDERGRAD STUDENTS
729 full-time, 22 part-time. Students come from 50 states and territories; 65 other countries; 75% are from out of state; 65% live on campus.

Freshmen:
Admission: 1,095 applied, 529 admitted.
Retention: 76% of full-time freshmen returned.

FACULTY
Total: 101, 38% full-time, 68% with terminal degrees.
Student/faculty ratio: 11:1.

ACADEMICS
Calendar: semesters. *Degrees:* bachelor's and master's.
Special study options: advanced placement credit, cooperative education, double majors, English as a second language, honors programs, independent study, internships, part-time degree program, services for LD students, study abroad, summer session for credit.
Computers: Students can access the following: computer help desk, free student e-mail accounts, online (class) grades, online (class) registration, online (class) schedules. Campuswide network is available. Wireless service is available via entire campus.
Library: Main Library plus 1 other. Students can reserve study rooms.

STUDENT LIFE
Housing options: men-only, women-only. Campus housing is provided by a third party. Freshman campus housing is guaranteed.
Activities and organizations: drama/theater group, student-run newspaper, choral group, Student Government, Campus Ambassadors, Student Magazine, Theatre Club, Babel Language Exchange.

Athletics *Intercollegiate sports:* soccer M. *Intramural sports:* baseball M/W, basketball M/W, cross-country running M/W, equestrian sports M/W, field hockey M/W, football M/W, golf M/W, lacrosse M/W, racquetball M/W, soccer M/W, squash M/W, swimming and diving M/W, tennis M/W, ultimate Frisbee M/W, volleyball M/W.
Campus security: 24-hour emergency response devices.
Student services: personal/psychological counseling.

COSTS
Costs (2018–19) *One-time required fee:* $225. *Comprehensive fee:* $28,260 includes full-time tuition ($20,460), mandatory fees ($180), and room and board ($7620). Part-time tuition and fees vary according to course load and degree level. *College room only:* $4600. Room and board charges vary according to housing facility. *Payment plan:* installment. *Waivers:* children of alumni and employees or children of employees.

APPLYING
Standardized Tests *Required for some:* IB, A-Levels, French Baccalaureate, Selectividad, Maturita, or Abitur.
Options: electronic application, deferred entrance.
Required: essay or personal statement, high school transcript, minimum 2.5 GPA. *Recommended:* 2 letters of recommendation.
Application deadlines: 5/31 (freshmen), 5/31 (transfers).
Notification: continuous (freshmen), continuous (transfers).

CONTACT
Ms. Heidi Buffington, Director of Admissions, Saint Louis University–Madrid Campus, Avenida del Valle, 34, Madrid 28003, Spain. *Phone:* -34 91-554-5858 Ext. 206. *Fax:* 34 91-554-6202. *E-mail:* heidi.buffington@slu.edu.

Schiller International University
Madrid, Spain
http://www.schiller.edu/

CONTACT
Ms. Kamala Dontamsetti, Associate Director of Admissions, Schiller International University, 300 East Bay Drive, Largo, FL 33700. *Phone:* 727-736-5082 Ext. 234. *Toll-free phone:* 800-261-9571 (in-state); 800-261-9751 (out-of-state). *Fax:* 727-734-0359. *E-mail:* admissions@schiller.edu.

SWITZERLAND

Ecole Hôtelière de Lausanne
Lausanne, Switzerland
http://www.ehl.edu/

CONTACT
Ecole Hôtelière de Lausanne, Route de Cojonnex 18, Le Chalet-a-Gobet, CH-1000 Lausanne 25, Switzerland. *Phone:* -41 21 785 1111.

Franklin University Switzerland
Sorengo, Switzerland
http://www.fus.edu/

- **Independent** comprehensive, founded 1969
- **Suburban** 7-acre campus with easy access to Milan, Italy
- **Coed** 395 undergraduate students, 100% full-time, 64% women, 36% men
- **Moderately difficult** entrance level, 55% of applicants were admitted

UNDERGRAD STUDENTS
395 full-time. 100% are from out of state; 100% international; 3% transferred in; 80% live on campus.

Freshmen:
Admission: 919 applied, 510 admitted, 204 enrolled. *Average high school GPA:* 3.4. *Test scores:* SAT evidence-based reading and writing scores over 500: 82%; SAT math scores over 500: 95%; ACT scores over 18: 100%; SAT evidence-based reading and writing scores over 600: 38%;

SAT math scores over 600: 57%; ACT scores over 24: 72%; SAT evidence-based reading and writing scores over 700: 19%; SAT math scores over 700: 19%; ACT scores over 30: 20%.
Retention: 88% of full-time freshmen returned.

FACULTY
Total: 47, 49% full-time, 96% with terminal degrees.
Student/faculty ratio: 9:1.

ACADEMICS
Calendar: semesters. *Degrees:* bachelor's and master's.

Special study options: accelerated degree program, advanced placement credit, double majors, English as a second language, honors programs, independent study, internships, part-time degree program, study abroad, summer session for credit.

Computers: Students can access the following: campus intranet, computer help desk, free student e-mail accounts, online (class) grades, online (class) registration, online (class) schedules, Live@EDU skydrive, learning management system, office online collaboration tools, LAN Storage space, student access to academic/financial records and portal available in student lounge and libraries. Campuswide network is available. 100% of college-owned or -operated housing units are wired for high-speed Internet access. Wireless service is available via entire campus.
Library: David R. Grace Library plus 2 others.

STUDENT LIFE
Housing options: on-campus residence required through sophomore year; coed. Campus housing is university owned and leased by the school. Freshman campus housing is guaranteed.

Activities and organizations: drama/theater group, student-run newspaper, Student Government Association, Newspaper, Literary Society, Drama Club, Peer Educators Program.

Athletics *Intramural sports:* basketball M(c)/W(c), skiing (downhill) M(c)/W(c), soccer M(c)/W(c), tennis M(c)/W(c), volleyball M(c)/W(c).

Campus security: 24-hour emergency response devices, student patrols, late-night transport/escort service, controlled dormitory access, late night patrols by professional security service personnel.

Student services: health clinic, personal/psychological counseling.

COSTS & FINANCIAL AID
Costs (2018–19) *Comprehensive fee:* $54,310 includes full-time tuition ($39,600), mandatory fees ($1420), and room and board ($13,290). *College room only:* $10,900.

Financial Aid Of all full-time matriculated undergraduates who enrolled in 2017, 147 applied for aid, 127 were judged to have need. In 2017, 82 non-need-based awards were made. *Average financial aid package:* $25,897. *Average need-based loan:* $4312. *Average need-based gift aid:* $20,157. *Average non-need-based aid:* $12,287.

APPLYING
Options: electronic application, deferred entrance.
Application fee: $90.
Required: essay or personal statement, high school transcript, minimum 2.0 GPA, 3 letters of recommendation. *Recommended:* interview.
Application deadlines: 3/15 (freshmen), 6/15 (transfers).
Notification: continuous (freshmen), continuous (transfers).

CONTACT
Franklin University Switzerland, Via Ponte Tresa 29, CH-6924 Sorengo, Switzerland.

Glion Institute of Higher Education
Glion-sur-Montreux, Switzerland
http://www.glion.edu/

CONTACT
Admissions, Glion Institute of Higher Education, Route de Glion 111, CH-1823 Glion-sur-Montreux, Switzerland. *Phone:* 41-0 21 989 26 77. *Fax:* 41-0 21 989 26 78. *E-mail:* info@glion.edu.

International University in Geneva
Geneva, Switzerland
http://www.iun.ch/

CONTACT
Ms. Virginie Morel, Admissions Officer, International University in Geneva, Geneva 1215, Switzerland. *Phone:* -41 22710-7110. *Fax:* 41 22710-7111. *E-mail:* bachelor@iun.ch.

Les Roches International School of Hotel Management
Bluche, Switzerland
http://www.lesroches.edu/

CONTACT
Enrollment Management Department, Les Roches International School of Hotel Management, CH-3975 Bluche, Switzerland. *Phone:* 41-021 989 26 44. *Fax:* 41-021 989 26 45. *E-mail:* info@lesroches.edu.

TAIWAN

Christ's College
Taipei, Taiwan
http://www.cct.edu.tw/

CONTACT
Ms. Lucy Li, Recruiter, Christ's College, No. 51, Ziqiang Road, Tamsui District, New Taipei City 251, Taiwan. *Phone:* -+886-2-2809-7661. *Fax:* +886-2-8809-1084. *E-mail:* lucyli@christs-college.org.

UNITED ARAB EMIRATES

The American University in Dubai
Dubai, United Arab Emirates
http://www.aud.edu/
- **Proprietary** comprehensive, founded 1995
- **Urban** campus
- **Coed** 1,997 undergraduate students
- 74% of applicants were admitted

UNDERGRAD STUDENTS
Students come from 105 other countries.

Freshmen:
Admission: 1,343 applied, 988 admitted.

FACULTY
Total: 171, 74% full-time, 64% with terminal degrees.
Student/faculty ratio: 15:1.

ACADEMICS
Calendar: semesters. *Degrees:* certificates, bachelor's, and master's.

Special study options: accelerated degree program, advanced placement credit, double majors, English as a second language, honors programs, independent study, internships, part-time degree program, services for LD students, study abroad, summer session for credit.

Computers: 631 computers/terminals are available on campus for general student use. Students can access the following: computer help desk, free student e-mail accounts, online (class) grades, online (class) registration, online (class) schedules. Campuswide network is available. 100% of college-owned or -operated housing units are wired for high-speed Internet access. Wireless service is available via entire campus.
Library: University Library. *Books:* 47,378 (physical), 300,000 (digital/electronic); *Serial titles:* 85 (physical); *Databases:* 48.

STUDENT LIFE

Housing options: men-only, women-only. Campus housing is university owned. Freshman campus housing is guaranteed.

Activities and organizations: drama/theater group, student-run newspaper, Student Government Association, Community Service Club, Drama Club, Music Club, Debate Club.

Athletics *Intercollegiate sports:* basketball M/W, soccer M/W, swimming and diving M/W, tennis M/W, volleyball M/W. *Intramural sports:* basketball M/W, football M/W, soccer M/W, squash M/W, swimming and diving M/W, table tennis M/W, tennis M/W, track and field M/W, volleyball M/W.

Campus security: 24-hour patrols.

Student services: health clinic, personal/psychological counseling.

APPLYING

Options: electronic application, early admission.

Application fee: 55 United Arab Emirates dirhams.

Required: high school transcript, minimum 2.0 GPA, 2 letters of recommendation. *Required for some:* interview. *Recommended:* essay or personal statement.

CONTACT

Mrs. Carol Maalouf, Director of Admissions, The American University in Dubai, PO Box 28282, Dubai, United Arab Emirates. *Phone:* -971 4 399 9000 Ext. 170. *Fax:* 971 4 399 8899. *E-mail:* admissions@aud.edu.

American University of Sharjah
Sharjah, United Arab Emirates
http://www.aus.edu/

CONTACT

American University of Sharjah, PO Box 26666, Sharjah, United Arab Emirates. *Phone:* -971 6 515-5555.

UNITED KINGDOM

Hult International Business School
London, United Kingdom
http://www.hult.edu/

- **Independent** comprehensive, founded 1959
- **Urban** campus with easy access to San Francisco, London
- **Coed**
- **Moderately difficult** entrance level

FACULTY

Student/faculty ratio: 15:1.

ACADEMICS

Calendar: 5-term academic calendar: required fall, winter, spring terms; optional Summer 1, Summer 2 terms. *Degrees:* bachelor's, master's, and doctoral.

Library: Main Library plus 2 others. *Books:* 1,815 (physical).

STUDENT LIFE

Housing options: on-campus residence required through sophomore year; coed. Campus housing is leased by the school. Freshman applicants given priority for college housing.

Activities and organizations: drama/theater group, student-run newspaper, choral group, Language Cafe, Model United Nations, International Law Society, Hult RISE (charity club), Consultancy Club.

Campus security: 24-hour emergency response devices and patrols, controlled dormitory access.

Student services: personal/psychological counseling.

COSTS

Costs (2017–18) *Tuition:* 24,900 British pounds full-time. Full-time tuition and fees vary according to course load and location. *Room only:* Room and board charges vary according to board plan, housing facility, location, and student level.

APPLYING

Standardized Tests *Required for some:* SAT or ACT (for admission), TOEFL, IELTS, or PTE for non-native English speakers.

Options: electronic application.

Application fee: 75 British pounds.

Required: essay or personal statement, high school transcript, 2 letters of recommendation. *Required for some:* interview.

CONTACT

Hult International Business School, 35 Commercial Road, London E1 1LD, United Kingdom. *Phone:* -44 207 341 8555. *E-mail:* bachelor@hult.edu.

London Metropolitan University
London, United Kingdom
http://www.londonmet.ac.uk/

CONTACT

London Metropolitan University, 166-220 Holloway Road, London N7 8DB, United Kingdom.

Open University
Milton Keynes, United Kingdom
http://www.open.ac.uk/

CONTACT

Open University, Walton Hall, Milton Keynes MK7 6AA, United Kingdom.

Regent's University London
London, United Kingdom
http://www.regents.ac.uk/

CONTACT

Admissions Director, Regent's University London, Inner Circle, Regent's Park, London NW1 4NS, United Kingdom. *Phone:* 44-0 207 487 7505. *Fax:* 44-0 207 487 7425. *E-mail:* bacl@regents.ac.uk.

Richmond, The American International University in London
Richmond, United Kingdom
http://www.richmond.ac.uk/

CONTACT

Mr. Nick Atkinson, Director of United States Admissions, Richmond, The American International University in London, 343 Congress Street, Suite 3100, Boston, MA 02210-1214. *Phone:* 617-450-5617. *Fax:* 617-450-5601. *E-mail:* us_admissions@richmond.ac.uk.

College Close-Ups

A ★ indicates that the school has detailed information with a Premium Profile on Petersons.com.

ACADEMY OF ART UNIVERSITY
SAN FRANCISCO, CALIFORNIA

 To read more about this school, visit http://petersons.to/academyofartuniversity

The College

In 1929, Academy of Art University founder Richard S. Stephens, who was the advertising Creative Director of *Sunset* magazine, acted on his belief that "aspiring artists and designers, given proper instruction, hard work, and dedication, can learn the skills needed to become successful professionals." His new School of Advertising Art consisted of 46 students meeting in one room on San Francisco's Kearny Street.

The instructors, who were professional artists, brought real-world problems, situations, solutions, and practical experience to the students. Based on this idea, the school's philosophy was formulated: Hire established professionals to teach the art and design professionals of tomorrow. At that time, advertising consisted primarily of illustrations, photos, and copy. Consequently, it became necessary to teach beginning students the fundamentals of drawing, painting, color, light, and photography as well as layout and typography.

When Richard A. Stephens succeeded his father as President in 1951, the Foundations Department was added, ensuring all students mastered the basic principles of traditional art and design. Illustration soon expanded to include fine arts (drawing, painting, sculpture, and printmaking), and advertising design led to the School of Graphic Design. A Fashion School (design, knitwear, textiles, and merchandising) and an Interior Design School were also added. In 1966, the Academy officially became a college, and a decade later began offering the Master of Fine Arts degree. Later, five more buildings were purchased, and by 1992, the student body comprised more than 2,500 students.

The leadership of the Academy was then turned over to the third generation. Dr. Elisa Stephens, granddaughter of the school's founder, quickly determined that the school's small School of Web Design & New Media had enormous potential to prepare students for multimedia careers with such companies as Pixar, Adobe, and Walt Disney Productions. It is now one of the largest departments at the Academy. In 2004, the name of the school was changed from Academy of Art College to Academy of Art University, in recognition of its depth, scope, and quality.

Today, Academy of Art University is the largest accredited private art and design university in the nation. Nearly one third of the student body is made up of international students. The Academy has over 30 facilities that house classrooms, studios, galleries, and residence halls. The students, who are admitted through an open-enrollment policy, aspire to earn A.A., B.A., B.F.A., B.S., B.Arch., M.A., M.F.A., or M.Arch. degrees or an Art Teaching Credential. Students can study in San Francisco or through the Academy's flexible online programs.

The Academy maintains a system of courtesy shuttles to connect the different points of the campus, all of which are located within the city limits of San Francisco, one of the world's most vibrant and beautiful cities. The instructors, who are working art and design professionals from around the world, are drawn to the Academy and to the creative and intellectual center that is the Bay Area. Extensive senior-year internship programs allow students to gain valuable experience and develop strong portfolios in their chosen field prior to graduation.

Academy of Art University is an accredited member of the WASC Senior College and University Commission (WSCUC), National Association of Schools of Art and Design (NASAD), Council for Interior Design Accreditation (CIDA) for B.F.A.-IAD and M.F.A.-IAD, National Architectural Accrediting Board (NAAB) for B.Arch. and M.Arch., and California Commission on Teacher Credentialing (CTC).

Location

The city of San Francisco is one of the great cultural centers of the world; a melting pot of diversity, culture, and creativity that has spawned major museums and galleries, world-class opera and theaters, dance companies, film production and recording studios, technological innovation, performing artists ranging from classical to popular music, and numerous other cultural opportunities. The city's status as a tourist mecca located on the Pacific Rim ensures that one encounters people from all corners of the world.

The climate is moderate and offers kaleidoscopic blends of sunshine and fog most of the year. The Northpoint campus is located at the historic Cannery building near world-famous Pier 39, where students can view Alcatraz Island from their classroom windows. In addition, four campus buildings are located two blocks from historic Union Square, in the commercial heart of the city, and three others are located near the Financial District. Shop 657, a store in Union Square, opened in December 2014 to display AAU designs and provide merchandising students real-world experience.

The city offers myriad locations for field trips and studio visits. World-renowned artists display their creations in the Academy's five nonprofit art galleries, which are open to the public. The Academy is an urban institution that both draws upon and contributes to the cultural wealth of the community in which it resides.

Majors

Academy of Art University offers A.A., B.A., B.F.A., B.S., B.Arch., M.A., M.F.A., and M.Arch. degrees and an Art Teaching Credential. Programs are available online and in San Francisco in the following: acting* (speech, improv, physical acting), advertising (creative strategy, art direction, copywriting, television commercials), animation & visual effects (background painting/layout design, character development, storyboard art, 3-D modeling, VFX/compositing), architecture (structures, materials and methods of construction, design process, structural and environmental systems), art education (learning to teach in museums, developmental psychology, teaching art in the community), art history (Renaissance art, American art history, ancient art history, looking at art, philosophy), art teaching credential (learning to teach both children and adults), communications & media technologies (journalism, editing, short-form documentary), costume design (design research, production bible, costume consistency, hair and makeup), fashion (design, knitwear, merchandising, textiles), fashion journalism (fashion writing, editorials for magazines, newspaper writing, fashion news, social media), fashion marketing (market research, analysis of business trends, digital and social media trends, effective branding, written communication), fashion merchandising (fashion business analysis, product selection, effective business plan), fashion product development (identify materials, manufacturing process, understanding of brand, consumer, and price point, technical drawings, knowledge of computer software), fashion styling (advanced skills for styling fashion products, photography, composition, lighting, hair styling, make-up artistry, art direction, production management), fashion textile design (design research, sketchbook, concept selection, original design production, trial and self-edit designs), fashion visual merchandising, research and concept development, visual presentation, creative merchandising concepts, verbal and written presentation), fine art (painting, printmaking, sculpture), game development (game engines, prototyping, level design, game art, 3-D modeling), game programming (engineering and programming techniques, math and object-oriented programming, complex algorithms, writing code), graphic design (corporate and brand identity, package design, print and collateral), illustration (children's books, editorial, comic books), industrial design (furniture design, product design, toy design, transportation design), interior architecture & design (commercial and residential design, furniture design), jewelry & metal arts (fashion jewelry design, enameling, stone setting, casting, welded and fabricated sculpture), landscape architecture (plant design, elements in landscape, grading and drainage, urban open spaces), motion pictures & television (cinematography, directing, editing, producing, production design, screenwriting), music production & sound design for visual media (harmony, arranging, orchestration, music production techniques, scoring for film), photography (architecture, advertising, digital documentary, editorial, fashion, fine art, landscape, photojournalism, portraiture), studio production for advertising & design, visual development (concept art for animation, film, and games; digital painting; character design; cinematic storytelling; Marquette sculpting; environment creation), web design & new media (user experience design, interactive design, new media, web design), and writing for film, television, & digital media. * Acting degree program is currently not available online.

Academic Programs

The Bachelor of Fine Arts degree requires foundations courses, major courses, art electives, and liberal arts courses. Fundamental courses are related specifically to students' majors to prepare them to begin intense focus courses in their field by the sophomore year. All major courses of study are structured so the student builds upon skills learned the previous semester and advances to the next level of technical or creative proficiency. Some related major courses may be taken concurrently.

Liberal arts courses teach practical applications for forging a professional career in art and design. International students who come from countries where English is not the primary language may take additional EAP (English for Art Purposes) classes, as determined by English language proficiency testing. Students are advised to meet with departmental directors at least once during the academic year to have their progress assessed. Portfolios are reviewed before the junior year to determine whether or not a student has progressed sufficiently to continue study at the Academy.

Academic Facilities

Academy of Art University's industry-standard facilities offer students the tools they need to prepare for professional careers in art and design. The Academy invests in top-notch equipment to ensure it remains on the cutting edge of technology. Learning on industry-standard equipment, students gain hands-on experience.

Academy of Art University students have access to an array of digital tools. The School of Game Development and the School of Animation & Visual Effects provide the latest equipment, as well as a video and Cintiq lab, green screen studio, and sound booth. The School of Web Design & New Media houses a usability lab with the most current software, while the School of Music Production & Sound Design for Visual Media offers the latest sound design and video editing tools and is proud to have a new flagship mixing console, the Avid S6. The Academy is the first university in California to offer this new console and the second organization in California other than Skywalker Sound to own the console.

The School of Advertising is designed to look, feel, and function like an ad agency. Located in the heart of San Francisco's Financial District, the School of Graphic Design has the latest industry tools that enable students to have a seamless transition into the world of work following graduation. And the School of Illustration is housed in a unique historic building in San Francisco's Union Square District. The original libraries, meeting rooms, theater, and a ballroom have been transformed into drawing/painting studios and classrooms.

Undergraduate and graduate students in Architecture, Interior Architecture & Design, and Landscape Architecture share an 800-square-foot materials library and plotting room, as well as a model shop. The School of Industrial Design offers multiple shop facilities and a 3-D computer lab. The School of Landscape Architecture benefits from being located in San Francisco, the hub of urban landscape design.

Fashion students have access to studio facilities for women's, men's and children's wear, as well as textile design, knitwear design, and fashion merchandising and marketing. Surrounded by world-renowned museums and galleries, the School of Fine Art and the School of Art History facilities include thousands of square feet of studio space with everything their students need to bring their individual visions to life.

The School of Motion Pictures & Television and the School of Acting facilities include a postproduction area, green screen studio, screenwriting lab, and several soundstage studios. Students of the School of Communications & Media Technologies have access to a cutting-edge radio studio and television studio, complete with robotic cameras, anchor desks and interview sets, teleprompters, and green screens. School of Photography facilities are equipped with both traditional and digital photographic technology.

The library provides advanced digital tools, making it possible for students to access extensive art and design image resources and information on demand. The Academy Resource Center offers all students free learning support services including study hall tutoring, academic coaching, English as second language support programs, a writing lab, and a multimedia language lab.

Costs

For Fall 2018, undergraduate tuition will be $873 per credit unit. Full-time students must carry at least 12 semester units per term. There is a nonrefunable $50 fee when applying. Lab fees run from $25 to $400 per semester, depending on the class. Tuition and fees are subject to change at any time. Art supplies can run from $250 to $1,500 per semester, depending on the major. The Academy has most of the expensive technical equipment available for students to borrow or use in a lab. Academy of Art University operates many residence halls within the city. Several housing options are offered, and costs vary based on the building and room/unit assigned. For further information, students may contact the Department of Housing and Residence Life directly at 415-618-6335

Financial Aid

The Academy offers financial aid packages consisting of grants, loans, and work-study to eligible students with a demonstrated need. Low-interest loans are available to all eligible students, regardless of need. As financial aid programs, procedures, and eligibility requirements change frequently, applicants should contact the Financial Aid Office at financialaid@academyart.edu or 800-544-2787 (toll-free, U.S. only).

Faculty

The Academy averages 1,404 instructors in fall/spring semester, most of whom are full-time art and design professionals and part-time teachers. The student-teacher ratio for undergraduate classes averages 14:1.

Student Government

Although there is no formal student government, each department has between two and three student representatives who meet with the President as needed throughout the semester to discuss any student issues.

Admission Requirements

Applicants for the A.A., B.A., B.F.A., B.S., and B.Arch. programs must have a high school diploma or equivalent. There is no portfolio requirement. M.A., M.F.A., and M.Arch. Applicants must have a bachelor's degree and submit a portfolio and statement of intent. International students take written and speech tests to determine which EAP (English for Art Purposes) classes may have to be completed. Most EAP classes can be taken in conjunction with art and design classes. All foundations classes offer specialized EAP sections with instructors trained for language assistance. The application fee is $50 for undergraduates. A $1,000 tuition deposit applies to international applicants.

What Sets Academy of Art University Apart

The Academy is one of the few art and design schools that believes in nurturing the whole artist; this includes developing athletic ability along with artistic talent. Students can participate in intercollegiate, intramural, and club sports. With Pacific West honors and national championships, the Academy offers basketball, baseball, softball, cross country, track and field, soccer, golf, volleyball, and tennis for its students to partake in. Furthermore, the Academy is proud to be the only art school in the NCAA Division II. Students have gone on to compete in the Olympics and have been drafted by professional leagues to play their sport professionally.

Application and Information

Students may apply to enter the Academy at the beginning of the spring, fall, or summer semesters. Information in this profile is subject to change. Students should contact Academy of Art University for current information or visit www.academyart.edu to learn about total costs, median student loan debt, potential occupations, and other information.

Academy of Art University
79 New Montgomery Street
San Francisco, California 94105
Phone: 415-274-2200
    800-544-2787 (U.S. only)
Fax: 415-618-6287
E-mail: info@academyart.edu
Website: www.academyart.edu
    https://www.facebook.com/AcademyofArtUniversity
    https://twitter.com/academy_of_art
    https://plus.google.com/+academyofartuniversity/posts
    http://www.pinterest.com/academyofartuni
    http://academyofartu.tumblr.com
    http://instagram.com/academy_of_art
    http://www.youtube.com/user/academyofartu
    http://weheartit.com/AcademyofArtU

Academy of Art University's downtown campus.

ALLEGHENY COLLEGE
MEADVILLE, PENNSYLVANIA

 To read more about this school, visit http://petersons.to/alleghenycollege

The College

One of Loren Pope's forty "Colleges That Change Lives," Allegheny is cited as the premiere college in the country for students with "unusual combinations" of interests and talents. On its historic campus—where the liberal arts and sciences have been taught for more than 200 years—students develop combinations of majors and minors in areas that may, at first glance, seem unrelated: biology and economics, political science and music, history and psychology. Allegheny students share an abiding passion for learning and life, a spirit of camaraderie, and a respect for shared inquiry that spans all areas of study. Neuroscience majors play in the Civic Symphony and build houses during Alternative Spring Break. Students prepare for law school while playing basketball and interning in Washington, D.C. Computer science majors present work in philosophy at national conferences.

Building on a combination of academic disciplines and passions, every student completes the comprehensive Senior Project under the guidance of a faculty adviser in his or her major field. The project demonstrates the skills most prized by employers and graduate schools: the ability to complete a major assignment, work independently, analyze and synthesize information, and to write and speak persuasively.

Allegheny students are encouraged to explore all of their interests and to look at academic disciplines from multiple perspectives, which leads them to extraordinary outcomes. Biochemistry majors use the skills they learned in communication arts to start marketing careers with the Environmental Protection Agency. English majors collaborate with the College's pre-health advisers and enjoy acceptance rates to medical school between 80 and 100 percent— twice the national average. And over 95 percent of Allegheny's job-seeking graduates find employment within six months.

Leaders in business, government, medicine, education, and community service frequently declare that the future belongs to individuals who are innovators, inventors, and big-picture thinkers, those who think both analytically and creatively. It is this preparation for the global marketplace, and for life, that Allegheny, with its emphasis on "unusual combinations," is nationally known for providing.

Location

Central campus looks like a traditional college with a rich liberal arts heritage and tradition, with its 79 acres of rolling lawns and brick walkways, historic buildings, and century-old oaks and elms. A 203-acre recreational complex and a 283-acre nature reserve complement state-of-the-art classrooms, labs, theaters, studios and other facilities.

The campus overlooks the town of Meadville, a county seat that features a courthouse, hospital, a variety of industries, and more. Allegheny students connect with the community in many ways, from running after-school programs to taking in the latest movies, from creating art installations to checking out live music.

Allegheny students live in a section of the country that most people get to see only on vacation. Northwest Pennsylvania is a nature-lover's paradise of verdant, undisturbed forests and streams and lakes that are gems of biodiversity. It's no wonder that the College has one of the oldest Outing Clubs in the country.

Allegheny is ideally situated within 2 hours of the social and transportation hubs of Pittsburgh, Cleveland, and Buffalo. Being just close enough to major cities allows for frequent excursions to major sporting events, concerts, and other attractions.

Majors and Degrees

Allegheny students can earn the Bachelor of Arts (B.A.) or the Bachelor of Science (B.S.) degree in the following programs of study: applied computing; art and technology; art (studio); art history; biochemistry; biology; business; chemistry; communication arts; community and justice studies; computer science; creative writing; economics; English; environmental geology; environmental science; environmental studies; French; geology; German; global health studies; history; international studies; mathematics; music; neuroscience; philosophy; physics; political science; psychology; religious studies; Spanish; theatre; women's, gender, and sexuality studies; and self-designed majors.

In addition to the above majors, minors are available in: art and the environment, Asian studies, astronomy, black studies, Chinese studies, classical studies, dance and movement studies, environmental writing, French studies, Jewish studies, journalism in the public interest, Latin, Latin American and Caribbean studies, medieval and Renaissance studies, Middle East and North African studies, music history, music performance, music theory, and writing.

Dedicated advisers are available for students interested in: pre-dental, pre-law, pre-medicine, pre-nursing, pre-pharmacy, and pre-veterinary.

Students may also take advantage of accelerated master's and doctoral degree programs, teacher certification programs, and engineering cooperative programs with other top institutions.

Academic Programs

Allegheny College believes so strongly in unusual combinations that they are built right into its curriculum; it is one of the few liberal arts colleges nationally that requires students to choose a minor as well as a major. In some ways, this may make school more difficult. But most students at Allegheny are individuals for whom the most difficult thing would be to give up some vital part of themselves. Some Allegheny students have majors and minors that complement each other in predictable ways—an international studies major with a minor in French, for example. But there are other students whose majors and minors represent very different aspects of themselves— an environmental studies major with a minor in creative writing or a chemistry major with a minor in history. Coupled with experiential learning and the distinctive Senior Project, seeing academic disciplines from multiple perspectives leads to extraordinary outcomes.

During the first two years, every Allegheny student participates in seminars that focus on written and oral communication as well as academic and career advising, and the faculty instructor serves as adviser for both years. This progressive course sequence, in addition to the Junior Seminar and Senior Project, helps students create a four-year experience to match all of their needs and goals.

Under the guidance of a faculty adviser in his or her major field, every student completes the Senior Project, a significant piece of original scholarly work with a creative, analytical, or experimental focus. The project mirrors a master's thesis and requires project management skills, independent work, writing and presentation skills, and the ability to analyze and synthesize information. Allegheny has required a senior capstone experience since the college's first commencement ceremony in 1821. The Council on Undergraduate Research recognized Allegheny as the top baccalaureate college in the nation for providing high-quality research experiences to undergraduates.

In the National Survey of Student Engagement, responses by college freshmen placed Allegheny within the top 10 percent in the United States for both a supportive campus environment and level of academic challenge.

Off-Campus Programs

Allegheny College recognizes the enormous academic, professional, and personal value of studying off-campus, nationally or internationally. Allegheny students can experience multiple off-campus adventures, learning with an eclectic group of students with diverse academic majors and interests. The Gateway facilitates a variety of opportunities through study abroad, career services, community service, and more.

The College sponsors semester and year-long study-away programs, some of which require skills in languages other than English, and others with no language requirements. More than 190 Allegheny students and faculty participate in forty Allegheny-sponsored study abroad programs in twenty countries.

In addition, faculty members lead students each year on intensive three-week experiential learning seminars. These for-credit, faculty-designed programs occur at the end of each spring semester. Recent excursions took students to Austria, the Czech Republic, England, Germany, India, Japan, Turkey, and South Africa.

The Office of Career Education maintains a database of 2,500 internship and shadowing opportunities, including especially popular ones in Boston, New York City, Los Angeles, and Washington, D.C. Students at Allegheny can choose among several kinds of internships, including academic internships taken for credit that often take place during a spring or fall semester and noncredit internships throughout the summer.

Academic Facilities

Allegheny boasts the nationally acclaimed Steffee Hall of Life Sciences, which incorporates state-of-the-art labs located right next to classrooms and faculty offices. A new environmental science center features the best in sustainable practices with a living wall, aquaponics equipment, and solar panels. Students also benefit from the GIS learning lab, planetarium, and seismographic network station.

The multimillion-dollar Vukovich Center for Communication Arts, which meets LEED certification standards and has a rooftop garden, features a learning theater, scene and costume shops, and video production facilities. Language students enjoy a multimedia learning lab, and dancers work in bright, functional studio and performance spaces. The Bowman, Penelec, and Megahan art galleries display student and faculty work as well as visiting exhibits.

Allegheny's Learning Commons provides academic support to all students through professional guidance, peer mentors, training, and effective learning tools. The center is housed in Pelletier Library, which offers more than 900,000 volumes, as well as extensive digital resources, research tools, and unique meeting spaces.

Costs

For 2017–18, tuition and fees were $45,970. Room and board was $11,650.

Financial Aid

Through the generous support of its alumni, Allegheny is able to provide over $43 million in achievement-based scholarships; need-based grant assistance; and aid awarded to students from federal, state, and private sources. Allegheny's financial assistance allows many students the opportunity to make a college choice based on value and fit, rather than financial constraints.

Allegheny's Trustee Scholarships are awarded without regard to financial need to students who have balanced academic excellence with other distinctive activities while in high school. Awards range up to $112,000, distributed equally over four years of study at Allegheny (up to $30,000 per year), and renew automatically.

Faculty

Whether it's conducting research, teaching a First-Year Seminar, leading a three-week study tour, co-authoring an article or making an authentic French dinner, faculty work and learn alongside students every day. There's no graduate school buffer between undergraduates and faculty. Students don't have to wait behind graduate students for research positions on faculty-led projects or compete against hundreds of other students for the lead roles in plays or an editorship at the literary magazine.

Of the 173 full-time faculty members, 91 percent have earned the highest degree in their fields. The student to faculty ratio is 11:1, and introductory classes have an average of 19 students. Advanced classes have an average of 12 students, and some seminars have fewer than 10. Of all classes, 88 percent have fewer than 30 students.

Every student has a faculty adviser for the first two years and a faculty adviser in his/her major field for the final two years. Culminating with their work guiding students through the Senior Project, faculty members are not only supportive and engaging teachers but true leaders and mentors.

Student Government

The Allegheny Student Government is the official voice and administrative unit of the student body. This extremely active and influential organization concerns itself with the quality of the educational, cultural, and social aspects of the Allegheny community. Its members organize and coordinate programs of a cocurricular and extracurricular nature and sponsor more than 120 student-run clubs and organizations.

Students serve on every major college committee, including faculty searches, sustainability efforts, and strategic planning. Their presence exemplifies the importance placed on student participation and represents the influence students have on the institution.

Admission Requirements

From the time a prospective student first contacts Allegheny, the college's holistic approach is directed to addressing his or her unique character, needs, and aspirations. During the application process, primary attention is focused on those criteria that indicate academic promise, including difficulty of high school classes, GPA, and class rank. Careful consideration is also given to those personal qualities that are important in the total success of the college experience: school and community activities, recommendation letters, and the personal essay. Students are encouraged to share additional information through the college's application supplement and an interview and visit. Allegheny embraces the concept that standardized test scores do not exclusively reflect a student's full range of abilities or potential to succeed in college. As a result, Allegheny is now test optional. ACT and SAT I scores are optional for U.S. citizens and permanent residents.

The result is a highly personalized approach to the selection of students that remains consistent with the aims of the college, respects the individuality of each applicant, and ensures equal consideration of every candidate. The College encourages diversity and actively seeks students from all ethnic, religious, racial, political, geographic, and socioeconomic backgrounds.

Application and Information

Office of Admissions
Allegheny College
520 North Main Street
Meadville, Pennsylvania 16335
Phone: 814-332-4351
      800-521-5293 (toll-free)
Fax: 814-337-0431
E-mail: admissions@allegheny.edu
Web site: http://www.allegheny.edu/admissions
      http://www.allegheny.edu/distinctions
      http://www.allegheny.edu/visit
      http://www.allegheny.edu/apply

Recognized among Loren Pope's *40 "Colleges That Change Lives,"* Allegheny College is one of the nation's most historic and innovative institutions of higher education. Allegheny is one of the only colleges in the country that requires students to choose both a major and minor, ensuring they develop the skills needed to be analytical and creative.

AQUINAS COLLEGE
GRAND RAPIDS, MICHIGAN

 To read more about this school, visit http://petersons.to/aquinascollege

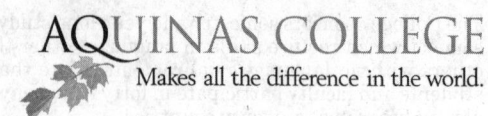
AQUINAS COLLEGE
Makes all the difference in the world.

The College

Recently named a Top 50 Catholic college, Aquinas is located on the eastern edge of the city of Grand Rapids. Aquinas enjoys all of the advantages of Michigan's second-largest city and is just a 3-hour drive from Detroit or Chicago. The Aquinas College campus is an interesting blend of early-nineteenth century architecture coupled with modern-day structures. The campus abounds with natural beauty; it has been called the most beautiful small campus in Michigan. Its 90 species of trees, winding woodland paths, and inviting creeks and ponds create a peaceful 117-acre environment that students of all ages find welcoming.

Founded by the Dominican Sisters of Grand Rapids in 1886, Aquinas has a Catholic heritage and a Christian tradition. For more than 130 years, Aquinas College has inspired students to transform the world by providing a liberal arts education infused with the Catholic Dominican values of prayer, study, service, and community. It is lived out by Aquinas students who volunteer their time and talents in the Grand Rapids community and by those who travel to places such as the Dominican Republic; Appalachia, Kentucky; or any of a dozen other service-learning project sites. An ability to see the world from different perspectives is the hallmark of an Aquinas-educated student.

An Aquinas education makes graduates more employable. Each year, hundreds of Aquinas students find businesses, government agencies, and other organizations eager to offer field experience and internship opportunities. Students can find employment and internships with organizations such as the American Cancer Society, Detroit Red Wings, Grand Rapids Art Museum, Meijer, Mercy Health, Steelcase, United States Senate, Van Andel Institute, and Walt Disney World, to name a few. Over 90 percent of Aquinas seniors find jobs or enroll in graduate school within six months after graduation.

Aquinas sees a liberal arts education as career preparation. The Aquinas general education plan exposes students to the necessary skills that enable them to become critical thinkers, articulate speakers, strong writers, and effective problem solvers. Aquinas faculty members insist that students carry values as well as skills into the workplace. The College's curriculum, with its more than 60 majors, is designed to provide students with both breadth and depth and to foster a thirst for knowledge and truth and a spirit of intellectual dialogue and inquiry. Coupled with nationally recognized internship programs, it prepares students to both live and work in the rapidly changing world of today and tomorrow.

Arriving from places as near as Grand Rapids, Chicago, and Detroit and as far as China and South America, the approximately 1,900 students include 1,300 full-time, 175 part-time, 150 graduate students, 100 dually enrolled high school students, and almost 200 students in nursing, which is a collaborative program with the University of Detroit Mercy. The Insignis program at Aquinas encourages students of exceptional academic ability to participate in social and intellectual activities such as lectures and receptions for visiting scholars and trips to places of cultural interest. Aquinas offers more than 70 student organizations, ranging from intramural teams and departmental clubs to a wide variety of musical groups, student publications, and service organizations.

In addition to its undergraduate degrees, Aquinas also offers Master in the Art of Teaching, Master of Art in Counseling, Master in Education, and Master of Management graduate degrees.

Location

Aquinas' location in Grand Rapids allows students to reap the benefits of west Michigan's economic, educational, and cultural center. The city was recently recognized as one of the "Top 52 Places to Go in the World" by *The New York Times*. Grand Rapids combines big-city excitement and small-town charm. There are cosmopolitan amenities ranging from four-star hotels and restaurants to top-notch cultural facilities and entertainment venues. Established attractions include ArtPrize, Laughfest, the Gerald R. Ford Presidential Museum, the Van Andel Public Museum, the 10,000-seat Fifth Third Park for Whitecaps minor-league baseball, the 70-acre Fredrik Meijer Gardens, and the 12,000-seat Van Andel Arena, home to the Grand Rapids Griffins AHL hockey team and a venue for nationally known music concerts and performances. With nearly half a million area residents, there are abundant recreation, arts, and cultural opportunities available.

Majors and Degrees

Aquinas College offers the following undergraduate degree programs: Bachelor of Arts, Bachelor of Fine Arts, Bachelor of Arts in general education, Bachelor of Music Education, Bachelor of Science, Bachelor of Science in Business Administration, Bachelor of Science in sustainable business, and Bachelor of Science in International Business. A Bachelor of Science in Nursing degree program is offered in collaboration with the University of Detroit Mercy and Mercy Health St. Mary's.

Majors and programs of study are offered in:

- accounting
- accounting/business administration
- art
- art/business administration
- art history
- biochemistry and molecular biology
- biology
- business administration
- business administration/chemistry
- business administration/communication
- business administration/music
- business administration/sport management
- chemical physics
- chemistry
- child life specialist
- communication
- community leadership
- computer information systems
- data analytics
- drawing
- economics
- education
- engineering
- English
- environmental studies
- exercise science
- French
- geography
- German
- health
- health science
- history
- international studies
- Irish studies
- Japanese
- journalism/publications
- learning disabilities
- management information systems
- marketing
- mathematics
- music
- organizational communication
- painting
- philosophy
- photography
- physical education and recreation
- physics
- political science
- printmaking
- psychology
- sculpture
- social science
- sociology
- Spanish
- studio art
- sustainable business
- theatre
- theatre for social change
- theology
- translation and interpretation
- urban studies
- visual arts administration
- women's studies
- world languages

Associate degrees are also available, including the Associate of Arts and the Associate of Science.

Pre-professional programs include dentistry, law, medicine, occupational therapy, physical therapy, physician's assistant studies, and veterinary science.

COLLEGE CLOSE-UPS

Academic Programs

In addition to their major and minor fields of study, students take a First Year Experience Course and an integrated skills course called Inquiry and Expression. This course spans the first semester of the freshman year and has an emphasis on writing integrated with reading critically, oral communication skills, critical thinking, library/electronic research methods, computer utilization, and basic quantitative reasoning. The thematic content is American Pluralism: The Individual in a Diverse America. As juniors, they are required to take 3 hours in Theological Foundation. Students are also required to be proficient in a second language through the 102 level. There also is a distribution plan in the general education plan covering social science, natural world, humanities, cross-cultural awareness, and mathematics. The Aquinas Advantage Center expands learning beyond the classroom by housing co-curricular opportunities for study away, internships, and faculty-guided research in one central department. Aquinas also accepts credit through CLEP, Advanced Placement, and International Baccalaureate.

Off-Campus Programs

Students have the option of participating in the Dominican College Campus Interchange Program. Cooperating colleges are Barry University in Miami, Florida; Dominican College in San Rafael, California; and St. Thomas Aquinas College in Sparkill, New York. Students can increase their language skills through Study Away programs in Costa Rica, France, Italy, Japan, Spain, London, or Germany. An Aquinas faculty member accompanies approximately 30 students to Aquinas' study center in Tully Cross, Ireland. Students have the opportunity to earn a full semester of credit while traveling abroad, and living in a rural Irish community. The curriculum is centered on several aspects of Irish studies.

Academic Facilities

The Albertus Magnus Hall of Science facility is currently undergoing a $32 million expansion and renovation that will pave the way for new programs, innovative research, and student engagement. The Grace Hauenstein Library is a $6-million facility with resources that include a public access catalog, audiovisual materials, circulation and course reserve materials, reference services, and interlibrary loan services (free access to more than 60 million books and documents from libraries across the country). Other facilities include the Cook Carriage House student center and the Art and Music Center, featuring a 200-seat recital hall, an art gallery, and a sculpture studio. The Aquinas Performing Arts Center is a $7-million facility providing a state-of-the-art theater venue. Five apartment buildings also provide great housing options for upperclassmen.

AQnet allows residents and commuters to wirelessly connect their personal computers or other devices to the Internet while on campus. Students will find centrally located kiosks and computer labs on campus in classrooms, residence halls, the Grace Hauenstein Library, and common areas.

Costs

For 2018–19, tuition is $31,976 and room and board are $9,338 for a total of $41,314. Annual fees are $598 per year. Other expenses, including books, travel, and personal supplies, average $2,000.

Financial Aid

Aquinas College awards both merit-based financial assistance and traditional need-based assistance to qualified students. The Spectrum Scholarship Program was developed to recognize students' achievements in academics, leadership, and service. More than 95 percent of entering freshmen receive some form of financial assistance. The College administers the traditional grant and loan programs, including Federal Direct Loans and Parent PLUS loans. Athletic grants are also available. The College participates in an automatic payment program. This plan assists students in paying costs over a period of time. To apply for financial assistance, students must complete the Free Application for Federal Student Aid (FAFSA).

Faculty

Aquinas faculty members are teachers first: while research plays an important part in the Aquinas faculty's development, teaching remains the number-one priority. In addition to teaching, faculty members serve as academic advisers, mentors, and advisers to various clubs and organizations on campus. With a student-professor ratio of 11:1, faculty members give individual attention and assistance to students. All classes and labs are taught by faculty members, not graduate assistants. More than 80 percent of Aquinas faculty members have doctoral or terminal degrees.

Student Government

The Student Senate is the governing body of Aquinas students. Senators are chosen by securing twenty-five signatures of students in support of their involvement. These students have both voice and vote on issues facing the College's Academic Assembly. The Senate is responsible for many of the academic, social, recreational, and cultural activities on the campus.

Admission Requirements

Freshman and transfer applications are received on a rolling basis. A candidate for admission to Aquinas is considered on the basis of academic preparation, scholarship, and character. Admission depends on a number of factors, including academic records and ACT or SAT test scores. The online application for admission does not require a fee. The admissions office reserves the right to review applications on a case-by-case basis. Curriculum, extracurricular activities, and any extenuating circumstances are considered in the decision. Letters of recommendation are encouraged but not required.

Application and Information

Prospective students may submit a free application for admission at https://www.aquinas.edu/undergraduate.

For further information, interested students should contact:

Angie Schlosser-Bacon
Director of Admissions
Aquinas College
1700 Fulton E
Grand Rapids, Michigan 49506-1801
Phone: 616-632-2900
      800-678-9593 (toll-free)
E-mail: admissions@aquinas.edu
Website: aquinas.edu

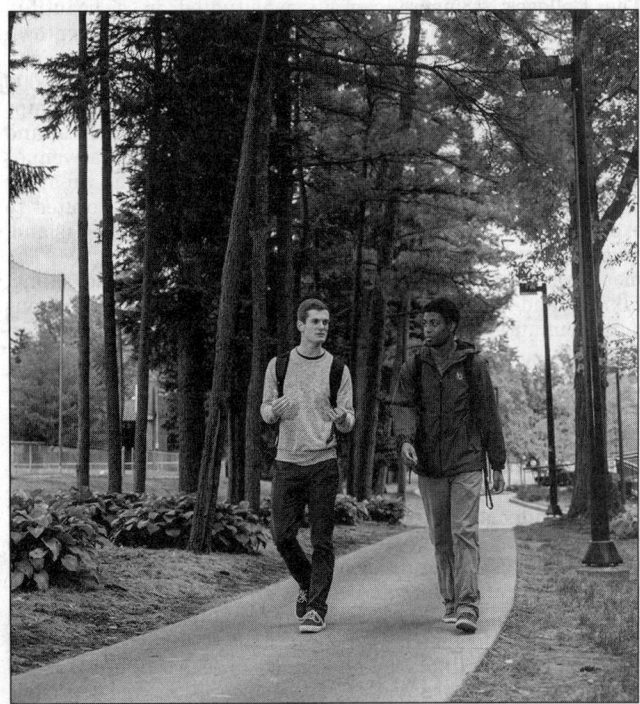

ASSUMPTION COLLEGE
WORCESTER, MASSACHUSETTS

 To read more about this school, visit http://petersons.to/assumptioncollege

The College

Assumption College, established in 1904 by the Augustinians of the Assumption, is a coeducational institution known for its classic liberal arts curriculum and strong academic programs in business and professional studies. The College's 2,000 undergraduates choose among 30 majors and 47 minors, gaining a depth and breadth of knowledge that serves as a foundation for personal fulfillment and lifelong success. Students' educational experience is grounded in the rich Catholic intellectual tradition, which cultivates both the mind and the personal values students require to meet the demands of a constantly changing world. Undergraduate and graduate students are guided by faculty and staff members in a thriving community that develops individuals known for critical intelligence, thoughtful citizenship, and compassionate service.

The academic journey is characterized by individual attention and the quest for personal excellence. With a student-faculty ratio of just 12:1, Assumption's professors serve as mentors who challenge students to ask questions, find their own answers, and grow—intellectually, socially, and spiritually. Students are encouraged to pursue hands-on experience at internships and to participate in individual research projects. The result? Ninety-four percent of the graduates who responded to a survey six months after graduation are either employed, enrolled in graduate school, or engaged in community service.

At Assumption, 90 percent of the undergraduates live on campus and housing is guaranteed for all four years. The campus is lively seven days a week with academic programming, activities sponsored by student clubs and organizations, community service opportunities, campus ministry programs, and intercollegiate, intramural, and club sports. The College's state-of-the-art recreation center offers a number of opportunities for students to exercise or participate in intramural sports.

Location

The College's 185-acre campus is situated in a beautiful, residential neighborhood just minutes from downtown Worcester, Massachusetts. Worcester, the second-largest city in New England, is a vibrant college town, home to 35,000 students. The city offers extensive opportunities for internships in virtually every field, as well as numerous entertainment and community service options. Great restaurants, cultural venues and programs, and retail shops provide students with an array of off-campus activities. Worcester is also centrally located to exciting urban areas such as Boston; Providence, Rhode Island; and Hartford, Connecticut only an hour's drive away. The mountains of Vermont and New Hampshire provide skiing, hiking, and sightseeing opportunities. There are numerous daily commuter trains to Boston as well as other transportation options.

Majors and Degrees

Assumption offers undergraduate and graduate degrees.

Undergraduates pursue Bachelor of Arts degrees. The most popular majors include English (concentrations in literature or writing and mass communications), history, political science, psychology, the natural sciences (biology, biotechnology and molecular biology, neuroscience, chemistry, and environmental science), education, human services and rehabilitation studies, and business disciplines such as accounting, international business, management, marketing, and organizational communication. Minors are offered in 47 areas. Pre-professional advising programs are available for medicine, law, and dentistry.

The College has also developed partnerships with a number of highly regarded institutions to provide students with additional options, including engineering with the University of Notre Dame and Washington University in St. Louis, environmental science with Duke University, and law (3+3 programs) with Duquesne, Vermont, University of St. Thomas, and Western New England law schools. There are agreements for numerous medical professions as well, and joint seven-year programs are also available for those interested in podiatry or optometry.

Assumption College offers graduate degrees in applied behavior analysis, business, special education, school counseling, clinical counseling psychology, health advocacy, and rehabilitation counseling. An accelerated 6-in-5 combined bachelor's and master's degree is offered in several programs.

Academic Programs

The College's classic liberal arts curriculum promotes lively discussion of the books, ideas, people, and events that have shaped civilization. Faculty members and students explore the rich Catholic intellectual tradition together as they seek truth and the nature of the world.

Assumption also offers academic programs and courses that help students achieve their full potential. The College's Honors Program and the Fortin and Gonthier Core Texts and Enduring Questions Program encourage students to challenge themselves intellectually through intensive study and independent research. The SOPHIA (SOPHomore Initiative at Assumption) program is designed to help students discover a deeper connection between their spiritual, personal, and professional lives. Air Force and Army ROTC are also available at a neighboring institution.

Assumption College follows a traditional two-semester calendar, from late August to mid-May, as well as an optional January intersession. The Graduate Studies programs and the Center for Continuing and Career Education also offer two summer sessions for students.

Undergraduates complete a core curriculum that provides a strong foundation in the liberal arts, in addition to developing the skills and knowledge necessary for their professional career. Students must complete 120 credit hours in all academic programs to earn a degree.

Off-Campus Programs

The College and eleven other institutions of higher learning compose the Colleges of Worcester Consortium, which combines resources to offer the 35,000 college students in the area even greater academic and social opportunities. Assumption students may cross-register for academic credit at any of the participating colleges and enjoy their social and cultural events. Free transportation to and from other participating institutions is available.

Eligible students may choose to spend a semester or a year abroad. Assumption opened a campus in Rome in February 2013. The campus provides the opportunity for a close learning community where students live, study, and travel together in the city that forged the foundations of Western Civilization. The College's students have studied abroad in Australia, Austria, Chile, China, Costa Rica, the Czech Republic, England, France, Germany, Greece, Ireland, Italy, Japan, the Netherlands, Spain, and other locations. There are also numerous one- and two-week international experiences led by Assumption faculty.

Eighty-one percent of Assumption students have undertaken at least one internship, where they explore their professional

COLLEGE CLOSE-UPS

choices and broaden their workplace skills at local, regional, national, and international sites. In recent years, they have interned at PBS, the U.S. House of Representatives, Ralph Lauren, the Hungarian Embassy, Smith Barney, Fidelity, *The Rachel Ray Show, The Daily Show with Jon Stewart,* ABC News, PricewaterhouseCoopers, AT&T, Sony Japan, and countless other organizations.

Campus Facilities

The recently constructed Tsotsis Family Academic Center is a 62,000-square-foot building that features 13 high-tech, flexible classrooms; seminar rooms; common study spaces; a 400-seat performance hall with a rehearsal room, both of which are equipped with a sophisticated sound system not found in any other higher education institution on the East Coast; and a multi-function space that can accommodate 400 people.

The Testa Science Center houses the Department of Natural Sciences and features multiuse classrooms with state-of-the-art technology, ten teaching laboratories, seven laboratories dedicated to faculty and student research, a greenhouse, and student lounge areas.

The Information Technology Center houses computer labs, technology-rich classrooms, and an experienced support staff. Students can learn Web authoring, graphics and animation, digital video, and multimedia production. The digital audio studio is available to all students and faculty members.

Assumption offers a variety of housing options to accommodate the 90 percent of students who choose to live on campus. There are traditional residence halls, suites, a living and learning residence, and apartments with full kitchens. All resident students have individual hard-wired and wireless Internet access in their rooms. The College's stadium and athletic facilities support Assumption's 24 NCAA Division II intercollegiate teams, recreational programs, and the physical well-being of the campus community.

Costs

For 2017–18, tuition was $38,850, room and board were $12,195, and student fees were $750. The board plan is required for all first-year students.

Financial Aid

The College offers financial aid based on demonstrated need and scholastic achievement. The College requires that students submit the Free Application for Federal Student Aid (FAFSA), which is available on October 1. This form should be filed by February 15, so that the College may consider the information as it makes financial aid awards.

All applicants for admission are considered for merit awards of up to $21,000 per year. Funds awarded through this program reflect the College's commitment to academic excellence and student leadership. The College also awards up to fifty $25,000 Light the Way Scholarships each year to students who are working to positively impact the work in their own meaningful way.

Faculty

More than 94 percent of the Assumption College faculty members hold the highest degree in their field. They are active scholars presenting their ideas and research at professional conferences, writing books and articles, and publishing in journals. With a student-to-faculty ratio of 12:1, professors work closely with students and challenge them to explore new paths of knowledge and make their own discoveries. All of Assumption's academic advisors are full-time faculty members.

Student Organizations and Government

There are more than 60 clubs and organizations on campus, offering students many opportunities in community service, sports, academics, leadership, and special interests. The Student Government Association (SGA), the elected representatives of the student body, coordinates official communication between the student community and the College administration and officially recognizes student clubs and activities.

Admission Requirements

All applicants must graduate from an accredited secondary school with a minimum of 18 academic units. These units should include 4 years of English, 3 years of mathematics, 2 years of a foreign language, 2 years of history, 2 years of science, and 5 additional academic units.

Admission to Assumption is test-score optional. When submitting an application, an essay and recommendations are required. Interviews are recommended, but not required.

The number of solid academic courses, including the number of honors-level or Advanced Placement–level courses, is considered during the application review process.

The Admissions Committee understands that grading standards vary from school to school and from one course to another. Class rank provides some context within which to place the grades of students applying from a given school, but is not the only factor weighed when considering a student for admission. Some schools also provide grade distribution charts. The Committee also considers whether the applicant's grade point average or rank in class is weighted or unweighted.

Application and Information

Campus visits are strongly recommended. Appointments can be scheduled Monday through Friday. Group Information Sessions are held most Saturdays in the fall.

Applicants must submit a completed application, a $50 application fee, official transcripts, a recommendation letter, and an essay. Applications for early action admission must be received by November 1. There is a second early action admission deadline of December 15. The deadline for regular admission is February 15. Students may complete the Common Application and Supplement at www.commonapp.org.

For more information, students should contact:

Office of Admissions
Assumption College
500 Salisbury Street
P.O. Box 15005
Worcester, Massachusetts 01609-1296
Phone: 508-767-7285
     866-477-7776 (toll-free)
E-mail: admissions@assumption.edu
Website: www.assumption.edu
     twitter.com/AssumptionNews
     facebook.com/assumptioncollege

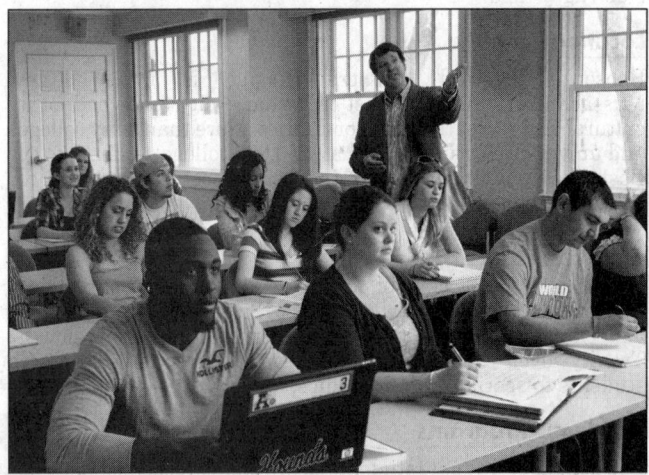

With a student-faculty ratio of just 12:1, Assumption's professors challenge students to ask questions, find their own answers, and grow.

BABSON COLLEGE
WELLESLEY, MASSACHUSETTS

 To read more about this school, visit http://petersons.to/babsoncollege

The College

Babson College is the educator, convener, and thought leader for Entrepreneurship of All Kinds™. As the only school to teach Entrepreneurial Thought and Action®, Babson shapes the leaders the world needs: those with strong functional knowledge and the skills and vision to navigate change, accommodate ambiguity, solve problems, and motivate teams in a common purpose. Every day, Babson students, faculty, and alumni address real-world business and societal problems, creating sustainable economic and social value in today's fast-paced global economy. Babson is accredited by the International Association for Management Education, AACSB International—The Association to Advance Collegiate Schools of Business, the New England Association of Schools and Colleges, and the European Quality Improvement System (EQUIS).

The 2017–18 undergraduate enrollment was 2,342 students with 48 percent women and 52 percent men. Babson is a residential college and is a fast-paced community alive with intellectual, cultural, athletic, and social activities. Approximately 85 percent of the undergraduate student body lives on campus all four years in fourteen residence halls. Housing options include fraternity and sorority housing, and entrepreneurial, service-oriented, and other specialty-themed housing.

Babson College is an NCAA Division III school. Most of the College's intercollegiate teams compete in the New England Women's and Men's Athletic Conference (NEWMAC). There are twenty-two men's and women's varsity sports teams, with additional club and intramural sports available to all students. More information is available at www.babsonathletics.com.

The Webster Center features an indoor, 200-meter, six-lane track; a field house; a gymnasium with three basketball courts; a racquetball court; a 25-yard, six-lane pool with 1- and 3-meter diving boards; a fitness center; squash courts; and a dance/aerobics studio. In fall 2017, Babson broke ground on a new, modern fitness and recreation facility designed to benefit the entire community. The Babson Recreation and Athletics Center is expected to open in 2019. The Babson Skating Center features a 600-seat skating arena. Outdoor facilities include eight tennis courts, an AstroTurf field, a game field, a renovated softball diamond, a baseball field, two sand-based varsity fields, and a club rugby field.

Location

Babson's beautiful 370-acre campus is in Wellesley, Massachusetts, 10 miles west of Boston, a city renowned for its cultural and recreational opportunities. More than sixty colleges and universities bring more than 250,000 college students to the Boston area, making it one of the world's best college towns for cultural exchange and research.

Majors and Degrees

Babson offers a Bachelor of Science degree, a Master of Business Administration degree, two Master of Science degree programs, and executive education programs for business professionals. Twenty-seven concentrations are available for undergraduate students to specialize their studies.

Academic Programs

Babson undergraduate students earn a highly respected Bachelor of Science degree, recognized around the world by employers who appreciate the powerful combination of deep functional knowledge and the entrepreneurial mindset of Babson graduates.

First-year courses at Babson lay the groundwork for students' future courses—and careers—starting with the Foundations of Management and Entrepreneurship (FME) course, a yearlong immersion into the business world. A team of 10–15 students develops and manages an actual business or service organization, studying organizational behavior, marketing, entrepreneurship, and operations, while emphasizing the integrated role these functions have in a business. Students will have the chance to dabble in all areas of the organization, testing what disciplines and possible careers they would like to pursue further.

Students will also take integrated liberal arts foundation courses providing them with valuable analytic and communication skills and an appreciation for the arts and humanities. Throughout the year, students will develop a deeper understanding (and appreciation) of themselves and their goals, as they continue to prepare to excel in business and in life.

A weekly First-Year Seminar will ease each student's transition to college life by helping them develop an awareness of campus resources, providing a support group for challenges that arise, and teaching communication and study skills. Members of the Babson community—including alumni, faculty, staff members, and peer mentors—provide personal and professional support throughout all four years.

Second-year students take an integrated series of courses in finance, economics, marketing, information technology, management accounting, and operations management. These courses offer functional knowledge of each discipline, and because they are thematically linked, they also provide the broad perspective of a CEO.

Students look at actual business problems via case studies and get real-world experience by studying, touring, interacting with, and presenting to local companies. Pursuing topics more intensively allows students to focus on certain areas of concentration and begin to formulate ideas on what to pursue in life after college.

Throughout the third and fourth years at Babson, students begin to think about issues with increased confidence, independence, and creativity. There is flexibility to reflect on career options and to pursue courses that align with personal and professional goals. In addition to management and liberal arts electives, students gain field experience via internships or consulting programs. Students may also opt to take their education abroad for a semester or short elective during schools breaks and apply it to real-life situations in countries around the world.

Babson offers twenty-seven optional concentrations in both business and liberal arts disciplines; descriptions can be found at www.babson.edu/concentrations. Students may focus their course of study by choosing a concentration in their areas of interest. Special programs, such as the Weissman Scholarship program, the Honors Program, the Center for Women's Entrepreneurial Leadership Scholars Program, the Management Consulting Field Experience, the Babson College Fund (student-managed endowment), Master of Science in Accounting (MSA), and independent research allow students to take advantage of customized learning opportunities at Babson.

Entering students may be granted credit or advanced course placement for successful scores on Advanced Placement (AP) examinations administered by the College Board as well as some courses in the International Baccalaureate (I.B.) curriculum.

Babson operates on a two-semester academic calendar. Semesters run from September to December and from late January through May. An optional credit-bearing three-week winter session is offered in January, and two summer sessions are offered—one from late May to early July and one from mid-July to mid-August.

Faculty

Because of Babson's close-knit community, students are able to form close relationships with the faculty. Of the 266 faculty members, 183 are full-time, and 89 percent of the full-time faculty members hold a doctoral degree or its equivalent. Faculty members are accomplished entrepreneurs, executives, scholars, authors, researchers, poets, and artists who bring an intellectual diversity that adds depth to Babson's educational programs and offers students a rich, challenging experience. Babson's student-faculty ratio is 11:1 and faculty members teach 100 percent of the courses. More information can be found at www.babson.edu/faculty.

Student Government

Students are encouraged to take an active role in campus activities and student government. The Student Government Association promotes students' interests; allocates funds to campus organizations for academic, social, and recreational activities; licenses student-run businesses; and helps formulate and maintain student regulations. There are over 115 student clubs and organizations currently on campus.

Off-Campus Programs

Babson has a partnership with Wellesley College and the Franklin W. Olin College of Engineering, an independent institution located on a 70-acre site adjacent to Babson. Babson, Olin, and Wellesley are collaborating inside and outside the classroom in order to provide extraordinary opportunities in all aspects of the student experience, including joint academic and research programming, student life programming, and lecture series.

Babson's vibrant education abroad programs enable students to spend a summer, semester, or school break abroad. Currently, 108 programs are offered in thirty-five countries, and full academic credit is given for approved management and liberal arts courses.

Academic Facilities

Horn Library houses an extensive business collection of print, media, and online information resources. Students have campus-wide access to library resources. Wireless access is available throughout the campus. Every incoming Babson undergraduate student receives a leased laptop computer, which is replaced after the sophomore year.

Other facilities are the Donald W. Reynolds Campus Center, the Richard W. Sorenson Family Visual Arts Center, the Stephen D. Cutler Center for Investments and Finance, The Leonard A. Schlesinger Innovation Center, the Glavin Family Chapel, the Center for Women's Entrepreneurial Leadership, and the Arthur M. Blank Center for Entrepreneurship.

Costs

For 2017–18, tuition was $49,664.

Financial Aid

Babson is committed to educating students from diverse backgrounds. Applying for financial aid does not affect a student's chances of being admitted to Babson College. Financial assistance is awarded on merit and demonstrated financial need.

Need-based financial assistance is available to U.S. citizens and permanent residents of the United States. A small number of need-based scholarships are awarded each year to international students as part of the Global Scholars Program. Babson's merit scholarships include Weissman Scholarships, Presidential Scholarships, The Center for Women's Entrepreneurial Leadership Scholarship, the Diversity Leadership Awards, Posse Scholarship, DECA Scholarship, Junior Achievement Scholarship, NFTE Scholarship, Sorenson Arts Scholarship, and Blank Entrepreneurship Scholarship. Application for aid is made by submitting the Free Application for Federal Student Aid (FAFSA) and the Financial Aid PROFILE of the College Scholarship Service. The application deadline for first-year undergraduate students is February 1. For transfer students the deadline is April 1 for September enrollment, and November 1 for January enrollment.

Admission Requirements

In selecting new students, the admission office considers each candidate based on academic factors such as high school record, recommendations, standardized test scores, and essays. Nonacademic factors are also considered, including extracurricular activities, demonstrated leadership abilities, character/personal qualities, volunteer work, work experience, creativity and enthusiasm, and a willingness to contribute to the Babson community in meaningful ways. Evaluation is based upon comparisons of the qualifications of those who apply. The degree of competition is set by the caliber of the applicants themselves. Consideration is given to the depth and rigor of each candidate's academic program, academic motivation and achievement, and progress from one year to the next. Prospective students are strongly encouraged to have completed or be currently enrolled in a pre-calculus math class.

Babson College offers three application plans: early decision, early action, and regular decision. For more information about these plans and their deadlines, prospective students should visit Babson's website at www.babson.edu/ugrad. Campus visits and group information sessions with an admission counselor are strongly recommended.

Application and Information

For further information or application forms, students should contact:

Office of Undergraduate Admission

Lunder Admission Center

Babson College

Babson Park, Massachusetts 02457-0310

Phone: 781-239-5522

     800-488-3696 (toll-free)

Fax: 781-239-4006

E-mail: ugradadmission@babson.edu

Website: www.babson.edu/ugrad

     www.facebook.com/babsonadmission

     www.instagram.com/babsonadmission

     www.twitter.com/BabsonAdmission

Tomasso Hall

BALDWIN WALLACE UNIVERSITY
BEREA, OHIO

 To read more about this school, visit http://petersons.to/baldwinwallaceuniversity

The University

Founded in 1845, Baldwin Wallace University (BW) in Berea, Ohio, is an accredited institution affiliated with the United Methodist Church that blends the hallmarks of a traditional arts and sciences education with an emphasis on professional preparation. Baldwin Wallace has a long history of diversity, as it was one of the first institutions of higher learning in the nation to admit students without regard to race or gender. That spirit of inclusiveness has flourished and evolved into a personalized approach to education, one that stresses individual growth as students learn to learn, respond to new ideas, adapt to new situations, and prepare for the certainty of change.

With an enrollment of approximately 3,000 full-time undergraduate students and a total campus population of nearly 4,000 students, BW offers unique opportunities for engaged, transformative learning. Within the incoming first-year class at BW, 28 states are represented with 30 percent of students coming from outside of Ohio, 22 percent are students of color, and 29 percent would be the first in their families to earn a four-year college degree. First-year students have an average high school GPA of 3.52, a composite ACT score of 24, and a combined SAT (evidence-based reading/writing + math) score of 1191.

Experiential learning is key to a BW education and is a requirement for all undergraduates. BW maintains a proven commitment to the arts and sciences—characterized by excellence in teaching and learning that provides a strong foundation for internships, faculty-directed research, performance, and service-learning programs. Students work with faculty and staff to combine these opportunities in a way that prepares graduates for success after college.

In a recent post-graduation alumni survey, 90 percent of respondents found rewarding jobs or entered the graduate or professional school of their choice within one year of graduation. Some programs—including communication disorders, music therapy, and neuroscience—have graduate school acceptance rates at or near 100 percent.

BW offers many distinctive academic programs. BW's neuroscience program has been nationally recognized by the *Society for Neuroscience*.

BW is also home to a world-renowned Conservatory of Music. The undergraduate-only nature of the Conservatory offers collaborative mentoring opportunities with a faculty of accomplished artists plus extraordinary opportunities for performance in a variety of ensembles. The University hosts the country's oldest collegiate Bach Festival.

BW has an early medical school acceptance agreement with Ohio University's Heritage College of Osteopathic Medicine, Lake Erie College of Osteopathic Medicine, and Northeast Ohio Medical University, aimed at developing a pipeline of pre-med students committed to primary care.

Location

Baldwin Wallace students enjoy the best of both worlds. Berea, Ohio, with its tree-lined streets, picturesque homes, and population of 19,000, is an ideal suburban college town. At the same time, students are only 20 minutes from the heart of Cleveland (known as the CLE), which is home to many *Fortune 500* companies and burgeoning tech and healthcare sectors. As such, Northeast Ohio provides students with outstanding internship and field experience opportunities that maximize real-world preparation and the value of a BW degree. Each year, approximately 350 BW students complete internships at business, nonprofit, and government sites in the area. Cleveland is also known for first-rate museums and galleries, professional sporting events, a world-class orchestra, exciting nightlife, an extensive park system with access to Lake Erie, and Playhouse Square—Cleveland's

Theater District—the largest performing arts center in the United States outside of New York.

Approximately 85 percent of first-year students live on campus in a variety of settings, including residential learning communities. Students 21 years or older also have access to University-owned apartments. A renovated residential complex featuring suite-style living is also available. All full-time students are required to live on campus during their first and second years, with residency exemptions available for commuting students who live with their families.

Majors and Degrees

Baldwin Wallace offers the Bachelor of Arts (B.A.), Bachelor of Science (B.S.), Bachelor of Science in Education (B.S.E.), Bachelor of Music (B.M.), Bachelor of Fine Arts (B.F.A.) and Bachelor of Music in Education (B.M.E.) degrees. A Bachelor of Science in Nursing (B.S.N.) degree is offered in an accelerated format to students who have previously completed a bachelor's degree. Majors include accounting, acting (B.F.A), art (studio), arts management & entrepreneurship, athletic training, biology, broadcasting & mass communication, business administration, chemistry, communication studies, computer network security, computer science, creative writing, criminal justice, digital media & design: graphic design or interactive design, economics, education, engineering (general), English, environmental science, exercise science, film studies, finance, French, German, healthcare management, health coaching & health promotion, health & physical education, history, human resource management, industrial & organizational psychology, innovation & entrepreneurship, international business, international studies, management, marketing, mathematics (applied), mathematics (pure), national security, neuroscience, philosophy, physics, political science, psychology, public health, public history, public & nonprofit management, public relations, religion, sociology, software engineering, Spanish, sport management, sustainability, and theatre: acting & directing, dance & movement, design & technical, or stage management. Pre-professional majors include communication sciences & disorders and physical therapy. Pre-professional pathways include dentistry, law, medicine, pharmacy, primary healthcare advancement, social work, and veterinary. Dozens of minors are offered. The BW Conservatory of Music offers majors in music composition, music education, music history & literature, music performance: keyboard, strings, voice, or woodwinds/brass/percussion, music theatre, music theory, music therapy, as well as two liberal arts in music (B.A.) majors, one with an academic emphasis and the other with an applied emphasis.

Academic Programs

Over eighty majors and several 3-2 cooperative and pre-professional programs and pre-professional pathways are available to traditional Baldwin Wallace undergraduates. The Honors Program offers innovative coursework and rigorous student-focused initiatives centered on fostering critical thinking, problem-solving and communication skills for approximately 250 high-achieving students.

International Programs

Baldwin Wallace sends over 30 percent of its full-time undergraduate student body abroad each year in over thirty different programs. BW offers long-term and short-term programs in Africa, Asia, Australia, Europe, and Latin and South America. BW has institutional (exchange) partnerships with institutions around the globe, where students can study for a semester, summer, or academic year. International options include Argentina, Australia, China, Ecuador, England, France, Germany, Ghana, India, Ireland, Italy, Japan, Morocco, Scotland, South Korea, Spain, Sweden, and Switzerland.

In addition to traditional exchange programs, BW features a series of focused full-semester seminars that are led by BW faculty and staff members and examine specific topics or geographic regions. Quite literally, students learn while on the road. Full-semester seminars are offered in alternating academic years. One example of a full-semester seminar is Seminar in Europe. Students travel through Europe experiencing different cultures across the continent.

BW also sponsors faculty-led two- to three-week seminars for credit in May, which are ideal for students who seek an international experience but do not want to be away for extended periods of time. BW has many short-term opportunities including a two-week immersion course in British theatre that includes a nine-day trip to London. Past and current programs include travel to Brazil, China, Germany, Guatemala, Ghana, England, Ireland, and India.

Academic Facilities

Baldwin Wallace continues to invest in facilities for student learning, including the Thomas Family Center for Science and Innovation, a facility featuring a combined 100,000 square-feet of comprehensive laboratory, research, and study space. This complex includes the Center for Innovation and Growth, a facility that prepares tomorrow's leaders to change their world as students learn—and practice—skills in creativity, innovation, and entrepreneurship.

The BW Conservatory of Music is housed within the Boesel Musical Arts Center, which provides students with world-class rehearsal and performance spaces. The BW Conservatory of Music is now designated as an All-Steinway School, ensuring students have access to the finest pianos in the world and best tools for success. The BW Conservatory of Music is also home to the Jones Music Library and the Riemenschneider Bach Institute, where priceless Bach-related manuscripts and first editions are stored.

These facilities complement the extensive offerings already available to students, including campus computer labs; a campus TV station and 4,000-watt radio station; recently renovated recreation and athletic facilities; an on-campus gallery showcasing the work of student, faculty, and area artists; and the Burrell Memorial Observatory. A new campus master plan, already being implemented, will enhance facilities to support BW's mission and create an even more pedestrian-friendly, environmentally responsible campus with inviting green spaces.

Costs

Baldwin Wallace's tuition ranks among the lowest and most affordable private colleges in Ohio. In 2018–19, full-time (12–18 credit hours) liberal arts student tuition is $32,586 per academic year and $11,282 for room and board (BW does not have fees). Conservatory student tuition is $35,302 for the 2018–19 academic year.

Baldwin Wallace offers a four-year graduation guarantee—a promise that academically prepared students who meet specified benchmarks during their study at BW will earn their bachelor's degrees in four years or fewer. If a student who follows the agreement does not graduate in four years, BW will pay up to one year's additional tuition for the additional course work needed to graduate.

Financial Aid

To help students and their families meet the cost of a high-quality education, Baldwin Wallace awards nearly $50 million annually to students in the form of scholarships, grants, loans, and work-study opportunities. About 82 percent of all BW full-time undergraduates have financial need. One hundred percent of all full-time undergraduate students with financial need received financial support from BW in 2017–18.

Renewable merit scholarships ranging from $10,000 to $17,000 are awarded to incoming first-year students who have demonstrated a commitment to academic preparation and achievement. The University also offers talent scholarships and special awards, as well as scholarships for transfer students.

Faculty

Close relationships are at the heart of the Baldwin Wallace experience. The student-faculty ratio is 12:1, allowing for a more personalized and collaborative academic environment. Professors share their wisdom and experience on a one-to-one basis, helping students choose classes or assisting students in their search for the perfect internship. From corporate executives and lifelong educators to environmentalists and practicing professionals, BW's 469 full-time and part-time faculty members bring impressive credentials from their fields and are dedicated and talented teachers who want to provide an educational experience that goes well beyond the textbook.

Student Clubs and Organizations

Baldwin Wallace students participate in more than 100 clubs, professional organizations, and honor societies, ranging from community service and political action groups to student government and student-run media to marching band to fraternities and sororities. Almost one in five undergraduate students competes in one of 23 NCAA Division III varsity sports in the competitive Ohio Athletic Conference (OAC), and many others participate in club sports, intramurals, and recreational activities.

Admission Requirements

When it comes to GPA, class rank or standardized test score requirements, Baldwin Wallace believes in giving balanced consideration to all aspects of a student's college preparation. BW reviews the following information for each applicant: completed application for admission (BW is a member of the Common Application and does not have an application fee for students submitting materials online), high school transcript, SAT/ACT test results (or a recently graded writing sample if student has a 3.0+ cumulative GPA and is eligible to be test-optional), and school report form. Applicants to the BW Conservatory of Music have additional requirements, as do applicants to the B.F.A. in acting program, including an audition.

Application and Information

Students may begin applying to BW for the following fall term as of August 1, though the first notifications for admission will not be sent until early October. Beginning in October, applicants are notified of admission decisions on a rolling basis within two to four weeks upon the completion of their application to BW. The priority application deadline is November 1. Applicants to the BW Conservatory of Music and/or to the B.F.A. in acting program may have separate deadlines to consider and should consult the BW website. Although students are encouraged to apply before May 1 so they are in a position to meet the priority student deposit deadline, applications will continue to be accepted on a space-available basis until the start of the fall semester.

Baldwin Wallace University
275 Eastland Road
Berea, Ohio 44017-2088
Phone: 440-826-2222
    877-BW-APPLY (toll-free)
Fax: 440-826-3830
E-mail: admission@bw.edu
Website: http://www.bw.edu/admission
Social Media: @BWadmission

Baldwin Wallace Class of 2021

BARNARD COLLEGE
NEW YORK, NEW YORK

 To read more about this school, visit http://petersons.to/barnardcollege

The College

The founders of Barnard College were among the pioneers in the late nineteenth-century crusade who sought to make access to higher education available to women. Founded in 1889 and formally partnered with Columbia University since 1900, the College serves more than 2,500 students today from almost every state and more than fifty countries. It offers the intimacy of a small college with the added advantages of a large research university. Barnard remains affiliated with Columbia, with students at both schools regularly cross-registering for courses taught at either institution. Barnard students have access to the University's resources and graduates receive their degree from Columbia. At the same time, Barnard College remains a small, independent liberal arts college, devoted solely to the undergraduate education of women. The College maintains its own Board of Trustees, faculty, administrative staff, endowment, admissions process, and sole ownership of its property and physical plant.

The self-contained Barnard campus occupies 4+ acres of urban property along Broadway between 116th and 120th streets and serves as an oasis from the hustle and bustle of New York City. Its location on the upper west side of Manhattan grants students access to thousands of internship opportunities in addition to unparalleled cultural, intellectual, and social resources. Barnard's diverse student body includes residents from nearly every state and more than fifty countries worldwide. Over 40 percent of the current first-year class identifies as students of color, and 15 percent of the class comes from non-college backgrounds.

Location

Barnard is located north of Central Park on the upper west side of Manhattan, in the safe and student-friendly Morningside Heights neighborhood. The campus is directly across from Columbia University, and has numerous educational and cultural institutions as neighbors, including the Jewish Theological Seminary, Bank Street School of Education, St. John the Divine church, and Grant's tomb. Abounding with cultural, educational, internship, and professional opportunities and more than 500,000 college students, New York is Barnard's laboratory.

Majors and Degrees

Students can earn a Bachelor of Arts (B.A.) in the following subjects: Africana studies, American studies, ancient studies, anthropology, architecture, art history, Asian and Middle Eastern cultures, astronomy, biochemistry, biological sciences, chemistry, classics (Greek and Latin), comparative literature, computer science, dance, economics, education, English, environmental biology science or studies, European studies, film studies, French, German, history, human rights, Italian, Jewish studies, mathematics and applied mathematics, medieval and Renaissance studies, music, neuroscience, philosophy, physics, political science, psychology, religion, Russian and Slavic studies, sociology, Spanish and Latin American cultures, statistics, theater, urban studies, and women's, gender, and sexuality studies. The College provides an excellent education program, leading to teaching certification with a specific urban studies track, and prepares students for programs in health and medicine, law, and business, as well as further study in a variety of graduate programs.

Barnard College also offers double- and joint-degree programs in cooperation with other schools within the Columbia community. These include a five-year M.P.A./M.I.A. (3-2) program offered in conjunction with the School of International and Public Affairs, a double-degree program with List College of the Jewish Theological Seminary, and through the Fu Foundation School of Engineering and Applied Science at Columbia, Barnard students can pursue a five-year (3-2) program in all branches of engineering.

Academic Programs

Two required courses, First-Year Seminar and First-Year Writing, set the foundation for a Barnard education with small seminar classes, limited to 16 and 12 students, respectively. In addition to these First Year Experience courses, Barnard's flexible general education requirements are organized around Foundation Requirements in four subject areas and Modes of Thinking that connect to six themes. A generous list of courses allows for students to choose which options interest them most. Barnard students shape their educational experience by choosing courses that enhance the way they view the world.

Advanced placement and I.B. credit are available. Barnard operates on a two-semester calendar, with classes beginning in early September. The fall semester ends in mid-December; classes resume for the spring semester in mid-January and end in mid-May.

Off-Campus Programs

As an independent partner of Columbia University, Barnard offers students open access to courses, libraries, and other facilities of the University. With special permission, students may also register for selected classes in Columbia's graduate and professional schools. In addition, two highly selective lesson exchange programs with the Juilliard School and the nearby Manhattan School of Music allow qualified Barnard students to take music lessons in a conservatory setting.

Barnard has a rich history and tradition of study abroad dating back to the 1930s. Today, qualified students are eligible to study in nearly 100 programs in more than fifty countries worldwide and nearly forty percent of Barnard students spend a semester or year abroad. Students are currently studying in Argentina, Australia, Austria, Bolivia, Brazil, Chile, China, Costa Rica, Czech Republic, Denmark, Ecuador, England, France, Germany, Greece, Hungary, Ireland, Israel, Italy, Japan, Jordan, Kenya, Madagascar, Netherlands, New Zealand, Panama, Peru, Russia, Scotland, Senegal, South Africa, Spain, Switzerland, and other locations. Students may also participate in a domestic exchange with Spelman College in Atlanta or Howard University in Washington, D.C.

Barnard's location offers its students a variety of work experiences through more than 2,500 internships. More than two thirds of Barnard students participate in internships throughout the academic year and/or summer.

Academic Facilities

Barnard's campus blends classic and modern architecture. Barnard Hall is home to the Ethel S. LeFrak ('41) and Samuel J. LeFrak Center (with a zine collection focused on feminism and femme identity by people of all genders with an emphasis on zines by women of color), the Barnard Center for Research on Women, and the Julius S. Held Lecture Hall, and stands opposite the main gates of the College. The south end of the campus, referred to as the Quad, contains the Brooks, Reid, Hewitt, and Sulzberger residence halls; first-year students are housed in the Quad. Additional housing (twelve residence halls in total) provides those entering as first-years guaranteed housing for four years of continuous enrollment at Barnard. The latest campus addition, the Diana Center, a 70,000 square-foot student center, added a new element of design in 2010. Its seven-story glass structure stretches across campus, linking the historic gates of the entrance at the south end of campus, to one of the original campus buildings, Milbank Hall, on the north.

Construction is underway for the Cheryl and Philip Milstein Teaching and Learning Center. The Milstein Center will serve as a new academic hub in the heart of the Barnard College campus. When the Milstein Center opens its doors, scheduled for August 2018, it will stand at the core of a Barnard education and at the center of the Morningside Heights campus. The 128,000 square-foot building will include a 40,000 square-foot library and centers for pedagogy, media, data analysis, movement, and design. The Center, which will be nearly double the size of the building it replaces, also will include the Vagelos Computational Science Center, homes for the Barnard Center for Research on Women and the Athena Center for Leadership Studies, and social and study spaces for students. Historic Milbank Hall anchors the north end of campus, topped by the 2,500-square-foot Arthur Ross Greenhouse, housing administrative and faculty offices in addition to the Minor Latham Playhouse. Sulzberger Tower and the residential quadrangle secure the south end of campus where most Barnard students reside.

Costs

Tuition and fees for 2017–18 were $50,882. Room and board costs are an additional $16,100.

Financial Aid

Financial aid at Barnard is awarded based upon demonstrated need. Federal funds and institutional grants are administered as determined by federal and institutional methodology. Barnard provides no merit or athletic scholarships. Once need has been established, Barnard covers 100 percent of demonstrated need with a combination of grants, loans, and work-study or student employment. Approximately 40 percent of the students at Barnard receive some form of financial aid.

Barnard College has a need-blind admission policy in which first-year applicants who are U.S. citizens or permanent residents are judged solely on merit without reference to financial circumstances. International and transfer students are considered for need-based aid from a limited pool of funding.

Faculty

Barnard College employs more than 300 teaching faculty members with a student-faculty ratio of 10:1. Barnard's faculty includes editors of leading scholarly journals, prize-winning novelists and translators, and frequent winners of awards from respected foundations, corporations, and government agencies. They are actively engaged in research and publication in their respective fields, but they regard teaching as their primary commitment. From the start of their time at the College, all students have faculty advisers who assist them in selecting courses and designing individual academic programs, in addition to a vast network of decanal, staff, and peer advising.

Student Life

Barnard women have access to more than eighty clubs and organizations on the College campus alone. Add to this list the hundreds of additional dually recognized clubs with members from both Barnard and Columbia, provided for through Barnard's long-standing partnership with the University, and strong friendships develop among students from both sides of Broadway. Student groups include performance groups, academic and pre-professional, ethnic and cultural, language, community service, and publications. Social interaction and cooperation between Barnard and Columbia groups is virtually seamless, with Barnard women regularly joining and leading a variety of Columbia organizations. Students, faculty members, and administrators also serve on tripartite committees and share responsibility for policy on curriculum, housing, financial aid, orientation, and the library.

On Barnard's campus, every student service is designed to meet the needs of a women-focused community. Primary Health Services, Furman Counseling Center, the academic advising program, and and a unique Career Development and graduate school/fellowships advising Center, called Beyond Barnard, create programs to provide the kind of support young women may need as they navigate their academic experiences and life beyond college. The Athena Center for Leadership studies also provides Barnard students with the unique opportunity to become an Athena scholar and dedicate a portion of their studies to leadership development, history, and skills, culminating in a senior capstone project.

Admission Requirements

The Committee on Admissions selects motivated women of proven academic strength who exhibit intellectual and personal maturity. Careful consideration is given to candidates' high school records, recommendations, writing skills, standardized test scores, special abilities and interests, and personal and educational context.

Admission to Barnard is highly selective and candidates for admission to the first-year class are expected to have taken a highly rigorous college-preparatory program. Students educated in a non-English-speaking setting or who have studied in English for less than four years must also take the TOEFL or IELTS exam. Interview opportunities are available for first-year students, but are not required. Interviews are not part of the transfer admission process.

Application and Information

Applicants for first-year admission should apply in the fall of their senior year of high school. Applications must be received by January 1 and must include the non-refundable application fee. Students are notified in late March. Well-qualified high school seniors who have selected Barnard as their first-choice college are encouraged to apply under the binding early decision plan. Early decision applications must be submitted by November 1. Barnard accepts sophomore and junior transfer students. Transfer applications must be submitted by March 15 for consideration for September entrance and by November 1 for consideration for January.

For more information about Barnard College, students should contact:

Jennifer Fondiller
Vice President for Enrollment
Barnard College, Office of Admissions
3009 Broadway
New York, New York 10027
Phone: 212-854-2014
Fax: 212-280-8797
E-mail: admissions@barnard.edu
Website: http://www.admissions.barnard.edu

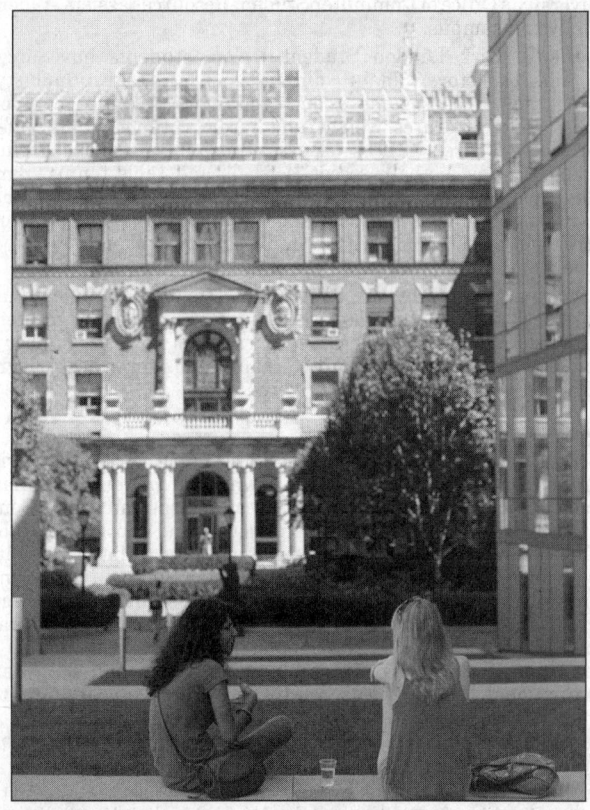

A view of Milbank Hall from the Diana, Barnard's multipurpose student center.

BARRY UNIVERSITY
MIAMI SHORES, FLORIDA

 To read more about this school, visit http://petersons.to/barryuniversity

The University

For more than 75 years, Barry University has been providing a higher education experience that focuses on inspiring and training the next generation of change agents and leaders. Barry graduates apply what's learned in the classroom to a constantly changing and diverse world, while promoting civic engagement for the betterment of humanity.

Barry University, located in sunny Miami, Florida, is comprised of eight colleges and schools offering more than 100 bachelor's, master's, and doctoral degree programs. A university that values diversity, Barry's community includes approximately 7,500 students from nearly all 50 states and 80 countries; more than 65,000 alumni worldwide; and 1,700 faculty and staff members. Barry students gain vital hands-on experience, both locally and internationally, as they prepare to advance their careers in today's global market. Barry's use of service learning, which integrates coursework with community needs, engages students with real-world issues, and encourages them to help find solutions.

With degree programs in the arts and sciences, business, education, health sciences, nursing, law, podiatric medicine, and social work, Barry students can quickly find their calling and acquire professional experience before graduation through internships and innovative service-learning programs.

Barry's palm-tree lined main campus is in Miami, but the university also includes the Dwayne O. Andreas School of Law in Orlando; adult and continuing education programs at 11 additional locations throughout Florida; and graduate programs in the Caribbean.

Barry students live on campus in 10 residence halls. Living-learning housing is available in five distinct areas: S.T.E.M., Honors Program, Transitions, Business Connections, and Pre-Nursing. The University's Office of Commuter Student Resources assists students who live off campus.

At the R. Kirk Landon Student Union, students have access to the bookstore, main dining hall, restaurant/pub-style dining, snack bar, game room, and more. A fully equipped fitness center features weight and cardio equipment and offers a variety of free fitness classes. Intramural sports include basketball, flag football, soccer, softball, and table tennis. Barry holds membership in 20 honor societies and hosts more than 60 student organizations, including the dance team, choir, Campus Activities Board, WBRY student radio station, student newspaper, as well as active fraternities and sororities.

Barry is accredited by the Southern Association of Colleges and Schools Commission on Colleges to award bachelor's, master's, specialist, and doctoral degrees. Barry also holds a number of accreditations from professional organizations for specific degree programs.

Location

Barry University is located within the dynamic South Florida community, just minutes from downtown Miami and Miami Beach. At the crossroads of the Americas and the gateway to South America, Miami offers limitless experiences and opportunities that reflect its broad diversity. The international city of Miami is a center for business, tourism, and entertainment, providing a wide range of internship options and a vibrant cultural scene. Yearly events include the world-famous Art Basel Miami Beach contemporary art festival; Calle Ocho, the largest Hispanic street festival in the nation; the Miami International Book Fair; and the Miami International Film Festival. The New World Symphony and the Miami City Ballet provide a full season of performances, while the nearby Wynwood Arts District hosts a free art walk every second Saturday of the month.

South Florida is also home to the Miami Heat basketball team, the Miami Dolphins football team, the Miami Marlins baseball team, and the Florida Panthers hockey team. Miami's warm climate allows for swimming, sailing, scuba diving, golf, tennis, soccer, and other outdoor activities year-round, while the natural beauty of the Florida Keys, Everglades, and coral reefs are just a few hours away. Barry University's Center for Student Involvement regularly coordinates trips to help students experience the best that South Florida has to offer.

Majors and Degrees

Barry offers the Bachelor of Arts degree in advertising, art (art history, graphic design, and studio art), broadcast and emerging media, communication and media studies, English (literature and professional writing), general studies, history, international studies, music, philosophy, photography (biomedical/forensic), pre-law, public relations, Spanish (language and literature and translation and interpretation), theater (acting, dance theater, technical theater), and theology.

The Bachelor of Science degree is offered in accounting, applied sport and exercise science, athletic training (five-year seamless B.S. to M.S.), biology (marine, preprofessional), cardiovascular perfusion, clinical biology (histotechnology, medical technology), chemistry (biochemistry, preprofessional), computer information sciences (computer security, multimedia), computer science, criminology, education (B.S. to M.S. option, infancy through early-childhood education, early- and middle-childhood education, special education), exercise physiology (five-year seamless B.S. to M.S., pre-med, pre–physical therapy), finance, international business, management, marketing, mathematical sciences (computational, general, and statistics/actuarial science), political science, psychology (forensic, industrial/organizational), sociology, and sport management.

Barry also offers the Bachelor of Science in Nursing, the Bachelor of Fine Arts (art and photography), the Bachelor of Music (instrumental performance, music education, vocal performance), and the Bachelor of Social Work.

Minor concentrations are available in specific subject areas as well as in the interdisciplinary areas of Africana studies, film studies, journalism, peace studies, social sciences, and women's studies. Certificates are also offered in Africana studies, photography, Spanish translation and interpretation, and women's studies.

Accelerated undergraduate degree programs are offered for working adults during evening and weekend programs through the university's School of Professional and Career Education (PACE).

Academic Programs

Barry operates on a semester plan. The first semester extends from the end of August to mid-December, and the second semester extends from mid-January to early May. Two 6-week sessions are offered during the summer. Students must maintain a minimum cumulative grade point average of 2.0 (or C) and earn a minimum of 120 credits for a degree. Of these 120 credits, 9 must be in philosophy and theology, 9 in communication—oral and written, 9 in humanities and arts, 9 in physical or natural sciences and mathematics, and 9 in social and behavioral sciences.

The traditional full-time academic load is 12 to 18 credits each semester and 6 credits each summer term. Candidates for degree programs may elect a major and area of specialization and must satisfy all requirements of the program that they choose to follow, including all professional preparation requirements. Internships are required for many majors.

An ELS Language Centers program is available to international students who need to increase language proficiency. The Center for Advanced Learning offers a program designed to assist students with learning disabilities who have the intellectual potential and motivation to complete a four-year degree.

The Honors Program offers an active, interdisciplinary honors curriculum designed to add breadth and depth to the educational experience.

Barry University

Community Service

Faithful to its traditions, the Barry University experience fosters individual and communal transformation where learning leads to knowledge and truth, reflection leads to informed action, and a commitment to social justice leads to collaborative service. Rooted in its Catholic heritage, Barry promotes community service through organizations, including Best Buddies International, Habitat for Humanity, Alternative Spring Break, and Pals-4-Paws animal rescue. Barry received the prestigious 2015 Community Engagement Classification from the Carnegie Foundation for the Advancement of Teaching. Colleges and universities that earn the distinction show evidence of improving and producing research that makes a difference in communities, revitalizing their civic and academic missions, and developing deeper community partnerships.

This is not the first time Barry has been recognized for its dedication to community service. Barry has consistently been named to the President's Honor Roll for Community Service after students logged more than 45,000 hours of community service. Barry's application process is managed by the Center for Community Service Initiatives, which serves as the university's community engagement clearinghouse and functions as a catalyst to foster civic engagement among members of the Barry community.

Academic Facilities

Academic facilities include multimedia classrooms, the Monsignor William Barry Memorial Library, the Glenn Hubert Learning Center, a performing arts center, a full-service digital television production studio, art studios, photography and digital imaging labs, a human performance lab, an athletic training room, a biomechanics lab, a nursing lab and resource center, and several other labs dedicated to Barry's health, science, and education programs.

Costs

The following were average costs of attending Barry for the 2017–18 academic year. Tuition for full-time undergraduate students for the academic year was $29,700. Room and board costs averaged $10,600, based on a double-occupancy room. Expenses such as books, supplies, laboratory fees, and transportation are not included in these costs.

Financial Aid

All undergraduate students, U.S. citizens, permanent residents, and international students are automatically considered for financial aid once they have been accepted. Assistance options include scholarships and grants, federal financial aid, Stamps Leadership Scholars Program, and the Federal Work-Study program. Florida students have access to a wide assortment of state-funded assistance programs to attend college in-state. Students may be eligible for funds from the Florida Bright Futures Scholarship program, the Florida Resident Access Grant (FRAG), and the Florida Student Assistance Grant (FSAG).

Barry makes every effort to offer financial aid to students through a variety of federal, state, and institutional packages. Nearly 90 percent of Barry students receive some form of financial aid.

For more information about receiving a financial aid at Barry, please visit: barry.edu/future-students/undergraduate/financial-aid.

Faculty

At Barry University, students experience a small community atmosphere where they can always rely on administrators and faculty for advice, encouragement, and personal attention. Barry has approximately 346 full-time faculty members, 80 percent of whom hold terminal degrees; and 476 part-time faculty members. The student-faculty ratio is 11:1.

Athletics

Barry fields 12 intercollegiate athletic teams that participate in the NCAA Division II and the Sunshine State Conference. Over the years, the Buccaneers have won 18 NCAA championships, 70 Sunshine State Conference Titles, and have had 341 All-Americans, 413 Scholar All-Americans, and nine NCAA Women of the Year finalists, the most of any Division II school.

Women's sports include basketball, golf, rowing, soccer, softball, tennis, and volleyball; men's sports include baseball, basketball, golf, soccer, and tennis. Barry's coaches have been awarded 64 "Coach of the Year" awards through the Sunshine State Conference, and have gone on to win 11 national awards.

Barry's intercollegiate athletics program aims at achieving athletic triumphs and also helps student-athletes excel academically.

Campus Life

Barry students enjoy a vibrant, lively, campus community where engaged learners organize and participate in a wide variety of academic, athletic, and social experiences. College life is not just about the classroom. At Barry, students enjoy a full range of extracurricular activities, including intramural sports, student government, and more than 60 clubs and organizations. The diversity of organizations and clubs on campus gives Barry students the chance to take the lessons they learn outside the classroom and make them part of their overall educational experience. From Founders' Week in the fall to Homecoming and Festival of Nations in the spring, tradition abounds at Barry. Students, faculty, staff, and alumni gather throughout the year to connect Barry's past with its present to create a meaningful future.

Admission Requirements

In reviewing the credentials of students seeking admission, Barry University considers an applicant's composite efforts. Candidates must provide the following materials: the completed application form, official high school or college transcripts, and the results of the SAT or ACT.

Application and Information

Barry has a rolling admissions policy and reviews applications as they are completed. Students are notified of their acceptance once the admissions staff has reviewed all required documents. Prospective students are advised to apply early and may submit their application any time after completion of their junior year in high school. The student's completed application form and supporting credentials should be sent to the Office of Admissions. Students may also apply online at barry.edu/apply.

Barry University
Division of Enrollment Services
11300 Northeast Second Avenue
Miami, Florida 33161-6695
Phone: 305-899-3100
      800-695-2279 (toll-free)
Fax: 305-899-2971
E-mail: admissions@barry.edu
Website: http://www.barry.edu
      http://facebook.com/BarryUniversity (Facebook)
      http://twitter.com/BarryUniversity (Twitter)
      https://www.instagram.com/barryuniversity (Instagram)

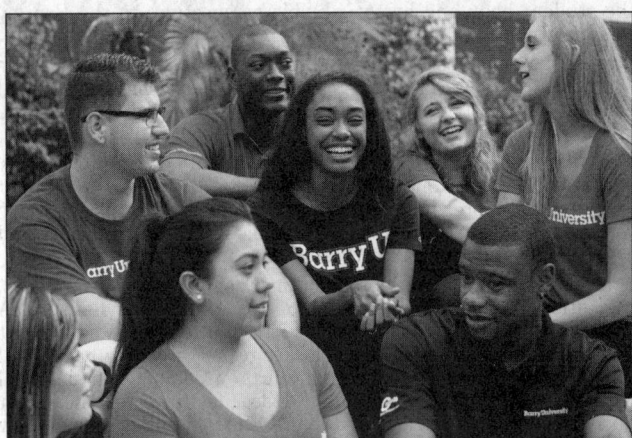

A transformational education that goes beyond the classroom.

BENTLEY UNIVERSITY
WALTHAM, MASSACHUSETTS

 To read more about this school, visit http://petersons.to/bentleyuniversity

The University

Bentley University provides a modern education to prepare students for today's complex business world. The Bentley experience has been designed to give students more: Business plus the arts and sciences. Classroom learning plus real-world experience. World-class technology plus global perspective. As a result, Bentley students are highly sought after by today's leading organizations because of their professionalism, exposure to state-of-the-art research tools, and diverse, real-world experience. In its 2016 "Best Undergraduate Business Schools" issue, *Bloomberg Businessweek* ranked Bentley 10th among the country's top undergraduate business programs.

Located on a classic New England campus minutes from Boston, Bentley offers a wide variety of majors and minors, as well as optional liberal studies and business studies majors designed to create a modern intersection of the arts and sciences and business that's unique in higher education. This fusion of business fundamentals and liberal arts enables Bentley students to think outside of the box when faced with critical decisions in the workplace.

Bentley was recently ranked #2 in the country for its career services office and #4 in the country for internship opportunities by the Princeton Review. The Office of Career Services offers resources including an on-campus recruiting program involving 1,000 national and international companies; an online job and internship database; career fairs; workshops on topics such as interviewing and networking; and a Career Development Seminar (CDI 101) for first-year students.

This approach works: In 2017, more than 97 percent of students found employment or enrolled in graduate school within six months of graduation. Their median annual salary was $57,000.

Approximately 98 percent of freshmen live on campus. Twenty-three residence halls provide a range of housing options: dorms, suites, and apartments. Housing is provided for all four years; all residence halls are air-conditioned and typically include study lounges, exercise facilities, TV lounges, and game rooms. Bentley has a variety of meal plans for students to choose from as they move into suites and apartments with kitchens. There are eleven places on campus to dine, offering an array of food options from buffet-style cafeterias to Currito and Dunkin' Donuts.

Students live and learn in a multicultural environment that prepares them to thrive in today's diverse world. International students representing nearly 100 countries make up 18 percent of the student body and bring valuable perspectives to the Bentley community.

Supporting Bentley's commitment to diversity are offices such as the Multicultural Center, Spiritual Life Center, Center for International Students and Scholars, Center for Women in Business, and the Women's Center.

The newly renovated Student Center is the hub of campus activity and is home to the main dining room, the pub, eateries, student services, and more than 100 student organizations. These groups represent academics, the arts and media, religions, fraternity and sorority life, and cultural interests.

Athletic programs are a Bentley hallmark and include intramurals, recreational sports, and more than 20 varsity teams in NCAA Divisions I and II. The Dana Athletic Center houses a weight and fitness complex, food court, locker rooms, a gym, a basketball court, volleyball and racquetball courts, a competition-size pool with a diving tank, and saunas. Outdoor facilities include soccer and baseball fields, a track, and tennis courts. Bentley's brand-new arena will house the school's Division I hockey team and other campus activities.

Location

Bentley's location in Waltham, Massachusetts—just minutes west of Boston—puts the city within easy reach. As the country's ultimate university town, Boston's options range from theater to art exhibits, dance clubs to concerts, and championship sports to world-class shopping. Bentley's free shuttle makes regular trips to Harvard Square in Cambridge, just a subway ride from Boston. Boston also offers many opportunities for internships and jobs after graduation.

Majors and Degrees

The Bentley curriculum is a ground-breaking integration of business and the arts and sciences that has been featured in the *Wall Street Journal*.

To that end, Bachelor of Science (B.S.) degree programs enable students to gain in-depth knowledge and skills in specific business disciplines: accountancy, actuarial science, computer information systems, corporate finance and accounting, creative industries, data analytics, economics–finance, finance, information design and corporate communication, information systems audit and control, management, managerial economics, marketing, mathematical sciences, and professional sales.

Bentley also offers Bachelor of Arts (B.A.) degree programs with majors in English, global studies, health sciences, history, liberal arts, media and culture, philosophy, public policy, Spanish studies, and sustainability science. All Bachelor of Arts students gain business experience through either the Business Studies Major (BSM) or minor. All students can also choose from one of 35 minors, including entrepreneurial studies, law, and sports management.

The Liberal Studies Major (LSM), an optional double major, can be combined with any business program. It provides students with a competitive edge by building meaningful connections across and within disciplines. To complete the LSM, students do not need to take any extra courses beyond those normally required. It allows students to add another credential to their degree, helping them stand out to employers. LSM concentrations include American studies; diversity and society; earth, environment, and global sustainability; ethics and social responsibility; global perspectives; health and industry; media arts and society; and quantitative perspectives.

Academic Programs

The Honors Program provides our most academically-talented students, selected each year from the top 10 percent of applicants, access to challenging, seminar-style courses each semester, small classes, as well as research funding and fellowships. Honors Program students also enjoy co-curricular activities designed to enhance the academic curriculum.

The Women's Leadership Program is sponsored by Bentley's Center for Women and Business, and gives participants the opportunity to participate in workshops, roundtables, and special events that explore critical gender equity issues on a deeper level, while developing effective leadership and communications skills. The program also includes a $10,000 annual award toward tuition, totaling $40,000 over four years.

The Falcon Fast-Track Program is a streamlined graduate school enrollment option for top-tier Bentley graduates with a GPA of 3.2 or higher. This new program allows qualified Bentley graduates to obtain a master's degree after completing a bachelor's degree (up to five years after graduation) without going through the traditional application process, including waiver of the GMAT or GRE, and no application fee.

Off-Campus Programs

Hands-on experience is emphasized across the curriculum. Internships, study abroad, service-learning, and corporate partnerships allow students to apply classroom theory in the community.

Each year, more than 92 percent of students complete at least one internship and 71 percent complete two or more, building valuable work experience and networking connections. Some of the top internship employers include Fidelity Investments, the TJX Companies, Liberty Mutual, Bain & Company, and all of the Big Four accounting firms.

Bentley students can gain insight into different cultures by studying abroad. Programs take place in more than 26 countries and vary in length from one week to a full academic year.

Through Bentley's Service-Learning Center, students build skills in business, communication, and teamwork while assisting nonprofit and community-based organizations both locally and internationally.

Academic Facilities

Concepts taught in the classroom are put to use in several high-tech learning laboratories.

Bentley's financial Trading Room combines state-of-the-art technology and real-time data to offer first-hand exposure to financial concepts in simulated trading sessions. Resources include Bloomberg, Capital IQ, Datastream, FactSet, Thomson One Analytics, Portfolio Analysis, MATLAB, S&P Compustat, and Worldscope.

The Center for Marketing Technology plays an integral role in marketing programs. Students gain a full grasp of software options, familiarity with research tools and techniques, and knowledge of new digital marketing frameworks.

The Accounting Center for Electronic Learning and Business Management (ACELAB) introduces cutting-edge technologies that are reshaping the accounting profession. Students have access to auditing and tax preparation software as well as other professional applications from industry leaders such as SAP and Oracle.

The Center for Languages and International Collaboration (CLIC) is a key resource for language courses, international studies majors, and students with an interest in global issues. The center promotes collaboration among Bentley students and their counterparts overseas.

The Media and Culture Labs and Studio feature resources for video production and editing as well as digital photography. The lab provides students with industry-standard software programs for screenwriting, sound mixing, graphic design, and DVD authoring.

The User Experience Center (UXC) features labs ideal for usability testing. Students use the applications employed by technical communicators, web developers, user-interface designers, and usability specialists.

The CIS Learning and Technology Sandbox is a collaborative space for learning new technologies. Its resources include Google TVs, Xbox 360 with Kinect, study spaces, large-screen TVs, a smart board, specialized networking equipment, and the latest in Windows, Linux, and Android development software.

The Bentley Library is outfitted with computer workstations, group study rooms, and wireless network access. It also has an exceptional number of online database resources, research guides, and consultation appointments are available to assist students with their projects.

Costs

Tuition for resident and nonresident students during the 2018–19 academic year is $48,180. Room and board (double room, meal plan) costs are $16,320. Additional expenses include books, supplies, technology fee, and personal and travel expenses.

Financial Aid

Bentley's financial aid program includes both scholarships based on academic achievement, which are awarded through the admission process, as well as grants based on financial need. Bentley administered nearly $100 million in aid to undergraduate students last year. More than 80 percent of aid awarded comes from Bentley-funded grants and scholarships. Currently, more than 70 percent of undergraduates receive some type of financial assistance—either grants, scholarships, loans, and/or work study.

Faculty

Bentley faculty members are teacher-scholars known for their classroom skills and cutting-edge research. They bring practical, real-world experience to the classroom, based on years of professional involvement in their fields. Faculty research focuses on issues of prime importance to current business practice. Much of the research is conducted in partnership with leading organizations. A student-faculty ratio of 11:1 and average class size of 26 ensure a personal experience for students. All courses are taught by professors; there are no teaching assistants. Students often note that professors are accessible to them outside of the classroom.

Student Government

Bentley has a number of student governing groups, including the Student Government Association, Residence Hall Association, and the Graduate Student Association.

Admission Requirements

Applicants are encouraged to complete a competitive university preparatory program. Recommendations include four years of English, four years of mathematics (preferably algebra I and II, geometry, and pre-calculus or its equivalent), and three to four years each of history, laboratory science, and a foreign language.

Along with the application, students must submit a secondary school transcript, letters of recommendation from a teacher and a counselor, and official scores of either the SAT or ACT. Bentley has a separate application for transfer students. Applicants who are nonnative speakers of English must also submit official scores of the Test of English as a Foreign Language (TOEFL).

Application and Information

Bentley University accepts the Common Application. Candidates for the fall semester are notified in late March; spring semester candidates and transfers are notified on a rolling basis.

Prospective students can visit bentley.edu/undergraduate/applying for application information and deadlines.

For more information, students should contact:
Office of Undergraduate Admission
Bentley University
175 Forest Street
Waltham, Massachusetts 02452-4705
Phone: 781-891-2244
        800-523-2354 (toll-free)
Fax: 781-891-3414
E-mail: ugadmission@bentley.edu
Website: bentley.edu/undergraduate
          facebook.com/bentleyadmission
          twitter.com/ugabentley

Bentley opened the new arena, home to the Division I hockey team, in February 2018.

BETHEL COLLEGE
MISHAWAKA, INDIANA

 For more information, visit http://petersons.to/bethelcollege

The College

Going to college is about much more than earning a degree. Bethel wants students to become completely connected: to understand, with depth and insight, the world and students' place in it. The experience is both rewarding and challenging, but Bethel offers all the resources students need to succeed.

Bethel is a Christian college affiliated with the Missionary Church. Its 1,500 students represent more than 20 denominational affiliations and come from 27 states and 41 different countries Twenty-three percent of the student body is multicultural.

As a college of the arts and sciences, Bethel provides students with skills they will use throughout their lifetime: effective communication, resourceful problem solving, teamwork, and critical thinking. This solid preparation means that students enjoy success as they pursue their careers or graduate school. With more than 50 areas of study, students are able to learn what they love and put it to use in the real world.

The solid preparation built into a Bethel education means graduates in every program enjoy exceptional success. Consider these facts:

- Bethel graduates have been admitted to top-ranking graduate and professional schools, including those at Indiana University, University of Notre Dame, Stanford University, the Peabody Institute of The Johns Hopkins University, Gordon-Conwell Seminary, Cornell University, and many others.

- Bethel has the highest percentage of alumni rated as "highly effective teachers" in the classroom of any other college in Indiana, according to a report by the Indiana Department of Education.

- 92 percent of Bethel students who have applied to medical school have been accepted, more than twice the national average of 45 percent.

- Sign language interpreting students achieved a 100 percent pass rate for the National Interpreter Certification (NIC) written exam.

Connection after connection, the people at Bethel—students, faculty, and staff—are a community. Individuals connect their faith with learning, science with scripture, revelation with research, and competition with compassion. Bethel College is the ground for spirited connections.

Location

Bethel is a suburban community in a vibrant location, rich with opportunity. The Mishawaka/South Bend area of Northern Indiana is home to 250,000 residents, five colleges, the second largest shopping district in the state, and 50 parks. Several local attractions, like the Potawatomi Zoo, South Bend Chocolate Café, The Morris Performing Arts Center, and the South Bend Cubs, are within minutes of campus. Students enjoy the serenity of a suburban campus setting, but they can also stand on the sandy beaches of Lake Michigan, which is less than an hour away, or visit the city of Chicago only 90 miles from campus. With more than 16,000 businesses in the region, students can pursue an internship or job at a major business, health care facility, church, social service agency, or governmental office.

Majors and Degrees

Bethel offers more than 50 different programs of study at the undergraduate, pre-professional and graduate level.

Undergraduate degree programs include: Accounting, Applied Politics, Art–Graphic Design, Art–Studio Arts, Biblical Languages*, Biblical Studies*, Biochemistry and Molecular Biology, Biology, Business Administration, Business Management*, Chemistry, Christian Ministries, Biblical Studies Track, Children's Ministries Track, Christian Ministries Track, Sports Ministries Track, TESOL Track, Youth Ministries Track, Communication, Computer Science*, Criminal Justice, Cross-Cultural Communication*, Deaf Studies*, Design*, Economics*, Economics and Finance, Education, Art, Early Childhood, Elementary, English, Health/Physical Education, Mathematics, Music, Science–Biology, Science–Chemistry, Social Studies, Special Education, Engineering and Management, English & Writing, Exercise Science, Family Studies*, Financial Services Professional, History, Humanities, Intercultural Studies, International Health, Leadership*, Liberal Studies, Marketing*, Mathematics, Mathematics/Physics (Engineering 3-2), Music (General), Music/Church Music*, Music Performance, Musical Theatre*, Nursing, Pastoral Ministries, Philosophy, Physics*, Psychology, Sign Language Interpreting, Sociology, Spanish*, Sport Management, Sport Studies, Teaching English to Students of Other Languages (TESOL), Theatre Arts, Undecided/Exploratory Studies, Worship Arts, and Youth Ministry*.

* Associate degree, minor, or concentration

Pre-professional programs are available in the following fields: Dentistry, Law, Medicine, Optometry, Pharmacy, Physical Therapy, Seminary, and Veterinary Medicine.

Bethel also offers several graduate degree programs, including the Master of Arts in Business Administration (MBA), Master of Arts in Counseling, Master of Arts in Education, Master of Arts in Ministry, Master of Arts in Pastoral Ministries, Master of Arts in School Administration, Master of Arts in Special Education, Master of Arts in Teaching, Master of Arts in Theological Studies, Master of Science in Nursing, and Transition to Teaching program. Additional information is available at BethelCollege.edu/Academics.

Academic Programs

Students who haven't made a decision about their major and want to explore the wide range of options available to them can do so through Bethel's unique exploratory studies program. The program offers time to exercise intellectual curiosity and define long-term academic and career goals. Students can start by taking The Bethel Core, 54 credit hours in liberal arts courses that are required for almost all majors.

Bethel's Center for Academic Success provides a range of support services: free tutoring, study spaces, the Disability Services office, and more.

Bethel College is accredited by the Higher Learning Commission, Indiana Division of Professional Standards, National Association of Schools of Music, National Council for Accreditation of Teacher Education, Accreditation Commission for Education in Nursing, and Indiana Professional Licensing Agency.

Off-Campus Programs

Bethel students aren't limited to the four walls of the classroom. They have the opportunity to gain a global vision by learning about the world, studying abroad, experiencing new cultures, and serving others. The Global Engagement Office exists to enable students to move beyond their current cultural, spiritual, academic and relational contexts. Through short-term and semester-length trips, students encounter fresh cultural experiences and service opportunities designed to challenge them academically, stretch their global outlook, and spur them on spiritually, all while growing in Christian community. Bethel offers educational opportunities across the country and around the world, with semester-abroad programs in Australia, Costa Rica, Jordan, Oxford, South Africa, and Uganda. There are also opportunities to travel during the summer to places like Spain or Indonesia or to go on week-long trips called Task Force Teams to places like Guatemala, Thailand, Alaska, or California. Additional information can be found at BethelCollege.edu/MoveBeyond.

Bethel has been named to the President's Higher Education Community Service Honor Roll by the Corporation for National and Community Service. Preparing servant leaders is central to Bethel's mission, so it shouldn't surprise one to learn the campus is home to a variety of community-focused ministries and missions. Students can act on their faith through service learning, which provides opportunities to tutor children, build houses, feed the hungry, and clean parks and neighborhoods. Students take part in an annual service workday, when classes are cancelled and Bethel students, faculty, and staff pitch in to serve the community. In addition, each dorm is matched to an organization in the community where they serve in a variety of ways.

Academic Facilities

A solid college of the arts and sciences, Bethel is emerging as a strong, innovative, and dynamic regional campus. Since 2000, more than 20 buildings have been added to Bethel's campus including Bridges Hall, a women's residence hall; Sufficient Grounds Café and Campus Store; Jenkins baseball stadium, an addition to Science Hall, Logan Village, and a ceramics studio.

The Otis Bowen Library is an integral part of Bethel and its educational systems. The library supports the various divisions within the undergraduate college, the graduate programs, and the professional growth of the professors and the recreational and general interest of the college. Special collections include the Education Resource Center, the Archives of Bethel College, the Missionary Church Archives and Historical Collection, and the Dr. Otis R. Bowen Museum and Archives.

Costs

In the 2018–19 academic year, tuition is $28,140. Room and board (14 meal/week plan) costs total $8,620. Actual direct costs may vary based on meal plan selection and housing assignment.

Financial Aid

More than 97 percent of Bethel students receive financial assistance. Upon admission, students are automatically considered for a merit award of up to $16,000 per year. Bethel also matches church scholarships dollar-for-dollar, up to $1,000 per year. There are also awards based on talent and ability through art, athletics, music, and theater. More details can be found at BethelCollege.edu/FinancialAid.

Faculty

Eighty-two percent of the full-time, tenured Bethel faculty hold a terminal degree in their field. They consider their primary role to be teachers and mentors to Bethel students. The student-faculty ratio is 12:1 and the average class has 16 students, which allows students more opportunity to receive personal attention from professors.

Student Life

More than 30 active student organizations provide ample opportunities for Bethel students to get involved. Students can stay active via intramural sports such as powder-puff and flag football, indoor and sand volleyball, League of Legends, 3 versus 3 and 5 versus 5 basketball, futsal (indoor soccer), dodgeball, and softball. They can connect with others who have similar interests by joining a club: American Sign Language Club, Black Student Fellowship, Enactus (business club), International Student Fellowship, Mu Alpha Theta (math club), Psychology Club, Student Council, Students for Life, and The Company (theater arts). There are also multiple vocal and instrumental ensembles that offer music scholarships for majors, minors, and talented nonmajor students.

The Bethel Pilots are perennial powerhouses, competing in the Crossroads League of the NAIA and in the National Christian College Athletic Association (NCCAA). The Pilots have won 35 national team championships since 1990. A broad spectrum of athletic teams for both men and women compete at Bethel: baseball (m), basketball (m/w), competitive cheerleading (m/w), cross-country (m/w), drumline (m/w), golf (m/w), lacrosse (w), rugby (m), soccer (m/w), softball (w), tennis (m/w), track and field (m/w), and volleyball (w).

Application and Information

Bethel accepts applications anytime online; there is no charge. Prospective students must submit a completed online application, official SAT or ACT sores, and an official high school transcript including at least six semesters (sent directly to Bethel). Transfer students need not submit test scores if they have passed college-level courses in both math and English, however official college transcripts from all colleges or universities attended are required. Bethel is recognized as a home-school-friendly college; a template for home school students' high school transcripts is available from the Bethel Admission Office. Further details are online at BethelCollege.edu/Apply.

Office of Admission
1001 Bethel Circle
Mishawaka, Indiana 46545
United States
Phone: 800-422-4101
E-mail: Admissions@BethelCollege.edu
Website: BethelCollege.edu/Info

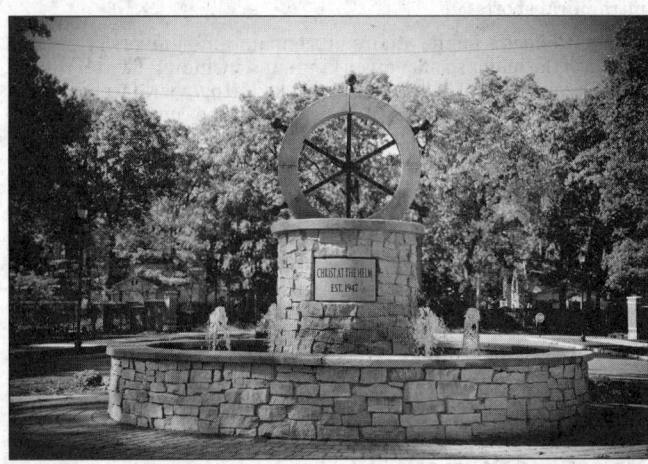

BOSTON COLLEGE
CHESTNUT HILL, MASSACHUSETTS

The University

Boston College (BC) was founded in 1863 by the Jesuits to serve the sons of Boston's Irish immigrants. Today a coeducational university on more than 239 acres in Chestnut Hill, BC may seem a world apart from the small school in the crowded heart of Boston that was its first home. Through more than fifteen decades of growth and change, however, BC has held fast to the Jesuit ideals that inspired its founders. A Jesuit education today, as a century ago, is grounded in the liberal arts and in a commitment to the service of others.

Undergraduates may enroll in the Morrissey College of Arts and Sciences, the Wallace E. Carroll School of Management, the Connell School of Nursing, or the Lynch School of Education.

BC's approximately 9,000 undergraduates come from many backgrounds. The university draws from nearly all fifty states and more than fifty-five countries. Students' religious and cultural backgrounds are similarly diverse. Today, the university's AHANA (African American, Hispanic, Asian, and Native American) and international students make up approximately 30 percent of the undergraduate student body.

In today's complex and increasingly diverse world, the university believes that the best education is one that broadens a student's capacity to reason, think, and make critical judgments in a wide range of areas. Thus, each BC student fulfills a core of liberal arts courses from which he or she can pursue degrees in more than fifty areas of study and choose from more than 1,400 course offerings throughout the university.

According to several recent national publications, BC is in the top tier of the nation's colleges and universities. The foundation for that achievement is the university's scholars and researchers—821 full-time professionals who make up the faculty. The kinship between teachers and students is one of the hallmarks of a BC education; that relationship is nurtured by a student-teacher ratio of 12.2:1. The median class size at the university is 20 students.

At BC, learning continues beyond the classroom in more than 225 student-run organizations. These include student government, honor societies, language and cultural organizations, performance ensembles, political groups, pre-professional clubs, publications, and service organizations. BC also sponsors thirteen varsity teams for men and sixteen for women, all of which compete at the NCAA Division I level. The College also supports over sixty club and intramural sports.

Boston College's public affairs office maintains university profiles on five of the major social networking sites, including Twitter (http://twitter.com/BostonCollege), Facebook (http://www.facebook.com/BostonCollege), YouTube (http://www.youtube.com/bostoncollege), Instagram (http://instagram.com/BostonCollege), and Google+ (https://plus.google.com/+bostoncollege).

Location

Located in the Chestnut Hill section of Newton, BC sits on the doorstep of one of America's great cities, a center of culture and education for more than three centuries. It is an energetic, cosmopolitan city that draws life and enthusiasm from the more than 200,000 college students in residence during the academic year. Located just 6 miles from downtown Boston and with easy access to the city via the trolley system that stops at the foot of the campus, BC offers the best of both worlds: a scenic suburban setting neighboring an exciting metropolitan center.

Majors and Degrees

The College of Arts and Sciences (A&S) is the oldest and largest of the four undergraduate schools at BC. A&S students must complete thirty-eight 1-semester courses, thirty-two of which are in A&S departments. The normal course load is five courses per semester for the first three years and four courses per semester

during the senior year. The undergraduate curriculum includes the university core curriculum and ten to twelve courses in the major field, with the remainder of courses chosen as electives. A&S offers degrees in the following areas: art history, biochemistry, biology, chemistry, classical studies, communication, computer science, economics, English, environmental geosciences, environmental studies, film studies, French, geology, geological studies, geophysics, German studies, Hispanic studies, history, independent major, international studies, Islamic civilizations and societies, Italian, linguistics, mathematics, music, philosophy, physics, political science, psychology, Russian, Slavic studies, sociology, studio art, theater, and theology. Pre-professional advisement is also available in medical, dental, veterinary, and legal programs. Students can also select from twenty-one departmental minors, or seventeen interdisciplinary minors.

The Carroll School of Management educates students to be leaders in business and industry and in public agencies, educational institutions, and service organizations. The Carroll School offers concentrations in accounting, accounting information systems, computer science, corporate reporting and analysis, economics, finance, general management, information systems, management and leadership, marketing, operations management, and new co-concentration options in entrepreneurship, business analytics, and managing for social impact and the public good.

The Lynch School of Education prepares students for education and human services professions. Programs provide a general education, professional preparation, and specialized education in the major field. Fieldwork in area schools is closely linked to course work in each specialization. The Lynch School awards degrees upon completion of thirty-eight courses, including the university core curriculum, a major field of study in education, and a second major in a subject field or an interdisciplinary area in A&S that complements the student's program. Areas of specialization include applied psychology and human development, elementary education, and secondary education. The Lynch School also offers interdisciplinary majors in American heritages, general science, mathematics/computer science, and perspectives on Spanish America.

The Connell School of Nursing offers a four-year program of study leading to a Bachelor of Science degree. The three major components to the curriculum are nursing major courses, electives, and the required university core curriculum. In all courses, principles of wellness, illness, rehabilitation, and health maintenance serve as a theoretical basis in preparing students for professional nursing practice. Nursing courses include traditional classes, simulated and audiovisual laboratory activities on campus, and clinical learning activities in health-care settings.

Academic Programs

Every BC education is centered on a core curriculum—a set of required courses. BC offers a core curriculum because it believes in the unity of knowledge. While the core, which is continually reviewed by a committee of faculty members, varies somewhat by school, its common elements include literature, natural science, writing, philosophy, theology, social science, history, mathematics, fine arts, and cultural diversity.

There are a wide variety of extraordinary academic programs available to BC students to enhance their educational experience. They include, among others, honors programs within each of the university's four undergraduate schools, Undergraduate Faculty Research Fellows, the Scholar of the College, PULSE, and Perspectives on Western Culture.

Off-Campus Programs

BC encourages all students to take part in internship programs. Approximately 80 percent of BC undergraduates participate in at least one internship or prepracticum placement during their college years. Internships can be paid or unpaid and may take place during the academic year or the summer; some carry academic credit.

BC students may take on the challenge of international study in more than sixty programs administered by BC at universities in more than forty countries. BC students who study abroad typically do so in their junior year, but there is also a range of full-year and summer-abroad opportunities. The Office of International Programs helps students with program selection and applications and maintains a library of reference books and professional evaluations of international study programs.

Academic Facilities

BC's eight libraries contain more than 3 million printed volumes, over 4 million items in microform, 817,757 e-books, 264,747 government documents, 45,837 serial subscriptions, and a wide collection of films and archival items. The resources of the library system range from some of Europe's earliest printed books to hundreds of computerized databases. Students with personal computers have dorm-room access to these databases as well as to Quest and other library information sources through Agora, the campus information network. BC also offers a 24/7 "Ask a Librarian" e-mail service and the capability to text questions to a librarian. In addition, all of BC's libraries and classrooms offer a wireless network that provides access to these resources and the Internet.

Research laboratories in the state-of-the-art science facilities have been specially designed to accommodate the advanced instrumentation required for modern science and to provide flexibility for accommodating new equipment. The $85-million expansion to the Higgins Biology and Physics Center was carefully designed to place classrooms, laboratories, computer facilities, and office space in proximity and to facilitate interaction among faculty members, researchers, and students. In addition to the Center's seventeen new teaching laboratories, special working labs are designed and outfitted for research and teaching in the fields of biology and physics.

Boston College opened Stokes Hall in January 2013. This $78-million facility was strategically designed to foster interdisciplinary collaboration among BC's humanities departments and enhanced student-faculty interaction, with thirty-six state-of-the-art classrooms and 200 faculty offices for the Classical Studies, English, History, Philosophy, and Theology departments. Stokes Hall also houses the Academic Advising Center, College of Arts and Sciences Honors Department, and Office of First Year Experience, as well as common areas, conference rooms, a coffee shop, and an outdoor garden and plaza that provide multiple meeting spaces to connect students and faculty.

In 2016, Boston College opened a new residence hall with 490 beds, as well as a new museum of art which hosts modern architecture with larger space for exhibits, functions, and meetings.

BC is currently constructing new athletics fields which should be open in the spring of 2018, as well as a new recreation complex which should be ready by the spring of 2019.

Costs

Tuition for the 2017–18 academic year was $52,500, which included a student activity fee and campus health fee of $846. The total for room and board was $14,142, which included the board plan. Freshman mandatory fees include a one-time required charge of $510 for first-year orientation and student identification.

Financial Aid

BC maintains a financial aid program to assist deserving and qualified students who might otherwise not be able to attend the university. Boston College is committed to providing funds to meet the full demonstrated need of every admitted student who applies for financial aid. Overall, 66 percent of students receive some form of financial aid with the University awarding over $130 million annually in need-based scholarships and grants. Assistance for freshmen alone included more than $20 million in need-based grants. The university offers financial aid to students based on need as demonstrated by completion of the College Scholarship Service's Financial Aid PROFILE and the Free Application for Federal Student Aid (FAFSA). All requirements and deadlines and complete instructions are available in BC admission literature. An application for financial aid in no way affects a decision on admission.

Each year, BC chooses 15 incoming freshmen as Presidential Scholars to receive merit-based, full-tuition scholarships. Students are selected from all candidates who apply through the early action program.

Faculty

BC has 821 full-time faculty members. Of these faculty members, 98 percent hold doctoral degrees. Approximately 50 Jesuits live on BC-owned property and make up one of the largest Apostolic Jesuit communities in the world. About a quarter of those members are active in the College's administration and teaching.

Student Government

The Undergraduate Government of Boston College (UGBC), formed in 1968, is led by the president and vice president, who are elected in the spring of each year by the entire student body. UGBC's goal is to serve the students by providing services and opportunities and by representing them in the best manner possible to the university community. To accomplish this goal, UGBC provides many educational, social, and cultural programs, such as concerts, lectures, roundtables, and more.

Admission Requirements

The undergraduate admission staff pays particular attention to students who have done well in a demanding college-preparatory curriculum, including Advanced Placement (AP) and honors courses when available. For the class of 2021, there were 28,454 applications for 2,412 places. The majority of incoming freshmen ranked comfortably in the top 10 percent of their high school class. The SAT scores of the middle half of admitted freshmen were 1320–1490. On the ACT, scores of the middle half were between 30 and 33.

Application and Information

Students applying to Boston College for a place in the freshman class must complete both the Common Application and the Boston College Supplemental Application. All applicants should submit the BC Supplemental Application as soon as they have decided to apply to Boston College. Students are encouraged to review the electronic application instructions on BC's website at http://www.bc.edu/content/bc/admission/undergrad/process.html and then apply at http://www.commonapp.org.

Students applying through the regular admission program must submit the Common Application and all other required forms, along with the $75 application fee, by January 1. Candidates are notified of action taken on their application in early April. Admitted students intending to matriculate are required to forward a confirmation fee to the Admission Office postmarked by May 1.

Students with superior academic credentials who view Boston College as a top choice may apply through the nonbinding early action program. These applicants must submit both application forms, along with the $75 application fee, by November 1. Candidates learn of their admission decision before December 25 but have the standard deadline (May 1) to reserve their places as freshmen. Boston College does permit students to apply under early action if they have applied to an early decision college.

BC accepts approximately 150 transfer students each year. Transfer candidates should request applications for transfer admission from the Office of Undergraduate Admission or via the website at http://www.bc.edu/transfer. In addition to high school records and standardized test results, transfer applicants must furnish transcripts from all postsecondary institutions they have attended.

For more information, students should contact:

Office of Undergraduate Admission
Devlin Hall 208
Boston College
Chestnut Hill, Massachusetts 02467
Phone: 617-552-3100
          800-360-2522 (toll-free)
Fax: 617-552-0798
Website: http://www.bc.edu

BOSTON UNIVERSITY
BOSTON, MASSACHUSETTS

The University

Boston University (BU) is a private teaching and research university ranked #37 in the nation and #39 in the world by *U.S. News & World Report*. With ten undergraduate schools and colleges; over 250 majors and minors; more than 600 in-depth, global courses; and 100+ study-abroad programs, the challenges at BU are vast and varied. BU students come from all fifty states and more than 100 countries; they are bright, driven, and inquisitive. Students study with world-renowned faculty, 90 percent of whom have a Ph.D. or equivalent. Faculty members include Fulbright scholars, Guggenheim scholars, Sloan Research fellows, Pulitzer Prize winners, a MacArthur fellow, and a former Poet Laureate. With an average class size of 27 and a 10:1 student-to-faculty ratio, these amazing professors become more than just a face students see in class. There are hundreds of research projects that allow undergraduates to work directly with faculty as early as freshman year through the Undergraduate Research Opportunities Program (UROP).

Location

Located in the heart of Boston, students experience the city as an extension of the campus. Boston provides an environment rich in intellectual and cultural stimuli; no other city in the world can compete with Boston's remarkable concentration of higher education institutions, world-renowned medical centers, and historic and cultural attractions. The city provides many opportunities for impressive internship and research positions and is home to world-class attractions including the Museum of Fine Arts, Fenway Park, the Boston Symphony Orchestra, and a thriving theater district. With four years of guaranteed campus housing, and 75 percent of undergraduates living on campus all four years, the campus feels like a true residential community in the heart of Boston.

Majors and Degrees

Of the University's seventeen schools and colleges, ten offer opportunities for undergraduate study.

As BU's largest academic division, the College of Arts & Sciences (CAS) offers a diverse learning community with world-class research faculty. Students may major in American studies; ancient Greek; ancient Greek and Latin; anthropology; anthropology and religion; archaeology; architectural studies; astronomy; astronomy and physics; biochemistry and molecular biology; biology; biology with a specialization in behavioral biology; biology with a specialization in cell biology, molecular biology, and genetics; biology with a specialization in ecology and conservation biology; biology with a specialization in neurobiology; chemistry; chemistry with specialization in biochemistry; chemistry with specialization in teaching; Chinese language and literature; cinema and media studies (also offered in COM); classical civilization; classics and philosophy; classics and religion; comparative literature; computer science; earth and environmental sciences; economics; economics and mathematics; English; environmental analysis and policy; French and linguistics; French studies; geophysics and planetary sciences; German language and literature; history; history of art and architecture; Italian studies; Japanese and linguistics; Japanese language and literature; Latin; linguistics; linguistics and philosophy; linguistics and speech, language, and hearing sciences (also offered in Sargent); marine science; mathematics (includes statistics); mathematics and computer science; mathematics and mathematics education; mathematics and philosophy; neuroscience; philosophy; philosophy and neuroscience; philosophy and physics; philosophy and political science; philosophy and psychology; philosophy and religion; physics; political science; pre-dentistry; pre-law; pre-medicine; pre–veterinary medicine; psychology; religion; Russian language and literature; sociology; Spanish; and Spanish and linguistics. Special curricula include seven-year accelerated programs in liberal arts and medicine or liberal arts and dentistry; the Modular Medical Integrated Curriculum (MMEDIC); the BU dual-degree program; the CFA/CAS double-degree program; the SED/CAS double-degree program; and various combined B.A./M.A. degree programs.

The College of Fine Arts (CFA) offers programs in the School of Music (composition and theory, music education, musicology, performance, and nonperformance), the School of Theatre (acting, design, stage management, production, and theater arts/performing), and the School of Visual Arts (art education, graphic design, painting, printmaking, and sculpture). There is also a double-degree program that allows students to earn two bachelor's degrees simultaneously in the CFA and the CAS.

The College of General Studies (CGS) offers spring admission to the January Boston-London Program. This demanding, two-year program in the liberal arts and sciences stresses an interdisciplinary and global approach to learning. Students begin course work in Boston in January with classes in the humanities, social sciences, and rhetoric, before gaining global perspectives in London during a six-week summer term of intensive study. Students complete the CGS curriculum in their sophomore year, then continue into one of BU's degree-granting schools or colleges to complete their studies. For students who are unable to go abroad, a similar program is offered during the summer in Boston.

Located in one of the largest media markets in the nation, the College of Communication (COM) offers majors in cinema and media studies (also offered in CAS); communication (advertising, public relations, communication studies); film and television (production, writing, management); and journalism (with specialization available in broadcast, magazine, news-editorial, online, and photojournalism).

Majors in the College of Engineering (ENG) include biomedical engineering (a program consistently ranked among the top in the country by *U.S. News & World Report*), computer engineering, electrical engineering, mechanical engineering, and mechanical engineering with specialization in aerospace.

The College of Health and Rehabilitation Sciences: Sargent College is one of the oldest and top-ranked health sciences schools in the country. It offers programs in behavior and health; health science; human physiology; linguistics and speech, language, and hearing sciences; nutrition; and speech, language, and hearing sciences. Also offered is a six-year B.S./D.P.T. program.

The Frederick S. Pardee School of Global Studies is housed within the College of Arts & Sciences and is dedicated to advancing human progress and educating the next generation of global leaders. The school's education, research, and initiatives aim to produce globally competent citizens and leaders. Consisting of two divisions—international studies and regional studies—the school offers programs in Asian studies, European studies, international relations, Latin American studies, and Middle East and North Africa studies.

Areas of concentration in the School of Education (SED) include bilingual education (includes TESOL), deaf studies, early childhood education, elementary education, English education, mathematics education, modern foreign languages education, science education, social studies education, and special education. The SED/CAS double-degree program is also offered.

Located in one of the hospitality and tourism capitals of the world, the School of Hospitality Administration (SHA) offers a rigorous program in the management of hotels, restaurants, food and beverage service, travel and tourism, and entertainment. SHA offers majors in hospitality and communication and hospitality administration, with concentrations in event management, hospitality marketing, and hospitality real estate development.

With a unique global curriculum, the Questrom School of Business (Questrom) offers concentrations in accounting, entrepreneurship, finance, general management (business), health and life sciences management, international management, law, management information systems, marketing, operations and technology management, organizational behavior, real estate, retailing, and strategy and innovation.

Academic Programs

A Boston University education combines the elements of a traditional liberal arts education with training for the professions. There are

250 programs of study to choose from, including BU's top-ranked biomedical engineering, occupational therapy, deaf studies, economics, international relations, management information systems, journalism, theatre, and archeology programs. Highly qualified freshmen may also be invited to participate in the prestigious Arvind and Chandan Nandlal Kilachand Honors College.

Students complete general education requirements through the BU Hub, an innovative new general education program that is integrated with majors and minors and enables students to develop six core capacities. Students take courses of interest while exploring areas ranging from global citizenship to scientific and social inquiry to ethical reasoning or digital communication. The Hub is robust in its options for experiential learning and co-curriculars, and its signature feature, the BU Cross-College Challenge, offers an opportunity to work with a team of students and faculty drawn from across BU's schools and colleges.

Boston University has more than 100 study-abroad opportunities that take students around the world for courses, internships, and fieldwork. Opportunities are offered on six continents, in over twenty-five countries, and in cities such as Auckland, Dresden, London, Los Angeles, Madrid, Paris, Shanghai, Sydney, and Washington, D.C. Programs offered include studies in art/architecture, business/economics, engineering, health and human services, journalism/communications, visual/performing arts, and many more. Fieldwork programs may be found in locations that include Ecuador and Spain.

Boston University operates on a calendar of two semesters and two summer terms. Students generally take four courses each semester.

Academic Facilities

The Yawkey Center for Student Services is home to BU's Center for Career Development, Educational Resource Center, Pre-Professional Advising Office with pre-med and pre-law advising services, and the two-story Marciano Commons dining hall. The Engineering Product Innovation Center (EPIC) is a 15,000-square-foot facility where undergraduates can experiment with developing new products, from design to manufacturing. The BUild Lab: IDG Capital Student Innovation Center fosters innovation and entrepreneurship across the campus and any area of study. Students can connect with advisers, find funding sources, collaborate with other students on projects, and get help with matters from design and prototyping to legal advice and marketing. West campus features the modern Student Village, including Agganis Arena; the Fitness and Recreation Center, complete with a 35-foot rock-climbing wall; and high-rise, apartment-style dorms. BU also has a life science and engineering facility with 187,000-square-feet of laboratory and research space for the biology, bioinformatics, chemistry, and bioengineering departments. The state-of-the-art Photonics Center features classroom and laboratory space for the College of Engineering as well as labs designed to support industry partners who seek to develop new photonics-based products. The Questrom School of Business building also offers technologically advanced educational facilities, with a dedicated career center and management library.

The new Joan & Edgar Booth Theatre and College of Fine Arts Production Center, studio space for visual arts students, practice rooms for music, and a 575-seat music performance center are indicative of BU's support for the arts. More than 2.8 million library volumes and over 4.7 million microform units are contained in Mugar Memorial Library, where the Twentieth-Century Archives are held, including the papers of Dr. Martin Luther King, Jr., Theodore Roosevelt, Robert Frost, and Bette Davis.

Costs

Tuition for 2018–19 is $52,816, estimated room and board costs are $15,720, and University and college fees are $1,132. These costs are exclusive of books, supplies, transportation, and personal expenses.

Financial Assistance

Boston University helps students realize their dreams with several different kinds of financial aid: BU scholarships, federal and state grants, federal loans, federal work-study awards, and financing and payment plan options. Financial aid is offered on the basis of calculated financial eligibility, and two or more types of aid are often combined in award packages. Students must submit the FAFSA and the CSS Profile by established deadlines to be considered. In addition, the Trustee Scholarship (full tuition) and the Presidential Scholarship ($20,000) are offered to the highest achieving students who apply for admission.

The University makes every effort to assist students with calculated financial eligibility, however funds are limited. All applicants who anticipate the need for financial aid are encouraged to apply.

Admission Requirements

The Board of Admissions considers each candidate individually. Primary emphasis is placed on the strength of the secondary school record, but required test scores, character, breadth of interest, school recommendations, and other personal qualifications are also carefully evaluated. Students are required to submit the SAT or the ACT, with the exception of those applying to the College of Fine Arts. A full listing of the standardized testing requirements can be found on the BU Admissions website at www.bu.edu/admissions/apply/. Secondary school graduation or an equivalency diploma is required of all candidates; for the College of Fine Arts a prescreening, audition, or a portfolio may be required, depending on the program of interest. For the accelerated medical and dental programs, interviews and SAT Subject Test scores are required. Boston University offers programs of early decision (binding agreement), early decision 2 (binding agreement), and deferred admission.

Transfer applicants are considered for September or January admission. Transfer students are not eligible for admission to the accelerated liberal arts medical or dental programs or the six-year, combined Bachelor of Science in Health Studies/Doctor of Physical Therapy program. January admission to the College of Fine Arts School of Theatre is also not available to transfer students.

Boston University admits qualified students to all its programs and activities regardless of their race, color, national origin, religion, sex, age, or disability.

Application and Information

Boston University requires the Common Application. Information on applying is available online at www.bu.edu/admissions/apply/. The deadline for regular decision applications is January 2. Applicants for early decision must apply by November 1. Accelerated medical and dental program applications are due November 15. The deadline for the Trustee Scholarship (full tuition) and the Presidential Scholarship ($20,000) is December 1. Regular decision students must submit the College Scholarship Service (CSS) Financial Aid Profile and the Free Application for Federal Student Aid (FAFSA) by February 1.

Transfer students applying for September admission should submit their applications, CSS Profile, and FAFSA forms by March 1 or by November 1 for January admission.

Boston University Admissions
233 Bay State Road
Boston, Massachusetts 02215
Phone: 617-353-2300
E-mail: admissions@bu.edu
Website: http://www.bu.edu/admissions
http://www.facebook.com/BUadmissions
https://twitter.com/ApplyToBU
https://www.instagram.com/applytobu

Students at Boston University find that nothing separates them from Boston's world-class museums, vibrant culture, legendary sports teams, rich history, or world-renowned scientific and medical communities.

BRYN MAWR COLLEGE
BRYN MAWR, PENNSYLVANIA

★ To read more about this school, visit http://petersons.to/brynmawrcollege

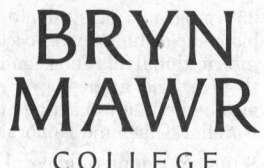

The College

Every year 1,300 undergraduate women and 400 graduate students from around the world gather on Bryn Mawr College's historic campus to study with leading scholars, conduct advanced research, and expand the boundaries of what's possible.

The undergraduate college is known as one of the most academically rigorous liberal-arts colleges in the nation and consistently ranks among the top feeder schools to the world's premier graduate programs and professional schools.

Bryn Mawr's, Leadership, Innovation and Liberal Arts Center (LILAC), Office of Civic Engagement, and the Praxis Program, which integrates fieldwork with theoretical study, provide students with extensive opportunities for internships in nearby Philadelphia and beyond, where they may apply their knowledge outside the classroom. Many students pursue independent and interdepartmental majors with faculty permission. Joint academic programs also exist with Haverford, Swarthmore, and the University of Pennsylvania.

Through advanced research projects, summer internships, and collaborative research with faculty members, students are involved in the local, national, and global communities.

Bryn Mawr offers a unique interdisciplinary experience, 360°, in which a cohort of students takes several courses together to engage multiple aspects of a topic or theme, giving students an opportunity to investigate thoroughly and thoughtfully a multitude of perspectives. Typical 360°s focus on the history, economic concerns, cultural intersections, and political impact of an era, decision, event, policy, or important scientific innovation. 360° participants hone their arguments and insights through writing and research, develop strategies for teamwork that push the limits of their talents and creativity, and work with professors and scholars to promote big-picture thinking.

Bryn Mawr's prestigious alumnae include the first woman to be president of Harvard University, one of the first women to receive the Nobel Peace Prize, the first woman neurosurgeon, and the first and only woman to receive four Academy Awards.

Diversity is central to Bryn Mawr's mission as an extraordinary liberal-arts college, improving the academic experience and enriching the campus community. Students of color and international students make up 56 percent of the undergraduate enrollment. Bryn Mawr's student body is composed of women from forty-five U.S. states, districts, and territories and sixty other countries.

Above all else, Bryn Mawr women share a tremendous respect for individual differences, not merely a passive tolerance of other lifestyles and points of view. The result is a community that resounds with the energy, healthy friction, and range of perspectives that can only come from true cultural and ideological diversity.

The diversity that Bryn Mawr students experience, in and out of the classroom, helps prepare them to be confident global citizens and leaders.

Bryn Mawr women share a commitment to a community that is based on inclusion and support, reinforced by the College's Honor Code, a set of principles stressing personal integrity and mutual respect. In the words of one graduating senior, "This is a place where being yourself makes you feel part of something larger than yourself. A strong sense of self is what we all have in common."

Bryn Mawr is a charter member of the Centennial Conference and is home to twelve NCAA varsity athletic teams. Students may compete in badminton, basketball, crew, cross-country, field hockey, lacrosse, soccer, swimming, tennis, indoor track and field, outdoor track and field, and volleyball. The Bern Schwartz Fitness and Athletic Center offers enhanced spaces for training, fitness, and aquatics.

Goodhart Hall serves as a hub for the College's performing arts scene and boasts a theater for 500+, a teaching theater, scene shop, music rooms, and several performance spaces. Other performance spaces include the Pembroke Dance Studio and the Denbigh Studio.

Bryn Mawr students participate in more than 100 active student organizations. The tri-college community of Haverford, Swarthmore, and Bryn Mawr also sponsors many student groups and activities.

Location

Students at Bryn Mawr have the best of it all in terms of location. The campus itself is such a picture-perfect example of Collegiate Gothic that it has been used as the backdrop for many motion pictures. A quick 5-minute walk into the suburban town of Bryn Mawr finds an eclectic mix of funky independent and favorite franchise coffee shops, eateries, and retailers; an historic movie theater; and a commuter train that can take students to the heart of Philadelphia in about 20 minutes.

Philadelphia has a bustling arts scene and nightlife and is home to more than 250,000 college students. Bryn Mawr women enjoy a rich academic and social life on their own campus and at neighboring tri-college partners, Haverford and Swarthmore Colleges, as well as the University of Pennsylvania.

Bryn Mawr's relationship with Haverford College is particularly close and students participate in many bi-college extracurricular activities, including the orchestra, the chorus, the drama program, and a bi-college newspaper. A 20-minute walk or a 5-minute ride on the bi-college Blue Bus brings students from one campus to the other.

Almost all students live on campus in one of thirteen main residence halls. Two of the buildings are listed on the National Register of Historic Places, and one is also a National Historic Landmark.

Majors and Degrees

Bryn Mawr College grants the Bachelor of Arts (A.B.) degree with majors, minors, and concentrations in more than forty areas: Africana studies; anthropology; astronomy; biochemistry; biology; chemistry; child and family studies; Chinese; classical and Near Eastern archaeology; classical culture and society; classical languages; comparative literature; computational methods; computer science; creative writing; dance; East Asian languages and cultures; economics; education; English; environmental studies; film studies; fine arts; French and Francophone studies; gender and sexuality; geoarchaeology; geology; German and German studies; Greek; growth and structure of cities; Hebrew and Judaic studies; health studies; history; history of art; international studies; Italian studies; Japanese; Latin; Latin American, Iberian, and Latina/o studies; linguistics; mathematics; Middle East studies; music; neurosciences; peace, conflict, and social justice studies; philosophy; physics; political science; psychology; religion; Romance languages; Russian; sociology; Spanish; and theater studies. In consultation with faculty and academic advisers, students may apply to partnership programs for combined undergraduate/graduate degrees from the University of Pennsylvania in engineering, education, city planning, and bioethics. Other partnership programs are available in public health from Boston University, and Chinese studies from Zhejiang University. Combined undergraduate programs in engineering are also available through Cal Tech and Columbia University.

There are approximately 3,000 course exchanges between Bryn Mawr and Haverford each year, selected from a jointly published course list. Bryn Mawr students may major in any of Haverford's coordinate departments or in astronomy, classics, fine arts, music, or religion while earning a Bachelor of Arts degree from Bryn Mawr. Students may also apply to obtain their master's through the combined A.B./M.A. program in chemistry, classical and Near Eastern archaeology, French, Greek studies, Latin language and Roman studies, classical studies, history of art, mathematics, and physics.

Academic Programs

The Bryn Mawr curriculum is designed to encourage breadth of learning and training in the fundamentals of scholarship. At some point during their first three years at Bryn Mawr, students are required to complete Approaches to Inquiry, a curriculum designed to introduce possibilities and problems in scientific investigation, critical interpretation, cross-cultural analysis, and inquiry into the past. Many options are available to fulfill these requirements and students are encouraged to explore many areas of interest. Innovative curricular options include interdisciplinary programs like the Growth and Structure of Cities and the Middle East Studies programs; 360° Course Clusters; and Focus Courses, which are demanding, half-semester courses that may ignite a new intellectual passion. Mature, sophisticated, in-depth study in a major program during the last two years is designed to prepare students for the lifelong pleasure and responsibility of educating themselves and playing an active role in contemporary society. The curriculum encourages independence within a rigorous but flexible framework. Each student chooses and plans her major in consultation with her dean and faculty adviser. Some students take advantage of this freedom to design an independent major, while others fashion their own intellectual perspectives by enrolling in courses that span academic fields or participating in independent research experiences.

With certain restrictions, full-time Bryn Mawr students may also take courses at Swarthmore College, the University of Pennsylvania, and Villanova University during the academic year without paying additional fees.

Off-Campus Programs

Bryn Mawr is only 20 minutes by car or seven short stops by train from the vast cultural and professional resources of Philadelphia, the nation's sixth-largest city. Philadelphia is an incredible resource for Bryn Mawr—a truly accessible city, rich with cultural and professional opportunities, including the Philadelphia Museum of Art, the Philadelphia Orchestra, the Pennsylvania Ballet, numerous theaters, professional sports teams, and some of the nation's most important historic sites. Students may also take advantage of internship opportunities in Center City law firms, art galleries, government agencies, hospitals, TV studios, banks, and schools. When Philadelphia seems too small, 1 in 3 Bryn Mawr students take advantage of one of Bryn Mawr's many study-abroad options.

Academic Facilities

Bryn Mawr ranks among the top 25 of all U.S. colleges and universities in the percentage of female graduates going on to earn a Ph.D. Bryn Mawr students have unlimited access to libraries and laboratories equal to those of many graduate programs, allowing students to pursue independent research at a level unavailable at most undergraduate institutions. These resources include an extensive array of laboratory equipment for the study of science, such as a robotics lab, laser with rangefinder, DNA analyzers, and a geological subsurface profiling system. The Park Science Building is currently under renovation to update and expand the many laboratory spaces and equipment. More than 1 million volumes in a network of open-stack libraries are available to Bryn Mawr students, as well as access to the libraries of both Haverford and Swarthmore Colleges via the Tripod Library System.

In addition, the College has recently enhanced several of its buildings to support student inquiry in all of the liberal arts, including a $19-million renovation of the Marjorie Goodhart Theater which consists of a new state-of-the-art theater, practice rooms, a teaching theater, and scene shop; the upgrade of Dalton Hall, home to Bryn Mawr's social science labs and classrooms; and Bettws-y-Coed, a center for the study of psychology complete with new labs, faculty offices, and meeting rooms. Four former faculty residences have also been renovated to house the student activities village, Cambrian Row.

Costs

In 2017–18, Bryn Mawr tuition, room and board, and fees totaled $66,410.

Financial Aid

To apply for financial aid, students must submit the Free Application for Federal Student Aid (FAFSA), the College Scholarship Service (CSS) PROFILE form, and if applicable, the CSS Noncustodial Parent PROFILE. The College also requires a signed copy of the custodial and noncustodial parents' prior year federal income tax returns, including W-2 forms, and all schedules and attachments. The student's federal income tax return is only required if the student is selected for verification. Tax returns must be submitted to The College Board's Institutional Documentation Service (IDOC). Applicants who are not citizens of the U.S. may file the (CSS) PROFILE. Non–U.S. citizens must also submit letters (in English) from their parents' employers stating gross income and the value of any perquisites, subsidies, and benefits directly to the Office of Financial Aid. Prospective first-year students are notified of admission and financial aid decisions simultaneously.

Faculty

The Bryn Mawr faculty has 152 full-time members, of whom 57 percent are women and 19 percent are professors of color. The College's student-faculty ratio is 8:1. Few colleges or universities can genuinely claim the intellectual curiosity, intensity, and passion found at Bryn Mawr. Classes are small (many have fewer than 15 students), and faculty members come to know their students as individuals. That means more than just being on a first-name basis. In fact, Bryn Mawr faculty members, world-renowned leaders in their fields, regard their students as junior colleagues, fully capable of working at a high level, developing their own ideas, and making important contributions. It is in this way that, perhaps more than at any other school, Bryn Mawr feels like a graduate school on an undergraduate level.

Student Government

Bryn Mawr's culture of innovative leadership dates back to 1892 and the founding of the Student Self-Government Association (SGA), the oldest undergraduate governing body in the country. SGA gives Bryn Mawr students the responsibility of running many campus organizations and activities and participating in discussions and resolutions of important issues, such as curriculum and faculty appointments.

Admission Requirements

Every year, Bryn Mawr receives many more outstanding applications for admission than can be admitted into the first-year class of about 360 students. As members of the Common Application and Coalition Application, Bryn Mawr practices holistic review, with admission decisions based on a number of factors. Strength of the applicant's high school curriculum within the context of the high school and academic performance are of significant importance. Other factors considered are a student's writing, recommendations from the high school counselor and academic teachers, test scores (optional), involvement in school and community, and diverse or unique perspectives and talents a student might bring to the Bryn Mawr community.

Basic high school academic requirements include 4 years of English, 3 years of mathematics, at least 1 year each of a laboratory science and history, and a solid foundation in at least one foreign language. However, most applicants are well prepared for the academic rigor of Bryn Mawr and have taken at least three lab science courses as well as mathematics courses that include trigonometry. Standardized test scores for U.S. applicants or U.S. permanent residents are not required. Non-U.S. citizens and non-U.S. permanent residents are required to submit standardized test scores (SAT I or ACT) as well as either the TOEFL or IELTS if their primary language is not English and/or their language of instruction over the past four years has not been English. Complete details may be found on the Bryn Mawr website.

An interview, either with an admissions representative or with a local alumnae representative, is strongly recommended, but not required.

Bryn Mawr accepts the Common Application and Coalition Application and waives the application fees when students apply online. Application forms should be submitted by November 15 for fall early decision applicants, by January 1 for winter early decision applicants, and by January 15 for regular decision applicants.

Transfer students must complete a minimum of two years of work at Bryn Mawr to qualify for the A.B. degree.

Application and Information

The Office of Admissions is open from 9 a.m. to 5 p.m. on weekdays and some Saturdays throughout the year. Please visit the College website http://www.brynmawr.edu/admissions to plan a visit. Bryn Mawr accepts both the Common Application (http://www.commonapplication.org) and the Coalition Application (http://www.coalitionforcollegeaccess.org/). For additional information, prospective students should contact:

Bryn Mawr College Office of Admissions
101 North Merion Avenue
Bryn Mawr, Pennsylvania 19010-2899
Phone: 610-526-5152
Fax: 610-526-7471
E-mail: admissions@brynmawr.edu
Websites: http://www.brynmawr.edu
http://www.brynmawr.edu/admissions/
http://www.facebook.com/BMCadmissions
http://twitter.com/BrynMawrCollege

Students walking outside the campus center.

CALIFORNIA UNIVERSITY OF PENNSYLVANIA
CALIFORNIA, PENNSYLVANIA

 For more information, visit http://petersons.to/calupenn

The University

Guided by a special mission in science and technology, California University of Pennsylvania (Cal U) offers professional, career-focused programs in the arts and sciences, technologies, and education that engage students in applied and active learning. At Cal U, highly trained faculty members, caring staff and exceptional facilities combine to help every student prepare for a meaningful career. A proud member of Pennsylvania's State System of Higher Education, Cal U serves more than 7,500 undergraduate and graduate students.

Location

The University is located on 294 acres in the borough of California, Pennsylvania, about 35 miles south of Pittsburgh on the banks of the Monongahela River.

Cal U's location in rural southwestern Pennsylvania makes it easy to enjoy camping, hiking, fishing, skiing, and other outdoor activities. The University is also within easy driving distance of architect Frank Lloyd Wright's Fallingwater, one of America's foremost architectural treasures.

For those who prefer city life, the campus offers ready access to the Pittsburgh metropolitan area and its many cultural attractions and sporting events. Shopping, concerts, museums, theater, and more are all just a short drive away. The University organizes regular trips to Pittsburgh and other locations, so students can experience a wide variety of performances and activities.

Majors and Degrees

California University of Pennsylvania offers more than 100 undergraduate majors and concentrations and 95 graduate and professional programs, on campus and 100 percent online. Academic programs are offered through Cal U's three Colleges and its School of Graduate Studies and Research.

Cal U's **Eberly College of Science and Technology** offers scientific, technological, and career-oriented degree programs to prepare students for the complex and evolving demands of the industrial, business, and healthcare fields, as well as for further study in graduate and professional schools.

To help students develop personally and professionally, the College has designed an enriching curriculum built around two education components. The general education component provides a well-rounded education to maximize effectiveness in the workplace and as socially responsible citizens. The professional component includes the critical technical, scientific, business, and support courses that form the foundation for immediate employment or advanced study in each student's chosen field.

Laboratory and workshop experiences supplement a foundation in theory, and many of Cal U's programs provide active learning and internship opportunities that integrate real-world experience with classroom learning.

The Eberly College of Science and Technology includes the following departments: Applied Engineering and Technology; Biological and Environmental Sciences; Business and Economics; Chemistry and Physics; Earth Science; Math, Computer Science, and Information Systems; Nursing; and Professional Studies.

Cal U's **College of Education and Human Services** offers career-oriented degree programs to prepare students for the complex demands of the education and human services fields, or for advanced-level study.

Teacher education is the historical mission of California University of Pennsylvania, and the university offers professional certification and degree programs in a variety of fields, including early childhood/elementary, middle level and secondary education, special education, and technology education.

In addition, the departments of TRIO and Academic Services, Communication Disorders, Counselor Education, Health Science, Exercise Science and Sport Studies, and Social Work provide professional degrees, certifications, and certificate programs.

By combining classroom learning and field experiences, the College of Education and Human Services helps to create a dynamic community of learners and self-assured graduates who are ready to make an impact on their chosen professions. All programs leading to licensure are accredited by their appropriate national organizations.

Cal U's **College of Liberal Arts** furthers intellectual development in the arts, humanities, and social sciences through the departments of Art and Languages; Communications, Design and Culture; Criminal Justice; English; History, Politics and Society; Music and Theatre; and Psychology.

In addition, the College houses the University Honors Program and offers a degree program in liberal studies, an interdisciplinary minor in leadership studies, and a minor in women's studies.

Liberal arts programs at Cal U give students a solid academic foundation in their chosen discipline while fostering skills that employers find essential in any field: critical and analytical thinking, problem solving, communication skills, teamwork, and individual initiative. These programs foster creativity and self-expression as they help students see connections—between the past and the present, the world we know and the ones we imagine, and the local community and the global society.

Cal U's **School of Graduate Studies and Research** offers professional doctorates, master's degrees, certifications, and certificate programs. Both on-campus and online options are available to students who want to add to their knowledge, enhance their resumes, or advance their careers.

Evening classes, accelerated programs, and Cal U Global Online, the University's 100 percent online learning community, make it easier for students to balance earning a degree or other credential with career and family demands. Dual-degree and certificate programs, as well as Cal U's professional doctorates, help students target advanced learning to meet their professional needs.

Highly qualified faculty in Cal U's School of Graduate Studies lead programs that combine rigorous coursework with practical, career-focused experience. Caring staff in the Graduate Admissions and Global Online offices work with students step by step to help them achieve their educational goals as quickly and affordably as possible.

Costs

In 2017–18, undergraduate tuition at Cal U was $7,492 for Pennsylvania residents and $11,238 for out-of-state residents. The average cost of room and board for an incoming freshman was $10,186, and fees were $3,148.80. Books, travel expenses, and other supplies are additional.

Financial Aid

More than 90 percent of all students attending Cal U receive some type of financial aid. The federal Free Application for Federal Student Aid (FAFSA), along with the cost of education, determines whether a student is eligible for need-based assistance. A variety of merit-based scholarships also are available. Cal U works individually with students to build a financial aid package customized to meet their needs.

Faculty

Cal U is a student-centered university that is committed above all to academic excellence and intellectual rigor. All courses are taught by faculty members, not teaching assistants or graduate students.

Stellar faculty are dedicated to helping students take important steps toward achieving their career goals. Among Cal U's professors are Fulbright Specialists, Frederick Douglass Scholars, and recipients of grants from prestigious organizations such as the National Science Foundation and the National Endowment for the Humanities. But at the end of the day, faculty members say that teaching, motivating, and inspiring students is what they do best.

Student Research

Cal U's Center for Undergraduate Research facilitates faculty-led research experiences for students in all majors, providing financial support for student proposals and a student travel fund to support presentations at local, regional, and national events.

Students and faculty showcase their research, scholarship, creative activity, and application at the annual Strike a Spark Conference, an opportunity to hone presentation skills and share their work with the entire campus community.

The SAI Farm, owned and operated by Cal U students, provides an outdoor setting for research projects just over a mile from campus. At community sites throughout western Pennsylvania, students put classroom skills into practice. And opportunities such as the Madagascar Field School give inquisitive scholars a global perspective—and an experience they never forget.

University Honors Program

The University Honors Program at Cal U gives a select group of students a safe, supportive community in which to excel academically, socially, and professionally.

Honors Program students pursue innovative research projects and join other ambitious students in classes taught by Cal U's most distinguished faculty. They have opportunities to make the most of their Cal U education and to position themselves to excel after graduation, whether they choose to begin a career or enter graduate or professional school.

Each semester the Honors Program organizes three- to five-day excursions that allow students to conduct hands-on research; visit libraries, archives, and museums related to their research and coursework; and visit important cultural and historical sites. Many students use an excursion to begin their Honors Program thesis.

In addition, Cal U students in the University Honors Program can receive a scholarship to travel abroad with other honors students from Pennsylvania's State System of Higher Education.

Four-Year Graduation Plan

Cal U's Four-Year Graduation Plan helps students stay on track to complete a bachelor's degree in four years. First-year students agree to stick to one major, take a full course load, and maintain an acceptable grade-point average. In turn, the University provides advising and counseling services every semester, and the Academic Scheduling Center helps students develop an academic plan and keep track of their progress.

Students who follow the Four-Year Graduation Plan do more than graduate on time—they save money by finishing their studies on schedule and getting started on a career.

Career Services

Cal U's Career and Professional Development Center helps students prepare for the future. The Career Advantage program guides students as they make choices about academic majors, explore career options, gain experience, and transition into the workforce. The Career Center staff maintain connections with the region's employers, who regularly visit campus for networking events, job fairs and career training programs.

The Internship Center links Cal U students with employers for a mutually beneficial experience. High-quality, supervised internships allow Cal U students to test-drive their future careers, hone professional skills, build resumes, network, and gain an edge in the job market.

Leadership Training

Cal U's prepares students to take the lead, no matter what field of study they choose to pursue. Students can add a leadership minor that teaches them to think critically about global issues and learn to become leaders in education, business, science, or the arts.

And when students practice effective leadership in class, through community service, and as members of clubs and organizations, the results are documented on an official Activities Transcript.

Student Government

Cal U's Student Government is the official governing body for students. The forum establishes channels of communication between students and administrators/faculty, and it sponsors programs and activities to enrich campus life.

Student Government is part of the Student Association Inc. (SAI), the nonprofit corporation owned and operated by students of Cal U. Along with serving the student body, SAI and Student Government provide opportunities for students to develop leadership and community service skills.

Admissions Requirements

Prospective freshmen students who want to be considered for admission to Cal U as a degree-seeking student must submit an application or admission with a $25 application fee, official high school transcripts or GED credential, and official SAT or ACT scores.

Applicants will be considered for admission to Cal U after careful review of high school record, class rank, academic coursework, and SAT/ACT scores. Attention is given to personal essays, extracurricular activities, and letters of recommendation, if submitted.

Graduate admission varies by program. Information is available at calu.edu.

Application and Information

Applicants may apply online at calu.edu or may contact the Office of Admissions.

California University of Pennsylvania
c/o Undergraduate Admissions–Box 94
250 University Ave.
California, Pennsylvania 15419
Phone: 888-412-0479 (toll-free)
E-mail: admissions@calu.edu
Website: www.calu.edu

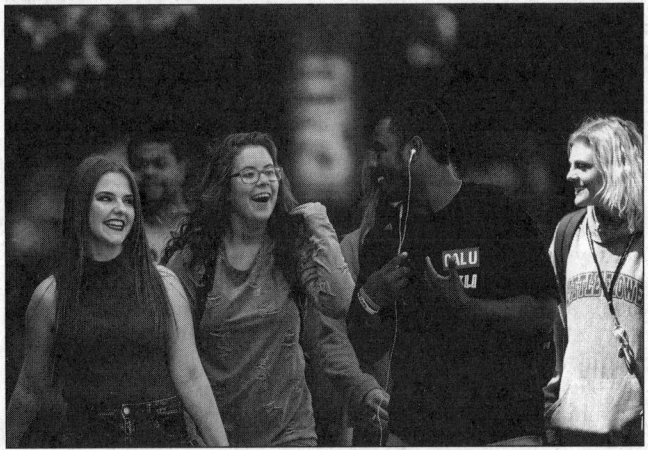

CASTLETON UNIVERSITY
CASTLETON, VERMONT

The University

Castleton University is dedicated to educating future leaders of Vermont and beyond, just as it has been since its founding in 1787. With more than 230 years of service to students, Castleton is the first institution of higher education in Vermont, and the eighteenth-oldest in the United States. Steeped in history, the University cherishes its long-standing traditions, with a focus on innovation through all facets of the student experience.

Sixty-five percent of Castleton's 2,000 students call Vermont home, while the remaining students come from across the United States and more than 40 countries. New England and the Middle Atlantic states are the most predominant areas represented in the University's out-of-state population.

Castleton students are positioned for success the moment they arrive on campus thanks to the First-Year Seminar, an immersive program designed to teach new students how to navigate and excel in their new educational pursuits. First-year students also benefit from an innovative cultural program known as Soundings, which introduces a world of theater, music, dance, film, debate, and lecture brought to Castleton by renowned performers and scholars.

Eleven residence halls on campus provide more than just housing to 1,100 students, they provide learning opportunities where students are challenged to build communities, interact with their peers, learn to respect and appreciate differences and become more involved in community governance. Each residence hall room has both wired and wireless high-speed internet free of charge, and is comfortably furnished. On-campus residence halls include corridor and suite options, and if students are looking for additional independence, the university's newest apartment-style living option in downtown Rutland offers just that. Off-campus housing is available through private landlords in Castleton and neighboring towns. Other amenities include ample free parking for all students, and meal plans that provide three location options for dining; Huden Dining Hall, The Fireside Café, and The Coffee Cottage.

Students further their experience outside of the classroom with more than 50 clubs and organizations including club sports; a nationally-recognized student newspaper; radio station; and clubs related to politics and government, academic majors, and community service. Vermont provides a majestic backdrop for an active student body that takes advantage of free skiing at nearby Pico Mountain, some of the best hiking and biking trails in the state, and countless other outdoor recreational opportunities provided by nearby Lake Bomoseen. At the varsity level, Castleton sponsors 28 NCAA Division III sports including men's and women's alpine skiing, baseball, men's and women's basketball, men's and women's cross-country, field hockey, football, men's golf, men's and women's ice hockey, men's and women's lacrosse, men's and women's Nordic skiing, men's and women's soccer, softball, men's and women's track and field, men's and women's tennis, women's volleyball, and men's wrestling. In addition to the more than 600 student-athletes participating in a varsity sport, there are also countless intramural opportunities throughout the year that serve the entire student population in a fun and supportive atmosphere.

With nearly $100 million in infrastructure improvements since 2002, Castleton's facilities are among the finest in New England as virtually every building on campus has either been built or renovated during that time. The largest project of the last decade was focused solely on the student experience, and resulted in a $25.7 million project that included a new multi-sport stadium, athletic complex, and campus center.

Location

Nestled at the base of the Green Mountains to the east and the Adirondacks to the west, Castleton is located in a quintessential Vermont village. The small-town feelings of safety and authenticity surround the University, but it is also just a short drive from Vermont's cities of Rutland and Burlington. Major cities such as New York, Boston, Hartford, and Montreal are all just a train ride or easy drive away, and students also have access to Rutland Airport with flights in and out of Boston several times each day.

Majors and Degrees

Castleton offers more than 75 programs of study for undergraduate and graduate students. Students may pursue B.A. or B.S. degrees in: accounting, American literature, art, biology, chemistry, children's literature, computer information systems, criminal justice, digital media, ecological studies, economics, elementary education, English, environmental science, exercise science, forensic psychology, geography, geology, global studies, graphic design, health education, health science, history, journalism, kinesiology, management, marketing, mass media, mathematics, music, music education, nursing, philosophy, physical education, political science, psychology, public relations, secondary education, social studies, social work, sociology, Spanish, special education, sport management, theater arts, world literature, and women's and gender studies. A.A. or A.S. degrees may be pursued in: business, media and communication, computer programming, criminal justice, and general studies.

Academic Programs

Castleton University is committed to providing a holistic educational experience, relying on a strong liberal arts foundation to provide its students with the critical thinking, problem-solving, and creative skills needed to succeed in tomorrow's workplace. This foundation is complimented by a focus on career preparation through experiential learning. With more than 400 partnerships in the region, Castleton offers students opportunities through civic engagement, internships, and research.

The only college or university in the country to operate a regional economic development corporation, Castleton students benefit from access to local employers, a state-of-the-art makerspace, and a flourishing entrepreneurial spirit in the region. In 2017 Castleton was the recipient of a five-year grant from the McNair Foundation worth more than $1 million to help its students gain entry into doctoral programs. This new addition complements the growing number of pre-professional offerings such as pre-law, pre-med, and pre-pharmacy as well as the countless research opportunities available through student-faculty partnerships, the Castleton Polling Institute, and other off-campus opportunities.

Castleton students typically enroll in five courses each 15-week semester. In addition to the traditional calendar, Castleton also offers summer and January terms to allow students to stay on track for degree completion.

Academic Facilities

The Calvin Coolidge Library is home to a 500,000-volume collection of books, periodicals, microforms, and nonprint media. Access includes outside scholarly resources through online databases and several inter-library relationships throughout the state of Vermont and beyond.

The Stafford Academic Center is a modern academic building that houses the largest lecture hall on campus, computing and media services, several computer labs, the nursing program's simulation lab, and is connected to the Calvin Coolidge Library. In addition to being a hub for student research and IT support, Stafford is also home to the mathematics, education, and nursing programs.

Leavenworth Hall is home to the social sciences, languages, and media and communication departments. The recently renovated building includes state-of-the-art video editing bays, a television studio, and student lounge among its highlights. The courtyard and outdoor classroom are among students' favorite places to hang out and catch up.

The university's award-winning student newspaper, *The Spartan*, provides communication students with an experiential learning opportunity as soon as their first year.

The Castleton Polling Institute, Vermont's premiere public survey research center, is located in Leavenworth Hall giving students the opportunity to participate in policy research, market research, and public opinion polling at the local and national level.

The Fine Arts Center is the hub of student creativity. Home to Castleton fine and performing arts, music, athletic bands, and graphic design programs, students have every opportunity to showcase talents of their own, or take in a show from a variety of world-renowned guest artists in the 500-seat Casella Theater.

The Jeffords Science Center houses the psychological sciences and natural sciences programs. Offering laboratory and classroom space, as well as a large lecture hall, greenhouse and gardens, Jeffords is well equipped to help students find solutions to the scientific questions of tomorrow.

Home to Glenbrook Gymnasium, two athletic training rooms, team rooms, and strength training facilities for all 600 student-athletes, the Spartan Athletic Complex is the hub for Spartan Pride as well as home to the athletic training, physical education, health education, and sport management programs.

Costs

Costs for 2018–19 are as follows: Vermont resident undergraduate tuition is $11,184 (per year), nonresident undergraduate tuition is $27,192 (per year); room and board is $10,598 (per year); and total fees are $1,360 (per year).

Financial Aid

More than 80 percent of Castleton University's full-time undergraduate students receive financial assistance from federal, state, and University programs or other public and private sources. Grants, loans, and student work programs are available for qualified students. Applicants for financial aid should file the Free Application for Federal Student Aid (FAFSA) form by April 1 of the senior year in high school. All financial aid awards are based on need. Castleton offers an array of need- and merit-based scholarships for first-year, transfer, international, and returning students.

Faculty

Castleton has nearly 100 full-time members of the faculty, 96 percent of whom hold terminal degrees in their chosen field. Part-time faculty members, many of whom are experienced experts in the professional world, complement the program offerings and bolster the learning experience. Students benefit from 1:1 faculty advising and a 14:1 student-faculty ratio in the classroom.

Student Government

The Student Government Association (SGA) operates with three distinctive branches: Congress, University Court, and Campus Activities Board (CAB). All students participating in any facet of these groups are considered active members of the SGA. The SGA represents the Castleton student body and administers the student activity fee which is assessed to all students to fund activities and the more than 50 clubs and organizations on campus.

Admission Requirements

Applicants are evaluated on the basis of their secondary school records, standardized test scores, and recommendations. Admission is granted to those applicants who have demonstrated their ability and potential to meet the challenges of a postsecondary learning experience.

Application and Information

Students may apply for admission through the Common Application. Under Castleton's rolling admission policy, applications are processed throughout the year, and candidates are notified of the admission decision as soon as their files are complete. Students are admitted in the fall and spring semesters.

For more information about Castleton University or to arrange a campus visit, students should contact:
Office of Admissions
Castleton University
Castleton, Vermont 05735
Phone: 802-468-1213
 800-639-8521 (toll-free)
Fax: 802-468-1476
E-mail: info@castleton.edu
Website: www.castleton.edu

The Castleton campus is nestled at the base of the Green Mountains, and has a panoramic view of every season.

THE CATHOLIC UNIVERSITY OF AMERICA

WASHINGTON, D.C.

THE
CATHOLIC UNIVERSITY
of AMERICA

The University

Located in the nation's capital, The Catholic University of America is a national research university with the comfortable feel of a nurturing educational community. Anchored by its Catholic identity and inspired by a rich intellectual tradition, the University welcomes undergraduate and graduate students from around the globe to study with world-class faculty at the forefront of their fields.

Catholic University's record of academic excellence is widely recognized by top scholars. Life outside the classroom is equally exciting: The University fields 25 varsity intercollegiate teams and offers a full array of recreational club sports, as well as a state-of-the-art fitness center. More than 70 majors and over 100 clubs mean there is always a way for the roughly 3,300 undergraduate students to explore their interests.

Visitors to campus are captivated by the University's tree-lined setting in an urban environment. Students at Catholic University have the best of both worlds: They study and live on the largest campus in Washington, D.C., where they can enjoy a complete collegiate experience, but they also are located in the heart of the nation's capital. Traveling by Metrorail, which is right next to campus, students are minutes away from the abundant array of educational, cultural, social, political, and professional opportunities that make Washington a unique laboratory for learning.

Location

The exciting attractions of the nation's capital are just minutes away from the University's residential college campus, the largest and greenest campus in the District of Columbia.

Washington, D.C., is one of the nation's largest college towns, with more than 100,000 students at colleges and universities in the region. The University participates in the Consortium of Universities of the Washington Metropolitan Area, so students have access to courses at other universities, including American, Georgetown, George Washington, Howard, and the University of Maryland College Park. With 91 stations throughout the city and surrounding areas, including Catholic University's own stop, the Metrorail system is safe, fast, and convenient.

Majors and Degrees

With more than 70 undergraduate majors, 10 academic schools that grant undergraduate degrees, and small class sizes, Catholic University offers remarkably diverse areas of study. Students can delve deeply into their major interests while rooting their studies in the enduring liberal arts.

Degree programs are offered in the following majors: accounting, anthropology, architecture, architecture and civil engineering, art history, art–studio art, biochemistry, biology, biomedical engineering, chemical physics, chemistry, city and regional studies, civil engineering, classical civilization, classical humanities, classics–Greek and Latin, computer science, construction engineering and management, drama, economics, education studies (non-teaching), education, electrical engineering, English language and literature, environmental chemistry, environmental engineering, environmental studies, finance, French and Francophone studies, German studies, Hispanic studies, history, instrumental performance, international business, international economics and finance, Italian studies, management, marketing, mathematics, mathematics and physics, mechanical engineering, media and communication studies, medieval and Byzantine studies, music composition, music education, music–general, music–instrumental performance, music–organ, music–piano, music–voice performance, musical theatre, nursing, organ, philosophy, physics, piano, politics, psychology, social work, sociology, Spanish, structural/geotechnical engineering, studio art, theology and religious studies, and voice performance.

Additional information on undergraduate majors can be found online at www.cua.edu/undergraduateprograms.

Academic Programs

Catholic University offers all of the benefits of a major research university within a nurturing educational community.

All undergraduates participate in the First-Year Experience (FYE), an introduction to the life of the mind through coursework and activities rooted in the liberal arts and the Catholic intellectual tradition. Within Learning Communities, students take a sequence of four core classes in philosophy, theology, and English. The FYE also goes beyond the classroom with service learning activities, class-based excursions into Washington, D.C., an annual Speaker Series, and one-on-one academic advising.

The Undergraduate Advising Center provides dynamic advising resources for all students. The Center for Academic Success offers a wide range of academic services designed to help students of all abilities strengthen their skills and take an active role in their education.

The University Honors Program (UHP) offers a challenging and inspiring liberal arts program to motivated students with outstanding academic promise. Through the give and take of intimate, seminar-style classes, UHP students find themselves pushed to be more broad-minded and rigorous, more thoughtful, quicker on their feet, more keenly critical, and more humane in their pursuit of the truth. In addition to an outstanding academic program, the UHP offers a variety of excellent social and cultural opportunities. Those who choose to live in the Centennial Village Honors Community enjoy even more opportunities for enrichment.

There are over 2,000 internship opportunities for students. On average, 67 percent of student internships are paid while the other 33 percent are done for class credit during the semester or summer. Students have recently had the advantage of internships with the FBI, Congress, JP Morgan, and Community Family Life Services, to name a few of the exciting opportunities for students from all schools and majors to develop skills in their chosen field. The Office of Career Services works with students throughout the job/internship process from resume workshops to mock interviews while connecting students with Catholic University alumni throughout the country and around the world. Catholic University students studying abroad in Brussels, Dublin, and London also have the opportunities to intern with the European Union, Irish Parliament, and British Parliament, respectively.

Off-Campus Programs

International outreach has been a central part of the University's mission since its founding. The Education Abroad Program continues that tradition. Any financial aid received on campus can be applied to an education abroad program. Students can choose to study and live in countries such as Australia, Belgium, Chile, China, England, France, Germany, Greece, Guatemala, Ireland, Italy, Mexico, Poland, and Spain, to name a few. With opportunities in more than 50 cities worldwide, students of any major can spend a summer, a semester, or a year abroad, immersed in a new culture.

The Rome Center of The Catholic University of America and Australian Catholic University offers semester-long programs, primarily for students enrolled in the schools of arts and sciences, business and economics, music, and architecture; a month-long Summer Experience Abroad for architecture majors; short courses in law, canon law, business and economics, and theology and religious studies; and a summer program for the First-Year Experience.

Costs

For the 2017–18 academic year, tuition was $43,300, room and board was $14,316, and fees totaled $760. Costs for books, transportation, and personal expenses are estimated at $4,106 for a total annual estimated cost of attendance of $62,842.

Financial Aid

Catholic University offers a comprehensive financial aid program that includes need-based aid, scholarships, federal work-study, and other forms of financial assistance. Over the last three years, 96 percent of first-year students received scholarships and/or grants directly from Catholic University. In that same three-year period, the average cost of tuition, room, and board for first-year students, after scholarships and grants, was $35,737. Catholic University compares very well with other private, national research institutions, though the value of a Catholic University of America education is incomparable.

Faculty

Professors at The Catholic University of America research compelling issues in their fields, connecting knowledge of the past to the promise of the future. The University's notable academic leadership has produced dozens of Fulbright, Guggenheim, Wilson, Mellon, and Oxford scholars. Catholic University stands out among research universities because undergraduate studies are a vital part of the faculty's interests. Four of every five professors teach at the undergraduate level.

Student Activities

Students are involved on campus and in the community in a wide array of activities. With more than 100 student organizations, Catholic University makes it easy for students to pursue their interests in virtually every field and activity imaginable. All activities are open to all students regardless of major or year in college. There are activities and organizations that emphasize academics, professions, community service, multiculturalism, politics, spiritual life, recreation, singing, dancing, student government, media, and more.

Admission Requirements

Prospective students are expected to have a rigorous and well-rounded academic background including 4 years of English, 4 years of social studies, 3 years of mathematics, 3 years of science (including at least 1 laboratory science), at least 2 years of a foreign language, and 1 year of fine arts or humanities.

The Catholic University of America is now test-optional for undergraduate admission. Submission of standardized test scores is optional for students applying for undergraduate admission. First-year and transfer applicants will receive full consideration for admission and merit-based scholarships regardless of whether they submit the results from the SAT or the ACT.

Application and Information

The Catholic University of America utilizes the Common Application. The Early Action application deadline is November 1 and the Early Decision application deadline is November 15; both Early Action and Early Decisions will receive notification on or around January 1. The regular decision application deadline is January 15, with notification on or around March 20.

The Catholic University of America invites prospective students and their families to visit the campus, meet admissions staff and current students, and learn about the many opportunities the University offers.

For more information, prospective students should contact:

Office of Undergraduate Admissions
The Catholic University of America
620 Michigan Avenue, N.E.
Washington, D.C. 20064
United States
Phone: 202-319-5305
      800-673-2772 (toll-free)
Fax: 202-319-6533
E-mail: cua-admissions@cua.edu
Website: http://admissions.cua.edu

Catholic University's 176-acre campus is the largest in Washington, D.C. The Basilica of the National Shrine of the Immaculate Conception is located adjacent to the University Mall.

CLEMSON UNIVERSITY
CLEMSON, SOUTH CAROLINA

★ To read more about this school, visit http://petersons.to/clemsonuniversity

The University

A top-23 public university with a reputation for excellence that's known worldwide, Clemson University leads the way in providing a hands-on education—in the lab, in the arts, and in the field. Clemson was founded in 1889 with a mission to be a "high seminary of learning" dedicated to teaching, research, and service. Today, Clemson is one of the country's most selective public research universities, and these three concepts remain prevalent, providing the framework for an exceptional educational experience.

At Clemson University, professors take the time to get to know students and explore innovative ways of teaching. Exceptional teaching is one reason Clemson's retention and graduation rates rank among the highest in the country for public universities.

Exceptional teaching is also why Clemson continues to attract an increasingly talented student body. In 2017, more than half of the entering freshmen were ranked in the top 10 percent of their high school classes, and the freshman class averaged 29 on the ACT, placing Clemson in the top seven public universities in the nation, as ranked by freshman ACT scores (*U.S. News & World Report*, 2017).

Clemson is committed to world-class research and is ranked in the highest research university category by the Carnegie Classification of Institutions of Higher Education. The University is also invested in the success of its students. Student retention at Clemson is consistently more than 90 percent. Much of this is due to the Academic Success Center (ASC). Established in 2001, the ASC has been recognized nationally and internationally by organizations related to tutoring, supplemental instruction, and collegiate learning. The ASC moved into a new, 35,000 square-foot facility in 2012 where it offers free one-on-one tutoring services for more than 80 courses and provides tutoring for additional courses as the need arises. Peer-assisted learning, academic skills workshops, and academic counseling are also available—free to all Clemson students. It is estimated that more than 50 percent of freshmen use ASC services during their first semester.

Clemson has also received national recognition for its innovative Communication Across the Curriculum (CAC) program. At Clemson, CAC is a standard teaching method used in nearly every department. Professors use CAC to focus on providing real-life challenges that require students to think and communicate effectively.

From cheering on the Tigers at a football game to socializing in the Hendrix Student Center, Clemson students can participate in a wide variety of activities outside the classroom. The more than 400 campus clubs and organizations include fraternities and sororities, as well as honorary, international, military, performing arts, political, professional, religious, service, social interest, special interest, sports and fitness, and student media programs and activities.

With 19 intercollegiate sports, Clemson offers exciting spectator sports year-round. Clemson is a charter member of the Atlantic Coast Conference (ACC) and is an NCAA Division I school. Admission to most regular-season home events is included in University fees for full-time students.

Clemson University is accredited by the Commission on Colleges of the Southern Association of Colleges and Schools to award bachelor's, master's, specialist, and doctoral degrees. Questions about the accreditation of Clemson University can be directed to the Commission on Colleges at 1866 Southern Lane, Decatur, Georgia 30033-4097; phone: 404-679-4500.

Location

Approximately midway between Charlotte, North Carolina, and Atlanta, Georgia, Clemson University is located on 1,400 acres in the foothills of the Blue Ridge Mountains and along the shores of Hartwell Lake. Great weather and proximity to natural wonders and large cities offer year-round recreational opportunities.

The University's enrollment of more than 24,000 undergraduate and graduate students makes it a defining presence in Clemson, South Carolina, a town of about 14,000. Students may live on campus in one of the 27 residence halls and five apartment communities, most of which are within a 15-minute walk to class or downtown. More than 99 percent of students live on campus their freshman year.

Majors and Degrees

Clemson offers more than 80 undergraduate and 119 graduate degree programs through seven academic colleges: Agriculture, Forestry, and Life Sciences; Architecture, Arts, and Humanities; Behavioral, Social and Health Sciences; Business; Engineering, Computing and Applied Sciences; Education; and Science. Undergraduate students can earn B.A., B.S., or preprofessional degrees in accounting; agribusiness; agricultural education; agricultural mechanization and business; animal and veterinary sciences; anthropology; architecture; art; biochemistry; bioengineering; biological sciences; biosystems engineering; chemical engineering; chemistry; civil engineering; communication; computer engineering; computer information systems; computer science; construction science and management; early childhood education; economics; electrical engineering; elementary education; English; environmental and natural resources; environmental engineering; financial management; food science and human nutrition; forest resource management; genetics; geology; graphic communications; health science; history; horticulture; industrial engineering; justice studies; landscape architecture; language and international health; language and international trade; management; marketing; materials science and engineering; mathematical sciences; mathematics teaching; mechanical engineering; microbiology; modern languages (American Sign Language, Chinese, French, German, Italian, Japanese, and Spanish); nursing; packaging science; Pan African studies; parks, recreation, and tourism management; philosophy; physics; plant and environmental sciences; political science; prepharmacy; preprofessional health studies; prerehabilitation sciences; preveterinary medicine; production studies in performing arts; psychology; religious studies; science teaching; secondary education; sociology; special education; sports communication; turfgrass; wildlife and fisheries biology; women's leadership; world cinema; and youth development studies.

Academic Programs

Clemson's academic year is divided into two semesters. The fall semester begins in mid-August and the spring semester starts in early January. Three summer sessions and four mini-semesters are also available. Students average 16 credit hours per semester, and Clemson requires all students to complete some general education classes specified by the University before graduation. The number of completed credit hours required for graduation varies, depending on the major.

Calhoun Honors College is a University-wide program that combines the strengths of a public, land-grant university with those of a highly selective small college. Calhoun scholars may choose to pursue departmental honors within their specific academic discipline. In addition, EUREKA! (Experiences in Undergraduate Research, Exploration, and Knowledge Advancement) is a unique and exciting program that enables honors students to pursue research and scholarly activities with faculty members across all disciplines. The advantages of membership in the Honors College include priority registration, extended library loan privileges, honors research grants, and a special living-learning community.

The National Scholars Program is a highly selective program for exceptional students who strive to meet their highest intellectual potential. One of its goals is to develop the interests and talents students need to compete for Rhodes, Marshall, and Truman scholarships; Fulbright Grants; National Science Foundation Graduate Fellowships; and other prestigious international fellowships. In 2016–17, 23 Clemson students received National Science Foundation Graduate Fellowships. Six Clemson graduates received Fulbright grants to conduct research or teach abroad, and three students were named Goldwater Scholars.

Clemson's Creative Inquiry (CI) program allows undergraduate students to engage in research about problems that spring from their own curiosity, from a professor's challenge, or from the pressing needs of the world around them. Team-based investigations are led by a faculty mentor and typically span two to four semesters. Students take ownership of their projects and take the risks necessary to solve problems and get answers. This invaluable experience produces exceptional graduates, capable of thinking critically, solving problems as a team, and communicating and presenting their ideas to others. In 2016–17, 4,802 students participated in 404 CI projects.

Clemson's nationally recognized Programs for Educational Enrichment and Retention (PEER) is committed to improving the academic performance of underrepresented students in engineering and science.

Off-Campus Programs

Clemson's students are strongly encouraged to incorporate a study-abroad experience in their overall Clemson journey. Programs are available on six continents for all disciplines and interests. These include faculty-led programs, exchange programs, and programs available through Clemson's partnerships with study-abroad providers and institutions.

Students in a variety of majors also have opportunities at other Clemson campuses around the world, including the Archbold Center in Dominica; the Daniel Center in Genoa, Italy; and the Clemson University Brussels Center in Belgium. There are other campuses around South Carolina, including Greenville, Greenwood, and Charleston.

The Cooperative Education program provides an opportunity for students to alternate periods of academic study with semesters of paid, career-related, engaged-learning experiences to bridge the gap between academic study and its application in professional practice. Clemson's Center for Career and Professional Development helps to pair students with companies seeking interns or co-op students. The Princeton Review ranks Clemson's career services program as the number-one career office in the nation, and with help from the career center, about 2,200 students participate in academic internships and co-ops annually. Because co-op experiences have been proven to enhance academic performance and provide a competitive edge when seeking full-time employment, Clemson students can now add on-campus internship experiences to their resumes. Students can work part- or full-time, with many in full-time positions having the option of earning credit. The University has made an investment to fund a portion of these experiences, so these on-campus jobs are paid positions.

Academic Facilities

The Clemson campus is a blend of historic buildings and advanced research facilities surrounded by stately trees and lush greenery.

Clemson's main library, the Robert M. Cooper Library, is located at the center of campus and provides a variety of services and up-to-date collections. The University's wireless networking capability lets students communicate with professors and classmates, read online course materials, check email, and conduct research—all from their own laptops.

The campus offers an array of facilities and programs designed to enhance a student's entire educational experience. These include the Pearce Center for Professional Communication, Class of 1941 Studio for Student Communication, Rutland Institute for Ethics, and the Academic Success Center.

Clemson real estate holdings also include more than 32,000 acres of forestry and agricultural lands throughout the state, most of which are dedicated to the University's research and service missions.

Costs

For the 2017–18 academic year, undergraduate tuition and fees were $15,116 for South Carolina residents and $36,058 for out-of-state residents. Room and board costs were approximately $9,592, and books and supplies were around $1,346. Estimated personal and transportation expenses were $3,520, and the one-time laptop computer cost was about $1,800.

Financial Aid

Financial aid is usually awarded based on need to supplement the amount students and their parents can contribute to college expenses. The University also awards some scholarships based entirely on academic merit. Clemson offers financial aid in the form of grants, scholarships, loans, and part-time employment, and 84 percent of all students receive financial aid at Clemson.

Entering freshmen are evaluated on a competitive basis for scholarships using the admission application. There is no separate scholarship application. For academic recruiting scholarships, selection of domestic students is based on test scores, high school class rank, and other academic factors. Stipends for in-state residents range from $500 per year to the full cost of attendance. Merit scholarships for out-of-state students range from $7,500 per year to the full cost of attendance. Academic recruiting scholarships are available only to entering freshmen and are renewable for three additional years if the minimum standards are maintained. The application for admission is the first step for prospective freshmen to be considered for merit awards.

General scholarships are awarded to both entering freshmen and upperclassmen. These may have special criteria set up by the donor, such as a certain residency, major, or career interest. Because of the restrictions on many of these scholarships, it is impossible to predict the recipients. The scholarship selection process is very competitive. Stipends range from $250 to $7,500.

Faculty

Clemson has more than 1,000 full-time faculty members, with around 86 percent holding a Ph.D. or terminal degree in their fields. In addition, the University has more than 100 part-time faculty members. Faculty honors include the Fulbright Scholarship, Guggenheim Fellowship, National Science Foundation CAREER Award, National Institutes of Health Senior Scientist Award, and membership in the American Academy of Arts and Sciences. The average class size is 31, and the student-to-faculty ratio is 16:1.

Admission Requirements

In 2017, the University received about 26,242 applications for a fall freshman class of 3,649. Transfer applications were received from 3,218 students, 1,572 of whom enrolled. Undergraduate applications are available online at clemson.edu/admissions.

For freshman applicants, the following factors are considered: class standing, standardized test scores (SAT or ACT), high school curriculum, grades, and choice of major. Entering freshmen must have completed 4 credits of English, 3 credits of mathematics, 3 credits of laboratory science, 3 credits of a foreign language (in the same language), 3 credits of social sciences, 1 credit of U.S. history, 1 credit of physical education or ROTC, and 1 credit of fine arts.

To be considered for transfer admission, candidates must have completed a full year of college study (a minimum of 30 semester hours or 45 quarter hours of transferable work completed after secondary school conclusion), earned a minimum cumulative GPA of at least 2.5 on a 4.0 scale (3.0 preferred), and completed freshman-level courses in English, science, and mathematics for their intended major at Clemson. Students may also transfer into Clemson after successful completion of their freshman year through the Bridge to Clemson program, a collaborative first-year academic and residential life partnership between Clemson University and Tri-County Technical College. Bridge is available by invitation only to qualified Clemson freshman applicants who have the potential to be successful at Clemson but, due to its competitive admissions landscape, could not be admitted directly into the University for their freshman year.

Application and Information

Application deadlines for freshman admissions are December 1 (priority date for fall semester), May 1 (fall semester), and December 15 (spring semester). For transfer admissions, the application deadlines are July 1 (fall semester) and December 15 (spring semester).

Office of Admissions
Clemson University
105 Sikes Hall, Box 345124
Clemson, South Carolina 29634-5124
Phone: 864-656-2287
Fax: 864-656-2464
E-mail: cuadmissions@clemson.edu
Website: http://www.clemson.edu/admissions

Hands-on problem solving and real-world experiences make Clemson students exceptionally prepared for postgraduate education and future career opportunities.

COLLEGE FOR CREATIVE STUDIES
DETROIT, MICHIGAN

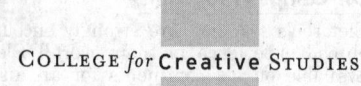

The College

The College for Creative Studies (CCS) is one of the nation's leading art and design education institutions. A private, fully accredited, four-year college located in Detroit, CCS offers Bachelor of Fine Arts degrees in eleven majors and Master of Fine Arts degrees in four majors. The College provides a dynamic learning environment in which students explore issues of art and design and the culture in which they exist while preparing for careers in the professional world. CCS is credited with having one of the world's most recognized programs in transportation design and for placing more graduates in automotive design careers than any other school.

The College is dedicated to providing an educational environment most conducive to the development of outstanding artists and designers. The teaching is directed not only toward developing technical excellence but also toward stimulating intellectual potential. Graduates are well prepared to join the professional world, have the overall ability to carry on their education as desired, are able to communicate effectively, and have a basic understanding of today's artistic, social, and intellectual world and its traditions. The current enrollment is more than 1,400 men and women.

Location

CCS' world-class facilities are located on two sites—the Walter and Josephine Ford Campus and the A. Alfred Taubman Center for Design Education, just a mile apart. At each site, students have access to the latest equipment and workspaces found in the leading creative companies. Twenty-eight major cultural and educational institutions are within easy walking distance. Students have full access to the Detroit Institute of Arts, one of the largest fine arts museums in the United States, and to the main branch of the Detroit Public Library, which offers more than 2 million volumes. Other available facilities include the New Detroit Science Center, Detroit Children's Museum, Detroit Historical Museum, and the Charles H. Wright Museum of African American History.

Majors and Degrees

The College for Creative Studies offers a four-year program leading to the Bachelor of Fine Arts (B.F.A.) degree and a two-year program granting a Master of Fine Arts (M.F.A.) degree. Bachelor's degrees can be earned in advertising–copywriting, advertising–design, art education, communication design, crafts (concentrations: ceramics, fiber design, glass, and metalsmithing and jewelry design), entertainment arts (concentrations: animation, game design, and film), fashion accessories design, fine arts (concentrations: painting, print media, and sculpture), illustration, interior design, photography, product design, and transportation design. Master's degrees can be earned in Color & Materials Design, Integrated Design, Interaction Design and Transportation Design. Minors in art history and art therapy are also available. Interdisciplinary studies in crafts and fine arts are permitted upon departmental recommendation.

Academic Programs

The B.F.A. degree requires completion of 126–127 credit hours: 78 in studio areas and 42–43 in general studies courses and 6 in general elective classes. In addition to course work in their chosen major, first-year students take courses in the Foundation Department, where they study drawing, color theory, and basic design. Students in all majors also take courses in the Liberal Arts Department, designed to provide them with an understanding of the larger social and cultural context in which they live. Typical weekly schedules for full-time students comprise 24 studio hours and six academic hours.

The M.F.A. degree requires completion of 60 credit hours and focuses on fostering critical thinking in a design context while keeping contemporary business reality in mind. CCS graduate classes are taught by industry leaders and an internationally recognized roster of visiting designers and artists with experience in design strategy, user-centric research, design execution and presentation, as well as entrepreneurial practices.

CCS' Continuing Education division offers a rich variety of high-quality art and design programs year-round to students of all ages and artistic backgrounds. High school sophomores, juniors, and seniors can earn college credit in CCS' Summer Experience Pre-College Program. Also available are portfolio preparation courses and professional development programs for teachers.

Off-Campus Programs

Independent study, internships, and study-abroad programs are available. Mobility programs, offered in cooperation with thirty-one other colleges in the Association of Independent Colleges of Art and Design (AICAD), allow students to take advantage of course offerings at other institutions while pursuing a degree at the College. In addition, seniors may study in a studio space in New York City to which CCS has access. Juniors and seniors also have the opportunity to spend a full year of study at an accredited institution abroad.

Academic Facilities

The CCS campus totals 16 acres, with approximately 1.5 million square feet of space. Located in midtown Detroit, the College is made up to two sites, the Walter and Josephine Ford Campus and the A. Alfred Taubman Center for Design Education.

The Walter and Josephine Ford Campus consists of the Kresge-Ford Building, Walter B. Ford II Building, the Manoogian Visual Resource Center, Yamasaki Building, and the Art Centre Building.

The Kresge-Ford Building was completed in 1975 and was a major addition to the College's classroom, studio, and office space. Currently the building houses the Art Education, Crafts, Fine Arts, Liberal Arts, and Photography departments. The Arts & Crafts Cafe, two student lounges and the Student Success Center are also located here.

The Walter B. Ford II Building, is a state-of-the art facility wired with a single digital network to carry voice, data, and video. The building houses the Entertainment Arts, Illustration, and Foundation departments and incorporates high-tech flexible classrooms with both traditional and computer workstations and a 250-seat auditorium equipped with LCD and HD projectors, VHS/DVD/Blu-ray technology, and 7.1 surround sound. In addition, the building also provides space on each floor for the exhibition of student work and includes numerous traditional animation labs, "The Stage"—a large production studio, a recording room and sound studios, figure and anatomy dry studios, and an Oxberry.

The Taubman Center is home to the College's six undergraduate design departments; graduate-degree programs in color and materials design, integrated design, interaction design, and transportation design; and the Henry Ford Academy: School for Creative Studies, an art and design charter school for middle and high school students. This second campus site has enabled CCS to expand its curriculum to include new areas of the creative industries, improve facilities for all of its departments, and connect with the local community through the Detroit Creative Corridor Center. It represents the College's commitment toward accelerating metro Detroit's transition to an innovation-based economy by renewing the infrastructure of an important urban neighborhood; attracting, developing, and retaining talent in the creative industries; spurring research in sustainable product development; and creating jobs and new business opportunities.

Costs

For the 2018–19 academic year, tuition is $1,423 per credit hour or $21,345 per semester for full-time enrollment (12 to 18 credits). Housing costs are $2,850 or $3,600 per semester. Meal plan options are $725 or $1,450 per semester. The estimated cost of materials and supplies is $2,500 in most fields of study.

Financial Aid

The College participates in the Federal Pell Grant, Federal Supplemental Educational Opportunity Grant, Federal Work-Study, Federal Stafford Student Loan, Federal PLUS loan, Michigan Tuition Grant, Michigan Competitive Scholarship, Michigan Work Study, Michigan Merit Award, Michigan Educational Trust, and Michigan Educational Savings Plan programs. The College also awards scholarships, based on artistic ability and academic excellence, to currently enrolled and prospective students.

The College attempts to financially assist qualified students who apply, contingent upon the availability of funds.

Faculty

The College has 425 faculty members. All members of the studio art faculty are professionals in their individual fields who bring diverse backgrounds and experiences to the classroom.

Student Government

Students participate in the leadership of the school in several ways. The Student Coalition is composed of representatives from each department and takes an active role in areas affecting student life. The coalition works with the Student Programming Coordinator to organize dances and other events during the year. The coalition was active in the founding of U245, the student-run gallery, and continues to support its activities.

Admission Requirements

The Office of Admissions at the College for Creative Studies is dedicated to assisting students in evaluating educational alternatives and career possibilities in the visual arts.

Applicants must have maintained a GPA of at least 2.5 in high school or successfully passed a high school equivalency examination and must submit SAT or ACT scores and a portfolio of representative work. Applicants who have had previous college experience are required to submit an official transcript from each institution attended. Personal interviews are available.

Application and Information

Applications for the fall term are accepted through August 1. Applications for the second semester should be submitted prior to December 1.

For application forms, catalogs, and additional information, students should contact:

Office of Admissions
College for Creative Studies
201 East Kirby
Detroit, Michigan 48202-4034
United States
Phone: 313-664-7425
        800-952-ARTS (toll-free)
Website: http://www.collegeforcreativestudies.edu

Aki Choklat, Chair of Fashion Accessories Design, works with students on the design of a new shoe.

THE COLLEGE OF NEW JERSEY
EWING TOWNSHIP, NEW JERSEY

 To read more about this school, visit http://petersons.to/tcnj

The College

The College of New Jersey (TCNJ) welcomes students who have the talent and motivation to succeed in a highly rigorous academic environment. Founded in 1855, the College enrolls about 6,500 full-time undergraduates, two thirds of whom reside on campus. Today it is heralded by *U.S. News & World Report* as well as *Barron's* as one of the most competitive and accomplished schools in the nation, public or private. TCNJ serves a diverse student body, preparing graduates to excel as leaders in their chosen fields.

TCNJ has set the standard for public higher education. Students appreciate the atmosphere they find at TCNJ, a school large enough to provide a full range of academic and extracurricular choices, yet small enough to be a genuine residential community of friends and fellow learners. With professors committed to collaboration in and out of the classroom and facilities of enviable quality, TCNJ represents an exceptional value in higher education.

In order to enhance student development and empowerment, TCNJ's curriculum is built around five key experiences which permeate every major in seven academic schools. Small classes prioritizing discussion and inquiry create a Personalized, Rigorous, and Collaborative Learning Environment where students and faculty work side by side in developing skills and applying concepts. Undergraduate Research, Mentored Internships, and Field Experiences give TCNJ students opportunities to get out of the classroom, develop their professional skill sets, and discover exciting career paths and academic endeavors. Passion for civic responsibility and a commitment to Community-Engaged Learning ensures that TCNJ graduates enter the professional world as top-notch scholars and citizens. Opportunities for Global Engagement found on the TCNJ campus and facilitated through internationally recognized study-abroad programs allow students to expand their internal scope and frame their academic goals and achievements in a truly global context. Finally, academic and extracurricular programs designed to foster Leadership Development help students build confidence and decision-making skills that they will need to solve the problems of tomorrow and build a brighter future.

All first- and second-year students at TCNJ are guaranteed on-campus housing, and most juniors and seniors continue to live on campus. Rooming arrangements are quite flexible, from doubles in freshman residence halls to suites and single rooms and on-campus town houses or apartments for upper class students. Over 200 student organizations on campus offer numerous opportunities for leadership development, community engagement, and the cultivation of lifelong friendships. Engaged and motivated within and beyond the classroom, an exceptional 96 percent of first-year students return for their sophomore year.

The arts flourish in two theaters, a recital hall, an art gallery, and numerous other campus venues. Student performances, professional groups on tour, and a large variety of films, lectures, local bands, and solo entertainers fill the academic year with opportunities for cultural enrichment.

Student wellness is given high priority at the College, with many facilities for recreation and physical conditioning. In fall 2015, TCNJ opened a brand-new student fitness center as part of the Campus Town project. This facility complements the workout spaces, 25-meter swimming and diving pool, and basketball court housed in Packer Hall; the weight room and indoor track in the Student Recreation Center; and the numerous, well-lit athletic fields across campus. In addition to these recreational resources, TCNJ employs dieticians, nutritionists, and other specialists committed to promoting healthy lifestyles and overall wellness in the realms of mind, body, and spirit.

As one of the top-ranked Division III members of the National Collegiate Athletic Association, TCNJ offers twenty sports: ten for men and ten for women. Since 1979, TCNJ student-athletes have amassed an aggregate of more than seventy first- and second-place finishes. TCNJ has produced over 40 individual national champions and more than 50 CoSIDA Academic All-Americans. In the past two decades, TCNJ has finished in the top ten of the Learfield Sports Director's Cup races more than fifteen times.

In addition to its NCAA athletics, TCNJ offers a wide variety of recreation programs for intramural competition and self-governing club sports teams. Each year, more than 3,500 students play with these less demanding, but still spirited and competitive organizations.

Location

Students at The College of New Jersey live and learn on a picturesque, 289-acre campus located in suburban Ewing Township, approximately 15 minutes from downtown Princeton; 10 minutes from Bucks County, Pennsylvania; and 5 miles from the state capital of Trenton. Woodlands and lakes surround major academic and residential buildings, which bear a distinctive Neoclassical Georgian Colonial aesthetic. The campus is 30 miles from the theaters and museums of Philadelphia and 60 miles from those in New York City, and public and mass transit services are easily accessible. In 2015, TCNJ completed the first phase of the Campus Town project. Adding an attractive downtown component to an already appealing campus, Campus Town offers students brand new residential opportunities, a pristine Barnes and Noble bookstore and café, and a comprehensive fitness center. Retail and dining establishments have been incorporated as well, with additional businesses scheduled to open throughout 2017 and into 2018.

Majors and Degrees

The College of New Jersey offers rigorous, personalized programs culminating in the Bachelor of Arts, Bachelor of Fine Arts, Bachelor of Music, Bachelor of Science, Bachelor of Science in Engineering, and Bachelor of Science in Nursing degrees.

TCNJ grants degrees in the following majors: Accountancy, African American Studies, Art Teacher Preparation (K–12); Art History; Biomedical Engineering; Biology*; Business Administration (specializations in finance, interdisciplinary business, management, and marketing); Chemistry*; Civil Engineering; Communication Studies; Computer Engineering; Computer Science; Criminology; Early Childhood Education; Education of the Deaf and Hard of Hearing; Economics*; Electrical Engineering; Elementary Education; Engineering Science (students may specialize in engineering management or policy and society); English*; Global Business; Health and Exercise Science; Health and Physical Education (teacher preparation K–12); History*; Interactive Multimedia; International Studies; i-STEM (integrative science, technology, engineering, and mathematics); Journalism and Professional Writing; Mathematics*; Mechanical Engineering; Music (options in performance and K–12 teacher preparation); Nursing; Philosophy; Physics*; Political Science; Psychology; Public Health; Sociology and Anthropology; Spanish*; Special Education; Speech Pathology; Technology Education /Pre-Engineering (K–12); Urban Education; Visual Arts (options in fine arts, graphic design, and lens-based art); and Women, Gender, and Sexuality Studies. *Programs in which students may prepare for teacher certification*

Specialized Programs: TCNJ offers a number of 5-year combined Master of Arts in Teaching degrees with dual certification in Elementary Education, and either Special Education, Urban Education, or Deaf and Hard-of-Hearing Education. Students may also enroll in a 7-year B.S./M.D. degree program with the New Jersey Medical School (Newark) or a 7-year B.S./O.D. degree program with the State University of New York College of Optometry. The College also offers a Medical Careers Advisory Committee for premed students and a Pre-Law Advisement Committee for students planning a career in law. Sixty-four percent of TCNJ undergraduates seeking admission to medical school and 88 percent seeking admission to law school are accepted into their top choice programs. Both of these figures significantly exceed national averages.

Academic Programs

All academic courses contain significant out-of-class requirements, which foster deeper student-faculty collaboration. All baccalaureate degrees require at least thirty-two courses, including a core curriculum in the traditional arts and sciences. The average class size is 23 students for upper-division lectures.

The thirty-week year is divided into fall and spring semesters; during the summer, courses are offered in two 5-week sessions and one 6-week session. Winter Session guarantees all of the benefits of full-time TCNJ courses in a more compact time frame, in addition to study-abroad opportunities. For those students who find that they cannot fit study abroad into their standard semester, Winter and Summer Session students travel everywhere from New Orleans to London.

Seminars, independent studies, and capstone courses give many students the opportunity for challenging advanced study in close collaboration with faculty mentors. Many TCNJ students publish the results of these endeavors or present them at national and regional conferences.

The College of New Jersey Honors Program offers top-tier students highly intensive academic experiences without adding extra obstructions on the path toward degree completion. Honors courses promote an interdisciplinary perspective and curriculum, concentrating on central themes relevant to cultural development. All honors classes are small, personalized, and stimulating.

Off-Campus Programs

TCNJ offers students a variety of full-year and one-semester programs of study abroad as well as study at other colleges and universities within the United States. Exchange programs are available in 80 cities in Australia, Austria, Canada, Denmark, France, Germany, Greece, Israel, Japan, Mexico, the United Kingdom, and numerous other countries. National exchanges are available at more than 130 participating institutions in the United States, the U.S. Virgin Islands, Puerto Rico, and Guam.

Academic Facilities

TCNJ has been nationally recognized as one of the most beautiful campuses in the nation. Within the past several years, the beautiful campus has grown with the addition of a Science Complex, Biology Building, Social Science Building, College Spiritual Center, Art and Interactive Media Building, Education Building, student apartments, and a state-of-the-art library, which serves as the intellectual and social hub of campus. In 2017 alone, TCNJ was proud to reopen the renovated Brower Student Center and an all new STEM (science, technology, engineering, and mathematics) complex. Campuswide networking provides full Internet accessibility from all residence hall rooms and more than twenty student computing laboratories.

Costs

For up-to-date information on in-state and out-of-state tuition and fees costs, as well as room and board figures, prospective students should head online and visit http://www.tcnj.edu/~sfs/tuition/index.html.

Financial Aid

Over 50 percent of full-time undergraduates receive some form of financial aid, such as federal, state, and institutional grants; merit scholarships; student employment; and loan assistance. The Free Application for Federal Student Aid (FAFSA) or Renewal FAFSA is used to apply for need-based aid at the federal and state levels.

Scholarships and grants include The College of New Jersey Merit Scholars Program, Founders Scholars, Provost Scholars, Bonner Scholars, Chairman of the Board Merit Scholars, the New Jersey Tuition Aid Grant, Federal Pell Grants, Federal Supplemental Educational Opportunity Grants (FSEOG), Educational Opportunity Fund (EOF) Promise Award, and Army and Air Force ROTC Scholarships, as well as other institutional scholarships. Loans include the Federal Subsidized and Unsubsidized Stafford Loans, the Federal Perkins Loan, the Federal Parent Loan for Undergraduate Students (PLUS), the New Jersey CLASS Loan, private/alternative loans, nursing loans, and short-term emergency loan funds. Student employment options include the need-based Federal Work-Study Program (on- and off-campus positions) as well as institutionally supported campus jobs.

Faculty

The approximately 335 full-time members of the College of New Jersey faculty are teachers and scholars possessing terminal degrees in their respective fields. They are also active researchers, authors, artists, performers, and regular contributors in their academic disciplines. All classes are led by full-time faculty members; there are no classes taught by graduate assistants. TCNJ boasts a student-faculty ratio of 13:1. From their first day, students work closely with faculty mentors, contributing to a wide array of projects. Members of the faculty have attracted many significant grants, fellowships, and awards, including the Bancroft Prize in History, Fulbright Scholarships, and grants from the National Science Foundation, the National Institute for Advanced Study, the Guggenheim Foundation, and the National Endowment for the Humanities. Faculty members mentor their students, preparing them for careers, graduate and professional schools, and prestigious fellowships such as the Fulbright, Truman, and Marshall Fellowships.

Student Governance and Programming

The Student Government Association at the College, is governed by elected representatives and works to support and empower all undergraduate students. Members of the Student Finance Board oversee and administer approximately $500,000 in student funds. The College Union Board sponsors a wide range of special events, including recent visits by Seth Meyers, Soledad O'Brien, Nick Offerman, and John Oliver.

Admission Requirements

The College of New Jersey seeks students who show intellectual curiosity, academic talent, and the potential to contribute to TCNJ's vibrant community. The College is committed to attracting students from diverse economic, racial, social, and geographic backgrounds. A high school record of college-preparatory credits, rigorous honors and Advanced Placement courses, high school class rank, SAT scores, special interests, skills, and qualities can be influential in application review. Certain departments, such as Art and Music, waive the SAT/ACT submission requirement and use additional criteria such as portfolio submissions and auditions to evaluate candidates seeking admission. The College of New Jersey reviews candidates holistically and takes into consideration the variations in high schools and communities from which the applicants hail.

Application and Information

The College of New Jersey is a member of the Common Application. The deadline for applications for Spring enrollment is November 1. The Regular Decision application deadline for Fall enrollment is February 1. There is a $75 application fee. Candidates who apply only to The College of New Jersey under the Early Decision agreement can apply up until November 1 to receive the earliest possible admissions notification on or before December 1. Early Decision applicants unable to complete and submit their application prior to November 1 may apply up until January 1 and receive notification on or before February 1. Students applying to the seven-year Accelerated Medical program must apply by December 1. For Fall enrollment, the College requires incoming students to pay an enrollment deposit of $600 no later than May 1.

For more information, students should contact:

The College of New Jersey
P.O. Box 7718
Ewing, New Jersey 08628-0718
United States
Phone: 609-771-2131
Website: http://www.tcnj.edu

The College of New Jersey, a marvel of Neoclassical Georgian Colonial architecture, welcomes students to one of the most beautiful campuses in the United States.

COLLEGE OF STATEN ISLAND OF THE CITY UNIVERSITY OF NEW YORK

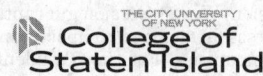

STATEN ISLAND, NEW YORK

⭐ To read more about this school, visit http://petersons.to/collegeofstatenisland

The College and the University

The College of Staten Island (CSI) is a four-year senior college within the City University of New York (CUNY) and is Staten Island's only public institution of higher learning. CSI is dedicated to access and excellence and currently serves over 13,500 students.

Offering over eighty programs and areas of study, the College ensures that students receive a thorough liberal arts education through core requirements that include classes in the arts and humanities, mathematics, sciences, and social sciences.

In addition to the exciting array of undergraduate degrees and majors available, CSI also awards master's degrees in the following disciplines: Accounting; Biology; Biology: Biotechnology Track; Business Management; Business Management: Large-Scale Data Analysis Track; Cinema and Media Studies; Clinical Mental Health Counseling; Computer Science; Education: Adolescence, Childhood, Special Education 1–6, and Special Education 7–12 tracks; Electrical Engineering; English; Environmental Science; Healthcare Management; History; Liberal Studies; Neuroscience; Nursing: Adult-Gerontological Health; Social Work; and Teaching of English to Speakers of Other Languages. CSI also offers the following post-master's and advanced certificates: Adult-Gerontological Health Nursing, Autism Spectrum Disorders, Bilingual Educaton, Business Analytics of Large-Scale Data, Leadership in Education, Public History, and Teaching of English to Speakers of Other Languages. CSI proudly confers the Clinical Doctorate in Physical Therapy (D.P.T.) and the Doctorate of Nurse Practice (D.N.P.).

Housing: CSI offers students an opportunity to live on campus in luxury apartment-style housing. Located in two brand-new buildings, Dolphin Cove North and South contain 133 furnished apartments housing 454 residents. The buildings offer both private and semi-private bedroom accommodations with semi-private bathrooms and full kitchens. Other amenities include a study lounge, fitness center, and convenient parking. Housing is filled on a first-come, first-served basis.

Location

Conveniently located in the heart of Staten Island, CSI's park-like 204-acre property is the largest single college campus, public or private, in New York City. Classrooms and academic offices are located in fourteen neo-Georgian buildings that form two quadrangles connected by the campus walk, which extends between the Library and the Campus Center. The Library, Dolphin Cove North and South, the Campus Center, the Biological Sciences/Chemical Sciences building, the Center for the Arts, and the Sports and Recreation Center provide outstanding facilities for scholastic and community activities.

CSI St. George, an extension of the CSI Willowbrook campus, located at 120 Stuyvesant Place, is home to a dynamic 16,000 square-foot facility a few blocks from the Staten Island Ferry, with convenient access for full- and part-time students from Staten Island, as well as commuters from Manhattan, Brooklyn, and the Bronx.

CSI's location offers students the better of two worlds, with Staten Island providing a suburban environment with some of the most interesting landscapes in the metropolitan area, and Manhattan, the center of cultural and social life in the city, being only 25 minutes from the Island by ferry. In addition, the Verrazano-Narrows Bridge provides direct access between Staten Island and Brooklyn.

Majors and Degrees

CSI offers the following associate degrees: Business (A.A.S.): Accounting, Finance, Information Systems, International Business, Management, and Marketing specializations; Computer Technology (A.A.S.): Programming and Information Science sequences;

Engineering Science (A.S.); Liberal Arts and Sciences (A.A./A.S.); and Nursing (A.A.S.).

CSI offers the following bachelor's degree programs: Accounting (B.S.); African and African Diaspora Studies (B.A.); American Studies (B.A.); Art (B.A./B.F.A.): Studio Art and Photography concentrations; Biochemistry (B.S.); Biology* (B.S.): Bioinformatics, Ecology, Evolution, and Behavioral Biology, Molecular, Cellular, and Developmental Biology, Neuroscience, and Health Science options; Business (B.S.): Finance, International Business, Management, and Marketing concentrations; Chemistry* (B.S.); Cinema Studies (B.A.): Critical Studies and Production concentrations; Communications (B.S.): Journalism, Media Studies, Design and Digital Media, and Corporate Communications concentrations; Computer Science (B.S.); Computer Science/Mathematics (B.S.); Drama (B.S.); Earth and Environmental Science (B.S.); Earth Science* (B.S.); Economics (B.A./B.S.): Business and Finance specializations; Education: Early Childhood, Childhood, and Adolescence programs; Electrical Engineering (B.S.); Engineering Science (B.S.): Computer and Mechanical specializations; English* (B.A.): Writing, Linguistics, Literature, and Dramatic Literature concentrations; Geography (B.A.); History* (B.A.); Information Systems and Informatics (B.S.); International Studies (B.A.); Italian Studies* (B.A.); Mathematics* (B.S.): Pure and Applied Mathematics emphases; Medical Technology (B.S.); Music (B.A./B.S.): Classical Performance, Literature and Theory, Music Technology, Jazz Studies, and Performance concentrations; Nursing (B.S.); Philosophy (B.A.); Philosophy and Political Science (B.A., dual major); Physics* (B.S.); Political Science (B.A.); Pre-Professional Preparation: Dentistry, Law, Medicine, Optometry, Physical Therapy, Chiropractic, and Podiatry programs; Psychology (B.A./B.S.); Science Letters and Society (B.A.): Early Childhood sequence (Birth–2) and Childhood sequence (1–6); Social Work (B.S.S.W.); Sociology–Anthropology (B.A.); Spanish* (B.A.); and Women's, Gender, and Sexuality Studies (B.A.).

*Adolescence Education track (grades 7–12) available.

Academic Programs

CSI offers two-year programs in career areas and in liberal arts and sciences, and four-year programs with majors in the traditional fields of study. General education requirements have been established for all degrees. Credit may be awarded for internships, research, and experiential learning. Students may graduate with honors in most bachelor's degree majors.

The College offers classes scheduled during both the day and evening, seven days a week, with a variety of course combinations leading to associate and bachelor's degrees, providing opportunities for nontraditional students to pursue a college education at more convenient times. CSI also offers intensive summer and winter sessions.

Honors Programs: The College offers several honors programs. Programs include Macaulay Honors College at CSI (MHC), the College's most selective full scholarship program*; The Verrazano School, a local honors program that creates learning communities and provides scholarships for study abroad; and Teacher Education Honors Academy at CSI (TEHA), a scholarship program designed to highly train select students to teach mathematics and science in New York City Department of Education middle and high schools.

*Scholarship receipt subject to eligibility requirements.

Off-Campus Programs

CSI students may use the resources of and receive credit for courses taken at other CUNY colleges to support their education. The College also gives a number of courses for credit at off-campus locations throughout the city through internships at major corporations and other sites. Exceptional study-abroad opportunities are available through CSI's Center for Global Engagement, which offers students the option of earning academic credit for study in Australia, Belgium, China, Costa Rica, Cuba, Denmark, Ecuador, England, France, Greece, Ireland, Israel, Italy, Japan, Morocco, Northern Ireland, Spain, Sweden, or St. John, U.S. Virgin Islands. Students may also pursue study-abroad programs in additional countries through the College Consortium for International Studies (CCIS).

Academic Facilities

The academic buildings are designed to house approximately 300 state-of-the-art laboratories and classrooms; each has its own computer lab, study lounge for students, and faculty offices.

The Campus Center is where students can relax, dine, and be entertained. The two-story rotunda at the heart of the structure contains the main dining facilities, the College's health services, a bookstore, offices for student organizations, study lounges, a small performance/café space, game rooms with the latest game consoles, and the state-of-the-art student-operated studios of WSIA 88.9, the only FM radio station on Staten Island.

The Center for the Arts complex provides facilities for teaching in the instructional wing and performance spaces in the public wing. The complex of public facilities includes a 911-seat auditorium, a 442-seat fully equipped theater, a 156-seat recital hall, a 143-seat lecture hall, an experimental Black Box Theater, art galleries, and a conference center. Classrooms, lecture halls, studios, screening rooms, and offices for faculty members are located in the instructional wing.

The CSI Library is staffed with librarians trained in every discipline offered at the College, who also hold faculty status and rank. The Library's total collection consists of approximately 532,189 books and ebooks, 77,283 electronic journals, 220 electronic resources, 19,800 streaming video titles, and 5,000 sound recordings. The Library's online catalog provides complete access to the collections, including access to holdings of other CUNY libraries. Students also have electronic access to database and research tools 24 hours a day via the Internet. In addition, the Library maintains a collection of current textbooks donated by the CSI Student Government. These and other course materials are available at the Reserve Desk. Wireless laptops are loaned to students for use throughout the Library. The Library building also houses the Office of Academic Support and the Cybercafé, which offers Starbucks® coffee.

The laboratory science building provides facilities for teaching and for two research centers: the Center for Environmental Science and the Center for Developmental Neuroscience and Developmental Disabilities. It consists of a research wing and an instructional wing. State-of-the-art laboratories serve students and faculty members in their teaching and research.

The CSI Astrophysical Observatory is a world-class resource that has been recognized by the International Astronomical Union as an official asteroid-tracking station.

CSI is dedicated to keeping its campus up-to-date during these technology-centric times. Planned updates include the highly innovative Interdisciplinary High-Performance Computational Center and expansions to the Library and Campus Center.

Costs

For 2018–19, undergraduate tuition for New York State (NYS) residents is $285 per credit for resident part-time matriculated students, $3,265 per semester for resident full-time matriculated students, and $415 per credit for resident non-degree students. Nonresident full- and part-time students are charged $580 per credit, and nonresident non-degree students are charged $865 per credit. Graduate NYS resident tuition is $5,225 per semester for students attending the College full-time and $440 per credit for resident part-time students. Nonresidents are charged $805 per credit for full- and part-time attendance.

Financial Aid

Financial aid is available through state and federal programs and includes the New York State Tuition Assistance Program (TAP) awards, Federal Pell Grants, Supplemental Educational Opportunity Grants (SEOG), Search for Elevation and Education through Knowledge (SEEK) awards, the Accelerated Study in

Associate Programs (ASAP) awards, Federal Work-Study Program awards, and student loan programs. Information about programs, application procedures, and deadlines is available from the Office of Student Financial Aid.

The CSI Scholarship is awarded annually to incoming freshmen, transfer, and current students with a 90.00 or 3.25 (or higher) GPA. Further information about scholarships is available from the Office of Fellowship and Scholarship Opportunities.

Faculty

The College has a full-time faculty of 406, of whom approximately 90 percent hold a doctoral degree or the highest attainable degree in their field. Numerous faculty members have made significant contributions in many areas of scholarship, creativity, and public service and have received prestigious grants and awards.

Student Government

A single body, the Senate, is composed of 25 elected students and represents the interests of the College's students, serving as liaison to faculty and administrators. The Senate derives funding from the Student Activity Fee and sponsors many academic and nonacademic programs benefiting students.

Admission Requirements

A freshman applicant seeking admission to a bachelor's degree program must pass the CUNY Assessment Tests (CATs) in reading, writing, and mathematics unless he or she qualifies for exemption based on their high SAT, ACT, or Regents Examination scores. Admission to a bachelor's degree program is determined by the applicant's high school courses, academic average, and the combined verbal and mathematics SAT scores. The College accepts applicants whose scores reach or exceed the College's minimum bachelor's degree program requirements. A faculty admissions committee may consider admitting applicants whose scores approach the College's minimum requirements. Entering first-year students may be admitted to associate-level programs if they have graduated from an accredited high school or have earned a high school equivalency diploma. A transfer applicant with 30 or more credits completed at the time of application must have a minimum cumulative GPA of 2.00. Applicants with fewer than 30 credits must have a GPA of at least 2.00 and must meet freshman entrance criteria.

Application and Information

Requests for further information and application materials should be directed to:

College of Staten Island/The City University of New York
Office of Recruitment and Admissions, Building 2A, Room 103
Staten Island, New York 10314
Phone: 718-982-2010
E-mail: admissions@csi.cuny.edu
Website: www.csi.cuny.edu

The CSI Library offers access to over 532,000 books and 77,000 electronic journals. All CSI students may also use the libraries and databases of other CUNY schools, allowing them access to millions of resources.

COLUMBIA UNIVERSITY
Columbia College/The Fu Foundation School of Engineering and Applied Science
NEW YORK, NEW YORK

The University

Columbia College and The Fu Foundation School of Engineering and Applied Science (Columbia Engineering) offer their students unique advantages; they are at the same time small, selective colleges and integral components of a major research university. Students benefit from over 250 years of rich history and distinction, easy access to the immense resources of New York City and a dynamic residential community where "Columbia Blue" is worn with pride at events ranging from Lions' basketball games to the World Leaders Forum, from the Varsity Show to late-night study sessions in the residence halls.

The Columbia College student body is composed of approximately 4,500 students; the Columbia Engineering student body has roughly 1,500. Students come from all fifty states and over ninety countries. They represent a dazzling array of ethnic, social, economic, cultural, religious, and geographic backgrounds. The diversity of Columbia's student body reflects the diversity of New York City, the world's most international city.

Columbia guarantees four years of on-campus housing to all entering first-year students. Nearly all undergraduates remain in University residence halls for all four years.

Columbia students take part in extracurricular groups of all kinds: artistic (theater, music, dance, film, and visual arts), athletic (thirty-one Division I varsity sports and dozens of club and intramural sports), communications (the *Columbia Daily Spectator,* the *Columbia Journal of Literary Criticism,* WKCR-FM, and many others), community service (Amnesty International, Big Brother/Big Sister programs, after-hours tutoring programs, a volunteer ambulance squad, and partnerships with dozens of hospitals, soup kitchens, and homeless shelters), and preprofessional (the Charles Drew Pre-Medical Society, the Society of Hispanic Professional Engineers, and more). Other groups represent students' ethnic, religious, political, and gender identities. There are thirty fraternities and sororities. Alfred Lerner Hall houses office and meeting space for student organizations, a black box theatre, a cinema, the James H. and Christine Turk Berick Center for Student Advising, and many dining options.

Location

Columbia shares its Manhattan neighborhood, Morningside Heights, with a number of other notable institutions: Barnard College, the Cathedral of St. John the Divine, Union Theological Seminary, Jewish Theological Seminary, and the Manhattan School of Music, to name a few. Many faculty members from Columbia and the other surrounding schools make their homes in the neighborhood. Morningside Heights is an area known for bookstores, wonderfully varied restaurants, and merchants that cater to student tastes, student budgets, and student hours.

Students are encouraged to and assisted in making full use of New York's breathtaking variety of cultural, recreational, and professional resources. Through the Columbia Arts Initiative, students can receive discounted tickets to Broadway shows, film screenings, art galleries, and a multitude of cultural events in New York City. Passport to NYC offers students free access to over thirty museums throughout the city. Columbia students can be found any day of the week exploring the Metropolitan Museum of Art, the Museum of Modern Art, the Guggenheim Museum, the Museum of African Art, the Museo del Barrio, or the Asia Society. They might be discovering the theatrical offerings on, off, or "off-off" Broadway (or on campus); attending the opera, ballet, or symphony at Lincoln Center; enjoying jazz in Greenwich Village or amateur night at the Apollo; sampling *pai gwat* in Chinatown;

or biking or jogging in Central Park. Columbia's Center for Career Education offers students opportunities to explore career pathways in depth; nowhere else in the world does the concentration of industries allow such a range of possibilities for internships and post-graduate employment. New York's public transportation system puts the entire city within easy reach of Columbia students; the campus is directly served by a subway line and five bus routes.

Majors and Degrees

Columbia College grants the B.A. degree in more than eighty programs of study in the humanities, social sciences, and pure sciences, including many interdisciplinary majors. Columbia Engineering grants the B.S. degree in sixteen engineering fields. A five-year program that begins in either school allows students to receive both a B.A. from Columbia College and a B.S. from Columbia Engineering.

Joint degree programs offer selected students the opportunity to combine their undergraduate work with study in Columbia University's schools of law and international affairs and with the Juilliard School.

Academic Programs

Columbia College is known for its Core Curriculum, a set of common courses required of all undergraduates and considered the necessary general education for students, irrespective of their choice in major. The communal learning—with all students encountering the same texts and issues at the same time—and the critical dialogue experienced in small seminars are the distinctive features of the Core. Begun in 1919, the Core Curriculum is one of the founding experiments in liberal higher education in the United States, and it remains vibrant nearly a century later. One of the signature courses in the Core is Contemporary Civilization, a year-long historical survey of Western civilization's religious, political, and moral philosophies; another is Literature Humanities, a year-long introduction to Western culture's most seminal and meaningful literary works. A second year of humanities offers a semester each of music and art appreciation, encouraging students to experience the cultural treasures of New York City. The Global Core requirement enlarges the scope of inquiry beyond the Western focus in order to promote learning and thought about the variety of cultures and the diversity of traditions that interact in the United States and the world today. Frontiers of Science outlines the approaches that scientists take to answer compelling problems in the natural world and introduces students to scientific research methods. University Writing equips students with the ability and thoughtfulness to read and write essays in order to participate in the academic conversations that form Columbia's intellectual community. The Core Curriculum exposes Columbia's multicultural student body to a variety of disciplines, preparing them for the complex questions and issues of modern society.

The strength of Columbia Engineering's education is in its unique vision—Engineering for Humanity—preparing students not only to be world-class engineers but also to be global leaders across industries who are equipped and motivated to address the most pressing global challenges in the areas of sustainability, health, security, connectivity, and creativity. In addition to taking rigorous math and science courses typically offered at top undergraduate programs, Columbia Engineering students benefit from programming that fosters innovation and entrepreneurship, and are also required to take courses in the liberal arts alongside their College counterparts, providing them with interdisciplinary tools for real-world problem solving. This type of broad academic exposure is what alumni often cite as the foundation of their later academic and professional success. Another hallmark of the Columbia Engineering education is the Art of Engineering, where first-year students are introduced to the field through interactive lectures, hands-on group projects, and guest speakers. Past examples of projects include mathematically modeling the U.S. elections, designing vital signs monitors, and modifying a laser pointer to transmit digital data over long distances. In addition to the technical issues discussed in the course, other key issues of importance in professional engineering such as ethics, project management, and societal impact are addressed.

Off-Campus Programs

Columbia maintains a network of global centers, developing opportunities for research, scholarship, teaching, and service across borders. With eight international locations ranging from Turkey to Chile and from Kenya to China, undergraduate options include summer Arabic language programs in Amman, Jordan or a semester-long French literature program in Paris at Columbia's Reid Hall. Columbia also has direct enrollment agreements with many partner institutions abroad, as well as a growing number of exchange programs with universities abroad.

Columbia was the first U.S. college to offer an integrated year-abroad program with the Universities of Oxford and Cambridge. Other programs allow students to work at the University of Kyoto in Japan or at the Free University of Berlin in Germany.

Altogether, Columbia students, with the help of advisers from the Office of Global Programs, may choose from over 150 study-abroad programs on nearly every continent.

Academic Facilities

Columbia has the fifth-largest research library system in the world, consisting of 12 million volumes and 26 million manuscripts within 3,000 collections. Included in the twenty-two libraries are the collections of the Avery Architectural and Fine Arts Library, the Starr East Asian Library, the Rare Book and Manuscript Library, and the Burke Library of Union Theological Seminary. All divisions are open to Columbia undergraduates. The LEED Gold–certified Northwest Corner Building houses cutting-edge labs that bring together researchers in biology, chemistry, physics, and engineering, as well as a science library, lecture hall, and café. Students may also make use of an electronic music lab, a cyclotron, an oral history collection, the facilities and programs of the Lamont-Doherty Earth Observatory, and oceanographic research ships.

Costs

Tuition for the 2017–18 academic year was $54,504. Room and board for all first-year students were $13,618. With typical fees, books, and supplies, the total cost of a year at Columbia was approximately $74,173.

Financial Aid

Columbia awards more than $150 million annually in scholarships and grants, and the average amount awarded in 2016–17 was $52,073. All first-year candidates who are U.S. citizens, have U.S. permanent resident or political refugee status, or are undocumented students who reside in the U.S. are considered for admission without regard to their financial need. International students who do not fit into the above categories should be aware that their admissions process is not need-blind; their financial need is taken into account at the time of admission. Regardless of citizenship, Columbia meets the full demonstrated need of every student admitted as a first-year or transfer student. All financial aid at Columbia is based on need, in the form of grants and student work only, not loans. Prospective students should go to http://cc-seas.financialaid.columbia.edu/ for information on specific requirements and deadlines.

Faculty

The student-to-faculty ratio is 6:1. Core Curriculum classes are capped at 22 students, and 80 percent of classes have 20 students or fewer. The Columbia faculty is committed to both teaching and research, and all faculty members, including the president of the University, teach undergraduates. All faculty members maintain office hours, and each student receives a faculty adviser from the department that they choose as a major.

Admission Requirements

The Columbia first-year class of 1,400 students is selected from a much larger pool of applicants through a holistic, committee-based review process. There are no specific course requirements for admission, but applicants must present evidence that they are prepared for college work in a variety of disciplines as required for the Columbia degree. Accordingly, the following preparation is strongly recommended: 4 years of English, including meaningful work in literature and writing; 3 (preferably 4) years of mathematics, including precalculus and calculus where offered; 3 (preferably 4) years of history and social studies; 3 or more years of the same foreign language; and 3 (preferably 4) years of laboratory science (including chemistry and physics where available). Modifying the preparatory program just outlined—by taking more work in some subjects and less in others—is not only acceptable but may be desirable in individual cases.

Standardized tests are required for admission, according to the following guidelines. Students must take *either* the SAT *or* the ACT, and they may self-report their scores. Students who take the SAT more than once are evaluated on the highest score they receive in any individual section. Applicants taking the ACT more than once are evaluated on the highest score received in any individual section. The writing component of both exams is not required. Only admitted students who choose to enroll at Columbia must have their official scores sent by the testing agency.

While Columbia does not require SAT or ACT writing tests or SAT Subject Tests, students who have taken these exams may submit their results if they wish them to be considered.

Transfer students may enter Columbia in the fall term only.

Columbia College and Columbia Engineering each have a Visiting Students Program, which allow students to attend for one or both semesters of their sophomore, junior, or senior year.

Application and Information

Students may apply via the Common Application or the Coalition Application. Students for whom Columbia is their definite first choice are encouraged to apply early decision. The early decision deadline is November 1, and candidates are notified by mid-December. Students admitted to Columbia under early decision are required to matriculate at Columbia and withdraw their applications to other colleges. The regular decision deadline is January 1, and candidates are notified by April 1. Admitted students must respond to Columbia's offer of admission by May 1.

For further information, interested students should contact:

Office of Undergraduate Admissions
Columbia University
1130 Amsterdam Avenue, MC 2807
New York, New York 10027
Phone: 212-854-2522
Fax: 212-854-1209
E-mail: ugrad-ask@columbia.edu
Website: http://undergrad.admissions.columbia.edu/
http://www.facebook.com/columbiaadmissions
http://www.twitter.com/hamiltonhall
http://www.instagram.com/columbiaadmissions

COLUMBIA UNIVERSITY SCHOOL OF GENERAL STUDIES

NEW YORK, NEW YORK

★ To read more about this school, visit http://petersons.to/columbiauniversitygs

The University and the School

The Columbia University School of General Studies (GS), founded in 1947, is the finest liberal arts college in the United States created specifically for returning and nontraditional students seeking a rigorous, traditional, Ivy League undergraduate education full or part time. Students come from a variety of backgrounds and, for personal or professional reasons, most have interrupted their educations, never attended college, or are only able to attend part time. GS is unique among colleges of its type, because its students are fully integrated into the Columbia undergraduate curriculum: they take the same courses, with the same faculty members, and earn the same degree as all other undergraduates at the University.

In the classroom, the diversity and varied personal experiences of the student body promote discussion and debate that is unparalleled in the Ivy League, fostering an environment of academic rigor and intellectual development. GS has more than 2,000 undergraduate degree candidates and more than 400 Postbac Premed students. The average age of the GS student body is 27, and more than 70 percent of GS students attend classes full time.

In addition to its bachelor's degree programs and the Columbia University Postbaccalaureate Premedical Program, GS offers combined undergraduate/graduate degree programs with Columbia's Schools of Engineering and Applied Science, Social Work, International and Public Affairs, Law, Business, Dental Medicine, and Public Health, as well as Teachers College and the College of Physicians and Surgeons. More than 70 percent of GS students go on to earn advanced degrees after graduation.

Location

Columbia University is located in Morningside Heights, on the Upper West Side of Manhattan. The University's neighbors include the Union Theological Seminary, the Jewish Theological Seminary, the Manhattan School of Music, Mount Sinai St. Luke's Hospital, Riverside Church, and the historic Cathedral of St. John the Divine, the largest cathedral in the world. The diversity of intellectual and social activities offered by these institutions is one of Columbia's great assets; another is New York City itself, which offers Columbia students a rich and almost boundless variety of social, cultural, and recreational opportunities that are themselves an education.

Majors and Degrees

The School of General Studies grants a B.A. degree and offers more than eighty majors and concentrations, including African American studies; American studies; ancient studies; anthropology; applied mathematics; archaeology; architecture; art history; astronomy; astrophysics; biochemistry; biology; biophysics; business management; chemical physics; chemistry; classics; comparative literature and society; computer science; creative writing; dance; data science; drama and theater arts; earth and environmental science; East Asian studies; economics; education; English; environmental biology; environmental chemistry; environmental science; ethnicity and race studies; evolutionary biology of the human species; film and media studies; financial economics; French; German literature and cultural history; Hispanic studies; history; human rights; information science; Italian cultural studies; Italian language and literature; jazz studies; Jewish studies; Latin American and Caribbean studies; Latin American and Iberian cultures; linguistics; mathematics; medieval and renaissance studies; Middle Eastern, South Asian, and African studies; modern Greek studies; music; neuroscience and behavior; philosophy; physics; political science; Portuguese studies; psychology; regional studies; religion; Russian language and culture; Russian literature and culture; Slavic studies; sociology; statistics; sustainable development; urban studies; visual arts; women's and gender studies; and Yiddish studies.

GS is home to the Columbia University Postbaccalaureate Premedical Program, the oldest and largest of its kind in the United States, as well as undergraduate dual-degree programs with the French University Sciences Po, Trinity College Dublin, City University of Hong Kong, and List College of the Jewish Theological Seminary.

The Dual BA Program between Columbia University and Sciences Po is an intensive, transatlantic course of study in which undergraduate students earn two bachelor's degrees in four years, once each from Sciences Po and Columbia University. Students begin by spending two years at one of three Sciences Po campuses, each of which is devoted to a particular region of the world and offers a heavy linguistic and cultural focus. After completing Sciences Po's interdisciplinary social sciences curriculum, students matriculate at GS to complete core and major requirements. Upon graduation, students are eligible for guaranteed admission to a graduate program at Sciences Po. Admission is highly competitive, and high school seniors are eligible to apply.

The Dual BA Program between Trinity College Dublin and Columbia University transcends traditional study-abroad opportunities by providing students the opportunity to pursue a rigorous undergraduate liberal arts education spanning two continents, at two world-renowned universities in the heart of Dublin and New York City. Upon completion of one of four programs at Trinity—English studies, European studies, history, or Middle Eastern and European languages and cultures—students matriculate at GS to complete core and major requirements. Admission is highly competitive, and high school seniors are eligible to apply.

Academic Programs

The School of General Studies offers a traditional liberal arts education designed to provide students with the broad knowledge and intellectual skills that foster continued education and growth in the years after college as well as providing a sound foundation for positions of responsibility in the professional world.

Requirements for the bachelor's degree comprise three elements: (1) core requirements, intended to develop critical skills in writing and quantitative reasoning while providing exposure to a range of knowledge and disciplines; (2) major requirements, designed to provide students sustained and coherent exposure to a particular discipline in an area of strong intellectual interest; and (3) elective courses. Students are required to complete a minimum of 124 points for the bachelor's degree; 60 of these may be in transfer credit, but at least 64 points (including the last 30 points) must be completed at Columbia.

Off-Campus Programs

Columbia students are encouraged to enhance their academic experiences through the more than 150 study-abroad programs offered in more than 100 cities around the world. Options include studying in Paris at the Columbia University Global Center, in Kyoto at the Consortium for Japanese Studies, in Kenya completing the Tropical Biology and Sustainability Program, or in Cuba taking courses at the University of Havana, to name a few.

Academic Facilities

The Columbia University Libraries constitute the nation's fifth-largest academic library system, with a collection of more than 13 million volumes, more than 160,000 journals and serials, and an extensive array of additional resources. Of the twenty-two libraries in the system, five are designated Distinctive Collections because of their unusual depth and nationally recognized excellence. The Fairchild Life Sciences Building houses research facilities, laboratories, electron microscopes, and a vast amount of biochemical equipment used for teaching and research. The University's physics building has been the scene of many important developments in the recent history of physics, including the invention of the laser and the first U.S. demonstration of nuclear fission.

Costs

For the 2017–18 academic year, tuition was $1,756 per point (credit), and annual living (room and board) and personal expenses (books, local commuting costs, and other expenses) were $23,765.

Financial Aid

The School of General Studies awards financial aid based upon need and academic ability. Approximately 70 percent of GS degree candidates receive some form of financial aid, including federal Pell grants, New York State grants, federal unsubsidized and subsidized loans, institutional scholarships, and Federal Work-Study Program awards. The average scholarship award ranges from $8,000 to $10,000 for first-year students.

Faculty

All undergraduate liberal arts courses at Columbia University are taught by members of the Columbia University Faculty of Arts and Sciences. These distinguished scholars in virtually every discipline also teach students in Columbia College, the Graduate School of Arts and Sciences, the School of the Arts, and the School of Professional Studies. The student-faculty ratio is 6:1, and GS students have many opportunities to work closely with faculty members, both in small classes and research projects. Faculty members also serve as departmental advisors to students majoring in their area of study and maintain regular office hours.

Student Government

One student represents GS in the University Senate, a decision-making body comprising students, faculty members, and administrative staff members from each division of the University. In addition, two GS students sit as voting members on the Committee on Instruction, which oversees the curriculum of the School. The General Studies Student Council elects officers each year and sponsors activities for students and the Premedical Association sponsors events related to the medical school admissions process.

Admission Requirements

The GS admission policy is geared to the maturity and varied backgrounds of its students. Aptitude and motivation are considered along with past academic performance, standardized test scores, and employment history. The School's admission decisions are based on a careful review of each application and reflect the Admissions Committee's considered judgment of the applicant's maturity, academic potential, and present ability to undertake course work at Columbia.

Admission requirements include a completed application form; an autobiographical statement; two letters of recommendation from academic or professional evaluators; official transcripts from all high schools, colleges, and universities attended; official SAT or ACT scores (some applicants may also take the General Studies Admissions Examination); and a nonrefundable application fee of $80.

Students from outside the United States may apply to the School of General Studies to start or complete a baccalaureate degree. In addition to the materials previously described, international applicants must submit official scores from the Duolingo English Test, TOEFL, or IELTS.

Application and Information

Fall early action applications completed by January 15 will receive a March 1 decision; applications completed by March 1 will receive a decision by May 1. Spring early action applications completed by September 1 will receive an October 1 decision; applications completed by October 1 will receive a decision by November 15.

For more information, students should contact:

Curtis M. Rodgers, Vice Dean
Office of Admissions and Educational Financing
School of General Studies
408 Lewisohn Hall
2970 Broadway
Columbia University, Mail Code 4101
New York, New York 10027
Phone: 212-854-2772
E-mail: gsdegree@columbia.edu
Website: http://gs.columbia.edu
 http://facebook.com/ColumbiaGS
 http://instagram.com/columbiageneralstudies
 http://twitter.com/ColumbiaGS
 http://youtube.com/GSColumbia

Morningside Campus, Columbia University.

DEAN COLLEGE
FRANKLIN, MASSACHUSETTS

The College

Founded in 1865, Dean is a unique New England college awarding both four-year baccalaureate and two-year associate degrees. Students may choose from over two-dozen academic programs supported by state-of-the-art facilities, a dedicated teaching faculty, and professional advising known for exceptional personalized academic support.

Located 45 minutes outside Boston in the town of Franklin, Massachusetts, Dean's attractive 100-acre campus is home to WGAO-FM, the Joan Phelps Palladino School of Dance, and several buildings listed on the National Register of Historic Places. There are two fitness centers, a gymnasium, and athletic fields, as well as a library learning commons, an advising center, a 214-seat theater, and numerous dance studios.

Nearly all of Dean's 1,200 full-time students live on campus, and housing is available for all four years. The student body is impressively diverse with more than 30 states and 25 countries represented (and an additional 500 part-time students). The College sponsors 15 NCAA Division III athletic teams, an Honors Program, internship and study abroad opportunities, an executive lecture series, and dozens of clubs, performance groups, and student organizations.

Dean College graduates are very successful. Of those receiving a bachelor's degree last year, 95 percent were employed or attending graduate school within a year. Among associate degree graduates, 98 percent were accepted as transfers to highly selective universities across the United States or had plans to continue their bachelor's degree at Dean.

Location

Dean's home town, Franklin, is a charming, historic Massachusetts community. The suburban setting is safe and convenient to downtown Boston with many local stores and restaurants to support an active college campus. The Commuter Rail—just three blocks from Dean—provides frequent train service to Boston, and students can reach popular destinations such as baseball's Fenway Park, the TD Garden, Museum of Fine Arts, and Harvard Square in less than an hour. Providence, Rhode Island, is even closer (40 minutes) where students can shop at Providence Place or see events at the Dunkin' Donuts Center and Rhode Island Center for the Performing Arts.

The area's biggest attractions are only minutes from Dean: Patriot Place and Gillette Stadium (home of the New England Patriots), the fashionable Wrentham Outlets, and Comcast Center outdoor amphitheater. For day trips, students can easily get to the beaches on Cape Cod, see Newport's mansions, or reach the mountains in nearby New Hampshire and Vermont.

Majors and Degrees

Dean College provides a wide range of programs across four academic schools: the School of Liberal Arts & Sciences, School of the Arts, School of Business, and the Joan Phelps Palladino School of Dance.

Bachelor's degrees are available in arts and entertainment management; business management; coaching and recreation; communications; criminal justice and homeland security management; dance; English; exercise science; history; liberal arts and studies; marketing; psychology; sociology; sport management; and theatre.

Dean also offers associate degree programs in pre-athletic training, business management, coaching, communications, criminal justice, dance, early childhood education, English, environmental studies, exercise science, general studies, health sciences, history, mathematics, physical education, pre-nursing, psychology, science, sociology, sport management, and theatre/musical theatre.

Academic Programs

Dean is accredited by the New England Association of Schools and Colleges. Graduation requirements include a 2.0 cumulative grade point average (GPA) and demonstrate competency in reading/writing, mathematics, and computers. Bachelor's degree candidates must complete a required internship or other experiential learning opportunity related to their major.

The Honors Program at Dean offers academically talented students an opportunity to engage in stimulating and challenging courses, seminars, and colloquia. Students who meet the honors entrance criteria enroll in special course sections reserved for honors students or may enhance non-honors courses with additional intensive readings and analysis approved by the instructors. The Honors Program also offers exciting academic and cultural activities outside the traditional classroom environment.

Study-abroad and study-away opportunities are increasingly popular at Dean. Students may choose programs across the globe through cooperative arrangements facilitated by the College or take advantage of Dean's relationship with the Washington Center Program for study and internships in Washington, D.C.

The Dean Leadership Institute sponsors an Executive Lecture Series that brings leaders in business, media, and the arts to campus. Featured speakers share their insights into post-graduate opportunities and help build each student's career network. Recent guests include Bert Jacobs (Life is Good), Bob Kraft (Kraft Group/New England Patriots), Anne Finucane (Bank of America), and Michael Spillane (Nike).

The Arch Learning Community provides comprehensive support for students with diagnosed learning differences. Arch students receive dedicated academic advising and a cohort educational model specially designed to help LD students maximize their academic and personal potential and find success within the rigors of a traditional college curriculum.

Academic Facilities

Students have access to a wide range of facilities, including the Green Family Library-Learning Commons and E. Ross Anderson Library, Berenson Writing Center, and Morton Family Learning Center—all housed under one roof. Together, these form the hub of Dean's academic support efforts. There are print and online resources for class projects, academic coaches to provide professional one-on-one mentoring, peer tutoring services, the Technology Service Center, and space for weekly faculty drop-in sessions where students can participate in group or individual advising.

Other academic facilities include the A.W. Pierce Technology and Science Center, which houses science and computer labs as well as the Alden Center high-tech master classroom; the Dean College Children's Center, an on-campus pre-school, which doubles as a learning laboratory for student teachers; and Campus Center, where students can find the Advising Center, Main Stage Theater, Guidrey Center, student activities office, and newly renovated classrooms featuring cutting-edge technology.

Costs

The basic costs related to attending Dean College for 2018–19 are $39,234 for tuition and fees and $16,836 for room and board.

Financial Aid

Dean College awards more than $20 million in scholarships and grants annually to assist their students in funding their educations. An astonishing 90 percent of Dean students receive some form of merit-based aid with an average award amount of $19,000 per year. These awards are based solely on the information students provide in their application for admission—not financial need—and help to reduce the average cost of attendance by over 30 percent. In addition, most students apply for—and receive—federal and state financial aid, which is separate from (and can be added to) Dean's scholarship awards.

Student financial aid packages are generally a combination of grants, loans, and work-study, contingent upon demonstrated need and the availability of funds. The College participates in all Federal Title IV and Federal Family Education Loan Programs. Students must submit the Free Application for Federal Student Aid (FAFSA) in order to be considered for need-based aid. Upon receipt of a valid FAFSA, full-time students are considered for all of the financial aid programs that Dean administers. Residents of Massachusetts and other reciprocal states may also be eligible for state scholarships, grants, or loans.

Faculty

Dean's dedicated faculty members, advisers, and educational specialists—some of the best in their respective fields—offer direct, personal involvement to help students obtain the full value of their college experience. The average class size is 18 students.

Student Government

The Student Government Association serves as a liaison between the student body and Dean College administration. It disseminates information about College policies, seeks out student opinion, allocates funds collected from the activities fee to clubs and organizations through a budget request process, and coordinates the activities of various clubs, groups, and organizations campus wide.

Admission Requirements

Every application to Dean is carefully reviewed by the Admission Committee. In addition to the application form, students must submit an official high school transcript. A letter of recommendation from a guidance counselor or teacher, a personal statement or essay, and SAT or ACT scores are all optional. Interviews are not required but are recommended. Students applying for the dance and theatre programs must audition.

Application and Information

Students who identify Dean as a top choice may choose to apply under the early action plan, with an application deadline of December 1. The College accepts applications on a rolling basis thereafter, though it is recommended that applications be submitted by March 15 to ensure access to the highest level of financial aid and priority in housing and class registration. Once an application is complete, an admissions decision is typically made within four weeks.

For more information, contact:

Office of Admissions
Dean College
99 Main Street
Franklin, Massachusetts 02038
Phone: 508-541-1508
    877-TRY-DEAN (toll-free)
E-mail: admissions@dean.edu
Website: http://www.dean.edu

Dean Hall, built in 1865 when Dean College was established.

DREXEL UNIVERSITY
PHILADELPHIA, PENNSYLVANIA

 To read more about this school, visit http://petersons.to/drexeluniversity

The University

Drexel University is a comprehensive global research university that has maintained a reputation for academic excellence since its founding in 1891. The University's use-inspired approach to learning prepares undergraduates for a variety of careers and graduate school. Cooperative education is a vital part of a Drexel education. Students gain professional experience in jobs related to their career interests by alternating classroom study with periods of meaningful employment. The 2017 undergraduate enrollment numbered 13,569 full-time students representing 48 states and 117 other countries. International students compose about 15.8 percent of the undergraduate population. Drexel University grants bachelor's, master's, and doctoral degrees—as well as certificates—in a variety of programs.

Drexel offers 18 Division I varsity athletic programs and competes in the Colonial Athletic Association Conference. The University also sponsors intramural and club sports.

There is always something to do on campus, including events such as dances, lectures, excursions, community service projects, free movie screenings from the Campus Activities Board (CAB), and other activities related to Drexel's more than 30 active fraternities and sororities. Students can also take part in performing arts groups in dance, theater, and music. In all, there are over 400 student organizations.

Location

Drexel is located in the heart of Philadelphia, the nation's sixth-largest city, and shares its University City neighborhood with five other universities. With thousands of college student residents, University City is a great place for students to spend their college years in an urban campus setting, surrounded by the amenities of the city and the diversity of their peers. Philadelphia is home to some of the nation's best historical and cultural attractions and offers a vibrant social and cultural scene, dynamic arts, and professional athletics of a first-class city. Drexel's location offers easy access to public transportation and the Drexel shuttle provides convenient, free transportation between campuses for Drexel students. Adjacent to Drexel's University City Campus, Amtrak's 30th Street Station is a hub for trains and buses to the Philadelphia suburbs, New York City, Washington, D.C., and the Philadelphia International Airport.

Academic Disciplines

Whatever their interests, students at Drexel are at the forefront of their fields. Drexel offers more than 80 undergraduate majors and over 20 accelerated degree programs. Academic majors include fields such as business, computing and informatics, design and art, education, engineering, entrepreneurship, health professions, hospitality, humanities and social sciences, nursing, public health, sciences, and undeclared.

Accelerated and joint degree programs allow students to earn both a bachelor's and an advanced degree in a shortened period of time. Drexel's accelerated and joint degree options include the BA/BS/JD in law; BA/BS+MD in medicine; BS/DPT in physical therapy; BS/MHS in physician assistant studies; BS/MPH in public health; BS/MBA programs in business, culinary arts and science, design and merchandising, entertainment and arts management, hospitality management, information systems, and music industry; BS/MS programs in accounting, biomedical engineering, communication, computing and informatics, education, engineering, and psychology; BS/MA in creative arts in therapy and dance/movement therapy; BA/BS/MS in science, technology, and security; and BA/BS in history/MS in library and information sciences.

Academic Enhancement Programs

Qualified students can apply to the Honors Program, one of many exciting opportunities offered by the Pennoni Honors College. The Honors Program offers enhanced academic and extracurricular options to talented students through course work, speakers, social activities, and travel. Honors students receive benefits such as small Honors classes, Honors housing, free tickets to cultural events in Philadelphia, Honors-specific advising and mentoring, and priority registration for classes. Students in the Honors Program who satisfy the requirements are eligible for Graduation with Honors, or, for the most accomplished students, Graduation with Distinction.

Drexel is a world-class comprehensive research institution committed to use-inspired research with real-world applications. Research at Drexel is driven by faculty from all disciplines and students are encouraged to seek opportunities to partner with world-renowned faculty or develop independent research projects. The STAR (Students Tackling Advanced Research) Scholars program invites qualified students to participate in faculty-mentored research projects in their chosen fields as early as freshman year. Students who take part in research may be eligible for stipends or academic credit.

Opportunities for Enrichment

Drexel's experiential learning model recognizes the importance of both academic and professional preparation. Drexel's cooperative education program (Drexel Co-op), provides professional employment experiences for students, giving them the opportunity to test-drive a career before they enter the workforce. The benefits are obvious – during their time at Drexel, students experience up to three different co-ops (up to 18 months). Drexel Co-op connects them with industry leaders and brings their cooperative education experiences back into the classroom. Because of this, Drexel students graduate having already built a professional network, and they typically receive higher starting salaries than their counterparts from other schools.

Drexel brings an international dimension to University life through its academic programs, study and cooperative education abroad, major research projects, global classrooms, conferences, and cultural events. Last year, more than 900 Drexel students had an international experience studying, doing research, and participating in service learning abroad. These students represented every major and took advantage of more than 80 program opportunities. With programs in Africa, Asia, Europe, Latin America, and the Pacific, locations are as varied as the interests of Drexel students.

Students can also become civically engaged and fulfill public service and leadership roles at Drexel's Lindy Center for Civic Engagement.

Academic Facilities

Drexel has three campus locations: University City Campus, Center City Campus, and Queen Lane Campus. The University's library system comprises the W. W. Hagerty Library, the Library Learning Terrace, the Legal Research Center, and three health sciences libraries. The W. W. Hagerty Library, the University's central library located on the University City campus, maintains subscriptions to nearly 12,000 electronic journals, which are accessed via the library website, along with academic journals and 200 databases. Students may borrow laptops for use in the library. The Library Learning Terrace, a 3,000-square-foot flexible learning space located in a residence hall and staffed by librarians, enables students to learn and research collaboratively through a variety of technologies. The Legal Research Center on the third floor of the Kline School of Law shares University databases while continuing to acquire new material. The additional libraries on the health sciences campuses provide study space, 75,000 books, and network access to the same set of online journals and databases.

The University comprises many state-of-the-art spaces for students. One popular student location is the twelve-story, 177,500-square-foot Gerri C. LeBow Hall, which houses the LeBow College of Business, along with the Chestnut Square complex, which features mixed-use housing and retail, including a Shake Shack. The URBN Center houses the Westphal College of Media Arts & Design and provides space for exhibitions, labs, studios, and a black box theater. The five-story, 130,000-square-foot Papadakis Integrated Sciences Building features classrooms and North America's largest biowall. In addition, The Summit at University City provides more student housing and mixed-use commercial space.

Costs

For the 2018–19 academic year, Drexel's estimated cost of attendance for a full-time undergraduate student starting as a freshman includes $50,874 in tuition, $2,405 in fees, and $14,079 in room and board. Students also incur additional costs for books (which vary by program), a computer for personal use, transportation, and miscellaneous personal costs.

Financial Aid

Freshmen eligible for merit and/or need-based funds were awarded financial aid in the 2017–18 academic year. The average financial aid awards for full-time degree-seeking undergraduates in the 2017–18 academic year, including all grant and scholarship sources, was $30,154. All incoming students are encouraged to submit both the CSS PROFILE and the Free Application for Federal Student Aid (FAFSA) by specific deadlines. Financial aid notifications to students begin mid-December for students accepted during Early Action and Early Decision. The Drexel Liberty Scholars Program also provides 50 full-tuition and fees scholarships to low-income students who live in or attend school in Philadelphia. The Drexel Global Scholar program grants full-tuition scholarships to exceptional international students who are also committed to global leadership.

Faculty

The University requires faculty members engaged in research and graduate-level teaching to also teach at the undergraduate level, allowing all students to benefit from the research activities of the faculty. Specially selected faculty members serve as advisors for freshmen. The student–faculty ratio is 11:1.

Admission Requirements

All colleges within the University require completion of a college-preparatory program in high school that includes at least 3 years of mathematics and 1 year of laboratory science. Students applying to a major in the sciences or business and engineering are required to take 4 years of mathematics (through trigonometry) and 2 years of laboratory science. Engineering requires 4 years of mathematics (through trigonometry and precalculus), chemistry, and physics. Biomedical engineering requires 1 year of calculus and 1 year of physics. Computer science and software engineering require 4 years of math (including trigonometry and calculus) and 2 years of lab science. The quality of academic performance is more important than merely meeting minimum requirements. The strength of preparation is judged primarily by rigor of course work or relative grade point average (GPA), by the degree of improvement in the quality of the academic record, and by the comments and recommendations from principals, school counselors, or teachers. Freshman applicants are required to submit standardized test scores—including the SAT, ACT, SAT Subject, AP, or IB—and can also utilize Drexel's flexible testing form of submission. Students who were admitted and enrolled in the fall of 2017 had an average SAT math score (25th–75th percentiles) of 580–690, and an average SAT critical reading score (25th–75th percentiles) of 580–670. The essay from the Common Application or personal statement is required of all full-time applicants (except nursing ACE). Design and Media majors may also be required to submit a writing supplement or portfolio. Transfer applicants should complete a minimum of 24 college credits from a regionally accredited institution. Transfer applicants who have fewer than 24 college credits prior to their application will also need to submit their high school transcript and SAT or ACT scores.

Application and Information

Applications for full-time undergraduate studies are accepted through the Common Application only. The application fee is $50, and all Common App waivers are honored. Freshman students may choose to apply under the Early Action, Early Decision, or Regular Decision options. Early Action admission is not binding. Early Decision is a binding application plan and, if accepted, students must withdraw all other active applications and commit to enrolling at Drexel. The Early Action and Early Decision deadlines are November 1, with admission decisions rendered in mid-December. Applications for Regular Decision full-time undergraduate status are due January 15, with admission decisions rendered no later than April 1. Applications for the BA/BS+MD early assurance degree program are due November 1. Drexel subscribes to the College Board candidates reply date of May 1. Transfer student deadlines vary by major and term of entry. For transfer application deadlines, please visit drexel.edu/undergrad/apply/deadlines.

Undergraduate Admissions
Drexel University
3141 Chestnut Street
Philadelphia, Pennsylvania 19104-2876
Phone: 215-895-2400
      800-2-DREXEL (toll-free)
Fax: 215-895-1285
E-mail: enroll@drexel.edu
Website: drexel.edu/admissions (admissions)
      drexel.edu/undergrad/apply (application)
      facebook.com/DrexelAdmission (Facebook)
      twitter.com/DrexelAdmission (Twitter)

Drexel students on Chestnut St. in University City, Philadephia, Pennsylvania.

EARLHAM COLLEGE
RICHMOND, INDIANA

 For more information, visit http://petersons.to/earlhamcollege

The College

Established in 1847, Earlham College is a selective, private liberal arts college. With its emphasis on experiential learning and profound inquiry, an Earlham education is excellent preparation not just for a first job, but a career and a lifetime of rewarding involvement.

Earlham has shaped its curriculum through an initiative called EPIC (Earlham Plan for Integrative Collaboration) in order to help its students connect their academic and personal passions with career preparation and opportunities to make a positive difference in the world. EPIC offers students multidisciplinary experiences that combine guided research opportunities, international education, and internships as well as academic centers devoted to entrepreneurship, global health, and social justice.

Among its distinctions, Earlham is committed to funding an internship, research experience or community-based project for every student. Called the EPIC Advantage, the program offers these funded experiences to help students connect high-impact experiences with their traditional course work and even extracurricular activities.

Earlham is a residential college of about 1,100 students. A global perspective comes naturally to the campus community. Earlham is ranked fifth by *U.S. News & World Report* among liberal arts colleges in the U.S. for the percentage of international students enrolled. With such a variety of students, campus life at Earlham is both lively and welcoming.

Besides traditional residence halls, Earlham has friendship and theme housing for those who share like interests. Yet one kind of housing isn't found at Earlham—sororities and fraternities. Earlham's inclusive community has never had them.

Founded by Quakers, Earlham College has prepared students to contribute to the social good since its inception. Earlham embraces cultural and individual differences alike and offers unparalleled opportunities for leadership, friendship, and community.

Earlham sponsors 20 NCAA Division III sports teams; most compete in the Heartland Collegiate Athletic Conference. The College also sponsors a hunt seat equestrian team, an Ultimate (Frisbee) team that competes on the club level, and numerous recreational sports.

Earlham is accredited by the Higher Learning Commission of the North Central Association of Colleges and Schools.

Location

The Earlham campus is located on 800 acres in the city of Richmond, Indiana. It is situated along the Indiana-Ohio border, about an hour's drive from Indianapolis, Cincinnati, or Dayton. Richmond, named the No. 1 small city in Indiana by *Cities Journal*, has a population of 36,000 and a rich heritage of music, culture, and architecture.

Majors and Degrees

Earlham offers a diverse range of degree programs including: African and African American Studies; ancient and classical studies; Arabic language and literature*; archaeology*; art; biochemistry; biology; chemistry; Chinese languages*; comparative languages and linguistics; computer science; economics; English; environmental sustainability; film studies*; French and Francophone studies; geology; German language and literature; global management (with tracks in finance,

international business, leadership and change, marketing, social entrepreneurship and social change, and supply chain and operations/management information technology); history; human development and social relations; international studies; Japanese language and linguistics*; Japanese studies; Jewish studies*; mathematics; museum studies*; music; neuroscience; peace and global studies; philosophy; physics and astronomy; politics; pre-engineering; pre-health; pre-law; psychology; public policy; Quaker studies*; religion; sociology/anthropology; Spanish and Hispanic studies; TESOL*; theatre arts; and women's, gender, sexuality studies. (*Indicates programs that are available as minors only.)

In addition to more than 40 undergraduate majors, Earlham offers two dual-degree programs: a 3+2 degree for engineering and a 3+1 degree programs that allows students to earn both a B.A. and a M.A.T. in just four years.

Academic Programs

Earlham is one of the only colleges in the United States to offer a funded summer internship, research experience, or community-based project to every student. Eligible experiences take place in the summer anytime between a student's first year and fourth year of enrollment. Earlham helps students create an opportunity to put their education into practice without having to worry about finances. Even if the opportunity is on another continent, EPIC Advantage will cover the travel expenses. Earlham's collaborative advising model, which includes a team of academic and career advisers, helps each student to consider the available opportunities and integrate their experiences into academic plans and career aspirations. There is also funding to support other high-impact learning experiences, including student-faculty research, so many Earlham students benefit from multiple opportunities.

Earlham's unique approach to academic life, high-impact experiences, teaching, and mentoring has been uncommonly effective:

Graduates from the past five years have earned such prestigious awards as the Rhodes Scholarship, Fulbright Scholarship, the Watson Fellowship, the National Science Foundation Pre-Doctoral Fellowship, the Samuel Huntington Public Service Award, and a Fellowship at the Carnegie Endowment for International Peace.

Of all colleges and universities in the U.S., Earlham also ranks in the top 2 percent for its percentage of graduates who go on to earn research doctorates.

A team of recent Earlham graduates won the 2016 Hult Prize, beating out 25,000 entrants in the world's largest student competition for the social good. They are using $1 million in prize money to launch a business that is already revolutionizing public transportation in several cities in Kenya.

Off-Campus Programs

Earlham's off-campus study programs send students all over the globe to explore new places and experience new cultures. In addition, Earlham's EPIC Advantage program provides another way to take part in off-campus experiences, including an internship, research opportunity, or a community-based project.

Semester-long programs include: Border Studies (Tucson), Ecuador, England, France/Senegal, Germany/Austria, Greece,

Japan, Middle East/Jordan, New Zealand, Spain, or Tibetan Studies (India).

May Term programs include: Bahamas, Benin, Berlin, Borneo, Canada, China, Costa Rica, Curaçao, England, Galápagos Islands, Greece, Hawaii, Iceland, Italy, Martinique, Spain, or Turkey.

Internship, research, and project locations funded by Earlham's EPIC Advantage include local, regional, U.S. and international sites.

Academic Facilities

Earlham's academic facilities are state-of-the-art and designed to foster collaboration. In recent years the College has invested more than $70 million in its campus, including new and renovated student center, science facilities, and a center for visual and performing arts.

Costs

Earlham College tuition and fees for the 2018–19 academic year are $56,850.

Financial Aid

Earlham believes that paying for college should not be a barrier to going to college and is committed to creating financial access to qualified students from all backgrounds. The College offers scholarships to high academic achievers (up to full tuition), to those who demonstrate a financial need and a commitment to volunteer service, to Quakers, and to highly qualified members of underrepresented racial and ethnic groups. Financial aid can also include loans and student employment.

Faculty

Recognized for their commitment to undergraduate teaching, Earlham's faculty members combine their love of scholarship with their teaching. It's a potent combination and it is the College's student body that benefits.

All Earlham professors also actively engage students as true partners in learning, and an unusually high number participate in scholarly or creative projects with their students. Eighty-five percent of Earlham professors include students in their research on some of the important challenges facing the world today, often leading to coauthored publications.

Students learn to be colleagues as part of their education. That's part of why everyone in the Earlham community is on a first-name basis, from students to staff, professors to the College president.

Most classes are small. Seventy percent have fewer than 15 students.

Student Life

With a long and varied list of active, student-led organizations to choose from, Earlham students have every chance to get involved outside of the classroom. Some of the more popular organizations include dance teams, Frisbee golf, Ultimate, cultural clubs, and political clubs. In addition, there are numerous co-ops on campus, including the Barn Co-op, home to Earlham's Equestrian Team horses and other horses boarded by students.

Besides the 20 varsity sports the College sponsors, there are numerous club teams and opportunities to participate in intramural sports. For those desiring a workout, Earlham has extensive wellness facilities, including a field house, swimming pool, weight room, climbing wall, exercise classes, and a walking track.

The activity calendar at Earlham is packed with speakers, theatre productions, art exhibits and much more. The campus also kicks off each school year with Sunsplash, an annual festival that includes live music from major bands, and wraps up each year with SpringFest, an outdoor event with inflatable games and other excuses to let loose.

Admission Requirements

Earlham is selective, with six applicants for every seat in the first-year class. The College seeks students who are academically prepared, intellectually curious, and who possess a variety of special talents and interests. Earlham also looks for students who are comfortable in their own skin and embrace differences.

Earlham takes a holistic approach in its review of students' applications for admission, giving consideration to academic achievement, writing ability (the essay is very important), and letters of recommendation from teachers and guidance counselors. In determining academic ability and college readiness, the College gives particular weight to a student's performance in high school courses and the quality of their chosen college preparatory academic program. Earlham also recognizes applicants' commitments, accomplishments and contributions beyond the classroom

Earlham uses the Common Application, which includes a guidance counselor recommendation and a teacher recommendation. Earlham expects high school applicants to have completed at least 15 academic high school units or the equivalent: 4 in English, 3 in mathematics, and 2 or more in a second language, science, and history or social studies. Experience in the area of studio or performing arts is very desirable. Earlham has a test-optional policy which means applicants are not required to submit any standardized test scores (Home-schooled and international students are required to submit standardized testing.)

Application and Information

Earlham College offers application plans for early decision (application materials due Nov. 15), early action (application materials due Dec. 1), and regular decision (application materials due Feb. 15). More information about these plans is available online at Earlham.edu/apply.

Contact Information

Office of Admissions
801 National Road West
Richmond, Indiana 47374
Phone: 765-983-1600
    800-EARLHAM (toll-free)
E-mail: admissions@earlham.edu
Website: earlham.edu/admissions
facebook.com/earlhamcollege

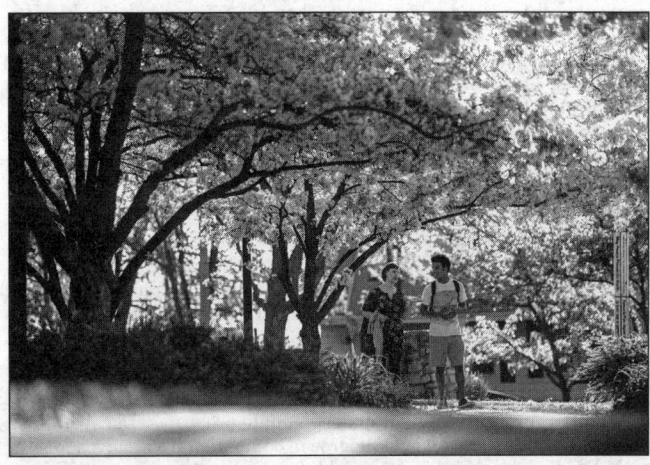

ELIZABETHTOWN COLLEGE
ELIZABETHTOWN, PENNSYLVANIA

 To read more about this school, visit http://petersons.to/elizabethtowncollege

The College

Founded in 1899, and located in historic Lancaster County, Pennsylvania, Elizabethtown College offers students more than 45 academic programs in liberal arts, sciences, and professional studies. A selective, private institution, the College is driven by its motto, "Educate for Service," and links classroom instruction with experiential learning through Signature Learning Experiences (SLEs), which supplement classroom learning and include choices in supervised research, cross-cultural experiences, community-based learning, internships, and capstone courses. SLEs prepare students for lives of purpose and are the hallmarks of the Elizabethtown experience.

Home to about 1,700 students in our traditional program, hailing from 28 states and 23 countries, approximately 84 percent live on the 204-acre campus in residence halls, townhouses and apartments, and college-owned houses called student-directed learning communities, where students commit to community-focused service work.

In addition to an active intramural and club sports program, Blue Jay Athletics fields 24 NCAA Division III teams for Men (Baseball, Basketball, Cross Country, Golf, Lacrosse, Soccer, Swimming, Tennis, indoor and outdoor Track & Field, Volleyball, Wrestling) and Women (Basketball, Cross Country, Field Hockey, Golf, Lacrosse, Soccer, Softball, Swimming, Tennis, indoor and outdoor Track & Field, Volleyball).

The Center for Student Success offers academic advising, individual academic coaching, tutoring, and writing support for all students. Student Wellness provides individual and group counseling in a diversity affirming environment, delivers health services in partnership with Penn State Health, and offers robust health promotion programs through The Well. Career Services assists with career exploration, job shadow, and internship options, and prepares students for the job search process. The Center for Student Involvement promotes strengths-based initiatives for cultivating lives of purpose and meaning including the Called to Lead program, civic and community engagement and interfaith programs.

The Office of Diversity is committed to valuing and fostering the diversity reflected in our life together and in the world beyond the campus. The Mosaic House serves as a gathering place for students of diverse backgrounds and interests.

The campus offers four dining venues: The Marketplace (traditional dining); The Jay's Nest (deli/quick-serve/convenience store); The Blue Bean (coffee shop); and The Jay Truck (food truck). Recreational spaces and offerings include The Body Shop, Thompson Gymnasium, fitness classes, an outdoor track, a pool, and lots of paths and green space. The KAV is a multipurpose entertainment and educational space. Leffler Chapel and Performance Center features an 840-seat auditorium. The campus events calendar boasts more than 125 arts and cultural happenings each academic year, not including student-run programming from OSA and the 80+ campus clubs. Opening in 2019 is the Bowers Center for Sports, Fitness and Well-being, a multi-use facility which includes living room spaces for students to gather, a 180-meter indoor track, smoothie café, food demonstration kitchen, fitness center, group fitness room with streaming fitness instruction, and wellness areas for meditation and yoga.

Elizabethtown holds accreditations from the Middle States Commission for Higher Education (MSCHE), American Chemical Society for Clinical Lab Services (ACS), National Association of Schools of Music (NASM), National Council on Social Work Education (CSWE), Accreditation Council for Occupational Therapy Education (ACOTE), Association of Collegiate Business Schools and Programs (ACBSP), and the Accreditation Board for Engineering and Technology Inc. for Computer Engineering and Engineering (ABET).

In addition to its traditional undergraduate programs, Elizabethtown also offers a Master of Science degree in occupational therapy; a Master of Public Policy; a Master of Special Education (4+1); a Master of Education in Curriculum and Instruction in Peace Education; and, through its School of Continuing and Professional Studies, Master of Business Administration (M.B.A.) and Master of Strategic Leadership degrees.

Location

Elizabethtown borough is a community of close to 12,000 people located in historic Lancaster County in south-central Pennsylvania, 20 minutes from Harrisburg (state capital), Hershey, and Lancaster; 90 minutes from Philadelphia and Baltimore; and a few hours from New York and Washington, D.C. The Amtrak station in Elizabethtown offers train service to and from New York, Philadelphia, and Pittsburgh. The Harrisburg International Airport is 15 minutes away.

Majors and Degrees

Bachelor of Arts degrees are awarded in communications, economics, English, fine arts, fine arts education, French, German, history, interfaith leadership studies, Japanese, legal studies, music, philosophy, political science, psychology, religious studies, sociology-anthropology, Spanish, Spanish education, and theatre.

Bachelor of Science degrees are offered in Accounting, Actuarial Science, Biochemistry, Biology (Allied Health, Biological Science, Pre-medicine, Secondary Education), Biotechnology, Business Administration (Accounting, Economics, Entrepreneurship and Family Business, Finance, Management, Marketing), Chemistry (ACS Professional, Chemical Physics, Chemistry Management, Forensic Science, Premedical, Secondary Education), Chemistry Laboratory Sciences, Communications (Public Relations, Mass) Computer Engineering, Computer Science, Criminal Justice, Data Science, Economics, Education/Early Childhood (Pre-K through 4, Dual Special EductationCertification), Education/Elementary & Middle-level(4-8), Engineering (Biomedical, Civil, Electrical, Environmental, Industrial and Systems, Mechanical), English (Literature, Professional Writing, Secondary Education), Environmental Science, Fine Arts (Art History, Studio Art, Art Education (K-12)), Finance, Financial Economics, French, German, Graphic Design, History, Information Systems, Interfaith Leadership Studies, International Business (Accounting, Economics, Entrepreneurship & Family Business, Finance, Management, Marketing, Self-Designed), Japanese, Legal Studies, Marketing, Mathematical Business, Mathematics (Applied Mathematics, Pure Mathematics, Secondary Education), Music, Music Education(K-12), Music Therapy, Occupational Therapy (5-year, entry level master's program), Philosophy, Physics (Secondary Education), Political Science, Psychology, Religious Studies, Social Work, Sociology and Anthropology(Anthropology, Criminology/Criminal Justice, Sociology), Spanish, Spanish Education (K-12), Theatre (Performance, Technology).

More than 108 minors, concentrations, endorsements, and certifications are offered.

The College offers a variety of cooperative programs that allow qualified students to combine undergraduate studies with direct admission into graduate school. These include a special partnership with Northumbria University in the UK; the Law Early Admissions Program with Drexel University Thomas R. Kline School of Law, Duquesne University School of Law, and Widener University Schools of Law; the 4+1 Masters in Molecular Medicine with Drexel University College of Medicine; a Masters of Public Health with Penn State College of Medicine; the Physician Assistant Program with Penn State College of Medicine; the Primary Care Program with Penn State College of Medicine; the Cardiovascular Invasive Specialty Program with Pennsylvania College of Health Sciences; the 3+4 or 4+4 Doctor of Dental Medicine with Lake Erie College of Osteopathic Medicine; 4+4 Doctor of Dental Surgery with West Virginia University School of Dentistry; and the 3+4 or 4+4 Doctor of Pharmaceutical with Lake Erie College of Osteopathic Medicine and the 3+3 Doctor of Physical Therapy with Thomas Jefferson University and Widener University.

Academic Programs

An interdisciplinary first-year seminar and a strong core curriculum create a solid foundation for a student's chosen area of study. The core develops critical analysis and communication skills that ensure adaptability in the ever-changing global marketplace. Independent and directed studies, undergraduate research, and internships are available.

The Elizabethtown College Honors Program offers top students a highly selective program of study with the opportunity for a stipend to fund professional development, research, or travel-related study.

Called to Lead is a leadership-building program that helps students aspire to lead purposeful lives. Scholarship and Creative Arts Days, held each spring, give students of all majors and class years the opportunity to showcase their research or creative works. The Center for Global Understanding and Peacemaking, Bowers Writers House, and The Young Center for Anabaptist and Pietist Studies all offer a variety of academic programming that further reinforce classroom experiences. The Social Enterprise Institute offers students the opportunity to collaborate with faculty and industry fellows to create sustainable social and economic value both domestically and internationally. The Momentum program, a pre-orientation program, helps first-generation college students prepare for the academic expectations of Elizabethtown.

Off-Campus Programs

During their time at Elizabethtown, each student is guaranteed to experience at least two of the following Signature Learning Experiences: undergraduate research, study abroad, community-based learning, internships/fieldwork, and capstone course work.

Students may study abroad for a semester in 45 different locations on six continents through the College's affiliate programs. Short-term academic study tours or service-learning trips are offered. The Center for Community and Civic Engagement offers numerous community-based learning experiences locally, regionally, and nationally.

Academic Facilities

The High Library contains more than 243,000 volumes and an extensive collection of journals and other research materials; computers and printers; conference rooms; and private, individual, and group study areas. Librarians help students with research projects and using library resources effectively.

The campus features numerous academic buildings, including the James B. Hoover Center for Business and The Masters Center for Science, Mathematics, and Engineering. The Baugher Student center is home to the Tempest Theatre and a dance studio, and Zug Memorial Hall houses a recital hall and private and group practice rooms. Steinman Center for Communications and Arts features a television studio, radio station, and office space for the College newspaper. The College houses three art galleries and the Masters Mineral Gallery.

Elizabethtown is home to The Young Center for Anabaptist and Pietist Studies, a world-renowned research center focusing on the Amish and other similar religions. The High Center, a local research and resource center for family-owned businesses, partners with academic departments for events and programs. The Social Enterprise Institute brings together faculty members, industry fellows of the Institute and students, to collaborate on social enterprise development initiatives.

Costs

For 2018–19, tuition is $46,940 and room and meals are $11,370, for a total comprehensive fee of $58,310. Students should also plan for an additional $2,150 for books, transportation, and personal expenses, for a total cost of $60,460. Financial aid is based on this figure.

Financial Aid

Elizabethtown College works with students and their families to make education affordable. About 97 percent of students receive some form of aid; packages typically combine scholarships, grants, loans, and student employment. About 86 percent of Elizabethtown's first-year students receive renewable merit-based scholarships, which are awarded on a competitive basis and without regard to need.

To apply for aid, students must file the Free Application for Federal Student Aid (FAFSA). Students are assigned a personal financial aid counselor to help them throughout their years at the College. Elizabethtown's deadline for financial consideration is March 15.

Faculty

Elizabethtown has a teaching faculty of 129 full-time professors. The student-faculty ratio is 13:1. Of the full-time faculty members, 95 percent hold a Ph.D. or the highest earned degree in their field. In addition to being assigned a faculty adviser for the First-Year Seminar program, when students declare a major, they are also assigned a new faculty adviser within the academic department of their declared major.

Student Government

Students play an active role in campus governance through Student Senate. Representative members of Student Senate are elected from each class. They advocate for students, coordinate special events, and allocate funds for student activities and the more than eighty student-directed clubs and organizations.

Admission Requirements

Elizabethtown believes the right fit is more than just SAT scores and GPA; other admission factors considered at the College are academic fit, cocurricular fit, and social fit. Admissions decisions are made without regard to sex, sexual orientation, race, religion, physical handicap, or place of residence. On average, 71 percent of all applicants are accepted. The middle 50 percent of enrolled students scored between 1080 and 1270 on the critical reading and mathematics sections of the SAT, and 60 percent were in the top 25 percent of their high school class.

The College is a diverse and exciting community, one that is composed of students who display leadership abilities and special talents. Campus interviews are highly recommended but not required for most students, although the College reserves the right to require interviews in special cases. Applicants to the Honors Program and occupational therapy program are required to interview. Auditions are required for music students.

Early admission is available for highly qualified high school juniors.

Application and Information

The College operates on a rolling admission basis—applications are processed as they are received—and the application deadline is April 1. Students can apply using the Common Application or online at the College's website. Applicants must submit a high school transcript, SAT or ACT scores, and a personal statement, essay, or graded paper. Early application is strongly recommended. Accepted students should notify the College of their decision to attend by May 1. Students who are interested in the Elizabethtown College Honors Program must submit a completed application by January 15.

For more information, students should contact:

Lauren Deibler, Director of Admissions
Elizabethtown College
One Alpha Drive
Elizabethtown, Pennsylvania 17022-2298
Phone: 717-361-1400
Fax: 717-361-1365
E-mail: admissions@etown.edu
Website: http://www.etown.edu

Elizabethtown College, home to about 1,700 students, offers more than forty-five majors and ninety minors and concentrations.

ELMHURST COLLEGE
ELMHURST, ILLINOIS

 To read more about this school, visit http://petersons.to/elmhurstcollege

The College

A private college in the heart of the Chicago metropolitan area, Elmhurst College is committed to helping students reach their full potential—in college and in the world beyond. An Elmhurst education is about more than courses and credits; it's about defining values, exploring the world, and preparing for a life of service, meaning, and achievement.

Elmhurst is one of the top 12 colleges in the Midwest, according to *U.S. News & World Report*, and it also ranks among the best values in the region. With more than 60 undergraduate majors and 15 graduate programs, Elmhurst boasts a student-to-faculty ratio of just 14 to 1. In small classes, professors get to know their students as individuals.

Beyond the classroom, students get plenty of opportunities to put their passions and talents into action in more than 100 campus activities. Elmhurst's 20 athletic teams compete in NCAA Division III and have won conference championships in five sports over the past decade.

More than 80 percent of Elmhurst undergraduates gain on-the-job experience through internships or service work, and nearly 94 percent of Elmhurst graduates find full-time employment or enter graduate school within a year of graduation. The College's robust career programs include more than 2,000 options for internships and other professional experiences.

Students come to Elmhurst from many states and countries, and from nearly every religious, racial and ethnic background. The student body comprises about 2,700 full-time undergraduate students, 250 adults pursuing an undergraduate degree and 600 graduate students.

Elmhurst College is accredited by the Department of Education of the State of Illinois, and by the Higher Learning Commission, a member of the North Central Association of Colleges and Schools. The baccalaureate degree in nursing and master's degree in nursing at Elmhurst College are accredited by the Commission on Collegiate Nursing Education (http://www.aacn.nche.edu/ccne-accreditation).

Location

Elmhurst's 48-acre grounds are an arboretum, with more than 800 varieties of trees, shrubs and other woody plants. The gorgeous campus is a green oasis in the heart of a quiet, safe suburb—but it's also just a few blocks from the Elmhurst Metra station, where students can catch the train for a 30-minute ride to downtown Chicago, providing easy access to world-class cultural, entertainment, and professional opportunities.

Academics

With more than 60 undergraduate majors and 16 pre-professional programs, Elmhurst boasts a student-to-faculty ratio of just 14 to 1. In small classes, students work closely with faculty members who are experts in their fields—and whose primary mission is teaching.

Many students collaborate with faculty on high-level research projects, studying subjects ranging from metastatic breast cancer to the effect of acting lessons on aging brains. An Honors Program offers special opportunities for students who are especially motivated by academic challenges.

Beyond the classroom, Elmhurst offers study-abroad opportunities in more than 60 countries. A special January Term offers undergraduate students the chance to undertake courses and field projects off campus.

Career Development

Elmhurst students gain real-world experience starting their first year. Internships, professional mentors, and shadowing experiences help them define their future and provide them the skills to succeed. Nearly 94 percent of Elmhurst College graduates are employed or in graduate school within a year of graduating.

Facilities

The Elmhurst campus combines the high-tech necessities of a modern education with the charm of a classic college campus. Its classic red-brick buildings boast wireless Internet access, smart classrooms, and more. In addition, the College has a long tradition of responsible stewardship of the environment. From low-impact lighting and permeable paving to a LEED-certified residence hall, Elmhurst incorporates green principles throughout campus life.

Costs

Full-time undergraduate tuition for 2018–19 is $36,755; basic room and board is $10,366.

Financial Aid

Elmhurst College is committed to making college affordable; 100 percent of new students receive financial aid in the form of grants, scholarships, loans, and work-study.

Campus Life

Students at Elmhurst find plenty of opportunities to put their passions and talents into action. The College offers more than 100 student organizations, including everything from Habitat for Humanity to the Black Student Union to religious groups and Greek life.

Many Elmhurst students live on campus, where they find all the amenities of home—plus the convenience of close proximity to classes, the library, the gym and all your favorite student activities. The College's six residence halls are equipped with full kitchens, cozy gathering spots, Internet access, and free cable TV. Each hall sponsors a variety of events—like movies, workshops, and barbecues—and has the support of an expert residence life staff.

Elmhurst also offers an array of services and resources designed to help students navigate the pressures of college life. Services in the Division of Student Affairs include individual counseling, support with housing issues, comprehensive health care services, transition assistance, and diversity education.

Admission Requirements

Elmhurst gives preference to students who have completed 16 academic units, including 3 units of English; 2 units each of mathematics, laboratory science, and social studies; and 7 units in additional college preparatory subjects.

Application and Information

To apply, prospective students should submit the following:

- **The application for admission.** Students may apply online at https://connect.elmhurst.edu/apply.

- **High school transcript** or GED test results.

- **Scores from the ACT or SAT,** sent directly from the testing corporation to Elmhurst. (Elmhurst's ACT code is 1020 and its SAT code is 1204).

- **A recommendation** from a high school faculty member (encouraged, but not required).

Elmhurst has an Early Action deadline (nonbinding) of November 1 with a December 1 notification. Rolling admission notifications begin mid-December.

Prospective students are encouraged to visit the campus, either individually or as part of a scheduled event. Admission events range from campus tours and open houses to information sessions and overnight visits.

The Office of Admission at Elmhurst College welcomes students' questions and comments.

For more information, please contact:

Office of Admission
Elmhurst College
190 Prospect Avenue
Elmhurst, Illinois 60126-3296
United States
Phone: 630-617-3400
      800-697-1871 (toll-free)
E-mail: admit@elmhurst.edu
Website: http://www.elmhurst.edu/admission

The Elmhurst College campus is within easy access of the limitless opportunities of downtown Chicago.

EMBRY-RIDDLE AERONAUTICAL UNIVERSITY

DAYTONA BEACH, FLORIDA

 To read more about this school, visit http://petersons.to/erau

The University

Embry-Riddle Aeronautical University's reputation as the leader in aviation and aerospace education is recognized worldwide. The University's history and legacy date back almost to the time of the Wright brothers. Embry-Riddle is a private, nonprofit university serving culturally diverse students seeking careers in aviation, aerospace, engineering, business, security and intelligence, and related fields. Residential campuses in Daytona Beach, Florida, and Prescott, Arizona, provide education in a traditional setting, while the Worldwide campus provides online learning options.

Approximately 5,700 undergraduate students and 600 graduate students are currently enrolled at the 185-acre Daytona Beach residential campus. Students come from all fifty states, and nearly 100 countries are represented, making Embry-Riddle a truly international university.

Currently 28 undergraduate degree programs, 16 graduate programs, and 7 doctoral programs are offered at the Daytona Beach campus. Embry-Riddle's premier aeronautical science (professional pilot) program and nationally ranked aerospace engineering program are the largest on campus and among the largest of their type in the nation.

Embry-Riddle conducts applied research and is leading the development of the Next Generation Air Transportation System along with the Federal Aviation Administration, Lockheed Martin, Boeing, and other high-tech organizations. Student research projects include development of green technologies like Embry-Riddle's EcoCAR and the world's first-of-its-kind hybrid aircraft. Alumni are leaders in every facet of the aviation and aerospace industries and serve as a strong network and resource for students.

Students at the Daytona Beach campus enjoy a wide array of activities and clubs, many focused on aviation and aerospace, as well as fraternities, sororities, and athletic opportunities. Thirty-four percent of students live on campus.

Embry-Riddle's award-winning precision flight demonstration teams offer students the opportunity to compete nationally in air and ground events. Embry-Riddle also has the largest all-volunteer Air Force ROTC detachment in the country and a prominent Naval ROTC unit and Army ROTC battalion. Embry-Riddle athletes compete in NCAA Division II sports, including baseball, basketball, crew, cross-country, golf, lacrosse, rowing, soccer, tennis, track, and volleyball; intramural options include rugby, wrestling, ice hockey, and more.

The University sports complex includes the ICI Center with two NCAA basketball courts, fitness center and weight room, two soccer fields, artificial turf fields, the Sliwa Stadium ballpark, the Crotty Tennis Center, and the Track and Field Complex. The Tine Davis Fitness Center is adjacent to the pool and features comprehensive fitness services and wellness programs.

The Center for Faith and Spirituality accommodates the variety of faiths represented by the student body of Embry-Riddle. It consists of a 140-seat nondenominational worship area and meditation space.

Location

The year-round clear flying weather and the resort communities surrounding Embry-Riddle's residential campus in Daytona Beach, Florida, offer students an excellent environment in which to study, fly, and enjoy recreational activities. The campus, adjacent to the Daytona Beach International Airport, is only 3 miles from what is labeled the world's most famous beach. The high-technology industries located in nearby Orlando and Kennedy Space Center provide the University with an outstanding support base. In addition, Walt Disney World and other theme parks are about an hour's drive from campus.

Majors and Degrees

Bachelor of Science degrees are offered in a variety of areas, each with a focus on the aviation, aerospace, security, technology, and related industries. A growing major in unmanned aircraft systems science (open only to U.S. citizens) combines Embry-Riddle's expertise in flight, air traffic management, safety and engineering. The College of Engineering offers majors in aerospace, civil, computer, electrical, mechanical, and software engineering. All engineering programs, including Engineering Physics, are ABET accredited.

Students who are interested in business administration gain in-demand industry specialization and may elect to major in management, accounting and finance, or marketing. An aviation business administration major is also available with majors in air transportation and supply chain management.

The College of Aviation awards degrees in aeronautical science (professional piloting), air traffic management, aviation maintenance science, aerospace and occupational safety, spaceflight operations, and meteorology. Other majors include astronomy and astrophysics, interdisciplinary studies (design your own major), communication, computational mathematics, global conflict studies, homeland security, human factors psychology, and space physics, all housed in the College of Arts & Sciences. The College's newest major, and the only one of its kind in the nation, is aerospace physiology, a pre-med program focused on the needs of the aviation and aerospace industry. Students entering Embry-Riddle with an undecided major have the opportunity to explore a variety of academic pursuits before making a commitment to a specific track.

Academic Programs

Study abroad offers students the opportunity to better understand the global nature of the aviation and aerospace industries. The Cooperative Education and Internship program adds value to the educational experience and allows students to gain real-world professional and networking skills. Hundreds of industry leaders, including Boeing, SpaceX, NASA, the airlines, and more recruit students for co-ops and full-time positions.

Academic Facilities

The multimillion-dollar simulation laboratories in the College of Aviation duplicate the components and functions in the national airspace system, including capabilities to replicate actual weather reporting, airports, airways, air traffic control, flow control, and pilot and aircraft performance as found in the national air transportation system. Flight instruction is provided in the Embry-Riddle fleet of sixty-plus aircraft and a wide array of flight training devices. Aircraft are equipped with Automatic Dependent Surveillance-Broadcast (ADS-B) technology that decreases hazards associated with traffic, weather, and terrain. The High-Altitude Normobaric Lab allows students to experience the symptoms of high-altitude hypoxia to better enable them to recognize and recover from this threat. Embry-Riddle is the first university in the nation to acquire this technology.

The Advanced Flight Simulation Center gives Embry-Riddle students the opportunity to train in world-class simulators. The center, with more than 20,000 square feet of space and four high bays, currently houses two advanced aviation training devices (AATDs), eight Cessna 172S NAVIIIs (Skyhawk), two Diamond DA42 TAE Twin Stars, two Diamond DA42 L360s, and one Canadair Regional Jet (CRJ-200). These devices duplicate the actual cockpit, adverse weather conditions, a full range of emergency situations, and virtually any flight pattern and complement flight training done in actual aircraft. Flight simulation enables students to learn aircraft performance, experience aerodynamic effects, and perform flight maneuvers immediately and without risk. Qualified to Level 6, the University's devices faithfully reproduce Embry-Riddle's fleet of single-engine and multiengine aircraft and are equipped with 220-degree panoramic visual theaters. In addition, the Aviation Building houses air traffic control and tower simulators, one motion-based disorientation trainer, and six basic aviation training devices (BATDs).

The James Hagedorn Aviation Complex includes 96,000 square feet in a three-building facility and is home to flight training operations, aircraft maintenance training, and a fleet maintenance hangar. The Emil Buehler Aviation Maintenance Science building's cutting-edge labs dedicated to aircraft systems, turbine engines, metallic and composite materials, and avionics electronics prepare students to become maintenance professionals. The facility includes classrooms, a licensed engine-repair station, a machine shop, and a third-floor observation deck overlooking the flight line and Daytona Beach International Airport runways.

The Lehman Engineering and Technology Center is home to the College of Engineering. Labs include the advanced vehicles green garage, wind tunnel lab, materials testing lab, clean energy systems lab, cybersecurity engineering lab, nanomaterials and composites labs, rocket lab, spacecraft development lab, and many more. Students use the labs to work in teams to develop hands-on projects. Research is conducted by faculty members and graduate and undergraduate students.

The newest academic facility is the 140,000 square-foot College of Arts & Sciences building, the largest structure on campus and home to the largest university-based telescope in the state of Florida. The building contains twenty-five labs dedicated to astronomy, astrophysics, atmospheric and space physics, biology, control theory, and engineering physics.

The College of Business academic building features the aviation operations simulation lab, which is used to develop and evaluate aviation/airline operational strategies and processes. In addition, the College's Teaching Airport, a partnership between Embry-Riddle and Daytona Beach International Airport, is focused on teaching, research, and public outreach.

The Capt. Willie Miller Instructional Center, a lecture auditorium and classroom complex, provides space for large audience events, including presentations by distinguished lecturers and speakers.

A new Student Union is scheduled to be completed in 2018 and will house the Jack R. Hunt Memorial Library and serve as the community hub with retail, food, and entertainment options. Not only will it be the largest building on campus, it will encompass numerous university and campus departments, facilities, and services.

Costs

For the 2018–19 academic year, tuition and fees are $18,057 per semester. Flight fees are charged in addition to tuition. On-campus room and board costs are approximately $5,719 per semester. Personal expenses, books, and fees are in addition to the above. Students who graduate from a Florida high school receive a discount of approximately 5 percent. Costs are subject to change.

Financial Aid

Applicants for financial aid are required to complete the Department of Education's Free Application for Federal Student Aid (FAFSA) and any other documents requested by the University. Students are encouraged to apply early if they wish to be considered for all types of programs. All applicants are automatically reviewed for merit scholarship eligibility.

Faculty

The faculty members provide an excellent balance of professional experience and academic achievement. Many faculty members who teach in the specialized and major programs have had professional experience in their areas of instruction. The student-faculty ratio is 17:1, and the average class size is 26. The primary concern of each faculty member is research, personalized teaching in classrooms and laboratories, on the flight line, and in student advising.

Student Government

The University places great emphasis on student self-government. The Student Government Association supports publication of the weekly newspaper and oversees the Touch-N-Go Office that organizes campus entertainment and broadcast of the student radio station, WIKD-FM.

Admission Requirements

Admission is open to any qualified applicant, regardless of creed, sex, race, national origin, handicap, or geographical location. When evaluating an applicant for admission, Embry-Riddle takes into consideration a student's high school academic record (both courses taken and overall grade point average), rank in class, and activities. Submission of standardized test scores (SAT or ACT) is optional for admission. Transfer students are required to submit official transcripts from all colleges and universities attended. High school transcripts are not required if the student has earned 30 college credits or more.

Application and Information

Embry-Riddle requires each applicant to submit an application form and fee, two letters of recommendation, and an official high school/college transcript. Flight students must provide an FAA Class I or Class II medical certificate. Embry-Riddle operates on a rolling admissions basis, and admission decisions are rendered throughout the year.

University Admissions
Embry-Riddle Aeronautical University
P.O. Box 11767
Daytona Beach, Florida 32120-1767
Phone: 386-226-6100
        800-862-2416 (toll-free nationwide)
E-mail: daytonabeach@erau.edu
Website: http://www.daytonabeach.erau.edu
        http://www.facebook.com/eraudb
        http://twitter.com/ERAU_Daytona
        http://www.youtube.com/EmbryRiddleUniv
        https://www.instagram.com/embryriddledaytona

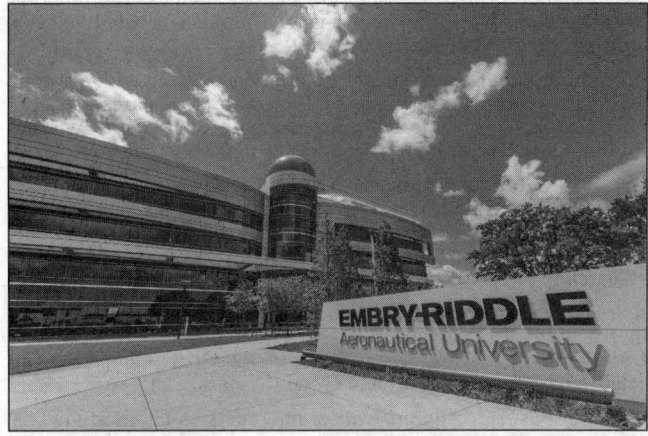

Embry-Riddle Aeronautical University, Daytona Beach, Florida, campus.

EMBRY-RIDDLE AERONAUTICAL UNIVERSITY

PRESCOTT, ARIZONA

EMBRY-RIDDLE
Aeronautical University
PRESCOTT, ARIZONA

The University

Embry-Riddle Aeronautical University's Prescott, Arizona campus is recognized and respected worldwide for cutting-edge instruction and training for tomorrow's aviation, aerospace, security and intelligence leaders.

Embry-Riddle is a private, four-year university accredited by SACS. The coed student population of just over 2,500 undergraduates comes from all fifty states and over thirty nations.

There are more than 100 student clubs and organizations including professional associations, fraternities, sororities, specialty clubs, and intramural sports. The National Association of Intercollegiate Athletics (NAIA) teams compete regionally and nationally as members of the CalPac Conference. Men's and women's teams include basketball, cross-country, golf, and soccer, along with men's wrestling, women's volleyball, and women's softball. The Golden Eagles flight team has consistently ranked among the top in the country in Safety and Flight Evaluation Conference (SAFECON) competitions, capturing the national championship title 11 times.

Within a year of graduation, 96 percent of graduates are either employed within their discipline or continuing their education.

Location

Prescott is a mile-high city and its climate reflects seasonable weather excellent for flying. Daytime averages are 80°F in the summer and 45°F in the winter. The local mountains reflect the spirit of the West, where students enjoy skiing, hiking, mountain biking, kayaking, rock climbing, and tours of the Grand Canyon.

Majors and Degrees

Twenty-five majors are offered through four different colleges: Arts and Sciences, Aviation, Engineering, and the nation's first College of Security and Intelligence.

Aeronautical Science, the professional pilot program, offers fixed-wing or rotary-wing flight options. The program emphasizes hands-on training to prepare students for a career in the aviation industry with airlines, corporate and commercial aviation, or the military.

Aeronautics builds upon pre-existing experience and training in aviation, or other technical fields. It also allows the flexibility to build a major with an aviation focus and a professional outcome.

Aerospace Engineering instructs the scientific principles that govern the design of airplanes, spacecraft, and jet engines. The program focuses primarily on the engineering of mission-oriented vehicles for atmospheric or space flight.

Air Traffic Management blends simulation training with rigorous academic study. Hands-on air traffic training prepares students for a career as an air traffic controller with the Federal Aviation Administration (FAA).

Applied Meteorology provides a practical understanding of the physics and dynamics of the atmosphere to forecast complex phenomena. This program offers areas of concentration in flight, meteorology for aviation operations, military meteorology, and research.

Astronomy emphasizes both a hands-on and theoretical education in the study of celestial objects and astrophysics. The Campus Observatory Complex, as well as Prescott's excellent viewing conditions, enhance education beyond the classroom.

Aviation Business Administration integrates in-depth studies of aviation, transportation, and government interface with a strong business foundation, and is approved by the Aviation Accreditation Board International (AABI).

Business Administration students experience a unique hands-on learning approach by taking their education outside the classroom and consulting with actual clients through a faculty-led student team. Students produce start-up business plans, strategic management plans, and conduct fraud-risk analysis.

Computer Engineering provides a background in the design of digital hardware and software systems including communications systems, computers, and devices that contain computers. A senior design project will closely follow the development of an engineering project in the industry.

Cyber Intelligence and Security empowers students to lead, manage, administer, and create organizations in cyber security. Students study computer forensics, information warfare, and technical intelligence while utilizing the University's state-of-the-art *Cyber Security Lab*.

Electrical Engineering is a systems-oriented program that includes analog and digital circuits, communication systems, computers, control systems, electromagnetic fields, energy sources and systems, and electronic materials and devices.

Forensic Accounting and Fraud Examination is where law enforcement meets the accounting world. Graduation prepares students for the Certified Fraud Examiner (CFE) exam and Certification, and incorporates criminal investigative skills with areas of accounting, including financial, managerial, information systems, governmental, auditing, tax accounting, and psychology.

Forensic Biology combines biology, chemistry, and law to give students experience in forensic science laboratories, law enforcement, and legal contexts. Hands-on activities include evidence collection, crime scene investigation, tissue sampling and analysis, and emphasis on DNA techniques. This major also fulfills pre-med requirements.

Forensic Psychology is the science of human behavior and prepares students to work in civil, legal, and criminal environments as experts in understanding, evaluating, and predicting human behavior. Training combines the study of global and cyber security, forensic science, the U.S. legal system and international affairs.

Global Business prepares students for international management. Classroom topics include global events and issues related to transportation, trade, public policy, technology, resources, energy, and the environment. Students study international cultures with a focus on emerging markets.

Global Security and Intelligence Studies gives graduates an expertise in terrorism, asymmetrical warfare, transportation security, threats to manufacturing facilities, corporate offices, computer systems, and telecommunications infrastructure. Students prepare for careers with the FBI, CIA, State Department, military intelligence, and private sectors. Options include Mandarin Chinese, Arabic, Spanish, and Russian.

Industrial Psychology and Safety explores the disciplines of aviation safety, occupational safety, industrial hygiene, ergonomics, and quantitative methods. The program delivers a foundation in human behavior and cognition as it relates to safety and organizational effectiveness.

Interdisciplinary Studies is a unique option allowing students to customize their undergraduate curriculum to match specific career goals by choosing three major areas of study to create their own major.

Mechanical Engineering focuses on the design of robotic, propulsion, and energy systems. The program prepares students for the vast career applications in this field including aerospace, automotive, robotics, thermal environmental control, recreational products, medicine, and manufacturing.

Simulation Science, Games and Animation instructs students to design and build technologies underlying aviation simulators, computer aided design (CAD) systems, computer animation software, streaming video networks, and computer games.

COLLEGE CLOSE-UPS

Software Engineering prepares students to work as programmers and software engineers, constructing software systems and developing system requirements. A unique cyber security track allows graduates to support the nation's need for cyber security to protect a company's proprietary information.

Space Physics is an applied physics program designed to prepare students for graduate studies in physics, astrophysics, and exotic propulsion systems, as well as for work in space and aerospace related industries.

Unmanned Aerial Systems focuses on the design, operation, and business components of the emerging unmanned aerial vehicles industry. This program emphasizes practical applications such as search and rescue, first responder, hazardous surveillance, or evaluation of emergencies.

Wildlife Science is the only undergraduate environmental science program in the country with a focus on the aviation and aerospace industries. Students with interest in wildlife biology, environmental science, and working in the outdoors should explore this growing and rewarding career field.

Academic Programs

Education at Embry-Riddle goes beyond the classroom. Through participation in internships and cooperative education arrangements, students in all fields of study gain valuable work experience with companies such as Delta Air Lines, the Federal Aviation Administration, Honeywell, Gulfstream, Lockheed Martin, NASA, the CIA, SpaceX, and more.

Army and Air Force Reserve Officer Training Corps (ROTC) courses are also available to all students. Embry-Riddle produces more Air Force officers and aviators than any institution except the Air Force Academy.

Faculty

Faculty, not graduate students, teach all classes. The average class size is 25, with a student-faculty ratio of 16:1. Faculty bring teaching and industry backgrounds to the classroom; most have extensive practical experience in their field and outstanding academic credentials.

Academic Facilities

Numerous laboratories and state-of-the-art equipment provide students many opportunities to explore, investigate, experiment, build, and participate in undergraduate research.

The Robertson Aviation Safety Center houses the nation's only university-level accident investigation laboratory. This outdoor facility allows for studying wreckage sites of actual aircraft accidents.

The Glen Doherty Center for Security and Intelligence serves as a laboratory for students of the nation's first College of Security and Intelligence to simulate exercises in emergency management and homeland security. Labs include Computer Security and Forensic Science, where students run forensic tests on cyber threats and crime scene evidence.

The recently completed STEM Education Center includes particle physics, exotic propulsion, optics, and remote sensing labs for space physics and astronomy majors, as well as advanced forensic, biology, chemistry, and robotics labs. It also contains a full-dome planetarium for use by all majors and the community. There is also a campus observatory housing a CCD (charged coupled device) debris telescope.

In the Aerospace Experimentation and Fabrication Building (AXFAB), students have access to a two-axis electromagnetic shaker, vacuum chambers to simulate space environment, and 3-D printers. Additionally, there is the Aerial Robotics Laboratory for research and development of unmanned systems; the Aerodynamics Laboratory which houses five wind tunnels; and the Propulsion Laboratory providing a micro-turbojet.

The King Engineering and Technology Center is home for the computer, electrical, and software engineering students. There is a design suite for autonomous vehicles as well as labs for communications, control theory, power, digital circuits, and linear circuits.

The Flight Training Center is located at the Prescott Municipal Airport 2 miles from campus. The fleet includes Cessna 172s, Diamond DA42 NGs, an American Champion Super Decathlon for extreme attitude recovery, and two Cessna 150s, furnished with Garmin G1000 navigation systems, for the flight team. All aircraft are ADS-b equipped. Also at the flight line are three Frasca 172 level 6 flight-training devices with 220° visual displays.

Additional College of Aviation facilities include an Air Traffic Control Lab, Student Innovation Lab for unmanned aerial systems research and development, and a Weather Center, which has radar and weather balloon launch capabilities.

Athletic facilities include indoor volleyball and basketball courts, fitness center, multipurpose gym, and matted wrestling room. Other facilities include a softball field, intercollegiate soccer field, tennis courts, sand volleyball courts, 25-yard swimming pool, racquetball courts, climbing wall, running track, and multisport recreation field. All facilities are available free of charge to all students.

Costs

The 2017–18 academic year tuition for all programs was $17,827 per semester for full-time students. Flight fees are charged in addition to tuition. The average on-campus housing rate for first-year students is $2,930 per semester; the required meal plan for freshmen is $2,304 per semester. Students also need to account for the cost of books, transportation, and personal expenses.

Financial Aid

Students can find many sources to assist with funding their education. Filing the FAFSA is important. Embry-Riddle also provides assistance in the form of academic scholarships, need-based grants, on-campus jobs, veterans' educational benefits (Embry-Riddle is a Yellow Ribbon school), and ROTC incentives.

Admission Requirements

Each student receives individual consideration for admission based on a variety of factors and circumstances. Completion of the application for admission begins this process; students also need to submit official transcripts, score reports for either the SAT or ACT (not required but highly recommended), and two letters of recommendation.

Application and Information

For additional information, students should contact:
Embry-Riddle Aeronautical University Admissions
3700 Willow Creek Road
Prescott, Arizona 86301
United States
Phone: 928-777-6600
        800-888-3728 (toll-free)
E-mail: prescott@erau.edu
Website: http://prescott.erau.edu

The beautiful Prescott, Arizona campus in front of its dramatic, picturesque Granite Mountain backdrop.

EMERSON COLLEGE
BOSTON, MASSACHUSETTS

 For more information, visit http://petersons.to/emersoncollege

The College

Founded in 1880 and located in the heart of Boston, Massachusetts, Emerson College is the nation's premier institution for the study of communication and the arts. Students may choose from nearly 30 undergraduate programs supported by state-of-the-art facilities and a nationally renowned faculty. Emerson's campus is home to WERS-FM, the oldest noncommercial radio station in Boston; the historic 1,200-seat Cutler Majestic Theatre; and *Ploughshares*, the award-winning literary journal for new writing.

Emerson College offers educational programs that prepare undergraduate and graduate men and women to assume positions of responsibility and leadership in communication and the arts and to pursue scholarship and work that brings innovation to these disciplines.

Originally a small, regional school of oratory, Emerson has evolved into a diverse, coeducational, and multifaceted degree-granting institution with a liberal arts rather than conservatory orientation. But its mission and focus remains largely the same: to explore and push the boundaries of communication, art, and culture and, thereby, to contribute to the advancement of society.

Many of the College's 37,000+ alumni remain active participants in the life of Emerson. Although concentrated in Massachusetts, California, and New York, Emersonians can be found working in virtually every major media, entertainment, or arts enterprise across the country.

The College's 3,810 undergraduate and 653 graduate students come from across the United States and forty-nine countries. Many undergraduate students live on campus, some in special learning communities, such as the Writers' Block, Film Immersion, and Performing Cultures. There is a fitness center, athletic field, and several residence halls, including a fourteen-story campus center and residence hall that houses a gymnasium and student-services offices. Emerson opened a new 18-story residence hall and a new 18,000 square-foot Dining Center in fall 2017.

Emerson is fully accredited by the New England Association of Schools and Colleges as authorized by the Commission on Institutions of Higher Education. Emerson is also accredited by the Council on Academic Accreditation of the American Speech-Language-Hearing Association and the Massachusetts Department of Education.

Location

Emerson College is located in Boston, Massachusetts, the most popular college city in the U.S. Emerson's campus is in the heart of downtown Boston and the city's Theatre District, just steps from the Massachusetts State House, Boston Common, the historic Freedom Trail, Boston Public Garden, Chinatown, and countless restaurants and museums.

Emerson College's Boston campus is located at the gateway to the city's bustling Theatre District, in close proximity to cultural resources, media outlets, and public transportation. It comprises a cluster of eleven buildings near the intersection of Boylston and Tremont Streets (adjacent to historic Boston Common) plus the magnificent Paramount Center, a performing arts and residence center on nearby Washington Street. The College also has facilities in Los Angeles and the Netherlands.

The Boston campus has been assembled during the past 30 years as the College moved to the Theatre District from the Back Bay. Since 1993, Emerson has invested more than $500 million in preserving and restoring historic spaces and also creating new facilities. Emerson's decision to create the "Campus on the Common" is widely credited with reviving and revitalizing this section of Boston, attracting the development of private residences, hotels, restaurants, and other retail spaces. Emerson is continuing its legacy of preservation and restoration through its plans to renovate the Little Building and the Colonial Theatre. When these projects are completed, the College will be able to house nearly 70 percent of its students and will have preserved several additional historic spaces for future generations.

Majors and Degrees

Boston's Emerson College offers Bachelor of Arts, Bachelor of Fine Arts, and Bachelor of Science degrees. Undergraduates can major in acting; business of creative enterprises; comedic arts; communication disorders; communication studies; creative writing; journalism; marketing communication; media arts production; media studies; musical theatre; political communication; production; sports communication; stage and production management; stage and screen design/technology; theatre; theatre design/technology; theatre education; theatre education and performance; theatre and performance; or writing, literature, and publishing. The individually-designed interdisciplinary program also allows students to create their own major from the multitude of programs offered in communication, arts, and the liberal arts with faculty approval.

Academic Programs

The Institute for Liberal Arts and Interdisciplinary Studies is also home to Emerson's highly competitive Honors Program. Emerson offers a wide range of student support services including the Academic Advising Center, Career Services, disability services, and the Lacerte Family Writing and Academic Resource Center.

Emerson College is committed to creating a campus environment that supports and promotes superior research, premier creative activities, and innovative scholarly pursuits. The mission of the Office of Research and Creative Scholarship (ORCS) is to serve the Emerson community by providing information, personal assistance, services, and programs to those who seek financial support for scholarly endeavors. The Office will also provide college-wide leadership in the development of research and sponsored program activities, and work closely with faculty, staff and senior administrators in shaping the effort to build a more robust program of grants and sponsored research.

Off-Campus Programs

Hundreds of internship placements exist throughout Boston and in major cities across the country, including Emerson College's Los Angeles center—a state-of-the-art facility home to a residential study and internship program in the hub of the global entertainment industry. Emerson also offers a semester-long program in Washington, DC. Students also have the option to register for courses with six other arts colleges in Boston through the ProArts Consortium.

The Office of Internationalization and Global Engagement (IGE) seeks to enhance global engagement by utilizing Emerson's collective talent, energy, human and financial resources to support compelling transformation and change in international education across disciplines and around the world. Students can study abroad at the college's castle in the Netherlands; 20+ additional study abroad opportunities in China, the Czech Republic, Greece, Spain, and more.

Academic Facilities

More than half of Emerson's facilities are new or renovated since 2002. Students have access to the highest quality equipment, clinical facilities devoted to communication disorders research and treatment, and an integrated digital newsroom for aspiring journalists.

The College also owns more performance space than any other institution in Boston. The eleven-story Tufte Performance and Production Center has rehearsal space, a theatre design/technology center, makeup lab, and costume shop. Emerson's Paramount Center performance facility houses a sound stage, black box theater, scene shop, film screening room, and residence hall. Other performance facilities include the Cutler Majestic Theatre, a 1,200-seat Broadway-style theatre, renovated in 2002, and the Bill Bordy Auditorium and Theater.

Emerson has one of the largest installations of film, video, and audio post-production facilities of any college in the country. Digital production labs contain workstations with multimedia production and digital video/audio applications. Emerson has been designated a New Media Center since 1995. Emerson also has numerous radio, television, and film outlets and facilities.

Clinical facilities include the Robbins Speech, Language and Hearing Center in the Department of Communication Sciences and Disorders. Graduate students work with patients and participate in a variety of Emerson-run clinics that are widely recognized in the field.

In addition, the Iwasaki Library houses more than 180,000 volumes and serial subscriptions, 10,000 microforms, 11,000 audiovisual materials, and 8,000 e-books. Students can access the resources of a dozen cooperating libraries through Emerson College's membership in the Fenway Library Consortium.

Costs

In the 2018–19 academic year, full-time undergraduate student tuition is $46,016, room and board (for a double room) is $17,690, and the student services fee is $836.

Financial Aid

Emerson offers a variety of financial assistance programs. Approximately 75 percent of Emerson's student body receives financial assistance to help pay for their education. Sources of support may include institutional gift aid, academic scholarships, need-based grants, loan programs, work-study, and payment plans. There are also merit scholarships available through the Office of Undergraduate Admission. All applicants are automatically reviewed for eligibility for these merit scholarships once they have submitted their application.

Faculty

With a student-faculty ratio of 13:1, students at Emerson College develop close relationships with remarkably talented and active instructors who are experts in their fields. Emerson's 479 full- and part-time faculty members are nationally recognized and award-winning authors, directors, researchers, producers, journalists, playwrights, actors, and more. The majority of the faculty has earned doctorates or the highest degree obtainable in their field.

Student Life

Emerson students are doers and learners, creating and collaborating even after class is over for the day. The college offers more than 80 student organizations and performance groups, student publications, and honor societies. Emerson also supports 14 NCAA Division III men's and women's athletic teams.

The College has four residence halls, three of which are newly renovated or brand new within the last eight years. The Little Building residence hall is undergoing a complete renovation and is slated to re-open in fall 2019. Students use the nearby Boston Common for relaxation and recreational activities such as tennis, softball, running, Quidditch, and ice-skating. The Field at Rotch Playground, located a mile from campus, serves as a practice and playing field while the Bobbi Brown and Steven Plofker Gym is the site for men's and women's basketball and volleyball games and other events.

Admission Requirements

Admission is competitive; each year, more than 12,900 applications are received for a class of approximately 870. Selection is based on academic promise as indicated by secondary school performance, recommendations, and writing competency. Emerson has a Test Optional admission policy. Students are welcome to submit SAT or ACT scores or may submit a test optional essay or major-related creative sample in their place. TOEFL, IELTS or other exams are required if English is not the first language. Emerson also considers personal qualities as seen in extracurricular activities, community involvement, and demonstrated leadership.

Application and Information

Emerson College accepts the Common Application and the Emerson Application. Students are required to complete all parts of their chosen application, including the Emerson-specific questions and writing supplement. There are additional requirements for students applying to Performing Arts programs, Comedic Arts, or Media Arts Production.

The deadline for fall admission for first-year students is January 15 (Early Action is November 1), and for transfer students, the priority deadline is March 15. The spring admission priority deadline is November 1 for first-year students and transfer students.

Emerson College Admissions
120 Boylston Street
Boston, Massachusetts 02116
United States
Phone: 617-824-8600
E-mail: admission@emerson.edu
Website: www.emerson.edu

ERSKINE COLLEGE
DUE WEST, SOUTH CAROLINA

 For more information, visit http://petersons.to/erskinecollege

The College

Erskine College has been preparing students to flourish in lives of learning, service, and leadership for more than 175 years. With its heritage of thoughtful scholarship, Christian commitment, and intentional community, Erskine offers a rich undergraduate experience. Founded by the Associate Reformed Presbyterian Church in 1839, it is the oldest four-year private Christian college in South Carolina and is accredited by the Southern Association of Colleges and Schools Commission on Colleges. Erskine provides an environment in which students can be challenged and inspired. Students work hard, think creatively and critically, and explore options across a variety of disciplines.

Erskine fields 15 intercollegiate teams in NCAA Division II as part of Conference Carolinas and offers intramural and recreational programs as well. Athletic facilities include a full court basketball gymnasium with an attached auxiliary gym and aerobics facility, racquetball courts, a rock climbing wall, a weight-training facility, baseball fields, softball fields, and two football-sized intramural activity fields. The Galloway gymnasium on campus houses a basketball arena along with volleyball and classroom facilities. Students have several dining options, including Moffatt Dining Hall, Snapper's Restaurant in the Watkins Student Center, and Erskine's own campus coffee shop, Java City.

Erskine is a residential campus offering more than 30 student organizations to complement the academic experience. Living on campus affords opportunities for fellowship and leadership through residence life, student government, and various student organizations, including Christian ministries, literary and honor societies, service clubs, and interest groups. Each residence hall provides fellowship opportunities, such as cookouts and movie nights. Erskine's small size means students can get to know just about everyone on campus, including their professors, who can become mentors and friends.

Location

Erskine College is located in Due West, a town of 1,200 residents located in historic Abbeville County, South Carolina, an area rich in colonial, Revolutionary War, and Civil War history. Erskine's 90-acre campus, with its tree-lined green spaces, gardens, and stately architecture, has been recognized as one of the 50 Most Beautiful Christian Colleges and Universities in the nation by Christian Universities Online.

The town and the college, with a number of antebellum buildings, are listed on the National Register of Historic Places. Erskine is located near lakes and recreational areas and within easy access to Interstate Routes 26 and 85 and the cities of Atlanta, Charlotte, Columbia, and Greenville. Due West is located about 30 minutes from the cities of Greenwood and Anderson, giving the town a calm and unplugged feeling. Greenville, an hour from Due West, is among the fastest growing cities in the country and is the site of many weekend activities, including AA Baseball games, as well as award-winning restaurants and a thriving downtown environment. Abbeville, with its quaint town square and historic playhouse, is only about 15 minutes from Due West.

Majors and Degrees

The College offers Bachelor of Arts (B.A.) and Bachelor of Science (B.S.) degrees. A B.A. candidate can choose from the following majors: American studies, Bible and religion, biology, chemistry, English, health science, history, mathematics, music, philosophy, political science, psychology, and social studies. A B.S. candidate can choose from the following majors: biology, business administration, chemistry, early childhood education, elementary education, health science, music education, physical education and coaching, psychology, special education, and sport management.

Students may choose from the following minors: Bible and religion, biology, business administration, chemistry, Christian education, Christian leadership, English, family studies, global studies, graphic design, health, healthcare management, history, information technology, mathematics, music, music studies, philosophy, physical education, physics, political science, psychology, secondary education, social entrepreneurship and innovation, theater, and visual art.

Erskine College maintains an engineering dual-degree program with Clemson University. Students in this program typically complete three years at Erskine and two to three years at Clemson, earning a B.S. degree in engineering from Clemson and a B.A. degree in biology, chemistry, or mathematics from Erskine.

Academic Programs

At Erskine, students are taught by professors, not graduate students, and the curriculum is based on the liberal arts tradition. Erskine also offers a number of pre-professional programs. More than 96 percent of Erskine's faculty members hold terminal degrees in their subject areas. Small class sizes, along with professors' efforts to promote mentoring relationships with students, help to spur Erskine students to achievement, enhance their academic growth, and prepare them for leadership. Students can work with faculty members to craft a course of study that suits their individual strengths and career interests.

Off-Campus Programs

Erskine offers opportunities for study abroad with the University of St. Andrews at St. Andrews in Scotland; with the OSAP program at Oxford University in England; with the University of Aix in Aix-en-Provence, France; with Tandem Escuela Internacional in Madrid, Spain; with the Universidad de Alicante in Alicante, Spain; and with the Universidad Veracruzana in Jalapa, Mexico. A student may choose to study abroad for either fall or spring semester or a full year.

Pre-professional externships at Erskine College are offered in several areas, including health-related fields (medicine, dentistry, medical technology, pharmacy, etc.), business, engineering, journalism, law and government, library science, ministry, social services, and veterinary medicine.

The college offers two summer semester terms in which students have the opportunity to travel with professors for course credit. In the past, students have traveled to Brazil, China, England, Germany, Lithuania, Scotland, and Spain. In the Department of Political Science, students are offered the chance to travel to the state capital of Columbia or to the nation's capital in Washington, D.C., where they meet with congressional and state representatives and form relationships for future experiences in government, nonprofits, and lobbying organizations.

Academic Facilities

All academic buildings on campus are wireless, and Erskine has developed innovative uses of technology to increase person-to-person communication and maximize student learning. Along with the successful use of technology, personal interaction that leads to lasting friendships and discovery within a community of learners continues as a primary focus on the Erskine campus.

Notable among Erskine's 11 academic buildings are the Bowie Arts Center, a 14,000-square-foot museum and gallery featuring an exhibit hall as well as a state-of-the-art classroom; the Daniel-Moultrie Science Center, a 46,000-square-foot facility featuring an auditorium, classrooms, state-of-the-art labs, a live animal room, and a greenhouse; the Moss Mathematics and Music Educational Facility, a 24,000-square-foot two-story building equipped with classrooms, computer labs, and state-of-the-art sound studios for vocal and instrumental performances; and Memorial Hall, which houses Erskine's musical performance theater and is directly connected to the Moss facility.

The climate-controlled McCain Library Department of Archives and Special Collections, located across from the McCain Library in Reid Hall and maintained by an archivist from the library staff, is used by both students and area historians. Reid Hall also houses the business department and contains a multimedia classroom.

Costs

For the 2018–19 academic year, Erskine's tuition is $36,150. Room and board charges are $11,350. Additional fees amount to approximately $1,000 annually.

Financial Aid

Financial aid is offered to a large percentage of Erskine's students through multiple endowed scholarships, grants, state aid, loans, and work-study assignments. Erskine offers merit scholarships to students that range from $7,500 to $14,000 based on high school academic performance. The school also accepts all applicable state aid programs from the state of South Carolina. Federal funds are available to students through the Federal Pell Grant, Federal work-study programs, Federal Supplemental Educational Opportunity Grants, and Federal Perkins Loan programs. Aid programs ranging up to $5,000 are also given to out-of-state students who may lack home state aid. Along with this, applicants can also apply for Erskine's Presidential Scholarship, an invitational academic competition that grants full scholarships (tuition, room, board, and fees) to two students per year. Students who apply for the Presidential Scholarship are also considered for the Solomon Award, which covers tuition for a four-year period.

Faculty

The Erskine full-time faculty numbers 40 men and women; 96 percent have earned the highest degree in their field. With an average class size of 20, a student-faculty ratio of 13:1, and private offices for all full-time faculty members, Erskine promotes a personal as well as an academic relationship between students and faculty members. All classroom instruction is done by faculty members and they are happy to assist and encourage students who wish to pursue undergraduate research through tutorials or summer research projects. These projects are carried out in an atmosphere free of competition from graduate students for books, laboratories, or professors' time. Erskine emphasizes advising and academic counseling for students throughout their four years.

Student Government

Erskine encourages students to get involved on campus. Positions of leadership are open to students of all class years in a variety of organizations. All students are represented by elected delegates to the Student Government Association's Student Senate and have formal representation at most college-wide committees involved in decision-making and policy formation.

Admission Requirements

Erskine College seeks students who are committed to serious academic study and critical thinking. Applicants are required to have completed at least 15 secondary school college preparatory units, 4 of which must be in English, 3 in mathematics, 3 in science, 3 in social studies, and 2 in a foreign language. Electives are also highly encouraged. Students applying to Erskine are required to submit scores from the SAT, ACT, or CLT for admission consideration. Students interested in the college's academic competition are encouraged to plan ahead and submit these scores before the month of November. Campus visits are strongly recommended; the admissions process is a personal one. Transfer students are accepted after submitting an application for admission and submitting a transcript from an accredited higher education institution showing at least 24 hours of course work completed at a 2.0 GPA. Out-of-state and international students are also encouraged to apply.

Application and Information

Erskine's application can be found online at http://know.erskine.edu. Students fill out a brief online inquiry form providing contact information and program interests. After this form is submitted, students will be directed to a personalized web page giving them more information about the college. On this page, students will find a link to the official application. Admission applications are reviewed and admissions decisions are made on a rolling basis beginning in August of the year prior to enrollment. The priority deadline for applications is May 1; all students who wish to be considered for academic merit scholarships should have a completed application on file in the Office of Undergraduate Admissions before this date. All students are encouraged to include Erskine (003432) on their FAFSA submission. Orientation programs for incoming first-year students take place in June and early July. Transfer student orientation programs are offered throughout the summer.

Robert J. Duran

Director of Admissions

Erskine College
P.O. Box 338
2 Washington Street
Due West, South Carolina 29639
Phone: 864-379-8838
E-mail: admissions@erskine.edu
Website: http://visit.erskine.edu

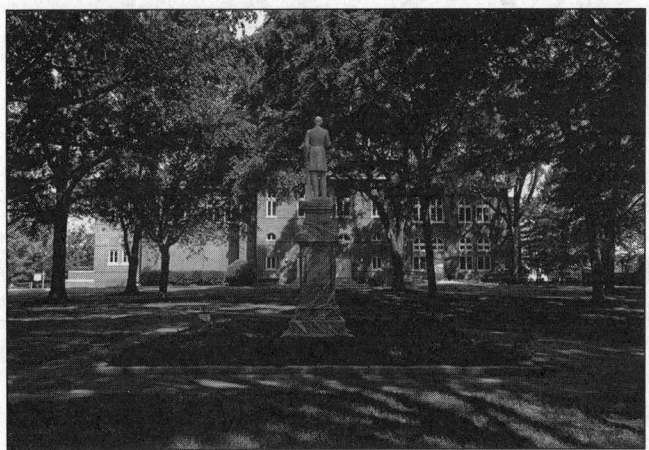

THE EVERGREEN STATE COLLEGE

OLYMPIA, WASHINGTON

 To learn more about this school, visit http://petersons.to/evergreenstate

The College

The Evergreen State College is a small, public liberal arts college located in Olympia, Washington, on a campus of forests and beaches. Evergreen's tradition is invention—and its learning model is a perfect fit for those who are inspired by the complexity of the ever-changing world, and excited to find and give the best of themselves.

Since opening its doors in 1971, Evergreen has established a national reputation for leadership in developing innovative, collaborative, team-taught academic programs. The college offers a vibrant undergraduate curriculum, three graduate programs, and public service centers that constitute a unique academic setting.

Evergreen has been a leader in environmental education from the beginning. In recent years, the school has stepped up its commitment to sustainability to reach beyond the classroom and even the campus—community partnerships for sustainability are integrated into programs through internship and outreach opportunities.

Evergreen values a student-centered learning environment, links between theory and practice, and a welcoming, multicultural community of faculty, students, and staff. Current enrollment is approximately 4,000.

Location

Evergreen is located in the heat of the Pacific Northwest, in Olympia, Washington. In one direction lies urban excitement. In another lies outdoor adventure. Evergreen students—known as "Greeners"—have easy access to oceans, mountains, rainforests, and some of America's hippest cities. Seattle and Portland are a short distance away, as is the Pacific Coast, Mount Rainier, skiing and snowboarding, state forests, nature preserves, and three national parks.

Olympia's diverse offerings include a farmers market and food co-op, the Olympia Film Society and Arts Walk, a rich music scene, the annual Procession of the Species event held on Earth Day, the state capital campus, and of course, a thriving coffee culture. Local parks provide trails, sports fields, beaches, a skate park, lakes, rivers, waterfalls, and woods.

Majors and Degrees

The Evergreen State College prepares creative minds for the way the world happens now. Like the world, Evergreen students focus instead of major, on layering disciplines into individual expressions of scholarship, and anticipating careers yet to be invented.

The college offers programs and courses in more than 60 fields of study, including: agriculture and food; anthropology; arts (dance, media, music, theater, visual); biology; botany; business and management; chemistry; communication; community studies; computer science; cultural and ethnic studies (African American, American, Asian, Hispanic/Mexicano, Latin American, Native American); earth science (geology/hydrology); ecology; economics; environmental studies; gender and Women's studies; geography; health; history; humanities; international studies; languages and linguistics (American Sign Language, Chinese, French, German, Japanese, Russian, Spanish); literature; marine science; mathematics; philosophy; physics; political economy and political science;pre-law; pre-medicine; psychology; social sciences; sociology; sustainability; writing; and zoology.

Academic Programs

At Evergreen, students experience a different way of learning. Like the world, everyone at Evergreen learns from each other, working in teams—from the science lab to the dorm room to the forests and beaches that surround them. Academic programs explore many sides of a theme or topic, and have fewer prerequisites. Narrative evaluations from faculty provide context and explanation, not simple solitary letters.

Students write an academic statement every year to review and connect common themes in their education each year as a road map they build along the way. This document does more than simply record academic achievements; it helps focus students' aspirations as they plot their unique path to a degree. Short essays help students to review, reflect upon, and connect common themes in their education; clarify academic goals so that they can get targeted support from faculty and academic advisers; plan their pathways and uncover the kinds of programs that meet their goals; and finally, to summarize what they have learned and done in their education in their own voice.

Most Evergreen classes, called programs, cover more than just one subject. Full-time programs combine subjects taught by several faculty members from different fields. A program connects these fields with an overarching theme, reflecting the interconnectedness of the real world.

Upper-level students can create their own programs—with the help of a faculty sponsor they set goals, and develop a syllabus as part of their individual learning contracts. They may also undertake research or internships. In addition, focused courses (2–6 credits) are available to complement their course of study. Students learn how to be an active, engaged citizen no matter which career they choose.

Ninety percent of Evergreen graduates find success in careers, service, or in grad schools across the globe within just one year after graduation. The school's three graduate programs—Master of Environmental Studies, Master of Public Administration, and Master in Teaching—ground students in values of service, community, social justice, and stewardship.

Academic Facilities

All Evergreen students can access top-tier equipment like nuclear magnetic resonance spectroscopes, 3-D printers, and studio cameras unlike other colleges that require upper-level experience or research clearance.

There are a variety of academic resources on campus, including the Center for Creative and Applied Media, sustainable agriculture lab building, organic farm and community gardens, Longhouse Education and Cultural Center, animation and design studio, ceramics studio, metal shop, wood shop, photography studios and darkrooms, and a living laboratory of 3,000 feet of waterfront property on the Puget Sound.

Costs

Evergreen's great education comes at a modest price. Greeners benefit from having the fastest time to degree completion among Washington's public four-year institutions. This means less in total costs for students. Those who borrow while attending Evergreen typically borrow below state and national averages (source: State of Washington Education Research and Data Center).

Estimated cost of attendance for the 2017–18 academic year included tuition ($6,678 for Washington residents and $24,138 for nonresidents); room and board, $9,681; books and supplies, $750; transportation, $1,155; and miscellaneous, $2,070; for a total of $20,334 (resident) or $37,794 (nonresident). The most current cost information is available at evergreen.edu/costs.

Financial Aid

Sixty-four percent of Greeners receive financial aid. The average award is $12,714. Financial aid counselors encourage all students to use the Free Application for Federal Student Aid (FAFSA) to apply for federal and state aid. Evergreen's priority deadline to receive complete and valid information from the federal processor is February 1. Evergreen's school code is 008155. Undocumented Washington resident students can apply through the Washington Application for State Financial Aid (WASFA). The priority deadline for the WASFA is also February 1.

Evergreen offers a variety of scholarships every year to new and continuing students. Some awards are based upon academic fields of study: the arts, computer studies, environmental studies, laboratory sciences and writing, for example. Students should review the scholarship application process and be prepared to submit their applications by the February 1 deadline.

Faculty

Evergreen's instructional faculty numbers 229, with 163 of those being full time. Of those, 78.2 percent have a Ph.D. or terminal degree in their field. The undergraduate student-to-faculty ratio is 21:1.

Campus Culture

The Evergreen experience is unique. The campus community is openhearted, real, and everyone is always learning from each other. Whether it's through athletics, recreation, or the arts, Greeners do things with an open mind and sense of community. Through the Geoduck Student Union, students are empowered to get involved in positive social and political change, shape campus culture, and make college life better, year after year.

When it comes to campus housing, students can choose what's right for their lifestyle. Whether students prefer same-gender living arrangements or vegan eating, Evergreen can accommodate most lifestyle pursuits. First-year students usually live in the residence halls. Apartments and modular housing become available after that.

Campus dining offers the community opportunities to spend quality time together. The Greenery, The Marketplace, The Flaming Eggplant, and other venues are ready to serve the dining and dietary needs of students.

Admission Requirements

Applicants must be high school graduates who have met basic college-preparatory standards (4 credits English, 3 credits mathematics, 3 credits social studies, 2 credits of a single foreign language, and 2 credits of science) and have taken challenging

electives beyond that. Grade point average and test scores will be used in the comprehensive admission review process. The average GPA for freshmen admitted in 2017 was 3.03. The average SAT composite (critical reading and math) score was 1130 and the average ACT composite test score was 24. Good standing in any college-level work attempted while in high school or after high school graduation is also required. The quality of the college work will be taken into consideration as well.

Requirements for home-school students, GED applicants, applicants with a high school proficiency exam, or who are 25 or older can be found on the college's website, http://www.evergreen.edu/admissions.

Application and Information

The priority admission application deadline is February 1 for fall quarter, October 1 for winter quarter, and December 1 for spring quarter. In most cases, admission decision letters are sent within 10 working days after the application file is complete and has been reviewed by the Admissions Committee. Potential students may apply online through the college's website. The application fee is $50; applicants may contact the office of admission about fee waivers.

Evergreen accepts e-transcripts from other schools and colleges that are registered members with Docufide, National Student Clearinghouse, Naviance, Parchment, and Scrip-Safe International. Official transcripts sent through the mail must arrive in a sealed envelope from the issuing school/college registrar. ACT or SAT scores for incoming freshmen should be sent by the testing agency. Evergreen's ACT school code is 4457 and the SAT school code is 4292.

For more information, students should contact:

The Evergreen State College
Office of Admissions
2700 Evergreen Parkway NW
Olympia, Washington 98505
Phone: 360-867-6170
Fax: 360-867-5114
E-mail: admissions@evergreen.edu
Website: http://evergreen.edu

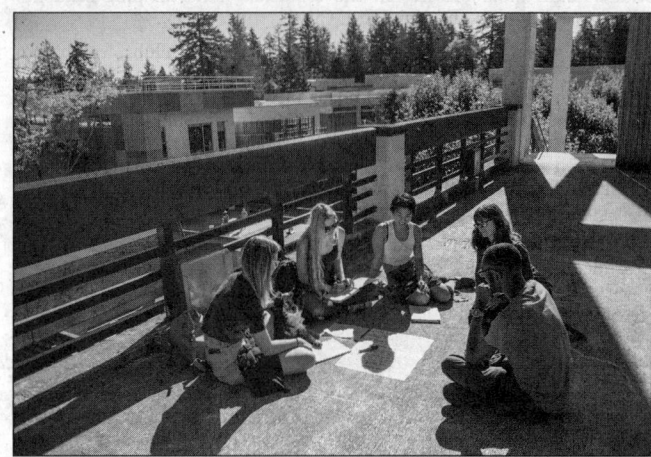

FASHION INSTITUTE OF TECHNOLOGY
State University of New York
NEW YORK, NEW YORK

 To read more about this school, visit http://petersons.to/fit

The College

The Fashion Institute of Technology, a college of the State University of New York, has been a leader in career education in art, design, business, and technology for nearly 75 years. FIT infuses its 47 majors with a comprehensive liberal arts education, providing a singular blend of practical experience and a pioneering curriculum that prepares students for success and leadership in the competitive global marketplace. FIT offers a range of innovative programs that are affordable and relevant to today's rapidly changing industries. Internationally renowned, FIT draws on its New York City location to provide a vibrant, creative community in which to learn. The schools of Art and Design, Business and Technology, and Liberal Arts offer Associate in Applied Science (A.A.S.), Bachelor of Fine Arts (B.F.A.), and Bachelor of Science (B.S.) degrees. The School of Graduate Studies offers Master of Arts (M.A.), Master of Fine Arts (M.F.A.), and Master of Professional Studies (M.P.S.) degrees. The college is accredited by the Middle States Commission on Higher Education, the National Association of Schools of Art and Design, and the Council for Interior Design Accreditation. FIT serves approximately 9,000 students from the greater metropolitan area, New York State, across the country, and around the world, providing full- and part-time study, evening/weekend degree programs, noncredit, certificate, and online courses.

FIT's faculty members bring high-level industry experience to the classroom, working as corporate executives, entrepreneurs, consultants, designers, artists, and authors. Both practitioners and scholars, they connect students with real-world practice in their fields, fostering collaboration, innovation, and a global perspective. Academic departments consult with industry leaders to ensure that the curriculum and classroom technology remain current with evolving professional practices.

FIT offers a complete college experience, with a vibrant campus life. Four residence halls house 2,300 students. Residential counselors and student staff members live in the residence halls, helping students adjust to college life and New York City.

The college hosts sixty student organizations and clubs, related to academics, athletics, special interests, and publications, including a campus newspaper, a fashion and beauty magazine, and an art and literary magazine. Intercollegiate teams and individual sports include cross-country, track and field, tennis, women's soccer, swimming and diving, and women's volleyball. Students take part in an array of fitness classes, including aerobics, dance, spin, and yoga, and they can work out in a 5,000 square-foot fitness center.

The David Dubinsky Student Center houses a dining hall and Starbucks café, game room, radio station, student-run boutique, student government and club offices, dance studio, health services, disability services, and counseling center.

Location

Occupying an entire block in Manhattan's Chelsea neighborhood, FIT's campus offers a vibrant urban experience. This location, at the heart of the fashion, advertising, visual arts, design, business, and communications industries, provides students unparalleled exposure to their fields through internships, field trips, mentorships, and industry-sponsored research and competitions. A wide range of cultural resources and entertainment options—from dining to museums to theater—are available within walking distance from campus, which is also convenient to subway and bus lines and major rail and bus transportation hubs.

Majors and Degrees

FIT offers fifteen Associate in Applied Science (A.A.S.) and twenty-six baccalaureate programs. All first-time students complete a two-year A.A.S. program in their major area of study and then typically continue in a related Bachelor of Fine Arts (B.F.A.) or Bachelor of Science (B.S.) program. Some students choose to begin their careers after earning the A.A.S., which qualifies them for entry-level positions in their chosen

field. All programs include a required liberal arts component. In addition, FIT offers a wide variety of minors that students may elect to complete.

The School of Art and Design offers ten A.A.S. and fourteen B.F.A. programs and two minors; the Jay and Patty Baker School of Business and Technology offers four A.A.S. and ten B.S. programs and one minor; and the School of Liberal Arts offers one A.A.S., two B.S. programs, and twenty-two minors. There is one interdisciplinary minor shared by all three undergraduate schools.

The fifteen A.A.S. programs, all of which provide the foundation for one or more corresponding baccalaureate-level programs, are accessories design*, advertising and marketing communications*, communication design foundation*, fashion design*, fashion business management* (with an online option), film and media, fine arts, illustration, interior design, jewelry design, menswear, photography and related media, production management: fashion and related industries, textile development and marketing*, and textile/surface design*. Programs with an * are also available as a one-year option for students with transfer credits, and the one-year fashion business management A.A.S. program is offered fully online.

The fourteen B.F.A. programs are accessories design, advertising design, computer animation and interactive media, fabric styling, fashion design (specializations in children's wear, intimate apparel, knitwear, special occasion, and sportswear), fine arts, graphic design, illustration, interior design, packaging design, photography and related media, textile/surface design, toy design, and visual presentation and exhibition design.

The twelve B.S. programs are advertising and marketing communications, art history and museum professions, cosmetics and fragrance marketing, direct and interactive marketing, entrepreneurship for the fashion and design industries, fashion business management, film and media, home products development, international trade and marketing for the fashion industries, production management: fashion and related industries, technical design, and textile development and marketing.

Nine of the degree programs are also available through evening/weekend study: advertising and marketing communications (A.A.S. and B.S.), communication design foundation (A.A.S.), fashion design (A.A.S.), fashion business management (A.A.S. and B.S.), graphic design (B.F.A.), illustration (B.F.A.), and international trade and marketing for the fashion industries (B.S.). The international trade and marketing program (B.S.) and the fashion business management program (A.A.S. only) are also available fully online.

Academic Programs

FIT's liberal arts courses hone critical thinking and communication skills, foster understanding of world cultures, and encourage students to become global citizens. Liberal arts courses are a key component of every major, and are adapted to the needs of each program. FIT's curriculum offers a range of subject-based and interdisciplinary minors that let students expand and deepen their major studies or explore additional interests. Liberal Arts minors include communication studies, dance, film and media, economics, international politics, Latin American studies, Mandarin Chinese, and women and gender studies; Art and Design minors are creative technology and design thinking; the Business and Technology minor is international trade and marketing; the ethics and sustainability minor is offered jointly through all three schools.

The Career and Internship Center offers lifetime placement services to graduates. Internships are a required element of many programs and are available to all students. Nearly one-third of FIT student interns are offered employment on completion of their internships.

The Presidential Scholars honors program, available to academically exceptional students in all disciplines, offers special liberal arts courses, projects, colloquiums, extracurricular activities, and off-campus visits designed to broaden horizons and stimulate discourse. Presidential

Scholars are also awarded priority course registration, an annual merit stipend and guaranteed access to housing in one of FIT's residence halls.

Precollege programs (fitnyc.edu/precollege) are available to middle and high school students during the fall, spring, and summer. More than 100 courses provide the chance to learn in an innovative environment, to develop art and design portfolios, to explore the business and technological sides of a wide range of creative careers, and to discover natural talents and abilities.

The Center for Continuing and Professional Studies (fitnyc.edu/ccps) provides courses for students and working professionals to pursue a certificate or further their knowledge in a particular area.

International Programs

FIT has two locations in Italy—one in Milan, one in Florence—and a third in South Korea, where students study fashion design or fashion business management and gain firsthand experience in the dynamics of international fashion. The study-abroad experience allows students to immerse themselves in diverse cultures and prepares them to live and work in a global community. Australia, China, England, France, and Mexico are some of the other countries where FIT offers study-abroad courses. Students can study abroad during the winter or summer sessions, or for a semester or a full academic year.

Academic Facilities

FIT provides its students with an urban campus of classrooms, laboratories, and studios that reflect the most advanced educational and professional practices. The Fred P. Pomerantz Art and Design Center houses studios, a printmaking room, display and exhibition design rooms, a model-making workshop, and a graphics printing service bureau. The Peter G. Scotese Computer-Aided Design and Communications Center allows students to explore the latest advancements in technology and their integration in design, photography, and computer graphics and animation. The fragrance studio, a professionally equipped fragrance development laboratory, is the only one of its kind on a U.S. college campus. Cutting and sewing laboratories offer the most advanced design and cutting machinery among educational facilities in the United States. The lighting laboratory, an educational and professional development facility, features more than 400 commercially available lighting fixtures. Other college facilities include a broadcasting studio, knitting and weaving labs, a multimedia foreign language laboratory, forty-six computer labs, and several additional labs with computers reserved for students in specific programs.

The Museum at FIT is New York City's only museum dedicated to fashion. Students, designers, and historians use it for research and inspiration. The museum, which is accredited by the American Alliance of Museums, operates year-round, and its exhibitions are free and open to the public. The Gladys Marcus Library provides more than 300,000 volumes of print, nonprint, and electronic materials. Students also have access to the library's Special Collections, a highly specialized repository of primary source research materials related to the fields of fashion and design. The library also offers specialized resources, such as clipping files, fashion and trend forecasting services, and sketch collections.

Costs

For 2017–18, the associate-level tuition per semester was $2,345 for in-state residents and $7,035 for nonresidents. Baccalaureate-level tuition per semester was $3,335 for in-state residents and $10,096 for nonresidents. Undergraduate housing costs ranged from $5,887 to $7,074 per semester for traditional residence hall accommodations with mandatory meal plan and from $6,299 to $10,495 for apartment-style accommodations. Meal plans varied from $1,915 to $2,451 per semester. Textbook costs and other nominal fees, such as locker rental or laboratory use, vary per program. Costs are subject to change.

Financial Aid

FIT attempts to remove financial barriers to college entrance by providing scholarships, grants, loans, and work-study employment for students in financial need. Over two-thirds of full-time, matriculated undergraduate students who complete the Free Application for Federal Student Aid (FAFSA) process receive some type of assistance through loans and/or grants. The college directly administers its own institutional grants and scholarships, which are provided by the FIT Foundation.

College-administered federal funding includes Federal Pell Grants, Federal Perkins Loans, Federal Supplemental Educational Opportunity Grants, Federal Work-Study, and Federal Family Educational Loans, which include student and parent loans. New York State residents who meet state guidelines for eligibility may also receive Tuition Assistance Program (TAP) and/or Educational Opportunity Program (EOP) grants.

Financial aid applicants must file the FAFSA. Students are also encouraged to apply for all available outside sources of aid. Additional documentation may be requested by the Financial Aid Services office. The FAFSA should be completed prior to February 15 for fall applicants or prior to November 1 for spring applicants.

Faculty

FIT's faculty is drawn from top professionals who bring their industry experience to the classroom and introduce students to the real-world opportunities and challenges of their disciplines through field trips, guest lectures, and sponsored competitions. Student-instructor interaction is encouraged, with no class larger than 25 and more often smaller. Courses are structured to foster participation, independent thinking, and self-expression.

Student Government

The FIT Student Government Association gives all students the privileges and responsibilities of citizens in a self-governing college community. Many faculty committees include student representatives, and the president of the student government sits on FIT's Board of Trustees.

Admission Requirements

Applicants for undergraduate admission must be either candidates for or recipients of a high school diploma or a General Educational Development (GED) certificate. Admission is based on strength and performance in college-preparatory course work and the student essay. A portfolio evaluation is required for art and design majors. Specific portfolio requirements are explained on FIT's website. SAT and ACT scores are required for placement in math and English classes and for students applying to the Presidential Scholars honors program. International applicants whose primary language of instruction was not English must submit scores from either the TOEFL, IELTS, or PTE examinations.

Transfer applicants must submit official transcripts from all post-secondary institutions attended for both admission and credit evaluation. Transfers students may qualify for the one-year A.A.S. option if they hold a baccalaureate degree from an accredited college or if they have a minimum of 30 transferable credits from an accredited college, including 24 credits that are equivalent to FIT's liberal arts requirements.

Students seeking admission to a B.F.A. or B.S. program must hold an A.A.S. degree from FIT or an equivalent degree from an accredited college. They must also meet the appropriate prerequisites for the specific major and must have completed FIT's liberal arts requirements. Further requirements may include an individual interview with a department committee, review of academic standing, and a portfolio review (for applicants to B.F.A. programs). Any student who applies for transfer to FIT from a four-year program must have completed a minimum of 60 credits, including the requisite art or technical courses and the liberal arts requirements.

Application and Information

Students interested in FIT's undergraduate programs are encouraged to attend an information session and take a student-led tour of the campus. The visit schedule is available online at fitnyc.edu/visitfit. A virtual tour of the campus can be found online at fitnyc.edu/virtualtour. Interested candidates may apply online at fitnyc.edu/admissions.

For more information, students should contact:

Undergraduate Admissions
Fashion Institute of Technology
227 West 27th Street, Room C139
New York, NY 10001-5992
Phone: 212-217-3760
E-mail: fitinfo@fitnyc.edu
Website: fitnyc.edu/admissions
facebook.com/FashionInstituteofTechnology
instagram.com/fitnyc
twitter.com/fit

FLORIDA SOUTHERN COLLEGE

LAKELAND, FLORIDA

 To read more about this school, visit http://petersons.to/floridasoutherncollege

The College

The oldest private college in the state, Florida Southern College (FSC) was chartered in 1883 and settled on the shores of the spectacular Lake Hollingsworth in Lakeland in 1922.

Today, Florida Southern is a nationally ranked residential, coeducational, and comprehensive college recognized for its commitment to providing engaged learning experiences to its students. Florida Southern's 2,500 undergraduate students represent nearly every state and fifty countries. Students choose Florida Southern because of its national reputation for dynamic, hands-on learning in an atmosphere that is friendly and personal.

An essential part of a Florida Southern education is allowing students to experience the world beyond the classroom. Florida Southern guarantees each student an internship and study abroad experience, along with providing ample opportunities to conduct lab and field research, become involved in community service, and perform on stage. Florida Southern also guarantees its students will graduate in four years.

Members of the community take great pride in the beautiful campus, a historic landmark and home to the world's largest single-site collection of buildings designed by renowned architect Frank Lloyd Wright.

As a residential community, Florida Southern provides its students with a wide range of housing options, including all-female and all-male halls, coed halls, suite-style living arrangements, and off-campus apartments. The College also dedicates spaces to various majors, honors students, and fraternity and sorority life. Accommodations are well equipped and feature stunning views of the lake, contemporary student lounges, modern kitchens and bathrooms, and wireless Internet access.

Athletic facilities are first rate. The George Jenkins Field House includes a three-court gymnasium, a weight room, and an athletic training room. The College recently completed a multimillion-dollar renovation to the Barnett Athletic Complex which provides state-of-the-art facilities for softball, soccer, and lacrosse. The popular Nina B. Hollis Wellness Center, the hub of student life, offers a fully equipped fitness center, an aerobics/dance studio, an intramural gymnasium, racquetball courts, and a competition-sized swimming pool. Directly across from the Wellness Center is Lake Hollingsworth, which offers kayaks, paddleboards, and water-skiing.

The student body is extremely involved. With more than 100 clubs, Florida Southern offers countless ways for students to pursue their interests while making lasting connections. Florida Southern is also home to 14 national fraternities and sororities. FSC's Moccasins are members of NCAA Division II. The 20 varsity programs, including men's and women's lacrosse teams, beach volleyball, a nationally ranked water-skiing team, and equestrian club, have won 30 national championship titles. The College also became the first school in Florida to join the National Association of Collegiate Esports (NACE), providing students opportunities to participate in competitive college video gaming. Other popular student activities are intramural sports, drama and music groups, publications, and organizations related to academic and political, religious, and social interests. A high percentage of students are involved in volunteer programs in the community, state, and internationally.

Location

Florida Southern's campus consists of approximately 113 acres on the shore of Lake Hollingsworth in Lakeland, Florida, a dynamic suburban community of about 120,000 residents in the heart of Florida's High Tech Corridor. The campus is within walking distance of Lakeland's historic downtown district. Lakeland is 40 miles east of Tampa and 50 miles west of Orlando, putting it within an hour's drive of the state's major recreational attractions, including Walt Disney World and award-winning beaches. The College is also ideally situated for internships and job opportunities with leading corporations that tap into one of the largest markets in the United States. Students enjoy Festival of Fine Arts series performances in music, dance, and drama, distinguished speakers, and business symposiums. The local Lakeland Center also offers many cultural and entertainment opportunities.

Majors and Degrees

Florida Southern College offers Bachelor of Arts, Bachelor of Fine Arts, Bachelor of Music, Bachelor of Music Education, Bachelor of Science, and Bachelor of Science in Nursing degrees in more than fifty majors including accounting, art (art education, art history, graphic design, and

studio art), biochemistry and molecular biology, biology, biotechnology, business administration (career tracks in finance, international business, management, and marketing), business and free enterprise, chemistry, citrus, communication (advertising and public relations, digital media, film studies, multimedia journalism, interpersonal and organizational communication, political communication, and sports communication), computer science, criminology, dance, economics and finance, education (elementary, music, and secondary), English, exercise science, history, healthcare administration, humanities, marine biology, mathematics, music (music education, music management, and music performance), nursing, philosophy, political economy, political science, psychology, religion, social science, Spanish, sports management, theater arts (musical theater, theater performance, and technical theater/design), and youth ministry.

Outstanding pre-professional programs are offered in dentistry, engineering, law, medicine, occupational therapy, optometry, pharmacy, physical therapy, physician assistant, theology, and veterinary medicine. Within a year of graduation, 97 percent of students report having achieved their post-baccalaureate degree goals by securing gainful employment or beginning an advanced degree program. Florida Southern's pre-law program boasts a 100 percent acceptance rate into law school, with similar results for pre-med students. One-hundred percent of accounting majors pass the CPA exam and go on to find jobs. The School of Education and School of Health Sciences boast exceptional first-time pass rates on licensure exams, as well as 100 percent placement rates for education and nursing majors.

FSC's Honors program provides special opportunities for a select group of entering first-year students to explore topics of common interest in an integrated and interdisciplinary fashion.

Academic Programs

Florida Southern's rigorous degree programs require the satisfactory completion of a minimum of 124 semester hours with a minimum grade point average of 2.0. Students and professors work together in discussion-based classes featuring debate, collaborative projects, and other forms of engaged learning. The College operates on the semester system, with two 15-week semesters, and summer sessions. The average course load is 16 hours per semester. Along with coursework in their major, students are required to complete a general education curriculum designed to help develop knowledge, communication, and critical thinking skills, as well as attitudes for lifelong success.

As part of FSC's engaged learning model, students work collaboratively with faculty on research, fieldwork, and service projects. For example, business students have established strategic plans and operational reports for corporate and nonprofit organizations. Nursing students have delivered babies in Tanzania, and chemistry students have collaborated with faculty members to become published in national academic journals, such as *The Journal of Physical Chemistry*. Fine arts students have performed alongside talented faculty and visiting performers. Regardless of their course of study, 100 percent of Florida Southern students graduate with the real-world experience employers seek.

The FSC experience is career focused from day one. The College's career counselors help students explore their strengths and provide continual evaluation of career options with personalized guidance on resume building, interviewing, and landing the ideal first post-college job.

Off-campus Programs

Entering first-year students are guaranteed a travel-study opportunity during their junior or senior year at Florida Southern. Students have traveled to Africa, the Caribbean, China, Costa Rica, England, France, Italy, Mexico, Washington, D.C., and other exciting destinations.

Florida Southern College is the only private institution of higher education in the state to affiliate with The Washington Center (TWC), a highly regarded, nonpartisan internship provider with international scope. Through this partnership, FSC students have access to prestigious and valuable field experiences. Programs include tailored academic seminars and internships with governmental, international, corporate, and nonprofit organizations.

Academic Facilities

The FSC campus combines beautiful landscape with modern buildings designed by world-famous architects.

The campus's newest addition is the Sharon and Jim France Admissions Center. The 18,800-square-foot building overlooking Lake Hollingsworth houses the Department of Enrollment Management and provides space to welcome prospective students and their families from across the world. Adjacent to the France Center stands the 40,000-square-foot Becker Business Building, designed by renowned architect Robert A. M. Stern. This premiere business education center features high-tech classrooms equipped with the latest educational technology. It also houses a simulated trading floor that functions as a laboratory in which students learn firsthand about investment analysis and trading strategies. The technologically advanced Joe K. and Alberta Blanton Nursing Building, home to the College's growing School of Nursing, features patient simulators in the state-of-the art treatment simulation laboratory. The Dr. Marcene H. and Robert E. Christoverson Humanities Building comprises contemporary classrooms along with language labs and the film studies center. The recently renovated Jack Berry Citrus building includes new collaboration spaces and modern computing facilities for computer science students. Frank Lloyd Wright's Polk Science Building is home to FSC's natural science and pre-medical programs and is outfitted with a wide range of cutting-edge instrumentation, such as a nuclear magnetic resonance spectrometer, the preeminent device in determining the structure of chemical compounds. The building also features the world's only Wright-designed planetarium.

The Marshall and Vera Lea Rinker Technology Center is the nucleus for learning on campus. It houses the College's main computer lab, classrooms, and small group study areas and provides students with the latest technologies.

An integral part of the intellectual life of the College, FSC's E. T. Roux Library provides access to a rich collection of materials, including print and digital books; periodicals; electronic databases; a media collection that includes CDs, DVDs, and CD-ROMs; a substantial microforms collection; and seating for almost 500 students. The Library is also home to TûTû's Cyber Café, a comfortable venue for club meetings as well as late-night study groups. Adjacent is the Sarah D. and L. Kirk McKay, Jr., Archives Center that houses the archival materials of the Florida Conference of the United Methodist Church, the Center for Florida History collection, the Florida Citrus Archives, along with the College's collection of Frank Lloyd Wright memorabilia.

The campus also boasts a fine arts complex that includes Branscomb Memorial Auditorium (seating 1,800 and nationally known for its perfect acoustics), the Marjorie M. McKinley Music Building, the Melvin Art Gallery, and the Loca Lee Buckner Theater.

Florida Southern is also home to a preschool lab and the Roberts Academy, the first transitional school for children with dyslexia in the state of Florida, each providing an opportunity for students majoring in elementary education to observe and teach.

Costs

The comprehensive cost for 2018–19 is $47,998 per year ($36,348 for tuition and standard fees and $11,650 for room and board). FSC estimates that $1,150 is adequate for books and supplies, and $1,500 should cover personal expenses, exclusive of travel to and from home.

Financial Aid

Consistently rated as a best value, 100 percent of all FSC students receive financial assistance. Each year, Florida Southern offers more than $45 million in college aid on the basis of academic merit; talent in athletics (baseball, basketball, beach volleyball, cross-country, golf, soccer, softball, swimming, tennis, volleyball, or lacrosse), fine arts, theater, leadership, or community service; or student need. The College's most talented applicants are invited to apply for several of the College's Prestige Scholarships, which cover up to the full cost of tuition and fees, as well as additional stipends for study abroad.

Florida Southern understands that everyone's financial situation is different and offers students assistance in meeting their educational expenses through scholarships, grants, loans, and campus employment. To demonstrate need, an applicant is required to file the Free Application for Federal Student Aid (FAFSA). Applicants for aid must reapply each year. Florida Southern participates in the William D. Ford Federal Direct Loan, Federal Perkins Loan, Federal Supplemental Educational Opportunity Grant, and Federal Work-Study college-based programs. All applicants are expected to apply for any entitlement grant for which they are eligible, such as a Federal Pell Grant and, for Florida residents, the Florida Student Assistance Grant. To be considered for these aid programs, a completed FAFSA must be filed; the priority-filing deadline is March 1.

Faculty

FSC faculty members are more than teachers—they also serve as advisors, mentors, and true partners in a student's learning. The student-faculty ratio is 15:1 and 80 percent of Florida Southern's faculty members have doctoral or other terminal degrees. Not only are they top scholars in their fields, but they are also devoted to providing students with personalized attention and a truly outstanding education. FSC professors are selected for their teaching abilities and their ability to relate to the needs and concerns of their students.

Admission Requirements

Florida Southern looks for two things in applicants: performance and promise. The majority of students who have been accepted have a weighted GPA of 3.7 or better in college-preparatory courses (including four courses in English, three in mathematics, and the balance divided among science, foreign language, and social science), and have earned an average SAT score of 1190 (combined reading and math scores) or a composite score of 26 on the ACT. All applicants must graduate from an accredited high school.

The Admissions Office is committed to reviewing individual applicants on their own merits based on the level of challenge attempted, patterns of grades over time, recommendations from references, and an applicant's own assessment of the learning environment best suited to his or her needs. Evidence of leadership and community service also are typical attributes of a successful applicant. Applicants are encouraged to visit campus and meet with an Admissions Counselor. (Qualified high school juniors may apply for early admission if they have the recommendation of their secondary school and have had a personal interview with the Director of Admissions.)

Florida Southern welcomes applications from students resuming their education and from older students who have delayed their entrance into college. The College typically enrolls 100 transfer students annually. Transfer applicants should have a minimum 2.5 grade point average and be eligible to return to or be graduates of their former institutions. Transfer students with fewer than 25 semester hours must submit high school transcripts and standardized test scores. Applicants who hold Associate of Arts degrees from regionally accredited two-year institutions are typically granted junior standing. All applicants are encouraged to interview (an interview may be required for some candidates).

Credit by examination is awarded on the basis of successful scores on Advanced Placement tests, the International Baccalaureate (I.B.), Advanced International Certificate of Education (AICE), and College-Level Examination Program (CLEP) tests.

Application and Information

An application is considered by the Admissions Committee when it has been received with required test scores, references, and transcripts from each school attended. Because all students are required to live on campus unless they are seniors, married, or living with their parents, early application is desirable to ensure that housing is available. The freshman application priority date is March 1. The deadline for early decision applicants is November 1.

For more information about Florida Southern College, prospective students should contact:

Office of Admissions
Florida Southern College
111 Lake Hollingsworth Drive
Lakeland, Florida 33801-5698
Phone: 800-274-4131 (toll-free)
E-mail: fscadm@flsouthern.edu
Website: http://www.flsouthern.edu

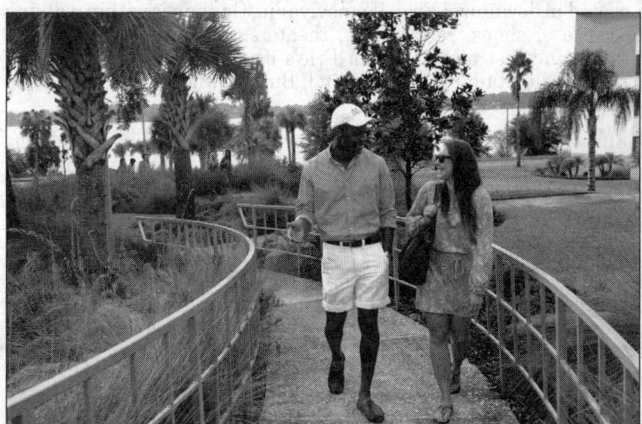

Signature opportunities, combined with our devoted faculty and stunning central Florida campus, create a college experience unlike any other.

GANNON UNIVERSITY

ERIE, PENNSYLVANIA

 To read more about this school, visit http://petersons.to/gannonuniversity

Believe in the possibilities.

The University

Gannon University is a place where lives are transformed, lifelong friendships made, and futures forged, a place where possibilities are discovered and become reality.

A Catholic, diocesan university founded in 1925, Gannon is more than a brick-and-mortar institution. It is a close-knit family of dedicated faculty, staff, and students inspired to solve problems, meet challenges, and make a difference in the process. It is a family that values faith, leadership, inclusiveness, and social responsibility—and puts those values into action locally and across the world.

Gannon's expert faculty and staff prepare students to be global citizens and leaders through innovative programs that are grounded in the liberal arts, sciences, and professional specializations and complemented by unique research, internship, and travel-abroad opportunities. Students don't have to imagine themselves interning at a Fortune 500 company, building an instrument for a NASA-funded project, or being immersed in the culture and history of Italy or Thailand or Spain. It happens at Gannon every day.

Gannon is consistently recognized by *U.S. News & World Report*; the 2018 edition of *America's Best Colleges* honored Gannon as one of the top 10 "Best Value Schools" among regional universities in the north. Gannon also earned national recognition as a 2017–18 Catholic College of Distinction, with special recognition of its nursing, business, engineering, and education programs.

But school pride doesn't end with academics. The entire Gannon community rallies around the Golden Knights and Lady Knights who excel in NCAA Division II athletics. Student-athletes can take their pick of 20 scholarship-granting varsity sports and year-round intramural and club sports. The campus includes the Recreation and Wellness Center, which recently underwent an expansion project that included a complete interior renovation, new cardio equipment, new locker rooms, and the addition of a 51,300 square-foot, indoor fieldhouse that features an 80-yard practice facility open to all students.

Students looking for a different kind of team can participate in service learning projects, or join any of more than 130 student clubs and organizations that offer a chance to bond with new friends over shared interests—two of the many ways Gannon students make memories that last a lifetime.

Location

Located in downtown Erie, Pennsylvania, Gannon is within walking distance of shops, restaurants, theaters, and professional sports venues and just minutes from Erie's bayfront and the beaches of Presque Isle State Park. Cleveland, Buffalo, and Pittsburgh all are within a two-hour drive.

Gannon's residence halls, apartments, academic buildings, administrative offices, and chapel are centered around the Waldron Campus Center—the heart of Gannon's campus—where members of the University's community meet, dine, study, and socialize. All campus housing is within three blocks of the cafeteria, Recreation and Wellness Center, library, and classrooms, creating a special, close-knit atmosphere in an urban setting. Students live and work near many of the businesses, organizations, and government agencies that are active partners in providing hands-on learning opportunities, including internships and service-learning experiences.

Majors and Degrees

The challenge at Gannon is not a lack of career paths—it's which one to choose. Students have their pick of more than 100 undergraduate, graduate, and online academic programs, all taught by faculty members who are experts in their field.

The College of Humanities, Education and Social Sciences offers programs in advertising communication, criminal justice, digital media communication, English, foreign language and international studies, foreign language and literature, history, interdisciplinary studies, journalism communications, legal studies, mortuary science, performance for media and stage, philosophy, political science, prelaw, a 3+3 prelaw program that includes early admission to Duquesne University, psychology, public relations, public service and global affairs, social work, theatre and communication arts, theatre technologies and design, or theology.

Future educators can chooese from several programs in the School of Education including early childhood education PreK–4, early childhood education PreK–4/special education PreK–8, middle level education 4–8 and middle level education 4–8/special education PreK–8, and secondary education (in biology, English, mathematics and social studies).

The Morosky College of Health Professions and Sciences offers the following degrees: athletic training (master's), medical laboratory science, nursing, nutrition and human performance, occupational therapy (five-year direct-entry master's and a doctorate offered at the Ruskin, Florida campus), physical therapy (direct-entry doctorate), physician assistant (five-year direct-entry master's), public health, radiologic sciences, respiratory care, sport and exercise science, and undecided health science.

Degrees are also offered in biochemistry, biology, chemical engineering (cooperative program), chemistry, forensic science, freshwater and marine biology, mathematics and science. Students who wish to enter chiropractic, dental, medical, optometry, pharmacy, podiatry, or veterinary school can choose from among 11 preprofessional programs.

The College of Engineering and Business offers degrees in biomedical engineering, computer science, electrical engineering (including a five-year co-op program), environmental engineering, industrial engineering, information systems, mechanical engineering (including a five-year co-op program), software engineering, and a dual-degree program in partnership with Esslingen University of Applied Sciences in which students earn bachelor's degrees in software engineering or computer science as well as software technology

Programs in the Dahlkemper School of Business include accounting, economics, entrepreneurship, finance, healthcare management, international management, management, management information systems, marketing, risk management and insurance, sport management and marketing, and supply chain management.

Academic Programs

Gannon's academic calendar consists of two full semesters running from August to December and from January to May, with optional summer classes. Basic graduation requirements for bachelor's degree candidates are 128 credit hours, including completion of requirements for the major and the liberal studies program. Associate degree students must complete 60 to 68 credit hours, depending on the program.

Academic Facilities

Nash Library, the hub of academic life at Gannon, reopened in 2017, following a complete exterior and interior renovation of the 82,000 square-foot building. The transformed library features new student study spaces, group collaboration spaces, the University's Writing and Research and S.T.E.M. centers, a full-service information technology help desk, new spaces for the university's archives and special collections, a reading room and a coffeehouse. The renovation follows the recent reopening of Beyer Hall after a 40,000 square-foot expansion project that created a collaborative space where students from around the world come together to learn, participate in campus life and organizations, and discover ways to engage the world.

Also new this year is the Donald M. and Judith C. Alstadt Environmental Center, waterfront property on 3.57 acres at the edge of the Allegheny National Forest that will be used by Gannon students and faculty to live, learn, and conduct research in a setting that offers unparalleled direct access to diverse ecosystems.

Gannon's academic facilities do more than house programs. They are the spaces where students learn by doing.

The Center for Business Ingenuity brings together the Dahlkemper School of business, Gannon's Small Business Development Center, and the Erie Technology Incubator under one roof, creating unprecedented collaboration between business students, entrepreneurs, business faculty, and consultants in a facility that looks and feels like a major corporate headquarters.

Gannon's mechanical, biomedical, and industrial engineering programs are located in another exceptional learning environment, the Center for Advanced Engineering, also home to the industrial engineering laboratory and the only biomedical engineering lab of its kind in the region.

Budding biologists, doctors, physicists, chemists, and engineers will spend much of their time in the Zurn Science Center, which houses laboratory space, an open-engineering computer lab, and 3-D printers for student use. Criminal justice students can investigate simulated crime scenes, conduct research in a state-of-the-art forensics lab, and train in interrogation rooms and a virtual reality firearms simulator in the forensic investigation center.

The Morosky College of Health Professions and Sciences is located in the Robert H. Morosky Academic Center, a 99,000 square-foot facility that includes classrooms, labs, and a state-of-the-art patient simulation center, the largest and most comprehensive one in the region. Nursing, respiratory care, radiologic science, physician assistant, and occupational therapy students come together at the center to take part in collaborative, hands-on learning.

Gannon's advertising, digital media communication, journalism, and theater programs, along with Gannon's award-winning radio station and student newspaper, are housed in the new Center for Communication Arts. Other academic buildings include the A. J. Palumbo Center, home to the College of Humanities, Education and Social Sciences, and Scottino Hall, home to the acclaimed Schuster Theatre.

Costs

Full-time tuition for 2017–18 was $15,090 per semester ($16,000 for engineering and health sciences), or $30,180 per academic year ($32,000 for engineering and health sciences). Tuition for part-time students was $730 to $785 per credit hour. Room and board range from $5,570 to $7,300 per semester. The total cost for the academic year at Gannon was $30,682 for commuting students and between $42,604 and $47,884 for resident students, depending on the program of study.

Financial Aid

Gannon is dedicated to ensuring a high-quality education is within everyone's reach: More than $27 million in student scholarship and financial aid is provided to 94 percent of undergraduate students. Students seeking financial aid can file the admissions and financial aid applications as early as October 1 and should file by the preferred deadline of March 15. Numerous employment and scholarship opportunities are available to qualified students. Each year the University offers its top incoming freshmen the ability to compete for full-tuition scholarships. The application deadline for this competition is December 15 with an on-campus competition in late January or early February.

Faculty

Gannon's faculty numbers more than 400 and 69 percent of the full-time faculty members have either doctoral or terminal degrees. The student-to-faculty ratio is 13:1, and average class size is approximately 25 students.

Admission Requirements

Gannon University actively recruits students of all races, faith traditions, and ages from all geographic regions of North America and abroad. Applicants must submit scores (including senior-year scores) on either the SAT or ACT; an up-to-date official transcript of the high school record (plus official college transcripts for transfer applicants); and a completed application form. Applications can be completed online at www.gannon.edu/apply or via the Common Application.

Admission decisions are based upon numerous factors, most importantly the high school record as demonstrated through grades and SAT and/or ACT scores and other test scores that may be available. Recommendations and personal statements also affect admission decisions. Transfer and international students should check with the admissions office for special application procedures.

Application and Information

Gannon operates on a rolling admissions basis; there is no deadline for filing applications with the exception of the physician assistant program, which has a deadline of December 1 for the fall semester. Due to the competitiveness of some programs, students interested in the nursing or occupational therapy programs are strongly encouraged to file applications in September. Early applications are recommended, as are enrollment deposits.

To find out more, contact:

Office of Admissions
Gannon University
109 University Square
Erie, Pennsylvania 16541
Phone: 814-871-7240
      800-GANNON-U (426-6668, toll-free)
Fax: 814-871-5803
E-mail: admissions@gannon.edu
Website: http://www.gannon.edu

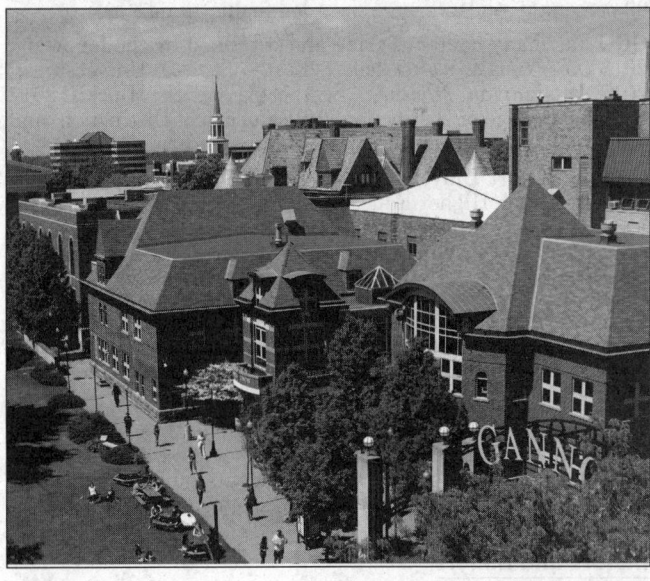

GEORGIAN COURT UNIVERSITY
LAKEWOOD, NEW JERSEY

★ To read more about this school, visit http://petersons.to/georgiancourtuniversity

The University

Georgian Court University (GCU) is a place where heart and intellect meet. GCU students learn to expand their possibilities while fostering their unique gifts and becoming more engaged citizens of the world. The historic 156-acre campus is home to over 2,000 students, creating a community of scholarship, empowerment, and professional relationships.

Georgian Court University is a four-year, private coeducational university located in Lakewood, New Jersey. GCU is set on a magnificent estate formerly belonging to financier George Jay Gould. The current GCU campus was sold to the Sisters of Mercy in 1924 from the heirs of George Jay Gould. The original estate featured an indoor swimming pool, court tennis court, and bowling alley, all housed in what is now called the Casino, which has been completely restored. Gould's estate also boasted a Japanese Garden, Formal Garden, and classical Italian Gardens, which still grace the campus with their natural and sculptural beauty.

As a forward-thinking university that supports diversity and academic excellence, GCU welcomes students of all faiths and backgrounds. The university offers a curriculum that is broad enough to be truly liberal, yet specialized enough to provide in-depth preparation for careers or further study.

As a coeducational institution, GCU continues to grow while maintaining a small-scale setting that provides a big value: a community based on the Mercy core values, including respect, integrity, justice, compassion, and service. Each GCU student shapes the experiential academic environment, which makes for a vibrant environment of teachers and learners.

GCU works to make its educational program available to all qualified students, regardless of financial need; in 2017–18, 99 percent of students were awarded financial aid.

GCU has many points of pride and is ranked by the following: 2018 *U.S. News & World Report* "Best Colleges & Universities;" 2017 *Washington Monthly* "Best Bang for the Buck;" 2017 Catholic College of Distinction; 2017 College of Distinction; and *Victory Media* declared GCU a 2017 Military-Friendly School.

Georgian Court University is accredited by the Middle States Commission on Higher Education.

Location

Georgian Court University's campus is conveniently situated 60 miles from New York and Philadelphia, and only 10 miles from the Jersey Shore. Bordering Lake Carasaljo, the site is a National Historic Landmark with alluring statuary, beautiful architecture, and lush gardens.

The campus is easily accessible from Route 9, the Garden State Parkway, and Interstate 195. New Jersey Transit bus access is within walking distance, giving students quick, inexpensive transportation to points of interest throughout the tristate area.

Majors and Minors

Georgian Court University offers degree programs in the following major disciplines:

Accounting; Applied Arts & Sciences; Art & Visual Studies; Biochemistry; Biology; Business Administration; Chemistry; Clinical Laboratory Sciences; Criminal Justice; Dance; Digital Communication; Digital Design; Education; English; Exercise Science, Wellness, & Sports; Finance; Graphic Design & Multimedia; Health Information Management; Health Profession Studies; Health Sciences; History; Interdisciplinary Studies; Latino Business Studies; Management; Marketing; Mathematics; Medical Imaging Sciences; Natural Sciences; Nursing; Pre-Professional Career Preparation (preparation for medical careers); Psychiatric Rehabilitation & Psychology; Psychology; Religious Studies; Social Work; Spanish; and Visual Art.

Minors are offered in: Accounting; American Studies; Anthropology; Biology; Business Administration; Chemistry; Coaching; Computer Information Systems; Criminal Justice; Dance; Dance Therapy; Digital Communication; Economics; English; Exercise Science, Wellness, & Sports; Finance; Gerontology; Global Justice & Society; Graphic Design; History; Integrative Health; International Area Studies; Latino/a and Caribbean Studies; Law Enforcement & Corrections; Management; Marketing; Mathematics; Psychology; Religious Studies; Social Media Marketing; Social Work; Spanish; Sports Management; Studio Art; Sustainability; The USA and the World; Women's Studies; and Writing.

Academic Programs

Every candidate for a B.A., B.S., B.S.W., or B.S.N. degree must complete a minimum of 120 credit hours to qualify for graduation. A minimum cumulative grade point average of C (2.0) must be maintained. Unless otherwise indicated for a specific major, a minimum cumulative GPA of 2.5 must be maintained in the major field.

GCU's academic calendar is available online at georgan.edu/academic-calendar.

GCU works to help students develop their academic skills in a supportive, caring environment. The Academic Development & Support Center (ADSC) offers tutoring and other academic support services so students can get the most out of their education. Disabilities Services, Peer Tutoring, and a fee-based support program for students with learning differences are also available.

Georgian Court University's Honors Program allows students to pursue academic honors and collaborate with faculty members in a variety of special courses. Honors students can benefit from courses that emphasize primary texts and sources, rigorous scholarly writing assignments and oral presentations, belonging to a committed community of scholars, preference in academic advisement and course registration, assistance with funding to present at regional and national conferences, and special advising regarding graduate and professional school applications and prestigious fellowship opportunities.

The Office of Career Services, Corporate Engagement and Continuing Education helps bridge the gap from being a student to becoming a professional and progressing through a career. The office has a wide array of tools and resources to help students find jobs and internships, identify and market their skill set, network, compile a resume, and prepare for interviews. These life-long, free services are available to both students and alumni.

Off-Campus Programs

The Office of Global Education Programs manages study abroad and travel abroad experiences. Study abroad trips last from a week to a year outside the United States, and students can earn credit. Georgian Court has formalized arrangements and discount agreements with several international universities. Travel abroad opportunities can satisfy an experiential learning or service requirement.

In addition to offering students opportunities to study abroad, Georgian Court University offers joint-degree programs allowing students to take courses at GCU and at a partner institution.

Academic Facilities

Jeffries Hall is Georgian Court's largest academic building, providing classrooms, seminar rooms, offices, art studios, and computer labs. The state-of-the-art Audrey Birish George Science Center offers the latest laboratory and instruction space for scientific study.

The Sister Mary Joseph Cunningham Library offers a wealth of resources to assist students in their studies and research pursuits. The library offers extensive online resources, special collections and archives, and spacious facilities for meetings and presentations.

Other campus buildings include the Raymond Hall Complex, which houses the School of Education, the Raymond Hall Computer Center, and the GCU Dining Hall. The School of Business and the Department of Psychology are based in Farley Center, which includes a computer lab, student lounge, and an International Collaboration Center. GCU's 67,000-square-foot Wellness Center Arena boasts two state-of-the-art dance studios for dance instruction.

Costs

For the 2017–18 academic year, tuition was $15,708 per semester for full-time students (12–18 credits); the nursing program tuition was $16,819. Part-time tuition (11 credits or fewer) was $718 per credit. Room and board was $5,404 per semester, with a $1,293 single room supplement. Fees included a full-time comprehensive fee of $730, a part-time comprehensive fee of $365, and a full-year parking fee of $193 (plus $13.27 New Jersey sales tax). Other small miscellaneous fees may be applicable.

Financial Aid

Georgian Court University is proud to meet the financial aid needs of its students with an annual budget of almost $20,000,000 in institutional aid. The University believes that a good education is a right—not a privilege. Through internal scholarships and outside scholarships, Georgian Court strives to make education attainable for all students.

In addition, there are GCU institutional, Federal, and State grants available for students who meet specific criteria. Students can also take advantage of the loan programs that are explained in further detail in the student loan section of the University's website. On-campus job opportunities include work study and freelance work.

Faculty

At GCU, more than 90 percent of the full-time faculty members hold doctoral degrees. From the freshman year on, students have the opportunity to take classes taught by department chairs, even school deans. Georgian Court features an average class size of 13, which promotes individual attention and open, thoughtful discourse among students and professors. All students receive individual counseling by a faculty adviser.

Student Government

The Student Government Association (SGA) of Georgian Court University is the official representative voice of the GCU student body. The SGA advocates on behalf of the students' interests and concerns. Through representation on University committees and other special meetings, the Student Government Association continues to play a vital role in fostering community and providing a direct link between students, faculty, and administration. The University also boasts several programs to help engage and develop students' leadership abilities, as well as a plethora of other clubs and organizations catering to a broad range of interests and lifestyles.

Admission Requirements

Georgian Court University welcomes applications from qualified students of all faiths and backgrounds who desire a liberal arts education. The University strives to enroll students who can benefit most from its academic program. In 2017, more than 40 percent of GCU's student population were first-generation college students. Entrance is based on individual merit. The high school record of achievement is of primary importance and must reflect solid performance. Applicants must have at least a 2.5 GPA for most majors, except nursing which requires a 3.0 GPA upon admittance. The majority of students at Georgian Court ranked in the upper half of their senior high school class. Transfer students are accepted into the freshman, sophomore, and junior classes for fall and spring semesters. All transfer applicants must be in good standing at their previous college. Applicants with fewer than 24 credits must fulfill all requirements for admission to the freshman class.

Further consideration is given to the applicant's extracurricular activities and the letters of recommendation submitted by teachers, counselors, employers, or similarly qualified people.

Application and Information

Applicants must submit their completed application (online via the Common Application or print and complete a paper application), a $40 application fee, their official high school transcript, SAT (GCU code: 2274) or ACT (GCU code: 2562) scores, two letters of recommendation, and an optional essay. Georgian Court has rolling deadlines for first-year students, so applications can be accepted throughout the year.

A campus interview is encouraged but not necessary. A guided tour of the campus is available at the interview.

For further information, prospective students should contact:

Office of Admissions
Georgian Court University
900 Lakewood Avenue
Lakewood, New Jersey 08701-2697
United States
Phone: 732-987-2700
      800-458-8422 Ext. 2700 (toll-free)
Fax: 732-987-2000
E-mail: admissions@georgian.edu
Website: georgian.edu/admissions

Georgian Court University's 67,000 square-foot, state-of-the-art Wellness Center Arena.

GRAND VIEW UNIVERSITY
DES MOINES, IOWA

★ To read more about this school, visit http://petersons.to/grandviewuniversity

The University

Grand View University is a liberal arts institution that offers a high-quality education to a diverse student body in a career-oriented, liberal arts–grounded curriculum at its campus in Des Moines, Iowa. Founded in 1896, Grand View welcomes traditional students, adult learners, and graduate students representing a wide range of ethnic, religious, and cultural backgrounds.

At Grand View, students find a winning combination of high-quality programs, experienced professors, and student experiences that will prepare them for successful careers. With 2,000 students and an average class size of 16, learning is an interactive process at Grand View—students engage in lively discussions, work on real-world projects, and participate in career-related work experiences.

Grand View stands out from other universities because of its partnerships with leading businesses and organizations in Des Moines, which has led to challenging internships and stellar job placement—for more than two decades nearly 100 percent of GV graduates have found jobs right after graduation or continued their education.

Students are encouraged to develop leadership and team skills through involvement in campus organizations, which include intercollegiate and intramural athletics, speech and theater groups, major department clubs, student government, musical ensembles, and honor societies. Grand View's student leadership program provides opportunities for students with or without leadership experience to seek and develop critical thinking, interpersonal, and networking skills.

Student athletes compete in men's baseball, basketball, bowling, competitive cheer (coed), cross-country, eSports, football, golf, shooting sports (coed), soccer, tennis, track and field, volleyball, and wrestling, and women's basketball, bowling, competitive dance, cross-country, golf, soccer, softball, tennis, track and field, and volleyball. Grand View is a member of the Heart of America Conference of the National Association of Intercollegiate Athletics. Athletic scholarships are available.

Location

Grand View is located in Des Moines, a metropolitan area of more than half a million people in central Iowa. In essence, Grand View's campus is the entire city of Des Moines because students aren't limited by the confines of a small campus or small town. Nationally recognized companies that have their corporate offices in Des Moines include DuPont/Pioneer, the Principal Financial Group, Meredith Corporation, Wells Fargo Home Mortgage, and the *Des Moines Register*.

The recreation and cultural options are endless. In a given day, students can catch an Iowa Cubs professional baseball doubleheader, head down to the Court Avenue district for great food and nightlife, or take in a concert at Wells Fargo Arena. A thriving arts program in Des Moines features the Des Moines Metro Opera, Ballet Iowa, the Des Moines Symphony, the Des Moines Art Center, the Des Moines Playhouse, and many others. The summer Des Moines Arts Festival is ranked third in the nation.

Majors and Degrees

Grand View University offers forty majors in areas such as accounting, applied mathematics, art education, biology, biochemistry, biotechnology, business administration (with concentrations in areas such as finance, game design, human resource management, management, and marketing), church music, computer science, criminal justice, digital media production, elementary education, English, graphic design, graphic journalism, kinesiology, history, human services, journalism and public relations, liberal arts, management information systems, multimedia communication, music, music education, nursing, organizational studies, paralegal studies, physical education, political studies (pre-law or public administration), psychology, secondary education, Spanish for careers and professionals, studio arts, theater arts, and theology.

The university also offers five master's degree programs: the Master of Science in Organizational Leadership, the Master of Science in Nursing (clinical nurse leadership, nursing education, and nurse leader), the Master of Education, Master of Science in Sport Management and Master of Science in Athletic Training.

Academic Programs

Grand View operates on a 4-4-1 academic calendar. The first semester runs from late August to December. The second semester begins in early January and ends in late April. Three one-month summer sessions are offered in May, June, and July, as is a summer trimester evening program.

Grand View's general education core takes an innovative, integrated approach to developing essential abilities employers seek in graduates, such as writing, speaking, analysis, problem-solving, and critical thinking. Through their coursework, students can gain the personal and intellectual depth that will help them thrive in today's knowledge-based economy and in their communities.

The Logos honors program augments the general education core. By invitation, freshmen and sophomores enrolled in this program complete a series of courses designed to challenge exceptional students.

An active study-abroad program gives students opportunities to learn in an international setting, particularly through a partnership with the Danish Institute for Study Abroad, IBA, and China's Tianfu University.

The Grand View academic mission is to provide a diverse student body with an academically rigorous education. In order to meet this commitment, Grand View provides a variety of learning environments and teaching techniques. Grand View's results on the 2015 National Survey of Student Engagement, a measure of educational quality used by 1,000 colleges and universities, ranked GV comparable to the top 10 percent of all NSSE schools on five out of the ten benchmarks for first-year students and in the top 50 percent on the remaining five.

Costs

For 2018–19, the comprehensive cost for first-year students living on campus is approximately $36,500, which includes tuition, an activity fee, a technology fee, a parking fee, and room and board. Students have several residential and meal plan options that affect cost. Health services and Internet access are also included in the comprehensive fee.

Financial Aid and Affordability

All incoming Grand View first-year students are automatically enrolled in GV COMPLETE, an innovative program that allows students to plan and finance their entire degree right from the beginning, with a four-year financing plan and a four-year academic plan. GV COMPLETE is designed to help make a Grand View education more affordable by limiting increases in tuition, room, and board over students' four years; to support students in making the most out of the scholarships, grants, and loans that will become key parts of their financing; and to encourage four-year graduation.

Most full-time Grand View students receive financial assistance. The average first-year full-time award package is usually around $27,500 with more than $20,000 in grants and scholarships, and the remainder in work-study and student loans. The amount of aid is determined through a combination of merit and analysis of need as determined through the Free Application for Federal Student Aid. The priority deadline for financial aid is January 15. Students receive notification of financial aid packages following acceptance of admission to the university and receipt of their financial aid analysis of need.

Faculty

There are approximately 94 full-time faculty members and 120 part-time faculty members. More than 62 percent of full-time faculty members hold terminal degrees. All classes are taught by professors; no graduate or teaching assistants instruct Grand View classes.

Student Government

Students participate in Grand View governance. The Student Activities Council and Viking Council plan student activities that promote educational, social, cultural, and recreational aspects of student life. Students serve as representatives on faculty and staff search committees, programming committees, and student life committees.

Admission Requirements

Applicants' files are reviewed to determine their preparation for a Grand View education. Official high school transcripts and submission of ACT or SAT scores are required for applicants with less than 24 semester hours of college credit. Applicants transferring from another college are required to submit official transcripts from all colleges previously attended.

Application and Information

For more information about Grand View, students should contact:
Admissions Office
Grand View University
1200 Grandview Avenue
Des Moines, Iowa 50316
Phone: 515-263-2810
          800-444-6083 (toll-free)
Fax: 515-263-2974
E-mail: admissions@grandview.edu
Website: http://www.grandview.edu
              https://www.facebook.com/GrandViewUniversity
              (Facebook)

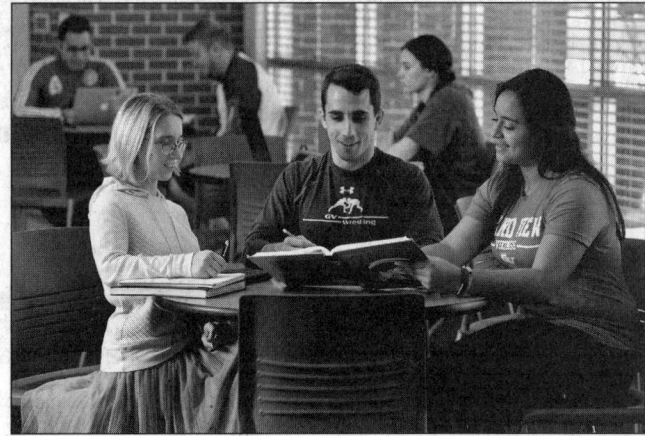

Grand View students in the Johnson Wellness Center.

GWYNEDD MERCY UNIVERSITY
GWYNEDD VALLEY, PENNSYLVANIA

 To read more about this school, visit http://petersons.to/gwyneddmercyuniversity

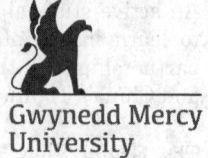
Gwynedd Mercy
University

The University

Gwynedd Mercy University (GMercyU) is a Catholic university with a strong foundation in the liberal arts and a deep commitment to the Mercy tradition of service to society. GMercyU believes that each person has the power to be a hero—to another individual, to a community, to the world. The University supports students in their quest to become their best selves with the help of a dedicated team of professors who take an interest in who they are, and who they aspire to be. Students are encouraged to join a growing team of *Distinctive Mercy Graduates* who are doing more than launching successful careers; they're living productive and meaningful lives. With excellent programs in nursing, health professions, arts and sciences, education, and business, GMercyU supports students in making a difference in their own lives and in the lives of others.

GMercyU is set on 160 beautiful acres in southeastern Pennsylvania and is home to nearly 2,000 undergraduate students, 19 NCAA Division III athletic teams, and dozens of clubs and organizations. The University is large enough to offer a vibrant campus life but small enough that students get the personal attention they need to achieve their goals.

In addition to taking classes toward graduation, students can join the University's nationally-renowned choir, join the Griffin Student Leadership Institute, improve the lives of others through Alternative Spring Break and Mercy Works programs, be part of a winning athletic team, hang out in the Late Nite Lounge, or choose from many other options. Students also can enjoy several on-campus dining choices or take a free shuttle to nearby restaurants when they're looking for a change of scene. Campus is just 30 minutes from Philadelphia, providing easy access to a wide array of cultural, entertainment, internship, career, and volunteer opportunities in one of the nation's most exciting cities.

With more than 20,000 alumni, Gwynedd Mercy University has a strong reputation for preparing *Distinctive Mercy Graduates* who make a difference in the world. PayScale named Gwynedd Mercy University as one of the "Top Colleges for Producing Graduates Who Make the World a Better Place" in 2014. In 2017, PayScale also ranked GMercyU in the Top 25 percent of schools nationwide for 20-year net return on investment, and the *Wall Street Journal/ Times Higher Education* College Rankings placed Gwynedd Mercy University among the top schools in the nation for the things that matter most, including student outcomes. Gwynedd Mercy University also is considered a College of Distinction, and is considered a military-friendly college.

Location

Gwynedd Mercy University's idyllic 160-acre campus is located in Gwynedd Valley, Pennsylvania, a suburb 30 miles from downtown Philadelphia. While on campus, students can enjoy beautiful outdoor spaces perfect for a long run, a friendly game of Frisbee, or a quiet lunch with friends under a tree. Philadelphia's Old City, South Street, sports arenas, and some of the best restaurants and concert venues around are just a 30-minute car or train ride from campus. The University also is just minutes from several major highways, including the Pennsylvania Turnpike and Interstate 95. In addition to the vibrant city life of Philadelphia, New Jersey beaches, the Pocono Mountains, Washington D.C., and New York City are just about two hours from campus. Students can take advantage of free shuttle service to the local train station or to the many shops, restaurants, and entertainment areas nearby.

Majors and Degrees

Gwynedd Mercy University offers baccalaureate degrees in accounting, behavioral/social gerontology, biology, digital communication, computer information science, criminal justice, education/special education, finance, history, human resource management, human services, management, marketing (with an emphasis on digital marketing), mathematics, medical laboratory science, nursing, occupational science/pre-OT, philosophy, psychology, radiologic technology, radiation therapy, respiratory care, social work, and sports management.

Associate degrees are awarded in liberal studies, natural science, and respiratory care. GMercyU also offers a number of master's degrees in business, education, and nursing, including a 4+1 MBA program on campus. Students who want to earn their doctorate degrees can choose from programs in education and nursing. Many graduate programs are offered in accelerated and/or online formats.

Academic Programs

The academic year is divided into two semesters, and most baccalaureate degree programs require the completion of a minimum of 120 credit hours. All of Gwynedd Mercy University's undergraduate programs include a strong focus on the liberal arts to ensure students develop some of today's most in-demand skills, including communication, critical thinking, and problem-solving. Liberal arts courses include language; literature and the fine arts; humanities; and behavioral, social, and natural sciences. Students have access to the Academic Resource Center for tutoring and writing assistance at no additional charge.

Individualized credit-bearing internships and work experience programs are available and recommended in all majors to give students firsthand experience in their chosen field before they graduate. Nearby Fortune 500 companies offer a variety of experiences to students in business and accounting, for example. TAP, the Teacher Apprentice Program, places every education major in the classroom one day a week beginning in their first year, and education students also complete pre-student teaching and student teaching experiences. All health professions and nursing programs require clinical experience. Students also have the opportunity to conduct research and present at academic and industry conferences, depending on their major. Students are encouraged to develop a global perspective through various study abroad and Alternative Spring Break service opportunities.

Off-Campus Programs

The excellent on-campus laboratory facilities are extended by affiliations with more than 200 hospitals and health care agencies in Pennsylvania, New Jersey, and Delaware, where nursing and health professions students may complete their clinical experiences. Merck provides a one-semester industrial laboratory experience for qualified biology majors. Gwynedd Mercy University also maintains a close relationship with nearby universities and companies, including Johnson & Johnson, McNeil, Sun Company, and Jefferson University, just to name a few.

Academic Facilities

Gwynedd Mercy University has expanded its physical facilities as its student enrollment has increased. Frances M. Maguire Hall is home to the Frances M. Maguire School of Nursing and Health Professions as well as the Division of Natural Sciences. This 50,000 square-foot state-of-the-art facility offers laboratories for areas such as nursing skills, respiratory care, radiation therapy, organic chemistry, and microbiology. The University's SIM® family includes newborn, infant, child, and adult simulation mannequins that allow students to practice techniques before performing them on real patients in clinical settings. An advanced video system also gives students real-time feedback on care techniques.

Gwynedd Mercy University continues to "discover the Next" with the addition of the newest academic building on campus, University Hall, which opened in the spring of 2014. The building is the home of the School of Business and Education. University Hall features state-of-the-art technology to further enhance educational opportunities, including a Financial Trading Room, equipped with a real-time stock ticker.

The Griffin Complex houses the University's recreation facilities, including a full gymnasium and track, racquetball court, cardio room, and weight room. The University's Julia Ball Auditorium is a 400-seat space for theatrical productions, musical events, and other cultural and academic programs. The Student Technology Center is equipped with personal computers and printers and the latest software for student use. The Valie Genuardi Hobbit House is a fully licensed academic lab school located right on campus. It is home to nursery and pre-kindergarten students, and also provides a place for students in the School of Business and Education to gain valuable hands-on experience.

The Keiss Library and Learning Commons links academic support services, library services, and career development services, providing a one-stop academic center that facilitates student success.

Costs

The published 2018–19 academic year tuition for full-time students (12 to 18 credits per semester) is $32,820. The published tuition for health professions and nursing students is $34,820. Room and board costs average $12,270. Professional liability fees for students enrolled in clinical components and lab fees are extra. The University offers generous scholarships ranging from $11,000 to full tuition, and other financial aid to qualified students.

Financial Aid

Gwynedd Mercy University's financial aid program is designed to provide financial assistance to academically qualified students whose resources are inadequate to meet the costs of attending the University. The student Financial Aid Committee assists as many students as possible, using Gwynedd Mercy University funds as well as federal, state, and other available funds. Aid is awarded on the basis of demonstrated financial need, academic proficiency, and responsible campus citizenship. In 2016–17, 100 percent of the University's first-time full-time students received some form of financial aid.

Faculty

The University's student-faculty ratio is 11:1, allowing for personal contact, advising, and after-class instruction. This is a widely acknowledged strength of the Gwynedd Mercy University experience. For nursing students in the clinical setting, there are never more than 8 students to 1 clinical adviser; in the health professions programs, there often is one-to-one instruction. The quality of teaching is enhanced by the diversified interests of the faculty. Faculty members teach both day and evening classes, allowing students the greatest flexibility in scheduling. Tutoring is available in all disciplines at no additional charge.

Student Government

All students are encouraged to take part in the responsibilities of student government. Student participation and shared responsibility for the welfare of the University are promoted through a framework of committees.

Admission Requirements

Admission to Gwynedd Mercy University is based on a student's high school record, rank in class, SAT or ACT scores, counselor's recommendation, and choice of major. Entrance requirements vary with the program. The rolling admission policy allows students to be informed of an admission decision within two to three weeks of submitting their completed application.

Gwynedd Mercy University awards credit for satisfactory completion of Advanced Placement courses, provided students receive an AP exam score of 3 or higher.

A minimum 2.0 grade point average (on a 4.0 scale) is generally required to transfer from another institution. Gwynedd Mercy University does, however, retain the right to require a higher GPA for admission to some programs.

Gwynedd Mercy University is committed to maintaining a positive learning, working, and living environment that is free from unlawful discrimination and harassment. Gwynedd Mercy University does not discriminate against any applicant for admission to or employment at the University because of race, religion, age, gender, sexual orientation, gender identity, national origin, disability, color, marital status, veteran status, genetic characteristics, or any other characteristic protected by federal, state or local law ("Protected Classes"). This includes, but is not limited to, admissions, financial aid, educational services, and student programs and activities, as well as to all terms and conditions of employment including, but not limited to, recruitment, selection, hiring, placement, transfer, promotion, training, compensation, benefits, discipline, and termination. The University will not tolerate unlawful acts of discrimination or harassment based upon Protected Classes, or related retaliation against or by any employee or student.

Application and Information

All prospective applicants are encouraged to visit the campus to meet with an admission counselor, dean, or program director. To apply for admission, applicants should complete the online application available at gmercyu.edu. First-time freshmen must also submit an official high school transcript or equivalency certificate; results of the SAT or ACT (for recent high school graduates); and a written recommendation from a principal, teacher, guidance counselor, or employer (optional but recommended). All applicants should verify that they meet the specific requirements and have the necessary high school prerequisites for admission.

Students who wish to transfer to Gwynedd Mercy University should submit the same online application, high school and college transcripts, and a letter of recommendation.

For additional information or to schedule campus tours and visits, students are encouraged to register with the Enrollment Support Services Office at admissions@gmercyu.edu or contact the office at 215-641-5510.

For more information, contact:

Office of Admissions
Gwynedd Mercy University
1325 Sumneytown Pike
P.O. Box 901
Gwynedd Valley, Pennsylvania 19437-9923
Phone: 800-342-5462 (toll-free)
      215-641-5510
E-mail: admissions@gmercycu.edu
Website: gmercyu.edu/admissions-aid/
      undergraduate-admissions
      twitter.com/GMercyU
      facebook.com/GMercyU
      instagram.com/gmercyu

Students walk to and from classes in University Hall, the newest academic building on campus.

HARDING UNIVERSITY
SEARCY, ARKANSAS

 To read more about this school, visit http://petersons.to/hardinguniversity

The University

Harding University was founded on Christian principles and a liberal arts tradition. Since 1924, Harding has challenged its students to pursue scholarship, service, teamwork, excellence, and commitment. The largest private university in Arkansas, it is ranked by *U.S. News and World Report* and Princeton Review as one of the top liberal arts universities in the South and attracts exceptional high school students representing every U.S. state and more than 54 nations and territories.

Harding University is accredited by the Higher Learning Commission and maintains specialized accreditation for its programs as appropriate to its educational purpose. Students have opportunities for hands-on learning whether it be engineering majors developing concept, design, and construction of an off-road vehicle; journalism majors managing, writing and editing for the student newspaper; or nursing majors conducting exam simulations on high-fidelity mannequins. With a student-teacher ratio of 14 to 1, strong relationships are built in and out of the classroom.

Students can cultivate friendships and interests with 120 academic and professional organizations and 31 social clubs. Ranging from the arts, music, politics, business, diversity, children, missions, service, and the environment, the clubs on campus offer a variety of interests to explore.

Provided with a Christian perspective through which to appreciate various disciplines, students excel as scholars and develop leadership skills. As a result, Harding alumni display character, conviction, and a competitive edge and are prepared for success at prestigious graduate schools and companies throughout the nation.

Location

Harding is located in Searcy, Arkansas, and offers students a hometown feeling with easy access to major cities. The University is about an hour away from Little Rock, Arkansas, and the Bill and Hillary Clinton National Airport and is about 2 hours away from Memphis, Tennessee. Located in The Natural State, University students have several nearby options such as the Little Red River, Pinnacle Mountain, and Petit Jean State Parks for fishing, camping, hiking, and other outdoor activities. Arkansas is home to 52 state parks.

Majors and Degrees

Housed within nine colleges, the University offers more than 100 academic majors, including 14 preprofessional programs, taught by top instructors.

Within the College of Allied Health, students may earn a Bachelor of Arts degree in communication sciences and disorders, a Bachelor of Science in exercise and sport sciences, a Master of Science degree in speech-language pathology, a Master of Science degree in physician assistant studies, and a Doctor of Physical Therapy degree.

The College of Arts and Humanities offers a wide range of degrees in the humanities, arts, communication, English language and literature, foreign language and international studies, history and political science, interior design, medical humanities, music, and theater.

In the College of Bible and Ministry, there are degrees in Bible and ministry, family ministry, leadership and ministry, missions, and preaching.

Students in the Paul R. Carter College of Business Administration may earn the Bachelor of Business Administration in accounting, finance, international business, information systems, management, marketing and professional sales, and a Master of Business Administration.

Those interested in teaching may earn degrees in birth–kindergarten early childhood/special education integrated, elementary education, middle level education English/language arts/math 4–8, middle level education English/language arts/science 4–8, middle level education English/language arts/social science 4–8, middle level math/science 4–8, middle level science/social sciences 4–8, middle level social sciences/math 4–8, secondary education, and special education in the Cannon-Clary College of Education. Students can also earn a Master of Arts, Master of Arts in Teaching, Master of Education, Master of Science, Master of Science in Education, Master of Science in Marriage and Family Therapy, educational specialist, and educational doctorate. Students can also earn several additional endorsements.

The Carr College of Nursing offers a Bachelor of Science in Nursing, enabling students to take the NCLEX-RN exam after graduation. There also is a Master of Science in Nursing degree program, preparing students to be family nurse practitioners.

Students can earn a Doctor of Pharmacy degree through the University's four-year program in the College of Pharmacy.

The College of Sciences allows students to study health sciences, behavioral sciences, biology, chemistry, computer science, engineering (civil, computer, electrical, and mechanical) and physics, exercise and sport sciences, family and consumer sciences, kinesiology, mathematics, medical humanities, medical laboratory science, psychology, and social work.

The Honors College offers a Bachelor of Arts in interdisciplinary studies for its students.

In addition, teaching licensure may be obtained in the following areas: art, biology, chemistry, drama/speech, English, family and consumer sciences, French, kinesiology, mathematics, music, social science, Spanish, and theater 7–12.

Academic Programs

For the basic requirements necessary for each degree, prospective students should visit the Harding University online catalog at www.harding.edu/catalog. Specific inquires may be addressed to catalog@harding.edu.

Students may apply and participate in the Honors College with acceptance based on acceptance to the University and an ACT score of 27 or higher or an SAT evidence-based reading and writing, plus math score of 1280 or higher. These students may take honors-level courses and graduate with honors.

Off-Campus Programs

Harding offers multiple study abroad programs in locations such as Australia, Chile, England, France, Greece, Italy, and Zambia that will help expand cultural awareness and understanding. Nearly 50 percent of each graduating class takes advantage of one of Harding's international experiences. At each location,

COLLEGE CLOSE-UPS

students are accompanied and taught by University faculty. Costs are based on 16 tuition hours and include housing and meals.

Academic Facilities

Harding's campus consists of 13 academic buildings, cafeteria, two auditoriums, a world-class recreation center, a library, a performing arts center, a student center, student health services, 14 residence halls, and six apartment complexes.

Costs

The basic undergraduate, on-campus cost for 2017–18 for 15 hours of enrollment per semester was $9,345 for a semester and $18,690 for the year. Tuition was $623 per course hour. Students paid $500 a year for a required technology fee, a one-time $195 first-year experience fee, $3,592 for a standard dorm room, and $3,310 for a standard meal plan of 190 meals plus a $225 declining cash balance. The overall total came to $26,092.

Financial Aid

On average, 92 percent of Harding University freshman students receive financial assistance. In 2016–17, Harding awarded students more than $14 million in institutional need-based grants and more than $24 million in institutional scholarships. In addition, students received nearly $8 million in federal, state, and externally funded scholarships and grants.

Admission Requirements

Students wishing to apply to Harding must have a 19 ACT or 900 SAT and 3.0 high school GPA (on a 4.0 scale). In addition, high school graduates should have completed at least 15 units in academic subjects. Specifically, an applicant should have completed 4 units of English, 3 units of mathematics (taken from general math, geometry, algebra, trigonometry, precalculus, or calculus), 3 units of social studies (taken from civics, American history, world history, or geography), and 2 units of natural science (taken from physical science, biology, physics, or chemistry). Students planning to major in any area of health care are strongly encouraged to take one or more chemistry courses while in high school. Although not required for admission, two years of foreign language is recommended. The additional units may come from any academic area.

Application and Information

Prospective students may apply online at www.harding.edu/apply/.

Because Harding receives so many applications, it recommends that students apply before fall of their senior year of high school—even if they haven't taken the ACT or SAT. Admissions advisers are glad to help students through this process.

For more information, prospective students should contact:

Harding University
Box 12255
Searcy, Arkansas 72149-5615
Phone: 501-279-4407
Website: http://www.harding.edu
http://www.facebook.com/HardingU
http://www.twitter.com/HardingU

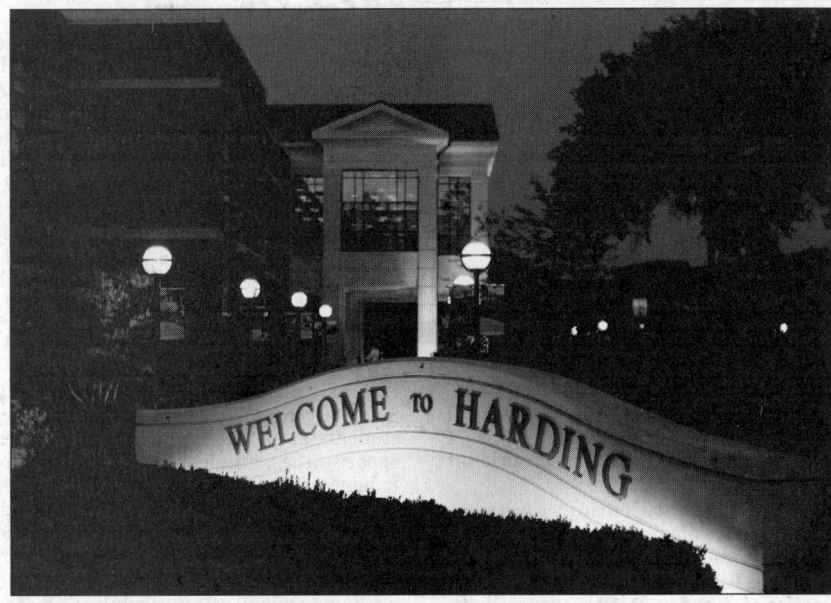

Harding University's student population represents all 50 states and 54 nations and territories. With more than 5,900 students, Harding is the largest private college or university in Arkansas.

HIGH POINT UNIVERSITY
HIGH POINT, NORTH CAROLINA

 For more information, visit http://petersons.to/highpoint

The University

At High Point University, every student receives an extraordinary education in an inspiring environment with caring people.®

U.S. News & World Report ranked High Point University #1 among Regional Colleges, the Most Innovative Regional College, and #1 for Best Undergraduate Teaching in Regional Colleges in its category. The environment of excellence transforms high school students into distinguished scholars who are prepared to tackle the challenges of the 21st century and thrive in an ever-changing global marketplace.

With more than 5,000 undergraduate students, High Point University (HPU) is a small liberal arts school with big-school facilities. Its 16 varsity teams play at the NCAA Division I level. Students come to HPU from 50 states and 37 countries, providing the school with great diversity in student history and experience. High Point University offers its students a safe community that feels like home, where the average class size is 17, and professors don't just know students' names—they know who they are and who they want to become.

The array of majors is vast, and each has been uniquely designed to challenge, inspire and transform. The academic programs include 50 undergraduate majors, 57 undergraduate minors, 12 pre-professional programs, and 13 graduate programs.

The curriculum emphasizes the study of the liberal arts in the belief that there is no better way to encourage communication skills, critical thinking, and personal integrity. The goal is to feed students' appetites for academic achievement and equip them for further education, the job market, or lives of service. Within the classroom environment, students find High Point University professors to be engaging mentors who are eager to share their own research and scholarly interests. Beyond the classroom, students are constantly met with opportunities to learn in a practical and innovative way. HPU's signature experiential learning program differentiates this collegiate experience from others and reinforces what is taught in the classroom while providing students with resources for professional networking and deep, practical knowledge of their fields.

Founded in 1924, High Point University has a strong academic history and is committed to building character, modeling values, and ensuring that students graduate with both expertise in their disciplines and the skills necessary to be successful in life.

Location

The cities of High Point, Greensboro, and Winston-Salem in North Carolina form the Piedmont Triad, with High Point University located in the center of the state. The Appalachian Mountains are 2 hours away, and the Atlantic coast is 3.5 hours away.

Majors and Degrees

High Point University offers Bachelor of Arts (B.A.) and Bachelor of Science (B.S.) degrees. Students may choose from the following majors and concentrations through the colleges listed below.

The School of Art and Design: Design Studies: Graphic Design, Interior Design, Studio Art, and Visual Merchandising Design.

The Earl N. Phillips School of Business: Accounting, International Business, Business Administration with an optional concentration in entrepreneurship; Marketing; and Sales, with an optional concentration in the furniture industry.

The Nido R. Qubein School of Communication: Electronic Media Production, Game and Interactive Media Design, Journalism, Media and Popular Culture Studies, and Strategic Communication.

The Stout School of Education: Elementary Education; Health and Physical Education; Secondary Education (9–12 licensure), with sub areas in biology, comprehensive science, English, history, and mathematics; Special Education (K–12 Licensure); Special Subjects (K–12 Licensure), with sub areas in art education and Spanish; and Education Studies.

The Congdon School of Health Sciences: Athletic training, Exercise Science, Physical Therapy, and Physician Assistant Studies.

The David R. Hayworth College of Arts and Sciences: Actuarial Science; Biochemistry; Biology; Chemistry; Computer Science; Criminal Justice; Dance; English with sub areas in literature and writing; History; Human Relations; International Relations; Mathematical Economics; Mathematics; French and Francophone Studies; Spanish; Music with sub areas in instrumental studies, piano/organ, and voice; Nonprofit Leadership and Management; Philosophy; Physics; Political Science; Psychology; Religion; Sociology; and Theatre with sub areas in performance, technical, dramatic writing, and collaborative theater.

The High Point University Graduate School offers the following programs: Strategic Communication (M.A.); Doctor of Education in Educational Leadership (Ed.D.); Educational Leadership (M.Ed.); Elementary Education (M.Ed.); Secondary Math (M.Ed.); Special Education (M.E.); Teaching Elementary Education K–6 (M.A.T.); Teaching Secondary Mathematics 9–12 (M.A.T.); Educational Administration (add-on license); History (M.A.); Master of Business Administration (M.B.A.); Nonprofit Management (M.A.); Master of Physician Assistant Studies (M.P.A.S.); and Doctor of Pharmacy (Pharm.D.).

Academic Programs

High Point University is committed to academic excellence. With small classes, caring professors and a myriad of student success stories, HPU has positioned itself as a place for scholars to thrive. A vibrant and engaging Honors Scholars Program recognizes and encourages creativity and academic achievement in top academic students.

Throughout their time at HPU, students are given real-world practical learning opportunities. The Office of Career and Professional Development helps students secure internships and jobs with companies such as NASA, MTV, Disney, Krispy Kreme, NBC, the Democratic and Republican National Conventions, and Merrill Lynch. The connections that students are exposed to during internships can often help lead them to full-time positions.

Off-Campus Programs

With a variety of extraordinary options at some of the most prestigious universities in the world, students at High Point University are encouraged to travel abroad as early as the summer after their freshman year. The university has partnerships with 25 different universities in 29 different countries including Argentina, Australia, Austria, the Czech Republic, Ecuador, Fiji, France, Germany, India, Italy, Japan, Russia, South Africa, Spain, and the United Kingdom.

An expanding Service Learning Program also provides more than a dozen courses with an off-campus service-learning component. These courses put students in community agencies committed to furthering the common good, where they can see and experience first-hand the issues they discuss in class.

Academic Facilities

Cottrell Hall, home to the Flanagan Center for Student Success, is a 40,000 square-foot facility that is the central hub of activity ,for students preparing for job interviews, seeking career development opportunities, and looking for ways to diversify their career skills. It houses the Office of Career and Professional Development, the Office of Study Abroad, the Office of Undergraduate Research and Creative Works, the Center for Entrepreneurship, Service Learning, the Freshman Success Program, and more.

The state-of-the-art 220,000 square-foot Congdon Hall features a pharmacology research lab, a gross anatomy lab, a human biomechanics and physiology lab, and more than a dozen simulation labs and spaces where real-world scenarios can come to life, including an operating room, emergency room, labor and delivery room, eight exam rooms, a pharmacy retail setting, and pharmacy hospital setting.

The Nido R. Qubein School of Communication features two high-definition TV studios, audio recording studios, a screening theater, editing labs, a student-operated radio station, a nationally-cited survey and research center, an interactive media and game design facility, and various computer labs. The school's Board of Advisers includes leaders in radio, television, newspaper, and magazine companies across the nation.

HPU's School of Art and Design emphasizes the importance of hand skills combined with technological proficiency in profession-specific software. Students studying in the School of Art and Design have access to cutting-edge equipment including a technology lab and several design-specific computer labs.

The 31,000 square-foot, LEED-Certified School of Education building houses the psychology department and the NCATE-accredited education school. It is equipped with simulated classrooms and clinical labs where psychology majors conduct hands-on testing and experiments.

The Plato S. Wilson School of Commerce houses the Center for Financial Research, which serves as a trading room and allows students to receive real-world, practical learning opportunities. The Center includes teaching and research technology, including financial databases, investment software, a stock ticker, and more.

Costs

For the 2018–19 academic year, High Point University's tuition and fees (including tuition, parking, laundry, entrance to athletic and cultural events, intramurals, Campus Concierge service, academic tutoring, library and media services, etc.) for full-time students is $35,118; room and board are $14,130.

Financial Aid

The Office of Student Financial Planning works diligently to assist students in their pursuit of postsecondary education at High Point University. Although the financial aid process can be complex, HPU's Financial Planning staff are well trained and highly qualified to make students' experiences positive and rewarding.

Interested students should submit the Free Application for Federal Student Aid (FAFSA) electronically via www.fafsa.ed.gov. The earliest that students may begin filing the FAFSA is October 1 of the senior year prior to entrance to HPU. The HPU school code is 002933.

The results from filing the FAFSA will be electronically transmitted to HPU for review. This form will produce an expected family contribution based on the family's financial data and will determine students' eligibility for HPU's need-based programs.

HPU will not be able to estimate students' eligibility for need-based aid until the FAFSA is filed. While there is not a deadline date to the FAFSA, it is important to file as early as possible; HPU disperses financial aid package information for students by March 1.

All major High Point University academic scholarships are awarded through the Presidential and High Point Scholarship programs. Each undergraduate admissions application also serves as an application for these scholarships.

Faculty

High Point University has a student-faculty ratio of 15:1 and an average class size of fewer than 17 students. More than 80 percent of faculty members have earned either the Ph.D. or other terminal degrees. Faculty members teach all classes; HPU does not use any graduate students or assistants to teach class. The Student Success Coaches are responsible for providing appropriate academic and transitional support to first-year students applicable to all aspects of the student's life tasks: academic, personal, social, and career. The coaches assist in this transition to college life and serve as the academic adviser for the first year. Students are assigned to success coaches based on their academic major.

Student Activities

With more than 100 student-led clubs and organizations represented on campus, HPU intentionally seeks to involve students in campus life through a diverse variety of platforms, including professional development associations, fine arts clubs, fraternities and sororities, honors societies, an active student government organization, religious life clubs, service organizations, special-interest groups, and more. In addition, HPU students annually provide more than 100,000 hours of voluntary service to the local community.

Admission Requirements

Freshman applicants must be graduates of accredited secondary schools and must meet the minimum course requirements which are as follows: 4 English units, 4 mathematics units, 3 science units, 3 social studies units, and 2 foreign language units. High Point University is a test-optional institution. As a result, official test scores are only required for Presidential Scholars consideration. Freshman applicants who want to be considered for the Presidential or High Point Scholars programs must submit their scores from the SAT or the ACT. International applicants should submit both TOEFL and SAT or ACT scores. Campus visits and personal interviews are strongly recommended.

Students who have completed Advanced Placement courses in high school and who have achieved scores of 4 or 5 on the Advanced Placement test administered by the College Board may receive credit at High Point University. Applicants may also receive credit for university-parallel courses successfully completed prior to enrollment at High Point University, including courses completed while in high school through dual-enrollment or International Baccalaureate programs.

Application and Information

The Office of Undergraduate Admissions accepts online applications for enrollment on a competitive basis using the Common Application. Freshmen deadlines are as follows:

- Early Decision (binding) application deadline: November 1
  Admissions notification date: November 28

- Early Action (nonbinding) application deadline: November 15
  Admissions notification date: December 15

- Early Decision II (binding) application deadline: February 1
  Admissions notification is rolling

- Regular Decision application deadline: March 15
  Admissions notification is rolling past February 1

Over 85 percent of enrolled students each year apply using one of the two early November application plans.

Official transcripts (high school and college, where applicable), one letter of recommendation, and a Counselor Report Form must be sent directly to the university by the appropriate school official. Students should request that copies of their SAT, ACT, or TOEFL scores be sent to the Office of Admissions at High Point University by the testing agency. All requests for application materials and information should be directed to:

Office of Undergraduate Admissions
High Point University
One University Parkway
High Point, North Carolina 27268-3598
United States of America
Phone: 336-841-9216
     800-345-6993 (toll-free)
E-mail: admiss@highpoint.edu
Website: http://www.highpoint.edu

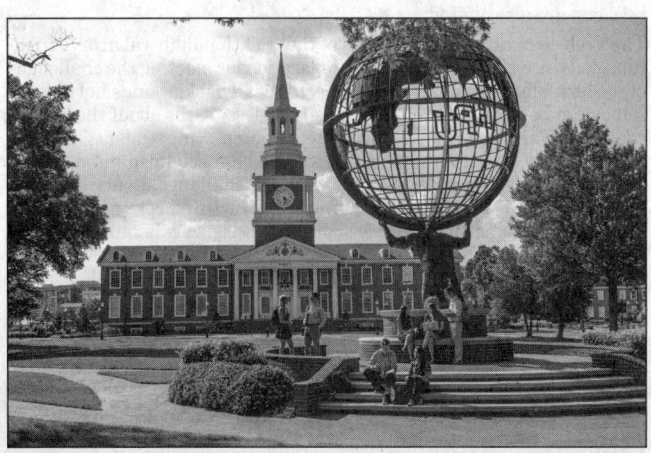

HILLSDALE COLLEGE
HILLSDALE, MICHIGAN

 For more information, visit http://petersons.to/hillsdalecollege

The College

Hillsdale College is a private, independent, nonsectarian, Christian institution of higher learning founded in 1844 by men and women who described themselves as "grateful to God for the inestimable blessings" resulting from civil and religious liberty and as "believing that the diffusion of sound learning is essential to the perpetuity of those blessings." The College has maintained institutional independence since its founding by refusing to accept aid from or control by federal authorities. Far-reaching private support from a national constituency has enabled Hillsdale to continue its trusteeship of the intellectual and spiritual inheritance tracing to Athens and Jerusalem, a heritage finding its clearest expression in the American experiment of self-government under law.

The undergraduate enrollment for fall 2017 was 1,463, of whom 51 percent were men and 49 percent were women. The College draws students from forty-nine states, the District of Columbia, and fourteen other countries. Approximately 34 percent of students are from Michigan. The entering freshman class in 2017 had the following mid-range scores: high school grade-point average of 3.82–4.0, ACT of 28–32, and SAT of 1280–1420. All Hillsdale students sign an Honor Code challenging self-government and committing them to honesty, duty, and respect.

Location

Hillsdale College is located amidst the hills, dales, and lakes of south-central Michigan. The Indiana and Ohio turnpikes are each 30 minutes away, and the College is within close reach of such metropolitan areas as Detroit, Chicago, Cleveland, Toledo, Ft. Wayne, and Indianapolis. The town of Hillsdale is a county seat with a population of 10,000. Stores, churches, restaurants, and movie theaters are all within walking distance of the campus.

Majors and Degrees

Hillsdale awards Bachelor of Arts and Bachelor of Science degrees in accounting, applied mathematics, art, biochemistry, biology, chemistry, classics, economics, English, exercise science, financial management, French, German, Greek, history, Latin, marketing/management, mathematics, music, philosophy, physical education, physics, politics, psychology, religion, rhetoric and public address, Spanish, speech, sport management, sport psychology, and theater. Interdisciplinary majors are available in American studies, Christian studies, comparative literature, European studies, international studies in business and foreign language, political economy, and sociology and social thought. Preprofessional programs are offered in allied health sciences (including optometry, pharmacy, and physical therapy), dentistry, education, engineering, environmental sciences, journalism, law, medicine and osteopathy, theology, and veterinary medicine. The Van Andel Graduate School of Statesmanship offers the Doctor of Philosophy in politics and the Master of Arts in politics.

The Academic Program

Hillsdale operates on a two-semester schedule, with the fall term beginning in late August and ending in mid-December and the spring term beginning in mid-January and ending in mid-May. Two 3-week summer sessions are also offered.

The College maintains its defense of the traditional liberal arts curriculum, convinced that it is the best preparation for meeting the challenges of modern life, and that it offers to people of all backgrounds not only an important body of knowledge, but also timeless truths about the human condition. The liberal arts are dedicated to stimulating students' intellectual curiosity, to encouraging the critical, well-disciplined mind, and to fostering personal growth through academic challenge. Every Hillsdale College student is required to complete a structured core of courses in the humanities, natural sciences, and social sciences. Required courses include Western and American Heritage, U.S. Constitution, Great Books in the Western and British/American Traditions, Classical Logic and Rhetoric, Western Philosophical Tradition, and Western Theological Tradition. All students declare a major by the end of the junior year. To graduate, students must complete a minimum 124 hours of course work

and fulfill the requirements of at least one major field. The B.A. program includes a foreign language proficiency requirement. The B.S. program requires additional studies in mathematics and the natural sciences.

The Center for Constructive Alternatives conducts four week-long symposia during the academic year and is one of the largest college lecture series in America. These programs, with themes ranging from historical to political, business, science, and the arts, bring to the campus distinguished scholars and public figures of national and international renown. All students are required to enroll in one seminar for credit.

The Collegiate Scholars Program enriches the academic experience of high-performing students by providing opportunities to become broadly and deeply versed in the contents and methods of inquiry of the liberal arts, preeminently of the Western intellectual tradition of humanistic and scientific learning in a manner consonant with the aims of the College's core curriculum. A combination of special seminars, campus lectures and discussions, retreats, subsidized foreign travel to a destination relevant to the program's purpose, and the completion of an interdisciplinary senior thesis help to meet this goal.

Off-Campus Programs

For forty years, the Washington Hillsdale Internship Program (WHIP) has provided students the opportunity to participate in full-time, academically intensive internships in the nation's capital. The program has been significantly bolstered with the 2008 establishment of the Hillsdale College Allan P. Kirby, Jr. Center for Constitutional Studies and Citizenship in Washington, D.C. Past interns and fellows have been placed in locations as challenging and rewarding as the U.S. House of Representatives, the U.S. Senate, the White House, various think tanks including the Heritage Foundation, news and media outlets, national security agencies, lobbying firms, international trade and relations organizations, and private sector companies.

Through the College's affiliations with the Center for Medieval and Renaissance Studies and the Oxford Study Abroad Program, Hillsdale students are able to study abroad for a summer or a year at one of the more than thirty colleges of Oxford University. Hillsdale offers a summer business program in cooperation with Regent's College in London, England, and the opportunity to study at the University of St. Andrews in St. Andrews, Scotland. Science students benefit from Hillsdale's 685-acre field research laboratory in northern Michigan, a marine biology program in the Florida Keys, and internship opportunities with the Omaha Zoo. Foreign language students frequently study abroad in Argentina, France, Germany, and Spain. Qualified individual students who wish to study in another country for a semester or a year are assisted by their faculty advisor and the registrar in planning a program that enables them to gain academic credit as well as take full advantage of their experience.

Academic Facilities

The Hillsdale College Mossey Library is a three-floor, 43,000-square-foot facility with a collection of 272,000 books, nearly two million electronic books, 22,000 audiovisual items, and subscriptions to 235 academic research databases, among other resources. In addition to the main study and research collections, the Library also contains a number of rare and special holdings, including the Ludwig von Mises, Russell Kirk, Richardson Heritage, Richard Weaver, and Carus Coin collections. Connected to other Michigan libraries through MelCat, and with college libraries nationwide via interlibrary loan, students have access to most any material necessary for on-campus research. Numerous individual study areas and group study rooms are available for students, as well as computer research terminals.

Lane and Kendall Halls at the front of campus serve as the primary academic facilities in the social sciences and humanities and contain classroom space and faculty offices, as well as a special laboratory for experimental psychology. The Strosacker Science Center houses the departments of biology, chemistry, and physics. The Joseph H. Moss Family Laboratory Wing is a 17,000-square-foot addition that includes a microbiology/cell biology lab, anatomy/physiology lab with human cadaver access, conservation genetics lab, water lab, greenhouse, and organic/general chemistry labs. The 32,000-square-foot Herbert Henry Dow Science Building provides additional classrooms, research laboratories, animal rooms, and a computer lab. Slayton Arboretum is a 48-acre campus garden and bird sanctuary used by students to practice field exercises and conduct research. The Mary Randall Preschool is a circular laboratory school in which nursery school children are taught by students specializing in early childhood education and psychology. Experts in the field have called this building "a model for the nation." The Hillsdale Academy, a K–12 private model school, provides additional opportunities for classroom observation.

The Roche Sports Complex is a facility available to varsity athletes and the general student body alike. The building houses the 60,000-square-foot Dawn Tibbetts Potter Arena, which features a student fitness center and basketball/volleyball courts. The building also houses the John "Jack" McAvoy Natatorium for swimming and diving, an exercise physiology and sports medicine facility, four racquetball courts, extensive locker room space, and a weight/fitness room. Adjacent is the 7,000-seat capacity Frank "Muddy" Waters Stadium, which features an artificial surface football field; all-weather, Olympic-quality eight-lane running track; outdoor tennis courts; and fields for soccer, baseball, and women's softball. Located northwest of the Roche Sports Complex, the 76,000-square-foot Margot V. Biermann Athletic Center houses four acrylic tennis courts and a six-lane, 200-meter NCAA regulation Mondo surface track.

The Sage Center for the Arts is home to the departments of art and theater. This 47,000-square-foot facility contains studios, classroom space, an exhibition gallery, a prop- and scene-construction shop, a sound studio, graphics lab, black box theatre, and the Markel Auditorium, a 353-seat performance hall (with orchestra pit). The 32,809-square-foot Howard Music Hall houses office, studio, classroom, rehearsal, and performance space for the John E. N. and Dede Howard Department of Music. Notable features include the McNamara Rehearsal Hall, Conrad Recital Hall, and studio space for percussion and jazz studies. Lower-level practice rooms are available to students during business hours without reservation.

The 53,000-square-foot Grewcock Student Union is the center of student life. The two-story structure houses the cafeteria, bookstore, student mail center, offices for student activities and publications, a lounge with a 100-inch flat-screen television, a formal lounge and conference room, AJ's Café, and a game area. Hayden Park sits at the northeastern perimeter of campus and encompasses 190 acres of rolling, partially wooded farmland. In addition to serving as a course for Hillsdale's cross-country teams, it provides a place for club and intramural sports, mountain biking, cross-country skiing, and general outdoor recreation. The 27,000-square-foot Christ Chapel is currently under construction and will be a center for spiritual life on campus and serve as a symbol of Hillsdale's Christian roots and identity.

Faculty

The faculty consists of 137 full-time members with a 10:1 student-teacher ratio and average class sizes of 15. No classes are taught by graduate students. The size and closeness of the College community enable personal attention and faculty mentorship inside the classroom and during office visits after class. Each student has a faculty advisor for core and major coursework who directs the program of study and provides academic and career counseling. Hillsdale's faculty considers teaching their first priority. Many faculty members also engage in research and scholarly writing, supported by summer and sabbatical leaves funded by the College, and are often invited to comment on the national scene in lecture programs and media outlets.

Athletics

Hillsdale's Charger athletes compete in 14 intercollegiate NCAA Division II varsity sports as part of the Great Midwest Athletic Conference. Hillsdale College sponsors varsity basketball, cross-country, swimming and diving, softball, tennis, indoor and outdoor track and field, and volleyball for women, and varsity baseball, basketball, cross-country, golf, football, tennis, and indoor and outdoor track and field for men. In 2016–17, 11 athletes earned All-American honors while 17 received Academic All-American awards. Hillsdale College boasts a 96 percent student-athlete Academic Success Rate. Fourteen club sports and eleven intramural sports are also available to students.

Student Life

Four national fraternities, three national sororities, a newspaper and radio station, and more than 100 other social, academic, spiritual, and service organizations provide Hillsdale students with a diverse array of cocurricular opportunities. A resident drama troupe and dance company, a concert choir and chamber chorale, a jazz program with big band and combos, instrumental chamber ensembles from string quartets to percussion ensemble, and a symphony orchestra and band constitute the College's performing arts organizations. The Student Activities Board hosts campus-wide social functions throughout the year, including marquee events like Garden Party, Homecoming, President's Ball, and Centralhallapalooza.

Hillsdale students are housed in dormitories, fraternity and sorority houses, and various off-campus dwellings. Single and double rooms are available on campus; there are no coed dormitories. Each College-owned residence hall is supervised by a resident director and resident advisers. All freshmen (except commuters) are required to live on campus; upper-class students seeking to live off campus must apply to the dean of men or dean of women for this privilege.

Special student services provided by the College include career planning and placement counseling; academic advising and tutoring; and a health service staffed by a physician, a resident nurse, and counselors.

Costs

Annual tuition for the 2017–18 academic year was $25,540, room was $5,240, board was $5,370, and mandatory fees were $1,202. Books, supplies, and personal expenses (including travel, recreation, and clothing) are estimated at $3,000 per year.

Financial Aid

Financial aid at Hillsdale is available in many forms. Academic scholarships are awarded on a competitive basis, regardless of financial need. The priority application deadline for academic scholarship consideration is January 1. The application for admission also serves as the Hillsdale application for merit-based aid. Athletic scholarships are awarded on a competitive basis in men's baseball, football, and golf; men's and women's basketball, tennis, track, and cross-country; and women's swimming, softball, and volleyball. The departments of art and music also award a select number of scholarships based on strength of portfolio/audition. To apply for aid on the basis of financial need, students are required to file Hillsdale's Confidential Family Financial Statement (CFFS). Because Hillsdale does not accept government funds, either directly for its operations or indirectly in the form of student aid, the FAFSA is not applicable; government funds are replaced with private dollars. Grants and loans are available from the College.

Admission Requirements

Admission to Hillsdale College is a privilege extended to students who are able to benefit by, and contribute to, the academic and social environment of the College. A formal application to Hillsdale College includes (1) a completed application form, (2) the scores from either the Scholastic Aptitude Test (SAT), the American College Test (ACT), or the Classic Learning Test, (3) an official transcript of high school grades (and post-secondary grades, if available), (4) thoughtful essay and short answer responses, (5) two academic letters of recommendation, and (6) a résumé of extracurricular activities, volunteerism, leadership, and work experience. An interview is recommended, but not required. Transfer students must include a Dean of Students Transfer Form and official college transcript(s). International students must submit all required documents in English; the ACT or SAT is required, the TOEFL is optional.

Application and Information

Students may apply to Hillsdale College any time after the completion of the junior year of high school. A formal application includes a completed application form accompanied by a nonrefundable fee of $35 (free if submitted online) and all required credentials. Application plans include early decision (November 1), spring admission (December 1), priority scholarship (January 1), and regular decision (April 1). Hillsdale College has been distinguished since its founding in 1844 by voluntarily adhering to a nondiscriminatory policy regarding race, religion, sex, and national or ethnic origin—long before the government began regulating such matters. All records and forms should be mailed to:

Admissions Office
Hillsdale College
33 East College Street
Hillsdale, Michigan 49242-1298
Phone: 517-607-2327
Fax: 517-607-2223
E-mail: admissions@hillsdale.edu
Website: http://www.hillsdale.edu

HOFSTRA UNIVERSITY
HEMPSTEAD, NEW YORK

 To read more about this school, visit http://petersons.to/hofstrauniversity

The University

Since its founding in 1935, Hofstra has evolved into an internationally renowned university that continues to achieve recognition as an institution of academic excellence. Hofstra has 27 academic accreditations and 30 total accreditations, and consistently earns recognition on the best college lists of *U.S. News & World Report*, The Princeton Review, *Fiske Guide to Colleges*, PayScale College ROI and Salary Reports, and *Forbes* magazine. Additionally, Hofstra has consistently been named to the President's Higher Education Community Service Honor Roll and is the only university to host three consecutive U.S. presidential debates (2008, 2012, and 2016).

Hofstra offers more than 160 undergraduate and more than 165 graduate program options. More than 100 dual-degree program options are also offered, giving students the opportunity to earn both a graduate and undergraduate degree in less time than if each degree was pursued separately. Students can choose from internationally recognized programs within Hofstra's various schools and colleges:

- Academic Health Sciences Center, including the Donald and Barbara Zucker School of Medicine at Hofstra/Northwell; the Hofstra Northwell School of Graduate Nursing and Physician Assistant Studies; and the School of Health Professions and Human Services.

- Frank G. Zarb School of Business

- Fred DeMatteis School of Engineering and Applied Science

- Hofstra College of Liberal Arts and Sciences, including the Peter S. Kalikow School of Government, Public Policy, and International Affairs; the School of Education; the School of Humanities, Fine and Performing Arts; and the School of Natural Sciences and Mathematics

- Honors College

- Lawrence Herbert School of Communication

- Maurice A. Deane School of Law

- Hofstra University Continuing Education

Hostra students live and learn in one of the university's 35 residence halls, each with a unique flair, community, and life of its own. There are also eleven living-learning communities, which give students the opportunity to live with others who share the same classes, or have similar passions for interests like leadership, health sciences, or the visual or performing arts.

Hofstra hosts hundreds of social, academic, and cultural events each year, drawing together scholars, business leaders, authors, celebrities, health care professionals, politicians, and journalists from across the nation and around the world. These events help foster the connection between in-classroom work and extracurricular interests.

The David S. Mack Sports and Exhibition Complex, a 93,000 square-foot facility, is home to the Hofstra Pride men's and women's basketball teams and wrestling team. It is also the site for events such as commencements, exhibitions, trade shows, televised political events—including U.S. presidential debates—and concerts. Other recreational and athletic facilities include an indoor, Olympic-size swimming pool; a state-of-the-art fitness center; and various athletic fields. In addition, Hofstra offers 17 intercollegiate athletic programs that compete at the NCAA Division I level; 33 local/national fraternities and sororities; and more than 200 academic, media, multicultural, performance, preprofessional, religious, social/political, and sports clubs and organizations.

Location

Hofstra's 244-acre suburban campus is a short train ride from all the cultural, recreational, internship, and career opportunities New York City has to offer—and only minutes from beautiful beaches, shopping malls, restaurants, and two airports.

Majors and Degrees

The Bachelor of Arts (B.A.) is awarded in African studies; American studies; anthropology; art history; Asian studies; biology; chemistry; Chinese; Chinese studies; classics; comparative literature and languages; computer science; criminology; dance; drama; early childhood education and childhood education (with dual major in another discipline); economics; elementary education; engineering science; English; English education; film studies and production; fine arts; foreign language education (French, German, Italian, Russian, Spanish); French; geography; geology; German; global studies; Hebrew; history; individually designed B.A. major in humanities, natural sciences, or social sciences;, Italian; Japanese and Japanese studies; Jewish studies; journalism; labor studies; Latin; Latin American and Caribbean studies; liberal arts; linguistics; mass media studies; math education (with a dual major in another discipline); mathematical economics; mathematics; music; philosophy; physics; political science; pre-health with a concentration in humanities and social sciences; psychology; public relations; public policy and public service; radio production and studies; religion; rhetorical studies; Russian; science education (biology, chemistry, earth science, physics); science technology, engineering and mathematics (STEM); social studies education (with a dual major in another discipline); sociology; Spanish; speech-language-hearing sciences; sustainability studies; television production and studies; urban ecology; and women's studies.

The Bachelor of Business Administration (B.B.A.) is awarded in accounting, business analytics, entrepreneurship, finance, information systems, international business, legal studies in business, management, marketing, and supply chain management.

The Bachelor of Science (B.S.) is offered in applied physics, athletic training, biochemistry, biology, business economics, chemistry, civil engineering, community health, computer engineering, computer science, computer science and mathematics (dual major), early childhood education/childhood education, electrical engineering, environmental resources, exercise science, fine arts, forensic science, geographic information systems, geology, health education, health science, industrial engineering, mathematical business economics, mathematical finance, mathematics, mechanical engineering, music, neuroscience, philosophy, physics, pre-medical, psychology, sustainability studies, urban ecology, video/television, video/television and business, video/television and film, and video/television.

The Bachelor of Science in Education (B.S.Ed.) is offered with specializations in dance, fine arts, music, and physical education.

The Bachelor of Engineering (B.E.) is offered in engineering science with specializations in biomedical engineering and civil engineering.

The Bachelor of Fine Arts (B.F.A.) is awarded in theater arts and dance.

Combined (dual) degrees offered include Bachelor of Arts/Juris Doctor (B.A./J.D.), in collaboration with the Maurice A. Deane School of Law; Juris Doctor/Master of Business Administration (J.D./MBA) in collaboration with the Maurice A. Deane School of Law and the Frank G. Zarb School of Business; Juris Doctor/Master of Public Health (J.D./M.P.H.) in collaboration with the Maurice A. Dean School of Law and the School of Health Professions and Human Services; Medical Doctorate/Master of Public Health in collaboration with the Donald and Barbara Zucker School of Medicine at Hofstra/Northwell and the School of Health Professions and Human Services; B.S./M.S. in physician assistant studies; B.S./M.D. and B.A./M.D., through the Donald and Barbara Zucker School of Medicine at Hofstra/Northwell; and various majors and concentrations leading to the B.A./MBA, B.S./MBA, B.A./M.S.Ed., B.A./M.A., B.A./M.S., B.S./M.S., B.B.A./M.S.Ed., B.B.A./M.S., B.B.A./MBA, B.S./M.S.Ed., B.S./M.A., B.A./M.F.A., M.A./MBA, and M.D./Ph.D.

Academic Programs

Requirements for graduation vary among schools and majors. A liberal arts core curriculum is an integral part of all areas of concentration. The University calendar is organized on a traditional fall and spring semester system, and offers an optional January session and three optional Summer sessions (between May and August).

Hofstra offers innovative programs designed to meet the needs of its diverse student body. These include Honors College, Legal Education Accelerated Program (LEAP), Hofstra 4+4 Program, First-Year Connections, and living/learning communities.

Honors College students can elect to study in any of the University's undergraduate programs and are involved in all fields of advanced study.

The Legal Education Accelerated Program allows students to earn both a B.A. and a J.D. in just six years.

The Hofstra 4+4 Program allows students to earn both a bachelor's degree (B.A. or B.S.) and M.D. in eight years in collaboration with the Donald and Barbara Zucker School of Medicine at Hofstra/Northwell.

First-Year Connections, an optional integrated academic and social program, helps first-year students connect with one another as well as with all the resources and opportunities offered at the University. The program offers seminars and course clusters, that satisfy general education requirements for all majors, and features small classes taught by distinguished faculty.

Through Hofstra's living/learning communities, students are exposed to environments that are intellectually stimulating, supportive, and conducive to building lasting friendships and a memorable first-year experience. These communities are associated with several first-year clusters and seminars, giving students the opportunity to live with students who are in their classes and who share their interests.

Off-Campus Programs

Hofstra extends learning beyond the classroom through varied internship programs and study-abroad opportunities. The internship programs take advantage of Hofstra's proximity to New York City, allowing students to gain real-life experience in areas such as finance, business, media, advertising, and entertainment. Through study-abroad programs in Europe, Asia, South America, and other locations, students can explore the world while earning college credits. More information is available at hofstra.edu/studyabroad.

Academic Facilities

Hofstra students have numerous opportunities for experiential learning, on and off campus. Students can conduct research with a distinguished professor in Hofstra's innovative labs, including a big data lab, a robotics and advanced manufacturing lab, and a cell and tissue engineering lab, or intern with top-tier companies in finance or media, the state Legislature, or Congress. Students also have access to cutting-edge facilities such as the Martin B. Greenberg Trading Room, equipped with 34 Bloomberg Professional terminals; or WRHU–88.7 FM, Radio Hofstra University, recipient of two prestigious Marconi Awards from the National Association of Broadcasters and one of the top college radio stations in the country (according to The Princeton Review Best Colleges 2015–2017).

Costs

The 2017–18 annual tuition and fees for a full-time undergraduate student are $43,960. The cost of a housing and dining plan is approximately $14,930. The full tuition and fees schedule is available at hofstra.edu/tuition.

Financial Aid

Hofstra University works hard to make a private college education affordable for students and families, and offers several financial aid options for new undergraduates, including interest-free payment plans and a four-year locked-in rate for tuition and fees (hofstra.edu/lockedintuitionrate) that can help students manage costs from admission through graduation. Detailed information can be found at hofstra.edu/FinancialAid.

Faculty

All classes at Hofstra are taught by distinguished faculty members who are committed to excellence in teaching, scholarly research, and service. With an average undergraduate class size of 20 and a student-faculty ratio of 13:1, students are encouraged to debate, question, conduct research, discuss, and think critically in an open, collaborative learning environment.

Student Government

The Student Government Association (SGA) is Hofstra University's student-run governing body and is comprised of full-time undergraduate students; the SGA acts as a liaison between Hofstra students and the University's faculty, administration, and Board of Trustees. In addition, SGA plans and executes multiple programs and initiatives throughout the academic year, and oversees and finances of more than 200 clubs and organizations.

Admission Requirements

Hofstra is a competitive institution that seeks to enroll students who demonstrate academic ability, intellectual curiosity, and the motivation to succeed and contribute to the campus community. Careful consideration is given to a student's high school record, types of courses taken, SAT or ACT scores (if applicable), letters of recommendation, extracurricular involvement, and the personal essay. Submitting standardized test scores to Hofstra is optional. Prospective students should visit hofstra.edu/testing policy for more information. The most competitive applicants will have followed a rigorous college preparatory curriculum and will have taken advantage of honors and advanced placement–level courses where appropriate. The Office of Admission prefers a high school curriculum that includes 4 years of English, 3 to 4 years of social studies, 2 to 3 years of foreign language, 3 years of mathematics (4 years for engineering applicants), and 3 years of science (4 years for engineering applicants). Campus visits are strongly recommended. Hofstra accepts applications from first-year, transfer, and international students.

Application and Information

For students whose first choice is Hofstra, there are two early action periods: (1) When an application is submitted by November 15, notification is made to the student by December 15; and (2) When an application is submitted by December 15, notification is made to the student by January 15. Students applying for regular decision are considered on a rolling basis.

First-year applicants must submit an application, $70 application fee, high school transcript, SAT or ACT scores (if applicable), essay, and letter of recommendation. Hofstra accepts applications via mail or online and participates in the Common Application.

For more information, contact:
Hofstra University
Office of Undergraduate Admission
100 Hofstra University
Hempstead, New York 11549-1000
Phone: 516-463-6700
Fax: 516-463-5100
E-mail: admission@hofstra.edu
Website: http://www.hofstra.edu/admission

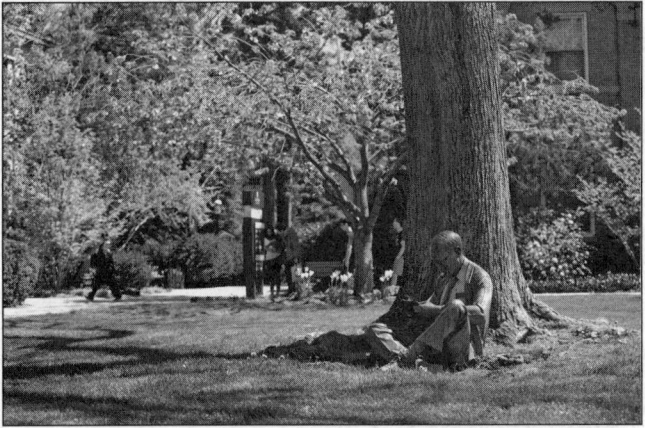

Hofstra students live and learn in the best of both worlds. Professors teach in traditional classroom settings, but lectures expand into the world beyond. With NYC only a 45-minute train ride away, students can immerse themselves in diverse cultural and entertainment activities, while applying what they learn in the classroom at internships and co-op programs.

HOLY NAMES UNIVERSITY
OAKLAND, CALIFORNIA

 For more information, visit http://petersons.to/holynamesu

The University

Founded in 1868, Holy Names University (HNU) empowers a diverse student body for leadership and service through liberal arts and professional education. It consistently ranks as one of the most diverse universities in the nation, and it receives the highest accreditation from the Western Association of Schools and Colleges.

Nearly 900 students have access to 15 bachelor's degrees, seven master's degrees, and four degree-completion programs. These rigorous programs along with small class sizes, dedicated teachers, personal attention, and focus on social justice prepare students for leadership and service roles.

Holy Names University's rigorous academic programs ensure that students graduate with the intelligence, experience, and confidence to obtain rewarding positions in their fields of interest.

Location

Holy Names University is situated on 60 wooded acres in the hills of Oakland, California. Its location offers a spectacular view of Oakland, San Francisco, and the Bay. The area's coastal climate provides temperate winters; clear, sunny fall and spring days; and sunny, breezy summers. The university's location amongst the hills provides a safe, beautiful, tranquil place to learn. Parks that surround the campus provide outdoor recreation like bicycling, hiking, and horseback riding.

HNU's close proximity to San Francisco provides easy access to urban amenities like museums, performing arts, and professional sporting events. Attractions like Carmel, Lake Tahoe, Monterey Bay, and Yosemite National Park are within driving distance

Majors and Degrees

Holy Names University is comprised of four schools, each of which offers the following programs of study:

The School of Liberal Arts: Communication Studies and self-designed major (may be across schools) with concentrations in English Literature, Latin American and Latino/a studies, Digital Arts, Music, Philosophy, Religious Studies, and Writing for Professionals.

The School of Nursing, Health, and Natural Sciences: Biology, Community Health Sciences (B.S.), Kinesiology (B.A. and B.S.), Nursing (post-licensure, RN to B.S.N.), and Nursing (pre-licensure, generic B.S.N.).

The School of Education: Liberal Studies (B.A.).

The School of Business and Applied Social Sciences: Accounting (B.S.); Business (B.A.) with the following emphases: Finance, International Business, Marketing, or Sports Management; Criminology; International Relations; Politics and History; Psychobiology; and Sociology.

Academic Programs

The Connections Project First-Year Experience (CP FYE) program is designed to help first-year students connect with the HNU community in meaningful ways that will support their social and academic transition into college life, including learning how to learn; learning how to serve; and learning how to lead.

Providing students with comprehensive support, the staff and departments in the Advising and Learning Resources area offer assistance with academic planning, tutoring and other learning supports, and disability services. The university strives to provide a wide range of resources for academic success and to work with students to identity and achieve their academic goals.

HNU's Center for Social Justice and Civic Engagement has increasingly been acknowledged as a model for aligning educational actions with institutional mission. The work of the Center has been recognized as enriching the understanding of social issues through personal exploration and socially responsible leadership at the University and within the local and global community.

Off-Campus Programs

HNU's Center for Social Justice and Civic Engagement organizes the following student trips each year:

HNU students and staff participate in the annual School of the Americas Watch Vigil and Protest, representing the HNU community in Nogales, Arizona. The delegation participates in activities to promote justice and peace, and to bring awareness to immigration policies.

HNU students travel with faculty and staff to Tutwiler, Mississippi, to work with Habitat for Humanity to build a home for a community resident. Students also visit several civil rights landmarks throughout the South, including the National Civil Rights Museum at the Lorraine Motel in Memphis, Tennessee, where Dr. Martin Luther King Jr. was assassinated.

Costs

For the 2018–19 academic year, full-time undergraduate tuition totals $38,800 with a campus fee of $516 per year. Residence hall room rates range from $6,812 to $9,906 per year and meal plans range from $5,942 to $6,378 per year, depending on the options selected.

Financial Aid

Holy Names University is one of the most affordable private universities in the San Francisco Bay Area. In fact, nearly all incoming freshman and day transfer students receive university grants and/or scholarships such as the following: Holy Names University Grants, athletic scholarships, Catholic High Schools scholarship, merit scholarships, music scholarships, and the Sister Marie Rose Durocher Scholarship.

Many undergraduate students also qualify for one or more of these financial aid resources: Cal Grant A & B (California state grants), Federal Pell Grant, Federal Direct Subsidized Stafford Loans, Federal Direct Unsubsidized Stafford Loans, Federal Parent Plus Loans, Federal Perkins Loans, private loans, and student employment.

Faculty

Holy Names University's faculty is highly qualified; 90 percent of full-time faculty members have the highest possible degree in their field. A low 13:1 student-faculty ratio facilitates interaction and involvement with students.

Faculty members bring unique experiences and perspectives to their classrooms. For example, students learn about Central America's history from a professor who grew up in El Salvador. They learn accounting and marketing strategies from a professor who's also a Certified Public Accountant and former entrepreneur.

As a licensed architect with more than 25 years of experience, Associate Professor of Management James Stryker, Ph.D. brings his own unique experiences to the classroom. His professional expertise includes starting and managing a design practice and working as the director of facility design and management for a Fortune 100 pharmaceutical company.

Student Life

Holy Names is a close-knit community where students build meaningful partnerships with faculty members. On-campus housing gives them the opportunity to create friendships and build strong ties with fellow students from diverse backgrounds and origins.

One of HNU's assets is its diversity. The student population is 64 percent female and 36 percent male; 34 percent are first-generation college students. The student body is 41.8 percent Hispanic, 20.5 percent black, 16.7 percent white, 10.1 percent Asian, 3.8 percent international, 2.5 percent Native Hawaiian/Pacific islander, and .4 percent American Indian or Alaskan.

Residential living also provides easy access to opportunities that enable students to express their creativity, have fun, help others, and take on leadership roles. Students can enjoy a wide range of activities—these are just a few options:

- Attend events like carnivals, dances, and NCAA intercollegiate athletic games

- Become peer mentors

- Engage in spiritual growth through the Campus Ministry

- Join student clubs and organizations, such as the HNU Black Student Union, Dance Force, Freaks and Geeks, and Latinos Unidos

- Participate in student government

- Pursue social justice work through the Center for Social Justice and Civic Engagement

Admission Requirements

Freshman applicants are considered for admission based on the overall strength of their high school preparation, SAT or ACT scores (SAT code is 4059 and ACT code is 0230), personal essay, letter of recommendation, extracurricular activities, and individual talents and achievements.

Application and Information

Applications are accepted on a rolling basis from October 1 to August 1. Eligible incoming freshman students who complete the Application for Admission by the March 2 priority deadline will be automatically awarded scholarships based on academic merit.

All applicants are strongly encouraged to complete the Free Application for Federal Student Aid (FAFSA) by the March 2 priority deadline. In addition, California residents should submit a GPA Verification Form to the California Student Aid Commission by March 2, the deadline for Cal Grant eligibility.

Online applications are free. Undergraduate paper applications are $20. Undergraduate applicants can also apply through The Common Application. Application forms and instructions and requirements for transfer and international students are available at https://www.hnu.edu/admissions/undergraduate/application-information:

For additional information, prospective students should contact:
Holy Names University
Office of Undergraduate Admission
3500 Mountain Boulevard
Oakland, California 94619
Phone: 510-436-1351
Fax: 510-436-1325
E-mail: admissions@hnu.edu
Website: https://www.hnu.edu

Holy Names University's location in the Oakland Hills provides wonderful views of the San Francisco Bay and infinite opportunities for personal and career development.

JOHN CABOT UNIVERSITY

ROME, ITALY

 To read more about this school, visit http://petersons.to/johncabotuniversity

The University

John Cabot University (JCU) was founded in 1972 and is the first overseas American university in Italy with regional accreditation by the Middle States Commission on Higher Education. JCU is a liberal arts university following the American system of education but with a distinctive European and international character. Located in the historic center of Rome, the University has unparalleled access to history, culture, and the active international communities associated with the United Nations organizations and embassies present in the city. With a commitment to a serious liberal arts education and a unique relationship with leading multinational corporations, media, and other cultural and international organizations, JCU provides degree-seeking students with the academic training and opportunities to participate in exclusive internships that will allow them to enter directly into challenging careers after graduation, or to continue their studies at prestigious graduate programs.

The University has a diverse and unique student body, comprised of American, Italian, and international degree-seeking students from more than seventy countries. This group is complemented by visiting American students from universities across the United States. The visiting students bring their own regional diversity, which enhances the international environment at JCU, resulting in a dynamic and engaging student body. JCU's commitment to creating a student community of both degree-seeking and visiting students results in the friendly, close community of a small campus, with the wide-ranging networks that come from studying with a large pool of students from across the United States.

The average class size is 15 students, and there are approximately 100 full- and part-time faculty members with advanced degrees from prestigious universities all over the world. Students work closely with professors and receive the individual attention needed to develop their academic abilities. JCU graduates are accepted into acclaimed graduate programs in the United States, the United Kingdom, and Europe, such as Columbia University, Johns Hopkins University, London School of Economics, and the University of Oxford.

The University is licensed by the Delaware Department of Education to award its degrees and is authorized by the Italian Ministry of Research and Instruction to operate as an institution of American higher education in Rome. John Cabot University was accredited in 2003 by the Middle States Commission on Higher Education (http://www.msche.org).

Location

John Cabot University is located in Rome, Italy, in the picturesque Trastevere neighborhood, just down the river from St. Peter's Basilica and the Vatican and a short walk from the Colosseum and Roman Forum. The University has three campuses within a 10-minute walk of each other and student residences with 24/7 security close to campus. The Frank J. Guarini Campus consists of a main building with three floors and an adjacent wing connected by terraces and courtyards. The property offers students a quiet atmosphere in which to study and interact, while historic, bustling Rome is just a few steps away. Surrounded by the gardens of the Accademia dei Lincei (the National Academy of Sciences, of which Galileo was an early member) and the Villa Farnesina of Raphael's famous frescoes, the Guarini Campus is buttressed by the Aurelian Wall of the Roman Empire. The Guarini Campus is approached through the Porta Settimiana, which was built in the third century and later rebuilt by Pope Alexander VI Borgia

in 1498. JCU also has spacious classrooms and a cafeteria in the Tiber Campus, which is located along the banks of the Tiber River. JCU's Critelli Campus, also along the Tiber, was opened in January 2018 and houses administrative offices as well as classrooms. All three campuses are equipped with WiFi, and classrooms are furnished with multimedia equipment. JCU's fine arts and art history classes often meet at famous monuments such as the Colosseum and the Forum. In essence, all of Rome is John Cabot University's campus, and students take advantage of JCU's urban setting, meeting with friends and faculty at local cafés as well as in many of the piazzas that are tucked away within the streets of Rome's historic center.

Majors and Degrees

John Cabot University offers the Bachelor of Arts degree in thirteen majors: art history, business administration, classical studies, communications, economics and finance, English literature, history, humanistic studies, international affairs, international business, Italian studies, marketing, and political science. JCU also offers a joint degree in communications with the University of Milan, as well as a dual degree in marketing with Pace University in New York City. Students may select minors in all of the major areas except international business, as well as in creative writing, entrepreneurship, philosophy, and psychology. John Cabot offers the Associate of Arts degree in all major fields of study. JCU also introduced a Master's degree in Art History in fall 2017, the first U.S.-accredited graduate degree program in art history based entirely in Rome.

Each of these programs is designed to offer a unique learning and living experience in a setting rich in history, culture, and geopolitical interaction. All majors are complemented by internship opportunities at the United Nations, museums, and international firms in Rome. JCU's Career Services Center offers support for students' preparation and transition into post-graduate activities, offering over 350 internship and job opportunities each year. JCU's 10,000-member alumni network spans 110 countries and includes business leaders, politicians, diplomats, artists, scholars, and entrepreneurs, providing additional opportunities for graduates to continue their career development through international connections.

Academic Programs

The American higher education system encourages experimentation and breadth, particularly during the first two years of the university experience. The curricula of the University's programs are divided into two basic categories: the general distribution requirements of the first two years of study, which give the student a broad exposure to the basic disciplines of the liberal arts educational experience, and the specific requirements of each degree awarded by the University.

The general distribution requirements and other introductory courses equip the student to select an area of specialization as a degree candidate. The degree requirements include ten to twelve core courses deemed by faculty members to be essential to the discipline of the degree. Other requisites include electives that support the core program and allow students to take courses in other discipline areas of particular interest.

The academic year is divided into two semesters of fifteen weeks each, beginning in late August and mid-January. In one semester, a student normally takes five courses, earning 15 credits in the semester and 30 credits in the year. Two 5-week summer sessions allow students to take one or two additional courses per summer session. To earn the Bachelor of Arts degree, a student must complete 120 credits (forty courses); to earn the Associate of Arts degree, a student must complete 60 credits (twenty courses).

JCU accepts up to 60 transfer credits, including the IB diploma, AP exams, UK A-Levels, and other college-level courses.

Special programs include English language preparation for university study (ENLUS) for non-native English speakers, after which students who successfully complete the program may transfer directly into one of JCU's degree programs.

Off-Campus Programs

The Go Global program at JCU offers degree-seeking students the opportunity to study at partner universities in the United States, Europe, Africa, Asia, and the Americas. This opportunity contributes to educational growth and cultural awareness, and helps prepare students for careers in international fields.

Academic Facilities

The Frohring Library provides the latest in online access to academic journals and indexes, and is the University center for research in support of the academic programs as well as a quiet place for study and pleasure reading. The University's four computer laboratories contain desktop computers (Macs and PCs) equipped with the latest software as well as printers and a full-color scanner. The University is equipped with high-speed WiFi across campus, a studio art facility, a fitness center, a cafeteria, and a digital media lab.

Costs

Tuition for 2018–19 is $24,900 and housing costs begin at $4,900 per semester.

Financial Aid

U.S. citizens and eligible non-citizens attending John Cabot University may apply for Title IV Federal Student Aid, including Federal Direct Subsidized, Unsubsidized, and Parent Loans for Undergraduate Students(PLUS). Academic scholarships are awarded by the University each year, based on merit and need; they include the Presidential Scholarship, the Italian Merit Scholarship, the Expansion Scholarship for Latin American students, the Dean's List Scholarship, and the assistance grant.

Faculty

The University has a distinguished faculty of professors from around the world who are actively engaged in research. In addition to teaching, faculty members take part in academic advising and co-curricular activities, such as field trips, lectures, and seminars.

Student Government

Student government at JCU contributes significantly to the quality of student life. A Student Senate is elected each year to coordinate activities. During the year, the Student Government sponsors a number of programs, such as the International Student Government Conference, which brings together student leaders from Italy, Europe, and the Middle East. The Student Government works with a faculty adviser and staff adviser in planning social, cultural, intellectual, and sports activities to respond to students' interests and needs.

Admission Requirements

Successful applicants must have a scholastic record demonstrating a commitment to their studies and the ability to succeed at college-level work.

The previous school's documentation of the applicant's academic ability, motivation, character, and contribution to school life is very important. The University does not prescribe a fixed secondary school course of study but considers both the quality and breadth of the student's record. Results of the SAT or the ACT are required for high school students graduating from an American secondary school.

The University is open to all applicants without regard to race, national origin, religion, or gender.

For applicants coming from the U.S. secondary school system, a standard college-preparatory program is expected. For applicants from other national systems, an essential requirement is successful completion of a secondary school program permitting university admission in the respective system. Students holding the Italian Diploma di Maturità, the International Baccalaureate, or other equivalent academic credentials may be granted advanced standing.

Applicants who did not attend an English-language secondary school or university for at least two years must demonstrate sufficient preparation in the English language. Standardized test scores, such as the Test of English as a Foreign Language (TOEFL) or the International English Language Testing System (IELTS), are required.

Application and Information

Admissions decisions are based on the review of official transcripts, results of standardized tests, the student's GPA, final examination results, a personal statement, an interview, and letters of recommendation from teachers or school counselors. A completed application must be accompanied by a nonrefundable application fee of $50. Students may complete the application online or apply through the Common Application. The University has three application deadlines for fall: November 15 (Early Action), March 1 (Regular Decision), and June 1 (Late Decision). The spring application deadline is October 15. Candidates are urged to submit their application and supporting documents as early as possible, as greater scholarship funds may be available.

Students may apply online at https://netcommunity.johncabot.edu/application#.

For additional information, prospective students should contact:

Admissions Office
John Cabot University
Caroline Critelli Guarini Campus
P.zza Giuseppe Gioachino Belli, 11
00153 Rome
Italy
Phone: 855-JCU ROMA
E-mail: admissions@johncabot.edu
Website: http://www.johncabot.edu
       https://www.facebook.com/JohnCabotUniversity
       http://twitter.com/JohnCabotRome
       http://instagram.com/johncabotuniversity

John Cabot University is located in the picturesque Trastevere neighborhood, just down the river from St. Peter's Basilica and the Vatican, and a short walk from the Colosseum and Roman Forum.

JOHNS HOPKINS UNIVERSITY
Krieger School of Arts and Sciences and Whiting School of Engineering
BALTIMORE, MARYLAND

 To read more about this school, visit http://petersons.to/johnshopkins

The University

As America's first research institution, Johns Hopkins University is well known for innovative advances in everything from technology to history and sociology. The university emphasizes the importance of exploration and discovery in the undergraduate experience. Learning occurs through hands-on experiences across all academic disciplines and within every subject imaginable. The academic experience is built around freedom, which allows students to create their own unique interdisciplinary paths. They choose classes they are genuinely interested in, not just required to take, so there's a real sense of curiosity around learning that extends beyond the classroom setting.

Collaborative learning is fundamental to the academic culture and cross-disciplinary partnerships occur between students of all academic areas. Hopkins professors, another invaluable resource, are enthusiastic about teaching and often include undergraduates in their own groundbreaking research. Students get to know their professors and classmates the way they would at a small liberal arts college but have all of the opportunities of a major research institution with a global reach. As a part of this community, undergraduates not only work alongside experts who share their interests but they also run with projects of their own design. In fact, the university remains a national leader of research funding and students in all programs within the Krieger School of Arts & Sciences and Whiting School of Engineering gain practical experiences through research conducted both on and off campus. Every day, faculty and students together create meaningful contributions to academic discourse and make important discoveries. Almost 75 percent of students across all disciplines participate in research, which takes place in labs, museums, and unconventional places throughout campus and the city of Baltimore.

The Homewood campus brings together students with varied interests. Diversity of thought, culture, and experiences cultivates a dynamic, open-minded environment. With over 300 student-run organizations, students find leadership opportunities and the chance to get involved on campus and in their local and global communities.

Location

Located in Baltimore, Maryland, the undergraduate Homewood campus is a traditional college campus with all the advantages of a major city just beyond its front gates. The 140-acre campus, featuring grassy quads and brick buildings, is surrounded by residential areas and neighborhoods that boast one-of-a-kind boutiques, restaurants, historic theaters, and a thriving arts and entertainment district. Baltimore's cultural and networking resources make it an extension of the classroom and an integral part of a Hopkins education. The experiences Hopkins students find in Baltimore create lasting memories and offer preparation for future success in a wide variety of industries. An entrepreneurial hub, Baltimore is the ideal environment to build professional networks, access coveted internships and careers, and get startups off the ground. Undergrads intern at major corporations, government agencies, and nonprofits and make lasting connections with help from the broader Hopkins network. Hopkins students also embrace the University's long-standing commitment to Baltimore and use their skills to make an impact on the city that becomes their second home.

Majors and Degrees

Academics at Hopkins are interdisciplinary and collaboration is encouraged—between students and faculty and across disciplines. The majority of programs combine different areas of study to enable students to make connections across academic boundaries and discover new interests. This establishes a dynamic, engaging learning environment where students from various backgrounds bring an array of perspectives to class discussions. More than 60 percent of Hopkins students pursue a double major or minor, often creating unique combinations like electrical engineering and romance languages or biomedical engineering and business. The full list of majors and minors can be found online at apply.jhu.edu/majors.

Academic Programs

Undergraduates in all programs in the Krieger School of Arts & Sciences and Whiting School of Engineering gain practical experience through innovative research. Several funded programs, such as the Provost's Undergraduate Research Award and the Woodrow Wilson Undergraduate Research Fellowship, are available to give participants the chance to complete projects of their own design. Students also encounter real-world experiences—like implementing marketing plans for local companies and heading startup businesses on campus through the Center for Leadership Education—as well as classes in business, marketing, and communications, accounting and financial management, and entrepreneurship and management. Students can pursue their creative interests through the Center for Visual Arts, which offers nearly 40 studio courses and state-of-the-art equipment for student use.

Students interested in pursuing law or medicine choose any major/minor combination but follow a pre-law or pre-med advising track offered through the Office of Pre-Professional Advising. The biomedical engineering (BME) program at Johns Hopkins, widely regarded as one of the best in the world, is the only undergraduate limited-enrollment major.

Several combined programs are available for undergraduates who want to broaden their educational experience. The Peabody Double Degree Program allows qualified students to simultaneously earn a bachelor of music from the Johns Hopkins Peabody Institute and a B.A or B.S. from Johns Hopkins University. The Direct Matriculation Programs: Master's in International Studies and Master's in Global Health Studies, allow qualified students displaying a strong interest in either area to pursue a combined bachelor's/master's degree with the Johns Hopkins School of Advanced International Studies (SAIS) or the Johns Hopkins Bloomberg School of Public Health. The University also offers the Army ROTC program on campus and the Air Force ROTC program in cooperation with the University of Maryland, College Park.

Off-Campus Programs

Off campus, the city of Baltimore provides unique academic, cultural, and pre-professional experiences. Some classes partner with local organizations to give students practical experiences that complement classroom lectures—like engineering a "fish ladder" at Maryland's Bloede Dam or replicating ancient Greek pottery work at Baltimore Clayworks. Due to the vast network of Hopkins schools and facilities that extends throughout Baltimore (and abroad), undergraduates have the chance to take courses and participate in research at the other renowned divisions of Johns Hopkins University, including the Peabody Conservatory, the School of Nursing, the Bloomberg School of Public Health, the Nitze School of Advanced International Studies, the School of Education, the Carey Business School, and the School of Medicine. In addition to local programs and opportunities, each year more than 500 students study abroad in nearly 30 countries all over the globe. The University also participates in a cooperative program with other colleges in the Baltimore area, such as the Maryland Institute College of Art (MICA), which Hopkins partnered with to open the Johns Hopkins–MICA Film Centre.

Academic Facilities

Collaborative learning is fundamental to the academic environment and many of the newest buildings were designed to foster collaboration across disciplines. Brody Learning Commons (BLC) is one of the most popular places for students to gather, study, and work together. Designed with student input, the building is directly connected to the library and contains the latest learning technology—like interactive projectors that allow students to write on walls and video teleconferencing capabilities—in an eco-friendly, energy-efficient space. The Undergraduate Teaching Labs (UTL), a 105,000-square-foot facility equipped with the latest lab technology, enables synergistic, cross-disciplinary partnerships and research opportunities. Malone Hall was built in 2014 and is a hub for the computer science department, where faculty and students work on innovative projects. The Milton S. Eisenhower Library on the Homewood campus is part of the University's Sheridan Libraries, which comprise the Milton S. Eisenhower Library (including the rare books collection), the John Work Garrett Library, the Albert D. Hutzler Undergraduate Reading Room, and the George Peabody Library. Together, these libraries provide one of the most comprehensive learning resources in the world. Two on-campus creative centers provide resources for students in the arts: the Mattin Student Arts Center contains theaters, a dance studio, music practice rooms, film and digital labs, darkrooms, and art studios; the Brown Foundation Digital Media Center offers digital tools like high-end computers and cameras that enable digital and audio composition and editing, animation, virtual painting, 3-D modeling, and workshops for programs like Adobe After Effects. Off campus, just a short shuttle ride away, the JHU Technology Ventures office allows student entrepreneurs to collaborate, strategize, and get their ideas off the ground.

Costs

Costs for 2018–19 are $53,740 for tuition and $15,836 for room and meals, plus personal expenses like books and travel. (Expenses such as travel and room and meals vary based on choices.)

Financial Aid

Johns Hopkins is dedicated to enrolling the strongest students each year regardless of financial need, and does so by offering a variety of financial support programs for all types of families as well as personalized guidance through the process of finding the right path for them. The University will meet 100 percent of calculated need and also offers a broad range of grants and support. Last year, students received over $100 million in grant money towards their Hopkins education, with an average need-based grant for first-year students of over $42,000. More details, including financial aid application requirements and deadlines and net price calculator tools, are available online at finaid.jhu.edu.

Faculty

As a global research university, Johns Hopkins attracts esteemed faculty. Hopkins professors are world-class scholars and experts in their fields who are constantly making important contributions to their industries and academia at large. They've accomplished impressive feats such as placing 100 percent of their class in finance jobs, winning Nobel Prizes, making scientific breakthroughs, leading global initiatives, and being granted awards for decades-long research studies. They're enthusiastic about teaching, often including undergraduates in their own groundbreaking research, and are always accessible to advise and assist students. Faculty are readily available to students and it's not unusual to brainstorm research ideas over coffee or debate philosophical theories during office hours.

Admission Requirements

Johns Hopkins seeks students who are eager to take advantage of the resources and opportunities at the University and who will contribute to the campus community. The student's academic character, intellectual curiosity, impact and initiative, and extracurricular involvement play a significant role in application review. A student's intellectual interests and accomplishments are of primary importance, and the admissions committee considers each applicant's scholastic record, standardized test results, essays, and recommendations from secondary school officials. In addition to the application and the Hopkins supplement, including a school-specific essay, other required documents include: two teacher recommendations, the secondary school report, and scores on the SAT or the ACT. The University enrolls a first-year class of approximately 1,300 men and women from across the globe. In addition, transfer students from other colleges and universities are admitted to the sophomore and junior classes. Prospective students should refer to apply.jhu.edu/apply for more information about the application process.

Application and Information

Johns Hopkins accepts the Coalition Application, the Common Application, and the Universal College Application, all with a Johns Hopkins supplement. Students who are certain Johns Hopkins is the place for them should consider applying under the Early Decision plan. This requires that the application be submitted by November 1. The deadline for the Regular Decision application is usually January 1. (Note: Deadlines can vary slightly from year to year; see apply.jhu.edu/apply for specific dates.) Notification is given by April 1 for Regular Decision students and by December 15 for those applying under the Early Decision plan. Students wishing to enroll in the biomedical engineering (BME) program must indicate BME as their first choice major on their application. Students applying to the Direct Matriculation Program: Master's in International Studies or Direct Matriculation Program: Master's in Global Health Studies (DMP) must submit an additional application and essay to be considered. First-year students who apply to the BME major or Direct Matriculation Program receive notification at the time of their admission to Johns Hopkins University. Students interested in pursuing a research project of their own design can also apply to the Woodrow Wilson Undergraduate Research Fellowship, which awards up to $10,000 to arts and sciences undergraduates. The Wilson Fellowship application deadline is in January and the date varies slightly from year to year.

Office of Undergraduate Admissions
Johns Hopkins University
Mason Hall
3400 N. Charles Street
Baltimore, Maryland 21218-2683
Phone: 410-516-8171
Fax: 410-516-6025
E-mail: gotojhu@jhu.edu
Website: http://apply.jhu.edu

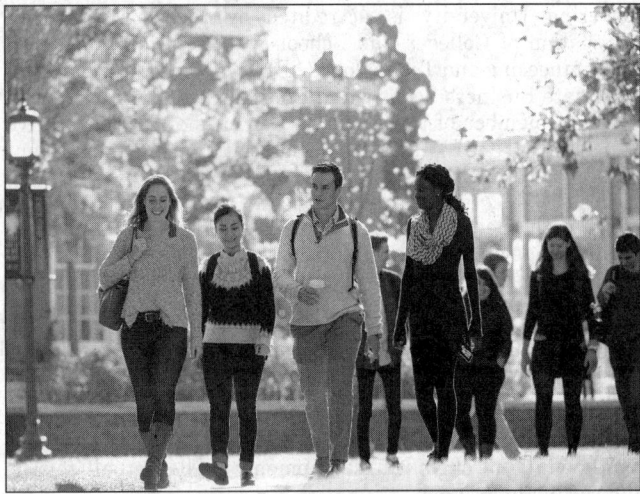

Johns Hopkins undergrads walking to class on the Homewood campus.

KETTERING UNIVERSITY
FLINT, MICHIGAN

 To read more about this school, visit http://petersons.to/ketteringuniversity

The University

Founded in 1919, Kettering University is a private university specializing in science, technology, engineering, math (STEM), and business degrees. The university enrolls about 2,500 undergraduate students and offers a 14:1 student-faculty ratio. Most classes have fewer than 20 students and are taught by Ph.D.-level professors, not teaching assistants. This combination of small class size and highly qualified teaching staff ensures students a much more personalized learning experience.

Kettering is a highly acclaimed university with the one of the country's most modern cooperative education and experiential learning programs. Students in all majors alternate between study terms and full-time work terms. During study terms, students learn material in small, intense classes and labs. During work terms, students work as paid professionals for major companies in industries related to their fields of study. Kettering students have done everything from testing ballistic systems for the U.S. government to reengineering crowd management at Disney World. Kettering has the only cooperative education and experiential learning program of its kind in the country, with students beginning to work in co-op positions as early as their freshman year. Students graduate from Kettering with 2½ years of professional experience and impressive resumes.

Kettering University's cooperative education and experiential learning program pairs hands-on education with real-world experience. This unique system of education prepares students to be business and industry leaders, innovators, and thinkers, with cutting-edge skills who are ready to compete in the global marketplace.

Kettering University is accredited by the North Central Association of Colleges and Schools, the Accreditation Board for Engineering and Technology (ABET), and the Association of Collegiate Business Schools and Programs (ACBSP). Kettering is also a member of the National Commission of Cooperative Education (NCCE) and the Association of Independent Technological Universities.

Along with their academic talents, Kettering students bring a wide range of skills and interests with them to campus. The university offers more than 50 student organizations, including 12 fraternities and 5 sororities, an active student government, a state-of-the-art recreation and fitness facility, and very competitive intramural sports, all aimed at nurturing all aspects of students' experience on campus. Recreation facilities include athletic fields, tennis courts, and a recreation center with an Olympic-size, six-lane swimming pool; aerobic fitness rooms; a full line of Nautilus equipment; and basketball, tennis, and racquetball courts.

Kettering also offers a number of in-demand Master of Science degree programs, including an M.B.A., which are available both on-campus and online. Professional counseling, support services, and healthcare services are available. More information about Kettering can be found on Facebook (facebook.com/ketteringu), Twitter at (@ketteringU), or Instagram (@KetteringU1919).

Location

Kettering University is located in Flint, Michigan, which is 60 miles north of Detroit and 60 miles west of Port Huron. Flint has approximately 100,000 residents and a metropolitan area population of 420,000. Flint is particularly proud of its Cultural Center, which is only 10 minutes from Kettering's campus. Built and endowed entirely by the gifts of private citizens, the Cultural Center includes the Alfred P. Sloan Museum, the Whiting Auditorium (home of the Flint Symphony and host to leading stage shows and entertainers), the Robert T. Longway Planetarium (Michigan's largest and best-equipped sky show facility), the Flint Institute of Arts, the F. A. Bower Theater, the Dort Institute of Music, Mott Community College, and the Flint Public Library. Nearby is the University of Michigan–Flint campus.

The area also offers numerous outdoor and indoor recreational opportunities, including access to county wide trail systems that pass through Kettering's campus. Within a few minutes' drive are downhill and cross-country skiing facilities, lakes for the entire range of water sports, a wide selection of good public golf courses, excellent indoor and outdoor skating rinks, and plentiful shopping facilities and restaurants.

Majors and Degrees

Kettering University offers a 4½-year, professional cooperative education and experiential learning program with Bachelor of Science degrees in applied biology, applied mathematics, applied physics, biochemistry, business administration, chemical engineering, chemistry, computer engineering, computer science, electrical engineering, engineering physics, industrial engineering, and mechanical engineering.

Kettering also offers a variety of dual-degree programs and more than 50 minors, specialties, and concentrations, to ensure that students' degrees are tailored to their interests and career goals. Examples include computer gaming, acoustics, medical physics, alternative energy, and a pre-med course of study.

Academic Programs

Although each program at Kettering University has its own requirements, 160 credit hours are generally required for graduation. The program involves nine academic terms and nine work terms, two of which are centered on the Cumulative Undergraduate Experience (CUE), which is a focused, major work project which displays tangible proof of the student's growth, knowledge, and mastery of real-world skills necessary for success. Students alternate between 11-week periods of academic study on the campus in Flint and twelve-week periods of related work experience with their corporate employer. The academic year consists of two 3-month academic terms on campus and two 3-month terms of paid work experience.

Academic Facilities

Kettering University offers innovative facilities, labs, and educational resources, and students start using them as early as their freshman year. The Crash Safety Center, for example, is the only facility of its kind in the nation used in an undergraduate program. The University also offers labs in areas such as fuel-cell research, polymer optimization, machining, acoustics, and more.

Kettering is fully networked and allows 24-hour access to computer resources and the Internet from dorms and labs. A 445-student residence hall and an apartment complex are located on the campus for student housing. The library offers more than 100,000 cataloged volumes and 540 periodicals. And through online resources like Kettering Connect and Blackboard, students can always be in touch with professors and university staff members.

Costs

For 2017-18, tuition costs were $42,490 and room and board cost $8,040. Kettering offers fixed-rate tuition, and was the first STEM university in Michigan to do so. For students making normal progress towards their degrees, tuition rates will not change during their course of study, removing some of the guesswork associated with budgeting for college costs.

Financial Aid

Kettering University invests in the academic success of its students through generous financial aid packages that include scholarships, loans, and work-study opportunities. Approximately 99 percent of Kettering students receive some sort of financial aid. Factor in co-op earnings—between $40,000 and $65,000 over the course of the college career—and the fixed-rate tuition guarantee, and students are able to take advantage of one of the best values in education today. In addition, Kettering's Merit Scholarship program awards students with extremely generous scholarship packages. Students should fill out the Free Application for Federal Student Aid (FAFSA) and request a copy of the analysis to be sent to Kettering University. The university works to create a financial aid package for based on those results.

Faculty

Kettering University's faculty members balance a commitment to teaching with focused applied research interests, many of which undergraduate students participate in. Most professors have industrial experience in addition to academic credentials and maintain contact with industry through consulting, sponsored research, and advising on student thesis projects. More than 84 percent of faculty members hold a Ph.D. Because only half of the students are on campus at any one time, class sizes are small, and opportunities for enrichment and extra help from faculty are readily available.

Admission Requirements

Admission to Kettering University is competitive and based on scholastic achievement and extracurricular interests, activities, and achievements. Applicants are required to have earned the following: 3 years of English, 2 years algebra, 1 year of geometry, 1 semester of trigonometry, 2 years of lab science (1 must be physics or chemistry; both are recommended). Applicants must submit results of the SAT or ACT (Kettering's ACT code number is 1998 and the SAT code number is 1246).

Most Kettering University students are in the top 10 percent of their graduating class. Kettering University also welcomes students wishing to transfer from other colleges and universities. The transfer alternative is an excellent way to gain admission for students who do not enroll as freshmen.

Application and Information

Students can apply online at http://www.kettering.edu/apply Students can apply online at http://www.kettering.edu/apply or through the Common Application. Students should call 800-955-4464 ext. 7865 for assistance. Kettering officials review applications and let students know if they have been accepted. Although Kettering accepts and processes applications throughout the year, it is best to apply as early as possible. Once accepted, students receive information on programs and the professional co-op program, which are only available to admitted students. Students should complete the co-op registration (resume) online and pay a $300 tuition deposit (to be credited to the first-semester tuition). The deposit shows that a student is as serious about Kettering as Kettering is about the student and ensures a place in the entering class and eligibility to begin the co-op employment search process.

For more information, prospective students should contact:

Admissions Office
Kettering University
1700 University Avenue
Flint, Michigan 48504
United States
Phone: 810-762-7865
      800-955-4464 Ext. 7865 (toll-free in the United States and Canada)
E-mail: admissions@kettering.edu
Website: https://www.kettering.edu
      https://www.facebook.com/KetteringUniversity
      https://www.twitter.com/KetteringU
      https://www.instagram.com/ketteringu1919

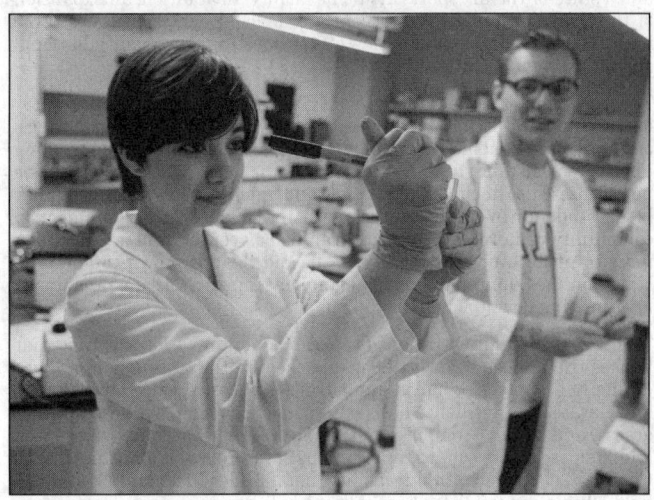

Kettering students major in experience.

KING'S COLLEGE
WILKES-BARRE, PENNSYLVANIA

 To read more about this school, visit http://petersons.to/kingscollege

The College

King's College is an independent, coed, four-year Catholic college with 2,400 students. Founded in 1946 by the Holy Cross Priests and Brothers from the University of Notre Dame, King's prepares students for a purposeful life, with an education that integrates the human values inherent in a broadly based liberal arts curriculum. The College encourages the religious, moral, personal, and social development of its students.

In addition to the undergraduate degrees, King's College offers a Master of Science (M.S.) degree in health-care administration, a Master of Education (M.Ed.) degree in reading or curriculum and instruction, and a five-year physician assistant studies program leading to a master's degree.

Academic advising begins before students enroll and continues with an innovative program of career development across the curriculum. King's Academic Skills Center includes a nationally certified tutoring program and a faculty-staffed writing center. More than 70 percent of students who attend King's graduate from the College, which is well above the national average, and 99 percent are employed or attend graduate school within six months of graduation.

The charming urban campus comprises eight city blocks and features many buildings and centers that house King's numerous academic programs, including the Charles E. and Mary Parente Life Sciences Center, the Mulligan Physical Sciences Center, and the William G. McGowan School of Business. The 15-acre campus also includes Monarch Court; the Sheehy-Farmer Campus Center, which offers an art gallery, an outdoor waterfall and patio, a student restaurant, and marketplace dining; the J. Carroll McCormick Campus Ministry Center; and the William S. Scandlon Physical Education Center, which features a 3,200-seat basketball arena, wrestling facilities, racquetball and handball courts, an Olympic-size swimming pool, a wellness center, and a state-of-the-art sports medicine facility. In addition, an expansion of the Scandlon Center was recently completed, which includes three multipurpose courts as well as new offices, meeting rooms, and additional sports medicine facilities.

The new King's on the Square facility is a vibrant and dynamic center for learning and living in the heart of downtown Wilkes-Barre. King's on the Square is home to a number of professional programs, including physician assistant studies, athletic training, and exercise science. The new center also includes attractive and safe student residences that bring students in direct contact with the downtown environment; a community-centered art and cultural display center; and a Chick-fil-A restaurant for students, faculty, staff, and the downtown community. King's on the Square has quickly established itself as a safe, productive, and bustling downtown anchor.

The six-story administration and science buildings form a unit that houses the College's newly renovated theater, the Susquehanna Place dining hall and coffee bar, administrative offices, science laboratories, and classrooms. Residence halls have cable television, wireless Internet access, and 24-hour computer labs. Many of King's athletic teams train and compete just two miles from campus at the Robert L. Betzler Athletic Complex, a 33.5-acre athletic facility that includes McCarthy Stadium; a field house; and fields for baseball, softball, men's and women's soccer, football, and field hockey.

More than fifty student organizations provide King's students with a wide range of opportunities to explore interests outside of the classroom. King's offers 27 NCAA Division III teams including men's baseball, basketball, football, golf, ice hockey, lacrosse, soccer, swimming, tennis, and wrestling; women's basketball, field hockey, ice hockey, lacrosse, soccer, softball, swimming, tennis, and volleyball; and coed cross-country.

The College offers cheerleading, ice hockey, and track and field as club sports. Intramural sports include basketball, flag football, indoor soccer, racquetball, and dodgeball. Other co-curricular activities include: academic clubs in almost every department, the King's Players (theater), Cantores Christi Regis (choir), Campus Ministry, the Experiencing the Arts Series, *The Crown* (student newspaper), the *Regis* (yearbook), and the *SCOP* (literary magazine).

Location

The King's campus is located in a residential area near downtown Wilkes-Barre, Pennsylvania, a city of approximately 50,000 on the banks of the Susquehanna River. A growing city, Wilkes-Barre has developed both economically and culturally, yet it has avoided many typical urban problems. Shopping malls, multiplex theaters, a brand new riverfront park, art galleries, and restaurants are nearby. Two blocks from King's is the F. M. Kirby Center, which has hosted national performances, music groups, traveling theater, and more. National recording acts regularly perform in nearby venues.

King's is a short drive from several ski resorts, state parks, and major lakes where students can participate in many seasonal outdoor activities. Students can also enjoy professional sports action including the New York Yankees' AAA baseball team, the Pocono International Raceway which hosts two NASCAR races each season, and the Pittsburgh Penguins' minor-league ice hockey team. The Mohegan Sun Arena is the host to many concerts and events, and is the site of the King's commencement. The campus is close to major metropolitan areas including New York City and Philadelphia (each a 2½-hour drive); Washington, D.C., and the attractions of New England are within a 4-hour drive.

Majors and Degrees

King's awards the Master of Science, Master of Education, Bachelor of Arts, Bachelor of Science, Associate of Arts, and Associate of Science degrees. The College's thirty-six major programs are offered in the arts and sciences and the William G. McGowan School of Business, which is accredited by AACSB International—The Association to Advance Collegiate Schools of Business.

Arts and sciences include the humanities and social sciences division (computers and information systems, criminal justice, economics, English–literature, English–professional writing, French, history, mass communications, philosophy, political science, psychology, sociology, Spanish, theater, and theology); the education division, which is accredited by NCATE (preschool–grade 4, secondary certification, and special education); the science division (biology, chemistry, computer science, engineering, environmental science, environmental studies, general science, mathematics, neuroscience, and physics); and the allied health division (clinical lab science, physician assistant studies, exercise science, and athletics training education/sports medicine accredited by CAAHEP). Beginning in the fall of 2018, the College also will offer a Bachelor of Science degree in nursing. Available majors in the William G. McGowan School of Business are accounting, finance, human resources management, international business, management, and marketing. King's offers pre-professional programs in chiropractic, dentistry, law, medicine, optometry, pharmacy, and veterinary science. The College offers civil and mechanical engineering programs, as well as a 3+2 dual-degree program with the University of Notre Dame.

Academic Programs

The general education program at King's is recognized nationwide by its peers. King's has been recognized in more than twengyt consecutive issues of U.S. News & World Report's Best Colleges Guide. The College was also recognized by the John Templeton Foundation Honor Roll for Character-Building Colleges, the Forbes/CCAP list of America's best colleges.

The honors program offers highly motivated students the challenge of learning in discussion-centered courses that explore distinctive subject matter with exciting and innovative approaches. Twenty honor societies encourage students to excel in their chosen fields and recognize students for their academic distinction; members are honored each year at the All-College Honors Convocation. Science students receive hands-on lab training much earlier than students at other institutions and work together with faculty members on real-world research projects.

Off-Campus Programs

Experiential learning (via internships) is available in conjunction with almost every major. King's students have interned at CNN, the New York Stock Exchange, PricewaterhouseCoopers, the U.S. House of Representatives, U.S. Senators' offices, the U.S. Department of Energy, Walt Disney World, and Xerox Corporation, among other places. Every year, students are placed with local, regional, and national companies around the globe.

Through the study-abroad program many of King's students have studied on campuses throughout Europe, Thailand, China, Australia, and various other countries.

Academic Facilities

King's facilities include the 51,000-square-foot, three-story D. Leonard Corgan Library, which contains several study rooms, a 160,000-volume collection, and a computerized catalog, which students can access from their home or residence hall. The library provides full-text databases from every computer on campus, and access to college and research libraries throughout the United States. Students and faculty members also have direct access to more than 1 million volumes through the local library cooperative (NEPBC).

King's features computer labs with more than 440 PCs, 24-hour labs in residence halls, e-mail accounts for all students, computerized library databases, multimedia classrooms with a variety of instructional aids, course discussions on Moodle, distance-learning facilities for teleconferencing, and cross-registration with area colleges that enables students to take courses complementary to their majors.

The Charles E. and Mary Parente Life Sciences Center, which contains a molecular biology laboratory and a genomics center, includes computer facilities, instrumentation rooms, a rooftop greenhouse, and environmental chambers. The Mulligan Physical Sciences Center includes modern research laboratories, computer facilities, and state-of-the-art instrumentation used for molecular identification. The five-year physician assistant studies program (master's degree) is located in the new King's on the Square facility, which includes a state-of-the-art gross anatomy lab, four clinical practice labs, and ten examination rooms.

Costs

For the 2017–18 academic year, tuition for full-time students was $35,830; average room and board total $12,408.

Financial Aid

King's assists all qualified students through its financial aid programs. Currently, more than 99 percent of King's students receive financial aid in the form of scholarships, grants, work-study, or loans. For 2017, the average financial aid award was $26,283, removing a significant amount of the financial obligation from students and their families. Aid is awarded on the basis of demonstrated financial need (the difference between the total cost of education and the expected family contribution).

In addition to financial aid programs, installment payment plans are available, offering students and/or their families the ability to make monthly payments throughout the academic year. Students who wish to be considered for financial aid must fill out the Free Application for Federal Student Aid (FAFSA) and the King's College Financial Aid Application. The preferred FAFSA filing deadline for first-year students is February 15.

Faculty

King's College has 131 full-time and 96 part-time faculty members. Eighty-five percent of the full-time faculty members have a Ph.D. or an equivalent terminal degree. Graduate assistants do not teach courses. The student-faculty ratio is 12.9:1.

Student Government

The student government coordinates and participates in numerous activities for both the student body and the surrounding community. It regularly holds open forums for students and senior administrators at the College, coordinates informal socials for the students with the College president, and makes presentations at each meeting of the Board of Directors. In addition, the student government sponsors events that foster awareness for social and justice issues and a celebration of cultural diversity.

Admission Requirements

King's encourages applications from qualified high school students and those who wish to transfer from another institution. To be considered for admission, students must be prepared to successfully pursue a program of study at the College, as evidenced by the quality of previous academic and extracurricular performance, the recommendation of school officials and character references, and the student's display of personal promise, maturity, and motivation. King's admits students of any race, sex, color, creed, or national or ethnic origin.

Admission decisions are made for both high school students and transfer students with the understanding that all current courses and examinations will be completed satisfactorily. Candidates should complete 4 years of mathematics (through trigonometry or pre-calculus). One year each of high school chemistry, biology, and physics is also strongly recommended.

The Office of Admission offers two methods for candidates to apply for admission: the SAT/ACT Traditional Choice and the Test Optional Choice. Applicants are required to state their preference prior to the application review, and the decision is nonreversible. Students who select the SAT/ACT Traditional Choice must submit a completed application, official high school transcripts, SAT or ACT scores, guidance counselor recommendation, an essay, and the $30 application fee, which is waived if students apply online. Students who choose the Test Optional Choice must submit a completed application, official high school transcripts, an official graded writing sample from either their junior or senior year—submitted and notarized by the high school guidance office, guidance counselor recommendation, an essay, and the $30 application fee, which is waived if students apply online.

Application and Information

Applicants should forward a completed application and the $30 fee to the Office of Admission or apply online at www.kings.edu in order to waive the application fee. Secondary and postsecondary (if applicable) transcripts must be sent. Admission decisions are not made until all credentials are received. King's subscribes to a rolling admission policy. Decisions are announced within two weeks from the date of application. Upon notification of acceptance, a $200 nonrefundable deposit is requested to reserve a place in the class. The deposit deadline is May 1 but may be extended upon request. To schedule an interview, obtain an application form, or for more information, students should contact:

Office of Admission
King's College
133 North River Street
Wilkes-Barre, Pennsylvania 18711
Phone: 570-208-5858
    888-KINGS-PA (toll-free)
E-mail: admissions@kings.edu
Website: http://www.kings.edu
    http://www.facebook.com/kingscollegepa
    http://twitter.com/KingsCollege_PA

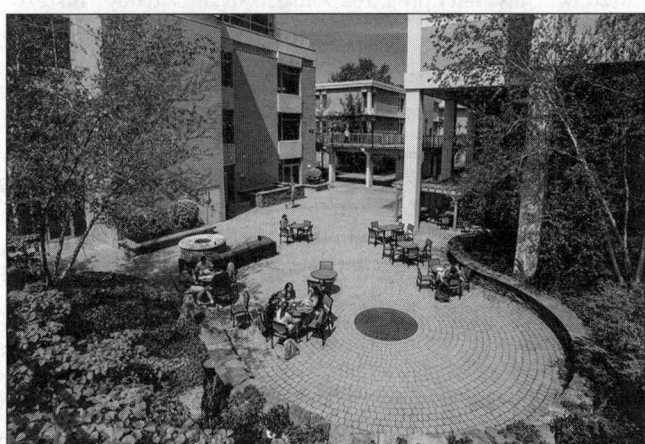

KUTZTOWN UNIVERSITY OF PENNSYLVANIA
KUTZTOWN, PENNSYLVANIA

★ To read more about this school, visit http://petersons.to/kutztownuniversity

The University

For the last 150 years, students who choose Kutztown University choose to become part of a community defined by bright, ambitious students; brilliant, dedicated faculty; and a diverse, vibrant learning atmosphere.

Kutztown University (KU) is a four-year public institution located 30 minutes from Allentown and Reading, 90 minutes from Philadelphia, and 2 hours from New York City. Founded in 1866, KU has nearly 9,000 undergraduate and graduate students, more than 100 areas of study, 200 student organizations, and 21 NCAA Division II athletic programs—all housed on a beautiful 289-acre campus.

Location

Kutztown offers the benefits of a safe, quaint, walkable community with access to the Northeast's best cities. The campus is a hub for public transportation with daily routes to Philadelphia and New York City. Students can check out the Philadelphia Zoo or Adventure Aquarium, catch the Art Bus to New York City to explore the Museum of Modern Art, or take a trip to Washington, D.C. to visit the Smithsonian. In addition to the opportunities for arts and entertainment, great opportunities for internships and career exploration and also within easy reach.

Locally, the beauty of the eastern Pennsylvania countryside offers easy access to hiking, biking, skiing, and other outdoor activities. Students can sample Pennsylvania Dutch culture both on and off campus, but when the conveniences of a major city are needed, Allentown and Reading are just a short drive away.

Majors and Degrees

When it comes to areas of study, there are many to choose from. Kutztown University prepares students to enter today's fastest-growing fields.

College of Business: Students learn the skills necessary and prepare to take on the global challenges of today's business environment through programs in accounting, finance, management, marketing, sports management, and leadership development. KU's business administration programs have earned the prestigious Association to Advance Collegiate Schools of Business (AACSB) International. AACSB accreditation is the hallmark of excellence in business education and positions KU's programs among the top 5 percent of business schools internationally. The Leisure and Sport Studies program, one of the largest and fastest growing at KU, received its Commission on Sport Management Accreditation (COSMA) in fall of 2015, placing it among the few accredited programs in the United States.

College of Education: Students can study and prepare for a career as a lifelong learner and teacher in elementary education (grades Pre-K–4 or 4–8), secondary education, special education, library science, instructional technology, and school counseling. KU has one of only four programs in the U.S. that offer a

major in special education with a focus on visual impairment. It also boasts one of the few clinically-based reading specialist programs as well as a new autism endorsement certification. Teacher education programs at Kutztown University are nationally accredited by the Council for the Accreditation of Educator Preparation (CAEP, formerly NCATE).

College of Liberal Arts and Sciences: From ancient civilizations to today's cultural norms, living things to fossilized remains, students can research and apply their natural curiosity to learn how and why people, languages, and processes exist as they do and what tomorrow may bring.

KU offers a wide variety of programs: anthropology, biological sciences, chemistry, computer science, criminal justice, English, environmental science, geography, geology, German studies, history, marine science, mathematics, paralegal studies, philosophy, physics, political science, psychology, public administration, professional writing, sociology, social work, or Spanish. A traditional liberal arts education has proven valuable to employers. Students develop the communication, writing, research, teamwork, and critical-thinking skills that are marketable in a wide range of fields. KU's commitment to undergraduate research ensures students have opportunities to present their findings at local and national meetings, and they may even be published in an academic journal alongside the professor's work. Internships are another opportunity to gain further work experience.

College of Visual and Performing Arts: Students can unleash their creativity as KU pushes them to their limits and beyond, whether craft the best piece for a portfolio or the soundtrack of their life.

The College of Visual and Performing Arts awards degrees in art history; music; music: commercial emphasis; communication studies; and cinema, television, and media production, and social media theory and strategy; as well as art education and music education. Fine Arts degrees are offered in applied digital arts, communication design (graphic design), crafts, and studio art with concentrations in digital media, drawing, painting, photography, print making, and sculpture. Minors offered in audio engineering, digital communication and new media, entrepreneurship, and jazz offer an eclectic opportunity to students pursuing the arts.

Academic Opportunities

Kutztown students can take advantage of a long list of unique academic opportunities such as undergraduate research, living and learning communities, experiential learning options, and practical application through student leadership and organizations. KU offers expert faculty and small, personalized learning opportunities both in class and in the field.

For students seeking a challenge, the Honors Program at KU provides challenges in new and exciting ways, while offering many perks and privileges. Honors students access specialized courses, internships, conferences, committees, and independent study programs. The Honors Program also offers a summer

Honors Study Abroad program and a number of merit-based scholarships.

KU's Career Development Center is available to all students and alumni and offer superior assistance with everything from choosing a major to finding an internship, or landing jobs after graduation and beyond.

Study Away

KU students can make the world their classroom, by choosing to study away from campus, nationally or internationally, through more than 150 student exchange programs. KU participates in international studies programs where students can immerse themselves in the history and culture of England, Spain, Austria, China, Ecuador, or South Africa, just to name a few, all while maintaining a focused area of study and earning credits toward graduation.

Costs

Kutztown University offers an excellent value to students via affordable tuition; numerous scholarship, grant, loan, and campus employment opportunities; and highly successful student outcomes. For the 2017–18 school year, tuition (up to 18 credits), fees, and on-campus room and meals for Pennsylvania residents was $20,269; for out-of-state students, the cost was $24,257.

Out-of-state students who are admitted to the university now receive a 40 percent reduction in the cost to attend, saving families more than $7,000 per academic year.

Financial Aid

The goal of financial aid is to place a quality education within reach. The goal of a college education is to get a great job and establish a career. KU grads do just that. The best part of investing in education is that its value will only increase. On average, a bachelor's degree increases lifetime earning potential by $1 million.

More than 80 percent of Kutztown University students finance their education with some form of financial aid. With numerous scholarship, grant, loan, and campus employment opportunities; affordable tuition; and highly successful student outcomes, Kutztown University offers a tremendous value.

Students seeking scholarships are encouraged to apply early. The only form needed to apply for financial aid is the FAFSA. KU must receive the completed and processed FAFSA by February 15 for applicants to be considered for scholarships or other awards.

Faculty

Although many professors at KU are involved in important research and are leaders in their fields, their primary interest is in the classroom. KU has more than 350 full-time instructors and the average class size is 25. Approximately 90 percent of the faculty members hold terminal degrees in their field of study. Upon enrollment in the University, each student is assigned a faculty adviser to help plan his or her academic career.

Campus Life

KU offers an array of living choices: traditional or suite-style residence halls, apartments, and townhouses. Students live on campus the first two years.

Involvement on campus is the key to having an enjoyable, fulfilling experience at KU. Students are encouraged to join a club, volunteer, cheer on Golden Bear athletics, and more.

Admission Requirements

Kutztown University operates on a rolling admissions basis, meaning applications are accepted throughout the year. Admission requirements are outlined on the Admissions page of the University's website. Admission decisions are based on grade point average and standardized test scores (both SAT and ACT scores are accepted). Certain academic programs have other admission requirements; those details are outlined on the website.

Application and Information

The completed application, $35 nonrefundable application fee, test scores, official final transcripts, and other required materials must be submitted to the Office of Admissions. To learn more, prospective students can visit www.kutztown.edu/apply. To speak with an admissions representative, contact:

Office of Admissions
Kutztown University of Pennsylvania
Kutztown, Pennsylvania 19530
United States
Phone: 610-683-4060
E-mail: admissions@kutztown.edu
Website: http://www.kutztown.edu/admissions

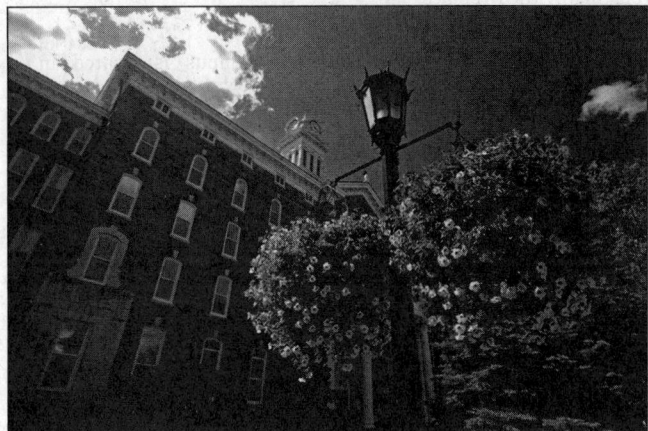

Old Main Clock Tower at Kutztown University.

LE MOYNE COLLEGE
SYRACUSE, NEW YORK

 To read more about this school, visit http://petersons.to/lemoynecollege

The College

Le Moyne College is a four-year, coeducational Jesuit college of approximately 2,800 undergraduate students that uniquely balances a comprehensive liberal arts education with preparation for specific career paths or graduate study. Founded by the Society of Jesus in 1946, Le Moyne is the second youngest of the twenty-eight Jesuit colleges and universities in the United States. Its emphasis is on the education of the whole person and on the search for meaning and value as integral parts of an intellectual life. Le Moyne's personal approach to education is reflected in the quality of contact between students and faculty members.

A wide range of student-directed activities, athletics, clubs, and service organizations complement the academic experience. Intramural sports are very popular with Le Moyne students; nearly 85 percent of the students participate. Le Moyne also has twenty-one NCAA intercollegiate teams (ten for men and eleven for women). Athletic facilities include a new soccer/lacrosse turf field, softball and baseball fields; basketball, and racquetball courts; a weight-training and fitness center; practice fields; and two gymnasiums. A recreation center houses an Olympic-size indoor swimming pool, jogging track, indoor tennis and volleyball courts, and additional basketball, racquetball, and fitness areas.

Around 85 percent of students live in residence halls, apartments, and town houses on campus. The Residence Hall Councils and the Le Moyne Student Programming Board organize a variety of campus activities, including concerts, dances, a weekly film series, student talent programs, and special lectures as well as off-campus trips and skiing excursions. The College also has a plaza, which houses its bookstore, a café, and a pizzeria. The new Dolphin Den, which features a food court and a convenience store, is a popular space for students to meet, have a bite to eat, or just spend a quiet moment relaxing by the fireplace.

Location

Le Moyne's 160-plus acre, tree-lined campus is located in a residential setting 10 minutes from downtown Syracuse, the heart of New York state, whose metropolitan population is about 700,000. Syracuse is convenient to most major cities throughout the Northeast, New England, and Canada and offers a wide array of shopping centers and restaurants, many near Le Moyne. Syracuse offers year-round entertainment in the form of rock concerts at the Landmark Theatre, professional baseball and hockey, Bristol Omnitheatre, Syracuse Stage, Everson Museum of Art, and the Armory Square district downtown, which offers one-of-a-kind eateries, pubs, and coffeehouses in addition to a wide variety of social and cultural events. All are easily accessible via the excellent public transportation service, which schedules regular stops on Le Moyne's campus. Just a few miles outside the city are the rolling hills, picturesque lakes, and miles of open country for which central New York is renowned. An extensive network of state and county parks, recreational areas, and other facilities offers an abundance of recreational opportunities, including swimming, boating, hiking, downhill and cross-country skiing, snowboarding, and golf.

Majors and Degrees

Le Moyne College awards the Bachelor of Arts degree in biological sciences, communication (advertising, filmmaking, journalism, media studies, music and culture, music industry, music journalism, public relations, television/radio), computer science, criminology (human services, international affairs, law enforcement, research), cybersecurity, economics, English (creative writing, literature), French, history, mathematics (actuarial science, pure mathematics, statistics), peace and global studies, philosophy, physics, political science, psychology, religious studies, sociology (anthropology, criminology, human services, research and theory), software applications and system development, Spanish, and theatre arts. The Bachelor of Science degree is awarded in biochemistry, biological sciences (health professions, molecular biology, neurobiology), chemistry, economics, environmental science systems, environmental studies, general science, physics, and psychology. The Bachelor of Science is also awarded in accounting, business analytics, finance, human resource management, information systems, management and leadership, and marketing. A Bachelor of Science in nursing is offered as well.

Students may minor in advanced writing, arts administration, business administration, classical humanities, film, gender and women's studies, Irish literature, Italian, Latin, legal studies, health information systems, medieval studies, music, urban and regional studies, or visual arts, as well as most of the major fields of study offered. Preprofessional programs are offered in dentistry, law, medicine, direct-entry occupational therapy studies, optometry, physical therapy, direct-entry physician assistant studies, podiatry, and veterinary science. Students may prepare for teaching careers through certification programs in adolescent education, dual adolescent/special education, dual childhood/special education, and TESOL.

Le Moyne College and the L. C. Smith College of Engineering and Computer Science at Syracuse University offer a dual-degree program in which students may earn a bachelor's degree from Le Moyne and a master's degree in engineering from Syracuse University. Concentrations include aerospace; chemical, electrical, and mechanical engineering; computer science; and other fields of engineering.

Formal accelerated 3-4 programs are offered in dentistry, optometry, and podiatry in cooperation with the State University of New York at Buffalo School of Dental Medicine, Pennsylvania College of Optometry at Salus University, and the New York College of Podiatric Medicine. Predental students may also participate in an early assurance program with the State University of New York at Buffalo School of Dental Medicine. Cooperative 3-2 dual-degree programs in engineering are available with Clarkson University, Manhattan College, and University of Detroit Mercy.

SUNY Upstate Medical University in Syracuse offers students pursuing careers in the health-related professions an accelerated 3-3 doctoral-level transfer program in physical therapy as well as two-year cooperative transfer programs in medical technology, and respiratory care. Premedical students at Le Moyne are also offered the opportunity to participate in a medical school early assurance program. An early assurance program for premedical students is also available through the State University of New York at Buffalo School of Medicine and formal agreements also exist with Fordham's School of Law and Syracuse University School of Law.

Academic Programs

While each major department has its own sequence requirements for the minimum 120 credit hours needed for the Le Moyne degree, the College is convinced that there is a fundamental intellectual discipline that should characterize the graduate of a superior liberal arts college. Le Moyne's core curriculum provides this foundation by including studies of English language and literature, philosophy, history, religious studies, natural sciences, and social sciences.

For exceptional students, Le Moyne offers an integral honors program that includes an interdisciplinary humanities sequence as well as departmental honors courses. Le Moyne also offers a part-time course of study during evening hours through its Center for Continuing Education.

Le Moyne students may enroll in Army and Air Force ROTC programs in conjunction with Syracuse University.

Off-Campus Programs

The study-abroad program allows qualified students to spend a semester or year in almost any country throughout the world. Le Moyne College has study-abroad programs or affiliations in the Czech Republic, Dominican Republic, England, Germany, Ireland, Scotland, and Spain. Students can also use partner programs to study in locations such as Australia, Costa Rica, Egypt, France,

COLLEGE CLOSE-UPS

Italy, Japan, and South Africa. Le Moyne is a participant in the sixty-member New York State Visiting Student Program. As part of the mission of preparing future leaders, Le Moyne College places a strong emphasis on career preparation through internships and other forms of experiential education. Academic departments and the Office of Career Advising and Development both provide programs and services for students interested in interning part time and full time, both locally and in major cities such as New York and Washington, D.C. The Offices of Service Learning and the Academic Deans are also involved in experiential education to promote learning outside the classroom. In the sciences, students take part in campus research with mentor faculty members. Others receive assistance in pursuing outstanding opportunities off campus in leading research laboratories and health-care settings. The College has maintained a long-standing relationship with the Washington Center internship programs, where students from all majors complete full-time semester-long internships in Washington, D.C., with government, business, or major nonprofit organizations. Faculty members in the Political Science Department assist students interested in opportunities in Albany, the state's seat of government, with either the New York State Senate or Assembly. Finally, the education programs at Le Moyne put students into school classrooms starting immediately as freshmen and continuing each year until graduation.

Academic Facilities

Le Moyne students benefit from an ongoing commitment to technological excellence. The College's forty-two buildings are equipped with accounting, biology, chemistry, computer science, physics, psychology, and statistics laboratories. The W. Carroll Coyne Center for the Performing Arts houses generous production, performance, and classroom space; the latest light and sound technology; scene and costume shops; an aerobics and dance studio; and rehearsal rooms for instrumental and choral music. Academic facilities also include an extensively renovated color television studio; a radio/recording studio; a receiver-antenna satellite dish; transmission and scanning electron microscopes; a nuclear magnetic resonance spectrometer; a gas chromatograph/mass spectrophotometer; a 240,000-volume, open-stack library; and extensive on-site computer facilities. A fiber-optic network enables students to access the library system, the campus network, and the Internet from several computer labs around the campus or from their personal computers in their rooms. All classrooms are smart classrooms, with multimedia capabilities that expand and enrich the learning process. Le Moyne students have access to other libraries through the Central New York Library Resources Council, and the campus Academic Support Center is available to students for instructional support. In addition, Le Moyne recently opened a 48,000-square-foot addition to its existing science complex, and the Madden School of Business, featuring a state-of-the-art trading floor and analytics lab.

Costs

For 2018–19, Le Moyne's tuition is $33,560. Room and board charges are $13,780. Additional fees amount to approximately $1,065.

Financial Aid

Financial aid is offered to a large percentage of Le Moyne's students through scholarships, grants, loans, and work-study assignments. Le Moyne offers a generous program of merit-based academic and athletic scholarships as well as financial aid based on a student's need and academic promise. Federal funds are available through the Federal Pell Grant, Federal Work-Study, Federal Supplemental Educational Opportunity Grant, and Federal Perkins Loan programs. A student's eligibility for need-based financial aid is determined from the Free Application for Federal Student Aid (FAFSA). It is recommended that the FAFSA be submitted by February 1.

Faculty

The Le Moyne full-time faculty numbers 150 men and women; 94 percent have earned the highest degree in their field. With an average class size of 20, a student-faculty ratio of 13:1, and private offices for all full-time faculty members, the College promotes a personal as well as an academic relationship between students and faculty members. All classroom instruction is done by faculty members, and they are happy to assist and encourage students who wish to pursue undergraduate research through tutorials or senior research projects. These projects are carried out in an atmosphere free of competition from graduate students for books, laboratories, or professors' time. Le Moyne emphasizes advising and academic counseling for students throughout their four years.

Student Government

The College encourages student leadership in all activities. Positions of leadership are open to students in all class years. Students are represented by a Student Senate and have formal representation through the senate on most College-wide committees involved in decision making and policy formation.

Admission Requirements

Le Moyne seeks qualified students who are well prepared for serious academic study. Secondary school preparation must have included at least 17 college-preparatory high school units, 4 of which must be in English, 4 in social studies, 3–4 in mathematics, 3–4 in foreign language, and 3–4 in science. It is also recommended that prospective science and mathematics majors complete 4 units of mathematics and science. Students applying to Le Moyne College have the option of submitting their SAT and ACT test scores or withholding them for consideration as part of the admission process. However, for those wishing to be considered for top academic scholarships, the SAT or ACT is required and should be taken no later than December or January of the senior year in high school. Campus visits are strongly recommended, as the admission process is a personal one. As bases for selection, academic achievement and secondary school recommendations are of primary importance. Out-of-state and international students are encouraged to apply.

Application and Information

Le Moyne offers students the opportunity to apply in two ways: early action or regular admission. The early action program is nonbinding and provides high school students the opportunity to receive an admission decision by December 15 of their senior year. The early action application deadline is November 15. Regular admission applications are reviewed and admission decisions are made on a rolling basis beginning January 1. The priority deadline for applications is February 1; all students who wish to be considered for academic merit scholarships should have a completed application on file in the Office of Admission before this date. All students are encouraged to include Le Moyne (002748) on their FAFSA submission. Transfer students are encouraged to apply before August 1 for the fall semester and December 1 for the spring semester. Orientation programs for incoming first-year students take place in June and early July. Transfer student orientation programs are offered throughout the summer.

Mary Chandler
Senior Director of Admission
Le Moyne College
Syracuse, New York 13214-1399
Phone: 315-445-4300
        800-333-4733 (toll-free)
E-mail: admission@lemoyne.edu
Website: http://www.lemoyne.edu
        facebook.com/lemoyne
        twitter.com/lemoynecollege
        instagram.com/lemoyne_college
        youtube.com/lemoynecollege

Grewen Hall, the College's oldest building, overlooks Le Moyne's beautiful 160-plus acre campus.

COLLEGE CLOSE-UPS

LINCOLN UNIVERSITY
LINCOLN UNIVERSITY, PENNSYLVANIA

 For more information, visit http://petersons.to/lincolnuniversity

The University

Founded in 1854, Lincoln University is the country's first degree-granting HBCU (Historically Black College and University). Since its beginning, the university has attracted an international and interracial student body from surrounding communities, the region, and other nations. Its most notable alumni include poet Langston Hughes ('29) and former Associate Justice of the Supreme Court of the United States Thurgood Marshall ('30).

The university continues to cultivate leaders and achievers. It offers approximately 2,000 students more than 35 liberal arts and science-based undergraduate programs; graduate programs in business, counseling, education, and human services.

Its learning environment emphasizes concern for each student, quality education, and small classes. As a result, students graduate prepared to create successful careers in today's fast-paced, technology-based, global environment.

Lincoln University is accredited by the Middle States Commission on Higher Education.

Location

The main campus is in Lincoln University, Pennsylvania, which is in the northeastern region of the United States. The beautiful campus is situated amid wooded hilltops and rolling farmlands. Located on 422 acres in southern Chester County, the campus marries tradition and modern facilities, with sweeping pathways that encourage walking and contemplation within a safe and scenic landscape.

Lincoln's close proximity to several major cities provides the tranquility of a rural setting and the excitement of the metropolis. The campus is 45 miles from Philadelphia, Pennsylvania; 55 miles from Baltimore, Maryland; 25 miles from Wilmington, Delaware; and 135 miles from Newark, New Jersey.

Majors and Degrees

Lincoln University's programs of study available include: accounting, anthropology, biochemistry and molecular biology, biology, black studies (minor), business and entrepreneurial studies for non-business majors (minor), chemistry, computer science, criminal justice, economics (minor), engineering science, English liberal arts, entrepreneurship (minor), finance, foreign languages, general science, health science, history, human services, information technology, international relations (minor), liberal studies, management, mass communications, mathematics, music, nursing pre-licensure B.S.N., nursing RN to B.S.N., Pan-Africana studies, philosophy, physics, political science, pre-law certificate program, psychology, religion, sociology, and visual arts.

Some of Lincoln University's most popular areas of study are the following:

The **Registered Nurse (RN) to Bachelor of Science in Nursing (B.S.N.)** program develops nurse leaders skilled at providing high quality, holistic, patient-centered nursing care. Areas of study include leadership, population health, professional roles and values, and research. The program is offered part-time either online or on-campus.

The **Bachelor of Science (B.S.) in Accounting** prepares students for careers as Certified Public Accountants (CPAs). Its curriculum provides professional and technical knowledge of accounting theory and practice. It also exposes students to specific areas of accounting including accounting information systems, audit, financial and managerial accounting, international accounting, and taxation.

The **Bachelor of Science (B.S.) in Biology** strengthens students' knowledge of foundational areas in biology at the molecular, cellular, organismal, and ecosystem levels. It also trains students to conduct original scientific investigations and communicate their research and findings to interested parties.

The **Bachelor of Science (B.S.) in Computer Science** trains students to design, develop, and test computer programs in languages like Assembly, C++, Java, and Visual BASIC. It also trains students to read, analyze, organize, store, and utilize data by creating graphical user interface forms, developing database design and modeling, and using data structures.

The **Bachelor of Science (B.S.) in Criminal Justice** provides students with in-depth information about how the criminal justice system works at the local, state, and federal levels. It explains how interactions between criminal justice institutions and the people in these settings change over time. It also provides awareness about how different social forces impact the types and rates of criminal behavior.

The **Bachelor of Science (B.S.) in Engineering Science** includes course work in civil, computer, electrical, and environmental engineering. It trains students to use engineering, mathematics, and science principles to solve problems. It also prepares them to design and conduct experiments as well as analyze and interpret data.

The **Bachelor of Arts (B.A.) in Music Performance** provides a creative and broad music curriculum that emphasizes band instrument, orchestral instrument, piano, and voice. Through research, lectures, and rigorous practice, students gain the performance skills and knowledge to pursue careers as educators and/or performers.

Academic Programs

Lincoln University offers undergraduate courses during two 15-week semesters and one or two six-week summer sessions each year.

Students have access to a broad range of academic, professional, and social resources including the following: Career Services, Center for Advising and Student Achievement, Horace Mann Bond Honors Program, international programs and services, Math Learning Center, placement assessment, Women's Center, Writing and Reading Center, and a writing proficiency program.

Costs

For the 2018–19 academic year, first-year tuition and fees total $12,479 for Pennsylvania residents and $18,395 for out-of-state students. Housing costs for the year are $5,264 and the most popular meal plan is $4,474. Costs for books and other supplies are estimated at about $2,000 per year.

Financial Aid

A college education is an important investment in the future. There are many options available for financial assistance, and more than 90 percent of students at Lincoln make use of these resources to meet their obligations. Lincoln University provides scholarships and participates in the following grant and loan programs: Federal Pell Grant, Federal Supplemental Educational Opportunity Grant, Federal Subsidized Direct Loan, Federal Unsubsidized Direct Loan, Federal PLUS Loan, and Pennsylvania State Grant.

The university also participates in financial assistance programs for veterans. Plus, it allows students who reside in the following states (and the District of Columbia) to use grants from their states to cover expenses: Connecticut, Delaware, Maine, Massachusetts, Ohio, Rhode Island, and West Virginia.

To be eligible for all forms of financial aid, including work-study and most university-funded scholarships, prospective students first need to complete the Free Application for Federal Student Aid (FAFSA). All FAFSA applications should be filed by April 1 for the following academic year to receive priority consideration for most types of financial assistance.

Faculty

Lincoln has 100 full-time faculty members; 76 percent of those hold a doctoral or highest academic degree in their field. The student-faculty ratio is 15:1 and 96 percent of all classes have fewer than 39 students.

The university's faculty members help students connect classroom experiences to industry. As leaders in their fields, they bring an extensive range of theoretical and practical experience to their teaching. They're also dedicated to helping students achieve both their academic and career goals.

Professor Marilyn Button, PhD serves as chair of the Department of Languages and Literature, Professor Monica Gray, whose credentials include a PhD, MPH, CPH, and PE, is advisor to several student-centered organizations, and Professor James Wadley, PhD is chair of the Counseling and Human Services deaprtment, are among the university's dedicated faculty.

Student Life

Students at Lincoln University enjoy countless opportunities to form supportive and lasting friendships with fellow students. Most of them live on campus, which makes socializing, studying, and working more convenient. They have access to more than 60 student clubs, organizations, fraternities, and sororities; community service projects; activities and events; intramural sports; and bands. There is also a recreation center, Wellness Center, health services, and counseling services.

The Lincoln Lions athletic teams compete in NCAA Division II and the Central Intercollegiate Athletic Association. Men's sports include baseball, basketball, cross-country, football, and track and field; women's sports are basketball, cross-country, soccer, softball, track and field, and volleyball.

Admission Requirements

Applicants to Lincoln University must submit: a completed application for admission; an official high school transcript or GED test results and certificate along with a high school transcript; scores from either the Scholastic Aptitude Test (SAT) or American College Test (ACT); and a $20 application fee. Recommended, but not required are two letters of recommendation and an application essay that the applicant writes about themselves and events in their life that have made a difference in the way they view themselves and others (minimum 250 words).

Application and Information

Freshman and transfer students may apply online via the university's website, or applications can be downloaded and mailed. When the application is received, the student will be notified by postcard. After all test scores, transcripts, application fee, recommendations, and other supporting documents have been received, the Admissions Office will review the application. It usually takes at least 14 business days to complete the evaluation process. Lincoln University has a rolling admission system; however, in order to obtain on-campus housing and a better financial aid package, students are advised to apply as quickly as possible. Priority deadlines are April 15 for the fall semester and December 15 for the spring semester.

For more information, prospective students should contact:

Lincoln University
Office of Undergraduate Admissions
Cannon House 103
1570 Baltimore Pike
Lincoln University, Pennsylvania 19352
Phone: 484-365-8000
      800-790-0191 (toll-free)
Fax: 484-365-8109
E-mail: admissions@lincoln.edu
Website: http://www.lincoln.edu

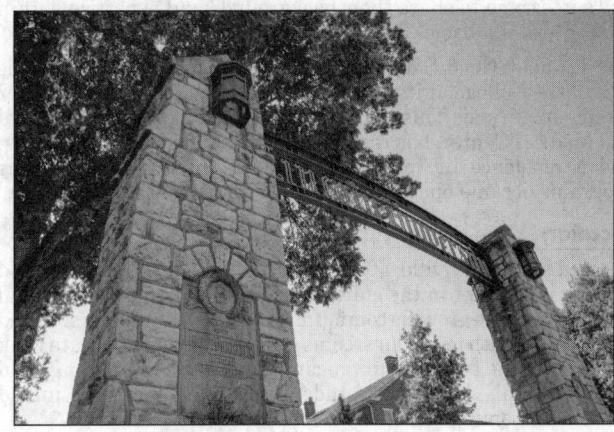

Memorial Arch, Lincoln University in Pennsylvania

LINFIELD COLLEGE
McMINNVILLE, OREGON

 To read more about this school, visit http://petersons.to/linfieldcollege

The College

Linfield College (1858) is an independent, coeducational, residential, comprehensive liberal arts and sciences college dedicated to providing an educational environment conducive to learning and participation. There are 1,700 full-time students on the McMinnville campus. These students come primarily from the thirteen Western states (twenty-four states overall) but also from nineteen other countries. Students of color make up 33 percent of the student body, and 4 percent of students are international. Most students are between 18 and 22. Linfield is primarily residential, with seventeen residence halls, each accommodating between 10 and 100 residents. Each hall establishes its own calendar of social, educational, and recreational events throughout the year. Students who reside on campus eat their meals in the College dining hall. Houses and apartments are available for upper-division students. Social clubs, professional organizations, four sororities and four fraternities, service clubs, and almost forty other organizations, including a new marching band, play an important role in the daily life of a Linfield student. Linfield's winning athletics tradition fosters participation at all levels of competition. Women compete in intercollegiate basketball, cross-country, golf, lacrosse, soccer, softball, swimming, tennis, track and field, and volleyball. Men compete in intercollegiate baseball, basketball, cross-country, football, golf, soccer, swimming, tennis, and track and field. Linfield also has an extensive and active year-round intramural program.

Linfield hosts the Oregon Nobel Laureate Symposium, one of five such symposiums worldwide. At each symposium, several Nobel laureates come to share their backgrounds and expertise within the context of a basic theme.

The Linfield–Good Samaritan School of Nursing, an academic unit of the College at its Portland campus, prepares students for careers in nursing. This campus, at the Good Samaritan Hospital and Medical Center, has residence facilities, food service options, and a residence life program. In 2006, the Portland campus programs became open only to transfer admission.

Location

Located in McMinnville, 40 miles southwest of Portland, Linfield College is a leader in the cultural, educational, and recreational events of the fast-growing community of 35,000. Linfield is situated on 189 acres with most classrooms no more than a 10-minute walk from any of the twenty-four on-campus apartment buildings and residence halls. With most students living on campus, Linfield offers a welcoming and lively community.

Coffeehouses, cinemas, boutiques, a community theater, the Evergreen Air and Space Museum (including an IMAX theater and water park), bowling alleys, and a wide variety of restaurants are within walking distance for Linfield students. The central Oregon coast is an hour to the west, and the outdoor activity areas of the Oregon Cascade Range, including year-round skiing at Mount Hood, are two hours to the east. Salem, the state capital of Oregon, is 25 miles to the southeast, and Eugene is 80 miles south. Rainfall in western Oregon averages 42 inches annually and the winter temperature averages 41°F.

Majors and Degrees

Linfield offers the Bachelor of Arts degree in communication arts, creative writing, electronic arts, Francophone African Studies, French studies, German, German studies, history, intercultural communication, international relations, Japanese, Japanese studies, Latin American/Latino studies, literature, mass communication, music, philosophy, political science, religious studies, sociology, Spanish, studio art, and theater arts. The Bachelor of Arts or Bachelor of Science degree is offered in accounting, anthropology, applied physics, biochemistry and molecular biology, biology, business, chemistry, computing science, economics, elementary education, environmental studies, exercise science, finance, international business, marketing, management, mathematics, physical activity and fitness studies, physical education, physics, and psychology. A Bachelor of Science in Nursing (B.S.N.) is also available. The College has programs to prepare students for advanced study in any health profession, including medicine, as well as law. The education department offers a strong program of teacher certification at the secondary and elementary levels.

Academic Programs

The academic year is divided into two 15-week semesters (fall and spring) and a four-week winter term in January. The January Term, required for first-year students, but optional for students in subsequent years, offers regular departmental courses and off-campus and international study. Academic courses are assigned 1–5 semester credit hours each; 125 credits are required for a B.A. or a B.S. degree. Students divide their time equally among required general education courses, a major area of study, and elective subjects. The Linfield Curriculum courses, selected to provide a solid foundation in the liberal arts, require students to take 3 semester hours in each of the six Modes of Inquiry as well as one upper-division course in one of these areas. These Modes of Inquiry are as follows: Vital Past; Ultimate Questions; Individuals, Systems, and Societies; Natural World; Creative Studies; and Quantitative Reasoning. In addition, students are required to take a writing-intensive course, a course addressing global pluralisms, and a course dealing with United States pluralism. Individually designed majors are available with faculty approval. Students majoring in a foreign language spend an academic year in a country in which the language being studied is the native tongue.

The College offers courses in English through the English Language and Culture Program. These courses are designed to help international students whose native language is not English to achieve competence in academic and social English skills, so that they may work effectively in their undergraduate classes at Linfield.

Off-Campus Programs

Off-campus educational experiences include the Semester Abroad program, involving four months of study in Australia, Austria, China, Ecuador, England, France, Germany, Hong Kong, Ireland, Japan, New Zealand, Norway, South Korea, and Spain. Transportation for the first round-trip is included in the cost of tuition, and most of these study programs cost the same as a semester on campus. January Term study-abroad programs for four weeks are also offered. Recent offerings included Health Care in Kenya; China's Solutions to Energy Issues in the Twenty-first Century; Art and Visual Culture of Catalonia, Spain; and Australia: From Colony to Asian Power.

Academic Facilities

In recent years, the College has opened two residence halls, six apartment buildings, the James F. Miller Fine Arts Center, the Marshall Theatre and communication arts facility, the Vivian A. Bull Center for Music, and the Nicholson Library. The library covers 56,000 square feet and combines traditional collections of books and journals with the new and changing digital and electronic technology to provide access to the web and web-based designs. The studio theater has an audience seating capacity of up to 140 and includes space for set construction and design.

In 2011, Linfield reopened the former library to provide new classroom and office space for the departments of business, economics, English, and philosophy. This state-of-the-art facility, T. J. Day Hall, includes the College's writing center and the Linfield Center for the Northwest (LCN). The LCN cultivates regionally relevant partnerships for training, research, service learning, and cultural or artistic exchanges. These opportunities promote student engagement in regional issues and produce real-world change. T. J. Day Hall is Linfield's first LEED-certified Gold building, underscoring the College's commitment to sustainability and conservation.

Murdock and Graf Halls house the biology, chemistry, and physics departments and up-to-date laboratories and equipment. Other facilities include art galleries and studios, a 250-watt FM radio station, an experimental psychology lab, dance and music studios, a preschool, and a 425-seat auditorium that houses a three-manual, 48-rank Casavant pipe organ.

Linfield students benefit from a communications and technology network that includes phone service, voice mail, e-mail, and wireless Internet connections in each residence hall room. In addition, there is wireless access in the library and all other areas of the campus.

The Health and Physical Education/Recreation Complex houses three gymnasiums; weight rooms; fitness laboratories with a hydrostatic weighing tank, a metabolic and pulmonary measuring system, and an electrocardiovascular exercise ECG system; an eight-lane, 25-yard indoor pool; handball and racquetball courts; classrooms; offices; and a 28,000-square-foot field house.

Costs

For 2017–18, tuition and fees were $41,100 per two-semester year, board was $5,370, and a double room was $6,400. There was a $245 per-credit fee for on-campus January Term classes, which is waived for first-year students.

Financial Aid

Eligibility for most of Linfield's assistance programs is based on need as determined by a federally approved needs analysis processor. The only form required for need-based programs is the Free Application for Federal Student Aid (FAFSA). Linfield participates in the federal grant, loan, and work programs, and other forms of financial assistance on the basis of demonstrated need.

The College awards scholarships to full-time students based on scholastic achievement, independent of financial need. These academic scholarships vary from 30 to 60 percent of tuition. A number of criteria are used when determining scholarships, including grade point average, strength of curriculum, and standardized test scores. Linfield sponsors special scholarships for National Merit finalists. The College also sponsors an annual Competitive Scholarship Day in February. Participation is limited to high school seniors who meet particular academic requirements and apply by December 1. Each academic department offers prizes ranging from $12,000 to $20,000, divided over the student's four years at Linfield. Scholarships are also available to students from the departments of music, theater, and communication who demonstrate outstanding leadership and community service. Financial assistance for non–U.S. citizens is limited to partial-tuition scholarships and the opportunity to work part-time on campus.

Faculty

There are 129 faculty members, each of whom is committed to undergraduate teaching and scholarship. Ninety-four percent have doctoral or other terminal degrees within their field. The student-faculty ratio is 11:1, and faculty members serve as academic advisers. There are no teaching assistants.

Student Government

Students have a significant voice in establishing and changing College policies and regulations. The Student Senate, chosen through campus elections, is the focus of student opinion and debate. Students are represented on most College governing councils and committees with faculty members and trustees, and they are encouraged to express and implement their ideas on academic or extracurricular matters.

Admission Requirements

Admission to Linfield College is selective. Admission is granted to students who are likely to grow and succeed in a personal and challenging liberal arts environment. Each applicant is judged on individual merit, based on high school performance, a writing sample, recommendations from teachers and counselors, precollege standardized test results (ACT or SAT), and the depth and quality of an applicant's involvement in community and school activities. Linfield is a member of the Common Application Association.

International students whose education has been in a language other than English must submit certified English translations of their academic work. Proficiency in English is required, as demonstrated by an official TOEFL score report or other English proficiency exam.

Application and Information

The early action deadline is November 1 (with notification by January 15) and the regular decision priority deadline is February 1 (with notification by April 1).

Interviews are not required, but students are encouraged to visit. Appointments should be made in advance and can be requested online at http://www.linfield.edu/stopby. The Linfield website provides students with information on academic programs, student life, and athletics.

Interested students are encouraged to contact:

Office of Admission
Linfield College
900 SE Baker Street
McMinnville, Oregon 97128
Phone: 503-883-2213
      800-640-2287 (toll-free)
Fax: 503-883-2472
E-mail: admission@linfield.edu
Website: http://www.linfield.edu/admission
      https://www.facebook.com/LinfieldCollege/
      https://twitter.com/linfieldcollege
      https://www.instagram.com/linfieldcollege/

Linfield College is located 1 hour southwest of Portland, Oregon's largest city, on nearly 200 acres. Nearly sixty buildings, many built in Georgian colonial style, house forty academic departments among a grove of oak trees.

LOYOLA UNIVERSITY MARYLAND
BALTIMORE, MARYLAND

 To read more about this school, visit http://petersons.to/loyolauniversityinmaryland

The University

Loyola University Maryland is a Jesuit, Catholic comprehensive university committed to the educational and spiritual traditions of the Society of Jesus and the development of the whole person. Accordingly, the University inspires students to learn, lead, and serve in a diverse and changing world.

Loyola's current full-time undergraduate enrollment is 4,104; 82 percent of the student body lives on campus, with all first-year students participating in Messina, Loyola's living learning program. The University encourages co-curricular activities that contribute to the academic, social, and spiritual growth of the student. These include social and cultural organizations, student government activities, an ROTC program, national honor societies, and Patriot League Division I athletic programs such as basketball, cross-country, golf, lacrosse, rowing, soccer, swimming and diving, tennis, track, and volleyball. The majority of the student body participates in the wide variety of club and intramural sports offered.

In recent years, Loyola's campus has undergone significant expansion. Thirteen apartment complexes and four first-year residence halls provide Loyola students with on-campus housing. In 2011, the Donnelly Science Center was expanded, making it the largest academic building on the Evergreen campus. The Andrew White Student Center offers several dining choices, as well as spacious meeting and recreational space. The Student Center also provides facilities for athletics, the communication department, and the fine arts, including the McManus Theatre and Reitz Arena, which holds as many as 3,000 people for various events. The Student Center also has an art gallery, classrooms, black box theatre, and music, photography, and studio art labs. Loyola's recreational sports facility is the Fitness and Aquatic Center. This state-of-the-art 115,000 square-foot athletic facility provides an indoor pool, basketball courts, squash courts, a climbing wall, fitness equipment, tracks, and outdoor playing fields. The Ridley Athletic Complex, completed in spring 2010, is a 6,000-seat grandstand stadium that hosts lacrosse, soccer, and rugby games. The adjacent McClure Tennis Center features eight lighted courts and a locker room facility.

Location

The Loyola campus is located in a residential area of north Baltimore, five miles from the city's Inner Harbor area. This location offers students the advantage of quiet residential living with the attractions and amenities of city life. Other colleges and universities in the vicinity help to expand the social calendar and academic life. The fourth-largest metropolitan area in the United States, Baltimore/Washington D.C. has a wide variety of theaters, museums, professional and intercollegiate sports events, and historical points of interest.

Majors and Degrees

Loyola offers more than 30 majors and more than 45 minors. The Bachelor of Arts degree is awarded in art history, classical civilization, classics, communication, comparative cultures and literary studies, computer science, economics, elementary education, English, fine arts, French, German, global studies, history, philosophy, political science, psychology, sociology, Spanish, speech-language-hearing sciences, theology, and writing. The Bachelor of Business Administration degree is awarded in accounting, business economics, finance, information systems, international business, management, and marketing. The Bachelor of Science degree is awarded in biology, chemistry, computer science, engineering (with concentrations in mechanical, computer, electrical, and materials), mathematics, statistics, and physics.

Academic Programs

The curriculum at Loyola is divided into three parts: the core, the major, and electives. The core contains those courses that Loyola considers essential to the liberal arts curriculum. These courses, which are required of all students regardless of major, are completed throughout the four years. The core consists of a classical or modern language, English literature, writing, mathematics and natural science, social science, fine arts, history, philosophy, ethics, and theology. Majors enable students to pursue their specialized area of study in depth. Electives give students the opportunity to broaden their intellectual and cultural background in areas of special interest. To prepare for graduate study, students may enroll in one of three pre-professional programs: pre-health, pre-medical, or pre-law.

Messina, Loyola's first-year experience, is designed to help students adjust quickly to college-level work and forge a clear path to success at Loyola and in the life and career that will follow. Messina offers a similarly distinctive and powerful beginning, an opportunity to explore a wide range of academic disciplines, appreciate their interconnectedness, and take to heart the importance of learning in a student's personal and intellectual growth.

Off-Campus Programs

Loyola University Maryland participates in a cooperative program with Notre Dame of Maryland University, Johns Hopkins University, Goucher College, Morgan State University, Towson University, the Peabody Conservatory of Music, Stevenson University, University of Maryland (Baltimore County), and the Maryland Institute College of Art. Loyola students may cross-register at any of these area colleges and universities.

Students in good academic standing may pursue studies abroad through Loyola's programs in Accra, Ghana; Alcalá, Spain; Athens, Greece; Auckland, New Zealand; Bangkok, Thailand; Beijing, China; Berlin, Germany; Cape Town, South Africa; Copenhagen, Denmark; Cork, Ireland; Dubai, United Arab Emirates; Glasgow, Scotland; Leuven, Belgium; Lyon, France; Melbourne, Australia; Newcastle, England; Paris, France; Rome, Italy; and San Salvador, El Salvador. Loyola also participates in exchange programs with eight other countries, offers summer and winter study tours, and assists students in applying to a variety of non-Loyola affiliated international study programs each year.

Academic Facilities

The Donnelly Science Center houses class laboratory spaces, research laboratories, offices, a conference room for the natural sciences, storage, a vivarium, a microscopy center, and a robotics laboratory. Spacious hallways connecting the building's wings on all levels include spaces for science displays and gathering areas for students and faculty in biology, chemistry, physics, computer science, and engineering.

The Sellinger School of Business and Management is Loyola's AACSB-accredited business school. Highlights of this school include experiential learning requirements, the Sellinger Scholars honors program, many student associations, and the Student Experiential Learning Lab, a state-of-the-art trading room that allows students access to the three most widely used databases in the finance industry—Reuters, Morningstar, and Bloomberg—and features a six-screen video display for breaking news and real-time market updates and a scrolling price ticker.

Costs

For 2018–19, tuition for all undergraduate students is $47,520 per year. Housing costs are $10,270 or $11,570, depending upon the specific residence hall in which the student lives. The base meal plan for first-year residential students is $4,160 per year and student fees are estimated at $1,400.

Financial Aid

The University strives to make a Loyola education accessible for qualified students of all socioeconomic backgrounds. Financial aid is awarded based on academic ability and financial need. Eighty-five percent of the student body receives financial assistance in the forms of Loyola University Maryland grants and scholarships, state scholarships, Federal Supplemental Educational Opportunity Grants, Federal Pell Grants, Federal Perkins Loans, and Federal Work-Study Program opportunities. To apply for financial assistance, students must submit the Free Application for Federal Student Aid (FAFSA) and the CSS/Financial Aid PROFILE through the College Scholarship Service. The financial aid application deadline is January 15.

Faculty

Loyola intends to maintain its faculty-student ratio of approximately 12:1 and an average class size of 20 students to ensure its continued focus on students as individuals. Of the 369 full-time faculty members, 73 percent are tenured or on the tenure track. Zero classes are taught by graduate students or teaching assistants.

Student Government

The Student Government serves three chief functions, which make its existence not only valuable but also necessary. These functions are to represent the student body outside the University, to provide leadership within the student body, and to perform services, both social and academic, for the students. Responsibility for budgeting activities also rests with the Student Government. The president of the Student Government is a member of the College Academic Council.

Admission Requirements

The admission evaluation at Loyola combines an analysis of academic information submitted along with a review of recommendations, the record of extracurricular involvement, and evidence of special talent, leadership, and service. The admission committee does not use a formula or have strict cutoffs. Instead, the admission office's goal is to conduct a balanced and holistic review, taking a number of factors into account. Submission of SAT and ACT scores is optional for all first-year applicants, excluding home-school students. Students who choose not to submit standardized test scores must submit an additional teacher letter of recommendation or personal essay. Students may apply early decision (binding), early action (nonbinding), or regular decision (nonbinding). The University welcomes applications from students of character, intelligence, and motivation, without discrimination on the grounds of race or religious belief.

Application and Information

Interested students seeking to enroll at Loyola may apply online using the Common Application. Each applicant must submit a school counselor letter of recommendation, a teacher letter of recommendation, and a personal statement. Applicants for financial aid must file the Free Application for Federal Student Aid (FAFSA) to be considered for federal student aid and also file the CSS Profile application to be considered for all forms of institutionally funded need-based aid. A $60 application fee must accompany the application for admission.

For additional information, students are encouraged to contact:

Undergraduate Admission Office
Loyola University Maryland
4501 North Charles Street
Baltimore, Maryland 21210-2699
Phone: 410-617-5012
    800-221-9107 (toll-free)
Website: http://www.loyola.edu/undergraduate
    http://www.facebook.com/
        LoyolaMarylandAdmission
    https://twitter.com/LOYOLAdmission
    https://instagram.com/LOYOLAdmission

Loyola University Maryland is located in residential Baltimore, five miles from the Inner Harbor and less than an hour from Washington, D.C., affording students access to an array of cultural events, internship opportunities, and field experiences.

LUTHER COLLEGE
DECORAH, IOWA

 To read more about this school, visit http://petersons.to/luthercollege

LUTHER
COLLEGE

The College

Luther College, founded in 1861 by Norwegian immigrants, is a four-year residential liberal arts college of the Lutheran church (ELCA). The College is an academic community of faith and learning where students of promise from all beliefs and backgrounds have the freedom to learn, to express themselves, to perform, to compete, and to grow. Located in Decorah, Iowa, the College is home to more than 2,050 students from 39 states and 74 countries. Twenty-seven percent of the students are from Iowa; 82 percent come from the four-state area of Iowa, Minnesota, Wisconsin, and Illinois. In 2017–18, 161 international students chose to study at Luther.

In keeping with its liberal arts tradition, the College requires students to develop a depth of knowledge in their chosen major and a breadth of knowledge through exposure to a wide range of subjects and intellectual approaches (general requirements). Learning at Luther is about engagement: faculty members who are passionate in their teaching and scholarship; students who are bright, active, and involved; and a College community characterized by personal attention, hands-on experiences, academic challenge, and community support. At Luther, all students become immersed in the liberal arts through the College's Paideia program. This program, which is uncommon in its approach, helps train students' minds and develop their research and writing skills as they explore human cultures and history. In addition, Luther offers a Phi Beta Kappa chapter and departmental honor societies, evidence of the quality of teaching and learning on campus.

At Luther, students are encouraged to seek out connections between their lives in the classroom and their lives outside the classroom. The College provides a stimulating cultural and educational atmosphere by bringing distinguished public figures, theatre groups, musicians, and educators to the campus. Cocurricular activities are an important part of college life. The College sponsors six choirs, three orchestras, three bands, two jazz bands, and a full theatre and dance program. Numerous student organizations and societies provide ample opportunities for student involvement in meaningful activities. As a community of faith, students can participate in chapel, weekly Sunday worship, and outreach teams.

Nineteen intercollegiate sports are offered. Men compete in ten intercollegiate sports: baseball, basketball, cross-country, football, golf, soccer, swimming, tennis, track and field, and wrestling. Women compete in nine intercollegiate sports: basketball, cross-country, golf, soccer, softball, swimming, tennis, track and field, and volleyball. Club sports include Ultimate Frisbee and rugby. Seventy percent of the student body is involved in an extensive intramural and recreational sports program. Available for recreational use are twelve newly renovated tennis courts, an eight-lane polyurethane 400-meter track, numerous cross-country running and ski trails, and 15 acres of intramural fields. The well-equipped Regents Center houses four hardwood basketball courts, a wrestling complex, three racquetball courts, and a 3,000-seat gymnasium. A sports forum accommodates a six-lane, 200-meter indoor track; six indoor tennis courts; locker rooms; and athletic training facilities. The Legends Fitness for Life Center provides the latest fitness equipment and a 30-foot-high rock-climbing wall. Luther offers an aquatic center, which opened in 2013 and features an eight-lane stainless steel pool complete with diving well. Legacy Field, a brand new football field installed in 2017, features distinctive blue turf.

Location

The College is located in Decorah, a city of 8,000 people in the scenic bluff country of northeast Iowa. The Upper Iowa River, which runs through the campus, is designated as a National Scenic and Recreational River. Rich in Scandinavian heritage, Decorah is a popular recreation area, providing opportunities for canoeing, kayaking, fishing, hunting, cross-country skiing, camping, hiking, biking, and spelunking. Three airports are located within a 75-mile radius of Decorah: in Rochester, Minnesota; Waterloo, Iowa; and La Crosse, Wisconsin.

Majors and Degrees

Luther College grants the Bachelor of Arts (B.A.) degree and offers majors in accounting, Africana Studies, anthropology, art, Biblical languages, biology, chemistry, classics, communication studies, computer science, data science, economics, elementary education, English, environmental studies, French, German, health and fitness promotion, history, international studies, management, mathematics, mathematics/statistics, music, neuroscience, Nordic studies, nursing, philosophy, physical education–exercise physiology, physics, political science, psychology, religion, Russian Studies, social work, sociology, Spanish, theatre, and women and gender studies. Preprofessional preparation is offered in dentistry, engineering, law, medicine, optometry, pharmacy, physical therapy, seminary, and veterinary medicine.

Academic Programs

Luther operates on a 4-1-4 academic calendar. The first semester runs from September to December, followed by a three-week January Term, and the second semester, which runs from February to May. Two four-week summer sessions are offered in June and July. All students must complete at least thirty regular courses and two January-term courses in order to graduate from Luther. Other requirements for graduation include four common foundational courses: Paideia (111 and 112); foreign language (typically one or two courses); religion (two courses, one of which must be in Biblical studies); and wellness (two 1-credit courses). In addition to a focused area of study (the major, which usually requires eight to ten courses), Luther requires all students to take courses in three general fields of inquiry: the natural world (two courses); human behavior (two courses); and human expression (two courses). Before graduating, students are required to bring together all they have learned in two culminating experiences: senior project (one course); and Paideia 450. Luther students also develop the perspectives and skills they will utilize in their lives as citizens and professionals equipped for distinguished service. Qualified students may develop interdisciplinary majors with faculty advisers.

Off-Campus Programs

Luther operates under the belief that the best education connects students with global issues and helps them engage with the larger world. Luther is consistently ranked among the top baccalaureate colleges in the nation for the number of students studying abroad prior to graduation.

Luther's off-campus programs not only span the globe, but also offer in-depth and immersive study in a wide variety of subjects. Students may participate in programs during fall and spring semesters, the January Term, and summer sessions.

The College's signature off-campus programs include an academic-year program in Nottingham, England; a semester program in Sliema, Malta; a semester program in Münster,

Germany; and a semester program in Coldigioco, Italy. In addition, Luther is part of a thirteen-college consortium which runs a successful Washington Semester in Washington, D.C. Students also have options for urban study at several centers in Chicago.

Each January Term, 300–400 Luther students study on eighteen to twenty-five faculty-led domestic and international programs.

Finally, Luther students have a wide variety of off-campus options through Luther-affiliated programs, such as those sponsored by the Associated Colleges of the Midwest, Institute for Study Abroad–Butler University, the Institute for the International Education of Students (IES), and International Studies Abroad (ISA), among others.

Academic Facilities

The 1,000-acre campus includes Preus Library, housing 340,812 volumes, over 800 print periodicals, 200,000 electronic books, and the College art collection. The library's circulation desk, Research Help Desk, Technology Help Desk, and Digital Media Center connect students with the resources they need. Two science teaching facilities, Sampson Hoffland Laboratories and Valders Hall of Science, feature modern, well-equipped labs as well as a planetarium, a greenhouse, an herbarium, a live-animal center, a human anatomy laboratory, a natural history museum, and a psychology sleep laboratory. Within easy walking distance of the campus, the field study area offers an ideal setting for studies in aquatic biology, ecology, and field biology. Five ponds, two reestablished prairies, marshes, wooded areas, and agricultural lands are available for classwork and independent study. The College has wired and wireless networking support throughout the campus. Residence halls, classrooms, and labs are outfitted with computers, printers, and academic software. Multiple connections to the Internet provide high bandwidth and reliable connectivity.

Luther College maintains radio station KWLC-AM, and the College's affiliate station, KLSE-FM, is part of the Minnesota Public Radio network. Luther is also home to one of the largest archaeological research centers in Iowa.

The Language Learning Center houses computer facilities and video screening rooms, as well as a foreign language media library with over 800 foreign language films, audio books, and print books for language learners.

The economics and business, mathematics, and computer science departments are located in Luther's high-tech, fully networked F. W. Olin Building.

The award-winning Jenson-Noble Hall of Music contains 32,000 square feet of classrooms, studios, practice rooms, and rehearsal rooms for keyboard, vocal, and instrumental music. The Center for Faith and Life (CFL) houses a 42-stop/62-rank organ in the 1,600-seat auditorium for the performing arts. A 200-seat recital hall, a 24-hour meditation chapel, and one of four campus art galleries are located in the CFL as well. The Center for the Arts serves as the home for theatre, dance, and the visual arts.

Costs

For 2018–19, the comprehensive fee is $51,750, which includes tuition, room, board, a technology fee, subscription to student publications, and admission to College-supported concerts, lectures, and other events. A room telephone, cable TV, computer access from residence hall rooms, and a health-service program are also included. Private music lessons are $510 per semester. It is estimated that an additional $3,015 is adequate for books, clothing, entertainment, and other personal expenses.

Financial Aid

More than 98 percent of all Luther students receive financial aid in the form of grants, scholarships, low-interest loans, and work-study jobs on campus. Luther awards Founders, President's, and Dean's Scholarships to students demonstrating superior academic achievement. The amount of aid given is determined by an analysis of the Free Application for Federal Student Aid (FAFSA).

Faculty

There are 175 full-time faculty members; 95 percent hold a Ph.D., first professional, or other terminal degree. The student-faculty ratio is 11:1.

Student Government

Students share in the governance of the College and participate in social and cultural programming. They have full membership on most College committees, majority representation in the Community Assembly, and nonvoting representation on the Board of Regents.

Admission Requirements

Admission is selective. An applicant must be a graduate of an accredited high school and have completed at least 4 units of English, 3 units of mathematics, 3 units of social science, and 2 units of natural science. It is strongly recommended that the applicant have at least two years of a foreign language. Transfer students may enroll at the beginning of the fall or spring semester or the January term.

Application and Information

An application, SAT or ACT scores, an educator's reference, a personal statement/essay, and a transcript of previous academic work are required for admission. On-campus interviews are recommended but not required. For more information about Luther, students should contact:
Admissions Office
Luther College
700 College Drive
Decorah, Iowa 52101-1042
Phone: 563-387-1287
        800-458-8437 (toll-free)
Fax: 563-387-2159
E-mail: admissions@luther.edu (admissions)
        finaid@luther.edu (financial aid)
        global@luther.edu (international)
Website: http://admissions.luther.edu
        http://www.facebook.com/luthercollege1861
        http://twitter.com/luthercollege

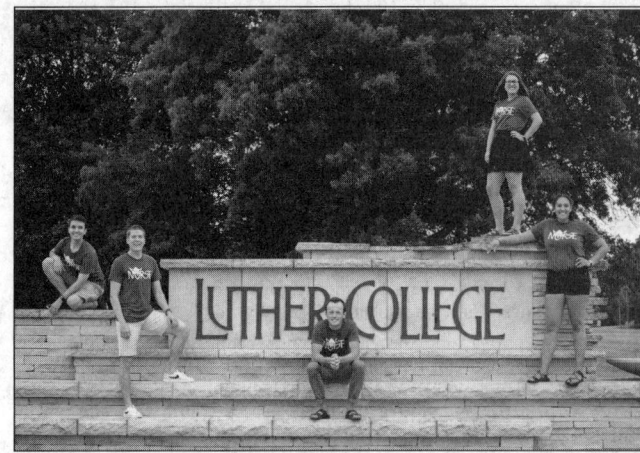

Luther College students learn in a community that emphasizes challenging academics, a world-class music program, competitive athletics, and opportunities to put their classroom learning to the test through internships, independent research, and study abroad. Typically, 97 percent of Luther graduates are employed, attending graduate school, or engaged in an internship or volunteer work within eight months of graduation.

LYNCHBURG COLLEGE
LYNCHBURG, VIRGINIA

 University *of* Lynchburg

The College

The University of Lynchburg is a vibrant learning community where students are empowered to discover their abilities and passions, connect with professors and the community, and achieve more than they dreamed possible. Formerly known as Lynchburg College (LC), a name change to the University of Lynchburg will go into effect in the fall of 2018. In claiming its university status, Lynchburg remains committed to its student-centered approach to instruction and has expanded on its institutional priority for active, engaged, and relevant learning opportunities across disciplines and throughout the University's curricula.

A fully accredited, coeducational, residential university affiliated with the Christian Church (Disciples of Christ), The University of Lynchburg offers 50 undergraduate majors, 60 minors, and 14 pre-professional programs, all supported by a strong liberal arts foundation. The University's graduate studies program includes three doctoral degrees and 14 master's programs. The University of Lynchburg is nationally recognized by such publications as The Princeton Review's The Best 376 Colleges: 2016 edition, *U.S. News & World Report* (Best Regional Universities category and Best Colleges for Veterans in the South), and the John Templeton Foundation's Honor Roll of Character-Building Colleges. Lynchburg is one of the 40 colleges and universities featured in Loren Pope's *Colleges That Change Lives*.

The University of Lynchburg is home to 2,800 undergraduate and graduate students, representing 38 states and 19 foreign countries. The University community is largely residential with 75 percent of the full-time undergraduate student body living on campus.

Located in the heart of Lynchburg, Virginia on 250 acres, the beautifully landscaped campus is a showplace. Set against a backdrop of the majestic Blue Ridge Mountains, the campus comprises more than 40 buildings, many of Georgian-style architecture. Buildings form an elliptical pattern with Hopwood Hall at the east end of campus and Snidow Chapel at the west end, symbolically linking the principles of faith and reason, the vision of Dr. Josephus Hopwood, the University's founder. The Drysdale Student Center is the hub for student activities with dining options, fitness room, club and student organization meeting space, the Campus Store, and Veterans Center.

The University community is a busy place, with a wide variety of activities including service and honor organizations, such as the national Bonner Leader Program; more than 100 clubs and organizations; 12 fraternities and sororities; and opportunities to participate in dramatic productions, student publications, religious activities, and musical performances. The Outdoor Leadership Program provides adventure-based leadership and team-building opportunities for individuals and groups. Community service (www.lynchburg.edu/volunteering-and-service) is a distinguishing feature of University of Lynchburg students, staff, and faculty, who last year contributed more than 70,000 volunteer hours to the community. The University has been on the President's Higher Education Community Service Honor Roll for the past seven years.

The University of Lynchburg encourages students to develop and maintain a sustainable lifestyle and supports sustainability initiatives on campus that include recycling, climate commitment, a community bike project, energy upgrades, and free bus rides for students.

The intercollegiate athletic program (www.lynchburgsports.com/landing/index) provides opportunities for men and women to compete in 21 sports in the NCAA Division III and the Old Dominion Athletic Conference (ODAC). In 2014, Lynchburg's women's soccer team won the NCAA Division III championship, bringing home the first team national championship in the history of the institution. Lynchburg students can also play a variety of intramural and club sports. The Turner Athletic Facility includes exercise and fitness areas, a dance studio, and one of the top exercise physiology labs in Virginia.

Shellenberger Field, named for Lynchburg's legendary soccer coach, is state-of-the-art with artificial turf, an eight-lane track, night lighting, and a 3,000-spectator capacity stadium with chair and bleacher seating. The field hosts men's and women's soccer, lacrosse, track and field, field hockey, and intramural and club sports. Moon Field is home to Lynchburg's softball team and the track and field events of javelin, hammer, shot put, and discus. Fox Field is one of the best baseball fields in the ODAC, with batting cages, a press box, and seating for up to 1,000 spectators.

Location

The University of Lynchburg (www.lynchburg.edu) is located in central Virginia, 100 miles from Richmond, Virginia, 180 miles southwest of Washington, D.C., and 50 miles east of Roanoke. Air, bus, and railroad transportation place Lynchburg within easy reach of any urban center. Greater Lynchburg is a growing business and industrial center with a population of more than 240,000. The city is noted for its climate, culture, historic landmarks, and proximity to the Blue Ridge Mountains.

Majors and Degrees

The University of Lynchburg offers the bachelor of arts degree in: accounting, art (graphic design or studio art), athletic training, business administration, communication studies (convergent journalism, social influence, electronic media or public relations), economics (financial or general), English (literature or writing), French, history, international relations, liberal arts studies, management, marketing, music (instrumental or vocal education, instrumental or vocal performance), philosophy, political science, religious studies, sociology (cultural studies, deviance and crime, human services), Spanish, sports management, and theater. The Bachelor of Science degree is offered in: biology, biomedical science, chemistry, computer science, environmental science, exercise physiology, health promotion, human development and learning (elementary education or special education), mathematics, nursing, physics, and psychology. More information is available at www.lynchburg.edu/majors-and-minors.

Pre-professional and professional courses are available in art therapy, dentistry, engineering, forestry and wildlife management, law, library science, medicine, ministry and ministry-related occupations, museum studies, occupational therapy, optometry, pharmacy, physical therapy, and veterinary medicine.

Academic Programs

To be eligible for a degree, a student must complete at least 124 semester hours of college-level academic work with a grade point average of at least 2.0 or higher on all work undertaken in the major field.

The curriculum at the University of Lynchburg is divided into two general areas: general education requirements and the major, providing students with breadth and depth of study. General education requirements are selected from the broad disciplines of world literature, fine arts, philosophy, religious studies, mathematics, history, social science, laboratory science, foreign languages, and health and movement science. Additional hours are available for students to explore coursework in free elective hours of their choice or students may devote their free elective hours to a minor.

The University's Westover Honors Program (www.lynchburg.edu/academics/westover-honors-program) is designed to attract, stimulate, challenge, and fulfill academically gifted students through a challenging curriculum that promotes intellectual curiosity and independent thinking and places strong emphasis on creative problem solving.

Off-Campus Programs

Lynchburg students are encouraged to engage in foreign-study programs, particularly Lynchburg's study-abroad program (www.lynchburg.edu/study-abroad).

More than 1,000 internships (www.lynchburg.edu/career-services) are available locally, nationally, and internationally, and are integral parts of a Lynchburg education. As members of the Tri-College Consortium of Virginia, Lynchburg College, Randolph College, and Sweet Briar College maintain cooperative relationships for sharing facilities and offerings.

Academic Facilities

The University of Lynchburg has 23 computer labs with both PCs and Macs. New students may bring a computer of their own or utilize one of the many available on campus. All students are assigned an e-mail account and have access to the internet. All residence hall rooms are wired for network access and the intranet, which serves the University community. Wireless internet access is available in most areas of the campus.

The University has several active learning classrooms where students can write on the walls, collaborate in the cloud with the help of Chromecast-enabled monitors, and easily rearrange the room thanks to wheeled tables and chairs.

The Hobbs-Sigler Science Center provides an outstanding learning environment for students studying biology, chemistry, physics, biomedical sciences, environmental science, psychology, mathematics, and computer science. A cadaver lab, cutting-edge research labs, online weather station, GIS and remote sensing software, and digitizer are just some of the learning tools available. This facility is also used during the summer by the Virginia Governor's School for Math and Science to provide programming for selected high school students.

Schewel Hall, a $12-million classroom and laboratory facility, houses the School of Business and Economics, the Communication Studies program, foreign languages, and performing arts. This 67,000 square-foot facility includes technology-based classrooms, computer laboratories, and specialized teaching-learning settings, including a model stock exchange room, a digital darkroom, and a multimedia development center with television and recording studios. Sydnor Performance Hall provides an excellent venue for concerts, lectures, and other programs, with seating for 250 people.

The Daura Gallery (www.lynchburg.edu/daura-gallery) is the major repository of more than 1,000 works of Pierre Daura, the Catalan-American artist for whom the Gallery is named. Each year, The Daura Gallery features traveling exhibitions throughout the academic year and is the site for the Senior Art Show where selected student works are exhibited.

The Claytor Nature Study Center located on nearly 500 acres in nearby Bedford County provides an outdoor classroom and laboratory for hands-on, field-based environmental study and research. Donated to the institution by the late A. Boyd Claytor III, a member of the Lynchburg Board of Trustees, the property features lakes, woodlands, wetlands, grasslands, rare plants, formal gardens, a primitive campground, and three miles of hiking trails. The land is now managed for environmental conservation and restoration through agreements with the Virginia Outdoors Foundation and the USDA's Natural Resources Conservation Service. The A. Boyd Claytor III Education and Research Facility, a 7,700 square-foot multipurpose building, offers Lynchburg students and regional K–12 students and teachers an ideal location for learning with seminar, laboratory, classroom, conference, and retreat space.

The Belk Astronomical Observatory sits at one of the highest points of the Claytor Center property (approximately 960 feet above sea level) and is one of the most publicly accessible dark sky observatories in Virginia. The observatory features an RC Optical Systems 20-inch (0.51 meter) Truss Ritchey-Chrétien telescope with a 177-square-foot dome housing, and an observation deck equipped with 12 piers for mounting smaller telescopes. The control room is equipped with instrumentation that allows Lynchburg to conduct extensive stellar and planetary research and pursue astronomical research with other regional colleges and universities.

The Chandler Eco-Lodge, a 16-bed facility at Claytor, provides overnight accommodations for students and researchers who wish to study outside the classroom. The 2,100 square-foot lodge is built with energy-efficiency and low-impact design and includes a constructed wetland to handle wastewater.

Costs

Total charges for resident students for the 2018–19 session are $40,360: $38,560 tuition, $10,800 room and board, and $970 student fees (www.lynchburg.edu/undergraduate-admission/tuition-fees).

Financial Aid

The University of Lynchburg administers a financial aid program of more than $40 million annually. These resources are awarded to students for meritorious achievement and/or for demonstrated need. The University of Lynchburg offers academic scholarships (www.lynchburg.edu/financial-aid/scholarships) that range from $10,000 to $21,000 and are based on performance and accomplishments at the high school or community university level. In addition, the University offers scholarship competitions with awards ranging from $1,000 to $5,000, which are awarded in conjunction with other academic scholarships. The competitions are based upon academic performance, leadership, community service and talent. These awards are renewable each year until the student graduates, as long as the recipient maintains a qualifying minimum academic average each year. Students are identified to receive these scholarships through the admission application; no separate application is necessary. Free early aid estimates are available for students. More than 98 percent of last year's entering class received academic and/or need-based financial aid. The average amount of aid received was $37,000.

To determine eligibility for need-based financial aid, the student should complete the Free Application for Federal Student Aid (FAFSA), which may be obtained at most high schools and at the University. The FAFSA results determine the student's eligibility for federally funded grants and loans and other support such as work-study opportunities. In addition, students from Virginia are eligible to apply for the Virginia Tuition Assistance grant.

Faculty

The University of Lynchburg's faculty members are outstanding scholars who are leaders in their disciplines. Of the 190 full-time members, 83 percent hold the doctorate or terminal degree in their fields. The student-faculty ratio is 11:1, which allows for personal attention and student-faculty collaborative research, both of which are essential to the Lynchburg experience. While Lynchburg faculty are involved in various research and writing projects, University policy requires that teaching is to be their top priority.

Admission Requirements

A candidate for admission to the University of Lynchburg (www.lynchburg.edu/undergraduate-admission) should be a graduate of an approved secondary school with a minimum of 16 academic units or the equivalent, as shown by examination. It is required that the academic work include major emphases in the areas of English, foreign language, social science, natural sciences, and mathematics. An applicant must demonstrate above-average academic ability in all areas of study, as admission is competitive. In support of the record, a student must present satisfactory scores on the ACT or SAT (critical reading and math scores are used to determine admission decisions and merit scholarship awards). It is recommended that all students have a personal interview and visit the campus beginning the spring semester of their junior year or during their senior year. Enrollment Office hours during the academic year are 9 a.m. to 5 p.m. Monday through Friday and 10 a.m. to noon on Saturday during the academic year.

Application and Information

The University operates on an early semester calendar. The first semester begins in late August and ends before Christmas, and the second semester runs from mid-January to early May. An optional winter term abroad is also offered.

Early decision admission applications must be received by November 15 (www.lynchburg.edu/undergraduate-admission/freshman-application-steps); notification of acceptance is made by December 15. All other applications are processed on a rolling admissions basis. Applicants are notified of the status of their application usually within two to four weeks of the date their application file is completed.

For information, students should contact:

Sharon Walters-Bower, Director of Admissions
The University of Lynchburg
1501 Lakeside Drive
Lynchburg, Virginia 24501
Phone: 434-544-8300
        800-426-8101 (toll-free)
Fax: 434-544-8653
E-mail: admissions@lynchburg.edu
Website: http://www.lynchburg.edu

The iconic LOVEworks sculpture at the University of Lynchburg serves as a visible reminder of the University's commitment to embracing all people and to our past as Lynchburg College (LC)..

MANHATTAN COLLEGE
RIVERDALE, NEW YORK

 To read more about this school, visit http://petersons.to/manhattancollege

The College

Manhattan College has more than sixty programs that build upon a strong liberal arts foundation and offer professional preparation in business, education and health, liberal arts, science, and engineering. Learning extends beyond the classroom through internships in New York City and beyond.

The College is one of only a few U.S. colleges to have chapters of all five of these distinguished national honor societies: Phi Beta Kappa, Beta Gamma Sigma, Kappa Delta Pi, Sigma Xi, and Beta Pi.

Manhattan College ranks among the top 15 Catholic colleges in the United States on Forbes' list of *Best Value Colleges 2017: The 300 Schools Worth the Investment.*

Following in the Lasallian Catholic tradition, many Manhattan College students actively define their commitment to social justice by balancing their traditional lifestyles with immersion and service experiences around the city, country, and world.

Each year, Campus Ministry and Social Action (CMSA) organizes several L.O.V.E. programs (Lasallian Outreach Volunteer Experience), which give students the opportunity to travel to some of the world's poorest areas in New Orleans, West Virginia, Kenya, Ecuador, and the Dominican Republic to volunteer with people of very different socioeconomic backgrounds.

Closer to home, the Lasallian Collegians volunteer on campus and in New York City by arranging school blood drives, toy drives, soup kitchen trips, and food runs. In addition, the Arches offers freshman students the opportunity to live in a community in Lee Hall and take one class together each semester of their freshman year that incorporates cultural excursions and service projects in New York City. Many former Arches students say the friendships they made through the program last well beyond graduation.

The tight-knit College community is comprised of 3,927 students. With a 12:1 student-to-faculty ratio, professors know students personally and care about their success. The majority of students live on the traditional collegiate campus, just a subway ride from midtown Manhattan.

Location

Manhattan College's 23-acre campus is located 10 miles north of midtown Manhattan in the suburban Riverdale section of the Bronx, about a mile from Westchester County. The College is located in the world's greatest cultural hub, where renowned museums and landmarks serve as off-campus classrooms. Students have access to internship and job opportunities at some of the country's most prestigious companies. From Fortune 500 companies to independent start-ups, students can find an organization in New York City to support their career goals.

Majors and Degrees

Business: The School of Business, accredited by AACSB International, has programs leading to a Bachelor of Science in Business Administration degree with majors in accounting, business analytics, computer information systems, economics, finance, global business studies, management, and marketing.

In addition, Manhattan College also offers the following graduate programs: the Bachelor of Science in Professional Accounting/Master of Business Administration and the Bachelor of Science in Business/Master of Business Administration, which offer students the opportunity to complete a five-year multiple award program.

Education and Health: The School of Education and Health offers a curriculum leading to a Bachelor of Arts degree in childhood education, childhood/special education (dual program), and adolescent education. The kinesiology curriculum leads to a Bachelor of Science degree in physical education and exercise science. The health curriculum leads to a Bachelor of Science degree in allied health, with a concentration in health care administration or general sciences. Curricula in radiological and health sciences lead to a Bachelor of Science in radiation therapy or nuclear medicine technology. In addition, the School of Education and Health offers the five-year childhood/special education program, which allows the student to receive a bachelor's and master's degree with eligibility to pursue certification for grades 1–6 in regular and special education. The School of Education and Health also offers master's degrees and professional diplomas in school counseling, mental health counseling, special education, and school building leadership. All programs are approved by the New York State Education Department and accredited by the Teacher Education Accreditation Council (TEAC).

Engineering: The School of Engineering has a well-deserved reputation as one of the best college engineering schools in the nation and offers programs leading to a Bachelor of Science degree in chemical, civil, computer, electrical, and mechanical engineering. The program is fully accredited by the Educational Accreditation Commission of ABET. Graduate programs are also available in chemical, civil, computer, electrical, environmental, and mechanical engineering.

Liberal Arts: The curriculum of the School of Liberal Arts provides programs that lead to a Bachelor of Arts or Bachelor of Science degree with majors in the humanities and the social sciences, including art history, communication, economics, English, French, government, history, labor studies, philosophy, psychology, religious studies, sociology, and Spanish. Interdisciplinary majors include international studies, peace studies, and urban studies.

Science: In the School of Science, programs lead to a Bachelor of Science or Bachelor of Arts degree with majors in biochemistry, biology, chemistry, computer science, environmental science, mathematics, and physics. Pre-medical, pre-dental, and pre–veterinary studies programs are also available. In addition, Manhattan College also offers the following graduate programs: Applied Mathematics–Data Analytics and Computer Science.

Academic Programs

The core curriculum shared by the Schools of Liberal Arts and Science studies some of the vital works of humankind, explores new ideas, examines the meaning of scientific experimentation, and encourages a student to develop his or her thinking and leadership abilities. The major programs offer advanced work in specific humanistic and scientific disciplines and opportunities to work on research projects in collaboration with faculty scholars.

In the School of Engineering, all engineering students follow a common core curriculum during the first two years and choose a major at the beginning of the junior year. Each curriculum includes a generous selection of courses in basic sciences, the engineering sciences, humanistic studies, and mathematics.

The School of Business prepares students for positions of executive responsibility in business, government, and nonprofit organizations. The business curriculum is based on a strong commitment to liberal education and is well balanced between professional business courses, humanities, sciences, and social sciences. This is a reflection of the school's belief that executives should be broadly educated and should involve themselves, as well as their organizations, in efforts to solve social problems.

The School of Education and Health prepares students for teaching, counseling, and health professions. Students complete the College's core curriculum in liberal arts and sciences and then complete a major in various programs in the school's three departments: education, kinesiology, and radiological and health professions. All programs include internships/practicums in schools, hospitals, or other institutions. Graduates of the school's teacher-preparation programs receive New York State provisional teaching certification. The school also offers a five-year B.A./M.S. program in childhood/special education and special education.

Off-Campus Programs

Manhattan College also offers study-abroad programs in many countries; arrangements can be made to study in a country of choice. Students in the School of Business may participate in the International Field Studies Seminar. As participants, they spend time in another country studying the effect of that environment on international firms. Career services and co-op education integrate classroom theory with the practical experience of a job in industry, business, the social services, the arts, or government. Portions of the education courses are conducted in New York City schools, so that student teachers may gain experience in urban education at an early stage.

Academic Facilities

There are more than forty scientific and engineering laboratories at Manhattan, including the Research and Learning Center, as well as a modern language laboratory and a computer information systems laboratory. Manhattan's O'Malley Library is a state-of-the-art facility featuring modern accommodations for study and research.

The Raymond W. Kelly ('63) Student Commons, which opened in the fall of 2014, is a 70,000-square-foot building, which has quickly become a focal point on campus. It enhances the College's ability to integrate academics and student life, and provides space for fitness and wellness programming, cultural and community events, dining, student activities, and student collaboration.

Costs

For 2017–18, the tuition for Manhattan College was $38,200 per year plus program fee. Room and board for the year was $15,600.

Financial Aid

Manhattan grants or administers financial assistance in the form of tuition awards to students on the basis of need and/or ability. Need is evaluated by submitting the FAFSA. In addition to a merit scholarship fund, Manhattan offers endowed scholarships, special category scholarships and student athletic grants, Federal Pell Grants, Federal Supplemental Educational Opportunity Grants, student loans, Federal Work-Study Program awards, and New York State financial assistance are also available to students who qualify. Forty-eight percent of all students receive merit aid with 94 percent of the students receiving aid.

Faculty

Manhattan's faculty has 219 full-time faculty members. Ninety-three percent of the faculty members hold doctorates. They are available to students for informal guidance and counseling and serve as official moderators of many campus organizations.

Admission Requirements and Application Information

An application for admission to Manhattan College may be submitted using the Common Application or a Manhattan College Application. An application fee of $75 is required.

In reviewing applications for admission, the most emphasis is placed upon student course selection and the rigor of the course curriculum as well as on cumulative grade point average. All applicants must have completed a minimum of 16 units in academic subjects to be qualified for admission.

Applicants for freshman admission need to submit SAT or ACT scores. Only a student's highest scores are considered for admission and scholarship eligibility.

Grades and examination scores alone do not adequately evaluate a student's ability to be successful in college. Therefore, appropriate character references are considered important when reviewing candidates for admission. One letter of recommendation from a teacher or guidance counselor is required. Applicants must also submit a brief personal statement or college essay.

Interviews are recommended but not required as part of the admissions process.

Applications are reviewed on a rolling admission basis. Manhattan will consider for admission any qualified student upon completion of the junior year. Students must continue to demonstrate progress at the same academic level in their senior year and that all secondary school graduation requirements must be met, and a diploma issued, in order to enroll. Junior college or other transfer students are welcome. Manhattan College requires applicants whose native language is not English to take the Test of English as a Foreign Language (TOEFL), IELTS, the SAT, or ACT exam. The average SAT score is 1100–1240.

The high school report, recommendation letters, and transcript must be submitted by the high school guidance counselor. There is a rolling admissions policy and a March 1 priority deadline for financial aid applications.

For more information, contact:

William J. Bisset, Ph.D.
Vice President for Enrollment Management
Manhattan College
Riverdale, New York 10471
United States
Phone: 718-862-7200
        800-MC2-XCEL (toll-free)
E-mail: admit@manhattan.edu
Website: http://www.manhattan.edu

Manhattan College centers a great deal of its campus activity around the main quadrangle.

MARLBORO COLLEGE
MARLBORO, VERMONT

 Marlboro College

 To read more about this school, visit http://petersons.to/marlborocollege

The College

Marlboro College is an intentionally small, intellectually demanding liberal arts college, where students with a passion for learning pursue their deepest interests. An exceptionally close-knit learning environment in the inspiring natural setting of Vermont's Green Mountains, Marlboro offers student-designed study through small classes and advanced individualized study. Rather than follow a prescribed academic program, Marlboro students work closely with faculty advisers to map out an individualized course of study based on their intellectual interests. Marlboro's goal is to teach students to think clearly and learn independently, develop a command of clear writing, and aspire to making a difference in the world, all while participating responsibly in a self-governing community.

Marlboro was founded in 1946, and the college's rural, 300-plus-acre campus includes the original cluster of barns and other farm buildings that were converted by the first students and faculty members into classrooms and dormitories. The campus also features 17 miles of trails, and the Outdoor Program offers instruction and equipment for backpacking, cross-country skiing, kayaking, rock climbing, snow-shoeing, and other outdoor recreational opportunities that bring students in touch with the surrounding environment. The soccer team competes with other colleges, and more impromptu gatherings of students play volleyball, basketball, softball, and Ultimate (Frisbee) on an informal basis. In addition, Marlboro's much-anticipated broomball tournament (a game akin to hockey, but with less skill and grace) takes place each winter, with prizes for the winning teams and those with the best costumes. Campus committees organize many events both on and off campus, including concerts, lectures, poetry and fiction readings, art shows, and trips to Boston, Montreal, and New York for museum visits, shopping, and baseball games. Other activities that enrich campus life include parties, dances, plays, and film screenings.

Marlboro is—and intends to remain—one of the nation's smallest liberal arts colleges, with some 300 students on average. They come from all across the United States and several other countries and represent a rich diversity of socioeconomic backgrounds, perspectives, and interests. Transfer students—who make up one quarter of each incoming class—bring an important wealth of perspective to the campus community. More than 80 percent of all students live in campus housing, which consists of small dormitories and several four-bedroom cottages.

Location

The center of Marlboro, just 2 miles from the college, is a quintessential Vermont village, with a post office, a town clerk's office, and an inn. The total population of the town is 1,200 residents, more in the summer during the famous Marlboro Music Festival. The town of Brattleboro, 12 miles away, is a lively cultural and commercial center with bookstores, restaurants, coffee shops, a community food cooperative, music venues, and a movie theater. The college is 2 hours by car from Boston and 4 hours from New York City and Montreal.

Areas of Study and Degrees

Marlboro confers Bachelor of Arts and Bachelor of Science degrees in 34 fields. Areas of study offered include American studies, anthropology, art history, Asian studies, biology, ceramics, chemistry and biochemistry, classics, computer science, cultural history, dance, economics, environmental studies, film/video studies, gender studies, history, languages, liberal studies, literature, mathematics, music, painting, philosophy, photography, physics and astronomy, politics, psychology, religion, sculpture, sociology, theater, visual arts, world studies, and writing.

Students at Marlboro have the freedom to design their own course of study based on these degree fields, with the support and guidance of inspiring faculty members, and are encouraged to make interdisciplinary connections and pursue individualized research. The college also offers Bachelor of Arts and Bachelor of Science degrees in international studies through its World Studies Program, which includes a six-to-eight month internship in another country. Marlboro confers master's degrees and related certificates in management and teaching which provides a practical and seamless next step for many undergraduate students.

Academic Programs

In the first two years, Marlboro students study broadly, discover new interests, and begin to see the connections that lead many to pursue interdisciplinary work. Each new student is paired with a faculty adviser and joins an advising group of students with similar interests that meets each week. Students learn from each other, as well as from their engaging professors, in seminar-style classes.

Marlboro believes that clear writing both reflects and engenders clear thinking. Whether their academic interests lean toward Russian literature or contemporary dance, students write prodigiously over the course of their time at Marlboro. The college requires each new student to pass a Clear Writing Requirement within three semesters of enrolling. Designated writing courses, faculty advisers, and student writing tutors all help new students meet the requirement. Whatever career paths Marlboro students forge, they all benefit from the ability to process complex information and effectively communicate their ideas to others.

More than any other academic component, Marlboro's Plan of Concentration sets the college apart from other undergraduate programs. Undertaken by all Marlboro students in their junior and senior years, the Plan is the collection of related projects and papers that form the final product of the student's academic work at Marlboro. It is an individualized program of classes, research, experiences, one-to-one study, and original thought, driven by the student's interests and academic goals and designed in close collaboration with faculty sponsors. Final evaluation of the student's Plan is conducted by her or his faculty advisers and an outside examiner who is a recognized expert in the student's field.

Off-Campus Programs

Marlboro College sponsors multiple academic adventures and service-learning trips each year, ranging from community work in South Carolina and Cambodia to interdisciplinary research in Cuba, China, Kenya, and Vietnam. Whether they are in the World Studies Program or not, students working on their Plan of Concentration often travel abroad or attend other institutions for a period of time to complement their academic work. Marlboro faculty members may help plan these pursuits and frequently aid students in securing internships in their academic fields.

Academic Facilities

Marlboro's academic facilities offer small classrooms and inviting faculty offices for students to meet in small groups and individually with their professors. Facilities are open 24 hours a day, supporting student research and creative explorations in a DNA lab, a black-and-white darkroom, a digital film-editing studio, art and pottery studios, and an astronomical observatory. The Rudolf and Irene Serkin Performing Arts Center offers more than 10,000 square feet for music, dance, and drama rehearsals and performances. Marlboro's Total Health Center provides additional space for medical and psychological counseling services as well as a fitness room. The new Snyder Center for the Visual Arts, which opened in 2016, includes studios, classrooms, gallery space, and a digital media lab.

Costs

Tuition and fees at Marlboro are $40,840 for the 2018–19 academic year. Room and board costs are $12,348.

Financial Aid

More than 90 percent of all full-time Marlboro students receive some form of financial help. The college is committed to helping any student who qualifies for admission assemble the financial resources necessary to attend, and need is not a factor in the admission decision. Merit scholarships and grants are also available.

Faculty

Marlboro's 40 full-time faculty members are committed first and foremost to teaching. The lively exchange of ideas between teachers and students is the cornerstone of the Marlboro curriculum. The college's 6:1 student-faculty ratio sparks dynamic exchanges between students and their teachers both in and out of the classroom, and fosters a close-knit community in which asking questions is more important than knowing the right answers.

Student Government

All students, faculty, and staff members are equal members of the college Town Meeting, when the community comes together each month to debate and decide budget initiatives, college policies, and other issues that affect daily life. A board of selectpersons, elected by the college community, serves the college's interests and is responsible for drafting the Town Meeting agenda. Students serve with faculty and staff members on more than 30 college committees, including those that make decisions on hiring faculty, housing policies, and special scholarships. Other important committees include the social committee and the Community Court, which is responsible for enforcing campus standards of conduct.

Admission Requirements

The Admissions Committee seeks students with intellectual promise; a high degree of motivation, self-discipline, personal stability, and social concern; and the ability and desire to contribute to the college community. All applicants are considered without regard to race, creed, sex, sexual orientation, gender identity or its expression, national or ethnic origin, age, or disability. Homeschoolers, transfers, veterans, and older or returning students are encouraged to apply.

Like most colleges, Marlboro requires students to submit several forms of documentation, from high school transcripts to teacher recommendations. SAT or ACT scores are optional, and whether they are submitted or not, the admissions office evaluates each applicant as a unique individual who possesses qualities that are not necessarily quantifiable.

A campus visit is strongly recommended for all applicants, and interviews are required. Marlboro does not use a formulaic approach in making admission decisions. Applicants are encouraged to demonstrate their particular strengths; the goal is a successful match between the student and the college.

Application and Information

New students and transfers are admitted for either the spring or the fall semester. Applicants for the fall semester have a choice of three admission plans. The early decision plan is for those students who have thoroughly researched Marlboro and for whom Marlboro is the first choice. Applicants should be aware that early decision is binding. The early decision deadline for first-year students to submit application materials is November 15, and applicants are notified by December 1. Early action, a nonbinding plan, has a deadline of January 15. These applicants are notified of a decision on February 1. The regular admission deadline is March 15. The deadline for transfer students to submit applications materials for the fall semester is rolling.

Students can apply to Marlboro through the Common Application or directly through Marlboro College's own application, found on the college website. All applications should include the Marlboro College supplement form with a "Why Marlboro" personal statement, a $50 application fee, complete transcripts from all secondary schools and colleges currently or previously attended, an analytical writing sample, and two letters of recommendation. SAT or ACT test scores are not required, but will be taken into consideration if submitted by the prospective student. In lieu of a high school transcript, homeschooled students must submit a detailed description of their curriculum (including reading lists and academic study areas).

Office of Admissions
Marlboro College, 2582 South Road
Marlboro, Vermont 05344-0300
United States
Phone: 802-257-4333
      800-343-0049 (toll-free)
Fax: 802-451-7555
E-mail: admissions@marlboro.edu
Website: http://www.marlboro.edu

Classes at Marlboro College are small and informal, enabling faculty members to bring an extraordinary degree of commitment, passion, and mentoring to their teaching.

MARYWOOD UNIVERSITY
SCRANTON, PENNSYLVANIA

 To read more about this school, visit http://petersons.to/marywooduniversity

The University

Marywood University enrolls more than 2,900 students in its undergraduate, graduate, and doctoral programs. Founded in 1915 by the Sisters, Servants of the Immaculate Heart of Mary, the University provides a framework for educational excellence that enables students to develop fully as persons and to master professional and leadership skills necessary for meeting human needs.

Students at Marywood have the opportunity to build on their academic interests and proactively shape their educational experience. Marywood believes in the power of the individual and in the premise that education is the most empowering tool.

Marywood is fully accredited by the Commission on Higher Education of the Middle States Association of Colleges and Schools. Program-specific accreditations are available to review online at www.marywood.edu/academics.

Marywood's athletic programs provide students with opportunities to play on competitive intercollegiate, club, and intramural teams. Students compete on an intercollegiate basis in baseball, basketball, cross-country, field hockey, golf, lacrosse, rugby, soccer, softball, swimming/diving, tennis, track and field, and volleyball. Marywood is a member of NCAA Division III, the Colonial States Athletic Conference (CSAC), and the Eastern College Athletic Conference.

Prospective students can connect with Marywood through social networks including Facebook (facebook.com/marywoodu), Twitter (twitter.com/marywoodu), and YouTube (youtube.com/marywoodu).

Location

Marywood's campus is part of an attractive residential area of Scranton, in northeastern Pennsylvania. With a population of 78,000, Scranton is the fifth-largest city in Pennsylvania. Marywood is close to many major cities of the Northeast; traveling by car, it is 2½ hours to New York and Philadelphia, 4 hours to Washington, D.C., and 5½ hours to Boston. Several airlines serve the Wilkes-Barre/Scranton International Airport, which is 20 minutes from the campus. The Pocono Mountains, offering spectacular scenery and an abundance of outdoor recreational opportunities, including downhill skiing, are a short distance from campus.

Academic Programs

All students are required to complete a core curriculum in the liberal arts in addition to the courses in their major. Opportunities for undergraduates abound through double majors, honors and independent-study programs, practicums, internships, and study abroad. Army and Air Force ROTC programs are available.

Majors and Degrees

At the undergraduate level, Marywood awards the Bachelor of Arts (B.A.), Bachelor of Architecture (B.Arch.), Bachelor of Business Administration (B.B.A.), Bachelor of Environmental Design in Architecture (B.E.D.A.), Bachelor of Fine Arts (B.F.A.), Bachelor of Interior Architecture (B.I.A.), Bachelor of Music (B.M.), Bachelor of Science (B.S.), Bachelor of Science in Nursing (B.S.N.), and Bachelor of Social Work (B.S.W.).

Marywood offers majors in the following areas of study: accounting, ad hoc (self-designed), advertising and public relations, architecture and interior architecture/design, art (studio: ceramics, painting, sculpture, illustration; design: graphic design, photography), art therapy, arts administration (art, music, theater), athletic training, aviation management, biology, biology secondary education, biotechnology, communication sciences and disorders (speech-language pathology), computer science, criminal justice, cyber security (information security), digital media and broadcast production (broadcast, corporate), early childhood and elementary education, early childhood and elementary education/special education, English (literature and writing), English secondary education, entrepreneurship, environmental science, exercise science, financial planning, health services administration, history, history/pre-law, history secondary education, hospitality management, international business, journalism, management, marketing, mathematics, mathematics secondary education, medical laboratory science, music education, music performance, music therapy, nursing, nutrition and dietetics, philosophy, pre-physician assistant studies, psychology, psychology/clinical practice, religious studies, retail business management, sociology, social work, Spanish, Spanish secondary education, and theater.

Off-Campus Programs

Study-abroad opportunities are available in countries such as Australia, Canada, England, France, Mexico, and Spain. Through Studio Art Centers International (SACI), art students may study in Florence, Italy.

Academic Facilities

In recent years, the University has made major improvements to campus, including new athletic, residence, and dining facilities, and one of the finest studio arts facilities in the northeast. The Learning Commons is a 21st century–style library featuring four levels of open, accessible, and technologically advanced facilities. The Insalaco Center for Studio Arts features 60,000 square feet of fully equipped studios, labs, and classroom spaces for a broad variety of artistic disciplines. The Center for Architectural Studies offers students two levels of studio space in a spacious, adaptive re-use of Marywood's former gymnasium and pool space. A Center for Communication Arts offers a wide range of media tools, including a soundstage for television production and audio recording, a radio station, video and editing rooms, an animation studio, and print journalism facilities.

Costs

Tuition for full-time students (12–18 credits per semester) for the 2018–19 academic year was a flat fee of $33,160. There is also a general fee of $1,500 for full-time students. Costs for room and board for a full academic year are approximately $14,000, depending on which meal plan is selected and the desired room occupancy.

Financial Aid

Marywood offers a comprehensive program of financial aid to assist students in meeting educational costs. Eligibility for federal and state programs is based on demonstrated financial need, as determined by a federal eligibility formula that analyzes family income and assets. In addition, approximately $29 million in institutional aid is awarded annually to Marywood students. Applicants to Marywood are considered for all financial assistance programs for which they qualify. Candidates are required to submit the Free Application for Federal Student Aid (FAFSA) and the Marywood application form.

Faculty

Among faculty members at Marywood, 141 are full-time, and 82 percent of these hold the Ph.D. or the highest degree in their field. The student-faculty ratio is 12:1. Faculty members are evaluated on their teaching and on their scholarly and artistic activities.

Student Government

All matriculated students in the undergraduate school are members of the Student Government Association (SGA). The SGA operates with a number of committees, including the Student Council, the Resident Committee, and the Commuter Committee. The association plays a key role in establishing a positive campus environment.

Admission Requirements

Candidates for admission should demonstrate reasonable progress toward graduation in an accredited secondary school, have graduated from a secondary school, or offer evidence of an equivalent secondary education. Each candidate should show satisfactory academic preparation in 16 units of subject matter, including 4 units of English, 3 units of social studies, 2 units of mathematics, 1 unit of science with laboratory, and 6 additional units. Prospective students should check with the Office of University Admissions regarding current standardized test requirements.

In addition to fulfilling general admission requirements, candidates for admission to a degree program in architecture, art, education, music, nursing, pre–physician assistant studies, and speech language pathology must meet special standards established by the department. Prior to enrollment, music, theater, and art candidates are required to audition or to present an art portfolio.

For certain programs, candidates without the recommended distribution of units may be eligible for admission if their course work as a whole and the results of their tests offer evidence of a strong foundation for college work. Candidates who are deficient in required course work may complete the appropriate work during the summer or first year in college.

A student who demonstrates satisfactory academic performance at another college may apply for admission as a transfer student. Academic courses presented for transfer should be equivalents of courses required by the programs of study at Marywood. Students should have earned a grade of C or higher in their course work; C– will not transfer. A student should expect to earn a minimum of 42 credits at Marywood; ordinarily, at least one half of the credits required for a major must also be earned at Marywood.

International candidates are required to meet the academic standards for admission, demonstrate proficiency in the use of the English language, and submit documentation of having sufficient funds to cover educational and living expenses for the duration of study. To certify proficiency in the use of English, international applicants whose primary language is not English must submit scores from the Test of English as a Foreign Language (TOEFL) or the IELTS.

Application and Information

Applications for admission are considered on a rolling basis; however, candidates are strongly encouraged to submit applications by March 1. Applications received after March 1 are considered on the basis of available space in particular programs. To be considered for admission, freshman applicants must submit to the Office of University Admissions a completed application, a nonrefundable $35 application fee (waived if applying online), an official high school transcript, an official report of scores from the SAT or ACT, and at least one letter of recommendation. Students can apply online at www.marywood.edu/admissions/applying.

Transfer students must submit a completed application, a nonrefundable $35 application fee (waived if applying online), an official high school transcript, official academic transcript(s) reflecting all college course work for which the candidate has enrolled, and at least one letter of recommendation.

All submitted credentials become the property of Marywood and are not returnable to the applicant. Admission standards and policies are free of discrimination on grounds of race, color, national origin, sex, age, or disability.

For further information, interested students should contact:

Christian DiGregorio, Senior Director
Office of University Admissions
Marywood University
2300 Adams Avenue
Scranton, Pennsylvania 18509
Phone: 866-279-9663
Fax: 570-961-4763
E-mail: yourfuture@marywood.edu
Website: http://www.marywood.edu/admissions
www.facebook.com/marywoodu
www.twitter.com/marywoodu
www.youtube.com/marywoodu

The majestic Rotunda located in the Liberal Arts Center on Marywood's campus.

MILLERSVILLE UNIVERSITY OF PENNSYLVANIA

MILLERSVILLE, PENNSYLVANIA

★ To read more about this school, visit http://petersons.to/millersvilleuniversityofpennsylvania

The University

Millersville University of Pennsylvania, nestled in the hills of Amish country, offers a wide range of programs and a commitment to high-quality undergraduate and graduate instruction. Millersville's student body of approximately 8,100, including 7,200 undergraduates, is large enough for the University to offer over 100 academic programs, plus master's and doctoral degree programs. The University is also small enough to provide friendly service and individual attention. Students report that the relaxed, friendly campus atmosphere is one component of their superior collegiate experience at Millersville. The campus features a beautiful green and flowered landscape, a pond with resident swans, and clean, well-maintained facilities.

Millersville University was established more than 150 years ago, in 1855, as a normal school, the first one in Pennsylvania. It remained a teachers college until 1962 when it was authorized to offer liberal arts degrees. It has been Millersville University of Pennsylvania since 1983.

Students most frequently cite Millersville's excellent academic reputation and affordable tuition as the top two reasons why they chose the University. Education, business administration, psychology, biology, English, speech communications, and sociology are among the most popular majors offered. Millersville's undergraduates are diverse; one in nine students attends part-time, 23 percent are members of a racial/ethnic minority group, and 10 percent are more than 25 years old. Thirty-three percent of Millersville undergraduates are from Lancaster County, 63 percent from elsewhere in Pennsylvania, 5 percent from out of state, and 2 percent from other countries.

The University offers 19 intercollegiate varsity sports in NCAA Division II as well as intramural and club sports. There are a wide range of special interest clubs, fraternities and sororities, musical organizations, publications, and broad cultural programs available.

Thirty-one percent of undergraduates live on campus in residence halls, with the rest commuting from home or living nearby. Coed dormitories and apartments are available for students. Freshmen and sophomores not commuting from home are required to live on campus. The possession, use, or sale of alcoholic beverages and illegal drugs is prohibited on the University campus. Smoking is prohibited in all academic and residential buildings on campus. Freshmen are permitted to have cars on campus.

Special services provided for students include free tutoring, academic advisement, career planning and placement, personal counseling, health services, wellness activities, and special facilities for commuters.

Location

Millersville is three miles from Lancaster City, a growing metropolitan area. Lancaster County is an exceptionally friendly and beautiful area with a large number of art galleries, stores, restaurants, theaters, parks, and tourist attractions. The campus is served by the area bus system, and Lancaster has Amtrak service for easy access to nearby cities like Philadelphia, which is an hour and a half away; Washington, D.C., which is two and a half hours away; and New York City, which is three hours away. Baltimore is also an easy hour and a half drive from campus. There is also air service nearby.

Lancaster County is one of the fastest-growing counties in Pennsylvania and has one of the lowest unemployment rates in the state. The local economy is sound and diverse. Sixty percent of Millersville graduates choose to settle within the county.

Majors and Degrees

Millersville offers the Bachelor of Arts degree in anthropology, art, biology, chemistry, earth sciences, economics, English, environmental geology, French, geography, German, government and political affairs, history, international studies, mathematics, music, philosophy, physics, psychology, social work, sociology, and Spanish.

The Bachelor of Science degree is offered in allied health technology; applied engineering, safety and technology; biology; business administration; chemistry; communications and theatre; computer science; geology; mathematics; meteorology; occupational safety and environmental health; ocean sciences and coastal sciences; and physics.

The Bachelor of Science in Education degree with teaching certification is offered in art education, biology, chemistry, earth sciences, Pre-K–4 education, English, French, German, mathematics, middle level education, music education, physics, social studies, Spanish, special education, and technology education. Millersville now offers degree programs in inclusive education, allowing students to specialize in an age group and subject area while also learning how to teach students with special needs.

The University also offers the Bachelor of Fine Arts degree in art; the Bachelor of Science in nursing degree for RNs only (fully online and on-campus options are available); and the Associate of Technology degree in applied engineering, safety and technology.

Other new academic programs have been added to Millersville's offerings to better serve the student body with specialized degrees. The multidisciplinary studies major allows students to work with a faculty advisor to combine their unique areas of interest and create a custom degree focus. The Paul H. Slaugh Jr. entrepreneurship minor allows students to combine entrepreneurship with a major of their choosing. Millersville now also offers degree programs in entertainment technology, sports journalism, and environmental hazards and emergency management. Students should refer to the website for a complete listing. More than 65 minors are offered along with engineering programs for chemistry majors. Special advisement is available for students interested in pre-medicine and pre-law.

Academic Programs

Millersville University places a strong emphasis on the liberal arts. Nearly half of the courses required for all its under-graduate degrees, including those with technical or professional majors, are in the liberal arts. This prepares students for a lifetime of learning and gives them a background in writing, speaking, analysis, and critical thinking across a broad range of subjects.

Millersville's baccalaureate degree programs have four common curricular elements: proficiency requirements in English composition and speech; the general education program, which constitutes about half the curriculum; the major field of study; and elective courses, if needed, to meet the minimum of 120 credits required for graduation. Within this framework, students have many choices in developing programs of study.

The general education program has requirements in writing, speaking, humanities, natural sciences and mathematics, social sciences, and interdisciplinary and/or multicultural study. There is also a health and physical education requirement.

Millersville offers a University Honors College, departmental honors programs, independent study, a pass/fail option, and a successful Exploratory Program for undeclared students who are deciding about a major.

The University operates on a 4-1-4 academic calendar with summer sessions.

Off-Campus Programs

An exchange agreement with Franklin & Marshall College allows Millersville students to take select Franklin & Marshall courses not offered at Millersville. Cooperative education internships are available to students in most majors, and some majors offer or require specialized internships. Millersville has study-abroad programs in Australia, Chile, China, England, France, Germany, Ireland, Japan, Peru, Scotland, South Africa, Spain, and other countries. Qualified students who wish to study abroad elsewhere may do so through the University's cooperative arrangements with other colleges and universities. Students may also choose to student teach or participate in an internship abroad.

Academic Facilities

With numerous study areas, classrooms, and even a café, the new Dr. Francine G. McNairy Library and Learning Forum is a relaxing and visually pleasing place where students can study and work. Materials from other libraries are available through interlibrary loan.

The University's computing facilities support both PC and Apple platforms. There are more than 400 terminals and computer stations available in multiple computer labs across campus. On-campus access to the Internet is available for all faculty members and students. Wireless access is available in all buildings, residence halls, classrooms, and offices.

Other University facilities include an extensive scientific instrumentation inventory, industry and technology laboratories, a variety of art studios and galleries, two visual and performing arts centers, a state-of-the-art sound studio, three gymnasiums, two swimming pools, radio and television production facilities, soundproof music practice modules, and a language laboratory.

Costs

Annual tuition and fees in 2017–18 were $11,858 (based on 15 credits per semester) for Pennsylvania residents and $21,560 for out-of-state students. Annual room and board charges for 2017–18 were $13,670.

Financial Aid

Approximately 82 percent of Millersville undergraduates receive financial aid through grants, scholarships, employment, and loans. Scholarships are available on the basis of academic performance. Federal Pell, Federal Supplemental Educational Opportunity grants, and Pennsylvania Higher Education Assistance Agency (PHEAA) grants are awarded on the basis of need. Students may also qualify for Federal Perkins Loans and Federal Stafford Student Loans. On-campus and off-campus job opportunities are plentiful, with nearly one-third of students holding an on-campus job.

Students applying for a federal or state grant, Federal Work-Study, or a Federal Perkins Loan must complete the Free Application for Federal Student Aid. The forms are available from high school guidance offices, from the Financial Aid Office, or online at http://www.fafsa.ed.gov. Deadlines are given in the forms' instructions.

Faculty

Millersville University faculty members are dedicated to teaching and to offering individual attention. In 2016–17 the University employed 475 full and part-time faculty. Ninety-eight percent of the full-time faculty members have earned the highest degree in their field. The University keeps a relatively low student-faculty ratio of 22:1 and an average class size of approximately 25. No classes are taught by graduate or teaching assistants.

Student Government

Millersville University students participate in University governance through the Student Senate, faculty-student committees, and representation on the Faculty Senate, the Council of Trustees, and the Millersville Borough Council. The Student Senate works with faculty members and the administration on major University policies.

Admission Requirements

Millersville University admits approximately 60 percent of its applicants. More than 80 percent of its full-time freshmen rank in the top 40 percent of their high school class. Academic records are the most important factor in admission decisions. Applicants must have successfully completed at least 4 years of high school English, 3 years of social studies, 3 years of mathematics, and 3 years of science (1 unit must be a lab). In addition, 2 years of foreign language is strongly recommended.

Since meeting people with different backgrounds and interests is an important part of the college experience, Millersville University is committed to recruiting a diversified student body. SAT or ACT scores are required. Letters of recommendations are encouraged. Out-of-state, international, nontraditional, and transfer applicants are welcome. Exceptional high school students may apply for early admission at the end of their junior year. Admitted applicants may request to defer their admission for up to two semesters. Advanced standing is offered through CLEP and AP examinations.

Application and Information

To apply, students should submit an online application with a $40 processing fee and official copies of the high school record and SAT or ACT scores (freshman applicants only, transfer students must submit official transcripts from all previous institutions). A 3–5 minute video essay can be submitted instead of a written application essay. The paper application fee is $50. The University has a rolling admission policy, and students are encouraged to apply early (by mid-November) in their senior year for fall admission. Applicants are usually notified of a decision within a month after a completed application and required materials are received. Students can apply to Millersville via the Pennsylvania State System of Higher Education App or the Common App.

For application forms and additional information, students should contact:

Office of Admissions
Millersville University of Pennsylvania
P.O. Box 1002
Millersville, Pennsylvania 17551-0302
Phone: 717-871-4625
      800-MU-ADMIT (toll-free)
E-mail: admissions@millersville.edu
Website: www.millersville.edu
YouTube: www.youtube.com/millersvilleu
Facebook: www.facebook.com/villeadmissions
Twitter: https://twitter.com/VilleAdmissions
Virtual tour: www.youvisit.com/millersville

Millersville University has more than 100 undergraduate programs available and state-of-the-art facilities. Students can find their path at a top-ranked public university that is committed to their future.

MILLS COLLEGE

OAKLAND, CALIFORNIA

MILLS

 To read more about this school, visit http://petersons.to/millscollege

The College

Located in the heart of the San Francisco Bay Area, Mills College helps students tap into their boldness and determination, creativity and conviction, with an education that changes lives. In an inclusive community of inspiring women, Mills students gain the skills, the confidence, and the power to make a statement in their careers and in their communities.

The 9:1 student-faculty ratio enables students to work closely with Mills professors, who are fiercely dedicated to teaching and mentoring independent thinkers. Students delve into their studies in interactive classes (17 is the average class size) that spark debate and engaged learning. The College encourages students to cross boundaries and explore how different fields inform and enhance each other, creating eclectic areas of interdisciplinary study such as dance and sociology or math and philosophy.

Outside of the classroom, the 135-acre Mills campus has something for everyone. Students can join a wide range of clubs, write for the student newspaper, attend experimental music concerts, take Zumba or karate classes, and just hang out at the outdoor pool. Many also become teammates as part of the College's six National Collegiate Athletic Association (NCAA) Division III sports teams, competing against other schools in cross-country, rowing, soccer, swimming, tennis, or volleyball. While the students and their interests are diverse in every way, the one constant is a commitment to supporting each other's success and improving the world around them.

Mills has been educating women since 1852, and in 1920, added innovative graduate programs for women and men to its academic offerings. Always a college of firsts, among women's colleges Mills was: the first west of the Rockies, the first to create a computer science major, one of the first to offer a modern dance major, and the first to enact an admission policy for transgender students. *U.S. News & World Report* ranks Mills among the top ten colleges in the West and #2 in Best Value Colleges. Mills is also ranked as one of the best colleges in the nation by The Princeton Review. The College has been home to alumnae who have gone on to excel as authors, composers, lawyers, professors, ambassadors, scientists, news anchors, governors, congresswomen, and activists.

Location

Mills students live and study in Oakland, California, one of the most ethnically diverse cities in the United States. Major media outlets, including the *New York Times* and *Forbes*, have ranked Oakland among the best cities in America. Students take full advantage of the area, enjoying the First Friday gallery crawls, hiking through Redwood Regional Park, and getting involved in the community through internships, volunteering, and service learning.

Beyond Oakland, students explore all the Bay Area has to offer, including Ocean Beach, the Golden Gate Bridge, the San Francisco Museum of Modern Art, and the California Academy of Sciences. Arts organizations, healthcare providers, tech giants, and nonprofits also call the Bay Area home, and the career services office at Mills keeps tabs on internships and job openings as one of the many ways it helps prepare students for future careers. Students have gained hands-on experience at organizations such as the American Civil Liberties Union, Children's Hospital Oakland, Google, and the Office of Congresswoman Barbara Lee, a proud Mills alumna.

Majors and Degrees

Mills offers a Bachelor of Arts or Bachelor of Science degree in a variety of majors that enable students to discover and dive deeply into the academic areas that most inspire them. Beginning in fall 2018, Mills will be offering a new signature academic experience—*M*POWER—that will be shared by students across all majors. *M*POWER unites transformative learning experiences, leadership development, community engagement, and career preparation. Students will work with an academic success team that will guide them in their area of interest and help them work towards realizing their career aspirations. Each student will participate in community-engaged learning opportunities and collaborate with faculty on creative, research, or other special projects. Throughout their academic journey, students will connect with Mills alumnae and our career services team for mentoring, career planning, and internship opportunities so students will be prepared for future success.

Mills offers the Bachelor of Arts (B.A.) degree in art and technology; art (history and studio); biochemistry and molecular biology; biology; biopsychology; business administration; business economics; chemistry; child development; communication; computer science; dance; data science; economics; English; environmental science; environmental studies; ethnic studies; global humanities and critical thought; history; international relations; mathematics; music; political science; politics, economics, policy, and law; psychology; public health and health equity; sociology; theater studies; and women's, gender and sexuality studies. The major in child development meets the requirements for a state child development permit for teaching in preschool and day-care centers and provides a strong basis for graduate school and for many other careers. Special pre-medical and pre-law advising is available.

Mills offers the Bachelor of Science (B.S.) degree in biochemistry and molecular biology, biology, biopsychology, chemistry, environmental science, mathematics, and public health and health equity. Mills has also partnered with Boston's Simmons College to provide the first two years of courses leading to a Bachelor of Science in Nursing (B.S.N.) degree. Upon successful completion of the two-year program at Mills, students are guaranteed admission into Simmon's rigorous B.S.N. program to pursue their professional training.

Students can also choose to create their own major, working with three faculty advisers to plan an individual program that draws together courses from across the curriculum and creates an integrated educational experience.

Mills offers ten unique programs that enable students to earn both a bachelor's and a master's degree in less time—increasing their career options after college. The bachelor's-to-master's accelerated degree programs are: B.A./M.A.E. applied economics, B.A./M.B.A. business administration, B.A./M.A. computer science, B.A./M.A. early childhood education, B.A./M.A. early childhood special education/teaching credential, B.A./M.A. education/teaching credential, B.A./M.A. infant mental health, B.A./M.M management, B.A./M.P.P. public policy, and B.A./Joint M.P.P./M.B.A.

Academic Programs

To earn a Mills bachelor's degree, students complete 120 semester credits (usually 15 credits each semester). Grading is traditional, and a pass-fail option is available outside the major.

The core curriculum at Mills prepares students to successfully pursue any career and educational opportunities that they choose throughout their lives. The principal goal is for students to graduate as fully engaged global citizens who combine confidence, the ability to think independently, and a sense of responsibility for the wider community and world. The core curriculum emphasizes the value of diverse perspectives, critical analysis, and knowledge as being essential to social change. The requirements fall into three outcome categories: foundational skills (critical analysis, information literacy, written and oral communication, and quantitative literacy), modes of inquiry (race, gender, and power; scientific inquiry; language other than English; and international perspectives), and contributions to knowledge and society (community engagement and creativity, innovation, and experimentation).

Faculty

Great professors don't lecture—they inspire. At Mills, students learn through lively discussions and hands-on exploration led by accomplished faculty who are dedicated to teaching and passionately engaged in research and creative endeavors. Nearly 75 percent of Mills faculty hold the highest degrees in their field; approximately 70 percent are women, and over one-third are faculty of color. The excellent student-faculty ratio gives students opportunities to work alongside these diverse, expert scholars to present at conferences, stage performances, contribute to original research, curate exhibitions, and coauthor journal articles. No matter what students are interested in, Mills professors encourage them to pursue their unique paths thoughtfully and enthusiastically.

Off-Campus Programs

Students can expand their learning off campus by signing up for the College's cross-registration program, which enables students to expand their perspective and their learning by taking a course at local schools such as California College of the Arts; California State University, East Bay; Saint Mary's College of California; or UC Berkeley. For an academic adventure within the United States, students can take advantage of the College's domestic study program. They may participate in exchange or visiting programs at schools including Barnard, Manhattanville, Mount Holyoke, Simmons, Spelman, and Wellesley.

The College's international study-abroad opportunities help students discover fresh ways of thinking, learn a new language, or explore a subject in its native land. With access to more than 20 institutions across the globe, recent Mills students have studied abroad in countries including Argentina, France, India, Ireland, New Zealand, and Scotland.

Student Clubs and Organizations

At Mills, students are part of an energetic campus community that strives for inclusion, growth, and cultural diversity through a variety of groups, clubs, and activities to explore throughout the year. The many clubs reflect social or political interests; celebrate shared identities; and explore academic interests, hobbies, or entertainment. The roster of student-led organizations includes the Black Student Collective, Earth CORPS, El Club de Español, Feminist Democrats, Hip Hop Dance Club, and the Mills Computer Club.

Academic Facilities

The facilities at Mills reflect and support the many passions, interests, and academic pursuits of its students. They can view the latest exhibition at the on-campus art museum, create experimental music in Littlefield Concert Hall, build an aquaponics system in the Botanic Garden, or create new forms of dance in Lisser Hall.

Students in STEM fields benefit from the state-of-the-art learning environment in the Betty Irene Moore Natural Sciences Building. In addition to high-tech classrooms, multiple teaching laboratories, and a research lab, the LEED-certified Platinum facility is a model of green construction. Next door, the Botanic Garden provides a living laboratory for ecological restoration and biology research.

The Jeannik Méquet Littlefield Concert Hall hosts a cutting-edge concert series, student-led fine arts performances, College ceremonies, and special community events. It features an expanded stage area and enhanced acoustic features for performances and recording. Newly renovated Lisser Hall contains a fully accessible, open-floor theater with mobile seating for 272; it also is home to the annual "Mills Got Talent" student showcases.

The highly regarded Children's School at Mills College provides an opportunity to engage in hands-on learning for students seeking careers in early childhood education. Students can also conduct research in the Early Childhood and Family Research Lab, Center for Play Research, and Language Development Lab on campus.

The Mills College Art Museum houses the largest permanent collection of any liberal arts college on the West Coast and attracts a wide array of innovative exhibitions, with an emphasis on female artists. Students also have the rare opportunity to work behind the scenes, documenting and digitizing priceless artwork, curating exhibitions, and leading the senior thesis art show.

The Special Collections at the F. W. Olin Library include historical and literary treasures such as a copy of Shakespeare's First Folio, a Mozart manuscript, and a leaf from a Gutenberg Bible. The library is also home to the Center for the Book, a forum for celebrating the powerful cultural impact of the book, in all of its forms.

Costs

Mills has added another first to its list of accomplishments by becoming the first private college in California to substantially reduce the cost of its undergraduate education. To make its top-ranked education more accessible to more students, Mills is reducing undergraduate tuition by 36 percent beginning in fall 2018. Tuition will be $28,765 (reduced from $44,765); room and board costs will be $13,448. Students will still be able to receive merit scholarships and need-based financial aid in addition to the tuition reduction.

Financial Aid

In the 2017–18 academic year, more than 80 percent of incoming Mills students received some form of financial aid. The College offers a variety of merit- and need-based scholarships that can total up to $10,000 for first-year students and transfer students. Additional aid is available through federal and state grants, private scholarships, loans, and work-study opportunities.

To be considered for government aid and need-based Mills scholarships, first-year and transfer students must file the Free Application for Federal Student Aid (FAFSA) by the appropriate deadline. California residents must also file the Cal Grant GPA Verification Form to be considered for a Cal Grant.

Mills recognizes students' academic achievements, demonstrated leadership skills, contributions to the community, and special talents through a wide variety of merit scholarships. All entering fall-term, full-time applicants who meet certain academic or talent eligibility requirements are considered for Mills scholarships, with no additional application form needed.

Admission Requirements

Admission to Mills is selective, yet holistic. The admission process is designed to allow students to share a complete picture of their experiences, passions, activities, and what they hope to achieve, in addition to their academic accomplishments.

Most first-year students admitted to Mills have a B+ average and have followed a full college-preparatory course in their secondary school, including 4 years of English, 3 to 4 years of mathematics, 2 to 4 years of foreign languages, 2 to 4 years of social sciences, and 2 to 4 years of a laboratory science. Additional course work in fine arts is given positive consideration, as are special talents or interests. Submission of SAT or ACT scores is not required. Course credit may be awarded for the College Board Advanced Placement tests and the International Baccalaureate program's higher-level examinations.

Mills welcomes applications from transfer students and women who have delayed their entrance to college or who wish to continue work on their bachelor's degrees. The high school transcript requirement is waived if 24 or more transferable semester units have been completed. For international students, TOEFL, IELTS, or ELS are required to satisfy English language proficiency requirements. Applications should be accompanied by transcripts, a letter of recommendation, and, for international students, language test scores.

An interview, either on campus or online through Skype or FaceTime, is strongly recommended for all applicants.

Application and Contact Information

First-year students: Fall admission application deadlines are November 15 for early action and January 15 for regular decision. All required materials are due by January 15.

Transfer students: Fall admission application deadlines are March 1 for priority scholarship consideration and April 1 for regular decision.

Spring admission application deadline: November 1 for both first-year and transfer students. Admission decisions are sent via e-mail and regular mail on a rolling basis.

For more information, students are invited to contact:

Office of Undergraduate Admissions
Mills College
5000 MacArthur Boulevard
Oakland, California 94613
Phone: 510-430-2135
    800-87-MILLS (toll-free)
Fax: 510-430-3298
E-mail: admission@mills.edu
Website: https://www.mills.edu
        https://www.facebook.com/millscollege (Facebook)
        https://twitter.com/millscollege (Twitter)
        https://youtube.com/millscollege (YouTube)

At Mills, students are encouraged to stand out, emboldened to think big, and empowered to make a statement.

MISERICORDIA UNIVERSITY
DALLAS, PENNSYLVANIA

 To read more about this school, visit http://petersons.to/misericordiauniversity

The University

Misericordia University is a high-quality liberal arts and professional studies institution rooted in service to others and committed to challenging academics and the personal attention students deserve. Founded by the Religious Sisters of Mercy in 1924, Misericordia offers undergraduate and graduate programs to resident and commuter students, as well as adult students. Current enrollment is more than 2,800 men and women.

The University cultivates a spirit of community service and a lifelong love of learning in its students through extracurricular activities, experiential learning, and challenging academic programs. In the National Survey of Student Engagement, Misericordia students say they are more involved in learning and have better relationships with faculty members and peers than students at other similar institutions. Misericordia is also ranked in the top tier of *U.S. News & World Report's* America's Best Regional Universities–North Category 2018.

Misericordia operates twelve residential facilities, including five residence halls, a town house complex, and off-campus housing, with a total capacity of more than 1,100 students. This includes three nearby homes are reserved for upper-level students. Residents have a number of options, including single rooms and wellness housing. Each residence hall offers study rooms, laundry facilities, and recreational lounges. The Metz Dining Hall is located in the Banks Student Life Center, which also houses a "We Proudly Brew Starbucks" coffee shop, a Chick-fil-A Express, and the Chopping Block restaurant, and the renovated Student Union that features flat-screen televisions as well as pool and foosball tables.

There are numerous campus activities. Besides Student Government, there are over 40 chartered student clubs and organizations. Cultural events, Campus Ministry, intramural and intercollegiate athletic programs, performing arts shows, art exhibits, and many other social activities complement the academic experience. The Metz Field House provides enhanced facilities for student athletes. In keeping with the University's tradition of Mercy, Service, Justice, and Hospitality, students have opportunities to develop leadership potential through service projects. Misericordia earned a spot on the President's National Community Service Honor Roll for the past several years.

On spring break, students have served the needy in rural Appalachia, the Gulf Coast, Texas, California, Philadelphia, and the South Bronx. Students have volunteered abroad in Jamaica, Guyana, and Romania.

Personalized attention is the key to the support available in the Student Success Center. A psychologist, counselors, therapists, and peer counselors conduct workshops each semester on a variety of topics, including test anxiety, stress management, time management, and goal setting. Many services are free of charge to students and contacts are confidential.

First-year students may join the Guaranteed Placement Program (GPP) through the Insalaco Center for Career Development. The GPP program includes academic standards, cocurricular activities (such as leadership and service projects), internships, resume development, etiquette development, and interviewing skills. If a student fulfills the program's requirements and is not employed in his or her field or enrolled in graduate or professional school within six months of graduation, a paid internship is assured. The center also co-presents the Choice Program, which offers special guidance for students who have not declared a major. Opportunities for career exploration, cooperative education, and internships help students develop the skills they need to be successful when they enter the working world.

Student Health Services staff members provide first aid, assessment and treatment of common illnesses, and referrals for more serious health conditions. Health center activities are directed by a nurse practitioner. A self-care room offers reference materials and up-to-date information on personal health concerns. All services are confidential.

A rapidly evolving world has increased the number of adults who seek higher education. Misericordia offers bachelor's, master's, and doctoral programs for adult learners in several formats. The Ruth Matthews Bourger Women with Children program provides housing and support services for single women with children who are working toward their undergraduate degree. Convenient evening, online, and weekend formats also are available for people with families and full-time jobs.

Master's degrees are available in education, nurse practitioner studies, occupational therapy, speech/language pathology, business administration, and organizational management. A doctoral program in physical therapy is available to students entering in a full-time format, and doctoral programs in occupational therapy and nursing practice are available for graduate students via part-time study, including online and in-class components.

The University is fully accredited by the Middle States Association of Colleges and Schools. The medical imaging, nursing, occupational therapy, physical therapy, social work, and speech-language pathology programs are accredited by the National League for Nursing Accrediting Commission, the Council on Social Work Education, the Joint Review Committee on Education in Radiologic Technology, the American Occupational Therapy Association, the American Physical Therapy Association, and the American Speech-Language and Hearing Association.

Location

Located in northeastern Pennsylvania, Misericordia University is the oldest four-year institution of higher education in Luzerne County. Expansive lawns and thick stands of trees dominate the 115-acre upper and expanding lower campuses. It is 9 miles from the city of Wilkes-Barre. The area offers shopping centers, malls, cinemas, skiing, professional sporting events, and a variety of cultural activities. Pennsylvania's largest natural lake and two state parks are nearby, as are Pocono ski resorts. Metropolitan New York and Philadelphia are each within a 3-hour drive. Public and university-sponsored transportation serves the campus.

Majors and Degrees

Misericordia University awards the Bachelor of Arts (B.A.) degree in English, history, government, law and national security, medical and health humanities, and philosophy. The Bachelor of Science (B.S.) degree is awarded in accounting, biochemistry, biology, business administration, chemistry, clinical laboratory science, computer science, diagnostic medical sonography, early childhood and special education, health care management, health science, information technology, mass communications and design, mathematics, medical imaging, middle level education, professional studies, psychology, secondary education, sport management, and statistics. The Bachelor of Science in Nursing (B.S.N.) is awarded to nursing majors, and a Bachelor of Social Work (B.S.W.) is awarded to social work majors. Specializations in exercise science, IT security, marketing, medical science, patient navigation, pre-law, respiratory therapy, sport communications, surgical technology, and preprofessional occupations are also available. Certification programs include addictions counseling, diagnostic medical sonography, post-professional pediatrics certificate for occupational therapists and physical therapists, and secondary education. These may be taken in support of several degrees offered by Misericordia or as stand-alone programs.

The University also offers five-year entry-level graduate majors in occupational therapy and speech-language pathology. Students graduate with a master's degree in speech-language pathology or occupational therapy and a bachelor's degree in health sciences. The physical therapy program is a 6½-year doctoral program. Students graduate with a bachelor's degree in one of several areas and a Doctor of Physical Therapy (D.P.T.) degree.

Academic Programs

Candidates for the B.A., B.S., B.S.N., or B.S.W. must fulfill a 49-credit liberal arts core curriculum in addition to the requirements of their chosen major to graduate. They must earn at least 36 credit hours in a chosen field. For regularly enrolled students, the average requirement for a baccalaureate degree is a total of 121 credits. Other options include minors, specializations, certifications, and electives. Other degrees have specialized requirements. Interested students should consult the academic catalog for the most current information.

Courses are offered on a semester basis, beginning in August and January and ending in December and May. Summer, weekend, online, and accelerated courses are also available.

Academic Facilities

The chemistry, physics, and biology departments all have fully equipped research laboratories available to students in these fields. State-of-the-art equipment includes high-performance liquid chromatography (HPLC), a rotary evaporator, and a new gas chromatograph mass spectrometer. The science building contains a gross anatomy laboratory, a rare asset for a university of this size. The University also houses an energized radiation laboratory for the medical imaging program. The Passan Hall–College of Health Sciences provides classrooms and high-tech laboratories for the occupational therapy, physical therapy, speech-language pathology, and nursing programs in a facility devoted to these majors.

In addition to the four main computer labs, most other campus buildings and common areas offer wireless Internet access. The University operates MyMU, a secure online portal where students can access e-mail, course schedules, class registration tools, and student account and registration information from a single sign-on.

Mercy Hall, the original administrative building, offers multi-purpose academic classrooms and facilities. Many key student service departments, including the registrar, student accounts, and financial aid are centralized in one area in Mercy Hall. Sandy and Marlene Insalaco Hall houses the Pauly Friedman Art Gallery, café, computer labs, an ensemble room, fine arts classroom, music teaching and practice areas, and the Assistive Technology Research Institute.

The new Michael and Tina MacDowell Residence Hall hosts three ultramodern classrooms on the first floor.

The three-story Mark Kintz Bevevino Library covers 37,500 square feet and houses stacks for 90,000 volumes. Materials include information and communication technology and a reference section that offers books, serials, and a variety of periodicals as well as reference search tools.

Costs

Full-time undergraduate tuition for 2017–18 was $30,030 per year. The general fee was $1,630. Housing options include traditional rooms, suites, town houses, and lower-campus housing. The median room cost was $8,082. The median board cost is $4,492.

Financial Aid

All students applying for financial aid must complete the Free Application for Federal Student Aid (FAFSA) by May 1, but it can be completed as early as October 1 of senior year. This is used for Federal Pell Grants, Federal Supplemental Educational Opportunity Grants (FSEOG), subsidized and unsubsidized Federal Direct Student Loans, Federal Perkins Loans, nursing loans, and the Federal Work-Study Program. This application is also the basis upon which state and institutional aid is awarded. The University also offers a no-interest monthly payment plan. Many scholarships are available including $20 million in presidential scholarships based on academic ability and $4.6 million in McAuley Awards for students who have experience in leadership roles and volunteer service.

Faculty

There are 137 full-time faculty members. A student-faculty ratio of 11.3:1 results in students receiving a great deal of individual attention from a highly qualified faculty; 78 percent of the faculty members hold doctorates. Besides student academic advising, the faculty members also serve as advisers to clubs.

Student Government

An active student government organization serves as a liaison between the students and the faculty and staff members. The administration enables students to become involved by serving as student representatives on various University committees.

Admission Requirements

Misericordia University admits applicants based on their secondary school record, high school recommendation, extracurricular activities, and personal promise. The University requires SAT or ACT scores.

Transfer students with a cumulative average of at least 2.0 (4.0 scale) may be considered for admission and may receive advanced standing. Some majors require a 2.5 or higher cumulative average. Transfer students must submit official high school transcripts and transcripts of work completed at other colleges and universities.

Application and Information

Applicants must submit the free online application, available at misericordia.edu/apply, transcripts, and SAT or ACT scores.

The University considers applications on a rolling basis. Usually, candidates are notified of the admission decision within three weeks of receipt of all required materials.

For more information, students should contact:

Office of Admissions
Misericordia University
301 Lake Street
Dallas, Pennsylvania 18612-1090
Phone: 570-674-6461
      866-262-6363 (toll free)
Fax: 570-675-2441
E-mail: admiss@misericordia.edu
Website: http://admissions.misericordia.edu
      www.twitter.com/misericordiaUAD
      www.facebook.com/misericordiauniversity
      www.facebook.com/misericoridau

Misericordia University offers multiple medical and health science degree options on the undergraduate and graduate levels.

MOLLOY COLLEGE
ROCKVILLE CENTRE, NEW YORK

 To read more about this school, visit http://petersons.to/molloycollege

The College

What college offers a great education with small classes, wonderful internships, community service projects, and international trips, plus an amazing campus life program to round out the college experience? Welcome to Molloy College.

Molloy, an independent, private Catholic college based in Rockville Centre, was founded in 1955 by the Sisters of Saint Dominic in Amityville, New York. The College serves a student population of more than 4,900 undergraduate and graduate students. Molloy students can earn degrees in a variety of outstanding academic programs, including nursing, business, education, social work, music therapy, and many more.

Prospective students are always looking for an academic environment that offers the best fit for the student and the best value for their tuition dollar. Molloy was ranked a Top 3 Value institution the last two years by *Money* magazine, the only college in the nation to claim that distinction. Molloy's top ranking was based on a variety of factors, including graduation rates and earnings of graduates.

Molloy continues to earn recognition in many areas. College Factual recently named Molloy the #1 college for health professions, as well as naming Molloy's undergraduate nursing program the best in the nation. Molloy's business students have the highest pass rate on Long Island for the CPA exam, and the College's music therapy program is ranked 16th in the nation by TheBestSchools.org. In addition, the College's residence halls were voted Best in New York by Niche.com, and these rankings also referenced Molloy's freshmen retention rate, which is among the highest in the country (85 percent). Also of note, Molloy graduates' starting salaries have ranked among the highest in the U.S. in surveys conducted by Georgetown University and PayScale.com.

Location and Environment

Molloy is located on the South Shore of Long Island in Rockville Centre. Its proximity to New York City—just a short train ride away from the 30-acre campus—allows students to benefit from the cultural and social opportunities that Manhattan has to offer. Molloy's location in the New York metro region provides its students with numerous opportunities for internships and clinical placements, critical for helping students land their first job upon graduation.

Molloy College also offers off-campus locations for study at the Suffolk Center in East Farmingdale and at area hospitals and schools, all designed to provide convenience for graduate and continuing education students. Most recently, Molloy opened a new facility at 50 Broadway in Manhattan's downtown Oculus District. The new building houses the Molloy/CAP21 B.F.A. musical conservatory program, in addition to hosting a variety of lectures and other academic programs.

Majors and Degrees

Molloy offers the A.A. degree in liberal arts; the A.A.S. degree in cardiovascular technology and respiratory care; and the B.A. or B.S. degree in accounting, art, biology, business management, communications, computer science, computer information systems, criminal justice, education, English, earth and environmental studies, finance, history, interdisciplinary studies, marketing, mathematics, modern languages, music, music therapy, new media, nuclear medicine technology, nursing, philosophy, political science, psychology, respiratory care, sociology, speech language pathology/audiology, and theology;

the B.S.W. degree in Social Work; and the B.F.A. in art, music, and theatre arts. Teacher certification programs are available in childhood (1–6), adolescence (7–12), special education, and birth–grade 2 childhood special education.

On the graduate level, Molloy offers a Master of Science degree as well as post-master's certification in nursing and education. M.B.A. programs are available in business, accounting, healthcare, marketing, and personal financial planning; a master's program in clinical mental health counseling was recently launched as well. A master's in social work is offered through Molloy's partnership with Fordham University. Molloy also offers graduate degrees in criminal justice, music therapy, and speech-language pathology. The College offers three doctoral programs: a Ph.D. in nursing and a Doctor of Nursing Practice (D.N.P.), as well as an Ed.D. in Education.

Students interested in pre-dental, pre-law, pre-medical, or pre-veterinary programs are offered special advisement.

Articulation agreements with community colleges and established transfer credit policies ensure ease of transferability. Experienced admissions counselors will evaluate transfer applicants' credits and help plan toward a path toward degree completion.

Academic Programs

At Molloy, small class size, engaging and experienced faculty, and renowned academic programs help ensure student success, both in the classroom and beyond.

Molloy strives to make the college experience convenient for all students. The College offers evening and weekend classes, many in online and hybrid formats, with accelerated schedules designed to accommodate students' busy schedules.

A minimum of 128 credit hours is required for a baccalaureate degree; these courses include a strong liberal arts general education curriculum for every major field of study. Students may choose a double major, and many minors are available. Molloy has a 4-1-4 academic calendar.

Students may earn CLEP and CPE credit, and advanced placement credit is granted for a score of 3 or better on the AP exam. Qualified full-time students may participate in the Army ROTC program at Hofstra University or St. John's University on a cross-enrolled basis. Molloy students may also elect Air Force ROTC on a cross-enrolled basis with New York Institute of Technology.

Off-Campus Programs

The vast majority of students at Molloy enjoy an internship at some point in their academic careers. These real-world experiences are a crucial part of the learning process and ensure that students enter their chosen field ready to make strong contributions. Molloy's location in the New York metro region provides its students with numerous opportunities for all-important internships and clinical placements that can lead to a full-time job.

Molloy students are also instilled with the belief that they can make a difference beyond the classroom. As part of Molloy's tradition of service, students become involved in projects that help underserved populations in New York City, New Orleans, Puerto Rico and Haiti, to name but a few locations. Through the College's international education program, students seek enrichment and greater understanding of the world by participating in trips to Europe, Japan, South America, and other locales around the globe.

Facilities

In recent years Molloy has added a number of new facilities, including two residence halls, a student center, and a performing arts theatre, all of which enhance the student experience. Additionally, Molloy recently opened the Barbara H. Hagan School of Nursing to support its nationally ranked nursing programs. The College is slated to open its newest residence hall in fall 2019.

Molloy is a wireless campus and its computer labs house more than 325 PCs. Many departments have their own computer labs with state-of-the-art equipment.

The James E. Tobin (JET) Library is the center of academic research on the Molloy College campus. Beyond the library's physical collection of books, media, and periodicals, it also provides 24/7 access to over 250,000 ebooks as well as full text to over 170 million articles contained within its 80+ subscription databases. The facility itself contains reference computers, three classrooms, a media center, and designated areas for both group and private study. The Information Commons, located in the Public Square, offers an additional 40 computers as well as four study rooms that can be reserved in advance. Reference services are available to both on-campus and remote researchers in a variety of ways, including a chat service that is available all of the hours the library is open. Additionally, the Public Square provides numerous music studios, for both individual and group study.

The Wilbur Arts Center features art studios, a cable television studio, and the Lucille B. Hays Theatre. The school also has six science labs, a language lab, the education resource center, new state-of-the-art nursing labs, and a behavioral sciences research facility.

Costs

For 2017–18, tuition was $29,110 and required fees were $1,190. Students can expect to spend about $1,400 on books.

Financial Aid

Financial aid, which is based on academic achievement and financial need, is awarded to more than 85 percent of the student body. Aid is awarded in the form of scholarships, grants, loans, and Federal Work-Study Program employment. Merit-based scholarships and grants are also available.

Students are required to complete the FAFSA application every year. Full- and partial-tuition scholarships are available through the following: Molloy Scholars, Presidential Dominican Scholarships, Presidential Business Scholarships, Dean Scholarships, Academic Achievement, Fine Arts Scholarships, Community Service Awards, and other funded scholarships. The Transfer Scholarship Program awards partial-tuition scholarships to students transferring into Molloy College with at least a 3.0 cumulative GPA. Nursing transfers are required to have a 3.3 GPA to be eligible for a transfer scholarship. Athletic grants (Division II only) are awarded to full-time students who show superior athletic ability in baseball, basketball, bowling, cross-country, equestrian, field hockey, indoor and outdoor track, lacrosse, soccer, softball, tennis, or volleyball.

Faculty

Molloy's 10:1 undergraduate student-faculty ratio reflects the College's commitment to its students. In addition, the College has increased the number of faculty members by more than 10 percent in recent years. Of those faculty members, more than 77 percent have doctoral degrees.

Student Organizations and Activities

Molloy offers plenty of opportunities for its 4,900+ undergraduate and graduate students.

There are more than 50 academic programs, approximately 60 clubs and honor societies, various service opportunities, and NCAA Division II athletics, providing abundant opportunities for each student to not only strive for academic excellence, but also explore new interests, pursue athletics, and enrich the community.

Admission Requirements

While Molloy is a selective college, admissions counselors respect each individual applicant and consider the whole student—not just test scores—when making admissions decision. Prospective freshmen must submit their high school credentials, SAT or ACT scores, the Molloy application, and a $40 nonrefundable application fee. While not required, a personal interview is strongly suggested.

Entrance requirements include graduation from high school or equivalent with 20.5 units, including the following: 4 units of English, 3 units of a foreign language, 3 units of mathematics, 4 units of social studies, and 3 units of science. Those who plan to major in mathematics must have 4 units of high school mathematics and 2 units of science, including either chemistry or physics. Biology majors must have biology, chemistry, physics, and 4 units of mathematics. Nursing majors must have biology and chemistry. Cardio-respiratory science majors must have biology, chemistry, and mathematics. Nuclear medicine majors must have high school algebra and biology. Applicants lacking above requirements are reviewed on an individual basis.

Application Information

Molloy College offers rolling admissions at the undergraduate level. Early action on admission will be made promptly on applications received by December 1 of the senior year from well-qualified students who have filed all their credentials with the admissions office.

Prospective students are invited to visit the campus. Questions or requests for more information can be directed to:

Undergraduate Admissions
Molloy College
1000 Hempstead Avenue
Rockville Centre, New York 11571
Phone: 516-323-4000
888-4-MOLLOY (toll-free)
E-mail: admissions@molloy.edu
Website: http://www.molloy.edu
        http://www.facebook.com/GoMolloy
        http://www.twitter.com/MolloyCollege

MONMOUTH UNIVERSITY
WEST LONG BRANCH, NEW JERSEY

 To read more about this school, visit http://petersons.to/monmouth

The College

Monmouth University is a first-tier, private university located along New Jersey's northern coastline that offers a welcoming and dynamic setting for student development. Innovative academic programs, individual faculty attention, and nationally ranked Division I athletics make this private university a great place for students to prepare for their futures.

Monmouth's beautiful coastal campus sits at the heart of a vibrant culture rich in history, the arts, technology, and entrepreneurship. Just an hour from New York and Philadelphia, the University provides a welcoming and dynamic setting that prepares students to succeed in life after graduation. Renowned faculty are actively involved in advancing academic research nationwide while encouraging meaningful community involvement and critical thinking for self-fulfillment.

A comprehensive selection of in-demand degree programs are led by innovative faculty in a small class setting, where students are active participants in their education.

Monmouth has a diverse student body comprising approximately 6,400 undergraduate and graduate students. While many are from the Northeast, students come from all across the United States, as well as nations around the world. Monmouth offers traditional residence halls and garden-style apartments. Some University-sponsored beachfront campus housing is also offered to students who meet certain requirements.

Students at Monmouth have an assortment of extracurricular activities to choose from, including more than 120 student-run clubs and organizations, such as the Student Government Association, the campus newspaper (The Outlook), the FM radio station (WMCX), the television station (Hawk TV), the online news portal (The Verge), the yearbook (Shadows), the literary magazine (Monmouth Review), and various sororities and fraternities. Special events are held throughout the year, including art exhibits, concerts, lectures, and sightseeing trips. Monmouth's Alternative Spring Break provides students with the opportunity to travel globally to take part in service projects and community building.

Students can also cheer on Monmouth's 23 NCAA Division I men's and women's athletic programs. The teams compete primarily in the Metro Atlantic Athletic Conference (MAAC), with the exception of football, which competes in the full-scholarship Big South Conference, and bowling, a member of the Southland Bowling League. The University's basketball and track and field teams compete in the 153,200-square-foot OceanFirst Bank Center, a 4,200-seat venue that opened in 2009. All Monmouth students have access to the arena, which also houses a 200-meter, six-lane indoor track; fitness center; conference space; the University Store; and luxury suites. The University's football, lacrosse, and outdoor track and field programs open their new home in fall 2017, with the debut of Monmouth Stadium. The new stadium will accommodate 4,200 fans and feature state-of-the-art media facilities and end zone to end zone seating.

Monmouth offers something for everyone, and it strives to ensure that students have the resources and support to pursue their goals. The Center for Student Success (CSS) assists students through a variety of academic and career counseling services and programs. Graduates benefit from continued relationships with the Monmouth family. Many return to campus to visit friends, discuss projects with faculty members, and even recruit the next generation of alumni.

Location

Monmouth's coastal campus provides a safe, suburban setting in one of the world's largest metropolitan regions, ideally positioned to help students develop and pursue their career interests while enjoying rich cultural opportunities. Approximately one hour from both New York City and Philadelphia, and one mile from the coastal beaches of the Atlantic Ocean, the University is also at the heart of the coast's vibrant tri-city region.

Economic and political centers of the country and the world are made real and accessible through fascinating internships, a robust study-abroad program, and multiple field experience opportunities. Corporate global headquarters, world-class museums, Madison Square Garden, the Barclays Center, and other sports hubs, shops, restaurants, and theaters are all within reach of the campus.

Majors and Degrees

Monmouth University offers 32 baccalaureate degree programs in six academic schools that share the University's commitment to providing a rigorous academic experience grounded in the liberal arts. The Leon Hess Business School awards bachelor's degrees in business administration with concentrations in accounting; economics; finance; economics and finance; international business; management and decision sciences; marketing; marketing, management, and decision sciences; and real estate. The School of Education awards bachelor's degrees that allow students to earn certification as elementary and secondary school teachers; the school also offers various endorsements, such as English as a second language and teacher of students with disabilities. The Wayne D. McMurray School of Humanities and Social Sciences awards bachelor's degrees in anthropology, art, communication, criminal justice, English, fine arts, foreign language, history, homeland security, music, political science, psychology, and sociology. A Spanish and international business B.A. degree is awarded jointly through the Leon Hess Business School and the School of Humanities and Social Sciences. The School of Science awards bachelor's degrees in biology, chemistry, clinical laboratory sciences, computer science, marine and environmental biology and policy, mathematics, medical laboratory science, and software engineering. The School of Social Work awards the Bachelor of Social Work degree. The Marjorie K. Unterberg School of Nursing and Health Studies awards bachelor's degrees in health studies and health and physical education, as well as the Bachelor of Science in Nursing. A pre-professional advising program is available for students who intend to pursue careers in medicine, dentistry, or other healthcare fields. Monmouth also offers a number of Five-Year Baccalaureate/Master's programs, which enable qualified students to earn a bachelor's and a master's degree in five years in business, computer science, criminal justice, education (select programs), English, history, social work, or software engineering.

Academic Programs

The curriculum at Monmouth University is focused on learning experiences that are both high impact and immersive, extending beyond the classroom, and designed to prepare students for life after college.

Monmouth challenges students in a demanding college environment built on a regimen of reading, deliberating, writing, experimenting, and discussion that ignites curiosity, helps uncover latent passions, and discover a greater sense of purpose.

Transformative learning extends beyond the lecture hall, through a campus-wide culture of teaching excellence that includes linked-learning communities, first-year and senior seminars, study abroad, common readings, experiential education opportunities, community-based participatory research and service-learning courses. Students study abroad in Australia, England, Italy, Spain, and more. Additionally, Monmouth's alternative break allows students to take part in service projects and community building activities in locales around the globe including Guatemala, Haiti, and Nicaragua.

Monmouth students have access to internships, practicums, and even employment opportunities during their course of study. Many students have internships in New York City and Philadelphia, with industry leaders including JPMorgan Chase, NBCUniversal, L'Oreal, and others. The University also partners with the Washington Center, allowing students to earn credit for experiential learning gained through internships and symposia in the nation's capital.

Monmouth's location and network provide tremendous academic opportunities to students. For example, students in Monmouth's music industry program interface with industry professionals in and beyond the classroom, managing their own record label, Blue Hawk Records. There is a real spirit of entrepreneurship on campus that comes to life through student activities like the student-managed investment fund Hawk Capital. Marine and environmental biology and policy students benefit from the University's proximity to coastal waterways.

Qualified students accepted to the University's Honors School participate in an educational environment that encourages and supports intellectual and personal excellence. First-year courses are clustered to enhance interactive learning, with professors who develop common themes and assignments. Honors classes are distinguished by in-depth coverage of material through discussion and writing, smaller class sizes, and a heightened student-faculty rapport. In their final year, each Honors School student researches, writes, and publicly presents an honors thesis, guided by a faculty member who serves as their academic mentor.

Academic Facilities

Monmouth's 55 buildings provide a synthesis of historical architecture and modern aesthetics. The campus' signature building is Woodrow Wilson Hall, a National Historic Landmark, which served as Daddy Warbucks' mansion in the 1982 film *Annie*. The library, the former mansion of Murry and Leonie Guggenheim, is listed on the National Register of History Places and holds 290,000 print and online monographs, 180 databases (abstracts and full-text, e-books, motion picture, image, tools), over 74,000 electronic and print journal subscriptions, and over 1,200 media items. The Lauren K. Woods Theatre, once the Guggenheim carriage house, is a showcase for professional and student performances and that offer students direct experience with all phases of the theater arts.

The Jules L. Plangere Jr. Center for Communication, which is home to the Department of Communication, provides state-of-the-art studios and editing facilities. Joan and Robert Rechnitz Hall houses the Department of Art and Design and features an art gallery, Mac labs, a reception area, and an animation and editing studio. The newest facility is Pozycki Hall, a two-story addition to the Samuel E. and Mollie Bey Hall and home to the Kislak Real Estate Institute. It includes a 150-seat lecture hall, student lounge, general and computer classrooms, and spacious meeting rooms.

Costs

For 2017–18, tuition and fees were approximately $36,733 per year. Annual room and board costs were approximately $13,451; actual costs are determined by the room and meal plan selected.

Financial Aid

At Monmouth, 99 percent of first-year students receive some form of financial aid; about 96 percent receive a scholarship or grant (federal, state, or University); the average scholarship/grant package is $22,521; and the average financial aid package, including student loans and work study, is approximately $26,944. All this, combined with the fact that Monmouth awards more than $59 million in institutional aid to students each year, makes Monmouth an affordable option for many families.

A wide range of University scholarships and grants are offered to all prospective full-time, first-year, and transfer students on the basis of academic performance.

The University participates in all federal and state grant and loan programs. To establish eligibility and to capitalize on available assistance, students should complete the Free Application for Federal Student Aid (FAFSA), which is available after October 1. Students and their families may call 732-571-3463, e-mail finaid@monmouth.edu, or visit the Financial Aid Office for assistance.

Students interested in attending Monmouth can get an estimate of their eligibility for federal, state, and institutional aid, even before submitting their application. To complete the University's Scholarship Inquiry Form and Net Price Calculator, visit www.monmouth.edu/scholarship and www.monmouth.edu/netpricecalculator

Faculty

The University's professors are leaders in their fields and contribute through research, publishing, and consulting services to their respective academic areas. There are 302 full-time and 385 part-time faculty members. Approximately 75 percent of full-time faculty members have doctorates or terminal degrees in their fields. The average class size is 21, and the student-faculty ratio is 13:1.

Student Government

The Student Government Association (SGA) is an important and necessary voice in the University community; its views are recognized and respected. Monmouth students who wish to get involved with SGA can also do so as general members. This flexible form of involvement does not require a student to run for a position or participate in any one of the elections that are sponsored by SGA. More information is available at www.monmouth.edu/sga.

Admission Requirements

Many factors are considered in an admission application. For first-year applicants, a committee evaluates the high school transcripts and SAT or ACT scores, one letter of recommendation, and a personal essay. A resume of activities including leadership positions held and other information supporting the application are also welcome. Campus tours and information sessions with admission counselors are available. Transfer students must submit official transcripts from all colleges attended. If transfer students have earned fewer than 24 transferable credits, they must fulfill first-year admission requirements as well. Nursing applicants must apply by December 1 and submit a nursing-specific essay.

Application and Information

Early action is a nonbinding option for students who wish to receive an early response from Monmouth. December 1 is the deadline for early action and nursing applicants, and admission decisions are mailed by January 15. The application deadline for regular decision is March 1, with an admission decision notification date prior to April 1. Applications received after March 1 are considered on a space-available basis. First-year housing is guaranteed for students who submit the required enrollment deposit, housing deposit, and housing contract by May 1. Students who submit their deposits and housing contract after May 1 may be placed on a wait list for admission and/or housing.

For further information, students should contact:

Office of Undergraduate Admissions
Monmouth University
400 Cedar Avenue
West Long Branch, New Jersey 0774-1898
Phone: 732-571-3456
        800-543-9671 (toll-free)
Fax: 732-263-5166
E-mail: admission@monmouth.edu
Website: http://www.monmouth.edu
        http://www.facebook.com/monmouthuniversity
        http://www.twitter.com/monmouthu
        http://www.youtube.com/monmouthuniversity

Monmouth University's Woodrow Wilson Hall is designated as a National Historic Landmark.

MOUNT ALOYSIUS COLLEGE

CRESSON, PENNSYLVANIA

 To read more about this school, visit http://petersons.to/mountaloysiuscollege

The College

Mount Aloysius College is a private, comprehensive, Catholic liberal arts college sponsored by the Sisters of Mercy. The College welcomes people of all faith traditions. Established in 1853, Mount Aloysius College offers both undergraduate and graduate education. Since the founding of the College, nearly 17,000 students have become proud Mount Aloysius alumni. The College is committed to providing small class sizes, and students benefit from accessible faculty and staff. Mount Aloysius students come mostly from throughout Pennsylvania and the mid-Atlantic Region. There are approximately 2,500 students enrolled (unduplicated headcount).

Mount Aloysius College is one of 17 Mercy Colleges nationwide. Students are encouraged to synthesize faith with learning, to develop competence with compassion, to apply their talents and gifts to the service of others, and to assume leadership in their community.

Student activities play a distinctive role in personal growth. At Mount Aloysius College, there are approximately 100 organized clubs, groups, honor societies, and an intramural sports program. Activities include a student newspaper, residence hall associations, student government, cheerleading, dance team, scholarship-funded theater and choir programs, and a student activities planning board. Mount Aloysius fun includes social events, intramural sports, athletic events, comedians, live music, theater, educational events, campus forums, and awesome guest lectures.

Mount Aloysius College is a member of NCAA Division III. Athletic programs involve both women and men and include basketball, cross-country, golf, soccer, and tennis. Men's baseball and women's bowling, softball, and volleyball are offered. Athletes benefit from the Ray S. and Louise S. Walker Athletic Field Complex, which includes a softball field and soccer field. The Calandra-Smith baseball complex houses the Mountie Stables which offer players and fans lockers, showers, a press box, and concession facilities.

Opened in autumn 2013, the Athletic Convocation and Wellness Center is a spectacular 87,400 square-foot multipurpose facility on the western edge of the beautiful 193-acre campus. This facility takes Mount Aloysius athletics to a new level and adds a welcomed special events venue to the southern Allegheny Mountains. This Center houses a main gymnasium and events venue with seating for over 2,500, home and visitor locker rooms, training facilities, high-tech classrooms, a conference center, and office space. On the ground floor, a new state-of-the-art wellness center offers both cardio and resistance training in a spacious, modern environment.

In spring 2014, an anonymous donor memorialized the late Sr. Virginia Bertschi, RSM by repurposing the former Health and Fitness Center. The new Bertschi Center and Technology Commons—with open architecture, vivid colors, and glass walls offering great views of the campus and surrounding mountains—is an additional social, technology, and special events venue that serves both commuter and resident students.

The main campus building is a picturesque structure dating to 1897. It houses the admissions, financial aid, security, health, and academic offices, along with the Office of the President, classrooms, the region's premiere nursing simulation center, and the Wolf-Kuhn Art Gallery. Cosgrave Center is the hub of campus life. The building contains the Dining Hall, Snack Bar, Bookstore, Childcare Center (part of the elementary education/early childhood program at the College), lounges, recreational rooms, student affairs offices, and meeting rooms. Residence halls include Ihmsen Hall; the Misciagna Residence—a state-of-the-art residence hall, providing 25 suites and private bathrooms; McAuley Hall featuring double and single rooms, a large multipurpose room, and study lounge; and Saint Gert's and Saint Joseph's residence halls. Alumni Hall is a historic, multipurpose facility used for College drama, musicals, lectures, and performing arts events. The College operates 12 months per year and opens its facilities to the Southern Allegheny community.

The College is 100 percent wireless, and smart classrooms are located throughout the campus.

Mount Aloysius is fully accredited by the Middle States Association of Colleges and Schools and approved by the Pennsylvania Department of Education. All nursing and health studies programs are fully accredited by their professional accrediting bodies, including the National League for Nursing Accrediting Commission, the Commission on Accreditation for Programs of Diagnostic Medical Sonography, the Commission on Accreditation in Physical Therapy Education, the American Association of Medical Assistants, and the Joint Commission on Accreditation for Programs of Surgical Technology.

In addition to its undergraduate programs—both associate and bachelor's degrees—Mount Aloysius offers master's degree programs in business administration, behavioral specialist consulting, community counseling, and psychology.

Location

Mount Aloysius College is located in the scenic Southern Allegheny Mountains of west-central Pennsylvania, in the town of Cresson. Convenient and accessible from U.S. Route 22, the College's setting is rural but mere minutes from State College, Altoona, Johnstown, and Pittsburgh, Pennsylvania. Outdoor lovers are at home here. The area has warm, beautiful summers; brisk, breathtaking autumns; invigorating winters; and cool, blooming springs. Facilities are available for biking, golfing, swimming, horseback riding, waterskiing, boating, hiking, spelunking, cross-country and downhill skiing, picnicking, and amusement parks. A well-kept system of State Parks is convenient to the College as are shopping malls, golf courses, and numerous historical sites.

Majors and Degrees

Mount Aloysius College awards bachelor's and associate degrees in the arts, sciences, and health studies fields in both career-oriented and traditional liberal arts programs. Baccalaureate degrees are available in accounting (includes a fifth-year MBA option), American Sign Language/English interpreter education, behavioral and social science, biology and general science, business administration (includes a fifth-year MBA option), computer science, criminology, dentistry (4-4), elementary/early childhood education and secondary education (with certifications), English, general science, history/political science, humanities, information technology, math/science, medical imaging, nursing (RN-BSN program), nursing (2+2), occupational therapy (3-2), osteopathic medicine (3-4), pharmacy (3-3), physical therapy (4-3), physician assistant studies (3-2), prelaw, psychology, ultrasonography, and undecided/exploratory. Associate degrees are offered in applied technology, business administration, criminology, early childhood studies, general studies, legal studies, liberal arts, medical assistant studies, nursing, physical therapist assistant studies, radiography/medical imaging, sign language/deaf studies, and surgical technology. The College also confers the MBA and a master's degree in counseling.

Academic Programs

Whether preparing students for careers upon graduation or for graduate school, Mount Aloysius recognizes the importance of a liberal education. In addition to receiving solid preparation for a chosen career, every student at the College receives a foundation in the arts, sciences, and humanities through an outstanding core curriculum. Strong emphasis is placed on the specialized courses within each program of study, and many academic programs combine classroom experience with internships and related training at area clinical sites, agencies, and institutions. In addition to its regular academic programs, Mount Aloysius offers independent and directed study with a commitment to service, a central component of a Mercy education. The College has an excellent honors program and academic services area. The academic calendar has two traditional semesters and optional summer sessions.

Off-Campus Programs

An important feature of many academic programs is off-campus training. The majority of the College's programs of study require credit-yielding practicums at partnering hospitals, public and private schools, or health or human service agencies. Students in all health programs benefit from required clinical training during their time at the College.

Academic Facilities

The Mount Aloysius College Library is a state-of-the-art learning and study facility offering unprecedented access to a world of information. With a Buhl Electronic Classroom and more than 80,000 print and nonprint titles, the Library is an impressive, 31,000 square-foot facility with ample seating, four group-study rooms, reading lounge, and an unparalleled 18,000-volume Ecumenical Collection donated by Pastor Gerald Myers. This facility is completely automated, with an online catalog and access to remote libraries and the Internet through more than 30 workstations. The Library also houses the Information Technology Center, home to 15 multimedia workstations and the latest educational software.

Pierce Hall serves as the campus science center and is undergoing a major expansion. When completed in August of 2018, over 45,000 square feet of new lab and classroom space will have been added. The facility will be officially renamed the Learning Center for Health Science & Technology.

Academic Hall is home to the College Honors Program. It houses classrooms, labs, seminar rooms, faculty offices, and electronic classrooms. The College is proud of its bridge to the past and its progress in providing 21st-century learning facilities.

Costs

Annual tuition and fees for the 2017–18 academic year for full-time students were $21,230; room and board were $9,880. Up-to-date cost information is available online at http://www.mtaloy.edu/tuition-fees/tuition-and-fees.

Financial Aid

Mount Aloysius prides itself on affordability. Many MAC students hail from proud families of modest means and many are first-generation students. The College understands the expense involved in acquiring a quality education and encourages students to apply for all available aid. Through the Office of Financial Aid, the College assists students in applying for state and federal grants, loans, work-study awards, merit scholarships and more. The College awards academic monies based on GPA and SAT or ACT scores. These awards are renewable over a four-year period and range from $3,000 to $14,000 per year. Mount Aloysius College participates in all federal and state programs; fully 94 percent of Mount Aloysius College students receive some form of financial aid. *U.S. News & World Report* has ranked Mount Aloysius College as one of the best-priced private liberal arts colleges in the United States.

Faculty

The Mount Aloysius faculty consists of approximately 175 members, whose primary responsibility is teaching and advising students. Many faculty members hold advanced or terminal degrees and are expected to maintain close instructional ties with students. Many professors hold national, professional certificates in such disciplines as criminology, education, law, and nursing. The Mount Aloysius student-faculty ratio of 14:1 allows close contact between students and faculty members, providing personal attention in a highly structured environment—a key ingredient in the College's academic philosophy.

Student Government

The Student Government Association (SGA) represents students on all issues that concern the College. The SGA appoints student representatives to all student-oriented College committees. The College encourages student participation in the general governance structure and other matters concerning the development and implementation of policies on residential student life.

Recognitions

Mount Aloysius was recently named one of 100 Best Value Colleges in the U.S. It is a College of Distinction and a Pennsylvania College of Distinction; three separate academic areas—business, education, and nursing—have also earned College of Distinction

status. Mount Aloysius was one of four colleges deemed "an engine of opportunity" in a White House Report. In the past year, the College's Theatre productions have earned several awards from the prestigious Kennedy Center. The Nursing Division is ranked sixth in Pennsylvania for NCLEX pass rates among nursing programs that test more than 85 students annually. The American Sign Language/English Interpreter program is one of only 13 accredited bachelor's programs in the nation.

Admission Requirements

The College enrolls a freshman class of approximately 350 students. The total class of 550 includes transfer students. Admission is selective, based on academic promise, as indicated by a student's secondary school performance and activities, standardized test scores, and special experience and talents. Applicants are required to have or expected to earn a diploma from an approved secondary school or a GED diploma. Submission of official transcripts and SAT or ACT scores is required. In addition to the general admission requirements, specific admission requirements exist for the health programs.

For further information, students should visit the College's website at http://www.mtaloy.edu. Prospective students are encouraged to visit the scenic 193-acre campus. The College is open Monday to Friday from 8:30 a.m. to 5 p.m. and on select Saturdays.

Application and Information

To apply for admission to Mount Aloysius College, candidates are encouraged to submit their application and $30 application fee to the Office of Undergraduate and Graduate Admissions. In addition, students may apply online.

For further information, students should contact:

Office of Undergraduate and Graduate Admissions
Mount Aloysius College
7373 Admiral Peary Highway
Cresson, Pennsylvania 16630
Phone: 814-886-6383
      888-823-2220 (toll-free)
Fax: 814-886-6441
E-mail: admissions@mtaloy.edu
Website: http://www.mtaloy.edu

Mount Aloysius College, located on a beautiful 193-acre campus in Cresson, Pennsylvania provides a safe, vibrant learning community. Nestled in the southern Allegheny Mountains, Mount Aloysius is one of 17 U.S. Mercy colleges and universities. Mount Aloysius offers year-round recreational and cultural opportunities. Students enjoy both the security of the campus and the proximity to State College to the east and Pittsburgh to the west. Mount Aloysius College is minutes away from all the amenities of Altoona and Johnstown, Pennsylvania. Interstate highways, the Pennsylvania Turnpike, AMTRAK train service, bus service, and several regional airports—including Pittsburgh International Airport—make Mount Aloysius College convenient from anywhere.

MT SIERRA COLLEGE
MONROVIA, CALIFORNIA

 To read more about this school, visit http://petersons.to/mtsierra

The College

Mt Sierra is a private, Southern California college located close to all the opportunities and attractions that Los Angeles has to offer. The College was founded in 1990 and for more than 25 years has been known for its focus on technology and the arts. The Bachelor's degree programs in media arts, network communications, and information technology prepare graduates for lifelong careers. Students acquire the cutting-edge knowledge and skills that today's world demands, while learning in a caring and supportive environment.

Mt Sierra prides itself on having small classes but big opportunities. Because of our small class sizes, each student is known and valued, students and professors get to know each other by name, and student interaction is commonplace. The College is dedicated to providing access to higher education and a practical, hands-on, quality learning environment that is flexible and accessible to a geographically diverse and multicultural population.

The College prepares students to become leaders in their fields because its curriculum is based on the current needs of the workplace, not just theory. The school helps each student find internships, so they can connect their learning to their career. If students are interested in starting their own company, Mt Sierra has an incubator on campus to link to mentors, partners, and potential investors. This career-oriented focus contributes to a smoother pathway to employment after graduation. Mt Sierra's commitment to its students doesn't stop at graduation. The school offers lifelong learning opportunities, which means graduates can return any time to take courses to update their skills, with no tuition charge.

Graduates of Mt Sierra College have gone on to work at a range of high-profile firms, including Apple, Xerox, IBM, JPL, Yahoo, Verizon, LinkedIn, Pepsi, Blizzard Entertainment, Electronic Arts, Activision, Marvel Studios, Lightstorm Entertainment, Blizzard Entertainment, Symantec, Gateway, Boeing, Caltech, AT&T, County of Los Angeles, Wells Fargo, Kaiser Permanente, ABC, Disney, MGM, NBC, CBS, Universal, Warner Brothers, and others.

Mt Sierra College is accredited by the Accrediting Commission of Career Schools and Colleges (ACCSC); 2101 Wilson Blvd., Suite 302, Arlington, Virginia 22201; phone: 703-247-4212.

The U.S. Department of Education recognizes the ACCSC as a national accrediting agency. More information can be found at www.accsc.org. The College is authorized by the Department of Homeland Security to issue i-20s and admit international students and is also authorized through the Department of Education to offer federal loans and grants to qualified students.

Mt Sierra College's approval to operate as a private post-secondary school in the State of California is based on provisions of the California Private Post-Secondary Education Act (CPPEA) of 2009, (California Education Code, Title 3, Division 10, Part 59, Chapter 8), effective January 1, 2010. The Act is administered by the Bureau for Private Postsecondary Education, under the Department of Consumer Affairs.

Location

Nestled in the picturesque foothills of the San Gabriel Mountains, Mt Sierra College is located near premier art and technology centers and the world-renown Los Angeles film and entertainment industries.

Majors and Degrees

Mt Sierra College offers a winning combination of technology and creativity in a caring and supporting environment. The dedicated faculty and staff at Mt Sierra College prepare students for meaningful, lifelong careers.

The College's bachelor's degree programs undergo continuous review to ensure that students are receiving the education they need to begin—and succeed in—their life-long careers.

The College offers Bachelor of Science (B.S.) degrees in computer information technology, network communications, and information security. A Bachelor of Arts (B.A.) degree is available in media arts with concentrations in visual design or game arts and design.

Each program has two components. First, the core curriculum for each degree provides students with a progressive foundation pertaining to their field of study. Most core courses include hands-on experience or lab simulations in a virtual environment to maximize each student's education. Second, the general education curriculum provides students with critical thinking skills, information literacy competencies, quantitative reasoning, as well as written and verbal communication skills. These skills are developed extensively throughout both curricula to ensure that students are equipped to express themselves effectively.

Academic Programs

Mt Sierra College offers a hands-on, experiential education that combines practical experience and a strong theoretical understanding of the principles that govern the application of technological, artistic, and business skills, preparing students for successful roles in their chosen field and in their community.

The College also provides students with opportunities to explore the world through a strong general education. Graduates leave Mt Sierra with a theoretical and practical basis for understanding the forces that shape society. They develop the ability to think critically and to communicate effectively using the written and spoken word;

The atmosphere at Mt Sierra promotes student success. Learning is enhanced through small class sizes, individual attention, student-centered support services, and the College's commitment to placing the educational needs of the student first.

The College utilizes a variety of learning resources. Students learn to identify problems and research solutions, supported by Mt Sierra's tools and programs, creating practical solutions through creative experiences. The College focuses on effective learning outcomes including internship opportunities and other experiences to enhance the students' education, professional development, and future employment.

Mt Sierra offers a flexible structure that recognizes the varied needs of today's students. Programs are offered through a variety of methods, including the use of distance education. The College understands the many barriers that face students and offers programs and services to support a range of needs. The learning environment encourages diversity by making programs accessible to a geographically diverse and multicultural population.

Academic Facilities

Mt Sierra College offers approximately 25,000 square-feet of space dedicated to student learning. Students learn in state-of-the-art laboratories as well as spacious, traditional classrooms, all networked using the latest technology.

The Mt Sierra College Learning Resources Center is in a dedicated facility with a collection of books and visual media available for reference or circulation exclusive to Mt Sierra College students. The library staff provides instruction on the use of the database as well as accessing all other available resources. The Learning Resources Center houses networked personal computers and Macs for student research as well as plug-in ports.

Costs

For the 2018–19 academic year, the estimated tuition per academic year (9 calendar months) is $14,220. Tuition does not include room and board, books, software, supplies, fees of any kind, or transportation to and from the College.

There is also a $50 application fee, a $100 registration fee, and lab fees that range from $50 to $456, depending on the course.

Financial Aid

Mt Sierra College students may be eligible for financial aid to help defray the costs of their education and related expenses. Financial aid is available in the form of grants, loans, and scholarships. Mt. Sierra College offers Full scholarship, MSC Scholarship, Transfer scholarship and International scholarship for those who qualify.

To establish eligibility for aid, applicants will need to complete the Free Application for Federal Student Aid (FAFSA). This application must be completed each fiscal year financial aid is requested at Mt Sierra College. More information about the FAFSA application process is available at qwww.fafsa.gov.

Active duty U.S. Military personnel or veterans and their spouses are eligible for a 15 percent tuition reduction. This benefit is open to all branches of the military, including the National Guard and Reserve members and spouses. Spouses are not eligible if legally separated or divorced.

Faculty

At Mt Sierra College students learn from industry professionals with real-world experience in their chosen field of study. Our degrees are industry-driven and designed to train students for the workplace of the future. All courses are made to stimulate and inspire while recreating the same tasks faced on the job.

Classes are small with an average of 13 students.

Student Life

Student housing options are available for out-of-state and international students. A variety of housing options are available in Monrovia and the neighboring cities of Duarte, Azusa, Arcadia, and Sierra Madre. Housing information is available through Student Services and International Development.

The college maintains a staff of highly qualified professionals to meet the needs of the students. The Student Services Department is available to answer questions, offer solutions, address concerns, and is dedicated to enhancing the college experience. The Student Services Department also includes Career Services. Services are provided free of charge to all students and alumni.

Mt Sierra provides organized student activities to promote student involvement. There is an active student council, a range of events for students both on and off campus, and opportunities for community involvement.

Admission Requirements

Acceptance to Mt Sierra College is based primarily upon a personal interview and a review of the applicant's high school and/or college transcripts.

To be eligible for admission, applicants must have earned a high school diploma or its recognized equivalent (i.e. GED). Applicants whose high school or college transcripts indicate a CGPA of 2.25 are eligible to apply for admission.

After acceptance, the Mathematics and Writing Assessments are used to determine placement in Mathematics and English courses.

Application and Information

Mt Sierra College offers year-round enrollment and applications are accepted for the fall, winter, spring, and summer quarters. Interested individuals are invited to schedule an interview with a Mt Sierra College Admissions Representative and tour the campus. Applicants must submit an application form and sign the enrollment agreement, accompanied by a nonrefundable application fee.

Potential students are invited to schedule a tour of Mt Sierra to experience what makes the campus, faculty, and curriculum special.

Mt Sierra College
800 Royal Oaks Drive
Suite 101
Monrovia, California 91016
Phone: 888-828-8800
626-873-2100
E-mail: admissions@mtsierra.edu
Website: mtsierra.edu

MUHLENBERG COLLEGE
ALLENTOWN, PENNSYLVANIA

 To read more about this school, visit http://petersons.to/muhlenbergcollege

The College

Founded in 1848, Muhlenberg College is a top-tier liberal arts college that offers a more comprehensive array of pre-professional programs than most institutions of its size. Its mission is to develop independent critical thinkers who are intellectually agile, characterized by a zeal for reasoned and civil debate, knowledgeable about the achievements and traditions of diverse civilizations and cultures, able to express ideas with clarity and grace, committed to lifelong learning, equipped with ethical values, and prepared for lives of leadership and service.

Muhlenberg students achieve the College's goals by assuming strong individual responsibility for intense involvement in academic work and for personal involvement within the College community. The more than 110 student organizations provide outlets for the diverse cultural, athletic, religious, social, leadership, and service interests of students. The campus is primarily residential; more than 90 percent of the 2,200 students live on campus. Muhlenberg students are smart, open-minded people of all backgrounds who care deeply about the world and each other. They love to learn, they are good citizens and friends, and they are motivated for professional success. But they don't take themselves too seriously. More than 9 of 10 first-year students return as sophomores.

Muhlenberg students are guided by an active Career Center and more than 1,800 alumni who are part of The Muhlenberg Network, in advising, mentoring, and opening doors to professional opportunities. More than 90 percent are employed and/or attending graduate school within one year of graduation. About one third of a typical graduating class proceeds immediately to graduate or professional school, while two thirds pursue a career immediately upon graduation.

Location

Located less than 90 miles west of New York City and 60 miles north of Philadelphia, Muhlenberg's campus in Allentown, Pennsylvania is beautiful and convenient. Allentown is Pennsylvania's third-largest and fastest-growing city. It is home to one of the best park systems in the United States—and thanks to more than $1 billion in recent investments, was recently honored as a finalist for a global award for excellence. It is a magnet for entrepreneurs and new businesses ranging from tech and design to logistics, finance, medicine, and biotechnology. These businesses offer internships and full-time employment to Muhlenberg students and alumni.

Majors and Degrees

Muhlenberg offers the Bachelor of Arts (A.B.) degree in the following fields: accounting, American studies, anthropology, art history, business administration, dance, economics, English, film studies, finance, French, history, international studies, Jewish studies, media and communication, music, philosophy, philosophy/political thought, political economy, political science, psychology, religious studies, Russian studies, sociology, Spanish, studio art, and theater. The Bachelor of Science (B.S.) degree is offered in the following fields: biochemistry, biology, chemistry, computer science, environmental science, mathematics, neuroscience, physical science, physics, and public health. Students may also design their own major.

Minors are offered in most of the major fields, as well as in Africana studies, creative writing, documentary storytelling, German studies, innovation and entrepreneurship, Italian studies, Latin American and Caribbean studies, women's and gender studies, public health, sustainability studies, and Asian traditions.

Muhlenberg also offers students cooperative programs with Boston University in medicine, public health and management; a 3-4 dental program with the University of Pennsylvania; a 3-3 B.S. program in physical therapy with Thomas Jefferson University; a 3-2 B.S./M.S. program in occupational therapy with Thomas Jefferson University; a 3-2/4-2 combined program in engineering, offered in cooperation with Columbia University; a 4-4 dual-admission program with SUNY College of Optometry; graduate programs at American University in finance; at Penn State College of Medicine in public health; and at Lehigh University in management. In addition, students may receive certification to teach at the elementary and secondary levels.

Academic Programs

Muhlenberg's academic programs emphasize breadth of study in the liberal arts as well as in-depth study of a particular academic major. All students must fulfill requirements in the arts, foreign culture, the humanities, social sciences, and natural sciences. Strong achievement on Advanced Placement examinations may enable a student to receive advanced placement, possibly with credit. Scores of 4 or 5 earn automatic credit.

Students work closely with academic advisers to formulate programs well suited to their individual interests, abilities, needs, and goals. Generally, students are expected to declare their major at the end of the sophomore year; however, many students later change their academic major with no difficulty. A double major is possible, and about a third of Muhlenberg students graduate with a double major. The College also enriches the freshman-year experience through more than 35 special-focus First-Year Seminars. Seniors have the opportunity to synthesize and integrate their academic experience through a Culminating Undergraduate Experience (CUE).

Off-Campus Programs

Study abroad is available through Muhlenberg's Semester-in-London Program, Netherlands semester, Dublin semester, or more than 160 affiliate agreements with international universities all over the world. More than half of Muhlenberg students choose to study abroad.

Students may participate in a variety of internships in local, national, and international businesses; health-care facilities; schools; public agencies; theaters; broadcasting stations; and magazines. Government internships in Harrisburg, Pennsylvania, and Washington, D.C., and an Ethics and Public Affairs semester in Washington, D.C., as well as a New York City semester at Jewish Theological Seminary also are available.

Students may enroll in courses offered at any of the five other member institutions of the Lehigh Valley Association of

Independent Colleges: Lafayette College, Lehigh University, Cedar Crest College, DeSales University, and Moravian College.

Academic Facilities

Muhlenberg's library collection, housed in the state-of-the-art Harry C. Trexler Library, contains more than 310,000 volumes as well as numerous government documents, periodicals, and electronic and online resources. Students may also use library materials owned by the other institutions participating in the Lehigh Valley Association of Independent Colleges.

The Baker Center for the Arts was designed for Muhlenberg by the well-known architect Philip Johnson. It houses a modern theater complex, a recital hall, classrooms, art studios, and a fine arts gallery. The Trexler Pavilion for Theater and Dance provides dance performance and studio space, a proscenium theater, a Black Box theater, a costume shop, and additional rehearsal spaces.

Life science facilities include numerous laboratories, classrooms, two electron microscopes, a DNA sequencer, an isolation room used for growing and studying viruses, and a museum of natural history. Facilities supporting students in the physical sciences include equipment for optics, electronics, and atomic, nuclear, and solid-state physics. The College supports both Microsoft and Apple applications throughout campus.

Costs

The comprehensive tuition and fees for the 2017–18 academic year was $50,830. The room and board fee averaged $11,300. The total cost for a resident student was approximately $62,130.

Financial Aid

Muhlenberg College endeavors to make its educational opportunities available to all qualified students regardless of their financial circumstances. While most financial aid at Muhlenberg is based on financial need as demonstrated by the College Scholarship Service Financial Aid PROFILE and FAFSA, there is also significant merit aid available. Typically, about 87 percent of Muhlenberg's students qualify for and receive aid from all sources (institutional, federal and state). The average gift aid for first-year students is $26,674. Merit scholarships range from $40,000 to $1,000.

Faculty

The Muhlenberg faculty consists of 185 full-time and 127 part-time members. While many faculty members are distinguished for their scholarly research, teaching is the main emphasis of their work. Professors at all levels work closely with students both inside and outside of the classroom. Many department heads teach introductory courses, and no courses are taught by graduate students or teaching assistants.

Student Government

Muhlenberg students are expected to demonstrate a high level of responsibility with regard to their own governance and to participate extensively in internal decision-making and communication processes throughout the campus. These responsibilities are coordinated by the Student Government, which transacts all business pertaining to the student body. This organization is in charge of a student activities budget

of more than $350,000. In addition, 2 students serve as representatives to the Board of Trustees, and students hold membership on many faculty committees.

Admission Requirements

The College's admissions process is holistic, selecting students who give evidence of ability and scholastic achievement, seriousness of purpose, and the capacity to make constructive contributions to the College community and the world. In terms of academic quality, the middle range for the SAT reading and writing is 570–680 and 560–570 for math. The ACT middle range is 25–30. Average GPA is 3.3 on a 4.0 unweighted scale.

Muhlenberg also has a long-standing test optional policy. An on-campus interview is strongly recommended for all applicants and required for students who choose not to submit standardized test scores.

Application and Information

Prospective first-year students may apply for admission under either the Early Decision or Regular Decision plan. About half of the first-year class is admitted through Early Decision. In addition, transfer admission is offered for both fall and spring semesters. Application requirements and deadlines for first-year and transfer admission can be found at muhlenberg.edu/apply.

For further information, interested students should contact:

Melissa W. Falk
Dean of Admissions and Financial Aid
Muhlenberg College
Allentown, Pennsylvania 18104-5586
Phone: 484-664-3200
E-mail: admissions@muhlenberg.edu
Website: www.muhlenberg.edu

Located 90 miles west of New York City and 60 miles north of Philadelphia, Muhlenberg's campus in Allentown, Pennsylvania, is beautiful and convenient.

NEUMANN UNIVERSITY
ASTON, PENNSYLVANIA

★ To read more about this school, visit http://petersons.to/neumannuniversity

The University

Neumann University (http://www.neumann.edu), a Catholic co-educational institution in the Franciscan tradition, recognizes the value of developing intellectual excellence, professional competence, and strong community life. As a university that balances the liberal arts with the professions, Neumann was founded to meet and expand the educational and professional horizons of men and women through instruction that is based on values, ethical behavior, and service to others. With its Living and Learning Center residence halls, Neumann University is able to serve a diverse geographic and demographic population.

Founded and sponsored by the Sisters of St. Francis of Philadelphia, the University is committed to a varied student body and welcomes students of all denominations. Enrollment is around 2,900.

The Life Center houses the Meagher Theatre, the Bruder Athletic Center, and the Crossroads Cafe dining facility. Intercollegiate sports include women's basketball, cross-country, field hockey, golf, ice hockey, indoor track, lacrosse, soccer, softball, swimming, tennis, track, and volleyball; and men's baseball, basketball, cross-country, golf, ice hockey, indoor track, lacrosse, soccer, tennis, track, and volleyball. Neumann University competes as a member of the National Collegiate Athletic Association (NCAA) Division III, the Colonial States Athletic Conference, and the Eastern Collegiate Athletic Conference (ECAC). Intramural sports and club teams are available to all members of the campus community.

The Living and Learning Center is designed to provide a state-of-the-art residential experience, with a focus on education within a real-world living environment. Technologically smart, the center connects students to both faculty members and friends via wireless Internet, which is available in every suite and apartment. The center also houses a separate computer lab, a fitness center, a reflection room, various study rooms with warming kitchens for group study or meetings, and a laundry.

The University provides a full range of services to students, including career placement, career and personal counseling, a tutoring program, and health services.

Neumann students are involved in a wide variety of campus and community activities. Major and special interest clubs are available for student participation. Clubs bring together students who share common interests and help foster new friendships.

At Neumann, the spiritual dimension of one's life is recognized as integral to total human development. The Ministry Team provides a pastoral presence on campus and promotes a sense of community. The entire University community is invited to serve the needs of the poor and neglected in society through various outreach programs, with special attention to the need for peace and justice in the world today.

Neumann is well positioned to respond to the academic and extracurricular needs of students who are of traditional or nontraditional age, commuters or residents, and full-time or part-time.

In addition to undergraduate programs, Neumann confers master's degrees in accounting, education, nursing, organizational and strategic leadership, pastoral counseling, and sport business as well as doctoral degrees in education (Ed.D.), pastoral counseling (Ph.D.), and physical therapy (D.P.T.).

Location

Neumann, with a beautiful 68-acre suburban campus in Aston, Delaware County, Pennsylvania, is a short distance from Philadelphia; Wilmington, Delaware; southern New Jersey; and Maryland. It is easily accessible from major arteries such as I-95, Route 476, Route 1, and the Pennsylvania Turnpike.

Majors and Degrees

Neumann offers strong academic majors leading to a Bachelor of Arts degree or a Bachelor of Science degree in accounting, arts production and performance, biology, business administration, communication and digital media, computer information systems, criminal justice, education, English, health sciences, liberal arts, marketing, nursing, political science, psychology, public safety administration, social work, and sport management. The education programs lead to teacher certification in early elementary (PK–4), special education (PK–8) or secondary education. Pre-professional programs in engineering, law, medicine, pharmacy, and physical therapy are also available. An accelerated evening program for adults leads to an Associate of Arts, Bachelor of Arts, or Bachelor of Science degree in liberal studies or professional studies.

Academic Programs

The academic program at Neumann University is composed of a core curriculum (required of all students), a major area of study (chosen by each student), and a wide range of elective offerings. Students may also choose a minor area of study. The University's broad base of liberal arts offerings prepares students for the intellectual and social challenges they will face in the employment marketplace and throughout their lives. The core is intended to provide basic knowledge of the liberal arts and sciences; develop verbal, written, and symbolic communication skills; and stimulate interest in a broad range of topics for the purpose of enhancing the individual's contributions to society, thereby enabling the individual to realize full human potential.

Classroom instruction is supplemented by field experience and internships, through which students can earn credit and gain experience by working in a job related to their career interest. Fieldwork and student teaching are required of all education majors. Clinical practice for the nursing major occurs in a variety of health-care facilities in the tri-state area.

The honors program is an opportunity for academically talented students to explore imaginative and innovative perspectives on learning. It is also an opportunity to stimulate and motivate students to expand their knowledge and interest and to strive for greater excellence. Moreover, it is a reward for prior perseverance and dedication as well as an obligation to use skills and abilities in service to others. Admission to the honors program is by invitation.

Neumann University has transfer articulation agreements with numerous schools throughout the area.

Academic Facilities

The Child Development Center is a state-of-the-art, octagonal-shaped building, specifically designed to house an educational program for preschoolers. As a state-licensed day-care facility, it enrolls children of Neumann students, the faculty, and the community. The Child Development Center is part of the Division of Education and Human Services. Students enrolled in education courses use the center for observation, practical experience, and student teaching.

The Academic Computing Center is located on the ground floor of the University. The computers are viewed as tools to support all fields of study and all students and faculty members. Neumann University provides wireless access across campus. Computers are available to all students, as is software related to various academic disciplines.

The University library contains a balanced collection of more than 55,000 physical volumes and films, 20,000 e-books, and nearly 100,000 electronic journals. E-books and journals can be accessed from anywhere with an Internet connection. Collaboration with faculty and membership in local consortia (TCLC, SEPCHE) ensures access to the most relevant resources for academic success. Professional librarians provide in-person research support seven days a week and also create online Research Guides and video tutorials for around-the-clock assistance. Librarians also provide cutting-edge instruction to help develop essential 21st-century skills like critical thinking, technological literacy, and information management. Quiet study rooms, collaborative group spaces, and an open computer lab and Wi-Fi collectively support student study needs.

Costs

Annual tuition and fees for full-time students (12 to 19 credits per semester) in 2018–19 is $31,400. Room and board is $13,020.

Financial Aid

Typically, about 95 percent of Neumann undergraduate students receive some form of financial aid (scholarships, grants, and student loans).

Neumann offers a variety of renewable scholarships each year to entering full-time freshmen and transfer students. Interested applicants should contact the Office of Admissions and Financial Aid as soon as possible to determine eligibility.

In addition to Neumann scholarships, funds are available through the Federal Pell Grant, Federal Supplemental Educational Opportunity Grant, and Federal Work-Study Programs. Many states provide grant money to attend Neumann (non-Pennsylvania residents should check with their state's higher education agency for details). Veterans Administration benefits can be received by qualified veterans or their dependents. Federal Stafford Student Loans and Federal PLUS Program loans are available and can be applied for through Neumann's preferred lender or any participating bank. Neumann also offers institutional need-based grants. All students requesting financial aid must complete the Free Application for Federal Student Aid (FAFSA) each year to determine eligibility. In order to expedite processing, the FAFSA should be submitted by March 15 for the following school year. Financial aid funds are renewable annually based on need, as determined by the FAFSA results.

Faculty

Neumann students describe faculty members as sincere, hard-working, determined, and energetic. Faculty members view themselves, first, as teachers and are proud partners in their students' journeys toward professional careers. Each student has a faculty adviser, who assists in arranging a program designed to meet the student's educational goals. Many faculty members serve as moderators of student clubs. The student-faculty ratio is 13:1.

Student Government

The Student Government Association (SGA) is the representative body for all students. Its function is to implement the aims and purposes of the University, foster cooperation in student relationships, assist the University in being responsive to the needs of the student body, and encourage personal responsibility for an intelligent system of student self-government. Through the Student Activities Board, social functions are planned throughout the year. Students serve on various University committees, including the Student Affairs Committee of the Board, Academic Advising Committee, Honors Program Committee, Registration/Orientation Task Force, and Student Judicial Board. For full-time students, a Student Government Association fee of $85 per semester is required.

Admission Requirements

Neumann has a rolling admission policy and accepts applications throughout the year. Applicants are considered on the basis of high school record, SAT or ACT scores, recommendations, class rank, and other indicators of potential to succeed in university-level studies. Applications for admission are reviewed without regard to sex, race, creed, color, national origin, age, sexual orientation, pregnancy, military status, religion, or disability. Applicants should be graduates of an accredited high school (or present equivalent credentials) and have a recommended curriculum of 16 units of high school course work, distributed as follows: 4 in English, 2 to 3 in science, 2 in mathematics, 2 in social studies, 2 in foreign language, and 4 in electives. Students intending to pursue a major in biology or clinical laboratory science must have at least 1 year of high school biology and chemistry, and high school physics is highly recommended.

Neumann participates in the Advanced Placement (AP) Program and the College-Level Examination Program (CLEP).

An interview and tour of the campus are highly recommended for all prospective students and parents. Visits can be arranged by contacting the Office of Admissions.

Application and Information

Applicants for freshman admission are requested to have SAT or ACT scores and high school transcripts sent to the Office of Admissions. A nonrefundable $35 application fee should accompany the completed application. A free application is available online at http://www.neumann.edu.

Neumann University welcomes applications from students who have attended or are currently attending either two-year or four-year regionally accredited institutions of higher learning.

For further information, students should contact:

Office of Admissions
Neumann University
One Neumann Drive
Aston, Pennsylvania 19014-1298
United States
Phone: 610-558-5616
        800-9NEUMANN (toll-free)
E-mail: neumann@neumann.edu
Website: http://www.neumann.edu

Students love the newest building on campus, the Mirenda Center for Sport, Spirituality, and Character Development.

NEUMONT COLLEGE OF COMPUTER SCIENCE
SALT LAKE CITY, UTAH

 To read more about this school, visit http://petersons.to/neumont

The College

Neumont College of Computer Science is different by design. To address shortcomings in traditional higher education, Neumont's founders met with educators and leading employers from around the country to design an innovative computer science curriculum that better prepares students to meet the needs of the rapidly evolving technology industry. The result is a computer science education that merges academic rigor, exposure to cutting-edge technologies, and relevant professional knowledge through a real-world project-based curriculum.

Neumont's mission is to provide a professional education that is rich in ideas, current in industry best practices, and deep in technological insight from the input of industry-leading partners. The institution is committed to a collaborative learning process, a high-quality learning environment, contributing broadly to students' lives, and bringing value to the enterprises it partners. Neumont graduates are known for their technology expertise and business acumen, their capacity to innovate, and their motivation to succeed. Employers that have hired Neumont graduates include Google, Microsoft, eBay, Oracle, 3M, HP, Amazon, Blizzard Entertainment, Dell EMC, and many others.

Neumont's original approach to computer science education has been featured in and cited by major news outlets from around the country for innovation in higher education. Neumont's unique curriculum combines classroom instruction and labs with a collaborative learning environment and real-world project experiences for companies like IBM, Nike, and eBay. The campus was custom-designed to fit the college's needs with a focus on interactive classrooms, study areas, project rooms, and labs.

Neumont's students come from all across the United States. In the fall of 2017, 81 percent of all current students came from outside the state of Utah. The student body is 89 percent male and 11 percent female, and the student-to-faculty ratio is 29:1.

The Office of Student Affairs assists students in creating groups that meet regularly for different activities and events. Clubs and organizations may focus on a single game (i.e., Magic the Gathering, Pathfinder, or billiards) or they may focus on a specific issue like fitness, women in technology, or equality.

Freshmen are required to live in Neumont-sponsored housing for their first four quarters. Students are housed in apartment complexes near the campus in downtown Salt Lake City. Every apartment comes with furnished bedrooms, kitchens, and living spaces. All utilities are included, as well as high-speed internet, on-site laundry, and access to fitness facilities.

Location

Neumont's convenient location offers a chance for our students to enjoy a little bit of everything. Salt Lake City offers a vibrant local scene where art, food, and music converge daily. Plus, it's just minutes away from world-class hiking, camping, skiing, and snowboarding.

The downtown campus is conveniently located on public transit lines, including TRAX, which offers service to the Salt Lake International Airport (SLC) and other points of interest. TRAX is Utah's light rail system that connects Neumont Student Housing with the academic center. Students are encouraged to walk, use TRAX, bike, or make use of the local bike sharing program. All apartment complexes are conveniently located near grocery stores, entertainment venues, and restaurants. In addition, Neumont offers a weekly van service to big box retailers.

Majors and Degrees

Neumont offers 180-credit Bachelor of Science degrees which can be completed in three years. Students attend classes year-round with a three-week break between each ten-week quarter. Students major in one of five areas of technology:

- B.S.C.S.: Bachelor of Science in Computer Science

- B.S.G.D.: Bachelor of Science in Software & Game Development

- B.S.I.S.: Bachelor of Science in Computer Information Systems

- B.S.T.M.: Bachelor of Science in Business Technology Operations Management

- B.S.W.D.: Bachelor of Science in Web Design & Development

Academic Programs

The Neumont academic model is simple: students learn to master technology in a project-based environment. In the tech industry, nearly all software is developed in a team, so students learn how to fill different roles, meet deadlines, manage requirements, and resolve conflicts.

The curriculum sequentially weaves increasingly complex projects and faculty mentoring into every aspect of a student's education. During their final quarters at Neumont, students participate in Enterprise Projects and develop real-world solutions for real companies.

Each degree program follows a project-based learning model that requires students to work in small teams to complete projects. Students in undergraduate programs are required to attend courses full-time and can earn a bachelor's degree in three years by attending class year-round.

Every student is assigned an advocate to help them make decisions regarding their career goals and degree choice and to ensure they are on track for graduation.

Costs

For the 2017–18 academic year, tuition was $7,650 per quarter, housing was $1,990 per quarter, and books and supplies were $400 per quarter. There is a one-time $2,500 charge for a laptop computer. The activities fee was $150 per quarter and the technology fee was $350 per quarter. Once a student progresses beyond the fourth quarter of study there are also some program-specific fees of up to $210 per quarter.

Financial Aid

Neumont's Office of Financial Aid works with each student to create a customized package of grants, loans, and scholarships to fund tuition, fees, housing, books, and living expenses. Every student is encouraged to submit the Free Application for Federal Student Aid (FAFSA). In addition to offering several scholarships and grants, Neumont participates in federal grant programs and federal and private loan programs.

There are also a variety of opportunities for student employment on and off campus. Students interested in pursuing Neumont-sponsored employment opportunities must be in good academic standing. All student employment is based on approval from their advocate and the Director of Student Affairs.

Faculty

Each member of Neumont's faculty is hired specifically for their professional experience and expertise in the computer science industry. Instructors are required to teach designated learning outcomes that allow students to work in a real-world, professional environment. All core computer science classes are taught by faculty members with experience in software engineering and a passion for teaching.

Admissions

The Admissions Committee evaluates applicants to determine if they have the qualifications and commitment needed to succeed in Neumont's rigorous academic environment. With an average acceptance rate of 83 percent, Neumont students are dedicated, driven, and tech-obsessed. The committee relies heavily on academic achievements, such as standardized test score (ACT and/or SAT) and cumulative high school GPA, to assess an applicant. On average, students who enrolled in the fall of 2017 had a cumulative high school GPA of 3.07, an average composite ACT score of 24, or an average combined math and reading SAT score of 1107.

Because not all of an applicant's strengths can be shown through a test score, the committee also evaluates life experience, personal essays, technology expertise, interest in technology, and proven work ethic. Applicants are invited to contact the Office of Admissions if there is something about their background beyond test scores and GPA that should be evaluated.

Neumont accepts applications for admission three times a year. Applications, including transcripts and test scores, must be submitted by the early, general, or late admission application deadlines. In addition to academic achievement, applicants will be evaluated based on their passion for technology and work ethic.

Interested students are invited to visit the campus or take a virtual tour at http://www.neumont.edu/campustour.

For more information, prospective students should contact:

Jasmine Pena, Associate Director of Admissions
Neumont College of Computer Science
143 South Main Street
Salt Lake City, Utah 84111
Phone: 888-638-6668
       801-302-2800
E-mail: admissions@neumont.edu
Website: www.neumont.edu
      www.facebook.com/neumont
      www.twitter.com/neumontcs
      www.instagram.com/neumontcs
      www.youtube.com/user/neumont

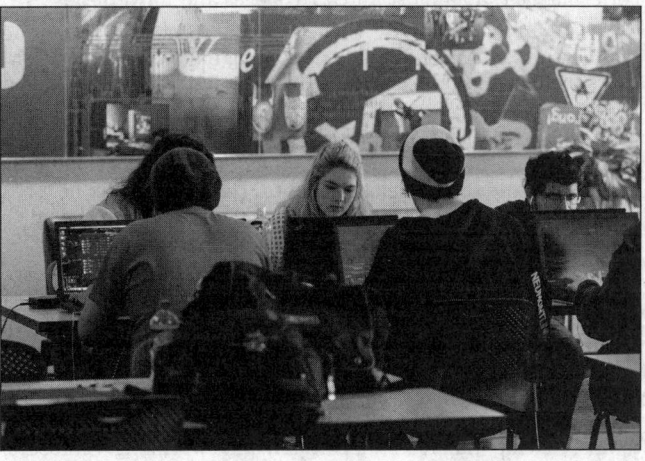

NEW COLLEGE OF FLORIDA
SARASOTA, FLORIDA

The College

New College of Florida offers serious students the opportunity to pursue rigorous academic study in an environment designed to promote depth in thinking, free exchange of ideas, and highly individualized interaction with faculty members. The College was founded as a private institution in 1960 with a devotion to the values implicit in a liberal arts and sciences education, and a dedication to creating an innovative academic program where talented students and outstanding faculty members could come together to pursue learning through small classes, seminars, and independent study, and to pursue advanced undergraduate research.

In 2001, New College was designated as the official Honors College in the liberal arts and sciences for the State University System of Florida. New College is regularly featured in guidebooks as being among the nation's leading educational values and as one of the country's top small, public colleges. New College is also known as one of the nation's top producers of Fulbright scholarship recipients, with 61 in the last decade alone, a better per-capita performance than almost all U.S. colleges and universities.

About 80 percent of New College graduates go on to pursue graduate or professional study at leading institutions, in recent years including Harvard, Yale, MIT, Georgetown, Berkeley, and Oxford.

New College's student population is 861, of whom approximately 62 percent are women. Approximately 20 percent of students are out-of-state or overseas residents. The College has begun a growth initiative and plans to gradually increase enrollment to 1,200 by 2023.

The College's 110-acre bayfront location near the Gulf of Mexico includes basketball, racquetball, tennis, and volleyball courts; a multipurpose soccer, softball, and athletic field; a running trail; a 25-meter swimming pool; and a comprehensive fitness center. The New College sailing team is part of the Inter-Collegiate Sailing Association of North America (ICSA). Students also compete in recreational and intramural sports including soccer, tennis, fencing, flag football, softball, and swimming. Sailboats, kayaks, and canoes are also available free of charge.

Location

On the coastline in southwest Florida, New College serves as the northern gateway to Sarasota, a bustling city 50 miles south of Tampa. Sarasota is noted for its recreational and cultural attractions, including beautiful white-sand beaches, professional theater, orchestra, opera, and ballet companies, and an abundance of art and music venues. Notably, New College sits adjacent to the world-famous John and Mable Ringling Museum of Art, which offers students free entry to view its Baroque and Renaissance art collections.

Many major airlines serve Sarasota-Bradenton International Airport, which is near the College. Buses link the campus to downtown, shopping malls, parks, and beaches, though bicycling is the favored means of transportation among students.

Majors and Degrees

New College awards the Bachelor of Arts degree in liberal arts and sciences. Each of the College's nearly forty different areas of concentration (majors) is an individualized program that students design in consultation with faculty members. These include anthropology; applied mathematics; art; art history; biochemistry; biology; biopsychology; chemistry; Chinese language and culture; classics; computer science; economics; English; environmental studies; European studies; French; gender studies; German studies/German language and literature; history; humanities; international and area studies; literature; marine biology; mathematics; medieval and Renaissance studies; music; natural sciences; neurobiology; philosophy; physics; political science; psychology; public policy; religion; Russian language and literature; social sciences; sociology; Spanish language, literature, and culture; and urban studies. Partial areas of concentration include theater. Students may also pursue special program areas of concentration with faculty approval. Pre-medical, pre-law, pre-M.B.A., pre-veterinary, and other advanced-degree program advising and guidelines are provided by faculty members and by the Center for Engagement and Opportunity. New College also offers a master's degree program in data science.

Academic Programs

New College's distinctive curriculum enables students, in close consultation with faculty members, to develop programs of seminars, tutorials, independent research, internships, and off-campus experiences that meet each student's personal academic interests and goals.

At the end of each semester, rather than grades, students receive detailed narrative evaluations as well as satisfactory/unsatisfactory assessments of their work from individual faculty members. Graduation requirements include satisfactory completion of seven academic contracts (a set of academic courses and other goals for the semester, planned by the student and faculty adviser), three independent-study projects, a senior thesis or project, and an oral baccalaureate examination. In addition to the requirements for individual majors, students must complete eight courses within the liberal arts curriculum, with at least one course each in the humanities, social sciences, natural sciences, and diverse perspectives. Students must also meet basic proficiency in mathematics and English language and advanced proficiency in written and oral English language.

The College operates on a 4-1-4 calendar year, including a January interterm when students undertake independent study projects, such as library, laboratory, or field research; internships; and performing arts projects, all of which they design and complete under faculty sponsorship.

Off-Campus Programs

New College believes that internships, fieldwork, and independent research can make a significant contribution to an undergraduate education, and facilitates such study through its flexible, individualized curriculum and special support services. New College is a member of the National Student Exchange, which provides access to nearly 200 universities with programs in the U.S. and abroad (many with comparable tuition costs) and the Consortium for Innovative Environments in Learning.

Academic Facilities

New College's Jane Bancroft Cook Library is befitting of one of the country's leading colleges and has an open stack arrangement that allows free access to most materials. With a resident collection of more than 285,000 items, and unmediated access to more than 11 million items from the State University System of Florida Libraries, Cook Library provides research-level collections to students and faculty. The library also boasts access to the University of South Florida electronic collections. In total, the library has access to more than 10,000 electronic serial titles, including scholarly journals, newspapers, digital images and videos, and datasets. A comprehensive online interlibrary loan system gives students convenient access to holdings of libraries worldwide. In addition, the library offers research instruction, digital services, data management and grant compliance services, and numerous workshops, lectures, seminars, and other offerings. Robust wireless network access is available to all users.

The Harry Sudakoff Conference Center hosts visiting lecturers, meetings of campus and community organizations, and special events. The Caples Fine Arts Complex includes the 264-seat Mildred Sainer Music and Arts Pavilion, which features student, local, and national performances; the Lota Mundy Music Building, which houses eight music practice rooms and the Benjamin and Barbara Slavin Electronic Music Studio; the Christianne Felsmann Fine Arts Building; the Betty Isermann Fine Arts Gallery and Studio; and a sculpture studio.

The R. V. Heiser Natural Sciences Complex houses laboratories, classrooms, offices, a state-of-the-art optical spectroscopy and nanomaterials laboratory, a research greenhouse, herbarium, a computer lab, two electron microscopes, and an auditorium. An $8 million addition that opened in fall 2017 expanded Heiser by 50 percent. The Rhoda and Jack Pritzker Marine Biology Research Center, one of the leading marine research centers in southwest Florida, features culture rooms, laboratories, and aquariums with water drawn from Sarasota Bay.

The College's 35,000 square-foot Academic Center, which opened in 2011, was awarded LEED Gold certification by the U.S. Green Building Council. It includes a state-of-the-art computer lab, classrooms, faculty offices, and a student lounge.

Costs

For the 2017–18 academic year, the estimated in-state tuition and fees at New College of Florida were $6,916 and out-of-state tuition and fees were $29,944. Room and board costs were $9,264.

Financial Aid

Most students receive scholarship funding from either New College of Florida or the New College Foundation. Approximately 96 percent of New College students receive some form of financial assistance, including academic scholarships and need-based financial aid. To apply for federal and need-based financial aid, students should file the Free Application for Federal Student Aid (FAFSA). November 1 is the priority date for need-based financial aid. No additional forms are required for most of the College's scholarship programs. New College of Florida guarantees an offer of scholarship funding to all admitted applicants with admission files completed by April 15, so long as they are US citizens or eligible non-citizens, and have not yet earned a bachelor's or advanced degree. The same deadline applies to freshmen, transfers, and internationals.

Faculty

Of New College's full-time faculty members, 97 percent hold the highest degree awarded in their field of study, usually the doctorate. They come to New College from the finest universities nationally and abroad, drawn to an environment that emphasizes excellence in teaching and fosters a close-knit community of scholars. Faculty members sponsor individual students in the formulation of their academic programs, gradually moving toward a form of mentorship through which joint research is sometimes pursued. A 10:1 student-faculty ratio is a key factor in the College's individualized approach to education. At New College, all classes are taught by faculty, not by teaching assistants.

Student Government

Student input is a decisive factor in campus governance. Elected student representatives serve on the Board of Trustees and most major policymaking committees, and are voting participants in divisional and campus-wide faculty meetings. The New College Student Alliance, the College's student government, has authority over funding for recreational events, social events, student clubs and organizations on campus, and allocation of the Green Fee for environmentally friendly projects.

Admission Requirements

New College of Florida seeks highly capable students eager to take responsibility for their own education. The admissions staff reviews each candidate individually, assessing his or her potential for success within, and contribution to, the College's unique environment. Course selection, academic record, and writing ability are focal points of the committee's review. The majority (57 percent) of the first-year students entering in fall 2017 ranked in the top 20 percent of their high school class. The middle 50 percent of SAT takers had a combined score of 1200–1360 on the evidence-based reading/writing and math sections. The middle 50 percent of ACT takers had a composite score of 25–30.

All prospective students may apply for entrance to the fall term. Only prospective transfer students may apply the spring term. Candidates must submit an admission application, fee or fee waiver, Self-reported Student Academic Record (SSAR), SAT or ACT scores, and a letter of recommendation. A campus visit and demonstrated interest are also recommended for all those with serious interest in applying.

Application and Information

Admissions application materials and descriptive literature are available through the New College Office of Admissions and Financial Aid. The deadline for priority admission is November 1. All students who meet this deadline will receive a decision by April 1, however some students will receive their decisions sooner. Applications will continue to be accepted on a rolling basis November 2 through April 15. Those students who apply during that time will receive their decisions on a rolling basis. A completed application and all supporting documents must be submitted to the Office of Admissions and Financial Aid before a candidate is considered for admission.

Inquiries and application requests should be directed to:

Joy Hamm
Dean of Admissions and Financial Aid
New College of Florida
5800 Bay Shore Road
Sarasota, Florida 34243-2109
United States
Phone: 941-487-5000
Fax: 941-487-5001
E-mail: admissions@ncf.edu
Website: http://www.ncf.edu
http://www.facebook.com/newcollegeofflorida
http://twitter.com/NewCollegeofFL
http://www.youtube.com/user/NewCollegeofFL

New College of Florida's historic waterfront campus features spectacular sunsets, wetlands, an intertidal lagoon, and boat access.

NIAGARA UNIVERSITY
NIAGARA UNIVERSITY, NEW YORK

 To read more about this school, visit http://petersons.to/niagarauniversity

The University

Niagara University (NU), founded in 1856, is a private, comprehensive university rooted in a Catholic and Vincentian tradition. The suburban campus combines the old and new; both ivy-covered buildings and modern architectural structures line its picturesque landscape. The University is easily accessible via the New York State Thruway, both the Buffalo and Niagara Falls international airports, and rail and bus service.

There are approximately 3,100 undergraduate and 850 graduate students enrolled at Niagara. A large percentage of these students take advantage of the more than 100 extracurricular and cocurricular activities offered. Volunteer work in the community is popular among the students and enhances learning and community relations.

University sports teams compete on the Division I level and are members of the NCAA, the Metro Atlantic Athletic Conference and the Atlantic Hockey Association. Intercollegiate sports for men include baseball, basketball, cross-country, golf, ice hockey, soccer, swimming and diving, and tennis. Intercollegiate sports for women include basketball, cross-country, golf, lacrosse, outdoor track and field, soccer, softball, swimming and diving, tennis, and volleyball. Club sports include cheerleading, danceline, hockey, rugby, skiing, wrestling, and many others. The Kiernan Recreation Center offers a variety of sports and recreational facilities, including a multipurpose gymnasium, a swimming and diving pool, an indoor track, racquetball courts, free weight and Nautilus rooms, and aerobics rooms. There are several outdoor athletic fields as well as basketball and tennis courts.

Additional student services include the Student Health Center; the Office of Academic Support, which provides free tutoring services; and the Office of Career Services, which offers professional and career counseling. Other services include counseling, new student orientation, academic support, and veterans' affairs.

Niagara University's housing accommodations include five residence halls, a grouping of five small cottages, and a student apartment complex.

The University offers graduate studies in business, counseling, criminal justice, education, finance, interdisciplinary studies, information security and digital forensics, sport management and a Ph.D. in leadership and policy.

Location

Niagara University's picturesque 160-acre campus is located in the town of Lewiston, New York, two minutes off the I-190 on Route 104. The campus is situated on Monteagle Ridge overlooking the lower Niagara River, which connects the two Great Lakes of Erie and Ontario. The University's suburban campus setting is just a few miles from the world-famous Niagara Falls, 20 minutes from Buffalo, which offers a variety of cultural events, sports, and entertainment opportunities, and just 90 minutes from Rochester and Toronto, Canada's largest metropolitan area. In addition, the University is minutes away from the quaint village of Lewiston, New York, and the city of Niagara Falls, New York.

Majors and Degrees

The **College of Arts and Sciences** offers the Bachelor of Arts degree in art history with museum studies, chemistry, communication studies, English, environmental science, French, gerontology, history, international studies, liberal arts, life sciences, mathematics, philosophy, political science, psychology, religious studies, social sciences, sociology, and Spanish. The Bachelor of Science degree is awarded in actuarial science, biochemistry, biology (with a concentration in biotechnology), chemistry, computer and information sciences, criminal justice, environmental science, mathematics, nursing, psychology, and social work. This division also offers the Bachelor of Fine Arts degree in theatre studies (with concentrations in performance, design and production, and theatre specializations). Preprofessional programs are offered in dentistry, law, medicine, pharmacy, veterinary medicine, and Army ROTC. An Associate of Arts degree is available in general studies. Enrichment courses in fine arts and languages are also available. A combination five-year B.S./M.S. program is available to students in the criminal justice program; psychology majors can engage in a

six-year B.A./M.S. program in clinical mental health counseling; and an accelerated nursing program and an R.N.-to-B.S.N. program is offered for students who already have their R.N.

Preprofessional Partnerships: NU offers a number of preprofessional partnerships. These include a 3+4 partnership in pharmacy with the State University of New York at Buffalo (SUNY), a 2+3 partnership in pharmacy with Lake Erie College of Osteopathic Medicine (LECOM), a 3+4 partnership in medicine with LECOM, and a 3+4 partnership in dentistry with SUNY at Buffalo. Qualified premedical Niagara students are eligible to apply for the early assurance program sponsored by the SUNY at Buffalo.

Niagara University's **College of Business Administration** is accredited by AACSB International—The Association to Advance Collegiate Schools of Business and offers a B.B.A. and a combination B.B.A./M.B.A. degree (five-year program) in accounting. This division offers B.S. degrees in economics, finance, management (with concentrations in human resources, international business, and supply chain management), and marketing (with a concentration in food marketing), as well as a B.A. in economics. In addition, an A.A.S. degree can be earned in business. Students gain real-world experiences through internships, study abroad, and via cooperative education programs as well as research being conducted in several business-focused campus centers.

Holding the highest accreditations possible in both the United States and Canada—the United States Council for the Accreditation of Educator Preparation (CAEP) and Canada's Ontario College of Teachers—Niagara University's **College of Education** provides students with an option of earning dual certification to teach in both countries. The College of Education offers bachelor's degree programs leading to New York state initial certification in early childhood and childhood (birth–grade 6), childhood (grades 1–6), childhood and middle childhood (grades 1–9), middle childhood and adolescence (grades 5–12), special education and childhood (grades 1–6), special education and adolescence (grades 7–12), and in Teaching English to Speakers of Other Languages (TESOL). All education majors pursue an academic concentration to establish expertise in one of the following subject areas: business, English language arts, French, liberal arts, mathematics, social studies, and Spanish. Business education is offered only for grades 5–12. The academic concentrations in biology, chemistry, or liberal arts can only be pursued in the early childhood and childhood (birth–grade 6), and special education and childhood (grades 1–6). Most other states, and Puerto Rico, have reciprocity agreements with New York, so an NU education would qualify education majors to teach in those states as well.

The **College of Hospitality and Tourism Management** provides a career-oriented curriculum leading to a B.S. degree in three specific areas: hotel and restaurant management (with concentrations in food and beverage management; luxury hospitality operations; and hotel planning, development, and operations), sport management (with concentrations in sport operations and revenue management), and tourism and recreation management (with concentrations in event and meeting management and tourism destination management). The College of Hospitality and Tourism Management offered the world's first bachelor's degree in tourism. NU's hotel and restaurant program, the second oldest in New York state, was the seventh program nationally to be accredited by the Accreditation Commission for Programs in Hospitality Administration by the Council of Hotel, Restaurant, and Institutional Education. The College introduces students to a comprehensive body of knowledge about the hotel, restaurant, tourism, and recreational areas and applies this knowledge to current industry challenges. The College requires that its students accumulate 800 hours of industry-related experience. These and other practical experiences offer NU students the knowledge necessary to advance in the field. Students work with industry leaders in classroom projects, join academic clubs and professional organizations, and participate in special trips to trade shows and conventions and specially designed study-abroad experiences, making NU a national leader in the area.

For students who are undecided about which major to choose, Niagara University offers its award-winning **Academic Exploration Program (AEP).** AEP provides a structured opportunity for students to participate in a thorough, organized process of selecting a major that meets their academic talents and career goals while fulfilling requirements to graduate with classmates on time.

Academic Programs

Niagara University's curricula enable students to pursue their academic preferences and to complete courses that lead to proficiency in other academic areas. The Honors program provides special academic opportunities that stimulate, encourage, and challenge participants. In addition, an accelerated three-year degree program is offered to qualified students.

Niagara grants credit for successful scores on the Advanced Placement, College-Level Examination Program, and the International Baccalaureate tests.

Internships, research, and independent study are available in many academic programs. An Army ROTC program is also offered.

NU is fully accredited by the Middle States Association of Colleges and Schools. The University's programs in the respective areas are accredited by the Council for the Accreditation of Educator Preparation, AACSB International–The Association to Advance Collegiate Schools of Business, and the Council on Social Work Education. The chemistry department has the approval of the American Chemical Society. The travel, hotel, and restaurant administration program is accredited by the Commission for Programs in Hospitality Administration.

Off-Campus Programs

For those students who wish to study abroad, the University offers programs in Argentina, Australia, Chile, China, England, France, Ireland, Italy, Japan, Spain, Thailand, and many other countries. Students may choose from more than 200 programs in more than 30 countries available through the University's membership in the American Institute for Foreign Studies, Center for Cross-Cultural Study, College Consortium for International Studies, Global Learning Semesters, and Semester at Sea.

Academic Facilities

In recent years, Niagara University has experienced a process of transformation that has significantly developed the physical character of the University's campus and its 21st-century approach to teaching and learning.

The $33 million B. Thomas Golisano Center for Integrated Sciences offers 50,000 square-feet of learning space and cutting-edge equipment that encourages collaboration among scientific disciplines. The Academic Complex, the home to the College of Education and the College of Business Administration (Bisgrove Hall), is a state-of-the-art learning facility, with a simulated trading floor. The newly renovated and expanded Russell J. Salvatore Dining Commons features presentation-style cooking, a variety of comfortable seating options, and bold colors and design elements that create an inviting environment for NU students to gather and enjoy meals.

Costs

Tuition for 2017–18 was $30,500. Room and board (with a choice of meal plans) cost an additional $12,950 per year. Fees were estimated at $1,450 per year. Niagara estimates that an additional $2,500 to $3,050 per year is adequate for books, laundry, and other essentials, such as travel to and from home.

Financial Aid

Ninety-nine percent of the entering freshmen and transfer students received a financial aid package which may include merit-based scholarships, loans, grants, or campus employment. Students seeking financial aid should file the Free Application for Federal Student Aid (FAFSA). New York state residents should also file a Tuition Assistance Program (TAP) application.

Faculty

Niagara University has a dedicated, accessible faculty that genuinely cares about the academic and personal growth of their students. Their commitment to teaching is their primary concern. A student-to-faculty ratio of 12:1 and an average class size of approximately 20 allow personal attention and classroom interaction.

Admission Requirements

Niagara University welcomes students who have demonstrated aptitude and academic achievement at the high school level. The university has adopted a test-optional admissions policy for most first-year undergraduate applicants, beginning with the fall 2018 entry year. Niagara has joined a growing number of the nation's most competitive and well-respected institutions by giving students the option to submit or withhold standardized test scores (SAT/ACT) as part of their admissions application. The Office of Undergraduate Admissions will continue to accept standardized test scores from students who believe their results are reflective of their academic abilities to succeed at the university. If they feel that it doesn't reflect their ability and academic skills, they have the option of not submitting.

The few exceptions to this test-optional policy include students who are seeking entrance into a nursing or biology major, those who wish to be considered for Trustees or Presidential Scholarships, students looking to apply for science-related scholarships such as NUSURF (Niagara University Science Undergraduate Research Fellowship), and home-schooled students.

International students are required to submit the results of their TOEFL examination and a translation of their academic documentation. Interviews are recommended. Transfer students are accepted in any semester. (Transfer credit is evaluated individually by the dean of each division.) Students who complete high school in less than four years are eligible for early admission. Students may also apply under an early action program. Economically and educationally disadvantaged students from New York State are eligible to apply for admission through the Higher Educational Opportunity Program (HEOP).

Application and Information

Niagara operates on a rolling admission basis and adheres to the College Board Candidates Reply Date. Nursing and theatre applicants are encouraged to apply by mid-December of their senior year. A visit to the campus is recommended, and overnight accommodations in a residence hall are available through the Niagara Nights program.

Information on all aspects of the University can be obtained by contacting the Office of Admissions or by visiting www.niagara.edu.

Mark Wojnowski
Director of Admissions
Niagara University
Niagara University, New York 14109-2011
Phone: 716-286-8700
　　　　800-462-2111 (toll-free)
Fax: 716-286-8710
E-mail: admissions@niagara.edu
Website: http://www.niagara.edu
　　　　http://www.facebook.com/niagarau
　　　　http://twitter.com/niagarauniv
　　　　http://instagram.com/NiagaraUniversity

Adjacent to the international border between the United States and Canada, Niagara University's 160-acre campus runs along the top of picturesque Monteagle Ridge, overlooking the Niagara River gorge just 4 miles north of the world-famous waterfalls.

COLLEGE CLOSE-UPS

NORTHEASTERN UNIVERSITY
BOSTON, MASSACHUSETTS

 Northeastern University

★ To read more about this school, visit http://petersons.to/northeasternuniv

The University

There's a certain energy about Northeastern University. It comes from the bright, ambitious students, exhibiting a strong sense of purpose in the classroom and while working or studying abroad. In the city of Boston—the ultimate college town—and across the globe, Northeastern students challenge themselves intellectually, investigate career options, participate in community service, and graduate both personally and professionally prepared for their future careers and graduate school.

Northeastern is a leader in interdisciplinary research, urban engagement, and the seamless integration of classroom learning with real-world experiences. The academic curriculum is enhanced by experiential learning opportunities including undergraduate research, professional work experience, global programs, and service-learning options. Anchored by the world's largest, most innovative cooperative education program, Northeastern prepares students for a lifetime of achievement.

The current undergraduate enrollment of 18,107 is made up of students of all backgrounds and interests, giving Northeastern its distinctive culture. Students can join a cultural club, participate in cutting-edge research with faculty from various disciplines, or perform with an award-winning acapella group. They can travel to nearby New Hampshire or Vermont for a ski club trip, play varsity or club basketball, tutor children in the community, volunteer at a local soup kitchen, and more. Students have countless opportunities to make lifelong friendships, to try something brand new—a class, a sport, or a career path—to hone their leadership skills, and have fun. Quiet corners of the campus feel far from city streets and give students a secluded haven to read, write, or relax in and around the 73-acre campus, a dynamic and welcoming stretch of leafy green in the heart of Boston.

Location

Northeastern's residential campus is located in the center of Boston, where the distinctive neighborhoods of the Back Bay, South End, Fenway, and Roxbury meet. Over half of the student body lives on campus and many of the residence halls have amazing views of the Boston skyline.

The Back Bay area, known for its many cultural and educational institutions, is just steps away from Symphony Hall, the New England Conservatory of Music, the Museum of Fine Arts, and the Isabella Stewart Gardner Museum. The South End is home to elegant Victorian row houses, a vibrant arts scene, hidden gardens, and some of the finest dining in Boston. The Fenway area, with its beautiful rose garden, bicycle and jogging paths, and Fenway Park (home of the Boston Red Sox) is also just a few blocks away.

Majors and Degrees

Northeastern's undergraduate programs are divided among eight colleges and programs.

The College of Arts, Media and Design awards degrees in architecture; arts, media arts and design; communication studies; game design; journalism; media and screen studies; as well as music/music industry; music composition and technology; studio art; and theatre.

The D'Amore-McKim School of Business offers two degree options: the Bachelor of Science in Business Administration (B.S.B.A.) and the Bachelor of Science in International Business (B.S.I.B.), which includes language instruction as well as international study and work. D'Amore-McKim offers concentrations in accounting; entrepreneurship and innovation; finance; international business, with six concentrations; management; management information systems; marketing; and supply chain management.

The College of Computer and Information Science awards degrees in computer science and information science and also offers combined majors that pair computer science with biology; business; cognitive psychology; communication studies; computer engineering; cyber operations; digital art; environmental science; game design; interactive media; journalism; mathematics; music; music composition and technology; and physics; and pair information science with business; cognitive psychology; environmental science; and journalism.

The College of Engineering offers degrees in bioengineering; chemical; civil; computer; electrical; industrial; and mechanical engineering.

The Bouvé College of Health Sciences awards degrees in health science; nursing; pharmacy; and physical therapy. The college also offers a six-year Doctor of Pharmacy degree and a six-year program leading to a Doctor of Physical Therapy.

The College of Science awards degrees in applied physics; behavioral neuroscience; biochemistry; biology; biomedical physics; chemistry; environmental science; environmental studies; linguistics; marine biology; mathematics; physics; and psychology.

The College of Social Sciences and Humanities awards undergraduate degrees in African American studies; American Sign Language; Asian studies; criminal justice; cultural anthropology; economics; English; history; human services; international affairs; Jewish studies (combined major only); philosophy; political science; religious studies; sociology; and Spanish.

The Explore Program for undeclared students offers a wide array of academic opportunities designed to help students who want to explore their options before committing to any major(s). The program provides the support and guidance students need to discover and eventually choose one of Northeastern's undergraduate programs.

Within Northeastern's 175+ majors are more than 95 defined combined majors—unique, blended programs designed to allow students to explore multiple fields, all within one integrated academic plan.

Academic Programs

Award-winning faculty mentors are at the heart of a Northeastern education, as well as a rigorous and innovative curriculum, undergraduate research opportunities, and global and professional experiences that challenge and transform. Northeastern's innovative programs encompass a wide range of majors, concentrations, and interdisciplinary studies along with honors, pre-professional, and study abroad programs.

Northeastern's approach to educating its students is to integrate a challenging academic curriculum with experiential learning opportunities including research, global experiences, service learning, and the university's signature cooperative education program (co-op), enabling students to make deep connections between their field of study and the world around them. At Northeastern, Rigorous Academics + Immersive Experiences = Experiential Learning.

After completing their first year, Northeastern students integrate classroom learning with immersive six-month periods of full-time professional work, global study, service, or research experiences related to their major or interests. Northeastern's flexibility enables students to choose a four- or five-year path with up to eighteen months of experience, strengthening their professional network and giving them confidence—and a significant edge in the job market. Students learn what career is a good fit for them—and what careers are not—all before graduating. In addition, half of the students in co-ops are offered full-time jobs from their co-op employer.

Northeastern partners with over 3,350 co-op employers around the globe, including some of the world's largest and most reputable companies: Pfizer, John Hancock, Google, Fidelity Investments, ESPN, IBM, General Electric, Massachusetts General Hospital, Microsoft, NASA, Disney, and the Boston Globe, just to name a few. Experiential learning opportunities have been available in 136 countries around the world since 2006.

The University Honors Program allows a select group of students to participate in enriched opportunities and offers experiences that include honors sections of academic courses, seminars, independent research, and specialized study abroad programs.

Academic Facilities

Northeastern is home to over 50 research centers and undergraduates have ample opportunities to work alongside their professors to aid and conduct research on a variety of topics. The new 220,000 square-foot Interdisciplinary Science and Engineering Complex has further evolved Northeastern's research enterprise by providing state-of-the-art infrastructure and fostering collaboration across disciplines.

The university library system is comprised of Snell Library, a 240,000 square-foot central library on the Boston campus, the School of Law Library, and a small supplemental collection at the Nahant Marine Science Center. Snell Library houses 530,566 printed books, 589,334 e-books, 98,654 licensed electronic journal titles, and 81,493 streaming audio and visual titles (as of June 2016).

Northeastern University provides a broad range of academic and administrative computer resources to students, faculty, and staff members. Many computing resources are available, including an extensive wireless network, technology-assisted classrooms, computer labs, and the myNortheastern Admitted Student Portal, which allows students to access many administrative and academic functions online.

Costs

For 2017–18, tuition was $48,560, and room and board fees were $15,660. Regardless of time to degree, tuition is charged only while students are earning course credit.

Financial Aid

The university operates a substantial aid program designed to make attendance feasible for all qualified students. By coordinating the resources of the university and various public and private scholarship programs, the Office of Student Financial Services was able to provide more than $263 million in grant and scholarship assistance this past year. More than 75 percent of students receive some form of financial aid. Northeastern participates in all federal aid programs. Financial aid is based on need and academic merit and may consist of grants, loans, work-study employment, or any combination of the three. To apply, students must file the Free Application for Federal Student Aid (FAFSA) and a CSS PROFILE form with the College Scholarship Service by the priority filing date for their chosen application deadline.

Faculty

The university has more than 1,300 full-time faculty members with a wide variety of research and teaching interests and specialties. Academic advisors in each college work closely with students to assist them in developing programs suited to their interests and abilities. Co-op advisors assist students in resume-building, honing interview skills and tactics, and developing contacts with businesses and employers to support networking and professional opportunities.

Admission Requirements

Students may enter the university with advanced credit on the basis of test scores on Advanced Placement (AP) examinations, the International Baccalaureate (I.B.) examinations, or with successful completion of accredited college-level courses. In addition to the application for admission, prospective freshmen must submit official high school transcript(s) (or official GED score reports); official transcripts for any college-level coursework taken while a secondary-school student; written recommendations from their secondary school counselor and a teacher; and scores from the SAT (Northeastern's College Board code is 3667) or ACT, including the writing section. Please visit the university's website for additional admission details for specific student populations and transfer admissions requirements (northeastern.edu/admissions).

Application and Information

Admission to Northeastern is selective and competitive. For the freshman class entering in fall 2018, the university received approximately 62,000 applications for 2,800 seats in the freshman class. Students are reviewed in the context of their environment, with attention paid to their academic course selection and rigor, academic achievement, extracurricular involvement and impact, and their potential fit with Northeastern, including the demonstration of personal traits like leadership, adaptability, a global perspective, or an entrepreneurial spirit.

November 1 is the deadline for both the Early Action admission program and the binding Early Decision I program. Students who have carefully explored their college options and have decided that Northeastern is where they want to enroll may choose to apply under the Early Decision I program. Admitted Early Decision I students are required to pay a deposit by January 15. Beginning with fall 2018 entry, Northeastern is introducing the Early Decision II option; Early Decision II allows students who realize that Northeastern is their first choice later in the application process to still show their high level of interest. Early Decision II is a binding decision. The deadline for Early Decision II and the regular admission program is January 1. Admitted students are required to pay a deposit by May 1 to secure a place in the class. For transfer students, the admission deadlines are April 1 for fall and October 1 for spring admission. Fall transfer and spring admission decisions are made on a space-available basis and are released online by June 1.

Northeastern offers a variety of visit options including information sessions and campus tours. For more information, or to register, visit northeastern.edu/admissions/connect/visit.

For more information, students should contact:
The Office of Undergraduate Admissions
240 West Village F
Northeastern University
360 Huntington Avenue
Boston, Massachusetts 02115
Phone: 617-373-2200
E-mail: admissions@northeastern.edu
Website: northeastern.edu/admissions

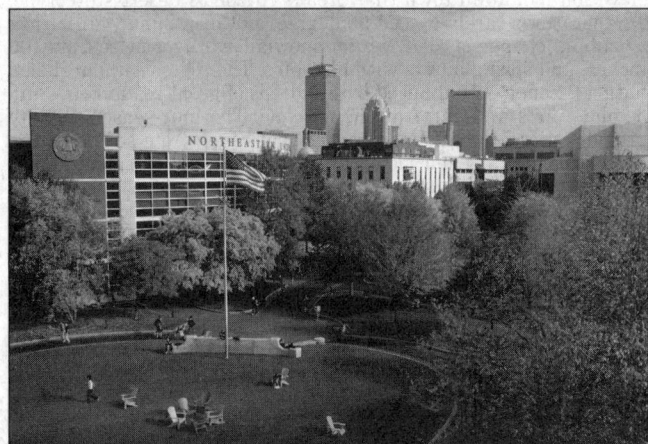

Northeastern's campus skyline and Centennial Common, a typical quad where students relax, study, and hang out with friends.

NORTHERN ARIZONA UNIVERSITY
FLAGSTAFF, ARIZONA

 To read more about this school, visit http://petersons.to/nau

The University

Founded in 1899, Northern Arizona University (NAU) is a fully accredited four-year public university centered on students. For those interested in a collaborative community with a breadth of stellar programs and a dedicated research agenda, NAU offers a comfortable university environment ideal for academic achievement, personal growth, professional outcomes, and adventure.

The university's Flagstaff campus offers the amenities of a big-campus environment with a small-campus feel—all in a beautiful mountain location that ranks among the best college towns in the nation. NAU also has innovative partnerships with numerous Arizona community colleges, which gives students affordable and convenient options for transferring into an NAU bachelor's degree program.

NAU offers a comprehensive range of nearly 100 majors to choose from and many nationally ranked programs taught by professors who recognize potential and will help students realize theirs. Students have an abundance of opportunities to participate in important research and creative and scholarly projects alongside faculty who bring their focus to their labs and their passion to the classrooms. Nearly 3,000 students participate in research and professional internships each year, placing them shoulder-to-shoulder at the brink of discovery. High-achieving students can even work simultaneously on select master's degrees and graduate in as few as five years with both a bachelor's and a master's degree. And students can find everything they need to accomplish their goals, including programs and support services that are second to none—from enrollment to graduation and beyond.

NAU also delivers a predictable price tag through its fixed tuition rate, known as The Pledge. Students who attend the Flagstaff campus will pay the same fixed tuition rate for up to four years with a no-increases guarantee. Students who live in one of 14 Western states can save nearly 40 percent on the out-of-state tuition rate through the Western Undergraduate Exchange (WUE). Every major is eligible for the WUE rate.

Location

With a population of around 70,000, Flagstaff is a vibrant high-elevation mountain town that breaks Arizona's desert stereotype. Temperatures rarely exceed 90 degrees in the summer, fall brings a brilliant change of color, winter snowfall averages more than 100 inches, and spring bursts with blossoms. The region's unparalleled natural scenery is enhanced by hundreds of great restaurants and a robust arts and entertainment scene. The four-season climate provides recreational opportunities that range from scenic hiking and biking to skiing and snowboarding. The campus sits just 75 miles south of the Grand Canyon—close enough that studies might bring students there to collect water samples from the Colorado River, discuss issues related to Native populations, participate in interactive painting workshops, or explore the art and culture of the region.

Flagstaff's charm, location, and recreational opportunities consistently pull in top honors and distinctions from national publications. Time. com named it one of the nation's happiest cities, and the American Institute for Economic Research's 2017 College Destinations Index named Flagstaff the No. 1 Best College Town in Arizona and No. 3 in the nation. *Outside Magazine* also has named Flagstaff among the best places to live in the United States. Prospective students can explore some of the most popular local sights through NAU's fully immersive online regional tour: nau.edu/explore.

In addition to Northern Arizona University's Flagstaff campus, NAU also has locations throughout the state that provide a convenient way for students to complete an NAU degree at an Arizona community college. Online options also allow students to take classes that work with their schedule.

Academics

NAU offers nearly 100 bachelor's degrees, about 64 master's degrees, 12 doctoral degrees, and a wide range of minors, certificates, and emphases, so students are sure to find a program that's right for them. Majors and programs are organized by academic discipline under nine colleges: the College of Arts and Letters; the College of Education; the College of Engineering, Informatics and Applied Sciences; The College of Forestry and Natural Sciences; the College of Health and Human Services; the College of Social and Behavioral Sciences; The W. A. Franke College of Business; the Honors College; and the Graduate College. Some of the university's most popular majors include biomedical science, criminology and criminal justice, nursing, mechanical engineering, and elementary education.

Through the Honors College, students can pursue a rewarding and enriching academic path that emphasizes small, interactive classes where students gain critical-thinking skills that appeal to employers and graduate schools. Academically motivated students are inspired by the meaningful engagement found by living and working among a group of motivated students who share a passion for learning.

To complete a bachelor's degree at NAU, students must complete 120 units of credit, including all liberal studies and capstone requirements, and all requirements for a student's specific academic plan. Other requirements, such as transfer credit restrictions and minimum GPA, also apply. Detailed information can be found at nau.edu/academics.

Beyond the Classroom

A degree from NAU represents a quality educational experience—one that incorporates a practical learning approach beyond any textbook. Nearly 600 NAU students each year travel to partner institutions in one of 61 foreign countries for a study-abroad experience. Those wishing to stay closer to home can study at one of 200 U.S. institutions through the National Student Exchange program. An internationalization strategy at NAU incorporates global cultures into every discipline. And the Interdisciplinary Global Programs in Business, Engineering, and International Affairs infuse language, culture, and a year abroad into students' studies—participants graduate with two degrees: one in their field of study and one in their chosen foreign language.

A signature of the NAU undergraduate experience is a focus on engaged and active learning. Nearly 3,000 students each year work alongside skilled faculty and mentors who provide practical research opportunities. More than 1,000 students convene each spring for the Undergraduate Symposium, a large-scale event where students share their research and discoveries and present scholarly and creative work to their peers, professors, and the Flagstaff community.

NAU also takes advantage of its prime location with world-class outdoor education opportunities. An interdisciplinary Grand Canyon semester offers students immersion in the science, culture, and politics of one of the truly unique regions of the U.S. Flagstaff is the world's first International Dark Sky City and offers unparalleled night skies and stargazing facilities for astronomical research, including the Discovery Channel Telescope, the world's fifth-largest. And the 50,000-acre Centennial Forest offers forestry majors and students in other environmental studies programs the chance to conduct research and practice maintenance of a variety of ecosystems.

Facilities

With nearly 90 percent of freshmen choosing to live on campus, students begin to build their community the moment they arrive at NAU. Freshman housing options are based upon each student's academic interests, so they select a room in the Residential College that aligns with their major and career interests and live alongside others who are on a similar journey. Multiple Academic Success Centers on campus provide distinct types of tutoring, most at no cost. And the 225,000-square-foot Cline Library offers an array of services, research materials, and study spaces, and students can reserve rooms, check out laptops, and get help with technology or writing.

The visually striking, five-story Science and Health Building serves as a symbol of the university's rise to scientific and research prominence. This is where students interested in medicine, dentistry, research, or science education will take some of their first steps toward a professional career. The university's one-of-a-kind Native American Cultural Center was built with input from 22 tribes and reflects NAU's commitment to Native American students and to helping others learn more about these cultures.

NAU's Aquatic and Tennis Complex attracts international athletes and Olympic teams for high-altitude training, and a world-class recreation facility at the Health and Learning Center offers a 38-foot climbing wall, an indoor jogging track, a fully equipped weight room, cardio studio, and much more.

A visit to campus is the best way to learn more about the university's impressive facilities; for those who can't make it to Flagstaff in person, NAU's online virtual tour is the next best thing: nau.edu/virtualtour.

Costs

NAU tuition and fees for 2018–19 are $11,564 per academic year for Arizona residents and $25,828 for nonresidents. Under the Western Undergraduate Exchange (WUE) program, students from 14 qualifying states pay a tuition rate nearly 40 percent lower than the out-of-state rate. The 2017–18 WUE tuition and fee rate is $16,759 per academic year. Tuition rates are set each spring by the Arizona Board of Regents. Room, board, books, transportation, and personal expenses vary by student and are not included in the tuition costs.

NAU makes financial planning for college easier with The Pledge, a four-year fixed-tuition guarantee. Students who attend on the Flagstaff campus will pay the same fixed-tuition rate for up to four years. In addition, students with a meal plan will have the same rates for up to two years. More details of The Pledge can be found at nau.edu/pledge.

Financial Aid

Students are automatically considered for merit scholarships when they apply and have submitted their test scores. Arizona residents might be eligible for the Lumberjack Scholars Award, which covers up to 100 percent of the cost of in-state tuition. Nonresidents might be eligible for a number of awards including the President's Excellence Scholarship, valued at $36,000 over four years. NAU's friendly financial aid staff is available to help students explore other opportunities such as private scholarships, grants, and loans in order to make their education as affordable as possible. More details regarding financial aid can be found at nau.edu/finaid.

Faculty

Northern Arizona University is designed for discovery. The faculty and staff care about student success and encourage students to push past their limits and develop new strengths. From biology to social sciences, professors weave interactive learning into NAU's curriculum, providing students with the hands-on experience they need to succeed and opportunities to make original contributions to a field of study.

NAU professors from a variety of disciplines are among the leading experts in their fields, such as astronomy professor David Trilling, who is one of the world's foremost asteroid researchers and works on several NASA-funded projects investigating hundreds of asteroids, including those that could strike Earth. Biology professor Kiisa Nishikawa's muscle function theory is improving prosthetic devices and neuromuscular disease treatment. And entomology professor Rich Hofstetter studies how loud rock music might slow the infestation of bark beetles, which destroy pine trees and increase wildfire danger in Southwestern forests.

Student Clubs and Organizations

Getting involved in campus life is one of the best ways students can gain leadership skills and define their own NAU experience. Northern Arizona University offers more than 375 clubs and organizations ranging from sport clubs and intramurals to sororities and fraternities. There is also a wide range of leadership, academic, and service organizations related to almost every hobby, passion, or academic interest students might have.

Studies have shown that students who are involved in campus activities are more likely to be successful; it's also a great way to meet new friends. NAU students can join organizations such as First Jacks, which empowers first-generation college students toward personal and academic success; or find a sense of *Ohana*, or family, with the HAPA Hawaiian Club. The university's thriving intramural sports program ranges from favorites such as basketball and soccer to unique sports such as Canoe Battleship and even Quidditch. NAU's ultra-competitive ice hockey team, the IceJacks, is one of nearly 40 club sports and ranks among the top teams in the American Collegiate Hockey Association's Western region. Whatever a student's interest, pursuits, or background, there is a club or organization offering a sense of community and a chance to get involved.

Admission Requirements and Application Information

NAU applicants will be offered admission if they demonstrate a 3.0 high school core GPA and have no deficiencies in the 16 required college preparatory courses. Students will be considered for admission if they have a 2.5 high school core GPA and no more than one deficiency in any two areas of the college preparatory courses.

Students can apply online. They are required to access their high school transcripts and self-report them on the online application. A $25 application fee is required, and NAU also requests that students send ACT and/or SAT scores in order to be considered for scholarships. Deadlines and additional details are available online at nau.edu/admissions.

Northern Arizona University
Undergraduate Admissions and Orientation
P.O. Box 4084
Student and Academic Services Building (#60)
Flagstaff, Arizona 86011-4084
Phone: 888-628-2968 (toll-free)
Fax: 928-523-6023
E-mail: admissions@nau.edu
Website: nau.edu

NORTHERN KENTUCKY UNIVERSITY

HIGHLAND HEIGHTS, KENTUCKY

The University

Northern Kentucky University (NKU) was founded in 1968 and is the newest of Kentucky's eight state universities. Nestled in a quiet suburb, NKU is just minutes from the entertainment and career opportunities of downtown Cincinnati. NKU has an enrollment of more than 14,500 students from forty-five states and sixty-one countries and is accredited by the Southern Association of Colleges and Schools. The Salmon P. Chase College of Law is accredited by both the American Bar Association and the Association of American Law Schools.

There are more than 220 student organizations and NKU's athletic teams compete in the NCAA Division I Horizon League Conference. Intercollegiate sports are offered for men and women in basketball, cross-country, track, golf, soccer, and tennis; for men in baseball; and for women in fast-pitch softball and volleyball. Intramural activities vary by semester, but include basketball, dodgeball, field hockey, flag football, ice hockey, racquetball, soccer, softball, taekwando, volleyball, and many others. A complete list can be found online at http://campusrec.nku.edu.

Majors and Degrees

NKU offers 72 bachelor's degrees, 2 associate degrees, 22 graduate programs, 10 doctoral and post master's programs, the Juris Doctor, as well as 28 graduate certificates.

Academic Programs

NKU operates on a semester calendar. To receive a bachelor's degree, students must complete a minimum of 120 credit hours. At least 60 credit hours are required for the associate degree.

The University offers a variety of career planning and placement, internship, independent study, work-study, and cooperative-education programs. There is also an advising, counseling, and testing Center available. Other programs include an honors program, a program that allows for the dual enrollment of high school students, a program where students can combine their career interests in the liberal arts and engineering fields, and University 101, an orientation program for freshmen and transfer students.

NKU recognizes credit earned through the Advanced Placement (AP) Program and the general, subject, and institutional tests of specific College-Level Examination Program (CLEP). A maximum of 45 credit hours may be applied toward the bachelor's degree from the AP and CLEP examinations. The International Baccalaureate program allows students to earn credit in science, mathematics, psychology, and languages.

Off-Campus Programs

More than 330 students participated in study-abroad programs in twenty-six countries worldwide.

Academic Facilities

Among the academic facilities at NKU are an anthropology museum, a biology museum, and an art gallery with rotating exhibits. NKU also has a laser projection planetarium; laboratories for nursing, respiratory care, and radiologic technology; the 9,000-seat BB&T Arena; and the James C. and Rachel M. Votruba Student Union, a student-centered facility, and focal point for campus programs and student organizations.

NKU's Griffin Hall, the home of the College of Informatics, is designed to help students interested in communication and media, computer science, information technology, or management information systems become the new generation of professionals who will build the region's information economy. The W. Frank Steely Library contains 311,155 book titles and maintains 1,729 paper periodical subscriptions (additional periodicals are available in electronic format). Computer laboratories offer students opportunities to learn and utilize a variety of software programs. The Computer Science Department and Criminal Justice Department have collaborated to offer students a computer forensics minor to teach students how to handle digital evidence and how to present such evidence in court.

Costs

Tuition and fees for 2018-2019 were $9,360 for Kentucky students, $13,520 for metro students, and $18,720 for nonresidents. Other costs included $7,700–$9,800 for room and meals, about $850 for books and supplies, and $3,000 for miscellaneous expenses.

Financial Aid

Northern Kentucky University awards more than $6 million in academic scholarships each year to the incoming freshman class. The University awards scholarships to highly motivated students who demonstrate strong academic performance. Students who achieve a 2.5 GPA and a 21 ACT or 1060 SAT are considered for academic awards. The University offers numerous scholarship levels. Each scholarship level has merit guidelines that students must meet to qualify. To be considered to academic scholarships, interested students need to apply for admission by February 15 (based on availability of funds). For fall 2018, there is no separate scholarship application for general Northern Kentucky University academic scholarships. Students who qualify for a scholarship receive an award letter upon acceptance to NKU. Prospective students can visit scholarships.nku.edu for information on additional scholarship opportunities that require an application, letters of recommendation, or an essay. There is no deadline for the University's financial aid application; however, students who wish to receive institutional aid must apply by February 1 for priority consideration. Applicants are notified of acceptance on a rolling basis.

Faculty

More than 82 percent of the faculty members at NKU hold a doctoral degree or the terminal degree in their field. Classes are small, with an average class size of 24 and a student-faculty ratio of 18:1. All classes are taught by faculty members; no classes are taught by graduate assistants.

Student Government

Student Government (SG) is the elected student assembly at Northern Kentucky University. It is the official student voice on campus and represents the student viewpoint on University committees. All SG meetings are open, and students are encouraged to attend.

Admission Requirements

Incoming freshmen must submit an application for admission; arrange for the official ACT, SAT, or COMPASS score report to be sent; and request that the high school send an official transcript. In order to be considered for regular admission, a student must meet precollege curriculum requirements for Kentucky and institutional admission standards. Out-of-state applicants must also meet the Kentucky precollege curriculum requirements.

Based on the review of official test results and the precollege curriculum, students are admitted into one of two categories: regular admission or admission with conditions. Students who have two or more deficiencies are encouraged to retake the ACT or SAT so an additional review can be completed. Students with two or more deficiencies may be asked to submit an essay, letters of recommendation, and an activities portfolio before an admission decision

can be rendered. Students with two or more deficiencies who are offered admission will be required to participate in the Pathfinders Program, which is designed to enhance student engagement and provide tools needed for future academic achievement. The program includes: mandatory advising, completion of University 101 (Introduction to College) course, participation in study tables, tutoring, and college success workshops. Some degree programs require that students meet additional criteria; more information is available in the current catalog (http://www.nku.edu).

Application and Information

The $40 paper application fee may be waived for applicants with demonstrated need. The fall semester early action and scholarship deadline is February 15, assured consideration deadline is February 15, enrollment confirmation deadline is May 1, and the final deadline is July 1. The priority application deadline for the nursing program is January 31. The priority application deadline for the respiratory care program is February 15.

For more information, students should contact:
Office of Admissions
Northern Kentucky University
Highland Heights, Kentucky 41099
Phone: 859-572-5220
      800-637-9948 (toll-free)
E-mail: beanorse@nku.edu
Website: http://admissions.nku.edu
      http://www.facebook.com/nkuedu
      http://twitter.com.nkuedu

Northern Kentucky University's modern campus is set in Highland Heights, just minutes from downtown Cincinnati.

NORTHERN VERMONT UNIVERSITY
JOHNSON, VERMONT AND LYNDONVILLE, VERMONT

 For more information, visit http://petersons.to/NorthernVermontU

The University

Set in the heart of Vermont's mountains, Northern Vermont University (NVU), with two campuses, at Johnson and Lyndon, and an online division, guides curious, motivated, engaged students on their path to success and their place in the world. The university boasts a 95 percent job placement rate for its graduates. NVU's 2,500 plus students hail from Vermont, New England, and around the world.

On July 1, 2018, Johnson State College and Lyndon State College joined to become Northern Vermont University. By combining more than 200 years of history in liberal arts and professional learning, NVU and its two campuses offer expanded access to a faculty with a broad range of expertise and experience.

Students collaborate with, and learn from, a network of peers and staff. Members of the strong alumni network live all over the world. On these close-knit campuses, relationships last a lifetime. Alumni help graduates get a foot in the door to launch their professions.

NVU offers in-demand degrees in business, criminal justice, education, psychology and human services, and specialized degrees in animation and illustration, atmospheric sciences, climate change science, electronic journalism arts, fine woodworking and furniture design, music business and industry, mountain recreation management, studio arts, and theater.

NVU students enroll at either campus. Students can take classes at both, on campus and via online and telepresence classrooms.

NVU–Lyndon: The Lyndon campus, located in Vermont's Northeast Kingdom, offers distinct professional programs based in a liberal arts core, where every degree is infused with career-ready skills. Programs such as atmospheric sciences, mountain recreation management, electronic journalism arts, music business and industry, and exercise science prepare students for career success through real-world experiences such as internships and practicums.

Music business and industry interns can be found working on concert tours for world-famous musicians. Atmospheric sciences students regularly take first place in national competitions. Electronic journalism arts students routinely win national awards for their daily live news broadcasts—including a coveted Emmy award.

NVU–Johnson: The Johnson campus, designated by COPLAC as Vermont's premier public liberal arts institution, offers an immersive, high-impact, liberal arts experience that prepares students for meaningful careers and lifelong growth. Students are prepared to thrive in an ever-changing world.

Faculty members are active scholars and researchers committed to student success. Cross-disciplinary learning—through research, internships, student teaching, and other forms of experiential learning—enhances the student experience. Environmental and social awareness is a fundamental component of an NVU–Johnson education.

Location

NVU and its two campuses are located in the northern tier of Vermont. The 350-acre Johnson campus sits on a breathtaking hilltop amidst the Green Mountain range. Situated near Stowe, the campus is 1 hour from Burlington (Vermont's largest city), 3.5 hours from Boston, 1.5 hours from Montreal, and has access to six major ski resorts.

The modern 174-acre Lyndon campus is in Lyndonville, high on a beautiful hillside overlooking Burke Mountain in the heart of Vermont's scenic Northeast Kingdom. Nearby are two major ski areas and the Kingdom Trails mountain biking network. Lyndon is easily accessible from all points by Interstate 91, 3 hours from Boston and Springfield, Massachusetts, and 2.5 hours from Montreal.

Majors and Degrees

NVU offers bachelor's degrees in accounting, animation and illustration, anthropology and sociology, art, atmospheric sciences, biology, business, childhood education, cinema production, climate change science, communications and community media, computer information systems, creative writing, criminal justice, early childhood education, electronic journalism arts, elementary education, English, environmental science, exercise science, explorations/undecided, fine woodworking and furniture design, global studies, graphic design, health science, history, interdisciplinary studies, liberal studies, mathematics, media arts, mountain recreation management, music, music business and industry, music education, musical theater, natural sciences, outdoor education, political science, psychology, psychology and human services, secondary education, sport management, studio arts, sustainability studies, and wellness and alternative medicine. NVU offers online bachelor's degrees in business, early childhood education, interdisciplinary studies, professional studies, psychology, and wellness and alternative medicine.

Associate's degrees are offered in business administration, cinema production, computing, electronic journalism arts, fine woodworking and furniture design, general studies, human services, management, mathematics, music business and industry, photography, pre-nursing, special education, technical theater, visual communications, and visual arts.

There are graduate programs in counseling, education, liberal arts, and studio arts.

Academics

Established in 1828, NVU–Johnson is designated by COPLAC as Vermont's premier public liberal arts institution with curriculum in professional programs and liberal arts and sciences.

Lyndon was established in 1911. Today, NVU–Lyndon is best known for innovative professional programs that combine real-world experience and career-ready skills, with a traditional education in the liberal arts.

NVU operates on a two-semester calendar plus a summer session and a two-week winter term. To graduate with a bachelor's degree, students must complete 120 credit hours and meet university and program requirements. Sixty credit hours are required for associate's degrees. Incoming students are tested for competence in writing and mathematics; deficiencies must be made up in noncredit classes during the first two semesters.

NVU's Academic Support Centers, Career Services, Financial Aid Offices, Student Life, and Health Services are just some of the entities that serve the needs and promote the well-being of students. Complete information can be found at NorthernVermont.edu.

Off-Campus Programs

Out-of-classroom and off-campus study is an integral part of the curriculum in the form of paid and unpaid internships, site visits, hands-on projects, research, independent study, field trips, and domestic and international study-away programs.

Academic Facilities

The NVU–Johnson campus has well-equipped facilities for arts, sciences, computing, and traditional classroom-based learning. The campus has one large lecture hall, a telepresence classroom, a geology lab, a chemistry lab, and an exercise physiology lab. There are seven computing labs for student use, including two all-Mac labs for media arts students. The recently renovated Visual Arts Center hosts facilities for traditional photography and ceramics, as well as two painting studios and a sculpture studio. Performing arts and theater tech students make their home in Dibden Center for the arts, which houses a 500-seat theater, practice rooms, and a MIDI lab and recording studio. The campus student center offers a game room, fireplace lounge, and a performance space for smaller events. The library holdings consist of more than 111,000 volumes, 6,500 e-books, 384 print journals, and 36,000 e-journals.

The NVU–Lyndon campus is modern and well-equipped. There are smart classrooms, two lecture halls, six computer classrooms, six science labs, and two general computer labs. There is a digital media, graphic design, video editing, and photo lab; a GIS-mapping lab; comprehensive weather center, atmospheric science lab, and observation deck; two exercise science labs; a recording studio/music business and industry lab; an instructional materials center for education majors; a psychology lab and reading lab; and the News7 broadcast production studio. The Alexander Twilight Theatre and Moore Community Room provide flexible space for gatherings, activities, and performances of all kinds. The library holdings include more than 60,000 print volumes and 100,000 managed electronic and print resources, including periodicals, e-books, and e-reference sources; and 10,000 audio visual materials including music, films, and documentaries.

Costs

The 2018–19 tuition for Vermont residents is $10,944 per year; for nonresidents, it is $24,264. The NEBHE regional program allows for a $6,500 discount for New England students in eligible programs (program eligibility by state can be found at NorthernVermont.edu/FinancialAid); there are also regionally based discounts ranging from $4,500–$6,500 for non-NEBHE students. Room and board (21-meal plan) for one academic year is $10,598. Required fees, not including health and accident insurance or the orientation/matriculation fee, total $1,130. Total expenses for a Vermont resident living on campus are $22,672; for a nonresident, $35,992. Complete information on costs can be found at NorthernVermont.edu/Tuition.

Financial Aid

Financial aid is available in the form of loans, grants, and campus employment under the Federal Work-Study program. Approximately 89 percent of the student population receives some type of financial aid from institutional and outside sources. Applicants for aid are required to complete the Free Application for Federal Student Aid (FAFSA). NVU offers merit-based scholarships as well.

Faculty

Northern Vermont University's faculty consists of 94 full-time and 168 part-time across the two campuses. The majority of NVU faculty hold the highest degree in their field. Some are successful entrepreneurs, offering real-world expertise to back up their classroom teaching. Faculty across both campuses are involved in research and offer research opportunities to NVU students.

Faculty members serve as academic advisors and mentors to students and student organizations. Student evaluation of teaching is a formal process and is used in personnel decisions.

Student Life

A full slate of cultural activities such as movies, lectures, theater, dance, and music keep students entertained. Campus events range from the intellectual to the physical, with abundant opportunities for learning and fun. A rich mix of off-campus travel, adventure programming, and community service is offered to enrich life outside the classroom.

There are more than thirty student organizations on each campus, including the campus radio stations; theater and dance groups; and numerous sports, social, service, and academic clubs.

Outdoor activities are around every corner. Students enjoy the three nearby ski areas, on Burke Mountain, Smugglers' Notch, and Jay Peak; run white water rivers; and bike Kingdom Trails, one of the best mountain biking networks in the U.S. The Long Trail System and other walking, hiking, and cross-country ski trails are nearby. On campus, there are indoor climbing centers, disc golf, ropes courses, terrain parks, biking and hiking trails, and skate parks.

On the Johnson campus, there are four residence halls and college apartments for both graduate and undergraduate students. Students who live on campus eat at the Stearns Dining Hall and the Common Grounds Cafe. All students are allowed to have vehicles on campus.

At Lyndon, there are eight residence halls, including a 132-unit, apartment-style hall for juniors and seniors. Students who live on campus eat at the Stevens Dining Hall and the Hornet's Nest Snack Bar. All students are allowed to have vehicles on campus.

Athletics

NVU boasts two athletic departments, one for each campus. Athletes compete in Division III at the varsity level, for either the Johnson Badgers or the Lyndon Hornets. Johnson Badgers: basketball (men, women), cross-country (men, women), golf (men), lacrosse (men), soccer (men, women), softball (women), tennis (men, women), track and field (men, women), triathlon (women), and volleyball (men, women). Lyndon Hornets: baseball (men), basketball (men, women), cross-country (men, women), lacrosse (men, women), soccer (men, women), softball (women), tennis (men, women), track and field (men, women), and volleyball (women). As Hornets or Badgers, the teams will even play each other!

Admission Requirements

NVU emphasizes academic success as reflected on high school or college transcripts, and social and academic potential as reflected in a letter of recommendation. NVU seeks applicants whose academic record reveals maturity and motivation as well as a sense of responsibility and leadership. International students can find detailed information on the university's website. The SAT is optional. Complete information about admissions requirements is available at NorthernVermont.edu/Apply.

Admission requirements for transfer students are the same as those for first-year applicants; an official transcript must also be obtained from each college-level institution that the applicant has attended.

Application and Information

Interested students can apply online at NorthernVermont.edu/Apply. A nonrefundable $50 fee must accompany each application. Northern Vermont University also accepts the Common Application.

For further information, students should contact:

Northern Vermont University
E-mail: Admissions@NorthernVermont.edu
Website: NorthernVermont.edu

Northern Vermont University–Johnson
Office of Admissions
337 College Hill
Johnson, Vermont 05056
Phone: 800-635-2356

Northern Vermont University–Lyndon
Office of Admissions
P.O. Box 919
1001 College Rd.
Lyndonville, Vermont 05851
Phone: 800-225-1998

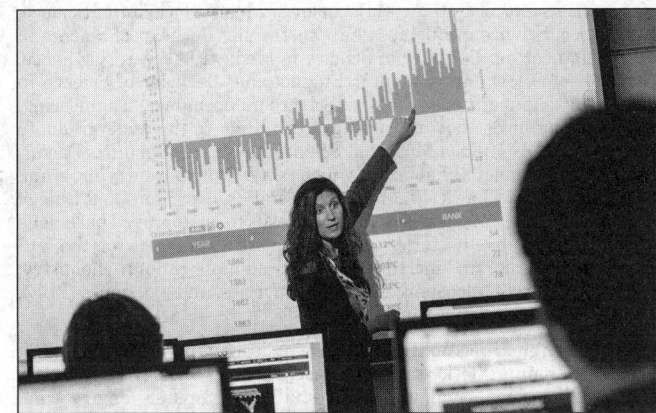

Climate Change Science is just one of the cutting-edge degrees offered at Northern Vermont University.

OHIO NORTHERN UNIVERSITY
ADA, OHIO

The University

Ohio Northern University (ONU) has a 94 percent job and graduate school placement rate. Its long-standing success is partly because of excellent professors, partly because of ambitious students, and partly because the University has always been rooted in the future. At ONU, students move toward a career long before they graduate—and ONU's alumni successes prove it. With top-ranked programs and opportunities outside the classroom, any path a student chooses at ONU will be grounded in concrete applications for the future. Established in 1871 and comprised of five colleges (Arts & Sciences, Business Administration, Engineering, Pharmacy, and Law), ONU's beautiful residential campus is made up of more than sixty modern residences and academic buildings and provides a vibrant campus experience.

Students can choose from a variety of campus activities including more than 200 student organizations; four national sororities and six national fraternities; fine arts, music, and theatrical events; and intramural and club sports. Residence hall living is an integral part of the educational program, contributing to a student's personal development. There are nine residence halls on campus as well as eight campus apartment complexes and an Affinity Housing complex.

The ONU Polar Bears compete successfully at the NCAA Division III level in twenty-three varsity sports as part of the highly respected Ohio Athletic Conference. ONU has twelve men's teams (baseball, basketball, cross-country, football, golf, lacrosse, soccer, swimming and diving, tennis, indoor and outdoor track, and wrestling) and eleven women's teams (basketball, cross-country, fast-pitch softball, golf, lacrosse, soccer, swimming and diving, tennis, indoor and outdoor track, and volleyball).

Location

Ohio Northern University's campus is situated on 342 beautiful acres in the village of Ada (population 5,500). Located in northwestern Ohio, ONU is easily accessible by major highways and conveniently located near major cities such as Columbus, Dayton, Toledo, and Fort Wayne, Indiana.

Majors and Degrees

Ohio Northern University offers the undergraduate degrees: Bachelor of Arts, Bachelor of Fine Arts, Bachelor of Music, Bachelor of Science, Bachelor of Science in Business Administration, Bachelor of Science in Civil Engineering, Bachelor of Science in Medical Laboratory Science, Bachelor of Science in Computer Engineering, Bachelor of Science in Electrical Engineering, Bachelor of Science in Mechanical Engineering, and Bachelor of Science in Nursing. In addition to the undergraduate programs, ONU offers a Master of Science in Accounting; Juris Doctor; Doctor of Pharmacy (Pharm.D.), which is a 0-6, direct entry program; and the Master of Laws (LL.M.) in Democratic Governance and Rule of Law. The 3+3 Law Admissions Program leads to an approved bachelor's degree plus a juris doctorate degree. Majors considered for the 3+3 Admissions Program include business administration; chemistry; English; history; philosophy; philosophy, politics, and economics (PPE); political science; religion; and sociology.

Majors are offered in accounting; advertising design; applied mathematics; art education; athletic training; biochemistry; biology; chemistry; civil engineering; communication studies; computer engineering; computer science; construction management; creative writing; criminal justice; early childhood education; electrical engineering; engineering education; engineering exploratory; environmental and field biology; exercise physiology; forensic biology; French; German; graphic design; history; international theatre and production; language arts education; literature; management; manufacturing technology; marketing; mathematical statistics; mathematics; mechanical engineering; medical laboratory science; middle childhood education; molecular biology; multimedia journalism; music; music education; musical theatre; music performance; nursing; pharmaceutical and healthcare business; pharmacy; philosophy; philosophy, politics, and economics; physics;

political science; professional writing; psychology; public health; public relations; religion; risk management and insurance; social studies; sociology; Spanish; sport management; studio arts; technology education; theatre; youth ministry; undecided business; undecided general studies; and undecided sciences.

Special preprofessional programs are available in dentistry, law, medicine, occupational therapy, physical therapy, physician assistant, seminary, and veterinary medicine. Teacher licensure programs are offered at the early childhood, middle childhood, adolescent/young adult, and multiage levels within 16 programs and two endorsement areas.

Changes in programs of study are updated at www.onu.edu.

Academic Programs

The Getty College of Arts & Sciences creatively combines a traditional liberal arts education with cutting-edge preprofessional studies. The college offers more than 50 majors in 17 academic departments, and students can earn a Bachelor of Arts, Bachelor of Fine Arts, Bachelor of Music, Bachelor of Science, Bachelor of Science in Medical Laboratory Science, or Bachelor of Science in Nursing.

Thirteen students in the sciences have been honored by the Barry M. Goldwater Scholarship and Excellence in Education Foundation in the past ten years. The college has also been recognized as one of the top 200 programs in the nation for creative students in *Creative Colleges: A Guide for Student Actors, Artists, Dancers, Musicians and Writers*.

Working closely with dedicated faculty members, students complete the general education requirements, delve deeply into advanced courses, and engage in high-impact learning through research, internships, practicum experiences, study abroad, and more.

The Dicke College of Business Administration focuses on creating ethical, entrepreneurial, and professional business and civic leaders. The college offers a rigorous academic curriculum with signature programs in pharmaceutical and healthcare business, and risk management and insurance. Internships are required by the college and are available year-round. There are international programs, including study abroad, work abroad, and study tours. An office of experiential learning supports students looking for these opportunities. The course of study for the Bachelor of Science in Business Administration includes a four-year business core experience themed around strategic business planning. Personal attention and mentoring from faculty members, small intimate classes, and active student organizations combine with an emphasis on experiential learning, global awareness, and the entrepreneurial spirit. The college is accredited by the AACSB International—The Association to Advance Collegiate Schools of Business. The Dicke College of Business Administration is ranked by *Bloomberg Businessweek* among the top 50 undergraduate business programs in the United States and the top private school business program in Ohio.

The T. J. Smull College of Engineering is noted for its hands-on learning; small, intimate classes; dedicated, accessible professors; and world-class, top-ranked instruction. Ranked twenty-ninth in the nation for undergraduate engineering programs by *U.S. News & World Report*, ONU's engineering and computer science programs prepare graduates who think critically, lead confidently, and have solid technical foundations upon which to build successful long-term careers. From strong lab components to a host of experiential learning opportunities, ONU's faculty is committed to helping its students achieve their educational goals and realize their dreams. The college features six accredited, disciplinary majors in civil, computer, electrical, and mechanical engineering; computer science; and engineering education, a degree option supporting the demand for high school math teachers with engineering degrees.

The courses for the first academic year are essentially the same for each degree program, offering students an easy track to move from one program to another if initially uncertain which disciplines they prefer to study.

An optional five-year co-op program is available for students in each program, provided they maintain a minimum 2.5 GPA. The college focuses on high-impact learning as an essential part of an engineering education; thus, in addition to a co-op program, students apply their classroom learning in freshman design projects, senior capstone projects, national design competitions, and numerous engineering projects in community service (EPICS). Further, many opportunities are available for valuable work experience through the co-op and internship programs, with a historically high job-placement rate for graduates.

For more than 130 years, the Raabe College of Pharmacy has offered distinctive, challenging, and comprehensive training for some of the nation's most talented pharmacists. This University signature program features a six-year Doctor of Pharmacy (Pharm.D.) degree accredited by the American Council on Pharmaceutical Education. This program is direct-entry, admitting students immediately from high school into the college's professional program. This approach enables students to take pharmacy courses from the very first day. A rigorous curriculum utilizes an innovative modular format to organize learning around the human body systems and patient care implementation.

Cutting-edge clinical facilities include the Pharmacy Skills Center, where students access state-of-the-art compounding/counseling pods with portable OTC simulation stations. Students gain considerable experience through a strong undergraduate research program and may pursue minors or dual majors in other areas. Faculty members are teaching-focused but remain current in their research disciplines. Upon graduation, students are well schooled in every aspect of pharmacy and have a high placement rate.

Off-Campus Programs

Many majors may take part in study-abroad programs developed in consultation with faculty members. Field experiences and internships are available to most majors. Externships are required of all pharmacy majors and place students in retail and clinical experiences. Teacher licensure requires one semester of primary or secondary classroom teaching experience under the supervision of practicing teachers. Additional opportunities include computer science and mathematics co-op programs (professional practice), engineering co-op programs (professional practice, domestic and international), and an honors program. All off-campus learning experiences carry credit.

Academic Facilities

Among the nineteen modern academic buildings on campus, the newest is the Mathile Center for the Natural Sciences, which expands the science-learning environment. This 95,145-square-foot student-centered academic research and learning facility blends hands-on teaching excellence with advanced technology in a functional modern environment.

The College of Business Administration's Dicke Hall offers students a modern setting for high-tech classrooms, meeting rooms and a 150-seat lecture forum.

ONU's Heterick Memorial Library and the Taggart Law Library provide information resources and services to support course offerings and foster independent study.

The Freed Center for the Performing Arts houses Communications and Theatre Arts classrooms and features a 550-seat theater/concert hall, a 120-seat studio theater, and television and radio production facilities. WONB-FM is the commercial-free voice of ONU.

Costs

Tuition and fees charges for the 2018–19 year are $32,260 for the colleges of Arts & Sciences and Business Administration; $36,810 for the College of Engineering; and $37,980 for the College of Pharmacy. These totals do not include room and board.

Financial Aid

Even with one of the highest returns on investment in the nation, ONU invests more than $45 million toward merit-based scholarships and need-based resources. To be considered, the student should submit the FAFSA to the University along with the admission application.

Faculty

More than 210 full-time faculty members bring extensive academic, work, travel, and life experience to their classrooms. Ohio Northern values excellence, innovation, technology, diversity, and its people. With an 11:1 student-faculty ratio, students get lots of personal attention from professors who are passionate about teaching and mentoring.

Student Government

The Student Senate provides self-government in many areas of student life and seeks to further ideals of character and service to the University. The Student Senate serves as the official representative group of the student body to the University administration and agencies in matters pertaining to the student body.

Admission Requirements

High school students applying for admission to the University should present an official transcript indicating at least 16 total units of study, including work in specific academic areas as indicated by each college. Applicants are also required to submit scores on the ACT and/or SAT. For scholarship purposes, the traditional sections of the ACT and the SAT are considered. An on-campus interview is also recommended.

Application and Information

In the colleges of Arts & Sciences, Business Administration, and Engineering, a student's file is considered complete when it contains the application, official high school transcript, and ACT and/or SAT scores. The College of Pharmacy requires a personal statement and a recommendation in addition to the previous items.

The College of Pharmacy's application deadline is December 1 for entering freshmen. A campus visit is strongly encouraged for consideration for admittance into this college.

Requests for catalogs or additional information should be directed to:

Office of Admissions
Ohio Northern University
525 South Main Street
Ada, Ohio 45810
Phone: 888-408-4668 (toll-free)
Fax: 419-772-2821
E-mail: admissions-ug@onu.edu
Website: www.onu.edu
　　　 www.facebook.com/ohionorthern
　　　 www.twitter.com/ohionorthern

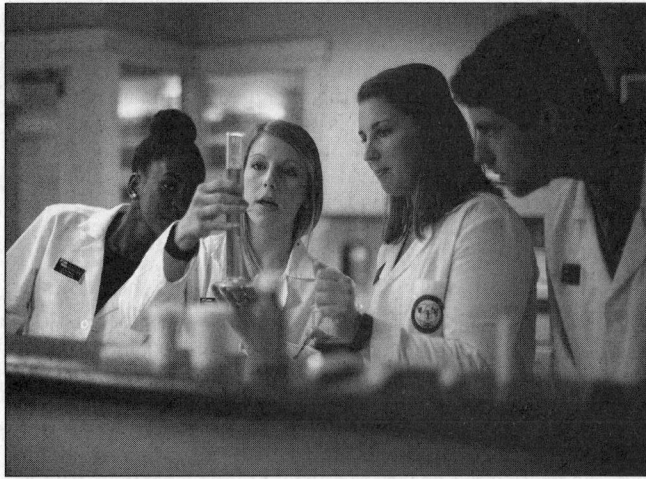

Pharmacy students (from left) Ruth Aminu, Emily Somerfield, Alicia Sawmiller, and Caleb VonStein work in the Pharmacy Skills Center of the Ohio Northern University College of Pharmacy. An Ohio Northern University education is based on experiential, hands-on learning, and students are guided by professors who know them personally and care about their lifelong success.

OHIO WESLEYAN UNIVERSITY

DELAWARE, OHIO

 For more information, visit http://petersons.to/ohiowesleyanu

Ohio
Wesleyan
University

The University

Ohio Wesleyan University (OWU) offers a liberal arts education that combines personal attention and guidance, a vast array of majors, global travel, research, and internships to help students find their passion and make it their career. Collaborating with professors on research projects, obtaining grants to explore new academic terrain, gaining practical experience from internships, and participating in sports and clubs are just some of the opportunities available at the university.

Students, who represent 45 U.S. states and territories and 26 countries, all participate in The OWU Connection, a personalized and expertly guided four-year program that includes a guaranteed, signature experience (travel, research, or internship) and opportunities to create a degree plan from more than 90 academic majors and 60 minors.

Because of its commitment to excellence in liberal arts education, Ohio Wesleyan is ranked among the top universities in the nation. *U.S. News & World Report* ranked it one of the best liberal arts colleges in its 2017 edition of America's Best Colleges. *The Princeton Review* listed it among the Best 381 Colleges and Best Midwestern colleges. *Forbes* magazine named it the most entrepreneurial college in Ohio and number 17 in the nation. Ohio Wesleyan is also features in the influential guidebook, *Colleges that Change Lives.*

Ohio Wesleyan's focus on providing rigorous academics and transforming theory into practice ensures that students graduate with the skills and experience that impress employers and graduate schools. Upon graduation, students join a network of successful alumni and obtain positions with employers in many industries, which recently have included JPMorgan Chase, Nationwide Financial, Lee Strasberg Theatre & Film Institute, Teach for America, Audubon Zoo, Democratic Party of Virginia, Cleveland Clinic, Cincinnati Children's Hospital, Cardinal Health, Battelle, Boehringer Ingelheim, M.D. Anderson Cancer Center, and graduate schools such as Harvard Law, Yale, University of Pennsylvania, University of Chicago, Boston University, Ohio University College of Osteopathic Medicine, and University of California Davis.

Location

Ohio Wesleyan is located in Delaware, Ohio, in the Midwestern region of the United States. Its beautiful 200-acre campus has 61 buildings and 11 locations on the National Register of Historic Places.

Students walk easily to downtown Delaware, where they find a variety of coffee shops, restaurants, and shopping venues. Attractions include the Strand Theatre and Whit's Frozen Custard, and events such as monthly First Friday celebrations and Farmers' Market Saturdays.

The campus is only 30 minutes from Columbus, Ohio, the 14th-largest city in America, with many recreational options including professional sports, restaurants, shopping, major concerts, and art galleries. It also provides outstanding work and internship opportunities.

Majors and Degrees

OWU's 90 academic majors combine focused study with expert faculty, real-world internship and research opportunities, and the expansive understanding that comes from studying the liberal arts. With the university's flexible structure, 27 percent of OWU students pursue at least two majors, one of the highest percentages in the country.

Available majors include: accounting; ancient studies; anthropology and sociology; astrophysics (B.S. and B.A.); biochemistry: general or ACS certified; biology; black world studies; botany; business administration; chemistry: general or ACS certified; classics; communication; comparative literature; computer science; dance; data analytics; earth science; East Asian studies; economics; education: early childhood, middle childhood, or special education; English: creative writing or literature; environmental science; environmental studies; finance economics; film studies; fine arts: art education, art history, studio art (B.A.), or studio art (B.F.A.); French; genetics; geography; geology (B.S. and B.A.); German; health and human kinetics: general, exercise science, health promotion, sports and exercise management; history: general or education; interdisciplinary (self-designed); international business; international studies: general, developing countries, or Europe; journalism; Latin American studies; management economics; mathematics: general or statistics; medieval studies; microbiology (B.S. and B.A.); Middle Eastern studies; music: B.A., composition, education, or performance; neuroscience; nutrition; philosophy; physics (B.S. and B.A.); planetary science; politics and government; pre-law; pre-medicine/pre-dentistry; pre-optometry; pre-public administration; pre-theology; pre-veterinary medicine; psychology; religion; renaissance studies; social justice; sociology/anthropology; Spanish; theatre; urban studies; women's and gender studies; and zoology: general or pre-professional.

Academic Programs

The OWU Connection, Ohio Wesleyan's unique academic program, connects traditional liberal arts with real-world experience. Interdisciplinary classes and programs explore areas where different fields blend; travel-learning courses augment classroom learning with international travel and study; Theory-to-Practice Grants allow students to conduct research and gain experience in settings around the globe; and meaningful internships and signature projects help students coalesce four years of learning. Only through The OWU Connection can students craft a personalized degree plan from more than 90 academic majors and with expert guidance from faculty mentors. Each student is guaranteed a signature research, travel-learning, or internship experience.

Ohio Wesleyan's Leland F. and Helen Schubert Honors Program offers students the opportunity to tailor their education to specific needs and interests, pursue advanced topics, master complex analytical and research skills, work independently, and widen career options.

Off-Campus Programs

More than half of all OWU students enrich their campus experience with travel-learning to more than 30 countries. OWU offers semester-long programs in Salamanca, Spain; Tanzania; and more. Internship programs include New York Arts and Wesleyan in Washington. Travel-Learning Courses go to Argentina, Ireland, Germany, Japan, Costa Rica, and more. Theory-to-Practice Grants fund student projects around the world.

Costs

The general fees at Ohio Wesleyan are comparable to those at institutions of similar size and reputation. For the 2017–18 academic year, residential tuition was $44,430; standard room was $6,450; average board was $5,500; and the activity fee was $260 for a total of $56,640.

Financial Aid

Ohio Wesleyan makes every effort to make earning a degree from a top-tier university affordable. About 97 percent of students receive financial aid from one or more of the following sources: need-based grants, government-sponsored student loans, merit scholarships and awards, and/or student employment through the Federal Work-Study and OWU Institutional Student Employment programs.

For 2018–19, prospective students who meet just two criteria—a minimum 3.4 GPA and an 1150 SAT or 23 ACT score—will receive $30,000 Branch Rickey Scholarships when they enroll at Ohio Wesleyan.

To be considered for all merit scholarships, the admission application must be received by the Regular Decision deadline of March 1. Priority consideration is given to applications received by the Early Action deadline of January 15. To be considered for all available need-based financial aid, the Free Application for Federal Student Aid (FAFSA) should be submitted.

Faculty

Students learn in small classes from faculty members who are accomplished teachers, excellent researchers, and skilled practitioners. There are no graduate teaching assistants at OWU. Ohio Wesleyan students consistently rate the faculty highly for quality of teaching, excitement about their academic disciplines, mentoring, commitment, and accessibility. There are 146 full-time faculty members. The average class size is 17 students, and the student-faculty ratio is 11:1. Every year students select 10 favorite professors to deliver 3-minute i^3 lectures, which can be seen on the OWU website.

Student Life

Ohio Wesleyan provides a diverse community where 30 percent of students are multicultural or come from other countries. Nearly every student lives on campus all four years, creating a close-knit community. Housing options include residence halls, Greek houses, and small living units (SLUs) that allow students passionate about a topic to live and learn together.

OWU offers 25 varsity sports and is a competitive member of the NCAA Division III and North Coast Athletic Conference.

A myriad of resources ensure that students can create a rewarding and memorable college experience. OWU is proud to offer its students more than 150 clubs and organizations; fraternities and sororities; fine, performing, and visual arts opportunities; spirituality and religious programs; community and global service opportunities; diversity and multicultural programs; and campus events and celebrations throughout the school year.

Admission Requirements

Ohio Wesleyan accepts the Common Application and the OWU Online Application. The application fee of $35 is waived for online applications. In addition to the application, OWU requires a secondary school report and counselor recommendation; official high school transcript; optional SAT or ACT scores (SAT code: 1594; ACT code: 3316), and an admission essay. A teacher evaluation form is strongly encouraged.

Ohio Wesleyan no longer requires high school students who have a cumulative GPA of 3.0 or higher by the end of the junior year to submit SAT or ACT scores for admission consideration. OWU believes that mastery of a rigorous college preparatory curriculum is a more significant predictor of college success than a single test on a single day. The university's holistic review process also considers recommendations from teachers and the quality of extracurricular involvement.

However, to be considered for a Branch Rickey Scholarship, or for invitation into the Honors Program, applicants may want to include test scores if they are above Ohio Wesleyan's average test scores.

Application and Information

The Early Decision application deadline is November 15, with notification November 30. Applicants also must complete and submit the Early Decision form with their application. The deadline for Early Action I is December 1, with notification December 15. The Early Decision II deadline is January 15, with notification January 30. The regular decision application is March 1, with notification March 15.

For more information, prospective students should contact:

Ohio Wesleyan University
61 South Sandusky Street
Delaware, Ohio 43015
Phone: 800-922-8953
Fax: 740-368-3314
E-mail: owuadmit@owu.edu
Website: www.owu.edu

Ohio Wesleyan's 200-acre campus offers endless opportunities for students to fully experience the richness and connectedness of a liberal arts education.

OLIVET NAZARENE UNIVERSITY
BOURBONNAIS, ILLINOIS

 To read more about this school, visit http://petersons.to/olivetnazareneuniversity

The University

Olivet Nazarene University (ONU) is a private, Christian liberal arts university with a strong emphasis on academic excellence and Christ-centered living. Olivet's 275-acre Bourbonnais campus offers world-class facilities for learning, personal development, entertainment, and all aspects of student life. The atmosphere promotes academic rigor, fun, relationship building, career preparation, and spiritual growth.

The student body of nearly 5,000—including 2,900 undergraduates—represents more than 40 denominations, most U.S. states, and more than 20 countries. Olivet operates on a two-semester schedule from August to May, and two summer sessions are available.

Faculty, staff, and administration are dedicated to teaching, encouraging, and mentoring each student as a whole person—academically, socially, and spiritually. Olivet's high retention, graduation, and employment/placement rates demonstrate the University's commitment to student success.

Outside the classroom, Olivet students participate in more than 90 clubs, ministries, honor societies, and organizations, including 20 intramural sports, the 195-member marching band, two orchestras, 21 musical ensembles, and theatre groups.

ONU competes in 21 intercollegiate men's and women's sports as a member of the National Association of Intercollegiate Athletics (NAIA), the National Christian College Athletic Association (NCCAA), and the Chicagoland Collegiate Athletic Conference (CCAC).

A signature structure on the Olivet campus is the 3,046-seat Betty and Kenneth Hawkins Centennial Chapel—the venue for chapel services, concerts, and campus events, and home to the Kankakee Valley Symphony Orchestra.

Facilities also include the 168,000-square-foot Douglas E. Perry Student Life and Recreation Center, featuring an eight-lane running track, two swimming pools, a four-story rock climbing wall, basketball courts, and other amenities that include workout facilities used by the Chicago Bears of the National Football League. The ONU campus is home to the Chicago Bears' summer training camp, which annually draws national and local media coverage as well as thousands of fans to Olivet's campus.

In addition to traditional undergraduate programs, Olivet offers 20 advanced degree programs, including the Doctor of Education in Ethical Leadership (Ed.D.) and degree-completion continuing studies programs through the School of Graduate and Continuing Studies (SGCS). Programs are designed to facilitate a seamless transition from undergraduate to master's programs. As it strives to meet the needs of adults returning to school, the SGCS also helps working adults complete degree requirements without interrupting their employment. Courses and programs also provide resources to help enhance students' personal and professional lives.

The SGCS offers courses on the main campus in Bourbonnais; Rolling Meadows and Oak Brook, Illinois; Indianapolis, Indiana; Grand Rapids and Grand Ledge, Michigan; Hong Kong; and at more than 100 learning locations throughout Chicagoland and the Midwest. Students benefit from robust online programming, as well as courses offered in more than 150 churches, schools, hospitals, and other locations convenient to their homes or workplaces.

The University is also home to Shine.FM, a top-rated contemporary Christian radio network. Olivet-owned Shine.FM broadcasts over the air in the Chicago area, Indianapolis, Northwest Indiana, and Lansing, Michigan, as well as online at Stations.Shine.FM; and via the Shine.FM app. Olivet students studying multimedia communication work alongside seasoned professionals in operating the station.

Location

Olivet's main campus is located just 50 miles south of Chicago's Loop, in the historic village of Bourbonnais, Illinois. The area offers shopping, restaurants, entertainment, and outdoor recreation through the Kankakee River State Park system.

Students benefit from ONU's proximity to Chicago's cultural, sports, and entertainment attractions. Numerous and varied professional internships and employment opportunities are additional advantages.

Majors and Degrees

Olivet confers Bachelor of Arts (B.A.) and/or Bachelor of Science (B.S.) degrees in more than 140 areas of study (majors, minors, and concentrations), including accounting, actuarial science, art, art–drawing/illustration, art–digital graphics, art–painting, art–photography, art education, athletic coaching, athletic training, biblical languages, biology, biology teaching, business administration, business–healthcare management, business–human resource management, business–management, business–not-for-profit/philanthropy, business–operations management, business–public administration, chemistry, chemistry–biochemistry, chemistry–forensics, chemistry teaching, child development, children's ministry, Christian education, communication studies, communication teaching, computer science, corporate communication, criminal justice, criminal justice–law enforcement, dietetics, early childhood education, earth and space science teaching, economics, economics and finance–applied economics, economics and finance–Certified Financial Planning, economics and finance–corporate finance, elementary education, engineering–architectural, engineering–chemical, engineering–civil, engineering–computer, engineering–electrical, engineering–environmental, engineering–industrial, engineering–mechanical, engineering–software, English, English as a Second Language, English as a Second Language teaching, English education, environmental science, exercise science, family and consumer sciences, family and consumer sciences–family studies, family and consumer sciences–hospitality, family and consumer sciences–education, fashion merchandising, finance, French, general studies, geography, geological science, Greek, health education, Hebrew, history, history teaching, information systems, information technology, intercultural studies, interior design, international business, leadership studies, legal studies, literature, management information systems, marketing, marketing–commercial graphics, marketing–international, marketing–management, marketing–public relations, mass communications, mathematics, mathematics education, military affairs, military science, ministerial missions, multimedia communication, multimedia communication–film studies, multimedia communication–journalism, multimedia communication–live event media management, multimedia communication–ministry media, multimedia communication–radio/record industry, multimedia communication–TV/video production, music, music composition, music education, music ministry, music performance, musical theatre, nursing, pastoral ministry, philosophy, physical education and health teaching, physical sciences, political science, pre-art therapy, pre-dental, pre-law, pre-medicine, pre-optometry, pre-pharmacy, pre-physical therapy, pre-physician's assistant, pre-seminary, pre-veterinary, psychology, psychology teaching, public policy–domestic, public policy–foreign, public relations and strategic communication, recreation, recreation/sport/fitness, religion, religion–biblical studies, religion–philosophy, religion–theology, religious studies, social science, social science education, social work, sociology, Spanish, Spanish education, special education, sport management–administration, sport management–marketing, theatre, writing, youth ministry, and zoology.

Academic Programs

Olivet is dedicated to "Education with a Christian Purpose." This commitment to Christ-centered learning mandates nothing less than the highest quality academic programs. Olivet's liberal arts curriculum requires that students complete 45 to 58 hours of general education courses. With the addition of major and minor programs of study, students must complete a minimum of 128 credit hours to earn a bachelor's degree. Credit may be earned through advanced placement (AP) and College Level Examination Program (CLEP) tests. Students may also participate in the on-campus U.S. Military Reserve Officers' Training Corps (ROTC).

Olivet offers 10 distinct accelerated bachelor's/master's (4+1 style) programs, in which students can obtain a bachelor's and a master's degree in approximately five years. These programs include majors in accounting; business administration; management information systems; economics/finance (with concentrations in certified financial planning, corporate finance, or public economics); international business or marketing leading to a Master of Business Administration; or a Master of Arts in Pastoral Ministry, Family Ministry, or Urban Ministry

In fine arts, Olivet's School of Music earned the Apple Distinguished Program designation for 2014 through 2016 for its iLearn@Olivet initiative, which provides an iPad to every member of the Tiger marching band and all music majors, as well as faculty and staff members. The Department of Art and Digital Design and the School of Education also utilize iPad and Apple technology for instruction and student projects.

Off-Campus Programs

Each semester, ONU offers off-campus study programs, including the Council for Christian Colleges and Universities BestSemester programs, such as American Studies Program in Washington, D.C.; Australia Studies Centre; Contemporary Music Center; Latin American Studies Program; Los Angeles Film Studies Center; Middle East Studies Program; Oxford Summer Programme; Uganda Studies Program; and Northern Ireland Program.

Other study programs include AuSable Institute of Environmental Studies, International Business Institute, ISA Spain (Barcelona), Nazarene International Language Institute, Oxford Summer Program, Quetzal Education Research Center (QERC), Environmental Studies (Costa Rica), Tokyo Christian University, and a wide range of locations available through Veritas Abroad and International Studies Abroad. Costs are often comparable to a semester at Olivet, and students earn academic credit for these programs. Some financial aid is available.

Numerous short-term educational and mission-oriented trips are available to ONU students during spring and summer breaks. More than 200 Olivet students participate in mission trips each year.

Academic Facilities

ONU continues to expand and refine its main campus facilities to anticipate the needs of the steadily increasing student population.

In 2014, to accommodate the growing engineering program, the University completed an expansion and renovation of Reed Hall of Science. The building now has a three-story wing dedicated to studying technology and innovation, as well as state-of-the-art engineering design labs for students in the Walker School of Engineering. Plans call for another Reed expansion—for the natural sciences program—as well as expansion and renovation of Larsen Fine Arts Center and Wisner Hall of Nursing and Health Sciences.

State-of-the-art academic facilities include Benner Library and Resource Center, information hub for digital and print research and communication; and Strickler Planetarium, renovated in 2008 with the same technology as Chicago's Adler Planetarium (one of the Midwest's few all-digital planetaria).

Costs

The cost of an Olivet education continues to be competitive for private colleges nationwide. A full year's tuition for 2017–18 was $32,950, based on 12 to 18 credit hours. Room and board are estimated at $7,900 for the year, based on double occupancy and a meal plan. Additional fees are $990 for the year. Olivet offers an interest-free payment plan with four equal payments per semester.

Financial Aid

Olivet participates in all federal and state financial aid programs while also offering institutional need-based assistance and various academic and extracurricular scholarships. For school year 2017–18, Olivet awarded more than $110 million in financial aid, with 99 percent of ONU's traditional undergraduates receiving a collective total of $60.9 million in federal and state grants and institutional grants and scholarships. The University participates in all federal and state financial aid programs. To apply for aid, students must fill out the Free Application for Federal Student Aid (FAFSA). Priority deadline for FAFSA filing is December 15. The University creates a financial aid package once a student is an accepted ONU applicant.

Faculty

For more than 120 full-time ONU faculty members, teaching is a ministry. These dedicated Christian leaders are the key to excellent education inside and outside the classroom. Olivet's 17:1 student-faculty ratio gives faculty the opportunity to teach, mentor, and encourage students with personal attention. Faculty members are deeply committed and involved in campus life, whether sponsoring social organizations and clubs, participating in talent shows, tutoring in their offices, or talking with students over lunch in the dining room. Faculty and ONU staff members also work side-by-side with students in local and regional ministry projects. Beyond spiritual modeling, course instruction, and service roles, faculty members maintain an agenda for professional growth through staying current in their respective fields of study, professional leadership, and published scholarship projects.

Student Government

The Associated Student Council (ASC) is the ONU student government organization on campus. The executive council consists of a president; executive officers for student relations, graphic design, marketing and content management, finance, events and programming, and spiritual life; executive editor of *The GlimmerGlass* student newspaper; and executive editor of the *Aurora* yearbook. These students work alongside the University's administrative team to ensure the welfare and promotion of campus activities and organizations.

Admission Requirements

Admission to Olivet is moderately difficult. Students are considered for admission on the basis of high school GPA and ACT or SAT scores. For international students, TOEFL results are also considered. Students with low test scores and/or GPA may be admitted on a provisional basis. A campus visit and interview are strongly recommended for all prospective students.

Application and Information

Applications are processed on a rolling basis. Application deadline is May 1. For some scholarships, an early decision is required. Students may apply through Olivet's website or by mail. The process includes the written or electronic application, high school transcripts, and ACT or SAT scores. An enrollment deposit is collected to prioritize student housing and class registration.

For more information or to arrange a campus visit, contact:

Office of Admissions
Olivet Nazarene University
One University Avenue
Bourbonnais, Illinois 60914
Phone: 800-648-1463 (toll-free)
E-mail: admissions@olivet.edu
Website: http://www.olivet.edu
  http://www.facebook.com/olivetnazareneuniversity
  http://twitter.com/OlivetNazareneU and
      http://twitter.com/ONUInsider
  http://www.youtube.com/olivetnazareneu
  http://instagram.com/olivetnazarene

Olivet Nazarene University is a place where top-tier academic instruction, social connection, and spiritual development intersect to prepare students for their careers, futures, and lives of service to God and humanity.

PACE UNIVERSITY
NEW YORK CITY AND WESTCHESTER, NEW YORK

 To read more about this school, visit http://petersons.to/paceuniversity

The University

Founded in 1906, Pace University is a leading private metropolitan university that offers an exceptional liberal arts education combined with superior professional preparation, two strategic undergraduate New York locations, and robust scholarships and financial aid. The diverse student population of 8,914 undergraduates (6,284 in New York City and 2,630 in Westchester) is enrolled in more than 3,000 courses across 100-plus majors and combined, accelerated bachelor's and graduate degree programs. These are offered through five undergraduate schools and colleges: the Lubin School of Business, the Dyson College of Arts and Sciences, the Seidenberg School of Computer Science and Information Systems, the School of Education, and the College of Health Professions. Pace facilitates more than 5,000 internships, co-op experiences, practicums, field experiences, and clinical assignments every year.

Many student-led clubs and organizations are active on the campus, including the Pace Advertising Club, African Students Association, the Pace Association for Collegiate Entrepreneurs, the Student Government Association, and the Collegiate Psychology Club. Pace also offers many campus activities, including student government associations, fraternities, sororities, two campus newspapers, two literary magazines, two yearbooks, and two campus broadcasting systems. Athletic facilities are available for students, and intercollegiate sports include baseball, basketball, cross-country, cheerleading, dance, women's field hockey, football, lacrosse, women's soccer, women's softball, swimming and diving, and women's volleyball.

The student body is diverse, representing forty-nine states, five U.S. territories, and more than 100 countries.

Location

Pace University is a multicampus institution with campuses in both New York City and Westchester, New York. Both locations are within reach of cultural, business, and social resources and opportunities. The New York City campus is located in the heart of the Financial District in lower Manhattan, and within a short walking distance of Wall Street and the South Street Seaport. Lincoln Center, Broadway theaters, museums, and many world-famous attractions are minutes away by public transportation. Located 35 miles north of New York City, the newly renovated Westchester campus offers a traditional college experience: state-of-the-art science and video production labs, competitive athletics, fraternities and sororities, and access to internship opportunities at many Fortune 500 companies.

Students can take courses at either campus, and housing is available in both New York City and Westchester residence halls.

Majors and Degrees

The following programs are offered at both the New York City and Westchester campuses. The Bachelor of Business Administration (B.B.A.) is offered with majors in accounting (with concentrations in forensic accounting and internal auditing), accounting–public, finance, general business, information systems, international management, management (with concentrations in business, entrepreneurship, health care, hospitality and tourism, and human resources), and marketing (with concentrations in advertising and integrated marketing communications, global marketing management, and sports marketing). In addition, a five-year combined B.B.A./M.B.A in public accounting is available for qualified students. The Bachelor of Arts (B.A.) degree is granted in adolescent education (with concentrations in biology, chemistry, earth science, English, history/social studies, mathematics, and Spanish), applied psychology and human relations, biology, childhood education, computer science, early childhood education, economics, environmental studies, film and screen studies, health science, history, information systems, liberal studies, mathematics, philosophy and religious studies, political science, and psychology. The Bachelor of Science (B.S.) degree is offered in biochemistry, biology, business economics, chemistry, computer science, criminal justice, economics, environmental science, health science, information systems, information systems, information technology, mathematics, professional computer studies, and professional studies.

Certain programs are available only on one campus. The B.S. programs in biology–pre-professional (occupational therapy, optometry, and podiatry) and forensic science; the B.B.A. programs in arts and entertainment management, and business analytics; the B.F.A. programs in acting, art, commercial dance, musical theater, and production and design for stage and screen; and the B.A. programs in acting; acting for film, television, voice-overs, and commercials; American studies; art; art history; communication science and disorders; communication studies; directing; English language and literature; language, culture, and world trade; global Asia studies; global professional studies; Latin American studies; modern languages and culture; peace and justice studies; sociology-anthropology; Spanish; stage management; teaching students with speech and language disabilities; theater arts (acting and design/technical); and women's and gender studies are offered only at the New York City campus. The B.A. programs in biological psychology, communication arts and journalism, communications, digital journalism, digital cinema and filmmaking, English, English and communications, education, global professional studies, and personality and social psychology, and the B.S. programs in nursing are available at the Westchester campus only.

Pace University offers a five-year engineering programs in cooperation with Manhattan College and Rensselaer Polytechnic Institute. Students attend Pace for three years and either Manhattan College or Rensselaer for two years. Upon successful completion, students receive a B.S. degree in chemistry from Pace and either a Bachelor of Chemical Engineering (B.C.E.) in chemical engineering from Manhattan or a B.S. degree in engineering from Rensselaer.

Academic Programs

The Pace Path is an innovative program unique to Pace University that helps each student become successful in college, career, and life. Each student develops strengths in managing oneself, interpersonal relations, and organizational awareness through co-curricular activities with an academic program. This is accomplished through collaboration with Pace faulty, advisers, staff, coaches, and mentors. The Pace Path is framed by Pace's historic mission of *Opportunitas* and prepares innovative thinkers through a powerful combination of knowledge in the professions, real-world experience, and rigorous liberal arts curriculum.

The Pforzheimer Honors College is a highly esteemed opportunity at Pace—a community of talented undergraduate scholars studying under the distinguished faculty of the University's five undergraduate schools and colleges. It is a place to excel and realize potential.

Pace University's internship program is nationally recognized and offers qualified students the opportunity to gain experience in their field of study while earning a four-year degree. Students can choose full-time, part-time, or summer positions working in an area directly related to their major course of study. Over 4,000 Pace students participate each year in internships, faculty-sponsored research, consulting projects, fieldwork, and practicums—Pace's Career Services team is one of the largest in the New York Metropolitan area.

Academic Facilities

Pace University opened its second new high-rise (34 stories) residence hall on its New York City campus in fall 2015. It is the tallest university residence hall in the world. In addition, there are brand new science labs, art studios, an honors student lounge, and School of Performing Arts studios. The Westchester campus had the most visible and dramatic changes with new modern residence halls, enlarged student centers, digital video/filmmaking facilities, new environmental center with indoor and outdoor classrooms, expanded athletic fields, and new field house.

Costs

For the 2018–19 academic year, undergraduate tuition is $43,624 per year for full-time study. The cost for an on-campus double-occupancy room and board is $16,600–$19,200, with different housing options available.

Financial Aid

Pace University strives to provide opportunities to students of diverse backgrounds and varied circumstances and is committed to offering financial aid to students to the fullest extent of its resources. University-sponsored scholarships are awarded to students on the basis of academic merit, service to the community, and financial need. The goal is to offer every student as much financial assistance as possible, based upon availability and need. Last year, ninety-two percent of first-year students received financial aid. Pace's comprehensive student financial aid assistance program includes scholarships, grants, on-campus employment, student loans (federal and alternative plans), and tuition payment plans. Pace participates in all federal financial aid programs and the New York State Tuition Assistance Program (TAP) and honors awards from other states' incentive grant programs.

Students should submit the Free Application for Federal Student Aid (FAFSA) by November 15 for priority consideration for the fall semester. Pace University's new Net Price Calculator (www.pace.edu/calculator) is an online tool designed to help students and their families estimate their financial aid package. Many find that Pace is actually more affordable than similar public and private colleges due to the scholarship and financial aid awards offered to families.

Faculty

First and foremost, Pace University professors are dedicated teachers. All Pace classes are taught by professors. Students will never take a course taught by a teaching assistant. Faculty members also bring real-world experience and scholarship into the classroom through their work with outside companies and organizations and by leading cutting-edge research projects. Faculty members come from the best graduate and doctoral programs in the country. Professors—90 percent of whom hold Ph.D.'s—have earned degrees from the University of Pennsylvania, Harvard, Brown, Columbia, and Yale. Pace professors work closely with students to not only broaden their academic horizons, but to show how their work in the classroom is applicable to their future careers.

Admission Requirements

A minimum of 16 academic units from an accredited secondary school, or equivalent, are required. Academic subjects in high school should be distributed as follows: 4 years of English, 3–4 years of college-preparatory mathematics, 2 years of foreign language, 3–4 years of history/social science, 2 years of laboratory science, and 2–3 units of academic electives. All domestic applicants are required to take either the SAT or ACT examination and have results forwarded to the University. International students are required to take the TOEFL, IELTS, or PTE.

Application and Information

Students can apply online at www.pace.edu/apply.

For more information contact:

Pace University
861 Bedford Road
Pleasantville, New York 10570-2799
Phone: 800-874-7223 (toll-free)
E-mail: infoctr@pace.edu
Website: http://www.pace.edu

PACIFIC UNIVERSITY
FOREST GROVE, OREGON

 To read more about this school, visit http://petersons.to/pacificuniversity

The University

Pacific University is a private, fully accredited university with more than sixty undergraduate fields of study and sixteen graduate and professional programs. With colleges in the Arts and Sciences, Business, Education, Health Professions, and Optometry, the University's four Oregon campuses draw more than 3,800 students.

Students come from around the United States and abroad for a wide variety of programs, but they share a common Pacific University experience: small classes, a nurturing environment, and personal attention. Students learn from the university's full-time faculty members, who are devoted to teaching and to forming close mentoring relationships with their students. Recent graduates at both the undergraduate and graduate level say that access to the high-quality faculty is a hallmark of the University.

As the first chartered university west of the Mississippi, Pacific University has a long history of excellence. At every level, its curriculum emphasizes real-world experience, service learning, and preparation to contribute to a global community.

The Forest Grove Campus is Pacific University's residential campus, where most undergraduate students study.

The campus is home to six residence halls and a student apartment complex; the newest residence hall opened in fall 2014. Many of the newer buildings feature double-occupancy rooms or suites, as well as shared study spaces, kitchens, and game rooms. The residential nature of the campus creates a vibrant living environment, where students develop close, lifelong friendships.

There are more than sixty student interest groups at Pacific University, including student media, academic societies, religious and political organizations, and service clubs. One of the largest student organizations, Na Haumana O Hawai'i, unites Pacific's significant population of students from Hawai'i and presents an authentic lu'au each year.

Pacific University also is a member of the NCAA Division III Northwest Conference. The campus athletic center houses a gymnasium, fitness center, state-of-the-art indoor field house featuring FieldTurf, handball/racquetball courts, wrestling room, and a sports medicine training facility. The Lincoln Park Athletic Complex, a partnership with the City of Forest Grove, features a 1,100-seat stadium with a nine-lane, 400-meter track, a FieldTurf soccer/football/lacrosse field, a Bond baseball field with turf infield, and a varsity softball field.

Almost a third of undergraduate students participate in varsity athletics. Men's sports include baseball, basketball, cross-country, football, golf, soccer, swimming, tennis, track and field, and wrestling. Women compete in basketball, cross-country, golf, lacrosse, rowing, soccer, softball, swimming, tennis, track and field, volleyball, and wrestling. Students also participate in junior varsity and club sports.

Informal sports also are a highlight of the Pacific University student experience. Students compete in intramural sports, and they also enjoy outdoor recreation opportunities through Outdoor Pursuits, which offers training, equipment, and organized trips for snowboarding and skiing, rock climbing, camping, kayaking, and much more. Students also can rent bicycles for a semester or for the year from Outdoor Pursuits to get around the bike-friendly Forest Grove area.

Locations

Pacific University was founded in Forest Grove, Oregon, in 1849. The historic college town, population 22,000, is now home to the 55-acre oak-covered campus on the west side of the Portland Metro Area. About 25 miles from downtown Portland and an hour from the Oregon Coast or Mount Hood, Forest Grove is the perfect home base for exploring the best of Oregon's urban and outdoor adventures.

Pacific University also offers health professions and graduate business programs on its growing campus in Hillsboro, Oregon, the fifth-largest city in the state. Located on the regional light-rail line in the Hillsboro Health and Education District, the Hillsboro Campus connects students with world-class learning opportunities and real-world experience as they connect with local businesses, hospitals, and nonprofit organizations.

Undergraduate and graduate teaching programs, as well as a Master of Social Work program, are offered at Pacific University's campus in Eugene.

Pacific University's newest campus is in Woodburn, one of the most diverse and fastest-growing communities in Oregon. The College of Education has a science, technology, engineering, and math teaching program embedded in the local school district and also offers a degree track in elementary education and English language learning at the Woodburn Campus.

Majors and Degrees

Pacific University is known for its excellent liberal arts foundation, as well as the superior preparation its students receive to go on to careers and advanced study. In particular, the University is heralded for its graduate programs in health professions, as well as its undergraduate preparation for healthcare fields and medical school. Pacific offers several advanced pathways into graduate programs, including three-year tracks to pharmacy and athletic training programs.

Pacific emphasizes the education benefits of research projects, internships, study-abroad experiences, and service learning. Most freshmen participate in a semester-long first-year seminar program designed to introduce students to college-level writing and research expectations. The core curriculum emphasizes writing, reasoning, and communication skills, as well as global perspectives and service. Pacific University also requires most students to complete a senior capstone, a year-long research project designed and implemented by students and culminating in a presentation to the University community.

Most undergraduate programs operate on a two-semester calendar with an optional short term and limited summer courses. Many graduate and professional programs have year-round calendars.

The Pacific University College of Arts and Sciences offers most undergraduate majors, including programs in anthropology/sociology, applied science, art, bioinformatics, biology, chemistry, computer science, criminal justice, dance, economics, English, environmental science, exercise science, history, international studies, mathematics, media arts, modern languages, music, philosophy, physics, politics and government, psychology, public health, social work, and theatre. The College of Arts and Sciences also offers a nationally recognized, low-residency Master of Fine Arts in writing program, and a new Master of Social Work program.

The College of Business offers undergraduate tracks in accounting, finance, international business, marketing, and business administration, as well as a one-year MBA program.

The College of Health Professions provides an undergraduate program in dental hygiene studies and an online bachelor of health science program, as well as graduate programs in athletic training, audiology, healthcare administration, occupational therapy, pharmacy, physical therapy, physician assistant studies, and professional psychology as well as a graduate-level certificate program in gerontology.

The College of Education offers an undergraduate major in education and learning, as well as a Bachelor of Education in elementary education and English language learning. Graduate programs in the College of Education include a fifth-year Master of Arts in Teaching, a Master of Arts in teaching special education, a Master of Education, and several endorsement options. Also available is a master's degree in speech-language pathology, as well as an undergraduate minor in communication sciences and disorders that prepares students for the speech-language pathology program.

The College of Optometry offers a Doctor of Optometry program, as well as master's and Ph.D. programs in vision science.

Costs

Tuition and fees for the 2017–18 school year were $41,624 for undergraduates in the College of Arts and Sciences. Room and board were $12,162 for a double room and a University meal plan.

Financial Aid

Financial assistance at Pacific is awarded on the basis of demonstrated need, academic merit, and talent. The Free Application for Federal Student Aid (FAFSA) is used in evaluating need. Prospective students are encouraged to apply for financial assistance by submitting the FAFSA to the federal processor as soon after October 1 as possible. Pacific provides financial assistance through grants, scholarships, loans, and part-time employment. For more information prospective students can e-mail financialaid@pacificu.edu.

Faculty

Pacific's outstanding faculty members provide the foundation for the University's academic program. A student-faculty ratio of 10:1 and an average class size of 19 students in undergraduate courses allows for personal attention from the professors. Pacific University does not use graduate or teaching assistants; all faculty members teach their own courses.

Admission Requirements

Pacific University is selective in considering new students. Primary consideration is given to a candidate's academic preparation and potential for successful study at the college level, as assessed by evaluating the student's transcripts of college-preparatory work, counselor and teacher recommendations, personal essay, SAT and/or ACT scores, and other student-submitted information. Transfer students must submit high school records and test scores if they have completed less than 30 semester hours, plus official transcripts from any institution previously attended.

Application and Information

Students may apply early and may be notified early through the modified rolling admissions plan. Pacific University is an exclusive member of the Common Application. For additional information, interested students should contact:

Office of Admissions
Pacific University
2043 College Way
Forest Grove, Oregon 97116
Phone: 503-352-2218
        800-677-6712 (toll-free)
E-mail: admissions@pacificu.edu
Website: http://www.pacificu.edu
         http://www.facebook.com/pacificu
         http://www.twitter.com/pacificu

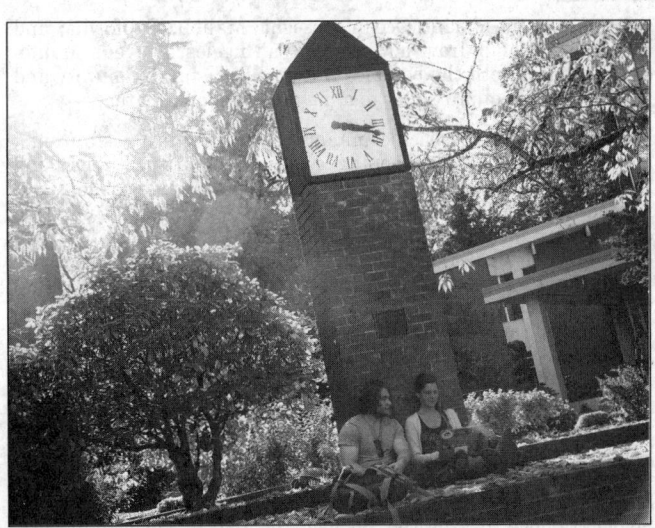

PEPPERDINE UNIVERSITY
Seaver College
MALIBU, CALIFORNIA

PEPPERDINE

The University and The College

Pepperdine University is a private, faith-based university committed to the highest standards of academic excellence and Christian values, where students are strengthened for lives of purpose, service, and leadership.

Seaver College, Pepperdine's undergraduate liberal arts college, is comprised of approximately 3,300 students, 54 percent of which come from California. Thirty-six percent hail from the other forty-nine states, and 10 percent are international. The 2017–18 freshmen class had an average high school GPA of 3.75. It's this diversity of backgrounds and worldviews that helps contribute to Pepperdine's unique educational experience.

Nestled between the Santa Monica Mountains and the Pacific Ocean, Pepperdine's Malibu campus provides fantastic on-campus housing options for all students. Students are required to live on campus during their first and second years, and also have premium residence halls available as upperclassmen.

Students have a wide range of extracurricular activities and organizations to choose from, including social, honor, service, spiritual, professional, divisional, and special interest clubs. Pepperdine provides students with interests in communications and media the chance to be involved with the campus radio station, weekly student newspaper and television broadcast.

Pepperdine has 17 Division One men's and women's athletic programs that have won an impressive 13 national team championships and 12 individual national championships. As a member of the West Coast Conference, the University houses a 3,500-seat gymnasium, an Olympic-size swimming pool, a tennis pavilion and sixteen additional tennis courts, an intramural field, and a 2,000-seat baseball stadium.

Pepperdine's graduate schools include the School of Law, School of Public Policy, School of Education and Psychology, and the George L. Graziado School of Business and Management. These distinguished programs offer master's degrees in law, dispute resolution, public policy, business, and more.

Location

Overlooking the Pacific Ocean in scenic Malibu, California, and less than an hour from downtown Los Angeles, Seaver's Malibu campus offers both the benefits of a small coastal community and the advantages of proximity to a major metropolitan area.

Malibu is a pristine beach community with excellent restaurants, a movie theater, and shopping centers complete with banking facilities and industry-leading brands. The winding seashore and rugged beauty of Malibu connects students to a litany of nightlife options in Santa Monica, Hollywood, and Los Angeles. Malibu's clean air provides an environment conducive to study, while the moderate climate permits year-round outdoor recreation. In addition to making use of the physical education facilities on campus, students can enjoy swimming, surfing, horseback riding, fishing, hiking, boating, kayaking, and other activities in the vicinity. As an international epicenter of culture, industry, and trade, Los Angeles provides students with a one-of-a-kind living experience.

Majors and Degrees

Students can choose from forty-five majors and thirty-seven minors. Seaver College awards the Bachelor of Arts in advertising, art, art history, biology, chemistry, communication, creative writing, economics, English, film studies, French, German, Hispanic studies (Spanish), history, integrated marketing communication, international studies, Italian, journalism, liberal arts, math education, media production, music, natural science, philosophy, political science, psychology, public relations, religion, sociology, sport administration, sports medicine, theater and music, theater and media production, and theater arts.

The Bachelor of Science is awarded in accounting, biology, business administration, chemistry, computer science and mathematics, international business, mathematics, nutritional science, physics, and sports medicine. A teacher education program offers credentials in single or multiple subjects.

Academic Programs

The academic programs at Seaver College provide students with a liberal arts education in a Christian atmosphere that sharpens critical thinking, improves information literacy, and builds a learning community. Students must complete 128 units for the B.A. or B.S. degree, including 64 units in general education requirements and 40 or more in upper-division studies.

Major requirements may be fulfilled through three basic arrangements. Students who specialize in a discipline must complete at least 24 units of upper-division work in their chosen discipline. Students may choose an interdisciplinary major, entailing at least 40 units of upper-division work, with courses ranging broadly across disciplinary lines within a division and on occasion crossing divisional lines, in one of the following fields of study: communication, English, humanities, international studies, liberal arts, or religion. Alternatively, students may initiate a contract major by presenting an application for specific upper-division courses to the Dean of Seaver College.

Seaver College functions on a semester plan; the regular academic year consists of two semesters from late August to April. In addition to the regular academic year, summer sessions run from early May to August.

At Seaver, instruction and study are adapted both to students' abilities and to the nature of the course content, instead of utilizing only the traditional lecture method. Programs involve several types of learning experiences: seminars, integrated lectures, individual study, fieldwork, and laboratories. Students are never taught by a teacher's assistant at Pepperdine; the average class size is 19 students and a student-to-faculty ratio of 13:1 fosters an environment where professors are invested in the growth and success of their students.

The Dean's List of undergraduate students is published each semester, comprised of the top 10 percent of the class with a grade point index no lower than 3.5. Other honors include cum laude for students graduating with a scholastic level of at least 3.5, magna cum laude for 3.7, and summa cum laude for 3.9.

Off-Campus Programs

At Seaver, students have the opportunity to study abroad in Buenos Aires, Argentina; Florence, Italy; Heidelberg, Germany; Lausanne, Switzerland; London, England; and Shanghai, China. The academic programs emphasize European, Latin American, or Asian history and culture. Seaver also offers an internship-based program in Washington, D.C. and summer special interest programs in Spain, Thailand, East Africa, and the Middle East. Classes are taught by Seaver faculty members. Serious study and the daily experiences of living in another country give students a special depth of understanding of other cultures and a broader world perspective.

The Buenos Aires program accommodates approximately 60 students who live in the homes of carefully selected host families. The Florence program houses approximately 55 students who live in a Florentine villa and residential complex with classrooms, a library, a computer facility, and recreational facilities. The Heidelberg program has space for approximately 50 students at the Moore Haus, located near the city's famous castle. Classes are held in modern facilities in downtown Heidelberg. The Lausanne program accommodates about 70 students. The Pepperdine facility is located in La Croisée near the center of Lausanne, which has a picturesque view of Lake Geneva and the French Alps. The London program has space for approximately 40 students in the Knightsbridge area. In addition to living quarters, the facility includes classrooms, a library, a computer room, offices, and a student center. The Shanghai program accommodates approximately 40 students who live in the Pepperdine-owned jia, meaning "house," which is located in the French Concession area near the American Consulate. The majority of the international program facilities are University-owned.

Academic Facilities

The Malibu campus is home to academic complexes containing seminar and lecture rooms, art studios, communication facilities, science and computer laboratories, mini-theaters, a recital hall, and administrative offices. The newly renovated Payson Library is the global gateway to knowledge and provides students access to thousands of online journals, articles, and periodicals through various databases. Payson Library serves as a sanctuary for study, learning, and research by encouraging discovery, contemplation, social discourse, and creative expression.

The 300-seat George Elkins Auditorium is used for public presentations and lectures. The Center for the Arts facility includes the renowned Frederick R. Weisman Museum of Art and the Smothers Theatre, which seats 450 people and is used for dance, music, and theater performances. The Center for Communication and Business building houses a state-of-the-art radio and television production center where students have the opportunity to work on Pepperdine's cable television and radio stations.

Costs

Costs for the 2017–18 academic year were $51,740 for tuition, $14,870 for room and board, and $252 for additional fees.

Financial Aid

Approximately 84 percent of Seaver's students receive some form of financial assistance through scholarships, loans, grants, work-study programs, or jobs within the University. To be eligible for financial assistance from institutional resources, an undergraduate student must be enrolled in at least 12 units. To ensure full consideration, the Free Application for Federal Student Aid (FAFSA) should be submitted by the priority deadlines of November 1 for early action and February 15 for regular decision for the fall semester and October 15 for the spring semester. Students who qualify should also apply for the Cal Grant (California residents only). Prospective students will receive their estimated financial assistance award after admission to the University but prior to the enrollment deadline.

Faculty

Seaver College's faculty includes men and women of high academic distinction whose primary focus is instruction with a secondary focus on research. Fifty-four percent of faculty members are full-time, and 87 percent of full-time faculty members hold a doctorate or terminal degree in their field. Upon enrollment, each student is assigned an academic adviser from among the faculty members. A qualified counseling staff is also available to assist with personal, professional, and academic needs.

Student Government

The Student Government Association (SGA) is composed of student leaders dedicated to providing Pepperdine's students with quality representation through innovative advocacy programs. SGA serves as the voice of the students to the Seaver administration and works in coordination with the Student Activities Office in establishing activities and maintaining school policies. Seaver has more than 1,000 programmed on-campus events each year including movies, sightseeing trips, guest performances, dances, speakers, and more. Pepperdine has eight nationally recognized sororities and five fraternities and there are over 110 different student clubs and organizations on campus that focus on a range of interests, including academic, language, art, music, dance, drama, sports, and politics.

Admission Requirements

Applicants are admitted on the basis of their academic record, SAT or ACT scores, and personal information and references. Transfer applicants are high school graduates who have taken any transferable college units after graduating high school. Students who took colleges courses prior to graduating high school are not considered transfer students and should apply as a first-year student. To ensure full consideration for the fall semester, students should apply by the early action deadline of November 1 or regular application deadline of January 15. October 15 is the regular deadline for the spring semester. Decision letter dates are announced in the current application form.

Seaver College seeks to enroll a diverse student body. As such, Pepperdine University does not unlawfully discriminate on the basis of any status or condition protected by applicable federal or state law in the administration of its educational policies, admission, financial assistance, employment, educational programs, or activities.

Application and Information

To request information, students should contact:

Office of Admission
Seaver College
Pepperdine University
Malibu, California 90263-4392
Phone: 310-506-4392
E-mail: admission-seaver@pepperdine.edu
Website: http://seaver.pepperdine.edu/admission
       https://seaver.pepperdine.edu/admission/risingtide
        (Docuseries)
       http://on.fb.me/Seaver_Admission (Facebook)
       http://twitter.com/#!/SeaverAdmission (Twitter)
       http://instagram.com/seaveradmission# (Instagram)
       http://bit.ly/YouTube_Pepperdine (YouTube)
       http://pinterest.com/seaveradmission/ (Pinterest)

The 830-acre Malibu campus of Pepperdine University, Seaver College, overlooks the Pacific Ocean, 30 miles west of Los Angeles, California.

PLATT COLLEGE SAN DIEGO

SAN DIEGO, CALIFORNIA

 For more information, visit http://petersons.to/platt-college-sandiego

The College

Built on the historic site of the original Jack in the Box, Platt College San Diego (PCSD), is the first and only accredited, degree-granting college that solely specializes in Graphic Design, Web Development, 3-D Modeling/Assets, and Digital Filmmaking/VFX within the greater San Diego area. With small class sizes, inverted curriculum, and project-based instruction, Platt College San Diego offers educational programs that are designed to empower and generate an atmosphere of creative learning and development.

Why Platt College San Diego?

- Small class sizes

- Complete design classes first to become marketable quickly

- One design class at a time

- Day or evening classes available

- No application, parking, or monthly material fees

- Books and supplies included

- Locked tuition cost with no hidden fees

- Easy transfer credit evaluation

- VA approved

Majors and Degrees

The Bachelor of Science degree in Media Arts with an emphasis on Web Design and Development, prepares students for careers in the web world. This program is structured to complement the revolutionary changes in interactive design that have catapulted the primarily print media area of graphic design into new arenas that combine audio, video, text, graphics, animation, and commerce.

The Bachelor of Science degree in Media Arts with an emphasis in 3D Modeling and Design prepares students for a broad range of design and technology skills. Mastering these skills results in artist's/designer's ability to express visual creativity through technology and the creative process.

The Bachelor of Science Degree in Media Arts with an emphasis in Digital Video Production offers solid knowledge enabling students to solve complex video production problems and create professional artistically unique products.

PCSD also offers an Associate of Applied Science: Graphic Design degree program and an Associate of Applied Science: Graphic Design degree program.

Facilities and Equipment

The 18,500 square-foot campus of classrooms, computer labs, library, and administrative offices is located in the metropolitan area of San Diego. The facilities for core curriculum courses (taught in computer labs) in terms 1–4 accommodate a maximum of 30 students. The core curriculum courses in terms 5 and 6 (upper division) accommodate a maximum of 12 students (in the computer labs). The general education lecture classrooms accommodate a maximum of 30 students. In all cases, class sizes are carefully controlled to provide individualized assistance, which is PCSD's hallmark.

The campus is accessible to the physically challenged with designated parking and an elevator. The facilities and equipment comply with all federal, state, and local ordinances relating to fire, building, and health and safety codes. Equipment typical of that used in today's industry is in place in the classrooms and is available for student use. A specific list of equipment utilized in each classroom can be requested from the admissions department. Internet access is available throughout the facilities.

Admission Requirements

Prior to the start date, candidates for enrollment in PCSD must provide evidence of high school completion in the form of an original diploma from a regionally accredited high school or the recognized equivalent (i.e. an original GED certificate or score report or California High School Proficiency Exam certificate or score report), or in the form of an official transcript.

All applicants must interview with an admissions representative prior to enrollment. Those interviewing in person will be given a tour of the facility to view classrooms, equipment, explore financial aid options (for those who qualify), and see examples of student work. Those unable to interview in person must have an admissions interview by phone.

PCSD uses an aptitude test to measure the candidate's academic preparedness to undertake college-level coursework in English and mathematics. Other nationally based exams, such as the SAT or ACT exam, will be considered. In addition, the applicant's past academic performance and work experience may be reviewed to determine if the individual can benefit from training at PCSD.

Transfer of Credit to Platt College

PCSD will consider the transfer of credits for completed coursework from other accredited institutions. Transcripts from all previously attended institutions, military transcripts, and AP/CLEP/DSST scores must be submitted to the College from the institution granting the credit and must be officially signed and sealed.

To be eligible for transfer of general education credit to PCSD, a minimum grade of "C" or a 2.0 in the transfer course must have been achieved, and the credit must be considered comparable to the level of coursework of the PCSD's program and non-remedial in nature. The College utilizes American Council on Education (ACE) recommended scores for CLEP and DSST.

Career Services

The ultimate goal of PCSD is for graduates to be employed in their field of training. The school maintains a career services program designed to assist qualified students and graduates in obtaining career goals. Leads for full or part-time job opportunities are solicited or contacted from a variety of industry sources and networking opportunities. Graduates and students are encouraged to utilize these employment opportunities as they become available.

The career services department advises students on interviewing skills, resume writing, and job search techniques.

Although the College cannot guarantee employment, many graduates who actively seek employment with the assistance of the career services department secure jobs in their field of training. A statistical report indicating placement percentages for each program is provided to each prospective student by the admissions department prior to enrollment.

Many companies have benefited from hiring PCSD alumni, such as: Activision/Blizzard, Apple, DC Comics, Digital Domain, Disney, Google, ILM, Infinity Ward, and Nike to name a few.

Costs

Platt College San Diego offers a locked tuition with no hidden fees. Books and supplies are included and there are no application, parking, or monthly material fees. Costs vary by program. The most up-to-date tuition information is available online at https://platt.edu/downloads/pcsd_tuition.pdf.

Financial Aid

Students applying for financial aid must submit the Free Application for Federal Student Aid (FAFSA). Students must meet the eligibility requirements of the program to qualify. PCSD participates in a variety of financial aid programs: the Federal Pell Grant, Federal Supplemental Educational Opportunity Grant (FSEOG), Veterans' Education Programs (Post911, the GI Bill, and the Yellow Ribbon Program), the Iraq and Afghanistan Service Grant, Cal Grants, the Federal Work-Study Program, the Stafford Loan Program, and the PLUS Loan Program.

The Platt College San Diego Academic Scholarship and PCSD Extended Opportunity Scholarship are also available to help qualified students pay for their education.

Student Life

Platt strives to balance the serious business in the classroom with fun outside of it. Often live media demonstrations, music, poetry, dance, raffle prizes, refreshments, and spontaneous opportunities to be creative can be enjoyed in the Platt Courtyard. Students, faculty, and staff gather often in the courtyard to celebrate holidays or bring awareness to cultural events.

Students are encouraged to showcase their artwork at galleries and exhibits throughout the San Diego area. Extracurricular activities, such as field trips, competitions, and cultural events, provide a variety of opportunities to become inspired outside of the classroom. Students have access to a master list of numerous community service opportunities and are encouraged to take part in charitable and community service throughout the year.

Accreditation and Approvals

The College is accredited by the Accrediting Commission of Career Schools and Colleges (ACCSC) is listed by the U.S. Department of Education as a nationally recognized accrediting agency.

Platt College San Diego is a private institution approved by the Bureau of Private Postsecondary Education (BPPE).

How to Get Started

Potential students can take their first step toward being part of the Platt College San Diego experience by calling 866-PLATTCOLLEGE or 866-752-8826 or going online at platt. edu to schedule a visit.

For more information, contact:

Steve Gallup, Director of Admissions/Marketing
Platt College San Diego—Digital Media Design
6250 El Cajon Boulevard
San Diego, California 92115
United States
Phone: 866-752-8826
Fax: 619-308-0570
E-mail: sgallup@platt.edu
Website: https://platt.edu

PRATT INSTITUTE
BROOKLYN, NEW YORK

 To read more about this school, visit http://petersons.to/prattinstitute

The Institute

Industrialist and philanthropist Charles Pratt founded Pratt Institute in 1887 to educate students for various professions on a non-degree level. As the educational preparation necessary for various professions expanded, Pratt Institute moved to offer baccalaureate degrees with its first granted in 1938 and its first graduate degree granted in 1950. Now, with twenty-seven undergraduate majors and concentrations, Pratt offers students a wide variety of programs in which to major or take elective courses.

With its undergraduate ranked programs in art, design, and architecture ranked among the top five or ten in the country, Pratt has been ranked among the top design schools in the United States by *Business Week*. Pratt was also ranked number one in the country for its fine arts and studio programs by *USA Today*.

In addition to the four-year programs on its Brooklyn campus, Pratt offers students several additional locations to pursue their education: a two-year program in Utica, New York, at PrattMWP; and an associate degree program in fine art, graphic design, illustration, and gaming as well as a two- and four-year degree in construction management in Manhattan.

Although the characteristics and educational requirements of the professions for which Pratt prepares students have changed over the course of a century, the Institute has succeeded in pursuing its abiding purpose—to blend theoretical learning with professional and humanistic development—and has kept its curricula current by hiring practicing professionals to teach. Standards are high, modeled after the professional world. Faculty members connect students with internships and eventually jobs after graduation. Industry projects and internships provide students with real-world experience. Eighty-seven percent of Pratt's graduates are working within the first year after graduation.

Pratt Institute offers four-year bachelor's, two-year associate's, and master's degrees. Pratt's national and international reputation attracts undergraduate and graduate students from forty-eight U.S. states and over eighty countries. Students who choose Pratt are committed to the study of art, design, architecture, or creative writing and to their career objectives.

A short subway or bus ride from the museums, galleries, and design centers of both Manhattan and Brooklyn, Pratt Institute's main campus in Brooklyn, New York features twenty-five buildings of differing architectural styles spread throughout a beautifully landscaped 25-acre campus. The campus was ranked by *Architectural Digest* as one of the top ten campuses nationwide with the best architecture. It includes a contemporary sculpture garden (ranked among the top ten campus art collections by *Public Art Review*), an athletic center, residence halls, dining halls, outstanding studio facilities, and historic buildings. Nineteen of the buildings house studios, classrooms, laboratories, administrative offices, auditoria, sports facilities, food services, and student centers. A new green LEED gold-certified building houses student administrative services including admissions, undergraduate and graduate digital arts programs, and various administrative offices, including student financial services and the registrar's offices. Six buildings are student residences, including the Stabile Hall freshman residence, which provides studio space on each floor; a new freshman residence hall is under construction. There is adequate parking for residents and commuters. Student services include career planning and placement, health and counseling, a disabilities office, a HEOP program, and student development. More than sixty student organizations are available including fraternities and sororities, honorary societies, professional societies, and clubs.

Location

Pratt Institute, the country's premier college of art, design, writing, and architecture, has its main campus in the Clinton Hill neighborhood of Brooklyn, just minutes from downtown Manhattan. Ninety percent of Pratt's freshmen and over half of its undergraduates live on the tree-lined Brooklyn campus. Close to the Brooklyn Museum and the Brooklyn Academy of Music, Pratt is ideally located, providing students with a green oasis just minutes from the art capital of the world, Manhattan. The Manhattan campus is located in Chelsea. The Utica campus, home to the first two years of Pratt's programs in fine art, communications design, photography, and art and design education (teacher certification) with automatic relocation to the Brooklyn campus for the junior year, is located in upstate New York.

Majors and Degrees

Pratt Institute offers the Bachelor of Architecture, Bachelor of Fine Arts, Bachelor of Art, Bachelor of Industrial Design, Bachelor of Professional Studies, Bachelor of Science, Associate of Occupational Studies, and Associate of Applied Science degrees.

The Bachelor of Architecture degree program is a five-year, accredited program. For the Bachelor of Fine Arts degree, a candidate may choose to major in art and design education (art teacher certification), history of art and design, communications design (advertising art direction, graphic design, and illustration), digital arts (3-D animation, 2-D animation, and interactive arts), fashion design, film, fine arts (ceramics, drawing, jewelry, painting, printmaking, sculpture, and integrated practice), interior design, photography, or writing. The Bachelor of Arts is offered in critical and visual studies and art history. The Bachelor of Industrial Design is offered for students interested in product and furniture design. In the Bachelor of Professional Studies degree program, the major is in construction management. Students seeking the Bachelor of Science degree can major in construction management or professional services management.

The two-year Associate of Occupational Studies degree is offered in game design and interactive media, graphic design, and illustration. The Associate of Applied Science is offered in painting/drawing and graphic design/illustration. The two-year Associate of Applied Science degree is transferable to a four-year program.

Students may also earn combined bachelor's/master's degrees. Programs include the B.F.A./M.S. in art and design education as well as art history.

Academic Programs

Educating artists and creative professionals to be responsible contributors to society has been the mission of Pratt Institute since it assembled its first group of students in 1887. Within the structure of that professional education, Pratt students are encouraged to acquire the diverse knowledge that is necessary for them to succeed in their chosen fields including sustainability. In addition to the professional studies, the curriculum in each of Pratt's schools includes a broad range of liberal arts courses. Students from all schools take these courses together and have the opportunity to examine the interrelationships of art, science, technology, and human need.

At the time of graduation, students in the associate degree programs have completed 67 credit hours of course work. In the bachelor's programs, credit-hour requirements are 126 credits with opportunities to take electives in other disciplines or minors, depending on the particular program. For the Bachelor of Architecture degree, 170 credits are required.

Pratt's academic calendar consists of two semesters plus optional summer terms that allow students to choose alternative courses or various options usually not offered during the fall or spring semester.

Off-Campus Programs

Pratt Institute offers credit for a wide variety of off-campus study programs. The internship program offers qualified students challenging on-the-job experience related to their major fields of interest; this extension of the classroom and laboratory into the professional world adds a practical dimension to periods of on-campus study.

International programs, available during all academic sessions, have included art and design offerings in the cities of Copenhagen and Rome and in the countries of England, France, Italy, and South Africa. Architecture programs have been held in Italy, Finland, and Japan. New programs are developed regularly in these and other countries. A semester-long program is offered in Rome each year.

Academic Facilities

Founded as the first free library in Brooklyn, the Pratt Institute Library has more than 176,674 bound volumes, 84,604 art books, 237 print and online art and art history journals, a rare book collection, and subscriptions to journals online through JSTOR, EBSCO, and others. The library also has serial backfiles and other material, including government documents; 251,603 audiovisual materials; and 3,996 microforms and subscribes to 925 periodicals—the largest collection of any independent art school. With their ID cards, Pratt students also have access to numerous college libraries in the metropolitan area.

Extensive studio and state-of-the-art computer lab facilities are provided for all Pratt students. In the School of Art and Design, these include studio, shop, and technical facilities for work in all media, from the traditional to the most experimental. Gallery space, both on campus and at Pratt Manhattan, is extensive, showing the work of students, alumni, faculty members, staff members, and other well-known artists, architects, and designers.

Costs

Tuition for the 2018–19 academic year is $49,810. Room charges are $8,862 per academic year. A meal plan is available, and costs about $3,760 for the year. The fees are approximately $2,060. The estimated cost of books and supplies is $1,750 per academic year. Students should allow an additional $3,000 for transportation and personal expenses. For an updated list of tuition and fees, prospective students should visit www.pratt.edu/admissions/financing-your-education/financing-undergraduate/cost-of-attendance.

Financial Aid

Pratt Institute offers an extensive program of merit-based scholarships, need-based grants, loans, and awards based on academic achievement, talent, financial need, or all three. More than 75 percent of Pratt students receive financial assistance through one or more of these kinds of aid.

Faculty

The faculty at Pratt Institute is exceptional in that a large number of practicing professionals augment the regular full-time faculty. There are 157 full-time and 991 part-time faculty members. In small classes and studios, students have easy access to professors whose natural environment is the design studio, the architectural office, or the industrial research department. Faculty members often connect students with internships and eventually jobs.

Student Government

The Student Government Association (SGA) maintains primary responsibility for all student interests and involvement at Pratt. All undergraduate students are encouraged to become involved in the SGA, whose main functions are allocating and administering funds collected through the student activities fee, scheduling student activities, and representing the student viewpoint to the rest of the Pratt community.

Admission Requirements

Pratt Institute attracts and enrolls highly motivated and talented students from diverse backgrounds. Applications are welcome from all qualified students, regardless of age, sex, race, color, religion, national origin, or handicap. Admission standards at Pratt are high. One of the major components for admission consideration in art, design, or architecture is the evaluation of a student's art or writing portfolio, which must be submitted along with the other required documents.

All applicants to four-year programs must submit official transcripts, test scores, and a visual or writing portfolio with the exception of construction management applicants who are not required to submit a portfolio. Instructions may be found at www.pratt.edu/apply.

The admission committee bases its decisions on careful reviews of all credentials submitted by applicants in relation to the requirements of the program to which students seek admission. International students must submit TOEFL or IELTS scores or SAT scores, but not both. In certain cases, extraordinary talent may offset a low grade or a test score.

Application and Information

Pratt has two admissions deadlines: November 1 for early action and January 5 for regular admissions. To receive full consideration, students must submit their applications by January 5 for anticipated entrance in the fall semester and by October 1 for anticipated entrance in the spring semester. Additional details regarding application deadlines can be found on Pratt's website: https://www.pratt.edu/admissions/applying/applying-undergraduate/ug-application-requirements.

For more information about Pratt Institute, students should contact:

Office of Admissions
Pratt Institute
200 Willoughby Avenue
Brooklyn, New York 11205
Phone: 718-636-3514
      800-331-0834 (toll-free)
E-mail: admissions@pratt.edu
Website: www.pratt.edu
      www.pratt.edu/request (Catalog request)
      www.pratt.edu/visit (Visit information and online
      campus tour registration)
      http://on.fb.me/pratt_admissions (Facebook)

Pratt's campus in the spring. © 2014 Bob Handelman

QUINNIPIAC UNIVERSITY
HAMDEN, CONNECTICUT

 To read more about this school, visit http://petersons.to/quinnipiac

Quinnipiac
UNIVERSITY

The University

Quinnipiac University offers four-year and graduate-level degree programs leading to careers in health sciences, nursing, business, communications, engineering, natural sciences, education, liberal arts, law, and medicine. A curriculum that combines a career focus with a globally oriented liberal arts background prepares graduates for the future, whether they start their careers right after commencement or opt to pursue advanced study.

Quinnipiac is coeducational and nonsectarian and currently enrolls 7,000 full-time undergraduates, 1,445 full-time graduate law and medical students, and 1,675 part-time students in its undergraduate, graduate, and professional programs. Twenty-five percent of the students are residents of Connecticut; the rest represent primarily the northeast corridor, in all thirty-one states including Alaska, California, and Texas and thirty countries. Quinnipiac is big enough to sustain a wide variety of people and programs but small enough to keep students from getting lost in the shuffle. Life on campus emphasizes students' personal, as well as academic, growth. The approximately 140 student organizations, 16 Greek chapters, and extracurricular activities, including intramural and intercollegiate (NCAA Division I) athletics, give students a chance to exercise their talents, muscles, and leadership skills. The University has a student newspaper, TV station, and an FM radio station (WQAQ) and twenty-one intercollegiate teams in men's baseball, basketball, cross-country, ice hockey, lacrosse, soccer, and tennis, and in women's acrobatics and tumbling, basketball, cross-country, field hockey, golf, ice hockey, lacrosse, rugby, soccer, softball, tennis, track (indoor and outdoor), and volleyball. Teams compete in the MAAC conference; men's and women's ice hockey teams in the ECAC; and women's field hockey in the Big East.

The University has three distinct campus settings. The 250-acre Mount Carmel campus has fifty buildings including the Arnold Bernhard Library, academic facilities, an athletic and recreation center, and twenty-five residence halls of different styles, mainly for freshmen and sophomores, with traditional double and quad (4-person) rooms, suites, and multilevel suites and apartments with kitchens. About 95 percent of all freshmen and 75 percent of the total undergraduate population live in Quinnipiac housing. The nearby 250-acre York Hill campus includes the Sports Center with twin 3,500-seat arenas for ice hockey and basketball; a suite-style, with singles and doubles, 1,500-bed residence hall and townhouses for juniors and seniors; "Rocky Top," a lodge-like student center; spectacular views; and a multilevel parking garage for 2,000 vehicles. Seniors may also live in University-owned houses or apartments. Senior-year housing is on a space-available basis. A free shuttle takes students between all three campuses.

Career planning takes place in each of the schools with assistance from the deans' offices. It begins with faculty advisement, along with career exploration, a strong focus on internships and clinical placements, consideration of various major and job fields, and exposure to prospective employers and job preparation. Approximately 30 percent of the undergraduate student population remains at Quinnipiac for their graduate degree in combined or direct entry majors, particularly in education, business, communications, physical and occupational therapy, physician assistant, and social work programs. The innovative Business 4-year (3+1) B.S./M.B.A. offers academically talented applicants the opportunity to complete both degrees in just four years. A similar 3+1 dual-degree program in the School of Communications offers students an undergraduate B.A. or B.F.A. and a graduate M.S. in 4 years. And academically strong students can complete a 3+3 B.A./J.D. degree in the School of Law in just 6 instead of the traditional 7 years. New programs include the 3+1 B.S./M.S. biology/molecular cell biology and a 3+2 B.A. or B.S./M.S.W. with undergraduate degrees in Health Science Studies or several majors in Arts and Sciences along with the School of Social Work.

Graduate programs lead to the Master of Science (M.S.) degree in accounting, business analytics, information technology, cyber-security (new), interactive media, journalism, molecular and cell biology, organizational leadership, public relations, and teacher leadership; the Master of Health Science in anesthesiologist assistant, medical lab sciences, cardiovascular perfusion, pathologist assistant, and physician assistant; the Doctor of Nursing Practice in adult and family nursing and nurse anesthesia; the Doctor of Physical Therapy; a Master of Health Sciences in Advanced Medical Imaging and Leadership; the Master of Business Administration; the Master of Business Administration in Health Care Management; the Master of Business Administration–Chartered Financial Analyst; the Master of Arts in Teaching; and the Master of Social Work. The Quinnipiac University School of Law offers full- and part-time programs leading to a J.D. degree or J.D./M.B.A. degree in combination with the School of Business. Several of the graduate degree programs are offered online or in a hybrid format. The Frank H. Netter MD School of Medicine focuses on developing doctors as part of a health-care team with a focus on primary care, rehabilitative medicine, and global health.

Location

Situated at the foot of Sleeping Giant Mountain in Hamden, Connecticut, Quinnipiac provides the best of the suburbs and the city. The University is only 8 miles from New Haven, 30 minutes from Hartford (the state capital), and less than 2 hours from New York City and Boston. Bordering the campus is the 1,700-acre Sleeping Giant State Park, for walking and hiking. The free campus shuttle takes students to nearby shopping and restaurants, as well as to New Haven, where they can visit various art and science museums, attend a performance at Yale Rep or the Shubert Theater, find great restaurants, and have easy access to Metro North and Amtrak at the New Haven train station.

Majors and Degrees

The Schools of Health Sciences and Nursing grant bachelor's degrees in athletic training, biomedical science, health science studies, microbiology/immunology, radiologic science (3-year accelerated B.S.), diagnostic medical sonography, and nursing. Combined B.S./graduate degree programs include occupational therapy (5½-year entry-level master's), physical therapy (6- or 7-year entry-level doctorate), and physician assistant studies (6-year freshman entry-level master's). Students who wish to prepare for entry into medical, dental, chiropractic, veterinary, or other medical schools work with a premed adviser and the pre-health advisory committee. The graduate MSW offers a 3+2 degree with the B.S. in Health Science Studies or several degrees in Arts and Sciences.

The School of Business (accredited by AACSB International and ranked in the top 100 Best Undergraduate Business Schools in 2014 *Bloomberg BusinessWeek*) offers bachelor's degree programs in accounting, biomedical marketing, entrepreneurship, finance, computer information systems, international business, management, and marketing. The school offers an innovative Business 4-year (3+1) B.S./M.B.A. program to highly qualified business students, also a fast-track, five-year combined-degree program in which students from all majors may gain preadmission to the M.B.A. program, allowing them to fast-track through their M.B.A. in 12–14 months after earning their bachelor's degree by taking several undergraduate and graduate business courses while undergraduates.

The School of Engineering's mechanical, civil, industrial, and software engineering programs are accredited by the Engineering Accreditation Commission of ABET. In addition, the School offers a B.S. in computer science.

The College of Arts and Sciences offers bachelor's degree programs in behavioral neuroscience, biochemistry, biology, chemistry, criminal justice, economics, English, gerontology, history, interdisciplinary studies, independent study, law in society, mathematics, philosophy, political science, psychology, sociology, Spanish, and theater. Qualified students can go on to the Master of Science in molecular and cell biology program or pursue graduate programs in education, business, law, health sciences, journalism, interactive media, medicine, and social work.

The School of Communications offers undergraduate majors in advertising and integrated communications, communications/media studies; film, television, and media arts; graphic and interactive design; journalism; and public relations, plus a B.F.A. in film and graduate programs in journalism, public relations, sports journalism, and interactive media. One highlight is "QU in LA," a Los Angeles location for summer/fall/spring internships for communications and business students in particular, but open to all undergraduate and graduate Quinnipiac students.

The School of Education's B.A./M.A.T. five-year program provides certification for teaching elementary (K–6) and secondary grades (7–12). The B.A./Master of Arts in Teaching (M.A.T.) program is accredited by CAEP the Council for the Accreditation of Education Preparation. Students complete a B.A. or B.S. in a subject area or in Interdisciplinary Studies in the College of Arts and Sciences; take the freshman course, Introduction to the Teaching Profession; and then continue the M.A.T. course work in their junior and senior years and complete the degree in a final graduate year.

Academic Programs

The Quinnipiac Learning Paradigm begins at orientation, involving students in identifying their strengths and goals, and follows through to graduation. Students begin their electronic portfolio to track their accomplishments and learning. The foundation of the University Curriculum encourages students to explore a variety of options when selecting a major, double major, major and minor, or combined undergraduate/graduate degrees. The Writing Across the Curriculum initiative (WAC) stresses the improvement in writing skills in all subject areas. The University honors program addresses the needs and interests of the most academically talented and committed students. Advanced placement, credit, or both are given for appropriate scores on Advanced Placement tests and CLEP general and subject examinations as well as for scores of 4 or higher in the International Baccalaureate higher-level subjects.

Off-Campus Programs

Students can study abroad in a variety of countries. Most students choose a study-abroad option in their sophomore or junior year, many at Quinnipiac's affiliated program in Ireland. Students in any of the six undergraduate schools can also get hands-on experience in their field through off-campus internships and clinical placements in the health sciences. Academic credit is available for internships and affiliations, which are often part of degree requirements.

Academic Facilities

Academic life focuses on the Bernhard Library which is open 24/7 during the fall and spring semesters. This attractive facility provides individual carrels and small rooms for group study. The Learning Commons offers individual tutoring assistance along with helpful learning workshops.

The School of Communications provides 4K (ultra-high-definition) cameras and editing rooms; multimedia and digital design labs; a high-definition TV production studio; audio production; print journalism; a news innovation center; and all the latest software for film, video, interactive media, websites, graphics, and animation. The Bloomberg terminals in the Financial Technology Center in the School of Business is a high-tech, simulated trading floor providing students with the opportunity to access real-time financial data, conduct interactive trading simulations, and develop financial models in preparation for careers in finance. The Center for Innovation and Entrepreneurship and the App Lab encourage students in all majors to think creatively.

Engineering uses a long list of workshops for hands-on learning: computer-aided engineering, biomedical, circuits and controls, environmental, fluids, geotechnical, hydraulics, rapid prototyping and performance optimization.

The Center for Medicine, Nursing, and Health Sciences on the North Haven campus provides state-of-the-art facilities for the Schools of Medicine, Nursing, Health Sciences, Law, and Education, such as movement study/motion analysis and biomechanics labs; the ergonomics and assistive technology lab; a model adaptive apartment; an orthopedics lab; several rehabilitative sciences labs; CT scan, MRI, radiography, ultrasound, and mammography facilities; and the latest clinical skills simulation labs for adults and pediatric/neonatal patients including an intensive care unit, physical diagnosis lab, physical exam suite, health assessment labs, human anatomy lab, and two operating suites.

Costs

The 2018–19 total direct costs are $62,500, of which tuition and student and technology fees total $47,960 (for students taking 12–16 credits per semester). Room and board average $14,540 (and includes $3,280 allocated as the base meal plan). Indirect expenses, estimated at $2,800 per year, include books, personal, and travel expenses.

Financial Aid and Scholarships

Quinnipiac designs financial aid packages to include need-based grants and merit-based scholarships that do not have to be repaid, plus self-help financial aid programs such as federal and University-based work study, and loans. Students and families seeking need-based aid will file the Free Application for Federal Student Aid (FAFSA), which is available October 1. Freshman scholarships are based on the overall academic GPA/class rank plus the highest SAT or ACT scores. Transfer students are encouraged to file the FAFSA and may receive scholarships based on their previous college work (minimum 3.0 GPA).

Faculty

The faculty is characterized by its teaching competence and outstanding academic qualifications. Of the 400 full-time faculty members, 85 percent have earned a Ph.D. or the appropriate terminal degree in their field. The faculty also includes a number of part-time teachers who are practicing professionals and experts in their fields. Classes are taught by these scholars and professionals and not by student instructors, and a low student-faculty ratio promotes close associations among faculty members and students.

Student Government

The Student Government is the student legislative body of Quinnipiac. It represents student opinion, promotes student welfare, supervises student organizations, appropriates funds for student groups, and provides student representation on the Board of Trustees.

Admission Requirements

Quinnipiac seeks students from a broad range of backgrounds. On average, freshman students have a 3.4 GPA or better average in college-preparatory courses (transfer students generally have a 2.5 GPA or higher), rank in the top 25 percent of their high school class, and have an average combined score of 1100 on the SAT (critical reading plus math) or an ACT composite of 22. Students are encouraged to submit test scores, but they are optional for those applying to the Schools of Business, Communications, Engineering, and the College of Arts and Sciences. They are however required if applying to the Schools of Health Sciences and Nursing. Visits to the campus for an interview, open house, group information session, or a campus tour are strongly encouraged and can be arranged at www. qu.edu/visit. Transfer students are welcome to make an appointment to discuss requirements and the transfer of credit from previous institutions. Quinnipiac sponsors six open house programs during the year and several Saturday morning information sessions followed by a campus tour, plus weekday individual interviews and student-led campus tours.

Application and Information

Quinnipiac generally receives about 23,000 applications for admission and enrolls an incoming class of 1,900 freshmen and 200 transfer students. Quinnipiac has a rolling admission policy for its undergraduate programs and therefore recommends that freshman applicants submit the application fairly early in the fall of their senior year, followed by their transcript, first marking period grades, and test scores (if required—see website for details) well before the deadline of February 1. Students applying to the 6-year physician assistant program should submit the application by October 15, and those applying to physical therapy, nursing, and occupational therapy programs should submit the application by November 15. An early decision (binding) option is available in all majors with an application deadline of November 1. Applications are reviewed as soon as they are complete, and the University begins notifying students of decisions in November. Quinnipiac is a member of the Common Application. Students placed on a waiting list are notified of any openings by June 1. Quinnipiac subscribes to the May 1 Candidates Reply Date Agreement. For information about full-time undergraduate study, students should contact:

Office of Undergraduate Admissions
Quinnipiac University
Hamden, Connecticut 06518-1940
Phone: 203-582-8600
      800-462-1944 (toll-free)
Fax: 203-582-8906
E-mail: admissions@qu.edu
Website: www.quinnipiac.edu
      www.facebook.com/QuinnipiacUniversity
      twitter.com/QU_Admissions
      quadmissions-blogspot.com/
      www.youtube.com/quinnipiacuniversity

For information regarding transfer and part-time study:

Office of Transfer and Part-time Admissions
Quinnipiac University
Hamden, Connecticut 06518-1940
Phone: 203-582-8612
Fax: 203-582-8906
E-mail: transferadmission@qu.edu

REED COLLEGE
PORTLAND, OREGON

 To read more about this school, visit http://petersons.to/reedcollege

The College

Referred to as one of the most intellectual colleges in the country, Reed is known for its high standards of scholarly practice, creative thinking, and engaged citizenship. A genuine enthusiasm for academic work and intellectual exchange is valued, and the Honor Principle, Reed's ethos that guides both academic and campus life, ensures personal responsibility and mutual respect for its small community of 1,410 students and 148 faculty members. More than four-fifths of Reed's students come from outside the Northwest, with one-fifth from the Northeast and one-tenth from outside of the United States. Over 30 percent of Reed's students identify with historically underrepresented racial and ethnic backgrounds. Reed's twenty-three residence halls enable approximately 70 percent of students to live on campus.

At its founding, Reed rejected fraternal societies and varsity sports. The goal was to foster a climate of inclusivity and collaboration focused on academics. This atmosphere persists, with student groups—social, religious, and cultural—open to all and fitness and the development of athletic skills taking precedence over competition.

Location

Reed's 116-acre wooded campus is located in a residential section of southeast Portland. The city, a welcoming metropolis, offers a thriving local music scene, diverse restaurants and food carts, tranquil Japanese and Chinese gardens, noisy downtown clubs, a plethora of bridges and bike paths, and the largest independent bookstore in the world. Just 90 minutes west of Portland are the wild beaches of the Pacific Ocean; 90 minutes east are the ski slopes of Mount Hood where Reed owns a ski cabin for use by the college community.

Majors and Degrees

Reed College awards the Bachelor of Arts degree in a variety of traditional fields, as well as in interdisciplinary combinations. Students may select from the following majors: American studies, anthropology, art, biochemistry and molecular biology, biology, chemistry, chemistry-physics, Chinese literature, Chinese studies, classics, classics-religion, comparative literature, computer science, dance, dance-theater, economics, English literature, environmental studies, French literature, German literature, history, history-literature, international and comparative policy studies, linguistics, literature-theater, mathematics, mathematics with concentrations in either computer science or statistics, mathematics-economics, mathematics-physics, music, neuroscience, philosophy, physics, political science, psychology, religion, Russian literature, sociology, Spanish literature, and theatre.

Students may also design their own interdisciplinary majors. The approval of such special programs, which link two or more disciplines, is reviewed by the student's adviser and the departments concerned.

Reed offers several combined 3-2 programs, which allow the student to earn both a bachelor's degree from Reed and a professional degree from the cooperating institution. Science programs and institutions include engineering, computer science (California Institute of Technology, Columbia University, and Rensselaer Polytechnic Institute), and forestry-environmental sciences (Duke University). The college also has a combined program in visual arts (Pacific Northwest College of Art).

Academic Programs

Hallmarks of academic life at Reed include the small-group conference method of teaching and its reliance on active student participation; a de-emphasizing of grades coupled with comprehensive narrative feedback; a yearlong interdisciplinary humanities program; and distribution requirements that balance breadth of learning with the depth of designing an in-depth senior thesis. In addition to fulfilling the requirements for the major, taking the humanities course, and writing the senior thesis, students must satisfy a distributional requirement, consisting of two core classes from each of the following academic groups: literature, philosophy, and the arts; history, social sciences, and psychology; the natural sciences; and math, foreign language, logic, and linguistics. Students must also take two classes from one other department outside their major course of study.

Off-Campus Programs

Reed participates in domestic exchange programs with Howard University in Washington, D.C.; Sarah Lawrence College in New York; and Sea Education Association in Massachusetts. In addition, Reed provides study-abroad opportunities for students in Australia, Argentina, Botswana, China, Costa Rica, Cuba, the Czech Republic, Ecuador, Egypt, France, Germany, Greece, Hungary, Ireland, Israel, Italy, Kenya, Lebanon, Morocco, Palestine, Russia, South Africa, Spain, Taiwan, Tanzania, Turkey, Turks and Caicos, and the United Kingdom. Students may also arrange independent study plans in consultation with appropriate faculty members, the director for off-campus studies, and the registrar.

Academic Facilities

Students have access to Reed's substantial library collection by searching the online catalog in the library or from any computer on the campus network. Through its participation in Summit, a union catalog of Oregon and Washington academic libraries, Reed provides online access to other library catalogs and databases. Students may borrow materials directly from academic libraries in the Portland area, as well as from collections worldwide through interlibrary loan. In addition, the Reed library accommodates a first-rate art gallery, a language lab, and a multimedia resource facility. The Reed library is open 18 hours most days and 24 hours a day during examinations.

The science laboratories at Reed are among the best equipped of any undergraduate college in the United States. These include the A. A. Knowlton Laboratory of Physics, the Arthur F. Scott Laboratory of Chemistry, and the L. E. Griffin Memorial Biology Building. Reed's nuclear research reactor (the only such reactor in the country that is staffed primarily by undergraduates) and radiochemistry lab are actively used for student research, instruction, and training. For those interested in the arts, the campus houses studio art facilities, performing arts facilities, twenty instrumental practice rooms, a computer music laboratory, a recording system, and an 800-seat auditorium. In fall 2013, Reed opened a new $28-million Performing Arts Building, representing a major step forward in the college's commitment to the important role the arts play at Reed. Other popular facilities include a radio station and Reed's newly expanded sports center, which offers a climbing wall and a nationally recognized outdoor program.

Costs

Tuition for 2017–18 was $53,900, and room and board was $13,670. The student body fee was $300, bringing the yearly total cost to approximately $67,870. The cost of books and incidental expenses averages approximately $2,000.

Financial Aid

Over half of the Reed student body receives financial assistance from the college. A full need-based financial aid program makes Reed accessible to students from a wide range of economic backgrounds. The college guarantees to meet the full demonstrated need of all continuing students in good academic standing who complete their financial aid applications on time. Reed's own funds are the primary source of grants to students, making up 83 percent of the average financial aid package in 2017–18. Reed also administers federal and state grants as well as federally subsidized loan programs. Campus employment and work-study programs are available. The size of a financial aid award is based solely upon analysis of the student's need. The average amount awarded to students receiving financial aid in 2016–17 was $44,798, which includes grants, loans, and work opportunities. Reed students' average graduating loan debt for all four years is $19,528, well below the national average.

Faculty

All classes at Reed are taught by professors rather than by teaching assistants. Classes are small, averaging about 15 students. The opportunity to work closely with faculty members is noted by students as one of the great benefits of a Reed education. Reed faculty members point to the opportunity to work with students who are serious scholars as one of the great benefits of teaching at Reed. Faculty members commit themselves primarily to teaching, with scholarly and scientific research furthering this primary goal; they view students as partners in learning, often serving as coauthors and co-investigators on professional papers and research projects. This close association is due, in large part, to a 10:1 student-faculty ratio and the one-on-one relationship between thesis adviser (a professor) and student during the senior year.

Student Government

The Student Senate is the central body in student governance. The Senate consists of the student body president, vice president, and 8 student representatives, all elected by the students. Its two primary functions are to allocate student body funds and to represent student interests and concerns to the faculty, administration, and Reed College Board of Trustees. The Senate distributes approximately $40,000 each semester to the many student organizations on campus. As agreed under the community constitution, students participate fully in discussions and decisions on a wide variety of issues. The Student Committee on Academic Policy and Planning participates in debate about the curriculum at Reed; many other committees, from the Library Board to the Reactor Committee, have substantial student input. The Senate and student body president make all student appointments to such committees.

Admission Requirements

Reed welcomes applications from freshman and transfer candidates who are genuinely committed to the pursuit of a liberal arts education and a rigorous academic program. Those applicants are admitted who, in the view of the Admission Committee, are most likely to become successful members of and contribute significantly and honorably to the Reed community. The college is committed to maintaining a student body distinguished by its intellectual passion and its diverse range of backgrounds, interests, and talents.

Admission decisions are based on many integrated factors, but academic accomplishments and talents are given the greatest weight in the selection process. A strong secondary school preparation, including honors and advanced courses where available, improves a student's chances for admission. Such a program usually includes: 4 years of English and 3 to 4 years of mathematics (through pre-calculus), science, foreign language, and history or social studies. Given the wide variation in high school programs and quality, however, there are no fixed requirements for secondary school courses. Applicants are expected to have obtained a secondary school diploma prior to enrollment, although exceptions are occasionally made. There are no cutoff points for high school or college grades or for test scores.

Reed recognizes the qualities of character—in particular, motivation, intellectual curiosity, individual responsibility, and community and social consciousness—as important considerations in the selection process, beyond a demonstrated commitment to academic excellence. Thus, the Admission Committee looks for students whose accomplishments and interests in various fields of endeavor will contribute to the overall liveliness of the Reed community. Personal interviews, either on or off campus, are not a requirement in the admission process but are recommended whenever possible. Applications for early decision should be submitted by November 15 (Option I) or December 20 (Option II), early action applications should be submitted by November 15, regular freshman admission by January 15, and transfer candidates by March 1.

Application and Information

The Office of Admission is open Monday through Friday from 8:30 a.m. until 5 p.m. (Pacific time) all year, except for major holidays. The Admission Office is also open on select Saturdays in the spring and fall. Reed College uses both the Coalition Application and the Common Application; students can find a complete list of application requirements online at reed.edu/apply/guide-to-applying.

For further information or to arrange a campus tour, overnight stay, information session, or interview, students should contact:

Office of Admission
Reed College
3203 Southeast Woodstock Boulevard
Portland, Oregon 97202-8199
Phone: 503-777-7511
       800-547-4750 (toll-free)
Fax: 503-777-7553
E-mail: admission@reed.edu
Website: reed.edu

Students at Reed College have a great appreciation for intellectual inquiry and passionate discussion, wherever it can be found.

REGIS COLLEGE
WESTON, MASSACHUSETTS

 For more information, visit http://petersons.to/regiscollege

The University

Regis is boldly empowering the next generation of leaders to change lives. A coed, Catholic university founded by the Sisters of Saint Joseph of Boston, Regis offers innovative programs in the arts and sciences, business and communication, health sciences, and nursing.

A foundation in the liberal arts ensures that Regis students are well-rounded and forward-thinking. The university offers more than 30 academic majors, minors, and pre-professional programs. These programs prepare students for careers in high-demand fields, including business, education, healthcare, and public service. Internships, clinical placements, student teaching, and research opportunities allow students to integrate their skills and the knowledge developed over the course of their studies into real-world experiences. Ninety-seven percent of the class of 2017 had secured professional employment or were enrolled in graduate school six months after graduation.

Regis provides a student-centered environment with a focus on highly personalized support and education for all students. The wide range of clubs, organizations, and opportunities offered reflect the strong diversity in the student body. More than 31 states and seven countries are represented in the student body.

The Princeton Review has named Regis among the top Northeast colleges in the nation for academic excellence. The university is recognized as a leader in interactive, participatory digital education. Regis was also named a "hidden gem" school by Colleges of Distinction for its excellence in providing outstanding teaching, offering vibrant communities, and engaging students.

Location

Located on a beautiful 132-acre suburban campus in Weston, students enjoy being a part of Regis's close-knit campus community. When they're ready to pursue an internship or explore a dynamic cultural center, they are only 12 miles away from Boston. Regis operates a regular shuttle to the area's MBTA rapid-transit system and provides car-sharing programs so students can take advantage of the many social and cultural activities in the area, including museums, historic landmarks, and sporting events.

Majors and Degrees

Undergraduate degrees from the School of Arts and Sciences: The School of Arts and Sciences at Regis offers bachelor's programs in a wide range of career-focused tracks. Programs combine a strong core curriculum with practical experience opportunities to help students develop knowledge, values, and professional skills.

Bachelor's degrees are offered in biology, biomedical engineering, criminal justice studies, cybersecurity, English, environmental sustainability, and interdisciplinary humanities.

Education with teacher licensure programs are available in early childhood education, elementary education, middle school education, and secondary school education.

Undergraduate degrees from the School of Health Sciences: The School of Health Sciences offers cutting-edge interdisciplinary programs designed to prepare students for successful careers in ever-changing fields.

Bachelor's degrees are offered in diagnostic medical sonography, exercise science, neuroscience, nuclear medicine, nutrition, psychology, public health, social work, sport management, and therapeutic recreation.

Undergraduate degrees from the School of Nursing: Regis is one of three schools in New England to be named a Center of Excellence in Nursing Education by the National League of Nursing, and one of only 35 to ever receive the honor. The designation was awarded to Regis for "creating environments that enhance student learning and professional development."

Students in the nursing program are able to bring their classroom experience to life during their clinical rotations. Regis nursing students are able to complete clinicals at some of the leading hospitals in the country. Past clinical placements include Massachusetts General Hospital, Boston Children's Hospital, and Newton-Wellesley Hospital.

Graduates of the nursing program at Regis are in high demand at hospitals, private and public clinics, as well as long-term care facilities. Many students choose to go directly into Regis' highly regarded master's programs. Students can take graduate nursing courses as electives at Regis and continue in the M.S. in Nursing after earning their undergraduate nursing degree.

Undergraduate degrees from the School of Business and Communication: Students in the School of Business and Communication represent the future of regional, national, and global industry leadership.

Bachelor's degrees offered include global business management and communication.

Students participate in cutting-edge seminars and focused, high-level internships at investment firms, hospitals, law firms, and other prestigious organizations. Professors bring real-world experience into the classroom to combine theory and practice, providing quality individual and seminar-style mentoring.

Students in the global business management program are preapproved to spend a semester studying in either Cyprus, Greece or Milan, Italy.

Academic Programs

The Learning Commons for Academic Student Support provides free academic support for students. The Learning Commons offers tutoring services, academic workshops, and various learning communities.

The Center for Internships and Career Placement actively reaches out to the community to provide part-time jobs, internships, and professional job opportunities. Using a curriculum that's unique to Regis, students are taught how to identify and land the job that's right for them. Other career assistance includes online tools and required courses, workshops, one-on-one counseling, and career development and recruitment events.

The Regis Honors Program provides qualified students with intellectually and personally stimulating experiences, including academically rigorous courses; participation in community leadership, service learning, and service; and personal enrichment opportunities. Honors students explore complex issues of civic responsibility and global citizenship, and develop skills in contributing to the betterment of society, a central goal of Regis' mission.

Academic Facilities

Modern facilities are centrally located in the heart of Regis' historic campus. Residence halls are steps away from classrooms, the library, dining facilities and cafes, fitness centers, and a beautiful quad.

Regis is revolutionizing the campus experience. In addition to state-of-the-art computer labs, every incoming student receives an iPad as part of a nationally acclaimed program. Regis also has Fit Bikes in the library so that students can work out and study at the same time.

Costs

For the 2018–19 academic year, tuition is $41,015 and room and board is $15,180. All charges and fees are determined by the Board of Trustees and are subject to change.

Financial Aid

Regis is committed to providing a quality education while keeping costs affordable. Every student who applies to Regis is automatically considered for a merit scholarship. More than 95 percent of students at Regis receive financial assistance in the form of merit scholarships or need-based institutional grants, state and federal grants, loans, and work-study jobs. Students who are not eligible Federal Work-Study funding may apply for employment on campus.

Merit scholarships are available for up to four years, as long as students maintain their renewal requirements. Regis offers full-tuition Presidential Catholic scholarships to outstanding students who attend Catholic high schools. The Alumni Scholarship is available to both first-year and transfer students, and the Phi Theta Kappa Scholarship is designated specifically for transfer students.

Faculty

Professors at Regis take a values-based approach to teaching that focuses on a student-centered experience. With a student-to-faculty ratio of 12:1, Regis students have opportunities to work alongside professors on complex research projects and learn in state-of-the-art simulation labs.

Student Life

Regis prides itself on a strong, caring community, with the right mix of challenge, support, and personalized attention. The comfortable campus provides a setting where it's easy to make friends and get to know professors. Regis' 18 NCAA Division III Athletics teams, known as the Pride, have 100 percent of their facilities located directly on campus, including a synthetic turf field, eight-lane track, indoor complex, tennis courts, and a softball complex. With more than 30 clubs and organizations, students have many opportunities to get involved.

Regis guarantees four-year, on-campus housing and many choose to live on campus as a way to experience Regis beyond the classroom. All Regis residence halls offer laundry facilities, kitchenettes, lounge areas, and study spaces, and are staffed by resident directors and assistants. More than 800 programs and events take place in the residence halls each year.

Admission Requirements

Regis considers each application holistically. Credentials are thoroughly evaluated and all aspects of every candidate's application are reviewed. Many factors are considered, including academic performance in a college preparatory curriculum and grades received; leadership qualities and participation in extracurricular activities; the required essay, demonstrating a student's ability to think critically and communicate effectively; letters of recommendation; SAT/ACT scores (optional for all academic programs except nursing); and an interview with an admission representative (highly recommended, but not required).

The following college preparatory credentials are recommended: English, 4 years; mathematics, 3 years (algebra I and II, geometry), natural science, 3 years (2 with a lab); social science, 3 years; foreign language, 2 years (same language); and electives, 3 or 4 years.

Regis welcomes applicants for admission without regard to race, color, religious affiliation, national or ethnic origin, or learning or physical disability.

Application and Information

Regis accepts the Common Application. In addition to this form, applicants must also submit their official secondary school transcript, a personal essay, one signed letter of recommendation from a secondary school counselor or teacher on official letterhead, and a nonrefundable $50 application fee. Regis is a test-optional institution, with the exception of home-schooled students, those interested in applying to the nursing major, and those interested in the St. George's University Accelerated Medical/Veterinary School Program. TOEFL scores may be requested if the student's native language is not English.

Regis has a rolling admission policy. Students may submit their application at any point during the year. Regis also has Early Action and Priority Application deadlines. Students who wish to be considered for Early Action must apply by November 15. The Priority Application deadline is February 1.

Admitted students should submit a nonrefundable enrollment deposit by the enrollment deposit deadline of May 1. Deposits received after May 1 will be accepted on a space-available basis. Admitted students applying for the spring semester (January) should submit a nonrefundable enrollment deposit by January 1. Deposits received after January 1 or May 1 will be accepted on a space-available basis.

A final high school transcript and an official indication of graduation must be received by the Office of Undergraduate Admission no later than July 15. Failure to submit these documents may result in the student's acceptance being rescinded and cancellation of the Financial Aid Award letter.

Office of Undergraduate Admission
Regis
235 Wellesley Street
Weston, Massachusetts 02493
Phone: 866-438-7344
E-mail: admission@regiscollege.edu
Website: http://www.regiscollege.edu

RIDER UNIVERSITY
LAWRENCEVILLE, NEW JERSEY

 To read more about this school, visit http://petersons.to/rideruniversity

The University

When students join Rider University's vibrant living-and-learning community, life—and learning—is never the same. Guided by Rider's gifted faculty and supported by its staff, Rider students discover powerful new ways to connect learning to the world around them.

The University is located in central New Jersey, easily accessible to New York City and Philadelphia, offering students great opportunities for exploration, culture, leadership development, internships, and jobs.

Students are at the heart of everything that happens at Rider. The University's student-centered commitment begins with professors who are focused on teaching and mentoring students. That commitment is shared by the entire University community, where every staff member is available to support students and their goals. It's a unique environment dedicated to giving students the self-confidence, skills and strong foundation essential for professional and personal success.

Students come to Rider from 38 states, three U.S. territories, and 68 countries. Each year, Rider enrolls 3,800 undergraduate and 1,000 graduate students.

The greatest legacy of a Rider education is measured by the success of its alumni. Rider alumni have gone on to great success at many of the country's top-ranked graduate and professional schools. They have competed for and won prestigious internships, research grants, scholarships, and fellowships—including numerous Fulbright Scholars.

The outcomes of a Rider education are clear: over 93 percent of Rider graduates are employed full- or part-time, pursuing graduate study, or involved in a volunteer or fellowship position within six months of graduating. And, 273 Rider alumni are presidents, CEOs, and leaders of national or international corporations or organizations.

Location

Rider's central location between two vibrant metropolitan centers—New York and Philadelphia—offers great opportunities for adventure, exploration, culture and shopping, plus internships and jobs. Rider is just minutes away from historic downtown Princeton, incredible nature trails, shopping malls, and more. Students can head an hour in any direction to laze at the beach, downhill ski, or enjoy the sights and sounds of the big city. Whether it's for sightseeing or shows, auditions or internships, Rider is only 90 minutes by train to the heart of Manhattan or an hour to downtown Philadelphia.

Majors and Degrees

At Rider, students can choose from nearly 70 undergraduate and 35 graduate programs through five colleges/schools: College of Business Administration; College of Liberal Arts and Sciences; College of Education and Human Services; School of Fine and Performing Arts; and College of Continuing Studies. Interdisciplinary majors are plentiful, and dual majors are encouraged.

Academic Programs

Lessons learned in the classroom at Rider are complemented and reinforced with rich hands-on experiences. Students have the opportunity to participate in impressive professional internships, student-faculty research, honors and study-abroad programs, and volunteer experiences.

Rider students do lab work, perform on stage, hold leadership roles on campus, and work at the TV station as early as freshman year. Education majors are guaranteed 700 hours of classroom experience through field placements that begin in the sophomore year. Each year, Rider students complete more than 1,000 internships, co-ops, and field placements as part of their degree studies. Rider's award-winning Model UN program, innovative Global Village class, and a wealth of study-abroad and international partnership programs provide opportunities for students to experience the world in a new way.

Learning is enhanced by course work that reflects the latest best practices and technology, and guest lectures by leading experts. With plenty of real-world opportunities in nearby New York and Philadelphia, these great cities are true learning laboratories for students.

By building on these experiences, achievements, credentials, and contacts, Rider students discover what they love to do most—and stand out from the competition when they graduate.

Each of Rider's colleges has a career adviser who specializes in providing the support and preparation needed to move students from their majors to relevant careers. Students begin planning for the future in their first semester, using the expert resources of the Career Development and Success Center to create a compelling professional portfolio and a targeted resume. More information is available online at www.rider.edu/careers.

Students also have opportunities to develop polished interview skills through interactive workshops and alumni videos, launch their job search through the Rider career "handshake" site, and shadow and network with Rider alumni. Rider also hosts career fairs attended each year by hundreds of employers who come to campus to recruit candidates.

Costs

Rider is proud to be private and affordable. Students benefit from the many advantages of Rider's private university experience, and generous scholarship and financial aid programs that focus on making its bottom-line costs extremely competitive with most public colleges and universities.

For the 2017–18 academic year, tuition was $40,570 for full-time students. There is a student activities fee of $145 per semester and a technology fee of $225 per semester. There may be additional fees associated with certain academic programs.

Housing options ranged from $4,820 to $6,380 per semester, depending on the type of residence selected. Meal plans ranged from $2,530 to $2,610 per semester. Additional details can be found online at http://www.rider.edu/offices-services/financial-aid-scholarships/tuition-fees/housing-and-dining-rates.

Financial Aid

Financial aid is personal and tailored to each student's needs and circumstances, starting with the assigning of a personal financial aid advisor to each student. Ninety-nine percent of Rider students receive various forms of financial aid and 98 percent receive Rider-funded scholarships and gift aid. The average annual student assistance package at Rider is more than $33,000. More information on financial aid and scholarship availability can be found at http://www.rider.edu/offices-services/financial-aid-scholarships.

Faculty

Rider's professors are passionate about their disciplines, but teaching is their top priority. They are distinguished authors, educators, scholars, scientists, performing artists, and researchers; an impressive 99 percent hold a doctorate or the highest degree in their field. With an average class size of 22 and a 11:1 student/faculty ratio, classes at Rider are small and collegial.

Student Life

Rider's focus on engaged learning helps students grow, professionally and personally, through abundant global and cultural experiences, honors and leadership development programs, service-learning opportunities, and exposure to the arts.

Rider's vibrant and active campus community includes student government, more than 150 student organizations, fraternities and sororities, plus 20 NCAA Division I men's and women's teams, and 28 club and intramural sports. Getting involved offers students the chance to inspire and lead others, manage budgets, plan successful events, and engage in big-picture thinking.

Admission Requirements

Rider University welcomes students with a variety of academic backgrounds. When reviewing an application for admission, the Undergraduate Admission Office takes a holistic approach by assessing academic performance, letters of recommendation, and admission essay. Once the committee has reviewed the entirety of the student's academic experience, an admission decision will be made.

Potential students must submit official transcripts from their high school or for any college work they may have completed while in high school, a letter of recommendation, scores from SAT or ACT test (writing section is not required), and a $50 nonrefundable application fee.

Application and Information

The application deadlines for the fall semester are the following: Early Action (nonbinding), November 15; musical theatre, December 15; and scholarship deadline, January 15. For spring admission, the scholarship deadline is December 15.

Campus tours are offered Monday through Friday at 10 a.m. and 1 p.m. and select Saturdays at 10 a.m. or 1 p.m. To register for a tour online, visit http://rider.edu/visit.

For details on application dates and more, visit http://www.rider.edu/applynow.
Office of Admission
Rider University
2083 Lawrenceville Road
Lawrenceville, New Jersey 08648
Phone: 609-896-5000 (Main)
      800-257-9026 (Admission)
E-mail: admissions@rider.edu
Website: http://www.rider.edu

Rider University's vibrant and engaged learning community brings together people from diverse backgrounds, talents, and perspectives to explore subjects, tackle problems, share ideas, embark on adventures, and create solutions.

RIPON COLLEGE
RIPON, WISCONSIN

The College

Established in 1851, Ripon College is Wisconsin's best-value private college and a national leader in liberal arts education, devoted to ensuring every student realizes their unique potential. Ripon's five-course, 20-credit Catalyst curriculum rigorously develops the 21st-century skills employers seek while streamlining the path to graduation. Students enjoy extensive freedom to pursue their passions and craft their own academic program of study. Students are overwhelmingly satisfied with the amount of personalized attention they receive from devoted faculty and staff. Within six months of graduation, 96 percent of alumni are employed, in graduate school or student-teaching.

Ripon is a member of the prestigious Associated Colleges of the Midwest (ACM). The College competes athletically as part of the Midwest Conference and offers 21 NCAA Division III varsity teams. Ripon has a student-to-faculty ratio of 12:1, and the average class size is fewer than 20 students. The brand new $23.5 million Willmore Center provides students with state-of-the-art facilities to train, work out, study, and learn, and boasts the best NCAA indoor track in Wisconsin. More information is available at ripon. edu/willmore-center.

Location

The College is in the historic city of Ripon, Wisconsin—a friendly, safe community of just under 8,000 people, 80 miles northwest of Milwaukee, 70 miles southwest of Green Bay, 73 miles northeast of Madison, 180 miles northwest of Chicago, and 255 miles southeast of the Twin Cities in Minnesota. The nearest airport is 40 minutes away in Appleton, Wisconsin.

The campus comprises 250 tree-lined acres and 27 buildings, 10 of which are listed on the National Register of Historic Places. A sustainable campus, Ripon is home to the Ceresco Prairie Conservancy with 130 acres of native prairie, oak savanna, and wetland habitat in the making.

Majors and Degrees

Ripon College offers a four-year graduation guarantee with 30 majors and 42 minors, including a variety of fast-track pre-professional programs. Every student graduates with a concentration in Applied Innovation upon completing the five-course, 20-credit Catalyst curriculum.

Majors include Anthropology, Art History, Biology, Business Management, Chemistry, Chemistry–Biology, Communication, Economics, Educational Studies, English, Environmental Studies, Exercise Science/Athletic Training Track, Foreign Languages, Global Studies, History, Mathematics, Music, Philosophy, Physical Education, Physical Science, Politics and Government, Psychobiology, Psychology, Recreation Physical Education, Religion, Sociology, Spanish, Sport Management, Studio Art, and Theatre.

Minors include American Studies, ARMS (Ancient, Renaissance, and Medieval Studies), Anthropology, Art History, Biology, Business Management, Chemistry, Classical Studies, Coaching, Communication, Criminal Justice, Dramatic Literature, Economics, Educational Studies, English, Entrepreneurship, Environmental Biology, Francophone Studies, French, Health, History, Latin American and Caribbean Studies, Law and Society, Mathematics, Military Leadership, Music, National Security Studies, Nonprofit Management, Philosophy, Physics, Politics and Government, Psychology, Religion, Socially Responsible Leadership, Sociology, Spanish, Studio Art, Theatre Production, and Women's and Gender Studies.

Ripon College offers fast-track programs that allow students to get professional degrees sooner in certain fields. There are currently fast-track programs in engineering with Washington University; law with Marquette University, American University, Mitchell Hamline University, and St. Thomas University; and osteopathic medicine with Lake Erie College of Osteopathic Medicine. Other pre-professional programs available include: Government Service, Journalism, Library and Information Science, Military Leadership, Ministry, Pre-Med and Health Sciences (medicine, dentistry, veterinary medicine, optometry, podiatry, physical therapy, pharmacy, nursing, chiropractic medicine, sports medicine), and Social Work.

Teacher certification is offered in Early Childhood, Elementary, Middle/Junior High, Secondary, Bilingual/ESL, and Special Education. In addition, Ripon offers licensure in 26 subject areas. Teacher certification programs approved by the Wisconsin Department of Public Instruction prepare students for licensure at the early childhood/middle childhood level (grades PK through 5), the middle childhood/early adolescence level (grades 1 through 8), the early adolescence/adolescence level (grades 6 through 12), and cross categorical special education (MC-EA). The educational studies department also offers PK–12 certification programs in Art, Foreign Languages (French and Spanish), Music, Physical Education, Physical Education and Health, and Theatre (pending program approval).

Academic Programs

Ripon's innovative new curriculum, Catalyst, began with the first-year class in fall 2016. The five-course, 20-credit curriculum rigorously develops the 21st-century skills that employers seek while streamlining the path to graduation. Catalyst ensures students have extensive freedom and are able to complete multiple majors and minors, study abroad, and hold internships in four years.

Ripon's liberal arts curriculum introduces students to a wide variety of disciplines. About 40 percent of students complete double or triple majors, while some create special self-designed majors. Hallmarks of a Ripon education are excellent writen and oral communication skills; critical-thinking and problem-solving skills; quantitative analysis; intercultural competence; collaboration;and informational literacy. Students enjoy limitless opportunities to explore serious research pursuits alongside faculty as an undergraduate, no matter what the student's major.

A Ripon education can take students anywhere, as demonstrated by the College's talented and well-known alumni. One student studied psychology and played basketball at Ripon, then become a seven-time Grammy winner: jazz singer Al Jarreau (1962). Another, Oliver Williamson (1954) earned a Nobel Prize in economics. Jeff Bantle (1980), a chief flight director with NASA, helped guide the space shuttle into orbit, and Gail Dobish (1976) is an international opera star. Neonatologist Dr. Jonathan Muraskas (1978) is credited with saving the world's smallest premature baby, and Richard Threlkeld (1959) covered the world as former Moscow correspondent for CBS News. Other entertainment notables include Harrison Ford (1964), Spencer Tracy (1924), and Justin Neibank (1978). Recent alumni Zach Morris (2002) studied at Oxford University as a Rhodes Scholar and also found time to play touch football with former President Bill Clinton and spend an evening at Buckingham Palace with Queen Elizabeth.

Off-Campus Programs

United States or abroad? Three weeks, one semester, two semesters? Students can choose from more than 40 programs, each officially sanctioned by and affiliated with Ripon. Although most programs are connected with a major or minor program, all are open to every Ripon student, regardless of major. Scholarships are available to pursue off-campus study.

Programs are offered throughout the United States, including Chicago; Knoxville, Tennessee; Nashville, Tennessee; a southwest Indian reservation; Washington, D.C.; Woods Hole, Massachusetts; and experiences at sea. International programs are offered in Europe, Africa, South America, Central America, India, and Asia.

Ripon College offers three-week Liberal Arts In Focus courses in January, May, and August. Taught in short, intensive blocks, In

Focus courses are designed as immersion experiences to provide a bridge between the theory and content of disciplines. Recent courses have included history lessons in Italy; intensive biology field studies in Costa Rica and the Wilderness Field Station near Ely, Minnesota; and a unique English course in Great Britain covering children's fantasy literature from Beatrix Potter to Harry Potter.

Academic Facilities

The 27 buildings on the Ripon campus include historic limestone structures and more modern facilities. Recent updates include a $23.5 million athletics, health, and wellness center; a brand new Center for Career and Professional Development; a completely renovated recital hall; an apartment-style residence hall; and enhancements to the student union, dining facilities, and student activity spaces.

The athletics, health, and wellness center features new high-tech classrooms, a state-of-the-art fitness center, an NCAA indoor track, performance courts, fitness studios, athletic training center, an open air atrium, new conference and meeting spaces, and other enhancements.

C. J. Rodman Center for the Arts is home to a theater with a state-of-the-art computerized lighting system, a recital hall with one of only 50 existing Bedient organs, an art gallery, a high-tech lab, and a sculpture garden.

Bovay's Study Bar & Mercantile opened in March 2017 in a historic building in downtown Ripon. This unique venue features a high-tech collaborative study space, a study bar with barista coffee service, a mercantile with official Ripon College apparel and gifts, and flexible meeting space. Bovay's is open late into the evening and features barista coffee service during peak study hours. Student interns working in the space will benefit from hands-on experiential training in marketing, merchandising, and small-business management.

Ripon College provides a secure, high-speed Wi-Fi network across campus and in every building. In addition, a state-of-the-art fiber optic network (10 Gb/s) connects all academic buildings, administrative buildings, and residence halls.

Students, faculty, and staff are issued a G Suite account that offers a variety of productivity tools (Gmail, Calendar, Drive, Docs, Forms, Hangouts) to enhance campus collaboration and communication. Multi-functional devices (MFDs) are located in every academic and administrative building to service the campus printing, copying and scanning needs. The College also has 3-D printers that several faculty have incorporated into their course curricula.

Open-use computer labs are located across campus, offering both Windows and Mac OS devices, projectors, and MFDs.

Ripon College has partnered with Apogee to provide a cutting-edge cable TV/video solution. With the revolutionary IPTV service, Stream2, students can view HD content live, on-demand, or recorded (20 hours of DVR storage per user) on their laptops, tablets, and smartphones.

Library staff provide friendly and efficient circulation, reference, instruction, and interlibrary loan services that aid in research. The library also houses the College archives, a computer lab, digital media stations, and more than 25 online databases. Library holdings include access to more than 300,000 physical and electronic books and 55,000 periodicals.

Costs

Tuition for the 2018–19 academic year is $43,508, room and board is $8,401, and fees are $300, for a total cost of $52,209.

Financial Aid

Pursuing a college degree is an important investment, so financial circumstances will never affect Ripon's admission decision. The College provides 100 percent of students with the financial assistance necessary to graduate and works to ensure a great economic value per every dollar spent.

Ripon offers its students competitive packages with funding from many sources: merit-based scholarships, need-based grants, educational loans, work-study, and scholarships from outside organizations. Academic scholarships range from $20,000 to $34,000 per year.

Student Organizations and Activities

From Love Your Melon to fencing, Ripon College hosts more than 60 student-run clubs and organizations. Students are encouraged to lead the programs, supported by the Student Senate's activity fee. This allows students to collaborate on conceiving, organizing, marketing, and developing unique activities.

Ripon's NCAA Division III Intercollegiate Teams compete in the Midwest Conference. Men's varsity sports include: baseball, basketball, cross-country, cycling, football, soccer, swimming and diving, tennis, and indoor and outdoor track and field. Women's varsity sports include: basketball, cross-country, cycling, dance, soccer, softball, swimming and diving, tennis, indoor and outdoor track and field, and volleyball.

In addition, Ripon offers a variety of intramural sports throughout the year, including kickball, dodgeball, flag football, indoor soccer, inner-tube water polo, basketball, bowling, badminton, whiffle ball, video games, volleyball, Ultimate Frisbee, and aerobics.

Admission Requirements

Ripon encourages applications from those students who are best prepared to benefit from and contribute to the academic and extracurricular programs that it offers. In evaluating applications, attention is paid to evidence of academic achievement, as indicated both by the distribution of courses taken in secondary school and by performance in those courses.

Ripon is test optional; test scores will be considered if the applicant chooses to submit them.

For further information, students should contact:

Leigh D. Mlodzik
Dean of Admission
Ripon College
300 Seward Street
P.O. Box 248
Ripon, Wisconsin 54971-0248
Phone: 800-947-4766 (toll-free)
E-mail: adminfo@ripon.edu
Website: http://www.ripon.edu

Ripon College's new $23.5 million Willmore Center was host to the 2018 Midwest Conference Indoor Track and Field and Women's Basketball Championships.

RIVIER UNIVERSITY
NASHUA, NEW HAMPSHIRE

 For more information, visit http://petersons.to/rivieruniversity

The University

Rivier University, a private Catholic university founded in 1933 by the Sisters of the Presentation of Mary, has earned a reputation for excellence with distinguished academic programs. Rivier offers many of the region's leading programs at the undergraduate, graduate, postgraduate, and doctoral levels.

Rivier's School of Undergraduate Studies enrolls approximately 1,400 students, including more than 870 full-time day students. With a 15:1 student-faculty ratio, day students have plenty of opportunities to connect with faculty and become active members of the academic community.

The majority of undergraduate students enroll from the six New England states. Rivier also attracts students from all over the United States as well as international students representing countries in Africa, Asia, Europe, and the Middle East. Students who live on campus reside in four modern residence halls, some with suite-style options. Rivier also provides substance-free housing and honors housing. The Dion Center features the University's student center and the newly renovated Dining Center which offers a healthy, upscale dining experience. The commuter lounge, a campus store, student development offices, and meeting rooms are also available in the Dion Center.

The Office of Student Affairs, the Student Government Association, and more than 13 student clubs and organizations provide a calendar of social, cultural, and recreational activities, including concerts, live entertainment, films, and sporting events. The University and student organizations frequently organize outings, including trips to locations such as Boston and New York. Students also enjoy performances by the Rivier Theater Company.

Rivier's orientation for new students introduces them to the University's wide array of services, such as academic advisers, the Academic Support Center, and peer tutors. The Health Services Center and the Wellness and Counseling Center ensure students' physical and emotional well-being. A full-time chaplain and Campus Ministry staff coordinate spiritual activities and service opportunities.

Be Remarkable

University programs feature a strong liberal arts foundation and proactive professional preparation. Students are encouraged to "Be Remarkable" through Rivier's unique combination of classroom learning, real-world experiences, and career preparation. Vocational exploration begins in the first year, and a personal, four-year academic and professional action plan is offered to each student, charting a path to achieving their goals. Close collaboration between academics, Student Advising, faculty, and the Career Development Center facilitates students' achievement and tracks progress on their plans.

Employment Promise Program

Rivier University has instituted an innovative Employment Promise Program to enhance career preparation and employability of students in all academic disciplines. The program demonstrates the University's confidence in its educational experience marked by distinctive academic programs, committed faculty, and active learning. Through this initiative, the University promises invested students that they will secure a job within nine months of graduation. If they do not, they will receive additional support in the form of payment of monthly federal subsidized student loans for up to one year or enrollment in up to six Rivier master's degree courses tuition-free. Rivier is the only institution in New Hampshire to offer this program.

Athletics

Rivier is a Division III member of the NCAA and sponsors 13 intercollegiate sports. Rivier Raiders compete in men's and women's soccer, volleyball, cross-country, basketball, and lacrosse; men's baseball; and women's field hockey and softball. The men's volleyball team has been nationally ranked every year since 2001. The Muldoon Health and Fitness Center is home to Rivier's varsity athletics, fitness activities, and recreation programs including volleyball, floor hockey, basketball, weight training, indoor soccer, and more. The campus also has a turf rectangular field and a natural grass softball field, as well as a beach volleyball court and cross-country trail. Student athletes can take advantage of an on-campus athletic training clinic for injury assessment and rehabilitation.

Location

Nashua (population approximately 87,000) is located in southern New Hampshire. The city of Boston lies within easy access 40 miles to the south. Local access to public transportation provides for easy travel to and from the campus. Recreational activities abound year-round at nearby lakes and ski areas, in the White Mountains to the north, and at the seacoast, just an hour's drive to the east. The Manchester airport is a 15-minute drive from campus, convenient for students who must access air travel.

Majors and Degrees

Rivier University awards Bachelor of Arts and Bachelor of Science degrees in the following areas: biology, biology education, biotechnology, business, criminal justice, early childhood education, education and community leadership, elementary education, English, English education, finance, global studies, history, homeland and international security, human development, liberal studies, marketing, mathematics, mathematics education, nursing, political science, psychology, public health, secondary education, social studies education, sociology, and special education. The University offers preprofessional programs in law, dentistry, medicine, and veterinary medicine.

Academic Programs

Professional studies and liberal arts programs prepare students for a rapidly changing, highly technological, and global society. The broad-based curriculum focuses on preparing students for rewarding careers and furthering their personal growth. The University launched a new core curriculum, offering opportunities for service learning, servant leadership, civic engagement, and community service to support the intellectual growth of students and enhance student leadership. Students choose from courses in three areas: humanities and social sciences, mathematics and natural sciences, and languages in the core complement. The new core is aligned with the Association of American Colleges and Universities' (AAC&U) essential learning outcomes, which provide Rivier graduates with the strong intellectual and practical skills that are in demand in the workplace. A bachelor's degree requires a minimum of 120 credits with a grade point average of at least 2.0. For an associate degree, the student must complete a minimum of 60 credits with a grade point average of at least 2.0.

All departments encourage qualified students to pursue internships in their field of study. Students in Rivier's public health major will work alongside public health professionals at local agencies, and a study-abroad component offers first-hand global perspective and experience. Education majors student teach in local schools. Nursing majors complete clinical rotations in healthcare facilities throughout southern New Hampshire and northern Massachusetts. History, law, and political science majors may work in a law office, business, legal-assistance agency, or government agency. Sociology and psychology majors work with local social service agencies. English and marketing majors work in public relations, broadcasting, or corporate communications positions. Business majors work in advertising, management, and technology.

Honors and awards for students include placement on the dean's list, membership in Kappa Gamma Pi or Psi Chi, listing in *Who's Who Among Students in American Universities and Colleges*, listing in *The National Dean's List*, and degrees with honors. Academically talented students may also apply to the four-year Global Scholars Honors Program.

The academic year is divided into two 14-week semesters. Students usually take five courses each semester. Additional courses are offered during the summer. Academic credit may be granted to incoming freshmen on the basis of Advanced Placement test and CLEP examination scores. Students may also "challenge" courses and receive credit by special examination.

Off-Campus Programs

Through Rivier University's membership in the New Hampshire College and University Council, a sixteen-member consortium of senior and two-year colleges, Rivier students may register for courses at any of the member colleges and receive transfer credits.

Academic Facilities

Academic facilities include Memorial Hall, which houses 14 classrooms, the Office of Global Engagement, faculty offices, a lecture hall, a behavioral science lab, and Rivier's art gallery. The Academic Computer Center features up to 68 workstations with a full range of cutting-edge software and Internet/email access. Regina Library provides access to more than 150,000 e-books and over 80 research databases, as well as more than 3 million volumes in 12 area libraries on virtually every academic subject. The Writing and Resource Center offers assistance from professional writing consultants as well as peer tutors. Other academic facilities include nursing and science laboratories; a physical assessment lab and nursing skills simulation lab, which provide nursing students with practical experience using blood pressure cuffs, ophthalmoscopes, IV pumps, high-fidelity patient simulators, and more; the McLean Center for Finance and Economics; the BAE Student Research Lab; a clinical psychology lab; electronic classrooms offering multimedia learning tools; and the Benoit Education Center, which houses the eight-classroom Landry Early Childhood Center, observation rooms, and an educational resource center.

Costs

Tuition and fees for the academic year 2018–19 are $31,040; room and board, $12,525; and books and supplies, approximately $1,400.

Financial Aid

Financial aid is awarded on the basis of the financial need of the student and family. Approximately 98 percent of Rivier's full-time undergraduate students receive financial aid from the University or from government or private sources. Federal aid includes Federal Pell Grants, Federal Supplemental Educational Opportunity Grants, Federal Perkins Loans, Federal Direct Stafford Student Loans, the Federal Direct PLUS loan program, and the Federal Work-Study Program. To be considered for financial aid, a student must file the Free Application for Federal Student Aid (FAFSA) with the federal government as soon as possible after October 1 for the coming year. FAFSA results should be on file with the University Financial Aid Office prior to March 1 for the following academic year. Each applicant is assessed individually to determine the best combination of grant, work, scholarship, and loan amounts to meet the need of the student. The University awards more than $10 million in institutional merit-based scholarships and grants annually. For more information, students should contact the Office of Financial Aid.

Faculty

The University employs 69 full-time faculty members. Part-time instructors in specialized areas are working professionals who bring current knowledge and expertise in their field to their classes. All classes are taught by faculty members, and department chairs serve as academic advisers to students in their major programs.

Student Government

Every full-time day student automatically becomes a member of the Student Government Association (SGA) upon registration and payment of the student activity fee. The SGA's main goals are to stimulate active participation in all University functions; to establish and maintain effective channels of communication among members of the University community and the community at large; to foster a mutual trust; to encourage a spirit of cooperation; and to initiate new endeavors. The SGA also supervises student clubs and organizations and oversees their finances. The SGA Executive Board serves as the channel of communication through which the views of the students on institutional policies reach the University administration.

Admission Requirements

Applicants for admission should ordinarily have completed, in an accredited high school, a minimum of 16 academic units, including 4 of English, 2 of a modern foreign language, 3 of mathematics, 2 of social science, 1 of laboratory science, and 3 of electives. The most successful candidates are in the upper half of their class, with at least a B average. The University does not require SAT or ACT scores as part of a student's overall admissions file, except for nursing students. While nursing students are required to provide SAT or ACT scores, all other students have the option to submit their scores. A personal interview is strongly recommended but not required.

Rivier welcomes applications from qualified transfer candidates from accredited institutions, as well as applications from international students. Transfer students must forward transcripts of all previous college work and a high school transcript. International students must fulfill the requirements for general admission; they may also be required to submit Test of English as a Foreign Language (TOEFL) scores. Deferred admission may be granted to students who wish to postpone entrance for up to one year, provided they have not been enrolled full-time at another postsecondary institution.

Application and Information

Applications must be accompanied by an essay, one letter of recommendation, and a high school transcript. The School of Undergraduate Studies employs a system of rolling admission that allows qualified students to be admitted approximately one month after their application is completed. Transfers should apply by June 1 for fall admission and by December 1 for spring admission. Those applying for financial aid should observe the March 1 deadline. Interviews are arranged through the Admissions Office. Students may apply online using the Common Application or the application on the University's website.

For an application or additional information, please contact:

Office of Undergraduate Admissions
Rivier University
420 South Main Street
Nashua, New Hampshire 03060
Phone: 603-897-8507
Fax: 603-891-1799
E-mail: admissions@rivier.edu
Website: http://www.rivier.edu

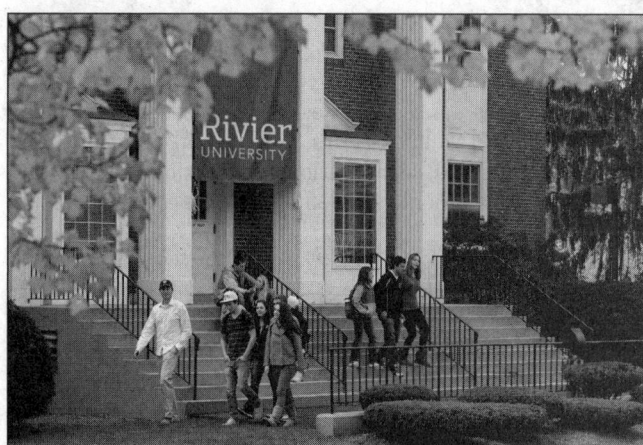

Students enjoy Rivier's great location in the heart of New England—approximately an hour's drive from Boston, the mountains, and the seacoast.

ROBERT MORRIS UNIVERSITY
MOON TOWNSHIP, PENNSYLVANIA

 To read more about this school, visit http://petersons.to/robertmorrisuniversity

The University

A private university in Pittsburgh's suburban hills, Robert Morris University (RMU) is a nationally ranked doctoral degree-granting university set on a 230-acre former estate that is a short drive from the cultural and commercial opportunities of a major city. Founded in 1921, RMU offers more than 80 undergraduate and graduate degree programs, including many online options, providing more than 5,000 students academic excellence with a professional focus.

The University built its reputation in the business fields of accounting, finance, marketing, and management. It has grown to include programs in communications, information systems, engineering, mathematics, science, education, social sciences, nursing, and health sciences. RMU uses a student engagement transcript to document internships, service-learning activities, study abroad, leadership roles, and other learning outside the classroom.

RMU is a teaching-centered institution featuring small classes taught by professors and a student-faculty ratio of 15:1. Recent years have seen the construction of new buildings for the School of Business, the School of Communications and Information Systems, and the School of Nursing and Health Sciences, along with major expansion and renovation of the School of Engineering, Mathematics, and Science, and the School of Education and Social Sciences. New residence halls accommodate a growing student population on a campus that has evolved from commuter to residential, with more than 85 percent of freshmen living in campus housing.

Visiting international scholars and a variety of opportunities to study abroad—for a semester or just a few weeks—enrich students' global perspectives. Students can participate in any of nearly 100 clubs and organizations. The Student Life Office organizes dances, parties, movie screenings, comedy acts, health and wellness fairs, educational programs, and day trips. Business organizations, professional clubs, and honor societies provide students with career preparation opportunities.

The University's competitive athletics program fields sixteen NCAA Division I teams, and the Colonials have won numerous titles and championships. The University is building the new UPMC Events Center on campus, opening in 2019, for its men's and women's basketball programs—the women have won the Northeast Conference title three of the last five years, while the men have the most conference titles in the NEC and won most recently in 2015. Nationally ranked Division I men's and women's ice hockey teams play at the RMU Island Sports Center, a 32-acre sports and recreation complex. Students can also participate in a number of club and intramural sports on campus.

Location

The 230-acre main campus is located in Moon Township, Pennsylvania, just 15 minutes from Pittsburgh International Airport and 17 miles from downtown Pittsburgh. The RMU Island Sports Center is 15 minutes from campus on Neville Island.

Majors and Degrees

Robert Morris University offers 51 undergraduate programs of study: accounting, actuarial science, advertising, biology, biomedical engineering, business, communication, competitive intelligence systems, computer information systems, corporate communication, criminal justice, cyber forensics and information security, economics, education (early childhood, special education, middle level, and business education), engineering, English, environmental science, finance, graphic design, health services administration, history, hospitality and tourism management, industrial engineering, information sciences, intelligence systems, journalism, management, manufacturing engineering, marketing, mathematics, mechanical engineering, media arts, nuclear medicine technology, nursing, organizational leadership, photography, political science, pre-medicine, professional communications/information systems, psychology, public relations, social science, sociology, software development, software engineering, special education, sport management, sport psychology, theater, TV/video production, web design, and writing.

Fully online bachelor's degree programs are available in business, criminal justice, cyber forensics and information security, English, health services administration, hospitality and tourism management, organizational leadership, psychology, and RN–M.S.N.

The University offers five-year integrated bachelor's/master's degree programs, medical school affiliation, cooperative education programs, an integrated 3+3 J.D. program with Duquesne University School of Law, and an honors program.

Academic Programs

Robert Morris operates on a two-semester schedule with various summer sessions. A total of 120 credits are required for most bachelor's degrees. Internship or co-op credits of 3 to 12 hours may be used toward degree requirements. The University participates in a cross-registration program with nine local colleges through the Pittsburgh Council on Higher Education consortium.

Academic Facilities

The 2016 completion of Scaife Hall, which includes a new nursing simulation center, means that each of the University's five schools has its own home, each fully equipped with learning technology, including state-of-the-art laboratories and studios, simulation equipment, and videoconferencing. Learning resources include a traditional library with more than 137,000 bound volumes, 80 reference databases, and 600 periodical subscriptions.

Costs

Annual tuition for the 2018–19 year is a $29,060 flat rate, based on a 24- to 36-credit, two-semester schedule. Annual room and board is $11,400 based on double occupancy and the Patriot meal plan.

Financial Aid

Ninety percent of RMU undergraduates who request it receive some sort of financial aid, including scholarships, grants, loans, and work-study programs. Both need-based and achievement-based awards are available. All applicants must complete the admissions application, the Free Application for Federal Student Aid, and the grant forms from their own state.

Faculty

The University has more than 480 full- and part-time faculty members; 87 percent of full-time faculty members hold terminal degrees. The student-faculty ratio is 15:1 and the average class size is 22. Students may take advantage of the expertise offered by the faculty in academic advisement and counseling, as well as counseling from the staff at the Center for Student Success.

Student Government

The Student Government Association represents all student organizations, including fraternities and sororities. Members participate in the planning of all social and cultural events on campus.

Admission Requirements

First-time freshmen must submit an application for admission with a $30 application fee (waived for online applicants), official high school transcripts or GED credential, and official SAT or ACT scores. Preference is given to applicants with a minimum 3.0 high school GPA and a combined SAT score of 1000 (Reading + Math) or a composite ACT score of 22.

Transfer students who have earned credits from another regionally accredited institution must submit transcripts from all postsecondary institutions attended and must have a minimum 2.0 GPA. Students with less than 30 college credits must also submit high school transcripts or GED credential.

Certain select academic programs have higher admissions criteria. Students are encouraged to arrange for a campus visit with an admissions counselor.

Application and Information

Students are encouraged to submit applications in the fall of their senior year of high school. Official transcripts and counselor recommendations should accompany the application; there is a $30 application processing fee that is waived for online applicants.

Robert Morris uses a rolling admission system; students are considered for acceptance as soon as all application materials have been received and evaluated.

For additional information and application materials, students should contact:

Kellie Laurenzi
Dean of Admissions
Robert Morris University
6001 University Boulevard
Moon Township, Pennsylvania 15108
Phone: 800-762-0097 (toll-free)
Website: http://www.rmu.edu
         http://www.facebook.com/RMUpgh
         http://twitter.com/rmu
         http://www.youtube.com/RMUNewsTube

RMU students engage in a campus tradition: taking selfies with "Bronze Bob," a statue of university namesake Robert Morris.

ROCHESTER INSTITUTE OF TECHNOLOGY

ROCHESTER, NEW YORK

R·I·T

The University

Rochester Institute of Technology (RIT) is among the world's leading career-oriented, technological universities. RIT offers more than ninety undergraduate programs in areas such as engineering, computing and information sciences, engineering technology, business, hospitality, science, art, design, photography, biomedical sciences, game design and development, and the liberal arts including psychology, advertising and public relations, and public policy. Students may choose from more than eighty different minors to develop personal and professional interests that complement their academic program. RIT is a world leader in experiential education, which includes cooperative education, internships, study abroad, and undergraduate research. As home to the National Technical Institute for the Deaf (NTID), RIT is a world leader in providing access services for deaf and hard-of-hearing students. RIT enrolls students from every state and more than 100 countries.

Close to 70 percent of RIT's approximately 15,400 full-time undergraduate students live on the campus in residence halls or campus apartments.

Each year, RIT's more than 300 student organizations sponsor over 1,300 on-campus activities. RIT offers 23 varsity sports, including Division I men's and women's hockey. Recreational facilities are exceptional and include two ice rinks, an aquatics center, a field house with an indoor track, and fitness facilities.

Location

The greater Rochester area has a population of about 800,000. Per-capita income is among the highest in the nation for metropolitan centers. The area's many internationally known industries employ a high proportion of scientists, technologists, and skilled workers. Rochester's industries have always been closely associated with RIT's programs and progress. Rochester is also a hub for higher education with twelve colleges and universities in the area.

Majors and Degrees

The College of Applied Science and Technology offers the Bachelor of Science (B.S.) degree in applied technical leadership (upper-division, online only), civil engineering technology, computer engineering technology, electrical engineering technology, electrical/mechanical engineering technology, manufacturing engineering technology, and mechanical engineering technology. It also grants the Bachelor of Science in environmental sustainability, health and safety, international hospitality and service management, and packaging science. An undeclared option allowing freshmen to delay selecting a major for up to a year is available in the School of Engineering Technology.

The E. Philip Saunders College of Business offers the B.S. in accounting, finance, new media marketing, international business, management, management information systems, and marketing. A 4+1 M.B.A. option is available, as are several minors, including entrepreneurship, digital business, and supply chain management. An undeclared option allowing freshmen to delay the selection of their major for up to one year is available.

The B. Thomas Golisano College of Computing and Information Sciences offers the B.S. in computer science, computing security, computing and information technologies, game design and development, human-centered computing, new media interactive development, software engineering, and web and mobile computing. The college also offers a computing exploration option for undeclared freshman students.

The Kate Gleason College of Engineering grants the B.S. in biomedical engineering, chemical engineering, computer engineering, electrical engineering, industrial and systems engineering, mechanical engineering, and microelectronic engineering. Degree options in aerospace, automotive, bioengineering, biomedical, energy and environment, ergonomics, information systems, manufacturing, and software engineering are also offered within the college. Accelerated B.S./M.S. options are available. The Engineering

Exploration Program, which allows freshmen to delay the selection of their major for up to one year, is available.

The College of Health Sciences and Technology offers B.S. programs in biomedical sciences, diagnostic medical sonography, exercise science, nutrition management, and a five-year physician assistant B.S./M.S. program.

The College of Imaging Arts and Sciences offers the Bachelor of Fine Arts in advertising photography, ceramics and ceramic sculpture, film and animation, fine art photography, studio arts, glass, graphic design, illustration, industrial design, interior design, medical illustration, metals and jewelry design, new media design and imaging, photojournalism, 3-D digital graphics, visual media, and woodworking. The college also offers B.S. programs in biomedical photographic communications, digital media, graphic media, imaging and photographic technology, motion picture science, and new media/publishing. An undeclared option allowing freshmen to delay the selection of their major for up to one year is available in the School of Art, the School of Design, the School for American Crafts, and the School of Photographic Arts and Sciences.

The College of Liberal Arts offers B.S. programs in advertising and public relations, communication, criminal justice, digital humanities and social sciences, economics, journalism, international and global studies, museum studies, philosophy, psychology, public policy, and sociology and anthropology. The Liberal Arts Exploration Program is designed to help undecided students formulate education and career plans.

The College of Science offers B.S. programs in applied mathematics, applied statistics and actuarial sciences, biology, biochemistry, bioinformatics, biotechnology and molecular bioscience, chemistry, computational mathematics, environmental science, imaging science, and physics. Special options are available in premedical studies (medicine, dentistry, veterinary medicine). Minors are available in astronomy, exercise science, imaging science, mathematics, physics, and statistics. Accelerated B.S./M.S. and B.S./M.B.A. programs are available. General Science Exploration allows freshmen to delay the selection of their major for up to one year.

Home of the National Technical Institute for the Deaf, RIT is a world leader in providing educational opportunities and access services for deaf and hard-of-hearing students. NTID awards associate degree programs and offers pre-baccalaureate studies for deaf and hard-of-hearing students. The associate degree programs prepare students for immediate employment after graduation or transfer into one of RIT's bachelor's degree programs. The pre-baccalaureate studies program prepares students for entry into RIT's bachelor's degree programs. Nearly 600 of the 1,150 deaf and hard-of-hearing students at RIT are enrolled in bachelor's degree programs in the other eight colleges.

Academic Programs

Most students entering as freshmen enroll directly in the academic program of their choice. Options for undeclared students are offered by most colleges as described above. A University Exploration program is available for entering freshmen who wish to explore programs in two or more colleges. Students interested in pre-law, pre-medical, and other pre-health professions may enroll in any major at RIT and take advantage of pre-professional advising programs that provide the guidance necessary to complete the admission requirements for graduate programs in law, medicine, and other health professions. Undergraduates may choose from more than eighty different minors. Double-majors and accelerated dual-degree (combined bachelor's/masters) options are available. The RIT honors program admits approximately 150 freshmen annually. Air Force and Army ROTC programs are available on the campus. A Naval ROTC program is offered jointly with the University of Rochester.

Every academic program at RIT offers some form of experiential education opportunity, including cooperative education, internships, study abroad, undergraduate research, and industry-sponsored projects. Co-op students alternate periods of full-time study with periods of full-time paid work experience directly related to their field of study and career interests. Last year, more than 4,400 students completed approximately 6,000 co-op assignments with nearly 2,300 employers, earning collectively in excess of $45 million.

Off-Campus Programs

RIT has four international locations. RIT Croatia is located in Dubrovnik and Zagreb, Croatia and offers undergraduate degree programs in hospitality and service management, information technology, and international business. RIT Kosovo in Pristina provides career-oriented programs that foster links between the university, industry, and government in support of workforce development. RIT Dubai offers graduate and undergraduate programs in business, engineering, service leadership, and information sciences.

Academic Facilities

Excellent facilities add to the quality of academic life. Students have access to some of the most up-to-date microelectronic, telecommunications, and computer engineering facilities in the U.S. RIT's Wallace Center is a true multimedia learning center. Its collections are exceptionally extensive in the areas of art and design, education for the deaf, photography, and printing.

Students use state-of-the-art computer equipment regardless of their major. Central computer systems can be accessed via a high-speed data network connecting the library, academic facilities, residence hall rooms, and on-campus apartments. There are more than sixty locations campuswide, with wireless networking connectivity utilizing 802.11b technology. The RIT campus network is served by two OC3 connections, each operating at a data rate of 155 Mbps, and one T3 connection operating at 45 Mbps. RIT is among a select group of institutions with access to the Internet2 research network, a collaborative research and development effort led by more than 170 U.S. universities working in partnership with industry and government.

Costs

For 2017–18, undergraduate tuition for the academic year (two semesters) was $39,506. Fees, including the activities and health fees, are $562. Room and board (twenty meals per week) cost $12,666.

Financial Aid

Approximately 77 percent of RIT's full-time undergraduates receive some form of financial aid that includes RIT scholarships, alumni or industry-supported scholarships, and state and federal government grants. A variety of loans and part-time work positions are available. The FAFSA must be submitted by March 1. Giving full recognition to scholarship apart from financial need, RIT awards a number of academic scholarships based on grades, test scores, and activities. Freshmen applying by January 15 and transfers applying by March 1 are considered for these scholarships.

Faculty

There are 1,023 full-time faculty members, 441 part-time faculty members, and an administrative and supporting staff of more than 2,200. Approximately 71 percent of the faculty members have earned a Ph.D. or the terminal degree in their field.

Student Government

The Student Government is the representative body for students. It works with RIT administration, faculty, and staff members to communicate the needs and desires of the student body and to communicate decisions of the administration to students. Fraternity and sorority members, off-campus and hearing-impaired students, and students from minority groups elect special representative bodies. All full-time and part-time undergraduate and graduate students are represented in Student Government.

Admission Requirements

Admission to RIT is competitive and varies from selective to highly selective depending on the desired program of study. The major factors determining freshman admission are strength of academic program, high school performance, and ACT or SAT test results. College performance is the main factor for transfer candidates. Students applying for programs in art, design, and crafts must submit a portfolio as part of the application process.

RIT promotes and values diversity and admits qualified men and women of any race, color, national or ethnic origin, religion, sexual orientation, gender identity, gender expression, or marital status. RIT does not discriminate on the basis of handicap in the recruitment or admission of students or in the operation of any of its programs or activities, as specified by federal laws and regulations.

Application and Information

An application, a nonrefundable processing fee of $65, official transcripts of all secondary school or college records, and SAT or ACT scores (for prospective freshmen) should be forwarded to RIT. Freshman applicants who provide all required materials for fall entry by January 15 receive admission notification by March 15. Prospective freshmen who apply after February 1 are considered on a space-available basis. A binding early decision plan is offered to prospective freshmen who have completed applications and filed credentials by November 15 to receive notification by January 1. Transfer applicants are strongly recommend to file their materials on or before March 1 for fall or summer admission and November 1 for spring admission. Fall applicants to the physician assistant program must have all application materials in by December 1.

For application forms, students should contact:

Director of Undergraduate Admissions
Rochester Institute of Technology
60 Lomb Memorial Drive
Rochester, New York 14623-5604
Phone: 585-475-6631
Fax: 585-475-7424
E-mail: admissions@rit.edu
Website: http://www.rit.edu
http://www.facebook.com/RITfb
http://twitter.com/RITAdmissions

A view of the campus.

SAINT ANSELM COLLEGE
MANCHESTER, NEW HAMPSHIRE

 To read more about this school, visit http://petersons.to/saintanselmcollege

The College

Saint Anselm College is a nationally-ranked private, Catholic, undergraduate institution with approximately 2,000 students. Founded in 1889 by the world's oldest religious order, the Benedictines—a Catholic order that has endured and thrived for more than 1,500 years—Saint Anselm is accredited by the New England Association of Schools and Colleges and holds membership in the Association of American Colleges, The American Council on Education, the National Catholic Educational Association, and the National Association of Independent Colleges and Universities. It is the third-oldest Catholic college in New England.

Saint Anselm College prepares students for life. With a liberal arts education, graduates are ready for real career experience, and for the challenges that lie ahead. They take their Saint Anselm experience with them to think critically, communicate effectively, and solve problems creatively.

Saint Anselm graduates are CEOs, doctors, lawyers, nurses, engineers, teachers, marketers, and researchers. They are humanitarians, healers, and philanthropists. They graduate Saint Anselm with the drive to achieve, empowered to make the world a better place. In fact, 99 percent of the class of 2016 was employed, in graduate school, or engaged in service within six months of graduation.

There's much to see and do on campus from open skate nights at Sullivan Arena to spring concerts on the quad. Academic buildings, such as the Goulet Science Center and Gadbois Hall, house innovative labs where remarkable research happens every day. There are cell culture labs, climate-controlled environmental chambers, a greenhouse, a sleep lab, SimMan labs, and more. In the library, students have access to the latest technological advances and a range of workspaces for individuals and groups.

Recreational facilities include the Carr Center with basketball courts and the 9,000 square-foot, three-level fitness center. Saint Anselm College boasts some of the top athletic facilities in the Northeast-10 Conference. The College's twenty intercollegiate athletic teams play all of their home contests on campus (with the exception of the golf team and the ski team) at Grappone Stadium, Sullivan Arena, or Melucci Field.

Ninety-one percent of Saint Anselm students live on campus in traditional residence halls, suites, townhouses, or apartments. A new 47,000-square-foot, 150-bed residence hall was completed in August 2014 offering students an innovative, living-learning community. Whether students live on campus or commute, everyone has access to Saint Anselm College's amazing food, ranked eighth in the nation by the Princeton Review.

New Hampshire Institute of Politics: Saint Anselm is home to the New Hampshire Institute of Politics & Political Library (NHIOP), which offers unparalleled opportunities for students to be in the front row of the democratic process. Its auditorium, West Wing, TV studio, and classrooms are where students meet today's prominent political policy thinkers and researchers, journalists and authors, scientists, industry executives, global leaders, and presidential candidates. The Institute, nationally known to political scholars and strategists, is an essential campaign stop for presidential candidates. All of the U.S. presidents in the last fifty years have visited Saint Anselm.

Location

Saint Anselm College is located on 380 acres in Manchester, New Hampshire and is an hour drive from Boston, the Atlantic Ocean and New Hampshire seacoast, and the White Mountains. Just minutes from downtown Manchester, students can find all the venues a small city has to offer: great restaurants and coffee shops, a theater, museum, minor league baseball and hockey teams, and a concert and sports arena to name a few. The Manchester-Boston Regional Airport is also just minutes from the College.

Majors and Degrees

At Saint Anselm College, students may earn a Bachelor of Arts degree in the following academic programs and majors: accounting, American studies, applied physics, archaeology, biochemistry, biology, business, chemistry, classics, communication, computer science, computer science with business, computer science with mathematics, criminal justice, economics, education studies: elementary and secondary, engineering physics (3-2 program), English, environmental science, environmental studies, finance, fine arts (art history, music, and studio art), forensic science, French, German studies, great books, history, international business, international relations, marketing, mathematics, mathematics with economics, natural science, peace and justice studies, philosophy, physics, politics, psychology, social work, sociology, Spanish, and theology. The College also offers a Bachelor of Science in Nursing (B.S.N.) through a traditional, undergraduate nursing program and a hybrid RN-to-B.S.N. program.

Saint Anselm students may pursue preprofessional programs in dentistry, law, medicine, theology, and veterinary medicine.

The engineering physics (3-2) program partners with the University of Notre Dame, University of Massachusetts-Lowell, Catholic University of America, and Manhattan College. More information is available online at www.anselm.edu/engineering.

Off-Campus Programs

At Saint Anselm College, a liberal arts education gives students a solid foundation for any career, but opportunities outside the classroom give students a competitive edge and real job experience.

Students find all kinds of experiential learning opportunities at Saint Anselm including internships, research, study abroad, and volunteering. Students of all majors and interests can find opportunities for internships through the Career Development Center, which also brings employers to campus and advises students throughout their job search.

Internships are offered in Boston, New York City, Washington, D.C., Manchester, and beyond. Some recent internships opportunities have included: the Boston Bruins, United States Secret Service, Fidelity Investments, the United States Senate, Fox News, and the American Cancer Society.

Many students work closely on research projects with faculty members on campus to gain valuable lab skills, but there are also opportunities at local hospitals and businesses.

Students interested in study abroad can travel the world visiting such places as Thailand, Morocco, and South Africa. In recent years, students have studied marine biology on Australia's Great

Barrier Reef, art history in the museums of Florence, finance in London, language in Spain and France, the culture of peace in Peru, and political history in Ireland. Saint Anselm College offers a semester abroad in Orvieto, Italy, with classes taught by Saint Anselm College faculty. If studying abroad for an entire semester seems too long, Saint Anselm students have traveled with faculty members on week-long trips to places such as China, Panama, and Vietnam.

Saint Anselm students have gained essential leadership and organizational skills through volunteering, doing everything from teaching English to new Americans to working the crisis hotline at the YWCA. In addition, every winter and spring break, Saint Anselm students travel to organizations around the country to volunteer at service sites through Service & Solidarity Mission trips. These service trips challenge students, giving them valuable perspectives and changing their views on the world.

Costs

For the 2018–19 academic year, tuition is $39,990, room and board is $14,500, and fees are $1,300.

Financial Aid

Saint Anselm provides students with financial aid opportunities through both private and federal aid programs. The College provides financial aid to offset the reasonable monetary investment that the student and family are expected to contribute. Ninety-seven percent of the College's undergraduates receive some degree of financial aid. Saint Anselm's financial aid opportunities include grants, loans, scholarships, and employment positions.

Merit scholarships are awarded to outstanding students. Two forms are required in applying for aid; the student must submit the CSS/Financial Aid PROFILE and the Free Application for Federal Student Aid (FAFSA).

Faculty

With an average class size of 18 and a student-faculty ratio of 10 to 1, students receive individual attention in small classes. With 220 professors and no teaching assistants, Saint Anselm faculty members are committed to the success of their students.

Student Life

With more than sixty clubs and organizations, twenty varsity athletic teams, a performing arts center, and an art gallery, Saint Anselm students have plenty of activities to explore. From the soccer club to the mock trial team to the Muslim Student Association, there is a club for every interest, cultural to academic.

Students interested in service will be right at home volunteering through the Meelia Center for Community Engagement or through Campus Ministry. Saint Anselm students volunteered more than 51,000 hours last year. Service & Solidarity Mission trips, held during each winter and spring break, allow Saint Anselm students to volunteer at locations around the country.

Saint Anselm College is part of the Division II Northeast-10 and ECAC Conferences and offers men's intercollegiate baseball, basketball, cross-country, football, golf, ice hockey, lacrosse, skiing, soccer, and tennis; and women's basketball, cross-country, field hockey, ice hockey, lacrosse, skiing, soccer, softball, tennis, and volleyball. Saint Anselm also has a variety of club, recreational, and intramural sports teams.

Admission Requirements

In reviewing applicants for the first-year class, admission considers each prospective student carefully. Counselors assess each applicant's secondary school performance, SAT or ACT scores (optional for non-nursing majors, nursing majors must submit scores), recommendation letters, and the written essay. Of highest priority is the applicant's secondary school transcript, with a specific focus on both the rigor of course study and the marks received. Saint Anselm invites transfer and international students to apply.

Saint Anselm College has the following admission deadlines:

• Early action—November 15

• Early decision—December 1

• Nursing majors—must apply by one of the early deadlines

• Regular decision—February 1

Saint Anselm College invites students and families to visit campus for a tour, information session, and/or interview.

For more information, prospective students should contact:

Office of Admission
Saint Anselm College
100 Saint Anselm Drive
Manchester, New Hampshire 03102
Phone: 603-641-7500
      888-426-7356 (toll-free)
E-mail: admission@anselm.edu
Website: http://www.anselm.edu

Saint Anselm's campus is home to students, instructors, researchers, and administrators, all striving to create a community where learning shapes living and where the search for knowledge takes place in an environment that values critical thinking, multicultural exchange, and service to humanity.

SAINT FRANCIS UNIVERSITY
LORETTO, PENNSYLVANIA

 To read more about this school, visit http://petersons.to/saintfrancisuniversity

The University

As the first Franciscan university in the nation, Saint Francis University has been has educating competent, caring professionals for 170 years. The private, Catholic, coeducational institution founded by the Franciscan Friars of the Third Order Regular, welcomes students of all faiths and currently enrolls more than 2,600 students from more than 20 countries.

The University offers highly targeted, career-focused programs grounded in the liberal arts tradition of inquiry and self-discovery. The values of respect, drive, generosity, and joy run deep in the University culture and help to prepare ethical, knowledgeable professionals with a passion to shape the world. This holistic approach to career preparation is supported by respected faculty who work closely with students in small settings to meet individual goals.

Saint Francis students are encouraged to make a difference through research and service projects, and many start as early as their freshman year. Undergraduate students work alongside Ph.D. faculty members conducting research and service projects as part of classes and through specialized learning centers such as the Center for Watershed Research and Service, The Keirn Family World War II Museum, the Center for the Study of Occupational Regulation, and the Center for Rural Cancer Survivorship.

Every student is encouraged to look beyond the classroom for career and personal growth through service leadership, undergraduate research, internships, and global opportunities. Saint Francis students graduate with a custom transcript in addition to their academic transcript known as their L.I.S.T. (Leadership, Involvement, Service Transcript) that quantifies these co-curricular accomplishments for employers.

The University is home to a vibrant campus life experience which capitalizes on its natural, rural setting as well as activities organized through student leaders. There are more than 50 official clubs and organizations including Campus Ministry, club sports, Greek Life, the Literary Guild, and marching band. Athletics also plays a major role in the student life with twenty-three NCAA Division I sports for men and women ranging from football to water polo.

Location

Saint Francis University's picturesque campus is situated on 600 acres in the heart of the Allegheny Mountains. The campus is located in the borough of Loretto, which has a population of approximately 1,400. The campus is 6 miles from the county seat of Ebensburg, which has a population of 4,000. The cities of Johnstown and Altoona are within 25 miles of Loretto and have populations of 35,000 and 55,000, respectively. The University is a 90-minute drive east of Pittsburgh.

Majors and Degrees

Saint Francis University offers more than 60 undergraduate majors and concentrations through four distinct academic schools. Each school couples classroom curriculum with embedded research and outreach centers for in-depth experiences.

School of Arts and Letters: Arts and Letters, Criminal Justice, Early Childhood Education, English, Environmental Studies, Fermentation, History, International Studies, Middle Childhood Education, Philosophy, Political Sciences, Pre-Law, Public Administration/Government Services, Religious Studies, Social Work, Sociology, Spanish, and Women's Studies.

School of Business: Accounting, Economics, Entrepreneurship Concentration, Finance, Healthcare Management, Management, Management Information Systems (M.I.S.), Marketing, and MBA (5-year, undergraduate entry).

School of Health Sciences: Exercise Physiology, Healthcare Studies (pre–allied health, pre-Occupational Therapy, Pre-Physician Assistant), Nursing, Occupational Therapy (5-year master's degree), Physical Therapy (6-year doctorate program), and Physician Assistant Sciences (5-year master's degree).

School of Sciences: Aquarium and Zoo Sciences, Biology, Biochemistry, Chemistry, Computer Science, Cybersecurity Administration, Engineering, Environmental Engineering, Mathematics, Petroleum and Natural Gas Engineering, and Pre-Professional (dentistry, optometry, pharmacy, veterinary).

The University is accredited by the Middle States Association of Colleges and Schools. Many departmental programs also hold program-level accreditations. A complete list of accreditations may be found in the University catalog or online at www.francis.edu.

Academic Programs

The program of study leading to a bachelor's degree is usually completed in eight semesters. To qualify for graduation, a student must follow a program of study approved by the Office of the Provost that totals at least 128 credits distributed among liberal arts courses, major requirements, collateral requirements, and general electives. All students, regardless of major, are required to complete the University's general education program of 58 credits. A majority of academic programs integrate hands-on learning opportunities using undergraduate research, clinical fieldwork experiences, study abroad, or independent study.

Off-Campus Programs

Students at Saint Francis University may, with permission of the University's administration, spend their junior year of study abroad or may earn credit for participation in summer programs conducted in Canada, France, Germany, Spain, and other countries by accredited American colleges and universities.

Students are encouraged to take advantage of the University's study abroad facility in Ambialet, France anytime throughout their academic career. The Semester in France program offers study for students within any major for the same tuition costs as studying on campus.

A number of departments offer students the opportunity for off-campus study. For some majors, such as nursing, occupational therapy, physical therapy, physician assistant science, education, medical technology, and social work, internships and/or clinical rotations are required. Saint Francis

University strongly encourages students in all other academic majors to complement their field of study with an internship, study abroad, a community service experience, or academic research with a faculty member.

Academic Facilities

The Campus Mall is flanked by academic buildings dedicated to each of the four academic schools. The newest construction projects include a re-imagined space for The Shields School of Business and a state-of-the art 70,000 square-foot science center. These projects complement the DiSepio Institute for Rural Health and Wellness Center which provides a clinical training area for health sciences. The University's Capital Campaign includes additional enhancements for health sciences. Students in the Arts and Letters conduct archival research in the newly opened Keirn Family World War II Museum.

Costs

For 2017–18, tuition was $33,856. In addition, there were fees for expenses associated with lodging, food, insurance, facilities, technology, orientation, and travel. The estimated total per student ranged from $45,784 to $47,626. Detailed cost breakdowns are available on the University website, www.francis.edu.

Financial Aid

Approximately 98 percent of the Saint Francis University student body receives financial aid. In addition to participating in federal and state need-based student aid programs, Saint Francis University offers its own substantial grant program and a generous scholarship program that is based on SAT or ACT scores, high school average, and class rank. Academic awards range from $1,000 to $18,000 annually.

Faculty

Faculty members are chosen for their knowledge of subject matter, as well as for their ability to communicate. Of the teaching faculty at Saint Francis University, 90 percent hold a doctorate or the highest degree attainable in their specific field of expertise. No teaching assistants or graduate students teach classes at Saint Francis University.

Student Clubs and Organizations

Saint Francis University offers an extensive list of co-curricular organizations for students. Over 60 clubs and organizations allow students to choose to become involved in areas of interest. A Greek life community, Student Government Association, and Student Activities Organization provide students additional leadership and involvement opportunities. Several club sport teams are available for students.

Admission Requirements

The admission committee considers applicants and renders decisions on the basis of the secondary school record, the recommendation of the secondary school principal or counselor, and the results of the SAT or ACT. Applicants to the School of Health Science should be aware of specified application requirements and deadlines. Applicants should have a minimum of 16 academic units and are strongly encouraged to visit the University campus for an admission interview and tour. Interviews and campus tours are available Monday through Friday throughout the year and select Saturday mornings while classes are in session.

Transfer students must submit a formal transfer application and a college clearance form in addition to official transcripts from each high school and college previously attended. Transfer students receive an advanced standing evaluation after an offer of admission has been made.

Saint Francis University, an equal opportunity/affirmative action employer, complies with applicable federal and state laws regarding nondiscrimination and affirmative action, including Title IX of the Educational Amendments of 1972, Titles VI and VII of the Civil Rights Act of 1964, and Section 504 of the Rehabilitation Act of 1973. Saint Francis University is committed to a policy of non-discrimination and equal opportunity in employment, education programs and activities, and admissions that includes all persons regardless of race, gender, color, religion, national origin or ancestry, age, marital status, disability, or Vietnam-era veteran status. Inquiries or complaints may be addressed to the University's Director of Human Resources/Affirmative Action/Title IX Coordinator, Saint Francis University, Loretto, Pennsylvania 15940; telephone: 814-472-3264.

For other University information, students should call 814-472-3000 or visit the website at www.francis.edu.

Application and Information

The University operates under a rolling admission policy. The occupational therapy and physical therapy programs have a January 15 priority application deadline. The Physician Assistant Sciences program has a November 15 priority application deadline. For more information about Saint Francis University, students should contact:
Vice President for Enrollment Management
Saint Francis University
P.O. Box 600
Loretto, Pennsylvania 15940
Phone: 814-472-3100
        866-342-5738 (toll-free)
E-mail: admissions@francis.edu
Website: http://www.francis.edu
        http://www.facebook.com/SaintFrancisUniversity
        http://twitter.com/SaintFrancisPA

In the fall of 2016, following a year-long $7 million renovation and expansion project, Schwab Hall welcomed students once more, this time re-imagined as home to The Shields School of Business. The project was funded entirely by donations from alumni and friends of the University.

SAINT JOSEPH'S UNIVERSITY
PHILADELPHIA, PENNSYLVANIA

 For more information, visit http://petersons.to/saintjosephsu

The University

Saint Joseph's University (SJU) is a nationally recognized, Catholic, Jesuit university. For 160 years, Saint Joseph's has advanced the professional and personal ambitions of men and women by providing a rigorous Jesuit education—one that demands high achievement, expands knowledge, deepens understanding, stresses effective reasoning and communication, develops moral and spiritual character, and imparts enduring pride. SJU's Haub School of Business is AACSB accredited, recognized by the National Honor Society Phi Beta Kappa chapter, and listed on the President's Higher Education Community Service Honor Roll. Saint Joseph's is the home to almost 5,000 undergraduate students and over 3,500 graduate and doctoral students.

As a Jesuit university, Saint Joseph's believes each student realizes his or her fullest potential through challenging classroom study, applied learning opportunities, and a commitment to excellence in all endeavors. The University also reinforces the individual's lifelong engagement with the greater world. Graduates of Saint Joseph's attain success in their careers with the help of an extensive network of alumni who have become leading figures in business, law, medicine, education, the arts, technology, government, and public service.

A Saint Joseph's education encompasses all aspects of personal growth and development, reflecting the Ignatian credo of *cura personalis*. Guided by faculty members who are committed to both teaching and scholarship, students develop intellectually through an intense liberal arts curriculum and advanced study in a chosen discipline. Students mature socially by participating in the University's campus life, noted for its rich variety of activities, infectious enthusiasm, and mutual respect. Students grow ethically and spiritually by *living greatly* both in the classroom and in the larger society beyond the campus.

Steeped in the Jesuit, Catholic tradition, Saint Joseph's provides a rigorous, intensive education that both disciplines and expands the mind. Students develop a lifelong desire to learn and grow while also acquiring the skills and knowledge necessary for success in their professional lives. At the core of this education is a general education program, which exposes students to primary fields of inquiry and the cultural values that shape their world. A Jesuit emphasis on engaged teaching and mentoring permeates the university. Faculty members at Saint Joseph's, many of whom are leading scholars in their disciplines, expect students to perform at the highest level and set demanding standards within the curriculum.

Saint Joseph's is at the forefront of utilizing innovative technologies to enhance and promote learning. These technologies are widely integrated into the educational process both in class and beyond, where they are also used for individual and collaborative research projects. By mastering these tools and achieving technological fluency, Saint Joseph's students gain a valuable edge in their careers.

Saint Joseph's students engage enthusiastically in all facets of campus life—academic, social, athletic, ethical, and spiritual. Their active participation creates a vibrant, dynamic campus community. In all their activities, students emphasize personal integrity as well as a respect and care for others. This produces a mutually supportive, humane, and tolerant environment for individual success and service to others.

Location

Located on the edge of metropolitan Philadelphia, Saint Joseph's provides ready access to the vast career opportunities and cultural resources of America's fifth-largest city, while affording students a cohesive and intimate campus experience.

Because of its location, Saint Joseph's has close ties to the professional opportunities and cultural life of Philadelphia. Students enjoy direct access to internships and cooperative education programs. Philadelphia also offers ample outlets for community involvement and service, and students can easily take advantage of Philadelphia's professional sports, entertainment, and cultural events. Philly is great for students.

Majors and Degrees

Saint Joseph's offers full-time baccalaureate degree programs in over fifty major fields of study and numerous specialty programs, which are administered by two separate colleges.

The College of Arts and Sciences awards bachelor's degrees in actuarial science, classical studies, art, art education, Asian studies, autism behavioral studies, biology, chemical biology, chemistry, communication studies, computer science, criminal justice, economics, education (early childhood/elementary PreK–4; early childhood/elementary PreK–4 + special education K–8 [double major]; elementary/middle years 4–8), English, environmental science, European studies, French, German, history, interdisciplinary health services, international relations, Italian, mathematics, music, philosophy, physics, political science, psychology, religious studies, sociology, Spanish, theater and film, and theology.

The Erivan K. Haub School of Business awards bachelor's degrees in accounting; business administration; business intelligence and analytics; entertainment marketing; family business and entrepreneurship; finance; food marketing; international business; leadership, ethics, and organizational sustainability; managing human capital; marketing; pharmaceutical and healthcare marketing; risk management and insurance; and sports marketing. A co-op program is available for all business majors.

Five-year B.S./M.S. programs are offered in education, international marketing, psychology, and writing studies. The University also offers special academic minors in advertising and public relations; Africana studies; American studies; animal studies; art history; behavioral neuroscience; business; Chinese language and culture; environmental and sustainability studies; faith-justice studies; gender studies; interdisciplinary health care ethics; Italian studies; journalism; justice and ethics in the law; Latin American studies; Medieval, renaissance, and reformation studies; music industry; real estate finance; special education; secondary education; and TESOL (teaching English to speakers of other languages). SJU works in partnership with Thomas Jefferson University on joint-degree programs in bioscience technologies, nursing, occupational therapy, physical therapy, and radiologic science.

Academic Programs

At Saint Joseph's University, the aim of providing the student with the qualities of a liberally educated individual is pursued through a threefold plan encompassing forty courses. The major concentration (ten to sixteen courses) is intended to provide students with depth in a given field in order to prepare them for effective work in that field or graduate study. The general education program (fifteen to eighteen courses) is intended to ensure that students have mastered basic skills necessary for further work, have been exposed to the main divisions of learning, have been introduced to several new fields of study, and have acquired an appreciation for diversity and an ethically-informed perspective. Art and literature, non-native languages, mathematics, natural sciences, history, social sciences, philosophy, and theology are among the areas of study included in the general education program. Electives (six to fifteen courses) are intended to provide flexibility by encouraging students to pursue studies in areas they have found interesting, to test their interest in an unexplored area, or to deepen their knowledge in the major field.

Within the Saint Joseph's honors program, the curriculum will challenge students' intellect, creativity, and time-management skills. Honors students attend special events, receptions, concerts, and lectures, and have opportunities to present research and creative work at national conferences and seminars.

Off-Campus Programs

Saint Joseph's encourages an internship or co-op experience and provides hundreds of ways for students to connect with the nation's top employers. SJU Summer Scholars gives students the opportunity to dive into a special research or creative project while working closely with a faculty mentor. Students may study abroad in places like China, Ireland, Italy, South Africa, and more. There are also many opportunities to gain a real-world understanding of human and social issues while taking part in the well-known service-learning programs.

Academic Facilities

The facilities at Saint Joseph's are a blend of the old and the new. Barbelin/Lonergan Hall is a fine example of collegiate Gothic architecture. Its spire carillon tower rises above the campus and is easily the most recognizable landmark at Saint Joseph's. Mandeville Hall, a modern international academic center, is the home of the Erivan K. Haub School of Business. Mandeville Hall offers classrooms with state-of-the-art technology, and a Wall Street trading room, with access to electronic sources of financial and investment data. The new Post Learning Commons has become a hub for students seeking space for collaboration, studying, and relaxation, with its floor-to-ceiling windows for spectacular views of the campus, expanded and varied study spaces, plush lounges, and a café. Villiger, the University's newest residence hall, and three other on-campus residence halls house the entire freshman class.

Costs

Current tuition for one academic year is $44,974. The average cost for room and board is $14,840. These costs do not include student fees associated with specific majors or residence halls.

Financial Aid

Many of Saint Joseph's students receive merit and/or federal financial assistance. More than 90 percent of the University's student body receives assistance in the form of academic and athletic scholarships, grants, loans, and work-study funds. In 2017, 97 percent of new freshmen were awarded grants and scholarships over the last five years combined.

Students are automatically considered for merit scholarships upon application to the University. Students who wish to be considered for federal financial assistance should submit the Free Application for Federal Student Aid (FAFSA). Residents from states other than Pennsylvania should file the FAFSA and the proper state grant application from the Education Assistance Agency of their resident state.

Faculty

Saint Joseph's esteemed research faculty is committed to undergraduate teaching. A student-faculty ratio of 14:1 and an average class size of 25 offer excellent opportunities for students and faculty members to interact, both inside and outside the classroom. One hundred percent of the full-time, tenure-track faculty members hold a doctorate or terminal degree in their field.

Student Leadership and Activities

The Office of Student Leadership and Activities is dedicated to enhancing the educational development of students by providing opportunities for involvement in co-curricular programs and services. These include athletics, leadership programs, student clubs and organizations, Greek life, event programming and planning, and the University Student Senate.

More than 98 percent of the Class of 2016 completed an experiential learning opportunity, from a co-op at Estée Lauder to an internship at IBM to a semester abroad in Spain.

SJU students are leaders. They assist in academic departments, participate in student government and are responsible for running Mass, large fundraising campaigns and events, and sometimes leading over 500 students on a service immersion trip to Appalachia each year.

Admission Requirements

Candidates for admission to the freshman class must submit evidence of academic achievement in a college-preparatory program. In addition to the application students must submit an official high school transcript, letter of recommendation, a $50 application fee, and a personal essay.

Application and Information

Merit scholarships are awarded within the context of a deadline admissions policy with an early decision I and early action application deadline of November 15, early decision II application deadline of January 15, and a regular decision deadline of February 1. More information is available online at sju.edu/apply.

Office of Undergraduate Admissions
Saint Joseph's University
5600 City Avenue
Philadelphia, Pennsylvania 19131-1395
Phone: 610-660-1300
E-mail: admit@sju.edu
Website: sju.edu
    facebook.com/sjuadmissions
    twitter.com/sjuadmissions
    instagram.com/sjuadmissions

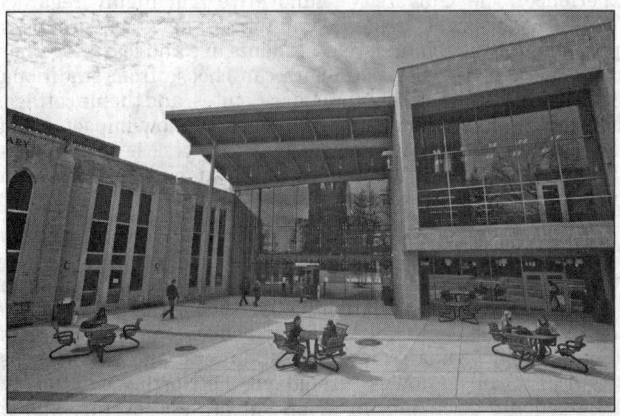

The Post Learning Commons Building at Saint Joseph's University is a hub of social and studious activity in the center of campus. (Photo credit: Melissa Kelly)

ST. LAWRENCE UNIVERSITY
CANTON, NEW YORK

 To read more about this school, visit http://petersons.to/stlawrenceuniversity

The University

St. Lawrence University invites students to learn new ways of seeing the world, voicing ideas, and connecting with others. Graduates have the tools with which to think clearly, express themselves persuasively, and step into the global community with an understanding of their responsibility to all people and to the planet. These tools have helped St. Lawrence graduates find success; nearly 97 percent of the most recent graduating class were employed or enrolled in graduate school less than a year after graduation.

Founded in 1856, St. Lawrence is the oldest continuously coeducational degree-granting institution of higher learning in New York State. Initially established as a theology school for the Universalist Church, it quickly evolved into the liberal arts college that it is today. St. Lawrence is a private, nonsectarian university of approximately 2,400 undergraduate men and women, with a small graduate program in education. St. Lawrence is known for its residential/academic First-Year Program, its international study opportunities and area studies programs, its students' strong interest in the environment and the outdoors, and its strong sense of community.

St. Lawrence students are self-starters. The self-designed major is popular, intramural sports leagues are always full, and more than 170 student clubs and organizations serve broad interests, from communication to community service and creativity to social action. The University routinely hosts well-known speakers, while concerts, plays, and films are regulars on the weekly events calendar.

St. Lawrence students have historically placed high value on athletic activity, and a large number participate in varsity, intramural, or club sports. Most of the 33 varsity men's and women's teams compete at the NCAA Division III level, with the exception of men's and women's ice hockey, which compete in Division I, and riding, Alpine skiing, Nordic skiing, squash, and men's crew. Recreational facilities include cross-country ski and running trails; indoor and outdoor tennis courts; an athletic complex with a gymnasium, two field houses, a 133-station fitness center, a three-story climbing wall, and a pool; an ice rink; an equestrian center; a boathouse; a golf course; a nine-lane all-weather track; an artificial-turf field for lacrosse and field hockey; ten squash courts; and performance fields for soccer, football, baseball, and softball.

Residential life is an important aspect of the St. Lawrence experience. The University's innovative and highly regarded First-Year Program creates communities in which groups of approximately 30–35 first-year students live and learn together. In the upperclass years, students can choose from traditional residence halls, Greek chapter houses, suites, and theme cottages that focus on student interests, such as low-impact living and community service. Seniors may also choose townhouses. St. Lawrence sponsors a full range of student services, from counseling to career planning.

Location

St. Lawrence is situated on a 1,000-acre campus in the village of Canton, New York (population 6,400), the seat of St. Lawrence County. Canton, with its Victorian homes, tree-lined streets, village green, farmer's market, restaurants, and small shops, is typical of college towns throughout the Northeast. Students and residents often mix in stores, at athletic events, and in community projects. Ottawa, Canada's capital, is 75 minutes to the north, while Lake Placid, one of America's hiking and skiing meccas, is 90 minutes to the southeast.

Majors and Degrees

St. Lawrence offers the Bachelor of Arts and Bachelor of Science degrees; students can choose from 69 majors and have the option of picking from 40 minors. Combined five-year programs with other institutions are in place in engineering and management, and specialized advising is offered in preparation for postgraduate work in dentistry, law, medicine, nursing, physical therapy, and veterinary medicine.

Academic Programs

St. Lawrence's foremost mission is to provide its students with a liberal arts education. Students complete requirements in eight areas and concentrated work in a major field as well as demonstrating competence in writing. Close faculty-student interaction is a hallmark of a St. Lawrence education. Every semester, many students engage in independent or honors projects, often working with professors on joint research projects that lead to publication in leading scholarly journals. A senior project is required in most majors.

Off-Campus Programs

St. Lawrence University supports a variety of off-campus programs on six continents that allow students to enrich their majors, expand their world, gain cross-cultural skills, and prepare to be responsible global citizens. Nearly 70 percent of St. Lawrence students study off campus during their collegiate careers. St. Lawrence operates or has partnered with other carefully selected programs in Australia, Austria, Canada, China, Costa Rica, the Czech Republic, Denmark, England, France, India, Italy, Japan, Jordan, Kenya, New Zealand, Spain, Thailand, and Trinidad and Tobago. The Kenya program is based at the University-owned and operated campus in the suburbs of Nairobi. The program strives to provide students with a unique study-abroad experience. In addition, the University's membership in the International Student Exchange Program (ISEP) permits students to directly enroll in universities in more than 50 additional countries. St. Lawrence also operates a program at Fisk University in Nashville, Tennessee, and administers its own Adirondack Semester Program, Sustainability Semester Program, and the Liberal Arts in New York City Semester Program. The University also enrolls students in The Washington Center internship program, located in Washington, D.C.

Academic Facilities

Owen D. Young Library and Launders Science Library contain more than a million volumes as well as electronic resources and ample space for reading and research. Griffiths Arts Center is the home of the University's art and art history, performance, and communication studies academic programs, as well as two theaters, an art gallery in which selections from St. Lawrence's 7,000-piece permanent collection are frequently shown, and the Peterson-Kermani Performance Hall, a 19,000-square-foot space for the performing arts. A unified science complex houses the departments of Biology, Chemistry, Physics, Psychology, Geology, and Mathematics, Computer Science, and Statistics, and is connected via a covered hallway to the science library and computing center. The 130,000-square-foot Johnson Hall of Science was the first LEED-certified gold science building in New York State. Richardson Hall, St. Lawrence's oldest building and on the National Register of Historic Places, is home to the English and religious studies departments. Other departments can be found in academic buildings clustered on one part of the campus, so classrooms are not far apart.

Costs

The comprehensive fee for 2018–19 is $68,890, including tuition, fees, room, and board.

Financial Aid

St. Lawrence awards both merit scholarships and need-based financial aid. More than 97 percent of the University's students receive some form of financial assistance, including scholarships, grants, student loans, and campus jobs. St. Lawrence is committed to assisting as many students as possible and recognizes academic and personal achievement in making financial aid decisions. To apply for need-based financial aid, students must file the Free Application for Federal Student Aid (FAFSA) between October 1 and February 1 and request that the results be sent directly to St. Lawrence.

Faculty

The 210 members of St. Lawrence's faculty are teachers and scholars who pride themselves on not just knowing student names, but knowing students. While teaching and advising are their primary responsibilities, they are also active researchers, artists, performers, and regular contributors in their academic disciplines. Faculty members teach all courses at St. Lawrence; no undergraduate courses are taught by graduate students. Active teaching assistants and tutoring programs, involving qualified upperclass students, are closely supervised by faculty members. The student-faculty ratio is about 11:1. Faculty members hold regular office hours, serve as academic advisers to students, and frequently take part in extracurricular activities on campus.

Student Government

The Thelomathesian Society, comprised of all students on campus, is governed by a senate of elected representatives. The senate distributes funds in support of student activities and provides two student delegates to the University's Board of Trustees.

Admission Requirements

St. Lawrence seeks students who can be successful in a demanding academic program and who can contribute to the quality of life of the community. The University is committed to enrolling students who represent the widest possible diversity of economic, social, ethnic, and geographic backgrounds. Academic preparation and ability are the most important criteria, but demonstrated ability in the creative arts, athletics, and/or social service is also a measure of a student's potential to benefit the St. Lawrence community. Candidates may choose whether to submit standardized test scores (SAT or ACT); University admissions are test-optional for domestic students. International students are required to submit SAT scores. A campus visit is strongly encouraged, and interviews may be scheduled on-campus or off-campus in certain areas.

Although there is no set distribution of required high school courses, successful applicants typically show strong preparation in the humanities, social sciences, mathematics, and natural sciences. Honors, Advanced Placement, and International Baccalaureate courses are opportunities for applicants to demonstrate intellectual maturity and curiosity, qualities highly valued in the admission process.

Application and Information

St. Lawrence uses the Common Application as its sole application form. The application processing fee is $60, which is waived if candidates have made an official visit to campus. Regular Decision applications should be submitted by February 1, with notification in mid-March. Students who decide that St. Lawrence is their first choice may apply Early Decision. The priority deadline for Early Decision begins November 1; students may commit to Early Decision up until February 1. Early Decision candidates will generally be notified within two weeks of receipt of a completed application.

Transfer candidates should submit applications no later than November 1 for the spring semester or March 1 for the fall semester.

For additional information, students should contact:

Office of Admissions and Financial Aid
St. Lawrence University
23 Romoda Drive
Canton, New York 13617
Phone: 315-229-5261 (admissions)
      800-285-1856 (admissions, toll-free)
      315-229-5265 (financial aid)
      800-355-0863 (financial aid, toll-free)
E-mail: admissions@stlawu.edu or finaid@stlawu.edu
Website: http://www.stlawu.edu
      http://www.facebook.com/StLawrenceU
      http://twitter.com/StLawrenceU
      http://instagram.com/StLawrenceU
      http://www.youtube.com/StLawrenceU
      https://www.snapchat.com/add/stlawrenceu

Located in the center of campus, the Sullivan Student Center is home to the Northstar Café, Career Services, the Campus Mailroom, Student Activities, Volunteer Services, Residence Life, and plenty of comfortable student study and meeting spaces.

SAINT MARY'S COLLEGE
NOTRE DAME, INDIANA

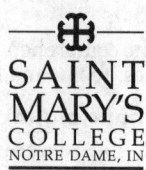

The College

Saint Mary's College is a Catholic undergraduate women's college located in Notre Dame, Indiana, offering graduate programs for women and men. The Sisters of the Holy Cross founded the College in 1844.

The undergraduate community is made up of bright, talented women who are on the path to self-discovery. Saint Mary's curriculum is challenging, not only in the student's chosen area of study, but also within the liberal arts. The Saint Mary's College experience includes its unique general education program (the Sophia Program), writing proficiency standards, senior comprehensive programs, and the development of exceptional critical thinking skills. Ninety-three percent of the school's graduates complete their degrees in four years, and whether they choose new careers, graduate school, or postgraduate service, Saint Mary's alumnae are prepared for life.

With just under 1,500 undergraduate students from approximately 42 states and about 10 countries, Saint Mary's brings together women from a wide range of backgrounds and experiences. International and diverse students compose 19 percent of the student body. One hundred and six women and men were enrolled in the graduate programs in 2017–18.

Saint Mary's unique relationship with the University of Notre Dame provides access to the exciting atmosphere of a large university—just across the street. Students at both schools can take courses at either institution. Saint Mary's students can audition for Notre Dame's legendary marching band or work for *The Observer*, the student newspaper for Saint Mary's and Notre Dame. In addition, students participate in dances, concerts, lectures, and social organizations on both campuses. Holy Cross College is also just next door to Saint Mary's College. Holy Cross congregations founded all three campuses.

Saint Mary's residential campus becomes the students' second home. Saint Mary's five residence halls include Opus Hall, which offers apartment-style living for seniors on campus. Residence halls host events and compete with each other in intramural athletics. Each hall also sponsors a local nonprofit organization that provides students with service opportunities. All residence halls have chapels, and the Church of Our Lady of Loretto, the main worship space, offers daily Mass on campus.

As an NCAA Division III school and a member of the Michigan Intercollegiate Athletic Association (MIAA), Saint Mary's sponsors varsity teams in basketball, cross-country, golf, lacrosse, soccer, softball, tennis, and volleyball. Club sports, co-sponsored with Notre Dame, include gymnastics and figure skating. In addition, Saint Mary's offers many intramural sports. The new Angela Athletic and Wellness Complex is scheduled to open in spring of 2018, complete with a training and fitness center with weight and cardio machines, an indoor track, fitness classes for every level, a cafe, and study spaces.

Location

Saint Mary's beautiful 100-acre campus, set alongside the Saint Joseph River, is across the street from the University of Notre Dame, next door to Holy Cross College, minutes north of the city of South Bend (population 101,000), 90 miles from Chicago and 140 miles from Indianapolis. The South Bend community provides opportunities for internships, field practicums, and volunteer service. Eighty percent of Saint Mary's students engage in service by the time they graduate (the national average is approximately 55 percent).

Majors and Degrees

Saint Mary's College offers seven undergraduate degree programs: Bachelor of Arts, Bachelor of Science, Bachelor of Science in Nursing, Bachelor of Social Work, Bachelor of Business Administration, Bachelor of Fine Arts, and Bachelor of Music, and more than 30 major areas of study. The College offers more than 40 minors, including American history, anthropology, computer science, environmental studies, justice studies, Latin American studies, and women's studies.

Saint Mary's also offers three coeducational graduate degrees: a Master of Science in Data Science, a Master of Science in Speech Language Pathology, and a Doctorate of Nursing Practice. A Master in Autism Studies was just recently approved to begin in 2019.

In addition, a five-year, dual-degree engineering program is offered in cooperation with the University of Notre Dame and leads to a bachelor's degree from Saint Mary's College and a Bachelor of Science in Engineering degree from Notre Dame in aerospace, chemical, civil, computer, electrical, environmental, or mechanical engineering.

Saint Mary's education department, accredited by the National Council for Accreditation of Teacher Education, offers an elementary education major (grades K–6) and a secondary education minor (grades 5–12). With an elementary education major, students can also receive mild intervention licensure (K–6) and an Indiana reading licensure (P–12). Saint Mary's also offers minors in English as a second language and early childhood education. In addition, the department offers programs for those interested in teaching the visual arts or music. Secondary education requires a major in one of the following: English, Spanish, mathematics, science (science majors must complete licensing requirements in chemistry or life science), history (history majors must complete additional course work in political science and one of the following: sociology, psychology, economics), and political science (political science majors must complete additional course work in history and one of the following: sociology, psychology, economics).

Academic Programs

In addition to completing the required credit hours in her chosen field, every undergraduate student completes a senior comprehensive in her major (a thesis, a research or creative project, or a written or oral examination). All undergraduate students must also complete a writing-intensive "W" course, usually in the first year, and an advanced portfolio of writing in the major discipline, usually in the senior year.

Off-Campus Programs

Intercultural competence is a cornerstone of the liberal arts education. Saint Mary's combines that with travel and adventure through study-abroad experiences in over 15 locations: Argentina, Australia, Austria, China, Ecuador, England, France, Greece, Honduras, Ireland, Italy, Jamaica, Morocco, South Africa, South Korea, Spain, and Uganda. Saint Mary's students may also study in other countries through a cooperative program with the University of Notre Dame. Domestic programs include a semester at American University in Washington, D.C. for political science majors, opportunities for student teachers in Native American communities, and the Catalyst Trip, a journey to sites significant to the history of social justice.

Academic Facilities

Several buildings have computer labs in addition to computer "collaboratories," where students and faculty members can conduct online research in classroom settings.

The Cushwa-Leighton Library houses a collection of more than 228,000 volumes. Also located in the library are the Trumper Computer Center, the Instructional Technology Resource Center, and a rare-book room.

Laboratory facilities are available for biology, chemistry, and physics in the newly renovated Science Hall, and for psychology and language students. Art studios, music practice rooms, O'Laughlin Auditorium, and Little Theatre provide space for fine arts creation, practice, and performance. Spes Unica Hall, an academic building, provides students with technology-equipped classrooms, group and individual study spaces, and presentation spaces.

The Early Childhood Development Center provides education and psychology majors with a unique opportunity to work with young children on campus.

Costs

Expenses for the 2017–18 academic year include tuition and fees, $40,800; room and board, $12,100 (average); and miscellaneous expenses (approximate cost of books, transportation, and living costs), $2,300.

Financial Aid

The College strives to make a Saint Mary's education available for every admitted student by offering financial aid packages that might include institutional need-based assistance, merit scholarships, and work-study opportunities in addition to state and federal grants and loans. One-hundred percent of admitted students receive some sort of financial aid in College grants and scholarships.

All applicants for financial aid must complete the Free Application for Federal Student Aid (FAFSA) by March 1 for each year that they desire assistance.

Faculty

Saint Mary's professors are experts in their fields of study and mentors to their students inside and outside the classroom. Of the full-time faculty members, 83 percent hold earned doctorates or other terminal degrees. Saint Mary's also has 70 part-time faculty members.

Student Government

The Student Government Association (SGA) is a dynamic student-led organization that sponsors extracurricular and co-curricular activities including service projects, social events, and learning experiences. It provides student participants with leadership opportunities that often include leadership training. SGA has voting representatives on the president's two highest advisory boards, the Student Affairs Council and the Academic Affairs Council. A student is also a voting member of the College's Board of Trustees.

Admission Requirements

Applicants for undergraduate admission to Saint Mary's College should be impending graduates of an accredited high school. Home-schooled students are also encouraged to apply. All applicants must complete a four-year, college-preparatory curriculum that consists of a minimum of 16 academic (Carnegie) units where one unit represents one full year of study. The minimum requirements are: 4 units of English, 2 units of the same foreign language, 3 units of college-preparatory mathematics (beginning with algebra I), 2 units of laboratory science, and 2 units of history or social science. The remaining required units should consist of three additional units in the above listed subjects.

Applications must include an academic transcript showing current rank and senior-year courses (if available), a secondary school report, SAT or ACT scores, and an essay. There is no application fee, and Saint Mary's is a member of the Common Application.

Saint Mary's encourages students to visit the campus for a tour and informational meeting with an admission counselor. Arrangements to attend classes, meet with coaches, stay overnight, or have an admission meeting via phone (for students who do not visit campus) can be made by contacting the Office of Admission.

Application and Information

Saint Mary's has two application and notification programs: early decision and modified rolling regular admission. Highly qualified students who have selected Saint Mary's as their first choice for admission may apply under the early decision program. The application deadline is November 15, and the notification date is December 15. Students who apply for modified rolling admission, and those whose application files are complete on or before December 1 are notified of the admission decision by mid-January. Applications received after December 1 are reviewed in the order in which they become complete. The priority application deadline for regular admission is February 15. Applications are accepted, however, as long as space is available.

Interested students are encouraged to contact:

Office of Admission
Saint Mary's College
Notre Dame, Indiana 46556-5001
Phone: 574-284-4587
      800-551-7621 (toll-free)
Fax: 574-284-4841
E-mail: admission@saintmarys.edu
Website: www.saintmarys.edu
      facebook.com/saintmaryscollegeadmission

We promise you discovery. Discovery of yourselves, discovery of the universe, and your place in it.
—Sister Madeleva Wolfe, CSC,
President of Saint Mary's College from 1934–1961

ST. NORBERT COLLEGE

DE PERE, WISCONSIN

The College

St. Norbert College is a private institution that was founded in 1898. It has a total undergraduate enrollment of 2,102 students on a scenic, riverfront campus that spans 112 acres in the metropolitan Green Bay area. At St. Norbert, the undergraduate curriculum is guided by a liberal arts core and the opportunity for students to pursue one of 40 majors, including pre-professional programs, or design their own.

St. Norbert College (SNC) is the only institution of higher education in the world sponsored by the Norbertines, a Catholic order devoted to living in community and serving others. The college welcomes students of all faiths who aspire to develop their full potential in understanding and serving the world. St. Norbert has grown to become an influential part of business, educational, service, theological and cultural experiences throughout northeastern Wisconsin. It is conveniently located within three hours of Chicago, Milwaukee, and Madison, Wisconsin.

St. Norbert's academic and student experience highlights include:

- 97 percent of SNC students receive financial aid

- SNC provides a four-year graduation guarantee

- Roughly 30 percent of SNC students study abroad via programs that span 29 countries

- Students can choose from 40 majors or design their own

- The student-to-faculty ratio is 13:1

- First-year students are eligible for collaborative research fellowships and internships

- International students from 20+ countries call SNC their home away from home

- SNC has more than 80 student organizations and clubs

- SNC has 22 varsity athletic teams and a distinguished history of Division III championships

- Students contribute 28,000+ hours of service annually

- Within nine months of graduation, 91 percent of SNC students are employed or attending graduate school

- SNC's chef-prepared meals are nationally ranked and recognized

The college's motto is *docere et exemplo*, to teach by word and example.

Students at St. Norbert exhibit a strong sense of community, school pride, and an appreciation for the diverse perspectives and global opportunities available to them. They often highlight the relationships they have developed with peers and faculty, as well as the rewards of volunteering in the local community.

Location

The 112-acre St. Norbert campus is located on the Fox River in De Pere, Wisconsin, just minutes south of Green Bay, a metropolitan area of about 300,000 people. Rich in industry, culture, arts, and entertainment, De Pere and the greater Green Bay area are recognized among the 100 best communities for young people by America's Promise Alliance. The campus is part of a vibrant 18-county region of 1.2 million people, home to Fortune 500

companies, hospitals, schools, and service organizations, many of which offer internships for students

Majors and Degrees

St. Norbert offers programs leading to the Bachelor of Arts, Bachelor of Science, Bachelor of Music, and Bachelor of Business Administration degrees.

Programs of study at St. Norbert include: accounting, American studies, art–fine arts, art–graphic design, biology–biomedical, biology–organismal, business administration, chemistry, chemistry–biochemistry, classical studies, communication and media studies, computer science, computer science–business information systems, computer science–graphic design and implementation, economics, education, English, English–creative writing, environmental science, French, geography, geology, German, history, human services (social work), international business and language area studies, international studies, Japanese, leadership studies, mathematics, military science/ROTC, music, natural sciences, nursing, peace and justice, philosophy, physics, political science, pre-dental, pre-engineering, pre-law, pre-medical, pre-pharmacy, pre-veterinary, psychology, religious studies, religious studies–youth ministry, sociology, Spanish, teacher education, theatre studies, and women's and gender studies.

Graduate Programs: Through its Donald J. Schneider School of Business & Economics, the college offers a Master of Business Administration degree. St. Norbert also offers Master of Arts in Liberal Studies and Master of Theological Studies degrees.

Academic Programs

As a liberal arts institution, St. Norbert equips students with exceptional communication, critical-thinking, problem-solving, and leadership skills. An honors program offers additional challenge for students who demonstrate exceptional academic ability.

The academic centers at St. Norbert enrich students' academic experience and serve as valuable resources for the community. The centers include the Center for Exceptional Leadership, the Center for Norbertine Studies, the Norman Miller Center for Peace, Justice & Public Understanding, the Sturzl Center for Service & Learning, the Center for Global Engagement, the Center for Business & Economic Analysis, and the Strategic Research Institute.

Off-Campus Programs

St. Norbert students, regardless of major, can spend a summer, a semester, or a year abroad. In fact, 30 percent of St. Norbert students spend at least one semester abroad compared to less than 4 percent nationally. The college has more than 75 study-abroad program sites in 29 countries on six continents. An international-study component is a part of majors in French, Spanish, and German, as well as both the international business program and the international studies major.

St. Norbert considers international experience vital to today's graduates and it is a key component of the college's educational mission. St. Norbert's international curriculum prepares students to live in a global society. A Washington semester is also available through American University in Washington, D.C.

First-year students still undecided about their life path can participate in the Gap Experience, which takes them from the Canadian north shore of Lake Superior to the natural wonders of Guatemala, all while earning college credit toward their degree.

Additional service-learning opportunities are available throughout the year, including the TRIPS (Turning Responsibility Into Powerful Service) program in local, national, and international locations.

Academic Facilities

The facilities that define St. Norbert's campus include buildings of rich historical significance as well as state-of-the art new construction.

The Mulva Library features 250,000 volumes, enhanced technology, flexible study and classroom spaces, and a 24-hour computer study area. A high-tech multimedia studio on the lower level of the library opened in 2013 and has become a favorite place for students to collaborate on group projects.

The F. K. Bemis International Center provides students with opportunities to prepare for careers with greater international emphasis. The center also serves as a resource for K–12 schools and Wisconsin businesses for language instruction, translation, and interpretation.

The stunning Gehl-Mulva Science Center, completed in 2015, is home to St. Norbert's science programs as well as the Medical College of Wisconsin's northeast Wisconsin campus. The 160,000-square-foot facility features classrooms and labs equipped with the latest technology.

A signature addition to the campus, the new Mulva Family Fitness & Sports Center is home to the college's indoor sports, health, and wellness facilities, and aquatics center. Schneider Stadium is an outdoor athletics complex that provides a modern venue for football, soccer, and track and field.

Michels Commons is a hub for student life with chef-prepared meals at Ruth's Marketplace and a popular gathering place in Dale's Sports Lounge. St. Norbert ranks in the top 3 percent of all colleges in the nation for its food.

The Cassandra Voss Center offers innovative, holistic programming about gender, identity, and diversity, attracting leading figures in the field as speakers.

Fifteen residence halls provide the link between living and learning for roughly 85 percent of St. Norbert students. Some residence halls focus on community service or feature campus programs, such as the honors program. An apartment-style residence hall offers upperclassmen a transitional experience to living on their own. Many halls have chapels for students.

Costs

For 2018–19, tuition and required fees for full-time students total $38,129 for the year. Room and board costs average $10,556 per year.

Financial Aid

Students share in more than $60 million of financial aid each year, including scholarships and grants, campus jobs, and educational loans. More than 97 percent of St. Norbert students receive financial aid, with an average aid amount of more than $24,000 per year. There are both need-based and merit-based awards as well as full Army ROTC scholarships each year. A multitude of work-study positions exist on campus, as well as paid community internships.

Need-based awards are made on the basis of the Free Application for Federal Student Aid (FAFSA; St. Norbert College's code is 003892) and the St. Norbert College institutional application for financial aid. First-year applicants should submit their FAFSA by Jan. 1 of their senior year of high school.

Faculty

Ninety-one percent of the 200 full-time faculty members at St. Norbert hold a doctoral or other terminal degree in their field. The student-to-faculty ratio is 13:1, and student success is the top priority of the faculty. They work closely with students in their major area of study, help students prepare for graduate school, write letters of recommendation, and work with those who seek independent study and research opportunities. Research fellowships and collaborations with faculty members are available to all students—as early as their first year—who may ultimately have the opportunity to present their research findings collaboratively with faculty members at national conferences.

Student Government

The Student Government Association is active on campus, with representation extending as far as the college's board of trustees. The president of the college and his cabinet respect the voice of the student body, and openly discuss issues that impact students and the college community. There are more than 80 organizations in which students can get involved.

Admission Requirements

St. Norbert College welcomes enrollment from a diverse group of students who are prepared academically and who will make a contribution to the college's living and learning community. Students who are likely to succeed are accepted based on their holistic achievements, not just grades and test scores. The average GPA of admitted students is 3.5, and the average ACT composite score is 25. Students with superior test scores and grades are invited to enroll in the honors program. The college encourages and welcomes applications from international, transfer, and diverse students.

Application and Information

Because St. Norbert gives preference to qualified students according to the date of admission and enrollment deposit, it benefits students to apply as early as possible in their senior year. Students are notified about admission decisions on a rolling basis beginning in late September. A $350 nonrefundable deposit is required to confirm enrollment.

For more information about St. Norbert College, students should contact:

Ed Lamm
Vice President for Enrollment Management and Communications
St. Norbert College
100 Grant Street
De Pere, Wisconsin 54115
Phone: 920-403-3005
      800-236-4878 (toll-free)
E-mail: admit@snc.edu
Website: http://www.snc.edu
      http://www.snc.edu/go/socialmedia

A welcoming, supportive community greets first-year students at Convocation.

ST. THOMAS AQUINAS COLLEGE
SPARKILL, NEW YORK

 To read more about this school, visit http://petersons.to/stthomasaquinascollege

The College

St. Thomas Aquinas College (STAC) was founded in 1952 as a three-year teacher-training college with 30 students. Today, the College offers more than 100 different majors, minors, specializations, and dual degree programs and has a total student body of 2,800 in all programs, on and off campus. Much growth and development has taken place over the College's history. The College offers a Master of Science in Education, with concentrations in autism, literacy, and special education, as well as postgraduate certificate programs in autism (online), literacy, and special education. The College also offers a Master of Business Administration (M.B.A.) program with concentrations in finance, management, and marketing; and an online M.B.A. in general studies. St. Thomas offers a Master of Science in Teaching program for individuals without a background in teacher education who are seeking a career change. The College is home to New York University's Master in Social Work program.

The suburban campus includes two residential complexes: Aquinas Village, which consists of self-contained townhouse units that house 300 students, and the McNelis Commons, which consists of townhouse residential units that house 375 students and a common dining hall and laundry building. Approximately 40 percent of the College's full-time student population resides on campus.

Extracurricular activities are provided through forty different organizations, including the Spartan Volunteers, a community service program; a student-run radio station (WSTK); the Laetare Players dramatic and musical club; and the student-edited campus newspaper and yearbook. The College has NCAA Division II teams in men's and women's cross-country, indoor and outdoor track and field, basketball, soccer, lacrosse, and tennis; women's field hockey and softball; and men's baseball and golf. They recently added Sprint Football, Women's Triathlon, Women's Bowling, and E-sports to their varsity sport roster. There are a number of club sports including ice hockey, cheerleading and dance, bowling, and ski and snowboarding, as well as intramural athletics.

The College has a campus ministry office, a health office, and residence life, career development, and counseling services.

Location

The College is located in Rockland County, just 15 miles north of New York City, giving students quick access to learning, cultural, internship, and career opportunities in one of the world's most exciting cities.

Majors and Degrees

St. Thomas Aquinas College's School of Business offers accounting (and accounting as a dual degree with an M.B.A. degree), finance, hospitality management, management, marketing, and sport management. Minors are offered in business management, marketing, economics, human resource management, international business, sport management, and management information systems. Specializations are in management relations/industrial and organizational psychology.

The School of Arts & Sciences offers degrees in the humanities, mathematics, natural sciences, and social sciences. Programs are available in art therapy, art and visual communications in graphic design or media art, communication arts, creative writing, English, journalism, philosophy and religious studies, Romance languages, Spanish, mathematics, computer sciences, biochemistry, biology, exercise science, forensic science, medical technology, natural sciences, criminal justice, psychology, therapeutic recreation, social science, and history. There are specializations in biology, chemistry, and physics. Minors include art therapy, biology, chemistry, communication arts, computer information science, criminal justice, English, fine arts, history, journalism, mathematics, performing arts, physics, public relations, religious studies, social media, sociology, Spanish, therapeutic recreation, and creative writing. A full listing of all programs can be found online at www.stac.edu.

The School of Education offers programs in grades 1–6 childhood education, the same plus special education, birth–6 early childhood and childhood education, and grades 7–12 adolescence education. An art education program with certifications in grades K–12 is offered as well as a middle school extension that adds to either the elementary or secondary degree, enabling the student to certify for all middle school grades. The School of Education also offers several dual-degree programs: B.S./B.A. and M.S.Ed. in childhood (B.S.) and special education (M.S.Ed.), grades 1–6; mathematics (B.S.) and special education (M.S.Ed.), grades 7–12; social sciences (B.S.) and special education (M.S.Ed.), grades 7–12; and Spanish (B.A.) and special education (M.S.Ed.), grades 7–12.

The College offers a five-year dual-degree program in mathematics/engineering with The George Washington University (GWU) or Manhattan College. Students study at St. Thomas for three years. After completion of their final two years at either GWU or Manhattan, they earn a B.S. in mathematics from STAC and a B.S. in engineering from one of the other two institutions. The College also offers several dual-degree options in biology: a dual degree in biology (B.S. from STAC) and biomedical engineering (M.S. from Polytechnic University), a dual degree in biology (B.S. from STAC) and physical therapy (D.P.T. from New York Medical College), a dual degree in biology (B.S. from STAC) and chiropractic (D.C. from New York Chiropractic College), and a dual degree in biology (B.S. from STAC) and podiatry (D.P.M. from New York College of Podiatric Medicine). There are several other strategic alliances, such as preferred admission to St. John's University School of Law in New York and a similar program with Barry University School of Law in Florida that includes scholarship funds. St. Thomas also has strategic agreements with St. John's University for an M.P.S. in sport management and a Master of Public Health.

Academic Programs

The College strives to develop students who are not only generally educated but also possess advanced knowledge in specialized areas, are prepared for further study, and have the background to undertake fulfilling careers. To earn a bachelor's degree, students must complete a total of 120 semester hours, including a minimum of 51 credits in a core curriculum; complete all requirements for the specific major; and complete the final 30 hours at St. Thomas. The College awards up to 30 credits for life experience and up to 30 credits for achievement on the College-Level Examination Program (CLEP). The College operates on a semester calendar (quarterly on the M.B.A. level). Students may enroll in classes in the fall, winter (a one-month session), spring, and summer (three separate sessions). Undergraduate students can apply for the fall and spring semesters. Graduate education students can apply for the fall, spring, and summer semesters. Classes are scheduled during the day and evening, and students are permitted considerable academic flexibility in planning their programs.

Students can pursue independent study and internships, and many majors require a field practicum. The College maintains an active Center for Academic Excellence as a resource for enhancing academic performance, and students are encouraged to meet regularly with faculty advisers for academic guidance and career direction.

The College has a widely recognized program for college-age learning-disabled students, called the Pathways Program (at an additional cost). The College also participates in the New York State Higher Education Opportunity Program and provides an honors program (freshman applicants only) for exceptionally qualified students with a limited number of 70 percent scholarships. The honors program includes summer study at Oxford University. The Aquinas Leaders Work Scholarship program is for qualified students (freshmen applicants only) with strong academic abilities and a desire to gain work experience each semester that can be related to academic pursuits. Aquinas Leaders receive financial awards that cover approximately 60 percent of tuition costs over four years.

Off-Campus Programs

The College offers a variety of degree programs to active-duty military personnel, spouses, and dependents at the United States Military Academy at West Point. Associate and bachelor's degree are offered in a variety of areas at a discounted tuition rate.

Through articulation agreements with high schools, students can take college-level courses for credit at their own high schools at a very discounted tuition rate. This program provides high school students an opportunity to get a jump-start on their college careers by immersing them in college-level coursework and providing them with transferrable college credits for it.

The study-abroad program provides opportunities at colleges and universities in such places as Brazil, Canada, England, France, Hungary, Ireland, Italy, Morocco, and Spain. Several other locations are also available.

Academic Facilities

Borelli Hall, a green-designed, LEED-certified Silver building, features new classrooms with interactive board technologies. Costello Hall houses the science laboratories, technology theaters, and Azarian-McCullough Art Gallery. Spellman Hall houses a multiroom technology corridor, with a state-of-the-art communication studio where students produce their own news show, and technology and language labs. Lougheed Library provides a variety of online research opportunities for students. The Bloomberg Professional Laboratory provides students with the same platform for news, data, analytics, and research used by the world's leading banks, corporations, government agencies and public policy makers, law firms, libraries, energy companies, and media outlets. Aquinas Hall houses athletic facilities and a fitness center. Maguire Hall is home to classrooms, art studios, and the Sullivan Theater. Additional meeting areas are provided in the Romano Student-Alumni Center and in the two residence complexes, McNelis Commons and Aquinas Village. There is an after-hours club in the McNelis Commons dining hall for student activities.

Costs

For 2018–19, the tuition for full-time study (12 to 16 credits per semester) is $31.150; annual fees are $800. Room and board at the College Commons are $13,250. Certain studio, laboratory, and computer courses carry fees.

Financial Aid

In 2017–18, 85 percent of the student body received financial aid. The College is committed to providing students with the resources necessary to continue their education. Students must submit the Free Application for Federal Student Aid (FAFSA) each year. The College awards academic and merit scholarships from $5,000 up to 70 percent scholarships and provides need-based aid from the College as well as athletic grants and all federal and New York State aid programs.

St. Thomas strives to partner with the student to make college education affordable. The College has one of the lowest private college tuition rates in New York State, and scholarships make it even more affordable. The College is also a member of the Yellow Ribbon program for veterans enabling a qualified veteran to study with a full tuition scholarship.

Faculty

The faculty has 70 full-time and 55 part-time members; 80 percent have terminal degrees. The student-faculty ratio is 18:1. All faculty members participate in the academic advising of students and serve on College committees. Many serve as advisers to extracurricular activities.

Student Government

The Student Government consists of elected members who officially represent the student body, are responsible for planning and implementing student-originated programs, and coordinate and oversee all extracurricular organizations. Through its various offices, students play a vital part in offering consultation on new policies, planning social and cultural events, managing student funds, and operating the judicial system. In addition, the College Forum, which is composed of elected students, faculty members, alumni, administrators, and trustees, meets regularly to discuss policies, procedures, long-range plans, and any problems affecting the College.

Admission Requirements

All applicants must have successfully completed an approved secondary school program or the equivalent, including 4 years in English, 3 years in mathematics, 3 years in science, 2 years of foreign language, and 4 years of social studies. Applicants whose high school background varies from the recommended pattern are considered. Freshman applicants must submit the application for admission, including an essay, high school transcripts, SAT and/or ACT scores, and a letter of recommendation. Transfer students must submit the application and official transcripts of all previous college work. An academic evaluation is prepared for every matriculant. The College is a member of the Common Application and students are strongly encouraged to apply online through that service.

Application and Information

Candidates should submit completed application forms to the Admissions and Financial Aid Office and must request that their official transcripts be sent to the Admissions Office from their school. Students are notified of the admission decision on a rolling basis upon receipt of all the necessary credentials. The College is a member of the Common Application and students can find the link to apply on its website, http://www.stac.edu/apply.

St. Thomas Aquinas College does not discriminate in its educational programs, activities or employment practices based on race, color, national origin, sex, sexual orientation or expression, disability, age, religion, ancestry, genetic information, marital status, veteran status or any other legally-protected category. Announcement of this policy is in accordance with State and with Federal law, including Title VI and Title VII of the Civil Rights Act of 1964, Title IX of the Education Amendments of 1972, Section 504 of the Rehabilitation Act of 1973, the Age Discrimination in Employment Act of 1967 and the Americans with Disabilities Act of 1990. For more information, please contact: EEO, Section 504/ADA and Title IX Compliance Officer, 125 Route 340, Sparkill, New York 10976; phone: 845-398-4044.

For more information or an application, students should contact:
Admissions and Financial Aid Office
St. Thomas Aquinas College
125 Route 340
Sparkill, New York 10976-1050
Phone: 845-398-4100
E-mail: admissions@stac.edu
Website: http://www.stac.edu

St. Thomas Aquinas College's Costello Hall in the fall.

SAINT VINCENT COLLEGE
LATROBE, PENNSYLVANIA

 To read more about this school, visit http://petersons.to/saintvincentcollege

The College

Founded in 1846, Saint Vincent College is the first Benedictine college in the United States. It is an educational community rooted in the tradition of the Catholic faith, the heritage of Benedictine monasticism, and the love of values inherent in the liberal approach to life and learning. There are 1,586 full-time undergraduate students and 60 part-time students, of whom 72 percent reside on campus. The College welcomes students from twenty-six states and eight other countries. In addition to more than fifty programs in the liberal arts and sciences, the College offers the Master of Science degrees in education: in counselor education, curriculum and instruction, instructional design and technology, special education, and school administration and supervision. The College also offers postbaccalaureate and certification programs in special education, instructional technology specialist, principal, early childhood director, English as a second language, and online teaching. Other graduate and professional programs include a Master of Science in management: operational excellence, a Master of Science in criminology, and a Doctor of Nurse Anesthesia Practice.

Student services include advising, athletics, career placement and planning, computer assistance, and a wellness center. Students choose from more than fifty social, political, cultural, service, recreational, and religious student organizations. Saint Vincent College is accredited by the Department of Education of the Commonwealth of Pennsylvania, the Middle States Association of Colleges and Schools, and the Association of Collegiate Business Schools and Programs.

Location

Saint Vincent College is located on 200 acres in the Laurel Highlands of southwestern Pennsylvania. Noted for its beautiful countryside, the region offers abundant opportunities for outdoor recreation and adventure. Excellent sites for hiking, mountain biking, skiing, camping, and white-water rafting are less than half an hour from the campus in ten state forests. Pittsburgh, a regional center of culture and the arts, is only 35 miles to the west. The city offers music, museums, theater, shopping, nightlife, and sports.

Majors and Degrees

The College offers more than fifty degree programs; the most popular majors are biology, criminology, psychology, management, and accounting. The College is organized into four schools: the Alex G. McKenna School of Business, Economics, and Government; the Herbert W. Boyer School of Natural Sciences, Mathematics, and Computing; the School of Humanities and Fine Arts; and the School of Social Sciences, Communication, and Education.

The McKenna School includes majors in the areas of accounting, business economics, business education, information technology, economics, finance, international business, joint economics and mathematics, management, marketing, politics, political science, and public policy. The School of Natural Sciences, Mathematics, and Computing offers degrees in biochemistry, bioinformatics, biology, chemistry, computer science, cybersecurity, engineering science, environmental chemistry, environmental science, information technology, integrated science, mathematics, mathematics/engineering, physics, and physics education. The School of Humanities and Fine Arts offers majors in arts administration (performing arts), art education, English, graphic design, history, liberal arts, music, music performance, philosophy, philosophy/politics, philosophy/theology, Spanish, studio arts, and theology. The School of Social Sciences, Communication, and Education offers degrees in anthropology, communication, criminology, law and society, education (early childhood or middle grades), pre-law, psychology and sociology. Middle grade certification is offered in language arts, mathematics, science, and social studies, while minors in K–12 and secondary education include art, biology, business computing and information technology, chemistry, Chinese, English, French, mathematics, physics, social studies, and Spanish.

The College offers a law school 3+3 program in cooperation with Duquesne University. Students complete their requirements in English, history, political science, public policy analysis, and sociology at Saint Vincent College. In addition, in conjunction with university schools of engineering, the College offers a five-year cooperative liberal arts and engineering program, as well as a four-year degree in engineering science.

Saint Vincent offers pre–health training in accelerated osteopathic medicine, accelerated podiatric medicine, allopathic medicine, chiropractic medicine, dental medicine, occupational therapy, optometry, pharmacy, physician assistant studies, physical therapy, and veterinary medicine in cooperation with various professional schools.

Students may select minor areas of study in accounting, anthropology, art history, arts administration, biochemistry, biology, biotechnology, chemistry, children's literature, children's studies, Chinese language and culture, communication, computing and information science, economics, education, English, environmental chemistry, environmental science, finance, fine arts, forensic science (computer security, financial investigations, or natural science), French, German, graphic arts, history, international business, international studies, Italian, Latin, liberal arts, management: operational excellence, marketing, mathematics, music, music history, peace and justice, philosophy, physics, political science, public administration, psychology, sociology, Spanish, studio arts, and theology.

Academic Programs

An academic year consists of two semesters, fall and spring, with the opportunity to earn credits in the summer. Saint Vincent College requires each student to complete a minimum of 124 credits, satisfy the requirements for the major(s) as specified by the department(s) or school(s), achieve an overall grade point average of at least 2.0 as well as a grade point average of at least 2.0 in the major, and satisfy the capstone requirement as specified by the major department(s) or school(s). Each student must complete a core curriculum. The core curriculum provides all students with a broadly based education that provides a general body of knowledge in the humanities, social sciences, natural sciences, and mathematics; an interdisciplinary view of that knowledge base; and the skills to increase that general body of knowledge throughout their lives. Special programs include national and international academic honor societies, an internship program, an interdisciplinary writing program, and an honors program. An annual Academic Conference allows students to showcase their work across a variety of disciplines.

Off-Campus Programs

Saint Vincent students may choose to learn in surrounding communities, those across the country, or around the world.

Service plays a prominent role in the life of the campus—nearly two-thirds of seniors take part in a service project, and every student organization completes at least one service project each year. There are numerous local service opportunities, as well as service trips to Alaska, Appalachia, New Jersey, and abroad in Brazil, China, Guatemala, Haiti, Italy, and Taiwan.

Students can study abroad for a semester, an academic year, summer, or spring break in places as diverse as Argentina, Australia, China, Egypt, Great Britain, France, India, Italy, Japan, Poland, Russia, South Africa, Taiwan, and Turkey. In addition to options in dozens of other countries, the College has affiliations with nine Chinese colleges and universities.

From the breadth of the liberal arts curriculum to the excitement of hands-on learning, Saint Vincent's goal is to encourage a love for learning that endures.

Academic Facilities

Saint Vincent College has invested more than $100 million in campus facilities during the past ten years, including the $45-million Dupré

Science Pavilion, where every student takes at least two laboratory classes. Its James F. Will Engineering and Biomedical Sciences, Hall, opened in 2017, is specifically designed for collaborative, interdisciplinary learning.

The result is a modern, student-friendly campus that features accessible computer laboratories and workstations; fiber-optic cabling between buildings; Wi-Fi across campus and specialized laboratories for the study of astronomy, ecology, genetics, geology, human anatomy, life sciences, microbiology, optics, organic chemistry, physiology, and other subjects. From the multimedia computer lab to the nature reserve (created by the late golfing legend and College supporter Arnold Palmer) to the $14-million Fred Rogers Center for Early Learning and Children's Media, Saint Vincent offers many resources to help students intensify their learning.

Traditionally, Benedictine institutions have granted a place of honor to the library. Open 89 hours a week, the Latimer Family Library offers access to more than 250,000 printed volumes; 99,000 microforms such as microfilm, microfiche, and cards; 3,000 musical scores; 400 periodical subscriptions; and online access to electronic journals through 19 different databases. The library also houses a collection of rare books and incunabula (pre-1500 imprints). It also provides plentiful space for quiet studying.

The Robert S. Carey Student Center, covering more than 2 acres, contains the Frank and Elizabeth Resnik Swimming Pool, a gymnasium, performing arts center, wellness center, bookstore, fitness center, locker rooms and training rooms, snack bar, student lounge, chapel, billiards room, art gallery, art studios, and music practice rooms.

Costs

Tuition and fees at Saint Vincent for 2017–18 were $17,516 per semester, and room and board costs average $5,568 per semester, depending on accommodations and meal plan. Books and supplies cost $1,000–$1,500 per year. Costs are subject to change.

Financial Aid

Saint Vincent College offers a comprehensive program of financial aid in the form of scholarships, grants, loans, part-time employment, and deferred-payment schedules and coordinates programs from the federal and state financial aid program. In 2017–18, 100 percent of first-year students who applied for financial aid were offered assistance. The College annually awards qualified freshmen academic scholarships of up to $20,500 per year, renewable for up to four years, for excellence in academic achievement. In addition, the College offers first-generation grants, out-of-state grants, and grants to graduates of Catholic high schools and Benedictine parishes, among others. Other financial aid opportunities include Federal Direct Student Loans and Federal PLUS loans. Residents of Pennsylvania may be eligible for the Pennsylvania Higher Education Assistance Agency Grant program. In order to be considered for financial aid, students must complete the Free Application for Federal Student Aid (FAFSA).

Faculty

The faculty numbers 102 members, of whom 91 percent hold terminal degrees. Members of the faculty have earned doctorates or terminal degrees at such schools as Catholic University of America, Cornell, Duke, Fordham, Northwestern, Notre Dame, NYU, Stanford, Yale, and the Universities of California, Chicago, and Pennsylvania. Faculty members are engaged as principal investigators in research and other projects funded through government agencies such as the National Science Foundation and the U.S. Department of Education and private foundations. The student-faculty ratio is 11:1, and no classes are taught by teaching assistants. Faculty members have chosen to teach at Saint Vincent in part because they value the quality of student-teacher interaction, specifically the emphasis on high standards, personalized learning, fieldwork, hands-on experience, and the high level of classroom participation.

Student Government and Student Activities

The Student Government Association (SGA) builds community at the College by providing opportunities for the students, faculty members, and administrators to share in their common interests. All class officers, senators, and representatives can vote in the unicameral senate that makes up the student government.

The sense of community that Saint Vincent is known for is fostered from the day students arrive on campus. Orientation lasts five weeks and involves more than 150 upperclassmen whose mission is to make freshmen feel at home. Every student is matched with an upperclassman who serves as a big brother or big sister throughout the first year. In the residence halls (where more than 70 percent of students live), trained prefects foster a safe living environment and provide guidance and advice, along with activities and educational programs.

The College community is proud of the Catholic, Benedictine tradition that has shaped life on the campus for more than 170 years. In keeping with the tradition of hospitality, Saint Vincent welcomes students of all faiths or of no faith. The campus includes places for prayer, as it is an important part of life for many of our administrators, faculty members, and students—no matter their faith traditions.

Admission Requirements

Saint Vincent College has a rolling admission policy. Adequate preparation for college is an important determinant for a successful college education. Fifteen secondary school academic units are required for admission to Saint Vincent College. These 15 units must include 4 units of English, 3 or more units of college-preparatory mathematics, 1 unit of laboratory science, and 3 units of social science; 2 units of a foreign language are preferred among 5 elective units. Engineering students must have 1 unit in plane geometry, 1 unit in intermediate algebra, 1 unit in physics, and ½ unit in trigonometry in addition to those listed above. Art education, art studio, and graphic design majors must submit a portfolio for acceptance to the Fine Arts Department, and music and music performance students must audition for acceptance.

Transfer students are invited to apply to Saint Vincent College, which awards generous scholarships to academically capable transfer students. The applicant's academic achievement and personal history at the postsecondary schools previously attended are of primary importance in the decision for admission.

Application and Information

To be considered for admission, a freshman applicant must submit a completed application form with the nonrefundable $25 application fee, an official transcript sent directly to Saint Vincent College from the guidance office at the secondary school of graduation, and an official copy of the test results from the SAT or ACT.

An application and additional information may be obtained by contacting:
Office of Admission and Financial Aid
Saint Vincent College
300 Fraser Purchase Road
Latrobe, Pennsylvania 15650-2690
Phone: 800-782-5549 (toll-free)
E-mail: admission@stvincent.edu
Website: http://www.stvincent.edu
https://www.facebook.com/saintvincentcollege (Facebook)
https://twitter.com/MySaintVincent (Twitter)
https://www.youtube.com/user/saintvincentcollege (YouTube)
https://instagram.com/SaintVincentCollege (Instagram)

Saint Vincent College offers a warm and welcoming atmosphere combined with technologically advanced facilities including the $45-million Sis and Herman Dupré Science Pavilion, dedicated in 2013 and expanded in 2017.

SETON HALL UNIVERSITY
SOUTH ORANGE, NEW JERSEY

 To read more about this school, visit http://petersons.to/setonhalluniversity

The University

As one of the nation's leading Catholic universities, Seton Hall provides great minds with rigorous and challenging academic opportunities in over ninety academic programs that are highly ranked by the Princeton Review, *U.S. News & World Report,* and *Bloomberg Businessweek.* Seton Hall offers all the advantages of a large research university—national reputation; challenging academic programs; notable alumni; state-of-the-art facilities; renowned faculty; and extensive opportunities for internships, research, and scholarship— with all the benefits of a small, supportive, and nurturing environment. The 14:1 student-to-faculty ratio and average class size of 21 students means faculty members know more about each student than just their name.

The University's accomplished faculty members include Fulbright Scholars, prominent researchers, authors, artists, filmmakers, former school superintendents and principals, leaders in nursing, former ambassadors, analysts, and lawmakers—all of whom are dedicated to their fields and their students. They have graduated from some of the nation's leading institutions, including Seton Hall, Harvard, Columbia, Yale, Princeton, and Dartmouth. While faculty members shine in the lecture halls and on the national stage every day, they also meet regularly with students outside the classroom and help them learn to think critically.

Seton Hall offers more than 17,000 internship opportunities, and over 81 percent of students have an internship—or two—on their resume before graduation. This is just one of the reasons Seton Hall graduates have an employment rate of over 90 percent and mid-career earnings 50 percent higher than the national average. Seton Hall was recently ranked in the top 5 in the nation for providing internship opportunities. This national reputation coupled with the University's stellar academic programs draws over 550 employers to campus each year to recruit graduates.

Seton Hall is a Catholic university with a 160-year tradition of educational excellence. A welcoming community, Seton Hall embraces students of all faiths and inspires them to become servant-leaders who make a difference in the world. The University community performs over 40,000 hours of community service annually.

Location

Nestled in the suburban village of South Orange, New Jersey, Seton Hall provides small-town charm combined with big-city opportunities. The University's 58-acre, suburban, park-like campus sits proudly in this picturesque town with tree-lined streets; historic, gracious homes; and quaint shops just 14 miles from New York City—close to all the action, but not engulfed by it.

The bustling town center—with diners, pizzerias, banks, pharmacies, Starbucks, Cold Stone Creamery, a gourmet marketplace, South Orange Performing Arts Center, a movie theater, and more—is just a 5-minute walk from campus. The train station, right in the center of town, provides a direct link to NYC's Penn Station, just 30 minutes away.

The University takes full advantage of all the Big Apple has to offer; after all, it's where the worlds of entertainment, art, publishing, global finance, international diplomacy, and fashion collide. NYC is also one of the world's largest job markets, brimming with internship and job placement opportunities in a variety of companies. Seton Hall students have interned at leading companies like Goldman Sachs, American Express, CNN, the U.S. Secret Service, the United Nations, The *New York Times,* Prudential, The Museum of Natural History, Lockheed Martin, NBC, Sony Music, JPMorgan Chase, Lincoln Center and more.

One of the wealthiest states in the nation, New Jersey is brimming with opportunity. Seton Hall's backyard boasts a powerhouse corporate corridor of more than fifty Fortune 500 companies, pharmaceutical giants, and major corporations. For students, this means networking, internships, and career opportunities.

Academic Programs

Seton Hall is a place where great minds are exposed to even greater opportunities. This is evident in the dozens of student and alumni national scholars and fellows, including nearly 20 prestigious Fulbright Scholars since 2009, as well as Rhodes, Udall, Pickering, Marshall, Critical Language, and Truman Scholars and more than 100,000 alumni who are now successful as CEOs, judges, doctors, principals, CFOs, journalists, nurses, diplomats, and more. About 1,000 Seton Hall graduates have served in executive positions at firms like Oppenheimer, Visiting Nurse Service of New York, American Express, and Merrill Lynch. They have served as elected officials in Washington, D.C., and in hundreds of state capitals and town halls throughout the country. In New Jersey alone, almost 20 percent of the state legislators holds a Seton Hall degree.

Seton Hall's commitment to academic excellence is evident in the more than ninety academic programs offered through six undergraduate schools and colleges. In addition, the University has recently announced plans to form a medical school in partnership with Hackensack University Medical Center; the first class is scheduled to begin in the fall of 2018. A joint degree program for direct admission as a freshman applicant is also planned.

Majors and Degrees

Accounting•
Accounting (5-year B.S./M.S. dual-degree∞)
Africana Studies•
American Humanics√
Ancient Greek†
Anthropology•
Applied Scientific Mathematics†
Arabic†
Archaeology†
Art (Art History•, Fine Arts•, Graphic Interactive and Advertising Design•)
Asian Studies•
Athletic Training (5-year B.S./M.S. or B.A./M.S. dual-degree)∞
Biochemistry
Biology (B.A. or B.S.)
Broadcasting, Visual and Interactive Media•
Business Administration•‡
Catholic Studies•‡
Catholic Theology•
Chemistry•
Classical Culture†
Classical Languages†
Classical Studies•
Communication•
Computer Graphics√
Computer Science•
Creative Writing
Criminal Justice•
Data Visualization and Analysis√
Digital Media and Video√
Digital Media Production for the Web√
Diplomacy and International Relations•
Early Childhood (integrated with elementary and special education)

Elementary Education (integrated with early childhood and special education)
Education with Speech Language Pathology (6-year B.S.E./M.S. dual- degree)∞
Economics (B.A. or B.S.)
Engineering (Biomedical, Chemical, Civil, Computer, Electrical, Industrial, Mechanical)§
English•
Entrepreneurial Studies√
Environmental Sciences†
Environmental Studies•
Ethics and Applied Ethics†
Finance
French•
Gerontology√
Graphic, Interactive, and Advertising Design
History•
Information Technologies√
Information Technology Management‡
International Business
International Relations
Italian•
Italian Studies†
Journalism•
Latin†
Latin America and Latino/ Latina Studies•
Law (3+3 program)∞
Legal Studies in Business†
Liberal Studies
Management
Marketing
Mathematical Finance
Mathematics•
M.B.A. (5-year B.S./M.B.A. or B.A./ M.B.A. dual-degree)∞
Modern Languages

Music (Comprehensive Music/ Music Education, Music Performance•)
Musical Theatre†
Nonprofit Studies†
Nursing
Occupational Therapy (6-year B.A./M.S. dual-degree)∞
Philosophical Theology√
Philosophy•
Physical Therapy (6-year B.S./D.P.T. dual-degree)∞
Physician Assistant (6-year B.S./M.S. dual-degree)∞
Physics (B.A. or B.S.)•
Political Science•
Pre-Dental*
Pre-Law*
Pre-Medical*
Pre-Optometry*
Pre-Veterinary*
Psychology (B.A. or B.S.)•
Public Relations
Religion•

Russian†
Russian and East European Studies†√
Secondary Education (optional integration with special education)
Social and Behavioral Sciences
Social Work•
Sociology•
Spanish•
Special Education (integrated with early childhood, elementary, and secondary education)
Speech Language Pathology (6-year B.S.E./M.S. dual- degree)∞
Sport Management•
Supply Chain Management√
Theatre and Performance•
Web Design√
Women and Gender Studies†
Writing†
Undecided

• Minor also available
† Minor only
√ Certificate program only
‡ Certificate program also available
§ Dual-degree program with New Jersey Institute of Technology
∞ Seton Hall dual-degree program
* Pre-professional programs (students must also select a major)

Campus Facilities

Seton Hall places a strong emphasis on the use of state-of-the-art technology, facilities, and support services to aid in its students' development. Many investments have been made to the campus infrastructure, including the recent construction of a new academic classroom building, new residence hall space, a new parking deck, a Dunkin' Donuts, and a new recreation and fitness center. In addition, the campus boasts a state-of-the-art research library complete with a computerized catalog and 200 computer terminals. The Science and Technology Center is home to state-of-the-future biology and chemistry labs, an atrium, and auditorium, as well as an observatory and greenhouse.

The campus also offers many unique learning labs, such as a Mock Trading Room, Patient Simulation Laboratory, Market Research Center, a student-run radio station (ranked the number-one noncommercial radio station by the National Association of Broadcasters), and Sport Polling Center. All incoming students are provided a new, fully loaded laptop computer.

Costs

Seton Hall offers a flat-tuition rate for students taking between 12 and 18 credit hours. The 2017–18 tuition and fees were $40,888. Room and board costs vary depending on meal plans; however, the average rate is $13,502.

Financial Aid

Paying for college is a major investment. Seton Hall University has been rated as one of the best schools in the nation for return on investment and is committed to providing students with the resources needed to make their dreams a reality. The University gives over $96 million in aid each year; 98 percent of students receive some form of financial aid, and 97 percent receive scholarships or grants directly from the University. Most scholarships are automatically awarded upon admission and do not require separate applications. However, there are also several special scholarships for which students can apply; more information on those is available online at www.shu.edu/ go/scholarships. Seton Hall also provides need-based aid to eligible students who complete the Free Application for Federal Student Aid (FAFSA) form by December 1.

Student Organizations and Activities

On campus, Seton Hall leaders learn to put their ideas into action; discover something new; become part of a community; and build trust, spirit, and lasting friendships. Extracurricular activities abound, with over 130 clubs and organizations, twenty-two Greek societies, fourteen Division 1 Big East athletic teams, and extensive club and intramural sports. Students can audition for one of the many theater productions each year; broadcast at the number-one ranked college radio station in the nation, WSOU-FM, which attracts more than 120,000 listeners a week from the NYC area; be part of the Brownson Speech and Debate team, which has been ranked among the top 20 college and university forensic teams for years; or write for one of three student newspapers. More than two thirds of Seton Hall students participate in clubs and organizations and over 50 percent participate in club or intramural sports.

Admissions Process

Seton Hall takes a holistic approach to reviewing applications for admission, considering academic performance in high school, grades and the rigor of the curriculum, and SAT and/or ACT scores. These are essential indicators of a potential student's ability to succeed at Seton Hall. A personal essay, recommendations, extracurricular activities, and interest in the University are also considerations. Students can apply using the Common Application or the Seton Hall application, located on the admission.shu.edu website.

The typical student who entered Seton Hall last year had an average GPA of 3.6 (B+), an average SAT score of 1150 (old SAT) or 1220 (new SAT), and/or an average ACT score of 25.

Application and Information

Potential students are encouraged to visit Seton Hall in person. Tours are offered Mondays through Fridays at 10 a.m. and 2 p.m. and on Saturdays at 10 a.m., noon, and 2 p.m. Open houses are offered in mid-October, mid-November, mid-February, and late April. Visits can be scheduled online at www.shu.edu/visiting

For more information, prospective students should contact:

Office of Undergraduate Admissions
Seton Hall University
400 South Orange Avenue
South Orange, New Jersey 07079
Phone: 800-THE-HALL (843-4255; toll-free)
E-mail: thehall@shu.edu
Website: http://www.admissions.shu.edu

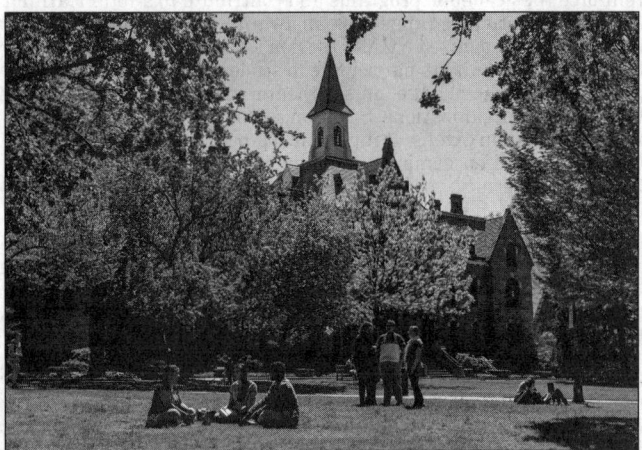

Students enjoy a spring day on the University Green, the scenic pathway located at the heart of Seton Hall's campus.

SIMPSON COLLEGE
INDIANOLA, IOWA

The College

Founded in 1860, Simpson College is a private liberal arts college affiliated with the United Methodist Church. Simpson produces successful students by combining the best of a liberal arts education with outstanding career preparation and extracurricular programs. With 1,300 full-time students and a student to faculty ratio of 13:1, students have the opportunity to work closely with their professors. Simpson's faculty members are as dedicated to their fields of study as they are to teaching—and it shows in the classroom. When this type of dedication and passion is combined with well-prepared and motivated students, the potential for success is unlimited.

The campus is located just minutes from Iowa's capital city, Des Moines, which was recently ranked as the top city for business and careers. The proximity to Des Moines allows Simpson students to take advantage of an abundance of internship opportunities. Whether working with Fortune 500 companies, spending time in an elementary school, or gaining resume-building experiences in a medical field, students learn to push their own boundaries. Simpson's excellent internship program gives students an advantage in today's competitive job market.

Simpson's beautiful, tree-lined campus in Indianola provides small-town friendliness and safety, while the campus facilities are continually enhanced and updated for academic and recreational opportunities. Within the last ten years, multimillion-dollar projects include the renovation and expansion of Blank Performing Arts Center, renovation of outdoor athletic facilities, the addition of a stunning new student center, and a $6-million expansion and renovation of the Simpson Athletic Complex and Steven Johnson Fitness Center.

Simpson's 4-4-1 academic calendar includes a May Term that provides students with unique learning opportunities in the classroom, an internship setting, or while studying abroad. Throughout the year, students take advantage of Simpson's innovative Engaged Citizenship Curriculum. The curriculum allows students to gain skills and experiences valued most by employers while choosing classes that interest them.

Extracurricular activities at Simpson are designed to supplement and reinforce the academic programs and contribute to a total learning experience. Activities range from an award-winning music program to nationally recognized NCAA Division III athletic teams. Students have the opportunity to participate in student government, campus publications, religious life, music, theater, departmental clubs, and various other organizations. Simpson competes in 19 intercollegiate sports and has an extensive intramural program. Simpson has eight Greek chapters on campus, including three national fraternities, one local fraternity, and four national sororities; each with their own house.

Location

Simpson is located in Indianola, a residential community with a population of 14,400. Indianola is 12 miles south of Des Moines, with easy access to Interstates 35 and 80. The Des Moines International Airport is 20 minutes from campus. Indianola is host to nationally known events including the Des Moines Metropolitan Opera and the National Balloon Classic. The vibrant, small-town community has many choices for entertainment and recreation including Lake Ahquabi State Park, Summerset Trail, and unique restaurants and shops within walking distance of campus. Indianola's proximity to Des Moines gives students plenty of distinct advantages. Within minutes, students are right in the heart of some of the best entertainment and employment options Iowa and the Midwest have to offer.

Majors and Degrees

Simpson College grants Bachelor of Arts and Bachelor of Music degrees. Majors include accounting, actuarial science, applied philosophy, art, biochemistry, biology, business management, chemistry, clinical health science, computer information systems, computer science, criminal justice, economics, education (elementary and secondary), English, environmental science, exercise science, forensic science/biochemistry, French, German, graphic design, health services leadership, history, human services, interactive media, interdisciplinary studies, international management, international relations, management information systems, mathematics, multimedia journalism, music, music education, music performance, neuroscience, philosophy, physical education, physics, political science, psychology, public relations, religion, social justice, sociology, Spanish, sports administration, sports communication, studio art, and theater arts.

Simpson also offers pre-professional programs in athletic training, chiropractic, dentistry, engineering, law, medicine, nursing, optometry, pharmacy, physical therapy, theology/ministry, and veterinary medicine. Concentration areas such as early childhood education and ethics are available, as well as many additional minors, including women's studies, human resources management, Latin American studies, and coaching endorsements.

Academic Programs

Simpson College operates on a 4-4-1 academic calendar. The first semester starts in late August and ends in mid-December; the second semester starts in mid-January and ends in late April. A three-week session takes place during the month of May. During this period, students participate in a field experience/internship, study abroad, or take a course on campus with a hands-on focus.

The First-Year Program is an extensive program of orientation, team building, mentoring, community service, advising, and course work structured to help new students adapt to their first year of college. The program begins with orientation and continues throughout the academic year. The academic component of the First-Year Program is the Simpson Colloquium, a joint classroom and advising concept that is unique among first-year programs. These courses are small in size—no more than 18 first-year students each—and all are taught by each student's faculty adviser.

With Simpson's Engaged Citizenship Curriculum, students delve deeper in their courses and focus more on projects that provide hands-on understanding of the subject matter. These courses allow students to work closely and build strong relationships with faculty members, one of the hallmarks of a Simpson education. The curriculum encourages students to take advantage of Simpson's community partnerships, hold internships, study abroad, or conduct independent research. It was developed in response to research that indicates future employers are looking for effective communicators, innovators, and problem solvers. Simpson is on the forefront of providing the kind of experiential, liberal arts education that college graduates need to succeed in their careers and achieve fulfillment in their lives.

Off-Campus Programs

Simpson provides many opportunities for studying abroad, with the choice of a semester-long program or a three-week May Term. Simpson's semester-long, faculty-led study abroad programs include England, Germany, Thailand, Tahiti, Australia, and Chile. Students also have the opportunity for semester study-abroad programs in France, Spain, Italy, and more locations.

In addition, 10 to 15 travel courses are offered each May Term. Recent destinations include Africa, Central America, Great Britain, France, Greece, Ireland, New Zealand, the Galapagos Islands, Brazil, Argentina, and Scandinavia. May Term study abroad courses are led by Simpson faculty members and give students the opportunity to experience a different culture while gaining a stronger global perspective. Over 40 percent of students travel abroad during their time at Simpson.

The Capitol Hill Internship Program (CHIP) provides students with the opportunity to spend either the fall or spring semester in Washington, D.C. Past participants have had various experiences including interning for members of Congress, the Smithsonian Institution, the Republican National Committee, the Justice Department, CNN, the Australian Embassy, and FOX News.

Academic Facilities

Simpson has a wireless campus network with high-speed Internet access. There are numerous computer labs throughout campus where students can use standard office suite applications or specialized, discipline-specific applications.

The Carver Science Center, named after Simpson's most distinguished alumnus George Washington Carver, provides state-of-the-art research facilities, computer labs, a cadaver lab, and classrooms.

The Henry H. and Thomas H. McNeill Hall houses classrooms for business management, accounting, health services leadership, and economics.

The Amy Robertson Music Center is home to Simpson's acclaimed music department and contains the Sven and Mildred Lekberg Recital Hall, ten studios, twenty-two practice rooms, a music computer lab, and the band rehearsal room. The Salsbury Wing includes a choral rehearsal room, a classroom, and studios.

Dunn Library, a modern academic learning resource center, contains over 175,000 books, periodicals, videos/DVDs, and CDs. Many resources (print and online) can be located from the library website. Additional materials for research can be obtained through a national interlibrary loan network. The Center for Academic Resources is also located in Dunn Library, which provides free academic support services to all students.

The A. H. and Theo Blank Performing Arts Center underwent a multimillion-dollar expansion and renovation in 2011. The center accommodates Simpson's well-known programs in theater arts and opera. It includes the magnificent 500-seat Pote Theatre, with both proscenium and hydraulically controlled thrust stages, a studio theater, the Barborka Gallery, technical facilities, and shops and classrooms.

Wallace Hall, named to the National Register of Historic Places, contains facilities for education, sociology, and applied social science.

Mary Berry Hall houses the psychology department which includes six labs, a control room for observation and data processing, and an animal care space. In addition, the building is home to humanities classrooms, a language lab, faculty offices, and the Farnham Art Galleries.

The Gaumer Center contains offices for multimedia communication and art and provides space for the college newspaper, *The Simpsonian*, and radio station KSTM.

Faculty

Simpson offers one professor for every 13 students. Simpson's faculty members serve as academic advisers as well as teachers. Their commitment goes beyond the classroom as they often attend college plays, operas, and athletic events, reinforcing their sincere interest in the lives of the students and their ultimate success.

Costs

Tuition and fees for 2018–19 are $39,144; room charges are $4,062; and board is $4,318. These figures do not include books, music fees, or personal expenses.

Financial Aid

Simpson College is dedicated to making it financially feasible for qualified students to experience the advantages of a Simpson education. In fact, 100 percent of full-time Simpson students receive financial assistance. Generous gifts from alumni, trustees, and friends of the College—in addition to state and federal student aid

programs—make this opportunity possible. Simpson offers financial assistance on both a need and non-need basis. Need is determined by filing the Free Application for Federal Student Aid.

Financial assistance granted on a non-need basis includes generous academic scholarships (awarded on the basis of prior academic records) and talent scholarships (available in theater, music, art, and speech/debate). The talent scholarships are determined by audition/portfolio or application.

In addition, specific scholarships such as the John C. Culver Fellowship, the Iowa History Center Scholarship, the George Washington Carver Fellowship, the Interfaith Fellowship, and the Wesley Service Scholarship can be obtained through application.

Admission Requirements

A strong academic record is essential. Applications are acted upon by an admissions committee, which is elected by the faculty. These faculty members consider the college-preparatory courses taken and the grades received in those courses (transcripts and cumulative GPA), and standardized test scores (ACT and/or SAT), including test sub scores, as well as a high school report form/counselor recommendation.

Transfer applicants are accepted on the basis of successful completion of academic work at an accredited college or university.

Application and Information

Applications are accepted on a rolling basis beginning in early fall and continuing on a space-available basis. Simpson's rolling admission policy allows flexibility; however, early application is recommended.

Application information can be found at www.simpson.edu/apply.

For additional information or to obtain application materials, students should contact:

Office of Admissions
Simpson College
701 North C Street
Indianola, Iowa 50125
Phone: 515-961-1624
      800-362-2454 Ext. 1624
E-mail: admiss@simpson.edu
Website: http://www.simpson.edu
      http://www.facebook.com/simpsoncollege
      http://twitter.com/simpsoncollege
      http://www.youtube.com/simpsonweb
      http://instagram.com/simpsoncollege

SKIDMORE COLLEGE
SARATOGA SPRINGS, NEW YORK

 To read more about this school, visit http://petersons.to/skidmorecollege

The College

Skidmore College is an independent liberal arts college of 2,500 students from 45 states and 67 countries that prides itself on its creative approaches to just about everything. Hence the College's belief that "Creative Thought Matters." About 60 percent of the student body is female and 40 percent male, with 22 percent being domestic students of color, 11 percent international students, and 13 percent first-generation students.

Students enjoy a full schedule of intellectual, cultural, and social activities, such as lectures, visiting scholars in residence, art exhibits, concerts, and dance and theater performances. There are approximately 120 student organizations, including a newspaper, radio and TV stations, ethnic and cultural associations, art and literary journals, and a volunteer network. There are no fraternities or sororities. A strong NCAA Division III intercollegiate sports program for men and women—19 teams in all—includes baseball, basketball, field hockey, golf, ice hockey, lacrosse, riding, rowing, soccer, softball, swimming and diving, tennis, and volleyball. Skidmore competes in the Liberty League, which also includes Bard, Clarkson, Hobart and William Smith, Ithaca, Rensselaer Polytechnic Institute, Rochester Institute of Technology, St. Lawrence, Union, and Vassar. The College has programs in intramural and club sports, health, fitness, and wellness.

Skidmore's campus includes more than 50 buildings. The Williamson Sports and Recreation Complex has a pool and diving well, racquet-sport courts, basketball and volleyball courts, several intramural gyms, three dance studios, a weight room, a fitness center, and a human performance laboratory. Adjacent to the complex are Wachenheim Field, a small stadium with an artificial turf field for soccer, lacrosse, and intramurals, and a 400-meter all-weather track; softball and field hockey turf fields; and the lighted Wenger Tennis Courts. The Frances Young Tang Teaching Museum and Art Gallery, unique in its interdisciplinary approach to exhibits and programming, opened in 2000.

The more than 1,000-acre campus, 300 acres of which consists of the recreation and research-rich North Woods, has been recently upgraded with renovations to athletics, dining, and residential facilities. Skidmore's newest academic building, opened in 2010, is the Zankel Music Center, featuring a spectacular 600-seat recital hall and state-of-the art recording studio. In addition, the Northwoods Apartments, opened in 2007 for upperclassmen, feature "green" apartments that use geothermal heating and cooling systems. The similar Sussman Village Apartments were completed in 2013. More than 40 percent of Skidmore's buildings are heated and cooled geothermally.

Location

Saratoga Springs, 30 miles north of Albany, New York's state capital, is perennially short-listed as one of the most interesting and vibrant small cities in the U.S. Famed for health, history, and horses—its mineral waters, Revolutionary War battlefield, and the nation's oldest thoroughbred racetrack—Saratoga is renowned as an arts and cultural destination. In recent years, *Travel + Leisure* named Saratoga Springs America's seventh-best college town and USA Today named it the seventh-best main street in the U.S. The Saratoga Performing Arts Center is summer home to the New York City Ballet, Philadelphia Orchestra, and Opera Saratoga, and is a performing venue for top rock and jazz musicians. Downtown is just a 10-minute walk from Skidmore and is brimming with galleries, clubs, shops, coffeehouses, and restaurants. Its location near the foothills of the Adirondack Mountains puts an abundance of recreational opportunities—ski areas, parks, lakes, and mountains from New York, Vermont, and Massachusetts—within an hour's drive. Boston, New York City, and Montreal are each approximately 180 miles from the campus.

Majors and Degrees

Skidmore College grants degrees in 43 academic disciplines, including a Bachelor of Arts degree in the following liberal arts subjects: American studies, anthropology, art history, Asian studies, biology, chemistry, classics, computer science, economics, English, environmental science, environmental studies, gender studies, geosciences, history, international affairs, mathematics, music, neuroscience, philosophy, physics, political science, psychology, religious studies, sociology, and world languages and literatures (French, German, and Spanish). The Bachelor of Science degree is granted in areas of a more professional nature, including business, dance, education studies, health and human physiological sciences, social work, studio art, and theater. There are seven interdepartmental majors, business-French and political-Spanish being just two examples. A self-determined major is also available. Most majors have corresponding minors. Minors are also available in arts administration, Chinese, intergroup relations, Italian, Japanese, Latin American studies, and media and film studies. In keeping with the College's creative spirit and the realities of the marketplace, about half of Skidmore students choose a second major or minor.

Through partnerships with other institutions, Skidmore offers enhanced program/degree offerings in business, education, engineering, nursing, and physical and occupational therapy. These include 4+1 M.B.A. programs with Rochester Institute of Technology, and Clarkson University Graduate School; the Whitman MBA Advantage program with Syracuse University; 4+1 M.S.A. and M.S.F. programs with Syracuse; dual-degree programs in engineering with Clarkson, Dartmouth College, and Rensselaer Polytechnic Institute; an M.S. in accountancy with Wake Forest University; dual-degree programs in physical therapy and occupational therapy with Sage Graduate School; an M.S. in Teaching with Clarkson; and a 4+1 nursing program (New York University School of Nursing). Skidmore also has certification programs in teaching and social work and preprofessional programs in law and medicine/health professions.

Academic Programs

The Skidmore journey begins with the First-Year Experience, which introduces students to the rigorous interdisciplinary academic program and overall approach to learning and connects them with a faculty adviser/mentor. Talented but economically disadvantaged students accepted into the Opportunity Program (Higher Education Opportunity Program and Academic Opportunity Program) participate in a month-long summer program. Some 250 students are members of Skidmore's Periclean Honors Forum on the basis of their academic achievement and aspirations, leadership qualities, and civic commitment.

Generally, students choose a major by the end of sophomore year. They are also expected to take one to two courses in both quantitative reasoning and expository writing, and at least one course of the following: natural science, social science, arts, humanities, and culture-centered inquiry. There is plenty of academic support through Student Academic Services. In their junior and senior years, students often add value to their courses of study through faculty-student collaborative research (academic year and summer program), internships (many funded and for credit), volunteerism, service-learning, and off-campus study.

Off-Campus Programs

About 60 percent of Skidmore's students spend a semester or year off campus. In addition to Skidmore programs in England, France, New Zealand, and Spain, students can access approximately 120 international programs through the College's Approved Programs structure, including programs in Africa, Asia, Europe, Latin America, and Australia. All academic majors and minors can be accommodated and transfer credits are guaranteed for students studying on an Approved Program. Financial aid is transferable to most off-campus study programs. Annually, nearly 25 percent of the student body members engage in research with a faculty mentor, including nearly 100 in the summer student-faculty research program. The College also offers a Washington Semester (internship in conjunction with

American University) and a semester at the Marine Biological Laboratory in Woods Hole, Massachusetts.

Academic Facilities

Skidmore's 1,000-acre campus is comprised of more than 50 buildings. The newest academic building, the Arthur Zankel Music Center, features a spectacular 600-seat recital hall and a state-of-the-art recording studio. Skidmore's visual and performing arts space includes the Saisselin Art Center, with studios and the Schick Art Gallery; the Janet Kinghorn Bernhard Theater, with a seating capacity of 350, and an experimental black box theater; and the Dance Center. The Frances Young Tang Teaching Museum and Art Gallery provides a focal point for cross-disciplinary study through the visual arts. The Dana Science Center offers state-of-the-art teaching and research space, including a microscopy center. Dana links the College's science departments to the Mathematics and Computer Science departments in neighboring Harder Hall, which features a Linux lab with more than 20 workstations for advanced computer science projects.

Costs

In 2017–18, tuition and fees were $52,446, a double dorm room was $8,278, and board was $5,726.

Financial Aid

Skidmore annually provides approximately $45 million in financial aid. The average 2017–18 first-year aid package was $42,000 and ranged from $2,000 to $65,000; 42 percent of students receive need-based grants; 50 percent receive some form of financial aid; and 50 percent are given the opportunity to work on campus. Average postcollege student debt (just under $23,000) is well below the national average. Students interested in applying for admission are encouraged to do so regardless of their intention to seek financial aid. The FAFSA, a copy of the federal income tax form, and the CSS Profile must be filed each year. The College hosts an annual Filene Music Scholarship Competition to award four to six $60,000 ($15,000 per year) scholarships on the basis of musical ability without regard to financial need. Five to seven $15,000 scholarships ($60,000 over four years) in math and science are also awarded annually. The Skidmore Scholars in Science and Mathematics program provides up to eight S3M scholars with demonstrated financial need annual financial-aid packages with no loan component in the first two years and with reduced loans in years three and four.

Faculty

Skidmore College has more than 300 full-time faculty members, 87 percent of whom hold a doctorate or the highest degree in their field. The student-to-faculty ratio is about 8:1 and the average class size is 16. Although actively engaged in research and publication in their individual fields, Skidmore faculty members regard teaching as their primary commitment. All students have faculty advisers who assist them in selecting courses and in designing individual academic programs.

Student Government

Students at Skidmore play an active role in College governance. Through the Student Government Association (SGA) and membership on a number of major College committees, they participate in academic and social life. The SGA operates under the authority granted by the Board of Trustees and is dedicated to democratic self-government and responsible citizenship. Elected faculty members and student representatives serve on the All-College Council, the Academic Integrity Board, and the Social Integrity Board. Broad concerns of the SGA include educational policy, elections, social and student events, first-year orientation, student publications, and student clubs and organizations.

Admission Requirements

Those seeking admission to Skidmore's first-year class should complete a secondary school curriculum that includes at least 16 credits in college-preparatory courses. The Admissions Committee is also pleased to consider applications from qualified high school juniors who plan to accelerate and enter college early. Applicants typically have completed 4 years of English, 4 years of a foreign language, 4 years of mathematics, 4 years of social studies, and 3 to 4 years of laboratory science. Applicants must provide a secondary school transcript, letters of recommendation from two teachers of academic subjects, and a report from their guidance counselor.

Although Skidmore is test optional (some exceptions for international and home-schooled students), students who wish to can submit their standardized test scores (SAT with writing or ACT with writing). A campus visit and interview is also recommended.

Through its participation in the Higher Education Opportunity Program, Skidmore enrolls capable, energetic, and ambitious New York state residents who, because of their academic and financial situations, would not otherwise gain admission to the College under traditional requirements. Skidmore's Academic Opportunity Program (AOP) recruits similar students who reside outside of New York. The programs are collectively referred to as the Opportunity Program.

Application and Information

Applicants for admission are requested to complete the Common Application—online at www.commonapp.org—and submit it with a $65 fee or request a fee waiver from their adviser. They may also apply through the Coalition for Access, Affordability, and Success, online at www.coalitionforcollegeaccess.org. All information should be postmarked by January 15. Applications from early decision candidates should be submitted by November 15 for the Round I early decision plan or by January 15 for the Round II early decision plan. Transfer candidates are urged to apply by April 1 for the next fall term and by November 1 for the next spring term. In addition to a high school transcript, transfer candidates are required to submit, by the appropriate deadlines, an official transcript of all college-level work completed, recommendations from two professors, and a statement regarding personal and academic standing from the dean of students at the current college. International students are given special attention throughout the admissions process. Applicants whose first language is not English are encouraged to submit the results of the Test of English as a Foreign Language (TOEFL). There are a limited number of need-based financial aid awards available for outstanding international students.

Mary Lou W. Bates
Vice President and Dean of Admissions and Financial Aid
Skidmore College
815 North Broadway
Saratoga Springs, New York 12866
Phone: 518-580-5570
        800-867-6007 (toll-free)
E-mail: admissions@skidmore.edu
Website: www.skidmore.edu
        www.facebook.com/SkidmoreCollege
        http://twitter.com/skidmorecollege
        https://www.instagram.com/skidmorecollege
        https://www.pinterest.com/skidmorecollege
        www.skidmore.edu/admissions/visit/youvisit.
            php#virtualtour
        www.skidmore.edu/videos/ www.youtube.com/
            skidmorecollege

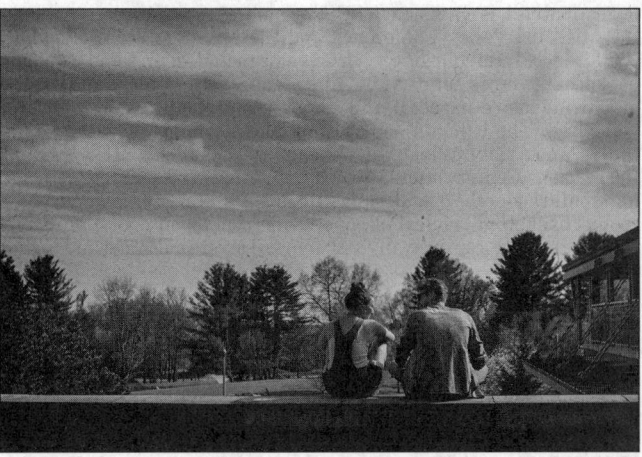

Students chat, with Haupt Pond and the southeastern corner of campus in the distance.

SOUTHERN ILLINOIS UNIVERSITY CARBONDALE
CARBONDALE, ILLINOIS

 To read more about this school, visit http://petersons.to/southernillinoisuniversitycarbondale

The University

Southern Illinois University Carbondale (SIU), chartered in 1869, is a comprehensive, state-supported institution with nationally and internationally recognized instructional, research, and service programs. SIU is fully accredited by the North Central Association of Colleges and Schools.

SIU offers more than 200 undergraduate majors, minors, and specializations; three associate degree programs; 95 baccalaureate degree programs; 80 master's degree programs; 34 doctoral programs; and professional degrees in law and medicine. SIU is a multicampus university that includes the Carbondale campus as well as the SIU School of Medicine at Springfield.

During the 2016 academic year, SIU's enrollment was 15,987, which included 12,182 undergraduate students, 3,183 graduate students, and 622 professional students. The average age of undergraduates is 23. International students account for 8.49 percent of SIU's total enrollment. Of U.S. undergraduate students, 17.91 percent are African-American, 0.21 percent are American Indian/Alaskan, 1.9 percent are Asian or Pacific Islander, and 9.19 percent are Hispanic.

Students who are ready to start college but not ready to commit to a specific major can enroll in SIU's Exploratory Student Advisement-Undeclared (EXPU) program. Advisers and career counselors help these students plan their education and careers. SIU faculty members, staff members, and alumni help students arrange internships, cooperative education programs, and work-study programs.

All single students under the age of 21 not residing with their parents or legal guardians, and with fewer than 26 credit hours earned after high school, are required to live in university-owned and operated residence halls. SIU offers three on-campus residential areas for single students, each with a dining hall, a post office, and laundry facilities. Learning Resource Centers, available on both sides of campus, offer writing centers, computer labs, and student lounges. University Housing Residence Hall Dining provides all-you-care-to-eat meals and late-night dining. Residence Hall Dining offers a variety of menus, vegetarian and light entrees, display cooking, and a full-time dietitian to help students with special dietary needs. Apartment housing is available for sophomore-, junior- and senior-level undergraduates, graduate students, and students with families.

SIU intercollegiate sports teams compete at the NCAA Division I level (football is Division I-FCS). Conference affiliations include the Missouri Valley Conference and the Missouri Valley Football Conference. Intercollegiate sports teams include men's and women's basketball, cross-country, diving, golf, swimming, and track and field; men's baseball and football; and women's softball and volleyball. The campus has various playing fields, several tennis courts, and a campus lake with a beach and boat dock. SIU's Student Recreation Center offers an Olympic-size pool; indoor tracks; handball/racquetball and squash courts; a climbing wall; weight rooms; basketball, volleyball, and tennis courts; outdoor equipment rental; an aerobic area; wallyball; martial arts; and dance and cardio studios.

The Student Center is one of the largest in the United States without a hotel. It holds a bookstore, several restaurants, a craft shop, facilities for bowling and billiards, headquarters for more than 275 student organizations and the student government office, four ballrooms, and an auditorium. On-campus events throughout the year include concerts, plays, festivals, guest speakers, and musicals.

Location

Carbondale is six hours south of Chicago, two hours southeast of St. Louis, and three hours north of Nashville, Tennessee. Four large recreational lakes, two great rivers (the Mississippi and the Ohio), and the 270,000-acre Shawnee National Forest are within reach of the campus. The mid-South climate is ideal for year-round outdoor activities.

Carbondale is a city of 26,000 that supports one large enclosed mall, several mini-malls, and theaters and restaurants. Students frequent the shops and restaurants that line Illinois Avenue and Grand Avenue.

Majors and Degrees

The university offers three Associate in Applied Science degree programs (aviation flight, physical therapist assistant, and radiologic sciences) at the College of Applied Sciences and Arts.

The College of Applied Sciences and Arts offers bachelor's degree programs in architectural studies; automotive technology; aviation management; aviation technologies; dental hygiene; electronic systems technologies; fashion design and merchandising; health care management; information systems technologies; interior design; mortuary science and funeral service; public safety management (off-campus only); radiologic sciences; and technical resource management.

The College of Agricultural Sciences offers bachelor's degree programs in agribusiness economics; agricultural systems and education*; animal science; crop, soil, and environmental management; forestry; horticulture; hospitality and tourism administration; and human nutrition and dietetics.

The College of Business offers bachelor's degree programs in accounting; business and administration (online only); business economics; finance; management; and marketing.

The College of Education and Human Services offers bachelor's degree programs in several undergraduate programs, many in conjunction with other colleges on campus. The programs include: art education*; behavior analysis and therapy; biological science education*; communication disorders and sciences; early childhood*; elementary education*; English teacher education*; exercise science; foreign languages (French, German, and Spanish)*; history education*; math education*; physical education teacher education*; public health; recreation; rehabilitation services; social science education*; social work; special education*; sport administration; and workforce education and development (* denotes educator licensure required through the university's Teacher Education program).

The College of Engineering offers bachelor's degree programs in civil engineering; computer engineering; electrical engineering; electrical engineering technology; industrial technology; mechanical engineering; and mining engineering.

The College of Liberal Arts offers bachelor's degrees in Africana studies; anthropology; art; classics; communication studies; criminology and criminal justice; design; economics; English; geography and environmental resources; history; languages, cultures, and international studies; linguistics; mathematics; music; musical theater; paralegal studies; philosophy; political science; psychology; sociology; theater; and university studies.

The College of Mass Communication and Media Arts offers bachelor's degrees in cinema and photography; journalism; and radio, television, and digital media.

The College of Science offers bachelor's degree programs in biological sciences; chemistry; computer science; geology; mathematics; microbiology; physics; physiology; plant biology; zoology; and pre-professional programs and advisement in the following areas: chiropractic; dental; medical; nursing; occupational therapy; optometry; osteopathic medicine; pharmacy; physical therapy; physician assistant; podiatry; and veterinary medicine.

In addition to the many majors offered at SIU, specializations are offered in all colleges in many areas.

Academic Programs

Each bachelor's degree candidate must earn a minimum of 120 semester hours of credit, including at least 42 at the 300–400 level at a 4-year institution and the last 30 at SIU. Each student must maintain at least a "C" average in all course work at SIU and must fulfill the university core curriculum and the specific requirements of their degree programs. SIU awards credit through qualifying extension and correspondence programs, military experience, the High School Advanced Placement program, the College-Level Examination Program (CLEP), SIU's proficiency examination program, and work experience.

SIU offers honors coursework and special recognition for students who demonstrate exceptional academic achievement. The Air Force and Army offer ROTC programs at SIU. SIU offers fall and spring semesters, as well as a summer term.

Off-Campus Programs

Southern Illinois University Carbondale is committed to serving statewide, national, and international needs. This commitment is reflected in SIU Extended Campus, which offers educational opportunities located off campus. SIU Extended Campus is present at 20 military installations and 17 nonmilitary locations across 14 states, offering 24 online degree programs, 15 off-campus programs, and five military programs.

Off-campus credit programs are designed to meet the educational needs of adults wishing to pursue a degree but who are unable to travel to the Carbondale campus.

Additional information can be found at extendedcampus.siu.edu.

Academic Facilities

In addition to the 2.6 million volumes, 3.6 million microfilms, and more than 43,000 current periodicals and serials available in Morris Library, students and faculty members have access to more than 200,000 e-books. More details are available online at lib.siu.edu.

Students learn and practice in the Transportation Education Center based at the Southern Illinois Airport, outdoor laboratories, the student-run *Daily Egyptian* newspaper, WSIU-TV, WSIU-FM, art and natural history museums, a literary magazine, McLeod Theater, Memorial Hospital, a vivarium, plant biology greenhouses, University Farms, and Touch of Nature Environmental Center.

Costs

Tuition and fee charges for the 2017–18 academic year (fall and spring) for students enrolled in 15 or more semester hours were $13,932 for Illinois residents and out-of-state domestic residents, and $28,107 international students. Room and board totaled $10,622. (All costs are subject to change.) The cost of books and school supplies varies among programs. The average cost is $1,100 per academic year. Beginning Fall 2017, SIU Carbondale is eliminating out-of-state tuition for undergraduate students and moving to an international/domestic rate structure.

Financial Aid

More than $284 million in financial aid was distributed to 16,631 SIU students in fiscal year 2016 through federal, state, and institutionally funded financial aid programs.

To apply for financial aid at SIU, students should complete the Free Application for Federal Student Aid (FAFSA). Applications that are filed before December 1 receive priority consideration for campus-based aid. The FAFSA can be completed online at fafsa.ed.gov, and students should list Southern Illinois University Carbondale (Federal School Code 001758) as a school of choice.

SIU has a large student employment program, with about 4,200 students employed each year in a variety of job classifications.

Faculty

Faculty members are dedicated to excellence in teaching and to their advancement of knowledge in a variety of disciplines and professions. Many faculty members are well-known nationally and internationally for their research contributions. The student-faculty ratio is 14.83:1. There are 762 full-time and 89 part-time instructional faculty members.

Teaching assistants at SIU are graduate students who assist faculty members in teaching.

Student Government

The Undergraduate Student Government (USG) represents the undergraduate student body at Southern Illinois University Carbondale in all matters pertaining to student welfare, student activities, and student participation in University planning and administration. The Undergraduate Student Government is composed of three separate branches: Judicial, Legislative, and Executive. The Executive branch consists of a president, vice president(s), chief of staff, and treasurer. The Legislative branch consists of 51 senators. Senators serve on various committees within USG including Internal Affairs, External Affairs, and the Funding Board. Senators also may serve on external campus advisory committees, representing the interests of the student body. The Judicial Board consists of five justices

Admission Requirements

Freshman applicants whose ACT composite score is at or above 23 (SAT score at or above 1130) and whose high school grade point average is at or above 2.0 (on a 4.0 scale) are admitted to the university. Applicants also can be admitted with an ACT composite score at or above 18 (SAT score at or above 940) and a high school GPA at or above 3.0 (on a 4.0 scale). All other applicants who meet the course subject pattern requirements will undergo a holistic review to determine potential admissibility. Admission of students who do not meet automatic admission requirements may be subject to conditions. Freshman applicants must meet course pattern requirements: 4 years of English, 3 years of mathematics, 3 years of laboratory science, 3 years of social science, and 2 years of electives.

Transfer applicants must have an overall grade point average of at least 2.0 on a 4.0 scale, based on work attempted at all institutions and calculated by SIU grading policies. Transfer applicants must also be eligible to continue at the last institution attended.

Some programs have higher admission requirements or require additional screening for admission. Undergraduates can apply online at admissions.siu.edu.

Application and Information

Admission is granted on a rolling basis. Application priority deadlines for freshmen and transfer students are May 1 for the summer term and fall semester, and Dec. 1 for the spring semester. The application fee is $40.

For more information, prospective students should contact:

Undergraduate Admissions
Mail Code 4710
1263 Lincoln Drive
Southern Illinois University Carbondale
Carbondale, Illinois 62901
Phone: 618-536-4405
E-mail: admissions@siu.edu
Website: http://www.siu.edu
http://www.facebook.com/SouthernIllinoisUniversityCarbondale
http://twitter.com/siuc

SIU Carbondale, ranked among the top 5 percent of the nation's public research institutions, offers more than 200 degree and certificate programs. Centrally located, diverse, and featuring remarkable amenities and hands-on learning opportunities, SIU provides 8,474 acres of possibilities.

SOUTHERN METHODIST UNIVERSITY
DALLAS, TEXAS

⭐ For more information, visit http://petersons.to/smu

The University

Southern Methodist University (SMU) is a nationally ranked global research university in the dynamic city of Dallas. SMU's alumni, faculty, and 11,000-plus students in seven degree-granting schools demonstrate an entrepreneurial spirit as they lead change in their professions, communities, and the world.

SMU celebrates diversity, with students from across the United States and nearly 90 nations, as well as a variety of ethnic, socioeconomic, and religious backgrounds. Sixty-five percent of SMU first-year students come from outside Texas. Fall 2017 undergraduate enrollment included 27 percent of students from diverse ethnic backgrounds.

Students can choose from more than 100 majors and 85 minors. One in five SMU students opts to pursue a double major. Students can customize their education by combining a major in the humanities or sciences with another in engineering, business or the arts for a dual degree. According to the Center for World University Rankings 2017, SMU is in the top 0.5 percent of world universities.

SMU hosts more than 400 performances, concerts, and exhibits on campus during the school year. The Tate Lecture Series brings world-changers and experts to campus. Recent speakers have included Condoleezza Rice, Robert Edsel, Scott Kelly, and Brandon Stanton.

Location

SMU students benefit from the University's proximity to the heart of Dallas, which is home to amazing restaurants, a world-renowned arts district, exciting nightlife, and professional sports.

SMU's location in Dallas—home to more than 20 Fortune 500 companies—offers students abundant internship opportunities. Dallas is also ranked number one for jobs by *Forbes* in 2017. The Dallas area is home to companies such as American Airlines, AT&T, Texas Instruments, Toyota, Southwest Airlines, and ExxonMobil. Ninety-three percent of May 2017 SMU graduates were employed or in graduate/professional school six months after graduation.

Dallas-Fort Worth is the nation's fourth-largest metropolitan area and home to about 7 million residents. Dallas offers top-tier museums and performance facilities, including the AT&T Performing Arts Center, Meyerson Symphony Center, Dallas Museum of Art, Nasher Sculpture Center, Perot Museum of Nature and Science, and SMU's Meadows Museum. The Dallas area is home to the Dallas Cowboys, Dallas Mavericks, Dallas Stars, Texas Rangers, FC Dallas, Lone Star Park, Texas Motor Speedway and professional golf tournaments.

Dallas-Fort Worth International Airport offers service to 149 domestic destinations—including access to every major city in the continental U.S. within four hours—and 57 international destinations. Dallas Love Field, home to Southwest Airlines, serves more than 42,000 passengers daily.

Majors and Degrees

SMU offers strong undergraduate, graduate, and professional programs through seven schools.

The **Dedman College of Humanities and Sciences** is SMU's largest and most diverse academic unit. It is home to the humanities and social, natural, and mathematical sciences—disciplines that are the core of higher education. Undergraduate students in Dedman College may major and minor in more than 50 programs. Dedman College offers 18 master's programs and 15 doctoral programs, plus numerous interdisciplinary programs.

The **Cox School of Business** equips students with the knowledge, skills, and experience needed to become business leaders. Major

publications, including *Bloomberg Businessweek, The Economist, Poets&Quants,* and *Forbes,* rank SMU Cox among the top business schools nationally and globally. Degrees offered by the Cox School include: Bachelor of Business Administration with majors in accounting, finance, financial consulting, general business, management, marketing, and real estate finance; Full-Time, Fast Track Professional, and Executive Master of Business Administration; and master's degrees in accounting, business analytics, finance, management,and sport management (in partnership with the Simmons School).

The **Lyle School of Engineering**, ranked among the top 10 percent of schools for highest-paid engineering graduates by College Factual 2018, prepares today's engineering students to be tomorrow's innovators equipped with both technical and leadership skills. Degree programs offered include bachelor's, master's, and doctoral degrees through the departments of Civil and Environmental Engineering; Computer Science and Engineering; Electrical Engineering; Engineering Management, Information and Systems; Mechanical Engineering; Multidisciplinary Studies; and dual- and joint-degree programs with other schools on campus, such as the Cox School of Business.

The **Meadows School of the Arts** prepares students to lead professional careers in the arts and communications and provides opportunities for all SMU students to grow in appreciation of the arts. A leader in innovative community engagement programs, Meadows challenges students to make a difference locally and globally by developing connections between arts entrepreneurship and social change. The School offers minors and bachelor's and master's degrees through 11 divisions: Temerlin Advertising Institute, Art, Art History (also offering a Ph.D.), Arts Management and Arts Entrepreneurship, Corporate Communication and Public Affairs, Creative Computation, Dance, Film and Media Arts, Journalism, Music, and Theatre.

The **Annette Caldwell Simmons School of Education and Human Development** prepares exemplary professionals and advances knowledge through evidence-based research. Undergraduate programs include a major and three different concentrations in applied physiology and sport management and a major in educational studies. The school offers three doctoral programs, about 10 master's degrees, and a number of graduate professional-preparation programs. Its academic departments include Teaching and Learning, Applied Physiology and Wellness, Dispute Resolution and Counseling, Education Policy and Leadership, and Liberal Studies.

Students at SMU can also opt to focus on specialized studies through degree-track programs such as pre-law, pre-health, physical therapy, and biomedical research.

SMU's undergraduate curriculum is complemented by the nationally recognized **Dedman School of Law**, offering a personalized legal education in a community of distinguished scholars, and **Perkins School of Theology**, which prepares women and men for faithful leadership in vital Christian ministry.

Academic Programs

Students benefit from small classes and opportunities for research, leadership development, and unique learning experiences on campus and around the world. Undergraduate students participate in scholarly research, civic engagement, professional internships, and creative activity related to education goals.

SMU faculty and students conduct research in the U.S. and worldwide in the sciences, engineering, education, arts, humanities, and business. Examples include natural hazards, water quality, cyber security, data analytics, learning disabilities, human performance, immigration, and the search for dark matter, as well as treatments for cancer, neurodegenerative diseases, diabetes, anxiety, and depression.

Off-Campus Programs

Students can expand their horizons with SMU Abroad's more than 150 programs in 50-plus countries to study for a semester, a summer, or a year. The unique SMU-in-Taos program brings history, science, and art to life at SMU's spectacular campus in Northern New Mexico.

Academic Facilities

SMU's campus includes 134 buildings featuring state-of-the-art teaching and learning facilities and equipment.

SMU's eight libraries house the largest private collection of research materials in the Southwest, with more than four million volumes.

The Meadows Museum houses one of the largest and most comprehensive collections of Spanish art outside Spain. A partnership with Madrid's Prado Museum includes the loan of major paintings from the Prado and an internship exchange.

SMU is also home to the George W. Bush Presidential Library and Museum. This is the first presidential library to share the campus of a private university.

Estimated Costs

For the 2017–18 academic year, undergraduate tuition and fees was $52,498; average housing and dining was $16,510.

Financial Aid

In addition to providing a valuable education with lifelong benefits, SMU partners with families to manage the cost of that education. Besides academic scholarships and customized financial aid packages for eligible students, SMU offers several payment plans. Three out of four SMU undergraduate students receive some form of financial assistance from the University, including academic or need-based aid. According to *Forbes* 2017 Best Value Colleges ranking, SMU is one of only 300 schools nationwide that are worth the investment. Competitive academic scholarships include the President's Scholars Program, the Nancy Ann and Ray L. Hunt Leadership Scholars Program, and scholarships offered by SMU's individual schools.

Faculty

SMU has 1,204 full- and part-time faculty members, and more than 80 percent of full-time faculty hold a Ph.D. or the highest degree in their field. The undergraduate student-to-faculty ratio is 11-to-1.

Student Life

Approximately 3,200 undergraduate and graduate students live on campus in 11 Residential Commons and six upperclass/graduate communities. The Residential Commons enable all first- and second-year students to live on campus and include on-site classes, social activities, and Faculty in Residence.

Students can make their mark, meet new people, and develop leadership skills through nearly 200 clubs and organizations spanning a variety of activities. They can also get involved in student government, campus programming, or community service. Annually, nearly 2,500 undergraduate volunteers make a difference through approximately 70 nonprofit agencies. Students also participate in Alternative Breaks national service projects. Other options for students include joining a religious or multicultural group, or getting involved in Greek life.

SMU has 17 NCAA Division I athletics programs, including the Mustang football team, which has played in four recent bowl games. Mustang spirit and traditions make for memories that will last a lifetime.

Students can stay in shape at the Dedman Center for Lifetime Sports with the latest health and fitness equipment. Students interested in sports can opt to participate in one or more of the 18 intramurals, such as flag football, basketball, and softball, as well as 15 club sports, including lacrosse, baseball, and hockey.

Admission Requirements

SMU carefully considers each application with the goal of adding dimension to its diverse, ambitious community of scholars. The strongest applications are not always those with the greatest number of accomplishments, but those that resonate with authenticity and passion.

Prospective students need to submit a completed application (either SMU's online application; The Common Application; ApplyTexas; or Coalition Application for first-year undergraduate applicants), the completed Early Decision agreement form (if applying Early Decision), a $60 nonrefundable application fee, an official high school transcript, official SAT or ACT scores—SMU does not require the SAT optional essay or the ACT writing test (students graduating outside of the U.S. and music, theatre, dance, studio art, and film B.F.A. applicants are not required to submit test scores), a personal essay, a counselor recommendation (required), a teacher recommendation (optional), an extracurricular resume (optional), and a Home School supplement (if applicable). Students applying for dance, music, theatre, art, or film programs should also review audition and portfolio requirements.

The Early Action (nonbinding) and Early Decision I (binding) deadline is November 1. The Regular Decision (nonbinding) and Early Decision II (binding) deadline is January 15.

Application and Information

The best way for students to get a feel for SMU is to visit. SMU offers many structured visits, such as Mustang Days and Academic Spotlights, where prospective students can meet current students, talk with academic representatives, and tour campus. Prospective students can also attend an information session, speak with an admission counselor, and tour on a weekday or selected Saturday. More information is available at smu.edu/visit.

For more information, prospective students should contact:
SMU Undergraduate Admission
Southern Methodist University
6425 Boaz Lane
P.O. Box 750100
Dallas, Texas 75275
Phone: 214-768-2058
      800-323-0672 (toll-free)
E-mail: ugadmission@smu.edu
Website: smu.edu/admission

SOUTHERN NEW HAMPSHIRE UNIVERSITY

MANCHESTER, NEW HAMPSHIRE

 To read more about this school, visit http://petersons.to/snhu

The University

At Southern New Hampshire University (SNHU), student success is the number-one priority. This sense of dedication to helping students achieve their education and career goals can be seen across the entire institution.

U.S. News and World Report has consistently ranked SNHU among the country's most innovative universities. This year, the publication ranked SNHU as the most innovative regional Tier 1 University in the northern United States—an impressive achievement for a school that is committed to consistently reinventing the way that education is delivered and received.

Academic programs are created with the real world in mind, so students are prepared to launch successful careers when they graduate. Classes are taught by highly credentialed faculty who have professional experience and remain current in their fields. Academic and personal support is readily available, both inside and outside the classroom. With small class sizes, students never feel like just a name or a number, and are able to get to know their professors. Students in need of help will find that faculty and staff are quick to rally around them and work toward furthering their understanding and success. With more than 50 undergraduate programs (in addition to more than 60 graduate programs), students can have meaningful experiences that will better prepare them for the real world in a wide range of fields.

A private university education can and should be affordable, and SNHU operates on the belief that college should change students' lives—not break the bank. That's why students with high school GPAs of 2.5 and higher can earn up to $20,000 in academic scholarships in addition to generous financial aid packages. More than 90 percent of the students at SNHU receive some type of financial aid.

SNHU is always looking to improve and provide state-of-the-art facilities that enhance the student experience. A new science and technology building opened in the fall of 2017, featuring a wind tunnel, robotics lab, machine shop, and more. Other recent additions to campus include the Gustafson Center, home to SNHU's Admission and Career Development departments, an athletic stadium, and a new 300-bed residence hall. Another residence hall is currently on the way, as well as a larger science and technology building that will enhance the university's existing facilities.

Students can get involved with over 70 student-run clubs and organizations at SNHU, or even start their own. Intercollegiate teams compete in the Northeast-10 Conference of the NCAA's Division II, and available sports include baseball, men's and women's basketball, cheerleading, men's and women's cross-country, men's golf, ice hockey, men's and women's lacrosse, men's and women's soccer, softball, men's and women's tennis, women's track and field, and women's volleyball. Intramural sports are also extremely popular. SNHU's powerful athletic teams have earned honors from the NCAA and *USA Today* for high grades and 100 percent graduation rates.

Athletic facilities include an indoor, 25-meter competition-size swimming pool, a racquetball court, an aerobic studio, and more. The university also recently finished construction of a brand-new athletic complex.

The Wellness Center provides short-term health care, health education, and counseling services for students, and develops a robust schedule of events around issues ranging from bullying and domestic violence prevention to nutrition and physical fitness. In addition, students with disabilities will find that SNHU ensures that all buildings and facilities on campus are handicapped-accessible.

The Career and Professional Development Center provides assistance with resume development, letter writing, company research, networking, and informational interviewing, in addition to facilitating internships and job opportunities. Lifetime counseling and career services are available to both current students and alumni.

Location

SNHU is conveniently located just five minutes from downtown Manchester, New Hampshire's largest city, and has been named one of the top college towns in the country. Public transportation is available, and students may keep cars on campus beginning in their freshman year. The mountains, beaches, and Boston are all just an hour away. CQ Press has repeatedly named New Hampshire one of the nation's most livable states.

Majors and Degrees

SNHU has three schools: the School of Arts and Sciences, the School of Business, and the School of Education, as well as the College of Engineering, Technology, and Aeronautics. The university offers associate, bachelor's, master's, and doctoral degrees. Undergraduate programs provide students with a strong general education foundation and the knowledge and skills they need to succeed in their careers.

The College of Engineering, Technology, and Aeronautics reflects the increased demand for graduates in STEM fields. SNHU has recently launched several new majors in these fields, including mechanical engineering, aeronautical engineering, computer science, electrical and computer engineering, air traffic management, and construction management. Once complete, the new science and technology building will provide additional resources in support of these programs.

The School of Arts and Sciences offers degrees in communication, creative writing, English language and literature, environmental science, game art and development, game programming and development, graphic design and media arts, history, justice studies, law and politics (pre-J.D. option), mathematics, psychology, and sociology. In addition, SNHU is adding a new biology major to better serve those students seeking to enter the health and biological research fields.

The School of Business majors include accounting, accounting/finance, business administration, business analytics, computer information technology, culinary and baking arts (A.S.), economics, fashion merchandising and management, hospitality business, hospitality management, international business, marketing, operations and project management, sport management, and technical management. SNHU also offers a unique Degree in Three track which is available for most programs in the School of Business. Through Degree in Three, students are able to earn their degree in three years through a blend of traditional academics and real-world experience. The goal of the program is to foster and enhance effective communication, critical thinking, and teamwork. The program enables students to save more than $40,000 in tuition and room and board; take a traditional course load of five classes per semester; graduate in six semesters with no night, weekend, or summer courses; secure internships and participate in community events; and pursue interests—such as graduate school, employment, or travelling abroad—instead of their fourth year.

The School of Education majors include early childhood education, elementary education, elementary education with certification in general special education, English education, middle school mathematics education, middle school science education, music education, secondary mathematics education, social studies education, and special education.

SNHU also offers an honors program, a prelaw program, and a pre-MBA program for students seeking additional academic challenges.

Off-Campus Programs

Southern New Hampshire University excels at mixing academic theory with practical experience both inside and outside of the classroom. Undergraduates participate in off-campus cooperative education experiences and internships, which can earn them up to 12 academic credits. Such opportunities are based on a student's major and career goals, and are typically undertaken during a student's junior or senior year. Students can work with faculty members and the Career and Professional Development Center to find appropriate assignments.

SNHU has established relationships with many respected, high-profile employers who provide internship and job opportunities, including Fidelity Investments, BAE, Rockstar Games, Walt Disney World, Marriott International, Enterprise Holdings, AmeriCorps, and prominent sports organizations such as Major League Soccer, the Boston Celtics, the Boston Red Sox, and more.

Students also work with real-world off-campus partners in their courses. For example, marketing students have created media campaigns for area businesses, while education students assist local teachers in their classrooms. SNHU graduates are always in demand because businesses know they have been prepared to contribute both on the job and in their communities.

At SNHU, students are able to go beyond the campus and enjoy opportunities for studying abroad at a number of partnering institutions in countries around the world. In terms of tuition and room and board, studying abroad costs no more than living on campus and SNHU will even pick up the tab for a student's flight (up to $1,000) and the full cost of travel health insurance. All of the credits and grades earned overseas at a partner university will apply directly towards an SNHU degree.

Costs

For the 2017–18 academic year, undergraduate tuition cost $31,136. For on-campus residents, the average room and board cost was $12,278. Students should plan to budget funds for books, supplies, travel, and personal expenses. In an effort to continue to remain an affordable private university option for as many students as possible, SNHU has frozen tuition for the 2018–19 academic year. Many families are surprised to learn that attending SNHU is often less expensive than seemingly lower-cost institutions.

Financial Aid

More than 90 percent of the SNHU students receive some form of financial aid, which may include need-based grants, academic and merit scholarships, and loans. SNHU also participates in the Federal Work-Study Program and the Federal Supplemental Educational Opportunity Grant Program. The school is also eligible under the Federal Stafford Student Loan Program and the Federal Pell Grant Program. Aid applicants should complete the Free Application for Federal Student Aid (FAFSA) by the priority deadline of March 15. Student Financial Services can provide the appropriate forms, or students can go online to http://www.fafsa.ed.gov. Academic, athletic, and leadership scholarships are also available for students who qualify.

Faculty

SNHU has more than 128 full-time faculty members and over 200 part-time instructors, with a student-faculty ratio of 15:1. A majority of the full-time faculty members at the university hold a Ph.D. or the equivalent degree in their area of expertise.

Programs at SNHU blend theory with practice to stimulate students' professional development and personal growth. Faculty members bring extensive academic, work, travel, and life experiences to their classrooms. Although their primary goal is teaching, faculty members remain current in their disciplines. Outside the classroom, faculty members are management consultants, CPAs, analysts, small-business owners, economists, accountants, marketing professionals, engineers, entrepreneurs, innkeepers, chefs, world travelers, artists, poets, novelists, psychologists, and much more.

Student Government

The Student Government Association is led by 25 students, including five officers, who represent all of the students at SNHU. Its primary function is to represent the student body in campus affairs and to distribute student activity funds. One student is appointed to represent the student body on the Board of Trustees. Students are also appointed to most other standing committees, including the Dining Services Committee, Residence Life Committee, Public Safety Committee, the Curriculum Advisory Committee, and the Library Committee.

Admission Requirements

Applicants for admission are evaluated individually on the basis of academic credentials and personal characteristics. When reviewing applicants, primary emphasis is placed on a student's academic record, as demonstrated by the quality and level of college-preparatory course work and achievement attained. Most successful candidates admitted to SNHU present a program of study consisting of 16 college-preparatory courses, including 4 years of English, 3 or more years of mathematics (up through successful completion of algebra II), 2 or more years of science, and 2 or more years of social science. Separate consideration is given to admission decisions for transfer, nontraditional, international, and Bradley Three-Year Honors Program in Business applicants.

Application and Information

Applicants for undergraduate day programs must submit an application (via the Common Application), college essay, $40 application fee, official high school transcript, and one letter of recommendation from a school counselor or teacher. SNHU is a test-optional institution and SAT/ACT scores are not required.

Freshman applicants can apply before November 15 to be considered for the early action deadline. SNHU operates on a rolling admission basis; however, the priority application deadline is February 1. Admission and scholarship decisions are made within 30 days of receiving all required admission materials.

For more information about Southern New Hampshire University, students should contact:

Office of Admission
Southern New Hampshire University
2500 North River Road
Manchester, New Hampshire 03106-1045
Phone: 603-645-9611
Fax: 603-645-9693
E-mail: admission@snhu.edu
Website: http://www.snhu.edu
　　　　http://www.facebook.com/snhuoncampus
　　　　http://www.twitter.com/snhuoncampus

SPRINGFIELD COLLEGE
SPRINGFIELD, MASSACHUSETTS

 To read more about this school, visit http://petersons.to/springfieldcollege

SPRINGFIELD
COLLEGE
▽

The College

Real-world experience through fieldwork and internships, combined with outstanding academic preparation, gives Springfield College graduates a competitive advantage when they move on to careers or graduate education. Students perform fieldwork, internships, or service learning as early as their first semester, gaining valuable experience while following the College's mission of leadership in service to others.

Internationally renowned for educating leaders in health sciences, human and social services, sports and movement studies, education, business, and the arts and sciences, Springfield College offers bachelor's, master's, and doctorate degree programs, and it is accredited by the New England Association of Schools and Colleges (NEASC) and numerous other disciplinary accrediting bodies. Springfield College is recognized in the top tier of Best Regional Universities—North Region, in the 2017 edition of *U.S. News & World Report*'s "Best Colleges."

The Mission: Springfield College is a private, coeducational institution that was founded in 1885 with its Humanics philosophy: "to educate students, in spirit, mind, and body for leadership in service to others." Humanics has remained the College mission to this day, and students, faculty members, and administration are committed to that mission.

The College has been named to the President's Higher Education Community Service Honor Roll, has received Carnegie Foundation Community Engagement Classification, and has won the Jostens/ NADIIIAA Award of Merit for community service by student athletes. The Institute for International Sport named it one of the fifteen most influential educators through sport in America. Springfield College is designated by the YMCA of the USA as a premier leadership development center.

Student Population: A diverse student body of 3,200 undergraduate and graduate students at the main campus comes from across the country and around the world.

Cocurricular Activities: Enriching the undergraduate experience is an array of cocurricular activities, health and wellness programs, arts and cultural events; an extensive campus recreation program; and one of the nation's largest athletics programs for a midsized college. There are more than 100 organizations and opportunities for involvement. More than 80 percent of undergraduates participate in some form of athletics, including varsity teams, intramurals, or club sports. Approximately 44 percent of males and 32 percent of females enrolled in the traditional undergraduate programs on the Springfield College campus participate in intercollegiate athletics. There are men's and women's teams in basketball, cross-country, gymnastics, lacrosse, soccer, swimming, diving, tennis, track and volleyball; women's teams in field hockey and softball; and men's teams in baseball, football, golf, and wrestling. Approximately 90 percent of the student body uses the Wellness Center and 35 to 40 percent of students participate in intramurals or clubs specifically.

Campus Facilities: Ten campus residence halls provide guaranteed on-campus housing. Options include traditional residence halls and suite-style accommodations with private rooms for 2 to 4 students along with a shared lounge, kitchen, and bathrooms. All residences are coeducational. Seniors may choose to live off campus. The main student dining facility features a range of fresh food options. There are snack and other light-fare services around the campus, including a food court in a two-story atrium.

Recreational Facilities: The award-winning Wellness & Recreation Complex facilities represent the best in collegiate recreational centers. The complex includes the Wellness Center, Field House, and Athletic Training/Exercise Science Complex with 160,560 square feet of instructional, athletic, and recreational space adjoining the Physical Education Complex and Art Linkletter Natatorium.

The buildings support the College's degree programs in athletic training, physical education, exercise science, sport management, and related areas. They also contain and support the center for campus recreation and wellness with its comprehensive programming serving the entire campus community.

Location

Springfield College's picturesque, 182-acre campus includes several new and newly renovated state-of-the-art facilities that blend with traditional campus architecture. On the shores of Lake Massasoit in the Pioneer Valley, Springfield College is located in Springfield, the third-largest city in Massachusetts and fourth-largest in New England (Boston, Worcester, and Providence are larger). A wide range of social, cultural, and athletic activities enhance the valley, as well as twelve other colleges and universities. For example, Springfield Symphony Hall is the site of concerts, plays, musicals, and dance performances; the MassMutual Center in Springfield is home to the American Hockey League's Springfield Thunderbirds; and the Naismith Memorial Basketball Hall of Fame is an international attraction.

Nearby cities and towns offer many additional attractions. Northampton bustles with trendy shops, coffee houses, galleries, theater productions, health food stores, nightclubs, and restaurants. The Berkshire Hills offer hiking, skiing, biking, and other outdoor activities. Boston lies 90 miles to the east, New York City is less than a 3-hour drive away, Vermont is 1 hour away, and Bradley International Airport is 20 miles south.

Majors and Degrees

Springfield College offers Bachelor of Science or Bachelor of Arts degrees in the following: accounting, American studies, applied exercise science, art, art therapy, athletic training, biology, business management (opportunity for a unique 4 + 1 program culminating in an M.B.A.), communications/sports journalism, communication sciences and disorders, computer and information sciences, computer graphics/digital arts, criminal justice, dance, early childhood education, elementary education, emergency medical services management, English, finance, general studies, health care management, health science, health promotion for schools and communities, history, marketing, mathematics, mathematics and computer technology, nutritional sciences, occupational therapy (entry-level 5½-year program culminating in a Master of Science degree), physical education (movement and sport studies), physical therapy (entry-level 6½-year program culminating in a Doctor of Physical Therapy degree), physician assistant (entry-level six-year program culminating in a Master of Science degree), psychology, recreation management, rehabilitation and disability studies, secondary education, sociology, special education, sport management, and sports biology. Undeclared majors receive help in determining their path in First-Year Seminar.

Academic Program

Consistent with the unique Springfield College Humanics philosophy, undergraduate education takes a holistic approach and prepares the student—in spirit, mind, and body—for a life of leadership in fields that help others.

The College has a two-semester academic calendar. To graduate, students must complete 120 credits including required courses for the major field of study, electives, and required courses for all students (writing, computer applications, arts and humanities, analytical and natural sciences, social sciences, international/multicultural studies, social justice, and physical education). Students may also earn credit for successful completion of Advanced Placement (AP) high school courses, and through the DANTES subject standard test and the College-Level Examination Program (CLEP) administered by the College Board.

Springfield College has agreements with several medical schools, which guarantee acceptance of its qualified students. In addition, many Springfield College programs allow undergraduates to take graduate-level courses.

There are campus chapters of the following honor societies: Beta Beta Beta (biology), Kappa Delta Pi (education), Phi Alpha (social work), Phi Epsilon Kappa (health, physical education, recreation or safety), and Psi Chi (psychology).

Off-Campus Programs

From their very first semester, Springfield students benefit from fieldwork, internships, and service learning. The College maintains relationships with businesses, nonprofits, public and private agencies, and schools, and students benefit from real-world experience early and often. Sites have included the Naismith Memorial Basketball Hall of Fame, American Hockey League, *The Boston Globe,* YMCAs, American Heart Association, MassMutual, Hilton Head Crowne Plaza, Reebok Health and Fitness Center, Baystate Medical Center, children's hospitals, parks and recreation departments, and more. The Springfield College Career Center assists students and alumni with exploring career options, identifying career-related experiential learning, refining job search skills, identifying employment opportunities, preparing for admission to graduate and professional schools, and networking with alumni.

Extensive study-abroad programs are available. Students may also enroll in courses at some of the other colleges in the Springfield area.

Academic Facilities

Technologically up-to-date, the campus is wireless and has smart classrooms, computer labs, a videoconferencing facility, a conference center, a language laboratory, a television studio, a journalism lab, a radio station, and more.

Science facilities include the Schoo-Bemis Science Center with state-of-the-art equipment; the Athletic Training/Exercise Science Complex, cited as one of the most outstanding in the nation; and the Health Sciences Center, with a human anatomy laboratory and sophisticated equipment for physical testing, analysis, and treatment. Herbert P. Blake Hall contains labs, testing, and treatment facilities, including the medical simulation laboratory, or sim lab, that features high-fidelity 3G adult and baby patient-simulator mannequins that respond like humans, allowing students to experience realistic, hands-on training and complicated medical techniques. Locklin Hall contains a well-equipped rehabilitation assessment and counseling services center.

For arts studies and programs, the renovated Fuller Arts Center and Appleton Auditorium is the site of performances, and the Visual Arts Center contains studio workspace and a public exhibition center.

The East Campus comprises an 82-acre forest ecosystem with camping facilities and lake shoreline. It supports the programs of Springfield College through purposefully designed, outdoor experiential-learning opportunities. The Springfield College Child Development Center is an exceptional fieldwork facility for students of education and psychology.

Babson Library, located in the newly renovated Learning Commons, is well known for its resources in physical education, psychology, education, and health and human services, contains a rich collection of full-text print and digital materials. Library staff members assist, and students have access to a full range of information sources.

Costs

For the 2018–19 academic year, tuition and fees are $37,445. Room and board costs are $12,550.

Financial Aid

Students are encouraged to apply for grants, loans, and student employment. Springfield College financial aid is awarded based on need and academic achievement. The College gives full consideration to students who submit the Free Application for Federal Student Aid (FAFSA). Students

not eligible for financial aid may be considered for campus employment.

Faculty

Most of the 208 faculty members hold doctorates or other terminal degrees. The student-teacher ratio is 15:1.

Student Government

The Student Government Association, managed by elected students, promotes students' interests and welfare. It guides and finances more than 30 student organizations, adopts policies affecting students, and is a liaison between students and the College administration.

Admission Requirements

Springfield College evaluates applicants on the basis of academic and personal factors. Applications for regular admission or early decision must be submitted to the Office of Undergraduate Admissions and include a completed application form, a high school transcript, one personal reference, and SAT or ACT scores. Transfer students must also submit a transcript and a transfer college report from each college attended.

Application due dates are as follows: undergraduate applicants, April 1; transfer students, August 1; physical therapy program, December 1; and occupational therapy program, January 15. Physician Assistant applicants must apply as early decision 1 (December 1) or early decision 2 (January 15).

Members of the Springfield College faculty and staff are interested in meeting each applicant and encourage candidates to visit the College and experience campus life. The College offers personal interviews, campus tours, and open-house programs and also facilitates contact with alumni and current students.

Application and Information

Springfield College accepts the Common Application. The Springfield College Admissions Committee reviews applications upon receiving them.

Information may be obtained from:

Office of Admissions
Springfield College
263 Alden Street
Springfield, Massachusetts 01109
Phone: 413-748-3136
     800-343-1257 (toll-free)
E-mail: admissions@springfieldcollege.edu
Website: springfieldcollege.edu

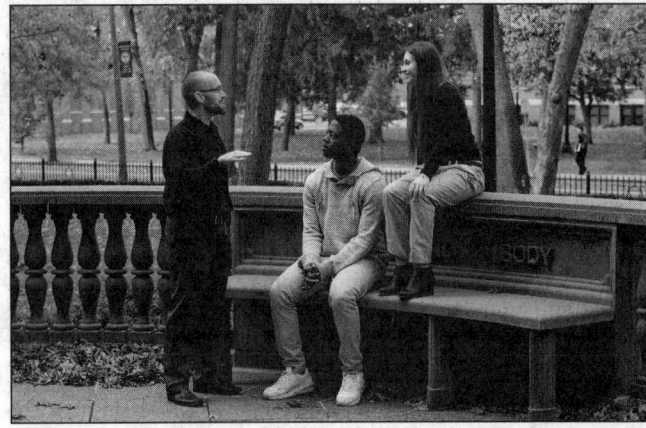

Faculty members make time so students make the grade. The student-to-faculty ratio is 15:1, so faculty members get to know their students, and can provide assistance and guidance throughout their studies at Springfield College.

COLLEGE CLOSE-UPS

STATE UNIVERSITY OF NEW YORK AT OSWEGO

OSWEGO, NEW YORK

 To read more about this school, visit http://petersons.to/sunyoswego

The University

Founded in 1861, SUNY Oswego is a comprehensive college with an excellent academic reputation and a commitment to teaching, learning, research, and service. Total enrollment, including part-time and graduate students, is approximately 8,000 students including 6,800 undergraduates. More than 110 liberal arts and career-oriented programs are offered through the College of Liberal Arts and Sciences; School of Business; School of Communication, Media, and the Arts; and School of Education.

Located on 696 acres on the southern shore of Lake Ontario, the spacious tree-lined campus consists of over fifty academic and residential buildings. Twelve residence halls and The Village townhouse complex offer a variety of on-campus housing opportunities. More than 200 registered extracurricular organizations cover a wide range of social, academic, cultural, and intellectual interests. Theater, art, film, music, dance, and discussion events fill the campus cultural calendar throughout the school year as well. There is a full slate of twenty-four NCAA Division III intercollegiate sports for men and women, along with a full complement of competitive club sports and intramural athletics.

SUNY Oswego receives more than 14,000 applications for some 2,000 freshman and transfer openings each fall. It has been recognized by a number of authoritative guides for its outstanding academic opportunities and high academic standards. In recent years, SUNY Oswego has been cited for excellence and selectivity in *U.S. News & World Report's Best Colleges Guide, Colleges of Distinction,* and in both the Princeton Review's *Best Northeastern Colleges* and their *Best Value Colleges* for 2018 for the sixth consecutive year. The Princeton Review and *USA Today* recently named SUNY Oswego to their "Best Value" listing of colleges and universities in the nation.

The Oswego campus is undergoing a facilities renaissance with over $800 million invested in campus construction and renovations in recent years. Recently completed projects include the $118-million Richard S. Shineman Center for Science, Engineering, and Innovation; a new Biological Field Station lab facility; renovation and conversion of Romney Field House; and major renovations and additions to the performing arts facility and the School of Education's Park and Wilber Halls.

Location

With a population of nearly 20,000, the city of Oswego is a modest-sized, friendly upstate New York community. It is the country's oldest freshwater port and one of the leading ports on the Great Lakes and St. Lawrence Seaway. The city and its surrounding area are known for summer and winter recreation, including camping, boating, sailing, fishing, tennis, golf, ice skating, alpine and cross-country skiing, snowboarding, and sledding. The campus is conveniently located 35 miles northwest of Syracuse and 65 miles east of Rochester. Students traveling by rail or air may utilize bus service to Oswego through the Regional Transportation Center located adjacent to one of the largest malls in the northeast, Destiny USA in Syracuse.

Majors and Degrees

SUNY Oswego awards the Bachelor of Arts (B.A.), Bachelor of Science (B.S.), and Bachelor of Fine Arts (B.F.A.) degrees.

Through the College of Liberal Arts and Sciences, students can earn a baccalaureate degree in American studies, anthropology, applied mathematics, applied mathematical economics, biochemistry, biology, chemistry, cinema and screen studies, cognitive science, computer science, creative writing, economics, electrical and computer engineering, English, French, gender and women's studies, geochemistry, geology, German, global and international studies, history, human development, information science, language and international trade, linguistics, mathematics, meteorology, philosophy, philosophy-psychology, physics, political science, psychology, public justice, sociology, software engineering, Spanish, and zoology.

The School of Business offers B.S. degree programs in accounting, business administration, finance, human resource management, marketing, operations management and information systems, and risk management and insurance.

The School of Communication, Media, and the Arts offers baccalaureate degree programs in art, broadcasting and mass communication, communication and social interaction, graphic design, journalism, music, public relations, and theater.

The School of Education offers B.S. degree programs in adolescence education, childhood education, teaching English to speakers of other languages (TESOL), technology education, technology management, vocational-teacher preparation, and wellness management.

In addition, three innovative five-year combined bachelor's and master's programs are available: a bachelor's degree in accounting with an M.B.A., a bachelor's in psychology with an M.B.A., and a bachelor's in psychology with a master's in human computer interaction.

Cooperative programs include a 2+2 program leading to a B.S. in medical imaging sciences, as well as a 3+3 program leading to a B.S./D.P.T. in physical therapy from SUNY Upstate Medical University; and a 3+4 pre-optometry program leading to a bachelor's in chemistry from Oswego and an O.D. in optometry from SUNY College of Optometry.

Academic Programs

Oswego offers students a broad range of courses in the liberal arts and in preprofessional and professional studies. In addition to core courses within a major, all students must satisfy general education requirements designed to strengthen basic writing and analytical proficiency, give students awareness of their cultural heritage, and provide a level of literacy in the social and behavioral sciences, natural sciences, and humanities.

Before arriving on campus, students are assigned an adviser from either their major area or the college's Student Advisement Center. Advisers assist students who have not declared a major; help with academic, personal, and career concerns; and collaborate in scheduling courses needed for graduation. In addition, most students are matched with a first-year peer adviser, an older student, to help them face the challenges of their first year. The college has more than 500 undeclared students; many drawn by Oswego's reputation for helping learners find their way in education and life.

Students may be selected for the college's honors program, which provides a challenging academic experience for high achievers regardless of major.

Off-Campus Programs

Opportunities exist for students to broaden their knowledge of other countries by participating in one of eighty different summer or semester overseas academic programs offered. A newer option is short study-abroad quarter courses offering an

COLLEGE CLOSE-UPS

intensive curriculum followed by a one-to-two-week experience in a foreign country.

Internships and other field experiences are available for students from all disciplines through the Center for Experiential Learning. In addition, a formalized cooperative education program (co-op) is available to students from over twenty-five major areas. Each year, more than 1,000 Oswego students participate in internships, co-ops, and other career-awareness activities on campus, in the local area, and throughout the world.

Academic Facilities

Penfield Library is a high-tech information center supporting the curriculum, teaching, and research of SUNY Oswego. Through Interlibrary Loan, Penfield can provide additional materials from libraries all over the world.

Campuswide computer technology services support students in their classroom, residence, and Internet activities. Wireless access is available throughout the campus. The campus maintains hundreds of Macintosh and Windows-based computers.

Adjacent to the campus, the college maintains the 330-acre Rice Creek Field Station, with its $5.5-million, modern, 7,200-square-foot lab facility which opened its doors in the fall of 2013. The facility has two lab/classrooms, a lecture room, and exhibit areas with an indoor viewing gallery, providing a unique vista of the creek and pond. College classes and community education programs are regularly held at the field station, which ranks among the five most extensively used facilities of its kind in the country.

Tyler Hall, Oswego's newly renovated fine arts center, has an art gallery that features annual traveling exhibitions, locally produced theme exhibitions, and the best work of students and faculty members. Tyler Hall's Waterman Theatre hosts student plays, musical performances, and productions by internationally renowned traveling artists.

The WRVO Stations, the college's 50,000-watt public radio outlet, provides outstanding on-campus internship opportunities. Communication Department facilities also include two new all-digital television studios, a modern radio lab, and two new journalism labs in Lanigan Hall. Student-run TV and radio stations and the college newspaper are located in the new Campus Center facilities.

Costs

Tuition for 2017–18 was $3,335 per semester for New York State residents and $8,160 per semester for nonresidents. Room and board charges were approximately $7,014 per semester for entering students, depending on the meal plan, and additional fees totaled approximately $1,490 per semester. SUNY Oswego guarantees that a student's initial first-year costs for room and board will be frozen for up to four consecutive years. Although many activities on campus are free of charge, students need to budget for personal expenses.

Financial Aid

Need-based financial assistance consists of grants, loans, and part-time employment. Oswego offers more than $84 million in aid to its students annually. Students interested in financial aid must file a Free Application for Federal Student Aid (FAFSA). New York State residents also need to file an application for the state's Tuition Assistance Program (TAP).

Oswego offers a very generous merit scholarship program. Students receive more than $6 million annually in merit scholarships and approximately 45 percent of the entering freshman class receives one. The average four-year renewable scholarship is more than $3,000 per year. Through New York State's Excelsior Scholarship program, a large number of New York students are also eligible for free tuition at SUNY Oswego. For scholarship qualifications and details, students should visit http://www.oswego.edu/admissions/scholarships.

Faculty

With approximately 88 percent of SUNY Oswego faculty holding doctoral or other terminal degrees, students can be assured of the opportunity for an outstanding undergraduate education. The student-faculty ratio is approximately 18:1. While dedicated to teaching first and foremost, Oswego's faculty members are also actively engaged in research—often in partnership with undergraduate students.

Admission Requirements

Admission to Oswego is competitive, with high school average, academic program, and standardized test scores being the most important criteria for applicants. Special talents such as artistic, musical, athletic, and creative writing skills are also considered. The Committee on Admissions accepts results of either the ACT or the SAT. A campus admissions visit is encouraged.

Transfer students in good standing are encouraged to apply for admission. The average GPA for entering transfer students is 3.0.

Application and Information

Oswego accepts both The Common Application and the SUNY Application for admission. Both applications are available online at http://www.oswego.edu/apply. Oswego evaluates applications as they are completed and as space remains available. Applications completed by January 15 for the fall term or October 15 for the spring term are ensured equal consideration. Applications received after those dates are welcomed, although considered as space remains available.

Prospective students and their parents are encouraged to visit the campus to participate in a student-guided tour and speak with an admissions counselor. Visits can be scheduled online at www.oswego.edu/admissions. Interested candidates can also call the Office of Admissions in advance to schedule a visit.

For further information, students should contact:

Office of Admissions
229 Sheldon Hall
SUNY Oswego
Oswego, New York 13126
Phone: 315-312-2250
Fax: 315-312-3260
E-mail: admiss@oswego.edu
Website: http://www.oswego.edu/admissions

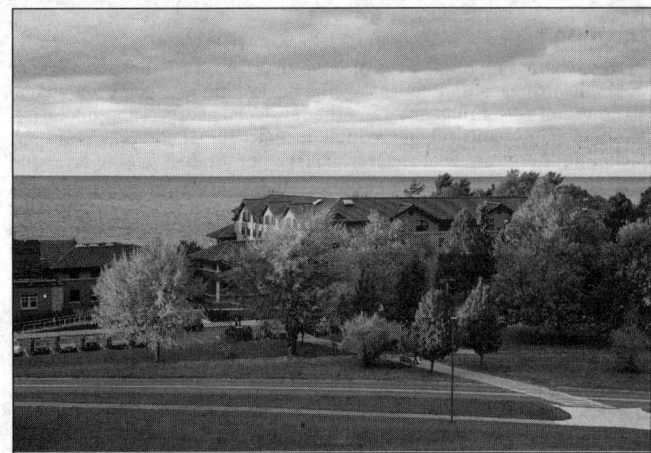

SUNY Oswego is located on 696 acres on the southern shore of Lake Ontario.

STATE UNIVERSITY OF NEW YORK COLLEGE OF ENVIRONMENTAL SCIENCE AND FORESTRY

SYRACUSE, NEW YORK

★ To read more about this school, visit http://petersons.to/sunyesf

The College

The SUNY College of Environmental Science and Forestry (ESF) is one of the nation's largest and most widely recognized environmental colleges. Founded in 1911, the College has grown beyond its original emphasis on forestry to include professional education in environmental science, landscape architecture, environmental studies, and engineering in addition to distinguished programs in the biological and physical sciences. Throughout its history, the College has focused on addressing the environmental issues of the time in its three mission areas—instruction, research, and public service. ESF graduates are well-prepared for environmental careers through specialized academic programs and a holistic approach to solving today's environmental and resource problems.

A leader in its field, ESF is one of the specialized doctoral degree–granting colleges within the State University of New York System. The College currently supports undergraduate and graduate degree programs in more than thirty environmentally-related disciplines. Graduate programs lead to the Master of Science (M.S.), Master of Landscape Architecture (M.L.A.), Master of Professional Studies (M.P.S.), and Doctor of Philosophy (Ph.D.) degrees. ESF's research program is conducted throughout the world and research funding totals more than $15 million per year.

ESF's main campus is located on 12 acres adjacent to Syracuse University and SUNY Upstate Medical University in an urban residential setting. There are 1,750 undergraduate and 550 graduate students enrolled at ESF. The College's unique partnership with Syracuse University offers ESF students the opportunity to take additional classes there for academic diversity and depth, and to participate in cultural events, student clubs, fraternities and sororities, and professional organizations.

ESF recently opened two new buildings on campus. Centennial Hall, is an environmentally friendly residence hall that houses more than 500 ESF students in a combination of double rooms and student apartments and the Gateway Center is a hub for campus events that serves as a showcase for the College's sustainability efforts. The center features a wood pellet–fueled heat-and-power plant designed to generate enough energy for five campus buildings.

Location

Syracuse, a metropolitan area of more than 730,000 people, is a leader in the health care and education industries and is recognized as one of the nation's emerging centers for the development of green technologies. It offers many cultural, recreational, and educational opportunities, including museums, live theater, college and professional sports, and historic points of interest. Syracuse is centrally located at the crossing point of two Northeast superhighways. The driving time to Syracuse from New York City, Philadelphia, Boston, Toronto, and Montreal is about 5 hours; from Buffalo and Albany, about 3 hours. The city is served by a modern international airport and major bus and rail lines.

Majors and Degrees

The SUNY College of Environmental Science and Forestry offers three undergraduate degrees: the Bachelor of Science (B.S.), the Bachelor of Landscape Architecture (B.L.A.), and the Associate in Applied Science (A.A.S.). The B.S. degree is awarded in aquatic and fisheries science, biochemistry, bioprocess engineering, biotechnology, chemistry, conservation biology, construction management, environmental biology, environmental education and interpretation, environmental health, environmental resources engineering, environmental science, environmental studies, forest ecosystem science, forest health, forest resources management, natural resources management, paper engineering, renewable materials science, sustainable energy management, and wildlife science. A number of options and concentrations are offered within specific curricula. The B.L.A. degree, which requires a semester of off-campus study, is awarded in landscape architecture. Two-year A.A.S. degrees are awarded in forest technology,

land surveying technology, and environmental and natural resources conservation at ESF's Ranger School campus in Wanakena, New York.

Academic Programs

All students at ESF have opportunities for specialized study as well as research and field experience. The Department of Environmental and Forest Biology is the largest department on campus and encompasses seven different majors, including biotechnology, conservation biology, wildlife science, aquatic and fisheries science, forest health, and environmental education and interpretation. Biology students are required to complete a four-week period of summer field study, usually at ESF's Cranberry Lake Biological Station, following their sophomore or junior year. Options for specialization within the chemistry program include biochemistry, environmental chemistry, and natural and synthetic polymer chemistry.

The construction management program teaches management, analysis, and design skills used in today's green construction process, with an emphasis on environmental and engineering issues.

Environmental resources engineering students learn skills in such areas as biological, environmental, and water resources engineering; mapping science; and geographic information systems.

The closely related environmental science program also deals with engineering science, along with areas of focus in watershed science, health and the environment, earth and atmospheric systems science, environmental analysis, and renewable energy. The new environmental health program focuses on the study of the intersection of human health and the physical environment. Analysis, prevention, and mitigation of potential environmental hazards are also studied.

Bioprocess engineering students focus on the engineering, biology, and chemistry of ecologically sound industrial technologies and processes, giving students career opportunities in areas such as chemical engineering and bioengineering, pharmaceuticals, and renewable energy.

The forest resources management curriculum offers areas of focus in forest management, measurement, and policy, along with forest ecology and biology. The program includes a minor in management offered in conjunction with Syracuse University. Natural resources management students can concentrate in specialized areas such as recreation or water resources management. Students in sustainable energy management focus on energy resources management, markets and policies, energy systems and sustainability, and renewable energy technologies. Forest and natural resources management students are required to complete a four-week period of summer field study at ESF's Wanakena campus prior to the junior year.

The environmental studies major offers specializations in environmental communication and society; biological science applications; and environmental policy, planning, and law.

The landscape architecture program is a five-year bachelor's degree that is accredited by the ASLA to provide preparation to enter this licensed profession. Students study site design, urban and regional planning, historic preservation, community and environmental design, and computer applications. During the first semester of the fifth year, the landscape architecture curriculum requires participation in off-campus independent study. Paper engineering students can study process and product design and environmental engineering applied to the pulp, paper, and related chemical industries, while paper science students focus on a variety of industry-specific research and management areas. In addition, ESF offers excellent preparation for graduate study in health professions, law, veterinary science, and medicine; the College has a joint admission agreement with the College of Medicine at nearby SUNY Upstate Medical University.

Academic Facilities

Specialized facilities and equipment include electron microscopes, plant-growth chambers, climate-controlled greenhouses, an animal environmental simulation chamber, a bioacoustical laboratory, a radioisotope laboratory, numerous computer labs, nuclear magnetic resonance spectrometers, gas chromatography apparatus, a mass spectrometer, ultracentrifuges, and X-ray and infrared spectrophotometers. The photogrammetric and geodetic facilities of the environmental resources engineering department are among the most extensive available in the United States. The paper science and engineering laboratory has a semi-commercial paper mill with accessory equipment. The sustainable construction management and engineering department has a strength-of-materials laboratory, a pilot-scale plywood laboratory, and a machining laboratory. The landscape architecture faculty has a one-of-a-kind environmental simulation laboratory. The greenhouses and forest insectary in Illick Hall are used to produce plant and insect materials for the classroom and laboratory. Extensive collections are available, including wood samples from all over the world, botanical materials, insects, birds, mammals, and fishes. The Roosevelt Wildlife Collection contains more than 10,000 species of well-preserved vertebrate and invertebrate animals and also recognizes the environmental interests and contributions of U.S. president Theodore Roosevelt.

The F. Franklin Moon Library includes the Academic Success Center for tutorial support in mathematics, writing, and other courses. Moon Library contains more than 100,000 specialized catalog items, including more than 1,800 research journals. The library also provides comprehensive abstract and indexing services relevant to the College's programs. Library facilities and services are supplemented by the collections at Syracuse University and the SUNY Upstate Medical University, both within walking distance.

ESF's regional campuses in Tully, Warrensburg, Cranberry Lake, Newcomb, and Wanakena, New York, offer a great diversity of forest sites that are used as outdoor teaching laboratories and for intensive research. ESF operates numerous field stations and provides students and faculty with access to over 25,000 acres of College-owned forest properties to support its instruction, research, and public service programs. These special properties make ESF one of the largest college campuses in the world.

Costs

Estimated costs for the 2017–18 academic year included resident tuition and fees of $8,604 and out-of-state tuition and fees of $18,254. Room and board expenses were $15,800. Books, personal expenses, and travel are estimated at $2,450.

Financial Aid

A wide variety of financial aid is available for ESF students, and more than 85 percent of the students receive some type of support. The forms of financial aid include merit- and need-based scholarships, grants, low-interest student loans, and student employment programs. All students are encouraged to apply for financial aid by completing the Free Application for Federal Student Aid (FAFSA).

Faculty

Faculty members at ESF are highly trained and dedicated to the College's teaching, research, and public-service missions. There are close to 140 full-time and 46 adjunct faculty members. Many are nationally and internationally recognized for their expertise in specialized fields. Nearly all regular faculty members hold twelve-month appointments. Just over 80 percent are tenured, and more than half are full professors, of whom 93 percent have earned doctorates. There is no distinction between the undergraduate and graduate faculty. Faculty members teach at both levels, and no courses are taught by teaching assistants. Faculty members serve as advisors to students and student groups and encourage excellence in scholarship and research. The student-faculty ratio is about 12:1.

Student Government

The College has a representative Undergraduate Student Association, and student representatives also participate in a counterpart association at Syracuse University. The ESF student government organizes and presents social activities, and its representatives attend College administrative meetings, communicate students' concerns and ideas to the administration, and serve as a conduit of information back to the student body. ESF students are obligated to abide by Syracuse University's rules and regulations when accessing classes or student services there.

Admission Requirements

Students who are interested in ESF have four enrollment options: early decision, regular freshman admission, guaranteed transfer admission, and regular transfer admission.

Outstanding high school seniors who have selected SUNY-ESF as their top choice may apply for early decision, a binding, first-choice application/early notification program for fall-entry freshmen. Students considering early decision admission must file an application and provide all supporting credentials to SUNY-ESF by the December 1 deadline. Students applying for early decision are notified by January 15.

Regular freshman admission is a second option for applicants who want to enroll immediately following high school. These candidates should demonstrate strong academic performance in a college-preparatory program, with emphasis on mathematics and science preparation. Students applying for regular freshmen entry are notified by March 1. All freshman candidates apply for admission to their intended programs of study.

Guaranteed transfer admission (GTA) candidates apply to ESF as high school seniors but are offered admission for either their sophomore or junior year. Students who plan to attend another college prior to transferring to ESF select this option to ensure a place at ESF for their chosen entry date. This option may also be offered to students who do not meet the freshman admission criteria. Those who are accepted for guaranteed transfer admission receive a letter of acceptance, contingent upon the successful completion of all the prerequisite courses required for the curriculum they have selected. The prerequisite courses are outlined and described in an enclosure with the student's acceptance letter and can also be found on the College's website at http://www.esf.edu.

Students are considered for admission to ESF on the basis of their previous college course work, overall academic aptitude, and interest in the College's programs. Consideration is given to both the quality and the appropriateness of each student's prior academic experience. The College has developed cooperative transfer programs with two-year colleges in New York, Connecticut, Massachusetts, New Jersey, and Pennsylvania.

Application and Information

Students may apply for fall or spring admission. Admission decisions are made on a rolling basis until the class is filled. ESF accepts either the State University of New York Application form or the Common Application. Links to both applications can be found online at http://www.esf.edu/admissions/freshman/apply.htm. Requests for more information should be directed to:

Office of Undergraduate Admissions
SUNY College of Environmental Science and Forestry
1 Forestry Drive
Syracuse, New York 13210-2779
Phone: 315-470-6600
Fax: 315-470-6933
E-mail: esfinfo@esf.edu
Website: http://www.esf.edu
http://www.facebook.com/sunyesf
http://twitter.com/sunyesf/
http://www.youtube.com/user/SUNYESFVIDEO

STERLING COLLEGE
CRAFTSBURY COMMON, VERMONT

Sterling College
Working Hands. Working Minds.

The College

"We have lived our lives by the assumption that what was good for us would be good for the world. We have been wrong. We must change our lives so that it will be possible to live by the contrary assumption, that what is good for the world will be good for us. And that requires that we make the effort to know the world and learn what is good for it."—Wendell Berry

Sterling College is *the* leading voice in environmental stewardship education. Environmental stewardship means loving the place where you live; taking care to know the landscape and the community; and making sustainable choices that protect the climate, water, soil, and wilderness while ensuring that the world's food system is healthful and just. Sterling College removes the barriers between living one's life and learning. It is for the student who wants to become an environmental steward and who looks forward to the rigor and challenge of working with both hands and mind.

Sterling students, faculty, and partners in the community co-create an innovative education that inspires, challenges, and pushes students to discover their own environmental stewardship vision, whether that entails conducting research in the Arctic, growing foods, drafting clean water legislation, or leading a youth group on a wilderness canoe trip. Students need to be ready to get their hands dirty, both literally and figuratively, when they arrive to the campus on Craftsbury Common in Vermont's Northeast Kingdom.

"At Sterling, there's a real history of being able to see where you've been, where you are now, and where you're going. Sterling is a really experiential place. Here, you can get a feel for the kind of world you want to live in, and what kind of world we can create." —Brighde Moffat '15

Academics: Sterling students are invested in solving the biggest issues of the 21st century: focusing on protecting and preserving soil, food, water, air, and climate. Working with faculty and staff, students are tackling how to rethink humanity's relationship with the natural world in place-based, hands-on classes where theory meets practice. Students spend about 40–50 percent of their class time outside the traditional classroom setting.

Sterling College offers Bachelor of Arts degrees in Ecology, Environmental Humanities, Outdoor Education, Sustainable Agriculture, and Sustainable Food Systems. Students can also choose to design their own majors—some examples include Agroecology, Environmental Justice, Human Geography of Seeds, Conservation Education, and International Agriculture. Curriculum at Sterling is strongly interdisciplinary and grounded in the liberal arts, with interrelated coursework drawn from all five majors. Core requirements include Ecology, A Sense of Place, Tools and their Applications, and a series of experiences focused on wilderness survival and group dynamics. All new students, accompanied by faculty members, take part in Winter Expedition, a four-day trek along the ridge of the nearby Lowell Mountain Range. Winter Expedition has been a tradition at Sterling College for over 50 years.

Classes at Sterling are small and foster experiential learning and deep inquiry through close relationships between faculty and students. The typical class size at Sterling is 10, and the student-to-faculty ratio is 7:1. Sterling's faculty is composed of 17 full-time members and approximately 17 adjuncts, and 85 percent of the faculty have advanced degrees. Sterling is also a destination for speakers, activists, and professionals who come to campus to share knowledge about sustainable systems and environmental stewardship.

Authentic Sustainability: Sterling believes that the well-being of humanity depends on small, interconnected communities committed to conscientious practices in agriculture and energy use, and in stewardship of the air, soil, and water. Sterling was among the very first colleges in the United States to link the liberal arts to ecology, outdoor education, environmental humanities, and sustainable agriculture.

In 2013, Sterling College became the first college in Vermont and the third in the nation to divest its endowment from fossil fuels. For three consecutive years, the Real Food Challenge has ranked Sterling as the top college in the United States serving food on campus that is local, sustainable, organic, humane, and fair trade, with the Sterling Farm producing 35 percent of the College's food. In 2016, Sterling was in the top 25 of *Sierra* magazine's Greenest Schools in America, with a rank of #23 overall. Sterling was also ranked #1 for sustainable food and dining, #3 for academics, and #6 for investments by *Sierra*. In 2017, Sterling received an updated STARS Gold rating from the Association for the Advancement of Sustainability in Higher Education, ranking first in sustainability performance in Vermont and third in all of North America.

Work: Sterling College is one of only nine colleges recognized by the federal government as a Work College and the only Work College in the Northeast. It doesn't matter what a student's financial aid award is—every student enrolls in the Work Program and works to keep the campus thriving. The Work Program equips students with real-world experiences and skills, and helps build a strong resume over the course of their time on campus. At Sterling, the community depends on the work of students, and the campus is a laboratory for gaining insight into the role of the individual in the health and welfare of the community.

Students are paid for their work and earn a minimum of $1,600 per semester toward their tuition with the possibility of higher earnings as students take on more significant leadership positions.

"I was drawn to Sterling because of the Work Program. I know that at the end of four years I will walk away from Sterling with a resume full of work and life experiences that any employer would find of interest. Returning to a sense of place, community, and local resilience is the next step in the environmental movement. Sterling is at the forefront of this movement; a college education here trains you to be a leader through engaged practice in community living." —Allyson Makuch '15

Community: At Sterling, students, faculty members, and staff members work to create community together. Sterling College strives to be an educational community in which people of all backgrounds and experiences feel at home, where differences are embraced, and where individuals take responsibility for furthering the dignity of all.

Sterling is small and will remain so by design. It is the only college in the nation where the entire community of students and faculty members sit together each week for Community Meeting. Everyone is on a first-name basis, including the President, Deans, and faculty members.

Sterling College currently has three athletic teams on campus: Nordic skiing, and the nation's first collegiate mountain and trail running team, the Skyrunners.

Community life is informal. Sterling students are likely to enjoy a long weekend of hiking, a lively evening of contra dancing, caring for beehives with friends, Nordic skiing at the Craftsbury Outdoor Center, or sitting by a bonfire at the College's woodland lean-tos above the Black River.

Location

Sterling's rural location is one of the College's most prized characteristics. The College stewards 430 acres which includes 300 acres of pristine boreal research forest.

The Northeast Kingdom of Vermont is a working landscape dotted with dairy farms, market gardens, and homesteads, and is an international destination for outdoor sports and adventure. There are four ski areas within 45 minutes of the College. When city life beckons, however, Burlington is about an hour or so away, and Montreal is only 2 hours from campus.

Majors and Degrees

Sterling College offers Bachelor of Arts degrees in Ecology, Environmental Humanities, Outdoor Education, Sustainable Agriculture, and Sustainable Food Systems. Students can also choose to design their own major.

Off-Campus Programs

Faculty-led, immersive, and environmentally focused, the Sterling College Global Field Studies and Wilderness Field Semester programs offers students the chance to discover the diversity of the planet's landscapes and explore the complex, ever-changing co-evolutionary relationships between people and place. Students take the field research methodologies they have practiced on campus and apply these methods to new places. Global Field Studies are included as part of a student's fees at Sterling and there is no additional cost to participate. Recent Global Field Studies classes have been held in Belize, the Bahamas, Arctic Canada, Great Britain, the Hudson River watershed, Mexico, Scandinavia, and the Sierra Nevada.

The Integrated Farming Practicum is a summer program for students majoring in Sustainable Agriculture or Sustainable Food Systems that provides intensive, hands-on training on the Sterling Farm. With visiting faculty, workshops, and electives that span value-added food production, grazing, animal husbandry and more, this program is ideal for students seeking to build their own agricultural skills.

In fall of 2019, Sterling is slated to launch the Wendell Berry Farming Program in New Castle, Kentucky in collaboration with The Berry Center. This program will provide 300–400 level curriculum for students interested in farming and community-building.

Academic Facilities

The campus has 18 residential, administrative, and classroom buildings. Facilities include a woodshop, computer labs, a draft animal barn, a blacksmithing and farrier shop, two greenhouses, a teaching kitchen, and the Brown Library.

Outdoor teaching facilities include a challenge course with a climbing wall, a managed woodlot and sugarbush, recreation and nature trails, large organic gardens, a sugarhouse, and the diversified Sterling Farm, powered by both tractor and animal power.

Costs

Tuition for the 2017–18 academic year was $33,570, room and board was $9,846, and fees were $4,468.

Financial Aid

Choosing to go to college is one of the most important events in a student's life. Sterling College is committed to make this transformative education accessible and does everything it can to work with students and their families to plan an affordable path to graduation.

Every year, Sterling commits more than $2 million to support student financial aid. From small semester grants to full scholarships, Sterling College works diligently to create an affordable academic experience.

The average Sterling grant for 2015–16 was $20,229. The average student loan debt for a graduate of Sterling College is $28,662. Ninety-eight percent of Sterling students receive some form of financial aid.

"I know that financial aid is crucial to the strength of Sterling. Over my years here, I have seen that sound financial aid allows us to enroll the right students in the College—students who care about the environment and community and who want to make a difference in the world we live in."—Ned Houston, Distinguished Professor and former Director of Financial Aid

Admission Requirements

Admission to Sterling College opens the door to a transformative and affordable education, valuable work experience, and an eclectic, diverse, and socially conscious community. Sterling College offers admission to both first-time college applicants and transfer applicants. There is also a significant population of student veterans and adult learners. The admission process at Sterling is highly individualized, characterized by significant one-on-one support from the College's admission counselors and financial aid team.

Sterling practices test-blind admission which means that standardized test scores are not considered during application review. An applicant's academic record is given equal weight with their work ethic, character, and passion for environmental stewardship.

Sterling requires an online application, a personal essay, two letters of recommendation, and a high school transcript or the equivalent. No student is granted admission to Sterling College until they have completed an interview—be it in person, over the phone, or via Skype.

Application and Information

High school seniors who wish to receive an early response to their application may apply for Early Decision or Early Action. For Early Decision, a completed application must be on file by November 15 to be notified of a decision on or before December 1. For Early Action I, a completed application must be on file on or before December 15 to be notified of a decision on or before January 1. For Early Action II, a completed application must be on file by January 15 for notification on or before February 1. All other applicants are encouraged to submit applications for Regular Decision by April 1 for notification by April 15. All deposits for Early Action I, Early Action II, and Regular Decision are due by May 1 for fall enrollment. Students may choose to defer for up to two semesters upon depositing.

Students should contact:

Tim Patterson, Director of Admission
Sterling College
P.O. Box 72
Craftsbury Common, Vermont 05827
United States
Phone: 802-586-7711
　　　　800-648-3591 (toll-free)
Fax: 802-586-2596
E-mail: admission@sterlingcollege.edu
Website: http://www.sterlingcollege.edu
　　　　www.facebook.com/SterlingCollegeVT
　　　　www.twitter.com/SterlingCollegeVT
　　　　www.instagram.com/sterlingcollegevt
　　　　www.instagram.com/thesterlingkitchen
　　　　www.instagram.com/thesterlingcollegefarm

Sterling College is the leading voice in higher education for environmental stewardship. It was among the first colleges to focus on sustainability. Sterling College students are invested in solving the biggest issues of the 21st century: food, water, air, soil, energy, and climate, as well as reshaping humanity's relationship with the natural world.

STOCKTON UNIVERSITY
GALLOWAY, NEW JERSEY

 To read more about this school, visit http://petersons.to/stocktonuniversity

The University

Thinking translates into doing at Stockton. Students gain hands-on experience in nursing, exercise science, occupational therapy, or physical therapy at the two hospitals on campus; use cutting-edge technology to preserve historic underwater wreck sites or analyze the seafloor's ecosystems at Stockton's Marine Science & Environmental Field Station; study artistic techniques firsthand through a partnership with the Noyes Museum of Art or at the Philadelphia Museum of Art; or bask in the beautiful, 2,000-acre campus in the Pinelands National Reserve just minutes from the ocean, a perfect setting for Stockton's nationally renowned environmental and marine science programs.

Stockton students engage with Fulbright Scholars, Guggenheim Fellows, and Pulitzer-awarded authors. Small classes are guided by professors who care as much about teaching as research, allowing for discussion, debate, and discovery in the classroom and beyond.

Rooted in a deep social and environmental consciousness, Stockton offers extensive service learning opportunities and has become an international leader in alternative energy research and conservation efforts.

Founded in 1969, The Richard Stockton College of New Jersey was named for one of the signers of the Declaration of Independence. In 2015, Stockton celebrated a new designation and name change to Stockton University. The University offers bachelor's, master's, and doctoral degree programs designed to challenge the brightest students, providing many of the academic, technological, and cultural advantages of a large university, but with the communal spirit typical of smaller colleges.

Stockton enrolls over 9,200 students from New Jersey, the Mid-Atlantic states, and foreign countries, providing unique educational programs with a curriculum focused on developing the students' analytic and creative capabilities through the encouragement of individually planned courses of study.

The Stockton experience is enhanced by more than 130 clubs and organizations, an active Greek life, honor societies, and athletics. In addition to extensive intramural and club sports, NCAA Division III sports teams offered include men's baseball, basketball, lacrosse, and soccer, women's basketball, crew, field hockey, golf, lacrosse, soccer, softball, tennis, and volleyball, and men's and women's cross-country and track and field. Students who participate in co-curricular activities have their experiences documented through the ULTRA (Undergraduate Learning, Training, and Awareness) program, culminating in a co-curricular transcript.

Stockton provides on-campus housing for more than 4,000 students in traditional residence halls, apartments, campus-owned facilities, and at the new residence hall on the Atlantic City boardwalk. All complexes are furnished and air conditioned, with cable TV and Internet. Others choose to live off campus in nearby apartment complexes or winter rentals in one of the local shore towns.

Beyond its undergraduate programs, Stockton offers the following graduate degrees: Doctor of Nursing Practice, Doctor of Physical Therapy, and Doctor of Education in organizational leadership; Master of Arts in American studies, criminal justice, Holocaust and genocide studies, education, educational leadership, and instructional technology; Master of Business Administration; Master of Science in communication disorders, computational science, data science and strategic analytics, nursing, and occupational therapy; Master of Social Work; and a Professional Science Master's in environmental science. Certificate and endorsement programs are offered in bilingual/bicultural education, ESL (English as a second language), family nurse practitioner, forensic psychology, health professions prep, homeland security, learning disabilities teacher consultant, middle school endorsement, New Jersey standard supervisor endorsement, preschool–grade 3 endorsement, reading specialist, special education, and student assistance coordinator.

Stockton University is accredited by the Commission on Higher Education of the Middle States Association of Colleges and Schools. In addition, the social work program is accredited by the Council on Social Work Education; teacher education is approved by the New Jersey Department of Education, the National Association of State Directors of Teacher Education and Certification, and the Teacher Education Accreditation Council; nursing is accredited by the New Jersey Board of Nursing and the Commission on Collegiate Nursing Education; chemistry is accredited by the American Chemical Society; physical therapy is accredited by the Commission on Accreditation in Physical Therapy Education of the American Physical Therapy Association; environmental health is accredited by the National Environmental Health Sciences and Protection Accreditation Council; health administration is accredited by the Association of University Programs in Health Administration; occupational therapy is accredited by the Accreditation Council for Occupational Therapy Education of the American Occupational Therapy Association; communication disorders is accredited by the American Speech-Language-Hearing Association and Council on Academic Accreditation in Audiology and Speech-Language Pathology; criminal justice is accredited by the Academy of Criminal Justice Sciences; and business is accredited by the Association to Advance Collegiate Schools of Business.

Location

Stockton's campus is located in Galloway, New Jersey, nestled in the environmentally protected Pinelands National Reserve, just minutes west of Atlantic City, an hour from Philadelphia, and 2 hours from New York City. Courses are also offered online and at the Atlantic City, Hammonton, Manahawkin, and Woodbine Instructional Sites. Collaboration with the Sam Azeez Museum of Woodbine Heritage and the Noyes Museum of Art provides enriching exhibitions and educational programs. The new Atlantic City Gateway campus, which includes an academic building, parking garage, and residential facility overlooking the Boardwalk, will allow Stockton to grow and support its surrounding communities as well as expand the hospitality and tourism management, business, social work, organizational/community leadership, and civic engagement programs.

Majors and Degrees

The Bachelor of Arts, Bachelor of Fine Arts, and Bachelor of Science degrees are offered in studies in the arts (visual and performing), biochemistry/molecular biology, biology, business (accounting, finance, financial planning, management, marketing), chemistry, communications, computer science, computing information systems, criminal justice (forensic psychology/investigation, homeland security), economics, education, environmental science, exercise science, geology, health sciences, historical studies, hospitality and tourism management, languages and culture studies, liberal studies, literature, marine science, mathematics, nursing, philosophy and religion, physics, political science, psychology, sociology and anthropology, social work, and sustainability.

Stockton also offers pre-professional preparation in dentistry, law, medicine, pharmacy, veterinary medicine, communication disorders (speech therapy), occupational therapy, physical therapy, and physician assistant studies, with the master's in occupational therapy, communication disorders, and doctorate in physical therapy completed at Stockton. The University also has an accelerated seven-year dual-degree articulation agreements with Rowan School of Osteopathic Medicine; an accelerated dual-degree program in pharmaceutical engineering with New Jersey Institute of Technology; and five-year, dual-degree programs with New Jersey Institute of Technology, Rowan University, and Rutgers University for engineering. In addition, students can graduate from Stockton with a Bachelor of Science degree in biochemistry/molecular biology or biology and finish their Doctor of Pharmacy degree through the Ernest Mario School of Pharmacy at Rutgers University.

Academic Programs

To earn a baccalaureate degree from Stockton, a student must satisfactorily complete a minimum of 128 semester credits. Degree programs include a combination of general studies and major studies. Bachelor of Arts students must earn 64 credits in general studies; Bachelor of Science students must earn 48. General studies courses are cross-disciplinary courses designed to introduce students to all major areas of the curriculum and to the intellectual skills necessary for success in college. Students must select courses from each major curricular area. The only required courses within general studies are basic studies (up to three); students may be exempt from these courses based on testing. Bachelor of Arts students must earn 64 credits in major studies; Bachelor of Science students must earn 80. Requirements are carefully structured and emphasize sequences of specific courses.

Stockton students have the opportunity to influence what and how they learn. The preceptorial system enables students to work closely with a faculty-staff preceptor in planning and evaluating courses and in exploring career paths.

Off-Campus Programs

Off-campus experiences for credit are a requirement for most programs, namely in the form of internships, research projects, and field studies. Stockton sends more students to the Washington Internship Program than any other college or university outside the Washington, D.C., area.

Study abroad, Semester at Sea, and an honors program provide additional opportunities.

The Career Center as well as academic offices coordinate off-campus internships; foreign study is coordinated by the Office of Global Engagement..

Academic Facilities

Stockton's campus serves as a living-learning center, with academic, recreational, and living spaces mixed to promote interaction among students, faculty, and staff. Facilities include interactive and electronic classrooms, an extensive library containing the Sara and Sam Schoffer Holocaust Resource Center, an art gallery, and performing arts center. New academic facilities for 2018 include a 58,000 square-foot addition to the current Unified Science Center as well as a new 38,000 square-foot structure for classroom and office space.

Costs

Costs for the 2017–18 academic year were $13,403 for in-state students and $20,357 for out-of-state students (flat-rate tuition up to 40 credits per year, fees); on-campus housing and board were $12,162 (double-occupancy residence room, Ultimate meal plan). Books, supplies, transportation, and personal items are extra. Costs are subject to change.

Financial Aid

Financial aid is available as scholarships, grants, loans, and work-study. Need-based financial aid is awarded according to student and family need. Students seeking financial aid should file the Free Application for Federal Student Aid (FAFSA) as soon as possible after October 1. Stockton offers aggressive and generous merit-based aid awards to academically talented freshman and transfer students based on standardized test scores, grade point average, high school class rank, and college-level performance.

Faculty

Stockton's faculty represent highly diverse academic, training, and social backgrounds, with 95 percent holding terminal degrees in their field. Faculty members work closely with students through individualized research opportunities, and share social, recreational, and cultural programs with students and staff. This arrangement supports the exceptional rapport and learning relationships among students and faculty members.

Student Government

The Stockton University Student Senate consists of 25 student members. The advisory council is made up of 1 faculty member and 2 staff members. Student senators hold office for one year. The Student Senate reviews and makes recommendations on budgets of funded student organizations and acts as the official representative of the student body.

Admission Requirements

Stockton operates on rolling admission. Fall admission deadline is May 1 for most freshmen, with special program deadlines posted on the university's website. Transfer deadline for fall admission is July 1. Spring (January) admission deadline for all students is December 1. Students may apply for admission to the fall or spring term and are notified of the decision as soon as their application file is completed and has been reviewed. Freshman applicants must submit ACT and/or SAT scores. All students must submit official transcripts from all educational institutions attended. Admission is selective.

Armed Services veterans and those who have been away from formal education for some time are encouraged to apply. Stockton makes no distinction between part- and full-time students in offering admission.

Stockton offers special admission to a limited number of New Jersey students from educationally and financially disadvantaged backgrounds. Students wishing to explore this opportunity should contact the Admissions Office.

Application and Information

For more information, contact:
Dean of Enrollment Management
Stockton University
101 Vera King Farris Drive
Galloway, New Jersey 08205-9441
Phone: 609-652-4261
      866-772-2885 (toll-free)
Fax: 609-626-5541
E-mail: admissions@stockton.edu
Website: Stockton.edu
      Facebook.com/StocktonUniversity
      Twitter.com/@Stockton_edu
      Instagram.com/stocktonuniversity

Stockton University offers quality, value, distinction, and location. The personal attention of a private, liberal arts institution and the value of a public education are combined at Stockton, New Jersey's distinctive public university.

TEMPLE UNIVERSITY
PHILADELPHIA, PENNSYLVANIA

★ To read more about this school, visit http://petersons.to/templeuniversity

The University

With a reputation for providing an affordable, high-quality education, Temple University prepares students to be successful in everything that they do. At this vibrant, urban, public research university, passionate students turn opportunities into accomplishments: World-class labs are the proving grounds for innovative ideas. A classroom doubles as the boardroom of a tech startup. Professors do more than teach, they become longtime mentors. Temple students are driven to take action, and at Temple they have everything they need to achieve their goals.

Cutting-edge facilities—including a 247,000-square-foot Science Education and Research Center, more than 3,800 engaged faculty members, and top-ranked programs combine to create a dynamic academic environment that attracts students from across the country and around the world. With 17 schools and colleges, eight campuses, and more than 40,000 students, Temple is the thirty-first largest university in the United States.

Living on campus puts students in the heart of the action. Nearly 80 percent of freshmen live on campus, where they are a short walk from class, fitness facilities, Temple's hallmark food trucks, and the many events that take place every day at Temple. The University boasts a 10,200-seat entertainment complex that hosts NCAA Division I basketball games as well as concerts—Fetty Wap, Sam Smith, and Bob Dylan have all performed there. With more than 300 student organizations and clubs to choose from, Temple students are never bored. From activism to student-powered media to yoga, campus life is always exciting.

But a Temple education goes far beyond campus. The city is an extension of the classroom, and opportunities for hands-on learning are everywhere, from museums and technology meet-ups to internships in business, healthcare, media and the arts. Learning from experts first-hand means students are ready for anything when they graduate, and the University's more than 320,000 alumni form a powerful support network.

Location

Each of Temple's distinct campuses has its own personality and environment, from urban to suburban to international. Temple's Main Campus is located just 1.5 miles from the center of Philadelphia, one of the largest cities on the East Coast. Philadelphia is among the most walkable cities in the U.S.—meaning students can easily access all the city has to offer, including more than 100 museums, a thriving restaurant scene, numerous sports teams, and the largest urban landscaped park in the country. The professional world is also right outside Temple's door: There are thousands of opportunities for hands-on learning and internships in the Philadelphia area, and the University's more than 100,000 alumni in the region love to hire Temple students.

Temple's other seven campuses include a location in Tokyo—the largest and oldest American university in Japan—and another in Rome, Italy. Temple University Harrisburg is located in the heart of Pennsylvania's capital city. The University's campus in Ambler, Pennsylvania, is the hub of the University's environmental programs and home to a 187-acre arboretum that serves as a living laboratory. In addition to Main Campus, Temple's Philadelphia campuses are the Health Sciences Center just north of Main Campus, and the Center City and Podiatric Medicine campuses, both a short subway ride away in downtown Philadelphia.

Majors and Degrees

Temple offers more than 140 undergraduate degree programs, making it easy for students to follow, or discover, their passion. Students who need time to decide on a major can explore their interests through the University Studies program. Those who would like to accelerate their education can apply to one of Temple's many dual-degree programs.

The **Tyler School of Art** offers a B.F.A. with concentrations in ceramics, glass, fibers and materials studies, graphic and interactive design, metals/jewelry/CAD-CAM, painting and drawing, photography, printmaking, and sculpture; a B.A. in art history, art therapy, and visual studies; and a B.S. in art education. Tyler's architecture program confers a B.S. in historic preservation, architecture (pre-professional), and facilities management. B.S. programs are offered in community development and in horticulture and landscape architecture. B.S. programs are offered in community and regional planning and in horticulture and landscape architecture.

The **Fox School of Business** offers a B.B.A. in accounting, actuarial science, business management, economics, entrepreneurship and innovation management, finance, financial planning, human resource management, international business, legal studies, management information systems, marketing, real estate, risk management and insurance, statistical science and data analytics, and supply chain management.

The **College of Education** offers a B.A. in adult and organizational development and a B.S. in career and technical education, early childhood–elementary education, human development and community engagement, middle-grades education (4–8), and secondary education.

The **College of Engineering** offers a B.S. in civil engineering, electrical engineering (computer), engineering (general program), environmental engineering, and mechanical engineering. A B.S. is also offered in bioengineering, construction management technology, and engineering technology.

The **College of Liberal Arts** offers a B.A. in Africology and African American studies; American studies; anthropology; Asian studies; Chinese; classics; criminal justice; economics; English; environmental studies; French; gender, sexuality, and women's studies; geography and urban studies; German; global studies; history; Italian; Jewish studies; Latin American studies; liberal studies; mathematical economics; neuroscience: systems, behaviors, and plasticity; philosophy; political science; psychology; religion; sociology; and Spanish.

The **Klein College of Media and Communication** offers a B.A. in advertising, communication and social influence, communication studies, journalism, media studies and production, and public relations.

The **Boyer College of Music and Dance** offers a B.S. in music and a B.M. in jazz studies/composition, jazz studies/performance (instrumental, keyboard, or vocal), music composition, music education, music education with jazz studies component, music history, music technology, music theory, music therapy, music therapy with jazz studies component, and performance (instrumental, keyboard, or vocal). A B.F.A. is offered in dance.

The **College of Public Health** offers a B.S. in exercise and sport science; health information management; health professions; kinesiology; nursing; public health; pre-health information management; public health; speech, language, and hearing science; and therapeutic recreation.

The **College of Science and Technology** offers a B.S. in applied mathematics; biochemistry; biology; biology with teaching; biophysics; chemistry; chemistry with teaching; computer science; computer science and physics; data science; earth and space science with teaching; environmental science; general science with teaching; geology; information science and technology; mathematical economics; mathematics; mathematics and computer science; mathematics and computer science with teaching; mathematics and physics; mathematics and technology with teaching; natural sciences; neuroscience (cell and molecular); physics; physics with teaching; and pre-pharmacy.

The **School of Social Work** offers the B.S.W. degree.

The **School of Theater, Film, and Media Arts** offers a B.A. and a B.F.A. in theater and in film and media arts, as well as a B.F.A. in musical theater.

The **School of Tourism and Hospitality Management** offers a B.S. in sport and recreation management and in tourism and hospitality management.

Academic Programs

Students passionate about learning are attracted to Temple because of its variety of academic programs: More than 570 are offered, including more than 140 bachelor's degree programs. The University provides all of the resources and opportunities of a large, world-class research institution and the individual attention of a small college—with a 15:1 student-to-faculty ratio.

All students complete the General Education curriculum, a cross-section of courses that forms the intellectual foundation of a Temple education. But every student's experience at Temple is unique and transformative.

Some students pursue common interests in Living and Learning Communities. Academically qualified students take on extra intellectual challenges through the Honors Program. Temple's study-abroad programs offer opportunities to take learning around the world. Students might find their niche earning course credit while running Temple's cooperative, locavore café. The Hatchery is the Tyler School of Art's design incubator, where entrepreneurial students transform projects into real products.

Students have opportunities to work directly with renowned faculty on research and creative projects and present at professional conferences, publish in peer-reviewed journals, and premiere music and dance at venues around the globe.

A degree from Temple doesn't simply fill a transcript or create lines on a résumé. Temple empowers students to spark change in themselves and prepares them to charge forward into the world.

Academic Facilities

Whether in a high-tech classroom or the University's Science Education and Research Center (SERC), Temple students learn in world-class facilities. At SERC, which is home to 68 research and teaching labs and leading-edge technologies, students work with faculty on real-world projects, making the connection between understanding science and putting advanced research techniques into practice.

At the TECH Center—among the largest student computer labs in the country—students can collaborate in breakout rooms, edit video in a specialized lab, get assistance from the 24-hour help desk, or work on one of 700 computers. There are more than 100 other computer labs on campus, 3,600 student workstations, and 450 technology-enabled classrooms.

With more than four million titles and an extensive special collection of rare books and archives, Temple's libraries rank among the top research libraries in North America. In spring 2016, the University broke ground on a new, state-of-the-art library that will feature a robotic book retrieval system and spaces devoted to traditional library activities, such as study and reading, as well as to technology-mediated activities, including data visualization and 3-D printing.

Costs

Tuition and fees for the 2017–18 academic year were $16,658 for Pennsylvania residents and $28,418 for out-of-state residents (tuition rates vary by major). Room and board for the academic year were about $10,810.

Financial Aid

Temple offers a multitude of options to help make college more affordable. A variety of scholarships, grants, loans, and work-study programs are available: 71 percent of first-year students receive need-based financial aid, and 44 percent receive academic scholarships. Four-year academic merit scholarships for talented freshmen range from $2,000 to full tuition, and several include summer stipends for research, internships, and study abroad.

Most incoming freshmen—93 percent—commit to Temple's Fly in 4 program, an innovative plan which helps students limit their debt and enter the workforce sooner by graduating in four years.

Faculty

Starting in their first semester, students at Temple have contact with faculty at the forefront of their fields—winners of prestigious teaching and research awards, scientists doing groundbreaking research, and working artists who exhibit all over the world.

Temple faculty members are also known for their practical experience—a marketing class may be led by a successful entrepreneur; music lessons by a member of the Philadelphia Orchestra. Marine biologists, newspaper editors, published authors, practicing architects, and healthcare professionals all bring their expertise to the classroom.

And the roster of outstanding faculty members is growing. On average, Temple has hired 57 new faculty members per year for the past decade, from leading universities and research centers including Princeton University, MIT, and the Cleveland Clinic.

Admission Requirements

The Temple Option is an admissions path for determined and tenacious students who have the ability to succeed in college but may not perform well on standardized tests. Students can opt to submit SAT or ACT scores, or they can choose the Temple Option and respond to short-answer questions.

For freshman admissions, high-school grades (quality of courses and grade trends), standardized test scores or the Temple Option responses, and other factors are considered. Temple uses a sliding scale rather than absolute cutoffs. SAT subject tests and personal interviews are not required. Official copies of high-school transcripts and standardized test scores must be sent directly to the admissions office.

The deadline for spring admission is November 1. Temple offers rolling admissions and early action decision plans for the fall semester. Those interested in early action must submit a completed application by November 1 and will receive notification by mid-January. The rolling admissions deadline is February 1; freshman decisions begin in early fall. Temple's admissions process is holistic; every aspect of the student's academic history is considered. Typically, students with a B+ average or better in a strong college-prep curriculum in grades 9–12 and in the top 30 percent of their graduating classes are accepted. For students submitting test scores, the average SAT score in 2017 was 1220, and the average ACT composite was 27.

The application fee is $55; most students apply online through Temple or the Common Application.

Applicants are considered transfer students if they have attempted 15 or more college-level credits after high school. If this is not the case, they should apply as freshman students. In admissions decisions, careful consideration is given to the quality of a student's program, number of credits earned, and GPA. The average GPA for new transfer students is 3.16 (on a 4.0 scale). The architecture, nursing, and pharmacy programs have higher minimum GPA requirements. For most programs, transfer students must complete the application process by June 1 for the fall semester or by November 1 for the spring semester. The fall priority deadline for the health information management and nursing programs is February 1. SAT or ACT scores are not required if an applicant has earned at least 15 college-level credits.

Application and Information

A completed file contains an application form accompanied by a nonrefundable application fee, a secondary-school transcript (sent by the student's school), and SAT or ACT scores (sent directly by the testing agencies) or responses to the Temple Option questions.

For additional information, students may contact:
Office of Undergraduate Admissions
Temple University
Philadelphia, Pennsylvania 19122-6096
United States
Phone: 215-204-7200
      888-340-2222 (toll-free)
E-mail: askanowl@temple.edu
Website: nextstop.temple.edu
Facebook: facebook.com/TempleU
Twitter: @admissionsTU
Instagram: @admissionsTU
Snapchat: @admissionsTU

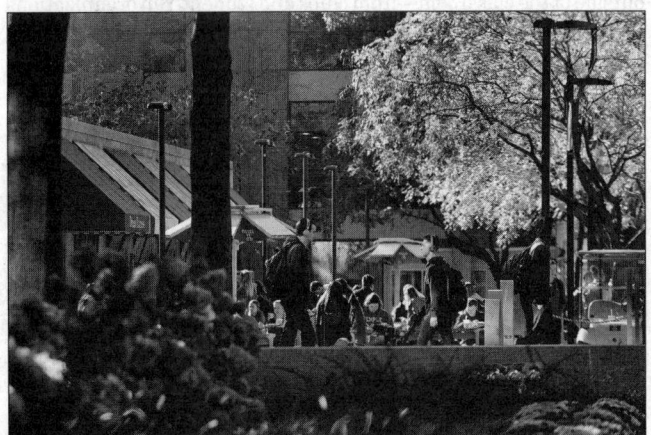

At Temple University, students get a full campus experience—complete with state-of-the-art facilities and labs, and bountiful, green social spaces—while being in the heart of a destination city.

THOMAS JEFFERSON UNIVERSITY
(Philadelphia University + Thomas Jefferson University)
PHILADELPHIA, PENNSYLVANIA

 To read more about this school, visit http://petersons.to/jefferson

The University

With the union of Philadelphia University and Thomas Jefferson University, Jefferson is a comprehensive national university with nine colleges and three schools, offering bachelor's, master's and doctoral degrees, and a history of prominence dating back to 1824. Yet Jefferson maintains an intimate campus community with 2,800 undergraduates on its East Falls Campus.

At Jefferson, personal attention and ongoing advisement are cornerstones. From the moment students enroll, they have a network of resources to help them transition to a university environment, find academic support, and facilitate their personal and professional development. These benefits, together with an emphasis on quality education, are the reasons why the school brings out the best in every student.

The Jefferson, East Falls Campus student body is academically, geographically, culturally, and economically diverse. The campus has 2,800 full- and part-time students from 47 states and 34 countries. More than 90 percent of Jefferson freshmen live in one of its residence halls. Class sizes average 18 students, allowing for lively discussions and fostering relationships between and among its students and its experienced and dedicated faculty. From day one, students are treated like professionals. They work on class projects alongside students from a variety of majors outside their own, mirroring what happens in the real world. At Jefferson, it's known as Nexus Learning.

Jefferson has established a phenomenal record of career success for its graduates; its career placement rate in major-related jobs has consistently been above 90 percent, within a few months of graduation, for more than twenty years. Ninety-six percent of Jefferson's 2017 graduates are working in their disciplines or have been accepted to the graduate school of their choice.

Jefferson offers many chances for its students to get involved outside of the classroom—from clubs and student-run organizations to campus-wide community service projects, from Open Mic nights to resume writing workshops—learning is integrated in all the University does.

In addition, Jefferson is a member of the CACC conference at the NCAA Division II level for the following sports: men's baseball, basketball, cross-country/track, golf, soccer, and tennis, and women's basketball, cross-country/track, golf, lacrosse, rowing, soccer, softball, tennis, and volleyball. An extensive intramural sports program is also available to all students.

Jefferson is a private institution of higher learning, fully accredited by the Middle States Association of Colleges and Schools.

Location

Jefferson (Philadelphia University + Thomas Jefferson University) East Falls Campus is located 15 minutes northwest of Center City Philadelphia, a rich and vibrant city in Pennsylvania. The 52 buildings on the University's 100-acre campus range from historic Victorian mansions to contemporary classroom, library, and residential facilities. Jefferson offers the best of both worlds: a beautiful campus with tree-lined walkways, spacious lawns, and classical architecture, just minutes away from its extended classroom—one the nation's most exciting and lively cities, filled with entertainment, cultural events, and more than 300 years of American history.

Majors and Degrees

Jefferson, East Falls offers more than 50 undergraduate and graduate degree programs leading to the Bachelor of Science, Bachelor of Architecture, Bachelor of Science in Engineering, Bachelor of Landscape Architecture, master's degrees, and doctoral degrees.

Jefferson's most popular degrees include fashion, architecture, engineering, health sciences, landscape architecture, textiles, digital media, fashion merchandising and management, marketing, physician assistant studies, business, psychology, and biology.

Academic Programs

Through a unique blend of liberal and specialized education with an interdisciplinary focus, the University prepares students for today's complex, global workplace. The University achieves this by focusing on innovation, innovative thinking and an award-winning Nexus Learning approach—active, collaborative learning that is connected to the real world and infused with the liberal arts.

Study-abroad and internship opportunities are available for fall, spring, and summer semesters at locations all around the world. Along with an exciting and memorable experience, students may receive credit for courses and positions that apply directly to their challenging, professional-oriented curricula.

Costs

For the 2018–19 academic year, tuition totals $39,495 and the general fee is $1,006. Room rates range from $6,295 to $9,285, depending on style of accommodations; meal plans range from $2,425 to $7,170. Books and supplies are estimated at $1,000. Costs are subject to change.

Financial Aid

Jefferson is committed to making a high-quality, professional education affordable for every qualified student. If meeting educational costs is a concern, applicants are encouraged to apply for financial aid, regardless of family financial circumstances. More than 90 percent of students receive aid in the form of grants, loans, campus employment and/or scholarships. Merit, need-based, and athletic scholarships are available. More information on scholarship opportunities is available on the University's website at http://eastfalls.jefferson.edu/financialaid/undergraduate/scholarships/.

Admission Requirements

To be considered for admission to Jefferson, first-year applicants must submit:

- $40 nonrefundable application fee

- Official high school transcript(s)

- SAT and/or ACT scores. The code for the SAT is 2666 and the ACT is 3668.

- Letter of recommendation from a teacher or counselor who can speak to academic preparation and college readiness. An academic recommendation form is available to download from the University's website.

- Essay of at least 250 words.

Jefferson does not require a portfolio review for first-year applicants. If an applicant has some college-level coursework, a portfolio review may be required to assess transferable credit.

Application and Information

Jefferson has an Early Action deadline of November 1 and a Regular Decision deadline of March 1 (with the exception of a December 15 deadline for the physician assistant studies program).

The Admissions Committee begins reviewing applications for fall terms in October and for spring terms in June. The Admissions Committee will review applications for a given term until all programs are filled. Some academic programs, as well as on-campus housing, may have limited capacity and may close earlier than others. For this reason, students are encouraged to apply early in the academic year prior to their desired enrollment term. After submitting all required application materials, applicants can expect to receive their admissions decision within 4 to 6 weeks.

The Admissions Committee reviews each candidate's application by examining a variety of factors, including high school and/or college academic performance, standardized test scores (SAT and/or ACT), counselor or teacher recommendation, and application essay. Involvement in extracurricular activities, volunteer or work experience relevant to a candidate's chosen major, and the level of the candidate's academic curriculum are also considered. Jefferson has a customized admissions application and also accepts the Common Application. To apply online to Jefferson as an undergraduate student, complete the Jefferson Online Application or Common Application.

Prospective students are encouraged to visit Jefferson. There are several types of visit opportunities available.

For more information, contact:

Office of Admissions
Jefferson (Philadelphia University + Thomas Jefferson University)
4201 Henry Avenue
Philadelphia, Pennsylvania 19144
Phone: 215-951-2800
E-mail: admissions@PhilaU.edu
Website: http://eastfalls.jefferson.edu/undergrad/

TRINE UNIVERSITY
ANGOLA, INDIANA

 To read more about this school, visit http://petersons.to/trineuniversity

The University

Trine University has a reputation for producing in-demand work-ready graduates, proven by Trine's 99.2 percent job placement rate over the past four years. Career opportunities are one reason students choose Trine, along with its well-maintained campus, welcoming community, and opportunities to excel.

Students can expect a well-rounded college experience with challenging courses taught by engaged, experienced faculty members, eager to help students succeed. Small class size and a 16:1 student-to-faculty ratio foster personalized attention and optimal classroom performance.

Trine is private, independent, and coeducational, offering associate, baccalaureate, master's and doctoral degrees to students in about 35 programs, including engineering, mathematics, forensic science, pre–physical therapy, business, education, psychology, exercise science, criminal justice, and sport management.

Trine has invested more than $155 million in campus upgrades since 2000. In fall 2017, the university opened the Thunder Ice Arena, home to its new men's and women's hockey teams as well as student and community activities. The new MTI Center, including basketball courts, a six-lane bowling alley, and esports arena, began hosting athletic, student, and entertainment events in January 2018. A new residence hall slated for fall 2018 will help meet the housing needs of a growing student body.

In fall 2017, Trine set an institutional enrollment record for the fourth straight year. Trine has 5,184 students with more than 2,100 on the main campus.

The Trine student body breaks down as follows:

- Academic averages for the freshman class include a 3.53 GPA, 1130 SAT, and 25 ACT. Twenty-three percent were in the top 10 percent of their high school graduating class and 51 percent were in the top 25 percent.
- Students represent 36 states and 27 countries.
- Engineering is the most popular program with 45 percent of students enrolled.
- More than 700 students are involved in NCAA Division III athletics.

The 450-acre campus offers an inviting, safe, vibrant atmosphere that complements the seriousness and determination with which Trine students pursue academic goals. Trine has more than 60 academic, cultural, service, and Greek organizations and 23 varsity athletic teams.

Trine is a member of National Collegiate Athletic Association (NCAA) Division III and the Michigan Intercollegiate Athletic Association (MIAA), the nation's oldest athletic conference. The NCAA hockey teams are members of the Northern Collegiate Hockey Association and the ACHA Division II team competes in the Great Midwest Hockey League. Men's sports include baseball, basketball, bowling, cross-country, esports, football, golf, hockey, lacrosse, soccer, tennis, track, volleyball, and wrestling. Women's sports include basketball, bowling, cross-country, esports, golf, hockey, lacrosse, soccer, softball, tennis, track, triathlon, and volleyball. Many students also participate on intramural sports teams.

Trine students excel on the field and in and out of the classroom.

- Chemical engineering seniors have won the American Institute of Chemical Engineers national individual design competition six times and the national design safety award numerous times.
- Trine's Tau Alpha Omicron chapter of the American Criminal Justice Association annually wins regional and national awards for marksmanship, crime scene investigation, and physical agility.
- In 2017, Trine's softball team made history by earning its second trip to the NCAA Division III National Championships. The team has appeared in the NCAA postseason every year since 2008, hosting its first Super Regional championship in 2016.
- Trine's 2016–17 women's basketball team won the MIAA Conference championship and advanced to the NCAA Division III tournament. The football team earned a conference championship and NCAA tournament berth in fall 2017.

- Trine's track and field program has sent at least two participants to national championship meets since the 2013–14 season, with an All-American honoree in every indoor and outdoor season since that date.
- During 2016–17, 48 Thunder student-athletes were recognized on all-conference teams. Trine boasted 130 student-athletes on the MIAA honor roll for having above a 3.5 grade-point average and lettering in a varsity sport.

Location

Trine is in Angola, the heart of northeast Indiana's scenic lake resort region, halfway between Chicago and Cleveland. Just a 45-minute drive from Indiana's second-largest city, Fort Wayne, Trine offers the safety and ease of a small-town environment, near some of the nation's most vital cities.

Majors and Degrees

The Allen School of Engineering & Technology awards Bachelor of Science degrees in biomedical, chemical and bioprocess, civil, computer, electrical, mechanical, and software engineering and design engineering technology. Minors are offered in aeronautical, biomedical, bioprocess, energy, environmental, metallurgical, plastics, software, and structural engineering.

The Ketner School of Business awards Bachelor of Science in business administration degrees with majors in accounting, business administration, golf management, management, marketing, and sport management.

The Franks School of Education awards Bachelor of Science degrees in elementary, English, health and physical, mathematics, science, and social studies education, as well as a dual licensure program in elementary education and special education/mild intervention K–6.

The Jannen School of Arts and Sciences awards Bachelor of Arts degrees with majors in communication, English, and general studies (pre-legal and self-designated), and Bachelor of Science degrees with majors in computer information science, criminal justice, mathematics, and psychology.

The Rinker-Ross School of Health Sciences offers Bachelor of Science degrees in biochemistry, biology, chemistry, exercise science, forensic science, and sport and recreation; and pre–physician assistant, pre–physical therapy, and pre-medical professional tracks, as well as a doctoral degree in physical therapy. The school plans to offer a Master of Physician Assistant Studies program beginning in August 2018.

The College of Graduate and Professional Studies, with eight education centers in Indiana and Michigan, awards associate's, bachelor's, and master's degrees in 10 programs. Graduate programs include a Master of Business Administration and Master of Science degrees in leadership, criminal justice, engineering management, and information studies.

Academic Programs

Students learn from professionals with advanced degrees and industry expertise, and get hands-on experience in laboratories stocked with state-of-the-art equipment. About 90 percent of Trine students complete an internship, co-op, or other experiential learning.

Trine University is accredited by the Higher Learning Commission and a member of the North Central Association (www.hlcommission.org; phone: 312-263-0456). Trine's programs in chemical engineering, civil engineering, computer engineering, electrical engineering, and mechanical engineering are accredited by the Engineering Accreditation Commission of ABET (111 Market Place, Suite 1050, Baltimore, Maryland 21202-4012; phone: 410-347-7700). All teacher preparation programs are accredited by the Council for the Accreditation of Educator Preparation (www.caepnet.org) and the Indiana Department Education/Office of Educator Licensing and Development (www.doe.ingov/licensing). The Ketner School of Business, Bachelor of Science in business administration program is accredited by the Accreditation Council for Business Schools and Programs (www.acbsp.org). Associate degree programs in accounting and business administration are also accredited.

The Doctor of Physical Therapy Program at Trine University is accredited by the Commission on Accreditation in Physical Therapy Education (CAPTE), 1111 North Fairfax Street, Alexandria, Virginia, 22314; phone: 703-706-3245; e-mail: accreditation@apta.org; website: http://capteonline.org).

Trine University has applied for Accreditation–Provisional from the Accreditation Review Commission on Education for the Physician Assistant (ARC-PA). Trine University anticipates matriculating its first class in August 2018, pending achieving Accreditation–Provisional status at the March 2018 ARC-PA meeting. Accreditation–Provisional is an accreditation status granted when the plans and resource allocation, if fully implemented as planned, of a proposed program that has not yet enrolled students appear to demonstrate the program's ability to meet the ARC-PA standards or when a program holding accreditation-provisional status appears to demonstrate continued progress in complying with the standards as it prepares for the graduation of the first class (cohort) of students. In the event that provisional accreditation is not received, the graduate PA program will not commence in August 2018 and graduate PA tuition deposits will be refunded. This does not apply to Trine University's undergraduate pre–PA curriculum, which can provide a foundational education for PA programs, regardless of the Trine University graduate PA program status.

Enhanced Learning

Trine's Innovation One provides opportunities for students to work with business and industry and even manage startup companies. Innovation One, located in the Jim and Joan Bock Center for Innovation and Biomedical Engineering, is an incubator for creativity, invention, and design that enhances education through experiential learning and fosters economic development by supporting new and existing businesses.

Off-Campus Programs

Trine's Employment Resource Center works with diverse companies to provide co-op and internship opportunities. Semesters of classroom study alternate with professional work experience, which can give students a competitive edge in the job market and offset college expenses. Often, co-ops and internships launch careers as they lead to full-time employment.

Academic Facilities

The John G. Best Hall of Science, home of the Rinker-Ross School of Health Sciences, contains classrooms and science laboratories. A $6.6 million, 26,000 square-foot addition opened in January 2017, housing seven laboratories, twelve offices and group study spaces.

The Jim and Joan Bock Center for Innovation and Biomedical Engineering houses laboratories to support the Allen School of Engineering & Technology and Innovation One. Experiential learning for students in all majors is also available through i1.

The Thomas L. Fawick Hall of Engineering, home to the Allen School of Engineering & Technology, features classrooms and laboratories, providing student access to technology from day one.

The Perry T. Ford Memorial Building, home of the Ketner School of Business, boasts technology-rich classrooms and a design that mimics a contemporary business setting.

The T. Furth Center for Performing Arts is home to Trine's music program and the Ryan Concert Hall is the venue for a variety of concerts, which include university instrumental and vocal ensembles, as well as nationally known entertainers like the Oak Ridge Boys, Michael Bolton, Wynonna Judd, Three Dog Night, Amy Grant, America, Kenny Rogers, and The Guess Who.

The Rick L. and Vicki L. James University Center is the hub for student activity, including a library stocked with computers, Fabiani Theatre, WEAX radio station, student health center, and the Whitney Commons dining hall.

William D. Shambaugh Hall, home of the Franks School of Education, offers a juvenile literature and school curriculum collection, kits, and audio-visual resource materials, as well as workspace and materials to support education students.

The Charles and Nancy Taylor Hall of Humanities houses the Department of Humanities & Communication as well as classrooms, the Wells Gallery, the Humanities Institute, the Fine Arts Library, and Wells Theater, home of the university's drama club.

Costs

Tuition for the academic year (two semesters) in 2018–19 is $31,700 ($34,200 for engineering). Room and standard meal plan (19 meals per week) for the academic year cost $10,810 (double occupancy).

Financial Aid

Financial aid may be awarded in the form of scholarships, grants, loans, or campus employment. Trine requires the Free Application for Federal Student Aid (FAFSA) and recommends submission by March 1.

Trine stands out in this area because:

- Ninety-six percent of undergraduate students receive some form of financial aid.
- More than $27 million is awarded in institutional aid.
- Average financial aid per student is $28,200.
- The school has been recognized for graduating students with the least amount of debt.

Faculty

Trine has 108 full-time faculty members; most have doctoral degrees and professional experience.

Student Government

The student senate is organized to provide funding and formulate policies for campus organizations. Each class elects representatives to the senate.

Admission Requirements

Graduation from an approved high school or equivalent preparation is required for admission. Selection is made without regard to race, religion, or gender. Applicants are required to take the ACT or SAT prior to approval for admission. Applicants' high school grade point average and class rank are also important factors.

Graduates of community or junior colleges and students who have attended other colleges and universities are eligible for transfer. Counselors work closely with those who wish to transfer to ensure a smooth transition to Trine. Credit may be allowed in subjects that parallel Trine programs, provided the student earned a C or better in the course.

Application and Information

Trine University's online application is free and available at trine.edu. The university admits applicants on the basis of scholastic achievement and academic potential. Admission decisions are made on a rolling basis. Applicants are notified of their status within two weeks of receipt of their application, high school record, and test scores. Transfer students must also submit an official copy of their college transcript(s).

Interested students and their parents are encouraged to visit the campus. Contact the Office of Admission to make arrangements.

For additional information, students should call or write:

Office of Admission
Trine University
One University Avenue
Angola, Indiana 46703-1764
Phone: 260-665-4100
     800-347-4878
E-mail: admit@trine.edu
Website: trine.edu
     facebook.com/trineadmissions
     youtube/trineuniversity

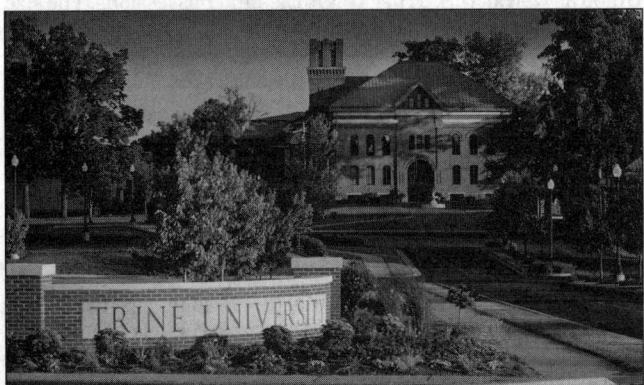

Trine University provides a safe, comfortable environment for learning and intellectual growth as well as for athletics and diverse activities.

UNITED STATES MERCHANT MARINE ACADEMY

KINGS POINT, NEW YORK

 For more information, visit http://petersons.to/merchantmarineacademy

The Academy

The United States Merchant Marine Academy is a federal service academy that educates individuals for careers as licensed Merchant Marine officers. Graduates serve America's marine transportation and defense needs. With 95 percent of the world's products transported over water, these leaders are vital to the effective operation of our merchant fleet for both commercial and military transport during war and peace.

The Academy is known for providing rigorous education and training. In fact, its bachelor degree program has more credit hours than programs in any other federal service academy. This challenging coursework is augmented by the Academy's Sea Year experience, which affords midshipmen (students) the opportunity to acquire hands-on, real-world experiences aboard working commercial vessels sailing to ports around the world. Midshipmen who master this demanding curriculum earn three credentials: a Bachelor of Science degree, a United States Coast Guard license, and an officer's commission in the United States armed forces.

Upon graduation, every graduate has a service obligation that offers more career options than any other federal academy. Graduates can work five years in the U.S. maritime industry and serve eight years as an officer in a reserve unit of any branch of the armed forces. Alternatively, they can choose to serve five years of active duty in any branch of the armed forces.

Academy graduates are highly sought after as officers in the military and the merchant marine. U.S. Merchant Marine graduates play a key role in the maritime industry, which is vital to America's economy and continued prosperity. The most important element in a productive merchant fleet and a strong transportation industry is people—men and women who can lead with integrity, honor, intelligence, dedication, and competence. The U.S. Merchant Marine Academy ensures that such people are available to the nation as shipboard officers and as leaders in the transportation field who will meet the challenges of the present and the future.

The Academy's Regiment of Midshipmen numbers approximately 950 young men and women who represent every state of the Union as well as U.S. Trust Territories and Possessions. The size of the student body contributes to a true sense of camaraderie among the members of the Regiment and permits the Academy to maintain an excellent student-teacher ratio.

The United States Merchant Marine Academy is accredited by the Middle States Commission on Higher Education (MSCHE), 3624 Market Street, Philadelphia, Pennsylvania 19104; 267-284-5000, http://www.msche.org.

Location

The United States Merchant Marine Academy is located in Kings Point, New York in the northeastern region of the United States. It's situated on Long Island's "Gold Coast" neighborhood and provides a stunning view of New York City's skyline.

The academy's 82-acre campus features the beautiful American Merchant Marine Museum, a swimming pool along the waterfront, numerous academic buildings including Gibbs Hall,

with its state-of-the-art engineering and science laboratories, Yocum Sailing Center, and an interfaith chapel.

Degree Programs

A sound college education is the foundation for every profession in our society and the mariner's profession is no exception. The academic curriculum at the Academy provides each midshipman with the broad college education required for a Bachelor of Science degree, a U.S. Coast Guard License as Merchant Marine Officer, and a Commission as Ensign in the Navy Reserve.

As part of the Bachelor of Science curriculum, midshipmen complete core courses, courses in their majors, and elective courses as well as hands-on experience at sea. Core courses provide in-depth knowledge in the following academic and professional areas: comparative literature and history, English, leadership and ethics, mathematics, and naval science.

The Academy offers the following five majors:

Marine Transportation—emphasizes nautical science and maritime business management.

Maritime Logistics and Security—emphasizes nautical science, managing complex maritime and intermodal supply chains, security challenges facing the marine transportation system.

Marine Engineering—emphasizes shipboard engineering operations.

Marine Engineering Systems—emphasizes design of shipboard systems and machinery.

Marine Engineering and Shipyard Management—emphasizes the management of shipyards, and the production and repair of marine vehicles.

The Academy challenges its midshipmen intellectually and physically. Freshman students make the transition from high school graduate to Academy midshipman. In their first few months, they learn many new terms, the quality of endurance, how to perform under pressure, and most importantly, how to successfully manage time. During sophomore year, and again during junior year, midshipmen are sent to sea for practical shipboard training. Aboard ship, sailing the trade routes of the world, they learn the value of self-reliance and initiative as they gain firsthand experience in the mariner's environment. In senior year, they fine-tune the skills learned in the classroom and at sea as they prepare to enter the professional world.

Career Opportunities

Graduates of the United States Merchant Marine Academy are fully equipped to take advantage of the many career opportunities that await them. They typically build their careers and fulfill the service obligation at sea or ashore as Merchant Marine officers and commission as Ensign in the Navy Reserve, or apply to any branch of the armed forces as active duty officers.

Employers are eager to hire them because of their exemplary character, hands-on experience, leadership and problem-solving skills, professional expertise, and self-discipline. Nearly 100 percent of the Academy's graduates secure well-paying jobs within three to six months of graduation.

Students acquire the tools to achieve long-term career success. A Standard and Poor's report ranked the United States Merchant Marine Academy eighteenth among the top 550 colleges and universities whose alumni include directors of U.S. companies, presidents, and vice presidents (in proportion to total number of graduates).

Facilities

The campus includes multiple buildings, including state-of-the-art classrooms and labs, dining facilities, recently renovated barracks (dorms), and recreational and physical fitness buildings. There are also extensive waterfront facilities and activities.

The Academy library is dedicated to providing information and services to further the education process at Kings Point by offering resources in a variety of formats from traditional to high tech. Easy access to resources quickly provides the reference, research, and reading material needed to support the curriculum.

Costs and Financial Aid

The federal government covers the cost of tuition, books, room and board, and uniforms. Midshipmen pay for an Academy-approved personal laptop, activity fees, licensing fees, personal and transportation expenses, and personal services (such as tailoring, laundry, personal grooming, etc.).

The Academy doesn't offer traditional institutional aid such as scholarships. However, all students, no matter their income levels, are eligible for federal financial aid. They can also seek scholarships from private sources.

Faculty

Faculty members are highly skilled teachers, mentors, and scholars. They help create a supportive, stimulating, and rigorous learning environment where students can reach their full potential.

Student Life

The Academy's 950 midshipmen lead regimented yet interesting and enjoyable lives. During the academic year, they follow a daily schedule Monday through Friday which includes meal times, room inspections, classes, athletics, and study time. On Friday afternoons and Saturday mornings they participate in inspections and regimental parades.

Midshipmen have access to more than 40 registered student organizations that host a variety of events and programs. They can also take on leadership roles such as campus activities board member, morale or diversity training officer, or petty officer. They can also participate in 27 varsity and intramural sports, including basketball, baseball, cross-country, football, lacrosse, swimming, track and field, volleyball, and wresting.

There are also plenty of opportunities to venture off campus to enjoy the culture of New York City and Long Island.

Admission Requirements

To be eligible to enter the Academy, candidates must be at least 17 years of age and no older than 25; be a citizen of the United States; meet the physical, security, suitability, and character requirements necessary for commission in the U.S. Navy Reserve; obtain a Congressional nomination to the Academy; submit a completed application; and qualify scholastically.

Candidates should pursue studies in high school that will prepare them for the Academy's rigorous program. Candidates must have satisfactorily completed their high school education at an accredited secondary school or its equivalent. They must have earned at least 16 units of credit: 4 units must be in English; 3 units in mathematics (from algebra, trigonometry, pre-calculus, and/or calculus); and 1 unit in physics or chemistry with a laboratory. The Academy strongly recommends that candidates take four years of mathematics and both physics and chemistry. Courses in mechanical drawing and machine shop are also desirable.

All candidates are required to take either the SAT or ACT test. The current minimum qualifying scores for the SAT Reasoning Test (taken after March 2016) are 30 Reading and 580 for Math. The current minimum qualifying scores for the ACT are 24 English and 24 Math and applicants must also achieve a minimum composite score of 23. Each of the three minimum scores must be achieved individually in order to meet the Academy's minimum test score requirements.

Satisfactory completion of the Candidate Fitness Assessment (CFA) is required for admission. Passing results must be received in the Admissions Office by the 1 March application deadline. The CFA is a test of strength, agility, speed and endurance. The examination may be administered by a J/ROTC instructor, physical education teacher, coach, or any commissioned/noncommissioned officer other than a parent/guardian.

Candidates must be nominated to the Academy by a U.S. Representative or Senator. The ideal time for a candidate to apply for a nomination is in May of junior year in high school.

Application and Information

Students may begin applying to the Academy on June 1 of their junior year of high school. The application deadline is March 1 of the year they wish to enter the Academy. U.S. candidates for admission to the Academy must apply online; however, all documents must be mailed, e-mailed or faxed and received in the Admissions Office by March 1. Documents cannot be uploaded onto the web portal.

For more information, prospective candidates may contact:
Admissions Office
United States Merchant Marine Academy
300 Steamboat Road
Kings Point, New York 11024
United States
Phone: 866-546-4778
Fax: 516-773-5390
E-mail: admissions@usmma.edu
Website: https://www.usmma.edu/

UNIVERSITY OF ALASKA FAIRBANKS
FAIRBANKS, ALASKA

★ To read more about this school, visit http://petersons.to/universityofalaskafairbanks

The University

The University of Alaska Fairbanks (UAF) draws students into a welcoming community, offering inspiring and transformational educational challenges—from the personal to the global—in the vast natural laboratory that is Alaska. Founded in 1917, UAF is Alaska's top teaching and research university. Total enrollment is nearly 10,000 students; 83 percent are from Alaska, with the rest coming from the United States and 44 other countries.

The 2,250-acre Fairbanks campus, located near the middle of Alaska, offers limitless opportunities for activity and recreation. Academic buildings and residences make up the core of campus, and just beyond are miles of trails, two lakes, and a boreal forest research and recreational area. Most of UAF's research institutes, including the Geophysical Institute and the International Arctic Research Center, are clustered on the West Ridge. The university's Agricultural and Forestry Experiment Station is on campus, as are a Cooperative Fish and Wildlife Research Unit and various state and federal agencies and laboratories. The Margaret Murie Building, with 100,000 square-feet of life science classrooms and laboratories, opened in 2013. A six-story engineering building, completed in 2017, features 40 modern labs, a cold-testing room that can be chilled to minus 50 degrees, and a 48-foot tall high bay with a 4-foot-thick floor to study large, heavy objects.

The Student Recreation Center and Patty Center house a variety of sports and physical activity facilities, including multipurpose areas for aerobics, badminton, calisthenics, dance, gymnastics, judo, karate, tennis, and volleyball; a rifle and pistol range; courts for basketball, handball, racquetball, and squash; an elevated 200-meter, three-lane jogging track; a swimming pool; weight-training and modern fitness equipment areas; an ice arena for recreational skating and hockey; a three-story indoor climbing wall; and an outdoor rock/ice climbing wall.

The student union, the William Ransom Wood Center, is the focus of numerous activities for students and faculty members. A major expansion in 2014 added a modern dining facility where students have numerous menu options, many of them featuring made-to-order items. The expansion also added a coffee shop with extensive lounge seating and a study area that can be reconfigured for performances and exhibits. The Wood Center houses meeting and exhibit rooms, lounges and television areas, and student government offices, as well as a campus information desk, pub, bowling alley, and games room.

Intercollegiate athletics include men's and women's basketball, cross-country running and skiing, men's ice hockey, and women's volleyball and swim teams. The university also has an outstanding rifle team that has produced several Olympic athletes and earned 10 NCAA championships.

Location

The University of Alaska Fairbanks campus sits on a ridge named Troth Yeddha', meaning "wild potato hill" in the local indigenous language. The campus offers beautiful views across the Tanana River valley to the Alaska Range, with 20,310-foot Denali on the southwest horizon. The Fairbanks area, population 100,000, serves as a major trade center for outlying towns and villages in Interior Alaska. The city is connected to the rest of the state and the lower 48 states by air and highway. Municipal buses, which UAF students can ride free, are available between downtown Fairbanks, the surrounding area, and campus. A convenient shuttle bus service is available on campus.

Fairbanks offers the amenities of larger cities while maintaining the atmosphere of a smaller, more personal town. Denali National Park and Preserve and other vast wilderness areas are close at hand, and Anchorage is 350 miles south via the Parks Highway. Members of the Fairbanks and UAF communities unite to perform in the Fairbanks Symphony Orchestra, Arctic Chamber Orchestra, and many other musical and theatrical programs.

Majors and Degrees

The University of Alaska Fairbanks awards occupational endorsements, certificates, A.A., A.S., A.A.S., B.A., B.A.S., B.A.A.S., B.B.A., B.E.M., B.F.A., B.M., and B.S. degrees in accounting; accounting technician; administrative assistant; airframe; airframe and powerplant; Alaska Native studies; anthropology; applied accounting; applied business; applied business management; apprenticeship technologies; Arctic and Northern studies; art; automotive technology; aviation maintenance; basic carpentry; biological sciences; bookkeeping technician; business administration; chemistry; child development and family studies; civil engineering; communication; community health; computer engineering; computer science; construction management; construction trades technology; culinary arts and hospitality; dental assistant; diesel/heavy equipment; digital journalism; drafting technology; early childhood education; earth science; electrical engineering; elementary education; English; environmental studies; Eskimo (Inupiaq and Yup'ik); ethnobotany; facility maintenance; film and performing arts; financial services representative; fire science; fisheries; fisheries and ocean sciences; foreign languages; general science; geography; geological engineering; geoscience; health care reimbursement; high latitude range management; history; homeland security; homeland security and emergency management; human services; information technology specialist; instrumentation technology; interdisciplinary studies; Japanese studies; justice; law enforcement academy; linguistics; mathematics; mechanical engineering; medical assistant; medical billing; medical coding; medical/dental reception; medical office reception; mining engineering; mining mill operations; music; Native language education; natural resources management (including forestry); nurse aide; paralegal studies; paramedicine; petroleum engineering; physics; political science; powerplant; pre-nursing qualifications; process technology; professional piloting; psychology; rural development; rural human services; rural human services behavioral health aide; rural surface water quality testing; rural utilities business management; rural waste management and spill response; safety, health, and environmental awareness technology; secondary education; social work; sustainable energy; tribal justice; tribal management; welding (entry level); wildland fire science; wildlife biology and conservation; Yup'ik language and culture; and Yup'ik language proficiency.

Academic Programs

The academic year is divided into two semesters; registration begins in early April for the fall semester and in November for the spring semester. In addition, there are three-week, six-week, and 12-week summer sessions and two-week between-semester sessions in January and May.

The university is organized into the colleges of Engineering and Mines, Fisheries and Ocean Sciences, Liberal Arts, Natural Science and Mathematics, and Rural and Community Development, and the schools of Education, Management, and Natural Resources and Extension. A minimum of 120 credits must be completed for the four-year baccalaureate degree programs.

Students who receive scores of 3 or higher on most of the College Board's Advanced Placement tests may be awarded credit by the university. Students graduating from any school offering the International Baccalaureate Programme should review a comprehensive list of transfer credits available at http://catalog.uaf.edu/getting-started/transferring-credits/. Enrolled students may challenge courses for credit by successfully completing College-Level Examination Program examinations or by completing locally prepared examinations. Requests for advanced placement credit and credit by examination are coordinated through the Office of the Registrar.

The Office of Undergraduate Research and Scholarly Activity supports and develops UAF's diverse and robust programs to engage undergraduate students in research and creative scholarship. URSA helps students pursue research from a single credit of first-year seminar to an independent scholarly investigation or senior thesis.

The Honors Program is for highly motivated undergraduate students who wish to acquire an advanced understanding of the natural and social sciences, arts, and humanities. Prospective honors students need a minimum ACT plus writing composite score of 27 or a minimum combined SAT score of 1300.

Off-Campus Programs

The university maintains active exchange programs with universities around the world. Membership in the UArctic's north2north exchange program gives UAF students an extensive array of opportunities throughout the circumpolar North. Additional study programs and internships are available through affiliates maintaining sites in numerous countries. UAF is also a member of the National Student Exchange, participating with more than 200 colleges and universities throughout the United States, in U.S. territories, and at 10 locations in Canada.

Academic Facilities

The Fine Arts Complex features a 480-seat theater, a 1,072-seat concert hall, FM public radio (KUAC) and educational television (PBS) studios, an art gallery, and the Elmer E. Rasmuson Library. The library collection contains more than 1.2 million items, including many in the prestigious Alaska and Polar Regions Collection and Archives. Electronic catalogs provide access to collections in 11,000 libraries nationwide.

Students have free use of the university's academic computing facilities and wireless network in labs, classrooms, dorm rooms, and other campus locations.

The University of Alaska Museum of the North attracts nearly 100,000 visitors each year to Interior Alaska and is located on the Fairbanks campus. The museum collects, preserves, and exhibits materials from Alaska and the North.

Costs

In 2016–17, annual tuition and fees were $7,798 for students taking 30 credits (full time) split evenly between lower and upper division courses. Nonresident students paid $23,055 annually for the 30 credits. Generally, to qualify as residents, students must show proof they have been living in Alaska for two years. Residents of Alaska and of foreign cities or provinces having sister agreements with any Alaska city, as well as military service members, veterans, and their dependents are eligible for resident tuition rates.

The approximate annual cost for books and supplies is $2,000. A double-occupancy residence hall room on campus and a meal plan cost $8,530 per academic year during the 2016–17 academic year. All costs are subject to change.

If the student lives in a Western Undergraduate Exchange state (http://www.uaf.edu/admissions/other/wue), tuition is approximately 1.5 times that of an Alaska resident.

Financial Aid

A large portion of financial aid is derived from the Alaska Supplemental Education Loan Program, which is available to all students attending UAF, regardless of residency. Three kinds of aid are available: grants and scholarships (which need not be repaid), loans, and part-time employment. Inquiries should be sent by e-mail to the Financial Aid Office at uaf-financialaid@alaska.edu. Academic merit and service scholarships are one-year scholarships ranging from $1,000–$15,000 that are awarded by the Office of Admissions. To apply, students should submit for review a scholarship application, an application for admission, a high school transcript, and test scores. Questions about this scholarship should be directed to the Office of Admissions. The deadline for University of Alaska and UAF-funded scholarships is February 15. Prospective students should check the financial aid website (www.uaf.edu/finaid/) for information about grants, loans, other aid, and applicable due dates.

Faculty

Seventy-seven percent of full-time faculty members and 50 percent of part-time faculty hold doctoral or terminal degrees, and many are engaged in research. In keeping with university policy, faculty members provide academic counseling for students. The combination of a student-faculty ratio of 11:1 and ready access to instructors for help outside of class leads to an excellent educational experience for students.

Admission Requirements

For admission to a baccalaureate program, applicants must be high school graduates with a GPA of at least 2.5 with 16 credits of high school core curriculum and a cumulative grade point average of at least 3.0. A GPA between 2.5 and 3.0 requires an ACT plus writing score of 18 or SAT score of 955. Transfer students must also have a minimum grade point average of 2.0 in all previous college work.

Applicants for a major in a scientific or technical field may be required to present a higher grade point average and to have completed specific background courses before being accepted into the major department.

Application and Information

The undergraduate application deadlines are May 1 for the summer semester, June 15 for the fall semester, and November 1 for the spring semester. A $50 application fee is required when the application is submitted. Applicants are notified of the admission decision once all application materials have been received.

For more information, applicants should contact:

Office of Admissions
University of Alaska Fairbanks
P.O. Box 757480
Fairbanks, Alaska 99775-7480
Phone: 907-474-7500
        800-478-1823 (toll-free)
E-mail: uaf-admissions@alaska.edu
Website: http://www.uaf.edu/admissions

UNIVERSITY OF CALGARY
CALGARY, ALBERTA, CANADA

 To read more about this school, visit http://petersons.to/universityofcalgary

The University

Located in Canada's fourth largest city, the University of Calgary (popularly known as UCalgary) is home to more than 32,000 students, including a diverse population of more than 3,800 international students. In 2015, QS World University Rankings named UCalgary the #1 young university in North America. In 2016, *Times Higher Education* ranked UCalgary as one of the top 200 most globally oriented universities in the world.

UCalgary offers small classes with an average undergraduate student to instructor ratio of 23:1. The university's 14 faculties include the Cumming School of Medicine, the Faculty of Arts, the Faculty of Environmental Design, the Faculty of Graduate Studies, Haskayne School of Business, the Faculty of Kinesiology, the Faculty of Law, the Faculty of Nursing, the Faculty of Science, the Faculty of Social Work, the Faculty of Veterinary Medicine, Schulich School of Engineering, and the Werklund School of Education.

What sets UCalgary apart are enhanced student experiences such as hands-on learning programs, unique research opportunities, and leadership development seminars. Programs focus on channeling the natural curiosity of students by giving them the tools to critically examine their surroundings and take part in hands-on solutions. These opportunities contribute to the university's strong record of preparing students for their future careers; UCalgary graduates have a 91 percent employment rate.

In addition to exceptional academic experiences, students have access to support services that are second to none. The University provides support to foster student success and encourage leadership through programs on campus, in the community, and abroad. UCalgary helps students nurture lifelong interests and prepare them to take on the challenges of current and emerging career paths.

Location

UCalgary's main campus is located on 526 park-like acres minutes from downtown Calgary. In addition to being a great place to study, Calgary is also a fun place to live, with numerous dining and shopping options, major sports teams, and a dynamic arts and culture scene. Calgary is ranked the fifth most-livable city worldwide (The Economist Intelligence Unit, 2015) and is one of the safest major cities in Canada (Statistics Canada, 2012). With the Canadian Rocky Mountains just an hour's drive away, UCalgary's world-class location puts students next door to some of the best hiking and skiing in the world, not to mention biking, rock climbing, kayaking, and more.

Majors and Degrees

UCalgary's 14 faculties grant degrees up to the doctoral level in most disciplines. UCalgary offers undergraduate programs in the following areas: accounting; actuarial science; ancient and medieval history; anthropology; archaeology; architecture; art history; astrophysics; biochemistry; bioinformatics; biological sciences; biomechanics; biomedical sciences; business technology management; Canadian studies; cellular, molecular, and microbial biology; chemical engineering; chemistry; civil engineering; communication and media studies; community rehabilitation and disability studies; computer science; dance; development studies; drama; earth science; East Asian language studies; East Asian studies; economics; ecology; education; electrical engineering; energy engineering; energy management; English; entrepreneurship and innovation; environmental science; exercise and health physiology; finance; film studies; French; general commerce; general mathematics; geography; geology; geomatics engineering; geophysics; German; Greek and Roman studies; health and society; history; international business strategy; international Indigenous studies; international relations; Italian studies; kinesiology; Latin American studies; law; law and society; leadership in pedagogy and coaching; linguistics; linguistics and language; marketing; mathematics; mechanical engineering; medicine; mind sciences in kinesiology; multidisciplinary; music; natural sciences; neuroscience; nursing; oil and gas engineering; operations management; organizational behavior and human resources; personal financial planning; petroleum land management; philosophy; physics; plant biology; political science; psychology; real estate; religious studies; risk management: insurance and finance; risk management and insurance; Russian; social work; sociology; software engineering; Spanish; supply chain management; urban studies; veterinary medicine; visual studies; women's studies; and zoology.

Undergraduate students can also complement their program of study with an embedded Certificate in Sustainability Studies or Creative Writing.

Teaching and Learning

As a comprehensive academic and research institution, UCalgary inspires and supports discovery, creativity and innovation across all disciplines. UCalgary is committed to its Eyes High Strategy, which entails sharpening the focus on research, enriching the quality and breadth of learning, integrating with the community, and offering a rich and multi-faceted student experience in an inclusive and respectful campus culture.

Through the Taylor Institute for Teaching and Learning, the university takes the lead in educational innovation by researching the most effective methods for engaging students, by supporting faculty to be the best teachers they can be, and by providing some of the most innovative learning spaces available in North America.

UCalgary has numerous programs and services provided on campus to help students achieve success, including Career Services, the Faith and Spirituality Centre, International Student Services, Student Accessibility Services, the Student Success Centre, Students' Union, the Welcome Centre, the Native Centre, and the Women's Resource Centre.

Academic Facilities

The University of Calgary's facilities support how students learn, collaborate, and experience, with more than 10.5 million square feet of space across four campuses, plus research field stations, and an international campus in Qatar.

UCalgary has demonstrated best practices in green building construction in 11 major buildings—one of the largest concentrations of green buildings on any post-secondary campus in Canada—and supports the ongoing improvement of the environmental sustainability of the school's research and innovation-related infrastructure through initiatives like the Utility Reduction Program.

The campus has been expanding since 1966. Recently built facilities include the Taylor Institute for Teaching and Learning, the Crowsnest and Aurora residence halls, and the expansion and renovation of the Schulich School of Engineering complex.

The libraries at UCalgary contain more than 7.8 million items, giving students access to the materials and resources they need.

As a comprehensive research institution, the university houses 73 Canada Research Chairs and more than 80 research institutes and centres, all working to find solutions to the challenging problems facing society today.

Costs

The average undergraduate tuition is Can$5,385.90 for full-time Canadian students. The rate for full-time international students is Can$18,338.40. First-year residence costs with a meal plan range from Can$8,705 to Can$12,381. More specific information regarding tuition and fees is available online at ucalgary.ca/pubs/calendar/current/p-1-1.html.

Financial Aid

UCalgary issues more than 11,000 awards, scholarships, and bursaries valued at $28 million annually to reward academic and extracurricular activities and support financial need.

Student Life

As a young vibrant campus community, UCalgary offers unforgettable celebrations and events, top-notch recreation facilities, extensive student services, and endless opportunities to meet new people.

Driven to become a global intellectual hub, UCalgary helps students engage internationally; each year more than 1,200 students enhance their academic experience through exchange, group study, and internship programs in over 40 countries.

UCalgary offers a variety of on-campus housing options in secured buildings. Whether students come from Canberra or Canterbury, they have a guaranteed home on campus for the first two years if they enter directly from high school and apply for residence by May 1. The university also offers various meals plans to suit individual needs, and fully-furnished rooms include features such as Wi-Fi, all utilities, access to student tutoring services, and more.

Students enjoy cheering on the university's Dinos sports teams, as well as staying active themselves. UCalgary athletes have won 45 USport national championships and 14 Olympic medals. Student fees include access to all the Active Living facilities and discounts on rentals from the Outdoor Centre, the largest facility of its kind in North America. Students can re-energize, create, and maintain a healthy, active lifestyle with access to the university's world-class health and recreation facilities.

The University Theatre hosts more than 175 events annually, including academic productions from the School of Creative and Performing Arts. Touring concerts and outside companies also enjoy frequent access to this spacious, well-designed theatre.

The SU Wellness Centre on campus provides an extensive list of services including family medicine, massage therapy, chiropractic, nutrition, dental services, personal counseling, and a walk-in clinic.

Admission Requirements

The UCalgary application process is completed online. Students can explore the programs offered, and view the requirements and deadlines at ucalgary.ca/future-students/undergraduate/apply.

English is the official language of instruction at UCalgary. All applicants must demonstrate English language proficiency to be considered for admission. Academically qualified applicants who do not meet UCalgary's English language proficiency requirement may be considered for the International Foundations Program (not all degree programs offer this option). Additional information regarding admissions requirements for international students, including English language proficiency requirements and the International Foundations Program, is available online at ucalgary.ca/future-students/undergraduate/international.

International Student Services (ISS) provides support services and customized advising for all international students preparing to study at UCalgary. Prospective students can visit ucalgary.ca/iss for more information about ISS. Any questions about the application or study permit process should be emailed to the Regulated Canadian Immigration Consultant in ISS at international.advice@ucalgary.ca.

Application and Information

UCalgary accepts undergraduate applications annually from October 1 to March 1. Applicants are able to change their program choices online through the application until March 1. Applicants are encouraged to also apply for scholarships and awards using the online submission process until the deadline of March 1. Applicants can track the status of the application through their My UCalgary portal. Upon receiving an offer of admission, students can also use their My UCalgary portal to accept the offer, pay the admission deposit, and register for courses.

For more information, prospective students should contact:
University of Calgary
Admissions Office, MB117
2500 University Drive, NW
Calgary, Alberta T2N 1N4
Canada
Phone: 403-210-7625
E-mail: future.students@ucalgary.ca
Website: http://www.ucalgary.ca/future-students/
undergraduate/contact
ucalgary.ca/futurestudents
@ucalgaryFS

University of Calgary students can pursue a lifelong interest, find a new passion, and prepare themselves for emerging career paths, all in one of the most vibrant, dynamic, and culturally diverse cities in the world.

UNIVERSITY OF CALIFORNIA SAN DIEGO

SAN DIEGO, CALIFORNIA

The University

Situated on a sunny cliff overlooking the Pacific Ocean, the University of California San Diego is a place that has reimagined the traditional path to knowledge. Established in 1960, UC San Diego is a public research university that has been shaped by exceptional scholars who aren't afraid to make waves—from creating the world's first algae-based surfboard to developing wireless health-monitoring tattoos and printing 3-D blood vessels.

The 1,200-acre campus is located in the La Jolla neighborhood of San Diego, Calif., in the heart of one of the most densely concentrated innovation hubs in the nation. The campus is consistently ranked among the top 10 best public universities in the nation and top 15 in the world for research, teaching, public service, and post-graduation career prospects.

The university is organized into six undergraduate residential colleges, five academic divisions—Arts and Humanities, Biological Sciences, Jacobs School of Engineering, Physical Sciences, and Social Sciences—and five professional and graduate schools, including the Rady School of Management, School of Global Policy and Strategy, School of Medicine, Scripps Institution of Oceanography/School of Marine Sciences, and Skaggs School of Pharmacy and Pharmaceutical Sciences.

Over the last 50 years, 16 Nobel laureates have taught on campus. Over 160 current faculty are members of one or more of the prestigious national academies, while numerous others have garnered such awards as the McArthur Fellowship, National Medal of Science, Pulitzer Prize, Fields Medal, and Academy Award.

UC San Diego's more than 185,000 alumni include National Medal of Science honoree J. Craig Venter, one of the first to sequence the human genome; Kate Rubins, NASA astronaut who recently conducted human health studies in space; Nathan East, one of the most recorded bassists in history; Albert Lin, an explorer using crowdsourcing and radar to find the lost tomb of Genghis Khan; and Guy "Bud" Tribble, who managed the original Macintosh software development team.

UC San Diego is committed to creating a climate of respect and understanding. Through innovative programs, the campus opens doors to higher education for first generation students and those from underserved communities. The university was recently ranked fourth in the nation for providing access to low-income students by *The New York Times*. In addition, UC San Diego graduates the largest percentage of women with STEM degrees, and has been named one of the top 10 most LGBTQ-friendly public universities.

Students are invited to engage in open dialogue, develop leadership skills, and learn about social issues at six campus community centers. In addition, students can take part in numerous cultural events and celebrations of diversity, from Raza Awareness Week to the annual UC San Diego Powwow and Martin Luther King Jr. Parade and Day of Service.

Majors and Degrees

The campus offers more than 100 undergraduate degree programs spanning five academic divisions, as well as master's and doctoral degree programs in 60 academic departments. A complete list of undergraduate degree programs can be found at http://ucsd.edu/academics-detail.html.

Academic Programs

UC San Diego's academic programs, taught by highly regarded scholars, prepare students to stand out and lead change. All UC San Diego undergraduates can find their community thanks to the college system, patterned after the small-college feel of Cambridge and Oxford. Each of the university's six colleges have distinct neighborhoods, residence facilities, staff, traditions, and general education requirements. Every UC San Diego undergraduate is assigned to one of six colleges when they are admitted to UC San Diego; furthermore, college assignments are not based on major. Students may select from the full range of available majors regardless of college assignment.

A student-centered university, UC San Diego offers supplemental learning, tutoring, and career development programs to equip students to thrive academically. Through services offered at the Teaching + Learning Commons, students develop transferable skills, participate in peer-facilitated study groups, and are matched with experiential learning projects.

In addition, nearly a dozen makerspaces and incubators offer resources, training, and mentorship opportunities to help students launch their big ideas. At The Basement, students gain business guidance and funding ideas from alumni and industry mentors. For hands-on projects, the EnVision Arts and Engineering Maker Studio contains tools to design, fabricate, and prototype, including 3-D printers, welding stations, and laser cutters.

Students apply their learning outside the classroom through faculty-mentored research, service learning projects, study abroad and professional internships. Undergraduates can explore opportunities through the Research Experience and Applied Learning Portal, get matched with real-world training opportunities through the Academic Internship Program, and become immersed in the culture of another country through the Study Abroad Office.

Costs

For the 2017–18 academic years, tuition and fees for California residents was $14,230; nonresidents pay a supplemental tuition of $28,014. The estimated cost of on-campus housing and meals is $13,254. Books and supplies are estimated at $1,198.

Financial Aid

For prospective students and their families, budgeting, costs and how to pay for college can seem complicated. UC San Diego offers information and advising to help students understand the big picture and the bottom line. Students may utilize a wide array of grants, loans, scholarships, veteran's benefits, work-study, and other means to finance their education.

Student Life

Life at UC San Diego is far from ordinary. In 2018, UC San Diego was ranked first nationally among "Top 10 Surf Colleges" by *Surfer* magazine. The campus features a competitive surf team, classes on the physics of surfing as well as opportunities to learn how to ride the salty swells.

When students aren't immersed in the sea, they unwind at one of dozens of campuswide events, including Triton Fest, a month-long fall kickoff experience that has featured a haunted trail, go-kart racing, and outdoor movie night; Winter Game Fest, the largest student-run gaming festival on the West Coast; and the Sun God Festival, a day-long carnival and concert.

The university features nearly 500 student organizations on campus, ranging from academic-focused and pre-professional groups to social and cultural clubs as well as spiritual and service groups. There are also more than 40 Greek organizations focused on academic excellence, service and leadership. In addition, UC San Diego students are very active in their community through a number of co-curricular community service programs; more than 70 student organizations have a primary focus on service. On average, nearly 20,000 UC San Diego students complete more than 3 million hours of change-making community service each year.

UC San Diego's Triton Athletics includes 23 intercollegiate sports teams, which have garnered 30 national championship titles. The university is reclassifying into NCAA Division I, and will begin a full Big West Conference competitive slate in the 2020–21 academic year. Facilities include a 5,000-seat arena, ballpark, aquatic center with two Olympic-sized pools, and a state-of-the-art athletic performance center. Students can also take part in dozens of sports clubs and intramural leagues, choose from hundreds of recreation classes, and venture into the wild with the campus's Outback Adventures.

Within the six residential colleges, students bond over shared classes and annual events, from the summertime watermelon drop—a fruity physics experiment—to the 1960s-inspired Muirstock concert and the annual chocolate festival. In addition, transfer students find community in the Village Apartments, comprised of 13 buildings dedicated to transfer student housing, including two high rises with ocean views; while graduate students have the option to reside in one of six housing communities on or nearby campus, with amenities for couples and students with children.

UC San Diego is an ever-evolving campus, with big transformational plans over the next five years to accommodate the growing needs of the university. New construction includes the arrival of light rail transit in 2021; the Torrey Pines Living and Learning Neighborhood, a mixed-use community with student housing and state-of-the-art academic facilities; and an Innovation and Design Center, a hub for creativity, collaboration, and entrepreneurship.

Admission Requirements

UC San Diego looks for students at the freshman level who are well-prepared to succeed in a rigorous and challenging academic setting. Admission is highly competitive and applicants must exceed the minimum requirements. Every application, including the personal insight questions, is reviewed by a minimum of two individuals.

In addition to the 14 factors that are detailed on the University of California admissions website, freshman applicants must earn a high school diploma (or equivalent); complete a rigorous array of college preparatory classes with a C grade or better (detailed on the university's website); earn a GPA of 3.0 or better

(California residents) or 3.4 or better (nonresidents); submit scores from either ACT Plus Writing, SAT Reasoning Test with critical reading, math, and writing; answers to UC San Diego's Personal Insight Questions; and a portfolio for students who want to major in history, literature, music, philosophy, theatre and dance, and visual arts. Meeting these requirements does not guarantee admission. Students admitted to UC San Diego exceed UC admission requirements.

Application and Information

The University of California application (available online) must be submitted by November 30. In December, applicants will receive an email that confirms receipt of their application. In January, applicants will receive instructions on how to log into UC San Diego's application status portal. The FAFSA or California Dream Act application must be filed by March 2. Freshman admission decisions will be posted by the end of March.

UC San Diego receives more than 90,000 freshman applications each year. Successful applicants must exceed minimum UC admission requirements. Enrollment goals are established annually. The campus does not select students on the basis of academic major or choice of UC San Diego undergraduate college.

For more information, prospective students may contact:

Office of Admissions
University of California San Diego
9500 Gilman Drive
La Jolla, California 92093
Phone: 858-534-4831
Fax: 858-534-5629
E-mail: admissionsreply@ucsd.edu
Website: www.ucsd.edu

UC San Diego Geisel Library

UNIVERSITY OF CENTRAL FLORIDA
ORLANDO, FLORIDA

The University

The University of Central Florida (UCF) is a comprehensive research university with more than 66,000 students. As one of the nation's fastest-growing and largest universities, UCF enrolls an academically talented and diverse student body representing all fifty states and more than 120 countries. The University offers educational and research programs that complement the regional economy, with strong components in aerospace engineering, business, education, film, health, hospitality management, medicine, nursing, and social sciences. UCF's programs in communication and the fine arts help to meet the cultural and recreational needs of a growing metropolitan area. The University also offers many graduate programs leading to master's and doctoral degrees. The UCF College of Medicine offers the M.D. degree.

UCF is accredited by the Commission on Colleges of the Southern Association of Colleges and Schools. In addition, a number of scientific, professional, and academic bodies confer accreditation in specific disciplines and groups of disciplines.

UCF has established extensive partnerships with businesses and industries in the central Florida area and beyond that provide students with exceptional research and learning experiences. These partnerships bring practical learning environments to UCF students through co-op, internship programs, and joint curriculum development strategies.

The on-campus and campus-affiliated housing facilities include traditional residence halls, apartment-style options, and Greek housing that accommodates approximately 11,500 students. In addition, several thousand students live in apartments located within walking distance of the campus.

Students participate in approximately 650 student organizations, including special-interest clubs, multicultural organizations, fraternities and sororities, honor societies, and academic and preprofessional organizations. The Office of Student Involvement schedules a wide array of extracurricular programs, including concerts, movies, and guest speakers.

The University of Central Florida is a member of the NCAA and competes in the American Athletic Conference (AAC). All teams compete on the NCAA Division I level. UCF's men's teams compete in intercollegiate baseball, basketball, football, golf, soccer, and tennis. Women's teams compete in basketball, cross-country, golf, rowing, soccer, softball, tennis, track and field, and volleyball. Intercollegiate coed club activities include championship cheerleading, crew, and waterskiing teams. The University offers an extensive intramural sports program.

Location

The University of Central Florida is located on 1,415 acres approximately 13 miles east of downtown Orlando. In addition to the academic programs offered on the Orlando campus, upper-division students can work toward a degree at eleven locations around the central Florida area.

Majors and Degrees

The University offers the degrees of Bachelor of Applied Science, Bachelor of Arts, Bachelor of Design, Bachelor of Fine Arts, Bachelor of Music, Bachelor of Music Education, Bachelor of Science, Bachelor of Science in Business Administration, Bachelor of Science in Education, Bachelor of Science in Engineering, Bachelor of Science in Nursing, Bachelor of Social Work, and Bachelor of Science in Social Sciences. These degrees are available in the colleges listed below, with majors or areas of specialization as indicated. The most up-to-date list of colleges, departments, majors, and minors is available at www.ucf.edu.

The College of Arts and Humanities offers degrees in art, architecture, digital media, English, film, French, history, humanities and cultural studies, Latin American studies, music, music education, philosophy, photography, religion and cultural studies, Spanish, theatre studies, and writing and rhetoric.

The College of Business Administration offers degrees in accounting, business economics, economics, finance, integrated business, management, marketing, and real estate.

The College of Education and Human Performance offers degrees in early childhood development and education, elementary education, exceptional student education, secondary education, sport and exercise science, teacher education, and technical education and industry training.

The College of Engineering and Computer Science offers degrees in aerospace engineering, civil engineering, computer engineering, computer science, construction engineering, electrical engineering, environmental engineering, industrial engineering, information technology, and mechanical engineering.

The College of Health and Public Affairs offers degrees in athletic training, communication sciences and disorders, criminal justice, health informatics and information management, health services administration, health sciences, legal studies, nonprofit management, public administration, and social work.

The College of Medicine and the Burnett School of Biomedical Sciences offers degrees in biomedical sciences, biotechnology, and medical laboratory sciences.

The College of Nursing offers degrees in nursing.

The College of Optics and Photonics offers degrees in photonic science and engineering.

The College of Sciences offers degrees in actuarial science, advertising/public relations, anthropology, biology, chemistry, communication and conflict, forensic science, human communication, international and global studies, journalism, mathematics, physics, political science, psychology, radio/television, sociology, social sciences, and statistics.

The Rosen College of Hospitality Management offers degrees in entertainment management, event management, hospitality management, and restaurant and foodservice management.

The College of Undergraduate Studies offers degrees in environmental studies and interdisciplinary studies.

Preprofessional programs are offered in chiropractic, dentistry, law, medicine, occupational therapy, optometry, pharmacy, physical therapy, physician assistant, podiatry, public health, and veterinary medicine.

Academic Programs

UCF provides a total education through a core curriculum of 36 hours of general education courses. In addition to fulfilling the general education requirement, each student must complete the necessary major and/or minor requirements to reach the minimum of 120 semester hours necessary for graduation.

Several special programs help students reach their academic and leadership potential. The Burnett Honors College at UCF encourages students to achieve academic excellence through small classes and interactive symposia. The innovative LEAD Scholars Academy fosters leadership and service commitment through a comprehensive student development program. The Major Exploration Program (MEP) helps entering freshmen define their career goals and develop an academic strategy to reach those goals. The University also offers online courses and degree programs.

UCF offers Air Force and Army ROTC programs.

Off-Campus Programs

Career Services and Experiential Learning provides comprehensive and coordinated career development, enhances academic study, and builds ongoing partnerships with employers and the community. The UCF Abroad Office offers study-abroad programs. UCF is also a participant in the National Student Exchange Consortium.

Academic Facilities

In addition to the academic programs offered on the Orlando campus, upper division students can work toward a degree at eleven campuses located throughout Central Florida. These regional campuses work cooperatively with local state colleges to provide all four years of course work in many academic areas. The library houses over 2 million print volumes and subscribes to more than 53,000 periodicals and journals (49,000 in electronic format). Students have access to an online computer catalog that provides information on the collections of the State University System libraries. An extensive online network of more than 600 computers (both PC and Mac) cover the campus. The Institute for Simulation and Training gives students the opportunity to pursue undergraduate research. The College of Optics and Photonics allows faculty members and students to work directly with industry personnel in conducting basic and applied research at the regional and national levels. The Central Florida Research Park, adjacent to the UCF campus, houses more than 125 high-technology firms and agencies. This proximity fosters relationships between industry and the University, which strengthens the academic programs at UCF.

Costs

For Florida residents, the cost of tuition and fees in 2017–18, based on a full-time course load, was $6,368 for the year; for out-of-state residents, the cost was $22,466. Room and board were approximately $9,764 per year, books and supplies cost approximately $1,152.

Financial Aid

Financial aid is awarded according to each student's demonstrated financial need in relation to college costs and may include grants, loans, scholarships, and part-time employment. Programs based upon need include the Federal Perkins Loan, Federal Pell Grant, Florida Student Assistance Grant, Federal Work-Study, Florida College Career Work-Study Program, and Federal Stafford Student Loan. To qualify for these programs, students must complete the Free Application for Federal Student Aid (FAFSA). The priority application deadline is December 1. Seventy-six percent of UCF students receive some form of financial assistance.

Faculty

The University's teaching faculty consists of 2,481 full-time members and adjunct members. Eighty-two percent of the full-time faculty members hold a doctoral or terminal degree. Undergraduate instruction is given primarily by the full-time and adjunct faculty members; graduate students play a minor role in undergraduate instruction. Students are assigned to a faculty adviser in their area of specialization for assistance in academic matters. The student-faculty ratio is 29.6:1.

Student Government

UCF's Student Government Association provides an opportunity for students to become involved at UCF. Every UCF student is encouraged to voice his or her opinion through senate representatives. Student Government is divided into three branches—the student-elected executive branch, the student-elected legislative branch, and the appointed judicial branch. Student Government is responsible for the allocation of all activity and service fees paid by students as a part of their tuition. This money goes toward student services, including the online Macintosh lab, homecoming activities, campus activities board, legal services, and funding for clubs and organizations. Admission is free to all events directly sponsored by the Student Government.

Admission Requirements

A freshman applicant is a student with fewer than 12 hours of college course work after high school graduation. The most important criteria in the admission decision for these applicants are the high school academic record, rigor of course work, grade point average, grade trends, and SAT or ACT test scores. UCF operates on a rolling admission basis. Students are generally notified of their initial admission decision within two to three weeks after receipt of the application and all official supporting documents. If the number of qualified applicants exceeds the number that the University is permitted to enroll, a waiting list is established.

All applicants must have earned a minimum of 18 high school academic units (yearlong courses that are not remedial in nature).

These include 4 units of English (3 must include substantial writing), 4 units of mathematics at or above algebra I, 3 units of natural science (2 must include a laboratory), 3 units of social science, 2 units of one world language, and 2 units of academic electives. Grades in honors, International Baccalaureate, Advanced Placement, AICE, dual-enrollment, pre-AP, pre-IB, and pre-AICE courses are given additional weight in the GPA computation. Students must meet the Florida Department of Education minimum eligibility to be considered for admission. Applicants should understand that the satisfaction of minimum requirements does not guarantee admission to UCF.

Admission requirements for transfer applicants vary by the number of college credit hours the student has successfully completed prior to enrolling at UCF. Complete details are available at http://admissions.ucf.edu/transfer. A transfer credit summary evaluation is provided to students once they are offered admission to UCF.

Application and Information

Students are encouraged to apply several months in advance. Transfers can apply online at http://admissions.ucf.edu and freshmen can apply at http://admissions.ucf.edu or through the Common Application. It is recommended that freshman students apply early during the fall semester of their senior year. Applications are accepted up to one year prior to the start of the term for which enrollment is desired. Priority application deadlines are May 1 for the fall term (July 1 for transfers), November 1 for the spring term, and March 1 for the summer term.

The Campus Visit Experience, which includes an information session and a campus tour, is offered Monday through Friday at 10 and 2 (except holidays). Students can sign up for a campus visit online at http://admissions.ucf.edu.

For more information, contact:

Office of Undergraduate Admissions
University of Central Florida
P.O. Box 160111
Orlando, Florida 32816-0111
Phone: 407-823-3000
E-mail: admission@.ucf.edu
Website: http://www.ucf.edu

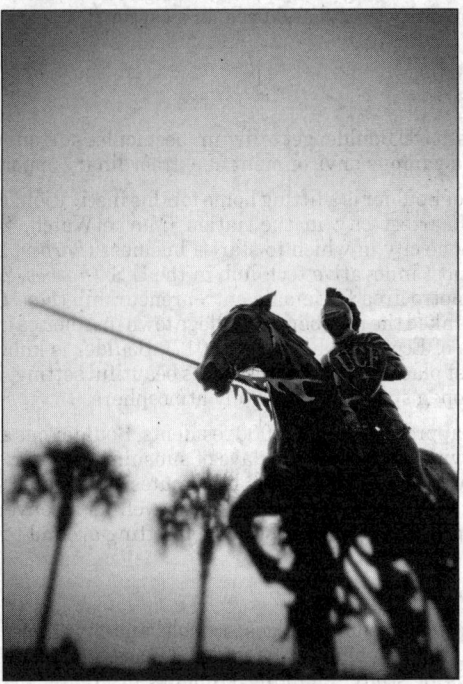

The Charging Knight symbolizes UCF's excellence in academics, partnerships, and athletics.

UNIVERSITY OF COLORADO BOULDER
BOULDER, COLORADO

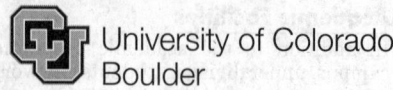

⭐ For more information, visit http://petersons.to/uofcoloradoboulder

The University

The University of Colorado Boulder (CU Boulder) is a dynamic community of scholars and learners situated on one of the most spectacular college campuses in the country. CU Boulder is one of thirty-four U.S. public institutions belonging to the prestigious Association of American Universities (AAU) and has an established reputation for world-class teaching, research, and service to the global society.

At the cornerstone of the university experience are CU Boulder's innovative academic programs, hands-on opportunities, and rigorous coursework that will prepare students for a complex global society. Within the supportive learning community, students will interact with world-renowned faculty—which include Nobel laureates, MacArthur "genius grant" fellows, U.S. Professor of the Year awardees, and National Medal of Science winners—who listen, question and help students refine their ideas to develop a broad understanding of the world, strong leadership skills, and an enhanced ability to think critically.

CU Boulder offers more than 110 undergraduate and graduate programs; 84 bachelor's majors; 34 concurrent bachelor's/master's degree programs; more than 30 minors and 29 certificate programs; 11 research institutes and nearly 90 research centers. More than 2,000 undergraduate students are directly involved in faculty research.

With hands-on experience, world-class education and the ability to think critically, globally, and creatively, CU Boulder graduates benefit from a strong salary potential, high employment rates and the opportunity to find and excel in a career they are passionate about.

Location

Students at CU Boulder get to live in spectacular surroundings and learn in a campus environment of extraordinary opportunities.

The city of Boulder is a fitting home for this institution. It's known as the smartest city in the nation (MarketWatch, 2015), the number-one city in which to start a business (*Forbes*, 2015), the second-most innovative tech hub in the U.S. (*Forbes*, 2015), and the top metro area for female entrepreneurship (*Fast Company*, 2015). Ranked the number-one college town in America (American Institute of Economic Research, 2017), Boulder is known as one of the best places to live because of its beautiful setting, its 45,000 acres of open space, and its lively atmosphere.

Home to approximately 100,000 residents, Boulder has a mild, dry climate with more than 300 days of sunshine per year. Over 300 miles of bike lanes, bike paths, bike routes, designated shoulders and paths in and around Boulder, as well as a convenient bus system, provide excellent options for getting around town.

Majors and Degrees

CU Boulder has eight colleges, schools, and programs. Amongst them, CU Boulder offers more than 3,900 academic courses across 150 fields of study, enabling students to create an academic experience that is unique.

College of Arts and Sciences: The oldest and largest college at CU Boulder and intellectual core of the university, conducting research, scholarship, creative work, and education in more than 60 fields. CU Boulder's research generates new knowledge, solving some of the world's most critical problems. The College offers 50 majors, 25 minors, and 10 certificate programs; there

are 10 different residential academic programs available to students during their first year of studies.

College of Engineering and Applied Science: The top-ranked engineering programs in Colorado and the entire Rocky Mountain region are found in this college, with a full range of degree programs that emphasize hands-on, active learning, and a tradition of research excellence. Engineers Without Borders began at CU in 2000, and has since grown to 206 chapters in 34 countries.

College of Media, Communication and Information: Students learn and prepare to be leaders in the ever-changing information society. CMCI students and faculty think across boundaries, innovate around emerging problems, and create culture that transcends convention. CU offers six student media outlets and six affiliated centers and labs.

College of Music: CU Boulder is the home of one of the country's top public music programs. A talented and active faculty of musicians, composers, and scholars teach an impressive series of programs, ranging from performance to music theory. The college offers 7 degree plans and more than 23 fields of study. The College of Music's library contains more than 150,000 volumes, scores, recordings, and periodicals.

Leeds School of Business: Students can earn undergraduate, master's and doctoral degrees from the top-ranked Colorado business school, also one of the best business schools in the Rocky Mountain and Midwest regions. Leeds has several points of pride: 88 percent of internships are paid; 92 percent of 2016 graduates were in a job within three months of graduation; and about 200 students annually take part in the Leeds First-Year Global Experience program (offered in 11 countries); and eight global initiative programs give students the opportunity to travel and learn about international business.

School of Education: CU Boulder is a proud national leader in the field of education, working professionally with colleagues and communities to deliver outstanding undergraduate and graduate programs for classroom teachers and future scholars alike. More than half of the college's alumni teach in Colorado public schools. Students log many hours of field experience and in turn, 98.5 percent of teacher licensure graduates are employed or in graduate school within a year.

Program in Environmental Design (ENVD): This program fosters an innovative interdisciplinary education to prepare students for practice and advanced study in numerous design-based fields, as well as to apply design thinking to a variety of other possible careers. ENVD houses a state-of-the-art design fabrication lab that includes woodworking tools, metal welding, and shaping equipment.

Preprofessional Study Programs in Health and Law: These programs prepare undergraduate students for future advanced education in their field of interest through specialized advising, resources, and networking opportunities—all of which help to determine if it is the right fit.

Academic Programs

CU Boulder offers students a wealth of opportunities to engage in hands-on learning and scholarly research in fields as diverse as literature and biology. Programs include the Undergraduate Research Opportunities program, which funds research projects and scholarly and creative work; the Engineering Active Learning Program, which gives students the chance to gain hands-on engineering experience while forging professional connections through internships; the Biological Sciences Initiative Scholars in STEM Undergraduate Research, which helps students gain research experience as paid research assistants; and the Herbst Program of Humanities for engineering students, a unique program that encourages engineering students to develop thinking skills that incorporate humanities disciplines.

A group of programs, referred to as Top Scholars, is designed to enhance the educational opportunities for high-achieving students who are seeking the challenge of becoming more critical and analytical thinkers.

The CU LEAD Alliance and Scholarship Program is a set of academic learning. LEAD stands for Leadership, Excellence, Achievement, and Diversity, and the students, faculty, and staff in these communities work together to help students from diverse and underrepresented backgrounds succeed at CU Boulder.

Off-Campus Programs

Studying abroad is a unique opportunity for students to learn from other cultures, enhance their resumes, travel the world, and grow as individuals. Education Abroad gives students the chance to earn academic credit while taking classes in another country. The Education Abroad Office administers 400 CU Boulder sponsored programs in 64 countries. More than 1,300 students study through CU Boulder programs annually.

Costs

Estimated tuition, fees, on-campus housing (double room), and meals (19 per week) for the 2017–18 academic year for Colorado residents ranges from $27,884 to $32,948, based on course of study. The totals for nonresidents ranges from $52,018 to $55,214, based on course of study.

In April 2016, the University of Colorado Board of Regents approved a four-year guarantee of tuition and mandatory fee costs for undergraduate resident and nonresident students. The purpose of this guarantee is to provide financial predictability for students and families. The CU Boulder Guarantee will allow students and families to understand not just first-year tuition and mandatory fee costs, but what these will cost in four years.

Financial Aid

Approximately 15,000 undergraduate students received over $255 million in federal, state, and university aid in 2014–15. Of that total, almost $100 million was in the form of grants, scholarships and work-study. Prospective students are encouraged to complete the Free Application for Federal Student Aid (FAFSA) by February 15 to ensure full consideration for limited funds. The FAFSA is available starting October 1 for the 2018–19 academic year and must be completed each year. Incoming students are automatically considered for some scholarships, but more are available via the CU Boulder Scholarship Application between October 1 and February 15.

Faculty

CU Boulder and its nationally and internationally ranked faculty have built a global reputation for outstanding teaching, research, and creative work across more than 150 academic fields. CU Boulder faculty members are leaders in their fields, but are also dedicated to working closely with undergraduate students. Among faculty members, there are: the 2004 and 2013 National Professor of the Year; 5 Nobel Laureates; 9 recipients of MacArthur Fellowships (also known as the "genius grant"); 19 Rhodes Scholars; 89 faculty who are part of the National Academies of Science, Arts and Sciences, Engineering, or

Education; and more than 100 Fulbright fellows. The student to faculty ratio is 18:1.

Student Life

Estimated CU Boulder's inclusive community offers many ways to get involved and make lifelong friends. CU Boulder has one of the most active college campuses in the nation, where recreation, sports, and student groups play a key role in the campus experience. More than 3,500 students are enrolled in Residential Academic Programs, Living and Learning communities, and First-Year Interest Groups. CU Boulder has 33 competitive club sports, including crew, hockey, snowboarding, and swimming, while 12+ intramural sports provide opportunity for campus competition in sports like broomball, inner-tube water polo, and flag football.

Students also have the opportunity to serve the greater good through volunteerism and civic engagement, whether it's around the world or across the street. More than 6,000 students serve each year through the CU Boulder Volunteer Resource Center.

Admission Requirements

CU Boulder's mission is to enroll an incoming class of highly qualified, intellectually curious, and actively involved students who have demonstrated high levels of maturity and personal integrity as well as a commitment to serving their communities. While admission is competitive, applicants will be considered on an individual basis relative to a prediction of academic success in the college to which they apply.

The primary factor in admission decisions is academic achievement: classroom performance in core academic and prerequisite courses, the rigor of those courses, and the best combination of scores on the SAT or ACT.

While academics and test scores play a large role in admission decisions, secondary factors, such as school and community involvement, also help assess the overall qualities of an applicant.

Application and Information

Materials needed for application include the online application, a $50 application fee, a personal essay and writing supplement, a letter of recommendation, high school transcript or equivalency, and SAT or ACT scores. The Early Action deadline is November 15 and the regular decision deadline is January 15.

Office of Admissions
University of Colorado at Boulder
552 UCB
Boulder, Colorado 80309
Phone: 303-492-6301
Fax: 303-492-7115
E-mail: admissions@colorado.edu
Website: http://www.colorado.edu

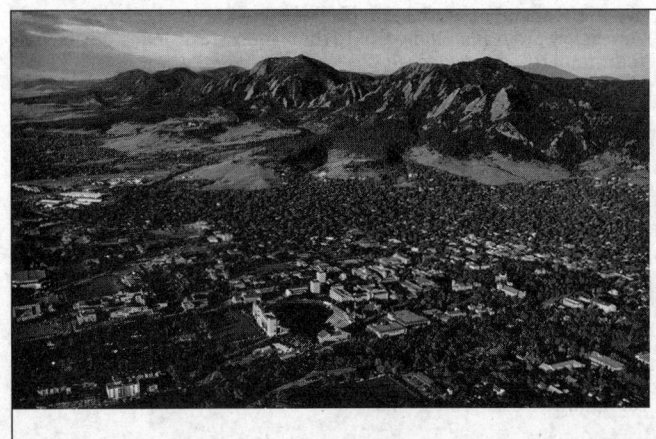

UNIVERSITY OF DENVER
DENVER, COLORADO

The University

Since its founding in 1864—2014 marked a sesquicentennial celebration of 150 years of tradition and legacy—the University of Denver (DU) has grown into one of the West's premier private universities, blending the friendliness and personal attention of a small liberal arts college with the resources and intellectual diversity of an advanced research institution. As the oldest private university in the Rocky Mountain region, the University is home to not only a top-ranked undergraduate program, but also to a number of world-renowned research centers and professional programs, including the Josef Korbel School of International Studies, the Sturm College of Law, and the Daniels College of Business.

The 125-acre campus brings together 5,754 traditional undergraduate students and 5,806 graduate students from 50 states and over 90 countries. In an environment that prizes innovation, cross-disciplinary study, and adventurous learning partnerships, students embark on a personalized educational journey inspired and framed by a spirit of exploration and openness.

Whatever their backgrounds and majors, DU students are engaged and active, taking advantage of the region's many recreation and cultural opportunities—everything from world-class skiing and white-water rafting to award-winning professional theater at the Denver Center for the Performing Arts and alternative music shows at Red Rocks Amphitheatre. On campus, students attend performances at the three-venue Newman Center for the Performing Arts and cheer for the 17 varsity teams that compete in NCAA Division I Athletics at the Ritchie Center for Sports & Wellness. DU has claimed many athletic successes over the years including eight national hockey titles, one lacrosse title, and 24 national championship skiing titles.

The University of Denver is accredited by the Higher Learning Commission. The Carnegie Foundation classifies the University of Denver as a Doctoral/Research University–Extensive.

Location

Located just eight miles from bustling downtown Denver and mere minutes from the Rocky Mountain foothills, the University of Denver's tree-shaded campus is surrounded by pleasant urban neighborhoods offering coffee shops, retail stores, and diverse restaurants. The institution is located along a light-rail line and major bus lines, providing access to the city's arts districts, shopping centers, sports arenas, and an extensive network of parks. DU students can ride all public transportation for free, using their University-supplied CollegePass smart cards.

Majors and Degrees

The University of Denver offers 12 bachelor's degrees in over 100 programs of study, including the arts, business, computer science, engineering, humanities, international studies, mathematics, natural sciences, and social sciences. Students who are interested in pre-professional programs can choose from law, medical, dental, and veterinary programs that prepare them for professional study beyond their undergraduate degree.

In addition, the University offers 4+1 and 3+2 dual-degree programs that allow students to complete both a bachelor's and master's degree in five years or less. These dual-degree programs are offered in education, social work, computer science, engineering, business, art history, international studies, public policy, and geographic information science. There is also a six-year B.A. or B.S./J.D. program in conjunction with DU's Sturm College of Law.

Academic Programs

Undergraduate programs at the University operate on the quarter system and emphasize experiential, dynamic, and cross-disciplinary learning, providing students with the culture and tools to create a positive impact and make meaningful, lasting contributions to their communities and professions.

First-year students enroll in a First-Year Seminar. Limited to 18 students, these seminars focus on a topic that reflects the professor's research interests. This professor, who serves as a mentor throughout the student's first year, introduces the class to university-level work and inquiry, while also advising students on everything from time management to University procedures. The seminar is complemented by a two-quarter writing sequence that trains students to conduct research, construct arguments, and write persuasively for the academic setting. The University's emphasis on writing continues throughout the next three years, with upper-division writing-intensive classes across the disciplines. By the time they graduate, DU students have developed the communication skills that are essential for career success.

Undergraduate students also complete foundations courses in mathematics and computer science, the arts and humanities, natural sciences, and social sciences. DU's Common Curriculum ensures students have a wide base of knowledge upon graduation.

Because the University believes in the value of hands-on learning, students are encouraged to collaborate with faculty members and peers on research projects and creative endeavors. Through the Partners in Scholarship (PinS) program, DU sponsors student work through grants that fund field studies, research trips, and special materials. At year's end, students share their research and findings at a special symposium for their peers.

Thanks to opportunities like these, the University's academic programs earn high marks from students. In the 2016 National Survey of Student Engagement (NSSE), first-year students and seniors at over 500 participating U.S. colleges and universities reported their satisfaction with their own campus. National results revealed that DU students reported significantly higher levels of satisfaction than the average of students at all other participating mid-size private schools for involvement in collaborative learning, quantitative reasoning, reflective and integrative learning, interaction with faculty members, and the quality of interactions on campus.

Off-Campus Programs

To prepare students for the challenges of global citizenship, the University of Denver sponsors Cherrington Global Scholars, a for-credit program that aims to send every eligible junior and senior abroad for at least a quarter of study. The University believes so strongly in this opportunity to expand understanding and foster connections that it ensures qualifying students pay no more for the experience than for a quarter spent on campus. The University budgets about $10 million each year in support of this outstanding program. On average, 70 percent of all DU students participate in study-abroad programs, one of the highest percentages in the nation.

Academic Facilities

The University has invested hundreds of millions of dollars in new buildings and learning centers to ensure that students can prepare for the challenges awaiting them after graduation. These include the Robert and Judi Newman Center for the Performing Arts, home to the University's celebrated Lamont School of Music and host to a performing arts series known for its adventurous offerings; the Daniels College of Business, which houses eleven case-style meeting rooms, nine seminar classrooms, and an Advanced Technology Center; the Knoebel School of Hospitality Management, home to a full-production kitchen, a beverage-management center, a 120-person dining hall, a student-run coffee shop, and a student-faculty-staff commons; and the Anderson Academic Commons, which serves as the library and hub of the University with a central campus location, multimedia software support services, and a full complement of individual and group study areas and rooms. DU recently opened the Daniel Felix Ritchie School of Engineering and Computer Science, which allows dramatic expansion of both current programming and new STEM initiatives, including the Knoebel Center for the Study of Aging as well as the Sie Complex, part of the Korbel School of International Studies. Both facilities make use of state-of-the-art tools to enhance the ability of students to gain the knowledge and skills needed to excel in their careers.

With a state-of-the-art fitness center, a natatorium, a field house, two ice arenas, a gymnastics venue, a lacrosse stadium, a soccer stadium, and a tennis pavilion, the Ritchie Center for Sports and Wellness brings students and members of the Denver community together to exercise, try new sports, and cheer on the Pioneer athletic teams to victory.

Three new physical spaces are scheduled to be completed by fall of 2020 as well, including a first-year residence hall; a Community Commons that will provide a gathering place for students, faculty, staff, and other community members; and the Pioneer Career Achievement Center, which will allow students and alumni to make more robust and intentional connections.

Costs

For the 2018–19 academic year, tuition will be $49,392, fees are estimated at $1,164, and on-campus room and board costs are $13,000, for a total of $63,561. Because the University of Denver is a private institution, costs are the same for in-state and out-of-state students.

Financial Aid

The University of Denver offers two types of financial assistance to students: need-based aid, which includes scholarships, grants, loans, and work-study based on financial need; and merit-based awards, which include scholarships based on merit or special talent. Each year, the Financial Aid office awards over $144 million in need- and merit-based assistance to undergraduate students. About 83 percent of full-time DU undergraduates receive some form of financial assistance.

To recognize achievement in the classroom, the sports arena, leadership, and in music, theatre, and art, the University sponsors a number of merit- and talent-based scholarships. Although the requirements vary from scholarship to scholarship, most are renewable each year if the student maintains a specified minimum GPA. More information regarding scholarships can be found at http://www.du.edu/financialaid.

Need-based financial aid is computed using a number of factors, including family income, assets, size, and the number of family members attending college at the same time. DU utilizes both the CSS Profile and the Free Application for Federal Student Aid (FAFSA) to determine need-based aid. Need-based awards generally combine scholarships, grants, loans, and work-study opportunities from a variety of federal, state, and institutional sources. The financial aid offer may also include any competitive scholarships the student has been awarded at the point of admission. To help determine how much need- and merit-based aid might be available to a prospective student and his or her family, DU offers access to a comprehensive net price calculator, found at www.du.edu/estimator.

The priority deadline for applying for financial aid is November 15 for Early Action and Early Decision I applicants, and February 1 for Regular Decision and Early Decision II applicants. Because financial aid funds are limited, students who complete their financial aid applications in a timely manner are more likely to maximize financial aid resources. The student's financial aid package cannot be determined until he or she is officially admitted to DU. More information on applying for financial aid at DU is available at http://www.du.edu/financialaid.

Faculty

DU professors teach more than 99 percent of undergraduate courses, ensuring students work closely with faculty members and the intensity of the learning environment is maximized. The average class size is 22 students; 80 percent of undergraduate classes have fewer than 30 students and 96 percent of classes have fewer than 50 students.

Committed teachers, innovative researchers, and prolific publishers, University of Denver professors often include undergraduate students in their research projects and fieldwork. It is not uncommon for an undergraduate student to share publication credit with a professor or to participate in groundbreaking research with tangible, transformational benefits for humankind.

Student Government

At the University of Denver, the student population is represented by the Undergraduate Student Government (USG), whose elected representatives participate in the University's legislative process and communicate student interests to the administration. In addition, USG oversees the allocation of the student activities fee and the licensing of DU's 150-plus student organizations. In the past few years this group has worked extensively on matters ranging from sustainability to diversity and academic affairs to spirit on campus.

USG includes senators from each major, each geographic area (on-campus, off-campus), and each class (senior, junior, etc.). The USG Executive Board includes an advisor, graduate advisor, president, vice president, and a cabinet of members.

Admission Requirements

Admission to the University of Denver is selective. Students are evaluated individually on the basis of their academic record, test scores, essay, and recommendations. In making its admission decisions, the University seeks to foster an academic community of geographically, ethnically, and economically diverse learners. The admission committee seeks students who are committed to integrity, innovation, inclusiveness, leadership, academic excellence, and community engagement.

Applicants are required to submit either the Common Application or the DU Pioneer Application—both are posted on the DU website. In addition, applicants are required to submit their high school transcripts, scores from either the SAT or ACT (DU uses the superscore system), an essay, and a high school counselor recommendation. Students may also submit a teacher recommendation and a ZeeMee profile, although neither is required.

Application and Information

The University of Denver offers four application programs for first-year domestic students seeking fall quarter admission. Early Action (deadline of November 1) is a nonbinding program leading to an admission decision in mid-December. Early Decision I (also a November 1 deadline) is a binding program leading to an admission decision in early December. Regular Decision and Early Decision II (deadline of January 15 for both), which are nonbinding and binding respectively, are the final admission programs for fall quarter consideration. Regular Decision applicants and Early Decision II applicants receive their admission decision in early to mid-March.

To learn more about the University of Denver, students should contact:

Undergraduate Admission
University of Denver
2197 South University Boulevard
Denver, Colorado, 80208-9401
United States
Phone: 303-871-2036
E-mail: admission@du.edu
Website: http://www.du.edu/admission
　　　　 http://www.youtube.com/uofdenver
　　　　 http://www.facebook.com/uofdenveradmission
　　　　 http://twitter.com/uofdenver

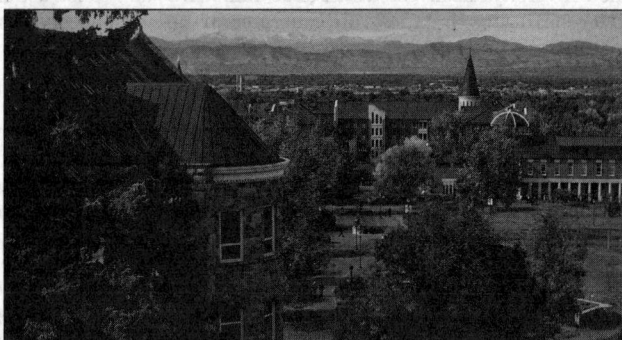

University of Denver

UNIVERSITY OF DUBUQUE
DUBUQUE, IOWA

⭐ To read more about this school, visit http://petersons.to/universityofdubuque

A Tradition of Professional and Theological Training

The University of Dubuque (UD) is a private, Presbyterian professional university that combines a broad study of liberal arts with hands-on experience. Students gain specialized knowledge and master particular skills within their major. Students develop critical abilities that serve them well in adapting to a changing world.

Located about 175 miles from Chicago, the University has been known throughout its 166-year history as a place of hope, opportunity, and promise for students coming from regional, national, and international locations.

UD is one of the most diverse campuses in the Midwest, representing students from 43 states and 22 countries. It is a college of community where Christian commitment, intellectual integrity, and academic excellence are the basis for learning. Students can adjust their mix of liberal arts and professional training in ways that suit their learning styles and that help achieve both personal and professional goals. More information is available online at http://www.dbq.edu/campuslife/officeofstudentlife.

Campus Setting and Surrounding Area

Situated on the Mississippi River where the borders of Wisconsin, Illinois, and Iowa meet, UD is located in Iowa's first city, Dubuque. This central location puts UD students within easy driving distance of cities such as Chicago, Illinois; Des Moines, Iowa; Madison, Wisconsin; and Rochester, Minnesota.

A lively cultural scene, Dubuque is home to the National Mississippi River Museum and Aquarium, the Dubuque Museum of Art, the Grand Opera House, the Dubuque Symphony Orchestra, and a variety of shops, restaurants, and event venues. The city boasts miles of trails for walking, hiking, biking, downhill and cross country skiing opportunities, and many Mississippi waterway and byway activities.

Surrounded by comfortable green spaces within a historic city, UD students enjoy the benefits of modern facilities. Since 1998, the University has invested over $250 million into new construction and renovations that integrate contemporary green spaces within historic architecture.

Required Freshman Courses

The first-year curriculum orients students into the rigor of upper-level course work, while building a community of new friends through the experiences they share with their peers. With the support of an enthusiastic community, new UD students are challenged to build upon their gifts through academic inquiry, social interactions, and spiritual exploration as they discover their place within a diverse campus community. Students and faculty together explore topics that influence global cultures within the context of the University's Christian tradition.

Undergraduate and Graduate Degrees at a Glance

The University of Dubuque developed Diamond, an education model that focuses all classroom learning around four key principles: academics, stewardship, vocation, and community and character. These features of Diamond set the standards for committed faculty and staff involvement, exciting and relevant course content, and inspirational spiritual guidance. Diamond helps students reach their full potential by promoting an environment that is student centered and individually focused. Students are prepared to manage change by building confidence, developing flexibility, and encouraging critical thinking.

The University's 14 departments outline the academic programs found within each area as well as options for interdisciplinary majors. UD also has options for individually designed majors and minors through consultation with academic advisers.

Undergraduate degrees within the Bachelor of Arts area of study include: criminal justice; dance; English; fine and performing arts; liberal studies; music; psychology; religious studies; sociology; sports marketing and management; and theatre.

Undergraduate degrees within the Bachelor of Business Administration field of study include: accounting, business administration, computer information systems, computer information technology, human resource management, and marketing.

Undergraduate degrees within the Bachelor of Science program include: aviation management; biology; communication; digital art and design; chemistry; digital forensics; elementary education; environmental science; flight operations; human health science; mathematics; natural and applied science; secondary education; nursing; pre-professional health science; philosophy; physical education; psychology; sociology; teacher education; and wellness and exercise science.

Graduates are eligible for certification where applicable. For example, the Bachelor of Science degree in Flight Operations is centered on a Pilot Training School certified under FAA 14 CFR Part 141, and prepares students for FAA certification (licensing) and ratings.

All students who complete the UD Teacher Education Program are eligible to apply for an Iowa Initial Teacher License.

Students who graduate with their Bachelor of Science in Nursing are eligible to take the licensure exam NCLEX (National Council [of State Boards of Nursing] Licensure Examination) to become registered nurses.

The University of Dubuque's academic strengths support and align with several prominent needs for graduate education both in the region and globally. Offered in a traditional semester-long course format, courses are taught by both University of Dubuque faculty as well as subject matter experts who are currently in the work world. Degrees include: Master of Arts in Communication, Master of Business Administration, Accelerated Adult MBA and MAC Degree (LIFE), Master in Physician Assistant Studies, and a Master of Arts in Christian Leadership.

The MBA degree gives students advanced business acumen with courses that integrate communication and knowledge management, finance, human capital, organizational management, and business strategy and modeling.

Research Fellowships

The Joseph and Linda Chlapaty Summer Research Fellowship and The Butler Fellowship are two examples of the research opportunities available to UD students. These fellowships help prepare undergraduate students for their postgraduate pursuits, no matter their discipline of study. Each year, over 30 upperclassmen are awarded a fellowship to conduct research over the course of a summer. The University of Dubuque works hard to ensure that these awards cover the costs of research supplies and travel, giving students free reign to explore and inquire within their area of study.

Heeding the Call to Theological Education and Service

The University of Dubuque Theological Seminary (UDTS), a seminary of the Presbyterian Church (U.S.A), is a vibrant and growing ecumenical community, with students and faculty from the Presbyterian Church (U.S.A), the United Methodist Church, the United Church of Christ, the Reformed Church of America, and a number of other denominations and cultures.

The seminary offers a variety of degrees in both residential and distance formats, along with unique programming options. UDTS is the only seminary in the Presbyterian Church (U.S.A) that is accredited by ATS to provide distance education programs, and is the only seminary that is part of a larger university.

UDTS offers three master's degrees: the Master of Divinity and the Master of Arts in Mission and Discipleship, in both residential and distance formats, and together with the larger university, the Master of Arts in Mission and Discipleship program which is offered completely online via distance education. Cooperative programs with the University include the 3/3, and 3/2 programs, along with the Young Adult Ministry Scholars (YAMS) program, which allows students to engage in ministry with young adults while earning either a Master of Divinity or Master of Arts in Mission and Discipleship at the same time. The YAMS program is a 100 percent tuition remission program.

Success Center Provides Every Kind of Help

The University's Academic Success Center connects students with the resources to achieve both academic and personal goals.

Services include individual tutoring, writing, disability accommodations, testing services, academic probation support services, English learning labs, math learning labs, peer-assisted learning study groups, and athletic study tables.

Student Life and Community Service

UD has four traditional residence halls and six apartment-style buildings for undergraduate students living on campus. Townhouses are available for seminary and graduate students.

Activities and events planned by over 60 clubs and organizations supplement students' academic life with valuable experience, fun, and friendship. Out-of-classroom programs provide opportunities for vocational growth, leadership training, community service, and personal development. Greek life also thrives at UD through numerous sororities and fraternities.

UD has been recognized nationally for its history of community service throughout the years. Students participate in service projects they plan both in the classroom and through co-curricular programs, fraternities or sororities, and in campus ministry.

Study Abroad Opportunities

UD Study-Abroad programs bring both long-term (semester) and short-term international experience to students. Students return, even from short study trips, with new knowledge about foreign societies and world viewpoints.

Costs

Tuition (based on a full academic year): $32,670; full-time student fees: $1,440; room and board: $9,780; room only: $4,860.

Academic and Career Guidance, Financial Aid, and ROTC

The University provides academic advising services that empower students to make informed decisions about their academic and professional aspirations. At the beginning of their first year, each student is assigned a Director of Advising who helps them plan their course schedules and enter the University with a platform for success. The University's Center for Vocation and Civic Engagement helps students direct their strengths to real-world experiences outside the college setting. The Center's staff guides students to discover their unique strengths and gifts, providing them with insight into their chosen vocation and directing them toward appropriate internships, potential employers, and possible graduate schools.

Eighty-five percent of UD's students receive financial assistance through scholarships, awards and grants, loans, or work-study programs.

An Army Reserve Officers' Training Corps (ROTC) program is available along with associated merit-based scholarships.

Faculty

UD faculty totals 216. The student-to-faculty ratio is 14:1.

Application Information

All applicants must submit their complete high school transcripts, an essay or personal statement, two letters of recommendation, and a $25 application fee. An average high school GPA of 2.5 is required for first-year students to be regularly admitted. UD offers rolling admissions.

For further information, prospective students should contact:

Robert D. Broshous
Associate Vice President and Dean of Admission
University of Dubuque
2000 University Avenue
Dubuque, Iowa 52001-5009
Phone: 563-589-3199
Fax: 563-589-3690
E-mail: admissns@dbq.edu
Website: http://www.dbq.edu

Heritage Center, the University's fine and performing arts, worship, and campus center, opened in May 2013.

UNIVERSITY OF EVANSVILLE
EVANSVILLE, IN

 For more information, visit http://petersons.to/evansville

The University

The University of Evansville (UE) is a United Methodist Church affiliated institution and maintains a strong relationship with the church. Both share a commitment to inclusiveness which students appreciate. Students also learn the impact of their personal and professional conduct.

Life at UE is diverse from its student body to its distinctive curriculum. UE's 2,514 students come from 44 states and over 50 counties, allowing a lot of interconnection. The curriculum is built on many perspectives. Students gain exposure to great ideas, timeless themes, significant questions, and many worldviews. Faculty members prepare students for success no matter where their careers may take them.

The University of Evansville has earned recognition in several areas. The 2018 *U.S. News & World Report* ranks UE as a best college for study abroad and the top Midwest school for international students, ranks its business and engineering programs among the best at small private universities, cites it as being a military-friendly school, and places it #3 as a best value in the Midwest. Other entities also rank UE as a top college, giving it high marks for value, study-abroad programs, and commitment to service and volunteering.

The University of Evansville is accredited by the Higher Learning Commission (230 South LaSalle Street, Suite 7-500, Chicago, Illinois, 60604-1411; 800-621-7440; hlcommission.org) and specific programs offered by the University of Evansville are accredited by their appropriate specialized professional organizations.

Location

UE is located in Evansville, Indiana, population 122,000, the third-largest city in the state. Evansville is 3 hours from St. Louis, 3 hours from Indianapolis, 2 hours from Nashville, 2 hours from Louisville, and 4 hours from Cincinnati. Major employers in Evansville include Mead Johnson Nutrition, Alcoa, Toyota, Mission Health Systems, T.J. Maxx, Deaconess Hospital, St. Vincent Hospital, and SABIC.

Majors and Degrees

Students can explore a wide selection of more than 80 undergraduate majors and six graduate programs. UE has three colleges and one school within the University: the Schroeder School of Business, the College of Education and Health Sciences, the College of Engineering and Computer Science, and the William L. Ridgway College of Arts and Sciences.

Programs of study include: accounting, archaeology, art (ceramics, painting, pre-art therapy, sculpture, visual communication design), art history, athletic training, baccalaureate to Doctor of Medicine, biochemistry, biology, business, chemistry (chemistry, chemistry-business administration), civil engineering, classical studies, clinical laboratory science, cognitive science, communication (advertising and public relations, health communication, journalism, multimedia, sport communication), computer engineering, computer science, creative writing, criminal justice, economics, education (elementary education, secondary education, special education, transition to teaching, transfer pathway),electrical engineering (biomedical option), English, environmental administration, environmental science, ethics and social change, exercise science (applied exercise science, pre-professional exercise science),finance, foreign languages and cultures (French, German, Greek [instruction], Hebrew [instruction], Latin [instruction], Russian [instruction], Spanish), global business, health services administration, history, international studies, literature, logistics and supply chain management, management, marketing, mathematics (actuarial science application, mathematics, pre-doctoral mathematics), mechanical engineering, music (music–general, music education, music management, music performance, music therapy), neuroscience, nursing (B.S. in Nursing, RN to B.S.N.), philosophy, physical therapy (Doctor of Physical Therapy, physical therapist assistant), physician assistant (Master of Physician Assistant Science), physics, political science, pre-ministry, pre-professional health programs (pre-dentistry, pre-medicine, pre-optometry, pre-pharmacy, pre-veterinary), psychology, public health, religion (pre-ministry),sociology (anthropology, general sociology), software engineering, statistics and data science, theatre (design and technology, stage management, theatre education, theatre generalist, theatre management, theatre performance), and undeclared (Major Discovery).

Academic Programs

Students from a wide range of majors and interests can apply to do undergraduate research through UE's UExplore program. Benefits of doing undergraduate research with UExplore include readiness for graduate school, professional and life experience, contact with faculty, in-depth exploration of topics in which the student has a personal interest, access to research grants, and a summer stipend and housing.

Another unique UE program is ChangeLab, an experiential program that bridges the gap between classroom instruction and real-world needs. Students join multidisciplinary teams to work side-by-side with top organizations on relevant, contemporary issues. Faculty coaches and outside experts guide participants on producing practical outcomes for their clients.

The ChangeLab program gives students opportunities to use their skills on real-world projects to make a positive impact. They can take an interdisciplinary approach and work alongside students in other majors. Participating in ChangeLab helps students gain confidence and acquire marketable skills.

UE's Honors Program offers students many benefits including special housing, early registration for classes, special networking opportunities, and the camaraderie of peers who enjoy being intellectually engaged. Honors students are eligible to apply for Honors Program research grants, given each year to support excellent research by Honors Program students.

Off-Campus Programs/Harlaxton College

The University of Evansville is nationally recognized for its dedication to international education. UE students can study in several countries, including England, Spain, Mexico, New Zealand, Israel, and others, giving students the opportunity to discover an interconnected global society and become vested participants in it.

The Harlaxton College study-abroad program in Grantham, England, is ranked as the number one study-abroad program in the nation (bestcollegereviews.org). Harlaxton College is a 100-room Victorian manor house in the rolling English countryside. It is not far outside of London, which allows students to experience both the country and metropolitan area. Students share the manor with a community of committed faculty and supportive staff. They can connect with fellow students from UE and partner colleges. There is also opportunity to have personal family visits.

The key part of the Harlaxton College curriculum is a British studies course which combines lectures, seminars, and travel for an interdisciplinary introduction to British life and culture.

Disciplines include literature, art history, economics, history, and political science. To further enhance the experience, the course is taught by British faculty. Courses from a wide range of other disciplines are also available, such as humanities, social science, engineering, and nursing.

Harlaxton students have many opportunities for experiential learning and can explore Britain their way. They may take part in the Meet-a-Family program to experience local life and there are a variety of sporting events where students can play with the locals. Students can also travel throughout the UK and Europe to gain personal experiences with different cultures and histories.

Harlaxton College offers a five-week summer session each year. The summer program has a wide-ranging curriculum and weekend travel opportunities.

Academic Facilities

The UE campus covers 75 acres and includes 31 major buildings. Olmsted Administration Hall is the oldest building on campus.

Two libraries provide information and research services that support the schools, colleges, and research of the University. The Clifford Memorial Library and the Bower-Suhrheinrich Library offer more than 22,000 unique e-journals, 170,000 e-books, 230,000 books and bound volumes, nearly 100 research databases, and 16 group study rooms and collaborative spaces.

Costs

For the 2018–19 academic year, full-time tuition at UE is $35,300 and fees for full-time students total $1,116. There is an additional cost of $1,640 per year for music majors. The average room and meal plan is $12,460 and books are estimated at $1,200 per academic year. Costs for transportation and additional living and personal expenses varies by student.

Financial Aid

The University of Evansville Office of Financial Aid provides personalized financial aid services to students and their families. All students are encouraged to file the Free Application for Federal Student Aid (FAFSA) to determine all available sources of financial aid for which they are eligible.

UE is proud that 100 percent of domestic freshman students receive merit-based scholarships. The average financial aid and scholarship package is $29,727. In addition to these scholarships, students may qualify for grants, loans, and work-study.

Faculty

UE's dedicated and qualified faculty is committed to serving the student population; there are no graduate assistants teaching any classes. Eighty-six percent of full-time faculty hold a doctorate or terminal degree. The average class size is 18 and the student-faculty ratio is 12:1, allowing students the opportunity to work closely with and get to know their professors.

Student Life

UE seeks to provide students with more than just housing, but rather a dynamic living community that enriches the college experience. The University of Evansville offers students a wide variety of options for on-campus living, with seven residence halls featuring living arrangements to suit each student's needs. The UE residential experience provides plenty of opportunities to support academic pursuits, personal growth, community involvement, and the chance to form lifelong friendships.

Students have access to a wide range of sports and exercise equipment and facilities at the Student Fitness Center. Other student services include a career center, health center, and counseling services. Religious life activities challenge students to articulate their own values and beliefs while at the same time appreciating the beliefs of others.

UE's Center for Student Engagement offers countless opportunities to meet and connect with students who share your hobbies and interests. There are more than 120 student groups on campus and 24 percent of the student body is socially Greek affiliated.

Admission Requirements

UE utilizes the Common Application. Candidates for admission to UE are expected to have studied a rigorous college preparatory curriculum, which includes high school subjects, at the minimum: English, 4 years; math, 3 years (4 highly recommended); lab sciences, 3 years (chemistry required for engineering and nursing); social sciences, 3 years; and foreign language, 2 years recommended, but not required for admission consideration.

Students applying for admission to the University of Evansville will be required to submit results from either the ACT Assessment with the ACT Writing Test, the SAT-I (critical reading, math, and writing), or the new SAT-R. Because UE values academic achievement, character, and initiative, it is optional for most applicants to submit their scores with their applications. Students must select test optional on their initial application to the University of Evansville. By selecting test optional, students will be reviewed based on the high school transcript to include but not limited to GPA, curriculum, and graduation track (AP, IB, Honors, etc.). In addition, students selecting test optional will be required to submit an essay. Test optional is unavailable for homeschooled students as well as applicants to the following programs: baccalaureate to M.D., direct-entry nursing, direct-entry physician assistant, direct-entry physical therapy, and engineering majors (except computer science).

All applicants are recommended to submit an essay of 250–500 words. Students interested in direct-entry physical therapy, direct-entry physician assistant, or physical therapist assistant are required to submit a program-specific essay.

Application and Information

The Early Action application deadline is December 1; admission and scholarship decisions will be mailed no later than December 15. Admission and scholarships will be offered on a space-available basis after December 1.

Students interested in the physical therapy, physician assistant, or nursing direct entry programs must submit a completed Application for Admission and Scholarship to UE by November 1, 2018.

Prospective students are encouraged to visit the campus and can do so by contacting:

University of Evansville
1800 Lincoln Avenue
Evansville, Indiana 47722
Phone: 812-488-2000, 833-232-6223
Fax: 812-488-4076
E-mail: admission@evansville.edu
Website: www.evansville.edu

UNIVERSITY OF MAINE
ORONO, MAINE

 For more information, visit http://petersons.to/universityofmaine

The University

The University of Maine (UMaine) offers the extensive academic opportunities expected from a major research university, with the close-knit feel of a small college. The University of Maine is Maine's Flagship University, offering the most comprehensive academic experience in the state. There are nearly 100 majors and academic programs, 75 master's degree programs, and 35 doctoral programs. All majors benefit from a strong foundation in the liberal arts. Top students are invited to join the Honors College, one of the country's oldest and most prestigious honors colleges in the nation. UMaine is also the state's only public research university, housing facilities with an international reputation for excellence. UMaine students have extraordinary opportunities to gain real-world experience through research and experiential learning. Undergraduates have the opportunity to collaborate with faculty, conduct fieldwork, and participate in internships around the world. Wildlife ecology majors learn about animal behavior by working in the field with wildlife biologists and black bear cubs. Many engineering students secure co-ops that typically lead to employment immediately after graduation. Education majors have the opportunity to take advantage of urban, rural, and international student-teaching opportunities. There are over 200 student organizations, such as the student investment club that manages a $2.3-million real-money portfolio, Greek Life, Division I athletics, and many more.

Location

There's no place like Maine. UMaine students are surrounded by the great outdoors and have ample opportunity to explore everything the state has to offer. Orono is nestled between the Stillwater and Penobscot rivers. The campus has a traditional New England feel with ivy-covered brick buildings, towering pines, and beautiful fall foliage. Some of the best skiing in the Northeast is within easy driving distance. Beautiful tourist attractions such as Bar Harbor, Acadia National Park, Baxter State Park, and the northern terminus of the Appalachian Trail are just a short drive from campus. The University of Maine is 10 minutes from the city of Bangor, Maine's third-largest city, with its own international airport.

Majors and Degrees

UMaine offers nearly 100 majors and programs across six colleges at the undergraduate level: the College of Education and Human Development; College of Engineering; College of Liberal Arts and Sciences; College of Natural Sciences, Forestry, and Agriculture; the Maine Business School; and the Honors College. In addition, UMaine offers the Explorations program, designed to help undecided students identify a major across the vast academic opportunities available and find the best fit for a degree program. The Division of Lifelong Learning offers online classes, Summer University, Winter Session, and distance-learning opportunities for students who need a flexible class schedule.

Academic Programs

UMaine provides a comprehensive academic and student experience, yielding graduates who are well-educated, well-adjusted, and well-prepared to succeed after graduation and assume leadership roles within their respective careers. The University seeks to foster excellence and innovation through inspired, dedicated teaching by ensuring there is a constant discovery of new knowledge for students. In addition to their major or concentration within their degree programs, University of Maine students benefit from a solid liberal arts foundation. Students develop and refine the qualities needed to fully engage with the world around them, regardless of their academic discipline.

Undergraduate research is a major component of the learning atmosphere. The University of Maine offers students true hands-on research experience, as early as their first year on campus. UMaine is the state's largest research university, providing rich and diverse opportunities for undergraduates to publish findings, travel the globe, and work alongside UMaine's world-class scholars and researchers. The Center for Undergraduate Research connects students with faculty projects applicable to their academic interests and future careers. The abundance of research opportunities also provides students with great mentoring connections between faculty and students that carry benefits beyond the classroom. The skills students develop through research creates applicants who are much more competitive in the workplace and graduate school.

Campus Programs

Students will get a full and enriching college experience at UMaine. The University of Maine hosts many on-campus programs and opportunities for students to explore and meet new people. There are over 200 clubs and organizations for students to get involved in, such as Greek Life, Woodsmen's Team, Robotics Club, Spanish Club, and more. The Campus Activities Board also puts on free events during the school year, including movies, karaoke, game nights, and astronomy shows. Students can join an athletic team or cheer the UMaine Black Bears Division I teams to victory for free during the year.

There are many ways to explore Maine off campus as well through outdoor recreation, music and food festivals, museums, and much more. Bangor, a 10-minute drive from campus, hosts Summer Concerts in the Park, the American Folk Festival, and a state fair.

Through UMaine study-abroad programs, students explore globally while enhancing their education by taking courses, researching or volunteering. UMaine students have traveled to China to study emerging financial markets, to Italy to learn about Renaissance art history, to Turkey to study film, and to Brazil to look at our world's diverse ecosystem.

Academic Facilities

The University of Maine is home to state-of-the-art research facilities, classrooms, and teaching laboratories. Fogler Library is the state's largest library and located in the heart of campus. It houses more than 1.4 million volumes, 1.6 million microforms, and 2.3 million U.S. and Canadian government publications. It's also the archive of papers written by famous UMaine Alumnus Stephen King. Students have access to UMaine's new Capital Markets Training Laboratory with state-of-the-art technology and 12 Bloomberg Terminals that provide hands-on learning in finance. The Virtual Environment and Multimodal Interaction Laboratory (VEMI) is a research facility that combines fully immersive virtual reality with augmented reality technologies in an integrated research and development environment. Students from all interests and majors collaborate in VEMI Lab research in areas such as aging, vision impairment, and virtual realities. The new, multi-million-dollar Innovative Media Research and Commercialization Center (IMRC) and the Wyeth Family Studio Art Center contain facilities for training, research, development, and commercialization. Students have access to many different labs, such as a fabrication studio, electronics lab, audio and video production labs, 3-D printing and design, and prototype production.

The University of Maine is also a cultural hub. It is home to the region's premier performing arts center, the Collins Center for the Arts, as well as several museums and galleries.

Costs

For the 2018–19 academic year, tuition for in-state undergraduate students is estimated at $8,580, and $27,960 for out-of-state residents. Canadian residents and students who qualify for the New England Regional Program (NEBHE) will pay an estimated $13,740 for tuition. The average credit load for full-time students is 15 credit hours per semester or 30 credit hours for the academic year. Required university fees are estimated at $2,322 per year for a full-time student. These fees include a variety of healthcare services and admission to cultural, recreational, and athletic events. Books and supplies cost, on average, about $1,000, and room and board estimated cost is $10,144 for one academic year.

Financial Aid

UMaine requires all financial aid applicants to file the Free Application for Federal Student Aid (FAFSA). The priority deadline to apply for aid is March 1. Awards usually consist of a combination of several types of aid, ranging from grants and scholarships to work-study jobs and student loans. Students are encouraged to apply by the Early Action deadline of December 1 to ensure admission in selective academic programs and receive merit scholarships based on high school achievement, as demonstrated by high school rank, grade point average, and standardized test results (SAT and ACT). Additional information on application deadlines and merit scholarships is available online at go.umaine.edu.

Faculty

UMaine is known for its beautiful and vast campus, large student body, and family atmosphere. Students will get to know each other quickly, but even more importantly, so will their professors. UMaine's professors have an open-door policy and encourage students to meet with them outside of class. Undergraduate classes are taught by professors, and many faculty go on to be academic and professional mentors for their students. Students have the opportunity to work alongside UMaine's renowned scholars and scientists in research and other academic ventures.

Student Government

Student Government, Inc. is the independent representative body for UMaine's undergraduate students. An elected president, vice president, and vice president of financial affairs direct and coordinate student clubs and programs at the University of Maine. Student Government works closely with the Office of the Vice President for Student Life and appoints 200 student representatives to various university committees. These students assist with the planning and implementation of residence hall programs, student discipline, athletics, and cultural activities on campus.

Admission Requirements

Admission to the University of Maine is a highly competitive and selective process. Successful applicants hold high scholastic achievement, intellectual curiosity, and extracurricular involvement that promise success at the University of Maine. The holistic selection process looks at the strength of the high school curriculum, grades received, class rank, counselor recommendation, and SAT or ACT scores for admission consideration. Additional information such as essays and community involvement may help the admissions committee evaluate student applications. UMaine recognizes advanced work completed in secondary schools in Advanced Placement tests, honors, or higher education courses. Students who pass examinations may be exempt from certain courses at UMaine.

Application and Information

Applicants may submit electronic or paper versions of the Common Application or the University of Maine Mobile Application. Required documents for all applicants include official high school or college transcripts, counselor recommendations, and SAT or ACT scores. Students above the age of 25 do not need to submit SAT or ACT test scores. Students are encouraged to apply by December 1 to ensure admission in selective academic programs and receive merit scholarship–based application review. More information on application deadlines and merit scholarships can be found on the University's website at go.umaine.edu. Applications and all supporting documents (i.e. SAT or ACT scores, transcripts, essays, etc.) should be sent to UMS Processing, P.O. Box 412, Bangor, ME 04402-0412.

For additional information on the application process, prospective students can contact the Office of Admissions at 207-581-1561 or umaineadmissions@maine.edu.

Office of Admissions
5713 Chadbourne Hall
University of Maine
Orono, Maine 04469-5713
Phone: 207-581-1561
Fax: 207-581-1213
E-mail: umaineadmissions@maine.edu
Website: go.umaine.edu
       facebook.com/UMaineAdmissions
       twitter.com@GoUMaine
       instagram.com@university.of.maine
       linkedin.com/edu/school?id=18586
       pinterest.com/GoUMaine/

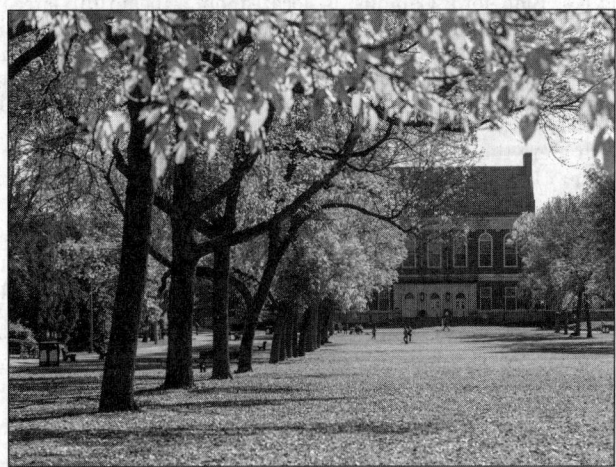

The Mall is the heart of the University of Maine campus.

UNIVERSITY OF NEW ENGLAND
BIDDEFORD AND PORTLAND, MAINE AND TANGIER, MOROCCO

★ To read more about this school, visit http://petersons.to/une

The University

The University of New England (UNE) is Maine's largest private university, an innovative educational community with two distinctive coastal Maine campuses, a vibrant new campus in Tangier, Morocco and a robust offering of degree and certificate programs online. UNE attracts internationally recognized scholars in the health sciences, life sciences, business, education, the social sciences, and the humanities, allowing both graduate and undergraduate students to engage in research and scholarship alongside dedicated faculty.

UNE is home to Maine's only medical and dental schools—part of a comprehensive health education mission built on a pioneering interprofessional approach that also includes pharmacy, nursing and an array of allied health professions. UNE offers an interdisciplinary academic environment with an emphasis on global engagement and hands-on learning experiences. As a community, UNE is committed to creating the future by nurturing well-rounded scholars and professionals who can adapt, prosper and lead in a rapidly evolving world.

UNE's 8,281 students are enrolled in a wide variety of academic programs at the undergraduate, graduate, and professional levels in six colleges: the College of Arts and Sciences, the College of Dental Medicine, the College of Osteopathic Medicine, the College of Pharmacy, the Westbrook College of Health Professions, and the online College of Graduate and Professional Studies. At the undergraduate level, UNE has approximately 2,377 students enrolled, from 39 different states, in more than 40 undergraduate degree programs.

UNE traces its history to 1831 with the founding of Westbrook College, one of Maine's oldest institutions of learning. Today's University represents a union of three unique higher education institutions through the combining of St. Francis College and the New England College of Osteopathic Medicine in 1978 and Westbrook College in 1996.

Location

UNE's Biddeford Campus is located on a beautiful site in Biddeford, Maine, where the Saco River meets the Atlantic Ocean. With more than 4,000 feet of water frontage, enjoying the ocean comes naturally to students. The campus is home to the College of Arts and Sciences and the College of Osteopathic Medicine, which offers the Doctor of Osteopathic Medicine (D.O.). With more than 540 acres, the Biddeford Campus is also home to the Harold Alfond Center for Health Sciences, a modern 80,000-square-foot science education facility, the Marine Science Center, and the Harold Alfond Forum.

UNE's quintessential historic New England campus in the city of Portland is home to the College of Dental Medicine, the College of Pharmacy, and the Westbrook College of Health Professions, which offers undergraduate programs in dental hygiene and nursing, among others, and graduate programs in nurse anesthesia, occupational therapy, physical therapy, physician assistant, public health, and social work. The College of Dental Medicine is housed in the state-of-the-art Oral Health Center. The 41-acre Portland Campus is also home to the Center for Global Humanities, the Art Gallery, and the Maine Women Writers Collection.

UNE's third campus is in Tangier, Morocco, and offers students the opportunity to spend a semester or academic year abroad, taking English-language classes in their regular courses of study while discovering the culture of Morocco and the city of Tangier at no additional cost. UNE's campus location offers easy access to downtown, the main beach, and the major cultural activities the city has to offer.

Majors and Degrees

UNE offers highly competitive undergraduate and graduate programs in a variety of areas.

UNE's undergraduate majors include animal behavior, applied exercise science, applied mathematics, applied social and cultural studies, aquaculture and aquarium science, art and design media, art education, athletic training, biochemistry, biological sciences, business, chemistry, communications, dental hygiene, elementary/middle education, English, environmental science, environmental studies, global studies, health, wellness and occupational studies, history, interdisciplinary studies in the humanities, laboratory science, marine affairs, marine entrepreneurship, marine sciences, medical biology (pre-dental medicine, pre-medicine, pre-optometry, pre–physician assistant, and pre–veterinary medicine), neuroscience, nursing, nutrition, political science, pre-pharmacy, pre–physical therapy, psychology, public health, secondary education, social work, sociology, sport and recreation management, and sustainability and business.

Master's degree programs include applied nutrition, athletic training, biological sciences, education, health informatics, marine sciences, nurse anesthesia, occupational therapy, physician assistant, public health, and social work.

Doctorates offered include dental medicine (D.M.D.), education leadership (Ed.D.), osteopathic medicine (D.O.), pharmacy (Pharm.D.), and physical therapy (D.P.T.).

Academic Programs

UNE's academic programs ensure that students have plenty of opportunities for extensive fieldwork, clinical experiences, research, internships, and global experiences at both the undergraduate and graduate levels. All undergraduate programs at UNE have a core curriculum that provides a foundation in the liberal arts. The core reflects the values of each college and is designed to prepare students for living informed, thoughtful, and active lives in a complex and changing society.

The Student Academic Success Center provides a comprehensive array of academic support services including placement testing, courses, workshops, tutoring, and individual consultations. The Office of Career Services provides academic and career exploration assistance, assistance in applying to graduate schools, self-assessment and personal interest exploration, resume help, and information and access to job listings and job fairs.

Off-Campus Programs

UNE is committed to supplementing the traditional learning process with practical applications. All students are encouraged to participate in cooperative education programs, field placements, and practicums. These experiences are required for graduation by most majors and provide valuable learning situations that increase a student's exposure to job-related opportunities. Students also have the opportunity for vibrant study-abroad experiences. Students can enjoy a semester abroad at UNE's Morocco campus or with partner universities in Spain, France, and Iceland for about the same cost as a semester in Maine. Courses are offered in the sciences, humanities, social sciences, business, and the arts and are taught in English by the host university. Faculty-led short-term travel courses offer other exciting opportunities to study abroad.

Student Organizations and Activities

The University offers a variety of cultural and social events and encourages students to become involved in activities, clubs, and sports. Popular interests include scuba diving, skiing, hiking, biking, varsity and intramural sports, swimming, surfing, music, theater, community service, and student leadership development programs. Opportunities for such activities are available at on-campus facilities, including the Campus Center and the Harold Alfond Forum, a 106,000-square-foot facility featuring an ice hockey rink, basketball court, classroom and lab space, fitness center, and multipurpose courts.

UNE's Department of Athletics operates an NCAA Division III varsity athletics program. Varsity sports for men are basketball, cross-country, golf, ice hockey, lacrosse, and soccer. Football will see its first varsity action beginning in 2018. Varsity sports for women are basketball, cross-country, field hockey, ice hockey, lacrosse, rugby, soccer, softball, swimming, and volleyball.

Academic Facilities

Both the Biddeford and Portland Campuses feature buildings with a variety of uses to support the needs of the University community. On the Biddeford Campus, classroom and office spaces are housed in several facilities across campus. Several research facilities are on campus, including the Marine Science Center; the Harold Alfond Center for Health Sciences, with biology and chemistry labs as well as lecture halls, classrooms, a gross anatomy lab, and UNE's medical school facilities; the Pickus Center for Biomedical Research; and Peter and Cécile Morgane Hall, a science center providing additional classrooms and an undergraduate teaching laboratory. The Danielle N. Ripich Commons offers study areas, relaxation spaces, a fire pit, outdoor patios, and a one-stop-shopping venue for student services—from academic advising to career services to financial aid.

On the Portland Campus, Ludcke Auditorium is used for a variety of academic programs. Coleman Dental Hygiene Building houses classroom, clinic, and faculty space. The Blewett Science Center, home to UNE's nursing program, consists of science labs and classrooms. UNE's Interprofessional Simulation and Innovation Center, which provides customized training and education for students and health professionals, is also on the Portland Campus. Proctor Hall is a classroom building and is home to the Proctor Learning and Career Center. The Josephine S. Abplanalp Library houses study space and a computer lab, as well as the Maine Women Writers Collection. The College of Pharmacy is a LEED-certified academic and research facility with teaching and research laboratories and a lecture hall. The College of Dental Medicine has its administration offices in historic Goddard Hall and its clinical home, the Oral Health Center, is a teaching clinic and simulation facility.

Faculty

The personal attention students receive from faculty both in and out of class, and the quality of faculty as experts in their fields are key strengths of the UNE experience. Students appreciate their faculty members as mentors, and trust them as accomplished scholars who impact their fields. From designing coastal trails and restoring wetlands on campus to caring for patients in need, UNE faculty members not only work side-by-side with their students, but are recognized by their peers and other leaders for their expertise. UNE faculty members are national award recipients, Fulbright scholars, authors, and world-class researchers, and they share their knowledge unselfishly with their students.

Costs

The costs for undergraduate students per academic year for 2017–18 were: tuition, $35,240; room and board, $13,580; and fees, $1,290.

Financial Aid

Approximately 98 percent of all full-time students received some form of financial assistance. The average package exceeds $24,000 including scholarships, grants, loans, and employment. The University of New England has an extensive academic scholarship program. Merit awards range from $4,000 to $20,000 per year.

Admission Requirements

Students applying for admission should submit a completed application, a $40 nonrefundable application fee, transcripts of all academic work (high school and college), and scores on either the ACT or SAT. Students who do not use English as their primary language must submit TOEFL scores. Students applying for admission should have completed a curriculum that includes English, mathematics, science, and social sciences. International students must also complete the International Student Supplemental Application. All prospective students are strongly encouraged to visit the University of New England at an open house or for an information session and tour. Information sessions and tours are held daily Monday through Friday; Saturday tours are also available. Prospective students can register for a tour at www.une.edu/visit.

Application and Information

The undergraduate freshman admission application deadline is February 15. Applications received after that date are reviewed on a space-available basis. There is a nonbinding December 1 early action application deadline with a December 31 notification date. Applications for the spring term are accepted through December 1.

For application information, students should contact:
University of New England
Office of Undergraduate Admissions
11 Hills Beach Road
Biddeford, Maine 04005
Phone: 207-602-2847
       800-477-4863 (toll-free)
Fax: 207-602-5900
E-mail: admissions@une.edu
Website: www.une.edu

With 4,000 feet of water frontage on UNE's Biddeford Campus, students' education and college experiences are enriched both inside and outside the classroom.

UNIVERSITY OF NEW HAVEN
WEST HAVEN, CONNECTICUT

 To read more about this school, visit http://petersons.to/universityofnewhaven

The University

The University of New Haven's mission is to prepare career-ready graduates for meaningful roles in today's global economy and to nurture the pursuit of lifelong learning. Founded in 1920, the University of New Haven is a private, independent institution focused on combining experience-based learning with liberal arts and sciences. The University is committed to student success through educational innovation, continuous improvement in career and professional education, and support of scholarship and personal development. The main campus moved to its present location in West Haven in 1960 and has since rapidly expanded its programs, facilities, and faculty, attracting a student body that now stands at over 6,800—including the current enrollment of 4,600 full-time undergraduates.

The University is fully accredited by the New England Association of Schools and Colleges (NEASC). Individual programs, departments, and schools hold various forms of national and professional accreditations, including the American Bar Association, American Dental Association, Forensic Science Education Programs Accreditation Commission, National Association of Schools of Art and Design, and the Association to Advance Collegiate Schools of Business. In addition, seven of the University of New Haven's bachelor's degree programs—chemical, civil, electrical, computer, industrial and systems, mechanical engineering, and computer science—are fully accredited by the Engineering Accreditation Commission of the Accreditation Board for Engineering and Technology, Inc. (EAC/ABET).

The main campus is in West Haven, Connecticut, on a hillside close to Long Island Sound. The main campus houses four academic colleges: the College of Arts and Sciences, the College of Business, the Tagliatela College of Engineering, and the Henry C. Lee College of Criminal Justice and Forensic Sciences. The University of New Haven also operates four satellite campuses: the Lyme Academy College of Fine Arts in Old Lyme, Connecticut; a graduate business campus in Orange, Connecticut; the M.S. National Security campus in Albuquerque, New Mexico; and an international campus in Prato, Italy. Following the addition of the Graduate School in 1969, New Haven College was designated a university. Thirty master's degree programs attract full- and part-time graduate students, while just over 100 associate and bachelor's degree programs are available to entering freshmen and transfer students in a great variety of academic disciplines.

Other main campus buildings include the Marvin K. Peterson Library, the Henry C. Lee Institute of Forensic Science, the Bayer Hall admissions building, the Campus Bookstore, new residence halls and apartments, and Bartels Hall, the campus center, which houses one of the dining facilities and student activities. Across the street from main campus is the Dental Hygiene Clinic and North Hall, which houses the arson investigation labs. The Charger Gymnasium, blue and gold turf of the football stadium, and athletic fields are located on the North Campus, just two short blocks from Maxcy Hall, the historic main administration building.

The University of New Haven has one of the most respected and successful NCAA Division II athletics programs in the country, with Charger teams combining to make over 120 post-season tournament appearances. The University is a member of the Northeast-10 Conference, one of the most prestigious and celebrated conferences in the nation. The University of New Haven and its student athletes have won numerous conference, regional, and national awards, both athletically and academically. The University offers seventeen varsity sports: men's baseball, basketball, cross-country, football, soccer, indoor and outdoor track and field; and women's basketball, cross-country, field hockey, lacrosse, soccer, softball, tennis, indoor and outdoor track and field, and volleyball.

Over 65 percent of the full-time undergraduate students live on campus in thirteen residence halls. More than 170 clubs and organizations are available to students. Included are student chapters of professional societies, religious organizations, social groups, special-interest clubs, student councils, cultural groups, and fraternities and sororities.

Location

West Haven is contiguous to New Haven. There are theaters that attract star performers from the entertainment world, a harbor and beaches, fine restaurants, museums, and galleries in the area. Numerous social and cultural programs are presented by the many colleges and universities in the area. New Haven is served by a local airport and major railroads, and its location at the junction of two interstate highways places the University of New Haven within easy driving distance of New York, Boston, Cape Cod, and the ski areas of New England.

Majors and Degrees

The College of Arts and Sciences offers a Bachelor of Arts degree in art, communication, English, global studies, history, marine affairs, mathematics, music, music and sound recording, music industry, political science, theater, and psychology; a Bachelor of Fine Arts degree in graphic design and interior design; and a Bachelor of Science degree in biology, communication, genetics and biotechnology, dental hygiene, environmental science, legal studies, marine biology, mathematics, music and sound recording, and nutrition and dietetics.

The College of Business offers the Bachelor of Science degree in accounting, business management, economics, finance, hospitality and tourism management, international business, marketing, and sport management. In addition, the College of Business offers a fast-track 3+1 study program allowing academically strong students the opportunity to earn a Bachelor of Science degree in business and a Master of Business Administration (M.B.A.) in just four years.

The Tagliatela College of Engineering offers a Bachelor of Science degree in chemical engineering, chemistry, civil engineering, computer engineering, computer science, cyber security and networks, electrical engineering, general engineering, industrial and systems engineering, and mechanical engineering.

The Henry C. Lee College of Criminal Justice and Forensic Sciences offers a Bachelor of Science degree in criminal justice, fire science, forensic science, national security studies, and paramedicine.

The Lyme Academy College of Fine Arts offers a Bachelor of Fine Arts degree in drawing, illustration, painting, and sculpture.

Academic Programs

The University of New Haven offers a broad range of programs in both liberal arts and professional areas. Experiential learning is emphasized, and there are diverse and numerous opportunities for internships, cooperative education, independent study, and industrial projects. Professional experiences are required for graduation in a number of degree programs. The University provides student-support services including the Center for

Student Success, Career Development, and a Center for Learning Resources, offering tutoring service open to all students.

The undergraduate division operates on a 4-1-4 calendar. Credit is given for successful scores on International Baccalaureate and Advanced Placement examinations. The University honors program provides outstanding study opportunities for high-achieving students. The residency requirement for all degrees is 30 credit hours.

The University of New Haven believes that all students pursuing a bachelor's degree should develop a common set of skills; its goal is to prepare all graduates for the complex lives they will lead in a changing world. This can best be done through the University Core Curriculum, which consists of a minimum of 40 credit hours in nine basic competencies.

Academic Facilities

The Marvin K. Peterson Library contains more than 400,000 volumes in hard copy and provides access to about 20,000 electronic books and 20,000 e-journals from the library website and Voyager online catalog. Databases are available on a wide variety of subjects, with a focus on business, criminal justice/forensic science, engineering, and psychology, as well as general arts and sciences. Through interlibrary loan services, the University community has access to the holdings of more than 8,650 other libraries. The building also includes study and social spaces on the upper levels.

The communication program allows students to utilize professional equipment and software in the Laurel Vlock Center for Convergent Media, as well as on-campus field and studio production labs, editing labs, a fully equipped television studio, and an award-winning radio station (WNHU 88.7 FM).

The University's Marine Biology students benefit from the brand-new 6,000 square-foot Marine Sciences Center built on the historic site of New Haven's Canal Dock shipping pier. The facility is built on a floating dock and features state-of-the-art marine research and teaching labs, a large wet lab, boathouse, and direct waterfront access.

The Tagliatela College of Engineering features labs with state-of-the-art hardware and software, including a Solar Testing and Training laboratory and University Makerspace. The University's cross-disciplinary cyber security and networks program allows students to experience virtual reality technology in the Cyber Forensics Research and Education Lab. Facilities for the internationally recognized forensic science and criminal justice programs were expanded with the addition of a Crime Scene Training House. This unique learning space allows faculty to replicate crime scenes and then use cameras to monitor each room as students independently process the scene from start to finish.

Costs

Full-time undergraduate tuition for the 2018–19 academic year, including all fees, is $38,170; room and board costs total $15,310.

Financial Aid

The University of New Haven offers a comprehensive financial aid program that includes University resources as well as state, federal, and private-aid programs. Approximately 95 percent of full-time undergraduate students receive some form of assistance. Students receive federal aid through the Federal Pell Grant, Federal Supplemental Educational Opportunity Grant, Federal Work-Study, Federal Direct Student Loan, and Federal Direct PLUS loan programs. The University also administers programs sponsored by the state of Connecticut for Connecticut residents attending the University. Some students also qualify for financial aid from other states and from private companies, organizations, and foundations.

Faculty

The University of New Haven prides itself that the majority of its full-time faculty members (more than 90 percent) hold terminal degrees in their disciplines. No classes are taught by teaching assistants. Faculty are available for students to meet with for advisement as well as collaborate with on undergraduate research. There are over 270 full-time and 400 part-time faculty members, making the student-faculty ratio 16:1.

Student Government

The Undergraduate Student Government Association supervises annual expenditures by undergraduate clubs and organizations, directs liaison committees, supports student publications and the student-operated FM radio station, and schedules cultural and social events. Student representatives are elected annually to the University's Board of Governors.

Admission Requirements

To be eligible for admission, one must be a high school graduate or present evidence of equivalent preparation and have submitted all necessary application documents for consideration. The admissions decision is based on an applicant's high school transcript, SAT or ACT scores, letter(s) of recommendation, and personal essay. The transfer admissions decision is based on an applicant's college transcript(s) and personal essay. Out-of-state residents are considered for admission on the same basis as in-state residents. The University of New Haven does not discriminate on the basis of age, color, sex, religion, race, sexual orientation, national origin, or disability in admission or treatment of students, administration or distribution of financial aid, or recruitment of employees.

Application and Information

To apply to the University of New Haven, one must submit a completed application via the Common Application (with $50 fee), official records of all academic enrollment, SAT or ACT results, a letter of recommendation (from an academic source), and a personal essay (250–650 words). International students are required to demonstrate proficiency in English and provide documentation of financial support. Applications are considered on a rolling admissions basis with the opportunity to apply for early action, early decision, and regular decision.

For more information, contact:

Office of Undergraduate Admissions
University of New Haven
300 Boston Post Road
West Haven, Connecticut 06516
Phone: 203-932-7319
E-mail: admissions@newhaven.edu
Website: http://www.newhaven.edu

Maxcy Hall on the campus of the University of New Haven.

THE UNIVERSITY OF NORTH CAROLINA WILMINGTON

WILMINGTON, NORTH CAROLINA

 To read more about this school, visit http://petersons.to/northcarolinawilmington

The University

The University of North Carolina Wilmington (UNCW), a public, comprehensive university, combines a small-college commitment to excellence in teaching with a research university's opportunities for student involvement in significant faculty scholarship. The University provides a personal learning environment that integrates teaching and mentoring with research and service, and promotes cultural diversity, community engagement, and individual growth and development. The school was named among 2016's Best Southeastern Schools by The Princeton Review for the tenth consecutive year, and was ranked among the top 20 Best Regional Universities in the South by *U.S. News & World Report*. UNCW offers 57 bachelor's degrees in 49 majors, 30 graduate degree programs, and four doctoral degrees. The University is accredited by the Commission on Colleges of the Southern Association of Colleges and Schools and is one of the seventeen constituent institutions that compose the public university system in the state of North Carolina.

UNCW enrolls nearly 16,500 students, with approximately 14,502 at the undergraduate level. Moreover, the University has the fourth-highest freshman SAT (critical reading and math only) average (1250), the fourth-highest freshman retention rate (87 percent), and the third-highest five-year graduation rate (69 percent) in the UNC system. With an average GPA of 4.18, incoming students have already demonstrated their motivation and ability to succeed in an academic setting.

At UNCW, students as well as faculty and staff members take full advantage of the University's proximity to the coast and its connections to the community. The internationally respected biology and marine biology programs have created promising research and development opportunities in the biotechnology, pharmacology, and mariculture fields. The Watson College of Education works closely with more than 100 area schools and agencies to improve the quality of public schools in the region. The School of Nursing is housed in a high-tech building equipped with patient simulation labs that replicate clinic, hospital, and home health care settings. The labs prepare students with extensive training prior to their placement in a wide range of clinical-practice experiences.

Campus life is a vibrant part of the UNCW experience. Students can live in one of 12 residential campus communities, with numerous options among residence halls, suites, and apartment buildings. Students enjoy a variety of cutting-edge cuisines at the University's 16 dining locations. Students may participate in more than 270 student organizations, including political, academic, professional, sports, service, ethnic, religious, and student media groups. As a member of NCAA Division I, UNCW fields 20 varsity teams, including men's and women's basketball, cross-country, golf, soccer, swimming and diving, and tennis; women's softball and volleyball; and men's baseball.

Several facilities serve as hubs for the entire campus community. The Fisher Student Center and the Fisher University Union include a two-story bookstore, a 360-seat movie theater, offices for student organizations, student lounges, a large game room, an art exhibition gallery and display spaces, a convenience store, and dining areas. Nearby, Randall Library's technology resource and assistance centers connect students, faculty, and staff to extensive collections of information, both on campus and in the world at large. The Campus Commons features a lake with lighted fountains, a network of sidewalks, a clock tower, and an open-air amphitheater. Monthly exhibitions of paintings, sculptures, and graphic arts are held in a variety of spaces on campus, including Claude Howell Gallery, Randall Library, Cultural Arts Building, Warwick Center, and the Ann Flack Boseman Gallery.

The Department of Campus Recreation offers numerous activities to support students' health and well-being. The 165,000 square-foot facility includes multipurpose courts; a group exercise room; climbing wall; an elevated, multilane walking and jogging track; a large selection of elliptical trainers, stair climbers, treadmills, and weight machines; and an indoor pool, outdoor leisure pool, and patio deck. Other recreational

facilities include the Gazebo Complex, which features four tennis courts, three basketball courts, two volleyball courts, and a softball field; and a natatorium with an eight-lane swimming pool and an adjacent diving tank.

Location

The campus occupies 660 acres in the southeastern part of North Carolina, midway between the Cape Fear River and the Atlantic Ocean. The city of Wilmington is situated on the east bank of the Cape Fear River, about 15 miles from Carolina Beach and 5 miles from Wrightsville Beach. Several main highways lead into the city, and a nearby airport (ILM) provides easy access from the city to other destinations.

Wilmington combines historical beauty and modern convenience. Visitors can visit many art galleries, museums, and historical landmarks; enjoy an evening of theater, music, and nightlife; or visit the city's many shops and restaurants. Ocean breezes and the nearness of the Gulf Stream give Wilmington an enjoyable year-round climate. Nature lovers can go biking, hiking, or bird watching in one of Wilmington's parks or play golf on one of the city's six courses. Wilmington's proximity to the river and the ocean makes it an ideal haven for water lovers, whether they prefer taking a riverboat cruise or spending the day surfing and swimming at the beach.

Majors and Degrees / Academic Programs

The College of Arts and Sciences offers degree programs in Anthropology, Art History, Biology, Chemistry, Communication Studies, Computer Science, Creative Writing, Criminology, Digital Arts, English, Environmental Science, Film Studies, French, Geography, Geology, Geosciences, German Studies, History, International Studies, Information Technology, Marine Biology, Mathematics, Music, Music Education, Oceanography, Philosophy and Religion, Physics, Political Science, Psychology, Sociology, Spanish, Statistics, Studio Art, and Theatre.

Degree programs in the College of Health and Human Services include Athletic Training; Exercise Science; Physical Education and Health; Public Health Studies; Recreation, Sport Leadership, and Tourism Management; Recreation Therapy; Clinical Research; Professional Nursing; RN to B.S.N. (online accelerated program), and Social Work.

Degree programs available in the Cameron School of Business include Accounting, Business Analytics, Economics, Entrepreneurship and Business Development, Finance, General Business, Human Resource Management, Information Technology, International Business, Management and Leadership, Management Information Systems, Marketing (Professional Selling or Marketing Strategy), and Supply Chain Management.

Degree programs available in the Watson College of Education include Education of Young Children, Elementary Education, Middle Grades Education, Special Education, and Secondary Education.

Off-Campus Programs

Academic areas across campus sponsor study-abroad programs that are designed to strengthen relationships between the University and the international community, including international students and institutions in other countries. For example, the Cameron School of Business offers an International Master of Business Administration (I.M.B.A.), the Watson College of Education conducts programs in Belize, and the School of Nursing partners with a rural health clinic in Peru. Many of the University's study abroad programs are coordinated by the Office of International Programs. These may last a few weeks, a semester, or an entire academic year; several occur during the summer. The University has developed more than 500 programs in over 50 countries, including Argentina, Ghana, Israel, Thailand, Italy, and China.

The University also coordinates travel experiences that include more than study, such as internships that may consist of a combination of coursework and/or supervised work experience in a government agency, profit or nonprofit agency, or company. Students and recent graduates may work abroad as family caretakers or English language teachers, either in exchange for room and board or for a salary. Volunteer opportunities in other countries may involve healthcare, agriculture, community development, language training, youth camps, or house-building projects.

Academic Facilities

The William Madison Randall Library holds more than 2.1 million items, including more than 1 million books, journals, and government documents; more than 65,000 multimedia items; and a vast microform collection. In addition, the library provides extensive indexes and full texts for thousands of journals and books, including NC LIVE, LexisNexis, Science Direct, and JSTOR. The library's specialized collections include the Rare Book Collection and the Southeastern North Carolina Collection, devoted to publications about or written by residents of the Lower Cape Fear region. In addition, the library is a selective depository for United States government publications and a full depository for North Carolina documents.

Costs

In 2017–18, full-time undergraduate tuition and fees totaled $7,048 per year for in-state residents and $21,064 for nonresidents. Students living on campus can also expect to spend up to $6,660 per academic year on room and board, $1,126 on books and supplies, $1,775 on transportation, $2,540 on health insurance if not covered under another policy, and $1,618 on miscellaneous costs. Room, board, and transportation costs for commuters vary. Students enrolled part-time pay according to the number of credit hours earned each semester; costs vary, depending on the number of credits and whether the student is a resident or nonresident.

Financial Aid

In order to be considered for the maximum amount of financial assistance, prospective students should submit the Free Application for Federal Student Aid (FAFSA) as early as possible; the priority deadline is March 1st. The University awards millions of dollars each year to assist students. Most of this aid is need-based, but a number of merit-based scholarships are available for the most outstanding students.

The University offers several scholarships—including scholarships specifically for incoming freshmen and students enrolled in specific programs—that have been generously donated in honor of individuals or organizations. Award amounts and eligibility criteria vary, but most of these scholarships are renewable as long as the student is enrolled in a degree program and continues to meet the eligibility requirements. For students with exceptional financial need, the University developed the S.O.A.R program designed to help eligible participants reduce student loan debt. The Federal Pell Grant Program and the Federal Supplemental Educational Opportunity Grant (FSEOG) Program, along with several North Carolina state programs, also help offset the cost of attendance for low-income families. Some programs are limited to in-state students only.

Several federal loan programs are available for students who require additional assistance. Loan amount limits are established by the federal government. Some students also participate in federal work-study, which awards money to students who work up to 20 hours per week on campus.

Faculty

The University seeks to attract and maintain a faculty of outstanding individuals who are capable of contributing to the enrichment of its diverse and comprehensive instructional and research programs. Of the nearly 1,000-strong faculty members, approximately 86 percent hold terminal degrees and more than 60 percent are tenured. Faculty members come from all geographic regions of the United States and several foreign countries, bringing a rich variety of educational experiences, training, and scholarly knowledge.

Student Government

The Student Government Association is devoted to the best interests of the University and committed to upholding a high standard of morals and conduct. Student activity fees support the Student Government Association in its objectives and activities. The student body president

and class representatives are elected by the student body, and the president appoints an executive board, which includes a chief of staff, treasurer, and secretary.

Admission Requirements

All prospective students must meet the following minimum course requirements for enrollment: 4 units in English; 2 units of the same foreign language; 4 units of mathematics (one for which algebra II is a prerequisite); 3 units in science (including at least 1 unit in biology, 1 unit in the physical sciences, and 1 laboratory course); and 2 units in social science (including 1 unit in United States history).

Prospective students are required to submit the following materials: a completed application for admission, official transcripts from all high schools attended, essay, short answer question on the application, an official SAT or ACT score, and an $80 application fee. Students have the option to submit a letter of recommendation. When reviewing a freshman application, the admissions committee looks carefully at the applicant's academic achievements including rigorous coursework, writing, grade point average, standardized test scores, and extracurricular activities. Students admitted to the University average a combined math and critical reading score of 1250 on the SAT and/or an ACT composite average of 25.

Application and Information

Students applying for early action should have their applications submitted online by November 1 or earlier, and are notified on or around January 20. Regular decision applications must be submitted by February 1; students are notified of the University's decision on or around April 1.

Transfer applicants applying for summer or fall entry must have their applications submitted by March 1, and by October 15 for spring. Decision letters are mailed on a rolling basis.

To receive information and updates about UNCW on a regular basis, students should create a SeaLevel account found on the UNCW website.

Office of Admissions
University of North Carolina Wilmington
601 South College Road
Wilmington, North Carolina 28403-5904
United States
Phone: 910-962-3243
Fax: 910-962-3038
E-mail: admissions@uncw.edu
Website: http://www.uncw.edu/
https://www.facebook.com/UNCWOfficeofAdmissions
https://twitter.com/UNCW_Admissions

UNCW offers a powerful academic experience that stimulates creative inquiry, critical thinking, thoughtful expression, and responsible citizenship.

UNIVERSITY OF PITTSBURGH AT BRADFORD

BRADFORD, PENNSYLVANIA

 University of Pittsburgh Bradford

you can go beyond

★ To read more about this school, visit http://petersons.to/universityofpittsburghatbradford

The University

The University of Pittsburgh at Bradford (Pitt-Bradford) can take students beyond—beyond the classroom by offering internships and research opportunities; beyond the degree by providing a robust Career Services Office and an informal alumni network; beyond 9-to-5 by offering an active student life, a friendly residence-life environment, excellent athletic and cultural facilities, and a wide range of recreational opportunities; beyond place by exposing students to the world and offering many study-abroad opportunities; and beyond students' expectations by giving them a college experience that can transform them.

At Pitt-Bradford, students live and learn on a safe, intimate campus, where they receive individual and personalized attention from committed professors who work at their side. In addition, students earn a degree from the University of Pittsburgh, which commands respect around the world.

Students can work out in a state-of-the-art fitness center or swim in the six-lane swimming pool in the Richard E. and Ruth McDowell Sport and Fitness Center. The building also houses facilities for intercollegiate and intramural athletic events.

The Frame-Westerberg Commons offers a place to eat, gather, and participate in campus life. The building houses the dining hall, where students can help themselves to a wide assortment of meals; a bookstore, which features an after-hours convenience store; offices for many student clubs and organizations; and areas to read or relax.

There are more than sixty clubs and organizations, from the campus radio station and newspaper to academic clubs, honor societies, and fraternities and sororities. Pitt-Bradford competes in Division III of the NCAA and fields seven men's teams in baseball, basketball, golf, soccer, swimming, tennis, and wrestling, and seven women's teams in basketball, bowling, soccer, softball, swimming, tennis, and volleyball.

Location

Pitt-Bradford encompasses 319 acres in the foothills of the Allegheny Mountains, only steps from the Allegheny National Forest. Pitt-Bradford also is a short drive from larger cities such as Buffalo, New York (80 miles north); Pittsburgh (160 miles southeast); and Erie, Pennsylvania (90 miles west). Pitt-Bradford can also be reached easily by car and plane.

At Pitt-Bradford, students have many opportunities to participate in co-curricular opportunities in the region, including cross-country and downhill skiing, snowboarding, snowshoeing, ice skating, biking, fishing, hiking, and hunting.

Majors and Degrees

Students may pursue four-year degrees in accounting, applied mathematics; athletic training; biology; biology education 7–12; broadcast communications; business, computer and information technology K–12; business management; chemistry; chemistry education 7–12; computer information systems and technology; criminal justice; early level education PreK–4; economics; energy science and technology; English; English education 7–12; environmental studies; exercise science; general studies; health and physical education K–12; history/political science; hospitality management; interdisciplinary arts; international affairs; mathematics education 7–12; nursing; physical sciences; psychology; public relations; radiological science; social studies education 7–12; sociology; sport and recreation management; and writing.

Pitt-Bradford also offers associate degrees in engineering science, information systems, liberal studies, nursing (RN), and petroleum technology.

Students may also study engineering for up to two years at Pitt-Bradford and then complete a program at the Oakland campus in bioengineering, chemical and petroleum engineering, civil and environmental engineering, electrical and computer engineering, industrial engineering, materials science and engineering, or mechanical engineering.

Pitt-Bradford also offers programs for students to continue their studies in many of the University of Pittsburgh's graduate and professional programs such as medicine, dentistry, and law.

Pitt-Bradford also offers the first two years of study leading to the doctorate in pharmacy. Students must complete the program at the Oakland campus, where admission is competitive. The Pittsburgh School of Pharmacy pre-admits some qualified high school seniors, pending completion of the first two years of the pre-professional program at Pitt-Bradford.

The University also has an agreement with Lake Erie College of Osteopathic Medicine (LECOM), which allows qualifying students to continue their education in medicine at LECOM after their third year at Pitt-Bradford. Students who have successfully completed their first year of medical school classes at LECOM will receive their bachelor's degree from Pitt-Bradford. They will then continue at LECOM to finish their medical studies.

Academic Programs

The academic programs stress critical-thinking and communication skills and encourage hands-on learning through field experience, internships, and faculty-student collaboration on research. A Pitt-Bradford bachelor's degree requires 120–128 credit hours (requirements differ slightly among programs). Students need to complete between 60 and 70 credit hours to earn an associate degree.

The accounting major prepares students for the workplace, which has a growing need for accountants. The major also prepares students to earn a master's degree in either professional accountancy or business administration.

The biology program prepares students for careers in health-related professions, education, and research; technical positions in governmental agencies; and careers with food, pharmaceutical, chemical, and biotechnology companies. Most students interested in medicine, dentistry, optometry, pharmacy, osteopathy, physical therapy, occupational therapy, podiatry, chiropractic medicine, veterinary medicine, preclinical dietetics and nutrition, and a variety of careers in health and rehabilitation sciences are biology majors.

Students who choose to major in broadcast communications, English, public relations, or writing are able to work on the award-winning student newspaper, *The Source;* broadcast over the college radio station, WDRQ; and publish original works in the award-winning student literary magazine, *Baily's Beads.* Students also have access to an all-digital television studio and two digital radio facilities.

Students who choose a major in computer information systems and technology will get a broad IT background and gain hands-on lab experiences. Students will learn programming applications, network development, systems design and analysis, web technologies, multimedia applications, database development, and systems administration.

In the criminal justice program, students are able to intern with local and regional police departments, county court and probation offices, and a federal prison. State-of-the-art crime-scene investigatory tools enable students to work a crime scene using many of the same tools as professional law enforcement agents. In the Crime Scene Investigation (CSI) House students can process simulated crime scenes and collect evidence just like the pros.

An education major prepares a student for a career as a teacher in a world of rapid political, economic, scientific, and cultural change. The Education Department seeks to graduate students who have general knowledge and specific content knowledge, as well as sound theory and practice.

The nursing program at Pitt-Bradford offers an Associate of Science degree that can be completed in two years and a Bachelor of Science in Nursing degree that requires two additional years. Students may commence this program upon completion of the associate degree.

In psychology, students gain knowledge in the scientific and theoretical aspects of psychology as well as the application of this knowledge. The major prepares students for graduate work in psychology and related disciplines and for employment in social service agencies, mental health centers, industries, and not-for-profit and governmental agencies.

Students may relocate to another University of Pittsburgh campus to complete academic programs not offered at Pitt-Bradford, but they may earn no more than 70 credits before transferring. All students in the arts and sciences may relocate, provided they are in good standing. Engineering students may relocate if they maintain a grade point average of at least 3.0.

Academic Facilities

In addition to the T. Edward and Tullah Hanley Library on campus, Pitt-Bradford students have online access to the entire University of Pittsburgh library system.

Blaisdell Hall, the fine arts and communication arts building, houses the art, communication arts, interdisciplinary arts, theater, and music programs and features state-of-the-art equipment. Students can find a computer graphics lab, two art studios, a music/theater rehearsal hall, and a radio and television studio. The building also houses a multipurpose theater and serves as the cultural center for the region by housing plays, concerts, lectures, and other arts-related events.

Fisher Hall houses the science programs, such as biology, chemistry, engineering, engineering science and technology, petroleum technology, and physics. The science labs are filled with up-to-date scientific equipment, enabling students to perform a variety of experiments. The building also has two computer-aided learning centers and, on the roof, a campus greenhouse.

In Swarts Hall, students take courses in business, education, sociology, anthropology, psychology, history/political science, languages, English, writing, and criminal justice. The building also houses a nursing suite and multimedia classrooms that can turn a typical class into an audio and visual experience.

There is more to the Richard E. and Ruth McDowell Sport and Fitness Center than sports. The building also houses the athletic training, exercise science, and sport and recreation management programs, along with a human performance lab and an athletic training room.

In the Ceramic Studio, students get their hands dirty—literally. Students have sixteen motorized pottery wheels, a manual kick wheel, a work table, and a kiln to help turn slabs of clay into art.

Costs

For 2017–18, tuition for full-time students was $6,470 per fifteen-week term for Pennsylvania residents and $12,092 for nonresidents. Nursing tuition was $8,289 per term for Pennsylvania residents and $15,419 for nonresidents. Room and board expenses were $4,529 per term. Other costs include an activity fee of $100 per term, a wellness fee of $75 per term, a parking and transportation fee of $40 per term, and a computer fee of $175 per term. Books and supplies cost approximately $500 per term.

Financial Aid

Pitt-Bradford believes that the cost of a college education should not be a deterrent to any student regardless of family financial circumstances. Nearly 99 percent of students who apply for assistance receive some form of financial aid, including grants, scholarships, loans and work-study opportunities administered through the Financial Aid Office. During 2017–18, the average financial aid award was roughly $16,374 for Pennsylvania students and $23,000 for out-of-state students. All aid applicants must submit the Free Application for Federal Student Aid (FAFSA) by March 1 to receive priority consideration. Pennsylvania residents who complete the FAFSA by March 1 are also eligible for Pennsylvania Higher Education Assistance Agency (PHEAA) grants. Students who live outside of Pennsylvania should contact their state agency to learn more about the prerequisites for grants.

The University awards merit-based scholarships to those who demonstrate exceptional academic achievement. The University ROTC program is another possible source of aid. The University encourages veterans to contact the VA about educational benefits.

To learn more about financial assistance, students should contact the Financial Aid Office or visit the financial aid website at http://www.upb.pitt.edu/financialaid.

Faculty

Pitt-Bradford's 74 full-time faculty members hold doctorates and master's degrees from some of the most prestigious universities in the nation, including Cornell, Harvard, Stanford, and the University of Pittsburgh. Teaching is the primary activity of the faculty, and personal attention is emphasized in the classroom. Faculty members welcome the chance to meet with their students and know them by name. The student-faculty ratio is 18:1.

Student Government

Because Pitt-Bradford is a personalized campus, opportunities for leadership abound. Many students become campus leaders as early as their sophomore year. Regardless of students' background or interests, most find many places to become involved at Pitt-Bradford.

The Student Activities Council schedules comedy performances, lectures, art exhibits, movies, and trips to such cities as Toronto, Niagara Falls, Cooperstown, and New York City.

Admission Requirements

The Admissions Committee considers three primary factors in evaluating an applicant's ability to succeed in college work: the high school record, the results of standardized tests (SAT or ACT), and the high school's recommendations. In addition, personal qualifications, extracurricular activities, and potential to contribute to the college community may be taken into consideration.

Application and Information

Pitt-Bradford has a rolling admissions program, and students may apply at any time. All candidates are notified as soon as action is taken on their application.

Candidates for admission should complete and return the paper application with a nonrefundable $45 fee. However, students can apply online at no charge. Students must also submit an official copy of their high school record and scores from either the SAT or ACT. In addition to fulfilling the above requirements, transfer applicants must submit all official college transcripts and must have a minimum cumulative grade point average of 2.0.

The Office of Admissions welcomes campus visits by students and their families; such visits help students arrive at a final decision about Pitt-Bradford. Interviews and tours are scheduled Monday through Friday, 9 a.m. to 3 p.m., and on selected Saturdays. Arrangements can be made by contacting the Office of Admissions or by going online to http://www.upb.pitt.edu/visit.

For application forms, catalogs, and further information, students should contact:

Office of Admissions
University of Pittsburgh at Bradford
300 Campus Drive
Bradford, Pennsylvania 16701-2898
Phone: 814-362-7555
      800-872-1787 (toll-free)
Website: http://www.upb.pitt.edu
      http://www.facebook.com/PittBradford
      https://twitter.com/PittBradford
      http://www.instagram.com/upittbradford
      http://www.snapchat.com/add/upittbradford

At Pitt-Bradford, students have small classes and get personalized attention from their professors.

UNIVERSITY OF REDLANDS
REDLANDS, CALIFORNIA

★ To read more about this school, visit http://petersons.to/universityofredlands

The University

For more than 100 years, the University of Redlands has offered its students a tradition of a superior liberal arts and sciences education. Its outstanding faculty provides students with extraordinary opportunities for learning and growth through close, informal interaction. These relationships are the foundation of the University's close-knit community.

The College of Arts and Sciences enrolls more than 2,400 students. Seventy-three percent of the freshman class comes from California and the remainder from 45 states and 43 countries of citizenship. In addition to a strong academic program in the liberal arts, sciences, pre-professional programs, and the arts, students benefit from many extracurricular programs, including music, drama, dance, and athletics. Internships are available for students in many academic programs. The School of Music and the Department of Theatre Arts provide a rich selection of cultural events throughout the year. Prominent speakers are invited to the campus each year to give major addresses and participate in classes and public discussion groups. Additional social functions are organized by Student Affairs and individual residence halls. Students also have the opportunity to join local nonresidential fraternities and sororities or any of the over 120 clubs offered. Students are encouraged to take advantage of ready access to personalized advice and support in the areas of career and personal counseling and academic support.

Seventy percent of students live on campus in residence halls that offer a variety of accommodations including single gender, coed by separate wings, and coed by alternate suites.

The University of Redlands is one of a select number of schools that has a chapter of Phi Beta Kappa, the nation's oldest and most prestigious academic honor society. In addition, 21 Redlands students have been awarded Fulbright awards within the past nine years.

The University of Redlands offers master's programs in the fields of business, communication sciences and disorders, education, geographic information systems, and music. The School of Education offers a Doctorate in Leadership for Educational Justice (Ed.D.).

Location

The University is located in the City of Redlands in Southern California, within an hour's drive of the beach, mountains, and deserts, allowing students to take full advantage of the outdoors. Overlooking the 160-acre campus are the two highest mountains in Southern California, Mt. San Gorgonio and Mt. San Bernardino. Redlands has a population of 70,000 and is situated at an elevation of 1,500 feet. Metropolitan Los Angeles to the west and Palm Springs to the east are both about an hour's drive away by freeway.

Majors and Degrees

The degree can be earned in the academic areas of accounting; Asian studies; biochemistry and molecular biology; biology; business administration; chemistry; communication sciences and disorders; computer science; creative writing; economics; education 4+1 credential/master's; engineering 3-2; English; environmental science; environmental studies; financial economics; French; German; global business; health, medicine, and society; history; international relations; Johnston Center for Integrative Studies; Latin American studies; liberal studies; management; mathematics; media and visual culture studies; philosophy; physics; political science; psychology; public policy; race and ethnic studies; religious studies; sociology and anthropology; Spanish; studio art; theatre arts; theatre business; and women, gender, and sexuality studies. Minors are offered in art history, astronomy, environmental chemistry, human-animal studies, physical education, and spatial studies. The professional degree of Bachelor of Music (B.M.) is offered by the School of Music. Primary and secondary credentials are granted by the School of Education. Strong integrated programs of study in pre-law and pre-health are available and advise students for pre-professional development.

Academic Programs

Academic majors are offered in the spirit of a liberal arts program, with an emphasis on developing the whole student. In addition to the standard academic program, study abroad programs, independent study, and an honors program are offered to provide greater diversity.

A liberal arts education exposes students to a wide variety of academic disciplines. Typically, such exposure carries no underlying theme but is distributed among broad categories such as the humanities, arts, social sciences, and natural sciences. The University of Redlands requires students to take courses that emphasize competence in writing, computing, problem solving, and creative skills—all of which are fundamental to a lifetime of learning and career development. In addition, first-year students participate in a seminar that integrates the academic program and helps build close relationships between students and faculty members. The overriding emphasis of this innovative curriculum is a thorough investigation of human values as they affect the individual and society. An examination of the worth of the individual, respect for nature and life, free inquiry, and the understanding of other cultures are a few of the topics covered through various courses. The University hopes that this experience will broaden each student's understanding and better equip them to deal with today's dynamic society.

The Johnston Center for Integrative Studies provides a nontraditional approach for a select group of highly motivated students. Johnston Center students are exempt from most of the academic structure of Redlands and instead negotiate their entire course of study with a faculty and peer committee. Drawing from the Redlands curriculum as well as from courses created each semester by the Johnston community, each student proposes an individually designed general studies program and an area of concentration. Course performance is evaluated in a narrative format rather than with letter grades. These students live in the Johnston Center Complex, a living and learning community that includes student rooms, faculty offices, classrooms, and space for weekly community meetings. Students who are enrolled in the Johnston Center are expected to contribute to the life of the center's community.

The academic calendar divides the school year into a 4-4-1 plan, providing a fall semester, a spring semester, and a May term. The four classes taken in the fall semester are completed prior to the third Friday in December. The spring semester begins in January and runs through April. The four-week May term offers students the chance to pursue one subject in depth. Extensive off-campus opportunities, including internships, study abroad, and on-campus independent study, are available.

Academic Facilities

The institution has facilities with a mix of Greek, Spanish, and modern Californian architecture. The ground floor of the Armacost Library includes rooms for collaboration and learning, the Fletcher Jones Computing Center, a student study area, the Bulldog Café, and a lounge. Other facilities include the Stauffer Complex for Science, Mathematics, and Environmental Studies; and the Center for the Arts, featuring the Glen Wallichs Theatre, Frederick Loewe Performance Hall, and an art gallery. The library houses 400,000 publications and online databases such as Dialog, ABI/INFORM, PsychLIT, ERIC, Wilson Indexes, and the Music Index.

Costs

Tuition for 2017–18 was $47,722, and room and board costs were $13,862.

Financial Aid

More than 90 percent of Redlands students receive some sort of financial aid. Financial aid is merit- and need-based. Students seeking financial assistance should submit the Free Application for Federal Student Aid (FAFSA) by March 2. Forms can be found online at www.fafsa.gov. Academic scholarships are also available based on grades and test scores. In 2015, the Richard and Virginia Hunsaker Scholarship award was presented to its first recipients. This scholarship program is awarded to approximately 8 incoming freshmen annually and recognizes exceptional applicants who exhibit outstanding academic achievement, leadership, and contributions to their schools and communities. The highly competitive award meets each recipient's full demonstrated financial need for all four years. Talent Awards of up to $3,000 may be given to students who submit additional work in studio art, creative writing, and theatre arts, and awards of up to $10,000 may be given to students auditioning for the School of Music.

Faculty

The wide variety of academic backgrounds represented in the faculty provides students with an excellent opportunity to live and work in an atmosphere of intellectual inquiry. Academic advising is handled by faculty members, and all students are assigned an adviser in the area of their major interest. Students will find faculty members to be passionate about their work and their students. Classes are rarely taught in a lecture style but rather in a discussion-based narrative including the original thoughts of the students.

Student Government

Authority and responsibility for student government is delegated to the Associated Students of the University of Redlands (ASUR) by the President and the faculty to make possible genuine participation by students in the governance of the University. The organization is composed of all students in the college, and its officers are chosen by the student body. More than 60 positions of representation are open to students on faculty, administrative, trustee, and alumni committees. Among other activities and responsibilities, the student government finances and operates a student-union complex, on-campus shuttle, convocation series, radio station, and newspaper.

Admission Requirements

Graduation from an accredited high school or the equivalent is necessary for admission. While no single academics schedule is required, it is strongly recommended that students take a college preparatory curriculum. This includes 4 years of English, 3 years of math (including algebra 2), 3 years of social science, 2 to 3 years of a foreign language, and 2 to 3 years of science, including 2 years of a lab science. An average grade of at least B should have been maintained in the high school program. Applicants are requested to submit the results of the SAT or the ACT. It is recommended that students should submit all scores from these tests as they are super-scored. SAT Subject Tests are not required. Standardized test scores are not required of transfers who bring at least 24 transferable units to the University. International students, for whom English is not their first language, must submit the results from any of the following exams: TOEFL, IELTS, or PTE-A.

Transfer students should have maintained a minimum 2.8 grade point average and may transfer up to 66 units of credit from a community college and 96 units from a four-year institution.

All students must submit their application using the Common Application. This can be found online at commonapp.org. The application fee is $50.

Application and Information

Freshmen admissions applications are processed in two phases and on a space-available basis. Those wishing to be considered for Early Action or Early Decision should apply by November 15. Students wanting to apply for Regular Decision should submit their application by January 15. Transfer applicants should apply by March 1 for priority fall semester admission or November 1 for spring semester admission. Applications made after this date are considered on a space-available basis.

Further inquiries should be addressed to:

Office of Admissions
University of Redlands
P.O. Box 3080
Redlands, California 92373-0999
Phone: 800-455-5064 (toll-free)
Fax: 909-335-4089
E-mail: admissions@redlands.edu
Website: http://www.redlands.edu

The University of Redlands has held steadfast to its mission since 1907 to educate the hearts and minds of its students.

UNIVERSITY OF SAN FRANCISCO
SAN FRANCISCO, CALIFORNIA

 To read more about this school, visit http://petersons.to/universityofsanfrancisco

The University

The University of San Francisco—a private, Jesuit university—reflects the diverse and dynamic city that surrounds it. USF provides students from all backgrounds an education that is intensely personalized, intellectually inspiring, and designed expressly to help them change the world for the better.

USF enrolls 6,745 undergraduate and 4,293 graduate students, offers more than 100 undergraduate and graduate degree programs, and boasts a network of over 110,000 alumni who live in all 50 states, six U.S. territories, and 135 countries. The school's campus, in the geographic heart of San Francisco, puts students right in the middle of everything San Francisco has to offer.

USF is one of the most diverse university campuses in the United States. Living and learning in a community that comprises students from 49 states and 96 countries is a unique opportunity. USF guarantees two semesters of housing to all first-time, first-year students who enroll for the fall semester. More than 90 percent of incoming first-years live on campus. Any new student who is not a first-time, first-year student may apply for housing and will be assigned housing based on space availability.

The University offers five on-campus residence halls, one on-campus house, two off-campus residence halls, and one on-campus apartment-style residence. Housing for first-time first-year students is in Gillson, Hayes-Healy, Lone Mountain, and Fromm. Housing for upper-division students under the age of 21 is in Toler and Pedro Arrupe, 12 blocks from campus. Housing for upper-division students ages 21+ is in Loyola Village (apartment-style living). Fulton House, a single-family home and cottage, is reserved for specific graduate student populations. St. Anne, in the Inner Sunset district, houses law students. Each residence hall has laundry facilities, study rooms/spaces, community kitchens, television lounges, and 24-hour front desk staff (except St. Anne and Fulton House, which do not have desk operations).

University Center, in the heart of campus, is home to the USF bookstore, Center for Academic and Student Achievement, Career Services Center, and the Cultural Centers, which bring students together to increase their understanding and embrace their roles as members of a diverse local and global community.

The Koret Health and Recreation Center provides facilities for court games, weight training, massage, personal training, and various aquatic activities in an Olympic-size pool. Spin, yoga, and Pilates mat are just some of the free classes offered at Koret. Outdoor adventures include horseback riding, skiing/snowboarding, and sea kayaking. Intramural and club sports include basketball, soccer, flag football, sailing, table tennis, karate, lacrosse, rugby, water polo, Ultimate (Frisbee), and volleyball. NCAA Division I sports include baseball, basketball, cross-country, golf, soccer, tennis, track and field, and women's volleyball and sand volleyball.

Dining venues are located all over campus. The Market Café in University Center offers a food court with a variety of choices, including global and vegetarian options. Other dining options include Wolf & Kettle Café, Crossroads Café, and Kendrick Café in the School of Law.

Location

USF's 55-acre campus is located in the center of one of the world's most dynamic cities, just minutes from the Financial District, Golden Gate Park, Fisherman's Wharf, and the Pacific Ocean. Students take advantage of the opportunities available in San Francisco including concerts, museums, theater, dining, the ballet, opera, and major sporting events. The city also offers a wide range of research, community involvement, internship, and employment opportunities.

Majors and Degrees

The College of Arts and Sciences offers both B.A. and B.S. degrees. The School of Management offers B.S. degrees. The School of Nursing and Health Professions offers a direct-entry, four-year B.S. in Nursing for qualified high school and transfer applicants. Major programs include accounting, advertising, architecture and community design, art history/arts management, Asian studies, biology, chemistry, communication studies, comparative literature and culture, computer science, critical diversity studies, data science, design, economics, English, entrepreneurship and innovation, environmental science, environmental studies, finance, fine arts, French studies, history, hospitality management, international business, international studies, Japanese studies, kinesiology, Latin American studies, marketing, management, mathematics, media studies, nursing, performing arts and social justice, philosophy, physics, politics, psychology, sociology, Spanish, theology and religious studies, and urban studies.

USF offers 71 minors and special programs, including astronomy; African studies; Asia Pacific studies; Catholic studies and social thought; ethnic studies; film studies; honors college; Jewish studies and social justice; Latin@/Chican@ studies; Middle Eastern studies; neuroscience; 4+3 dual degrees in law, premedical, and other pre-professional health studies; public relations; a five-year dual-degree teacher preparation program that results in teacher certification at the elementary or secondary level; and the School of Management honors cohort program.

Academic Programs

The University of San Francisco offers a well-rounded education that prepares students not only for successful careers but also for fulfilling lives. A baccalaureate degree is issued upon the successful completion of a 128-credit curriculum consisting of 44 credits in core requirements chosen from six specified categories, with the remainder of credits being taken as part of major requirements and electives. The academic year is based on two semesters, with summer sessions and a winter intersession also available. USF101, a 1-unit course available to first-semester undergraduates, helps students learn about USF's Jesuit mission, join the campus community, navigate the university's academic requirements and resources, and map their individual paths to graduation.

USF accepts Advanced Placement (AP) credits, as certified by the College Board's Advanced Placement Program exams; the International Baccalaureate program courses; and the College-Level Examination Program (CLEP). Students in the College of Arts and Sciences may earn a bachelor's degree in three years with a combination of Advanced Placement credits and an academically rigorous schedule.

The USF Pre-Professional Health Committee serves to guide and recommend students to medical and dental professional schools as well as to schools for pharmacy, optometry, veterinary medicine, and podiatry. A student may complete the premedical or other pre–health science requirements as part of, or in addition to, the requirements of an academic major. The Pre-Professional Health Committee assists students with the application process, collects and mails recommendations to professional schools, conducts interviews in preparation for application, and endorses approved candidates via a committee letter of recommendation sent to all professional schools selected by the student.

The St. Ignatius Institute offers a core curriculum based on the great books of Western civilization. Any undergraduate student, regardless of major, may take Institute courses to meet core curriculum requirements. The University also offers Army ROTC, which offers scholarships for qualified applicants and continuing students.

Off-Campus Programs

The USF Center for Global Education offers over 130 semester-long programs including exchange programs with Jesuit and Catholic-affiliated universities in Argentina, Australia, Brazil, Chile, China, Colombia, Ecuador, England, France, Greece, Ireland, Japan, Korea, Mexico, Netherlands, Peru, Philippines, Spain, Taiwan, Turkey, and Uruguay. The Center also offers internship-specific programs in a broad range of fields including arts, business, hospitality, international relations, plus field study programs focused on global issues such as sustainable development, public health, human rights, and climate change.

Because all USF students are encouraged to give back and to change the world in ways both small and large, the Leo T. McCarthy Center for Public Service and the Common Good forms partnerships between local communities and USF. Students participate in service-learning projects that include socially just urban design, outreach to underserved children in local schools, and habitat restoration.

Academic Facilities

USF students have access to Gleeson Library's 2.2 million holdings and to Lo Schiavo Center for Science and Innovation, which houses a digital lecture hall; spaces for collaborative learning; and labs for chemistry, toxicology, advanced biotechnology, and mathematics. Cowell Hall, the base for nursing classes and the Nursing Skills Laboratory, includes the Instructional Media Center. Malloy Hall, headquarters for the School of Management, houses a computer lab and special seminar rooms. Kalmanovitz Hall houses all programs in the humanities and social sciences and features state-of-the-art classrooms, a rooftop sculpture garden, and seventeen laboratories for language, writing, media, and psychology. The 281 Masonic building is home to the Performing Arts and Social Justice department, the first program in the nation that trains young artists to create a humane and just society through their craft. The Presentation Theater and Lone Mountain Studio Theater offer space for theatrical productions and guest speakers.

Costs

Tuition and fees for the 2017–18 school year were $46,229. Room and board were $14,330 for the academic year.

Financial Aid

A variety of financial aid programs are available at the University, including scholarships, grants, loans, and campus employment. Domestic students who wish to be considered for financial aid must file the Free Application for Federal Student Aid (FAFSA) and College Scholarship Service Profile (CSS) by February 15. More than two thirds of all USF students receive some type of financial aid. In addition to need-based financial aid, the University has a generous academic scholarship program based on the applicant's high school record and test scores. Eligible students are identified during the admission process and can apply as early action, early decision, or regular action applicants. Scholarship recipients are expected to maintain a competitive GPA while enrolled at USF.

Faculty

The University has 1,239 full- and part-time faculty members; 95.6 percent of full-time faculty hold doctoral or terminal degrees in the fields they teach. USF fosters a close relationship between students and faculty members. This is reflected in the small classes (fewer than 25 students), the low student-to-faculty ratio (14:1), and the faculty members' availability for advising. The central focus of faculty is on classroom teaching and working with students on research. Classes are not taught by student teachers or teachers' assistants.

Student Clubs and Organizations

Undergraduates participate in over 100 student associations, including fraternities and sororities, honor societies, student media,

performing arts groups, and culturally focused clubs. Annual events sponsored by student organizations range from Campus Movie Fest to theater productions and cultural events such as Black Cultural Dinner, Barrio Fiesta, Lu'au, Culturescape, and Dia de la Mujer. Students also participate in Campus Activities Board–sponsored events including Fright Night, Holiday Roller Rink, Donaroo Spring Concert, Spring Carnival, and Late Nights at Crossroads.

All undergraduates are members of the Associated Students of the University of San Francisco (ASUSF). ASUSF Senate is the official representative body of undergraduate students at USF, composed of an executive board and student senators. The ASUSF government has three functions: to represent the official student viewpoint, to recommend policies, and to fund activities and services.

Admission Requirements

The University seeks students who are sincerely interested in pursuing a well-rounded education and who hope to make a positive difference in the world. The admission process is selective, and each application is reviewed individually. To enhance the quality and diversity of its student body, USF welcomes men and women of all races, nationalities, and religious beliefs—or no religious belief—to apply. Eligibility is based on high school course work and GPA, the application essay, an academic recommendation, extracurricular involvement, and test scores. Domestic applicants are required to submit SAT or ACT test scores. International applicants are required to submit TOEFL or IELTS test scores; however, if an international applicant submits sufficient SAT or ACT test scores, the TOEFL or IELTS may be waived.

Application and Information

A completed application includes the application form, the application fee, a personal essay, all academic transcripts, standardized test scores, and one letter of recommendation. For the fall semester, the application deadlines are: November 1 for early action and early decision (freshmen), January 15 for regular decision (freshmen), and March 1 (transfers).

Inquiries should be addressed to:

Office of Admission
University of San Francisco
2130 Fulton Street
San Francisco, California 94117-1080
Phone: 415-422-6563
        800-CALL-USF (toll-free outside California)
Fax: 415-422-2217
E-mail: admission@usfca.edu
Website: http://www.usfca.edu
        http://www.facebook.com/University.of.San.Francisco
        http://twitter.com/USFCA
        http://www.youtube.com/usfcalifornia

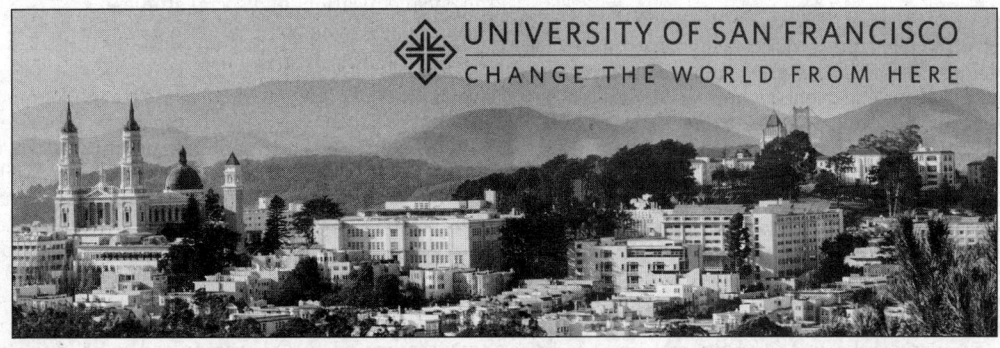

UNIVERSITY OF SAN FRANCISCO
CHANGE THE WORLD FROM HERE

UNIVERSITY OF SCIENCE AND ARTS OF OKLAHOMA

CHICKASHA, OKLAHOMA

The College for the Curious Mind

Curious minds challenge the world. At the University of Science and Arts of Oklahoma, the state's only public liberal arts college, students get a distinctive educational experience that combines an innovative and creative interdisciplinary core curriculum with superior instruction in major fields of study. This prepares students to challenge and change the world in which they live— forging a future of their own.

Small class sizes. Approachable faculty. A beautiful historic campus. USAO provides students with experiences and opportunities unlike any other public institution in Oklahoma. Students have the chance to work hands-on conducting original research, participating in practicums, and designing and implementing projects that will not only prepare them for their chosen career, but ensure they excel.

USAO graduates are living proof that this rigorous liberal arts model enables students to learn, exercise critical thinking and communicate effectively. Within one year of receiving their degree, a higher percentage of graduates from USAO are employed than from any other university in Oklahoma. Regardless of a student's path of study, the skills gained at USAO are time-tested and designed to last a lifetime.

USAO's unusual status and superior performance as a public institution has attracted extensive independent and unsolicited recognition from multiple national observers of higher education. They praise the value of the school's combination of academic quality, accessibility, and affordability, as well as its record of enhancing the social, economic, and financial prospects of its graduates.

USAO is recognized by the American Council of Trustees and Alumni as one of only 24 universities nationwide, and the only university in Oklahoma, to receive an "A" grade from the national "What Will They Learn?" initiative for superior curriculum. USAO achieved this distinction by meeting the highest standards, requiring every student to have a solid foundation in math, science, literature, history and other core subjects.

Washington Monthly ranked USAO 5th, the highest ranked school in Oklahoma, on its 2017 list of the 100 Best Bang for the Buck colleges and universities among southern states. They also ranked USAO in the top 100 Liberal Arts Colleges nationwide; one of only six public institutions listed.

As part of its annual best value in public colleges report, *Kiplinger Personal Finance Magazine* placed USAO on its list of 100 best values in public colleges in the nation for in-state attendees, one of only three Oklahoma universities to make the grade.

Student Life

An important part of college life is discovering new interests, hobbies and friendships. At USAO, we are committed to creating a vibrant residential college experience where students can be themselves and enjoy all the university has to offer. The opportunities are endless here. We work hard to keep the calendar filled with exciting events to get students out of their room and into something fun year-round. Popular events include theatrical and musical productions, Inter-Tribal Heritage Club powwows, guest speakers, world-class performing artists, and sporting events. USAO also has more than 40 clubs and student organizations. No matter a student's interests, they are able to customize their campus experience. There are plenty of places on campus to spend time with friends, hang out and relax. Students who want to be

more active can spend time in USAO's state-of-the-art Nobbs Wellness Center.

Student Success

A top priority at USAO is ensuring students have the tools and support needed to achieve great things. USAO's Student Success Center helps make the transition from high school to college easier by providing both academic and social support for students.

The first of its kind in Oklahoma, the Neill-Wint Center for Neurodiversity assists students with autism spectrum disorder (ASD) adapt to college life and helps ensure postsecondary success. Varying levels of academic, social and residential support aid students in meeting their personal and professional goals.

Athletics

USAO takes pride in developing scholar-athletes who demonstrate the valuable relationship between academics and athletics—a relationship that characterizes great liberal arts colleges everywhere. USAO's nationally-ranked teams compete among the most elite divisions in small college athletics. USAO offers men's and women's soccer, cross-country, track and field, and basketball. There is also men's baseball and women's softball and volleyball. USAO's coaches are committed to establishing nationally-known athletic programs that compete for conference and national championships on a regular basis.

Location

Located in Chickasha, Oklahoma, USAO is within 35 minutes of urban shopping and entertainment in three directions. USAO is a National Historic District and is the only college or university in Oklahoma to be on the National Register of Historic Places. It was given this status because of its antiquity and the preservation of numerous original buildings on campus.

Majors and Degrees

Students attending USAO can major in a variety of degree programs including art, biology, business, chemistry, communication, deaf education, early childhood education, economics, elementary education, English, fine art, history, mathematics, music, natural science, physical education, physics, political science, psychology, public policy, sociology, speech-language pathology, and theatre arts. For students looking to attend a professional school, USAO offers undergraduate degrees to prepare students for such programs: pre-dentistry, pre-medicine, pre-nursing, pre-veterinary, pre-optometry, and pre-pharmacy. Students can also receive their teacher certification in art, English, math, music, natural science, physical education, and social studies.

Academic Programs

As Oklahoma's only public liberal arts university, USAO provides students a broad educational experience, grounded in the sciences and humanities, that reinforces communication, critical thinking and problem solving. The USAO experience is built on an Interdisciplinary Studies (IDS) core curriculum—the required sequence of courses that will introduce students to key ideas across a range of disciplines including history, science, art, mathematics, literature, philosophy, economics, art, and theatre. USAO works to make sure students graduate with a degree that makes them employable, trainable and flexible enough to succeed in the 21st century economy. USAO is committed to helping students complete a traditional four-year baccalaureate degree in no more than four years. Completion of 124 credit hours is required for graduation.

The small campus environment fosters relationships. The student-to-faculty member ratio of 13:1 creates an environment where students have access to their professors and everyone knows one another.

The academic year consists of two 15-week trimesters, August through December and January through April. The third trimester consists of a 5-week Independent Study term, April through May, and a 10-week summer session, May through August.

USAO recognizes students whose GPA is 3.5 or higher for 12 or more hours of class work in the fall and spring trimesters and for all summer-term hours enrolled. The Regents Honor Roll recognizes those who meet the same criteria and who have been enrolled full-time for three consecutive trimesters. The University further recognizes and encourages academic excellence through graduation with honors.

Off-Campus Programs

The opportunities available at USAO reach far beyond the walls of Troutt Hall, the campus' administrative heart. Through study abroad programs, students can take learning beyond the classroom and across borders. Whether a student chooses to participate in a semester-long or short-term study abroad program, they'll be able to explore their major, other countries and cultures in new and exciting ways.

Students can take part in many volunteer programs while at USAO. The most popular opportunity is Drover Difference Day, the university's annual day of community service. Students volunteer throughout Chickasha, reflect on their service experience, and provide feedback about what they learned, all while helping others.

USAO offers leadership development opportunities for emerging and current student leaders to prepare for authoritative roles on campus, in the community and around the world. Students will engage in a combination of theoretical and practical experiences to gain a more meaningful understanding of leadership topics and have an opportunity to join the Leadership Academy Program. The Leadership Academy is open to all students with leadership interests

Academic Facilities

Academic facilities at USAO are designed for both traditional and hands-on learning experiences. The classrooms in Troutt Hall have been designated learning spaces for students since 1911. Today however, the campus hosts a multitude of educational spaces. Drawing rooms, Apple computer labs, and insulated rehearsal rooms for instrumental and vocal practice all allow students the opportunity to practice their crafts. The accredited child development center allows teacher education students the chance to work one-on-one with preschool-age children during their undergraduate studies.

Costs

Per term, the 2017–18 tuition and fees for a full-time undergraduate resident student were $3,600. The cost of housing and dining plan was approximately $2,930 per term. Books and supplies cost approximately $600. For the full tuition and fees schedule, students should visit usao.edu/financial-aid/.

Financial Aid

The University believes that no student should avoid college because he or she doesn't have the money. In 2016–17, 91 percent of USAO's students received some type of financial aid assistance through scholarships, loans, grants, and work-study programs. The overall total awarded for that year was $10,588,152. In addition, 76 percent of incoming freshmen were awarded an institutional scholarship for fall 2016. For more information, students should visit usao.edu/financial-aid.

Faculty

USAO's mission attracts highly qualified faculty. Nearly 90 percent of USAO's faculty members have terminal degrees in their fields and no classes are taught by teaching assistants. Faculty members come from prestigious graduate schools from across the country.

Student Government

The USAO Student Government Association is composed of student leaders dedicated to providing students with quality representation. SGA serves as the voice of the students to the USAO administration and works in coordination with the Student Services Office.

Admission Requirements

USAO strives to recruit creative, intelligent, and driven students who will make a great addition to the university, as well as take advantage of a liberal arts education. There are many different factors that might make someone an outstanding student at USAO, and the university's application process reflects this diversity. USAO uses a combination of various qualities to assess each individual for admission. More information about the admissions requirements for freshmen, transfer, international, homeschool, and adult students is available online at usao.edu/future-students.

Application and Information

Students can apply online at usao.edu/apply.

For additional information, students may contact:

Admissions Office
University of Science and Arts of Oklahoma
1727 West Alabama
Chickasha, Oklahoma 73018
Phone: 405-574-1357
　　　　800-933-8726 (toll-free)
E-mail: usao-admissions@usao.edu
Website: http://www.usao.edu

The University of Science and Arts of Oklahoma provides bright and talented students an affordable, high-quality education usually found at elite expensive institutions. Its central educational purpose is to develop critically needed talent to serve an ever-changing workforce and the requirements of responsible citizenship.

THE UNIVERSITY OF TULSA

TULSA, OKLAHOMA

The University

The University of Tulsa (TU) is a private, comprehensive degree-granting university that provides high-quality education in the arts, humanities, sciences, engineering, business, education, applied health sciences, and law. Fully accredited by the North Central Association of Colleges and Universities, TU comprises the Kendall College of Arts and Sciences, the Collins College of Business, the College of Engineering and Natural Sciences, the Oxley College of Health Sciences, the College of Law, and a Graduate School.

The university is an NCAA Division IA participant currently in the American Athletic Conference. TU, which maintains a covenant relationship with the Presbyterian Church (U.S.A.), is a force for good locally, through its True Blue Neighbors initiatives (with more than 70,000 volunteer hours per year), as well as through various student programs that include projects such as producing assistive devices for locally disabled people and working on international projects that provide self-sustaining sources of energy and hot water.

TU's 11:1 student-faculty ratio, average class size of 20, and emphasis on individual attention anchor an educational culture where students receive both rigorous challenges and comprehensive support. In 2016, TU graduates had a 93 percent placement rate in full-time jobs or graduate/professional schools.

Extracurricular opportunities include intramural sports, special interest clubs, preprofessional organizations, national fraternities and sororities, community service organizations, student government, departmental honorary groups, and campus ministries.

Total fall 2017 enrollment was 4,433, with 3,343 undergraduates and 1,090 graduate and 346 law students. The ratio of men to women is 56:44, 17 percent of the students are multicultural, and 26 percent international. TU's diverse student population comes from Oklahoma, 48 states and the District of Columbia, and 68 countries.

Based on academic reputation and other factors, the *U.S. News & World Report*'s *2016 Best Colleges* ranks TU eighty-sixth among doctoral/research universities in the United States.

Location

TU is a 220-acre residential campus in midtown Tulsa, Oklahoma. Tulsa's prominent industries include energy, telecommunications, technology, data processing, manufacturing, health care, aerospace, transportation, and education, all of which provide TU students with opportunities for internships and employment after graduation. The Tulsa metropolitan area has about 550,000 residents. Cultural assets include the Performing Arts Center, BOK Center (venue for popular entertainers), acclaimed ballet and opera companies, a symphony, Philbrook Museum, Gilcrease Museum, Brady Arts District, and cultural festivals. Professional sports in Tulsa include baseball, basketball, and hockey. The River Parks system provides facilities for outdoor activities with jogging and biking trails, while Guthrie Green is a popular arts, music, and food truck destination.

Majors and Degrees

The Kendall College of Arts and Sciences grants the Bachelor of Arts, Bachelor of Fine Arts, Bachelor of Music, Bachelor of Music Education, and Bachelor of Science degrees with majors in anthropology, art, art history, arts management, Chinese studies, creative writing, deaf education, earth and environmental sciences, economics, education, English, environmental policy, film studies, French, German, history, media studies, music, musical theatre, organizational studies, philosophy, political science, psychology, religion, Russian studies, sociology, Spanish, theatre, women's and gender studies, and self-designed majors.

The Collins College of Business awards the Bachelor of Science in Business Administration degree in accounting, business administration (accelerated master's), computer information systems, economics, energy management, finance, management, and marketing; and a Bachelor of Science in international business and language. Certificate programs are available in accounting, finance, management information systems, not-for-profit

administration, and sports administration. Management majors may choose specializations in business law, entrepreneurship and family business management, or human resource management. The college is home to several specialized centers, including the Energy Management Program, Family Owned Business Institute, the Genave King Rogers Center for Business Law, and the Williams Risk Management Center.

The Oxley College of Health Sciences offers the Bachelor of Science degree in nursing, athletic training, exercise and sport science, and a Bachelor of Arts degree in speech-language pathology.

The College of Engineering and Natural Sciences offers the Bachelor of Arts degree in biology and the Bachelor of Science degree in applied mathematics, biochemistry, biogeosciences, biological science (options in pre-medicine, pre-dentistry, and pre-veterinary science), chemical engineering, chemistry, computer science, computer simulation and gaming, cyber security, electrical and computer engineering, electrical engineering, engineering physics, geology, geophysics, geosciences, information technology, mathematics, mechanical engineering, petroleum engineering, and physics. The college features state-of-the-art research facilities for all majors. Since 1995, more than 50 TU engineering students have received the prestigious Barry M. Goldwater Scholarship, the nation's premier award for undergraduate students in engineering, math, or science.

Minors are available in major fields of study, as well as advertising; African American studies; ancient Greek; bioinformatics; biomedical engineering; business administration; business analytics; Chinese; coaching; computational sciences; creative writing; cyber security; dance; digital studies; early intervention; energy and environmental resources management; energy business; film scoring; geology; healthcare informatics; high performance computing; innovation and entrepreneurship; international business; Latin; law, policy and social justice; linguistics; medieval and early modern studies; Portuguese; Russian; and sport management.

Academic Programs

The Tulsa Curriculum links a broad, humanities-based core and writing-across-the-curriculum approach for all students with a highly flexible group of majors, minors, concentrations, and certificate programs. TU students can receive an education that is well-rounded, in-depth, and uniquely personalized. Candidates for graduation must complete at least 124 semester hours of course work, with more hours required of engineering and business administration majors.

The Honors Program engages students in a critical examination of the major epochs and ideas of Western thought and culture through careful study of primary texts. The acclaimed Tulsa Undergraduate Research Challenge (TURC) program combines advanced research in most disciplines, scholarship, and community service.

The TU Institute for Information Security is developing defenses against cyber-attacks and comprised infrastructure. The center supports the university's National Security Agency (NSA)–accredited certificate program in information assurance, a curriculum that integrates information security with computer law and policy issues. TU has been designated a Center of Excellence in information assurance by the NSA and is one of six pioneer institutions selected by the National Science Foundation for the Federal Cyber Service Initiative (Cyber Corps).

Air Force ROTC is available through a satellite program.

Qualified students may receive credit through Advanced Placement testing. Students who complete the International Baccalaureate diploma can receive up to 30 college credit hours.

The University of Tulsa operates on a semester calendar. The fall term begins in late August and the spring term in mid-January.

Off-Campus Programs

The university is supportive of study-abroad and internship experiences. The Center for Global Education helps students locate the perfect program, whether for TU credit or as an intern or volunteer. Students choose from hundreds of opportunities offered around the world through a direct exchange with an international university, an affiliate-sponsored program, or as part of a faculty-led course. Internship opportunities are also available in Tulsa and throughout the nation.

Academic Facilities

TU's libraries, historic McFarlin Library and Mabee Legal Information Center, house more than 4 million items. McFarlin holdings include over 920,000 volumes, 620,000 titles, 120,000 e-books, 40,000 electronic periodicals, 7,500 videos, and 10,000 recordings. McFarlin's special collections rare book holdings number over 125,000 volumes and are internationally recognized, particularly for holdings of Native American history and law, along with nineteenth- and twentieth-century Irish, English, and American literature. McFarlin is home to the papers of 2001 Nobel Laureate V. S. Naipaul. The 12,000 square-foot Academic Technology Center annex was dedicated in 2009, adding computer labs, a coffee shop, and restored reading rooms.

The College of Engineering and Natural Sciences added J. Newton Rayzor Hall, a $14-million home for the Tandy School of Computer Science and Department of Electrical Engineering with 24 integrated classrooms and state-of-the-art teaching/research laboratories; and Stephenson Hall, the 38,600 square-foot home for the Department of Mechanical Engineering and McDougall School of Petroleum Engineering. The university's flagship Keplinger Hall is undergoing renovation. Additional research facilities are housed at Tulsa's North Campus where government- and industry-funded research consortia explore innovations and solve problems faced by the petroleum industry while fostering student learning.

Helmerich Hall, which houses the Collins College of Business, includes innovative learning spaces such as the Williams Students Services Center and Studio Blue. The Williams Risk Management Center combines the latest in trading-floor technology and advanced study in risk management theories and techniques.

The Roxana Rózsa and Robert Eugene Lorton Performance Center houses the School of Music and the Department of Film Studies. The 77,000 square-foot facility includes a 600-seat concert hall, specialized rehearsal and practice rooms, and a film production suite with postproduction editing and scoring capabilities.

Most recently, the Oxley College of Health Sciences moved to downtown Tulsa, occupying 50,000 square feet of the building at 1215 South Boulder. To accommodate travel between the main campus and the college, the university will operate continuous shuttle routes for students, faculty, and staff. The new building expands TU's downtown presence, which also includes the Henry Zarrow Center for Art and Education in the Brady Arts District.

The Donald W. Reynolds Center is the campus arena and convocation center, home for TU basketball and volleyball, and includes cutting-edge facilities for video editing and training.

The Allen Chapman Student Union offers dining options and meeting spaces. Meals and snacks are also available in the Pat Case Dining Center, the Collins Fitness Center, and the McFarlin Library Café.

The 29,000 square-foot Case Athletic Complex is home to the Golden Hurricane football program and adjoins the H. A. Chapman Stadium where players enjoy one of the nation's elite college football training and playing environments.

The university's 34-acre sports and recreation complex features a 64,000 square-foot fitness center, the Michael Case Tennis Center, track, NCAA soccer and softball fields, and intramural fields.

TU manages the city's Gilcrease Museum, home to the world's largest collection of art and artifacts of the American West. The two entities have expanded into Tulsa's Brady Arts District to open the Henry Zarrow Center for Art and Education, providing classes and studio space. In 2014, the university opened the Helmerich Center for American Research at Gilcrease Museum to house the museum's library and archive. Visiting faculty, students, and scholars from around the world visit the 25,000 square-foot facility to conduct research and present symposia on their research topics.

Costs

For 2017–18, the typical cost for students living on campus was $52,625, including $40,484 for tuition, $11,116 for room and board, and fees of $1,025. Additional miscellaneous expenses (including books) average about $4,500 per year.

Financial Aid

In 2016, 94 percent of entering students received some form of financial aid (including grants, scholarships, work-study, and loans). TU offers a limited number of highly competitive Presidential Scholarships that cover full tuition, room, and board. All applicants may be considered for a range of University scholarships based on academic merit. Performance scholarships are available in music and theater by audition. The University of Tulsa participates in National Merit and National Achievement Scholarship Corporation's Finalist program and the National Hispanic Scholar Program. Applicants for aid should submit the Free Application for Federal Student Aid (FAFSA) by January 15 for priority consideration.

Faculty

The University has 348 full-time faculty members, with 96 percent having earned the highest degree in their field of study. The faculty is primarily a teaching faculty, although most of its members are also involved in funded research or publishing activities.

Admission Requirements

The University of Tulsa seeks students whose academic background indicates potential for success in the university's rigorous academic environment. Performance in high school college-preparatory subjects and scores on the SAT or ACT are key factors in the admission evaluation, but each applicant is reviewed holistically. Each applicant's counselor recommendation; extracurricular activities; and indicators of leadership, creativity, and focus are all taken into consideration. Campus visits and interviews are highly recommended but not required.

Application and Information

TU has a nonbinding, early action freshman admission plan with an application deadline of November 1. Decisions are mailed within five weeks. Applications received after November 1 are reviewed under a rolling admission process with notifications made on an ongoing basis in early January.

An application, high school transcript, ACT or SAT score results, and a guidance counselor recommendation are required. TU accepts the Common Application or its own online or paper application form. TU adheres to the national Candidate's Reply Date of May 1.

For more information, students should contact:

Office of Undergraduate Admission
The University of Tulsa
800 South Tucker Drive
Tulsa, Oklahoma 74104-3189
Phone: 918-631-2307 (in Tulsa)
   800-331-3050 (toll-free)
Fax: 918-631-5008
E-mail: admission@utulsa.edu
Website: https://admission.utulsa.edu

Bayless Plaza is home to the iconic Kendall Bell.

UTICA COLLEGE
UTICA, NEW YORK

The College

A private, independent college founded in 1946, Utica College (UC) is known for its excellent academic programs, outstanding faculty, personal attention, and diverse student population. The hallmarks of Utica College's academic programs are the integration of liberal and professional studies and a strong emphasis on internships, research, and other experiential learning opportunities, but UC is best known for the close, personal relationship students have with both faculty and staff members. More than 4,000 undergraduate and graduate students attend UC, including students from a wide variety of socioeconomic and cultural backgrounds. While most students come from New York, New England, and the middle Atlantic states, students are drawn to UC from all parts of the United States, and there is a growing international student population.

Utica College offers a broad selection of undergraduate majors, minors, and special programs, as well as graduate programs in rapidly growing professions such as cybersecurity, financial crime, physical therapy, and health care administration. UC also offers a robust selection of study-abroad opportunities as well as preprofessional programs and an honors program.

In fall of 2016, Utica College ushered in a new era for college affordability, reducing the cost of undergraduate tuition and fees by 42 percent for all new and returning students in the on-campus undergraduate program. The 2017–18 published price of tuition and fees is $20,677, and when the average room and board of $10,828 is added in, the approximate total cost of attendance is $31,505 per year, before financial aid.

Located in a suburban residential area of Utica, New York, Utica College's modern, 128-acre campus offers excellent learning, living, and recreational facilities. Half of UC's students live on campus in residence halls that feature a variety of housing options, modern amenities, and lounges for studying or relaxing with friends. Freshmen primarily live in North and South Halls, which offer double- and triple-occupancy rooms. Dining options on campus satisfy a wide variety of tastes, including American and international cuisines, vegetarian meals, a large salad bar, and lighter fare such as burgers and pizza. Students enjoy a range of dining venues on campus, from the main dining commons in Strebel Student Center, which recently underwent a $4 million overhaul, to convenient cafes in the Library and academic buildings, plus customizable Mexican entrees at Tres Habaneros, located in the Pioneer Cafe.

Whether students live on or off campus, they can take advantage of more than eighty student organizations, focusing on community service, music, theater, and politics as well as fraternities, sororities, and major-related clubs that provide opportunities for students to organize academic and career-related events. Students can write for the student newspaper, work at the College's radio station, submit entries for the literary magazine, or work on the yearbook. Students also have the opportunity to enjoy lectures, concerts, poetry readings, art exhibits, plays, and nationally recognized speakers.

Utica College offers twenty-six NCAA Division III varsity sports, including men's baseball, basketball, cross-country, football, golf, ice hockey, lacrosse, soccer, swimming and diving, tennis, and track and field; and women's basketball, cross-country, field hockey, golf, ice hockey, lacrosse, soccer, softball, swimming and diving, tennis, track and field, volleyball, and water polo. UC also offers club sports and a wide variety of intramural opportunities. Utica College is a member of the Empire 8 Athletic Conference and the Eastern College Athletic Conference. Nearly a third of all UC students participate in at least one Division III intercollegiate sport, and more than 45 percent are active in intramural or nonvarsity club sports.

Athletic facilities include the 1,200-seat multisport Gaetano Stadium with a state-of-the-art field turf synthetic grass playing surface; the Clark Athletic Center, which contains a large gymnasium, racquetball courts, a swimming pool, saunas, a recently renovated 6,400-square-foot free-weight room and fully equipped fitness facility, and the Todd and Jen Hutton Sports and Recreation Center, a 135,000-square-foot multi-sport dome that is one of the largest facilities of its kind in North America. Ice hockey games are played at the recently upgraded Adirondack Bank Center, a 4,000-seat arena in downtown Utica featuring pro-style hockey locker rooms and training facilities.

Location

The city of Utica is located in the heart of the historic Mohawk Valley in the center of New York State. Just 90 miles west of Albany and 50 miles east of Syracuse, Utica has a thriving arts community, beautiful parks, and expanding shopping centers featuring national retailers. Utica College is conveniently located just 10 minutes from the nearest bus and Amtrak station, and only 50 miles east of Hancock International Airport in Syracuse. There are numerous recreational facilities, including a municipal ski slope and an excellent golf course less than a mile from the Utica College campus. Other nearby recreational opportunities include tennis, swimming, boating, fishing, hiking, and camping.

Academic Programs

Utica College offers undergraduate degree programs in accounting, animal behavior, biochemistry, biology, business economics and finance, business management, chemistry, communication and media, computer science, construction management, criminal intelligence analysis, criminal justice, cyber-security and information assurance, economics, English, foreign language, fraud and financial crime investigation, French, geoscience, government and politics, health care management, health studies, history, international studies, liberal studies, mathematics, neuroscience, nursing (traditional, RN to B.S.N., and accelerated), occupational therapy, philosophy, physical therapy, physics, psychobiology, psychology, psychology–child life, public relations, sociology and anthropology, Spanish, sports management, teacher education, therapeutic recreation, and wellness and adventure education. Preprofessional programs include dentistry, law, medicine, optometry, podiatry, and veterinary medicine.

Occupational therapy and physical therapy majors earn a bachelor's degree in health studies with direct entry into UC's graduate programs, as long as academic requirements are met. Utica College offers a master's degree in occupational therapy and a doctorate in physical therapy (D.P.T.).

A complete list of programs, including undergraduate minors, can be found online at www.utica.edu/programs.

For those students who are undecided, professionals in the Office of Student Success, Career Services, and Residence Life facilitate exploratory programs, academic advising, and career counseling.

Utica College offers the Higher Education Opportunity Program (HEOP), the Collegiate Science and Technology Entry Program (CSTEP), and Summer Institute, which serves as an academic bridge between high school and college.

Off-Campus Programs

UC's study-abroad programs give students opportunities to widen their global perspectives through exchange programs with universities in Spain, Italy, Poland, Finland, Hungary, Peru, Scotland, and Wales, as well as American College in Dublin, Ireland, among other options. Special study-abroad opportunities include the College's annual forensic anthropology field school in Albania as well as learning experiences in London and elsewhere.

Students are encouraged to complete internships and field placements to gain professional experience with businesses and organizations while they are earning college credit. Utica College's cooperative education program allows students to earn money while gaining professional experience.

Academic Facilities

The Frank E. Gannett Memorial Library includes a collection of some 172,000 volumes, 800 serial subscriptions, hundreds of online journals, and other resources, as well as the new Kelly Teaching and Learning Center, which contains the College's Writing and Math Centers. Located on the lower level of the library are the Media Center, computer labs, the Edith Langley Barrett Fine Art Gallery, and a large concourse—the site of special events, such as musical recitals, receptions, and guest lectures.

Along with smart classrooms and faculty offices, UC's main academic complex features advanced new laboratories for biology, chemistry, and zoology. F. Eugene Romano Hall provides state-of-the-art classroom, laboratory, and clinical space, as well as learning technology for students in the health sciences. The Economic Crime, Justice Studies, and Cybersecurity Building supports cutting-edge research and advanced learning at both the undergraduate and graduate levels in these very dynamic disciplines. The Professor Raymond Simon Convergence Media Center features a high-definition broadcast facility, control room, and edit suite. Located in the heart of Utica's revitalized downtown financial district, the recently completed Robert Brvenik Center for Business Education features a fully functional trading room with live stock ticker, smart classrooms, a large student lounge, and other resources to support students enrolled in the college's business and economics programs.

In addition to wireless Internet available across campus, Utica College maintains computer laboratories with both Windows and Macintosh computers.

Costs

In the fall of 2016, Utica College's "Bold Move For Tomorrow" affordability initiative took effect, reducing the tuition price by 42 percent, with a substantial reduction in room and board costs. For 2017–18, tuition is $20,677. Average room and board costs are $10,828. Student activity and technology fees will total $550. Books and supplies average $1,400 per year.

Financial Aid

Keeping quality, private education affordable is central to Utica College's mission. More than 90 percent of UC freshmen typically receive financial aid. The College also awards numerous merit scholarships.

Almost every federal and state financial aid program is available through Utica College. Students apply for institutional and governmental financial aid by filing the Free Application for Federal Student Aid (FAFSA).

Faculty

Utica College's faculty is diverse, energetic, accomplished, and devoted to their students. The vast majority of faculty members have earned their Ph.D. or other terminal degree, and while many are involved in research, the primary focus of faculty members is teaching. The typical class size is 20 students, the student-faculty ratio is 11:1, and all faculty members are involved in assisting students with their academic planning.

Student Government

One of Utica College's strongest traditions is student participation in the College's governance structure. Students may serve on a number of student governing bodies, and students also serve on all standing committees of the College.

Admission Requirements

Utica College admits students who can best benefit from the educational opportunities the College offers. The Admission Committee gives each application individual attention, and the potential for a student's success at UC is measured primarily by an evaluation of past academic performance, scholastic ability, and personal characteristics. Freshman applicants must have completed 16 academic units, including 4 years of English. Students should follow a college-preparatory program, including 3 units of mathematics, 3 units of science, 2 units of foreign language, and 3 units of social studies.

Application and Information

Students may apply for fall, spring, or summer admission. Materials required include a completed Utica College application form, official high school or college transcripts, one letter of recommendation, a personal statement, and a $40 application fee. Utica College is test-optional and therefore does not require SAT or ACT scores, with the exception of the programs listed below. A personal interview for all applications is strongly suggested.

Occupational therapy, physical therapy, nursing, and joint health professions program applicants must submit SAT or ACT scores. International students must complete the international student application form. The application fee is waived for students who apply to HEOP or CSTEP; however, SAT or ACT scores are required to be considered for either program.

The College offers three admissions programs: early decision, early action, and rolling admissions.

Additional admissions information can be found online at http://www.utica.edu/admissions.

Inquiries should be sent to:

Office of Undergraduate Admissions
Utica College
1600 Burrstone Road
Utica, New York 13502-4892
Phone: 315-792-3006
      800-782-8884 (toll-free)
E-mail: admiss@utica.edu
Website: http://www.utica.edu
      http://www.facebook.com/UticaCollegeAdmissions
      http://twitter.com/uticacollege

With help from Sodexo and Connor Architecture, Utica College completed a $4 million overhaul of its main dining commons in 2017 featuring a fully redesigned space with new tables, chairs, TVs and couches, and themed dining stations, each named after a meaningful aspect of Utica College lore.

VANDERBILT UNIVERSITY
NASHVILLE, TENNESSEE

VANDERBILT
UNIVERSITY

The University

In 1873, on the heels of the Civil War, "Commodore" Cornelius Vanderbilt gave $1 million to the university that now bears his name, with the hope that it would "contribute to strengthening the ties which should exist between all sections of our common country." Since then, Vanderbilt has consistently enrolled intelligent and talented students and challenged them daily to expand their intellectual horizons in an inclusive environment based on open inquiry and respect. Vanderbilt's comprehensive interdisciplinary approach to education allows students to pursue a wide array of academic and curricular interests outside of their main focus of study, and the University's Opportunity Vanderbilt financial aid program ensures that Vanderbilt is often cited among the country's best values.

Consistently ranked among the top 20 universities in the country by *U.S. News & World Report,* Vanderbilt is a private research university that features ten schools including four undergraduate schools. Each year, 1,600 first-year students join the University, bringing the total undergraduate population to approximately 6,900 students. Vanderbilt students come from across the country and around the world, and represent a rich diversity of backgrounds. Among undergraduates, 7.7 percent are international students, 39.3 percent are minority students, and 66 percent receive some type of financial assistance.

Vanderbilt's 7:1 student-faculty ratio gives students access to faculty members of prominence in every area of academic study. More than 50 percent of undergraduates collaborate with professors on research spanning almost every academic field, including natural and social sciences, humanities, engineering, and education. Faculty members share their perspectives as instructors and advisers with the goal of providing a challenging, comprehensive education that encourages broad perspectives and critical thinking.

A park-like campus located in the heart of Nashville, Vanderbilt offers a top-ranked residential experience for its undergraduates, nearly all of whom live on campus all four years. First-year students live and learn on The Martha Rivers Ingram Commons, a collection of ten residence halls, or Houses, clustered along one side of campus. The Ingram Commons incorporates more than just bricks and mortar. Faculty members—including the dean of The Commons and faculty heads of house—and their families live there, facilitating easy and meaningful interactions between students and professors. Frequent educational and social programming at The Commons invites students and faculty to explore current events and social issues. After their first year, students have many housing options, including apartment-style living and two new residential colleges, Warren and Moore.

Vanderbilt students take full advantage of student life in over 430 student organizations, a full range of study-abroad programs, Division I Athletics, and a variety of internship opportunities.

Location

Vanderbilt University is located in Nashville, the capital of Tennessee. Ranked one of the Best Places to Go in 2017 by *Frommer's Travel Guide,* Nashville boasts a rich mosaic of cultures, vibrant arts, business, health, and technology sectors, and an array of recreational opportunities. Nashville hosts thousands of live concerts each year in every conceivable genre and is recognized as a top college city in America and an excellent location for businesses. Nashville's booming cultural scene, striking natural beauty, and thriving economy attract people from around the world.

Majors and Degrees

College of Arts and Science: African American and Diaspora Studies; American Studies; Anthropology; Art; Asian Studies; Biochemistry and Chemical Biology; Biological Sciences; Chemistry; Cinema and Media Arts; Classical and Mediterranean Studies; Communication of Science and Technology; Communication Studies; Earth and Environmental Sciences; Ecology, Evolution, and Organismal Biology; Economics; Economics and History; English; Environmental Sociology; European Studies; French; French and European Studies; German Studies; German and European Studies; History; History of Art; Italian

and European Studies; Jewish Studies; Latin American Studies; Latino and Latina Studies; Law, History, and Society; Mathematics; Medicine, Health, and Society; Molecular and Cellular Biology; Neuroscience; Philosophy; Physics; Political Science; Psychology; Public Policy Studies; Religious Studies; Russian; Russian and European Studies; Sociology; Spanish; Spanish and European Studies; Spanish and Portuguese; Spanish, Portuguese, and European Studies; Theatre; and Women's and Gender Studies.

Blair School of Music: Composition; Integrated Studies; Integrated Studies/Teacher Education; and Performance.

School of Engineering: Biomedical Engineering; Chemical Engineering; Civil Engineering; Computer Engineering; Computer Science; Electrical Engineering; Engineering Science; and Mechanical Engineering.

Peabody College of Education and Human Development: Child Development; Child Studies; Cognitive Studies; Early Childhood and Elementary Education; Human and Organizational Development; Secondary Education; and Special Education.

Graduate/Professional Schools: Divinity School; Graduate School; Law School; Owen Graduate School of Management; Peabody College of Education and Human Development; School of Engineering; School of Medicine; and School of Nursing.

Pre-professional advising is available for undergraduate students interested in pursuing graduate degrees in architecture, business, law, or health professions.

Academic Programs

Students apply for admission to one of four undergraduate schools: the College of Arts and Science, the School of Engineering, Peabody College of Education and Human Development, or the Blair School of Music. In all four schools, honors programs and opportunities for research, independent study, and internships are available. About 30 percent of undergraduate students pursue double majors within or across the four undergraduate schools, and about half add an optional minor.

The College of Arts and Science offers a wide spectrum of courses in the humanities, social sciences, and natural sciences, and has majors in 50 departments and interdisciplinary areas. Students in A&S achieve both breadth and depth in their education by satisfying a set of liberal arts and science courses through AXLE (Achieving eXcellence in Liberal Education), and by completing at least one major.

The Blair School of Music offers conservatory-level music training in a strong liberal arts environment. Vanderbilt is one of only four top-twenty universities in the nation to offer an accredited undergraduate school of music, and the only one whose school of music is solely for undergraduates. The curriculum combines intensive musical training with liberal arts studies and students take approximately one-third of their courses outside of the music school. The Blair School also offers a music minor and a wide variety of courses, private instruction, and performing organizations for non-majors.

For more than 125 years, the School of Engineering has educated engineers for practice in industry, government, consulting, teaching, and research careers. In addition to technical courses, each student's program includes a rich complement of course work in the humanities and social sciences, resulting in a balanced foundation for future achievement and the assumption of leadership roles in their chosen fields. All programs leading to a Bachelor of Engineering degree are ABET-accredited, and students can earn a Bachelor of Science degree while majoring in Computer Science or Engineering Science.

Ranked one of the top seven graduate schools of education (according to *U.S. News & World Report*) for more than fifteen consecutive years, Peabody College offers degree programs in education and human development. The degree reflects a strong liberal arts foundation combined with a solid program of pre-professional courses and a multitude of internship and practicum opportunities. All undergraduates must complete requirements in communications, the humanities, mathematics, the natural sciences, and the social sciences. Moreover, students have an abundance of field experiences throughout their four years.

Regardless of school or major, the academic experience at Vanderbilt goes well beyond the traditional classroom. Across all four undergraduate schools, students engage in hands-on learning that complements and furthers their academic experience at Vanderbilt. Immersion Vanderbilt calls for each undergraduate student to participate in an intensive learning experience that takes place in and beyond the classroom and culminates in the creation of a final project. Students will engage in a civic and professional, creative expression, international, or research immersion experience.

Off-Campus Programs

Study-abroad programs allow students to immerse themselves in languages and cultures around the world. Vanderbilt offers more than 120 programs in countries such as Argentina, Australia, Austria, Chile, China, Cuba, Czech Republic, Denmark, the Dominican Republic, Egypt, England, France, Israel, Italy, Japan, Russia, Singapore, South Africa, and Spain. In these Vanderbilt-approved programs, students receive direct credit for their courses, and the cost of tuition is usually the same as for study on campus in Nashville. In addition, any scholarships, grants, or loans a student has been awarded apply to Vanderbilt study-abroad programs. Students may also participate in programs sponsored by other universities by working with an adviser.

Academic Facilities

The newest academic facilities on campus are the Engineering and Science Building and the adjacent Innovation Pavilion. The Engineering and Science Building is a 230,000 square-foot, seven-story teaching and research building designed to foster project teamwork and promote interdisciplinary research. Next door in the Innovation Pavilion is the Wond'ry, Vanderbilt's new epicenter for innovation and entrepreneurship. Through collaborative work environments, maker spaces, and curricular programming, the Wond'ry is the place where abstract ideas are transformed into concrete realities that will make differences in people's lives.

Costs

The estimated costs for 2018–19 include: tuition, $48,592; housing, $10,550; meals, $5,614; books and supplies, $1,294; student activities and recreation fee, $1,216; personal expenses allowance, $2,802; first-year experience fee, $799; new student transcript fee, $100; engineering lab fee*, $800; and engineering laptop allowance*, $1,600. Travel allowances are variable. *The engineering laptop allowance and laboratory fee apply to engineering students only. First-year engineering students are required to either purchase a laptop from Vanderbilt or provide their own computer that meets published requirements.

Financial Aid

Through Opportunity Vanderbilt, the University makes three important commitments reflecting a strong dedication to making a Vanderbilt education possible: Vanderbilt is need-blind for all U.S. citizens and eligible non-citizens; Vanderbilt meets 100 percent of demonstrated need for all admitted students; and Vanderbilt's financial aid packages do not include loans. Also, there are no income cutoffs that limit eligibility. These three commitments combined place Vanderbilt among a small number of universities to adopt such progressive policies. Need-based aid is awarded according to the evaluation of the FAFSA and the CSS/Financial Aid PROFILE.

Vanderbilt also awards merit-based scholarships to selected first-year applicants who demonstrate exceptional accomplishment and intellectual promise. Three signature scholarship programs comprise the majority of these honor scholarships: the Ingram Scholarship Program, the Cornelius Vanderbilt Scholarship, and the Chancellor's Scholarship. To be considered for the Cornelius Vanderbilt Scholarship, a separate application is required. To be considered for the Ingram or Chancellor's Scholarship, a separate application is strongly encouraged.

In the 2017–18 school year, 66 percent of Vanderbilt undergraduates received some type of financial assistance.

Faculty

Vanderbilt University has 975 full-time instructional faculty members. All undergraduate faculty members teach undergraduate students and many also serve as research mentors and academic advisers. A low student-faculty ratio provides for an intimate academic experience between students and professors who are recognized nationally and worldwide for their research. Ninety-one percent of classes have fewer than 50 students.

Student Government

The Vanderbilt Student Government (VSG) provides students with an opportunity to participate actively in maintaining a high quality of life on campus. It works with student organizations to bring nationally prominent speakers to campus and provides an interesting and diverse array of programming throughout the year. A vital part of life at Vanderbilt is the honor system, governed entirely by students through representatives on the Honor Council. Each year, a senior is selected as a Young Alumni Trustee of the University's Board of Trust.

Admission Requirements

Vanderbilt uses a holistic admissions process—there are no cutoffs based on standardized testing or grade point averages. The Admissions Committee evaluates students' academic records, test scores (either the SAT or ACT is required), extracurricular involvement, counselor and teacher recommendations, and personal essay. Applicants to the Blair School of Music are required to submit a separate application and a prescreening video, and selected applicants are invited to an on-campus audition.

Vanderbilt seeks students with high standards of scholarship and character. Most competitive applicants have a strong academic profile—including excellent grades in the context of a rigorous course load, strong test scores, and positive academic letters of recommendation. In addition, most successful applicants demonstrate significant levels of engagement and leadership outside the classroom.

Application and Information

Students whose first choice is Vanderbilt may apply under one of Vanderbilt's early decision plans. Applications are due by November 1 for Early Decision I and by January 1 for Early Decision II; notification is made by mid-December for Early Decision I and by mid-February for Early Decision II. Regular Decision applications are due January 1 and admission decisions are available by the end of March. The priority application deadline for students seeking transfer admission is March 15 for the following fall semester entry.

Office of Undergraduate Admissions
Vanderbilt University
2305 West End Avenue
Nashville, Tennessee 37203-1727
Phone: 615-322-2561
　　　　800-288-0432 (toll-free)
E-mail: admissions@vanderbilt.edu
Website: admissions.vanderbilt.edu
　　　　facebook.com/vanderbiltadmissions
　　　　twitter.com/vanderbiltu
　　　　instagram.com/vanderbiltadmissions
　　　　vanderbiltadmissions.tumblr.com

Kirkland Hall, Vanderbilt's oldest and most historic building.

WAYNE STATE UNIVERSITY
DETROIT, MICHIGAN

 For more information, visit http://petersons.to/waynestateu

The University

While some colleges offer a semester in the city, Wayne State University (WSU) offers every day in Detroit. The 200-acre traditional and high-tech campus is in the heart of Midtown, offering unparalleled access to cultural experiences, community involvement, and corporate career opportunities.

Wayne State students get more than a diploma—they get hands-on experience that helps them soar into a bright future. More than 27,000 students come from every U.S. state and nearly 80 countries to form Michigan's most diverse campus where education is not confined to the classroom. Wayne State's standing as a premier urban research university results in plenty of opportunities for students to get into the lab and explore, as early as their first year. Detroit is rich with opportunity for experiential learning in a range of fields. Whether students are looking for an internship or a full-time job, Wayne State can help them find their best match.

For those interested in continuing their studies, Wayne State's renowned graduate school offers certificates as well as master's, doctoral, and professional degrees in hundreds of fields, including law, medicine, business, social work, and more.

Upon graduation, Wayne State Warriors automatically become part of an alumni network that's 260,000 strong and stretches across the globe, eager to help fellow Warriors with career opportunities and camaraderie.

Wayne State is a nationally recognized urban center of excellence in research, having received the Carnegie Foundation's highest classifications for research and community engagement, with annual research expenditures of more than $221 million.

The university offers an immersive educational experience where students work alongside people from different countries, cultures, and socioeconomic backgrounds in a microcosm of today's interconnected world. Wayne State students gain a distinct advantage as they prepare to build successful careers in a complex global marketplace.

Location

Wayne State is located in Midtown Detroit, the city center and one of the country's fastest-growing neighborhoods. The campus features 200 acres of green space, walking paths, and state-of-the-art facilities surrounded by renowned cultural institutions and industry-leading employers. Students benefit from a traditional college experience in a nontraditional setting. Just a few steps from campus is a vibrant city bustling with entertainment and enrichment opportunities.

Wayne State students can enroll in courses on the main campus in Midtown or on one of five satellite campuses in Clinton Township, Farmington Hills, Livonia, and two in Warren. Satellite campuses offer students the convenience of taking classes close to home or work, and at a variety of times. Both undergraduate and graduate courses and degree programs in a wide range of disciplines are available at satellite campuses and are taught by Wayne State faculty members, providing off-campus students with the same academic experience as those in Midtown.

Majors and Degrees

Whether students come to campus knowing exactly what they want to do with their lives or are searching for their purpose, Wayne State stands ready with hundreds of undergraduate program options (wayne.edu/programs) in the following schools and colleges:

Mike Ilitch School of Business: With a move to a new state-of-the-art building in the heart of The District Detroit on the horizon, the Mike Ilitch School of Business prepares students for challenging and rewarding careers. Entrepreneurial programming and collaboration with the region's business community are two reasons why the Ilitch School is consistently named a best business school by The Princeton Review.

College of Education: With an urban focus and mission behind its commitment to excellence, inclusion, and social justice, the College of Education offers degree programs in 37 areas. Many are award winning and have received national recognition for their innovative, field-based practices. Wayne State teacher certification graduates are hired soon after graduation and typically remain in the metro Detroit area, although alumni can be found in countries around the globe.

College of Engineering: Wayne State's engineering curriculum leads the nation in game-changing fields such as electric-drive vehicle technology and alternative energy. Students learn from faculty experts who engineer the physical world at all levels, from nanoscale biomedical innovations to colossal manufacturing plants. Ninety-four percent of 2015 graduates were employed within six months of graduation.

College of Fine, Performing, and Communication Arts (CFPCA): CFPCA students benefit from seamless access to Detroit's cultural riches such as museums and theaters. Equally important are numerous internship opportunities in industry, advertising, public relations, and journalism. Alumni include a Pulitzer prize-winning journalist and recipients of and nominees for the Grammy, Emmy, Tony, Golden Globe, Obie, Screen Actors Guild, and Caldecott awards.

College of Liberal Arts and Sciences (CLAS): With 19 departments and more than 40 degree programs, CLAS is the largest and most comprehensive of Wayne State's schools and colleges, producing well-rounded students with a passion for lifelong learning and the skills to succeed at whatever they choose to do. It's where the humanities meets history, where Plato meets plate tectonics, and where students come for the richest educational experience on campus.

College of Nursing: The College of Nursing is committed to providing a world-class educational experience through B.S.N., M.S.N., Ph.D., D.N.P., and graduate certificate programs. A dedication to student success and a state-of-the-art learning environment combine to produce graduates who are prepared to be nurse leaders in research, education, and practice. Faculty and students serve Detroit's diverse populations while promoting community and urban health.

Eugene Applebaum College of Pharmacy and Health Sciences (EACPHS): Devoted to educating the modern health care team, EACPHS offers more than 25 degrees and certificates through 11 academic programs. Its learning environment extends beyond the classroom into underserved communities and hospitals. At EACPHS, students are well prepared to respond effectively in a rapidly changing health care system in their respective fields.

School of Social Work: Consistent with its long history of identifying and addressing emerging social issues, the School of Social Work has risen to the challenges of 21st century society, applying technology to cutting-edge research and evidence-based practices, training practitioners within a global context, and marshaling the social and health sciences in interdisciplinary programs that approach complex issues of economic, behavioral, and social well-being from multiple perspectives.

Academic Programs

Academic excellence and pioneering research are central to the university's mission and a primary reason why graduate and undergraduate students alike choose to attend. Wayne State is one of the 50 largest public universities in the nation and a member of the state's University Research Corridor along with the University of Michigan and Michigan State University, generating 95 percent of research in the state and supporting economic growth throughout Michigan.

Wayne State's centers and institutes play an integral role in the university's emphasis on encouraging innovative scholarship, providing service to society, and strengthening its performance as a nationally recognized research university. These centers and institutes embrace the multidisciplinary nature of scholarship and research within the university, and expand university boundaries by fostering collaborations with government, industry and organizations to enhance economic growth and the quality of life locally, nationally and globally.

The university's Office of Diversity and Inclusion is a unique resource dedicated to supporting the entire university community. This committed group of individuals is focused on sustaining Wayne State's inclusive campus and can provide assistance on a number of issues.

Off-Campus Programs

Wayne State students have the opportunity to apply their learning for the betterment of the community and the city as a whole. Wayne State and its active student body take pride in being a key player in the city's unique urban renaissance. From student startups to service learning, students make a meaningful impact on the city they call home.

Costs

Wayne State students are assessed tuition each semester based on their residency, credit hours, year in school, division status, academic program, and school or college. Updated information is available at wayne.edu/tuition.

Financial Aid

A range of resources, including grants, scholarships, work-study, and several types of loans are available to help students finance their Wayne State education. All applicants should file the annual Free Application for Federal Student Aid (FAFSA) early to help determine eligibility. New undergraduates will be considered for a merit award when their admissions application is received. Students may qualify for other specialized types of financial aid based on a variety of factors.

Faculty

WSU faculty members are renowned for innovation and expertise in their fields, crafting hands-on curricula to take students out of the classroom and into the real world.

Student Life

Wayne State offers hundreds of student organizations that sponsor everything from cultural celebrations and political debates to volunteer events. Comfortable and convenient student housing offers numerous amenities and plenty of space for studying and socializing.

With nearly 20 collegiate teams, Wayne State Warriors compete in most major sports, from football to fencing (wsuathletics.com). Students flock to the Warrior Zone cheering section, and can get in the game themselves at the Mort Harris Recreation and Fitness Center on campus, with its full gym, sport courts, three-lane track, 30-foot rock wall, and access to intramural and club sports.

Application and Information

WSU delivers an exemplary education to students who want to go beyond the books and make a difference. Interested students can apply using the university application or the Common Application. Transcripts are also required and there is a $25 application fee. Students can submit their SAT score using the WSU code 1898 or ACT score using the WSU code 2064. Those who plan to major in music, theater, or dance should schedule an audition and/or interview with the department.

All application materials for students who plan to start classes in the fall are due by August 1. Deadline for winter semester is December 1, and for spring/summer semester is April 1. Applicants should receive an admission decision within two to three weeks after submitting all required materials.

Wayne State University
42 West Warren Avenue
P.O. Box 02759
Detroit, Michigan 48202
Phone: 313-577-2100
Fax: 313-577-7536
E-mail: studentservice@wayne.edu
Website: wayne.edu

At Wayne State University, students prepare for a bright future led by esteemed faculty members in company with a diverse collection of classmates. They do so on a bustling urban campus within walking distance of world-class cultural, entertainment and experiential learning opportunities.

WEBB INSTITUTE
GLEN COVE, NEW YORK

Webb Institute

Webb was founded by the great, entrepreneurial nineteenth-century shipbuilder William H. Webb in 1889. Since its inception, the following traditions have made the Webb experience an unparalleled one:

- A full-tuition scholarship is awarded to every enrolled student who is a U.S. citizen or permanent resident.

- All students graduate with a dual Bachelor of Science degree in Naval Architecture and Marine Engineering.

- Paid internships are provided for all students in every academic year, giving every student approximately eight months of work experience in the marine industry prior to graduation.

- Upon graduating, students have a 100 percent job placement rate or graduate school acceptance rate.

- With just 98 students, faculty are accessible (8:1 student-to-faculty ratio), and the opportunities for leadership, extra-curricular activities, hands-on experiences, intercollegiate sports, etc. are limitless.

- Located only an hour from New York City by train, students are provided with unlimited opportunities to take advantage of what the city offers.

- Students are governed by an Honor Code System.

Location

Webb is located in Glen Cove on Long Island's North Shore, about 25 miles east of New York City. Convenient train service from Glen Cove to New York City brings a variety of cultural, educational, and recreational activities within reach of Webb students.

Academic Program

All students at Webb graduate with a dual Bachelor of Science degree in Naval Architecture and Marine Engineering, which encompasses several engineering disciplines. Webb's 146-credit curriculum is based on a systems approach to engineering and provides each student with rich experiences in mathematics, engineering, naval architecture, and design. Students also take one humanities course in each semester as part of the mission not only to offer a first-rate engineering education but also to encourage development of the whole person and lifelong learning. The depth and quality of this rigorous curriculum is made to ensure that all graduates are prepared to pursue careers in the maritime industry or beyond, or to continue their education in premier graduate programs. Each semester includes at least one course in naval architecture or marine engineering that serves to tie the program together from the beginning to end.

Webb's academic experience also includes the following unique programs:

- The Classroom Experience—Each of the four classes at Webb has its own classroom, which includes a lecture area in the front, and individual work stations in the back. This environment encourages students to work collaboratively as well as to help one another.

- Winter Work Term—Between the fall and spring semesters, all students take part in a practical work term. These eight-week winter work terms provide students with first-hand experiences in the industry and encourage attitudes and work habits that contribute to a sense of professional excellence. Students have pursued Winter Work Term experiences in each of the seven continents.

- Monday Lecture Series—In addition to formal courses, all students attend Webb's weekly Monday Lecture, during which invited speakers discuss a variety of topics from the technical to historic to current events. The weekly lecture is designed to expand Webb students' education in both technical and non-technical subject areas.

- Zeien Lecture Series—Twice per year, the Webb community and invited guests congregate for a special evening presentation as part of the Zeien Lecture Series, which brings noted individuals from industry, academia, the arts, and government to Webb's campus to share their stories, experiences, insights, and knowledge.

- Senior Thesis—During the junior year, Webb students, under the guidance of members of the faculty, choose a topic for their senior thesis, a requirement for graduation. This process includes developing an approach and presenting a formal proposal for consideration and approval of the faculty. Throughout their last year and a half at Webb, the students conduct research, perform tests, study data, and write their theses, ultimately presenting them to the Webb community at the end of their senior year.

- University of Southampton Exchange Program (SOTON)— Students are given the opportunity to enrich their study of naval architecture and marine engineering as well as to experience the rich culture of Great Britain and Europe with Webb's University of Southampton Exchange Program. Webb students are invited to this premier university during their first semester of sophomore year, and selected students from Southampton are invited to join the Webb administration, faculty, staff and student body in the spring.

Facilities

Webb's 26-acre, ocean-front campus, the former estate of Herbert L. Pratt, includes beautiful historic buildings as well as unique and state-of-the-art facilities. These facilities include:

Haeberle Lab—Houses several state-of-the-art laboratories that are designed to help students further explore and master naval architecture and marine engineering. These laboratories include marine engineering, mechanical engineering, materials testing and structural engineering, and electrical engineering labs, as well as aerodynamics and hydrodynamics labs.

The Robinson Model Basin—Built in 1947, the basin houses a shop model towing tank and an instrumentation room. The 93-foot-long model tank is used for student coursework, academic instruction, consulting work, and research for the US Navy. The tank features a full-height viewing window which allows for observations to be made above and below the water line.

The Machine Shop and Carpenter Shop—The shops house various tools available for student use. The woodshop has a table saw, compound mitre saw, jointer, bandsaw, drill press, a suite of hand power tools, and the Webb model cutter, a ShopBot three-axis CNC router. Webb's Machine Shop houses a set of MIG, TIG, and arc-welding stations, lathes and milling machines (including a CNC mill), as well as saws grinders, drill presses, and many smaller items typically found in a shop. It also contains an aluminum shop for cold forming aluminum sheets.

Goldbach Boathouse—Located on Webb's private beach and pier, the boathouse stores supplies for the fleet of 420s, Boston Whalers, rowing sculls, windsurfers, and kayaks.

The Livingston Library—Contains extensive resources in naval architecture, marine engineering, science and general engineering, as well as collections in literature, social sciences, and the arts.

The Couch Computer Lab—The lab includes several multi-core processing computers that support the use of high-end engineering software for Finite Element Analysis (FEA), computational fluid dynamics, and physicist-based modeling and simulation. The lab also has printing and plotting capabilities, including 3-D printing.

The Advanced Learning Classroom (ALC)—The state-of-the-art ALC was designed to support new learning technologies together with distance learning capabilities. The classroom is outfitted with a video conferencing system, cameras, speakers, and microphones that support the receipt and delivery of lectures from remote and local participants, as well as remote collaboration with industry and academia.

Costs

All U.S. citizens and permanent residents who are enrolled at Webb Institute receive a scholarship covering the full cost of tuition. Students must pay for room, board, and an annual fee. The room and board charge is $15,180 for 2018–19, and the annual fee is $425. Noncitizens are charged tuition of $49,750 in addition to the room and board charge and annual fee. Freshmen are required to purchase a laptop through Webb Institute.

Financial Aid

In addition to the full-tuition scholarship for all U.S. citizens and permanent residents enrolled at Webb, students can be awarded internal scholarships for their other costs. Approximately a quarter of the student body are awarded additional need-based and non-need-based scholarships annually. The required winter work internship in the industry during the months of January and February provides income for students that assists in covering additional expenses. Supplementary aid opportunities are available through the Federal Pell Grant, Federal Stafford Student Loan Program, and other external scholarship programs. Students requiring financial assistance must submit the Free Application for Federal Student Aid (FAFSA) two weeks after submitting their application.

Faculty

Webb Institute has an inspiring faculty with extensive industry experience whose primary commitment at Webb is teaching. In addition to being involved in campus life, many members of the faculty possess professional engineer's licenses and engage in sponsored research programs, consult for commercial firms, do research, create reports, and present papers at conferences. Classes are limited to 28 students, and with a student-faculty ratio of 8:1, are also very accessible. Each student is assigned a faculty advisor upon enrolling at Webb, and faculty members also serve as mentors for the students' senior thesis projects.

Student Government and Honor Code

The Student Organization (SO) at Webb is highly active in student administrative, social, and educational affairs. It is supplemented by an Honor Council and Honor Code. Together, these entities provide students with a high degree of responsibility for student life activities. Students also serve on many faculty committees and attend Board Meetings.

Admissions Requirements

To be considered for admission to Webb Institute, applicants must submit the following:

- Webb Institute Application

- A nonrefundable application fee (fee waivers available)

- Secondary School Report Form and Official High School or College Transcript

- The following official standardized test scores:

    SAT or ACT (SAT Code: 2970, ACT Code: 2987)

    SAT Subject Test: Math Level 1 or Math Level 2 or an AP/IB exam in calculus

    Optional, but highly recommended: SAT Subject Test in physics or chemistry OR an AP/IB exam in physics or chemistry

- Two letters of recommendation from teachers

- To be considered for the Webb Institute full-tuition scholarship, a copy of the applicant's birth certificate, valid U.S. passport, or U.S. Permanent Resident card

Application Process

Admission to Webb is a highly personalized and holistic process. To be considered for admission, prospective students must submit their applications and accompanying documents by the following deadlines: Early Decision, October 15 or regular decision, February 1.

The Admissions Committee will review every application, and select students with diverse perspectives who value intellectual rigor, curiosity, and integrity to be finalists. Finalists are then invited to take part in an overnight experience, during which they are interviewed by the president of the college and a faculty member. A portion of these finalists are accepted to Webb's freshman class.

Transfer applicants are reviewed on an individual basis in the context of the entire applicant pool. Their requirements for admission are, therefore, the same. However, it is important to note that Webb does not accept college credits from other institutions or from AP exams. Regardless of previous college coursework or scores on AP exams, all students enter Webb as first-semester freshmen.

Contact Information:

Webb Institute
Office of Admissions and Student Affairs
298 Crescent Beach Road
Glen Cove, New York 11542
Phone: 516-671-8355
E-mail: admissions@webb.edu
Website: http://www.webb.edu

Webb Institute is located approximately 25 miles east of Manhattan, directly on the Long Island Sound.

WENTWORTH INSTITUTE OF TECHNOLOGY

BOSTON, MASSACHUSETTS

⭐ To read more about this school, visit http://petersons.to/wentworthinstituteoftechnology

The Institute

Founded in 1904, Wentworth's core purpose and mission is to empower, inspire, and innovate through experiential learning. The Institute's core values reflect that it is student-centered, with a passion for real-life, hands-on teaching and learning, and that innovation and creativity are at the center of its mission.

To ensure students gain exceptional preparation for career success and stand ready to tackle problems that have never been solved before, Wentworth offers a unique combination of five factors: focused academics, cooperative learning, innovation and entrepreneurship, collaboration and partnerships, and ideal location.

Focused Academics: At Wentworth, academics serve as a foundation—an exceptionally sturdy foundation—intended to be built upon by other learning opportunities, such as labs and co-op experiences. Honoring a tradition of out-of-classroom learning, all undergraduate students are required to spend a minimum of two semesters in a co-op program, regardless of the college or their major. This multifaceted academic approach stems from Wentworth's commitment to the tenets of EPIC (externally collaborative, project-based, interdisciplinary culture) Learning.

EPIC Learning provides an educational experience that closely mirrors the environments and challenges found in real workplaces—the pace, the unpredictability, and the need for creative problem-solving and collaboration. Through hands-on, experiential learning activities, students put theory into practice and gain competence and confidence as they engage in trial-and-error exercises in real-world situations. They emerge with a newfound understanding of their own abilities and the impact they can make in the world.

Bachelor of Science (B.S.) degrees are awarded in the following majors: applied mathematics (three-year program with a four-year option), applied science (beginning fall 2019), architecture, biological engineering, biomedical engineering, business management (optional concentrations in entrepreneurship or project management), civil engineering, computer engineering, computer information systems, computer networking, computer science, construction management (concentration in facilities management), electromechanical engineering (5-year program), electrical engineering, engineering (interdisciplinary), industrial design, interior design, and mechanical engineering. Baccalaureate degrees in architecture and interior design are designated as first professional degrees. Minors are also offered in varied disciplines.

In addition to Wentworth's 19 undergraduate programs, master's degree programs are awarded in applied computer science, architecture, civil engineering, construction management, facility management, project management, and technology management.

Co-operative Learning: Active for more than 40 years, Wentworth's cooperative education programs is one of the largest and most comprehensive of its kind in the nation: two semesters of co-op employment are required for graduation; one additional (summer) semester of co-op is optional. Wentworth students hit the ground running and achieve academic success because they already have extensive experience applying classroom knowledge in real-world situations.

Co-op experiences are directly related to a student's major course of study. They typically begin after the second year at Wentworth (architecture majors do their first co-op in their sophomore year), ensuring that the student has a solid foundation of skills and knowledge to apply in the field. During co-op terms, students earn income yet do not pay tuition; furthermore, if the co-op placement is local, students can choose to live on campus, maintaining close connections to friends and to Wentworth activities.

Though a majority of co-ops take place in New England, there are no geographic limits. Recently, students have worked in the mid-Atlantic states, Arizona, California, Florida, North Carolina, Texas, and Washington, as well as outside the U.S. in such countries as Australia, China, and France.

Innovation and Entrepreneurship: Accelerate, Wentworth Innovation + Entrepreneurship Center was conceived as a logical extension of Wentworth's existing strengths and disciplines to drive thought partnerships, interdisciplinary engagement, and out-of-the-box ideas among students, alumni, industry, and the Boston community. Being in Boston means that students are learning and working amid one of the country's leading hubs of innovation, home to a thriving and fast-paced start-up ecosystem that includes research centers, venture capitalists, and business and technology experts.

Ideal Location: Wentworth's Boston campus, located in one of America's leading centers of learning and discovery, is moments away from world-renowned schools, art museums, and dozens of major historic sites.

Boston provides Wentworth students with an expanded learning laboratory, rich with resident experts and examples of excellence in a range of fields. Design students can visit the city's premier buildings (featuring architecture from the Revolutionary War era to modern revolutionaries like Frank Gehry), study its sites, and learn from local experts as part of their studios. Engineering and construction students engage with the city's sophisticated culture of technology and its infrastructure, including the iconic Zakim Bridge, the widest cable-stayed span in the world.

Wentworth's thirty buildings house classrooms, studios, laboratories, administrative offices, and other facilities. Beatty Hall houses the Flanagan Campus Center, Schumann Fitness Center, Alumni Library, cafeteria, computer center, classrooms, recreation room, and office space. State-of-the-art laboratories, such as the High-Tech Highway, Center for Sciences and Biomedical Engineering and the Manufacturing Center, are situated throughout the campus. A new multipurpose academic building is scheduled to open in spring 2019.

Living on Wentworth's 31-acre campus has many benefits; students are required to live on campus for their freshman and sophomore year (unless a student meets one of several reasons for an exception to this policy). Wentworth guarantees housing for the length of a student's program.

Students also have opportunities for study abroad, including established programs in Ireland, Switzerland, Australia, England, Spain, France, or the Netherlands; faculty-led travel; and the Colleges of the Fenway Global Education Opportunities Center for independent study.

Collaboration and Partnerships: Wentworth collaborates with leading universities, corporations, and other partners on a wide range of projects. These opportunities provide students with hands-on experience and valuable professional connections as they interact with and serve the needs of industries that seek out fresh ideas from Wentworth undergraduates. Wentworth also makes it a priority to engage students in projects that benefit the local community.

Wentworth's membership in the Colleges of the Fenway (COF) gives students the intimacy of a small college community and the resources of a major university. The COF consortium members are Emmanuel College, Massachusetts College of Art and Design, Massachusetts College of Pharmacy and Health Sciences University, Simmons College, and Wentworth Institute of Technology. The consortium offers the benefits of cross-registration and access to social events, intramural teams, dance and theater troupes, a chorus and orchestra, professional activities, libraries, and campus facilities within walking distance of one another. The COF's Global Education Opportunities Center provides access to exchange programs and overseas institutions as well as cross-registration for faculty-led travel courses.

Costs

For 2018–19, tuition is $33,950, books and supplies are approximately $1,500, and the average room and board cost is approximately $13,850 (this figure varies according to accommodation). Tuition includes a brand-new laptop that is outfitted with the complete suite of software used in the student's academic program.

Financial Aid

Merit-based scholarships are awarded to accepted students. Wentworth also provides federal and state financial assistance, such as Federal Pell and Federal Supplemental Educational Opportunity Grants, Federal Perkins Loans, Federal Work-Study Program awards, Gilbert Matching Grants, and Massachusetts No-Interest Loans, to students with financial need in accordance with federal and state guidelines.

Wentworth participates in the Federal Direct Lending program. As a result, students are eligible to borrow under the Federal Direct Stafford Student Loan program and parents may borrow under the Federal Direct PLUS program. Individuals participating in these programs borrow money directly from the federal government rather than through lending institutions.

In addition to these need-based programs, Wentworth also participates in the MEFA loan program sponsored by the Massachusetts Educational Financing Authority. Wentworth offers several payment options through payment plans and alternative loan financing.

To apply for financial aid, new students should complete the Free Application for Federal Student Aid (FAFSA) by March 1. Applications received after that date are considered as funds allow.

Faculty

Wentworth's faculty includes 145 full-time and 165 part-time members. The primary responsibility of every faculty member is teaching. Although professors may engage in some research and related work, student development remains the central mission of Wentworth's faculty. Upon entering Wentworth, every student is assigned a faculty adviser.

Student Government

Wentworth's Student Government performs an essential function as the official representative of the student body. Its purposes are to receive and express student opinion, to advance the best interests of the student body with the administration and faculty and with other institutions and associations, to support all extracurricular activities of the student body, and to serve as a bond between the student body and the faculty to foster cooperation and understanding. The Student Government is made up of elected representatives from each class section and the officers elected by the student body at large. The Student Government sponsors social functions and student organizations and serves as an advocate for student concerns.

Athletics

Wentworth is a NCAA Division III university with 17 teams. Wentworth also offers several club sports and intramural sports are offered through the Colleges of the Fenway.

Admission Requirements

Applicants must be a high school graduate (or have passed the GED test) and must meet specific entrance requirements. All programs require four years of English, a laboratory science, and mathematics through algebra II in a college-preparatory program. All engineering majors, the computer science, applied science and applied math programs require a background in precalculus. All programs require the submission of SAT or ACT scores. International students and transfers are welcome.

Application and Information

Students are admitted to Wentworth for September and January enrollment. Notification of admission is made on a rolling basis. Students can apply via the Common Application, the Universal College Application or at http://www.wit.edu/apply. The online application fee is $50. An application form, the application fee, transcripts from the secondary school and any colleges previously attended, SAT or ACT scores, a personal statement, and a letter of recommendation should be sent to:
Admissions Office
Wentworth Institute of Technology
550 Huntington Avenue
Boston, Massachusetts 02115
Phone: 617-989-4000
　　　　800-556-0610 (toll-free)
Fax: 617-989-4010
E-mail: admissions@wit.edu
Website: http://www.wit.edu
　　　　http://twitter.com/WITadmissions
　　　　http://facebook.com/wentworthadmissions

WESTERN CONNECTICUT STATE UNIVERSITY

DANBURY, CONNECTICUT

 To read more about this school, visit http://petersons.to/westernconnecticutstateuniversity

The University

Western Connecticut State University (WCSU) in Danbury, Connecticut, is a mid-size, academically rich, affordably priced public university conveniently located just off Interstate 84 on Connecticut's border with New York State. Comprising four schools and a graduate studies division, it has an enrollment of close to 6,000 students.

The university has progressed from its beginnings as a small teacher-training school in 1903, through more than a century of program development and multimillion-dollar infrastructure expansion to become the respected, full-service university it is today.

Two Campuses, Each Unique

Only an hour north of New York City, the school's traditional Midtown campus is complemented by the sweeping landscapes of the campus at Westside. Though separated by a short drive, the two are totally in sync with one another. Students develop leadership skills in more than 80 clubs, organizations, and residence hall associations, and participate in activities ranging from sports to fundraisers to carnivals and festivals on whichever campus they're held.

The 35-acre Midtown campus is home to stately Old Main, the school's original structure, which was built in 1904. On the whole, however, Midtown's varied architecture tells a modern story. From the construction of Fairfield Hall in the 1920s, to the nearly $100-million infrastructure infusion that culminated in the "green," technology-rich, LEED-certified Science Building in 2006, Midtown's history has mirrored the extraordinary changes and growth of America's 20th century.

Westside's 364-acre campus boasts a large sports complex and a wide range of beautifully designed campus buildings, including the recently opened 130,000-square-foot Visual and Performing Arts Center (VPAC), home to the School of Visual and Performing Arts. With its state-of-the-art performance, studio, recording, and classroom facilities, the center draws audiences from all over to its productions.

Collegedegreesearch.net, a Web-based search engine, rated VPAC ninth on its list of the nation's "25 Most Amazing Campus Arts Centers." *Connecticut Magazine* called it the best college performing arts venue in the state for 2015. "It is rare that the moment you walk into a theater or concert hall a standing ovation seems in order, but that's the case," stated the magazine. "The main theater and separate acoustically designed musical hall are, in a word, breathtaking."

Great Programs, Accomplished Faculty, and Endless Opportunity

Students at Western gain the foundational knowledge, professional training, critical-thinking, and communication skills essential to compete successfully in today's competitive job market. Experienced professors who understand the present-day applications of their discipline prepare students in 39 programs. Majors, concentrations, and options add up to 90 choices of paths students can follow to a bachelor's degree.

Testimonials Confirm the Value of a Western Degree

"She is exceptional....She leads by example, provides forward momentum for the business, and is an absolute asset," wrote one employer to Western's Career Center about a recent WCSU-grad hire. The center provides guidance and services to students preparing to enter the job market. Other employers send comments such as "He has far exceeded his peers, and our expectations," and "She has been the lead on several projects. Wish I had five more like her!"

Graduates themselves agree. Sam Kantrow '09, a popular on-air meteorologist at WTNH News 8 (New Haven, Connecticut), praised the groundbreaking meteorology program he pursued at Western. "Without the knowledge provided by WCSU, I never would have acquired the skill set needed to succeed on the air in a top-30 television market," he said.

Opportunities to Go Beyond the Campus

The faculty members at Western make the most of the university's location by providing their students with off-campus experiences. Eye-opening visits to world-famous museums in New York City for art majors, tours of Wall Street firms for business students, doing field research locally and abroad as scientists-in-training—these are learning events where the classroom is the world.

On their own, as well, WCSU students enjoy proximity to the attractions of the tri-state area. Growing their independence, they take day trips to New York's Broadway or Greenwich Village, or head out to historic cities like Boston.

Aware of being where so many giants of commerce, entertainment, and global geopolitics meet or make their headquarters, students aim for internships, jobs, and future careers at the many corporations and organizations headquartered from Manhattan on up—some located in or close to Danbury!

Cory Paris '14, a political science major, transferred to WCSU from a college in Kansas, attracted by the many opportunities the region holds. "Being just an hour from New York allowed me to pursue an internship with the Clinton Global Initiative in Manhattan," said Paris, who was later offered a role with that organization.

The World Comes to Western

Over the years, many well-known artists, lecturers, and performers have found Western a great university at which to speak or perform. Oscar-winning actors have appeared, as have famous sports figures, jazz musicians, scientists, and writers. The university has even been host to powerful politicians and world leaders.

"Meeting His Holiness the Dalai Lama at Western and attending his talks about compassion was so memorable for me," said Sheldon Poole, a student in Western's respected Kathwari Honors Program. Poole graduated with a degree in political science. The event he refers to drew audiences from everywhere and culminated, through the generosity of the Dalai Lama, in the establishment of Western's Center for Compassion, Creativity, and Innovation.

Brittany Chengeri '15, a community health major, emphasized how her instructors helped her develop the confidence to participate in a health volunteer program in Africa while studying at WCSU. "I couldn't have asked for more encouraging, dedicated professors and advisers," she said.

Campus Life and Local Attractions

Students who choose to live on campus at Western are housed in six residence halls, three per campus. Safe, with 24/7 University Police presence and full security systems, accommodations range from classic dorm-style living to full apartments for up to five. Midtown's Student Center offers dining facilities, lounges, rec rooms, a bookstore selling various supplies, and various rooms where clubs and organizations have meetings and events. At Westside, the recently built Campus Center provides similar facilities.

Students may have their cars on campus, where there is free, safe, and well-lighted parking. Continuous complimentary shuttle service is available between campuses and to the Danbury Fair Mall, one of the region's largest indoor malls. Buses, trains, and taxis offer additional options for traveling off campus to cities such as New York.

Danbury's many restaurants are known for their various distinctive cuisines. Several are located just a short walk from Midtown or quick ride down beautiful University Avenue at Westside. For movie lovers, choices range from art films to blockbusters at the nearby Danbury Lowes 16-theater complex, the Cinema in neighboring Bethel, or theaters just minutes over the border in New York.

Outdoors, there are several area hiking trails and the glorious nature walk at Westside's own Nature Preserve. Beautiful nearby Candlewood Lake, the state's largest body of fresh water, offers picnicking, hiking and seasonal water sports.

Students Get Involved and Get Productive

From the Adventure Club to the Zeta Beta Tau (ZBT) fraternity, a broad range of clubs and organizations at WCSU bring together individuals with common interests to participate in memory- and friendship-making experiences. Often these include community outreach projects that lead to character and leadership building as well as personal satisfaction. Opportunities to network are inherently part of these experiences. Students are introduced to new challenges and often discover talents they didn't know they had.

Western encourages participation in all areas of collegiate life, supporting student interest in myriad topics from preservation of the natural environment on a global scale—for example, in WCSU's chapter of Jane Goodall's Roots and Shoots organization—to performance groups such the university's dance, acting, and puppetry clubs.

Athletics, club sports and personal fitness are also a great part of the Western experience. About 350 students participate in intercollegiate team sports. With Colonial Chuck as their mascot and spirited fans to cheer them on, WCSU's Colonials meet challengers on home courts and fields, in the 2,500-seat stadium of the Athletic Complex, or away at rival schools. There are men's teams compete in baseball, basketball, football, lacrosse, soccer, and tennis; women's teams compete in basketball, field hockey, lacrosse, soccer softball, swimming, tennis, and volleyball.

In addition, Westside's 80,000-square-foot O'Neill Center houses a pool, arena, courts, and workout facilities for students to participate in numerous intramural and club sports. At Midtown, the WesternRec program and Colonial Fitness Zone provide perfect venues for participation in intramural sports, attending special events and meeting the challenge of staying fit.

Bright Futures Begin at Western

Spirited, talented, and full of promise, students at Western respond to the many opportunities the university offers them. As the future opens on ever-expanding vistas of career and personal possibilities, discovering and developing the unique potential of each of its students will continue to remain priority one for WCSU.

Costs

As part of the Connecticut State Colleges & Universities system, Western provides a high-quality private university education at an exceptionally reasonable public school cost. In the 2017–18 academic year, in-state tuition and required fees totaled $5,229 per semester. Tuition and required fees for Students in the New England Regional Student Program totaled $6,429 per semester. For other out-of-state students, tuition and fees totaled $11,573.50 per semester. One-time fees, miscellaneous fees, books, laboratory fees, health insurance, and personal expenses are not included in these estimates.

Housing costs range from $3,337 to $5,204 per semester. Meal plans range from $1,075.50 to $2,654 per semester.

Financial Aid

Western Connecticut State University offers financial aid to help qualified students meet their educational expenses. The staff of Financial Aid and Student Employment is available to assist students in determining their eligibility for the various sources of aid available.

For more information, students should contact the Financial Aid Office at 203-837-8580 or wcsufinancialaid@wcsu.edu.

Admission Requirements

Western requires that candidates for admission have a high school diploma from an accredited secondary school or an equivalency diploma. General Educational Development (GED) scores must be converted into a State of Connecticut Equivalency Diploma. Each applicant is assessed individually, but the following guidelines must also be met: SAT (1000 guideline), ACT also accepted; top one-third rank in graduating class; and a B- average in 4 years of English, 3 years math (algebra 1, geometry, algebra 2), 2 years social sciences, including U.S. history, 2 years of laboratory sciences, and 2 to 3 years of foreign language (3 recommended). Nursing, education, and business applicants may have higher requirements. Auditions are required for applicants to the Department of Music.

Applicants must submit the completed application form, a $50 nonrefundable application fee, SAT or ACT test scores, and official high school transcript or equivalency diploma.

Application and Information

For those applying for the fall semester, notification of admission begins on December 1 and continues on a rolling basis. A reply to an offer of admission must be received by May 1. Rolling admissions for the spring semester begins on October 1. Note that although most freshmen enter WSCU in the fall, roughly 10 percent enter in other semesters.

For more information, students should contact:

Undergraduate Admissions Office
Western Connecticut State University
181 White Street
Danbury, Connecticut 06810
Phone: 203-837-9000
      877-837-WCSU (toll-free)
E-mail: admissions@wcsu.edu
Website: http://www.wcsu.edu
      http://www.facebook.com/WestConn
      http://twitter.com/West

WESTMONT COLLEGE
SANTA BARBARA, CALIFORNIA

The College

Westmont College helps students unite both spirit and mind through a liberal arts education that offers rigorous training in every area of human knowledge and fosters a deep love of God. The college's nationally ranked program focuses entirely on undergraduates, and helps them develop deep relationships by living in a residential Christian community. Westmont professors lead semesters on four continents to help students develop a global perspective.

Learning at Westmont extends beyond the classroom as students participate in a variety of student clubs, activities and service projects. Athletes can compete with a Warrior team or play for a club sport or intramural league. Musicians have the opportunity to perform with accomplished choirs and instrumental groups, the theater program stages classic plays and an exciting Fringe Festival, and art students study in beautifully designed studios and exhibit artwork in the Westmont Ridley-Tree Museum of Art. Other possibilities include the student newspaper, literary magazine, or yearbook; intercultural clubs and political organizations; or volunteer opportunities in the community. Chapel, an integral part of a Westmont education, features inspiring speakers who encourage students to grow in their faith. Attendance is required three days a week.

Westmont's Office of Career Planning and Calling helps students discover their strengths and weaknesses, then prepare for a career by facilitating internships. Westmont's professors and classes also provide preparation for graduate school; Westmont alumni have attended some of the finest universities in the world, such as UCLA, Stanford, Harvard, Yale, Princeton, Cambridge, the University of Chicago, and others.

The college's 1,200 students come from more than 30 states and 16 countries, with the highest percentage from California. About 61 percent are women, 25 percent are students of color, and 2 percent are international students. Ninety-five percent of students live in the six residence halls on campus or the apartment complex off campus.

Westmont belongs to the National Association of Intercollegiate Athletics and the Golden State Athletic Conference and competes in intercollegiate sports for men and women in basketball, cross-country, soccer, tennis, and track and field and in baseball (men) and volleyball (women). Club teams for men include polo, rugby, soccer, volleyball, Ultimate (Frisbee), and golf; women's club teams are polo, cheer, and golf. Both men and women can participate in intramural sports.

Location

Located in scenic Santa Barbara, Westmont's 111-acre wooded campus lies between the Santa Ynez Mountains and the Pacific Ocean. Students enjoy the beach and mountain trails year-round. The local community offers a wealth of culture, including museums, theaters, libraries, concerts, lectures, and historic sites.

Majors and Degrees

Westmont awards Bachelor of Arts (B.A.) and Bachelor of Science (B.S.) degrees in more than 100 academic majors, minors, and programs: alternative major, art, art history, biology, chemistry, communication studies, computer science, economics and business, data analytics, education, engineering physics, English, English and modern languages, European studies, French, history, kinesiology, liberal studies, mathematics, music, philosophy, physics, political science, psychology, religious studies, social science, sociology and anthropology, Spanish, and theater arts. The California Commission for Teacher Preparation and Licensing accredits the teacher-preparation program, and students may qualify for either the single-subject or the multiple-subject credential. Pre-professional programs include athletic training, dentistry, engineering, law,

medicine, ministry and missionary studies, pharmacy, physical therapy, and veterinary studies.

Academic Programs

All majors and programs of study feature thought-provoking and inspiring ways to integrate belief, thought, and action to reach a deeper, more accurate understanding of the world and achieve a wider impact. Professors demand critical thinking and encourage exploration of the world of ideas through a wide range of opportunities and organizations. For example, students consider issues of science and religion through the Pascal Society and attend lectures in the humanities sponsored by the Erasmus Society. At Westmont, an exclusively undergraduate college, students can engage in significant research projects in the sciences and all disciplines by assisting professors in their scholarly work and completing independent study. Professors, staff members, and alumni seek to help students grow through their questions toward an ever-deeper faith.

Global Education

Westmont professors lead the college's global education programs, including **Europe Semester**, which offers the broadest geographical scope. **England Semester** combines travel and residential study of literature in the British Isles. At **Westmont in Cairo** students live in a developing world megalopolis at the heart of the Islamic world. **Westmont in Jerusalem** lets students explore the ancient world of Jesus and modern Israel-Palestine. Through **Westmont in Mexico**, students gain skills for effective cross-cultural living and improve their Spanish-speaking skills. **Westmont in East Asia** takes participants to Seoul, Shanghai, and Singapore to learn about globalization, culture, society, and Christianity. **Westmont in Northern Europe** features extended stays in London, Berlin, and Northern Ireland and focuses on conflict and peace-making. **Global Health: Uganda** gives medical and public-health-related majors an international field placement at a local organization in Uganda. Students can take part in a meaningful internship during **Westmont in San Francisco** and grapple with big questions while staying in a historic mansion in a vibrant area of the city. At **Westmont Downtown**, participants live in downtown Santa Barbara, study social entrepreneurship, and spend 20 hours a week in a significant internship. Westmont's membership in the Christian College Consortium (CCC) lets students explore additional opportunities and programs led by other colleges, such as language and cultural study in places such as France, Spain, and Latin America; a Washington Semester in the nation's capital; and the Consortium Visitor Program, in which students spend a semester at another of the CCC's 13 campuses.

Academic Facilities

Westmont's newest buildings include the Global Leadership Center, Adams Center for the Visual Arts, which features the Westmont Ridley-Tree Museum of Art, Winter Hall for Science and Mathematics, and the Westmont Observatory with the powerful Keck Telescope. The tri-level Roger John Voskuyl Library, named for Westmont's third president, provides resources and services that support the teaching and research needs of faculty, staff, students, and the surrounding community. The library collections include 237,000 books, media items, music scores, and microforms; 300 print periodical titles; 105 online databases with access to 12,000 online periodicals; and access to additional resources through the Gold Coast Library Network, Camino, and Interlibrary Loan Services. Westmont's network consists of both wired and wireless components. Wireless coverage extends to all campus buildings and most outdoor areas, with a total Internet bandwidth of 135 Mb/s. Students obtain Google Apps accounts through Westmont, providing email, a calendar, document sharing, and 4 GB of storage per student. The college provides a computer lab with 27 dual-platform iMacs located on the main floor of the library. Westmont's Learning Commons, a 21st-century space in the library, brings together library, technology, and other campus services in an environment that fosters collaborative and creative work and social interaction. Voskuyl Library also houses departments that provide student support services: Academic Advising and Disability Services, Internship Programs, Writer's Corner, and Information Technology. Porter Theatre contains state-of-the-art equipment for dramatic productions and concerts, including the Black Box Theatre. Mericos H. Whittier Science Building and Winter Hall for Science and Mathematics house the college's science program and equipment, including an ultracentrifuge, a liquid scintillation counter for measuring radioactivity, physiographic units, and other equipment for advanced physiological studies.

Costs

Tuition and fees for 2017–18 were $44,044, and room and board for the academic year are $13,886. The cost of books and personal expenses are estimated at $3,000.

Financial Aid

Westmont provides generous financial aid and encourages all students to apply regardless of their financial resources. Eighty-five percent of students receive some form of financial assistance. Westmont offers awards worth 85 percent of tuition through the Augustinian Scholarship and Honors Program to 60 students each year, available only to first-year applicants who apply via nonbinding early action. A select group of these applicants participate in a formal competition on campus; interested students should contact the Office of Admissions for more information. Other merit awards in the financial aid program—President's, Ruth Kerr, Wallace L. Emerson, and Founders Scholarships and the Warrior Academic Award—range from $12,000 to $22,000. Transfer students may be eligible for scholarships ranging from $9,000 to $15,000, offered to students with impressive academic achievement. Westmont also gives awards to those who demonstrate strength in art, music, theater arts, dance, cultural diversity, and athletics. After submitting the Free Application for Federal Student Aid (FAFSA), students may be eligible for state grants, aid from federal programs, institutional grants, loans, and work-study programs.

Faculty

One of Westmont's highest priorities is attracting and retaining Christian teachers and scholars with outstanding credentials and a love for students. Students get to know professors personally and will likely spend time with them outside of class. The college's 93 full-time and 54 part-time professors are dedicated to integrating faith and learning and being actively involved in the lives of students. The student-faculty ratio is 12:1; the average class size is 18. Ninety-six percent of tenure-track faculty members hold a terminal degree. Professors are committed to teaching at the undergraduate level and advise either incoming first-year students or majors in their department. Although teaching is their primary scholarly activity, many professors engage in research, write books, and publish articles in leading journals and periodicals.

Student Government

The Westmont College Student Association (WCSA) is a self-governing body. Students elect WCSA representatives, who are responsible for organizing social, cultural, and educational activities. They actively participate as voting members on most faculty committees, and allocate the student budget to various clubs and organizations. Westmont Student Ministries, another student-managed organization, organizes a range of outreach programs and ministries on and off campus.

Admission Requirements

Westmont selects candidates for admission from prospective students who demonstrate their preparation for the academic stimulation and spiritual vitality central to Westmont's character. All applicants must submit one academic letter of recommendation, official high school or college transcripts, and official SAT or ACT scores. A pastoral/character reference is optional. An interview is strongly encouraged. For transfer students from an accredited two- or four-year college or university or a Bible college or university that is accredited by the American Association of Bible Colleges, the evaluation is based on achievement in solid, transferable course work; an assessment of the personal areas covered by the application

(as stated above); and the quality of the written responses. High school records must also be submitted.

Application and Information

Students may enroll at Westmont at the beginning of either the fall or spring semester. The college offers an early-action plan. High school seniors interested in applying Early Action 1 must submit an application by October 15, and those interested in applying Early Action 2 must submit an application by November 15. Notifications are mailed by December 1 and January 1, respectively. The priority deadline for regular decision is February 15 for first-year applicants and March 15 for transfers. Notifications are mailed on a rolling basis. Applications should be submitted online via the Common Application or the Westmont Application with an application fee of $50. The Office of Admission encourages prospective students to complete the application process as early as possible.

Visitors are welcome any time. Guests may stay overnight in the residence halls, attend classes and chapel, speak with professors or coaches, audition for a music program, share a portfolio with the art department, interview with an admissions counselor, and eat meals with Westmont students. Several Preview Day events are held each semester. Westmont seeks to enroll a well-rounded and varied first-year class while creating a dynamic and culturally and traditionally diverse community of learners possessing a variety of attributes, accomplishments, backgrounds, and interests.

For more information regarding admissions students should contact:

Office of Admission
Westmont College
955 La Paz Road
Santa Barbara, California 93108
Phone: 800-777-9011 (toll-free)
Fax: 805-565-6234
E-mail: admissions@westmont.edu
Website: http://www.westmont.edu/
http://www.facebook.com/westmont
http://twitter.com/westmontnews

Nestled in the beautiful hills of Santa Barbara, California, Westmont is home to 1,200 undergraduate scholars, all seeking to engage the academy, church, and world.

WEST VIRGINIA WESLEYAN COLLEGE
BUCKHANNON, WEST VIRGINIA

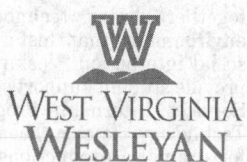

The College

Founded in 1890, West Virginia Wesleyan College is a coeducational, residential, liberal arts college in Buckhannon, West Virginia. The College has an enrollment of 1,350 undergraduate students from thirty-five states and twenty-one countries. The average class size is 19 and the student-faculty ratio is 13:1. More than 80 percent of the faculty members hold the highest degree in their respective teaching field. Each fall, West Virginia Wesleyan enrolls approximately 415 freshmen and 50 transfers. Fifty percent of students originate from out-of-state, and the ratio of men to women is 1:1. Approximately 17 percent of the students are minority or international students. More than 85 percent of students live on campus, and housing is required for all four years of study. Housing options include residence halls, suites, on-campus apartments, and campus-adjacent residence units.

Among the many services available to students is the Learning Center, which provides comprehensive learning resources for all students, as well as robust services for students with diagnosed learning differences and is one of the foremost programs of its type in the country.

In addition to challenging academic curriculum and innovative technology, Wesleyan offers a balanced and comprehensive student-life program. Co-curricular activities include twenty-two NCAA Division II varsity sports, intramurals, and outdoor recreation adventures. More than seventy campus organizations include vocal and instrumental musical ensembles, theatre arts, dance, community service, clubs, special interest groups, Greek life, and spiritual and religious life programming. On-campus media opportunities include a campus radio station, student newspaper, and yearbook. The student-run Bobcat Entertainment Board schedules cultural and social entertainment every week during the academic year.

Location

Situated in the foothills of the Allegheny Mountains, Wesleyan's picturesque 100-acre campus is located in the historic town of Buckhannon, West Virginia. Buckhannon is located two hours south of Pittsburgh, Pennsylvania, and 90 minutes north of Charleston, West Virginia. It is easily accessible by interstate highways. Buckhannon has been included in Norman Crampton's book, *The Top 100 Best Small Towns in America* and *The 120 Best College Towns in America*. Students are drawn to the attractive and friendly setting and the many restaurants, social events, and outdoor adventures available within a short distance from campus.

Majors and Degrees

The College awards Bachelor of Arts, Bachelor of Science, Bachelor of Science in Nursing, and Bachelor of Music Education degrees, in addition to a number of master's-level degrees. Majors include: accounting, art, arts administration, athletic training, biology, business administration, five-year bachelor's + master's in business administration, chemistry, Christian formation, communication studies, computer information science, computer science, criminal justice, economics, education (combined elementary/secondary, elementary, or secondary), engineering 3-2, English (literature, education, or writing), environmental science, environmental studies, exercise science, gender studies, graphic design, history, international business, international studies, management, marketing, mathematics, music (applied or theory), music education, musical theatre, nursing, painting and drawing, philosophy, physics, political science, psychology, public relations, religion, sociology, sport business, and theatre arts.

Preprofessional study programs are offered in dentistry, law, medicine, optometry, pharmacy, physical therapy, and veterinary medicine. The degrees are determined by the content of the student's program.

West Virginia Wesleyan also offers the following master's degrees: Master of Science in Athletic Training, Master of Business Administration, Master of Fine Arts in Creative Writing, and Master of Science in Nursing.

Academic Programs

Students are required to complete 120 credit hours of course work to become eligible for graduation. Approximately one third of those hours are taken in a student's major, one third in the general studies curriculum requirement, and one third in electives. The general studies and elective courses are taken to develop and enhance a student's worldview.

Wesleyan operates on a traditional semester system. The optional May Term is a three-week intensive period of study giving students the opportunity to earn three credit hours. International travel opportunities are popular options during May Term.

The honors program is offered for superior students who meet the specific requirements and are willing to commit themselves to a rigorous and enriching curriculum that affirms the highest ideals of a liberal arts institution. Challenging classes and cultural outings are an integral part of the honors program and are offered throughout the academic year.

Advanced credit is available for students who achieve required scores on Advanced Placement exams, International Baccalaureate exams, and CLEP tests.

New students are assigned a faculty adviser who assists with course selection and student concerns. All first-year students are required to successfully complete a four-hour First Year Seminar course. In addition to helping students adapt to college life, the First Year Seminar courses are topical and apply credit toward a general studies requirement.

Off-Campus Programs

Study abroad is highly encouraged and is an important part of the Wesleyan student's experience. In the recent past, students have studied in such countries as Australia, Austria, Bolivia, Bulgaria, England, Ireland, Italy, Kenya, Korea, Spain, and Wales, but there are a number of other countries in which students may study. Internships are required for many majors and highly encouraged for others. They are available locally, as well as in cities such as Pittsburgh, New York, Washington, D.C., and others around the globe. These off-campus opportunities can be taken for a complete semester, during the May Term, or during the summer.

Academic Facilities

Wesleyan's twenty-four buildings, including eleven modern residence hall units, house some of the most impressive facilities in the region. Residence hall facilities include Fleming Hall, which was completely remodeled in 2008; Dunn Hall, a new residence hall that opened to students in 2011; and Doney Hall (single rooms) that opened in 2013. Other recent campus construction includes the Virginia Thomas Law Center for the Performing Arts and the Reemsnyder Research Center for the sciences. A brand-new wellness center with Nautilus equipment, full cardio theater, separate workout rooms, and locker room facilities opened in 2012. In 2014 the College opened a new Welcome Center and over the next five years will remodel every major academic classroom through funding received from a Title III grant program. This $10-million grant also provides for a Student Success Center and Center for Teaching and Learning, providing Wesleyan unparalleled support services.

The Annie Merner Pfeiffer Library houses more than 105,000 volumes, 700 periodicals, and 10,000 media materials. More than 220 million additional resources worldwide can be accessed through a number of online databases from students' own residence halls 24 hours a day. Located in the center of the campus is Wesley Chapel, the largest sanctuary in West Virginia, and the Martin Religious Center. The Benedum Campus and Community Center houses a convenience store, bookstore, swimming pool, the Cat's Claw restaurant, the campus radio station, and student services offices.

The Rockefeller Health and Physical Education Center includes a main gymnasium that seats 3,700, an intramural gymnasium, weight-training rooms, and an indoor Astroturf training and recreational area. Other key campus buildings include Christopher Hall of Science and the adjacent Reemsnyder Research Center, which houses state-of-the-art laboratories and classrooms to complement the Christopher's planetarium, herbarium, and greenhouse; Loar Hall, which includes a 165-seat recital hall and state-of-the-art computer music lab; Middleton Hall, which houses the department of nursing; Haymond Hall of Science; and the Lynch-Raine Administration Building.

Costs

The College's 2018–19 tuition and fees will be $30,461 and room and board will be $8,856. Wesleyan offers a 10-month interest-free payment plan.

Financial Aid

Wesleyan allocates nearly $15 million each year to help supplement the financial needs of students and their families. Merit scholarships are available for students who demonstrate excellence in the classroom, as well as those who demonstrate talent in the arts and athletics. Scholarship opportunities are available for students who have a strong commitment to community service and for those who have a comprehensive co-curricular resume. A variety of need-based programs are also available, including government grants and loans, institutional grants, and student employment. All students and their families should file the Free Application for Federal Student Aid by February 15. The institutional code for West Virginia Wesleyan is 003830.

Faculty

The faculty members at Wesleyan have a primary goal of teaching and advising. More than 80 percent of the full-time faculty members hold the highest degree in their respective fields. With a 13:1 student-faculty ratio, classes are small, and personal attention is evident in all departments. Not only are faculty members teachers and advisers, but they are also mentors and friends.

Student Government

The Student Senate is structured to encourage and promote student participation. The four peer-elected officers are elected by their respective classes or representative student organizations. Student Senate meets biweekly, along with faculty members, administration, and staff members, and is recognized as the driving force behind many initiatives and decisions on campus.

Admission Requirements

Wesleyan seeks students who have proven academic credentials, combined with achievements and talents that enhance the quality of life on campus. Students are selected by the Office of Admission on the basis of their high school transcripts, college entrance exam results, letters of recommendation, campus interviews, and other supportive information. All applicants must take the SAT or ACT and submit secondary school transcripts from all schools attended, along with the application for admission. Candidates are considered on an individual basis without regard to race, color, national origin, sex, sexual orientation, age, disability, or religious affiliation. Essays and campus interviews are strongly encouraged and may be required in some instances.

Transfer students from accredited institutions are considered for admission. All official college transcripts must be submitted, along with high school transcripts and college entrance exam results.

Applicants who complete their secondary education through an alternative program (e.g., home schooling) must present evidence that they have been adequately prepared for college work to be considered for admission. SAT or ACT results are also required.

Application and Information

Applicants must submit an application for admission, official transcripts, and ACT or SAT scores. The application review period opens each year on September 1. Applying online is free of charge at http://apply.wvwc.edu. Wesleyan is also a Common Application school and applicants may apply free of charge. A paper application is also available. Admission decisions are made on a rolling basis, and students are notified within three weeks of receipt of all required documents. The preferred application deadline is March 1 for the fall semester, and December 1 for the spring semester. Applicants who wish to be considered for merit scholarships must apply before March 1. Interviews, campus tours, faculty and staff appointments, and class visits are encouraged and may be arranged through the Office of Admission.

For additional information, students should contact admissions@wvwc.edu and:

Office of Admission
West Virginia Wesleyan College
59 College Avenue
Buckhannon, West Virginia 26201
Phone: 304-473-8510
      800-722-9933 (toll-free)
E-mail: admission@wvwc.edu
Website: http://www.wvwc.edu

The Central Campus Green is one of many outdoor gathering spaces where students meet, study, and pass through on their way to classes and co-curricular activities.

WHEATON COLLEGE
WHEATON, ILLINOIS

The College

Ranked by *U.S. News & World Report* as one of the nation's top liberal arts colleges, Wheaton College attracts exceptional students from all fifty states and more than ninety countries. An interdenominational Christian liberal arts college, Wheaton takes the pursuit of faith and learning seriously. In addition to upholding an academically rigorous curriculum, Wheaton is committed to being a community that fearlessly pursues God's truth; invests in developing whole, well-rounded students; and prepares its graduates to lead lives that make a difference in the world.

The student body at Wheaton College consists of approximately 2,400 undergraduates (including 150+ students in the Conservatory of Music), approximately 80 percent of which come from outside Illinois.

Wheaton College's nearly 160-year history demonstrates the benefits of stable leadership in private Christian higher education—it has had only 8 presidents since it was founded in 1860. Wheaton has been faithful to its original precepts, and its legacy is shown in the lives of its graduates. Many distinguished graduate schools currently enroll Wheaton graduates, including Notre Dame, Princeton, SMU, Yale, and the Universities of Chicago and Missouri–Kansas City; several of the Big Ten music schools; and the A.R.T./MXAT Institute for Advanced Theater Training at Harvard. Wheaton alumni also excel in a wealth of endeavors around the world, with many holding positions in business and finance, government and foreign service, teaching, ministry, law, medicine, and the arts. Wheaton graduates actively contribute to their communities and churches, and no matter what position they hold, they strive to make a difference in the world around them.

Wheaton offers a rich, life-changing education, with graduates trained for life, not just jobs. Students are taught to think, reason, and express themselves effectively. They are equipped to attain knowledge and measure it against the truth of God's word, understand the importance of service, and value faith that embraces both theological accuracy and actively living it out. Developing strong, life-long relationships—with classmates, professors, and Jesus Christ—is a priority. Graduates are well-positioned for whatever they want to pursue and prepared to face the challenges of life. The Wheaton experience is distinctive, and living and learning at Wheaton is extraordinary. As a visiting lecturer recently observed, "I was so impressed by the enthusiasm of the Wheaton students to shape the world, and to make it a better place. And they are approaching this goal in practical ways. Some colleges are full of dour cynics. Wheaton is the opposite—brimming with optimists!"

Location

Wheaton's 80-acre campus is located in a residential suburb (population 55,000) 25 miles west of Chicago. The educational and cultural features of the Chicago metropolitan area are easily accessible by train and regularly visited by students.

Majors and Degrees

Wheaton grants the Bachelor of Arts and Bachelor of Science degrees and, through the Wheaton Conservatory of Music, the Bachelor of Music and Bachelor of Music Education degrees.

The following majors are available in the arts and sciences: ancient languages, anthropology, applied health science, archaeology, art, biblical and theological studies, biology, business/economics, chemistry, Christian education and ministry, communication, computer science, economics, education, English, environmental studies, geology, history, interdisciplinary studies, international relations, mathematics, modern languages (French, German, and Spanish), music, philosophy, physics, political science, psychology, sociology, and urban studies.

The Wheaton Conservatory of Music offers a full range of professional music majors, including composition, education, history/literature,

performance, music with elective studies in an outside field, and music with an emphasis in a music-related field (such as media/film music, pedagogy, conducting, and collaborative piano). Students seeking these professional music degrees are accepted directly into the program by audition.

An on-campus program in military science leads to a commission in the U.S. Army at graduation. In addition to the majors offered, Wheaton has programs leading to teacher certification and to athletic training certification as well as programs preparing students for careers in business, health professions, law, and ministry.

Academic Programs

Wheaton's academic curriculum combines with artistic, athletic, religious, service, and social activities to achieve a lively interaction of faith, learning, and living. Because of the College's strong commitment to developing effective servant/leaders for society worldwide and the church, there is a particularly strong integration of faith and learning in all degree programs. A new general education curriculum, Christ at the Core, implemented in fall '16, brings a well-rounded, Christ-centered academic experience while allowing increased freedom and flexibility among cohorts.

Students must demonstrate competence (either by examination or by taking prescribed courses) in foreign language, mathematics, speech, and writing. All students must complete area requirements in applied health science, art, biblical studies, history, literature, music, natural science, philosophy, and social science. A student may be granted advanced placement or college credit on the basis of examination (including SAT Subject Tests, AP, or IB).

Wheaton offers ten natural science majors—applied health science, biology, chemistry, computer science, environmental studies, geology, liberal arts engineering, liberal arts nursing, mathematics, and physics—in six academic departments. Also, 3-2 programs are offered in engineering and nursing, alongside a five-year cooperative engineering program with Illinois Institute of Technology and other engineering schools. The Wheaton faculty members engage the study of science authoritatively, enthusiastically, and creatively in the classrooms and laboratories and beyond the campus. They are creative and offer more than two dozen general education courses in the natural sciences as well as the majors listed above. The programming includes the use of state-of-the-art technologies and techniques on the main Wheaton campus, cutting edge geological and biological studies in a large science station in the scientifically rich area of the Black Hills of South Dakota, and marine biology studies in Belize.

Off-Campus Programs

Wheaton offers a variety of off-campus opportunities to enhance students' programs of study. The Wheaton Passage program is a popular experience available to new students at the College's Northwoods Campus in the wilderness of northern Wisconsin prior to orientation. Another program, Human Needs and Global Resources (HNGR), combines classroom study with a six-month, field-based, service-learning internship in the Global South. A similar program in urban studies, Wheaton in Chicago, focuses on urban issues in U.S. cities and includes a semester living in College-owned housing in urban Chicago.

Other special summer programs for credit include field study at the Wheaton College Science Station in the Black Hills of South Dakota; working with youth at HoneyRock Camp; interdisciplinary study in East Asia; the study of English literature in England; language study in France, Germany, and Spain; the Wheaton in the Holy Lands program, involving biblical and archaeological studies; the Arts in London program, which includes course work in music, theater, and art; and an international study program based in England and the Netherlands, offering courses in economics, political science, and psychology. Wheaton is a member of the Council of Christian Colleges and Universities, based in Washington, D.C. The council's activities increase students' learning opportunities by bringing special programs to campus and by providing off-campus study.

Off-campus programs include American Studies in Washington, D.C.; the Washington Journalism Center in Washington, D.C.; the Los Angeles Film Studies Center; the Contemporary Music Center in Martha's Vineyard; Latin American Studies in Costa Rica; Middle East Studies in Cairo; the Australia Studies Center; China Studies Program; the Scholar's Semester in Oxford; Russia Studies Program; and Uganda Studies Program. Wheaton has also recently affiliated with the International Sustainable Development Studies Institute in Thailand. In addition, Wheaton's membership in the Christian College Consortium allows students a semester of study at one of the other twelve consortium colleges.

Cooperative programs in social science are available at American and Drew Universities, and students may participate in a European seminar conducted by Gordon College.

Academic Facilities

A new Admissions Welcome Center building and the new Armerding Center for Music and the Arts opened in Fall 2017, with the new Concert Hall to follow in 2019.

An $80-million science and mathematics facility opened in Fall 2010. The 128,000-square-feet of space includes eight teaching labs and research space designed to promote collaborative teacher-student research.

In 2009, an $11 million renovation of Adams Hall added art gallery and studio space. Edman Chapel, often the venue for concerts by world-class musicians, has undergone a $9 million renovation that added rehearsal space, including a large rehearsal room named for alum John Nelson, former conductor of Ensemble Orchestral de Paris.

In 2008, Wheaton's Memorial Student Center reopened after an extensive renovation to house the Wheaton Center for Faith, Politics and Economics. The facility provides classroom, research, and public discussion space geared toward the study of economics, politics, and values in business, government, and ministry. Other recent additions to campus facilities include the Todd Beamer Student Center (2004); the Wade Center (2001), which houses the books and papers of seven British authors, including C. S. Lewis and J. R. R. Tolkien; and the Sports and Recreation Complex (2000).

Costs

Tuition for the 2017–18 year is $36,420; room and board for the year are $10,180. The Wheaton Fund subsidizes students' education expenses by nearly a third.

Financial Aid

Realizing that a private college education is a sizable investment, Wheaton is committed to providing the necessary need-based financial aid so students can attend. Last year Wheaton awarded over $30 million in grants and scholarships.

For first-time, full-time freshman who have financial need and were awarded any financial aid, the average amount of need-based scholarship or grant awarded for 2017–18 was $23,361.

The Center for Vocation and Career helps students to secure part-time jobs, as well as future employment, including Canvas to engage sophomores, employer recruiting, job fairs, professional development, and Wheaton in Network (WiN) alumni networking resources for upperclass students.

Faculty

95 percent of Wheaton's 222 full-time faculty members hold terminal degrees. The professors' primary commitment as educators and advisers is enriched by their considerable research, publishing, and artistic activities. In addition, the professors are active Christians who strive to show how a profound commitment to God's word structures a vision of all of life, including intellectual life. They are dedicated to honoring a Christian perspective and to modeling Christ's love to their students.

All undergraduate courses are taught by faculty members.

To ensure a rich range of perspectives and expertise, every department at Wheaton has at least 3 full-time professors, and most have 5 to 10. The student-faculty ratio is 11:1.

Student Government

Student Government ensures a student voice in institutional affairs and provides a wide range of opportunities to develop leadership abilities. Student Government's vision is "To further the educational, spiritual, and relational development of the Wheaton College community as elected servant leaders representing student initiative, concern, creativity, and enthusiasm."

Besides Student Government, there are over forty academic, cultural, social justice, and entertainment student groups on campus. In addition, the Office of Christian Outreach provides opportunities for student ministry through student-run mission trips and ministries in urban and suburban Chicago.

Admission Requirements

Wheaton is a selective college that seeks to enroll students who evidence a vital Christian experience, high moral character, personal integrity, social concern, strong academic ability and motivation, and the desire to pursue Christian higher education as defined in the aims and objectives of the College. These qualities are evaluated by consideration of each applicant's academic record, autobiographical essays, test scores, recommendations, optional interview, and participation in extracurricular activities. For students applying to the Conservatory of Music, strong consideration is given to the evaluation of the required audition.

Applicants must have a high school diploma or the equivalent, and at the time of graduation should have completed a college-preparatory curriculum with a minimum of 18 acceptable units.

Satisfactory scores on the SAT or on the ACT examination are required of all applicants to the freshman class. The middle 50 percent range of scores for those admitted is 27–32 (ACT) and 1250–1400 composite score on the SAT.

Application and Information

An application packet, complete with detailed instructions and requirements, can be obtained from the Admissions Office or online. For early action (nonbinding), students seeking admission in the fall term should apply to either the College of Arts and Sciences or the Conservatory of Music by November 1. The regular action deadline is January 10; the transfer application deadline is March 1. An admissions counselor can provide more information about Wheaton in general or the application process in particular.

Further information is available from:

Admissions Office
Wheaton College
501 College Avenue
Wheaton, Illinois 60187
Phone: 630-752-5005
        800-222-2419
E-mail: admissions@wheaton.edu
Website: wheaton.edu
         wheaton.edu/connect

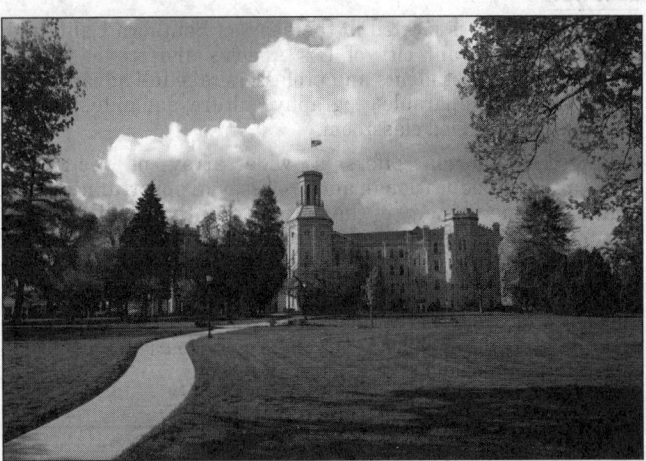

Historic Blanchard Hall overlooks Wheaton's front of campus.

WHITTIER COLLEGE

WHITTIER, CALIFORNIA

For more information, visit http://petersons.to/whittiercollege

The College

Whittier College is a private, four-year liberal arts college located in Whittier, California. The school—which has an enrollment of over 1,600 students—offers small class sizes, personalized degree programs, and ample opportunities for real-world learning experiences.

Whittier has earned a reputation for providing a high-quality liberal arts education. The Princeton Review recently named Whittier as one of the country's best institutions for undergraduate education, and it included Whittier in the 2016 edition of "The Best 380 Colleges." Whittier is also among 200 schools listed in "Colleges of Distinction," a national college guidebook that showcases colleges that offer engaged students, great teaching, a vibrant community, and successful outcomes.

Whittier takes on the liberal arts in a distinctly West Coast way—with a fresh eye toward how ideas intersect across disciplines. The College places an emphasis on providing students with a truly interdisciplinary liberal arts education. Whittier students are encouraged to think critically and to learn about other perspectives and cultures through cross-curricular courses and experiential learning activities such as internships and study-abroad opportunities.

The value of a Whittier College education lies in Whittier's core mission: to prepare students from diverse backgrounds for success in a complex global society. Whittier's approach to education produces graduates with skills that are highly valued by employers and graduate schools alike.

With a low faculty-to-student ratio, Whittier students receive the one-on-one attention that helps them stay focused and on-track. Because there are no impacted majors or programs, students can choose their major freely without the stress of competing for a spot.

Eighty-nine percent of Whittier graduates complete their degree in four years. With access to hundreds of semester courses and an interim term, Whittier students can fulfill major requirements without delays.

Whittier College is accredited by the Western Association of Schools and Colleges (WASC).

Location

Whittier College is located in the heart of Southern California, between the vibrant city of Los Angeles and scenic Orange County. Whittier students and professors take full advantage of the region's incomparable geography, culture, and industry, and use it as an extended classroom.

Southern California offers a wide array of recreation, entertainment, educational, and professional opportunities. The region is home to many of the nation's and the world's leading cultural and industry influencers. Hollywood's production studios, Anaheim's theme parks, and the South Bay's aerospace industry are all a short drive from Whittier College.

Just a few blocks from the College, Uptown Whittier boasts cafes and restaurants, a movie theater, a farmer's market, and dozens more shops for students to explore and enjoy.

Majors and Degrees

Students at Whittier College may choose from 30 majors, 37 minors, and 3 pre-professional programs, including anthropology, history, mathematics, political science, economics, English, and business administration. Programs of study include: anthropology, art (art history, studio art, or digital art and design), biochemistry, biology, business administration (accounting, finance, international business, management, or marketing concentrations), chemistry, child development, Chinese, economics (business economics, general distributive, or pre-professional economics options), engineering 3-2 (chemistry, mathematics, physics, or science and letters options), English (creative writing emphasis available), environmental science (environmental studies or environmental science tracks), French, global and cultural studies (culture, geographical area, issues, or national/transnational institutions options), health sciences (pre-med, pre-vet, or pre-pharm), history, kinesiology and nutrition science (pre–physical therapy or sports management emphasis), mathematics (teaching credential emphasis available), mathematics–business, music, applied philosophy, philosophy, physics (astronomy emphasis available), political science (international relations track available), pre-law, pre-therapy (physical, occupational, or recreational), psychology, religious studies, social work, sociology, Spanish, and theatre and communication arts (design and technology or performance emphasis).

Whittier College also provides students with opportunities to pursue self-designed majors through its Whittier Scholars Program (WSP). WSP students work closely with faculty members to develop a highly personalized course of study in specific areas of interest. This program culminates in the research, presentation, and defense of senior projects. Approximately 12 percent of Whittier students participate in WSP.

Academic Programs

In addition to completing the required course work for their major, all Whittier students are required to complete six hours of course work each in the areas of natural science, social science, fine arts, and humanities. The College's paired classes help students see the interconnectedness of ideas. Students take at least two paired classes while at Whittier, and in these classes they explore subjects that intersect in provocative ways.

All Whittier College students are required to complete several specialized courses designed to help them improve and refine their writing skills. The required writing course work begins with a first-year writing seminar and culminates in a paper-in-the-major, which each student completes during his or her senior year of study. The paper-in-the-major, which is developed with the guidance of a faculty member, is often used as a writing sample by students applying to graduate programs.

Whittier provides a wide range of services and programs designed to help new students adjust to college life. All first-year students participate in a linked class, two courses that are taken together during the first semester. These small classes of no more than 16 students help to create a common intellectual experience. In addition, each student is assigned a faculty mentor to provide advising and mentoring during their first semester. They also have a peer mentor who connects them to the College.

First-year students also live in close proximity; they are placed in three residence halls, forming a residential community. Resident Advisers in these communities will intentionally coordinate programs that will assist students in their transition to college. Additional activities, such as orientation and pre-orientation, also play a key role in ensuring student success.

Off-Campus Programs

Because Whittier College is located within driving distance to Los Angeles and Orange County, students have access to a wide range of internships with companies in industries ranging from entertainment to business. Whittier students have completed internships with Sony Pictures, Merrill Lynch, the J. Paul Getty Museum, EMI Music Publishing, New Line Cinema, First Heritage Bank, Southern California Edison, and the U.S. Department of Education.

Students may also choose to gain hands-on work experience through one of Whittier's many partnerships with community and government organizations such as the Boys and Girls Club of Whittier. Students in fields such as education, child psychology, and social work can participate in work-study programs at Broadoaks Children's School, Whittier's private, nonprofit demonstration school.

Whittier College provides many opportunities for students interested in learning about other cultures. Each student may choose to spend a semester, a year, or a summer living and studying in a variety of locations around the world. Whittier also offers several study-abroad opportunities through its faculty-led JanTerm and MayTerm programs. Past and upcoming study-abroad opportunities include a course on managing multinational corporations in Mexico; a study of Islamic culture in Morocco; an examination of race, religion, and gender in South America; and an anthropology course in Tanzania. Whittier's Global Poet Scholarship (GPS) gives every student $2,000 to study abroad.

Academic Facilities

The campus boasts an eclectic mix of historic architecture and state-of-the art amenities including a 400-seat performing arts center, an art gallery, an outdoor amphitheater, a recently upgraded library, a 7,000-seat sports stadium with a new track and field, and a beautiful aquatics center. The College also opened a new Science & Learning Center in fall 2016.

Costs

For the 2018–19 academic year, tuition is $47,496 with fees of $590. The cost of a double room is $7,666 and the 15-weekly meal plan is $6,076.

Financial Aid

Scholarships and financial aid are available, and over 90 percent of Whittier students receive a combination of grants, scholarships, and loans. More than $8.5 million in aid was awarded to Whittier students in 2017–18. Students will automatically be considered for a wide range of academic awards when they apply. In addition, there are talent scholarships in art, music, and theater that students can pursue without having to major or even minor in those academic disciplines.

Faculty

At Whittier, professors, students, and staff support each other and come together to share in the thrill of discovery, the joy of learning, and the gratification that comes with contributing to society. Students work with professors and staff to tap into their unique abilities, talents, and aspirations. Together, they design a complete college experience that combines academics, internships, fellowships, and service learning.

The College's full-time faculty numbers 109. The average class size is 19, with a student-faculty ratio of 12:1.

Student Life

Students interested in getting involved in extracurricular activities can choose from a wide variety of options. Whittier is home to nearly 100 academic, cultural, political, and general-interest clubs and organizations, as well as several service-oriented fraternities and sororities, called societies at Whittier. The school also has a student newspaper, yearbook, literary magazine, video production studio, and radio station. Through the Leadership Experience and Programs (LEAP) Office, there are opportunities for involvement in student government, community service, and a number of programs dedicated to helping students develop their leadership skills.

Whittier is home to 22 intercollegiate sports teams, including men's and women's basketball, cross-country, track and field, swimming and diving, water polo, soccer, lacrosse, golf, and tennis. Whittier also offers men's baseball and football and women's volleyball and softball.

Admission Requirements

Students interested in applying to Whittier College must submit a completed application (available at www.commonapp.org), a $50 application fee, transcripts, SAT I or ACT scores (test optional for students with a cumulative GPA of 3.0 and higher), a personal statement/essay, counselor evaluation, and letter of recommendation from a current or former teacher. Students interested in transferring to Whittier from another college or university must also submit college transcripts and letters of recommendation from two former or current professors.

Application and Information

Students are encouraged to apply early to ensure consideration for the fullest range of scholarship opportunities. Applications are reviewed on a rolling basis as they are completed.

The application filing date for Early Action candidates (nonbinding early deadline) is November 15. The priority application filing date for Regular Decision candidates is February 1 and the deadline for financial aid applicants to file the Free Application for Federal Student Aid (FAFSA) and for California Residents to apply for the Cal Grant Program is March 2.

Whittier College Admission Office
13406 East Philadelphia Street
P.O. Box 634
Whittier, California 90608
United States
Phone: 562-907-4238
      888-200-0369 (toll-free)
Fax: 562-907-4870
E-mail: admissions@whittier.edu
Website: https://www.whittier.edu
      https://www.facebook.com/WhittierCollege
      https://www.instagram.com/whittiercollege
      https://twitter.com/whittiercollege

WILKES UNIVERSITY
WILKES-BARRE, PENNSYLVANIA

The University

Wilkes University offers the opportunities of a large university and the personal attention of a small institution. Its unique program mix and variety of extracurricular activities let students build their educational experience to suit their goals and interests.

Students may notice something unexpected: professors genuinely interested in their thoughts and aspirations. All Wilkes students have opportunities to gain real-world experience, whether starting a business, conducting research, or using high-tech instruments that even graduate students at other institutions rarely touch.

Located at the foothills of the Pocono Mountains, along the shore of the Susquehanna River and within walking distance of downtown Wilkes-Barre, Pennsylvania, Wilkes University is a private, comprehensive institution with more than 2,400 undergraduate students.

The University includes the College of Arts, Humanities, and Social Sciences; the College of Science and Engineering; the Nesbitt School of Pharmacy; the Passan School of Nursing; the Sidhu School of Business and Leadership; the School of Education; and University College (for undecided students). Wilkes offers bachelor's and master's degrees in the humanities, social and natural sciences, engineering, business administration, nursing, and education as well as the Master of Fine Arts, Doctor of Pharmacy, Doctor of Education, and Doctor of Nursing Practice degrees.

The Wilkes campus features a parklike quadrangle surrounded by modern classroom buildings and historic nineteenth-century mansions that have been restored as student residences and academic buildings. Facilities include the Cohen Science Center, a sports and conference center, a financial trading room, and a new media and communication center. New engineering facilities are slated to open in summer 2018.

Programs provide students with a liberal arts foundation that cultivates independent thinking and prepares them for professional life or for graduate or professional school. Academic advising integrated with career planning is stressed, and hands-on experiences are provided in laboratory, internship, and cooperative education settings. Free tutorial services are available to all students.

The University is accredited by the Middle States Association of Colleges and Schools and has specialized accreditation in the sciences, engineering, nursing, education, and business. Ninety-six percent of students are employed or attending graduate/professional school within one year of receiving their degrees.

First-year students enrolling prior to May 1 are guaranteed housing, and all students may have cars on campus. Campus housing is available for all four years. Residence halls include modern, multifloor buildings and historic mansions.

Student activities complement academic life. Intercollegiate athletics encompass 24 Division III sports, including swimming and women's and men's ice hockey. About 100 clubs and organizations recognize student achievement and provide opportunities for leadership development, professional growth, and community service. The award-winning e-mentor program links current students with incoming freshmen to ease the transition to college life.

Location

Wilkes-Barre is a medium-sized city of about 43,000. Nearby recreational facilities include Pocono Mountain ski resorts; PNC Field, home of a Triple A baseball team; the Mohegan Sun Arena, home to a professional hockey team; golf courses; state parks; tennis courts; and harness racing.

The University is located in the historic district, which features a performing arts center, the Wilkes University/King's College Barnes and Noble bookstore, a fourteen-screen movie complex, and numerous shops and restaurants. Other offerings include art galleries, ethnic and community festivals, and libraries and museums. The city is approximately 2 hours from New York City and Philadelphia.

Wilkes-Barre lies near the intersection of Interstates 80, 81, and 476 and within 6 hours of Washington, D.C. and Boston. The Wilkes-Barre/Scranton International Airport is about 20 minutes from campus.

Majors and Degrees

Wilkes University offers Bachelor of Arts, Bachelor of Fine Arts, Bachelor of Business Administration, and Bachelor of Science degrees, as well as a guaranteed-seat Doctor of Pharmacy program. Majors offered are: accounting; applied and engineering sciences; biochemistry; biology; chemistry; communication studies; computer information systems; computer science; criminology; digital design and media art; earth and environmental sciences; electrical engineering; education (elementary and early childhood, middle-level, secondary with a subject-area major, and special education certification); engineering management; English; entrepreneurship; environmental engineering; finance; geology; history; hospitality leadership; international studies; management; marketing; mathematics; mechanical engineering; medical laboratory sciences; musical theatre; neuroscience; nursing; philosophy; physics; political science; psychology; public administration; sociology; Spanish; sports management; theatre arts; and theatre design and technology. Wilkes also offers the six-year guaranteed-seat pharmacy program, a five-year B.A./M.B.A. in industrial/organizational psychology, and a 4+1 B.S./M.S. in bioengineering.

Premedical and prelaw preparation programs are strong. Other preprofessional programs include dentistry, occupational therapy, optometry, physical therapy, physician assistant, podiatry, and veterinary science. A full-time director of health sciences and student success advises students who wish to continue study in a professional health-care field. The University offers an affiliated program in medicine with the Penn State College of Medicine at Hershey; in optometry with the Pennsylvania College of Optometry and the State University of New York (SUNY) College of Optometry; in podiatry with Temple University School of Podiatric Medicine; in occupational therapy with Temple University; in physical therapy with Drexel University, Temple University, and Widener University; and in medical technology/medical laboratory sciences with Robert Packer Hospital.

Academic Programs

Through a rigorous curriculum that emphasizes hands-on experience, Wilkes helps prepare students in all majors to adapt to a technologically and socially evolving world. To graduate, students must complete a core curriculum from 120 to 136 credits, depending on their major.

The University operates on a dual-semester calendar, with optional summer sessions and a January intersession. Advanced Placement test credits, College Level Examination Program (CLEP) credits, and International Baccalaureate (I.B.) credits are accepted.

Off-Campus Programs

A cooperative education (internship) program is available to all students, with credit applicable in most majors. Many government offices and private businesses in northeastern Pennsylvania, as well as in New York City, Philadelphia, Harrisburg, and Washington, D.C., employ Wilkes students. A study-abroad adviser works with interested students, placing them in the situation best suited to their academic pursuits. Students have recently attended programs in Costa Rica, England, Spain, Tanzania, and Uganda.

Academic Facilities

New engineering laboratories are scheduled to be ready for use in summer 2018 and the new Karambelas Media and Communication Center opened in fall 2017. The Cohen Science Center and clinical nursing simulation center opened in 2013. The modern Eugene

S. Farley Library offers wireless Internet access and areas for both independent study and group collaboration. Complete laboratory facilities are available for biology, chemistry, earth and environmental sciences, engineering, nursing, pharmacy, and psychology. Student-produced programming is broadcast from WCLH-FM and a television studio. The Dorothy Dickson Darte Center contains a 500-seat main theater and a 45-seat black box theater. The unique NeuroTraining and Research Center is located in Breiseth Hall.

Costs

For the 2018–19 academic year, tuition is $34,454 per year, and room and board are $14,682. Fees are $1,880 annually.

Financial Aid

Financial aid is available to students who demonstrate quality academic ability and/or financial need, as verified by the Free Application for Federal Student Aid (FAFSA). Merit-based and need-based aid is available for qualified students. Scholarships ranging from $13,000 to $19,000 per year are available to students based on academic ability, regardless of financial need. Approximately 90 percent of students receive some type of financial assistance.

Faculty

Wilkes University has a nationally recruited full-time faculty of 182 members, approximately 91 percent of whom have earned Ph.D.'s or terminal degrees in their chosen field. Faculty evaluation criteria emphasize teaching excellence and effective advising, while recognizing continued scholarly activities. The student-faculty ratio is 13:1.

Admission Requirements

SAT or ACT scores are required. In cases where a student has taken the examination more than once, scores from the highest testing in each category are used. Freshman applicants should either have completed or be in the process of completing a college-preparatory course of study, including 3 to 4 years of mathematics, social studies, science, and English. Additional courses should be elected in academic subjects according to individual interests. Acceptable electives include foreign language and computing, among others. Students who have not followed this pattern may still qualify for admission if there is other strong evidence of preparation for college work. Letters of recommendation are not required but may be submitted. Students intending to pursue a major in pharmacy should have completed algebra I and II, geometry, and trigonometry prior to enrollment. Students intending to major in nursing should have completed courses in biology and chemistry. An audition is required for all prospective musical theatre and theatre arts students. Transfer students must submit a transcript from every college previously attended.

Wilkes University is an Equal Opportunity/Affirmative Action institution. No applicant shall be denied admission to the University because of race, color, gender, religion, national or ethnic origin, sexual orientation, or handicap.

Application and Information

Applications for admission should be completed early in the senior year of secondary school. Applications are reviewed after all of the student's credentials have been received. Notification of the University's decision reaches the student two to four weeks after the application file is complete. Priority deadline for all applications is March 1; applications for the Guaranteed Seat Pharmacy Program must be received by February 1. Other health science programs may have additional deadlines.

Contact the Admissions Office for more information.

Admissions Office
Wilkes University
84 West South Street
Wilkes-Barre, Pennsylvania 18766
Phone: 570-408-4400
        800-945-5378 Ext. 4400 (toll-free)
Website: http://www.wilkes.edu

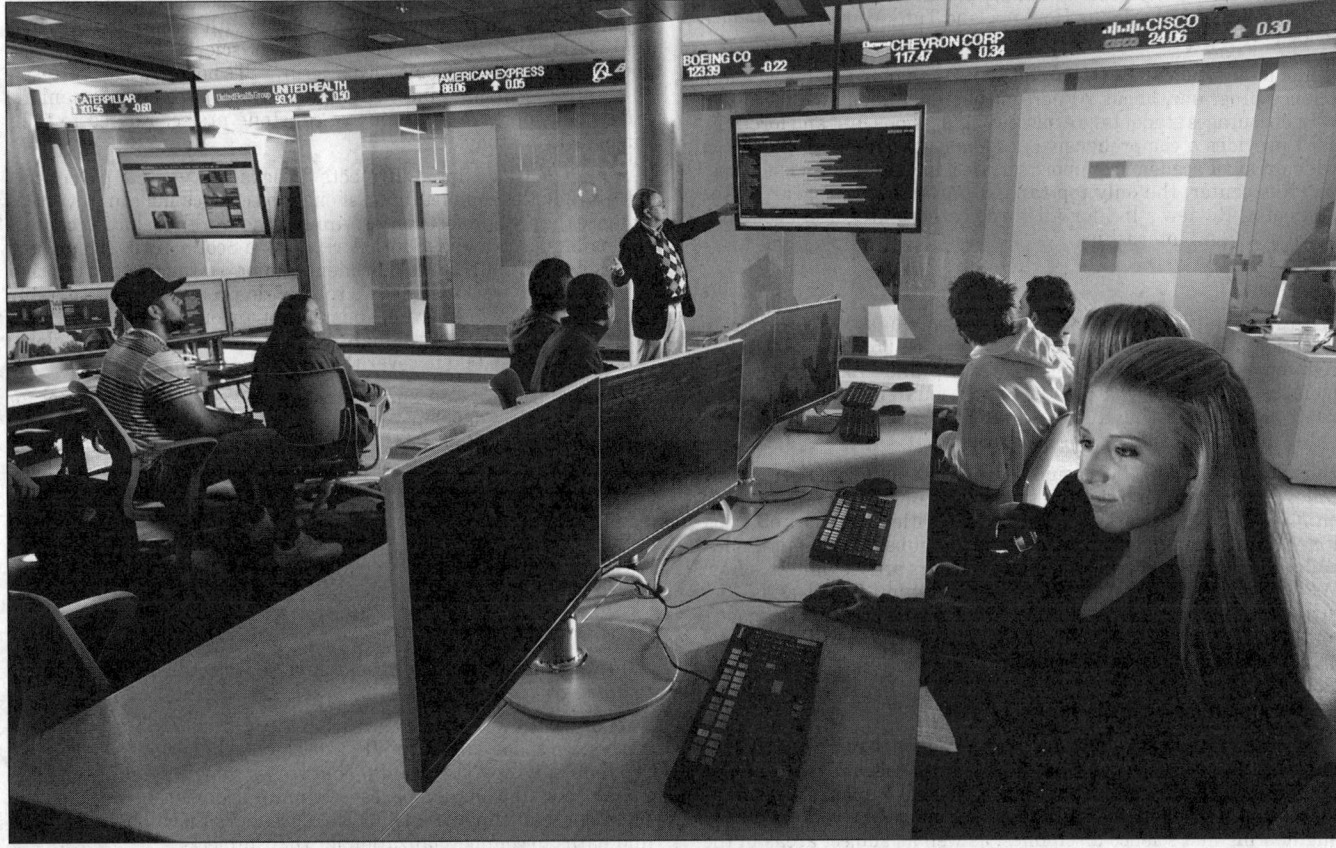

The Sidhu School of Business and Leadership's home includes a financial trading room, complete with stock ticker.

WORCESTER POLYTECHNIC INSTITUTE
WORCESTER, MASSACHUSETTS

 To read more about this school, visit http://petersons.to/wpi

The University

Following its founding motto of "Theory and Practice," Worcester Polytechnic Institute (WPI) offers a unique project-based curriculum that prepares students to take on the world's great challenges. Students not only take rigorous classes, but also complete distinctive hands-on projects that address real issues in communities across the globe. In addition, small classes, one-on-one interaction with professors, non-punitive grading, and a spirit of innovation and teamwork encourage students to think creatively, collaborate across disciplines, and put their ideas into practice.

WPI has been widely recognized for its research-based academic programs and the success of its graduates. It is consistently ranked among the top national universities by *U.S. News & World Report* and the Princeton Review. The *Wall Street Journal* ranked WPI No. 1 for faculty combining research and teaching. According to the National Association of Colleges and Employers, the starting salaries of WPI graduates are 32 percent higher than those of many other college graduates. WPI was also ranked fifteenth in the nation for return on investment by *Forbes* and seventh by CNBC for colleges where students go on to earn the most money. The Princeton Review has also ranked WPI one of the 10-best study-abroad programs four years running, the only technological school to be so recognized.

Top-tier employers seek out WPI graduates for their real-world experience and ability to work collaboratively. More than 90 percent of students are in full-time jobs or attending graduate school within several months of graduation. Students are recruited by leading organizations such as Amazon Robotics, Pfizer, General Electric, Fidelity Investments, Johnson & Johnson, and Tesla. Each year, WPI graduates are accepted at many prestigious graduate schools, including MIT, Yale, Johns Hopkins, and Tufts University Medical School.

While many students attend WPI for its top-notch engineering and science programs, about 20 percent of students enter undeclared. WPI encourages students to explore their passions first and foremost. WPI provides a comprehensive academic advising program and a wide array of academic support services, including a robust career services center, the only top-ranked university to appear on the Princeton Review's list for all three career categories (services, placement, and internships).

Location

With its beautiful architecture and grassy quad, WPI provides a traditional New England campus situated on 95 acres in a hilltop residential neighborhood. Students stop and chat with faculty members on tree-lined paths, study by the fountain in Reunion Plaza, grab a coffee at the Rubin Campus Center, and watch live entertainment at the Goat's Head restaurant.

Home to nine other colleges and universities and more than 38,000 college students, Worcester is a true college town. It is ranked ninth on *Forbes*' list of "America's Most Livable Cities" and part of Axios' top-10 list for up-and-coming tech startup hubs. Late-night diners, clubs, museums, concert venues, and theaters are just minutes from WPI. Boston is less than an hour away by commuter rail, and major attractions in the region, including New York, Cape Cod, Providence, and the Berkshires, are easily accessible. There is also skiing and snowboarding at nearby Wachusett Mountain.

Majors and Degrees

WPI offers Bachelor of Science (B.S.) and Bachelor of Art (B.A.) degrees, as well as a combined B.S./M.S. program that enables students to begin studying toward, or even complete, a master's degree in their senior year. Students can major in a wide variety of engineering and science disciplines, as well as subject areas in the humanities and arts, social sciences, and business. They can also design their own majors or choose from interdisciplinary programs such as interactive media and game development, bioinformatics and computational biology, and robotics engineering (WPI's was the first undergraduate program in robotics in the nation). Additional information is available online at wpi.edu/academics.

WPI also offers preprofessional programs in dentistry, law, medicine, and veterinary medicine; see wpi.edu/+prehealth. The university also offers teacher licensure (wpi.edu/+teach).

Academic Programs

At WPI, most students take three courses during each of the four 7-week terms (two in the fall and two in the spring). Classes aim to provide a balance between academic content and hands-on projects and group work. WPI's academic program also encourages collaboration, not competition—students can get grades of A, B, C, or no credit, but do not receive failing grades.

Regardless of their majors, all students must meet a humanities and arts requirement that encourages them to broaden their thinking and explore new areas of performance, creativity, and culture by taking courses in disciplines such as music, art, theatre, foreign language, history, and literature.

Paid internships and co-ops are available to advance education and earn income. Hundreds of opportunities are available each year with global companies like Boston Scientific, ExxonMobil, General Electric, and SpaceX. *U.S. News & World Report* cited WPI's internship/co-ops as 1 of 17 programs to look for.

WPI Projects Program

Projects are at the heart of the WPI curriculum. All students complete a junior-year project in which they work with a team to address a real-world problem at the intersection of science, technology, and society—from designing bicycle paths in WPI's hometown of Worcester to creating an ambulance-dispatch system in Venice. As seniors, students undertake an intensive capstone project related to their major field of study.

Through WPI's Global Projects Program, over 60 percent of undergraduates complete at least one project off campus and overseas at more than 40 project centers around the world, including centers in Thailand, Australia, South Africa, Nova Scotia, Switzerland, and all over the United States. Students immerse themselves in other cultures while working to solve real-world problems in partnership with government, corporate, and nonprofit sponsors. The experience is on WPI—each undergraduate student receives a one-time global scholarship of $5,000 to cover the costs of studying abroad.

Students, alumni, and employers praise WPI's project model for helping students develop professional and personal skills including strategically managing projects, problem solving, teamwork, communication, and leadership abilities, as well as increased global awareness and enriched personal lives. WPI's off-campus programs were recently recognized by the Princeton Review, which ranked WPI first for most popular study abroad program in its 2016 edition of the best colleges. Additional information is available at admissions.wpi.edu/+global.

Academic Facilities

There are many teaching, research, and project facilities available to undergraduates at WPI.

The brand-new Foisie Innovation Studio is a state-of-the-art innovation space suited for WPI's distinctive hands-on collaborative problem-solving. The Studio contains a robotics lab, high-tech classrooms, and makerspaces—communal inventing workspaces. The Center for Innovation and Entrepreneurship will help students find paths to commercialization for their projects.

In addition, undergraduates have access to over 40 state-of-the-art research centers and laboratories, including two atomic-force microscopes, medical imaging laboratories, a fire science laboratory, a laser holography lab, a computer music lab, a satellite navigation lab, and a research library with over half a million print and digital resources.

The Life Sciences and Bioengineering Center at Gateway Park is a state-of-the-art 130,000 square-foot facility for research and teaching in biology and biotechnology, biomedical engineering, chemistry and biochemistry, and chemical engineering.

WPI also has an exceptional computer and networking infrastructure, including hundreds of computers in open-access 24/7 labs, powerful UNIX workstations, access to specialized scientific and engineering software, and a campuswide high-speed data network.

Costs

For 2016–17, full-time tuition for first-year undergraduates was $46,364. Room and board charges were $13,736.

Financial Aid

Approximately 97 percent of students at WPI receive financial assistance in the form of need- and merit-based aid. Need-based aid includes financial aid packages, on-campus jobs, and loan programs. WPI has one of the nation's best loan repayment rates, a marker of its graduates' return on investment. More information is available from WPI's Office of Student Aid & Financial Literacy at wpi.edu/+finaid.

All admitted applicants to WPI are also considered for academic scholarships based upon academic performance, leadership, extracurricular involvement, and community service. More information is available at wpi.edu/+scholarships.

Faculty

WPI's full- and part-time faculty members are passionate teachers as well as committed researchers and scholars with world-class credentials. They are leading contributors to the fields of bioengineering, cybersecurity, robotics, energy and sustainability, materials science, and more. Thirteen members of the current faculty are Fulbright Scholars and more than 20 have won the CAREER Award, the National Science Foundation's most prestigious honor for young faculty members.

With a 13:1 student-faculty ratio, WPI facilitates small classes where students have ample opportunity to join discussions, work in teams, and interact with professors, as evidenced by the *Wall Street Journal* ranking WPI number one in "Faculty That Best Combine Scholarly Research and Classroom Instruction." WPI ranks number one for student-faculty interaction (National Survey of Student Engagement), and *U.S. News & World Report* ranks WPI as a top-50 college among national universities for faculty resources, including salary, class size, and student-faculty ratio.

Student Activities

At WPI, students work hard but play hard too—undergraduates at all levels take part in more than 200 clubs and organizations, ranging from music and theater ensembles to cultural and religious organizations, community service clubs, and professional groups.

WPI "gets Greek life right," according to BestCollegesOnline.com—more than 30 percent of students participate in one of the 19 fraternities and sororities on campus, performing over 30,000 hours of community service per year. The Student Government Association also gives a voice to undergraduates within WPI's close-knit community.

More than 80 percent of students are involved in sports programs, including twenty varsity (NCAA Division III) athletics teams and nearly forty club and intramural sports. Students also work out at the university's state-of-the art sports and recreation center, one of the finest university athletic facilities in the Northeast, built in 2012 and featuring a four-court gymnasium, indoor jogging track, racquetball and squash courts, and competition pool. The Rec Center is also a reflection of WPI's commitment to support the environment with its green design and sustainable attributes.

Admission Requirements

WPI has high standards for applicants and looks for more than just outstanding academic performance. They take care to admit students who will thrive at the university. These students tend to be creative and curious; like to work in teams; are comfortable making their own decisions; love math and science but feel just as passionate about literature, music, movies, and the arts; and are ready to make a positive impact on the world around them.

As a test-optional university, applicants are not required to submit SAT or ACT scores. WPI will accept scores if they are sent, but admission decisions will not be influenced by the exclusion of standardized test scores. Full admissions requirements can be found at admissions.wpi.edu.

Application and Information

The Common Application is the only way to apply to WPI. The deadline for Early Action round 1 is November 1, with notification by December 20. The deadline for Early Action round 2 is January 1, with notification by February 10. The regular decision deadline is February 1, with notification by April 1. More information is available at admissions.wpi.edu/apply.

Students are encouraged to visit the WPI campus to learn more about the university, see its facilities, and hear firsthand about the WPI experience. Many students call the visit to campus the most influential decision on determining their fit at WPI. Students can also view a VR-enabled virtual tour at wpi.edu/+tour.

To schedule a visit or request more information, students should contact:

Undergraduate Admissions
Bartlett Center
Worcester Polytechnic Institute
100 Institute Road
Worcester, Massachusetts 01609-2280
Phone: 508-831-5286
Fax: 508-831-5875
E-mail: admissions@wpi.edu
Website: admissions.wpi.edu
Facebook: facebook.com/WPI
Instagram: instagram.com/WPI
Twitter: twitter.com/WPI

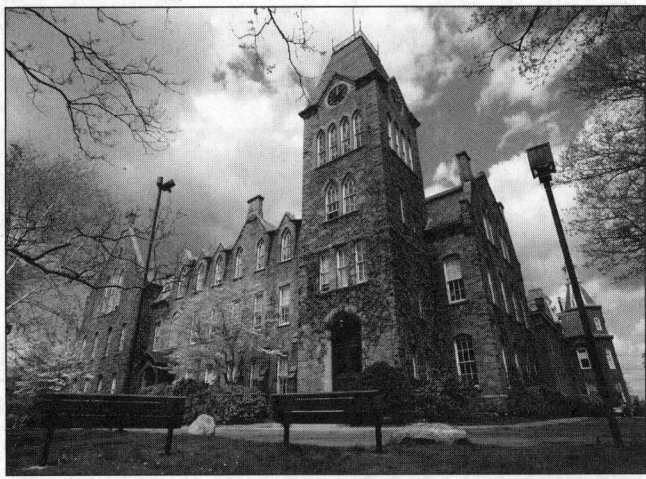

WPI is situated on a 95-acre campus, 40 miles west of Boston in a residential section of Worcester, Massachusetts, the second largest city in New England and home to nine colleges.

Indexes

Majors

ACCOUNTING

Abilene Christian U (TX)
Academy Coll (MN)
Adams State U (CO)
Adelphi U (NY)
Alabama State U (AL)
Albion Coll (MI)
Albright Coll (PA)
Alcorn State U (MS)
Alfred U (NY)
Alma Coll (MI)
American Intl Coll (MA)
American Public U System (WV)
American U (DC)
The American U in Cairo (Egypt)
Anderson U (IN)
Anderson U (SC)
Andrews U (MI)
Angelo State U (TX)
Appalachian State U (NC)
Aquinas Coll (MI)
Arcadia U (PA)
Arizona State U at the Tempe
    campus (AZ)
Arizona State U at the West
    campus (AZ)
Arkansas Tech U (AR)
Asbury U (KY)
Ashland U (OH)
Assumption Coll (MA)
Athabasca U (AB, Canada)
Athens State U (AL)
Auburn U (AL)
Auburn U at Montgomery (AL)
Augsburg U (MN)
Augustana Coll (IL)
Augustana U (SD)
Aurora U (IL)
Austin Peay State U (TN)
Averett U (VA)
Avila U (MO)
Azusa Pacific U (CA)
Babson Coll (MA)
Baker U (KS)
Baldwin Wallace U (OH)
Ball State U (IN)
Barry U (FL)
Baruch Coll of the City U of New
    York (NY)
Baylor U (TX)
Bay Path U (MA)
Belhaven U (MS)
Bellarmine U (KY)
Belmont U (TN)
Bemidji State U (MN)
Benedictine Coll (KS)
Benedictine U (IL)
Bentley U (MA)
Berry Coll (GA)
Bethel Coll (IN)
Bethune-Cookman U (FL)
Binghamton U, State U of New
    York (NY)
Biola U (CA)
Blackburn Coll (IL)
Black Hills State U (SD)
Bloomsburg U of Pennsylvania (PA)
Bluefield Coll (VA)
Bluffton U (OH)
Bob Jones U (SC)
Boise State U (ID)
Boston Coll (MA)
Boston U (MA)
Bowie State U (MD)
Bowling Green State U (OH)
Bradley U (IL)
Brenau U (GA)
Brescia U (KY)
Brewton-Parker Coll (GA)
Bridgewater State U (MA)
Brigham Young U–Idaho (ID)
Brock U (ON, Canada)
Bryant U (RI)
Buena Vista U (IA)
Butler U (IN)
Cairn U (PA)
Caldwell U (NJ)
California Baptist U (CA)
California Lutheran U (CA)

California State U, Dominguez Hills
    (CA)
California State U, Fullerton (CA)
California State U, Long Beach
    (CA)
California State U, Northridge (CA)
California State U, San Bernardino
    (CA)
California State U, San Marcos
    (CA)
California State U, Stanislaus (CA)
Calumet Coll of Saint Joseph (IN)
Calvin Coll (MI)
Cameron U (OK)
Campbellsville U (KY)
Canisius Coll (NY)
Capital U (OH)
Cardinal Stritch U (WI)
Caribbean U (PR)
Carlow U (PA)
Carroll Coll (MT)
Carroll U (WI)
Carson-Newman U (TN)
Carthage Coll (WI)
Case Western Reserve U (OH)
Catawba Coll (NC)
The Catholic U of America (DC)
Cedar Crest Coll (PA)
Cedarville U (OH)
Centenary Coll of Louisiana (LA)
Central Connecticut State U (CT)
Central Methodist U (MO)
Central Michigan U (MI)
Central Penn Coll (PA)
Central State U (OH)
Champlain Coll (VT)
Chapman U (CA)
Charleston Southern U (SC)
Chatham U (PA)
Chestnut Hill Coll (PA)
Chowan U (NC)
Christian Brothers U (TN)
Christopher Newport U (VA)
Claremont McKenna Coll (CA)
Clarion U of Pennsylvania (PA)
Clark Atlanta U (GA)
Clarke U (IA)
Clayton State U (GA)
Clemson U (SC)
Cleveland State U (OH)
Coastal Carolina U (SC)
Coe Coll (IA)
Colegio Universitario de San Juan,
    San Juan (PR)
The Coll at Brockport, State U of
    New York (NY)
Coll of Charleston (SC)
The Coll of Idaho (ID)
The Coll of New Jersey (NJ)
Coll of Saint Benedict (MN)
The Coll of Saint Rose (NY)
The Coll of St. Scholastica (MN)
Coll of Staten Island of the City U of
    New York (NY)
Coll of the Holy Cross (MA)
Coll of the Ozarks (MO)
The Coll of Westchester (NY)
The Coll of William and Mary (VA)
Colorado Christian U (CO)
Colorado Mesa U (CO)
Colorado State U–Pueblo (CO)
Columbia Coll (MO)
Columbia Coll (SC)
Columbus State U (GA)
Concordia Coll–New York (NY)
Concordia U (QC, Canada)
Concordia U Chicago (IL)
Concordia U, Nebraska (NE)
Concordia U, St. Paul (MN)
Concordia U Wisconsin (WI)
Converse Coll (SC)
Corban U (OR)
Cornerstone U (MI)
Creighton U (NE)
Culver-Stockton Coll (MO)
Curry Coll (MA)
Daemen Coll (NY)
Dakota State U (SD)
Dallas Baptist U (TX)
Davenport U, Grand Rapids (MI)

Defiance Coll (OH)
Delaware State U (DE)
DePaul U (IL)
DeSales U (PA)
Dickinson State U (ND)
Doane U (NE)
Dominican Coll (NY)
Dominican U (IL)
Drake U (IA)
Drexel U (PA)
Drury U (MO)
Duquesne U (PA)
D'Youville Coll (NY)
East Carolina U (NC)
East Central U (OK)
Eastern Mennonite U (VA)
Eastern Michigan U (MI)
Eastern Nazarene Coll (MA)
Eastern New Mexico U (NM)
Eastern Washington U (WA)
East Tennessee State U (TN)
East Texas Baptist U (TX)
ECPI U, Virginia Beach (VA)
Edgewood Coll (WI)
Elizabethtown Coll (PA)
Elmhurst Coll (IL)
Elms Coll (MA)
Elon U (NC)
Emmanuel Coll (MA)
Emory & Henry Coll (VA)
Emory U (GA)
Emporia State U (KS)
Endicott Coll (MA)
Excelsior Coll (NY)
Fairfield U (CT)
Fairleigh Dickinson U, Florham
    Campus (NJ)
Fairleigh Dickinson U, Metropolitan
    Campus (NJ)
Fayetteville State U (NC)
Felician U (NJ)
Fisher Coll (MA)
Fitchburg State U (MA)
Flagler Coll (FL)
Florida Ag and Mech U (FL)
Florida Atlantic U (FL)
Florida Gulf Coast U (FL)
Florida Inst of Technology (FL)
Florida Intl U (FL)
Florida National U (FL)
Florida Southern Coll (FL)
Florida State U (FL)
Fordham U (NY)
Fort Lewis Coll (CO)
Framingham State U (MA)
Francis Marion U (SC)
Franklin Coll (IN)
Franklin Pierce U (NH)
Friends U (KS)
Frostburg State U (MD)
Furman U (SC)
Gannon U (PA)
Geneva Coll (PA)
George Mason U (VA)
Georgetown Coll (KY)
Georgetown U (DC)
The George Washington U (DC)
Georgia Coll & State U (GA)
Georgian Court U (NJ)
Georgia Southern U (GA)
Georgia Southwestern State U
    (GA)
Georgia State U (GA)
Golden Gate U (CA)
Gonzaga U (WA)
Gordon Coll (MA)
Goshen Coll (IN)
Governors State U (IL)
Graceland U (IA)
Grambling State U (LA)
Grand Valley State U (MI)
Grand View U (IA)
Greensboro Coll (NC)
Greenville U (IL)
Grove City Coll (PA)
Guilford Coll (NC)
Gustavus Adolphus Coll (MN)
Gwynedd Mercy U (PA)
Hamline U (MN)
Hampton U (VA)

Hannibal-LaGrange U (MO)
Harding U (AR)
Hardin-Simmons U (TX)
Harris-Stowe State U (MO)
Hartwick Coll (NY)
HEC Montreal (QC, Canada)
Heidelberg U (OH)
Hendrix Coll (AR)
High Point U (NC)
Hilbert Coll (NY)
Hillsdale Coll (MI)
Hofstra U (NY)
Holy Family U (PA)
Holy Names U (CA)
Hood Coll (MD)
Hope Coll (MI)
Houston Baptist U (TX)
Howard Payne U (TX)
Hunter Coll of the City U of New
    York (NY)
Huntingdon Coll (AL)
Husson U (ME)
Huston-Tillotson U (TX)
Idaho State U (ID)
Illinois Coll (IL)
Illinois State U (IL)
Illinois Wesleyan U (IL)
Immaculata U (PA)
Indiana State U (IN)
Indiana Tech (IN)
Indiana U of Pennsylvania (PA)
Indiana Wesleyan U (IN)
Inter American U of Puerto Rico,
    Aguadilla Campus (PR)
Inter American U of Puerto Rico,
    Barranquitas Campus (PR)
Inter American U of Puerto Rico,
    Bayamón Campus (PR)
Inter American U of Puerto Rico,
    Fajardo Campus (PR)
Inter American U of Puerto Rico,
    Metropolitan Campus (PR)
Inter American U of Puerto Rico,
    San Germán Campus (PR)
Iona Coll (NY)
Iowa State U of Science and
    Technology (IA)
Ithaca Coll (NY)
Jackson State U (MS)
Jacksonville U (FL)
James Madison U (VA)
John Brown U (AR)
John Carroll U (OH)
Judson U (IL)
Juniata Coll (PA)
Kansas State U (KS)
Kansas Wesleyan U (KS)
Kean U (NJ)
Keiser U, Fort Lauderdale (FL)
Kennesaw State U (GA)
Kent State U (OH)
King's Coll (PA)
LaGrange Coll (GA)
Lamar U (TX)
Langston U (OK)
La Roche Coll (PA)
La Salle U (PA)
Lasell Coll (MA)
La Sierra U (CA)
Lawrence Technological U (MI)
Lebanon Valley Coll (PA)
Lee U (TN)
Lehigh U (PA)
Lehman Coll of the City U of New
    York (NY)
Le Moyne Coll (NY)
Lenoir-Rhyne U (NC)
LeTourneau U (TX)
Lewis U (IL)
Liberty U (VA)
Limestone Coll (SC)
Lincoln Memorial U (TN)
Lincoln U (MO)
Lincoln U (PA)
Lindenwood U (MO)
Linfield Coll (OR)
Lipscomb U (TN)
Lock Haven U of Pennsylvania (PA)
Long Island U–LIU Brooklyn (NY)
Long Island U–LIU Post (NY)

Loras Coll (IA)
Louisiana Coll (LA)
Louisiana State U and A&M Coll
    (LA)
Loyola Marymount U (CA)
Loyola U Chicago (IL)
Loyola U New Orleans (LA)
Lubbock Christian U (TX)
Luther Coll (IA)
Lycoming Coll (PA)
Lynchburg Coll (VA)
Madonna U (MI)
Malone U (OH)
Manchester U (IN)
Manhattan Coll (NY)
Manhattanville Coll (NY)
Mansfield U of Pennsylvania (PA)
Maranatha Baptist U (WI)
Marian U (IN)
Marian U (WI)
Marietta Coll (OH)
Marist Coll (NY)
Marquette U (WI)
Marshall U (WV)
Maryville U of Saint Louis (MO)
Marywood U (PA)
Massachusetts Coll of Liberal
    Arts (MA)
The Master's U (CA)
McKendree U (IL)
McMurry U (TX)
McNeese State U (LA)
McPherson Coll (KS)
Medgar Evers Coll of the City U of
    New York (NY)
Mercer U, Macon (GA)
Mercy Coll (NY)
Mercyhurst U (PA)
Meredith Coll (NC)
Merrimack Coll (MA)
Messiah Coll (PA)
Metropolitan State U of Denver
    (CO)
Miami U (OH)
Michigan State U (MI)
Michigan Technological U (MI)
MidAmerica Nazarene U (KS)
Middle Tennessee State U (TN)
Milligan Coll (TN)
Millikin U (IL)
Millsaps Coll (MS)
Minnesota State U Moorhead (MN)
Minot State U (ND)
Misericordia U (PA)
Mississippi State U (MS)
Missouri Baptist U (MO)
Missouri State U (MO)
Missouri Valley Coll (MO)
Missouri Western State U (MO)
Molloy Coll (NY)
Monmouth Coll (IL)
Montclair State U (NJ)
Moravian Coll (PA)
Morehead State U (KY)
Mount Aloysius Coll (PA)
Mount Marty Coll (SD)
Mount Mary U (WI)
Mount Mercy U (IA)
Mount St. Joseph U (OH)
Mount Saint Mary Coll (NY)
Mount Saint Mary's U (CA)
Mount St. Mary's U (MD)
Mount Vernon Nazarene U (OH)
Muhlenberg Coll (PA)
Murray State U (KY)
Muskingum U (OH)
National U (CA)
Nazareth Coll of Rochester (NY)
Neumann U (PA)
Newberry Coll (SC)
New Jersey City U (NJ)
Newman U (KS)
New Mexico Highlands U (NM)
New Mexico State U (NM)
New York Inst of Technology (NY)
New York U (NY)
Niagara U (NY)
Nichols Coll (MA)
North Carolina Central U (NC)
North Carolina State U (NC)

North Carolina Wesleyan Coll (NC)
North Central Coll (IL)
North Dakota State U (ND)
Northeastern State U (OK)
Northeastern U (MA)
Northern Arizona U (AZ)
Northern Illinois U (IL)
Northern Kentucky U (KY)
Northern Michigan U (MI)
Northern State U (SD)
Northern Vermont U—Lyndon (VT)
North Greenville U (SC)
Northwest Christian U (OR)
Northwestern Coll (IA)
Northwestern Oklahoma State U (OK)
Northwestern State U of Louisiana (LA)
Northwest Missouri State U (MO)
Northwest Nazarene U (ID)
Northwest U (WA)
Nova Southeastern U (FL)
Nyack Coll (NY)
Oakland U (MI)
Oglethorpe U (GA)
Ohio Dominican U (OH)
Ohio Northern U (OH)
The Ohio State U (OH)
Ohio U (OH)
Ohio Wesleyan U (OH)
Oklahoma Baptist U (OK)
Oklahoma Christian U (OK)
Oklahoma City U (OK)
Oklahoma State U (OK)
Old Dominion U (VA)
Olivet Nazarene U (IL)
Oral Roberts U (OK)
Oregon Inst of Technology (OR)
Oregon State U (OR)
Ottawa U (KS)
Otterbein U (OH)
Ouachita Baptist U (AR)
Our Lady of the Lake U (TX)
Pace U (NY)
Pace U, Pleasantville Campus (NY)
Palm Beach Atlantic U (FL)
Peirce Coll (PA)
Penn State Abington (PA)
Penn State Altoona (PA)
Penn State Beaver (PA)
Penn State Berks (PA)
Penn State Brandywine (PA)
Penn State DuBois (PA)
Penn State Erie, The Behrend Coll (PA)
Penn State Fayette, The Eberly Campus (PA)
Penn State Greater Allegheny (PA)
Penn State Hazleton (PA)
Penn State Lehigh Valley (PA)
Penn State Mont Alto (PA)
Penn State New Kensington (PA)
Penn State Schuylkill (PA)
Penn State Shenango (PA)
Penn State U Park (PA)
Penn State Wilkes-Barre (PA)
Penn State Worthington Scranton (PA)
Penn State York (PA)
Pennsylvania Coll of Technology (PA)
Pepperdine U, Malibu (CA)
Pfeiffer U (NC)
Pittsburg State U (KS)
Point Loma Nazarene U (CA)
Point Park U (PA)
Point U (GA)
Portland State U (OR)
Post U (CT)
Prairie View A&M U (TX)
Providence Coll (RI)
Purdue U (IN)
Purdue U Northwest (IN)
Queens Coll of the City U of New York (NY)
Quinnipiac U (CT)
Radford U (VA)
Ramapo Coll of New Jersey (NJ)
Randolph-Macon Coll (VA)
Rasmussen Coll Bloomington (MN)
Rasmussen Coll Brooklyn Park (MN)
Rasmussen Coll Eagan (MN)
Rasmussen Coll Fargo (ND)
Rasmussen Coll Mankato (MN)
Rasmussen Coll New Port Richey (FL)

Rasmussen Coll Ocala (FL)
Rasmussen Coll Rockford (IL)
Rasmussen Coll St. Cloud (MN)
Redeemer U Coll (ON, Canada)
Regent U (VA)
Regis U (CO)
Rhode Island Coll (RI)
Rider U (NJ)
Robert Morris U (PA)
Robert Morris U Illinois (IL)
Roberts Wesleyan Coll (NY)
Rochester Inst of Technology (NY)
Rockford U (IL)
Rocky Mountain Coll (MT)
Roger Williams U (RI)
Roosevelt U (IL)
Rosemont Coll (PA)
Rutgers U–Camden (NJ)
Rutgers U–Newark (NJ)
Rutgers U–New Brunswick (NJ)
Sacred Heart U (CT)
The Sage Colls (NY)
Saginaw Valley State U (MI)
St. Ambrose U (IA)
Saint Anselm Coll (NH)
Saint Augustine's U (NC)
St. Bonaventure U (NY)
St. Catherine U (MN)
Saint Francis U (PA)
St. John Fisher Coll (NY)
Saint John's U (MN)
St. John's U (NY)
St. Joseph's Coll, Long Island Campus (NY)
St. Joseph's Coll, New York (NY)
Saint Joseph's U (PA)
Saint Leo U (FL)
Saint Louis U (MO)
Saint Louis U–Madrid Campus (Spain)
Saint Martin's U (WA)
Saint Mary-of-the-Woods Coll (IN)
Saint Mary's Coll of California (CA)
St. Mary's U (TX)
Saint Mary's U of Minnesota (MN)
Saint Michael's Coll (VT)
St. Norbert Coll (WI)
Saint Peter's U (NJ)
St. Thomas Aquinas Coll (NY)
St. Thomas U (FL)
Saint Vincent Coll (PA)
Salisbury U (MD)
Salve Regina U (RI)
Samford U (AL)
Sam Houston State U (TX)
San Diego State U (CA)
San Francisco State U (CA)
Santa Clara U (CA)
Schreiner U (TX)
Scripps Coll (CA)
Seattle Pacific U (WA)
Seattle U (WA)
Seton Hill U (PA)
Shawnee State U (OH)
Shaw U (NC)
Shepherd U (WV)
Shippensburg U of Pennsylvania (PA)
Shorter U (GA)
Silver Lake Coll of the Holy Family (WI)
Simpson Coll (IA)
Slippery Rock U of Pennsylvania (PA)
Southeastern Louisiana U (LA)
Southeastern Oklahoma State U (OK)
Southeastern U (FL)
Southeast Missouri State U (MO)
Southern Adventist U (TN)
Southern Arkansas U–Magnolia (AR)
Southern Illinois U Carbondale (IL)
Southern Illinois U Edwardsville (IL)
Southern Methodist U (TX)
Southern Utah U (UT)
Southwest Baptist U (MO)
Southwestern Adventist U (TX)
Southwestern Assemblies of God U (TX)
Southwestern Coll (KS)
Spring Hill Coll (AL)
State U of New York at Fredonia (NY)
State U of New York at New Paltz (NY)

State U of New York at Oswego (NY)
State U of New York at Plattsburgh (NY)
State U of New York Coll at Geneseo (NY)
State U of New York Coll at Old Westbury (NY)
State U of New York Coll at Oneonta (NY)
State U of New York Polytechnic Inst (NY)
Stephen F. Austin State U (TX)
Stetson U (FL)
Stevenson U (MD)
Stonehill Coll (MA)
Suffolk U (MA)
Sullivan U (KY)
Susquehanna U (PA)
Syracuse U (NY)
Tarleton State U (TX)
Taylor U (IN)
Temple U (PA)
Tennessee Technological U (TN)
Tennessee Wesleyan U (TN)
Texas A&M Intl U (TX)
Texas A&M U (TX)
Texas A&M U–Central Texas (TX)
Texas A&M U–Commerce (TX)
Texas A&M U–Corpus Christi (TX)
Texas A&M U–Kingsville (TX)
Texas A&M U–Texarkana (TX)
Texas Christian U (TX)
Texas Lutheran U (TX)
Texas State U (TX)
Texas Tech U (TX)
Texas Woman's U (TX)
Thomas Edison State U (NJ)
Thomas U (GA)
Tiffin U (OH)
Towson U (MD)
Transylvania U (KY)
Trevecca Nazarene U (TN)
Trine U (IN)
Trinity Christian Coll (IL)
Trinity U (TX)
Troy U (AL)
Truman State U (MO)
Tulane U (LA)
Union Coll (NE)
Union U (TN)
Université de Sherbrooke (QC, Canada)
U at Albany, State U of New York (NY)
U at Buffalo, the State U of New York (NY)
The U of Akron (OH)
The U of Alabama (AL)
The U of Alabama at Birmingham (AL)
U of Alaska Fairbanks (AK)
The U of Arizona (AZ)
U of Arkansas (AR)
U of Bridgeport (CT)
U of Central Arkansas (AR)
U of Central Florida (FL)
U of Central Oklahoma (OK)
U of Charleston (WV)
U of Cincinnati (OH)
U of Colorado Boulder (CO)
U of Dayton (OH)
U of Denver (CO)
U of Dubuque (IA)
U of Evansville (IN)
The U of Findlay (OH)
U of Florida (FL)
U of Georgia (GA)
U of Guam (GU)
U of Guelph (ON, Canada)
U of Hartford (CT)
U of Hawaii at Manoa (HI)
U of Houston (TX)
U of Houston–Clear Lake (TX)
U of Houston–Downtown (TX)
U of Idaho (ID)
U of Illinois at Chicago (IL)
U of Illinois at Springfield (IL)
U of Jamestown (ND)
The U of Kansas (KS)
U of Kentucky (KY)
U of La Verne (CA)
U of Louisiana at Monroe (LA)
U of Louisville (KY)
U of Maine (ME)
U of Maine at Machias (ME)
U of Mary Hardin-Baylor (TX)

U of Maryland, Coll Park (MD)
U of Maryland Eastern Shore (MD)
U of Maryland U Coll (MD)
U of Massachusetts Amherst (MA)
U of Massachusetts Dartmouth (MA)
U of Memphis (TN)
U of Miami (FL)
U of Michigan–Dearborn (MI)
U of Michigan–Flint (MI)
U of Minnesota, Crookston (MN)
U of Minnesota, Duluth (MN)
U of Minnesota, Twin Cities Campus (MN)
U of Missouri (MO)
U of Missouri–St. Louis (MO)
U of Mobile (AL)
U of Montana (MT)
U of Montevallo (AL)
U of Mount Union (OH)
U of Nebraska–Lincoln (NE)
U of Nevada, Las Vegas (NV)
U of Nevada, Reno (NV)
U of New Haven (CT)
U of New Orleans (LA)
U of North Alabama (AL)
U of North Carolina at Asheville (NC)
The U of North Carolina at Charlotte (NC)
The U of North Carolina at Greensboro (NC)
The U of North Carolina at Pembroke (NC)
U of North Dakota (ND)
U of Northern Iowa (IA)
U of North Florida (FL)
U of North Georgia (GA)
U of North Texas (TX)
U of Notre Dame (IN)
U of Oklahoma (OK)
U of Oregon (OR)
U of Pennsylvania (PA)
U of Pittsburgh (PA)
U of Pittsburgh at Bradford (PA)
U of Pittsburgh at Greensburg (PA)
U of Providence (MT)
U of Puerto Rico–Humacao (PR)
U of Regina (SK, Canada)
U of Rhode Island (RI)
U of Richmond (VA)
U of St. Francis (IL)
U of Saint Francis (IN)
U of Saint Joseph (CT)
U of Saint Mary (KS)
U of St. Thomas (MN)
U of St. Thomas (TX)
U of San Diego (CA)
U of San Francisco (CA)
U of Saskatchewan (SK, Canada)
The U of Scranton (PA)
U of Sioux Falls (SD)
U of South Alabama (AL)
U of South Carolina (SC)
U of South Dakota (SD)
U of Southern California (CA)
U of Southern Indiana (IN)
U of Southern Maine (ME)
U of Southern Mississippi (MS)
U of South Florida, St. Petersburg (FL)
U of South Florida Sarasota-Manatee (FL)
The U of Tampa (FL)
The U of Tennessee (TN)
The U of Tennessee at Martin (TN)
The U of Texas at Austin (TX)
The U of Texas at Dallas (TX)
The U of Texas at El Paso (TX)
The U of Texas at San Antonio (TX)
The U of Texas of the Permian Basin (TX)
The U of Texas Rio Grande Valley (TX)
U of the Incarnate Word (TX)
U of the Potomac (DC)
U of the Virgin Islands (VI)
The U of Toledo (OH)
U of Toronto (ON, Canada)
The U of Tulsa (OK)
U of Utah (UT)
The U of Virginia's Coll at Wise (VA)
U of Washington (WA)
U of Washington, Bothell (WA)
U of Washington, Tacoma (WA)
U of Waterloo (ON, Canada)

The U of West Alabama (AL)
U of West Georgia (GA)
U of Wisconsin–Eau Claire (WI)
U of Wisconsin–La Crosse (WI)
U of Wisconsin–Madison (WI)
U of Wisconsin–Milwaukee (WI)
U of Wisconsin–Parkside (WI)
U of Wisconsin–Platteville (WI)
U of Wisconsin–River Falls (WI)
U of Wisconsin–Stevens Point (WI)
U of Wisconsin–Superior (WI)
U of Wisconsin–Whitewater (WI)
U of Wyoming (WY)
Upper Iowa U (IA)
Ursuline Coll (OH)
Utah State U (UT)
Utah Valley U (UT)
Utica Coll (NY)
Valdosta State U (GA)
Valparaiso U (IN)
Vanguard U of Southern California (CA)
Villanova U (PA)
Virginia Commonwealth U (VA)
Virginia Polytechnic Inst and State U (VA)
Wagner Coll (NY)
Wake Forest U (NC)
Walsh Coll of Accountancy and Business Administration (MI)
Walsh U (OH)
Wartburg Coll (IA)
Washington & Jefferson Coll (PA)
Washington State U (WA)
Washington State U–Global Campus (WA)
Washington State U–Tri-Cities (WA)
Washington State U–Vancouver (WA)
Washington U in St. Louis (MO)
Waynesburg U (PA)
Wayne State U (MI)
Webber Intl U (FL)
Weber State U (UT)
Webster U (MO)
West Chester U of Pennsylvania (PA)
Western Connecticut State U (CT)
Western Illinois U (IL)
Western Kentucky U (KY)
Western Michigan U (MI)
Western New England U (MA)
Western State Colorado U (CO)
Western Washington U (WA)
Westminster Coll (PA)
Westminster Coll (UT)
West Texas A&M U (TX)
West Virginia U (WV)
West Virginia U Inst of Technology (WV)
West Virginia Wesleyan Coll (WV)
Whitworth U (WA)
Wichita State U (KS)
Widener U (PA)
Wilkes U (PA)
William Jewell Coll (MO)
William Paterson U of New Jersey (NJ)
William Penn U (IA)
William Woods U (MO)
Wilmington U (DE)
Winona State U (MN)
Wisconsin Lutheran Coll (WI)
Wittenberg U (OH)
Wofford Coll (SC)
Woodbury U (CA)
Wright State U (OH)
Wright State U–Lake Campus (OH)
Xavier U of Louisiana (LA)
York Coll of Pennsylvania (PA)
Youngstown State U (OH)

ACCOUNTING AND BUSINESS/MANAGEMENT

Babson Coll (MA)
Bethel U (TN)
Bryant U (RI)
Canisius Coll (NY)
Chaminade U of Honolulu (HI)
Chestnut Hill Coll (PA)
East Carolina U (NC)
Eastern Nazarene Coll (MA)
EDP U of Puerto Rico (PR)
EDP U of Puerto Rico–San Sebastian (PR)
Emory U (GA)

Hope Coll (MI)
Husson U (ME)
Maranatha Baptist U (WI)
McPherson Coll (KS)
Mercy Coll (NY)
Northcentral U (CA)
Rasmussen Coll New Port Richey (FL)
Rasmussen Coll Ocala (FL)
Rocky Mountain Coll (MT)
Santa Clara U (CA)
Sierra Nevada Coll (NV)
Touro U Worldwide (CA)
U of Providence (MT)
Washington and Lee U (VA)
Western State Colorado U (CO)

ACCOUNTING AND COMPUTER SCIENCE
Fordham U (NY)
Grove City Coll (PA)
Saint Mary-of-the-Woods Coll (IN)

ACCOUNTING AND FINANCE
Albright Coll (PA)
Babson Coll (MA)
Bentley U (MA)
Bethel U (MN)
Bridgewater State U (MA)
Bucknell U (PA)
Clarkson U (NY)
DEREE - The American Coll of Greece (Greece)
Drake U (IA)
East Central U (OK)
Eastern Nazarene Coll (MA)
Eastern U (PA)
Ferris State U (MI)
Granite State Coll (NH)
Hiram Coll (OH)
Holy Family U (PA)
Maryville Coll (TN)
McPherson Coll (KS)
Northern Michigan U (MI)
Northwest U (WA)
Ohio Christian U (OH)
Saint Francis U (PA)
U of North Dakota (ND)
U of Southern Maine (ME)
U of Waterloo (ON, Canada)
Western New England U (MA)
Western State Colorado U (CO)

ACCOUNTING RELATED
Bentley U (MA)
Brigham Young U (UT)
Eastern Michigan U (MI)
Eastern Nazarene Coll (MA)
Guilford Coll (NC)
Gwynedd Mercy U (PA)
Maryville U of Saint Louis (MO)
McDaniel Coll (MD)
McPherson Coll (KS)
North Dakota State U (ND)
Northern Michigan U (MI)
Rocky Mountain Coll (MT)
Saint Mary's Coll of California (CA)
State U of New York at New Paltz (NY)
State U of New York at Oswego (NY)
U of New Haven (CT)
Washington State U (WA)

ACCOUNTING TECHNOLOGY AND BOOKKEEPING
Ferris State U (MI)
Missouri Valley Coll (MO)
Rowan U (NJ)
Trine U (IN)
The U of Akron (OH)

ACOUSTICS
Columbia Coll Chicago (IL)

ACTING
Academy of Art U (CA)
Anderson U (SC)
Arcadia U (PA)
Ashland U (OH)
Augsburg U (MN)
Baldwin Wallace U (OH)
Barry U (FL)
Baylor U (TX)
Belmont U (TN)
Bennington Coll (VT)
Boston U (MA)
Bradley U (IL)
Brenau U (GA)

Brigham Young U (UT)
California Baptist U (CA)
California State U, Long Beach (CA)
Central Michigan U (MI)
Chapman U (CA)
Coker Coll (SC)
Coll of the Ozarks (MO)
Columbia Coll Chicago (IL)
DePaul U (IL)
Drake U (IA)
Elon U (NC)
Emerson Coll (MA)
Emory & Henry Coll (VA)
Florida Southern Coll (FL)
Florida State U (FL)
Gannon U (PA)
Greensboro Coll (NC)
Hofstra U (NY)
Illinois Wesleyan U (IL)
Ithaca Coll (NY)
Kean U (NJ)
Keene State Coll (NH)
Lindenwood U (MO)
Lipscomb U (TN)
Marlboro Coll (VT)
Marymount Manhattan Coll (NY)
Michigan State U (MI)
Minnesota State U Moorhead (MN)
New World School of the Arts (FL)
Oakland U (MI)
Ohio U (OH)
Oklahoma City U (OK)
Oral Roberts U (OK)
Pace U (NY)
Penn State Abington (PA)
Penn State Altoona (PA)
Penn State Beaver (PA)
Penn State Berks (PA)
Penn State Brandywine (PA)
Penn State DuBois (PA)
Penn State Erie, The Behrend Coll (PA)
Penn State Fayette, The Eberly Campus (PA)
Penn State Greater Allegheny (PA)
Penn State Hazleton (PA)
Penn State Lehigh Valley (PA)
Penn State Mont Alto (PA)
Penn State New Kensington (PA)
Penn State Schuylkill (PA)
Penn State Shenango (PA)
Penn State U Park (PA)
Penn State Wilkes-Barre (PA)
Penn State Worthington Scranton (PA)
Penn State York (PA)
Pepperdine U, Malibu (CA)
Point Park U (PA)
Purdue U (IN)
Regent U (VA)
Rhode Island Coll (RI)
Roosevelt U (IL)
Seton Hill U (PA)
Shenandoah U (VA)
Stevenson U (MD)
Syracuse U (NY)
Temple U (PA)
Texas Christian U (TX)
Towson U (MD)
Trinity U (TX)
U of Cincinnati (OH)
U of Hartford (CT)
U of Maryland, Baltimore County (MD)
U of Nevada, Las Vegas (NV)
U of Northern Iowa (IA)
U of Regina (SK, Canada)
U of Southern California (CA)
The U of Texas at Austin (TX)
The U of the Arts (PA)
U of Washington (WA)
Webster U (MO)
Western Michigan U (MI)
Whitworth U (WA)
Wright State U (OH)

ACTUARIAL SCIENCE
Anderson U (SC)
Appalachian State U (NC)
Arcadia U (PA)
Arizona State U at the Tempe campus (AZ)
Ashland U (OH)
Assumption Coll (MA)
Aurora U (IL)
Ball State U (IN)

Baruch Coll of the City U of New York (NY)
Bellarmine U (KY)
Bentley U (MA)
Bob Jones U (SC)
Bowling Green State U (OH)
Bradley U (IL)
Brigham Young U (UT)
Bryant U (RI)
Butler U (IN)
California Baptist U (CA)
Calvin Coll (MI)
Carnegie Mellon U (PA)
Carroll U (WI)
Central Michigan U (MI)
Concordia U (QC, Canada)
Concordia U Wisconsin (WI)
DePaul U (IL)
Drake U (IA)
Eastern Michigan U (MI)
Elmhurst Coll (IL)
Ferris State U (MI)
Florida State U (FL)
Franklin Coll (IN)
Georgia State U (GA)
Hartwick Coll (NY)
High Point U (NC)
Indiana U Northwest (IN)
Indiana U South Bend (IN)
Lebanon Valley Coll (PA)
Lycoming Coll (PA)
Maryville U of Saint Louis (MO)
Messiah Coll (PA)
Michigan State U (MI)
Milwaukee School of Eng (WI)
Minnesota State U Moorhead (MN)
Mount Mercy U (IA)
New York U (NY)
Niagara U (NY)
North Central Coll (IL)
Northwestern Coll (IA)
Oakland U (MI)
Ohio Northern U (OH)
The Ohio State U (OH)
Ohio U (OH)
Olivet Nazarene U (IL)
Penn State Abington (PA)
Penn State Altoona (PA)
Penn State Beaver (PA)
Penn State Berks (PA)
Penn State Brandywine (PA)
Penn State DuBois (PA)
Penn State Erie, The Behrend Coll (PA)
Penn State Fayette, The Eberly Campus (PA)
Penn State Greater Allegheny (PA)
Penn State Hazleton (PA)
Penn State Lehigh Valley (PA)
Penn State Mont Alto (PA)
Penn State New Kensington (PA)
Penn State Schuylkill (PA)
Penn State Shenango (PA)
Penn State Wilkes-Barre (PA)
Penn State Worthington Scranton (PA)
Penn State York (PA)
Purdue U (IN)
Queens Coll of the City U of New York (NY)
Roanoke Coll (VA)
Robert Morris U (PA)
Roosevelt U (IL)
St. John's U (NY)
St. Joseph's Coll, New York (NY)
Saint Joseph's U (PA)
Saint Mary's U of Minnesota (MN)
Siena Coll (NY)
Simon Fraser U (BC, Canada)
Simpson Coll (IA)
Temple U (PA)
Texas Christian U (TX)
U at Albany, State U of New York (NY)
U of California, Santa Barbara (CA)
U of Central Florida (FL)
U of Central Oklahoma (OK)
U of Maine at Farmington (ME)
U of Michigan–Flint (MI)
U of Missouri–St. Louis (MO)
U of Nebraska–Lincoln (NE)
U of Pennsylvania (PA)
U of Regina (SK, Canada)
U of St. Thomas (MN)
The U of Texas at Dallas (TX)
The U of Texas at San Antonio (TX)
U of Toronto (ON, Canada)

U of Waterloo (ON, Canada)
U of Wisconsin–Madison (WI)
U of Wisconsin–Milwaukee (WI)
Valparaiso U (IN)
Wartburg Coll (IA)
Western New England U (MA)

ADMINISTRATIVE ASSISTANT AND SECRETARIAL SCIENCE
Campbellsville U (KY)
EDP U of Puerto Rico (PR)
EDP U of Puerto Rico–San Sebastian (PR)
Idaho State U (ID)
The U of North Carolina at Greensboro (NC)
U of Puerto Rico–Humacao (PR)
Valdosta State U (GA)
Weber State U (UT)

ADULT AND CONTINUING EDUCATION
Auburn U (AL)
Brock U (ON, Canada)
Eastern Washington U (WA)
Louisiana State U and A&M Coll (LA)
U of Regina (SK, Canada)
U of the Fraser Valley (BC, Canada)
Welch Coll (TN)

ADULT AND CONTINUING EDUCATION ADMINISTRATION
Concordia Coll–New York (NY)
Penn State Abington (PA)
Penn State Altoona (PA)
Penn State Beaver (PA)
Penn State Berks (PA)
Penn State Brandywine (PA)
Penn State DuBois (PA)
Penn State Erie, The Behrend Coll (PA)
Penn State Fayette, The Eberly Campus (PA)
Penn State Greater Allegheny (PA)
Penn State Hazleton (PA)
Penn State Lehigh Valley (PA)
Penn State Mont Alto (PA)
Penn State New Kensington (PA)
Penn State Schuylkill (PA)
Penn State Shenango (PA)
Penn State Wilkes-Barre (PA)
Penn State Worthington Scranton (PA)
Penn State York (PA)

ADULT DEVELOPMENT AND AGING
Madonna U (MI)
Rhode Island Coll (RI)
St. Thomas U (NB, Canada)
U of Guelph (ON, Canada)

ADULT HEALTH NURSING
Concordia Coll–New York (NY)
King U (TN)
Long Island U–LIU Brooklyn (NY)
U of Rochester (NY)
Worcester State U (MA)

ADVERTISING
Adams State U (CO)
Appalachian State U (NC)
ArtCenter Coll of Design (CA)
Ball State U (IN)
Barry U (FL)
Bowling Green State U (OH)
Bradley U (IL)
Brigham Young U (UT)
California State U, Fullerton (CA)
Central Michigan U (MI)
Columbia Coll Chicago (IL)
Drake U (IA)
Emerson Coll (MA)
Fashion Inst of Technology (NY)
Ferris State U (MI)
Florida State U (FL)
Franklin Pierce U (NH)
Gannon U (PA)
Grand Valley State U (MI)
Hampton U (VA)
Harding U (AR)
Iona Coll (NY)
Iowa State U of Science and Technology (IA)
Kent State U (OH)
Lamar U (TX)

Lee U (TN)
Lindenwood U (MO)
Loyola U Chicago (IL)
Marquette U (WI)
Michigan State U (MI)
Minnesota State U Moorhead (MN)
Murray State U (KY)
New York Inst of Technology (NY)
Northwest Missouri State U (MO)
Ohio Northern U (OH)
Oklahoma Christian U (OK)
Pace U (NY)
Pace U, Pleasantville Campus (NY)
Penn State Abington (PA)
Penn State Altoona (PA)
Penn State Beaver (PA)
Penn State Berks (PA)
Penn State Brandywine (PA)
Penn State DuBois (PA)
Penn State Erie, The Behrend Coll (PA)
Penn State Fayette, The Eberly Campus (PA)
Penn State Greater Allegheny (PA)
Penn State Hazleton (PA)
Penn State Lehigh Valley (PA)
Penn State Mont Alto (PA)
Penn State New Kensington (PA)
Penn State Schuylkill (PA)
Penn State Shenango (PA)
Penn State U Park (PA)
Penn State Wilkes-Barre (PA)
Penn State Worthington Scranton (PA)
Penn State York (PA)
Pepperdine U, Malibu (CA)
Portland State U (OR)
Quinnipiac U (CT)
Rider U (NJ)
Rochester Inst of Technology (NY)
Rowan U (NJ)
St. John's U (NY)
Sam Houston State U (TX)
San Diego State U (CA)
Southern Adventist U (TN)
Southern Methodist U (TX)
Suffolk U (MA)
Syracuse U (NY)
Temple U (PA)
Texas Christian U (TX)
Texas State U (TX)
Texas Tech U (TX)
Union U (TN)
The U of Alabama (AL)
U of Central Florida (FL)
U of Florida (FL)
U of Georgia (GA)
U of Houston (TX)
U of Idaho (ID)
U of Miami (FL)
U of Missouri (MO)
U of Oklahoma (OK)
U of Oregon (OR)
U of San Francisco (CA)
U of South Carolina (SC)
U of Southern Indiana (IN)
U of Southern Mississippi (MS)
The U of Tennessee (TN)
The U of Texas at Austin (TX)
Washington State U (WA)
Washington U in St. Louis (MO)
Waynesburg U (PA)
Webster U (MO)
Western Kentucky U (KY)
Western Michigan U (MI)
Western New England U (MA)
Widener U (PA)
Youngstown State U (OH)

AERONAUTICAL/AEROSPACE ENGINEERING TECHNOLOGY
American Public U System (WV)
Bowling Green State U (OH)
Idaho State U (ID)
Kent State U (OH)
LeTourneau U (TX)
Purdue U (IN)
Saint Louis U–Madrid Campus (Spain)
Utah State U (UT)

AERONAUTICS/AVIATION/ AEROSPACE SCIENCE AND TECHNOLOGY
Arizona State U at the Polytechnic campus (AZ)
Averett U (VA)
Bowling Green State U (OH)

Bridgewater State U (MA)
Delaware State U (DE)
Embry-Riddle Aeronautical U–Daytona (FL)
Florida Inst of Technology (FL)
Indiana State U (IN)
Kansas State U (KS)
Kent State U (OH)
LeTourneau U (TX)
Lewis U (IL)
Liberty U (VA)
Metropolitan State U of Denver (CO)
Middle Tennessee State U (TN)
The Ohio State U (OH)
Ohio U (OH)
Oklahoma State U (OK)
Polk State Coll (FL)
Saint Louis U (MO)
Texas A&M U–Central Texas (TX)
Texas Lutheran U (TX)
U of Minnesota, Crookston (MN)
U of North Texas (TX)
U of Oklahoma (OK)
Vaughn Coll of Aeronautics and Technology (NY)

AEROSPACE, AERONAUTICAL AND ASTRONAUTICAL/SPACE ENGINEERING
Arizona State U at the Tempe campus (AZ)
Auburn U (AL)
California Polytechnic State U, San Luis Obispo (CA)
California State Polytechnic U, Pomona (CA)
California State U, Long Beach (CA)
Case Western Reserve U (OH)
Clarkson U (NY)
Concordia U (QC, Canada)
Embry-Riddle Aeronautical U–Daytona (FL)
Florida Inst of Technology (FL)
Georgia Inst of Technology (GA)
Iowa State U of Science and Technology (IA)
Kent State U (OH)
Massachusetts Inst of Technology (MA)
Mississippi State U (MS)
Missouri U of Science and Technology (MO)
New Mexico State U (NM)
North Carolina State U (NC)
The Ohio State U (OH)
Oklahoma State U (OK)
Penn State Abington (PA)
Penn State Altoona (PA)
Penn State Beaver (PA)
Penn State Berks (PA)
Penn State Brandywine (PA)
Penn State DuBois (PA)
Penn State Erie, The Behrend Coll (PA)
Penn State Fayette, The Eberly Campus (PA)
Penn State Greater Allegheny (PA)
Penn State Hazleton (PA)
Penn State Lehigh Valley (PA)
Penn State Mont Alto (PA)
Penn State New Kensington (PA)
Penn State Schuylkill (PA)
Penn State Shenango (PA)
Penn State U Park (PA)
Penn State Wilkes-Barre (PA)
Penn State Worthington Scranton (PA)
Penn State York (PA)
Purdue U (IN)
Rensselaer Polytechnic Inst (NY)
Rochester Inst of Technology (NY)
Saint Louis U (MO)
San Diego State U (CA)
Stanford U (CA)
Syracuse U (NY)
Texas A&M U (TX)
U at Buffalo, the State U of New York (NY)
The U of Alabama (AL)
The U of Arizona (AZ)
U of California, Davis (CA)
U of California, Irvine (CA)
U of California, Los Angeles (CA)
U of California, San Diego (CA)
U of Central Florida (FL)

U of Cincinnati (OH)
U of Colorado Boulder (CO)
U of Florida (FL)
The U of Kansas (KS)
U of Maryland, Coll Park (MD)
U of Miami (FL)
U of Michigan (MI)
U of Minnesota, Twin Cities Campus (MN)
U of Notre Dame (IN)
U of Oklahoma (OK)
U of Southern California (CA)
The U of Tennessee (TN)
The U of Texas at Austin (TX)
U of Toronto (ON, Canada)
U of Virginia (VA)
U of Washington (WA)
Utah State U (UT)
Virginia Polytechnic Inst and State U (VA)
Western Michigan U (MI)
West Virginia U (WV)
West Virginia U Inst of Technology (WV)
Wichita State U (KS)
Worcester Polytechnic Inst (MA)

AEROSPACE GROUND EQUIPMENT TECHNOLOGY
Liberty U (VA)

AEROSPACE PHYSIOLOGY AND MEDICINE
Embry-Riddle Aeronautical U–Daytona (FL)

AFRICAN AMERICAN/BLACK STUDIES
American U (DC)
Amherst Coll (MA)
Arizona State U at the Tempe campus (AZ)
Bates Coll (ME)
Berea Coll (KY)
Binghamton U, State U of New York (NY)
Bowling Green State U (OH)
Brandeis U (MA)
California State U, Dominguez Hills (CA)
California State U, Fullerton (CA)
California State U, Long Beach (CA)
California State U, Los Angeles (CA)
California State U, Northridge (CA)
City Coll of the City U of New York (NY)
Claremont McKenna Coll (CA)
Clemson U (SC)
Cleveland State U (OH)
Coe Coll (IA)
Colby Coll (ME)
The Coll at Brockport, State U of New York (NY)
Coll of Charleston (SC)
The Coll of New Jersey (NJ)
Coll of Staten Island of the City U of New York (NY)
The Coll of William and Mary (VA)
The Coll of Wooster (OH)
Columbia U (NY)
Cornell U (NY)
Dartmouth Coll (NH)
Denison U (OH)
DePaul U (IL)
DePauw U (IN)
Dominican U (IL)
Drew U (NJ)
Earlham Coll (IN)
East Carolina U (NC)
Eastern Michigan U (MI)
Emory U (GA)
Florida Ag and Mech U (FL)
Florida State U (FL)
Fordham U (NY)
Georgia State U (GA)
Gettysburg Coll (PA)
Guilford Coll (NC)
Hamilton Coll (NY)
Hampshire Coll (MA)
Harvard U (MA)
Hobart and William Smith Colls (NY)
Hunter Coll of the City U of New York (NY)
Indiana State U (IN)
Indiana U Bloomington (IN)

Indiana U Northwest (IN)
Indiana U–Purdue U Indianapolis (IN)
Iowa State U of Science and Technology (IA)
Johns Hopkins U (MD)
Kent State U (OH)
Knox Coll (IL)
Lehman Coll of the City U of New York (NY)
Loyola Marymount U (CA)
Loyola U Chicago (IL)
Luther Coll (IA)
Marquette U (WI)
Mercer U, Macon (GA)
Metropolitan State U of Denver (CO)
Miami U (OH)
Middle Tennessee State U (TN)
Morehouse Coll (GA)
Mount Holyoke Coll (MA)
New York U (NY)
Northeastern U (MA)
Northwestern U (IL)
Oberlin Coll (OH)
Occidental Coll (CA)
The Ohio State U (OH)
Ohio U (OH)
Ohio Wesleyan U (OH)
Old Dominion U (VA)
Penn State Abington (PA)
Penn State Altoona (PA)
Penn State Beaver (PA)
Penn State Berks (PA)
Penn State Brandywine (PA)
Penn State DuBois (PA)
Penn State Erie, The Behrend Coll (PA)
Penn State Fayette, The Eberly Campus (PA)
Penn State Greater Allegheny (PA)
Penn State Hazleton (PA)
Penn State Lehigh Valley (PA)
Penn State Mont Alto (PA)
Penn State New Kensington (PA)
Penn State Schuylkill (PA)
Penn State Shenango (PA)
Penn State U Park (PA)
Penn State Wilkes-Barre (PA)
Penn State Worthington Scranton (PA)
Penn State York (PA)
Pitzer Coll (CA)
Pomona Coll (CA)
Portland State U (OR)
Princeton U (NJ)
Purdue U (IN)
Queens Coll of the City U of New York (NY)
Ramapo Coll of New Jersey (NJ)
Rhode Island Coll (RI)
Rhodes Coll (TN)
Roosevelt U (IL)
Rutgers U–Camden (NJ)
Rutgers U–Newark (NJ)
Rutgers U–New Brunswick (NJ)
Saint Louis U (MO)
San Diego State U (CA)
San Francisco State U (CA)
Smith Coll (MA)
Sonoma State U (CA)
Southern Illinois U Carbondale (IL)
Southern Methodist U (TX)
Stanford U (CA)
State U of New York at New Paltz (NY)
State U of New York Coll at Cortland (NY)
State U of New York Coll at Geneseo (NY)
Stony Brook U, State U of New York (NY)
Syracuse U (NY)
Temple U (PA)
Tufts U (MA)
U at Albany, State U of New York (NY)
U at Buffalo, the State U of New York (NY)
The U of Alabama (AL)
The U of Alabama at Birmingham (AL)
The U of Arizona (AZ)
U of California, Davis (CA)
U of California, Irvine (CA)
U of California, Los Angeles (CA)
U of California, Riverside (CA)

U of California, Santa Barbara (CA)
U of Central Arkansas (AR)
U of Cincinnati (OH)
U of Florida (FL)
U of Georgia (GA)
U of Illinois at Chicago (IL)
The U of Kansas (KS)
U of Louisville (KY)
U of Maryland, Baltimore County (MD)
U of Maryland, Coll Park (MD)
U of Massachusetts Amherst (MA)
U of Massachusetts Boston (MA)
U of Memphis (TN)
U of Miami (FL)
U of Michigan (MI)
U of Michigan–Dearborn (MI)
U of Michigan–Flint (MI)
U of Minnesota, Twin Cities Campus (MN)
U of Montana (MT)
U of Nevada, Las Vegas (NV)
U of New Mexico (NM)
The U of North Carolina at Chapel Hill (NC)
The U of North Carolina at Charlotte (NC)
The U of North Carolina at Greensboro (NC)
U of Northern Colorado (CO)
U of Notre Dame (IN)
U of Oklahoma (OK)
U of Pennsylvania (PA)
U of Pittsburgh (PA)
U of Puget Sound (WA)
U of Rhode Island (RI)
U of Rochester (NY)
U of South Carolina (SC)
U of Southern California (CA)
The U of Texas at Austin (TX)
The U of Toledo (OH)
U of Virginia (VA)
U of Wisconsin–Madison (WI)
U of Wisconsin–Milwaukee (WI)
U of Wyoming (WY)
Vanderbilt U (TN)
Virginia Commonwealth U (VA)
Washington U in St. Louis (MO)
Wayne State U (MI)
Wellesley Coll (MA)
Wesleyan U (CT)
Western Michigan U (MI)
Wheaton Coll (MA)
William Paterson U of New Jersey (NJ)

AFRICAN LANGUAGES
U of California, Los Angeles (CA)
U of Wisconsin–Madison (WI)

AFRICAN STUDIES
Agnes Scott Coll (GA)
Augustana Coll (IL)
Bard Coll (NY)
Barnard Coll (NY)
Bowdoin Coll (ME)
Bowling Green State U (OH)
Carleton Coll (MN)
Columbia U (NY)
Connecticut Coll (CT)
Dartmouth Coll (NH)
Davidson Coll (NC)
Dickinson Coll (PA)
Emory U (GA)
Fordham U (NY)
Franklin & Marshall Coll (PA)
Hampshire Coll (MA)
Haverford Coll (PA)
Hobart and William Smith Colls (NY)
Hofstra U (NY)
Illinois Wesleyan U (IL)
Kennesaw State U (GA)
Kentucky State U (KY)
Lehigh U (PA)
Lincoln U (PA)
Marlboro Coll (VT)
Middlebury Coll (VT)
Northwestern U (IL)
Ohio U (OH)
Portland State U (OR)
Queens Coll of the City U of New York (NY)
Rowan U (NJ)
Rutgers U–New Brunswick (NJ)
Sarah Lawrence Coll (NY)
Simmons Coll (MA)

Tufts U (MA)
Tulane U (LA)
Union Coll (NY)
United States Military Acad (NY)
The U of Kansas (KS)
U of Pennsylvania (PA)
U of Richmond (VA)
U of Toronto (ON, Canada)
Vassar Coll (NY)
Washington U in St. Louis (MO)
Wellesley Coll (MA)
Willamette U (OR)

AGRIBUSINESS
Abilene Christian U (TX)
Adams State U (CO)
American U of Beirut (Lebanon)
Andrews U (MI)
Angelo State U (TX)
Arkansas Tech U (AR)
Brigham Young U (UT)
Delaware Valley U (PA)
Eastern New Mexico U (NM)
Florida Ag and Mech U (FL)
Greenville U (IL)
Iowa State U of Science and Technology (IA)
Kent State U at Tuscarawas (OH)
Middle Tennessee State U (TN)
Mississippi State U (MS)
Missouri State U (MO)
New Mexico State U (NM)
North Carolina State U (NC)
North Dakota State U (ND)
Northwest Missouri State U (MO)
Penn State Abington (PA)
Penn State Altoona (PA)
Penn State Beaver (PA)
Penn State Berks (PA)
Penn State Brandywine (PA)
Penn State DuBois (PA)
Penn State Erie, The Behrend Coll (PA)
Penn State Fayette, The Eberly Campus (PA)
Penn State Greater Allegheny (PA)
Penn State Hazleton (PA)
Penn State Lehigh Valley (PA)
Penn State Mont Alto (PA)
Penn State New Kensington (PA)
Penn State Schuylkill (PA)
Penn State Shenango (PA)
Penn State U Park (PA)
Penn State Wilkes-Barre (PA)
Penn State Worthington Scranton (PA)
Penn State York (PA)
Sam Houston State U (TX)
Southeast Missouri State U (MO)
Stephen F. Austin State U (TX)
Tarleton State U (TX)
Texas A&M U (TX)
Texas A&M U–Commerce (TX)
Texas A&M U–Kingsville (TX)
Texas State U (TX)
U of Arkansas (AR)
U of Central Missouri (MO)
U of Georgia (GA)
U of Idaho (ID)
U of Minnesota, Crookston (MN)
U of Saskatchewan (SK, Canada)
U of Wisconsin–Platteville (WI)
U of Wisconsin–River Falls (WI)
U of Wyoming (WY)
Vermont Tech Coll (VT)
Washington State U (WA)
West Texas A&M U (TX)

AGRICULTURAL AND DOMESTIC ANIMAL SERVICES RELATED
Saint Mary-of-the-Woods Coll (IN)

AGRICULTURAL AND EXTENSION EDUCATION
Louisiana State U and A&M Coll (LA)
New Mexico State U (NM)
North Carolina State U (NC)
Northwestern Oklahoma State U (OK)
The Ohio State U (OH)
Penn State Abington (PA)
Penn State Altoona (PA)
Penn State Beaver (PA)
Penn State Berks (PA)
Penn State Brandywine (PA)
Penn State DuBois (PA)

Penn State Erie, The Behrend Coll (PA)
Penn State Fayette, The Eberly Campus (PA)
Penn State Greater Allegheny (PA)
Penn State Hazleton (PA)
Penn State Lehigh Valley (PA)
Penn State Mont Alto (PA)
Penn State New Kensington (PA)
Penn State Schuylkill (PA)
Penn State Shenango (PA)
Penn State Wilkes-Barre (PA)
Penn State Worthington Scranton (PA)
Penn State York (PA)
Tarleton State U (TX)
U of Arkansas (AR)
The U of Tennessee (TN)

AGRICULTURAL AND FOOD PRODUCTS PROCESSING
Angelo State U (TX)
Kansas State U (KS)
Morningside Coll (IA)
The Ohio State U (OH)
Texas A&M U (TX)
U of Nebraska–Lincoln (NE)
Washington State U (WA)

AGRICULTURAL AND HORTICULTURAL PLANT BREEDING
Delaware State U (DE)
Washington State U (WA)

AGRICULTURAL BUSINESS AND MANAGEMENT
Alcorn State U (MS)
Brigham Young U (UT)
Brigham Young U–Idaho (ID)
California Polytechnic State U, San Luis Obispo (CA)
California State Polytechnic U, Pomona (CA)
Clemson U (SC)
Coll of the Ozarks (MO)
Delaware State U (DE)
Florida Southern Coll (FL)
Graceland U (IA)
Iowa State U of Science and Technology (IA)
Kansas State U (KS)
Louisiana State U and A&M Coll (LA)
Michigan State U (MI)
Missouri Valley Coll (MO)
Oklahoma State U (OK)
Oregon State U (OR)
Purdue U (IN)
Southern Arkansas U–Magnolia (AR)
Tennessee Technological U (TN)
Texas A&M U (TX)
Texas Tech U (TX)
The U of Arizona (AZ)
U of Guelph (ON, Canada)
U of Idaho (ID)
U of Louisiana at Monroe (LA)
U of Maryland Eastern Shore (MD)
U of Missouri (MO)
U of Nebraska at Kearney (NE)
U of Nebraska–Lincoln (NE)
The U of Tennessee (TN)
The U of Tennessee at Martin (TN)
U of the Fraser Valley (BC, Canada)
U of Wisconsin–Madison (WI)
Upper Iowa U (IA)
Utah State U (UT)
Washington State U (WA)
West Texas A&M U (TX)

AGRICULTURAL BUSINESS AND MANAGEMENT RELATED
Delaware State U (DE)
Penn State New Kensington (PA)
U of California, Davis (CA)
U of Minnesota, Twin Cities Campus (MN)
Utah State U (UT)

AGRICULTURAL BUSINESS TECHNOLOGY
Brigham Young U–Idaho (ID)
The U of Arizona (AZ)
U of Minnesota, Crookston (MN)
U of Wisconsin–Platteville (WI)

AGRICULTURAL COMMUNICATION/ JOURNALISM
Auburn U (AL)
California Polytechnic State U, San Luis Obispo (CA)
Kansas State U (KS)
North Dakota State U (ND)
Oklahoma State U (OK)
Purdue U (IN)
Sam Houston State U (TX)
Texas A&M U (TX)
Texas Tech U (TX)
U of Georgia (GA)
U of Idaho (ID)
U of Nebraska–Lincoln (NE)
U of Wisconsin–Madison (WI)
U of Wyoming (WY)
Washington State U (WA)
West Texas A&M U (TX)

AGRICULTURAL ECONOMICS
Alcorn State U (MS)
Auburn U (AL)
Brigham Young U (UT)
Brigham Young U–Idaho (ID)
Clemson U (SC)
Colorado State U (CO)
Cornell U (NY)
Kansas State U (KS)
Mississippi State U (MS)
North Dakota State U (ND)
The Ohio State U (OH)
Oklahoma State U (OK)
Oregon State U (OR)
Purdue U (IN)
Southern Illinois U Carbondale (IL)
Tarleton State U (TX)
Texas A&M U (TX)
Texas Tech U (TX)
U of Florida (FL)
U of Georgia (GA)
U of Guelph (ON, Canada)
U of Idaho (ID)
U of Kentucky (KY)
U of Maryland, Coll Park (MD)
U of Missouri (MO)
U of Nebraska–Lincoln (NE)
U of Saskatchewan (SK, Canada)
U of Wisconsin–Madison (WI)
Utah State U (UT)
Virginia Polytechnic Inst and State U (VA)
Washington State U (WA)
West Virginia U (WV)

AGRICULTURAL ENGINEERING
Auburn U (AL)
California Polytechnic State U, San Luis Obispo (CA)
Clemson U (SC)
Cornell U (NY)
Florida Ag and Mech U (FL)
Iowa State U of Science and Technology (IA)
Kansas State U (KS)
Michigan State U (MI)
Missouri U of Science and Technology (MO)
North Carolina State U (NC)
North Dakota State U (ND)
The Ohio State U (OH)
Oklahoma State U (OK)
Oregon State U (OR)
Penn State Abington (PA)
Penn State Beaver (PA)
Penn State Brandywine (PA)
Penn State DuBois (PA)
Penn State Erie, The Behrend Coll (PA)
Penn State Fayette, The Eberly Campus (PA)
Penn State Greater Allegheny (PA)
Penn State Hazleton (PA)
Penn State Lehigh Valley (PA)
Penn State Mont Alto (PA)
Penn State New Kensington (PA)
Penn State Schuylkill (PA)
Penn State Shenango (PA)
Penn State U Park (PA)
Penn State Wilkes-Barre (PA)
Penn State Worthington Scranton (PA)
Penn State York (PA)
Purdue U (IN)
Rutgers U–New Brunswick (NJ)
Tennessee Technological U (TN)

Texas A&M U (TX)
U of Arkansas (AR)
U of California, Los Angeles (CA)
U of Georgia (GA)
U of Hawaii at Manoa (HI)
U of Maryland, Coll Park (MD)
U of Nebraska–Lincoln (NE)
The U of Tennessee (TN)
U of Wisconsin–Madison (WI)
Utah State U (UT)
Washington State U (WA)

AGRICULTURAL/FARM SUPPLIES RETAILING AND WHOLESALING
Dickinson State U (ND)
Tarleton State U (TX)
Texas A&M U (TX)

AGRICULTURAL MECHANICS AND EQUIPMENT TECHNOLOGY
Washington State U (WA)

AGRICULTURAL MECHANIZATION
California Polytechnic State U, San Luis Obispo (CA)
Iowa State U of Science and Technology (IA)
Kansas State U (KS)
North Carolina State U (NC)
North Dakota State U (ND)
Penn State Abington (PA)
Penn State Altoona (PA)
Penn State Beaver (PA)
Penn State Berks (PA)
Penn State Brandywine (PA)
Penn State DuBois (PA)
Penn State Erie, The Behrend Coll (PA)
Penn State Fayette, The Eberly Campus (PA)
Penn State Greater Allegheny (PA)
Penn State Hazleton (PA)
Penn State Lehigh Valley (PA)
Penn State Mont Alto (PA)
Penn State New Kensington (PA)
Penn State Schuylkill (PA)
Penn State Shenango (PA)
Penn State Wilkes-Barre (PA)
Penn State Worthington Scranton (PA)
Penn State York (PA)
Purdue U (IN)
Sam Houston State U (TX)
Stephen F. Austin State U (TX)
Tarleton State U (TX)
U of Idaho (ID)
U of Minnesota, Crookston (MN)
U of Missouri (MO)
U of Nebraska–Lincoln (NE)
U of Wisconsin–River Falls (WI)
Washington State U (WA)

AGRICULTURAL POWER MACHINERY OPERATION
U of Minnesota, Crookston (MN)

AGRICULTURAL PRODUCTION
Stephen F. Austin State U (TX)
Washington State U (WA)

AGRICULTURAL PUBLIC SERVICES RELATED
Oklahoma State U (OK)
U of Kentucky (KY)

AGRICULTURAL TEACHER EDUCATION
Arkansas Tech U (AR)
Auburn U (AL)
California Polytechnic State U, San Luis Obispo (CA)
California State Polytechnic U, Pomona (CA)
Central State U (OH)
Clemson U (SC)
Coll of the Ozarks (MO)
Colorado State U (CO)
Delaware State U (DE)
Eastern New Mexico U (NM)
Iowa State U of Science and Technology (IA)
Kansas State U (KS)
Michigan State U (MI)
Mississippi State U (MS)
Missouri State U (MO)
New Mexico State U (NM)

North Carolina State U (NC)
North Dakota State U (ND)
Northwest Missouri State U (MO)
The Ohio State U (OH)
Purdue U (IN)
Sam Houston State U (TX)
Southeast Missouri State U (MO)
Southern Arkansas U–Magnolia (AR)
State U of New York at Oswego (NY)
Tennessee Technological U (TN)
U of Arkansas (AR)
U of Florida (FL)
U of Georgia (GA)
U of Idaho (ID)
U of Maryland Eastern Shore (MD)
U of Minnesota, Twin Cities Campus (MN)
U of Missouri (MO)
U of Nebraska–Lincoln (NE)
The U of Tennessee at Martin (TN)
U of Wisconsin–Platteville (WI)
U of Wisconsin–River Falls (WI)
U of Wyoming (WY)
Utah State U (UT)
Washington State U (WA)
West Virginia U (WV)

AGRICULTURE
Alcorn State U (MS)
American U of Beirut (Lebanon)
Angelo State U (TX)
Auburn U (AL)
Austin Peay State U (TN)
Berea Coll (KY)
Brigham Young U–Idaho (ID)
California State U, Stanislaus (CA)
Cameron U (OK)
Cornell U (NY)
Delaware State U (DE)
Dickinson State U (ND)
Eastern New Mexico U (NM)
Florida Ag and Mech U (FL)
Hampshire Coll (MA)
Illinois State U (IL)
Iowa State U of Science and Technology (IA)
Kentucky State U (KY)
Lincoln U (MO)
McNeese State U (LA)
Missouri State U (MO)
Morehead State U (KY)
New Mexico State U (NM)
North Carolina State U (NC)
North Dakota State U (ND)
Northwestern Oklahoma State U (OK)
Northwest Missouri State U (MO)
Oregon State U (OR)
Penn State Abington (PA)
Penn State Altoona (PA)
Penn State Beaver (PA)
Penn State Berks (PA)
Penn State Brandywine (PA)
Penn State DuBois (PA)
Penn State Erie, The Behrend Coll (PA)
Penn State Fayette, The Eberly Campus (PA)
Penn State Greater Allegheny (PA)
Penn State Hazleton (PA)
Penn State Lehigh Valley (PA)
Penn State Mont Alto (PA)
Penn State New Kensington (PA)
Penn State Schuylkill (PA)
Penn State Shenango (PA)
Penn State U Park (PA)
Penn State Wilkes-Barre (PA)
Penn State Worthington Scranton (PA)
Penn State York (PA)
Prairie View A&M U (TX)
Purdue U (IN)
Rutgers U–New Brunswick (NJ)
Sam Houston State U (TX)
Southern Arkansas U–Magnolia (AR)
Southern Illinois U Carbondale (IL)
Southern Utah U (UT)
Stephen F. Austin State U (TX)
Tarleton State U (TX)
Tennessee Technological U (TN)
Texas A&M U (TX)
Texas A&M U–Commerce (TX)
Texas A&M U–Kingsville (TX)
Texas State U (TX)

Texas Tech U (TX)
Truman State U (MO)
U of Georgia (GA)
U of Guam (GU)
U of Maryland, Coll Park (MD)
U of Maryland Eastern Shore (MD)
U of Missouri (MO)
U of Nebraska–Lincoln (NE)
U of Nevada, Reno (NV)
The U of Tennessee at Martin (TN)
U of Vermont (VT)
U of Wisconsin–River Falls (WI)
Utah State U (UT)
Washington State U (WA)
Western Illinois U (IL)
Western Kentucky U (KY)
West Texas A&M U (TX)

AGRICULTURE AND AGRICULTURE OPERATIONS RELATED
California State U, Stanislaus (CA)
Coll of the Atlantic (ME)
Emmanuel Coll (GA)
Murray State U (KY)
The Ohio State U (OH)
Penn State U Park (PA)
The U of Arizona (AZ)
U of California, Davis (CA)
U of Kentucky (KY)
U of Nebraska–Lincoln (NE)
U of Saskatchewan (SK, Canada)

AGROECOLOGY AND SUSTAINABLE AGRICULTURE
Central State U (OH)
Delaware Valley U (PA)
The Evergreen State Coll (WA)
Goshen Coll (IN)
Green Mountain Coll (VT)
Guilford Coll (NC)
Mississippi State U (MS)
Purdue U (IN)
Unity Coll (ME)
U of Idaho (ID)
U of Maine (ME)
U of Massachusetts Amherst (MA)
U of Minnesota, Crookston (MN)
U of New Hampshire (NH)
U of Rhode Island (RI)
U of Wyoming (WY)
Washington State U (WA)

AGRONOMY AND CROP SCIENCE
Auburn U (AL)
Brigham Young U–Idaho (ID)
California Polytechnic State U, San Luis Obispo (CA)
Coll of the Ozarks (MO)
Delaware State U (DE)
Delaware Valley U (PA)
Iowa State U of Science and Technology (IA)
Kansas State U (KS)
Mississippi State U (MS)
Missouri State U (MO)
New Mexico State U (NM)
North Carolina State U (NC)
Northwest Missouri State U (MO)
Oregon State U (OR)
Penn State Abington (PA)
Penn State Altoona (PA)
Penn State Beaver (PA)
Penn State Berks (PA)
Penn State Brandywine (PA)
Penn State DuBois (PA)
Penn State Erie, The Behrend Coll (PA)
Penn State Fayette, The Eberly Campus (PA)
Penn State Greater Allegheny (PA)
Penn State Hazleton (PA)
Penn State Mont Alto (PA)
Penn State New Kensington (PA)
Penn State Shenango (PA)
Penn State Wilkes-Barre (PA)
Penn State Worthington Scranton (PA)
Penn State York (PA)
Purdue U (IN)
Tarleton State U (TX)
Tennessee Technological U (TN)
Texas A&M U (TX)
Texas A&M U–Kingsville (TX)
The U of Arizona (AZ)
U of Arkansas (AR)
U of Georgia (GA)

U of Guelph (ON, Canada)
U of Kentucky (KY)
U of Minnesota, Crookston (MN)
U of Nebraska–Lincoln (NE)
U of Saskatchewan (SK, Canada)
The U of Tennessee at Martin (TN)
U of Vermont (VT)
U of Wisconsin–Madison (WI)
U of Wisconsin–Platteville (WI)
U of Wisconsin–River Falls (WI)
Utah State U (UT)
Virginia Polytechnic Inst and State U (VA)
Washington State U (WA)
West Texas A&M U (TX)

AIR AND SPACE OPERATIONS TECHNOLOGY
Embry-Riddle Aeronautical U–Daytona (FL)

AIRCRAFT POWERPLANT TECHNOLOGY
Idaho State U (ID)

AIRFRAME MECHANICS AND AIRCRAFT MAINTENANCE TECHNOLOGY
Antelope Valley Coll (CA)
Kansas State U (KS)
Southeastern Oklahoma State U (OK)
Vaughn Coll of Aeronautics and Technology (NY)

AIRLINE FLIGHT ATTENDANT
California Baptist U (CA)

AIRLINE PILOT AND FLIGHT CREW
Academy Coll (MN)
Auburn U (AL)
Baylor U (TX)
Bridgewater State U (MA)
California Baptist U (CA)
Delaware State U (DE)
Eastern Michigan U (MI)
Embry-Riddle Aeronautical U–Daytona (FL)
Farmingdale State Coll (NY)
Indiana State U (IN)
Jacksonville U (FL)
Kansas State U (KS)
LeTourneau U (TX)
Lynn U (FL)
Purdue U (IN)
Rocky Mountain Coll (MT)
Southeastern Oklahoma State U (OK)
Tarleton State U (TX)
Texas A&M U–Central Texas (TX)
U of Dubuque (IA)
U of Louisiana at Monroe (LA)
U of Minnesota, Crookston (MN)
U of North Dakota (ND)
Utah Valley U (UT)
Western Michigan U (MI)
Westminster Coll (UT)

AIR TRAFFIC CONTROL
Arizona State U at the Polytechnic campus (AZ)
Embry-Riddle Aeronautical U–Daytona (FL)
Hampton U (VA)
LeTourneau U (TX)
Lewis U (IL)
Lynn U (FL)
U of Maryland Eastern Shore (MD)
U of North Dakota (ND)

AIR TRANSPORTATION RELATED
California Baptist U (CA)
Florida Inst of Technology (FL)
Inter American U of Puerto Rico, Bayamón Campus (PR)
U of North Dakota (ND)

ALGEBRA AND NUMBER THEORY
Marlboro Coll (VT)

ALLIED HEALTH AND MEDICAL ASSISTING SERVICES RELATED
Cedarville U (OH)
Coll of Saint Elizabeth (NJ)
The Ohio State U (OH)
The Ohio State U at Lima (OH)
Ramapo Coll of New Jersey (NJ)

U of Vermont (VT)
Widener U (PA)

ALLIED HEALTH DIAGNOSTIC, INTERVENTION, AND TREATMENT PROFESSIONS RELATED
Coll of Saint Elizabeth (NJ)
Fairleigh Dickinson U, Florham Campus (NJ)
Fairleigh Dickinson U, Metropolitan Campus (NJ)
Georgian Court U (NJ)
Hofstra U (NY)
Immaculata U (PA)
Millersville U of Pennsylvania (PA)
Northern Michigan U (MI)
Point Loma Nazarene U (CA)
Rutgers U–Newark (NJ)
Rutgers U–New Brunswick (NJ)
Sacred Heart U (CT)
Tennessee Wesleyan U (TN)
Thomas Edison State U (NJ)
Thomas Jefferson U (PA)
Touro U Worldwide (CA)
U of Nebraska at Kearney (NE)
The U of North Carolina at Charlotte (NC)
Weber State U (UT)

ALTERNATIVE AND COMPLEMENTARY MEDICINE
American Coll of Healthcare Sciences (OR)

ALTERNATIVE AND COMPLEMENTARY MEDICINE RELATED
Metropolitan State U of Denver (CO)

AMERICAN GOVERNMENT AND POLITICS
Arizona Christian U (AZ)
Bridgewater State U (MA)
Emmanuel Coll (MA)
Emory & Henry Coll (VA)
Fitchburg State U (MA)
La Salle U (PA)
Lenoir-Rhyne U (NC)
Marlboro Coll (VT)
The Master's U (CA)
Misericordia U (PA)
Oklahoma Christian U (OK)
United States Military Acad (NY)
The U of Akron (OH)
U of Montana (MT)
Wayland Baptist U (TX)
Western Michigan U (MI)

AMERICAN HISTORY
Bryant U (RI)
Charleston Southern U (SC)
Florida Coll (FL)
Gettysburg Coll (PA)
Howard Payne U (TX)
Keene State Coll (NH)
Morningside Coll (IA)
Sarah Lawrence Coll (NY)
United States Military Acad (NY)
U of Washington, Tacoma (WA)
William Peace U (NC)

AMERICAN INDIAN/NATIVE AMERICAN STUDIES
Arizona State U at the Tempe campus (AZ)
Augsburg U (MN)
Bemidji State U (MN)
Black Hills State U (SD)
Brandon U (MB, Canada)
Colgate U (NY)
Concordia U (QC, Canada)
Dartmouth Coll (NH)
East Central U (OK)
The Evergreen State Coll (WA)
Fort Lewis Coll (CO)
Hampshire Coll (MA)
Humboldt State U (CA)
Inst of American Indian Arts (NM)
Iowa State U of Science and Technology (IA)
Northeastern State U (OK)
Northern Arizona U (AZ)
Northland Coll (WI)
Northwest U (WA)
Portland State U (OR)
St. Thomas U (NB, Canada)
San Diego State U (CA)

San Francisco State U (CA)
Sonoma State U (CA)
Stanford U (CA)
Trent U (ON, Canada)
U of Alaska Fairbanks (AK)
The U of Arizona (AZ)
U of California, Davis (CA)
U of California, Los Angeles (CA)
U of California, Riverside (CA)
U of Hawaii at Manoa (HI)
U of Minnesota, Duluth (MN)
U of Minnesota, Morris (MN)
U of Minnesota, Twin Cities Campus (MN)
U of Montana (MT)
U of New Mexico (NM)
The U of North Carolina at Pembroke (NC)
U of North Dakota (ND)
U of Oklahoma (OK)
U of Regina (SK, Canada)
U of Saskatchewan (SK, Canada)
U of Science and Arts of Oklahoma (OK)
U of South Dakota (SD)
U of Toronto (ON, Canada)
U of Washington (WA)
U of Wisconsin–Eau Claire (WI)
U of Wyoming (WY)
Western New England U (MA)

AMERICAN LITERATURE
Bryant U (RI)
Marlboro Coll (VT)
U of California, Los Angeles (CA)
Washington U in St. Louis (MO)
Whittier Coll (CA)

AMERICAN NATIVE/NATIVE AMERICAN EDUCATION
The Coll of St. Scholastica (MN)
Northeastern State U (OK)
U of Regina (SK, Canada)

AMERICAN NATIVE/NATIVE AMERICAN LANGUAGES
Bemidji State U (MN)
U of Alaska Fairbanks (AK)
U of Minnesota, Twin Cities Campus (MN)
U of Regina (SK, Canada)

AMERICAN SIGN LANGUAGE (ASL)
Augustana U (SD)
Bethel Coll (IN)
California State U, Sacramento (CA)
Kent State U (OH)
Lamar U (TX)
Liberty U (VA)
Madonna U (MI)
Maryville Coll (TN)
Northeastern U (MA)
Rochester Inst of Technology (NY)
St. Catherine U (MN)
U of Houston (TX)
U of Rochester (NY)
U of Wisconsin–Milwaukee (WI)
Utah Valley U (UT)
William Woods U (MO)

AMERICAN STUDIES
Albright Coll (PA)
American U (DC)
Amherst Coll (MA)
Ashland U (OH)
Augustana U (SD)
Austin Coll (TX)
Bard Coll (NY)
Barnard Coll (NY)
Bates Coll (ME)
Baylor U (TX)
Bennington Coll (VT)
Bethany Lutheran Coll (MN)
Boston U (MA)
Bowling Green State U (OH)
Brandeis U (MA)
Bryant U (RI)
California State Polytechnic U, Pomona (CA)
California State U, Fullerton (CA)
California State U, Long Beach (CA)
California State U, San Bernardino (CA)
Carleton Coll (MN)
Case Western Reserve U (OH)
Chowan U (NC)

Christopher Newport U (VA)
Claremont McKenna Coll (CA)
Coe Coll (IA)
Colby Coll (ME)
Coll of Coastal Georgia (GA)
Coll of Staten Island of the City U of New York (NY)
The Coll of William and Mary (VA)
Columbia Coll (MO)
Columbia U (NY)
Connecticut Coll (CT)
Cornell U (NY)
Creighton U (NE)
DePaul U (IL)
Dickinson Coll (PA)
Dominican U (IL)
Eckerd Coll (FL)
Elmhurst Coll (IL)
Emmanuel Coll (MA)
Emory U (GA)
Fairfield U (CT)
Fordham U (NY)
Franklin & Marshall Coll (PA)
Franklin Pierce U (NH)
Georgetown Coll (KY)
Georgetown U (DC)
The George Washington U (DC)
Gettysburg Coll (PA)
Hamilton Coll (NY)
Hampshire Coll (MA)
Hendrix Coll (AR)
Hillsdale Coll (MI)
Hobart and William Smith Colls (NY)
Hofstra U (NY)
Illinois Wesleyan U (IL)
Indiana U Bloomington (IN)
Kansas State U (KS)
Keene State Coll (NH)
Kent State U (OH)
Kenyon Coll (OH)
Knox Coll (IL)
Lafayette Coll (PA)
La Salle U (PA)
Lehman Coll of the City U of New York (NY)
Lenoir-Rhyne U (NC)
Lesley U (MA)
Lindsey Wilson Coll (KY)
Lipscomb U (TN)
Long Island U–LIU Post (NY)
Lycoming Coll (PA)
Manhattanville Coll (NY)
Marist Coll (NY)
Marlboro Coll (VT)
Miami U (OH)
Middlebury Coll (VT)
Mount Saint Mary's U (CA)
Muhlenberg Coll (PA)
Muskingum U (OH)
Nazareth Coll of Rochester (NY)
Northwestern U (IL)
Occidental Coll (CA)
Oglethorpe U (GA)
Oklahoma State U (OK)
Oregon State U (OR)
Pace U (NY)
Pace U, Pleasantville Campus (NY)
Penn State Abington (PA)
Penn State Berks (PA)
Penn State Brandywine (PA)
Penn State Erie, The Behrend Coll (PA)
Penn State Harrisburg (PA)
Penn State Lehigh Valley (PA)
Penn State Schuylkill (PA)
Penn State Worthington Scranton (PA)
Penn State York (PA)
Pitzer Coll (CA)
Pomona Coll (CA)
Providence Coll (RI)
Purdue U (IN)
Queens Coll of the City U of New York (NY)
Ramapo Coll of New Jersey (NJ)
Reed Coll (OR)
Rider U (NJ)
Roger Williams U (RI)
Rollins Coll (FL)
Rowan U (NJ)
Rutgers U–Newark (NJ)
Rutgers U–New Brunswick (NJ)
Saint Francis U (PA)
St. John Fisher Coll (NY)
Saint Louis U (MO)
Saint Mary's Coll of California (CA)

Saint Michael's Coll (VT)
St. Olaf Coll (MN)
Saint Peter's U (NJ)
Salve Regina U (RI)
San Francisco State U (CA)
Scripps Coll (CA)
Sewanee: The U of the South (TN)
Siena Coll (NY)
Skidmore Coll (NY)
Smith Coll (MA)
Sonoma State U (CA)
Stanford U (CA)
State U of New York at Oswego (NY)
State U of New York Coll at Geneseo (NY)
State U of New York Coll at Old Westbury (NY)
Stetson U (FL)
Stonehill Coll (MA)
Stony Brook U, State U of New York (NY)
Temple U (PA)
Tennessee Wesleyan U (TN)
Towson U (MD)
Tufts U (MA)
Tulane U (LA)
Union Coll (NY)
U at Buffalo, the State U of New York (NY)
The U of Alabama (AL)
U of Arkansas (AR)
U of California, Davis (CA)
U of Hawaii at Manoa (HI)
The U of Kansas (KS)
U of Maryland, Baltimore County (MD)
U of Maryland, Coll Park (MD)
U of Massachusetts Boston (MA)
U of Massachusetts Lowell (MA)
U of Miami (FL)
U of Michigan (MI)
U of Michigan–Dearborn (MI)
U of Minnesota, Twin Cities Campus (MN)
U of New Mexico (NM)
The U of North Carolina at Chapel Hill (NC)
U of Notre Dame (IN)
U of Pennsylvania (PA)
U of Pittsburgh at Greensburg (PA)
U of Richmond (VA)
U of Rochester (NY)
U of San Francisco (CA)
U of Southern California (CA)
U of Southern Mississippi (MS)
The U of Texas at Austin (TX)
The U of Texas at Dallas (TX)
The U of Texas at San Antonio (TX)
The U of Toledo (OH)
U of Toronto (ON, Canada)
U of Washington, Bothell (WA)
U of Washington, Tacoma (WA)
U of Wyoming (WY)
Ursinus Coll (PA)
Utah State U (UT)
Valparaiso U (IN)
Vanderbilt U (TN)
Vassar Coll (NY)
Virginia Wesleyan U (VA)
Warner Pacific Coll (OR)
Washington Coll (MD)
Washington State U (WA)
Washington U in St. Louis (MO)
Wellesley Coll (MA)
Wesleyan U (CT)
Western Connecticut State U (CT)
Western Washington U (WA)
Wheaton Coll (MA)
Whitworth U (WA)
Williams Coll (MA)

ANALYSIS AND FUNCTIONAL ANALYSIS
Marlboro Coll (VT)

ANALYTICAL CHEMISTRY
North Central Coll (IL)
West Chester U of Pennsylvania (PA)

ANATOMY
Andrews U (MI)
Bryant U (RI)
Oakland U (MI)
Tulane U (LA)

ANCIENT/CLASSICAL GREEK
Amherst Coll (MA)
Augustana Coll (IL)
Bard Coll (NY)
Barnard Coll (NY)
Baylor U (TX)
Boston U (MA)
Brigham Young U (UT)
Brock U (ON, Canada)
Bryn Mawr Coll (PA)
California State U, Long Beach
  (CA)
Canisius Coll (NY)
Carleton Coll (MN)
Dartmouth Coll (NH)
DePauw U (IN)
Duquesne U (PA)
Emory U (GA)
Franklin & Marshall Coll (PA)
Gettysburg Coll (PA)
Hampden-Sydney Coll (VA)
Hillsdale Coll (MI)
Hobart and William Smith Colls
  (NY)
Hunter Coll of the City U of New
  York (NY)
Indiana U Bloomington (IN)
Kalamazoo Coll (MI)
Kenyon Coll (OH)
Knox Coll (IL)
Loyola U Chicago (IL)
Loyola U New Orleans (LA)
Marlboro Coll (VT)
Monmouth Coll (IL)
Mount Holyoke Coll (MA)
Multnomah U (OR)
Queens Coll of the City U of New
  York (NY)
Randolph Coll (VA)
Randolph-Macon Coll (VA)
Rice U (TX)
Rutgers U–New Brunswick (NJ)
St. Olaf Coll (MN)
Samford U (AL)
Santa Clara U (CA)
Sarah Lawrence Coll (NY)
Sewanee: The U of the South (TN)
Smith Coll (MA)
Southwestern U (TX)
Stanford U (CA)
Tufts U (MA)
U of California, Los Angeles (CA)
U of Michigan (MI)
U of New Hampshire (NH)
The U of North Carolina at
  Greensboro (NC)
U of Notre Dame (IN)
U of Richmond (VA)
The U of Texas at Austin (TX)
U of Vermont (VT)
U of Washington (WA)
Wabash Coll (IN)
Wake Forest U (NC)
Washington U in St. Louis (MO)
Wellesley Coll (MA)
Whitman Coll (WA)

ANCIENT NEAR EASTERN AND BIBLICAL LANGUAGES
Baylor U (TX)
Belmont U (TN)
Carson-Newman U (TN)
Concordia U Chicago (IL)
Concordia U Irvine (CA)
Concordia U Wisconsin (WI)
Geneva Coll (PA)
Houston Baptist U (TX)
Howard Payne U (TX)
Luther Coll (IA)
The Master's U (CA)
Northwest Nazarene U (ID)
Northwest U (WA)
Oklahoma Baptist U (OK)
Toccoa Falls Coll (GA)
Union U (TN)
U of Toronto (ON, Canada)
U of Washington (WA)

ANCIENT STUDIES
Bates Coll (ME)
Boston U (MA)
Bowdoin Coll (ME)
Colby Coll (ME)
Columbia U (NY)
Concordia U (QC, Canada)
Eckerd Coll (FL)
Emory U (GA)
Lehigh U (PA)

Loyola Marymount U (CA)
Mount Holyoke Coll (MA)
Ohio Wesleyan U (OH)
Purdue U (IN)
Rollins Coll (FL)
Rutgers U–Newark (NJ)
Saint Joseph's U (PA)
St. Olaf Coll (MN)
Santa Clara U (CA)
Southwestern Assemblies of God U
  (TX)
The U of Kansas (KS)
U of Maryland, Baltimore County
  (MD)
U of Michigan (MI)
U of Nebraska–Lincoln (NE)
U of Richmond (VA)
The U of Texas at Austin (TX)
Vanderbilt U (TN)
Washington U in St. Louis (MO)
Wheaton Coll (MA)

ANIMAL-ASSISTED THERAPY
Aurora U (IL)
Averett U (VA)
Carroll Coll (MT)

ANIMAL BEHAVIOR AND ETHOLOGY
Bucknell U (PA)
Canisius Coll (NY)
Carroll U (WI)
Franklin & Marshall Coll (PA)
Hampshire Coll (MA)
Indiana U Bloomington (IN)
U of New England (ME)
U of Toronto (ON, Canada)

ANIMAL GENETICS
Clemson U (SC)
Dartmouth Coll (NH)
Ohio Wesleyan U (OH)
Rutgers U–New Brunswick (NJ)
U of Toronto (ON, Canada)

ANIMAL HEALTH
Brigham Young U–Idaho (ID)
U of Georgia (GA)

ANIMAL/LIVESTOCK HUSBANDRY AND PRODUCTION
Delaware Valley U (PA)
Rutgers U–New Brunswick (NJ)
Tarleton State U (TX)
Texas A&M U (TX)

ANIMAL PHYSIOLOGY
Rutgers U–New Brunswick (NJ)
Sonoma State U (CA)
The U of Akron (OH)
U of Toronto (ON, Canada)
Utah State U (UT)

ANIMAL SCIENCES
Abilene Christian U (TX)
Angelo State U (TX)
Auburn U (AL)
Brigham Young U–Idaho (ID)
California Polytechnic State U, San
  Luis Obispo (CA)
California State Polytechnic U,
  Pomona (CA)
Clemson U (SC)
Coll of the Ozarks (MO)
Colorado State U (CO)
Cornell U (NY)
Delaware State U (DE)
Delaware Valley U (PA)
Iowa State U of Science and
  Technology (IA)
Kansas State U (KS)
Langston U (OK)
Louisiana State U and A&M Coll
  (LA)
Lubbock Christian U (TX)
Michigan State U (MI)
Middle Tennessee State U (TN)
Mississippi State U (MS)
Missouri State U (MO)
New Mexico State U (NM)
North Carolina State U (NC)
North Dakota State U (ND)
Northwest Missouri State U (MO)
The Ohio State U (OH)
Oklahoma State U (OK)
Oregon State U (OR)
Penn State Abington (PA)
Penn State Altoona (PA)

Penn State Beaver (PA)
Penn State Berks (PA)
Penn State Brandywine (PA)
Penn State DuBois (PA)
Penn State Erie, The Behrend Coll
  (PA)
Penn State Fayette, The Eberly
  Campus (PA)
Penn State Greater Allegheny (PA)
Penn State Hazleton (PA)
Penn State Lehigh Valley (PA)
Penn State Mont Alto (PA)
Penn State New Kensington (PA)
Penn State Schuylkill (PA)
Penn State Shenango (PA)
Penn State U Park (PA)
Penn State Wilkes-Barre (PA)
Penn State Worthington Scranton
  (PA)
Penn State York (PA)
Purdue U (IN)
Rutgers U–New Brunswick (NJ)
Sam Houston State U (TX)
Southern Illinois U Carbondale (IL)
Stephen F. Austin State U (TX)
Tarleton State U (TX)
Tennessee Technological U (TN)
Texas A&M U (TX)
Texas A&M U–Commerce (TX)
Texas A&M U–Kingsville (TX)
Texas State U (TX)
Texas Tech U (TX)
The U of Arizona (AZ)
U of Arkansas (AR)
U of California, Davis (CA)
The U of Findlay (OH)
U of Florida (FL)
U of Georgia (GA)
U of Guelph (ON, Canada)
U of Hawaii at Manoa (HI)
U of Idaho (ID)
U of Kentucky (KY)
U of Maine (ME)
U of Maryland, Coll Park (MD)
U of Massachusetts Amherst (MA)
U of Minnesota, Crookston (MN)
U of Minnesota, Twin Cities
  Campus (MN)
U of Missouri (MO)
U of Nebraska–Lincoln (NE)
U of New Hampshire (NH)
U of Rhode Island (RI)
U of Saskatchewan (SK, Canada)
The U of Tennessee (TN)
The U of Tennessee at Martin (TN)
U of Vermont (VT)
U of Wisconsin–Madison (WI)
U of Wisconsin–Platteville (WI)
U of Wisconsin–River Falls (WI)
U of Wyoming (WY)
Utah State U (UT)
Virginia Polytechnic Inst and State
  U (VA)
Washington State U (WA)
West Texas A&M U (TX)
West Virginia U (WV)

ANIMAL SCIENCES RELATED
Delaware Valley U (PA)
Penn State Abington (PA)
Penn State Beaver (PA)
Penn State Brandywine (PA)
Penn State DuBois (PA)
Penn State Erie, The Behrend Coll
  (PA)
Penn State Fayette, The Eberly
  Campus (PA)
Penn State Greater Allegheny (PA)
Penn State Hazleton (PA)
Penn State Lehigh Valley (PA)
Penn State Mont Alto (PA)
Penn State New Kensington (PA)
Penn State Schuylkill (PA)
Penn State Shenango (PA)
Penn State Wilkes-Barre (PA)
Penn State Worthington Scranton
  (PA)
Penn State York (PA)
U of California, Davis (CA)

ANIMATION, INTERACTIVE TECHNOLOGY, VIDEO GRAPHICS AND SPECIAL EFFECTS
Academy of Art U (CA)
American Acad of Art (IL)
American Intl Coll (MA)
ArtCenter Coll of Design (CA)

Bennington Coll (VT)
Bradley U (IL)
Brigham Young U (UT)
Buena Vista U (IA)
California Coll of the Arts (CA)
Coll of the Atlantic (ME)
Columbia Coll Chicago (IL)
Concordia U (QC, Canada)
Davenport U, Grand Rapids (MI)
DePaul U (IL)
DigiPen Inst of Technology (WA)
Eastern Michigan U (MI)
East Tennessee State U (TN)
Elmhurst Coll (IL)
Fashion Inst of Technology (NY)
Ferris State U (MI)
Florida State U (FL)
George Mason U (VA)
Kansas City Art Inst (MO)
Laguna Coll of Art & Design (CA)
Lawrence Technological U (MI)
Loyola Marymount U (CA)
Lynn U (FL)
Massachusetts Coll of Art and
  Design (MA)
Middle Tennessee State U (TN)
Minneapolis Coll of Art and Design
  (MN)
Missouri Western State U (MO)
New England Inst of Technology
  (RI)
New Mexico State U (NM)
North Central Coll (IL)
Northeastern U (MA)
Pennsylvania Coll of Art & Design
  (PA)
Point Park U (PA)
Regent U (VA)
Ringling Coll of Art and Design (FL)
Rochester Inst of Technology (NY)
Sam Houston State U (TX)
Savannah Coll of Art and Design
  (GA)
State U of New York Coll of
  Technology at Alfred (NY)
U of Idaho (ID)
U of the Incarnate Word (TX)
Villa Maria Coll (NY)
Webster U (MO)

ANTHROPOLOGY
Adelphi U (NY)
Agnes Scott Coll (GA)
Albion Coll (MI)
Albright Coll (PA)
Alma Coll (MI)
American U (DC)
The American U in Cairo (Egypt)
Amherst Coll (MA)
Antioch Coll, Yellow Springs (OH)
Appalachian State U (NC)
Arizona State U at the Tempe
  campus (AZ)
Athabasca U (AB, Canada)
Auburn U (AL)
Augustana Coll (IL)
Augustana U (SD)
Austin Coll (TX)
Ball State U (IN)
Bard Coll (NY)
Barnard Coll (NY)
Bates Coll (ME)
Baylor U (TX)
Beloit Coll (WI)
Bennington Coll (VT)
Binghamton U, State U of New York
  (NY)
Biola U (CA)
Bloomsburg U of Pennsylvania (PA)
Boise State U (ID)
Boston U (MA)
Bowdoin Coll (ME)
Brandeis U (MA)
Bridgewater State U (MA)
Bryn Mawr Coll (PA)
Bucknell U (PA)
Buffalo State Coll, State U of New
  York (NY)
Butler U (IN)
California State Polytechnic U,
  Pomona (CA)
California State U, Dominguez Hills
  (CA)
California State U, East Bay (CA)
California State U, Fullerton (CA)
California State U, Long Beach
  (CA)

California State U, Los Angeles
  (CA)
California State U, Northridge (CA)
California State U, Sacramento
  (CA)
California State U, San Bernardino
  (CA)
California State U, San Marcos
  (CA)
California State U, Stanislaus (CA)
California U of Pennsylvania (PA)
Carleton Coll (MN)
Case Western Reserve U (OH)
The Catholic U of America (DC)
Central Connecticut State U (CT)
Central Michigan U (MI)
City Coll of the City U of New York
  (NY)
Clarion U of Pennsylvania (PA)
Clemson U (SC)
Cleveland State U (OH)
Colby Coll (ME)
Colgate U (NY)
The Coll at Brockport, State U of
  New York (NY)
Coll of Charleston (SC)
The Coll of Idaho (ID)
Coll of the Holy Cross (MA)
The Coll of William and Mary (VA)
The Coll of Wooster (OH)
The Colorado Coll (CO)
Colorado State U (CO)
Columbia U (NY)
Concordia U (QC, Canada)
Connecticut Coll (CT)
Cornell Coll (IA)
Cornell U (NY)
Creighton U (NE)
Dartmouth Coll (NH)
Davidson Coll (NC)
Denison U (OH)
DePaul U (IL)
DePauw U (IN)
Dickinson Coll (PA)
Drake U (IA)
Drew U (NJ)
Drexel U (PA)
Earlham Coll (IN)
East Carolina U (NC)
Eastern Michigan U (MI)
Eastern New Mexico U (NM)
Eastern Washington U (WA)
East Tennessee State U (TN)
Eckerd Coll (FL)
Elon U (NC)
Emory U (GA)
Florida Atlantic U (FL)
Florida Gulf Coast U (FL)
Florida State U (FL)
Fordham U (NY)
Fort Lewis Coll (CO)
Franklin & Marshall Coll (PA)
Franklin Pierce U (NH)
Furman U (SC)
George Mason U (VA)
Georgetown U (DC)
The George Washington U (DC)
Georgia Southern U (GA)
Georgia State U (GA)
Gettysburg Coll (PA)
Grand Valley State U (MI)
Grinnell Coll (IA)
Gustavus Adolphus Coll (MN)
Hamilton Coll (NY)
Hamline U (MN)
Hampshire Coll (MA)
Hartwick Coll (NY)
Harvard U (MA)
Haverford Coll (PA)
Hawai`i Pacific U (HI)
Hendrix Coll (AR)
Hobart and William Smith Colls
  (NY)
Hofstra U (NY)
Humboldt State U (CA)
Hunter Coll of the City U of New
  York (NY)
Idaho State U (ID)
Illinois State U (IL)
Illinois Wesleyan U (IL)
Indiana U Bloomington (IN)
Indiana U Northwest (IN)
Indiana U of Pennsylvania (PA)
Indiana U–Purdue U Indianapolis
  (IN)
Indiana U South Bend (IN)

Inter American U of Puerto Rico, San Germán Campus (PR)
Iowa State U of Science and Technology (IA)
Ithaca Coll (NY)
James Madison U (VA)
John Jay Coll of Criminal Justice of the City U of New York (NY)
Johns Hopkins U (MD)
Juniata Coll (PA)
Kansas State U (KS)
Kennesaw State U (GA)
Kent State U (OH)
Kenyon Coll (OH)
Knox Coll (IL)
Kutztown U of Pennsylvania (PA)
Lafayette Coll (PA)
Lawrence U (WI)
Lee U (TN)
Lehigh U (PA)
Lehman Coll of the City U of New York (NY)
Lincoln U (PA)
Lindenwood U (MO)
Linfield Coll (OR)
Longwood U (VA)
Louisiana State U and A&M Coll (LA)
Loyola U Chicago (IL)
Luther Coll (IA)
Macalester Coll (MN)
Marlboro Coll (VT)
Marquette U (WI)
Massachusetts Inst of Technology (MA)
Mercyhurst U (PA)
Metropolitan State U of Denver (CO)
Miami U (OH)
Michigan State U (MI)
Michigan Technological U (MI)
Middle Tennessee State U (TN)
Millersville U of Pennsylvania (PA)
Minnesota State U Moorhead (MN)
Mississippi State U (MS)
Missouri State U (MO)
Monmouth Coll (IL)
Montclair State U (NJ)
Mount Holyoke Coll (MA)
Muhlenberg Coll (PA)
Muskingum U (OH)
Nazareth Coll of Rochester (NY)
New Coll of Florida (FL)
New Mexico State U (NM)
New York U (NY)
North Carolina State U (NC)
North Central Coll (IL)
North Dakota State U (ND)
Northern Arizona U (AZ)
Northern Illinois U (IL)
Northern Kentucky U (KY)
Northern Vermont U–Lyndon (VT)
Northwestern U (IL)
Oakland U (MI)
Oberlin Coll (OH)
The Ohio State U (OH)
Ohio U (OH)
Oklahoma Baptist U (OK)
Oregon State U (OR)
Pacific Lutheran U (WA)
Penn State Abington (PA)
Penn State Altoona (PA)
Penn State Beaver (PA)
Penn State Berks (PA)
Penn State Brandywine (PA)
Penn State DuBois (PA)
Penn State Erie, The Behrend Coll (PA)
Penn State Fayette, The Eberly Campus (PA)
Penn State Greater Allegheny (PA)
Penn State Hazleton (PA)
Penn State Lehigh Valley (PA)
Penn State Mont Alto (PA)
Penn State New Kensington (PA)
Penn State Schuylkill (PA)
Penn State Shenango (PA)
Penn State U Park (PA)
Penn State Wilkes-Barre (PA)
Penn State Worthington Scranton (PA)
Penn State York (PA)
Pitzer Coll (CA)
Pomona Coll (CA)
Portland State U (OR)
Princeton U (NJ)

Purchase Coll, State U of New York (NY)
Purdue U (IN)
Queens Coll of the City U of New York (NY)
Radford U (VA)
Reed Coll (OR)
Rhode Island Coll (RI)
Rhodes Coll (TN)
Rice U (TX)
Ripon Coll (WI)
Rollins Coll (FL)
Rutgers U–Newark (NJ)
Rutgers U–New Brunswick (NJ)
Saint Francis U (PA)
St. John Fisher Coll (NY)
St. John's U (NY)
St. Lawrence U (NY)
Saint Louis U (MO)
Saint Louis U–Madrid Campus (Spain)
Saint Martin's U (WA)
Saint Mary's Coll of California (CA)
St. Mary's Coll of Maryland (MD)
St. Thomas U (NB, Canada)
Saint Vincent Coll (PA)
San Diego State U (CA)
San Francisco State U (CA)
Santa Clara U (CA)
Sarah Lawrence Coll (NY)
Scripps Coll (CA)
Seattle U (WA)
Sewanee: The U of the South (TN)
Skidmore Coll (NY)
Smith Coll (MA)
Sonoma State U (CA)
Southern Illinois U Carbondale (IL)
Southern Illinois U Edwardsville (IL)
Southern Methodist U (TX)
Southern Utah U (UT)
Southwestern U (TX)
Stanford U (CA)
State U of New York at New Paltz (NY)
State U of New York at Oswego (NY)
State U of New York at Plattsburgh (NY)
State U of New York Coll at Cortland (NY)
State U of New York Coll at Geneseo (NY)
State U of New York Coll at Oneonta (NY)
State U of New York Coll at Potsdam (NY)
Stony Brook U, State U of New York (NY)
Susquehanna U (PA)
Sweet Briar Coll (VA)
Syracuse U (NY)
Temple U (PA)
Texas A&M U (TX)
Texas Christian U (TX)
Texas State U (TX)
Texas Tech U (TX)
Transylvania U (KY)
Trent U (ON, Canada)
Trinity U (TX)
Troy U (AL)
Tufts U (MA)
Tulane U (LA)
Union Coll (NY)
U at Albany, State U of New York (NY)
U at Buffalo, the State U of New York (NY)
The U of Akron (OH)
The U of Alabama (AL)
The U of Alabama at Birmingham (AL)
U of Alaska Fairbanks (AK)
The U of Arizona (AZ)
U of Arkansas (AR)
U of California, Davis (CA)
U of California, Irvine (CA)
U of California, Los Angeles (CA)
U of California, Riverside (CA)
U of California, San Diego (CA)
U of California, Santa Barbara (CA)
U of California, Santa Cruz (CA)
U of Central Florida (FL)
U of Chicago (IL)
U of Cincinnati (OH)
U of Colorado Boulder (CO)

U of Colorado Colorado Springs (CO)
U of Colorado Denver (CO)
U of Denver (CO)
U of Florida (FL)
U of Georgia (GA)
U of Guam (GU)
U of Guelph (ON, Canada)
U of Hawaii at Manoa (HI)
U of Houston (TX)
U of Houston–Clear Lake (TX)
U of Idaho (ID)
U of Illinois at Chicago (IL)
The U of Kansas (KS)
U of Kentucky (KY)
U of King's Coll (NS, Canada)
U of La Verne (CA)
U of Louisville (KY)
U of Maine (ME)
U of Maryland, Baltimore County (MD)
U of Maryland, Coll Park (MD)
U of Mary Washington (VA)
U of Massachusetts Amherst (MA)
U of Massachusetts Boston (MA)
U of Memphis (TN)
U of Miami (FL)
U of Michigan (MI)
U of Michigan–Dearborn (MI)
U of Michigan–Flint (MI)
U of Minnesota, Duluth (MN)
U of Minnesota, Morris (MN)
U of Minnesota, Twin Cities Campus (MN)
U of Missouri (MO)
U of Missouri–St. Louis (MO)
U of Montana (MT)
U of Nebraska–Lincoln (NE)
U of Nevada, Las Vegas (NV)
U of Nevada, Reno (NV)
U of New Hampshire (NH)
U of New Mexico (NM)
U of New Orleans (LA)
U of North Carolina at Asheville (NC)
The U of North Carolina at Chapel Hill (NC)
The U of North Carolina at Charlotte (NC)
The U of North Carolina at Greensboro (NC)
The U of North Carolina Wilmington (NC)
U of North Dakota (ND)
U of Northern Colorado (CO)
U of Northern Iowa (IA)
U of North Florida (FL)
U of North Texas (TX)
U of Notre Dame (IN)
U of Oklahoma (OK)
U of Oregon (OR)
U of Pennsylvania (PA)
U of Pittsburgh (PA)
U of Pittsburgh at Greensburg (PA)
U of Regina (SK, Canada)
U of Rhode Island (RI)
U of Richmond (VA)
U of Rochester (NY)
U of San Diego (CA)
U of Saskatchewan (SK, Canada)
U of South Alabama (AL)
U of South Carolina (SC)
U of South Dakota (SD)
U of Southern California (CA)
U of Southern Indiana (IN)
U of Southern Mississippi (MS)
U of South Florida, St. Petersburg (FL)
The U of Tennessee (TN)
The U of Texas at Austin (TX)
The U of Texas at El Paso (TX)
The U of Texas at San Antonio (TX)
The U of Texas Rio Grande Valley (TX)
U of the Fraser Valley (BC, Canada)
The U of Toledo (OH)
U of Toronto (ON, Canada)
The U of Tulsa (OK)
U of Utah (UT)
U of Vermont (VT)
U of Virginia (VA)
U of Washington (WA)
U of Waterloo (ON, Canada)
U of West Georgia (GA)
U of Wisconsin–Madison (WI)
U of Wisconsin–Milwaukee (WI)

U of Wyoming (WY)
Utah State U (UT)
Vanderbilt U (TN)
Vanguard U of Southern California (CA)
Vassar Coll (NY)
Virginia Commonwealth U (VA)
Wagner Coll (NY)
Wake Forest U (NC)
Washington Coll (MD)
Washington State U (WA)
Washington State U–Vancouver (WA)
Washington U in St. Louis (MO)
Wayne State U (MI)
Weber State U (UT)
Wellesley Coll (MA)
Wells Coll (NY)
Wesleyan U (CT)
West Chester U of Pennsylvania (PA)
Western Connecticut State U (CT)
Western Illinois U (IL)
Western Kentucky U (KY)
Western Michigan U (MI)
Western Oregon U (OR)
Western State Colorado U (CO)
Western Washington U (WA)
Westmont Coll (CA)
Wheaton Coll (IL)
Wheaton Coll (MA)
Whitman Coll (WA)
Whittier Coll (CA)
Wichita State U (KS)
Widener U (PA)
Willamette U (OR)
William Paterson U of New Jersey (NJ)
William Peace U (NC)
Williams Coll (MA)
Wisconsin Lutheran Coll (WI)
Wright State U (OH)
Wright State U–Lake Campus (OH)
Youngstown State U (OH)

ANTHROPOLOGY RELATED
Bridgewater State U (MA)
Butler U (IN)
California Baptist U (CA)
U of Michigan (MI)
Western Washington U (WA)

APPAREL AND ACCESSORIES MARKETING
U of Rhode Island (RI)
Woodbury U (CA)

APPAREL AND TEXTILE MANUFACTURING
Academy of Art U (CA)
Ball State U (IN)
Fashion Inst of Technology (NY)
FIDM/Fashion Inst of Design & Merchandising, Los Angeles Campus (CA)
Michigan State U (MI)

APPAREL AND TEXTILE MARKETING MANAGEMENT
Academy of Art U (CA)
Auburn U (AL)
Colorado State U (CO)
Indiana Tech (IN)
Iowa State U of Science and Technology (IA)
Savannah Coll of Art and Design (GA)
U of Central Oklahoma (OK)
U of the Incarnate Word (TX)
Wayne State U (MI)

APPAREL AND TEXTILES
Academy of Art U (CA)
Appalachian State U (NC)
Auburn U (AL)
Bowling Green State U (OH)
California State Polytechnic U, Pomona (CA)
California State U, Long Beach (CA)
Delaware State U (DE)
East Carolina U (NC)
Framingham State U (MA)
Georgia Southern U (GA)
Illinois State U (IL)
Indiana State U (IN)
Indiana U Bloomington (IN)
Iowa State U of Science and Technology (IA)

Kansas State U (KS)
Lamar U (TX)
Liberty U (VA)
Lipscomb U (TN)
Louisiana State U and A&M Coll (LA)
Michigan State U (MI)
Middle Tennessee State U (TN)
Mississippi State U (MS)
Missouri State U (MO)
New Mexico State U (NM)
North Dakota State U (ND)
Northern Illinois U (IL)
The Ohio State U (OH)
Ohio U (OH)
Oregon State U (OR)
Rhode Island School of Design (RI)
Seattle Pacific U (WA)
Southern Illinois U Carbondale (IL)
Tennessee Technological U (TN)
Texas A&M U–Kingsville (TX)
The U of Akron (OH)
The U of Alabama (AL)
U of Arkansas (AR)
U of California, Davis (CA)
U of Hawaii at Manoa (HI)
U of Idaho (ID)
U of Kentucky (KY)
U of Minnesota, Twin Cities Campus (MN)
U of Missouri (MO)
U of Nebraska–Lincoln (NE)
The U of North Carolina at Greensboro (NC)
U of Northern Iowa (IA)
U of Rhode Island (RI)
U of Southern Mississippi (MS)
The U of Texas at Austin (TX)
U of Wisconsin–Madison (WI)
U of Wisconsin–Stout (WI)
Virginia Polytechnic Inst and State U (VA)
Washington State U (WA)
Western Kentucky U (KY)

APPAREL AND TEXTILES RELATED
Savannah Coll of Art and Design (GA)

APPLIED AND PROFESSIONAL ETHICS
Carnegie Mellon U (PA)
Carson-Newman U (TN)
Drexel U (PA)
Mount Saint Mary's U (CA)
Simpson Coll (IA)
U of Michigan–Flint (MI)
Western Michigan U (MI)

APPLIED BEHAVIOR ANALYSIS
Ball State U (IN)
Cairn U (PA)
Florida Inst of Technology (FL)
Saint Joseph's U (PA)
U of North Texas (TX)
Western Michigan U (MI)

APPLIED ECONOMICS
Allegheny Coll (PA)
Augsburg U (MN)
Binghamton U, State U of New York (NY)
Bowling Green State U (OH)
Brigham Young U (UT)
Bryant U (RI)
Carnegie Mellon U (PA)
Concordia U (QC, Canada)
Farmingdale State Coll (NY)
HEC Montreal (QC, Canada)
Ithaca Coll (NY)
Penn State Abington (PA)
Penn State Beaver (PA)
Penn State Brandywine (PA)
Penn State DuBois (PA)
Penn State Erie, The Behrend Coll (PA)
Penn State Fayette, The Eberly Campus (PA)
Penn State Greater Allegheny (PA)
Penn State Hazleton (PA)
Penn State Lehigh Valley (PA)
Penn State Mont Alto (PA)
Penn State New Kensington (PA)
Penn State Schuylkill (PA)
Penn State Shenango (PA)
Penn State Wilkes-Barre (PA)

Penn State Worthington Scranton (PA)
Penn State York (PA)
The U of Akron (OH)
The U of Arizona (AZ)
U of Central Oklahoma (OK)
U of Dayton (OH)
U of Massachusetts Amherst (MA)
U of Minnesota, Twin Cities Campus (MN)
U of Northern Iowa (IA)
U of San Francisco (CA)
U of Waterloo (ON, Canada)
Ursinus Coll (PA)
Wabash Coll (IN)

APPLIED HORTICULTURE/ HORTICULTURAL BUSINESS SERVICES RELATED
Delaware Valley U (PA)
North Dakota State U (ND)
U of Rhode Island (RI)

APPLIED HORTICULTURE/ HORTICULTURE OPERATIONS
Colorado State U (CO)
Farmingdale State Coll (NY)
Kent State U at Salem (OH)
North Carolina State U (NC)
Texas A&M U (TX)
U of Maine (ME)
U of Massachusetts Amherst (MA)

APPLIED LINGUISTICS
Caldwell U (NJ)
Corban U (OR)
Marlboro Coll (VT)
Mid-Atlantic Christian U (NC)
Portland State U (OR)
U of Idaho (ID)

APPLIED MATHEMATICS
American U (DC)
American U of Beirut (Lebanon)
Arizona State U at the Polytechnic campus (AZ)
Arizona State U at the West campus (AZ)
Auburn U (AL)
Augustana Coll (IL)
Azusa Pacific U (CA)
Baldwin Wallace U (OH)
Baylor U (TX)
Biola U (CA)
Boise State U (ID)
Bowie State U (MD)
Brescia U (KY)
Brigham Young U–Idaho (ID)
Brock U (ON, Canada)
Bryant U (RI)
California State U, Fullerton (CA)
California State U, Long Beach (CA)
Carroll Coll (MT)
Carroll U (WI)
Case Western Reserve U (OH)
Central Michigan U (MI)
Charleston Southern U (SC)
Christopher Newport U (VA)
Clarkson U (NY)
Coastal Carolina U (SC)
Colgate U (NY)
The Coll of Idaho (ID)
Columbia U (NY)
East Central U (OK)
Elizabethtown Coll (PA)
Elon U (NC)
Emmaus Bible Coll (IA)
Emory U (GA)
Endicott Coll (MA)
Farmingdale State Coll (NY)
Ferris State U (MI)
Fitchburg State U (MA)
Florida Inst of Technology (FL)
Florida State U (FL)
Geneva Coll (PA)
The George Washington U (DC)
Georgia Inst of Technology (GA)
Grand View U (IA)
Hampden-Sydney Coll (VA)
Harvard U (MA)
Hillsdale Coll (MI)
Humboldt State U (CA)
Huntington U (AL)
Indiana U South Bend (IN)
Inter American U of Puerto Rico, San Germán Campus (PR)
Iona Coll (NY)

Johns Hopkins U (MD)
Kennesaw State U (GA)
Kent State U (OH)
Kettering U (MI)
La Salle U (PA)
Lasell Coll (MA)
Lee U (TN)
Lipscomb U (TN)
Long Island U–LIU Post (NY)
Loyola Marymount U (CA)
Marist Coll (NY)
Marlboro Coll (VT)
Mary Baldwin U (VA)
Maryville U of Saint Louis (MO)
The Master's U (CA)
Millsaps Coll (MS)
Missouri U of Science and Technology (MO)
New Coll of Florida (FL)
New Jersey Inst of Technology (NJ)
North Carolina State U (NC)
North Central Coll (IL)
Northern Illinois U (IL)
Northwestern U (IL)
Ohio Northern U (OH)
Ohio U (OH)
Penn State Harrisburg (PA)
Post U (CT)
Purdue U (IN)
Quinnipiac U (CT)
Rice U (TX)
Robert Morris U (PA)
Rockhurst U (MO)
Roger Williams U (RI)
Rutgers U–Newark (NJ)
Saginaw Valley State U (MI)
St. Thomas Aquinas Coll (NY)
San Diego State U (CA)
San Francisco State U (CA)
Simon Fraser U (BC, Canada)
Sonoma State U (CA)
State U of New York at Oswego (NY)
State U of New York Coll at Geneseo (NY)
State U of New York Polytechnic Inst (NY)
Stony Brook U, State U of New York (NY)
Syracuse U (NY)
Temple U (PA)
Texas A&M U (TX)
Texas State U (TX)
Thomas Edison State U (NJ)
Trent U (ON, Canada)
Trevecca Nazarene U (TN)
Tufts U (MA)
U at Buffalo, the State U of New York (NY)
The U of Akron (OH)
U of California, Davis (CA)
U of California, Los Angeles (CA)
U of California, San Diego (CA)
U of Central Oklahoma (OK)
U of Colorado Boulder (CO)
The U of Findlay (OH)
U of Houston–Downtown (TX)
U of Idaho (ID)
U of Jamestown (ND)
U of Massachusetts Lowell (MA)
U of Miami (FL)
U of New England (ME)
U of New Hampshire (NH)
U of New Haven (CT)
The U of North Carolina at Chapel Hill (NC)
U of North Florida (FL)
U of Pittsburgh (PA)
U of Pittsburgh at Bradford (PA)
U of Pittsburgh at Greensburg (PA)
U of Rochester (NY)
U of Saint Mary (KS)
The U of Scranton (PA)
U of Sioux Falls (SD)
U of South Carolina Aiken (SC)
The U of Tennessee at Chattanooga (TN)
The U of Texas at El Paso (TX)
U of the Virgin Islands (VI)
U of Toronto (ON, Canada)
The U of Tulsa (OK)
U of Utah (UT)
U of Waterloo (ON, Canada)
U of Wisconsin–Madison (WI)
U of Wisconsin–Milwaukee (WI)
U of Wisconsin–Stout (WI)
U of Wisconsin–Superior (WI)

Valdosta State U (GA)
Washington State U (WA)
Washington State U–Vancouver (WA)
Washington U in St. Louis (MO)
Weber State U (UT)
Wentworth Inst of Technology (MA)
Western Michigan U (MI)
Western Washington U (WA)
Wheaton Coll (IL)
William Penn U (IA)

APPLIED MATHEMATICS RELATED
Arizona State U at the Tempe campus (AZ)
Averett U (VA)
Belmont U (TN)
Berea Coll (KY)
Bucknell U (PA)
Carroll U (WI)
Elizabethtown Coll (PA)
Georgia Inst of Technology (GA)
Inter American U of Puerto Rico, Bayamón Campus (PR)
Inter American U of Puerto Rico, Metropolitan Campus (PR)
Keene State Coll (NH)
Louisiana Coll (LA)
Lycoming Coll (PA)
Mount St. Joseph U (OH)
Temple U (PA)
U of California, Santa Barbara (CA)
U of Washington (WA)
U of Waterloo (ON, Canada)
U of Wisconsin–Milwaukee (WI)
Whitworth U (WA)
Willamette U (OR)

APPLIED PSYCHOLOGY
Arizona State U at the Polytechnic campus (AZ)
Belhaven U (MS)
Bryant U (RI)
Carson-Newman U (TN)
Christian Brothers U (TN)
Embry-Riddle Aeronautical U– Daytona (FL)
Farmingdale State Coll (NY)
Georgia Southern U–Armstrong Campus (GA)
Gwynedd Mercy U (PA)
Judson U (IL)
Kansas Wesleyan U (KS)
Loyola U Chicago (IL)
Mount Saint Mary's U (CA)
Multnomah U (OR)
New York U (NY)
Oregon Inst of Technology (OR)
Pace U (NY)
Pace U, Pleasantville Campus (NY)
Palo Alto U (CA)
State U of New York Coll of Technology at Canton (NY)
United States Military Acad (NY)
U of Saint Mary (KS)

AQUACULTURE
Auburn U (AL)
Clemson U (SC)
U of New England (ME)

AQUATIC BIOLOGY/ LIMNOLOGY
Florida Inst of Technology (FL)
Gannon U (PA)
State U of New York Coll of Environmental Science and Forestry (NY)
Stetson U (FL)
Texas State U (TX)
U of South Carolina (SC)
Western Michigan U (MI)

ARABIC
American U (DC)
Bard Coll (NY)
Baylor U (TX)
Binghamton U, State U of New York (NY)
California U of Pennsylvania (PA)
Dartmouth Coll (NH)
DePaul U (IL)
Emory U (GA)
Georgetown U (DC)
Lebanese American U (Lebanon)
Marlboro Coll (VT)
Michigan State U (MI)
Middlebury Coll (VT)

Montclair State U (NJ)
The Ohio State U (OH)
Portland State U (OR)
Tufts U (MA)
United States Military Acad (NY)
The U of Arizona (AZ)
U of California, Los Angeles (CA)
U of Cincinnati (OH)
U of Georgia (GA)
U of Maryland, Coll Park (MD)
U of Notre Dame (IN)
U of Oklahoma (OK)
The U of Texas at Austin (TX)
U of Toronto (ON, Canada)
Washington U in St. Louis (MO)
Western Kentucky U (KY)

ARCHEOLOGY
The American U in Cairo (Egypt)
American U of Beirut (Lebanon)
Biola U (CA)
Boston U (MA)
Bowdoin Coll (ME)
Bridgewater State U (MA)
Brock U (ON, Canada)
Bryn Mawr Coll (PA)
Coll of Charleston (SC)
The Coll of Wooster (OH)
Columbia U (NY)
Cornell Coll (IA)
Cornell U (NY)
Dartmouth Coll (NH)
Dickinson Coll (PA)
Franklin Pierce U (NH)
The George Washington U (DC)
Hamilton Coll (NY)
Haverford Coll (PA)
Hunter Coll of the City U of New York (NY)
Johns Hopkins U (MD)
Kent State U (OH)
Lycoming Coll (PA)
Mercyhurst U (PA)
New York U (NY)
Oberlin Coll (OH)
Penn State Abington (PA)
Penn State Altoona (PA)
Penn State Beaver (PA)
Penn State Berks (PA)
Penn State Brandywine (PA)
Penn State DuBois (PA)
Penn State Erie, The Behrend Coll (PA)
Penn State Fayette, The Eberly Campus (PA)
Penn State Greater Allegheny (PA)
Penn State Hazleton (PA)
Penn State Lehigh Valley (PA)
Penn State Mont Alto (PA)
Penn State New Kensington (PA)
Penn State Schuylkill (PA)
Penn State Shenango (PA)
Penn State U Park (PA)
Penn State Wilkes-Barre (PA)
Penn State Worthington Scranton (PA)
Penn State York (PA)
Saint Mary's Coll of California (CA)
Simon Fraser U (BC, Canada)
Southern Adventist U (TN)
Stanford U (CA)
State U of New York Coll at Potsdam (NY)
Sweet Briar Coll (VA)
Tufts U (MA)
U of California, San Diego (CA)
U of Cincinnati (OH)
U of Evansville (IN)
U of Missouri (MO)
The U of North Carolina at Chapel Hill (NC)
U of Saskatchewan (SK, Canada)
U of Southern California (CA)
The U of Texas at Austin (TX)
U of Toronto (ON, Canada)
U of Wisconsin–La Crosse (WI)
Washington U in St. Louis (MO)
Wesleyan U (CT)
Western Washington U (WA)
Wheaton Coll (IL)

ARCHITECTURAL AND BUILDING SCIENCES
ArtCenter Coll of Design (CA)
Georgia Inst of Technology (GA)
Lawrence Technological U (MI)
New York Inst of Technology (NY)

Savannah Coll of Art and Design (GA)
State U of New York Coll of Technology at Delhi (NY)
Syracuse U (NY)
Temple U (PA)
U of Massachusetts Amherst (MA)
Washington U in St. Louis (MO)

ARCHITECTURAL DRAFTING AND CAD/CADD
Academy of Art U (CA)

ARCHITECTURAL ENGINEERING
Andrews U (MI)
Auburn U (AL)
California Polytechnic State U, San Luis Obispo (CA)
Drexel U (PA)
Kansas State U (KS)
Lawrence Technological U (MI)
Milwaukee School of Eng (WI)
Missouri U of Science and Technology (MO)
Oklahoma State U (OK)
Penn State Abington (PA)
Penn State Altoona (PA)
Penn State Beaver (PA)
Penn State Berks (PA)
Penn State Brandywine (PA)
Penn State DuBois (PA)
Penn State Erie, The Behrend Coll (PA)
Penn State Fayette, The Eberly Campus (PA)
Penn State Greater Allegheny (PA)
Penn State Hazleton (PA)
Penn State Lehigh Valley (PA)
Penn State Mont Alto (PA)
Penn State New Kensington (PA)
Penn State Schuylkill (PA)
Penn State Shenango (PA)
Penn State U Park (PA)
Penn State Wilkes-Barre (PA)
Penn State Worthington Scranton (PA)
Penn State York (PA)
Rutgers U–New Brunswick (NJ)
Texas A&M U–Kingsville (TX)
Tufts U (MA)
The U of Alabama (AL)
U of Cincinnati (OH)
U of Colorado Boulder (CO)
The U of Kansas (KS)
U of Miami (FL)
U of Nebraska–Lincoln (NE)
U of Oklahoma (OK)
The U of Texas at Austin (TX)
U of Wyoming (WY)
Worcester Polytechnic Inst (MA)

ARCHITECTURAL ENGINEERING TECHNOLOGY
Delaware State U (DE)
Farmingdale State Coll (NY)
Ferris State U (MI)
Fitchburg State U (MA)
Indiana U–Purdue U Indianapolis (IN)
New England Inst of Technology (RI)
Purdue U (IN)
Seminole State Coll of Florida (FL)
State U of New York Coll of Technology at Alfred (NY)
U of Hartford (CT)
U of Southern Mississippi (MS)
Vermont Tech Coll (VT)
Washington U in St. Louis (MO)

ARCHITECTURAL HISTORY AND CRITICISM
Boston U (MA)
Coll of the Holy Cross (MA)
Cornell U (NY)
DePaul U (IL)
Iowa State U of Science and Technology (IA)
Savannah Coll of Art and Design (GA)
Syracuse U (NY)
The U of Kansas (KS)
U of Miami (FL)
U of San Diego (CA)
The U of Texas at Austin (TX)
U of Virginia (VA)

ARCHITECTURAL TECHNOLOGY
Indiana State U (IN)
New York Inst of Technology (NY)
Washington U in St. Louis (MO)
Western Kentucky U (KY)

ARCHITECTURE
Academy of Art U (CA)
American U of Beirut (Lebanon)
Andrews U (MI)
Arizona State U at the Tempe campus (AZ)
Auburn U (AL)
Ball State U (IN)
Barnard Coll (NY)
Benedictine Coll (KS)
Bennington Coll (VT)
Boston Architectural Coll (MA)
California Baptist U (CA)
California Coll of the Arts (CA)
California Polytechnic State U, San Luis Obispo (CA)
California State Polytechnic U, Pomona (CA)
Carnegie Mellon U (PA)
The Catholic U of America (DC)
City Coll of the City U of New York (NY)
Clemson U (SC)
Columbia U (NY)
Cooper Union for the Advancement of Science and Art (NY)
Cornell Coll (IA)
Cornell U (NY)
Drexel U (PA)
Drury U (MO)
Dunwoody Coll of Technology (MN)
Florida Ag and Mech U (FL)
Florida Atlantic U (FL)
Florida Intl U (FL)
Georgia Inst of Technology (GA)
Hampshire Coll (MA)
Hampton U (VA)
Hobart and William Smith Colls (NY)
Inter American U of Puerto Rico, San Germán Campus (PR)
Ithaca Coll (NY)
Judson U (IL)
Kean U (NJ)
Keene State Coll (NH)
Kennesaw State U (GA)
Kent State U (OH)
Lebanese American U (Lebanon)
Lehigh U (PA)
Louisiana State U and A&M Coll (LA)
Marywood U (PA)
Massachusetts Coll of Art and Design (MA)
Massachusetts Inst of Technology (MA)
Miami U (OH)
Middlebury Coll (VT)
Mississippi State U (MS)
New Jersey Inst of Technology (NJ)
New York Inst of Technology (NY)
North Carolina State U (NC)
Northeastern U (MA)
The Ohio State U (OH)
Oklahoma State U (OK)
Penn State U Park (PA)
Polytechnic U of Puerto Rico (PR)
Portland State U (OR)
Prairie View A&M U (TX)
Pratt Inst (NY)
Princeton U (NJ)
Rensselaer Polytechnic Inst (NY)
Rhode Island School of Design (RI)
Rice U (TX)
Roger Williams U (RI)
Sarah Lawrence Coll (NY)
Smith Coll (MA)
Southern Illinois U Carbondale (IL)
State U of New York Coll of Technology at Alfred (NY)
Temple U (PA)
Texas A&M U (TX)
Texas Tech U (TX)
Tulane U (LA)
U at Buffalo, the State U of New York (NY)
The U of Arizona (AZ)
U of Arkansas (AR)
U of California, Los Angeles (CA)
U of Central Florida (FL)

U of Cincinnati (OH)
U of Colorado Denver (CO)
U of Florida (FL)
U of Hawaii at Manoa (HI)
U of Houston (TX)
U of Idaho (ID)
U of Illinois at Chicago (IL)
The U of Kansas (KS)
U of Kentucky (KY)
U of Maryland, Coll Park (MD)
U of Memphis (TN)
U of Miami (FL)
U of Michigan (MI)
U of Minnesota, Twin Cities Campus (MN)
U of Nebraska–Lincoln (NE)
U of Nevada, Las Vegas (NV)
U of New Mexico (NM)
The U of North Carolina at Charlotte (NC)
U of Notre Dame (IN)
U of Oklahoma (OK)
U of Oregon (OR)
U of Pennsylvania (PA)
U of San Francisco (CA)
U of Southern California (CA)
The U of Tennessee (TN)
The U of Texas at Austin (TX)
The U of Texas at San Antonio (TX)
U of Toronto (ON, Canada)
U of Utah (UT)
U of Virginia (VA)
U of Washington (WA)
U of Waterloo (ON, Canada)
U of Wisconsin–Milwaukee (WI)
Virginia Polytechnic Inst and State U (VA)
Washington State U (WA)
Washington U in St. Louis (MO)
Wellesley Coll (MA)
Wentworth Inst of Technology (MA)
Woodbury U (CA)

ARCHITECTURE RELATED
Ball State U (IN)
Case Western Reserve U (OH)
Connecticut Coll (CT)
Eugene Lang Coll of Liberal Arts (NY)
Lipscomb U (TN)
Mount Holyoke Coll (MA)
New Jersey Inst of Technology (NJ)
Northern Michigan U (MI)
Parsons School of Design (NY)
The U of Arizona (AZ)
U of Illinois at Chicago (IL)
U of Utah (UT)
Washington U in St. Louis (MO)

AREA STUDIES RELATED
Augsburg U (MN)
Boston U (MA)
Bridgewater State U (MA)
Eastern Michigan U (MI)
Gannon U (PA)
Gettysburg Coll (PA)
Hofstra U (NY)
Illinois Wesleyan U (IL)
Iowa State U of Science and Technology (IA)
Lycoming Coll (PA)
Marlboro Coll (VT)
Millersville U of Pennsylvania (PA)
New York U (NY)
Northeastern State U (OK)
Northwestern U (IL)
Queens Coll of the City U of New York (NY)
Ramapo Coll of New Jersey (NJ)
Stanford U (CA)
State U of New York at Plattsburgh (NY)
U of Alaska Fairbanks (AK)
U of California, Santa Barbara (CA)
U of Michigan–Dearborn (MI)
U of Oklahoma (OK)
U of Pittsburgh (PA)
U of San Francisco (CA)
U of Virginia (VA)
U of Washington (WA)
Utah State U (UT)
Virginia Commonwealth U (VA)
Washington U in St. Louis (MO)
Williams Coll (MA)

ARMY ROTC/MILITARY SCIENCE
Iowa State U of Science and Technology (IA)
Northwest U (WA)

ARMY ROTC, MILITARY SCIENCE AND OPERATIONS RELATED
Calvary U (MO)
Western Kentucky U (KY)

ART
Alabama State U (AL)
Alberta Coll of Art & Design (AB, Canada)
Albion Coll (MI)
Albright Coll (PA)
Alfred U (NY)
Allegheny Coll (PA)
Alma Coll (MI)
Alverno Coll (WI)
American Acad of Art (IL)
The American U in Cairo (Egypt)
Andrews U (MI)
Appalachian State U (NC)
Aquinas Coll (MI)
Arcadia U (PA)
Arizona State U at the Tempe campus (AZ)
Arkansas Tech U (AR)
Athens State U (AL)
Auburn U at Montgomery (AL)
Augustana Coll (IL)
Augustana U (SD)
Aurora U (IL)
Austin Coll (TX)
Austin Peay State U (TN)
Averett U (VA)
Avila U (MO)
Azusa Pacific U (CA)
Baldwin Wallace U (OH)
Ball State U (IN)
Barton Coll (NC)
Bates Coll (ME)
Baylor U (TX)
Belhaven U (MS)
Belmont U (TN)
Bemidji State U (MN)
Benedictine Coll (KS)
Berea Coll (KY)
Berry Coll (GA)
Bethany Lutheran Coll (MN)
Bethel U (MN)
Binghamton U, State U of New York (NY)
Biola U (CA)
Birmingham-Southern Coll (AL)
Blackburn Coll (IL)
Black Hills State U (SD)
Bluefield Coll (VA)
Bluffton U (OH)
Bowie State U (MD)
Bowling Green State U (OH)
Bradley U (IL)
Brescia U (KY)
Brigham Young U–Idaho (ID)
Brock U (ON, Canada)
Bucknell U (PA)
Buena Vista U (IA)
Buffalo State Coll, State U of New York (NY)
Cairn U (PA)
Caldwell U (NJ)
California Coll of the Arts (CA)
California Lutheran U (CA)
California State Polytechnic U, Pomona (CA)
California State U, Dominguez Hills (CA)
California State U, East Bay (CA)
California State U, Fullerton (CA)
California State U, Long Beach (CA)
California State U, Los Angeles (CA)
California State U, Monterey Bay (CA)
California State U, Northridge (CA)
California State U, Sacramento (CA)
California State U, San Bernardino (CA)
California State U, Stanislaus (CA)
California U of Pennsylvania (PA)
Calvin Coll (MI)
Cameron U (OK)
Campbellsville U (KY)

Capital U (OH)
Cardinal Stritch U (WI)
Carnegie Mellon U (PA)
Carroll U (WI)
Carson-Newman U (TN)
The Catholic U of America (DC)
Cedar Crest Coll (PA)
Centenary Coll of Louisiana (LA)
Central Connecticut State U (CT)
Central Michigan U (MI)
Central State U (OH)
Chapman U (CA)
City Coll of the City U of New York (NY)
Clarion U of Pennsylvania (PA)
Clark Atlanta U (GA)
Clemson U (SC)
Cleveland State U (OH)
Coe Coll (IA)
Colby Coll (ME)
Colgate U (NY)
The Coll at Brockport, State U of New York (NY)
The Coll of Idaho (ID)
The Coll of New Jersey (NJ)
Coll of Saint Benedict (MN)
Coll of Saint Elizabeth (NJ)
Coll of Saint Mary (NE)
The Coll of St. Scholastica (MN)
Coll of the Atlantic (ME)
The Coll of William and Mary (VA)
Colorado Mesa U (CO)
Columbia Coll (MO)
Concordia Coll–New York (NY)
Concordia U Chicago (IL)
Concordia U Irvine (CA)
Concordia U, Nebraska (NE)
Concordia U, St. Paul (MN)
Concordia U Wisconsin (WI)
Converse Coll (SC)
Cornell Coll (IA)
Cornish Coll of the Arts (WA)
Creighton U (NE)
Culver-Stockton Coll (MO)
Daemen Coll (NY)
Dallas Baptist U (TX)
Davidson Coll (NC)
Delaware State U (DE)
Denison U (OH)
DePaul U (IL)
Dickinson State U (ND)
Doane U (NE)
Dominican U of California (CA)
Drake U (IA)
Earlham Coll (IN)
East Central U (OK)
Eastern Mennonite U (VA)
Eastern Michigan U (MI)
Eastern New Mexico U (NM)
Eastern Oregon U (OR)
East Tennessee State U (TN)
Edgewood Coll (WI)
Elmhurst Coll (IL)
Elms Coll (MA)
Elon U (NC)
Emporia State U (KS)
Evangel U (MO)
The Evergreen State Coll (WA)
Fairleigh Dickinson U, Metropolitan Campus (NJ)
Fayetteville State U (NC)
Felician U (NJ)
Florida Atlantic U (FL)
Florida Gulf Coast U (FL)
Florida Intl U (FL)
Fort Lewis Coll (CO)
Framingham State U (MA)
Francis Marion U (SC)
Franklin Pierce U (NH)
Friends U (KS)
The George Washington U (DC)
Georgia Coll & State U (GA)
Georgian Court U (NJ)
Georgia Southern U (GA)
Georgia Southern U–Armstrong Campus (GA)
Georgia Southwestern State U (GA)
Gettysburg Coll (PA)
Gonzaga U (WA)
Gordon Coll (MA)
Goshen Coll (IN)
Governors State U (IL)
Graceland U (IA)
Green Mountain Coll (VT)
Greensboro Coll (NC)
Greenville U (IL)

Grinnell Coll (IA)
Guilford Coll (NC)
Gustavus Adolphus Coll (MN)
Hampton U (VA)
Hannibal-LaGrange U (MO)
Hartwick Coll (NY)
Haverford Coll (PA)
Hendrix Coll (AR)
Hillsdale Coll (MI)
Hiram Coll (OH)
Hobart and William Smith Colls (NY)
Hollins U (VA)
Hood Coll (MD)
Howard Payne U (TX)
Humboldt State U (CA)
Hunter Coll of the City U of New York (NY)
Idaho State U (ID)
Illinois Coll (IL)
Illinois State U (IL)
Illinois Wesleyan U (IL)
Indiana State U (IN)
Indiana U Bloomington (IN)
Indiana U East (IN)
Indiana U Kokomo (IN)
Indiana U of Pennsylvania (PA)
Indiana U South Bend (IN)
Indiana U Southeast (IN)
Indiana Wesleyan U (IN)
Inter American U of Puerto Rico, San Germán Campus (PR)
Iowa State U of Science and Technology (IA)
Ithaca Coll (NY)
Jacksonville U (FL)
James Madison U (VA)
Judson U (IL)
Juniata Coll (PA)
Kalamazoo Coll (MI)
Kansas State U (KS)
Kean U (NJ)
Kennesaw State U (GA)
Knox Coll (IL)
Lafayette Coll (PA)
Laguna Coll of Art & Design (CA)
La Sierra U (CA)
Lebanon Valley Coll (PA)
Lehigh U (PA)
Lehman Coll of the City U of New York (NY)
Lesley U (MA)
Lewis U (IL)
Lincoln Memorial U (TN)
Lindenwood U (MO)
Linfield Coll (OR)
Lock Haven U of Pennsylvania (PA)
Luther Coll (IA)
Lycoming Coll (PA)
Lynchburg Coll (VA)
Lyon Coll (AR)
Macalester Coll (MN)
Manchester U (IN)
Marian U (IN)
Marietta Coll (OH)
Marist Coll (NY)
Marlboro Coll (VT)
Marshall U (WV)
Mary Baldwin U (VA)
Marylhurst U (OR)
Marymount Manhattan Coll (NY)
Massachusetts Coll of Liberal Arts (MA)
McDaniel Coll (MD)
McNeese State U (LA)
McPherson Coll (KS)
Mercer U, Macon (GA)
Mercyhurst U (PA)
Metropolitan State U of Denver (CO)
Miami U (OH)
Michigan State U (MI)
Middle Tennessee State U (TN)
Millersville U of Pennsylvania (PA)
Minnesota State U Moorhead (MN)
Minot State U (ND)
Missouri State U (MO)
Missouri Valley Coll (MO)
Monmouth Coll (IL)
Montclair State U (NJ)
Moravian Coll (PA)
Morehouse Coll (GA)
Mount Mary U (WI)
Mount Mercy U (IA)
Mount St. Joseph U (OH)
Mount Saint Mary's U (CA)
Mount Vernon Nazarene U (OH)

Muhlenberg Coll (PA)
Muskingum U (OH)
Nazareth Coll of Rochester (NY)
Newberry Coll (SC)
New Jersey City U (NJ)
New Jersey Inst of Technology (NJ)
Newman U (KS)
New Mexico Highlands U (NM)
North Carolina Central U (NC)
North Central Coll (IL)
North Dakota State U (ND)
Northeastern State U (OK)
Northeastern U (MA)
Northern Illinois U (IL)
Northern Michigan U (MI)
Northern State U (SD)
Northern Vermont U–Lyndon (VT)
Northwestern Coll (IA)
Northwestern U (IL)
Northwest Nazarene U (ID)
Notre Dame de Namur U (CA)
Oakland City U (IN)
Oberlin Coll (OH)
Occidental Coll (CA)
Oglethorpe U (GA)
Ohio Dominican U (OH)
Ohio Northern U (OH)
The Ohio State U (OH)
Ohio U (OH)
Oklahoma Baptist U (OK)
Oklahoma Christian U (OK)
Oklahoma City U (OK)
Oklahoma State U (OK)
Old Dominion U (VA)
Olivet Nazarene U (IL)
Oral Roberts U (OK)
Oregon State U (OR)
Ottawa U (KS)
Otterbein U (OH)
Our Lady of the Lake U (TX)
Penn State Abington (PA)
Penn State Altoona (PA)
Penn State Beaver (PA)
Penn State Berks (PA)
Penn State Brandywine (PA)
Penn State DuBois (PA)
Penn State Erie, The Behrend Coll (PA)
Penn State Fayette, The Eberly Campus (PA)
Penn State Greater Allegheny (PA)
Penn State Hazleton (PA)
Penn State Lehigh Valley (PA)
Penn State Mont Alto (PA)
Penn State New Kensington (PA)
Penn State Schuylkill (PA)
Penn State Shenango (PA)
Penn State U Park (PA)
Penn State Wilkes-Barre (PA)
Penn State Worthington Scranton (PA)
Penn State York (PA)
Pepperdine U, Malibu (CA)
Piedmont Coll (GA)
Pittsburg State U (KS)
Pitzer Coll (CA)
Pomona Coll (CA)
Portland State U (OR)
Pratt Inst (NY)
Presbyterian Coll (SC)
Purchase Coll, State U of New York (NY)
Radford U (VA)
Randolph Coll (VA)
Redeemer U Coll (ON, Canada)
Reed Coll (OR)
Regis U (CO)
Rhodes Coll (TN)
Rice U (TX)
Rider U (NJ)
Ringling Coll of Art and Design (FL)
Ripon Coll (WI)
Roanoke Coll (VA)
Roberts Wesleyan Coll (NY)
Rockford U (IL)
Rocky Mountain Coll (MT)
Roger Williams U (RI)
Rollins Coll (FL)
Rutgers U–Camden (NJ)
Rutgers U–Newark (NJ)
Rutgers U–New Brunswick (NJ)
Sacred Heart U (CT)
Saginaw Valley State U (MI)
St. Ambrose U (IA)
St. Andrews U (NC)
Saint Anselm Coll (NH)
St. Catherine U (MN)

Saint John's U (MN)
Saint Joseph's U (PA)
St. Lawrence U (NY)
Saint Louis U–Madrid Campus (Spain)
Saint Mary's Coll of California (CA)
St. Mary's Coll of Maryland (MD)
Saint Michael's Coll (VT)
St. Norbert Coll (WI)
St. Olaf Coll (MN)
Saint Peter's U (NJ)
St. Thomas Aquinas Coll (NY)
Salisbury U (MD)
Samford U (AL)
Sam Houston State U (TX)
San Diego State U (CA)
San Francisco State U (CA)
Scripps Coll (CA)
Seattle Pacific U (WA)
Shawnee State U (OH)
Shepherd U (WV)
Shippensburg U of Pennsylvania (PA)
Shorter U (GA)
Sierra Nevada Coll (NV)
Silver Lake Coll of the Holy Family (WI)
Simmons Coll (MA)
Simon Fraser U (BC, Canada)
Simpson Coll (IA)
Skidmore Coll (NY)
Slippery Rock U of Pennsylvania (PA)
Smith Coll (MA)
Sonoma State U (CA)
Southeastern Louisiana U (LA)
Southeastern Oklahoma State U (OK)
Southeast Missouri State U (MO)
Southern Adventist U (TN)
Southern Arkansas U–Magnolia (AR)
Southern Illinois U Carbondale (IL)
Southern Illinois U Edwardsville (IL)
Southern Utah U (UT)
Southwest Baptist U (MO)
Stanford U (CA)
State U of New York at Fredonia (NY)
State U of New York at Oswego (NY)
State U of New York at Plattsburgh (NY)
State U of New York Coll at Old Westbury (NY)
State U of New York Coll at Oneonta (NY)
State U of New York Empire State Coll (NY)
Stephen F. Austin State U (TX)
Stetson U (FL)
Stony Brook U, State U of New York (NY)
Susquehanna U (PA)
Tarleton State U (TX)
Taylor U (IN)
Tennessee Technological U (TN)
Texas A&M U–Corpus Christi (TX)
Texas Lutheran U (TX)
Texas State U (TX)
Texas Tech U (TX)
Texas Woman's U (TX)
Tiffin U (OH)
Towson U (MD)
Transylvania U (KY)
Trinity U (TX)
Troy U (AL)
Truman State U (MO)
Tulane U (LA)
Union U (TN)
U at Albany, State U of New York (NY)
U at Buffalo, the State U of New York (NY)
The U of Alabama at Birmingham (AL)
U of Alaska Fairbanks (AK)
U of Arkansas (AR)
U of California, Los Angeles (CA)
U of California, Riverside (CA)
U of California, San Diego (CA)
U of California, Santa Cruz (CA)
U of Central Arkansas (AR)
U of Central Florida (FL)
U of Charleston (WV)
U of Dallas (TX)

U of Denver (CO)
U of Evansville (IN)
The U of Findlay (OH)
U of Georgia (GA)
U of Hawaii at Manoa (HI)
U of Houston (TX)
U of Idaho (ID)
U of Jamestown (ND)
U of La Verne (CA)
U of Maine at Farmington (ME)
U of Maine at Machias (ME)
U of Maine at Presque Isle (ME)
U of Massachusetts Boston (MA)
U of Memphis (TN)
U of Miami (FL)
U of Michigan (MI)
U of Minnesota, Duluth (MN)
U of Minnesota, Twin Cities Campus (MN)
U of Missouri (MO)
U of Mobile (AL)
U of Montana (MT)
U of Montevallo (AL)
U of Mount Union (OH)
U of Nebraska at Kearney (NE)
U of Nevada, Las Vegas (NV)
U of Nevada, Reno (NV)
U of New Hampshire (NH)
U of New Mexico (NM)
U of North Alabama (AL)
U of North Carolina at Asheville (NC)
The U of North Carolina at Charlotte (NC)
The U of North Carolina at Greensboro (NC)
U of North Dakota (ND)
U of Northern Iowa (IA)
U of North Florida (FL)
U of North Georgia (GA)
U of North Texas (TX)
U of Oklahoma (OK)
U of Oregon (OR)
U of Pikeville (KY)
U of Providence (MT)
U of Puget Sound (WA)
U of Rhode Island (RI)
U of Saint Mary (KS)
U of San Diego (CA)
U of Science and Arts of Oklahoma (OK)
U of Sioux Falls (SD)
U of South Alabama (AL)
U of South Dakota (SD)
U of Southern California (CA)
U of Southern Indiana (IN)
U of South Florida, St. Petersburg (FL)
The U of Tampa (FL)
The U of Tennessee at Chattanooga (TN)
The U of Texas at Austin (TX)
The U of Texas at San Antonio (TX)
The U of Texas of the Permian Basin (TX)
The U of Texas Rio Grande Valley (TX)
U of the Incarnate Word (TX)
U of the Pacific (CA)
The U of Toledo (OH)
U of Utah (UT)
U of Virginia (VA)
The U of Virginia's Coll at Wise (VA)
U of Washington (WA)
U of West Georgia (GA)
U of Wisconsin–Eau Claire (WI)
U of Wisconsin–La Crosse (WI)
U of Wisconsin–Madison (WI)
U of Wisconsin–Milwaukee (WI)
U of Wisconsin–Parkside (WI)
U of Wisconsin–Platteville (WI)
U of Wisconsin–River Falls (WI)
U of Wisconsin–Stevens Point (WI)
U of Wisconsin–Whitewater (WI)
U of Wyoming (WY)
Upper Iowa U (IA)
Ursinus Coll (PA)
Utah State U (UT)
Valdosta State U (GA)
Valley City State U (ND)
Valparaiso U (IN)
Villa Maria Coll (NY)
Virginia Polytechnic Inst and State U (VA)
Virginia Wesleyan U (VA)
Wabash Coll (IN)

Wagner Coll (NY)
Walsh U (OH)
Wartburg Coll (IA)
Washington & Jefferson Coll (PA)
Washington Coll (MD)
Washington U in St. Louis (MO)
Wayland Baptist U (TX)
Waynesburg U (PA)
Wayne State Coll (NE)
Wayne State U (MI)
Weber State U (UT)
Webster U (MO)
Wells Coll (NY)
West Chester U of Pennsylvania (PA)
Western Connecticut State U (CT)
Western Illinois U (IL)
Western Michigan U (MI)
Western Oregon U (OR)
Western State Colorado U (CO)
Western Washington U (WA)
Westfield State U (MA)
Westminster Coll (UT)
Westmont Coll (CA)
West Texas A&M U (TX)
West Virginia State U (WV)
West Virginia U (WV)
West Virginia Wesleyan Coll (WV)
Wheaton Coll (IL)
Whitman Coll (WA)
Whittier Coll (CA)
Whitworth U (WA)
Wichita State U (KS)
Willamette U (OR)
William Paterson U of New Jersey (NJ)
Williams Coll (MA)
William Woods U (MO)
Winona State U (MN)
Winthrop U (SC)
Wisconsin Lutheran Coll (WI)
Wittenberg U (OH)
Wright State U (OH)
Wright State U–Lake Campus (OH)
Xavier U of Louisiana (LA)
Youngstown State U (OH)

ART HISTORY, CRITICISM AND CONSERVATION

Academy of Art U (CA)
Adams State U (CO)
Adelphi U (NY)
Agnes Scott Coll (GA)
Albion Coll (MI)
Allegheny Coll (PA)
American U (DC)
The American U of Paris (France)
Aquinas Coll (MI)
Arcadia U (PA)
Augsburg U (MN)
Augustana Coll (IL)
Baker U (KS)
Bard Coll (NY)
Barnard Coll (NY)
Baylor U (TX)
Belmont U (TN)
Beloit Coll (WI)
Bennington Coll (VT)
Binghamton U, State U of New York (NY)
Birmingham-Southern Coll (AL)
Bloomsburg U of Pennsylvania (PA)
Boston Coll (MA)
Boston U (MA)
Bowdoin Coll (ME)
Bowling Green State U (OH)
Bradley U (IL)
Brandeis U (MA)
Bridgewater State U (MA)
Bryn Mawr Coll (PA)
Bucknell U (PA)
Buffalo State Coll, State U of New York (NY)
California State Polytechnic U, Pomona (CA)
California State U, Dominguez Hills (CA)
California State U, East Bay (CA)
California State U, Fullerton (CA)
California State U, Long Beach (CA)
California State U, Stanislaus (CA)
Calvary U (MO)
Carleton Coll (MN)
Carthage Coll (WI)
Case Western Reserve U (OH)
The Catholic U of America (DC)

Centre Coll (KY)
Chapman U (CA)
Chatham U (PA)
City Coll of the City U of New York (NY)
Clarke U (IA)
Clark U (MA)
Coastal Carolina U (SC)
Coe Coll (IA)
Colby Coll (ME)
Coll of Charleston (SC)
The Coll of New Jersey (NJ)
Coll of the Holy Cross (MA)
The Coll of William and Mary (VA)
The Coll of Wooster (OH)
The Colorado Coll (CO)
Columbia Coll Chicago (IL)
Columbia U (NY)
Columbus State U (GA)
Concordia U (QC, Canada)
Connecticut Coll (CT)
Converse Coll (SC)
Cornell Coll (IA)
Cornell U (NY)
Dartmouth Coll (NH)
Denison U (OH)
DePaul U (IL)
DePauw U (IN)
DEREE - The American Coll of Greece (Greece)
Dominican U (IL)
Dominican U of California (GA)
Drake U (IA)
Drew U (NJ)
Drury U (MO)
Duquesne U (PA)
East Carolina U (NC)
Eastern Michigan U (MI)
Eastern Washington U (WA)
Elon U (NC)
Emory U (GA)
Fairfield U (CT)
Ferris State U (MI)
Flagler Coll (FL)
Florida Intl U (FL)
Florida Southern Coll (FL)
Florida State U (FL)
Fordham U (NY)
Franklin & Marshall Coll (PA)
Franklin Coll (IN)
Franklin U Switzerland (Switzerland)
Furman U (SC)
George Mason U (VA)
Georgetown U (DC)
The George Washington U (DC)
Gettysburg Coll (PA)
Grand Valley State U (MI)
Gustavus Adolphus Coll (MN)
Hamilton Coll (NY)
Hamline U (MN)
Hampshire Coll (MA)
Hartwick Coll (NY)
Harvard U (MA)
Haverford Coll (PA)
Hiram Coll (OH)
Hobart and William Smith Colls (NY)
Hofstra U (NY)
Hollins U (VA)
Hope Coll (MI)
Humboldt State U (CA)
Hunter Coll of the City U of New York (NY)
Indiana U Bloomington (IN)
Indiana U–Purdue U Indianapolis (IN)
Ithaca Coll (NY)
Jacksonville U (FL)
James Madison U (VA)
John Cabot U (Italy)
John Carroll U (OH)
Johns Hopkins U (MD)
Juniata Coll (PA)
Kalamazoo Coll (MI)
Kansas City Art Inst (MO)
Kennesaw State U (GA)
Kent State U (OH)
Kenyon Coll (OH)
Knox Coll (IL)
Kutztown U of Pennsylvania (PA)
Lafayette Coll (PA)
La Salle U (PA)
Lawrence U (WI)
Lehigh U (PA)
Lehman Coll of the City U of New York (NY)

Lindenwood U (MO)
Long Island U–LIU Post (NY)
Loyola Marymount U (CA)
Loyola U Chicago (IL)
Lycoming Coll (PA)
Manhattanville Coll (NY)
Mansfield U of Pennsylvania (PA)
Marist Coll (NY)
Marlboro Coll (VT)
Maryland Inst Coll of Art (MD)
Marymount Manhattan Coll (NY)
Massachusetts Coll of Art and
  Design (MA)
McDaniel Coll (MD)
Merrimack Coll (MA)
Messiah Coll (PA)
Metropolitan State U of Denver
  (CO)
Miami U (OH)
Michigan State U (MI)
Middlebury Coll (VT)
Millsaps Coll (MS)
Mills Coll (CA)
Minnesota State U Moorhead (MN)
Missouri State U (MO)
Mount Holyoke Coll (MA)
Muhlenberg Coll (PA)
Nazareth Coll of Rochester (NY)
New Coll of Florida (FL)
New York U (NY)
Niagara U (NY)
North Carolina State U (NC)
North Central Coll (IL)
Northern Illinois U (IL)
Northern Michigan U (MI)
Northwestern U (IL)
Oakland U (MI)
Oberlin Coll (OH)
Oglethorpe U (GA)
The Ohio State U (OH)
Ohio U (OH)
Ohio Wesleyan U (OH)
Old Dominion U (VA)
Pace U (NY)
Pacific Lutheran U (WA)
Paris Coll of Art (France)
Penn State Abington (PA)
Penn State Altoona (PA)
Penn State Beaver (PA)
Penn State Berks (PA)
Penn State Brandywine (PA)
Penn State DuBois (PA)
Penn State Erie, The Behrend Coll
  (PA)
Penn State Fayette, The Eberly
  Campus (PA)
Penn State Greater Allegheny (PA)
Penn State Hazleton (PA)
Penn State Lehigh Valley (PA)
Penn State Mont Alto (PA)
Penn State New Kensington (PA)
Penn State Schuylkill (PA)
Penn State Shenango (PA)
Penn State U Park (PA)
Penn State Wilkes-Barre (PA)
Penn State Worthington Scranton
  (PA)
Penn State York (PA)
Pepperdine U, Malibu (CA)
Pitzer Coll (CA)
Pomona Coll (CA)
Portland State U (OR)
Pratt Inst (NY)
Presbyterian Coll (SC)
Princeton U (NJ)
Principia Coll (IL)
Providence Coll (RI)
Purchase Coll, State U of New York
  (NY)
Purdue U (IN)
Queens Coll of the City U of New
  York (NY)
Randolph Coll (VA)
Randolph-Macon Coll (VA)
Regis U (CO)
Rhode Island Coll (RI)
Rice U (TX)
Roanoke Coll (VA)
Rockford U (IL)
Roger Williams U (RI)
Rollins Coll (FL)
Rosemont Coll (PA)
Rutgers U–Camden (NJ)
Rutgers U–New Brunswick (NJ)
St. Catherine U (MN)
Saint Louis U (MO)

Saint Louis U–Madrid Campus
  (Spain)
Saint Mary's Coll of California (CA)
St. Mary's Coll of Maryland (MD)
St. Olaf Coll (MN)
Saint Peter's U (NJ)
Saint Vincent Coll (PA)
Salve Regina U (RI)
San Diego State U (CA)
San Francisco Art Inst (CA)
Santa Clara U (CA)
Sarah Lawrence Coll (NY)
Savannah Coll of Art and Design
  (GA)
Scripps Coll (CA)
Seattle U (WA)
Seton Hill U (PA)
Sewanee: The U of the South (TN)
Skidmore Coll (NY)
Smith Coll (MA)
Sonoma State U (CA)
Southern Methodist U (TX)
Southern Utah U (UT)
Southwestern U (TX)
Stanford U (CA)
State U of New York at Fredonia
  (NY)
State U of New York at New Paltz
  (NY)
State U of New York Coll at
  Cortland (NY)
State U of New York Coll at
  Geneseo (NY)
State U of New York Coll at
  Oneonta (NY)
Stephen F. Austin State U (TX)
Stetson U (FL)
Stonehill Coll (MA)
Stony Brook U, State U of New York
  (NY)
Suffolk U (MA)
Susquehanna U (PA)
Sweet Briar Coll (VA)
Syracuse U (NY)
Temple U (PA)
Texas Christian U (TX)
Texas State U (TX)
Towson U (MD)
Transylvania U (KY)
Trinity U (TX)
Tufts U (MA)
Tulane U (LA)
U at Albany, State U of New York
  (NY)
U at Buffalo, the State U of New
  York (NY)
The U of Akron (OH)
The U of Alabama (AL)
The U of Arizona (AZ)
U of California, Davis (CA)
U of California, Irvine (CA)
U of California, Los Angeles (CA)
U of California, Riverside (CA)
U of California, San Diego (CA)
U of California, Santa Barbara (CA)
U of California, Santa Cruz (CA)
U of Central Oklahoma (OK)
U of Chicago (IL)
U of Cincinnati (OH)
U of Colorado Boulder (CO)
U of Dallas (TX)
U of Dayton (OH)
U of Denver (CO)
U of Evansville (IN)
U of Florida (FL)
U of Georgia (GA)
U of Guelph (ON, Canada)
U of Hartford (CT)
U of Houston (TX)
U of Illinois at Chicago (IL)
The U of Kansas (KS)
U of Kentucky (KY)
U of La Verne (CA)
U of Louisville (KY)
U of Maine (ME)
U of Maryland, Coll Park (MD)
U of Mary Washington (VA)
U of Massachusetts Amherst (MA)
U of Massachusetts Dartmouth
  (MA)
U of Memphis (TN)
U of Miami (FL)
U of Michigan (MI)
U of Michigan–Dearborn (MI)
U of Michigan–Flint (MI)
U of Minnesota, Duluth (MN)
U of Minnesota, Morris (MN)

U of Minnesota, Twin Cities
  Campus (MN)
U of Missouri (MO)
U of Missouri–St. Louis (MO)
U of Nebraska–Lincoln (NE)
U of Nevada, Las Vegas (NV)
U of Nevada, Reno (NV)
U of New Mexico (NM)
U of New Orleans (LA)
U of North Carolina at Asheville
  (NC)
The U of North Carolina at Chapel
  Hill (NC)
The U of North Carolina at
  Charlotte (NC)
The U of North Carolina at
  Greensboro (NC)
The U of North Carolina
  Wilmington (NC)
U of Northern Iowa (IA)
U of North Florida (FL)
U of North Texas (TX)
U of Notre Dame (IN)
U of Oklahoma (OK)
U of Oregon (OR)
U of Pennsylvania (PA)
U of Pittsburgh (PA)
U of Regina (SK, Canada)
U of Rhode Island (RI)
U of Richmond (VA)
U of Rochester (NY)
U of Saint Francis (IN)
U of Saint Joseph (CT)
U of St. Thomas (MN)
U of San Diego (CA)
U of San Francisco (CA)
U of Saskatchewan (SK, Canada)
U of South Carolina (SC)
U of Southern California (CA)
The U of Tennessee (TN)
The U of Texas at Austin (TX)
The U of Texas at San Antonio (TX)
U of the Pacific (CA)
The U of Toledo (OH)
The U of Tulsa (OK)
U of Utah (UT)
U of Vermont (VT)
U of Washington (WA)
U of Waterloo (ON, Canada)
U of Wisconsin–Madison (WI)
U of Wisconsin–Milwaukee (WI)
U of Wisconsin–Superior (WI)
U of Wyoming (WY)
Ursinus Coll (PA)
Ursuline Coll (OH)
Vanderbilt U (TN)
Vassar Coll (NY)
Villanova U (PA)
Virginia Commonwealth U (VA)
Wake Forest U (NC)
Walsh U (OH)
Washington and Lee U (VA)
Washington U in St. Louis (MO)
Wayne State U (MI)
Webster U (MO)
Wellesley Coll (MA)
Wells Coll (NY)
Wesleyan U (CT)
Western Kentucky U (KY)
Western Michigan U (MI)
Western Washington U (WA)
West Virginia U (WV)
Wheaton Coll (MA)
Whitman Coll (WA)
Whitworth U (WA)
Willamette U (OR)
William Paterson U of New Jersey
  (NJ)
Williams Coll (MA)
Winthrop U (SC)
Wittenberg U (OH)
Wofford Coll (SC)
Wright State U (OH)
Wright State U–Lake Campus (OH)
Youngstown State U (OH)

ARTIFICIAL INTELLIGENCE
Indiana U Bloomington (IN)

**ARTS, ENTERTAINMENT, AND
MEDIA MANAGEMENT**
Albright Coll (PA)
Anderson U (IN)
Belmont U (TN)
Butler U (IN)
Champlain Coll (VT)
Columbia Coll Chicago (IL)
Concordia U, Nebraska (NE)

Dean Coll (MA)
Drexel U (PA)
Drury U (MO)
Elon U (NC)
Judson U (IL)
Kansas Wesleyan U (KS)
Long Island U–LIU Post (NY)
National U (CA)
Schreiner U (TX)
Shenandoah U (VA)
State U of New York at Fredonia
  (NY)
Stonehill Coll (MA)
U of Central Florida (FL)
U of Central Oklahoma (OK)
The U of Findlay (OH)
U of Kentucky (KY)
U of North Alabama (AL)
The U of Tulsa (OK)
Western New England U (MA)

**ARTS, ENTERTAINMENT, AND
MEDIA MANAGEMENT
RELATED**
Belmont U (TN)
Loyola U New Orleans (LA)
U of Southern California (CA)

ART TEACHER EDUCATION
Academy of Art U (CA)
Adams State U (CO)
Adelphi U (NY)
Albright Coll (PA)
Alfred U (NY)
Alverno Coll (WI)
Anderson U (SC)
Andrews U (MI)
Appalachian State U (NC)
Arkansas Tech U (AR)
Asbury U (KY)
Ashland U (OH)
Augustana Coll (IL)
Augustana U (SD)
Averett U (VA)
Baker U (KS)
Baylor U (TX)
Belmont U (TN)
Beloit Coll (WI)
Bemidji State U (MN)
Benedictine Coll (KS)
Berry Coll (GA)
Bethany Lutheran Coll (MN)
Bethel Coll (IN)
Bethel U (MN)
Birmingham-Southern Coll (AL)
Boise State U (ID)
Boston U (MA)
Bowling Green State U (OH)
Bradley U (IL)
Brescia U (KY)
Bridgewater State U (MA)
Brigham Young U–Idaho (ID)
Buena Vista U (IA)
Buffalo State Coll, State U of New
  York (NY)
California Lutheran U (CA)
California State U, Long Beach
  (CA)
Calvin Coll (MI)
Campbellsville U (KY)
Capital U (OH)
Carlow U (PA)
Carroll U (WI)
Carson-Newman U (TN)
Case Western Reserve U (OH)
Central Connecticut State U (CT)
Central Michigan U (MI)
Central State U (OH)
City Coll of the City U of New York
  (NY)
Clarke U (IA)
Coe Coll (IA)
Coker Coll (SC)
The Coll of New Jersey (NJ)
The Coll of New Rochelle (NY)
Coll of Saint Mary (NE)
Coll of the Ozarks (MO)
Columbus State U (GA)
Concordia U (QC, Canada)
Concordia U Chicago (IL)
Concordia U, Nebraska (NE)
Concordia U, St. Paul (MN)
Concordia U Wisconsin (WI)
Converse Coll (SC)
Culver-Stockton Coll (MO)
Daemen Coll (NY)
Delaware State U (DE)
DePaul U (IL)

Dickinson State U (ND)
East Carolina U (NC)
East Central U (OK)
Eastern Michigan U (MI)
Eastern Washington U (WA)
Edgewood Coll (WI)
Elmhurst Coll (IL)
Emory & Henry Coll (VA)
Escuela de Artes Plasticas y
  Diseño de Puerto Rico (PR)
Evangel U (MO)
Fayetteville State U (NC)
Ferris State U (MI)
Flagler Coll (FL)
Florida Intl U (FL)
Florida Southern Coll (FL)
Framingham State U (MA)
Francis Marion U (SC)
Franklin Pierce U (NH)
Friends U (KS)
Georgia Southern U–Armstrong
  Campus (GA)
Georgia State U (GA)
Goshen Coll (IN)
Graceland U (IA)
Grand Valley State U (MI)
Green Mountain Coll (VT)
Greensboro Coll (NC)
Gustavus Adolphus Coll (MN)
Hampton U (VA)
Hannibal-LaGrange U (MO)
Harding U (AR)
Hardin-Simmons U (TX)
Hofstra U (NY)
Holy Family U (PA)
Hope Coll (MI)
Houston Baptist U (TX)
Howard Payne U (TX)
Humboldt State U (CA)
Indiana State U (IN)
Indiana U Bloomington (IN)
Indiana U–Purdue U Indianapolis
  (IN)
Indiana U South Bend (IN)
Indiana Wesleyan U (IN)
Inter American U of Puerto Rico,
  San Germán Campus (PR)
Ithaca Coll (NY)
Jacksonville U (FL)
Kansas State U (KS)
Kennesaw State U (GA)
Kent State U (OH)
Kutztown U of Pennsylvania (PA)
Lee U (TN)
Lehman Coll of the City U of New
  York (NY)
Lincoln Memorial U (TN)
Lincoln U (MO)
Lindenwood U (MO)
Lindsey Wilson Coll (KY)
Lipscomb U (TN)
Long Island U–LIU Brooklyn (NY)
Long Island U–LIU Post (NY)
Louisiana Coll (LA)
Lubbock Christian U (TX)
Manchester U (IN)
Manhattanville Coll (NY)
Maryland Inst Coll of Art (MD)
Maryville U of Saint Louis (MO)
Marywood U (PA)
Massachusetts Coll of Art and
  Design (MA)
McKendree U (IL)
McMurry U (TX)
Mercyhurst U (PA)
Meredith Coll (NC)
Messiah Coll (PA)
Metropolitan State U of Denver
  (CO)
Miami U (OH)
Michigan State U (MI)
Middle Tennessee State U (TN)
Millikin U (IL)
Minnesota State U Moorhead (MN)
Minot State U (ND)
Missouri State U (MO)
Missouri Western State U (MO)
Molloy Coll (NY)
Morningside Coll (IA)
Mount Mary U (WI)
Mount Mercy U (IA)
Mount St. Joseph U (OH)
Mount Vernon Nazarene U (OH)
Muskingum U (OH)
Nazareth Coll of Rochester (NY)
New Jersey City U (NJ)
North Central Coll (IL)

Northeastern State U (OK)
Northern Illinois U (IL)
Northern Michigan U (MI)
Northern State U (SD)
Northwestern Coll (IA)
Northwest Missouri State U (MO)
Northwest Nazarene U (ID)
Nova Southeastern U (FL)
Ohio Dominican U (OH)
Ohio Northern U (OH)
The Ohio State U (OH)
Ohio Wesleyan U (OH)
Olivet Nazarene U (IL)
Oral Roberts U (OK)
Otterbein U (OH)
Ouachita Baptist U (AR)
Palm Beach Atlantic U (FL)
Penn State Abington (PA)
Penn State Altoona (PA)
Penn State Beaver (PA)
Penn State Berks (PA)
Penn State Brandywine (PA)
Penn State DuBois (PA)
Penn State Erie, The Behrend Coll (PA)
Penn State Fayette, The Eberly Campus (PA)
Penn State Greater Allegheny (PA)
Penn State Hazleton (PA)
Penn State Lehigh Valley (PA)
Penn State Mont Alto (PA)
Penn State New Kensington (PA)
Penn State Schuylkill (PA)
Penn State Shenango (PA)
Penn State Worthington Scranton (PA)
Penn State U Park (PA)
Penn State Wilkes-Barre (PA)
Penn State Worthington Scranton (PA)
Penn State York (PA)
Piedmont Coll (GA)
Point Loma Nazarene U (CA)
Pratt Inst (NY)
Purdue U (IN)
Queens Coll of the City U of New York (NY)
Rhode Island Coll (RI)
Rocky Mountain Coll (MT)
Saginaw Valley State U (MI)
St. Ambrose U (IA)
St. Catherine U (MN)
Saint Joseph's U (PA)
Saint Louis U–Madrid Campus (Spain)
Saint Mary-of-the-Woods Coll (IN)
St. Mary's U (TX)
Saint Michael's Coll (VT)
Saint Vincent Coll (PA)
Seton Hill U (PA)
Shawnee State U (OH)
Silver Lake Coll of the Holy Family (WI)
Simpson Coll (IA)
Southeastern Oklahoma State U (OK)
Southeast Missouri State U (MO)
Southern Adventist U (TN)
Southern Arkansas U–Magnolia (AR)
Southern Utah U (UT)
Southwest Baptist U (MO)
State U of New York at New Paltz (NY)
Syracuse U (NY)
Taylor U (IN)
Temple U (PA)
Tennessee Technological U (TN)
Texas Christian U (TX)
Texas Lutheran U (TX)
Towson U (MD)
Transylvania U (KY)
Trinity Christian Coll (IL)
Union U (TN)
The U of Akron (OH)
The U of Arizona (AZ)
U of Central Missouri (MO)
U of Central Oklahoma (OK)
U of Cincinnati (OH)
U of Dayton (OH)
U of Denver (CO)
U of Evansville (IN)
The U of Findlay (OH)
U of Florida (FL)
U of Idaho (ID)
U of Illinois at Chicago (IL)
The U of Kansas (KS)
U of Kentucky (KY)
U of Maine (ME)

U of Mary Hardin-Baylor (TX)
U of Maryland, Coll Park (MD)
U of Maryland Eastern Shore (MD)
U of Massachusetts Dartmouth (MA)
U of Michigan–Flint (MI)
U of Minnesota, Duluth (MN)
U of Missouri (MO)
U of New Mexico (NM)
The U of North Carolina at Greensboro (NC)
The U of North Carolina at Pembroke (NC)
U of North Florida (FL)
U of North Georgia (GA)
U of Providence (MT)
U of Regina (SK, Canada)
U of St. Francis (IL)
U of Saint Francis (IN)
U of Sioux Falls (SD)
U of South Carolina (SC)
U of South Dakota (SD)
U of Southern Maine (ME)
The U of Tennessee at Chattanooga (TN)
The U of Texas at Austin (TX)
U of Vermont (VT)
U of Wisconsin–Madison (WI)
U of Wisconsin–Milwaukee (WI)
U of Wisconsin–River Falls (WI)
U of Wisconsin–Stout (WI)
U of Wisconsin–Superior (WI)
U of Wisconsin–Whitewater (WI)
Upper Iowa U (IA)
Ursuline Coll (OH)
Utah Valley U (UT)
Valdosta State U (GA)
Valley City State U (ND)
Valparaiso U (IN)
Virginia Commonwealth U (VA)
Virginia Wesleyan U (VA)
Wartburg Coll (IA)
Washington & Jefferson Coll (PA)
Washington U in St. Louis (MO)
Wayne State Coll (NE)
Weber State U (UT)
Western Michigan U (MI)
Western State Colorado U (CO)
Western Washington U (WA)
Westmont Coll (CA)
West Virginia Wesleyan Coll (WV)
Whitworth U (WA)
William Woods U (MO)
Winona State U (MN)
Xavier U of Louisiana (LA)
Youngstown State U (OH)

ART THERAPY
Alverno Coll (WI)
Arcadia U (PA)
Bluffton U (OH)
Bowling Green State U (OH)
Cairn U (PA)
Capital U (OH)
Carlow U (PA)
Cedar Crest Coll (PA)
Chowan U (NC)
The Coll of New Rochelle (NY)
Concordia U Chicago (IL)
Concordia U, Nebraska (NE)
Converse Coll (SC)
Edgewood Coll (WI)
Emmanuel Coll (MA)
Harding U (AR)
Houston Baptist U (TX)
Indiana Wesleyan U (IN)
Kansas Wesleyan U (KS)
Lesley U (MA)
Lipscomb U (TN)
Long Island U–LIU Post (NY)
Marywood U (PA)
Mercyhurst U (PA)
Millikin U (IL)
Mount Mary U (WI)
Naropa U (CO)
Nazareth Coll of Rochester (NY)
St. Thomas Aquinas Coll (NY)
Seton Hill U (PA)
Sierra Nevada Coll (NV)
Southern Adventist U (TN)
Taylor U (IN)
Trinity Christian Coll (IL)
U of Saint Francis (IN)
The U of Tampa (FL)
U of Wisconsin–Superior (WI)
Ursuline Coll (OH)
West Virginia Wesleyan Coll (WV)

ASIAN AMERICAN STUDIES
Arizona State U at the Tempe campus (AZ)
Binghamton U, State U of New York (NY)
California State U, Fullerton (CA)
California State U, Long Beach (CA)
California State U, Los Angeles (CA)
California State U, Northridge (CA)
Columbia U (NY)
Pitzer Coll (CA)
Pomona Coll (CA)
San Francisco State U (CA)
Scripps Coll (CA)
Stanford U (CA)
U of California, Davis (CA)
U of California, Irvine (CA)
U of California, Los Angeles (CA)
U of California, Riverside (CA)
U of California, Santa Barbara (CA)
U of Denver (CO)
U of Southern California (CA)

ASIAN HISTORY
Gettysburg Coll (PA)
Sarah Lawrence Coll (NY)
U of Washington, Tacoma (WA)

ASIAN STUDIES
Amherst Coll (MA)
Arizona State U at the Tempe campus (AZ)
Augustana Coll (IL)
Austin Coll (TX)
Bard Coll (NY)
Barnard Coll (NY)
Baylor U (TX)
Belmont U (TN)
Bennington Coll (VT)
Berea Coll (KY)
Binghamton U, State U of New York (NY)
Birmingham-Southern Coll (AL)
Boston U (MA)
Bowdoin Coll (ME)
Bowling Green State U (OH)
California State U, Long Beach (CA)
California State U, Los Angeles (CA)
California State U, Sacramento (CA)
Calvin Coll (MI)
Carleton Coll (MN)
Carthage Coll (WI)
Case Western Reserve U (OH)
City Coll of the City U of New York (NY)
Claremont McKenna Coll (CA)
Clark U (MA)
Coe Coll (IA)
Colgate U (NY)
Coll of Saint Benedict (MN)
Coll of the Holy Cross (MA)
The Colorado Coll (CO)
Cornell U (NY)
Dartmouth Coll (NH)
Florida Intl U (FL)
Florida State U (FL)
Furman U (SC)
The George Washington U (DC)
Gonzaga U (WA)
Hamilton Coll (NY)
Hobart and William Smith Colls (NY)
Illinois Wesleyan U (IL)
Indiana U of Pennsylvania (PA)
John Carroll U (OH)
Kean U (NJ)
Kennesaw State U (GA)
Kenyon Coll (OH)
Knox Coll (IL)
Lehigh U (PA)
Loyola Marymount U (CA)
Macalester Coll (MN)
Manhattanville Coll (NY)
Marlboro Coll (VT)
McDaniel Coll (MD)
Mount Holyoke Coll (MA)
Nazareth Coll of Rochester (NY)
Northeastern U (MA)
Northwestern U (IL)
Ohio U (OH)
Old Dominion U (VA)
Pace U (NY)
Penn State U Park (PA)

Pepperdine U, Malibu (CA)
Pitzer Coll (CA)
Pomona Coll (CA)
Purdue U (IN)
Randolph-Macon Coll (VA)
Rice U (TX)
Rollins Coll (FL)
Saint John's U (MN)
St. John's U (NY)
Saint Joseph's U (PA)
St. Mary's Coll of Maryland (MD)
St. Olaf Coll (MN)
San Diego State U (CA)
Sarah Lawrence Coll (NY)
Scripps Coll (CA)
Seattle U (WA)
Sewanee: The U of the South (TN)
Skidmore Coll (NY)
State U of New York at New Paltz (NY)
Stony Brook U, State U of New York (NY)
Suffolk U (MA)
Temple U (PA)
Trinity U (TX)
Tufts U (MA)
Tulane U (LA)
Union Coll (NY)
U at Albany, State U of New York (NY)
U at Buffalo, the State U of New York (NY)
U of California, Riverside (CA)
U of California, Santa Barbara (CA)
U of Cincinnati (OH)
U of Colorado Boulder (CO)
U of Hawaii at Manoa (HI)
U of Louisville (KY)
U of Maryland, Baltimore County (MD)
U of Maryland U Coll (MD)
U of Massachusetts Boston (MA)
U of Michigan (MI)
U of Montana (MT)
U of Nevada, Las Vegas (NV)
U of New Mexico (NM)
The U of North Carolina at Chapel Hill (NC)
U of Northern Colorado (CO)
U of Oregon (OR)
U of Richmond (VA)
U of San Francisco (CA)
The U of Texas at Austin (TX)
The U of Toledo (OH)
U of Toronto (ON, Canada)
U of Utah (UT)
U of Vermont (VT)
U of Washington (WA)
U of Wisconsin–Madison (WI)
Utah State U (UT)
Vanderbilt U (TN)
Vassar Coll (NY)
Washington State U (WA)
Washington U in St. Louis (MO)
Western Kentucky U (KY)
Whitman Coll (WA)
Willamette U (OR)
William Paterson U of New Jersey (NJ)
Williams Coll (MA)

ASIAN STUDIES (EAST)
Austin Coll (TX)
Bates Coll (ME)
Binghamton U, State U of New York (NY)
Boston U (MA)
Brandeis U (MA)
Bryn Mawr Coll (PA)
Bucknell U (PA)
Colby Coll (ME)
Columbia U (NY)
Connecticut Coll (CT)
Davidson Coll (NC)
Denison U (OH)
DePaul U (IL)
DePauw U (IN)
Dickinson Coll (PA)
Emory U (GA)
The George Washington U (DC)
Gettysburg Coll (PA)
Grand Valley State U (MI)
Hampshire Coll (MA)
Harvard U (MA)
Haverford Coll (PA)
Hofstra U (NY)
Indiana U Bloomington (IN)

John Carroll U (OH)
Johns Hopkins U (MD)
Kalamazoo Coll (MI)
Lawrence U (WI)
Marlboro Coll (VT)
Miami U (OH)
Middlebury Coll (VT)
Minnesota State U Moorhead (MN)
Mount Holyoke Coll (MA)
New Coll of Florida (FL)
New York U (NY)
North Central Coll (IL)
Oberlin Coll (OH)
Occidental Coll (CA)
Ohio Wesleyan U (OH)
Penn State Abington (PA)
Penn State Altoona (PA)
Penn State Beaver (PA)
Penn State Berks (PA)
Penn State Brandywine (PA)
Penn State DuBois (PA)
Penn State Erie, The Behrend Coll (PA)
Penn State Fayette, The Eberly Campus (PA)
Penn State Greater Allegheny (PA)
Penn State Hazleton (PA)
Penn State Lehigh Valley (PA)
Penn State Mont Alto (PA)
Penn State New Kensington (PA)
Penn State Schuylkill (PA)
Penn State Shenango (PA)
Penn State Worthington Scranton (PA)
Penn State York (PA)
Portland State U (OR)
Princeton U (NJ)
Queens Coll of the City U of New York (NY)
Rutgers U–New Brunswick (NJ)
Simmons Coll (MA)
Smith Coll (MA)
Stanford U (CA)
Trinity U (TX)
Tufts U (MA)
United States Military Acad (NY)
U at Albany, State U of New York (NY)
The U of Arizona (AZ)
U of Bridgeport (CT)
U of California, Davis (CA)
U of California, Irvine (CA)
U of Missouri (MO)
U of Montana (MT)
U of Pennsylvania (PA)
U of Rochester (NY)
U of Southern California (CA)
U of Toronto (ON, Canada)
Ursinus Coll (PA)
Valparaiso U (IN)
Washington U in St. Louis (MO)
Wayne State U (MI)
Wellesley Coll (MA)
Wesleyan U (CT)
Western Washington U (WA)
Willamette U (OR)
Wittenberg U (OH)

ASIAN STUDIES (SOUTH)
Binghamton U, State U of New York (NY)
Concordia U (QC, Canada)
Gettysburg Coll (PA)
Hampshire Coll (MA)
Indiana U Bloomington (IN)
Middlebury Coll (VT)
Mount Holyoke Coll (MA)
U of Missouri (MO)
U of Pennsylvania (PA)
U of Toronto (ON, Canada)
U of Washington (WA)

ASIAN STUDIES (SOUTHEAST)
Tufts U (MA)
U of Washington (WA)

ASIAN STUDIES (URAL-ALTAIC AND CENTRAL)
Indiana U Bloomington (IN)

ASTRONOMY
Amherst Coll (MA)
Ball State U (IN)
Barnard Coll (NY)
Baylor U (TX)
Benedictine Coll (KS)
Bennington Coll (VT)
Boston U (MA)

Brigham Young U (UT)
Bryn Mawr Coll (PA)
Case Western Reserve U (OH)
Central Michigan U (MI)
Colgate U (NY)
Columbia U (NY)
Cornell U (NY)
Dartmouth Coll (NH)
Drake U (IA)
Franklin & Marshall Coll (PA)
George Mason U (VA)
Hampshire Coll (MA)
Haverford Coll (PA)
Indiana U Bloomington (IN)
Lehigh U (PA)
Lycoming Coll (PA)
Marlboro Coll (VT)
Mount Holyoke Coll (MA)
Northern Arizona U (AZ)
Northwestern U (IL)
The Ohio State U (OH)
Ohio Wesleyan U (OH)
Penn State Abington (PA)
Penn State Altoona (PA)
Penn State Beaver (PA)
Penn State Berks (PA)
Penn State Brandywine (PA)
Penn State DuBois (PA)
Penn State Erie, The Behrend Coll (PA)
Penn State Fayette, The Eberly Campus (PA)
Penn State Greater Allegheny (PA)
Penn State Hazleton (PA)
Penn State Lehigh Valley (PA)
Penn State Mont Alto (PA)
Penn State New Kensington (PA)
Penn State Schuylkill (PA)
Penn State Shenango (PA)
Penn State U Park (PA)
Penn State Wilkes-Barre (PA)
Penn State Worthington Scranton (PA)
Penn State York (PA)
Pomona Coll (CA)
Rice U (TX)
San Diego State U (CA)
San Francisco State U (CA)
Smith Coll (MA)
State U of New York at New Paltz (NY)
Stonehill Coll (MA)
Stony Brook U, State U of New York (NY)
Tufts U (MA)
Union Coll (NY)
The U of Arizona (AZ)
U of Colorado Boulder (CO)
U of Florida (FL)
U of Georgia (GA)
U of Hawaii at Manoa (HI)
The U of Kansas (KS)
U of Maryland, Coll Park (MD)
U of Massachusetts Amherst (MA)
U of Michigan (MI)
U of Montana (MT)
U of Oklahoma (OK)
U of Pittsburgh (PA)
U of Southern California (CA)
The U of Texas at Austin (TX)
The U of Toledo (OH)
U of Virginia (VA)
U of Washington (WA)
Valdosta State U (GA)
Valparaiso U (IN)
Vassar Coll (NY)
Villanova U (PA)
Wayne State U (MI)
Wellesley Coll (MA)
Wesleyan U (CT)
Whitman Coll (WA)
Williams Coll (MA)
Youngstown State U (OH)

ASTRONOMY AND ASTROPHYSICS RELATED

Butler U (IN)
Coll of Charleston (SC)
Embry-Riddle Aeronautical U–Daytona (FL)
Emory U (GA)
Florida Inst of Technology (FL)
Harvard U (MA)
Texas Christian U (TX)
U of Wyoming (WY)
Whitman Coll (WA)

ASTROPHYSICS

Agnes Scott Coll (GA)
Barnard Coll (NY)
Baylor U (TX)
Boston U (MA)
California Inst of Technology (CA)
Carnegie Mellon U (PA)
Colgate U (NY)
Columbia U (NY)
Florida State U (FL)
Franklin & Marshall Coll (PA)
Haverford Coll (PA)
Lehigh U (PA)
Lycoming Coll (PA)
Marlboro Coll (VT)
Michigan State U (MI)
Ohio U (OH)
Ohio Wesleyan U (OH)
Princeton U (NJ)
Rice U (TX)
Rutgers U–New Brunswick (NJ)
San Francisco State U (CA)
Tufts U (MA)
United States Military Acad (NY)
U of California, Los Angeles (CA)
U of California, Santa Cruz (CA)
U of Cincinnati (OH)
U of Hawaii at Manoa (HI)
U of Minnesota, Twin Cities Campus (MN)
U of New Mexico (NM)
U of Oklahoma (OK)
U of Wisconsin–Madison (WI)
Villanova U (PA)
Wellesley Coll (MA)
Whitman Coll (WA)
Williams Coll (MA)

ATHLETIC TRAINING

Alfred U (NY)
Alma Coll (MI)
Anderson U (IN)
Anderson U (SC)
Appalachian State U (NC)
Aquinas Coll (MI)
Ashland U (OH)
Augustana U (SD)
Aurora U (IL)
Averett U (VA)
Azusa Pacific U (CA)
Baldwin Wallace U (OH)
Ball State U (IN)
Benedictine Coll (KS)
Bethel Coll (KS)
Bethel U (MN)
Boston U (MA)
Bowling Green State U (OH)
Bridgewater State U (MA)
Brigham Young U (UT)
Buena Vista U (IA)
California State U, Fullerton (CA)
California State U, Long Beach (CA)
California State U, Northridge (CA)
California U of Pennsylvania (PA)
Canisius Coll (NY)
Capital U (OH)
Carroll U (WI)
Carthage Coll (WI)
Catawba Coll (NC)
Cedarville U (OH)
Central Connecticut State U (CT)
Central Methodist U (MO)
Central Michigan U (MI)
Chapman U (CA)
Clarke U (IA)
Coe Coll (IA)
The Coll at Brockport, State U of New York (NY)
Colorado Mesa U (CO)
Colorado State U–Pueblo (CO)
Concordia U Irvine (CA)
Concordia U Wisconsin (WI)
Concord U (WV)
Culver-Stockton Coll (MO)
Defiance Coll (OH)
DePauw U (IN)
Dominican Coll (NY)
Duquesne U (PA)
East Carolina U (NC)
East Central U (OK)
Eastern Michigan U (MI)
Eastern U (PA)
Eastern Washington U (WA)
East Stroudsburg U of Pennsylvania (PA)
East Texas Baptist U (TX)

Emory & Henry Coll (VA)
Emporia State U (KS)
Endicott Coll (MA)
Florida Gulf Coast U (FL)
Florida Southern Coll (FL)
Florida State U (FL)
Fort Lewis Coll (CO)
Frostburg State U (MD)
George Mason U (VA)
Georgetown Coll (KY)
Georgia Coll & State U (GA)
Georgia Southern U (GA)
Grand Valley State U (MI)
Greensboro Coll (NC)
Gustavus Adolphus Coll (MN)
Harding U (AR)
Hardin-Simmons U (TX)
Heidelberg U (OH)
Hofstra U (NY)
Hope Coll (MI)
Houston Baptist U (TX)
Howard Payne U (TX)
Illinois State U (IL)
Immaculata U (PA)
Indiana State U (IN)
Indiana U Bloomington (IN)
Indiana Wesleyan U (IN)
Iowa State U of Science and Technology (IA)
Ithaca Coll (NY)
James Madison U (VA)
Kansas State U (KS)
Kean U (NJ)
Keene State Coll (NH)
Kent State U (OH)
King's Coll (PA)
King U (TN)
Lasell Coll (MA)
Lee U (TN)
Lewis U (IL)
Liberty U (VA)
Limestone Coll (SC)
Lincoln Memorial U (TN)
Lindenwood U (MO)
Linfield Coll (OR)
Long Island U–LIU Brooklyn (NY)
Longwood U (VA)
Loras Coll (IA)
Louisiana Coll (LA)
Louisiana State U and A&M Coll (LA)
Lubbock Christian U (TX)
Lynchburg Coll (VA)
Manchester U (IN)
Marietta Coll (OH)
Marist Coll (NY)
Marquette U (WI)
Marshall U (WV)
Marywood U (PA)
Massachusetts Coll of Liberal Arts (MA)
McKendree U (IL)
McMurry U (TX)
Mercyhurst U (PA)
Messiah Coll (PA)
Miami U (OH)
Michigan State U (MI)
MidAmerica Nazarene U (KS)
Middle Tennessee State U (TN)
Millikin U (IL)
Minnesota State U Moorhead (MN)
Minot State U (ND)
Missouri State U (MO)
Missouri Valley Coll (MO)
Montclair State U (NJ)
Mount St. Joseph U (OH)
Muskingum U (OH)
Neumann U (PA)
New Mexico State U (NM)
North Carolina Central U (NC)
North Central Coll (IL)
Northern Illinois U (IL)
Northern Kentucky U (KY)
Northern Michigan U (MI)
Northwestern Coll (IA)
Northwest Nazarene U (ID)
Ohio Northern U (OH)
The Ohio State U (OH)
Ohio U (OH)
Oklahoma Baptist U (OK)
Olivet Nazarene U (IL)
Otterbein U (OH)
Palm Beach Atlantic U (FL)
Penn State U Park (PA)
Pfeiffer U (NC)
Piedmont Coll (GA)
Point Loma Nazarene U (CA)

Quinnipiac U (CT)
Radford U (VA)
Rowan U (NJ)
Sacred Heart U (CT)
Saginaw Valley State U (MI)
Saint Louis U–Madrid Campus (Spain)
Salisbury U (MD)
Samford U (AL)
Sam Houston State U (TX)
San Diego State U (CA)
Shawnee State U (OH)
Slippery Rock U of Pennsylvania (PA)
Southeastern Louisiana U (LA)
Southeast Missouri State U (MO)
Southern Arkansas U–Magnolia (AR)
Southern Utah U (UT)
Southwest Baptist U (MO)
Southwestern Coll (KS)
State U of New York Coll at Cortland (NY)
Stony Brook U, State U of New York (NY)
Tabor Coll (KS)
Texas A&M U–Corpus Christi (TX)
Texas Christian U (TX)
Texas Lutheran U (TX)
Texas State U (TX)
Tiffin U (OH)
Towson U (MD)
Troy U (AL)
Truman State U (MO)
Tusculum Coll (TN)
Union U (TN)
Université de Sherbrooke (QC, Canada)
The U of Akron (OH)
The U of Alabama (AL)
U of Central Arkansas (AR)
U of Central Florida (FL)
U of Cincinnati (OH)
U of Evansville (IN)
U of Florida (FL)
U of Georgia (GA)
U of Idaho (ID)
The U of Kansas (KS)
U of La Verne (CA)
U of Maine (ME)
U of Maine at Presque Isle (ME)
U of Miami (FL)
U of Michigan (MI)
U of Minnesota, Duluth (MN)
U of Mobile (AL)
U of Montana (MT)
U of Mount Union (OH)
U of Nebraska–Lincoln (NE)
U of Nevada, Las Vegas (NV)
U of New England (ME)
U of New Hampshire (NH)
The U of North Carolina at Charlotte (NC)
The U of North Carolina at Pembroke (NC)
The U of North Carolina Wilmington (NC)
U of North Dakota (ND)
U of Northern Colorado (CO)
U of Northern Iowa (IA)
U of North Florida (FL)
U of North Georgia (GA)
U of Pittsburgh at Bradford (PA)
U of Southern Maine (ME)
U of Southern Mississippi (MS)
The U of Tampa (FL)
The U of Tennessee at Martin (TN)
The U of Texas at Austin (TX)
The U of Texas of the Permian Basin (TX)
U of the Incarnate Word (TX)
The U of Tulsa (OK)
U of Utah (UT)
U of Vermont (VT)
The U of West Alabama (AL)
U of Wisconsin–Eau Claire (WI)
U of Wisconsin–La Crosse (WI)
U of Wisconsin–Madison (WI)
U of Wisconsin–Milwaukee (WI)
U of Wisconsin–Stevens Point (WI)
Upper Iowa U (IA)
Valdosta State U (GA)
Valley City State U (ND)
Vanguard U of Southern California (CA)
Warner Pacific Coll (OR)
Washington State U (WA)

Waynesburg U (PA)
Wayne State Coll (NE)
Weber State U (UT)
Welch Coll (TN)
West Chester U of Pennsylvania (PA)
Western Illinois U (IL)
Western Michigan U (MI)
Westfield State U (MA)
West Texas A&M U (TX)
West Virginia Wesleyan Coll (WV)
Whitworth U (WA)
Wichita State U (KS)
William Paterson U of New Jersey (NJ)
William Woods U (MO)
Winona State U (MN)
Wright State U (OH)
Wright State U–Lake Campus (OH)
Youngstown State U (OH)

ATMOSPHERIC CHEMISTRY AND CLIMATOLOGY

Northern Vermont U–Lyndon (VT)
Rutgers U–New Brunswick (NJ)

ATMOSPHERIC SCIENCES AND METEOROLOGY

Ball State U (IN)
The Coll at Brockport, State U of New York (NY)
Cornell U (NY)
Embry-Riddle Aeronautical U–Daytona (FL)
George Mason U (VA)
Iowa State U of Science and Technology (IA)
Jackson State U (MS)
Millersville U of Pennsylvania (PA)
North Carolina State U (NC)
Northern Illinois U (IL)
The Ohio State U (OH)
Ohio U (OH)
Penn State Abington (PA)
Penn State Altoona (PA)
Penn State Beaver (PA)
Penn State Berks (PA)
Penn State Brandywine (PA)
Penn State DuBois (PA)
Penn State Erie, The Behrend Coll (PA)
Penn State Fayette, The Eberly Campus (PA)
Penn State Greater Allegheny (PA)
Penn State Hazleton (PA)
Penn State Lehigh Valley (PA)
Penn State Mont Alto (PA)
Penn State New Kensington (PA)
Penn State Schuylkill (PA)
Penn State Shenango (PA)
Penn State U Park (PA)
Penn State Wilkes-Barre (PA)
Penn State Worthington Scranton (PA)
Penn State York (PA)
Purdue U (IN)
Rutgers U–New Brunswick (NJ)
Saint Louis U (MO)
State U of New York at Oswego (NY)
State U of New York Coll at Oneonta (NY)
State U of New York Maritime Coll (NY)
Stony Brook U, State U of New York (NY)
Texas A&M U (TX)
Texas A&M U–Corpus Christi (TX)
U at Albany, State U of New York (NY)
U of California, Davis (CA)
U of Colorado Boulder (CO)
U of Georgia (GA)
The U of Kansas (KS)
U of Louisiana at Monroe (LA)
U of Louisville (KY)
U of Miami (FL)
U of Michigan (MI)
U of Missouri (MO)
U of Nebraska–Lincoln (NE)
U of Nevada, Reno (NV)
U of North Carolina at Asheville (NC)
U of North Dakota (ND)
U of Utah (UT)
U of Washington (WA)
U of Waterloo (ON, Canada)
U of Wisconsin–Madison (WI)

Valparaiso U (IN)
Western Connecticut State U (CT)

ATMOSPHERIC SCIENCES AND METEOROLOGY RELATED
East Carolina U (NC)
U of California, Los Angeles (CA)

ATOMIC/MOLECULAR PHYSICS
San Diego State U (CA)
U of Waterloo (ON, Canada)

AUDIOLOGY
Biola U (CA)
California State U, Long Beach (CA)
Cleveland State U (OH)
Northwestern U (IL)
The Ohio State U (OH)
Stephen F. Austin State U (TX)
U of Montevallo (AL)
Western Michigan U (MI)

AUDIOLOGY AND SPEECH-LANGUAGE PATHOLOGY
Adelphi U (NY)
Andrews U (MI)
Auburn U (AL)
Auburn U at Montgomery (AL)
Augustana U (SD)
Ball State U (IN)
Biola U (CA)
Bloomsburg U of Pennsylvania (PA)
Bluffton U (OH)
Boston U (MA)
Bowling Green State U (OH)
Brescia U (KY)
Buffalo State Coll, State U of New York (NY)
California State U, East Bay (CA)
California State U, Long Beach (CA)
California State U, Sacramento (CA)
Calvin Coll (MI)
The Coll of Idaho (ID)
The Coll of Saint Rose (NY)
East Carolina U (NC)
Eastern New Mexico U (NM)
Elmhurst Coll (IL)
Emerson Coll (MA)
The George Washington U (DC)
Hardin-Simmons U (TX)
Hofstra U (NY)
Hunter Coll of the City U of New York (NY)
Idaho State U (ID)
Illinois State U (IL)
Indiana State U (IN)
Indiana U Bloomington (IN)
Indiana U of Pennsylvania (PA)
Iona Coll (NY)
Ithaca Coll (NY)
Kent State U (OH)
Lehman Coll of the City U of New York (NY)
Long Island U–LIU Brooklyn (NY)
Long Island U–LIU Post (NY)
Longwood U (VA)
Louisiana State U and A&M Coll (LA)
Marymount Manhattan Coll (NY)
Marywood U (PA)
Mercy Coll (NY)
Miami U (OH)
Middle Tennessee State U (TN)
Minnesota State U Moorhead (MN)
Missouri State U (MO)
Murray State U (KY)
Nazareth Coll of Rochester (NY)
New York U (NY)
Northeastern State U (OK)
Northwestern U (IL)
Ohio U (OH)
Old Dominion U (VA)
Purdue U (IN)
Queens Coll of the City U of New York (NY)
St. John's U (NY)
Southeastern Louisiana U (LA)
Southern Illinois U Edwardsville (IL)
State U of New York at Fredonia (NY)
State U of New York at Plattsburgh (NY)

State U of New York Coll at Cortland (NY)
Temple U (PA)
Texas Woman's U (TX)
Towson U (MD)
U at Buffalo, the State U of New York (NY)
The U of Alabama (AL)
U of Arkansas (AR)
U of Central Arkansas (AR)
U of Central Florida (FL)
U of Florida (FL)
U of Kentucky (KY)
U of Louisiana at Monroe (LA)
U of Minnesota, Twin Cities Campus (MN)
U of Montana (MT)
U of New Mexico (NM)
The U of North Carolina at Greensboro (NC)
U of Northern Colorado (CO)
U of North Texas (TX)
U of Pittsburgh (PA)
U of Southern Mississippi (MS)
The U of Tennessee (TN)
The U of Texas at Austin (TX)
The U of Texas at Dallas (TX)
The U of Texas at El Paso (TX)
U of the Pacific (CA)
The U of Tulsa (OK)
U of Utah (UT)
U of Virginia (VA)
U of Wisconsin–Madison (WI)
U of Wisconsin–Milwaukee (WI)
U of Wisconsin–Stevens Point (WI)
U of Wyoming (WY)
Utah State U (UT)
Washington State U (WA)
Washington State U–Spokane (WA)
West Chester U of Pennsylvania (PA)
Western Michigan U (MI)
West Virginia U (WV)

AUDIOVISUAL COMMUNICATIONS TECHNOLOGIES RELATED
Husson U (ME)
Webster U (MO)

AUDITING
Babson Coll (MA)
Bradley U (IL)
Carlow U (PA)
Davenport U, Grand Rapids (MI)
Inter American U of Puerto Rico, Bayamón Campus (PR)
State U of New York Coll of Technology at Delhi (NY)

AUTOBODY/COLLISION AND REPAIR TECHNOLOGY
Idaho State U (ID)
Pennsylvania Coll of Technology (PA)

AUTOMATION ENGINEER TECHNOLOGY
ECPI U, Virginia Beach (VA)
Millersville U of Pennsylvania (PA)
State U of New York Coll of Technology at Delhi (NY)

AUTOMOBILE/AUTOMOTIVE MECHANICS TECHNOLOGY
Brigham Young U–Idaho (ID)
Idaho State U (ID)
McPherson Coll (KS)
New England Inst of Technology (RI)

AUTOMOTIVE ENGINEERING TECHNOLOGY
ArtCenter Coll of Design (CA)
Colorado State U–Pueblo (CO)
Ferris State U (MI)
Indiana State U (IN)
Pennsylvania Coll of Technology (PA)
Pittsburg State U (KS)
Southern Illinois U Carbondale (IL)
Weber State U (UT)
Western Washington U (WA)

AVIATION/AIRWAY MANAGEMENT
Auburn U (AL)
Averett U (VA)
Baylor U (TX)

Bridgewater State U (MA)
California Baptist U (CA)
California State U, Los Angeles (CA)
Delaware State U (DE)
Eastern Michigan U (MI)
Eastern New Mexico U (NM)
Farmingdale State Coll (NY)
Florida Inst of Technology (FL)
Hallmark U (TX)
Hampton U (VA)
Indiana State U (IN)
Inter American U of Puerto Rico, Bayamón Campus (PR)
Jacksonville U (FL)
LeTourneau U (TX)
Lewis U (IL)
Liberty U (VA)
Lynn U (FL)
Marywood U (PA)
Metropolitan State U of Denver (CO)
Middle Georgia State U (GA)
The Ohio State U (OH)
Ohio U (OH)
Purdue U (IN)
Rocky Mountain Coll (MT)
Saint Louis U–Madrid Campus (Spain)
Southern Illinois U Carbondale (IL)
Texas A&M–Central Texas (TX)
Thomas Edison State U (NJ)
U of Dubuque (IA)
U of North Dakota (ND)
U of the Fraser Valley (BC, Canada)
Vaughn Coll of Aeronautics and Technology (NY)
Western Michigan U (MI)
Westminster Coll (UT)
West Virginia U Inst of Technology (WV)
Wilmington U (DE)

AVIONICS MAINTENANCE TECHNOLOGY
Pennsylvania Coll of Technology (PA)
Southern Illinois U Carbondale (IL)
Vaughn Coll of Aeronautics and Technology (NY)
Western Michigan U (MI)

AYURVEDIC MEDICINE
Maharishi U of Management (IA)

BALLET
Brigham Young U (UT)
Friends U (KS)
Indiana U Bloomington (IN)
Marymount Manhattan Coll (NY)
Texas Christian U (TX)
U of Utah (UT)

BANKING AND FINANCIAL SUPPORT SERVICES
Brescia U (KY)
Buena Vista U (IA)
Delaware State U (DE)
Hardin-Simmons U (TX)
Husson U (ME)
Northern State U (SD)
Saint Peter's U (NJ)
Sam Houston State U (TX)
Stephen F. Austin State U (TX)
U of North Florida (FL)
U of the Incarnate Word (TX)
Youngstown State U (OH)

BEHAVIORAL ASPECTS OF HEALTH
Oregon Inst of Technology (OR)
Point U (GA)
Taylor U (IN)
U of Houston–Downtown (TX)
U of Southern California (CA)
The U of Texas at Austin (TX)

BEHAVIORAL SCIENCES
Ambrose U (AB, Canada)
American Baptist Coll (TN)
Andrews U (MI)
Athens State U (AL)
Bemidji State U (MN)
California Baptist U (CA)
California State U, Dominguez Hills (CA)
Carnegie Mellon U (PA)
Chaminade U of Honolulu (HI)

Columbia Coll (SC)
Columbia Southern U (AL)
Concordia Coll–New York (NY)
Concordia U Irvine (CA)
Concordia U, Nebraska (NE)
Duquesne U (PA)
Evangel U (MO)
Gwynedd Mercy U (PA)
Inter American U of Puerto Rico, San Germán Campus (PR)
Johns Hopkins U (MD)
Marlboro Coll (VT)
Metropolitan State U of Denver (CO)
Missouri Baptist U (MO)
Northern Michigan U (MI)
Nova Southeastern U (FL)
Point Park U (PA)
Purdue U Northwest (IN)
Rider U (NJ)
Rowan U (NJ)
Saint Augustine's U (NC)
Tabor Coll (KS)
Tennessee Wesleyan U (TN)
Trevecca Nazarene U (TN)
Tufts U (MA)
U of Houston–Clear Lake (TX)
The U of Kansas (KS)
U of La Verne (CA)
U of Maine at Fort Kent (ME)
U of Maine at Machias (ME)
U of Missouri (MO)
Walsh U (OH)
Widener U (PA)
Wilmington U (DE)
York Coll of Pennsylvania (PA)

BIBLICAL STUDIES
Abilene Christian U (TX)
Alaska Bible Coll (AK)
Amridge U (AL)
Anderson U (SC)
Andrews U (MI)
Appalachian Bible Coll (WV)
Arizona Christian U (AZ)
Arlington Baptist U (TX)
Asbury U (KY)
Austin Graduate School of Theology (TX)
Azusa Pacific U (CA)
The Baptist Coll of Florida (FL)
Baptist U of the Americas (TX)
Barclay Coll (KS)
Belhaven U (MS)
Belmont U (TN)
Bethel U (MN)
Beulah Heights U (GA)
Biola U (CA)
Bluefield Coll (VA)
Blue Mountain Coll (MS)
Bluffton U (OH)
Bob Jones U (SC)
Bryan Coll (TN)
Cairn U (PA)
California Baptist U (CA)
Calvary U (MO)
Calvin Coll (MI)
Campbellsville U (KY)
Canisius Coll (NY)
Carolina Christian Coll (NC)
Carson-Newman U (TN)
Cedarville U (PA)
Charlotte Christian Coll and Theological Sem (NC)
Coll of Biblical Studies–Houston (TX)
Coll of the Ozarks (MO)
Corban U (OR)
Cornerstone U (MI)
Covenant Coll (GA)
Criswell Coll (TX)
Dallas Baptist U (TX)
Eastern Mennonite U (VA)
Eastern U (PA)
East Texas Baptist U (TX)
Emmaus Bible Coll (IA)
Evangel U (MO)
Florida Coll (FL)
Geneva Coll (PA)
Goshen Coll (IN)
Hannibal-LaGrange U (MO)
Harding U (AR)
Hardin-Simmons U (TX)
Hobe Sound Bible Coll (FL)
Hope Intl U (CA)
Horizon U (IN)
Houston Baptist U (TX)

Howard Payne U (TX)
Indiana Wesleyan U (IN)
Johnson U (TN)
Johnson U Florida (FL)
Judson U (IL)
Kentucky Mountain Bible Coll (KY)
King U (TN)
Lee U (TN)
LeTourneau U (TX)
Liberty U (VA)
Lincoln Christian U (IL)
Lipscomb U (TN)
Louisiana Coll (LA)
Lubbock Christian U (TX)
Luther Rice Coll & Sem (GA)
Malone U (OH)
Maranatha Baptist U (WI)
Marlboro Coll (VT)
Master's Coll and Sem (ON, Canada)
The Master's U (CA)
Messiah Coll (PA)
MidAmerica Nazarene U (KS)
Mid-Atlantic Christian U (NC)
Milligan Coll (TN)
Mount Vernon Nazarene U (OH)
Multnomah U (OR)
North Greenville U (SC)
Northwest Christian U (OR)
Northwest Nazarene U (ID)
Northwest U (WA)
Nyack Coll (NY)
Oklahoma Baptist U (OK)
Oklahoma Christian U (OK)
Olivet Nazarene U (IL)
Oral Roberts U (OK)
Ouachita Baptist U (AR)
Palm Beach Atlantic U (FL)
Point Loma Nazarene U (CA)
Point U (GA)
Redeemer U Coll (ON, Canada)
Roberts Wesleyan Coll (NY)
Shiloh U (IA)
Southeastern U (FL)
Southern Adventist U (TN)
Southwest Baptist U (MO)
Southwestern Assemblies of God U (TX)
Taylor U (IN)
Theological U of the Caribbean (PR)
Toccoa Falls Coll (GA)
Trinity Christian Coll (IL)
Truett McConnell U (GA)
Union Coll (NE)
Union U (TN)
The U of Findlay (OH)
U of Minnesota, Twin Cities Campus (MN)
Vanguard U of Southern California (CA)
Waynesburg U (PA)
Welch Coll (TN)
Wheaton Coll (IL)
Whitworth U (WA)

BILINGUAL AND MULTILINGUAL EDUCATION
Boston U (MA)
California State U, Stanislaus (CA)
Calvin Coll (MI)
Canisius Coll (NY)
Houston Baptist U (TX)
Loyola U Chicago (IL)
Our Lady of the Lake U (TX)
Queens Coll of the City U of New York (NY)
State U of New York Coll at Old Westbury (NY)
Texas A&M Intl U (TX)
Texas Christian U (TX)
U of Guam (GU)
U of Regina (SK, Canada)
U of San Francisco (CA)
The U of Texas at San Antonio (TX)
U of Wisconsin–Milwaukee (WI)
Western Illinois U (IL)

BIOCHEMICAL ENGINEERING
Christian Brothers U (TN)
U of Colorado Boulder (CO)
U of Georgia (GA)

BIOCHEMISTRY
Abilene Christian U (TX)
Adams State U (CO)
Adelphi U (NY)
Agnes Scott Coll (GA)

Albion Coll (MI)
Albright Coll (PA)
Allegheny Coll (PA)
Alma Coll (MI)
American Intl Coll (MA)
American U (DC)
Anderson U (IN)
Andrews U (MI)
Arizona State U at the Tempe campus (AZ)
Asbury U (KY)
Auburn U (AL)
Augustana Coll (IL)
Augustana U (SD)
Austin Coll (TX)
Azusa Pacific U (CA)
Barnard Coll (NY)
Bates Coll (ME)
Baylor U (TX)
Beloit Coll (WI)
Benedictine Coll (KS)
Berry Coll (GA)
Bethany Lutheran Coll (MN)
Binghamton U, State U of New York (NY)
Biola U (CA)
Boston Coll (MA)
Bowdoin Coll (ME)
Bowling Green State U (OH)
Bradley U (IL)
Brandeis U (MA)
Bridgewater Coll (VA)
Bridgewater State U (MA)
Brock U (ON, Canada)
Bryant U (RI)
Bucknell U (PA)
Buena Vista U (IA)
Butler U (IN)
California Lutheran U (CA)
California Polytechnic State U, San Luis Obispo (CA)
California State U, Dominguez Hills (CA)
California State U, East Bay (CA)
California State U, Fullerton (CA)
California State U, Long Beach (CA)
California State U, Los Angeles (CA)
California State U, Northridge (CA)
California State U, San Marcos (CA)
Calvin Coll (MI)
Canisius Coll (NY)
Capital U (OH)
Carroll U (WI)
Carson-Newman U (TN)
Case Western Reserve U (OH)
Cedar Crest Coll (PA)
Centenary Coll of Louisiana (LA)
Central Connecticut State U (CT)
Central Michigan U (MI)
Chaminade U of Honolulu (HI)
Chapman U (CA)
Charleston Southern U (SC)
Chatham U (PA)
Chestnut Hill Coll (PA)
Christian Brothers U (TN)
Christopher Newport U (VA)
City Coll of the City U of New York (NY)
Claremont McKenna Coll (CA)
Clarke U (IA)
Clark U (MA)
Clemson U (SC)
Coastal Carolina U (SC)
Coe Coll (IA)
Colby Coll (ME)
Colgate U (NY)
The Coll at Brockport, State U of New York (NY)
Coll of Mount Saint Vincent (NY)
Coll of Saint Benedict (MN)
Coll of Saint Elizabeth (NJ)
The Coll of Saint Rose (NY)
The Coll of St. Scholastica (MN)
Coll of Staten Island of the City U of New York (NY)
The Coll of Wooster (OH)
The Colorado Coll (CO)
Colorado State U (CO)
Columbia Coll (SC)
Columbia U (NY)
Connecticut Coll (CT)
Converse Coll (SC)
Cornell Coll (IA)

Curry Coll (MA)
Daemen Coll (NY)
Dartmouth Coll (NH)
Denison U (OH)
DePaul U (IL)
DePauw U (IN)
DeSales U (PA)
Dickinson Coll (PA)
Doane U (NE)
Dominican U (IL)
Drake U (IA)
Drew U (NJ)
Duquesne U (PA)
Earlham Coll (IN)
East Carolina U (NC)
Eastern Mennonite U (VA)
Eastern Michigan U (MI)
Eastern Nazarene Coll (MA)
Eastern New Mexico U (NM)
Eastern U (PA)
East Stroudsburg U of Pennsylvania (PA)
Eckerd Coll (FL)
Elizabethtown Coll (PA)
Elmhurst Coll (IL)
Elon U (NC)
Emmanuel Coll (MA)
Fairfield U (CT)
Fairleigh Dickinson U, Florham Campus (NJ)
Fairleigh Dickinson U, Metropolitan Campus (NJ)
Ferris State U (MI)
Florida Gulf Coast U (FL)
Florida Inst of Technology (FL)
Florida State U (FL)
Fort Lewis Coll (CO)
Franklin & Marshall Coll (PA)
Gannon U (PA)
Geneva Coll (PA)
Georgetown Coll (KY)
Georgetown U (DC)
Georgia Inst of Technology (GA)
Georgian Court U (NJ)
Georgia Southern U–Armstrong Campus (GA)
Gettysburg Coll (PA)
Gonzaga U (WA)
Grand Valley State U (MI)
Grand View U (IA)
Grinnell Coll (IA)
Grove City Coll (PA)
Gustavus Adolphus Coll (MN)
Hamilton Coll (NY)
Hamline U (MN)
Harding U (AR)
Hartwick Coll (NY)
Harvard U (MA)
Haverford Coll (PA)
Hawai`i Pacific U (HI)
Heidelberg U (OH)
High Point U (NC)
Hillsdale Coll (MI)
Hiram Coll (OH)
Hobart and William Smith Colls (NY)
Hofstra U (NY)
Holy Family U (PA)
Hood Coll (MD)
Humboldt State U (CA)
Huntingdon Coll (AL)
Husson U (ME)
Idaho State U (ID)
Illinois State U (IL)
Indiana U Bloomington (IN)
Indiana U East (IN)
Indiana U Kokomo (IN)
Indiana U Northwest (IN)
Indiana U of Pennsylvania (PA)
Indiana U South Bend (IN)
Indiana Wesleyan U (IN)
Iona Coll (NY)
Iowa State U of Science and Technology (IA)
Ithaca Coll (NY)
John Brown U (AR)
Judson U (IL)
Juniata Coll (PA)
Kansas State U (KS)
Kennesaw State U (GA)
Kent State U (OH)
Kenyon Coll (OH)
Kettering U (MI)
King U (TN)
Knox Coll (IL)
Kutztown U of Pennsylvania (PA)
Lafayette Coll (PA)

LaGrange Coll (GA)
Lamar U (TX)
La Roche Coll (PA)
La Salle U (PA)
La Sierra U (CA)
Lawrence Technological U (MI)
Lawrence U (WI)
Lee U (TN)
Lehigh U (PA)
Lehman Coll of the City U of New York (NY)
Le Moyne Coll (NY)
Lewis U (IL)
Liberty U (VA)
Lipscomb U (TN)
Long Island U–LIU Brooklyn (NY)
Loras Coll (IA)
Louisiana State U and A&M Coll (LA)
Loyola Marymount U (CA)
Loyola U Chicago (IL)
Loyola U New Orleans (LA)
Lubbock Christian U (TX)
Lycoming Coll (PA)
Madonna U (MI)
Malone U (OH)
Manchester U (IN)
Manhattan Coll (NY)
Manhattanville Coll (NY)
Mansfield U of Pennsylvania (PA)
Marietta Coll (OH)
Marist Coll (NY)
Marlboro Coll (VT)
Mary Baldwin U (VA)
Marymount U (VA)
Maryville Coll (TN)
Maryville U of Saint Louis (MO)
McMurry U (TX)
McPherson Coll (KS)
Mercer U, Macon (GA)
Mercyhurst U (PA)
Merrimack Coll (MA)
Messiah Coll (PA)
Metropolitan State U of Denver (CO)
Miami U (OH)
Michigan State U (MI)
Middlebury Coll (VT)
Millsaps Coll (MS)
Mills Coll (CA)
Misericordia U (PA)
Mississippi State U (MS)
Missouri Baptist U (MO)
Missouri Western State U (MO)
Monmouth Coll (IL)
Montclair State U (NJ)
Moravian Coll (PA)
Mount Holyoke Coll (MA)
Mount Mercy U (IA)
Mount St. Joseph U (OH)
Mount Saint Mary's U (CA)
Mount St. Mary's U (MD)
Muhlenberg Coll (PA)
Nazareth Coll of Rochester (NY)
New Coll of Florida (FL)
New Jersey Inst of Technology (NJ)
Newman U (KS)
New Mexico State U (NM)
New York U (NY)
Niagara U (NY)
North Carolina State U (NC)
North Central Coll (IL)
Northeastern U (MA)
Northern Michigan U (MI)
Northwestern Coll (IA)
Northwestern U (IL)
Northwest Nazarene U (ID)
Oakland U (MI)
Oberlin Coll (OH)
Occidental Coll (CA)
Ohio Northern U (OH)
The Ohio State U (OH)
Oklahoma Baptist U (OK)
Oklahoma Christian U (OK)
Oklahoma City U (OK)
Oklahoma State U (OK)
Old Dominion U (VA)
Oral Roberts U (OK)
Otterbein U (OH)
Pace U (NY)
Pace U, Pleasantville Campus (NY)
Penn State Abington (PA)
Penn State Altoona (PA)
Penn State Beaver (PA)
Penn State Berks (PA)
Penn State Brandywine (PA)
Penn State DuBois (PA)

Penn State Erie, The Behrend Coll (PA)
Penn State Fayette, The Eberly Campus (PA)
Penn State Greater Allegheny (PA)
Penn State Hazleton (PA)
Penn State Lehigh Valley (PA)
Penn State Mont Alto (PA)
Penn State New Kensington (PA)
Penn State Schuylkill (PA)
Penn State Shenango (PA)
Penn State U Park (PA)
Penn State Wilkes-Barre (PA)
Penn State Worthington Scranton (PA)
Penn State York (PA)
Pitzer Coll (CA)
Point Loma Nazarene U (CA)
Portland State U (OR)
Presbyterian Coll (SC)
Providence Coll (RI)
Purchase Coll, State U of New York (NY)
Purdue U (IN)
Quinnipiac U (CT)
Ramapo Coll of New Jersey (NJ)
Reed Coll (OR)
Regis U (CO)
Rhode Island Coll (RI)
Rice U (TX)
Rider U (NJ)
Ripon Coll (WI)
Roanoke Coll (VA)
Roberts Wesleyan Coll (NY)
Rochester Inst of Technology (NY)
Rockford U (IL)
Rockhurst U (MO)
Roger Williams U (RI)
Rollins Coll (FL)
Roosevelt U (IL)
Rose-Hulman Inst of Technology (IN)
Rosemont Coll (PA)
Rowan U (NJ)
Rutgers U–New Brunswick (NJ)
Sacred Heart U (CT)
The Sage Colls (NY)
Saginaw Valley State U (MI)
Saint Anselm Coll (NH)
St. Bonaventure U (NY)
St. Catherine U (MN)
Saint John's U (MN)
Saint Joseph's U (PA)
St. Lawrence U (NY)
Saint Louis U (MO)
Saint Mary's Coll of California (CA)
St. Mary's Coll of Maryland (MD)
St. Mary's U (TX)
Saint Mary's U of Minnesota (MN)
Saint Michael's Coll (VT)
Saint Peter's U (NJ)
Saint Vincent Coll (PA)
Samford U (AL)
San Francisco State U (CA)
Santa Clara U (CA)
Schreiner U (TX)
Scripps Coll (CA)
Seattle Pacific U (WA)
Seattle U (WA)
Seton Hill U (PA)
Sewanee: The U of the South (TN)
Siena Coll (NY)
Simon Fraser U (BC, Canada)
Simpson Coll (IA)
Smith Coll (MA)
Southern Adventist U (TN)
Southern Methodist U (TX)
Southwestern Adventist U (TX)
Southwestern Coll (KS)
Southwestern U (TX)
Spelman Coll (GA)
Spring Hill Coll (AL)
State U of New York at Fredonia (NY)
State U of New York at New Paltz (NY)
State U of New York at Oswego (NY)
State U of New York at Plattsburgh (NY)
State U of New York Coll at Geneseo (NY)
State U of New York Coll at Old Westbury (NY)
State U of New York Coll at Oneonta (NY)

State U of New York Coll at Potsdam (NY)
Stephen F. Austin State U (TX)
Stetson U (FL)
Stevens Inst of Technology (NJ)
Stevenson U (MD)
Stockton U (NJ)
Stonehill Coll (MA)
Stony Brook U, State U of New York (NY)
Suffolk U (MA)
Susquehanna U (PA)
Syracuse U (NY)
Tabor Coll (KS)
Taylor U (IN)
Temple U (PA)
Tennessee Technological U (TN)
Texas A&M U (TX)
Texas Christian U (TX)
Texas State U (TX)
Texas Tech U (TX)
Texas Woman's U (TX)
Trent U (ON, Canada)
Trine U (IN)
Trinity Christian Coll (IL)
Trinity U (TX)
Tufts U (MA)
Tulane U (LA)
Union Coll (NY)
Université de Sherbrooke (QC, Canada)
U at Albany, State U of New York (NY)
U at Buffalo, the State U of New York (NY)
The U of Akron (OH)
The U of Arizona (AZ)
U of California, Los Angeles (CA)
U of California, Riverside (CA)
U of California, San Diego (CA)
U of California, Santa Cruz (CA)
U of Charleston (WV)
U of Cincinnati (OH)
U of Colorado Boulder (CO)
U of Colorado Colorado Springs (CO)
U of Dallas (TX)
U of Dayton (OH)
U of Denver (CO)
U of Evansville (IN)
U of Guelph (ON, Canada)
U of Hawaii at Manoa (HI)
U of Houston (TX)
U of Idaho (ID)
U of Illinois at Chicago (IL)
U of Illinois at Springfield (IL)
U of Jamestown (ND)
The U of Kansas (KS)
U of King's Coll (NS, Canada)
U of Maine (ME)
U of Mary Hardin-Baylor (TX)
U of Maryland, Coll Park (MD)
U of Massachusetts Boston (MA)
U of Miami (FL)
U of Michigan (MI)
U of Michigan–Dearborn (MI)
U of Michigan–Flint (MI)
U of Minnesota, Duluth (MN)
U of Minnesota, Twin Cities Campus (MN)
U of Missouri (MO)
U of Missouri–St. Louis (MO)
U of Montana (MT)
U of Mount Union (OH)
U of Nebraska–Lincoln (NE)
U of Nevada, Las Vegas (NV)
U of Nevada, Reno (NV)
U of New England (ME)
U of New Hampshire (NH)
U of New Mexico (NM)
The U of North Carolina at Greensboro (NC)
U of Northern Iowa (IA)
U of North Texas (TX)
U of Notre Dame (IN)
U of Oklahoma (OK)
U of Oregon (OR)
U of Pennsylvania (PA)
U of Puget Sound (WA)
U of Regina (SK, Canada)
U of St. Francis (IL)
U of Saint Joseph (CT)
U of St. Thomas (MN)
U of St. Thomas (TX)
U of San Diego (CA)
U of Saskatchewan (SK, Canada)
The U of Scranton (PA)

U of Southern California (CA)
U of Southern Indiana (IN)
The U of Tampa (FL)
The U of Texas at Austin (TX)
The U of Texas at Dallas (TX)
The U of Texas at San Antonio (TX)
U of the Incarnate Word (TX)
U of the Pacific (CA)
The U of Toledo (OH)
U of Toronto (ON, Canada)
The U of Tulsa (OK)
U of Vermont (VT)
U of Washington (WA)
U of Washington, Bothell (WA)
U of Waterloo (ON, Canada)
U of Wisconsin–La Crosse (WI)
U of Wisconsin–Madison (WI)
U of Wisconsin–Milwaukee (WI)
U of Wisconsin–Stevens Point (WI)
Ursinus Coll (PA)
Valparaiso U (IN)
Vanguard U of Southern California (CA)
Vassar Coll (NY)
Villanova U (PA)
Virginia Polytechnic Inst and State U (VA)
Wabash Coll (IN)
Wartburg Cell (IA)
Washington & Jefferson Coll (PA)
Washington and Lee U (VA)
Washington State U (WA)
Washington U in St. Louis (MO)
Weber State U (UT)
Wellesley Coll (MA)
Wells Coll (NY)
West Chester U of Pennsylvania (PA)
Western Kentucky U (KY)
Western Michigan U (MI)
Western State Colorado U (CO)
Western Washington U (WA)
Westminster Coll (PA)
West Virginia U (WV)
Wheaton Coll (MA)
Whitman Coll (WA)
Whittier Coll (CA)
Whitworth U (WA)
Widener U (PA)
Wilkes U (PA)
William Jewell Coll (MO)
Winona State U (MN)
Wisconsin Lutheran Coll (WI)
Worcester Polytechnic Inst (MA)
Wright State U (OH)
Wright State U–Lake Campus (OH)
Xavier U of Louisiana (LA)
Youngstown State U (OH)

BIOCHEMISTRY AND MOLECULAR BIOLOGY
Anderson U (SC)
Aquinas Coll (MI)
Bellarmine U (KY)
Belmont U (TN)
Benedictine U (IL)
Bethel Coll (IN)
Boston U (MA)
Bryn Mawr Coll (PA)
California State U, Long Beach (CA)
Carroll Coll (MT)
Centre Coll (KY)
Connecticut Coll (CT)
Culver-Stockton Coll (MO)
The Evergreen State Coll (WA)
Florida Southern Coll (FL)
Hampden-Sydney Coll (VA)
Harding U (AR)
Hardin-Simmons U (TX)
Hendrix Coll (AR)
Hope Coll (MI)
Houston Baptist U (TX)
Lebanon Valley Coll (PA)
Lincoln U (PA)
Linfield Coll (OR)
Marquette U (WI)
McPherson Coll (KS)
Michigan State U (MI)
Michigan Technological U (MI)
Middlebury Coll (VT)
Minnesota State U Moorhead (MN)
North Dakota State U (ND)
Oregon State U (OR)
Purdue U (IN)
Rhodes Coll (TN)
Salve Regina U (RI)

Simmons Coll (MA)
U of California, Irvine (CA)
U of Georgia (GA)
U of Maryland, Baltimore County (MD)
U of Massachusetts Amherst (MA)
U of Minnesota, Duluth (MN)
U of New Hampshire (NH)
U of Regina (SK, Canada)
U of Waterloo (ON, Canada)
Whitman Coll (WA)
Wittenberg U (OH)

BIOCHEMISTRY, BIOPHYSICS AND MOLECULAR BIOLOGY RELATED
Amherst Coll (MA)
Blackburn Coll (IL)
California Baptist U (CA)
Indiana U Kokomo (IN)
Marlboro Coll (VT)
Rensselaer Polytechnic Inst (NY)
St. Mary's U (TX)
Sweet Briar Coll (VA)
Towson U (MD)
U of Miami (FL)
U of Waterloo (ON, Canada)
Wichita State U (KS)

BIOENGINEERING AND BIOMEDICAL ENGINEERING
Alabama State U (AL)
Alfred U (NY)
Arizona State U at the Tempe campus (AZ)
Binghamton U, State U of New York (NY)
Boston U (MA)
Bucknell U (PA)
California Baptist U (CA)
California Inst of Technology (CA)
California Polytechnic State U, San Luis Obispo (CA)
California State U, Long Beach (CA)
Case Western Reserve U (OH)
The Catholic U of America (DC)
Central Michigan U (MI)
City Coll of the City U of New York (NY)
Clemson U (SC)
The Coll of New Jersey (NJ)
Colorado State U (CO)
Columbia U (NY)
Dartmouth Coll (NH)
Delaware State U (DE)
Drexel U (PA)
Duquesne U (PA)
Elon U (NC)
Endicott Coll (MA)
Fairfield U (CT)
Florida Gulf Coast U (FL)
Florida Inst of Technology (FL)
Florida Intl U (FL)
Gannon U (PA)
George Mason U (VA)
Georgia Inst of Technology (GA)
Harding U (AR)
Harvard U (MA)
Hofstra U (NY)
Indiana Tech (IN)
Indiana U–Purdue U Indianapolis (IN)
Iowa State U of Science and Technology (IA)
Johns Hopkins U (MD)
Lawrence Technological U (MI)
Lehigh U (PA)
LeTourneau U (TX)
Louisiana State U and A&M Coll (LA)
Loyola U Chicago (IL)
Marquette U (WI)
Massachusetts Inst of Technology (MA)
Miami U (OH)
Michigan Technological U (MI)
Milwaukee School of Eng (WI)
Mississippi State U (MS)
New Jersey Inst of Technology (NJ)
New York U (NY)
North Carolina State U (NC)
Northwestern U (IL)
The Ohio State U (OH)
Oral Roberts U (OK)
Oregon State U (OR)
Penn State Abington (PA)
Penn State Altoona (PA)

Penn State Beaver (PA)
Penn State Berks (PA)
Penn State Brandywine (PA)
Penn State DuBois (PA)
Penn State Erie, The Behrend Coll (PA)
Penn State Fayette, The Eberly Campus (PA)
Penn State Greater Allegheny (PA)
Penn State Hazleton (PA)
Penn State Lehigh Valley (PA)
Penn State Mont Alto (PA)
Penn State New Kensington (PA)
Penn State Schuylkill (PA)
Penn State Shenango (PA)
Penn State U Park (PA)
Penn State Wilkes-Barre (PA)
Penn State Worthington Scranton (PA)
Penn State York (PA)
Purdue U (IN)
Rensselaer Polytechnic Inst (NY)
Rice U (TX)
Rochester Inst of Technology (NY)
Rose-Hulman Inst of Technology (IN)
Rowan U (NJ)
Rutgers U–New Brunswick (NJ)
Saint Louis U (MO)
Saint Louis U–Madrid Campus (Spain)
Santa Clara U (CA)
Stanford U (CA)
Stevens Inst of Technology (NJ)
Stony Brook U, State U of New York (NY)
Syracuse U (NY)
Temple U (PA)
Texas A&M U (TX)
Trine U (IN)
Tufts U (MA)
Tulane U (LA)
Union Coll (NY)
U at Buffalo, the State U of New York (NY)
The U of Akron (OH)
The U of Alabama at Birmingham (AL)
The U of Arizona (AZ)
U of Arkansas (AR)
U of California, Davis (CA)
U of California, Irvine (CA)
U of California, Riverside (CA)
U of California, San Diego (CA)
U of California, Santa Cruz (CA)
U of Central Oklahoma (OK)
U of Cincinnati (OH)
U of Colorado Denver (CO)
U of Florida (FL)
U of Guelph (ON, Canada)
U of Houston (TX)
U of Illinois at Chicago (IL)
U of Louisville (KY)
U of Maine (ME)
U of Massachusetts Amherst (MA)
U of Massachusetts Dartmouth (MA)
U of Massachusetts Lowell (MA)
U of Memphis (TN)
U of Miami (FL)
U of Michigan (MI)
U of Michigan–Dearborn (MI)
U of Minnesota, Twin Cities Campus (MN)
U of Mount Union (OH)
U of Nevada, Reno (NV)
U of New Hampshire (NH)
U of North Texas (TX)
U of Oklahoma (OK)
U of Pennsylvania (PA)
U of Pittsburgh (PA)
U of Rhode Island (RI)
U of Rochester (NY)
U of South Carolina (SC)
U of Southern California (CA)
The U of Tennessee (TN)
The U of Texas at Austin (TX)
The U of Texas at Dallas (TX)
The U of Texas at San Antonio (TX)
U of the Pacific (CA)
The U of Toledo (OH)
U of Toronto (ON, Canada)
U of Utah (UT)
U of Vermont (VT)
U of Virginia (VA)
U of Washington (WA)
U of Waterloo (ON, Canada)

U of Wisconsin–Madison (WI)
Vanderbilt U (TN)
Virginia Commonwealth U (VA)
Washington State U (WA)
Washington U in St. Louis (MO)
Wayne State U (MI)
Wentworth Inst of Technology (MA)
Western New England U (MA)
West Virginia U (WV)
Wichita State U (KS)
Widener U (PA)
Worcester Polytechnic Inst (MA)
Wright State U (OH)
Wright State U–Lake Campus (OH)

BIOETHICS/MEDICAL ETHICS
Houston Baptist U (TX)
U of Miami (FL)
U of Richmond (VA)
U of Rochester (NY)

BIOINFORMATICS
Arizona State U at the Tempe campus (AZ)
Baylor U (TX)
California State U, San Bernardino (CA)
Canisius Coll (NY)
Davenport U, Grand Rapids (MI)
Gannon U (PA)
Inter American U of Puerto Rico, Bayamón Campus (PR)
Iowa State U of Science and Technology (IA)
Kettering U (MI)
Lebanese American U (Lebanon)
Loyola U Chicago (IL)
Marquette U (WI)
Michigan Technological U (MI)
New Jersey Inst of Technology (NJ)
Portland State U (OR)
Ramapo Coll of New Jersey (NJ)
Rensselaer Polytechnic Inst (NY)
Rochester Inst of Technology (NY)
Rowan U (NJ)
St. Bonaventure U (NY)
Saint Vincent Coll (PA)
Stevens Inst of Technology (NJ)
Trinity Christian Coll (IL)
U at Buffalo, the State U of New York (NY)
The U of Arizona (AZ)
U of California, San Diego (CA)
U of California, Santa Cruz (CA)
U of Denver (CO)
U of Maryland, Baltimore County (MD)
U of Memphis (TN)
U of Pennsylvania (PA)
U of Pittsburgh (PA)
U of St. Thomas (TX)
U of Saskatchewan (SK, Canada)
U of Waterloo (ON, Canada)
Virginia Commonwealth U (VA)
Wheaton Coll (MA)
Whitworth U (WA)
Worcester State U (MA)

BIOLOGICAL AND BIOMEDICAL SCIENCES RELATED
Baptist Coll of Health Sciences (TN)
Bethel U (MN)
Biola U (CA)
Boston U (MA)
Central Michigan U (MI)
Charleston Southern U (SC)
Christopher Newport U (VA)
Cornell U (NY)
Dakota State U (SD)
Delaware State U (DE)
Franciscan Missionaries of Our Lady U (LA)
Gordon State Coll (GA)
Grand Valley State U (MI)
Guilford Coll (NC)
Holy Names U (CA)
Indiana U Bloomington (IN)
Indiana U East (IN)
Kent State U (OH)
Mount Aloysius Coll (PA)
New York Inst of Technology (NY)
Oklahoma City U (OK)
Penn State Abington (PA)
Penn State Altoona (PA)
Penn State Beaver (PA)
Penn State Berks (PA)

Penn State Brandywine (PA)
Penn State DuBois (PA)
Penn State Erie, The Behrend Coll (PA)
Penn State Fayette, The Eberly Campus (PA)
Penn State Greater Allegheny (PA)
Penn State Hazleton (PA)
Penn State Lehigh Valley (PA)
Penn State Mont Alto (PA)
Penn State New Kensington (PA)
Penn State Schuylkill (PA)
Penn State Shenango (PA)
Penn State U Park (PA)
Penn State Wilkes-Barre (PA)
Penn State Worthington Scranton (PA)
Penn State York (PA)
Rochester Inst of Technology (NY)
Rutgers U–Newark (NJ)
The Sage Colls (NY)
Saint Mary's Coll of California (CA)
Siena Coll (NY)
Trevecca Nazarene U (TN)
Union Coll (NY)
U of Cincinnati (OH)
U of Maryland U Coll (MD)
U of Michigan (MI)
U of North Dakota (ND)
U of Wisconsin–Parkside (WI)
Ursuline Coll (OH)
Utah State U (UT)
Washington U in St. Louis (MO)
Western State Colorado U (CO)
Whitman Coll (WA)

BIOLOGICAL AND PHYSICAL SCIENCES
Adelphi U (NY)
Alaska Pacific U (AK)
Alfred U (NY)
Alice Lloyd Coll (KY)
Allegheny Coll (PA)
Arcadia U (PA)
Athabasca U (AB, Canada)
Averett U (VA)
Baldwin Wallace U (OH)
Bemidji State U (MN)
Bennington Coll (VT)
Brock U (ON, Canada)
Calumet Coll of Saint Joseph (IN)
Calvin Coll (MI)
Charleston Southern U (SC)
Clarion U of Pennsylvania (PA)
Coll of Saint Benedict (MN)
Coll of the Atlantic (ME)
Colorado Christian U (CO)
Concordia U Chicago (IL)
Cottey Coll (MO)
Covenant Coll (GA)
Dominican U (IL)
Drexel U (PA)
Eastern Michigan U (MI)
Eastern Nazarene Coll (MA)
East Stroudsburg U of Pennsylvania (PA)
Emory U (GA)
Eugene Lang Coll of Liberal Arts (NY)
The Evergreen State Coll (WA)
Fairleigh Dickinson U, Metropolitan Campus (NJ)
Fordham U (NY)
Gettysburg Coll (PA)
Indiana U Kokomo (IN)
Indiana U of Pennsylvania (PA)
Indiana U–Purdue U Indianapolis (IN)
John Carroll U (OH)
Johns Hopkins U (MD)
Keene State Coll (NH)
King's Coll (PA)
Lawrence U (WI)
Le Moyne Coll (NY)
Long Island U–LIU Brooklyn (NY)
Mansfield U of Pennsylvania (PA)
Maryville U of Saint Louis (MO)
The Master's U (CA)
Michigan State U (MI)
Middle Tennessee State U (TN)
Mississippi State U (MS)
Moravian Coll (PA)
New Coll of Florida (FL)
North Carolina Wesleyan Coll (NC)
North Central Coll (IL)
Northwestern U (IL)
Northwest Missouri State U (MO)

Penn State Abington (PA)
Penn State Altoona (PA)
Penn State Beaver (PA)
Penn State Berks (PA)
Penn State Brandywine (PA)
Penn State DuBois (PA)
Penn State Erie, The Behrend Coll (PA)
Penn State Fayette, The Eberly Campus (PA)
Penn State Greater Allegheny (PA)
Penn State Hazleton (PA)
Penn State Lehigh Valley (PA)
Penn State Mont Alto (PA)
Penn State New Kensington (PA)
Penn State Schuylkill (PA)
Penn State Shenango (PA)
Penn State U Park (PA)
Penn State Wilkes-Barre (PA)
Penn State Worthington Scranton (PA)
Penn State York (PA)
Portland State U (OR)
Purdue U (IN)
Quinnipiac U (CT)
Ramapo Coll of New Jersey (NJ)
Roberts Wesleyan Coll (NY)
Rockford U (IL)
Rutgers U–Camden (NJ)
Saint Anselm Coll (NH)
Saint John's U (MN)
Saint Louis U–Madrid Campus (Spain)
St. Mary's Coll of Maryland (MD)
St. Norbert Coll (WI)
Saint Peter's U (NJ)
Sam Houston State U (TX)
San Francisco State U (CA)
Sierra Nevada Coll (NV)
Simon Fraser U (BC, Canada)
Southern Arkansas U–Magnolia (AR)
State U of New York at Fredonia (NY)
Stony Brook U, State U of New York (NY)
Texas State U (TX)
Texas Tech U (TX)
Thomas Edison State U (NJ)
Trent U (ON, Canada)
Troy U (AL)
Union Coll (NY)
Union U (TN)
The U of Alabama at Birmingham (AL)
U of Alaska Fairbanks (AK)
U of Central Arkansas (AR)
U of Denver (CO)
U of Georgia (GA)
U of Houston–Downtown (TX)
U of Massachusetts Amherst (MA)
U of Northern Iowa (IA)
U of Notre Dame (IN)
U of Oregon (OR)
U of Pittsburgh (PA)
U of Puget Sound (WA)
U of Regina (SK, Canada)
U of Southern Indiana (IN)
U of Southern Mississippi (MS)
The U of Texas at San Antonio (TX)
U of Waterloo (ON, Canada)
The U of West Alabama (AL)
U of Wisconsin–Platteville (WI)
U of Wisconsin–River Falls (WI)
U of Wisconsin–Stevens Point (WI)
U of Wisconsin–Superior (WI)
Upper Iowa U (IA)
Vanguard U of Southern California (CA)
Virginia Commonwealth U (VA)
Walsh U (OH)
Warner Pacific Coll (OR)
Washington State U (WA)
Washington State U–Tri-Cities (WA)
Washington U in St. Louis (MO)
Western Washington U (WA)

BIOLOGICAL/BIOSYSTEMS ENGINEERING
Auburn U (AL)
Iowa State U of Science and Technology (IA)
Oakland U (MI)
The U of Arizona (AZ)
U of Arkansas (AR)
U of California, San Diego (CA)

U of Florida (FL)
U of Georgia (GA)
U of Guelph (ON, Canada)
U of Idaho (ID)
U of Nebraska–Lincoln (NE)

BIOLOGY/BIOLOGICAL SCIENCES
Abilene Christian U (TX)
Acadia U (NS, Canada)
Adams State U (CO)
Adelphi U (NY)
Agnes Scott Coll (GA)
Alabama State U (AL)
Albion Coll (MI)
Albright Coll (PA)
Alcorn State U (MS)
Alfred U (NY)
Alice Lloyd Coll (KY)
Allegheny Coll (PA)
Alma Coll (MI)
Alverno Coll (WI)
Ambrose U (AB, Canada)
American Intl Coll (MA)
American U (DC)
The American U in Cairo (Egypt)
Amherst Coll (MA)
Anderson U (IN)
Anderson U (SC)
Andrews U (MI)
Angelo State U (TX)
Appalachian State U (NC)
Aquinas Coll (MI)
Arcadia U (PA)
Arizona Christian U (AZ)
Arizona State U at the Polytechnic campus (AZ)
Arizona State U at the Tempe campus (AZ)
Arizona State U at the West campus (AZ)
Arkansas Tech U (AR)
Asbury U (KY)
Ashland U (OH)
Assumption Coll (MA)
Athens State U (AL)
Auburn U (AL)
Auburn U at Montgomery (AL)
Augsburg U (MN)
Augustana Coll (IL)
Augustana U (SD)
Aurora U (IL)
Austin Coll (TX)
Austin Peay State U (TN)
Averett U (VA)
Avila U (MO)
Azusa Pacific U (CA)
Baker U (KS)
Baldwin Wallace U (OH)
Ball State U (IN)
Bard Coll (NY)
Barnard Coll (NY)
Barry U (FL)
Barton Coll (NC)
Bates Coll (ME)
Baylor U (TX)
Bay Path U (MA)
Becker Coll (MA)
Belhaven U (MS)
Bellarmine U (KY)
Belmont U (TN)
Beloit Coll (WI)
Bemidji State U (MN)
Benedictine Coll (KS)
Benedictine U (IL)
Bennett Coll (NC)
Bennington Coll (VT)
Berea Coll (KY)
Berry Coll (GA)
Bethany Lutheran Coll (MN)
Bethel Coll (IN)
Bethel Coll (KS)
Bethel U (MN)
Bethel U (TN)
Bethune-Cookman U (FL)
Binghamton U, State U of New York (NY)
Biola U (CA)
Birmingham-Southern Coll (AL)
Blackburn Coll (IL)
Black Hills State U (SD)
Bloomsburg U of Pennsylvania (PA)
Bluefield Coll (VA)
Blue Mountain Coll (MS)
Bluffton U (OH)
Bob Jones U (SC)
Boise State U (ID)

Boston Coll (MA)
Boston U (MA)
Bowdoin Coll (ME)
Bowie State U (MD)
Bowling Green State U (OH)
Bradley U (IL)
Brandeis U (MA)
Brandon U (MB, Canada)
Brenau U (GA)
Brescia U (KY)
Brewton-Parker Coll (GA)
Bridgewater Coll (VA)
Bridgewater State U (MA)
Brigham Young U–Idaho (ID)
Brock U (ON, Canada)
Bryan Coll (TN)
Bryant U (RI)
Bryn Athyn Coll of the New Church (PA)
Bryn Mawr Coll (PA)
Bucknell U (PA)
Buena Vista U (IA)
Buffalo State Coll, State U of New York (NY)
Butler U (IN)
Caldwell U (NJ)
California Baptist U (CA)
California Inst of Technology (CA)
California Lutheran U (CA)
California Polytechnic State U, San Luis Obispo (CA)
California State Polytechnic U, Pomona (CA)
California State U, Dominguez Hills (CA)
California State U, East Bay (CA)
California State U, Fullerton (CA)
California State U, Long Beach (CA)
California State U, Los Angeles (CA)
California State U, Monterey Bay (CA)
California State U, Northridge (CA)
California State U, Sacramento (CA)
California State U, San Bernardino (CA)
California State U, San Marcos (CA)
California State U, Stanislaus (CA)
California U of Pennsylvania (PA)
Calvin Coll (MI)
Cameron U (OK)
Campbellsville U (KY)
Canisius Coll (NY)
Capital U (OH)
Cardinal Stritch U (WI)
Carleton Coll (MN)
Carlow U (PA)
Carnegie Mellon U (PA)
Carroll Coll (MT)
Carroll U (WI)
Carson-Newman U (TN)
Carthage Coll (WI)
Case Western Reserve U (OH)
Catawba Coll (NC)
The Catholic U of America (DC)
Cazenovia Coll (NY)
Cedar Crest Coll (PA)
Cedarville U (OH)
Centenary Coll of Louisiana (LA)
Central Connecticut State U (CT)
Central Methodist U (MO)
Central Michigan U (MI)
Central State U (OH)
Centre Coll (KY)
Chaminade U of Honolulu (HI)
Chapman U (CA)
Charleston Southern U (SC)
Chatham U (PA)
Chestnut Hill Coll (PA)
Chowan U (NC)
Christian Brothers U (TN)
Christopher Newport U (VA)
The Citadel, The Military Coll of South Carolina (SC)
City Coll of the City U of New York (NY)
Claremont McKenna Coll (CA)
Clark Atlanta U (GA)
Clarke U (IA)
Clarkson U (NY)
Clark U (MA)
Clayton State U (GA)
Clemson U (SC)
Cleveland State U (OH)

Coastal Carolina U (SC)
Coe Coll (IA)
Coker Coll (SC)
Colby Coll (ME)
Colgate U (NY)
The Coll at Brockport, State U of New York (NY)
Coll of Charleston (SC)
Coll of Coastal Georgia (GA)
The Coll of Idaho (ID)
Coll of Mount Saint Vincent (NY)
The Coll of New Jersey (NJ)
The Coll of New Rochelle (NY)
Coll of Saint Benedict (MN)
Coll of Saint Elizabeth (NJ)
Coll of Saint Mary (NE)
The Coll of Saint Rose (NY)
The Coll of St. Scholastica (MN)
Coll of Staten Island of the City U of New York (NY)
Coll of the Atlantic (ME)
Coll of the Holy Cross (MA)
The Coll of William and Mary (VA)
The Coll of Wooster (OH)
Colorado Christian U (CO)
Colorado Mesa U (CO)
Colorado State U (CO)
Colorado State U–Pueblo (CO)
Columbia Coll (MO)
Columbia Coll (SC)
Columbia U (NY)
Columbus State U (GA)
Concordia Coll–New York (NY)
Concordia U (QC, Canada)
Concordia U Chicago (IL)
Concordia U Irvine (CA)
Concordia U, Nebraska (NE)
Concordia U of Edmonton (AB, Canada)
Concordia U, St. Paul (MN)
Concordia U Wisconsin (WI)
Concord U (WV)
Connecticut Coll (CT)
Converse Coll (SC)
Cornell Coll (IA)
Cornell U (NY)
Cornerstone U (MI)
Covenant Coll (GA)
Creighton U (NE)
Culver-Stockton Coll (MO)
Curry Coll (MA)
Daemen Coll (NY)
Dallas Baptist U (TX)
Dartmouth Coll (NH)
Davidson Coll (NC)
Defiance Coll (OH)
Delaware State U (DE)
Delaware Valley U (PA)
Denison U (OH)
DePaul U (IL)
DePauw U (IN)
DeSales U (PA)
Dickinson Coll (PA)
Dickinson State U (ND)
Doane U (NE)
Dominican Coll (NY)
Dominican U (IL)
Dominican U of California (CA)
Drake U (IA)
Drew U (NJ)
Drexel U (PA)
Duquesne U (PA)
D'Youville Coll (NY)
Earlham Coll (IN)
East Carolina U (NC)
East Central U (OK)
Eastern Mennonite U (VA)
Eastern Michigan U (MI)
Eastern Nazarene Coll (MA)
Eastern New Mexico U (NM)
Eastern Oregon U (OR)
Eastern U (PA)
Eastern Washington U (WA)
East Stroudsburg U of Pennsylvania (PA)
East Tennessee State U (TN)
East Texas Baptist U (TX)
Eckerd Coll (FL)
Edgewood Coll (WI)
Elizabethtown Coll (PA)
Elmhurst Coll (IL)
Elms Coll (MA)
Elon U (NC)
Emmanuel Coll (GA)
Emmanuel Coll (MA)
Emory & Henry Coll (VA)
Emory U (GA)

Emporia State U (KS)
Evangel U (MO)
The Evergreen State Coll (WA)
Excelsior Coll (NY)
Fairfield U (CT)
Fairleigh Dickinson U, Florham Campus (NJ)
Fairleigh Dickinson U, Metropolitan Campus (NJ)
Farmingdale State Coll (NY)
Fayetteville State U (NC)
Felician U (NJ)
Ferris State U (MI)
Fisher Coll (MA)
Fitchburg State U (MA)
Florida Ag and Mech U (FL)
Florida Atlantic U (FL)
Florida Gulf Coast U (FL)
Florida Inst of Technology (FL)
Florida Intl U (FL)
Florida Southern Coll (FL)
Florida State U (FL)
Fordham U (NY)
Framingham State U (MA)
Franciscan Missionaries of Our Lady U (LA)
Francis Marion U (SC)
Franklin & Marshall Coll (PA)
Franklin Coll (IN)
Franklin Pierce U (NH)
Friends U (KS)
Frostburg State U (MD)
Furman U (SC)
Gannon U (PA)
Geneva Coll (PA)
George Mason U (VA)
Georgetown Coll (KY)
Georgetown U (DC)
The George Washington U (DC)
Georgia Coll & State U (GA)
Georgia Gwinnett Coll (GA)
Georgia Inst of Technology (GA)
Georgian Court U (NJ)
Georgia Southern U (GA)
Georgia Southern U–Armstrong Campus (GA)
Georgia Southwestern State U (GA)
Georgia State U (GA)
Gettysburg Coll (PA)
Gonzaga U (WA)
Gordon Coll (MA)
Goshen Coll (IN)
Governors State U (IL)
Graceland U (IA)
Grambling State U (LA)
Grand Valley State U (MI)
Grand View U (IA)
Green Mountain Coll (VT)
Greensboro Coll (NC)
Greenville U (IL)
Grinnell Coll (IA)
Grove City Coll (PA)
Guilford Coll (NC)
Gustavus Adolphus Coll (MN)
Gwynedd Mercy U (PA)
Hamilton Coll (NY)
Hamline U (MN)
Hampden-Sydney Coll (VA)
Hampshire Coll (MA)
Hampton U (VA)
Hannibal-LaGrange U (MO)
Harding U (AR)
Hardin-Simmons U (TX)
Harrisburg U of Science and Technology (PA)
Harris-Stowe State U (MO)
Hartwick Coll (NY)
Harvard U (MA)
Harvey Mudd Coll (CA)
Haverford Coll (PA)
Hawai'i Pacific U (HI)
Heidelberg U (OH)
Hendrix Coll (AR)
High Point U (NC)
Hillsdale Coll (MI)
Hiram Coll (OH)
Hobart and William Smith Colls (NY)
Hofstra U (NY)
Hollins U (VA)
Holy Family U (PA)
Holy Names U (CA)
Hood Coll (MD)
Hope Coll (MI)
Houston Baptist U (TX)
Howard Payne U (TX)

Humboldt State U (CA)
Hunter Coll of the City U of New York (NY)
Huntingdon Coll (AL)
Husson U (ME)
Huston-Tillotson U (TX)
Idaho State U (ID)
Illinois Coll (IL)
Illinois State U (IL)
Illinois Wesleyan U (IL)
Immaculata U (PA)
Indiana State U (IN)
Indiana U Bloomington (IN)
Indiana U East (IN)
Indiana U Kokomo (IN)
Indiana U Northwest (IN)
Indiana U of Pennsylvania (PA)
Indiana U–Purdue U Indianapolis (IN)
Indiana U South Bend (IN)
Indiana U Southeast (IN)
Indiana Wesleyan U (IN)
Inter American U of Puerto Rico, Aguadilla Campus (PR)
Inter American U of Puerto Rico, Barranquitas Campus (PR)
Inter American U of Puerto Rico, Bayamón Campus (PR)
Inter American U of Puerto Rico, Fajardo Campus (PR)
Inter American U of Puerto Rico, Metropolitan Campus (PR)
Inter American U of Puerto Rico, San Germán Campus (PR)
Iona Coll (NY)
Iowa State U of Science and Technology (IA)
Ithaca Coll (NY)
Jackson State U (MS)
Jacksonville U (FL)
James Madison U (VA)
John Brown U (AR)
John Carroll U (OH)
Johns Hopkins U (MD)
Johnson C. Smith U (NC)
Judson U (IL)
Juniata Coll (PA)
Kalamazoo Coll (MI)
Kansas State U (KS)
Kansas Wesleyan U (KS)
Kean U (NJ)
Keene State Coll (NH)
Kennesaw State U (GA)
Kent State U (OH)
Kent State U at Stark (OH)
Kentucky State U (KY)
Kenyon Coll (OH)
Kettering U (MI)
King's Coll (PA)
King U (TN)
Knox Coll (IL)
Kutztown U of Pennsylvania (PA)
Lafayette Coll (PA)
LaGrange Coll (GA)
Lamar U (TX)
Langston U (OK)
La Roche Coll (PA)
La Salle U (PA)
La Sierra U (CA)
Lawrence U (WI)
Lebanese American U (Lebanon)
Lebanon Valley Coll (PA)
Lee U (TN)
Lehigh U (PA)
Lehman Coll of the City U of New York (NY)
Le Moyne Coll (NY)
Lenoir-Rhyne U (NC)
LeTourneau U (TX)
Lewis U (IL)
Liberty U (VA)
Life U (GA)
Limestone Coll (SC)
Lincoln Memorial U (TN)
Lincoln U (MO)
Lincoln U (PA)
Lindenwood U (MO)
Lindsey Wilson Coll (KY)
Linfield Coll (OR)
Lipscomb U (TN)
Lock Haven U of Pennsylvania (PA)
Logan U (MO)
Long Island U–LIU Brooklyn (NY)
Long Island U–LIU Post (NY)
Longwood U (VA)
Loras Coll (IA)
Louisiana Coll (LA)

Louisiana State U and A&M Coll (LA)
Loyola Marymount U (CA)
Loyola U Chicago (IL)
Loyola U New Orleans (LA)
Lubbock Christian U (TX)
Luther Coll (IA)
Lycoming Coll (PA)
Lynchburg Coll (VA)
Lynn U (FL)
Lyon Coll (AR)
Macalester Coll (MN)
Madonna U (MI)
Malone U (OH)
Manchester U (IN)
Manhattan Coll (NY)
Manhattanville Coll (NY)
Mansfield U of Pennsylvania (PA)
Maranatha Baptist U (WI)
Marian U (IN)
Marian U (WI)
Marietta Coll (OH)
Marist Coll (NY)
Marlboro Coll (VT)
Marquette U (WI)
Marshall U (WV)
Mary Baldwin U (VA)
Marymount California U (CA)
Marymount Manhattan Coll (NY)
Marymount U (VA)
Maryville Coll (TN)
Maryville U of Saint Louis (MO)
Marywood U (PA)
Massachusetts Coll of Liberal Arts (MA)
Massachusetts Inst of Technology (MA)
The Master's U (CA)
McDaniel Coll (MD)
McKendree U (IL)
McMurry U (TX)
McNeese State U (LA)
McPherson Coll (KS)
Medgar Evers Coll of the City U of New York (NY)
Mercer U, Macon (GA)
Mercy Coll (NY)
Mercy Coll of Ohio (OH)
Mercyhurst U (PA)
Meredith Coll (NC)
Merrimack Coll (MA)
Messiah Coll (PA)
Metropolitan State U of Denver (CO)
Miami Dade Coll (FL)
Miami U (OH)
Michigan State U (MI)
Michigan Technological U (MI)
Mid-America Christian U (OK)
MidAmerica Nazarene U (KS)
Mid-Atlantic Christian U (NC)
Middlebury Coll (VT)
Middle Georgia State U (GA)
Middle Tennessee State U (TN)
Millersville U of Pennsylvania (PA)
Milligan Coll (TN)
Millikin U (IL)
Millsaps Coll (MS)
Mills Coll (CA)
Minnesota State U Moorhead (MN)
Minot State U (ND)
Misericordia U (PA)
Mississippi State U (MS)
Missouri Baptist U (MO)
Missouri State U (MO)
Missouri U of Science and Technology (MO)
Missouri Valley Coll (MO)
Missouri Western State U (MO)
Molloy Coll (NY)
Monmouth Coll (IL)
Montana Tech of The U of Montana (MT)
Montclair State U (NJ)
Moravian Coll (PA)
Morehead State U (KY)
Morehouse Coll (GA)
Morningside Coll (IA)
Morris Coll (SC)
Mount Aloysius Coll (PA)
Mount Holyoke Coll (MA)
Mount Marty Coll (SD)
Mount Mary U (WI)
Mount Mercy U (IA)
Mount St. Joseph U (OH)
Mount Saint Mary Coll (NY)
Mount Saint Mary's U (CA)

Mount St. Mary's U (MD)
Mount Vernon Nazarene U (OH)
Muhlenberg Coll (PA)
Murray State U (KY)
National U (CA)
Nazareth Coll of Rochester (NY)
Neumann U (PA)
Newberry Coll (SC)
New Coll of Florida (FL)
New Jersey City U (NJ)
New Jersey Inst of Technology (NJ)
Newman U (KS)
New Mexico Highlands U (NM)
New Mexico Inst of Mining and Technology (NM)
New Mexico State U (NM)
New York Inst of Technology (NY)
New York U (NY)
Niagara U (NY)
North Carolina Central U (NC)
North Carolina State U (NC)
North Carolina Wesleyan Coll (NC)
North Central Coll (IL)
North Dakota State U (ND)
Northeastern State U (OK)
Northeastern U (MA)
Northern Arizona U (AZ)
Northern Illinois U (IL)
Northern Kentucky U (KY)
Northern Michigan U (MI)
Northern State U (SD)
Northern Vermont U–Lyndon (VT)
North Greenville U (SC)
Northland Coll (WI)
Northwest Christian U (OR)
Northwestern Coll (IA)
Northwestern Oklahoma State U (OK)
Northwestern State U of Louisiana (LA)
Northwestern U (IL)
Northwest Missouri State U (MO)
Northwest Nazarene U (ID)
Northwest U (WA)
Notre Dame de Namur U (CA)
Nova Southeastern U (FL)
Nyack Coll (NY)
Oakland City U (IN)
Oakland U (MI)
Oberlin Coll (OH)
Occidental Coll (CA)
Oglethorpe U (GA)
Ohio Dominican U (OH)
Ohio Northern U (OH)
The Ohio State U (OH)
The Ohio State U at Lima (OH)
The Ohio State U at Marion (OH)
Ohio U (OH)
Ohio Wesleyan U (OH)
Oklahoma Baptist U (OK)
Oklahoma Christian U (OK)
Oklahoma City U (OK)
Oklahoma State U (OK)
Old Dominion U (VA)
Olivet Nazarene U (IL)
Oral Roberts U (OK)
Oregon Inst of Technology (OR)
Oregon State U (OR)
Ottawa U (KS)
Otterbein U (OH)
Ouachita Baptist U (AR)
Our Lady of the Lake U (TX)
Pace U (NY)
Pace U, Pleasantville Campus (NY)
Pacific Lutheran U (WA)
Palm Beach Atlantic U (FL)
Penn State Abington (PA)
Penn State Altoona (PA)
Penn State Beaver (PA)
Penn State Berks (PA)
Penn State Brandywine (PA)
Penn State DuBois (PA)
Penn State Erie, The Behrend Coll (PA)
Penn State Fayette, The Eberly Campus (PA)
Penn State Greater Allegheny (PA)
Penn State Hazleton (PA)
Penn State Lehigh Valley (PA)
Penn State Mont Alto (PA)
Penn State New Kensington (PA)
Penn State Schuylkill (PA)
Penn State Shenango (PA)
Penn State U Park (PA)
Penn State Wilkes-Barre (PA)
Penn State Worthington Scranton (PA)

Penn State York (PA)
Pepperdine U, Malibu (CA)
Pfeiffer U (NC)
Piedmont Coll (GA)
Pine Manor Coll (MA)
Pittsburg State U (KS)
Pitzer Coll (CA)
Point Loma Nazarene U (CA)
Point Park U (PA)
Point U (GA)
Pomona Coll (CA)
Portland State U (OR)
Post U (CT)
Prairie View A&M U (TX)
Presbyterian Coll (SC)
Principia Coll (IL)
Providence Coll (RI)
Purchase Coll, State U of New York (NY)
Purdue U (IN)
Purdue U Northwest (IN)
Queens Coll of the City U of New York (NY)
Quinnipiac U (CT)
Radford U (VA)
Ramapo Coll of New Jersey (NJ)
Randolph Coll (VA)
Randolph-Macon Coll (VA)
Redeemer U Coll (ON, Canada)
Reed Coll (OR)
Regis U (CO)
Rensselaer Polytechnic Inst (NY)
Rhode Island Coll (RI)
Rhodes Coll (TN)
Rice U (TX)
Rider U (NJ)
Ripon Coll (WI)
Rivier U (NH)
Roanoke Coll (VA)
Robert Morris U (PA)
Roberts Wesleyan Coll (NY)
Rochester Inst of Technology (NY)
Rockford U (IL)
Rockhurst U (MO)
Rocky Mountain Coll (MT)
Rogers State U (OK)
Roger Williams U (RI)
Rollins Coll (FL)
Roosevelt U (IL)
Rose-Hulman Inst of Technology (IN)
Rosemont Coll (PA)
Rowan U (NJ)
Rust Coll (MS)
Rutgers U–Camden (NJ)
Rutgers U–Newark (NJ)
Rutgers U–New Brunswick (NJ)
Sacred Heart U (CT)
The Sage Colls (NY)
Saginaw Valley State U (MI)
St. Ambrose U (IA)
St. Andrews U (NC)
Saint Anselm Coll (NH)
Saint Augustine's U (NC)
St. Bonaventure U (NY)
St. Catherine U (MN)
Saint Francis U (PA)
St. John Fisher Coll (NY)
Saint John's U (MN)
St. John's U (NY)
Saint Joseph's Coll, Long Island Campus (NY)
St. Joseph's Coll, New York (NY)
Saint Joseph's U (PA)
St. Lawrence U (NY)
Saint Leo U (FL)
Saint Louis U (MO)
Saint Martin's U (WA)
Saint Mary-of-the-Woods Coll (IN)
Saint Mary's Coll of California (CA)
St. Mary's Coll of Maryland (MD)
St. Mary's U (TX)
Saint Mary's U of Minnesota (MN)
Saint Michael's Coll (VT)
St. Norbert Coll (WI)
St. Olaf Coll (MN)
Saint Peter's U (NJ)
St. Thomas Aquinas Coll (NY)
St. Thomas U (FL)
Saint Vincent Coll (PA)
Salisbury U (MD)
Salve Regina U (RI)
Samford U (AL)
Sam Houston State U (TX)
San Diego State U (CA)
San Francisco State U (CA)
Santa Clara U (CA)

Sarah Lawrence Coll (NY)
Schreiner U (TX)
Scripps Coll (CA)
Seattle Pacific U (WA)
Seattle U (WA)
Seton Hill U (PA)
Sewanee: The U of the South (TN)
Shawnee State U (OH)
Shaw U (NC)
Shenandoah U (VA)
Shepherd U (WV)
Shippensburg U of Pennsylvania (PA)
Shorter U (GA)
Siena Coll (NY)
Silver Lake Coll of the Holy Family (WI)
Simmons Coll (MA)
Simon Fraser U (BC, Canada)
Simpson Coll (IA)
Skidmore Coll (NY)
Slippery Rock U of Pennsylvania (PA)
Smith Coll (MA)
Sonoma State U (CA)
Southeastern Louisiana U (LA)
Southeastern Oklahoma State U (OK)
Southeastern U (FL)
Southeast Missouri State U (MO)
Southern Adventist U (TN)
Southern Arkansas U–Magnolia (AR)
Southern Illinois U Carbondale (IL)
Southern Illinois U Edwardsville (IL)
Southern Methodist U (TX)
Southern Utah U (UT)
Southern Vermont Coll (VT)
Southwest Baptist U (MO)
Southwestern Adventist U (TX)
Southwestern Coll (KS)
Southwestern U (TX)
Spelman Coll (GA)
Spring Hill Coll (AL)
Stanford U (CA)
State U of New York at Fredonia (NY)
State U of New York at New Paltz (NY)
State U of New York at Oswego (NY)
State U of New York at Plattsburgh (NY)
State U of New York Coll at Cortland (NY)
State U of New York Coll at Geneseo (NY)
State U of New York Coll at Old Westbury (NY)
State U of New York Coll at Oneonta (NY)
State U of New York Coll at Potsdam (NY)
State U of New York Polytechnic Inst (NY)
Stephen F. Austin State U (TX)
Stetson U (FL)
Stevens Inst of Technology (NJ)
Stevenson U (MD)
Stockton U (NJ)
Stonehill Coll (MA)
Stony Brook U, State U of New York (NY)
Suffolk U (MA)
Susquehanna U (PA)
Sweet Briar Coll (VA)
Syracuse U (NY)
Tabor Coll (KS)
Tarleton State U (TX)
Taylor U (IN)
Temple U (PA)
Tennessee Technological U (TN)
Tennessee Wesleyan U (TN)
Texas A&M Intl U (TX)
Texas A&M U (TX)
Texas A&M U–Commerce (TX)
Texas A&M U–Corpus Christi (TX)
Texas A&M U–Kingsville (TX)
Texas A&M U–Texarkana (TX)
Texas Christian U (TX)
Texas Lutheran U (TX)
Texas State U (TX)
Texas Tech U (TX)
Texas Woman's U (TX)
Thomas U (GA)
Toccoa Falls Coll (GA)

Towson U (MD)
Transylvania U (KY)
Trent U (ON, Canada)
Trevecca Nazarene U (TN)
Trine U (IN)
Trinity Christian Coll (IL)
Trinity U (TX)
Troy U (AL)
Truett McConnell U (GA)
Truman State U (MO)
Tufts U (MA)
Tulane U (LA)
Tusculum Coll (TN)
Union Coll (NE)
Union Coll (NY)
Union U (TN)
United States Military Acad (NY)
Université de Sherbrooke (QC, Canada)
U at Albany, State U of New York (NY)
U at Buffalo, the State U of New York (NY)
The U of Akron (OH)
The U of Alabama (AL)
The U of Alabama at Birmingham (AL)
U of Alaska Fairbanks (AK)
The U of Arizona (AZ)
U of Arkansas (AR)
U of Bridgeport (CT)
U of California, Davis (CA)
U of California, Irvine (CA)
U of California, Los Angeles (CA)
U of California, Riverside (CA)
U of California, San Diego (CA)
U of California, Santa Barbara (CA)
U of California, Santa Cruz (CA)
U of Central Arkansas (AR)
U of Central Florida (FL)
U of Central Missouri (MO)
U of Central Oklahoma (OK)
U of Charleston (WV)
U of Chicago (IL)
U of Cincinnati (OH)
U of Colorado Colorado Springs (CO)
U of Colorado Denver (CO)
U of Dallas (TX)
U of Dayton (OH)
U of Denver (CO)
U of Dubuque (IA)
U of Evansville (IN)
The U of Findlay (OH)
U of Florida (FL)
U of Georgia (GA)
U of Guam (GU)
U of Guelph (ON, Canada)
U of Hartford (CT)
U of Hawaii at Manoa (HI)
U of Houston (TX)
U of Houston–Clear Lake (TX)
U of Houston–Downtown (TX)
U of Idaho (ID)
U of Illinois at Chicago (IL)
U of Illinois at Springfield (IL)
U of Jamestown (ND)
The U of Kansas (KS)
U of Kentucky (KY)
U of King's Coll (NS, Canada)
U of La Verne (CA)
U of Louisiana at Monroe (LA)
U of Louisville (KY)
U of Maine (ME)
U of Maine at Farmington (ME)
U of Maine at Fort Kent (ME)
U of Maine at Machias (ME)
U of Maine at Presque Isle (ME)
U of Mary Hardin-Baylor (TX)
U of Maryland, Baltimore County (MD)
U of Maryland, Coll Park (MD)
U of Maryland Eastern Shore (MD)
U of Mary Washington (VA)
U of Massachusetts Amherst (MA)
U of Massachusetts Boston (MA)
U of Massachusetts Dartmouth (MA)
U of Massachusetts Lowell (MA)
U of Memphis (TN)
U of Miami (FL)
U of Michigan (MI)
U of Michigan–Dearborn (MI)
U of Michigan–Flint (MI)
U of Minnesota, Crookston (MN)
U of Minnesota, Duluth (MN)
U of Minnesota, Morris (MN)

U of Minnesota, Twin Cities Campus (MN)
U of Missouri (MO)
U of Missouri–St. Louis (MO)
U of Mobile (AL)
U of Montana (MT)
U of Montevallo (AL)
U of Mount Union (OH)
U of Nebraska at Kearney (NE)
U of Nebraska–Lincoln (NE)
U of Nevada, Las Vegas (NV)
U of Nevada, Reno (NV)
U of New England (ME)
U of New Hampshire (NH)
U of New Haven (CT)
U of New Mexico (NM)
U of New Orleans (LA)
U of North Alabama (AL)
U of North Carolina at Asheville (NC)
The U of North Carolina at Chapel Hill (NC)
The U of North Carolina at Charlotte (NC)
The U of North Carolina at Greensboro (NC)
The U of North Carolina at Pembroke (NC)
The U of North Carolina Wilmington (NC)
U of North Dakota (ND)
U of Northern Colorado (CO)
U of Northern Iowa (IA)
U of North Florida (FL)
U of North Georgia (GA)
U of North Texas (TX)
U of Notre Dame (IN)
U of Oregon (OR)
U of Pennsylvania (PA)
U of Pikeville (KY)
U of Pittsburgh (PA)
U of Pittsburgh at Bradford (PA)
U of Pittsburgh at Greensburg (PA)
U of Providence (MT)
U of Puerto Rico–Humacao (PR)
U of Puget Sound (WA)
U of Regina (SK, Canada)
U of Rhode Island (RI)
U of Richmond (VA)
U of Rochester (NY)
U of St. Francis (IL)
U of Saint Francis (IN)
U of Saint Joseph (CT)
U of Saint Mary (KS)
U of St. Thomas (MN)
U of St. Thomas (TX)
U of San Diego (CA)
U of San Francisco (CA)
U of Saskatchewan (SK, Canada)
U of Science and Arts of Oklahoma (OK)
The U of Scranton (PA)
U of Sioux Falls (SD)
U of South Carolina (SC)
U of South Carolina Aiken (SC)
U of South Dakota (SD)
U of Southern California (CA)
U of Southern Indiana (IN)
U of Southern Maine (ME)
U of Southern Mississippi (MS)
U of South Florida, St. Petersburg (FL)
U of South Florida Sarasota-Manatee (FL)
The U of Tampa (FL)
The U of Tennessee (TN)
The U of Tennessee at Chattanooga (TN)
The U of Tennessee at Martin (TN)
The U of Texas at Austin (TX)
The U of Texas at Dallas (TX)
The U of Texas at El Paso (TX)
The U of Texas at San Antonio (TX)
The U of Texas of the Permian Basin (TX)
The U of Texas Rio Grande Valley (TX)
U of the Fraser Valley (BC, Canada)
U of the Incarnate Word (TX)
U of the Pacific (CA)
U of the Virgin Islands (VI)
The U of Toledo (OH)
U of Toronto (ON, Canada)
The U of Tulsa (OK)
U of Utah (UT)
U of Vermont (VT)

U of Virginia (VA)
The U of Virginia's Coll at Wise (VA)
U of Washington (WA)
U of Washington, Bothell (WA)
U of Waterloo (ON, Canada)
The U of West Alabama (AL)
U of West Georgia (GA)
U of Wisconsin–Eau Claire (WI)
U of Wisconsin–La Crosse (WI)
U of Wisconsin–Madison (WI)
U of Wisconsin–Milwaukee (WI)
U of Wisconsin–Platteville (WI)
U of Wisconsin–River Falls (WI)
U of Wisconsin–Stevens Point (WI)
U of Wisconsin–Superior (WI)
U of Wisconsin–Whitewater (WI)
U of Wyoming (WY)
Upper Iowa U (IA)
Ursinus Coll (PA)
Ursuline Coll (OH)
Utah State U (UT)
Utah Valley U (UT)
Utica Coll (NY)
Valdosta State U (GA)
Valley City State U (ND)
Valparaiso U (IN)
Vanderbilt U (TN)
Vanguard U of Southern California (CA)
Vassar Coll (NY)
Villanova U (PA)
Virginia Commonwealth U (VA)
Virginia Military Inst (VA)
Virginia Polytechnic Inst and State U (VA)
Virginia Wesleyan U (VA)
Wabash Coll (IN)
Wagner Coll (NY)
Wake Forest U (NC)
Waldorf U (IA)
Walsh U (OH)
Wartburg Coll (IA)
Washington & Jefferson Coll (PA)
Washington and Lee U (VA)
Washington Coll (MD)
Washington State U (WA)
Washington State U–Tri-Cities (WA)
Washington State U–Vancouver (WA)
Washington U in St. Louis (MO)
Wayland Baptist U (TX)
Waynesburg U (PA)
Wayne State Coll (NE)
Wayne State U (MI)
Webster U (MO)
Wellesley Coll (MA)
Wells Coll (NY)
Wesleyan U (CT)
West Chester U of Pennsylvania (PA)
Western Connecticut State U (CT)
Western Illinois U (IL)
Western Kentucky U (KY)
Western Michigan U (MI)
Western New England U (MA)
Western Oregon U (OR)
Western State Colorado U (CO)
Western Washington U (WA)
Westfield State U (MA)
Westminster Coll (PA)
Westminster Coll (UT)
Westmont Coll (CA)
West Texas A&M U (TX)
West Virginia State U (WV)
West Virginia U (WV)
West Virginia U Inst of Technology (WV)
West Virginia Wesleyan Coll (WV)
Wheaton Coll (IL)
Wheaton Coll (MA)
Whitman Coll (WA)
Whittier Coll (CA)
Whitworth U (WA)
Wichita State U (KS)
Widener U (PA)
Wilkes U (PA)
Willamette U (OR)
William Jewell Coll (MO)
William Paterson U of New Jersey (NJ)
William Peace U (NC)
William Penn U (IA)
Williams Coll (MA)
William Woods U (MO)
Winona State U (MN)

Winthrop U (SC)
Wisconsin Lutheran Coll (WI)
Wittenberg U (OH)
Wofford Coll (SC)
Worcester Polytechnic Inst (MA)
Worcester State U (MA)
Wright State U (OH)
Xavier U of Louisiana (LA)
York Coll of Pennsylvania (PA)
Youngstown State U (OH)

BIOLOGY/BIOTECHNOLOGY LABORATORY TECHNICIAN

Cleveland State U (OH)
Davenport U, Grand Rapids (MI)
Delaware State U (DE)
Penn State Abington (PA)
Penn State Altoona (PA)
Penn State Beaver (PA)
Penn State Berks (PA)
Penn State Brandywine (PA)
Penn State DuBois (PA)
Penn State Erie, The Behrend Coll (PA)
Penn State Fayette, The Eberly Campus (PA)
Penn State Greater Allegheny (PA)
Penn State Hazleton (PA)
Penn State Lehigh Valley (PA)
Penn State Mont Alto (PA)
Penn State New Kensington (PA)
Penn State Schuylkill (PA)
Penn State Shenango (PA)
Penn State U Park (PA)
Penn State Wilkes-Barre (PA)
Penn State Worthington Scranton (PA)
Penn State York (PA)
State U of New York at Fredonia (NY)
State U of New York Coll at Oneonta (NY)
Ursuline Coll (OH)

BIOLOGY TEACHER EDUCATION

Abilene Christian U (TX)
Adams State U (CO)
Albion Coll (MI)
Aquinas Coll (MI)
Arizona Christian U (AZ)
Arkansas Tech U (AR)
Ashland U (OH)
Augustana U (IL)
Ball State U (IN)
Baylor U (TX)
Bay Path U (MA)
Bethel Coll (IN)
Bethune-Cookman U (FL)
Biola U (CA)
Blackburn Coll (IL)
Bluefield Coll (VA)
Blue Mountain Coll (MS)
Bowling Green State U (OH)
Bradley U (IL)
Bridgewater State U (MA)
Brigham Young U–Idaho (ID)
Bryan Coll (TN)
Buena Vista U (IA)
California State U, Long Beach (CA)
Calvin Coll (MI)
Campbellsville U (KY)
Canisius Coll (NY)
Carroll Coll (MT)
Carroll U (WI)
Cedarville U (OH)
Central Methodist U (MO)
Central Michigan U (MI)
City Coll of the City U of New York (NY)
Coker Coll (SC)
The Coll of New Jersey (NJ)
Coll of Saint Mary (NE)
The Coll of Saint Rose (NY)
Coll of Staten Island of the City U of New York (NY)
Coll of the Ozarks (MO)
Concordia U Chicago (IL)
Concordia U, St. Paul (MN)
Corban U (OR)
Cornerstone U (MI)
Culver-Stockton Coll (MO)
Daemen Coll (NY)
Dakota State U (SD)
Daytona State Coll (FL)
Delaware State U (DE)
Dickinson State U (ND)

Dominican Coll (NY)
East Central U (OK)
Eastern Michigan U (MI)
Eastern Nazarene Coll (MA)
Eastern Washington U (WA)
East Texas Baptist U (TX)
Edgewood Coll (WI)
Elmhurst Coll (IL)
Emory & Henry Coll (VA)
Evangel U (MO)
Ferris State U (MI)
Fitchburg State U (MA)
Florida Inst of Technology (FL)
Florida Southern Coll (FL)
Florida State U (FL)
Fort Lewis Coll (CO)
Franklin Coll (IN)
Friends U (KS)
Gordon State Coll (GA)
Goshen Coll (IN)
Grand Valley State U (MI)
Green Mountain Coll (VT)
Greensboro Coll (NC)
Greenville U (IL)
Grove City Coll (PA)
Gustavus Adolphus Coll (MN)
Gwynedd Mercy U (PA)
Harding U (AR)
Hofstra U (NY)
Holy Family U (PA)
Hope Coll (MI)
Houston Baptist U (TX)
Howard Payne U (TX)
Hunter Coll of the City U of New York (NY)
Huntingdon Coll (AL)
Illinois State U (IL)
Immaculata U (PA)
Indiana U Bloomington (IN)
Indiana U Northwest (IN)
Indiana U South Bend (IN)
Indiana U Southeast (IN)
Indiana Wesleyan U (IN)
Inter American U of Puerto Rico, Aguadilla Campus (PR)
Inter American U of Puerto Rico, Barranquitas Campus (PR)
Inter American U of Puerto Rico, Fajardo Campus (PR)
Inter American U of Puerto Rico, San Germán Campus (PR)
Iona Coll (NY)
Ithaca Coll (NY)
Juniata Coll (PA)
Kansas Wesleyan U (KS)
Kennesaw State U (GA)
Lee U (TN)
Le Moyne Coll (NY)
Lincoln Memorial U (TN)
Lincoln U (MO)
Lindenwood U (MO)
Lindsey Wilson Coll (KY)
Lipscomb U (TN)
Long Island U–LIU Brooklyn (NY)
Long Island U–LIU Post (NY)
Louisiana Coll (LA)
Madonna U (MI)
Manchester U (IN)
Manhattanville Coll (NY)
Maranatha Baptist U (WI)
Marist Coll (NY)
Maryville Coll (TN)
Marywood U (PA)
McMurry U (TX)
Mercyhurst U (PA)
Merrimack Coll (MA)
Messiah Coll (PA)
Miami Dade Coll (FL)
Miami U (OH)
Michigan State U (MI)
MidAmerica Nazarene U (KS)
Millikin U (IL)
Minnesota State U Moorhead (MN)
Minot State U (ND)
Misericordia U (PA)
Missouri State U (MO)
Morningside Coll (IA)
Morris Coll (SC)
Mount Mary U (WI)
Mount Vernon Nazarene U (OH)
Nazareth Coll of Rochester (NY)
Niagara U (NY)
North Dakota State U (ND)
Northern Michigan U (MI)
Northern State U (SD)
Northwestern Coll (IA)
Northwest Missouri State U (MO)

Northwest Nazarene U (ID)
Northwest U (WA)
Oakland City U (IN)
Ohio Dominican U (OH)
Ohio Northern U (OH)
Ohio Wesleyan U (OH)
Pace U (NY)
Pace U, Pleasantville Campus (NY)
Palm Beach Atlantic U (FL)
Pittsburg State U (KS)
Point Park U (PA)
Providence Coll (RI)
Queens Coll of the City U of New York (NY)
Rivier U (NH)
Roberts Wesleyan Coll (NY)
Rocky Mountain Coll (MT)
Rust Coll (MS)
Saginaw Valley State U (MI)
St. Catherine U (MN)
Saint Francis U (PA)
St. John Fisher Coll (NY)
St. John's U (NY)
St. Joseph's Coll, Long Island Campus (NY)
St. Joseph's Coll, New York (NY)
Saint Joseph's U (PA)
Saint Mary's U of Minnesota (MN)
Salve Regina U (RI)
Schreiner U (TX)
Seattle U (WA)
Seton Hill U (PA)
Southeastern U (FL)
Southern Adventist U (TN)
Southern Utah U (UT)
Southwest Baptist U (MO)
Southwestern Adventist U (TX)
Spring Hill Coll (AL)
State U of New York at New Paltz (NY)
State U of New York at Plattsburgh (NY)
State U of New York Coll at Cortland (NY)
State U of New York Coll at Old Westbury (NY)
State U of New York Coll at Oneonta (NY)
State U of New York Coll at Potsdam (NY)
Syracuse U (NY)
Taylor U (IN)
Trevecca Nazarene U (TN)
Trine U (IN)
Trinity Christian Coll (IL)
Union Coll (NE)
U of California, Irvine (CA)
U of Central Oklahoma (OK)
U of Dubuque (IA)
U of Evansville (IN)
The U of Findlay (OH)
U of Illinois at Chicago (IL)
U of Jamestown (ND)
U of Louisiana at Monroe (LA)
U of Maine (ME)
U of Maine at Farmington (ME)
U of Maine at Machias (ME)
U of Mary Hardin-Baylor (TX)
U of Maryland, Baltimore County (MD)
U of Missouri (MO)
U of Mobile (AL)
U of Nebraska-Lincoln (NE)
The U of North Carolina at Greensboro (NC)
U of Providence (MT)
U of Regina (SK, Canada)
U of Sioux Falls (SD)
U of South Dakota (SD)
The U of Tennessee at Martin (TN)
U of Waterloo (ON, Canada)
U of Wisconsin-Superior (WI)
Utah State U (UT)
Utah Valley U (UT)
Utica Coll (NY)
Valley City State U (ND)
Valparaiso U (IN)
Washington U in St. Louis (MO)
Waynesburg U (PA)
Wayne State Coll (NE)
Weber State U (UT)
Welch Coll (TN)
Western Michigan U (MI)
Western State Colorado U (CO)
Western Washington U (WA)
Westfield State U (MA)
Widener U (PA)

William Woods U (MO)
Winona State U (MN)
Xavier U of Louisiana (LA)
York Coll of Pennsylvania (PA)
Youngstown State U (OH)

BIOMATHEMATICS, BIOINFORMATICS, AND COMPUTATIONAL BIOLOGY RELATED
Florida Inst of Technology (FL)
Florida State U (FL)
Harvey Mudd Coll (CA)
La Sierra U (CA)
U of California, Los Angeles (CA)
Walsh U (OH)
Washington U in St. Louis (MO)
Worcester Polytechnic Inst (MA)

BIOMEDICAL SCIENCES
Adventist U of Health Sciences (FL)
Alverno Coll (WI)
Antioch Coll, Yellow Springs (OH)
Auburn U (AL)
Bradley U (IL)
Bridgewater State U (MA)
Brigham Young U (UT)
Brock U (ON, Canada)
Central Michigan U (MI)
Charles R. Drew U of Medicine and Science (CA)
Christian Brothers U (TN)
City Coll of the City U of New York (NY)
Coll of the Ozarks (MO)
Colorado State U (CO)
Concordia Coll–New York (NY)
Concordia U Wisconsin (WI)
Edgewood Coll (WI)
Fitchburg State U (MA)
Florida Inst of Technology (FL)
Franciscan Missionaries of Our Lady U (LA)
Hiram Coll (OH)
Jefferson Coll of Health Sciences (VA)
Keiser U, Fort Lauderdale (FL)
La Sierra U (CA)
Lewis U (IL)
Liberty U (VA)
Lubbock Christian U (TX)
Lynchburg Coll (VA)
Madonna U (MI)
Marist Coll (NY)
Marquette U (WI)
Marymount Manhattan Coll (NY)
Maryville U of Saint Louis (MO)
McMurry U (TX)
Minnesota State U Moorhead (MN)
Morehead State U (KY)
Multnomah U (OR)
New Mexico Inst of Mining and Technology (NM)
North Carolina Central U (NC)
North Carolina Wesleyan Coll (NC)
Northern Arizona U (AZ)
Oakland U (MI)
The Ohio State U (OH)
Oklahoma City U (OK)
Rochester Inst of Technology (NY)
Rowan U (NJ)
Rutgers U–New Brunswick (NJ)
St. John's U (NY)
Saint Leo U (FL)
St. Louis Coll of Pharmacy (MO)
Sam Houston State U (TX)
State U of New York at Fredonia (NY)
Susquehanna U (PA)
Tarleton State U (TX)
Texas A&M U (TX)
Texas A&M U–Corpus Christi (TX)
Texas A&M U–Kingsville (TX)
Trent U (ON, Canada)
Troy U (AL)
Union Coll (NE)
U at Buffalo, the State U of New York (NY)
U of California, Riverside (CA)
U of California, Santa Cruz (CA)
U of Central Florida (FL)
U of Central Oklahoma (OK)
U of Colorado Denver (CO)
U of Guelph (ON, Canada)
U of Michigan–Flint (MI)
U of Minnesota, Duluth (MN)
U of New England (ME)

U of New Hampshire (NH)
U of Northern Iowa (IA)
U of Pennsylvania (PA)
U of Rhode Island (RI)
U of Saint Mary (KS)
U of Saskatchewan (SK, Canada)
U of South Alabama (AL)
U of South Carolina Aiken (SC)
U of South Dakota (SD)
The U of Texas at Austin (TX)
The U of Texas Rio Grande Valley (TX)
U of Washington, Tacoma (WA)
Washington State U (WA)
Western Michigan U (MI)

BIOMEDICAL TECHNOLOGY
Andrews U (MI)
Cleveland State U (OH)
Indiana U–Purdue U Indianapolis (IN)
Kent State U (OH)
Long Island U–LIU Post (NY)
Rutgers U–Camden (NJ)

BIOMETRY/BIOMETRICS
Carnegie Mellon U (PA)
Cornell U (NY)
Rutgers U–New Brunswick (NJ)
Stanford U (CA)

BIOPHYSICS
Andrews U (MI)
Arizona State U at the Tempe campus (AZ)
Augsburg U (MN)
Brandeis U (MA)
Brigham Young U (UT)
Carnegie Mellon U (PA)
Claremont McKenna Coll (CA)
Columbia U (NY)
Elon U (NC)
Emory U (GA)
Haverford Coll (PA)
Iowa State U of Science and Technology (IA)
Johns Hopkins U (MD)
La Sierra U (CA)
Lipscomb U (TN)
Loyola U Chicago (IL)
Loyola U New Orleans (LA)
Marquette U (WI)
Miami U (OH)
New Jersey Inst of Technology (NJ)
Northeastern U (MA)
Oakland U (MI)
Pitzer Coll (CA)
Regent U (VA)
Rowan U (NJ)
St. Lawrence U (NY)
Scripps Coll (CA)
Southern Adventist U (TN)
Southern Methodist U (TX)
State U of New York Coll at Geneseo (NY)
Syracuse U (NY)
Temple U (PA)
U at Buffalo, the State U of New York (NY)
U of California, Los Angeles (CA)
U of California, San Diego (CA)
U of Michigan (MI)
U of Pennsylvania (PA)
U of San Diego (CA)
U of San Francisco (CA)
The U of Scranton (PA)
U of Southern California (CA)
U of Southern Indiana (IN)
U of Toronto (ON, Canada)
Washington & Jefferson Coll (PA)
Washington U in St. Louis (MO)
Whitman Coll (WA)
Whitworth U (WA)

BIOPSYCHOLOGY
Augsburg U (MN)
Bucknell U (PA)
Geneva Coll (PA)
Grand Valley State U (MI)
Immaculata U (PA)
Liberty U (VA)
Life U (GA)
Messiah Coll (PA)
Monmouth Coll (IL)
Morningside Coll (IA)
New Coll of Florida (FL)
Oglethorpe U (GA)
Ohio Dominican U (OH)

Rider U (NJ)
Spring Hill Coll (AL)
Tufts U (MA)
U of California, Santa Barbara (CA)
U of Guelph (ON, Canada)
Wagner Coll (NY)
Washington U in St. Louis (MO)

BIOSTATISTICS
Emmanuel Coll (MA)
Indiana U–Purdue U Indianapolis (IN)
Saint Louis U (MO)
Simmons Coll (MA)
Tulane U (LA)
The U of North Carolina at Chapel Hill (NC)
The U of Scranton (PA)

BIOTECHNOLOGY
Alma Coll (MI)
Auburn U (AL)
Bay Path U (MA)
Brock U (ON, Canada)
California State Polytechnic U, Pomona (CA)
California State U, San Marcos (CA)
City Coll of the City U of New York (NY)
Colorado State U (CO)
Delaware State U (DE)
East Stroudsburg U of Pennsylvania (PA)
Elizabethtown Coll (PA)
Endicott Coll (MA)
Ferris State U (MI)
Fitchburg State U (MA)
Florida Gulf Coast U (FL)
Florida Southern Coll (FL)
Grand View U (IA)
Hunter Coll of the City U of New York (NY)
Indiana U Bloomington (IN)
Indiana U East (IN)
Indiana U–Purdue U Indianapolis (IN)
Inter American U of Puerto Rico, Aguadilla Campus (PR)
Inter American U of Puerto Rico, Barranquitas Campus (PR)
Inter American U of Puerto Rico, Bayamón Campus (PR)
James Madison U (VA)
Keiser U, Fort Lauderdale (FL)
Kennesaw State U (GA)
Kent State U (OH)
Manhattan Coll (NY)
Marywood U (PA)
Massachusetts Coll of Liberal Arts (MA)
Missouri Baptist U (MO)
New York Inst of Technology (NY)
North Dakota State U (ND)
Oregon State U (OR)
Point Park U (PA)
Rochester Inst of Technology (NY)
Roosevelt U (IL)
Rutgers U–New Brunswick (NJ)
Southeastern Oklahoma State U (OK)
State U of New York Coll of Environmental Science and Forestry (NY)
Stevenson U (MD)
Syracuse U (NY)
Tufts U (MA)
U at Buffalo, the State U of New York (NY)
U of California, Davis (CA)
U of California, San Diego (CA)
U of Central Florida (FL)
U of Georgia (GA)
U of Hawaii at Manoa (HI)
U of Houston (TX)
U of Houston–Downtown (TX)
The U of Kansas (KS)
U of Kentucky (KY)
U of Nevada, Reno (NV)
The U of North Carolina at Pembroke (NC)
U of Saskatchewan (SK, Canada)
U of Waterloo (ON, Canada)
U of Wisconsin–River Falls (WI)
Ursuline Coll (OH)
Utah Valley U (UT)
Washington State U (WA)

Western Kentucky U (KY)
West Texas A&M U (TX)
William Paterson U of New Jersey (NJ)
Worcester State U (MA)

BLOOD BANK TECHNOLOGY
Rasmussen Coll St. Cloud (MN)

BOTANY/PLANT BIOLOGY
Andrews U (MI)
Auburn U (AL)
Bennington Coll (VT)
Brandon U (MB, Canada)
California State U, Long Beach (CA)
Coll of the Atlantic (ME)
Connecticut Coll (CT)
Humboldt State U (CA)
Iowa State U of Science and Technology (IA)
Kent State U (OH)
Marlboro Coll (VT)
Miami U (OH)
Michigan State U (MI)
North Carolina State U (NC)
North Dakota State U (ND)
Ohio U (OH)
Ohio Wesleyan U (OH)
Oklahoma State U (OK)
Oregon State U (OR)
Purdue U (IN)
Rutgers U–Newark (NJ)
San Francisco State U (CA)
Sonoma State U (CA)
Southern Illinois U Carbondale (IL)
The U of Akron (OH)
U of California, Davis (CA)
U of California, Riverside (CA)
U of Florida (FL)
U of Georgia (GA)
U of Hawaii at Manoa (HI)
U of Maine (ME)
U of Nebraska–Lincoln (NE)
U of New Hampshire (NH)
U of Oklahoma (OK)
U of Providence (MT)
The U of Texas at Austin (TX)
U of Toronto (ON, Canada)
U of Vermont (VT)
U of Washington (WA)
U of Wisconsin–Madison (WI)
U of Wyoming (WY)
Utah State U (UT)
Utah Valley U (UT)
Washington State U (WA)
Weber State U (UT)

BOTANY/PLANT BIOLOGY RELATED
Frostburg State U (MD)
Marlboro Coll (VT)
U of Hawaii at Manoa (HI)
U of Minnesota, Twin Cities Campus (MN)

BRASS INSTRUMENTS
Conservatorio de Musica de Puerto Rico (PR)
Liberty U (VA)
San Francisco Conservatory of Music (CA)
The U of Kansas (KS)
U of Southern California (CA)
Vanderbilt U (TN)
Youngstown State U (OH)

BROADCAST JOURNALISM
Auburn U (AL)
Barry U (FL)
Belmont U (TN)
Bemidji State U (MN)
Biola U (CA)
Bluffton U (OH)
Bowie State U (MD)
Bowling Green State U (OH)
Brigham Young U (UT)
Buffalo State Coll, State U of New York (NY)
California State U, Long Beach (CA)
Cameron U (OK)
Central State U (OH)
Chapman U (CA)
The Coll at Brockport, State U of New York (NY)
Concordia U Chicago (IL)
Delaware State U (DE)

Drake U (IA)
Elon U (NC)
Emerson Coll (MA)
Evangel U (MO)
Gettysburg Coll (PA)
Gonzaga U (WA)
Goshen Coll (IN)
Grand View U (IA)
Hampton U (VA)
Hannibal-LaGrange U (MO)
Harding U (AR)
Humboldt State U (CA)
Ithaca Coll (NY)
Langston U (OK)
Manchester U (IN)
Marywood U (PA)
Massachusetts Coll of Liberal Arts (MA)
Minnesota State U Moorhead (MN)
Mount Vernon Nazarene U (OH)
Northern Kentucky U (KY)
North Greenville U (SC)
Ohio Wesleyan U (OH)
Oklahoma Christian U (OK)
Oklahoma City U (OK)
Point Park U (PA)
Quinnipiac U (CT)
Rust Coll (MS)
Southern Adventist U (TN)
State U of New York at Oswego (NY)
Suffolk U (MA)
Syracuse U (NY)
Trevecca Nazarene U (TN)
Union U (TN)
U of Central Oklahoma (OK)
U of Miami (FL)
U of Missouri (MO)
U of Nebraska–Lincoln (NE)
U of North Texas (TX)
U of Oklahoma (OK)
The U of Scranton (PA)
U of South Carolina (SC)
U of Southern California (CA)
The U of Texas at El Paso (TX)
Wartburg Coll (IA)
Washington State U (WA)
Western Kentucky U (KY)
West Texas A&M U (TX)
Youngstown State U (OH)

BUDDHIST STUDIES
Marlboro Coll (VT)

BUILDING/CONSTRUCTION FINISHING, MANAGEMENT, AND INSPECTION RELATED
California State U, Long Beach (CA)
Pratt Inst (NY)
U of Maryland Eastern Shore (MD)

BUILDING/CONSTRUCTION SITE MANAGEMENT
Pennsylvania Coll of Technology (PA)
Rowan U (NJ)
Southern Utah U (UT)
The U of Texas at San Antonio (TX)

BUSINESS ADMINISTRATION AND MANAGEMENT
Abilene Christian U (TX)
Academy Coll (MN)
Acadia U (NS, Canada)
Adams State U (CO)
Adelphi U (NY)
Agnes Scott Coll (GA)
Alabama State U (AL)
Alaska Pacific U (AK)
Albion Coll (MI)
Albright Coll (PA)
Alcorn State U (MS)
Alfred U (NY)
Alice Lloyd Coll (KY)
Alliant Intl U–San Diego (CA)
Alma Coll (MI)
Alverno Coll (WI)
Ambrose U (AB, Canada)
American Coll (MN)
American Intl Coll (MA)
American Public U System (WV)
American U (DC)
American U in Bulgaria (Bulgaria)
The American U in Cairo (Egypt)
The American U of Paris (France)
Amridge U (AL)
Anderson U (IN)
Anderson U (SC)
Angelo State U (TX)

Antioch U Los Angeles (CA)
Antioch U Midwest (OH)
Appalachian State U (NC)
Aquinas Coll (MI)
Arcadia U (PA)
Arizona Christian U (AZ)
Arizona State U at the Polytechnic campus (AZ)
Arizona State U at the Tempe campus (AZ)
Arizona State U at the West campus (AZ)
Arkansas Tech U (AR)
Ashland U (OH)
Assumption Coll (MA)
Athabasca U (AB, Canada)
Athens State U (AL)
Auburn U (AL)
Auburn U at Montgomery (AL)
Augsburg U (MN)
Augustana Coll (IL)
Augustana U (SD)
Aurora U (IL)
Austin Coll (TX)
Averett U (VA)
Avila U (IL)
Azusa Pacific U (CA)
Babson Coll (MA)
Baldwin Wallace U (OH)
Ball State U (IN)
The Baptist Coll of Florida (FL)
Baptist U of the Americas (TX)
Barclay Coll (KS)
Barry U (FL)
Barton Coll (NC)
Baruch Coll of the City U of New York (NY)
Baylor U (TX)
Bay Path U (MA)
Beacon Coll (FL)
Becker Coll (MA)
Belhaven U (MS)
Belmont U (TN)
Bemidji State U (MN)
Benedictine Coll (KS)
Bennett Coll (NC)
Bentley U (MA)
Berea Coll (KY)
Berry Coll (GA)
Bethany Lutheran Coll (MN)
Bethel Coll (IN)
Bethel U (MN)
Bethel U (TN)
Bethune-Cookman U (FL)
Beulah Heights U (GA)
Binghamton U, State U of New York (NY)
Biola U (CA)
Birmingham-Southern Coll (AL)
Black Hills State U (SD)
Bloomsburg U of Pennsylvania (PA)
Bluefield Coll (VA)
Blue Mountain Coll (MS)
Bluffton U (OH)
Bob Jones U (SC)
Boise State U (ID)
Boston Coll (MA)
Boston U (MA)
Bowie State U (MD)
Bowling Green State U (OH)
Bowling Green State U–Firelands Coll (OH)
Bradley U (IL)
Brandman U (CA)
Brandon U (MB, Canada)
Brewton-Parker Coll (GA)
Bridgewater Coll (VA)
Bridgewater State U (MA)
Brigham Young U–Idaho (ID)
Brock U (ON, Canada)
Bryan Coll (TN)
Bryant U (RI)
Bucknell U (PA)
Buena Vista U (IA)
Buffalo State Coll, State U of New York (NY)
Cairn U (PA)
Caldwell U (NJ)
California Lutheran U (CA)
California Polytechnic State U, San Luis Obispo (CA)
California State Polytechnic U, Pomona (CA)
California State U, Dominguez Hills (CA)
California State U, East Bay (CA)
California State U, Fullerton (CA)

California State U, Long Beach (CA)
California State U, Los Angeles (CA)
California State U Maritime Acad (CA)
California State U, Monterey Bay (CA)
California State U, Northridge (CA)
California State U, Sacramento (CA)
California State U, San Bernardino (CA)
California State U, San Marcos (CA)
California State U, Stanislaus (CA)
California U of Pennsylvania (PA)
Calumet Coll of Saint Joseph (IN)
Calvary U (MO)
Calvin Coll (MI)
Cameron U (OK)
Campbellsville U (KY)
Canisius Coll (NY)
Capital U (OH)
Cardinal Stritch U (WI)
Caribbean U (PR)
Carlow U (PA)
Carnegie Mellon U (PA)
Carroll Coll (MT)
Carroll U (WI)
Carson-Newman U (TN)
Carthage Coll (WI)
Case Western Reserve U (OH)
Catawba Coll (NC)
The Catholic U of America (DC)
Cazenovia Coll (NY)
Cedar Crest Coll (PA)
Cedarville U (OH)
Centenary Coll of Louisiana (LA)
Central Connecticut State U (CT)
Central Methodist U (MO)
Central Michigan U (MI)
Central Penn Coll (PA)
Chaminade U of Honolulu (HI)
Champlain Coll (VT)
Chapman U (CA)
Charleston Southern U (SC)
Charter Oak State Coll (CT)
Chestnut Hill Coll (PA)
Chipola Coll (FL)
Chowan U (NC)
Christian Brothers U (TN)
Christopher Newport U (VA)
The Citadel, The Military Coll of South Carolina (SC)
City Coll of the City U of New York (NY)
Clarion U of Pennsylvania (PA)
Clark Atlanta U (GA)
Clarke U (IA)
Clarkson U (NY)
Clark U (MA)
Clayton State U (GA)
Clemson U (SC)
Cleveland State U (OH)
Coastal Carolina U (SC)
Coe Coll (IA)
Cogswell Polytechnical Coll (CA)
Coker Coll (SC)
The Coll at Brockport, State U of New York (NY)
Coll of Business and Technology–Main Campus (FL)
Coll of Business and Technology–Miami Gardens (FL)
Coll of Charleston (SC)
Coll of Coastal Georgia (GA)
The Coll of Idaho (ID)
The Coll of New Jersey (NJ)
Coll of Saint Benedict (MN)
Coll of Saint Elizabeth (NJ)
Coll of Saint Mary (NE)
The Coll of Saint Rose (NY)
The Coll of St. Scholastica (MN)
Coll of the Ozarks (MO)
The Coll of Westchester (NY)
The Coll of William and Mary (VA)
Colorado Christian U (CO)
Colorado State U (CO)
Columbia Coll (MO)
Columbia Coll (SC)
Columbia Southern U (AL)
Columbus State U (GA)
Concordia Coll–New York (NY)
Concordia U (QC, Canada)
Concordia U Chicago (IL)
Concordia U Irvine (CA)

Concordia U of Edmonton (AB, Canada)
Concordia U, St. Paul (MN)
Concordia U Wisconsin (WI)
Concord U (WV)
Converse Coll (SC)
Corban U (OR)
Cornerstone U (MI)
Cottey Coll (MO)
Creighton U (NE)
Culver-Stockton Coll (MO)
Curry Coll (MA)
Daemen Coll (NY)
Dakota State U (SD)
Dallas Baptist U (TX)
Davenport U, Grand Rapids (MI)
Dean Coll (MA)
Defiance Coll (OH)
Delaware State U (DE)
Delaware Valley U (PA)
DePaul U (IL)
DEREE - The American Coll of Greece (Greece)
Dickinson State U (ND)
Doane U (NE)
Dominican Coll (NY)
Dominican U (IL)
Dominican U of California (CA)
Drake U (IA)
Drew U (NJ)
Drury U (MO)
Dunwoody Coll of Technology (MN)
D'Youville Coll (NY)
East Carolina U (NC)
Eastern Mennonite U (VA)
Eastern Michigan U (MI)
Eastern Nazarene Coll (MA)
Eastern New Mexico U (NM)
Eastern U (PA)
Eastern Washington U (WA)
East Stroudsburg U of Pennsylvania (PA)
East Tennessee State U (TN)
East Texas Baptist U (TX)
Eckerd Coll (FL)
ECPI U, Virginia Beach (VA)
Edgewood Coll (WI)
EDP U of Puerto Rico (PR)
Elizabethtown Coll (PA)
Elmhurst Coll (IL)
Elon U (NC)
Emmanuel Coll (MA)
Emmaus Bible Coll (IA)
Emory & Henry Coll (VA)
Emory U (GA)
Emporia State U (KS)
Endicott Coll (MA)
Evangel U (MO)
Excelsior Coll (NY)
Fairfield U (CT)
Fairleigh Dickinson U, Florham Campus (NJ)
Fairleigh Dickinson U, Metropolitan Campus (NJ)
Farmingdale State Coll (NY)
Fayetteville State U (NC)
Felician U (NJ)
Ferris State U (MI)
Fisher Coll (MA)
Fitchburg State U (MA)
Flagler Coll (FL)
Florida Atlantic U (FL)
Florida Coll (FL)
Florida Gulf Coast U (FL)
Florida Inst of Technology (FL)
Florida Intl U (FL)
Florida National U (FL)
Florida Southern Coll (FL)
Florida State U (FL)
Fordham U (NY)
Fort Lewis Coll (CO)
Francis Marion U (SC)
Franklin & Marshall Coll (PA)
Franklin Pierce U (NH)
Friends U (KS)
Frostburg State U (MD)
Furman U (SC)
Gannon U (PA)
Geneva Coll (PA)
George Mason U (VA)
Georgetown Coll (KY)
Georgetown U (DC)
The George Washington U (DC)
Georgia Coll & State U (GA)
Georgia Inst of Technology (GA)
Georgia Military Coll (GA)
Georgian Court U (NJ)

Georgia Southern U (GA)
Georgia Southwestern State U (GA)
Georgia State U (GA)
Gettysburg Coll (PA)
Golden Gate U (CA)
Gonzaga U (WA)
Gordon Coll (MA)
Gordon State Coll (GA)
Goshen Coll (IN)
Governors State U (IL)
Graceland U (IA)
Grambling State U (LA)
Grand View U (IA)
Granite State Coll (NH)
Green Mountain Coll (VT)
Greensboro Coll (NC)
Greenville U (IL)
Grove City Coll (PA)
Guilford Coll (NC)
Gustavus Adolphus Coll (MN)
Hallmark U (TX)
Hamline U (MN)
Hampton U (VA)
Hannibal-LaGrange U (MO)
Harding U (AR)
Hardin-Simmons U (TX)
Harris-Stowe State U (MO)
Hartwick Coll (NY)
Hawai'i Pacific U (HI)
HEC Montreal (QC, Canada)
Heidelberg U (OH)
High Point U (NC)
Hilbert Coll (NY)
Hiram Coll (OH)
Hofstra U (NY)
Holy Family U (PA)
Holy Names U (CA)
Hood Coll (MD)
Hope Coll (MI)
Hope Intl U (CA)
Houston Baptist U (TX)
Howard Payne U (TX)
Humboldt State U (CA)
Huntingdon Coll (AL)
Husson U (ME)
Huston-Tillotson U (TX)
Idaho State U (ID)
Illinois Coll (IL)
Illinois State U (IL)
Illinois Wesleyan U (IL)
Immaculata U (PA)
Indiana State U (IN)
Indiana Tech (IN)
Indiana U of Pennsylvania (PA)
Indiana Wesleyan U (IN)
Inter American U of Puerto Rico, Fajardo Campus (PR)
Inter American U of Puerto Rico, Metropolitan Campus (PR)
Inter American U of Puerto Rico, San Germán Campus (PR)
Iona Coll (NY)
Iowa State U of Science and Technology (IA)
Ithaca Coll (NY)
Jackson State U (MS)
Jacksonville U (FL)
James Madison U (VA)
John Brown U (AR)
John Cabot U (Italy)
John Carroll U (OH)
Johnson C. Smith U (NC)
Johnson U (TN)
Johnson U Florida (FL)
John Wesley U (NC)
Judson U (IL)
Kansas State U (KS)
Kansas Wesleyan U (KS)
Kean U (NJ)
Keene State Coll (NH)
Keiser U, Fort Lauderdale (FL)
Kennesaw State U (GA)
Kent State U (OH)
Kent State U at Ashtabula (OH)
Kent State U at Geauga (OH)
Kent State U at Salem (OH)
Kent State U at Stark (OH)
Kent State U at Trumbull (OH)
Kent State U at Tuscarawas (OH)
Kentucky State U (KY)
Kettering U (MI)
The King's Coll (NY)
King's Coll (PA)
Kutztown U of Pennsylvania (PA)
LaGrange Coll (GA)
Langston U (OK)

La Salle U (PA)
Lasell Coll (MA)
La Sierra U (CA)
Lawrence Technological U (MI)
Lebanese American U (Lebanon)
Lebanon Valley Coll (PA)
Lee U (TN)
Lehman Coll of the City U of New York (NY)
Lenoir-Rhyne U (NC)
Lesley U (MA)
LeTourneau U (TX)
Lewis U (IL)
Liberty U (VA)
Limestone Coll (SC)
Lincoln Coll (IL)
Lincoln Memorial U (TN)
Lincoln U (CA)
Lincoln U (MO)
Lincoln U (PA)
Lindenwood U (MO)
Lindsey Wilson Coll (KY)
Linfield Coll (OR)
Lipscomb U (TN)
Lock Haven U of Pennsylvania (PA)
Long Island U–LIU Brooklyn (NY)
Long Island U–LIU Post (NY)
Longwood U (VA)
Loras Coll (IA)
Louisiana Coll (LA)
Louisiana State U and A&M Coll (LA)
Loyola U Chicago (IL)
Loyola U New Orleans (LA)
Lubbock Christian U (TX)
Luther Coll (IA)
Lycoming Coll (PA)
Lynchburg Coll (VA)
Lynn U (FL)
Lyon Coll (AR)
Madonna U (MI)
Maharishi U of Management (IA)
Malone U (OH)
Manchester U (IN)
Manhattanville Coll (NY)
Mansfield U of Pennsylvania (PA)
Maranatha Baptist U (WI)
Marian U (IN)
Marian U (WI)
Marietta Coll (OH)
Marist Coll (NY)
Marquette U (WI)
Marshall U (WV)
Mary Baldwin U (VA)
Marylhurst U (OR)
Marymount California U (CA)
Marymount Manhattan Coll (NY)
Marymount U (VA)
Maryville Coll (TN)
Maryville U of Saint Louis (MO)
Marywood U (PA)
Massachusetts Coll of Liberal Arts (MA)
The Master's U (CA)
McDaniel Coll (MD)
McKendree U (IL)
McMurry U (TX)
McNeese State U (LA)
McPherson Coll (KS)
Mercy Coll (NY)
Mercyhurst U (PA)
Meredith Coll (NC)
Merrimack Coll (MA)
Messenger Coll (TX)
Messiah Coll (PA)
Metropolitan State U of Denver (CO)
Miami U (OH)
Michigan State U (MI)
Michigan Technological U (MI)
Mid-America Christian U (OK)
MidAmerica Nazarene U (KS)
Mid-Atlantic Christian U (NC)
Middle Georgia State U (GA)
Middle Tennessee State U (TN)
Midland Coll (TX)
Millersville U of Pennsylvania (PA)
Milligan Coll (TN)
Millikin U (IL)
Millsaps Coll (MS)
Milwaukee School of Eng (WI)
Minnesota State U Moorhead (MN)
Minot State U (ND)
Misericordia U (PA)
Mississippi State U (MS)
Missouri Baptist U (MO)
Missouri State U (MO)

Missouri U of Science and Technology (MO)
Missouri Valley Coll (MO)
Missouri Western State U (MO)
Molloy Coll (NY)
Monmouth Coll (IL)
Montclair State U (NJ)
Moravian Coll (PA)
Morehead State U (KY)
Morehouse Coll (GA)
Morningside Coll (IA)
Morris Coll (SC)
Mount Aloysius Coll (PA)
Mount Marty Coll (SD)
Mount Mary U (WI)
Mount Mercy U (IA)
Mount St. Joseph U (OH)
Mount Saint Mary Coll (NY)
Mount Saint Mary's U (CA)
Mount Vernon Nazarene U (OH)
Muhlenberg Coll (PA)
Murray State U (KY)
Muskingum U (OH)
National Louis U (IL)
National Paralegal Coll (AZ)
National U (CA)
Nazareth Coll of Rochester (NY)
Neumann U (PA)
Newberry Coll (SC)
New England Inst of Technology (RI)
New Jersey City U (NJ)
New Jersey Inst of Technology (NJ)
Newman U (KS)
New Mexico Highlands U (NM)
New Mexico Inst of Mining and Technology (NM)
New Mexico State U (NM)
New York Inst of Technology (NY)
Niagara U (NY)
Nichols Coll (MA)
North American U (TX)
North Carolina Central U (NC)
North Carolina State U (NC)
North Carolina Wesleyan Coll (NC)
North Central Coll (IL)
Northcentral U (CA)
North Dakota State U (ND)
Northeastern State U (OK)
Northeastern U (MA)
Northern Arizona U (AZ)
Northern Illinois U (IL)
Northern Kentucky U (KY)
Northern Michigan U (MI)
Northern State U (SD)
Northern Vermont U–Lyndon (VT)
North Greenville U (SC)
Northland Coll (WI)
Northwest Christian U (OR)
Northwestern Coll (IA)
Northwestern Oklahoma State U (OK)
Northwestern State U of Louisiana (LA)
Northwest Missouri State U (MO)
Northwest Nazarene U (ID)
Northwest U (WA)
Notre Dame de Namur U (CA)
Nova Southeastern U (FL)
Nyack Coll (NY)
Oakland City U (IN)
Oglethorpe U (GA)
Ohio Christian U (OH)
Ohio Dominican U (OH)
Ohio Northern U (OH)
The Ohio State U (OH)
The Ohio State U at Lima (OH)
The Ohio State U at Mansfield (OH)
The Ohio State U at Marion (OH)
The Ohio State U at Newark (OH)
Ohio U (OH)
Ohio Wesleyan U (OH)
Oklahoma Christian U (OK)
Oklahoma City U (OK)
Oklahoma State U (OK)
Old Dominion U (VA)
Olivet Nazarene U (IL)
Oral Roberts U (OK)
Oregon State U (OR)
Ottawa U (KS)
Otterbein U (OH)
Ouachita Baptist U (AR)
Our Lady of the Lake U (TX)
Pace U (NY)
Pacific Lutheran U (WA)
Palm Beach Atlantic U (FL)
Palm Beach State Coll (FL)

Peirce Coll (PA)
Penn State Beaver (PA)
Penn State Brandywine (PA)
Penn State DuBois (PA)
Penn State Erie, The Behrend Coll (PA)
Penn State Fayette, The Eberly Campus (PA)
Penn State Greater Allegheny (PA)
Penn State Harrisburg (PA)
Penn State Hazleton (PA)
Penn State Mont Alto (PA)
Penn State New Kensington (PA)
Penn State Shenango (PA)
Penn State Wilkes-Barre (PA)
Penn State Worthington Scranton (PA)
Penn State York (PA)
Pennsylvania Coll of Technology (PA)
Pepperdine U, Malibu (CA)
Pfeiffer U (NC)
Piedmont Coll (GA)
Pine Manor Coll (MA)
Pittsburgh Tech Coll (PA)
Point Loma Nazarene U (CA)
Point Park U (PA)
Point U (GA)
Polk State Coll (FL)
Polytechnic U of Puerto Rico (PR)
Polytechnic U of Puerto Rico, Miami Campus (FL)
Portland State U (OR)
Post U (CT)
Potomac State Coll of West Virginia U (WV)
Prairie View A&M U (TX)
Presbyterian Coll (SC)
Principia Coll (IL)
Providence Coll (RI)
Purdue U (IN)
Purdue U Northwest (IN)
Quinnipiac U (CT)
Radford U (VA)
Ramapo Coll of New Jersey (NJ)
Rasmussen Coll Bloomington (MN)
Rasmussen Coll Brooklyn Park (MN)
Rasmussen Coll Eagan (MN)
Rasmussen Coll Fargo (ND)
Rasmussen Coll Mankato (MN)
Rasmussen Coll New Port Richey (FL)
Rasmussen Coll Ocala (FL)
Rasmussen Coll Rockford (IL)
Rasmussen Coll St. Cloud (MN)
Redeemer U Coll (ON, Canada)
Regent U (VA)
Regis U (CO)
Rensselaer Polytechnic Inst (NY)
Rhode Island Coll (RI)
Rhodes Coll (TN)
Rice U (TX)
Rider U (NJ)
Ripon Coll (WI)
Rivier U (NH)
Roanoke Coll (VA)
Robert Morris U (PA)
Robert Morris U Illinois (IL)
Roberts Wesleyan Coll (NY)
Rochester Inst of Technology (NY)
Rockford U (IL)
Rockhurst U (MO)
Rocky Mountain Coll (MT)
Rogers State U (OK)
Roger Williams U (RI)
Rollins Coll (FL)
Rosemont Coll (PA)
Rowan U (NJ)
Rust Coll (MS)
Rutgers U–Camden (NJ)
Rutgers U–Newark (NJ)
Rutgers U–New Brunswick (NJ)
Sacred Heart U (CT)
The Sage Colls (NY)
Saginaw Valley State U (MI)
St. Andrews U (NC)
Saint Augustine's U (NC)
St. Bonaventure U (NY)
St. Catherine U (MN)
Saint Francis U (PA)
St. John Fisher Coll (NY)
Saint John's U (MN)
St. John's U (NY)
St. Joseph's Coll, Long Island Campus (NY)
St. Joseph's Coll, New York (NY)

Saint Joseph's U (PA)
Saint Leo U (FL)
Saint Louis U (MO)
Saint Louis U–Madrid Campus (Spain)
Saint Martin's U (WA)
Saint Mary-of-the-Woods Coll (IN)
Saint Mary's Coll of California (CA)
St. Mary's U (TX)
Saint Michael's Coll (VT)
St. Norbert Coll (WI)
Saint Peter's U (NJ)
St. Thomas Aquinas Coll (NY)
St. Thomas U (FL)
Saint Vincent Coll (PA)
Salisbury U (MD)
Salve Regina U (RI)
Samford U (AL)
Sam Houston State U (TX)
San Diego State U (CA)
San Francisco State U (CA)
Schreiner U (TX)
Seattle Pacific U (WA)
Seattle U (WA)
Seminole State Coll of Florida (FL)
Seton Hill U (PA)
Shawnee State U (OH)
Shaw U (NC)
Shenandoah U (VA)
Shepherd U (WV)
Shippensburg U of Pennsylvania (PA)
Shorter U (GA)
Sierra Nevada Coll (NV)
Silver Lake Coll of the Holy Family (WI)
Simmons Coll (MA)
Simon Fraser U (BC, Canada)
Simpson Coll (IA)
Slippery Rock U of Pennsylvania (PA)
Sonoma State U (CA)
Southeastern Louisiana U (LA)
Southeastern Oklahoma State U (OK)
Southeastern U (FL)
Southeast Missouri State U (MO)
Southern Adventist U (TN)
Southern Arkansas U–Magnolia (AR)
Southern Illinois U Carbondale (IL)
Southern Illinois U Edwardsville (IL)
Southern Methodist U (TX)
Southern Utah U (UT)
Southern Vermont Coll (VT)
Southwest Baptist U (MO)
Southwestern Assemblies of God U (TX)
Southwestern Coll (KS)
Spring Hill Coll (AL)
State U of New York at Fredonia (NY)
State U of New York at New Paltz (NY)
State U of New York at Oswego (NY)
State U of New York at Plattsburgh (NY)
State U of New York Coll at Geneseo (NY)
State U of New York Coll at Old Westbury (NY)
State U of New York Coll at Potsdam (NY)
State U of New York Coll of Technology at Alfred (NY)
State U of New York Coll of Technology at Canton (NY)
State U of New York Coll of Technology at Delhi (NY)
State U of New York Polytechnic Inst (NY)
Stephen F. Austin State U (TX)
Stetson U (FL)
Stevens Inst of Technology (NJ)
Stevenson U (MD)
Stevens–The Inst of Business & Arts (MO)
Stockton U (NJ)
Stonehill Coll (MA)
Stony Brook U, State U of New York (NY)
Suffolk U (MA)
Sullivan U (KY)
Susquehanna U (PA)
Syracuse U (NY)

Tarleton State U (TX)
Taylor U (IN)
Tennessee Technological U (TN)
Tennessee Wesleyan U (TN)
Texas A&M Intl U (TX)
Texas A&M U (TX)
Texas A&M U–Central Texas (TX)
Texas A&M U–Commerce (TX)
Texas A&M U–Corpus Christi (TX)
Texas A&M U–Kingsville (TX)
Texas A&M U–Texarkana (TX)
Texas Lutheran U (TX)
Texas State U (TX)
Texas Tech U (TX)
Texas Woman's U (TX)
Thomas Edison State U (NJ)
Thomas U (GA)
Tiffin U (OH)
Toccoa Falls Coll (GA)
Touro Coll Los Angeles (CA)
Towson U (MD)
Trent U (ON, Canada)
Trevecca Nazarene U (TN)
Trine U (IN)
Trinity U (TX)
Troy U (AL)
Truett McConnell U (GA)
Truman State U (MO)
Tulane U (LA)
Tusculum Coll (TN)
Union Coll (NE)
Union U (TN)
United States Military Acad (NY)
Unity Coll (ME)
Université de Sherbrooke (QC, Canada)
U at Albany, State U of New York (NY)
U at Buffalo, the State U of New York (NY)
The U of Akron (OH)
The U of Alabama (AL)
The U of Alabama at Birmingham (AL)
U of Alaska Fairbanks (AK)
The U of Arizona (AZ)
U of Arkansas (AR)
U of California, Irvine (CA)
U of California, Riverside (CA)
U of Central Arkansas (AR)
U of Central Florida (FL)
U of Central Missouri (MO)
U of Central Oklahoma (OK)
U of Cincinnati (OH)
U of Colorado Boulder (CO)
U of Colorado Colorado Springs (CO)
U of Colorado Denver (CO)
U of Dallas (TX)
U of Denver (CO)
U of Dubuque (IA)
U of Evansville (IN)
The U of Findlay (OH)
U of Florida (FL)
U of Georgia (GA)
U of Guam (GU)
U of Hartford (CT)
U of Hawaii at Manoa (HI)
U of Houston (TX)
U of Houston–Clear Lake (TX)
U of Houston–Downtown (TX)
U of Idaho (ID)
U of Illinois at Chicago (IL)
U of Illinois at Springfield (IL)
U of Jamestown (ND)
The U of Kansas (KS)
U of La Verne (CA)
U of Louisiana at Monroe (LA)
U of Maine (ME)
U of Maine at Fort Kent (ME)
U of Maine at Machias (ME)
U of Management and Technology (VA)
U of Mary Hardin-Baylor (TX)
U of Maryland Eastern Shore (MD)
U of Maryland U Coll (MD)
U of Mary Washington (VA)
U of Massachusetts Amherst (MA)
U of Massachusetts Boston (MA)
U of Massachusetts Lowell (MA)
U of Memphis (TN)
U of Miami (FL)
U of Michigan (MI)
U of Michigan–Dearborn (MI)
U of Michigan–Flint (MI)
U of Minnesota, Crookston (MN)
U of Minnesota, Duluth (MN)

U of Minnesota, Morris (MN)
U of Missouri (MO)
U of Mobile (AL)
U of Montevallo (AL)
U of Mount Union (OH)
U of Nebraska at Kearney (NE)
U of Nebraska–Lincoln (NE)
U of Nevada, Las Vegas (NV)
U of Nevada, Reno (NV)
U of New England (ME)
U of New Hampshire (NH)
U of New Haven (CT)
U of New Mexico (NM)
U of New Orleans (LA)
U of North Alabama (AL)
U of North Carolina at Asheville (NC)
The U of North Carolina at Chapel Hill (NC)
The U of North Carolina at Charlotte (NC)
The U of North Carolina at Greensboro (NC)
The U of North Carolina at Pembroke (NC)
The U of North Carolina Wilmington (NC)
U of North Dakota (ND)
U of Northern Colorado (CO)
U of Northern Iowa (IA)
U of North Florida (FL)
U of North Georgia (GA)
U of Oklahoma (OK)
U of Pennsylvania (PA)
U of Pikeville (KY)
U of Pittsburgh at Bradford (PA)
U of Pittsburgh at Greensburg (PA)
U of Providence (MT)
U of Puerto Rico–Humacao (PR)
U of Puget Sound (WA)
U of Regina (SK, Canada)
U of Rhode Island (RI)
U of Richmond (VA)
U of St. Francis (IL)
U of Saint Francis (IN)
U of Saint Joseph (CT)
U of Saint Mary (KS)
U of St. Thomas (MN)
U of St. Thomas (TX)
U of San Diego (CA)
U of San Francisco (CA)
U of Saskatchewan (SK, Canada)
The U of Scranton (PA)
U of Sioux Falls (SD)
U of South Alabama (AL)
U of South Carolina (SC)
U of South Carolina Aiken (SC)
U of South Dakota (SD)
U of Southern California (CA)
U of Southern Indiana (IN)
U of Southern Maine (ME)
U of Southern Mississippi (MS)
U of South Florida, St. Petersburg (FL)
U of South Florida Sarasota-Manatee (FL)
The U of Tampa (FL)
The U of Tennessee (TN)
The U of Tennessee at Chattanooga (TN)
The U of Tennessee at Martin (TN)
The U of Texas at Austin (TX)
The U of Texas at El Paso (TX)
The U of Texas at San Antonio (TX)
The U of Texas of the Permian Basin (TX)
The U of Texas Rio Grande Valley (TX)
U of the Fraser Valley (BC, Canada)
U of the Incarnate Word (TX)
U of the Pacific (CA)
U of the Potomac (DC)
U of the Virgin Islands (VI)
The U of Toledo (OH)
U of Toronto (ON, Canada)
The U of Tulsa (OK)
U of Utah (UT)
U of Valley Forge (PA)
U of Vermont (VT)
The U of Virginia's Coll at Wise (VA)
U of Washington (WA)
U of Washington, Bothell (WA)
U of Washington, Tacoma (WA)
U of Waterloo (ON, Canada)
The U of West Alabama (AL)

U of West Georgia (GA)
U of Wisconsin–Eau Claire (WI)
U of Wisconsin–La Crosse (WI)
U of Wisconsin–Madison (WI)
U of Wisconsin–Parkside (WI)
U of Wisconsin–River Falls (WI)
U of Wisconsin–Stevens Point (WI)
U of Wisconsin–Stout (WI)
U of Wisconsin–Superior (WI)
U of Wisconsin–Whitewater (WI)
U of Wyoming (WY)
Upper Iowa U (IA)
Ursuline Coll (OH)
Utah State U (UT)
Utah Valley U (UT)
Utica Coll (NY)
Valdosta State U (GA)
Valley City State U (ND)
Vanguard U of Southern California (CA)
Vermont Tech Coll (VT)
Villa Maria Coll (NY)
Villanova U (PA)
Virginia Polytechnic Inst and State U (VA)
Virginia Wesleyan U (VA)
Wagner Coll (NY)
Walsh Coll of Accountancy and Business Administration (MI)
Walsh U (OH)
Warner Pacific Coll (OR)
Wartburg Coll (IA)
Washington and Lee U (VA)
Washington Coll (MD)
Washington State U (WA)
Washington State U–Global Campus (WA)
Washington State U–Spokane (WA)
Washington State U–Tri-Cities (WA)
Washington State U–Vancouver (WA)
Washington U in St. Louis (MO)
Wayland Baptist U (TX)
Waynesburg U (PA)
Wayne State Coll (NE)
Webber Intl U (FL)
Weber State U (UT)
Webster U (MO)
Welch Coll (TN)
Wells Coll (NY)
West Chester U of Pennsylvania (PA)
Western Connecticut State U (CT)
Western Illinois U (IL)
Western Kentucky U (KY)
Western Michigan U (MI)
Western New England U (MA)
Western State Colorado U (CO)
Western Washington U (WA)
Westfield State U (MA)
Westminster Coll (PA)
West Texas A&M U (TX)
West Virginia State U (WV)
West Virginia U (WV)
West Virginia U Inst of Technology (WV)
West Virginia Wesleyan Coll (WV)
Wheaton Coll (MA)
Whittier Coll (CA)
Whitworth U (WA)
Wichita State U (KS)
Widener U (PA)
Wilkes U (PA)
William Jewell Coll (MO)
William Paterson U of New Jersey (NJ)
William Peace U (NC)
William Woods U (MO)
Wilmington U (DE)
Winona State U (MN)
Winthrop U (SC)
Wisconsin Lutheran Coll (WI)
Wittenberg U (OH)
Woodbury U (CA)
Worcester State U (MA)
Wright State U (OH)
Xavier U of Louisiana (LA)
York Coll of Pennsylvania (PA)
Youngstown State U (OH)

BUSINESS ADMINISTRATION, MANAGEMENT AND OPERATIONS RELATED
Adams State U (CO)
Alverno Coll (WI)

Augsburg U (MN)
Austin Coll (TX)
Babson Coll (MA)
Bay Path U (MA)
Benedictine U (IL)
Bethel U (TN)
Blackburn Coll (IL)
Bowling Green State U (OH)
California State U, San Bernardino (CA)
Calumet Coll of Saint Joseph (IN)
Capital U (OH)
Carnegie Mellon U (PA)
Cazenovia Coll (NY)
Central Michigan U (MI)
Charleston Southern U (SC)
Clayton State U (GA)
Coll of Central Florida (FL)
Colorado Christian U (CO)
Colorado Mesa U (CO)
Columbia Coll (SC)
Cornerstone U (MI)
Davenport U, Grand Rapids (MI)
Daytona State Coll (FL)
Delaware State U (DE)
Dominican U of California (CA)
Eastern Oregon U (OR)
Embry-Riddle Aeronautical U–Daytona (FL)
Florida Inst of Technology (FL)
Florida Keys Comm Coll (FL)
Gettysburg Coll (PA)
Hallmark U (TX)
Hofstra U (NY)
Howard Payne U (TX)
Huntingdon Coll (AL)
Inter American U of Puerto Rico, Metropolitan Campus (PR)
Jacksonville U (FL)
Judson U (IL)
Kettering U (MI)
La Roche Coll (PA)
Le Moyne Coll (NY)
Limestone Coll (SC)
Lincoln Christian U (IL)
Lincoln Coll of New England, Southington (CT)
Lincoln Memorial U (TN)
Malone U (OH)
Mercer U, Macon (GA)
Metropolitan State U of Denver (CO)
Miami Dade Coll (FL)
Millikin U (IL)
Missouri Baptist U (MO)
Missouri State U (MO)
Morris Coll (SC)
North Dakota State U (ND)
Northwest U (WA)
Oakland U (MI)
Ohio Northern U (OH)
Pennsylvania Coll of Technology (PA)
Pensacola State Coll (FL)
Polk State Coll (FL)
Rider U (NJ)
Roosevelt U (IL)
St. Thomas U (FL)
Shenandoah U (VA)
Siena Coll (NY)
South Florida State Coll (FL)
Spring Hill Coll (AL)
State U of New York at New Paltz (NY)
Texas Tech U (TX)
Thomas Edison State U (NJ)
Trine U (IN)
Trinity Christian Coll (IL)
Unity Coll (ME)
The U of Alabama at Birmingham (AL)
U of Charleston (WV)
U of Houston–Clear Lake (TX)
U of Illinois at Springfield (IL)
U of Louisville (KY)
U of Maine at Farmington (ME)
U of Maryland, Baltimore County (MD)
U of Maryland U Coll (MD)
U of Miami (FL)
U of North Georgia (GA)
U of Pennsylvania (PA)
U of Southern Maine (ME)
The U of Texas at Austin (TX)
U of Waterloo (ON, Canada)
U of Wyoming (WY)
Washington U in St. Louis (MO)

Waynesburg U (PA)
Western New England U (MA)
Wichita State U (KS)
Widener U (PA)
Wisconsin Lutheran Coll (WI)

BUSINESS AUTOMATION/TECHNOLOGY/DATA ENTRY
Mount Vernon Nazarene U (OH)
Point U (GA)
The U of Tampa (FL)

BUSINESS/COMMERCE
Adams State U (CO)
Alice Lloyd Coll (KY)
American Coll of Thessaloniki (Greece)
Anderson U (SC)
Asbury U (KY)
Auburn U at Montgomery (AL)
Austin Coll (TX)
Avila U (MO)
Azusa Pacific U (CA)
Baker U (KS)
Ball State U (IN)
Baylor U (TX)
Bellarmine U (KY)
Belmont U (TN)
Bethel Coll (IN)
Bethel Coll (KS)
Bloomsburg U of Pennsylvania (PA)
Bowling Green State U (OH)
Brandeis U (MA)
Brenau U (GA)
Brescia U (KY)
Brock U (ON, Canada)
Bryn Athyn Coll of the New Church (PA)
Bucknell U (PA)
California Baptist U (CA)
California State U, Dominguez Hills (CA)
Canisius Coll (NY)
Cardinal Stritch U (WI)
Caribbean U (PR)
The Catholic U of America (DC)
Central State U (OH)
Champlain Coll (VT)
Christian Brothers U (TN)
Clayton State U (GA)
Coll of Central Florida (FL)
Coll of Coastal Georgia (GA)
The Coll of New Rochelle (NY)
Coll of Staten Island of the City U of New York (NY)
Colorado Mesa U (CO)
Colorado State U–Pueblo (CO)
Columbia Central U, Caguas (PR)
Columbia Central U, Yauco (PR)
Columbia Coll (MO)
Columbus State U (GA)
Concordia U, Nebraska (NE)
Covenant Coll (GA)
Davenport U, Grand Rapids (MI)
Dickinson State U (ND)
Drake U (IA)
Drexel U (PA)
Earlham Coll (IN)
East Central U (OK)
Eastern Michigan U (MI)
Eastern Nazarene Coll (MA)
East Texas Baptist U (TX)
Edgewood Coll (WI)
The Evergreen State Coll (WA)
Excelsior Coll (NY)
Framingham State U (MA)
Franklin Coll (IN)
Georgia Gwinnett Coll (GA)
Goshen Coll (IN)
Grand Valley State U (MI)
HEC Montreal (QC, Canada)
Hofstra U (NY)
Hollins U (VA)
Howard Payne U (TX)
Huntingdon Coll (AL)
Husson U (ME)
Idaho State U (ID)
Indiana State U (IN)
Indiana U Bloomington (IN)
Indiana U East (IN)
Indiana U Kokomo (IN)
Indiana U Northwest (IN)
Indiana U of Pennsylvania (PA)
Indiana U–Purdue U Indianapolis (IN)
Indiana U South Bend (IN)
Indiana U Southeast (IN)

Iowa State U of Science and Technology (IA)
Ithaca Coll (NY)
Jacksonville U (FL)
John Brown U (AR)
Johns Hopkins U (MD)
Juniata Coll (PA)
Kalamazoo Coll (MI)
Kansas State U (KS)
Kentucky State U (KY)
King U (TN)
Lamar U (TX)
La Salle U (PA)
La Sierra U (CA)
Liberty U (VA)
LIM Coll (NY)
Limestone Coll (SC)
Louisiana Coll (LA)
Manchester U (IN)
Marymount Manhattan Coll (NY)
Maryville U of Saint Louis (MO)
Massachusetts Inst of Technology (MA)
McMurry U (TX)
Medgar Evers Coll of the City U of New York (NY)
Mercer U, Macon (GA)
Metropolitan Coll of New York (NY)
MidAmerica Nazarene U (KS)
Missouri State U (MO)
Montana Tech of The U of Montana (MT)
Morehead State U (KY)
Mount Mercy U (IA)
Mount St. Mary's U (MD)
Mount Vernon Nazarene U (OH)
Multnomah U (OR)
Murray State U (KY)
New Mexico State U (NM)
New York U (NY)
Niagara U (NY)
Nichols Coll (MA)
Northeastern U (MA)
Northern Illinois U (IL)
Northern Kentucky U (KY)
Northwest Christian U (OR)
Northwest U (WA)
Oakland U (MI)
Ohio Northern U (OH)
The Ohio State U (OH)
The Ohio State U at Lima (OH)
The Ohio State U at Mansfield (OH)
The Ohio State U at Marion (OH)
The Ohio State U at Newark (OH)
Ohio Wesleyan U (OH)
Oklahoma Christian U (OK)
Pace U (NY)
Pace U, Pleasantville Campus (NY)
Penn State Abington (PA)
Penn State Altoona (PA)
Penn State Berks (PA)
Penn State Lehigh Valley (PA)
Penn State Schuylkill (PA)
Pittsburg State U (KS)
Purdue U Northwest (IN)
Randolph Coll (VA)
Randolph-Macon Coll (VA)
Rochester Inst of Technology (NY)
Roosevelt U (IL)
Saginaw Valley State U (MI)
Saint Anselm Coll (NH)
St. Lawrence U (NY)
Saint Mary's Coll of California (CA)
St. Thomas U (FL)
Saint Vincent Coll (PA)
Sam Houston State U (TX)
Santa Clara U (CA)
Schreiner U (TX)
Seattle Pacific U (WA)
Seattle U (WA)
Siena Coll (NY)
Skidmore Coll (NY)
Southern Arkansas U–Magnolia (AR)
Southwestern U (TX)
State U of New York at New Paltz (NY)
State U of New York at Plattsburgh (NY)
State U of New York Empire State Coll (NY)
Stephen F. Austin State U (TX)
Sullivan U (KY)
Sweet Briar Coll (VA)
Tabor Coll (KS)
Tarleton State U (TX)
Temple U (PA)

Texas A&M U–Commerce (TX)
Texas A&M U–Corpus Christi (TX)
Texas A&M U–Kingsville (TX)
Texas A&M U–Texarkana (TX)
Texas Tech U (TX)
Texas Woman's U (TX)
Transylvania U (KY)
Trine U (IN)
Trinity Christian Coll (IL)
The U of Akron (OH)
The U of Arizona (AZ)
U of Arkansas (AR)
U of Bridgeport (CT)
U of Central Arkansas (AR)
U of Central Florida (FL)
U of Cincinnati (OH)
U of Denver (CO)
U of Georgia (GA)
U of Hawaii at Manoa (HI)
U of Houston–Clear Lake (TX)
U of Houston–Downtown (TX)
The U of Kansas (KS)
U of Kentucky (KY)
U of Maine at Fort Kent (ME)
U of Maryland, Coll Park (MD)
U of Massachusetts Dartmouth (MA)
U of Missouri–St. Louis (MO)
U of Montana (MT)
U of Nevada, Reno (NV)
U of North Texas (TX)
U of Notre Dame (IN)
U of Oregon (OR)
U of Pittsburgh (PA)
U of Puget Sound (WA)
U of Regina (SK, Canada)
U of Rhode Island (RI)
U of Rochester (NY)
U of Saint Francis (IN)
U of Science and Arts of Oklahoma (OK)
U of South Alabama (AL)
U of South Dakota (SD)
U of South Florida Sarasota-Manatee (FL)
The U of Texas at Austin (TX)
The U of Texas at Dallas (TX)
The U of Texas at San Antonio (TX)
The U of Tulsa (OK)
U of Utah (UT)
U of Virginia (VA)
U of Wisconsin–Milwaukee (WI)
U of Wisconsin–Platteville (WI)
U of Wisconsin–Whitewater (WI)
Utah State U (UT)
Villa Maria Coll (NY)
Virginia Commonwealth U (VA)
Wake Forest U (NC)
Waldorf U (IA)
Walsh Coll of Accountancy and Business Administration (MI)
Washington & Jefferson Coll (PA)
Washington State U (WA)
Washington U in St. Louis (MO)
Webber Intl U (FL)
Welch Coll (TN)
Western New England U (MA)
Western Oregon U (OR)
Westmont Coll (CA)
West Texas A&M U (TX)
West Virginia U (WV)
West Virginia U Inst of Technology (WV)
Worcester Polytechnic Inst (MA)
Wright State U (OH)
Wright State U–Lake Campus (OH)
Youngstown State U (OH)

BUSINESS/CORPORATE COMMUNICATIONS

Aquinas Coll (MI)
Augustana U (SD)
Babson Coll (MA)
Bentley U (MA)
Brock U (ON, Canada)
Bryant U (RI)
Calvin Coll (MI)
Central Penn Coll (PA)
Chestnut Hill Coll (PA)
Christian Brothers U (TN)
Concordia U Chicago (IL)
Concordia U, Nebraska (NE)
Duquesne U (PA)
Elon U (NC)
Holy Names U (CA)
Inter American U of Puerto Rico, Metropolitan Campus (PR)

Lycoming Coll (PA)
Marietta Coll (OH)
Marquette U (WI)
MidAmerica Nazarene U (KS)
Morningside Coll (IA)
National U (CA)
Nichols Coll (MA)
North Dakota State U (ND)
Penn State Abington (PA)
Point Loma Nazarene U (CA)
Rockhurst U (MO)
Roosevelt U (IL)
Saint Leo U (FL)
Stephen F. Austin State U (TX)
Stevenson U (MD)
Trinity Christian Coll (IL)
U of Houston (TX)
U of New England (ME)
Walsh U (OH)

BUSINESS FAMILY AND CONSUMER SCIENCES/ HUMAN SCIENCES

Brigham Young U (UT)
U of Houston (TX)
Virginia Polytechnic Inst and State U (VA)

BUSINESS, MANAGEMENT, AND MARKETING RELATED

Adelphi U (NY)
Alfred U (NY)
American U (DC)
Arizona State U at the Polytechnic campus (AZ)
Arizona State U at the Tempe campus (AZ)
Arizona State U at the West campus (AZ)
Arlington Baptist U (TX)
Athens State U (AL)
Benedictine U (IL)
Bentley U (MA)
Bowling Green State U (OH)
Bradley U (IL)
Bridgewater State U (MA)
California State U, Dominguez Hills (CA)
Concordia Coll–New York (NY)
Corban U (OR)
Duquesne U (PA)
Eastern Nazarene Coll (MA)
Eastern U (PA)
Elms Coll (MA)
FIDM/Fashion Inst of Design & Merchandising, Los Angeles Campus (CA)
FIDM/Fashion Inst of Design & Merchandising, San Francisco Campus (CA)
Franklin U Switzerland (Switzerland)
Hamline U (MN)
Hofstra U (NY)
Howard Payne U (TX)
Loyola U Chicago (IL)
Mercyhurst U (PA)
Messiah Coll (PA)
Missouri U of Science and Technology (MO)
Multnomah U (OR)
Neumann U (PA)
New Jersey Inst of Technology (NJ)
New York U (NY)
Oregon Inst of Technology (OR)
Penn State U Park (PA)
Point Park U (PA)
Polytechnic U of Puerto Rico (PR)
Roberts Wesleyan Coll (NY)
Saint Anselm Coll (NH)
Saint Mary's U of Minnesota (MN)
Seton Hill U (PA)
Sierra Nevada Coll (NV)
Skidmore Coll (NY)
Southwestern Coll (KS)
State U of New York at Plattsburgh (NY)
State U of New York Coll of Technology at Alfred (NY)
State U of New York Coll of Technology at Canton (NY)
State U of New York Coll of Technology at Delhi (NY)
State U of New York Maritime Coll (NY)
Susquehanna U (PA)
Trevecca Nazarene U (TN)
Troy U (AL)

U of Minnesota, Crookston (MN)
U of Southern Mississippi (MS)
U of Wisconsin–Stout (WI)
U of Wisconsin–Whitewater (WI)
Utica Coll (NY)
Western State Colorado U (CO)
Worcester Polytechnic Inst (MA)

BUSINESS/MANAGERIAL ECONOMICS

Allegheny Coll (PA)
Andrews U (MI)
Arkansas Tech U (AR)
Auburn U (AL)
Ball State U (IN)
Bard Coll (NY)
Baruch Coll of the City U of New York (NY)
Baylor U (TX)
Belmont U (TN)
Beloit Coll (WI)
Benedictine U (IL)
Bentley U (MA)
Berry Coll (GA)
Boise State U (ID)
Boston Coll (MA)
Bowling Green State U (OH)
Bradley U (IL)
Brock U (ON, Canada)
Bryant U (RI)
California Inst of Technology (CA)
California State U, Fullerton (CA)
California State U, Long Beach (CA)
Campbellsville U (KY)
Canisius Coll (NY)
Capital U (OH)
Carson-Newman U (TN)
Cedarville U (OH)
Chapman U (CA)
Charleston Southern U (SC)
Chatham U (PA)
Clarion U of Pennsylvania (PA)
Clark Atlanta U (GA)
Cleveland State U (OH)
Coastal Carolina U (SC)
Coll of Mount Saint Vincent (NY)
The Coll of Saint Rose (NY)
The Coll of Wooster (OH)
Colorado State U–Pueblo (CO)
Converse Coll (SC)
Delaware State U (DE)
DePaul U (IL)
Duquesne U (PA)
Eastern Michigan U (MI)
Eastern Washington U (WA)
East Tennessee State U (TN)
Fairleigh Dickinson U, Florham Campus (NJ)
Fairleigh Dickinson U, Metropolitan Campus (NJ)
Fordham U (NY)
Fort Lewis Coll (CO)
Francis Marion U (SC)
Georgetown Coll (KY)
The George Washington U (DC)
Georgia Coll & State U (GA)
Georgia Inst of Technology (GA)
Georgia Southern U (GA)
Georgia Southern U–Armstrong Campus (GA)
Georgia State U (GA)
Grambling State U (LA)
Grand Valley State U (MI)
Green Mountain Coll (VT)
Greensboro Coll (NC)
Grove City Coll (PA)
Gustavus Adolphus Coll (MN)
Hampden-Sydney Coll (VA)
HEC Montreal (QC, Canada)
Hofstra U (NY)
Hope Coll (MI)
Husson U (ME)
Illinois Coll (IL)
Inter American U of Puerto Rico, Bayamón Campus (PR)
Inter American U of Puerto Rico, Metropolitan Campus (PR)
Inter American U of Puerto Rico, San Germán Campus (PR)
Iowa State U of Science and Technology (IA)
Ithaca Coll (NY)
Jackson State U (MS)
James Madison U (VA)
Kennesaw State U (GA)
Kent State U (OH)

Lamar U (TX)
Lehigh U (PA)
Lewis U (IL)
Limestone Coll (SC)
Lincoln Memorial U (TN)
Lipscomb U (TN)
Louisiana Coll (LA)
Louisiana State U and A&M Coll (LA)
Loyola U Chicago (IL)
Loyola U New Orleans (LA)
Marquette U (WI)
Marshall U (WV)
Mary Baldwin U (VA)
Marymount Manhattan Coll (NY)
Miami U (OH)
Middle Tennessee State U (TN)
Mississippi State U (MS)
Missouri Valley Coll (MO)
New York U (NY)
Niagara U (NY)
Nichols Coll (MA)
North Carolina State U (NC)
Northern Arizona U (AZ)
Northern Kentucky U (KY)
Northwest Missouri State U (MO)
Oakland U (MI)
Oglethorpe U (GA)
The Ohio State U (OH)
The Ohio State U at Lima (OH)
The Ohio State U at Mansfield (OH)
The Ohio State U at Marion (OH)
The Ohio State U at Newark (OH)
Ohio U (OH)
Ohio Wesleyan U (OH)
Oklahoma State U (OK)
Old Dominion U (VA)
Otterbein U (OH)
Pace U (NY)
Pace U, Pleasantville Campus (NY)
Penn State Abington (PA)
Penn State Altoona (PA)
Penn State Beaver (PA)
Penn State Berks (PA)
Penn State Brandywine (PA)
Penn State DuBois (PA)
Penn State Erie, The Behrend Coll (PA)
Penn State Fayette, The Eberly Campus (PA)
Penn State Greater Allegheny (PA)
Penn State Hazleton (PA)
Penn State Lehigh Valley (PA)
Penn State Mont Alto (PA)
Penn State New Kensington (PA)
Penn State Schuylkill (PA)
Penn State Shenango (PA)
Penn State Wilkes-Barre (PA)
Penn State Worthington Scranton (PA)
Penn State York (PA)
Pfeiffer U (NC)
Point Loma Nazarene U (CA)
Presbyterian Coll (SC)
Quinnipiac U (CT)
Rider U (NJ)
Saginaw Valley State U (MI)
Saint Anselm Coll (NH)
Saint Peter's U (NJ)
Salisbury U (MD)
Samford U (AL)
Sam Houston State U (TX)
Santa Clara U (CA)
Seattle U (WA)
Shenandoah U (VA)
Shorter U (GA)
Sonoma State U (CA)
Southern Illinois U Carbondale (IL)
Southern Illinois U Edwardsville (IL)
Spring Hill Coll (AL)
State U of New York at Plattsburgh (NY)
State U of New York Coll at Oneonta (NY)
State U of New York Coll at Potsdam (NY)
Stephen F. Austin State U (TX)
Stetson U (FL)
Suffolk U (MA)
Tarleton State U (TX)
Taylor U (IN)
Tennessee Technological U (TN)
Texas A&M U–Corpus Christi (TX)
Texas State U (TX)
Troy U (AL)
Union Coll (NY)

Union U (TN)
The U of Alabama (AL)
The U of Alabama at Birmingham (AL)
The U of Arizona (AZ)
U of Arkansas (AR)
U of California, Irvine (CA)
U of California, Los Angeles (CA)
U of California, Riverside (CA)
U of California, Santa Cruz (CA)
U of Central Florida (FL)
U of Central Oklahoma (OK)
U of Dayton (OH)
U of Denver (CO)
U of Georgia (GA)
U of Guelph (ON, Canada)
U of Idaho (ID)
U of Kentucky (KY)
U of Louisville (KY)
U of Maine at Farmington (ME)
U of Mary Hardin-Baylor (TX)
U of Memphis (TN)
U of Miami (FL)
U of Missouri (MO)
U of Nebraska–Lincoln (NE)
U of Nevada, Reno (NV)
U of North Alabama (AL)
The U of North Carolina at Charlotte (NC)
The U of North Carolina at Greensboro (NC)
U of North Dakota (ND)
U of North Florida (FL)
U of North Texas (TX)
U of Oklahoma (OK)
U of Rochester (NY)
U of San Diego (CA)
U of San Francisco (CA)
U of Saskatchewan (SK, Canada)
U of South Carolina (SC)
U of Southern Mississippi (MS)
U of South Florida, St. Petersburg (FL)
The U of Tennessee (TN)
The U of Tennessee at Martin (TN)
The U of Texas at San Antonio (TX)
U of the Incarnate Word (TX)
U of West Georgia (GA)
U of Wyoming (WY)
Utica Coll (NY)
Valdosta State U (GA)
Villanova U (PA)
Virginia Commonwealth U (VA)
Virginia Polytechnic Inst and State U (VA)
Washington State U (WA)
Washington U in St. Louis (MO)
Weber State U (UT)
West Chester U of Pennsylvania (PA)
Western Illinois U (IL)
Western Kentucky U (KY)
Western Michigan U (MI)
Western State Colorado U (CO)
Westminster Coll (UT)
Westmont Coll (CA)
West Texas A&M U (TX)
West Virginia U (WV)
West Virginia Wesleyan Coll (WV)
Wheaton Coll (IL)
Wichita State U (KS)
Widener U (PA)
Wofford Coll (SC)
Wright State U (OH)
Wright State U–Lake Campus (OH)
Youngstown State U (OH)

BUSINESS OPERATIONS SUPPORT AND SECRETARIAL SERVICES RELATED

Delaware State U (DE)
State U of New York at New Paltz (NY)

BUSINESS STATISTICS

Ball State U (IN)
Baylor U (TX)
Ferris State U (MI)
HEC Montreal (QC, Canada)
Hofstra U (NY)
Loyola U New Orleans (LA)
Marian U (IN)
Maryville U of Saint Louis (MO)
U of Central Missouri (MO)
U of Denver (CO)
The U of Tennessee (TN)
The U of Tulsa (OK)

BUSINESS TEACHER EDUCATION
Adams State U (CO)
Arizona Christian U (AZ)
Arkansas Tech U (AR)
Auburn U (AL)
Avila U (MO)
Ball State U (IN)
Baylor U (TX)
Bethune-Cookman U (FL)
Black Hills State U (SD)
Bluefield Coll (VA)
Bowling Green State U (OH)
Buena Vista U (IA)
Buffalo State Coll, State U of New York (NY)
California State U, Dominguez Hills (CA)
Campbellsville U (KY)
Canisius Coll (NY)
Carson-Newman U (TN)
Coll of Saint Mary (NE)
Concordia U Wisconsin (WI)
Corban U (OR)
Dakota State U (SD)
Delaware State U (DE)
Dickinson State U (ND)
Doane U (NE)
East Central U (OK)
Eastern Michigan U (MI)
Eastern Washington U (WA)
Edgewood Coll (WI)
Emmanuel Coll (GA)
Emory & Henry Coll (VA)
Evangel U (MO)
Fayetteville State U (NC)
Ferris State U (MI)
Friends U (KS)
Goshen Coll (IN)
Gwynedd Mercy U (PA)
Hampton U (VA)
Hannibal-LaGrange U (MO)
Hofstra U (NY)
Howard Payne U (TX)
Illinois State U (IL)
Immaculata U (PA)
Indiana State U (IN)
Lee U (TN)
Lehman Coll of the City U of New York (NY)
LeTourneau U (TX)
Lincoln U (MO)
Lindenwood U (MO)
Louisiana Coll (LA)
Maranatha Baptist U (WI)
Middle Tennessee State U (TN)
Minot State U (ND)
Mississippi State U (MS)
Missouri Baptist U (MO)
Missouri State U (MO)
Morehead State U (KY)
Mount Vernon Nazarene U (OH)
Nazareth Coll of Rochester (NY)
Niagara U (NY)
Northwestern Coll (IA)
Northwest Missouri State U (MO)
Oakland City U (IN)
Ohio Wesleyan U (OH)
Oral Roberts U (OK)
Rider U (NJ)
Robert Morris U (PA)
Rust Coll (MS)
Saint Vincent Coll (PA)
Sam Houston State U (TX)
Southern Arkansas U–Magnolia (AR)
Southern Utah U (UT)
Southwestern Adventist U (TX)
Trevecca Nazarene U (TN)
Trinity Christian Coll (IL)
Union U (TN)
U of Central Arkansas (AR)
U of Central Missouri (MO)
U of Maine at Machias (ME)
U of Maryland Eastern Shore (MD)
U of Minnesota, Twin Cities Campus (MN)
U of Missouri (MO)
U of Nebraska at Kearney (NE)
U of Nebraska–Lincoln (NE)
The U of North Carolina at Greensboro (NC)
U of Northern Iowa (IA)
U of Regina (SK, Canada)
U of Southern Mississippi (MS)
The U of Tennessee at Martin (TN)
U of Wisconsin–Whitewater (WI)
Upper Iowa U (IA)
Utah State U (UT)
Utah Valley U (UT)
Utica Coll (NY)
Valley City State U (ND)
Wayland Baptist U (TX)
Wayne State Coll (NE)
Weber State U (UT)
Western Kentucky U (KY)
Western Michigan U (MI)
Winona State U (MN)

CAD/CADD DRAFTING/ DESIGN TECHNOLOGY
Academy of Art U (CA)
Eastern Michigan U (MI)
Idaho State U (ID)
Murray State U (KY)
Trine U (IN)

CANADIAN LITERATURE
Marlboro Coll (VT)

CANADIAN STUDIES
Acadia U (NS, Canada)
Athabasca U (AB, Canada)
Brandon U (MB, Canada)
Brock U (ON, Canada)
Concordia U of Edmonton (AB, Canada)
Trent U (ON, Canada)
Université Sainte-Anne (NS, Canada)
U of Toronto (ON, Canada)
U of Washington (WA)
U of Waterloo (ON, Canada)
Western Washington U (WA)

CARDIOVASCULAR TECHNOLOGY
Louisiana State U Health Sciences Center (LA)
Piedmont Coll (GA)
Saint Mary's U of Minnesota (MN)
Weber State U (UT)

CARIBBEAN STUDIES
Hofstra U (NY)
Northwestern U (IL)

CASINO MANAGEMENT
Central Michigan U (MI)

CELL AND MOLECULAR BIOLOGY
Adams State U (CO)
Bennington Coll (VT)
Binghamton U, State U of New York (NY)
Bradley U (IL)
Bridgewater State U (MA)
Bryant U (RI)
Bucknell U (PA)
Canisius Coll (NY)
Cedarville U (OH)
Christopher Newport U (VA)
The Colorado Coll (CO)
Concordia U (QC, Canada)
Fort Lewis Coll (CO)
Grand Valley State U (MI)
Harvard U (MA)
John Jay Coll of Criminal Justice of the City U of New York (NY)
Johns Hopkins U (MD)
Liberty U (VA)
Limestone Coll (SC)
Loyola U New Orleans (LA)
Marymount U (VA)
Minnesota State U Moorhead (MN)
Missouri State U (MO)
Northeastern State U (OK)
Northwest Nazarene U (ID)
Ohio U (OH)
Oklahoma City U (OK)
Purdue U (IN)
Sacred Heart U (CT)
Seattle Pacific U (WA)
Seattle U (WA)
Texas A&M U (TX)
Texas Tech U (TX)
Université Sainte-Anne (NS, Canada)
The U of Arizona (AZ)
U of California, Irvine (CA)
U of California, Los Angeles (CA)
U of California, Santa Cruz (CA)
U of Colorado Boulder (CO)
U of Hawaii at Manoa (HI)
U of Michigan (MI)

U of Puget Sound (WA)
U of Regina (SK, Canada)
U of Rhode Island (RI)
The U of Tennessee at Martin (TN)
The U of Texas at Austin (TX)
U of Washington (WA)
Western Washington U (WA)

CELL BIOLOGY AND ANATOMICAL SCIENCES RELATED
Rutgers U–New Brunswick (NJ)
Tulane U (LA)
U of Mary Hardin-Baylor (TX)

CELL BIOLOGY AND ANATOMY
Dallas Baptist U (TX)
Huntingdon Coll (AL)
U of Saskatchewan (SK, Canada)
Western State Colorado U (CO)

CELL BIOLOGY AND HISTOLOGY
Beloit Coll (WI)
California State U, Dominguez Hills (CA)
California State U, Long Beach (CA)
California State U, San Marcos (CA)
The Coll of Saint Rose (NY)
Humboldt State U (CA)
Johns Hopkins U (MD)
Mansfield U of Pennsylvania (PA)
Marlboro Coll (VT)
Northwestern U (IL)
Rutgers U–New Brunswick (NJ)
San Francisco State U (CA)
Sonoma State U (CA)
Tulane U (LA)
U of California, Davis (CA)
U of California, San Diego (CA)
U of Georgia (GA)
U of Minnesota, Twin Cities Campus (MN)

CELTIC LANGUAGES
U of Notre Dame (IN)

CERAMIC ARTS AND CERAMICS
Adams State U (CO)
Alberta Coll of Art & Design (AB, Canada)
Alfred U (NY)
Anderson U (SC)
Aquinas Coll (MI)
Arcadia U (PA)
Bennington Coll (VT)
Bowling Green State U (OH)
Bradley U (IL)
Brigham Young U (UT)
California Coll of the Arts (CA)
California State U, Long Beach (CA)
Coll of the Atlantic (ME)
Coll of the Ozarks (MO)
Columbia Coll (MO)
Concordia U (QC, Canada)
Franklin Pierce U (NH)
Hofstra U (NY)
Indiana Wesleyan U (IN)
Inter American U of Puerto Rico, San Germán Campus (PR)
Kansas City Art Inst (MO)
Marlboro Coll (VT)
Maryland Inst Coll of Art (MD)
Marywood U (PA)
Massachusetts Coll of Art and Design (MA)
New Hampshire Inst of Art (NH)
Northern Michigan U (MI)
Northwest Nazarene U (ID)
Ohio Northern U (OH)
Pratt Inst (NY)
Providence Coll (RI)
Rhode Island Coll (RI)
Rhode Island School of Design (RI)
Rochester Inst of Technology (NY)
Rutgers U–New Brunswick (NJ)
Seton Hill U (PA)
State U of New York at New Paltz (NY)
Syracuse U (NY)
Temple U (PA)
Texas Christian U (TX)
The U of Akron (OH)
U of Dallas (TX)

U of Hartford (CT)
The U of Kansas (KS)
U of Massachusetts Dartmouth (MA)
U of Miami (FL)
U of Michigan (MI)
U of Oregon (OR)
U of Regina (SK, Canada)
U of Washington (WA)
Washington U in St. Louis (MO)
Western State Colorado U (CO)

CERAMIC SCIENCES AND ENGINEERING
Alfred U (NY)
Missouri U of Science and Technology (MO)
Rutgers U–New Brunswick (NJ)

CHEMICAL AND BIOMOLECULAR ENGINEERING
Florida State U (FL)
Johns Hopkins U (MD)
Massachusetts Inst of Technology (MA)
Milwaukee School of Eng (WI)
New York U (NY)
Stony Brook U, State U of New York (NY)
U of Washington (WA)

CHEMICAL ENGINEERING
American U of Beirut (Lebanon)
Arizona State U at the Tempe campus (AZ)
Auburn U (AL)
Bucknell U (PA)
California Baptist U (CA)
California Inst of Technology (CA)
California State Polytechnic U, Pomona (CA)
California State U, Long Beach (CA)
Calvin Coll (MI)
Carnegie Mellon U (PA)
Case Western Reserve U (OH)
Christian Brothers U (TN)
City Coll of the City U of New York (NY)
Clarkson U (NY)
Clemson U (SC)
Cleveland State U (OH)
Colorado State U (CO)
Columbia U (NY)
Cooper Union for the Advancement of Science and Art (NY)
Cornell U (NY)
Drexel U (PA)
Elon U (NC)
Florida Ag and Mech U (FL)
Florida Inst of Technology (FL)
Florida State U (FL)
Georgia Inst of Technology (GA)
Hampton U (VA)
Iowa State U of Science and Technology (IA)
Johns Hopkins U (MD)
Kansas State U (KS)
Kettering U (MI)
Lafayette Coll (PA)
Lamar U (TX)
Lehigh U (PA)
Louisiana State U and A&M Coll (LA)
Manhattan Coll (NY)
Massachusetts Inst of Technology (MA)
Miami U (OH)
Michigan State U (MI)
Michigan Technological U (MI)
Mississippi State U (MS)
Missouri U of Science and Technology (MO)
New Jersey Inst of Technology (NJ)
New Mexico Inst of Mining and Technology (NM)
New Mexico State U (NM)
New York U (NY)
North Carolina State U (NC)
Northeastern U (MA)
Northwestern U (IL)
The Ohio State U (OH)
Ohio U (OH)
Oklahoma State U (OK)
Oregon State U (OR)
Pace U (NY)
Penn State Abington (PA)

Penn State Altoona (PA)
Penn State Beaver (PA)
Penn State Berks (PA)
Penn State Brandywine (PA)
Penn State DuBois (PA)
Penn State Erie, The Behrend Coll (PA)
Penn State Fayette, The Eberly Campus (PA)
Penn State Greater Allegheny (PA)
Penn State Hazleton (PA)
Penn State Lehigh Valley (PA)
Penn State Mont Alto (PA)
Penn State New Kensington (PA)
Penn State Schuylkill (PA)
Penn State Shenango (PA)
Penn State U Park (PA)
Penn State Wilkes-Barre (PA)
Penn State Worthington Scranton (PA)
Penn State York (PA)
Polytechnic U of Puerto Rico (PR)
Prairie View A&M U (TX)
Princeton U (NJ)
Purdue U (IN)
Rensselaer Polytechnic Inst (NY)
Rice U (TX)
Rochester Inst of Technology (NY)
Rose-Hulman Inst of Technology (IN)
Rowan U (NJ)
Rutgers U–New Brunswick (NJ)
Saint Louis U–Madrid Campus (Spain)
Stanford U (CA)
Stevens Inst of Technology (NJ)
Syracuse U (NY)
Tennessee Technological U (TN)
Texas A&M U (TX)
Texas A&M U–Kingsville (TX)
Texas Tech U (TX)
Trine U (IN)
Tufts U (MA)
Tulane U (LA)
United States Military Acad (NY)
Université de Sherbrooke (QC, Canada)
U at Buffalo, the State U of New York (NY)
The U of Akron (OH)
The U of Alabama (AL)
The U of Arizona (AZ)
U of Arkansas (AR)
U of California, Davis (CA)
U of California, Irvine (CA)
U of California, Los Angeles (CA)
U of California, Riverside (CA)
U of California, San Diego (CA)
U of California, Santa Barbara (CA)
U of Cincinnati (OH)
U of Colorado Boulder (CO)
U of Dayton (OH)
U of Florida (FL)
U of Houston (TX)
U of Idaho (ID)
U of Illinois at Chicago (IL)
The U of Kansas (KS)
U of Kentucky (KY)
U of Louisville (KY)
U of Maine (ME)
U of Maryland, Baltimore County (MD)
U of Maryland, Coll Park (MD)
U of Massachusetts Amherst (MA)
U of Massachusetts Lowell (MA)
U of Michigan (MI)
U of Minnesota, Duluth (MN)
U of Minnesota, Twin Cities Campus (MN)
U of Missouri (MO)
U of Nebraska–Lincoln (NE)
U of Nevada, Reno (NV)
U of New Hampshire (NH)
U of New Haven (CT)
U of New Mexico (NM)
U of North Dakota (ND)
U of Notre Dame (IN)
U of Oklahoma (OK)
U of Pennsylvania (PA)
U of Pittsburgh (PA)
U of Rhode Island (RI)
U of Rochester (NY)
U of Saskatchewan (SK, Canada)
U of South Alabama (AL)
U of South Carolina (SC)
U of Southern California (CA)
The U of Tennessee (TN)

The U of Tennessee at Chattanooga (TN)
The U of Texas at Austin (TX)
The U of Texas at San Antonio (TX)
The U of Toledo (OH)
U of Toronto (ON, Canada)
The U of Tulsa (OK)
U of Utah (UT)
U of Virginia (VA)
U of Washington (WA)
U of Waterloo (ON, Canada)
U of Wisconsin–Madison (WI)
U of Wisconsin–Stevens Point (WI)
U of Wyoming (WY)
Vanderbilt U (TN)
Villanova U (PA)
Virginia Commonwealth U (VA)
Virginia Polytechnic Inst and State U (VA)
Washington State U (WA)
Washington U in St. Louis (MO)
Wayne State U (MI)
Western Michigan U (MI)
West Virginia U (WV)
West Virginia U Inst of Technology (WV)
Widener U (PA)
Worcester Polytechnic Inst (MA)
Youngstown State U (OH)

CHEMICAL ENGINEERING RELATED
State U of New York Coll of Environmental Science and Forestry (NY)

CHEMICAL ENGINEERING TECHNOLOGY
United States Military Acad (NY)

CHEMICAL PHYSICS
Adams State U (CO)
Aquinas Coll (MI)
Augustana U (SD)
Bowdoin Coll (ME)
Carnegie Mellon U (PA)
Centre Coll (KY)
Columbia U (NY)
Hamilton Coll (NY)
Harvard U (MA)
Hendrix Coll (AR)
Michigan State U (MI)
Saginaw Valley State U (MI)
Simon Fraser U (BC, Canada)
Susquehanna U (PA)
U of Guelph (ON, Canada)
U of Waterloo (ON, Canada)

CHEMICAL TECHNOLOGY
U of Cincinnati (OH)
U of Regina (SK, Canada)

CHEMISTRY
Abilene Christian U (TX)
Acadia U (NS, Canada)
Adams State U (CO)
Adelphi U (NY)
Agnes Scott Coll (GA)
Alabama State U (AL)
Albion Coll (MI)
Albright Coll (PA)
Alcorn State U (MS)
Alfred U (NY)
Allegheny Coll (PA)
Alma Coll (MI)
Alverno Coll (WI)
American Intl Coll (MA)
American U (DC)
The American U in Cairo (Egypt)
American U of Beirut (Lebanon)
Amherst Coll (MA)
Anderson U (IN)
Andrews U (MI)
Angelo State U (TX)
Appalachian State U (NC)
Aquinas Coll (MI)
Arcadia U (PA)
Arizona State U at the Tempe campus (AZ)
Arkansas Tech U (AR)
Asbury U (KY)
Ashland U (OH)
Assumption Coll (MA)
Athens State U (AL)
Auburn U (AL)
Auburn U at Montgomery (AL)
Augsburg U (MN)
Augustana Coll (IL)
Augustana U (SD)

Austin Coll (TX)
Austin Peay State U (TN)
Averett U (VA)
Azusa Pacific U (CA)
Baker U (KS)
Baldwin Wallace U (OH)
Ball State U (IN)
Bard Coll (NY)
Barnard Coll (NY)
Barry U (FL)
Barton Coll (NC)
Bates Coll (ME)
Baylor U (TX)
Belhaven U (MS)
Bellarmine U (KY)
Belmont U (TN)
Beloit Coll (WI)
Bemidji State U (MN)
Benedictine Coll (KS)
Benedictine U (IL)
Bennett Coll (NC)
Bennington Coll (VT)
Berea Coll (KY)
Berry Coll (GA)
Bethany Lutheran Coll (MN)
Bethel Coll (IN)
Bethel Coll (KS)
Bethel U (MN)
Bethel U (TN)
Bethune-Cookman U (FL)
Binghamton U, State U of New York (NY)
Biola U (CA)
Birmingham-Southern Coll (AL)
Blackburn Coll (IL)
Black Hills State U (SD)
Bloomsburg U of Pennsylvania (PA)
Bluefield Coll (VA)
Bluffton U (OH)
Bob Jones U (SC)
Boise State U (ID)
Boston Coll (MA)
Boston U (MA)
Bowdoin Coll (ME)
Bowling Green State U (OH)
Bradley U (IL)
Brandeis U (MA)
Brandon U (MB, Canada)
Brescia U (KY)
Bridgewater Coll (VA)
Bridgewater State U (MA)
Brigham Young U–Idaho (ID)
Brock U (ON, Canada)
Bryn Mawr Coll (PA)
Bucknell U (PA)
Buena Vista U (IA)
Buffalo State Coll, State U of New York (NY)
Butler U (IN)
Caldwell U (NJ)
California Baptist U (CA)
California Inst of Technology (CA)
California Lutheran U (CA)
California Polytechnic State U, San Luis Obispo (CA)
California State Polytechnic U, Pomona (CA)
California State U, Dominguez Hills (CA)
California State U, East Bay (CA)
California State U, Fullerton (CA)
California State U, Long Beach (CA)
California State U, Los Angeles (CA)
California State U, Northridge (CA)
California State U, Sacramento (CA)
California State U, San Bernardino (CA)
California State U, San Marcos (CA)
California State U, Stanislaus (CA)
California U of Pennsylvania (PA)
Calvin Coll (MI)
Cameron U (OK)
Campbellsville U (KY)
Canisius Coll (NY)
Capital U (OH)
Cardinal Stritch U (WI)
Carleton Coll (MN)
Carlow U (PA)
Carnegie Mellon U (PA)
Carroll Coll (MT)
Carroll U (WI)
Carson-Newman U (TN)
Carthage Coll (WI)

Case Western Reserve U (OH)
Catawba Coll (NC)
The Catholic U of America (DC)
Cedar Crest Coll (PA)
Cedarville U (OH)
Centenary Coll of Louisiana (LA)
Central Connecticut State U (CT)
Central Methodist U (MO)
Central Michigan U (MI)
Central State U (OH)
Centre Coll (KY)
Chapman U (CA)
Charleston Southern U (SC)
Chatham U (PA)
Chestnut Hill Coll (PA)
Christian Brothers U (TN)
Christopher Newport U (VA)
The Citadel, The Military Coll of South Carolina (SC)
City Coll of the City U of New York (NY)
Claremont McKenna Coll (CA)
Clarion U of Pennsylvania (PA)
Clark Atlanta U (GA)
Clarke U (IA)
Clarkson U (NY)
Clark U (MA)
Clayton State U (GA)
Clemson U (SC)
Cleveland State U (OH)
Coastal Carolina U (SC)
Coe Coll (IA)
Coker Coll (SC)
Colby Coll (ME)
Colgate U (NY)
The Coll at Brockport, State U of New York (NY)
Coll of Charleston (SC)
The Coll of Idaho (ID)
Coll of Mount Saint Vincent (NY)
The Coll of New Jersey (NJ)
The Coll of New Rochelle (NY)
Coll of Saint Benedict (MN)
Coll of Saint Elizabeth (NJ)
Coll of Saint Mary (NE)
The Coll of Saint Rose (NY)
The Coll of St. Scholastica (MN)
Coll of Staten Island of the City U of New York (NY)
Coll of the Holy Cross (MA)
Coll of the Ozarks (MO)
The Coll of William and Mary (VA)
The Coll of Wooster (OH)
The Colorado Coll (CO)
Colorado Mesa U (CO)
Colorado State U (CO)
Colorado State U–Pueblo (CO)
Columbia Coll (MO)
Columbia Coll (SC)
Columbia U (NY)
Columbus State U (GA)
Concordia U (QC, Canada)
Concordia U Chicago (IL)
Concordia U Irvine (CA)
Concordia U, Nebraska (NE)
Concordia U of Edmonton (AB, Canada)
Concordia U, St. Paul (MN)
Concord U (WV)
Connecticut Coll (CT)
Converse Coll (SC)
Cornell Coll (IA)
Cornell U (NY)
Covenant Coll (GA)
Creighton U (NE)
Culver-Stockton Coll (MO)
Dartmouth Coll (NH)
Davidson Coll (NC)
Delaware State U (DE)
Delaware Valley U (PA)
Denison U (OH)
DePaul U (IL)
DePauw U (IN)
DeSales U (PA)
Dickinson Coll (PA)
Dickinson State U (ND)
Doane U (NE)
Dominican U (IL)
Dominican U of California (CA)
Drake U (IA)
Drew U (NJ)
Drexel U (PA)
Drury U (MO)
Duquesne U (PA)
D'Youville Coll (NY)
Earlham Coll (IN)
East Carolina U (NC)

East Central U (OK)
Eastern Mennonite U (VA)
Eastern Michigan U (MI)
Eastern Nazarene Coll (MA)
Eastern New Mexico U (NM)
Eastern U (PA)
Eastern Washington U (WA)
East Stroudsburg U of Pennsylvania (PA)
East Tennessee State U (TN)
East Texas Baptist U (TX)
Eckerd Coll (FL)
Edgewood Coll (WI)
Elizabethtown Coll (PA)
Elmhurst Coll (IL)
Elms Coll (MA)
Elon U (NC)
Emmanuel Coll (MA)
Emory & Henry Coll (VA)
Emory U (GA)
Emporia State U (KS)
Evangel U (MO)
Fairfield U (CT)
Fairleigh Dickinson U, Florham Campus (NJ)
Fairleigh Dickinson U, Metropolitan Campus (NJ)
Fayetteville State U (NC)
Ferris State U (MI)
Fitchburg State U (MA)
Florida Ag and Mech U (FL)
Florida Atlantic U (FL)
Florida Gulf Coast U (FL)
Florida Inst of Technology (FL)
Florida Intl U (FL)
Florida Southern Coll (FL)
Florida State U (FL)
Fordham U (NY)
Fort Lewis Coll (CO)
Framingham State U (MA)
Francis Marion U (SC)
Franklin & Marshall Coll (PA)
Franklin Coll (IN)
Friends U (KS)
Frostburg State U (MD)
Furman U (SC)
Gannon U (PA)
Geneva Coll (PA)
George Mason U (VA)
Georgetown Coll (KY)
Georgetown U (DC)
The George Washington U (DC)
Georgia Coll & State U (GA)
Georgia Gwinnett Coll (GA)
Georgia Inst of Technology (GA)
Georgian Court U (NJ)
Georgia Southern U (GA)
Georgia Southern U–Armstrong Campus (GA)
Georgia Southwestern State U (GA)
Georgia State U (GA)
Gettysburg Coll (PA)
Gonzaga U (WA)
Gordon Coll (MA)
Goshen Coll (IN)
Governors State U (IL)
Graceland U (IA)
Grambling State U (LA)
Grand Valley State U (MI)
Greensboro Coll (NC)
Greenville U (IL)
Grinnell Coll (IA)
Grove City Coll (PA)
Guilford Coll (NC)
Gustavus Adolphus Coll (MN)
Hamilton Coll (NY)
Hamline U (MN)
Hampden-Sydney Coll (VA)
Hampshire Coll (MA)
Hampton U (VA)
Harding U (AR)
Hardin-Simmons U (TX)
Hartwick Coll (NY)
Harvard U (MA)
Harvey Mudd Coll (CA)
Haverford Coll (PA)
Hawai'i Pacific U (HI)
Heidelberg U (OH)
Hendrix Coll (AR)
High Point U (NC)
Hillsdale Coll (MI)
Hiram Coll (OH)
Hobart and William Smith Colls (NY)
Hofstra U (NY)
Hollins U (VA)

Hood Coll (MD)
Hope Coll (MI)
Houston Baptist U (TX)
Howard Payne U (TX)
Humboldt State U (CA)
Hunter Coll of the City U of New York (NY)
Huntingdon Coll (AL)
Huston-Tillotson U (TX)
Idaho State U (ID)
Illinois Coll (IL)
Illinois State U (IL)
Illinois Wesleyan U (IL)
Immaculata U (PA)
Indiana State U (IN)
Indiana U Bloomington (IN)
Indiana U Kokomo (IN)
Indiana U Northwest (IN)
Indiana U of Pennsylvania (PA)
Indiana–Purdue U Indianapolis (IN)
Indiana U South Bend (IN)
Indiana U Southeast (IN)
Indiana Wesleyan U (IN)
Inter American U of Puerto Rico, Metropolitan Campus (PR)
Inter American U of Puerto Rico, San Germán Campus (PR)
Iona Coll (NY)
Iowa State U of Science and Technology (IA)
Ithaca Coll (NY)
Jackson State U (MS)
Jacksonville U (FL)
James Madison U (VA)
John Brown U (AR)
John Carroll U (OH)
Johns Hopkins U (MD)
Johnson C. Smith U (NC)
Judson U (IL)
Juniata Coll (PA)
Kalamazoo Coll (MI)
Kansas State U (KS)
Kansas Wesleyan U (KS)
Kean U (NJ)
Keene State Coll (NH)
Kennesaw State U (GA)
Kent State U (OH)
Kentucky State U (KY)
Kenyon Coll (OH)
Kettering U (MI)
King's Coll (PA)
King U (TN)
Knox Coll (IL)
Kutztown U of Pennsylvania (PA)
Lafayette Coll (PA)
LaGrange Coll (GA)
Lamar U (TX)
Langston U (OK)
La Roche Coll (PA)
La Salle U (PA)
La Sierra U (CA)
Lawrence Technological U (MI)
Lawrence U (WI)
Lebanese American U (Lebanon)
Lebanon Valley Coll (PA)
Lee U (TN)
Lehigh U (PA)
Lehman Coll of the City U of New York (NY)
Le Moyne Coll (NY)
Lenoir-Rhyne U (NC)
LeTourneau U (TX)
Lewis U (IL)
Liberty U (VA)
Limestone Coll (SC)
Lincoln Memorial U (TN)
Lincoln U (MO)
Lincoln U (PA)
Lindenwood U (MO)
Linfield Coll (OR)
Lipscomb U (TN)
Lock Haven U of Pennsylvania (PA)
Long Island U–LIU Brooklyn (NY)
Long Island U–LIU Post (NY)
Longwood U (VA)
Loras Coll (IA)
Louisiana Coll (LA)
Louisiana State U and A&M Coll (LA)
Loyola Marymount U (CA)
Loyola U Chicago (IL)
Loyola U New Orleans (LA)
Lubbock Christian U (TX)
Luther Coll (IA)
Lycoming Coll (PA)
Lynchburg Coll (VA)

Lyon Coll (AR)
Macalester Coll (MN)
Madonna U (MI)
Malone U (OH)
Manchester U (IN)
Manhattan Coll (NY)
Manhattanville Coll (NY)
Mansfield U of Pennsylvania (PA)
Marian U (IN)
Marian U (WI)
Marietta Coll (OH)
Marist Coll (NY)
Marlboro Coll (VT)
Marquette U (WI)
Marshall U (WV)
Mary Baldwin U (VA)
Maryville Coll (TN)
Maryville U of Saint Louis (MO)
Massachusetts Coll of Liberal Arts (MA)
Massachusetts Inst of Technology (MA)
McDaniel Coll (MD)
McKendree U (IL)
McMurry U (TX)
McNeese State U (LA)
McPherson Coll (KS)
MCPHS U (MA)
Mercer U, Macon (GA)
Mercyhurst U (PA)
Meredith Coll (NC)
Merrimack Coll (MA)
Messiah Coll (PA)
Metropolitan State U of Denver (CO)
Miami U (OH)
Michigan State U (MI)
Michigan Technological U (MI)
MidAmerica Nazarene U (KS)
Middlebury Coll (VT)
Middle Tennessee State U (TN)
Millersville U of Pennsylvania (PA)
Milligan Coll (TN)
Millikin U (IL)
Millsaps Coll (MS)
Mills Coll (CA)
Minnesota State U Moorhead (MN)
Minot State U (ND)
Misericordia U (PA)
Mississippi State U (MS)
Missouri Baptist U (MO)
Missouri State U (MO)
Missouri U of Science and Technology (MO)
Missouri Western State U (MO)
Monmouth Coll (IL)
Montana Tech of The U of Montana (MT)
Montclair State U (NJ)
Moravian Coll (PA)
Morehead State U (KY)
Morehouse Coll (GA)
Morningside Coll (IA)
Mount Holyoke Coll (MA)
Mount Marty Coll (SD)
Mount Mary U (WI)
Mount Mercy U (IA)
Mount St. Joseph U (OH)
Mount Saint Mary Coll (NY)
Mount Saint Mary's U (CA)
Mount St. Mary's U (MD)
Mount Vernon Nazarene U (OH)
Muhlenberg Coll (PA)
Murray State U (KY)
Muskingum U (OH)
Nazareth Coll of Rochester (NY)
Newberry Coll (SC)
New Coll of Florida (FL)
New Jersey City U (NJ)
New Jersey Inst of Technology (NJ)
Newman U (KS)
New Mexico Highlands U (NM)
New Mexico Inst of Mining and Technology (NM)
New Mexico State U (NM)
New York Inst of Technology (NY)
New York U (NY)
Niagara U (NY)
North Carolina Central U (NC)
North Carolina State U (NC)
North Carolina Wesleyan Coll (NC)
North Central Coll (IL)
North Dakota State U (ND)
Northeastern State U (OK)
Northeastern U (MA)
Northern Arizona U (AZ)
Northern Illinois U (IL)

Northern Kentucky U (KY)
Northern Michigan U (MI)
Northern State U (SD)
Northland Coll (WI)
Northwestern Coll (IA)
Northwestern Oklahoma State U (OK)
Northwestern U (IL)
Northwest Missouri State U (MO)
Northwest Nazarene U (ID)
Nova Southeastern U (FL)
Oakland U (MI)
Oberlin Coll (OH)
Occidental Coll (CA)
Oglethorpe U (GA)
Ohio Dominican U (OH)
Ohio Northern U (OH)
The Ohio State U (OH)
Ohio U (OH)
Ohio Wesleyan U (OH)
Oklahoma Baptist U (OK)
Oklahoma Christian U (OK)
Oklahoma State U (OK)
Old Dominion U (VA)
Olivet Nazarene U (IL)
Oral Roberts U (OK)
Oregon State U (OR)
Otterbein U (OH)
Ouachita Baptist U (AR)
Our Lady of the Lake U (TX)
Pace U (NY)
Pace U, Pleasantville Campus (NY)
Pacific Lutheran U (WA)
Penn State Abington (PA)
Penn State Altoona (PA)
Penn State Beaver (PA)
Penn State Berks (PA)
Penn State Brandywine (PA)
Penn State DuBois (PA)
Penn State Erie, The Behrend Coll (PA)
Penn State Fayette, The Eberly Campus (PA)
Penn State Greater Allegheny (PA)
Penn State Hazleton (PA)
Penn State Lehigh Valley (PA)
Penn State Mont Alto (PA)
Penn State New Kensington (PA)
Penn State Schuylkill (PA)
Penn State Shenango (PA)
Penn State Park (PA)
Penn State Wilkes-Barre (PA)
Penn State Worthington Scranton (PA)
Penn State York (PA)
Pepperdine U, Malibu (CA)
Pfeiffer U (NC)
Piedmont Coll (GA)
Pittsburg State U (KS)
Pitzer Coll (CA)
Point Loma Nazarene U (CA)
Pomona Coll (CA)
Portland State U (OR)
Prairie View A&M U (TX)
Presbyterian Coll (SC)
Princeton U (NJ)
Principia Coll (IL)
Providence Coll (RI)
Purchase Coll, State U of New York (NY)
Purdue U (IN)
Purdue U Northwest (IN)
Queens Coll of the City U of New York (NY)
Quinnipiac U (CT)
Radford U (VA)
Ramapo Coll of New Jersey (NJ)
Randolph Coll (VA)
Randolph-Macon Coll (VA)
Redeemer U Coll (ON, Canada)
Reed Coll (OR)
Regis U (CO)
Rensselaer Polytechnic Inst (NY)
Rhode Island Coll (RI)
Rhodes Coll (TN)
Rice U (TX)
Rider U (NJ)
Ripon Coll (WI)
Roanoke Coll (VA)
Roberts Wesleyan Coll (NY)
Rochester Inst of Technology (NY)
Rockford U (IL)
Rockhurst U (MO)
Rocky Mountain Coll (MT)
Roger Williams U (RI)
Rollins Coll (FL)
Roosevelt U (IL)

Rose-Hulman Inst of Technology (IN)
Rosemont Coll (PA)
Rowan U (NJ)
Rust Coll (MS)
Rutgers U–Camden (NJ)
Rutgers U–Newark (NJ)
Rutgers U–New Brunswick (NJ)
Sacred Heart U (CT)
The Sage Colls (NY)
Saginaw Valley State U (MI)
St. Ambrose U (IA)
Saint Anselm Coll (NH)
St. Bonaventure U (NY)
St. Catherine U (MN)
Saint Francis U (PA)
St. John Fisher Coll (NY)
Saint John's U (MN)
St. John's U (NY)
St. Joseph's Coll, Long Island Campus (NY)
St. Joseph's Coll, New York (NY)
Saint Joseph's U (PA)
St. Lawrence U (NY)
Saint Louis U (MO)
Saint Louis U–Madrid Campus (Spain)
Saint Martin's U (WA)
Saint Mary's Coll of California (CA)
St. Mary's Coll of Maryland (MD)
St. Mary's U (TX)
Saint Mary's U of Minnesota (MN)
Saint Michael's Coll (VT)
St. Norbert Coll (WI)
St. Olaf Coll (MN)
Saint Peter's U (NJ)
St. Thomas U (FL)
Saint Vincent Coll (PA)
Salisbury U (MD)
Salve Regina U (RI)
Samford U (AL)
Sam Houston State U (TX)
San Diego State U (CA)
San Francisco State U (CA)
Santa Clara U (CA)
Sarah Lawrence Coll (NY)
Schreiner U (TX)
Scripps Coll (CA)
Seattle Pacific U (WA)
Seattle U (WA)
Seton Hill U (PA)
Sewanee: The U of the South (TN)
Shawnee State U (OH)
Shaw U (NC)
Shenandoah U (VA)
Shepherd U (WV)
Shippensburg U of Pennsylvania (PA)
Shorter U (GA)
Siena Coll (NY)
Simmons Coll (MA)
Simon Fraser U (BC, Canada)
Simpson Coll (IA)
Skidmore Coll (NY)
Slippery Rock U of Pennsylvania (PA)
Smith Coll (MA)
Sonoma State U (CA)
Southeastern Louisiana U (LA)
Southeastern Oklahoma State U (OK)
Southeast Missouri State U (MO)
Southern Adventist U (TN)
Southern Arkansas U–Magnolia (AR)
Southern Illinois U Carbondale (IL)
Southern Illinois U Edwardsville (IL)
Southern Methodist U (TX)
Southern Utah U (UT)
Southwest Baptist U (MO)
Southwestern Adventist U (TX)
Southwestern Coll (KS)
Southwestern U (TX)
Spelman Coll (GA)
Spring Hill Coll (AL)
Stanford U (CA)
State U of New York at Fredonia (NY)
State U of New York at New Paltz (NY)
State U of New York at Oswego (NY)
State U of New York at Plattsburgh (NY)

State U of New York Coll at Cortland (NY)
State U of New York Coll at Geneseo (NY)
State U of New York Coll at Old Westbury (NY)
State U of New York Coll at Oneonta (NY)
State U of New York Coll at Potsdam (NY)
State U of New York Coll of Environmental Science and Forestry (NY)
Stephen F. Austin State U (TX)
Stetson U (FL)
Stevens Inst of Technology (NJ)
Stevenson U (MD)
Stockton U (NJ)
Stonehill Coll (MA)
Stony Brook U, State U of New York (NY)
Suffolk U (MA)
Susquehanna U (PA)
Sweet Briar Coll (VA)
Syracuse U (NY)
Tabor Coll (KS)
Tarleton State U (TX)
Taylor U (IN)
Temple U (PA)
Tennessee Technological U (TN)
Tennessee Wesleyan U (TN)
Texas A&M Intl U (TX)
Texas A&M U (TX)
Texas A&M U–Commerce (TX)
Texas A&M U–Corpus Christi (TX)
Texas A&M U–Kingsville (TX)
Texas Christian U (TX)
Texas Lutheran U (TX)
Texas State U (TX)
Texas Tech U (TX)
Texas Woman's U (TX)
Towson U (MD)
Transylvania U (KY)
Trent U (ON, Canada)
Trevecca Nazarene U (TN)
Trine U (IN)
Trinity Christian Coll (IL)
Trinity U (TX)
Troy U (AL)
Truman State U (MO)
Tufts U (MA)
Tulane U (LA)
Tusculum Coll (TN)
Union Coll (NE)
Union Coll (NY)
Union U (TN)
United States Military Acad (NY)
Université de Sherbrooke (QC, Canada)
U at Albany, State U of New York (NY)
U at Buffalo, the State U of New York (NY)
The U of Akron (OH)
The U of Alabama (AL)
The U of Alabama at Birmingham (AL)
U of Alaska Fairbanks (AK)
The U of Arizona (AZ)
U of Arkansas (AR)
U of California, Davis (CA)
U of California, Irvine (CA)
U of California, Los Angeles (CA)
U of California, Riverside (CA)
U of California, San Diego (CA)
U of California, Santa Barbara (CA)
U of California, Santa Cruz (CA)
U of Central Arkansas (AR)
U of Central Florida (FL)
U of Central Missouri (MO)
U of Central Oklahoma (OK)
U of Charleston (WV)
U of Chicago (IL)
U of Cincinnati (OH)
U of Colorado Boulder (CO)
U of Colorado Colorado Springs (CO)
U of Colorado Denver (CO)
U of Dallas (TX)
U of Dayton (OH)
U of Denver (CO)
U of Dubuque (IA)
U of Evansville (IN)
The U of Findlay (OH)
U of Florida (FL)
U of Georgia (GA)
U of Guam (GU)

U of Guelph (ON, Canada)
U of Hartford (CT)
U of Hawaii at Manoa (HI)
U of Houston (TX)
U of Houston–Clear Lake (TX)
U of Houston–Downtown (TX)
U of Idaho (ID)
U of Illinois at Chicago (IL)
U of Illinois at Springfield (IL)
U of Jamestown (ND)
The U of Kansas (KS)
U of Kentucky (KY)
U of King's Coll (NS, Canada)
U of La Verne (CA)
U of Louisville (KY)
U of Maine (ME)
U of Mary Hardin-Baylor (TX)
U of Maryland, Baltimore County (MD)
U of Maryland, Coll Park (MD)
U of Maryland Eastern Shore (MD)
U of Mary Washington (VA)
U of Massachusetts Amherst (MA)
U of Massachusetts Boston (MA)
U of Massachusetts Dartmouth (MA)
U of Massachusetts Lowell (MA)
U of Memphis (TN)
U of Miami (FL)
U of Michigan (MI)
U of Michigan–Dearborn (MI)
U of Michigan–Flint (MI)
U of Minnesota, Duluth (MN)
U of Minnesota, Morris (MN)
U of Minnesota, Twin Cities Campus (MN)
U of Missouri (MO)
U of Missouri–St. Louis (MO)
U of Montana (MT)
U of Montevallo (AL)
U of Mount Union (OH)
U of Nebraska at Kearney (NE)
U of Nebraska–Lincoln (NE)
U of Nevada, Las Vegas (NV)
U of New England (ME)
U of New Hampshire (NH)
U of New Haven (CT)
U of New Mexico (NM)
U of New Orleans (LA)
U of North Alabama (AL)
U of North Carolina at Asheville (NC)
The U of North Carolina at Chapel Hill (NC)
The U of North Carolina at Charlotte (NC)
The U of North Carolina at Greensboro (NC)
The U of North Carolina at Pembroke (NC)
The U of North Carolina Wilmington (NC)
U of North Dakota (ND)
U of Northern Colorado (CO)
U of Northern Iowa (IA)
U of North Florida (FL)
U of North Georgia (GA)
U of North Texas (TX)
U of Notre Dame (IN)
U of Oklahoma (OK)
U of Oregon (OR)
U of Pennsylvania (PA)
U of Pikeville (KY)
U of Pittsburgh (PA)
U of Pittsburgh at Bradford (PA)
U of Pittsburgh at Greensburg (PA)
U of Providence (MT)
U of Puerto Rico–Humacao (PR)
U of Puget Sound (WA)
U of Regina (SK, Canada)
U of Rhode Island (RI)
U of Richmond (VA)
U of Rochester (NY)
U of Saint Francis (IN)
U of Saint Joseph (CT)
U of Saint Mary (KS)
U of St. Thomas (MN)
U of St. Thomas (TX)
U of San Diego (CA)
U of San Francisco (CA)
U of Saskatchewan (SK, Canada)
U of Science and Arts of Oklahoma (OK)
The U of Scranton (PA)
U of Sioux Falls (SD)
U of South Alabama (AL)
U of South Carolina (SC)

U of South Carolina Aiken (SC)
U of South Dakota (SD)
U of Southern California (CA)
U of Southern Indiana (IN)
U of Southern Maine (ME)
U of Southern Mississippi (MS)
The U of Tampa (FL)
The U of Tennessee (TN)
The U of Tennessee at Chattanooga (TN)
The U of Tennessee at Martin (TN)
The U of Texas at Austin (TX)
The U of Texas at Dallas (TX)
The U of Texas at El Paso (TX)
The U of Texas at San Antonio (TX)
The U of Texas of the Permian Basin (TX)
The U of Texas Rio Grande Valley (TX)
U of the Fraser Valley (BC, Canada)
U of the Incarnate Word (TX)
U of the Pacific (CA)
U of the Virgin Islands (VI)
The U of Toledo (OH)
The U of Tulsa (OK)
U of Utah (UT)
U of Vermont (VT)
U of Virginia (VA)
The U of Virginia's Coll at Wise (VA)
U of Washington (WA)
U of Washington, Bothell (WA)
U of Waterloo (ON, Canada)
The U of West Alabama (AL)
U of West Georgia (GA)
U of Wisconsin–Eau Claire (WI)
U of Wisconsin–La Crosse (WI)
U of Wisconsin–Madison (WI)
U of Wisconsin–Milwaukee (WI)
U of Wisconsin–Parkside (WI)
U of Wisconsin–Platteville (WI)
U of Wisconsin–River Falls (WI)
U of Wisconsin–Stevens Point (WI)
U of Wisconsin–Superior (WI)
U of Wisconsin–Whitewater (WI)
U of Wyoming (WY)
Upper Iowa U (IA)
Ursinus Coll (PA)
Utah State U (UT)
Utah Valley U (UT)
Utica Coll (NY)
Valdosta State U (GA)
Valley City State U (ND)
Valparaiso U (IN)
Vanderbilt U (TN)
Vanguard U of Southern California (CA)
Vassar Coll (NY)
Villanova U (PA)
Virginia Commonwealth U (VA)
Virginia Military Inst (VA)
Virginia Polytechnic Inst and State U (VA)
Virginia Wesleyan U (VA)
Wabash Coll (IN)
Wagner Coll (NY)
Wake Forest U (NC)
Walsh U (OH)
Wartburg Coll (IA)
Washington & Jefferson Coll (PA)
Washington and Lee U (VA)
Washington Coll (MD)
Washington State U (WA)
Washington U in St. Louis (MO)
Wayland Baptist U (TX)
Waynesburg U (PA)
Wayne State Coll (NE)
Wayne State U (MI)
Weber State U (UT)
Wellesley Coll (MA)
Wells Coll (NY)
Wesleyan U (CT)
West Chester U of Pennsylvania (PA)
Western Connecticut State U (CT)
Western Illinois U (IL)
Western Kentucky U (KY)
Western Michigan U (MI)
Western New England U (MA)
Western Oregon U (OR)
Western State Colorado U (CO)
Western Washington U (WA)
Westfield State U (MA)
Westminster Coll (PA)
Westminster Coll (UT)
Westmont Coll (CA)

West Texas A&M U (TX)
West Virginia State U (WV)
West Virginia U (WV)
West Virginia U Inst of Technology (WV)
West Virginia Wesleyan Coll (WV)
Wheaton Coll (IL)
Wheaton Coll (MA)
Whitman Coll (WA)
Whittier Coll (CA)
Whitworth U (WA)
Wichita State U (KS)
Widener U (PA)
Wilkes U (PA)
Willamette U (OR)
William Jewell Coll (MO)
William Paterson U of New Jersey (NJ)
Williams Coll (MA)
Winona State U (MN)
Winthrop U (SC)
Wisconsin Lutheran Coll (WI)
Wittenberg U (OH)
Wofford Coll (SC)
Worcester Polytechnic Inst (MA)
Worcester State U (MA)
Wright State U (OH)
Xavier U of Louisiana (LA)
York Coll of Pennsylvania (PA)
Youngstown State U (OH)

CHEMISTRY RELATED

Boston U (MA)
Bridgewater Coll (VA)
Bridgewater State U (MA)
Carnegie Mellon U (PA)
Case Western Reserve U (OH)
Chatham U (PA)
Coll of Charleston (SC)
Dartmouth Coll (NH)
Delaware State U (DE)
Duquesne U (PA)
Eastern Nazarene Coll (MA)
Eastern Oregon U (OR)
Eastern U (PA)
East Stroudsburg U of Pennsylvania (PA)
Ferris State U (MI)
Florida Inst of Technology (FL)
Harvard U (MA)
Inter American U of Puerto Rico, Bayamón Campus (PR)
Kansas Wesleyan U (KS)
Keene State Coll (NH)
LeTourneau U (TX)
Marlboro Coll (VT)
Mercer U, Macon (GA)
Michigan Technological U (MI)
Mount St. Joseph U (OH)
Northern Michigan U (MI)
Ohio Northern U (OH)
Palm Beach Atlantic U (FL)
Saginaw Valley State U (MI)
Saint Anselm Coll (NH)
Saint Mary's Coll of California (CA)
Saint Vincent Coll (PA)
Sam Houston State U (TX)
Stony Brook U, State U of New York (NY)
U at Buffalo, the State U of New York (NY)
U of California, Santa Barbara (CA)
U of Chicago (IL)
U of Denver (CO)
U of Notre Dame (IN)
U of Puerto Rico–Humacao (PR)
The U of Scranton (PA)
U of Southern Mississippi (MS)
U of the Pacific (CA)
U of Wisconsin–Eau Claire (WI)
U of Wisconsin–Milwaukee (WI)
Washington U in St. Louis (MO)
Wayne State U (MI)
Western Illinois U (IL)
Western Michigan U (MI)
Western State Colorado U (CO)
West Virginia Wesleyan Coll (WV)
Whitman Coll (WA)

CHEMISTRY TEACHER EDUCATION

Adams State U (CO)
Albion Coll (MI)
Aquinas Coll (MI)
Arkansas Tech U (AR)
Ashland U (OH)
Augustana Coll (IL)
Ball State U (IN)

Baylor U (TX)
Bethel Coll (IN)
Bluefield Coll (VA)
Boston U (MA)
Bowling Green State U (OH)
Bradley U (IL)
Brigham Young U–Idaho (ID)
Buena Vista U (IA)
Calvin Coll (MI)
Campbellsville U (KY)
Canisius Coll (NY)
Carroll Coll (MT)
Carroll U (WI)
Cedarville U (OH)
Central Methodist U (MO)
Central Michigan U (MI)
City Coll of the City U of New York (NY)
Coker Coll (SC)
The Coll of New Jersey (NJ)
Coll of Saint Mary (NE)
Coll of Staten Island of the City U of New York (NY)
Coll of the Ozarks (MO)
Concordia U Chicago (IL)
Concordia U, St. Paul (MN)
Daytona State Coll (FL)
Delaware State U (DE)
Dickinson State U (ND)
East Central U (OK)
Eastern Michigan U (MI)
Eastern Nazarene Coll (MA)
Eastern Washington U (WA)
Edgewood Coll (WI)
Elmhurst Coll (IL)
Emory & Henry Coll (VA)
Evangel U (MO)
Ferris State U (MI)
Florida Inst of Technology (FL)
Fort Lewis Coll (CO)
Geneva Coll (PA)
Goshen Coll (IN)
Grand Valley State U (MI)
Greenville U (IL)
Grove City Coll (PA)
Gustavus Adolphus Coll (MN)
Hofstra U (NY)
Holy Family U (PA)
Hope Coll (MI)
Huntingdon Coll (AL)
Immaculata U (PA)
Indiana U Bloomington (IN)
Indiana U Northwest (IN)
Indiana U South Bend (IN)
Indiana Wesleyan U (IN)
Inter American U of Puerto Rico, San Germán Campus (PR)
Ithaca Coll (NY)
Juniata Coll (PA)
Kansas Wesleyan U (KS)
Kent State U (OH)
Lee U (TN)
Le Moyne Coll (NY)
Lincoln Memorial U (TN)
Lincoln U (MO)
Lindenwood U (MO)
Lipscomb U (TN)
Long Island U–LIU Brooklyn (NY)
Long Island U–LIU Post (NY)
Louisiana Coll (LA)
Madonna U (MI)
Manchester U (IN)
Manhattanville Coll (NY)
Marist Coll (NY)
Martin Luther Coll (MN)
Maryville Coll (TN)
McMurry U (TX)
Mercyhurst U (PA)
Merrimack Coll (MA)
Messiah Coll (PA)
Miami Dade Coll (FL)
Miami U (OH)
Michigan State U (MI)
Millikin U (IL)
Minnesota State U Moorhead (MN)
Minot State U (ND)
Misericordia U (PA)
Missouri State U (MO)
Morningside Coll (IA)
Mount Marty Coll (SD)
Mount Mary U (ND)
Mount Vernon Nazarene U (OH)
Nazareth Coll of Rochester (NY)
New York U (NY)
Niagara U (NY)
North Dakota State U (ND)
Northern Michigan U (MI)

Northern State U (SD)
Northwest Missouri State U (MO)
Northwest Nazarene U (ID)
Ohio Dominican U (OH)
Ohio Northern U (OH)
Ohio Wesleyan U (OH)
Pace U (NY)
Pace U, Pleasantville Campus (NY)
Pepperdine U, Malibu (CA)
Pittsburg State U (KS)
Providence Coll (RI)
Queens Coll of the City U of New York (NY)
Rhode Island Coll (RI)
Roberts Wesleyan Coll (NY)
Saginaw Valley State U (MI)
St. Catherine U (MN)
Saint Francis U (PA)
St. John Fisher Coll (NY)
St. Joseph's Coll, Long Island Campus (NY)
St. Joseph's Coll, New York (NY)
Saint Joseph's U (PA)
Saint Mary's U of Minnesota (MN)
Schreiner U (TX)
Seattle U (WA)
Seton Hill U (PA)
Southern Adventist U (TN)
Southern Utah U (UT)
Southwest Baptist U (MO)
Southwestern Adventist U (TX)
State U of New York at New Paltz (NY)
State U of New York at Plattsburgh (NY)
State U of New York Coll at Cortland (NY)
State U of New York Coll at Old Westbury (NY)
State U of New York Coll at Oneonta (NY)
State U of New York Coll at Potsdam (NY)
Syracuse U (NY)
Taylor U (IN)
Transylvania U (KY)
Trevecca Nazarene U (TN)
Trine U (IN)
Trinity Christian Coll (IL)
Union Coll (NE)
U of California, San Diego (CA)
U of Central Oklahoma (OK)
U of Dubuque (IA)
U of Evansville (IN)
U of Illinois at Chicago (IL)
U of Jamestown (ND)
U of Louisiana at Monroe (LA)
U of Maine (ME)
U of Maine at Farmington (ME)
U of Mary Hardin-Baylor (TX)
U of Maryland, Baltimore County (MD)
U of Michigan–Dearborn (MI)
U of Missouri (MO)
U of Nebraska–Lincoln (NE)
U of Providence (MT)
U of Regina (SK, Canada)
U of St. Thomas (MN)
U of Sioux Falls (SD)
The U of Tennessee at Martin (TN)
U of Waterloo (ON, Canada)
U of Wisconsin–Stevens Point (WI)
U of Wisconsin–Superior (WI)
U of Wisconsin–Whitewater (WI)
Utah State U (UT)
Utah Valley U (UT)
Utica Coll (NY)
Valley City State U (ND)
Valparaiso U (IN)
Washington U in St. Louis (MO)
Waynesburg U (PA)
Wayne State Coll (NE)
Weber State U (UT)
Western Michigan U (MI)
Western State Colorado U (CO)
Western Washington U (WA)
Westfield State U (MA)
Widener U (PA)
Winona State U (MN)
Xavier U of Louisiana (LA)

CHILD-CARE AND SUPPORT SERVICES MANAGEMENT

Brigham Young U (UT)
Chestnut Hill Coll (PA)
Ferris State U (MI)
Idaho State U (ID)

CHILD-CARE PROVISION

Brigham Young U (UT)
Colorado Mesa U (CO)
Southeastern Oklahoma State U (OK)
Wayne State Coll (NE)

National Louis U (IL)
Newberry Coll (SC)
Rust Coll (MS)
Seton Hill U (PA)
State U of New York Coll of Technology at Canton (NY)
Texas Tech U (TX)
The U of Texas Rio Grande Valley (TX)
U of the Fraser Valley (BC, Canada)

CHILD DEVELOPMENT

Alcorn State U (MS)
Appalachian State U (NC)
Aquinas Coll (MI)
Auburn U (AL)
Bennington Coll (VT)
Bluffton U (OH)
Bowling Green State U (OH)
Brigham Young U (UT)
Brigham Young U–Idaho (ID)
California State U, Long Beach (CA)
California State U, Los Angeles (CA)
California State U, Northridge (CA)
California State U, Sacramento (CA)
Cameron U (OK)
Carson-Newman U (TN)
Central Michigan U (MI)
Coll of the Ozarks (MO)
Concordia U, St. Paul (MN)
Delaware State U (DE)
Eastern Washington U (WA)
East Tennessee State U (TN)
Hampton U (VA)
Hannibal-LaGrange U (MO)
Harding U (AR)
Humboldt State U (CA)
Iowa State U of Science and Technology (IA)
Kansas State U (KS)
Lesley U (MA)
Madonna U (MI)
Meredith Coll (NC)
Michigan State U (MI)
Missouri Baptist U (MO)
Mount Saint Mary's U (CA)
Oklahoma Christian U (OK)
Olivet Nazarene U (IL)
Point Loma Nazarene U (CA)
Point U (GA)
Portland State U (OR)
Post U (CT)
Quinnipiac U (CT)
St. Bonaventure U (NY)
Santa Clara U (CA)
Seton Hill U (PA)
State U of New York Coll at Oneonta (NY)
Tennessee Technological U (TN)
Texas Tech U (TX)
Texas Woman's U (TX)
Trent U (ON, Canada)
Tufts U (MA)
The U of Akron (OH)
U of Alaska Fairbanks (AK)
U of Guelph (ON, Canada)
U of Houston–Clear Lake (TX)
U of La Verne (CA)
U of Maryland Eastern Shore (MD)
The U of North Carolina at Greensboro (NC)
U of Saint Joseph (CT)
U of Saint Mary (KS)
The U of Tennessee at Martin (TN)
The U of Texas at Dallas (TX)
U of Virginia (VA)
Vanderbilt U (TN)
Weber State U (UT)
Western Michigan U (MI)
West Virginia U (WV)
Whittier Coll (CA)
Youngstown State U (OH)

CHILDREN'S AND ADOLESCENT LITERATURE

Central Michigan U (MI)
Marlboro Coll (VT)

CHINESE
Ball State U (IN)
Bard Coll (NY)
Bates Coll (ME)
Beloit Coll (WI)
Bennington Coll (VT)
Boston U (MA)
Bryant U (RI)
California State U, Long Beach (CA)
California State U, Los Angeles (CA)
Calvin Coll (MI)
Carnegie Mellon U (PA)
Carthage Coll (WI)
Case Western Reserve U (OH)
Colgate U (NY)
Coll of the Holy Cross (MA)
Dartmouth Coll (NH)
Davidson Coll (NC)
Emory U (GA)
Florida State U (FL)
Georgetown U (DC)
The George Washington U (DC)
Grinnell Coll (IA)
Hamilton Coll (NY)
Hobart and William Smith Colls (NY)
Hofstra U (NY)
Hunter Coll of the City U of New York (NY)
Iowa State U of Science and Technology (IA)
Lawrence U (WI)
Lehigh U (PA)
Macalester Coll (MN)
Marlboro Coll (VT)
Messiah Coll (PA)
Michigan State U (MI)
Middlebury Coll (VT)
Nazareth Coll of Rochester (NY)
New Coll of Florida (FL)
North Central Coll (IL)
Occidental Coll (CA)
The Ohio State U (OH)
Penn State U Park (PA)
Pomona Coll (CA)
Portland State U (OR)
Queens Coll of the City U of New York (NY)
Reed Coll (OR)
Rutgers U–New Brunswick (NJ)
St. Olaf Coll (MN)
San Francisco State U (CA)
Sarah Lawrence Coll (NY)
Scripps Coll (CA)
Southern Methodist U (TX)
Stanford U (CA)
Temple U (PA)
Trinity U (TX)
Tufts U (MA)
Union Coll (NY)
United States Military Acad (NY)
U of California, Davis (CA)
U of California, Los Angeles (CA)
U of California, San Diego (CA)
U of California, Santa Barbara (CA)
U of Colorado Boulder (CO)
U of Georgia (GA)
U of Hawaii at Manoa (HI)
U of Houston (TX)
U of Kentucky (KY)
U of Maryland, Coll Park (MD)
U of Massachusetts Amherst (MA)
U of Notre Dame (IN)
U of Oklahoma (OK)
U of Oregon (OR)
U of Pittsburgh (PA)
U of Puget Sound (WA)
U of Regina (SK, Canada)
U of Rhode Island (RI)
U of Utah (UT)
U of Vermont (VT)
U of Washington (WA)
U of Wisconsin–Madison (WI)
Vassar Coll (NY)
Wake Forest U (NC)
Washington State U (WA)
Washington U in St. Louis (MO)
Wellesley Coll (MA)
Western Kentucky U (KY)
Western Washington U (WA)
Whittier Coll (CA)
Williams Coll (MA)
Wisconsin Lutheran Coll (WI)
Wofford Coll (SC)

CHINESE STUDIES
Ball State U (IN)
The Coll of William and Mary (VA)
DePaul U (IL)
Drew U (NJ)
Furman U (SC)
Gettysburg Coll (PA)
Marlboro Coll (VT)
Morehouse Coll (GA)
Oakland U (MI)
Pacific Lutheran U (WA)
U at Albany, State U of New York (NY)
U of California, Irvine (CA)
U of Minnesota, Duluth (MN)
U of North Dakota (ND)
U of Richmond (VA)
The U of Tulsa (OK)
U of Washington (WA)
Willamette U (OR)

CHRISTIAN STUDIES
Ambrose U (AB, Canada)
Anderson U (SC)
Bethel U (TN)
Bluefield Coll (VA)
Brewton-Parker Coll (GA)
Bryan Coll (TN)
California Baptist U (CA)
Canisius Coll (NY)
Coll of Biblical Studies–Houston (TX)
The Coll of St. Scholastica (MN)
Coll of the Holy Cross (MA)
Concordia U Wisconsin (WI)
Gordon Coll (MA)
Hardin-Simmons U (TX)
Hillsdale Coll (MI)
Houston Baptist U (TX)
Lee U (TN)
Liberty U (VA)
Louisiana Coll (LA)
Loyola U Chicago (IL)
Loyola U New Orleans (LA)
Marian U (IN)
Marlboro Coll (VT)
McMurry U (TX)
Messenger Coll (TX)
Missouri Baptist U (MO)
Oklahoma Baptist U (OK)
Ouachita Baptist U (AR)
Point Loma Nazarene U (CA)
Roanoke Coll (VA)
Saint Mary's U of Minnesota (MN)
St. Thomas U (NB, Canada)
Southwestern Coll (KS)
Stonehill Coll (MA)
Tabor Coll (KS)
Tennessee Wesleyan U (TN)
Toccoa Falls Coll (GA)
Truett McConnell U (GA)
U of Dubuque (IA)
U of Mary Hardin-Baylor (TX)
Ursuline Coll (OH)
Whitworth U (WA)

CINEMATOGRAPHY AND FILM/VIDEO PRODUCTION
Academy of Art U (CA)
American U (DC)
Anderson U (IN)
ArtCenter Coll of Design (CA)
Belmont U (TN)
Bennington Coll (VT)
Binghamton U, State U of New York (NY)
Biola U (CA)
Bob Jones U (SC)
Brigham Young U (UT)
California State U, Long Beach (CA)
California State U, Northridge (CA)
Chapman U (CA)
City Coll of the City U of New York (NY)
Clayton State U (GA)
Cleveland State U (OH)
Columbia Coll Chicago (IL)
Compass Coll of Cinematic Arts (MI)
Concordia U (QC, Canada)
Cornerstone U (MI)
DePaul U (IL)
Drexel U (PA)
Eastern New Mexico U (NM)
Eastern Washington U (WA)
Emerson Coll (MA)
The Evergreen State Coll (WA)

Fairleigh Dickinson U, Florham Campus (NJ)
Fashion Inst of Technology (NY)
FIDM/Fashion Inst of Design & Merchandising, Los Angeles Campus (CA)
Fitchburg State U (MA)
George Mason U (VA)
Goshen Coll (IN)
Humboldt State U (CA)
Hunter Coll of the City U of New York (NY)
Inst of American Indian Arts (NM)
Ithaca Coll (NY)
John Brown U (AR)
John Paul the Great Catholic U (CA)
Keene State Coll (NH)
Keiser U, Fort Lauderdale (FL)
La Sierra U (CA)
Liberty U (VA)
Long Island U–LIU Post (NY)
Loyola Marymount U (CA)
Loyola U New Orleans (LA)
Lynn U (FL)
Maharishi U of Management (IA)
Massachusetts Coll of Art and Design (MA)
Messiah Coll (PA)
Miami Dade Coll (FL)
Minneapolis Coll of Art and Design (MN)
Montclair State U (NJ)
Mount Saint Mary's U (CA)
New England Inst of Technology (RI)
New Mexico Highlands U (NM)
New Mexico State U (NM)
New York U (NY)
Northern Michigan U (MI)
Northern Vermont U–Lyndon (VT)
Oakland U (MI)
Ohio U (OH)
Oklahoma City U (OK)
Pace U, Pleasantville Campus (NY)
Palm Beach Atlantic U (FL)
Point Park U (PA)
Pratt Inst (NY)
Purchase Coll, State U of New York (NY)
Quinnipiac U (CT)
Regent U (VA)
Ringling Coll of Art and Design (FL)
Rochester Inst of Technology (NY)
Rutgers U–Newark (NJ)
San Francisco Art Inst (CA)
Sarah Lawrence Coll (NY)
Savannah Coll of Art and Design (GA)
School of Visual Arts (NY)
Southeastern U (FL)
Southern Adventist U (TN)
Southern Illinois U Carbondale (IL)
Southern Methodist U (TX)
Southwestern Assemblies of God U (TX)
Stanford U (CA)
Stevenson U (MD)
Syracuse U (NY)
Taylor U (IN)
Temple U (PA)
U of Central Arkansas (AR)
U of Central Florida (FL)
U of Illinois at Chicago (IL)
U of Miami (FL)
U of Montana (MT)
U of North Carolina School of the Arts (NC)
The U of North Carolina Wilmington (NC)
U of Regina (SK, Canada)
U of Rhode Island (RI)
U of Southern California (CA)
The U of the Arts (PA)
Vanguard U of Southern California (CA)
Villa Maria Coll (NY)
Virginia Commonwealth U (VA)
Wayne State U (MI)
Webster U (MO)
Wilmington U (DE)
Wisconsin Lutheran Coll (WI)
Woodbury U (CA)

CITY/URBAN, COMMUNITY AND REGIONAL PLANNING
Appalachian State U (NC)

Arizona State U at the Tempe campus (AZ)
Ball State U (IN)
Bridgewater State U (MA)
Buffalo State Coll, State U of New York (NY)
California Polytechnic State U, San Luis Obispo (CA)
California State Polytechnic U, Pomona (CA)
Concordia U (QC, Canada)
Cornell U (NY)
East Carolina U (NC)
Eastern Michigan U (MI)
Eastern Washington U (WA)
Florida Atlantic U (FL)
Frostburg State U (MD)
Indiana U of Pennsylvania (PA)
Iowa State U of Science and Technology (IA)
Jacksonville U (FL)
Massachusetts Inst of Technology (MA)
Miami U (OH)
Michigan State U (MI)
Missouri State U (MO)
The Ohio State U (OH)
Parsons School of Design (NY)
Portland State U (OR)
Rowan U (NJ)
Rutgers U–New Brunswick (NJ)
Salisbury U (MD)
Temple U (PA)
Texas A&M U (TX)
Texas State U (TX)
Tufts U (MA)
The U of Akron (OH)
The U of Arizona (AZ)
U of California, Davis (CA)
U of Cincinnati (OH)
U of New Hampshire (NH)
U of Saskatchewan (SK, Canada)
The U of Texas at Austin (TX)
U of Virginia (VA)
U of Washington (WA)
U of Waterloo (ON, Canada)
West Chester U of Pennsylvania (PA)
Western Michigan U (MI)
Westfield State U (MA)

CIVIL ENGINEERING
American U of Beirut (Lebanon)
Angelo State U (TX)
Arizona State U at the Tempe campus (AZ)
Auburn U (AL)
Boise State U (ID)
Bradley U (IL)
Bucknell U (PA)
California Baptist U (CA)
California Polytechnic State U, San Luis Obispo (CA)
California State Polytechnic U, Pomona (CA)
California State U, Long Beach (CA)
California State U, Los Angeles (CA)
California State U, Northridge (CA)
California State U, Sacramento (CA)
Calvin Coll (MI)
Caribbean U (PR)
Carnegie Mellon U (PA)
Carroll Coll (MT)
Case Western Reserve U (OH)
The Catholic U of America (DC)
Central Connecticut State U (CT)
Christian Brothers U (TN)
The Citadel, The Military Coll of South Carolina (SC)
City Coll of the City U of New York (NY)
Clarkson U (NY)
Clemson U (SC)
Cleveland State U (OH)
The Coll of New Jersey (NJ)
Colorado State U (CO)
Columbia U (NY)
Concordia U (QC, Canada)
Cooper Union for the Advancement of Science and Art (NY)
Cornell U (NY)
Delaware State U (DE)
Drexel U (PA)
Florida Ag and Mech U (FL)

Florida Atlantic U (FL)
Florida Gulf Coast U (FL)
Florida Inst of Technology (FL)
Florida Intl U (FL)
Florida State U (FL)
George Mason U (VA)
The George Washington U (DC)
Georgia Inst of Technology (GA)
Georgia Southern U (GA)
Gonzaga U (WA)
Hofstra U (NY)
Idaho State U (ID)
Iowa State U of Science and Technology (IA)
Jackson State U (MS)
Johns Hopkins U (MD)
Kansas State U (KS)
Kennesaw State U (GA)
King's Coll (PA)
Lafayette Coll (PA)
Lamar U (TX)
Lawrence Technological U (MI)
Lebanese American U (Lebanon)
Lehigh U (PA)
LeTourneau U (TX)
Lipscomb U (TN)
Louisiana State U and A&M Coll (LA)
Loyola Marymount U (CA)
Manhattan Coll (NY)
Marquette U (WI)
Massachusetts Inst of Technology (MA)
Merrimack Coll (MA)
Michigan State U (MI)
Michigan Technological U (MI)
Milwaukee School of Eng (WI)
Mississippi State U (MS)
Missouri U of Science and Technology (MO)
Montana Tech of The U of Montana (MT)
New Jersey Inst of Technology (NJ)
New Mexico Inst of Mining and Technology (NM)
New Mexico State U (NM)
New York U (NY)
North Carolina State U (NC)
North Dakota State U (ND)
Northeastern U (MA)
Northern Arizona U (AZ)
Northwestern U (IL)
Ohio Northern U (OH)
The Ohio State U (OH)
Ohio U (OH)
Oklahoma State U (OK)
Old Dominion U (VA)
Oregon Inst of Technology (OR)
Oregon State U (OR)
Penn State Abington (PA)
Penn State Altoona (PA)
Penn State Beaver (PA)
Penn State Berks (PA)
Penn State Brandywine (PA)
Penn State DuBois (PA)
Penn State Erie, The Behrend Coll (PA)
Penn State Fayette, The Eberly Campus (PA)
Penn State Greater Allegheny (PA)
Penn State Harrisburg (PA)
Penn State Hazleton (PA)
Penn State Lehigh Valley (PA)
Penn State Mont Alto (PA)
Penn State New Kensington (PA)
Penn State Schuylkill (PA)
Penn State Shenango (PA)
Penn State U Park (PA)
Penn State Wilkes-Barre (PA)
Penn State Worthington Scranton (PA)
Penn State York (PA)
Polytechnic U of Puerto Rico (PR)
Portland State U (OR)
Prairie View A&M U (TX)
Princeton U (NJ)
Purdue U (IN)
Purdue U Northwest (IN)
Quinnipiac U (CT)
Rensselaer Polytechnic Inst (NY)
Rice U (TX)
Rockhurst U (MO)
Roger Williams U (RI)
Rose-Hulman Inst of Technology (IN)
Rowan U (NJ)
Rutgers U–New Brunswick (NJ)

Saint Louis U (MO)
Saint Louis U–Madrid Campus (Spain)
Saint Martin's U (WA)
San Diego State U (CA)
San Francisco State U (CA)
Santa Clara U (CA)
Seattle U (WA)
Southern Illinois U Carbondale (IL)
Southern Illinois U Edwardsville (IL)
Southern Methodist U (TX)
Stanford U (CA)
State U of New York Polytechnic Inst (NY)
Stevens Inst of Technology (NJ)
Stony Brook U, State U of New York (NY)
Syracuse U (NY)
Tarleton State U (TX)
Temple U (PA)
Tennessee Technological U (TN)
Texas A&M U (TX)
Texas A&M U–Kingsville (TX)
Texas Tech U (TX)
Trine U (IN)
Tufts U (MA)
United States Coast Guard Acad (CT)
United States Military Acad (NY)
Université de Sherbrooke (QC, Canada)
U at Buffalo, the State U of New York (NY)
The U of Akron (OH)
The U of Alabama (AL)
The U of Alabama at Birmingham (AL)
U of Alaska Fairbanks (AK)
The U of Arizona (AZ)
U of Arkansas (AR)
U of California, Davis (CA)
U of California, Irvine (CA)
U of California, Los Angeles (CA)
U of Central Florida (FL)
U of Cincinnati (OH)
U of Colorado Boulder (CO)
U of Colorado Denver (CO)
U of Dayton (OH)
U of Evansville (IN)
U of Florida (FL)
U of Georgia (GA)
U of Hartford (CT)
U of Hawaii at Manoa (HI)
U of Houston (TX)
U of Idaho (ID)
U of Illinois at Chicago (IL)
The U of Kansas (KS)
U of Kentucky (KY)
U of Louisville (KY)
U of Maine (ME)
U of Maryland, Coll Park (MD)
U of Massachusetts Amherst (MA)
U of Massachusetts Dartmouth (MA)
U of Massachusetts Lowell (MA)
U of Memphis (TN)
U of Miami (FL)
U of Michigan (MI)
U of Minnesota, Duluth (MN)
U of Minnesota, Twin Cities Campus (MN)
U of Missouri (MO)
U of Missouri–St. Louis (MO)
U of Mount Union (OH)
U of Nebraska–Lincoln (NE)
U of Nevada, Las Vegas (NV)
U of Nevada, Reno (NV)
U of New Hampshire (NH)
U of New Haven (CT)
U of New Mexico (NM)
U of New Orleans (LA)
The U of North Carolina at Charlotte (NC)
U of North Dakota (ND)
U of North Florida (FL)
U of Notre Dame (IN)
U of Oklahoma (OK)
U of Pittsburgh (PA)
U of Rhode Island (RI)
U of Saskatchewan (SK, Canada)
U of South Alabama (AL)
U of South Carolina (SC)
U of Southern California (CA)
The U of Tennessee (TN)
The U of Tennessee at Chattanooga (TN)

The U of Texas at Austin (TX)
The U of Texas at El Paso (TX)
The U of Texas at San Antonio (TX)
The U of Texas Rio Grande Valley (TX)
U of the Pacific (CA)
The U of Toledo (OH)
U of Toronto (ON, Canada)
U of Utah (UT)
U of Vermont (VT)
U of Virginia (VA)
U of Washington (WA)
U of Waterloo (ON, Canada)
U of Wisconsin–Madison (WI)
U of Wisconsin–Milwaukee (WI)
U of Wisconsin–Platteville (WI)
U of Wyoming (WY)
Utah State U (UT)
Valparaiso U (IN)
Vanderbilt U (TN)
Villanova U (PA)
Virginia Military Inst (VA)
Virginia Polytechnic Inst and State U (VA)
Washington State U (WA)
Washington State U–Tri-Cities (WA)
Wayne State U (MI)
Wentworth Inst of Technology (MA)
Western Kentucky U (KY)
Western Michigan U (MI)
Western New England U (MA)
West Texas A&M U (TX)
West Virginia U (WV)
West Virginia U Inst of Technology (WV)
Widener U (PA)
William Jewell Coll (MO)
Worcester Polytechnic Inst (MA)
Youngstown State U (OH)

CIVIL ENGINEERING RELATED
California Polytechnic State U, San Luis Obispo (CA)
Embry-Riddle Aeronautical U–Daytona (FL)
Ohio Northern U (OH)
U of Southern California (CA)

CIVIL ENGINEERING TECHNOLOGY
Cedarville U (OH)
Central Connecticut State U (CT)
Colorado State U–Pueblo (CO)
Delaware State U (DE)
Fairleigh Dickinson U, Metropolitan Campus (NJ)
Idaho State U (ID)
Indiana State U (IN)
Kennesaw State U (GA)
Lincoln U (MO)
Metropolitan State U of Denver (CO)
Murray State U (KY)
Oklahoma State U Inst of Technology (OK)
Pennsylvania Coll of Technology (PA)
Point Park U (PA)
Rochester Inst of Technology (NY)
State U of New York Coll of Technology at Canton (NY)
State U of New York Polytechnic Inst (NY)
Temple U (PA)
United States Military Acad (NY)
U of Houston–Downtown (TX)
U of Maine (ME)
U of Massachusetts Lowell (MA)
The U of North Carolina at Charlotte (NC)
Youngstown State U (OH)

CLASSICAL, ANCIENT MEDITERRANEAN AND NEAR EASTERN STUDIES AND ARCHAEOLOGY
Bard Coll (NY)
Bowdoin Coll (ME)
Butler U (IN)
Calvin Coll (MI)
Colgate U (NY)
Emory U (GA)
Florida State U (FL)
Hampshire Coll (MA)
Kalamazoo Coll (MI)
Lycoming Coll (PA)
Randolph-Macon Coll (VA)

Saint Anselm Coll (NH)
Syracuse U (NY)
U of California, Davis (CA)
U of California, Los Angeles (CA)
U of Illinois at Chicago (IL)
U of Michigan (MI)
U of St. Thomas (MN)
U of Toronto (ON, Canada)

CLASSICS AND CLASSICAL LANGUAGES
Acadia U (NS, Canada)
Agnes Scott Coll (GA)
Amherst Coll (MA)
Asbury U (KY)
Augustana Coll (IL)
Augustana U (SD)
Austin Coll (TX)
Ball State U (IN)
Barnard Coll (NY)
Baylor U (TX)
Beloit Coll (WI)
Binghamton U, State U of New York (NY)
Boston Coll (MA)
Boston U (MA)
Bowdoin Coll (ME)
Bowling Green State U (OH)
Brandeis U (MA)
Bryn Mawr Coll (PA)
Bucknell U (PA)
Carleton Coll (MN)
Carroll Coll (MT)
Carthage Coll (WI)
Case Western Reserve U (OH)
The Catholic U of America (DC)
Centre Coll (KY)
Christendom Coll (VA)
Christopher Newport U (VA)
Claremont McKenna Coll (CA)
Clark U (MA)
Colby Coll (ME)
Colgate U (NY)
Coll of Charleston (SC)
Coll of Saint Benedict (MN)
Coll of the Holy Cross (MA)
The Coll of William and Mary (VA)
The Coll of Wooster (OH)
The Colorado Coll (CO)
Columbia U (NY)
Concordia U (QC, Canada)
Connecticut Coll (CT)
Cornell Coll (IA)
Cornell U (NY)
Creighton U (NE)
Dartmouth Coll (NH)
Davidson Coll (NC)
Denison U (OH)
DePauw U (IN)
Dickinson Coll (PA)
Drew U (NJ)
Duquesne U (PA)
Earlham Coll (IN)
Emory U (GA)
The Evergreen State Coll (WA)
Fordham U (NY)
Franklin & Marshall Coll (PA)
Furman U (SC)
Georgetown U (DC)
The George Washington U (DC)
Gettysburg Coll (PA)
Grand Valley State U (MI)
Grinnell Coll (IA)
Gustavus Adolphus Coll (MN)
Hamilton Coll (NY)
Hampden-Sydney Coll (VA)
Harvard U (MA)
Haverford Coll (PA)
Hendrix Coll (AR)
Hillsdale Coll (MI)
Hobart and William Smith Colls (NY)
Hofstra U (NY)
Hollins U (VA)
Hope Coll (MI)
Houston Baptist U (TX)
Hunter Coll of the City U of New York (NY)
Illinois Wesleyan U (IL)
Indiana U Bloomington (IN)
John Cabot U (Italy)
John Carroll U (OH)
Johns Hopkins U (MD)
Kent State U (OH)
Kenyon Coll (OH)
Knox Coll (IL)
Lawrence U (WI)

Lehigh U (PA)
Lehman Coll of the City U of New York (NY)
Loyola U Chicago (IL)
Luther Coll (IA)
Macalester Coll (MN)
Manhattan Coll (NY)
Marlboro Coll (VT)
Marquette U (WI)
Mercer U, Macon (GA)
Miami U (OH)
Middlebury Coll (VT)
Millsaps Coll (MS)
Monmouth Coll (IL)
Montclair State U (NJ)
Mount Holyoke Coll (MA)
New York U (NY)
North Central Coll (IL)
Northwestern U (IL)
Oberlin Coll (OH)
The Ohio State U (OH)
Ohio U (OH)
Ohio Wesleyan U (OH)
Pacific Lutheran U (WA)
Penn State Abington (PA)
Penn State Altoona (PA)
Penn State Beaver (PA)
Penn State Berks (PA)
Penn State Brandywine (PA)
Penn State DuBois (PA)
Penn State Erie, The Behrend Coll (PA)
Penn State Fayette, The Eberly Campus (PA)
Penn State Greater Allegheny (PA)
Penn State Hazleton (PA)
Penn State Lehigh Valley (PA)
Penn State Mont Alto (PA)
Penn State New Kensington (PA)
Penn State Schuylkill (PA)
Penn State Shenango (PA)
Penn State U Park (PA)
Penn State Wilkes-Barre (PA)
Penn State Worthington Scranton (PA)
Penn State York (PA)
Pitzer Coll (CA)
Pomona Coll (CA)
Princeton U (NJ)
Queens Coll of the City U of New York (NY)
Randolph Coll (VA)
Randolph-Macon Coll (VA)
Reed Coll (OR)
Rhodes Coll (TN)
Rice U (TX)
Rockford U (IL)
Rutgers U–Newark (NJ)
Rutgers U–New Brunswick (NJ)
Saint Anselm Coll (NH)
Saint John's U (MN)
Saint Louis U (MO)
Saint Louis U–Madrid Campus (Spain)
Saint Michael's Coll (VT)
St. Olaf Coll (MN)
Saint Peter's U (NJ)
Samford U (AL)
San Diego State U (CA)
San Francisco State U (CA)
Santa Clara U (CA)
Scripps Coll (CA)
Sewanee: The U of the South (TN)
Siena Coll (NY)
Skidmore Coll (NY)
Smith Coll (MA)
Southwestern U (TX)
Stanford U (CA)
Sweet Briar Coll (VA)
Syracuse U (NY)
Temple U (PA)
Texas A&M U (TX)
Texas Tech U (TX)
Transylvania U (KY)
Trent U (ON, Canada)
Trinity U (TX)
Truman State U (MO)
Tufts U (MA)
Tulane U (LA)
Union Coll (NY)
U at Buffalo, the State U of New York (NY)
The U of Akron (OH)
The U of Arizona (AZ)
U of Arkansas (AR)
U of California, Irvine (CA)
U of California, San Diego (CA)

U of California, Santa Barbara (CA)
U of California, Santa Cruz (CA)
U of Chicago (IL)
U of Cincinnati (OH)
U of Colorado Boulder (CO)
U of Dallas (TX)
U of Evansville (IN)
U of Florida (FL)
U of Georgia (GA)
U of Guelph (ON, Canada)
U of Hawaii at Manoa (HI)
U of Illinois at Chicago (IL)
The U of Kansas (KS)
U of Kentucky (KY)
U of King's Coll (NS, Canada)
U of Maryland, Coll Park (MD)
U of Mary Washington (VA)
U of Massachusetts Amherst (MA)
U of Massachusetts Boston (MA)
U of Miami (FL)
U of Michigan (MI)
U of Minnesota, Twin Cities Campus (MN)
U of Missouri (MO)
U of Montana (MT)
U of Nebraska–Lincoln (NE)
U of New Hampshire (NH)
U of New Mexico (NM)
U of North Carolina at Asheville (NC)
The U of North Carolina at Chapel Hill (NC)
The U of North Carolina at Greensboro (NC)
U of North Dakota (ND)
U of Notre Dame (IN)
U of Oklahoma (OK)
U of Oregon (OR)
U of Pennsylvania (PA)
U of Pittsburgh (PA)
U of Puget Sound (WA)
U of Regina (SK, Canada)
U of Rhode Island (RI)
U of Rochester (NY)
U of St. Thomas (MN)
The U of Scranton (PA)
U of South Carolina (SC)
U of Southern California (CA)
The U of Tennessee (TN)
The U of Texas at Austin (TX)
U of the Pacific (CA)
U of Toronto (ON, Canada)
U of Utah (UT)
U of Vermont (VT)
U of Virginia (VA)
U of Washington (WA)
U of Waterloo (ON, Canada)
U of Wisconsin–Madison (WI)
U of Wisconsin–Milwaukee (WI)
Valparaiso U (IN)
Vanderbilt U (TN)
Vassar Coll (NY)
Villanova U (PA)
Virginia Wesleyan U (VA)
Wabash Coll (IN)
Wake Forest U (NC)
Washington and Lee U (VA)
Washington State U (WA)
Washington U in St. Louis (MO)
Wayne State U (MI)
Wellesley Coll (MA)
Wesleyan U (CT)
Wheaton Coll (MA)
Whitman Coll (WA)
Willamette U (OR)
Williams Coll (MA)
Wright State U (OH)

CLASSICS AND CLASSICAL LANGUAGES RELATED
Austin Coll (TX)
California State U, Long Beach (CA)
Eckerd Coll (FL)
Florida State U (FL)
Gonzaga U (WA)
Lee U (TN)
Loyola U New Orleans (LA)
Marlboro Coll (VT)
Marquette U (WI)
New Coll of Florida (FL)
Ohio U (OH)
Rutgers U–Newark (NJ)
Tulane U (LA)
U of California, Los Angeles (CA)
U of Chicago (IL)
Wheaton Coll (IL)

Wheaton Coll (MA)

CLINICAL, COUNSELING AND APPLIED PSYCHOLOGY RELATED
Northern Vermont U–Lyndon (VT)

CLINICAL LABORATORY SCIENCE/MEDICAL TECHNOLOGY
Anderson U (IN)
Andrews U (MI)
Arkansas Tech U (AR)
Auburn U (AL)
Augustana U (SD)
Austin Peay State U (TN)
Ball State U (IN)
Barry U (FL)
Baylor U (TX)
Bellarmine U (KY)
Bemidji State U (MN)
Benedictine U (IL)
Blackburn Coll (IL)
Blue Mountain Coll (MS)
Bowling Green State U (OH)
Bradley U (IL)
Brescia U (KY)
Brigham Young U (UT)
Caldwell U (NJ)
California State U, Dominguez Hills (CA)
Campbellsville U (KY)
Canisius Coll (NY)
Carroll U (WI)
The Catholic U of America (DC)
Clarion U of Pennsylvania (PA)
Coker Coll (SC)
The Coll at Brockport, State U of New York (NY)
Coll of Saint Elizabeth (NJ)
Coll of Saint Mary (NE)
The Coll of Saint Rose (NY)
Coll of Staten Island of the City U of New York (NY)
Coll of the Ozarks (MO)
DePaul U (IL)
East Carolina U (NC)
East Central U (OK)
Eastern Mennonite U (VA)
Eastern Michigan U (MI)
Eastern New Mexico U (NM)
East Stroudsburg U of Pennsylvania (PA)
Elmhurst Coll (IL)
Evangel U (MO)
Fairleigh Dickinson U, Florham Campus (NJ)
Fairleigh Dickinson U, Metropolitan Campus (NJ)
Farmingdale State Coll (NY)
Ferris State U (MI)
Florida Gulf Coast U (FL)
Florida Southern Coll (FL)
Franciscan Missionaries of Our Lady U (LA)
Gannon U (PA)
George Mason U (VA)
The George Washington U (DC)
Georgian Court U (NJ)
Georgia Southern U–Armstrong Campus (GA)
Greensboro Coll (NC)
Hartwick Coll (NY)
Holy Family U (PA)
Idaho State U (ID)
Illinois Coll (IL)
Illinois State U (IL)
Indiana State U (IN)
Indiana U of Pennsylvania (PA)
Indiana U–Purdue U Indianapolis (IN)
Indiana U South Bend (IN)
Indiana U Southeast (IN)
Indiana Wesleyan U (IN)
Inter American U of Puerto Rico, Metropolitan Campus (PR)
Inter American U of Puerto Rico, San Germán Campus (PR)
Jacksonville U (FL)
Jefferson Coll of Health Sciences (VA)
Kansas State U (KS)
Kean U (NJ)
Kent State U (OH)
King's Coll (PA)
King U (TN)
Lebanon Valley Coll (PA)
Lincoln Memorial U (TN)

Lincoln U (MO)
Long Island U–LIU Brooklyn (NY)
Long Island U–LIU Post (NY)
Louisiana Coll (LA)
Louisiana State U Health Sciences Center (LA)
Lubbock Christian U (TX)
Malone (OH)
Manchester U (IN)
Mansfield U of Pennsylvania (PA)
Marian U (IN)
Marist Coll (NY)
Marquette U (WI)
Marshall U (WV)
Mary Baldwin U (VA)
Maryville U of Saint Louis (MO)
Marywood U (PA)
McNeese State U (LA)
Mercy Coll (NY)
Miami U (OH)
Michigan State U (MI)
Michigan Technological U (MI)
Minot State U (ND)
Mississippi State U (MS)
Missouri State U (MO)
Missouri Western State U (MO)
Morningside Coll (IA)
Mount Marty Coll (SD)
Mount Mercy U (IA)
Muskingum U (OH)
National U (CA)
Nazareth Coll of Rochester (NY)
North Dakota State U (ND)
Northeastern State U (OK)
Northern Illinois U (IL)
Northern Michigan U (MI)
Northern State U (SD)
Northwestern Coll (IA)
Northwest Missouri State U (MO)
Oakland U (MI)
Ohio Northern U (OH)
The Ohio State U (OH)
Oklahoma Christian U (OK)
Old Dominion U (VA)
Oral Roberts U (OK)
Pittsburg State U (KS)
Purdue U (IN)
Purdue U Northwest (IN)
Ramapo Coll of New Jersey (NJ)
Roberts Wesleyan Coll (NY)
Rochester Inst of Technology (NY)
Rockhurst U (MO)
Roosevelt U (IL)
Rutgers U–Camden (NJ)
Rutgers U–Newark (NJ)
Rutgers U–New Brunswick (NJ)
Saginaw Valley State U (MI)
St. Catherine U (MN)
Saint Francis U (PA)
St. John's U (NY)
St. Joseph's Coll, Long Island Campus (NY)
St. Joseph's Coll, New York (NY)
Saint Louis U (MO)
Saint Mary-of-the-Woods Coll (IN)
Saint Mary's U of Minnesota (MN)
St. Thomas Aquinas Coll (NY)
Salisbury U (MD)
Salve Regina U (RI)
Sam Houston State U (TX)
Seton Hill U (PA)
Southeast Missouri State U (MO)
Southern Adventist U (TN)
Southern Arkansas U–Magnolia (AR)
Southwest Baptist U (MO)
Southwestern Adventist U (TX)
Spencerian Coll (KY)
State U of New York at Fredonia (NY)
State U of New York at Plattsburgh (NY)
Stevenson U (MD)
Stony Brook U, State U of New York (NY)
Tarleton State U (TX)
Texas A&M U–Corpus Christi (TX)
Texas State U (TX)
Texas Woman's U (TX)
Thomas Jefferson U (PA)
Union Coll (NE)
Union U (TN)
U at Buffalo, the State U of New York (NY)
The U of Akron (OH)
The U of Alabama at Birmingham (AL)

U of Bridgeport (CT)
U of Central Arkansas (AR)
U of Central Florida (FL)
U of Central Missouri (MO)
U of Central Oklahoma (OK)
U of Cincinnati (OH)
U of Evansville (IN)
The U of Findlay (OH)
U of Hartford (CT)
U of Hawaii at Manoa (HI)
U of Illinois at Springfield (IL)
U of Jamestown (ND)
The U of Kansas (KS)
U of Kentucky (KY)
U of Louisiana at Monroe (LA)
U of Maine (ME)
U of Maryland Eastern Shore (MD)
U of Massachusetts Dartmouth (MA)
U of Massachusetts Lowell (MA)
U of Michigan–Flint (MI)
U of Montana (MT)
U of Mount Union (OH)
U of New England (ME)
U of New Hampshire (NH)
The U of North Carolina at Chapel Hill (NC)
The U of North Carolina at Greensboro (NC)
U of North Dakota (ND)
U of North Texas (TX)
U of Regina (SK, Canada)
U of Rhode Island (RI)
U of St. Francis (IL)
U of Saint Francis (IN)
U of Sioux Falls (SD)
U of South Dakota (SD)
U of Southern Mississippi (MS)
The U of Tennessee (TN)
The U of Texas at Austin (TX)
The U of Texas at El Paso (TX)
The U of Texas Rio Grande Valley (TX)
The U of Toledo (OH)
U of Utah (UT)
U of Vermont (VT)
The U of Virginia's Coll at Wise (VA)
U of Washington (WA)
U of Wisconsin–La Crosse (WI)
U of Wisconsin–Milwaukee (WI)
U of Wisconsin–Stevens Point (WI)
U of Wyoming (WY)
Utah State U (UT)
Valley City State U (ND)
Virginia Commonwealth U (VA)
Wake Forest U (NC)
Walsh U (OH)
Wartburg Coll (IA)
Wayne State U (MI)
Weber State U (UT)
Western Connecticut State U (CT)
Western Illinois U (IL)
Western Kentucky U (KY)
West Virginia U (WV)
Wichita State U (KS)
Wilkes U (PA)
Winona State U (MN)
Wright State U (OH)
Wright State U–Lake Campus (OH)
York Coll of Pennsylvania (PA)
Youngstown State U (OH)

CLINICAL/MEDICAL LABORATORY ASSISTANT
Baptist Coll of Health Sciences (TN)

CLINICAL/MEDICAL LABORATORY SCIENCE AND ALLIED PROFESSIONS RELATED
Allen Coll (IA)
Auburn U (AL)
Blackburn Coll (IL)
The Coll of Idaho (ID)
Gwynedd Mercy U (PA)
Hunter Coll of the City U of New York (NY)
Misericordia U (PA)
New Jersey Inst of Technology (NJ)
Roosevelt U (IL)
Rutgers U–Newark (NJ)
Rutgers U–New Brunswick (NJ)
Saint Louis U (MO)
U of Minnesota, Twin Cities Campus (MN)
U of Saint Mary (KS)

CLINICAL/MEDICAL LABORATORY TECHNOLOGY
Auburn U (AL)
Auburn U at Montgomery (AL)
Barry U (FL)
Boston U (MA)
Delaware State U (DE)
Fairleigh Dickinson U, Metropolitan Campus (NJ)
Penn State DuBois (PA)
Rhode Island Coll (RI)
St. Thomas Aquinas Coll (NY)
Sonoma State U (CA)
U of Maryland Eastern Shore (MD)
U of Montana (MT)
U of New Mexico (NM)
U of Science and Arts of Oklahoma (OK)
Weber State U (UT)

CLINICAL/MEDICAL SOCIAL WORK
Eastern New Mexico U (NM)
New Mexico Highlands U (NM)

CLINICAL NURSE SPECIALIST
LeTourneau U (TX)
The U of Texas at Austin (TX)

CLINICAL NUTRITION
Kent State U (OH)
La Salle U (PA)
Life U (GA)
Long Island U–LIU Post (NY)
Messiah Coll (PA)
Southern Illinois U Edwardsville (IL)
U of North Dakota (ND)

CLINICAL PSYCHOLOGY
Augsburg U (MN)
Biola U (CA)
Eastern Nazarene Coll (MA)
Redeemer U Coll (ON, Canada)
Sam Houston State U (TX)
Simon Fraser U (BC, Canada)
Southern Adventist U (TN)
Tufts U (MA)
U of Mary Hardin-Baylor (TX)
The U of Texas at Austin (TX)
Western State Colorado U (CO)

COGNITIVE PSYCHOLOGY AND PSYCHOLINGUISTICS
Dartmouth Coll (NH)
Emory U (GA)
Fitchburg State U (MA)
Northwestern U (IL)
Scripps Coll (CA)
State U of New York at Oswego (NY)
Tulane U (LA)
U of California, San Diego (CA)
Vassar Coll (NY)
Washington U in St. Louis (MO)
Welch Coll (TN)
Wellesley Coll (MA)

COGNITIVE SCIENCE
California State U, Stanislaus (CA)
Canisius Coll (NY)
Carnegie Mellon U (PA)
Case Western Reserve U (OH)
Hampshire Coll (MA)
Indiana U Bloomington (IN)
Johns Hopkins U (MD)
Lehigh U (PA)
Loyola U New Orleans (LA)
Massachusetts Inst of Technology (MA)
Millsaps Coll (MS)
Occidental Coll (CA)
Pomona Coll (CA)
Rensselaer Polytechnic Inst (NY)
Sarah Lawrence Coll (NY)
Simmons Coll (MA)
Simon Fraser U (BC, Canada)
State U of New York at Oswego (NY)
Susquehanna U (PA)
United States Military Acad (NY)
U of California, Irvine (CA)
U of California, Los Angeles (CA)
U of California, San Diego (CA)
U of California, Santa Cruz (CA)
U of Evansville (IN)
U of Georgia (GA)
U of Michigan (MI)
U of Pennsylvania (PA)

U of Richmond (VA)
U of Southern California (CA)
The U of Texas at Dallas (TX)
Vanderbilt U (TN)
Virginia Polytechnic Inst and State U (VA)
Washington U in St. Louis (MO)

COLLEGE STUDENT COUNSELING AND PERSONNEL SERVICES
Bowling Green State U (OH)

COMMERCIAL AND ADVERTISING ART
Academy of Art U (CA)
Alberta Coll of Art & Design (AB, Canada)
American Acad of Art (IL)
ArtCenter Coll of Design (CA)
Ashland U (OH)
Ball State U (IN)
Bemidji State U (MN)
Biola U (CA)
Black Hills State U (SD)
Bowling Green State U (OH)
Buena Vista U (IA)
Buffalo State Coll, State U of New York (NY)
California Coll of the Arts (CA)
California State U, Long Beach (CA)
California U of Pennsylvania (PA)
Carroll U (WI)
Carson-Newman U (TN)
Clark U (MA)
The Coll of New Jersey (NJ)
The Coll of Saint Rose (NY)
The Coll of Westchester (NY)
Columbia Coll Chicago (IL)
Concordia U Chicago (IL)
Concordia U Wisconsin (WI)
Dominican U (IL)
Drake U (IA)
Fashion Inst of Technology (NY)
Franklin Pierce U (NH)
Graceland U (IA)
Hampton U (VA)
Iowa State U of Science and Technology (IA)
Jacksonville U (FL)
Keene State Coll (NH)
Kent State U (OH)
Kutztown U of Pennsylvania (PA)
Laguna Coll of Art & Design (CA)
Lewis U (IL)
Lipscomb U (TN)
Lycoming Coll (PA)
Marietta Coll (OH)
Marymount Manhattan Coll (NY)
Massachusetts Coll of Art and Design (MA)
Mercy Coll (NY)
Miami U (OH)
Millikin U (IL)
Minnesota State U Moorhead (MN)
New York Inst of Technology (NY)
Northern Kentucky U (KY)
Northwest Nazarene U (ID)
Ohio Northern U (OH)
Oklahoma Christian U (OK)
Oral Roberts U (OK)
Pennsylvania Coll of Art & Design (PA)
Pennsylvania Coll of Technology (PA)
Portland State U (OR)
Pratt Inst (NY)
Purchase Coll, State U of New York (NY)
Rochester Inst of Technology (NY)
Rutgers U–New Brunswick (NJ)
St. Norbert Coll (WI)
St. Thomas Aquinas Coll (NY)
Sam Houston State U (TX)
School of Visual Arts (NY)
Seattle U (WA)
Seton Hill U (PA)
Southwest Baptist U (MO)
State U of New York at Fredonia (NY)
State U of New York at Oswego (NY)
Syracuse U (NY)
U of Central Missouri (MO)
U of Cincinnati (OH)
U of Minnesota, Duluth (MN)
U of New Haven (CT)

U of North Georgia (GA)
U of San Francisco (CA)
The U of Tennessee (TN)
The U of Texas at El Paso (TX)
U of the Pacific (CA)
U of Wisconsin–Stevens Point (WI)
Upper Iowa U (IA)
Wartburg Coll (IA)
Washington U in St. Louis (MO)
Waynesburg U (PA)
Weber State U (UT)
Woodbury U (CA)
York Coll of Pennsylvania (PA)

COMMERCIAL PHOTOGRAPHY
Appalachian State U (NC)
Fashion Inst of Technology (NY)
Nossi Coll of Art (TN)
Rochester Inst of Technology (NY)
School of Visual Arts (NY)

COMMUNICATION
Albion Coll (MI)
Albright Coll (PA)
Arizona Christian U (AZ)
Asbury U (KY)
Ashland U (OH)
Averett U (VA)
Bethany Lutheran Coll (MN)
Bethel Coll (IN)
Bethel U (MN)
Biola U (CA)
Blackburn Coll (IL)
Bob Jones U (SC)
Boston Coll (MA)
Boston U (MA)
Bradley U (IL)
Brenau U (GA)
Brigham Young U–Idaho (ID)
California State U, Northridge (CA)
Carlow U (PA)
Carthage Coll (WI)
Cazenovia Coll (NY)
Centenary Coll of Louisiana (LA)
Cleveland State U (OH)
The Coll of New Jersey (NJ)
Coll of the Ozarks (MO)
Colorado Christian U (CO)
Columbia Coll Chicago (IL)
Columbus State U (GA)
Concordia U Irvine (CA)
Concordia U, Nebraska (NE)
Cornell U (NY)
Dallas Baptist U (TX)
DEREE - The American Coll of Greece (Greece)
DeSales U (PA)
Dominican Coll (NY)
Eastern New Mexico U (NM)
Edgewood Coll (WI)
Florida Coll (FL)
Florida Inst of Technology (FL)
Fordham U (NY)
Frostburg State U (MD)
Geneva Coll (PA)
Gonzaga U (WA)
Goshen Coll (IN)
Granite State Coll (NH)
Hannibal-LaGrange U (MO)
Hawai`i Pacific U (HI)
High Point U (NC)
Hiram Coll (OH)
Huntingdon Coll (AL)
Indiana Wesleyan U (IN)
John Brown U (AR)
John Cabot U (Italy)
Kansas Wesleyan U (KS)
Kent State U (OH)
Kutztown U of Pennsylvania (PA)
Lamar U (TX)
La Salle U (PA)
Lasell Coll (MA)
Lebanese American U (Lebanon)
Le Moyne Coll (NY)
Lenoir-Rhyne U (NC)
Liberty U (VA)
Limestone Coll (SC)
Lincoln Christian U (IL)
Lycoming Coll (PA)
Marist Coll (NY)
Marquette U (WI)
Marymount Manhattan Coll (NY)
Marymount U (VA)
Massachusetts Coll of Liberal Arts (MA)
McPherson Coll (KS)
Michigan State U (MI)

Milligan Coll (TN)
Misericordia U (PA)
National Louis U (IL)
New Mexico State U (NM)
New York Inst of Technology (NY)
Northwest Christian U (OR)
Northwest Missouri State U (MO)
Northwest U (WA)
Nyack Coll (NY)
Oakland City U (IN)
Oakland U (MI)
Oklahoma City U (OK)
Oregon Inst of Technology (OR)
Pepperdine U, Malibu (CA)
Portland State U (OR)
Post U (CT)
Purdue U (IN)
Randolph-Macon Coll (VA)
Regent U (VA)
Roanoke Coll (VA)
Rowan U (NJ)
Sacred Heart U (CT)
Saint Anselm Coll (NH)
St. John Fisher Coll (NY)
Saint Joseph's U (PA)
Saint Louis U (MO)
Saint Louis U–Madrid Campus (Spain)
Saint Martin's U (WA)
Simpson Coll (IA)
Slippery Rock U of Pennsylvania (PA)
Southeastern U (FL)
Southern Vermont Coll (VT)
Southwestern Coll (KS)
Spring Hill Coll (AL)
Stetson U (FL)
Susquehanna U (PA)
Tarleton State U (TX)
Tennessee Wesleyan U (TN)
Texas A&M U (TX)
Texas A&M U–Corpus Christi (TX)
Texas A&M U–Kingsville (TX)
Toccoa Falls Coll (GA)
Towson U (MD)
Trinity U (TX)
U of California, San Diego (CA)
U of California, Santa Barbara (CA)
U of Central Oklahoma (OK)
U of Colorado Colorado Springs (CO)
U of Dubuque (IA)
U of Evansville (IN)
U of Houston–Clear Lake (TX)
U of Houston–Downtown (TX)
U of Illinois at Chicago (IL)
U of Illinois at Springfield (IL)
U of Maine (ME)
U of Mary Hardin-Baylor (TX)
U of Massachusetts Amherst (MA)
U of Massachusetts Boston (MA)
U of Michigan–Flint (MI)
U of Minnesota, Crookston (MN)
U of Mobile (AL)
U of Mount Union (OH)
U of North Dakota (ND)
U of Saint Francis (IN)
U of San Diego (CA)
The U of Scranton (PA)
The U of Tampa (FL)
The U of Tennessee at Chattanooga (TN)
The U of Texas at San Antonio (TX)
The U of Texas of the Permian Basin (TX)
The U of Toledo (OH)
U of Utah (UT)
U of Wisconsin–Eau Claire (WI)
U of Wisconsin–Stevens Point (WI)
U of Wisconsin–Whitewater (WI)
Westminster Coll (PA)
Whitworth U (WA)
Wichita State U (KS)
William Peace U (NC)
William Penn U (IA)
Woodbury U (CA)
Youngstown State U (OH)

COMMUNICATION AND JOURNALISM RELATED
Auburn U (AL)
Augustana Coll (IL)
Benedictine U (IL)
Berry Coll (GA)
Bob Jones U (SC)
Bowling Green State U (OH)
Brigham Young U (UT)

Buena Vista U (IA)
California Lutheran U (CA)
Carlow U (PA)
Chestnut Hill Coll (PA)
Clarke U (IA)
Concordia U (QC, Canada)
Dominican Coll (NY)
Dominican U of California (CA)
Drexel U (PA)
Eastern Nazarene Coll (MA)
Endicott Coll (MA)
Farmingdale State Coll (NY)
Florida Inst of Technology (FL)
Friends U (KS)
Hannibal-LaGrange U (MO)
Immaculata U (PA)
Lehman Coll of the City U of New York (NY)
Madonna U (MI)
Malone U (OH)
Manhattanville Coll (NY)
Marquette U (WI)
Mercer U, Macon (GA)
Merrimack Coll (MA)
Minot State U (ND)
Morehead State U (KY)
Newberry Coll (SC)
Notre Dame de Namur U (CA)
Ohio Northern U (OH)
The Ohio State U (OH)
Oklahoma Christian U (OK)
Our Lady of the Lake U (TX)
Penn State Abington (PA)
Penn State Altoona (PA)
Penn State Beaver (PA)
Penn State Berks (PA)
Penn State Brandywine (PA)
Penn State DuBois (PA)
Penn State Erie, The Behrend Coll (PA)
Penn State Fayette, The Eberly Campus (PA)
Penn State Greater Allegheny (PA)
Penn State Hazleton (PA)
Penn State Lehigh Valley (PA)
Penn State Mont Alto (PA)
Penn State New Kensington (PA)
Penn State Schuylkill (PA)
Penn State Shenango (PA)
Penn State U Park (PA)
Penn State Wilkes-Barre (PA)
Penn State Worthington Scranton (PA)
Penn State York (PA)
Quinnipiac U (CT)
Rosemont Coll (PA)
Sacred Heart U (CT)
Saint Mary's Coll of California (CA)
Southeastern Oklahoma State U (OK)
State U of New York Polytechnic Inst (NY)
Tennessee Technological U (TN)
Trevecca Nazarene U (TN)
U of Guam (GU)
U of Miami (FL)
U of Minnesota, Duluth (MN)
U of Minnesota, Twin Cities Campus (MN)
Virginia Polytechnic Inst and State U (VA)
Washington U in St. Louis (MO)
Webster U (MO)
West Virginia U (WV)
Wisconsin Lutheran Coll (WI)

COMMUNICATION AND MEDIA RELATED
Academy of Art U (CA)
Adelphi U (NY)
Ashland U (OH)
Athabasca U (AB, Canada)
Auburn U (AL)
Austin Coll (TX)
Belmont U (TN)
Bennington Coll (VT)
Biola U (CA)
Butler U (IN)
Cameron U (OK)
Canisius Coll (NY)
Carthage Coll (WI)
The Coll of Saint Rose (NY)
Concordia U (QC, Canada)
Curry Coll (MA)
DePaul U (IL)
DeSales U (PA)
Eastern Mennonite U (VA)

Elon U (NC)
Emory U (GA)
Fairleigh Dickinson U, Metropolitan Campus (NJ)
Florida State U (FL)
Franklin U Switzerland (Switzerland)
Georgetown Coll (KY)
Granite State Coll (NH)
Greenville U (IL)
Hood Coll (MD)
Judson U (IL)
Kennesaw State U (GA)
King's Coll (PA)
La Roche Coll (PA)
Lasell Coll (MA)
Loyola U Chicago (IL)
Lycoming Coll (PA)
Lynn U (FL)
Marquette U (WI)
Marymount Manhattan Coll (NY)
Middle Georgia State U (GA)
Milligan Coll (TN)
Missouri Baptist U (MO)
Molloy Coll (NY)
Montclair State U (NJ)
Morehead State U (KY)
Neumann U (PA)
Newberry Coll (SC)
New Jersey Inst of Technology (NJ)
New York U (NY)
Northeastern U (MA)
Northwestern U (IL)
Ohio Northern U (OH)
Oklahoma City U (OK)
Pace U (NY)
Pace U, Pleasantville Campus (NY)
Penn State Erie, The Behrend Coll (PA)
Point Park U (PA)
Rochester Inst of Technology (NY)
Roger Williams U (RI)
Rollins Coll (FL)
St. Thomas U (FL)
Salve Regina U (RI)
Slippery Rock U of Pennsylvania (PA)
Southern Methodist U (TX)
Southwestern Coll (KS)
Stanford U (CA)
Trent U (ON, Canada)
Unity Coll (ME)
Université de Sherbrooke (QC, Canada)
U of Central Missouri (MO)
U of Colorado Boulder (CO)
U of Evansville (IN)
U of Miami (FL)
U of Mobile (AL)
U of North Georgia (GA)
The U of Texas at Dallas (TX)
The U of West Alabama (AL)
U of Wisconsin–Stevens Point (WI)
U of Wisconsin–Superior (WI)
Virginia Wesleyan U (VA)
Waldorf U (IA)
Walsh U (OH)
Washington & Jefferson Coll (PA)

COMMUNICATION DISORDERS SCIENCES AND SERVICES RELATED
Elms Coll (MA)
Marquette U (WI)
Ouachita Baptist U (AR)
U of Missouri (MO)
U of New Hampshire (NH)

COMMUNICATION SCIENCES AND DISORDERS
Appalachian State U (NC)
Arizona State U at the Tempe campus (AZ)
Auburn U (AL)
Augustana Coll (IL)
Baldwin Wallace U (OH)
Baylor U (TX)
Biola U (CA)
Bob Jones U (SC)
Bowling Green State U (OH)
Bridgewater State U (MA)
Brock U (ON, Canada)
Butler U (IN)
California State U, East Bay (CA)
California State U, Fullerton (CA)
California State U, Long Beach (CA)

California State U, Los Angeles (CA)
California State U, Northridge (CA)
California U of Pennsylvania (PA)
Carlos Albizu U (PR)
Case Western Reserve U (OH)
Central Michigan U (MI)
Emerson Coll (MA)
Florida State U (FL)
Governors State U (IL)
Hampton U (VA)
Harding U (AR)
Ithaca Coll (NY)
Jacksonville U (FL)
Kansas State U (KS)
Lamar U (TX)
La Salle U (PA)
Lebanon Valley Coll (PA)
Maryville U of Saint Louis (MO)
Metropolitan State U of Denver (CO)
Minot State U (ND)
Mount Vernon Nazarene U (OH)
Northern Illinois U (IL)
Northwestern U (IL)
Our Lady of the Lake U (TX)
Pace U (NY)
Penn State Abington (PA)
Penn State Altoona (PA)
Penn State Beaver (PA)
Penn State Berks (PA)
Penn State Brandywine (PA)
Penn State DuBois (PA)
Penn State Erie, The Behrend Coll (PA)
Penn State Fayette, The Eberly Campus (PA)
Penn State Greater Allegheny (PA)
Penn State Hazleton (PA)
Penn State Lehigh Valley (PA)
Penn State Mont Alto (PA)
Penn State New Kensington (PA)
Penn State Schuylkill (PA)
Penn State Shenango (PA)
Penn State U Park (PA)
Penn State Wilkes-Barre (PA)
Penn State Worthington Scranton (PA)
Penn State York (PA)
Portland State U (OR)
Queens Coll of the City U of New York (NY)
Radford U (VA)
Rhode Island Coll (RI)
Saint Louis U (MO)
Samford U (AL)
San Diego State U (CA)
San Francisco State U (CA)
Shaw U (NC)
Southeastern U (FL)
Southeast Missouri State U (MO)
Southern Illinois U Carbondale (IL)
State U of New York at Fredonia (NY)
State U of New York at New Paltz (NY)
Stephen F. Austin State U (TX)
Syracuse U (NY)
Texas A&M Intl U (TX)
Texas A&M U–Kingsville (TX)
Texas State U (TX)
Truman State U (MO)
The U of Akron (OH)
The U of Arizona (AZ)
U of Cincinnati (OH)
U of Colorado Boulder (CO)
U of Georgia (GA)
U of Houston (TX)
The U of Kansas (KS)
U of Maine (ME)
U of Maryland, Coll Park (MD)
U of Massachusetts Amherst (MA)
U of Minnesota, Duluth (MN)
U of Nebraska at Kearney (NE)
U of North Dakota (ND)
U of Oklahoma Health Sciences Center (OK)
U of Oregon (OR)
U of Rhode Island (RI)
U of South Alabama (AL)
U of South Dakota (SD)
U of South Florida Sarasota-Manatee (FL)
The U of Texas at Austin (TX)
The U of Texas Rio Grande Valley (TX)
U of Vermont (VT)

U of Wisconsin–Eau Claire (WI)
U of Wisconsin–River Falls (WI)
U of Wisconsin–Stevens Point (WI)
U of Wisconsin–Whitewater (WI)
Wayne State U (MI)
Western Illinois U (IL)
Western Kentucky U (KY)
Western Washington U (WA)
West Texas A&M U (TX)
Wichita State U (KS)
William Paterson U of New Jersey (NJ)
Winthrop U (SC)
Worcester State U (MA)
Xavier U of Louisiana (LA)

COMMUNICATIONS TECHNOLOGIES AND SUPPORT SERVICES RELATED
Alverno Coll (WI)
Chestnut Hill Coll (PA)
Framingham State U (MA)
Lesley U (MA)
Minot State U (ND)
Trinity Christian Coll (IL)
U of Central Oklahoma (OK)
U of Wisconsin–Platteville (WI)

COMMUNICATIONS TECHNOLOGY
Eastern Michigan U (MI)
East Stroudsburg U of Pennsylvania (PA)
Inter American U of Puerto Rico, Bayamón Campus (PR)
Messiah Coll (PA)
Northern Vermont U–Lyndon (VT)
Southern Adventist U (TN)

COMMUNITY HEALTH AND PREVENTIVE MEDICINE
Ball State U (IN)
Bowling Green State U (OH)
Canisius Coll (NY)
Carroll Coll (MT)
Charles R. Drew U of Medicine and Science (CA)
Florida Gulf Coast U (FL)
Florida State U (FL)
George Mason U (VA)
Georgia Coll & State U (GA)
Governors State U (IL)
Hiram Coll (OH)
Hofstra U (NY)
Indiana U Bloomington (IN)
Kent State U (OH)
Mansfield U of Pennsylvania (PA)
Moravian Coll (PA)
Murray State U (KY)
National U (CA)
Pine Manor Coll (MA)
Portland State U (OR)
Tufts U (MA)
U of Florida (FL)
U of La Verne (CA)
U of Maryland, Coll Park (MD)
U of the Incarnate Word (TX)
U of Wisconsin–Eau Claire (WI)
U of Wisconsin–La Crosse (WI)
Western Kentucky U (KY)

COMMUNITY HEALTH SERVICES COUNSELING
Becker Coll (MA)
Canisius Coll (NY)
Carroll Coll (MT)
Central Michigan U (MI)
Cornerstone U (MI)
Delaware State U (DE)
Eastern Washington U (WA)
Indiana State U (IN)
James Madison U (VA)
Johnson C. Smith U (NC)
Massachusetts Coll of Liberal Arts (MA)
Morris Coll (SC)
New Mexico State U (NM)
Northern Illinois U (IL)
Northern Michigan U (MI)
Ohio U (OH)
Rhode Island Coll (RI)
Texas A&M U (TX)
The U of Arizona (AZ)
U of Central Arkansas (AR)
The U of Kansas (KS)
U of Maine at Farmington (ME)
U of Massachusetts Lowell (MA)
U of Michigan–Dearborn (MI)
U of Pennsylvania (PA)

Western Connecticut State U (CT)
Western Washington U (WA)
Whitworth U (WA)
Worcester State U (MA)
Wright State U (OH)
Wright State U–Lake Campus (OH)
Youngstown State U (OH)

COMMUNITY ORGANIZATION AND ADVOCACY
Acadia U (NS, Canada)
Allegheny Coll (PA)
Alverno Coll (WI)
Arizona State U at the Downtown Phoenix campus (AZ)
Arizona State U at the West campus (AZ)
Bemidji State U (MN)
Bryant U (RI)
Central Michigan U (MI)
Columbia Coll (SC)
Emory & Henry Coll (VA)
Guilford Coll (NC)
Indiana Wesleyan U (IN)
Metropolitan Coll of New York (NY)
Middle Georgia State U (GA)
Nazareth Coll of Rochester (NY)
New York U (NY)
Northland Coll (WI)
Northwestern U (IL)
Providence Coll (RI)
Rockhurst U (MO)
Southern Arkansas U–Magnolia (AR)
State U of New York Empire State Coll (NY)
U of Alaska Fairbanks (AK)
U of California, Santa Cruz (CA)
U of Colorado Boulder (CO)
U of Hartford (CT)
U of Massachusetts Boston (MA)
U of New Mexico (NM)
West Virginia U Inst of Technology (WV)

COMMUNITY PSYCHOLOGY
Clayton State U (GA)
Northwestern U (IL)
Rogers State U (OK)
U of Miami (FL)
U of Washington, Bothell (WA)

COMPARATIVE LITERATURE
The American U in Cairo (Egypt)
The American U of Paris (France)
Barnard Coll (NY)
Barry U (FL)
Beloit Coll (WI)
Binghamton U, State U of New York (NY)
Boston U (MA)
Brandeis U (MA)
Brock U (ON, Canada)
Bryn Mawr Coll (PA)
California State U, Fullerton (CA)
California State U, Long Beach (CA)
Case Western Reserve U (OH)
Chowan U (NC)
City Coll of the City U of New York (NY)
Clark U (MA)
Coll of the Atlantic (ME)
Coll of the Holy Cross (MA)
The Coll of Wooster (OH)
The Colorado Coll (CO)
Columbia U (NY)
Cornell U (NY)
Dartmouth Coll (NH)
Earlham Coll (IN)
Eckerd Coll (FL)
Emory U (GA)
Fordham U (NY)
Franklin Pierce U (NH)
Franklin U Switzerland (Switzerland)
Georgetown U (DC)
Gettysburg Coll (PA)
Harvard U (MA)
Haverford Coll (PA)
Hillsdale Coll (MI)
Hobart and William Smith Colls (NY)
Hofstra U (NY)
Hunter Coll of the City U of New York (NY)
Indiana U Bloomington (IN)

Inter American U of Puerto Rico, San Germán Campus (PR)
John Cabot U (Italy)
John Carroll U (OH)
Lycoming Coll (PA)
Manchester U (IN)
Marlboro Coll (VT)
Middlebury Coll (VT)
New Coll of Florida (FL)
New York U (NY)
Northwestern U (IL)
Northwest U (WA)
Oberlin Coll (OH)
The Ohio State U (OH)
Ohio Wesleyan U (OH)
Penn State Abington (PA)
Penn State Altoona (PA)
Penn State Beaver (PA)
Penn State Berks (PA)
Penn State Brandywine (PA)
Penn State DuBois (PA)
Penn State Erie, The Behrend Coll (PA)
Penn State Fayette, The Eberly Campus (PA)
Penn State Greater Allegheny (PA)
Penn State Hazleton (PA)
Penn State Lehigh Valley (PA)
Penn State Mont Alto (PA)
Penn State New Kensington (PA)
Penn State Schuylkill (PA)
Penn State Shenango (PA)
Penn State U Park (PA)
Penn State Wilkes-Barre (PA)
Penn State Worthington Scranton (PA)
Penn State York (PA)
Princeton U (NJ)
Purchase Coll, State U of New York (NY)
Purdue U (IN)
Queens Coll of the City U of New York (NY)
Quinnipiac U (CT)
Ramapo Coll of New Jersey (NJ)
Reed Coll (OR)
Rockford U (IL)
Rutgers U–New Brunswick (NJ)
St. Catherine U (MN)
Saint Francis U (PA)
Saint Mary's Coll of California (CA)
San Diego State U (CA)
San Francisco State U (CA)
Sarah Lawrence Coll (NY)
Smith Coll (MA)
Sonoma State U (CA)
Stanford U (CA)
State U of New York Coll at Geneseo (NY)
State U of New York Coll at Old Westbury (NY)
Stony Brook U, State U of New York (NY)
Tufts U (MA)
U of California, Davis (CA)
U of California, Irvine (CA)
U of California, Los Angeles (CA)
U of California, San Diego (CA)
U of California, Santa Barbara (CA)
U of California, Santa Cruz (CA)
U of Chicago (IL)
U of Georgia (GA)
U of Massachusetts Amherst (MA)
U of Michigan (MI)
U of Minnesota, Twin Cities Campus (MN)
U of New Mexico (NM)
The U of North Carolina at Chapel Hill (NC)
U of Oregon (OR)
U of Pennsylvania (PA)
U of Pittsburgh at Greensburg (PA)
U of Rochester (NY)
U of St. Thomas (MN)
U of San Francisco (CA)
U of South Carolina (SC)
U of Southern California (CA)
The U of Texas at Austin (TX)
The U of Texas at Dallas (TX)
U of Toronto (ON, Canada)
U of Utah (UT)
U of Virginia (VA)
U of Washington (WA)
U of Wisconsin–Madison (WI)
U of Wisconsin–Milwaukee (WI)
Washington U in St. Louis (MO)
Wellesley Coll (MA)

Willamette U (OR)
Williams Coll (MA)

COMPUTATIONAL AND APPLIED MATHEMATICS
American Public U System (WV)
Bryant U (RI)
Florida State U (FL)
Harrisburg U of Science and Technology (PA)
Maryville U of Saint Louis (MO)
Oregon Inst of Technology (OR)
Purdue U (IN)
Shepherd U (WV)
U of Notre Dame (IN)
U of Southern California (CA)
The U of Texas at Austin (TX)
Virginia Polytechnic Inst and State U (VA)
William Jewell Coll (MO)
Wittenberg U (OH)

COMPUTATIONAL BIOLOGY
Carnegie Mellon U (PA)
Case Western Reserve U (OH)
Colby Coll (ME)
Florida State U (FL)
Lipscomb U (TN)
Massachusetts Inst of Technology (MA)
Rutgers U–Camden (NJ)

COMPUTATIONAL MATHEMATICS
Arizona State U at the Tempe campus (AZ)
Asbury U (KY)
California Inst of Technology (CA)
Carnegie Mellon U (PA)
Christopher Newport U (VA)
Coll of Saint Benedict (MN)
Embry-Riddle Aeronautical U–Daytona (FL)
Loyola U New Orleans (LA)
Marquette U (WI)
McKendree U (IL)
Michigan State U (MI)
The Ohio State U (OH)
Rochester Inst of Technology (NY)
Saint John's U (MN)
Siena Coll (NY)
Simmons Coll (MA)
Southwestern U (TX)
Stevens Inst of Technology (NJ)
U of California, Davis (CA)
U of California, Los Angeles (CA)
U of California, San Diego (CA)
U of Puerto Rico–Humacao (PR)
U of Washington (WA)
U of Waterloo (ON, Canada)

COMPUTATIONAL SCIENCE
American U (DC)
Canisius Coll (NY)
Florida State U (FL)
Hood Coll (MD)
Iowa State U of Science and Technology (IA)
Siena Coll (NY)
U of Michigan–Dearborn (MI)
The U of Texas at Austin (TX)
The U of Texas Rio Grande Valley (TX)
U of Wisconsin–River Falls (WI)
U of Wisconsin–Stevens Point (WI)
Washington State U (WA)
Washington State U–Global Campus (WA)
Washington State U–Vancouver (WA)
Winona State U (MN)

COMPUTER AND INFORMATION SCIENCES
Academy Coll (MN)
Adelphi U (NY)
Albright Coll (PA)
Alcorn State U (MS)
Alverno Coll (WI)
American U (DC)
American U in Bulgaria (Bulgaria)
Anderson U (IN)
Andrews U (MI)
Angelo State U (TX)
Aquinas Coll (MI)
Arcadia U (PA)
Arizona State U at the Tempe campus (AZ)
Arkansas Tech U (AR)

Assumption Coll (MA)
Athabasca U (AB, Canada)
Athens State U (AL)
Auburn U (AL)
Austin Coll (TX)
Avila U (MO)
Azusa Pacific U (CA)
Ball State U (IN)
Barnard Coll (NY)
Beacon Coll (FL)
Becker Coll (MA)
Bellarmine U (KY)
Belmont U (TN)
Bennett Coll (NC)
Bennington Coll (VT)
Bentley U (MA)
Berea Coll (KY)
Bethel U (MN)
Binghamton U, State U of New York (NY)
Boston Coll (MA)
Bowie State U (MD)
Bowling Green State U (OH)
Bradley U (IL)
Brandman U (CA)
Bryant U (RI)
Bucknell U (PA)
Butler U (IN)
Cairn U (PA)
Caldwell U (NJ)
California Lutheran U (CA)
California State U, Los Angeles (CA)
California U of Pennsylvania (PA)
Carroll Coll (MT)
Carroll U (WI)
Carthage Coll (WI)
Catawba Coll (NC)
The Catholic U of America (DC)
Central Connecticut State U (CT)
Champlain Coll (VT)
Chapman U (CA)
Chestnut Hill Coll (PA)
Chowan U (NC)
The Citadel, The Military Coll of South Carolina (SC)
Clarion U of Pennsylvania (PA)
Clark Atlanta U (GA)
Clarke U (IA)
Clemson U (SC)
Cleveland State U (OH)
Coastal Carolina U (SC)
Coleman U, San Diego (CA)
The Coll at Brockport, State U of New York (NY)
Coll of Charleston (SC)
The Coll of New Jersey (NJ)
The Coll of St. Scholastica (MN)
The Coll of William and Mary (VA)
Colorado Christian U (CO)
Colorado Mesa U (CO)
Colorado State U (CO)
Columbia Coll (MO)
Columbia Coll (SC)
Columbus State U (GA)
Concordia U Chicago (IL)
Cornell U (NY)
Covenant Coll (GA)
Curry Coll (MA)
Dakota State U (SD)
Dallas Baptist U (TX)
Delaware State U (DE)
DEREE - The American Coll of Greece (Greece)
Dickinson Coll (PA)
Dickinson State U (ND)
Doane U (NE)
Dominican Coll (NY)
Earlham Coll (IN)
East Central U (OK)
Eastern Michigan U (MI)
Eastern New Mexico U (NM)
Eastern Oregon U (OR)
Eastern Washington U (WA)
East Stroudsburg U of Pennsylvania (PA)
East Tennessee State U (TN)
Edgewood Coll (WI)
Elizabethtown Coll (PA)
Elms Coll (MA)
Elon U (NC)
Emmanuel Coll (GA)
Emmaus Bible Coll (IA)
Emporia State U (KS)
The Evergreen State Coll (WA)
Fairfield U (CT)

Fairleigh Dickinson U, Florham Campus (NJ)
Fairleigh Dickinson U, Metropolitan Campus (NJ)
Felician U (NJ)
Fisher Coll (MA)
Fitchburg State U (MA)
Florida Atlantic U (FL)
Florida Gulf Coast U (FL)
Florida Intl U (FL)
Florida State U (FL)
Fordham U (NY)
Framingham State U (MA)
Francis Marion U (SC)
Franklin & Marshall Coll (PA)
Friends U (KS)
Gannon U (PA)
Geneva Coll (PA)
George Mason U (VA)
Georgetown Coll (KY)
The George Washington U (DC)
Georgia Inst of Technology (GA)
Georgia Southern U (GA)
Georgia Southern U–Armstrong Campus (GA)
Georgia State U (GA)
Graceland U (IA)
Grand Valley State U (MI)
Grand View U (IA)
Greenville U (IL)
Guilford Coll (NC)
Gwynedd Mercy U (PA)
Hamilton Coll (NY)
Hannibal-LaGrange U (MO)
Harrisburg U of Science and Technology (PA)
Hartwick Coll (NY)
Hope Coll (MI)
Howard Payne U (TX)
Husson U (ME)
Huston-Tillotson U (TX)
Indiana State U (IN)
Indiana U of Pennsylvania (PA)
Indiana Wesleyan U (IN)
Inter American U of Puerto Rico, Barranquitas Campus (PR)
Inter American U of Puerto Rico, Fajardo Campus (PR)
Ithaca Coll (NY)
Jackson State U (MS)
Jacksonville U (FL)
James Madison U (VA)
John Jay Coll of Criminal Justice of the City U of New York (NY)
Johns Hopkins U (MD)
Johnson C. Smith U (NC)
Juniata Coll (PA)
Kalamazoo Coll (MI)
Kansas State U (KS)
Kean U (NJ)
Keene State Coll (NH)
Keiser U, Fort Lauderdale (FL)
Kennesaw State U (GA)
Kent State U (OH)
Kentucky State U (KY)
King's Coll (PA)
Kutztown U of Pennsylvania (PA)
Lamar U (TX)
La Roche Coll (PA)
La Salle U (PA)
Lebanon Valley Coll (PA)
Lehman Coll of the City U of New York (NY)
Le Moyne Coll (NY)
Lenoir-Rhyne U (NC)
Liberty U (VA)
Lincoln Memorial U (TN)
Lincoln U (PA)
Lindenwood U (MO)
Lock Haven U of Pennsylvania (PA)
Long Island U–LIU Brooklyn (NY)
Loyola Marymount U (CA)
Loyola U Chicago (IL)
Loyola U New Orleans (LA)
Lubbock Christian U (TX)
Macalester Coll (MN)
Mansfield U of Pennsylvania (PA)
Marist Coll (NY)
Marlboro Coll (VT)
Marquette U (WI)
Marshall U (WV)
Maryville Coll (TN)
Massachusetts Coll of Liberal Arts (MA)
The Master's U (CA)
McDaniel Coll (MD)
McMurry U (TX)

Mercy Coll (NY)
Mercyhurst U (PA)
Metropolitan State U of Denver (CO)
Miami Dade Coll (FL)
Miami U (OH)
Michigan State U (MI)
Middle Georgia State U (GA)
Millersville U of Pennsylvania (PA)
Milligan Coll (TN)
Mills Coll (CA)
Minot State U (ND)
Misericordia U (PA)
Mississippi State U (MS)
Missouri U of Science and Technology (MO)
Missouri Western State U (MO)
Molloy Coll (NY)
Montclair State U (NJ)
Morehead State U (KY)
Morehouse Coll (GA)
Mount St. Joseph U (OH)
Mount St. Mary's U (MD)
Neumann U (PA)
New England Inst of Technology (RI)
New Jersey City U (NJ)
New Jersey Inst of Technology (NJ)
New Mexico Highlands U (NM)
New Mexico State U (NM)
New York Inst of Technology (NY)
New York U (NY)
Niagara U (NY)
North American U (TX)
North Carolina Wesleyan Coll (NC)
Northeastern U (MA)
Northern Kentucky U (KY)
Northern Michigan U (MI)
Northern Vermont U–Lyndon (VT)
Northwestern U (IL)
Northwest Missouri State U (MO)
Notre Dame de Namur U (CA)
Nova Southeastern U (FL)
Oakland U (MI)
Occidental Coll (CA)
The Ohio State U (OH)
Ohio U (OH)
Oklahoma Baptist U (OK)
Oklahoma City U (OK)
Oklahoma State U (OK)
Old Dominion U (VA)
Oral Roberts U (OK)
Our Lady of the Lake U (TX)
Pace U (NY)
Pace U, Pleasantville Campus (NY)
Palm Beach Atlantic U (FL)
Penn State Abington (PA)
Penn State Altoona (PA)
Penn State Beaver (PA)
Penn State Berks (PA)
Penn State Brandywine (PA)
Penn State DuBois (PA)
Penn State Erie, The Behrend Coll (PA)
Penn State Fayette, The Eberly Campus (PA)
Penn State Greater Allegheny (PA)
Penn State Harrisburg (PA)
Penn State Hazleton (PA)
Penn State Lehigh Valley (PA)
Penn State Mont Alto (PA)
Penn State New Kensington (PA)
Penn State Schuylkill (PA)
Penn State Shenango (PA)
Penn State U Park (PA)
Penn State Wilkes-Barre (PA)
Penn State Worthington Scranton (PA)
Penn State York (PA)
Pittsburg State U (KS)
Polytechnic U of Puerto Rico (PR)
Polytechnic U of Puerto Rico, Miami Campus (FL)
Portland State U (OR)
Prairie View A&M U (TX)
Principia Coll (IL)
Ramapo Coll of New Jersey (NJ)
Regis U (CO)
Rhode Island Coll (RI)
Rice U (TX)
Rider U (NJ)
Roanoke Coll (VA)
Rochester Inst of Technology (NY)
Roger Williams U (RI)
Rollins Coll (FL)
Rowan U (NJ)
Rutgers U–Camden (NJ)

Rutgers U–Newark (NJ)
Rutgers U–New Brunswick (NJ)
Sacred Heart U (CT)
Saginaw Valley State U (MI)
Saint Augustine's U (NC)
St. Catherine U (MN)
St. John Fisher Coll (NY)
St. John's U (NY)
Saint Joseph's U (PA)
St. Lawrence U (NY)
Saint Leo U (FL)
Saint Louis U (MO)
Saint Louis U–Madrid Campus (Spain)
Saint Mary-of-the-Woods Coll (IN)
St. Mary's Coll of Maryland (MD)
St. Mary's U (TX)
St. Norbert Coll (WI)
Saint Peter's U (NJ)
St. Thomas Aquinas Coll (NY)
Saint Vincent Coll (PA)
Salisbury U (MD)
Sam Houston State U (TX)
Shaw U (NC)
Shepherd U (WV)
Shippensburg U of Pennsylvania (PA)
Shorter U (GA)
Siena Coll (NY)
Sierra Nevada Coll (NV)
Simmons Coll (MA)
Simpson Coll (IA)
Skidmore Coll (NY)
Slippery Rock U of Pennsylvania (PA)
Southeastern Oklahoma State U (OK)
Southeast Missouri State U (MO)
Southern Arkansas U–Magnolia (AR)
Southern Illinois U Edwardsville (IL)
Southern Utah U (UT)
Southwest Baptist U (MO)
Southwestern U (TX)
Spelman Coll (GA)
Spring Hill Coll (AL)
State U of New York at New Paltz (NY)
State U of New York at Plattsburgh (NY)
State U of New York Coll at Old Westbury (NY)
State U of New York Polytechnic Inst (NY)
Stephen F. Austin State U (TX)
Stetson U (FL)
Stevenson U (MD)
Stony Brook U, State U of New York (NY)
Suffolk U (MA)
Syracuse U (NY)
Tarleton State U (TX)
Temple U (PA)
Tennessee Wesleyan U (TN)
Texas A&M U–Central Texas (TX)
Texas A&M U–Commerce (TX)
Texas A&M U–Corpus Christi (TX)
Texas A&M U–Kingsville (TX)
Texas Christian U (TX)
Texas State U (TX)
Texas Tech U (TX)
Texas Woman's U (TX)
Tiffin U (OH)
Transylvania U (KY)
Trinity Christian Coll (IL)
Trinity U (TX)
Troy U (AL)
Truman State U (MO)
Tufts U (MA)
Tulane U (LA)
Union Coll (NE)
Union Coll (NY)
United States Military Acad (NY)
U at Albany, State U of New York (NY)
The U of Alabama (AL)
The U of Alabama at Birmingham (AL)
U of Alaska Fairbanks (AK)
The U of Arizona (AZ)
U of Arkansas (AR)
U of California, Irvine (CA)
U of California, Los Angeles (CA)
U of Central Arkansas (AR)
U of Central Florida (FL)
U of Central Missouri (MO)

U of Central Oklahoma (OK)
U of Cincinnati (OH)
U of Colorado Denver (CO)
U of Dayton (OH)
U of Denver (CO)
U of Dubuque (IA)
The U of Findlay (OH)
U of Florida (FL)
U of Hartford (CT)
U of Hawaii at Manoa (HI)
U of Houston (TX)
U of Houston–Clear Lake (TX)
U of Houston–Downtown (TX)
The U of Kansas (KS)
U of Kentucky (KY)
U of La Verne (CA)
U of Mary Hardin-Baylor (TX)
U of Maryland U Coll (MD)
U of Mary Washington (VA)
U of Massachusetts Boston (MA)
U of Massachusetts Dartmouth (MA)
U of Michigan (MI)
U of Michigan–Dearborn (MI)
U of Missouri (MO)
U of Mobile (AL)
U of Montana (MT)
U of Nebraska at Kearney (NE)
U of Nebraska–Lincoln (NE)
U of Nevada, Reno (NV)
U of New Hampshire (NH)
U of New Haven (CT)
U of New Mexico (NM)
U of North Alabama (AL)
U of North Dakota (ND)
U of North Florida (FL)
U of North Georgia (GA)
U of North Texas (TX)
U of Notre Dame (IN)
U of Oregon (OR)
U of Pikeville (KY)
U of Pittsburgh at Greensburg (PA)
U of Providence (MT)
U of Puget Sound (WA)
U of Rhode Island (RI)
U of Richmond (VA)
U of Saint Mary (KS)
U of San Francisco (CA)
U of South Carolina (SC)
U of South Dakota (SD)
U of Southern Indiana (IN)
U of Southern Mississippi (MS)
The U of Tampa (FL)
The U of Texas at Austin (TX)
The U of Texas at San Antonio (TX)
The U of Texas of the Permian Basin (TX)
U of the Fraser Valley (BC, Canada)
U of the Incarnate Word (TX)
U of the Potomac (DC)
U of Virginia (VA)
The U of Virginia's Coll at Wise (VA)
U of Washington, Bothell (WA)
U of Washington, Tacoma (WA)
U of West Georgia (GA)
U of Wisconsin–Eau Claire (WI)
U of Wisconsin–La Crosse (WI)
U of Wisconsin–Madison (WI)
U of Wisconsin–Milwaukee (WI)
U of Wisconsin–Platteville (WI)
U of Wisconsin–River Falls (WI)
U of Wisconsin–Stevens Point (WI)
U of Wisconsin–Whitewater (WI)
Utah State U (UT)
Utica Coll (NY)
Valdosta State U (GA)
Valley City State U (ND)
Vassar Coll (NY)
Virginia Commonwealth U (VA)
Virginia Polytechnic Inst and State U (VA)
Wake Forest U (NC)
Walsh Coll of Accountancy and Business Administration (MI)
Wartburg Coll (IA)
Washington State U (WA)
Washington State U–Tri-Cities (WA)
Washington State U–Vancouver (WA)
Washington U in St. Louis (MO)
Waynesburg U (PA)
Wayne State Coll (NE)
Wayne State U (MI)
Webber Intl U (FL)

Weber State U (UT)
Webster U (MO)
West Chester U of Pennsylvania (PA)
Western Illinois U (IL)
Western Kentucky U (KY)
Western Michigan U (MI)
Western Washington U (WA)
Westminster Coll (PA)
Westminster Coll (UT)
West Texas A&M U (TX)
West Virginia U Inst of Technology (WV)
West Virginia Wesleyan Coll (WV)
Widener U (PA)
Wilkes U (PA)
Willamette U (OR)
William Paterson U of New Jersey (NJ)
William Penn U (IA)
Worcester State U (MA)
Wright State U (OH)
Wright State U–Lake Campus (OH)
Xavier U of Louisiana (LA)
Youngstown State U (OH)

COMPUTER AND INFORMATION SCIENCES AND SUPPORT SERVICES RELATED

Amridge U (AL)
Arizona State U at the West campus (AZ)
California State U, Los Angeles (CA)
Coll of Staten Island of the City U of New York (NY)
DePaul U (IL)
Ferris State U (MI)
Hilbert Coll (NY)
Hofstra U (NY)
Indiana Tech (IN)
Indiana U–Purdue U Indianapolis (IN)
Lehigh U (PA)
Limestone Coll (SC)
Long Island U–LIU Post (NY)
Missouri U of Science and Technology (MO)
Northern Kentucky U (KY)
Purdue U Northwest (IN)
St. Bonaventure U (NY)
Southern Adventist U (TN)
Talladega Coll (AL)
United States Military Acad (NY)
U at Albany, State U of New York (NY)
U of Mount Union (OH)
U of Northern Iowa (IA)
U of Notre Dame (IN)
U of Pittsburgh (PA)
U of Providence (MT)
U of the Potomac (DC)
U of Washington, Bothell (WA)
Utah State U (UT)
Washington U in St. Louis (MO)

COMPUTER AND INFORMATION SCIENCES RELATED

Buena Vista U (IA)
California State U, Dominguez Hills (CA)
California State U, Monterey Bay (CA)
Carnegie Mellon U (PA)
Coll of Charleston (SC)
The Colorado Coll (CO)
Granite State Coll (NH)
Gwynedd Mercy U (PA)
Hofstra U (NY)
Limestone Coll (SC)
Maryville Coll (TN)
Mercer U, Macon (GA)
Missouri State U (MO)
Northern Kentucky U (KY)
Taylor U (IN)
Temple U (PA)
Université de Sherbrooke (QC, Canada)
U of New Haven (CT)
U of Northern Iowa (IA)
U of Providence (MT)
U of Wisconsin–Stout (WI)
Wagner Coll (NY)
West Virginia U (WV)

COMPUTER AND INFORMATION SYSTEMS SECURITY

American Public U System (WV)
Anderson U (IN)
Arkansas Tech U (AR)
Aurora U (IL)
Bay Path U (MA)
Bentley U (MA)
Central Penn Coll (PA)
Charter Oak State Coll (CT)
Coleman U, San Diego (CA)
Columbia Southern U (AL)
Dakota State U (SD)
Davenport U, Grand Rapids (MI)
DePaul U (IL)
Donnelly Coll (KS)
Drexel U (PA)
East Stroudsburg U of Pennsylvania (PA)
ECPI U, Virginia Beach (VA)
Excelsior Coll (NY)
Ferris State U (MI)
Frostburg State U (MD)
Guilford Coll (NC)
Hallmark U (TX)
Hilbert Coll (NY)
Illinois State U (IL)
Immaculata U (PA)
Indiana Tech (IN)
Iowa State U of Science and Technology (IA)
Kennesaw State U (GA)
LeTourneau U (TX)
Lewis U (IL)
Limestone Coll (SC)
Lindenwood U (MO)
Lipscomb U (TN)
Loyola U Chicago (IL)
Marshall U (WV)
Marywood U (PA)
Mercy Coll (NY)
Mount St. Mary's U (MD)
Oklahoma State U Inst of Technology (OK)
Pennsylvania Coll of Technology (PA)
Pensacola State Coll (FL)
Pittsburgh Tech Coll (PA)
Rasmussen Coll Bloomington (MN)
Rasmussen Coll Brooklyn Park (MN)
Rasmussen Coll Eagan (MN)
Rasmussen Coll Fargo (ND)
Rasmussen Coll Mankato (MN)
Rasmussen Coll New Port Richey (FL)
Rasmussen Coll Ocala (FL)
Rasmussen Coll St. Cloud (MN)
Rochester Inst of Technology (NY)
Roosevelt U (IL)
St. Ambrose U (IA)
St. John's U (NY)
Saint Leo U (FL)
Sam Houston State U (TX)
Southeast Missouri State U (MO)
State U of New York Coll of Technology at Alfred (NY)
State U of New York Coll of Technology at Canton (NY)
State U of New York Polytechnic Inst (NY)
Stevens Inst of Technology (NJ)
Sullivan U (KY)
Taylor U (IN)
Trine U (IN)
U of Cincinnati (OH)
U of Colorado Colorado Springs (CO)
U of Illinois at Springfield (IL)
U of Maryland U Coll (MD)
U of Miami (FL)
U of Michigan–Dearborn (MI)
U of Providence (MT)
U of Saint Francis (IN)
U of St. Thomas (MN)
The U of Tampa (FL)
The U of Texas at Austin (TX)
The U of Texas at San Antonio (TX)
U of the Potomac (DC)
The U of Tulsa (OK)
Weber State U (UT)
Western Illinois U (IL)
Western Washington U (WA)
Wilmington U (DE)

COMPUTER ENGINEERING

Anderson U (IN)

Arizona State U at the Tempe campus (AZ)
Auburn U (AL)
Bellarmine U (KY)
Bethune-Cookman U (FL)
Binghamton U, State U of New York (NY)
Boston U (MA)
Bowling Green State U (OH)
Bradley U (IL)
Brigham Young U–Idaho (ID)
Bucknell U (PA)
California Baptist U (CA)
California Polytechnic State U, San Luis Obispo (CA)
California State Polytechnic U, Pomona (CA)
California State U, East Bay (CA)
California State U, Fullerton (CA)
California State U, Long Beach (CA)
California State U, Northridge (CA)
California State U, Sacramento (CA)
California State U, San Bernardino (CA)
Capital U (OH)
Case Western Reserve U (OH)
Cedarville U (OH)
Central Michigan U (MI)
Christian Brothers U (TN)
Christopher Newport U (VA)
Clarkson U (NY)
Clemson U (SC)
Cleveland State U (OH)
The Coll of New Jersey (NJ)
Coll of Saint Elizabeth (NJ)
Colorado State U (CO)
Columbia U (NY)
Concordia U (QC, Canada)
DigiPen Inst of Technology (WA)
Drexel U (PA)
Eastern Nazarene Coll (MA)
Elizabethtown Coll (PA)
Elon U (NC)
Embry-Riddle Aeronautical U–Daytona (FL)
Fairfield U (CT)
Florida Ag and Mech U (FL)
Florida Atlantic U (FL)
Florida Inst of Technology (FL)
Florida Intl U (FL)
Florida State U (FL)
George Mason U (VA)
The George Washington U (DC)
Georgia Inst of Technology (GA)
Gonzaga U (WA)
Grand Valley State U (MI)
Harding U (AR)
Hofstra U (NY)
Indiana Tech (IN)
Indiana U–Purdue U Indianapolis (IN)
Inter American U of Puerto Rico, Bayamón Campus (PR)
Iowa State U of Science and Technology (IA)
Jackson State U (MS)
Johns Hopkins U (MD)
Johnson C. Smith U (NC)
Kansas State U (KS)
Kettering U (MI)
Lawrence Technological U (MI)
Lebanese American U (Lebanon)
Lehigh U (PA)
LeTourneau U (TX)
Lewis U (IL)
Liberty U (VA)
Lipscomb U (TN)
Louisiana State U and A&M Coll (LA)
Loyola U Chicago (IL)
Manhattan Coll (NY)
Marquette U (WI)
Merrimack Coll (MA)
Miami U (OH)
Michigan State U (MI)
Michigan Technological U (MI)
Milwaukee School of Eng (WI)
Mississippi State U (MS)
Missouri U of Science and Technology (MO)
New Jersey Inst of Technology (NJ)
New York U (NY)
North Carolina State U (NC)
North Central Coll (IL)
North Dakota State U (ND)

Northeastern U (MA)
Northwestern U (IL)
Oakland U (MI)
Ohio Northern U (OH)
The Ohio State U (OH)
Oklahoma Christian U (OK)
Oklahoma State U (OK)
Old Dominion U (VA)
Oral Roberts U (OK)
Penn State Abington (PA)
Penn State Altoona (PA)
Penn State Beaver (PA)
Penn State Berks (PA)
Penn State Brandywine (PA)
Penn State DuBois (PA)
Penn State Erie, The Behrend Coll (PA)
Penn State Fayette, The Eberly Campus (PA)
Penn State Greater Allegheny (PA)
Penn State Hazleton (PA)
Penn State Lehigh Valley (PA)
Penn State Mont Alto (PA)
Penn State New Kensington (PA)
Penn State Schuylkill (PA)
Penn State Shenango (PA)
Penn State U Park (PA)
Penn State Wilkes-Barre (PA)
Penn State Worthington Scranton (PA)
Penn State York (PA)
Polytechnic U of Puerto Rico (PR)
Portland State U (OR)
Prairie View A&M U (TX)
Princeton U (NJ)
Purdue U (IN)
Purdue U Northwest (IN)
Rice U (TX)
Rochester Inst of Technology (NY)
Roger Williams U (RI)
Rose-Hulman Inst of Technology (IN)
Rutgers U–New Brunswick (NJ)
Sacred Heart U (CT)
Saint Louis U (MO)
Saint Louis U–Madrid Campus (Spain)
St. Mary's U (TX)
San Diego State U (CA)
San Francisco State U (CA)
Santa Clara U (CA)
Shepherd U (WV)
Southern Illinois U Carbondale (IL)
Southern Illinois U Edwardsville (IL)
Southern Methodist U (TX)
State U of New York at New Paltz (NY)
Stevens Inst of Technology (NJ)
Suffolk U (MA)
Syracuse U (NY)
Taylor U (IN)
Tennessee Technological U (TN)
Texas A&M U (TX)
Texas Tech U (TX)
Trine U (IN)
Tufts U (MA)
Université de Sherbrooke (QC, Canada)
U at Albany, State U of New York (NY)
U at Buffalo, the State U of New York (NY)
The U of Akron (OH)
U of Alaska Fairbanks (AK)
U of Arkansas (AR)
U of Bridgeport (CT)
U of California, Irvine (CA)
U of California, Los Angeles (CA)
U of California, Riverside (CA)
U of California, San Diego (CA)
U of California, Santa Barbara (CA)
U of California, Santa Cruz (CA)
U of Central Florida (FL)
U of Cincinnati (OH)
U of Colorado Boulder (CO)
U of Colorado Colorado Springs (CO)
U of Dayton (OH)
U of Denver (CO)
U of Evansville (IN)
U of Florida (FL)
U of Georgia (GA)
U of Guelph (ON, Canada)
U of Hartford (CT)
U of Houston (TX)
U of Houston–Clear Lake (TX)

U of Idaho (ID)
U of Illinois at Chicago (IL)
The U of Kansas (KS)
U of Kentucky (KY)
U of Louisville (KY)
U of Maine (ME)
U of Maryland, Baltimore County (MD)
U of Maryland, Coll Park (MD)
U of Massachusetts Amherst (MA)
U of Massachusetts Boston (MA)
U of Massachusetts Dartmouth (MA)
U of Massachusetts Lowell (MA)
U of Memphis (TN)
U of Miami (FL)
U of Michigan (MI)
U of Michigan–Dearborn (MI)
U of Minnesota, Twin Cities Campus (MN)
U of Missouri (MO)
U of Mount Union (OH)
U of Nebraska–Lincoln (NE)
U of Nevada, Las Vegas (NV)
U of Nevada, Reno (NV)
U of New Hampshire (NH)
U of New Haven (CT)
U of New Mexico (NM)
The U of North Carolina at Charlotte (NC)
U of North Texas (TX)
U of Notre Dame (IN)
U of Oklahoma (OK)
U of Pennsylvania (PA)
U of Pittsburgh (PA)
U of Rhode Island (RI)
U of St. Thomas (MN)
U of Saskatchewan (SK, Canada)
The U of Scranton (PA)
U of South Alabama (AL)
U of South Carolina (SC)
U of Southern California (CA)
The U of Tennessee (TN)
The U of Texas at Dallas (TX)
The U of Texas at San Antonio (TX)
The U of Texas Rio Grande Valley (TX)
U of the Pacific (CA)
The U of Toledo (OH)
U of Toronto (ON, Canada)
The U of Tulsa (OK)
U of Utah (UT)
U of Virginia (VA)
U of Washington (WA)
U of Washington, Bothell (WA)
U of Waterloo (ON, Canada)
U of Wisconsin–Madison (WI)
U of Wisconsin–Milwaukee (WI)
U of Wisconsin–Stout (WI)
U of Wyoming (WY)
Utah State U (UT)
Valparaiso U (IN)
Vanderbilt U (TN)
Villanova U (PA)
Virginia Commonwealth U (VA)
Virginia Polytechnic Inst and State U (VA)
Washington State U (WA)
Washington U in St. Louis (MO)
Weber State U (UT)
Wentworth Inst of Technology (MA)
Western Michigan U (MI)
Western New England U (MA)
West Virginia U (WV)
West Virginia U Inst of Technology (WV)
Wichita State U (KS)
Wright State U (OH)
Wright State U–Lake Campus (OH)
Xavier U of Louisiana (LA)
York Coll of Pennsylvania (PA)

COMPUTER ENGINEERING RELATED

Auburn U (AL)
Ohio Northern U (OH)
U of California, Santa Cruz (CA)

COMPUTER ENGINEERING TECHNOLOGIES RELATED

Inter American U of Puerto Rico, Bayamón Campus (PR)
Oregon Inst of Technology (OR)
U of Guelph (ON, Canada)

COMPUTER ENGINEERING TECHNOLOGY

Ball State U (IN)

Brock U (ON, Canada)
California State U, Long Beach (CA)
California U of Pennsylvania (PA)
Central Connecticut State U (CT)
Eastern Michigan U (MI)
Farmingdale State Coll (NY)
Indiana State U (IN)
Indiana U–Purdue U Indianapolis (IN)
Kennesaw State U (GA)
LeTourneau U (TX)
Prairie View A&M U (TX)
Rochester Inst of Technology (NY)
Sam Houston State U (TX)
Shawnee State U (OH)
State U of New York Coll of Technology at Alfred (NY)
State U of New York Polytechnic Inst (NY)
U of Cincinnati (OH)
U of Dayton (OH)
U of Hartford (CT)
U of Houston (TX)
U of Houston–Downtown (TX)
U of Memphis (TN)
U of Southern Mississippi (MS)
Utah State U (UT)
Vermont Tech Coll (VT)
Weber State U (UT)

COMPUTER GRAPHICS

Academy of Art U (CA)
AIC Coll of Design (OH)
Alberta Coll of Art & Design (AB, Canada)
Bowie State U (MD)
Champlain Coll (VT)
Coleman U, San Diego (CA)
Coll of the Atlantic (ME)
Concordia U (QC, Canada)
Dakota State U (SD)
DePaul U (IL)
Elms Coll (MA)
Indiana Wesleyan U (IN)
Lindenwood U (MO)
Pratt Inst (NY)
Purdue U (IN)
Purdue U Northwest (IN)
Rochester Inst of Technology (NY)
Rogers State U (OK)
State U of New York at Fredonia (NY)
State U of New York Coll at Oneonta (NY)
Texas A&M U (TX)
U of Dubuque (IA)
U of Houston (TX)
U of Mary Hardin-Baylor (TX)
U of Pennsylvania (PA)
U of Providence (MT)
Walsh U (OH)
Whitworth U (WA)
Wilmington U (DE)

COMPUTER HARDWARE ENGINEERING

Auburn U (AL)
Utah Valley U (UT)

COMPUTER/INFORMATION TECHNOLOGY SERVICES ADMINISTRATION RELATED

Bloomsburg U of Pennsylvania (PA)
Chestnut Hill Coll (PA)
Concordia U, St. Paul (MN)
DeSales U (PA)
Friends U (KS)
Golden Gate U (CA)
Holy Names U (CA)
Limestone Coll (SC)
Long Island U–LIU Brooklyn (NY)
Marywood U (PA)
Missouri State U (MO)
Point Park U (PA)
Robert Morris U (PA)
St. Joseph's Coll, Long Island Campus (NY)
St. Joseph's Coll, New York (NY)
Southwestern Coll (KS)
U of California, Santa Cruz (CA)
The U of Findlay (OH)
U of Guam (GU)
U of Maryland, Baltimore County (MD)
U of Northern Iowa (IA)
U of Providence (MT)
Washington U in St. Louis (MO)

COMPUTER INSTALLATION AND REPAIR TECHNOLOGY
Inter American U of Puerto Rico, Bayamón Campus (PR)

COMPUTER PROGRAMMING
Andrews U (MI)
Brock U (ON, Canada)
Caribbean U (PR)
Champlain Coll (VT)
Cogswell Polytechnical Coll (CA)
Columbia Coll Chicago (IL)
Davenport U, Grand Rapids (MI)
DePaul U (IL)
EDP U of Puerto Rico (PR)
Farmingdale State Coll (NY)
Franklin Pierce U (NH)
Gannon U (PA)
Hardin-Simmons U (TX)
Husson U (ME)
Inter American U of Puerto Rico, San Germán Campus (PR)
La Salle U (PA)
Le Moyne Coll (NY)
Limestone Coll (SC)
Marlboro Coll (VT)
Missouri Valley Coll (MO)
New England Inst of Technology (RI)
Rowan U (NJ)
Saint Francis U (PA)
Southeast Missouri State U (MO)
Southwestern Coll (KS)
Tufts U (MA)
Université de Sherbrooke (QC, Canada)
The U of Akron (OH)
U of Michigan–Dearborn (MI)
U of Mount Union (OH)
U of Providence (MT)
Youngstown State U (OH)

COMPUTER PROGRAMMING RELATED
Curry Coll (MA)
Marlboro Coll (VT)
The U of Akron (OH)

COMPUTER PROGRAMMING (SPECIFIC APPLICATIONS)
Academy of Art U (CA)
Central Penn Coll (PA)
DePaul U (IL)
DigiPen Inst of Technology (WA)
ECPI U, Virginia Beach (VA)
Jacksonville U (FL)
Kennesaw State U (GA)
State U of New York Coll of Technology at Alfred (NY)
U of Washington, Bothell (WA)

COMPUTER SCIENCE
Abilene Christian U (TX)
Acadia U (NS, Canada)
Adams State U (CO)
Alabama State U (AL)
Albright Coll (PA)
Allegheny Coll (PA)
Alma Coll (MI)
American Coll of Thessaloniki (Greece)
The American U in Cairo (Egypt)
American U of Beirut (Lebanon)
The American U of Paris (France)
Amherst Coll (MA)
Anderson U (IN)
Andrews U (MI)
Appalachian State U (NC)
Arcadia U (PA)
Arizona State U at the Tempe campus (AZ)
Ashland U (OH)
Athens State U (AL)
Auburn U at Montgomery (AL)
Augsburg U (MN)
Augustana Coll (IL)
Augustana U (SD)
Aurora U (IL)
Austin Coll (TX)
Austin Peay State U (TN)
Azusa Pacific U (CA)
Baker U (KS)
Baldwin Wallace U (OH)
Bard Coll (NY)
Barry U (FL)
Baylor U (TX)
Becker Coll (MA)
Belhaven U (MS)
Beloit Coll (WI)

Bemidji State U (MN)
Benedictine Coll (KS)
Benedictine U (IL)
Bennington Coll (VT)
Bethany Lutheran Coll (MN)
Bethune-Cookman U (FL)
Binghamton U, State U of New York (NY)
Biola U (CA)
Blackburn Coll (IL)
Bloomsburg U of Pennsylvania (PA)
Bob Jones U (SC)
Boise State U (ID)
Boston Coll (MA)
Boston U (MA)
Bowdoin Coll (ME)
Bradley U (IL)
Brandeis U (MA)
Brandon U (MB, Canada)
Bridgewater Coll (VA)
Bridgewater State U (MA)
Brigham Young U–Idaho (ID)
Brock U (ON, Canada)
Bryn Mawr Coll (PA)
Buena Vista U (IA)
Cairn U (PA)
California Baptist U (CA)
California Inst of Technology (CA)
California Lutheran U (CA)
California Polytechnic State U, San Luis Obispo (CA)
California State Polytechnic U, Pomona (CA)
California State U, Dominguez Hills (CA)
California State U, East Bay (CA)
California State U, Fullerton (CA)
California State U, Long Beach (CA)
California State U, Los Angeles (CA)
California State U, Northridge (CA)
California State U, Sacramento (CA)
California State U, San Bernardino (CA)
California State U, San Marcos (CA)
California State U, Stanislaus (CA)
Calvary U (MO)
Calvin Coll (MI)
Cameron U (OK)
Canisius Coll (NY)
Capital U (OH)
Cardinal Stritch U (WI)
Carleton Coll (MN)
Carnegie Mellon U (PA)
Carroll Coll (MT)
Carson-Newman U (TN)
Carthage Coll (WI)
Case Western Reserve U (OH)
The Catholic U of America (DC)
Cedarville U (OH)
Central Methodist U (MO)
Central Michigan U (MI)
Central State U (OH)
Centre Coll (KY)
Champlain Coll (VT)
Chapman U (CA)
Charleston Southern U (SC)
Christian Brothers U (TN)
Christopher Newport U (VA)
City Coll of the City U of New York (NY)
Clark Atlanta U (GA)
Clarkson U (NY)
Clark U (MA)
Clayton State U (GA)
Coe Coll (IA)
Coker Coll (SC)
Colby Coll (ME)
Colgate U (NY)
Coll of Saint Benedict (MN)
Coll of Saint Elizabeth (NJ)
The Coll of Saint Rose (NY)
Coll of Staten Island of the City U of New York (NY)
Coll of the Holy Cross (MA)
Coll of the Ozarks (MO)
The Coll of Wooster (OH)
Columbia Coll (MO)
Columbia U (NY)
Concordia U (QC, Canada)
Concordia U, Nebraska (NE)
Concordia U, St. Paul (MN)
Concordia U Wisconsin (WI)
Connecticut Coll (CT)

Cornell Coll (IA)
Cornell U (NY)
Creighton U (NE)
Dallas Baptist U (TX)
Dartmouth Coll (NH)
Delaware State U (DE)
Denison U (OH)
DePaul U (IL)
DePauw U (IN)
DeSales U (PA)
Doane U (NE)
Dominican U (IL)
Drake U (IA)
Drew U (NJ)
Drexel U (PA)
Dunwoody Coll of Technology (MN)
Duquesne U (PA)
East Carolina U (NC)
Eastern Mennonite U (VA)
Eastern Michigan U (MI)
Eastern U (PA)
Eckerd Coll (FL)
Elon U (NC)
Embry-Riddle Aeronautical U–Daytona (FL)
Emory U (GA)
Endicott Coll (MA)
Evangel U (MO)
Fairleigh Dickinson U, Metropolitan Campus (NJ)
Fayetteville State U (NC)
Felician U (NJ)
Fitchburg State U (MA)
Florida Inst of Technology (FL)
Florida Southern Coll (FL)
Fordham U (NY)
Franklin Coll (IN)
Franklin Pierce U (NH)
Frostburg State U (MD)
Furman U (SC)
Gannon U (PA)
George Mason U (VA)
Georgetown U (DC)
The George Washington U (DC)
Georgia Coll & State U (GA)
Georgia Southwestern State U (GA)
Georgia State U (GA)
Gettysburg Coll (PA)
Gonzaga U (WA)
Gordon Coll (MA)
Goshen Coll (IN)
Governors State U (IL)
Graceland U (IA)
Grambling State U (LA)
Grand View U (IA)
Grinnell Coll (IA)
Grove City Coll (PA)
Gustavus Adolphus Coll (MN)
Hampden-Sydney Coll (VA)
Hampshire Coll (MA)
Hampton U (VA)
Harding U (AR)
Harvard U (MA)
Harvey Mudd Coll (CA)
Haverford Coll (PA)
Hawai'i Pacific U (HI)
Heidelberg U (OH)
Hendrix Coll (AR)
High Point U (NC)
Hiram Coll (OH)
Hobart and William Smith Colls (NY)
Hofstra U (NY)
Hood Coll (MD)
Humboldt State U (CA)
Hunter Coll of the City U of New York (NY)
Huston-Tillotson U (TX)
Idaho State U (ID)
Illinois Coll (IL)
Illinois State U (IL)
Illinois Wesleyan U (IL)
Indiana Tech (IN)
Indiana U Bloomington (IN)
Indiana U Kokomo (IN)
Indiana U Northwest (IN)
Indiana U–Purdue U Indianapolis (IN)
Indiana U South Bend (IN)
Indiana U Southeast (IN)
Inter American U of Puerto Rico, Aguadilla Campus (PR)
Inter American U of Puerto Rico, Barranquitas Campus (PR)
Inter American U of Puerto Rico, Bayamón Campus (PR)

Inter American U of Puerto Rico, Metropolitan Campus (PR)
Inter American U of Puerto Rico, San Germán Campus (PR)
Iona Coll (NY)
Iowa State U of Science and Technology (IA)
Ithaca Coll (NY)
John Carroll U (OH)
Kennesaw State U (GA)
Kent State U (OH)
Kettering U (MI)
King's Coll (PA)
Knox Coll (IL)
Lafayette Coll (PA)
Langston U (OK)
La Roche Coll (PA)
La Salle U (PA)
La Sierra U (CA)
Lawrence Technological U (MI)
Lebanese American U (Lebanon)
Lehigh U (PA)
Lehman Coll of the City U of New York (NY)
LeTourneau U (TX)
Lewis U (IL)
Limestone Coll (SC)
Lindenwood U (MO)
Linfield Coll (OR)
Lipscomb U (TN)
Long Island U–LIU Post (NY)
Longwood U (VA)
Loras Coll (IA)
Louisiana State U and A&M Coll (LA)
Luther Coll (IA)
Lynchburg Coll (VA)
Madonna U (MI)
Maharishi U of Management (IA)
Malone U (OH)
Manchester U (IN)
Manhattan Coll (NY)
Manhattanville Coll (NY)
Mansfield U of Pennsylvania (PA)
Marietta Coll (OH)
Marist Coll (NY)
Marlboro Coll (VT)
Marywood U (PA)
Massachusetts Coll of Liberal Arts (MA)
Massachusetts Inst of Technology (MA)
McKendree U (IL)
McNeese State U (LA)
Mercer U, Macon (GA)
Mercy Coll (NY)
Mercyhurst U (PA)
Meredith Coll (NC)
Merrimack Coll (MA)
Messiah Coll (PA)
Metropolitan State U of Denver (CO)
Michigan Technological U (MI)
MidAmerica Nazarene U (KS)
Middlebury Coll (VT)
Middle Tennessee State U (TN)
Milligan Coll (TN)
Millsaps Coll (MS)
Mills Coll (CA)
Milwaukee School of Eng (WI)
Minnesota State U Moorhead (MN)
Minot State U (ND)
Missouri State U (MO)
Missouri U of Science and Technology (MO)
Missouri Valley Coll (MO)
Monmouth Coll (IL)
Montana Tech of The U of Montana (MT)
Moravian Coll (PA)
Mount Holyoke Coll (MA)
Mount St. Joseph U (OH)
Mount Vernon Nazarene U (OH)
Murray State U (KY)
Muskingum U (OH)
National U (CA)
Neumont Coll of Computer Science (UT)
New Coll of Florida (FL)
New England Inst of Technology (RI)
New Jersey Inst of Technology (NJ)
New Mexico Inst of Mining and Technology (NM)
North Carolina State U (NC)
North Central Coll (IL)
Northcentral U (CA)

North Dakota State U (ND)
Northeastern State U (OK)
Northeastern U (MA)
Northern Arizona U (AZ)
Northern Illinois U (IL)
Northwestern Coll (IA)
Northwestern Oklahoma State U (OK)
Northwestern U (IL)
Northwest Nazarene U (ID)
Nova Southeastern U (FL)
Nyack Coll (NY)
Oberlin Coll (OH)
Ohio Dominican U (OH)
Ohio Northern U (OH)
Ohio U (OH)
Ohio Wesleyan U (OH)
Oklahoma Baptist U (OK)
Oklahoma Christian U (OK)
Olivet Nazarene U (IL)
Oral Roberts U (OK)
Oregon State U (OR)
Ouachita Baptist U (AR)
Pace U (NY)
Pace U, Pleasantville Campus (NY)
Pacific Lutheran U (WA)
Palm Beach Atlantic U (FL)
Penn State Erie, The Behrend Coll (PA)
Pitzer Coll (CA)
Polytechnic U of Puerto Rico (PR)
Pomona Coll (CA)
Portland State U (OR)
Prairie View A&M U (TX)
Providence Coll (RI)
Purdue U (IN)
Purdue U Northwest (IN)
Queens Coll of the City U of New York (NY)
Quinnipiac U (CT)
Radford U (VA)
Randolph-Macon Coll (VA)
Rasmussen Coll Bloomington (MN)
Rasmussen Coll Brooklyn Park (MN)
Rasmussen Coll Eagan (MN)
Rasmussen Coll Fargo (ND)
Rasmussen Coll Mankato (MN)
Rasmussen Coll New Port Richey (FL)
Rasmussen Coll Ocala (FL)
Rasmussen Coll St. Cloud (MN)
Redeemer U Coll (ON, Canada)
Reed Coll (OR)
Regent U (OR)
Regis U (CO)
Rensselaer Polytechnic Inst (NY)
Renton Tech Coll (WA)
Rhode Island Coll (RI)
Rhodes Coll (TN)
Roanoke Coll (VA)
Rochester Inst of Technology (NY)
Rockford U (IL)
Rocky Mountain Coll (MT)
Roger Williams U (RI)
Roosevelt U (IL)
Rose-Hulman Inst of Technology (IN)
Rowan U (NJ)
Rust Coll (MS)
Saginaw Valley State U (MI)
St. Ambrose U (IA)
Saint Anselm Coll (NH)
Saint Augustine's U (NC)
St. Bonaventure U (NY)
Saint Francis U (PA)
Saint John's U (MN)
St. Joseph's Coll, Long Island Campus (NY)
St. Joseph's Coll, New York (NY)
Saint Louis U (MO)
Saint Martin's U (WA)
St. Mary's U (TX)
Saint Mary's U of Minnesota (MN)
Saint Michael's Coll (VT)
St. Norbert Coll (WI)
St. Olaf Coll (MN)
St. Thomas U (FL)
Samford U (AL)
San Diego State U (CA)
San Francisco State U (CA)
Sarah Lawrence Coll (NY)
Scripps Coll (CA)
Seattle U (WA)
Seton Hill U (PA)
Sewanee: The U of the South (TN)
Shaw U (NC)

Silver Lake Coll of the Holy Family (WI)
Simon Fraser U (BC, Canada)
Simpson Coll (IA)
Smith Coll (MA)
Sonoma State U (CA)
Southeastern Louisiana U (LA)
Southern Adventist U (TN)
Southern Illinois U Carbondale (IL)
Southern Illinois U Edwardsville (IL)
Southern Methodist U (TX)
Southwest Baptist U (MO)
Southwestern Adventist U (TX)
Southwestern Coll (KS)
Stanford U (CA)
State U of New York at Fredonia (NY)
State U of New York at Oswego (NY)
State U of New York Coll at Old Westbury (NY)
State U of New York Coll at Oneonta (NY)
Stetson U (FL)
Stevens Inst of Technology (NJ)
Stonehill Coll (MA)
Suffolk U (MA)
Susquehanna U (PA)
Tarleton State U (TX)
Taylor U (IN)
Tennessee Technological U (TN)
Texas A&M U (TX)
Texas Lutheran U (TX)
Texas State U (TX)
Tiffin U (OH)
Towson U (MD)
Trent U (ON, Canada)
Trine U (IN)
Trinity Christian Coll (IL)
Tufts U (MA)
Tulane U (LA)
Tusculum Coll (TN)
Union Coll (NE)
Union U (TN)
Université de Sherbrooke (QC, Canada)
U at Albany, State U of New York (NY)
U at Buffalo, the State U of New York (NY)
The U of Akron (OH)
U of Alaska Fairbanks (AK)
The U of Arizona (AZ)
U of Arkansas (AR)
U of Bridgeport (CT)
U of California, Irvine (CA)
U of California, Riverside (CA)
U of California, San Diego (CA)
U of California, Santa Barbara (CA)
U of California, Santa Cruz (CA)
U of Chicago (IL)
U of Colorado Boulder (CO)
U of Colorado Colorado Springs (CO)
U of Dayton (OH)
U of Denver (CO)
U of Evansville (IN)
The U of Findlay (OH)
U of Georgia (GA)
U of Guam (GU)
U of Guelph (ON, Canada)
U of Hawaii at Manoa (HI)
U of Houston–Clear Lake (TX)
U of Idaho (ID)
U of Illinois at Chicago (IL)
U of Illinois at Springfield (IL)
U of Jamestown (ND)
U of King's Coll (NS, Canada)
U of La Verne (CA)
U of Louisiana at Monroe (LA)
U of Maine (ME)
U of Maine at Farmington (ME)
U of Maine at Fort Kent (ME)
U of Management and Technology (VA)
U of Mary Hardin-Baylor (TX)
U of Maryland, Baltimore County (MD)
U of Maryland, Coll Park (MD)
U of Maryland Eastern Shore (MD)
U of Massachusetts Amherst (MA)
U of Massachusetts Lowell (MA)
U of Memphis (TN)
U of Miami (FL)
U of Michigan–Flint (MI)
U of Minnesota, Duluth (MN)

U of Minnesota, Morris (MN)
U of Minnesota, Twin Cities Campus (MN)
U of Missouri (MO)
U of Missouri–St. Louis (MO)
U of Montana (MT)
U of Nevada, Las Vegas (NV)
U of Nevada, Reno (NV)
U of New Haven (CT)
U of New Orleans (LA)
U of North Carolina at Asheville (NC)
The U of North Carolina at Chapel Hill (NC)
The U of North Carolina at Charlotte (NC)
The U of North Carolina at Greensboro (NC)
The U of North Carolina at Pembroke (NC)
The U of North Carolina Wilmington (NC)
U of Northern Iowa (IA)
U of Oklahoma (OK)
U of Pittsburgh (PA)
U of Pittsburgh at Bradford (PA)
U of Providence (MT)
U of Puget Sound (WA)
U of Regina (SK, Canada)
U of Rochester (NY)
U of St. Francis (IL)
U of St. Thomas (MN)
U of St. Thomas (TX)
U of San Diego (CA)
U of San Francisco (CA)
U of Saskatchewan (SK, Canada)
The U of Scranton (PA)
U of Sioux Falls (SD)
U of South Alabama (AL)
U of Southern California (CA)
U of Southern Indiana (IN)
U of Southern Maine (ME)
The U of Tennessee (TN)
The U of Tennessee at Chattanooga (TN)
The U of Tennessee at Martin (TN)
The U of Texas at Dallas (TX)
The U of Texas at El Paso (TX)
The U of Texas Rio Grande Valley (TX)
U of the Pacific (CA)
U of the Virgin Islands (VI)
U of Toronto (ON, Canada)
The U of Tulsa (OK)
U of Utah (UT)
U of Vermont (VT)
U of Washington (WA)
U of Washington, Bothell (WA)
U of Waterloo (ON, Canada)
U of Wisconsin–Milwaukee (WI)
U of Wisconsin–Parkside (WI)
U of Wisconsin–Superior (WI)
U of Wyoming (WY)
Ursinus Coll (PA)
Utah Valley U (UT)
Valparaiso U (IN)
Vanderbilt U (TN)
Villanova U (PA)
Virginia Military Inst (VA)
Virginia Polytechnic Inst and State U (VA)
Virginia Wesleyan U (VA)
Wagner Coll (NY)
Walsh U (OH)
Wartburg Coll (IA)
Washington and Lee U (VA)
Washington Coll (MD)
Washington State U (WA)
Washington State U–Tri-Cities (WA)
Washington State U–Vancouver (WA)
Washington U in St. Louis (MO)
Wayland Baptist U (TX)
Weber State U (UT)
Webster U (MO)
Wellesley Coll (MA)
Wells Coll (NY)
Wentworth Inst of Technology (MA)
Wesleyan U (CT)
Western Connecticut State U (CT)
Western Michigan U (MI)
Western New England U (MA)
Western Oregon U (OR)
Western State Colorado U (CO)
Westfield State U (MA)
Westminster Coll (PA)

Westminster Coll (UT)
Westmont Coll (CA)
West Texas A&M U (TX)
West Virginia State U (WV)
West Virginia U (WV)
West Virginia U Inst of Technology (WV)
West Virginia Wesleyan Coll (WV)
Wheaton Coll (IL)
Wheaton Coll (MA)
Whitworth U (WA)
Widener U (PA)
Willamette U (OR)
William Penn U (IA)
Williams Coll (MA)
Winona State U (MN)
Wisconsin Lutheran Coll (WI)
Wittenberg U (OH)
Wofford Coll (SC)
Worcester Polytechnic Inst (MA)
Xavier U of Louisiana (LA)
York Coll of Pennsylvania (PA)
Youngstown State U (OH)

COMPUTER SOFTWARE AND MEDIA APPLICATIONS RELATED
Academy of Art U (CA)
ArtCenter Coll of Design (CA)
Champlain Coll (VT)
Coll of Charleston (SC)
DePaul U (IL)
Duquesne U (PA)
Elms Coll (MA)
Franklin Coll (IN)
Holy Names U (CA)
Iowa State U of Science and Technology (IA)
LeTourneau U (TX)
Limestone Coll (SC)
Loyola U Chicago (IL)
Pace U, Pleasantville Campus (NY)
U of Denver (CO)
U of Providence (MT)
U of Wisconsin–Stout (WI)
Worcester Polytechnic Inst (MA)

COMPUTER SOFTWARE ENGINEERING
Allegheny Coll (PA)
Arizona State U at the Polytechnic campus (AZ)
Auburn U (AL)
Baldwin Wallace U (OH)
Bowling Green State U (OH)
Brock U (ON, Canada)
California Baptist U (CA)
Carroll U (WI)
Clarkson U (NY)
Concordia U (QC, Canada)
DigiPen Inst of Technology (WA)
Drexel U (PA)
Dunwoody Coll of Technology (MN)
Embry-Riddle Aeronautical U–Daytona (FL)
Fairfield U (CT)
Florida Gulf Coast U (FL)
Florida Inst of Technology (FL)
Indiana Tech (IN)
Indiana Wesleyan U (IN)
Iowa State U of Science and Technology (IA)
Keiser U, Fort Lauderdale (FL)
Kennesaw State U (GA)
Lawrence Technological U (MI)
Loyola U Chicago (IL)
Manchester U (IN)
Miami U (OH)
Michigan Technological U (MI)
Milwaukee School of Eng (WI)
Montana Tech of The U of Montana (MT)
New Hampshire Inst of Art (NH)
Nova Southeastern U (FL)
Ohio Dominican U (OH)
Oklahoma City U (OK)
Penn State Erie, The Behrend Coll (PA)
Point Loma Nazarene U (CA)
Quinnipiac U (CT)
Robert Morris U (PA)
Rochester Inst of Technology (NY)
Rose-Hulman Inst of Technology (IN)
St. Mary's U (TX)
Shippensburg U of Pennsylvania (PA)

State U of New York at Oswego (NY)
Stevens Inst of Technology (NJ)
Trine U (IN)
U of California, Irvine (CA)
U of Central Oklahoma (OK)
U of Evansville (IN)
U of Guelph (ON, Canada)
U of Miami (FL)
U of Minnesota, Crookston (MN)
U of Nebraska–Lincoln (NE)
U of Northern Colorado (CO)
U of Regina (SK, Canada)
The U of Scranton (PA)
The U of Texas at Dallas (TX)
U of Toronto (ON, Canada)
U of Waterloo (ON, Canada)
U of Wisconsin–Platteville (WI)
Upper Iowa U (IA)
Utah Valley U (UT)
Valley City State U (ND)
Vermont Tech Coll (VT)
Washington State U (WA)
Wichita State U (KS)
William Penn U (IA)

COMPUTER SOFTWARE TECHNOLOGY
Cogswell Polytechnical Coll (CA)
Farmingdale State Coll (NY)
Oregon Inst of Technology (OR)
Sam Houston State U (TX)

COMPUTER SYSTEMS ANALYSIS
Arizona State U at the Polytechnic campus (AZ)
Arkansas Tech U (AR)
Baldwin Wallace U (OH)
Buena Vista U (IA)
California Polytechnic State U, San Luis Obispo (CA)
Concordia U (QC, Canada)
Davenport U, Grand Rapids (MI)
HEC Montreal (QC, Canada)
Kent State U (OH)
Northern Arizona U (AZ)
Pittsburg State U (KS)
Rochester Inst of Technology (NY)
Saginaw Valley State U (MI)
St. Ambrose U (IA)
Seattle Pacific U (WA)
Shippensburg U of Pennsylvania (PA)
Taylor U (IN)
Texas Christian U (TX)
Tiffin U (OH)
U of Denver (CO)
U of Houston (TX)
U of Illinois at Springfield (IL)
U of Minnesota, Twin Cities Campus (MN)
U of North Dakota (ND)
U of Providence (MT)
U of Vermont (VT)
U of Washington, Bothell (WA)
West Virginia U Inst of Technology (WV)

COMPUTER SYSTEMS NETWORKING AND TELECOMMUNICATIONS
Baldwin Wallace U (OH)
Centennial Coll (ON, Canada)
Champlain Coll (VT)
Chowan U (NC)
Coleman U, San Diego (CA)
Concordia U (QC, Canada)
Davenport U, Grand Rapids (MI)
DePaul U (IL)
EDP U of Puerto Rico (PR)
EDP U of Puerto Rico–San Sebastian (PR)
Ferris State U (MI)
Idaho State U (ID)
Illinois State U (IL)
Indiana Tech (IN)
Inter American U of Puerto Rico, Aguadilla Campus (PR)
Inter American U of Puerto Rico, Bayamón Campus (PR)
Iona Coll (NY)
Johns Hopkins U (MD)
Kansas State U (KS)
Kean U (NJ)
Keiser U, Fort Lauderdale (FL)
Lindenwood U (MO)

Montana Tech of The U of Montana (MT)
Mount Vernon Nazarene U (OH)
Northern Michigan U (MI)
Northwestern Oklahoma State U (OK)
Ohio U (OH)
Pennsylvania Coll of Technology (PA)
Rochester Inst of Technology (NY)
Stevenson U (MD)
Tiffin U (OH)
The U of Akron (OH)
U of Minnesota, Duluth (MN)
U of Minnesota, Twin Cities Campus (MN)
The U of North Carolina at Greensboro (NC)
U of Pennsylvania (PA)
U of Providence (MT)
U of Toronto (ON, Canada)
U of Wisconsin–Stout (WI)
Utah Valley U (UT)
Weber State U (UT)
Wentworth Inst of Technology (MA)
Western State Colorado U (CO)
Whitworth U (WA)

COMPUTER TEACHER EDUCATION
Abilene Christian U (TX)
Aquinas Coll (MI)
Arkansas Tech U (AR)
Baylor U (TX)
Bowling Green State U (OH)
Buena Vista U (IA)
Concordia U Chicago (IL)
Dakota State U (SD)
Eastern Michigan U (MI)
Edgewood Coll (WI)
Grand Valley State U (MI)
Howard Payne U (TX)
McMurry U (TX)
Michigan State U (MI)
U of Nebraska–Lincoln (NE)
U of Wisconsin–Superior (WI)
Utica Coll (NY)

COMPUTER TECHNOLOGY/COMPUTER SYSTEMS TECHNOLOGY
ECPI U, Virginia Beach (VA)
Excelsior Coll (NY)
Florida Atlantic U (FL)
New England Inst of Technology (RI)
Point Loma Nazarene U (CA)
Rensselaer Polytechnic Inst (NY)
Wayne State U (MI)

CONDENSED MATTER AND MATERIALS PHYSICS
Kansas Wesleyan U (KS)
Michigan Technological U (MI)
Rowan U (NJ)

CONDUCTING
Chapman U (CA)
Ithaca Coll (NY)
McMurry U (TX)
The New School Coll of Performing Arts (NY)
The U of Texas at Austin (TX)

CONSERVATION BIOLOGY
Boston U (MA)
Bryant U (RI)
Cedar Crest Coll (PA)
Colorado State U (CO)
Florida Inst of Technology (FL)
Grove City Coll (PA)
Lincoln Coll (IL)
St. Lawrence U (NY)
Seattle U (WA)
State U of New York Coll of Environmental Science and Forestry (NY)
U of Idaho (ID)
U of Maine at Machias (ME)
U of Wisconsin–Madison (WI)

CONSTRUCTION ENGINEERING
The American U in Cairo (Egypt)
American U of Beirut (Lebanon)
Arizona State U at the Tempe campus (AZ)
Bowling Green State U (OH)
Bradley U (IL)

California State U, Long Beach (CA)
Concordia U (QC, Canada)
Kennesaw State U (GA)
Lamar U (TX)
Marquette U (WI)
National U (CA)
New York U (NY)
North Carolina State U (NC)
North Dakota State U (ND)
Oregon State U (OR)
Purdue U (IN)
Texas A&M U–Commerce (TX)
Texas Tech U (TX)
The U of Alabama (AL)
U of Nebraska–Lincoln (NE)
U of New Mexico (NM)
Washington State U (WA)

CONSTRUCTION ENGINEERING TECHNOLOGY
Bemidji State U (MN)
Bowling Green State U (OH)
Bradley U (IL)
California Baptist U (CA)
California State Polytechnic U, Pomona (CA)
California State U, Long Beach (CA)
California State U, Sacramento (CA)
Central Michigan U (MI)
Colorado Mesa U (CO)
Colorado State U (CO)
Fairleigh Dickinson U, Metropolitan Campus (NJ)
Farmingdale State Coll (NY)
Fitchburg State U (MA)
Florida Ag and Mech U (FL)
Florida Inst of Technology (FL)
Florida Intl U (FL)
Georgia Southern U (GA)
Kansas State U (KS)
Michigan State U (MI)
Missouri Western State U (MO)
Northern Michigan U (MI)
Oklahoma State U (OK)
Pittsburg State U (KS)
Prairie View A&M U (TX)
Purdue U Northwest (IN)
Sam Houston State U (TX)
San Diego State U (CA)
Seminole State Coll of Florida (FL)
Southern Illinois U Edwardsville (IL)
Tarleton State U (TX)
Texas A&M U (TX)
Texas State U (TX)
The U of Akron (OH)
U of Florida (FL)
U of Houston (TX)
U of Maryland Eastern Shore (MD)
U of Nebraska–Lincoln (NE)
U of Nevada, Las Vegas (NV)
U of North Florida (FL)
U of North Texas (TX)
The U of Toledo (OH)
Wayne State U (MI)
Western Kentucky U (KY)

CONSTRUCTION MANAGEMENT
Appalachian State U (NC)
Arizona State U at the Tempe campus (AZ)
Ball State U (IN)
Boise State U (ID)
Brigham Young U–Idaho (ID)
California State U, East Bay (CA)
California State U, Northridge (CA)
Central Connecticut State U (CT)
Clemson U (SC)
Colorado State U–Pueblo (CO)
Drexel U (PA)
Dunwoody Coll of Technology (MN)
Eastern Michigan U (MI)
Ferris State U (MI)
Illinois State U (IL)
Indiana State U (IN)
John Brown U (AR)
Kennesaw State U (GA)
Kent State U (OH)
Lawrence Technological U (MI)
Louisiana State U and A&M Coll (LA)
Michigan State U (MI)
Michigan Technological U (MI)
Middle Tennessee State U (TN)

Milwaukee School of Eng (WI)
Minnesota State U Moorhead (MN)
Mississippi State U (MS)
Missouri State U (MO)
Montana Tech of The U of Montana (MT)
National U (CA)
New England Inst of Technology (RI)
North Dakota State U (ND)
Northern Arizona U (AZ)
Northern Kentucky U (KY)
Ohio Northern U (OH)
Pittsburg State U (KS)
Roger Williams U (RI)
State U of New York Coll of Environmental Science and Forestry (NY)
State U of New York Coll of Technology at Alfred (NY)
State U of New York Coll of Technology at Delhi (NY)
U of Louisiana at Monroe (LA)
U of Minnesota, Twin Cities Campus (MN)
U of Nevada, Las Vegas (NV)
U of Northern Iowa (IA)
U of Oklahoma (OK)
U of Wisconsin–Stout (WI)
Utah Valley U (UT)
Vermont Tech Coll (VT)
Virginia Polytechnic Inst and State U (VA)
Washington State U (WA)
Weber State U (UT)
Wentworth Inst of Technology (MA)
Western Illinois U (IL)
West Virginia U Inst of Technology (WV)

CONSTRUCTION TRADES
Utica Coll (NY)

CONSTRUCTION TRADES RELATED
Weber State U (UT)

CONSUMER ECONOMICS
Delaware State U (DE)
U of Georgia (GA)
U of Kentucky (KY)
The U of Tennessee (TN)
U of Utah (UT)

CONSUMER MERCHANDISING/ RETAILING MANAGEMENT
Academy of Art U (CA)
Bradley U (IL)
HEC Montreal (QC, Canada)
Oregon State U (OR)
Purdue U (IN)
San Francisco State U (CA)
Savannah Coll of Art and Design (GA)
Simmons Coll (MA)
Syracuse U (NY)
U of Memphis (TN)

CONSUMER SERVICES AND ADVOCACY
Carson-Newman U (TN)
State U of New York Coll at Oneonta (NY)
Texas State U (TX)

CORRECTIONS
Adams State U (CO)
Bowling Green State U (OH)
California State U, Stanislaus (CA)
California U of Pennsylvania (PA)
Hardin-Simmons U (TX)
John Jay Coll of Criminal Justice of the City U of New York (NY)
Langston U (OK)
Lee U (TN)
Mercyhurst U (PA)
Missouri Valley Coll (MO)
Southeast Missouri State U (MO)
Stephen F. Austin State U (TX)
Texas State U (TX)
Tiffin U (OH)
U of Central Oklahoma (OK)
U of Minnesota, Crookston (MN)
U of New Mexico (NM)
U of Pittsburgh (PA)
U of Providence (MT)
Weber State U (UT)
Western Oregon U (OR)
Youngstown State U (OH)

CORRECTIONS ADMINISTRATION
Inter American U of Puerto Rico, Barranquitas Campus (PR)
U of Providence (MT)

CORRECTIONS AND CRIMINAL JUSTICE RELATED
Anderson U (SC)
Averett U (VA)
Bethune-Cookman U (FL)
Cameron U (OK)
Cedarville U (OH)
Delaware State U (DE)
Emporia State U (KS)
Gwynedd Mercy U (PA)
Indiana Tech (IN)
John Jay Coll of Criminal Justice of the City U of New York (NY)
Keene State Coll (NH)
La Roche Coll (PA)
Limestone Coll (SC)
Muskingum U (OH)
Newberry Coll (SC)
Northwestern Coll (IA)
Oakland U (MI)
Rasmussen Coll Bloomington (MN)
Rasmussen Coll Brooklyn Park (MN)
Rasmussen Coll Eagan (MN)
Rasmussen Coll Fargo (ND)
Rasmussen Coll Mankato (MN)
Rasmussen Coll New Port Richey (FL)
Rasmussen Coll Ocala (FL)
Rasmussen Coll St. Cloud (MN)
Robert Morris U (PA)
Roger Williams U (RI)
Saint Mary's U of Minnesota (MN)
Sam Houston State U (TX)
State U of New York Coll of Technology at Canton (NY)
The U of Alabama at Birmingham (AL)
U of Alaska Fairbanks (AK)
U of Michigan–Flint (MI)
U of Providence (MT)
U of Saint Joseph (CT)
Warner Pacific Coll (OR)
Weber State U (UT)

COSTUME DESIGN
Academy of Art U (CA)
Albright Coll (PA)
Brenau U (GA)
Greensboro Coll (NC)
Marymount Manhattan Coll (NY)
Webster U (MO)

COUNSELING PSYCHOLOGY
Arizona Christian U (AZ)
Averett U (VA)
Avila U (MO)
Bob Jones U (SC)
Coker Coll (SC)
Cornerstone U (MI)
Delaware Valley U (PA)
Eastern Nazarene Coll (MA)
Eastern Washington U (WA)
Emmanuel Coll (MA)
Emmaus Bible Coll (IA)
Fort Lewis Coll (CO)
Geneva Coll (PA)
Hobe Sound Bible Coll (FL)
Hope Intl U (CA)
Lesley U (MA)
Maryville Coll (TN)
Mid-Atlantic Christian U (NC)
Morningside Coll (IA)
Mount Saint Mary's U (CA)
Newman U (KS)
Northwestern U (IL)
Point U (GA)
Saint Leo U (FL)
Southwestern Assemblies of God U (TX)
Toccoa Falls Coll (GA)
Trinity Coll of Florida (FL)
U of Chicago (IL)
U of Jamestown (ND)
Wayne State Coll (NE)

COUNSELOR EDUCATION/ SCHOOL COUNSELING AND GUIDANCE
Bowling Green State U (OH)
Brandon U (MB, Canada)
East Central U (OK)
Sam Houston State U (TX)

Université de Sherbrooke (QC, Canada)
U of South Dakota (SD)

CRAFTS, FOLK ART AND ARTISANRY
Bowling Green State U (OH)
Bridgewater State U (MA)
Brigham Young U (UT)
Kutztown U of Pennsylvania (PA)
Malone U (OH)
Rochester Inst of Technology (NY)
The U of the Arts (PA)
Virginia Commonwealth U (VA)

CREATIVE WRITING
Adams State U (CO)
Agnes Scott Coll (GA)
Albion Coll (MI)
Allegheny Coll (PA)
The American U of Paris (France)
Anderson U (SC)
Arcadia U (PA)
Arkansas Tech U (AR)
Asbury U (KY)
Ashland U (OH)
Augsburg U (MN)
Augustana Coll (IL)
Austin Coll (TX)
Baldwin Wallace U (OH)
Bard Coll (NY)
Belhaven U (MS)
Beloit Coll (WI)
Bennington Coll (VT)
Berry Coll (GA)
Binghamton U, State U of New York (NY)
Biola U (CA)
Blackburn Coll (IL)
Bowie State U (MD)
Bowling Green State U (OH)
Bradley U (IL)
Brandeis U (MA)
Bridgewater State U (MA)
Bucknell U (PA)
Butler U (IN)
California Baptist U (CA)
California Coll of the Arts (CA)
California State U, Long Beach (CA)
Calvary U (MO)
Canisius Coll (NY)
Capital U (OH)
Carlow U (PA)
Carnegie Mellon U (PA)
Carroll U (WI)
Carson-Newman U (TN)
Catawba Coll (NC)
Central Michigan U (MI)
Chapman U (CA)
Chatham U (PA)
Christian Brothers U (TN)
City Coll of the City U of New York (NY)
Coe Coll (IA)
Colby Coll (ME)
The Coll of Idaho (ID)
Coll of the Atlantic (ME)
Colorado Christian U (CO)
The Colorado Coll (CO)
Columbia Coll Chicago (IL)
Columbia U (NY)
Concordia U (QC, Canada)
Converse Coll (SC)
Corban U (OR)
Cornell Coll (IA)
Dartmouth Coll (NH)
Denison U (OH)
Dominican U of California (CA)
Drew U (NJ)
Eastern Michigan U (MI)
Eckerd Coll (FL)
Emerson Coll (MA)
Emory & Henry Coll (VA)
Emory U (GA)
Fairleigh Dickinson U, Florham Campus (NJ)
Florida Southern Coll (FL)
Florida State U (FL)
Franklin & Marshall Coll (PA)
Franklin Coll (IN)
Franklin Pierce U (NH)
Franklin U Switzerland (Switzerland)
George Mason U (VA)
Gettysburg Coll (PA)
Green Mountain Coll (VT)
Guilford Coll (NC)

Hamilton Coll (NY)
Hamline U (MN)
Hampshire Coll (MA)
Hartwick Coll (NY)
Hiram Coll (OH)
Hofstra U (NY)
Hollins U (VA)
Indiana Wesleyan U (IN)
Inst of American Indian Arts (NM)
Ithaca Coll (NY)
Johns Hopkins U (MD)
Kansas City Art Inst (MO)
Knox Coll (IL)
Lebanon Valley Coll (PA)
Lee U (TN)
Lehman Coll of the City U of New York (NY)
Linfield Coll (OR)
Loras Coll (IA)
Loyola U New Orleans (LA)
Lubbock Christian U (TX)
Lycoming Coll (PA)
Malone U (OH)
Marlboro Coll (VT)
Massachusetts Coll of Liberal Arts (MA)
Massachusetts Inst of Technology (MA)
McMurry U (TX)
Mercer U, Macon (GA)
Miami U (OH)
Morehead State U (KY)
Mount St. Joseph U (OH)
Murray State U (KY)
New Hampshire Inst of Art (NH)
The New School for Public Engagement (NY)
North Central Coll (IL)
Northeastern State U (OK)
Northern Michigan U (MI)
Northern Vermont U–Lyndon (VT)
Northland Coll (WI)
Oakland U (MI)
Oberlin Coll (OH)
Ohio Northern U (OH)
Ohio U (OH)
Ohio Wesleyan U (OH)
Oklahoma Christian U (OK)
Pepperdine U, Malibu (CA)
Pratt Inst (NY)
Providence Coll (RI)
Purchase Coll, State U of New York (NY)
Purdue U (IN)
Randolph Coll (VA)
Redeemer U Coll (ON, Canada)
Rhode Island Coll (RI)
Ringling Coll of Art and Design (FL)
Roanoke Coll (VA)
Rocky Mountain Coll (MT)
Roger Williams U (RI)
Saginaw Valley State U (MI)
St. Bonaventure U (NY)
St. Catherine U (MN)
Saint Mary-of-the-Woods Coll (IN)
St. Thomas Aquinas Coll (NY)
San Francisco State U (CA)
Sarah Lawrence Coll (NY)
Seattle U (WA)
Seton Hill U (PA)
Sierra Nevada Coll (NV)
Southeastern U (FL)
Southern Methodist U (TX)
Southern Vermont Coll (VT)
Southwestern Coll (KS)
State U of New York at Oswego (NY)
State U of New York Coll at Potsdam (NY)
Stephen F. Austin State U (TX)
Susquehanna U (PA)
Sweet Briar Coll (VA)
Texas Christian U (TX)
Truman State U (MO)
The U of Arizona (AZ)
U of California, Riverside (CA)
U of California, San Diego (CA)
U of Central Oklahoma (OK)
U of Cincinnati (OH)
U of Denver (CO)
U of Evansville (IN)
The U of Findlay (OH)
U of Houston (TX)
U of Idaho (ID)
U of La Verne (CA)
U of Maine at Farmington (ME)
U of Maine at Machias (ME)

U of Miami (FL)
U of Michigan (MI)
U of Montana (MT)
U of Mount Union (OH)
The U of North Carolina Wilmington (NC)
U of Pittsburgh (PA)
U of Pittsburgh at Bradford (PA)
U of Pittsburgh at Greensburg (PA)
U of Providence (MT)
U of Puget Sound (WA)
U of Regina (SK, Canada)
U of St. Thomas (MN)
U of Southern California (CA)
The U of Texas at Austin (TX)
The U of Texas at El Paso (TX)
The U of the Arts (PA)
Valparaiso U (IN)
Villa Maria Coll (NY)
Waldorf U (IA)
Washington U in St. Louis (MO)
Waynesburg U (PA)
Weber State U (UT)
Wells Coll (NY)
Western Michigan U (MI)
Western New England U (MA)
Western State Colorado U (CO)
Western Washington U (WA)
West Virginia Wesleyan Coll (WV)
Wheaton Coll (MA)
Wichita State U (KS)

CRIMINALISTICS AND CRIMINAL SCIENCE
Alabama State U (AL)
Bay Path U (MA)
Indiana Tech (IN)
Saint Leo U (FL)
Seattle U (WA)
Tiffin U (OH)
Weber State U (UT)

CRIMINAL JUSTICE/LAW ENFORCEMENT ADMINISTRATION
Abilene Christian U (TX)
Adams State U (CO)
Alfred U (NY)
Anderson U (IN)
Anderson U (SC)
Arizona State U at the Downtown Phoenix campus (AZ)
Arizona State U at the West campus (AZ)
Athens State U (AL)
Austin Peay State U (TN)
Averett U (VA)
Azusa Pacific U (CA)
Barton Coll (NC)
Bay Path U (MA)
Becker Coll (MA)
Belhaven U (MS)
Bemidji State U (MN)
Bethel U (TN)
Blackburn Coll (IL)
Bluefield Coll (VA)
Boise State U (ID)
Bowie State U (MD)
Bowling Green State U (OH)
Bradley U (IL)
Brewton-Parker Coll (GA)
Buffalo State Coll, State U of New York (NY)
California Baptist U (CA)
California Lutheran U (CA)
California State U, East Bay (CA)
California State U, Long Beach (CA)
California State U, Sacramento (CA)
Calvary U (MO)
Campbellsville U (KY)
Canisius Coll (NY)
Carthage Coll (WI)
Catawba Coll (NC)
Central Penn Coll (PA)
Charter Oak State Coll (CT)
Chestnut Hill Coll (PA)
The Citadel, The Military Coll of South Carolina (SC)
Clarion U of Pennsylvania (PA)
Colegio Universitario de San Juan, San Juan (PR)
The Coll of New Jersey (NJ)
The Coll of Saint Rose (NY)
Columbia Coll (MO)
Concordia U Wisconsin (WI)
Corban U (OR)

Culver-Stockton Coll (MO)
Delaware State U (DE)
Delaware Valley U (PA)
Drexel U (PA)
Eastern Nazarene Coll (MA)
East Tennessee State U (TN)
East Texas Baptist U (TX)
Elms Coll (MA)
Emmanuel Coll (GA)
Evangel U (MO)
Excelsior Coll (NY)
Fairleigh Dickinson U, Metropolitan Campus (NJ)
Fayetteville State U (NC)
Felician U (NJ)
Ferris State U (MI)
Florida National U (FL)
Franklin Pierce U (NH)
The George Washington U (DC)
Georgia Coll & State U (GA)
Georgia Southwestern State U (GA)
Graceland U (IA)
Grand Valley State U (MI)
Grand View U (IA)
Greenville U (IL)
Gustavus Adolphus Coll (MN)
Hampton U (VA)
Hannibal-LaGrange U (MO)
Harris-Stowe State U (MO)
Hartwick Coll (NY)
Hawai`i Pacific U (HI)
Huntingdon Coll (AL)
Husson U (ME)
Huston-Tillotson U (TX)
Indiana Tech (IN)
Indiana U East (IN)
Iona Coll (NY)
John Jay Coll of Criminal Justice of the City U of New York (NY)
Kansas Wesleyan U (KS)
Kean U (NJ)
Keiser U, Fort Lauderdale (FL)
Limestone Coll (SC)
Lincoln Coll (IL)
Lincoln Coll of New England, Southington (CT)
Lincoln Memorial U (TN)
Lincoln U (MO)
Lindsey Wilson Coll (KY)
Lock Haven U of Pennsylvania (PA)
Long Island U–LIU Post (NY)
Lubbock Christian U (TX)
Lynn U (FL)
Mansfield U of Pennsylvania (PA)
Marist Coll (NY)
Marymount California U (CA)
Marymount U (VA)
Marywood U (PA)
Mercy Coll (NY)
Merrimack Coll (MA)
Michigan State U (MI)
Mid-America Christian U (OK)
MidAmerica Nazarene U (KS)
Middle Tennessee State U (TN)
Millikin U (IL)
Missouri Valley Coll (MO)
Morris Coll (SC)
Mount Aloysius Coll (PA)
Mount Mary U (WI)
Mount Mercy U (IA)
Mount Vernon Nazarene U (OH)
Muskingum U (OH)
National U (CA)
New England Inst of Technology (RI)
Newman U (KS)
New York Inst of Technology (NY)
Nichols Coll (MA)
North Carolina Wesleyan Coll (NC)
Northcentral U (CA)
Northeastern State U (OK)
North Greenville U (SC)
Northwest Christian U (OR)
Northwest Nazarene U (ID)
Northwest U (WA)
Ohio Northern U (OH)
Ohio U–Zanesville (OH)
Oklahoma City U (OK)
Olivet Nazarene U (IL)
Pace U (NY)
Pace U, Pleasantville Campus (NY)
Penn State Abington (PA)
Penn State Altoona (PA)
Penn State Beaver (PA)
Penn State Berks (PA)
Penn State Brandywine (PA)

Penn State DuBois (PA)
Penn State Erie, The Behrend Coll (PA)
Penn State Fayette, The Eberly Campus (PA)
Penn State Greater Allegheny (PA)
Penn State Hazleton (PA)
Penn State Lehigh Valley (PA)
Penn State Mont Alto (PA)
Penn State New Kensington (PA)
Penn State Schuylkill (PA)
Penn State Shenango (PA)
Penn State U Park (PA)
Penn State Wilkes-Barre (PA)
Penn State Worthington Scranton (PA)
Penn State York (PA)
Pfeiffer U (NC)
Piedmont Coll (GA)
Portland State U (OR)
Regent U (VA)
Rivier U (NH)
Roberts Wesleyan Coll (NY)
Rochester Inst of Technology (NY)
Rockhurst U (MO)
Rogers State U (OK)
Roger Williams U (RI)
Rutgers U–New Brunswick (NJ)
Sacred Heart U (CT)
Saint Augustine's U (NC)
Saint Francis U (PA)
St. John's U (NY)
St. Joseph's Coll, Long Island Campus (NY)
St. Joseph's Coll, New York (NY)
St. Mary's U (TX)
St. Thomas Aquinas Coll (NY)
St. Thomas U (FL)
Salve Regina U (RI)
Sam Houston State U (TX)
San Francisco State U (CA)
Shenandoah U (VA)
Simpson Coll (IA)
Sonoma State U (CA)
Southern Vermont Coll (VT)
Southwest Baptist U (MO)
Southwestern Assemblies of God U (TX)
State U of New York at Fredonia (NY)
State U of New York at Oswego (NY)
State U of New York Coll of Technology at Canton (NY)
Stevenson U (MD)
Talladega Coll (AL)
Tarleton State U (TX)
Thomas U (GA)
Tiffin U (OH)
Toccoa Falls Coll (GA)
Trevecca Nazarene U (TN)
Trine U (IN)
Trinity Christian Coll (IL)
Tusculum Coll (TN)
U at Albany, State U of New York (NY)
U of Central Missouri (MO)
U of Central Oklahoma (OK)
U of Colorado Colorado Springs (CO)
U of Colorado Denver (CO)
U of Dayton (OH)
The U of Findlay (OH)
U of Georgia (GA)
U of Guam (GU)
U of Guelph (ON, Canada)
U of Louisville (KY)
U of Maine at Presque Isle (ME)
U of Management and Technology (VA)
U of Mary Hardin-Baylor (TX)
U of Maryland Eastern Shore (MD)
U of Massachusetts Lowell (MA)
U of Memphis (TN)
U of Minnesota, Crookston (MN)
U of New Haven (CT)
U of North Alabama (AL)
U of Northern Iowa (IA)
U of Oklahoma (OK)
U of Pittsburgh at Bradford (PA)
U of Pittsburgh at Greensburg (PA)
U of Providence (MT)
U of Regina (SK, Canada)
U of St. Francis (IL)
U of South Alabama (AL)
U of South Carolina (SC)
U of South Dakota (SD)

The U of Tennessee at Chattanooga (TN)
The U of Tennessee at Martin (TN)
The U of Texas at El Paso (TX)
U of the Incarnate Word (TX)
U of Wisconsin–Parkside (WI)
Utah Valley U (UT)
Utica Coll (NY)
Villanova U (PA)
Virginia Commonwealth U (VA)
Waldorf U (IA)
Waynesburg U (PA)
Webber Intl U (FL)
Western Illinois U (IL)
Western Oregon U (OR)
Westminster Coll (PA)
West Virginia U Inst of Technology (WV)
West Virginia Wesleyan Coll (WV)
Whitworth U (WA)
Widener U (PA)
William Peace U (NC)
Wilmington U (DE)
York Coll of Pennsylvania (PA)
Youngstown State U (OH)

CRIMINAL JUSTICE/POLICE SCIENCE
Athabasca U (AB, Canada)
Bemidji State U (MN)
Bowling Green State U (OH)
California State U, East Bay (CA)
Caribbean U (PR)
Colorado Mesa U (CO)
Columbia Southern U (AL)
East Central U (OK)
Eastern Nazarene Coll (MA)
Ferris State U (MI)
George Mason U (VA)
Georgia Southern U–Armstrong Campus (GA)
Gwynedd Mercy U (PA)
Hilbert Coll (NY)
Idaho State U (ID)
Inter American U of Puerto Rico, Metropolitan Campus (PR)
Inter American U of Puerto Rico, San Germán Campus (PR)
John Jay Coll of Criminal Justice of the City U of New York (NY)
Malone U (OH)
Marian U (WI)
Middle Tennessee State U (TN)
Northwestern Oklahoma State U (OK)
Ohio Northern U (OH)
Oklahoma Baptist U (OK)
Oklahoma City U (OK)
Rowan U (NJ)
Sam Houston State U (TX)
Southern Utah U (UT)
Stephen F. Austin State U (TX)
Texas A&M Intl U (TX)
Texas State U (TX)
U of Hartford (CT)
U of Pittsburgh at Greensburg (PA)
U of Providence (MT)
U of Regina (SK, Canada)
U of the Virgin Islands (VI)
U of Toronto (ON, Canada)
U of Washington, Tacoma (WA)
Washington State U (WA)
Washington State U–Global Campus (WA)
Washington State U–Vancouver (WA)
Weber State U (UT)
Western Connecticut State U (CT)
Western Oregon U (OR)

CRIMINAL JUSTICE/SAFETY
Adelphi U (NY)
Alabama State U (AL)
Alcorn State U (MS)
American Intl Coll (MA)
American Public U System (WV)
American U (DC)
Angelo State U (TX)
Antioch U Los Angeles (CA)
Appalachian State U (NC)
Athens State U (AL)
Auburn U at Montgomery (AL)
Aurora U (IL)
Baldwin Wallace U (OH)
Ball State U (IN)
Barton Coll (NC)
Bellarmine U (KY)
Benedictine U (IL)

Bethel Coll (IN)
Bloomsburg U of Pennsylvania (PA)
Blue Mountain Coll (MS)
Bluffton U (OH)
Bob Jones U (SC)
Boston U (MA)
Bowling Green State U (OH)
Bowling Green State U–Firelands Coll (OH)
Brandman U (CA)
Bridgewater State U (MA)
Bryan Coll (TN)
Buena Vista U (IA)
Cairn U (PA)
Caldwell U (NJ)
California State U, Dominguez Hills (CA)
California State U, Fullerton (CA)
California State U, Los Angeles (CA)
California State U, San Bernardino (CA)
California State U, Stanislaus (CA)
California U of Pennsylvania (PA)
Calumet Coll of Saint Joseph (IN)
Cardinal Stritch U (WI)
Cazenovia Coll (NY)
Central Methodist U (MO)
Central Penn Coll (PA)
Central State U (OH)
Chaminade U of Honolulu (HI)
Champlain Coll (VT)
Charleston Southern U (SC)
Charter Oak State Coll (CT)
Chowan U (NC)
Clark Atlanta U (GA)
Clayton State U (GA)
Coe Coll (IA)
The Coll at Brockport, State U of New York (NY)
Coll of Coastal Georgia (GA)
Coll of the Ozarks (MO)
Colorado Mesa U (CO)
Columbia Coll (SC)
Columbus State U (GA)
Concordia U, Nebraska (NE)
Concordia U, St. Paul (MN)
Curry Coll (MA)
Dallas Baptist U (TX)
Davenport U, Grand Rapids (MI)
Dean Coll (MA)
Defiance Coll (OH)
DeSales U (PA)
Dominican Coll (NY)
East Carolina U (NC)
Eastern Nazarene Coll (MA)
Eastern New Mexico U (NM)
East Stroudsburg U of Pennsylvania (PA)
ECPI U, Virginia Beach (VA)
Edgewood Coll (WI)
Endicott Coll (MA)
Fisher Coll (MA)
Fitchburg State U (MA)
Florida Ag and Mech U (FL)
Florida Atlantic U (FL)
Florida Gulf Coast U (FL)
Florida Intl U (FL)
Friends U (KS)
Frostburg State U (MD)
Gannon U (PA)
Georgia Gwinnett Coll (GA)
Georgian Court U (NJ)
Georgia Southern U (GA)
Georgia State U (GA)
Governors State U (IL)
Graceland U (IA)
Grambling State U (LA)
Grand View U (IA)
Granite State Coll (NH)
Greensboro Coll (NC)
Guilford Coll (NC)
Harding U (AR)
Hardin-Simmons U (TX)
Harris-Stowe State U (MO)
High Point U (NC)
Hilbert Coll (NY)
Holy Family U (PA)
Hood Coll (MD)
Houston Baptist U (TX)
Husson U (ME)
Huston-Tillotson U (TX)
Illinois State U (IL)
Immaculata U (PA)
Indiana U Bloomington (IN)
Indiana U Kokomo (IN)
Indiana U Northwest (IN)

Indiana U–Purdue U Indianapolis (IN)
Indiana U South Bend (IN)
Indiana U Southeast (IN)
Indiana Wesleyan U (IN)
Inter American U of Puerto Rico, Aguadilla Campus (PR)
Inter American U of Puerto Rico, Barranquitas Campus (PR)
Inter American U of Puerto Rico, Fajardo Campus (PR)
Iowa State U of Science and Technology (IA)
Jackson State U (MS)
Keiser U, Fort Lauderdale (FL)
Kennesaw State U (GA)
Kent State U (OH)
Kent State U at Ashtabula (OH)
Kent State U at East Liverpool (OH)
Kent State U at Salem (OH)
Kent State U at Stark (OH)
Kent State U at Trumbull (OH)
Kent State U at Tuscarawas (OH)
Kentucky State U (KY)
King's Coll (PA)
King U (TN)
Kutztown U of Pennsylvania (PA)
Lamar U (TX)
La Roche Coll (PA)
La Salle U (PA)
La Sierra U (CA)
Lenoir-Rhyne U (NC)
Lewis U (IL)
Liberty U (VA)
Limestone Coll (SC)
Lincoln Coll (IL)
Lincoln U (PA)
Lindenwood U (MO)
Lipscomb U (TN)
Longwood U (VA)
Loras Coll (IA)
Louisiana Coll (LA)
Loyola U Chicago (IL)
Lycoming Coll (PA)
Madonna U (MI)
Manchester U (IN)
Marshall U (WV)
McNeese State U (LA)
Mercer U, Macon (GA)
Mercyhurst U (PA)
Messiah Coll (PA)
Metropolitan State U of Denver (CO)
Michigan State U (MI)
Middle Georgia State U (GA)
Minnesota State U Moorhead (MN)
Minot State U (ND)
Missouri Baptist U (MO)
Missouri Western State U (MO)
Molloy Coll (NY)
Mount Marty Coll (SD)
Mount Vernon Nazarene U (OH)
Murray State U (KY)
Neumann U (PA)
New Jersey City U (NJ)
New Mexico Highlands U (NM)
New Mexico State U (NM)
Nichols Coll (MA)
North Carolina Central U (NC)
North Dakota State U (ND)
Northeastern U (MA)
Northern Kentucky U (KY)
Northern Michigan U (MI)
Northern Vermont U–Lyndon (VT)
Northwestern State U of Louisiana (LA)
Northwest U (WA)
Nova Southeastern U (FL)
Nyack Coll (NY)
Oakland City U (IN)
Ohio Christian U (OH)
Ohio Northern U (OH)
Oklahoma Christian U (OK)
Olivet Nazarene U (IL)
Our Lady of the Lake U (TX)
Penn State Abington (PA)
Penn State Altoona (PA)
Penn State Erie, The Behrend Coll (PA)
Penn State Fayette, The Eberly Campus (PA)
Penn State Harrisburg (PA)
Penn State Schuylkill (PA)
Penn State Wilkes-Barre (PA)
Pittsburg State U (KS)
Point Park U (PA)
Point U (GA)

Polk State Coll (FL)
Post U (CT)
Potomac State Coll of West Virginia U (WV)
Prairie View A&M U (TX)
Quinnipiac U (CT)
Radford U (VA)
Rhode Island Coll (RI)
Rider U (NJ)
Roanoke Coll (VA)
Rochester Inst of Technology (NY)
Roosevelt U (IL)
Rosemont Coll (PA)
Rowan U (NJ)
Rutgers U–Camden (NJ)
Rutgers U–Newark (NJ)
Rutgers U–New Brunswick (NJ)
Sacred Heart U (CT)
Saginaw Valley State U (MI)
St. Ambrose U (IA)
Saint Anselm Coll (NH)
Saint Leo U (FL)
Saint Louis U (MO)
Saint Martin's U (WA)
Saint Peter's U (NJ)
St. Thomas U (FL)
Samford U (AL)
Sam Houston State U (TX)
San Diego State U (CA)
Seattle U (WA)
Seton Hill U (PA)
Shaw U (NC)
Shippensburg U of Pennsylvania (PA)
Southeastern Louisiana U (LA)
Southeastern Oklahoma State U (OK)
Southeastern U (FL)
Southern Arkansas U–Magnolia (AR)
Southern Illinois U Edwardsville (IL)
Southwestern Coll (KS)
State U of New York at Plattsburgh (NY)
State U of New York Coll at Oneonta (NY)
State U of New York Coll at Potsdam (NY)
State U of New York Coll of Technology at Delhi (NY)
Sullivan U (KY)
Tarleton State U (TX)
Temple U (PA)
Tennessee Wesleyan U (TN)
Texas A&M U–Central Texas (TX)
Texas A&M U–Commerce (TX)
Texas A&M U–Corpus Christi (TX)
Texas A&M U–Kingsville (TX)
Texas A&M U–Texarkana (TX)
Texas Christian U (TX)
Texas State U (TX)
Texas Woman's U (TX)
Troy U (AL)
Truett McConnell U (GA)
Truman State U (MO)
The U of Akron (OH)
The U of Alabama (AL)
U of Arkansas (AR)
U of Bridgeport (CT)
U of Central Florida (FL)
U of Central Oklahoma (OK)
U of Cincinnati (OH)
U of Dubuque (IA)
U of Evansville (IN)
U of Houston–Downtown (TX)
U of Illinois at Chicago (IL)
U of Illinois at Springfield (IL)
U of Jamestown (ND)
U of Louisiana at Monroe (LA)
U of Maryland U Coll (MD)
U of Massachusetts Boston (MA)
U of Michigan–Dearborn (MI)
U of Mount Union (OH)
U of Nebraska at Kearney (NE)
U of Nevada, Las Vegas (NV)
The U of North Carolina at Charlotte (NC)
The U of North Carolina at Pembroke (NC)
U of North Dakota (ND)
U of Northern Colorado (CO)
U of North Florida (FL)
U of North Georgia (GA)
U of North Texas (TX)
U of Pikeville (KY)
U of Providence (MT)

U of Regina (SK, Canada)
U of Saint Francis (IN)
The U of Scranton (PA)
U of South Dakota (SD)
U of Southern Indiana (IN)
U of Southern Mississippi (MS)
The U of Texas at San Antonio (TX)
The U of Texas of the Permian Basin (TX)
The U of Texas Rio Grande Valley (TX)
U of the Fraser Valley (BC, Canada)
U of the Incarnate Word (TX)
The U of Toledo (OH)
U of Valley Forge (PA)
The U of Virginia's Coll at Wise (VA)
U of Wisconsin–Eau Claire (WI)
U of Wisconsin–Milwaukee (WI)
U of Wisconsin–Platteville (WI)
U of Wisconsin–Superior (WI)
U of Wyoming (WY)
Valdosta State U (GA)
Virginia Wesleyan U (VA)
Wayne State Coll (NE)
Wayne State U (MI)
Weber State U (UT)
West Chester U of Pennsylvania (PA)
Western Michigan U (MI)
Western New England U (MA)
Westfield State U (MA)
Westminster Coll (UT)
West Texas A&M U (TX)
West Virginia State U (WV)
Wichita State U (KS)
Wilkes U (PA)
William Paterson U of New Jersey (NJ)
William Woods U (MO)
Winona State U (MN)
Woodbury U (CA)
Worcester State U (MA)
Youngstown State U (OH)

CRIMINOLOGY
Adams State U (CO)
Albright Coll (PA)
Arcadia U (PA)
Assumption Coll (MA)
Auburn U (AL)
Avila U (MO)
Barry U (FL)
Benedictine Coll (KS)
Biola U (CA)
Butler U (IN)
California State U, San Marcos (CA)
California State U, Stanislaus (CA)
Capital U (OH)
Carlow U (PA)
Cedar Crest Coll (PA)
Central Connecticut State U (CT)
Chatham U (PA)
Cleveland State U (OH)
Coker Coll (SC)
The Coll of New Jersey (NJ)
Concordia U Chicago (IL)
Cottey Coll (MO)
Delaware State U (DE)
DePaul U (IL)
Dominican U (IL)
Drexel U (PA)
Eastern Michigan U (MI)
Eastern U (PA)
Eastern Washington U (WA)
Elmhurst Coll (IL)
Emmanuel Coll (MA)
Fairleigh Dickinson U, Florham Campus (NJ)
Flagler Coll (FL)
Florida Southern Coll (FL)
Florida State U (FL)
Framingham State U (MA)
Geneva Coll (PA)
Gonzaga U (WA)
Hamline U (MN)
Heidelberg U (OH)
Hofstra U (NY)
Howard Payne U (TX)
Humboldt State U (CA)
Husson U (ME)
Indiana State U (IN)
Indiana U of Pennsylvania (PA)
John Jay Coll of Criminal Justice of the City U of New York (NY)

Johnson C. Smith U (NC)
Lasell Coll (MA)
Lebanon Valley Coll (PA)
Lee U (TN)
Le Moyne Coll (NY)
LeTourneau U (TX)
Loyola U New Orleans (LA)
Lycoming Coll (PA)
Lynchburg Coll (VA)
Marquette U (WI)
Mary Baldwin U (VA)
Maryville Coll (TN)
Maryville U of Saint Louis (MO)
McMurry U (TX)
Meredith Coll (NC)
Mississippi State U (MS)
Missouri State U (MO)
Mount St. Joseph U (OH)
Mount Saint Mary Coll (NY)
Mount Saint Mary's U (CA)
Mount St. Mary's U (MD)
National Louis U (IL)
Niagara U (NY)
North Carolina State U (NC)
Northern Arizona U (AZ)
Ohio Dominican U (OH)
The Ohio State U (OH)
The Ohio State U at Mansfield (OH)
The Ohio State U at Marion (OH)
Ohio U (OH)
Old Dominion U (VA)
Regis U (CO)
Rivier U (NH)
Saint Francis U (PA)
St. John Fisher Coll (NY)
Saint Joseph's U (PA)
Saint Mary-of-the-Woods Coll (IN)
St. Mary's U (TX)
St. Thomas U (NB, Canada)
Saint Vincent Coll (PA)
Simon Fraser U (BC, Canada)
Slippery Rock U of Pennsylvania (PA)
Spring Hill Coll (AL)
State U of New York Coll at Cortland (NY)
State U of New York Coll at Old Westbury (NY)
Stockton U (NJ)
Stonehill Coll (MA)
Suffolk U (MA)
Tabor Coll (KS)
Texas A&M U–Kingsville (TX)
Thomas U (GA)
The U of Akron (OH)
The U of Alabama (AL)
U of California, Irvine (CA)
U of Denver (CO)
U of Florida (FL)
U of Houston–Clear Lake (TX)
U of La Verne (CA)
U of Maryland, Coll Park (MD)
U of Massachusetts Dartmouth (MA)
U of Memphis (TN)
U of Miami (FL)
U of Minnesota, Duluth (MN)
U of Minnesota, Twin Cities Campus (MN)
U of Missouri–St. Louis (MO)
U of Mount Union (OH)
U of Nevada, Reno (NV)
U of New Hampshire (NH)
The U of North Carolina Wilmington (NC)
U of Northern Iowa (IA)
U of Rhode Island (RI)
U of Saint Mary (KS)
U of St. Thomas (MN)
U of St. Thomas (TX)
U of Sioux Falls (SD)
U of Southern Maine (ME)
U of South Florida, St. Petersburg (FL)
U of South Florida Sarasota-Manatee (FL)
The U of Tampa (FL)
The U of Texas at Dallas (TX)
The U of Texas of the Permian Basin (TX)
U of Toronto (ON, Canada)
U of West Georgia (GA)
U of Wisconsin–River Falls (WI)
U of Wisconsin–Whitewater (WI)
Upper Iowa U (IA)
Valparaiso U (IN)
Virginia Wesleyan U (VA)

Walsh U (OH)
Western Kentucky U (KY)
Western State Colorado U (CO)
West Virginia U (WV)
Wilkes U (PA)
William Penn U (IA)
Wittenberg U (OH)
Wright State U (OH)
Wright State U–Lake Campus (OH)

CRISIS/EMERGENCY/DISASTER MANAGEMENT
Adelphi U (NY)
American Public U System (WV)
Arkansas Tech U (AR)
Columbia Coll (SC)
Immaculata U (PA)
Kansas Wesleyan U (KS)
North Dakota State U (ND)
Northwest Missouri State U (MO)
Ohio Christian U (OH)
Pennsylvania Coll of Technology (PA)
Post U (CT)
Rowan U (NJ)
Saint Louis U (MO)
Southeast Missouri State U (MO)
State U of New York Coll of Technology at Canton (NY)
Truckee Meadows Comm Coll (NV)
U at Albany, State U of New York (NY)
U of Alaska Fairbanks (AK)
U of Northern Iowa (IA)
U of North Texas (TX)
Upper Iowa U (IA)
Waldorf U (IA)

CRITICAL INFRASTRUCTURE PROTECTION
Anderson U (SC)
Excelsior Coll (NY)
George Mason U (VA)
Idaho State U (ID)

CROP PRODUCTION
Delaware Valley U (PA)
North Dakota State U (ND)
U of Minnesota, Crookston (MN)
Washington State U (WA)

CULINARY ARTS
Coll of the Ozarks (MO)
Drexel U (PA)

CULINARY ARTS RELATED
U of Nevada, Las Vegas (NV)
U of North Alabama (AL)

CULINARY SCIENCE
The Culinary Inst of America (NY)
Iowa State U of Science and Technology (IA)
Mississippi State U (MS)
Texas Woman's U (TX)

CULTURAL ANTHROPOLOGY
Arcadia U (PA)
Eugene Lang Coll of Liberal Arts (NY)
Webster U (MO)

CULTURAL RESOURCE MANAGEMENT AND POLICY ANALYSIS
California State U, Dominguez Hills (CA)
U of Waterloo (ON, Canada)

CULTURAL STUDIES/CRITICAL THEORY AND ANALYSIS
American Public U System (WV)
Arizona State U at the West campus (AZ)
Bryant U (RI)
Excelsior Coll (NY)
Howard Payne U (TX)
Northern Arizona U (AZ)
Rollins Coll (FL)
The U of Tampa (FL)
Western Kentucky U (KY)
Willamette U (OR)

CURRICULUM AND INSTRUCTION
Curry Coll (MA)
Eastern Washington U (WA)
Franklin Pierce U (NH)
Lasell Coll (MA)
Randolph Coll (VA)

Sam Houston State U (TX)
U of South Dakota (SD)
The U of Texas at Austin (TX)
Utah State U (UT)
Welch Coll (TN)

CUSTOMER SERVICE MANAGEMENT
Drexel U (PA)
Ohio U (OH)
Southwest Baptist U (MO)

CYBER/COMPUTER FORENSICS AND COUNTERTERRORISM
Bloomsburg U of Pennsylvania (PA)
Champlain Coll (VT)
Chestnut Hill Coll (PA)
Christian Brothers U (TN)
Davenport U, Grand Rapids (MI)
Excelsior Coll (NY)
Farmingdale State Coll (NY)
Kansas Wesleyan U (KS)
Keiser U, Fort Lauderdale (FL)
National U (CA)
Northeastern State U (OK)
Oakland U (MI)
Regent U (VA)
Robert Morris U (PA)
Roger Williams U (RI)
Sullivan U (KY)
U of Central Oklahoma (OK)
U of the Incarnate Word (TX)
U of the Potomac (DC)

CYBER/ELECTRONIC OPERATIONS AND WARFARE
Excelsior Coll (NY)
LeTourneau U (TX)
Maryville U of Saint Louis (MO)
Northern Michigan U (MI)

CYTOGENETICS/GENETICS/ CLINICAL GENETICS TECHNOLOGY
Northern Michigan U (MI)

CYTOTECHNOLOGY
Barry U (FL)
Edgewood Coll (WI)
Illinois Coll (IL)
Indiana U–Purdue U Indianapolis (IN)
Marian U (WI)
Marshall U (WV)
Oakland U (MI)
Rutgers U–New Brunswick (NJ)
Saint Louis U (MO)
Saint Mary's U of Minnesota (MN)
State U of New York at Plattsburgh (NY)
Thomas Jefferson U (PA)
U of North Texas (TX)

CZECH
The U of Texas at Austin (TX)

DAIRY SCIENCE
California Polytechnic State U, San Luis Obispo (CA)
Delaware Valley U (PA)
Eastern New Mexico U (NM)
Iowa State U of Science and Technology (IA)
U of Georgia (GA)
U of New Hampshire (NH)
U of Wisconsin–Madison (WI)
U of Wisconsin–River Falls (WI)
Utah State U (UT)
Virginia Polytechnic Inst and State U (VA)

DANCE
Adelphi U (NY)
Agnes Scott Coll (GA)
Alabama State U (AL)
Amherst Coll (MA)
Anderson U (IN)
Anderson U (SC)
Appalachian State U (NC)
Arizona State U at the Tempe campus (AZ)
Baldwin Wallace U (OH)
Ball State U (IN)
Bard Coll (NY)
Barnard Coll (NY)
Bates Coll (ME)
Belhaven U (MS)
Beloit Coll (WI)
Bennington Coll (VT)

Bowling Green State U (OH)
Brenau U (GA)
Brigham Young U–Idaho (ID)
Butler U (IN)
California State U, East Bay (CA)
California State U, Fullerton (CA)
California State U, Long Beach (CA)
California State U, Los Angeles (CA)
California State U, Sacramento (CA)
Case Western Reserve U (OH)
Cedar Crest Coll (PA)
Chapman U (CA)
The Coll at Brockport, State U of New York (NY)
Coll of Charleston (SC)
The Colorado Coll (CO)
Colorado Mesa U (CO)
Colorado State U (CO)
Columbia Coll (SC)
Columbia Coll Chicago (IL)
Columbia U (NY)
Concordia U (QC, Canada)
Connecticut Coll (CT)
Cornish Coll of the Arts (WA)
Dean Coll (MA)
Denison U (OH)
DeSales U (PA)
Dickinson Coll (PA)
Dominican U of California (CA)
East Carolina U (NC)
Eastern Michigan U (MI)
Elon U (NC)
Emory U (GA)
Florida Southern Coll (FL)
Florida State U (FL)
Fordham U (NY)
Franklin & Marshall Coll (PA)
George Mason U (VA)
The George Washington U (DC)
Georgian Court U (NJ)
Grand Valley State U (MI)
Gustavus Adolphus Coll (MN)
Hamilton Coll (NY)
Hampshire Coll (MA)
High Point U (NC)
Hobart and William Smith Colls (NY)
Hofstra U (NY)
Hollins U (VA)
Hope Coll (MI)
Hunter Coll of the City U of New York (NY)
Idaho State U (ID)
Indiana U Bloomington (IN)
Iowa State U of Science and Technology (IA)
Jacksonville U (FL)
Johnson C. Smith U (NC)
The Juilliard School (NY)
Keene State Coll (NH)
Kennesaw State U (GA)
Kent State U (OH)
Kenyon Coll (OH)
La Roche Coll (PA)
Lehman Coll of the City U of New York (NY)
Lindenwood U (MO)
Long Island U–LIU Brooklyn (NY)
Long Island U–LIU Post (NY)
Loyola Marymount U (CA)
Loyola U Chicago (IL)
Manhattanville Coll (NY)
Marlboro Coll (VT)
Marymount Manhattan Coll (NY)
Mercyhurst U (PA)
Meredith Coll (NC)
Messiah Coll (PA)
Middlebury Coll (VT)
Mills Coll (CA)
Missouri Valley Coll (MO)
Montclair State U (NJ)
Mount Holyoke Coll (MA)
Muhlenberg Coll (PA)
Nazareth Coll of Rochester (NY)
New Mexico State U (NM)
New World School of the Arts (FL)
New York U (NY)
Northwestern U (IL)
Nova Southeastern U (FL)
Oakland U (MI)
Oberlin Coll (OH)
The Ohio State U (OH)
Ohio U (OH)
Oklahoma City U (OK)

Oral Roberts U (OK)
Pace U (NY)
Palm Beach Atlantic U (FL)
Pitzer Coll (CA)
Point Park U (PA)
Pomona Coll (CA)
Purchase Coll, State U of New York (NY)
Radford U (VA)
Randolph Coll (VA)
Reed Coll (OR)
Rhode Island Coll (RI)
Rider U (NJ)
Rockford U (IL)
Roger Williams U (RI)
Rowan U (NJ)
Rutgers U–New Brunswick (NJ)
Saint Louis U–Madrid Campus (Spain)
Saint Mary's Coll of California (CA)
St. Olaf Coll (MN)
Sam Houston State U (TX)
San Diego State U (CA)
San Francisco State U (CA)
Sarah Lawrence Coll (NY)
Scripps Coll (CA)
Seton Hill U (PA)
Shenandoah U (VA)
Simon Fraser U (BC, Canada)
Skidmore Coll (NY)
Slippery Rock U of Pennsylvania (PA)
Smith Coll (MA)
Southern Methodist U (TX)
Southern Utah U (UT)
Spelman Coll (GA)
State U of New York at Fredonia (NY)
State U of New York Coll at Potsdam (NY)
Stephen F. Austin State U (TX)
Sweet Briar Coll (VA)
Temple U (PA)
Texas Christian U (TX)
Texas State U (TX)
Texas Tech U (TX)
Texas Woman's U (TX)
Towson U (MD)
Troy U (AL)
Tulane U (LA)
U at Buffalo, the State U of New York (NY)
The U of Akron (OH)
The U of Alabama (AL)
The U of Arizona (AZ)
U of California, Irvine (CA)
U of California, Los Angeles (CA)
U of California, San Diego (CA)
U of California, Santa Barbara (CA)
U of Central Oklahoma (OK)
U of Cincinnati (OH)
U of Colorado Boulder (CO)
U of Florida (FL)
U of Georgia (GA)
U of Hartford (CT)
U of Hawaii at Manoa (HI)
U of Houston (TX)
U of Idaho (ID)
The U of Kansas (KS)
U of Maryland, Baltimore County (MD)
U of Maryland, Coll Park (MD)
U of Massachusetts Amherst (MA)
U of Michigan (MI)
U of Michigan–Flint (MI)
U of Minnesota, Twin Cities Campus (MN)
U of Montana (MT)
U of Nebraska–Lincoln (NE)
U of Nevada, Las Vegas (NV)
U of Nevada, Reno (NV)
U of New Mexico (NM)
The U of North Carolina at Charlotte (NC)
The U of North Carolina at Greensboro (NC)
U of North Carolina School of the Arts (NC)
U of North Texas (TX)
U of Oklahoma (OK)
U of Oregon (OR)
U of Richmond (VA)
U of Rochester (NY)
U of Saint Francis (IN)
U of South Carolina (SC)
U of Southern California (CA)
U of Southern Mississippi (MS)

The U of Tampa (FL)
The U of Texas at Austin (TX)
The U of Texas Rio Grande Valley (TX)
The U of the Arts (PA)
U of Utah (UT)
U of Washington (WA)
U of Wisconsin–Madison (WI)
U of Wisconsin–Milwaukee (WI)
U of Wisconsin–Stevens Point (WI)
Ursinus Coll (PA)
Utah State U (UT)
Utah Valley U (UT)
Valdosta State U (GA)
Virginia Commonwealth U (VA)
Washington U in St. Louis (MO)
Wayne State U (MI)
Weber State U (UT)
Webster U (MO)
Wells Coll (NY)
Wesleyan U (CT)
Western Kentucky U (KY)
Western Michigan U (MI)
Western Oregon U (OR)
Western Washington U (WA)
Westminster Coll (UT)
West Texas A&M U (TX)
Winthrop U (SC)
Wittenberg U (OH)
Wright State U (OH)
Wright State U–Lake Campus (OH)

DANCE RELATED
Anderson U (IN)
Brigham Young U (UT)
California State U, Long Beach (CA)
Coker Coll (SC)
Drexel U (PA)
Marlboro Coll (VT)
Marymount Manhattan Coll (NY)
Western Michigan U (MI)
Youngstown State U (OH)

DANISH
U of Washington (WA)

DATA MODELING/ WAREHOUSING AND DATABASE ADMINISTRATION
Aquinas Coll (MI)
Bryant U (RI)
Limestone Coll (SC)
Marist Coll (NY)
Pennsylvania Coll of Technology (PA)
Rochester Inst of Technology (NY)
U of Michigan (MI)

DATA PROCESSING AND DATA PROCESSING TECHNOLOGY
Bemidji State U (MN)
California State U, San Marcos (CA)
Delaware State U (DE)
Dickinson State U (ND)
U of Arkansas (AR)
U of Dubuque (IA)
U of San Francisco (CA)
U of Southern Mississippi (MS)

DEAF STUDIES
California State U, Northridge (CA)
Coll of the Holy Cross (MA)
Columbia Coll Chicago (IL)
Towson U (MD)
U of Valley Forge (PA)

DENTAL ASSISTING
Delaware State U (DE)

DENTAL HYGIENE
Ball State U (IN)
Clayton State U (GA)
Eastern Washington U (WA)
East Tennessee State U (TN)
Farmingdale State Coll (NY)
Ferris State U (MI)
Georgia Highlands Coll (GA)
Idaho State U (ID)
Indiana U Northwest (IN)
Indiana U–Purdue U Indianapolis (IN)
Indiana U South Bend (IN)
Lewis U (IL)
Lincoln Coll of New England, Southington (CT)

Louisiana State U Health Sciences Center (LA)
MCPHS U (MA)
New York U (NY)
Northern Arizona U (AZ)
The Ohio State U (OH)
Old Dominion U (VA)
Oregon Inst of Technology (OR)
Pennsylvania Coll of Technology (PA)
Rhode Island Coll (RI)
Southern Illinois U Carbondale (IL)
Texas Woman's U (TX)
Tyler Jr Coll (TX)
U of Bridgeport (CT)
U of Hawaii at Manoa (HI)
U of Louisiana at Monroe (LA)
U of Louisville (KY)
U of Michigan (MI)
U of Minnesota, Twin Cities Campus (MN)
U of New England (ME)
U of New Haven (CT)
U of New Mexico (NM)
The U of North Carolina at Chapel Hill (NC)
U of Oklahoma Health Sciences Center (OK)
U of South Dakota (SD)
U of Southern California (CA)
U of Southern Indiana (IN)
U of Washington (WA)
U of Wyoming (WY)
Utah Valley U (UT)
Vermont Tech Coll (VT)
Virginia Commonwealth U (VA)
Weber State U (UT)
Western Kentucky U (KY)
West Virginia U (WV)
Wichita State U (KS)
Youngstown State U (OH)

DENTAL LABORATORY TECHNOLOGY
Boston U (MA)

DENTAL SERVICES AND ALLIED PROFESSIONS RELATED
Delaware State U (DE)
Indiana U–Purdue U Indianapolis (IN)

DESIGN AND APPLIED ARTS RELATED
Alverno Coll (WI)
Antioch U Los Angeles (CA)
Arizona State U at the Tempe campus (AZ)
Asbury U (KY)
Athabasca U (AB, Canada)
Auburn U (AL)
Augsburg U (MN)
Azusa Pacific U (CA)
Bemidji State U (MN)
Buffalo State Coll, State U of New York (NY)
Butler U (IN)
California Coll of the Arts (CA)
Concordia U (QC, Canada)
Converse Coll (SC)
Drexel U (PA)
Eugene Lang Coll of Liberal Arts (NY)
Farmingdale State Coll (NY)
Fashion Inst of Technology (NY)
Ferris State U (MI)
Franklin Pierce U (NH)
Guilford Coll (NC)
Hampshire Coll (MA)
Harding U (AR)
Hofstra U (NY)
Houston Baptist U (TX)
Inter American U of Puerto Rico, San Germán Campus (PR)
Iowa State U of Science and Technology (IA)
Laguna Coll of Art & Design (CA)
Mansfield U of Pennsylvania (PA)
Maryland Inst Coll of Art (MD)
McMurry U (TX)
Merrimack Coll (MA)
Montclair State U (NJ)
New York Inst of Technology (NY)
Parsons School of Design (NY)
Penn State Altoona (PA)
Penn State Berks (PA)
Penn State U Park (PA)

Portland State U (OR)
Pratt Inst (NY)
Roberts Wesleyan Coll (NY)
School of Visual Arts (NY)
Schreiner U (TX)
Shawnee State U (OH)
Southern Methodist U (TX)
State U of New York at Fredonia (NY)
U of California, Los Angeles (CA)
The U of Findlay (OH)
U of Illinois at Chicago (IL)
U of Oregon (OR)
U of Wisconsin–Stout (WI)
Washington U in St. Louis (MO)

DESIGN AND VISUAL COMMUNICATIONS
Alberta Coll of Art & Design (AB, Canada)
American U (DC)
Anderson U (IN)
Auburn U (AL)
Barton Coll (NC)
Bellarmine U (KY)
Belmont U (TN)
Bennington Coll (VT)
Biola U (CA)
Boise State U (ID)
Bowling Green State U (OH)
Bowling Green State U–Firelands Coll (OH)
Bryant U (RI)
Buffalo State Coll, State U of New York (NY)
California Coll of the Arts (CA)
California State U, Monterey Bay (CA)
Carnegie Mellon U (PA)
Cazenovia Coll (NY)
Cedarville U (OH)
Central Connecticut State U (CT)
Coll of the Ozarks (MO)
Concordia U, St. Paul (MN)
EDP U of Puerto Rico (PR)
Endicott Coll (MA)
Escuela de Artes Plasticas y Diseño de Puerto Rico (PR)
Eugene Lang Coll of Liberal Arts (NY)
Farmingdale State Coll (NY)
Ferris State U (MI)
Franklin U Switzerland (Switzerland)
Graceland U (IA)
Houston Baptist U (TX)
Indiana U Bloomington (IN)
Inter American U of Puerto Rico, Metropolitan Campus (PR)
Iowa State U of Science and Technology (IA)
Jacksonville U (FL)
Kean U (NJ)
Laguna Coll of Art & Design (CA)
La Roche Coll (PA)
Lawrence Technological U (MI)
Lehigh U (PA)
Lewis U (IL)
LIM Coll (NY)
Linfield Coll (OR)
Loyola U Chicago (IL)
Loyola U New Orleans (LA)
Lubbock Christian U (TX)
Madonna U (MI)
Marymount U (VA)
Maryville Coll (TN)
Massachusetts Coll of Art and Design (MA)
Millersville U of Pennsylvania (PA)
Missouri State U (MO)
Mount St. Joseph U (OH)
Muskingum U (OH)
Nazareth Coll of Rochester (NY)
New Hampshire Inst of Art (NH)
New Mexico Highlands U (NM)
North Carolina State U (NC)
Northern Arizona U (AZ)
Ohio Northern U (OH)
The Ohio State U (OH)
Oral Roberts U (OK)
Oregon State U (OR)
Paris Coll of Art (France)
Purdue U (IN)
Radford U (VA)
Rensselaer Polytechnic Inst (NY)
Robert Morris U (PA)
Rochester Inst of Technology (NY)

Saginaw Valley State U (MI)
Saint Mary-of-the-Woods Coll (IN)
San Francisco State U (CA)
Savannah Coll of Art and Design (GA)
Seattle Pacific U (WA)
Southern Illinois U Carbondale (IL)
Stevenson U (MD)
Syracuse U (NY)
Texas Christian U (TX)
Texas State U (TX)
U of Arkansas (AR)
U of Cincinnati (OH)
U of Dayton (OH)
U of Evansville (IN)
U of Hartford (CT)
The U of Kansas (KS)
U of Mary Hardin-Baylor (TX)
U of Maryland, Baltimore County (MD)
U of Massachusetts Dartmouth (MA)
U of Michigan–Flint (MI)
U of North Texas (TX)
U of Notre Dame (IN)
U of Oklahoma (OK)
U of Saint Francis (IN)
U of San Francisco (CA)
The U of Tennessee at Martin (TN)
The U of Texas at Austin (TX)
U of Washington (WA)
U of Wisconsin–Stevens Point (WI)
Ursuline Coll (OH)
Utah Valley U (UT)
Washington U in St. Louis (MO)
Weber State U (UT)
Western Washington U (WA)
West Virginia U (WV)
Wilmington U (DE)
Wisconsin Lutheran Coll (WI)

DESKTOP PUBLISHING AND DIGITAL IMAGING DESIGN
California Baptist U (CA)
Chowan U (NC)
La Salle U (PA)
New England Inst of Technology (RI)
Rochester Inst of Technology (NY)
Wilmington U (DE)

DEVELOPMENTAL AND CHILD PSYCHOLOGY
Antioch U Midwest (OH)
Bay Path U (MA)
Boston Coll (MA)
Bridgewater State U (MA)
California State U, Stanislaus (CA)
Carson-Newman U (TN)
Cornerstone U (MI)
Eastern Nazarene Coll (MA)
Eastern Washington U (WA)
East Texas Baptist U (TX)
Emmanuel Coll (MA)
Fitchburg State U (MA)
Hampton U (VA)
Marlboro Coll (VT)
Maryville Coll (TN)
Metropolitan State U of Denver (CO)
Mills Coll (CA)
Mount Saint Mary's U (CA)
Northern Michigan U (MI)
Quinnipiac U (CT)
Saint Leo U (FL)
Sonoma State U (CA)
Texas Christian U (TX)
Tufts U (MA)
U of California, San Diego (CA)
U of Minnesota, Twin Cities Campus (MN)
U of Saint Francis (IN)
The U of Texas at Dallas (TX)
Utica Coll (NY)
Vanderbilt U (TN)
Western Washington U (WA)

DEVELOPMENTAL BIOLOGY AND EMBRYOLOGY
U of California, Santa Barbara (CA)

DEVELOPMENT ECONOMICS AND INTERNATIONAL DEVELOPMENT
Calvin Coll (MI)
Clark U (MA)
Marlboro Coll (VT)
Messiah Coll (PA)
Penn State Altoona (PA)

Penn State Berks (PA)
Point Loma Nazarene U (CA)
Sarah Lawrence Coll (NY)
Seattle Pacific U (WA)
U of California, Los Angeles (CA)
U of Dayton (OH)
U of Guelph (ON, Canada)
U of King's Coll (NS, Canada)
U of Richmond (VA)
U of St. Thomas (TX)
U of San Francisco (CA)
U of the Fraser Valley (BC, Canada)
U of Vermont (VT)

DIAGNOSTIC MEDICAL SONOGRAPHY AND ULTRASOUND TECHNOLOGY
Adventist U of Health Sciences (FL)
Allen Coll (IA)
Baptist Coll of Health Sciences (TN)
Benedictine U (IL)
The George Washington U (DC)
Grand Valley State U (MI)
Lewis U (IL)
Long Island U–LIU Brooklyn (NY)
Marian U (WI)
Misericordia U (PA)
Nebraska Methodist Coll (NE)
Newman U (KS)
Nova Southeastern U (FL)
Oregon Inst of Technology (OR)
Rhode Island Coll (RI)
Rochester Inst of Technology (NY)
Roosevelt U (IL)
Seattle U (WA)
Thomas Jefferson U (PA)
The U of Findlay (OH)
U of Missouri (MO)
U of Oklahoma Health Sciences Center (OK)
Weber State U (UT)

DIESEL MECHANICS TECHNOLOGY
Idaho State U (ID)

DIETETICS
Abilene Christian U (TX)
Acadia U (NS, Canada)
Andrews U (MI)
Appalachian State U (NC)
Ashland U (OH)
Ball State U (IN)
Bowling Green State U (OH)
Bradley U (IL)
Buffalo State Coll, State U of New York (NY)
California Polytechnic State U, San Luis Obispo (CA)
California State Polytechnic U, Pomona (CA)
California State U, Long Beach (CA)
California State U, Los Angeles (CA)
California State U, San Bernardino (CA)
Carson-Newman U (TN)
Case Western Reserve U (OH)
Central Michigan U (MI)
Coll of Saint Elizabeth (NJ)
Coll of the Ozarks (MO)
Delaware State U (DE)
Dominican U (IL)
D'Youville Coll (NY)
East Carolina U (NC)
Eastern Michigan U (MI)
Florida Intl U (FL)
Florida State U (FL)
Georgia State U (GA)
Harding U (AR)
Idaho State U (ID)
Illinois State U (IL)
Immaculata U (PA)
Indiana State U (IN)
Iowa State U of Science and Technology (IA)
Kansas State U (KS)
Keene State Coll (NH)
Keiser U, Fort Lauderdale (FL)
Lebanese American U (Lebanon)
Lehman Coll of the City U of New York (NY)
Life U (GA)
Lipscomb U (TN)

Mansfield U of Pennsylvania (PA)
Marshall U (WV)
Marywood U (PA)
Meredith Coll (NC)
Miami U (OH)
Michigan State U (MI)
Missouri State U (MO)
Mount Mary U (WI)
New Mexico State U (NM)
North Dakota State U (ND)
Northeastern State U (OK)
Northern Illinois U (IL)
Northwest Missouri State U (MO)
The Ohio State U (OH)
Olivet Nazarene U (IL)
Ouachita Baptist U (AR)
Point Loma Nazarene U (CA)
Purdue U (IN)
Queens Coll of the City U of New York (NY)
Rowan U (NJ)
Rutgers U–New Brunswick (NJ)
St. Catherine U (MN)
Saint Louis U (MO)
San Diego State U (CA)
San Francisco State U (CA)
Seton Hill U (PA)
Simmons Coll (MA)
State U of New York Coll at Oneonta (NY)
Tennessee Technological U (TN)
Texas A&M U–Kingsville (TX)
Texas Christian U (TX)
Texas Tech U (TX)
The U of Akron (OH)
U of Central Missouri (MO)
U of Cincinnati (OH)
U of Dayton (OH)
U of Florida (FL)
U of Georgia (GA)
U of Illinois at Chicago (IL)
U of Maryland Eastern Shore (MD)
U of Missouri (MO)
U of New Haven (CT)
U of North Dakota (ND)
U of Northern Colorado (CO)
U of North Florida (FL)
U of Oklahoma Health Sciences Center (OK)
U of Pittsburgh (PA)
U of Rhode Island (RI)
U of Southern Mississippi (MS)
The U of Tennessee at Martin (TN)
The U of Texas at San Antonio (TX)
U of Vermont (VT)
U of Wisconsin–Stevens Point (WI)
U of Wisconsin–Stout (WI)
Wayne State U (MI)
West Chester U of Pennsylvania (PA)
Western Illinois U (IL)
Youngstown State U (OH)

DIETETICS AND CLINICAL NUTRITION SERVICES RELATED
Bowling Green State U (OH)
Madonna U (MI)
Texas Christian U (TX)
Western Michigan U (MI)

DIGITAL ARTS
Academy of Art U (CA)
Albright Coll (PA)
Antioch Coll, Yellow Springs (OH)
Arizona State U at the Tempe campus (AZ)
Ashland U (OH)
Austin Coll (TX)
Bethany Lutheran Coll (MN)
Blackburn Coll (IL)
Bowling Green State U (OH)
Carthage Coll (WI)
Champlain Coll (VT)
Concordia U (QC, Canada)
Daemen Coll (NY)
DeSales U (PA)
Escuela de Artes Plasticas y Diseño de Puerto Rico (PR)
Florida Southern Coll (FL)
Georgian Court U (NJ)
Greenville U (IL)
Hamline U (MN)
Kansas Wesleyan U (KS)
Kennesaw State U (GA)
King U (TN)
Kutztown U of Pennsylvania (PA)
La Salle U (PA)

Lipscomb U (TN)
Long Island U–LIU Post (NY)
Manchester U (IN)
Marlboro Coll (VT)
Marymount California U (CA)
Marymount Manhattan Coll (NY)
Minnesota State U Moorhead (MN)
The New School–Parsons Paris (France)
Northeastern U (MA)
Northern Vermont U–Lyndon (VT)
Pacific Northwest Coll of Art (OR)
Pennsylvania Coll of Art & Design (PA)
Point Loma Nazarene U (CA)
Rhode Island Coll (RI)
Roberts Wesleyan Coll (NY)
San Francisco Art Inst (CA)
Southwestern Coll (KS)
Stetson U (FL)
Tiffin U (OH)
Trinity Christian Coll (IL)
U of Central Florida (FL)
U of Florida (FL)
U of Massachusetts Dartmouth (MA)
U of New Mexico (NM)
U of North Carolina at Asheville (NC)
U of Puget Sound (WA)
U of Saint Francis (IN)
U of Southern California (CA)
The U of Tampa (FL)
The U of Texas at Austin (TX)
The U of Toledo (OH)
U of Wisconsin–Stout (WI)
U of Wisconsin–Whitewater (WI)
Wartburg Coll (IA)
Whitworth U (WA)
Woodbury U (CA)

DIGITAL COMMUNICATION AND MEDIA/MULTIMEDIA
Abilene Christian U (TX)
Academy of Art U (CA)
Albright Coll (PA)
Alma Coll (MI)
Anderson U (SC)
Ashland U (OH)
Baldwin Wallace U (OH)
Ball State U (IN)
Baylor U (TX)
Bennington Coll (VT)
Bethany Lutheran Coll (MN)
Bluffton U (OH)
Bowling Green State U (OH)
Bradley U (IL)
Bryant U (RI)
Buena Vista U (IA)
Butler U (IN)
California Coll of the Arts (CA)
California Lutheran U (CA)
California State U, Dominguez Hills (CA)
Calvin Coll (MI)
Canisius Coll (NY)
Carson-Newman U (TN)
Cedar Crest Coll (PA)
Cedarville U (OH)
Clarkson U (NY)
Cleveland State U (OH)
Columbia Coll Chicago (IL)
Concordia Coll–New York (NY)
Concordia U Wisconsin (WI)
Corban U (OR)
Cornerstone U (MI)
Dallas Baptist U (TX)
Eastern Mennonite U (VA)
Eugene Lang Coll of Liberal Arts (NY)
The Evergreen State Coll (WA)
Fitchburg State U (MA)
Florida Atlantic U (FL)
Florida Gulf Coast U (FL)
Florida State U (FL)
Georgia Inst of Technology (GA)
Georgian Court U (NJ)
Georgia Southern U (GA)
Grand Valley State U (MI)
Granite State Coll (NH)
Harding U (AR)
Hawai`i Pacific U (HI)
Hilbert Coll (NY)
Howard Payne U (TX)
Indiana U Bloomington (IN)
Indiana U Kokomo (IN)

Indiana U–Purdue U Indianapolis (IN)
Indiana U South Bend (IN)
Inter American U of Puerto Rico, Bayamón Campus (PR)
Keene State Coll (NH)
Kent State U (OH)
Kutztown U of Pennsylvania (PA)
Lawrence Technological U (MI)
Lebanon Valley Coll (PA)
Lee U (TN)
Lewis U (IL)
Liberty U (VA)
Limestone Coll (SC)
Lincoln U (PA)
Lindenwood U (MO)
Long Island U–LIU Brooklyn (NY)
Loyola U Chicago (IL)
Loyola U New Orleans (LA)
Lubbock Christian U (TX)
Lycoming Coll (PA)
Lynn U (FL)
Manhattanville Coll (NY)
Marquette U (WI)
Marywood U (PA)
Messiah Coll (PA)
Miami U (OH)
Middle Tennessee State U (TN)
Minneapolis Coll of Art and Design (MN)
Minnesota State U Moorhead (MN)
Mount Mercy U (IA)
Muskingum U (OH)
National U (CA)
New York Inst of Technology (NY)
New York U (NY)
Northern Michigan U (MI)
Northern Vermont U–Lyndon (VT)
North Greenville U (SC)
Ohio U (OH)
Oregon State U (OR)
Point Park U (PA)
Rensselaer Polytechnic Inst (NY)
Rochester Inst of Technology (NY)
Saginaw Valley State U (MI)
St. Bonaventure U (NY)
St. John Fisher Coll (NY)
San Diego State U (CA)
Savannah Coll of Art and Design (GA)
Seattle U (WA)
Simpson Coll (IA)
Southeastern U (FL)
Southwestern Coll (KS)
State U of New York at New Paltz (NY)
State U of New York Coll of Technology at Canton (NY)
Stevenson U (MD)
Texas A&M U (TX)
Texas State U (TX)
Texas Tech U (TX)
Tiffin U (OH)
Trevecca Nazarene U (TN)
U of Cincinnati (OH)
U of Denver (CO)
U of Georgia (GA)
U of Idaho (ID)
U of Maine (ME)
U of Miami (FL)
U of Northern Iowa (IA)
U of North Georgia (GA)
U of Puerto Rico–Humacao (PR)
U of Rochester (NY)
U of Saskatchewan (SK, Canada)
The U of Tampa (FL)
The U of Texas at Dallas (TX)
U of the Incarnate Word (TX)
U of Toronto (ON, Canada)
U of Valley Forge (PA)
U of Waterloo (ON, Canada)
Valdosta State U (GA)
Valparaiso U (IN)
Villa Maria Coll (NY)
Walsh U (OH)
Washington State U (WA)
Washington State U–Tri-Cities (WA)
Washington State U–Vancouver (WA)
Webster U (MO)
Wellesley Coll (MA)
Westminster Coll (PA)
West Texas A&M U (TX)
Whitworth U (WA)
Wilkes U (PA)
William Jewell Coll (MO)

DIRECT ENTRY MIDWIFERY
Midwives Coll of Utah (UT)

DIRECTING AND THEATRICAL PRODUCTION
Anderson U (SC)
Augsburg U (MN)
Baldwin Wallace U (OH)
Belmont U (TN)
Bennington Coll (VT)
Binghamton U, State U of New York (NY)
Boston U (MA)
Bradley U (IL)
Brigham Young U (UT)
California State U, Long Beach (CA)
Columbia Coll Chicago (IL)
Cornish Coll of the Arts (WA)
Drake U (IA)
Emory & Henry Coll (VA)
Hofstra U (NY)
Juniata Coll (PA)
Keene State Coll (NH)
Lipscomb U (TN)
Marlboro Coll (VT)
Marymount Manhattan Coll (NY)
Pace U (NY)
Pepperdine U, Malibu (CA)
Point Park U (PA)
Rider U (NJ)
Texas Christian U (TX)
U of Miami (FL)
The U of the Arts (PA)
U of Washington (WA)
Webster U (MO)
Whitworth U (WA)

DISABILITY STUDIES
Aurora U (IL)
Florida State U (FL)
The U of Toledo (OH)

DISPUTE RESOLUTION
Life U (GA)

DIVINITY/MINISTRY
Anderson U (SC)
Azusa Pacific U (CA)
The Baptist Coll of Florida (FL)
Barclay Coll (KS)
Belmont U (TN)
Bethel Coll (IN)
Biola U (CA)
Bluefield Coll (VA)
Calvary U (MO)
Campbellsville U (KY)
Carson-Newman U (TN)
Corban U (OR)
Eastern Nazarene Coll (MA)
Houston Baptist U (TX)
Indiana Wesleyan U (IN)
Johnson U (TN)
John Wesley U (NC)
Judson U (IL)
Kansas Wesleyan U (KS)
Master's Coll and Sem (ON, Canada)
The Master's U (CA)
Messenger Coll (TX)
Mid-America Christian U (OK)
Nebraska Christian Coll of Hope Intl U (NE)
Northwest Nazarene U (ID)
Northwest U (WA)
Ohio Christian U (OH)
Oklahoma Baptist U (OK)
Providence Coll (RI)
Regent U (VA)
Roberts Wesleyan Coll (NY)
Shiloh U (IA)
Shorter U (GA)
Southeastern U (FL)
Southwestern Assemblies of God U (TX)
Toccoa Falls Coll (GA)
Trevecca Nazarene U (TN)
U of Valley Forge (PA)

DOCUMENTARY PRODUCTION
Columbia Coll Chicago (IL)
High Point U (NC)
Ithaca Coll (NY)
Marlboro Coll (VT)
Mount Saint Mary's U (CA)
Spelman Coll (GA)
U at Albany, State U of New York (NY)

DRAFTING AND DESIGN TECHNOLOGY
Academy of Art U (CA)
East Carolina U (NC)
East Central U (OK)
Northern Michigan U (MI)
Sam Houston State U (TX)
Trine U (IN)
Weber State U (UT)
Western Michigan U (MI)

DRAFTING/DESIGN ENGINEERING TECHNOLOGIES RELATED
Central Michigan U (MI)
Weber State U (UT)

DRAMA AND DANCE TEACHER EDUCATION
Adams State U (CO)
Austin Coll (TX)
Ball State U (IN)
Belmont U (TN)
Boise State U (ID)
Bridgewater State U (MA)
Catawba Coll (NC)
Central Connecticut State U (CT)
Coll of the Ozarks (MO)
Columbia Coll (SC)
Columbus State U (GA)
East Carolina U (NC)
East Texas Baptist U (TX)
Edgewood Coll (WI)
Emerson Coll (MA)
Greensboro Coll (NC)
Hardin-Simmons U (TX)
Hofstra U (NY)
Hope Coll (MI)
Howard Payne U (TX)
Jacksonville U (FL)
Keene State Coll (NH)
Lee U (TN)
Lipscomb U (TN)
Lubbock Christian U (TX)
Maryville Coll (TN)
Meredith Coll (NC)
Missouri Baptist U (MO)
Montclair State U (NJ)
Ohio Wesleyan U (OH)
Piedmont Coll (GA)
Point Park U (PA)
St. Catherine U (MN)
Southern Utah U (UT)
Southwestern Assemblies of God U (TX)
State U of New York Coll at Potsdam (NY)
Trevecca Nazarene U (TN)
The U of Akron (OH)
U of Central Oklahoma (OK)
U of Evansville (IN)
The U of North Carolina at Greensboro (NC)
U of Regina (SK, Canada)
U of South Dakota (SD)
U of Wisconsin–Whitewater (WI)
Utah Valley U (UT)
Valparaiso U (IN)
Washington U in St. Louis (MO)
Wayne State Coll (NE)
Weber State U (UT)

DRAMATIC/THEATER ARTS
Abilene Christian U (TX)
Acadia U (NS, Canada)
Adelphi U (NY)
Agnes Scott Coll (GA)
Alabama State U (AL)
Albion Coll (MI)
Albright Coll (PA)
Alfred U (NY)
Allegheny Coll (PA)
Alma Coll (MI)
American Intl Coll (MA)
American U (DC)
The American U in Cairo (Egypt)
Amherst Coll (MA)
Anderson U (SC)
Angelo State U (TX)
Appalachian State U (NC)
Aquinas Coll (MI)
Arcadia U (PA)
Arizona State U at the Tempe campus (AZ)
Asbury U (KY)
Ashland U (OH)
Auburn U (AL)
Augsburg U (MN)

Augustana Coll (IL)
Augustana U (SD)
Aurora U (IL)
Austin Peay State U (TN)
Averett U (VA)
Avila U (MO)
Baker U (KS)
Ball State U (IN)
Bard Coll (NY)
Barnard Coll (NY)
Barry U (FL)
Barton Coll (NC)
Bates Coll (ME)
Baylor U (TX)
Belhaven U (MS)
Bellarmine U (KY)
Belmont U (TN)
Beloit Coll (WI)
Bemidji State U (MN)
Benedictine Coll (KS)
Bennington Coll (VT)
Berea Coll (KY)
Bethany Lutheran Coll (MN)
Bethel Coll (IN)
Bethel U (MN)
Bethel U (TN)
Binghamton U, State U of New York (NY)
Biola U (CA)
Birmingham-Southern Coll (AL)
Blackburn Coll (IL)
Bloomsburg U of Pennsylvania (PA)
Bluefield Coll (VA)
Bob Jones U (SC)
Boise State U (ID)
Boston Coll (MA)
Boston U (MA)
Bowling Green State U (OH)
Bradley U (IL)
Brandeis U (MA)
Brenau U (GA)
Bridgewater State U (MA)
Brigham Young U–Idaho (ID)
Brock U (ON, Canada)
Bryan Coll (TN)
Bucknell U (PA)
Buffalo State Coll, State U of New York (NY)
Butler U (IN)
California Baptist U (CA)
California Lutheran U (CA)
California Polytechnic State U, San Luis Obispo (CA)
California State Polytechnic U, Pomona (CA)
California State U, Dominguez Hills (CA)
California State U, East Bay (CA)
California State U, Fullerton (CA)
California State U, Long Beach (CA)
California State U, Los Angeles (CA)
California State U, Northridge (CA)
California State U, Sacramento (CA)
California State U, San Bernardino (CA)
California State U, Stanislaus (CA)
California U of Pennsylvania (PA)
Calvary U (MO)
Capital U (OH)
Cardinal Stritch U (WI)
Carleton Coll (MN)
Carnegie Mellon U (PA)
Carroll Coll (MT)
Carroll U (WI)
Carson-Newman U (TN)
Carthage Coll (WI)
Case Western Reserve U (OH)
Catawba Coll (NC)
The Catholic U of America (DC)
Cedar Crest Coll (PA)
Cedarville U (OH)
Centenary Coll of Louisiana (LA)
Central Connecticut State U (CT)
Central Methodist U (MO)
Centre Coll (KY)
Chapman U (CA)
Chowan U (NC)
Christopher Newport U (VA)
City Coll of the City U of New York (NY)
Claremont McKenna Coll (CA)
Clarion U of Pennsylvania (PA)
Clarke U (IA)
Clark U (MA)

Cleveland State U (OH)
Coastal Carolina U (SC)
Coe Coll (IA)
Coker Coll (SC)
Colby Coll (ME)
Colgate U (NY)
The Coll at Brockport, State U of New York (NY)
Coll of Charleston (SC)
The Coll of Idaho (ID)
Coll of Saint Benedict (MN)
Coll of Staten Island of the City U of New York (NY)
Coll of the Holy Cross (MA)
Coll of the Ozarks (MO)
The Coll of William and Mary (VA)
The Coll of Wooster (OH)
The Colorado Coll (CO)
Colorado Mesa U (CO)
Colorado State U (CO)
Columbia Coll Chicago (IL)
Columbia U (NY)
Columbus State U (GA)
Concordia U (QC, Canada)
Concordia U Chicago (IL)
Concordia U Irvine (CA)
Concordia U, Nebraska (NE)
Concordia U, St. Paul (MN)
Connecticut Coll (CT)
Converse Coll (SC)
Cornell Coll (IA)
Cornell U (NY)
Cornish Coll of the Arts (WA)
Covenant Coll (GA)
Creighton U (NE)
Culver-Stockton Coll (MO)
Daemen Coll (NY)
Dartmouth Coll (NH)
Davidson Coll (NC)
Dean Coll (MA)
Denison U (OH)
DePaul U (IL)
DePauw U (IN)
DeSales U (PA)
Dickinson Coll (PA)
Dickinson State U (ND)
Doane U (NE)
Dominican U (IL)
Drake U (IA)
Drew U (NJ)
Drury U (MO)
Duquesne U (PA)
Earlham Coll (IN)
East Carolina U (NC)
East Central U (OK)
Eastern Mennonite U (VA)
Eastern Michigan U (MI)
Eastern Nazarene Coll (MA)
Eastern New Mexico U (NM)
Eastern Oregon U (OR)
Eastern Washington U (WA)
East Stroudsburg U of Pennsylvania (PA)
East Tennessee State U (TN)
East Texas Baptist U (TX)
Eckerd Coll (FL)
Edgewood Coll (WI)
Elizabethtown Coll (PA)
Elmhurst Coll (IL)
Elon U (NC)
Emerson Coll (MA)
Emory & Henry Coll (VA)
Emory U (GA)
Emporia State U (KS)
Eugene Lang Coll of Liberal Arts (NY)
The Evergreen State Coll (WA)
Fairfield U (CT)
Fairleigh Dickinson U, Florham Campus (NJ)
Fairleigh Dickinson U, Metropolitan Campus (NJ)
Fitchburg State U (MA)
Flagler Coll (FL)
Florida Ag and Mech U (FL)
Florida Atlantic U (FL)
Florida Gulf Coast U (FL)
Florida Intl U (FL)
Florida Southern Coll (FL)
Florida State U (FL)
Fordham U (NY)
Fort Lewis Coll (CO)
Francis Marion U (SC)
Franklin & Marshall Coll (PA)
Franklin Coll (IN)
Franklin Pierce U (NH)
Friends U (KS)

Frostburg State U (MD)
Furman U (SC)
Gannon U (PA)
George Mason U (VA)
Georgetown Coll (KY)
The George Washington U (DC)
Georgia Coll & State U (GA)
Georgia Southern U (GA)
Georgia Southern U–Armstrong Campus (GA)
Georgia Southwestern State U (GA)
Gettysburg Coll (PA)
Gonzaga U (WA)
Gordon Coll (MA)
Goshen Coll (IN)
Governors State U (IL)
Grand View U (IA)
Greensboro Coll (NC)
Grinnell Coll (IA)
Guilford Coll (NC)
Gustavus Adolphus Coll (MN)
Hamilton Coll (NY)
Hamline U (MN)
Hampshire Coll (MA)
Hampton U (VA)
Hannibal-LaGrange U (MO)
Harding U (AR)
Hardin-Simmons U (TX)
Hartwick Coll (NY)
Heidelberg U (OH)
Hendrix Coll (AR)
High Point U (NC)
Hillsdale Coll (MI)
Hiram Coll (OH)
Hofstra U (NY)
Hollins U (VA)
Hope Coll (MI)
Howard Payne U (TX)
Humboldt State U (CA)
Hunter Coll of the City U of New York (NY)
Idaho State U (ID)
Illinois Coll (IL)
Illinois State U (IL)
Illinois Wesleyan U (IL)
Indiana State U (IN)
Indiana U Bloomington (IN)
Indiana U Northwest (IN)
Indiana U of Pennsylvania (PA)
Indiana U South Bend (IN)
Iowa State U of Science and Technology (IA)
Ithaca Coll (NY)
Jacksonville U (FL)
James Madison U (VA)
The Juilliard School (NY)
Juniata Coll (PA)
Kalamazoo Coll (MI)
Kansas State U (KS)
Kansas Wesleyan U (KS)
Kean U (NJ)
Kennesaw State U (GA)
Kent State U (OH)
Kenyon Coll (OH)
King's Coll (PA)
King U (TN)
Knox Coll (IL)
Lafayette Coll (PA)
LaGrange Coll (GA)
Lamar U (TX)
Lawrence U (WI)
Lehigh U (PA)
Lehman Coll of the City U of New York (NY)
Le Moyne Coll (NY)
Lenoir-Rhyne U (NC)
Lewis U (IL)
Liberty U (VA)
Limestone Coll (SC)
Lincoln Coll (IL)
Lindenwood U (MO)
Linfield Coll (OR)
Lipscomb U (TN)
Lock Haven U of Pennsylvania (PA)
Long Island U–LIU Post (NY)
Louisiana Coll (LA)
Louisiana State U and A&M Coll (LA)
Loyola Marymount U (CA)
Loyola U Chicago (IL)
Loyola U New Orleans (LA)
Luther Coll (IA)
Lycoming Coll (PA)
Lynchburg Coll (VA)
Lynn U (FL)
Lyon Coll (AR)

Macalester Coll (MN)
Manchester U (IN)
Marietta Coll (OH)
Marlboro Coll (VT)
Marquette U (WI)
Marymount Manhattan Coll (NY)
Maryville Coll (TN)
Marywood U (PA)
Massachusetts Inst of Technology (MA)
McDaniel Coll (MD)
McMurry U (TX)
McPherson Coll (KS)
Mercer U, Macon (GA)
Meredith Coll (NC)
Merrimack Coll (MA)
Messiah Coll (PA)
Metropolitan State U of Denver (CO)
Miami U (OH)
Michigan State U (MI)
Middlebury Coll (VT)
Middle Tennessee State U (TN)
Millikin U (IL)
Mills Coll (CA)
Minnesota State U Moorhead (MN)
Missouri Baptist U (MO)
Missouri State U (MO)
Missouri Valley Coll (MO)
Missouri Western State U (MO)
Molloy Coll (NY)
Monmouth Coll (IL)
Montclair State U (NJ)
Morehead State U (KY)
Morehouse Coll (GA)
Morningside Coll (IA)
Mount Holyoke Coll (MA)
Mount Marty Coll (SD)
Mount Vernon Nazarene U (OH)
Muhlenberg Coll (PA)
Murray State U (KY)
Muskingum U (OH)
Naropa U (CO)
Nazareth Coll of Rochester (NY)
Newberry Coll (SC)
New Coll of Florida (FL)
New Mexico State U (NM)
The New School Coll of Performing Arts (NY)
New World School of the Arts (FL)
New York U (NY)
Niagara U (NY)
North Carolina Central U (NC)
North Carolina Wesleyan Coll (NC)
North Central Coll (IL)
North Dakota State U (ND)
Northeastern State U (OK)
Northeastern U (MA)
Northern Arizona U (AZ)
Northern Illinois U (IL)
Northern Kentucky U (KY)
Northern Michigan U (MI)
Northern State U (SD)
Northern Vermont U–Lyndon (VT)
North Greenville U (SC)
Northwestern Coll (IA)
Northwestern State U of Louisiana (LA)
Northwestern U (IL)
Northwest Missouri State U (MO)
Northwest U (WA)
Notre Dame de Namur U (CA)
Nova Southeastern U (FL)
Oakland U (MI)
Oberlin Coll (OH)
Occidental Coll (CA)
Ohio Northern U (OH)
The Ohio State U (OH)
The Ohio State U at Lima (OH)
Ohio U (OH)
Ohio Wesleyan U (OH)
Oklahoma Baptist U (OK)
Oklahoma Christian U (OK)
Oklahoma City U (OK)
Oklahoma State U (OK)
Old Dominion U (VA)
Oral Roberts U (OK)
Ottawa U (KS)
Otterbein U (OH)
Ouachita Baptist U (AR)
Our Lady of the Lake U (TX)
Pacific Lutheran U (WA)
Palm Beach Atlantic U (FL)
Pepperdine U, Malibu (CA)
Piedmont Coll (GA)
Pitzer Coll (CA)
Point Park U (PA)

Pomona Coll (CA)
Portland State U (OR)
Prairie View A&M U (TX)
Presbyterian Coll (SC)
Principia Coll (IL)
Providence Coll (RI)
Purchase Coll, State U of New York (NY)
Purdue U (IN)
Queens Coll of the City U of New York (NY)
Quinnipiac U (CT)
Radford U (VA)
Ramapo Coll of New Jersey (NJ)
Randolph Coll (VA)
Randolph-Macon Coll (VA)
Redeemer U Coll (ON, Canada)
Reed Coll (OR)
Rhode Island Coll (RI)
Rhodes Coll (TN)
Ripon Coll (WI)
Roanoke Coll (VA)
Rockford U (IL)
Rocky Mountain Coll (MT)
Roger Williams U (RI)
Roosevelt U (IL)
Rutgers U–Camden (NJ)
Rutgers U–Newark (NJ)
Rutgers U–New Brunswick (NJ)
Sacred Heart U (CT)
The Sage Colls (NY)
Saginaw Valley State U (MI)
St. Ambrose U (IA)
St. Bonaventure U (NY)
St. Catherine U (MN)
Saint John's U (MN)
Saint Louis U (MO)
Saint Louis U–Madrid Campus (Spain)
Saint Martin's U (WA)
Saint Mary's Coll of California (CA)
St. Mary's Coll of Maryland (MD)
Saint Mary's U of Minnesota (MN)
Saint Michael's Coll (VT)
St. Norbert Coll (WI)
St. Olaf Coll (MN)
Salisbury U (MD)
Salve Regina U (RI)
Samford U (AL)
Sam Houston State U (TX)
San Diego State U (CA)
San Francisco State U (CA)
Santa Clara U (CA)
Sarah Lawrence Coll (NY)
Savannah Coll of Art and Design (GA)
Schreiner U (TX)
Scripps Coll (CA)
Seattle Pacific U (WA)
Seattle U (WA)
Seton Hill U (PA)
Sewanee: The U of the South (TN)
Shepherd U (WV)
Shorter U (GA)
Simon Fraser U (BC, Canada)
Simpson Coll (IA)
Skidmore Coll (NY)
Slippery Rock U of Pennsylvania (PA)
Smith Coll (MA)
Sonoma State U (CA)
Southeastern Oklahoma State U (OK)
Southeast Missouri State U (MO)
Southern Arkansas U–Magnolia (AR)
Southern Illinois U Carbondale (IL)
Southern Illinois U Edwardsville (IL)
Southern Methodist U (TX)
Southern Utah U (UT)
Southwest Baptist U (MO)
Southwestern Assemblies of God U (TX)
Southwestern Coll (KS)
Southwestern U (TX)
Spring Hill Coll (AL)
Stanford U (CA)
State U of New York at Fredonia (NY)
State U of New York at New Paltz (NY)
State U of New York at Oswego (NY)
State U of New York at Plattsburgh (NY)

State U of New York Coll at Geneseo (NY)
State U of New York Coll at Oneonta (NY)
State U of New York Coll at Potsdam (NY)
Stephen F. Austin State U (TX)
Stetson U (FL)
Stevenson U (MD)
Stony Brook U, State U of New York (NY)
Suffolk U (MA)
Susquehanna U (PA)
Sweet Briar Coll (VA)
Syracuse U (NY)
Tabor Coll (KS)
Tarleton State U (TX)
Tennessee Wesleyan U (TN)
Texas A&M U (TX)
Texas A&M U–Commerce (TX)
Texas A&M U–Corpus Christi (TX)
Texas A&M U–Kingsville (TX)
Texas Christian U (TX)
Texas Lutheran U (TX)
Texas State U (TX)
Texas Tech U (TX)
Texas Woman's U (TX)
Towson U (MD)
Transylvania U (KY)
Trevecca Nazarene U (TN)
Trinity U (TX)
Truman State U (MO)
Tufts U (MA)
Tulane U (LA)
Union U (TN)
U at Albany, State U of New York (NY)
U at Buffalo, the State U of New York (NY)
The U of Akron (OH)
The U of Alabama (AL)
The U of Alabama at Birmingham (AL)
The U of Arizona (AZ)
U of Arkansas (AR)
U of California, Irvine (CA)
U of California, Los Angeles (CA)
U of California, Riverside (CA)
U of California, San Diego (CA)
U of California, Santa Barbara (CA)
U of California, Santa Cruz (CA)
U of Central Arkansas (AR)
U of Central Florida (FL)
U of Central Missouri (MO)
U of Central Oklahoma (OK)
U of Cincinnati (OH)
U of Colorado Boulder (CO)
U of Colorado Denver (CO)
U of Dallas (TX)
U of Dayton (OH)
U of Denver (CO)
U of Evansville (IN)
The U of Findlay (OH)
U of Florida (FL)
U of Georgia (GA)
U of Guelph (ON, Canada)
U of Hawaii at Manoa (HI)
U of Houston (TX)
U of Idaho (ID)
U of Illinois at Chicago (IL)
U of Illinois at Springfield (IL)
U of Jamestown (ND)
The U of Kansas (KS)
U of Kentucky (KY)
U of King's Coll (NS, Canada)
U of La Verne (CA)
U of Louisville (KY)
U of Maine (ME)
U of Maine at Machias (ME)
U of Maryland, Baltimore County (MD)
U of Maryland, Coll Park (MD)
U of Massachusetts Amherst (MA)
U of Massachusetts Boston (MA)
U of Memphis (TN)
U of Miami (FL)
U of Michigan (MI)
U of Michigan–Flint (MI)
U of Minnesota, Duluth (MN)
U of Minnesota, Morris (MN)
U of Minnesota, Twin Cities Campus (MN)
U of Missouri (MO)
U of Missouri–St. Louis (MO)
U of Mobile (AL)
U of Montana (MT)
U of Montevallo (AL)

U of Mount Union (OH)
U of Nebraska at Kearney (NE)
U of Nebraska–Lincoln (NE)
U of Nevada, Las Vegas (NV)
U of Nevada, Reno (NV)
U of New Hampshire (NH)
U of New Mexico (NM)
U of New Orleans (LA)
U of North Alabama (AL)
U of North Carolina at Asheville (NC)
The U of North Carolina at Chapel Hill (NC)
The U of North Carolina at Charlotte (NC)
The U of North Carolina at Greensboro (NC)
The U of North Carolina at Pembroke (NC)
U of North Carolina School of the Arts (NC)
The U of North Carolina Wilmington (NC)
U of North Dakota (ND)
U of Northern Colorado (CO)
U of Northern Iowa (IA)
U of North Texas (TX)
U of Notre Dame (IN)
U of Oklahoma (OK)
U of Oregon (OR)
U of Pennsylvania (PA)
U of Pittsburgh (PA)
U of Puget Sound (WA)
U of Regina (SK, Canada)
U of Rhode Island (RI)
U of Richmond (VA)
U of Saint Mary (KS)
U of St. Thomas (TX)
U of San Diego (CA)
U of Saskatchewan (SK, Canada)
U of Science and Arts of Oklahoma (OK)
The U of Scranton (PA)
U of South Alabama (AL)
U of South Carolina (SC)
U of South Dakota (SD)
U of Southern California (CA)
U of Southern Indiana (IN)
U of Southern Maine (ME)
U of Southern Mississippi (MS)
The U of Tampa (FL)
The U of Tennessee (TN)
The U of Tennessee at Chattanooga (TN)
The U of Tennessee at Martin (TN)
The U of Texas at Austin (TX)
The U of Texas at El Paso (TX)
The U of Texas Rio Grande Valley (TX)
U of the Fraser Valley (BC, Canada)
U of the Incarnate Word (TX)
U of the Pacific (CA)
The U of Toledo (OH)
U of Tulsa (OK)
U of Utah (UT)
U of Vermont (VT)
U of Virginia (VA)
The U of Virginia's Coll at Wise (VA)
U of Washington (WA)
U of Waterloo (ON, Canada)
U of West Georgia (GA)
U of Wisconsin–Eau Claire (WI)
U of Wisconsin–La Crosse (WI)
U of Wisconsin–Madison (WI)
U of Wisconsin–Milwaukee (WI)
U of Wisconsin–Parkside (WI)
U of Wisconsin–River Falls (WI)
U of Wisconsin–Stevens Point (WI)
U of Wisconsin–Whitewater (WI)
U of Wyoming (WY)
Ursinus Coll (PA)
Utah State U (UT)
Utah Valley U (UT)
Valdosta State U (GA)
Valparaiso U (IN)
Vanderbilt U (TN)
Vanguard U of Southern California (CA)
Vassar Coll (NY)
Virginia Commonwealth U (VA)
Virginia Polytechnic Inst and State U (VA)
Virginia Wesleyan U (VA)
Wabash Coll (IN)
Wagner Coll (NY)

Wake Forest U (NC)
Waldorf U (IA)
Washington and Lee U (VA)
Washington Coll (MD)
Washington State U (WA)
Washington U in St. Louis (MO)
Wayland Baptist U (TX)
Wayne State Coll (NE)
Wayne State U (MI)
Weber State U (UT)
Webster U (MO)
Wellesley Coll (MA)
Wells Coll (NY)
Wesleyan U (CT)
West Chester U of Pennsylvania (PA)
Western Connecticut State U (CT)
Western Illinois U (IL)
Western Kentucky U (KY)
Western Oregon U (OR)
Western State Colorado U (CO)
Western Washington U (WA)
Westfield State U (MA)
Westminster Coll (PA)
Westminster Coll (UT)
Westmont Coll (CA)
West Texas A&M U (TX)
West Virginia U (WV)
West Virginia Wesleyan Coll (WV)
Whitman Coll (WA)
Whittier Coll (CA)
Whitworth U (WA)
Wichita State U (KS)
Wilkes U (PA)
Willamette U (OR)
William Jewell Coll (MO)
William Peace U (NC)
Williams Coll (MA)
William Woods U (MO)
Winona State U (MN)
Winthrop U (SC)
Wisconsin Lutheran Coll (WI)
Wittenberg U (OH)
Wofford Coll (SC)
Wright State U (OH)
Wright State U–Lake Campus (OH)
York Coll of Pennsylvania (PA)
Youngstown State U (OH)

DRAMATIC/THEATER ARTS AND STAGECRAFT RELATED
Adams State U (CO)
Aquinas Coll (MI)
Benedictine Coll (KS)
Brenau U (GA)
Brigham Young U (UT)
Catawba Coll (NC)
Charleston Southern U (SC)
Coastal Carolina U (SC)
Columbia Coll Chicago (IL)
DePaul U (IL)
Drake U (IA)
Fayetteville State U (NC)
Indiana U South Bend (IN)
Lee U (TN)
Lindenwood U (MO)
Marlboro Coll (VT)
Pepperdine U, Malibu (CA)
Saint Augustine's U (NC)
Seton Hill U (PA)
Southern Illinois U Carbondale (IL)
Southwestern Coll (KS)
Syracuse U (NY)
U of Michigan–Flint (MI)
U of Northern Colorado (CO)
U of Southern California (CA)
Webster U (MO)
Western Kentucky U (KY)
Western Michigan U (MI)
Wheaton Coll (MA)

DRAWING
Adams State U (CO)
Alberta Coll of Art & Design (AB, Canada)
American Acad of Art (IL)
Aquinas Coll (MI)
Bennington Coll (VT)
Biola U (CA)
Birmingham-Southern Coll (AL)
Bowling Green State U (OH)
Bradley U (IL)
Brigham Young U (UT)
Buffalo State Coll, State U of New York (NY)
California Coll of the Arts (CA)
California State U, Long Beach (CA)

Carson-Newman U (TN)
Coll of the Atlantic (ME)
Columbus State U (GA)
Concord U (WV)
Drake U (IA)
Ferris State U (MI)
Georgia State U (GA)
Inter American U of Puerto Rico, San Germán Campus (PR)
Laguna Coll of Art & Design (CA)
Lewis U (IL)
Lindenwood U (MO)
Marlboro Coll (VT)
Maryland Inst Coll of Art (MD)
Minneapolis Coll of Art and Design (MN)
Northern Michigan U (MI)
Oakland U (MI)
Portland State U (OR)
Pratt Inst (NY)
Providence Coll (RI)
Rutgers U–New Brunswick (NJ)
School of Visual Arts (NY)
Seton Hill U (PA)
Sonoma State U (CA)
State U of New York at Fredonia (NY)
U of Hartford (CT)
U of Michigan (MI)
U of New Haven (CT)
U of Regina (SK, Canada)
Washington U in St. Louis (MO)
West Virginia Wesleyan Coll (WV)

EARLY CHILDHOOD EDUCATION
Adams State U (CO)
Alabama State U (AL)
Alma Coll (MI)
Antioch U Midwest (OH)
Aquinas Coll (MI)
Arcadia U (PA)
Arizona State U at the Tempe campus (AZ)
Arkansas Tech U (AR)
Arlington Baptist U (TX)
Auburn U (AL)
Baldwin Wallace U (OH)
Ball State U (IN)
Barton Coll (NC)
Baylor U (TX)
Bay Path U (MA)
Becker Coll (MA)
Belmont U (TN)
Berry Coll (GA)
Bethel Coll (IN)
Bloomsburg U of Pennsylvania (PA)
Bluffton U (OH)
Bob Jones U (SC)
Boise State U (ID)
Boston U (MA)
Bradley U (IL)
Brandman U (CA)
Brewton-Parker Coll (GA)
Bridgewater State U (MA)
Brigham Young U (UT)
Brigham Young U–Idaho (ID)
Bucknell U (PA)
Butler U (IN)
California Baptist U (CA)
California State U, Dominguez Hills (CA)
California State U, Los Angeles (CA)
California State U, San Bernardino (CA)
California State U, San Marcos (CA)
California State U, Stanislaus (CA)
California U of Pennsylvania (PA)
Calvin Coll (MI)
Cameron U (OK)
Capital U (OH)
Cardinal Stritch U (WI)
Carlow U (PA)
Carroll U (WI)
Carson-Newman U (TN)
The Catholic U of America (DC)
Cazenovia Coll (NY)
Cedar Crest Coll (PA)
Cedarville U (OH)
Central Connecticut State U (CT)
Central Methodist U (MO)
Central Michigan U (MI)
Central State U (OH)
Chaminade U of Honolulu (HI)
Champlain Coll (VT)

Charleston Southern U (SC)
Chatham U (PA)
Chestnut Hill Coll (PA)
Christian Brothers U (TN)
City Coll of the City U of New York (NY)
Clarion U of Pennsylvania (PA)
Clark Atlanta U (GA)
Clemson U (SC)
Cleveland State U (OH)
Coastal Carolina U (SC)
Coker Coll (SC)
Coll of Central Florida (FL)
Coll of Charleston (SC)
Coll of Coastal Georgia (GA)
The Coll of New Jersey (NJ)
The Coll of Saint Rose (NY)
Coll of the Ozarks (MO)
Colorado State U (CO)
Columbia Coll (SC)
Columbus State U (GA)
Concordia Coll–New York (NY)
Concordia U Chicago (IL)
Concordia U, Nebraska (NE)
Concordia U, St. Paul (MN)
Curry Coll (MA)
Delaware State U (DE)
DePaul U (IL)
DeSales U (PA)
Dominican U (IL)
Duquesne U (PA)
East Central U (OK)
Eastern Michigan U (MI)
Eastern Nazarene Coll (MA)
Eastern New Mexico U (NM)
Eastern Oregon U (OR)
Eastern U (PA)
Eastern Washington U (WA)
East Stroudsburg U of Pennsylvania (PA)
Edgewood Coll (WI)
Elizabethtown Coll (PA)
Elms Coll (MA)
Elon U (NC)
Endicott Coll (MA)
Evangel U (MO)
Fayetteville State U (NC)
Fitchburg State U (MA)
Florida Ag and Mech U (FL)
Florida Atlantic U (FL)
Florida Gulf Coast U (FL)
Florida Intl U (FL)
Fort Lewis Coll (CO)
Framingham State U (MA)
Francis Marion U (SC)
Frostburg State U (MD)
Gannon U (PA)
Georgia Coll & State U (GA)
Georgia Gwinnett Coll (GA)
Georgia Southern U–Armstrong Campus (GA)
Gordon Coll (MA)
Gordon State Coll (GA)
Governors State U (IL)
Granite State Coll (NH)
Greensboro Coll (NC)
Grove City Coll (PA)
Hannibal-LaGrange U (MO)
Harding U (AR)
Hardin-Simmons U (TX)
Harris-Stowe State U (MO)
Hiram Coll (OH)
Hofstra U (NY)
Holy Family U (PA)
Hood Coll (MD)
Idaho State U (ID)
Illinois Coll (IL)
Illinois State U (IL)
Indiana U Bloomington (IN)
Indiana U Kokomo (IN)
Indiana U of Pennsylvania (PA)
Indiana U–Purdue U Indianapolis (IN)
Inter American U of Puerto Rico, San Germán Campus (PR)
Iona Coll (NY)
Iowa State U of Science and Technology (IA)
Judson U (IL)
Keene State Coll (NH)
Kennesaw State U (GA)
Kent State U (OH)
Kent State U at Salem (OH)
Kent State U at Tuscarawas (OH)
King's Coll (PA)
Kutztown U of Pennsylvania (PA)
LaGrange Coll (GA)

La Salle U (PA)
Lasell Coll (MA)
Lebanon Valley Coll (PA)
Lee U (TN)
Liberty U (VA)
Limestone Coll (SC)
Lindenwood U (MO)
Lock Haven U of Pennsylvania (PA)
Long Island U–LIU Brooklyn (NY)
Long Island U–LIU Post (NY)
Louisiana State U and A&M Coll (LA)
Loyola U Chicago (IL)
Lubbock Christian U (TX)
Lynn U (FL)
Madonna U (MI)
Malone U (OH)
Maranatha Baptist U (WI)
Marian U (WI)
Martin Luther Coll (MN)
Marywood U (PA)
McMurry U (TX)
McNeese State U (LA)
Merrimack Coll (MA)
Messiah Coll (PA)
Miami Dade Coll (FL)
Miami U (OH)
Michigan State U (MI)
Middle Tennessee State U (TN)
Millersville U of Pennsylvania (PA)
Millikin U (IL)
Minnesota State U Moorhead (MN)
Misericordia U (PA)
Missouri Baptist U (MO)
Missouri State U (MO)
Missouri Valley Coll (MO)
Missouri Western State U (MO)
Morehead State U (KY)
Morehouse Coll (GA)
Morris Coll (SC)
Mount Aloysius Coll (PA)
Mount St. Joseph U (OH)
Mount Saint Mary Coll (NY)
Mount Vernon Nazarene U (OH)
Murray State U (KY)
Muskingum U (OH)
Naropa U (CO)
National Louis U (IL)
National U (CA)
Newberry Coll (SC)
New Jersey City U (NJ)
Newman U (KS)
New Mexico State U (NM)
New York U (NY)
Northeastern State U (OK)
Northern Arizona U (AZ)
Northern Illinois U (IL)
North Greenville U (SC)
Northwest Christian U (OR)
Northwestern Oklahoma State U (OK)
Northwestern State U of Louisiana (LA)
Nyack Coll (NY)
Oakland City U (IN)
Ohio Christian U (OH)
Ohio Dominican U (OH)
Ohio Northern U (OH)
Ohio U (OH)
Ohio Wesleyan U (OH)
Oklahoma Baptist U (OK)
Oklahoma Christian U (OK)
Oklahoma City U (OK)
Olivet Nazarene U (IL)
Oral Roberts U (OK)
Ouachita Baptist U (AR)
Pine Manor Coll (MA)
Point U (GA)
Polk State Coll (FL)
Presbyterian Coll (SC)
Purdue U (IN)
Purdue U Northwest (IN)
Regent U (VA)
Rhode Island Coll (RI)
Ripon Coll (WI)
Rivier U (NH)
Roberts Wesleyan Coll (NY)
Rockford U (IL)
Roosevelt U (IL)
Rowan U (NJ)
St. Ambrose U (IA)
Saint Vincent Coll (PA)
Salisbury U (MD)
Salve Regina U (RI)
San Diego State U (CA)
San Francisco State U (CA)
Schreiner U (TX)

Shawnee State U (OH)
Shippensburg U of Pennsylvania (PA)
Silver Lake Coll of the Holy Family (WI)
Slippery Rock U of Pennsylvania (PA)
Southeastern Louisiana U (LA)
Southeastern U (FL)
Southern Arkansas U–Magnolia (AR)
Southern Illinois U Carbondale (IL)
Southern Illinois U Edwardsville (IL)
Southwest Baptist U (MO)
Southwestern Coll (KS)
Spelman Coll (GA)
Spring Hill Coll (AL)
State U of New York Coll at Geneseo (NY)
State U of New York Coll at Old Westbury (NY)
State U of New York Coll at Potsdam (NY)
Stevenson U (MD)
Stonehill Coll (MA)
Susquehanna U (PA)
Tennessee Technological U (TN)
Tennessee Wesleyan U (TN)
Texas Christian U (TX)
Thomas U (GA)
Towson U (MD)
Trevecca Nazarene U (TN)
Tufts U (MA)
The U of Akron (OH)
The U of Alabama at Birmingham (AL)
U of Arkansas (AR)
U of Central Florida (FL)
U of Central Oklahoma (OK)
U of Cincinnati (OH)
U of Colorado Colorado Springs (CO)
U of Dayton (OH)
U of Georgia (GA)
U of Guam (GU)
U of Hartford (CT)
U of Hawaii at Manoa (HI)
The U of Kansas (KS)
U of Kentucky (KY)
U of Maine at Farmington (ME)
U of Massachusetts Boston (MA)
U of Michigan–Dearborn (MI)
U of Michigan–Flint (MI)
U of Minnesota, Crookston (MN)
U of Missouri (MO)
U of Missouri–St. Louis (MO)
U of Mobile (AL)
U of Mount Union (OH)
U of Nevada, Las Vegas (NV)
U of New Mexico (NM)
The U of North Carolina at Chapel Hill (NC)
The U of North Carolina at Greensboro (NC)
U of North Dakota (ND)
U of Northern Colorado (CO)
U of North Florida (FL)
U of North Georgia (GA)
U of Oklahoma (OK)
U of Regina (SK, Canada)
U of Science and Arts of Oklahoma (OK)
The U of Scranton (PA)
U of South Alabama (AL)
U of South Carolina Aiken (SC)
U of Southern Indiana (IN)
The U of Tennessee at Chattanooga (TN)
U of the Virgin Islands (VI)
The U of Tulsa (OK)
U of Valley Forge (PA)
U of Vermont (VT)
U of Wisconsin–Milwaukee (WI)
U of Wisconsin–Parkside (WI)
U of Wisconsin–River Falls (WI)
U of Wisconsin–Stevens Point (WI)
U of Wisconsin–Stout (WI)
U of Wisconsin–Whitewater (WI)
Ursuline Coll (OH)
Valdosta State U (GA)
Vanderbilt U (TN)
Walsh U (OH)
Warner Pacific Coll (OR)
Wayland Baptist U (TX)
Wayne State Coll (NE)
Weber State U (UT)

Webster U (MO)
Welch Coll (TN)
Wells Coll (NY)
West Chester U of Pennsylvania (PA)
Western Kentucky U (KY)
Western Michigan U (MI)
Western Washington U (WA)
Wheaton Coll (MA)
Widener U (PA)
William Paterson U of New Jersey (NJ)
Wilmington U (DE)
Wisconsin Lutheran Coll (WI)
Worcester State U (MA)
Wright State U (OH)
Wright State U–Lake Campus (OH)
Xavier U of Louisiana (LA)
York Coll of Pennsylvania (PA)
Youngstown State U (OH)

EARTH SCIENCE EDUCATION
Albion Coll (MI)
Ball State U (IN)
Boise State U (ID)
Brigham Young U–Idaho (ID)
Calvin Coll (MI)
Central Michigan U (MI)
Florida Inst of Technology (FL)
Long Island U–LIU Post (NY)
Minnesota State U Moorhead (MN)
Pace U (NY)
Pace U, Pleasantville Campus (NY)
Queens Coll of the City U of New York (NY)
State U of New York Coll at Potsdam (NY)
Syracuse U (NY)
U of Maine at Farmington (ME)
Western Michigan U (MI)
Western Washington U (WA)
Winona State U (MN)

EAST ASIAN LANGUAGES
Arizona State U at the Tempe campus (AZ)
Austin Coll (TX)
Columbia U (NY)
Eckerd Coll (FL)
Indiana U Bloomington (IN)
Smith Coll (MA)
U of Georgia (GA)
The U of Kansas (KS)
U of Pennsylvania (PA)
U of Puget Sound (WA)
U of Southern California (CA)
The U of Texas at Austin (TX)
Washington and Lee U (VA)

EAST ASIAN LANGUAGES RELATED
Boston U (MA)
Dartmouth Coll (NH)
Northwestern U (IL)
U of Chicago (IL)
U of Florida (FL)
U of Minnesota, Twin Cities Campus (MN)
Washington U in St. Louis (MO)

ECOLOGY
Barry U (FL)
Beloit Coll (WI)
Bemidji State U (MN)
Bennington Coll (VT)
Brigham Young U–Idaho (ID)
Bryant U (RI)
California State U, Dominguez Hills (CA)
California State U, Long Beach (CA)
California State U, San Marcos (CA)
Christian Brothers U (TN)
Clark U (MA)
Coll of the Ozarks (MO)
Colorado State U (CO)
Columbia U (NY)
Concordia Coll–New York (NY)
Concordia U (QC, Canada)
Dartmouth Coll (NH)
Defiance Coll (OH)
The Evergreen State Coll (WA)
Fort Lewis Coll (CO)
Georgetown U (KY)
Greensboro Coll (NC)
Iowa State U of Science and Technology (IA)

Le Moyne Coll (NY)
Manchester U (IN)
Marlboro Coll (VT)
Medgar Evers Coll of the City U of New York (NY)
Molloy Coll (NY)
New Mexico State U (NM)
New York U (NY)
Northern Michigan U (MI)
Northern State U (SD)
Northwestern U (IL)
Oberlin Coll (OH)
Ohio U (OH)
Oklahoma State U (OK)
Olivet Nazarene U (IL)
Princeton U (NJ)
Rice U (TX)
Rutgers U–New Brunswick (NJ)
Salisbury U (MD)
San Diego State U (CA)
San Francisco State U (CA)
Seattle Pacific U (WA)
Siena Coll (NY)
Sierra Nevada Coll (NV)
Sonoma State U (CA)
State U of New York at Plattsburgh (NY)
Stony Brook U, State U of New York (NY)
Susquehanna U (PA)
Tufts U (MA)
Tulane U (LA)
Université de Sherbrooke (QC, Canada)
The U of Akron (OH)
U of California, Los Angeles (CA)
U of California, San Diego (CA)
U of California, Santa Barbara (CA)
U of California, Santa Cruz (CA)
U of Denver (CO)
U of Georgia (GA)
U of Guelph (ON, Canada)
U of Maine at Machias (ME)
U of Maryland, Coll Park (MD)
U of Maryland Eastern Shore (MD)
U of Minnesota, Twin Cities Campus (MN)
U of Northern Iowa (IA)
U of North Texas (TX)
U of Pittsburgh (PA)
U of Saskatchewan (SK, Canada)
U of Waterloo (ON, Canada)
Utah State U (UT)
Washington U in St. Louis (MO)

ECOLOGY AND EVOLUTIONARY BIOLOGY
Angelo State U (TX)
Bradley U (IL)
Case Western Reserve U (OH)
Colby Coll (ME)
The Colorado Coll (CO)
Minnesota State U Moorhead (MN)
Purdue U (IN)
The U of Arizona (AZ)
U of California, Irvine (CA)
U of California, San Diego (CA)
U of Colorado Boulder (CO)
U of Michigan (MI)
U of Pittsburgh (PA)
The U of Texas at Austin (TX)
Vanderbilt U (TN)

ECOLOGY, EVOLUTION, SYSTEMATICS AND POPULATION BIOLOGY RELATED
Brewton-Parker Coll (GA)
Hofstra U (NY)
Pitzer Coll (CA)
U of California, Davis (CA)
U of Colorado Boulder (CO)
U of Guelph (ON, Canada)
U of New Hampshire (NH)
U of Regina (SK, Canada)
U of Washington (WA)

E-COMMERCE
Delaware State U (DE)
Harrisburg U of Science and Technology (PA)
Lewis U (IL)
Limestone Coll (SC)
Maryville U of Saint Louis (MO)
Seattle U (WA)
Towson U (MD)
Trevecca Nazarene U (TN)
The U of Akron (OH)

U of La Verne (CA)
U of Pennsylvania (PA)
The U of Scranton (PA)
U of the Incarnate Word (TX)
The U of Toledo (OH)
U of Toronto (ON, Canada)
Washington State U (WA)
Western Michigan U (MI)
Winthrop U (SC)

ECONOMETRICS AND QUANTITATIVE ECONOMICS
Baldwin Wallace U (OH)
Bowdoin Coll (ME)
Bryant U (RI)
Bucknell U (PA)
Carnegie Mellon U (PA)
Colgate U (NY)
The Colorado Coll (CO)
Columbia U (NY)
Drexel U (PA)
Hampden-Sydney Coll (VA)
High Point U (NC)
Hofstra U (NY)
Ithaca Coll (NY)
Marquette U (WI)
Massachusetts Inst of Technology (MA)
Providence Coll (RI)
Southern Methodist U (TX)
State U of New York at Oswego (NY)
U of California, Irvine (CA)
U of California, Santa Barbara (CA)
U of Dayton (OH)
U of Guelph (ON, Canada)
U of Minnesota, Twin Cities Campus (MN)
U of Northern Iowa (IA)
U of Rhode Island (RI)
Wake Forest U (NC)
Weber State U (UT)
Western Kentucky U (KY)
Youngstown State U (OH)

ECONOMICS
Acadia U (NS, Canada)
Adams State U (CO)
Adelphi U (NY)
Agnes Scott Coll (GA)
Albion Coll (MI)
Albright Coll (PA)
Allegheny Coll (PA)
Alma Coll (MI)
American U (DC)
American U in Bulgaria (Bulgaria)
The American U in Cairo (Egypt)
American U of Beirut (Lebanon)
Amherst Coll (MA)
Andrews U (MI)
Appalachian State U (NC)
Aquinas Coll (MI)
Arizona State U at the Tempe campus (AZ)
Ashland U (OH)
Assumption Coll (MA)
Auburn U (AL)
Auburn U at Montgomery (AL)
Augsburg U (MN)
Augustana Coll (IL)
Augustana U (SD)
Austin Coll (TX)
Babson Coll (MA)
Baker U (KS)
Baldwin Wallace U (OH)
Ball State U (IN)
Bard Coll (NY)
Barnard Coll (NY)
Barry U (FL)
Baruch Coll of the City U of New York (NY)
Bates Coll (ME)
Baylor U (TX)
Bellarmine U (KY)
Beloit Coll (WI)
Bemidji State U (MN)
Benedictine Coll (KS)
Benedictine U (IL)
Bennington Coll (VT)
Berea Coll (KY)
Bethel Coll (IN)
Bethel U (MN)
Binghamton U, State U of New York (NY)
Birmingham-Southern Coll (AL)
Bloomsburg U of Pennsylvania (PA)
Bluffton U (OH)
Boise State U (ID)

Boston Coll (MA)
Boston U (MA)
Bowdoin Coll (ME)
Bowie State U (MD)
Bowling Green State U (OH)
Bradley U (IL)
Brandeis U (MA)
Brandon U (MB, Canada)
Bridgewater Coll (VA)
Bridgewater State U (MA)
Brigham Young U–Idaho (ID)
Brock U (ON, Canada)
Bryant U (RI)
Bryn Mawr Coll (PA)
Bucknell U (PA)
Buffalo State Coll, State U of New York (NY)
Butler U (IN)
Caldwell U (NJ)
California Inst of Technology (CA)
California Lutheran U (CA)
California Polytechnic State U, San Luis Obispo (CA)
California State Polytechnic U, Pomona (CA)
California State U, East Bay (CA)
California State U, Fullerton (CA)
California State U, Long Beach (CA)
California State U, Los Angeles (CA)
California State U, Northridge (CA)
California State U, Sacramento (CA)
California State U, San Bernardino (CA)
California State U, San Marcos (CA)
California State U, Stanislaus (CA)
Calvin Coll (MI)
Campbellsville U (KY)
Canisius Coll (NY)
Capital U (OH)
Carleton Coll (MN)
Carnegie Mellon U (PA)
Carthage Coll (WI)
Case Western Reserve U (OH)
Catawba Coll (NC)
The Catholic U of America (DC)
Centenary Coll of Louisiana (LA)
Central Connecticut State U (CT)
Central Michigan U (MI)
Central State U (OH)
Centre Coll (KY)
Charleston Southern U (SC)
Chowan U (NC)
Christopher Newport U (VA)
City Coll of the City U of New York (NY)
Claremont McKenna Coll (CA)
Clarion U of Pennsylvania (PA)
Clark U (MA)
Clemson U (SC)
Cleveland State U (OH)
Coastal Carolina U (SC)
Coe Coll (IA)
Colby Coll (ME)
Colgate U (NY)
Coll of Charleston (SC)
Coll of Mount Saint Vincent (NY)
The Coll of New Jersey (NJ)
The Coll of New Rochelle (NY)
Coll of Saint Benedict (MN)
Coll of Staten Island of the City U of New York (NY)
Coll of the Atlantic (ME)
Coll of the Holy Cross (MA)
The Coll of William and Mary (VA)
The Coll of Wooster (OH)
Colorado Christian U (CO)
The Colorado Coll (CO)
Colorado State U (CO)
Columbia U (NY)
Concordia U (QC, Canada)
Concordia U Irvine (CA)
Concordia U Wisconsin (WI)
Connecticut Coll (CT)
Converse Coll (SC)
Cornell Coll (IA)
Cornell U (NY)
Cornerstone U (MI)
Creighton U (NE)
Dartmouth Coll (NH)
Davidson Coll (NC)
Denison U (OH)
DePaul U (IL)
DePauw U (IN)

DEREE - The American Coll of Greece (Greece)
DeSales U (PA)
Dickinson Coll (PA)
Doane U (NE)
Dominican U (IL)
Drew U (NJ)
Drexel U (PA)
Drury U (MO)
Duquesne U (PA)
Earlham Coll (IN)
East Carolina U (NC)
Eastern Mennonite U (VA)
Eastern Michigan U (MI)
Eastern Oregon U (OR)
Eastern Washington U (WA)
East Stroudsburg U of Pennsylvania (PA)
East Tennessee State U (TN)
Eckerd Coll (FL)
Edgewood Coll (WI)
Elizabethtown Coll (PA)
Elmhurst Coll (IL)
Elon U (NC)
Emmanuel Coll (MA)
Emory & Henry Coll (VA)
Emory U (GA)
Emporia State U (KS)
Eugene Lang Coll of Liberal Arts (NY)
Fairfield U (CT)
Fairleigh Dickinson U, Florham Campus (NJ)
Fairleigh Dickinson U, Metropolitan Campus (NJ)
Fitchburg State U (MA)
Flagler Coll (FL)
Florida Ag and Mech U (FL)
Florida Atlantic U (FL)
Florida Gulf Coast U (FL)
Florida Intl U (FL)
Florida Southern Coll (FL)
Florida State U (FL)
Fordham U (NY)
Fort Lewis Coll (CO)
Framingham State U (MA)
Francis Marion U (SC)
Franklin & Marshall Coll (PA)
Franklin Coll (IN)
Frostburg State U (MD)
Furman U (SC)
George Mason U (VA)
Georgetown Coll (KY)
Georgetown U (DC)
The George Washington U (DC)
Georgia Southern U (GA)
Georgia Southern U–Armstrong Campus (GA)
Georgia State U (GA)
Gettysburg Coll (PA)
Gonzaga U (WA)
Gordon Coll (MA)
Governors State U (IL)
Graceland U (IA)
Grand Valley State U (MI)
Grinnell Coll (IA)
Grove City Coll (PA)
Guilford Coll (NC)
Gustavus Adolphus Coll (MN)
Hamilton Coll (NY)
Hamline U (MN)
Hampden-Sydney Coll (VA)
Hampshire Coll (MA)
Hampton U (VA)
Harding U (AR)
Hardin-Simmons U (TX)
Hartwick Coll (NY)
Harvard U (MA)
Haverford Coll (PA)
Heidelberg U (OH)
Hendrix Coll (AR)
Hillsdale Coll (MI)
Hiram Coll (OH)
Hobart and William Smith Colls (NY)
Hofstra U (NY)
Hollins U (VA)
Hood Coll (MD)
Hope Coll (MI)
Humboldt State U (CA)
Hunter Coll of the City U of New York (NY)
Idaho State U (ID)
Illinois Coll (IL)
Illinois State U (IL)
Illinois Wesleyan U (IL)
Indiana State U (IN)

Indiana U Bloomington (IN)
Indiana U Northwest (IN)
Indiana U of Pennsylvania (PA)
Indiana U–Purdue U Indianapolis (IN)
Indiana U South Bend (IN)
Indiana U Southeast (IN)
Indiana Wesleyan U (IN)
Inter American U of Puerto Rico, San Germán Campus (PR)
Iona Coll (NY)
Iowa State U of Science and Technology (IA)
Ithaca Coll (NY)
Jacksonville U (FL)
James Madison U (VA)
John Cabot U (Italy)
John Carroll U (OH)
John Jay Coll of Criminal Justice of the City U of New York (NY)
Johns Hopkins U (MD)
Johnson C. Smith U (NC)
Juniata Coll (PA)
Kalamazoo Coll (MI)
Kansas State U (KS)
Kean U (NJ)
Keene State Coll (NH)
Kent State U (OH)
Kenyon Coll (OH)
King's Coll (PA)
Knox Coll (IL)
Lafayette Coll (PA)
La Salle U (PA)
La Sierra U (CA)
Lawrence U (WI)
Lebanese American U (Lebanon)
Lebanon Valley Coll (PA)
Lehman Coll of the City U of New York (NY)
Le Moyne Coll (NY)
Lenoir-Rhyne U (NC)
Limestone Coll (SC)
Lincoln Memorial U (TN)
Lindenwood U (MO)
Linfield Coll (OR)
Long Island U–LIU Brooklyn (NY)
Long Island U–LIU Post (NY)
Longwood U (VA)
Loras Coll (IA)
Louisiana State U and A&M Coll (LA)
Loyola Marymount U (CA)
Loyola U New Orleans (LA)
Lubbock Christian U (TX)
Luther Coll (IA)
Lycoming Coll (PA)
Lynchburg Coll (VA)
Lyon Coll (AR)
Macalester Coll (MN)
Manchester U (IN)
Manhattan Coll (NY)
Manhattanville Coll (NY)
Marietta Coll (OH)
Marist Coll (NY)
Marlboro Coll (VT)
Marquette U (WI)
Marshall U (WV)
Mary Baldwin U (VA)
Marymount U (VA)
Maryville Coll (TN)
Massachusetts Inst of Technology (MA)
McDaniel Coll (MD)
McKendree U (IL)
Mercer U, Macon (GA)
Meredith Coll (NC)
Merrimack Coll (MA)
Messiah Coll (PA)
Metropolitan State U of Denver (CO)
Miami U (OH)
Michigan State U (MI)
Michigan Technological U (MI)
Middlebury Coll (VT)
Middle Tennessee State U (TN)
Millersville U of Pennsylvania (PA)
Milligan Coll (TN)
Millsaps Coll (MS)
Mills Coll (CA)
Minnesota State U Moorhead (MN)
Mississippi State U (MS)
Missouri State U (MO)
Missouri U of Science and Technology (MO)
Missouri Valley Coll (MO)
Missouri Western State U (MO)
Monmouth Coll (IL)

Montclair State U (NJ)
Moravian Coll (PA)
Morehouse Coll (GA)
Mount Holyoke Coll (MA)
Mount St. Mary's U (MD)
Muhlenberg Coll (PA)
Murray State U (KY)
Muskingum U (OH)
Nazareth Coll of Rochester (NY)
New Coll of Florida (FL)
New Jersey City U (NJ)
New Mexico State U (NM)
New York U (NY)
Niagara U (NY)
Nichols Coll (MA)
North Central Coll (IL)
North Dakota State U (ND)
Northeastern U (MA)
Northern Illinois U (IL)
Northern Michigan U (MI)
Northern State U (SD)
Northwestern Coll (IA)
Northwestern U (IL)
Northwest Missouri State U (MO)
Oakland U (MI)
Oberlin Coll (OH)
Occidental Coll (CA)
Oglethorpe U (GA)
Ohio Dominican U (OH)
The Ohio State U (OH)
Ohio U (OH)
Ohio Wesleyan U (OH)
Oklahoma City U (OK)
Oklahoma State U (OK)
Old Dominion U (VA)
Olivet Nazarene U (IL)
Oregon State U (OR)
Otterbein U (OH)
Our Lady of the Lake U (TX)
Pace U (NY)
Pace U, Pleasantville Campus (NY)
Pacific Lutheran U (WA)
Penn State Abington (PA)
Penn State Altoona (PA)
Penn State Beaver (PA)
Penn State Berks (PA)
Penn State Brandywine (PA)
Penn State DuBois (PA)
Penn State Erie, The Behrend Coll (PA)
Penn State Fayette, The Eberly Campus (PA)
Penn State Greater Allegheny (PA)
Penn State Hazleton (PA)
Penn State Lehigh Valley (PA)
Penn State Mont Alto (PA)
Penn State New Kensington (PA)
Penn State Schuylkill (PA)
Penn State Shenango (PA)
Penn State U Park (PA)
Penn State Wilkes-Barre (PA)
Penn State Worthington Scranton (PA)
Penn State York (PA)
Pepperdine U, Malibu (CA)
Pfeiffer U (NC)
Pittsburg State U (KS)
Pitzer Coll (CA)
Point Park U (PA)
Pomona Coll (CA)
Portland State U (OR)
Princeton U (NJ)
Principia Coll (IL)
Providence Coll (RI)
Purchase Coll, State U of New York (NY)
Purdue U (IN)
Queens Coll of the City U of New York (NY)
Quinnipiac U (CT)
Radford U (VA)
Ramapo Coll of New Jersey (NJ)
Randolph Coll (VA)
Randolph-Macon Coll (VA)
Reed Coll (OR)
Regis U (CO)
Rensselaer Polytechnic Inst (NY)
Rhode Island Coll (RI)
Rhodes Coll (TN)
Rice U (TX)
Rider U (NJ)
Ripon Coll (WI)
Roanoke Coll (VA)
Robert Morris U (PA)
Rochester Inst of Technology (NY)
Rockford U (IL)
Rockhurst U (MO)

Roger Williams U (RI)
Rollins Coll (FL)
Roosevelt U (IL)
Rose-Hulman Inst of Technology (IN)
Rowan U (NJ)
Rutgers U–Camden (NJ)
Rutgers U–Newark (NJ)
Rutgers U–New Brunswick (NJ)
Sacred Heart U (CT)
Saginaw Valley State U (MI)
St. Ambrose U (IA)
Saint Anselm Coll (NH)
St. Catherine U (MN)
Saint Francis U (PA)
St. John Fisher Coll (NY)
Saint John's U (MN)
St. John's U (NY)
Saint Joseph's U (PA)
St. Lawrence U (NY)
Saint Leo U (FL)
Saint Louis U–Madrid Campus (Spain)
Saint Mary's Coll of California (CA)
St. Mary's Coll of Maryland (MD)
St. Mary's U (TX)
Saint Michael's Coll (VT)
St. Norbert Coll (WI)
St. Olaf Coll (MN)
Saint Peter's U (NJ)
St. Thomas U (FL)
St. Thomas U (NB, Canada)
Saint Vincent Coll (PA)
Salisbury U (MD)
Salve Regina U (RI)
San Diego State U (CA)
San Francisco State U (CA)
Santa Clara U (CA)
Sarah Lawrence Coll (NY)
Scripps Coll (CA)
Seattle Pacific U (WA)
Seattle U (WA)
Seton Hill U (PA)
Sewanee: The U of the South (TN)
Shepherd U (WV)
Shippensburg U of Pennsylvania (PA)
Shorter U (GA)
Siena Coll (NY)
Simmons Coll (MA)
Simon Fraser U (BC, Canada)
Simpson Coll (IA)
Skidmore Coll (NY)
Smith Coll (MA)
Sonoma State U (CA)
Southeast Missouri State U (MO)
Southern Illinois U Carbondale (IL)
Southern Illinois U Edwardsville (IL)
Southern Methodist U (TX)
Southern Utah U (UT)
Southwestern U (TX)
Spelman Coll (GA)
Stanford U (CA)
State U of New York at Fredonia (NY)
State U of New York at New Paltz (NY)
State U of New York at Oswego (NY)
State U of New York at Plattsburgh (NY)
State U of New York Coll at Cortland (NY)
State U of New York Coll at Geneseo (NY)
State U of New York Coll at Oneonta (NY)
State U of New York Coll at Potsdam (NY)
Stephen F. Austin State U (TX)
Stetson U (FL)
Stockton U (NJ)
Stonehill Coll (MA)
Stony Brook U, State U of New York (NY)
Suffolk U (MA)
Susquehanna U (PA)
Sweet Briar Coll (VA)
Syracuse U (NY)
Tarleton State U (TX)
Temple U (PA)
Tennessee Technological U (TN)
Texas A&M U (TX)
Texas A&M U–Central Texas (TX)
Texas A&M U–Corpus Christi (TX)
Texas Christian U (TX)

Texas Lutheran U (TX)
Texas State U (TX)
Texas Tech U (TX)
Towson U (MD)
Transylvania U (KY)
Trent U (ON, Canada)
Trinity U (TX)
Troy U (AL)
Truman State U (MO)
Tufts U (MA)
Tulane U (LA)
Union Coll (NY)
Union U (TN)
United States Military Acad (NY)
U at Albany, State U of New York (NY)
U at Buffalo, the State U of New York (NY)
The U of Akron (OH)
U of Alaska Fairbanks (AK)
The U of Arizona (AZ)
U of Arkansas (AR)
U of California, Davis (CA)
U of California, Irvine (CA)
U of California, Los Angeles (CA)
U of California, Riverside (CA)
U of California, San Diego (CA)
U of California, Santa Barbara (CA)
U of California, Santa Cruz (CA)
U of Central Arkansas (AR)
U of Central Florida (FL)
U of Central Missouri (MO)
U of Chicago (IL)
U of Cincinnati (OH)
U of Colorado Boulder (CO)
U of Colorado Colorado Springs (CO)
U of Colorado Denver (CO)
U of Dallas (TX)
U of Dayton (OH)
U of Denver (CO)
U of Evansville (IN)
The U of Findlay (OH)
U of Florida (FL)
U of Georgia (GA)
U of Guelph (ON, Canada)
U of Hartford (CT)
U of Hawaii at Manoa (HI)
U of Houston (TX)
U of Idaho (ID)
U of Illinois at Chicago (IL)
U of Illinois at Springfield (IL)
The U of Kansas (KS)
U of Kentucky (KY)
U of King's Coll (NS, Canada)
U of La Verne (CA)
U of Louisville (KY)
U of Maine (ME)
U of Maryland, Baltimore County (MD)
U of Maryland, Coll Park (MD)
U of Mary Washington (VA)
U of Massachusetts Amherst (MA)
U of Massachusetts Boston (MA)
U of Massachusetts Dartmouth (MA)
U of Massachusetts Lowell (MA)
U of Memphis (TN)
U of Miami (FL)
U of Michigan (MI)
U of Michigan–Dearborn (MI)
U of Michigan–Flint (MI)
U of Minnesota, Duluth (MN)
U of Minnesota, Morris (MN)
U of Minnesota, Twin Cities Campus (MN)
U of Missouri (MO)
U of Missouri–St. Louis (MO)
U of Montana (MT)
U of Mount Union (OH)
U of Nebraska at Kearney (NE)
U of Nebraska–Lincoln (NE)
U of Nevada, Las Vegas (NV)
U of New Hampshire (NH)
U of New Haven (CT)
U of New Mexico (NM)
U of North Carolina at Asheville (NC)
The U of North Carolina at Chapel Hill (NC)
The U of North Carolina at Greensboro (NC)
The U of North Carolina Wilmington (NC)
U of North Dakota (ND)
U of Northern Colorado (CO)
U of Northern Iowa (IA)

U of North Florida (FL)
U of North Texas (TX)
U of Notre Dame (IN)
U of Oklahoma (OK)
U of Oregon (OR)
U of Pennsylvania (PA)
U of Pittsburgh (PA)
U of Pittsburgh at Bradford (PA)
U of Puget Sound (WA)
U of Regina (SK, Canada)
U of Rhode Island (RI)
U of Richmond (VA)
U of Rochester (NY)
U of St. Thomas (MN)
U of St. Thomas (TX)
U of San Diego (CA)
U of San Francisco (CA)
U of Saskatchewan (SK, Canada)
U of Science and Arts of Oklahoma (OK)
The U of Scranton (PA)
U of South Carolina (SC)
U of South Dakota (SD)
U of Southern California (CA)
U of Southern Indiana (IN)
U of Southern Maine (ME)
U of South Florida, St. Petersburg (FL)
The U of Tampa (FL)
The U of Tennessee (TN)
The U of Tennessee at Chattanooga (TN)
The U of Tennessee at Martin (TN)
The U of Texas at Austin (TX)
The U of Texas at Dallas (TX)
The U of Texas at El Paso (TX)
The U of Texas Rio Grande Valley (TX)
U of the Fraser Valley (BC, Canada)
U of the Pacific (CA)
The U of Toledo (OH)
U of Toronto (ON, Canada)
The U of Tulsa (OK)
U of Utah (UT)
U of Vermont (VT)
U of Virginia (VA)
The U of Virginia's Coll at Wise (VA)
U of Washington (WA)
U of Waterloo (ON, Canada)
U of West Georgia (GA)
U of Wisconsin–Eau Claire (WI)
U of Wisconsin–La Crosse (WI)
U of Wisconsin–Madison (WI)
U of Wisconsin–Milwaukee (WI)
U of Wisconsin–Parkside (WI)
U of Wisconsin–Platteville (WI)
U of Wisconsin–River Falls (WI)
U of Wisconsin–Stevens Point (WI)
U of Wisconsin–Superior (WI)
U of Wisconsin–Whitewater (WI)
Utah State U (UT)
Utah Valley U (UT)
Utica Coll (NY)
Valparaiso U (IN)
Vanderbilt U (TN)
Vassar Coll (NY)
Villanova U (PA)
Virginia Military Inst (VA)
Virginia Polytechnic Inst and State U (VA)
Wabash Coll (IN)
Wagner Coll (NY)
Wake Forest U (NC)
Wartburg Coll (IA)
Washington & Jefferson Coll (PA)
Washington and Lee U (VA)
Washington Coll (MD)
Washington State U (WA)
Washington State U–Global Campus (WA)
Washington U in St. Louis (MO)
Wayne State U (MI)
Weber State U (UT)
Webster U (MO)
Wellesley Coll (MA)
Wells Coll (NY)
Wesleyan U (CT)
Western Connecticut State U (CT)
Western Illinois U (IL)
Western Kentucky U (KY)
Western Michigan U (MI)
Western New England U (MA)
Western Oregon U (OR)
Western State Colorado U (CO)
Western Washington U (WA)

Westfield State U (MA)
Westminster Coll (UT)
Westmont Coll (CA)
West Virginia State U (WV)
West Virginia U (WV)
West Virginia Wesleyan Coll (WV)
Wheaton Coll (IL)
Wheaton Coll (MA)
Whitman Coll (WA)
Whittier Coll (CA)
Whitworth U (WA)
Wichita State U (KS)
Widener U (PA)
Willamette U (OR)
William Jewell Coll (MO)
William Paterson U of New Jersey (NJ)
Williams Coll (MA)
Winona State U (MN)
Wittenberg U (OH)
Wofford Coll (SC)
Worcester Polytechnic Inst (MA)
Worcester State U (MA)
Wright State U (OH)
Wright State U–Lake Campus (OH)
York Coll of Pennsylvania (PA)
Youngstown State U (OH)

ECONOMICS RELATED
American Intl Coll (MA)
Augsburg U (MN)
Centre Coll (KY)
Colorado Christian U (CO)
The Colorado Coll (CO)
Emory & Henry Coll (VA)
Florida Southern Coll (FL)
Lindenwood U (MO)
Marlboro Coll (VT)
Muhlenberg Coll (PA)
Regis U (CO)
U of Maine (ME)
U of Minnesota, Duluth (MN)
U of Regina (SK, Canada)
U of Richmond (VA)
U of San Francisco (CA)
U of Wisconsin–Whitewater (WI)
Valparaiso U (IN)
Washington & Jefferson Coll (PA)
Wayne State U (MI)
Western Washington U (WA)
Westminster Coll (PA)
Wittenberg U (OH)

EDUCATION
Acadia U (NS, Canada)
Alma Coll (MI)
Alverno Coll (WI)
Andrews U (MI)
Arcadia U (PA)
Arlington Baptist U (TX)
Ashland U (OH)
Augsburg U (MN)
Avila U (MO)
The Baptist Coll of Florida (FL)
Barnard Coll (NY)
Barry U (FL)
Baylor U (TX)
Bay Path U (PA)
Beloit Coll (WI)
Bemidji State U (MN)
Bennington Coll (VT)
Berea Coll (KY)
Bethany Lutheran Coll (MN)
Bethel Coll (IN)
Biola U (CA)
Birmingham-Southern Coll (AL)
Bluefield Coll (VA)
Bowdoin Coll (ME)
Bowie State U (MD)
Bowling Green State U (OH)
Bowling Green State U–Firelands Coll (OH)
Bradley U (IL)
Brandeis U (MA)
Brandon U (MB, Canada)
Brenau U (GA)
Brewton-Parker Coll (GA)
Brock U (ON, Canada)
Bucknell U (PA)
Canisius Coll (NY)
Carroll U (WI)
Carson-Newman U (TN)
The Catholic U of America (DC)
Cedar Crest Coll (PA)
Central Methodist U (MO)
Chapman U (CA)

Chipola Coll (FL)
Chowan U (NC)
Christian Brothers U (TN)
City Coll of the City U of New York (NY)
Clark Atlanta U (GA)
Clark U (MA)
Coe Coll (IA)
Coker Coll (SC)
Colby Coll (ME)
Colgate U (NY)
Coll of Mount Saint Vincent (NY)
The Coll of New Rochelle (NY)
Coll of Saint Mary (NE)
Coll of the Atlantic (ME)
The Colorado Coll (CO)
Columbia Coll (SC)
Columbia U (NY)
Concordia Coll–New York (NY)
Concordia U (QC, Canada)
Concordia U Chicago (IL)
Concordia U of Edmonton (AB, Canada)
Concordia U, St. Paul (MN)
Concordia U Wisconsin (WI)
Concord U (WV)
Converse Coll (SC)
Corban U (OR)
Curry Coll (MA)
Defiance Coll (OH)
Dominican Coll (NY)
Duquesne U (PA)
Eastern Nazarene Coll (MA)
Eastern Washington U (WA)
East Texas Baptist U (TX)
Elmhurst Coll (IL)
Elms Coll (MA)
Elon U (NC)
Emory U (GA)
The Evergreen State Coll (WA)
Felician U (NJ)
Fitchburg State U (MA)
Fordham U (NY)
Franklin Pierce U (NH)
Furman U (SC)
Gettysburg Coll (PA)
Goshen Coll (IN)
Graceland U (IA)
Greensboro Coll (NC)
Guilford Coll (NC)
Gustavus Adolphus Coll (MN)
Gwynedd Mercy U (PA)
Hampshire Coll (MA)
Hampton U (VA)
Hannibal-LaGrange U (MO)
Harris-Stowe State U (MO)
Haverford Coll (PA)
Heidelberg U (OH)
Hiram Coll (OH)
Humboldt State U (CA)
Huston-Tillotson U (TX)
Illinois Coll (IL)
Illinois Wesleyan U (IL)
Indiana Wesleyan U (IN)
Inter American U of Puerto Rico, Barranquitas Campus (PR)
Inter American U of Puerto Rico, San Germán Campus (PR)
Iowa State U of Science and Technology (IA)
Jacksonville U (FL)
John Carroll U (OH)
Juniata Coll (PA)
Kent State U (OH)
Knox Coll (IL)
Langston U (OK)
Lebanese American U (Lebanon)
Lesley U (MA)
Liberty U (VA)
Limestone Coll (SC)
Lincoln Memorial U (TN)
Lindenwood U (MO)
Lindsey Wilson Coll (KY)
Lipscomb U (TN)
Lycoming Coll (PA)
Macalester Coll (MN)
Manchester U (IN)
Manhattan Coll (NY)
Manhattanville Coll (NY)
Mansfield U of Pennsylvania (PA)
Marian U (IN)
Marietta Coll (OH)
Maryville Coll (TN)
Massachusetts Coll of Liberal Arts (MA)
The Master's U (CA)
McPherson Coll (KS)

Mercyhurst U (PA)
Merrimack Coll (MA)
Miami Dade Coll (FL)
Michigan State U (MI)
Millsaps Coll (MS)
Missouri Baptist U (MO)
Missouri Valley Coll (MO)
Mount Marty Coll (SD)
Mount Mary U (WI)
Mount St. Joseph U (OH)
Mount Saint Mary's U (CA)
Mount Vernon Nazarene U (OH)
Muskingum U (OH)
Nazareth Coll of Rochester (NY)
Neumann U (PA)
Newman U (KS)
Niagara U (NY)
North Carolina State U (NC)
North Carolina Wesleyan Coll (NC)
North Central Coll (IL)
Northeastern U (MA)
Northern Illinois U (IL)
Northwestern U (IL)
Northwest U (WA)
Nova Southeastern U (FL)
Ohio Christian U (OH)
Ohio Dominican U (OH)
Ohio Northern U (OH)
The Ohio State U (OH)
Ohio Wesleyan U (OH)
Oklahoma Baptist U (OK)
Oklahoma City U (OK)
Oregon State U (OR)
Otterbein U (OH)
Pacific Lutheran U (WA)
Pfeiffer U (NC)
Piedmont Coll (GA)
Purdue U Northwest (IN)
Quinnipiac U (CT)
Redeemer U Coll (ON, Canada)
Regent U (VA)
Regis U (CO)
Rhodes Coll (TN)
Ripon Coll (WI)
Rivier U (NH)
Rockford U (IL)
Roger Williams U (RI)
Rosemont Coll (PA)
Rowan U (NJ)
Sacred Heart U (CT)
Saginaw Valley State U (MI)
St. Ambrose U (IA)
St. Catherine U (MN)
Saint Francis U (PA)
Saint Louis U (MO)
Saint Martin's U (WA)
Saint Michael's Coll (VT)
St. Thomas Aquinas Coll (NY)
St. Thomas U (NB, Canada)
Schreiner U (TX)
Seattle Pacific U (WA)
Shawnee State U (OH)
Simmons Coll (MA)
Simon Fraser U (BC, Canada)
Simpson Coll (IA)
Skidmore Coll (NY)
Smith Coll (MA)
Southeastern U (FL)
Southern Methodist U (TX)
Southwestern Assemblies of God U (TX)
Southwestern U (TX)
State U of New York at Fredonia (NY)
State U of New York at Oswego (NY)
State U of New York at Plattsburgh (NY)
State U of New York Coll at Geneseo (NY)
State U of New York Coll at Oneonta (NY)
State U of New York Empire State Coll (NY)
Stetson U (FL)
Stonehill Coll (MA)
Syracuse U (NY)
Tabor Coll (KS)
Taylor U (IN)
Tennessee Technological U (TN)
Tennessee Wesleyan U (TN)
Texas Lutheran U (TX)
Tiffin U (OH)
Trent U (ON, Canada)
Trine U (IN)
Trinity Christian Coll (IL)
Tufts U (MA)

Union U (TN)
Université de Sherbrooke (QC, Canada)
Université Sainte-Anne (NS, Canada)
U of Arkansas (AR)
U of California, Irvine (CA)
U of Central Missouri (MO)
U of Charleston (WV)
U of Colorado Denver (CO)
U of Dallas (TX)
U of Hawaii at Manoa (HI)
U of Maine at Machias (ME)
U of Maryland Eastern Shore (MD)
U of Massachusetts Amherst (MA)
U of Massachusetts Boston (MA)
U of Miami (FL)
U of Michigan–Dearborn (MI)
U of Michigan–Flint (MI)
U of Minnesota, Duluth (MN)
U of Missouri (MO)
U of Missouri–St. Louis (MO)
U of Montana (MT)
U of Nevada, Las Vegas (NV)
U of North Texas (TX)
U of Oregon (OR)
U of Pittsburgh at Greensburg (PA)
U of Regina (SK, Canada)
U of Saint Francis (IN)
U of Saint Mary (KS)
U of St. Thomas (TX)
U of San Francisco (CA)
U of Saskatchewan (SK, Canada)
U of South Dakota (SD)
The U of Texas at San Antonio (TX)
U of the Pacific (CA)
U of Toronto (ON, Canada)
The U of Tulsa (OK)
U of Utah (UT)
U of Vermont (VT)
U of Washington, Bothell (WA)
U of Washington, Tacoma (WA)
U of Wisconsin–Milwaukee (WI)
U of Wisconsin–Platteville (WI)
Upper Iowa U (IA)
Ursinus Coll (PA)
Vanderbilt U (TN)
Vanguard U of Southern California (CA)
Vassar Coll (NY)
Wagner Coll (NY)
Walsh U (OH)
Washington & Jefferson Coll (PA)
Washington State U (WA)
Washington U in St. Louis (MO)
Webster U (MO)
Welch Coll (TN)
Wells Coll (NY)
Westminster Coll (PA)
Westmont Coll (CA)
West Texas A&M U (TX)
West Virginia Wesleyan Coll (WV)
Whitworth U (WA)
Wilkes U (PA)
William Peace U (NC)
William Woods U (MO)
Winona State U (MN)
Wisconsin Lutheran Coll (WI)
Wittenberg U (OH)
Xavier U of Louisiana (LA)
Youngstown State U (OH)

EDUCATIONAL ADMINISTRATION AND SUPERVISION RELATED
Canisius Coll (NY)

EDUCATIONAL ASSESSMENT, EVALUATION, AND RESEARCH RELATED
Blackburn Coll (IL)
Penn State Altoona (PA)
Penn State Berks (PA)
Penn State U Park (PA)

EDUCATIONAL, INSTRUCTIONAL, AND CURRICULUM SUPERVISION
Canisius Coll (NY)
Millikin U (IL)
Sam Houston State U (TX)

EDUCATIONAL/ INSTRUCTIONAL TECHNOLOGY
Academy of Art U (CA)
Bowling Green State U (OH)
Bridgewater State U (MA)
Canisius Coll (NY)

Eastern Washington U (WA)
Inter American U of Puerto Rico, Barranquitas Campus (PR)
Iowa State U of Science and Technology (IA)
Jackson State U (MS)
LeTourneau U (TX)
Rhode Island Coll (RI)
Sam Houston State U (TX)
U of Michigan–Dearborn (MI)
Wayne State U (MI)
Western Oregon U (OR)
Widener U (PA)
Wilmington U (DE)

EDUCATIONAL LEADERSHIP AND ADMINISTRATION
Avila U (MO)
Bradley U (IL)
Canisius Coll (NY)
Eastern Washington U (WA)
Sam Houston State U (TX)
U of Minnesota, Crookston (MN)
U of San Francisco (CA)
The U of Texas at Austin (TX)
Welch Coll (TN)

EDUCATIONAL PSYCHOLOGY
Mississippi State U (MS)
Saint Vincent Coll (PA)
U of Pittsburgh (PA)
The U of Texas at Austin (TX)

EDUCATIONAL STATISTICS AND RESEARCH METHODS
Bucknell U (PA)

EDUCATION (MULTIPLE LEVELS)
Adams State U (CO)
Anderson U (SC)
Arcadia U (PA)
Assumption Coll (MA)
Augustana U (SD)
Austin Peay State U (TN)
Averett U (VA)
Biola U (CA)
Birmingham-Southern Coll (AL)
Bowling Green State U (OH)
Canisius Coll (NY)
Central State U (OH)
Coll of Charleston (SC)
Coll of Coastal Georgia (GA)
Coll of Saint Elizabeth (NJ)
Coll of Saint Mary (NE)
The Coll of St. Scholastica (MN)
Columbia U (NY)
Concordia U Chicago (IL)
Concordia U, Nebraska (NE)
Concordia U Wisconsin (WI)
DePaul U (IL)
Dominican U (IL)
Eastern Nazarene Coll (MA)
Eastern Washington U (WA)
Emory & Henry Coll (VA)
Felician U (NJ)
Florida Southern Coll (FL)
Frostburg State U (MD)
Gannon U (PA)
Geneva Coll (PA)
Gwynedd Mercy U (PA)
Hamline U (MN)
Harding U (AR)
Hofstra U (NY)
Huston-Tillotson U (TX)
Illinois Coll (IL)
Indiana Wesleyan U (IN)
Ithaca Coll (NY)
John Carroll U (OH)
Lindenwood U (MO)
Manchester U (IN)
Manhattan Coll (NY)
Merrimack Coll (MA)
Middle Tennessee State U (TN)
Missouri Baptist U (MO)
Molloy Coll (NY)
Mount Mary U (WI)
Mount Saint Mary Coll (NY)
Niagara U (NY)
North American U (TX)
Northland Coll (WI)
Northwestern Coll (IA)
Nyack Coll (NY)
Ohio Northern U (OH)
Ohio Wesleyan U (OH)
Piedmont Coll (GA)
Redeemer U Coll (ON, Canada)
Saint Augustine's U (NC)

Saint Mary-of-the-Woods Coll (IN)
Samford U (AL)
Shawnee State U (OH)
Slippery Rock U of Pennsylvania (PA)
Spelman Coll (GA)
Stockton U (NJ)
Tennessee Technological U (TN)
Tennessee Wesleyan U (TN)
Texas A&M U–Central Texas (TX)
Texas Lutheran U (TX)
Troy U (AL)
U of Central Florida (FL)
U of Louisville (KY)
U of Maine at Fort Kent (ME)
U of Memphis (TN)
U of Michigan–Flint (MI)
U of Minnesota, Duluth (MN)
U of Nebraska–Lincoln (NE)
U of North Alabama (AL)
U of Providence (MT)
U of Saskatchewan (SK, Canada)
U of South Florida, St. Petersburg (FL)
The U of Tennessee at Martin (TN)
The U of Toledo (OH)
The U of West Alabama (AL)
Utah State U (UT)
Virginia Wesleyan U (VA)
Wake Forest U (NC)
Washington U in St. Louis (MO)
Wayland Baptist U (TX)
Western Kentucky U (KY)
West Virginia Wesleyan Coll (WV)
William Jewell Coll (MO)
Wisconsin Lutheran Coll (WI)

EDUCATION RELATED

Arcadia U (PA)
Arizona State U at the Polytechnic campus (AZ)
Arizona State U at the Tempe campus (AZ)
Arizona State U at the West campus (AZ)
Becker Coll (MA)
Blackburn Coll (IL)
Bob Jones U (SC)
Bowling Green State U (OH)
Brigham Young U (UT)
California State Polytechnic U, Pomona (CA)
Central State U (OH)
Colorado Christian U (CO)
Concordia U, St. Paul (MN)
Delaware State U (DE)
DePaul U (IL)
Eastern Oregon U (OR)
Edgewood Coll (WI)
Graceland U (IA)
Indiana U Bloomington (IN)
Jackson State U (MS)
Lee U (TN)
Lindsey Wilson Coll (KY)
Louisiana Coll (LA)
Mercer U, Macon (GA)
Mount Holyoke Coll (MA)
Northwest Missouri State U (MO)
Northwest Nazarene U (ID)
Ohio Northern U (OH)
Piedmont Coll (GA)
Point Park U (PA)
Rowan U (NJ)
Saginaw Valley State U (MI)
Saint Mary-of-the-Woods Coll (IN)
Saint Mary's U of Minnesota (MN)
Shaw U (NC)
Southern Adventist U (TN)
State U of New York at New Paltz (NY)
Towson U (MD)
Union Coll (NE)
U of Maine at Presque Isle (ME)
U of Miami (FL)
U of Minnesota, Duluth (MN)
U of Minnesota, Twin Cities Campus (MN)
U of Nevada, Reno (NV)
U of Northern Iowa (IA)
U of Puerto Rico–Humacao (PR)
U of South Alabama (AL)
U of Washington (WA)
U of Waterloo (ON, Canada)
Vanderbilt U (TN)

EDUCATION (SPECIFIC LEVELS AND METHODS) RELATED

Appalachian State U (NC)
Brigham Young U (UT)
Cairn U (PA)
Concordia Coll–New York (NY)
Delaware State U (DE)
Eastern Nazarene Coll (MA)
Emory & Henry Coll (VA)
Immaculata U (PA)
Inter American U of Puerto Rico, Metropolitan Campus (PR)
Inter American U of Puerto Rico, San Germán Campus (PR)
Lenoir-Rhyne U (NC)
Lynchburg Coll (VA)
Rowan U (NJ)
Washington U in St. Louis (MO)
Western Washington U (WA)

EDUCATION (SPECIFIC SUBJECT AREAS) RELATED

Anderson U (SC)
Appalachian State U (NC)
Augsburg U (MN)
Averett U (VA)
Avila U (MO)
Ball State U (IN)
Baylor U (TX)
Bowling Green State U (OH)
Brigham Young U (UT)
Cairn U (PA)
Eastern Michigan U (MI)
Eastern Nazarene Coll (MA)
Edgewood Coll (WI)
Florida Inst of Technology (FL)
Florida State U (FL)
Graceland U (IA)
Indiana U Bloomington (IN)
Madonna U (MI)
Marywood U (PA)
Minot State U (ND)
Missouri State U (MO)
Missouri Western State U (MO)
Murray State U (KY)
Northern Michigan U (MI)
Northwest Missouri State U (MO)
Old Dominion U (VA)
Piedmont Coll (GA)
Pittsburg State U (KS)
Point Park U (PA)
Union Coll (NE)
U of Central Oklahoma (OK)
U of Kentucky (KY)
U of Minnesota, Duluth (MN)
U of Nebraska–Lincoln (NE)
U of Regina (SK, Canada)
The U of Texas at Austin (TX)
U of Wisconsin–Eau Claire (WI)
U of Wisconsin–Stout (WI)
Utah State U (UT)
Wartburg Coll (IA)
Wayne State Coll (NE)
Weber State U (UT)
Western Washington U (WA)
William Woods U (MO)

ELECTRICAL AND ELECTRONIC ENGINEERING TECHNOLOGIES RELATED

Excelsior Coll (NY)
LeTourneau U (TX)
Penn State Berks (PA)
Pennsylvania Coll of Technology (PA)
Point Park U (PA)
Rochester Inst of Technology (NY)
Southern Illinois U Carbondale (IL)
Vaughn Coll of Aeronautics and Technology (NY)
West Virginia U Inst of Technology (WV)

ELECTRICAL AND ELECTRONICS ENGINEERING

American Public U System (WV)
The American U in Cairo (Egypt)
Anderson U (IN)
Arizona State U at the Tempe campus (AZ)
Arkansas Tech U (AR)
Auburn U (AL)
Baylor U (TX)
Binghamton U, State U of New York (NY)
Bloomsburg U of Pennsylvania (PA)
Boise State U (ID)
Boston U (MA)

Bradley U (IL)
Bucknell U (PA)
California Inst of Technology (CA)
California Polytechnic State U, San Luis Obispo (CA)
California State Polytechnic U, Pomona (CA)
California State U, Fullerton (CA)
California State U, Long Beach (CA)
California State U, Los Angeles (CA)
California State U, Northridge (CA)
California State U, Sacramento (CA)
Calvin Coll (MI)
Caribbean U (PR)
Carnegie Mellon U (PA)
Case Western Reserve U (OH)
The Catholic U of America (DC)
Cedarville U (OH)
Central Michigan U (MI)
Christian Brothers U (TN)
Christopher Newport U (VA)
The Citadel, The Military Coll of South Carolina (SC)
City Coll of the City U of New York (NY)
Clarkson U (NY)
Clemson U (SC)
Cleveland State U (OH)
The Coll of New Jersey (NJ)
Colorado State U (CO)
Columbia U (NY)
Concordia U (QC, Canada)
Cooper Union for the Advancement of Science and Art (NY)
Cornell U (NY)
Delaware State U (DE)
Dominican U (IL)
Drexel U (PA)
Eastern Nazarene Coll (MA)
Eastern Washington U (WA)
Embry-Riddle Aeronautical U–Daytona (FL)
Fairfield U (CT)
Fairleigh Dickinson U, Metropolitan Campus (NJ)
Florida Ag and Mech U (FL)
Florida Atlantic U (FL)
Florida Inst of Technology (FL)
Florida Intl U (FL)
Florida State U (FL)
Franklin W. Olin Coll of Eng (MA)
Gannon U (PA)
George Mason U (VA)
The George Washington U (DC)
Georgia Inst of Technology (GA)
Georgia Southern U (GA)
Gonzaga U (WA)
Grand Valley State U (MI)
Grove City Coll (PA)
Hampton U (VA)
Harding U (AR)
Hofstra U (NY)
Idaho State U (ID)
Indiana Tech (IN)
Indiana U–Purdue U Indianapolis (IN)
Inter American U of Puerto Rico, Bayamón Campus (PR)
Iowa State U of Science and Technology (IA)
Jackson State U (MS)
Jacksonville U (FL)
Johns Hopkins U (MD)
Kansas State U (KS)
Kennesaw State U (GA)
Kettering U (MI)
Lafayette Coll (PA)
Lamar U (TX)
Lawrence Technological U (MI)
Lebanese American U (Lebanon)
Lehigh U (PA)
LeTourneau U (TX)
Liberty U (VA)
Louisiana State U and A&M Coll (LA)
Loyola Marymount U (CA)
Manhattan Coll (NY)
Marquette U (WI)
Marshall U (WV)
Massachusetts Inst of Technology (MA)
Merrimack Coll (MA)
Miami U (OH)
Michigan State U (MI)

Michigan Technological U (MI)
Milligan Coll (TN)
Milwaukee School of Eng (WI)
Mississippi State U (MS)
Missouri U of Science and Technology (MO)
Montana Tech of The U of Montana (MT)
Mount Vernon Nazarene U (OH)
National U (CA)
New England Inst of Technology (RI)
New Jersey Inst of Technology (NJ)
New Mexico Highlands U (NM)
New Mexico Inst of Mining and Technology (NM)
New Mexico State U (NM)
New York Inst of Technology (NY)
New York U (NY)
North Carolina State U (NC)
North Central Coll (IL)
North Dakota State U (ND)
Northeastern U (MA)
Northern Arizona U (AZ)
Northern Illinois U (IL)
Northwestern U (IL)
Oakland U (MI)
Ohio Northern U (OH)
The Ohio State U (OH)
Ohio U (OH)
Oklahoma Christian U (OK)
Oklahoma State U (OK)
Old Dominion U (VA)
Oral Roberts U (OK)
Oregon Inst of Technology (OR)
Oregon State U (OR)
Penn State Abington (PA)
Penn State Altoona (PA)
Penn State Beaver (PA)
Penn State Berks (PA)
Penn State Brandywine (PA)
Penn State DuBois (PA)
Penn State Erie, The Behrend Coll (PA)
Penn State Fayette, The Eberly Campus (PA)
Penn State Greater Allegheny (PA)
Penn State Harrisburg (PA)
Penn State Hazleton (PA)
Penn State Lehigh Valley (PA)
Penn State Mont Alto (PA)
Penn State New Kensington (PA)
Penn State Schuylkill (PA)
Penn State Shenango (PA)
Penn State U Park (PA)
Penn State Wilkes-Barre (PA)
Penn State Worthington Scranton (PA)
Penn State York (PA)
Point Park U (PA)
Polytechnic U of Puerto Rico (PR)
Portland State U (OR)
Prairie View A&M U (TX)
Princeton U (NJ)
Purdue U (IN)
Purdue U Northwest (IN)
Rensselaer Polytechnic Inst (NY)
Rice U (TX)
Rochester Inst of Technology (NY)
Rockhurst U (MO)
Roger Williams U (RI)
Rose-Hulman Inst of Technology (IN)
Rowan U (NJ)
Rutgers U–New Brunswick (NJ)
Saginaw Valley State U (MI)
Saint Louis U–Madrid Campus (Spain)
St. Mary's U (TX)
San Diego State U (CA)
San Francisco State U (CA)
Santa Clara U (CA)
Seattle Pacific U (WA)
Seattle U (WA)
Shippensburg U of Pennsylvania (PA)
Southern Illinois U Carbondale (IL)
Southern Illinois U Edwardsville (IL)
Southern Methodist U (TX)
Stanford U (CA)
State U of New York at New Paltz (NY)
State U of New York at Oswego (NY)
State U of New York Maritime Coll (NY)

Michigan Technological U (MI)
State U of New York Polytechnic Inst (NY)
Stevens Inst of Technology (NJ)
Stony Brook U, State U of New York (NY)
Syracuse U (NY)
Tarleton State U (TX)
Temple U (PA)
Tennessee Technological U (TN)
Texas A&M U (TX)
Texas A&M U–Commerce (TX)
Texas A&M U–Corpus Christi (TX)
Texas A&M U–Kingsville (TX)
Texas State U (TX)
Texas Tech U (TX)
Trine U (IN)
Tufts U (MA)
Tulane U (LA)
Union Coll (NY)
United States Coast Guard Acad (CT)
United States Military Acad (NY)
Université de Sherbrooke (QC, Canada)
U at Buffalo, the State U of New York (NY)
The U of Akron (OH)
The U of Alabama (AL)
The U of Alabama at Birmingham (AL)
U of Alaska Fairbanks (AK)
U of Arkansas (AR)
U of Bridgeport (CT)
U of California, Davis (CA)
U of California, Irvine (CA)
U of California, Los Angeles (CA)
U of California, Riverside (CA)
U of California, San Diego (CA)
U of California, Santa Barbara (CA)
U of California, Santa Cruz (CA)
U of Central Florida (FL)
U of Central Oklahoma (OK)
U of Cincinnati (OH)
U of Colorado Boulder (CO)
U of Colorado Colorado Springs (CO)
U of Colorado Denver (CO)
U of Dayton (OH)
U of Denver (CO)
U of Evansville (IN)
U of Florida (FL)
U of Georgia (GA)
U of Hartford (CT)
U of Hawaii at Manoa (HI)
U of Houston (TX)
U of Idaho (ID)
U of Illinois at Chicago (IL)
The U of Kansas (KS)
U of Kentucky (KY)
U of Louisville (KY)
U of Maine (ME)
U of Maryland, Coll Park (MD)
U of Massachusetts Amherst (MA)
U of Massachusetts Boston (MA)
U of Massachusetts Dartmouth (MA)
U of Massachusetts Lowell (MA)
U of Memphis (TN)
U of Miami (FL)
U of Michigan (MI)
U of Michigan–Dearborn (MI)
U of Minnesota, Duluth (MN)
U of Minnesota, Twin Cities Campus (MN)
U of Missouri (MO)
U of Missouri–St. Louis (MO)
U of Mount Union (OH)
U of Nebraska–Lincoln (NE)
U of Nevada, Las Vegas (NV)
U of Nevada, Reno (NV)
U of New Hampshire (NH)
U of New Haven (CT)
U of New Mexico (NM)
U of New Orleans (LA)
The U of North Carolina at Charlotte (NC)
U of North Dakota (ND)
U of North Florida (FL)
U of North Texas (TX)
U of Notre Dame (IN)
U of Oklahoma (OK)
U of Pennsylvania (PA)
U of Pittsburgh (PA)
U of Regina (SK, Canada)
U of Rhode Island (RI)
U of Rochester (NY)
U of St. Thomas (MN)

U of San Diego (CA)
U of Saskatchewan (SK, Canada)
The U of Scranton (PA)
U of South Alabama (AL)
U of South Carolina (SC)
U of Southern California (CA)
U of Southern Maine (ME)
The U of Tennessee (TN)
The U of Tennessee at Chattanooga (TN)
The U of Texas at Austin (TX)
The U of Texas at Dallas (TX)
The U of Texas at El Paso (TX)
The U of Texas at San Antonio (TX)
The U of Texas Rio Grande Valley (TX)
U of the Pacific (CA)
The U of Toledo (OH)
U of Toronto (ON, Canada)
The U of Tulsa (OK)
U of Utah (UT)
U of Vermont (VT)
U of Virginia (VA)
U of Washington (WA)
U of Washington, Bothell (WA)
U of Washington, Tacoma (WA)
U of Waterloo (ON, Canada)
U of Wisconsin–Madison (WI)
U of Wisconsin–Milwaukee (WI)
U of Wisconsin–Platteville (WI)
U of Wyoming (WY)
Utah State U (UT)
Valparaiso U (IN)
Vanderbilt U (TN)
Villanova U (PA)
Virginia Commonwealth U (VA)
Virginia Military Inst (VA)
Virginia Polytechnic Inst and State U (VA)
Washington State U (WA)
Washington State U–Global Campus (WA)
Washington State U–Tri-Cities (WA)
Washington State U–Vancouver (WA)
Washington U in St. Louis (MO)
Wayne State U (MI)
Weber State U (UT)
Wentworth Inst of Technology (MA)
Western Kentucky U (KY)
Western Michigan U (MI)
Western New England U (MA)
Western Washington U (WA)
Westminster Coll (PA)
West Texas A&M U (TX)
West Virginia U (WV)
West Virginia U Inst of Technology (WV)
Wichita State U (KS)
Widener U (PA)
Wilkes U (PA)
Worcester Polytechnic Inst (MA)
Wright State U (OH)
Wright State U–Lake Campus (OH)
Youngstown State U (OH)

ELECTRICAL, ELECTRONIC AND COMMUNICATIONS ENGINEERING TECHNOLOGY
Arizona State U at the Polytechnic campus (AZ)
Bowling Green State U (OH)
Brigham Young U–Idaho (ID)
Buffalo State Coll, State U of New York (NY)
California State Polytechnic U, Pomona (CA)
California State U, Long Beach (CA)
California U of Pennsylvania (PA)
Central Connecticut State U (CT)
Cleveland State U (OH)
Delaware State U (DE)
Eastern Michigan U (MI)
Fairleigh Dickinson U, Metropolitan Campus (NJ)
Farmingdale State Coll (NY)
Ferris State U (MI)
Fitchburg State U (MA)
Florida Ag and Mech U (FL)
Hampton U (VA)
Idaho State U (ID)
Indiana State U (IN)
Indiana U–Purdue U Indianapolis (IN)

Inter American U of Puerto Rico, Aguadilla Campus (PR)
Inter American U of Puerto Rico, San Germán Campus (PR)
Kennesaw State U (GA)
LeTourneau U (TX)
Metropolitan State U of Denver (CO)
Miami Dade Coll (FL)
Michigan Technological U (MI)
Middle Tennessee State U (TN)
Missouri Western State U (MO)
Northern Kentucky U (KY)
Northwestern State U of Louisiana (LA)
Oklahoma State U (OK)
Oregon Inst of Technology (OR)
Penn State Erie, The Behrend Coll (PA)
Pittsburg State U (KS)
Prairie View A&M U (TX)
Purdue U (IN)
Purdue U Northwest (IN)
Sam Houston State U (TX)
State U of New York Coll of Technology at Alfred (NY)
State U of New York Coll of Technology at Canton (NY)
State U of New York Polytechnic Inst (NY)
Texas A&M U (TX)
Texas A&M U–Corpus Christi (TX)
Troy U (AL)
The U of Akron (OH)
U of Central Missouri (MO)
U of Cincinnati (OH)
U of Dayton (OH)
U of Hartford (CT)
U of Houston (TX)
U of Maine (ME)
U of Maryland Eastern Shore (MD)
U of Massachusetts Lowell (MA)
U of Memphis (TN)
The U of North Carolina at Charlotte (NC)
U of North Texas (TX)
U of Southern Mississippi (MS)
Valencia Coll (FL)
Vaughn Coll of Aeronautics and Technology (NY)
Vermont Tech Coll (VT)
Wayne State U (MI)
Weber State U (UT)
Youngstown State U (OH)

ELECTRICAL, ELECTRONICS AND COMMUNICATIONS ENGINEERING RELATED
Marquette U (WI)
The U of Arizona (AZ)

ELECTROMECHANICAL AND INSTRUMENTATION AND MAINTENANCE TECHNOLOGIES RELATED
Excelsior Coll (NY)

ELECTROMECHANICAL ENGINEERING
Wentworth Inst of Technology (MA)

ELECTROMECHANICAL TECHNOLOGY
Buffalo State Coll, State U of New York (NY)
Excelsior Coll (NY)
Murray State U (KY)
Purdue U Northwest (IN)
Rochester Inst of Technology (NY)
U of Northern Iowa (IA)
The U of Toledo (OH)
Vermont Tech Coll (VT)
Wayne State U (MI)

ELEMENTARY AND MIDDLE SCHOOL ADMINISTRATION/ PRINCIPALSHIP
Charleston Southern U (SC)
The Ohio State U (OH)
The Ohio State U at Lima (OH)
The Ohio State U at Mansfield (OH)
The Ohio State U at Marion (OH)
The Ohio State U at Newark (OH)

ELEMENTARY EDUCATION
Abilene Christian U (TX)
Acadia U (NS, Canada)
Alabama State U (AL)
Alcorn State U (MS)
Alfred U (NY)

Alice Lloyd Coll (KY)
Alma Coll (MI)
Alverno Coll (WI)
American Samoa Comm Coll (AS)
American U (DC)
Anderson U (IN)
Anderson U (SC)
Andrews U (MI)
Appalachian State U (NC)
Aquinas Coll (MI)
Arcadia U (PA)
Arizona Christian U (AZ)
Arizona State U at the Polytechnic campus (AZ)
Arizona State U at the Tempe campus (AZ)
Arizona State U at the West campus (AZ)
Arkansas Tech U (AR)
Arlington Baptist U (TX)
Asbury U (KY)
Ashland U (OH)
Athens State U (AL)
Auburn U (AL)
Auburn U at Montgomery (AL)
Augsburg U (MN)
Augustana Coll (IL)
Augustana U (SD)
Aurora U (IL)
Austin Coll (TX)
Avila U (MO)
Baker U (KS)
Ball State U (IN)
The Baptist Coll of Florida (FL)
Barclay Coll (KS)
Barry U (FL)
Barton Coll (NC)
Baylor U (TX)
Bay Path U (MA)
Belhaven U (MS)
Bellarmine U (KY)
Belmont U (TN)
Beloit Coll (WI)
Bemidji State U (MN)
Benedictine Coll (KS)
Benedictine U (IL)
Bennett Coll (NC)
Bethany Lutheran Coll (MN)
Bethel Coll (IN)
Bethel Coll (KS)
Bethel U (MN)
Bethel U (TN)
Bethune-Cookman U (FL)
Biola U (CA)
Birmingham-Southern Coll (AL)
Blackburn Coll (IL)
Black Hills State U (SD)
Bluefield Coll (VA)
Blue Mountain Coll (MS)
Bob Jones U (SC)
Boise State U (ID)
Boston Coll (MA)
Boston U (MA)
Bowie State U (MD)
Bowling Green State U (OH)
Bradley U (IL)
Brandman U (CA)
Brandon U (MB, Canada)
Brenau U (GA)
Brescia U (KY)
Bridgewater State U (MA)
Brigham Young U–Idaho (ID)
Brock U (ON, Canada)
Bryan Coll (TN)
Bryn Athyn Coll of the New Church (PA)
Bucknell U (PA)
Buena Vista U (IA)
Buffalo State Coll, State U of New York (NY)
Butler U (IN)
Cairn U (PA)
Caldwell U (NJ)
California U of Pennsylvania (PA)
Calumet Coll of Saint Joseph (IN)
Calvary U (MO)
Calvin Coll (MI)
Cameron U (OK)
Campbellsville U (KY)
Cardinal Stritch U (WI)
Caribbean U (PR)
Carroll Coll (MT)
Carroll U (WI)
Carson-Newman U (TN)
Carthage Coll (WI)
Catawba Coll (NC)
The Catholic U of America (DC)

Cedar Crest Coll (PA)
Central Connecticut State U (CT)
Central Methodist U (MO)
Central Michigan U (MI)
Chaminade U of Honolulu (HI)
Champlain Coll (VT)
Charleston Southern U (SC)
Chatham U (PA)
Chestnut Hill Coll (PA)
Chowan U (NC)
City Coll of the City U of New York (NY)
Clarke U (IA)
Clark U (MA)
Clemson U (SC)
Coastal Carolina U (SC)
Coe Coll (IA)
Coker Coll (SC)
Coll of Charleston (SC)
Coll of Mount Saint Vincent (NY)
The Coll of New Jersey (NJ)
The Coll of New Rochelle (NY)
Coll of Saint Benedict (MN)
Coll of Saint Mary (NE)
The Coll of Saint Rose (NY)
The Coll of St. Scholastica (MN)
Coll of Staten Island of the City U of New York (NY)
Coll of the Atlantic (ME)
Coll of the Ozarks (MO)
Colorado Christian U (CO)
Columbia Coll (SC)
Concordia Coll–New York (NY)
Concordia U (QC, Canada)
Concordia U Chicago (IL)
Concordia U, Nebraska (NE)
Concordia U of Edmonton (AB, Canada)
Concordia U, St. Paul (MN)
Concordia U Wisconsin (WI)
Concord U (WV)
Converse Coll (SC)
Corban U (OR)
Cornell Coll (IA)
Cornerstone U (MI)
Covenant Coll (GA)
Creighton U (NE)
Criswell Coll (TX)
Culver-Stockton Coll (MO)
Curry Coll (MA)
Daemen Coll (NY)
Dakota State U (SD)
Dallas Baptist U (TX)
Daytona State Coll (FL)
Defiance Coll (OH)
Delaware State U (DE)
DePaul U (IL)
DeSales U (PA)
Dickinson State U (ND)
Doane U (NE)
Dominican Coll (NY)
Dominican U (IL)
Donnelly Coll (KS)
Drake U (IA)
Drexel U (PA)
Drury U (MO)
D'Youville Coll (NY)
East Carolina U (NC)
East Central U (OK)
Eastern Michigan U (MI)
Eastern Nazarene Coll (MA)
Eastern New Mexico U (NM)
East Texas Baptist U (TX)
Edgewood Coll (WI)
Elmhurst Coll (IL)
Elms Coll (MA)
Elon U (NC)
Emmanuel Coll (GA)
Emmanuel Coll (MA)
Emmaus Bible Coll (IA)
Emporia State U (KS)
Endicott Coll (MA)
Evangel U (MO)
Fayetteville State U (NC)
Felician U (NJ)
Ferris State U (MI)
Fitchburg State U (MA)
Flagler Coll (FL)
Florida Atlantic U (FL)
Florida Coll (FL)
Florida Gulf Coast U (FL)
Florida Intl U (FL)
Florida Southern Coll (FL)
Florida State U (FL)
Fordham U (NY)
Fort Lewis Coll (CO)
Framingham State U (MA)

Francis Marion U (SC)
Franklin Coll (IN)
Franklin Pierce U (NH)
Friends U (KS)
Frostburg State U (MD)
Furman U (SC)
Geneva Coll (PA)
Georgetown Coll (KY)
Georgian Court U (NJ)
Georgia Southern U (GA)
Georgia Southwestern State U (GA)
Gettysburg Coll (PA)
Gonzaga U (WA)
Gordon Coll (MA)
Gordon State Coll (GA)
Goshen Coll (IN)
Governors State U (IL)
Graceland U (IA)
Grambling State U (LA)
Grand Valley State U (MI)
Grand View U (IA)
Granite State Coll (NH)
Green Mountain Coll (VT)
Greensboro Coll (NC)
Greenville U (IL)
Guilford Coll (NC)
Gustavus Adolphus Coll (MN)
Hamline U (MN)
Hampton U (VA)
Hannibal-LaGrange U (MO)
Harding U (AR)
Harris-Stowe State U (MO)
Hawai`i Pacific U (HI)
Heidelberg U (OH)
High Point U (NC)
Hobe Sound Bible Coll (FL)
Hofstra U (NY)
Holy Family U (PA)
Hope Coll (MI)
Hope Intl U (CA)
Houston Baptist U (TX)
Howard Payne U (TX)
Humboldt State U (CA)
Hunter Coll of the City U of New York (NY)
Huntingdon Coll (AL)
Husson U (ME)
Huston-Tillotson U (TX)
Idaho State U (ID)
Illinois Coll (IL)
Illinois State U (IL)
Illinois Wesleyan U (IL)
Indiana State U (IN)
Indiana Tech (IN)
Indiana U Bloomington (IN)
Indiana U East (IN)
Indiana U Kokomo (IN)
Indiana U Northwest (IN)
Indiana U–Purdue U Indianapolis (IN)
Indiana U South Bend (IN)
Indiana U Southeast (IN)
Indiana Wesleyan U (IN)
Inter American U of Puerto Rico, Aguadilla Campus (PR)
Inter American U of Puerto Rico, Barranquitas Campus (PR)
Inter American U of Puerto Rico, Fajardo Campus (PR)
Inter American U of Puerto Rico, Metropolitan Campus (PR)
Inter American U of Puerto Rico, San Germán Campus (PR)
Iona Coll (NY)
Iowa State U of Science and Technology (IA)
Jackson State U (MS)
Jacksonville U (FL)
John Brown U (AR)
John Carroll U (OH)
Johnson U (TN)
Johnson U Florida (FL)
John Wesley U (NC)
Judson U (IL)
Kansas State U (KS)
Kansas Wesleyan U (KS)
Kean U (NJ)
Keene State Coll (NH)
Keiser U, Fort Lauderdale (FL)
Kennesaw State U (GA)
Kentucky Mountain Bible Coll (KY)
Kentucky State U (KY)
King's Coll (PA)
King U (TN)
Knox Coll (IL)
Langston U (OK)

La Roche Coll (PA)
Lasell Coll (MA)
La Sierra U (CA)
Lee U (TN)
Le Moyne Coll (NY)
Lenoir-Rhyne U (NC)
Lesley U (MA)
LeTourneau U (TX)
Lewis U (IL)
Liberty U (VA)
Limestone Coll (SC)
Lincoln Memorial U (TN)
Lincoln U (MO)
Lindenwood U (MO)
Lindsey Wilson Coll (KY)
Linfield Coll (OR)
Lipscomb U (TN)
Long Island U–LIU Brooklyn (NY)
Long Island U–LIU Post (NY)
Loras Coll (IA)
Louisiana Coll (LA)
Louisiana State U and A&M Coll (LA)
Loyola U Chicago (IL)
Luther Coll (IA)
Lynchburg Coll (VA)
Lynn U (FL)
Madonna U (MI)
Maharishi U of Management (IA)
Manchester U (IN)
Manhattan Coll (NY)
Manhattanville Coll (NY)
Mansfield U of Pennsylvania (PA)
Maranatha Baptist U (WI)
Marian U (IN)
Marian U (WI)
Marietta Coll (OH)
Marquette U (WI)
Marshall U (WV)
Martin Luther Coll (MN)
Marymount U (VA)
Maryville U of Saint Louis (MO)
Marywood U (PA)
The Master's U (CA)
McKendree U (IL)
McMurry U (TX)
McNeese State U (LA)
Medgar Evers Coll of the City U of New York (NY)
Mercer U, Macon (GA)
Mercyhurst U (PA)
Merrimack Coll (MA)
Messiah Coll (PA)
Michigan State U (MI)
Mid-America Christian U (OK)
MidAmerica Nazarene U (KS)
Mid-Atlantic Christian U (NC)
Middle Georgia State U (GA)
Millikin U (IL)
Minnesota State U Moorhead (MN)
Minot State U (ND)
Mississippi State U (MS)
Missouri Baptist U (MO)
Missouri State U (MO)
Missouri Valley Coll (MO)
Missouri Western State U (MO)
Molloy Coll (NY)
Monmouth Coll (IL)
Morehead State U (KY)
Morningside Coll (IA)
Morris Coll (SC)
Mount Marty Coll (SD)
Mount Mercy U (IA)
Mount Saint Mary's U (CA)
Mount St. Mary's U (MD)
Multnomah U (OR)
Murray State U (KY)
Naropa U (CO)
National Louis U (IL)
National U (CA)
Nazareth Coll of Rochester (NY)
Neumann U (PA)
Newberry Coll (SC)
New Jersey City U (NJ)
Newman U (KS)
New Mexico Highlands U (NM)
New Mexico State U (NM)
New York U (NY)
Niagara U (NY)
North Carolina Central U (NC)
North Carolina State U (NC)
North Carolina Wesleyan Coll (NC)
North Central Coll (IL)
Northcentral U (CA)
Northeastern State U (OK)
Northern Arizona U (AZ)
Northern Illinois U (IL)

Northern Kentucky U (KY)
Northern Michigan U (MI)
Northern State U (SD)
Northern Vermont U–Lyndon (VT)
North Greenville U (SC)
Northwest Christian U (OR)
Northwestern Coll (IA)
Northwestern Oklahoma State U (OK)
Northwestern State U of Louisiana (LA)
Northwest Nazarene U (ID)
Northwest U (WA)
Nova Southeastern U (FL)
Nyack Coll (NY)
Oakland City U (IN)
Oakland U (MI)
The Ohio State U (OH)
The Ohio State U at Lima (OH)
The Ohio State U at Mansfield (OH)
The Ohio State U at Marion (OH)
The Ohio State U at Newark (OH)
Ohio U–Zanesville (OH)
Ohio Wesleyan U (OH)
Oklahoma Baptist U (OK)
Oklahoma Christian U (OK)
Oklahoma City U (OK)
Oklahoma State U (OK)
Olivet Nazarene U (IL)
Oral Roberts U (OK)
Ottawa U (KS)
Otterbein U (OH)
Pace U (NY)
Pace U, Pleasantville Campus (NY)
Palm Beach Atlantic U (FL)
Penn State Abington (PA)
Penn State Altoona (PA)
Penn State Beaver (PA)
Penn State Berks (PA)
Penn State Brandywine (PA)
Penn State DuBois (PA)
Penn State Erie, The Behrend Coll (PA)
Penn State Fayette, The Eberly Campus (PA)
Penn State Greater Allegheny (PA)
Penn State Harrisburg (PA)
Penn State Hazleton (PA)
Penn State Lehigh Valley (PA)
Penn State Mont Alto (PA)
Penn State New Kensington (PA)
Penn State Schuylkill (PA)
Penn State Shenango (PA)
Penn State U Park (PA)
Penn State Wilkes-Barre (PA)
Penn State Worthington Scranton (PA)
Penn State York (PA)
Pfeiffer U (NC)
Pittsburg State U (KS)
Point Loma Nazarene U (CA)
Point Park U (PA)
Polk State Coll (FL)
Presbyterian Coll (SC)
Purdue U (IN)
Purdue U Northwest (IN)
Queens Coll of the City U of New York (NY)
Redeemer U Coll (ON, Canada)
Regis U (CO)
Rhode Island Coll (RI)
Rider U (NJ)
Ripon Coll (WI)
Rivier U (NH)
Robert Morris U (PA)
Rockford U (IL)
Rockhurst U (MO)
Rocky Mountain Coll (MT)
Roger Williams U (RI)
Rollins Coll (FL)
Roosevelt U (IL)
Rosemont Coll (PA)
Rowan U (NJ)
Rust Coll (MS)
Sacred Heart U (CT)
The Sage Colls (NY)
Saginaw Valley State U (MI)
St. Ambrose U (IA)
St. Andrews U (NC)
Saint Anselm Coll (NH)
St. Bonaventure U (NY)
St. Catherine U (MN)
Saint Francis U (PA)
St. John Fisher Coll (NY)
Saint John's U (MN)
St. John's U (NY)

St. Joseph's Coll, Long Island Campus (NY)
St. Joseph's Coll, New York (NY)
Saint Joseph's U (PA)
Saint Leo U (FL)
Saint Martin's U (WA)
Saint Mary-of-the-Woods Coll (IN)
Saint Mary's U of Minnesota (MN)
Saint Michael's Coll (VT)
St. Norbert Coll (WI)
Saint Peter's U (NJ)
St. Thomas Aquinas Coll (NY)
St. Thomas U (FL)
Salisbury U (MD)
Salve Regina U (RI)
Samford U (AL)
Schreiner U (TX)
Seton Hill U (PA)
Shaw U (NC)
Shepherd U (WV)
Shorter U (GA)
Silver Lake Coll of the Holy Family (WI)
Simmons Coll (MA)
Simpson Coll (IA)
Skidmore Coll (NY)
Southeastern Louisiana U (LA)
Southeastern Oklahoma State U (OK)
Southeastern U (FL)
Southeast Missouri State U (MO)
Southern Adventist U (TN)
Southern Illinois U Carbondale (IL)
Southern Illinois U Edwardsville (IL)
Southern Utah U (UT)
South Florida State Coll (FL)
Southwest Baptist U (MO)
Southwestern Adventist U (TX)
Southwestern Assemblies of God U (TX)
Southwestern Coll (KS)
Spring Hill Coll (AL)
State U of New York at Fredonia (NY)
State U of New York at New Paltz (NY)
State U of New York at Oswego (NY)
State U of New York at Plattsburgh (NY)
State U of New York Coll at Cortland (NY)
State U of New York Coll at Geneseo (NY)
State U of New York Coll at Old Westbury (NY)
State U of New York Coll at Oneonta (NY)
State U of New York Coll at Potsdam (NY)
Stetson U (FL)
Stevenson U (MD)
Stonehill Coll (MA)
Tabor Coll (KS)
Taylor U (IN)
Temple U (PA)
Tennessee Technological U (TN)
Tennessee Wesleyan U (TN)
Texas Christian U (TX)
Texas Lutheran U (TX)
Toccoa Falls Coll (GA)
Towson U (MD)
Transylvania U (KY)
Trent U (ON, Canada)
Trevecca Nazarene U (TN)
Trine U (IN)
Trinity Christian Coll (IL)
Trinity Coll of Florida (FL)
Troy U (AL)
Truett McConnell U (GA)
Tufts U (MA)
Union Coll (NE)
Union U (TN)
Université de Sherbrooke (QC, Canada)
Université Sainte-Anne (NS, Canada)
The U of Alabama (AL)
The U of Alabama at Birmingham (AL)
U of Alaska Fairbanks (AK)
The U of Arizona (AZ)
U of Arkansas (AR)
U of Central Florida (FL)
U of Central Missouri (MO)
U of Central Oklahoma (OK)

U of Charleston (WV)
U of Cincinnati (OH)
U of Colorado Boulder (CO)
U of Colorado Colorado Springs (CO)
U of Dallas (TX)
U of Dubuque (IA)
U of Evansville (IN)
The U of Findlay (OH)
U of Florida (FL)
U of Guam (GU)
U of Hartford (CT)
U of Hawaii at Manoa (HI)
U of Idaho (ID)
U of Illinois at Chicago (IL)
U of Illinois at Springfield (IL)
U of Jamestown (ND)
The U of Kansas (KS)
U of Kentucky (KY)
U of Louisiana at Monroe (LA)
U of Louisville (KY)
U of Maine (ME)
U of Maine at Farmington (ME)
U of Maine at Machias (ME)
U of Maine at Presque Isle (ME)
U of Mary Hardin-Baylor (TX)
U of Maryland, Coll Park (MD)
U of Maryland Eastern Shore (MD)
U of Miami (FL)
U of Michigan (MI)
U of Michigan–Dearborn (MI)
U of Michigan–Flint (MI)
U of Minnesota, Crookston (MN)
U of Minnesota, Morris (MN)
U of Minnesota, Twin Cities Campus (MN)
U of Missouri (MO)
U of Missouri–St. Louis (MO)
U of Mobile (AL)
U of Montana (MT)
U of Montevallo (AL)
U of Nebraska at Kearney (NE)
U of Nebraska–Lincoln (NE)
U of Nevada, Las Vegas (NV)
U of Nevada, Reno (NV)
U of New England (ME)
U of New Mexico (NM)
U of New Orleans (LA)
U of North Alabama (AL)
The U of North Carolina at Chapel Hill (NC)
The U of North Carolina at Charlotte (NC)
The U of North Carolina at Greensboro (NC)
The U of North Carolina at Pembroke (NC)
The U of North Carolina Wilmington (NC)
U of North Dakota (ND)
U of Northern Colorado (CO)
U of Northern Iowa (IA)
U of North Florida (FL)
U of Oklahoma (OK)
U of Pennsylvania (PA)
U of Pikeville (KY)
U of Pittsburgh at Bradford (PA)
U of Providence (MT)
U of Puerto Rico–Humacao (PR)
U of Regina (SK, Canada)
U of Rhode Island (RI)
U of St. Francis (IL)
U of Saint Francis (IN)
U of Saint Mary (KS)
U of St. Thomas (TX)
U of San Francisco (CA)
U of Science and Arts of Oklahoma (OK)
The U of Scranton (PA)
U of Sioux Falls (SD)
U of South Alabama (AL)
U of South Carolina (SC)
U of South Carolina Aiken (SC)
U of South Dakota (SD)
U of Southern Indiana (IN)
U of Southern Mississippi (MS)
U of South Florida, St. Petersburg (FL)
U of South Florida Sarasota-Manatee (FL)
The U of Tampa (FL)
The U of Tennessee at Martin (TN)
The U of Texas at San Antonio (TX)
U of the Incarnate Word (TX)
U of the Virgin Islands (VI)
The U of Tulsa (OK)
U of Utah (UT)

U of Vermont (VT)
U of West Georgia (GA)
U of Wisconsin–Eau Claire (WI)
U of Wisconsin–La Crosse (WI)
U of Wisconsin–Madison (WI)
U of Wisconsin–Milwaukee (WI)
U of Wisconsin–Parkside (WI)
U of Wisconsin–Platteville (WI)
U of Wisconsin–River Falls (WI)
U of Wisconsin–Stevens Point (WI)
U of Wisconsin–Superior (WI)
U of Wisconsin–Whitewater (WI)
U of Wyoming (WY)
Upper Iowa U (IA)
Utah State U (UT)
Utah Valley U (UT)
Utica Coll (NY)
Valley City State U (ND)
Valparaiso U (IN)
Vanderbilt U (TN)
Vanguard U of Southern California (CA)
Virginia Wesleyan U (VA)
Wagner Coll (NY)
Waldorf U (IA)
Warner Pacific Coll (OR)
Wartburg Coll (IA)
Washington State U (WA)
Washington State U–Tri-Cities (WA)
Washington State U–Vancouver (WA)
Washington U in St. Louis (MO)
Wayland Baptist U (TX)
Waynesburg U (PA)
Wayne State Coll (NE)
Wayne State U (MI)
Webber Intl U (FL)
Weber State U (UT)
Webster U (MO)
Welch Coll (TN)
Wells Coll (NY)
Western Connecticut State U (CT)
Western Illinois U (IL)
Western Kentucky U (KY)
Western Michigan U (MI)
Western New England U (MA)
Western Washington U (WA)
Westfield State U (MA)
Westminster Coll (PA)
Westminster Coll (UT)
Westmont Coll (CA)
West Virginia State U (WV)
West Virginia U (WV)
West Virginia Wesleyan Coll (WV)
Wheaton Coll (IL)
Wheaton Coll (MA)
Whitworth U (WA)
Wichita State U (KS)
Widener U (PA)
Wilkes U (PA)
William Jewell Coll (MO)
William Paterson U of New Jersey (NJ)
William Penn U (IA)
William Woods U (MO)
Wilmington U (DE)
Winona State U (MN)
Winthrop U (SC)
Wisconsin Lutheran Coll (WI)
Worcester State U (MA)
Wright State U–Lake Campus (OH)
Xavier U of Louisiana (LA)
Youngstown State U (OH)

EMERGENCY MEDICAL TECHNOLOGY (EMT PARAMEDIC)

Brigham Young U–Idaho (ID)
Columbia Southern U (AL)
Concordia U Chicago (IL)
Creighton U (NE)
Franklin Pierce U (NH)
The George Washington U (DC)
Jefferson Coll of Health Sciences (VA)
Oregon Inst of Technology (OR)
Pennsylvania Coll of Technology (PA)
U of Maryland, Baltimore County (MD)
U of New Haven (CT)
U of New Mexico (NM)
U of Sioux Falls (SD)
U of South Alabama (AL)
U of Washington (WA)

ENERGY MANAGEMENT AND SYSTEMS TECHNOLOGY
Creighton U (NE)
Excelsior Coll (NY)
Ferris State U (MI)
Fitchburg State U (MA)
Idaho State U (ID)
Illinois State U (IL)
Iowa State U of Science and Technology (IA)
Unity Coll (ME)
Vermont Tech Coll (VT)

ENGINEERING
Abilene Christian U (TX)
Albion Coll (MI)
Arcadia U (PA)
Arizona State U at the Polytechnic campus (AZ)
Auburn U (AL)
Augsburg U (MN)
Azusa Pacific U (CA)
Baldwin Wallace U (OH)
Ball State U (IN)
Barry U (FL)
Bates Coll (ME)
Baylor U (TX)
Beloit Coll (WI)
Benedictine Coll (KS)
Bethany Lutheran Coll (MN)
Bethel Coll (IN)
Binghamton U, State U of New York (NY)
Biola U (CA)
Bob Jones U (SC)
Boston U (MA)
Bradley U (IL)
Buffalo State Coll, State U of New York (NY)
California Baptist U (CA)
California Inst of Technology (CA)
California State Polytechnic U, Pomona (CA)
California State U, Long Beach (CA)
California State U, Los Angeles (CA)
Calvin Coll (MI)
Carthage Coll (WI)
Case Western Reserve U (OH)
The Catholic U of America (DC)
Clarkson U (NY)
Clark U (MA)
Coll of Staten Island of the City U of New York (NY)
Coll of the Ozarks (MO)
Colorado State U–Pueblo (CO)
Cooper Union for the Advancement of Science and Art (NY)
Cornell Coll (IA)
Cornell U (NY)
Cornerstone U (MI)
Dartmouth Coll (NH)
Dominican U (IL)
Drexel U (PA)
East Carolina U (NC)
East Central U (OK)
Eastern Mennonite U (VA)
Eastern Nazarene Coll (MA)
Elizabethtown Coll (PA)
Elon U (NC)
Florida Inst of Technology (FL)
Franklin W. Olin Coll of Eng (MA)
Frostburg State U (MD)
Geneva Coll (PA)
The George Washington U (DC)
Gonzaga U (WA)
Harvard U (MA)
Harvey Mudd Coll (CA)
Hope Coll (MI)
Indiana State U (IN)
Indiana U Bloomington (IN)
Indiana U–Purdue U Indianapolis (IN)
Inter American U of Puerto Rico, San Germán Campus (PR)
Iowa State U of Science and Technology (IA)
Jacksonville U (FL)
James Madison U (VA)
John Brown U (AR)
Johns Hopkins U (MD)
Lafayette Coll (PA)
LaGrange Coll (GA)
LeTourneau U (TX)
Manchester U (IN)
Manhattan Coll (NY)

Marian U (IN)
Marshall U (WV)
Maryville Coll (TN)
McNeese State U (LA)
Mercer U, Macon (GA)
Messiah Coll (PA)
Miami U (OH)
Michigan State U (MI)
Michigan Technological U (MI)
Milwaukee School of Eng (WI)
Missouri U of Science and Technology (MO)
Montana Tech of The U of Montana (MT)
New Mexico Highlands U (NM)
North Carolina State U (NC)
Northeastern U (MA)
Northland Coll (WI)
Northwestern U (IL)
Oglethorpe U (GA)
Ohio Northern U (OH)
Oklahoma Christian U (OK)
Old Dominion U (VA)
Olivet Nazarene U (IL)
Oral Roberts U (OK)
Pacific Lutheran U (WA)
Pfeiffer U (NC)
Princeton U (NJ)
Purdue U Northwest (IN)
Quinnipiac U (CT)
Rensselaer Polytechnic Inst (NY)
Robert Morris U (PA)
Rochester Inst of Technology (NY)
Roger Williams U (RI)
Rowan U (NJ)
Rutgers U–Camden (NJ)
Rutgers U–Newark (NJ)
Saginaw Valley State U (MI)
Saint Anselm Coll (NH)
Saint Augustine's U (NC)
Saint Francis U (PA)
Saint Louis U (MO)
Saint Louis U–Madrid Campus (Spain)
Saint Mary's Coll of California (CA)
Saint Michael's Coll (VT)
Saint Vincent Coll (PA)
San Diego State U (CA)
Santa Clara U (CA)
Schreiner U (TX)
Seattle Pacific U (WA)
Seattle U (WA)
Spelman Coll (GA)
Stanford U (CA)
State U of New York Polytechnic Inst (NY)
Stevens Inst of Technology (NJ)
Stony Brook U, State U of New York (NY)
Tarleton State U (TX)
Taylor U (IN)
Temple U (PA)
Texas Christian U (TX)
Trine U (IN)
Tufts U (MA)
U at Buffalo, the State U of New York (NY)
The U of Akron (OH)
U of California, Irvine (CA)
U of California, San Diego (CA)
U of Cincinnati (OH)
U of Colorado Boulder (CO)
U of Denver (CO)
U of Hartford (CT)
U of Hawaii at Manoa (HI)
U of Mary Hardin-Baylor (TX)
U of Maryland, Baltimore County (MD)
U of Michigan (MI)
U of Nebraska–Lincoln (NE)
U of Nevada, Las Vegas (NV)
U of New Haven (CT)
U of North Carolina at Asheville (NC)
U of Oklahoma (OK)
U of Regina (SK, Canada)
U of Rochester (NY)
U of San Diego (CA)
U of Southern Indiana (IN)
The U of Tennessee at Chattanooga (TN)
The U of Tennessee at Martin (TN)
U of the Incarnate Word (TX)
U of Toronto (ON, Canada)
U of Utah (UT)
U of Vermont (VT)
U of Virginia (VA)

U of Wisconsin–Platteville (WI)
Vaughn Coll of Aeronautics and Technology (NY)
Wake Forest U (NC)
Washington and Lee U (VA)
Washington U in St. Louis (MO)
Wells Coll (NY)
Wentworth Inst of Technology (MA)
Western Illinois U (IL)
Whitworth U (WA)
Widener U (PA)
Wilkes U (PA)
Winona State U (MN)
Wright State U (OH)
Youngstown State U (OH)

ENGINEERING CHEMISTRY
Oakland U (MI)

ENGINEERING FIELDS RELATED
ArtCenter Coll of Design (CA)

ENGINEERING/INDUSTRIAL MANAGEMENT
Arizona State U at the Tempe campus (AZ)
Bethel Coll (IN)
Bowling Green State U (OH)
California State U, Long Beach (CA)
Christian Brothers U (TN)
Claremont McKenna Coll (CA)
Clarkson U (NY)
Eastern Michigan U (MI)
Fort Lewis Coll (CO)
Grove City Coll (PA)
Iowa State U of Science and Technology (IA)
Kansas State U (KS)
Kennesaw State U (GA)
Miami U (OH)
Michigan Technological U (MI)
Middle Tennessee State U (TN)
Missouri State U (MO)
Missouri U of Science and Technology (MO)
Morehead State U (KY)
New York Inst of Technology (NY)
Pittsburg State U (KS)
Purdue U (IN)
Purdue U Northwest (IN)
Saginaw Valley State U (MI)
St. Mary's U (TX)
Stanford U (CA)
State U of New York Coll of Technology at Canton (NY)
Stevens Inst of Technology (NJ)
Texas State U (TX)
Trine U (IN)
United States Merchant Marine Acad (NY)
United States Military Acad (NY)
The U of Arizona (AZ)
U of Illinois at Chicago (IL)
U of Management and Technology (VA)
The U of Scranton (PA)
The U of Tennessee at Chattanooga (TN)
The U of Texas at Austin (TX)
U of the Incarnate Word (TX)
U of the Pacific (CA)
U of Vermont (VT)
Western Michigan U (MI)
Widener U (PA)
Wilkes U (PA)

ENGINEERING MECHANICS
Carroll Coll (MT)
Columbia U (NY)
Iowa State U of Science and Technology (IA)
Johns Hopkins U (MD)
Lehigh U (PA)
U of Cincinnati (OH)
The U of Texas at Austin (TX)
U of Wisconsin–Madison (WI)
Virginia Polytechnic Inst and State U (VA)

ENGINEERING PHYSICS/ APPLIED PHYSICS
Adams State U (CO)
Anderson U (IN)
Arizona State U at the Polytechnic campus (AZ)
Arkansas Tech U (AR)
Augustana Coll (IL)

Augustana U (SD)
Belmont U (TN)
Bemidji State U (MN)
Biola U (CA)
California Inst of Technology (CA)
Carroll U (WI)
Case Western Reserve U (OH)
Christian Brothers U (TN)
Columbia U (NY)
Cornell U (NY)
Dartmouth Coll (NH)
Delaware State U (DE)
Doane U (NE)
Eastern Michigan U (MI)
Eastern Nazarene Coll (MA)
Elon U (NC)
Embry-Riddle Aeronautical U–Daytona (FL)
Fordham U (NY)
Fort Lewis Coll (CO)
Goshen Coll (IN)
Hampden-Sydney Coll (VA)
Jacksonville U (FL)
John Carroll U (OH)
Juniata Coll (PA)
Kansas Wesleyan U (KS)
Kettering U (MI)
Lehigh U (PA)
LeTourneau U (TX)
Linfield Coll (OR)
Loras Coll (IA)
Loyola Marymount U (CA)
Miami U (OH)
Minnesota State U Moorhead (MN)
Morehouse Coll (GA)
Morningside Coll (IA)
Murray State U (KY)
New Mexico State U (NM)
New York U (NY)
Northeastern State U (OK)
Northwest Nazarene U (ID)
Oakland U (MI)
The Ohio State U (OH)
Oral Roberts U (OK)
Otterbein U (OH)
Point Loma Nazarene U (CA)
Providence Coll (RI)
Randolph Coll (VA)
Randolph-Macon Coll (VA)
Rensselaer Polytechnic Inst (NY)
Rose-Hulman Inst of Technology (IN)
St. Ambrose U (IA)
Saint Louis U (MO)
Saint Louis U–Madrid Campus (Spain)
Saint Mary's U of Minnesota (MN)
Samford U (AL)
Santa Clara U (CA)
Southeast Missouri State U (MO)
Stephen F. Austin State U (TX)
Stevens Inst of Technology (NJ)
Tarleton State U (TX)
Taylor U (IN)
Trevecca Nazarene U (TN)
Tufts U (MA)
U at Buffalo, the State U of New York (NY)
U of California, San Diego (CA)
U of Central Oklahoma (OK)
U of Colorado Boulder (CO)
U of Illinois at Chicago (IL)
The U of Kansas (KS)
U of Maine (ME)
U of Massachusetts Boston (MA)
U of Michigan (MI)
U of Minnesota, Duluth (MN)
U of Nevada, Reno (NV)
U of New Hampshire (NH)
U of Oklahoma (OK)
U of Pittsburgh (PA)
U of Saskatchewan (SK, Canada)
U of the Pacific (CA)
The U of Tulsa (OK)
U of Wisconsin–Madison (WI)
U of Wisconsin–Platteville (WI)
Westminster Coll (PA)
Westmont Coll (CA)
Whittier Coll (CA)
Whitworth U (WA)
Worcester Polytechnic Inst (MA)
Wright State U (OH)

ENGINEERING RELATED
Agnes Scott Coll (GA)
Alfred U (NY)
Auburn U (AL)

Benedictine Coll (KS)
California State U, Long Beach (CA)
Claremont McKenna Coll (CA)
The Coll of Idaho (ID)
Colorado State U–Pueblo (CO)
Gettysburg Coll (PA)
Indiana U–Purdue U Indianapolis (IN)
Lehigh U (PA)
Madonna U (MI)
Maryville U of Saint Louis (MO)
Massachusetts Maritime Acad (MA)
Michigan State U (MI)
Mississippi State U (MS)
New York U (NY)
Northern Michigan U (MI)
Northwestern U (IL)
Ohio Northern U (OH)
The Ohio State U (OH)
Ohio Wesleyan U (OH)
Oregon Inst of Technology (OR)
Oregon State U (OR)
Penn State Altoona (PA)
Penn State Berks (PA)
Penn State U Park (PA)
Polytechnic U of Puerto Rico (PR)
Principia Coll (IL)
Purdue U (IN)
Rochester Inst of Technology (NY)
Rose-Hulman Inst of Technology (IN)
State U of New York at Oswego (NY)
State U of New York Polytechnic Inst (NY)
Stevens Inst of Technology (NJ)
Tufts U (MA)
U at Albany, State U of New York (NY)
U of California, Davis (CA)
U of Colorado Colorado Springs (CO)
U of Maryland, Coll Park (MD)
U of Miami (FL)
U of Michigan–Dearborn (MI)
U of New Hampshire (NH)
U of Pennsylvania (PA)
The U of Virginia's Coll at Wise (VA)
U of Washington (WA)
U of Waterloo (ON, Canada)
U of Wisconsin–Madison (WI)
Washington U in St. Louis (MO)
Waynesburg U (PA)
Western Michigan U (MI)
Wheaton Coll (IL)
York Coll of Pennsylvania (PA)

ENGINEERING-RELATED TECHNOLOGIES
Rochester Inst of Technology (NY)
United States Merchant Marine Acad (NY)

ENGINEERING SCIENCE
Arizona State U at the Polytechnic campus (AZ)
Benedictine U (IL)
Bethel U (MN)
California Polytechnic State U, San Luis Obispo (CA)
Carroll Coll (MT)
Coastal Carolina U (SC)
The Coll of New Jersey (NJ)
Colorado State U (CO)
Concordia U, St. Paul (MN)
Cornell Coll (IA)
Emory U (GA)
Hofstra U (NY)
Lincoln U (PA)
Morehouse Coll (GA)
Muskingum U (OH)
New Jersey Inst of Technology (NJ)
Northwestern U (IL)
Ohio Wesleyan U (OH)
Penn State Abington (PA)
Penn State Altoona (PA)
Penn State Beaver (PA)
Penn State Berks (PA)
Penn State Brandywine (PA)
Penn State DuBois (PA)
Penn State Erie, The Behrend Coll (PA)
Penn State Fayette, The Eberly Campus (PA)
Penn State Greater Allegheny (PA)

Penn State Hazleton (PA)
Penn State Lehigh Valley (PA)
Penn State Mont Alto (PA)
Penn State New Kensington (PA)
Penn State Schuylkill (PA)
Penn State Shenango (PA)
Penn State U Park (PA)
Penn State Wilkes-Barre (PA)
Penn State Worthington Scranton (PA)
Penn State York (PA)
Rensselaer Polytechnic Inst (NY)
Rutgers U–New Brunswick (NJ)
St. Mary's U (TX)
St. Thomas Aquinas Coll (NY)
Shepherd U (WV)
Simon Fraser U (BC, Canada)
Smith Coll (MA)
Sonoma State U (CA)
Southern Utah U (UT)
State U of New York Coll at Oneonta (NY)
Sweet Briar Coll (VA)
Trinity U (TX)
Tufts U (MA)
Tulane U (LA)
U of California, San Diego (CA)
U of Miami (FL)
U of Michigan (MI)
U of Michigan–Flint (MI)
U of New Mexico (NM)
U of Pittsburgh (PA)
U of Pittsburgh at Bradford (PA)
U of Rochester (NY)
U of South Carolina (SC)
U of Toronto (ON, Canada)
Vanderbilt U (TN)
Wartburg Coll (IA)
Washington and Lee U (VA)
Wright State U (OH)
Wright State U–Lake Campus (OH)

ENGINEERING TECHNOLOGIES AND ENGINEERING RELATED
Ball State U (IN)
Bowling Green State U (OH)
California State U Maritime Acad (CA)
Cameron U (OK)
Daytona State Coll (FL)
East Carolina U (NC)
East Central U (OK)
Eastern Washington U (WA)
Excelsior Coll (NY)
Indiana State U (IN)
Keene State Coll (NH)
Morehead State U (KY)
New York Inst of Technology (NY)
Northeastern State U (OK)
Northern Kentucky U (KY)
Old Dominion U (VA)
Pennsylvania Coll of Technology (PA)
Pittsburg State U (KS)
Rogers State U (OK)
Shawnee State U (OH)
U of Hartford (CT)
The U of North Carolina at Charlotte (NC)
The U of West Alabama (AL)

ENGINEERING TECHNOLOGY
Austin Peay State U (TN)
Berry Coll (GA)
Buffalo State Coll, State U of New York (NY)
California State Polytechnic U, Pomona (CA)
California State U, Long Beach (CA)
California U of Pennsylvania (PA)
Drexel U (PA)
Eastern New Mexico U (NM)
East Tennessee State U (TN)
Grambling State U (LA)
Illinois State U (IL)
Indiana State U (IN)
Kansas State U (KS)
Kennesaw State U (GA)
Kent State U (OH)
Kent State U at Tuscarawas (OH)
Lawrence Technological U (MI)
Lenoir-Rhyne U (NC)
Middle Tennessee State U (TN)
Morehead State U (KY)
New Jersey Inst of Technology (NJ)
New Mexico State U (NM)

New York Inst of Technology (NY)
Northern Illinois U (IL)
Southeastern Louisiana U (LA)
Southeast Missouri State U (MO)
Southern Illinois U Carbondale (IL)
Southern Utah U (UT)
Temple U (PA)
Tennessee Technological U (TN)
Texas A&M U (TX)
Texas State U (TX)
U of Hartford (CT)
U of Maryland Eastern Shore (MD)
U of Memphis (TN)
U of North Alabama (AL)
U of Rochester (NY)
The U of Texas Rio Grande Valley (TX)
The U of West Alabama (AL)
U of Wisconsin–Stout (WI)
Wentworth Inst of Technology (MA)
Western Illinois U (IL)
West Texas A&M U (TX)
West Virginia U Inst of Technology (WV)
Wichita State U (KS)
William Penn U (IA)
Youngstown State U (OH)

ENGLISH
Abilene Christian U (TX)
Acadia U (NS, Canada)
Adams State U (CO)
Adelphi U (NY)
Agnes Scott Coll (GA)
Alabama State U (AL)
Albion Coll (MI)
Albright Coll (PA)
Alcorn State U (MS)
Alfred U (NY)
Alice Lloyd Coll (KY)
Allegheny Coll (PA)
Alma Coll (MI)
Alverno Coll (WI)
American Coll of Thessaloniki (Greece)
American Intl Coll (MA)
American Public U System (WV)
The American U in Cairo (Egypt)
Amherst Coll (MA)
Anderson U (IN)
Anderson U (SC)
Andrews U (MI)
Angelo State U (TX)
Appalachian State U (NC)
Aquinas Coll (MI)
Arcadia U (PA)
Arizona State U at the Polytechnic campus (AZ)
Arizona State U at the Tempe campus (AZ)
Arizona State U at the West campus (AZ)
Arkansas Tech U (AR)
Asbury U (KY)
Ashland U (OH)
Assumption Coll (MA)
Athabasca U (AB, Canada)
Athens State U (AL)
Auburn U (AL)
Auburn U at Montgomery (AL)
Augsburg U (MN)
Augustana Coll (IL)
Augustana U (SD)
Aurora U (IL)
Austin Coll (TX)
Austin Peay State U (TN)
Averett U (VA)
Avila U (MO)
Azusa Pacific U (CA)
Baker U (KS)
Baldwin Wallace U (OH)
Ball State U (IN)
Bard Coll (NY)
Barnard Coll (NY)
Barry U (FL)
Barton Coll (NC)
Baruch Coll of the City U of New York (NY)
Bates Coll (ME)
Baylor U (TX)
Belhaven U (MS)
Bellarmine U (KY)
Belmont U (TN)
Beloit Coll (WI)
Bemidji State U (MN)
Benedictine Coll (KS)
Benedictine U (IL)

Bennett Coll (NC)
Bennington Coll (VT)
Bentley U (MA)
Berea Coll (KY)
Berry Coll (GA)
Bethany Lutheran Coll (MN)
Bethel Coll (IN)
Bethel Coll (KS)
Bethel U (MN)
Bethel U (TN)
Bethune-Cookman U (FL)
Binghamton U, State U of New York (NY)
Biola U (CA)
Birmingham-Southern Coll (AL)
Blackburn Coll (IL)
Black Hills State U (SD)
Bloomsburg U of Pennsylvania (PA)
Bluefield Coll (VA)
Blue Mountain Coll (MS)
Bluffton U (OH)
Bob Jones U (SC)
Boise State U (ID)
Boston Coll (MA)
Boston U (MA)
Bowdoin Coll (ME)
Bowie State U (MD)
Bowling Green State U (OH)
Bradley U (IL)
Brandeis U (MA)
Brandon U (MB, Canada)
Brenau U (GA)
Brescia U (KY)
Brewton-Parker Coll (GA)
Bridgewater Coll (VA)
Bridgewater State U (MA)
Brigham Young U–Idaho (ID)
Brock U (ON, Canada)
Bryan Coll (TN)
Bryant U (RI)
Bryn Athyn Coll of the New Church (PA)
Bryn Mawr Coll (PA)
Bucknell U (PA)
Buena Vista U (IA)
Buffalo State Coll, State U of New York (NY)
Butler U (IN)
Cairn U (PA)
Caldwell U (NJ)
California Baptist U (CA)
California Inst of Technology (CA)
California Lutheran U (CA)
California Polytechnic State U, San Luis Obispo (CA)
California State Polytechnic U, Pomona (CA)
California State U, Dominguez Hills (CA)
California State U, East Bay (CA)
California State U, Fullerton (CA)
California State U, Long Beach (CA)
California State U, Los Angeles (CA)
California State U, Northridge (CA)
California State U, Sacramento (CA)
California State U, San Bernardino (CA)
California State U, San Marcos (CA)
California State U, Stanislaus (CA)
California U of Pennsylvania (PA)
Calumet Coll of Saint Joseph (IN)
Calvary U (MO)
Calvin Coll (MI)
Cameron U (OK)
Campbellsville U (KY)
Canisius Coll (NY)
Capital U (OH)
Cardinal Stritch U (WI)
Carleton Coll (MN)
Carlow U (PA)
Carnegie Mellon U (PA)
Carroll Coll (MT)
Carroll U (WI)
Carson-Newman U (TN)
Carthage Coll (WI)
Case Western Reserve U (OH)
Catawba Coll (NC)
The Catholic U of America (DC)
Cazenovia Coll (NY)
Cedar Crest Coll (PA)
Cedarville U (OH)
Centenary Coll of Louisiana (LA)
Central Connecticut State U (CT)

Central Methodist U (MO)
Central Michigan U (MI)
Central State U (OH)
Centre Coll (KY)
Chaminade U of Honolulu (HI)
Chapman U (CA)
Charleston Southern U (SC)
Chatham U (PA)
Chestnut Hill Coll (PA)
Chowan U (NC)
Christendom Coll (VA)
Christian Brothers U (TN)
Christopher Newport U (VA)
The Citadel, The Military Coll of South Carolina (SC)
City Coll of the City U of New York (NY)
Claremont McKenna Coll (CA)
Clarion U of Pennsylvania (PA)
Clark Atlanta U (GA)
Clarke U (IA)
Clark U (MA)
Clayton State U (GA)
Clemson U (SC)
Cleveland State U (OH)
Coastal Carolina U (SC)
Coe Coll (IA)
Coker Coll (SC)
Colby Coll (ME)
Colgate U (NY)
The Coll at Brockport, State U of New York (NY)
Coll of Charleston (SC)
The Coll of Idaho (ID)
Coll of Mount Saint Vincent (NY)
The Coll of New Jersey (NJ)
The Coll of New Rochelle (NY)
Coll of Saint Benedict (MN)
Coll of Saint Elizabeth (NJ)
Coll of Saint Mary (NE)
The Coll of Saint Rose (NY)
The Coll of St. Scholastica (MN)
Coll of Staten Island of the City U of New York (NY)
Coll of the Atlantic (ME)
Coll of the Holy Cross (MA)
Coll of the Ozarks (MO)
The Coll of William and Mary (VA)
The Coll of Wooster (OH)
Colorado Christian U (CO)
The Colorado Coll (CO)
Colorado Mesa U (CO)
Colorado State U (CO)
Colorado State U–Pueblo (CO)
Columbia Coll (MO)
Columbia Coll (SC)
Columbia U (NY)
Columbus State U (GA)
Concordia Coll–New York (NY)
Concordia U (QC, Canada)
Concordia U Chicago (IL)
Concordia U Irvine (CA)
Concordia U, Nebraska (NE)
Concordia U of Edmonton (AB, Canada)
Concordia U, St. Paul (MN)
Concordia U Wisconsin (WI)
Concord U (WV)
Connecticut Coll (CT)
Converse Coll (SC)
Corban U (OR)
Cornell Coll (IA)
Cornell U (NY)
Cornerstone U (MI)
Cottey Coll (MO)
Covenant Coll (GA)
Creighton U (NE)
Culver-Stockton Coll (MO)
Curry Coll (MA)
Daemen Coll (NY)
Dallas Baptist U (TX)
Dartmouth Coll (NH)
Davidson Coll (NC)
Dean Coll (MA)
Defiance Coll (OH)
Delaware State U (DE)
Delaware Valley U (PA)
Denison U (OH)
DePaul U (IL)
DePauw U (IN)
DEREE - The American Coll of Greece (Greece)
DeSales U (PA)
Dickinson Coll (PA)
Dickinson State U (ND)
Doane U (NE)
Dominican Coll (NY)

Dominican U (IL)
Dominican U of California (CA)
Drake U (IA)
Drew U (NJ)
Duquesne U (PA)
D'Youville Coll (NY)
Earlham Coll (IN)
East Carolina U (NC)
East Central U (OK)
Eastern Mennonite U (VA)
Eastern Michigan U (MI)
Eastern New Mexico U (NM)
Eastern Oregon U (OR)
Eastern Washington U (WA)
East Tennessee State U (TN)
East Texas Baptist U (TX)
Eckerd Coll (FL)
Edgewood Coll (WI)
Elizabethtown Coll (PA)
Elmhurst Coll (IL)
Elms Coll (MA)
Elon U (NC)
Emmanuel Coll (GA)
Emmanuel Coll (MA)
Emory & Henry Coll (VA)
Emory U (GA)
Emporia State U (KS)
Endicott Coll (MA)
Evangel U (MO)
The Evergreen State Coll (WA)
Fairfield U (CT)
Fairleigh Dickinson U, Florham Campus (NJ)
Fairleigh Dickinson U, Metropolitan Campus (NJ)
Fayetteville State U (NC)
Felician U (NJ)
Fitchburg State U (MA)
Flagler Coll (FL)
Florida Ag and Mech U (FL)
Florida Atlantic U (FL)
Florida Gulf Coast U (FL)
Florida Intl U (FL)
Florida State U (FL)
Fordham U (NY)
Fort Lewis Coll (CO)
Framingham State U (MA)
Francis Marion U (SC)
Franklin & Marshall Coll (PA)
Franklin Coll (IN)
Franklin Pierce U (NH)
Friends U (KS)
Frostburg State U (MD)
Furman U (SC)
Geneva Coll (PA)
George Mason U (VA)
Georgetown Coll (KY)
Georgetown U (DC)
The George Washington U (DC)
Georgia Coll & State U (GA)
Georgia Gwinnett Coll (GA)
Georgian Court U (NJ)
Georgia Southern U (GA)
Georgia Southern U–Armstrong Campus (GA)
Georgia Southwestern State U (GA)
Georgia State U (GA)
Gettysburg Coll (PA)
Gonzaga U (WA)
Gordon Coll (MA)
Gordon State Coll (GA)
Goshen Coll (IN)
Governors State U (IL)
Graceland U (IA)
Grambling State U (LA)
Grand Valley State U (MI)
Grand View U (IA)
Granite State Coll (NH)
Green Mountain Coll (VT)
Greensboro Coll (NC)
Greenville U (IL)
Grinnell Coll (IA)
Guilford Coll (NC)
Gustavus Adolphus Coll (MN)
Gwynedd Mercy U (PA)
Hamline U (MN)
Hampden-Sydney Coll (VA)
Hampshire Coll (MA)
Hampton U (VA)
Hannibal-LaGrange U (MO)
Harding U (AR)
Hardin-Simmons U (TX)
Hartwick Coll (NY)
Harvard U (MA)
Haverford Coll (PA)
Hawai`i Pacific U (HI)

Heidelberg U (OH)
Hendrix Coll (AR)
High Point U (NC)
Hilbert Coll (NY)
Hillsdale Coll (MI)
Hiram Coll (OH)
Hobart and William Smith Colls (NY)
Hofstra U (NY)
Hollins U (VA)
Holy Family U (PA)
Holy Names U (CA)
Hood Coll (MD)
Hope Coll (MI)
Hope Intl U (CA)
Houston Baptist U (TX)
Howard Payne U (TX)
Humboldt State U (CA)
Hunter Coll of the City U of New York (NY)
Huntingdon Coll (AL)
Husson U (ME)
Huston-Tillotson U (TX)
Idaho State U (ID)
Illinois Coll (IL)
Illinois State U (IL)
Immaculata U (PA)
Indiana State U (IN)
Indiana U Bloomington (IN)
Indiana U East (IN)
Indiana U Kokomo (IN)
Indiana U Northwest (IN)
Indiana U of Pennsylvania (PA)
Indiana U–Purdue U Indianapolis (IN)
Indiana U South Bend (IN)
Indiana U Southeast (IN)
Indiana Wesleyan U (IN)
Inter American U of Puerto Rico, Metropolitan Campus (PR)
Inter American U of Puerto Rico, San Germán Campus (PR)
Iona Coll (NY)
Iowa State U of Science and Technology (IA)
Ithaca Coll (NY)
Jackson State U (MS)
Jacksonville U (FL)
James Madison U (VA)
John Brown U (AR)
John Cabot U (Italy)
John Carroll U (OH)
John Jay Coll of Criminal Justice of the City U of New York (NY)
Johns Hopkins U (MD)
Johnson C. Smith U (NC)
Judson U (IL)
Juniata Coll (PA)
Kalamazoo Coll (MI)
Kansas State U (KS)
Kansas Wesleyan U (KS)
Kean U (NJ)
Keene State Coll (NH)
Kennesaw State U (GA)
Kent State U (OH)
Kent State U at Ashtabula (OH)
Kent State U at East Liverpool (OH)
Kent State U at Geauga (OH)
Kent State U at Salem (OH)
Kent State U at Stark (OH)
Kent State U at Trumbull (OH)
Kent State U at Tuscarawas (OH)
Kentucky State U (KY)
Kenyon Coll (OH)
The King's Coll (NY)
King's Coll (PA)
King U (TN)
Knox Coll (IL)
Kutztown U of Pennsylvania (PA)
Lafayette Coll (PA)
LaGrange Coll (GA)
Lamar U (TX)
Langston U (OK)
La Roche Coll (PA)
La Salle U (PA)
Lasell Coll (MA)
La Sierra U (CA)
Lawrence Technological U (MI)
Lawrence U (WI)
Lebanese American U (Lebanon)
Lebanon Valley Coll (PA)
Lee U (TN)
Lehigh U (PA)
Lehman Coll of the City U of New York (NY)
Le Moyne Coll (NY)
Lenoir-Rhyne U (NC)

Lesley U (MA)
LeTourneau U (TX)
Lewis U (IL)
Liberty U (VA)
Limestone Coll (SC)
Lincoln Memorial U (TN)
Lincoln U (MO)
Lincoln U (PA)
Lindenwood U (MO)
Lindsey Wilson Coll (KY)
Lipscomb U (TN)
Lock Haven U of Pennsylvania (PA)
Long Island U–LIU Brooklyn (NY)
Long Island U–LIU Post (NY)
Longwood U (VA)
Loras Coll (IA)
Louisiana Coll (LA)
Louisiana State U and A&M Coll (LA)
Loyola Marymount U (CA)
Loyola U Chicago (IL)
Lubbock Christian U (TX)
Luther Coll (IA)
Lycoming Coll (PA)
Lynchburg Coll (VA)
Lyon Coll (AR)
Macalester Coll (MN)
Madonna U (MI)
Maharishi U of Management (IA)
Malone U (OH)
Manchester U (IN)
Manhattan Coll (NY)
Manhattanville Coll (NY)
Mansfield U of Pennsylvania (PA)
Maranatha Baptist U (WI)
Marian U (IN)
Marian U (WI)
Marietta Coll (OH)
Marist Coll (NY)
Marlboro Coll (VT)
Marquette U (WI)
Marshall U (WV)
Mary Baldwin U (VA)
Marylhurst U (OR)
Marymount Manhattan Coll (NY)
Marymount U (VA)
Maryville Coll (TN)
Maryville U of Saint Louis (MO)
Marywood U (PA)
Massachusetts Coll of Liberal Arts (MA)
Massachusetts Inst of Technology (MA)
The Master's U (CA)
McDaniel Coll (MD)
McKendree U (IL)
McMurry U (TX)
McNeese State U (LA)
McPherson Coll (KS)
Mercer U, Macon (GA)
Mercy Coll (NY)
Mercyhurst U (PA)
Meredith Coll (NC)
Merrimack Coll (MA)
Messiah Coll (PA)
Metropolitan State U of Denver (CO)
Miami U (OH)
Michigan State U (MI)
Michigan Technological U (MI)
Mid-America Christian U (OK)
MidAmerica Nazarene U (KS)
Middle Georgia State U (GA)
Middle Tennessee State U (TN)
Millersville U of Pennsylvania (PA)
Milligan Coll (TN)
Millikin U (IL)
Millsaps Coll (MS)
Mills Coll (CA)
Minnesota State U Moorhead (MN)
Minot State U (ND)
Misericordia U (PA)
Mississippi State U (MS)
Missouri Baptist U (MO)
Missouri State U (MO)
Missouri U of Science and Technology (MO)
Missouri Valley Coll (MO)
Missouri Western State U (MO)
Molloy Coll (NY)
Monmouth Coll (IL)
Montclair State U (NJ)
Moravian Coll (PA)
Morehead State U (KY)
Morehouse Coll (GA)
Morningside Coll (IA)
Morris Coll (SC)

Mount Aloysius Coll (PA)
Mount Holyoke Coll (MA)
Mount Marty Coll (SD)
Mount Mary U (WI)
Mount Mercy U (IA)
Mount St. Joseph U (OH)
Mount Saint Mary Coll (NY)
Mount Saint Mary's U (CA)
Mount St. Mary's U (MD)
Mount Vernon Nazarene U (OH)
Muhlenberg Coll (PA)
Multnomah U (OR)
Murray State U (KY)
Muskingum U (OH)
Naropa U (CO)
National U (CA)
Nazareth Coll of Rochester (NY)
Neumann U (PA)
Newberry Coll (SC)
New Coll of Florida (FL)
New Jersey City U (NJ)
Newman U (KS)
New Mexico Highlands U (NM)
New Mexico State U (NM)
New York Inst of Technology (NY)
New York U (NY)
Niagara U (NY)
North Carolina Central U (NC)
North Carolina State U (NC)
North Carolina Wesleyan Coll (NC)
North Central Coll (IL)
North Dakota State U (ND)
Northeastern State U (OK)
Northeastern U (MA)
Northern Arizona U (AZ)
Northern Illinois U (IL)
Northern Kentucky U (KY)
Northern Michigan U (MI)
Northern State U (SD)
Northern Vermont U–Lyndon (VT)
North Greenville U (SC)
Northland Coll (WI)
Northwest Christian U (OR)
Northwestern Coll (IA)
Northwestern Oklahoma State U (OK)
Northwestern State U of Louisiana (LA)
Northwestern U (IL)
Northwest Missouri State U (MO)
Northwest Nazarene U (ID)
Northwest U (WA)
Notre Dame de Namur U (CA)
Nova Southeastern U (FL)
Nyack Coll (NY)
Oakland City U (IN)
Oakland U (MI)
Oberlin Coll (OH)
Occidental Coll (CA)
Oglethorpe U (GA)
Ohio Christian U (OH)
Ohio Dominican U (OH)
The Ohio State U (OH)
The Ohio State U at Lima (OH)
The Ohio State U at Mansfield (OH)
The Ohio State U at Marion (OH)
The Ohio State U at Newark (OH)
Ohio U (OH)
Ohio Wesleyan U (OH)
Oklahoma Christian U (OK)
Oklahoma City U (OK)
Oklahoma State U (OK)
Old Dominion U (VA)
Olivet Nazarene U (IL)
Oral Roberts U (OK)
Oregon State U (OR)
Ottawa U (KS)
Otterbein U (OH)
Ouachita Baptist U (AR)
Our Lady of the Lake U (TX)
Pace U (NY)
Pace U, Pleasantville Campus (NY)
Pacific Lutheran U (WA)
Palm Beach Atlantic U (FL)
Penn State Abington (PA)
Penn State Altoona (PA)
Penn State Beaver (PA)
Penn State Berks (PA)
Penn State Brandywine (PA)
Penn State DuBois (PA)
Penn State Erie, The Behrend Coll (PA)
Penn State Fayette, The Eberly Campus (PA)
Penn State Greater Allegheny (PA)
Penn State Harrisburg (PA)
Penn State Hazleton (PA)

Penn State Lehigh Valley (PA)
Penn State Mont Alto (PA)
Penn State New Kensington (PA)
Penn State Schuylkill (PA)
Penn State Shenango (PA)
Penn State U Park (PA)
Penn State Wilkes-Barre (PA)
Penn State Worthington Scranton (PA)
Penn State York (PA)
Pepperdine U, Malibu (CA)
Pfeiffer U (NC)
Piedmont Coll (GA)
Pine Manor Coll (MA)
Pittsburg State U (KS)
Pitzer Coll (CA)
Point Loma Nazarene U (CA)
Point Park U (PA)
Point U (GA)
Pomona Coll (CA)
Portland State U (OR)
Prairie View A&M U (TX)
Presbyterian Coll (SC)
Princeton U (NJ)
Principia Coll (IL)
Providence Coll (RI)
Purdue U (IN)
Purdue U Northwest (IN)
Queens Coll of the City U of New York (NY)
Quinnipiac U (CT)
Radford U (VA)
Randolph Coll (VA)
Randolph-Macon Coll (VA)
Redeemer U Coll (ON, Canada)
Reed Coll (OR)
Regent U (VA)
Regis U (CO)
Rhode Island Coll (RI)
Rhodes Coll (TN)
Rice U (TX)
Rider U (NJ)
Ripon Coll (WI)
Rivier U (NH)
Roanoke Coll (VA)
Robert Morris U (PA)
Roberts Wesleyan Coll (NY)
Rockford U (IL)
Rockhurst U (MO)
Rocky Mountain Coll (MT)
Roger Williams U (RI)
Rollins Coll (FL)
Roosevelt U (IL)
Rosemont Coll (PA)
Rowan U (NJ)
Rust Coll (MS)
Rutgers U–Camden (NJ)
Rutgers U–Newark (NJ)
Rutgers U–New Brunswick (NJ)
Sacred Heart U (CT)
The Sage Colls (NY)
Saginaw Valley State U (MI)
St. Ambrose U (IA)
St. Andrews U (NC)
Saint Anselm Coll (NH)
Saint Augustine's U (NC)
St. Bonaventure U (NY)
St. Catherine U (MN)
Saint Francis U (PA)
St. John Fisher Coll (NY)
Saint John's U (MN)
St. John's U (NY)
St. Joseph's Coll, Long Island Campus (NY)
St. Joseph's Coll, New York (NY)
Saint Joseph's U (PA)
St. Lawrence U (NY)
Saint Leo U (FL)
Saint Louis U (MO)
Saint Louis U–Madrid Campus (Spain)
Saint Martin's U (WA)
Saint Mary-of-the-Woods Coll (IN)
Saint Mary's Coll of California (CA)
St. Mary's Coll of Maryland (MD)
St. Mary's U (TX)
Saint Michael's Coll (VT)
St. Norbert Coll (WI)
St. Olaf Coll (MN)
Saint Peter's U (NJ)
St. Thomas Aquinas Coll (NY)
St. Thomas U (FL)
St. Thomas U (NB, Canada)
Saint Vincent Coll (PA)
Salisbury U (MD)
Salve Regina U (RI)
Samford U (AL)

Sam Houston State U (TX)
San Diego State U (CA)
San Francisco State U (CA)
Santa Clara U (CA)
Schreiner U (TX)
Scripps Coll (CA)
Seattle Pacific U (WA)
Seattle U (WA)
Seton Hill U (PA)
Sewanee: The U of the South (TN)
Shawnee State U (OH)
Shaw U (NC)
Shenandoah U (VA)
Shepherd U (WV)
Shippensburg U of Pennsylvania (PA)
Shorter U (GA)
Siena Coll (NY)
Sierra Nevada Coll (NV)
Silver Lake Coll of the Holy Family (WI)
Simmons Coll (MA)
Simon Fraser U (BC, Canada)
Simpson Coll (IA)
Skidmore Coll (NY)
Slippery Rock U of Pennsylvania (PA)
Smith Coll (MA)
Sonoma State U (CA)
Southeastern Louisiana U (LA)
Southeastern Oklahoma State U (OK)
Southeastern U (FL)
Southeast Missouri State U (MO)
Southern Adventist U (TN)
Southern Arkansas U–Magnolia (AR)
Southern Illinois U Carbondale (IL)
Southern Illinois U Edwardsville (IL)
Southern Methodist U (TX)
Southern Utah U (UT)
Southern Vermont Coll (VT)
Southwest Baptist U (MO)
Southwestern Adventist U (TX)
Southwestern Assemblies of God U (TX)
Southwestern U (TX)
Spelman Coll (GA)
Spring Hill Coll (AL)
Stanford U (CA)
State U of New York at Fredonia (NY)
State U of New York at New Paltz (NY)
State U of New York at Oswego (NY)
State U of New York at Plattsburgh (NY)
State U of New York Coll at Cortland (NY)
State U of New York Coll at Geneseo (NY)
State U of New York Coll at Oneonta (NY)
State U of New York Coll at Potsdam (NY)
Stephen F. Austin State U (TX)
Stetson U (FL)
Stevens Inst of Technology (NJ)
Stevenson U (MD)
Stockton U (NJ)
Stonehill Coll (MA)
Stony Brook U, State U of New York (NY)
Suffolk U (MA)
Susquehanna U (PA)
Sweet Briar Coll (VA)
Syracuse U (NY)
Tabor Coll (KS)
Tarleton State U (TX)
Taylor U (IN)
Temple U (PA)
Tennessee Technological U (TN)
Tennessee Wesleyan U (TN)
Texas A&M Intl U (TX)
Texas A&M U (TX)
Texas A&M U–Central Texas (TX)
Texas A&M U–Commerce (TX)
Texas A&M U–Corpus Christi (TX)
Texas A&M U–Kingsville (TX)
Texas A&M U–Texarkana (TX)
Texas Christian U (TX)
Texas Lutheran U (TX)
Texas State U (TX)
Texas Tech U (TX)
Texas Woman's U (TX)

Thomas U (GA)
Tiffin U (OH)
Toccoa Falls Coll (GA)
Towson U (MD)
Transylvania U (KY)
Trent U (ON, Canada)
Trevecca Nazarene U (TN)
Trine U (IN)
Trinity Christian Coll (IL)
Trinity U (TX)
Troy U (AL)
Truett McConnell U (GA)
Truman State U (MO)
Tufts U (MA)
Tulane U (LA)
Tusculum Coll (TN)
Union Coll (NE)
Union Coll (NY)
Union U (TN)
United States Military Acad (NY)
Université de Sherbrooke (QC, Canada)
Université Sainte-Anne (NS, Canada)
U at Albany, State U of New York (NY)
U at Buffalo, the State U of New York (NY)
The U of Akron (OH)
The U of Alabama (AL)
The U of Alabama at Birmingham (AL)
U of Alaska Fairbanks (AK)
The U of Arizona (AZ)
U of Arkansas (AR)
U of Bridgeport (CT)
U of California, Davis (CA)
U of California, Irvine (CA)
U of California, Los Angeles (CA)
U of California, Riverside (CA)
U of California, San Diego (CA)
U of California, Santa Barbara (CA)
U of Central Arkansas (AR)
U of Central Florida (FL)
U of Central Missouri (MO)
U of Central Oklahoma (OK)
U of Charleston (WV)
U of Chicago (IL)
U of Cincinnati (OH)
U of Colorado Boulder (CO)
U of Colorado Colorado Springs (CO)
U of Colorado Denver (CO)
U of Dallas (TX)
U of Dayton (OH)
U of Denver (CO)
U of Dubuque (IA)
U of Evansville (IN)
U of Florida (FL)
U of Georgia (GA)
U of Guam (GU)
U of Guelph (ON, Canada)
U of Hartford (CT)
U of Hawaii at Manoa (HI)
U of Houston (TX)
U of Houston–Clear Lake (TX)
U of Houston–Downtown (TX)
U of Idaho (ID)
U of Illinois at Chicago (IL)
U of Illinois at Springfield (IL)
U of Jamestown (ND)
The U of Kansas (KS)
U of Kentucky (KY)
U of King's Coll (NS, Canada)
U of La Verne (CA)
U of Louisiana at Monroe (LA)
U of Louisville (KY)
U of Maine (ME)
U of Maine at Farmington (ME)
U of Maine at Fort Kent (ME)
U of Maine at Machias (ME)
U of Maine at Presque Isle (ME)
U of Mary Hardin-Baylor (TX)
U of Maryland, Baltimore County (MD)
U of Maryland, Coll Park (MD)
U of Maryland Eastern Shore (MD)
U of Maryland U Coll (MD)
U of Mary Washington (VA)
U of Massachusetts Amherst (MA)
U of Massachusetts Boston (MA)
U of Massachusetts Dartmouth (MA)
U of Massachusetts Lowell (MA)
U of Memphis (TN)
U of Miami (FL)
U of Michigan (MI)

U of Michigan–Dearborn (MI)
U of Michigan–Flint (MI)
U of Minnesota, Duluth (MN)
U of Minnesota, Morris (MN)
U of Minnesota, Twin Cities Campus (MN)
U of Missouri (MO)
U of Missouri–St. Louis (MO)
U of Mobile (AL)
U of Montana (MT)
U of Montevallo (AL)
U of Mount Union (OH)
U of Nebraska at Kearney (NE)
U of Nebraska–Lincoln (NE)
U of Nevada, Las Vegas (NV)
U of Nevada, Reno (NV)
U of New England (ME)
U of New Hampshire (NH)
U of New Haven (CT)
U of New Mexico (NM)
U of New Orleans (LA)
U of North Alabama (AL)
U of North Carolina at Asheville (NC)
The U of North Carolina at Chapel Hill (NC)
The U of North Carolina at Charlotte (NC)
The U of North Carolina at Greensboro (NC)
The U of North Carolina at Pembroke (NC)
The U of North Carolina Wilmington (NC)
U of North Dakota (ND)
U of Northern Colorado (CO)
U of Northern Iowa (IA)
U of North Florida (FL)
U of North Georgia (GA)
U of North Texas (TX)
U of Notre Dame (IN)
U of Oklahoma (OK)
U of Oregon (OR)
U of Pennsylvania (PA)
U of Pikeville (KY)
U of Pittsburgh at Bradford (PA)
U of Pittsburgh at Greensburg (PA)
U of Providence (MT)
U of Puget Sound (WA)
U of Regina (SK, Canada)
U of Rhode Island (RI)
U of Richmond (VA)
U of Rochester (NY)
U of St. Francis (IL)
U of Saint Francis (IN)
U of Saint Joseph (CT)
U of Saint Mary (KS)
U of St. Thomas (MN)
U of St. Thomas (TX)
U of San Diego (CA)
U of San Francisco (CA)
U of Saskatchewan (SK, Canada)
U of Science and Arts of Oklahoma (OK)
The U of Scranton (PA)
U of Sioux Falls (SD)
U of South Alabama (AL)
U of South Carolina (SC)
U of South Carolina Aiken (SC)
U of South Dakota (SD)
U of Southern California (CA)
U of Southern Indiana (IN)
U of Southern Maine (ME)
U of Southern Mississippi (MS)
U of South Florida, St. Petersburg (FL)
U of South Florida Sarasota-Manatee (FL)
The U of Tampa (FL)
The U of Tennessee (TN)
The U of Tennessee at Chattanooga (TN)
The U of Tennessee at Martin (TN)
The U of Texas at Austin (TX)
The U of Texas at El Paso (TX)
The U of Texas at San Antonio (TX)
The U of Texas of the Permian Basin (TX)
The U of Texas Rio Grande Valley (TX)
U of the Fraser Valley (BC, Canada)
U of the Incarnate Word (TX)
U of the Pacific (CA)
U of the Virgin Islands (VI)
The U of Toledo (OH)
U of Toronto (ON, Canada)

The U of Tulsa (OK)
U of Utah (UT)
U of Valley Forge (PA)
U of Vermont (VT)
U of Virginia (VA)
The U of Virginia's Coll at Wise (VA)
U of Washington (WA)
U of Waterloo (ON, Canada)
The U of West Alabama (AL)
U of West Georgia (GA)
U of Wisconsin–Eau Claire (WI)
U of Wisconsin–La Crosse (WI)
U of Wisconsin–Madison (WI)
U of Wisconsin–Milwaukee (WI)
U of Wisconsin–Parkside (WI)
U of Wisconsin–Platteville (WI)
U of Wisconsin–River Falls (WI)
U of Wisconsin–Stevens Point (WI)
U of Wisconsin–Superior (WI)
U of Wisconsin–Whitewater (WI)
U of Wyoming (WY)
Upper Iowa U (IA)
Ursinus Coll (PA)
Ursuline Coll (OH)
Utah State U (UT)
Utah Valley U (UT)
Utica Coll (NY)
Valdosta State U (GA)
Valley City State U (ND)
Valparaiso U (IN)
Vanderbilt U (TN)
Vanguard U of Southern California (CA)
Vassar Coll (NY)
Villanova U (PA)
Virginia Commonwealth U (VA)
Virginia Military Inst (VA)
Virginia Polytechnic Inst and State U (VA)
Virginia Wesleyan U (VA)
Wabash Coll (IN)
Wagner Coll (NY)
Wake Forest U (NC)
Waldorf U (IA)
Walsh U (OH)
Warner Pacific Coll (OR)
Wartburg Coll (IA)
Washington & Jefferson Coll (PA)
Washington and Lee U (VA)
Washington Coll (MD)
Washington State U (WA)
Washington State U–Tri-Cities (WA)
Washington State U–Vancouver (WA)
Washington U in St. Louis (MO)
Wayland Baptist U (TX)
Waynesburg U (PA)
Wayne State Coll (NE)
Wayne State U (MI)
Weber State U (UT)
Webster U (MO)
Welch Coll (TN)
Wellesley Coll (MA)
Wells Coll (NY)
Wesleyan U (CT)
West Chester U of Pennsylvania (PA)
Western Connecticut State U (CT)
Western Illinois U (IL)
Western Kentucky U (KY)
Western Michigan U (MI)
Western New England U (MA)
Western Oregon U (OR)
Western State Colorado U (CO)
Western Washington U (WA)
Westfield State U (MA)
Westminster Coll (PA)
Westminster Coll (UT)
Westmont Coll (CA)
West Texas A&M U (TX)
West Virginia State U (WV)
West Virginia U (WV)
West Virginia Wesleyan Coll (WV)
Wheaton Coll (IL)
Wheaton Coll (MA)
Whitman Coll (WA)
Whittier Coll (CA)
Whitworth U (WA)
Wichita State U (KS)
Widener U (PA)
Wilkes U (PA)
Willamette U (OR)
William Jewell Coll (MO)
William Paterson U of New Jersey (NJ)

William Peace U (NC)
William Penn U (IA)
Williams Coll (MA)
William Woods U (MO)
Winona State U (MN)
Winthrop U (SC)
Wisconsin Lutheran Coll (WI)
Wittenberg U (OH)
Wofford Coll (SC)
Worcester State U (MA)
Wright State U (OH)
Wright State U–Lake Campus (OH)
Xavier U of Louisiana (LA)
York Coll of Pennsylvania (PA)
Youngstown State U (OH)

ENGLISH AS A SECOND/ FOREIGN LANGUAGE (TEACHING)

American U (DC)
Augsburg U (MN)
Bethel Coll (IN)
Bethel U (MN)
Bluffton U (OH)
Brigham Young U (UT)
Brock U (ON, Canada)
California State U, Stanislaus (CA)
Calvin Coll (MI)
Carroll Coll (MT)
The Catholic U of America (DC)
Concordia U (QC, Canada)
Concordia U, Nebraska (NE)
Concordia U, St. Paul (MN)
Concordia U Wisconsin (WI)
Doane U (NE)
Eastern Washington U (WA)
Goshen Coll (IN)
Hawai'i Pacific U (HI)
Indiana Wesleyan U (IN)
Inter American U of Puerto Rico, Aguadilla Campus (PR)
Inter American U of Puerto Rico, Barranquitas Campus (PR)
Inter American U of Puerto Rico, Fajardo Campus (PR)
Inter American U of Puerto Rico, Metropolitan Campus (PR)
Inter American U of Puerto Rico, San Germán Campus (PR)
Iowa State U of Science and Technology (IA)
Kent State U (OH)
Lee U (TN)
Le Moyne Coll (NY)
Liberty U (VA)
Maryville Coll (TN)
Minnesota State U Moorhead (MN)
Molloy Coll (NY)
Multnomah U (OR)
Niagara U (NY)
Northwest U (WA)
Nyack Coll (NY)
The Ohio State U (OH)
Oklahoma Christian U (OK)
Oklahoma City U (OK)
Queens Coll of the City U of New York (NY)
Roberts Wesleyan Coll (NY)
Saint Joseph's U (PA)
Salisbury U (MD)
Simmons Coll (MA)
Southern Adventist U (TN)
Union U (TN)
U of Guam (GU)
U of Hawaii at Manoa (HI)
U of Northern Iowa (IA)
U of Puerto Rico–Humacao (PR)
The U of Texas at San Antonio (TX)
U of Wisconsin–Milwaukee (WI)
U of Wisconsin–River Falls (WI)
Winona State U (MN)

ENGLISH/FRENCH AS A SECOND/FOREIGN LANGUAGE (TEACHING) RELATED

Kent State U (OH)

ENGLISH LANGUAGE AND LITERATURE RELATED

The Baptist Coll of Florida (FL)
Binghamton U, State U of New York (NY)
Concordia Coll–New York (NY)
Dakota State U (SD)
Doane U (NE)
Drexel U (PA)
Eastern U (PA)
Emmanuel Coll (MA)

Florida State U (FL)
Fort Lewis Coll (CO)
Harvard U (MA)
Hofstra U (NY)
John Cabot U (Italy)
Loyola U New Orleans (LA)
Marlboro Coll (VT)
Middlebury Coll (VT)
Milligan Coll (TN)
Ohio U (OH)
Saint Leo U (FL)
Saint Mary's Coll of California (CA)
Saint Mary's U of Minnesota (MN)
Southeastern U (FL)
State U of New York Empire State Coll (NY)
U of Michigan (MI)
U of Pennsylvania (PA)
U of Providence (MT)
Washington U in St. Louis (MO)
Webster U (MO)
Western Kentucky U (KY)

ENGLISH/LANGUAGE ARTS TEACHER EDUCATION

Abilene Christian U (TX)
Adams State U (CO)
Albion Coll (MI)
Alice Lloyd Coll (KY)
Alverno Coll (WI)
Anderson U (IN)
Anderson U (SC)
Appalachian State U (NC)
Aquinas Coll (MI)
Arizona Christian U (AZ)
Arkansas Tech U (AR)
Arlington Baptist U (TX)
Auburn U (AL)
Augustana Coll (IL)
Averett U (VA)
Ball State U (IN)
The Baptist Coll of Florida (FL)
Barry U (FL)
Baylor U (TX)
Bethany Lutheran Coll (MN)
Bethel Coll (IN)
Bethel U (MN)
Bethune-Cookman U (FL)
Blackburn Coll (IL)
Bluefield Coll (VA)
Blue Mountain Coll (MS)
Bob Jones U (SC)
Boise State U (ID)
Boston U (MA)
Bowling Green State U (OH)
Bradley U (IL)
Bridgewater State U (MA)
Brigham Young U–Idaho (ID)
Bryan Coll (TN)
Buena Vista U (IA)
Buffalo State Coll, State U of New York (NY)
Cairn U (PA)
California State U, Long Beach (CA)
Cameron U (OK)
Campbellsville U (KY)
Canisius Coll (NY)
Capital U (OH)
Carroll Coll (MT)
Carroll U (WI)
The Catholic U of America (DC)
Cedarville U (OH)
Central Michigan U (MI)
Charleston Southern U (SC)
Christian Brothers U (TN)
Coker Coll (SC)
The Coll of New Jersey (NJ)
Coll of Saint Mary (NE)
The Coll of Saint Rose (NY)
Coll of Staten Island of the City U of New York (NY)
Coll of the Ozarks (MO)
Colorado Christian U (CO)
Columbus State U (GA)
Concordia U Chicago (IL)
Corban U (OR)
Cornerstone U (MI)
Covenant Coll (GA)
Culver-Stockton Coll (MO)
Daemen Coll (NY)
Dakota State U (SD)
Delaware State U (DE)
Dickinson State U (ND)
Dominican Coll (NY)
Duquesne U (PA)
East Carolina U (NC)

East Central U (OK)
Eastern Michigan U (MI)
Eastern Washington U (WA)
East Texas Baptist U (TX)
Edgewood Coll (WI)
Elmhurst Coll (IL)
Emmanuel Coll (GA)
Emory & Henry Coll (VA)
Ferris State U (MI)
Fitchburg State U (MA)
Flagler Coll (FL)
Florida Ag and Mech U (FL)
Florida Atlantic U (FL)
Florida Southern Coll (FL)
Florida State U (FL)
Fort Lewis Coll (CO)
Franklin Coll (IN)
Friends U (KS)
Georgia Southern U–Armstrong
  Campus (GA)
Gordon State Coll (GA)
Goshen Coll (IN)
Grambling State U (LA)
Grand Valley State U (MI)
Grand View U (IA)
Granite State Coll (NH)
Green Mountain Coll (VT)
Greensboro Coll (NC)
Greenville U (IL)
Grove City Coll (PA)
Hannibal-LaGrange U (MO)
Harding U (AR)
Hardin-Simmons U (TX)
Hiram Coll (OH)
Hobe Sound Bible Coll (FL)
Hofstra U (NY)
Holy Family U (PA)
Hope Coll (MI)
Houston Baptist U (TX)
Howard Payne U (TX)
Huntingdon Coll (AL)
Husson U (ME)
Immaculata U (PA)
Indiana U Bloomington (IN)
Indiana U Northwest (IN)
Indiana U–Purdue U Indianapolis
  (IN)
Indiana U South Bend (IN)
Indiana Wesleyan U (IN)
Inter American U of Puerto Rico,
  San Germán Campus (PR)
Iona Coll (NY)
Ithaca Coll (NY)
John Brown U (AR)
Juniata Coll (PA)
Kansas Wesleyan U (KS)
Kennesaw State U (GA)
Lee U (TN)
Le Moyne Coll (NY)
LeTourneau U (TX)
Limestone Coll (SC)
Lincoln U (MO)
Lipscomb U (TN)
Long Island U–LIU Brooklyn (NY)
Long Island U–LIU Post (NY)
Louisiana Coll (LA)
Madonna U (MI)
Malone U (OH)
Manchester U (IN)
Manhattanville Coll (NY)
Maranatha Baptist U (WI)
Marian U (WI)
Marist Coll (NY)
Martin Luther Coll (MN)
Maryville Coll (TN)
Marywood U (PA)
McMurry U (TX)
Mercyhurst U (PA)
Merrimack Coll (MA)
Messiah Coll (PA)
Miami U (OH)
MidAmerica Nazarene U (KS)
Millikin U (IL)
Minnesota State U Moorhead (MN)
Minot State U (ND)
Misericordia U (PA)
Missouri State U (MO)
Missouri Western State U (MO)
Morningside Coll (IA)
Morris Coll (SC)
Mount Marty Coll (SD)
Mount Mary U (WI)
Mount Vernon Nazarene U (OH)
National U (CA)
Nazareth Coll of Rochester (NY)
Niagara U (NY)
North Dakota State U (ND)

Northeastern State U (OK)
Northern Michigan U (MI)
Northern State U (SD)
North Greenville U (SC)
Northwestern U (IA)
Northwestern Oklahoma State U
  (OK)
Northwest Missouri State U (MO)
Northwest Nazarene U (ID)
Northwest U (WA)
Nova Southeastern U (FL)
Nyack Coll (NY)
Oakland City U (IN)
Ohio Dominican U (OH)
Ohio Northern U (OH)
The Ohio State U (OH)
The Ohio State U at Lima (OH)
The Ohio State U at Mansfield (OH)
The Ohio State U at Marion (OH)
The Ohio State U at Newark (OH)
Oklahoma Baptist U (OK)
Oklahoma Christian U (OK)
Oklahoma City U (OK)
Olivet Nazarene U (IL)
Oral Roberts U (OK)
Pace U (NY)
Pace U, Pleasantville Campus (NY)
Palm Beach Atlantic U (FL)
Pepperdine U, Malibu (CA)
Piedmont Coll (GA)
Pittsburg State U (KS)
Point Park U (PA)
Providence Coll (RI)
Purdue U (IN)
Queens Coll of the City U of New
  York (NY)
Rhode Island Coll (RI)
Rivier U (NH)
Roberts Wesleyan Coll (NY)
Rocky Mountain Coll (MT)
Roger Williams U (RI)
Rust Coll (MS)
Saginaw Valley State U (MI)
St. Ambrose U (IA)
St. Catherine U (MN)
Saint Francis U (PA)
St. John Fisher Coll (NY)
St. John's U (NY)
St. Joseph's Coll, Long Island
  Campus (NY)
St. Joseph's Coll, New York (NY)
Saint Mary's U of Minnesota (MN)
Salve Regina U (RI)
Schreiner U (TX)
Seattle Pacific U (WA)
Seton Hill U (PA)
Slippery Rock U of Pennsylvania
  (PA)
Southeastern Louisiana U (LA)
Southeastern Oklahoma State U
  (OK)
Southeastern U (FL)
Southeast Missouri State U (MO)
Southern Adventist U (TN)
Southern Utah U (UT)
Southwest Baptist U (MO)
Southwestern Adventist U (TX)
Southwestern Assemblies of God U
  (TX)
Southwestern Coll (KS)
Spring Hill Coll (AL)
State U of New York at New Paltz
  (NY)
State U of New York at Plattsburgh
  (NY)
State U of New York Coll at
  Oneonta (NY)
State U of New York Coll at
  Potsdam (NY)
Syracuse U (NY)
Taylor U (IN)
Temple U (PA)
Texas Christian U (TX)
Tiffin U (OH)
Toccoa Falls Coll (GA)
Trevecca Nazarene U (TN)
Trine U (IN)
Trinity Christian Coll (IL)
Union Coll (NE)
The U of Akron (OH)
U of Central Oklahoma (OK)
U of Dubuque (IA)
U of Evansville (IN)
The U of Findlay (OH)
U of Georgia (GA)
U of Idaho (ID)
U of Illinois at Chicago (IL)

U of Jamestown (ND)
U of Louisiana at Monroe (LA)
U of Maine (ME)
U of Maine at Farmington (ME)
U of Maine at Machias (ME)
U of Mary Hardin-Baylor (TX)
U of Michigan–Flint (MI)
U of Mobile (AL)
The U of North Carolina at
  Greensboro (NC)
The U of North Carolina at
  Pembroke (NC)
U of Oklahoma (OK)
U of Providence (MT)
U of Puerto Rico–Humacao (PR)
U of Regina (SK, Canada)
U of St. Francis (IL)
U of St. Thomas (MN)
U of Sioux Falls (SD)
U of South Dakota (SD)
The U of Tennessee at Martin (TN)
U of Vermont (VT)
U of Wisconsin–Milwaukee (WI)
U of Wisconsin–Stevens Point (WI)
U of Wisconsin–Superior (WI)
U of Wisconsin–Whitewater (WI)
Ursuline Coll (OH)
Utah Valley U (UT)
Utica Coll (NY)
Valley City State U (ND)
Valparaiso U (IN)
Washington U in St. Louis (MO)
Wayland Baptist U (TX)
Waynesburg U (PA)
Wayne State Coll (NE)
Weber State U (UT)
Webster U (MO)
Welch Coll (TN)
Western Michigan U (MI)
Western State Colorado U (CO)
Westfield State U (MA)
Westmont Coll (CA)
West Virginia Wesleyan Coll (WV)
Widener U (PA)
William Woods U (MO)
Wilmington U (DE)
Winona State U (MN)
Wisconsin Lutheran Coll (WI)
York Coll of Pennsylvania (PA)
Youngstown State U (OH)

ENGLISH LITERATURE (BRITISH AND COMMONWEALTH)
Ambrose U (AB, Canada)
Bennington Coll (VT)
Concordia U (QC, Canada)
Gannon U (PA)
Hunter Coll of the City U of New
  York (NY)
Marian U (WI)
Marlboro Coll (VT)
New York U (NY)
Pace U (NY)
U of Pittsburgh (PA)
Washington U in St. Louis (MO)
Whittier Coll (CA)

ENTOMOLOGY
Cornell U (NY)
Iowa State U of Science and
  Technology (IA)
Michigan State U (MI)
The Ohio State U (OH)
Oklahoma State U (OK)
Purdue U (IN)
Rutgers U–New Brunswick (NJ)
Texas A&M U (TX)
U of California, Davis (CA)
U of California, Riverside (CA)
U of Florida (FL)
U of Georgia (GA)
U of Nebraska–Lincoln (NE)
U of Wisconsin–Madison (WI)
Utah State U (UT)
Washington State U (WA)

ENTREPRENEURIAL AND SMALL BUSINESS RELATED
Babson Coll (MA)
Fairleigh Dickinson U, Florham
  Campus (NJ)
Fairleigh Dickinson U, Metropolitan
  Campus (NJ)
Fashion Inst of Technology (NY)
Lipscomb U (TN)
Loyola U Chicago (IL)
New York Inst of Technology (NY)

Penn State U Park (PA)
State U of New York at Plattsburgh
  (NY)
U of St. Thomas (MN)

ENTREPRENEURSHIP
American Baptist Coll (TN)
American Public U System (WV)
The American U of Paris (France)
Arizona State U at the Tempe
  campus (AZ)
Ashland U (OH)
Auburn U at Montgomery (AL)
Avila U (MO)
Azusa Pacific U (CA)
Babson Coll (MA)
Baldwin Wallace U (OH)
Ball State U (IN)
Baylor U (TX)
Bay Path U (MA)
Belmont U (TN)
Binghamton U, State U of New York
  (NY)
Bradley U (IL)
Brigham Young U (UT)
Bryant U (RI)
Buena Vista U (IA)
Butler U (IN)
California Baptist U (CA)
California State U, Dominguez Hills
  (CA)
California State U, Fullerton (CA)
Canisius Coll (NY)
Carnegie Mellon U (PA)
Carthage Coll (WI)
Central Michigan U (MI)
Clarkson U (NY)
Coll of the Atlantic (ME)
Dallas Baptist U (TX)
Davenport U, Grand Rapids (MI)
DEREE - The American Coll of
  Greece (Greece)
Drexel U (PA)
Duquesne U (PA)
East Central U (OK)
Eastern Michigan U (MI)
Eastern U (PA)
Elon U (NC)
Emerson Coll (MA)
Endicott Coll (MA)
Florida State U (FL)
Gannon U (PA)
Governors State U (IL)
Grand Valley State U (MI)
Grove City Coll (PA)
Hampshire Coll (MA)
HEC Montreal (QC, Canada)
High Point U (NC)
Hofstra U (NY)
Husson U (ME)
Illinois Wesleyan U (IL)
Indiana Wesleyan U (IN)
Inter American U of Puerto Rico,
  Aguadilla Campus (PR)
Inter American U of Puerto Rico,
  Barranquitas Campus (PR)
Inter American U of Puerto Rico,
  Bayamón Campus (PR)
Inter American U of Puerto Rico,
  Metropolitan Campus (PR)
Inter American U of Puerto Rico,
  San Germán Campus (PR)
Iowa State U of Science and
  Technology (IA)
Jackson State U (MS)
Jacksonville U (FL)
John Paul the Great Catholic U
  (CA)
Juniata Coll (PA)
Kansas State U (KS)
Kennesaw State U (GA)
Kent State U (OH)
Lamar U (TX)
Lasell Coll (MA)
Lenoir-Rhyne U (NC)
Lincoln Coll (IL)
Lindenwood U (MO)
Lipscomb U (TN)
Long Island U–LIU Brooklyn (NY)
Louisiana State U and A&M Coll
  (LA)
Loyola Marymount U (CA)
Lynn U (FL)
Marquette U (WI)
Marymount Manhattan Coll (NY)
Mercer U, Macon (GA)
Mercy Coll (NY)

Metropolitan State U of Denver
  (CO)
Middle Tennessee State U (TN)
Millikin U (IL)
Minneapolis Coll of Art and Design
  (MN)
Missouri State U (MO)
Mount St. Mary's U (MD)
Northeastern State U (OK)
Northeastern U (MA)
Northern Kentucky U (KY)
Northern Michigan U (MI)
Northern Vermont U–Lyndon (VT)
Northland Coll (WI)
Ohio Northern U (OH)
Oklahoma State U (OK)
Oregon Inst of Technology (OR)
Pace U (NY)
Pace U, Pleasantville Campus (NY)
Point Loma Nazarene U (CA)
Purdue U Northwest (IN)
Quinnipiac U (CT)
Rider U (NJ)
Rollins Coll (FL)
Rowan U (NJ)
Saint Louis U (MO)
Saint Louis U–Madrid Campus
  (Spain)
St. Mary's U (TX)
Saint Mary's U of Minnesota (MN)
Samford U (AL)
Sam Houston State U (TX)
Seton Hill U (PA)
Shenandoah U (VA)
Shippensburg U of Pennsylvania
  (PA)
Sierra Nevada Coll (NV)
Southern Vermont Coll (VT)
Stetson U (FL)
Suffolk U (MA)
Syracuse U (NY)
Temple U (PA)
Texas Christian U (TX)
Trine U (IN)
Trinity Christian Coll (IL)
The U of Arizona (AZ)
U of Central Arkansas (AR)
U of Dayton (OH)
U of Hartford (CT)
U of Hawaii at Manoa (HI)
U of Houston (TX)
U of Illinois at Chicago (IL)
U of Maine at Machias (ME)
U of Miami (FL)
U of Michigan–Flint (MI)
U of Minnesota, Crookston (MN)
U of Minnesota, Duluth (MN)
U of Nevada, Las Vegas (NV)
U of New England (ME)
The U of North Carolina at
  Greensboro (NC)
The U of North Carolina at
  Pembroke (NC)
U of North Dakota (ND)
U of North Texas (TX)
U of Pittsburgh at Bradford (PA)
U of Regina (SK, Canada)
U of St. Francis (IL)
U of St. Thomas (MN)
U of San Francisco (CA)
U of Sioux Falls (SD)
U of South Dakota (SD)
U of South Florida, St. Petersburg
  (FL)
The U of Tampa (FL)
The U of Texas at San Antonio (TX)
The U of Texas Rio Grande Valley
  (TX)
The U of Toledo (OH)
U of Utah (UT)
U of Vermont (VT)
U of Washington (WA)
U of Wisconsin–Whitewater (WI)
Washington State U (WA)
Washington U in St. Louis (MO)
Waynesburg U (PA)
Western Kentucky U (KY)
Western Michigan U (MI)
Western New England U (MA)
Western State Colorado U (CO)
West Virginia U (WV)
Wichita State U (KS)
Wilkes U (PA)
Wittenberg U (OH)
York Coll of Pennsylvania (PA)

ENVIRONMENTAL BIOLOGY

Barnard Coll (NY)
Beloit Coll (WI)
Bennington Coll (VT)
Blackburn Coll (IL)
Boston U (MA)
Bridgewater State U (MA)
California State Polytechnic U, Pomona (CA)
Cazenovia Coll (NY)
Cedar Crest Coll (PA)
Chowan U (NC)
Christopher Newport U (VA)
Colby Coll (ME)
Colgate U (NY)
Coll of the Atlantic (ME)
Columbia U (NY)
Cornerstone U (MI)
East Stroudsburg U of Pennsylvania (PA)
Elizabethtown Coll (PA)
Ferris State U (MI)
Fitchburg State U (MA)
Fort Lewis Coll (CO)
Franklin Pierce U (NH)
Friends U (KS)
Greenville U (IL)
Heidelberg U (OH)
Humboldt State U (CA)
Inter American U of Puerto Rico, Bayamón Campus (PR)
Iona Coll (NY)
Liberty U (VA)
Lindenwood U (MO)
Manchester U (IN)
Marlboro Coll (VT)
The Master's U (CA)
McDaniel Coll (MD)
Michigan State U (MI)
Northern Arizona U (AZ)
Northwestern Coll (IA)
Ohio Northern U (OH)
Otterbein U (OH)
Roberts Wesleyan Coll (NY)
Saint Mary's U of Minnesota (MN)
Sewanee: The U of the South (TN)
State U of New York Coll at Cortland (NY)
State U of New York Coll of Environmental Science and Forestry (NY)
Texas A&M U (TX)
Tulane U (LA)
Unity Coll (ME)
Université Sainte-Anne (NS, Canada)
U of Dayton (OH)
U of Guelph (ON, Canada)
U of La Verne (CA)
U of Mount Union (OH)
U of Regina (SK, Canada)
U of Saskatchewan (SK, Canada)
The U of Tennessee at Martin (TN)
Washington U in St. Louis (MO)
Western State Colorado U (CO)

ENVIRONMENTAL CHEMISTRY

Beloit Coll (WI)
Colby Coll (ME)
Florida State U (FL)
Lawrence Technological U (MI)
Rhode Island Coll (RI)
Roberts Wesleyan Coll (NY)
U of California, San Diego (CA)

ENVIRONMENTAL CONTROL TECHNOLOGIES RELATED

Delaware State U (DE)

ENVIRONMENTAL DESIGN/ ARCHITECTURE

Arizona State U at the Tempe campus (AZ)
ArtCenter Coll of Design (CA)
Auburn U (AL)
Ball State U (IN)
Bennington Coll (VT)
Boston Architectural Coll (MA)
Bowling Green State U (OH)
Coll of the Atlantic (ME)
Cornell U (NY)
Delaware Valley U (PA)
Florida Atlantic U (FL)
Green Mountain Coll (VT)
Marywood U (PA)
North Carolina State U (NC)
North Dakota State U (ND)

Rutgers U–New Brunswick (NJ)
Stony Brook U, State U of New York (NY)
U at Buffalo, the State U of New York (NY)
U of Colorado Boulder (CO)
U of Hawaii at Manoa (HI)
U of Houston (TX)
U of Massachusetts Amherst (MA)
U of Memphis (TN)
U of Minnesota, Twin Cities Campus (MN)
U of New Mexico (NM)
U of Oklahoma (OK)
U of Pennsylvania (PA)
The U of Texas at Austin (TX)

ENVIRONMENTAL EDUCATION

Coll of the Atlantic (ME)
Juniata Coll (PA)
Sonoma State U (CA)
U of Dubuque (IA)
U of Maine at Machias (ME)
Whitworth U (WA)

ENVIRONMENTAL ENGINEERING TECHNOLOGY

Bowling Green State U (OH)
California State U, Long Beach (CA)
City Coll of the City U of New York (NY)
Florida State U (FL)
Kennesaw State U (GA)
North Carolina State U (NC)
Shawnee State U (OH)
Tufts U (MA)
United States Military Acad (NY)
The U of Findlay (OH)
U of Guelph (ON, Canada)
U of Wisconsin–Whitewater (WI)

ENVIRONMENTAL/ ENVIRONMENTAL HEALTH ENGINEERING

Arizona State U at the Polytechnic campus (AZ)
Arizona State U at the Tempe campus (AZ)
Bucknell U (PA)
California Inst of Technology (CA)
California Polytechnic State U, San Luis Obispo (CA)
Central State U (OH)
Clarkson U (NY)
Clemson U (SC)
Colorado State U (CO)
Columbia U (NY)
Drexel U (PA)
East Central U (OK)
Elon U (NC)
Florida Gulf Coast U (FL)
Florida Intl U (FL)
Gannon U (PA)
The George Washington U (DC)
Georgia Inst of Technology (GA)
Humboldt State U (CA)
Indiana Tech (IN)
Johns Hopkins U (MD)
Kennesaw State U (GA)
Lafayette Coll (PA)
Lehigh U (PA)
Louisiana State U and A&M Coll (LA)
Loyola U Chicago (IL)
Manhattan Coll (NY)
Marquette U (WI)
Massachusetts Inst of Technology (MA)
Michigan Technological U (MI)
Missouri U of Science and Technology (MO)
Montana Tech of The U of Montana (MT)
New Jersey Inst of Technology (NJ)
New Mexico Inst of Mining and Technology (NM)
North Carolina State U (NC)
Northern Arizona U (AZ)
Northwestern U (IL)
The Ohio State U (OH)
Oral Roberts U (OK)
Oregon State U (OR)
Penn State Abington (PA)
Penn State Altoona (PA)
Penn State Beaver (PA)
Penn State Berks (PA)

Penn State Brandywine (PA)
Penn State DuBois (PA)
Penn State Erie, The Behrend Coll (PA)
Penn State Fayette, The Eberly Campus (PA)
Penn State Greater Allegheny (PA)
Penn State Harrisburg (PA)
Penn State Hazleton (PA)
Penn State Lehigh Valley (PA)
Penn State Mont Alto (PA)
Penn State New Kensington (PA)
Penn State Schuylkill (PA)
Penn State Shenango (PA)
Penn State U Park (PA)
Penn State Wilkes-Barre (PA)
Penn State Worthington Scranton (PA)
Penn State York (PA)
Polytechnic U of Puerto Rico (PR)
Purdue U (IN)
Rensselaer Polytechnic Inst (NY)
Rice U (TX)
Roger Williams U (RI)
San Diego State U (CA)
Seattle U (WA)
Southern Methodist U (TX)
Stanford U (CA)
State U of New York Coll of Environmental Science and Forestry (NY)
Stevens Inst of Technology (NJ)
Suffolk U (MA)
Syracuse U (NY)
Tarleton State U (TX)
Taylor U (IN)
Temple U (PA)
Texas A&M U–Kingsville (TX)
Texas Tech U (TX)
Tufts U (MA)
Tulane U (LA)
United States Military Acad (NY)
U at Buffalo, the State U of New York (NY)
The U of Alabama (AL)
The U of Arizona (AZ)
U of California, Irvine (CA)
U of California, Riverside (CA)
U of Central Florida (FL)
U of Cincinnati (OH)
U of Colorado Boulder (CO)
U of Florida (FL)
U of Georgia (GA)
U of Miami (FL)
U of Michigan (MI)
U of Minnesota, Twin Cities Campus (MN)
U of Nevada, Reno (NV)
U of New Hampshire (NH)
U of North Dakota (ND)
U of Notre Dame (IN)
U of Oklahoma (OK)
U of Pennsylvania (PA)
U of Pittsburgh (PA)
U of Regina (SK, Canada)
U of Saskatchewan (SK, Canada)
U of Southern California (CA)
The U of Texas at Austin (TX)
The U of Toledo (OH)
U of Vermont (VT)
U of Washington (WA)
U of Waterloo (ON, Canada)
U of Wisconsin–Platteville (WI)
Utah State U (UT)
West Texas A&M U (TX)
Wilkes U (PA)
Worcester Polytechnic Inst (MA)

ENVIRONMENTAL HEALTH

American U of Beirut (Lebanon)
Baylor U (TX)
Boise State U (ID)
Bowling Green State U (OH)
Brewton-Parker Coll (GA)
California State U, Northridge (CA)
Central Michigan U (MI)
Colorado State U (CO)
Concordia U of Edmonton (AB, Canada)
Dickinson State U (ND)
East Carolina U (NC)
East Central U (OK)
East Tennessee State U (TN)
Illinois State U (IL)
Indiana U Bloomington (IN)
Oakland U (MI)
Ohio U (OH)

Old Dominion U (VA)
Rhode Island Coll (RI)
State U of New York Coll of Environmental Science and Forestry (NY)
U of Georgia (GA)
U of Massachusetts Lowell (MA)
The U of North Carolina at Chapel Hill (NC)
U of Regina (SK, Canada)
U of Washington (WA)
West Chester U of Pennsylvania (PA)
Western Kentucky U (KY)
Willamette U (OR)

ENVIRONMENTAL SCIENCE

Abilene Christian U (TX)
Albion Coll (MI)
Albright Coll (PA)
Allegheny Coll (PA)
Alverno Coll (WI)
American Public U System (WV)
American U (DC)
The American U of Paris (France)
Antioch Coll, Yellow Springs (OH)
Appalachian State U (NC)
Arizona State U at the West campus (AZ)
Arkansas Tech U (AR)
Ashland U (OH)
Assumption Coll (MA)
Auburn U (AL)
Auburn U at Montgomery (AL)
Averett U (VA)
Baldwin Wallace U (OH)
Ball State U (IN)
Barnard Coll (NY)
Baylor U (TX)
Bellarmine U (KY)
Belmont U (TN)
Benedictine U (IL)
Bennington Coll (VT)
Berry Coll (GA)
Bethel U (MN)
Bethune-Cookman U (FL)
Biola U (CA)
Boston U (MA)
Bradley U (IL)
Bridgewater Coll (VA)
Brigham Young U (UT)
Bryant U (RI)
Bucknell U (PA)
Buena Vista U (IA)
California Baptist U (CA)
California Lutheran U (CA)
California State U, East Bay (CA)
California State U, Long Beach (CA)
California State U, Monterey Bay (CA)
California U of Pennsylvania (PA)
Calvin Coll (MI)
Canisius Coll (NY)
Capital U (OH)
Carroll U (WI)
Carthage Coll (WI)
Catawba Coll (NC)
Cedarville U (OH)
Central Methodist U (MO)
Central Michigan U (MI)
Chatham U (PA)
Chestnut Hill Coll (PA)
Clarion U of Pennsylvania (PA)
Clarkson U (NY)
Cleveland State U (OH)
Coe Coll (IA)
Colby Coll (ME)
Colgate U (NY)
The Coll at Brockport, State U of New York (NY)
The Coll of Wooster (OH)
The Colorado Coll (CO)
Colorado Mesa U (CO)
Columbia Coll (MO)
Columbia U (NY)
Concordia U (QC, Canada)
Concordia U Chicago (IL)
Concordia U, Nebraska (NE)
Concordia U of Edmonton (AB, Canada)
Creighton U (NE)
Dallas Baptist U (TX)
Delaware State U (DE)
DePaul U (IL)
DEREE - The American Coll of Greece (Greece)

Dickinson Coll (PA)
Dickinson State U (ND)
Dominican U (IL)
Drake U (IA)
Drexel U (PA)
Duquesne U (PA)
Earlham Coll (IN)
Eastern Nazarene Coll (MA)
Eastern New Mexico U (NM)
Eastern U (PA)
Eastern Washington U (WA)
Edgewood Coll (WI)
Elon U (NC)
Emory & Henry Coll (VA)
Endicott Coll (MA)
The Evergreen State Coll (WA)
Fairleigh Dickinson U, Metropolitan Campus (NJ)
Flagler Coll (FL)
Florida Ag and Mech U (FL)
Florida Inst of Technology (FL)
Florida State U (FL)
Fordham U (NY)
Framingham State U (MA)
Franklin & Marshall Coll (PA)
Frostburg State U (MD)
Gannon U (PA)
Geneva Coll (PA)
George Mason U (VA)
Georgia Coll & State U (GA)
Georgia Gwinnett Coll (GA)
Gettysburg Coll (PA)
Goshen Coll (IN)
Green Mountain Coll (VT)
Hardin-Simmons U (TX)
Hartwick Coll (NY)
Hawai'i Pacific U (HI)
Heidelberg U (OH)
Hollins U (VA)
Humboldt State U (CA)
Hunter Coll of the City U of New York (NY)
Husson U (ME)
Idaho State U (ID)
Indiana U Bloomington (IN)
Indiana U–Purdue U Indianapolis (IN)
Inter American U of Puerto Rico, Bayamón Campus (PR)
Inter American U of Puerto Rico, San Germán Campus (PR)
Iowa State U of Science and Technology (IA)
Johns Hopkins U (MD)
Juniata Coll (PA)
Kennesaw State U (GA)
King's Coll (PA)
Kutztown U of Pennsylvania (PA)
Lamar U (TX)
La Salle U (PA)
La Sierra U (CA)
Lebanon Valley Coll (PA)
Lewis U (IL)
Lincoln Coll (IL)
Lincoln U (PA)
Linfield Coll (OR)
Lipscomb U (TN)
Longwood U (VA)
Louisiana State U and A&M Coll (LA)
Loyola Marymount U (CA)
Loyola U Chicago (IL)
Loyola U New Orleans (LA)
Lynchburg Coll (VA)
Madonna U (MI)
Marietta Coll (OH)
Marshall U (WV)
Maryville U of Saint Louis (MO)
Marywood U (PA)
Massachusetts Coll of Liberal Arts (MA)
Massachusetts Maritime Acad (MA)
McDaniel Coll (MD)
McMurry U (TX)
Merrimack Coll (MA)
Messiah Coll (PA)
Metropolitan State U of Denver (CO)
Miami U (OH)
Michigan State U (MI)
Michigan Technological U (MI)
Mills Coll (CA)
Monmouth Coll (IL)
Moravian Coll (PA)
Muhlenberg Coll (PA)
Muskingum U (OH)

Nazareth Coll of Rochester (NY)
New Jersey Inst of Technology (NJ)
New Mexico State U (NM)
Niagara U (NY)
North Carolina State U (NC)
Northeastern U (MA)
Northern Arizona U (AZ)
Northern Kentucky U (KY)
Northern Michigan U (MI)
Northern Vermont U–Lyndon (VT)
Northwestern U (IL)
Northwest U (WA)
Nova Southeastern U (FL)
Oakland U (MI)
Ohio Dominican U (OH)
The Ohio State U (OH)
Oklahoma State U (OK)
Oregon Inst of Technology (OR)
Oregon State U (OR)
Pace U (NY)
Pace U, Pleasantville Campus (NY)
Pfeiffer U (NC)
Piedmont Coll (GA)
Pitzer Coll (CA)
Point Loma Nazarene U (CA)
Post U (CT)
Queens Coll of the City U of New York (NY)
Ramapo Coll of New Jersey (NJ)
Randolph Coll (VA)
Regis U (CO)
Rensselaer Polytechnic Inst (NY)
Rhodes Coll (TN)
Rider U (NJ)
Rochester Inst of Technology (NY)
Rocky Mountain Coll (MT)
Roger Williams U (RI)
Rutgers U–Newark (NJ)
Rutgers U–New Brunswick (NJ)
Saint Francis U (PA)
Saint Louis U (MO)
Saint Louis U–Madrid Campus (Spain)
St. Mary's U (TX)
St. Norbert Coll (WI)
Saint Vincent Coll (PA)
Salisbury U (MD)
Samford U (AL)
Sam Houston State U (TX)
San Diego State U (CA)
San Francisco State U (CA)
Santa Clara U (CA)
Scripps Coll (CA)
Seattle U (WA)
Siena Coll (NY)
Sierra Nevada Coll (NV)
Simmons Coll (MA)
Simon Fraser U (BC, Canada)
Simpson Coll (IA)
Skidmore Coll (NY)
Southeast Missouri State U (MO)
Southern Illinois U Edwardsville (IL)
Southern Methodist U (TX)
Spelman Coll (GA)
State U of New York Coll at Cortland (NY)
State U of New York Coll of Environmental Science and Forestry (NY)
Stephen F. Austin State U (TX)
Stetson U (FL)
Stevenson U (MD)
Stonehill Coll (MA)
Suffolk U (MA)
Sweet Briar Coll (VA)
Tarleton State U (TX)
Taylor U (IN)
Temple U (PA)
Texas A&M U (TX)
Texas A&M U–Commerce (TX)
Texas A&M U–Corpus Christi (TX)
Texas Christian U (TX)
Texas State U (TX)
Trinity Christian Coll (IL)
Troy U (AL)
Tusculum Coll (TN)
United States Military Acad (NY)
Unity Coll (ME)
U at Albany, State U of New York (NY)
The U of Alabama (AL)
The U of Arizona (AZ)
U of Arkansas (AR)
U of California, Irvine (CA)
U of California, Los Angeles (CA)
U of California, Riverside (CA)

U of California, San Diego (CA)
U of Denver (CO)
U of Dubuque (IA)
U of Evansville (IN)
U of Florida (FL)
U of Guelph (ON, Canada)
U of Hawaii at Manoa (HI)
U of Houston (TX)
U of Houston–Clear Lake (TX)
U of Idaho (ID)
U of Illinois at Chicago (IL)
U of La Verne (CA)
U of Maine (ME)
U of Maine at Farmington (ME)
U of Maine at Presque Isle (ME)
U of Maryland, Baltimore County (MD)
U of Maryland, Coll Park (MD)
U of Massachusetts Amherst (MA)
U of Massachusetts Boston (MA)
U of Massachusetts Lowell (MA)
U of Michigan–Dearborn (MI)
U of Michigan–Flint (MI)
U of Minnesota, Duluth (MN)
U of Minnesota, Twin Cities Campus (MN)
U of Mount Union (OH)
U of Nevada, Reno (NV)
U of New England (ME)
U of New Hampshire (NH)
U of New Haven (CT)
U of New Mexico (NM)
The U of North Carolina at Chapel Hill (NC)
The U of North Carolina at Pembroke (NC)
The U of North Carolina Wilmington (NC)
U of Northern Iowa (IA)
U of Notre Dame (IN)
U of Oklahoma (OK)
U of Oregon (OR)
U of Rhode Island (RI)
U of Rochester (NY)
U of St. Francis (IL)
U of Saint Francis (IN)
U of St. Thomas (MN)
U of St. Thomas (TX)
U of San Diego (CA)
U of San Francisco (CA)
U of Saskatchewan (SK, Canada)
The U of Scranton (PA)
U of South Carolina (SC)
U of Southern California (CA)
U of Southern Indiana (IN)
U of Southern Maine (ME)
U of South Florida, St. Petersburg (FL)
The U of Tennessee at Chattanooga (TN)
The U of Texas at San Antonio (TX)
The U of Texas Rio Grande Valley (TX)
U of the Incarnate Word (TX)
The U of Toledo (OH)
U of Vermont (VT)
U of Virginia (VA)
U of Washington (WA)
U of Washington, Bothell (WA)
U of Washington, Tacoma (WA)
U of Waterloo (ON, Canada)
U of Wisconsin–Madison (WI)
U of Wisconsin–Milwaukee (WI)
U of Wisconsin–Stout (WI)
U of Wisconsin–Superior (WI)
U of Wisconsin–Whitewater (WI)
Upper Iowa U (IA)
Utah Valley U (UT)
Valley City State U (ND)
Valparaiso U (IN)
Vassar Coll (NY)
Villanova U (PA)
Walsh U (OH)
Wartburg Coll (IA)
Washington & Jefferson Coll (PA)
Washington Coll (MD)
Washington State U (WA)
Washington State U–Tri-Cities (WA)
Washington State U–Vancouver (WA)
Washington U in St. Louis (MO)
Wayland Baptist U (TX)
Wayne State U (MI)
Western Washington U (WA)
Westfield State U (MA)
Westminster Coll (PA)

West Texas A&M U (TX)
West Virginia Wesleyan Coll (WV)
Wheaton Coll (IL)
Wheaton Coll (MA)
Whittier Coll (CA)
Willamette U (OR)
Williams Coll (MA)
Wilmington U (DE)
Winthrop U (SC)
Wisconsin Lutheran Coll (WI)
Wittenberg U (OH)
Worcester State U (MA)
Wright State U (OH)
Wright State U–Lake Campus (OH)
Youngstown State U (OH)

ENVIRONMENTAL STUDIES

Acadia U (NS, Canada)
Adelphi U (NY)
Albion Coll (MI)
Albright Coll (PA)
Alfred U (NY)
Allegheny Coll (PA)
Alma Coll (MI)
American U (DC)
The American U of Paris (France)
Amherst Coll (MA)
Appalachian State U (NC)
Aquinas Coll (MI)
Arizona State U at the Polytechnic campus (AZ)
Arizona State U at the Tempe campus (AZ)
Augsburg U (MN)
Augustana Coll (IL)
Austin Coll (TX)
Bard Coll (NY)
Bates Coll (ME)
Baylor U (TX)
Bellarmine U (KY)
Beloit Coll (WI)
Bemidji State U (MN)
Bennington Coll (VT)
Bethel U (MN)
Binghamton U, State U of New York (NY)
Birmingham-Southern Coll (AL)
Blackburn Coll (IL)
Black Hills State U (SD)
Boise State U (ID)
Boston Coll (MA)
Bowdoin Coll (ME)
Bowling Green State U (OH)
Brandeis U (MA)
Bryant U (RI)
Bucknell U (PA)
California State U, East Bay (CA)
California State U, Monterey Bay (CA)
California State U, Sacramento (CA)
California State U, San Marcos (CA)
Calvin Coll (MI)
Canisius Coll (NY)
Carleton Coll (MN)
Carroll Coll (MT)
Case Western Reserve U (OH)
Catawba Coll (NC)
Central Michigan U (MI)
Centre Coll (KY)
Chaminade U of Honolulu (HI)
Champlain Coll (VT)
Chatham U (PA)
Christopher Newport U (VA)
Claremont McKenna Coll (CA)
Clarke U (IA)
Cleveland State U (OH)
Coe Coll (IA)
Colby Coll (ME)
Colgate U (NY)
Coll of Coastal Georgia (GA)
The Coll of Idaho (ID)
The Coll of New Rochelle (NY)
Coll of Saint Benedict (MN)
Coll of the Atlantic (ME)
Coll of the Holy Cross (MA)
The Coll of William and Mary (VA)
The Colorado Coll (CO)
Columbia Coll (SC)
Columbia Southern U (AL)
Columbia U (NY)
Concordia U, Nebraska (NE)
Concordia U Wisconsin (WI)
Connecticut Coll (CT)
Cornell Coll (IA)
Cottey Coll (MO)

Dartmouth Coll (NH)
Davidson Coll (NC)
Denison U (OH)
DePauw U (IN)
DEREE - The American Coll of Greece (Greece)
Dickinson Coll (PA)
Doane U (NE)
Drake U (IA)
Drew U (NJ)
Drexel U (PA)
Earlham Coll (IN)
Eastern Mennonite U (VA)
Eastern Nazarene Coll (MA)
Eckerd Coll (FL)
Elmhurst Coll (IL)
Elon U (NC)
Emory & Henry Coll (VA)
Emory U (GA)
Eugene Lang Coll of Liberal Arts (NY)
The Evergreen State Coll (WA)
Excelsior Coll (NY)
Fairfield U (CT)
Florida Ag and Mech U (FL)
Florida Gulf Coast U (FL)
Florida Intl U (FL)
Florida Southern Coll (FL)
Florida State U (FL)
Fort Lewis Coll (CO)
Franklin & Marshall Coll (PA)
Franklin Pierce U (NH)
Franklin U Switzerland (Switzerland)
Furman U (SC)
Georgetown U (DC)
The George Washington U (DC)
Gettysburg Coll (PA)
Gonzaga U (WA)
Green Mountain Coll (VT)
Guilford Coll (NC)
Gustavus Adolphus Coll (MN)
Hamilton Coll (NY)
Hamline U (MN)
Hampshire Coll (MA)
Hampton U (VA)
Harvard U (MA)
Hawai`i Pacific U (HI)
Heidelberg U (OH)
Hendrix Coll (AR)
Hiram Coll (OH)
Hobart and William Smith Colls (NY)
Hofstra U (NY)
Hollins U (VA)
Hood Coll (MD)
Humboldt State U (CA)
Huston-Tillotson U (TX)
Illinois Coll (IL)
Illinois Wesleyan U (IL)
Indiana U Bloomington (IN)
Indiana U South Bend (IN)
Indiana U Southeast (IN)
Inter American U of Puerto Rico, San Germán Campus (PR)
Iowa State U of Science and Technology (IA)
Ithaca Coll (NY)
Jacksonville U (FL)
John Carroll U (OH)
Johns Hopkins U (MD)
Juniata Coll (PA)
Kansas Wesleyan U (KS)
Keene State Coll (NH)
Kent State U (OH)
Kenyon Coll (OH)
King's Coll (PA)
Knox Coll (IL)
Lasell Coll (MA)
Lawrence U (WI)
Lehigh U (PA)
Le Moyne Coll (NY)
Lenoir-Rhyne U (NC)
Lesley U (MA)
Lincoln Memorial U (TN)
Linfield Coll (OR)
Loyola U Chicago (IL)
Loyola U New Orleans (LA)
Luther Coll (IA)
Lynchburg Coll (VA)
Lynn U (FL)
Macalester Coll (MN)
Maharishi U of Management (IA)
Malone U (OH)
Manchester U (IN)
Manhattanville Coll (NY)
Mansfield U of Pennsylvania (PA)

Marietta Coll (OH)
Marlboro Coll (VT)
Marquette U (WI)
Marymount Manhattan Coll (NY)
Maryville Coll (TN)
Maryville U of Saint Louis (MO)
Massachusetts Coll of Liberal Arts (MA)
McDaniel Coll (MD)
McKendree U (IL)
McPherson Coll (KS)
Meredith Coll (NC)
Michigan State U (MI)
Middlebury Coll (VT)
Millikin U (IL)
Mills Coll (CA)
Minnesota State U Moorhead (MN)
Moravian Coll (PA)
Mount Holyoke Coll (MA)
Mount St. Mary's U (MD)
Muskingum U (OH)
Naropa U (CO)
New Coll of Florida (FL)
New Mexico Highlands U (NM)
New Mexico Inst of Mining and Technology (NM)
The New School for Public Engagement (NY)
New York U (NY)
North Carolina Wesleyan Coll (NC)
North Central Coll (IL)
Northeastern U (MA)
Northern Arizona U (AZ)
Northern Illinois U (IL)
Northland Coll (WI)
Northwestern U (IL)
Oberlin Coll (OH)
Occidental Coll (CA)
Ohio Northern U (OH)
Ohio U (OH)
Ohio Wesleyan U (OH)
Oklahoma City U (OK)
Pace U (NY)
Pace U, Pleasantville Campus (NY)
Pacific Lutheran U (WA)
Penn State Altoona (PA)
Penn State U Park (PA)
Pfeiffer U (NC)
Pomona Coll (CA)
Portland State U (OR)
Principia Coll (IL)
Purchase Coll, State U of New York (NY)
Queens Coll of the City U of New York (NY)
Ramapo Coll of New Jersey (NJ)
Randolph Coll (VA)
Randolph-Macon Coll (VA)
Redeemer U Coll (ON, Canada)
Reed Coll (OR)
Regis U (CO)
Rhode Island Coll (RI)
Ripon Coll (WI)
Roanoke Coll (VA)
Robert Morris U (PA)
Rocky Mountain Coll (MT)
Rollins Coll (FL)
Rowan U (NJ)
Rutgers U–New Brunswick (NJ)
Saint Anselm Coll (NH)
St. Bonaventure U (NY)
Saint Francis U (PA)
Saint John's U (MN)
St. John's U (NY)
Saint Joseph's U (PA)
St. Lawrence U (NY)
Saint Martin's U (WA)
St. Mary's Coll of Maryland (MD)
Saint Michael's Coll (VT)
St. Olaf Coll (MN)
St. Thomas U (NB, Canada)
Saint Vincent Coll (PA)
Salve Regina U (RI)
San Diego State U (CA)
San Francisco State U (CA)
Santa Clara U (CA)
Seattle U (WA)
Sewanee: The U of the South (TN)
Shenandoah U (VA)
Shepherd U (WV)
Shippensburg U of Pennsylvania (PA)
Shorter U (GA)
Siena Coll (NY)
Skidmore Coll (NY)
Smith Coll (MA)
Sonoma State U (CA)

Southern Methodist U (TX)
Southwestern U (TX)
Spelman Coll (GA)
Stanford U (CA)
State U of New York at Fredonia (NY)
State U of New York at Plattsburgh (NY)
State U of New York Coll at Cortland (NY)
State U of New York Coll at Oneonta (NY)
State U of New York Coll at Potsdam (NY)
State U of New York Coll of Environmental Science and Forestry (NY)
Stockton U (NJ)
Stonehill Coll (MA)
Stony Brook U, State U of New York (NY)
Suffolk U (MA)
Susquehanna U (PA)
Sweet Briar Coll (VA)
Temple U (PA)
Tennessee Technological U (TN)
Tennessee Wesleyan U (TN)
Texas A&M U (TX)
Trent U (ON, Canada)
Trine U (IN)
Trinity U (TX)
Tufts U (MA)
Tulane U (LA)
Tusculum Coll (TN)
United States Military Acad (NY)
Université de Sherbrooke (QC, Canada)
The U of Arizona (AZ)
U of California, Davis (CA)
U of California, Irvine (CA)
U of California, San Diego (CA)
U of California, Santa Barbara (CA)
U of California, Santa Cruz (CA)
U of Central Arkansas (AR)
U of Central Florida (FL)
U of Chicago (IL)
U of Cincinnati (OH)
U of Colorado Boulder (CO)
U of Denver (CO)
U of Dubuque (IA)
U of Evansville (IN)
U of Guelph (ON, Canada)
U of Illinois at Springfield (IL)
The U of Kansas (KS)
U of Kentucky (KY)
U of Maine at Farmington (ME)
U of Maine at Fort Kent (ME)
U of Maine at Machias (ME)
U of Maine at Presque Isle (ME)
U of Maryland, Baltimore County (MD)
U of Maryland Eastern Shore (MD)
U of Michigan (MI)
U of Michigan–Dearborn (MI)
U of Minnesota, Duluth (MN)
U of Minnesota, Morris (MN)
U of Missouri (MO)
U of Montana (MT)
U of Nebraska–Lincoln (NE)
U of Nevada, Las Vegas (NV)
U of New England (ME)
U of North Carolina at Asheville (NC)
The U of North Carolina at Chapel Hill (NC)
The U of North Carolina at Pembroke (NC)
The U of North Carolina Wilmington (NC)
U of North Dakota (ND)
U of North Georgia (GA)
U of Oklahoma (OK)
U of Oregon (OR)
U of Pennsylvania (PA)
U of Pittsburgh at Bradford (PA)
U of Puget Sound (WA)
U of Regina (SK, Canada)
U of Rhode Island (RI)
U of Richmond (VA)
U of Rochester (NY)
U of St. Thomas (MN)
U of St. Thomas (TX)
U of San Diego (CA)
U of San Francisco (CA)
U of Southern California (CA)
U of Southern Indiana (IN)
U of Southern Maine (ME)

The U of Tampa (FL)
The U of Tennessee at Martin (TN)
U of the Pacific (CA)
The U of Toledo (OH)
U of Toronto (ON, Canada)
The U of Tulsa (OK)
U of Utah (UT)
U of Vermont (VT)
The U of Virginia's Coll at Wise (VA)
U of Washington (WA)
U of Washington, Bothell (WA)
U of Washington, Tacoma (WA)
U of Waterloo (ON, Canada)
U of Wisconsin–Madison (WI)
U of Wisconsin–Superior (WI)
U of Wyoming (WY)
Ursinus Coll (PA)
Vassar Coll (NY)
Villanova U (PA)
Virginia Commonwealth U (VA)
Virginia Polytechnic Inst and State U (VA)
Virginia Wesleyan U (VA)
Washington & Jefferson Coll (PA)
Washington and Lee U (VA)
Washington Coll (MD)
Washington U in St. Louis (MO)
Waynesburg U (PA)
Wellesley Coll (MA)
Wells Coll (NY)
Wesleyan U (CT)
Western Michigan U (MI)
Western State Colorado U (CO)
Western Washington U (WA)
Westminster Coll (UT)
Whitman Coll (WA)
Whittier Coll (CA)
Widener U (PA)
William Paterson U of New Jersey (NJ)
William Peace U (NC)
Williams Coll (MA)
Wisconsin Lutheran Coll (WI)
Wofford Coll (SC)

ENVIRONMENTAL TOXICOLOGY
Bryant U (RI)
Clarkson U (NY)
U of California, Davis (CA)

EPIDEMIOLOGY
Indiana U Bloomington (IN)
U of Rochester (NY)

EQUESTRIAN STUDIES
Asbury U (KY)
Averett U (VA)
Becker Coll (MA)
Colorado State U (CO)
Delaware Valley U (PA)
Emory & Henry Coll (VA)
North Dakota State U (ND)
Otterbein U (OH)
Post U (CT)
Rocky Mountain Coll (MT)
Rutgers U–New Brunswick (NJ)
Saint Mary-of-the-Woods Coll (IN)
Savannah Coll of Art and Design (GA)
Texas A&M U–Commerce (TX)
The U of Findlay (OH)
West Texas A&M U (TX)

ETHICS
Bridgewater State U (MA)
Carroll Coll (MT)
Drake U (IA)
Marlboro Coll (VT)
Syracuse U (NY)
U of Evansville (IN)
U of Washington, Bothell (WA)

ETHNIC, CULTURAL MINORITY, GENDER, AND GROUP STUDIES RELATED
Albion Coll (MI)
Allegheny Coll (PA)
American U (DC)
The American U of Paris (France)
Beloit Coll (WI)
Bethel U (MN)
Boise State U (ID)
Bowdoin Coll (ME)
Bowling Green State U (OH)
California Polytechnic State U, San Luis Obispo (CA)

California State Polytechnic U, Pomona (CA)
California State U, East Bay (CA)
California State U, Stanislaus (CA)
Central Michigan U (MI)
Chatham U (PA)
Christian Brothers U (TN)
The Colorado Coll (CO)
Colorado State U (CO)
Columbia Coll Chicago (IL)
Cornell Coll (IA)
Cottey Coll (MO)
Davidson Coll (NC)
The Evergreen State Coll (WA)
Grinnell Coll (IA)
Guilford Coll (NC)
Hampshire Coll (MA)
Humboldt State U (CA)
Indiana U Bloomington (IN)
Indiana U South Bend (IN)
John Jay Coll of Criminal Justice of the City U of New York (NY)
Kalamazoo Coll (MI)
Lawrence U (WI)
Marlboro Coll (VT)
Metropolitan State U of Denver (CO)
Mills Coll (CA)
Mount Holyoke Coll (MA)
New Coll of Florida (FL)
New York U (NY)
The Ohio State U (OH)
Saint Michael's Coll (VT)
San Diego State U (CA)
Santa Clara U (CA)
Sarah Lawrence Coll (NY)
Skidmore Coll (NY)
Southern Adventist U (TN)
Stanford U (CA)
Stonehill Coll (MA)
U at Buffalo, the State U of New York (NY)
U of California, Irvine (CA)
U of Chicago (IL)
U of Colorado Colorado Springs (CO)
U of Dayton (OH)
U of Denver (CO)
U of Hawaii at Manoa (HI)
U of Houston (TX)
U of Illinois at Chicago (IL)
U of Kentucky (KY)
U of Minnesota, Duluth (MN)
U of Nebraska–Lincoln (NE)
U of Pittsburgh (PA)
U of Southern California (CA)
U of Utah (UT)
U of Washington, Tacoma (WA)
Washington State U (WA)
Washington U in St. Louis (MO)
Wayne State U (MI)
Wellesley Coll (MA)
Western Kentucky U (KY)
Westfield State U (MA)
Whitman Coll (WA)
Williams Coll (MA)

ETHNIC STUDIES
Arizona State U at the West campus (AZ)
Columbia U (NY)
Edgewood Coll (WI)
Kansas State U (KS)
Messiah Coll (PA)
Oregon State U (OR)
Reed Coll (OR)
St. Olaf Coll (MN)
Santa Clara U (CA)
Sarah Lawrence Coll (NY)
U of California, San Diego (CA)
U of California, Santa Cruz (CA)
U of Colorado Boulder (CO)
U of Colorado Denver (CO)
U of Oregon (OR)
U of San Diego (CA)
The U of Texas at Austin (TX)
Willamette U (OR)

EUROPEAN HISTORY
Charleston Southern U (SC)
Gettysburg Coll (PA)
Howard Payne U (TX)
Keene State Coll (NH)
Sarah Lawrence Coll (NY)
U of Idaho (ID)
U of Washington, Tacoma (WA)

EUROPEAN STUDIES
American U in Bulgaria (Bulgaria)
Amherst Coll (MA)
Barnard Coll (NY)
Bennington Coll (VT)
Boston U (MA)
Bowling Green State U (OH)
Brandeis U (MA)
Canisius Coll (NY)
Carroll U (WI)
Coll of Saint Benedict (MN)
Emory & Henry Coll (VA)
Fort Lewis Coll (CO)
Georgetown Coll (KY)
The George Washington U (DC)
Gettysburg Coll (PA)
Gonzaga U (WA)
Hampshire Coll (MA)
Hillsdale Coll (MI)
Hobart and William Smith Colls (NY)
Loyola Marymount U (CA)
Marlboro Coll (VT)
Middlebury Coll (VT)
Millsaps Coll (MS)
New Coll of Florida (FL)
New York U (NY)
Ohio U (OH)
Pepperdine U, Malibu (CA)
Portland State U (OR)
Rutgers U–New Brunswick (NJ)
Saint John's U (MN)
Saint Joseph's U (PA)
Saint Mary's Coll of California (CA)
San Diego State U (CA)
Scripps Coll (CA)
Seattle Pacific U (WA)
Stony Brook U, State U of New York (NY)
Trinity U (TX)
Tufts U (MA)
United States Military Acad (NY)
U of California, Irvine (CA)
U of California, Los Angeles (CA)
U of Guelph (ON, Canada)
The U of Kansas (KS)
U of King's Coll (NS, Canada)
U of Minnesota, Morris (MN)
U of Missouri (MO)
U of New Mexico (NM)
The U of North Carolina at Chapel Hill (NC)
U of Richmond (VA)
U of South Carolina (SC)
The U of Texas at Austin (TX)
U of Toronto (ON, Canada)
U of Vermont (VT)
U of Washington (WA)
Vanderbilt U (TN)
Washington U in St. Louis (MO)
Webster U (MO)

EUROPEAN STUDIES (WESTERN)
Bates Coll (ME)
Illinois Wesleyan U (IL)
Seattle U (WA)
Tufts U (MA)
Willamette U (OR)

EVOLUTIONARY BIOLOGY
Bennington Coll (VT)
Case Western Reserve U (OH)
Coll of the Atlantic (ME)
Columbia U (NY)
Dartmouth Coll (NH)
Harvard U (MA)
Rice U (TX)
Rutgers U–New Brunswick (NJ)
Tulane U (LA)

EXECUTIVE ASSISTANT/ EXECUTIVE SECRETARY
Bowling Green State U (OH)
Caribbean U (PR)
U of Puerto Rico–Humacao (PR)

EXERCISE PHYSIOLOGY
Anderson U (SC)
Auburn U (AL)
Baldwin Wallace U (OH)
Baylor U (TX)
Biola U (CA)
Brigham Young U–Idaho (ID)
California Baptist U (CA)
Chestnut Hill Coll (PA)
Coll of Charleston (SC)
The Coll of St. Scholastica (MN)

Concordia U Wisconsin (WI)
East Carolina U (NC)
Fitchburg State U (MA)
Florida Southern Coll (FL)
Gonzaga U (WA)
Gordon Coll (MA)
Lynchburg Coll (VA)
Marquette U (WI)
Merrimack Coll (MA)
Northwest Christian U (OR)
Ohio Northern U (OH)
Ohio U (OH)
Pfeiffer U (NC)
Saint Francis U (PA)
Shenandoah U (VA)
Skidmore Coll (NY)
Taylor U (IN)
U at Buffalo, the State U of New York (NY)
U of California, Davis (CA)
U of California, Irvine (CA)
U of Colorado Colorado Springs (CO)
U of Dayton (OH)
U of Florida (FL)
U of Massachusetts Amherst (MA)
U of Miami (FL)
U of Minnesota, Twin Cities Campus (MN)
U of Southern Maine (ME)
The U of Toledo (OH)
U of Wisconsin–Superior (WI)
Ursinus Coll (PA)
Washington State U (WA)
Washington State U–Spokane (WA)
West Virginia U (WV)

EXPERIMENTAL PSYCHOLOGY
Georgia Southern U–Armstrong Campus (GA)
Marlboro Coll (VT)
Northern Michigan U (MI)
Purdue U (IN)
Redeemer U Coll (ON, Canada)
Saint Leo U (FL)
Tiffin U (OH)
Tufts U (MA)
U of California, Santa Barbara (CA)
U of Chicago (IL)
U of Mary Hardin-Baylor (TX)
U of Michigan (MI)
U of Rochester (NY)
U of South Carolina (SC)

FACILITIES PLANNING AND MANAGEMENT
Eastern Michigan U (MI)
Missouri State U (MO)
New England Inst of Technology (RI)

FAMILY AND COMMUNITY SERVICES
Andrews U (MI)
Bowling Green State U (OH)
East Carolina U (NC)
Harding U (AR)
Iowa State U of Science and Technology (IA)
John Brown U (AR)
La Roche Coll (PA)
Messiah Coll (PA)
Michigan State U (MI)
Mount St. Mary's U (MD)
Oklahoma Baptist U (OK)
Oklahoma Christian U (OK)
Stevenson U (MD)
Texas Tech U (TX)
Toccoa Falls Coll (GA)
Union U (TN)
U of Florida (FL)
U of Maine at Machias (ME)
U of Maryland, Coll Park (MD)
U of Miami (FL)
U of Michigan–Dearborn (MI)
U of Northern Iowa (IA)
U of Wisconsin–Madison (WI)
Western Michigan U (MI)
Youngstown State U (OH)

FAMILY AND CONSUMER ECONOMICS RELATED
Andrews U (MI)
Bowling Green State U (OH)
Brigham Young U (UT)
California State U, Sacramento (CA)

Carson-Newman U (TN)
U of Hawaii at Manoa (HI)
U of Maryland Eastern Shore (MD)
U of Minnesota, Twin Cities Campus (MN)
U of Missouri (MO)
U of Nebraska at Kearney (NE)
U of Nebraska–Lincoln (NE)
U of Northern Iowa (IA)
Utah State U (UT)

FAMILY AND CONSUMER SCIENCES/HOME ECONOMICS TEACHER EDUCATION
Ball State U (IN)
Baylor U (TX)
Bowling Green State U (OH)
Bradley U (IL)
Carson-Newman U (TN)
East Carolina U (NC)
East Central U (OK)
Hampton U (VA)
Harding U (AR)
Iowa State U of Science and Technology (IA)
Langston U (OK)
Messiah Coll (PA)
Missouri State U (MO)
New Mexico State U (NM)
North Dakota State U (ND)
The Ohio State U at Lima (OH)
Ohio U (OH)
Pittsburg State U (KS)
Queens Coll of the City U of New York (NY)
St. Catherine U (MN)
Seton Hill U (PA)
Southeast Missouri State U (MO)
Southern Utah U (UT)
State U of New York Coll at Oneonta (NY)
Tennessee Technological U (TN)
The U of Akron (OH)
U of Central Arkansas (AR)
U of Central Oklahoma (OK)
U of Georgia (GA)
U of Maryland Eastern Shore (MD)
U of Saskatchewan (SK, Canada)
The U of Tennessee at Martin (TN)
U of Wisconsin–Stevens Point (WI)
U of Wisconsin–Stout (WI)
Utah State U (UT)
Virginia Polytechnic Inst and State U (VA)
Wayne State Coll (NE)
Western Kentucky U (KY)
Western Michigan U (MI)
Winthrop U (SC)

FAMILY AND CONSUMER SCIENCES/HUMAN SCIENCES
Auburn U (AL)
Ball State U (IN)
Baylor U (TX)
Berea Coll (KY)
Bowling Green State U (OH)
Bradley U (IL)
Bridgewater Coll (VA)
Brigham Young U (UT)
Brigham Young U–Idaho (ID)
California State U, Long Beach (CA)
California State U, Northridge (CA)
Carson-Newman U (TN)
Coll of the Atlantic (ME)
Colorado State U (CO)
Delaware State U (DE)
East Tennessee State U (TN)
Florida State U (FL)
Harding U (AR)
Idaho State U (ID)
Illinois State U (IL)
Indiana U of Pennsylvania (PA)
Iowa State U of Science and Technology (IA)
Kansas State U (KS)
Liberty U (VA)
Lipscomb U (TN)
Louisiana State U and A&M Coll (LA)
Madonna U (MI)
The Master's U (CA)
Meredith Coll (NC)
Miami U (OH)
Mississippi State U (MS)
Montclair State U (NJ)
New Mexico Highlands U (NM)
North Carolina Central U (NC)

Northeastern State U (OK)
Northwestern State U of Louisiana (LA)
Olivet Nazarene U (IL)
Pittsburg State U (KS)
Prairie View A&M U (TX)
Purdue U (IN)
Queens Coll of the City U of New York (NY)
Rutgers U–New Brunswick (NJ)
St. Catherine U (MN)
Sam Houston State U (TX)
San Francisco State U (CA)
Seattle Pacific U (WA)
Seton Hill U (PA)
Shepherd U (WV)
Southeastern Louisiana U (LA)
Southeast Missouri State U (MO)
Southern Utah U (UT)
State U of New York Coll at Oneonta (NY)
Tarleton State U (TX)
Tennessee Technological U (TN)
Texas A&M U–Kingsville (TX)
Texas Tech U (TX)
Texas Woman's U (TX)
The U of Alabama (AL)
U of Arkansas (AR)
U of California, San Diego (CA)
U of Central Arkansas (AR)
U of Central Missouri (MO)
U of Kentucky (KY)
U of Maryland Eastern Shore (MD)
U of Montevallo (AL)
U of New Mexico (NM)
U of North Alabama (AL)
The U of North Carolina at Greensboro (NC)
U of Saint Joseph (CT)
The U of Tennessee at Martin (TN)
The U of Texas at Austin (TX)
U of Wyoming (WY)
Washington State U (WA)
Wayne State Coll (NE)
Youngstown State U (OH)

FAMILY AND CONSUMER SCIENCES/HUMAN SCIENCES BUSINESS SERVICES RELATED
Brigham Young U (UT)

FAMILY AND CONSUMER SCIENCES/HUMAN SCIENCES COMMUNICATION
U of Georgia (GA)

FAMILY AND CONSUMER SCIENCES/HUMAN SCIENCES RELATED
Auburn U (AL)
California State U, Long Beach (CA)

FAMILY PRACTICE NURSING
Graceland U (IA)
Grand Valley State U (MI)
Michigan State U (MI)
Pace U (NY)
Pace U, Pleasantville Campus (NY)
Texas A&M U–Commerce (TX)
The U of Texas at Austin (TX)
The U of Virginia's Coll at Wise (VA)

FAMILY PSYCHOLOGY
Arizona Christian U (AZ)
Corban U (OR)
Cornerstone U (MI)
Kansas Wesleyan U (KS)

FAMILY RESOURCE MANAGEMENT
Arizona State U at the Tempe campus (AZ)
Brigham Young U (UT)
Iowa State U of Science and Technology (IA)
Middle Tennessee State U (TN)
New Mexico State U (NM)
The Ohio State U (OH)
Ohio U (OH)
Texas Tech U (TX)
The U of Alabama (AL)
U of Georgia (GA)

FAMILY SYSTEMS
Anderson U (IN)
Ball State U (IN)
Bowling Green State U (OH)
Central Michigan U (MI)

Lipscomb U (TN)
Lubbock Christian U (TX)
Mid-Atlantic Christian U (NC)
Southern Adventist U (TN)
Towson U (MD)
The U of Akron (OH)
U of Southern Mississippi (MS)
Weber State U (UT)
Western Michigan U (MI)

FARM AND RANCH MANAGEMENT
Iowa State U of Science and Technology (IA)
Purdue U (IN)
Texas A&M U (TX)
Texas Christian U (TX)
U of Minnesota, Crookston (MN)

FASHION AND FABRIC CONSULTING
Academy of Art U (CA)

FASHION/APPAREL DESIGN
Academy of Art U (CA)
Albright Coll (PA)
Arizona State U at the Tempe campus (AZ)
Baylor U (TX)
Belmont U (TN)
Bennington Coll (VT)
Bob Jones U (SC)
Bowling Green State U (OH)
Brenau U (GA)
Buffalo State Coll, State U of New York (NY)
Cairn U (PA)
California Coll of the Arts (CA)
Carson-Newman U (TN)
Cazenovia Coll (NY)
Clark Atlanta U (GA)
Columbia Coll Chicago (IL)
Dominican U (IL)
Drexel U (PA)
EDP U of Puerto Rico (PR)
Escuela de Artes Plasticas y Diseño de Puerto Rico (PR)
Eugene Lang Coll of Liberal Arts (NY)
Fashion Inst of Technology (NY)
Ferris State U (MI)
FIDM/Fashion Inst of Design & Merchandising, Los Angeles Campus (CA)
Hampton U (VA)
Indiana U Bloomington (IN)
Iowa State U of Science and Technology (IA)
Jacksonville U (FL)
Kent State U (OH)
Lasell Coll (MA)
Lebanese American U (Lebanon)
Lindenwood U (MO)
Marist Coll (NY)
Marymount U (VA)
Massachusetts Coll of Art and Design (MA)
Meredith Coll (NC)
Michigan State U (MI)
Montclair State U (NJ)
Mount Mary U (WI)
The New School–Parsons Paris (France)
O'More Coll of Design (TN)
Paris Coll of Art (France)
Parsons School of Design (NY)
Pratt Inst (NY)
Purdue U (IN)
St. Catherine U (MN)
Savannah Coll of Art and Design (GA)
Stevenson U (MD)
Syracuse U (NY)
Texas Tech U (TX)
Texas Woman's U (TX)
U of Cincinnati (OH)
U of Maryland Eastern Shore (MD)
U of North Texas (TX)
U of San Francisco (CA)
U of the Incarnate Word (TX)
Ursuline Coll (OH)
Villa Maria Coll (NY)
Virginia Commonwealth U (VA)
Wade Coll (TX)
Washington U in St. Louis (MO)
Western Michigan U (MI)
Woodbury U (CA)

FASHION MERCHANDISING
Academy of Art U (CA)
Albright Coll (PA)
Ashland U (OH)
Baylor U (TX)
Belmont U (TN)
Bowling Green State U (OH)
Brenau U (GA)
Buffalo State Coll, State U of New York (NY)
California State U, Long Beach (CA)
Carson-Newman U (TN)
Cazenovia Coll (NY)
Central Michigan U (MI)
Columbia Coll (SC)
Delaware State U (DE)
Dominican U (IL)
East Central U (OK)
Eastern Michigan U (MI)
Fashion Inst of Technology (NY)
Fisher Coll (MA)
Hampton U (VA)
Harding U (AR)
Immaculata U (PA)
Indiana U of Pennsylvania (PA)
Kent State U (OH)
Lasell Coll (MA)
LIM Coll (NY)
Lipscomb U (TN)
Long Island U–LIU Post (NY)
Lynn U (FL)
Marymount Manhattan Coll (NY)
Marymount U (VA)
Mercyhurst U (PA)
Meredith Coll (NC)
Mount Mary U (WI)
Olivet Nazarene U (IL)
O'More Coll of Design (TN)
St. Catherine U (MN)
Sam Houston State U (TX)
State U of New York Coll at Oneonta (NY)
Stephen F. Austin State U (TX)
Stevenson U (MD)
Tennessee Technological U (TN)
Texas Christian U (TX)
Texas State U (TX)
Texas Tech U (TX)
Texas Woman's U (TX)
U of Bridgeport (CT)
U of Central Missouri (MO)
U of Georgia (GA)
U of Maryland Eastern Shore (MD)
U of North Texas (TX)
The U of Tennessee at Martin (TN)
Ursuline Coll (OH)
Utah State U (UT)
Western Illinois U (IL)
Western Michigan U (MI)
Youngstown State U (OH)

FIBER, TEXTILE AND WEAVING ARTS
Adams State U (CO)
Alberta Coll of Art & Design (AB, Canada)
Bowling Green State U (OH)
California Coll of the Arts (CA)
California State U, Long Beach (CA)
Cornell U (NY)
Kansas City Art Inst (MO)
Maryland Inst Coll of Art (MD)
Massachusetts Coll of Art and Design (MA)
Rhode Island School of Design (RI)
Savannah Coll of Art and Design (GA)
Syracuse U (NY)
Temple U (PA)
The U of Kansas (KS)
U of Massachusetts Dartmouth (MA)
U of Michigan (MI)
U of Oregon (OR)

FILIPINO/TAGALOG
U of Hawaii at Manoa (HI)

FILM/CINEMA/VIDEO STUDIES
The American U in Cairo (Egypt)
The American U of Paris (France)
Augsburg U (MN)
Baldwin Wallace U (OH)
Bard Coll (NY)
Barnard Coll (NY)
Belhaven U (MS)

Bennington Coll (VT)
Biola U (CA)
Boston Coll (MA)
Boston U (MA)
Bowling Green State U (OH)
Brandeis U (MA)
Brigham Young U (UT)
Brock U (ON, Canada)
California Baptist U (CA)
California Coll of the Arts (CA)
California State U, Long Beach (CA)
California State U, Northridge (CA)
California State U, Sacramento (CA)
Carleton Coll (MN)
Carson-Newman U (TN)
Champlain Coll (VT)
Chapman U (CA)
Claremont McKenna Coll (CA)
Clark U (MA)
Coe Coll (IA)
Coll of Staten Island of the City U of New York (NY)
The Colorado Coll (CO)
Columbia U (NY)
Concordia U (QC, Canada)
Connecticut Coll (CT)
Cornell U (NY)
Dartmouth Coll (NH)
Denison U (OH)
DeSales U (PA)
Dominican U (IL)
Eastern Michigan U (MI)
Eastern Washington U (WA)
Eckerd Coll (FL)
Emerson Coll (MA)
Emory U (GA)
Eugene Lang Coll of Liberal Arts (NY)
The Evergreen State Coll (WA)
Fashion Inst of Technology (NY)
Fordham U (NY)
Georgia State U (GA)
Grand Valley State U (MI)
Hamilton Coll (NY)
Houston Baptist U (TX)
Hunter Coll of the City U of New York (NY)
Iowa State U of Science and Technology (IA)
Ithaca Coll (NY)
Jacksonville U (FL)
Johns Hopkins U (MD)
Keene State Coll (NH)
Kenyon Coll (OH)
Lafayette Coll (PA)
La Sierra U (CA)
Lawrence U (WI)
Lipscomb U (TN)
Lycoming Coll (PA)
Marlboro Coll (VT)
Maryland Inst Coll of Art (MD)
Marymount Manhattan Coll (NY)
McDaniel Coll (MD)
Miami U (OH)
Michigan State U (MI)
Middlebury Coll (VT)
Minnesota State U Moorhead (MN)
Morehouse Coll (GA)
Mount Holyoke Coll (MA)
Muhlenberg Coll (PA)
National U (CA)
New York U (NY)
Northwestern U (IL)
Northwest U (WA)
Oakland U (MI)
The Ohio State U (OH)
Pace U (NY)
Pace U, Pleasantville Campus (NY)
Penn State Abington (PA)
Penn State Altoona (PA)
Penn State Beaver (PA)
Penn State Berks (PA)
Penn State Brandywine (PA)
Penn State DuBois (PA)
Penn State Erie, The Behrend Coll (PA)
Penn State Fayette, The Eberly Campus (PA)
Penn State Greater Allegheny (PA)
Penn State Hazleton (PA)
Penn State Lehigh Valley (PA)
Penn State Mont Alto (PA)
Penn State New Kensington (PA)
Penn State Schuylkill (PA)
Penn State Shenango (PA)

Penn State U Park (PA)
Penn State Wilkes-Barre (PA)
Penn State Worthington Scranton (PA)
Penn State York (PA)
Pepperdine U, Malibu (CA)
Pitzer Coll (CA)
Purchase Coll, State U of New York (NY)
Purdue U (IN)
Queens Coll of the City U of New York (NY)
Quinnipiac U (CT)
Rhode Island Coll (RI)
Rutgers U–New Brunswick (NJ)
Saint Augustine's U (NC)
San Francisco State U (CA)
Sarah Lawrence Coll (NY)
School of Visual Arts (NY)
Seattle U (WA)
Simon Fraser U (BC, Canada)
Smith Coll (MA)
Southwestern Coll (KS)
Stanford U (CA)
State U of New York at Fredonia (NY)
Stevenson U (MD)
Temple U (PA)
Tufts U (MA)
U at Buffalo, the State U of New York (NY)
U of Alaska Fairbanks (AK)
The U of Arizona (AZ)
U of California, Davis (CA)
U of California, Irvine (CA)
U of California, Los Angeles (CA)
U of California, San Diego (CA)
U of California, Santa Barbara (CA)
U of Chicago (IL)
U of Cincinnati (OH)
U of Colorado Boulder (CO)
U of Denver (CO)
U of Georgia (GA)
U of Hartford (CT)
The U of Kansas (KS)
U of Mary Hardin-Baylor (TX)
U of Maryland, Coll Park (MD)
U of Michigan (MI)
U of Nebraska–Lincoln (NE)
U of Nevada, Las Vegas (NV)
U of New Mexico (NM)
U of Oklahoma (OK)
U of Oregon (OR)
U of Pennsylvania (PA)
U of Pikeville (KY)
U of Pittsburgh (PA)
U of Regina (SK, Canada)
U of Richmond (VA)
U of Rochester (NY)
U of Southern California (CA)
The U of Tampa (FL)
The U of the Arts (PA)
The U of Toledo (OH)
The U of Tulsa (OK)
U of Utah (UT)
U of Vermont (VT)
U of Washington (WA)
U of Waterloo (ON, Canada)
U of Wisconsin–Milwaukee (WI)
Vanderbilt U (TN)
Vassar Coll (NY)
Washington U in St. Louis (MO)
Wayne State U (MI)
Webster U (MO)
Wellesley Coll (MA)
Wells Coll (NY)
Wesleyan U (CT)
Wheaton Coll (MA)
Whitman Coll (WA)
Winona State U (MN)
Wright State U (OH)
Wright State U–Lake Campus (OH)

FILM/VIDEO AND PHOTOGRAPHIC ARTS RELATED

Arizona State U at the Tempe campus (AZ)
Birmingham-Southern Coll (AL)
Brigham Young U (UT)
Calvary U (MO)
Chatham U (PA)
Cleveland State U (OH)
Coe Coll (IA)
Coll of the Atlantic (ME)
Fairfield U (CT)
Florida State U (FL)

Hampshire Coll (MA)
Hollins U (VA)
Kansas City Art Inst (MO)
La Roche Coll (PA)
Louisiana State U and A&M Coll (LA)
Marlboro Coll (VT)
Maryland Inst Coll of Art (MD)
Mount Saint Mary's U (CA)
Northern Michigan U (MI)
Nossi Coll of Art (TN)
The Ohio State U (OH)
Oklahoma City U (OK)
Portland State U (OR)
Pratt Inst (NY)
Rhode Island School of Design (RI)
Saint Joseph's U (PA)
School of Visual Arts (NY)
U of California, Santa Cruz (CA)
U of Illinois at Chicago (IL)
U of Minnesota, Twin Cities Campus (MN)
The U of the Arts (PA)
Wellesley Coll (MA)
Western Michigan U (MI)
Woodbury U (CA)

FINANCE

Abilene Christian U (TX)
Adams State U (CO)
Adelphi U (NY)
Alabama State U (AL)
Albion Coll (MI)
Albright Coll (PA)
Alfred U (NY)
Alma Coll (MI)
American U (DC)
Anderson U (IN)
Angelo State U (TX)
Appalachian State U (NC)
Arcadia U (PA)
Arizona State U at the Tempe campus (AZ)
Ashland U (OH)
Auburn U (AL)
Auburn U at Montgomery (AL)
Augsburg U (MN)
Aurora U (IL)
Austin Coll (TX)
Austin Peay State U (TN)
Avila U (MO)
Babson Coll (MA)
Baldwin Wallace U (OH)
Ball State U (IN)
Barry U (FL)
Baruch Coll of the City U of New York (NY)
Baylor U (TX)
Bellarmine U (KY)
Belmont U (TN)
Benedictine Coll (KS)
Benedictine U (IL)
Bentley U (MA)
Berry Coll (GA)
Bethune-Cookman U (FL)
Binghamton U, State U of New York (NY)
Boise State U (ID)
Boston Coll (MA)
Bowling Green State U (OH)
Bradley U (IL)
Brescia U (KY)
Bridgewater State U (MA)
Brigham Young U–Idaho (ID)
Brock U (ON, Canada)
Bryant U (RI)
Butler U (IN)
California State U, Dominguez Hills (CA)
California State U, Long Beach (CA)
California State U, Northridge (CA)
California State U, San Marcos (CA)
California State U, Stanislaus (CA)
Canisius Coll (NY)
Carnegie Mellon U (PA)
Carroll Coll (MT)
Carroll U (WI)
Carthage Coll (WI)
Case Western Reserve U (OH)
Cedarville U (OH)
Central Connecticut State U (CT)
Central Michigan U (MI)
Central Penn Coll (PA)
Charleston Southern U (SC)

Christopher Newport U (VA)
Clarion U of Pennsylvania (PA)
Clemson U (SC)
Cleveland State U (OH)
Coastal Carolina U (SC)
The Coll at Brockport, State U of New York (NY)
Coll of Charleston (SC)
The Coll of Saint Rose (NY)
The Coll of St. Scholastica (MN)
The Coll of William and Mary (VA)
Colorado Christian U (CO)
Columbia Coll (MO)
Columbus State U (GA)
Concordia U (QC, Canada)
Concordia U, St. Paul (MN)
Converse Coll (SC)
Corban U (OR)
Cornerstone U (MI)
Creighton U (NE)
Culver-Stockton Coll (MO)
Dakota State U (SD)
Dallas Baptist U (TX)
Davenport U, Grand Rapids (MI)
Delaware State U (DE)
DePaul U (IL)
DEREE - The American Coll of Greece (Greece)
DeSales U (PA)
Dickinson State U (ND)
Dominican U (IL)
Drake U (IA)
Drexel U (PA)
Drury U (MO)
Duquesne U (PA)
East Carolina U (NC)
East Central U (OK)
Eastern Michigan U (MI)
Eastern Washington U (WA)
East Tennessee State U (TN)
Elmhurst Coll (IL)
Elon U (NC)
Emmanuel Coll (MA)
Endicott Coll (MA)
Fairfield U (CT)
Fairleigh Dickinson U, Florham Campus (NJ)
Fairleigh Dickinson U, Metropolitan Campus (NJ)
Fayetteville State U (NC)
Ferris State U (MI)
Fisher Coll (MA)
Fitchburg State U (MA)
Flagler Coll (FL)
Florida Atlantic U (FL)
Florida Gulf Coast U (FL)
Florida Intl U (FL)
Florida State U (FL)
Fordham U (NY)
Fort Lewis Coll (CO)
Framingham State U (MA)
Francis Marion U (SC)
Franklin Pierce U (NH)
Friends U (KS)
Gannon U (PA)
George Mason U (VA)
Georgetown Coll (KY)
Georgetown U (DC)
The George Washington U (DC)
Georgian Court U (NJ)
Georgia Southern U (GA)
Georgia State U (GA)
Gonzaga U (WA)
Gordon Coll (MA)
Grand Valley State U (MI)
Grove City Coll (PA)
Hamline U (MN)
Hampton U (VA)
Harding U (AR)
Hardin-Simmons U (TX)
HEC Montreal (QC, Canada)
High Point U (NC)
Hillsdale Coll (MI)
Hofstra U (NY)
Holy Family U (PA)
Houston Baptist U (TX)
Howard Payne U (TX)
Husson U (ME)
Idaho State U (ID)
Illinois Coll (IL)
Illinois State U (IL)
Immaculata U (PA)
Indiana State U (IN)
Indiana U of Pennsylvania (PA)
Indiana Wesleyan U (IN)
Inter American U of Puerto Rico, Bayamón Campus (PR)

Inter American U of Puerto Rico, Metropolitan Campus (PR)
Inter American U of Puerto Rico, San Germán Campus (PR)
Iona Coll (NY)
Iowa State U of Science and Technology (IA)
Ithaca Coll (NY)
Jackson State U (MS)
Jacksonville U (FL)
James Madison U (VA)
John Cabot U (Italy)
John Carroll U (OH)
Juniata Coll (PA)
Kansas State U (KS)
Kean U (NJ)
Keiser U, Fort Lauderdale (FL)
Kennesaw State U (GA)
Kent State U (OH)
The King's Coll (NY)
King's Coll (PA)
Lamar U (TX)
La Roche Coll (PA)
La Salle U (PA)
Lasell Coll (MA)
La Sierra U (CA)
Lawrence Technological U (MI)
Lebanon Valley Coll (PA)
Lehigh U (PA)
Le Moyne Coll (NY)
Lenoir-Rhyne U (NC)
LeTourneau U (TX)
Lewis U (IL)
Lincoln Memorial U (TN)
Lincoln U (PA)
Lindenwood U (MO)
Linfield Coll (OR)
Long Island U–LIU Brooklyn (NY)
Loras Coll (IA)
Louisiana State U and A&M Coll (LA)
Loyola Marymount U (CA)
Loyola U Chicago (IL)
Loyola U New Orleans (LA)
Lubbock Christian U (TX)
Malone U (OH)
Manchester U (IN)
Manhattan Coll (NY)
Manhattanville Coll (NY)
Marian U (IN)
Marian U (WI)
Marietta Coll (OH)
Marquette U (WI)
Marshall U (WV)
Marymount Manhattan Coll (NY)
Massachusetts Inst of Technology (MA)
The Master's U (CA)
McMurry U (TX)
McNeese State U (LA)
McPherson Coll (KS)
Mercer U, Macon (GA)
Merrimack Coll (MA)
Messiah Coll (PA)
Metropolitan State U of Denver (CO)
Miami U (OH)
Michigan State U (MI)
Michigan Technological U (MI)
Middle Tennessee State U (TN)
Minnesota State U Moorhead (MN)
Minot State U (ND)
Mississippi State U (MS)
Missouri State U (MO)
Missouri Valley Coll (MO)
Missouri Western State U (MO)
Molloy Coll (NY)
Morehead State U (KY)
Mount Mercy U (IA)
Mount St. Joseph U (OH)
Mount Vernon Nazarene U (OH)
Murray State U (KY)
National U (CA)
Nazareth Coll of Rochester (NY)
New Jersey City U (NJ)
New Mexico Highlands U (NM)
New Mexico State U (NM)
New York Inst of Technology (NY)
New York U (NY)
Nichols Coll (MA)
North Central Coll (IL)
North Dakota State U (ND)
Northeastern State U (OK)
Northeastern U (MA)
Northern Arizona U (AZ)
Northern Illinois U (IL)
Northern Kentucky U (KY)

Northern Michigan U (MI)
Northern State U (SD)
Northwest Missouri State U (MO)
Northwest Nazarene U (ID)
Nova Southeastern U (FL)
Oakland U (MI)
Ohio Dominican U (OH)
The Ohio State U (OH)
Ohio U (OH)
Oklahoma Baptist U (OK)
Oklahoma Christian U (OK)
Oklahoma City U (OK)
Oklahoma State U (OK)
Old Dominion U (VA)
Oral Roberts U (OK)
Oregon State U (OR)
Otterbein U (OH)
Our Lady of the Lake U (TX)
Pace U (NY)
Pace U, Pleasantville Campus (NY)
Palm Beach Atlantic U (FL)
Penn State Abington (PA)
Penn State Altoona (PA)
Penn State Beaver (PA)
Penn State Berks (PA)
Penn State Brandywine (PA)
Penn State DuBois (PA)
Penn State Erie, The Behrend Coll (PA)
Penn State Fayette, The Eberly Campus (PA)
Penn State Greater Allegheny (PA)
Penn State Harrisburg (PA)
Penn State Hazleton (PA)
Penn State Lehigh Valley (PA)
Penn State Mont Alto (PA)
Penn State New Kensington (PA)
Penn State Schuylkill (PA)
Penn State Shenango (PA)
Penn State U Park (PA)
Penn State Wilkes-Barre (PA)
Penn State Worthington Scranton (PA)
Penn State York (PA)
Pepperdine U, Malibu (CA)
Pfeiffer U (NC)
Pittsburg State U (KS)
Point Loma Nazarene U (CA)
Polytechnic U of Puerto Rico (PR)
Portland State U (OR)
Post U (CT)
Prairie View A&M U (TX)
Providence Coll (RI)
Purdue U (IN)
Purdue U Northwest (IN)
Queens Coll of the City U of New York (NY)
Quinnipiac U (CT)
Radford U (VA)
Regis U (CO)
Rhode Island Coll (RI)
Rider U (NJ)
Rivier U (NH)
Robert Morris U (PA)
Rochester Inst of Technology (NY)
Rockford U (IL)
Roger Williams U (RI)
Roosevelt U (IL)
Rosemont Coll (PA)
Rowan U (NJ)
Rutgers U–Camden (NJ)
Rutgers U–Newark (NJ)
Rutgers U–New Brunswick (NJ)
Sacred Heart U (CT)
Saginaw Valley State U (MI)
St. Ambrose U (IA)
Saint Anselm Coll (NH)
St. Bonaventure U (NY)
Saint Francis U (PA)
St. John Fisher Coll (NY)
St. John's U (NY)
Saint Joseph's U (PA)
Saint Louis U (MO)
Saint Louis U–Madrid Campus (Spain)
St. Mary's U (TX)
Saint Mary's U of Minnesota (MN)
St. Thomas Aquinas Coll (NY)
St. Thomas U (FL)
Saint Vincent Coll (PA)
Salisbury U (MD)
Salve Regina U (RI)
Samford U (AL)
Sam Houston State U (TX)
San Diego State U (CA)
San Francisco State U (CA)
Santa Clara U (CA)

Schreiner U (TX)
Seattle U (WA)
Shippensburg U of Pennsylvania (PA)
Siena Coll (NY)
Sierra Nevada Coll (NV)
Simmons Coll (MA)
Slippery Rock U of Pennsylvania (PA)
Southeastern Louisiana U (LA)
Southeastern Oklahoma State U (OK)
Southeastern U (FL)
Southeast Missouri State U (MO)
Southern Adventist U (TN)
Southern Illinois U Carbondale (IL)
Southern Methodist U (TX)
Southern Utah U (UT)
Southwest Baptist U (MO)
Southwestern Adventist U (TX)
Southwestern Coll (KS)
State U of New York at Fredonia (NY)
State U of New York at New Paltz (NY)
State U of New York at Oswego (NY)
State U of New York at Plattsburgh (NY)
State U of New York Coll at Old Westbury (NY)
State U of New York Coll of Technology at Canton (NY)
Stephen F. Austin State U (TX)
Stetson U (FL)
Stonehill Coll (MA)
Suffolk U (MA)
Susquehanna U (PA)
Syracuse U (NY)
Tarleton State U (TX)
Taylor U (IN)
Temple U (PA)
Tennessee Technological U (TN)
Tennessee Wesleyan U (TN)
Texas A&M Intl U (TX)
Texas A&M U (TX)
Texas A&M U–Central Texas (TX)
Texas A&M U–Commerce (TX)
Texas A&M U–Corpus Christi (TX)
Texas A&M U–Kingsville (TX)
Texas A&M U–Texarkana (TX)
Texas Christian U (TX)
Texas Lutheran U (TX)
Texas State U (TX)
Texas Tech U (TX)
Texas Woman's U (TX)
Thomas Edison State U (NJ)
Tiffin U (OH)
Trine U (IN)
Trinity Christian Coll (IL)
Trinity U (TX)
Tulane U (LA)
Union U (TN)
Université de Sherbrooke (QC, Canada)
The U of Alabama (AL)
The U of Alabama at Birmingham (AL)
The U of Arizona (AZ)
U of Arkansas (AR)
U of Bridgeport (CT)
U of Central Arkansas (AR)
U of Central Florida (FL)
U of Central Missouri (MO)
U of Central Oklahoma (OK)
U of Charleston (WV)
U of Cincinnati (OH)
U of Colorado Boulder (CO)
U of Dayton (OH)
U of Denver (CO)
U of Evansville (IN)
The U of Findlay (OH)
U of Florida (FL)
U of Georgia (GA)
U of Guelph (ON, Canada)
U of Hartford (CT)
U of Hawaii at Manoa (HI)
U of Houston (TX)
U of Houston–Clear Lake (TX)
U of Houston–Downtown (TX)
U of Idaho (ID)
U of Illinois at Chicago (IL)
The U of Kansas (KS)
U of Kentucky (KY)
U of Louisiana at Monroe (LA)
U of Louisville (KY)
U of Maine (ME)

U of Mary Hardin-Baylor (TX)
U of Maryland, Coll Park (MD)
U of Maryland U Coll (MD)
U of Massachusetts Amherst (MA)
U of Massachusetts Dartmouth (MA)
U of Memphis (TN)
U of Miami (FL)
U of Michigan–Dearborn (MI)
U of Michigan–Flint (MI)
U of Minnesota, Duluth (MN)
U of Minnesota, Twin Cities Campus (MN)
U of Missouri (MO)
U of Montana (MT)
U of Montevallo (AL)
U of Mount Union (OH)
U of Nebraska–Lincoln (NE)
U of Nevada, Las Vegas (NV)
U of Nevada, Reno (NV)
U of New Haven (CT)
U of New Orleans (LA)
U of North Alabama (AL)
The U of North Carolina at Charlotte (NC)
The U of North Carolina at Greensboro (NC)
U of North Dakota (ND)
U of Northern Iowa (IA)
U of North Florida (FL)
U of North Georgia (GA)
U of North Texas (TX)
U of Notre Dame (IN)
U of Oklahoma (OK)
U of Pennsylvania (PA)
U of Pittsburgh (PA)
U of Regina (SK, Canada)
U of Rhode Island (RI)
U of St. Francis (IL)
U of Saint Francis (IN)
U of St. Thomas (MN)
U of St. Thomas (TX)
U of San Diego (CA)
U of San Francisco (CA)
U of Saskatchewan (SK, Canada)
The U of Scranton (PA)
U of South Alabama (AL)
U of South Carolina (SC)
U of South Dakota (SD)
U of Southern Indiana (IN)
U of Southern Maine (ME)
U of Southern Mississippi (MS)
U of South Florida, St. Petersburg (FL)
U of South Florida Sarasota-Manatee (FL)
The U of Tampa (FL)
The U of Tennessee (TN)
The U of Tennessee at Martin (TN)
The U of Texas at Austin (TX)
The U of Texas at Dallas (TX)
The U of Texas at El Paso (TX)
The U of Texas at San Antonio (TX)
The U of Texas of the Permian Basin (TX)
The U of Texas Rio Grande Valley (TX)
U of the Incarnate Word (TX)
The U of Toledo (OH)
U of Toronto (ON, Canada)
The U of Tulsa (OK)
U of Utah (UT)
U of Washington (WA)
U of Washington, Tacoma (WA)
The U of West Alabama (AL)
U of West Georgia (GA)
U of Wisconsin–Eau Claire (WI)
U of Wisconsin–La Crosse (WI)
U of Wisconsin–Madison (WI)
U of Wisconsin–Milwaukee (WI)
U of Wisconsin–Whitewater (WI)
U of Wyoming (WY)
Utah State U (UT)
Utah Valley U (UT)
Valdosta State U (GA)
Valparaiso U (IN)
Vanguard U of Southern California (CA)
Villanova U (PA)
Virginia Polytechnic Inst and State U (VA)
Wagner Coll (NY)
Wake Forest U (NC)
Walsh Coll of Accountancy and Business Administration (MI)
Walsh U (OH)
Wartburg Coll (IA)

Washington State U (WA)
Washington State U–Vancouver (WA)
Washington U in St. Louis (MO)
Waynesburg U (PA)
Wayne State U (MI)
Webber Intl U (FL)
Weber State U (UT)
Webster U (MO)
West Chester U of Pennsylvania (PA)
Western Connecticut State U (CT)
Western Illinois U (IL)
Western Kentucky U (KY)
Western Michigan U (MI)
Western New England U (MA)
Western Washington U (WA)
Westminster Coll (UT)
West Texas A&M U (TX)
West Virginia U (WV)
Whitworth U (WA)
Wichita State U (KS)
Wilkes U (PA)
William Paterson U of New Jersey (NJ)
Wilmington U (DE)
Winona State U (MN)
Wittenberg U (OH)
Wofford Coll (SC)
Wright State U (OH)
Wright State U–Lake Campus (OH)
York Coll of Pennsylvania (PA)
Youngstown State U (OH)

FINANCE AND FINANCIAL MANAGEMENT SERVICES RELATED
Babson Coll (MA)
Brenau U (GA)
Dominican Coll (NY)
Hofstra U (NY)
James Madison U (VA)
Minot State U (ND)
Point U (GA)
Saint Mary's Coll of California (CA)
Simmons Coll (MA)
State U of New York at New Paltz (NY)
U of Northern Iowa (IA)
The U of Tampa (FL)
Virginia Commonwealth U (VA)
Westminster Coll (UT)

FINANCIAL FORENSICS AND FRAUD INVESTIGATION
Champlain Coll (VT)
Hilbert Coll (NY)
John Jay Coll of Criminal Justice of the City U of New York (NY)
Keiser U, Fort Lauderdale (FL)
Mount St. Mary's U (MD)

FINANCIAL MATHEMATICS
American U (DC)
Anderson U (IN)
Asbury U (KY)
Blackburn Coll (IL)
Carnegie Mellon U (PA)
Hofstra U (NY)
Knox Coll (IL)
Lee U (TN)
LeTourneau U (TX)
Massachusetts Inst of Technology (MA)
Mount St. Joseph U (OH)
Purdue U (IN)
Trinity U (TX)
U of California, Los Angeles (CA)
U of Cincinnati (OH)
U of Kentucky (KY)
U of Mount Union (OH)

FINANCIAL PLANNING AND SERVICES
Baylor U (TX)
Bethel Coll (IN)
Brigham Young U (UT)
Bryant U (RI)
Central Michigan U (MI)
The Coll of Saint Rose (NY)
HEC Montreal (QC, Canada)
Kansas State U (KS)
Lubbock Christian U (TX)
Maryville U of Saint Louis (MO)
Marywood U (PA)
Merrimack Coll (MA)
Northern Michigan U (MI)
Purdue U (IN)
Roger Williams U (RI)

Saint Joseph's U (PA)
St. Mary's U (TX)
San Diego State U (CA)
Southern Methodist U (TX)
State U of New York Coll of Technology at Alfred (NY)
Temple U (PA)
The U of Akron (OH)
U of Jamestown (ND)
U of Minnesota, Duluth (MN)
U of Mount Union (OH)
U of Wisconsin–Madison (WI)
Utah Valley U (UT)
Western Michigan U (MI)
Widener U (PA)
William Paterson U of New Jersey (NJ)
Youngstown State U (OH)

FINE AND STUDIO ARTS MANAGEMENT
Albright Coll (PA)
Aquinas Coll (MI)
Baldwin Wallace U (OH)
Belhaven U (MS)
Bellarmine U (KY)
Bluefield Coll (VA)
Buena Vista U (IA)
Butler U (IN)
Chatham U (PA)
Coll of Charleston (SC)
The Coll of Idaho (ID)
Columbia Coll Chicago (IL)
Concordia U Chicago (IL)
Culver-Stockton Coll (MO)
Daemen Coll (NY)
Delaware State U (DE)
DePaul U (IL)
Dickinson State U (ND)
Eastern Michigan U (MI)
Fashion Inst of Technology (NY)
Fort Lewis Coll (CO)
Indiana U Bloomington (IN)
Ithaca Coll (NY)
Lasell Coll (MA)
Lenoir-Rhyne U (NC)
Lipscomb U (TN)
Mary Baldwin U (VA)
Marywood U (PA)
Massachusetts Coll of Liberal Arts (MA)
Mercyhurst U (PA)
Messiah Coll (PA)
Miami U (OH)
Minot State U (ND)
The New School–Parsons Paris (France)
North Carolina State U (NC)
Parsons School of Design (NY)
Pfeiffer U (NC)
Purchase Coll, State U of New York (NY)
Randolph-Macon Coll (VA)
Rider U (NJ)
Ringling Coll of Art and Design (FL)
Saint Vincent Coll (PA)
Seton Hill U (PA)
Simmons Coll (MA)
Spring Hill Coll (AL)
State U of New York at Fredonia (NY)
Syracuse U (NY)
The U of North Carolina at Greensboro (NC)
The U of Tulsa (OK)
U of Waterloo (ON, Canada)
U of Wisconsin–Stevens Point (WI)
Upper Iowa U (IA)
Wagner Coll (NY)
Waynesburg U (PA)
Westminster Coll (UT)
Whitworth U (WA)

FINE ARTS RELATED
Academy of Art U (CA)
Adelphi U (NY)
Alfred U (NY)
Allegheny Coll (PA)
ArtCenter Coll of Design (CA)
Ball State U (IN)
Benedictine U (IL)
Binghamton U, State U of New York (NY)
Birmingham-Southern Coll (AL)
Bowdoin Coll (ME)
Bowling Green State U (OH)
Bryn Athyn Coll of the New Church (PA)

California State U, Long Beach (CA)
The Coll of Saint Rose (NY)
Cornish Coll of the Arts (WA)
Covenant Coll (GA)
DeSales U (PA)
Ferris State U (MI)
Grand View U (IA)
Hampshire Coll (MA)
Huntingdon Coll (AL)
Indiana Wesleyan U (IN)
Jacksonville U (FL)
Kansas Wesleyan U (KS)
Kenyon Coll (OH)
Lindenwood U (MO)
Madonna U (MI)
Manhattanville Coll (NY)
Marlboro Coll (VT)
Maryland Inst Coll of Art (MD)
New York U (NY)
Northern Michigan U (MI)
Oakland U (MI)
The Ohio State U (OH)
Oklahoma City U (OK)
Pratt Inst (NY)
Providence Coll (RI)
Purchase Coll, State U of New York (NY)
Rhode Island School of Design (RI)
Rutgers U–Newark (NJ)
St. John's U (NY)
Seattle U (WA)
Seton Hill U (PA)
Skidmore Coll (NY)
Stevens Inst of Technology (NJ)
The U of Akron (OH)
U of California, Los Angeles (CA)
U of Denver (CO)
U of Guam (GU)
U of Hartford (CT)
U of Maryland, Baltimore County (MD)
U of Mary Washington (VA)
U of Massachusetts Lowell (MA)
U of Michigan (MI)
U of New Haven (CT)
U of Regina (SK, Canada)
The U of the Arts (PA)
U of Washington (WA)
U of Wisconsin–Milwaukee (WI)
U of Wisconsin–Superior (WI)
Widener U (PA)

FINE/STUDIO ARTS
Abilene Christian U (TX)
Academy of Art U (CA)
Agnes Scott Coll (GA)
Alberta Coll of Art & Design (AB, Canada)
Albion Coll (MI)
Albright Coll (PA)
Alfred U (NY)
Allegheny Coll (PA)
American U (DC)
The American U of Paris (France)
Amherst Coll (MA)
Angelo State U (TX)
Antioch Coll, Yellow Springs (OH)
Appalachian State U (NC)
Aquinas Coll (MI)
Arcadia U (PA)
ArtCenter Coll of Design (CA)
Asbury U (KY)
Ashland U (OH)
Auburn U (AL)
Augsburg U (MN)
Baker U (KS)
Baldwin Wallace U (OH)
Bard Coll (NY)
Barton Coll (NC)
Baylor U (TX)
Beacon Coll (FL)
Bellarmine U (KY)
Belmont U (TN)
Beloit Coll (WI)
Bemidji State U (MN)
Benedictine U (IL)
Bennington Coll (VT)
Bethany Lutheran Coll (MN)
Bethel Coll (IN)
Bethel Coll (KS)
Bethel U (MN)
Binghamton U, State U of New York (NY)
Biola U (CA)
Birmingham-Southern Coll (AL)
Bloomsburg U of Pennsylvania (PA)

Bob Jones U (SC)
Boston Coll (MA)
Bowdoin Coll (ME)
Bowling Green State U (OH)
Bradley U (IL)
Brandeis U (MA)
Brenau U (GA)
Bridgewater Coll (VA)
Bridgewater State U (MA)
Brigham Young U (UT)
Brigham Young U–Idaho (ID)
Brock U (ON, Canada)
Bryn Mawr Coll (PA)
Bucknell U (PA)
Buffalo State Coll, State U of New York (NY)
Caldwell U (NJ)
California Coll of the Arts (CA)
California Polytechnic State U, San Luis Obispo (CA)
California State U, East Bay (CA)
California State U, Fullerton (CA)
California State U, Long Beach (CA)
California State U, Stanislaus (CA)
Calvin Coll (MI)
Canisius Coll (NY)
Carleton Coll (MN)
Carlow U (PA)
Carroll U (WI)
Carthage Coll (WI)
Cazenovia Coll (NY)
Cedarville U (OH)
Centenary Coll of Louisiana (LA)
Central Michigan U (MI)
Centre Coll (KY)
Chapman U (CA)
Chatham U (PA)
Chestnut Hill Coll (PA)
Chowan U (NC)
Christian Brothers U (TN)
Christopher Newport U (VA)
Clarke U (IA)
Clark U (MA)
Coastal Carolina U (SC)
Coe Coll (IA)
Coker Coll (SC)
Colby Coll (ME)
Coll of Charleston (SC)
The Coll of Idaho (ID)
The Coll of New Jersey (NJ)
The Coll of New Rochelle (NY)
Coll of Staten Island of the City U of New York (NY)
Coll of the Holy Cross (MA)
The Coll of Wooster (OH)
The Colorado Coll (CO)
Colorado State U (CO)
Colorado State U–Pueblo (CO)
Columbia Coll (SC)
Columbia Coll Chicago (IL)
Concordia U (QC, Canada)
Concordia U, Nebraska (NE)
Concordia U, St. Paul (MN)
Concord U (WV)
Connecticut Coll (CT)
Converse Coll (SC)
Cooper Union for the Advancement of Science and Art (NY)
Cornell U (NY)
Cornish Coll of the Arts (WA)
Creighton U (NE)
Culver-Stockton Coll (MO)
Curry Coll (MA)
Daemen Coll (NY)
Dartmouth Coll (NH)
Denison U (OH)
DePauw U (IN)
Dickinson Coll (PA)
Dominican U (IL)
Drake U (IA)
Drew U (NJ)
Drury U (MO)
East Carolina U (NC)
Eastern Washington U (WA)
Elizabethtown Coll (PA)
Emmanuel Coll (MA)
Emory & Henry Coll (VA)
Emory U (GA)
Endicott Coll (MA)
Eugene Lang Coll of Liberal Arts (NY)
The Evergreen State Coll (WA)
Fairfield U (CT)
Fashion Inst of Technology (NY)
Flagler Coll (FL)
Florida Ag and Mech U (FL)

Florida Intl U (FL)
Florida Southern Coll (FL)
Florida State U (FL)
Franklin & Marshall Coll (PA)
Franklin Pierce U (NH)
Frostburg State U (MD)
Furman U (SC)
Georgetown Coll (KY)
Georgetown U (DC)
The George Washington U (DC)
Gettysburg Coll (PA)
Gordon Coll (MA)
Graceland U (IA)
Grand View U (IA)
Green Mountain Coll (VT)
Grinnell Coll (IA)
Guilford Coll (NC)
Hamilton Coll (NY)
Hamline U (MN)
Hampden-Sydney Coll (VA)
Harding U (AR)
Hardin-Simmons U (TX)
High Point U (NC)
Hobart and William Smith Colls (NY)
Hofstra U (NY)
Holy Family U (PA)
Hope Coll (MI)
Houston Baptist U (TX)
Howard Payne U (TX)
Humboldt State U (CA)
Hunter Coll of the City U of New York (NY)
Huntingdon Coll (AL)
Illinois State U (IL)
Indiana State U (IN)
Indiana U Bloomington (IN)
Indiana U Kokomo (IN)
Indiana U Northwest (IN)
Indiana U of Pennsylvania (PA)
Indiana U–Purdue U Indianapolis (IN)
Indiana U South Bend (IN)
Indiana U Southeast (IN)
Inst of American Indian Arts (NM)
Ithaca Coll (NY)
Jacksonville U (FL)
Judson U (IL)
Juniata Coll (PA)
Kansas State U (KS)
Kean U (NJ)
Keene State Coll (NH)
Kent State U (OH)
Kentucky State U (KY)
Kenyon Coll (OH)
Knox Coll (IL)
Kutztown U of Pennsylvania (PA)
Lafayette Coll (PA)
Laguna Coll of Art & Design (CA)
Lamar U (TX)
La Sierra U (CA)
Lebanese American U (Lebanon)
Lee U (TN)
Liberty U (VA)
Limestone Coll (SC)
Lincoln U (MO)
Lincoln U (PA)
Lindenwood U (MO)
Lindsey Wilson Coll (KY)
Linfield Coll (OR)
Lipscomb U (TN)
Lock Haven U of Pennsylvania (PA)
Long Island U–LIU Brooklyn (NY)
Long Island U–LIU Post (NY)
Louisiana Coll (LA)
Louisiana State U and A&M Coll (LA)
Loyola Marymount U (CA)
Loyola U Chicago (IL)
Loyola U New Orleans (LA)
Lubbock Christian U (TX)
Lycoming Coll (PA)
Maharishi U of Management (IA)
Manchester U (IN)
Manhattanville Coll (NY)
Marietta Coll (OH)
Marist Coll (NY)
Marlboro Coll (VT)
Maryland Inst Coll of Art (MD)
Marylhurst U (OR)
Marymount Manhattan Coll (NY)
Marymount U (VA)
Maryville Coll (TN)
Maryville U of Saint Louis (MO)
Massachusetts Coll of Art and Design (MA)
McKendree U (IL)

McMurry U (TX)
McPherson Coll (KS)
Mercyhurst U (PA)
Meredith Coll (NC)
Messiah Coll (PA)
Michigan State U (MI)
Middlebury Coll (VT)
Millikin U (IL)
Millsaps Coll (MS)
Mills Coll (CA)
Minneapolis Coll of Art and Design (MN)
Missouri Western State U (MO)
Molloy Coll (NY)
Morehead State U (KY)
Morningside Coll (IA)
Mount Holyoke Coll (MA)
Mount St. Joseph U (OH)
Muhlenberg Coll (PA)
Murray State U (KY)
Naropa U (CO)
Nazareth Coll of Rochester (NY)
New Coll of Florida (FL)
New Hampshire Inst of Art (NH)
New York U (NY)
Northeastern U (MA)
Northern Arizona U (AZ)
Northern Illinois U (IL)
Northern Kentucky U (KY)
Northern Vermont U–Lyndon (VT)
North Greenville U (SC)
Northland Coll (WI)
Northwestern State U of Louisiana (LA)
Northwest Missouri State U (MO)
Notre Dame de Namur U (CA)
Nova Southeastern U (FL)
Oberlin Coll (OH)
Ohio Northern U (OH)
Ohio U (OH)
Ohio Wesleyan U (OH)
Oklahoma Baptist U (OK)
Oklahoma City U (OK)
Oral Roberts U (OK)
Ouachita Baptist U (AR)
Pace U (NY)
Pacific Lutheran U (WA)
Pacific Northwest Coll of Art (OR)
Paier Coll of Art, Inc. (CT)
Palm Beach Atlantic U (FL)
Paris Coll of Art (France)
Parsons School of Design (NY)
Pennsylvania Coll of Art & Design (PA)
Piedmont Coll (GA)
Pitzer Coll (CA)
Pratt Inst (NY)
Principia Coll (IL)
Providence Coll (RI)
Purdue U (IN)
Queens Coll of the City U of New York (NY)
Randolph Coll (VA)
Randolph-Macon Coll (VA)
Reed Coll (OR)
Rice U (TX)
Ringling Coll of Art and Design (FL)
Rochester Inst of Technology (NY)
Roger Williams U (RI)
Rosemont Coll (PA)
The Sage Colls (NY)
Saginaw Valley State U (MI)
St. Ambrose U (IA)
St. Catherine U (MN)
St. Joseph's Coll, Long Island Campus (NY)
Saint Louis U (MO)
Saint Louis U–Madrid Campus (Spain)
St. Mary's Coll of Maryland (MD)
Saint Mary's U of Minnesota (MN)
Saint Peter's U (NJ)
St. Thomas Aquinas Coll (NY)
Saint Vincent Coll (PA)
Salisbury U (MD)
Salve Regina U (RI)
Sam Houston State U (TX)
San Diego State U (CA)
Santa Clara U (CA)
Sarah Lawrence Coll (NY)
School of Visual Arts (NY)
Scripps Coll (CA)
Seattle U (WA)
Seton Hill U (PA)
Sewanee: The U of the South (TN)
Shawnee State U (OH)
Shorter U (GA)

Sierra Nevada Coll (NV)
Simpson Coll (IA)
Smith Coll (MA)
Sonoma State U (CA)
Southern Arkansas U–Magnolia (AR)
Southern Illinois U Carbondale (IL)
Southern Methodist U (TX)
Southern Utah U (UT)
Southwestern U (TX)
Spring Hill Coll (AL)
Stanford U (CA)
State U of New York at Fredonia (NY)
State U of New York Coll at Cortland (NY)
State U of New York Coll at Oneonta (NY)
Stockton U (NJ)
Stonehill Coll (MA)
Suffolk U (MA)
Susquehanna U (PA)
Sweet Briar Coll (VA)
Syracuse U (NY)
Tabor Coll (KS)
Tarleton State U (TX)
Taylor U (IN)
Tennessee Technological U (TN)
Texas A&M Intl U (TX)
Texas A&M U–Commerce (TX)
Texas A&M U–Kingsville (TX)
Texas Christian U (TX)
Texas State U (TX)
Towson U (MD)
Trinity Christian Coll (IL)
Truman State U (MO)
Tufts U (MA)
Tulane U (LA)
Union Coll (NY)
Unity Coll (ME)
U at Buffalo, the State U of New York (NY)
The U of Akron (OH)
The U of Alabama (AL)
The U of Arizona (AZ)
U of California, Davis (CA)
U of California, Irvine (CA)
U of California, Riverside (CA)
U of California, San Diego (CA)
U of California, Santa Barbara (CA)
U of Central Florida (FL)
U of Central Missouri (MO)
U of Central Oklahoma (OK)
U of Cincinnati (OH)
U of Colorado Boulder (CO)
U of Colorado Denver (CO)
U of Dallas (TX)
U of Dayton (OH)
U of Florida (FL)
U of Georgia (GA)
U of Guelph (ON, Canada)
U of Houston–Clear Lake (TX)
U of Idaho (ID)
U of Illinois at Chicago (IL)
U of Illinois at Springfield (IL)
U of Jamestown (ND)
The U of Kansas (KS)
U of Kentucky (KY)
U of La Verne (CA)
U of Louisiana at Monroe (LA)
U of Louisville (KY)
U of Maine (ME)
U of Maine at Presque Isle (ME)
U of Mary Hardin-Baylor (TX)
U of Maryland, Baltimore County (MD)
U of Maryland, Coll Park (MD)
U of Massachusetts Amherst (MA)
U of Miami (FL)
U of Michigan–Flint (MI)
U of Minnesota, Duluth (MN)
U of Minnesota, Morris (MN)
U of Missouri–St. Louis (MO)
U of Nebraska–Lincoln (NE)
U of New England (ME)
U of New Hampshire (NH)
U of New Orleans (LA)
U of North Carolina at Asheville (NC)
The U of North Carolina at Chapel Hill (NC)
The U of North Carolina at Charlotte (NC)
The U of North Carolina at Greensboro (NC)
The U of North Carolina at Pembroke (NC)

The U of North Carolina Wilmington (NC)
U of Northern Colorado (CO)
U of Northern Iowa (IA)
U of North Florida (FL)
U of North Georgia (GA)
U of North Texas (TX)
U of Notre Dame (IN)
U of Oklahoma (OK)
U of Oregon (OR)
U of Pennsylvania (PA)
U of Pittsburgh (PA)
U of Providence (MT)
U of Regina (SK, Canada)
U of Rhode Island (RI)
U of Richmond (VA)
U of Rochester (NY)
U of Saint Francis (IN)
U of St. Thomas (TX)
U of San Francisco (CA)
U of Saskatchewan (SK, Canada)
U of Science and Arts of Oklahoma (OK)
U of South Carolina (SC)
U of South Carolina Aiken (SC)
U of Southern California (CA)
U of Southern Maine (ME)
U of Southern Mississippi (MS)
The U of Tennessee (TN)
The U of Texas at Austin (TX)
The U of Texas at San Antonio (TX)
The U of the Arts (PA)
U of the Fraser Valley (BC, Canada)
U of the Incarnate Word (TX)
U of the Pacific (CA)
The U of Tulsa (OK)
U of Vermont (VT)
U of Waterloo (ON, Canada)
Vanderbilt U (TN)
Vassar Coll (NY)
Wake Forest U (NC)
Washington and Lee U (VA)
Washington State U (WA)
Washington State U–Tri-Cities (WA)
Washington U in St. Louis (MO)
Wayland Baptist U (TX)
Webster U (MO)
Wellesley Coll (MA)
Wells Coll (NY)
Wesleyan U (CT)
West Chester U of Pennsylvania (PA)
Western Illinois U (IL)
Western Kentucky U (KY)
Western Michigan U (MI)
Western State Colorado U (CO)
Westminster Coll (PA)
Westminster Coll (UT)
West Texas A&M U (TX)
West Virginia Wesleyan Coll (WV)
Wheaton Coll (MA)
Whitman Coll (WA)
Whitworth U (WA)
Wichita State U (KS)
Willamette U (OR)
William Paterson U of New Jersey (NJ)
Wittenberg U (OH)
Wright State U–Lake Campus (OH)
York Coll of Pennsylvania (PA)
Youngstown State U (OH)

FIRE PREVENTION AND SAFETY TECHNOLOGY
Athens State U (AL)
Delaware State U (DE)
Jefferson Coll of Health Sciences (VA)
Oklahoma State U (OK)
U of New Haven (CT)

FIRE PROTECTION RELATED
The U of Akron (OH)
U of New Haven (CT)

FIRE SCIENCE/FIREFIGHTING
Coll of the Ozarks (MO)
Columbia Coll (SC)
Columbia Southern U (AL)
Hampton U (VA)
Idaho State U (ID)
John Jay Coll of Criminal Justice of the City U of New York (NY)
Madonna U (MI)
New Jersey City U (NJ)
Providence Coll (RI)

U of Florida (FL)
Utah Valley U (UT)

FIRE SERVICES ADMINISTRATION
Bowling Green State U (OH)
California State U, Los Angeles (CA)
Colorado State U (CO)
Columbia Southern U (AL)
Eastern Oregon U (OR)
Fayetteville State U (NC)
Holy Family U (PA)
John Jay Coll of Criminal Justice of the City U of New York (NY)
Lindenwood U (MO)
Metropolitan State U of Denver (CO)
St. Thomas U (FL)
Southern Illinois U Carbondale (IL)
U of Cincinnati (OH)
The U of North Carolina at Charlotte (NC)
Waldorf U (IA)
Western Illinois U (IL)
Western Oregon U (OR)

FISHING AND FISHERIES SCIENCES AND MANAGEMENT
Delaware State U (DE)
Humboldt State U (CA)
Iowa State U of Science and Technology (IA)
Mansfield U of Pennsylvania (PA)
Michigan State U (MI)
The Ohio State U (OH)
Oregon State U (OR)
Purdue U (IN)
Texas A&M U (TX)
U of Alaska Fairbanks (AK)
U of Idaho (ID)
U of Minnesota, Twin Cities Campus (MN)
U of Missouri (MO)
U of Rhode Island (RI)
The U of Tennessee at Martin (TN)
U of Wisconsin–Stevens Point (WI)

FLIGHT INSTRUCTION
U of North Dakota (ND)

FOLKLORE
Indiana U Bloomington (IN)
U of Oregon (OR)

FOODS AND NUTRITION RELATED
California State U, Long Beach (CA)
Samford U (AL)
Schoolcraft Coll (MI)
U of Guelph (ON, Canada)
U of Minnesota, Twin Cities Campus (MN)
Utah State U (UT)

FOOD SCIENCE
Acadia U (NS, Canada)
Auburn U (AL)
Bay Path U (MA)
California Polytechnic State U, San Luis Obispo (CA)
California State Polytechnic U, Pomona (CA)
Clarke U (IA)
Clemson U (SC)
Cornell U (NY)
Delaware Valley U (PA)
Dominican U (IL)
Framingham State U (MA)
Iowa State U of Science and Technology (IA)
Kansas State U (KS)
Michigan State U (MI)
Mississippi State U (MS)
Mount Mary U (WI)
North Carolina State U (NC)
North Dakota State U (ND)
The Ohio State U (OH)
Oklahoma State U (OK)
Oregon State U (OR)
Penn State Abington (PA)
Penn State Altoona (PA)
Penn State Beaver (PA)
Penn State Berks (PA)
Penn State Brandywine (PA)
Penn State DuBois (PA)

Penn State Erie, The Behrend Coll (PA)
Penn State Fayette, The Eberly Campus (PA)
Penn State Greater Allegheny (PA)
Penn State Hazleton (PA)
Penn State Lehigh Valley (PA)
Penn State Mont Alto (PA)
Penn State New Kensington (PA)
Penn State Schuylkill (PA)
Penn State Shenango (PA)
Penn State U Park (PA)
Penn State Wilkes-Barre (PA)
Penn State Worthington Scranton (PA)
Penn State York (PA)
Purdue U (IN)
Rutgers U–New Brunswick (NJ)
Simmons Coll (MA)
Texas Tech U (TX)
U of Arkansas (AR)
U of California, Davis (CA)
U of Florida (FL)
U of Georgia (GA)
U of Guelph (ON, Canada)
U of Idaho (ID)
U of Kentucky (KY)
U of Maine (ME)
U of Maryland, Coll Park (MD)
U of Massachusetts Amherst (MA)
U of Minnesota, Twin Cities Campus (MN)
U of Missouri (MO)
U of Nebraska–Lincoln (NE)
U of Saskatchewan (SK, Canada)
The U of Tennessee (TN)
U of Wisconsin–Madison (WI)
U of Wisconsin–River Falls (WI)
Virginia Polytechnic Inst and State U (VA)
Washington State U (WA)
Western Michigan U (MI)

FOOD SCIENCE AND TECHNOLOGY RELATED
Appalachian State U (NC)
Middle Tennessee State U (TN)
North Dakota State U (ND)
Virginia Polytechnic Inst and State U (VA)

FOOD SERVICE AND DINING ROOM MANAGEMENT
Michigan State U (MI)

FOOD SERVICE SYSTEMS ADMINISTRATION
Dominican U (IL)
Lamar U (TX)
Lipscomb U (TN)
The Ohio State U (OH)
Ohio U (OH)
Point Loma Nazarene U (CA)
Rochester Inst of Technology (NY)
Sam Houston State U (TX)
Simmons Coll (MA)
State U of New York Coll at Oneonta (NY)
The U of North Carolina at Greensboro (NC)
U of Wisconsin–Stout (WI)
Western Michigan U (MI)

FOODS, NUTRITION, AND WELLNESS
Acadia U (NS, Canada)
Alcorn State U (MS)
Andrews U (MI)
Arizona State U at the Downtown Phoenix campus (AZ)
Auburn U (AL)
Benedictine U (IL)
Bluffton U (OH)
Bowling Green State U (OH)
Bradley U (IL)
California State U, Los Angeles (CA)
Carson-Newman U (TN)
Cedar Crest Coll (PA)
Charles R. Drew U of Medicine and Science (CA)
Coll of the Ozarks (MO)
Delaware State U (DE)
Dominican U (IL)
Framingham State U (MA)
Georgia Southern U (GA)
Hunter Coll of the City U of New York (NY)
Indiana State U (IN)

Indiana U of Pennsylvania (PA)
Iowa State U of Science and Technology (IA)
Ithaca Coll (NY)
James Madison U (VA)
Lehman Coll of the City U of New York (NY)
Life U (GA)
Lincoln U (MO)
Long Island U–LIU Post (NY)
Madonna U (MI)
Middle Tennessee State U (TN)
Montclair State U (NJ)
Murray State U (KY)
New Mexico State U (NM)
The New School for Public Engagement (NY)
New York U (NY)
Northern Illinois U (IL)
Ohio U (OH)
Oklahoma State U (OK)
Oregon State U (OR)
Point Loma Nazarene U (CA)
Prairie View A&M U (TX)
Radford U (VA)
St. Catherine U (MN)
Samford U (AL)
Sam Houston State U (TX)
Seattle Pacific U (WA)
State U of New York at Plattsburgh (NY)
Stephen F. Austin State U (TX)
Syracuse U (NY)
Tennessee Technological U (TN)
Texas A&M U (TX)
Texas State U (TX)
Texas Woman's U (TX)
The U of Akron (OH)
U of Arkansas (AR)
U of Central Arkansas (AR)
U of Georgia (GA)
U of Idaho (ID)
U of Kentucky (KY)
U of Missouri (MO)
U of Nebraska–Lincoln (NE)
U of New Mexico (NM)
The U of North Carolina at Chapel Hill (NC)
U of Saint Joseph (CT)
The U of Tennessee (TN)
The U of Texas at Austin (TX)
U of Toronto (ON, Canada)
Virginia Polytechnic Inst and State U (VA)
Waldorf U (IA)
Washington State U (WA)
Wayne State U (MI)
Western Illinois U (IL)
Youngstown State U (OH)

FOOD TECHNOLOGY AND PROCESSING
Brigham Young U (UT)
Iowa State U of Science and Technology (IA)
New Mexico State U (NM)

FOREIGN LANGUAGES AND LITERATURES
Arkansas Tech U (AR)
Auburn U (AL)
Auburn U at Montgomery (AL)
Augustana U (SD)
Austin Peay State U (TN)
Benedictine Coll (KS)
Bennington Coll (VT)
Bloomsburg U of Pennsylvania (PA)
California Polytechnic State U, San Luis Obispo (CA)
Cameron U (OK)
The Citadel, The Military Coll of South Carolina (SC)
Clemson U (SC)
Colorado State U (CO)
Colorado State U–Pueblo (CO)
Concordia U of Edmonton (AB, Canada)
Covenant Coll (GA)
Duquesne U (PA)
East Carolina U (NC)
East Tennessee State U (TN)
Elon U (NC)
Emporia State U (KS)
The Evergreen State Coll (WA)
Framingham State U (MA)
Francis Marion U (SC)
Frostburg State U (MD)
Gannon U (PA)

George Mason U (VA)
Georgia Coll & State U (GA)
Georgia Inst of Technology (GA)
Gordon Coll (MA)
Hamilton Coll (NY)
Jackson State U (MS)
James Madison U (VA)
Juniata Coll (PA)
Kansas State U (KS)
Kenyon Coll (OH)
Knox Coll (IL)
Lamar U (TX)
Lock Haven U of Pennsylvania (PA)
Long Island U–LIU Brooklyn (NY)
Long Island U–LIU Post (NY)
Longwood U (VA)
Louisiana Coll (LA)
Lycoming Coll (PA)
Manchester U (IN)
Marshall U (WV)
Massachusetts Inst of Technology (MA)
Mercyhurst U (PA)
Metropolitan State U of Denver (CO)
Middle Tennessee State U (TN)
Mississippi State U (MS)
Missouri Western State U (MO)
New Coll of Florida (FL)
New Mexico State U (NM)
New York U (NY)
North Carolina State U (NC)
Northern Arizona U (AZ)
Oakland U (MI)
Old Dominion U (VA)
Pace U (NY)
Penn State Berks (PA)
Penn State Lehigh Valley (PA)
Piedmont Coll (GA)
Pitzer Coll (CA)
Presbyterian Coll (SC)
Principia Coll (IL)
Purdue U Northwest (IN)
Radford U (VA)
Roger Williams U (RI)
Rutgers U–New Brunswick (NJ)
St. Mary's Coll of Maryland (MD)
Saint Peter's U (NJ)
Samford U (AL)
Scripps Coll (CA)
Slippery Rock U of Pennsylvania (PA)
Southern Adventist U (TN)
Southern Illinois U Carbondale (IL)
Southern Illinois U Edwardsville (IL)
Stanford U (CA)
State U of New York Coll at Old Westbury (NY)
Stephen F. Austin State U (TX)
Stockton U (NJ)
Stonehill Coll (MA)
Suffolk U (MA)
Syracuse U (NY)
Tennessee Technological U (TN)
Texas A&M U (TX)
Texas Tech U (TX)
Towson U (MD)
Tufts U (MA)
Tulane U (LA)
Union Coll (NE)
Union Coll (NY)
Union U (TN)
The U of Alabama (AL)
The U of Alabama at Birmingham (AL)
U of Alaska Fairbanks (AK)
U of California, Riverside (CA)
U of California, San Diego (CA)
U of California, Santa Cruz (CA)
U of Dayton (OH)
U of Florida (FL)
U of Hartford (CT)
U of Houston (TX)
U of Idaho (ID)
U of Louisiana at Monroe (LA)
U of Maryland, Baltimore County (MD)
U of Mary Washington (VA)
U of Massachusetts Lowell (MA)
U of Memphis (TN)
U of Minnesota, Twin Cities Campus (MN)
U of Missouri–St. Louis (MO)
U of Montevallo (AL)
U of New Mexico (NM)
U of New Orleans (LA)

U of North Alabama (AL)
The U of North Carolina at Chapel Hill (NC)
The U of North Carolina at Greensboro (NC)
U of North Dakota (ND)
U of Northern Colorado (CO)
U of North Georgia (GA)
U of Saskatchewan (SK, Canada)
The U of Scranton (PA)
U of South Alabama (AL)
U of Southern Mississippi (MS)
U of South Florida, St. Petersburg (FL)
U of Tennessee (TN)
The U of Tennessee at Chattanooga (TN)
The U of Texas at San Antonio (TX)
The U of Virginia's Coll at Wise (VA)
U of Wisconsin–Platteville (WI)
U of Wisconsin–River Falls (WI)
Utica Coll (NY)
Virginia Commonwealth U (VA)
Washington Coll (MD)
Washington State U (WA)
Wayne State Coll (NE)
Wayne State U (MI)
Webster U (MO)
West Chester U of Pennsylvania (PA)
Western Illinois U (IL)
Western Washington U (WA)
West Virginia U (WV)
Wichita State U (KS)
Widener U (PA)
Winthrop U (SC)
Wright State U (OH)
Youngstown State U (OH)

FOREIGN LANGUAGES RELATED
Arizona State U at the Tempe campus (AZ)
Augustana U (SD)
Averett U (VA)
Binghamton U, State U of New York (NY)
Clemson U (SC)
Georgia Southern U (GA)
Indiana State U (IN)
Kennesaw State U (GA)
Marlboro Coll (VT)
Miami U (OH)
New York U (NY)
Northeastern U (MA)
Occidental Coll (CA)
Purchase Coll, State U of New York (NY)
Queens Coll of the City U of New York (NY)
St. Lawrence U (NY)
Saint Mary's Coll of California (CA)
United States Military Acad (NY)
U of Alaska Fairbanks (AK)
U of California, Los Angeles (CA)
U of Hawaii at Manoa (HI)
U of West Georgia (GA)
Wayne State U (MI)
Western Washington U (WA)

FOREIGN LANGUAGE TEACHER EDUCATION
Arkansas Tech U (AR)
Ashland U (OH)
Auburn U (AL)
Ball State U (IN)
Baylor U (TX)
Boston U (MA)
Bowling Green State U (OH)
Buffalo State Coll, State U of New York (NY)
Calvin Coll (MI)
Carroll U (WI)
Coll of Staten Island of the City U of New York (NY)
DePaul U (IL)
Eastern Michigan U (MI)
Florida Southern Coll (FL)
Grand Valley State U (MI)
Greensboro Coll (NC)
Hofstra U (NY)
Iona Coll (NY)
Long Island U–LIU Post (NY)
Manchester U (IN)
Mercyhurst U (PA)
Messiah Coll (PA)
Miami U (OH)

Nazareth Coll of Rochester (NY)
New York U (NY)
Ohio Northern U (OH)
The Ohio State U (OH)
Ohio Wesleyan U (OH)
Oral Roberts U (OK)
Pace U, Pleasantville Campus (NY)
Penn State Abington (PA)
Penn State Altoona (PA)
Penn State Beaver (PA)
Penn State Berks (PA)
Penn State Brandywine (PA)
Penn State DuBois (PA)
Penn State Erie, The Behrend Coll (PA)
Penn State Fayette, The Eberly Campus (PA)
Penn State Greater Allegheny (PA)
Penn State Mont Alto (PA)
Penn State Shenango (PA)
Penn State U Park (PA)
Penn State Worthington Scranton (PA)
Penn State York (PA)
Piedmont Coll (GA)
Providence Coll (RI)
Queens Coll of the City U of New York (NY)
Rhode Island Coll (RI)
Roger Williams U (RI)
Saint Francis U (PA)
Seton Hill U (PA)
Southeast Missouri State U (MO)
State U of New York Coll at Old Westbury (NY)
Temple U (PA)
U of Dayton (OH)
The U of Findlay (OH)
U of Georgia (GA)
U of Maine (ME)
U of Mary Hardin-Baylor (TX)
U of Minnesota, Duluth (MN)
U of Nebraska–Lincoln (NE)
U of Oklahoma (OK)
U of South Dakota (SD)
U of Vermont (VT)
U of Wisconsin–Milwaukee (WI)
U of Wisconsin–Stevens Point (WI)
Valparaiso U (IN)
Vanderbilt U (TN)
Virginia Wesleyan U (VA)
Wayne State Coll (NE)
Youngstown State U (OH)

FORENSIC CHEMISTRY
Alabama State U (AL)
Arizona State U at the West campus (AZ)
Ashland U (OH)
Bowling Green State U (OH)
Chestnut Hill Coll (PA)
Delaware State U (DE)
Emmanuel Coll (MA)
Lamar U (TX)
LeTourneau U (TX)
Loyola U New Orleans (LA)
Maryville U of Saint Louis (MO)
MidAmerica Nazarene U (KS)
Missouri Baptist U (MO)
Mount Mercy U (IA)
Palm Beach Atlantic U (FL)
U of Central Oklahoma (OK)
U of Rhode Island (RI)
U of Saint Francis (IN)
Western New England U (MA)

FORENSIC PSYCHOLOGY
Bay Path U (MA)
Canisius Coll (NY)
The Coll of Saint Rose (NY)
Corban U (OR)
Florida Inst of Technology (FL)
John Jay Coll of Criminal Justice of the City U of New York (NY)
National Louis U (IL)
Oklahoma Baptist U (OK)
St. Ambrose U (IA)
Tiffin U (OH)
U of New Haven (CT)
Western State Colorado U (CO)

FORENSIC SCIENCE AND TECHNOLOGY
American Public U System (WV)
Bay Path U (MA)
Becker Coll (MA)
Bluefield Coll (VA)
Bryant U (RI)

Buffalo State Coll, State U of New York (NY)
Cedar Crest Coll (PA)
Cedarville U (OH)
Chaminade U of Honolulu (HI)
Chestnut Hill Coll (PA)
The Coll of Saint Rose (NY)
Columbia Coll (MO)
Defiance Coll (OH)
Delaware State U (DE)
Eastern Nazarene Coll (MA)
Eastern New Mexico U (NM)
EDP U of Puerto Rico (PR)
Farmingdale State Coll (NY)
Fayetteville State U (NC)
Florida Gulf Coast U (FL)
Friends U (KS)
Gannon U (PA)
George Mason U (VA)
Hilbert Coll (NY)
Hofstra U (NY)
Husson U (ME)
Indiana U–Purdue U Indianapolis (IN)
Inter American U of Puerto Rico, Aguadilla Campus (PR)
Inter American U of Puerto Rico, Barranquitas Campus (PR)
Inter American U of Puerto Rico, Bayamón Campus (PR)
John Jay Coll of Criminal Justice of the City U of New York (NY)
King U (TN)
Lewis U (IL)
Liberty U (VA)
Long Island U–LIU Post (NY)
Loyola U Chicago (IL)
Lynn U (FL)
Madonna U (MI)
Marian U (WI)
Mercyhurst U (PA)
Middle Tennessee State U (TN)
Mount Marty Coll (SD)
Newman U (KS)
New Mexico Highlands U (NM)
Northwest Nazarene U (ID)
Pace U (NY)
Penn State Altoona (PA)
Penn State Berks (PA)
Penn State U Park (PA)
Piedmont Coll (GA)
Point Park U (PA)
Roberts Wesleyan Coll (NY)
Roger Williams U (RI)
St. Andrews U (NC)
Saint Francis U (PA)
Saint Louis U (MO)
St. Mary's U (TX)
St. Thomas Aquinas Coll (NY)
Sam Houston State U (TX)
Seton Hill U (PA)
Simpson Coll (IA)
State U of New York Coll of Technology at Alfred (NY)
Syracuse U (NY)
Texas A&M U (TX)
Tiffin U (OH)
Towson U (MD)
Trine U (IN)
U of Central Florida (FL)
U of Central Oklahoma (OK)
U of Dubuque (IA)
The U of Findlay (OH)
U of Maryland U Coll (MD)
U of Nebraska–Lincoln (NE)
U of New Haven (CT)
U of North Dakota (ND)
U of Pittsburgh at Bradford (PA)
U of Providence (MT)
The U of Scranton (PA)
U of Southern Mississippi (MS)
The U of Tampa (FL)
U of Toronto (ON, Canada)
U of Wisconsin–Platteville (WI)
Utah Valley U (UT)
Virginia Commonwealth U (VA)
Waynesburg U (PA)
Weber State U (UT)
Western New England U (MA)
West Virginia U (WV)
West Virginia U Inst of Technology (WV)
Wichita State U (KS)
York Coll of Pennsylvania (PA)
Youngstown State U (OH)

FOREST ENGINEERING
Oregon State U (OR)

FOREST/FOREST RESOURCES MANAGEMENT
Clemson U (SC)
Elizabethtown Coll (PA)
North Carolina State U (NC)
State U of New York Coll of Environmental Science and Forestry (NY)
Stephen F. Austin State U (TX)
U of Idaho (ID)
U of Montana (MT)
U of Nevada, Reno (NV)
U of Toronto (ON, Canada)
U of Wisconsin–Stevens Point (WI)
West Virginia U (WV)
Whitman Coll (WA)

FORESTRY
Albright Coll (PA)
Beloit Coll (WI)
California Polytechnic State U, San Luis Obispo (CA)
Delaware State U (DE)
Humboldt State U (CA)
Iowa State U of Science and Technology (IA)
Lenoir-Rhyne U (NC)
Michigan State U (MI)
Michigan Technological U (MI)
New Mexico Highlands U (NM)
Purdue U (IN)
Southern Illinois U Carbondale (IL)
State U of New York Coll of Environmental Science and Forestry (NY)
Stephen F. Austin State U (TX)
Texas A&M U (TX)
U of Florida (FL)
U of Georgia (GA)
U of Idaho (ID)
U of Maine (ME)
U of Missouri (MO)
U of Montana (MT)
U of New Hampshire (NH)
The U of Tennessee (TN)
U of Toronto (ON, Canada)
U of Vermont (VT)
U of Wisconsin–Stevens Point (WI)
Utah State U (UT)
Virginia Polytechnic Inst and State U (VA)
Washington State U (WA)

FORESTRY RELATED
Auburn U (AL)
Northland Coll (WI)
Northwest Missouri State U (MO)
U of Minnesota, Twin Cities Campus (MN)
U of Montana (MT)
U of Wisconsin–Parkside (WI)
U of Wisconsin–Stevens Point (WI)
Utah State U (UT)

FOREST SCIENCES AND BIOLOGY
Auburn U (AL)
Colorado State U (CO)
Iowa State U of Science and Technology (IA)
Mississippi State U (MS)
Northern Arizona U (AZ)
Ohio Northern U (OH)
Penn State Abington (PA)
Penn State Altoona (PA)
Penn State Beaver (PA)
Penn State Berks (PA)
Penn State Brandywine (PA)
Penn State DuBois (PA)
Penn State Erie, The Behrend Coll (PA)
Penn State Fayette, The Eberly Campus (PA)
Penn State Greater Allegheny (PA)
Penn State Hazleton (PA)
Penn State Lehigh Valley (PA)
Penn State Mont Alto (PA)
Penn State New Kensington (PA)
Penn State Schuylkill (PA)
Penn State Shenango (PA)
Penn State U Park (PA)
Penn State Wilkes-Barre (PA)
Penn State Worthington Scranton (PA)
Penn State York (PA)

Sewanee: The U of the South (TN)
State U of New York Coll of Environmental Science and Forestry (NY)
U of Idaho (ID)
U of Kentucky (KY)
U of Wisconsin–Madison (WI)

FOREST TECHNOLOGY
Penn State Abington (PA)
Penn State Altoona (PA)
Penn State Beaver (PA)
Penn State Berks (PA)
Penn State Brandywine (PA)
Penn State DuBois (PA)
Penn State Erie, The Behrend Coll (PA)
Penn State Fayette, The Eberly Campus (PA)
Penn State Greater Allegheny (PA)
Penn State Hazleton (PA)
Penn State Lehigh Valley (PA)
Penn State Mont Alto (PA)
Penn State New Kensington (PA)
Penn State Schuylkill (PA)
Penn State Shenango (PA)
Penn State Wilkes-Barre (PA)
Penn State Worthington Scranton (PA)
Penn State York (PA)

FRANCHISING
St. Catherine U (MN)

FRENCH
Acadia U (NS, Canada)
Adelphi U (NY)
Agnes Scott Coll (GA)
Albion Coll (MI)
Albright Coll (PA)
Allegheny Coll (PA)
Alma Coll (MI)
American U (DC)
Amherst Coll (MA)
Andrews U (MI)
Aquinas Coll (MI)
Arizona State U at the Tempe campus (AZ)
Asbury U (KY)
Ashland U (OH)
Athabasca U (AB, Canada)
Auburn U (AL)
Augsburg U (MN)
Augustana Coll (IL)
Augustana U (SD)
Austin Coll (TX)
Baker U (KS)
Baldwin Wallace U (OH)
Ball State U (IN)
Bard Coll (NY)
Barnard Coll (NY)
Barry U (FL)
Bates Coll (ME)
Baylor U (TX)
Belmont U (TN)
Beloit Coll (WI)
Benedictine Coll (KS)
Bennington Coll (VT)
Berea Coll (KY)
Berry Coll (GA)
Binghamton U, State U of New York (NY)
Boise State U (ID)
Boston Coll (MA)
Boston U (MA)
Bowling Green State U (OH)
Bradley U (IL)
Brandon U (MB, Canada)
Bridgewater Coll (VA)
Brock U (ON, Canada)
Bryant U (RI)
Bryn Mawr Coll (PA)
Bucknell U (PA)
Buffalo State Coll, State U of New York (NY)
Butler U (IN)
California Lutheran U (CA)
California State U, East Bay (CA)
California State U, Fullerton (CA)
California State U, Long Beach (CA)
California State U, Los Angeles (CA)
California State U, Northridge (CA)
California State U, Sacramento (CA)
California State U, San Bernardino (CA)

Calvin Coll (MI)
Capital U (OH)
Carleton Coll (MN)
Carnegie Mellon U (PA)
Carroll Coll (MT)
Carthage Coll (WI)
Case Western Reserve U (OH)
The Catholic U of America (DC)
Centenary Coll of Louisiana (LA)
Central Connecticut State U (CT)
Central Michigan U (MI)
Centre Coll (KY)
Chapman U (CA)
Chestnut Hill Coll (PA)
Christopher Newport U (VA)
City Coll of the City U of New York (NY)
Claremont McKenna Coll (CA)
Clarion U of Pennsylvania (PA)
Clark Atlanta U (GA)
Clark U (MA)
Clayton State U (GA)
Cleveland State U (OH)
Coe Coll (IA)
Colby Coll (ME)
Colgate U (NY)
The Coll at Brockport, State U of New York (NY)
Coll of Charleston (SC)
Coll of Coastal Georgia (GA)
Coll of Mount Saint Vincent (NY)
The Coll of New Rochelle (NY)
Coll of Saint Benedict (MN)
Coll of the Holy Cross (MA)
The Coll of William and Mary (VA)
The Coll of Wooster (OH)
The Colorado Coll (CO)
Columbia U (NY)
Concordia U (QC, Canada)
Concordia U of Edmonton (AB, Canada)
Connecticut Coll (CT)
Cornell Coll (IA)
Cornell U (NY)
Creighton U (NE)
Daemen Coll (NY)
Dartmouth Coll (NH)
Davidson Coll (NC)
Delaware State U (DE)
Denison U (OH)
DePaul U (IL)
DePauw U (IN)
Dickinson Coll (PA)
Doane U (NE)
Dominican U (IL)
Drew U (NJ)
Drury U (MO)
Earlham Coll (IN)
Eastern Michigan U (MI)
Eastern Washington U (WA)
Eckerd Coll (FL)
Edgewood Coll (WI)
Elizabethtown Coll (PA)
Elmhurst Coll (IL)
Elon U (NC)
Emory & Henry Coll (VA)
Fairfield U (CT)
Fairleigh Dickinson U, Florham Campus (NJ)
Fairleigh Dickinson U, Metropolitan Campus (NJ)
Florida Atlantic U (FL)
Florida Intl U (FL)
Florida State U (FL)
Fordham U (NY)
Franklin & Marshall Coll (PA)
Franklin Coll (IN)
Furman U (SC)
Georgetown Coll (KY)
Georgetown U (DC)
The George Washington U (DC)
Georgia Southern U–Armstrong Campus (GA)
Georgia State U (GA)
Gettysburg Coll (PA)
Gonzaga U (WA)
Gordon Coll (MA)
Grand Valley State U (MI)
Greensboro Coll (NC)
Grinnell Coll (IA)
Grove City Coll (PA)
Guilford Coll (NC)
Gustavus Adolphus Coll (MN)
Hamilton Coll (NY)
Hampden-Sydney Coll (VA)
Harding U (AR)
Hartwick Coll (NY)

Haverford Coll (PA)
Hendrix Coll (AR)
High Point U (NC)
Hillsdale Coll (MI)
Hiram Coll (OH)
Hobart and William Smith Colls (NY)
Hofstra U (NY)
Hollins U (VA)
Hood Coll (MD)
Hope Coll (MI)
Humboldt State U (CA)
Hunter Coll of the City U of New York (NY)
Idaho State U (ID)
Illinois Coll (IL)
Illinois State U (IL)
Illinois Wesleyan U (IL)
Indiana U Bloomington (IN)
Indiana U Northwest (IN)
Indiana U–Purdue U Indianapolis (IN)
Indiana U South Bend (IN)
Indiana U Southeast (IN)
Iona Coll (NY)
Iowa State U of Science and Technology (IA)
Ithaca Coll (NY)
Jacksonville U (FL)
John Carroll U (OH)
Johns Hopkins U (MD)
Johnson C. Smith U (NC)
Juniata Coll (PA)
Kalamazoo Coll (MI)
Keene State Coll (NH)
Kent State U (OH)
Kenyon Coll (OH)
King's Coll (PA)
King U (TN)
Knox Coll (IL)
Lafayette Coll (PA)
Lawrence U (WI)
Lebanon Valley Coll (PA)
Lee U (TN)
Lehigh U (PA)
Lehman Coll of the City U of New York (NY)
Le Moyne Coll (NY)
Lincoln U (PA)
Lindenwood U (MO)
Linfield Coll (OR)
Lipscomb U (TN)
Louisiana Coll (LA)
Louisiana State U and A&M Coll (LA)
Loyola Marymount U (CA)
Loyola U Chicago (IL)
Loyola U New Orleans (LA)
Luther Coll (IA)
Lycoming Coll (PA)
Lynchburg Coll (VA)
Macalester Coll (MN)
Manchester U (IN)
Manhattan Coll (NY)
Manhattanville Coll (NY)
Marist Coll (NY)
Marlboro Coll (VT)
McDaniel Coll (MD)
Mercer U, Macon (GA)
Merrimack Coll (MA)
Messiah Coll (PA)
Miami U (OH)
Michigan State U (MI)
Middlebury Coll (VT)
Millersville U of Pennsylvania (PA)
Missouri State U (MO)
Monmouth Coll (IL)
Montclair State U (NJ)
Moravian Coll (PA)
Morehouse Coll (GA)
Mount Holyoke Coll (MA)
Mount Saint Mary's U (CA)
Mount St. Mary's U (MD)
Muhlenberg Coll (PA)
Murray State U (KY)
Muskingum U (OH)
Nazareth Coll of Rochester (NY)
New Coll of Florida (FL)
New York U (NY)
Niagara U (NY)
North Carolina State U (NC)
North Central Coll (IL)
North Dakota State U (ND)
Northern Illinois U (IL)
Northern Kentucky U (KY)
Northern Michigan U (MI)

Northern State U (SD)
Northwestern U (IL)
Oakland U (MI)
Oberlin Coll (OH)
Occidental Coll (CA)
Oglethorpe U (GA)
Ohio Northern U (OH)
The Ohio State U (OH)
Ohio U (OH)
Ohio Wesleyan U (OH)
Oklahoma City U (OK)
Oklahoma State U (OK)
Oral Roberts U (OK)
Oregon State U (OR)
Otterbein U (OH)
Pacific Lutheran U (WA)
Penn State Abington (PA)
Penn State Altoona (PA)
Penn State Beaver (PA)
Penn State Berks (PA)
Penn State Brandywine (PA)
Penn State DuBois (PA)
Penn State Erie, The Behrend Coll (PA)
Penn State Fayette, The Eberly Campus (PA)
Penn State Greater Allegheny (PA)
Penn State Hazleton (PA)
Penn State Lehigh Valley (PA)
Penn State Mont Alto (PA)
Penn State New Kensington (PA)
Penn State Schuylkill (PA)
Penn State Shenango (PA)
Penn State U Park (PA)
Penn State Wilkes-Barre (PA)
Penn State Worthington Scranton (PA)
Penn State York (PA)
Pepperdine U, Malibu (CA)
Pittsburg State U (KS)
Pitzer Coll (CA)
Point Loma Nazarene U (CA)
Pomona Coll (CA)
Portland State U (OR)
Presbyterian Coll (SC)
Princeton U (NJ)
Principia Coll (IL)
Providence Coll (RI)
Purchase Coll, State U of New York (NY)
Purdue U (IN)
Queens Coll of the City U of New York (NY)
Randolph Coll (VA)
Randolph-Macon Coll (VA)
Redeemer U Coll (ON, Canada)
Reed Coll (OR)
Regis U (CO)
Rhode Island Coll (RI)
Rhodes Coll (TN)
Rice U (TX)
Rider U (NJ)
Roanoke Coll (VA)
Rockford U (IL)
Rockhurst U (MO)
Rutgers U–Camden (NJ)
Rutgers U–Newark (NJ)
Rutgers U–New Brunswick (NJ)
Saginaw Valley State U (MI)
St. Ambrose U (IA)
Saint Anselm Coll (NH)
St. Catherine U (MN)
St. John Fisher Coll (NY)
Saint John's U (MN)
St. John's U (NY)
Saint Joseph's U (PA)
St. Lawrence U (NY)
Saint Louis U (MO)
Saint Louis U–Madrid Campus (Spain)
Saint Mary's Coll of California (CA)
Saint Michael's Coll (VT)
St. Norbert Coll (WI)
St. Olaf Coll (MN)
St. Thomas U (NB, Canada)
Saint Vincent Coll (PA)
Salisbury U (MD)
Salve Regina U (RI)
Samford U (AL)
Sam Houston State U (TX)
San Diego State U (CA)
San Francisco State U (CA)
Santa Clara U (CA)
Sarah Lawrence Coll (NY)
Scripps Coll (CA)
Seattle U (WA)
Sewanee: The U of the South (TN)

Shippensburg U of Pennsylvania (PA)
Siena Coll (NY)
Simmons Coll (MA)
Simon Fraser U (BC, Canada)
Simpson Coll (IA)
Skidmore Coll (NY)
Slippery Rock U of Pennsylvania (PA)
Smith Coll (MA)
Sonoma State U (CA)
Southern Adventist U (TN)
Southern Methodist U (TX)
Southern Utah U (UT)
Southwestern U (TX)
Spelman Coll (GA)
Stanford U (CA)
State U of New York at Fredonia (NY)
State U of New York at New Paltz (NY)
State U of New York at Oswego (NY)
State U of New York at Plattsburgh (NY)
State U of New York Coll at Cortland (NY)
State U of New York Coll at Geneseo (NY)
State U of New York Coll at Oneonta (NY)
State U of New York Coll at Potsdam (NY)
Stetson U (FL)
Stonehill Coll (MA)
Stony Brook U, State U of New York (NY)
Susquehanna U (PA)
Sweet Briar Coll (VA)
Syracuse U (NY)
Temple U (PA)
Tennessee Technological U (TN)
Tennessee Wesleyan U (TN)
Texas A&M U (TX)
Texas Christian U (TX)
Texas State U (TX)
Texas Tech U (TX)
Transylvania U (KY)
Trent U (ON, Canada)
Trinity U (TX)
Truman State U (MO)
Tufts U (MA)
Tulane U (LA)
Union Coll (NY)
Union U (TN)
United States Military Acad (NY)
Université de Sherbrooke (QC, Canada)
Université Sainte-Anne (NS, Canada)
U at Buffalo, the State U of New York (NY)
The U of Akron (OH)
The U of Arizona (AZ)
U of Arkansas (AR)
U of California, Davis (CA)
U of California, Irvine (CA)
U of California, Los Angeles (CA)
U of California, Riverside (CA)
U of California, San Diego (CA)
U of California, Santa Barbara (CA)
U of Central Arkansas (AR)
U of Central Florida (FL)
U of Central Missouri (MO)
U of Central Oklahoma (OK)
U of Cincinnati (OH)
U of Colorado Boulder (CO)
U of Colorado Denver (CO)
U of Dallas (TX)
U of Dayton (OH)
U of Denver (CO)
U of Evansville (IN)
U of Florida (FL)
U of Georgia (GA)
U of Hawaii at Manoa (HI)
U of Houston (TX)
U of Idaho (ID)
U of Illinois at Chicago (IL)
U of Jamestown (ND)
The U of Kansas (KS)
U of Kentucky (KY)
U of King's Coll (NS, Canada)
U of La Verne (CA)
U of Louisville (KY)
U of Maine (ME)
U of Maine at Fort Kent (ME)
U of Maryland, Coll Park (MD)

U of Massachusetts Amherst (MA)
U of Massachusetts Boston (MA)
U of Massachusetts Dartmouth (MA)
U of Miami (FL)
U of Michigan (MI)
U of Michigan–Dearborn (MI)
U of Michigan–Flint (MI)
U of Minnesota, Duluth (MN)
U of Minnesota, Morris (MN)
U of Minnesota, Twin Cities Campus (MN)
U of Missouri (MO)
U of Montana (MT)
U of Mount Union (OH)
U of Nebraska at Kearney (NE)
U of Nebraska–Lincoln (NE)
U of Nevada, Las Vegas (NV)
U of Nevada, Reno (NV)
U of New Hampshire (NH)
U of New Mexico (NM)
U of North Alabama (AL)
U of North Carolina at Asheville (NC)
The U of North Carolina at Charlotte (NC)
The U of North Carolina at Greensboro (NC)
The U of North Carolina Wilmington (NC)
U of North Dakota (ND)
U of North Texas (TX)
U of Notre Dame (IN)
U of Oklahoma (OK)
U of Oregon (OR)
U of Pennsylvania (PA)
U of Pittsburgh (PA)
U of Puget Sound (WA)
U of Regina (SK, Canada)
U of Rhode Island (RI)
U of Richmond (VA)
U of Rochester (NY)
U of St. Thomas (MN)
U of St. Thomas (TX)
U of San Diego (CA)
U of San Francisco (CA)
U of Saskatchewan (SK, Canada)
The U of Scranton (PA)
U of South Carolina (SC)
U of South Dakota (SD)
U of Southern California (CA)
U of Southern Indiana (IN)
U of Southern Maine (ME)
The U of Tennessee (TN)
The U of Tennessee at Martin (TN)
The U of Texas at Austin (TX)
The U of Texas at El Paso (TX)
U of the Pacific (CA)
The U of Toledo (OH)
U of Toronto (ON, Canada)
The U of Tulsa (OK)
U of Utah (UT)
U of Vermont (VT)
U of Virginia (VA)
The U of Virginia's Coll at Wise (VA)
U of Washington (WA)
U of Waterloo (ON, Canada)
U of Wisconsin–Eau Claire (WI)
U of Wisconsin–La Crosse (WI)
U of Wisconsin–Madison (WI)
U of Wisconsin–Milwaukee (WI)
U of Wisconsin–Stevens Point (WI)
U of Wisconsin–Whitewater (WI)
U of Wyoming (WY)
Ursinus Coll (PA)
Utah State U (UT)
Valdosta State U (GA)
Valparaiso U (IN)
Vanderbilt U (TN)
Vassar Coll (NY)
Villanova U (PA)
Virginia Polytechnic Inst and State U (VA)
Virginia Wesleyan U (VA)
Wabash Coll (IN)
Wake Forest U (NC)
Walsh U (OH)
Washington & Jefferson Coll (PA)
Washington and Lee U (VA)
Washington Coll (MD)
Washington State U (WA)
Washington U in St. Louis (MO)
Weber State U (UT)
Webster U (MO)
Wellesley Coll (MA)

West Chester U of Pennsylvania (PA)
Western Kentucky U (KY)
Western Michigan U (MI)
Western Washington U (WA)
Westminster Coll (PA)
Westmont Coll (CA)
Wheaton Coll (IL)
Wheaton Coll (MA)
Whitman Coll (WA)
Whittier Coll (CA)
Whitworth U (WA)
Widener U (PA)
Willamette U (OR)
Williams Coll (MA)
Wittenberg U (OH)
Wofford Coll (SC)
Wright State U (OH)
Wright State U–Lake Campus (OH)
Xavier U of Louisiana (LA)

**FRENCH AS A SECOND/
FOREIGN LANGUAGE
(TEACHING)**
Saginaw Valley State U (MI)
U of Toronto (ON, Canada)
U of Wisconsin–Milwaukee (WI)
Whitworth U (WA)

**FRENCH LANGUAGE
TEACHER EDUCATION**
Albion Coll (MI)
Ashland U (OH)
Auburn U (AL)
Augustana Coll (IL)
Austin Coll (TX)
Boise State U (ID)
California Lutheran U (CA)
Calvin Coll (MI)
Canisius Coll (NY)
The Catholic U of America (DC)
Central Michigan U (MI)
Daemen Coll (NY)
Delaware State U (DE)
Eastern Michigan U (MI)
Eastern Washington U (WA)
Edgewood Coll (WI)
Elmhurst Coll (IL)
Emory & Henry Coll (VA)
Grand Valley State U (MI)
Grove City Coll (PA)
Harding U (AR)
Hofstra U (NY)
Holy Family U (PA)
Hope Coll (MI)
Indiana U South Bend (IN)
Iona Coll (NY)
Ithaca Coll (NY)
Juniata Coll (PA)
Lee U (TN)
Le Moyne Coll (NY)
Lindenwood U (MO)
Lipscomb U (TN)
Long Island U–LIU Post (NY)
Louisiana Coll (LA)
Manchester U (IN)
Manhattanville Coll (NY)
Marist Coll (NY)
Merrimack Coll (MA)
Messiah Coll (PA)
Miami U (OH)
Michigan State U (MI)
Missouri State U (MO)
Missouri Western State U (MO)
New York U (NY)
Niagara U (NY)
North Dakota State U (ND)
Northern Michigan U (MI)
Ohio Northern U (OH).
Ohio U (OH)
Ohio Wesleyan U (OH)
Pittsburg State U (KS)
Providence Coll (RI)
Queens Coll of the City U of New York (NY)
Rhode Island Coll (RI)
St. Catherine U (MN)
St. John Fisher Coll (NY)
Saint Joseph's U (PA)
Salve Regina U (RI)
Southern Adventist U (TN)
Southern Utah U (UT)
State U of New York at Plattsburgh (NY)
State U of New York Coll at Cortland (NY)
State U of New York Coll at Oneonta (NY)

State U of New York Coll at
  Potsdam (NY)
Université Sainte-Anne (NS,
  Canada)
The U of Akron (OH)
U of Central Oklahoma (OK)
U of Evansville (IN)
U of Illinois at Chicago (IL)
U of Maine (ME)
U of Michigan–Flint (MI)
U of Nebraska–Lincoln (NE)
The U of North Carolina at
  Greensboro (NC)
U of Regina (SK, Canada)
U of St. Thomas (MN)
U of South Dakota (SD)
The U of Tennessee at Martin (TN)
U of Toronto (ON, Canada)
U of Waterloo (ON, Canada)
U of Wisconsin–Whitewater (WI)
Valparaiso U (IN)
Washington U in St. Louis (MO)
Weber State U (UT)
Western Illinois U (IL)
Western Michigan U (MI)
Western Washington U (WA)
Widener U (PA)
Xavier U of Louisiana (LA)

FRENCH STUDIES
American U (DC)
Arcadia U (PA)
Bard Coll (NY)
Barnard Coll (NY)
Bowdoin Coll (ME)
Brandeis U (MA)
Brock U (ON, Canada)
Carleton Coll (MN)
Case Western Reserve U (OH)
Coe Coll (IA)
The Colorado Coll (CO)
Columbia U (NY)
Emory & Henry Coll (VA)
Emory U (GA)
Fordham U (NY)
Franklin U Switzerland
  (Switzerland)
Linfield Coll (OR)
Mills Coll (CA)
Moravian Coll (PA)
Pitzer Coll (CA)
Rhode Island Coll (RI)
Saint Joseph's U (PA)
Skidmore Coll (NY)
Smith Coll (MA)
Southern Methodist U (TX)
U of Guelph (ON, Canada)
U of New Hampshire (NH)
U of North Florida (FL)
U of Waterloo (ON, Canada)
Wagner Coll (NY)
Wellesley Coll (MA)
Wesleyan U (CT)
Wheaton Coll (MA)

**FUNERAL DIRECTION/
SERVICE**
Wayne State U (MI)

**FUNERAL SERVICE AND
MORTUARY SCIENCE**
Gannon U (PA)
Lincoln Coll of New England,
  Southington (CT)
Point Park U (PA)
Southern Illinois U Carbondale (IL)
U of Central Oklahoma (OK)
U of Minnesota, Twin Cities
  Campus (MN)
Upper Iowa U (IA)

**FURNITURE DESIGN AND
MANUFACTURING**
Minneapolis Coll of Art and Design
  (MN)
Rhode Island School of Design (RI)

**GAME AND INTERACTIVE
MEDIA DESIGN**
Abilene Christian U (TX)
Academy of Art U (CA)
Albright Coll (PA)
Arkansas Tech U (AR)
ArtCenter Coll of Design (CA)
Becker Coll (MA)
Boise State U (ID)
Bradley U (IL)
Brock U (ON, Canada)
Cardinal Stritch U (WI)

Champlain Coll (VT)
Cogswell Polytechnical Coll (CA)
Coleman U, San Diego (CA)
Columbia Coll Chicago (IL)
Dakota State U (SD)
DePaul U (IL)
DeSales U (PA)
Drexel U (PA)
Grand View U (IA)
Indiana U Bloomington (IN)
Indiana Wesleyan U (IN)
Inter American U of Puerto Rico,
  Barranquitas Campus (PR)
Inter American U of Puerto Rico,
  Bayamón Campus (PR)
Keiser U, Fort Lauderdale (FL)
Kennesaw State U (GA)
Laguna Coll of Art & Design (CA)
Long Island U–LIU Post (NY)
Marist Coll (NY)
Maryland Inst Coll of Art (MD)
New England Inst of Technology
  (RI)
Oklahoma Christian U (OK)
Quinnipiac U (CT)
Ringling Coll of Art and Design (FL)
Rochester Inst of Technology (NY)
Sacred Heart U (CT)
Sarah Lawrence Coll (NY)
Savannah Coll of Art and Design
  (GA)
Shawnee State U (OH)
Southern Arkansas U–Magnolia
  (AR)
Southwestern Coll (KS)
State U of New York Polytechnic
  Inst (NY)
U of California, Irvine (CA)
U of California, Santa Cruz (CA)
U of Denver (CO)
U of Saint Francis (IN)
U of Southern California (CA)
The U of Texas at Dallas (TX)
The U of the Arts (PA)
U of Wisconsin–Whitewater (WI)
Webster U (MO)
Wichita State U (KS)
William Peace U (NC)
Wilmington U (DE)
Woodbury U (CA)
Worcester Polytechnic Inst (MA)

GAY/LESBIAN STUDIES
Bennington Coll (VT)
Bryant U (RI)
Cornell U (NY)
Hampshire Coll (MA)
Marlboro Coll (VT)
Mills Coll (CA)
Sarah Lawrence Coll (NY)

GENERAL STUDIES
Alfred U (NY)
Ambrose U (AB, Canada)
American Public U System (WV)
Antioch U Midwest (OH)
Aquinas Coll (MI)
Athabasca U (AB, Canada)
Austin Coll (TX)
Austin Peay State U (TN)
Azusa Pacific U (CA)
Belmont U (TN)
Boise State U (ID)
Brandon U (MB, Canada)
Brenau U (GA)
Brewton-Parker Coll (GA)
Buffalo State Coll, State U of New
  York (NY)
California State U, San Bernardino
  (CA)
California State U, San Marcos
  (CA)
Calumet Coll of Saint Joseph (IN)
Cameron U (OK)
The Catholic U of America (DC)
Champlain Coll (VT)
Clarion U of Pennsylvania (PA)
Coll of the Ozarks (MO)
Colorado Christian U (CO)
Colorado State U (CO)
Columbia Coll (MO)
Columbia Coll Chicago (IL)
Concordia U-Chicago (IL)
Concordia U, St. Paul (MN)
Concordia U Wisconsin (WI)
Concord U (WV)
Cornell U (NY)

Dean Coll (MA)
DePaul U (IL)
Drexel U (PA)
East Carolina U (NC)
East Central U (OK)
Eastern Nazarene Coll (MA)
Eastern New Mexico U (NM)
East Tennessee State U (TN)
Emory & Henry Coll (VA)
Emporia State U (KS)
Fairfield U (CT)
Fairleigh Dickinson U, Florham
  Campus (NJ)
Fairleigh Dickinson U, Metropolitan
  Campus (NJ)
Ferris State U (MI)
Florida Inst of Technology (FL)
Fort Lewis Coll (CO)
George Mason U (VA)
Georgia Southern U (GA)
Graceland U (IA)
Granite State Coll (NH)
Hampton U (VA)
Harding U (AR)
Holy Family U (PA)
Howard Payne U (TX)
Humboldt State U (CA)
Idaho State U (ID)
Illinois State U (IL)
Indiana State U (IN)
Indiana Wesleyan U (IN)
Iowa State U of Science and
  Technology (IA)
Jacksonville U (FL)
Kansas Wesleyan U (KS)
Keene State Coll (NH)
Kent State U (OH)
Kent State U at Ashtabula (OH)
Kent State U at East Liverpool (OH)
Kent State U at Geauga (OH)
Kent State U at Salem (OH)
Kent State U at Stark (OH)
Kent State U at Trumbull (OH)
Kent State U at Tuscarawas (OH)
LaGrange Coll (GA)
Lamar U (TX)
La Roche Coll (PA)
La Salle U (PA)
La Sierra U (CA)
Lee U (TN)
Le Moyne Coll (NY)
Lewis U (IL)
Liberty U (VA)
Lincoln Christian U (IL)
Lindenwood U (MO)
Lipscomb U (TN)
Louisiana Coll (LA)
Loyola U Chicago (IL)
Madonna U (MI)
Marshall U (WV)
Marywood U (PA)
McNeese State U (LA)
Middle Tennessee State U (TN)
Minot State U (ND)
Misericordia U (PA)
Missouri Baptist U (MO)
Missouri Valley Coll (MO)
Molloy Coll (NY)
Montana Tech of The U of Montana
  (MT)
Morehead State U (KY)
Mount Marty Coll (SD)
Mount Mary U (WI)
Mount St. Joseph U (OH)
Murray State U (KY)
National U (CA)
New Jersey Inst of Technology (NJ)
New Mexico Inst of Mining and
  Technology (NM)
New Mexico State U (NM)
North Carolina Wesleyan Coll (NC)
Northeastern State U (OK)
Northern Kentucky U (KY)
Northern Vermont U–Lyndon (VT)
North Greenville U (SC)
Northwestern Oklahoma State U
  (OK)
Northwestern State U of Louisiana
  (LA)
Northwestern U (IL)
Northwest U (WA)
Nova Southeastern U (FL)
Oakland City U (IN)
Ohio Northern U (OH)
Ohio Wesleyan U (OH)
Oklahoma State U (OK)
Palm Beach Atlantic U (FL)

Pepperdine U, Malibu (CA)
Providence Coll (RI)
Roberts Wesleyan Coll (NY)
Rowan U (NJ)
Sacred Heart U (CT)
Saginaw Valley State U (MI)
St. Lawrence U (NY)
Saint Louis U (MO)
Samford U (AL)
Sam Houston State U (TX)
San Diego State U (CA)
Seattle Pacific U (WA)
Seton Hill U (PA)
Shawnee State U (OH)
Shenandoah U (VA)
Shepherd U (WV)
Shorter U (GA)
Simmons Coll (MA)
Simon Fraser U (BC, Canada)
Slippery Rock U of Pennsylvania
  (PA)
Southeastern Louisiana U (LA)
Southeastern Oklahoma State U
  (OK)
Southeastern U (FL)
Southeast Missouri State U (MO)
Southern Arkansas U–Magnolia
  (AR)
Southern Utah U (UT)
Southwestern Adventist U (TX)
Southwestern Assemblies of God U
  (TX)
Southwestern Coll (KS)
Spring Hill Coll (AL)
State U of New York at New Paltz
  (NY)
State U of New York Coll of
  Technology at Alfred (NY)
State U of New York Maritime Coll
  (NY)
State U of New York Polytechnic
  Inst (NY)
Tarleton State U (TX)
Tennessee Technological U (TN)
Texas A&M U–Commerce (TX)
Texas A&M U–Texarkana (TX)
Texas Christian U (TX)
Texas State U (TX)
Texas Tech U (TX)
Texas Woman's U (TX)
Tiffin U (OH)
Toccoa Falls Coll (GA)
Trevecca Nazarene U (TN)
Trinity Coll of Florida (FL)
Union Coll (NE)
The U of Arizona (AZ)
U of Bridgeport (CT)
U of Central Florida (FL)
U of Central Oklahoma (OK)
U of Charleston (WV)
U of Cincinnati (OH)
U of Dayton (OH)
U of Hartford (CT)
U of Idaho (ID)
U of Kentucky (KY)
U of La Verne (CA)
U of Louisiana at Monroe (LA)
U of Maine at Machias (ME)
U of Management and Technology
  (VA)
U of Mary Hardin-Baylor (TX)
U of Massachusetts Amherst (MA)
U of Memphis (TN)
U of Miami (FL)
U of Michigan (MI)
U of Michigan–Dearborn (MI)
U of Missouri (MO)
U of Mobile (AL)
U of Nebraska at Kearney (NE)
U of Nevada, Reno (NV)
U of New Mexico (NM)
U of North Dakota (ND)
U of Northern Iowa (IA)
U of North Texas (TX)
U of St. Thomas (TX)
U of San Francisco (CA)
U of South Florida Sarasota-
  Manatee (FL)
The U of Tampa (FL)
The U of Tennessee at Martin (TN)
The U of Texas at San Antonio (TX)
U of the Fraser Valley (BC,
  Canada)
The U of Toledo (OH)
U of Washington (WA)
U of Washington, Bothell (WA)
U of Washington, Tacoma (WA)

U of Wisconsin–Stevens Point (WI)
Valley City State U (ND)
Western Kentucky U (KY)
West Texas A&M U (TX)
West Virginia State U (WV)
West Virginia U (WV)
West Virginia U Inst of Technology
  (WV)
Whitworth U (WA)
Wichita State U (KS)
Widener U (PA)
Wilmington U (DE)
Worcester State U (MA)
York Coll of Pennsylvania (PA)
Youngstown State U (OH)

GENETICS
Cedar Crest Coll (PA)
Iowa State U of Science and
  Technology (IA)
New Mexico State U (NM)
North Carolina State U (NC)
Ohio Wesleyan U (OH)
Purdue U (IN)
U of California, Davis (CA)
U of California, Irvine (CA)
U of Georgia (GA)
U of New Hampshire (NH)
U of Wisconsin–Madison (WI)
Washington State U (WA)

GENETICS RELATED
The George Washington U (DC)

**GENOME SCIENCES/
GENOMICS**
Florida Inst of Technology (FL)
Northwestern Coll (IA)
U of New Haven (CT)

GEOCHEMISTRY
Bowling Green State U (OH)
Bridgewater State U (MA)
California Inst of Technology (CA)
Grand Valley State U (MI)
State U of New York at Fredonia
  (NY)
State U of New York at New Paltz
  (NY)
State U of New York at Oswego
  (NY)
State U of New York Coll at
  Cortland (NY)
State U of New York Coll at
  Geneseo (NY)
U of Waterloo (ON, Canada)
Washington U in St. Louis (MO)
Western Michigan U (MI)
Whitman Coll (WA)

**GEOGRAPHIC INFORMATION
SCIENCE AND CARTOGRAPHY**
Arizona State U at the Tempe
  campus (AZ)
Auburn U at Montgomery (AL)
Binghamton U, State of New York
  (NY)
Brigham Young U (UT)
Central Michigan U (MI)
East Central U (OK)
Hofstra U (NY)
Iowa State U of Science and
  Technology (IA)
Kennesaw State U (GA)
Metropolitan State U of Denver
  (CO)
Michigan State U (MI)
Northern Michigan U (MI)
Northwest Missouri State U (MO)
The Ohio State U (OH)
Oklahoma State U (OK)
Radford U (VA)
Rowan U (NJ)
State U of New York Coll at
  Oneonta (NY)
Stephen F. Austin State U (TX)
Tarleton State U (TX)
Texas A&M U (TX)
Texas State U (TX)
United States Military Acad (NY)
U at Buffalo, the State U of New
  York (NY)
The U of Akron (OH)
The U of Arizona (AZ)
U of Cincinnati (OH)
U of Idaho (ID)
U of Maryland, Coll Park (MD)
U of Minnesota, Duluth (MN)
U of North Alabama (AL)

U of Oklahoma (OK)
The U of Texas at Dallas (TX)
U of Utah (UT)
U of Wisconsin–Eau Claire (WI)
U of Wisconsin–Madison (WI)
Western Kentucky U (KY)

GEOGRAPHY

Adams State U (CO)
Appalachian State U (NC)
Aquinas Coll (MI)
Arizona State U at the Tempe campus (AZ)
Auburn U (AL)
Augustana Coll (IL)
Ball State U (IN)
Bemidji State U (MN)
Boston U (MA)
Bowling Green State U (OH)
Brandon U (MB, Canada)
Bridgewater State U (MA)
Brock U (ON, Canada)
Bucknell U (PA)
Buffalo State Coll, State U of New York (NY)
California State Polytechnic U, Pomona (CA)
California State U, Dominguez Hills (CA)
California State U, East Bay (CA)
California State U, Fullerton (CA)
California State U, Long Beach (CA)
California State U, Los Angeles (CA)
California State U, Northridge (CA)
California State U, Sacramento (CA)
California State U, San Bernardino (CA)
California State U, Stanislaus (CA)
California U of Pennsylvania (PA)
Calvin Coll (MI)
Carthage Coll (WI)
Central Connecticut State U (CT)
Central Michigan U (MI)
City Coll of the City U of New York (NY)
Clark U (MA)
Colgate U (NY)
Coll of Staten Island of the City U of New York (NY)
Concordia U (QC, Canada)
Concordia U Chicago (IL)
Concordia U, Nebraska (NE)
Concord U (WV)
Dartmouth Coll (NH)
DePaul U (IL)
East Carolina U (NC)
Eastern Michigan U (MI)
Eastern Washington U (WA)
East Tennessee State U (TN)
Elmhurst Coll (IL)
Emory & Henry Coll (VA)
Fayetteville State U (NC)
Fitchburg State U (MA)
Florida Atlantic U (FL)
Florida Intl U (FL)
Florida State U (FL)
Framingham State U (MA)
Frostburg State U (MD)
George Mason U (VA)
The George Washington U (DC)
Georgia Coll & State U (GA)
Georgia Southern U (GA)
Grand Valley State U (MI)
Gustavus Adolphus Coll (MN)
Harrisburg U of Science and Technology (PA)
Hofstra U (NY)
Humboldt State U (CA)
Hunter Coll of the City U of New York (NY)
Illinois State U (IL)
Indiana State U (IN)
Indiana U Bloomington (IN)
Indiana U of Pennsylvania (PA)
Indiana U–Purdue U Indianapolis (IN)
Indiana U Southeast (IN)
Jacksonville U (FL)
James Madison U (VA)
Johns Hopkins U (MD)
Kansas State U (KS)
Keene State Coll (NH)
Kennesaw State U (GA)
Kent State U (OH)
Kutztown U of Pennsylvania (PA)
Lehman Coll of the City U of New York (NY)
Long Island U–LIU Post (NY)
Louisiana State U and A&M Coll (LA)
Macalester Coll (MN)
Marshall U (WV)
Metropolitan State U of Denver (CO)
Miami U (OH)
Michigan State U (MI)
Middlebury Coll (VT)
Millersville U of Pennsylvania (PA)
Missouri State U (MO)
Montclair State U (NJ)
Mount Holyoke Coll (MA)
New Mexico State U (NM)
Northeastern State U (OK)
Northern Arizona U (AZ)
Northern Illinois U (IL)
Northern Kentucky U (KY)
Northern Michigan U (MI)
Northwestern U (IL)
Northwest Missouri State U (MO)
The Ohio State U (OH)
Ohio U (OH)
Ohio Wesleyan U (OH)
Oklahoma State U (OK)
Old Dominion U (VA)
Olivet Nazarene U (IL)
Penn State Abington (PA)
Penn State Altoona (PA)
Penn State Beaver (PA)
Penn State Berks (PA)
Penn State Brandywine (PA)
Penn State DuBois (PA)
Penn State Erie, The Behrend Coll (PA)
Penn State Fayette, The Eberly Campus (PA)
Penn State Greater Allegheny (PA)
Penn State Hazleton (PA)
Penn State Lehigh Valley (PA)
Penn State Mont Alto (PA)
Penn State New Kensington (PA)
Penn State Schuylkill (PA)
Penn State Shenango (PA)
Penn State U Park (PA)
Penn State Wilkes-Barre (PA)
Penn State Worthington Scranton (PA)
Penn State York (PA)
Pittsburg State U (KS)
Portland State U (OR)
Rhode Island Coll (RI)
Rowan U (NJ)
Rutgers U–New Brunswick (NJ)
Saginaw Valley State U (MI)
Salisbury U (MD)
Samford U (AL)
Sam Houston State U (TX)
San Diego State U (CA)
San Francisco State U (CA)
Sarah Lawrence Coll (NY)
Shippensburg U of Pennsylvania (PA)
Simon Fraser U (BC, Canada)
Slippery Rock U of Pennsylvania (PA)
Sonoma State U (CA)
Southern Illinois U Carbondale (IL)
Southern Illinois U Edwardsville (IL)
State U of New York at New Paltz (NY)
State U of New York at Plattsburgh (NY)
State U of New York Coll at Cortland (NY)
State U of New York Coll at Geneseo (NY)
State U of New York Coll at Oneonta (NY)
Stephen F. Austin State U (TX)
Syracuse U (NY)
Taylor U (IN)
Texas A&M U (TX)
Texas Christian U (TX)
Texas State U (TX)
Texas Tech U (TX)
Towson U (MD)
Trent U (ON, Canada)
United States Military Acad (NY)
U at Albany, State U of New York (NY)
U at Buffalo, the State U of New York (NY)
The U of Akron (OH)
The U of Alabama (AL)
U of Alaska Fairbanks (AK)
The U of Arizona (AZ)
U of Arkansas (AR)
U of California, Los Angeles (CA)
U of California, Santa Barbara (CA)
U of Central Arkansas (AR)
U of Central Missouri (MO)
U of Central Oklahoma (OK)
U of Chicago (IL)
U of Cincinnati (OH)
U of Colorado Boulder (CO)
U of Colorado Colorado Springs (CO)
U of Colorado Denver (CO)
U of Denver (CO)
U of Florida (FL)
U of Georgia (GA)
U of Guelph (ON, Canada)
U of Hawaii at Manoa (HI)
U of Houston–Clear Lake (TX)
U of Idaho (ID)
The U of Kansas (KS)
U of Kentucky (KY)
U of Louisville (KY)
U of Maine at Farmington (ME)
U of Maryland, Baltimore County (MD)
U of Mary Washington (VA)
U of Massachusetts Amherst (MA)
U of Memphis (TN)
U of Miami (FL)
U of Minnesota, Duluth (MN)
U of Minnesota, Twin Cities Campus (MN)
U of Missouri (MO)
U of Montana (MT)
U of Nebraska at Kearney (NE)
U of Nebraska–Lincoln (NE)
U of Nevada, Reno (NV)
U of New Hampshire (NH)
U of New Mexico (NM)
U of North Alabama (AL)
The U of North Carolina at Chapel Hill (NC)
The U of North Carolina at Charlotte (NC)
The U of North Carolina at Greensboro (NC)
The U of North Carolina Wilmington (NC)
U of North Dakota (ND)
U of Northern Colorado (CO)
U of Northern Iowa (IA)
U of North Texas (TX)
U of Oklahoma (OK)
U of Oregon (OR)
U of Regina (SK, Canada)
U of Richmond (VA)
U of St. Thomas (MN)
U of Saskatchewan (SK, Canada)
U of South Alabama (AL)
U of South Carolina (SC)
U of Southern California (CA)
U of Southern Mississippi (MS)
U of South Florida, St. Petersburg (FL)
The U of Tennessee (TN)
The U of Tennessee at Martin (TN)
The U of Texas at Austin (TX)
The U of Texas at San Antonio (TX)
U of the Fraser Valley (BC, Canada)
The U of Toledo (OH)
U of Toronto (ON, Canada)
U of Vermont (VT)
U of Washington (WA)
U of Waterloo (ON, Canada)
U of West Georgia (GA)
U of Wisconsin–Eau Claire (WI)
U of Wisconsin–La Crosse (WI)
U of Wisconsin–Madison (WI)
U of Wisconsin–Milwaukee (WI)
U of Wisconsin–Parkside (WI)
U of Wisconsin–Platteville (WI)
U of Wisconsin–River Falls (WI)
U of Wisconsin–Rock County (WI)
U of Wisconsin–Stevens Point (WI)
U of Wisconsin–Whitewater (WI)
U of Wyoming (WY)
Utah State U (UT)
Valparaiso U (IN)
Vassar Coll (NY)
Villanova U (PA)
Virginia Polytechnic Inst and State U (VA)
Wayne State Coll (NE)
Weber State U (UT)
West Chester U of Pennsylvania (PA)
Western Illinois U (IL)
Western Kentucky U (KY)
Western Michigan U (MI)
Western Oregon U (OR)
Western Washington U (WA)
West Virginia U (WV)
William Paterson U of New Jersey (NJ)
Worcester State U (MA)
Wright State U (OH)
Wright State U–Lake Campus (OH)
Youngstown State U (OH)

GEOGRAPHY RELATED

Arkansas Tech U (AR)
Bridgewater State U (MA)
Brigham Young U (UT)
Emory & Henry Coll (VA)
Northern Michigan U (MI)
Ohio U (OH)
Temple U (PA)
U of California, Los Angeles (CA)

GEOGRAPHY TEACHER EDUCATION

Aquinas Coll (MI)
Calvin Coll (MI)
Grand Valley State U (MI)
Michigan State U (MI)
Northern Michigan U (MI)
Rhode Island Coll (RI)
The U of Tennessee at Martin (TN)
U of Wisconsin–Whitewater (WI)
Valparaiso U (IN)
Wayne State Coll (NE)
Weber State U (UT)

GEOLOGICAL AND EARTH SCIENCES/GEOSCIENCES RELATED

Allegheny Coll (PA)
Boston U (MA)
Bridgewater State U (MA)
Brigham Young U (UT)
California State U, Dominguez Hills (CA)
California State U, Fullerton (CA)
Cedarville U (OH)
The Coll of Wooster (OH)
Earlham Coll (IN)
Eckerd Coll (FL)
Georgia Inst of Technology (GA)
Hamilton Coll (NY)
Harrisburg U of Science and Technology (PA)
Lehigh U (PA)
Minnesota State U Moorhead (MN)
Missouri U of Science and Technology (MO)
Muskingum U (OH)
Old Dominion U (VA)
Oregon State U (OR)
Penn State Abington (PA)
Penn State Altoona (PA)
Penn State Beaver (PA)
Penn State Berks (PA)
Penn State Brandywine (PA)
Penn State DuBois (PA)
Penn State Erie, The Behrend Coll (PA)
Penn State Fayette, The Eberly Campus (PA)
Penn State Greater Allegheny (PA)
Penn State Hazleton (PA)
Penn State Lehigh Valley (PA)
Penn State Mont Alto (PA)
Penn State New Kensington (PA)
Penn State Schuylkill (PA)
Penn State Shenango (PA)
Penn State U Park (PA)
Penn State Wilkes-Barre (PA)
Penn State Worthington Scranton (PA)
Penn State York (PA)
Princeton U (NJ)
Rocky Mountain Coll (MT)
Salisbury U (MD)
Stanford U (CA)
Texas A&M U (TX)
Texas Christian U (TX)
Towson U (MD)
Union Coll (NY)
U at Buffalo, the State U of New York (NY)
U of Guelph (ON, Canada)
U of Miami (FL)
U of Pittsburgh (PA)
U of Rhode Island (RI)
U of Utah (UT)
U of Washington (WA)
U of Wyoming (WY)
Utica Coll (NY)
Western State Colorado U (CO)
Whitman Coll (WA)

GEOLOGICAL/GEOPHYSICAL ENGINEERING

Michigan Technological U (MI)
Missouri U of Science and Technology (MO)
Montana Tech of The U of Montana (MT)
New Jersey Inst of Technology (NJ)
Rutgers U–Newark (NJ)
Tufts U (MA)
U of Alaska Fairbanks (AK)
U of California, Los Angeles (CA)
U of Michigan (MI)
U of Minnesota, Twin Cities Campus (MN)
U of Nevada, Reno (NV)
U of North Dakota (ND)
U of Rochester (NY)
U of Saskatchewan (SK, Canada)
The U of Texas at Austin (TX)
U of Toronto (ON, Canada)
U of Utah (UT)
U of Waterloo (ON, Canada)
U of Wisconsin–Madison (WI)

GEOLOGY/EARTH SCIENCE

Acadia U (NS, Canada)
Adams State U (CO)
Albion Coll (MI)
Alfred U (NY)
Allegheny Coll (PA)
Amherst Coll (MA)
Angelo State U (TX)
Appalachian State U (NC)
Arkansas Tech U (AR)
Ashland U (OH)
Auburn U (AL)
Augustana Coll (IL)
Austin Peay State U (TN)
Ball State U (IN)
Bates Coll (ME)
Baylor U (TX)
Beloit Coll (WI)
Bemidji State U (MN)
Binghamton U, State U of New York (NY)
Bloomsburg U of Pennsylvania (PA)
Boise State U (ID)
Boston Coll (MA)
Boston U (MA)
Bowdoin Coll (ME)
Bowling Green State U (OH)
Brandon U (MB, Canada)
Bridgewater State U (MA)
Brigham Young U–Idaho (ID)
Brock U (ON, Canada)
Bryn Mawr Coll (PA)
Bucknell U (PA)
Buffalo State Coll, State U of New York (NY)
California Inst of Technology (CA)
California Lutheran U (CA)
California Polytechnic State U, San Luis Obispo (CA)
California State Polytechnic U, Pomona (CA)
California State U, East Bay (CA)
California State U, Fullerton (CA)
California State U, Long Beach (CA)
California State U, Los Angeles (CA)
California State U, Northridge (CA)
California State U, Sacramento (CA)
California State U, San Bernardino (CA)
California State U, Stanislaus (CA)
California U of Pennsylvania (PA)
Calvin Coll (MI)
Carleton Coll (MN)
Case Western Reserve U (OH)
Cedarville U (OH)
Centenary Coll of Louisiana (LA)
Central Connecticut State U (CT)

Central Michigan U (MI)
City Coll of the City U of New York (NY)
Clarion U of Pennsylvania (PA)
Clark U (MA)
Clemson U (SC)
Colby Coll (ME)
Colgate U (NY)
The Coll at Brockport, State U of New York (NY)
Coll of Charleston (SC)
The Coll of William and Mary (VA)
The Coll of Wooster (OH)
The Colorado Coll (CO)
Colorado Mesa U (CO)
Colorado State U (CO)
Columbia U (NY)
Columbus State U (GA)
Concordia U Chicago (IL)
Concord U (WV)
Cornell Coll (IA)
Dartmouth Coll (NH)
Denison U (OH)
DePauw U (IN)
Dickinson Coll (PA)
Drexel U (PA)
East Carolina U (NC)
Eastern Michigan U (MI)
Eastern New Mexico U (NM)
Eastern Washington U (WA)
East Stroudsburg U of Pennsylvania (PA)
East Tennessee State U (TN)
Emporia State U (KS)
Florida Atlantic U (FL)
Florida Intl U (FL)
Florida State U (FL)
Fort Lewis Coll (CO)
Framingham State U (MA)
Franklin & Marshall Coll (PA)
Frostburg State U (MD)
George Mason U (VA)
The George Washington U (DC)
Georgia Southern U (GA)
Georgia Southwestern State U (GA)
Georgia State U (GA)
Guilford Coll (NC)
Gustavus Adolphus Coll (MN)
Hamilton Coll (NY)
Hardin-Simmons U (TX)
Hartwick Coll (NY)
Harvard U (MA)
Haverford Coll (PA)
Hobart and William Smith Colls (NY)
Hofstra U (NY)
Hope Coll (MI)
Humboldt State U (CA)
Idaho State U (ID)
Illinois State U (IL)
Indiana State U (IN)
Indiana U Bloomington (IN)
Indiana U Northwest (IN)
Indiana U of Pennsylvania (PA)
Indiana U–Purdue U Indianapolis (IN)
Iowa State U of Science and Technology (IA)
Jackson State U (MS)
James Madison U (VA)
Johns Hopkins U (MD)
Juniata Coll (PA)
Kansas State U (KS)
Kean U (NJ)
Keene State Coll (NH)
Kent State U (OH)
Kutztown U of Pennsylvania (PA)
Lafayette Coll (PA)
Lamar U (TX)
Lawrence U (WI)
Lehman Coll of the City U of New York (NY)
Lock Haven U of Pennsylvania (PA)
Long Island U–LIU Post (NY)
Louisiana State U and A&M Coll (LA)
Macalester Coll (MN)
Marietta Coll (OH)
Marshall U (WV)
Massachusetts Inst of Technology (MA)
Mercyhurst U (PA)
Metropolitan State U of Denver (CO)
Miami U (OH)
Michigan State U (MI)

Michigan Technological U (MI)
Middlebury Coll (VT)
Middle Tennessee State U (TN)
Millersville U of Pennsylvania (PA)
Millsaps Coll (MS)
Minot State U (ND)
Mississippi State U (MS)
Missouri State U (MO)
Missouri U of Science and Technology (MO)
Montclair State U (NJ)
Moravian Coll (PA)
Morehead State U (KY)
Mount Holyoke Coll (MA)
Murray State U (KY)
Muskingum U (OH)
New Jersey City U (NJ)
New Mexico Highlands U (NM)
New Mexico Inst of Mining and Technology (NM)
New Mexico State U (NM)
North Carolina State U (NC)
North Dakota State U (ND)
Northeastern U (MA)
Northern Arizona U (AZ)
Northern Illinois U (IL)
Northern Kentucky U (KY)
Northern Michigan U (MI)
Northland Coll (WI)
Northwestern U (IL)
Northwest Missouri State U (MO)
Oberlin Coll (OH)
Occidental Coll (CA)
The Ohio State U (OH)
Ohio U (OH)
Ohio Wesleyan U (OH)
Oklahoma State U (OK)
Olivet Nazarene U (IL)
Pacific Lutheran U (WA)
Penn State Abington (PA)
Penn State Altoona (PA)
Penn State Beaver (PA)
Penn State Berks (PA)
Penn State Brandywine (PA)
Penn State DuBois (PA)
Penn State Erie, The Behrend Coll (PA)
Penn State Fayette, The Eberly Campus (PA)
Penn State Greater Allegheny (PA)
Penn State Hazleton (PA)
Penn State Lehigh Valley (PA)
Penn State Mont Alto (PA)
Penn State New Kensington (PA)
Penn State Schuylkill (PA)
Penn State Shenango (PA)
Penn State U Park (PA)
Penn State Wilkes-Barre (PA)
Penn State Worthington Scranton (PA)
Penn State York (PA)
Piedmont Coll (GA)
Pitzer Coll (CA)
Pomona Coll (CA)
Portland State U (OR)
Purdue U (IN)
Queens Coll of the City U of New York (NY)
Radford U (VA)
Rensselaer Polytechnic Inst (NY)
Rice U (TX)
Rider U (NJ)
Rocky Mountain Coll (MT)
Rowan U (NJ)
Rutgers U–Newark (NJ)
Rutgers U–New Brunswick (NJ)
St. Lawrence U (NY)
Saint Louis U (MO)
St. Norbert Coll (WI)
Sam Houston State U (TX)
San Diego State U (CA)
San Francisco State U (CA)
Scripps Coll (CA)
Sewanee: The U of the South (TN)
Shawnee State U (OH)
Shippensburg U of Pennsylvania (PA)
Skidmore Coll (NY)
Slippery Rock U of Pennsylvania (PA)
Smith Coll (MA)
Sonoma State U (CA)
Southern Illinois U Carbondale (IL)
Southern Methodist U (TX)
Southern Utah U (UT)
Stanford U (CA)

State U of New York at Fredonia (NY)
State U of New York at New Paltz (NY)
State U of New York at Oswego (NY)
State U of New York at Plattsburgh (NY)
State U of New York Coll at Cortland (NY)
State U of New York Coll at Geneseo (NY)
State U of New York Coll at Oneonta (NY)
Stephen F. Austin State U (TX)
Stockton U (NJ)
Stony Brook U, State U of New York (NY)
Susquehanna U (PA)
Syracuse U (NY)
Tarleton State U (TX)
Temple U (PA)
Tennessee Technological U (TN)
Texas A&M U (TX)
Texas A&M U–Corpus Christi (TX)
Texas A&M U–Kingsville (TX)
Texas Christian U (TX)
Texas Tech U (TX)
Towson U (MD)
Trinity U (TX)
Tufts U (MA)
Tulane U (LA)
Union Coll (NY)
U at Buffalo, the State U of New York (NY)
The U of Akron (OH)
The U of Alabama (AL)
U of Alaska Fairbanks (AK)
The U of Arizona (AZ)
U of Arkansas (AR)
U of California, Davis (CA)
U of California, Irvine (CA)
U of California, Los Angeles (CA)
U of California, Riverside (CA)
U of California, San Diego (CA)
U of California, Santa Barbara (CA)
U of California, Santa Cruz (CA)
U of Central Missouri (MO)
U of Cincinnati (OH)
U of Colorado Boulder (CO)
U of Dayton (OH)
U of Florida (FL)
U of Georgia (GA)
U of Hawaii at Manoa (HI)
U of Houston (TX)
U of Houston–Downtown (TX)
U of Idaho (ID)
U of Illinois at Chicago (IL)
The U of Kansas (KS)
U of Kentucky (KY)
U of King's Coll (NS, Canada)
U of Maine (ME)
U of Maine at Farmington (ME)
U of Maryland, Coll Park (MD)
U of Massachusetts Amherst (MA)
U of Massachusetts Boston (MA)
U of Memphis (TN)
U of Miami (FL)
U of Michigan (MI)
U of Michigan–Dearborn (MI)
U of Minnesota, Duluth (MN)
U of Minnesota, Morris (MN)
U of Minnesota, Twin Cities Campus (MN)
U of Missouri (MO)
U of Montana (MT)
U of Mount Union (OH)
U of Nebraska–Lincoln (NE)
U of Nevada, Las Vegas (NV)
U of Nevada, Reno (NV)
U of New Hampshire (NH)
U of New Mexico (NM)
U of New Orleans (LA)
The U of North Carolina at Chapel Hill (NC)
The U of North Carolina at Charlotte (NC)
The U of North Carolina at Greensboro (NC)
The U of North Carolina Wilmington (NC)
U of North Dakota (ND)
U of Northern Colorado (CO)
U of Northern Iowa (IA)
U of Oklahoma (OK)
U of Oregon (OR)
U of Pennsylvania (PA)

U of Pittsburgh (PA)
U of Puget Sound (WA)
U of Regina (SK, Canada)
U of Rhode Island (RI)
U of Rochester (NY)
U of St. Thomas (MN)
U of Saskatchewan (SK, Canada)
U of South Alabama (AL)
U of South Carolina (SC)
U of South Dakota (SD)
U of Southern California (CA)
U of Southern Indiana (IN)
U of Southern Mississippi (MS)
The U of Tennessee (TN)
The U of Tennessee at Chattanooga (TN)
The U of Tennessee at Martin (TN)
The U of Texas at Austin (TX)
The U of Texas at Dallas (TX)
The U of Texas at El Paso (TX)
The U of Texas at San Antonio (TX)
The U of Texas of the Permian Basin (TX)
U of the Pacific (CA)
The U of Toledo (OH)
The U of Tulsa (OK)
U of Utah (UT)
U of Vermont (VT)
U of Washington (WA)
U of Waterloo (ON, Canada)
U of West Georgia (GA)
U of Wisconsin–Eau Claire (WI)
U of Wisconsin–Madison (WI)
U of Wisconsin–Milwaukee (WI)
U of Wisconsin–Parkside (WI)
U of Wisconsin–River Falls (WI)
U of Wisconsin–Stevens Point (WI)
U of Wyoming (WY)
Utah State U (UT)
Utah Valley U (UT)
Valdosta State U (GA)
Valparaiso U (IN)
Vanderbilt U (TN)
Vassar Coll (NY)
Virginia Polytechnic Inst and State U (VA)
Virginia Wesleyan U (VA)
Washington and Lee U (VA)
Washington State U (WA)
Washington State U–Tri-Cities (WA)
Washington State U–Vancouver (WA)
Washington U in St. Louis (MO)
Wayland Baptist U (TX)
Wayne State U (MI)
Weber State U (UT)
Wellesley Coll (MA)
West Chester U of Pennsylvania (PA)
Western Connecticut State U (CT)
Western Illinois U (IL)
Western Kentucky U (KY)
Western Michigan U (MI)
Western State Colorado U (CO)
Westminster Coll (UT)
West Virginia U (WV)
Wheaton Coll (IL)
Whitman Coll (WA)
Wichita State U (KS)
Wilkes U (PA)
William Paterson U of New Jersey (NJ)
Williams Coll (MA)
Winona State U (MN)
Wittenberg U (OH)
Wright State U (OH)
Youngstown State U (OH)

GEOPHYSICS AND SEISMOLOGY
Baylor U (TX)
Boise State U (ID)
Boston Coll (MA)
Boston U (MA)
Bowling Green State U (OH)
California Inst of Technology (CA)
Eastern Michigan U (MI)
Michigan Technological U (MI)
Missouri U of Science and Technology (MO)
New Mexico Inst of Mining and Technology (NM)
Rice U (TX)
St. Lawrence U (NY)
Southern Methodist U (TX)
Stanford U (CA)

State U of New York at Fredonia (NY)
State U of New York Coll at Geneseo (NY)
Texas A&M U (TX)
The U of Akron (OH)
U of California, Los Angeles (CA)
U of California, Riverside (CA)
U of California, Santa Barbara (CA)
U of Chicago (IL)
U of Houston (TX)
U of Nevada, Reno (NV)
U of Oklahoma (OK)
U of Saskatchewan (SK, Canada)
U of South Carolina (SC)
The U of Texas at Austin (TX)
The U of Texas at El Paso (TX)
The U of Tulsa (OK)
U of Utah (UT)
U of Washington (WA)
U of Waterloo (ON, Canada)
Washington U in St. Louis (MO)
Western Michigan U (MI)
Western Washington U (WA)
Whitman Coll (WA)

GERIATRIC NURSING
Graceland U (IA)

GERMAN
Agnes Scott Coll (GA)
Albion Coll (MI)
Allegheny Coll (PA)
Alma Coll (MI)
American U (DC)
Amherst Coll (MA)
Aquinas Coll (MI)
Arizona State U at the Tempe campus (AZ)
Auburn U (AL)
Augsburg U (MN)
Augustana Coll (IL)
Augustana U (SD)
Austin Coll (TX)
Baker U (KS)
Baldwin Wallace U (OH)
Ball State U (IN)
Bard Coll (NY)
Barnard Coll (NY)
Bates Coll (ME)
Baylor U (TX)
Belmont U (TN)
Beloit Coll (WI)
Bemidji State U (MN)
Berea Coll (KY)
Berry Coll (GA)
Binghamton U, State U of New York (NY)
Boise State U (ID)
Boston Coll (MA)
Boston U (MA)
Bowdoin Coll (ME)
Bowling Green State U (OH)
Brock U (ON, Canada)
Bryn Mawr Coll (PA)
Bucknell U (PA)
Butler U (IN)
California Lutheran U (CA)
California State U, Long Beach (CA)
Calvin Coll (MI)
Carleton Coll (MN)
Carnegie Mellon U (PA)
Carthage Coll (WI)
Case Western Reserve U (OH)
The Catholic U of America (DC)
Central Connecticut State U (CT)
Central Michigan U (MI)
Centre Coll (KY)
Christopher Newport U (VA)
Coe Coll (IA)
Colby Coll (ME)
Colgate U (NY)
Coll of Charleston (SC)
Coll of Saint Benedict (MN)
Coll of the Holy Cross (MA)
The Coll of William and Mary (VA)
The Colorado Coll (CO)
Columbia U (NY)
Concordia U Wisconsin (WI)
Converse Coll (SC)
Cornell Coll (IA)
Cornell U (NY)
Creighton U (NE)
Dartmouth Coll (NH)
Davidson Coll (NC)
Delaware State U (DE)

Denison U (OH)
DePaul U (IL)
DePauw U (IN)
Dickinson Coll (PA)
Doane U (NE)
Drew U (NJ)
Earlham Coll (IN)
Eastern Michigan U (MI)
Elizabethtown Coll (PA)
Elmhurst Coll (IL)
Fairfield U (CT)
Florida State U (FL)
Fordham U (NY)
Franklin & Marshall Coll (PA)
Furman U (SC)
Georgetown U (DC)
The George Washington U (DC)
Georgia State U (GA)
Gettysburg Coll (PA)
Gordon Coll (MA)
Grinnell Coll (IA)
Guilford Coll (NC)
Gustavus Adolphus Coll (MN)
Hamline U (MN)
Hampden-Sydney Coll (VA)
Harvard U (MA)
Haverford Coll (PA)
Heidelberg U (OH)
Hendrix Coll (AR)
Hillsdale Coll (MI)
Hofstra U (NY)
Hood Coll (MD)
Hope Coll (MI)
Hunter Coll of the City U of New York (NY)
Idaho State U (ID)
Illinois Coll (IL)
Illinois State U (IL)
Illinois Wesleyan U (IL)
Indiana U–Purdue U Indianapolis (IN)
Indiana U South Bend (IN)
Indiana U Southeast (IN)
Ithaca Coll (NY)
John Carroll U (OH)
Johns Hopkins U (MD)
Juniata Coll (PA)
Kalamazoo Coll (MI)
Kent State U (OH)
Kenyon Coll (OH)
Knox Coll (IL)
Lafayette Coll (PA)
Lawrence U (WI)
Lebanon Valley Coll (PA)
Lehigh U (PA)
Lenoir-Rhyne U (NC)
Linfield Coll (OR)
Lipscomb U (TN)
Luther Coll (IA)
Lycoming Coll (PA)
Macalester Coll (MN)
Marquette U (WI)
McDaniel Coll (MD)
Mercer U, Macon (GA)
Messiah Coll (PA)
Miami U (OH)
Michigan State U (MI)
Middlebury Coll (VT)
Millersville U of Pennsylvania (PA)
Minot State U (ND)
Missouri State U (MO)
Montclair State U (NJ)
Moravian Coll (PA)
Mount St. Mary's U (MD)
Murray State U (KY)
Muskingum U (OH)
Nazareth Coll of Rochester (NY)
New Coll of Florida (FL)
New York U (NY)
North Central Coll (IL)
Northern Illinois U (IL)
Northern Kentucky U (KY)
Northern State U (SD)
Northwestern U (IL)
Oakland U (MI)
Oberlin Coll (OH)
The Ohio State U (OH)
Ohio U (OH)
Ohio Wesleyan U (OH)
Oklahoma State U (OK)
Oregon State U (OR)
Pacific Lutheran U (WA)
Penn State Abington (PA)
Penn State Altoona (PA)
Penn State Beaver (PA)
Penn State Berks (PA)
Penn State Brandywine (PA)

Penn State DuBois (PA)
Penn State Erie, The Behrend Coll (PA)
Penn State Fayette, The Eberly Campus (PA)
Penn State Greater Allegheny (PA)
Penn State Hazleton (PA)
Penn State Lehigh Valley (PA)
Penn State Mont Alto (PA)
Penn State New Kensington (PA)
Penn State Schuylkill (PA)
Penn State Shenango (PA)
Penn State U Park (PA)
Penn State Wilkes-Barre (PA)
Penn State Worthington Scranton (PA)
Penn State York (PA)
Pomona Coll (CA)
Portland State U (OR)
Princeton U (NJ)
Purdue U (IN)
Queens Coll of the City U of New York (NY)
Randolph-Macon Coll (VA)
Reed Coll (OR)
Rhodes Coll (TN)
Rice U (TX)
Rider U (NJ)
Rutgers U–Camden (NJ)
Rutgers U–Newark (NJ)
Rutgers U–New Brunswick (NJ)
Saint John's U (MN)
Saint Joseph's U (PA)
Saint Louis U (MO)
Saint Louis U–Madrid Campus (Spain)
Saint Mary's Coll of California (CA)
St. Norbert Coll (WI)
St. Olaf Coll (MN)
Samford U (AL)
Sam Houston State U (TX)
San Diego State U (CA)
San Francisco State U (CA)
Santa Clara U (CA)
Sarah Lawrence Coll (NY)
Scripps Coll (CA)
Sewanee: The U of the South (TN)
Simpson Coll (IA)
Skidmore Coll (NY)
Smith Coll (MA)
Southern Methodist U (TX)
Southern Utah U (UT)
Southwestern U (TX)
State U of New York at Oswego (NY)
State U of New York Coll at Cortland (NY)
Stetson U (FL)
Stony Brook U, State U of New York (NY)
Susquehanna U (PA)
Syracuse U (NY)
Temple U (PA)
Tennessee Technological U (TN)
Texas A&M U (TX)
Texas Christian U (TX)
Texas State U (TX)
Texas Tech U (TX)
Transylvania U (KY)
Trent U (ON, Canada)
Trinity U (TX)
Truman State U (MO)
Tufts U (MA)
Tulane U (LA)
Union Coll (NY)
United States Military Acad (NY)
U at Buffalo, the State U of New York (NY)
The U of Arizona (AZ)
U of Arkansas (AR)
U of California, Davis (CA)
U of California, Los Angeles (CA)
U of California, San Diego (CA)
U of California, Santa Barbara (CA)
U of California, Santa Cruz (CA)
U of Central Missouri (MO)
U of Central Oklahoma (OK)
U of Chicago (IL)
U of Cincinnati (OH)
U of Dallas (TX)
U of Dayton (OH)
U of Denver (CO)
U of Evansville (IN)
U of Florida (FL)
U of Hawaii at Manoa (HI)
U of Jamestown (ND)
U of Kentucky (KY)

U of King's Coll (NS, Canada)
U of Maryland, Coll Park (MD)
U of Miami (FL)
U of Michigan (MI)
U of Minnesota, Duluth (MN)
U of Missouri (MO)
U of Montana (MT)
U of Mount Union (OH)
U of Nebraska at Kearney (NE)
U of Nebraska–Lincoln (NE)
U of Nevada, Las Vegas (NV)
U of New Hampshire (NH)
U of New Mexico (NM)
U of North Alabama (AL)
U of North Carolina at Asheville (NC)
The U of North Carolina at Charlotte (NC)
The U of North Carolina at Greensboro (NC)
The U of North Carolina Wilmington (NC)
U of North Dakota (ND)
U of North Texas (TX)
U of Notre Dame (IN)
U of Oregon (OR)
U of Pennsylvania (PA)
U of Pittsburgh (PA)
U of Puget Sound (WA)
U of Regina (SK, Canada)
U of Rhode Island (RI)
U of Rochester (NY)
U of St. Thomas (MN)
The U of Scranton (PA)
U of South Carolina (SC)
U of South Dakota (SD)
U of Southern Indiana (IN)
The U of Tennessee (TN)
The U of Texas at Austin (TX)
U of the Pacific (CA)
The U of Toledo (OH)
U of Toronto (ON, Canada)
The U of Tulsa (OK)
U of Utah (UT)
U of Vermont (VT)
U of Virginia (VA)
U of Waterloo (ON, Canada)
U of Wisconsin–La Crosse (WI)
U of Wisconsin–Stevens Point (WI)
U of Wisconsin–Whitewater (WI)
U of Wyoming (WY)
Ursinus Coll (PA)
Utah State U (UT)
Valparaiso U (IN)
Vanderbilt U (TN)
Vassar Coll (NY)
Virginia Polytechnic Inst and State U (VA)
Virginia Wesleyan U (VA)
Wabash Coll (IN)
Wake Forest U (NC)
Wartburg Coll (IA)
Washington & Jefferson Coll (PA)
Washington and Lee U (VA)
Washington Coll (MD)
Washington State U (WA)
Washington U in St. Louis (MO)
Wayne State U (MI)
Weber State U (UT)
Webster U (MO)
Wellesley Coll (MA)
Wesleyan U (CT)
West Chester U of Pennsylvania (PA)
Western Kentucky U (KY)
Western Michigan U (MI)
Western Oregon U (OR)
Western Washington U (WA)
Wheaton Coll (IL)
Wheaton Coll (MA)
Whitman Coll (WA)
Willamette U (OR)
Williams Coll (MA)
Wisconsin Lutheran Coll (WI)
Wittenberg U (OH)
Wofford Coll (SC)
Wright State U (OH)
Wright State U–Lake Campus (OH)

GERMANIC LANGUAGES
Columbia U (NY)
Eastern Michigan U (MI)
Grand Valley State U (MI)
Indiana U Bloomington (IN)
Jacksonville U (FL)
U of Colorado Boulder (CO)
The U of Kansas (KS)

U of Oklahoma (OK)
The U of Texas at Austin (TX)
U of Washington (WA)
U of Wisconsin–Eau Claire (WI)
U of Wisconsin–Madison (WI)
U of Wisconsin–Milwaukee (WI)
Washington U in St. Louis (MO)

GERMANIC LANGUAGES RELATED
Calvin Coll (MI)
Ohio Northern U (OH)
U of Minnesota, Twin Cities Campus (MN)
Wisconsin Lutheran Coll (WI)

GERMAN LANGUAGE TEACHER EDUCATION
Albion Coll (MI)
Auburn U (AL)
Augustana Coll (IL)
Ball State U (IN)
Boise State U (ID)
California Lutheran U (CA)
Calvin Coll (MI)
Canisius Coll (NY)
The Catholic U of America (DC)
Concordia U Wisconsin (WI)
Delaware State U (DE)
Eastern Michigan U (MI)
Elmhurst Coll (IL)
Grand Valley State U (MI)
Hofstra U (NY)
Hope Coll (MI)
Hunter Coll of the City U of New York (NY)
Indiana U South Bend (IN)
Ithaca Coll (NY)
Messiah Coll (PA)
Miami U (OH)
Michigan State U (MI)
Minot State U (ND)
Missouri State U (MO)
Montclair State U (NJ)
Ohio Northern U (OH)
Ohio U (OH)
Ohio Wesleyan U (OH)
Queens Coll of the City U of New York (NY)
Saint Joseph's U (PA)
Southern Utah U (UT)
U of Central Oklahoma (OK)
U of Evansville (IN)
U of Illinois at Chicago (IL)
U of Nebraska–Lincoln (NE)
The U of North Carolina at Greensboro (NC)
U of St. Thomas (MN)
U of South Dakota (SD)
The U of Tennessee at Martin (TN)
U of Wisconsin–Milwaukee (WI)
U of Wisconsin–Stevens Point (WI)
U of Wisconsin–Whitewater (WI)
Valparaiso U (IN)
Washington U in St. Louis (MO)
Weber State U (UT)
Western Michigan U (MI)
Western Washington U (WA)

GERMAN STUDIES
American U (DC)
Bard Coll (NY)
Barnard Coll (NY)
Brandeis U (MA)
Brock U (ON, Canada)
Case Western Reserve U (OH)
Coe Coll (IA)
The Coll of Wooster (OH)
Columbia U (NY)
Connecticut Coll (CT)
Cornell U (NY)
Emory U (GA)
Fordham U (NY)
Franklin & Marshall Coll (PA)
Hamilton Coll (NY)
Ithaca Coll (NY)
Kutztown U of Pennsylvania (PA)
Linfield Coll (OR)
Moravian Coll (PA)
Mount Holyoke Coll (MA)
North Carolina State U (NC)
Northern Michigan U (MI)
Pomona Coll (CA)
Smith Coll (MA)
Stanford U (CA)
U of California, Irvine (CA)
U of California, Riverside (CA)
U of California, San Diego (CA)

U of Illinois at Chicago (IL)
The U of Kansas (KS)
U of Massachusetts Amherst (MA)
U of Pittsburgh (PA)
U of Richmond (VA)
Wellesley Coll (MA)
Wheaton Coll (MA)

GERONTOLOGY
Alfred U (NY)
Barton Coll (NC)
Bethune-Cookman U (FL)
Bowling Green State U (OH)
California State U, Sacramento (CA)
California U of Pennsylvania (PA)
Case Western Reserve U (OH)
Gwynedd Mercy U (PA)
Iowa State U of Science and Technology (IA)
Ithaca Coll (NY)
John Carroll U (OH)
Madonna U (MI)
Miami U (OH)
Minnesota State U Moorhead (MN)
Missouri State U (MO)
Mount Saint Mary's U (CA)
Niagara U (NY)
Quinnipiac U (CT)
Regent U (VA)
St. Thomas U (NB, Canada)
San Diego State U (CA)
State U of New York Coll at Oneonta (NY)
U of Maryland U Coll (MD)
U of Massachusetts Boston (MA)
U of Northern Iowa (IA)
U of North Texas (TX)
U of Regina (SK, Canada)
U of Southern California (CA)
Weber State U (UT)
Youngstown State U (OH)

GOLF COURSE OPERATION AND GROUNDS MANAGEMENT
Trine U (IN)
U of the Incarnate Word (TX)

GRAPHIC AND PRINTING EQUIPMENT OPERATION/ PRODUCTION
Chowan U (NC)
Western Illinois U (IL)

GRAPHIC COMMUNICATIONS
Arizona State U at the Polytechnic campus (AZ)
Bradley U (IL)
California Polytechnic State U, San Luis Obispo (CA)
Carroll U (WI)
Chowan U (NC)
Eastern Washington U (WA)
Grand View U (IA)
Illinois State U (IL)
Murray State U (KY)
New England Inst of Technology (RI)
Rochester Inst of Technology (NY)
Roger Williams U (RI)
Sam Houston State U (TX)
The U of Findlay (OH)
U of Maryland U Coll (MD)
U of North Dakota (ND)
U of Northern Iowa (IA)

GRAPHIC COMMUNICATIONS RELATED
Bowling Green State U (OH)
Rasmussen Coll Bloomington (MN)
Rasmussen Coll Brooklyn Park (MN)
Rasmussen Coll Eagan (MN)
Rasmussen Coll Fargo (ND)
Rasmussen Coll Mankato (MN)
Rasmussen Coll New Port Richey (FL)
Rasmussen Coll Ocala (FL)
Rasmussen Coll Rockford (IL)
Rasmussen Coll St. Cloud (MN)
U of Wisconsin–Stout (WI)

GRAPHIC DESIGN
Abilene Christian U (TX)
Academy of Art U (CA)
Adams State U (CO)
Alberta Coll of Art & Design (AB, Canada)

American Acad of Art (IL)
American U (DC)
American U of Beirut (Lebanon)
Anderson U (SC)
Appalachian State U (NC)
Arcadia U (PA)
Arizona State U at the Tempe campus (AZ)
Arkansas Tech U (AR)
ArtCenter Coll of Design (CA)
Assumption Coll (MA)
Auburn U (AL)
Augsburg U (MN)
Augustana Coll (IL)
Baldwin Wallace U (OH)
Becker Coll (MA)
Belhaven U (MS)
Benedictine U (IL)
Bethel Coll (IN)
Bethel U (MN)
Bluffton U (OH)
Bob Jones U (SC)
Boise State U (ID)
Boston U (MA)
Bradley U (IL)
Brescia U (KY)
Bridgewater State U (MA)
Brigham Young U (UT)
Cairn U (PA)
Caldwell U (NJ)
California State Polytechnic U, Pomona (CA)
California State U, Dominguez Hills (CA)
California State U, Long Beach (CA)
California State U, Sacramento (CA)
California U of Pennsylvania (PA)
Calvin Coll (MI)
Cardinal Stritch U (WI)
Carson-Newman U (TN)
Carthage Coll (WI)
Cedarville U (OH)
Central Michigan U (MI)
Champlain Coll (VT)
Chapman U (CA)
Chatham U (PA)
Chowan U (NC)
City Coll of the City U of New York (NY)
Clarke U (IA)
Coastal Carolina U (SC)
Coker Coll (SC)
Coll of the Ozarks (MO)
Colorado Mesa U (CO)
Columbia Coll (MO)
Columbia Coll Chicago (IL)
Concordia U Irvine (CA)
Concordia U, Nebraska (NE)
Concordia U Wisconsin (WI)
Concord U (WV)
Cornish Coll of the Arts (WA)
Creative Center (NE)
Creighton U (NE)
Culver-Stockton Coll (MO)
Curry Coll (MA)
Daemen Coll (NY)
Defiance Coll (OH)
DePaul U (IL)
DEREE - The American Coll of Greece (Greece)
Doane U (NE)
Dominican U of California (CA)
Drake U (IA)
Drexel U (PA)
East Central U (OK)
Eastern Washington U (WA)
Edgewood Coll (WI)
Elmhurst Coll (IL)
Emmanuel Coll (MA)
Emory & Henry Coll (VA)
Endicott Coll (MA)
Eugene Lang Coll of Liberal Arts (NY)
Fairleigh Dickinson U, Florham Campus (NJ)
Fashion Inst of Technology (NY)
Ferris State U (MI)
FIDM/Fashion Inst of Design & Merchandising, Los Angeles Campus (CA)
FIDM/Fashion Inst of Design & Merchandising, San Francisco Campus (CA)
Fitchburg State U (MA)
Flagler Coll (FL)

Florida Ag and Mech U (FL)
Franklin Coll (IN)
Georgia Southern U (GA)
Grand View U (IA)
Harding U (AR)
Hardin-Simmons U (TX)
High Point U (NC)
Holy Family U (PA)
Inter American U of Puerto Rico, San Germán Campus (PR)
Iowa State U of Science and Technology (IA)
John Brown U (AR)
Judson U (IL)
Kansas City Art Inst (MO)
Kansas Wesleyan U (KS)
Keene State Coll (NH)
Laguna Coll of Art & Design (CA)
Lamar U (TX)
Lasell Coll (MA)
La Sierra U (CA)
Lebanese American U (Lebanon)
Lenoir-Rhyne U (NC)
Liberty U (VA)
Limestone Coll (SC)
Louisiana Coll (LA)
Lynn U (FL)
Madonna U (MI)
Malone U (OH)
Mansfield U of Pennsylvania (PA)
Marian U (WI)
Marietta Coll (OH)
Maryland Inst Coll of Art (MD)
Marymount Manhattan Coll (NY)
Maryville U of Saint Louis (MO)
Marywood U (PA)
McPherson Coll (KS)
Mercer U, Macon (GA)
Mercyhurst U (PA)
Meredith Coll (NC)
Michigan State U (MI)
MidAmerica Nazarene U (KS)
Milligan Coll (TN)
Minnesota State U Moorhead (MN)
Missouri Western State U (MO)
Montclair State U (NJ)
Morningside Coll (IA)
Mount Mary U (WI)
Mount Mercy U (IA)
Mount St. Joseph U (OH)
Mount Vernon Nazarene U (OH)
Newberry Coll (SC)
New Hampshire Inst of Art (NH)
North Carolina State U (NC)
North Central Coll (IL)
Northeastern U (MA)
Northern Michigan U (MI)
Northern Vermont U–Lyndon (VT)
Northland Coll (WI)
Northwestern Coll (IA)
Northwest Nazarene U (ID)
Nossi Coll of Art (TN)
Oakland U (MI)
Ohio Northern U (OH)
Ohio U (OH)
Oklahoma Baptist U (OK)
O'More Coll of Design (TN)
Oral Roberts U (OK)
Ouachita Baptist U (AR)
Pacific Northwest Coll of Art (OR)
Paier Coll of Art, Inc. (CT)
Palm Beach Atlantic U (FL)
Parsons School of Design (NY)
Penn State Abington (PA)
Penn State Altoona (PA)
Penn State Beaver (PA)
Penn State Berks (PA)
Penn State Brandywine (PA)
Penn State DuBois (PA)
Penn State Erie, The Behrend Coll (PA)
Penn State Fayette, The Eberly Campus (PA)
Penn State Greater Allegheny (PA)
Penn State Hazleton (PA)
Penn State Lehigh Valley (PA)
Penn State Mont Alto (PA)
Penn State New Kensington (PA)
Penn State Schuylkill (PA)
Penn State Shenango (PA)
Penn State U Park (PA)
Penn State Wilkes-Barre (PA)
Penn State Worthington Scranton (PA)
Penn State York (PA)
Pennsylvania Coll of Art & Design (PA)

Pensacola State Coll (FL)
Point Loma Nazarene U (CA)
Portland State U (OR)
Prairie View A&M U (TX)
Pratt Inst (NY)
Queens Coll of the City U of New York (NY)
Rhode Island Coll (RI)
Rhode Island School of Design (RI)
Rider U (NJ)
Ringling Coll of Art and Design (FL)
Robert Morris U Illinois (IL)
Rochester Inst of Technology (NY)
The Sage Colls (NY)
Saginaw Valley State U (MI)
St. John's U (NY)
Saint Mary's U of Minnesota (MN)
St. Norbert Coll (WI)
St. Thomas Aquinas Coll (NY)
Saint Vincent Coll (PA)
Samford U (AL)
San Diego State U (CA)
School of Visual Arts (NY)
Schreiner U (TX)
Simpson Coll (IA)
Southeastern U (FL)
Southern Adventist U (TN)
Southern Utah U (UT)
Spring Hill Coll (AL)
State U of New York at New Paltz (NY)
State U of New York Coll of Technology at Canton (NY)
Stevens–The Inst of Business & Arts (MO)
Stonehill Coll (MA)
Suffolk U (MA)
Susquehanna U (PA)
Tabor Coll (KS)
Taylor U (IN)
Temple U (PA)
Texas A&M U–Commerce (TX)
Texas A&M U–Corpus Christi (TX)
Texas Christian U (TX)
Trinity Christian Coll (IL)
Union Coll (NE)
The U of Akron (OH)
U of Bridgeport (CT)
U of Central Oklahoma (OK)
U of Dayton (OH)
U of Denver (CO)
U of Florida (FL)
U of Hartford (CT)
U of Houston (TX)
U of Illinois at Chicago (IL)
U of Mary Hardin-Baylor (TX)
U of Miami (FL)
U of Michigan (MI)
U of Minnesota, Twin Cities Campus (MN)
U of Nebraska–Lincoln (NE)
U of Nevada, Las Vegas (NV)
U of North Dakota (ND)
U of Northern Iowa (IA)
U of San Francisco (CA)
U of South Florida, St. Petersburg (FL)
The U of Tampa (FL)
The U of Tennessee at Martin (TN)
The U of the Arts (PA)
U of the Incarnate Word (TX)
U of Wisconsin–Parkside (WI)
U of Wisconsin–Stout (WI)
Villa Maria Coll (NY)
Virginia Commonwealth U (VA)
Walsh U (OH)
Washington U in St. Louis (MO)
Wayne State Coll (NE)
Weber State U (UT)
Western Michigan U (MI)
Western Colorado State U (CO)
West Texas A&M U (TX)
Whitworth U (WA)
Wichita State U (KS)
William Woods U (MO)
Youngstown State U (OH)

GREENHOUSE MANAGEMENT
U of Minnesota, Crookston (MN)

HEALTH AND MEDICAL ADMINISTRATIVE SERVICES RELATED
Brenau U (GA)
Concordia Coll–New York (NY)
Concordia U, St. Paul (MN)
Eastern Oregon U (OR)
Indiana U East (IN)

Indiana U Kokomo (IN)
Indiana U Northwest (IN)
Indiana U South Bend (IN)
Indiana U Southeast (IN)
Mount Mercy U (IA)
National Louis U (IL)
Northeastern U (MA)
Pennsylvania Coll of Technology (PA)
Samford U (AL)
State U of New York Coll of Technology at Canton (NY)
Western Michigan U (MI)

HEALTH AND PHYSICAL EDUCATION/FITNESS
Austin Peay State U (TN)
Averett U (VA)
Baker U (KS)
Baldwin Wallace U (OH)
Barton Coll (NC)
Baylor U (TX)
Berea Coll (KY)
Bethel Coll (KS)
Bethel U (TN)
Biola U (CA)
Blackburn Coll (IL)
Black Hills State U (SD)
Bluffton U (OH)
Bob Jones U (SC)
Boise State U (ID)
Bridgewater Coll (VA)
Bryan Coll (TN)
California Polytechnic State U, San Luis Obispo (CA)
California State Polytechnic U, Pomona (CA)
California State U, Dominguez Hills (CA)
California State U, East Bay (CA)
California State U, Fullerton (CA)
California State U, Monterey Bay (CA)
California State U, San Bernardino (CA)
California State U, San Marcos (CA)
California State U, Stanislaus (CA)
Cameron U (OK)
Capital U (OH)
Carroll Coll (MT)
Carroll U (WI)
Catawba Coll (NC)
Charleston Southern U (SC)
Cleveland State U (OH)
The Coll of William and Mary (VA)
Concordia U Irvine (CA)
Concordia U, Nebraska (NE)
Concordia U, St. Paul (MN)
Concordia U Wisconsin (WI)
Dallas Baptist U (TX)
Dean Coll (MA)
Delaware State U (DE)
Doane U (NE)
Eastern Michigan U (MI)
Eastern Oregon U (OR)
Eastern Washington U (WA)
East Tennessee State U (TN)
East Texas Baptist U (TX)
Elmhurst Coll (IL)
Emory & Henry Coll (VA)
Emory U (GA)
Evangel U (MO)
Florida Ag and Mech U (FL)
Friends U (KS)
Graceland U (IA)
Grand View U (IA)
Greensboro Coll (NC)
Guilford Coll (NC)
Hillsdale Coll (MI)
Howard Payne U (TX)
Humboldt State U (CA)
Husson U (ME)
Indiana U Bloomington (IN)
Indiana U of Pennsylvania (PA)
Iowa State U of Science and Technology (IA)
Ithaca Coll (NY)
Jacksonville U (FL)
James Madison U (VA)
Keene State Coll (NH)
King U (TN)
La Sierra U (CA)
Lee U (TN)
Liberty U (VA)
Lincoln Memorial U (TN)
Linfield Coll (OR)

Louisiana Coll (LA)
Lubbock Christian U (TX)
Luther Coll (IA)
Lynchburg Coll (VA)
Marian U (IN)
Maryville Coll (TN)
Marywood U (PA)
The Master's U (CA)
McDaniel Coll (MD)
McPherson Coll (KS)
MidAmerica Nazarene U (KS)
Middle Tennessee State U (TN)
Milligan Coll (TN)
Minnesota State U Moorhead (MN)
Missouri Western State U (MO)
Monmouth Coll (IL)
Morehouse Coll (GA)
Muskingum U (OH)
North Carolina Central U (NC)
North Carolina Wesleyan Coll (NC)
Northern Illinois U (IL)
Northern Michigan U (MI)
Northern State U (SD)
Northern Vermont U–Lyndon (VT)
Northwestern State U of Louisiana (LA)
Northwest Nazarene U (ID)
Northwest U (WA)
Oakland City U (IN)
The Ohio State U (OH)
Ohio U (OH)
Oklahoma Baptist U (OK)
Oral Roberts U (OK)
Palm Beach Atlantic U (FL)
Point Loma Nazarene U (CA)
Randolph Coll (VA)
Redeemer U Coll (ON, Canada)
Rhode Island Coll (RI)
Rocky Mountain Coll (MT)
Rowan U (NJ)
St. Catherine U (MN)
Saint Mary's Coll of California (CA)
Sam Houston State U (TX)
San Diego State U (CA)
Shawnee State U (OH)
Slippery Rock U of Pennsylvania (PA)
Southeast Missouri State U (MO)
Southwest Baptist U (MO)
Southwestern Adventist U (TX)
Syracuse U (NY)
Tabor Coll (KS)
Tennessee Technological U (TN)
Tennessee Wesleyan U (TN)
Texas A&M U–Kingsville (TX)
Texas Christian U (TX)
Truman State U (MO)
Union Coll (NE)
U of Arkansas (AR)
U of Dubuque (IA)
The U of Findlay (OH)
U of Georgia (GA)
U of Guam (GU)
U of Hawaii at Manoa (HI)
The U of Kansas (KS)
U of Louisville (KY)
U of Massachusetts Boston (MA)
U of Michigan (MI)
U of Mobile (AL)
U of Montevallo (AL)
U of New Orleans (LA)
The U of North Carolina at Chapel Hill (NC)
The U of North Carolina at Charlotte (NC)
The U of North Carolina at Pembroke (NC)
The U of North Carolina Wilmington (NC)
U of Northern Iowa (IA)
U of Providence (MT)
U of Regina (SK, Canada)
U of St. Thomas (MN)
U of San Francisco (CA)
U of Science and Arts of Oklahoma (OK)
U of Southern Maine (ME)
U of Southern Mississippi (MS)
The U of Tampa (FL)
The U of Tennessee at Martin (TN)
The U of Texas at Austin (TX)
U of Toronto (ON, Canada)
U of Utah (UT)
U of Wisconsin–Stevens Point (WI)
U of Wisconsin–Superior (WI)
Utah Valley U (UT)
Valley City State U (ND)

Valparaiso U (IN)
Vanguard U of Southern California (CA)
Walsh U (OH)
Wayland Baptist U (TX)
Weber State U (UT)
Welch Coll (TN)
West Chester U of Pennsylvania (PA)
Westfield State U (MA)
West Texas A&M U (TX)
West Virginia State U (WV)
West Virginia U (WV)
West Virginia Wesleyan Coll (WV)
Whittier Coll (CA)
Whitworth U (WA)
Youngstown State U (OH)

HEALTH AND PHYSICAL EDUCATION RELATED
Adelphi U (NY)
Arizona State U at the Downtown Phoenix campus (AZ)
Averett U (VA)
Avila U (MO)
Bloomsburg U of Pennsylvania (PA)
Bowling Green State U (OH)
Bridgewater State U (MA)
California State U, Long Beach (CA)
Coe Coll (IA)
Coker Coll (SC)
Concordia U Wisconsin (WI)
Cornell Coll (IA)
East Carolina U (NC)
Greensboro Coll (NC)
Gustavus Adolphus Coll (MN)
Ithaca Coll (NY)
La Sierra U (CA)
Limestone Coll (SC)
Lock Haven U of Pennsylvania (PA)
Mount Marty Coll (SD)
Mount Vernon Nazarene U (OH)
Naropa U (CO)
North Greenville U (SC)
Saint Mary's Coll of California (CA)
Texas Lutheran U (TX)
Union Coll (NE)
U of North Georgia (GA)
U of Wisconsin–Superior (WI)
Valdosta State U (GA)
Wayne State Coll (NE)
Weber State U (UT)

HEALTH AND WELLNESS
American Coll of Healthcare Sciences (OR)
Antioch U Midwest (OH)
Arizona State U at the Downtown Phoenix campus (AZ)
Arizona State U at the West campus (AZ)
Bowling Green State U (OH)
Brewton-Parker Coll (GA)
Canisius Coll (NY)
Cardinal Stritch U (WI)
Cedar Crest Coll (PA)
Chatham U (PA)
Creighton U (NE)
Culver-Stockton Coll (MO)
Daemen Coll (NY)
DeSales U (PA)
Fairleigh Dickinson U, Metropolitan Campus (NJ)
Georgetown Coll (KY)
Granite State Coll (NH)
Heidelberg U (OH)
Huntingdon Coll (AL)
Indiana U Kokomo (IN)
Indiana U South Bend (IN)
Indiana Wesleyan U (IN)
Keene State Coll (NH)
Lamar U (TX)
Lenoir-Rhyne U (NC)
Maryville U of Saint Louis (MO)
Missouri Baptist U (MO)
Mount St. Joseph U (OH)
New York Inst of Technology (NY)
North Dakota State U (ND)
Northern Vermont U–Lyndon (VT)
North Greenville U (SC)
Northwest U (WA)
Oakland U (MI)
The Ohio State U (OH)
Point Loma Nazarene U (CA)
Prairie View A&M U (TX)
Purdue U (IN)
Rhode Island Coll (RI)

Rowan U (NJ)
Sam Houston State U (TX)
Slippery Rock U of Pennsylvania (PA)
Texas A&M U (TX)
Texas A&M U–Commerce (TX)
Texas Woman's U (TX)
Towson U (MD)
Tulane U (LA)
U of Houston (TX)
U of Nevada, Reno (NV)
U of New England (ME)
U of Saint Francis (IN)
The U of Texas at San Antonio (TX)
The U of Texas Rio Grande Valley (TX)
U of Vermont (VT)
U of West Georgia (GA)
U of Wisconsin–La Crosse (WI)
U of Wisconsin–River Falls (WI)
U of Wisconsin–Stout (WI)
U of Wisconsin–Superior (WI)
Wichita State U (KS)

HEALTH COMMUNICATION
Ashland U (OH)
Cornerstone U (MI)
Grand Valley State U (MI)
Juniata Coll (PA)
Northern Kentucky U (KY)
San Diego State U (CA)
Southeast Missouri State U (MO)
Trinity Christian Coll (IL)
U of Evansville (IN)
U of Houston (TX)
Winona State U (MN)

HEALTH/HEALTH-CARE ADMINISTRATION
Adams State U (CO)
Adventist U of Health Sciences (FL)
Alma Coll (MI)
Alverno Coll (WI)
Appalachian State U (NC)
Arcadia U (PA)
Arizona State U at the Downtown Phoenix campus (AZ)
Arizona State U at the West campus (AZ)
Auburn U (AL)
Augustana U (SD)
Baldwin Wallace U (OH)
Baptist Coll of Health Sciences (TN)
Barton Coll (NC)
Belhaven U (MS)
Benedictine U (IL)
Black Hills State U (SD)
Bluffton U (OH)
Bowling Green State U (OH)
Brigham Young U–Idaho (ID)
Brock U (ON, Canada)
Butler U (IN)
Caldwell U (NJ)
California Baptist U (CA)
California State U, Dominguez Hills (CA)
California State U, Long Beach (CA)
Carlow U (PA)
Central Michigan U (MI)
Central Penn Coll (PA)
Charter Oak State Coll (CT)
Chestnut Hill Coll (PA)
Coastal Carolina U (SC)
Coll of Saint Elizabeth (NJ)
The Coll of Westchester (NY)
Columbia Coll (MO)
Columbia Coll (SC)
Columbia Southern U (AL)
Concordia U Chicago (IL)
Concordia U Irvine (CA)
Concordia U, St. Paul (MN)
Concordia U Wisconsin (WI)
Converse Coll (SC)
Creighton U (NE)
Dallas Baptist U (TX)
Davenport U, Grand Rapids (MI)
Drexel U (PA)
East Carolina U (NC)
East Central U (OK)
Eastern Michigan U (MI)
Eastern Washington U (WA)
ECPI U, Virginia Beach (VA)
Fayetteville State U (NC)
Ferris State U (MI)
Fisher Coll (MA)

Florida Ag and Mech U (FL)
Florida Atlantic U (FL)
Florida Intl U (FL)
Florida Southern Coll (FL)
Franciscan Missionaries of Our Lady U (LA)
Gannon U (PA)
Georgia Highlands Coll (GA)
Graceland U (IA)
Granite State Coll (NH)
Harding U (AR)
Harris-Stowe State U (MO)
Heidelberg U (OH)
Idaho State U (ID)
Immaculata U (PA)
Indiana U–Purdue U Indianapolis (IN)
Iona Coll (NY)
Ithaca Coll (NY)
Jackson State U (MS)
James Madison U (VA)
Jefferson Coll of Health Sciences (VA)
King U (TN)
Langston U (OK)
La Sierra U (CA)
Lebanon Valley Coll (PA)
Lee U (TN)
Lehman Coll of the City U of New York (NY)
LeTourneau U (TX)
Lewis U (IL)
Liberty U (VA)
Limestone Coll (SC)
Lincoln Coll (IL)
Lindenwood U (MO)
Long Island U–LIU Brooklyn (NY)
Long Island U–LIU Post (NY)
Loyola U Chicago (IL)
Madonna U (MI)
Maria Coll (NY)
Marian U (WI)
Mary Baldwin U (VA)
Marywood U (PA)
Mercy Coll of Ohio (OH)
Metropolitan State U of Denver (CO)
Middle Georgia State U (GA)
Midland Coll (TX)
Minnesota State U Moorhead (MN)
Misericordia U (PA)
Mississippi State U (MS)
Missouri Baptist U (MO)
Mount Mercy U (IA)
Muskingum U (OH)
National U (CA)
Nebraska Methodist Coll (NE)
Newberry Coll (SC)
New England Inst of Technology (RI)
Ohio U (OH)
Our Lady of the Lake U (TX)
Peirce Coll (PA)
Penn State Abington (PA)
Penn State Altoona (PA)
Penn State Beaver (PA)
Penn State Berks (PA)
Penn State Brandywine (PA)
Penn State DuBois (PA)
Penn State Erie, The Behrend Coll (PA)
Penn State Fayette, The Eberly Campus (PA)
Penn State Greater Allegheny (PA)
Penn State Hazleton (PA)
Penn State Lehigh Valley (PA)
Penn State Mont Alto (PA)
Penn State New Kensington (PA)
Penn State Schuylkill (PA)
Penn State Shenango (PA)
Penn State U Park (PA)
Penn State Wilkes-Barre (PA)
Penn State Worthington Scranton (PA)
Penn State York (PA)
Pennsylvania Coll of Health Sciences (PA)
Piedmont Coll (GA)
Providence Coll (RI)
Rasmussen Coll Bloomington (MN)
Rasmussen Coll Brooklyn Park (MN)
Rasmussen Coll Eagan (MN)
Rasmussen Coll Fargo (ND)
Rasmussen Coll Mankato (MN)
Rasmussen Coll New Port Richey (FL)

Rasmussen Coll Ocala (FL)
Rasmussen Coll Rockford (IL)
Rasmussen Coll St. Cloud (MN)
Regent U (VA)
Regis U (CO)
Rhode Island Coll (RI)
Roberts Wesleyan Coll (NY)
Roger Williams U (RI)
Rutgers U–New Brunswick (NJ)
Saint Leo U (FL)
Saint Louis U (MO)
Saint Mary-of-the-Woods Coll (IN)
Saint Peter's U (NJ)
Salve Regina U (RI)
Sam Houston State U (TX)
Shippensburg U of Pennsylvania (PA)
Simpson Coll (IA)
Southeast Missouri State U (MO)
Southern Adventist U (TN)
Southern Illinois U Carbondale (IL)
Southern Vermont Coll (VT)
Southwestern Coll (KS)
State U of New York Coll of Technology at Alfred (NY)
State U of New York Coll of Technology at Canton (NY)
Stonehill Coll (MA)
Texas State U (TX)
Tiffin U (OH)
Towson U (MD)
Trevecca Nazarene U (TN)
Trine U (IN)
The U of Alabama at Birmingham (AL)
U of Central Florida (FL)
U of Cincinnati (OH)
U of Dubuque (IA)
U of Evansville (IN)
U of Houston–Clear Lake (TX)
U of Kentucky (KY)
U of La Verne (CA)
U of Management and Technology (VA)
U of Maryland U Coll (MD)
U of Massachusetts Dartmouth (MA)
U of Miami (FL)
U of Michigan–Dearborn (MI)
U of Michigan–Flint (MI)
U of Minnesota, Crookston (MN)
U of Minnesota, Duluth (MN)
U of Minnesota, Twin Cities Campus (MN)
U of Nevada, Las Vegas (NV)
U of New Hampshire (NH)
The U of North Carolina at Chapel Hill (NC)
The U of North Carolina at Charlotte (NC)
U of North Florida (FL)
U of Pennsylvania (PA)
U of Providence (MT)
U of Rhode Island (RI)
U of St. Francis (IN)
U of Saint Francis (IN)
The U of Scranton (PA)
U of Southern Indiana (IN)
The U of Texas at Dallas (TX)
U of the Potomac (DC)
U of Virginia (VA)
U of Wisconsin–Eau Claire (WI)
Upper Iowa U (IA)
Ursuline Coll (OH)
Valdosta State U (GA)
Valparaiso U (IN)
Waldorf U (IA)
Washington U in St. Louis (MO)
Waynesburg U (PA)
Weber State U (UT)
Western Illinois U (IL)
Western Kentucky U (KY)
West Virginia U Inst of Technology (WV)
Wichita State U (KS)
Winona State U (MN)

HEALTH INFORMATION/ MEDICAL RECORDS ADMINISTRATION
Alabama State U (AL)
American Public U System (WV)
Arkansas Tech U (AR)
Bowling Green State U (OH)
Charter Oak State Coll (CT)
Coll of Coastal Georgia (GA)
The Coll of St. Scholastica (MN)

Dakota State U (SD)
Davenport U, Grand Rapids (MI)
Duquesne U (PA)
East Carolina U (NC)
East Central U (OK)
Eastern Washington U (WA)
Fairleigh Dickinson U, Metropolitan Campus (NJ)
Ferris State U (MI)
Fisher Coll (MA)
Florida Ag and Mech U (FL)
Georgian Court U (NJ)
Gordon State Coll (GA)
Grand Valley State U (MI)
Granite State Coll (NH)
Gwynedd Mercy U (PA)
Illinois State U (IL)
Indiana U Northwest (IN)
Indiana U–Purdue U Indianapolis (IN)
Indiana U Southeast (IN)
Kean U (NJ)
Keiser U, Fort Lauderdale (FL)
Long Island U–LIU Post (NY)
Metropolitan Coll of New York (NY)
Missouri Western State U (MO)
The Ohio State U (OH)
The Ohio State U at Lima (OH)
Oregon Inst of Technology (OR)
Peirce Coll (PA)
Pennsylvania Coll of Technology (PA)
Rasmussen Coll Bloomington (MN)
Rasmussen Coll Brooklyn Park (MN)
Rasmussen Coll Eagan (MN)
Rasmussen Coll Fargo (ND)
Rasmussen Coll Mankato (MN)
Rasmussen Coll New Port Richey (FL)
Rasmussen Coll Ocala (FL)
Rasmussen Coll Rockford (IL)
Rasmussen Coll St. Cloud (MN)
Regis U (CO)
Rutgers U–Newark (NJ)
Rutgers U–New Brunswick (NJ)
Saint Louis U (MO)
State U of New York Polytechnic Inst (NY)
Sullivan U (KY)
Texas State U (TX)
Thomas Edison State U (NJ)
Trevecca Nazarene U (TN)
The U of Alabama at Birmingham (AL)
U of Central Florida (FL)
U of Cincinnati (OH)
U of Illinois at Chicago (IL)
The U of Kansas (KS)
U of Maine at Farmington (ME)
U of Pittsburgh (PA)
U of Southern Indiana (IN)
The U of Toledo (OH)
U of Washington (WA)
U of Wisconsin–La Crosse (WI)
U of Wisconsin–Parkside (WI)
Weber State U (UT)
Western Kentucky U (KY)

HEALTH INFORMATION/ MEDICAL RECORDS TECHNOLOGY
East Central U (OK)
Excelsior Coll (NY)
Fisher Coll (MA)
Idaho State U (ID)
Keiser U, Fort Lauderdale (FL)
Resurrection U (IL)
St. John's U (NY)
U of Saint Mary (KS)

HEALTH/MEDICAL PHYSICS
Belmont U (TN)
Bloomsburg U of Pennsylvania (PA)
California State U, Dominguez Hills (CA)
California State U, Northridge (CA)
Oregon State U (OR)
U of Guelph (ON, Canada)
U of Nevada, Las Vegas (NV)

HEALTH/MEDICAL PREPARATORY PROGRAMS RELATED
Abilene Christian U (TX)
Allegheny Coll (PA)
Aquinas Coll (MI)

Arizona State U at the Downtown Phoenix campus (AZ)
Arizona State U at the West campus (AZ)
Asbury U (KY)
Aurora U (IL)
Avila U (MO)
Baylor U (TX)
Benedictine U (IL)
Blackburn Coll (IL)
Bloomsburg U of Pennsylvania (PA)
Cleveland State U (OH)
Corban U (OR)
Cornerstone U (MI)
Duquesne U (PA)
Emory & Henry Coll (VA)
Frostburg State U (MD)
Gannon U (PA)
Grove City Coll (PA)
Guilford Coll (NC)
Hofstra U (NY)
Iowa State U of Science and Technology (IA)
Ithaca Coll (NY)
Kansas Wesleyan U (KS)
Kent State U (OH)
Kent State U at Ashtabula (OH)
Lee U (TN)
Le Moyne Coll (NY)
Lenoir-Rhyne U (NC)
Lipscomb U (TN)
Lock Haven U of Pennsylvania (PA)
Louisiana Coll (LA)
Lubbock Christian U (TX)
Madonna U (MI)
Marshall U (WV)
Maryville U of Saint Louis (MO)
Mercer U, Macon (GA)
Mercyhurst U (PA)
Meredith Coll (NC)
Mount Marty Coll (SD)
Northern Illinois U (IL)
Northern Michigan U (MI)
Northern Vermont U–Lyndon (VT)
Oakland U (MI)
Oregon State U (OR)
Point Park U (PA)
Saginaw Valley State U (MI)
Seattle Pacific U (WA)
Seattle U (WA)
Southwestern Coll (KS)
The U of Findlay (OH)
U of Michigan–Flint (MI)
U of Missouri (MO)
U of Regina (SK, Canada)
U of South Alabama (AL)
U of Waterloo (ON, Canada)
U of Wisconsin–Parkside (WI)
Utica Coll (NY)
Valley City State U (ND)
Weber State U (UT)
Western Washington U (WA)

HEALTH/MEDICAL PSYCHOLOGY
Averett U (VA)
Bridgewater State U (MA)
Greenville U (IL)
Jefferson Coll of Health Sciences (VA)
Kansas Wesleyan U (KS)
MCPHS U (MA)
U of Mary Hardin-Baylor (TX)

HEALTH OCCUPATIONS TEACHER EDUCATION
Northwest U (WA)

HEALTH POLICY ANALYSIS
Brandeis U (MA)
Mount Saint Mary's U (CA)

HEALTH PROFESSIONS RELATED
Athens State U (AL)
Azusa Pacific U (CA)
Baldwin Wallace U (OH)
Boise State U (ID)
Boston U (MA)
Bowling Green State U (OH)
Bradley U (IL)
Brock U (ON, Canada)
California State U, East Bay (CA)
California State U, Long Beach (CA)
California State U, Los Angeles (CA)

California State U, Sacramento (CA)
Caribbean U (PR)
Clemson U (SC)
Cleveland State U (OH)
Coll of Coastal Georgia (GA)
Concordia Coll–New York (NY)
Cornell U (NY)
Curry Coll (MA)
DePaul U (IL)
East Tennessee State U (TN)
Elizabethtown Coll (PA)
Ferris State U (MI)
Fisher Coll (MA)
Florida State U (FL)
Furman U (SC)
Gannon U (PA)
George Mason U (VA)
Georgetown U (DC)
Georgia Southern U–Armstrong Campus (GA)
Gettysburg Coll (PA)
Grand Valley State U (MI)
King's Coll (PA)
Lock Haven U of Pennsylvania (PA)
Long Island U–LIU Brooklyn (NY)
Long Island U–LIU Post (NY)
Manchester U (IN)
Maryville Coll (TN)
Maryville U of Saint Louis (MO)
Marywood U (PA)
MCPHS U (MA)
Merrimack Coll (MA)
Molloy Coll (NY)
Mount St. Mary's U (MD)
Muskingum U (OH)
New Jersey City U (NJ)
Newman U (KS)
New York Inst of Technology (NY)
Northeastern State U (OK)
Northern Illinois U (IL)
Nova Southeastern U (FL)
Oakland U (MI)
Old Dominion U (VA)
Point Park U (PA)
Purdue U (IN)
Randolph Coll (VA)
Rowan U (NJ)
Rutgers U–New Brunswick (NJ)
The Sage Colls (NY)
Saint Augustine's U (NC)
St. John's U (NY)
St. Joseph's Coll, Long Island Campus (NY)
St. Joseph's Coll, New York (NY)
Saint Joseph's U (PA)
Saint Mary-of-the-Woods Coll (IN)
Samford U (AL)
San Francisco State U (CA)
Sonoma State U (CA)
Southern Methodist U (TX)
State U of New York Coll at Cortland (NY)
Tennessee Wesleyan U (TN)
Thomas Edison State U (NJ)
Thomas Jefferson U (PA)
U of Bridgeport (CT)
U of Central Arkansas (AR)
U of Charleston (WV)
U of Cincinnati (OH)
U of Hartford (CT)
U of Louisiana at Monroe (LA)
U of Maryland, Baltimore County (MD)
U of New England (ME)
The U of North Carolina at Charlotte (NC)
The U of North Carolina Wilmington (NC)
U of Northern Iowa (IA)
U of Pennsylvania (PA)
U of Pittsburgh (PA)
The U of Tennessee at Martin (TN)
The U of Texas at El Paso (TX)
U of Waterloo (ON, Canada)
U of Wisconsin–Parkside (WI)
U of Wisconsin–Stevens Point (WI)
Washington U in St. Louis (MO)
Wayne State U (MI)
Weber State U (UT)
West Virginia State U (WV)
Worcester State U (MA)
Youngstown State U (OH)

HEALTH SERVICES ADMINISTRATION
Anderson U (SC)

Arizona State U at the Downtown Phoenix campus (AZ)
Arizona State U at the West campus (AZ)
Bentley U (MA)
Chapman U (CA)
D'Youville Coll (NY)
Florida National U (FL)
Indiana U Northwest (IN)
Indiana U–Purdue U Indianapolis (IN)
Indiana U South Bend (IN)
Keiser U, Fort Lauderdale (FL)
McNeese State U (LA)
Northeastern State U (OK)
Ohio Northern U (OH)
Rider U (NJ)
Robert Morris U (PA)
Rutgers U–New Brunswick (NJ)
U of New Orleans (LA)
U of San Francisco (CA)
U of Washington, Tacoma (WA)

HEALTH SERVICES/ALLIED HEALTH/HEALTH SCIENCES
Adventist U of Health Sciences (FL)
Albion Coll (MI)
American Intl Coll (MA)
Angelo State U (TX)
Aquinas Coll (MI)
Aultman Coll of Nursing and Health Sciences (OH)
Bay Path U (MA)
Biola U (CA)
Bob Jones U (SC)
Boston U (MA)
Bradley U (IL)
Brigham Young U–Idaho (ID)
Butler U (IN)
California Baptist U (CA)
California State U, Dominguez Hills (CA)
California State U, Fullerton (CA)
California State U, Northridge (CA)
California State U, San Bernardino (CA)
Canisius Coll (NY)
Carroll Coll (MT)
Cedar Crest Coll (PA)
Chowan U (NC)
Clarion U of Pennsylvania (PA)
Clayton State U (GA)
The Coll at Brockport, State U of New York (NY)
The Coll of Idaho (ID)
The Coll of St. Scholastica (MN)
Coll of the Ozarks (MO)
Colorado Christian U (CO)
Columbus State U (GA)
DePaul U (IL)
Doane U (NE)
East Texas Baptist U (TX)
The Evergreen State Coll (WA)
Fairleigh Dickinson U, Florham Campus (NJ)
Florida Ag and Mech U (FL)
Florida Gulf Coast U (FL)
Friends U (KS)
Graceland U (IA)
Granite State Coll (NH)
Greensboro Coll (NC)
Heidelberg U (OH)
Hendrix Coll (AR)
Hofstra U (NY)
Husson U (ME)
Idaho State U (ID)
Keiser U, Fort Lauderdale (FL)
Lasell Coll (MA)
Lee U (TN)
Lincoln U (CA)
Lincoln U (PA)
Madonna U (MI)
Maria Coll (NY)
Marian U (IN)
Mary Baldwin U (VA)
Marymount U (VA)
Marywood U (PA)
Massachusetts Coll of Liberal Arts (MA)
McKendree U (IL)
McPherson Coll (KS)
Mercy Coll (NY)
Mercy Coll of Ohio (OH)
Mercyhurst U (PA)
Merrimack Coll (MA)
Messiah Coll (PA)

Miami Dade Coll (FL)
Milligan Coll (TN)
Misericordia U (PA)
Moravian Coll (PA)
National U (CA)
Nebraska Methodist Coll (NE)
Northern Kentucky U (KY)
Northwestern State U of Louisiana (LA)
Pace U (NY)
Pace U, Pleasantville Campus (NY)
Pennsylvania Coll of Health Sciences (PA)
Piedmont Coll (GA)
Purdue U Northwest (IN)
Quinnipiac U (CT)
Rhode Island Coll (RI)
Rider U (NJ)
Rutgers U–Camden (NJ)
Rutgers U–Newark (NJ)
Rutgers U–New Brunswick (NJ)
The Sage Colls (NY)
Saginaw Valley State U (MI)
Saint Joseph's U (PA)
Saint Louis U (MO)
St. Luke's Coll (IA)
Sam Houston State U (TX)
San Diego State U (CA)
Southeast Missouri State U (MO)
Spelman Coll (GA)
Spring Hill Coll (AL)
State U of New York Coll of Technology at Alfred (NY)
Stephen F. Austin State U (TX)
Stetson U (FL)
Stockton U (NJ)
Stonehill Coll (MA)
Stony Brook U, State U of New York (NY)
Taylor U (IN)
Texas A&M U–Corpus Christi (TX)
Texas Woman's U (TX)
Towson U (MD)
Union Coll (NE)
U of Central Florida (FL)
U of Colorado Colorado Springs (CO)
U of Florida (FL)
U of Hartford (CT)
U of Kentucky (KY)
U of Miami (FL)
U of Michigan–Flint (MI)
U of Minnesota, Crookston (MN)
U of New Haven (CT)
U of Northern Colorado (CO)
U of North Florida (FL)
U of Oklahoma Health Sciences Center (OK)
U of San Francisco (CA)
U of South Dakota (SD)
U of Southern California (CA)
U of Southern Mississippi (MS)
U of South Florida, St. Petersburg (FL)
The U of Tampa (FL)
The U of Texas at Dallas (TX)
The U of Texas Rio Grande Valley (TX)
U of the Incarnate Word (TX)
U of Utah (UT)
U of Washington, Bothell (WA)
The U of West Alabama (AL)
Valparaiso U (IN)
Washington U in St. Louis (MO)
West Chester U of Pennsylvania (PA)
Western Kentucky U (KY)
Western New England U (MA)
Westminster Coll (UT)
West Texas A&M U (TX)
West Virginia Wesleyan Coll (WV)
Wheaton Coll (IL)
Whitworth U (WA)
Widener U (PA)
William Paterson U of New Jersey (NJ)
Wilmington U (DE)
Youngstown State U (OH)

HEALTH TEACHER EDUCATION
Alverno Coll (WI)
Auburn U (AL)
Augsburg U (MN)
Averett U (VA)
Ball State U (IN)
Bemidji State U (MN)

Bethel U (MN)
Bluefield Coll (VA)
Bowling Green State U (OH)
Bridgewater State U (MA)
California State U, Stanislaus (CA)
Campbellsville U (KY)
Capital U (OH)
Carroll U (WI)
Central Michigan U (MI)
Concordia U, St. Paul (MN)
Defiance Coll (OH)
Delaware State U (DE)
Eastern Washington U (WA)
East Stroudsburg U of Pennsylvania (PA)
Elon U (NC)
George Mason U (VA)
Graceland U (IA)
Grand Valley State U (MI)
Gustavus Adolphus Coll (MN)
Hampton U (VA)
Harding U (AR)
Hofstra U (NY)
Hunter Coll of the City U of New York (NY)
Idaho State U (ID)
Illinois State U (IL)
Indiana U Bloomington (IN)
Inter American U of Puerto Rico, Barranquitas Campus (PR)
Inter American U of Puerto Rico, San Germán Campus (PR)
Iowa State U of Science and Technology (IA)
Ithaca Coll (NY)
Kansas Wesleyan U (KS)
Kent State U (OH)
Lee U (TN)
Lehman Coll of the City U of New York (NY)
Lincoln Memorial U (TN)
Linfield Coll (OR)
Long Island U–LIU Post (NY)
Maryville Coll (TN)
Michigan State U (MI)
Minnesota State U Moorhead (MN)
Missouri Baptist U (MO)
Missouri Valley Coll (MO)
Montclair State U (NJ)
Morehead State U (KY)
Murray State U (KY)
Muskingum U (OH)
New Mexico Highlands U (NM)
North Carolina Central U (NC)
North Dakota State U (ND)
Northern Illinois U (IL)
Northern Michigan U (MI)
Northwestern Oklahoma State U (OK)
Ohio Wesleyan U (OH)
Oral Roberts U (OK)
Otterbein U (OH)
Portland State U (OR)
Purdue U (IN)
Queens Coll of the City U of New York (NY)
Rhode Island Coll (RI)
Salisbury U (MD)
Sam Houston State U (TX)
Southwest Baptist U (MO)
State U of New York at Oswego (NY)
State U of New York Coll at Cortland (NY)
Tennessee Technological U (TN)
Troy U (AL)
The U of Akron (OH)
The U of Alabama at Birmingham (AL)
U of Cincinnati (OH)
U of Dubuque (IA)
The U of Findlay (OH)
U of Kentucky (KY)
U of Maine at Farmington (ME)
U of Mount Union (OH)
U of Nevada, Las Vegas (NV)
U of New Mexico (NM)
The U of North Carolina at Greensboro (NC)
U of Providence (MT)
U of Regina (SK, Canada)
U of South Dakota (SD)
U of Toronto (ON, Canada)
U of Wisconsin–La Crosse (WI)
U of Wisconsin–Superior (WI)
Utah State U (UT)
Utah Valley U (UT)

Valley City State U (ND)
Virginia Commonwealth U (VA)
Washington State U (WA)
Wayne State U (MI)
Western Connecticut State U (CT)
Western Michigan U (MI)
West Virginia Wesleyan Coll (WV)
William Penn U (IA)
Winona State U (MN)
Youngstown State U (OH)

HEAVY EQUIPMENT MAINTENANCE TECHNOLOGY
Ferris State U (MI)

HEBREW
Baruch Coll of the City U of New York (NY)
Binghamton U, State U of New York (NY)
Brigham Young U (UT)
Concordia U Wisconsin (WI)
Dartmouth Coll (NH)
Hofstra U (NY)
Hunter Coll of the City U of New York (NY)
Lehman Coll of the City U of New York (NY)
Multnomah U (OR)
New York U (NY)
The Ohio State U (OH)
Queens Coll of the City U of New York (NY)
U of Cincinnati (OH)
The U of Texas at Austin (TX)
Washington U in St. Louis (MO)

HIGHER EDUCATION/HIGHER EDUCATION ADMINISTRATION
Geneva Coll (PA)

HISPANIC-AMERICAN, PUERTO RICAN, AND MEXICAN-AMERICAN/ CHICANO STUDIES
Arizona State U at the Tempe campus (AZ)
Boston Coll (MA)
Bowling Green State U (OH)
California State U, Dominguez Hills (CA)
California State U, Fullerton (CA)
California State U, Long Beach (CA)
California State U, Los Angeles (CA)
California State U, Northridge (CA)
Claremont McKenna Coll (CA)
The Colorado Coll (CO)
Columbia U (NY)
Dartmouth Coll (NH)
Gettysburg Coll (PA)
Hunter Coll of the City U of New York (NY)
Loyola Marymount U (CA)
Metropolitan State U of Denver (CO)
Mills Coll (CA)
Our Lady of the Lake U (TX)
Pepperdine U, Malibu (CA)
Pitzer Coll (CA)
Pomona Coll (CA)
Rutgers U–Newark (NJ)
Rutgers U–New Brunswick (NJ)
San Diego State U (CA)
San Francisco State U (CA)
Scripps Coll (CA)
Sonoma State U (CA)
Southern Methodist U (TX)
Stanford U (CA)
State U of New York Coll at Oneonta (NY)
Trent U (ON, Canada)
Tulane U (LA)
U at Albany, State U of New York (NY)
The U of Arizona (AZ)
U of California, Davis (CA)
U of California, Irvine (CA)
U of California, Riverside (CA)
U of California, Santa Barbara (CA)
U of California, Santa Cruz (CA)
U of Michigan (MI)
U of Minnesota, Twin Cities Campus (MN)
U of New Mexico (NM)
U of Northern Colorado (CO)

U of Southern California (CA)
The U of Texas at Austin (TX)
The U of Texas at El Paso (TX)
The U of Texas at San Antonio (TX)
The U of Texas Rio Grande Valley (TX)
Vanderbilt U (TN)
Wheaton Coll (MA)

HISPANIC AND LATIN AMERICAN LANGUAGES
Boston U (MA)
Hamilton Coll (NY)
Loyola U New Orleans (LA)
Marlboro Coll (VT)
Molloy Coll (NY)
Pacific Lutheran U (WA)
Purdue U (IN)
Roger Williams U (RI)
Saint Louis U–Madrid Campus (Spain)
The U of Texas at Austin (TX)
U of Washington, Tacoma (WA)

HISTOLOGIC TECHNICIAN
Tarleton State U (TX)

HISTOLOGIC TECHNOLOGY/ HISTOTECHNOLOGIST
Oakland U (MI)
Roosevelt U (IL)

HISTORIC PRESERVATION AND CONSERVATION
Coll of Charleston (SC)
Delaware State U (DE)
Roger Williams U (RI)
Salve Regina U (RI)
Savannah Coll of Art and Design (GA)
Southeast Missouri State U (MO)
U of Mary Washington (VA)
The U of Texas at Austin (TX)
Ursuline Coll (OH)

HISTORY
Abilene Christian U (TX)
Acadia U (NS, Canada)
Adams State U (CO)
Adelphi U (NY)
Agnes Scott Coll (GA)
Alabama State U (AL)
Albion Coll (MI)
Albright Coll (PA)
Alcorn State U (MS)
Alfred U (NY)
Alice Lloyd Coll (KY)
Allegheny Coll (PA)
Alma Coll (MI)
Alverno Coll (WI)
Ambrose U (AB, Canada)
American Intl Coll (MA)
American Public U System (WV)
American U (DC)
American U in Bulgaria (Bulgaria)
The American U in Cairo (Egypt)
American U of Beirut (Lebanon)
The American U of Paris (France)
Amherst Coll (MA)
Anderson U (IN)
Anderson U (SC)
Andrews U (MI)
Angelo State U (TX)
Antioch Coll, Yellow Springs (OH)
Appalachian State U (NC)
Aquinas Coll (MI)
Arcadia U (PA)
Arizona State U at the Polytechnic campus (AZ)
Arizona State U at the Tempe campus (AZ)
Arizona State U at the West campus (AZ)
Arkansas Tech U (AR)
Asbury U (KY)
Ashland U (OH)
Assumption Coll (MA)
Athabasca U (AB, Canada)
Athens State U (AL)
Auburn U (AL)
Auburn U at Montgomery (AL)
Augsburg U (MN)
Augustana Coll (IL)
Augustana U (SD)
Aurora U (IL)
Austin Coll (TX)
Austin Peay State U (TN)
Averett U (VA)
Avila U (MO)

Azusa Pacific U (CA)
Baker U (KS)
Baldwin Wallace U (OH)
Ball State U (IN)
The Baptist Coll of Florida (FL)
Bard Coll (NY)
Barnard Coll (NY)
Barry U (FL)
Barton Coll (NC)
Baruch Coll of the City U of New York (NY)
Bates Coll (ME)
Baylor U (TX)
Belhaven U (MS)
Bellarmine U (KY)
Belmont U (TN)
Beloit Coll (WI)
Bemidji State U (MN)
Benedictine Coll (KS)
Benedictine U (IL)
Bennington Coll (VT)
Bentley U (MA)
Berea Coll (KY)
Berry Coll (GA)
Bethany Lutheran Coll (MN)
Bethel Coll (IN)
Bethel Coll (KS)
Bethel U (MN)
Bethel U (TN)
Binghamton U, State U of New York (NY)
Biola U (CA)
Birmingham-Southern Coll (AL)
Blackburn Coll (IL)
Black Hills State U (SD)
Bloomsburg U of Pennsylvania (PA)
Bluefield Coll (VA)
Blue Mountain Coll (MS)
Bluffton U (OH)
Bob Jones U (SC)
Boise State U (ID)
Boston Coll (MA)
Boston U (MA)
Bowdoin Coll (ME)
Bowie State U (MD)
Bowling Green State U (OH)
Bradley U (IL)
Brandeis U (MA)
Brandon U (MB, Canada)
Brenau U (GA)
Brescia U (KY)
Brewton-Parker Coll (GA)
Bridgewater Coll (VA)
Bridgewater State U (MA)
Brigham Young U–Idaho (ID)
Brock U (ON, Canada)
Bryan Coll (TN)
Bryant U (RI)
Bryn Mawr Coll (PA)
Bucknell U (PA)
Buena Vista U (IA)
Buffalo State Coll, State U of New York (NY)
Butler U (IN)
Cairn U (PA)
Caldwell U (NJ)
California Baptist U (CA)
California Inst of Technology (CA)
California Lutheran U (CA)
California Polytechnic State U, San Luis Obispo (CA)
California State Polytechnic U, Pomona (CA)
California State U, Dominguez Hills (CA)
California State U, East Bay (CA)
California State U, Fullerton (CA)
California State U, Long Beach (CA)
California State U, Los Angeles (CA)
California State U, Northridge (CA)
California State U, Sacramento (CA)
California State U, San Bernardino (CA)
California State U, San Marcos (CA)
California State U, Stanislaus (CA)
California U of Pennsylvania (PA)
Calvary U (MO)
Calvin Coll (MI)
Cameron U (OK)
Campbellsville U (KY)
Canisius Coll (NY)
Capital U (OH)
Cardinal Stritch U (WI)

Carleton Coll (MN)
Carlow U (PA)
Carroll Coll (MT)
Carroll U (WI)
Carson-Newman U (TN)
Carthage Coll (WI)
Case Western Reserve U (OH)
Catawba Coll (NC)
The Catholic U of America (DC)
Cedar Crest Coll (PA)
Cedarville U (OH)
Centenary Coll of Louisiana (LA)
Central Connecticut State U (CT)
Central Methodist U (MO)
Central Michigan U (MI)
Central State U (OH)
Centre Coll (KY)
Chapman U (CA)
Charleston Southern U (SC)
Chatham U (PA)
Chestnut Hill Coll (PA)
Chowan U (NC)
Christendom Coll (VA)
Christian Brothers U (TN)
Christopher Newport U (VA)
The Citadel, The Military Coll of South Carolina (SC)
City Coll of the City U of New York (NY)
Claremont McKenna Coll (CA)
Clarion U of Pennsylvania (PA)
Clark Atlanta U (GA)
Clarke U (IA)
Clarkson U (NY)
Clark U (MA)
Clayton State U (GA)
Clemson U (SC)
Cleveland State U (OH)
Coastal Carolina U (SC)
Coe Coll (IA)
Coker Coll (SC)
Colby Coll (ME)
Colgate U (NY)
The Coll at Brockport, State U of New York (NY)
Coll of Charleston (SC)
The Coll of Idaho (ID)
Coll of Mount Saint Vincent (NY)
The Coll of New Jersey (NJ)
The Coll of New Rochelle (NY)
Coll of Saint Benedict (MN)
Coll of Saint Elizabeth (NJ)
The Coll of Saint Rose (NY)
The Coll of St. Scholastica (MN)
Coll of Staten Island of the City U of New York (NY)
Coll of the Holy Cross (MA)
Coll of the Ozarks (MO)
The Coll of William and Mary (VA)
The Coll of Wooster (OH)
The Colorado Coll (CO)
Colorado Mesa U (CO)
Colorado State U (CO)
Colorado State U–Pueblo (CO)
Columbia Coll (MO)
Columbia U (NY)
Columbus State U (GA)
Concordia Coll–New York (NY)
Concordia U (QC, Canada)
Concordia U Chicago (IL)
Concordia U Irvine (CA)
Concordia U, Nebraska (NE)
Concordia U of Edmonton (AB, Canada)
Concordia U, St. Paul (MN)
Concordia U Wisconsin (WI)
Concord U (WV)
Connecticut Coll (CT)
Converse Coll (SC)
Corban U (OR)
Cornell Coll (IA)
Cornell U (NY)
Cornerstone U (MI)
Covenant Coll (GA)
Creighton U (NE)
Culver-Stockton Coll (MO)
Daemen Coll (NY)
Dallas Baptist U (TX)
Dartmouth Coll (NH)
Davidson Coll (NC)
Dean Coll (MA)
Defiance Coll (OH)
Delaware State U (DE)
Denison U (OH)
DePaul U (IL)
DePauw U (IN)

DEREE - The American Coll of Greece (Greece)
DeSales U (PA)
Dickinson Coll (PA)
Dickinson State U (ND)
Doane U (NE)
Dominican Coll (NY)
Dominican U (IL)
Dominican U of California (CA)
Drake U (IA)
Drew U (NJ)
Drexel U (PA)
Duquesne U (PA)
D'Youville Coll (NY)
Earlham Coll (IN)
East Carolina U (NC)
East Central U (OK)
Eastern Mennonite U (VA)
Eastern Michigan U (MI)
Eastern Nazarene Coll (MA)
Eastern New Mexico U (NM)
Eastern Oregon U (OR)
Eastern U (PA)
Eastern Washington U (WA)
East Stroudsburg U of Pennsylvania (PA)
East Tennessee State U (TN)
East Texas Baptist U (TX)
Eckerd Coll (FL)
Edgewood Coll (WI)
Elizabethtown Coll (PA)
Elmhurst Coll (IL)
Elms Coll (MA)
Elon U (NC)
Emmanuel Coll (MA)
Emory & Henry Coll (VA)
Emory U (GA)
Emporia State U (KS)
Endicott Coll (MA)
Eugene Lang Coll of Liberal Arts (NY)
Evangel U (MO)
Excelsior Coll (NY)
Fairfield U (CT)
Fairleigh Dickinson U, Florham Campus (NJ)
Fairleigh Dickinson U, Metropolitan Campus (NJ)
Fayetteville State U (NC)
Felician U (NJ)
Ferris State U (MI)
Fitchburg State U (MA)
Flagler Coll (FL)
Florida Ag and Mech U (FL)
Florida Atlantic U (FL)
Florida Coll (FL)
Florida Gulf Coast U (FL)
Florida Intl U (FL)
Florida Southern Coll (FL)
Florida State U (FL)
Fordham U (NY)
Fort Lewis Coll (CO)
Framingham State U (MA)
Francis Marion U (SC)
Franklin & Marshall Coll (PA)
Franklin Coll (IN)
Franklin Pierce U (NH)
Franklin U Switzerland (Switzerland)
Friends U (KS)
Frostburg State U (MD)
Furman U (SC)
Gannon U (PA)
Geneva Coll (PA)
George Mason U (VA)
Georgetown Coll (KY)
Georgetown U (DC)
The George Washington U (DC)
Georgia Coll & State U (GA)
Georgia Gwinnett Coll (GA)
Georgian Court U (NJ)
Georgia Southern U (GA)
Georgia Southern U–Armstrong Campus (GA)
Georgia Southwestern State U (GA)
Georgia State U (GA)
Gettysburg Coll (PA)
Gonzaga U (WA)
Gordon Coll (MA)
Gordon State Coll (GA)
Goshen Coll (IN)
Governors State U (IL)
Graceland U (IA)
Grambling State U (LA)
Grand Valley State U (MI)
Grand View U (IA)

Granite State Coll (NH)
Green Mountain Coll (VT)
Greensboro Coll (NC)
Greenville U (IL)
Grinnell Coll (IA)
Grove City Coll (PA)
Guilford Coll (NC)
Gustavus Adolphus Coll (MN)
Gwynedd Mercy U (PA)
Hamilton Coll (NY)
Hamline U (MN)
Hampden-Sydney Coll (VA)
Hampshire Coll (MA)
Hampton U (VA)
Hannibal-LaGrange U (MO)
Harding U (AR)
Hardin-Simmons U (TX)
Hartwick Coll (NY)
Harvard U (MA)
Haverford Coll (PA)
Hawai`i Pacific U (HI)
Heidelberg U (OH)
Hendrix Coll (AR)
High Point U (NC)
Hillsdale Coll (MI)
Hiram Coll (OH)
Hobart and William Smith Colls
   (NY)
Hofstra U (NY)
Hollins U (VA)
Holy Family U (PA)
Holy Names U (CA)
Hood Coll (MD)
Hope Coll (MI)
Houston Baptist U (TX)
Howard Payne U (TX)
Humboldt State U (CA)
Hunter Coll of the City U of New
   York (NY)
Huntingdon Coll (AL)
Huston-Tillotson U (TX)
Idaho State U (ID)
Illinois Coll (IL)
Illinois State U (IL)
Illinois Wesleyan U (IL)
Immaculata U (PA)
Indiana State U (IN)
Indiana U Bloomington (IN)
Indiana U East (IN)
Indiana U Northwest (IN)
Indiana U of Pennsylvania (PA)
Indiana U–Purdue U Indianapolis
   (IN)
Indiana U South Bend (IN)
Indiana U Southeast (IN)
Indiana Wesleyan U (IN)
Inter American U of Puerto Rico,
   Metropolitan Campus (PR)
Inter American U of Puerto Rico,
   San Germán Campus (PR)
Iona Coll (NY)
Iowa State U of Science and
   Technology (IA)
Ithaca Coll (NY)
Jackson State U (MS)
Jacksonville U (FL)
James Madison U (VA)
John Brown U (AR)
John Cabot U (Italy)
John Carroll U (OH)
John Jay Coll of Criminal Justice of
   the City U of New York (NY)
Johns Hopkins U (MD)
Johnson C. Smith U (NC)
Judson U (IL)
Juniata Coll (PA)
Kalamazoo Coll (MI)
Kansas State U (KS)
Kansas Wesleyan U (KS)
Kean U (NJ)
Keene State Coll (NH)
Kennesaw State U (GA)
Kent State U (OH)
Kent State U at Stark (OH)
Kenyon Coll (OH)
King's Coll (PA)
King U (TN)
Knox Coll (IL)
Kutztown U of Pennsylvania (PA)
Lafayette Coll (PA)
LaGrange Coll (GA)
Lamar U (TX)
La Roche Coll (PA)
La Salle U (PA)
La Sierra U (CA)
Lasell Coll (MA)
La Sierra U (CA)
Lawrence U (WI)

Lebanese American U (Lebanon)
Lebanon Valley Coll (PA)
Lee U (TN)
Lehigh U (PA)
Lehman Coll of the City U of New
   York (NY)
Le Moyne Coll (NY)
Lenoir-Rhyne U (NC)
Lewis U (IL)
Liberty U (VA)
Limestone Coll (SC)
Lincoln Memorial U (TN)
Lincoln U (MO)
Lincoln U (PA)
Lindenwood U (MO)
Lindsey Wilson Coll (KY)
Linfield Coll (OR)
Lipscomb U (TN)
Lock Haven U of Pennsylvania (PA)
Long Island U–LIU Brooklyn (NY)
Long Island U–LIU Post (NY)
Longwood U (VA)
Loras Coll (IA)
Louisiana Coll (LA)
Louisiana State U and A&M Coll
   (LA)
Loyola Marymount U (CA)
Loyola U Chicago (IL)
Loyola U New Orleans (LA)
Lubbock Christian U (TX)
Luther Coll (IA)
Lycoming Coll (PA)
Lynchburg Coll (VA)
Lyon Coll (AR)
Macalester Coll (MN)
Madonna U (MI)
Malone U (OH)
Manchester U (IN)
Manhattan Coll (NY)
Manhattanville Coll (NY)
Mansfield U of Pennsylvania (PA)
Marian U (IN)
Marian U (WI)
Marietta Coll (OH)
Marist Coll (NY)
Marlboro Coll (VT)
Marquette U (WI)
Marshall U (WV)
Mary Baldwin U (VA)
Marymount U (VA)
Maryville Coll (TN)
Maryville U of Saint Louis (MO)
Marywood U (PA)
Massachusetts Coll of Liberal Arts
   (MA)
Massachusetts Inst of Technology
   (MA)
The Master's U (CA)
McDaniel Coll (MD)
McKendree U (IL)
McMurry U (TX)
McNeese State U (LA)
Mercer U, Macon (GA)
Mercy Coll (NY)
Mercyhurst U (PA)
Meredith Coll (NC)
Merrimack Coll (MA)
Messiah Coll (PA)
Metropolitan State U of Denver
   (CO)
Miami U (OH)
Michigan State U (MI)
Michigan Technological U (MI)
Mid-America Christian U (OK)
MidAmerica Nazarene U (KS)
Middlebury Coll (VT)
Middle Georgia State U (GA)
Middle Tennessee State U (TN)
Millersville U of Pennsylvania (PA)
Milligan Coll (TN)
Millikin U (IL)
Millsaps Coll (MS)
Mills Coll (CA)
Minnesota State U Moorhead (MN)
Minot State U (ND)
Misericordia U (PA)
Mississippi State U (MS)
Missouri Baptist U (MO)
Missouri State U (MO)
Missouri U of Science and
   Technology (MO)
Missouri Valley Coll (MO)
Missouri Western State U (MO)
Molloy Coll (NY)
Monmouth Coll (IL)
Montclair State U (NJ)
Moravian Coll (PA)

Morehead State U (KY)
Morehouse Coll (GA)
Morningside Coll (IA)
Morris Coll (SC)
Mount Holyoke Coll (MA)
Mount Marty Coll (SD)
Mount Mary U (WI)
Mount Mercy U (IA)
Mount St. Joseph U (OH)
Mount Saint Mary Coll (NY)
Mount Saint Mary's U (CA)
Mount St. Mary's U (MD)
Mount Vernon Nazarene U (OH)
Muhlenberg Coll (PA)
Multnomah U (OR)
Murray State U (KY)
Muskingum U (OH)
National U (CA)
Nazareth Coll of Rochester (NY)
Newberry Coll (SC)
New Coll of Florida (FL)
New Jersey City U (NJ)
New Jersey Inst of Technology (NJ)
Newman U (KS)
New Mexico Highlands U (NM)
New Mexico State U (NM)
New York U (NY)
Niagara U (NY)
Nichols Coll (MA)
North Carolina Central U (NC)
North Carolina State U (NC)
North Carolina Wesleyan Coll (NC)
North Central Coll (IL)
North Dakota State U (ND)
Northeastern State U (OK)
Northeastern U (MA)
Northern Arizona U (AZ)
Northern Illinois U (IL)
Northern Kentucky U (KY)
Northern Michigan U (MI)
Northern State U (SD)
Northern Vermont U–Lyndon (VT)
North Greenville U (SC)
Northland Coll (WI)
Northwest Christian U (OR)
Northwestern Coll (IA)
Northwestern Oklahoma State U
   (OK)
Northwestern State U of Louisiana
   (LA)
Northwestern U (IL)
Northwest Missouri State U (MO)
Northwest Nazarene U (ID)
Northwest U (WA)
Notre Dame de Namur U (CA)
Nova Southeastern U (FL)
Nyack Coll (NY)
Oakland City U (IN)
Oakland U (MI)
Oberlin Coll (OH)
Occidental Coll (CA)
Oglethorpe U (GA)
Ohio Christian U (OH)
Ohio Dominican U (OH)
Ohio Northern U (OH)
The Ohio State U (OH)
The Ohio State U at Lima (OH)
The Ohio State U at Mansfield (OH)
The Ohio State U at Marion (OH)
The Ohio State U at Newark (OH)
Ohio U (OH)
Ohio Wesleyan U (OH)
Oklahoma Baptist U (OK)
Oklahoma Christian U (OK)
Oklahoma City U (OK)
Oklahoma State U (OK)
Old Dominion U (VA)
Olivet Nazarene U (IL)
Oral Roberts U (OK)
Oregon State U (OR)
Ottawa U (KS)
Otterbein U (OH)
Ouachita Baptist U (AR)
Our Lady of the Lake U (TX)
Pace U (NY)
Pace U, Pleasantville Campus (NY)
Pacific Lutheran U (WA)
Palm Beach Atlantic U (FL)
Penn State Abington (PA)
Penn State Altoona (PA)
Penn State Beaver (PA)
Penn State Berks (PA)
Penn State Brandywine (PA)
Penn State DuBois (PA)
Penn State Erie, The Behrend Coll
   (PA)

Penn State Fayette, The Eberly
   Campus (PA)
Penn State Greater Allegheny (PA)
Penn State Hazleton (PA)
Penn State Lehigh Valley (PA)
Penn State Mont Alto (PA)
Penn State New Kensington (PA)
Penn State Schuylkill (PA)
Penn State Shenango (PA)
Penn State U Park (PA)
Penn State Wilkes-Barre (PA)
Penn State Worthington Scranton
   (PA)
Penn State York (PA)
Pepperdine U, Malibu (CA)
Pfeiffer U (NC)
Piedmont Coll (GA)
Pittsburg State U (KS)
Pitzer Coll (CA)
Point Loma Nazarene U (CA)
Point Park U (PA)
Point U (GA)
Pomona Coll (CA)
Portland State U (OR)
Prairie View A&M U (TX)
Presbyterian Coll (SC)
Princeton U (NJ)
Principia Coll (IL)
Providence Coll (RI)
Purchase Coll, State U of New York
   (NY)
Purdue U (IN)
Purdue U Northwest (IN)
Queens Coll of the City U of New
   York (NY)
Quinnipiac U (CT)
Radford U (VA)
Ramapo Coll of New Jersey (NJ)
Randolph Coll (VA)
Randolph-Macon Coll (VA)
Redeemer U Coll (ON, Canada)
Reed Coll (OR)
Regent U (VA)
Regis U (CO)
Rhode Island Coll (RI)
Rhodes Coll (TN)
Rice U (TX)
Rider U (NJ)
Ripon Coll (WI)
Rivier U (NH)
Roanoke Coll (VA)
Roberts Wesleyan Coll (NY)
Rockford U (IL)
Rockhurst U (MO)
Rocky Mountain Coll (MT)
Rogers State U (OK)
Roger Williams U (RI)
Rollins Coll (FL)
Roosevelt U (IL)
Rosemont Coll (PA)
Rowan U (NJ)
Rutgers U–Camden (NJ)
Rutgers U–Newark (NJ)
Rutgers U–New Brunswick (NJ)
Sacred Heart U (CT)
The Sage Colls (NY)
Saginaw Valley State U (MI)
St. Ambrose U (IA)
Saint Anselm Coll (NH)
St. Bonaventure U (NY)
St. Catherine U (MN)
Saint Francis U (PA)
St. John Fisher Coll (NY)
Saint John's U (MN)
St. John's U (NY)
St. Joseph's Coll, Long Island
   Campus (NY)
St. Joseph's Coll, New York (NY)
Saint Joseph's U (PA)
St. Lawrence U (NY)
Saint Leo U (FL)
Saint Louis U (MO)
Saint Louis U–Madrid Campus
   (Spain)
Saint Martin's U (WA)
Saint Mary's Coll of California (CA)
St. Mary's Coll of Maryland (MD)
St. Mary's U (TX)
Saint Mary's U of Minnesota (MN)
Saint Michael's Coll (VT)
St. Norbert Coll (WI)
St. Olaf Coll (MN)
Saint Peter's U (NJ)
St. Thomas Aquinas Coll (NY)
St. Thomas U (FL)
St. Thomas U (NB, Canada)
Saint Vincent Coll (PA)

Salisbury U (MD)
Salve Regina U (RI)
Samford U (AL)
Sam Houston State U (TX)
San Diego State U (CA)
San Francisco State U (CA)
Santa Clara U (CA)
Sarah Lawrence Coll (NY)
Schreiner U (TX)
Scripps Coll (CA)
Seattle Pacific U (WA)
Seattle U (WA)
Seton Hill U (PA)
Sewanee: The U of the South (TN)
Shawnee State U (OH)
Shenandoah U (VA)
Shepherd U (WV)
Shippensburg U of Pennsylvania
   (PA)
Shorter U (GA)
Siena Coll (NY)
Silver Lake Coll of the Holy Family
   (WI)
Simmons Coll (MA)
Simon Fraser U (BC, Canada)
Simpson Coll (IA)
Skidmore Coll (NY)
Slippery Rock U of Pennsylvania
   (PA)
Smith Coll (MA)
Sonoma State U (CA)
Southeastern Louisiana U (LA)
Southeastern Oklahoma State U
   (OK)
Southeastern U (FL)
Southeast Missouri State U (MO)
Southern Adventist U (TN)
Southern Arkansas U–Magnolia
   (AR)
Southern Illinois U Carbondale (IL)
Southern Illinois U Edwardsville
   (IL)
Southern Methodist U (TX)
Southern Utah U (UT)
Southern Vermont Coll (VT)
Southwest Baptist U (MO)
Southwestern Adventist U (TX)
Southwestern Assemblies of God U
   (TX)
Southwestern Coll (KS)
Southwestern U (TX)
Spelman Coll (GA)
Spring Hill Coll (AL)
Stanford U (CA)
State U of New York at Fredonia
   (NY)
State U of New York at New Paltz
   (NY)
State U of New York at Oswego
   (NY)
State U of New York at Plattsburgh
   (NY)
State U of New York Coll at
   Cortland (NY)
State U of New York Coll at
   Geneseo (NY)
State U of New York Coll at Old
   Westbury (NY)
State U of New York Coll at
   Oneonta (NY)
State U of New York Coll at
   Potsdam (NY)
State U of New York Empire State
   Coll (NY)
Stephen F. Austin State U (TX)
Stetson U (FL)
Stevens Inst of Technology (NJ)
Stevenson U (MD)
Stockton U (NJ)
Stonehill Coll (MA)
Stony Brook U, State U of New York
   (NY)
Suffolk U (MA)
Susquehanna U (PA)
Sweet Briar Coll (VA)
Syracuse U (NY)
Tabor Coll (KS)
Tarleton State U (TX)
Taylor U (IN)
Temple U (PA)
Tennessee Technological U (TN)
Tennessee Wesleyan U (TN)
Texas A&M Intl U (TX)
Texas A&M U (TX)
Texas A&M U–Central Texas (TX)
Texas A&M U–Commerce (TX)
Texas A&M U–Corpus Christi (TX)

Texas A&M U–Kingsville (TX)
Texas A&M U–Texarkana (TX)
Texas Christian U (TX)
Texas Lutheran U (TX)
Texas State U (TX)
Texas Tech U (TX)
Texas Woman's U (TX)
Tiffin U (OH)
Toccoa Falls Coll (GA)
Towson U (MD)
Transylvania U (KY)
Trent U (ON, Canada)
Trevecca Nazarene U (TN)
Trinity Christian Coll (IL)
Trinity U (TX)
Troy U (AL)
Truett McConnell U (GA)
Truman State U (MO)
Tufts U (MA)
Tulane U (LA)
Tusculum Coll (TN)
Union Coll (NE)
Union Coll (NY)
Union U (TN)
Université de Sherbrooke (QC, Canada)
Université Sainte-Anne (NS, Canada)
U at Albany, State U of New York (NY)
U at Buffalo, the State U of New York (NY)
The U of Akron (OH)
The U of Alabama (AL)
The U of Alabama at Birmingham (AL)
U of Alaska Fairbanks (AK)
The U of Arizona (AZ)
U of Arkansas (AR)
U of California, Davis (CA)
U of California, Irvine (CA)
U of California, Los Angeles (CA)
U of California, Riverside (CA)
U of California, San Diego (CA)
U of California, Santa Barbara (CA)
U of California, Santa Cruz (CA)
U of Central Arkansas (AR)
U of Central Florida (FL)
U of Central Missouri (MO)
U of Central Oklahoma (OK)
U of Chicago (IL)
U of Cincinnati (OH)
U of Colorado Boulder (CO)
U of Colorado Colorado Springs (CO)
U of Colorado Denver (CO)
U of Dallas (TX)
U of Dayton (OH)
U of Denver (CO)
U of Evansville (IN)
The U of Findlay (OH)
U of Florida (FL)
U of Georgia (GA)
U of Guam (GU)
U of Guelph (ON, Canada)
U of Hartford (CT)
U of Hawaii at Manoa (HI)
U of Houston (TX)
U of Houston–Clear Lake (TX)
U of Houston–Downtown (TX)
U of Idaho (ID)
U of Illinois at Chicago (IL)
U of Illinois at Springfield (IL)
U of Jamestown (ND)
The U of Kansas (KS)
U of Kentucky (KY)
U of King's Coll (NS, Canada)
U of La Verne (CA)
U of Louisiana at Monroe (LA)
U of Louisville (KY)
U of Maine (ME)
U of Maine at Farmington (ME)
U of Maine at Machias (ME)
U of Maine at Presque Isle (ME)
U of Mary Hardin-Baylor (TX)
U of Maryland, Baltimore County (MD)
U of Maryland, Coll Park (MD)
U of Maryland Eastern Shore (MD)
U of Maryland U Coll (MD)
U of Mary Washington (VA)
U of Massachusetts Amherst (MA)
U of Massachusetts Boston (MA)
U of Massachusetts Dartmouth (MA)
U of Massachusetts Lowell (MA)
U of Memphis (TN)

U of Miami (FL)
U of Michigan (MI)
U of Michigan–Dearborn (MI)
U of Michigan–Flint (MI)
U of Minnesota, Duluth (MN)
U of Minnesota, Morris (MN)
U of Minnesota, Twin Cities Campus (MN)
U of Missouri (MO)
U of Missouri–St. Louis (MO)
U of Mobile (AL)
U of Montana (MT)
U of Montevallo (AL)
U of Mount Union (OH)
U of Nebraska at Kearney (NE)
U of Nebraska–Lincoln (NE)
U of Nevada, Las Vegas (NV)
U of Nevada, Reno (NV)
U of New England (ME)
U of New Hampshire (NH)
U of New Haven (CT)
U of New Mexico (NM)
U of New Orleans (LA)
U of North Alabama (AL)
U of North Carolina at Asheville (NC)
The U of North Carolina at Chapel Hill (NC)
The U of North Carolina at Charlotte (NC)
The U of North Carolina at Greensboro (NC)
The U of North Carolina at Pembroke (NC)
The U of North Carolina Wilmington (NC)
U of North Dakota (ND)
U of Northern Colorado (CO)
U of Northern Iowa (IA)
U of North Florida (FL)
U of North Georgia (GA)
U of North Texas (TX)
U of Notre Dame (IN)
U of Oklahoma (OK)
U of Oregon (OR)
U of Pennsylvania (PA)
U of Pikeville (KY)
U of Pittsburgh (PA)
U of Pittsburgh at Bradford (PA)
U of Providence (MT)
U of Puget Sound (WA)
U of Regina (SK, Canada)
U of Rhode Island (RI)
U of Richmond (VA)
U of Rochester (NY)
U of St. Francis (IL)
U of Saint Francis (IN)
U of Saint Joseph (CT)
U of Saint Mary (KS)
U of St. Thomas (MN)
U of St. Thomas (TX)
U of San Diego (CA)
U of San Francisco (CA)
U of Saskatchewan (SK, Canada)
U of Science and Arts of Oklahoma (OK)
The U of Scranton (PA)
U of Sioux Falls (SD)
U of South Alabama (AL)
U of South Carolina (SC)
U of South Carolina Aiken (SC)
U of South Dakota (SD)
U of Southern California (CA)
U of Southern Indiana (IN)
U of Southern Maine (ME)
U of Southern Mississippi (MS)
U of Southern Oregon (OR)
U of South Florida, St. Petersburg (FL)
U of South Florida Sarasota-Manatee (FL)
The U of Tampa (FL)
The U of Tennessee (TN)
The U of Tennessee at Chattanooga (TN)
The U of Tennessee at Martin (TN)
The U of Texas at Austin (TX)
The U of Texas at Dallas (TX)
The U of Texas at El Paso (TX)
The U of Texas at San Antonio (TX)
The U of Texas of the Permian Basin (TX)
The U of Texas Rio Grande Valley (TX)
U of the Fraser Valley (BC, Canada)
U of the Incarnate Word (TX)
U of the Pacific (CA)

The U of Toledo (OH)
U of Toronto (ON, Canada)
The U of Tulsa (OK)
U of Utah (UT)
U of Vermont (VT)
U of Virginia (VA)
The U of Virginia's Coll at Wise (VA)
U of Washington (WA)
U of Washington, Tacoma (WA)
U of Waterloo (ON, Canada)
The U of West Alabama (AL)
U of West Georgia (GA)
U of Wisconsin–Eau Claire (WI)
U of Wisconsin–La Crosse (WI)
U of Wisconsin–Madison (WI)
U of Wisconsin–Milwaukee (WI)
U of Wisconsin–Parkside (WI)
U of Wisconsin–Platteville (WI)
U of Wisconsin–River Falls (WI)
U of Wisconsin–Stevens Point (WI)
U of Wisconsin–Superior (WI)
U of Wisconsin–Whitewater (WI)
U of Wyoming (WY)
Ursinus Coll (PA)
Ursuline Coll (OH)
Utah State U (UT)
Utah Valley U (UT)
Utica Coll (NY)
Valdosta State U (GA)
Valley City State U (ND)
Valparaiso U (IN)
Vanderbilt U (TN)
Vanguard U of Southern California (CA)
Vassar Coll (NY)
Villanova U (PA)
Virginia Commonwealth U (VA)
Virginia Military Inst (VA)
Virginia Polytechnic Inst and State U (VA)
Virginia Wesleyan U (VA)
Wabash Coll (IN)
Wagner Coll (NY)
Wake Forest U (NC)
Waldorf U (IA)
Walsh U (OH)
Warner Pacific Coll (OR)
Wartburg Coll (IA)
Washington & Jefferson Coll (PA)
Washington and Lee U (VA)
Washington Coll (MD)
Washington State U (WA)
Washington State U–Tri-Cities (WA)
Washington State U–Vancouver (WA)
Washington U in St. Louis (MO)
Wayland Baptist U (TX)
Waynesburg U (PA)
Wayne State Coll (NE)
Wayne State U (MI)
Weber State U (UT)
Webster U (MO)
Welch Coll (TN)
Wellesley Coll (MA)
Wells Coll (NY)
Wesleyan U (CT)
West Chester U of Pennsylvania (PA)
Western Connecticut State U (CT)
Western Illinois U (IL)
Western Kentucky U (KY)
Western Michigan U (MI)
Western New England U (MA)
Western Oregon U (OR)
Western State Colorado U (CO)
Western Washington U (WA)
Westfield State U (MA)
Westminster Coll (PA)
Westminster Coll (UT)
Westmont Coll (CA)
West Texas A&M U (TX)
West Virginia State U (WV)
West Virginia U (WV)
West Virginia U Inst of Technology (WV)
West Virginia Wesleyan Coll (WV)
Wheaton Coll (IL)
Wheaton Coll (MA)
Whitman Coll (WA)
Whittier Coll (CA)
Whitworth U (WA)
Wichita State U (KS)
Widener U (PA)
Wilkes U (PA)
Willamette U (OR)

William Jewell Coll (MO)
William Paterson U of New Jersey (NJ)
William Penn U (IA)
Williams Coll (MA)
William Woods U (MO)
Winona State U (MN)
Winthrop U (SC)
Wisconsin Lutheran Coll (WI)
Wittenberg U (OH)
Wofford Coll (SC)
Worcester State U (MA)
Wright State U (OH)
Xavier U of Louisiana (LA)
York Coll of Pennsylvania (PA)
Youngstown State U (OH)

HISTORY AND PHILOSOPHY OF SCIENCE AND TECHNOLOGY
Bard Coll (NY)
California Inst of Technology (CA)
Case Western Reserve U (OH)
Georgia Inst of Technology (GA)
Harvard U (MA)
Johns Hopkins U (MD)
Michigan State U (MI)
Stevens Inst of Technology (NJ)
U of Chicago (IL)
U of Oklahoma (OK)
U of Pennsylvania (PA)
U of Pittsburgh (PA)
U of Toronto (ON, Canada)
U of Washington (WA)
U of Wisconsin–Madison (WI)

HISTORY RELATED
The American U of Paris (France)
Bentley U (MA)
Bridgewater Coll (VA)
Bridgewater State U (MA)
Bryn Athyn Coll of the New Church (PA)
Carnegie Mellon U (PA)
Chaminade U of Honolulu (HI)
Delaware State U (DE)
Harvard U (MA)
Indiana U Kokomo (IN)
Lebanon Valley Coll (PA)
LeTourneau U (TX)
Marquette U (WI)
Mercyhurst U (PA)
The Ohio State U (OH)
The Ohio State U at Mansfield (OH)
The Ohio State U at Marion (OH)
The Ohio State U at Newark (OH)
Regent U (VA)
Saint Mary's U of Minnesota (MN)
Sarah Lawrence Coll (NY)
United States Military Acad (NY)
U at Albany, State U of New York (NY)
U of California, Santa Barbara (CA)
U of Southern California (CA)
U of Washington (WA)
U of Washington, Tacoma (WA)
Vanderbilt U (TN)
Virginia Wesleyan U (VA)
Woodbury U (CA)

HISTORY TEACHER EDUCATION
Abilene Christian U (TX)
Albion Coll (MI)
Appalachian State U (NC)
Aquinas Coll (MI)
Auburn U (AL)
Augustana Coll (IL)
Biola U (CA)
Bluefield Coll (VA)
Boise State U (ID)
Bowling Green State U (OH)
Bradley U (IL)
Brigham Young U–Idaho (ID)
Bryan Coll (TN)
Buena Vista U (IA)
California Lutheran U (CA)
Calvin Coll (MI)
Campbellsville U (KY)
Carroll Coll (MT)
Carroll U (WI)
The Catholic U of America (DC)
Central Michigan U (MI)
Charleston Southern U (SC)
Christian Brothers U (TN)
The Coll of New Jersey (NJ)
Coll of Staten Island of the City U of New York (NY)

Coll of the Ozarks (MO)
Colorado Christian U (CO)
Concordia Chicago (IL)
Concordia U Wisconsin (WI)
Cornerstone U (MI)
Covenant Coll (GA)
Culver-Stockton Coll (MO)
Dickinson State U (ND)
Dominican Coll (NY)
Dominican U (IL)
East Central U (OK)
Eastern Michigan U (MI)
Eastern Nazarene Coll (MA)
East Texas Baptist U (TX)
Elmhurst Coll (IL)
Emory & Henry Coll (VA)
Evangel U (MO)
Ferris State U (MI)
Fitchburg State U (MA)
Florida Southern Coll (FL)
Friends U (KS)
Geneva Coll (PA)
Georgia Southern U–Armstrong Campus (GA)
Gordon State Coll (GA)
Grand Valley State U (MI)
Greenville U (IL)
Gwynedd Mercy U (PA)
Hannibal-LaGrange U (MO)
Hardin-Simmons U (TX)
Hobe Sound Bible Coll (FL)
Holy Family U (PA)
Hope Coll (MI)
Houston Baptist U (TX)
Howard Payne U (TX)
Huntingdon Coll (AL)
Inter American U of Puerto Rico, Metropolitan Campus (PR)
Inter American U of Puerto Rico, San Germán Campus (PR)
Ithaca Coll (NY)
Kansas Wesleyan U (KS)
Keene State Coll (NH)
Lee U (TN)
LeTourneau U (TX)
Lincoln Memorial U (TN)
Lindenwood U (MO)
Lipscomb U (TN)
Long Island U–LIU Post (NY)
Manchester (IN)
Maranatha Baptist U (WI)
Maryville Coll (TN)
McKendree U (IL)
McMurry U (TX)
Merrimack Coll (MA)
Michigan State U (MI)
MidAmerica Nazarene U (KS)
Minot State U (ND)
Missouri State U (MO)
Morningside Coll (IA)
Mount Marty Coll (SD)
Mount Mary U (WI)
Mount Vernon Nazarene U (OH)
Nazareth Coll of Rochester (NY)
North Dakota State U (ND)
Northern Michigan U (MI)
Northern State U (SD)
Northwest Nazarene U (ID)
Oakland City U (IN)
Ohio Northern U (OH)
Ohio Wesleyan U (OH)
Piedmont Coll (GA)
Pittsburg State U (KS)
Providence Coll (RI)
Rhode Island Coll (RI)
Rocky Mountain Coll (MT)
Roger Williams U (RI)
Saginaw Valley State U (MI)
St. Ambrose U (IA)
Saint Francis U (PA)
St. John Fisher Coll (NY)
Saint Joseph's U (PA)
Salve Regina U (RI)
Schreiner U (TX)
Southern Adventist U (TN)
Southern Utah U (UT)
Spring Hill Coll (AL)
Texas Lutheran U (TX)
Tiffin U (OH)
Toccoa Falls Coll (GA)
Trevecca Nazarene U (TN)
Trinity Christian Coll (IL)
Union Coll (NE)
The U of Akron (OH)
U of Central Oklahoma (OK)
U of Illinois at Chicago (IL)
U of Jamestown (ND)

U of Maine (ME)
U of Maine at Machias (ME)
U of Mary Hardin-Baylor (TX)
U of Mobile (AL)
U of Providence (MT)
U of Sioux Falls (SD)
U of South Dakota (SD)
The U of Tennessee at Martin (TN)
U of Wisconsin–Superior (WI)
U of Wisconsin–Whitewater (WI)
Utah Valley U (UT)
Utica Coll (NY)
Valley City State U (ND)
Valparaiso U (IN)
Wartburg Coll (IA)
Washington U in St. Louis (MO)
Wayne State Coll (NE)
Weber State U (UT)
Welch Coll (TN)
Western Michigan U (MI)
Western State Colorado U (CO)
Western Washington U (WA)
Westfield State U (MA)
Widener U (PA)
William Woods U (MO)
Xavier U of Louisiana (LA)

HOLISTIC HEALTH
Northern Vermont U–Lyndon (VT)

HOLOCAUST AND RELATED STUDIES
Keene State Coll (NH)
Marlboro Coll (VT)

HOME FURNISHINGS AND EQUIPMENT INSTALLATION
Brigham Young U (UT)

HOMELAND SECURITY
American Public U System (WV)
Anderson U (SC)
Angelo State U (TX)
Central Penn Coll (PA)
Columbia Southern U (AL)
DeSales U (PA)
Embry-Riddle Aeronautical U–Daytona (FL)
Excelsior Coll (NY)
Keiser U, Fort Lauderdale (FL)
Mercy Coll (NY)
National U (CA)
Northcentral U (CA)
Northeastern State U (OK)
Oakland U (MI)
Regent U (VA)
Saint Leo U (FL)
Slippery Rock U of Pennsylvania (PA)
State U of New York Coll of Technology at Canton (NY)
Tulane U (LA)
U at Albany, State U of New York (NY)
The U of Arizona (AZ)
U of Management and Technology (VA)
U of New Hampshire (NH)
Waldorf U (IA)
Wichita State U (KS)

HOMELAND SECURITY, LAW ENFORCEMENT, FIREFIGHTING AND PROTECTIVE SERVICES RELATED
Anderson U (SC)
Chestnut Hill Coll (PA)
Clayton State U (GA)
Eastern Michigan U (MI)
Florida Atlantic U (FL)
Idaho State U (ID)
Madonna U (MI)
Marian U (WI)
Massachusetts Maritime Acad (MA)
Miami Dade Coll (FL)
Neumann U (PA)
North Dakota State U (ND)
Northwestern Oklahoma State U (OK)
Oklahoma State U–Oklahoma City (OK)
Penn State Altoona (PA)
Penn State Berks (PA)
Point Park U (PA)
Roberts Wesleyan Coll (NY)
Thomas Edison State U (NJ)
Tiffin U (OH)

The U of West Alabama (AL)
Virginia Commonwealth U (VA)

HOMELAND SECURITY RELATED
Rivier U (NH)

HORSE HUSBANDRY/EQUINE SCIENCE AND MANAGEMENT
Averett U (VA)
Becker Coll (MA)
Delaware Valley U (PA)
Feather River Coll (CA)
Saint Mary-of-the-Woods Coll (IN)
Tiffin U (OH)
U of Guelph (ON, Canada)
U of Kentucky (KY)
U of Minnesota, Crookston (MN)
U of New Hampshire (NH)
Vermont Tech Coll (VT)
William Woods U (MO)

HORTICULTURAL SCIENCE
Auburn U (AL)
Brigham Young U–Idaho (ID)
Clemson U (SC)
Coll of the Ozarks (MO)
Colorado State U (CO)
Delaware Valley U (PA)
Iowa State U of Science and Technology (IA)
Kansas State U (KS)
Michigan State U (MI)
Mississippi State U (MS)
Missouri State U (MO)
New Mexico State U (NM)
North Carolina State U (NC)
Northwest Missouri State U (MO)
Oklahoma State U (OK)
Oregon State U (OR)
Penn State Abington (PA)
Penn State Altoona (PA)
Penn State Beaver (PA)
Penn State Berks (PA)
Penn State Brandywine (PA)
Penn State DuBois (PA)
Penn State Erie, The Behrend Coll (PA)
Penn State Fayette, The Eberly Campus (PA)
Penn State Greater Allegheny (PA)
Penn State Hazleton (PA)
Penn State Lehigh Valley (PA)
Penn State Mont Alto (PA)
Penn State New Kensington (PA)
Penn State Schuylkill (PA)
Penn State Shenango (PA)
Penn State Wilkes-Barre (PA)
Penn State Worthington Scranton (PA)
Penn State York (PA)
Purdue U (IN)
Sam Houston State U (TX)
Stephen F. Austin State U (TX)
Temple U (PA)
Tennessee Technological U (TN)
U of Cincinnati (OH)
U of Florida (FL)
U of Georgia (GA)
U of Idaho (ID)
U of Minnesota, Crookston (MN)
U of Nebraska–Lincoln (NE)
U of Saskatchewan (SK, Canada)
U of Vermont (VT)
U of Wisconsin–Madison (WI)
U of Wisconsin–Platteville (WI)
U of Wisconsin–River Falls (WI)
Utah State U (UT)
Virginia Polytechnic Inst and State U (VA)
Washington State U (WA)
Washington State U–Tri-Cities (WA)

HOSPITAL AND HEALTH-CARE FACILITIES ADMINISTRATION
American Intl Coll (MA)
Avila U (MO)
Black Hills State U (SD)
Champlain Coll (VT)
Clayton State U (GA)
Governors State U (IL)
Ithaca Coll (NY)
Metropolitan Coll of New York (NY)
Newman U (KS)
St. Joseph's Coll, Long Island Campus (NY)
St. Joseph's Coll, New York (NY)

Saint Joseph's U (PA)
Tiffin U (OH)
The U of Alabama (AL)
U of Oklahoma (OK)
U of St. Francis (IL)
U of South Dakota (SD)
The U of Toledo (OH)
U of Wisconsin–Milwaukee (WI)
Youngstown State U (OH)

HOSPITALITY ADMINISTRATION
American Public U System (WV)
Appalachian State U (NC)
Arkansas Tech U (AR)
Ashland U (OH)
Auburn U (AL)
Ball State U (IN)
Beacon Coll (FL)
Bethune-Cookman U (FL)
Boston U (MA)
Bowling Green State U (OH)
Buffalo State Coll, State U of New York (NY)
California State Polytechnic U, Pomona (CA)
Cardinal Stritch U (WI)
Central Connecticut State U (CT)
Central Michigan U (MI)
Coll of Charleston (SC)
Coll of Coastal Georgia (GA)
Coll of the Ozarks (MO)
Colorado Mesa U (CO)
Columbia Coll (SC)
Columbia Southern U (AL)
Concordia U, St. Paul (MN)
Concord U (WV)
Dallas Baptist U (TX)
Delaware State U (DE)
DePaul U (IL)
East Carolina U (NC)
Eastern Michigan U (MI)
East Stroudsburg U of Pennsylvania (PA)
ECPI U, Virginia Beach (VA)
Endicott Coll (MA)
Fairleigh Dickinson U, Florham Campus (NJ)
Fairleigh Dickinson U, Metropolitan Campus (NJ)
Ferris State U (MI)
Fisher Coll (MA)
Flagler Coll (FL)
Florida Atlantic U (FL)
Florida Intl U (FL)
Georgia State U (GA)
Grand Valley State U (MI)
Granite State Coll (NH)
Husson U (ME)
Indiana U Kokomo (IN)
Indiana U of Pennsylvania (PA)
Iowa State U of Science and Technology (IA)
James Madison U (VA)
Kansas State U (KS)
Kent State U (OH)
Kent State U at Ashtabula (OH)
Lasell Coll (MA)
Lebanese American U (Lebanon)
Lynn U (FL)
Madonna U (MI)
Marylhurst U (OR)
Marywood U (PA)
Mercyhurst U (PA)
Metropolitan State U of Denver (CO)
Michigan State U (MI)
Missouri State U (MO)
Montclair State U (NJ)
New Mexico State U (NM)
Nichols Coll (MA)
North Carolina Central U (NC)
North Dakota State U (ND)
Northern Arizona U (AZ)
Northern Michigan U (MI)
Northern Vermont U–Lyndon (VT)
Northwestern State U of Louisiana (LA)
Oklahoma State U (OK)
Oregon State U (OR)
Purdue U Northwest (IN)
Robert Morris U (PA)
Rochester Inst of Technology (NY)
Roosevelt U (IL)
Rutgers U–Camden (NJ)
St. John's U (NY)

St. Joseph's Coll, Long Island Campus (NY)
St. Joseph's Coll, New York (NY)
Saint Leo U (FL)
St. Thomas U (FL)
San Diego State U (CA)
San Francisco State U (CA)
Seton Hill U (PA)
Southeastern U (FL)
Southern Utah U (UT)
State U of New York Coll of Technology at Delhi (NY)
Stephen F. Austin State U (TX)
Stockton U (NJ)
Sullivan U (KY)
Syracuse U (NY)
Temple U (PA)
Tiffin U (OH)
The U of Alabama (AL)
U of Central Florida (FL)
U of Cincinnati (OH)
U of Denver (CO)
The U of Findlay (OH)
U of Kentucky (KY)
U of Massachusetts Amherst (MA)
U of Memphis (TN)
U of Nebraska–Lincoln (NE)
U of Nevada, Las Vegas (NV)
U of New Hampshire (NH)
U of New Haven (CT)
U of New Orleans (LA)
The U of North Carolina at Greensboro (NC)
U of North Texas (TX)
U of Pittsburgh at Bradford (PA)
U of San Francisco (CA)
U of South Alabama (AL)
U of South Carolina (SC)
U of South Florida Sarasota-Manatee (FL)
U of the Potomac (DC)
U of the Virgin Islands (VI)
U of Wisconsin–Stout (WI)
Utah Valley U (UT)
Washington State U (WA)
Washington State U–Global Campus (WA)
Washington State U–Tri-Cities (WA)
Washington State U–Vancouver (WA)
Webber Intl U (FL)
Western Illinois U (IL)
Western Kentucky U (KY)
West Virginia U (WV)
York Coll of Pennsylvania (PA)
Youngstown State U (OH)

HOSPITALITY ADMINISTRATION RELATED
Auburn U (AL)
California State U, Dominguez Hills (CA)
California State U, East Bay (CA)
California State U, Fullerton (CA)
Delaware State U (DE)
DEREE - The American Coll of Greece (Greece)
Florida State U (FL)
Penn State Abington (PA)
Penn State Altoona (PA)
Penn State Beaver (PA)
Penn State Berks (PA)
Penn State Brandywine (PA)
Penn State DuBois (PA)
Penn State Erie, The Behrend Coll (PA)
Penn State Fayette, The Eberly Campus (PA)
Penn State Greater Allegheny (PA)
Penn State Hazleton (PA)
Penn State Lehigh Valley (PA)
Penn State Mont Alto (PA)
Penn State New Kensington (PA)
Penn State Schuylkill (PA)
Penn State Shenango (PA)
Penn State U Park (PA)
Penn State Wilkes-Barre (PA)
Penn State Worthington Scranton (PA)
Penn State York (PA)
Purdue U Northwest (IN)
Southern Illinois U Carbondale (IL)
U of Central Florida (FL)
U of Nevada, Las Vegas (NV)
U of Southern Mississippi (MS)
Widener U (PA)

HOSPITALITY AND RECREATION MARKETING
Ferris State U (MI)
Husson U (ME)
Rochester Inst of Technology (NY)
Saint Joseph's U (PA)

HOTEL/MOTEL ADMINISTRATION
Ashland U (OH)
Auburn U (AL)
Bethune-Cookman U (FL)
Buffalo State Coll, State U of New York (NY)
California State U, Long Beach (CA)
Concord U (WV)
Cornell U (NY)
Drexel U (PA)
Ferris State U (MI)
Grand Valley State U (MI)
Hampton U (VA)
Husson U (ME)
Inter American U of Puerto Rico, Aguadilla Campus (PR)
Kansas State U (KS)
Metropolitan State U of Denver (CO)
New York U (NY)
The Ohio State U (OH)
Pace U (NY)
Purdue U (IN)
Purdue U Northwest (IN)
Rochester Inst of Technology (NY)
State U of New York at Plattsburgh (NY)
State U of New York Coll of Technology at Delhi (NY)
Texas Tech U (TX)
U of Central Missouri (MO)
U of Denver (CO)
U of Guelph (ON, Canada)
U of Houston (TX)
U of Maine at Machias (ME)
U of Maryland Eastern Shore (MD)
U of Memphis (TN)
U of Missouri (MO)
U of New Haven (CT)
U of Southern Mississippi (MS)
The U of Tennessee (TN)
Virginia Polytechnic Inst and State U (VA)
Washington State U (WA)
Widener U (PA)

HOTEL, MOTEL, AND RESTAURANT MANAGEMENT
Endicott Coll (MA)
New York Inst of Technology (NY)
Niagara U (NY)

HOUSING AND HUMAN ENVIRONMENTS
Harding U (AR)
Missouri State U (MO)
Ohio U (OH)
Oklahoma State U (OK)
The U of Akron (OH)
U of Georgia (GA)
U of Minnesota, Twin Cities Campus (MN)
U of Missouri (MO)
Utah State U (UT)

HOUSING AND HUMAN ENVIRONMENTS RELATED
Bob Jones U (SC)

HUMAN BIOLOGY
Baker U (KS)
Biola U (CA)
Hamline U (MN)
Indiana U–Purdue U Indianapolis (IN)
Johns Hopkins U (MD)
Pitzer Coll (CA)
Scripps Coll (CA)
U of California, Irvine (CA)
U of California, Los Angeles (CA)
U of California, San Diego (CA)
The U of Kansas (KS)
U of Saint Mary (KS)
U of Southern California (CA)

HUMAN COMPUTER INTERACTION
DigiPen Inst of Technology (WA)
Milwaukee School of Eng (WI)
Savannah Coll of Art and Design (GA)

Stony Brook U, State U of New York (NY)
U of Guelph (ON, Canada)
U of Wisconsin–Stevens Point (WI)
Whitworth U (WA)

HUMAN DEVELOPMENT AND FAMILY STUDIES
Abilene Christian U (TX)
Antioch U Midwest (OH)
Auburn U (AL)
Baylor U (TX)
Bowling Green State U (OH)
Brigham Young U (UT)
California State U, East Bay (CA)
California State U, Long Beach (CA)
California State U, San Bernardino (CA)
California State U, San Marcos (CA)
Colorado State U (CO)
Columbia Coll (SC)
Concordia U, St. Paul (MN)
Connecticut Coll (CT)
Cornell U (NY)
Eckerd Coll (FL)
George Mason U (VA)
Georgia Southern U (GA)
Hope Intl U (CA)
Howard Payne U (TX)
Illinois State U (IL)
Indiana State U (IN)
Indiana U of Pennsylvania (PA)
Kansas State U (KS)
Kent State U (OH)
Kent State U at Salem (OH)
Kent State U at Stark (OH)
Kentucky State U (KY)
Lamar U (TX)
Lesley U (MA)
Liberty U (VA)
Miami U (OH)
Michigan State U (MI)
Mississippi State U (MS)
Missouri State U (MO)
New Mexico State U (NM)
Niagara U (NY)
North Dakota State U (ND)
Northern Illinois U (IL)
Nova Southeastern U (FL)
The Ohio State U (OH)
Ohio U (OH)
Oklahoma State U (OK)
Oregon State U (OR)
Penn State Abington (PA)
Penn State Altoona (PA)
Penn State Beaver (PA)
Penn State Berks (PA)
Penn State Brandywine (PA)
Penn State DuBois (PA)
Penn State Erie, The Behrend Coll (PA)
Penn State Fayette, The Eberly Campus (PA)
Penn State Greater Allegheny (PA)
Penn State Harrisburg (PA)
Penn State Hazleton (PA)
Penn State Lehigh Valley (PA)
Penn State Mont Alto (PA)
Penn State New Kensington (PA)
Penn State Schuylkill (PA)
Penn State Shenango (PA)
Penn State U Park (PA)
Penn State Wilkes-Barre (PA)
Penn State Worthington Scranton (PA)
Penn State York (PA)
Purdue U (IN)
Purdue U Northwest (IN)
Rockford U (IL)
St. Joseph's Coll, Long Island Campus (NY)
St. Joseph's Coll, New York (NY)
Samford U (AL)
Seattle Pacific U (WA)
State U of New York at Oswego (NY)
State U of New York at Plattsburgh (NY)
Syracuse U (NY)
Temple U (PA)
Texas A&M U–Kingsville (TX)
Texas State U (TX)
Texas Tech U (TX)
Texas Woman's U (TX)

U at Albany, State U of New York (NY)
The U of Alabama (AL)
The U of Arizona (AZ)
U of Arkansas (AR)
U of California, Davis (CA)
U of California, San Diego (CA)
U of Central Oklahoma (OK)
U of Colorado Denver (CO)
U of Georgia (GA)
U of Guelph (ON, Canada)
U of Houston (TX)
U of Idaho (ID)
U of Kentucky (KY)
U of Maine (ME)
U of Memphis (TN)
U of Missouri (MO)
U of Nevada, Reno (NV)
U of New Hampshire (NH)
U of New Mexico (NM)
The U of North Carolina at Greensboro (NC)
U of North Texas (TX)
U of Rhode Island (RI)
U of St. Thomas (MN)
The U of Tennessee (TN)
The U of Texas at Austin (TX)
The U of Texas of the Permian Basin (TX)
U of Utah (UT)
U of Vermont (VT)
U of Waterloo (ON, Canada)
U of Wisconsin–Madison (WI)
Utah State U (UT)
Vanguard U of Southern California (CA)
Virginia Polytechnic Inst and State U (VA)
Warner Pacific Coll (OR)
Washington State U (WA)
Washington State U–Global Campus (WA)
Washington State U–Vancouver (WA)
Westminster Coll (PA)
Youngstown State U (OH)

HUMAN DEVELOPMENT AND FAMILY STUDIES RELATED
Auburn U (AL)
Binghamton U, State U of New York (NY)
Bowling Green State U (OH)
Clemson U (SC)
Harding U (AR)
Hope Intl U (CA)
LaGrange Coll (GA)
Merrimack Coll (MA)
Rowan U (NJ)
The U of Alabama (AL)
U of Valley Forge (PA)

HUMANITIES
Adelphi U (NY)
Antioch U Midwest (OH)
Athens State U (AL)
Baptist U of the Americas (TX)
Bard Coll (NY)
Baylor U (TX)
Belhaven U (MS)
Bemidji State U (MN)
Benedictine U (IL)
Bennington Coll (VT)
Bethel Coll (IN)
Biola U (CA)
Bob Jones U (SC)
Brigham Young U–Idaho (ID)
Brock U (ON, Canada)
Bucknell U (PA)
Buffalo State Coll, State U of New York (NY)
California State Polytechnic U, Pomona (CA)
California State U, Monterey Bay (CA)
California State U, Northridge (CA)
California State U, Sacramento (CA)
California State U, San Bernardino (CA)
Chaminade U of Honolulu (HI)
Charleston Southern U (SC)
Chowan U (NC)
Clarkson U (NY)
Coastal Carolina U (SC)
Coll of Saint Mary (NE)
The Coll of St. Scholastica (MN)
Concordia U (QC, Canada)

Concordia U Irvine (CA)
Concordia U Wisconsin (WI)
Corban U (OR)
Cornerstone U (MI)
Dominican Coll (NY)
Dominican U of California (CA)
Drexel U (PA)
Eastern Washington U (WA)
Eckerd Coll (FL)
Emory U (GA)
The Evergreen State Coll (WA)
Excelsior Coll (NY)
Fairleigh Dickinson U, Florham Campus (NJ)
Fairleigh Dickinson U, Metropolitan Campus (NJ)
Felician U (NJ)
Florida Inst of Technology (FL)
Florida Southern Coll (FL)
Florida State U (FL)
Fort Lewis Coll (CO)
Franciscan Missionaries of Our Lady U (LA)
The George Washington U (DC)
Harding U (AR)
Harrison Middleton U (AZ)
Holy Family U (PA)
Holy Names U (CA)
Hunter Coll of the City U of New York (NY)
Indiana U East (IN)
Indiana U Kokomo (IN)
Inter American U of Puerto Rico, Metropolitan Campus (PR)
Jacksonville U (FL)
John Cabot U (Italy)
John Carroll U (OH)
John Jay Coll of Criminal Justice of the City U of New York (NY)
John Paul the Great Catholic U (CA)
Johnson U Florida (FL)
Juniata Coll (PA)
Kansas State U (KS)
Kent State U (OH)
The King's Coll (NY)
Lasell Coll (MA)
Lawrence Technological U (MI)
Lee U (TN)
Lesley U (MA)
Lincoln Memorial U (TN)
Long Island U–LIU Brooklyn (NY)
Loyola Marymount U (CA)
Lubbock Christian U (TX)
Maranatha Baptist U (WI)
Marlboro Coll (VT)
Marshall U (WV)
Marymount Manhattan Coll (NY)
Michigan State U (MI)
Milligan Coll (TN)
Montclair State U (NJ)
Muskingum U (OH)
New Coll of Florida (FL)
New York U (NY)
North Central Coll (IL)
Northland Coll (WI)
Northwestern Coll (IA)
Northwestern U (IL)
Northwest Nazarene U (ID)
Nova Southeastern U (FL)
Oakland City U (IN)
The Ohio State U (OH)
Ohio Wesleyan U (OH)
Oklahoma Baptist U (OK)
Penn State Harrisburg (PA)
Point U (GA)
Portland State U (OR)
Providence Coll (RI)
Purdue U (IN)
Roberts Wesleyan Coll (NY)
Rockford U (IL)
Roger Williams U (RI)
Rollins Coll (FL)
The Sage Colls (NY)
St. Andrews U (NC)
St. Lawrence U (NY)
Saint Mary-of-the-Woods Coll (IN)
St. Norbert Coll (WI)
Saint Peter's U (NJ)
St. Thomas Aquinas Coll (NY)
Sam Houston State U (TX)
San Diego State U (CA)
San Francisco State U (CA)
Scripps Coll (CA)
Seattle U (WA)
Sierra Nevada Coll (NV)
Simon Fraser U (BC, Canada)

State U of New York Coll at Old Westbury (NY)
Stevens Inst of Technology (NJ)
Thomas Edison State U (NJ)
Thomas U (GA)
Trent U (ON, Canada)
Trinity U (TX)
Union Coll (NY)
United States Military Acad (NY)
U at Buffalo, the State U of New York (NY)
The U of Akron (OH)
U of Bridgeport (CT)
U of California, Irvine (CA)
U of California, Riverside (CA)
U of Central Florida (FL)
U of Central Oklahoma (OK)
U of Chicago (IL)
U of Cincinnati (OH)
U of Colorado Boulder (CO)
U of Houston–Clear Lake (TX)
U of Houston–Downtown (TX)
The U of Kansas (KS)
U of Louisville (KY)
U of Massachusetts Amherst (MA)
U of Michigan (MI)
U of Michigan–Dearborn (MI)
U of Mobile (AL)
U of New Hampshire (NH)
U of New Mexico (NM)
U of Northern Iowa (IA)
U of Oklahoma (OK)
U of Oregon (OR)
U of Pennsylvania (PA)
U of Pittsburgh (PA)
U of Pittsburgh at Bradford (PA)
U of Pittsburgh at Greensburg (PA)
U of Puerto Rico–Humacao (PR)
U of Regina (SK, Canada)
U of Richmond (VA)
U of San Diego (CA)
U of Southern Maine (ME)
The U of Tennessee at Chattanooga (TN)
The U of Texas at Austin (TX)
The U of Texas at San Antonio (TX)
The U of Texas of the Permian Basin (TX)
U of the Virgin Islands (VI)
U of Toronto (ON, Canada)
U of Washington (WA)
U of Washington, Bothell (WA)
U of Washington, Tacoma (WA)
U of Wyoming (WY)
Ursuline Coll (OH)
Valparaiso U (IN)
Villanova U (PA)
Virginia Wesleyan U (VA)
Wabash Coll (IN)
Washington Coll (MD)
Washington State U (WA)
Washington State U–Global Campus (WA)
Washington State U–Tri-Cities (WA)
Washington State U–Vancouver (WA)
Washington U in St. Louis (MO)
Webster U (MO)
Welch Coll (TN)
Wesleyan U (CT)
Western Oregon U (OR)
Western Washington U (WA)
Widener U (PA)
Willamette U (OR)
Wofford Coll (SC)
Worcester Polytechnic Inst (MA)

HUMAN/MEDICAL GENETICS
American Intl Coll (MA)

HUMAN NUTRITION
Baylor U (TX)
Bridgewater Coll (VA)
Case Western Reserve U (OH)
Cedar Crest Coll (PA)
Iowa State U of Science and Technology (IA)
Kansas State U (KS)
Kent State U (OH)
Metropolitan State U of Denver (CO)
The Ohio State U (OH)
Penn State Abington (PA)
Penn State Altoona (PA)
Penn State Beaver (PA)
Penn State Berks (PA)

Penn State Brandywine (PA)
Penn State DuBois (PA)
Penn State Erie, The Behrend Coll (PA)
Penn State Fayette, The Eberly Campus (PA)
Penn State Greater Allegheny (PA)
Penn State Hazleton (PA)
Penn State Lehigh Valley (PA)
Penn State Mont Alto (PA)
Penn State New Kensington (PA)
Penn State Schuylkill (PA)
Penn State Shenango (PA)
Penn State Wilkes-Barre (PA)
Penn State Worthington Scranton (PA)
Penn State York (PA)
Rochester Inst of Technology (NY)
Southern Utah U (UT)
Syracuse U (NY)
The U of Alabama (AL)
U of Dayton (OH)
U of Guelph (ON, Canada)
U of Houston (TX)
U of Kentucky (KY)
U of New England (ME)
Washington State U (WA)
Weber State U (UT)

HUMAN RESOURCES DEVELOPMENT
Blackburn Coll (IL)
Bryant U (RI)
Hawai‘i Pacific U (HI)
Limestone Coll (SC)
Nichols Coll (MA)
Northern Kentucky U (KY)
Oakland U (MI)
Southwestern Coll (KS)
Texas A&M U (TX)
U of Arkansas (AR)
U of Houston (TX)
U of Wisconsin–Milwaukee (WI)

HUMAN RESOURCES MANAGEMENT
Anderson U (SC)
Antioch U Midwest (OH)
Athabasca U (AB, Canada)
Athens State U (AL)
Auburn U (AL)
Auburn U at Montgomery (AL)
Avila U (MO)
Baldwin Wallace U (OH)
Ball State U (IN)
Baylor U (TX)
Belhaven U (MS)
Black Hills State U (SD)
Boston Coll (MA)
Bowling Green State U (OH)
Bradley U (IL)
Brenau U (GA)
Brescia U (KY)
Brigham Young U (UT)
Brock U (ON, Canada)
Bryant U (RI)
Buena Vista U (IA)
California State U, Long Beach (CA)
Canisius Coll (NY)
Carroll U (WI)
The Catholic U of America (DC)
Central Michigan U (MI)
Chestnut Hill Coll (PA)
The Coll of Saint Rose (NY)
Columbia Coll (MO)
Columbia Southern U (AL)
Concordia U (QC, Canada)
Concordia U, St. Paul (MN)
Converse Coll (SC)
Cornell Coll (IA)
Davenport U, Grand Rapids (MI)
Delaware State U (DE)
DeSales U (PA)
Dickinson State U (ND)
East Central U (OK)
Eastern Washington U (WA)
Ferris State U (MI)
Fisher Coll (MA)
Florida Intl U (FL)
Florida State U (FL)
Friends U (KS)
The George Washington U (DC)
Georgia Southwestern State U (GA)
Golden Gate U (CA)
Granite State Coll (NH)
Gwynedd Mercy U (PA)

HEC Montreal (QC, Canada)
Holy Family U (PA)
Holy Names U (CA)
Idaho State U (ID)
Immaculata U (PA)
Indiana State U (IN)
Indiana U of Pennsylvania (PA)
Inter American U of Puerto Rico, Aguadilla Campus (PR)
Inter American U of Puerto Rico, Barranquitas Campus (PR)
Inter American U of Puerto Rico, Bayamón Campus (PR)
Inter American U of Puerto Rico, Fajardo Campus (PR)
Inter American U of Puerto Rico, Metropolitan Campus (PR)
Inter American U of Puerto Rico, San Germán Campus (PR)
John Carroll U (OH)
Juniata Coll (PA)
Keiser U, Fort Lauderdale (FL)
Kent State U (OH)
King's Coll (PA)
Lamar U (TX)
La Salle U (PA)
La Sierra U (CA)
Le Moyne Coll (NY)
Lewis U (IL)
Limestone Coll (SC)
Lindenwood U (MO)
Lipscomb U (TN)
Loyola U Chicago (IL)
Lynchburg Coll (VA)
Madonna U (MI)
Mansfield U of Pennsylvania (PA)
Marian U (WI)
Marquette U (WI)
Marymount Manhattan Coll (NY)
Maryville Coll (TN)
McKendree U (IL)
Mercer U, Macon (GA)
Mercyhurst U (PA)
Merrimack Coll (MA)
Michigan State U (MI)
MidAmerica Nazarene U (KS)
Mount Mercy U (IA)
Nazareth Coll of Rochester (NY)
New York Inst of Technology (NY)
Nichols Coll (MA)
North Central Coll (IL)
Northcentral U (CA)
Oakland U (MI)
The Ohio State U (OH)
Ohio U (OH)
Otterbein U (OH)
Our Lady of the Lake U (TX)
Pace U (NY)
Pace U, Pleasantville Campus (NY)
Peirce Coll (PA)
Point Park U (PA)
Portland State U (OR)
Purdue U Northwest (IN)
Quinnipiac U (CT)
Rasmussen Coll Bloomington (MN)
Rasmussen Coll Brooklyn Park (MN)
Rasmussen Coll Eagan (MN)
Rasmussen Coll Mankato (MN)
Rasmussen Coll New Port Richey (FL)
Rasmussen Coll Ocala (FL)
Regent U (VA)
Regis U (CO)
Rhode Island Coll (RI)
Roberts Wesleyan Coll (NY)
Roosevelt U (IL)
Rowan U (NJ)
Rutgers U–New Brunswick (NJ)
Saint Francis U (PA)
St. Joseph's Coll, Long Island Campus (NY)
St. Joseph's Coll, New York (NY)
Saint Joseph's U (PA)
Saint Mary-of-the-Woods Coll (IN)
Saint Mary's U of Minnesota (MN)
Sam Houston State U (TX)
San Diego State U (CA)
Seton Hill U (PA)
Silver Lake Coll of the Holy Family (WI)
Southern Adventist U (TN)
Southwestern Assemblies of God U (TX)
State U of New York at Oswego (NY)

State U of New York Coll of Technology at Alfred (NY)
State U of New York Coll of Technology at Delhi (NY)
Stephen F. Austin State U (TX)
Sullivan U (KY)
Tarleton State U (TX)
Temple U (PA)
Tennessee Wesleyan U (TN)
Texas A&M U–Central Texas (TX)
Texas A&M U–Texarkana (TX)
Texas Woman's U (TX)
Thomas Edison State U (NJ)
Tiffin U (OH)
Trinity Christian Coll (IL)
The U of Akron (OH)
The U of Arizona (AZ)
U of Central Oklahoma (OK)
U of Cincinnati (OH)
U of Dubuque (IA)
The U of Findlay (OH)
U of Guelph (ON, Canada)
U of Hawaii at Manoa (HI)
U of Idaho (ID)
U of Maryland U Coll (MD)
U of Miami (FL)
U of Michigan–Dearborn (MI)
U of Michigan–Flint (MI)
U of Minnesota, Duluth (MN)
U of Minnesota, Twin Cities Campus (MN)
The U of North Carolina at Chapel Hill (NC)
U of North Dakota (ND)
U of Pennsylvania (PA)
U of Puerto Rico–Humacao (PR)
U of Regina (SK, Canada)
U of St. Francis (IL)
U of St. Thomas (MN)
U of Saskatchewan (SK, Canada)
The U of Scranton (PA)
U of Southern Mississippi (MS)
The U of Tennessee (TN)
The U of Tennessee at Martin (TN)
The U of Texas at San Antonio (TX)
U of the Incarnate Word (TX)
The U of Toledo (OH)
U of Valley Forge (PA)
U of Washington (WA)
U of Waterloo (ON, Canada)
U of Wisconsin–Whitewater (WI)
Upper Iowa U (IA)
Ursuline Coll (OH)
Utah State U (UT)
Washington State U (WA)
Washington U in St. Louis (MO)
Weber State U (UT)
Webster U (MO)
Western Illinois U (IL)
Western Michigan U (MI)
Westminster Coll (PA)
Wichita State U (KS)
William Penn U (IA)
Wilmington U (DE)
Winona State U (MN)
Wright State U (OH)
Wright State U–Lake Campus (OH)
Youngstown State U (OH)

HUMAN RESOURCES MANAGEMENT AND SERVICES RELATED
Carlow U (PA)
Concordia U of Edmonton (AB, Canada)
Grand Valley State U (MI)
Immaculata U (PA)
Michigan State U (MI)
Oakland City U (IN)
Stevens Inst of Technology (NJ)
Trine U (IN)
U of Hartford (CT)
U of Mount Union (OH)
U of Oklahoma (OK)
U of Pittsburgh (PA)
Widener U (PA)

HUMAN SERVICES
American Baptist Coll (TN)
Anderson U (SC)
Antioch U Midwest (OH)
Beacon Coll (FL)
Bethel U (TN)
Black Hills State U (SD)
California State U, Dominguez Hills (CA)
California State U, Fullerton (CA)
California State U, Monterey Bay (CA)

California State U, San Bernardino (CA)
Calumet Coll of Saint Joseph (IN)
Cardinal Stritch U (WI)
Carson-Newman U (TN)
Cazenovia Coll (NY)
Chestnut Hill Coll (PA)
Columbia Coll (MO)
Doane U (NE)
Dominican U (IL)
East Tennessee State U (TN)
Elon U (NC)
Emmanuel Coll (MA)
Fisher Coll (MA)
Fitchburg State U (MA)
Geneva Coll (PA)
The George Washington U (DC)
Gordon State Coll (GA)
Grand View U (IA)
Granite State Coll (NH)
Gwynedd Mercy U (PA)
Hardin-Simmons U (TX)
Hawai'i Pacific U (HI)
Hilbert Coll (NY)
Holy Names U (CA)
Indiana Tech (IN)
Judson U (IL)
Kennesaw State U (GA)
Lasell Coll (MA)
Lenoir-Rhyne U (NC)
Lesley U (MA)
LeTourneau U (TX)
Liberty U (VA)
Lincoln Coll (IL)
Lincoln Coll of New England, Southington (CT)
Lincoln U (PA)
Lindsey Wilson Coll (KY)
Loyola U Chicago (IL)
Marian U (WI)
Mercer U, Macon (GA)
Metropolitan State U of Denver (CO)
Missouri Baptist U (MO)
Missouri Valley Coll (MO)
Mount Marty Coll (SD)
Mount Saint Mary Coll (NY)
Northeastern U (MA)
Northern Illinois U (IL)
Notre Dame de Namur U (CA)
Nova Southeastern U (FL)
Ottawa U (KS)
Pfeiffer U (NC)
Post U (CT)
Quinnipiac U (CT)
St. Joseph's Coll, Long Island Campus (NY)
St. Joseph's Coll, New York (NY)
Saint Mary-of-the-Woods Coll (IN)
Saint Mary's U of Minnesota (MN)
Seton Hill U (PA)
Simpson Coll (IA)
Southeastern U (FL)
Southern Vermont Coll (VT)
Southwest Baptist U (MO)
Southwestern Assemblies of God U (TX)
Spelman Coll (GA)
State U of New York Coll at Cortland (NY)
Syracuse U (NY)
Tennessee Wesleyan U (TN)
Texas A&M U–Kingsville (TX)
Thomas Edison State U (NJ)
Towson U (MD)
U of Bridgeport (CT)
U of Hartford (CT)
U of Maine at Machias (ME)
U of Massachusetts Boston (MA)
U of Minnesota, Morris (MN)
U of Nevada, Las Vegas (NV)
U of North Georgia (GA)
U of North Texas (TX)
U of Oregon (OR)
U of Providence (MT)
The U of Scranton (PA)
Upper Iowa U (IA)
Valley City State U (ND)
Virginia Wesleyan U (VA)
Wayland Baptist U (TX)
Waynesburg U (PA)
Western Washington U (WA)
William Penn U (IA)
Wisconsin Lutheran Coll (WI)

HYDROLOGY AND WATER RESOURCES SCIENCE
The Coll at Brockport, State U of New York (NY)
Northland Coll (WI)
Rensselaer Polytechnic Inst (NY)
State U of New York Coll at Oneonta (NY)
Tarleton State U (TX)
The U of Arizona (AZ)
U of California, Davis (CA)
U of California, Santa Barbara (CA)
U of New Hampshire (NH)
The U of Texas at Austin (TX)
U of Toronto (ON, Canada)
U of Wisconsin–Stevens Point (WI)
Western Michigan U (MI)

ILLUSTRATION
Academy of Art U (CA)
Alberta Coll of Art & Design (AB, Canada)
American Acad of Art (IL)
Arcadia U (PA)
ArtCenter Coll of Design (CA)
Boise State U (ID)
Brigham Young U (UT)
California Coll of the Arts (CA)
California State U, Long Beach (CA)
Columbia Coll Chicago (IL)
Cornish Coll of the Arts (WA)
Eugene Lang Coll of Liberal Arts (NY)
Fashion Inst of Technology (NY)
Ferris State U (MI)
Indiana Wesleyan U (IN)
John Brown U (AR)
Kansas City Art Inst (MO)
Laguna Coll of Art & Design (CA)
Maryland Inst Coll of Art (MD)
Marywood U (PA)
Minneapolis Coll of Art and Design (MN)
New Hampshire Inst of Art (NH)
Northern Michigan U (MI)
Nossi Coll of Art (TN)
Pacific Northwest Coll of Art (OR)
Paier Coll of Art, Inc. (CT)
Paris Coll of Art (France)
Parsons School of Design (NY)
Pennsylvania Coll of Art & Design (PA)
Pratt Inst (NY)
Rhode Island School of Design (RI)
Ringling Coll of Art and Design (FL)
Rochester Inst of Technology (NY)
St. John's U (NY)
Savannah Coll of Art and Design (GA)
School of Visual Arts (NY)
Syracuse U (NY)
U of Hartford (CT)
The U of Kansas (KS)
U of Massachusetts Dartmouth (MA)
U of Michigan (MI)
U of New Haven (CT)
U of San Francisco (CA)
The U of the Arts (PA)
Virginia Commonwealth U (VA)
Washington U in St. Louis (MO)

INDUSTRIAL AND ORGANIZATIONAL PSYCHOLOGY
Avila U (MO)
Baldwin Wallace U (OH)
Baruch Coll of the City U of New York (NY)
Bridgewater State U (MA)
Canisius Coll (NY)
Concordia U Irvine (CA)
Excelsior Coll (NY)
Fitchburg State U (MA)
Fort Lewis Coll (CO)
Holy Family U (PA)
Ithaca Coll (NY)
Maryville U of Saint Louis (MO)
Marywood U (PA)
Middle Tennessee State U (TN)
Morningside Coll (IA)
Multnomah U (OR)
Northwest Missouri State U (MO)
Palo Alto U (CA)
St. Joseph's Coll, Long Island Campus (NY)
St. Joseph's Coll, New York (NY)

Saint Mary's Coll of California (CA)
Southern Adventist U (TN)
United States Military Acad (NY)
The U of Tennessee at Martin (TN)
Washington U in St. Louis (MO)

INDUSTRIAL AND PHYSICAL PHARMACY AND COSMETIC SCIENCES
The U of Toledo (OH)

INDUSTRIAL AND PRODUCT DESIGN
Academy of Art U (CA)
Appalachian State U (NC)
Arizona State U at the Tempe campus (AZ)
ArtCenter Coll of Design (CA)
Auburn U (AL)
California Coll of the Arts (CA)
California State U, Long Beach (CA)
Cedarville U (OH)
Clemson U (SC)
Drexel U (PA)
Escuela de Artes Plasticas y Diseño de Puerto Rico (PR)
Eugene Lang Coll of Liberal Arts (NY)
Fashion Inst of Technology (NY)
Ferris State U (MI)
FIDM/Fashion Inst of Design & Merchandising, Los Angeles Campus (CA)
Georgia Inst of Technology (GA)
Iowa State U of Science and Technology (IA)
Kean U (NJ)
Lawrence Technological U (MI)
Lebanon Valley Coll (PA)
Maryland Inst Coll of Art (MD)
Massachusetts Coll of Art and Design (MA)
Metropolitan State U of Denver (CO)
Montclair State U (NJ)
New Jersey Inst of Technology (NJ)
North Carolina State U (NC)
The Ohio State U (OH)
Parsons School of Design (NY)
Pennsylvania Coll of Technology (PA)
Pratt Inst (NY)
Purdue U (IN)
Rhode Island School of Design (RI)
Rochester Inst of Technology (NY)
San Francisco State U (CA)
Savannah Coll of Art and Design (GA)
Stanford U (CA)
Syracuse U (NY)
U of Bridgeport (CT)
U of Cincinnati (OH)
U of Houston (TX)
U of Illinois at Chicago (IL)
The U of Kansas (KS)
U of Michigan (MI)
U of Minnesota, Twin Cities Campus (MN)
U of San Francisco (CA)
The U of the Arts (PA)
U of Washington (WA)
U of Wisconsin–Stout (WI)
Virginia Polytechnic Inst and State U (VA)
Wentworth Inst of Technology (MA)
Western Michigan U (MI)
Western Washington U (WA)

INDUSTRIAL ELECTRONICS TECHNOLOGY
Pennsylvania Coll of Technology (PA)

INDUSTRIAL ENGINEERING
American U of Beirut (Lebanon)
Aquinas Coll (MI)
Arizona State U at the Tempe campus (AZ)
Auburn U (AL)
Binghamton U, State U of New York (NY)
Bradley U (IL)
California Baptist U (CA)
California Polytechnic State U, San Luis Obispo (CA)
California State Polytechnic U, Pomona (CA)

California State U, East Bay (CA)
California State U, Long Beach (CA)
Caribbean U (PR)
Clemson U (SC)
Colorado State U–Pueblo (CO)
Columbia U (NY)
Concordia U (QC, Canada)
Eastern Nazarene Coll (MA)
Florida Ag and Mech U (FL)
Florida State U (FL)
Francis Marion U (SC)
Gannon U (PA)
Georgia Inst of Technology (GA)
Hofstra U (NY)
Indiana Tech (IN)
Inter American U of Puerto Rico, Bayamón Campus (PR)
Iowa State U of Science and Technology (IA)
Kansas State U (KS)
Kettering U (MI)
Lamar U (TX)
Lawrence Technological U (MI)
Lebanese American U (Lebanon)
Lehigh U (PA)
Liberty U (VA)
Louisiana State U and A&M Coll (LA)
Milwaukee School of Eng (WI)
Mississippi State U (MS)
Missouri U of Science and Technology (MO)
New Jersey Inst of Technology (NJ)
New Mexico State U (NM)
North Carolina State U (NC)
North Dakota State U (ND)
Northeastern U (MA)
Northern Illinois U (IL)
Northwestern U (IL)
Oakland U (MI)
The Ohio State U (OH)
Ohio U (OH)
Oklahoma State U (OK)
Oregon State U (OR)
Penn State Abington (PA)
Penn State Altoona (PA)
Penn State Beaver (PA)
Penn State Berks (PA)
Penn State Brandywine (PA)
Penn State DuBois (PA)
Penn State Erie, The Behrend Coll (PA)
Penn State Fayette, The Eberly Campus (PA)
Penn State Greater Allegheny (PA)
Penn State Hazleton (PA)
Penn State Lehigh Valley (PA)
Penn State Mont Alto (PA)
Penn State New Kensington (PA)
Penn State Schuylkill (PA)
Penn State Shenango (PA)
Penn State Worthington Scranton (PA)
Penn State York (PA)
Polytechnic U of Puerto Rico (PR)
Purdue U (IN)
Quinnipiac U (CT)
Rensselaer Polytechnic Inst (NY)
Rochester Inst of Technology (NY)
Rutgers U–New Brunswick (NJ)
St. Ambrose U (IA)
St. Mary's U (TX)
Slippery Rock U of Pennsylvania (PA)
Southern Illinois U Edwardsville (IL)
Stanford U (CA)
State U of New York Maritime Coll (NY)
Texas A&M U (TX)
Texas A&M U–Commerce (TX)
Texas A&M U–Kingsville (TX)
Texas State U (TX)
Texas Tech U (TX)
U at Buffalo, the State U of New York (NY)
The U of Arizona (AZ)
U of Arkansas (AR)
U of Central Florida (FL)
U of Cincinnati (OH)
U of Dayton (OH)
U of Houston (TX)
U of Illinois at Chicago (IL)
U of Louisville (KY)

U of Massachusetts Amherst (MA)
U of Miami (FL)
U of Michigan (MI)
U of Michigan–Dearborn (MI)
U of Minnesota, Duluth (MN)
U of Minnesota, Twin Cities Campus (MN)
U of Missouri (MO)
U of New Haven (CT)
U of Oklahoma (OK)
U of Pittsburgh (PA)
U of Regina (SK, Canada)
U of Rhode Island (RI)
U of San Diego (CA)
U of South Carolina Aiken (SC)
U of Southern California (CA)
The U of Tennessee (TN)
The U of Texas at Austin (TX)
The U of Texas at El Paso (TX)
U of Toronto (ON, Canada)
U of Vermont (VT)
U of Washington (WA)
U of Wisconsin–Madison (WI)
U of Wisconsin–Milwaukee (WI)
U of Wisconsin–Platteville (WI)
Virginia Polytechnic Inst and State U (VA)
Wayne State U (MI)
Western Michigan U (MI)
Western New England U (MA)
West Virginia U (WV)
Wichita State U (KS)
Worcester Polytechnic Inst (MA)
Youngstown State U (OH)

INDUSTRIAL PRODUCTION TECHNOLOGIES RELATED
Bowling Green State U (OH)
Delaware State U (DE)
Ferris State U (MI)
Kennesaw State U (GA)
Millersville U of Pennsylvania (PA)
Mississippi State U (MS)
Missouri State U (MO)
Northwest Missouri State U (MO)
Pennsylvania Coll of Technology (PA)
Saginaw Valley State U (MI)
Valdosta State U (GA)
Wayne State Coll (NE)

INDUSTRIAL RADIOLOGIC TECHNOLOGY
Concordia U Wisconsin (WI)
U of Maryland Eastern Shore (MD)

INDUSTRIAL SAFETY TECHNOLOGY
Mansfield U of Pennsylvania (PA)
Northeastern State U (OK)
U of Houston–Downtown (TX)

INDUSTRIAL TECHNOLOGY
Ball State U (IN)
Bemidji State U (MN)
Black Hills State U (SD)
Bowling Green State U (OH)
Buffalo State Coll, State U of New York (NY)
California Polytechnic State U, San Luis Obispo (CA)
California State U, Long Beach (CA)
California State U, Los Angeles (CA)
Central Connecticut State U (CT)
Central State U (OH)
Clarion U of Pennsylvania (PA)
East Carolina U (NC)
Eastern Michigan U (MI)
Farmingdale State Coll (NY)
Ferris State U (MI)
Fitchburg State U (MA)
Illinois State U (IL)
Indiana State U (IN)
Iowa State U of Science and Technology (IA)
Jackson State U (MS)
Lamar U (TX)
Millersville U of Pennsylvania (PA)
Mississippi State U (MS)
Northern Illinois U (IL)
Northern Michigan U (MI)
Northwestern State U of Louisiana (LA)
Ohio U (OH)
Pittsburg State U (KS)
Purdue U Northwest (IN)

Roger Williams U (RI)
Sam Houston State U (TX)
Southeastern Louisiana U (LA)
Southeast Missouri State U (MO)
Southern Illinois U Carbondale (IL)
Tarleton State U (TX)
Tennessee Technological U (TN)
Texas A&M U–Commerce (TX)
Texas A&M U–Kingsville (TX)
Texas State U (TX)
U of Dayton (OH)
U of Idaho (ID)
U of Massachusetts Lowell (MA)
U of North Dakota (ND)
U of Northern Iowa (IA)
U of Southern Maine (ME)
U of Southern Mississippi (MS)
The U of Texas of the Permian Basin (TX)
Vincennes U (IN)
Washington State U (WA)
Western Kentucky U (KY)
West Virginia U Inst of Technology (WV)
William Penn U (IA)

INFORMATICS
American Coll of Thessaloniki (Greece)
Arizona State U at the Tempe campus (AZ)
Assumption Coll (MA)
Brigham Young U–Idaho (ID)
Dominican U (IL)
Drexel U (PA)
Goshen Coll (IN)
Indiana U Bloomington (IN)
Indiana U East (IN)
Indiana U Kokomo (IN)
Indiana U Northwest (IN)
Indiana U–Purdue U Indianapolis (IN)
Indiana U South Bend (IN)
Indiana U Southeast (IN)
Liberty U (VA)
Northern Arizona U (AZ)
Texas Woman's U (TX)
Trine U (IN)
U at Buffalo, the State U of New York (NY)
U of California, Irvine (CA)
U of Michigan (MI)
U of Washington (WA)

INFORMATION RESOURCES MANAGEMENT
Abilene Christian U (TX)
Athens State U (AL)
Chestnut Hill Coll (PA)
Juniata Coll (PA)
Lawrence Technological U (MI)
Lewis U (IL)
Lipscomb U (TN)
Lubbock Christian U (TX)
Michigan State U (MI)
Mount St. Mary's U (MD)
Rasmussen Coll New Port Richey (FL)
Rasmussen Coll Ocala (FL)
U of California, Irvine (CA)
U of Wisconsin–Eau Claire (WI)
Western Michigan U (MI)
Wilmington U (DE)

INFORMATION SCIENCE/ STUDIES
Adelphi U (NY)
Alabama State U (AL)
Albright Coll (PA)
Andrews U (MI)
Ashland U (OH)
Athabasca U (AB, Canada)
Averett U (VA)
Barry U (FL)
Baruch Coll of the City U of New York (NY)
Bemidji State U (MN)
Benedictine U (IL)
Bethune-Cookman U (FL)
Boise State U (ID)
Bowling Green State U (OH)
Bradley U (IL)
Brock U (ON, Canada)
Buffalo State Coll, State U of New York (NY)
California Lutheran U (CA)
California State U, Northridge (CA)
California State U, Stanislaus (CA)

Campbellsville U (KY)
Carroll U (WI)
Carson-Newman U (TN)
Case Western Reserve U (OH)
Chowan U (NC)
Christian Brothers U (TN)
Christopher Newport U (VA)
Clarion U of Pennsylvania (PA)
Clayton State U (GA)
Clemson U (SC)
Coastal Carolina U (SC)
Colegio Universitario de San Juan, San Juan (PR)
Coll of Charleston (SC)
Coll of Staten Island of the City U of New York (NY)
Colorado State U (CO)
Colorado State U–Pueblo (CO)
Columbia U (NY)
Concord U (WV)
Dakota State U (SD)
Davenport U, Grand Rapids (MI)
Delaware State U (DE)
DePaul U (IL)
Doane U (NE)
Drexel U (PA)
East Carolina U (NC)
Elizabethtown Coll (PA)
Elmhurst Coll (IL)
Elon U (NC)
Emporia State U (KS)
Excelsior Coll (NY)
Fordham U (NY)
Friends U (KS)
Frostburg State U (MD)
Georgia Southern U (GA)
Georgia Southern U–Armstrong Campus (GA)
Goshen Coll (IN)
Grambling State U (LA)
Grand Valley State U (MI)
Grand View U (IA)
Hampton U (VA)
Harris-Stowe State U (MO)
HEC Montreal (QC, Canada)
Heidelberg U (OH)
Idaho State U (ID)
Illinois Coll (IL)
Immaculata U (PA)
Inter American U of Puerto Rico, San Germán Campus (PR)
Jacksonville U (FL)
James Madison U (VA)
Kansas State U (KS)
Kennesaw State U (GA)
La Sierra U (CA)
Lenoir-Rhyne U (NC)
LeTourneau U (TX)
Limestone Coll (SC)
Lincoln U (MO)
Lipscomb U (TN)
Long Island U–LIU Post (NY)
Luther Coll (IA)
Mansfield U of Pennsylvania (PA)
Marietta Coll (OH)
McKendree U (IL)
Medgar Evers Coll of the City U of New York (NY)
Mercer U, Macon (GA)
Mercy Coll (NY)
Mercyhurst U (PA)
MidAmerica Nazarene U (KS)
Minnesota State U Moorhead (MN)
Missouri U of Science and Technology (MO)
Molloy Coll (NY)
Murray State U (KY)
New Jersey Inst of Technology (NJ)
Newman U (KS)
New Mexico Highlands U (NM)
Northeastern U (MA)
Northern Kentucky U (KY)
Northwestern Oklahoma State U (OK)
Northwestern State U of Louisiana (LA)
Northwestern U (IL)
Oklahoma Baptist U (OK)
Oklahoma Christian U (OK)
Olivet Nazarene U (IL)
Ottawa U (KS)
Pace U (NY)
Penn State Abington (PA)
Penn State Altoona (PA)
Penn State Beaver (PA)

Penn State Berks (PA)
Penn State Brandywine (PA)
Penn State DuBois (PA)
Penn State Erie, The Behrend Coll (PA)
Penn State Fayette, The Eberly Campus (PA)
Penn State Greater Allegheny (PA)
Penn State Harrisburg (PA)
Penn State Lehigh Valley (PA)
Penn State Mont Alto (PA)
Penn State New Kensington (PA)
Penn State Schuylkill (PA)
Penn State Shenango (PA)
Penn State U Park (PA)
Penn State Wilkes-Barre (PA)
Penn State Worthington Scranton (PA)
Penn State York (PA)
Portland State U (OR)
Quinnipiac U (CT)
Radford U (VA)
Ramapo Coll of New Jersey (NJ)
Robert Morris U (PA)
Rutgers U–Newark (NJ)
Rutgers U–New Brunswick (NJ)
The Sage Colls (NY)
Saint Joseph's U (PA)
St. Mary's U (TX)
Saint Michael's Coll (VT)
Saint Peter's U (NJ)
St. Thomas Aquinas Coll (NY)
Salisbury U (MD)
San Francisco State U (CA)
Silver Lake Coll of the Holy Family (WI)
Simmons Coll (MA)
Slippery Rock U of Pennsylvania (PA)
Southeastern Oklahoma State U (OK)
Southern Illinois U Carbondale (IL)
State U of New York at Fredonia (NY)
State U of New York at Oswego (NY)
State U of New York Coll at Old Westbury (NY)
State U of New York Polytechnic Inst (NY)
Stevenson U (MD)
Stockton U (NJ)
Stony Brook U, State U of New York (NY)
Suffolk U (MA)
Susquehanna U (PA)
Syracuse U (NY)
Tennessee Technological U (TN)
Texas A&M Intl U (TX)
Texas A&M U–Central Texas (TX)
Texas A&M U–Commerce (TX)
Texas Lutheran U (TX)
Texas Tech U (TX)
Towson U (MD)
Trine U (IN)
Tufts U (MA)
Tulane U (LA)
Union U (TN)
Université de Sherbrooke (QC, Canada)
U at Albany, State U of New York (NY)
U of Cincinnati (OH)
U of Colorado Boulder (CO)
U of Hartford (CT)
U of Houston (TX)
U of Illinois at Chicago (IL)
U of Kentucky (KY)
U of Management and Technology (VA)
U of Mary Hardin-Baylor (TX)
U of Maryland, Baltimore County (MD)
U of Maryland, Coll Park (MD)
U of Maryland U Coll (MD)
U of Massachusetts Lowell (MA)
U of Miami (FL)
U of Michigan (MI)
U of Michigan–Flint (MI)
U of Nevada, Las Vegas (NV)
The U of North Carolina at Chapel Hill (NC)
U of North Georgia (GA)
U of North Texas (TX)
U of Oklahoma (OK)
U of Pittsburgh (PA)
U of Providence (MT)

U of St. Thomas (MN)
The U of Scranton (PA)
U of South Alabama (AL)
U of South Carolina (SC)
The U of Texas at Austin (TX)
The U of Texas at El Paso (TX)
The U of Texas of the Permian
  Basin (TX)
The U of Texas Rio Grande Valley
  (TX)
U of the Pacific (CA)
The U of Toledo (OH)
The U of Tulsa (OK)
U of Utah (UT)
U of Washington, Bothell (WA)
U of Wisconsin–Milwaukee (WI)
Utah State U (UT)
Utah Valley U (UT)
Valdosta State U (GA)
Virginia Commonwealth U (VA)
Virginia Polytechnic Inst and State
  U (VA)
Wayne State Coll (NE)
Wayne State U (MI)
Weber State U (UT)
Webster U (MO)
Wentworth Inst of Technology (MA)
Westfield State U (MA)
West Virginia Wesleyan Coll (WV)
Widener U (PA)
Wilkes U (PA)

INFORMATION TECHNOLOGY
Abilene Christian U (TX)
American Public U System (WV)
Anderson U (SC)
Arkansas Tech U (AR)
Austin Peay State U (TN)
Baylor U (TX)
Bluefield Coll (VA)
Bluffton U (OH)
Bob Jones U (SC)
Boise State U (ID)
Bradley U (IL)
Brandman U (CA)
Brigham Young U (UT)
Brigham Young U–Idaho (ID)
Bryant U (RI)
Buena Vista U (IA)
Cairn U (PA)
Caldwell U (NJ)
California Baptist U (CA)
California State U, Dominguez Hills
  (CA)
California State U, Fullerton (CA)
California State U, Los Angeles
  (CA)
California State U, San Bernardino
  (CA)
California State U, Stanislaus (CA)
Cameron U (OK)
Central Michigan U (MI)
Central Penn Coll (PA)
Christopher Newport U (VA)
Clayton State U (GA)
Coastal Carolina U (SC)
The Coll of Saint Rose (NY)
Coll of the Ozarks (MO)
The Coll of Westchester (NY)
Columbia Southern U (AL)
Columbus State U (GA)
Cornell U (NY)
Creighton U (NE)
Daytona State Coll (FL)
DePaul U (IL)
DEREE - The American Coll of
  Greece (Greece)
DeSales U (PA)
Duquesne U (PA)
East Carolina U (NC)
Fairleigh Dickinson U, Metropolitan
  Campus (NJ)
Ferris State U (MI)
Florida Ag and Mech U (FL)
Florida Intl U (FL)
Florida State U (FL)
Frostburg State U (MD)
Furman U (SC)
George Mason U (VA)
Georgia Gwinnett Coll (GA)
Georgia Southwestern State U
  (GA)
Golden Gate U (CA)
Governors State U (IL)
Granite State Coll (NH)
Harding U (AR)
HEC Montreal (QC, Canada)

Illinois State U (IL)
Indiana State U (IN)
Inter American U of Puerto Rico,
  Bayamón Campus (PR)
Inter American U of Puerto Rico,
  Metropolitan Campus (PR)
Johnson C. Smith U (NC)
Juniata Coll (PA)
Kansas Wesleyan U (KS)
Keiser U, Fort Lauderdale (FL)
Kennesaw State U (GA)
Kentucky State U (KY)
King U (TN)
La Roche Coll (PA)
La Salle U (PA)
La Sierra U (CA)
Lawrence Technological U (MI)
Lee U (TN)
Lehigh U (PA)
Liberty U (VA)
Life U (GA)
Limestone Coll (SC)
Lincoln U (PA)
Lindenwood U (MO)
Lipscomb U (TN)
Long Island U–LIU Post (NY)
Loyola U Chicago (IL)
Marian U (WI)
Marist Coll (NY)
Marquette U (WI)
Marymount U (VA)
McKendree U (IL)
McMurry U (TX)
Merrimack Coll (MA)
Miami Dade Coll (FL)
Misericordia U (PA)
Missouri Baptist U (MO)
Missouri Western State U (MO)
Montclair State U (NJ)
Mount Aloysius Coll (PA)
Mount Saint Mary Coll (NY)
Murray State U (KY)
New England Inst of Technology
  (RI)
New Jersey Inst of Technology (NJ)
New Mexico Inst of Mining and
  Technology (NM)
New Mexico State U (NM)
New York Inst of Technology (NY)
Northern Kentucky U (KY)
Northwest U (WA)
Oakland U (MI)
Oklahoma State U (OK)
Oregon Inst of Technology (OR)
Ottawa U (KS)
Peirce Coll (PA)
Point Loma Nazarene U (CA)
Point Park U (PA)
Purdue U (IN)
Purdue U Northwest (IN)
Regent U (VA)
Rensselaer Polytechnic Inst (NY)
Rivier U (NH)
Robert Morris U Illinois (IL)
Rochester Inst of Technology (NY)
Sacred Heart U (CT)
St. Joseph's Coll, Long Island
  Campus (NY)
St. Joseph's Coll, New York (NY)
Saint Joseph's U (PA)
Saint Louis U–Madrid Campus
  (Spain)
Saint Martin's U (WA)
San Diego State U (CA)
Seminole State Coll of Florida (FL)
Simmons Coll (MA)
Slippery Rock U of Pennsylvania
  (PA)
State U of New York Coll of
  Technology at Canton (NY)
State U of New York Polytechnic
  Inst (NY)
Stephen F. Austin State U (TX)
Stevens Inst of Technology (NJ)
Sullivan U (KY)
Tarleton State U (TX)
Temple U (PA)
Texas Christian U (TX)
Thomas Edison State U (NJ)
Tiffin U (OH)
Towson U (MD)
Trevecca Nazarene U (TN)
Tusculum Coll (TN)
United States Military Acad (NY)
Université de Sherbrooke (QC,
  Canada)
U of Central Florida (FL)

U of Central Oklahoma (OK)
U of Cincinnati (OH)
U of Denver (CO)
U of Houston–Clear Lake (TX)
U of Jamestown (ND)
The U of Kansas (KS)
U of La Verne (CA)
U of Management and Technology
  (VA)
U of Massachusetts Boston (MA)
U of New Hampshire (NH)
The U of North Carolina at
  Pembroke (NC)
The U of North Carolina
  Wilmington (NC)
U of North Texas (TX)
U of Providence (MT)
U of St. Francis (IL)
U of San Francisco (CA)
The U of Scranton (PA)
U of South Alabama (AL)
U of South Florida Sarasota-
  Manatee (FL)
The U of Texas at Dallas (TX)
The U of Tulsa (OK)
U of Washington (WA)
U of Washington, Tacoma (WA)
U of Wisconsin–Stevens Point (WI)
U of Wisconsin–Superior (WI)
U of Wisconsin–Whitewater (WI)
Vanguard U of Southern California
  (CA)
Vermont Tech Coll (VT)
Wade Coll (TX)
Washington & Jefferson Coll (PA)
Western Illinois U (IL)
Western Kentucky U (KY)
Western New England U (MA)
Whitworth U (WA)
William Paterson U of New Jersey
  (NJ)
William Penn U (IA)
Wilmington U (DE)
Youngstown State U (OH)

**INFORMATION TECHNOLOGY
PROJECT MANAGEMENT**
American Public U System (WV)
Arizona State U at the Polytechnic
  campus (AZ)
Davenport U, Grand Rapids (MI)
Michigan State U (MI)
National U (CA)
Pace U (NY)
Pace U, Pleasantville Campus (NY)

INORGANIC CHEMISTRY
Central Connecticut State U (CT)

**INSTRUMENTATION
TECHNOLOGY**
Northern Michigan U (MI)
Oklahoma State U Inst of
  Technology (OK)
U at Albany, State U of New York
  (NY)

INSURANCE
Appalachian State U (NC)
Ball State U (IN)
Baylor U (TX)
Bowling Green State U (OH)
Butler U (IN)
Ferris State U (MI)
Florida State U (FL)
Gannon U (PA)
Georgia State U (GA)
Hilbert Coll (NY)
Idaho State U (ID)
Illinois State U (IL)
Illinois Wesleyan U (IL)
Indiana State U (IN)
Mississippi State U (MS)
Missouri State U (MO)
Northern Michigan U (MI)
Ohio Dominican U (OH)
Ohio Northern U (OH)
The Ohio State U (OH)
St. John's U (NY)
Saint Joseph's U (PA)
Southern Methodist U (TX)
Temple U (PA)
U of Central Arkansas (AR)
U of Central Oklahoma (OK)
U of Cincinnati (OH)
U of Georgia (GA)
U of Hartford (CT)
U of Houston–Downtown (TX)

U of Louisiana at Monroe (LA)
U of Minnesota, Twin Cities
  Campus (MN)
U of North Texas (TX)
U of Pennsylvania (PA)
U of Saint Francis (IN)
U of South Carolina (SC)
U of Wisconsin–Madison (WI)
Washington State U (WA)
William Penn U (IA)

INTELLIGENCE
Coastal Carolina U (SC)
Mercyhurst U (PA)

**INTERCULTURAL/
MULTICULTURAL AND
DIVERSITY STUDIES**
Bethel Coll (IN)
Biola U (CA)
Bryant U (RI)
Calvary U (MO)
Concordia U (QC, Canada)
Evangel U (MO)
The Evergreen State Coll (WA)
Indiana Wesleyan U (IN)
Judson U (IL)
Macalester Coll (MN)
MidAmerica Nazarene U (KS)
Missouri Valley Coll (MO)
Northwest U (WA)
Nyack Coll (NY)
St. Catherine U (MN)
Sarah Lawrence Coll (NY)
Southeastern U (FL)
Trevecca Nazarene U (TN)
U of Mobile (AL)
U of Regina (SK, Canada)
U of the Incarnate Word (TX)
Vanguard U of Southern California
  (CA)
Villanova U (PA)
Western Oregon U (OR)
Wofford Coll (SC)
Wright State U (OH)
Wright State U–Lake Campus (OH)

INTERDISCIPLINARY STUDIES
Agnes Scott Coll (GA)
Alfred U (NY)
Amherst Coll (MA)
Arizona State U at the West
  campus (AZ)
Auburn U (AL)
Auburn U at Montgomery (AL)
Averett U (VA)
Bard Coll (NY)
Barnard Coll (NY)
Bay Path U (MA)
Beloit Coll (WI)
Berry Coll (GA)
Bethel Coll (IN)
Biola U (CA)
Birmingham-Southern Coll (AL)
Blackburn Coll (IL)
Bloomsburg U of Pennsylvania (PA)
Bluefield Coll (VA)
Bob Jones U (SC)
Boston Coll (MA)
Brandman U (CA)
Brock U (ON, Canada)
Bryn Athyn Coll of the New Church
  (PA)
Bucknell U (PA)
California Lutheran U (CA)
California State U, East Bay (CA)
California State U, Long Beach
  (CA)
California State U, Los Angeles
  (CA)
Calvin Coll (MI)
Carleton Coll (MN)
Carson-Newman U (TN)
Centenary Coll of Louisiana (LA)
Central Methodist U (MO)
Chowan U (NC)
Christian Brothers U (TN)
Clark U (MA)
Coe Coll (IA)
Coll of Coastal Georgia (GA)
Coll of the Atlantic (ME)
The Coll of William and Mary (VA)
The Coll of Wooster (OH)
Connecticut Coll (CT)
Corban U (OR)
Cornell Coll (IA)
DePauw U (IN)
Doane U (NE)

Drexel U (PA)
Earlham Coll (IN)
East Stroudsburg U of
  Pennsylvania (PA)
Eckerd Coll (FL)
Elmhurst Coll (IL)
Embry-Riddle Aeronautical U–
  Daytona (FL)
Emerson Coll (MA)
Fairleigh Dickinson U, Florham
  Campus (NJ)
Fairleigh Dickinson U, Metropolitan
  Campus (NJ)
FIDM/Fashion Inst of Design &
  Merchandising, Los Angeles
  Campus (CA)
FIDM/Fashion Inst of Design &
  Merchandising, San Francisco
  Campus (CA)
Florida Ag and Mech U (FL)
Florida Gulf Coast U (FL)
Florida Inst of Technology (FL)
Geneva Coll (PA)
Georgetown U (DC)
The George Washington U (DC)
Georgian Court U (NJ)
Gettysburg Coll (PA)
Goshen Coll (IN)
Green Mountain Coll (VT)
Greensboro Coll (NC)
Grinnell Coll (IA)
Gustavus Adolphus Coll (MN)
Hamilton Coll (NY)
Harrisburg U of Science and
  Technology (PA)
Harris-Stowe State U (MO)
Hendrix Coll (AR)
Hollins U (VA)
Houston Baptist U (TX)
Huston-Tillotson U (TX)
Illinois Coll (IL)
Indiana U Bloomington (IN)
Indiana U East (IN)
Indiana U Kokomo (IN)
Indiana U Northwest (IN)
Indiana U–Purdue U Indianapolis
  (IN)
Indiana U South Bend (IN)
Indiana U Southeast (IN)
Iowa State U of Science and
  Technology (IA)
Ithaca Coll (NY)
Jacksonville U (FL)
John Carroll U (OH)
Johns Hopkins U (MD)
Kalamazoo Coll (MI)
Keiser U, Fort Lauderdale (FL)
Lehman Coll of the City U of New
  York (NY)
Liberty U (VA)
Life U (GA)
Lipscomb U (TN)
Loyola U New Orleans (LA)
Lynchburg Coll (VA)
Maranatha Baptist U (WI)
Marist Coll (NY)
Marlboro Coll (VT)
Marymount Manhattan Coll (NY)
Massachusetts Coll of Liberal Arts
  (MA)
McPherson Coll (KS)
Merrimack Coll (MA)
MidAmerica Nazarene U (KS)
Middle Georgia State U (GA)
Millersville U of Pennsylvania (PA)
Mills Coll (CA)
Minnesota State U Moorhead (MN)
Misericordia U (PA)
Mount Saint Mary Coll (NY)
Mount Saint Mary's U (CA)
National U (CA)
North Dakota State U (ND)
Northern Arizona U (AZ)
North Greenville U (SC)
Northland Coll (WI)
Northwestern U (IL)
Northwest U (WA)
Nyack Coll (NY)
Oberlin Coll (OH)
Oglethorpe U (GA)
Ohio Christian U (OH)
Ohio Dominican U (OH)
Oklahoma Baptist U (OK)
Pennsylvania Coll of Technology
  (PA)
Piedmont Coll (GA)
Purdue U Northwest (IN)

Queens Coll of the City U of New York (NY)
Rhode Island Coll (RI)
Rhodes Coll (TN)
Ripon Coll (WI)
Roanoke Coll (VA)
Rochester Inst of Technology (NY)
Rutgers U–New Brunswick (NJ)
Sacred Heart U (CT)
St. Andrews U (NC)
Saint Mary's Coll of California (CA)
St. Thomas U (NB, Canada)
Shiloh U (IA)
Siena Coll (NY)
Sierra Nevada Coll (NV)
Simpson Coll (IA)
Slippery Rock U of Pennsylvania (PA)
Smith Coll (MA)
Sonoma State U (CA)
Southern Illinois U Edwardsville (IL)
Southwestern Coll (KS)
Stanford U (CA)
State U of New York at Fredonia (NY)
State U of New York Coll at Oneonta (NY)
Stevenson U (MD)
Sweet Briar Coll (VA)
Syracuse U (NY)
Tennessee Technological U (TN)
Tennessee Wesleyan U (TN)
Texas A&M U–Texarkana (TX)
Texas Christian U (TX)
Towson U (MD)
Trent U (ON, Canada)
Trinity Coll of Florida (FL)
Université de Sherbrooke (QC, Canada)
U at Albany, State U of New York (NY)
The U of Alabama (AL)
The U of Arizona (AZ)
U of Arkansas (AR)
U of Bridgeport (CT)
U of California, San Diego (CA)
U of California, Santa Barbara (CA)
U of Central Florida (FL)
U of Colorado Colorado Springs (CO)
U of Dubuque (IA)
U of Evansville (IN)
U of Hartford (CT)
U of Kentucky (KY)
U of Memphis (TN)
U of Michigan–Flint (MI)
U of Minnesota, Duluth (MN)
U of Missouri (MO)
U of Montana (MT)
U of Mount Union (OH)
U of New Mexico (NM)
U of North Alabama (AL)
U of North Dakota (ND)
U of North Florida (FL)
U of Oklahoma (OK)
U of Puget Sound (WA)
U of Saint Francis (IN)
U of Saint Mary (KS)
U of San Francisco (CA)
U of Science and Arts of Oklahoma (OK)
U of South Alabama (AL)
The U of Tennessee at Chattanooga (TN)
The U of Tennessee at Martin (TN)
The U of Texas at Dallas (TX)
U of the Fraser Valley (BC, Canada)
U of the Pacific (CA)
The U of Toledo (OH)
The U of Tulsa (OK)
The U of Virginia's Coll at Wise (VA)
U of Washington, Tacoma (WA)
U of Waterloo (ON, Canada)
The U of West Alabama (AL)
Vanguard U of Southern California (CA)
Vassar Coll (NY)
Virginia Polytechnic Inst and State U (VA)
Virginia Wesleyan U (VA)
Wayne State Coll (NE)
Western Illinois U (IL)
Western Oregon U (OR)
Western State Colorado U (CO)

Western Washington U (WA)
Whitworth U (WA)
William Woods U (MO)
Wittenberg U (OH)

INTERIOR ARCHITECTURE
Auburn U (AL)
Benedictine Coll (KS)
Boston Architectural Coll (MA)
Bowling Green State U (OH)
California Coll of the Arts (CA)
Chatham U (PA)
Indiana State U (IN)
La Roche Coll (PA)
Lawrence Technological U (MI)
Lebanese American U (Lebanon)
Louisiana State U and A&M Coll (LA)
Miami U (OH)
Mississippi State U (MS)
Rhode Island School of Design (RI)
Sam Houston State U (TX)
Stephen F. Austin State U (TX)
Syracuse U (NY)
Texas Tech U (TX)
U of Houston (TX)
The U of Kansas (KS)
U of Missouri (MO)
U of Nebraska–Lincoln (NE)
U of Nevada, Las Vegas (NV)
U of New Haven (CT)
U of North Texas (TX)
U of Oregon (OR)
U of San Francisco (CA)
U of Southern Mississippi (MS)
The U of Texas at San Antonio (TX)
Woodbury U (CA)

INTERIOR DESIGN
Abilene Christian U (TX)
Academy of Art U (CA)
Anderson U (SC)
Appalachian State U (NC)
Arizona State U at the Tempe campus (AZ)
ArtCenter Coll of Design (CA)
Auburn U (AL)
Ball State U (IN)
Baylor U (TX)
Bay Path U (MA)
Belmont U (TN)
Brenau U (GA)
Brigham Young U–Idaho (ID)
California State U, Long Beach (CA)
California State U, Sacramento (CA)
Carson-Newman U (TN)
Cazenovia Coll (NY)
Chaminade U of Honolulu (HI)
Colorado State U (CO)
Columbia Coll Chicago (IL)
Concordia U Wisconsin (WI)
Converse Coll (SC)
Cornish Coll of the Arts (WA)
Design Inst of San Diego (CA)
Drexel U (PA)
Dunwoody Coll of Technology (MN)
East Carolina U (NC)
Eastern Michigan U (MI)
East Tennessee State U (TN)
EDP U of Puerto Rico (PR)
Endicott Coll (MA)
Eugene Lang Coll of Liberal Arts (NY)
Fashion Inst of Technology (NY)
Ferris State U (MI)
FIDM/Fashion Inst of Design & Merchandising, Los Angeles Campus (CA)
FIDM/Fashion Inst of Design & Merchandising, San Francisco Campus (CA)
Florida Intl U (FL)
Florida State U (FL)
Georgia Southern U (GA)
Hampton U (VA)
Harding U (AR)
High Point U (NC)
Illinois State U (IL)
Indiana U Bloomington (IN)
Indiana U of Pennsylvania (PA)
Indiana U–Purdue U Indianapolis (IN)
Indiana Wesleyan U (IN)
Iowa State U of Science and Technology (IA)

Judson U (IL)
Kansas State U (KS)
Kean U (NJ)
Kent State U (OH)
Lebanese American U (Lebanon)
Marist Coll (NY)
Maryland Inst Coll of Art (MD)
Marylhurst U (OR)
Marymount U (VA)
Maryville U of Saint Louis (MO)
Marywood U (PA)
McPherson Coll (KS)
Mercyhurst U (PA)
Meredith Coll (NC)
Michigan State U (MI)
Middle Tennessee State U (TN)
Mount Mary U (WI)
New England Inst of Technology (RI)
New Jersey Inst of Technology (NJ)
New York Inst of Technology (NY)
North Dakota State U (ND)
Northern Arizona U (AZ)
The Ohio State U (OH)
Oklahoma Christian U (OK)
Olivet Nazarene U (IL)
O'More Coll of Design (TN)
Oregon State U (OR)
Paier Coll of Art, Inc. (CT)
Paris Coll of Art (France)
Parsons School of Design (NY)
Polytechnic U of Puerto Rico (PR)
Pratt Inst (NY)
Purdue U (IN)
Ringling Coll of Art and Design (FL)
Rochester Inst of Technology (NY)
The Sage Colls (NY)
Samford U (AL)
San Diego State U (CA)
San Francisco State U (CA)
Savannah Coll of Art and Design (GA)
School of Visual Arts (NY)
Seattle Pacific U (WA)
Seminole State Coll of Florida (FL)
Southern Illinois U Carbondale (IL)
Stevens–The Inst of Business & Arts (MO)
Suffolk U (MA)
Texas Christian U (TX)
Texas State U (TX)
The U of Alabama (AL)
U of Arkansas (AR)
U of Bridgeport (CT)
U of Central Arkansas (AR)
U of Central Missouri (MO)
U of Central Oklahoma (OK)
U of Cincinnati (OH)
U of Florida (FL)
U of Idaho (ID)
U of Kentucky (KY)
U of Minnesota, Twin Cities Campus (MN)
The U of North Carolina at Greensboro (NC)
U of Northern Iowa (IA)
U of Oklahoma (OK)
U of San Francisco (CA)
The U of Tennessee (TN)
The U of Tennessee at Chattanooga (TN)
The U of Tennessee at Martin (TN)
The U of Texas at Austin (TX)
U of the Incarnate Word (TX)
U of Wisconsin–Madison (WI)
U of Wisconsin–Stevens Point (WI)
U of Wisconsin–Stout (WI)
Utah State U (UT)
Valdosta State U (GA)
Villa Maria Coll (NY)
Virginia Commonwealth U (VA)
Virginia Polytechnic Inst and State U (VA)
Wade Coll (TX)
Washington State U (WA)
Washington State U–Spokane (WA)
Weber State U (UT)
Wentworth Inst of Technology (MA)
Western Michigan U (MI)

INTERMEDIA/MULTIMEDIA
Alberta Coll of Art & Design (AB, Canada)
ArtCenter Coll of Design (CA)
Bennington Coll (VT)
Biola U (CA)

Calumet Coll of Saint Joseph (IN)
City Coll of the City U of New York (NY)
The Coll of New Jersey (NJ)
Columbia Coll Chicago (IL)
Concordia U (QC, Canada)
Emerson Coll (MA)
The Evergreen State Coll (WA)
Indiana U of Pennsylvania (PA)
Jacksonville U (FL)
Laguna Coll of Art & Design (CA)
Luther Coll (IA)
Marist Coll (NY)
Marlboro Coll (VT)
Maryland Inst Coll of Art (MD)
Massachusetts Coll of Art and Design (MA)
Mills Coll (CA)
Missouri State U (MO)
Pacific Northwest Coll of Art (OR)
Providence Coll (RI)
Purchase Coll, State U of New York (NY)
Ramapo Coll of New Jersey (NJ)
Rochester Inst of Technology (NY)
State U of New York at Fredonia (NY)
State U of New York Coll of Technology at Alfred (NY)
Tufts U (MA)
U of Hartford (CT)
U of Maine at Farmington (ME)
U of Oregon (OR)
U of Regina (SK, Canada)
U of the Incarnate Word (TX)
The U of Toledo (OH)
Weber State U (UT)

INTERNATIONAL AGRICULTURE
Coll of the Ozarks (MO)
Cornell U (NY)
Iowa State U of Science and Technology (IA)
U of California, Davis (CA)
U of Missouri (MO)
Utah State U (UT)

INTERNATIONAL AND COMPARATIVE EDUCATION
Avila U (MO)

INTERNATIONAL AND INTERCULTURAL COMMUNICATION
The American U of Paris (France)
Becker Coll (MA)
DePaul U (IL)
Linfield Coll (OR)
Michigan Technological U (MI)
Pepperdine U, Malibu (CA)
Saint Louis U–Madrid Campus (Spain)
Suffolk U (MA)
U of Valley Forge (PA)
Whitworth U (WA)

INTERNATIONAL BUSINESS/ TRADE/COMMERCE
Adams State U (CO)
Alverno Coll (WI)
American Intl Coll (MA)
The American U of Paris (France)
Anderson U (IN)
Anderson U (SC)
Angelo State U (TX)
Appalachian State U (NC)
Aquinas Coll (MI)
Arcadia U (PA)
Arizona State U at the West campus (AZ)
Assumption Coll (MA)
Auburn U (AL)
Auburn U at Montgomery (AL)
Augsburg U (MN)
Augustana Coll (IL)
Austin Coll (TX)
Avila U (MO)
Azusa Pacific U (CA)
Babson Coll (MA)
Baker U (KS)
Baldwin Wallace U (OH)
Ball State U (IN)
Barry U (FL)
Baruch Coll of the City U of New York (NY)
Baylor U (TX)
Belmont U (TN)
Benedictine Coll (KS)

Benedictine U (IL)
Berry Coll (GA)
Binghamton U, State U of New York (NY)
Biola U (CA)
Birmingham-Southern Coll (AL)
Bloomsburg U of Pennsylvania (PA)
Boise State U (ID)
Bowling Green State U (OH)
Bradley U (IL)
Bridgewater State U (MA)
Brock U (ON, Canada)
Bryant U (RI)
Bucknell U (PA)
Butler U (IN)
Caldwell U (NJ)
California State U, Dominguez Hills (CA)
California State U, Fullerton (CA)
California State U, Long Beach (CA)
California State U, San Marcos (CA)
Canisius Coll (NY)
Cardinal Stritch U (WI)
Carnegie Mellon U (PA)
The Catholic U of America (DC)
Cedarville U (OH)
Central Michigan U (MI)
Chaminade U of Honolulu (HI)
Champlain Coll (VT)
Chatham U (PA)
Chestnut Hill Coll (PA)
Clarion U of Pennsylvania (PA)
Cleveland State U (OH)
The Coll at Brockport, State U of New York (NY)
Coll of Charleston (SC)
The Coll of Idaho (ID)
Columbia Coll (MO)
Columbia Coll (SC)
Concordia Coll–New York (NY)
Concordia U (QC, Canada)
Concordia U, St. Paul (MN)
Concordia U Wisconsin (WI)
Converse Coll (SC)
Cornell Coll (IA)
Cornerstone U (MI)
Cottey Coll (MO)
Creighton U (NE)
Davenport U, Grand Rapids (MI)
Denison U (OH)
DEREE - The American Coll of Greece (Greece)
DeSales U (PA)
Dickinson Coll (PA)
Dickinson State U (ND)
Dominican U (IL)
Drake U (IA)
Drexel U (PA)
Duquesne U (PA)
D'Youville Coll (NY)
East Central U (OK)
Eastern Mennonite U (VA)
Eastern Michigan U (MI)
Eastern U (PA)
Eckerd Coll (FL)
Elizabethtown Coll (PA)
Elmhurst Coll (IL)
Elms Coll (MA)
Elon U (NC)
Emory & Henry Coll (VA)
Endicott Coll (MA)
Fairfield U (CT)
Farmingdale State Coll (NY)
Felician U (NJ)
Florida Atlantic U (FL)
Florida Inst of Technology (FL)
Florida Intl U (FL)
Fordham U (NY)
Fort Lewis Coll (CO)
Franklin U Switzerland (Switzerland)
Friends U (KS)
Gannon U (PA)
Georgetown U (DC)
The George Washington U (DC)
Georgian Court U (NJ)
Georgia Southern U (GA)
Gettysburg Coll (PA)
Gonzaga U (WA)
Grand Valley State U (MI)
Grove City Coll (PA)
Gustavus Adolphus Coll (MN)
Hamline U (MN)
Harding U (AR)
HEC Montreal (QC, Canada)

High Point U (NC)
Hilbert Coll (NY)
Hillsdale Coll (MI)
Hofstra U (NY)
Holy Family U (PA)
Houston Baptist U (TX)
Husson U (ME)
Illinois State U (IL)
Illinois Wesleyan U (IL)
Indiana U of Pennsylvania (PA)
Iona Coll (NY)
Iowa State U of Science and
    Technology (IA)
Ithaca Coll (NY)
Jacksonville U (FL)
James Madison U (VA)
John Brown U (AR)
John Cabot U (Italy)
John Carroll U (OH)
Juniata Coll (PA)
Kean U (NJ)
Keiser U, Fort Lauderdale (FL)
Kennesaw State U (GA)
King's Coll (PA)
La Roche Coll (PA)
La Salle U (PA)
Lasell Coll (MA)
Lebanon Valley Coll (PA)
Lenoir-Rhyne U (NC)
Lewis U (IL)
LIM Coll (NY)
Lindenwood U (MO)
Linfield Coll (OR)
Lipscomb U (TN)
Louisiana State U and A&M Coll
    (LA)
Loyola U Chicago (IL)
Loyola U New Orleans (LA)
Lynn U (FL)
Madonna U (MI)
Mansfield U of Pennsylvania (PA)
Marietta Coll (OH)
Marshall U (WV)
Marymount Manhattan Coll (NY)
Maryville Coll (TN)
Maryville U of Saint Louis (MO)
Marywood U (PA)
Massachusetts Coll of Liberal Arts
    (MA)
Massachusetts Maritime Acad
    (MA)
McPherson Coll (KS)
Mercer U, Macon (GA)
Merrimack Coll (MA)
Messiah Coll (PA)
Millikin U (IL)
Minot State U (ND)
Monmouth Coll (IL)
Moravian Coll (PA)
Mount Mercy U (IA)
Mount Saint Mary's U (CA)
Mount Vernon Nazarene U (OH)
Muskingum U (OH)
Nazareth Coll of Rochester (NY)
New Jersey Inst of Technology (NJ)
New Mexico State U (NM)
New York Inst of Technology (NY)
New York U (NY)
Nichols Coll (MA)
North Central Coll (IL)
Northeastern State U (OK)
Northeastern U (MA)
Northern Kentucky U (KY)
Northern State U (SD)
North Greenville U (SC)
Northwest Missouri State U (MO)
Northwest Nazarene U (ID)
Ohio Northern U (OH)
The Ohio State U (OH)
Ohio U (OH)
Ohio Wesleyan U (OH)
Oklahoma Baptist U (OK)
Oklahoma State U (OK)
Olivet Nazarene U (IL)
Oral Roberts U (OK)
Otterbein U (OH)
Pace U (NY)
Pace U, Pleasantville Campus (NY)
Palm Beach Atlantic U (FL)
Penn State DuBois (PA)
Penn State Erie, The Behrend Coll
    (PA)
Penn State Harrisburg (PA)
Penn State Lehigh Valley (PA)
Penn State Schuylkill (PA)
Pepperdine U, Malibu (CA)
Pfeiffer U (NC)

Pittsburg State U (KS)
Post U (CT)
Queens Coll of the City U of New
    York (NY)
Quinnipiac U (CT)
Ramapo Coll of New Jersey (NJ)
Rhode Island Coll (RI)
Rhodes Coll (TN)
Rider U (NJ)
Rochester Inst of Technology (NY)
Roger Williams U (RI)
Rollins Coll (FL)
Rosemont Coll (PA)
Saginaw Valley State U (MI)
St. Ambrose U (IA)
Saint Anselm Coll (NH)
St. Catherine U (MN)
Saint Francis U (PA)
St. John's U (NY)
Saint Joseph's U (PA)
Saint Louis U (MO)
Saint Louis U–Madrid Campus
    (Spain)
Saint Mary's Coll of California (CA)
St. Mary's U (TX)
Saint Mary's U of Minnesota (MN)
St. Norbert Coll (WI)
Saint Peter's U (NJ)
St. Thomas U (FL)
Saint Vincent Coll (PA)
Salisbury U (MD)
Samford U (AL)
Sam Houston State U (TX)
San Diego State U (CA)
San Francisco State U (CA)
Seattle U (WA)
Seton Hill U (PA)
Sierra Nevada Coll (NV)
Simpson Coll (IA)
Southeastern U (FL)
Southeast Missouri State U (MO)
Southern Adventist U (TN)
Southwestern Adventist U (TX)
Spring Hill Coll (AL)
State U of New York at New Paltz
    (NY)
State U of New York at Plattsburgh
    (NY)
Stephen F. Austin State U (TX)
Stetson U (FL)
Stonehill Coll (MA)
Suffolk U (MA)
Susquehanna U (PA)
Tarleton State U (TX)
Taylor U (IN)
Temple U (PA)
Tennessee Technological U (TN)
Texas A&M U–Central Texas (TX)
Texas A&M U–Kingsville (TX)
Texas A&M U–Texarkana (TX)
Texas Christian U (TX)
Texas Tech U (TX)
Tiffin U (OH)
Trevecca Nazarene U (TN)
Trine U (IN)
Trinity U (TX)
U at Buffalo, the State U of New
    York (NY)
The U of Akron (OH)
U of Arkansas (AR)
U of Bridgeport (CT)
U of California, San Diego (CA)
U of Cincinnati (OH)
U of Dayton (OH)
U of Denver (CO)
U of Evansville (IN)
The U of Findlay (OH)
U of Georgia (GA)
U of Hawaii at Manoa (HI)
U of Houston–Downtown (TX)
U of Jamestown (ND)
U of La Verne (CA)
U of Mary Hardin-Baylor (TX)
U of Maryland, Coll Park (MD)
U of Memphis (TN)
U of Miami (FL)
U of Michigan–Flint (MI)
U of Minnesota, Twin Cities
    Campus (MN)
U of Missouri (MO)
U of Montana (MT)
U of Mount Union (OH)
U of Nebraska–Lincoln (NE)
U of Nevada, Las Vegas (NV)
U of Nevada, Reno (NV)
U of New Haven (CT)

The U of North Carolina at
    Charlotte (NC)
The U of North Carolina at
    Greensboro (NC)
U of North Florida (FL)
U of Pennsylvania (PA)
U of Pittsburgh (PA)
U of Puerto Rico–Humacao (PR)
U of Puget Sound (WA)
U of Regina (SK, Canada)
U of Rhode Island (RI)
U of St. Francis (IL)
U of St. Thomas (MN)
U of San Diego (CA)
U of San Francisco (CA)
The U of Scranton (PA)
U of South Alabama (AL)
U of South Carolina (SC)
U of Southern California (CA)
U of Southern Mississippi (MS)
U of South Florida, St. Petersburg
    (FL)
The U of Tampa (FL)
The U of Tennessee at Martin (TN)
The U of Texas at Dallas (TX)
The U of Texas at San Antonio (TX)
The U of Texas Rio Grande Valley
    (TX)
U of the Incarnate Word (TX)
U of the Potomac (DC)
The U of Toledo (OH)
The U of Tulsa (OK)
U of Waterloo (ON, Canada)
U of Wisconsin–Eau Claire (WI)
U of Wisconsin–La Crosse (WI)
U of Wisconsin–Madison (WI)
U of Wisconsin–Superior (WI)
U of Wisconsin–Whitewater (WI)
Utica Coll (NY)
Valdosta State U (GA)
Valparaiso U (IN)
Vanguard U of Southern California
    (CA)
Villanova U (PA)
Waldorf U (IA)
Wartburg Coll (IA)
Washington & Jefferson Coll (PA)
Washington State U (WA)
Washington U in St. Louis (MO)
Waynesburg U (PA)
Wayne State U (MI)
West Chester U of Pennsylvania
    (PA)
Western Kentucky U (KY)
Western New England U (MA)
Western Washington U (WA)
Westminster Coll (PA)
Westminster Coll (UT)
Whitworth U (WA)
Wichita State U (KS)
Widener U (PA)
William Paterson U of New Jersey
    (NJ)
Wright State U (OH)

INTERNATIONAL ECONOMICS

Albion Coll (MI)
The American U of Paris (France)
Austin Coll (TX)
Belmont U (TN)
Brock U (ON, Canada)
Bryant U (RI)
Carthage Coll (WI)
The Coll of Idaho (ID)
The Colorado Coll (CO)
Elon U (NC)
Fitchburg State U (MA)
Franklin U Switzerland
    (Switzerland)
Georgetown U (DC)
Georgia State U (GA)
Gettysburg Coll (PA)
HEC Montreal (QC, Canada)
John Carroll U (OH)
La Salle U (PA)
Marlboro Coll (VT)
Rhodes Coll (TN)
Rockford U (IL)
St. Catherine U (MN)
Salve Regina U (RI)
State U of New York at Oswego
    (NY)
Texas Christian U (TX)
Texas Tech U (TX)
Trinity U (TX)
U of California, San Diego (CA)

U of California, Santa Cruz (CA)
U of New Haven (CT)
U of Puget Sound (WA)
U of Richmond (VA)
U of West Georgia (GA)
Valparaiso U (IN)
Washington U in St. Louis (MO)
Weber State U (UT)
Youngstown State U (OH)

INTERNATIONAL FINANCE

The American U of Paris (France)
Babson Coll (MA)
Brigham Young U (UT)
Bryant U (RI)
The Catholic U of America (DC)
Franklin U Switzerland
    (Switzerland)
HEC Montreal (QC, Canada)
Lenoir-Rhyne U (NC)
Texas Christian U (TX)
U of New Haven (CT)
Washington U in St. Louis (MO)

INTERNATIONAL/GLOBAL STUDIES

Abilene Christian U (TX)
Adelphi U (NY)
Albion Coll (MI)
Alfred U (NY)
American Public U System (WV)
Appalachian State U (NC)
Arcadia U (PA)
Arizona State U at the Tempe
    campus (AZ)
Arkansas Tech U (AR)
Assumption Coll (MA)
Auburn U at Montgomery (AL)
Baker U (KS)
Baldwin Wallace U (OH)
Bard Coll (NY)
Belhaven U (MS)
Benedictine Coll (KS)
Benedictine U (IL)
Bennington Coll (VT)
Bentley U (MA)
Boston Coll (MA)
Bowling Green State U (OH)
Brandeis U (MA)
Brigham Young U–Idaho (ID)
Bryant U (RI)
Bryn Mawr Coll (PA)
California Baptist U (CA)
California Lutheran U (CA)
Carnegie Mellon U (PA)
Carroll U (WI)
Case Western Reserve U (OH)
Cazenovia Coll (NY)
Cedar Crest Coll (PA)
Cedarville U (OH)
Central Connecticut State U (CT)
Centre Coll (KY)
Chatham U (PA)
Chestnut Hill Coll (PA)
City Coll of the City U of New York
    (NY)
Colby Coll (ME)
Coll of Charleston (SC)
The Coll of New Rochelle (NY)
Coll of Saint Elizabeth (NJ)
The Coll of St. Scholastica (MN)
Coll of Staten Island of the City U of
    New York (NY)
Coll of the Holy Cross (MA)
Colorado Christian U (CO)
Colorado State U (CO)
Concordia Coll–New York (NY)
Concordia U Irvine (CA)
Concordia U, Nebraska (NE)
Culver-Stockton Coll (MO)
Doane U (NE)
Dominican U of California (CA)
Drexel U (PA)
East Texas Baptist U (TX)
Emmanuel Coll (MA)
Endicott Coll (MA)
Eugene Lang Coll of Liberal Arts
    (NY)
The Evergreen State Coll (WA)
Flagler Coll (FL)
Framingham State U (MA)
Frostburg State U (MD)
Gannon U (PA)
Georgia Inst of Technology (GA)
Graceland U (IA)
Grand Valley State U (MI)
Greenville U (IL)
Guilford Coll (NC)

Hamline U (MN)
Hampshire Coll (MA)
Harding U (AR)
Hartwick Coll (NY)
Hawai'i Pacific U (HI)
Hofstra U (NY)
Hood Coll (MD)
Hope Coll (MI)
Humboldt State U (CA)
Illinois Wesleyan U (IL)
John Brown U (AR)
Juniata Coll (PA)
Kenyon Coll (OH)
Knox Coll (IL)
La Sierra U (CA)
Lawrence U (WI)
Lebanon Valley Coll (PA)
Lee U (TN)
Lehigh U (PA)
Le Moyne Coll (NY)
Liberty U (VA)
Long Island U–LIU Post (NY)
Louisiana State U and A&M Coll
    (LA)
Luther Coll (IA)
Lycoming Coll (PA)
Macalester Coll (MN)
Malone U (OH)
Manchester U (IN)
Manhattanville Coll (NY)
Marlboro Coll (VT)
Marymount Manhattan Coll (NY)
Maryville U of Saint Louis (MO)
McKendree U (IL)
Mercyhurst U (PA)
Meredith Coll (NC)
Michigan State U (MI)
Middle Tennessee State U (TN)
Minnesota State U Moorhead (MN)
Missouri State U (MO)
Missouri Western State U (MO)
Monmouth Coll (IL)
Morehead State U (KY)
Morningside Coll (IA)
Mount Mary U (WI)
Multnomah U (OR)
National U (CA)
New Coll of Florida (FL)
The New School for Public
    Engagement (NY)
New York U (NY)
North Carolina State U (NC)
North Central Coll (IL)
North Dakota State U (ND)
Northwest U (WA)
The Ohio State U (OH)
Oklahoma State U (OK)
Oregon State U (OR)
Pace U, Pleasantville Campus (NY)
Pacific Lutheran U (WA)
Pepperdine U, Malibu (CA)
Pitzer Coll (CA)
Point Loma Nazarene U (CA)
Point Park U (PA)
Presbyterian Coll (SC)
Providence Coll (RI)
Randolph Coll (VA)
Randolph-Macon Coll (VA)
Regent U (VA)
Rhode Island Coll (RI)
Rockford U (IL)
Rockhurst U (MO)
Roger Williams U (RI)
Rowan U (NJ)
Saginaw Valley State U (MI)
St. Bonaventure U (NY)
St. Lawrence U (NY)
Saint Leo U (FL)
Saint Mary's U of Minnesota (MN)
St. Norbert Coll (WI)
St. Thomas U (FL)
Salisbury U (MD)
Salve Regina U (RI)
Samford U (AL)
Sarah Lawrence Coll (NY)
Scripps Coll (CA)
Seattle U (WA)
Sewanee: The U of the South (TN)
Shippensburg U of Pennsylvania
    (PA)
Sierra Nevada Coll (NV)
Southeast Missouri State U (MO)
Southern Illinois U Edwardsville
    (IL)
Southern Methodist U (TX)
Spelman Coll (GA)

State U of New York Coll at Cortland (NY)
Susquehanna U (PA)
Tabor Coll (KS)
Tarleton State U (TX)
Temple U (PA)
Tennessee Wesleyan U (TN)
Texas A&M U (TX)
Texas State U (TX)
Texas Tech U (TX)
U at Albany, State U of New York (NY)
The U of Arizona (AZ)
U of California, Irvine (CA)
U of California, Los Angeles (CA)
U of California, Riverside (CA)
U of California, Santa Barbara (CA)
U of Central Arkansas (AR)
U of Central Florida (FL)
U of Colorado Boulder (CO)
U of Colorado Denver (CO)
U of Dayton (OH)
U of Florida (FL)
U of Illinois at Springfield (IL)
The U of Kansas (KS)
U of Kentucky (KY)
U of Maine at Farmington (ME)
U of Maryland, Baltimore County (MD)
U of Michigan (MI)
U of Nebraska–Lincoln (NE)
U of New England (ME)
U of New Haven (CT)
U of New Mexico (NM)
U of New Orleans (LA)
The U of North Carolina at Charlotte (NC)
The U of North Carolina Wilmington (NC)
U of North Dakota (ND)
U of Northern Colorado (CO)
U of Northern Iowa (IA)
U of North Florida (FL)
U of North Texas (TX)
U of Notre Dame (IN)
U of Oklahoma (OK)
U of Oregon (OR)
U of Pennsylvania (PA)
U of Regina (SK, Canada)
U of Saint Joseph (CT)
U of San Francisco (CA)
U of Saskatchewan (SK, Canada)
U of South Alabama (AL)
U of South Dakota (SD)
U of Southern California (CA)
The U of Tampa (FL)
The U of Texas at Austin (TX)
U of Utah (UT)
U of Vermont (VT)
U of Washington, Bothell (WA)
U of Washington, Tacoma (WA)
U of Waterloo (ON, Canada)
U of Wisconsin–Madison (WI)
U of Wisconsin–Milwaukee (WI)
U of Wisconsin–Platteville (WI)
U of Wisconsin–River Falls (WI)
U of Wisconsin–Stevens Point (WI)
U of Wisconsin–Whitewater (WI)
U of Wyoming (WY)
Valparaiso U (IN)
Villanova U (PA)
Virginia Polytechnic Inst and State U (VA)
Washington & Jefferson Coll (PA)
Webster U (MO)
Western Michigan U (MI)
Western New England U (MA)
Westminster Coll (PA)
West Virginia State U (WV)
Whitman Coll (WA)
Whittier Coll (CA)
Willamette U (OR)
William Peace U (NC)
Winona State U (MN)
Wright State U (OH)
Wright State U–Lake Campus (OH)

INTERNATIONAL MARKETING
Bryant U (RI)
Fashion Inst of Technology (NY)
Husson U (ME)
Oklahoma Baptist U (OK)
Oral Roberts U (OK)
Pace U, Pleasantville Campus (NY)
Texas Christian U (TX)
U of New Haven (CT)
U of Northern Iowa (IA)

INTERNATIONAL POLICY ANALYSIS
Southern Methodist U (TX)
Waynesburg U (PA)

INTERNATIONAL PUBLIC HEALTH
Allegheny Coll (PA)
American U (DC)
Bethel Coll (IN)
California Baptist U (CA)
La Sierra U (CA)
Mercer U, Macon (GA)
Union Coll (NE)
U of Southern California (CA)

INTERNATIONAL RELATIONS AND AFFAIRS
Agnes Scott Coll (GA)
Albright Coll (PA)
Allegheny Coll (PA)
Alverno Coll (WI)
American Coll of Thessaloniki (Greece)
American Intl Coll (MA)
American Public U System (WV)
American U (DC)
Anderson U (IN)
Aquinas Coll (MI)
Augsburg U (MN)
Augustana U (SD)
Austin Coll (TX)
Azusa Pacific U (CA)
Barry U (FL)
Baylor U (TX)
Belmont U (TN)
Beloit Coll (WI)
Benedictine U (IL)
Bennington Coll (VT)
Berry Coll (GA)
Bethel U (MN)
Bethune-Cookman U (FL)
Binghamton U, State U of New York (NY)
Bob Jones U (SC)
Boston U (MA)
Bowling Green State U (OH)
Bradley U (IL)
Bridgewater Coll (VA)
Bridgewater State U (MA)
Bryant U (RI)
Bucknell U (PA)
Butler U (IN)
California Lutheran U (CA)
California State U, East Bay (CA)
California State U, Long Beach (CA)
California State U, Monterey Bay (CA)
California State U, San Marcos (CA)
Calvin Coll (MI)
Canisius Coll (NY)
Capital U (OH)
Carleton Coll (MN)
Carnegie Mellon U (PA)
Carroll Coll (MT)
Carroll U (WI)
Case Western Reserve U (OH)
Central Michigan U (MI)
Chaminade U of Honolulu (HI)
Chatham U (PA)
City Coll of the City U of New York (NY)
Claremont McKenna Coll (CA)
Clark U (MA)
Cleveland State U (OH)
Colgate U (NY)
The Coll at Brockport, State U of New York (NY)
The Coll of Idaho (ID)
The Coll of New Jersey (NJ)
The Coll of William and Mary (VA)
The Coll of Wooster (OH)
Concordia Coll–New York (NY)
Connecticut Coll (CT)
Cornell Coll (IA)
Cottey Coll (MO)
Creighton U (NE)
Denison U (OH)
DePaul U (IL)
Dickinson Coll (PA)
Dominican U (IL)
Drake U (IA)
Drew U (NJ)
Duquesne U (PA)
Eastern Michigan U (MI)
Eastern Washington U (WA)

East Tennessee State U (TN)
Eckerd Coll (FL)
Edgewood Coll (WI)
Elon U (NC)
Emmanuel Coll (MA)
Emory U (GA)
Excelsior Coll (NY)
Fairfield U (CT)
Fairleigh Dickinson U, Metropolitan Campus (NJ)
Fitchburg State U (MA)
Florida Intl U (FL)
Florida State U (FL)
Fordham U (NY)
Francis Marion U (SC)
Franklin U Switzerland (Switzerland)
George Mason U (VA)
Georgetown U (DC)
The George Washington U (DC)
Georgia Inst of Technology (GA)
Georgia Southern U (GA)
Gettysburg Coll (PA)
Gonzaga U (WA)
Gordon Coll (MA)
Graceland U (IA)
Grand Valley State U (MI)
Hamilton Coll (NY)
Hampden-Sydney Coll (VA)
Hampshire Coll (MA)
Heidelberg U (OH)
Hendrix Coll (AR)
High Point U (NC)
Hobart and William Smith Colls (NY)
Hollins U (VA)
Holy Names U (CA)
Howard Payne U (TX)
Idaho State U (ID)
Illinois Coll (IL)
Illinois Wesleyan U (IL)
Immaculata U (PA)
Indiana U Bloomington (IN)
Indiana U East (IN)
Indiana U of Pennsylvania (PA)
Indiana U–Purdue U Indianapolis (IN)
Indiana U Southeast (IN)
Indiana Wesleyan U (IN)
Iona Coll (NY)
Iowa State U of Science and Technology (IA)
Jacksonville U (FL)
James Madison U (VA)
John Cabot U (Italy)
John Carroll U (OH)
Johns Hopkins U (MD)
Juniata Coll (PA)
Kalamazoo Coll (MI)
Kennesaw State U (GA)
Kent State U (OH)
Knox Coll (IL)
Lafayette Coll (PA)
La Roche Coll (PA)
Lebanese American U (Lebanon)
Lehigh U (PA)
Lenoir-Rhyne U (NC)
Lewis U (IL)
Liberty U (VA)
Lindenwood U (MO)
Linfield Coll (OR)
Lock Haven U of Pennsylvania (PA)
Loras Coll (IA)
Loyola Marymount U (CA)
Loyola U Chicago (IL)
Lynchburg Coll (VA)
Manhattan Coll (NY)
Marlboro Coll (VT)
Marquette U (WI)
Marshall U (WV)
Mary Baldwin U (VA)
Marymount Manhattan Coll (NY)
Maryville Coll (TN)
McKendree U (IL)
Mercer U, Macon (GA)
Mercy Coll (NY)
Meredith Coll (NC)
Miami U (OH)
Michigan State U (MI)
Middlebury Coll (VT)
Middle Tennessee State U (TN)
Mills Coll (CA)
Morningside Coll (IA)
Mount Holyoke Coll (MA)
Mount Mercy U (IA)
Mount St. Mary's U (MD)
Muhlenberg Coll (PA)

Murray State U (KY)
Muskingum U (OH)
Nazareth Coll of Rochester (NY)
Newberry Coll (SC)
New York U (NY)
Niagara U (NY)
Northeastern U (MA)
Northern Arizona U (AZ)
Northern Kentucky U (KY)
Northern Michigan U (MI)
Northern Vermont U–Lyndon (VT)
Northwestern U (IL)
Northwest Nazarene U (ID)
Nova Southeastern U (FL)
Oakland U (MI)
Occidental Coll (CA)
Oglethorpe U (GA)
Ohio Northern U (OH)
The Ohio State U (OH)
Ohio U (OH)
Ohio Wesleyan U (OH)
Oklahoma Baptist U (OK)
Old Dominion U (VA)
Oral Roberts U (OK)
Otterbein U (OH)
Penn State Abington (PA)
Penn State Altoona (PA)
Penn State Beaver (PA)
Penn State Berks (PA)
Penn State Brandywine (PA)
Penn State DuBois (PA)
Penn State Erie, The Behrend Coll (PA)
Penn State Fayette, The Eberly Campus (PA)
Penn State Greater Allegheny (PA)
Penn State Hazleton (PA)
Penn State Lehigh Valley (PA)
Penn State Mont Alto (PA)
Penn State New Kensington (PA)
Penn State Schuylkill (PA)
Penn State Shenango (PA)
Penn State U Park (PA)
Penn State Wilkes-Barre (PA)
Penn State Worthington Scranton (PA)
Penn State York (PA)
Pitzer Coll (CA)
Pomona Coll (CA)
Portland State U (OR)
Quinnipiac U (CT)
Redeemer U Coll (ON, Canada)
Reed Coll (OR)
Rhodes Coll (TN)
Rider U (NJ)
Roanoke Coll (VA)
Rochester Inst of Technology (NY)
Rockhurst U (MO)
Roger Williams U (RI)
Rollins Coll (FL)
Roosevelt U (IL)
Saginaw Valley State U (MI)
Saint Anselm Coll (NH)
St. Catherine U (MN)
Saint Francis U (PA)
St. John Fisher Coll (NY)
Saint Joseph's U (PA)
Saint Louis U (MO)
Saint Mary's Coll of California (CA)
St. Mary's U (TX)
Saint Michael's Coll (VT)
St. Norbert Coll (WI)
St. Thomas U (NB, Canada)
Samford U (AL)
San Diego State U (CA)
San Francisco State U (CA)
Sarah Lawrence Coll (NY)
Seton Hill U (PA)
Shawnee State U (OH)
Simmons Coll (MA)
Simpson Coll (IA)
Skidmore Coll (NY)
Sonoma State U (CA)
Southwestern Adventist U (TX)
Southwestern U (TX)
Spring Hill Coll (AL)
Stanford U (CA)
State U of New York at New Paltz (NY)
State U of New York at Oswego (NY)
State U of New York Coll at Cortland (NY)
State U of New York Coll at Geneseo (NY)
State U of New York Coll at Oneonta (NY)

Stetson U (FL)
Sweet Briar Coll (VA)
Syracuse U (NY)
Taylor U (IN)
Texas Christian U (TX)
Texas State U (TX)
Tiffin U (OH)
Towson U (MD)
Trent U (ON, Canada)
Trinity U (TX)
Tufts U (MA)
Tulane U (LA)
United States Military Acad (NY)
The U of Alabama (AL)
U of Arkansas (AR)
U of Bridgeport (CT)
U of California, Davis (CA)
U of Chicago (IL)
U of Cincinnati (OH)
U of Denver (CO)
U of Evansville (IN)
U of Georgia (GA)
U of Hartford (CT)
U of Idaho (ID)
U of La Verne (CA)
U of Maine (ME)
U of Mary Washington (VA)
U of Massachusetts Boston (MA)
U of Memphis (TN)
U of Miami (FL)
U of Minnesota, Duluth (MN)
U of Minnesota, Twin Cities Campus (MN)
U of Missouri–St. Louis (MO)
U of Mount Union (OH)
U of Nebraska at Kearney (NE)
U of Nevada, Reno (NV)
U of New Hampshire (NH)
U of North Georgia (GA)
U of Pennsylvania (PA)
U of Pittsburgh at Bradford (PA)
U of Puget Sound (WA)
U of Richmond (VA)
U of Rochester (NY)
U of St. Thomas (MN)
U of St. Thomas (TX)
U of San Diego (CA)
U of San Francisco (CA)
The U of Scranton (PA)
U of South Carolina (SC)
U of Southern California (CA)
U of Southern Indiana (IN)
U of Southern Mississippi (MS)
The U of Tennessee at Martin (TN)
U of the Incarnate Word (TX)
U of the Pacific (CA)
The U of Toledo (OH)
U of Toronto (ON, Canada)
U of Virginia (VA)
U of Waterloo (ON, Canada)
U of West Georgia (GA)
U of Wisconsin–Parkside (WI)
Ursinus Coll (PA)
Utica Coll (NY)
Valparaiso U (IN)
Vassar Coll (NY)
Virginia Military Inst (VA)
Virginia Polytechnic Inst and State U (VA)
Virginia Wesleyan U (VA)
Wagner Coll (NY)
Walsh U (OH)
Wartburg Coll (IA)
Washington Coll (MD)
Washington State U (WA)
Washington U in St. Louis (MO)
Webster U (MO)
Wellesley Coll (MA)
Wells Coll (NY)
Western Kentucky U (KY)
Western Oregon U (OR)
Westminster Coll (PA)
West Virginia Wesleyan Coll (WV)
Wheaton Coll (IL)
Wheaton Coll (MA)
Whitworth U (WA)
Widener U (PA)
Wilkes U (PA)
William Jewell Coll (MO)
Wittenberg U (OH)
Worcester Polytechnic Inst (MA)
York Coll of Pennsylvania (PA)

INTERNATIONAL RELATIONS AND NATIONAL SECURITY RELATED
Indiana U Bloomington (IN)

King U (TN)
San Diego State U (CA)
U of Mount Union (OH)
Virginia Polytechnic Inst and State U (VA)

INVESTMENTS AND SECURITIES
Babson Coll (MA)
Lynn U (FL)
Marymount Manhattan Coll (NY)
U of North Dakota (ND)
U of Northern Iowa (IA)

IRANIAN LANGUAGES
U of Maryland, Coll Park (MD)
The U of Texas at Austin (TX)

IRISH STUDIES
Bard Coll (NY)
Canisius Coll (NY)

ISLAMIC STUDIES
Boston Coll (MA)
Connecticut Coll (CT)
DePaul U (IL)
Marlboro Coll (VT)
The Ohio State U (OH)
Sarah Lawrence Coll (NY)
The U of Texas at Austin (TX)
U of Washington (WA)
Villanova U (PA)
Washington U in St. Louis (MO)
Wellesley Coll (MA)

ITALIAN
Arizona State U at the Tempe campus (AZ)
Bard Coll (NY)
Barnard Coll (NY)
Bennington Coll (VT)
Binghamton U, State U of New York (NY)
Boston Coll (MA)
Brock U (ON, Canada)
Bryn Mawr Coll (PA)
California State U, Long Beach (CA)
Central Connecticut State U (CT)
Coll of Staten Island of the City U of New York (NY)
Coll of the Holy Cross (MA)
The Colorado Coll (CO)
Columbia U (NY)
Concordia U (QC, Canada)
Cornell U (NY)
Dartmouth Coll (NH)
DePaul U (IL)
Dominican U (IL)
Drew U (NJ)
Fairfield U (CT)
Florida Intl U (FL)
Florida State U (FL)
Fordham U (NY)
Franklin & Marshall Coll (PA)
Georgetown U (DC)
Gettysburg Coll (PA)
Gonzaga U (WA)
Haverford Coll (PA)
Hofstra U (NY)
Hunter Coll of the City U of New York (NY)
Indiana U Bloomington (IN)
Iona Coll (NY)
Ithaca Coll (NY)
Johns Hopkins U (MD)
Lehman Coll of the City U of New York (NY)
Loyola U Chicago (IL)
Marist Coll (NY)
Middlebury Coll (VT)
Montclair State U (NJ)
Mount Holyoke Coll (MA)
Nazareth Coll of Rochester (NY)
New York U (NY)
Northwestern U (IL)
The Ohio State U (OH)
Penn State Abington (PA)
Penn State Altoona (PA)
Penn State Beaver (PA)
Penn State Berks (PA)
Penn State Brandywine (PA)
Penn State DuBois (PA)
Penn State Erie, The Behrend Coll (PA)
Penn State Fayette, The Eberly Campus (PA)
Penn State Greater Allegheny (PA)

Penn State Hazleton (PA)
Penn State Lehigh Valley (PA)
Penn State Mont Alto (PA)
Penn State New Kensington (PA)
Penn State Schuylkill (PA)
Penn State Shenango (PA)
Penn State U Park (PA)
Penn State Wilkes-Barre (PA)
Penn State Worthington Scranton (PA)
Penn State York (PA)
Pepperdine U, Malibu (CA)
Providence Coll (RI)
Queens Coll of the City U of New York (NY)
Rutgers U–Newark (NJ)
Rutgers U–New Brunswick (NJ)
St. John's U (NY)
Saint Joseph's U (PA)
Saint Mary's Coll of California (CA)
San Francisco State U (CA)
Santa Clara U (CA)
Sarah Lawrence Coll (NY)
Scripps Coll (CA)
Smith Coll (MA)
Stanford U (CA)
Stony Brook U, State U of New York (NY)
Susquehanna U (PA)
Syracuse U (NY)
Temple U (PA)
Tufts U (MA)
Tulane U (LA)
U at Buffalo, the State U of New York (NY)
The U of Arizona (AZ)
U of California, Davis (CA)
U of California, Los Angeles (CA)
U of California, San Diego (CA)
U of Colorado Boulder (CO)
U of Denver (CO)
U of Houston (TX)
U of Illinois at Chicago (IL)
U of Maryland, Coll Park (MD)
U of Massachusetts Amherst (MA)
U of Massachusetts Boston (MA)
U of Michigan (MI)
U of Minnesota, Twin Cities Campus (MN)
U of New Hampshire (NH)
U of Notre Dame (IN)
U of Oklahoma (OK)
U of Oregon (OR)
U of Pennsylvania (PA)
U of Pittsburgh (PA)
U of Rhode Island (RI)
U of San Francisco (CA)
The U of Scranton (PA)
U of Southern California (CA)
The U of Tennessee (TN)
The U of Texas at Austin (TX)
U of Toronto (ON, Canada)
U of Virginia (VA)
U of Washington (WA)
U of Wisconsin–Madison (WI)
U of Wisconsin–Milwaukee (WI)
Vassar Coll (NY)
Villanova U (PA)
Washington U in St. Louis (MO)
Wellesley Coll (MA)
Youngstown State U (OH)

ITALIAN STUDIES
Arcadia U (PA)
Bard Coll (NY)
Boston U (MA)
Brock U (ON, Canada)
The Colorado Coll (CO)
Columbia U (NY)
Connecticut Coll (CT)
Dickinson Coll (PA)
Emory U (GA)
Fordham U (NY)
Franklin U Switzerland (Switzerland)
John Cabot U (Italy)
Merrimack Coll (MA)
Miami U (OH)
Purdue U (IN)
Saint Joseph's U (PA)
Scripps Coll (CA)
Southern Methodist U (TX)
Tufts U (MA)
Tulane U (LA)
U of California, Santa Barbara (CA)
U of California, Santa Cruz (CA)
U of Richmond (VA)

U of San Diego (CA)
The U of Texas at Austin (TX)
U of Vermont (VT)
Wellesley Coll (MA)
Wesleyan U (CT)
Wheaton Coll (MA)

JAPANESE
Ball State U (IN)
Bard Coll (NY)
Bates Coll (ME)
Beloit Coll (WI)
Bennington Coll (VT)
Boston U (MA)
California State U, Fullerton (CA)
California State U, Long Beach (CA)
California State U, Los Angeles (CA)
California State U, Monterey Bay (CA)
Calvin Coll (MI)
Carnegie Mellon U (PA)
Carthage Coll (WI)
Colgate U (NY)
Dartmouth Coll (NH)
Eastern Michigan U (MI)
Elizabethtown Coll (PA)
Emory U (GA)
Florida State U (FL)
Georgetown U (DC)
Gettysburg Coll (PA)
Gustavus Adolphus Coll (MN)
Hobart and William Smith Colls (NY)
Hofstra U (NY)
Lehigh U (PA)
Linfield Coll (OR)
Macalester Coll (MN)
Michigan State U (MI)
Middlebury Coll (VT)
Murray State U (KY)
North Central Coll (IL)
Oakland U (MI)
Occidental Coll (CA)
The Ohio State U (OH)
Penn State Abington (PA)
Penn State Altoona (PA)
Penn State Beaver (PA)
Penn State Berks (PA)
Penn State Brandywine (PA)
Penn State DuBois (PA)
Penn State Erie, The Behrend Coll (PA)
Penn State Fayette, The Eberly Campus (PA)
Penn State Greater Allegheny (PA)
Penn State Hazleton (PA)
Penn State Lehigh Valley (PA)
Penn State Mont Alto (PA)
Penn State New Kensington (PA)
Penn State Schuylkill (PA)
Penn State Shenango (PA)
Penn State U Park (PA)
Penn State Wilkes-Barre (PA)
Penn State Worthington Scranton (PA)
Penn State York (PA)
Pomona Coll (CA)
Portland State U (OR)
Purdue U (IN)
St. Olaf Coll (MN)
San Diego State U (CA)
San Francisco State U (CA)
Sarah Lawrence Coll (NY)
Scripps Coll (CA)
Stanford U (CA)
Tufts U (MA)
U of Alaska Fairbanks (AK)
U of California, Davis (CA)
U of California, Irvine (CA)
U of California, Los Angeles (CA)
U of California, San Diego (CA)
U of California, Santa Barbara (CA)
U of Colorado Boulder (CO)
The U of Findlay (OH)
U of Hawaii at Manoa (HI)
U of Kentucky (KY)
U of Maryland, Coll Park (MD)
U of Massachusetts Amherst (MA)
U of Montana (MT)
U of Mount Union (OH)
The U of North Carolina at Charlotte (NC)
U of Notre Dame (IN)
U of Oklahoma (OK)
U of Oregon (OR)

U of Pittsburgh (PA)
U of Puget Sound (WA)
U of Regina (SK, Canada)
U of Rochester (NY)
U of San Francisco (CA)
U of the Pacific (CA)
U of Vermont (VT)
U of Washington (WA)
U of Wisconsin–Madison (WI)
Vassar Coll (NY)
Wake Forest U (NC)
Washington State U (WA)
Washington U in St. Louis (MO)
Wellesley Coll (MA)
Western Michigan U (MI)
Western Washington U (WA)
Williams Coll (MA)

JAPANESE STUDIES
Case Western Reserve U (OH)
Earlham Coll (IN)
Gettysburg Coll (PA)
Gustavus Adolphus Coll (MN)
Hofstra U (NY)
Hope Coll (MI)
Linfield Coll (OR)
Oakland U (MI)
U at Albany, State U of New York (NY)
U of California, San Diego (CA)
U of Washington (WA)
U of Wisconsin–Whitewater (WI)
Willamette U (OR)

JAZZ/JAZZ STUDIES
Bard Coll (NY)
Bennington Coll (VT)
Brigham Young U (UT)
Butler U (IN)
Capital U (OH)
Central State U (OH)
City Coll of the City U of New York (NY)
Columbia U (NY)
Concordia U (QC, Canada)
Conservatorio de Musica de Puerto Rico (PR)
Cornish Coll of the Arts (WA)
DePaul U (IL)
Drake U (IA)
Eugene Lang Coll of Liberal Arts (NY)
Florida State U (FL)
Hampton U (VA)
Hofstra U (NY)
Hope Coll (MI)
Ithaca Coll (NY)
Jacksonville U (FL)
Liberty U (VA)
Limestone Coll (SC)
Lincoln Coll (IL)
Loyola U New Orleans (LA)
Michigan State U (MI)
Minnesota State U Moorhead (MN)
The New School Coll of Performing Arts (NY)
North Carolina Central U (NC)
North Central Coll (IL)
Northwestern U (IL)
Oberlin Coll (OH)
The Ohio State U (OH)
Roosevelt U (IL)
Rutgers U–New Brunswick (NJ)
San Francisco Conservatory of Music (CA)
Shenandoah U (VA)
Temple U (PA)
The U of Akron (OH)
U of Central Oklahoma (OK)
U of Hartford (CT)
U of Maryland, Baltimore County (MD)
U of Miami (FL)
U of Michigan (MI)
U of North Carolina at Asheville (NC)
The U of North Carolina at Greensboro (NC)
U of Northern Iowa (IA)
U of North Florida (FL)
U of North Texas (TX)
U of Oregon (OR)
U of Rochester (NY)
U of Southern California (CA)
The U of Texas at Austin (TX)
U of Washington (WA)
Webster U (MO)

Western Michigan U (MI)
Whitman Coll (WA)
Whitworth U (WA)
Youngstown State U (OH)

JEWISH/JUDAIC STUDIES
American U (DC)
Arizona State U at the Tempe campus (AZ)
Bard Coll (NY)
Barnard Coll (NY)
Bennington Coll (VT)
Binghamton U, State U of New York (NY)
California State U, Northridge (CA)
City Coll of the City U of New York (NY)
Clark U (MA)
Coll of Charleston (SC)
Concordia U (QC, Canada)
Dickinson Coll (PA)
Emory U (GA)
Florida Atlantic U (FL)
The George Washington U (DC)
Gettysburg Coll (PA)
Hofstra U (NY)
Hunter Coll of the City U of New York (NY)
Indiana U Bloomington (IN)
Lehman Coll of the City U of New York (NY)
Marlboro Coll (VT)
Muhlenberg Coll (PA)
Northeastern U (MA)
Oberlin Coll (OH)
The Ohio State U (OH)
Ohr Somayach/Joseph Tanenbaum Educational Center (NY)
Penn State Abington (PA)
Penn State Altoona (PA)
Penn State Beaver (PA)
Penn State Berks (PA)
Penn State Brandywine (PA)
Penn State DuBois (PA)
Penn State Erie, The Behrend Coll (PA)
Penn State Fayette, The Eberly Campus (PA)
Penn State Greater Allegheny (PA)
Penn State Hazleton (PA)
Penn State Lehigh Valley (PA)
Penn State Mont Alto (PA)
Penn State New Kensington (PA)
Penn State Schuylkill (PA)
Penn State Shenango (PA)
Penn State U Park (PA)
Penn State Wilkes-Barre (PA)
Penn State Worthington Scranton (PA)
Penn State York (PA)
Purdue U (IN)
Queens Coll of the City U of New York (NY)
Rutgers U–New Brunswick (NJ)
San Diego State U (CA)
San Francisco State U (CA)
Sarah Lawrence Coll (NY)
Scripps Coll (CA)
Syracuse U (NY)
Temple U (PA)
Touro Coll Los Angeles (CA)
Tufts U (MA)
Tulane U (LA)
U at Buffalo, the State U of New York (NY)
The U of Arizona (AZ)
U of California, Los Angeles (CA)
U of California, San Diego (CA)
U of California, Santa Cruz (CA)
U of Chicago (IL)
U of Colorado Boulder (CO)
U of Florida (FL)
U of Hartford (CT)
The U of Kansas (KS)
U of Maryland, Coll Park (MD)
U of Massachusetts Amherst (MA)
U of Miami (FL)
U of Michigan (MI)
U of Minnesota, Twin Cities Campus (MN)
U of Oklahoma (OK)
U of Oregon (OR)
U of Pennsylvania (PA)
U of Southern California (CA)
The U of Texas at Austin (TX)
U of Washington (WA)
U of Wisconsin–Madison (WI)

U of Wisconsin–Milwaukee (WI)
Vanderbilt U (TN)
Vassar Coll (NY)
Washington U in St. Louis (MO)
Wellesley Coll (MA)

JOURNALISM
Academy of Art U (CA)
Albright Coll (PA)
American U (DC)
The American U in Cairo (Egypt)
The American U of Paris (France)
Andrews U (MI)
Angelo State U (TX)
Appalachian State U (NC)
Arkansas Tech U (AR)
Asbury U (KY)
Ashland U (OH)
Auburn U (AL)
Augustana U (SD)
Averett U (VA)
Ball State U (IN)
Barry U (FL)
Baruch Coll of the City U of New York (NY)
Baylor U (TX)
Belmont U (TN)
Bemidji State U (MN)
Benedictine Coll (KS)
Bethel U (MN)
Biola U (CA)
Boston U (MA)
Bowling Green State U (OH)
Bradley U (IL)
Brigham Young U (UT)
Buffalo State Coll, State U of New York (NY)
Butler U (IN)
California Baptist U (CA)
California Lutheran U (CA)
California Polytechnic State U, San Luis Obispo (CA)
California State U, Dominguez Hills (CA)
California State U, Fullerton (CA)
California State U, Long Beach (CA)
California State U, Northridge (CA)
California State U, Sacramento (CA)
Campbellsville U (KY)
Canisius Coll (NY)
Carroll U (WI)
Cedarville U (OH)
Central Connecticut State U (CT)
Central Michigan U (MI)
Central State U (OH)
Chatham U (PA)
Cleveland State U (OH)
The Coll of New Jersey (NJ)
The Coll of St. Scholastica (MN)
Coll of the Ozarks (MO)
Colorado State U (CO)
Columbia Coll Chicago (IL)
Concordia U (QC, Canada)
Concordia U Chicago (IL)
Concord U (WV)
Corban U (OR)
Creighton U (NE)
Delaware State U (DE)
DePaul U (IL)
Doane U (NE)
Dominican U (IL)
Drake U (IA)
Drury U (MO)
Duquesne U (PA)
East Central U (OK)
Eastern Michigan U (MI)
Eastern Nazarene Coll (MA)
Eastern Washington U (WA)
Elon U (NC)
Emerson Coll (MA)
Flagler Coll (FL)
Florida Ag and Mech U (FL)
Fordham U (NY)
Franklin Coll (IN)
Franklin Pierce U (NH)
Gannon U (PA)
The George Washington U (DC)
Georgia Coll & State U (GA)
Georgia Southern U (GA)
Georgia State U (GA)
Gettysburg Coll (PA)
Gonzaga U (WA)
Goshen Coll (IN)
Grand Valley State U (MI)
Grand View U (IA)

Hampton U (VA)
Harding U (AR)
Hofstra U (NY)
Humboldt State U (CA)
Illinois State U (IL)
Indiana U Bloomington (IN)
Indiana U of Pennsylvania (PA)
Indiana U–Purdue U Indianapolis (IN)
Indiana U Southeast (IN)
Indiana Wesleyan U (IN)
Iona Coll (NY)
Iowa State U of Science and Technology (IA)
Ithaca Coll (NY)
Kansas State U (KS)
Keene State Coll (NH)
Kennesaw State U (GA)
Kent State U (OH)
Lebanese American U (Lebanon)
Lee U (TN)
Lehigh U (PA)
Lewis U (IL)
Liberty U (VA)
Lincoln U (MO)
Lindenwood U (MO)
Long Island U–LIU Brooklyn (NY)
Long Island U–LIU Post (NY)
Louisiana Coll (LA)
Loyola U Chicago (IL)
Loyola U New Orleans (LA)
Lubbock Christian U (TX)
Madonna U (MI)
Marietta Coll (OH)
Marquette U (WI)
Marshall U (WV)
Massachusetts Coll of Liberal Arts (MA)
Mercer U, Macon (GA)
Messiah Coll (PA)
Metropolitan State U of Denver (CO)
Miami U (OH)
Michigan State U (MI)
Middle Tennessee State U (TN)
Minnesota State U Moorhead (MN)
Missouri State U (MO)
Montclair State U (NJ)
Mount Mercy U (IA)
Mount Saint Mary's U (CA)
Mount Vernon Nazarene U (OH)
Murray State U (KY)
Muskingum U (OH)
New Mexico State U (NM)
New York U (NY)
North Central Coll (IL)
Northeastern State U (OK)
Northeastern U (MA)
Northern Arizona U (AZ)
Northern Illinois U (IL)
Northern Kentucky U (KY)
North Greenville U (SC)
Northwestern U (IL)
Oakland U (MI)
Ohio Northern U (OH)
The Ohio State U (OH)
Ohio U (OH)
Ohio Wesleyan U (OH)
Oklahoma Baptist U (OK)
Oklahoma Christian U (OK)
Otterbein U (OH)
Pace U, Pleasantville Campus (NY)
Palm Beach Atlantic U (FL)
Penn State Abington (PA)
Penn State Altoona (PA)
Penn State Beaver (PA)
Penn State Berks (PA)
Penn State Brandywine (PA)
Penn State DuBois (PA)
Penn State Erie, The Behrend Coll (PA)
Penn State Fayette, The Eberly Campus (PA)
Penn State Greater Allegheny (PA)
Penn State Hazleton (PA)
Penn State Lehigh Valley (PA)
Penn State Mont Alto (PA)
Penn State New Kensington (PA)
Penn State Schuylkill (PA)
Penn State Shenango (PA)
Penn State U Park (PA)
Penn State Wilkes-Barre (PA)
Penn State Worthington Scranton (PA)
Penn State York (PA)
Pepperdine U, Malibu (CA)
Pfeiffer U (NC)

Point Loma Nazarene U (CA)
Point Park U (PA)
Purchase Coll, State U of New York (NY)
Quinnipiac U (CT)
Radford U (VA)
Rider U (NJ)
Rochester Inst of Technology (NY)
Roosevelt U (IL)
Rowan U (NJ)
Rust Coll (MS)
Rutgers U–Newark (NJ)
Rutgers U–New Brunswick (NJ)
St. Ambrose U (IA)
Saint Augustine's U (NC)
St. Bonaventure U (NY)
St. Catherine U (MN)
Saint Francis U (PA)
St. John's U (NY)
St. Joseph's Coll, Long Island Campus (NY)
St. Joseph's Coll, New York (NY)
St. Thomas Aquinas Coll (NY)
St. Thomas U (NB, Canada)
Samford U (AL)
Sam Houston State U (TX)
San Diego State U (CA)
San Francisco State U (CA)
Seattle U (WA)
Seton Hill U (PA)
Shippensburg U of Pennsylvania (PA)
Southeastern U (FL)
Southern Adventist U (TN)
Southern Arkansas U–Magnolia (AR)
Southern Illinois U Carbondale (IL)
Southern Methodist U (TX)
Southwestern Adventist U (TX)
Southwestern Coll (KS)
Spring Hill Coll (AL)
State U of New York at New Paltz (NY)
State U of New York at Oswego (NY)
State U of New York at Plattsburgh (NY)
Stony Brook U, State U of New York (NY)
Suffolk U (MA)
Syracuse U (NY)
Taylor U (IN)
Temple U (PA)
Tennessee Technological U (TN)
Texas A&M U–Commerce (TX)
Texas Christian U (TX)
Texas State U (TX)
Texas Tech U (TX)
Tiffin U (OH)
Trent U (ON, Canada)
Trevecca Nazarene U (TN)
Troy U (AL)
Union U (TN)
U at Albany, State U of New York (NY)
U of Alaska Fairbanks (AK)
The U of Arizona (AZ)
U of Arkansas (AR)
U of Bridgeport (CT)
U of Central Arkansas (AR)
U of Central Florida (FL)
U of Central Missouri (MO)
U of Cincinnati (OH)
U of Denver (CO)
U of Evansville (IN)
The U of Findlay (OH)
U of Florida (FL)
U of Georgia (GA)
U of Hawaii at Manoa (HI)
U of Houston (TX)
U of Idaho (ID)
The U of Kansas (KS)
U of Kentucky (KY)
U of King's Coll (NS, Canada)
U of La Verne (CA)
U of Maine (ME)
U of Maryland, Coll Park (MD)
U of Massachusetts Amherst (MA)
U of Memphis (TN)
U of Miami (FL)
U of Minnesota, Duluth (MN)
U of Minnesota, Twin Cities Campus (MN)
U of Missouri (MO)
U of Montana (MT)
U of Nebraska at Kearney (NE)
U of Nevada, Reno (NV)

U of New Mexico (NM)
U of Northern Colorado (CO)
U of North Texas (TX)
U of Oklahoma (OK)
U of Oregon (OR)
U of Pittsburgh at Greensburg (PA)
U of Regina (SK, Canada)
U of Rhode Island (RI)
U of Richmond (VA)
U of South Carolina (SC)
U of Southern California (CA)
U of Southern Indiana (IN)
U of Southern Mississippi (MS)
The U of Tennessee (TN)
The U of Texas at Austin (TX)
The U of Texas at El Paso (TX)
U of the Incarnate Word (TX)
U of Washington (WA)
U of West Georgia (GA)
U of Wisconsin–Eau Claire (WI)
U of Wisconsin–Madison (WI)
U of Wisconsin–River Falls (WI)
U of Wisconsin–Whitewater (WI)
U of Wyoming (WY)
Utah State U (UT)
Utica Coll (NY)
Wartburg Coll (IA)
Washington and Lee U (VA)
Washington State U (WA)
Washington U in St. Louis (MO)
Waynesburg U (PA)
Wayne State U (MI)
Weber State U (UT)
Webster U (MO)
Western Illinois U (IL)
Western Kentucky U (KY)
Western Michigan U (MI)
Western Washington U (WA)
West Texas A&M U (TX)
West Virginia U (WV)
Whitworth U (WA)
Youngstown State U (OH)

JOURNALISM RELATED
Abilene Christian U (TX)
Arizona State U at the Downtown Phoenix campus (AZ)
Benedictine U (IL)
Bennett Coll (NC)
Bowling Green State U (OH)
California State U, Long Beach (CA)
Calvary U (MO)
Central Michigan U (MI)
Columbia Coll (SC)
Fairfield U (CT)
Florida Inst of Technology (FL)
Kentucky State U (KY)
Marymount Manhattan Coll (NY)
Missouri Baptist U (MO)
Oklahoma State U (OK)
Point Park U (PA)
Roosevelt U (IL)
Simpson Coll (IA)
Southern Adventist U (TN)
Syracuse U (NY)
Taylor U (IN)
The U of Akron (OH)
U of California, Irvine (CA)
U of Colorado Boulder (CO)
U of Nebraska–Lincoln (NE)
Webster U (MO)
Western Washington U (WA)
Westminster Coll (PA)

JUVENILE CORRECTIONS
Harris-Stowe State U (MO)
Prairie View A&M U (TX)

KEYBOARD INSTRUMENTS
Acadia U (NS, Canada)
Anderson U (SC)
Andrews U (MI)
Ashland U (OH)
Baldwin Wallace U (OH)
Barry U (FL)
Birmingham-Southern Coll (AL)
Bob Jones U (SC)
Boston U (MA)
Bowling Green State U (OH)
Brigham Young U (UT)
California Baptist U (CA)
Calvary U (MO)
Campbellsville U (KY)
Capital U (OH)
Carson-Newman U (TN)
The Catholic U of America (DC)
Chapman U (CA)

Coker Coll (SC)
Coll of the Ozarks (MO)
Conservatorio de Musica de Puerto Rico (PR)
Converse Coll (SC)
Cornish Coll of the Arts (WA)
Dallas Baptist U (TX)
Drake U (IA)
East Central U (OK)
Hardin-Simmons U (TX)
Heidelberg U (OH)
Hope Coll (MI)
Houston Baptist U (TX)
Howard Payne U (TX)
Illinois Wesleyan U (IL)
Ithaca Coll (NY)
Jacksonville U (FL)
Liberty U (VA)
Lipscomb U (TN)
Madonna U (MI)
The Master's U (CA)
The New School Coll of Performing Arts (NY)
New York U (NY)
Northwestern U (IL)
Nyack Coll (NY)
Oakland U (MI)
Oberlin Coll (OH)
Ohio U (OH)
Oklahoma City U (OK)
Oral Roberts U (OK)
Ouachita Baptist U (AR)
Palm Beach Atlantic U (FL)
Point Loma Nazarene U (CA)
Rider U (NJ)
Roberts Wesleyan Coll (NY)
Roosevelt U (IL)
Samford U (AL)
San Francisco Conservatory of Music (CA)
Shenandoah U (VA)
Shorter U (GA)
Southeastern U (FL)
Southern Methodist U (TX)
State U of New York at Fredonia (NY)
Stetson U (FL)
Syracuse U (NY)
Texas Christian U (TX)
Union U (TN)
The U of Akron (OH)
U of Central Oklahoma (OK)
U of Cincinnati (OH)
The U of Kansas (KS)
U of Miami (FL)
U of Southern California (CA)
The U of Tennessee at Martin (TN)
U of the Pacific (CA)
The U of Tulsa (OK)
U of Washington (WA)
Valparaiso U (IN)
Vanderbilt U (TN)
Weber State U (UT)
Western Michigan U (MI)
Whitworth U (WA)
Wichita State U (KS)
Willamette U (OR)
Xavier U of Louisiana (LA)
Youngstown State U (OH)

KINDERGARTEN/PRESCHOOL EDUCATION
Arcadia U (PA)
Ashland U (OH)
Athens State U (AL)
Barry U (FL)
Baylor U (TX)
Black Hills State U (SD)
Bluefield Coll (VA)
Bowie State U (MD)
Bowling Green State U (OH)
Brandon U (MB, Canada)
Bucknell U (PA)
Buffalo State Coll, State U of New York (NY)
Cairn U (PA)
California Polytechnic State U, San Luis Obispo (CA)
Carson-Newman U (TN)
Catawba Coll (NC)
Central Connecticut State U (CT)
Central Methodist U (MO)
Concordia U (QC, Canada)
Concordia U Wisconsin (WI)
Concord U (WV)
Converse Coll (SC)
Delaware State U (DE)

East Carolina U (NC)
Eastern Nazarene Coll (MA)
Elmhurst Coll (IL)
Evangel U (MO)
Georgia State U (GA)
Greensboro Coll (NC)
Hampton U (VA)
Hunter Coll of the City U of New York (NY)
Illinois State U (IL)
Inter American U of Puerto Rico, Aguadilla Campus (PR)
Inter American U of Puerto Rico, Barranquitas Campus (PR)
Inter American U of Puerto Rico, Metropolitan Campus (PR)
Inter American U of Puerto Rico, San Germán Campus (PR)
John Carroll U (OH)
Kean U (NJ)
Lesley U (MA)
Lincoln Memorial U (TN)
Long Island U–LIU Post (NY)
Mansfield U of Pennsylvania (PA)
Marshall U (WV)
McPherson Coll (KS)
Michigan State U (MI)
New Jersey City U (NJ)
New Mexico Highlands U (NM)
North Carolina Central U (NC)
Northern Kentucky U (KY)
Northwestern Oklahoma State U (OK)
Ohio Northern U (OH)
Ohio Wesleyan U (OH)
Oklahoma Baptist U (OK)
Oklahoma Christian U (OK)
Olivet Nazarene U (IL)
Piedmont Coll (GA)
Post U (CT)
St. Catherine U (MN)
St. Thomas Aquinas Coll (NY)
Shaw U (NC)
Southeastern Oklahoma State U (OK)
State U of New York at Fredonia (NY)
State U of New York Coll at Cortland (NY)
State U of New York Coll at Oneonta (NY)
Susquehanna U (PA)
Tennessee Technological U (TN)
Thomas U (GA)
Tufts U (MA)
Union U (TN)
Université de Sherbrooke (QC, Canada)
The U of Arizona (AZ)
U of Arkansas (AR)
U of Central Arkansas (AR)
U of Cincinnati (OH)
U of Maine at Farmington (ME)
U of Maryland, Coll Park (MD)
U of Maryland Eastern Shore (MD)
U of Minnesota, Crookston (MN)
U of Minnesota, Duluth (MN)
U of Minnesota, Twin Cities Campus (MN)
U of Missouri (MO)
The U of North Carolina at Charlotte (NC)
The U of North Carolina at Pembroke (NC)
The U of North Carolina Wilmington (NC)
U of Northern Iowa (IA)
U of Providence (MT)
U of Regina (SK, Canada)
The U of Tennessee at Martin (TN)
The U of Toledo (OH)
Utah State U (UT)
Wagner Coll (NY)
Walsh U (OH)
Wartburg Coll (IA)
Westfield State U (MA)
West Virginia Wesleyan Coll (WV)
Widener U (PA)

KINESIOLOGY AND EXERCISE SCIENCE
Acadia U (NS, Canada)
Adams State U (CO)
Albion Coll (MI)
Anderson U (IN)
Anderson U (SC)
Angelo State U (TX)

Appalachian State U (NC)
Aquinas Coll (MI)
Arizona State U at the Downtown Phoenix campus (AZ)
Asbury U (KY)
Auburn U at Montgomery (AL)
Augsburg U (MN)
Augustana U (SD)
Aurora U (IL)
Avila U (MO)
Baker U (KS)
Ball State U (IN)
Barry U (FL)
Barton Coll (NC)
Baylor U (TX)
Becker Coll (MA)
Belhaven U (MS)
Bellarmine U (KY)
Belmont U (TN)
Berry Coll (GA)
Bethel Coll (IN)
Bethel U (MN)
Biola U (CA)
Bluefield Coll (VA)
Blue Mountain Coll (MS)
Bob Jones U (SC)
Boise State U (ID)
Brenau U (GA)
Bridgewater State U (MA)
Brigham Young U (UT)
Brock U (ON, Canada)
Buffalo State Coll, State U of New York (NY)
California Baptist U (CA)
California Lutheran U (CA)
California State U, East Bay (CA)
California State U, Long Beach (CA)
California State U, Los Angeles (CA)
California State U, Northridge (CA)
California State U, Sacramento (CA)
California State U, San Marcos (CA)
Calvin Coll (MI)
Capital U (OH)
Carroll U (WI)
Carson-Newman U (TN)
Carthage Coll (WI)
Catawba Coll (NC)
Cedar Crest Coll (PA)
Cedarville U (OH)
Central Connecticut State U (CT)
Central Michigan U (MI)
Central State U (OH)
Chatham U (PA)
Chowan U (NC)
The Citadel, The Military Coll of South Carolina (SC)
Coastal Carolina U (SC)
Coker Coll (SC)
The Coll at Brockport, State U of New York (NY)
The Coll of Idaho (ID)
Coll of Saint Mary (NE)
Colorado Mesa U (CO)
Colorado State U (CO)
Colorado State U–Pueblo (CO)
Columbia Coll (SC)
Columbus State U (GA)
Concordia U (QC, Canada)
Concordia U Chicago (IL)
Concordia U, Nebraska (NE)
Concordia U, St. Paul (MN)
Corban U (OR)
Cornell Coll (IA)
Cornerstone U (MI)
Creighton U (NE)
Dakota State U (SD)
Dean Coll (MA)
Defiance Coll (OH)
DePaul U (IL)
DePauw U (IN)
DeSales U (PA)
Dickinson State U (ND)
East Central U (OK)
Eastern Mennonite U (VA)
Eastern Michigan U (MI)
Eastern U (PA)
Eastern Washington U (WA)
East Stroudsburg U of Pennsylvania (PA)
East Texas Baptist U (TX)
Elmhurst Coll (IL)
Elon U (NC)
Emmanuel Coll (GA)

Endicott Coll (MA)
Fitchburg State U (MA)
Florida Atlantic U (FL)
Florida Gulf Coast U (FL)
Florida State U (FL)
Franklin Coll (IN)
Frostburg State U (MD)
Gannon U (PA)
George Mason U (VA)
Georgetown Coll (KY)
The George Washington U (DC)
Georgia Coll & State U (GA)
Georgia Gwinnett Coll (GA)
Georgian Court U (NJ)
Georgia Southern U (GA)
Gonzaga U (WA)
Goshen Coll (IN)
Grand Valley State U (MI)
Grand View U (IA)
Greensboro Coll (NC)
Greenville U (IL)
Grove City Coll (PA)
Guilford Coll (NC)
Hamline U (MN)
Hannibal-LaGrange U (MO)
Harding U (AR)
Hardin-Simmons U (TX)
High Point U (NC)
Hillsdale Coll (MI)
Hiram Coll (OH)
Hope Coll (MI)
Houston Baptist U (TX)
Humboldt State U (CA)
Huntingdon Coll (AL)
Husson U (ME)
Huston-Tillotson U (TX)
Illinois State U (IL)
Immaculata U (PA)
Indiana State U (IN)
Indiana U Bloomington (IN)
Indiana U–Purdue U Indianapolis (IN)
Indiana Wesleyan U (IN)
Iowa State U of Science and Technology (IA)
Ithaca Coll (NY)
Jacksonville U (FL)
Jefferson Coll of Health Sciences (VA)
John Brown U (AR)
Kansas State U (KS)
Kansas Wesleyan U (KS)
Keene State Coll (NH)
Keiser U, Fort Lauderdale (FL)
Kennesaw State U (GA)
Kent State U (OH)
Kentucky State U (KY)
King's Coll (PA)
King U (TN)
LaGrange Coll (GA)
Lamar U (TX)
La Roche Coll (PA)
Lasell Coll (MA)
La Sierra U (CA)
Lebanon Valley Coll (PA)
Lee U (TN)
Lenoir-Rhyne U (NC)
LeTourneau U (TX)
Lewis U (IL)
Liberty U (VA)
Life U (GA)
Lincoln Coll (IL)
Lincoln Memorial U (TN)
Lindenwood U (MO)
Linfield Coll (OR)
Lipscomb U (TN)
Long Island U–LIU Brooklyn (NY)
Longwood U (VA)
Loras Coll (IA)
Louisiana Coll (LA)
Malone U (OH)
Manchester U (IN)
Marian U (IN)
Marian U (WI)
Marshall U (WV)
Maryville Coll (TN)
Maryville U of Saint Louis (MO)
The Master's U (CA)
McDaniel Coll (MD)
McKendree U (IL)
McMurry U (TX)
McNeese State U (LA)
Mercy Coll (NY)
Meredith Coll (NC)
Miami U (OH)
Michigan State U (MI)
Michigan Technological U (MI)

MidAmerica Nazarene U (KS)
Middle Tennessee State U (TN)
Minnesota State U Moorhead (MN)
Mississippi State U (MS)
Missouri Baptist U (MO)
Missouri State U (MO)
Missouri Valley Coll (MO)
Monmouth Coll (IL)
Montclair State U (NJ)
Morehead State U (KY)
Mount Vernon Nazarene U (OH)
Murray State U (KY)
New Mexico State U (NM)
North Carolina Wesleyan Coll (NC)
North Central Coll (IL)
North Dakota State U (ND)
Northeastern State U (OK)
Northern Arizona U (AZ)
Northern Michigan U (MI)
Northern Vermont U–Lyndon (VT)
Northwestern Coll (IA)
Northwest Nazarene U (ID)
Notre Dame de Namur U (CA)
Nova Southeastern U (FL)
Occidental Coll (CA)
Ohio Dominican U (OH)
Ohio Northern U (OH)
The Ohio State U (OH)
Oklahoma Baptist U (OK)
Oklahoma State U (OK)
Olivet Nazarene U (IL)
Oral Roberts U (OK)
Oregon State U (OR)
Ottawa U (KS)
Ouachita Baptist U (AR)
Our Lady of the Lake U (TX)
Pacific Lutheran U (WA)
Palm Beach Atlantic U (FL)
Penn State Abington (PA)
Penn State Altoona (PA)
Penn State Beaver (PA)
Penn State Berks (PA)
Penn State Brandywine (PA)
Penn State DuBois (PA)
Penn State Erie, The Behrend Coll (PA)
Penn State Fayette, The Eberly Campus (PA)
Penn State Greater Allegheny (PA)
Penn State Hazleton (PA)
Penn State Lehigh Valley (PA)
Penn State Mont Alto (PA)
Penn State New Kensington (PA)
Penn State Schuylkill (PA)
Penn State Shenango (PA)
Penn State U Park (PA)
Penn State Wilkes-Barre (PA)
Penn State Worthington Scranton (PA)
Penn State York (PA)
Pepperdine U, Malibu (CA)
Piedmont Coll (GA)
Pittsburg State U (KS)
Point U (GA)
Prairie View A&M U (TX)
Purdue U (IN)
Queens Coll of the City U of New York (NY)
Redeemer U Coll (ON, Canada)
Regis U (CO)
Rice U (TX)
Roanoke Coll (VA)
Roberts Wesleyan Coll (NY)
Rockford U (IL)
Rocky Mountain Coll (MT)
Rutgers U–New Brunswick (NJ)
Saginaw Valley State U (MI)
Saint Augustine's U (NC)
Saint Louis U (MO)
Saint Mary's Coll of California (CA)
St. Mary's U (TX)
St. Olaf Coll (MN)
Salisbury U (MD)
Samford U (AL)
Sam Houston State U (TX)
San Diego State U (CA)
San Francisco State U (CA)
Schreiner U (TX)
Seattle Pacific U (WA)
Seattle U (WA)
Seton Hill U (PA)
Shaw U (NC)
Shippensburg U of Pennsylvania (PA)
Simmons Coll (MA)
Simon Fraser U (BC, Canada)
Simpson Coll (IA)

Sonoma State U (CA)
Southeastern U (FL)
Southern Adventist U (TN)
Southern Arkansas U–Magnolia (AR)
Southern Illinois U Carbondale (IL)
Southern Illinois U Edwardsville (IL)
Southern Utah U (UT)
Southwest Baptist U (MO)
Southwestern Adventist U (TX)
Southwestern U (TX)
State U of New York Coll at Cortland (NY)
Stephen F. Austin State U (TX)
Stockton U (NJ)
Syracuse U (NY)
Tabor Coll (KS)
Tarleton State U (TX)
Taylor U (IN)
Temple U (PA)
Tennessee Wesleyan U (TN)
Texas A&M Intl U (TX)
Texas A&M U (TX)
Texas A&M U–Commerce (TX)
Texas A&M U–Corpus Christi (TX)
Texas A&M U–Kingsville (TX)
Texas Lutheran U (TX)
Texas State U (TX)
Texas Tech U (TX)
Texas Woman's U (TX)
Towson U (MD)
Transylvania U (KY)
Trent U (ON, Canada)
Trine U (IN)
Trinity Christian Coll (IL)
Troy U (AL)
Truett McConnell U (GA)
Truman State U (MO)
Tusculum Coll (TN)
Union Coll (NE)
Union U (TN)
United States Military Acad (NY)
United States Sports Acad (AL)
Université de Sherbrooke (QC, Canada)
U of Central Arkansas (AR)
U of Central Oklahoma (OK)
U of Charleston (WV)
U of Dayton (OH)
U of Dubuque (IA)
U of Evansville (IN)
U of Georgia (GA)
U of Guelph (ON, Canada)
U of Hawaii at Manoa (HI)
U of Houston (TX)
U of Houston–Clear Lake (TX)
U of Idaho (ID)
U of Illinois at Chicago (IL)
U of Illinois at Springfield (IL)
U of Jamestown (ND)
The U of Kansas (KS)
U of La Verne (CA)
U of Louisiana at Monroe (LA)
U of Mary Hardin-Baylor (TX)
U of Maryland, Coll Park (MD)
U of Memphis (TN)
U of Michigan (MI)
U of Minnesota, Duluth (MN)
U of Mount Union (OH)
U of Nevada, Las Vegas (NV)
U of New England (ME)
U of New Hampshire (NH)
The U of North Carolina at Greensboro (NC)
The U of North Carolina Wilmington (NC)
U of North Dakota (ND)
U of Northern Colorado (CO)
U of North Texas (TX)
U of Oklahoma (OK)
U of Pittsburgh at Bradford (PA)
U of Puget Sound (WA)
U of Regina (SK, Canada)
U of Rhode Island (RI)
U of Saint Mary (KS)
U of San Francisco (CA)
U of Saskatchewan (SK, Canada)
The U of Scranton (PA)
U of Sioux Falls (SD)
U of South Carolina (SC)
U of South Carolina Aiken (SC)
U of Southern Indiana (IN)
The U of Tennessee (TN)
The U of Tennessee at Chattanooga (TN)
The U of Texas at Austin (TX)

The U of Texas at San Antonio (TX)
The U of Texas of the Permian Basin (TX)
The U of Texas Rio Grande Valley (TX)
U of the Fraser Valley (BC, Canada)
U of the Incarnate Word (TX)
U of the Pacific (CA)
The U of Toledo (OH)
The U of Tulsa (OK)
U of Utah (UT)
U of Vermont (VT)
U of Virginia (VA)
U of Waterloo (ON, Canada)
The U of West Alabama (AL)
U of Wisconsin–Eau Claire (WI)
U of Wisconsin–La Crosse (WI)
U of Wisconsin–Madison (WI)
U of Wisconsin–Milwaukee (WI)
U of Wisconsin–Parkside (WI)
U of Wyoming (WY)
Upper Iowa U (IA)
Valparaiso U (IN)
Vanguard U of Southern California (CA)
Wake Forest U (NC)
Walsh U (OH)
Warner Pacific Coll (OR)
Washington State U (WA)
Waynesburg U (PA)
Webster U (MO)
Western Illinois U (IL)
Western Kentucky U (KY)
Western Michigan U (MI)
Western Oregon U (OR)
Western State Colorado U (CO)
Western Washington U (WA)
Westmont Coll (CA)
West Texas A&M U (TX)
West Virginia Wesleyan Coll (WV)
Whittier Coll (CA)
Whitworth U (WA)
Wichita State U (KS)
Willamette U (OR)
William Paterson U of New Jersey (NJ)
William Peace U (NC)
William Penn U (IA)
William Woods U (MO)
Winona State U (MN)
Wisconsin Lutheran Coll (WI)
Wittenberg U (OH)
Wright State U (OH)
Wright State U–Lake Campus (OH)
Youngstown State U (OH)

KINESIOTHERAPY
Boston U (MA)
Bridgewater State U (MA)
California State U, Long Beach (CA)
Shaw U (NC)

KNOWLEDGE MANAGEMENT
Framingham State U (MA)
Saint Joseph's U (PA)
Syracuse U (NY)

KOREAN
Brigham Young U (UT)
The Ohio State U (OH)
U of California, Irvine (CA)
U of California, Los Angeles (CA)
U of Hawaii at Manoa (HI)
U of Washington (WA)

KOREAN STUDIES
U of Washington (WA)

LABOR AND INDUSTRIAL RELATIONS
Athabasca U (AB, Canada)
Bowling Green State U (OH)
Brock U (ON, Canada)
Clarion U of Pennsylvania (PA)
Cleveland State U (OH)
Cornell U (NY)
New York U (NY)
Penn State Abington (PA)
Penn State Altoona (PA)
Penn State Beaver (PA)
Penn State Berks (PA)
Penn State Brandywine (PA)
Penn State DuBois (PA)
Penn State Erie, The Behrend Coll (PA)

Penn State Fayette, The Eberly Campus (PA)
Penn State Greater Allegheny (PA)
Penn State Hazleton (PA)
Penn State Lehigh Valley (PA)
Penn State Mont Alto (PA)
Penn State New Kensington (PA)
Penn State Schuylkill (PA)
Penn State Shenango (PA)
Penn State U Park (PA)
Penn State Wilkes-Barre (PA)
Penn State Worthington Scranton (PA)
Penn State York (PA)
Rider U (NJ)
Rutgers U–New Brunswick (NJ)
Saint Francis U (PA)
San Francisco State U (CA)
State U of New York at Fredonia (NY)
State U of New York Coll at Old Westbury (NY)
State U of New York Empire State Coll (NY)
Tennessee Technological U (TN)
U of Bridgeport (CT)
U of Cincinnati (OH)
U of Massachusetts Boston (MA)
U of Minnesota, Twin Cities Campus (MN)
U of Toronto (ON, Canada)
Wayne State U (MI)

LABOR STUDIES
California State U, Dominguez Hills (CA)
Eastern Michigan U (MI)
Hofstra U (NY)
Indiana U Bloomington (IN)
Indiana U Kokomo (IN)
Indiana U Northwest (IN)
Indiana U–Purdue U Indianapolis (IN)
Indiana U South Bend (IN)
Queens Coll of the City U of New York (NY)

LANDSCAPE ARCHITECTURE
Academy of Art U (CA)
American U of Beirut (Lebanon)
Arizona State U at the Tempe campus (AZ)
Ball State U (IN)
Boston Architectural Coll (MA)
California Polytechnic State U, San Luis Obispo (CA)
California State Polytechnic U, Pomona (CA)
Clemson U (SC)
Coll of the Atlantic (ME)
Colorado State U (CO)
Cornell U (NY)
Delaware Valley U (PA)
Iowa State U of Science and Technology (IA)
Louisiana State U and A&M Coll (LA)
Michigan State U (MI)
Mississippi State U (MS)
North Dakota State U (ND)
Northeastern U (MA)
The Ohio State U (OH)
Oklahoma State U (OK)
Penn State Brandywine (PA)
Penn State Lehigh Valley (PA)
Penn State Schuylkill (PA)
Penn State U Park (PA)
Penn State Wilkes-Barre (PA)
Purdue U (IN)
Rutgers U–New Brunswick (NJ)
State U of New York Coll of Environmental Science and Forestry (NY)
Temple U (PA)
Texas A&M U (TX)
Texas Tech U (TX)
U of Arkansas (AR)
U of California, Davis (CA)
U of Florida (FL)
U of Georgia (GA)
U of Idaho (ID)
U of Kentucky (KY)
U of Maryland, Coll Park (MD)
U of Massachusetts Amherst (MA)
U of Nebraska–Lincoln (NE)
U of Nevada, Las Vegas (NV)
U of Oregon (OR)

U of Rhode Island (RI)
The U of Texas at Austin (TX)
U of Washington (WA)
U of Wisconsin–Madison (WI)
Utah State U (UT)
Virginia Polytechnic Inst and State U (VA)
Washington State U (WA)
West Virginia U (WV)

LANDSCAPING AND GROUNDSKEEPING
Andrews U (MI)
Delaware Valley U (PA)
Iowa State U of Science and Technology (IA)
Mississippi State U (MS)
Oklahoma State U (OK)
Penn State Abington (PA)
Penn State Altoona (PA)
Penn State Beaver (PA)
Penn State Berks (PA)
Penn State Brandywine (PA)
Penn State DuBois (PA)
Penn State Erie, The Behrend Coll (PA)
Penn State Fayette, The Eberly Campus (PA)
Penn State Greater Allegheny (PA)
Penn State Hazleton (PA)
Penn State Lehigh Valley (PA)
Penn State Mont Alto (PA)
Penn State New Kensington (PA)
Penn State Schuylkill (PA)
Penn State Shenango (PA)
Penn State U Park (PA)
Penn State Wilkes-Barre (PA)
Penn State Worthington Scranton (PA)
Penn State York (PA)
Tennessee Technological U (TN)
U of Minnesota, Crookston (MN)
U of Nebraska–Lincoln (NE)
Washington State U (WA)

LAND USE PLANNING AND MANAGEMENT
Central Michigan U (MI)
Marietta Coll (OH)
Metropolitan State U of Denver (CO)
U of Saskatchewan (SK, Canada)
U of Wisconsin–River Falls (WI)
West Virginia U (WV)

LANGUAGE INTERPRETATION AND TRANSLATION
Aquinas Coll (MI)
Brigham Young U (UT)
Concordia U (QC, Canada)
Kent State U (OH)
Lebanese American U (Lebanon)
Marlboro Coll (VT)
Northwestern Coll (IA)
Oklahoma State U–Oklahoma City (OK)
The U of Texas Rio Grande Valley (TX)

LASER AND OPTICAL ENGINEERING
Delaware State U (DE)
U of Central Florida (FL)
U of Rochester (NY)

LASER AND OPTICAL TECHNOLOGY
Oregon Inst of Technology (OR)

LATIN
Acadia U (NS, Canada)
Amherst Coll (MA)
Augustana Coll (IL)
Austin Coll (TX)
Bard Coll (NY)
Barnard Coll (NY)
Baylor U (TX)
Binghamton U, State U of New York (NY)
Boston U (MA)
Bowling Green State U (OH)
Bryn Mawr Coll (PA)
Canisius Coll (NY)
Carleton Coll (MN)
The Catholic U of America (DC)
Colgate U (NY)
Dartmouth Coll (NH)
DePauw U (IN)
Duquesne U (PA)

Emory U (GA)
Florida State U (FL)
Fordham U (NY)
Franklin & Marshall Coll (PA)
Furman U (SC)
Gettysburg Coll (PA)
Hampden-Sydney Coll (VA)
Haverford Coll (PA)
Hillsdale Coll (MI)
Hobart and William Smith Colls (NY)
Hofstra U (NY)
Hunter Coll of the City U of New York (NY)
John Carroll U (OH)
Kalamazoo Coll (MI)
Kenyon Coll (OH)
Knox Coll (IL)
Lehman Coll of the City U of New York (NY)
Loyola U Chicago (IL)
Loyola U New Orleans (LA)
Marlboro Coll (VT)
Mercer U, Macon (GA)
Missouri State U (MO)
Monmouth Coll (IL)
Montclair State U (NJ)
Mount Holyoke Coll (MA)
New York U (NY)
Oberlin Coll (OH)
Queens Coll of the City U of New York (NY)
Randolph Coll (VA)
Randolph-Macon Coll (VA)
Rice U (TX)
Rockford U (IL)
Rutgers U–New Brunswick (NJ)
Saint Joseph's U (PA)
Saint Mary's Coll of California (CA)
St. Olaf Coll (MN)
Samford U (AL)
Santa Clara U (CA)
Sarah Lawrence Coll (NY)
Sewanee: The U of the South (TN)
Smith Coll (MA)
Southwestern U (TX)
Trinity U (TX)
Tufts U (MA)
Tulane U (LA)
U of California, Los Angeles (CA)
U of Michigan (MI)
U of Missouri (MO)
U of New Hampshire (NH)
The U of North Carolina at Greensboro (NC)
U of Richmond (VA)
U of St. Thomas (MN)
The U of Scranton (PA)
The U of Texas at Austin (TX)
U of Toronto (ON, Canada)
U of Vermont (VT)
U of Washington (WA)
U of Wisconsin–Madison (WI)
Virginia Wesleyan U (VA)
Wabash Coll (IN)
Wake Forest U (NC)
Washington U in St. Louis (MO)
Wellesley Coll (MA)
Western Michigan U (MI)
Westminster Coll (PA)
Whitman Coll (WA)
Wright State U (OH)
Wright State U–Lake Campus (OH)

LATIN AMERICAN AND CARIBBEAN STUDIES
Coll of Charleston (SC)
Florida State U (FL)
Iowa State U of Science and Technology (IA)
Linfield Coll (OR)
Mount Holyoke Coll (MA)
Rollins Coll (FL)
Union Coll (NY)
U of Georgia (GA)
The U of Kansas (KS)
U of Michigan (MI)
U of Wisconsin–Madison (WI)
U of Wisconsin–Milwaukee (WI)

LATIN AMERICAN STUDIES
Adelphi U (NY)
Albion Coll (MI)
Albright Coll (PA)
Alverno Coll (WI)
American U (DC)
Arizona State U at the West campus (AZ)

Assumption Coll (MA)
Bard Coll (NY)
Barnard Coll (NY)
Bates Coll (ME)
Baylor U (TX)
Bennington Coll (VT)
Binghamton U, State U of New York (NY)
Boston U (MA)
Bowdoin Coll (ME)
Bowling Green State U (OH)
Brandeis U (MA)
Bucknell U (PA)
California State U, Fullerton (CA)
California State U, Los Angeles (CA)
California State U, Northridge (CA)
Canisius Coll (NY)
Carleton Coll (MN)
City Coll of the City U of New York (NY)
Colby Coll (ME)
Colgate U (NY)
Coll of the Holy Cross (MA)
The Coll of William and Mary (VA)
Columbia U (NY)
Connecticut Coll (CT)
Cornell Coll (IA)
Dartmouth Coll (NH)
Davidson Coll (NC)
Denison U (OH)
DePaul U (IL)
Dickinson Coll (PA)
Earlham Coll (IN)
Emory U (GA)
Flagler Coll (FL)
Fordham U (NY)
George Mason U (VA)
The George Washington U (DC)
Gettysburg Coll (PA)
Gonzaga U (WA)
Gustavus Adolphus Coll (MN)
Hamline U (MN)
Hampshire Coll (MA)
Haverford Coll (PA)
Hobart and William Smith Colls (NY)
Hofstra U (NY)
Hood Coll (MD)
Hunter Coll of the City U of New York (NY)
Illinois Wesleyan U (IL)
Iowa State U of Science and Technology (IA)
John Jay Coll of Criminal Justice of the City U of New York (NY)
Johns Hopkins U (MD)
Knox Coll (IL)
Lehigh U (PA)
Lehman Coll of the City U of New York (NY)
Macalester Coll (MN)
Marlboro Coll (VT)
Marquette U (WI)
Miami U (OH)
Middlebury Coll (VT)
Millsaps Coll (MS)
New York U (NY)
Oakland U (MI)
Oberlin Coll (OH)
Occidental Coll (CA)
Ohio U (OH)
Ohio Wesleyan U (OH)
Pace U (NY)
Penn State Abington (PA)
Penn State Altoona (PA)
Penn State Beaver (PA)
Penn State Berks (PA)
Penn State Brandywine (PA)
Penn State DuBois (PA)
Penn State Erie, The Behrend Coll (PA)
Penn State Fayette, The Eberly Campus (PA)
Penn State Greater Allegheny (PA)
Penn State Hazleton (PA)
Penn State Lehigh Valley (PA)
Penn State Mont Alto (PA)
Penn State New Kensington (PA)
Penn State Schuylkill (PA)
Penn State Shenango (PA)
Penn State U Park (PA)
Penn State Wilkes-Barre (PA)
Penn State Worthington Scranton (PA)
Penn State York (PA)
Pepperdine U, Malibu (CA)

Pomona Coll (CA)
Portland State U (OR)
Queens Coll of the City U of New York (NY)
Rhode Island Coll (RI)
Rhodes Coll (TN)
Rice U (TX)
Rutgers U–New Brunswick (NJ)
Saint Mary's Coll of California (CA)
St. Olaf Coll (MN)
Samford U (AL)
San Diego State U (CA)
Sarah Lawrence Coll (NY)
Scripps Coll (CA)
Seattle Pacific U (WA)
Smith Coll (MA)
Southwestern U (TX)
Stanford U (CA)
State U of New York at New Paltz (NY)
State U of New York at Plattsburgh (NY)
Syracuse U (NY)
Temple U (PA)
Trinity U (TX)
Tufts U (MA)
Tulane U (LA)
United States Military Acad (NY)
U at Albany, State U of New York (NY)
The U of Arizona (AZ)
U of California, Los Angeles (CA)
U of California, Riverside (CA)
U of California, San Diego (CA)
U of California, Santa Cruz (CA)
U of Central Florida (FL)
U of Chicago (IL)
U of Cincinnati (OH)
U of Denver (CO)
U of Idaho (ID)
U of Illinois at Chicago (IL)
U of Kentucky (KY)
U of Louisville (KY)
U of Miami (FL)
U of Minnesota, Duluth (MN)
U of Minnesota, Morris (MN)
U of Missouri (MO)
U of Nebraska–Lincoln (NE)
U of Nevada, Las Vegas (NV)
U of New Mexico (NM)
The U of North Carolina at Chapel Hill (NC)
The U of North Carolina at Charlotte (NC)
U of Oregon (OR)
U of Pennsylvania (PA)
U of Rhode Island (RI)
U of Richmond (VA)
U of San Francisco (CA)
The U of Scranton (PA)
U of South Carolina (SC)
The U of Texas at Austin (TX)
U of Toronto (ON, Canada)
U of Utah (UT)
U of Vermont (VT)
U of Washington (WA)
U of Wisconsin–Eau Claire (WI)
Vanderbilt U (TN)
Vassar Coll (NY)
Villanova U (PA)
Washington Coll (MD)
Washington U in St. Louis (MO)
Wellesley Coll (MA)
Wesleyan U (CT)
Westminster Coll (UT)
Whittier Coll (CA)
Willamette U (OR)
William Paterson U of New Jersey (NJ)

LATIN TEACHER EDUCATION
Ball State U (IN)
Boston U (MA)
Brigham Young U (UT)
Duquesne U (PA)
Miami U (OH)
Missouri State U (MO)
Montclair State U (NJ)
Ohio Wesleyan U (OH)
Queens Coll of the City U of New York (NY)
Western Michigan U (MI)

LAW ENFORCEMENT INTELLIGENCE ANALYSIS
ECPI U, Virginia Beach (VA)

LAY MINISTRY
Arizona Christian U (AZ)
Bethel Coll (IN)
Bethel U (MN)
Coll of Biblical Studies–Houston (TX)
Horizon U (IN)
Huntingdon Coll (AL)
Liberty U (VA)
Point Loma Nazarene U (CA)
Saint Mary's U of Minnesota (MN)
Trevecca Nazarene U (TN)
Trinity Christian Coll (IL)
U of Saint Francis (IN)
U of St. Thomas (MN)

LEARNING SCIENCES
Purdue U (IN)
The U of Arizona (AZ)

LEGAL ASSISTANT/PARALEGAL
Bay Path U (MA)
Boston U (MA)
Champlain Coll (VT)
Clarion U of Pennsylvania (PA)
Clayton State U (GA)
Coll of Saint Mary (NE)
Concordia U Wisconsin (WI)
Daemen Coll (NY)
Davenport U, Grand Rapids (MI)
East Central U (OK)
Eastern Michigan U (MI)
Elms Coll (MA)
Florida Gulf Coast U (FL)
Gannon U (PA)
Grand Valley State U (MI)
Hamline U (MN)
Hampton U (VA)
Hilbert Coll (NY)
Husson U (ME)
Idaho State U (ID)
Illinois State U (IL)
Indiana U–Purdue U Indianapolis (IN)
Kent State U (OH)
Lewis U (IL)
Liberty U (VA)
Loyola U Chicago (IL)
Madonna U (MI)
Maryville U of Saint Louis (MO)
Mercy Coll (NY)
Minnesota State U Moorhead (MN)
Mount St. Joseph U (OH)
National U (CA)
Northern Michigan U (MI)
Nova Southeastern U (FL)
Peirce Coll (PA)
Quinnipiac U (CT)
Regent U (VA)
Roger Williams U (RI)
Roosevelt U (IL)
Saint Mary-of-the-Woods Coll (IN)
Southern Illinois U Carbondale (IL)
State U of New York Coll of Technology at Canton (NY)
Stephen F. Austin State U (TX)
Stevenson U (MD)
Suffolk U (MA)
Sullivan U (KY)
Texas A&M U–Commerce (TX)
Tiffin U (OH)
U of Central Florida (FL)
U of Hartford (CT)
U of Houston–Clear Lake (TX)
U of La Verne (CA)
U of North Georgia (GA)
U of Providence (MT)
U of Southern Mississippi (MS)
The U of Tennessee at Chattanooga (TN)
Ursuline Coll (OH)
Valdosta State U (GA)
Western Kentucky U (KY)
William Woods U (MO)
Winona State U (MN)

LEGAL PROFESSIONS AND STUDIES RELATED
Ball State U (IN)
Bay Path U (MA)
Brenau U (GA)
California U of Pennsylvania (PA)
Drexel U (PA)
Georgia Southern U–Armstrong Campus (GA)
John Jay Coll of Criminal Justice of the City U of New York (NY)

Maryville U of Saint Louis (MO)
Montclair State U (NJ)
New Jersey Inst of Technology (NJ)
Ramapo Coll of New Jersey (NJ)
Roger Williams U (RI)
St. John's U (NY)
Syracuse U (NY)
Temple U (PA)
Tulane U (LA)
The U of Arizona (AZ)
U of Illinois at Springfield (IL)
U of Nebraska–Lincoln (NE)
U of Pennsylvania (PA)
The U of Tulsa (OK)
U of Wisconsin–Superior (WI)
Western Michigan U (MI)
William Woods U (MO)

LEGAL STUDIES
Adams State U (CO)
American Public U System (WV)
American U (DC)
Amherst Coll (MA)
Anderson U (SC)
Arizona State U at the Tempe campus (AZ)
Bay Path U (MA)
Bethany Lutheran Coll (MN)
Blackburn Coll (IL)
Brandman U (CA)
Bridgewater State U (MA)
Central Michigan U (MI)
Central Penn Coll (PA)
Coll of the Atlantic (ME)
Culver-Stockton Coll (MO)
DeSales U (PA)
Dickinson Coll (PA)
Doane U (NE)
Dominican U (IL)
Elms Coll (MA)
Emory & Henry Coll (VA)
Florida National U (FL)
Hamline U (MN)
Hampshire Coll (MA)
Harding U (AR)
Houston Baptist U (TX)
Illinois State U (IL)
John Jay Coll of Criminal Justice of the City U of New York (NY)
Keiser U, Fort Lauderdale (FL)
Lasell Coll (MA)
Lipscomb U (TN)
Mercy Coll (NY)
Morehead State U (KY)
Mount St. Joseph U (OH)
National Paralegal Coll (AZ)
Nazareth Coll of Rochester (NY)
Northeastern State U (OK)
Northwestern U (IL)
Northwest U (WA)
Oberlin Coll (OH)
Point Park U (PA)
Post U (CT)
Quinnipiac U (CT)
St. John Fisher Coll (NY)
St. John's U (NY)
Saint Joseph's U (PA)
Samford U (AL)
Scripps Coll (CA)
Southeastern U (FL)
State U of New York at Fredonia (NY)
Stevenson U (MD)
United States Military Acad (NY)
Université de Sherbrooke (QC, Canada)
U of Arkansas (AR)
U of California, Santa Cruz (CA)
U of Central Florida (FL)
U of Central Oklahoma (OK)
U of Denver (CO)
U of Hartford (CT)
The U of Kansas (KS)
U of La Verne (CA)
U of Maryland U Coll (MD)
U of Massachusetts Amherst (MA)
U of Miami (FL)
U of Montana (MT)
U of New Haven (CT)
U of Pittsburgh (PA)
The U of Texas at San Antonio (TX)
U of Washington (WA)
U of Washington, Tacoma (WA)
U of Wisconsin–Madison (WI)
Webster U (MO)
Western New England U (MA)

William Paterson U of New Jersey (NJ)
Wilmington U (DE)
Winona State U (MN)

LEGAL SUPPORT SERVICES RELATED
U of Cincinnati (OH)

LIBERAL ARTS AND SCIENCES AND HUMANITIES RELATED
Anderson U (IN)
Anderson U (SC)
Antioch Coll, Yellow Springs (OH)
Auburn U (AL)
Augsburg U (MN)
Belhaven U (MS)
Blue Mountain Coll (MS)
Brigham Young U (UT)
Bryan Coll (TN)
Butler U (IN)
California Polytechnic State U, San Luis Obispo (CA)
California State U, Dominguez Hills (CA)
Centre Coll (KY)
Coll of Saint Mary (NE)
The Colorado Coll (CO)
Drexel U (PA)
Duquesne U (PA)
Elms Coll (MA)
Fairfield U (CT)
Fairleigh Dickinson U, Florham Campus (NJ)
Florida Atlantic U (FL)
George Mason U (VA)
Georgia Coll & State U (GA)
Georgia Southern U–Armstrong Campus (GA)
Graceland U (IA)
Hampshire Coll (MA)
Hobe Sound Bible Coll (FL)
Hofstra U (NY)
Indiana U Bloomington (IN)
Indiana U East (IN)
Indiana U Kokomo (IN)
Indiana U Northwest (IN)
Indiana U–Purdue U Indianapolis (IN)
Indiana U South Bend (IN)
Indiana U Southeast (IN)
Iowa State U of Science and Technology (IA)
Johns Hopkins U (MD)
Kansas Wesleyan U (KS)
Kent State U at Ashtabula (OH)
Kent State U at East Liverpool (OH)
Kent State U at Geauga (OH)
Kent State U at Salem (OH)
Kent State U at Stark (OH)
Kent State U at Trumbull (OH)
Kent State U at Tuscarawas (OH)
The King's Coll (NY)
La Sierra U (CA)
Loyola U New Orleans (LA)
Malone U (OH)
Marlboro Coll (VT)
Marymount California U (CA)
Missouri Baptist U (MO)
Molloy Coll (NY)
Mount Aloysius Coll (PA)
New Coll of Florida (FL)
North Carolina State U (NC)
Northern Vermont U–Lyndon (VT)
Oakland U (MI)
Ohio U (OH)
Oklahoma City U (OK)
Pepperdine U, Malibu (CA)
Purchase Coll, State U of New York (NY)
Saint Anselm Coll (NH)
Saint Mary's Coll of California (CA)
Seattle U (WA)
Southern Methodist U (TX)
Southern Vermont Coll (VT)
Stevens Inst of Technology (NJ)
Tarleton State U (TX)
Trine U (IN)
Truett McConnell U (GA)
Tulane U (LA)
Union Coll (NE)
The U of Akron (OH)
U of California, Los Angeles (CA)
U of California, Santa Barbara (CA)
U of Maine at Farmington (ME)
U of Maryland U Coll (MD)
U of Mary Washington (VA)
U of Massachusetts Amherst (MA)

U of Oklahoma (OK)
U of Rhode Island (RI)
U of San Francisco (CA)
The U of Texas at Austin (TX)
The U of Texas at San Antonio (TX)
U of Utah (UT)
U of Wisconsin–Milwaukee (WI)
U of Wisconsin–Platteville (WI)
U of Wisconsin–River Falls (WI)
U of Wisconsin–Whitewater (WI)
Valdosta State U (GA)
Vassar Coll (NY)
Walsh U (OH)
Wayland Baptist U (TX)
Western Illinois U (IL)
Westminster Coll (UT)
West Virginia U Inst of Technology (WV)
Worcester Polytechnic Inst (MA)

LIBERAL ARTS AND SCIENCES/LIBERAL STUDIES
Abilene Christian U (TX)
Adams State U (CO)
Alaska Pacific U (AK)
Albion Coll (MI)
Alcorn State U (MS)
Alverno Coll (WI)
American Intl Coll (MA)
American U (DC)
Amridge U (AL)
Andrews U (MI)
Antioch U Los Angeles (CA)
Antioch U Midwest (OH)
Antioch U Santa Barbara (CA)
Appalachian State U (NC)
Aquinas Coll (MI)
Arcadia U (PA)
Arizona State U at the Polytechnic campus (AZ)
Ashland U (OH)
Athabasca U (AB, Canada)
Athens State U (AL)
Augsburg U (MN)
Augustana Coll (IL)
Augustana U (SD)
Aurora U (IL)
Austin Peay State U (TN)
Averett U (VA)
Azusa Pacific U (CA)
Ball State U (IN)
Barry U (FL)
Barton Coll (NC)
Baruch Coll of the City U of New York (NY)
Bay Path U (MA)
Beacon Coll (FL)
Becker Coll (MA)
Bellarmine U (KY)
Belmont U (TN)
Bemidji State U (MN)
Benedictine Coll (KS)
Bennington Coll (VT)
Bentley U (MA)
Bethany Lutheran Coll (MN)
Bethel Coll (IN)
Bethune-Cookman U (FL)
Biola U (CA)
Bluefield Coll (VA)
Boston U (MA)
Bowling Green State U (OH)
Bowling Green State U–Firelands Coll (OH)
Bradley U (IL)
Brandman U (CA)
Brandon U (MB, Canada)
Brenau U (GA)
Brescia U (KY)
Bridgewater Coll (VA)
Brigham Young U (UT)
Brigham Young U–Idaho (ID)
Brock U (ON, Canada)
Bryan Coll (TN)
Buffalo State Coll, State U of New York (NY)
Cairn U (PA)
California Baptist U (CA)
California Lutheran U (CA)
California Polytechnic State U, San Luis Obispo (CA)
California State Polytechnic U, Pomona (CA)
California State U, Dominguez Hills (CA)
California State U, East Bay (CA)
California State U, Fullerton (CA)

California State U, Long Beach (CA)
California State U, Los Angeles (CA)
California State U, Monterey Bay (CA)
California State U, Northridge (CA)
California State U, Sacramento (CA)
California State U, San Bernardino (CA)
California State U, San Marcos (CA)
California State U, Stanislaus (CA)
California U of Pennsylvania (PA)
Canisius Coll (NY)
Carlow U (PA)
Carnegie Mellon U (PA)
Carson-Newman U (TN)
The Catholic U of America (DC)
Cazenovia Coll (NY)
Cedarville U (OH)
Central Michigan U (MI)
Champlain Coll (VT)
Chapman U (CA)
Charter Oak State Coll (CT)
Chatham U (PA)
Chestnut Hill Coll (PA)
Christian Brothers U (TN)
Clarke U (IA)
Clarkson U (NY)
Clayton State U (GA)
Cleveland State U (OH)
Coastal Carolina U (SC)
Coe Coll (IA)
The Coll at Brockport, State U of New York (NY)
Coll of Mount Saint Vincent (NY)
The Coll of New Rochelle (NY)
The Coll of Saint Rose (NY)
Coll of the Atlantic (ME)
Colorado Christian U (CO)
Colorado Mesa U (CO)
Colorado State U (CO)
Colorado State U–Pueblo (CO)
Columbia Coll (SC)
Columbus State U (GA)
Conception Sem Coll (MO)
Concordia Coll–New York (NY)
Concordia U Irvine (CA)
Concordia U Wisconsin (WI)
Corban U (OR)
Cornell Coll (IA)
Culver-Stockton Coll (MO)
Curry Coll (MA)
Daemen Coll (NY)
Dakota State U (SD)
Dean Coll (MA)
Defiance Coll (OH)
DeSales U (PA)
Dominican U of California (CA)
Drexel U (PA)
Duquesne U (PA)
East Carolina U (NC)
Eastern Mennonite U (VA)
Eastern Nazarene Coll (MA)
Eastern New Mexico U (NM)
Eastern Oregon U (OR)
East Tennessee State U (TN)
Elon U (NC)
Emmanuel Coll (MA)
Emory & Henry Coll (VA)
Emory U (GA)
Endicott Coll (MA)
Eugene Lang Coll of Liberal Arts (NY)
The Evergreen State Coll (WA)
Excelsior Coll (NY)
Fayetteville State U (NC)
Felician U (NJ)
Fisher Coll (MA)
Fitchburg State U (MA)
Flagler Coll (FL)
Florida Atlantic U (FL)
Florida Coll (FL)
Florida Gulf Coast U (FL)
Florida Intl U (FL)
Florida National U (FL)
Fort Lewis Coll (CO)
Framingham State U (MA)
Francis Marion U (SC)
Franklin Pierce U (NH)
Friends U (KS)
Frostburg State U (MD)
Gannon U (PA)
George Mason U (VA)
Georgetown U (DC)

The George Washington U (DC)
Gettysburg Coll (PA)
Golden Gate U (CA)
Governors State U (IL)
Graceland U (IA)
Grand Valley State U (MI)
Grand View U (IA)
Granite State Coll (NH)
Green Mountain Coll (VT)
Greenville U (IL)
Gutenberg Coll (OR)
Hannibal-LaGrange U (MO)
Harris-Stowe State U (MO)
Harvard U (MA)
Hofstra U (NY)
Holy Names U (CA)
Hope Intl U (CA)
Houston Baptist U (TX)
Howard Payne U (TX)
Humboldt State U (CA)
Husson U (ME)
Illinois Coll (IL)
Illinois State U (IL)
Illinois Wesleyan U (IL)
Immaculata U (PA)
Indiana State U (IN)
Indiana U Bloomington (IN)
Indiana U of Pennsylvania (PA)
Indiana U Southeast (IN)
Iona Coll (NY)
Iowa State U of Science and Technology (IA)
Ithaca Coll (NY)
Jacksonville U (FL)
James Madison U (VA)
Johns Hopkins U (MD)
Juniata Coll (PA)
Kentucky State U (KY)
Kutztown U of Pennsylvania (PA)
Langston U (OK)
La Roche Coll (PA)
La Sierra U (CA)
Lee U (TN)
Lenoir-Rhyne U (NC)
Lesley U (MA)
Lewis U (IL)
Liberty U (VA)
Limestone Coll (SC)
Lincoln Coll (IL)
Lincoln Memorial U (TN)
Lincoln U (MO)
Lincoln U (PA)
Lindenwood U (MO)
Lock Haven U of Pennsylvania (PA)
Long Island U–LIU Post (NY)
Longwood U (VA)
Loras Coll (IA)
Louisiana State U and A&M Coll (LA)
Loyola Marymount U (CA)
Loyola U Chicago (IL)
Lynn U (FL)
Manchester U (IN)
Manhattan Coll (NY)
Manhattanville Coll (NY)
Mansfield U of Pennsylvania (PA)
Maria Coll (NY)
Marian U (WI)
Marietta Coll (OH)
Marist Coll (NY)
Marlboro Coll (VT)
Mary Baldwin U (VA)
Marymount California U (CA)
Marymount Manhattan Coll (NY)
Marymount U (VA)
Maryville U of Saint Louis (MO)
Massachusetts Coll of Liberal Arts (MA)
Massachusetts Inst of Technology (MA)
The Master's U (CA)
McNeese State U (LA)
Mercy Coll (NY)
Merrimack Coll (MA)
Miami U (OH)
Michigan Technological U (MI)
Middlebury Coll (VT)
Middle Tennessee State U (TN)
Mississippi State U (MS)
Monmouth Coll (IL)
Montana Tech of The U of Montana (MT)
Morris Coll (SC)
Mount Aloysius Coll (PA)
Mount Marty Coll (SD)
Mount Mary U (WI)
Mount St. Joseph U (OH)

Mount Saint Mary's U (CA)
Murray State U (KY)
Neumann U (PA)
Newman U (KS)
New Mexico Highlands U (NM)
New Mexico State U (NM)
New Saint Andrews Coll (ID)
The New School for Public Engagement (NY)
New York U (NY)
Niagara U (NY)
North Carolina State U (NC)
North Carolina Wesleyan Coll (NC)
North Central Coll (IL)
Northern Arizona U (AZ)
Northern Illinois U (IL)
Northern Kentucky U (KY)
Northern Michigan U (MI)
Northern State U (SD)
Northern Vermont U–Lyndon (VT)
North Greenville U (SC)
Northwestern Coll (IA)
Northwestern State U of Louisiana (LA)
Northwestern U (IL)
Northwest Nazarene U (ID)
Notre Dame de Namur U (CA)
Oakland U (MI)
Oklahoma Christian U (OK)
Oklahoma City U (OK)
Oklahoma State U (OK)
Olivet Nazarene U (IL)
Oral Roberts U (OK)
Oregon State U (OR)
Pace U (NY)
Pace U, Pleasantville Campus (NY)
Parsons School of Design (NY)
Penn State Abington (PA)
Penn State Altoona (PA)
Penn State Beaver (PA)
Penn State Berks (PA)
Penn State Brandywine (PA)
Penn State DuBois (PA)
Penn State Erie, The Behrend Coll (PA)
Penn State Fayette, The Eberly Campus (PA)
Penn State Greater Allegheny (PA)
Penn State Lehigh Valley (PA)
Penn State Mont Alto (PA)
Penn State New Kensington (PA)
Penn State Schuylkill (PA)
Penn State Shenango (PA)
Penn State U Park (PA)
Penn State Wilkes-Barre (PA)
Penn State Worthington Scranton (PA)
Penn State York (PA)
Pepperdine U, Malibu (CA)
Pittsburg State U (KS)
Point Loma Nazarene U (CA)
Point Park U (PA)
Portland State U (OR)
Providence Coll (RI)
Purchase Coll, State U of New York (NY)
Purdue U Northwest (IN)
Quinnipiac U (CT)
Ramapo Coll of New Jersey (NJ)
Randolph Coll (VA)
Regis U (CO)
Rhode Island Coll (RI)
Rider U (NJ)
Rivier U (NH)
Roberts Wesleyan Coll (NY)
Rogers State U (OK)
Roger Williams U (RI)
Roosevelt U (IL)
Rowan U (NJ)
Rutgers U–Camden (NJ)
Rutgers U–New Brunswick (NJ)
The Sage Colls (NY)
St. John Fisher Coll (NY)
St. John's Coll (MD)
St. John's Coll (NM)
St. John's U (NY)
St. Joseph's Coll, Long Island Campus (NY)
St. Joseph's Coll, New York (NY)
Saint Joseph's U (PA)
St. Lawrence U (NY)
St. Louis Coll of Pharmacy (MO)
Saint Mary-of-the-Woods Coll (IN)
Saint Mary's Coll of California (CA)
St. Olaf Coll (MN)
Saint Peter's U (NJ)
St. Thomas U (FL)

Saint Vincent Coll (PA)
Salisbury U (MD)
Salve Regina U (RI)
San Diego State U (CA)
San Francisco State U (CA)
Santa Clara U (CA)
Sarah Lawrence Coll (NY)
Schreiner U (TX)
Seattle Pacific U (WA)
Seattle U (WA)
Shaw U (NC)
Shenandoah U (VA)
Shippensburg U of Pennsylvania (PA)
Shorter U (GA)
Simon Fraser U (BC, Canada)
Skidmore Coll (NY)
Soka U of America (CA)
Sonoma State U (CA)
Southern Illinois U Carbondale (IL)
Southern Illinois U Edwardsville (IL)
Southwestern Coll (KS)
Spring Hill Coll (AL)
State U of New York at Fredonia (NY)
State U of New York at New Paltz (NY)
State U of New York at Plattsburgh (NY)
State U of New York Coll at Old Westbury (NY)
State U of New York Coll at Oneonta (NY)
Stephen F. Austin State U (TX)
Stevens Inst of Technology (NJ)
Stockton U (NJ)
Sweet Briar Coll (VA)
Syracuse U (NY)
Tarleton State U (TX)
Temple U (PA)
Tennessee Technological U (TN)
Texas A&M U–Central Texas (TX)
Texas A&M U–Commerce (TX)
Texas Tech U (TX)
Thomas Aquinas Coll (CA)
Thomas Edison State U (NJ)
Thomas Jefferson U (PA)
Thomas More Coll of Liberal Arts (NH)
Thomas U (GA)
Trent U (ON, Canada)
Trine U (IN)
Troy U (AL)
Tufts U (MA)
Tulane U (LA)
Union Coll (NY)
U at Albany, State U of New York (NY)
The U of Akron (OH)
U of Alaska Fairbanks (AK)
U of Bridgeport (CT)
U of California, Riverside (CA)
U of California, Santa Barbara (CA)
U of Central Arkansas (AR)
U of Central Oklahoma (OK)
U of Cincinnati (OH)
U of Dubuque (IA)
U of Evansville (IN)
U of Hartford (CT)
U of Hawaii at Manoa (HI)
U of Houston (TX)
U of Illinois at Springfield (IL)
The U of Kansas (KS)
U of La Verne (CA)
U of Louisville (KY)
U of Maine (ME)
U of Maine at Farmington (ME)
U of Maine at Fort Kent (ME)
U of Maine at Presque Isle (ME)
U of Maryland Eastern Shore (MD)
U of Mary Washington (VA)
U of Massachusetts Dartmouth (MA)
U of Massachusetts Lowell (MA)
U of Memphis (TN)
U of Michigan–Dearborn (MI)
U of Missouri–St. Louis (MO)
U of Montana (MT)
U of Nebraska–Lincoln (NE)
U of Nevada, Las Vegas (NV)
U of New England (ME)
U of New Haven (CT)
U of New Mexico (NM)
U of North Carolina at Asheville (NC)

The U of North Carolina at Chapel Hill (NC)
The U of North Carolina at Charlotte (NC)
The U of North Carolina at Greensboro (NC)
U of Northern Iowa (IA)
U of Notre Dame (IN)
U of Oklahoma (OK)
U of Pennsylvania (PA)
U of Pittsburgh (PA)
U of Pittsburgh at Bradford (PA)
U of Regina (SK, Canada)
U of Rochester (NY)
U of St. Francis (IL)
U of Saint Francis (IN)
U of Saint Mary (KS)
U of St. Thomas (TX)
U of San Diego (CA)
U of San Francisco (CA)
The U of Scranton (PA)
U of Sioux Falls (SD)
U of South Carolina (SC)
U of South Carolina Aiken (SC)
U of South Dakota (SD)
U of Southern Indiana (IN)
U of Southern Maine (ME)
The U of Tampa (FL)
The U of Texas at Austin (TX)
U of the Incarnate Word (TX)
The U of Toledo (OH)
The U of Tulsa (OK)
U of Vermont (VT)
U of Virginia (VA)
The U of Virginia's Coll at Wise (VA)
U of Waterloo (ON, Canada)
U of Wisconsin–Eau Claire (WI)
U of Wisconsin–Parkside (WI)
U of Wisconsin–Stevens Point (WI)
U of Wisconsin–Waukesha (WI)
U of Wisconsin–Whitewater (WI)
Utah State U (UT)
Utica Coll (NY)
Villanova U (PA)
Walsh U (OH)
Warner Pacific Coll (OR)
Washington Coll (MD)
Washington State U (WA)
Washington U in St. Louis (MO)
Weber State U (UT)
West Chester U of Pennsylvania (PA)
Western Connecticut State U (CT)
Western Illinois U (IL)
Western New England U (MA)
Westfield State U (MA)
Westmont Coll (CA)
West Virginia U (WV)
Whittier Coll (CA)
Wichita State U (KS)
Wilkes U (PA)
Willamette U (OR)
William Jewell Coll (MO)
William Paterson U of New Jersey (NJ)
William Peace U (NC)
Wittenberg U (OH)

LIBRARY AND INFORMATION SCIENCE
Clarion U of Pennsylvania (PA)
Emory & Henry Coll (VA)
Kutztown U of Pennsylvania (PA)
Sam Houston State U (TX)
U of Southern Mississippi (MS)

LIBRARY SCIENCE RELATED
Delaware State U (DE)
U of Providence (MT)

LICENSED PRACTICAL/ VOCATIONAL NURSE TRAINING
Campbellsville U (KY)
Lindenwood U (MO)
York Coll of Pennsylvania (PA)

LINGUISTIC AND COMPARATIVE LANGUAGE STUDIES RELATED
Appalachian State U (NC)
Boston U (MA)
Brigham Young U (UT)
Iowa State U of Science and Technology (IA)
Rowan U (NJ)
U of California, Los Angeles (CA)
U of California, San Diego (CA)

U of California, Santa Barbara (CA)
U of Kentucky (KY)
U of Southern California (CA)

LINGUISTICS
Baylor U (TX)
Bethel U (MN)
Binghamton U, State U of New York (NY)
Biola U (CA)
Boston U (MA)
Brandeis U (MA)
Brock U (ON, Canada)
Bryn Mawr Coll (PA)
Bucknell U (PA)
California State U, Dominguez Hills (CA)
California State U, Fullerton (CA)
California State U, Monterey Bay (CA)
California State U, Northridge (CA)
Calvin Coll (MI)
Carleton Coll (MN)
Carnegie Mellon U (PA)
Carson-Newman U (TN)
Cedarville U (OH)
City Coll of the City U of New York (NY)
Cleveland State U (OH)
The Coll of William and Mary (VA)
Columbia U (NY)
Concordia U (QC, Canada)
Cornell U (NY)
Cornerstone U (MI)
Dartmouth Coll (NH)
Eastern Michigan U (MI)
Emory U (GA)
Florida Atlantic U (FL)
Georgetown U (DC)
Georgia State U (GA)
Gordon Coll (MA)
Hampshire Coll (MA)
Harvard U (MA)
Hofstra U (NY)
Indiana U Bloomington (IN)
Iowa State U of Science and Technology (IA)
Lawrence U (WI)
Lehman Coll of the City U of New York (NY)
Macalester Coll (MN)
Marlboro Coll (VT)
Massachusetts Inst of Technology (MA)
Metropolitan State U of Denver (CO)
Miami U (OH)
Michigan State U (MI)
Mid-Atlantic Christian U (NC)
Montclair State U (NJ)
New York U (NY)
Northeastern U (MA)
Northwestern U (IL)
Oakland U (MI)
The Ohio State U (OH)
Ohio U (OH)
Pitzer Coll (CA)
Pomona Coll (CA)
Portland State U (OR)
Purdue U (IN)
Queens Coll of the City U of New York (NY)
Reed Coll (OR)
Rice U (TX)
Rutgers U–New Brunswick (NJ)
Saint Joseph's U (PA)
San Diego State U (CA)
Scripps Coll (CA)
Seattle Pacific U (WA)
Simon Fraser U (BC, Canada)
Southern Illinois U Carbondale (IL)
Stanford U (CA)
State U of New York at Oswego (NY)
Stony Brook U, State U of New York (NY)
Syracuse U (NY)
Truman State U (MO)
Tulane U (LA)
U at Albany, State U of New York (NY)
U at Buffalo, the State U of New York (NY)
U of Alaska Fairbanks (AK)
The U of Arizona (AZ)
U of California, Davis (CA)
U of California, Irvine (CA)

U of California, Los Angeles (CA)
U of California, Riverside (CA)
U of California, San Diego (CA)
U of California, Santa Barbara (CA)
U of California, Santa Cruz (CA)
U of Chicago (IL)
U of Cincinnati (OH)
U of Colorado Boulder (CO)
U of Florida (FL)
U of Georgia (GA)
U of Houston (TX)
The U of Kansas (KS)
U of Kentucky (KY)
U of King's Coll (NS, Canada)
U of Maryland, Coll Park (MD)
U of Massachusetts Amherst (MA)
U of Michigan (MI)
U of Michigan–Flint (MI)
U of Minnesota, Duluth (MN)
U of Minnesota, Twin Cities Campus (MN)
U of Missouri (MO)
U of Nevada, Las Vegas (NV)
U of New Hampshire (NH)
U of New Mexico (NM)
The U of North Carolina at Chapel Hill (NC)
U of North Texas (TX)
U of Oklahoma (OK)
U of Oregon (OR)
U of Pennsylvania (PA)
U of Pittsburgh (PA)
U of Regina (SK, Canada)
U of Rochester (NY)
U of Saskatchewan (SK, Canada)
U of Southern California (CA)
U of Southern Maine (ME)
The U of Texas at Austin (TX)
The U of Texas at El Paso (TX)
U of Toronto (ON, Canada)
U of Vermont (VT)
U of Washington (WA)
U of Wisconsin–Madison (WI)
U of Wisconsin–Milwaukee (WI)
Washington State U (WA)
Washington U in St. Louis (MO)
Wayne State U (MI)
Wellesley Coll (MA)
Western Washington U (WA)

LITERATURE
American U (DC)
Antioch Coll, Yellow Springs (OH)
Bradley U (IL)
Bryant U (RI)
Cairn U (PA)
Calvin Coll (MI)
Carson-Newman U (TN)
Central Michigan U (MI)
Colorado Christian U (CO)
Concordia U, St. Paul (MN)
Eugene Lang Coll of Liberal Arts (NY)
Excelsior Coll (NY)
Florida Southern Coll (FL)
Franklin U Switzerland (Switzerland)
Grove City Coll (PA)
Hamilton Coll (NY)
Linfield Coll (OR)
Lipscomb U (TN)
Loyola U New Orleans (LA)
Lubbock Christian U (TX)
Marlboro Coll (VT)
Marymount Manhattan Coll (NY)
Massachusetts Coll of Liberal Arts (MA)
New Coll of Florida (FL)
New York U (NY)
Occidental Coll (CA)
Ohio Northern U (OH)
Saint Mary's U of Minnesota (MN)
Sarah Lawrence Coll (NY)
Southwestern Coll (KS)
Stevens Inst of Technology (NJ)
The U of Findlay (OH)
U of Michigan–Flint (MI)
The U of Texas at Dallas (TX)
Washington U in St. Louis (MO)
Whitworth U (WA)

LITERATURE RELATED
Colorado Christian U (CO)
Marlboro Coll (VT)
Ohio Northern U (OH)

LIVESTOCK MANAGEMENT
The Ohio State U (OH)

Tarleton State U (TX)

LOGIC
Carnegie Mellon U (PA)
Marlboro Coll (VT)
U of Pennsylvania (PA)

LOGISTICS, MATERIALS, AND SUPPLY CHAIN MANAGEMENT
American Public U System (WV)
Anderson U (SC)
Athens State U (AL)
Auburn U (AL)
Baylor U (TX)
Binghamton U, State U of New York (NY)
Bloomsburg U of Pennsylvania (PA)
Boise State U (ID)
Bowling Green State U (OH)
Bradley U (IL)
Brigham Young U (UT)
Bryant U (RI)
California State U, Dominguez Hills (CA)
Central Michigan U (MI)
Clarkson U (NY)
Clayton State U (GA)
Coll of Charleston (SC)
Concordia U (QC, Canada)
DEREE - The American Coll of Greece (Greece)
DeSales U (PA)
Duquesne U (PA)
Eastern Michigan U (MI)
Elmhurst Coll (IL)
Gannon U (PA)
Georgia Highlands Coll (GA)
Georgia Southern U (GA)
Grand Valley State U (MI)
HEC Montreal (QC, Canada)
Hofstra U (NY)
Iowa State U of Science and Technology (IA)
Kennesaw State U (GA)
Lehigh U (PA)
Lincoln Coll (IL)
Miami Dade Coll (FL)
Michigan State U (MI)
Minnesota State U Moorhead (MN)
Missouri State U (MO)
Missouri Western State U (MO)
Murray State U (KY)
Niagara U (NY)
Northeastern State U (OK)
Northeastern U (MA)
Oakland U (MI)
The Ohio State U (OH)
Penn State Beaver (PA)
Penn State Brandywine (PA)
Penn State Fayette, The Eberly Campus (PA)
Penn State Greater Allegheny (PA)
Penn State Hazleton (PA)
Penn State Lehigh Valley (PA)
Penn State New Kensington (PA)
Penn State Schuylkill (PA)
Penn State Shenango (PA)
Penn State York (PA)
Portland State U (OR)
Rider U (NJ)
Rutgers U–Newark (NJ)
Rutgers U–New Brunswick (NJ)
Shippensburg U of Pennsylvania (PA)
Southeastern Louisiana U (LA)
Syracuse U (NY)
Temple U (PA)
Texas A&M U (TX)
Texas Christian U (TX)
Texas Tech U (TX)
Tiffin U (OH)
Truckee Meadows Comm Coll (NV)
United States Merchant Marine Acad (NY)
U of Arkansas (AR)
U of Evansville (IN)
The U of Findlay (OH)
The U of Kansas (KS)
U of Maryland, Coll Park (MD)
U of Massachusetts Amherst (MA)
U of Memphis (TN)
U of Michigan–Dearborn (MI)
U of Michigan–Flint (MI)
U of Nebraska–Lincoln (NE)
U of Northern Iowa (IA)
U of North Texas (TX)
U of Pittsburgh (PA)

U of Rhode Island (RI)
U of St. Francis (IL)
The U of Scranton (PA)
The U of Tennessee (TN)
The U of Texas at Austin (TX)
The U of Texas at Dallas (TX)
The U of Texas Rio Grande Valley (TX)
The U of Toledo (OH)
U of Washington (WA)
U of Wisconsin–Platteville (WI)
U of Wisconsin–Stout (WI)
U of Wisconsin–Superior (WI)
U of Wisconsin–Whitewater (WI)
Weber State U (UT)
Western Illinois U (IL)
Western Michigan U (MI)
West Virginia U (WV)
Wright State U (OH)
Wright State U–Lake Campus (OH)
York Coll of Pennsylvania (PA)

LONG TERM CARE ADMINISTRATION
Bowling Green State U (OH)
Weber State U (UT)

MACHINE TOOL TECHNOLOGY
Idaho State U (ID)

MAGNETIC RESONANCE IMAGING (MRI) TECHNOLOGY
Saint Louis U (MO)
Weber State U (UT)

MANAGEMENT INFORMATION SYSTEMS
Adams State U (CO)
The American U of Paris (France)
Angelo State U (TX)
Appalachian State U (NC)
Aquinas Coll (MI)
Auburn U (AL)
Auburn U at Montgomery (AL)
Augsburg U (MN)
Augustana U (SD)
Avila U (MO)
Azusa Pacific U (CA)
Babson Coll (MA)
Ball State U (IN)
Barry U (FL)
Baylor U (TX)
Belmont U (TN)
Bethel U (TN)
Bethune-Cookman U (FL)
Binghamton U, State U of New York (NY)
Biola U (CA)
Boston Coll (MA)
Bowling Green State U (OH)
Bradley U (IL)
Brewton-Parker Coll (GA)
Bridgewater Coll (VA)
Bridgewater State U (MA)
Bryant U (RI)
Butler U (IN)
California State U, Long Beach (CA)
Calvin Coll (MI)
Canisius Coll (NY)
Carson-Newman U (TN)
Catawba Coll (NC)
Cedarville U (OH)
Central Connecticut State U (CT)
Central Michigan U (MI)
Charleston Southern U (SC)
Clarkson U (NY)
Cleveland State U (OH)
Colorado Christian U (CO)
Colorado Mesa U (CO)
Columbia Coll (MO)
Columbus State U (GA)
Concordia U (QC, Canada)
Concordia U Chicago (IL)
Concordia U, Nebraska (NE)
Cornerstone U (MI)
Dallas Baptist U (TX)
DePaul U (IL)
DEREE - The American Coll of Greece (Greece)
DeSales U (PA)
Dominican Coll (NY)
Drexel U (PA)
East Carolina U (NC)
East Central U (OK)
Eastern Michigan U (MI)
Eastern New Mexico U (NM)
Eastern Washington U (WA)

Edgewood Coll (WI)
Elmhurst Coll (IL)
Fairfield U (CT)
Fayetteville State U (NC)
Felician U (NJ)
Florida Atlantic U (FL)
Florida Inst of Technology (FL)
Florida Intl U (FL)
Florida State U (FL)
Fordham U (NY)
Francis Marion U (SC)
Gannon U (PA)
Georgia Southern U (GA)
Gonzaga U (WA)
Governors State U (IL)
Graceland U (IA)
Grand View U (IA)
Greenville U (IL)
Hardin-Simmons U (TX)
Harris-Stowe State U (MO)
HEC Montreal (QC, Canada)
Hofstra U (NY)
Holy Family U (PA)
Howard Payne U (TX)
Husson U (ME)
Illinois Coll (IL)
Illinois State U (IL)
Immaculata U (PA)
Indiana State U (IN)
Indiana U of Pennsylvania (PA)
Inter American U of Puerto Rico, Aguadilla Campus (PR)
Inter American U of Puerto Rico, Barranquitas Campus (PR)
Iona Coll (NY)
Iowa State U of Science and Technology (IA)
Jacksonville U (FL)
Keiser U, Fort Lauderdale (FL)
Lamar U (TX)
La Salle U (PA)
Le Moyne Coll (NY)
Lewis U (IL)
Liberty U (VA)
Linfield Coll (OR)
Loras Coll (IA)
Loyola Marymount U (CA)
Loyola U Chicago (IL)
Luther Coll (IA)
Madonna U (MI)
Marshall U (WV)
Maryville U of Saint Louis (MO)
Massachusetts Coll of Liberal Arts (MA)
The Master's U (CA)
McMurry U (TX)
Mercer U, Macon (GA)
Miami U (OH)
Michigan Technological U (MI)
Mid-America Christian U (OK)
Middle Tennessee State U (TN)
Millikin U (IL)
Minot State U (ND)
Mississippi State U (MS)
Missouri State U (MO)
Morehead State U (KY)
Mount Mercy U (IA)
Mount Vernon Nazarene U (OH)
National Louis U (IL)
National U (CA)
Neumont Coll of Computer Science (UT)
Newman U (KS)
New Mexico Highlands U (NM)
North Dakota State U (ND)
Northeastern State U (OK)
Northeastern U (MA)
Northern Arizona U (AZ)
Northern Illinois U (IL)
Northern Kentucky U (KY)
Northern Michigan U (MI)
Northern State U (SD)
Northwest Missouri State U (MO)
Oakland U (MI)
Ohio Northern U (OH)
The Ohio State U (OH)
Ohio U (OH)
Oklahoma Baptist U (OK)
Old Dominion U (VA)
Olivet Nazarene U (IL)
Oral Roberts U (OK)
Oregon State U (OR)
Penn State Abington (PA)
Penn State Altoona (PA)
Penn State Beaver (PA)
Penn State Berks (PA)
Penn State Brandywine (PA)

Penn State DuBois (PA)
Penn State Erie, The Behrend Coll (PA)
Penn State Fayette, The Eberly Campus (PA)
Penn State Greater Allegheny (PA)
Penn State Harrisburg (PA)
Penn State Hazleton (PA)
Penn State Lehigh Valley (PA)
Penn State Mont Alto (PA)
Penn State New Kensington (PA)
Penn State Schuylkill (PA)
Penn State Shenango (PA)
Penn State U Park (PA)
Penn State Wilkes-Barre (PA)
Penn State Worthington Scranton (PA)
Penn State York (PA)
Pfeiffer U (NC)
Point Loma Nazarene U (CA)
Post U (CT)
Prairie View A&M U (TX)
Purdue U Northwest (IN)
Regent U (VA)
Rhode Island Coll (RI)
Robert Morris U (PA)
Rochester Inst of Technology (NY)
Rockford U (IL)
Roger Williams U (RI)
Rowan U (NJ)
Rutgers U–Newark (NJ)
St. Catherine U (MN)
Saint Francis U (PA)
Saint Joseph's U (PA)
Saint Louis U (MO)
Sam Houston State U (TX)
Santa Clara U (CA)
Schreiner U (TX)
Seattle Pacific U (WA)
Seton Hill U (PA)
Shawnee State U (OH)
Simon Fraser U (BC, Canada)
Simpson Coll (IA)
Southern Adventist U (TN)
Southwestern Coll (KS)
State U of New York at Plattsburgh (NY)
State U of New York Coll at Old Westbury (NY)
Stetson U (FL)
Stevenson U (MD)
Texas A&M Intl U (TX)
Texas A&M U (TX)
Texas A&M U–Central Texas (TX)
Texas A&M U–Commerce (TX)
Texas A&M U–Corpus Christi (TX)
Texas A&M U–Kingsville (TX)
Texas A&M U–Texarkana (TX)
The U of Akron (OH)
The U of Alabama (AL)
The U of Alabama at Birmingham (AL)
The U of Arizona (AZ)
U of Arkansas (AR)
U of Bridgeport (CT)
U of Central Arkansas (AR)
U of Central Missouri (MO)
U of Central Oklahoma (OK)
U of Colorado Boulder (CO)
U of Dayton (OH)
U of Denver (CO)
U of Georgia (GA)
U of Hartford (CT)
U of Hawaii at Manoa (HI)
U of Houston (TX)
U of Houston–Downtown (TX)
U of Idaho (ID)
U of Jamestown (ND)
The U of Kansas (KS)
U of Louisiana at Monroe (LA)
U of Louisville (KY)
U of Mary Hardin-Baylor (TX)
U of Massachusetts Dartmouth (MA)
U of Memphis (TN)
U of Michigan–Dearborn (MI)
U of Missouri (MO)
U of Montana (MT)
U of Nevada, Las Vegas (NV)
U of North Alabama (AL)
The U of North Carolina at Charlotte (NC)
U of Northern Iowa (IA)
U of North Texas (TX)
U of Notre Dame (IN)
U of Oklahoma (OK)
U of Pennsylvania (PA)

U of Puget Sound (WA)
U of Rhode Island (RI)
U of Saint Francis (IN)
U of San Francisco (CA)
U of Sioux Falls (SD)
U of Southern Mississippi (MS)
U of South Florida, St. Petersburg (FL)
The U of Tennessee at Martin (TN)
The U of Texas at Austin (TX)
The U of Texas at San Antonio (TX)
The U of Texas Rio Grande Valley (TX)
U of the Incarnate Word (TX)
U of the Virgin Islands (VI)
The U of Tulsa (OK)
U of Washington (WA)
The U of West Alabama (AL)
U of West Georgia (GA)
U of Wisconsin–Eau Claire (WI)
U of Wisconsin–La Crosse (WI)
U of Wisconsin–Madison (WI)
U of Wisconsin–Milwaukee (WI)
Upper Iowa U (IA)
Valley City State U (ND)
Villanova U (PA)
Wake Forest U (NC)
Washington State U (WA)
Washington State U–Global Campus (WA)
Washington State U–Vancouver (WA)
Wayne State U (MI)
Weber State U (UT)
Western Connecticut State U (CT)
Western Kentucky U (KY)
Western New England U (MA)
Western State Colorado U (CO)
Western Washington U (WA)
West Texas A&M U (TX)
West Virginia U (WV)
Wichita State U (KS)
William Woods U (MO)
Winona State U (MN)
Worcester Polytechnic Inst (MA)
Wright State U (OH)
Wright State U–Lake Campus (OH)
York Coll of Pennsylvania (PA)
Youngstown State U (OH)

MANAGEMENT INFORMATION SYSTEMS AND SERVICES RELATED
Bowling Green State U (OH)
Cardinal Stritch U (WI)
DeSales U (PA)
ECPI U, Virginia Beach (VA)
Fordham U (NY)
Montana Tech of The U of Montana (MT)
Newberry Coll (SC)
Northern Michigan U (MI)
Purdue U Northwest (IN)
Rogers State U (OK)
Temple U (PA)
Tiffin U (OH)
U of Pittsburgh (PA)
Western New England U (MA)
Westminster Coll (UT)
Widener U (PA)

MANAGEMENT SCIENCE
American Intl Coll (MA)
Arizona State U at the Tempe campus (AZ)
Auburn U (AL)
Averett U (VA)
Becker Coll (MA)
Bridgewater State U (MA)
Brigham Young U–Idaho (ID)
Bryant U (RI)
California State U, Northridge (CA)
The Catholic U of America (DC)
Central Methodist U (MO)
Denison U (OH)
DePaul U (IL)
Duquesne U (PA)
Elon U (NC)
Fitchburg State U (MA)
Florida State U (FL)
Grand Valley State U (MI)
Hamline U (MN)
Hardin-Simmons U (TX)
HEC Montreal (QC, Canada)
Illinois State U (IL)
Jacksonville U (FL)
Keiser U, Fort Lauderdale (FL)
La Roche Coll (PA)

La Salle U (PA)
Lehigh U (PA)
Lenoir-Rhyne U (NC)
Loras Coll (IA)
Louisiana State U and A&M Coll (LA)
Manhattan Coll (NY)
McKendree U (IL)
Miami U (OH)
Mid-America Christian U (OK)
Minnesota State U Moorhead (MN)
National Louis U (IL)
Northern Illinois U (IL)
Ohio Northern U (OH)
Oklahoma Baptist U (OK)
Olivet Nazarene U (IL)
Oral Roberts U (OK)
Point Loma Nazarene U (CA)
Portland State U (OR)
Rider U (NJ)
Rocky Mountain Coll (MT)
Roosevelt U (IL)
Rutgers U–New Brunswick (NJ)
St. Ambrose U (IA)
Saint Louis U (MO)
Salve Regina U (RI)
Siena Coll (NY)
Simon Fraser U (BC, Canada)
Southeastern Oklahoma State U (OK)
Southern Adventist U (TN)
Southern Illinois U Carbondale (IL)
Southwestern Assemblies of God U (TX)
State U of New York at Oswego (NY)
Trinity U (TX)
United States Coast Guard Acad (CT)
The U of Alabama (AL)
U of Arkansas (AR)
U of California, San Diego (CA)
U of Cincinnati (OH)
U of Florida (FL)
U of Illinois at Chicago (IL)
The U of Kansas (KS)
U of Kentucky (KY)
U of Maryland, Coll Park (MD)
U of Memphis (TN)
U of Miami (FL)
U of Missouri–St. Louis (MO)
U of Notre Dame (IN)
U of Providence (MT)
U of St. Francis (IL)
U of South Carolina (SC)
The U of Tennessee at Martin (TN)
The U of Texas at Austin (TX)
The U of Texas at Dallas (TX)
The U of Texas at San Antonio (TX)
U of the Fraser Valley (BC, Canada)
U of Washington, Bothell (WA)
U of Washington, Tacoma (WA)
U of Wyoming (WY)
Valparaiso U (IN)
Vaughn Coll of Aeronautics and Technology (NY)
Virginia Polytechnic Inst and State U (VA)
Wake Forest U (NC)
Washington State U (WA)
Western Kentucky U (KY)
Western Michigan U (MI)
William Paterson U of New Jersey (NJ)

MANAGEMENT SCIENCES AND QUANTITATIVE METHODS RELATED
Arkansas Tech U (AR)
Canisius Coll (NY)
Cornell Coll (IA)
George Mason U (VA)
HEC Montreal (QC, Canada)
Indiana State U (IN)
Massachusetts Inst of Technology (MA)
Mercer U, Macon (GA)
Miami U (OH)
Pace U (NY)
Penn State Lehigh Valley (PA)
Penn State Schuylkill (PA)
Purdue U (IN)
Rutgers U–New Brunswick (NJ)
Texas A&M U–Commerce (TX)
U of North Texas (TX)
U of Pennsylvania (PA)

U of South Dakota (SD)
The U of Texas at Austin (TX)

MANUFACTURING ENGINEERING
Arizona State U at the Polytechnic campus (AZ)
Boston U (MA)
Bradley U (IL)
Brigham Young U (UT)
California Polytechnic State U, San Luis Obispo (CA)
California State Polytechnic U, Pomona (CA)
California State U, Northridge (CA)
Central State U (OH)
Dunwoody Coll of Technology (MN)
Ferris State U (MI)
Georgia Southern U (GA)
Grand Valley State U (MI)
Hofstra U (NY)
Miami U (OH)
National U (CA)
New Jersey Inst of Technology (NJ)
North Dakota State U (ND)
Northwestern U (IL)
Oregon State U (OR)
Robert Morris U (PA)
Savannah Coll of Art and Design (GA)
Texas State U (TX)
U of Michigan–Dearborn (MI)
U of Southern Indiana (IN)
The U of Texas Rio Grande Valley (TX)
U of Toronto (ON, Canada)
U of Wisconsin–Milwaukee (WI)
U of Wisconsin–Stout (WI)
Washington State U (WA)
Washington State U–Vancouver (WA)
Western Washington U (WA)
Wichita State U (KS)
Youngstown State U (OH)

MANUFACTURING ENGINEERING TECHNOLOGY
Bradley U (IL)
California State U, Long Beach (CA)
Central Connecticut State U (CT)
Central Michigan U (MI)
East Carolina U (NC)
Eastern Michigan U (MI)
Farmingdale State Coll (NY)
Fitchburg State U (MA)
Idaho State U (ID)
Indiana State U (IN)
Missouri Western State U (MO)
Morehead State U (KY)
Murray State U (KY)
Northern Kentucky U (KY)
Ohio Northern U (OH)
Oregon Inst of Technology (OR)
Pennsylvania Coll of Technology (PA)
Pittsburg State U (KS)
Purdue U (IN)
Rochester Inst of Technology (NY)
Sam Houston State U (TX)
Tarleton State U (TX)
Texas A&M U (TX)
Texas State U (TX)
The U of Akron (OH)
U of Dayton (OH)
U of Memphis (TN)
U of Northern Iowa (IA)
U of Southern Indiana (IN)
U of Wisconsin–Platteville (WI)
Wayne State U (MI)
Weber State U (UT)
Western Kentucky U (KY)
Western Michigan U (MI)
Western Washington U (WA)

MARINE BIOLOGY AND BIOLOGICAL OCEANOGRAPHY
Alabama State U (AL)
Auburn U (AL)
Barry U (FL)
Bemidji State U (MN)
Boston U (MA)
California State U, Long Beach (CA)
Coastal Carolina U (SC)
Coll of Charleston (SC)
Coll of the Atlantic (ME)

East Stroudsburg U of Pennsylvania (PA)
Eckerd Coll (FL)
Fairleigh Dickinson U, Florham Campus (NJ)
Fairleigh Dickinson U, Metropolitan Campus (NJ)
Florida Inst of Technology (FL)
Florida Intl U (FL)
Florida Southern Coll (FL)
Gettysburg Coll (PA)
Hampton U (VA)
Hawai`i Pacific U (HI)
Humboldt State U (CA)
Jacksonville U (FL)
Loyola U New Orleans (LA)
Montclair State U (NJ)
New Coll of Florida (FL)
Northeastern U (MA)
Northwest Missouri State U (MO)
Nova Southeastern U (FL)
Roger Williams U (RI)
Rollins Coll (FL)
Rutgers U–New Brunswick (NJ)
Sacred Heart U (CT)
Saint Francis U (PA)
Samford U (AL)
San Francisco State U (CA)
Sonoma State U (CA)
Southwestern Coll (KS)
Spring Hill Coll (AL)
Stockton U (NJ)
Stony Brook U, State U of New York (NY)
Texas A&M U (TX)
Troy U (AL)
Unity Coll (ME)
The U of Alabama (AL)
U of California, Los Angeles (CA)
U of California, Santa Barbara (CA)
U of California, Santa Cruz (CA)
U of Guelph (ON, Canada)
U of Hawaii at Manoa (HI)
U of King's Coll (NS, Canada)
U of Maine at Machias (ME)
U of Maryland Eastern Shore (MD)
U of Miami (FL)
U of Mobile (AL)
U of New England (ME)
U of New Haven (CT)
U of North Alabama (AL)
The U of North Carolina Wilmington (NC)
U of Puerto Rico–Humacao (PR)
U of Rhode Island (RI)
U of San Diego (CA)
U of South Carolina (SC)
U of Southern Mississippi (MS)
The U of Tampa (FL)
The U of Texas Rio Grande Valley (TX)
U of the Virgin Islands (VI)
The U of West Alabama (AL)
Waynesburg U (PA)
Western Washington U (WA)
Whitman Coll (WA)
Wisconsin Lutheran Coll (WI)

MARINE MAINTENANCE AND SHIP REPAIR TECHNOLOGY
California State U Maritime Acad (CA)

MARINE SCIENCE/MERCHANT MARINE OFFICER
Hampton U (VA)
Massachusetts Maritime Acad (MA)
State U of New York Maritime Coll (NY)
Texas A&M U (TX)
United States Merchant Marine Acad (NY)
U of South Carolina (SC)

MARINE SCIENCES
California State U, Monterey Bay (CA)
Goshen Coll (IN)
Rider U (NJ)
Texas A&M U (TX)
U of Maine (ME)
The U of Texas at Austin (TX)

MARINE TRANSPORTATION RELATED
United States Merchant Marine Acad (NY)

MARITIME STUDIES
Coll of the Atlantic (ME)
DEREE - The American Coll of Greece (Greece)
Texas A&M U (TX)

MARKETING/MARKETING MANAGEMENT
Abilene Christian U (TX)
Adams State U (CO)
Adelphi U (NY)
Alabama State U (AL)
Albright Coll (PA)
Alfred U (NY)
Alma Coll (MI)
American Intl Coll (MA)
American Public U System (WV)
The American U of Paris (France)
Anderson U (IN)
Anderson U (SC)
Andrews U (MI)
Angelo State U (TX)
Appalachian State U (NC)
Arcadia U (PA)
Arizona State U at the Tempe campus (AZ)
Asbury U (KY)
Ashland U (OH)
Assumption Coll (MA)
Athabasca U (AB, Canada)
Auburn U (AL)
Auburn U at Montgomery (AL)
Augsburg U (MN)
Aurora U (IL)
Austin Peay State U (TN)
Averett U (VA)
Avila U (MO)
Azusa Pacific U (CA)
Babson Coll (MA)
Baldwin Wallace U (OH)
Ball State U (IN)
Barry U (FL)
Baylor U (TX)
Bay Path U (MA)
Becker Coll (MA)
Belmont U (TN)
Benedictine Coll (KS)
Benedictine U (IL)
Bentley U (MA)
Berry Coll (GA)
Binghamton U, State U of New York (NY)
Biola U (CA)
Blackburn Coll (IL)
Black Hills State U (SD)
Bluffton U (OH)
Boise State U (ID)
Boston Coll (MA)
Bowie State U (MD)
Bowling Green State U (OH)
Bradley U (IL)
Brenau U (GA)
Bridgewater State U (MA)
Brock U (ON, Canada)
Bryant U (RI)
Bucknell U (PA)
Buena Vista U (IA)
Butler U (IN)
Caldwell U (NJ)
California Baptist U (CA)
California Lutheran U (CA)
California State U, Dominguez Hills (CA)
California State U, Fullerton (CA)
California State U, Long Beach (CA)
California State U, Northridge (CA)
California State U, Sacramento (CA)
California State U, San Marcos (CA)
California State U, Stanislaus (CA)
Calvary U (MO)
Campbellsville U (KY)
Canisius Coll (NY)
Capital U (OH)
Cardinal Stritch U (WI)
Caribbean U (PR)
Carnegie Mellon U (PA)
Carroll U (WI)
Carson-Newman U (TN)
Carthage Coll (WI)
Case Western Reserve U (OH)
Catawba Coll (NC)
The Catholic U of America (DC)
Cedarville U (OH)
Central Connecticut State U (CT)

Central Michigan U (MI)
Central Penn Coll (PA)
Champlain Coll (VT)
Charleston Southern U (SC)
Chatham U (PA)
Chestnut Hill Coll (PA)
Chowan U (NC)
Christopher Newport U (VA)
Clarion U of Pennsylvania (PA)
Clayton State U (GA)
Clemson U (SC)
Cleveland State U (OH)
Coastal Carolina U (SC)
The Coll at Brockport, State U of New York (NY)
Coll of Charleston (SC)
The Coll of Saint Rose (NY)
The Coll of St. Scholastica (MN)
Coll of the Ozarks (MO)
The Coll of William and Mary (VA)
Colorado Christian U (CO)
Columbia Coll (MO)
Columbia Coll Chicago (IL)
Columbia Southern U (AL)
Columbus State U (GA)
Concordia U (QC, Canada)
Concordia U Chicago (IL)
Concordia U, Nebraska (NE)
Concordia U, St. Paul (MN)
Concordia U Wisconsin (WI)
Converse Coll (SC)
Cornerstone U (MI)
Creighton U (NE)
Culver-Stockton Coll (MO)
Dakota State U (SD)
Dallas Baptist U (TX)
Davenport U, Grand Rapids (MI)
Delaware State U (DE)
DePaul U (IL)
DEREE - The American Coll of Greece (Greece)
DeSales U (PA)
Dominican Coll (NY)
Dominican U (IL)
Drake U (IA)
Drexel U (PA)
Drury U (MO)
Duquesne U (PA)
East Carolina U (NC)
East Central U (OK)
Eastern Michigan U (MI)
Eastern Nazarene Coll (MA)
Eastern Washington U (WA)
East Tennessee State U (TN)
East Texas Baptist U (TX)
Elmhurst Coll (IL)
Elon U (NC)
Emerson Coll (MA)
Emmanuel Coll (MA)
Emporia State U (KS)
Endicott Coll (MA)
Evangel U (MO)
Fairfield U (CT)
Fairleigh Dickinson U, Florham Campus (NJ)
Fairleigh Dickinson U, Metropolitan Campus (NJ)
Fayetteville State U (NC)
Felician U (NJ)
Ferris State U (MI)
Fisher Coll (MA)
Fitchburg State U (MA)
Florida Atlantic U (FL)
Florida Gulf Coast U (FL)
Florida Inst of Technology (FL)
Florida Intl U (FL)
Fordham U (NY)
Fort Lewis Coll (CO)
Framingham State U (MA)
Francis Marion U (SC)
Franklin Pierce U (NH)
Friends U (KS)
Gannon U (PA)
George Mason U (VA)
Georgetown Coll (KY)
Georgetown U (DC)
The George Washington U (DC)
Georgia Coll & State U (GA)
Georgian Court U (NJ)
Georgia Southern U (GA)
Georgia Southwestern State U (GA)
Georgia State U (GA)
Golden Gate U (CA)
Gonzaga U (WA)
Goshen Coll (IN)
Grambling State U (LA)

Grand Valley State U (MI)
Grand View U (IA)
Granite State Coll (NH)
Greenville U (IL)
Grove City Coll (PA)
Hamline U (MN)
Hampton U (VA)
Hannibal-LaGrange U (MO)
Harding U (AR)
Hardin-Simmons U (TX)
HEC Montreal (QC, Canada)
High Point U (NC)
Hillsdale Coll (MI)
Hofstra U (NY)
Holy Family U (PA)
Holy Names U (CA)
Houston Baptist U (TX)
Howard Payne U (TX)
Husson U (ME)
Idaho State U (ID)
Illinois State U (IL)
Immaculata U (PA)
Indiana State U (IN)
Indiana U of Pennsylvania (PA)
Indiana Wesleyan U (IN)
Inter American U of Puerto Rico, Aguadilla Campus (PR)
Inter American U of Puerto Rico, Bayamón Campus (PR)
Inter American U of Puerto Rico, Fajardo Campus (PR)
Inter American U of Puerto Rico, Metropolitan Campus (PR)
Inter American U of Puerto Rico, San Germán Campus (PR)
Iona Coll (NY)
Iowa State U of Science and Technology (IA)
Ithaca Coll (NY)
Jackson State U (MS)
Jacksonville U (FL)
James Madison U (VA)
John Brown U (AR)
John Cabot U (Italy)
John Carroll U (OH)
Judson U (IL)
Juniata Coll (PA)
Kansas State U (KS)
Kansas Wesleyan U (KS)
Kean U (NJ)
Keiser U, Fort Lauderdale (FL)
Kennesaw State U (GA)
Kent State U (OH)
Kent State U at Stark (OH)
King's Coll (PA)
Lamar U (TX)
La Roche Coll (PA)
La Salle U (PA)
Lasell Coll (MA)
La Sierra U (CA)
Lehigh U (PA)
Le Moyne Coll (NY)
Lenoir-Rhyne U (NC)
LeTourneau U (TX)
Lewis U (IL)
LIM Coll (NY)
Limestone Coll (SC)
Lincoln Memorial U (TN)
Lindenwood U (MO)
Linfield Coll (OR)
Lipscomb U (TN)
Loras Coll (IA)
Louisiana State U and A&M Coll (LA)
Loyola Marymount U (CA)
Loyola U Chicago (IL)
Loyola U New Orleans (LA)
Lubbock Christian U (TX)
Lynchburg Coll (VA)
Lynn U (FL)
Madonna U (MI)
Malone U (OH)
Manchester U (IN)
Manhattan Coll (NY)
Manhattanville Coll (NY)
Mansfield U of Pennsylvania (PA)
Maranatha Baptist U (WI)
Marian U (IN)
Marian U (WI)
Marietta Coll (OH)
Marquette U (WI)
Marshall U (WV)
Mary Baldwin U (VA)
Marymount Manhattan Coll (NY)
Maryville Coll (TN)
Maryville U of Saint Louis (MO)
Marywood U (PA)

Massachusetts Coll of Liberal Arts (MA)
McKendree U (IL)
McMurry U (TX)
McNeese State U (LA)
Mercer U, Macon (GA)
Mercy Coll (NY)
Mercyhurst U (PA)
Merrimack Coll (MA)
Messiah Coll (PA)
Metropolitan State U of Denver (CO)
Miami U (OH)
Michigan State U (MI)
Michigan Technological U (MI)
Mid-America Christian U (OK)
MidAmerica Nazarene U (KS)
Middle Tennessee State U (TN)
Millikin U (IL)
Minot State U (ND)
Mississippi State U (MS)
Missouri Baptist U (MO)
Missouri State U (MO)
Missouri Valley Coll (MO)
Missouri Western State U (MO)
Molloy Coll (NY)
Morehead State U (KY)
Mount Mary U (WI)
Mount Mercy U (IA)
Mount Saint Mary's U (CA)
Mount Vernon Nazarene U (OH)
Murray State U (KY)
Muskingum U (OH)
Nazareth Coll of Rochester (NY)
Neumann U (PA)
New Mexico Highlands U (NM)
New Mexico State U (NM)
New York Inst of Technology (NY)
New York U (NY)
Niagara U (NY)
Nichols Coll (MA)
North Carolina Wesleyan Coll (NC)
North Central Coll (IL)
Northcentral U (CA)
North Dakota State U (ND)
Northeastern State U (OK)
Northeastern U (MA)
Northern Arizona U (AZ)
Northern Illinois U (IL)
Northern Kentucky U (KY)
Northern Michigan U (MI)
Northern State U (SD)
Northern Vermont U–Lyndon (VT)
North Greenville U (SC)
Northwest Missouri State U (MO)
Northwest Nazarene U (ID)
Northwest U (WA)
Nova Southeastern U (FL)
Oakland U (MI)
Ohio Northern U (OH)
The Ohio State U (OH)
Ohio U (OH)
Oklahoma Baptist U (OK)
Oklahoma Christian U (OK)
Oklahoma City U (OK)
Oklahoma State U (OK)
Old Dominion U (VA)
Olivet Nazarene U (IL)
Oral Roberts U (OK)
Oregon Inst of Technology (OR)
Oregon State U (OR)
Otterbein U (OH)
Pace U (NY)
Pace U, Pleasantville Campus (NY)
Palm Beach Atlantic U (FL)
Penn State Abington (PA)
Penn State Altoona (PA)
Penn State Beaver (PA)
Penn State Berks (PA)
Penn State Brandywine (PA)
Penn State DuBois (PA)
Penn State Erie, The Behrend Coll (PA)
Penn State Fayette, The Eberly Campus (PA)
Penn State Greater Allegheny (PA)
Penn State Harrisburg (PA)
Penn State Hazleton (PA)
Penn State Lehigh Valley (PA)
Penn State Mont Alto (PA)
Penn State New Kensington (PA)
Penn State Schuylkill (PA)
Penn State Shenango (PA)
Penn State U Park (PA)
Penn State Wilkes-Barre (PA)
Penn State Worthington Scranton (PA)

Penn State York (PA)
Pfeiffer U (NC)
Pittsburg State U (KS)
Point Loma Nazarene U (CA)
Point U (GA)
Polytechnic U of Puerto Rico (PR)
Portland State U (OR)
Post U (CT)
Prairie View A&M U (TX)
Providence Coll (RI)
Purdue U (IN)
Purdue U Northwest (IN)
Quinnipiac U (CT)
Radford U (VA)
Rasmussen Coll Bloomington (MN)
Rasmussen Coll Brooklyn Park (MN)
Rasmussen Coll Eagan (MN)
Rasmussen Coll Mankato (MN)
Rasmussen Coll New Port Richey (FL)
Rasmussen Coll Ocala (FL)
Rasmussen Coll St. Cloud (MN)
Redeemer U Coll (ON, Canada)
Regent U (VA)
Regis U (CO)
Rhode Island Coll (RI)
Rider U (NJ)
Rivier U (NH)
Robert Morris U (PA)
Roberts Wesleyan Coll (NY)
Rochester Inst of Technology (NY)
Rockford U (IL)
Roger Williams U (RI)
Roosevelt U (IL)
Rosemont Coll (PA)
Rowan U (NJ)
Rutgers U–Camden (NJ)
Rutgers U–Newark (NJ)
Rutgers U–New Brunswick (NJ)
Sacred Heart U (CT)
Saginaw Valley State U (MI)
St. Ambrose U (IA)
St. Bonaventure U (NY)
St. Catherine U (MN)
Saint Francis U (PA)
St. John's U (NY)
St. Joseph's Coll, Long Island Campus (NY)
St. Joseph's Coll, New York (NY)
Saint Joseph's U (PA)
Saint Leo U (FL)
Saint Louis U (MO)
Saint Mary-of-the-Woods Coll (IN)
St. Mary's U (TX)
Saint Mary's U of Minnesota (MN)
Saint Peter's U (NJ)
St. Thomas Aquinas Coll (NY)
St. Thomas U (FL)
Saint Vincent Coll (PA)
Salisbury U (MD)
Salve Regina U (RI)
Samford U (AL)
Sam Houston State U (TX)
San Diego State U (CA)
San Francisco State U (CA)
Santa Clara U (CA)
Schreiner U (TX)
Seattle U (WA)
Seton Hill U (PA)
Shippensburg U of Pennsylvania (PA)
Siena Coll (NY)
Simmons Coll (MA)
Simpson Coll (IA)
Slippery Rock U of Pennsylvania (PA)
Southeastern Louisiana U (LA)
Southeastern Oklahoma State U (OK)
Southeastern U (FL)
Southeast Missouri State U (MO)
Southern Adventist U (TN)
Southern Illinois U Carbondale (IL)
Southern Methodist U (TX)
Southern Utah U (UT)
Southwest Baptist U (MO)
Southwestern Adventist U (TX)
Southwestern Assemblies of God U (TX)
Southwestern Coll (KS)
Spring Hill Coll (AL)
State U of New York at Fredonia (NY)
State U of New York at New Paltz (NY)

State U of New York at Oswego (NY)
State U of New York at Plattsburgh (NY)
State U of New York Coll at Old Westbury (NY)
Stephen F. Austin State U (TX)
Stetson U (FL)
Stonehill Coll (MA)
Suffolk U (MA)
Susquehanna U (PA)
Syracuse U (NY)
Tarleton State U (TX)
Taylor U (IN)
Temple U (PA)
Tennessee Technological U (TN)
Tennessee Wesleyan U (TN)
Texas A&M U (TX)
Texas A&M U–Central Texas (TX)
Texas A&M U–Commerce (TX)
Texas A&M U–Corpus Christi (TX)
Texas A&M U–Kingsville (TX)
Texas A&M U–Texarkana (TX)
Texas Christian U (TX)
Texas State U (TX)
Texas Tech U (TX)
Texas Woman's U (TX)
Thomas Edison State U (NJ)
Tiffin U (OH)
Trevecca Nazarene U (TN)
Trine U (IN)
Trinity Christian Coll (IL)
Trinity U (TX)
Tulane U (LA)
Union U (TN)
Université de Sherbrooke (QC, Canada)
The U of Akron (OH)
The U of Alabama (AL)
The U of Alabama at Birmingham (AL)
The U of Arizona (AZ)
U of Arkansas (AR)
U of Bridgeport (CT)
U of Central Arkansas (AR)
U of Central Florida (FL)
U of Central Missouri (MO)
U of Central Oklahoma (OK)
U of Charleston (WV)
U of Cincinnati (OH)
U of Colorado Boulder (CO)
U of Dayton (OH)
U of Denver (CO)
U of Dubuque (IA)
U of Evansville (IN)
The U of Findlay (OH)
U of Florida (FL)
U of Georgia (GA)
U of Guelph (ON, Canada)
U of Hawaii at Manoa (HI)
U of Houston (TX)
U of Houston–Clear Lake (TX)
U of Houston–Downtown (TX)
U of Idaho (ID)
U of Illinois at Chicago (IL)
U of Jamestown (ND)
The U of Kansas (KS)
U of Kentucky (KY)
U of La Verne (CA)
U of Louisiana at Monroe (LA)
U of Louisville (KY)
U of Maine (ME)
U of Maine at Machias (ME)
U of Mary Hardin-Baylor (TX)
U of Maryland, Coll Park (MD)
U of Maryland U Coll (MD)
U of Massachusetts Amherst (MA)
U of Massachusetts Dartmouth (MA)
U of Memphis (TN)
U of Miami (FL)
U of Michigan–Dearborn (MI)
U of Michigan–Flint (MI)
U of Minnesota, Crookston (MN)
U of Minnesota, Duluth (MN)
U of Minnesota, Twin Cities Campus (MN)
U of Missouri (MO)
U of Montana (MT)
U of Montevallo (AL)
U of Mount Union (OH)
U of Nebraska–Lincoln (NE)
U of Nevada, Las Vegas (NV)
U of Nevada, Reno (NV)
U of New Haven (CT)
U of New Orleans (LA)
U of North Alabama (AL)

The U of North Carolina at Charlotte (NC)
U of North Dakota (ND)
U of Northern Iowa (IA)
U of North Florida (FL)
U of North Georgia (GA)
U of North Texas (TX)
U of Notre Dame (IN)
U of Oklahoma (OK)
U of Pennsylvania (PA)
U of Pittsburgh (PA)
U of Providence (MT)
U of Regina (SK, Canada)
U of Rhode Island (RI)
U of St. Francis (IL)
U of Saint Francis (IN)
U of St. Thomas (MN)
U of St. Thomas (TX)
U of San Diego (CA)
U of San Francisco (CA)
U of Saskatchewan (SK, Canada)
The U of Scranton (PA)
U of South Alabama (AL)
U of South Carolina (SC)
U of South Dakota (SD)
U of Southern Indiana (IN)
U of Southern Maine (ME)
U of Southern Mississippi (MS)
U of South Florida, St. Petersburg (FL)
U of South Florida Sarasota-Manatee (FL)
The U of Tampa (FL)
The U of Tennessee (TN)
The U of Tennessee at Martin (TN)
The U of Texas at Austin (TX)
The U of Texas at Dallas (TX)
The U of Texas at El Paso (TX)
The U of Texas at San Antonio (TX)
The U of Texas of the Permian Basin (TX)
The U of Texas Rio Grande Valley (TX)
U of the Incarnate Word (TX)
U of the Virgin Islands (VI)
The U of Toledo (OH)
The U of Tulsa (OK)
U of Utah (UT)
U of Washington (WA)
U of Washington, Bothell (WA)
U of Washington, Tacoma (WA)
The U of West Alabama (AL)
U of West Georgia (GA)
U of Wisconsin–Eau Claire (WI)
U of Wisconsin–La Crosse (WI)
U of Wisconsin–Madison (WI)
U of Wisconsin–Milwaukee (WI)
U of Wisconsin–Parkside (WI)
U of Wisconsin–Superior (WI)
U of Wisconsin–Whitewater (WI)
U of Wyoming (WY)
Upper Iowa U (IA)
Ursuline Coll (OH)
Utah State U (UT)
Utah Valley U (UT)
Valdosta State U (GA)
Valparaiso U (IN)
Vanguard U of Southern California (CA)
Villanova U (PA)
Virginia Commonwealth U (VA)
Virginia Polytechnic Inst and State U (VA)
Walsh Coll of Accountancy and Business Administration (MI)
Walsh U (OH)
Wartburg Coll (IA)
Washington State U (WA)
Washington State U–Vancouver (WA)
Washington U in St. Louis (MO)
Waynesburg U (PA)
Wayne State U (MI)
Webber Intl U (FL)
Weber State U (UT)
Webster U (MO)
Western Connecticut State U (CT)
Western Illinois U (IL)
Western Kentucky U (KY)
Western Michigan U (MI)
Western New England U (MA)
Western State Colorado U (CO)
Western Washington U (WA)
Westminster Coll (PA)
Westminster Coll (UT)
West Texas A&M U (TX)
West Virginia U (WV)

West Virginia Wesleyan Coll (WV)
Whitworth U (WA)
Wichita State U (KS)
Widener U (PA)
Wilkes U (PA)
William Paterson U of New Jersey (NJ)
Wilmington U (DE)
Winona State U (MN)
Wittenberg U (OH)
Woodbury U (CA)
Wright State U (OH)
Wright State U–Lake Campus (OH)
Xavier U of Louisiana (LA)
York Coll of Pennsylvania (PA)
Youngstown State U (OH)

MARKETING RELATED
Anderson U (IN)
Babson Coll (MA)
Bowling Green State U (OH)
Colorado Christian U (CO)
Delaware State U (DE)
Duquesne U (PA)
Eastern Nazarene Coll (MA)
Eastern U (PA)
Florida State U (FL)
Mount Mercy U (IA)
Mount St. Joseph U (OH)
Newberry Coll (SC)
Niagara U (NY)
Ohio Northern U (OH)
Our Lady of the Lake U (TX)
Saginaw Valley State U (MI)
Saint Louis U–Madrid Campus (Spain)
State U of New York at New Paltz (NY)
Stevenson U (MD)
U of Michigan–Dearborn (MI)
U of Minnesota, Duluth (MN)
U of Southern Mississippi (MS)
Washington U in St. Louis (MO)
Western Michigan U (MI)
Western New England U (MA)

MARKETING RESEARCH
Ashland U (OH)
Bowling Green State U (OH)
Bryant U (RI)
Fashion Inst of Technology (NY)
Husson U (ME)
Ithaca Coll (NY)
Lawrence Technological U (MI)
Mercyhurst U (PA)
Ohio Northern U (OH)

MARRIAGE AND FAMILY THERAPY/COUNSELING
DeSales U (PA)
Johnson U (TN)
Johnson U Florida (FL)
Oklahoma Baptist U (OK)
U of Mobile (AL)

MASSAGE THERAPY
Idaho State U (ID)

MASS COMMUNICATION/ MEDIA
Adams State U (CO)
Alcorn State U (MS)
Allegheny Coll (PA)
American Intl Coll (MA)
American U (DC)
American U in Bulgaria (Bulgaria)
The American U in Cairo (Egypt)
Andrews U (MI)
Arcadia U (PA)
Arizona State U at the Downtown Phoenix campus (AZ)
Ashland U (OH)
Auburn U (AL)
Augustana Coll (IL)
Austin Coll (TX)
Austin Peay State U (TN)
Baker U (KS)
Baldwin Wallace U (OH)
Barry U (FL)
Barton Coll (NC)
Belmont U (TN)
Beloit Coll (WI)
Bemidji State U (MN)
Benedictine Coll (KS)
Bentley U (MA)
Berea Coll (KY)
Bethel Coll (KS)
Bethel U (MN)
Bethune-Cookman U (FL)

Black Hills State U (SD)
Bloomsburg U of Pennsylvania (PA)
Bluefield Coll (VA)
Bowie State U (MD)
Brandman U (CA)
Brenau U (GA)
Bridgewater Coll (VA)
Brock U (ON, Canada)
Bryant U (RI)
Buena Vista U (IA)
Buffalo State Coll, State U of New York (NY)
California Lutheran U (CA)
California State U, East Bay (CA)
California State U, Long Beach (CA)
California State U, Sacramento (CA)
California State U, San Marcos (CA)
Calvary U (MO)
Calvin Coll (MI)
Campbellsville U (KY)
Carson-Newman U (TN)
Cedar Crest Coll (PA)
Central Connecticut State U (CT)
Chestnut Hill Coll (PA)
City Coll of the City U of New York (NY)
Clark U (MA)
Coll of Mount Saint Vincent (NY)
The Coll of New Rochelle (NY)
The Coll of Wooster (OH)
Colorado Mesa U (CO)
Colorado State U–Pueblo (CO)
Concordia U (QC, Canada)
Concordia U, St. Paul (MN)
Concordia U Wisconsin (WI)
Concord U (WV)
Culver-Stockton Coll (MO)
Dean Coll (MA)
Defiance Coll (OH)
Delaware Valley U (PA)
Denison U (OH)
DePaul U (IL)
DePauw U (IN)
Drake U (IA)
Drew U (NJ)
East Central U (OK)
Eastern Nazarene Coll (MA)
East Tennessee State U (TN)
East Texas Baptist U (TX)
Elizabethtown Coll (PA)
Emerson Coll (MA)
Emmanuel Coll (GA)
Emory & Henry Coll (VA)
Endicott Coll (MA)
Eugene Lang Coll of Liberal Arts (NY)
Felician U (NJ)
Fisher Coll (MA)
Flagler Coll (FL)
Florida Gulf Coast U (FL)
Florida Intl U (FL)
Florida Southern Coll (FL)
Fordham U (NY)
Francis Marion U (SC)
Franklin Pierce U (NH)
Frostburg State U (MD)
The George Washington U (DC)
Gonzaga U (WA)
Governors State U (IL)
Grambling State U (LA)
Grand View U (IA)
Green Mountain Coll (VT)
Greenville U (IL)
Gustavus Adolphus Coll (MN)
Hampton U (VA)
Hawai'i Pacific U (HI)
Heidelberg U (OH)
Hobart and William Smith Colls (NY)
Hofstra U (NY)
Hollins U (VA)
Holy Family U (PA)
Houston Baptist U (TX)
Hunter Coll of the City U of New York (NY)
Huston-Tillotson U (TX)
Illinois Coll (IL)
Illinois State U (IL)
Indiana U Bloomington (IN)
Indiana Wesleyan U (IN)
Iona Coll (NY)
Iowa State U of Science and Technology (IA)

Ithaca Coll (NY)
Jackson State U (MS)
Jacksonville U (FL)
John Cabot U (Italy)
John Carroll U (OH)
Johnson C. Smith U (NC)
Johnson U (TN)
Kutztown U of Pennsylvania (PA)
Lehman Coll of the City U of New York (NY)
LeTourneau U (TX)
Lincoln Memorial U (TN)
Lindenwood U (MO)
Lindsey Wilson Coll (KY)
Linfield Coll (OR)
Lipscomb U (TN)
Lock Haven U of Pennsylvania (PA)
Loras Coll (IA)
Louisiana Coll (LA)
Louisiana State U and A&M Coll (LA)
Lubbock Christian U (TX)
Lynn U (FL)
Macalester Coll (MN)
Manchester U (IN)
Mansfield U of Pennsylvania (PA)
Marist Coll (NY)
Marquette U (WI)
Marylhurst U (OR)
Maryville U of Saint Louis (MO)
Massachusetts Inst of Technology (MA)
The Master's U (CA)
McNeese State U (LA)
Mercer U, Macon (GA)
Mercy Coll (NY)
Meredith Coll (NC)
Miami U (OH)
Michigan State U (MI)
MidAmerica Nazarene U (KS)
Middle Tennessee State U (TN)
Missouri State U (MO)
Missouri Valley Coll (MO)
Morris Coll (SC)
Mount Saint Mary Coll (NY)
Muskingum U (OH)
Newman U (KS)
The New School for Public Engagement (NY)
North Carolina Central U (NC)
North Greenville U (SC)
Northwestern Oklahoma State U (OK)
Northwest Nazarene U (ID)
Oklahoma Baptist U (OK)
Oklahoma Christian U (OK)
Oklahoma City U (OK)
Olivet Nazarene U (IL)
Ottawa U (KS)
Ouachita Baptist U (AR)
Pace U (NY)
Palm Beach Atlantic U (FL)
Piedmont Coll (GA)
Point Loma Nazarene U (CA)
Point Park U (PA)
Pomona Coll (CA)
Principia Coll (IL)
Queens Coll of the City U of New York (NY)
Quinnipiac U (CT)
Rhode Island Coll (RI)
Robert Morris U (PA)
Roberts Wesleyan Coll (NY)
Roosevelt U (IL)
Rutgers U–New Brunswick (NJ)
St. Catherine U (MN)
Saint Francis U (PA)
Saint Mary-of-the-Woods Coll (IN)
Saint Michael's Coll (VT)
St. Norbert Coll (WI)
St. Thomas Aquinas Coll (NY)
Sam Houston State U (TX)
Scripps Coll (CA)
Shaw U (NC)
Sonoma State U (CA)
Southern Illinois U Edwardsville (IL)
Southwestern Assemblies of God U (TX)
State U of New York at Fredonia (NY)
State U of New York at Oswego (NY)
State U of New York Coll at Oneonta (NY)
Stephen F. Austin State U (TX)
Suffolk U (MA)

Temple U (PA)
Texas A&M U–Corpus Christi (TX)
Texas A&M U–Texarkana (TX)
Texas State U (TX)
Texas Tech U (TX)
Towson U (MD)
Trevecca Nazarene U (TN)
Tufts U (MA)
Tulane U (LA)
Union U (TN)
U at Albany, State U of New York (NY)
U of Bridgeport (CT)
U of California, San Diego (CA)
U of Charleston (WV)
U of Colorado Boulder (CO)
U of Denver (CO)
U of Houston (TX)
U of Jamestown (ND)
U of Louisiana at Monroe (LA)
U of Maine (ME)
U of Mary Hardin-Baylor (TX)
U of Maryland, Baltimore County (MD)
U of Maryland Eastern Shore (MD)
U of Memphis (TN)
U of Michigan–Dearborn (MI)
U of Missouri (MO)
U of Missouri–St. Louis (MO)
U of Nebraska at Kearney (NE)
U of Nevada, Las Vegas (NV)
U of New Mexico (NM)
U of North Alabama (AL)
U of North Carolina at Asheville (NC)
The U of North Carolina at Chapel Hill (NC)
The U of North Carolina at Greensboro (NC)
The U of North Carolina at Pembroke (NC)
U of Northern Iowa (IA)
U of North Florida (FL)
U of Pittsburgh (PA)
U of Pittsburgh at Greensburg (PA)
U of St. Francis (IL)
U of San Francisco (CA)
U of Sioux Falls (SD)
U of Southern Indiana (IN)
U of Southern Maine (ME)
U of South Florida, St. Petersburg (FL)
The U of Texas Rio Grande Valley (TX)
U of the Incarnate Word (TX)
U of Toronto (ON, Canada)
U of Washington, Bothell (WA)
U of Washington, Tacoma (WA)
U of Wisconsin–Eau Claire (WI)
U of Wisconsin–Milwaukee (WI)
U of Wisconsin–Superior (WI)
Upper Iowa U (IA)
Ursinus Coll (PA)
Valdosta State U (GA)
Vassar Coll (NY)
Villanova U (PA)
Virginia Commonwealth U (VA)
Virginia Wesleyan U (VA)
Wartburg Coll (IA)
Washington State U (WA)
Wayland Baptist U (TX)
Wayne State Coll (NE)
Webster U (MO)
Western New England U (MA)
Westminster Coll (PA)
Whitworth U (WA)
Widener U (PA)
Winona State U (MN)
Winthrop U (SC)
Worcester State U (MA)
Wright State U (OH)
Xavier U of Louisiana (LA)
York Coll of Pennsylvania (PA)

MATERIALS ENGINEERING
Alfred U (NY)
Arizona State U at the Tempe campus (AZ)
Auburn U (AL)
Boise State U (ID)
California Inst of Technology (CA)
California Polytechnic State U, San Luis Obispo (CA)
California State U, Long Beach (CA)
Case Western Reserve U (OH)
Clemson U (SC)

Columbia U (NY)
Cornell U (NY)
Drexel U (PA)
Florida State U (FL)
Georgia Inst of Technology (GA)
Iowa State U of Science and Technology (IA)
Johns Hopkins U (MD)
Lehigh U (PA)
Massachusetts Inst of Technology (MA)
Michigan State U (MI)
Michigan Technological U (MI)
New Mexico Inst of Mining and Technology (NM)
North Carolina State U (NC)
Northwestern U (IL)
The Ohio State U (OH)
Purdue U (IN)
Rensselaer Polytechnic Inst (NY)
Rice U (TX)
U at Albany, State U of New York (NY)
The U of Alabama at Birmingham (AL)
U of California, Davis (CA)
U of California, Irvine (CA)
U of California, Los Angeles (CA)
U of Cincinnati (OH)
U of Florida (FL)
U of Idaho (ID)
U of Kentucky (KY)
U of Maryland, Coll Park (MD)
U of Michigan (MI)
U of Minnesota, Twin Cities Campus (MN)
U of North Texas (TX)
U of Pennsylvania (PA)
U of Pittsburgh (PA)
The U of Tennessee (TN)
The U of Texas at Austin (TX)
U of Toronto (ON, Canada)
U of Utah (UT)
U of Washington (WA)
U of Wisconsin–Eau Claire (WI)
U of Wisconsin–Madison (WI)
U of Wisconsin–Milwaukee (WI)
Virginia Polytechnic Inst and State U (VA)
Washington State U (WA)
Winona State U (MN)
Wright State U (OH)
Wright State U–Lake Campus (OH)

MATERIALS SCIENCE
Carnegie Mellon U (PA)
Case Western Reserve U (OH)
Columbia U (NY)
Johns Hopkins U (MD)
Northwestern U (IL)
Penn State Abington (PA)
Penn State Altoona (PA)
Penn State Beaver (PA)
Penn State Berks (PA)
Penn State Brandywine (PA)
Penn State DuBois (PA)
Penn State Erie, The Behrend Coll (PA)
Penn State Fayette, The Eberly Campus (PA)
Penn State Greater Allegheny (PA)
Penn State Hazleton (PA)
Penn State Lehigh Valley (PA)
Penn State Mont Alto (PA)
Penn State New Kensington (PA)
Penn State Schuylkill (PA)
Penn State Shenango (PA)
Penn State U Park (PA)
Penn State Wilkes-Barre (PA)
Penn State Worthington Scranton (PA)
Penn State York (PA)
Rice U (TX)
Stanford U (CA)
The U of Arizona (AZ)
U of California, Los Angeles (CA)
U of California, Riverside (CA)
U of Pennsylvania (PA)
U of Toronto (ON, Canada)
U of Wisconsin–Eau Claire (WI)

MATHEMATICAL BIOLOGY
Averett U (VA)
LeTourneau U (TX)
U of Houston (TX)
U of Idaho (ID)
U of Pittsburgh (PA)

MATHEMATICAL STATISTICS AND PROBABILITY
Albion Coll (MI)
Bryant U (RI)
Calvin Coll (MI)
Carnegie Mellon U (PA)
Concordia Coll–New York (NY)
Concordia U (QC, Canada)
Marquette U (WI)
Purdue U (IN)
U of California, San Diego (CA)
U of the Incarnate Word (TX)

MATHEMATICS
Abilene Christian U (TX)
Acadia U (NS, Canada)
Adams State U (CO)
Adelphi U (NY)
Agnes Scott Coll (GA)
Alabama State U (AL)
Albion Coll (MI)
Albright Coll (PA)
Alcorn State U (MS)
Alfred U (NY)
Allegheny Coll (PA)
Alma Coll (MI)
Alverno Coll (WI)
American U (DC)
American U in Bulgaria (Bulgaria)
The American U in Cairo (Egypt)
American U of Beirut (Lebanon)
Amherst Coll (MA)
Anderson U (IN)
Anderson U (SC)
Andrews U (MI)
Angelo State U (TX)
Antioch U Midwest (OH)
Appalachian State U (NC)
Aquinas Coll (MI)
Arcadia U (PA)
Arizona State U at the Tempe campus (AZ)
Arkansas Tech U (AR)
Asbury U (KY)
Ashland U (OH)
Assumption Coll (MA)
Athens State U (AL)
Auburn U (AL)
Auburn U at Montgomery (AL)
Augsburg U (MN)
Augustana Coll (IL)
Augustana U (SD)
Aurora U (IL)
Austin Coll (TX)
Austin Peay State U (TN)
Averett U (VA)
Avila U (MO)
Azusa Pacific U (CA)
Baker U (KS)
Baldwin Wallace U (OH)
Ball State U (IN)
Bard Coll (NY)
Barnard Coll (NY)
Barry U (FL)
Barton Coll (NC)
Baruch Coll of the City U of New York (NY)
Bates Coll (ME)
Baylor U (TX)
Belhaven U (MS)
Bellarmine U (KY)
Belmont U (TN)
Beloit Coll (WI)
Bemidji State U (MN)
Benedictine Coll (KS)
Benedictine U (IL)
Bennett Coll (NC)
Bennington Coll (VT)
Bentley U (MA)
Berea Coll (KY)
Berry Coll (GA)
Bethany Lutheran Coll (MN)
Bethel Coll (IN)
Bethel Coll (KS)
Bethel U (MN)
Bethel U (TN)
Bethune-Cookman U (FL)
Binghamton U, State U of New York (NY)
Biola U (CA)
Birmingham-Southern Coll (AL)
Blackburn Coll (IL)
Black Hills State U (SD)
Bloomsburg U of Pennsylvania (PA)
Bluefield Coll (VA)
Blue Mountain Coll (MS)
Bluffton U (OH)

Bob Jones U (SC)
Boise State U (ID)
Boston Coll (MA)
Boston U (MA)
Bowdoin Coll (ME)
Bowie State U (MD)
Bowling Green State U (OH)
Bradley U (IL)
Brandeis U (MA)
Brandon U (MB, Canada)
Bridgewater Coll (VA)
Bridgewater State U (MA)
Brock U (ON, Canada)
Bryan Coll (TN)
Bryn Mawr Coll (PA)
Bucknell U (PA)
Buena Vista U (IA)
Buffalo State Coll, State U of New York (NY)
Butler U (IN)
Cairn U (PA)
Caldwell U (NJ)
California Baptist U (CA)
California Inst of Technology (CA)
California Lutheran U (CA)
California Polytechnic State U, San Luis Obispo (CA)
California State Polytechnic U, Pomona (CA)
California State U, Dominguez Hills (CA)
California State U, East Bay (CA)
California State U, Fullerton (CA)
California State U, Long Beach (CA)
California State U, Los Angeles (CA)
California State U, Monterey Bay (CA)
California State U, Northridge (CA)
California State U, Sacramento (CA)
California State U, San Bernardino (CA)
California State U, San Marcos (CA)
California State U, Stanislaus (CA)
California U of Pennsylvania (PA)
Calvary U (MO)
Calvin Coll (MI)
Cameron U (OK)
Campbellsville U (KY)
Capital U (OH)
Cardinal Stritch U (WI)
Carleton Coll (MN)
Carlow U (PA)
Carnegie Mellon U (PA)
Carroll Coll (MT)
Carroll U (WI)
Carson-Newman U (TN)
Carthage Coll (WI)
Case Western Reserve U (OH)
Catawba Coll (NC)
The Catholic U of America (DC)
Cedar Crest Coll (PA)
Cedarville U (OH)
Centenary Coll of Louisiana (LA)
Central Connecticut State U (CT)
Central Methodist U (MO)
Central Michigan U (MI)
Central State U (OH)
Centre Coll (KY)
Chapman U (CA)
Charleston Southern U (SC)
Chatham U (PA)
Chestnut Hill Coll (PA)
Chowan U (NC)
Christendom Coll (VA)
Christian Brothers U (TN)
Christopher Newport U (VA)
The Citadel, The Military Coll of South Carolina (SC)
City Coll of the City U of New York (NY)
Claremont McKenna Coll (CA)
Clarion U of Pennsylvania (PA)
Clark Atlanta U (GA)
Clarke U (IA)
Clarkson U (NY)
Clark U (MA)
Clayton State U (GA)
Clemson U (SC)
Cleveland State U (OH)
Coe Coll (IA)
Coker Coll (SC)
Colby Coll (ME)
Colgate U (NY)

The Coll at Brockport, State U of New York (NY)
Coll of Charleston (SC)
Coll of Coastal Georgia (GA)
The Coll of Idaho (ID)
Coll of Mount Saint Vincent (NY)
The Coll of New Jersey (NJ)
The Coll of New Rochelle (NY)
Coll of Saint Benedict (MN)
Coll of Saint Elizabeth (NJ)
Coll of Saint Mary (NE)
The Coll of Saint Rose (NY)
The Coll of St. Scholastica (MN)
Coll of Staten Island of the City U of New York (NY)
Coll of the Holy Cross (MA)
Coll of the Ozarks (MO)
The Coll of William and Mary (VA)
The Coll of Wooster (OH)
The Colorado Coll (CO)
Colorado Mesa U (CO)
Colorado State U (CO)
Colorado State U–Pueblo (CO)
Columbia Coll (MO)
Columbia Coll (SC)
Columbia U (NY)
Columbus State U (GA)
Concordia Coll–New York (NY)
Concordia U (QC, Canada)
Concordia U Chicago (IL)
Concordia U Irvine (CA)
Concordia U, Nebraska (NE)
Concordia U of Edmonton (AB, Canada)
Concordia U, St. Paul (MN)
Concordia U Wisconsin (WI)
Concord U (WV)
Connecticut Coll (CT)
Converse Coll (SC)
Corban U (OR)
Cornell Coll (IA)
Cornell U (NY)
Cornerstone U (MI)
Covenant Coll (GA)
Creighton U (NE)
Culver-Stockton Coll (MO)
Daemen Coll (NY)
Dallas Baptist U (TX)
Dartmouth Coll (NH)
Davidson Coll (NC)
Defiance Coll (OH)
Delaware State U (DE)
Denison U (OH)
DePaul U (IL)
DePauw U (IN)
DeSales U (PA)
Dickinson Coll (PA)
Dickinson State U (ND)
Doane U (NE)
Dominican Coll (NY)
Dominican U (IL)
Drake U (IA)
Drew U (NJ)
Drexel U (PA)
Duquesne U (PA)
D'Youville Coll (NY)
Earlham Coll (IN)
East Carolina U (NC)
East Central U (OK)
Eastern Mennonite U (VA)
Eastern Michigan U (MI)
Eastern Nazarene Coll (MA)
Eastern New Mexico U (NM)
Eastern Oregon U (OR)
Eastern U (PA)
Eastern Washington U (WA)
East Stroudsburg U of Pennsylvania (PA)
East Tennessee State U (TN)
East Texas Baptist U (TX)
Eckerd Coll (FL)
Edgewood Coll (WI)
Elizabethtown Coll (PA)
Elmhurst Coll (IL)
Elms Coll (MA)
Elon U (NC)
Emmanuel Coll (GA)
Emmanuel Coll (MA)
Emory & Henry Coll (VA)
Emory U (GA)
Emporia State U (KS)
Endicott Coll (MA)
Evangel U (MO)
Fairfield U (CT)
Fairleigh Dickinson U, Florham Campus (NJ)

Fairleigh Dickinson U, Metropolitan Campus (NJ)
Fayetteville State U (NC)
Felician U (NJ)
Fitchburg State U (MA)
Florida Ag and Mech U (FL)
Florida Atlantic U (FL)
Florida Gulf Coast U (FL)
Florida Inst of Technology (FL)
Florida Intl U (FL)
Florida Southern Coll (FL)
Florida State U (FL)
Fordham U (NY)
Fort Lewis Coll (CO)
Framingham State U (MA)
Francis Marion U (SC)
Franklin & Marshall Coll (PA)
Franklin Coll (IN)
Franklin Pierce U (NH)
Friends U (KS)
Frostburg State U (MD)
Furman U (SC)
Gannon U (PA)
George Mason U (VA)
Georgetown Coll (KY)
Georgetown U (DC)
The George Washington U (DC)
Georgia Coll & State U (GA)
Georgia Gwinnett Coll (GA)
Georgian Court U (NJ)
Georgia Southern U (GA)
Georgia Southern U–Armstrong Campus (GA)
Georgia Southwestern State U (GA)
Georgia State U (GA)
Gettysburg Coll (PA)
Gonzaga U (WA)
Gordon Coll (MA)
Gordon State Coll (GA)
Goshen Coll (IN)
Governors State U (IL)
Graceland U (IA)
Grand Valley State U (MI)
Greensboro Coll (NC)
Greenville U (IL)
Grinnell Coll (IA)
Grove City Coll (PA)
Guilford Coll (NC)
Gustavus Adolphus Coll (MN)
Gwynedd Mercy U (PA)
Hamilton Coll (NY)
Hamline U (MN)
Hampden-Sydney Coll (VA)
Hampshire Coll (MA)
Hampton U (VA)
Hannibal-LaGrange U (MO)
Harding U (AR)
Harris-Stowe State U (MO)
Hartwick Coll (NY)
Harvard U (MA)
Harvey Mudd Coll (CA)
Haverford Coll (PA)
Hawai'i Pacific U (HI)
Heidelberg U (OH)
Hendrix Coll (AR)
High Point U (NC)
Hillsdale Coll (MI)
Hiram Coll (OH)
Hobart and William Smith Colls (NY)
Hofstra U (NY)
Hollins U (VA)
Holy Family U (PA)
Hood Coll (MD)
Hope Coll (MI)
Houston Baptist U (TX)
Howard Payne U (TX)
Humboldt State U (CA)
Hunter Coll of the City U of New York (NY)
Huntingdon Coll (AL)
Huston-Tillotson U (TX)
Idaho State U (ID)
Illinois Coll (IL)
Illinois State U (IL)
Illinois Wesleyan U (IL)
Indiana State U (IN)
Indiana U Bloomington (IN)
Indiana U East (IN)
Indiana U Kokomo (IN)
Indiana U Northwest (IN)
Indiana U of Pennsylvania (PA)
Indiana U–Purdue U Indianapolis (IN)
Indiana U South Bend (IN)

Indiana U Southeast (IN)
Indiana Wesleyan U (IN)
Inter American U of Puerto Rico, Bayamón Campus (PR)
Inter American U of Puerto Rico, Metropolitan Campus (PR)
Inter American U of Puerto Rico, San Germán Campus (PR)
Iona Coll (NY)
Iowa State U of Science and Technology (IA)
Ithaca Coll (NY)
Jackson State U (MS)
Jacksonville U (FL)
James Madison U (VA)
John Brown U (AR)
John Carroll U (OH)
Johns Hopkins U (MD)
Johnson C. Smith U (NC)
Judson U (IL)
Juniata Coll (PA)
Kalamazoo Coll (MI)
Kansas State U (KS)
Kansas Wesleyan U (KS)
Kean U (NJ)
Keene State Coll (NH)
Kennesaw State U (GA)
Kent State U (OH)
Kent State U at Stark (OH)
Kentucky State U (KY)
Kenyon Coll (OH)
King's Coll (PA)
King U (TN)
Knox Coll (IL)
Kutztown U of Pennsylvania (PA)
Lafayette Coll (PA)
LaGrange Coll (GA)
Lamar U (TX)
Langston U (OK)
La Roche Coll (PA)
La Salle U (PA)
La Sierra U (CA)
Lawrence Technological U (MI)
Lawrence U (WI)
Lebanese American U (Lebanon)
Lebanon Valley Coll (PA)
Lee U (TN)
Lehigh U (PA)
Lehman Coll of the City U of New York (NY)
Le Moyne Coll (NY)
Lenoir-Rhyne U (NC)
LeTourneau U (TX)
Lewis U (IL)
Liberty U (VA)
Limestone Coll (SC)
Lincoln Memorial U (TN)
Lincoln U (MO)
Lincoln U (PA)
Lindenwood U (MO)
Linfield Coll (OR)
Lipscomb U (TN)
Lock Haven U of Pennsylvania (PA)
Long Island U–LIU Brooklyn (NY)
Long Island U–LIU Post (NY)
Longwood U (VA)
Loras Coll (IA)
Louisiana Coll (LA)
Louisiana State U and A&M Coll (LA)
Loyola Marymount U (CA)
Loyola U Chicago (IL)
Loyola U New Orleans (LA)
Lubbock Christian U (TX)
Luther Coll (IA)
Lycoming Coll (PA)
Lynchburg Coll (VA)
Lyon Coll (AR)
Macalester Coll (MN)
Madonna U (MI)
Maharishi U of Management (IA)
Malone U (OH)
Manchester U (IN)
Manhattan Coll (NY)
Manhattanville Coll (NY)
Mansfield U of Pennsylvania (PA)
Marian U (IN)
Marian U (WI)
Marietta Coll (OH)
Marist Coll (NY)
Marlboro Coll (VT)
Marquette U (WI)
Marshall U (WV)
Mary Baldwin U (VA)
Marymount U (VA)
Maryville Coll (TN)
Maryville U of Saint Louis (MO)

Marywood U (PA)
Massachusetts Coll of Liberal Arts (MA)
Massachusetts Inst of Technology (MA)
The Master's U (CA)
McDaniel Coll (MD)
McKendree U (IL)
McMurry U (TX)
McNeese State U (LA)
McPherson Coll (KS)
Mercer U, Macon (GA)
Mercy Coll (NY)
Mercyhurst U (PA)
Meredith Coll (NC)
Merrimack Coll (MA)
Messiah Coll (PA)
Metropolitan State U of Denver (CO)
Miami U (OH)
Michigan State U (MI)
Michigan Technological U (MI)
Mid-America Christian U (OK)
MidAmerica Nazarene U (KS)
Middlebury Coll (VT)
Middle Georgia State U (GA)
Middle Tennessee State U (TN)
Millersville U of Pennsylvania (PA)
Milligan Coll (TN)
Millikin U (IL)
Millsaps Coll (MS)
Mills Coll (CA)
Minnesota State U Moorhead (MN)
Minot State U (ND)
Misericordia U (PA)
Mississippi State U (MS)
Missouri Baptist U (MO)
Missouri State U (MO)
Missouri Valley Coll (MO)
Missouri Western State U (MO)
Molloy Coll (NY)
Monmouth Coll (IL)
Montana Tech of The U of Montana (MT)
Montclair State U (NJ)
Moravian Coll (PA)
Morehead State U (KY)
Morehouse Coll (GA)
Morningside Coll (IA)
Morris Coll (SC)
Mount Holyoke Coll (MA)
Mount Marty Coll (SD)
Mount Mary U (WI)
Mount Mercy U (IA)
Mount St. Joseph U (OH)
Mount Saint Mary Coll (NY)
Mount Saint Mary's U (CA)
Mount St. Mary's U (MD)
Mount Vernon Nazarene U (OH)
Muhlenberg Coll (PA)
Murray State U (KY)
Muskingum U (OH)
National U (CA)
Nazareth Coll of Rochester (NY)
Neumann U (PA)
Newberry Coll (SC)
New Coll of Florida (FL)
New Jersey City U (NJ)
New Jersey Inst of Technology (NJ)
Newman U (KS)
New Mexico Highlands U (NM)
New Mexico Inst of Mining and Technology (NM)
New Mexico State U (NM)
New York U (NY)
Niagara U (NY)
Nichols Coll (MA)
North Carolina Central U (NC)
North Carolina State U (NC)
North Carolina Wesleyan Coll (NC)
North Central Coll (IL)
North Dakota State U (ND)
Northeastern State U (OK)
Northeastern U (MA)
Northern Arizona U (AZ)
Northern Illinois U (IL)
Northern Kentucky U (KY)
Northern Michigan U (MI)
Northern State U (SD)
Northern Vermont U–Lyndon (VT)
North Greenville U (SC)
Northland Coll (WI)
Northwest Christian U (OR)
Northwestern Coll (IA)
Northwestern Oklahoma State U (OK)

Northwestern State U of Louisiana (LA)
Northwestern U (IL)
Northwest Missouri State U (MO)
Northwest Nazarene U (ID)
Northwest U (WA)
Nyack Coll (NY)
Oakland City U (IN)
Oakland U (MI)
Oberlin Coll (OH)
Occidental Coll (CA)
Oglethorpe U (GA)
Ohio Dominican U (OH)
Ohio Northern U (OH)
The Ohio State U (OH)
Ohio U (OH)
Ohio Wesleyan U (OH)
Oklahoma Baptist U (OK)
Oklahoma Christian U (OK)
Oklahoma City U (OK)
Oklahoma State U (OK)
Old Dominion U (VA)
Olivet Nazarene U (IL)
Oral Roberts U (OK)
Oregon State U (OR)
Ottawa U (KS)
Otterbein U (OH)
Ouachita Baptist U (AR)
Our Lady of the Lake U (TX)
Pace U (NY)
Pace U, Pleasantville Campus (NY)
Pacific Lutheran U (WA)
Palm Beach Atlantic U (FL)
Penn State Abington (PA)
Penn State Altoona (PA)
Penn State Beaver (PA)
Penn State Berks (PA)
Penn State Brandywine (PA)
Penn State DuBois (PA)
Penn State Erie, The Behrend Coll (PA)
Penn State Fayette, The Eberly Campus (PA)
Penn State Greater Allegheny (PA)
Penn State Hazleton (PA)
Penn State Lehigh Valley (PA)
Penn State Mont Alto (PA)
Penn State New Kensington (PA)
Penn State Schuylkill (PA)
Penn State Shenango (PA)
Penn State U Park (PA)
Penn State Wilkes-Barre (PA)
Penn State Worthington Scranton (PA)
Penn State York (PA)
Pepperdine U, Malibu (CA)
Pfeiffer U (NC)
Piedmont Coll (GA)
Pittsburg State U (KS)
Pitzer Coll (CA)
Point Loma Nazarene U (CA)
Pomona Coll (CA)
Portland State U (OR)
Prairie View A&M U (TX)
Presbyterian Coll (SC)
Princeton U (NJ)
Principia Coll (IL)
Providence Coll (RI)
Purchase Coll, State U of New York (NY)
Purdue U (IN)
Purdue U Northwest (IN)
Queens Coll of the City U of New York (NY)
Quinnipiac U (CT)
Radford U (VA)
Ramapo Coll of New Jersey (NJ)
Randolph U (VA)
Randolph-Macon Coll (VA)
Redeemer U Coll (ON, Canada)
Reed Coll (OR)
Regent U (VA)
Regis U (CO)
Rensselaer Polytechnic Inst (NY)
Rhode Island Coll (RI)
Rhodes Coll (TN)
Rice U (TX)
Rider U (NJ)
Ripon Coll (WI)
Rivier U (NH)
Roanoke Coll (VA)
Roberts Wesleyan Coll (NY)
Rochester Inst of Technology (NY)
Rockford U (IL)
Rockhurst U (MO)
Rocky Mountain Coll (MT)
Roger Williams U (RI)

Rollins Coll (FL)
Roosevelt U (IL)
Rose-Hulman Inst of Technology (IN)
Rosemont Coll (PA)
Rowan U (NJ)
Rust Coll (MS)
Rutgers U–Camden (NJ)
Rutgers U–Newark (NJ)
Rutgers U–New Brunswick (NJ)
Sacred Heart U (CT)
Saginaw Valley State U (MI)
St. Ambrose U (IA)
Saint Anselm Coll (NH)
Saint Augustine's U (NC)
St. Bonaventure U (NY)
St. Catherine U (MN)
Saint Francis U (PA)
St. John Fisher Coll (NY)
Saint John's U (MN)
St. John's U (NY)
St. Joseph's Coll, Long Island Campus (NY)
St. Joseph's Coll, New York (NY)
St. Joseph's U (PA)
St. Lawrence U (NY)
Saint Leo U (FL)
Saint Louis U (MO)
Saint Louis–Madrid Campus (Spain)
Saint Martin's U (WA)
Saint Mary-of-the-Woods Coll (IN)
Saint Mary's Coll of California (CA)
St. Mary's Coll of Maryland (MD)
St. Mary's U (TX)
Saint Mary's U of Minnesota (MN)
Saint Michael's Coll (VT)
St. Norbert Coll (WI)
St. Olaf Coll (MN)
Saint Peter's U (NJ)
St. Thomas Aquinas Coll (NY)
St. Thomas U (FL)
St. Thomas U (NB, Canada)
Saint Vincent Coll (PA)
Salisbury U (MD)
Salve Regina U (RI)
Samford U (AL)
Sam Houston State U (TX)
San Diego State U (CA)
San Francisco State U (CA)
Santa Clara U (CA)
Sarah Lawrence Coll (NY)
Schreiner U (TX)
Scripps Coll (CA)
Seattle Pacific U (WA)
Seattle U (WA)
Seton Hill U (PA)
Sewanee: The U of the South (TN)
Shawnee State U (OH)
Shaw U (NC)
Shenandoah U (VA)
Shepherd U (WV)
Shippensburg U of Pennsylvania (PA)
Shorter U (GA)
Siena Coll (NY)
Silver Lake Coll of the Holy Family (WI)
Simmons Coll (MA)
Simon Fraser U (BC, Canada)
Simpson Coll (IA)
Skidmore Coll (NY)
Slippery Rock U of Pennsylvania (PA)
Smith Coll (MA)
Sonoma State U (CA)
Southeastern Louisiana U (LA)
Southeastern Oklahoma State U (OK)
Southeastern U (FL)
Southeast Missouri State U (MO)
Southern Adventist U (TN)
Southern Arkansas U–Magnolia (AR)
Southern Illinois U Carbondale (IL)
Southern Illinois U Edwardsville (IL)
Southern Methodist U (TX)
Southern Utah U (UT)
Southwest Baptist U (MO)
Southwestern Adventist U (TX)
Southwestern Assemblies of God U (TX)
Southwestern Coll (KS)
Southwestern U (TX)
Spelman Coll (GA)
Spring Hill Coll (AL)

Stanford U (CA)
State U of New York at Fredonia (NY)
State U of New York at New Paltz (NY)
State U of New York at Oswego (NY)
State U of New York at Plattsburgh (NY)
State U of New York Coll at Cortland (NY)
State U of New York Coll at Geneseo (NY)
State U of New York Coll at Old Westbury (NY)
State U of New York Coll at Oneonta (NY)
State U of New York Coll at Potsdam (NY)
Stephen F. Austin State U (TX)
Stetson U (FL)
Stevens Inst of Technology (NJ)
Stockton U (NJ)
Stonehill Coll (MA)
Stony Brook U, State U of New York (NY)
Suffolk U (MA)
Susquehanna U (PA)
Sweet Briar Coll (VA)
Syracuse U (NY)
Tabor Coll (KS)
Tarleton State U (TX)
Taylor U (IN)
Temple U (PA)
Tennessee Technological U (TN)
Tennessee Wesleyan U (TN)
Texas A&M Intl U (TX)
Texas A&M U (TX)
Texas A&M U–Central Texas (TX)
Texas A&M U–Commerce (TX)
Texas A&M U–Corpus Christi (TX)
Texas A&M U–Kingsville (TX)
Texas A&M U–Texarkana (TX)
Texas Christian U (TX)
Texas Lutheran U (TX)
Texas State U (TX)
Texas Tech U (TX)
Texas Woman's U (TX)
Towson U (MD)
Transylvania U (KY)
Trent U (ON, Canada)
Trevecca Nazarene U (TN)
Trine U (IN)
Trinity Christian Coll (IL)
Trinity U (TX)
Troy U (AL)
Truman State U (MO)
Tufts U (MA)
Tulane U (LA)
Tusculum Coll (TN)
Union Coll (NE)
Union Coll (NY)
Union U (TN)
United States Military Acad (NY)
Université de Sherbrooke (QC, Canada)
U at Albany, State U of New York (NY)
U at Buffalo, the State U of New York (NY)
The U of Akron (OH)
The U of Alabama (AL)
The U of Alabama at Birmingham (AL)
U of Alaska Fairbanks (AK)
The U of Arizona (AZ)
U of Arkansas (AR)
U of Bridgeport (CT)
U of California, Davis (CA)
U of California, Irvine (CA)
U of California, Los Angeles (CA)
U of California, Riverside (CA)
U of California, San Diego (CA)
U of California, Santa Barbara (CA)
U of California, Santa Cruz (CA)
U of Central Arkansas (AR)
U of Central Florida (FL)
U of Central Missouri (MO)
U of Central Oklahoma (OK)
U of Cincinnati (OH)
U of Colorado Boulder (CO)
U of Colorado Colorado Springs (CO)
U of Colorado Denver (CO)
U of Dallas (TX)
U of Dayton (OH)
U of Denver (CO)

U of Dubuque (IA)
U of Evansville (IN)
The U of Findlay (OH)
U of Florida (FL)
U of Georgia (GA)
U of Guam (GU)
U of Hartford (CT)
U of Hawaii at Manoa (HI)
U of Houston (TX)
U of Houston–Clear Lake (TX)
U of Houston–Downtown (TX)
U of Idaho (ID)
U of Illinois at Chicago (IL)
U of Illinois at Springfield (IL)
U of Jamestown (ND)
The U of Kansas (KS)
U of Kentucky (KY)
U of King's Coll (NS, Canada)
U of La Verne (CA)
U of Louisiana at Monroe (LA)
U of Louisville (KY)
U of Maine (ME)
U of Maine at Farmington (ME)
U of Maine at Presque Isle (ME)
U of Mary Hardin-Baylor (TX)
U of Maryland, Baltimore County (MD)
U of Maryland, Coll Park (MD)
U of Maryland Eastern Shore (MD)
U of Mary Washington (VA)
U of Massachusetts Amherst (MA)
U of Massachusetts Boston (MA)
U of Massachusetts Dartmouth (MA)
U of Massachusetts Lowell (MA)
U of Memphis (TN)
U of Miami (FL)
U of Michigan (MI)
U of Michigan–Dearborn (MI)
U of Michigan–Flint (MI)
U of Minnesota, Duluth (MN)
U of Minnesota, Morris (MN)
U of Minnesota, Twin Cities Campus (MN)
U of Missouri (MO)
U of Missouri–St. Louis (MO)
U of Mobile (AL)
U of Montana (MT)
U of Montevallo (AL)
U of Mount Union (OH)
U of Nebraska at Kearney (NE)
U of Nebraska–Lincoln (NE)
U of Nevada, Las Vegas (NV)
U of Nevada, Reno (NV)
U of New England (ME)
U of New Hampshire (NH)
U of New Haven (CT)
U of New Mexico (NM)
U of New Orleans (LA)
U of North Alabama (AL)
U of North Carolina at Asheville (NC)
The U of North Carolina at Chapel Hill (NC)
The U of North Carolina at Charlotte (NC)
The U of North Carolina at Greensboro (NC)
The U of North Carolina at Pembroke (NC)
The U of North Carolina Wilmington (NC)
U of North Dakota (ND)
U of Northern Colorado (CO)
U of Northern Iowa (IA)
U of North Florida (FL)
U of North Georgia (GA)
U of North Texas (TX)
U of Notre Dame (IN)
U of Oklahoma (OK)
U of Oregon (OR)
U of Pennsylvania (PA)
U of Pikeville (KY)
U of Pittsburgh (PA)
U of Providence (MT)
U of Puget Sound (WA)
U of Regina (SK, Canada)
U of Rhode Island (RI)
U of Richmond (VA)
U of Rochester (NY)
U of St. Francis (IL)
U of Saint Francis (IN)
U of Saint Joseph (CT)
U of Saint Mary (KS)
U of St. Thomas (MN)
U of St. Thomas (TX)
U of San Diego (CA)

U of San Francisco (CA)
U of Saskatchewan (SK, Canada)
U of Science and Arts of Oklahoma (OK)
The U of Scranton (PA)
U of Sioux Falls (SD)
U of South Carolina (SC)
U of South Dakota (SD)
U of Southern California (CA)
U of Southern Indiana (IN)
U of Southern Maine (ME)
U of Southern Mississippi (MS)
The U of Tampa (FL)
The U of Tennessee (TN)
The U of Tennessee at Chattanooga (TN)
The U of Tennessee at Martin (TN)
The U of Texas at Austin (TX)
The U of Texas at Dallas (TX)
The U of Texas at El Paso (TX)
The U of Texas at San Antonio (TX)
The U of Texas of the Permian Basin (TX)
The U of Texas Rio Grande Valley (TX)
U of the Fraser Valley (BC, Canada)
U of the Incarnate Word (TX)
U of the Pacific (CA)
U of the Virgin Islands (VI)
The U of Toledo (OH)
The U of Tulsa (OK)
U of Utah (UT)
U of Vermont (VT)
U of Virginia (VA)
The U of Virginia's Coll at Wise (VA)
U of Washington (WA)
U of Washington, Bothell (WA)
U of Waterloo (ON, Canada)
The U of West Alabama (AL)
U of West Georgia (GA)
U of Wisconsin–Eau Claire (WI)
U of Wisconsin–La Crosse (WI)
U of Wisconsin–Madison (WI)
U of Wisconsin–Milwaukee (WI)
U of Wisconsin–Parkside (WI)
U of Wisconsin–Platteville (WI)
U of Wisconsin–River Falls (WI)
U of Wisconsin–Stevens Point (WI)
U of Wisconsin–Superior (WI)
U of Wisconsin–Whitewater (WI)
U of Wyoming (WY)
Upper Iowa U (IA)
Ursinus Coll (PA)
Ursuline Coll (OH)
Utah State U (UT)
Utah Valley U (UT)
Utica Coll (NY)
Valdosta State U (GA)
Valley City State U (ND)
Valparaiso U (IN)
Vanderbilt U (TN)
Vanguard U of Southern California (CA)
Vassar Coll (NY)
Villanova U (PA)
Virginia Commonwealth U (VA)
Virginia Military Inst (VA)
Virginia Polytechnic Inst and State U (VA)
Virginia Wesleyan U (VA)
Wabash Coll (IN)
Wagner Coll (NY)
Wake Forest U (NC)
Walsh U (OH)
Wartburg Coll (IA)
Washington & Jefferson Coll (PA)
Washington and Lee U (VA)
Washington Coll (MD)
Washington State U (WA)
Washington State U–Tri-Cities (WA)
Washington U in St. Louis (MO)
Wayland Baptist U (TX)
Waynesburg U (PA)
Wayne State Coll (NE)
Wayne State U (MI)
Weber State U (UT)
Webster U (MO)
Wellesley Coll (MA)
Wells Coll (NY)
Wesleyan U (CT)
West Chester U of Pennsylvania (PA)
Western Connecticut State U (CT)
Western Illinois U (IL)

Western Kentucky U (KY)
Western Michigan U (MI)
Western New England U (MA)
Western Oregon U (OR)
Western State Colorado U (CO)
Western Washington U (WA)
Westfield State U (MA)
Westminster Coll (PA)
Westminster Coll (UT)
Westmont Coll (CA)
West Texas A&M U (TX)
West Virginia State U (WV)
West Virginia U (WV)
West Virginia U Inst of Technology (WV)
West Virginia Wesleyan Coll (WV)
Wheaton Coll (IL)
Wheaton Coll (MA)
Whitman Coll (WA)
Whittier Coll (CA)
Whitworth U (WA)
Wichita State U (KS)
Widener U (PA)
Wilkes U (PA)
Willamette U (OR)
William Jewell Coll (MO)
William Paterson U of New Jersey (NJ)
William Penn U (IA)
Williams Coll (MA)
William Woods U (MO)
Winona State U (MN)
Winthrop U (SC)
Wisconsin Lutheran Coll (WI)
Wittenberg U (OH)
Wofford Coll (SC)
Worcester Polytechnic Inst (MA)
Worcester State U (MA)
Wright State U (OH)
Wright State U–Lake Campus (OH)
Xavier U of Louisiana (LA)
York Coll of Pennsylvania (PA)
Youngstown State U (OH)

MATHEMATICS AND COMPUTER SCIENCE

Albright Coll (PA)
Anderson U (IN)
Bennington Coll (VT)
Biola U (CA)
Bowdoin Coll (ME)
Brandon U (MB, Canada)
Brescia U (KY)
Bryan Coll (TN)
Calvin Coll (MI)
Chestnut Hill Coll (PA)
Christian Brothers U (TN)
Colgate U (NY)
The Colorado Coll (CO)
Columbia U (NY)
Delaware State U (DE)
DePaul U (IL)
Dominican U (IL)
Emory U (GA)
George Mason U (VA)
Hampden-Sydney Coll (VA)
Hofstra U (NY)
Immaculata U (PA)
Ithaca Coll (NY)
Lawrence Technological U (MI)
Lawrence U (WI)
LeTourneau U (TX)
Loyola U Chicago (IL)
Manchester U (IN)
Marlboro Coll (VT)
Massachusetts Inst of Technology (MA)
Palm Beach Atlantic U (FL)
Pepperdine U, Malibu (CA)
Pfeiffer U (NC)
Purdue U (IN)
Redeemer U Coll (ON, Canada)
Rochester Inst of Technology (NY)
Saint Francis U (PA)
Saint Mary's Coll of California (CA)
Santa Clara U (CA)
Stanford U (CA)
Temple U (PA)
Tufts U (MA)
U at Albany, State U of New York (NY)
The U of Akron (OH)
U of California, Irvine (CA)
The U of Findlay (OH)
U of Illinois at Chicago (IL)
U of Massachusetts Amherst (MA)

U of Massachusetts Dartmouth (MA)
U of Oregon (OR)
U of Regina (SK, Canada)
U of St. Francis (IL)
The U of Tampa (FL)
The U of Texas at Austin (TX)
U of Vermont (VT)
U of Waterloo (ON, Canada)
Valparaiso U (IN)
Washington U in St. Louis (MO)
Western Washington U (WA)
Wheaton Coll (MA)
Whitman Coll (WA)

MATHEMATICS AND STATISTICS

Canisius Coll (NY)
Colby Coll (ME)
Dakota State U (SD)
Emory U (GA)
The Evergreen State Coll (WA)
Luther Coll (IA)
Marlboro Coll (VT)
Reed Coll (OR)
Southeastern U (FL)
U of Notre Dame (IN)
U of South Alabama (AL)
U of Washington, Tacoma (WA)
Western Washington U (WA)

MATHEMATICS AND STATISTICS RELATED

Anderson U (IN)
Carnegie Mellon U (PA)
Chatham U (PA)
Delaware State U (DE)
Emory U (GA)
Hofstra U (NY)
Lycoming Coll (PA)
Marlboro Coll (VT)
Montana Tech of The U of Montana (MT)
New York U (NY)
Purchase Coll, State U of New York (NY)
St. Joseph's Coll, Long Island Campus (NY)
St. Joseph's Coll, New York (NY)
Saint Mary's Coll of California (CA)
Seattle Pacific U (WA)
Siena Coll (NY)
Tulane U (LA)
U of New Hampshire (NH)
The U of North Carolina at Charlotte (NC)
U of Notre Dame (IN)
U of Pittsburgh (PA)
U of Regina (SK, Canada)
U of Rochester (NY)
Western State Colorado U (CO)
Worcester Polytechnic Inst (MA)

MATHEMATICS RELATED

Agnes Scott Coll (GA)
Berry Coll (GA)
Eastern Nazarene Coll (MA)
Grambling State U (LA)
Long Island U–LIU Post (NY)
Louisiana Coll (LA)
Marlboro Coll (VT)
Ohio Northern U (OH)
Seton Hill U (PA)
Temple U (PA)
United States Military Acad (NY)
U of California, Los Angeles (CA)
U of Pittsburgh (PA)
U of Washington (WA)
U of Waterloo (ON, Canada)
Wheaton Coll (MA)

MATHEMATICS TEACHER EDUCATION

Abilene Christian U (TX)
Adams State U (CO)
Albion Coll (MI)
Alice Lloyd Coll (KY)
Anderson U (IN)
Anderson U (SC)
Aquinas Coll (MI)
Arizona Christian U (AZ)
Arkansas Tech U (AR)
Auburn U (AL)
Augustana Coll (IL)
Averett U (VA)
Baylor U (TX)
Berry Coll (GA)
Bethany Lutheran Coll (MN)

Bethel Coll (IN)
Bethel U (MN)
Biola U (CA)
Blackburn Coll (IL)
Black Hills State U (SD)
Bluefield Coll (VA)
Blue Mountain Coll (MS)
Bob Jones U (SC)
Boston U (MA)
Bowdoin Coll (ME)
Bowling Green State U (OH)
Bradley U (IL)
Brigham Young U–Idaho (ID)
Brock U (ON, Canada)
Bryan Coll (TN)
Buena Vista U (IA)
Buffalo State Coll, State U of New York (NY)
Cairn U (PA)
California Baptist U (CA)
California Lutheran U (CA)
California State U, Long Beach (CA)
Calvin Coll (MI)
Campbellsville U (KY)
Canisius Coll (NY)
Capital U (OH)
Carroll Coll (MT)
Carroll U (WI)
The Catholic U of America (DC)
Cedarville U (OH)
Central Michigan U (MI)
Charleston Southern U (SC)
Chipola Coll (FL)
Christian Brothers U (TN)
City Coll of the City U of New York (NY)
Clemson U (SC)
Coker Coll (SC)
The Coll of New Jersey (NJ)
Coll of Saint Mary (NE)
The Coll of Saint Rose (NY)
Coll of Staten Island of the City U of New York (NY)
Coll of the Ozarks (MO)
Columbus State U (GA)
Concordia U Chicago (IL)
Concordia U, St. Paul (MN)
Corban U (OR)
Cornerstone U (MI)
Covenant Coll (GA)
Culver-Stockton Coll (MO)
Curry Coll (MA)
Daemen Coll (NY)
Dakota State U (SD)
Daytona State Coll (FL)
Delaware State U (DE)
Dickinson State U (ND)
Dominican Coll (NY)
Duquesne U (PA)
East Carolina U (NC)
East Central U (OK)
Eastern Michigan U (MI)
Eastern Washington U (WA)
East Texas Baptist U (TX)
Edgewood Coll (WI)
Elmhurst Coll (IL)
Emmanuel Coll (GA)
Emory & Henry Coll (VA)
Felician U (NJ)
Ferris State U (MI)
Fitchburg State U (MA)
Florida Ag and Mech U (FL)
Florida Atlantic U (FL)
Florida Inst of Technology (FL)
Florida Southern Coll (FL)
Florida State U (FL)
Franklin Coll (IN)
Geneva Coll (PA)
Georgia Southern U–Armstrong Campus (GA)
Gordon State Coll (GA)
Goshen Coll (IN)
Grambling State U (LA)
Grand Valley State U (MI)
Granite State Coll (NH)
Greensboro Coll (NC)
Greenville U (IL)
Grove City Coll (PA)
Gustavus Adolphus Coll (MN)
Gwynedd Mercy U (PA)
Hannibal-LaGrange U (MO)
Harding U (AR)
Hardin-Simmons U (TX)
Hobe Sound Bible Coll (FL)
Hofstra U (NY)

Holy Family U (PA)
Hope Coll (MI)
Houston Baptist U (TX)
Howard Payne U (TX)
Hunter Coll of the City U of New York (NY)
Huntingdon Coll (AL)
Indiana U Bloomington (IN)
Indiana U Northwest (IN)
Indiana U South Bend (IN)
Indiana U Southeast (IN)
Indiana Wesleyan U (IN)
Inter American U of Puerto Rico, Metropolitan Campus (PR)
Inter American U of Puerto Rico, San Germán Campus (PR)
Iona Coll (NY)
Ithaca Coll (NY)
Jackson State U (MS)
John Brown U (AR)
Juniata Coll (PA)
Kansas Wesleyan U (KS)
Keene State Coll (NH)
Kennesaw State U (GA)
Kent State U (OH)
LaGrange Coll (GA)
Lee U (TN)
Le Moyne Coll (NY)
LeTourneau U (TX)
Limestone Coll (SC)
Lincoln Memorial U (TN)
Lincoln U (MO)
Lindenwood U (MO)
Lindsey Wilson Coll (KY)
Lipscomb U (TN)
Long Island U–LIU Brooklyn (NY)
Long Island U–LIU Post (NY)
Louisiana Coll (LA)
Loyola U Chicago (IL)
Madonna U (MI)
Manchester U (IN)
Manhattanville Coll (NY)
Maranatha Baptist U (WI)
Marist Coll (NY)
Marquette U (WI)
Martin Luther Coll (MN)
Maryville Coll (TN)
Marywood U (PA)
McMurry U (TX)
Mercyhurst U (PA)
Merrimack Coll (MA)
Messiah Coll (PA)
Miami Dade Coll (FL)
Miami U (OH)
Michigan State U (MI)
MidAmerica Nazarene U (KS)
Millikin U (IL)
Minnesota State U Moorhead (MN)
Minot State U (ND)
Misericordia U (PA)
Missouri State U (MO)
Morningside Coll (IA)
Morris Coll (SC)
Mount Marty Coll (SD)
Mount Mary U (WI)
Mount Vernon Nazarene U (OH)
National U (CA)
Nazareth Coll of Rochester (NY)
New York U (NY)
Niagara U (NY)
North Carolina State U (NC)
North Dakota State U (ND)
Northeastern State U (OK)
Northern Michigan U (MI)
Northern State U (SD)
North Greenville U (SC)
Northwestern Oklahoma State U (OK)
Northwestern U (IL)
Northwest Missouri State U (MO)
Northwest Nazarene U (ID)
Northwest U (WA)
Nova Southeastern U (FL)
Nyack Coll (NY)
Oakland City U (IN)
Ohio Dominican U (OH)
Ohio Northern U (OH)
Ohio Wesleyan U (OH)
Oklahoma Baptist U (OK)
Oklahoma Christian U (OK)
Olivet Nazarene U (IL)
Oral Roberts U (OK)
Pace U (NY)
Pace U, Pleasantville Campus (NY)
Palm Beach Atlantic U (FL)
Pepperdine U, Malibu (CA)
Piedmont Coll (GA)

Pittsburg State U (KS)
Point Park U (PA)
Providence Coll (RI)
Queens Coll of the City U of New York (NY)
Rhode Island Coll (RI)
Rivier U (NH)
Roberts Wesleyan Coll (NY)
Rocky Mountain Coll (MT)
Roger Williams U (RI)
Rust Coll (MS)
Saginaw Valley State U (MI)
St. Ambrose U (IA)
St. Catherine U (MN)
Saint Francis U (PA)
St. John Fisher Coll (NY)
St. John's U (NY)
St. Joseph's Coll, Long Island Campus (NY)
St. Joseph's Coll, New York (NY)
Saint Mary's U of Minnesota (MN)
Salve Regina U (RI)
Schreiner U (TX)
Seattle U (WA)
Seton Hill U (PA)
Shawnee State U (OH)
Shorter U (GA)
Southeastern Oklahoma State U (OK)
Southeastern U (FL)
Southeast Missouri State U (MO)
Southern Adventist U (TN)
Southern Utah U (UT)
Southwest Baptist U (MO)
Southwestern Assemblies of God U (TX)
Southwestern Coll (KS)
Spring Hill Coll (AL)
State U of New York at New Paltz (NY)
State U of New York Coll at Cortland (NY)
State U of New York Coll at Old Westbury (NY)
State U of New York Coll at Oneonta (NY)
State U of New York Coll at Potsdam (NY)
Syracuse U (NY)
Taylor U (IN)
Temple U (PA)
Texas Christian U (TX)
Texas Lutheran U (TX)
Trevecca Nazarene U (TN)
Trine U (IN)
Trinity Christian Coll (IL)
Union Coll (NE)
The U of Akron (OH)
The U of Arizona (AZ)
U of California, San Diego (CA)
U of Central Arkansas (AR)
U of Central Oklahoma (OK)
U of Dubuque (IA)
U of Evansville (IN)
The U of Findlay (OH)
U of Georgia (GA)
U of Hartford (CT)
U of Illinois at Chicago (IL)
U of Jamestown (ND)
U of Louisiana at Monroe (LA)
U of Maine (ME)
U of Maine at Farmington (ME)
U of Maine at Machias (ME)
U of Mary Hardin-Baylor (TX)
U of Michigan–Dearborn (MI)
U of Michigan–Flint (MI)
U of Minnesota, Duluth (MN)
U of Missouri (MO)
U of Mobile (AL)
U of Nebraska–Lincoln (NE)
U of New Hampshire (NH)
The U of North Carolina at Greensboro (NC)
The U of North Carolina at Pembroke (NC)
U of Northern Iowa (IA)
U of North Florida (FL)
U of Oklahoma (OK)
U of Providence (MT)
U of Regina (SK, Canada)
U of St. Francis (IL)
U of St. Thomas (MN)
U of Sioux Falls (SD)
U of South Dakota (SD)
U of Southern Maine (ME)
The U of Tennessee at Martin (TN)
The U of Tulsa (OK)

U of Vermont (VT)
U of Waterloo (ON, Canada)
U of Wisconsin–Milwaukee (WI)
U of Wisconsin–Stevens Point (WI)
U of Wisconsin–Superior (WI)
U of Wisconsin–Whitewater (WI)
Ursuline Coll (OH)
Utah State U (UT)
Utah Valley U (UT)
Utica Coll (NY)
Valley City State U (ND)
Valparaiso U (IN)
Vincennes U (IN)
Walsh U (OH)
Wartburg Coll (IA)
Washington U in St. Louis (MO)
Waynesburg U (PA)
Wayne State Coll (NE)
Weber State U (UT)
Western Michigan U (MI)
Western State Colorado U (CO)
Western Washington U (WA)
Westfield State U (MA)
Westmont Coll (CA)
West Virginia Wesleyan Coll (WV)
Whitworth U (WA)
Widener U (PA)
William Woods U (MO)
Wilmington U (DE)
Winona State U (MN)
York Coll of Pennsylvania (PA)
Youngstown State U (OH)

MECHANICAL DRAFTING AND CAD/CADD
Indiana U–Purdue U Indianapolis (IN)
Purdue U Northwest (IN)

MECHANICAL ENGINEERING
Alfred U (NY)
The American U in Cairo (Egypt)
American U of Beirut (Lebanon)
Anderson U (IN)
Andrews U (MI)
Arizona State U at the Tempe campus (AZ)
Arkansas Tech U (AR)
Auburn U (AL)
Baylor U (TX)
Benedictine Coll (KS)
Boise State U (ID)
Boston U (MA)
Bradley U (IL)
Bucknell U (PA)
California Baptist U (CA)
California Inst of Technology (CA)
California Polytechnic State U, San Luis Obispo (CA)
California State Polytechnic U, Pomona (CA)
California State U, Fullerton (CA)
California State U, Long Beach (CA)
California State U, Los Angeles (CA)
California State U Maritime Acad (CA)
California State U, Northridge (CA)
California State U, Sacramento (CA)
Calvin Coll (MI)
Carnegie Mellon U (PA)
Case Western Reserve U (OH)
The Catholic U of America (DC)
Cedarville U (OH)
Central Connecticut State U (CT)
Central Michigan U (MI)
Christian Brothers U (TN)
The Citadel, The Military Coll of South Carolina (SC)
City Coll of the City U of New York (NY)
Clarkson U (NY)
Clemson U (SC)
Cleveland State U (OH)
The Coll of New Jersey (NJ)
Colorado State U (CO)
Columbia U (NY)
Concordia U (QC, Canada)
Cooper Union for the Advancement of Science and Art (NY)
Cornell U (NY)
Delaware State U (DE)
Drexel U (PA)
Dunwoody Coll of Technology (MN)
Eastern Nazarene Coll (MA)
Eastern Washington U (WA)

Embry-Riddle Aeronautical U–Daytona (FL)
Fairfield U (CT)
Fairleigh Dickinson U, Metropolitan Campus (NJ)
Florida Ag and Mech U (FL)
Florida Atlantic U (FL)
Florida Inst of Technology (FL)
Florida Intl U (FL)
Florida State U (FL)
Franklin W. Olin Coll of Eng (MA)
Gannon U (PA)
George Mason U (VA)
The George Washington U (DC)
Georgia Inst of Technology (GA)
Georgia Southern U (GA)
Gonzaga U (WA)
Grand Valley State U (MI)
Grove City Coll (PA)
Harding U (AR)
Hofstra U (NY)
Idaho State U (ID)
Indiana Tech (IN)
Indiana U–Purdue U Indianapolis (IN)
Inter American U of Puerto Rico, Bayamón Campus (PR)
Iowa State U of Science and Technology (IA)
Jacksonville U (FL)
Johns Hopkins U (MD)
Kansas State U (KS)
Kennesaw State U (GA)
Kettering U (MI)
King's Coll (PA)
Lafayette Coll (PA)
Lamar U (TX)
Lawrence Technological U (MI)
Lebanese American U (Lebanon)
Lehigh U (PA)
LeTourneau U (TX)
Liberty U (VA)
Lipscomb U (TN)
Louisiana State U and A&M Coll (LA)
Loyola Marymount U (CA)
Manhattan Coll (NY)
Marquette U (WI)
Marshall U (WV)
Massachusetts Inst of Technology (MA)
Merrimack Coll (MA)
Miami U (OH)
Michigan State U (MI)
Michigan Technological U (MI)
Milwaukee School of Eng (WI)
Mississippi State U (MS)
Missouri U of Science and Technology (MO)
Montana Tech of The U of Montana (MT)
Mount Vernon Nazarene U (OH)
New England Inst of Technology (RI)
New Jersey Inst of Technology (NJ)
New Mexico Inst of Mining and Technology (NM)
New Mexico State U (NM)
New York Inst of Technology (NY)
New York U (NY)
North Carolina State U (NC)
North Central Coll (IL)
North Dakota State U (ND)
Northeastern U (MA)
Northern Arizona U (AZ)
Northern Illinois U (IL)
Northwestern U (IL)
Oakland U (MI)
Ohio Northern U (OH)
The Ohio State U (OH)
Ohio U (OH)
Oklahoma Christian U (OK)
Oklahoma State U (OK)
Old Dominion U (VA)
Oral Roberts U (OK)
Oregon Inst of Technology (OR)
Oregon State U (OR)
Penn State Abington (PA)
Penn State Altoona (PA)
Penn State Beaver (PA)
Penn State Berks (PA)
Penn State Brandywine (PA)
Penn State DuBois (PA)
Penn State Erie, The Behrend Coll (PA)
Penn State Fayette, The Eberly Campus (PA)

Penn State Greater Allegheny (PA)
Penn State Harrisburg (PA)
Penn State Hazleton (PA)
Penn State Lehigh Valley (PA)
Penn State Mont Alto (PA)
Penn State New Kensington (PA)
Penn State Schuylkill (PA)
Penn State Shenango (PA)
Penn State U Park (PA)
Penn State Wilkes-Barre (PA)
Penn State Worthington Scranton (PA)
Penn State York (PA)
Point Park U (PA)
Polytechnic U of Puerto Rico (PR)
Portland State U (OR)
Prairie View A&M U (TX)
Princeton U (NJ)
Purdue U (IN)
Purdue U Northwest (IN)
Quinnipiac U (CT)
Rensselaer Polytechnic Inst (NY)
Rice U (TX)
Rochester Inst of Technology (NY)
Rockhurst U (MO)
Roger Williams U (RI)
Rose-Hulman Inst of Technology (IN)
Rowan U (NJ)
Rutgers U–New Brunswick (NJ)
Saginaw Valley State U (MI)
Saint Louis U (MO)
Saint Louis U–Madrid Campus (Spain)
Saint Martin's U (WA)
St. Mary's U (TX)
San Diego State U (CA)
San Francisco State U (CA)
Santa Clara U (CA)
Seattle U (WA)
Shippensburg U of Pennsylvania (PA)
Southern Illinois U Carbondale (IL)
Southern Illinois U Edwardsville (IL)
Southern Methodist U (TX)
Stanford U (CA)
State U of New York at New Paltz (NY)
State U of New York Maritime Coll (NY)
State U of New York Polytechnic Inst (NY)
Stevens Inst of Technology (NJ)
Stony Brook U, State U of New York (NY)
Syracuse U (NY)
Temple U (PA)
Tennessee Technological U (TN)
Texas A&M U (TX)
Texas A&M U–Corpus Christi (TX)
Texas A&M U–Kingsville (TX)
Texas Tech U (TX)
Trine U (IN)
Tufts U (MA)
Union Coll (NY)
United States Coast Guard Acad (CT)
United States Military Acad (NY)
Université de Sherbrooke (QC, Canada)
U at Buffalo, the State U of New York (NY)
The U of Akron (OH)
The U of Alabama (AL)
The U of Alabama at Birmingham (AL)
U of Alaska Fairbanks (AK)
The U of Arizona (AZ)
U of Arkansas (AR)
U of Bridgeport (CT)
U of California, Davis (CA)
U of California, Irvine (CA)
U of California, Los Angeles (CA)
U of California, Riverside (CA)
U of California, San Diego (CA)
U of California, Santa Barbara (CA)
U of Central Florida (FL)
U of Central Oklahoma (OK)
U of Cincinnati (OH)
U of Colorado Boulder (CO)
U of Colorado Colorado Springs (CO)
U of Colorado Denver (CO)
U of Dayton (OH)
U of Denver (CO)
U of Evansville (IN)

U of Florida (FL)
U of Georgia (GA)
U of Guelph (ON, Canada)
U of Hartford (CT)
U of Hawaii at Manoa (HI)
U of Houston (TX)
U of Houston–Clear Lake (TX)
U of Idaho (ID)
U of Illinois at Chicago (IL)
U of Jamestown (ND)
The U of Kansas (KS)
U of Kentucky (KY)
U of Louisville (KY)
U of Maine (ME)
U of Maryland, Baltimore County (MD)
U of Maryland, Coll Park (MD)
U of Massachusetts Amherst (MA)
U of Massachusetts Dartmouth (MA)
U of Massachusetts Lowell (MA)
U of Memphis (TN)
U of Miami (FL)
U of Michigan (MI)
U of Michigan–Dearborn (MI)
U of Michigan–Flint (MI)
U of Minnesota, Duluth (MN)
U of Minnesota, Twin Cities Campus (MN)
U of Missouri (MO)
U of Missouri–St. Louis (MO)
U of Mount Union (OH)
U of Nebraska–Lincoln (NE)
U of Nevada, Las Vegas (NV)
U of Nevada, Reno (NV)
U of New Hampshire (NH)
U of New Haven (CT)
U of New Mexico (NM)
U of New Orleans (LA)
The U of North Carolina at Charlotte (NC)
U of North Dakota (ND)
U of North Florida (FL)
U of North Texas (TX)
U of Notre Dame (IN)
U of Oklahoma (OK)
U of Pennsylvania (PA)
U of Pittsburgh (PA)
U of Rhode Island (RI)
U of Rochester (NY)
U of St. Thomas (MN)
U of San Diego (CA)
U of Saskatchewan (SK, Canada)
U of South Alabama (AL)
U of South Carolina (SC)
U of Southern California (CA)
U of Southern Indiana (IN)
U of Southern Maine (ME)
The U of Tennessee (TN)
The U of Tennessee at Chattanooga (TN)
The U of Texas at Austin (TX)
The U of Texas at Dallas (TX)
The U of Texas at El Paso (TX)
The U of Texas at San Antonio (TX)
The U of Texas of the Permian Basin (TX)
The U of Texas Rio Grande Valley (TX)
U of the Pacific (CA)
The U of Toledo (OH)
U of Toronto (ON, Canada)
The U of Tulsa (OK)
U of Utah (UT)
U of Vermont (VT)
U of Virginia (VA)
U of Washington (WA)
U of Washington, Bothell (WA)
U of Waterloo (ON, Canada)
U of Wisconsin–Madison (WI)
U of Wisconsin–Milwaukee (WI)
U of Wisconsin–Platteville (WI)
U of Wyoming (WY)
Utah State U (UT)
Valparaiso U (IN)
Vanderbilt U (TN)
Villanova U (PA)
Virginia Commonwealth U (VA)
Virginia Military Inst (VA)
Virginia Polytechnic Inst and State U (VA)
Washington State U (WA)
Washington State U–Global Campus (WA)
Washington State U–Tri-Cities (WA)

Washington State U–Vancouver (WA)
Washington U in St. Louis (MO)
Wayne State U (MI)
Wentworth Inst of Technology (MA)
Western Illinois U (IL)
Western Kentucky U (KY)
Western Michigan U (MI)
Western New England U (MA)
West Texas A&M U (TX)
West Virginia U (WV)
West Virginia U Inst of Technology (WV)
Wichita State U (KS)
Widener U (PA)
Wilkes U (PA)
William Penn U (IA)
Worcester Polytechnic Inst (MA)
Wright State U (OH)
Wright State U–Lake Campus (OH)
York Coll of Pennsylvania (PA)
Youngstown State U (OH)

MECHANICAL ENGINEERING/ MECHANICAL TECHNOLOGY
Arizona State U at the Polytechnic campus (AZ)
Bowling Green State U (OH)
Buffalo State Coll, State U of New York (NY)
California State U, Long Beach (CA)
California State U, Sacramento (CA)
Central Connecticut State U (CT)
Central Michigan U (MI)
Colorado Mesa U (CO)
Delaware State U (DE)
Eastern Michigan U (MI)
Eastern Washington U (WA)
ECPI U, Virginia Beach (VA)
Fairleigh Dickinson U, Metropolitan Campus (NJ)
Farmingdale State Coll (NY)
Ferris State U (MI)
Idaho State U (ID)
Kennesaw State U (GA)
LeTourneau U (TX)
Metropolitan State U of Denver (CO)
Michigan Technological U (MI)
Northern Michigan U (MI)
Oklahoma State U (OK)
Oregon Inst of Technology (OR)
Penn State Erie, The Behrend Coll (PA)
Pennsylvania Coll of Technology (PA)
Pittsburg State U (KS)
Point Park U (PA)
Purdue U (IN)
Purdue U Northwest (IN)
State U of New York Coll of Technology at Alfred (NY)
State U of New York Polytechnic Inst (NY)
Tarleton State U (TX)
Texas A&M U–Corpus Christi (TX)
United States Military Acad (NY)
The U of Akron (OH)
U of Dayton (OH)
U of Hartford (CT)
U of Houston (TX)
U of Maine (ME)
The U of North Carolina at Charlotte (NC)
U of North Texas (TX)
The U of Toledo (OH)
Wayne State U (MI)
Weber State U (UT)
Youngstown State U (OH)

MECHANICAL ENGINEERING TECHNOLOGIES RELATED
Cleveland State U (OH)
Delaware State U (DE)
Indiana State U (IN)
Indiana U–Purdue U Indianapolis (IN)
LeTourneau U (TX)
Pennsylvania Coll of Technology (PA)
Purdue U Northwest (IN)
State U of New York Coll of Technology at Canton (NY)
U of Massachusetts Lowell (MA)
Vaughn Coll of Aeronautics and Technology (NY)

MECHANIC AND REPAIR TECHNOLOGIES RELATED
Colorado State U–Pueblo (CO)

MECHANICS AND REPAIR
Idaho State U (ID)

MECHATRONICS, ROBOTICS, AND AUTOMATION ENGINEERING
California U of Pennsylvania (PA)
Lawrence Technological U (MI)
Lebanese American U (Lebanon)
Middle Tennessee State U (TN)
Simon Fraser U (BC, Canada)
Southern Illinois U Edwardsville (IL)
U of Michigan–Dearborn (MI)
U of Washington (WA)
Worcester Polytechnic Inst (MA)

MEDICAL ANTHROPOLOGY
Creighton U (NE)
Lycoming Coll (PA)
U of Miami (FL)
Washington U in St. Louis (MO)

MEDICAL/CLINICAL ASSISTANT
Idaho State U (ID)

MEDICAL/HEALTH MANAGEMENT AND CLINICAL ASSISTANT
Davenport U, Grand Rapids (MI)
Elms Coll (MA)
Nebraska Methodist Coll (NE)
Rider U (NJ)
The U of Texas at Dallas (TX)

MEDICAL ILLUSTRATION
Arcadia U (PA)
Iowa State U of Science and Technology (IA)
Rochester Inst of Technology (NY)
Rowan U (NJ)

MEDICAL INFORMATICS
Idaho State U (ID)
King U (TN)
LeTourneau U (TX)
Metropolitan State U of Denver (CO)
Montana Tech of The U of Montana (MT)
Northern Kentucky U (KY)
Simmons Coll (MA)
State U of New York at Plattsburgh (NY)
Texas Woman's U (TX)
U of South Alabama (AL)
U of Waterloo (ON, Canada)
Western Michigan U (MI)

MEDICAL MICROBIOLOGY AND BACTERIOLOGY
Adams State U (CO)
Auburn U (AL)
Bowling Green State U (OH)
California Polytechnic State U, San Luis Obispo (CA)
Mississippi State U (MS)
New Mexico State U (NM)
Ohio Wesleyan U (OH)
Penn State Abington (PA)
Penn State Altoona (PA)
Penn State Beaver (PA)
Penn State Berks (PA)
Penn State Brandywine (PA)
Penn State DuBois (PA)
Penn State Erie, The Behrend Coll (PA)
Penn State Fayette, The Eberly Campus (PA)
Penn State Greater Allegheny (PA)
Penn State Hazleton (PA)
Penn State Lehigh Valley (PA)
Penn State Mont Alto (PA)
Penn State New Kensington (PA)
Penn State Schuylkill (PA)
Penn State Shenango (PA)
Penn State U Park (PA)
Penn State Wilkes-Barre (PA)
Penn State Worthington Scranton (PA)
Penn State York (PA)
Quinnipiac U (CT)
Rutgers U–New Brunswick (NJ)
San Francisco State U (CA)
Sonoma State U (CA)

Université de Sherbrooke (QC, Canada)
U of California, San Diego (CA)
U of Florida (FL)
U of Kentucky (KY)
U of King's Coll (NS, Canada)
U of Minnesota, Twin Cities Campus (MN)
U of Montana (MT)
U of Saskatchewan (SK, Canada)
U of Toronto (ON, Canada)
Utah State U (UT)
Wagner Coll (NY)
Xavier U of Louisiana (LA)

MEDICAL OFFICE ASSISTANT
Concordia U Wisconsin (WI)

MEDICAL RADIOLOGIC TECHNOLOGY
Averett U (VA)
Avila U (MO)
Baptist Coll of Health Sciences (TN)
Bellarmine U (KY)
Bloomsburg U of Pennsylvania (PA)
Boise State U (ID)
California State U, Long Beach (CA)
Carroll U (WI)
Clarion U of Pennsylvania (PA)
Concordia U Wisconsin (WI)
Creighton U (NE)
Emory U (GA)
Fairleigh Dickinson U, Florham Campus (NJ)
Georgia Southern U–Armstrong Campus (GA)
Grand Valley State U (MI)
Gwynedd Mercy U (PA)
Idaho State U (ID)
Indiana U Kokomo (IN)
Indiana U Northwest (IN)
Indiana–Purdue U Indianapolis (IN)
Indiana U South Bend (IN)
Inter American U of Puerto Rico, San Germán Campus (PR)
Kent State U at Salem (OH)
La Roche Coll (PA)
Long Island U–LIU Post (NY)
MCPHS U (MA)
Minot State U (ND)
Misericordia U (PA)
Morehead State U (KY)
Mount Aloysius Coll (PA)
Mount Marty Coll (SD)
National U (CA)
North Central Coll (IL)
Oakland U (MI)
The Ohio State U (OH)
Roosevelt U (IL)
Saint Louis U (MO)
Southern Illinois U Carbondale (IL)
Texas State U (TX)
U of Central Arkansas (AR)
U of Hartford (CT)
U of Michigan–Flint (MI)
U of Missouri (MO)
U of Nevada, Las Vegas (NV)
U of New Mexico (NM)
The U of North Carolina at Chapel Hill (NC)
U of Oklahoma Health Sciences Center (OK)
U of St. Francis (IL)
U of Sioux Falls (SD)
U of Southern Indiana (IN)
U of Vermont (VT)
U of Wisconsin–La Crosse (WI)
Valencia Coll (FL)
Wayne State U (MI)
Weber State U (UT)

MEDICAL STAFF SERVICES TECHNOLOGY
Converse Coll (SC)

MEDICINAL AND PHARMACEUTICAL CHEMISTRY
Michigan Technological U (MI)
U of California, San Diego (CA)
U of Dayton (OH)
U of Guelph (ON, Canada)
U of Michigan (MI)

MEDIEVAL AND RENAISSANCE STUDIES
Augsburg U (MN)
Bard Coll (NY)
Barnard Coll (NY)
Binghamton U, State U of New York (NY)
The Catholic U of America (DC)
Cleveland State U (OH)
The Coll of William and Mary (VA)
Columbia U (NY)
Cornell Coll (IA)
Dickinson Coll (PA)
Fordham U (NY)
Georgetown U (DC)
Lycoming Coll (PA)
Marlboro Coll (VT)
Mount Holyoke Coll (MA)
New Coll of Florida (FL)
New York U (NY)
The Ohio State U (OH)
Ohio Wesleyan U (OH)
Penn State Abington (PA)
Penn State Altoona (PA)
Penn State Beaver (PA)
Penn State Berks (PA)
Penn State Brandywine (PA)
Penn State DuBois (PA)
Penn State Erie, The Behrend Coll (PA)
Penn State Fayette, The Eberly Campus (PA)
Penn State Greater Allegheny (PA)
Penn State Hazleton (PA)
Penn State Lehigh Valley (PA)
Penn State Mont Alto (PA)
Penn State New Kensington (PA)
Penn State Schuylkill (PA)
Penn State Shenango (PA)
Penn State U Park (PA)
Penn State Wilkes-Barre (PA)
Penn State Worthington Scranton (PA)
Penn State York (PA)
Pomona Coll (CA)
Purdue U (IN)
Rutgers U–New Brunswick (NJ)
St. Olaf Coll (MN)
Sewanee: The U of the South (TN)
Smith Coll (MA)
Southern Methodist U (TX)
Tulane U (LA)
U at Albany, State U of New York (NY)
U of California, Santa Barbara (CA)
U of Chicago (IL)
U of Michigan (MI)
U of Nebraska–Lincoln (NE)
U of Notre Dame (IN)
U of Oregon (OR)
U of Regina (SK, Canada)
U of Saskatchewan (SK, Canada)
U of Waterloo (ON, Canada)
Vassar Coll (NY)
Washington and Lee U (VA)
Wellesley Coll (MA)

MEETING AND EVENT PLANNING
Central Michigan U (MI)
Coll of the Ozarks (MO)
Fisher Coll (MA)
Iowa State U of Science and Technology (IA)
Lasell Coll (MA)
Lynn U (FL)
Metropolitan State U of Denver (CO)
U of Central Florida (FL)

MENTAL AND SOCIAL HEALTH SERVICES AND ALLIED PROFESSIONS RELATED
Clarion U of Pennsylvania (PA)
Northern Kentucky U (KY)
Old Dominion U (VA)
Pennsylvania Coll of Technology (PA)
Roger Williams U (RI)
Southwestern Assemblies of God U (TX)

MENTAL HEALTH COUNSELING
Brandon U (MB, Canada)
Canisius Coll (NY)
Iona Coll (NY)
Suffolk U (MA)

MERCHANDISING, SALES, AND MARKETING OPERATIONS RELATED (GENERAL)
Eastern Michigan U (MI)
Georgia State U (GA)
High Point U (NC)
Lincoln U (MO)
U of Hartford (CT)
Washington U in St. Louis (MO)

MERCHANDISING, SALES, AND MARKETING OPERATIONS RELATED (SPECIALIZED)
Baylor U (TX)
Fashion Inst of Technology (NY)
Graceland U (IA)
High Point U (NC)
Saint Joseph's U (PA)
Wade Coll (TX)

METAL AND JEWELRY ARTS
Academy of Art U (CA)
Adams State U (CO)
Alberta Coll of Art & Design (AB, Canada)
Arcadia U (PA)
Bowling Green State U (OH)
California Coll of the Arts (CA)
California State U, Long Beach (CA)
Ferris State U (MI)
Hofstra U (NY)
Massachusetts Coll of Art and Design (MA)
Northern Michigan U (MI)
Pratt Inst (NY)
Rhode Island Coll (RI)
Rhode Island School of Design (RI)
Rochester Inst of Technology (NY)
Savannah Coll of Art and Design (GA)
Seton Hill U (PA)
State U of New York at New Paltz (NY)
Syracuse U (NY)
Temple U (PA)
The U of Akron (OH)
The U of Kansas (KS)
U of Massachusetts Dartmouth (MA)
U of Michigan (MI)
U of Oregon (OR)
Western State Colorado U (CO)

METALLURGICAL ENGINEERING
LeTourneau U (TX)
Missouri U of Science and Technology (MO)
Montana Tech of The U of Montana (MT)
The U of Alabama (AL)
U of Cincinnati (OH)
U of Nevada, Reno (NV)
The U of Texas at El Paso (TX)
U of Toronto (ON, Canada)
U of Utah (UT)

METEOROLOGY
Central Michigan U (MI)
Coll of Charleston (SC)
Florida Inst of Technology (FL)
Florida State U (FL)
Iowa State U of Science and Technology (IA)
Metropolitan State U of Denver (CO)
Northern Vermont U–Lyndon (VT)
Northland Coll (WI)
Rutgers U–New Brunswick (NJ)
U of Hawaii at Manoa (HI)
U of Miami (FL)
The U of North Carolina at Charlotte (NC)
U of Oklahoma (OK)
U of South Alabama (AL)
U of the Incarnate Word (TX)
U of Wisconsin–Milwaukee (WI)
Virginia Polytechnic Inst and State U (VA)
Western Illinois U (IL)
Western Kentucky U (KY)

MICROBIOLOGICAL SCIENCES AND IMMUNOLOGY RELATED
U of California, Los Angeles (CA)

MICROBIOLOGY
Arizona State U at the Tempe campus (AZ)
Auburn U (AL)
Bowling Green State U (OH)
Brigham Young U (UT)
California State U, Dominguez Hills (CA)
California State U, Long Beach (CA)
California State U, Los Angeles (CA)
Clemson U (SC)
Colorado State U (CO)
Concordia U Chicago (IL)
Idaho State U (ID)
Indiana U Bloomington (IN)
Inter American U of Puerto Rico, Aguadilla Campus (PR)
Inter American U of Puerto Rico, Bayamón Campus (PR)
Inter American U of Puerto Rico, Metropolitan Campus (PR)
Inter American U of Puerto Rico, San Germán Campus (PR)
Iowa State U of Science and Technology (IA)
Kansas State U (KS)
Louisiana State U and A&M Coll (LA)
Miami U (OH)
Michigan State U (MI)
North Carolina State U (NC)
North Dakota State U (ND)
Northern Arizona U (AZ)
Northern Michigan U (MI)
Northwestern State U of Louisiana (LA)
The Ohio State U (OH)
Ohio U (OH)
Oklahoma State U (OK)
Oregon State U (OR)
Rutgers U–New Brunswick (NJ)
San Diego State U (CA)
Southern Illinois U Carbondale (IL)
Texas A&M U (TX)
Texas State U (TX)
Texas Tech U (TX)
The U of Akron (OH)
The U of Alabama (AL)
The U of Arizona (AZ)
U of California, Davis (CA)
U of California, San Diego (CA)
U of California, Santa Barbara (CA)
U of Georgia (GA)
U of Guelph (ON, Canada)
U of Hawaii at Manoa (HI)
U of Idaho (ID)
The U of Kansas (KS)
U of Maine (ME)
U of Maryland, Coll Park (MD)
U of Massachusetts Amherst (MA)
U of Michigan (MI)
U of Michigan–Dearborn (MI)
U of Nebraska–Lincoln (NE)
U of Oklahoma (OK)
U of Pittsburgh (PA)
U of Puerto Rico–Humacao (PR)
U of Rhode Island (RI)
The U of Texas at Austin (TX)
U of Toronto (ON, Canada)
U of Vermont (VT)
U of Washington (WA)
U of Wisconsin–La Crosse (WI)
U of Wisconsin–Madison (WI)
U of Wisconsin–Milwaukee (WI)
U of Wyoming (WY)
Washington State U (WA)
Weber State U (UT)

MICROBIOLOGY AND IMMUNOLOGY
Purdue U (IN)
U of California, Irvine (CA)
U of Miami (FL)
U of Nevada, Reno (NV)
U of Saskatchewan (SK, Canada)
The U of Texas at San Antonio (TX)
West Virginia U (WV)

MIDDLE/NEAR EASTERN AND SEMITIC LANGUAGES
Indiana U Bloomington (IN)
Pepperdine U, Malibu (CA)
U of Pennsylvania (PA)
The U of Texas at Austin (TX)

MIDDLE/NEAR EASTERN AND SEMITIC LANGUAGES RELATED
Florida State U (FL)
U of Chicago (IL)
U of Michigan (MI)
U of Washington (WA)
Wayne State U (MI)

MIDDLE SCHOOL EDUCATION
Alice Lloyd Coll (KY)
Alverno Coll (WI)
Appalachian State U (NC)
Arkansas Tech U (AR)
Arlington Baptist U (TX)
Asbury U (KY)
Ashland U (OH)
Austin Coll (TX)
Avila U (MO)
Baker U (KS)
Baldwin Wallace U (OH)
Barton Coll (NC)
Bellarmine U (KY)
Belmont U (TN)
Berea Coll (KY)
Berry Coll (GA)
Bethel Coll (IN)
Black Hills State U (SD)
Bloomsburg U of Pennsylvania (PA)
Bluefield Coll (VA)
Bluffton U (OH)
Bob Jones U (SC)
Bowling Green State U (OH)
Brandon U (MB, Canada)
Brenau U (GA)
Brescia U (KY)
Brewton-Parker Coll (GA)
California U of Pennsylvania (PA)
Capital U (OH)
Carlow U (PA)
Carroll U (WI)
Carson-Newman U (TN)
Catawba Coll (NC)
Cedarville U (OH)
Central Methodist U (MO)
Central State U (OH)
Champlain Coll (VT)
Clark U (MA)
Clayton State U (GA)
Cleveland State U (OH)
Coastal Carolina U (SC)
Coll of Charleston (SC)
Coll of Coastal Georgia (GA)
Coll of the Atlantic (ME)
Columbia Coll (SC)
Columbus State U (GA)
Concordia Coll–New York (NY)
Concordia U, Nebraska (NE)
Concordia U, St. Paul (MN)
Concordia U Wisconsin (WI)
Delaware State U (DE)
DePaul U (IL)
Duquesne U (PA)
East Carolina U (NC)
Eastern Nazarene Coll (MA)
Eastern U (PA)
East Stroudsburg U of Pennsylvania (PA)
Elizabethtown Coll (PA)
Elon U (NC)
Emmanuel Coll (GA)
Evangel U (MO)
Fayetteville State U (NC)
Fitchburg State U (MA)
Florida Inst of Technology (FL)
Francis Marion U (SC)
Gannon U (PA)
Georgetown Coll (KY)
Georgia Coll & State U (GA)
Georgia Southern U (GA)
Georgia Southern U–Armstrong Campus (GA)
Georgia Southwestern State U (GA)
Gettysburg Coll (PA)
Gordon Coll (MA)
Gordon State Coll (GA)
Grand Valley State U (MI)
Granite State Coll (NH)
Greensboro Coll (NC)
Hampton U (VA)
Harding U (AR)
Harris-Stowe State U (MO)
High Point U (NC)
Hiram Coll (OH)
Indiana U of Pennsylvania (PA)
Indiana Wesleyan U (IN)
Ithaca Coll (NY)
Johnson U (TN)
Kennesaw State U (GA)
Kent State U (OH)
Kent State U at Geauga (OH)
Kent State U at Stark (OH)
Kutztown U of Pennsylvania (PA)
La Salle U (PA)
Lee U (TN)
Lenoir-Rhyne U (NC)
Lesley U (MA)
Lewis U (IL)
Lincoln U (MO)
Lindenwood U (MO)
Lindsey Wilson Coll (KY)
Lipscomb U (TN)
Lock Haven U of Pennsylvania (PA)
Lubbock Christian U (TX)
Malone U (OH)
Manchester U (IN)
Manhattan Coll (NY)
Marian U (WI)
Maryville Coll (TN)
Maryville U of Saint Louis (MO)
The Master's U (CA)
McMurry U (TX)
Mercer U, Macon (GA)
Merrimack Coll (MA)
Messiah Coll (PA)
Miami U (OH)
Michigan State U (MI)
MidAmerica Nazarene U (KS)
Millersville U of Pennsylvania (PA)
Misericordia U (PA)
Missouri Baptist U (MO)
Missouri State U (MO)
Missouri Valley Coll (MO)
Morehead State U (KY)
Mount Aloysius Coll (PA)
Mount Mary U (WI)
Mount Mercy U (IA)
Mount St. Joseph U (OH)
Mount Vernon Nazarene U (OH)
Murray State U (KY)
Muskingum U (OH)
Newberry Coll (SC)
North Carolina Central U (NC)
North Carolina State U (NC)
North Carolina Wesleyan Coll (NC)
Northern Kentucky U (KY)
Northwest Christian U (OR)
Northwest Missouri State U (MO)
Ohio Christian U (OH)
Ohio Dominican U (OH)
Ohio Northern U (OH)
The Ohio State U (OH)
The Ohio State U at Lima (OH)
The Ohio State U at Mansfield (OH)
The Ohio State U at Marion (OH)
The Ohio State U at Newark (OH)
Ohio Wesleyan U (OH)
Otterbein U (OH)
Ouachita Baptist U (AR)
Piedmont Coll (GA)
Point U (GA)
Presbyterian Coll (SC)
Rockhurst U (MO)
Roosevelt U (IL)
Saint Leo U (FL)
Saint Vincent Coll (PA)
Schreiner U (TX)
Shippensburg U of Pennsylvania (PA)
Shorter U (GA)
Southeastern Louisiana U (LA)
Southeast Missouri State U (MO)
Southern Arkansas U–Magnolia (AR)
Southern Illinois U–Edwardsville (IL)
Southwest Baptist U (MO)
State U of New York Coll at Cortland (NY)
State U of New York Coll at Old Westbury (NY)
State U of New York Coll at Oneonta (NY)
Stevenson U (MD)
Temple U (PA)
Texas Lutheran U (TX)
Thomas U (GA)
Toccoa Falls Coll (GA)
Towson U (MD)
Transylvania U (KY)
Trinity Christian Coll (IL)
Truett McConnell U (GA)
The U of Akron (OH)

U of Central Arkansas (AR)
U of Central Missouri (MO)
U of Cincinnati (OH)
U of Dayton (OH)
The U of Findlay (OH)
The U of Kansas (KS)
U of Kentucky (KY)
U of Maryland, Coll Park (MD)
U of Minnesota, Duluth (MN)
U of Missouri (MO)
U of Mount Union (OH)
The U of North Carolina at Chapel Hill (NC)
The U of North Carolina at Charlotte (NC)
The U of North Carolina at Greensboro (NC)
The U of North Carolina at Pembroke (NC)
The U of North Carolina Wilmington (NC)
U of North Dakota (ND)
U of Northern Iowa (IA)
U of North Florida (FL)
U of North Georgia (GA)
U of Pikeville (KY)
U of Providence (MT)
U of Regina (SK, Canada)
U of St. Thomas (MN)
The U of Scranton (PA)
U of Sioux Falls (SD)
U of South Carolina (SC)
U of South Carolina Aiken (SC)
The U of Tennessee at Chattanooga (TN)
The U of Texas at San Antonio (TX)
U of Valley Forge (PA)
U of Vermont (VT)
U of Wisconsin–Milwaukee (WI)
Ursuline Coll (OH)
Valdosta State U (GA)
Virginia Wesleyan U (VA)
Walsh U (OH)
Warner Pacific Coll (OR)
Washington U in St. Louis (MO)
Wayland Baptist U (TX)
Wayne State Coll (NE)
Webster U (MO)
West Chester U of Pennsylvania (PA)
Western Illinois U (IL)
Western Kentucky U (KY)
West Virginia Wesleyan Coll (WV)
Wilkes U (PA)
Wilmington U (DE)
Wright State U (OH)
Wright State U–Lake Campus (OH)
Xavier U of Louisiana (LA)
Youngstown State U (OH)

MILITARY APPLIED SCIENCES RELATED
United States Military Acad (NY)

MILITARY HISTORY
American Public U System (WV)
Hawai`i Pacific U (HI)
Marquette U (WI)
Rogers State U (OK)
United States Military Acad (NY)

MILITARY STUDIES
American Public U System (WV)

MILITARY TECHNOLOGIES AND APPLIED SCIENCES RELATED
Alcorn State U (MS)

MINING AND MINERAL ENGINEERING
Missouri U of Science and Technology (MO)
Montana Tech of The U of Montana (MT)
New Mexico Inst of Mining and Technology (NM)
Penn State Abington (PA)
Penn State Altoona (PA)
Penn State Beaver (PA)
Penn State Berks (PA)
Penn State Brandywine (PA)
Penn State DuBois (PA)
Penn State Erie, The Behrend Coll (PA)
Penn State Fayette, The Eberly Campus (PA)
Penn State Greater Allegheny (PA)
Penn State Hazleton (PA)
Penn State Lehigh Valley (PA)
Penn State Mont Alto (PA)
Penn State New Kensington (PA)
Penn State Schuylkill (PA)
Penn State Shenango (PA)
Penn State U Park (PA)
Penn State Wilkes-Barre (PA)
Penn State Worthington Scranton (PA)
Penn State York (PA)
Southern Illinois U Carbondale (IL)
U of Alaska Fairbanks (AK)
The U of Arizona (AZ)
U of Kentucky (KY)
U of Nevada, Reno (NV)
U of Toronto (ON, Canada)
U of Utah (UT)
Virginia Polytechnic Inst and State U (VA)
West Virginia U (WV)

MISSIONARY STUDIES AND MISSIOLOGY
Anderson U (SC)
Arizona Christian U (AZ)
Asbury U (KY)
The Baptist Coll of Florida (FL)
Bethel Coll (IN)
Biola U (CA)
Bob Jones U (SC)
Brewton-Parker Coll (GA)
California Baptist U (CA)
Calvary U (MO)
Carson-Newman U (TN)
Cedarville U (OH)
Charlotte Christian Coll and Theological Sem (NC)
Concordia U, St. Paul (MN)
Concordia U Wisconsin (WI)
Cornerstone U (MI)
Dallas Baptist U (TX)
Eastern U (PA)
East Texas Baptist U (TX)
Emmaus Bible Coll (IA)
Geneva Coll (PA)
Harding U (AR)
Hobe Sound Bible Coll (FL)
Hope Intl U (CA)
Indiana Wesleyan U (IN)
Johnson U (TN)
Johnson U Florida (FL)
Kentucky Mountain Bible Coll (KY)
Lee U (TN)
Lincoln Christian U (IL)
Lipscomb U (TN)
Lubbock Christian U (TX)
Maranatha Baptist U (WI)
MidAmerica Nazarene U (KS)
Mid-Atlantic Christian U (NC)
Mount Vernon Nazarene U (OH)
Multnomah U (OR)
North Greenville U (SC)
Northwest Christian U (OR)
Northwest Nazarene U (ID)
Northwest U (WA)
Ohio Christian U (OH)
Oklahoma Christian U (OK)
Olivet Nazarene U (IL)
Oral Roberts U (OK)
Ouachita Baptist U (AR)
Palm Beach Atlantic U (FL)
Southeastern U (FL)
Southern Adventist U (TN)
Southwest Baptist U (MO)
Southwestern Assemblies of God U (TX)
Toccoa Falls Coll (GA)
Trinity Coll of Florida (FL)
Truett McConnell U (GA)
U of Valley Forge (PA)
Vanguard U of Southern California (CA)
Wayland Baptist U (TX)
Welch Coll (TN)

MODELING, VIRTUAL ENVIRONMENTS AND SIMULATION
Academy of Art U (CA)
Albright Coll (PA)
Cogswell Polytechnical Coll (CA)
DigiPen Inst of Technology (WA)
Pennsylvania Coll of Technology (PA)
State U of New York Coll of Technology at Canton (NY)
U of Colorado Colorado Springs (CO)
U of Idaho (ID)
U of Southern California (CA)

MODERN GREEK
Colgate U (NY)
Concordia U Wisconsin (WI)
Furman U (SC)
John Carroll U (OH)
Lehman Coll of the City U of New York (NY)
Oberlin Coll (OH)
The Ohio State U (OH)
Tufts U (MA)
Tulane U (LA)
U of Michigan (MI)
U of Toronto (ON, Canada)
Wright State U (OH)
Wright State U–Lake Campus (OH)

MODERN LANGUAGES
Beloit Coll (WI)
Bemidji State U (MN)
Clark U (MA)
Coll of Mount Saint Vincent (NY)
The Coll of William and Mary (VA)
Cornell Coll (IA)
Fordham U (NY)
Franklin U Switzerland (Switzerland)
Gettysburg Coll (PA)
Hampton U (VA)
Marlboro Coll (VT)
Metropolitan State U of Denver (CO)
Nazareth Coll of Rochester (NY)
Presbyterian Coll (SC)
Purchase Coll, State U of New York (NY)
Rivier U (NH)
Saint Francis U (PA)
Saint Mary's Coll of California (CA)
Saint Peter's U (NJ)
St. Thomas Aquinas Coll (NY)
Trent U (ON, Canada)
U of Toronto (ON, Canada)
Virginia Military Inst (VA)
Walsh U (OH)
Washington U in St. Louis (MO)
Westmont Coll (CA)
Widener U (PA)

MOLECULAR BIOCHEMISTRY
Bob Jones U (SC)
Bryant U (RI)
Clarkson U (NY)
Simon Fraser U (BC, Canada)
U of California, Davis (CA)
U of Richmond (VA)
Wesleyan U (CT)

MOLECULAR BIOLOGY
Alverno Coll (WI)
Arizona State U at the Tempe campus (AZ)
Assumption Coll (MA)
Auburn U (AL)
Beloit Coll (WI)
Blackburn Coll (IL)
Boston U (MA)
California Lutheran U (CA)
Central Connecticut State U (CT)
Chestnut Hill Coll (PA)
Claremont McKenna Coll (CA)
Clarion U of Pennsylvania (PA)
Clark U (MA)
Coe Coll (IA)
Colby Coll (ME)
Colgate U (NY)
The Coll of Wooster (OH)
Dartmouth Coll (NH)
Florida Inst of Technology (FL)
Gettysburg Coll (PA)
Goshen Coll (IN)
Grove City Coll (PA)
Hampton U (VA)
Humboldt State U (CA)
Johns Hopkins U (MD)
Kenyon Coll (OH)
Lawrence Technological U (MI)
Lehigh U (PA)
Marlboro Coll (VT)
Messiah Coll (PA)
Millikin U (IL)
Montclair State U (NJ)
Muskingum U (OH)
Northwestern U (IL)
Ohio Northern U (OH)
Pitzer Coll (CA)
Pomona Coll (CA)
Princeton U (NJ)
Rollins Coll (FL)
Rutgers U–New Brunswick (NJ)
San Francisco State U (CA)
Scripps Coll (CA)
Simon Fraser U (BC, Canada)
Stetson U (FL)
Tulane U (LA)
U at Albany, State U of New York (NY)
U of California, San Diego (CA)
U of California, Santa Barbara (CA)
U of California, Santa Cruz (CA)
U of Denver (CO)
U of Guelph (ON, Canada)
U of Idaho (ID)
The U of Kansas (KS)
U of Maine (ME)
U of Michigan (MI)
U of Michigan–Flint (MI)
U of North Dakota (ND)
U of Pittsburgh (PA)
The U of Texas at Dallas (TX)
U of Toronto (ON, Canada)
U of Vermont (VT)
U of Wisconsin–Eau Claire (WI)
U of Wisconsin–Madison (WI)
U of Wisconsin–Parkside (WI)
U of Wyoming (WY)
Vanderbilt U (TN)
Wayland Baptist U (TX)
Wells Coll (NY)
Westminster Coll (PA)
Whitman Coll (WA)
William Jewell Coll (MO)

MOLECULAR GENETICS
Michigan State U (MI)
The Ohio State U (OH)
Rutgers U–New Brunswick (NJ)
Texas A&M U (TX)
U of Guelph (ON, Canada)
Washington State U (WA)

MOVEMENT THERAPY AND MOVEMENT EDUCATION
Brock U (ON, Canada)
Eastern Nazarene Coll (MA)
Texas Christian U (TX)

MULTICULTURAL EDUCATION
Fort Lewis Coll (CO)
Indiana Wesleyan U (IN)
U of St. Thomas (TX)

MULTI/INTERDISCIPLINARY STUDIES RELATED
Abilene Christian U (TX)
Adams State U (CO)
Adelphi U (NY)
Agnes Scott Coll (GA)
Alabama State U (AL)
Albion Coll (MI)
Allegheny Coll (PA)
Alverno Coll (WI)
American U (DC)
Anderson U (IN)
Angelo State U (TX)
Arcadia U (PA)
Arizona State U at the Downtown Phoenix campus (AZ)
Arizona State U at the Polytechnic campus (AZ)
Arizona State U at the Tempe campus (AZ)
Arizona State U at the West campus (AZ)
Arkansas Tech U (AR)
Athens State U (AL)
Austin Coll (TX)
Baldwin Wallace U (OH)
Barton Coll (NC)
Bates Coll (ME)
Baylor U (TX)
Belmont U (TN)
Bennett Coll (NC)
Bennington Coll (VT)
Berea Coll (KY)
Berry Coll (GA)
Bethel U (MN)
Bethel U (TN)
Binghamton U, State U of New York (NY)
Bluffton U (OH)
Boston U (MA)
Bowdoin Coll (ME)
Bowling Green State U (OH)
Brandeis U (MA)
Bryn Mawr Coll (PA)
Bucknell U (PA)
Buena Vista U (IA)
Buffalo State Coll, State U of New York (NY)
Caldwell U (NJ)
California Baptist U (CA)
California Inst of Integral Studies (CA)
California Inst of Technology (CA)
California Lutheran U (CA)
California Polytechnic State U, San Luis Obispo (CA)
California State U, Dominguez Hills (CA)
California State U, East Bay (CA)
California State U, Long Beach (CA)
California State U, Los Angeles (CA)
California State U, Monterey Bay (CA)
California State U, San Bernardino (CA)
California State U, San Marcos (CA)
California State U, Stanislaus (CA)
Calvary U (MO)
Cameron U (OK)
Capital U (OH)
Carroll Coll (MT)
Catawba Coll (NC)
Cedarville U (OH)
Central Connecticut State U (CT)
Chestnut Hill Coll (PA)
Christopher Newport U (VA)
Claremont McKenna Coll (CA)
Clarkson U (NY)
Cleveland State U (OH)
Colby Coll (ME)
Coll of Charleston (SC)
The Coll of Idaho (ID)
The Coll of New Jersey (NJ)
The Coll of New Rochelle (NY)
Coll of Saint Elizabeth (NJ)
The Coll of William and Mary (VA)
The Coll of Wooster (OH)
The Colorado Coll (CO)
Columbia Coll Chicago (IL)
Concord U (WV)
Cornell Coll (IA)
Covenant Coll (GA)
Criswell Coll (TX)
The Culinary Inst of America (NY)
Curry Coll (MA)
Dallas Baptist U (TX)
Dartmouth Coll (NH)
Davidson Coll (NC)
Delaware Valley U (PA)
DePauw U (IN)
Dickinson State U (ND)
D'Youville Coll (NY)
Earlham Coll (IN)
Eastern Mennonite U (VA)
Eastern Michigan U (MI)
Eastern Washington U (WA)
East Tennessee State U (TN)
East Texas Baptist U (TX)
Edgewood Coll (WI)
Emmanuel Coll (MA)
Emory U (GA)
Emporia State U (KS)
The Evergreen State Coll (WA)
Fairleigh Dickinson U, Metropolitan Campus (NJ)
Florida Inst of Technology (FL)
Florida Intl U (FL)
Florida Southern Coll (FL)
Franklin & Marshall Coll (PA)
Gannon U (PA)
Georgetown Coll (KY)
Georgetown U (DC)
Georgia Inst of Technology (GA)
Georgian Court U (NJ)
Georgia State U (GA)
Granite State Coll (NH)
Greenville U (IL)
Guilford Coll (NC)
Hamline U (MN)
Hampshire Coll (MA)
Harris-Stowe State U (MO)
Hawai`i Pacific U (HI)
High Point U (NC)
Hood Coll (MD)
Hope Coll (MI)

Howard Payne U (TX)
Humboldt State U (CA)
Idaho State U (ID)
Illinois Wesleyan U (IL)
Immaculata U (PA)
Indiana State U (IN)
Indiana U–Purdue U Indianapolis (IN)
Indiana U Southeast (IN)
Iowa State U of Science and Technology (IA)
Ithaca Coll (NY)
Jackson State U (MS)
Jacksonville U (FL)
John Brown U (AR)
Johnson C. Smith U (NC)
Juniata Coll (PA)
Kalamazoo Coll (MI)
Keene State Coll (NH)
Kennesaw State U (GA)
Kenyon Coll (OH)
King U (TN)
Knox Coll (IL)
Lamar U (TX)
Lasell Coll (MA)
Lawrence U (WI)
Lebanon Valley Coll (PA)
Lee U (TN)
LeTourneau U (TX)
Liberty U (VA)
Long Island U–LIU Brooklyn (NY)
Louisiana Coll (LA)
Louisiana State U and A&M Coll (LA)
Loyola Marymount U (CA)
Loyola U Chicago (IL)
Loyola U New Orleans (LA)
Luther Coll (IA)
Lycoming Coll (PA)
Macalester Coll (MN)
Manchester U (IN)
Manhattan Coll (NY)
Marian U (WI)
Marquette U (WI)
Mary Baldwin U (VA)
Marylhurst U (OR)
Maryville Coll (TN)
McDaniel Coll (MD)
McMurry U (TX)
McPherson Coll (KS)
Mercer U, Macon (GA)
Mercyhurst U (PA)
Meredith Coll (NC)
Messiah Coll (PA)
Metropolitan State U of Denver (CO)
Miami U (OH)
Michigan State U (MI)
Middle Tennessee State U (TN)
Millikin U (IL)
Millsaps Coll (MS)
Minnesota State U Moorhead (MN)
Mississippi State U (MS)
Missouri Baptist U (MO)
Missouri Western State U (MO)
Montclair State U (NJ)
Mount Holyoke Coll (MA)
Mount Mary U (WI)
Mount Mercy U (IA)
Mount St. Mary's U (MD)
Naropa U (CO)
National Louis U (IL)
Newman U (KS)
New York Inst of Technology (NY)
North Central Coll (IL)
Northeastern State U (OK)
Northern Illinois U (IL)
Northwest Christian U (OR)
Northwestern Oklahoma State U (OK)
Northwestern State U of Louisiana (LA)
Northwestern U (IL)
Northwest U (WA)
The Ohio State U (OH)
Ohio Wesleyan U (OH)
Old Dominion U (VA)
Otterbein U (OH)
Our Lady of the Lake U (TX)
Pace U (NY)
Pacific Lutheran U (WA)
Palm Beach Atlantic U (FL)
Penn State Erie, The Behrend Coll (PA)
Penn State Harrisburg (PA)
Pepperdine U, Malibu (CA)
Pittsburg State U (KS)

Point Park U (PA)
Prairie View A&M U (TX)
Princeton U (NJ)
Providence Coll (RI)
Radford U (VA)
Regis U (CO)
Rice U (TX)
Robert Morris U (PA)
Robert Morris U Illinois (IL)
Rogers State U (OK)
Roger Williams U (RI)
Rollins Coll (FL)
Rowan U (NJ)
Rutgers U–Camden (NJ)
Rutgers U–Newark (NJ)
Rutgers U–New Brunswick (NJ)
Saginaw Valley State U (MI)
Saint Anselm Coll (NH)
Saint Martin's U (WA)
Saint Mary's Coll of California (CA)
St. Mary's Coll of Maryland (MD)
Salisbury U (MD)
Samford U (AL)
Sam Houston State U (TX)
San Diego State U (CA)
San Francisco State U (CA)
Santa Clara U (CA)
Scripps Coll (CA)
Sewanee: The U of the South (TN)
Shippensburg U of Pennsylvania (PA)
Simmons Coll (MA)
Slippery Rock U of Pennsylvania (PA)
Sonoma State U (CA)
Southeastern Oklahoma State U (OK)
Southeastern U (FL)
Southeast Missouri State U (MO)
Southern Adventist U (TN)
Southern Arkansas U–Magnolia (AR)
Southern Illinois U Carbondale (IL)
Southern Methodist U (TX)
Southern Utah U (UT)
Southwestern Adventist U (TX)
Spelman Coll (GA)
State U of New York Empire State Coll (NY)
State U of New York Maritime Coll (NY)
Stephen F. Austin State U (TX)
Stevens Inst of Technology (NJ)
Stonehill Coll (MA)
Stony Brook U, State U of New York (NY)
Syracuse U (NY)
Tarleton State U (TX)
Taylor U (IN)
Temple U (PA)
Tennessee Technological U (TN)
Tennessee Wesleyan U (TN)
Texas A&M U (TX)
Texas A&M U–Central Texas (TX)
Texas A&M U–Commerce (TX)
Texas A&M U–Corpus Christi (TX)
Texas A&M U–Kingsville (TX)
Texas A&M U–Texarkana (TX)
Texas State U (TX)
Texas Tech U (TX)
Texas Woman's U (TX)
Thomas Edison State U (NJ)
Towson U (MD)
Trevecca Nazarene U (TN)
Trinity U (TX)
Truett McConnell U (GA)
Truman State U (MO)
Tulane U (LA)
Tusculum Coll (TN)
U at Albany, State U of New York (NY)
U at Buffalo, the State U of New York (NY)
The U of Akron (OH)
U of Alaska Fairbanks (AK)
U of California, Davis (CA)
U of California, Irvine (CA)
U of California, Los Angeles (CA)
U of California, Santa Barbara (CA)
U of Central Arkansas (AR)
U of Cincinnati (OH)
U of Colorado Boulder (CO)
U of Colorado Denver (CO)
U of Denver (CO)
U of Florida (FL)
U of Houston (TX)
U of Houston–Clear Lake (TX)

U of Houston–Downtown (TX)
U of Idaho (ID)
U of Kentucky (KY)
U of King's Coll (NS, Canada)
U of Maine (ME)
U of Maine at Farmington (ME)
U of Maryland, Baltimore County (MD)
U of Maryland, Coll Park (MD)
U of Maryland U Coll (MD)
U of Mary Washington (VA)
U of Massachusetts Amherst (MA)
U of Massachusetts Boston (MA)
U of Massachusetts Dartmouth (MA)
U of Memphis (TN)
U of Michigan (MI)
U of Michigan–Dearborn (MI)
U of Michigan–Flint (MI)
U of Minnesota, Crookston (MN)
U of Minnesota, Duluth (MN)
U of Minnesota, Morris (MN)
U of Minnesota, Twin Cities Campus (MN)
U of Missouri–St. Louis (MO)
U of Montevallo (AL)
U of Nevada, Las Vegas (NV)
U of New Hampshire (NH)
U of New Orleans (LA)
The U of North Carolina at Greensboro (NC)
The U of North Carolina at Pembroke (NC)
U of North Dakota (ND)
U of Northern Colorado (CO)
U of North Texas (TX)
U of Pikeville (KY)
U of Pittsburgh (PA)
U of Rhode Island (RI)
U of Richmond (VA)
U of Rochester (NY)
U of St. Francis (IL)
U of Saint Joseph (CT)
U of San Francisco (CA)
U of South Dakota (SD)
U of Southern California (CA)
U of Southern Mississippi (MS)
The U of Tennessee (TN)
The U of Texas at Austin (TX)
The U of Texas at San Antonio (TX)
The U of Texas of the Permian Basin (TX)
The U of Texas Rio Grande Valley (TX)
U of Virginia (VA)
U of Washington, Bothell (WA)
U of Washington, Tacoma (WA)
U of Waterloo (ON, Canada)
The U of West Alabama (AL)
U of Wisconsin–Milwaukee (WI)
U of Wisconsin–Platteville (WI)
U of Wisconsin–River Falls (WI)
U of Wisconsin–Stevens Point (WI)
U of Wisconsin–Superior (WI)
U of Wisconsin–Whitewater (WI)
U of Wyoming (WY)
Ursinus Coll (PA)
Utah State U (UT)
Utah Valley U (UT)
Valparaiso U (IN)
Vanderbilt U (TN)
Vassar Coll (NY)
Villanova U (PA)
Virginia Commonwealth U (VA)
Virginia Wesleyan U (VA)
Washington & Jefferson Coll (PA)
Washington and Lee U (VA)
Washington Coll (MD)
Washington State U (WA)
Washington U in St. Louis (MO)
Waynesburg U (PA)
Western Kentucky U (KY)
Western Michigan U (MI)
Western Washington U (WA)
Westminster Coll (PA)
West Texas A&M U (TX)
West Virginia U (WV)
West Virginia U Inst of Technology (WV)
Wheaton Coll (IL)
Wheaton Coll (MA)
Wichita State U (KS)
Wilkes U (PA)
William Jewell Coll (MO)
Williams Coll (MA)
Winona State U (MN)
Wisconsin Lutheran Coll (WI)

Woodbury U (CA)
Wright State U (OH)
Wright State U–Lake Campus (OH)

MUSEUM STUDIES
Beloit Coll (WI)
Coll of the Atlantic (ME)
Inst of American Indian Arts (NM)
Juniata Coll (PA)
Middlebury Coll (VT)
Randolph Coll (VA)
Tusculum Coll (TN)
U of Saint Francis (IN)
Walsh U (OH)

MUSIC
Abilene Christian U (TX)
Acadia U (NS, Canada)
Adams State U (CO)
Adelphi U (NY)
Agnes Scott Coll (GA)
Alabama State U (AL)
Albion Coll (MI)
Alcorn State U (MS)
Allegheny Coll (PA)
Alma Coll (MI)
Alverno Coll (WI)
Ambrose U (AB, Canada)
American U (DC)
Amherst Coll (MA)
Anderson U (IN)
Anderson U (SC)
Andrews U (MI)
Angelo State U (TX)
Aquinas Coll (MI)
Arizona State U at the Tempe campus (AZ)
Arkansas Tech U (AR)
Arlington Baptist U (TX)
Asbury U (KY)
Ashland U (OH)
Assumption Coll (MA)
Auburn U (AL)
Augsburg U (MN)
Augustana Coll (IL)
Augustana U (SD)
Aurora U (IL)
Austin Coll (TX)
Austin Peay State U (TN)
Averett U (VA)
Avila U (MO)
Azusa Pacific U (CA)
Baker U (KS)
Baldwin Wallace U (OH)
Ball State U (IN)
Baptist U of the Americas (TX)
Bard Coll (NY)
Barnard Coll (NY)
Baruch Coll of the City U of New York (NY)
Bates Coll (ME)
Baylor U (TX)
Belhaven U (MS)
Bellarmine U (KY)
Belmont U (TN)
Bemidji State U (MN)
Benedictine Coll (KS)
Benedictine U (IL)
Bennett Coll (NC)
Bennington Coll (VT)
Berea Coll (KY)
Berry Coll (GA)
Bethany Lutheran Coll (MN)
Bethel Coll (IN)
Bethel U (MN)
Bethel U (TN)
Bethune-Cookman U (FL)
Binghamton U, State U of New York (NY)
Biola U (CA)
Birmingham-Southern Coll (AL)
Blackburn Coll (IL)
Black Hills State U (SD)
Bloomsburg U of Pennsylvania (PA)
Bluefield Coll (VA)
Blue Mountain Coll (MS)
Bluffton U (OH)
Boise State U (ID)
Boston Coll (MA)
Boston U (MA)
Bowdoin Coll (ME)
Bowling Green State U (OH)
Bradley U (IL)
Brandeis U (MA)
Brandon U (MB, Canada)
Brenau U (GA)
Bridgewater State U (MA)

Brigham Young U–Idaho (ID)
Brock U (ON, Canada)
Bryan Coll (TN)
Bryn Mawr Coll (PA)
Bucknell U (PA)
Buffalo State Coll, State U of New York (NY)
Butler U (IN)
Cairn U (PA)
Caldwell U (NJ)
California Baptist U (CA)
California Lutheran U (CA)
California Polytechnic State U, San Luis Obispo (CA)
California State Polytechnic U, Pomona (CA)
California State U, Dominguez Hills (CA)
California State U, East Bay (CA)
California State U, Fullerton (CA)
California State U, Long Beach (CA)
California State U, Los Angeles (CA)
California State U, Monterey Bay (CA)
California State U, Northridge (CA)
California State U, Sacramento (CA)
California State U, San Bernardino (CA)
California State U, San Marcos (CA)
California State U, Stanislaus (CA)
Calvin Coll (MI)
Cameron U (OK)
Campbellsville U (KY)
Capital U (OH)
Carleton Coll (MN)
Carnegie Mellon U (PA)
Carroll U (WI)
Carson-Newman U (TN)
Carthage Coll (WI)
Case Western Reserve U (OH)
Catawba Coll (NC)
The Catholic U of America (DC)
Cedarville U (OH)
Centenary Coll of Louisiana (LA)
Central Connecticut State U (CT)
Central Methodist U (MO)
Central Michigan U (MI)
Centre Coll (KY)
Chapman U (CA)
Charleston Southern U (SC)
Chatham U (PA)
Chestnut Hill Coll (PA)
Chowan U (NC)
City Coll of the City U of New York (NY)
Clark Atlanta U (GA)
Clark U (MA)
Cleveland State U (OH)
Coastal Carolina U (SC)
Coe Coll (IA)
Colby Coll (ME)
Colgate U (NY)
Coll of Charleston (SC)
The Coll of Idaho (ID)
The Coll of New Jersey (NJ)
Coll of Saint Benedict (MN)
The Coll of Saint Rose (NY)
Coll of Staten Island of the City U of New York (NY)
Coll of the Atlantic (ME)
Coll of the Holy Cross (MA)
Coll of the Ozarks (MO)
The Coll of William and Mary (VA)
The Coll of Wooster (OH)
Colorado Christian U (CO)
The Colorado Coll (CO)
Colorado Mesa U (CO)
Colorado State U (CO)
Colorado State U–Pueblo (CO)
Columbia Coll (SC)
Columbia Coll Chicago (IL)
Columbia U (NY)
Columbus State U (GA)
Concordia Coll–New York (NY)
Concordia U (QC, Canada)
Concordia U Chicago (IL)
Concordia U, Nebraska (NE)
Concordia U of Edmonton (AB, Canada)
Concordia U, St. Paul (MN)
Concordia U Wisconsin (WI)
Connecticut Coll (CT)
Converse Coll (SC)

Corban U (OR)
Cornell Coll (IA)
Cornell U (NY)
Cornerstone U (MI)
Cornish Coll of the Arts (WA)
Covenant Coll (GA)
Creighton U (NE)
Culver-Stockton Coll (MO)
Dallas Baptist U (TX)
Dartmouth Coll (NH)
Davidson Coll (NC)
Delaware State U (DE)
Denison U (OH)
DePaul U (IL)
DePauw U (IN)
DEREE - The American Coll of
  Greece (Greece)
Dickinson Coll (PA)
Dickinson State U (ND)
Doane U (NE)
Dominican U (IL)
Dominican U of California (CA)
Drake U (IA)
Drew U (NJ)
Drury U (MO)
Duquesne U (PA)
Earlham Coll (IN)
East Carolina U (NC)
East Central U (OK)
Eastern Mennonite U (VA)
Eastern Michigan U (MI)
Eastern New Mexico U (NM)
Eastern Oregon U (OR)
Eastern U (PA)
Eastern Washington U (WA)
East Tennessee State U (TN)
East Texas Baptist U (TX)
Eckerd Coll (FL)
Edgewood Coll (WI)
Elizabethtown Coll (PA)
Elmhurst Coll (IL)
Elon U (NC)
Emmanuel Coll (GA)
Emory U (GA)
Emporia State U (KS)
Evangel U (MO)
Fairfield U (CT)
Fayetteville State U (NC)
Felician U (NJ)
Florida Ag and Mech U (FL)
Florida Atlantic U (FL)
Florida Coll (FL)
Florida Intl U (FL)
Florida Southern Coll (FL)
Fordham U (NY)
Fort Lewis Coll (CO)
Francis Marion U (SC)
Franklin & Marshall Coll (PA)
Franklin Coll (IN)
Franklin Pierce U (NH)
Friends U (KS)
Frostburg State U (MD)
Furman U (SC)
Geneva Coll (PA)
The George Washington U (DC)
Georgia Coll & State U (GA)
Georgia Southern U (GA)
Georgia Southern U–Armstrong
  Campus (GA)
Georgia Southwestern State U
  (GA)
Gettysburg Coll (PA)
Gordon Coll (MA)
Goshen Coll (IN)
Graceland U (IA)
Grambling State U (LA)
Grand Valley State U (MI)
Grand View U (IA)
Greensboro Coll (NC)
Greenville U (IL)
Grinnell Coll (IA)
Grove City Coll (PA)
Guilford Coll (NC)
Gustavus Adolphus Coll (MN)
Hamilton Coll (NY)
Hamline U (MN)
Hampshire Coll (MA)
Hampton U (VA)
Hannibal-LaGrange U (MO)
Harding U (AR)
Hardin-Simmons U (TX)
Hartwick Coll (NY)
Harvard U (MA)
Haverford Coll (PA)
Heidelberg U (OH)
Hendrix Coll (AR)
High Point U (NC)

Hillsdale Coll (MI)
Hiram Coll (OH)
Hobart and William Smith Colls
  (NY)
Hofstra U (NY)
Hollins U (VA)
Holy Names U (CA)
Hood Coll (MD)
Hope Coll (MI)
Houston Baptist U (TX)
Humboldt State U (CA)
Hunter Coll of the City U of New
  York (NY)
Huston-Tillotson U (TX)
Idaho State U (ID)
Illinois Coll (IL)
Illinois Wesleyan U (IL)
Immaculata U (PA)
Indiana State U (IN)
Indiana U of Pennsylvania (PA)
Indiana U South Bend (IN)
Indiana U Southeast (IN)
Inter American U of Puerto Rico,
  San Germán Campus (PR)
Iowa State U of Science and
  Technology (IA)
Ithaca Coll (NY)
Jacksonville U (FL)
John Brown U (AR)
Johns Hopkins U (MD)
Johnson C. Smith U (NC)
The Juilliard School (NY)
Kalamazoo Coll (MI)
Kansas State U (KS)
Kansas Wesleyan U (KS)
Kean U (NJ)
Keene State Coll (NH)
Kennesaw State U (GA)
Kent State U (OH)
Kentucky State U (KY)
Kenyon Coll (OH)
King U (TN)
Knox Coll (IL)
Kutztown U of Pennsylvania (PA)
Lafayette Coll (PA)
LaGrange Coll (GA)
Lamar U (TX)
Langston U (OK)
La Sierra U (CA)
Lawrence U (WI)
Lee U (TN)
Lehigh U (PA)
Lehman Coll of the City U of New
  York (NY)
Lenoir-Rhyne U (NC)
Lewis U (IL)
Liberty U (VA)
Limestone Coll (SC)
Lincoln U (PA)
Lindenwood U (MO)
Linfield Coll (OR)
Lipscomb U (TN)
Lock Haven U of Pennsylvania (PA)
Loras Coll (IA)
Louisiana Coll (LA)
Louisiana State U and A&M Coll
  (LA)
Loyola Marymount U (CA)
Loyola U Chicago (IL)
Loyola U New Orleans (LA)
Lubbock Christian U (TX)
Luther Coll (IA)
Lycoming Coll (PA)
Lynchburg Coll (VA)
Lyon Coll (AR)
Macalester Coll (MN)
Madonna U (MI)
Malone U (OH)
Manchester U (IN)
Manhattanville Coll (NY)
Mansfield U of Pennsylvania (PA)
Marian U (IN)
Marian U (WI)
Marietta Coll (OH)
Marlboro Coll (VT)
Marylhurst U (OR)
Maryville Coll (TN)
Massachusetts Coll of Liberal Arts
  (MA)
Massachusetts Inst of Technology
  (MA)
The Master's U (CA)
McDaniel Coll (MD)
McKendree U (IL)
McMurry U (TX)
Mercer U, Macon (GA)
Mercyhurst U (PA)

Meredith Coll (NC)
Messiah Coll (PA)
Metropolitan State U of Denver
  (CO)
Miami U (OH)
Michigan State U (MI)
Mid-America Christian U (OK)
MidAmerica Nazarene U (KS)
Middlebury Coll (VT)
Middle Georgia State U (GA)
Middle Tennessee State U (TN)
Millersville U of Pennsylvania (PA)
Millikin U (IL)
Millsaps Coll (MS)
Mills Coll (CA)
Minnesota State U Moorhead (MN)
Minot State U (ND)
Mississippi State U (MS)
Missouri Baptist U (MO)
Missouri State U (MO)
Missouri Valley Coll (MO)
Missouri Western State U (MO)
Molloy Coll (NY)
Monmouth Coll (IL)
Montclair State U (NJ)
Moravian Coll (PA)
Morehead State U (KY)
Morehouse Coll (GA)
Morningside Coll (IA)
Mount Holyoke Coll (MA)
Mount Marty Coll (SD)
Mount Mercy U (IA)
Mount St. Joseph U (OH)
Mount Saint Mary's U (CA)
Mount Vernon Nazarene U (OH)
Muhlenberg Coll (PA)
Murray State U (KY)
Muskingum U (OH)
Naropa U (CO)
Nazareth Coll of Rochester (NY)
Newberry Coll (SC)
New Coll of Florida (FL)
New Jersey City U (NJ)
New Mexico Highlands U (NM)
New York U (NY)
North Carolina Central U (NC)
North Central Coll (IL)
North Dakota State U (ND)
Northeastern State U (OK)
Northeastern U (MA)
Northern Arizona U (AZ)
Northern Illinois U (IL)
Northern Kentucky U (KY)
Northern Michigan U (MI)
Northern State U (SD)
Northern Vermont U–Lyndon (VT)
North Greenville U (SC)
Northwestern Coll (IA)
Northwestern Oklahoma State U
  (OK)
Northwestern U (IL)
Northwest Missouri State U (MO)
Northwest Nazarene U (ID)
Northwest U (WA)
Notre Dame de Namur U (CA)
Nova Southeastern U (FL)
Nyack Coll (NY)
Oakland City U (IN)
Oakland U (MI)
Oberlin Coll (OH)
Occidental Coll (CA)
Ohio Northern U (OH)
The Ohio State U (OH)
Ohio Wesleyan U (OH)
Oklahoma Baptist U (OK)
Oklahoma Christian U (OK)
Oklahoma City U (OK)
Oklahoma State U (OK)
Olivet Nazarene U (IL)
Oral Roberts U (OK)
Oregon State U (OR)
Ottawa U (KS)
Otterbein U (OH)
Ouachita Baptist U (AR)
Our Lady of the Lake U (TX)
Pacific Lutheran U (WA)
Palm Beach Atlantic U (FL)
Penn State Altoona (PA)
Penn State Beaver (PA)
Penn State Berks (PA)
Penn State Brandywine (PA)
Penn State DuBois (PA)
Penn State Greater Allegheny (PA)
Penn State Hazleton (PA)
Penn State Mont Alto (PA)
Penn State New Kensington (PA)
Penn State Shenango (PA)

Penn State U Park (PA)
Penn State Wilkes-Barre (PA)
Penn State Worthington Scranton
  (PA)
Penn State York (PA)
Pepperdine U, Malibu (CA)
Pfeiffer U (NC)
Piedmont Coll (GA)
Pitzer Coll (CA)
Point Loma Nazarene U (CA)
Point U (GA)
Pomona Coll (CA)
Portland State U (OR)
Prairie View A&M U (TX)
Presbyterian Coll (SC)
Princeton U (NJ)
Principia Coll (IL)
Providence Coll (RI)
Radford U (VA)
Ramapo Coll of New Jersey (NJ)
Randolph-Macon Coll (VA)
Redeemer U Coll (ON, Canada)
Reed Coll (OR)
Rhode Island Coll (RI)
Rhodes Coll (TN)
Rice U (TX)
Rider U (NJ)
Ripon Coll (WI)
Roanoke Coll (VA)
Roberts Wesleyan Coll (NY)
Rockford U (IL)
Rocky Mountain Coll (MT)
Rollins Coll (FL)
Roosevelt U (IL)
Rowan U (NJ)
Rutgers U–Camden (NJ)
Rutgers U–Newark (NJ)
Rutgers U–New Brunswick (NJ)
Saginaw Valley State U (MI)
St. Ambrose U (IA)
Saint Augustine's U (NC)
St. Catherine U (MN)
Saint John's U (MN)
Saint Joseph's U (PA)
St. Lawrence U (NY)
Saint Louis U (MO)
Saint Louis U–Madrid Campus
  (Spain)
Saint Martin's U (WA)
Saint Mary-of-the-Woods Coll (IN)
Saint Mary's Coll of California (CA)
St. Mary's Coll of Maryland (MD)
St. Mary's U (TX)
Saint Mary's U of Minnesota (MN)
Saint Michael's Coll (VT)
St. Norbert Coll (WI)
St. Olaf Coll (MN)
Saint Vincent Coll (PA)
Salisbury U (MD)
Salve Regina U (RI)
Samford U (AL)
Sam Houston State U (TX)
San Diego State U (CA)
San Francisco State U (CA)
Santa Clara U (CA)
Sarah Lawrence Coll (NY)
Schreiner U (TX)
Scripps Coll (CA)
Seattle Pacific U (WA)
Seattle U (WA)
Seton Hill U (PA)
Sewanee: The U of the South (TN)
Shaw U (NC)
Shepherd U (WV)
Shorter U (GA)
Silver Lake Coll of the Holy Family
  (WI)
Simmons Coll (MA)
Simon Fraser U (BC, Canada)
Simpson Coll (IA)
Slippery Rock U of Pennsylvania
  (PA)
Smith Coll (MA)
Sonoma State U (CA)
Southeastern Oklahoma State U
  (OK)
Southeast Missouri State U (MO)
Southern Adventist U (TN)
Southern Arkansas U–Magnolia
  (AR)
Southern Illinois U Carbondale (IL)
Southern Illinois U Edwardsville
  (IL)
Southern Methodist U (TX)
Southern Utah U (UT)
Southwest Baptist U (MO)
Southwestern Adventist U (TX)

Southwestern Coll (KS)
Southwestern U (TX)
Spelman Coll (GA)
Stanford U (CA)
State U of New York at Fredonia
  (NY)
State U of New York at New Paltz
  (NY)
State U of New York at Oswego
  (NY)
State U of New York at Plattsburgh
  (NY)
State U of New York Coll at
  Geneseo (NY)
State U of New York Coll at
  Oneonta (NY)
State U of New York Coll at
  Potsdam (NY)
Stephen F. Austin State U (TX)
Stetson U (FL)
Stony Brook U, State U of New York
  (NY)
Susquehanna U (PA)
Sweet Briar Coll (VA)
Syracuse U (NY)
Talladega Coll (AL)
Tarleton State U (TX)
Taylor U (IN)
Temple U (PA)
Tennessee Technological U (TN)
Tennessee Wesleyan U (TN)
Texas A&M Intl U (TX)
Texas A&M U (TX)
Texas A&M U–Commerce (TX)
Texas A&M U–Corpus Christi (TX)
Texas A&M U–Kingsville (TX)
Texas Christian U (TX)
Texas Lutheran U (TX)
Texas State U (TX)
Texas Tech U (TX)
Texas Woman's U (TX)
Tiffin U (OH)
Toccoa Falls Coll (GA)
Towson U (MD)
Trinity Christian Coll (IL)
Trinity U (TX)
Troy U (AL)
Truett McConnell U (GA)
Truman State U (MO)
Tufts U (MA)
Tulane U (LA)
Union Coll (NE)
Union U (TN)
U at Albany, State U of New York
  (NY)
U at Buffalo, the State U of New
  York (NY)
The U of Akron (OH)
The U of Alabama (AL)
The U of Alabama at Birmingham
  (AL)
U of Alaska Fairbanks (AK)
The U of Arizona (AZ)
U of Bridgeport (CT)
U of California, Davis (CA)
U of California, Irvine (CA)
U of California, Los Angeles (CA)
U of California, Riverside (CA)
U of California, San Diego (CA)
U of California, Santa Barbara (CA)
U of California, Santa Cruz (CA)
U of Central Arkansas (AR)
U of Central Missouri (MO)
U of Central Oklahoma (OK)
U of Chicago (IL)
U of Cincinnati (OH)
U of Colorado Boulder (CO)
U of Colorado Denver (CO)
U of Dayton (OH)
U of Denver (CO)
U of Evansville (IN)
U of Florida (FL)
U of Georgia (GA)
U of Guelph (ON, Canada)
U of Hartford (CT)
U of Hawaii at Manoa (HI)
U of Houston (TX)
U of Illinois at Chicago (IL)
U of Jamestown (ND)
The U of Kansas (KS)
U of King's Coll (NS, Canada)
U of La Verne (CA)
U of Louisville (KY)
U of Maine (ME)
U of Maine at Farmington (ME)
U of Maine at Machias (ME)
U of Mary Hardin-Baylor (TX)

U of Maryland, Baltimore County (MD)
U of Maryland, Coll Park (MD)
U of Mary Washington (VA)
U of Massachusetts Amherst (MA)
U of Massachusetts Boston (MA)
U of Massachusetts Dartmouth (MA)
U of Massachusetts Lowell (MA)
U of Memphis (TN)
U of Miami (FL)
U of Michigan (MI)
U of Michigan–Flint (MI)
U of Minnesota, Duluth (MN)
U of Minnesota, Morris (MN)
U of Minnesota, Twin Cities Campus (MN)
U of Missouri (MO)
U of Missouri–St. Louis (MO)
U of Mobile (AL)
U of Montana (MT)
U of Montevallo (AL)
U of Mount Union (OH)
U of Nebraska at Kearney (NE)
U of Nebraska–Lincoln (NE)
U of Nevada, Las Vegas (NV)
U of Nevada, Reno (NV)
U of New Hampshire (NH)
U of New Haven (CT)
U of New Orleans (LA)
U of North Alabama (AL)
U of North Carolina at Asheville (NC)
The U of North Carolina at Chapel Hill (NC)
The U of North Carolina at Charlotte (NC)
The U of North Carolina at Greensboro (NC)
The U of North Carolina at Pembroke (NC)
The U of North Carolina Wilmington (NC)
U of North Dakota (ND)
U of Northern Colorado (CO)
U of Northern Iowa (IA)
U of North Texas (TX)
U of Notre Dame (IN)
U of Oklahoma (OK)
U of Oregon (OR)
U of Pennsylvania (PA)
U of Pittsburgh (PA)
U of Puget Sound (WA)
U of Regina (SK, Canada)
U of Rhode Island (RI)
U of Richmond (VA)
U of Rochester (NY)
U of St. Francis (IL)
U of Saint Mary (KS)
U of St. Thomas (MN)
U of St. Thomas (TX)
U of San Diego (CA)
U of Saskatchewan (SK, Canada)
U of Science and Arts of Oklahoma (OK)
U of Sioux Falls (SD)
U of South Alabama (AL)
U of South Carolina (SC)
U of South Dakota (SD)
U of Southern California (CA)
U of Southern Maine (ME)
U of Southern Mississippi (MS)
The U of Tampa (FL)
The U of Tennessee (TN)
The U of Tennessee at Chattanooga (TN)
The U of Tennessee at Martin (TN)
The U of Texas at Austin (TX)
The U of Texas at El Paso (TX)
The U of Texas at San Antonio (TX)
The U of Texas of the Permian Basin (TX)
U of the Incarnate Word (TX)
U of the Pacific (CA)
The U of Toledo (OH)
The U of Tulsa (OK)
U of Utah (UT)
U of Vermont (VT)
U of Virginia (VA)
U of Washington (WA)
U of Waterloo (ON, Canada)
U of Wisconsin–Eau Claire (WI)
U of Wisconsin–La Crosse (WI)
U of Wisconsin–Madison (WI)
U of Wisconsin–Milwaukee (WI)
U of Wisconsin–Parkside (WI)
U of Wisconsin–Platteville (WI)

U of Wisconsin–River Falls (WI)
U of Wisconsin–Stevens Point (WI)
U of Wisconsin–Superior (WI)
U of Wisconsin–Whitewater (WI)
U of Wyoming (WY)
Utah State U (UT)
Utah Valley U (UT)
Valdosta State U (GA)
Valley City State U (ND)
Valparaiso U (IN)
Vanderbilt U (TN)
Vanguard U of Southern California (CA)
Vassar Coll (NY)
Villa Maria Coll (NY)
Virginia Polytechnic Inst and State U (VA)
Virginia Wesleyan U (VA)
Wabash Coll (IN)
Wagner Coll (NY)
Wake Forest U (NC)
Waldorf U (IA)
Walsh U (OH)
Warner Pacific Coll (OR)
Wartburg Coll (IA)
Washington & Jefferson Coll (PA)
Washington and Lee U (VA)
Washington Coll (MD)
Washington State U (WA)
Washington U in St. Louis (MO)
Wayland Baptist U (TX)
Wayne State Coll (NE)
Wayne State U (MI)
Weber State U (UT)
Webster U (MO)
Welch Coll (TN)
Wellesley Coll (MA)
West Chester U of Pennsylvania (PA)
Western Connecticut State U (CT)
Western Michigan U (MI)
Western Oregon U (OR)
Western State Colorado U (CO)
Western Washington U (WA)
Westfield State U (MA)
Westminster Coll (PA)
Westminster Coll (UT)
Westmont Coll (CA)
West Texas A&M U (TX)
West Virginia U (WV)
West Virginia Wesleyan Coll (WV)
Wheaton Coll (IL)
Wheaton Coll (MA)
Whitman Coll (WA)
Whittier Coll (CA)
Whitworth U (WA)
Wichita State U (KS)
Willamette U (OR)
William Jewell Coll (MO)
William Paterson U of New Jersey (NJ)
Williams Coll (MA)
Winona State U (MN)
Winthrop U (SC)
Wisconsin Lutheran Coll (WI)
Wittenberg U (OH)
Wright State U (OH)
Wright State U–Lake Campus (OH)
Xavier U of Louisiana (LA)
York Coll of Pennsylvania (PA)
Youngstown State U (OH)

MUSICAL INSTRUMENT FABRICATION AND REPAIR
Delaware State U (DE)

MUSICAL THEATER
American U (DC)
Anderson U (IN)
Anderson U (SC)
Aurora U (IL)
Blackburn Coll (IL)
Brenau U (GA)
Carthage Coll (WI)
Central Michigan U (MI)
Clarke U (IA)
Columbia Coll Chicago (IL)
Converse Coll (SC)
Creighton U (NE)
Culver-Stockton Coll (MO)
Elon U (NC)
Emory & Henry Coll (VA)
Florida Southern Coll (FL)
Florida State U (FL)
Indiana U Bloomington (IN)
Ithaca Coll (NY)
Kansas Wesleyan U (KS)
LaGrange Coll (GA)

Limestone Coll (SC)
Lindenwood U (MO)
Loyola U New Orleans (LA)
Marywood U (PA)
McKendree U (IL)
McPherson Coll (KS)
Messiah Coll (PA)
Millikin U (IL)
Minnesota State U Moorhead (MN)
Missouri Baptist U (MO)
The New School for Public Engagement (NY)
North Central Coll (IL)
Northern Vermont U–Lyndon (VT)
Oakland U (MI)
Ohio Northern U (OH)
Pace U (NY)
Point Park U (PA)
Rhode Island Coll (RI)
Roosevelt U (IL)
Shenandoah U (VA)
Southwestern Coll (KS)
Sweet Briar Coll (VA)
Syracuse U (NY)
Taylor U (IN)
Texas Christian U (TX)
Texas State U (TX)
U at Buffalo, the State U of New York (NY)
The U of Arizona (AZ)
U of California, Irvine (CA)
U of Michigan (MI)
U of Mobile (AL)
U of North Dakota (ND)
U of Oklahoma (OK)
The U of Tampa (FL)
The U of the Arts (PA)
Wayland Baptist U (TX)
Weber State U (UT)
Western Michigan U (MI)
West Texas A&M U (TX)
William Jewell Coll (MO)
William Peace U (NC)

MUSIC HISTORY, LITERATURE, AND THEORY
American U (DC)
Baldwin Wallace U (OH)
Baylor U (TX)
Bennington Coll (VT)
Birmingham-Southern Coll (AL)
Bowling Green State U (OH)
Brandon U (MB, Canada)
Bridgewater Coll (VA)
Brigham Young U (UT)
Bucknell U (PA)
Cairn U (PA)
California State U, Long Beach (CA)
Calvin Coll (MI)
The Catholic U of America (DC)
The Coll of Wooster (OH)
Concordia Coll–New York (NY)
Converse Coll (SC)
Eugene Lang Coll of Liberal Arts (NY)
Hofstra U (NY)
Jacksonville U (FL)
Lehigh U (PA)
Liberty U (VA)
Marlboro Coll (VT)
Nazareth Coll of Rochester (NY)
New Coll of Florida (FL)
Northwestern U (IL)
Oberlin Coll (OH)
The Ohio State U (OH)
Ouachita Baptist U (AR)
Randolph Coll (VA)
Rice U (TX)
Rider U (NJ)
St. Bonaventure U (NY)
Skidmore Coll (NY)
State U of New York at Fredonia (NY)
Syracuse U (NY)
Temple U (PA)
Tufts U (MA)
The U of Akron (OH)
U of California, Los Angeles (CA)
U of California, San Diego (CA)
U of Cincinnati (OH)
U of Hartford (CT)
U of Idaho (ID)
U of Kentucky (KY)
U of Michigan (MI)
The U of North Carolina at Greensboro (NC)

U of Regina (SK, Canada)
U of the Pacific (CA)
U of Toronto (ON, Canada)
U of Washington (WA)
Ursinus Coll (PA)
Washington U in St. Louis (MO)
Western Washington U (WA)
Wheaton Coll (IL)
Whitman Coll (WA)
Wright State U (OH)
Wright State U–Lake Campus (OH)
Youngstown State U (OH)

MUSIC MANAGEMENT
Albright Coll (PA)
Anderson U (IN)
Anderson U (SC)
Appalachian State U (NC)
Augsburg U (MN)
Belmont U (TN)
Berry Coll (GA)
Bethel U (TN)
Bradley U (IL)
Buena Vista U (IA)
Capital U (OH)
Chowan U (NC)
Columbia Coll Chicago (IL)
Concordia U, St. Paul (MN)
Dallas Baptist U (TX)
DePaul U (IL)
DePauw U (IN)
Drake U (IA)
Drexel U (PA)
Edgewood Coll (WI)
Elmhurst Coll (IL)
Ferris State U (MI)
Florida Atlantic U (FL)
Florida Southern Coll (FL)
Francis Marion U (SC)
Geneva Coll (PA)
Greenville U (IL)
Grove City Coll (PA)
Hardin-Simmons U (TX)
Heidelberg U (OH)
Hofstra U (NY)
Jacksonville U (FL)
Judson U (IL)
Lamar U (TX)
Lebanon Valley Coll (PA)
Lee U (TN)
Lewis U (IL)
Liberty U (VA)
Lindenwood U (MO)
Loyola U New Orleans (LA)
Lubbock Christian U (TX)
Madonna U (MI)
Mansfield U of Pennsylvania (PA)
The Master's U (CA)
Messiah Coll (PA)
Middle Tennessee State U (TN)
Missouri Baptist U (MO)
Murray State U (KY)
Nazareth Coll of Rochester (NY)
Northwest Christian U (OR)
Northwest U (WA)
Oklahoma City U (OK)
Simmons Coll (MA)
Southeastern U (FL)
State U of New York at Fredonia (NY)
State U of New York Coll at Oneonta (NY)
State U of New York Coll at Potsdam (NY)
Syracuse U (NY)
Trevecca Nazarene U (TN)
Union U (TN)
U of Evansville (IN)
U of Hartford (CT)
U of Idaho (ID)
U of Memphis (TN)
U of New Haven (CT)
U of Puget Sound (WA)
U of Southern California (CA)
U of Southern Mississippi (MS)
The U of the Arts (PA)
U of the Incarnate Word (TX)
U of the Pacific (CA)
Valley City State U (ND)
Villa Maria Coll (NY)
Warner Pacific Coll (OR)
Western State Colorado U (CO)
Winona State U (MN)

MUSICOLOGY AND ETHNOMUSICOLOGY
Bennington Coll (VT)
Boston U (MA)

Bowling Green State U (OH)
Converse Coll (SC)
East Tennessee State U (TN)
Liberty U (VA)
Marlboro Coll (VT)
Northwestern U (IL)
Roger Williams U (RI)
Tufts U (MA)
U of California, Los Angeles (CA)
U of Denver (CO)
The U of Kansas (KS)

MUSIC PEDAGOGY
Anderson U (SC)
Baylor U (TX)
Bob Jones U (SC)
Brigham Young U (UT)
Calvary U (MO)
Cedarville U (OH)
Holy Names U (CA)
Ithaca Coll (NY)
Liberty U (VA)
Maranatha Baptist U (WI)
Michigan State U (MI)
MidAmerica Nazarene U (KS)
Oakland U (MI)
Samford U (AL)
Temple U (PA)
Union Coll (NE)
U of Maryland, Baltimore County (MD)
U of Oklahoma (OK)
The U of Tennessee at Martin (TN)
Weber State U (UT)
Wheaton Coll (IL)
Whitworth U (WA)
Willamette U (OR)

MUSIC PERFORMANCE
Adams State U (CO)
Albion Coll (MI)
Alcorn State U (MS)
Allegheny Coll (PA)
Anderson U (IN)
Appalachian State U (NC)
Aquinas Coll (MI)
Arizona State U at the Tempe campus (AZ)
Augsburg U (MN)
Augustana Coll (IL)
Avila U (MO)
Baldwin Wallace U (OH)
Baylor U (TX)
Belmont U (TN)
Bennington Coll (VT)
Bethel Coll (IN)
Bethel U (MN)
Bethune-Cookman U (FL)
Binghamton U, State U of New York (NY)
Biola U (CA)
Black Hills State U (SD)
Bob Jones U (SC)
Boise State U (ID)
Boston U (MA)
Bowling Green State U (OH)
Bradley U (IL)
Brandon U (MB, Canada)
Bucknell U (PA)
Buena Vista U (IA)
Butler U (IN)
California Baptist U (CA)
California State U, Fullerton (CA)
California State U, Long Beach (CA)
California State U, Los Angeles (CA)
California State U, Stanislaus (CA)
Calvary U (MO)
Calvin Coll (MI)
Capital U (OH)
Cardinal Stritch U (WI)
Carnegie Mellon U (PA)
Carson-Newman U (TN)
Catawba Coll (NC)
The Catholic U of America (DC)
Cedarville U (OH)
Central Methodist U (MO)
Central State U (OH)
Chapman U (CA)
Charleston Southern U (SC)
Christopher Newport U (VA)
City Coll of the City U of New York (NY)
Clarke U (IA)
Coe Coll (IA)
The Coll of St. Scholastica (MN)

The Coll of Wooster (OH)
Colorado Christian U (CO)
Colorado Mesa U (CO)
Columbia Coll Chicago (IL)
Columbus State U (GA)
Concordia Coll–New York (NY)
Concordia U (QC, Canada)
Concordia U Chicago (IL)
Conservatorio de Musica de Puerto Rico (PR)
Converse Coll (SC)
Corban U (OR)
Cornerstone U (MI)
Covenant Coll (GA)
Dallas Baptist U (TX)
DePaul U (IL)
DePauw U (IN)
Drake U (IA)
Duquesne U (PA)
Eastern Michigan U (MI)
Elmhurst Coll (IL)
Elon U (NC)
Emory & Henry Coll (VA)
Florida Gulf Coast U (FL)
Florida Southern Coll (FL)
Florida State U (FL)
Fort Lewis Coll (CO)
Friends U (KS)
George Mason U (VA)
Georgia State U (GA)
Gonzaga U (WA)
Gordon Coll (MA)
Graceland U (IA)
Greensboro Coll (NC)
Grove City Coll (PA)
Gustavus Adolphus Coll (MN)
Hamline U (MN)
Hofstra U (NY)
Holy Names U (CA)
Hope Coll (MI)
Howard Payne U (TX)
Huntingdon Coll (AL)
Idaho State U (ID)
Illinois Wesleyan U (IL)
Indiana State U (IN)
Indiana U Bloomington (IN)
Indiana U of Pennsylvania (PA)
Indiana U South Bend (IN)
Indiana Wesleyan U (IN)
Inter American U of Puerto Rico, Metropolitan Campus (PR)
Ithaca Coll (NY)
Jackson State U (MS)
Jacksonville U (FL)
James Madison U (VA)
Johnson C. Smith U (NC)
Judson U (IL)
The Juilliard School (NY)
Kansas Wesleyan U (KS)
Kean U (NJ)
Keene State Coll (NH)
Kennesaw State U (GA)
Kentucky State U (KY)
LaGrange Coll (GA)
La Sierra U (CA)
Lawrence U (WI)
Lebanon Valley Coll (PA)
Lee U (TN)
Lenoir-Rhyne U (NC)
Liberty U (VA)
Limestone Coll (SC)
Lipscomb U (TN)
Long Island U–LIU Brooklyn (NY)
Long Island U–LIU Post (NY)
Louisiana Coll (LA)
Louisiana State U and A&M Coll (LA)
Loyola U New Orleans (LA)
Lynn U (FL)
Madonna U (MI)
Manchester U (IN)
Mansfield U of Pennsylvania (PA)
Maranatha Baptist U (WI)
Marian U (IN)
Marlboro Coll (VT)
Maryville Coll (TN)
Marywood U (PA)
McNeese State U (LA)
McPherson Coll (KS)
Mercer U, Macon (GA)
Mercyhurst U (PA)
Messiah Coll (PA)
Miami U (OH)
Michigan State U (MI)
MidAmerica Nazarene U (KS)
Millikin U (IL)
Missouri Baptist U (MO)

Missouri State U (MO)
Montclair State U (NJ)
Morningside Coll (IA)
Mount Vernon Nazarene U (OH)
Naropa U (CO)
Nazareth Coll of Rochester (NY)
Newberry Coll (SC)
New Mexico State U (NM)
The New School Coll of Performing Arts (NY)
New World School of the Arts (FL)
New York U (NY)
Northern Arizona U (AZ)
Northern Illinois U (IL)
North Greenville U (SC)
Northwestern State U of Louisiana (LA)
Northwestern U (IL)
Northwest Nazarene U (ID)
Notre Dame de Namur U (CA)
Nyack Coll (NY)
Oakland U (MI)
Ohio Northern U (OH)
The Ohio State U (OH)
Ohio U (OH)
Ohio Wesleyan U (OH)
Oklahoma Baptist U (OK)
Oklahoma City U (OK)
Old Dominion U (VA)
Olivet Nazarene U (IL)
Oral Roberts U (OK)
Otterbein U (OH)
Ouachita Baptist U (AR)
Palm Beach Atlantic U (FL)
Penn State U Park (PA)
Piedmont Coll (GA)
Pittsburg State U (KS)
Point Loma Nazarene U (CA)
Portland State U (OR)
Queens Coll of the City U of New York (NY)
Randolph Coll (VA)
Rhode Island Coll (RI)
Rice U (TX)
Rockford U (IL)
Rocky Mountain Coll (MT)
Roosevelt U (IL)
Rowan U (NJ)
Rutgers U–New Brunswick (NJ)
Saint Mary's U of Minnesota (MN)
St. Olaf Coll (MN)
Saint Vincent Coll (PA)
Samford U (AL)
Sam Houston State U (TX)
San Diego State U (CA)
San Francisco State U (CA)
Seton Hill U (PA)
Shenandoah U (VA)
Simpson Coll (IA)
Slippery Rock U of Pennsylvania (PA)
Southeastern Louisiana U (LA)
Southeastern Oklahoma State U (OK)
Southeastern U (FL)
Southern Adventist U (TN)
Southern Methodist U (TX)
Southwestern Adventist U (TX)
Southwestern Assemblies of God U (TX)
Southwestern Coll (KS)
Southwestern U (TX)
State U of New York Coll at Potsdam (NY)
Stetson U (FL)
Susquehanna U (PA)
Syracuse U (NY)
Tarleton State U (TX)
Taylor U (IN)
Temple U (PA)
Texas A&M U–Commerce (TX)
Texas A&M U–Kingsville (TX)
Texas Christian U (TX)
Texas State U (TX)
Toccoa Falls Coll (GA)
Transylvania U (KY)
Trevecca Nazarene U (TN)
Trinity U (TX)
Truman State U (MO)
Tulane U (LA)
Union Coll (NE)
Union U (TN)
U at Buffalo, the State U of New York (NY)
The U of Akron (OH)
U of Alaska Fairbanks (AK)
The U of Arizona (AZ)

U of Arkansas (AR)
U of California, Irvine (CA)
U of Central Arkansas (AR)
U of Central Florida (FL)
U of Cincinnati (OH)
U of Colorado Boulder (CO)
U of Dayton (OH)
U of Denver (CO)
U of Evansville (IN)
U of Georgia (GA)
U of Hartford (CT)
U of Houston (TX)
U of Idaho (ID)
U of Jamestown (ND)
The U of Kansas (KS)
U of Kentucky (KY)
U of Louisiana at Monroe (LA)
U of Maine (ME)
U of Mary Hardin-Baylor (TX)
U of Maryland, Baltimore County (MD)
U of Maryland, Coll Park (MD)
U of Massachusetts Amherst (MA)
U of Massachusetts Lowell (MA)
U of Miami (FL)
U of Michigan (MI)
U of Michigan–Flint (MI)
U of Minnesota, Duluth (MN)
U of Nevada, Reno (NV)
U of New Mexico (NM)
The U of North Carolina at Chapel Hill (NC)
The U of North Carolina at Charlotte (NC)
The U of North Carolina at Greensboro (NC)
The U of North Carolina at Pembroke (NC)
U of North Carolina School of the Arts (NC)
U of North Dakota (ND)
U of Northern Iowa (IA)
U of North Florida (FL)
U of North Georgia (GA)
U of North Texas (TX)
U of Oregon (OR)
U of Puget Sound (WA)
U of Rochester (NY)
U of St. Francis (IL)
U of St. Thomas (MN)
U of South Dakota (SD)
U of Southern California (CA)
U of Southern Maine (ME)
The U of Tampa (FL)
The U of Tennessee at Martin (TN)
The U of Texas at Austin (TX)
The U of the Arts (PA)
The U of Tulsa (OK)
U of Valley Forge (PA)
U of Vermont (VT)
U of Washington (WA)
U of West Georgia (GA)
U of Wisconsin–Madison (WI)
U of Wisconsin–Stevens Point (WI)
U of Wisconsin–Superior (WI)
U of Wyoming (WY)
Utah Valley U (UT)
Valdosta State U (GA)
Valparaiso U (IN)
Vanguard U of Southern California (CA)
Villa Maria Coll (NY)
Virginia Commonwealth U (VA)
Wartburg Coll (IA)
Washington State U (WA)
Wayland Baptist U (TX)
Weber State U (UT)
Webster U (MO)
Welch Coll (TN)
West Chester U of Pennsylvania (PA)
Western Connecticut State U (CT)
Western Illinois U (IL)
Western Kentucky U (KY)
Western Michigan U (MI)
Western Washington U (WA)
Wheaton Coll (IL)
Whitman Coll (WA)
Whitworth U (WA)
Wichita State U (KS)
William Jewell Coll (MO)
William Paterson U of New Jersey (NJ)
William Penn U (IA)
Wright State U (OH)
Wright State U–Lake Campus (OH)

Xavier U of Louisiana (LA)
Youngstown State U (OH)

MUSIC RELATED
Alverno Coll (WI)
Ball State U (IN)
Bellarmine U (KY)
Belmont U (TN)
Bethel Coll (KS)
Biola U (CA)
Bowling Green State U (OH)
Brewton-Parker Coll (GA)
Brigham Young U (UT)
Capital U (OH)
Coker Coll (SC)
Colorado Christian U (CO)
Columbia Coll Chicago (IL)
Concordia U Irvine (CA)
Cornerstone U (MI)
DePaul U (IL)
Duquesne U (PA)
Florida State U (FL)
Friends U (KS)
Greenville U (IL)
Grove City Coll (PA)
Hampton U (VA)
Illinois Wesleyan U (IL)
Indiana U Bloomington (IN)
Indiana U South Bend (IN)
Jacksonville U (FL)
Kent State U at Stark (OH)
Lipscomb U (TN)
McKendree U (IL)
Mercer U, Macon (GA)
Messiah Coll (PA)
Missouri Western State U (MO)
Morehead State U (KY)
Murray State U (KY)
Northern Vermont U–Lyndon (VT)
Northwestern U (IL)
Northwest U (WA)
Ohio Northern U (OH)
Palm Beach Atlantic U (FL)
Saint Mary's U of Minnesota (MN)
Tiffin U (OH)
Trevecca Nazarene U (TN)
Trinity Christian Coll (IL)
Truett McConnell U (GA)
U of Central Oklahoma (OK)
U of Denver (CO)
U of Hartford (CT)
U of Massachusetts Lowell (MA)
U of Memphis (TN)
U of Miami (FL)
U of Minnesota, Duluth (MN)
U of North Carolina at Asheville (NC)
U of Northern Iowa (IA)
U of Southern California (CA)
The U of Tulsa (OK)
U of Washington (WA)
Valparaiso U (IN)
Vanderbilt U (TN)
Wesleyan U (CT)
Western Illinois U (IL)
Western Kentucky U (KY)
West Virginia U (WV)
Wheaton Coll (IL)
Whitworth U (WA)
Wichita State U (KS)

MUSIC TEACHER EDUCATION
Abilene Christian U (TX)
Acadia U (NS, Canada)
Adams State U (CO)
Adelphi U (NY)
Alabama State U (AL)
Albion Coll (MI)
Alma Coll (MI)
Alverno Coll (WI)
Anderson U (IN)
Anderson U (SC)
Andrews U (MI)
Appalachian State U (NC)
Aquinas Coll (MI)
Arizona State U at the Tempe campus (AZ)
Arkansas Tech U (AR)
Arlington Baptist U (TX)
Asbury U (KY)
Ashland U (OH)
Auburn U (AL)
Augsburg U (MN)
Augustana Coll (IL)
Augustana U (SD)
Baker U (KS)
Baldwin Wallace U (OH)

Ball State U (IN)
The Baptist Coll of Florida (FL)
Baylor U (TX)
Belmont U (TN)
Beloit Coll (WI)
Bemidji State U (MN)
Benedictine Coll (KS)
Benedictine U (IL)
Berry Coll (GA)
Bethel Coll (IN)
Bethel U (MN)
Bethel U (TN)
Bethune-Cookman U (FL)
Biola U (CA)
Birmingham-Southern Coll (AL)
Bluefield Coll (VA)
Blue Mountain Coll (MS)
Bluffton U (OH)
Bob Jones U (SC)
Boise State U (ID)
Boston U (MA)
Bowling Green State U (OH)
Bradley U (IL)
Brandon U (MB, Canada)
Brenau U (GA)
Bridgewater State U (MA)
Brigham Young U–Idaho (ID)
Brock U (ON, Canada)
Bryan Coll (TN)
Bucknell U (PA)
Buena Vista U (IA)
Buffalo State Coll, State U of New York (NY)
Butler U (IN)
California Baptist U (CA)
California Lutheran U (CA)
California State U, Fullerton (CA)
Calvary U (MO)
Calvin Coll (MI)
Cameron U (OK)
Campbellsville U (KY)
Capital U (OH)
Carroll U (WI)
Carson-Newman U (TN)
Carthage Coll (WI)
Case Western Reserve U (OH)
Catawba Coll (NC)
Cedarville U (OH)
Central Connecticut State U (CT)
Central Methodist U (MO)
Central State U (OH)
Chapman U (CA)
Charleston Southern U (SC)
Chestnut Hill Coll (PA)
Chowan U (NC)
City Coll of the City U of New York (NY)
Clarion U of Pennsylvania (PA)
Clarke U (IA)
Coe Coll (IA)
Coker Coll (SC)
The Coll of New Jersey (NJ)
The Coll of Saint Rose (NY)
Coll of the Ozarks (MO)
The Coll of Wooster (OH)
Colorado Christian U (CO)
Colorado Mesa U (CO)
Columbus State U (GA)
Concordia U Chicago (IL)
Concordia U, Nebraska (NE)
Concordia U, St. Paul (MN)
Concordia U Wisconsin (WI)
Conservatorio de Musica de Puerto Rico (PR)
Converse Coll (SC)
Corban U (OR)
Cornell Coll (IA)
Cornerstone U (MI)
Culver-Stockton Coll (MO)
Dallas Baptist U (TX)
Delaware State U (DE)
DePaul U (IL)
DePauw U (IN)
Dickinson State U (ND)
Drake U (IA)
Duquesne U (PA)
East Carolina U (NC)
East Central U (OK)
Eastern Michigan U (MI)
Eastern Washington U (WA)
East Texas Baptist U (TX)
Edgewood Coll (WI)
Elmhurst Coll (IL)
Elon U (NC)
Emmanuel Coll (GA)
Emmaus Bible Coll (IA)
Emory & Henry Coll (VA)

Emporia State U (KS)
Evangel U (MO)
Florida Ag and Mech U (FL)
Florida Atlantic U (FL)
Florida Gulf Coast U (FL)
Florida Southern Coll (FL)
Florida State U (FL)
Fort Lewis Coll (CO)
Friends U (KS)
Furman U (SC)
Geneva Coll (PA)
Georgia Coll & State U (GA)
Georgia Southern U (GA)
Georgia Southern U–Armstrong Campus (GA)
Gettysburg Coll (PA)
Gonzaga U (WA)
Gordon Coll (MA)
Goshen Coll (IN)
Graceland U (IA)
Grand Valley State U (MI)
Grand View U (IA)
Greensboro Coll (NC)
Greenville U (IL)
Grove City Coll (PA)
Gustavus Adolphus Coll (MN)
Hampton U (VA)
Hannibal-LaGrange U (MO)
Harding U (AR)
Hardin-Simmons U (TX)
Hartwick Coll (NY)
Heidelberg U (OH)
Hobe Sound Bible Coll (FL)
Hofstra U (NY)
Hope Coll (MI)
Houston Baptist U (TX)
Howard Payne U (TX)
Humboldt State U (CA)
Huntingdon Coll (AL)
Idaho State U (ID)
Illinois Wesleyan U (IL)
Immaculata U (PA)
Indiana U Bloomington (IN)
Indiana U South Bend (IN)
Indiana Wesleyan U (IN)
Inter American U of Puerto Rico, San Germán Campus (PR)
Iowa State U of Science and Technology (IA)
Ithaca Coll (NY)
Jackson State U (MS)
Jacksonville U (FL)
John Brown U (AR)
Kansas State U (KS)
Kansas Wesleyan U (KS)
Kean U (NJ)
Keene State Coll (NH)
Kennesaw State U (GA)
Kent State U (OH)
Kentucky State U (KY)
King U (TN)
Kutztown U of Pennsylvania (PA)
Langston U (OK)
La Sierra U (CA)
Lawrence U (WI)
Lebanon Valley Coll (PA)
Lee U (TN)
Lenoir-Rhyne U (NC)
Limestone Coll (SC)
Lindenwood U (MO)
Lipscomb U (TN)
Long Island U–LIU Brooklyn (NY)
Long Island U–LIU Post (NY)
Loras Coll (IA)
Louisiana Coll (LA)
Louisiana State U and A&M Coll (LA)
Loyola U New Orleans (LA)
Lubbock Christian U (TX)
Lynchburg Coll (VA)
Madonna U (MI)
Malone U (OH)
Manchester U (IN)
Manhattanville Coll (NY)
Mansfield U of Pennsylvania (PA)
Maranatha Baptist U (WI)
Marian U (IN)
Marietta Coll (OH)
Martin Luther Coll (MN)
Maryville Coll (TN)
Marywood U (PA)
The Master's U (CA)
McKendree U (IL)
Mercer U, Macon (GA)
Mercyhurst U (PA)
Meredith Coll (NC)
Messiah Coll (PA)

Metropolitan State U of Denver (CO)
Miami U (OH)
Michigan State U (MI)
Mid-America Christian U (OK)
MidAmerica Nazarene U (KS)
Millikin U (IL)
Minnesota State U Moorhead (MN)
Minot State U (ND)
Mississippi State U (MS)
Missouri Baptist U (MO)
Missouri State U (MO)
Missouri Western State U (MO)
Molloy Coll (NY)
Morningside Coll (IA)
Mount Marty Coll (SD)
Mount Mercy U (IA)
Mount Vernon Nazarene U (OH)
Muskingum U (OH)
Nazareth Coll of Rochester (NY)
Newberry Coll (SC)
New Jersey City U (NJ)
New Mexico State U (NM)
New York U (NY)
North Central Coll (IL)
North Dakota State U (ND)
Northeastern State U (OK)
Northern Arizona U (AZ)
Northern Kentucky U (KY)
Northern Michigan U (MI)
Northern State U (SD)
Northern Vermont U–Lyndon (VT)
North Greenville U (SC)
Northwestern Coll (IA)
Northwestern Oklahoma State U (OK)
Northwestern State U of Louisiana (LA)
Northwestern U (IL)
Northwest Missouri State U (MO)
Northwest Nazarene U (ID)
Northwest U (WA)
Nyack Coll (NY)
Oakland U (MI)
Oberlin Coll (OH)
Ohio Christian U (OH)
Ohio Northern U (OH)
The Ohio State U (OH)
Ohio Wesleyan U (OH)
Oklahoma Baptist U (OK)
Oklahoma Christian U (OK)
Oklahoma State U (OK)
Olivet Nazarene U (IL)
Oral Roberts U (OK)
Otterbein U (OH)
Ouachita Baptist U (AR)
Pacific Lutheran U (WA)
Palm Beach Atlantic U (FL)
Penn State U Park (PA)
Pepperdine U, Malibu (CA)
Pfeiffer U (NC)
Piedmont Coll (GA)
Pittsburg State U (KS)
Point Loma Nazarene U (CA)
Providence Coll (RI)
Queens Coll of the City U of New York (NY)
Rhode Island Coll (RI)
Rider U (NJ)
Ripon Coll (WI)
Roberts Wesleyan Coll (NY)
Rocky Mountain Coll (MT)
Roosevelt U (IL)
Rowan U (NJ)
Rutgers U–New Brunswick (NJ)
Saginaw Valley State U (MI)
St. Ambrose U (IA)
St. Catherine U (MN)
Saint Mary's U of Minnesota (MN)
St. Norbert Coll (WI)
St. Olaf Coll (MN)
Salve Regina U (RI)
Samford U (AL)
Sam Houston State U (TX)
San Diego State U (CA)
Schreiner U (TX)
Seton Hill U (PA)
Shenandoah U (VA)
Shorter U (GA)
Silver Lake Coll of the Holy Family (WI)
Simpson Coll (IA)
Sonoma State U (CA)
Southeastern Oklahoma State U (OK)
Southeastern U (FL)
Southeast Missouri State U (MO)

Southern Adventist U (TN)
Southern Arkansas U–Magnolia (AR)
Southern Methodist U (TX)
Southern Utah U (UT)
Southwest Baptist U (MO)
Southwestern Assemblies of God U (TX)
Southwestern Coll (KS)
State U of New York at Fredonia (NY)
State U of New York Coll at Potsdam (NY)
Stetson U (FL)
Susquehanna U (PA)
Syracuse U (NY)
Tabor Coll (KS)
Taylor U (IN)
Temple U (PA)
Tennessee Technological U (TN)
Texas Christian U (TX)
Texas Lutheran U (TX)
Toccoa Falls Coll (GA)
Towson U (MD)
Transylvania U (KY)
Trevecca Nazarene U (TN)
Trinity Christian Coll (IL)
Trinity U (TX)
Truett McConnell U (GA)
Union Coll (NE)
Union U (TN)
The U of Akron (OH)
The U of Alabama (AL)
The U of Arizona (AZ)
U of Central Missouri (MO)
U of Central Oklahoma (OK)
U of Cincinnati (OH)
U of Colorado Boulder (CO)
U of Dayton (OH)
U of Evansville (IN)
U of Florida (FL)
U of Georgia (GA)
U of Hartford (CT)
U of Idaho (ID)
U of Jamestown (ND)
The U of Kansas (KS)
U of Kentucky (KY)
U of Louisville (KY)
U of Maine (ME)
U of Mary Hardin-Baylor (TX)
U of Maryland, Coll Park (MD)
U of Maryland Eastern Shore (MD)
U of Miami (FL)
U of Michigan (MI)
U of Michigan–Flint (MI)
U of Minnesota, Duluth (MN)
U of Minnesota, Twin Cities Campus (MN)
U of Missouri (MO)
U of Missouri–St. Louis (MO)
U of Mobile (AL)
U of Mount Union (OH)
U of Nebraska–Lincoln (NE)
U of Nevada, Reno (NV)
U of New Mexico (NM)
The U of North Carolina at Greensboro (NC)
The U of North Carolina at Pembroke (NC)
The U of North Carolina Wilmington (NC)
U of North Dakota (ND)
U of Northern Colorado (CO)
U of Northern Iowa (IA)
U of North Florida (FL)
U of North Georgia (GA)
U of Oklahoma (OK)
U of Oregon (OR)
U of Puget Sound (WA)
U of Regina (SK, Canada)
U of Rochester (NY)
U of St. Thomas (MN)
U of St. Thomas (TX)
U of Saskatchewan (SK, Canada)
U of Sioux Falls (SD)
U of South Carolina (SC)
U of South Carolina Aiken (SC)
U of South Dakota (SD)
U of Southern Maine (ME)
U of Southern Mississippi (MS)
The U of Tampa (FL)
The U of Tennessee at Martin (TN)
The U of Texas at Austin (TX)
U of the Incarnate Word (TX)
U of the Pacific (CA)
U of the Virgin Islands (VI)
U of Toronto (ON, Canada)

The U of Tulsa (OK)
U of Valley Forge (PA)
U of Vermont (VT)
U of Washington (WA)
U of West Georgia (GA)
U of Wisconsin–Madison (WI)
U of Wisconsin–Milwaukee (WI)
U of Wisconsin–River Falls (WI)
U of Wisconsin–Stevens Point (WI)
U of Wisconsin–Superior (WI)
U of Wyoming (WY)
Utah State U (UT)
Utah Valley U (UT)
Valley City State U (ND)
Valparaiso U (IN)
Vanderbilt U (TN)
VanderCook Coll of Music (IL)
Vanguard U of Southern California (CA)
Waldorf U (IA)
Warner Pacific Coll (OR)
Wartburg Coll (IA)
Wayland Baptist U (TX)
Wayne State Coll (NE)
Weber State U (UT)
Webster U (MO)
Welch Coll (TN)
Western Connecticut State U (CT)
Western Michigan U (MI)
Western State Colorado U (CO)
Western Washington U (WA)
Westfield State U (MA)
Westminster Coll (PA)
West Virginia Wesleyan Coll (WV)
Wheaton Coll (IL)
Whitworth U (WA)
Wichita State U (KS)
Winona State U (MN)
Winthrop U (SC)
Wright State U (OH)
Wright State U–Lake Campus (OH)
Xavier U of Louisiana (LA)
York Coll of Pennsylvania (PA)
Youngstown State U (OH)

MUSIC TECHNOLOGY

American U (DC)
California U of Pennsylvania (PA)
Carnegie Mellon U (PA)
Cogswell Polytechnical Coll (CA)
The Coll of Saint Rose (NY)
Columbia Coll Chicago (IL)
Connecticut Coll (CT)
Converse Coll (SC)
Culver-Stockton Coll (MO)
Edgewood Coll (WI)
Elon U (NC)
Indiana U–Purdue U Indianapolis (IN)
Iowa State U of Science and Technology (IA)
Keene State Coll (NH)
LaGrange Coll (GA)
La Sierra U (CA)
Lebanon Valley Coll (PA)
Mercy Coll (NY)
Northwest Christian U (OR)
Rowan U (NJ)
San Francisco Conservatory of Music (CA)
Shenandoah U (VA)
Stetson U (FL)
Stevens Inst of Technology (NJ)
Syracuse U (NY)
Transylvania U (KY)
U of Denver (CO)
U of Maryland, Baltimore County (MD)
U of Michigan (MI)
U of New Haven (CT)
U of North Carolina at Asheville (NC)
U of Northern Iowa (IA)
U of St. Francis (IL)
U of Saint Francis (IN)
U of Valley Forge (PA)
Utah Valley U (UT)
Western Michigan U (MI)

MUSIC THEORY AND COMPOSITION

Academy of Art U (CA)
Adams State U (CO)
Anderson U (IN)
Arizona State U at the Tempe campus (AZ)
Augustana Coll (IL)
Baldwin Wallace U (OH)

Baylor U (TX)
Belmont U (TN)
Bennington Coll (VT)
Biola U (CA)
Birmingham-Southern Coll (AL)
Boise State U (ID)
Boston U (MA)
Bowling Green State U (OH)
Bradley U (IL)
Brandon U (MB, Canada)
Bucknell U (PA)
Butler U (IN)
California Baptist U (CA)
California State U, Long Beach (CA)
Calvin Coll (MI)
Capital U (OH)
Carnegie Mellon U (PA)
Carson-Newman U (TN)
The Catholic U of America (DC)
Cedarville U (OH)
Central Michigan U (MI)
Chapman U (CA)
City Coll of the City U of New York (NY)
Coe Coll (IA)
Coll of the Ozarks (MO)
The Coll of Wooster (OH)
Columbia Coll Chicago (IL)
Concordia U (QC, Canada)
Concordia U Chicago (IL)
Conservatorio de Musica de Puerto Rico (PR)
Dallas Baptist U (TX)
DePaul U (IL)
DePauw U (IN)
DigiPen Inst of Technology (WA)
Florida State U (FL)
Hardin-Simmons U (TX)
Hofstra U (NY)
Hope Coll (MI)
Illinois Wesleyan U (IL)
Indiana Wesleyan U (IN)
Ithaca Coll (NY)
Jacksonville U (FL)
Keene State Coll (NH)
Lawrence U (WI)
Lipscomb U (TN)
Loyola U New Orleans (LA)
Lynn U (FL)
Madonna U (MI)
Manchester U (IN)
Marlboro Coll (VT)
Marylhurst U (OR)
Maryville Coll (TN)
Michigan State U (MI)
Newberry Coll (SC)
The New School Coll of Performing Arts (NY)
Northwestern U (IL)
Northwest Nazarene U (ID)
Northwest U (WA)
Nyack Coll (NY)
Oberlin Coll (OH)
Ohio Northern U (OH)
The Ohio State U (OH)
Ohio U (OH)
Oklahoma Baptist U (OK)
Oklahoma City U (OK)
Olivet Nazarene U (IL)
Oral Roberts U (OK)
Ouachita Baptist U (AR)
Palm Beach Atlantic U (FL)
Pepperdine U, Malibu (CA)
Point Loma Nazarene U (CA)
Randolph Coll (VA)
Rice U (TX)
Rider U (NJ)
Roosevelt U (IL)
Rowan U (NJ)
St. Olaf Coll (MN)
Samford U (AL)
Sam Houston State U (TX)
San Francisco Conservatory of Music (CA)
Shenandoah U (VA)
Southern Adventist U (TN)
Southern Methodist U (TX)
Southwestern U (TX)
Stetson U (FL)
Susquehanna U (PA)
Syracuse U (NY)
Taylor U (IN)
Temple U (PA)
Texas Christian U (TX)
Trevecca Nazarene U (TN)
Trinity U (TX)

Tufts U (MA)
Tulane U (LA)
The U of Akron (OH)
U of California, Santa Barbara (CA)
U of Central Missouri (MO)
U of Cincinnati (OH)
U of Dayton (OH)
U of Denver (CO)
U of Georgia (GA)
U of Idaho (ID)
The U of Kansas (KS)
U of Maryland, Baltimore County (MD)
U of Miami (FL)
U of Michigan (MI)
U of Minnesota, Duluth (MN)
The U of North Carolina at Greensboro (NC)
U of Northern Iowa (IA)
U of North Texas (TX)
U of Oregon (OR)
U of Regina (SK, Canada)
U of Rochester (NY)
U of Southern California (CA)
The U of Texas at Austin (TX)
The U of the Arts (PA)
U of the Pacific (CA)
The U of Tulsa (OK)
U of Washington (WA)
U of West Georgia (GA)
Valparaiso U (IN)
Vanderbilt U (TN)
Wartburg Coll (IA)
Washington State U (WA)
Washington U in St. Louis (MO)
Webster U (MO)
Western Connecticut State U (CT)
Western Michigan U (MI)
Western Washington U (WA)
Wheaton Coll (IL)
Whitman Coll (WA)
Whitworth U (WA)
Wichita State U (KS)
Willamette U (OR)
William Jewell Coll (MO)
Youngstown State U (OH)

MUSIC THERAPY
Alverno Coll (WI)
Appalachian State U (NC)
Arizona State U at the Tempe campus (AZ)
Augsburg U (MN)
Baldwin Wallace U (OH)
Belmont U (TN)
Charleston Southern U (SC)
The Coll of Wooster (OH)
Concordia U, Nebraska (NE)
Concordia U Wisconsin (WI)
Converse Coll (SC)
Drury U (MO)
Duquesne U (PA)
Eastern Michigan U (MI)
Edgewood Coll (WI)
Elizabethtown Coll (PA)
Florida Gulf Coast U (FL)
Florida State U (FL)
Georgia Coll & State U (GA)
Immaculata U (PA)
Indiana U–Purdue U Indianapolis (IN)
Loyola U New Orleans (LA)
Marylhurst U (OR)
Maryville U of Saint Louis (MO)
Marywood U (PA)
Mercyhurst U (PA)
Molloy Coll (NY)
Montclair State U (NJ)
Nazareth Coll of Rochester (NY)
Saint Mary-of-the-Woods Coll (IN)
Sam Houston State U (TX)
Seattle Pacific U (WA)
Seton Hill U (PA)
Shenandoah U (VA)
Slippery Rock U of Pennsylvania (PA)
Southern Methodist U (TX)
State U of New York at Fredonia (NY)
Temple U (PA)
Texas Woman's U (TX)
U of Dayton (OH)
U of Evansville (IN)
U of Georgia (GA)
The U of Kansas (KS)
U of Louisville (KY)
U of Miami (FL)

U of Minnesota, Twin Cities Campus (MN)
U of North Dakota (ND)
U of the Incarnate Word (TX)
U of the Pacific (CA)
Utah State U (UT)
Wartburg Coll (IA)
Western Michigan U (MI)
Willamette U (OR)

NANOTECHNOLOGY
Excelsior Coll (NY)
U of Guelph (ON, Canada)
U of Wisconsin–Platteville (WI)
Virginia Polytechnic Inst and State U (VA)

NATIONAL SECURITY POLICY
Anderson U (IN)
Angelo State U (TX)
Baldwin Wallace U (OH)
Excelsior Coll (NY)
U of New Haven (CT)
U of North Georgia (GA)

NATURAL RESOURCE ECONOMICS
Baldwin Wallace U (OH)
Juniata Coll (PA)
Malone U (OH)
Michigan State U (MI)
New Mexico State U (NM)
U of Guelph (ON, Canada)
U of New Hampshire (NH)
U of Rhode Island (RI)
U of Saskatchewan (SK, Canada)
The U of Tennessee (TN)

NATURAL RESOURCE RECREATION AND TOURISM
Unity Coll (ME)
U of Georgia (GA)
U of Idaho (ID)

NATURAL RESOURCES AND CONSERVATION RELATED
Bowling Green State U (OH)
California Polytechnic State U, San Luis Obispo (CA)
Mount Mercy U (IA)
Northland Coll (WI)
Penn State Abington (PA)
Penn State Altoona (PA)
Penn State Beaver (PA)
Penn State Berks (PA)
Penn State Brandywine (PA)
Penn State DuBois (PA)
Penn State Erie, The Behrend Coll (PA)
Penn State Fayette, The Eberly Campus (PA)
Penn State Greater Allegheny (PA)
Penn State Hazleton (PA)
Penn State Lehigh Valley (PA)
Penn State Mont Alto (PA)
Penn State New Kensington (PA)
Penn State Schuylkill (PA)
Penn State Shenango (PA)
Penn State U Park (PA)
Penn State Wilkes-Barre (PA)
Penn State Worthington Scranton (PA)
Penn State York (PA)
State U of New York Coll of Technology at Canton (NY)
U of Alaska Fairbanks (AK)
U of California, Davis (CA)
U of Wisconsin–Stevens Point (WI)
Utah State U (UT)

NATURAL RESOURCES/ CONSERVATION
Carroll U (WI)
Central Michigan U (MI)
Clemson U (SC)
Colorado State U (CO)
Colorado State U–Pueblo (CO)
Cornell U (NY)
The Evergreen State Coll (WA)
Grand Valley State U (MI)
Green Mountain Coll (VT)
Gustavus Adolphus Coll (MN)
Humboldt State U (CA)
Kent State U (OH)
Lubbock Christian U (TX)
Manchester U (IN)
Marlboro Coll (VT)
Mississippi State U (MS)

Muskingum U (OH)
North Carolina State U (NC)
Northern Michigan U (MI)
The Ohio State U (OH)
Penn State Abington (PA)
Penn State Altoona (PA)
Penn State Beaver (PA)
Penn State Berks (PA)
Penn State Brandywine (PA)
Penn State DuBois (PA)
Penn State Erie, The Behrend Coll (PA)
Penn State Fayette, The Eberly Campus (PA)
Penn State Greater Allegheny (PA)
Penn State Hazleton (PA)
Penn State Lehigh Valley (PA)
Penn State Mont Alto (PA)
Penn State New Kensington (PA)
Penn State Schuylkill (PA)
Penn State Shenango (PA)
Penn State U Park (PA)
Penn State Wilkes-Barre (PA)
Penn State Worthington Scranton (PA)
Penn State York (PA)
Purdue U (IN)
Rutgers U–New Brunswick (NJ)
Sewanee: The U of the South (TN)
Southeastern Oklahoma State U (OK)
State U of New York at Plattsburgh (NY)
State U of New York Coll of Environmental Science and Forestry (NY)
Texas A&M U (TX)
Texas Tech U (TX)
Towson U (MD)
Tusculum Coll (TN)
U of Alaska Fairbanks (AK)
The U of Arizona (AZ)
U of California, Davis (CA)
U of Kentucky (KY)
U of Maryland, Coll Park (MD)
U of Maryland U Coll (MD)
U of Massachusetts Amherst (MA)
U of Michigan (MI)
U of Minnesota, Crookston (MN)
U of Missouri (MO)
U of Montana (MT)
U of Nebraska–Lincoln (NE)
U of New Hampshire (NH)
U of Vermont (VT)
U of Wisconsin–River Falls (WI)
U of Wisconsin–Stevens Point (WI)
Upper Iowa U (IA)
Washington State U (WA)
Washington U in St. Louis (MO)

NATURAL RESOURCES/ CONSERVATION RELATED
Colby Coll (ME)
Miami U (OH)
Northland Coll (WI)
Sierra Nevada Coll (NV)
Stanford U (CA)
U of Michigan–Flint (MI)

NATURAL RESOURCES LAW ENFORCEMENT AND PROTECTIVE SERVICES
Texas Tech U (TX)
Unity Coll (ME)
U of Minnesota, Crookston (MN)

NATURAL RESOURCES MANAGEMENT AND POLICY
Alaska Pacific U (AK)
Angelo State U (TX)
Auburn U (AL)
Bowling Green State U (OH)
Bryant U (RI)
Clark U (MA)
Delaware State U (DE)
Dominican U of California (CA)
Humboldt State U (CA)
Iowa State U of Science and Technology (IA)
Kansas State U (KS)
Louisiana State U and A&M Coll (LA)
Marist Coll (NY)
Michigan Technological U (MI)
New Mexico Highlands U (NM)
North Carolina State U (NC)
North Dakota State U (ND)
The Ohio State U (OH)

Oregon State U (OR)
Purdue U (IN)
Rochester Inst of Technology (NY)
Rocky Mountain Coll (MT)
Rutgers U–New Brunswick (NJ)
State U of New York Coll of Environmental Science and Forestry (NY)
U of Guelph (ON, Canada)
U of Hawaii at Manoa (HI)
U of La Verne (CA)
U of Miami (FL)
U of Minnesota, Crookston (MN)
U of Nebraska–Lincoln (NE)
U of New Haven (CT)
U of Rhode Island (RI)
The U of Tennessee at Martin (TN)
U of Wisconsin–Stevens Point (WI)
Washington State U (WA)
Washington U in St. Louis (MO)

NATURAL RESOURCES MANAGEMENT AND POLICY RELATED
Delaware State U (DE)
Humboldt State U (CA)
The Ohio State U (OH)
Rutgers U–New Brunswick (NJ)
U of Saskatchewan (SK, Canada)
The U of Tennessee at Martin (TN)
Western Washington U (WA)

NATURAL SCIENCES
American Public U System (WV)
Athens State U (AL)
Azusa Pacific U (CA)
Bemidji State U (MN)
Benedictine Coll (KS)
Bethel Coll (KS)
California State U, Dominguez Hills (CA)
California State U, Los Angeles (CA)
Calvin Coll (MI)
Carthage Coll (WI)
Case Western Reserve U (OH)
Christian Brothers U (TN)
Colgate U (NY)
Coll of Saint Benedict (MN)
Coll of Saint Mary (NE)
The Coll of St. Scholastica (MN)
Coll of the Atlantic (ME)
Colorado State U (CO)
Concordia U Chicago (IL)
Concordia U, Nebraska (NE)
Daemen Coll (NY)
Dallas Baptist U (TX)
Defiance Coll (OH)
Doane U (NE)
Dominican U (IL)
Edgewood Coll (WI)
The Evergreen State Coll (WA)
Excelsior Coll (NY)
Felician U (NJ)
Fordham U (NY)
Georgian Court U (NJ)
Harrisburg U of Science and Technology (PA)
Hofstra U (NY)
Humboldt State U (CA)
Indiana U East (IN)
Inter American U of Puerto Rico, Metropolitan Campus (PR)
Inter American U of Puerto Rico, San Germán Campus (PR)
Johns Hopkins U (MD)
Judson U (IL)
Juniata Coll (PA)
Kansas State U (KS)
Lesley U (MA)
Logan U (MO)
Loyola Marymount U (CA)
Madonna U (MI)
Marlboro Coll (VT)
The Master's U (CA)
McPherson Coll (KS)
Mount St. Joseph U (OH)
Mount Saint Mary Coll (NY)
Muhlenberg Coll (PA)
New Coll of Florida (FL)
Northern Vermont U–Lyndon (VT)
Oklahoma Baptist U (OK)
Pepperdine U, Malibu (CA)
Saint John's U (MN)
Saint Peter's U (NJ)
St. Thomas Aquinas Coll (NY)
Saint Vincent Coll (PA)
Santa Clara U (CA)

Shorter U (GA)
State U of New York Coll at Geneseo (NY)
Temple U (PA)
Trent U (ON, Canada)
U of La Verne (CA)
U of Pennsylvania (PA)
U of Pittsburgh at Greensburg (PA)
U of Puget Sound (WA)
U of Science and Arts of Oklahoma (OK)
U of Washington (WA)
U of Wisconsin–Stevens Point (WI)
Virginia Wesleyan U (VA)
Washington U in St. Louis (MO)
Western Oregon U (OR)

NAVAL ARCHITECTURE AND MARINE ENGINEERING
Massachusetts Maritime Acad (MA)
State U of New York Maritime Coll (NY)
Stevens Inst of Technology (NJ)
Texas A&M U (TX)
United States Coast Guard Acad (CT)
United States Merchant Marine Acad (NY)
U of Michigan (MI)
U of New Orleans (LA)
Webb Inst (NY)

NAVY/MARINE CORPS ROTC/ NAVAL SCIENCE
Hampton U (VA)
Iowa State U of Science and Technology (IA)

NEAR AND MIDDLE EASTERN STUDIES
American U (DC)
The American U in Cairo (Egypt)
Bard Coll (NY)
Boston U (MA)
Brandeis U (MA)
Claremont McKenna Coll (CA)
Colgate U (NY)
Columbia U (NY)
Cornell U (NY)
Dartmouth Coll (NH)
Dickinson Coll (PA)
Emory & Henry Coll (VA)
Emory U (GA)
Fordham U (NY)
The George Washington U (DC)
Hampshire Coll (MA)
Harvard U (MA)
Hood Coll (MD)
Johns Hopkins U (MD)
Marlboro Coll (VT)
McDaniel Coll (MD)
Middlebury Coll (VT)
Mount Holyoke Coll (MA)
New York U (NY)
Oberlin Coll (OH)
Pomona Coll (CA)
Portland State U (OR)
Princeton U (NJ)
Queens Coll of the City U of New York (NY)
Rutgers U–New Brunswick (NJ)
Sarah Lawrence Coll (NY)
Scripps Coll (CA)
Smith Coll (MA)
Syracuse U (NY)
Trinity U (TX)
Tufts U (MA)
United States Military Acad (NY)
The U of Arizona (AZ)
U of California, Santa Barbara (CA)
U of Massachusetts Amherst (MA)
U of Michigan (MI)
U of Richmond (VA)
The U of Texas at Austin (TX)
The U of Toledo (OH)
U of Toronto (ON, Canada)
U of Utah (UT)
Washington U in St. Louis (MO)
Wellesley Coll (MA)
Williams Coll (MA)

NETWORK AND SYSTEM ADMINISTRATION
Central Connecticut State U (CT)
Central Penn Coll (PA)
Champlain Coll (VT)
Columbia Central U, Caguas (PR)
Kansas Wesleyan U (KS)

Michigan Technological U (MI)
Rochester Inst of Technology (NY)
Simmons Coll (MA)
U of Providence (MT)
Walsh U (OH)

NEUROBIOLOGY AND ANATOMY
Andrews U (MI)
Georgetown U (DC)
Harvard U (MA)
New Coll of Florida (FL)
Purdue U (IN)
U of California, Davis (CA)
U of California, Irvine (CA)
U of Washington (WA)

NEUROBIOLOGY AND BEHAVIOR
Fitchburg State U (MA)
La Sierra U (CA)

NEUROBIOLOGY AND NEUROSCIENCES RELATED
U of Southern California (CA)

NEUROSCIENCE
Adelphi U (NY)
Agnes Scott Coll (GA)
Allegheny Coll (PA)
American U (DC)
Amherst Coll (MA)
Augustana Coll (IL)
Baldwin Wallace U (OH)
Barnard Coll (NY)
Bates Coll (ME)
Baylor U (TX)
Bay Path U (MA)
Belmont U (TN)
Binghamton U, State U of New York (NY)
Boston U (MA)
Bowdoin Coll (ME)
Bowling Green State U (OH)
Brandeis U (MA)
Brock U (ON, Canada)
Bucknell U (PA)
California Inst of Technology (CA)
Carnegie Mellon U (PA)
Carthage Coll (WI)
Centenary Coll of Louisiana (LA)
Central Michigan U (MI)
Christopher Newport U (VA)
Claremont McKenna Coll (CA)
Clark U (MA)
Coe Coll (IA)
Colby Coll (ME)
Colgate U (NY)
The Coll of William and Mary (VA)
The Coll of Wooster (OH)
The Colorado Coll (CO)
Colorado State U (CO)
Columbia U (NY)
Concordia U (QC, Canada)
Connecticut Coll (CT)
Creighton U (NE)
DePaul U (IL)
Dickinson Coll (PA)
Dominican U (IL)
Drake U (IA)
Drew U (NJ)
Earlham Coll (IN)
Edgewood Coll (WI)
Emmanuel Coll (MA)
Emory U (GA)
Fordham U (NY)
Franklin & Marshall Coll (PA)
Furman U (SC)
George Mason U (VA)
Georgia State U (GA)
Grand Valley State U (MI)
Grove City Coll (PA)
Hamilton Coll (NY)
Hamline U (MN)
Hampshire Coll (MA)
High Point U (NC)
Hiram Coll (OH)
Hofstra U (NY)
Indiana U Bloomington (IN)
Indiana U–Purdue U Indianapolis (IN)
Indiana U Southeast (IN)
John Carroll U (OH)
Johns Hopkins U (MD)
Kenyon Coll (OH)
King's Coll (PA)
King U (TN)

Knox Coll (IL)
La Sierra U (CA)
Lawrence U (WI)
Lebanon Valley Coll (PA)
Lehigh U (PA)
Loras Coll (IA)
Luther Coll (IA)
Lycoming Coll (PA)
Macalester Coll (MN)
Marymount Manhattan Coll (NY)
Maryville Coll (TN)
Massachusetts Inst of Technology (MA)
Mercer U, Macon (GA)
Miami U (OH)
Michigan State U (MI)
Middlebury Coll (VT)
Moravian Coll (PA)
Morehead State U (KY)
Mount Holyoke Coll (MA)
Mount St. Joseph U (OH)
Muhlenberg Coll (PA)
Muskingum U (OH)
New York U (NY)
Northeastern U (MA)
Northern Kentucky U (KY)
Northern Michigan U (MI)
Northwestern U (IL)
Northwest Nazarene U (ID)
Oberlin Coll (OH)
The Ohio State U (OH)
Ohio U (OH)
Ohio Wesleyan U (OH)
Pitzer Coll (CA)
Pomona Coll (CA)
Princeton U (NJ)
Randolph-Macon Coll (VA)
Reed Coll (OR)
Regis U (CO)
Rhodes Coll (TN)
Rice U (TX)
Sacred Heart U (CT)
Saginaw Valley State U (MI)
St. Lawrence U (NY)
Saint Louis U (MO)
Saint Michael's Coll (VT)
Santa Clara U (CA)
Scripps Coll (CA)
Skidmore Coll (NY)
Smith Coll (MA)
State U of New York Coll at Geneseo (NY)
Stonehill Coll (MA)
Syracuse U (NY)
Temple U (PA)
Texas Christian U (TX)
Transylvania U (KY)
Trinity U (TX)
Tulane U (LA)
Union Coll (NY)
The U of Alabama at Birmingham (AL)
The U of Arizona (AZ)
U of California, Riverside (CA)
U of California, San Diego (CA)
U of California, Santa Cruz (CA)
U of Chicago (IL)
U of Cincinnati (OH)
U of Colorado Boulder (CO)
U of Evansville (IN)
U of Illinois at Chicago (IL)
U of King's Coll (NS, Canada)
U of Miami (FL)
U of Michigan (MI)
U of Minnesota, Twin Cities Campus (MN)
U of Montana (MT)
U of Mount Union (OH)
U of Nevada, Reno (NV)
U of New England (ME)
U of New Hampshire (NH)
U of Notre Dame (IN)
U of Pennsylvania (PA)
U of Pittsburgh (PA)
U of Rochester (NY)
U of St. Thomas (MN)
U of San Diego (CA)
The U of Scranton (PA)
U of Southern California (CA)
The U of Texas at Austin (TX)
The U of Texas at Dallas (TX)
U of Vermont (VT)
U of Wisconsin–River Falls (WI)
Ursinus Coll (PA)
Vanderbilt U (TN)
Villanova U (PA)

Virginia Polytechnic Inst and State U (VA)
Wartburg Coll (IA)
Washington & Jefferson Coll (PA)
Washington and Lee U (VA)
Washington State U (WA)
Washington State U–Vancouver (WA)
Washington U in St. Louis (MO)
Wellesley Coll (MA)
Western New England U (MA)
Western Washington U (WA)
Westminster Coll (PA)
Westminster Coll (UT)
Westmont Coll (CA)
Wheaton Coll (MA)
Wilkes U (PA)
Willamette U (OR)

NONPROFIT MANAGEMENT
Arizona State U at the Downtown Phoenix campus (AZ)
Aurora U (IL)
Austin Coll (TX)
Austin Peay State U (TN)
Bryant U (RI)
Cleveland State U (OH)
Concordia U Chicago (IL)
Concordia U Irvine (CA)
Cornerstone U (MI)
Donnelly Coll (KS)
Duquesne U (PA)
Gettysburg Coll (PA)
Granite State Coll (NH)
Hardin-Simmons U (TX)
High Point U (NC)
Johnson U Florida (FL)
Lenoir-Rhyne U (NC)
Mercy Coll (NY)
Missouri Valley Coll (MO)
Moravian Coll (PA)
Morningside Coll (IA)
Point Loma Nazarene U (CA)
Polytechnic U of Puerto Rico, Miami Campus (FL)
Rogers State U (OK)
Southeastern U (FL)
Southern Adventist U (TN)
Tiffin U (OH)
Toccoa Falls Coll (GA)
Trevecca Nazarene U (TN)
U of Central Florida (FL)
U of Denver (CO)
U of Minnesota, Twin Cities Campus (MN)
William Jewell Coll (MO)

NORWEGIAN
Brigham Young U (UT)
Pacific Lutheran U (WA)
St. Olaf Coll (MN)
U of North Dakota (ND)
U of Washington (WA)

NUCLEAR AND INDUSTRIAL RADIOLOGIC TECHNOLOGIES RELATED
Manhattan Coll (NY)

NUCLEAR ENGINEERING
Georgia Inst of Technology (GA)
Idaho State U (ID)
Iowa State U of Science and Technology (IA)
Massachusetts Inst of Technology (MA)
Missouri U of Science and Technology (MO)
North Carolina State U (NC)
Oregon State U (OR)
Penn State Abington (PA)
Penn State Altoona (PA)
Penn State Beaver (PA)
Penn State Berks (PA)
Penn State Brandywine (PA)
Penn State DuBois (PA)
Penn State Erie, The Behrend Coll (PA)
Penn State Fayette, The Eberly Campus (PA)
Penn State Greater Allegheny (PA)
Penn State Hazleton (PA)
Penn State Lehigh Valley (PA)
Penn State Mont Alto (PA)
Penn State New Kensington (PA)
Penn State Schuylkill (PA)
Penn State Shenango (PA)
Penn State U Park (PA)

Penn State Wilkes-Barre (PA)
Penn State Worthington Scranton (PA)
Penn State York (PA)
Purdue U (IN)
Rensselaer Polytechnic Inst (NY)
Texas A&M U (TX)
United States Military Acad (NY)
U of Cincinnati (OH)
U of Florida (FL)
U of Massachusetts Lowell (MA)
U of Michigan (MI)
U of New Mexico (NM)
The U of Tennessee (TN)
U of Wisconsin–Madison (WI)

NUCLEAR ENGINEERING TECHNOLOGY
Excelsior Coll (NY)
Idaho State U (ID)
United States Military Acad (NY)

NUCLEAR MEDICAL TECHNOLOGY
Adventist U of Health Sciences (FL)
Baptist Coll of Health Sciences (TN)
Barry U (FL)
Benedictine U (IL)
Cedar Crest Coll (PA)
East Central U (OK)
Ferris State U (MI)
Indiana U of Pennsylvania (PA)
Indiana U–Purdue U Indianapolis (IN)
Lewis U (IL)
Manhattan Coll (NY)
MCPHS U (MA)
Molloy Coll (NY)
North Central Coll (IL)
Oakland U (MI)
Old Dominion U (VA)
Oregon Inst of Technology (OR)
Rhode Island Coll (RI)
Robert Morris U (PA)
Roosevelt U (IL)
Saint Louis U (MO)
Saint Mary's U of Minnesota (MN)
U at Buffalo, the State U of New York (NY)
The U of Alabama at Birmingham (AL)
U of Central Arkansas (AR)
U of Cincinnati (OH)
The U of Findlay (OH)
U of Missouri (MO)
U of Nevada, Las Vegas (NV)
U of Oklahoma Health Sciences Center (OK)
U of St. Francis (IL)
U of the Incarnate Word (TX)
U of Wisconsin–La Crosse (WI)
Weber State U (UT)
York Coll of Pennsylvania (PA)

NUCLEAR/NUCLEAR POWER TECHNOLOGY
Excelsior Coll (NY)
U of North Texas (TX)

NUCLEAR PHYSICS
Arkansas Tech U (AR)

NURSE MIDWIFE/NURSING MIDWIFERY
U of Toronto (ON, Canada)

NURSING ADMINISTRATION
Augsburg U (MN)
Northwest Christian U (OR)
Nova Southeastern U (FL)
Ohio Northern U (OH)
U of San Francisco (CA)

NURSING EDUCATION
Bradley U (IL)
Graceland U (IA)
Ohio Northern U (OH)

NURSING PRACTICE
Alaska Pacific U (AK)
American U of Health Sciences (CA)
Ball State U (IN)
Benedictine Coll (KS)
Bluefield Coll (VA)
Brenau U (GA)
Christian Brothers U (TN)
Concordia Coll–New York (NY)

Concordia U, St. Paul (MN)
Eastern U (PA)
Hiram Coll (OH)
Lebanese American U (Lebanon)
Misericordia U (PA)
Sentara Coll of Health Sciences (VA)
The U of Texas at Austin (TX)
William Penn U (IA)

NURSING SCIENCE
Aquinas Coll (MI)
Averett U (VA)
Brandon U (MB, Canada)
Brock U (ON, Canada)
Carson-Newman U (TN)
Cedar Crest Coll (PA)
Central Penn Coll (PA)
Coll of Saint Elizabeth (NJ)
Duquesne U (PA)
EDP U of Puerto Rico (PR)
EDP U of Puerto Rico–San Sebastian (PR)
Florida State U (FL)
Holy Names U (CA)
Inter American U of Puerto Rico, Barranquitas Campus (PR)
Kean U (NJ)
Millersville U of Pennsylvania (PA)
New Jersey City U (NJ)
Ohio Christian U (OH)
Oklahoma City U (OK)
Pensacola State Coll (FL)
Rutgers U–Newark (NJ)
Rutgers U–New Brunswick (NJ)
Sacred Heart U (CT)
Saint Louis U–Madrid Campus (Spain)
Saint Peter's U (NJ)
Siena Coll (NY)
Texas A&M U–Central Texas (TX)
U of California, Irvine (CA)
U of Illinois at Chicago (IL)
The U of Texas at Austin (TX)
Wayne State U (MI)

NUTRITION SCIENCES
Auburn U (AL)
Boston U (MA)
Bowling Green State U (OH)
California Baptist U (CA)
California State U, Los Angeles (CA)
Canisius Coll (NY)
Case Western Reserve U (OH)
Coll of Saint Benedict (MN)
Colorado State U (CO)
Cornell U (NY)
Drexel U (PA)
Elmhurst Coll (IL)
Huntington Coll of Health Sciences (TN)
Iowa State U of Science and Technology (IA)
Keiser U, Fort Lauderdale (FL)
La Salle U (PA)
Lebanese American U (Lebanon)
Long Island U–LIU Post (NY)
Louisiana State U and A&M Coll (LA)
Merrimack Coll (MA)
Metropolitan State U of Denver (CO)
Michigan State U (MI)
New York U (NY)
North Carolina State U (NC)
The Ohio State U (OH)
Pepperdine U, Malibu (CA)
Purdue U (IN)
Rutgers U–New Brunswick (NJ)
The Sage Colls (NY)
Saint John's U (MN)
Simmons Coll (MA)
Southern Illinois U Carbondale (IL)
Syracuse U (NY)
Texas Tech U (TX)
Texas Woman's U (TX)
The U of Arizona (AZ)
U of California, Davis (CA)
U of Central Oklahoma (OK)
U of Cincinnati (OH)
U of Florida (FL)
U of Guelph (ON, Canada)
U of Hawaii at Manoa (HI)
U of Illinois at Chicago (IL)
U of Massachusetts Amherst (MA)
U of Massachusetts Lowell (MA)

U of Minnesota, Twin Cities
  Campus (MN)
U of Nevada, Las Vegas (NV)
U of Nevada, Reno (NV)
U of New Hampshire (NH)
The U of North Carolina at
  Greensboro (NC)
U of Northern Colorado (CO)
U of Oklahoma Health Sciences
  Center (OK)
U of Saint Francis (IN)
U of Saskatchewan (SK, Canada)
U of Southern Indiana (IN)
The U of Texas at Austin (TX)
U of the Incarnate Word (TX)
U of Vermont (VT)
U of Wisconsin–Madison (WI)
U of Wisconsin–Milwaukee (WI)
U of Wisconsin–Stevens Point (WI)

**OCCUPATIONAL HEALTH
AND INDUSTRIAL HYGIENE**
Grand Valley State U (MI)
Illinois State U (IL)
Montana Tech of The U of Montana
  (MT)
Ohio U (OH)
U of Central Oklahoma (OK)

**OCCUPATIONAL SAFETY
AND HEALTH TECHNOLOGY**
Columbia Southern U (AL)
Embry-Riddle Aeronautical U–
  Daytona (FL)
Grand Valley State U (MI)
Indiana State U (IN)
Indiana U of Pennsylvania (PA)
Keene State Coll (NH)
Marshall U (WV)
Millersville U of Pennsylvania (PA)
Murray State U (KY)
Pittsburg State U (KS)
Rochester Inst of Technology (NY)
Slippery Rock U of Pennsylvania
  (PA)
Southeastern Louisiana U (LA)
Southeastern Oklahoma State U
  (OK)
Southwest Baptist U (MO)
U of Central Missouri (MO)
U of Wisconsin–Whitewater (WI)
Waldorf U (IA)

**OCCUPATIONAL THERAPIST
ASSISTANT**
Idaho State U (ID)
Pennsylvania Coll of Technology
  (PA)
Rutgers U–Newark (NJ)

OCCUPATIONAL THERAPY
Alabama State U (AL)
American Intl Coll (MA)
Bay Path U (MA)
Calvin Coll (MI)
Carthage Coll (WI)
Concordia U Wisconsin (WI)
Dominican Coll (NY)
Dominican U of California (CA)
Duquesne U (PA)
D'Youville Coll (NY)
Eastern Michigan U (MI)
Eastern Washington U (WA)
Elizabethtown Coll (PA)
Elmhurst Coll (IL)
Gannon U (PA)
Grand Valley State U (MI)
Illinois Coll (IL)
Ithaca Coll (NY)
Long Island U–LIU Brooklyn (NY)
Louisiana Coll (LA)
McKendree U (IL)
Mount Mary U (WI)
Nazareth Coll of Rochester (NY)
Penn State Mont Alto (PA)
Quinnipiac U (CT)
Sacred Heart U (CT)
Saginaw Valley State U (MI)
St. Catherine U (MN)
Saint Francis U (PA)
Saint Louis U (MO)
Saint Vincent Coll (PA)
Shawnee State U (OH)
Towson U (MD)
U at Buffalo, the State U of New
  York (NY)
U of Missouri (MO)
U of New Hampshire (NH)

The U of Scranton (PA)
U of Southern California (CA)
U of Southern Indiana (IN)
U of Wisconsin–Milwaukee (WI)
Wartburg Coll (IA)
Western Michigan U (MI)
West Virginia U (WV)
Worcester State U (MA)

OCEAN ENGINEERING
California State U, Long Beach
  (CA)
Florida Atlantic U (FL)
Florida Inst of Technology (FL)
Texas A&M U (TX)
U of New Hampshire (NH)
U of Rhode Island (RI)
Virginia Polytechnic Inst and State
  U (VA)

**OCEANOGRAPHY (CHEMICAL
AND PHYSICAL)**
Coll of the Atlantic (ME)
Florida Inst of Technology (FL)
Hawai`i Pacific U (HI)
Humboldt State U (CA)
Kutztown U of Pennsylvania (PA)
Louisiana State U and A&M Coll
  (LA)
Millersville U of Pennsylvania (PA)
North Carolina State U (NC)
United States Coast Guard Acad
  (CT)
U of Miami (FL)
U of Michigan (MI)
The U of North Carolina
  Wilmington (NC)
U of South Carolina (SC)
U of Southern Mississippi (MS)
U of Washington (WA)
Whitman Coll (WA)

OFFICE MANAGEMENT
Adams State U (CO)
Babson Coll (MA)
Bowling Green State U (OH)
Clayton State U (GA)
East Central U (OK)
Eastern Michigan U (MI)
Inter American U of Puerto Rico,
  Aguadilla Campus (PR)
Inter American U of Puerto Rico,
  Barranquitas Campus (PR)
Inter American U of Puerto Rico,
  Fajardo Campus (PR)
Inter American U of Puerto Rico,
  Metropolitan Campus (PR)
Inter American U of Puerto Rico,
  San Germán Campus (PR)
Loyola U Chicago (IL)
Maranatha Baptist U (WI)
National U (CA)
Point Loma Nazarene U (CA)
Rider U (NJ)
Roosevelt U (IL)
Southwest Baptist U (MO)
Tarleton State U (TX)
Texas A&M U–Central Texas (TX)
U of Central Missouri (MO)
U of South Carolina (SC)
Valley City State U (ND)

**OFFICE OCCUPATIONS AND
CLERICAL SERVICES**
East Central U (OK)

OPERATIONS MANAGEMENT
Arizona State U at the Polytechnic
  campus (AZ)
Auburn U (AL)
Avila U (MO)
Babson Coll (MA)
Ball State U (IN)
Boston Coll (MA)
Bowling Green State U (OH)
California State U, Dominguez Hills
  (CA)
California State U, Long Beach
  (CA)
California State U, Stanislaus (CA)
Carnegie Mellon U (PA)
Central Connecticut State U (CT)
Central Michigan U (MI)
Cleveland State U (OH)
Concordia U (QC, Canada)
Drexel U (PA)
Ferris State U (MI)
Fort Lewis Coll (CO)
Golden Gate U (CA)

Gonzaga U (WA)
Governors State U (IL)
Grand Valley State U (MI)
Granite State Coll (NH)
Indiana U–Purdue U Indianapolis
  (IN)
Inter American U of Puerto Rico,
  Bayamón Campus (PR)
Inter American U of Puerto Rico,
  Metropolitan Campus (PR)
Lamar U (TX)
Le Moyne Coll (NY)
Loyola U Chicago (IL)
Marian U (WI)
Miami U (OH)
Minnesota State U Moorhead (MN)
Mount Mercy U (IA)
Northeastern State U (OK)
Northern Illinois U (IL)
Oakland City U (IN)
Oakland U (MI)
The Ohio State U (OH)
Oregon Inst of Technology (OR)
Oregon State U (OR)
Purdue U Northwest (IN)
Rhode Island Coll (RI)
Roger Williams U (RI)
Saginaw Valley State U (MI)
Sam Houston State U (TX)
San Diego State U (CA)
Southwestern Coll (KS)
Tennessee Technological U (TN)
Thomas Edison State U (NJ)
Trine U (IN)
The U of Akron (OH)
The U of Arizona (AZ)
U of Central Oklahoma (OK)
U of Cincinnati (OH)
U of Dayton (OH)
U of Houston (TX)
U of Massachusetts Dartmouth
  (MA)
U of Minnesota, Crookston (MN)
U of Minnesota, Twin Cities
  Campus (MN)
U of Nebraska at Kearney (NE)
The U of North Carolina at
  Charlotte (NC)
U of North Dakota (ND)
U of North Texas (TX)
U of Pennsylvania (PA)
U of St. Thomas (MN)
U of Saskatchewan (SK, Canada)
The U of Scranton (PA)
U of Southern Indiana (IN)
U of Utah (UT)
U of Wisconsin–Madison (WI)
U of Wisconsin–Milwaukee (WI)
U of Wisconsin–Stout (WI)
U of Wisconsin–Whitewater (WI)
Utah State U (UT)
Utah Valley U (UT)
Washington State U (WA)
Washington State U–Global
  Campus (WA)
Washington State U–Tri-Cities
  (WA)
Washington State U–Vancouver
  (WA)
Washington U in St. Louis (MO)
Wentworth Inst of Technology (MA)
Western Washington U (WA)
Widener U (PA)
Youngstown State U (OH)

OPERATIONS RESEARCH
Babson Coll (MA)
Bowling Green State U (OH)
Bryant U (RI)
California State U, Fullerton (CA)
Canisius Coll (NY)
Carnegie Mellon U (PA)
Columbia U (NY)
Cornell U (NY)
HEC Montreal (QC, Canada)
New York U (NY)
Princeton U (NJ)
Southern Methodist U (TX)
United States Coast Guard Acad
  (CT)
United States Military Acad (NY)
U of Toronto (ON, Canada)
U of Washington (WA)
U of Waterloo (ON, Canada)

**OPHTHALMIC AND
OPTOMETRIC SUPPORT**

**SERVICES AND ALLIED
PROFESSIONS RELATED**
Tennessee Wesleyan U (TN)

OPTICAL SCIENCES
Albright Coll (PA)
The Ohio State U (OH)
Saginaw Valley State U (MI)
The U of Arizona (AZ)
U of Rochester (NY)

ORGANIC CHEMISTRY
Concordia U (QC, Canada)
U of California, Santa Barbara (CA)

ORGANIZATIONAL BEHAVIOR
Athabasca U (AB, Canada)
Benedictine U (IL)
Bluffton U (OH)
Bowling Green State U (OH)
Carroll U (WI)
Coe Coll (IA)
The Coll of St. Scholastica (MN)
Concordia U Chicago (IL)
Eastern Mennonite U (VA)
Edgewood Coll (WI)
Greenville U (IL)
High Point U (NC)
Manhattan Coll (NY)
Mount St. Joseph U (OH)
National U (CA)
Northern Kentucky U (KY)
Northwestern U (IL)
Nyack Coll (NY)
Oral Roberts U (OK)
Palm Beach Atlantic U (FL)
Penn State Abington (PA)
Penn State Altoona (PA)
Penn State Beaver (PA)
Penn State Berks (PA)
Penn State Brandywine (PA)
Penn State DuBois (PA)
Penn State Erie, The Behrend Coll
  (PA)
Penn State Fayette, The Eberly
  Campus (PA)
Penn State Greater Allegheny (PA)
Penn State Harrisburg (PA)
Penn State Hazleton (PA)
Penn State Lehigh Valley (PA)
Penn State Mont Alto (PA)
Penn State New Kensington (PA)
Penn State Schuylkill (PA)
Penn State Shenango (PA)
Penn State U Park (PA)
Penn State Wilkes-Barre (PA)
Penn State Worthington Scranton
  (PA)
Penn State York (PA)
Pitzer Coll (CA)
Rider U (NJ)
Robert Morris U (PA)
Roosevelt U (IL)
Saint Joseph's U (PA)
Saint Louis U (MO)
Santa Clara U (CA)
Scripps Coll (CA)
Union Coll (NE)
United States Military Acad (NY)
U of Cincinnati (OH)
U of Michigan (MI)
U of North Texas (TX)
U of Oklahoma (OK)
U of Richmond (VA)
U of St. Francis (IL)
U of San Francisco (CA)
U of the Incarnate Word (TX)
The U of Toledo (OH)
The U of Tulsa (OK)
Waldorf U (IA)
Wayne State U (MI)
Wilmington U (DE)

**ORGANIZATIONAL
COMMUNICATION**
Aquinas Coll (MI)
Assumption Coll (MA)
Bloomsburg U of Pennsylvania (PA)
Bradley U (IL)
Brigham Young U (UT)
Buena Vista U (IA)
Butler U (IN)
Calvin Coll (MI)
Capital U (OH)
Cleveland State U (OH)
Concordia U, Nebraska (NE)
Creighton U (NE)
DePaul U (IL)

Emmanuel Coll (GA)
Florida Coll (FL)
Florida Southern Coll (FL)
Howard Payne U (TX)
Idaho State U (ID)
Lewis U (IL)
Lubbock Christian U (TX)
Marian U (WI)
Marylhurst U (OR)
McKendree U (IL)
Missouri State U (MO)
Murray State U (KY)
Muskingum U (OH)
Nichols Coll (MA)
North Central Coll (IL)
Northwest Missouri State U (MO)
Northwest U (WA)
Ohio Northern U (OH)
Olivet Nazarene U (IL)
Pepperdine U, Malibu (CA)
Pfeiffer U (NC)
Providence Coll (RI)
Roosevelt U (IL)
St. Ambrose U (IA)
Shorter U (GA)
Southeast Missouri State U (MO)
Suffolk U (MA)
Temple U (PA)
Trevecca Nazarene U (TN)
The U of Akron (OH)
U of Central Oklahoma (OK)
U of Idaho (ID)
U of Mount Union (OH)
The U of Texas at Austin (TX)
Weber State U (UT)
Western Kentucky U (KY)
Western Michigan U (MI)

**ORGANIZATIONAL
LEADERSHIP**
Alverno Coll (WI)
Anderson U (SC)
Arizona State U at the Polytechnic
  campus (AZ)
Auburn U at Montgomery (AL)
Averett U (VA)
Avila U (MO)
Bay Path U (MA)
Belhaven U (MS)
Bethel Coll (IN)
Beufah Heights U (GA)
Blackburn Coll (IL)
Bradley U (IL)
Brandman U (CA)
Brenau U (GA)
Bryant U (RI)
California Baptist U (CA)
Calvary U (MO)
Cardinal Stritch U (WI)
Carroll U (WI)
Chestnut Hill Coll (PA)
Cleveland State U (OH)
Coll of Biblical Studies–Houston
  (TX)
Columbia Southern U (AL)
Cottey Coll (MO)
Creighton U (NE)
Davenport U, Grand Rapids (MI)
Eastern U (PA)
Fisher Coll (MA)
Florida Inst of Technology (FL)
Graceland U (IA)
Hilbert Coll (NY)
Horizon U (IN)
Indiana Tech (IN)
Indiana Wesleyan U (IN)
La Salle U (PA)
Lewis U (IL)
Lincoln Christian U (IL)
Lipscomb U (TN)
Lubbock Christian U (TX)
Marquette U (WI)
MidAmerica Nazarene U (KS)
Missouri Baptist U (MO)
National U (CA)
North Carolina Wesleyan Coll (NC)
Ohio Christian U (OH)
Oral Roberts U (OK)
Point U (GA)
Providence Coll (RI)
Purdue U (IN)
Purdue U Northwest (IN)
Regent U (VA)
Saint Louis U (MO)
St. Thomas U (FL)
Salve Regina U (RI)
Samford U (AL)

Seattle U (WA)
Southeastern Louisiana U (LA)
Southeastern U (FL)
Southwestern Coll (KS)
Spring Hill Coll (AL)
Syracuse U (NY)
Toccoa Falls Coll (GA)
Trinity Coll of Florida (FL)
U of Central Oklahoma (OK)
U of Dayton (OH)
U of Evansville (IN)
U of Houston (TX)
U of La Verne (CA)
U of Louisiana at Monroe (LA)
U of Maine at Farmington (ME)
U of Mary Hardin-Baylor (TX)
U of Northern Iowa (IA)
U of South Dakota (SD)
U of West Georgia (GA)
U of Wisconsin–Platteville (WI)
Valdosta State U (GA)
Western Kentucky U (KY)
Woodbury U (CA)
Wright State U (OH)
Wright State U–Lake Campus (OH)

ORNAMENTAL HORTICULTURE
Delaware Valley U (PA)
Tarleton State U (TX)
Texas A&M U (TX)
U of Arkansas (AR)

ORTHOPTICS
St. Catherine U (MN)

ORTHOTICS/PROSTHETICS
Concordia U, St. Paul (MN)
U of Washington (WA)

OUTDOOR EDUCATION
Liberty U (VA)
Messiah Coll (PA)
Murray State U (KY)
Northern Vermont U–Lyndon (VT)
Northland Coll (WI)
Sierra Nevada Coll (NV)
Toccoa Falls Coll (GA)
Unity Coll (ME)
Weber State U (UT)

PACIFIC AREA/PACIFIC RIM STUDIES
Hawai`i Pacific U (HI)
U of Guam (GU)
U of Hawaii at Manoa (HI)

PACKAGING SCIENCE
Clemson U (SC)
Indiana State U (IN)
Michigan State U (MI)
U of Wisconsin–Stout (WI)

PAINTING
Adams State U (CO)
Alberta Coll of Art & Design (AB, Canada)
American Acad of Art (IL)
Anderson U (SC)
Aquinas Coll (MI)
Arcadia U (PA)
Bennington Coll (VT)
Biola U (CA)
Birmingham-Southern Coll (AL)
Boston U (MA)
Bowling Green State U (OH)
Bradley U (IL)
Brigham Young U (UT)
Buffalo State Coll, State U of New York (NY)
California Coll of the Arts (CA)
California State U, Long Beach (CA)
Carson-Newman U (TN)
Coe Coll (IA)
Coll of the Ozarks (MO)
Columbia Coll (MO)
Concordia U (QC, Canada)
Drake U (IA)
Escuela de Artes Plasticas y Diseño de Puerto Rico (PR)
Ferris State U (MI)
Franklin Coll (IN)
Harding U (AR)
Hofstra U (NY)
Indiana Wesleyan U (IN)
Inter American U of Puerto Rico, San Germán Campus (PR)
Kansas City Art Inst (MO)

Laguna Coll of Art & Design (CA)
Lewis U (IL)
Marlboro Coll (VT)
Maryland Inst Coll of Art (MD)
Marywood U (PA)
Massachusetts Coll of Art and Design (MA)
Minneapolis Coll of Art and Design (MN)
Northern Michigan U (MI)
Northwest Nazarene U (ID)
Oakland U (MI)
Ohio Northern U (OH)
Pacific Northwest Coll of Art (OR)
Pratt Inst (NY)
Providence Coll (RI)
Rhode Island Coll (RI)
Rhode Island School of Design (RI)
Rochester Inst of Technology (NY)
Rutgers U–New Brunswick (NJ)
St. Ambrose U (IA)
San Francisco Art Inst (CA)
Savannah Coll of Art and Design (GA)
School of Visual Arts (NY)
Seton Hill U (PA)
State U of New York at New Paltz (NY)
Syracuse U (NY)
Temple U (PA)
Texas Christian U (TX)
U of Dallas (TX)
U of Hartford (CT)
U of Houston (TX)
U of Illinois at Chicago (IL)
The U of Kansas (KS)
U of Massachusetts Dartmouth (MA)
U of Miami (FL)
U of New Haven (CT)
U of Oregon (OR)
U of Puget Sound (WA)
U of Regina (SK, Canada)
U of San Francisco (CA)
The U of Tampa (FL)
U of Washington (WA)
Virginia Commonwealth U (VA)
Washington U in St. Louis (MO)
Western State Colorado U (CO)
West Virginia Wesleyan Coll (WV)
Youngstown State U (OH)

PALEONTOLOGY
Bowling Green State U (OH)

PALLIATIVE CARE NURSING
Madonna U (MI)

PAPER SCIENCE AND ENGINEERING
U of Wisconsin–Stevens Point (WI)
Western Michigan U (MI)

PARASITOLOGY
Bowling Green State U (OH)

PARKS, RECREATION AND LEISURE
Alaska Pacific U (AK)
Alcorn State U (MS)
Arizona State U at the Downtown Phoenix campus (AZ)
Asbury U (KY)
Aurora U (IL)
Bemidji State U (MN)
Biola U (CA)
Black Hills State U (SD)
Bowling Green State U (OH)
Bridgewater State U (MA)
Brock U (ON, Canada)
California Polytechnic State U, San Luis Obispo (CA)
California State U, East Bay (CA)
California State U, Long Beach (CA)
California State U, Northridge (CA)
California State U, Sacramento (CA)
Campbellsville U (KY)
Catawba Coll (NC)
Central Michigan U (MI)
Central State U (OH)
Concordia U (QC, Canada)
East Carolina U (NC)
East Central U (OK)
Eastern Washington U (WA)
Elon U (NC)
Emporia State U (KS)
Evangel U (MO)

Fort Lewis Coll (CO)
Frostburg State U (MD)
Georgia Coll & State U (GA)
Georgia Southern U (GA)
Gordon Coll (MA)
Grambling State U (LA)
Green Mountain Coll (VT)
Humboldt State U (CA)
Indiana U Bloomington (IN)
Ithaca Coll (NY)
Kutztown U of Pennsylvania (PA)
Limestone Coll (SC)
Lindenwood U (MO)
Lindsey Wilson Coll (KY)
Manchester U (IN)
Messiah Coll (PA)
Metropolitan State U of Denver (CO)
Michigan State U (MI)
Missouri State U (MO)
Missouri Valley Coll (MO)
Morris Coll (SC)
Newberry Coll (SC)
New Mexico Highlands U (NM)
Northern Arizona U (AZ)
Northern Michigan U (MI)
North Greenville U (SC)
Northwest Nazarene U (ID)
Ohio U (OH)
Oklahoma Baptist U (OK)
Oklahoma State U (OK)
Olivet Nazarene U (IL)
Oregon State U (OR)
Pittsburg State U (KS)
Radford U (VA)
Rhode Island Coll (RI)
St. Andrews U (NC)
St. Thomas Aquinas Coll (NY)
Salisbury U (MD)
San Diego State U (CA)
San Francisco State U (CA)
Shaw U (NC)
Shepherd U (WV)
Shorter U (GA)
Southeastern Oklahoma State U (OK)
Southeast Missouri State U (MO)
Southern Illinois U Carbondale (IL)
Southern Utah U (UT)
Southwest Baptist U (MO)
State U of New York Coll at Cortland (NY)
Texas A&M U (TX)
U of Arkansas (AR)
U of Central Missouri (MO)
U of Central Oklahoma (OK)
U of Maine at Machias (ME)
U of Minnesota, Duluth (MN)
U of Minnesota, Twin Cities Campus (MN)
U of Missouri (MO)
U of Montana (MT)
U of Nebraska at Kearney (NE)
U of Nevada, Las Vegas (NV)
The U of North Carolina at Greensboro (NC)
U of Northern Iowa (IA)
U of South Alabama (AL)
U of South Dakota (SD)
U of Southern Mississippi (MS)
U of Utah (UT)
U of Waterloo (ON, Canada)
Upper Iowa U (IA)
Utah State U (UT)
Virginia Wesleyan U (VA)
Washington State U (WA)
Western State Colorado U (CO)
Western Washington U (WA)
York Coll of Pennsylvania (PA)

PARKS, RECREATION AND LEISURE FACILITIES MANAGEMENT
Alabama State U (AL)
Appalachian State U (NC)
Arkansas Tech U (AR)
Brigham Young U–Idaho (ID)
California State U, Sacramento (CA)
California U of Pennsylvania (PA)
Carroll U (WI)
Central Michigan U (MI)
Clemson U (SC)
The Coll at Brockport, State U of New York (NY)
Coll of the Ozarks (MO)
Colorado State U (CO)

PARKS, RECREATION AND LEISURE FACILITIES MANAGEMENT RELATED
Emmaus Bible Coll (IA)

Concord U (WV)
Delaware State U (DE)
Eastern Michigan U (MI)
Eastern Washington U (WA)
East Stroudsburg U of Pennsylvania (PA)
Florida Intl U (FL)
Franklin Pierce U (NH)
Hannibal-LaGrange U (MO)
Humboldt State U (CA)
Husson U (ME)
Illinois State U (IL)
Indiana State U (IN)
Indiana Wesleyan U (IN)
Kansas State U (KS)
Kean U (NJ)
Kent State U (OH)
Lock Haven U of Pennsylvania (PA)
Marshall U (WV)
Middle Tennessee State U (TN)
Missouri Valley Coll (MO)
Missouri Western State U (MO)
Mount Marty Coll (SD)
New Mexico Highlands U (NM)
New York U (NY)
North Carolina Central U (NC)
North Carolina State U (NC)
Northern Vermont U–Lyndon (VT)
Northwest Missouri State U (MO)
Old Dominion U (VA)
Oral Roberts U (OK)
Penn State Abington (PA)
Penn State Altoona (PA)
Penn State Beaver (PA)
Penn State Berks (PA)
Penn State Brandywine (PA)
Penn State DuBois (PA)
Penn State Erie, The Behrend Coll (PA)
Penn State Fayette, The Eberly Campus (PA)
Penn State Greater Allegheny (PA)
Penn State Hazleton (PA)
Penn State Lehigh Valley (PA)
Penn State Mont Alto (PA)
Penn State New Kensington (PA)
Penn State Schuylkill (PA)
Penn State Shenango (PA)
Penn State U Park (PA)
Penn State Wilkes-Barre (PA)
Penn State Worthington Scranton (PA)
Penn State York (PA)
St. Joseph's Coll, Long Island Campus (NY)
St. Joseph's Coll, New York (NY)
Slippery Rock U of Pennsylvania (PA)
State U of New York Coll at Cortland (NY)
State U of New York Coll of Technology at Delhi (NY)
Texas A&M U (TX)
Texas State U (TX)
Thomas U (GA)
Trine U (IN)
Trinity Christian Coll (IL)
Union U (TN)
U of Florida (FL)
U of Idaho (ID)
U of Maine (ME)
U of Maine at Machias (ME)
U of Minnesota, Crookston (MN)
U of New Hampshire (NH)
The U of North Carolina Wilmington (NC)
U of North Dakota (ND)
U of Northern Colorado (CO)
U of North Texas (TX)
U of St. Francis (IL)
U of Waterloo (ON, Canada)
U of West Georgia (GA)
U of Wisconsin–La Crosse (WI)
Wayland Baptist U (TX)
Western Illinois U (IL)
Western Kentucky U (KY)
Western Michigan U (MI)
Western State Colorado U (CO)
West Virginia State U (WV)
West Virginia U (WV)
Winona State U (MN)

Trine U (IN)

PARKS, RECREATION, LEISURE, AND FITNESS STUDIES RELATED
Belhaven U (MS)
Brigham Young U (UT)
Coker Coll (SC)
Ottawa U (KS)
Trinity Christian Coll (IL)
U of North Alabama (AL)
U of Waterloo (ON, Canada)
Utah State U (UT)
Western State Colorado U (CO)

PASTORAL COUNSELING AND SPECIALIZED MINISTRIES RELATED
Bethel Coll (IN)
Brescia U (KY)
Calvary U (MO)
John Brown U (AR)
Judson U (IL)
Lee U (TN)
Lipscomb U (TN)
Madonna U (MI)
Malone U (OH)
Maranatha Baptist U (WI)
Messenger Coll (TX)
Mid-America Christian U (OK)
Multnomah U (OR)
Ouachita Baptist U (AR)

PASTORAL STUDIES/COUNSELING
The Baptist Coll of Florida (FL)
Barclay Coll (KS)
Biola U (CA)
Calvary U (MO)
Campbellsville U (KY)
Charlotte Christian Coll and Theological Sem (NC)
Coll of Biblical Studies–Houston (TX)
Concordia U Wisconsin (WI)
Corban U (OR)
Dallas Baptist U (TX)
Dominican U (IL)
Eastern Nazarene Coll (MA)
East Texas Baptist U (TX)
Emmanuel Coll (GA)
Greenville U (IL)
Indiana Wesleyan U (IN)
Johnson U Florida (FL)
John Wesley U (NC)
Kentucky Mountain Bible Coll (KY)
Lee U (TN)
Liberty U (VA)
Loyola U Chicago (IL)
Maranatha Baptist U (WI)
Marian U (IN)
Master's Coll and Sem (ON, Canada)
The Master's U (CA)
Messenger Coll (TX)
MidAmerica Nazarene U (KS)
Mount St. Joseph U (OH)
Mount Vernon Nazarene U (OH)
Multnomah U (OR)
Nebraska Christian Coll of Hope Intl U (NE)
Newman U (KS)
Northwest Christian U (OR)
Northwest Nazarene U (ID)
Northwest U (WA)
Olivet Nazarene U (IL)
Oral Roberts U (OK)
Ouachita Baptist U (AR)
Providence Coll (RI)
Saint Francis U (PA)
Southwest Baptist U (MO)
Southwestern Assemblies of God U (TX)
Taylor U (IN)
Theological U of the Caribbean (PR)
Trinity Coll of Florida (FL)
U of Mary Hardin-Baylor (TX)
U of Saint Mary (KS)
U of St. Thomas (TX)
U of the Incarnate Word (TX)
U of Valley Forge (PA)
Vanguard U of Southern California (CA)
Walsh U (OH)
Welch Coll (TN)

PATHOLOGIST ASSISTANT
Wayne State U (MI)

PATHOLOGY/EXPERIMENTAL PATHOLOGY
Penn State Berks (PA)

PEACE STUDIES AND CONFLICT RESOLUTION
Arcadia U (PA)
Bennington Coll (VT)
Berea Coll (KY)
Bethel U (MN)
Butler U (IN)
California State U, Dominguez Hills (CA)
Chapman U (CA)
Clark U (MA)
Colgate U (NY)
Coll of Saint Benedict (MN)
The Coll of St. Scholastica (MN)
Creighton U (NE)
DePaul U (IL)
DePauw U (IN)
Earlham Coll (IN)
Eastern Mennonite U (VA)
Embry-Riddle Aeronautical U–Daytona (FL)
George Mason U (VA)
Gettysburg Coll (PA)
Goshen Coll (IN)
Guilford Coll (NC)
Hamline U (MN)
Hampshire Coll (MA)
Haverford Coll (PA)
John Carroll U (OH)
Juniata Coll (PA)
Kent State U (OH)
Manchester U (IN)
Manhattan Coll (NY)
Marquette U (WI)
Messiah Coll (PA)
Nazareth Coll of Rochester (NY)
Pace U (NY)
Regis U (CO)
Saint Anselm Coll (NH)
Saint John's U (MN)
Salisbury U (MD)
Tufts U (MA)
U of Massachusetts Lowell (MA)
U of Missouri (MO)
The U of North Carolina at Chapel Hill (NC)
The U of North Carolina at Greensboro (NC)
U of St. Thomas (MN)
U of Toronto (ON, Canada)
U of Utah (UT)
Wartburg Coll (IA)
Wellesley Coll (MA)
Whitworth U (WA)
Willamette U (OR)

PEDIATRIC NURSING
Youngstown State U (OH)

PERCUSSION INSTRUMENTS
Acadia U (NS, Canada)
Conservatorio de Musica de Puerto Rico (PR)
Northwestern U (IL)
Oberlin Coll (OH)
Oklahoma Christian U (OK)
Roosevelt U (IL)
San Francisco Conservatory of Music (CA)
State U of New York at Fredonia (NY)
Syracuse U (NY)
The U of Kansas (KS)
U of Southern California (CA)
U of Washington (WA)
Vanderbilt U (TN)
Xavier U of Louisiana (LA)
Youngstown State U (OH)

PERFUSION TECHNOLOGY
Carlow U (PA)

PERSONALITY PSYCHOLOGY
Pace U, Pleasantville Campus (NY)

PETROLEUM ENGINEERING
The American U in Cairo (Egypt)
Lebanese American U (Lebanon)
Louisiana State U and A&M Coll (LA)
Marietta Coll (OH)
Mississippi State U (MS)
Missouri U of Science and Technology (MO)

Montana Tech of The U of Montana (MT)
New Mexico Inst of Mining and Technology (NM)
Penn State Abington (PA)
Penn State Altoona (PA)
Penn State Beaver (PA)
Penn State Berks (PA)
Penn State Brandywine (PA)
Penn State DuBois (PA)
Penn State Erie, The Behrend Coll (PA)
Penn State Fayette, The Eberly Campus (PA)
Penn State Greater Allegheny (PA)
Penn State Hazleton (PA)
Penn State Lehigh Valley (PA)
Penn State Mont Alto (PA)
Penn State New Kensington (PA)
Penn State Schuylkill (PA)
Penn State Shenango (PA)
Penn State U Park (PA)
Penn State Wilkes-Barre (PA)
Penn State Worthington Scranton (PA)
Penn State York (PA)
Saint Francis U (PA)
Slippery Rock U of Pennsylvania (PA)
Stanford U (CA)
Texas A&M U (TX)
Texas A&M U–Kingsville (TX)
Texas Tech U (TX)
U of Alaska Fairbanks (AK)
U of Houston (TX)
The U of Kansas (KS)
U of North Dakota (ND)
U of Oklahoma (OK)
U of Regina (SK, Canada)
The U of Texas at Austin (TX)
The U of Texas of the Permian Basin (TX)
U of Toronto (ON, Canada)
The U of Tulsa (OK)
U of Wyoming (WY)
West Virginia U (WV)

PETROLEUM TECHNOLOGY
Mercyhurst U (PA)
Muskingum U (OH)

PHARMACEUTICAL MARKETING AND MANAGEMENT
DeSales U (PA)
Western New England U (MA)

PHARMACEUTICAL SCIENCES
Belmont U (TN)
Cedarville U (OH)
Cleveland State U (OH)
Duquesne U (PA)
D'Youville Coll (NY)
Lebanese American U (Lebanon)
U of California, Irvine (CA)
U of Georgia (GA)
U of Michigan (MI)
U of Pittsburgh (PA)
The U of Texas at Austin (TX)
West Virginia Wesleyan Coll (WV)

PHARMACEUTICS AND DRUG DESIGN
Purdue U (IN)
Temple U (PA)
U of Montana (MT)
U of Rhode Island (RI)
The U of Toledo (OH)
West Chester U of Pennsylvania (PA)

PHARMACOLOGY
Maryville Coll (TN)
Stony Brook U, State U of New York (NY)
U of California, Santa Barbara (CA)
U of Saskatchewan (SK, Canada)

PHARMACOLOGY AND TOXICOLOGY
Arizona State U at the West campus (AZ)
Iowa State U of Science and Technology (IA)
U at Buffalo, the State U of New York (NY)
The U of Toledo (OH)
U of Wisconsin–Madison (WI)

PHARMACOLOGY AND TOXICOLOGY RELATED
The George Washington U (DC)
MCPHS U (MA)
U at Buffalo, the State U of New York (NY)

PHARMACY
Butler U (IN)
The Coll of Idaho (ID)
Drake U (IA)
Manchester U (IN)
MCPHS U (MA)
Northeastern U (MA)
The Ohio State U (OH)
Presbyterian Coll (SC)
St. John's U (NY)
Saint Vincent Coll (PA)
Samford U (AL)
U of Cincinnati (OH)
The U of Kansas (KS)
U of Kentucky (KY)
U of Louisiana at Monroe (LA)
U of Montana (MT)
U of Oklahoma Health Sciences Center (OK)
U of Saskatchewan (SK, Canada)
The U of Texas at Austin (TX)
U of the Pacific (CA)
The U of Toledo (OH)
U of Toronto (ON, Canada)
Washington State U (WA)
Washington State U–Spokane (WA)

PHARMACY ADMINISTRATION AND PHARMACY POLICY AND REGULATORY AFFAIRS
Drake U (IA)
U of Michigan (MI)

PHARMACY, PHARMACEUTICAL SCIENCES, AND ADMINISTRATION RELATED
Alverno Coll (WI)
American U of Health Sciences (CA)
Duquesne U (PA)
Francis Marion U (SC)
Long Island U–LIU Brooklyn (NY)
MCPHS U (MA)
North Dakota State U (ND)
Ohio Northern U (OH)

PHARMACY TECHNICIAN
Columbia Central U, Caguas (PR)

PHILOSOPHY
Acadia U (NS, Canada)
Adelphi U (NY)
Agnes Scott Coll (GA)
Albion Coll (MI)
Albright Coll (PA)
Alfred U (NY)
Allegheny Coll (PA)
Alma Coll (MI)
Alverno Coll (WI)
American U (DC)
The American U in Cairo (Egypt)
American U of Beirut (Lebanon)
The American U of Paris (France)
Amherst Coll (MA)
Angelo State U (TX)
Antioch Coll, Yellow Springs (OH)
Appalachian State U (NC)
Aquinas Coll (MI)
Arcadia U (PA)
Arizona State U at the Tempe campus (AZ)
Asbury U (KY)
Ashland U (OH)
Assumption Coll (MA)
Auburn U (AL)
Augsburg U (MN)
Augustana Coll (IL)
Augustana U (SD)
Aurora U (IL)
Austin Coll (TX)
Austin Peay State U (TN)
Azusa Pacific U (CA)
Baker U (KS)
Baldwin Wallace U (OH)
Ball State U (IN)
Bard Coll (NY)
Barnard Coll (NY)
Barry U (FL)

Baruch Coll of the City U of New York (NY)
Bates Coll (ME)
Baylor U (TX)
Belhaven U (MS)
Bellarmine U (KY)
Belmont U (TN)
Beloit Coll (WI)
Bemidji State U (MN)
Benedictine Coll (KS)
Benedictine U (IL)
Bennington Coll (VT)
Bentley U (MA)
Berea Coll (KY)
Bethel Coll (IN)
Bethel U (MN)
Binghamton U, State U of New York (NY)
Biola U (CA)
Birmingham-Southern Coll (AL)
Bloomsburg U of Pennsylvania (PA)
Boise State U (ID)
Boston Coll (MA)
Boston U (MA)
Bowdoin Coll (ME)
Bowling Green State U (OH)
Bradley U (IL)
Brandeis U (MA)
Brandon U (MB, Canada)
Bridgewater State U (MA)
Brock U (ON, Canada)
Bryn Mawr Coll (PA)
Bucknell U (PA)
Buffalo State Coll, State U of New York (NY)
Butler U (IN)
California Baptist U (CA)
California Inst of Technology (CA)
California Lutheran U (CA)
California Polytechnic State U, San Luis Obispo (CA)
California State Polytechnic U, Pomona (CA)
California State U, Dominguez Hills (CA)
California State U, East Bay (CA)
California State U, Fullerton (CA)
California State U, Long Beach (CA)
California State U, Los Angeles (CA)
California State U, Northridge (CA)
California State U, Sacramento (CA)
California State U, San Bernardino (CA)
California State U, Stanislaus (CA)
California U of Pennsylvania (PA)
Calvin Coll (MI)
Canisius Coll (NY)
Capital U (OH)
Carleton Coll (MN)
Carlow U (PA)
Carnegie Mellon U (PA)
Carroll Coll (MT)
Carson-Newman U (TN)
Carthage Coll (WI)
Case Western Reserve U (OH)
The Catholic U of America (DC)
Centenary Coll of Louisiana (LA)
Central Connecticut State U (CT)
Central Methodist U (MO)
Central Michigan U (MI)
Centre Coll (KY)
Chapman U (CA)
Christendom Coll (VA)
Christopher Newport U (VA)
City Coll of the City U of New York (NY)
Claremont McKenna Coll (CA)
Clarion U of Pennsylvania (PA)
Clark Atlanta U (GA)
Clarke U (IA)
Clark U (MA)
Clayton State U (GA)
Clemson U (SC)
Cleveland State U (OH)
Coastal Carolina U (SC)
Coe Coll (IA)
Colby Coll (ME)
Colgate U (NY)
The Coll at Brockport, State U of New York (NY)
Coll of Charleston (SC)
The Coll of Idaho (ID)
Coll of Mount Saint Vincent (NY)
The Coll of New Jersey (NJ)

The Coll of New Rochelle (NY)
Coll of Saint Benedict (MN)
The Coll of St. Scholastica (MN)
Coll of Staten Island of the City U of New York (NY)
Coll of the Atlantic (ME)
Coll of the Holy Cross (MA)
The Coll of William and Mary (VA)
The Coll of Wooster (OH)
The Colorado Coll (CO)
Colorado State U (CO)
Columbia Coll (MO)
Columbia U (NY)
Conception Sem Coll (MO)
Concordia Coll–New York (NY)
Concordia U (QC, Canada)
Concordia U Chicago (IL)
Concordia U of Edmonton (AB, Canada)
Connecticut Coll (CT)
Converse Coll (SC)
Cornell Coll (IA)
Cornell U (NY)
Cornerstone U (MI)
Covenant Coll (GA)
Creighton U (NE)
Curry Coll (MA)
Dallas Baptist U (TX)
Dartmouth Coll (NH)
Davidson Coll (NC)
Delaware State U (DE)
Denison U (OH)
DePaul U (IL)
DePauw U (IN)
DEREE - The American Coll of Greece (Greece)
DeSales U (PA)
Dickinson Coll (PA)
Doane U (NE)
Dominican U (IL)
Drake U (IA)
Drew U (NJ)
Drexel U (PA)
Drury U (MO)
Duquesne U (PA)
D'Youville Coll (NY)
Earlham Coll (IN)
East Carolina U (NC)
Eastern Michigan U (MI)
Eastern U (PA)
Eastern Washington U (WA)
East Stroudsburg U of Pennsylvania (PA)
East Tennessee State U (TN)
Eckerd Coll (FL)
Elizabethtown Coll (PA)
Elmhurst Coll (IL)
Elon U (NC)
Emmanuel Coll (MA)
Emory & Henry Coll (VA)
Emory U (GA)
Eugene Lang Coll of Liberal Arts (NY)
The Evergreen State Coll (WA)
Fairfield U (CT)
Fairleigh Dickinson U, Florham Campus (NJ)
Fairleigh Dickinson U, Metropolitan Campus (NJ)
Felician U (NJ)
Florida Atlantic U (FL)
Florida Gulf Coast U (FL)
Florida Intl U (FL)
Florida Southern Coll (FL)
Florida State U (FL)
Fordham U (NY)
Fort Lewis Coll (CO)
Franklin & Marshall Coll (PA)
Franklin Coll (IN)
Frostburg State U (MD)
Furman U (SC)
Gannon U (PA)
Geneva Coll (PA)
George Mason U (VA)
Georgetown Coll (KY)
Georgetown U (DC)
The George Washington U (DC)
Georgia Coll & State U (GA)
Georgia Southern U (GA)
Georgia State U (GA)
Gettysburg Coll (PA)
Gonzaga U (WA)
Gordon Coll (MA)
Grand Valley State U (MI)
Green Mountain Coll (VT)
Greenville U (IL)
Grinnell Coll (IA)

Grove City Coll (PA)
Guilford Coll (NC)
Gustavus Adolphus Coll (MN)
Gwynedd Mercy U (PA)
Hamilton Coll (NY)
Hamline U (MN)
Hampden-Sydney Coll (VA)
Hampshire Coll (MA)
Hardin-Simmons U (TX)
Hartwick Coll (NY)
Harvard U (MA)
Haverford Coll (PA)
Heidelberg U (OH)
Hendrix Coll (AR)
High Point U (NC)
Hillsdale Coll (MI)
Hiram Coll (OH)
Hobart and William Smith Colls (NY)
Hofstra U (NY)
Hollins U (VA)
Hood Coll (MD)
Hope Coll (MI)
Houston Baptist U (TX)
Howard Payne U (TX)
Humboldt State U (CA)
Hunter Coll of the City U of New York (NY)
Idaho State U (ID)
Illinois Coll (IL)
Illinois State U (IL)
Illinois Wesleyan U (IL)
Indiana State U (IN)
Indiana U Bloomington (IN)
Indiana U Northwest (IN)
Indiana U of Pennsylvania (PA)
Indiana U–Purdue U Indianapolis (IN)
Indiana U South Bend (IN)
Indiana U Southeast (IN)
Indiana Wesleyan U (IN)
Iona Coll (NY)
Iowa State U of Science and Technology (IA)
Ithaca Coll (NY)
Jacksonville U (FL)
John Brown U (AR)
John Carroll U (OH)
John Jay Coll of Criminal Justice of the City U of New York (NY)
Johns Hopkins U (MD)
Juniata Coll (PA)
Kalamazoo Coll (MI)
Kansas State U (KS)
Kansas Wesleyan U (KS)
Kennesaw State U (GA)
Kent State U (OH)
Kenyon Coll (OH)
King's Coll (PA)
King U (TN)
Knox Coll (IL)
Kutztown U of Pennsylvania (PA)
Lafayette Coll (PA)
La Salle U (PA)
Lawrence U (WI)
Lebanese American U (Lebanon)
Lebanon Valley Coll (PA)
Lee U (TN)
Lehigh U (PA)
Lehman Coll of the City U of New York (NY)
Le Moyne Coll (NY)
Lenoir-Rhyne U (NC)
Lewis U (IL)
Liberty U (VA)
Lincoln Christian U (IL)
Lincoln U (PA)
Lindenwood U (MO)
Linfield Coll (OR)
Lipscomb U (TN)
Lock Haven U of Pennsylvania (PA)
Long Island U–LIU Brooklyn (NY)
Long Island U–LIU Post (NY)
Loras Coll (IA)
Louisiana State U and A&M Coll (LA)
Loyola Marymount U (CA)
Loyola U Chicago (IL)
Loyola U New Orleans (LA)
Luther Coll (IA)
Lycoming Coll (PA)
Lynchburg Coll (VA)
Macalester Coll (MN)
Malone U (OH)
Manchester U (IN)
Manhattan Coll (NY)
Manhattanville Coll (NY)

Mansfield U of Pennsylvania (PA)
Marian U (IN)
Marietta Coll (OH)
Marist Coll (NY)
Marlboro Coll (VT)
Marquette U (WI)
Marymount U (VA)
Maryville Coll (TN)
Marywood U (PA)
Massachusetts Coll of Liberal Arts (MA)
Massachusetts Inst of Technology (MA)
McDaniel Coll (MD)
McKendree U (IL)
McPherson Coll (KS)
Mercer U, Macon (GA)
Mercyhurst U (PA)
Merrimack Coll (MA)
Messiah Coll (PA)
Metropolitan State U of Denver (CO)
Miami U (OH)
Michigan State U (MI)
Middlebury Coll (VT)
Middle Tennessee State U (TN)
Millersville U of Pennsylvania (PA)
Millikin U (IL)
Millsaps Coll (MS)
Mills Coll (CA)
Minnesota State U Moorhead (MN)
Misericordia U (PA)
Mississippi State U (MS)
Missouri State U (MO)
Missouri U of Science and Technology (MO)
Missouri Valley Coll (MO)
Missouri Western State U (MO)
Molloy Coll (NY)
Monmouth Coll (IL)
Montclair State U (NJ)
Moravian Coll (PA)
Morehead State U (KY)
Morehouse Coll (GA)
Morningside Coll (IA)
Mount Holyoke Coll (MA)
Mount Mary U (WI)
Mount Mercy U (IA)
Mount Saint Mary's U (CA)
Mount St. Mary's U (MD)
Mount Vernon Nazarene U (OH)
Muhlenberg Coll (PA)
Muskingum U (OH)
Nazareth Coll of Rochester (NY)
New Coll of Florida (FL)
New Jersey City U (NJ)
Newman U (KS)
New Mexico State U (NM)
New York U (NY)
Niagara U (NY)
North Carolina State U (NC)
North Central Coll (IL)
North Dakota State U (ND)
Northeastern U (MA)
Northern Arizona U (AZ)
Northern Illinois U (IL)
Northern Kentucky U (KY)
Northern Michigan U (MI)
Northwestern Coll (IA)
Northwestern U (IL)
Northwest Missouri State U (MO)
Northwest Nazarene U (ID)
Northwest U (WA)
Nova Southeastern U (FL)
Nyack Coll (NY)
Oakland U (MI)
Oberlin Coll (OH)
Occidental Coll (CA)
Oglethorpe U (GA)
Ohio Dominican U (OH)
Ohio Northern U (OH)
The Ohio State U (OH)
Ohio U (OH)
Ohio Wesleyan U (OH)
Oklahoma Baptist U (OK)
Oklahoma City U (OK)
Oklahoma State U (OK)
Old Dominion U (VA)
Olivet Nazarene U (IL)
Oregon State U (OR)
Otterbein U (OH)
Ouachita Baptist U (AR)
Pacific Lutheran U (WA)
Palm Beach Atlantic U (FL)
Penn State Abington (PA)
Penn State Altoona (PA)
Penn State Beaver (PA)

Penn State Berks (PA)
Penn State Brandywine (PA)
Penn State DuBois (PA)
Penn State Erie, The Behrend Coll (PA)
Penn State Fayette, The Eberly Campus (PA)
Penn State Greater Allegheny (PA)
Penn State Hazleton (PA)
Penn State Lehigh Valley (PA)
Penn State Mont Alto (PA)
Penn State New Kensington (PA)
Penn State Schuylkill (PA)
Penn State Shenango (PA)
Penn State U Park (PA)
Penn State Wilkes-Barre (PA)
Penn State Worthington Scranton (PA)
Penn State York (PA)
Pepperdine U, Malibu (CA)
Piedmont Coll (GA)
Pitzer Coll (CA)
Point Loma Nazarene U (CA)
Pomona Coll (CA)
Portland State U (OR)
Presbyterian Coll (SC)
Princeton U (NJ)
Principia Coll (IL)
Providence Coll (RI)
Purchase Coll, State U of New York (NY)
Purdue U (IN)
Purdue U Northwest (IN)
Queens Coll of the City U of New York (NY)
Quinnipiac U (CT)
Randolph Coll (VA)
Randolph-Macon Coll (VA)
Redeemer U Coll (ON, Canada)
Reed Coll (OR)
Regis U (CO)
Rensselaer Polytechnic Inst (NY)
Rhode Island Coll (RI)
Rhodes Coll (TN)
Rice U (TX)
Rider U (NJ)
Ripon Coll (WI)
Roanoke Coll (VA)
Rochester Inst of Technology (NY)
Rockford U (IL)
Rockhurst U (MO)
Roger Williams U (RI)
Rollins Coll (FL)
Roosevelt U (IL)
Rosemont Coll (PA)
Rutgers U–Camden (NJ)
Rutgers U–Newark (NJ)
Rutgers U–New Brunswick (NJ)
Sacred Heart U (CT)
St. Ambrose U (IA)
Saint Anselm Coll (NH)
St. Bonaventure U (NY)
St. Catherine U (MN)
Saint Charles Borromeo Sem, Overbrook (PA)
Saint Francis U (PA)
St. John Fisher Coll (NY)
Saint John's U (MN)
St. John's U (NY)
Saint Joseph's U (PA)
St. Lawrence U (NY)
Saint Louis U (MO)
Saint Louis U–Madrid Campus (Spain)
Saint Mary's Coll of California (CA)
St. Mary's Coll of Maryland (MD)
St. Mary's U (TX)
Saint Mary's U of Minnesota (MN)
Saint Michael's Coll (VT)
St. Norbert Coll (WI)
St. Olaf Coll (MN)
Saint Peter's U (NJ)
St. Thomas Aquinas Coll (NY)
St. Thomas U (NB, Canada)
Saint Vincent Coll (PA)
Salisbury U (MD)
Salve Regina U (RI)
Samford U (AL)
Sam Houston State U (TX)
San Diego State U (CA)
San Francisco State U (CA)
Santa Clara U (CA)
Sarah Lawrence Coll (NY)
Scripps Coll (CA)
Seattle Pacific U (WA)
Seattle U (WA)
Sewanee: The U of the South (TN)

Siena Coll (NY)
Simmons Coll (MA)
Simon Fraser U (BC, Canada)
Simpson Coll (IA)
Skidmore Coll (NY)
Slippery Rock U of Pennsylvania (PA)
Smith Coll (MA)
Sonoma State U (CA)
Southeast Missouri State U (MO)
Southern Illinois U Carbondale (IL)
Southern Illinois U Edwardsville (IL)
Southern Methodist U (TX)
Southern Utah U (UT)
Southwestern U (TX)
Spelman Coll (GA)
Spring Hill Coll (AL)
Stanford U (CA)
State U of New York at Fredonia (NY)
State U of New York at New Paltz (NY)
State U of New York at Oswego (NY)
State U of New York at Plattsburgh (NY)
State U of New York Coll at Cortland (NY)
State U of New York Coll at Geneseo (NY)
State U of New York Coll at Old Westbury (NY)
State U of New York Coll at Oneonta (NY)
State U of New York Coll at Potsdam (NY)
Stephen F. Austin State U (TX)
Stetson U (FL)
Stevens Inst of Technology (NJ)
Stonehill Coll (MA)
Stony Brook U, State U of New York (NY)
Suffolk U (MA)
Susquehanna U (PA)
Sweet Briar Coll (VA)
Syracuse U (NY)
Taylor U (IN)
Temple U (PA)
Texas A&M U (TX)
Texas A&M U–Corpus Christi (TX)
Texas Christian U (TX)
Texas Lutheran U (TX)
Texas State U (TX)
Texas Tech U (TX)
Toccoa Falls Coll (GA)
Towson U (MD)
Transylvania U (KY)
Trent U (ON, Canada)
Trinity Christian Coll (IL)
Trinity U (TX)
Tufts U (MA)
Tulane U (LA)
Union Coll (NY)
Union U (TN)
United States Military Acad (NY)
Université de Sherbrooke (QC, Canada)
U at Albany, State U of New York (NY)
U at Buffalo, the State U of New York (NY)
The U of Akron (OH)
The U of Alabama (AL)
The U of Alabama at Birmingham (AL)
U of Alaska Fairbanks (AK)
The U of Arizona (AZ)
U of Arkansas (AR)
U of California, Davis (CA)
U of California, Irvine (CA)
U of California, Los Angeles (CA)
U of California, Riverside (CA)
U of California, San Diego (CA)
U of California, Santa Barbara (CA)
U of California, Santa Cruz (CA)
U of Central Arkansas (AR)
U of Central Florida (FL)
U of Central Oklahoma (OK)
U of Chicago (IL)
U of Cincinnati (OH)
U of Colorado Boulder (CO)
U of Colorado Colorado Springs (CO)
U of Colorado Denver (CO)
U of Dallas (TX)
U of Dayton (OH)

U of Denver (CO)
U of Dubuque (IA)
U of Evansville (IN)
The U of Findlay (OH)
U of Florida (FL)
U of Georgia (GA)
U of Guam (GU)
U of Guelph (ON, Canada)
U of Hartford (CT)
U of Hawaii at Manoa (HI)
U of Houston (TX)
U of Houston–Downtown (TX)
U of Idaho (ID)
U of Illinois at Chicago (IL)
U of Illinois at Springfield (IL)
The U of Kansas (KS)
U of Kentucky (KY)
U of King's Coll (NS, Canada)
U of La Verne (CA)
U of Louisville (KY)
U of Maine (ME)
U of Maryland, Baltimore County (MD)
U of Maryland, Coll Park (MD)
U of Massachusetts Amherst (MA)
U of Massachusetts Boston (MA)
U of Massachusetts Dartmouth (MA)
U of Massachusetts Lowell (MA)
U of Memphis (TN)
U of Miami (FL)
U of Michigan (MI)
U of Michigan–Dearborn (MI)
U of Michigan–Flint (MI)
U of Minnesota, Duluth (MN)
U of Minnesota, Morris (MN)
U of Minnesota, Twin Cities Campus (MN)
U of Missouri (MO)
U of Montana (MT)
U of Mount Union (OH)
U of Nebraska at Kearney (NE)
U of Nebraska–Lincoln (NE)
U of Nevada, Las Vegas (NV)
U of Nevada, Reno (NV)
U of New Hampshire (NH)
U of New Mexico (NM)
U of New Orleans (LA)
U of North Carolina at Asheville (NC)
The U of North Carolina at Chapel Hill (NC)
The U of North Carolina at Charlotte (NC)
The U of North Carolina at Greensboro (NC)
U of North Dakota (ND)
U of Northern Colorado (CO)
U of Northern Iowa (IA)
U of North Florida (FL)
U of North Texas (TX)
U of Notre Dame (IN)
U of Oklahoma (OK)
U of Oregon (OR)
U of Pennsylvania (PA)
U of Pittsburgh (PA)
U of Puget Sound (WA)
U of Regina (SK, Canada)
U of Rhode Island (RI)
U of Richmond (VA)
U of Rochester (NY)
U of Saint Francis (IN)
U of Saint Joseph (CT)
U of St. Thomas (MN)
U of St. Thomas (TX)
U of San Diego (CA)
U of San Francisco (CA)
U of Saskatchewan (SK, Canada)
The U of Scranton (PA)
U of South Alabama (AL)
U of South Carolina (SC)
U of South Dakota (SD)
U of Southern California (CA)
U of Southern Indiana (IN)
U of Southern Maine (ME)
U of Southern Mississippi (MS)
The U of Tampa (FL)
The U of Tennessee (TN)
The U of Tennessee at Martin (TN)
The U of Texas at Austin (TX)
The U of Texas at El Paso (TX)
The U of Texas at San Antonio (TX)
The U of Texas Rio Grande Valley (TX)
U of the Fraser Valley (BC, Canada)
U of the Incarnate Word (TX)

U of the Pacific (CA)
The U of Toledo (OH)
The U of Tulsa (OK)
U of Utah (UT)
U of Vermont (VT)
U of Virginia (VA)
U of Washington (WA)
U of Waterloo (ON, Canada)
U of West Georgia (GA)
U of Wisconsin–Eau Claire (WI)
U of Wisconsin–La Crosse (WI)
U of Wisconsin–Madison (WI)
U of Wisconsin–Milwaukee (WI)
U of Wisconsin–Parkside (WI)
U of Wisconsin–Platteville (WI)
U of Wisconsin–Stevens Point (WI)
U of Wyoming (WY)
Ursinus Coll (PA)
Ursuline Coll (OH)
Utah State U (UT)
Utah Valley U (UT)
Utica Coll (NY)
Valparaiso U (IN)
Vanderbilt U (TN)
Vassar Coll (NY)
Villanova U (PA)
Virginia Commonwealth U (VA)
Virginia Polytechnic Inst and State U (VA)
Virginia Wesleyan U (VA)
Wabash Coll (IN)
Wagner Coll (NY)
Wake Forest U (NC)
Walsh U (OH)
Wartburg Coll (IA)
Washington & Jefferson Coll (PA)
Washington and Lee U (VA)
Washington Coll (MD)
Washington State U (WA)
Washington U in St. Louis (MO)
Wayne State U (MI)
Weber State U (UT)
Webster U (MO)
Wellesley Coll (MA)
Wells Coll (NY)
Wesleyan U (CT)
West Chester U of Pennsylvania (PA)
Western Michigan U (MI)
Western New England U (MA)
Western Oregon U (OR)
Western Washington U (WA)
Westminster Coll (PA)
Westminster Coll (UT)
Westmont Coll (CA)
West Virginia U (WV)
West Virginia Wesleyan Coll (WV)
Wheaton Coll (IL)
Wheaton Coll (MA)
Whitman Coll (WA)
Whittier Coll (CA)
Whitworth U (WA)
Wichita State U (KS)
Wilkes U (PA)
Willamette U (OR)
William Jewell Coll (MO)
William Paterson U of New Jersey (NJ)
Williams Coll (MA)
Wisconsin Lutheran Coll (WI)
Wittenberg U (OH)
Wofford Coll (SC)
Wright State U (OH)
Wright State U–Lake Campus (OH)
Xavier U of Louisiana (LA)
York Coll of Pennsylvania (PA)
Youngstown State U (OH)

PHILOSOPHY AND RELIGIOUS STUDIES
Arizona State U at the West campus (AZ)
Barton Coll (NC)
Belmont U (TN)
Berry Coll (GA)
Bethune-Cookman U (FL)
Christian Brothers U (TN)
Concordia Coll–New York (NY)
Flagler Coll (FL)
Hillsdale Coll (MI)
LaGrange Coll (GA)
Marist Coll (NY)
Marlboro Coll (VT)
Marymount Manhattan Coll (NY)
Muskingum U (OH)
Oklahoma City U (OK)
Pace U (NY)

Pace U, Pleasantville Campus (NY)
Point Loma Nazarene U (CA)
St. Andrews U (NC)
St. Joseph's Coll, Long Island Campus (NY)
St. Joseph's Coll, New York (NY)
Southwestern Assemblies of God U (TX)
Southwestern Coll (KS)
Stockton U (NJ)
U of Maine at Farmington (ME)
U of North Dakota (ND)
U of Wisconsin–Stevens Point (WI)
Valdosta State U (GA)

PHILOSOPHY AND RELIGIOUS STUDIES RELATED
Barton Coll (NC)
Berry Coll (GA)
Bridgewater Coll (VA)
Butler U (IN)
Conception Sem Coll (MO)
Covenant Coll (GA)
Eastern Mennonite U (VA)
Eastern Nazarene Coll (MA)
Florida Ag and Mech U (FL)
Friends U (KS)
Hendrix Coll (AR)
James Madison U (VA)
Lyon Coll (AR)
Marlboro Coll (VT)
McPherson Coll (KS)
Millsaps Coll (MS)
Newberry Coll (SC)
Northwest U (WA)
Ouachita Baptist U (AR)
Radford U (VA)
Roberts Wesleyan Coll (NY)
Rocky Mountain Coll (MT)
Rowan U (NJ)
Samford U (AL)
San Francisco State U (CA)
Shawnee State U (OH)
Shaw U (NC)
State U of New York at Oswego (NY)
Syracuse U (NY)
Truman State U (MO)
Union U (TN)
U of Mary Washington (VA)
The U of North Carolina at Pembroke (NC)
The U of North Carolina Wilmington (NC)
U of Notre Dame (IN)
The U of Tennessee at Chattanooga (TN)
Washington U in St. Louis (MO)
West Virginia Wesleyan Coll (WV)
William Jewell Coll (MO)
Winthrop U (SC)

PHILOSOPHY RELATED
Butler U (IN)
Coll of Staten Island of the City U of New York (NY)
Lewis U (IL)
Loyola U New Orleans (LA)
Marlboro Coll (VT)
Mount Vernon Nazarene U (OH)
Ohio Northern U (OH)
The U of Arizona (AZ)
U of Massachusetts Boston (MA)
U of Pennsylvania (PA)
U of Southern California (CA)
U of Wisconsin–Stevens Point (WI)
Washington U in St. Louis (MO)

PHOTOGRAPHIC AND FILM/VIDEO TECHNOLOGY
Coll of the Ozarks (MO)
Husson U (ME)
Rochester Inst of Technology (NY)
St. John's U (NY)
Wilmington U (DE)

PHOTOGRAPHY
Adams State U (CO)
Alberta Coll of Art & Design (AB, Canada)
American Acad of Art (IL)
Andrews U (MI)
Aquinas Coll (MI)
Arcadia U (PA)
ArtCenter Coll of Design (CA)
Bard Coll (NY)
Barry U (FL)
Bennington Coll (VT)

Bowling Green State U (OH)
Bradley U (IL)
Bridgewater State U (MA)
Buffalo State Coll, State U of New York (NY)
California Baptist U (CA)
California Coll of the Arts (CA)
California State U, Long Beach (CA)
California State U, Sacramento (CA)
Calvary U (MO)
Cardinal Stritch U (WI)
Carroll U (WI)
Carson-Newman U (TN)
Cazenovia Coll (NY)
Chatham U (PA)
Coe Coll (IA)
Coker Coll (SC)
Columbia Coll (MO)
Columbia Coll Chicago (IL)
Concordia U (QC, Canada)
Concordia U Wisconsin (WI)
Dominican U (IL)
Drexel U (PA)
Eastern Mennonite U (VA)
Endicott Coll (MA)
Eugene Lang Coll of Liberal Arts (NY)
Ferris State U (MI)
Fitchburg State U (MA)
Grand Valley State U (MI)
Grand View U (IA)
Hampton U (VA)
Hofstra U (NY)
Indiana Wesleyan U (IN)
Inter American U of Puerto Rico, San Germán Campus (PR)
Ithaca Coll (NY)
John Brown U (AR)
Judson U (IL)
Kansas City Art Inst (MO)
Kansas Wesleyan U (KS)
Long Island U–LIU Post (NY)
Marlboro Coll (VT)
Maryland Inst Coll of Art (MD)
Marymount Manhattan Coll (NY)
Marywood U (PA)
Massachusetts Coll of Art and Design (MA)
Minneapolis Coll of Art and Design (MN)
Morningside Coll (IA)
New Hampshire Inst of Art (NH)
New York U (NY)
Northern Arizona U (AZ)
Northern Michigan U (MI)
Oakland U (MI)
Oklahoma City U (OK)
Pacific Northwest Coll of Art (OR)
Paier Coll of Art, Inc. (CT)
Paris Coll of Art (France)
Parsons School of Design (NY)
Pennsylvania Coll of Art & Design (PA)
Point Park U (PA)
Pratt Inst (NY)
Providence Coll (RI)
Purchase Coll, State U of New York (NY)
Purdue U (IN)
Rhode Island Coll (RI)
Rhode Island School of Design (RI)
Ringling Coll of Art and Design (FL)
Rutgers U–New Brunswick (NJ)
St. John's U (NY)
Sam Houston State U (TX)
San Francisco Art Inst (CA)
Savannah Coll of Art and Design (GA)
School of Visual Arts (NY)
Seattle U (WA)
Southern Adventist U (TN)
Spelman Coll (GA)
State U of New York at New Paltz (NY)
Syracuse U (NY)
Temple U (PA)
Texas A&M U–Commerce (TX)
Texas Christian U (TX)
Texas State U (TX)
The U of Akron (OH)
U of Central Florida (FL)
U of Central Missouri (MO)
U of Dayton (OH)
U of Hartford (CT)
U of Houston (TX)

U of Illinois at Chicago (IL)
U of La Verne (CA)
U of Massachusetts Dartmouth (MA)
U of Miami (FL)
U of Oregon (OR)
U of San Francisco (CA)
The U of the Arts (PA)
U of Washington (WA)
Villa Maria Coll (NY)
Virginia Commonwealth U (VA)
Washington U in St. Louis (MO)
Weber State U (UT)
Western State Colorado U (CO)
Youngstown State U (OH)

PHOTOJOURNALISM
Barton Coll (NC)
Bradley U (IL)
Central Michigan U (MI)
Columbia Coll Chicago (IL)
Minnesota State U Moorhead (MN)
Ohio U (OH)
Point Loma Nazarene U (CA)
Point Park U (PA)
Rochester Inst of Technology (NY)
St. John's U (NY)
Sierra Nevada Coll (NV)
Syracuse U (NY)
U of Central Oklahoma (OK)
U of Missouri (MO)
Western Kentucky U (KY)

PHYSICAL AND BIOLOGICAL ANTHROPOLOGY
U of Washington (WA)

PHYSICAL CHEMISTRY
LeTourneau U (TX)
Rice U (TX)
Whitworth U (WA)

PHYSICAL EDUCATION TEACHING AND COACHING
Adams State U (CO)
Adelphi U (NY)
Alabama State U (AL)
Alice Lloyd Coll (KY)
Anderson U (IN)
Appalachian State U (NC)
Aquinas Coll (MI)
Arkansas Tech U (AR)
Asbury U (KY)
Athens State U (AL)
Auburn U (AL)
Augsburg U (MN)
Augustana U (SD)
Aurora U (IL)
Austin Coll (TX)
Azusa Pacific U (CA)
Ball State U (IN)
Barry U (FL)
Baylor U (TX)
Bemidji State U (MN)
Benedictine Coll (KS)
Benedictine U (IL)
Bethel Coll (IN)
Bethel U (MN)
Bethune-Cookman U (FL)
Biola U (CA)
Blackburn Coll (IL)
Bluefield Coll (VA)
Blue Mountain Coll (MS)
Boise State U (ID)
Boston U (MA)
Bowling Green State U (OH)
Bridgewater State U (MA)
Brock U (ON, Canada)
Bryan Coll (TN)
Buena Vista U (IA)
Cairn U (PA)
California Lutheran U (CA)
California State U, Long Beach (CA)
California State U, Stanislaus (CA)
Calvin Coll (MI)
Campbellsville U (KY)
Canisius Coll (NY)
Capital U (OH)
Caribbean U (PR)
Carroll Coll (MT)
Carroll U (WI)
Carson-Newman U (TN)
Carthage Coll (WI)
Catawba Coll (NC)
Cedarville U (OH)
Central Connecticut State U (CT)
Central Methodist U (MO)

Central Michigan U (MI)
Charleston Southern U (SC)
Chowan U (NC)
The Citadel, The Military Coll of South Carolina (SC)
Coastal Carolina U (SC)
Coe Coll (IA)
Coker Coll (SC)
The Coll at Brockport, State U of New York (NY)
Coll of Charleston (SC)
The Coll of Idaho (ID)
The Coll of New Jersey (NJ)
Coll of the Ozarks (MO)
Columbus State U (GA)
Concordia U Chicago (IL)
Concordia U, St. Paul (MN)
Concordia U Wisconsin (WI)
Concord U (WV)
Corban U (OR)
Cornell Coll (IA)
Cornerstone U (MI)
Culver-Stockton Coll (MO)
Dakota State U (SD)
Dallas Baptist U (TX)
Defiance Coll (OH)
Delaware State U (DE)
Denison U (OH)
DePaul U (IL)
DePauw U (IN)
DeSales U (PA)
Dickinson State U (ND)
Doane U (NE)
East Carolina U (NC)
Eastern Mennonite U (VA)
Eastern Michigan U (MI)
Eastern Nazarene Coll (MA)
Eastern New Mexico U (NM)
East Stroudsburg U of Pennsylvania (PA)
East Texas Baptist U (TX)
Elmhurst Coll (IL)
Elon U (NC)
Emory & Henry Coll (VA)
Endicott Coll (MA)
Evangel U (MO)
Fayetteville State U (NC)
Florida Intl U (FL)
Fort Lewis Coll (CO)
Franklin Coll (IN)
Friends U (KS)
Frostburg State U (MD)
George Mason U (VA)
Georgia Southern U (GA)
Georgia Southern U–Armstrong Campus (GA)
Georgia Southwestern State U (GA)
Georgia State U (GA)
Gettysburg Coll (PA)
Gonzaga U (WA)
Goshen Coll (IN)
Graceland U (IA)
Grambling State U (LA)
Grand Valley State U (MI)
Grand View U (IA)
Greensboro Coll (NC)
Greenville U (IL)
Gustavus Adolphus Coll (MN)
Hampton U (VA)
Hannibal-LaGrange U (MO)
Hardin-Simmons U (TX)
High Point U (NC)
Hofstra U (NY)
Hope Coll (MI)
Houston Baptist U (TX)
Howard Payne U (TX)
Humboldt State U (CA)
Hunter Coll of the City U of New York (NY)
Huntingdon Coll (AL)
Huston-Tillotson U (TX)
Idaho State U (ID)
Illinois Coll (IL)
Illinois State U (IL)
Indiana State U (IN)
Indiana Tech (IN)
Indiana Wesleyan U (IN)
Inter American U of Puerto Rico, Aguadilla Campus (PR)
Inter American U of Puerto Rico, Metropolitan Campus (PR)
Inter American U of Puerto Rico, San Germán Campus (PR)
Ithaca Coll (NY)
Jackson State U (MS)
Jacksonville U (FL)

John Carroll U (OH)
Judson U (IL)
Kean U (NJ)
Keene State Coll (NH)
Kennesaw State U (GA)
Kent State U (OH)
Kentucky State U (KY)
Langston U (OK)
LeTourneau U (TX)
Limestone Coll (SC)
Lincoln Memorial U (TN)
Lincoln U (MO)
Lindenwood U (MO)
Lindsey Wilson Coll (KY)
Linfield Coll (OR)
Lipscomb U (TN)
Long Island U–LIU Brooklyn (NY)
Long Island U–LIU Post (NY)
Louisiana Coll (LA)
Louisiana State U and A&M Coll (LA)
Lubbock Christian U (TX)
Madonna U (MI)
Manchester U (IN)
Manhattan Coll (NY)
Maranatha Baptist U (WI)
Marshall U (WV)
Martin Luther Coll (MN)
Maryville Coll (TN)
Marywood U (PA)
The Master's U (CA)
McKendree U (IL)
McMurry U (TX)
McNeese State U (LA)
McPherson Coll (KS)
Meredith Coll (NC)
Messiah Coll (PA)
Metropolitan State U of Denver (CO)
Michigan State U (MI)
MidAmerica Nazarene U (KS)
Millikin U (IL)
Minnesota State U Moorhead (MN)
Minot State U (ND)
Missouri Baptist U (MO)
Missouri State U (MO)
Missouri Valley Coll (MO)
Monmouth Coll (IL)
Montclair State U (NJ)
Muskingum U (OH)
New Mexico Highlands U (NM)
North Central Coll (IL)
North Dakota State U (ND)
Northeastern State U (OK)
Northern Illinois U (IL)
Northern Kentucky U (KY)
Northern Michigan U (MI)
Northern State U (SD)
Northwestern Coll (IA)
Northwestern Oklahoma State U (OK)
Northwestern State U of Louisiana (LA)
Northwest Missouri State U (MO)
Northwest Nazarene U (ID)
Nova Southeastern U (FL)
Oakland City U (IN)
The Ohio State U (OH)
Oklahoma Baptist U (OK)
Oklahoma Christian U (OK)
Oklahoma City U (OK)
Oklahoma State U (OK)
Old Dominion U (VA)
Olivet Nazarene U (IL)
Oral Roberts U (OK)
Otterbein U (OH)
Ouachita Baptist U (AR)
Palm Beach Atlantic U (FL)
Pfeiffer U (NC)
Pittsburg State U (KS)
Purdue U (IN)
Queens Coll of the City U of New York (NY)
Radford U (VA)
Redeemer U Coll (ON, Canada)
Rhode Island Coll (RI)
Ripon Coll (WI)
Roanoke Coll (VA)
Roberts Wesleyan Coll (NY)
Rockford U (IL)
Rocky Mountain Coll (MT)
Rowan U (NJ)
The Sage Colls (NY)
Saginaw Valley State U (MI)
St. Andrews U (NC)
St. Bonaventure U (NY)
St. Catherine U (MN)

Salisbury U (MD)
Sam Houston State U (TX)
San Francisco State U (CA)
Schreiner U (TX)
Shenandoah U (VA)
Simpson Coll (IA)
Sonoma State U (CA)
Southeastern Louisiana U (LA)
Southeastern Oklahoma State U (OK)
Southeast Missouri State U (MO)
Southern Adventist U (TN)
Southern Arkansas U–Magnolia (AR)
Southern Utah U (UT)
Southwest Baptist U (MO)
Southwestern Assemblies of God U (TX)
Southwestern Coll (KS)
State U of New York Coll at Cortland (NY)
Syracuse U (NY)
Tabor Coll (KS)
Taylor U (IN)
Tennessee Technological U (TN)
Texas Christian U (TX)
Texas Lutheran U (TX)
Towson U (MD)
Transylvania U (KY)
Trevecca Nazarene U (TN)
Trine U (IN)
Trinity Christian Coll (IL)
Union Coll (NE)
Union U (TN)
United States Sports Acad (AL)
Université de Sherbrooke (QC, Canada)
The U of Akron (OH)
The U of Alabama (AL)
The U of Alabama at Birmingham (AL)
U of Central Arkansas (AR)
U of Central Florida (FL)
U of Central Missouri (MO)
U of Central Oklahoma (OK)
U of Dubuque (IA)
U of Guam (GU)
U of Idaho (ID)
U of Jamestown (ND)
The U of Kansas (KS)
U of Kentucky (KY)
U of La Verne (CA)
U of Louisiana at Monroe (LA)
U of Maine (ME)
U of Maine at Presque Isle (ME)
U of Mary Hardin-Baylor (TX)
U of Maryland, Coll Park (MD)
U of Maryland Eastern Shore (MD)
U of Memphis (TN)
U of Minnesota, Duluth (MN)
U of Missouri–St. Louis (MO)
U of Mobile (AL)
U of Montana (MT)
U of Mount Union (OH)
U of Nebraska at Kearney (NE)
U of Nebraska–Lincoln (NE)
U of New Mexico (NM)
The U of North Carolina at Greensboro (NC)
The U of North Carolina at Pembroke (NC)
U of Northern Iowa (IA)
U of North Florida (FL)
U of Pittsburgh (PA)
U of Pittsburgh at Bradford (PA)
U of Providence (MT)
U of Regina (SK, Canada)
U of Rhode Island (RI)
U of St. Thomas (MN)
U of San Francisco (CA)
U of Saskatchewan (SK, Canada)
U of South Alabama (AL)
U of South Carolina (SC)
U of Southern Indiana (IN)
U of Southern Mississippi (MS)
The U of Tampa (FL)
The U of Texas at Austin (TX)
U of the Incarnate Word (TX)
U of Vermont (VT)
The U of West Alabama (AL)
U of West Georgia (GA)
U of Wisconsin–Madison (WI)
U of Wisconsin–Platteville (WI)
U of Wisconsin–River Falls (WI)
U of Wisconsin–Stevens Point (WI)
U of Wisconsin–Superior (WI)
U of Wisconsin–Whitewater (WI)

U of Wyoming (WY)
Upper Iowa U (IA)
Utah State U (UT)
Utah Valley U (UT)
Valdosta State U (GA)
Valley City State U (ND)
Valparaiso U (IN)
Vanguard U of Southern California (CA)
Waldorf U (IA)
Walsh U (OH)
Warner Pacific Coll (OR)
Wartburg Coll (IA)
Wayland Baptist U (TX)
Wayne State Coll (NE)
Wayne State U (MI)
Weber State U (UT)
Welch Coll (TN)
Western Illinois U (IL)
Western Kentucky U (KY)
Western Michigan U (MI)
Western State Colorado U (CO)
Western Washington U (WA)
Westfield State U (MA)
Westmont Coll (CA)
West Virginia U (WV)
West Virginia U Inst of Technology (WV)
West Virginia Wesleyan Coll (WV)
Whitworth U (WA)
Wichita State U (KS)
William Paterson U of New Jersey (NJ)
William Penn U (IA)
William Woods U (MO)
Winona State U (MN)
Winthrop U (SC)
Wright State U (OH)
Wright State U–Lake Campus (OH)
Xavier U of Louisiana (LA)
Youngstown State U (OH)

PHYSICAL FITNESS TECHNICIAN
Averett U (VA)
Central Methodist U (MO)
Clarion U of Pennsylvania (PA)
Trevecca Nazarene U (TN)

PHYSICAL SCIENCES
Anderson U (IN)
Arizona State U at the Tempe campus (AZ)
Arkansas Tech U (AR)
Bemidji State U (MN)
Bennington Coll (VT)
Bethany Lutheran Coll (MN)
Biola U (CA)
Black Hills State U (SD)
Brock U (ON, Canada)
California State U, Sacramento (CA)
California State U, Stanislaus (CA)
California U of Pennsylvania (PA)
Calvin Coll (MI)
Chowan U (NC)
Coe Coll (IA)
Colgate U (NY)
Colorado Mesa U (CO)
Concordia U Chicago (IL)
Concordia U, Nebraska (NE)
Cottey Coll (MO)
Dakota State U (SD)
Defiance Coll (OH)
Doane U (NE)
Emporia State U (KS)
The Evergreen State Coll (WA)
Florida State U (FL)
Graceland U (IA)
Hampshire Coll (MA)
Hampton U (VA)
Kansas State U (KS)
La Sierra U (CA)
Lincoln U (PA)
The Master's U (CA)
Michigan State U (MI)
Minot State U (ND)
Montana Tech of The U of Montana (MT)
Mount Vernon Nazarene U (OH)
Muhlenberg Coll (PA)
New Mexico Inst of Mining and Technology (NM)
Northwestern State U of Louisiana (LA)
Olivet Nazarene U (IL)
Otterbein U (OH)

Penn State Erie, The Behrend Coll (PA)
Purdue U Northwest (IN)
Ripon Coll (WI)
Rowan U (NJ)
St. John's U (NY)
Saint Vincent Coll (PA)
Salisbury U (MD)
Sam Houston State U (TX)
San Diego State U (CA)
San Francisco State U (CA)
Seattle Pacific U (WA)
Seattle U (WA)
Southern Utah U (UT)
Suffolk U (MA)
Trent U (ON, Canada)
Trine U (IN)
United States Military Acad (NY)
U of California, Riverside (CA)
U of Chicago (IL)
U of Dayton (OH)
U of Guelph (ON, Canada)
U of Maryland, Coll Park (MD)
U of North Dakota (ND)
U of Pittsburgh (PA)
U of Pittsburgh at Bradford (PA)
U of San Francisco (CA)
U of Southern California (CA)
U of Southern Maine (ME)
The U of Texas Rio Grande Valley (TX)
U of the Pacific (CA)
U of Utah (UT)
U of Wyoming (WY)
Villanova U (PA)
Warner Pacific Coll (OR)
Washington State U (WA)
Washington State U–Tri-Cities (WA)
Wesleyan U (CT)
Western Kentucky U (KY)
Westfield State U (MA)
Worcester State U (MA)
Wright State U (OH)
Wright State U–Lake Campus (OH)
Youngstown State U (OH)

PHYSICAL SCIENCES RELATED
Bowling Green State U (OH)
The Coll of St. Scholastica (MN)
Covenant Coll (GA)
Eastern Michigan U (MI)
George Mason U (VA)
Rochester Inst of Technology (NY)
Saginaw Valley State U (MI)
State U of New York Empire State Coll (NY)
Stevens Inst of Technology (NJ)
Stony Brook U, State U of New York (NY)
Temple U (PA)
Union Coll (NY)
U of California, Davis (CA)
U of Cincinnati (OH)
U of Mary Washington (VA)
U of Miami (FL)
U of North Alabama (AL)
The U of North Carolina at Chapel Hill (NC)
U of Utah (UT)
Wayne State U (MI)

PHYSICAL SCIENCE TECHNOLOGIES RELATED
Delaware State U (DE)

PHYSICAL THERAPY
American Intl Coll (MA)
Andrews U (MI)
Ball State U (IN)
Bellarmine U (KY)
Biola U (CA)
Bowling Green State U (OH)
Concordia U (QC, Canada)
Concordia U Wisconsin (WI)
Dominican U (IL)
Duquesne U (PA)
Elmhurst Coll (IL)
Georgia Southern U–Armstrong Campus (GA)
Grand Valley State U (MI)
Gustavus Adolphus Coll (MN)
Hampton U (VA)
Ithaca Coll (NY)
Langston U (OK)
Loyola U Chicago (IL)
Maryville U of Saint Louis (MO)

Mount Saint Mary Coll (NY)
Muskingum U (OH)
Nazareth Coll of Rochester (NY)
Northeastern U (MA)
Northern Illinois U (IL)
Northern Vermont U–Lyndon (VT)
Northwest Nazarene U (ID)
Quinnipiac U (CT)
Sacred Heart U (CT)
Saint Francis U (PA)
Saint Vincent Coll (PA)
Simmons Coll (MA)
Tarleton State U (TX)
Trine U (IN)
The U of Akron (OH)
U of Cincinnati (OH)
U of Hartford (CT)
U of Maryland Eastern Shore (MD)
U of Minnesota, Morris (MN)
The U of Scranton (PA)
Vanguard U of Southern California (CA)

PHYSICAL THERAPY TECHNOLOGY
Idaho State U (ID)
Union Coll (NE)

PHYSICIAN ASSISTANT
Bethel U (TN)
Butler U (IN)
Cleveland State U (OH)
DeSales U (PA)
Duquesne U (PA)
D'Youville Coll (NY)
Gannon U (PA)
The George Washington U (DC)
Grand Valley State U (MI)
Pennsylvania Coll of Technology (PA)
Quinnipiac U (CT)
Rochester Inst of Technology (NY)
Saint Francis U (PA)
St. John's U (NY)
Saint Mary's U of Minnesota (MN)
Saint Vincent Coll (PA)
Seton Hill U (PA)
Southern Illinois U Carbondale (IL)
Union Coll (NE)
U of Kentucky (KY)
U of South Dakota (SD)
U of Washington (WA)
Wagner Coll (NY)

PHYSICS
Abilene Christian U (TX)
Acadia U (NS, Canada)
Adams State U (CO)
Adelphi U (NY)
Agnes Scott Coll (GA)
Alabama State U (AL)
Albion Coll (MI)
Albright Coll (PA)
Alfred U (NY)
Allegheny Coll (PA)
Alma Coll (MI)
American U (DC)
The American U in Cairo (Egypt)
American U of Beirut (Lebanon)
Amherst Coll (MA)
Anderson U (IN)
Andrews U (MI)
Angelo State U (TX)
Appalachian State U (NC)
Arizona State U at the Tempe campus (AZ)
Arkansas Tech U (AR)
Ashland U (OH)
Auburn U (AL)
Augsburg U (MN)
Augustana Coll (IL)
Augustana U (SD)
Austin Coll (TX)
Austin Peay State U (TN)
Azusa Pacific U (CA)
Baker U (KS)
Baldwin Wallace U (OH)
Ball State U (IN)
Bard Coll (NY)
Barnard Coll (NY)
Bates Coll (ME)
Baylor U (TX)
Bellarmine U (KY)
Belmont U (TN)
Beloit Coll (WI)
Bemidji State U (MN)
Benedictine Coll (KS)
Benedictine U (IL)

Bennington Coll (VT)
Berea Coll (KY)
Berry Coll (GA)
Bethel U (MN)
Binghamton U, State U of New York (NY)
Biola U (CA)
Birmingham-Southern Coll (AL)
Bloomsburg U of Pennsylvania (PA)
Bluffton U (OH)
Bob Jones U (SC)
Boise State U (ID)
Boston Coll (MA)
Boston U (MA)
Bowdoin Coll (ME)
Bowling Green State U (OH)
Bradley U (IL)
Brandeis U (MA)
Brandon U (MB, Canada)
Bridgewater Coll (VA)
Bridgewater State U (MA)
Brigham Young U–Idaho (ID)
Brock U (ON, Canada)
Bryn Mawr Coll (PA)
Bucknell U (PA)
Buena Vista U (IA)
Buffalo State Coll, State U of New York (NY)
Butler U (IN)
California Inst of Technology (CA)
California Lutheran U (CA)
California Polytechnic State U, San Luis Obispo (CA)
California State Polytechnic U, Pomona (CA)
California State U, Dominguez Hills (CA)
California State U, East Bay (CA)
California State U, Fullerton (CA)
California State U, Long Beach (CA)
California State U, Los Angeles (CA)
California State U, Northridge (CA)
California State U, Sacramento (CA)
California State U, San Bernardino (CA)
California State U, Stanislaus (CA)
California U of Pennsylvania (PA)
Calvin Coll (MI)
Cameron U (OK)
Canisius Coll (NY)
Carleton Coll (MN)
Carnegie Mellon U (PA)
Carroll Coll (MT)
Carroll U (WI)
Carson-Newman U (TN)
Carthage Coll (WI)
Case Western Reserve U (OH)
The Catholic U of America (DC)
Cedarville U (OH)
Central Connecticut State U (CT)
Central Methodist U (MO)
Central Michigan U (MI)
Centre Coll (KY)
Chatham U (PA)
Christian Brothers U (TN)
The Citadel, The Military Coll of South Carolina (SC)
City Coll of the City U of New York (NY)
Claremont McKenna Coll (CA)
Clarion U of Pennsylvania (PA)
Clark Atlanta U (GA)
Clarkson U (NY)
Clark U (MA)
Clemson U (SC)
Cleveland State U (OH)
Coastal Carolina U (SC)
Coe Coll (IA)
Colby Coll (ME)
Colgate U (NY)
The Coll at Brockport, State U of New York (NY)
Coll of Charleston (SC)
The Coll of Idaho (ID)
The Coll of New Jersey (NJ)
Coll of Saint Benedict (MN)
Coll of Staten Island of the City U of New York (NY)
Coll of the Holy Cross (MA)
The Coll of William and Mary (VA)
The Coll of Wooster (OH)
The Colorado Coll (CO)
Colorado Mesa U (CO)
Colorado State U (CO)

Colorado State U–Pueblo (CO)
Columbia U (NY)
Concordia U (QC, Canada)
Concordia U Irvine (CA)
Concordia U, Nebraska (NE)
Connecticut Coll (CT)
Cornell Coll (IA)
Cornell U (NY)
Covenant Coll (GA)
Creighton U (NE)
Dartmouth Coll (NH)
Davidson Coll (NC)
Delaware State U (DE)
Denison U (OH)
DePaul U (IL)
DePauw U (IN)
Dickinson Coll (PA)
Doane U (NE)
Drake U (IA)
Drew U (NJ)
Drury U (MO)
Duquesne U (PA)
Earlham Coll (IN)
East Carolina U (NC)
East Central U (OK)
Eastern Michigan U (MI)
Eastern Nazarene Coll (MA)
Eastern Washington U (WA)
East Stroudsburg U of Pennsylvania (PA)
East Tennessee State U (TN)
Eckerd Coll (FL)
Edgewood Coll (WI)
Elizabethtown Coll (PA)
Elmhurst Coll (IL)
Elon U (NC)
Emory & Henry Coll (VA)
Emory U (GA)
Emporia State U (KS)
Fairfield U (CT)
Fairleigh Dickinson U, Metropolitan Campus (NJ)
Florida Ag and Mech U (FL)
Florida Atlantic U (FL)
Florida Inst of Technology (FL)
Florida Intl U (FL)
Florida State U (FL)
Fordham U (NY)
Francis Marion U (SC)
Franklin & Marshall Coll (PA)
Frostburg State U (MD)
Furman U (SC)
Geneva Coll (PA)
George Mason U (VA)
Georgetown Coll (KY)
Georgetown U (DC)
The George Washington U (DC)
Georgia Coll & State U (GA)
Georgia Inst of Technology (GA)
Georgia Southern U (GA)
Georgia Southern U–Armstrong Campus (GA)
Georgia State U (GA)
Gettysburg Coll (PA)
Gonzaga U (WA)
Gordon Coll (MA)
Goshen Coll (IN)
Grand Valley State U (MI)
Greenville U (IL)
Grinnell Coll (IA)
Grove City Coll (PA)
Guilford Coll (NC)
Gustavus Adolphus Coll (MN)
Hamilton Coll (NY)
Hamline U (MN)
Hampden-Sydney Coll (VA)
Hampshire Coll (MA)
Hampton U (VA)
Harding U (AR)
Hardin-Simmons U (TX)
Hartwick Coll (NY)
Harvard U (MA)
Harvey Mudd Coll (CA)
Haverford Coll (PA)
Hendrix Coll (AR)
High Point U (NC)
Hillsdale Coll (MI)
Hiram Coll (OH)
Hobart and William Smith Colls (NY)
Hofstra U (NY)
Hope Coll (MI)
Houston Baptist U (TX)
Humboldt State U (CA)
Hunter Coll of the City U of New York (NY)
Idaho State U (ID)

Illinois Coll (IL)
Illinois State U (IL)
Illinois Wesleyan U (IL)
Indiana State U (IN)
Indiana U Bloomington (IN)
Indiana U of Pennsylvania (PA)
Indiana U–Purdue U Indianapolis (IN)
Indiana U South Bend (IN)
Indiana U Southeast (IN)
Iona Coll (NY)
Iowa State U of Science and Technology (IA)
Ithaca Coll (NY)
Jackson State U (MS)
Jacksonville U (FL)
James Madison U (VA)
John Carroll U (OH)
Johns Hopkins U (MD)
Juniata Coll (PA)
Kalamazoo Coll (MI)
Kansas State U (KS)
Kansas Wesleyan U (KS)
Kennesaw State U (GA)
Kent State U (OH)
Kenyon Coll (OH)
Kettering U (MI)
King U (TN)
Knox Coll (IL)
Kutztown U of Pennsylvania (PA)
Lafayette Coll (PA)
Lamar U (TX)
La Sierra U (CA)
Lawrence Technological U (MI)
Lawrence U (WI)
Lebanon Valley Coll (PA)
Lehigh U (PA)
Lehman Coll of the City U of New York (NY)
Le Moyne Coll (NY)
Lenoir-Rhyne U (NC)
Lewis U (IL)
Lincoln U (MO)
Lincoln U (PA)
Linfield Coll (OR)
Lipscomb U (TN)
Lock Haven U of Pennsylvania (PA)
Long Island U–LIU Brooklyn (NY)
Long Island U–LIU Post (NY)
Longwood U (VA)
Louisiana State U and A&M Coll (LA)
Loyola Marymount U (CA)
Loyola U Chicago (IL)
Loyola U New Orleans (LA)
Luther Coll (IA)
Lycoming Coll (PA)
Lynchburg Coll (VA)
Macalester Coll (MN)
Manchester U (IN)
Manhattan Coll (NY)
Marietta Coll (OH)
Marlboro Coll (VT)
Marquette U (WI)
Marshall U (WV)
Mary Baldwin U (VA)
Massachusetts Coll of Liberal Arts (MA)
Massachusetts Inst of Technology (MA)
McDaniel Coll (MD)
McMurry U (TX)
Mercer U, Macon (GA)
Merrimack Coll (MA)
Messiah Coll (PA)
Metropolitan State U of Denver (CO)
Miami U (OH)
Michigan State U (MI)
Michigan Technological U (MI)
MidAmerica Nazarene U (KS)
Middlebury Coll (VT)
Middle Tennessee State U (TN)
Millersville U of Pennsylvania (PA)
Millikin U (IL)
Millsaps Coll (MS)
Minnesota State U Moorhead (MN)
Minot State U (ND)
Mississippi State U (MS)
Missouri State U (MO)
Missouri U of Science and Technology (MO)
Monmouth Coll (IL)
Montclair State U (NJ)
Moravian Coll (PA)
Morehead State U (KY)
Morehouse Coll (GA)

Morningside Coll (IA)
Mount Holyoke Coll (MA)
Muhlenberg Coll (PA)
Murray State U (KY)
Muskingum U (OH)
New Coll of Florida (FL)
New Jersey City U (NJ)
New Jersey Inst of Technology (NJ)
New Mexico Highlands U (NM)
New Mexico Inst of Mining and Technology (NM)
New Mexico State U (NM)
New York U (NY)
North Carolina Central U (NC)
North Carolina State U (NC)
North Central Coll (IL)
North Dakota State U (ND)
Northeastern U (MA)
Northern Arizona U (AZ)
Northern Illinois U (IL)
Northern Kentucky U (KY)
Northern Michigan U (MI)
Northwestern U (IL)
Northwest Nazarene U (ID)
Oakland U (MI)
Oberlin Coll (OH)
Occidental Coll (CA)
Oglethorpe U (GA)
Ohio Northern U (OH)
The Ohio State U (OH)
Ohio U (OH)
Ohio Wesleyan U (OH)
Oklahoma Baptist U (OK)
Oklahoma City U (OK)
Oklahoma State U (OK)
Old Dominion U (VA)
Oral Roberts U (OK)
Oregon State U (OR)
Otterbein U (OH)
Ouachita Baptist U (AR)
Pace U, Pleasantville Campus (NY)
Pacific Lutheran U (WA)
Penn State Abington (PA)
Penn State Altoona (PA)
Penn State Beaver (PA)
Penn State Berks (PA)
Penn State Brandywine (PA)
Penn State DuBois (PA)
Penn State Erie, The Behrend Coll (PA)
Penn State Fayette, The Eberly Campus (PA)
Penn State Greater Allegheny (PA)
Penn State Hazleton (PA)
Penn State Lehigh Valley (PA)
Penn State Mont Alto (PA)
Penn State New Kensington (PA)
Penn State Schuylkill (PA)
Penn State Shenango (PA)
Penn State U Park (PA)
Penn State Wilkes-Barre (PA)
Penn State Worthington Scranton (PA)
Penn State York (PA)
Pepperdine U, Malibu (CA)
Piedmont Coll (GA)
Pittsburg State U (KS)
Pitzer Coll (CA)
Point Loma Nazarene U (CA)
Pomona Coll (CA)
Portland State U (OR)
Presbyterian Coll (SC)
Princeton U (NJ)
Principia Coll (IL)
Purchase Coll, State U of New York (NY)
Purdue U (IN)
Purdue U Northwest (IN)
Queens Coll of the City U of New York (NY)
Radford U (VA)
Ramapo Coll of New Jersey (NJ)
Randolph Coll (VA)
Randolph-Macon Coll (VA)
Reed Coll (OR)
Regis U (CO)
Rensselaer Polytechnic Inst (NY)
Rhode Island Coll (RI)
Rhodes Coll (TN)
Rice U (TX)
Roanoke Coll (VA)
Roberts Wesleyan Coll (NY)
Rockhurst U (MO)
Rocky Mountain Coll (MT)
Rollins Coll (FL)
Rose-Hulman Inst of Technology (IN)

Rowan U (NJ)
Rutgers U–Camden (NJ)
Rutgers U–Newark (NJ)
Rutgers U–New Brunswick (NJ)
Saginaw Valley State U (MI)
Saint Anselm Coll (NH)
St. Catherine U (MN)
St. John Fisher Coll (NY)
Saint John's U (MN)
St. John's U (NY)
Saint Joseph's U (PA)
St. Lawrence U (NY)
Saint Louis U (MO)
Saint Mary's Coll of California (CA)
St. Mary's Coll of Maryland (MD)
St. Mary's U (TX)
Saint Mary's U of Minnesota (MN)
Saint Michael's Coll (VT)
St. Norbert Coll (WI)
St. Olaf Coll (MN)
Saint Peter's U (NJ)
Saint Vincent Coll (PA)
Salisbury U (MD)
Samford U (AL)
Sam Houston State U (TX)
San Diego State U (CA)
San Francisco State U (CA)
Santa Clara U (CA)
Sarah Lawrence Coll (NY)
Scripps Coll (CA)
Seattle Pacific U (WA)
Seattle U (WA)
Sewanee: The U of the South (TN)
Shippensburg U of Pennsylvania (PA)
Siena Coll (NY)
Simmons Coll (MA)
Simon Fraser U (BC, Canada)
Simpson Coll (IA)
Skidmore Coll (NY)
Slippery Rock U of Pennsylvania (PA)
Smith Coll (MA)
Sonoma State U (CA)
Southeastern Louisiana U (LA)
Southeast Missouri State U (MO)
Southern Adventist U (TN)
Southern Arkansas U–Magnolia (AR)
Southern Illinois U Carbondale (IL)
Southern Illinois U Edwardsville (IL)
Southern Methodist U (TX)
Southwestern U (TX)
Spelman Coll (GA)
Stanford U (CA)
State U of New York at Fredonia (NY)
State U of New York at New Paltz (NY)
State U of New York at Oswego (NY)
State U of New York at Plattsburgh (NY)
State U of New York Coll at Cortland (NY)
State U of New York Coll at Geneseo (NY)
State U of New York Coll at Oneonta (NY)
State U of New York Coll at Potsdam (NY)
Stephen F. Austin State U (TX)
Stetson U (FL)
Stevens Inst of Technology (NJ)
Stockton U (NJ)
Stonehill Coll (MA)
Stony Brook U, State U of New York (NY)
Suffolk U (MA)
Susquehanna U (PA)
Sweet Briar Coll (VA)
Syracuse U (NY)
Tarleton State U (TX)
Taylor U (IN)
Temple U (PA)
Tennessee Technological U (TN)
Texas A&M U (TX)
Texas A&M U–Central Texas (TX)
Texas A&M U–Commerce (TX)
Texas A&M U–Corpus Christi (TX)
Texas A&M U–Kingsville (TX)
Texas Christian U (TX)
Texas Lutheran U (TX)
Texas State U (TX)
Texas Tech U (TX)
Towson U (MD)

Transylvania U (KY)
Trent U (ON, Canada)
Trevecca Nazarene U (TN)
Trinity U (TX)
Troy U (AL)
Truman State U (MO)
Tufts U (MA)
Tulane U (LA)
Union Coll (NE)
Union Coll (NY)
Union U (TN)
United States Military Acad (NY)
Université de Sherbrooke (QC, Canada)
U at Albany, State U of New York (NY)
U at Buffalo, the State U of New York (NY)
The U of Akron (OH)
The U of Alabama (AL)
The U of Alabama at Birmingham (AL)
U of Alaska Fairbanks (AK)
The U of Arizona (AZ)
U of Arkansas (AR)
U of California, Davis (CA)
U of California, Irvine (CA)
U of California, Los Angeles (CA)
U of California, Riverside (CA)
U of California, San Diego (CA)
U of California, Santa Barbara (CA)
U of California, Santa Cruz (CA)
U of Central Arkansas (AR)
U of Central Florida (FL)
U of Central Missouri (MO)
U of Chicago (IL)
U of Cincinnati (OH)
U of Colorado Boulder (CO)
U of Colorado Colorado Springs (CO)
U of Colorado Denver (CO)
U of Dallas (TX)
U of Dayton (OH)
U of Denver (CO)
U of Evansville (IN)
U of Florida (FL)
U of Georgia (GA)
U of Guelph (ON, Canada)
U of Hartford (CT)
U of Hawaii at Manoa (HI)
U of Houston (TX)
U of Houston–Clear Lake (TX)
U of Idaho (ID)
U of Illinois at Chicago (IL)
The U of Kansas (KS)
U of Kentucky (KY)
U of King's Coll (NS, Canada)
U of La Verne (CA)
U of Louisville (KY)
U of Maine (ME)
U of Maryland, Baltimore County (MD)
U of Maryland, Coll Park (MD)
U of Mary Washington (VA)
U of Massachusetts Amherst (MA)
U of Massachusetts Boston (MA)
U of Massachusetts Dartmouth (MA)
U of Massachusetts Lowell (MA)
U of Memphis (TN)
U of Miami (FL)
U of Michigan (MI)
U of Michigan–Dearborn (MI)
U of Michigan–Flint (MI)
U of Minnesota, Duluth (MN)
U of Minnesota, Morris (MN)
U of Minnesota, Twin Cities Campus (MN)
U of Missouri (MO)
U of Missouri–St. Louis (MO)
U of Montana (MT)
U of Mount Union (OH)
U of Nebraska at Kearney (NE)
U of Nebraska–Lincoln (NE)
U of Nevada, Las Vegas (NV)
U of Nevada, Reno (NV)
U of New Hampshire (NH)
U of New Mexico (NM)
U of New Orleans (LA)
U of North Alabama (AL)
U of North Carolina at Asheville (NC)
The U of North Carolina at Chapel Hill (NC)
The U of North Carolina at Charlotte (NC)

The U of North Carolina at Greensboro (NC)
The U of North Carolina at Pembroke (NC)
The U of North Carolina Wilmington (NC)
U of North Dakota (ND)
U of Northern Colorado (CO)
U of Northern Iowa (IA)
U of North Florida (FL)
U of North Georgia (GA)
U of North Texas (TX)
U of Notre Dame (IN)
U of Oklahoma (OK)
U of Oregon (OR)
U of Pennsylvania (PA)
U of Pittsburgh (PA)
U of Puerto Rico–Humacao (PR)
U of Puget Sound (WA)
U of Regina (SK, Canada)
U of Rhode Island (RI)
U of Richmond (VA)
U of Rochester (NY)
U of St. Thomas (MN)
U of San Diego (CA)
U of San Francisco (CA)
U of Saskatchewan (SK, Canada)
U of Science and Arts of Oklahoma (OK)
The U of Scranton (PA)
U of South Alabama (AL)
U of South Carolina (SC)
U of South Dakota (SD)
U of Southern California (CA)
U of Southern Maine (ME)
U of Southern Mississippi (MS)
The U of Tampa (FL)
The U of Tennessee (TN)
The U of Tennessee at Chattanooga (TN)
The U of Texas at Austin (TX)
The U of Texas at Dallas (TX)
The U of Texas at El Paso (TX)
The U of Texas at San Antonio (TX)
The U of Texas Rio Grande Valley (TX)
U of the Fraser Valley (BC, Canada)
U of the Pacific (CA)
U of the Virgin Islands (VI)
The U of Toledo (OH)
The U of Tulsa (OK)
U of Utah (UT)
U of Vermont (VT)
U of Virginia (VA)
U of Washington (WA)
U of Waterloo (ON, Canada)
U of West Georgia (GA)
U of Wisconsin–Eau Claire (WI)
U of Wisconsin–La Crosse (WI)
U of Wisconsin–Madison (WI)
U of Wisconsin–Milwaukee (WI)
U of Wisconsin–Parkside (WI)
U of Wisconsin–River Falls (WI)
U of Wisconsin–Stevens Point (WI)
U of Wisconsin–Whitewater (WI)
U of Wyoming (WY)
Ursinus Coll (PA)
Utah State U (UT)
Utah Valley U (UT)
Utica Coll (NY)
Valdosta State U (GA)
Valparaiso U (IN)
Vanderbilt U (TN)
Vassar Coll (NY)
Villanova U (PA)
Virginia Commonwealth U (VA)
Virginia Military Inst (VA)
Virginia Polytechnic Inst and State U (VA)
Wabash Coll (IN)
Wagner Coll (NY)
Wake Forest U (NC)
Wartburg Coll (IA)
Washington & Jefferson Coll (PA)
Washington and Lee U (VA)
Washington Coll (MD)
Washington State U (WA)
Washington U in St. Louis (MO)
Wayne State U (MI)
Weber State U (UT)
Wellesley Coll (MA)
Wells Coll (NY)
Wesleyan U (CT)
West Chester U of Pennsylvania (PA)
Western Illinois U (IL)

Western Kentucky U (KY)
Western Michigan U (MI)
Western State Colorado U (CO)
Western Washington U (WA)
Westminster Coll (PA)
Westminster Coll (UT)
Westmont Coll (CA)
West Texas A&M U (TX)
West Virginia U (WV)
West Virginia Wesleyan Coll (WV)
Wheaton Coll (IL)
Wheaton Coll (MA)
Whitman Coll (WA)
Whittier Coll (CA)
Whitworth U (WA)
Wichita State U (KS)
Widener U (PA)
Wilkes U (PA)
Willamette U (OR)
William Jewell Coll (MO)
Williams Coll (MA)
Winona State U (MN)
Wisconsin Lutheran Coll (WI)
Wittenberg U (OH)
Wofford Coll (SC)
Worcester Polytechnic Inst (MA)
Wright State U (OH)
Wright State U–Lake Campus (OH)
Xavier U of Louisiana (LA)
Youngstown State U (OH)

PHYSICS RELATED
Albion Coll (MI)
Augsburg U (MN)
Berry Coll (GA)
Bridgewater Coll (VA)
Bridgewater State U (MA)
Brigham Young U (UT)
Buena Vista U (IA)
California State U, San Marcos (CA)
Christopher Newport U (VA)
Coll of Saint Benedict (MN)
Delaware State U (DE)
Drexel U (PA)
Embry-Riddle Aeronautical U–Daytona (FL)
Emory U (GA)
Florida Inst of Technology (FL)
Fort Lewis Coll (CO)
Francis Marion U (SC)
Lawrence Technological U (MI)
Ohio Northern U (OH)
Presbyterian Coll (SC)
Rensselaer Polytechnic Inst (NY)
Rutgers U–Camden (NJ)
Rutgers U–Newark (NJ)
Saint John's U (MN)
Saint Mary's U of Minnesota (MN)
Southern Arkansas U–Magnolia (AR)
U of California, Davis (CA)
U of California, Irvine (CA)
U of Dayton (OH)
U of Notre Dame (IN)
U of Puerto Rico–Humacao (PR)
U of Regina (SK, Canada)
U of Rhode Island (RI)
U of Rochester (NY)
U of San Francisco (CA)
Whitman Coll (WA)

PHYSICS TEACHER EDUCATION
Abilene Christian U (TX)
Albion Coll (MI)
Arkansas Tech U (AR)
Auburn U (AL)
Augustana Coll (IL)
Ball State U (IN)
Bowdoin Coll (ME)
Bowling Green State U (OH)
Bradley U (IL)
Brigham Young U–Idaho (ID)
Buena Vista U (IA)
Canisius Coll (NY)
Cedarville U (OH)
Central Methodist U (MO)
Central Michigan U (MI)
City Coll of the City U of New York (NY)
The Coll of New Jersey (NJ)
Daytona State Coll (FL)
Delaware State U (DE)
East Central U (OK)
Eastern Michigan U (MI)
Eastern Nazarene Coll (MA)
Eastern Washington U (WA)

Elmhurst Coll (IL)
Emory & Henry Coll (VA)
Goshen Coll (IN)
Grand Valley State U (MI)
Greenville U (IL)
Grove City Coll (PA)
Gustavus Adolphus Coll (MN)
Hofstra U (NY)
Hope Coll (MI)
Indiana U Bloomington (IN)
Indiana U South Bend (IN)
Ithaca Coll (NY)
Juniata Coll (PA)
Kansas Wesleyan U (KS)
Kennesaw State U (GA)
Le Moyne Coll (NY)
Lincoln U (MO)
Lipscomb U (TN)
Madonna U (MI)
Manchester U (IN)
Martin Luther Coll (MN)
Merrimack Coll (MA)
Messiah Coll (PA)
Miami Dade Coll (FL)
Michigan State U (MI)
Minnesota State U Moorhead (MN)
Minot State U (ND)
Missouri State U (MO)
Morningside Coll (IA)
Mount Vernon Nazarene U (OH)
Muskingum U (OH)
North Dakota State U (ND)
Northern Michigan U (MI)
Northwest U (WA)
Ohio Northern U (OH)
Ohio Wesleyan U (OH)
Pittsburg State U (KS)
Providence Coll (RI)
Queens Coll of the City U of New York (NY)
Rhode Island Coll (RI)
Roberts Wesleyan Coll (NY)
Saginaw Valley State U (MI)
St. John Fisher Coll (NY)
St. John's U (NY)
Saint Joseph's U (PA)
Saint Mary's U of Minnesota (MN)
Saint Vincent Coll (PA)
Seattle U (WA)
Southern Adventist U (TN)
Southwestern Adventist U (TX)
State U of New York at New Paltz (NY)
State U of New York Coll at Cortland (NY)
State U of New York Coll at Oneonta (NY)
State U of New York Coll at Potsdam (NY)
Syracuse U (NY)
Taylor U (IN)
Trevecca Nazarene U (TN)
Union Coll (NE)
U of California, San Diego (CA)
U of Central Missouri (MO)
U of Central Oklahoma (OK)
U of Evansville (IN)
U of Illinois at Chicago (IL)
U of Maine at Farmington (ME)
U of Maryland, Baltimore County (MD)
U of Missouri (MO)
U of Nebraska–Lincoln (NE)
U of Regina (SK, Canada)
U of St. Thomas (MN)
U of South Dakota (SD)
U of Waterloo (ON, Canada)
U of Wisconsin–Stevens Point (WI)
U of Wisconsin–Whitewater (WI)
Utah State U (UT)
Utica Coll (NY)
Valparaiso U (IN)
Washington U in St. Louis (MO)
Weber State U (UT)
Western Michigan U (MI)
Winona State U (MN)

PHYSIOLOGICAL PSYCHOLOGY/ PSYCHOBIOLOGY
Albright Coll (PA)
Averett U (VA)
Binghamton U, State U of New York (NY)
Centre Coll (KY)
Florida Atlantic U (FL)
Holy Family U (PA)

Holy Names U (CA)
La Sierra U (CA)
Mills Coll (CA)
Oberlin Coll (OH)
Pace U, Pleasantville Campus (NY)
Quinnipiac U (CT)
Ripon Coll (WI)
Saint Mary's Coll of California (CA)
Southern Adventist U (TN)
U of California, Los Angeles (CA)
U of California, Santa Barbara (CA)
U of Colorado Denver (CO)
U of Michigan (MI)
Vassar Coll (NY)
Washington Coll (MD)

PHYSIOLOGY
Brigham Young U (UT)
California State U, Long Beach (CA)
California State U, San Marcos (CA)
Emmanuel Coll (MA)
Marquette U (WI)
Michigan State U (MI)
Northern Michigan U (MI)
Oklahoma Baptist U (OK)
Oklahoma State U (OK)
Seattle Pacific U (WA)
Southern Illinois U Carbondale (IL)
The U of Arizona (AZ)
U of California, Los Angeles (CA)
U of California, Santa Barbara (CA)
U of Colorado Boulder (CO)
U of Minnesota, Twin Cities Campus (MN)
U of Oregon (OR)
U of Saskatchewan (SK, Canada)
The U of Scranton (PA)
U of Washington (WA)
U of Wyoming (WY)

PLANETARY ASTRONOMY AND SCIENCE
California Inst of Technology (CA)
Florida Inst of Technology (FL)
Iowa State U of Science and Technology (IA)
Stonehill Coll (MA)
U of Waterloo (ON, Canada)

PLANT GENETICS
Purdue U (IN)

PLANT NURSERY MANAGEMENT
Washington State U (WA)

PLANT PATHOLOGY/ PHYTOPATHOLOGY
New Mexico State U (NM)
The Ohio State U (OH)
U of Wisconsin–Madison (WI)

PLANT PROTECTION AND INTEGRATED PEST MANAGEMENT
California State Polytechnic U, Pomona (CA)
Iowa State U of Science and Technology (IA)
U of Hawaii at Manoa (HI)
Washington State U (WA)

PLANT SCIENCES
Auburn U (AL)
Cornell U (NY)
Louisiana State U and A&M Coll (LA)
Middle Tennessee State U (TN)
The Ohio State U (OH)
Penn State U Park (PA)
Rutgers U–New Brunswick (NJ)
Southern Illinois U Carbondale (IL)
State U of New York Coll of Environmental Science and Forestry (NY)
Texas Tech U (TX)
The U of Arizona (AZ)
U of California, Santa Cruz (CA)
U of Florida (FL)
U of Guelph (ON, Canada)
U of Massachusetts Amherst (MA)
U of Minnesota, Crookston (MN)
U of Minnesota, Twin Cities Campus (MN)
U of Missouri (MO)
The U of Tennessee (TN)
Utah State U (UT)
Washington State U (WA)

PLANT SCIENCES RELATED
Auburn U (AL)
U of Hawaii at Manoa (HI)
Utah State U (UT)
West Virginia U (WV)

PLASTICS AND POLYMER ENGINEERING TECHNOLOGY
Eastern Michigan U (MI)
Ferris State U (MI)
Pennsylvania Coll of Technology (PA)
Pittsburg State U (KS)
Shawnee State U (OH)
Weber State U (UT)

PLAYWRITING AND SCREENWRITING
Academy of Art U (CA)
Bennington Coll (VT)
Brigham Young U (UT)
Chapman U (CA)
Columbia Coll Chicago (IL)
Concordia U (QC, Canada)
DePaul U (IL)
Drexel U (PA)
Emerson Coll (MA)
Emory U (GA)
Judson U (IL)
La Sierra U (CA)
Loyola Marymount U (CA)
Marymount Manhattan Coll (NY)
Ohio U (OH)
Point Park U (PA)
Purchase Coll, State U of New York (NY)
U of Southern California (CA)
The U of the Arts (PA)

POLISH
U of Illinois at Chicago (IL)
U of Michigan (MI)
U of Pittsburgh (PA)
U of Wisconsin–Madison (WI)

POLITICAL COMMUNICATION
Emerson Coll (MA)
Florida Southern Coll (FL)
Regent U (VA)
St. Thomas U (NB, Canada)
Suffolk U (MA)
U of Washington (WA)
Weber State U (UT)

POLITICAL ECONOMY
Antioch Coll, Yellow Springs (OH)
Arizona State U at the Tempe campus (AZ)
Augsburg U (MN)
Bryant U (RI)
Eastern Oregon U (OR)
The Evergreen State Coll (WA)
Hillsdale Coll (MI)
Marlboro Coll (VT)
Ohio Northern U (OH)
Rhodes Coll (TN)
Rollins Coll (FL)
Sarah Lawrence Coll (NY)
U of Southern California (CA)
The U of Texas at Dallas (TX)
U of Washington, Bothell (WA)
U of Washington, Tacoma (WA)
Williams Coll (MA)

POLITICAL SCIENCE AND GOVERNMENT
Abilene Christian U (TX)
Acadia U (NS, Canada)
Adams State U (CO)
Adelphi U (NY)
Agnes Scott Coll (GA)
Alabama State U (AL)
Albion Coll (MI)
Albright Coll (PA)
Alcorn State U (MS)
Alfred U (NY)
Allegheny Coll (PA)
Alma Coll (MI)
Alverno Coll (WI)
American Intl Coll (MA)
American Public U System (WV)
American U (DC)
The American U in Cairo (Egypt)
The American U of Paris (France)
Amherst Coll (MA)
Anderson U (IN)
Andrews U (MI)
Angelo State U (TX)
Appalachian State U (NC)

Aquinas Coll (MI)
Arcadia U (PA)
Arizona State U at the Polytechnic campus (AZ)
Arizona State U at the Tempe campus (AZ)
Arizona State U at the West campus (AZ)
Arkansas Tech U (AR)
Asbury U (KY)
Ashland U (OH)
Assumption Coll (MA)
Athabasca U (AB, Canada)
Athens State U (AL)
Auburn U (AL)
Auburn U at Montgomery (AL)
Augsburg U (MN)
Augustana Coll (IL)
Augustana U (SD)
Aurora U (IL)
Austin Coll (TX)
Austin Peay State U (TN)
Averett U (VA)
Avila U (MO)
Azusa Pacific U (CA)
Baldwin Wallace U (OH)
Ball State U (IN)
Bard Coll (NY)
Barnard Coll (NY)
Barry U (FL)
Barton Coll (NC)
Baruch Coll of the City U of New York (NY)
Bates Coll (ME)
Baylor U (TX)
Belhaven U (MS)
Bellarmine U (KY)
Belmont U (TN)
Beloit Coll (WI)
Bemidji State U (MN)
Benedictine Coll (KS)
Benedictine U (IL)
Bennett Coll (NC)
Bennington Coll (VT)
Berea Coll (KY)
Berry Coll (GA)
Bethel U (MN)
Bethune-Cookman U (FL)
Binghamton U, State U of New York (NY)
Biola U (CA)
Birmingham-Southern Coll (AL)
Blackburn Coll (IL)
Black Hills State U (SD)
Bloomsburg U of Pennsylvania (PA)
Boise State U (ID)
Boston Coll (MA)
Boston U (MA)
Bowdoin Coll (ME)
Bowie State U (MD)
Bowling Green State U (OH)
Bradley U (IL)
Brandon U (MB, Canada)
Brescia U (KY)
Brewton-Parker Coll (GA)
Bridgewater Coll (VA)
Bridgewater State U (MA)
Brigham Young U–Idaho (ID)
Brock U (ON, Canada)
Bryan Coll (TN)
Bryant U (RI)
Bryn Mawr Coll (PA)
Bucknell U (PA)
Buena Vista U (IA)
Buffalo State Coll, State U of New York (NY)
Butler U (IN)
Caldwell U (NJ)
California Baptist U (CA)
California Inst of Technology (CA)
California Lutheran U (CA)
California Polytechnic State U, San Luis Obispo (CA)
California State Polytechnic U, Pomona (CA)
California State U, Dominguez Hills (CA)
California State U, East Bay (CA)
California State U, Fullerton (CA)
California State U, Long Beach (CA)
California State U, Los Angeles (CA)
California State U, Northridge (CA)
California State U, Sacramento (CA)

California State U, San Bernardino (CA)
California State U, San Marcos (CA)
California State U, Stanislaus (CA)
California U of Pennsylvania (PA)
Calvary U (MO)
Calvin Coll (MI)
Cameron U (OK)
Campbellsville U (KY)
Canisius Coll (NY)
Capital U (OH)
Cardinal Stritch U (WI)
Carleton Coll (MN)
Carlow U (PA)
Carroll Coll (MT)
Carroll U (WI)
Carson-Newman U (TN)
Carthage Coll (WI)
Case Western Reserve U (OH)
Catawba Coll (NC)
The Catholic U of America (DC)
Cedar Crest Coll (PA)
Cedarville U (OH)
Centenary Coll of Louisiana (LA)
Central Connecticut State U (CT)
Central Methodist U (MO)
Central Michigan U (MI)
Central State U (OH)
Centre Coll (KY)
Chapman U (CA)
Charleston Southern U (SC)
Chatham U (PA)
Chestnut Hill Coll (PA)
Christendom Coll (VA)
Christopher Newport U (VA)
The Citadel, The Military Coll of South Carolina (SC)
City Coll of the City U of New York (NY)
Claremont McKenna Coll (CA)
Clarion U of Pennsylvania (PA)
Clark Atlanta U (GA)
Clarkson U (NY)
Clark U (MA)
Clayton State U (GA)
Clemson U (SC)
Cleveland State U (OH)
Coastal Carolina U (SC)
Coe Coll (IA)
Coker Coll (SC)
Colby Coll (ME)
Colgate U (NY)
The Coll at Brockport, State U of New York (NY)
Coll of Charleston (SC)
The Coll of Idaho (ID)
The Coll of New Jersey (NJ)
The Coll of New Rochelle (NY)
Coll of Saint Benedict (MN)
The Coll of Saint Rose (NY)
Coll of Staten Island of the City U of New York (NY)
Coll of the Holy Cross (MA)
The Coll of William and Mary (VA)
The Coll of Wooster (OH)
Colorado Christian U (CO)
The Colorado Coll (CO)
Colorado Mesa U (CO)
Colorado State U (CO)
Colorado State U–Pueblo (CO)
Columbia Coll (MO)
Columbia Coll (SC)
Columbia U (NY)
Columbus State U (GA)
Concordia U (QC, Canada)
Concordia U Chicago (IL)
Concordia U Irvine (CA)
Concordia U of Edmonton (AB, Canada)
Concordia U Wisconsin (WI)
Concord U (WV)
Connecticut Coll (CT)
Converse Coll (SC)
Corban U (OR)
Cornell Coll (IA)
Cornell U (NY)
Creighton U (NE)
Culver-Stockton Coll (MO)
Daemen Coll (NY)
Dallas Baptist U (TX)
Dartmouth Coll (NH)
Davidson Coll (NC)
Delaware State U (DE)
Denison U (OH)
DePaul U (IL)
DePauw U (IN)

DeSales U (PA)
Dickinson Coll (PA)
Dickinson State U (ND)
Doane U (NE)
Dominican U (IL)
Dominican U of California (CA)
Drake U (IA)
Drew U (NJ)
Drexel U (PA)
Drury U (MO)
Duquesne U (PA)
Earlham Coll (IN)
East Carolina U (NC)
East Central U (OK)
Eastern Michigan U (MI)
Eastern New Mexico U (NM)
Eastern U (PA)
Eastern Washington U (WA)
East Stroudsburg U of Pennsylvania (PA)
East Tennessee State U (TN)
East Texas Baptist U (TX)
Eckerd Coll (FL)
Edgewood Coll (WI)
Elizabethtown Coll (PA)
Elmhurst Coll (IL)
Elon U (NC)
Emmanuel Coll (MA)
Emory & Henry Coll (VA)
Emory U (GA)
Emporia State U (KS)
Endicott Coll (MA)
Eugene Lang Coll of Liberal Arts (NY)
Evangel U (MO)
The Evergreen State Coll (WA)
Fairfield U (CT)
Fairleigh Dickinson U, Florham Campus (NJ)
Fairleigh Dickinson U, Metropolitan Campus (NJ)
Fayetteville State U (NC)
Felician U (NJ)
Ferris State U (MI)
Fitchburg State U (MA)
Flagler Coll (FL)
Florida Ag and Mech U (FL)
Florida Atlantic U (FL)
Florida Gulf Coast U (FL)
Florida Intl U (FL)
Florida Southern Coll (FL)
Florida State U (FL)
Fordham U (NY)
Fort Lewis Coll (CO)
Framingham State U (MA)
Francis Marion U (SC)
Franklin & Marshall Coll (PA)
Franklin Coll (IN)
Franklin Pierce U (NH)
Friends U (KS)
Frostburg State U (MD)
Furman U (SC)
Gannon U (PA)
Geneva Coll (PA)
Georgetown Coll (KY)
Georgetown U (DC)
The George Washington U (DC)
Georgia Coll & State U (GA)
Georgia Gwinnett Coll (GA)
Georgia Southern U–Armstrong Campus (GA)
Georgia Southwestern State U (GA)
Georgia State U (GA)
Gettysburg Coll (PA)
Gonzaga U (WA)
Gordon Coll (MA)
Governors State U (IL)
Grambling State U (LA)
Grand Valley State U (MI)
Grand View U (IA)
Greensboro Coll (NC)
Grinnell Coll (IA)
Grove City Coll (PA)
Guilford Coll (NC)
Gustavus Adolphus Coll (MN)
Hamilton Coll (NY)
Hamline U (MN)
Hampden-Sydney Coll (VA)
Hampshire Coll (MA)
Hampton U (VA)
Harding U (AR)
Hardin-Simmons U (TX)
Harris-Stowe State U (MO)
Hartwick Coll (NY)
Harvard U (MA)
Haverford Coll (PA)

Hawai`i Pacific U (HI)
Heidelberg U (OH)
Hendrix Coll (AR)
High Point U (NC)
Hilbert Coll (NY)
Hillsdale Coll (MI)
Hiram Coll (OH)
Hobart and William Smith Colls (NY)
Hofstra U (NY)
Hollins U (VA)
Holy Family U (PA)
Hood Coll (MD)
Hope Coll (MI)
Houston Baptist U (TX)
Howard Payne U (TX)
Humboldt State U (CA)
Hunter Coll of the City U of New York (NY)
Huntingdon Coll (AL)
Huston-Tillotson U (TX)
Idaho State U (ID)
Illinois Coll (IL)
Illinois State U (IL)
Illinois Wesleyan U (IL)
Immaculata U (PA)
Indiana State U (IN)
Indiana U Bloomington (IN)
Indiana U East (IN)
Indiana U Northwest (IN)
Indiana U of Pennsylvania (PA)
Indiana U–Purdue U Indianapolis (IN)
Indiana U South Bend (IN)
Indiana U Southeast (IN)
Indiana Wesleyan U (IN)
Inter American U of Puerto Rico, Metropolitan Campus (PR)
Inter American U of Puerto Rico, San Germán Campus (PR)
Iona Coll (NY)
Iowa State U of Science and Technology (IA)
Ithaca Coll (NY)
Jackson State U (MS)
Jacksonville U (FL)
James Madison U (VA)
John Brown U (AR)
John Cabot U (Italy)
John Carroll U (OH)
John Jay Coll of Criminal Justice of the City U of New York (NY)
Johns Hopkins U (MD)
Johnson C. Smith U (NC)
Juniata Coll (PA)
Kalamazoo Coll (MI)
Kansas State U (KS)
Kean U (NJ)
Keene State Coll (NH)
Keiser U, Fort Lauderdale (FL)
Kennesaw State U (GA)
Kent State U (OH)
Kentucky State U (KY)
Kenyon Coll (OH)
King's Coll (PA)
King U (TN)
Knox Coll (IL)
Kutztown U of Pennsylvania (PA)
Lafayette Coll (PA)
LaGrange Coll (GA)
Lamar U (TX)
La Roche Coll (PA)
La Salle U (PA)
Lawrence U (WI)
Lebanese American U (Lebanon)
Lebanon Valley Coll (PA)
Lee U (TN)
Lehigh U (PA)
Lehman Coll of the City U of New York (NY)
Le Moyne Coll (NY)
Lenoir-Rhyne U (NC)
LeTourneau U (TX)
Lewis U (IL)
Liberty U (VA)
Lincoln U (MO)
Lincoln U (PA)
Lindenwood U (MO)
Linfield Coll (OR)
Lipscomb U (TN)
Lock Haven U of Pennsylvania (PA)
Long Island U–LIU Brooklyn (NY)
Long Island U–LIU Post (NY)
Longwood U (VA)
Loras Coll (IA)
Louisiana State U and A&M Coll (LA)

Loyola Marymount U (CA)
Loyola U Chicago (IL)
Loyola U New Orleans (LA)
Luther Coll (IA)
Lycoming Coll (PA)
Lynchburg Coll (VA)
Lynn U (FL)
Lyon Coll (AR)
Macalester Coll (MN)
Malone U (OH)
Manchester U (IN)
Manhattan Coll (NY)
Manhattanville Coll (NY)
Mansfield U of Pennsylvania (PA)
Marian U (IN)
Marietta Coll (OH)
Marist Coll (NY)
Marlboro Coll (VT)
Marquette U (WI)
Marshall U (WV)
Mary Baldwin U (VA)
Marymount Manhattan Coll (NY)
Marymount U (VA)
Maryville Coll (TN)
Massachusetts Coll of Liberal Arts (MA)
Massachusetts Inst of Technology (MA)
The Master's U (CA)
McDaniel Coll (MD)
McKendree U (IL)
McMurry U (TX)
McNeese State U (LA)
McPherson Coll (KS)
Mercer U, Macon (GA)
Mercy Coll (NY)
Mercyhurst U (PA)
Meredith Coll (NC)
Merrimack Coll (MA)
Messiah Coll (PA)
Metropolitan State U of Denver (CO)
Miami U (OH)
Michigan State U (MI)
Middlebury Coll (VT)
Middle Tennessee State U (TN)
Millersville U of Pennsylvania (PA)
Milligan Coll (TN)
Millikin U (IL)
Millsaps Coll (MS)
Mills Coll (CA)
Minnesota State U Moorhead (MN)
Mississippi State U (MS)
Missouri State U (MO)
Missouri Valley Coll (MO)
Missouri Western State U (MO)
Molloy Coll (NY)
Monmouth Coll (IL)
Montclair State U (NJ)
Moravian Coll (PA)
Morehead State U (KY)
Morehouse Coll (GA)
Morningside Coll (IA)
Morris Coll (SC)
Mount Holyoke Coll (MA)
Mount Mercy U (IA)
Mount Saint Mary Coll (NY)
Mount Saint Mary's U (CA)
Mount St. Mary's U (MD)
Mount Vernon Nazarene U (OH)
Muhlenberg Coll (PA)
Murray State U (KY)
Muskingum U (OH)
National U (CA)
Nazareth Coll of Rochester (NY)
Neumann U (PA)
Newberry Coll (SC)
New Coll of Florida (FL)
New Jersey City U (NJ)
New Mexico Highlands U (NM)
New Mexico State U (NM)
New York Inst of Technology (NY)
New York U (NY)
Niagara U (NY)
North Carolina Central U (NC)
North Carolina State U (NC)
North Carolina Wesleyan Coll (NC)
North Central Coll (IL)
North Dakota State U (ND)
Northeastern State U (OK)
Northeastern U (MA)
Northern Arizona U (AZ)
Northern Illinois U (IL)
Northern Kentucky U (KY)
Northern Michigan U (MI)
Northern State U (SD)
Northern Vermont U–Lyndon (VT)

North Greenville U (SC)
Northwestern Coll (IA)
Northwestern Oklahoma State U (OK)
Northwestern U (IL)
Northwest Missouri State U (MO)
Northwest Nazarene U (ID)
Northwest U (WA)
Notre Dame de Namur U (CA)
Nova Southeastern U (FL)
Oakland U (MI)
Oberlin Coll (OH)
Occidental Coll (CA)
Oglethorpe U (GA)
Ohio Christian U (OH)
Ohio Dominican U (OH)
Ohio Northern U (OH)
The Ohio State U (OH)
Ohio U (OH)
Ohio Wesleyan U (OH)
Oklahoma Baptist U (OK)
Oklahoma City U (OK)
Oklahoma State U (OK)
Old Dominion U (VA)
Olivet Nazarene U (IL)
Oral Roberts U (OK)
Oregon State U (OR)
Otterbein U (OH)
Ouachita Baptist U (AR)
Pace U (NY)
Pace U, Pleasantville Campus (NY)
Pacific Lutheran U (WA)
Palm Beach Atlantic U (FL)
Penn State Abington (PA)
Penn State Altoona (PA)
Penn State Beaver (PA)
Penn State Berks (PA)
Penn State Brandywine (PA)
Penn State DuBois (PA)
Penn State Erie, The Behrend Coll (PA)
Penn State Fayette, The Eberly Campus (PA)
Penn State Greater Allegheny (PA)
Penn State Hazleton (PA)
Penn State Lehigh Valley (PA)
Penn State Mont Alto (PA)
Penn State New Kensington (PA)
Penn State Schuylkill (PA)
Penn State Shenango (PA)
Penn State U Park (PA)
Penn State Wilkes-Barre (PA)
Penn State Worthington Scranton (PA)
Penn State York (PA)
Pepperdine U, Malibu (CA)
Pfeiffer U (NC)
Piedmont Coll (GA)
Pine Manor Coll (MA)
Pittsburg State U (KS)
Pitzer Coll (CA)
Point Loma Nazarene U (CA)
Point Park U (PA)
Pomona Coll (CA)
Portland State U (OR)
Prairie View A&M U (TX)
Presbyterian Coll (SC)
Princeton U (NJ)
Principia Coll (IL)
Providence Coll (RI)
Purchase Coll, State U of New York (NY)
Purdue U (IN)
Purdue U Northwest (IN)
Queens Coll of the City U of New York (NY)
Quinnipiac U (CT)
Radford U (VA)
Ramapo Coll of New Jersey (NJ)
Randolph Coll (VA)
Randolph-Macon Coll (VA)
Redeemer U Coll (ON, Canada)
Reed Coll (OR)
Regis U (CO)
Rhode Island Coll (RI)
Rhodes Coll (TN)
Rice U (TX)
Rider U (NJ)
Ripon Coll (WI)
Rivier U (NH)
Roanoke Coll (VA)
Rochester Inst of Technology (NY)
Rockford U (IL)
Rockhurst U (MO)
Rocky Mountain Coll (MT)
Roger Williams U (RI)
Rollins Coll (FL)

Roosevelt U (IL)
Rosemont Coll (PA)
Rowan U (NJ)
Rust Coll (MS)
Rutgers U–Camden (NJ)
Rutgers U–Newark (NJ)
Rutgers U–New Brunswick (NJ)
Sacred Heart U (CT)
Saginaw Valley State U (MI)
St. Ambrose U (IA)
Saint Anselm Coll (NH)
Saint Augustine's U (NC)
St. Bonaventure U (NY)
St. Catherine U (MN)
Saint Francis U (PA)
St. John Fisher Coll (NY)
Saint John's U (MN)
St. John's U (NY)
St. Joseph's Coll, Long Island Campus (NY)
St. Joseph's Coll, New York (NY)
Saint Joseph's U (PA)
St. Lawrence U (NY)
Saint Leo U (FL)
Saint Louis U (MO)
Saint Martin's U (WA)
Saint Mary's Coll of California (CA)
St. Mary's Coll of Maryland (MD)
St. Mary's U (TX)
Saint Michael's Coll (VT)
St. Norbert Coll (WI)
St. Olaf Coll (MN)
Saint Peter's U (NJ)
St. Thomas U (FL)
St. Thomas U (NB, Canada)
Saint Vincent Coll (PA)
Salisbury U (MD)
Salve Regina U (RI)
Samford U (AL)
Sam Houston State U (TX)
San Diego State U (CA)
San Francisco State U (CA)
Santa Clara U (CA)
Sarah Lawrence Coll (NY)
Schreiner U (TX)
Scripps Coll (CA)
Seattle Pacific U (WA)
Seattle U (WA)
Seton Hill U (PA)
Sewanee: The U of the South (TN)
Shaw U (NC)
Shenandoah U (VA)
Shepherd U (WV)
Shippensburg U of Pennsylvania (PA)
Siena Coll (NY)
Simmons Coll (MA)
Simon Fraser U (BC, Canada)
Simpson Coll (IA)
Skidmore Coll (NY)
Slippery Rock U of Pennsylvania (PA)
Smith Coll (MA)
Sonoma State U (CA)
Southeastern Louisiana U (LA)
Southeastern Oklahoma State U (OK)
Southeastern U (FL)
Southeast Missouri State U (MO)
Southern Illinois U Carbondale (IL)
Southern Illinois U Edwardsville (IL)
Southern Methodist U (TX)
Southern Utah U (UT)
Southwest Baptist U (MO)
Southwestern U (TX)
Spelman Coll (GA)
Spring Hill Coll (AL)
Stanford U (CA)
State U of New York at Fredonia (NY)
State U of New York at New Paltz (NY)
State U of New York at Oswego (NY)
State U of New York at Plattsburgh (NY)
State U of New York Coll at Cortland (NY)
State U of New York Coll at Geneseo (NY)
State U of New York Coll at Oneonta (NY)
State U of New York Coll at Potsdam (NY)
Stephen F. Austin State U (TX)
Stetson U (FL)

Stockton U (NJ)
Stonehill Coll (MA)
Stony Brook U, State U of New York (NY)
Suffolk U (MA)
Susquehanna U (PA)
Sweet Briar Coll (VA)
Syracuse U (NY)
Tarleton State U (TX)
Temple U (PA)
Tennessee Technological U (TN)
Texas A&M U (TX)
Texas A&M U–Central Texas (TX)
Texas A&M U–Commerce (TX)
Texas A&M U–Corpus Christi (TX)
Texas A&M U–Kingsville (TX)
Texas A&M U–Texarkana (TX)
Texas Christian U (TX)
Texas Lutheran U (TX)
Texas State U (TX)
Texas Tech U (TX)
Texas Woman's U (TX)
Thomas U (GA)
Towson U (MD)
Transylvania U (KY)
Trent U (ON, Canada)
Trinity U (TX)
Troy U (AL)
Truman State U (MO)
Tufts U (MA)
Tulane U (LA)
Tusculum Coll (TN)
Union Coll (NY)
Union U (TN)
United States Coast Guard Acad (CT)
United States Military Acad (NY)
U at Albany, State U of New York (NY)
U at Buffalo, the State U of New York (NY)
The U of Akron (OH)
The U of Alabama (AL)
The U of Alabama at Birmingham (AL)
U of Alaska Fairbanks (AK)
The U of Arizona (AZ)
U of Arkansas (AR)
U of California, Davis (CA)
U of California, Irvine (CA)
U of California, Los Angeles (CA)
U of California, Riverside (CA)
U of California, San Diego (CA)
U of California, Santa Barbara (CA)
U of California, Santa Cruz (CA)
U of Central Arkansas (AR)
U of Central Florida (FL)
U of Central Missouri (MO)
U of Central Oklahoma (OK)
U of Charleston (WV)
U of Chicago (IL)
U of Cincinnati (OH)
U of Colorado Boulder (CO)
U of Colorado Colorado Springs (CO)
U of Colorado Denver (CO)
U of Dallas (TX)
U of Dayton (OH)
U of Denver (CO)
U of Evansville (IN)
The U of Findlay (OH)
U of Florida (FL)
U of Georgia (GA)
U of Guam (GU)
U of Hartford (CT)
U of Hawaii at Manoa (HI)
U of Houston (TX)
U of Houston–Downtown (TX)
U of Idaho (ID)
U of Illinois at Chicago (IL)
U of Illinois at Springfield (IL)
U of Jamestown (ND)
The U of Kansas (KS)
U of Kentucky (KY)
U of King's Coll (NS, Canada)
U of La Verne (CA)
U of Louisiana at Monroe (LA)
U of Louisville (KY)
U of Maine (ME)
U of Maine at Farmington (ME)
U of Maine at Presque Isle (ME)
U of Mary Hardin-Baylor (TX)
U of Maryland, Baltimore County (MD)
U of Maryland, Coll Park (MD)
U of Maryland U Coll (MD)
U of Mary Washington (VA)

U of Massachusetts Amherst (MA)
U of Massachusetts Boston (MA)
U of Massachusetts Dartmouth (MA)
U of Massachusetts Lowell (MA)
U of Memphis (TN)
U of Miami (FL)
U of Michigan (MI)
U of Michigan–Dearborn (MI)
U of Michigan–Flint (MI)
U of Minnesota, Duluth (MN)
U of Minnesota, Morris (MN)
U of Minnesota, Twin Cities Campus (MN)
U of Missouri (MO)
U of Missouri–St. Louis (MO)
U of Mobile (AL)
U of Montevallo (AL)
U of Mount Union (OH)
U of Nebraska at Kearney (NE)
U of Nebraska–Lincoln (NE)
U of Nevada, Las Vegas (NV)
U of Nevada, Reno (NV)
U of New England (ME)
U of New Hampshire (NH)
U of New Haven (CT)
U of New Mexico (NM)
U of New Orleans (LA)
U of North Alabama (AL)
U of North Carolina at Asheville (NC)
The U of North Carolina at Chapel Hill (NC)
The U of North Carolina at Charlotte (NC)
The U of North Carolina at Greensboro (NC)
The U of North Carolina at Pembroke (NC)
The U of North Carolina Wilmington (NC)
U of North Dakota (ND)
U of Northern Colorado (CO)
U of Northern Iowa (IA)
U of North Florida (FL)
U of North Georgia (GA)
U of North Texas (TX)
U of Notre Dame (IN)
U of Oklahoma (OK)
U of Oregon (OR)
U of Pennsylvania (PA)
U of Pittsburgh (PA)
U of Pittsburgh at Bradford (PA)
U of Pittsburgh at Greensburg (PA)
U of Providence (MT)
U of Puget Sound (WA)
U of Regina (SK, Canada)
U of Rhode Island (RI)
U of Richmond (VA)
U of Rochester (NY)
U of St. Francis (IL)
U of Saint Francis (IN)
U of Saint Mary (KS)
U of St. Thomas (MN)
U of St. Thomas (TX)
U of San Diego (CA)
U of San Francisco (CA)
U of Saskatchewan (SK, Canada)
U of Science and Arts of Oklahoma (OK)
The U of Scranton (PA)
U of South Alabama (AL)
U of South Carolina (SC)
U of South Carolina Aiken (SC)
U of South Dakota (SD)
U of Southern California (CA)
U of Southern Indiana (IN)
U of Southern Maine (ME)
U of Southern Mississippi (MS)
U of South Florida, St. Petersburg (FL)
The U of Tampa (FL)
The U of Tennessee (TN)
The U of Tennessee at Chattanooga (TN)
The U of Tennessee at Martin (TN)
The U of Texas at Austin (TX)
The U of Texas at Dallas (TX)
The U of Texas at El Paso (TX)
The U of Texas at San Antonio (TX)
The U of Texas of the Permian Basin (TX)
The U of Texas Rio Grande Valley (TX)
U of the Fraser Valley (BC, Canada)
U of the Incarnate Word (TX)

U of the Pacific (CA)
The U of Toledo (OH)
U of Toronto (ON, Canada)
The U of Tulsa (OK)
U of Utah (UT)
U of Vermont (VT)
U of Virginia (VA)
The U of Virginia's Coll at Wise (VA)
U of Washington (WA)
U of Waterloo (ON, Canada)
U of West Georgia (GA)
U of Wisconsin–Eau Claire (WI)
U of Wisconsin–La Crosse (WI)
U of Wisconsin–Madison (WI)
U of Wisconsin–Milwaukee (WI)
U of Wisconsin–Parkside (WI)
U of Wisconsin–Platteville (WI)
U of Wisconsin–River Falls (WI)
U of Wisconsin–Stevens Point (WI)
U of Wisconsin–Whitewater (WI)
U of Wyoming (WY)
Ursinus Coll (PA)
Ursuline Coll (OH)
Utah State U (UT)
Utah Valley U (UT)
Utica Coll (NY)
Valdosta State U (GA)
Valparaiso U (IN)
Vanderbilt U (TN)
Vanguard U of Southern California (CA)
Vassar Coll (NY)
Villanova U (PA)
Virginia Commonwealth U (VA)
Virginia Polytechnic Inst and State U (VA)
Virginia Wesleyan U (VA)
Wabash Coll (IN)
Wagner Coll (NY)
Wake Forest U (NC)
Walsh U (OH)
Wartburg Coll (IA)
Washington & Jefferson Coll (PA)
Washington and Lee U (VA)
Washington Coll (MD)
Washington State U (WA)
Washington State U–Vancouver (WA)
Washington U in St. Louis (MO)
Wayne State Coll (NE)
Wayne State U (MI)
Weber State U (UT)
Webster U (MO)
Wellesley Coll (MA)
Wells Coll (NY)
Wesleyan U (CT)
West Chester U of Pennsylvania (PA)
Western Connecticut State U (CT)
Western Illinois U (IL)
Western Kentucky U (KY)
Western Michigan U (MI)
Western New England U (MA)
Western Oregon U (OR)
Western State Colorado U (CO)
Western Washington U (WA)
Westfield State U (MA)
Westminster Coll (PA)
Westminster Coll (UT)
Westmont Coll (CA)
West Texas A&M U (TX)
West Virginia State U (WV)
West Virginia U (WV)
West Virginia U Inst of Technology (WV)
West Virginia Wesleyan Coll (WV)
Wheaton Coll (IL)
Wheaton Coll (MA)
Whitman Coll (WA)
Whittier Coll (CA)
Whitworth U (WA)
Wichita State U (KS)
Widener U (PA)
Wilkes U (PA)
Willamette U (OR)
William Jewell Coll (MO)
William Paterson U of New Jersey (NJ)
Williams Coll (MA)
Wilmington U (DE)
Winona State U (MN)
Winthrop U (SC)
Wittenberg U (OH)
Wofford Coll (SC)
Wright State U (OH)

Wright State U–Lake Campus (OH)
Xavier U of Louisiana (LA)
York Coll of Pennsylvania (PA)
Youngstown State U (OH)

POLITICAL SCIENCE AND GOVERNMENT RELATED
American U in Bulgaria (Bulgaria)
The American U of Paris (France)
Belmont U (TN)
Bethel Coll (IN)
Blackburn Coll (IL)
Brandeis U (MA)
Buena Vista U (IA)
Capital U (OH)
Colorado Christian U (CO)
Delaware State U (DE)
Emory & Henry Coll (VA)
George Mason U (VA)
Georgetown Coll (KY)
McDaniel Coll (MD)
Muhlenberg Coll (PA)
Ohio Northern U (OH)
Our Lady of the Lake U (TX)
Pitzer Coll (CA)
Saint Mary's Coll of California (CA)
Saint Mary's U of Minnesota (MN)
Shenandoah U (VA)
U of California, Davis (CA)
U of Guelph (ON, Canada)
U of Northern Iowa (IA)
U of Washington (WA)
U of Wisconsin–Whitewater (WI)
Western Michigan U (MI)
Whitman Coll (WA)
William Peace U (NC)

POLYMER CHEMISTRY
Pittsburg State U (KS)
The U of Akron (OH)

POLYMER/PLASTICS ENGINEERING
Auburn U (AL)
Case Western Reserve U (OH)
Penn State Erie, The Behrend Coll (PA)
The U of Akron (OH)
U of Massachusetts Lowell (MA)
U of Southern Mississippi (MS)
U of Wisconsin–Stout (WI)
Western Washington U (WA)

POLYSOMNOGRAPHY
Stony Brook U, State U of New York (NY)

PORTUGUESE
Florida Intl U (FL)
Georgetown U (DC)
Indiana U Bloomington (IN)
The Ohio State U (OH)
Pitzer Coll (CA)
Rhode Island Coll (RI)
Rutgers U–Newark (NJ)
Rutgers U–New Brunswick (NJ)
Smith Coll (MA)
Tulane U (LA)
United States Military Acad (NY)
U of California, Los Angeles (CA)
U of California, Santa Barbara (CA)
U of Florida (FL)
U of Massachusetts Amherst (MA)
U of Massachusetts Dartmouth (MA)
U of New Mexico (NM)
The U of Texas at Austin (TX)
U of Toronto (ON, Canada)
U of Wisconsin–Madison (WI)

POULTRY SCIENCE
Auburn U (AL)
Delaware State U (DE)
Mississippi State U (MS)
North Carolina State U (NC)
Stephen F. Austin State U (TX)
Texas A&M U (TX)
U of Arkansas (AR)
U of Georgia (GA)
U of Maryland Eastern Shore (MD)
U of Wisconsin–Madison (WI)
Virginia Polytechnic Inst and State U (VA)

PRACTICAL NURSING, VOCATIONAL NURSING AND NURSING ASSISTANTS RELATED
Caribbean U (PR)

PRE-CHIROPRACTIC
Ashland U (OH)
Augustana U (SD)
Ball State U (IN)
Coll of Saint Benedict (MN)
Millikin U (IL)
Saint John's U (MN)
U of Regina (SK, Canada)
U of Sioux Falls (SD)

PRE-DENTISTRY STUDIES
Abilene Christian U (TX)
Acadia U (NS, Canada)
Albright Coll (PA)
Allegheny Coll (PA)
American U (DC)
Anderson U (IN)
Ashland U (OH)
Auburn U (AL)
Augustana U (SD)
Baldwin Wallace U (OH)
Ball State U (IN)
Barry U (FL)
Birmingham-Southern Coll (AL)
Boise State U (ID)
Boston U (MA)
Bowling Green State U (OH)
Bradley U (IL)
Brandon U (MB, Canada)
Buffalo State Coll, State U of New York (NY)
Calvin Coll (MI)
Campbellsville U (KY)
Carroll U (WI)
Carthage Coll (WI)
Cedar Crest Coll (PA)
Chapman U (CA)
City Coll of the City U of New York (NY)
Clark U (MA)
Clemson U (SC)
Coe Coll (IA)
Coll of Mount Saint Vincent (NY)
Coll of Saint Benedict (MN)
Concordia U Chicago (IL)
Defiance Coll (OH)
Drake U (IA)
Eastern Nazarene Coll (MA)
Elmhurst Coll (IL)
Evangel U (MO)
Florida Southern Coll (FL)
Fordham U (NY)
Franklin Pierce U (NH)
Furman U (SC)
The George Washington U (DC)
Gettysburg Coll (PA)
Graceland U (IA)
Grand Valley State U (MI)
Gustavus Adolphus Coll (MN)
Hamline U (MN)
Hampton U (VA)
Heidelberg U (OH)
Hobart and William Smith Colls (NY)
Hofstra U (NY)
Illinois Coll (IL)
Indiana Wesleyan U (IN)
Iowa State U of Science and Technology (IA)
John Carroll U (OH)
King's Coll (PA)
Lehigh U (PA)
Le Moyne Coll (NY)
Limestone Coll (SC)
Lindenwood U (MO)
Lindsey Wilson Coll (KY)
Lipscomb U (TN)
Lubbock Christian U (TX)
Madonna U (MI)
Manchester U (IN)
Maryville U of Saint Louis (MO)
Mercyhurst U (PA)
Millikin U (IL)
Missouri Valley Coll (MO)
Mount Mercy U (IA)
Mount Vernon Nazarene U (OH)
Muskingum U (OH)
Nazareth Coll of Rochester (NY)
Newman U (KS)
North Central Coll (IL)
Northern Michigan U (MI)
Northwestern Oklahoma State U (OK)
Northwest Nazarene U (ID)
Oglethorpe U (GA)
Ohio Northern U (OH)
Ohio Wesleyan U (OH)

Ouachita Baptist U (AR)
Quinnipiac U (CT)
Rhode Island Coll (RI)
Ripon Coll (WI)
Rivier U (NH)
Roberts Wesleyan Coll (NY)
Rochester Inst of Technology (NY)
Rockford U (IL)
Rutgers U–New Brunswick (NJ)
Saginaw Valley State U (MI)
Saint Anselm Coll (NH)
St. Catherine U (MN)
Saint Francis U (PA)
Saint John's U (MN)
Simpson Coll (IA)
Sonoma State U (CA)
State U of New York at Oswego (NY)
State U of New York Coll at Cortland (NY)
State U of New York Coll at Geneseo (NY)
State U of New York Coll at Oneonta (NY)
State U of New York Coll of Environmental Science and Forestry (NY)
Stetson U (FL)
Stevens Inst of Technology (NJ)
Susquehanna U (PA)
Syracuse U (NY)
Tarleton State U (TX)
Tennessee Technological U (TN)
Trinity U (TX)
Union Coll (NE)
Union U (TN)
U of Bridgeport (CT)
U of Central Missouri (MO)
U of Cincinnati (OH)
U of Dallas (TX)
U of Dayton (OH)
U of Illinois at Chicago (IL)
U of Maryland, Coll Park (MD)
U of Maryland Eastern Shore (MD)
U of Massachusetts Amherst (MA)
U of Minnesota, Morris (MN)
U of Nebraska–Lincoln (NE)
U of New England (ME)
U of Regina (SK, Canada)
U of St. Francis (IL)
U of Sioux Falls (SD)
The U of Tampa (FL)
The U of Tennessee at Martin (TN)
U of Wisconsin–Parkside (WI)
Upper Iowa U (IA)
Utah State U (UT)
Utica Coll (NY)
Virginia Wesleyan U (VA)
Wagner Coll (NY)
Walsh U (OH)
Washington Coll (MD)
Washington U in St. Louis (MO)
Waynesburg U (PA)
Wells Coll (NY)
Westminster Coll (PA)
Westmont Coll (CA)
West Virginia Wesleyan Coll (WV)
Whitworth U (WA)
Widener U (PA)
Youngstown State U (OH)

PRE-ENGINEERING
Anderson U (SC)
Asbury U (KY)
Augustana U (SD)
Azusa Pacific U (CA)
Baldwin Wallace U (OH)
Bethel U (TN)
Canisius Coll (NY)
Colorado State U (CO)
Delaware State U (DE)
Drake U (IA)
Eastern Nazarene Coll (MA)
Hamline U (MN)
Inter American U of Puerto Rico, San Germán Campus (PR)
Le Moyne Coll (NY)
Northwest Nazarene U (ID)
Ouachita Baptist U (AR)
Roberts Wesleyan Coll (NY)
Scripps Coll (CA)
Simpson Coll (IA)
Spring Hill Coll (AL)
U of Montana (MT)
The U of Scranton (PA)
U of Wisconsin–Parkside (WI)
Ursinus Coll (PA)

Wagner Coll (NY)
Waynesburg U (PA)
West Texas A&M U (TX)

PRE-LAW STUDIES
Abilene Christian U (TX)
Acadia U (NS, Canada)
Albright Coll (PA)
Allegheny Coll (PA)
Anderson U (IN)
Andrews U (MI)
Arcadia U (PA)
Ashland U (OH)
Auburn U (AL)
Augustana U (SD)
Azusa Pacific U (CA)
Babson Coll (MA)
Ball State U (IN)
Bard Coll (NY)
Barry U (FL)
Baylor U (TX)
Becker Coll (MA)
Bemidji State U (MN)
Bennington Coll (VT)
Binghamton U, State U of New York (NY)
Biola U (CA)
Birmingham-Southern Coll (AL)
Bowling Green State U (OH)
Brandon U (MB, Canada)
Bryant U (RI)
Buena Vista U (IA)
Buffalo State Coll, State U of New York (NY)
California State U, Dominguez Hills (CA)
Calvin Coll (MI)
Campbellsville U (KY)
Carthage Coll (WI)
Cedar Crest Coll (PA)
Cedarville U (OH)
Champlain Coll (VT)
City Coll of the City U of New York (NY)
Clark U (MA)
Coe Coll (IA)
Coll of Mount Saint Vincent (NY)
The Coll of New Rochelle (NY)
Coll of Saint Benedict (MN)
The Coll of Saint Rose (NY)
Colorado Christian U (CO)
Concordia Coll–New York (NY)
Concordia U Chicago (IL)
Concordia U Wisconsin (WI)
Corban U (OR)
Defiance Coll (OH)
DeSales U (PA)
Dominican U (IL)
Drake U (IA)
Eastern Nazarene Coll (MA)
Elmhurst Coll (IL)
Emmanuel Coll (GA)
Emory & Henry Coll (VA)
Evangel U (MO)
Florida Inst of Technology (FL)
Florida Southern Coll (FL)
Fordham U (NY)
Franklin Pierce U (NH)
Furman U (SC)
The George Washington U (DC)
Gettysburg Coll (PA)
Grand View U (IA)
Gustavus Adolphus Coll (MN)
Hamline U (MN)
Hampton U (VA)
Hartwick Coll (NY)
Heidelberg U (OH)
Hobart and William Smith Colls (NY)
Hofstra U (NY)
Howard Payne U (TX)
Illinois Coll (IL)
Indiana Tech (IN)
Indiana Wesleyan U (IN)
Iowa State U of Science and Technology (IA)
Ithaca Coll (NY)
John Carroll U (OH)
Judson U (IL)
King's Coll (PA)
Le Moyne Coll (NY)
Limestone Coll (SC)
Lincoln Memorial U (TN)
Lindenwood U (MO)
Lindsey Wilson Coll (KY)
Lipscomb U (TN)
Louisiana Coll (LA)

Madonna U (MI)
Manchester U (IN)
Mansfield U of Pennsylvania (PA)
Marlboro Coll (VT)
Massachusetts Coll of Liberal Arts (MA)
The Master's U (CA)
Michigan State U (MI)
Millikin U (IL)
Missouri Valley Coll (MO)
Mount Mercy U (IA)
Mount Vernon Nazarene U (OH)
Muskingum U (OH)
National U (CA)
Nazareth Coll of Rochester (NY)
Newman U (KS)
North Central Coll (IL)
Northern Arizona U (AZ)
Northern Michigan U (MI)
Northwestern Oklahoma State U (OK)
Northwest Nazarene U (ID)
Notre Dame de Namur U (CA)
Nova Southeastern U (FL)
Oglethorpe U (GA)
Ohio Northern U (OH)
Ohio Wesleyan U (OH)
Oklahoma Christian U (OK)
Oklahoma City U (OK)
Ouachita Baptist U (AR)
Palm Beach Atlantic U (FL)
Pfeiffer U (NC)
Quinnipiac U (CT)
Rensselaer Polytechnic Inst (NY)
Rhode Island Coll (RI)
Ripon Coll (WI)
Rivier U (NH)
Roberts Wesleyan Coll (NY)
Rochester Inst of Technology (NY)
Rockford U (IL)
Rutgers U–New Brunswick (NJ)
Saginaw Valley State U (MI)
Saint Anselm Coll (NH)
St. Catherine U (MN)
Saint Francis U (PA)
Saint John's U (MN)
St. Thomas U (FL)
Seton Hill U (PA)
Simpson Coll (IA)
Smith Coll (MA)
Sonoma State U (CA)
State U of New York at Fredonia (NY)
State U of New York at Oswego (NY)
State U of New York Coll at Cortland (NY)
State U of New York Coll at Geneseo (NY)
State U of New York Coll at Oneonta (NY)
State U of New York Coll of Environmental Science and Forestry (NY)
Stetson U (FL)
Stevens Inst of Technology (NJ)
Susquehanna U (PA)
Syracuse U (NY)
Tennessee Technological U (TN)
Trine U (IN)
Trinity U (TX)
Union Coll (NE)
Union U (TN)
U of Bridgeport (CT)
U of Cincinnati (OH)
U of Dallas (TX)
The U of Findlay (OH)
U of Maryland, Coll Park (MD)
U of Maryland Eastern Shore (MD)
U of Minnesota, Morris (MN)
U of Montana (MT)
U of Pittsburgh at Greensburg (PA)
U of Regina (SK, Canada)
U of St. Francis (IL)
U of Sioux Falls (SD)
The U of Tampa (FL)
U of Wisconsin–Parkside (WI)
U of Wisconsin–Superior (WI)
Utah State U (UT)
Utica Coll (NY)
Wagner Coll (NY)
Warner Pacific Coll (OR)
Washington Coll (MD)
Wayland Baptist U (TX)
Waynesburg U (PA)
Wells Coll (NY)
Western State Colorado U (CO)

Westminster Coll (PA)
Westmont Coll (CA)
West Texas A&M U (TX)
West Virginia Wesleyan Coll (WV)
Whittier Coll (CA)
Whitworth U (WA)
William Peace U (NC)
Xavier U of Louisiana (LA)
Youngstown State U (OH)

PREMEDICAL STUDIES
Abilene Christian U (TX)
Acadia U (NS, Canada)
Alaska Pacific U (AK)
Albright Coll (PA)
Allegheny Coll (PA)
American U (DC)
Anderson U (IN)
Andrews U (MI)
Arcadia U (PA)
Arizona State U at the Downtown Phoenix campus (AZ)
Arizona State U at the West campus (AZ)
Ashland U (OH)
Auburn U (AL)
Augustana Coll (IL)
Augustana U (SD)
Averett U (VA)
Avila U (MO)
Baldwin Wallace U (OH)
Ball State U (IN)
Bard Coll (NY)
Barry U (FL)
Bemidji State U (MN)
Bennington Coll (VT)
Binghamton U, State U of New York (NY)
Birmingham-Southern Coll (AL)
Bluffton U (OH)
Bob Jones U (SC)
Boise State U (ID)
Boston U (MA)
Bowling Green State U (OH)
Bradley U (IL)
Brandon U (MB, Canada)
Bryant U (RI)
Buffalo State Coll, State U of New York (NY)
Calvin Coll (MI)
Campbellsville U (KY)
Caribbean U (PR)
Carroll U (WI)
Carthage Coll (WI)
Cedar Crest Coll (PA)
Chapman U (CA)
City Coll of the City U of New York (NY)
Clark U (MA)
Clemson U (SC)
Coe Coll (IA)
Coll of Mount Saint Vincent (NY)
The Coll of New Rochelle (NY)
Coll of Saint Benedict (MN)
Colorado Christian U (CO)
Concordia U Chicago (IL)
Cornerstone U (MI)
Defiance Coll (OH)
Dominican U (IL)
Drake U (IA)
Earlham Coll (IN)
Eastern Nazarene Coll (MA)
Elmhurst Coll (IL)
Evangel U (MO)
Florida Southern Coll (FL)
Fordham U (NY)
Franklin Pierce U (NH)
Furman U (SC)
The George Washington U (DC)
Gettysburg Coll (PA)
Graceland U (IA)
Gustavus Adolphus Coll (MN)
Hamline U (MN)
Hampton U (VA)
Hartwick Coll (NY)
Heidelberg U (OH)
Hobart and William Smith Colls (NY)
Hofstra U (NY)
Illinois Coll (IL)
Immaculata U (PA)
Indiana Wesleyan U (IN)
Iowa State U of Science and Technology (IA)
Ithaca Coll (NY)
John Carroll U (OH)
King's Coll (PA)

La Salle U (PA)
Lehigh U (PA)
Le Moyne Coll (NY)
Lenoir-Rhyne U (NC)
Limestone Coll (SC)
Lincoln Memorial U (TN)
Lindenwood U (MO)
Lindsey Wilson Coll (KY)
Lipscomb U (TN)
Lubbock Christian U (TX)
Madonna U (MI)
Manchester U (IN)
Marlboro Coll (VT)
Maryville U of Saint Louis (MO)
Massachusetts Coll of Liberal Arts (MA)
The Master's U (CA)
MCPHS U (MA)
Mercer U, Macon (GA)
Miami U (OH)
Michigan State U (MI)
Millikin U (IL)
Missouri Valley Coll (MO)
Mount Mercy U (IA)
Mount St. Joseph U (OH)
Mount Vernon Nazarene U (OH)
Muskingum U (OH)
Nazareth Coll of Rochester (NY)
Newman U (KS)
North Carolina Wesleyan Coll (NC)
North Central Coll (IL)
Northern Michigan U (MI)
Northwestern Oklahoma State U (OK)
Northwestern U (IL)
Northwest Nazarene U (ID)
Notre Dame de Namur U (CA)
Oglethorpe U (GA)
Ohio Northern U (OH)
Ohio Wesleyan U (OH)
Oklahoma City U (OK)
Ouachita Baptist U (AR)
Pacific Lutheran U (WA)
Penn State Abington (PA)
Penn State Altoona (PA)
Penn State Beaver (PA)
Penn State Berks (PA)
Penn State Brandywine (PA)
Penn State DuBois (PA)
Penn State Erie, The Behrend Coll (PA)
Penn State Fayette, The Eberly Campus (PA)
Penn State Greater Allegheny (PA)
Penn State Hazleton (PA)
Penn State Lehigh Valley (PA)
Penn State Mont Alto (PA)
Penn State New Kensington (PA)
Penn State Schuylkill (PA)
Penn State Shenango (PA)
Penn State U Park (PA)
Penn State Wilkes-Barre (PA)
Penn State Worthington Scranton (PA)
Penn State York (PA)
Pfeiffer U (NC)
Quinnipiac U (CT)
Rensselaer Polytechnic Inst (NY)
Rhode Island Coll (RI)
Ripon Coll (WI)
Rivier U (NH)
Roberts Wesleyan Coll (NY)
Rochester Inst of Technology (NY)
Rockford U (IL)
Rutgers U–New Brunswick (NJ)
Saginaw Valley State U (MI)
St. Andrews U (NC)
Saint Anselm Coll (NH)
St. Catherine U (MN)
Saint Francis U (PA)
Saint John's U (MN)
St. Thomas Aquinas Coll (NY)
St. Thomas U (FL)
Samford U (AL)
Sarah Lawrence Coll (NY)
Simpson Coll (IA)
Smith Coll (MA)
Sonoma State U (CA)
Southeastern U (FL)
State U of New York at Fredonia (NY)
State U of New York at Oswego (NY)
State U of New York Coll at Cortland (NY)
State U of New York Coll at Geneseo (NY)

State U of New York Coll at Oneonta (NY)
State U of New York Coll of Environmental Science and Forestry (NY)
Stetson U (FL)
Stevens Inst of Technology (NJ)
Susquehanna U (PA)
Syracuse U (NY)
Tennessee Technological U (TN)
Texas Lutheran U (TX)
Trine U (IN)
Trinity U (TX)
Union Coll (NE)
Union U (TN)
Université de Sherbrooke (QC, Canada)
The U of Akron (OH)
U of Arkansas (AR)
U of Bridgeport (CT)
U of Central Missouri (MO)
U of Cincinnati (OH)
U of Dallas (TX)
U of Dayton (OH)
U of Hartford (CT)
U of Maine at Machias (ME)
U of Maryland Eastern Shore (MD)
U of Massachusetts Amherst (MA)
U of Minnesota, Morris (MN)
U of Montana (MT)
U of Nebraska–Lincoln (NE)
U of New England (ME)
U of Notre Dame (IN)
U of Regina (SK, Canada)
U of St. Francis (IL)
U of Sioux Falls (SD)
The U of Tampa (FL)
The U of Tennessee at Martin (TN)
U of Wisconsin–Milwaukee (WI)
U of Wisconsin–Parkside (WI)
U of Wisconsin–Superior (WI)
Upper Iowa U (IA)
Utah State U (UT)
Utica Coll (NY)
Vanguard U of Southern California (CA)
Virginia Wesleyan U (VA)
Wagner Coll (NY)
Walsh U (OH)
Warner Pacific Coll (OR)
Washington Coll (MD)
Washington U in St. Louis (MO)
Waynesburg U (PA)
Wells Coll (NY)
West Chester U of Pennsylvania (PA)
Westminster Coll (PA)
Westmont Coll (CA)
West Virginia Wesleyan Coll (WV)
Whittier Coll (CA)
Whitworth U (WA)
Widener U (PA)
Xavier U of Louisiana (LA)
Youngstown State U (OH)

PRENURSING STUDIES
Allegheny Coll (PA)
Arcadia U (PA)
Arizona State U at the Downtown Phoenix campus (AZ)
Averett U (VA)
Baylor U (TX)
Berry Coll (GA)
Biola U (CA)
Brigham Young U (UT)
California State U, Fullerton (CA)
Cleveland State U (OH)
The Coll of Idaho (ID)
Concordia U Chicago (IL)
Delaware State U (DE)
Eastern Nazarene Coll (MA)
Gettysburg Coll (PA)
Hardin-Simmons U (TX)
Jacksonville U (FL)
La Salle U (PA)
Limestone Coll (SC)
Lindenwood U (MO)
Lipscomb U (TN)
Lubbock Christian U (TX)
Madonna U (MI)
Missouri Valley Coll (MO)
Mount St. Joseph U (OH)
Oklahoma City U (OK)
Ouachita Baptist U (AR)
St. Thomas U (FL)
Seattle U (WA)
Simpson Coll (IA)

Tennessee Wesleyan U (TN)
U of Michigan–Flint (MI)
U of Montana (MT)

PRE-OCCUPATIONAL THERAPY
Arcadia U (PA)
Ashland U (OH)
Augustana U (SD)
Bradley U (IL)
Coll of Saint Benedict (MN)
Cornerstone U (MI)
Gwynedd Mercy U (PA)
Lubbock Christian U (TX)
Millikin U (IL)
Mount Vernon Nazarene U (OH)
Pace U (NY)
Saint John's U (MN)
Trevecca Nazarene U (TN)
U of Regina (SK, Canada)
U of St. Francis (IL)
Walsh U (OH)

PRE-OPTOMETRY
Ashland U (OH)
Augustana U (SD)
Ball State U (IN)
Calvin Coll (MI)
Lehigh U (PA)
Le Moyne Coll (NY)
Madonna U (MI)
Millikin U (IL)
Pace U (NY)
Rhode Island Coll (RI)
Simpson Coll (IA)
U of Regina (SK, Canada)
U of St. Francis (IL)
U of Wisconsin–Parkside (WI)

PRE-PHARMACY STUDIES
Allegheny Coll (PA)
Ashland U (OH)
Auburn U (AL)
Augustana U (SD)
Baldwin Wallace U (OH)
Barry U (FL)
Benedictine U (IL)
Bethel U (TN)
Butler U (IN)
Calvin Coll (MI)
Carroll U (WI)
Chapman U (CA)
Clemson U (SC)
Coll of Saint Benedict (MN)
Cornerstone U (MI)
Dominican U (IL)
Eastern Nazarene Coll (MA)
Elmhurst Coll (IL)
Emmanuel Coll (GA)
Emory & Henry Coll (VA)
Gettysburg Coll (PA)
Hamline U (MN)
Husson U (ME)
King's Coll (PA)
Le Moyne Coll (NY)
Limestone Coll (SC)
Lindsey Wilson Coll (KY)
Lipscomb U (TN)
Lubbock Christian U (TX)
Manchester U (IN)
Millikin U (IL)
Missouri Valley Coll (MO)
Mount Vernon Nazarene U (OH)
Muskingum U (OH)
Northern Michigan U (MI)
Northwest Nazarene U (ID)
Ouachita Baptist U (AR)
Roberts Wesleyan Coll (NY)
Saint John's U (MN)
Saint Michael's Coll (VT)
Simpson Coll (IA)
Union U (TN)
U of Central Missouri (MO)
U of Charleston (WV)
U of Minnesota, Morris (MN)
U of Montana (MT)
U of Nebraska–Lincoln (NE)
U of New England (ME)
U of Regina (SK, Canada)
U of St. Francis (IL)
The U of Tennessee at Martin (TN)
U of the Incarnate Word (TX)
U of Wisconsin–Parkside (WI)
Walsh U (OH)
Washington State U (WA)
Washington U in St. Louis (MO)
Westmont Coll (CA)
West Virginia Wesleyan Coll (WV)

Youngstown State U (OH)

PRE-PHYSICAL THERAPY
Anderson U (SC)
Arcadia U (PA)
Asbury U (KY)
Ashland U (OH)
Augustana U (SD)
Becker Coll (MA)
Blue Mountain Coll (MS)
Bradley U (IL)
California Baptist U (CA)
Calvin Coll (MI)
Coll of Saint Benedict (MN)
Hamline U (MN)
Kansas Wesleyan U (KS)
Lubbock Christian U (TX)
Massachusetts Coll of Liberal Arts (MA)
Merrimack Coll (MA)
Millikin U (IL)
Mount St. Joseph U (OH)
Mount Vernon Nazarene U (OH)
Northern Vermont U–Lyndon (VT)
Pace U (NY)
Rockford U (IL)
Saint John's U (MN)
Saint Mary's U of Minnesota (MN)
Simpson Coll (IA)
Trevecca Nazarene U (TN)
U of Dayton (OH)
The U of Findlay (OH)
U of Kentucky (KY)
U of Mary Hardin-Baylor (TX)
U of Montana (MT)
U of Regina (SK, Canada)
U of St. Francis (IL)
U of Sioux Falls (SD)
U of Wisconsin–Parkside (WI)
Walsh U (OH)
Western Washington U (WA)

PRE-THEOLOGY/PRE-MINISTERIAL STUDIES
Ashland U (OH)
Augustana U (SD)
Calvin Coll (MI)
Coll of Biblical Studies–Houston (TX)
Coll of Saint Benedict (MN)
Concordia Coll–New York (NY)
Concordia U Chicago (IL)
Concordia U of Edmonton (AB, Canada)
Corban U (OR)
Doane U (NE)
Eastern Nazarene Coll (MA)
Emmaus Bible Coll (IA)
Geneva Coll (PA)
Lee U (TN)
Manchester U (IN)
Martin Luther Coll (MN)
Mid-Atlantic Christian U (NC)
Nyack Coll (NY)
Ohio Northern U (OH)
Ohio Wesleyan U (OH)
Oral Roberts U (OK)
Point U (GA)
Saint John's U (MN)
Shorter U (GA)
Simpson Coll (IA)
Tabor Coll (KS)
Tennessee Wesleyan U (TN)
Trinity Coll of Florida (FL)
U of Dallas (TX)
Waynesburg U (PA)
Westmont Coll (CA)

PRE-VETERINARY STUDIES
Abilene Christian U (TX)
Acadia U (NS, Canada)
Albright Coll (PA)
Allegheny Coll (PA)
American U (DC)
Anderson U (IN)
Andrews U (MI)
Ashland U (OH)
Auburn U (AL)
Augustana U (SD)
Baldwin Wallace U (OH)
Ball State U (IN)
Barry U (FL)
Becker Coll (MA)
Bemidji State U (MN)
Binghamton U, State U of New York (NY)
Boise State U (ID)
Bradley U (IL)

Brandon U (MB, Canada)
Buffalo State Coll, State U of New York (NY)
Calvin Coll (MI)
Campbellsville U (KY)
Carroll U (WI)
Carthage Coll (WI)
Cedar Crest Coll (PA)
Chapman U (CA)
City Coll of the City U of New York (NY)
Clark U (MA)
Clemson U (SC)
Coe Coll (IA)
Coll of Saint Benedict (MN)
Coll of the Atlantic (ME)
Concordia Coll–New York (NY)
Defiance Coll (OH)
Delaware State U (DE)
Drake U (IA)
Eastern Nazarene Coll (MA)
Elmhurst Coll (IL)
Emory & Henry Coll (VA)
Evangel U (MO)
Florida Southern Coll (FL)
Fordham U (NY)
Franklin Pierce U (NH)
Furman U (SC)
Gettysburg Coll (PA)
Grand Valley State U (MI)
Gustavus Adolphus Coll (MN)
Hamline U (MN)
Hampton U (VA)
Hartwick Coll (NY)
Heidelberg U (OH)
Hobart and William Smith Colls (NY)
Hofstra U (NY)
Illinois Coll (IL)
Indiana Wesleyan U (IN)
Iowa State U of Science and Technology (IA)
John Carroll U (OH)
King's Coll (PA)
Le Moyne Coll (NY)
Limestone Coll (SC)
Lincoln Memorial U (TN)
Lindenwood U (MO)
Lindsey Wilson Coll (KY)
Lipscomb U (TN)
Lubbock Christian U (TX)
Madonna U (MI)
Manchester U (IN)
Marlboro Coll (VT)
Maryville U of Saint Louis (MO)
Mercy Coll (NY)
Mercyhurst U (PA)
Michigan State U (MI)
Millikin U (IL)
Missouri Valley Coll (MO)
Mount Mercy U (IA)
Mount Vernon Nazarene U (OH)
Muskingum U (OH)
Nazareth Coll of Rochester (NY)
Newman U (KS)
North Central Coll (IL)
Northern Michigan U (MI)
Northwest Missouri State U (MO)
Northwest Nazarene U (ID)
Oglethorpe U (GA)
Ohio Northern U (OH)
Ohio Wesleyan U (OH)
Ouachita Baptist U (AR)
Penn State U Park (PA)
Quinnipiac U (CT)
Rhode Island Coll (RI)
Ripon Coll (WI)
Rivier U (NH)
Roberts Wesleyan Coll (NY)
Rochester Inst of Technology (NY)
Rockford U (IL)
St. Andrews U (NC)
St. Catherine U (MN)
Saint Francis U (PA)
Saint John's U (MN)
Simpson Coll (IA)
Sonoma State U (CA)
State U of New York at Fredonia (NY)
State U of New York at Oswego (NY)
State U of New York Coll at Geneseo (NY)
State U of New York Coll at Oneonta (NY)

State U of New York Coll of Environmental Science and Forestry (NY)
State U of New York Coll of Technology at Canton (NY)
Stetson U (FL)
Susquehanna U (PA)
Syracuse U (NY)
Tennessee Technological U (TN)
Trinity U (TX)
The U of Arizona (AZ)
U of Bridgeport (CT)
U of Central Missouri (MO)
The U of Findlay (OH)
U of Illinois at Chicago (IL)
U of Maryland, Coll Park (MD)
U of Massachusetts Amherst (MA)
U of Minnesota, Crookston (MN)
U of Minnesota, Morris (MN)
U of Nebraska–Lincoln (NE)
U of Nevada, Reno (NV)
U of Regina (SK, Canada)
U of St. Francis (IL)
U of Sioux Falls (SD)
The U of Tampa (FL)
The U of Tennessee at Martin (TN)
U of Wisconsin–Parkside (WI)
Upper Iowa U (IA)
Utah State U (UT)
Utica Coll (NY)
Virginia Wesleyan U (VA)
Walsh U (OH)
Warner Pacific Coll (OR)
Washington Coll (MD)
Washington U in St. Louis (MO)
Waynesburg U (PA)
Wells Coll (NY)
Westminster Coll (PA)
Westmont Coll (CA)
West Virginia Wesleyan Coll (WV)
Whitworth U (WA)
Widener U (PA)
Youngstown State U (OH)

PRINTING MANAGEMENT
Carroll U (WI)
Coll of the Ozarks (MO)
Ferris State U (MI)
Pittsburg State U (KS)
Rochester Inst of Technology (NY)
U of Minnesota, Duluth (MN)

PRINTMAKING
Adams State U (CO)
Alberta Coll of Art & Design (AB, Canada)
Aquinas Coll (MI)
Arcadia U (PA)
Bennington Coll (VT)
Birmingham-Southern Coll (AL)
Boston U (MA)
Bowling Green State U (OH)
Bradley U (IL)
Brigham Young U (UT)
Buffalo State Coll, State U of New York (NY)
California Coll of the Arts (CA)
California State U, Long Beach (CA)
Columbia Coll (MO)
Concordia U (QC, Canada)
Drake U (IA)
Escuela de Artes Plasticas y Diseño de Puerto Rico (PR)
Ferris State U (MI)
Indiana Wesleyan U (IN)
Inter American U of Puerto Rico, San Germán Campus (PR)
Kansas City Art Inst (MO)
Laguna Coll of Art & Design (CA)
Maryland Inst Coll of Art (MD)
Massachusetts Coll of Art and Design (MA)
Minneapolis Coll of Art and Design (MN)
New Hampshire Inst of Art (NH)
Northern Michigan U (MI)
Northwest Nazarene U (ID)
Ohio Northern U (OH)
Pacific Northwest Coll of Art (OR)
Pratt Inst (NY)
Providence Coll (RI)
Purchase Coll, State U of New York (NY)
Rhode Island Coll (RI)
Rhode Island School of Design (RI)
Rutgers U–New Brunswick (NJ)

San Francisco Art Inst (CA)
Savannah Coll of Art and Design (GA)
School of Visual Arts (NY)
Seton Hill U (PA)
Sonoma State U (CA)
State U of New York at New Paltz (NY)
Syracuse U (NY)
Temple U (PA)
Texas Christian U (TX)
U of Dallas (TX)
U of Hartford (CT)
The U of Kansas (KS)
U of Miami (FL)
U of Michigan (MI)
U of North Dakota (ND)
U of Oregon (OR)
U of Puget Sound (WA)
U of Regina (SK, Canada)
U of San Francisco (CA)
The U of Texas at El Paso (TX)
Washington U in St. Louis (MO)
Western State Colorado U (CO)
Youngstown State U (OH)

PROFESSIONAL, TECHNICAL, BUSINESS, AND SCIENTIFIC WRITING
Albion Coll (MI)
Arizona State U at the Polytechnic campus (AZ)
Baylor U (TX)
Blackburn Coll (IL)
Boise State U (ID)
Bowling Green State U (OH)
Brescia U (KY)
Carnegie Mellon U (PA)
Cedarville U (OH)
Chatham U (PA)
Coker Coll (SC)
Concordia U, St. Paul (MN)
Eastern Michigan U (MI)
Eastern Washington U (WA)
Emory & Henry Coll (VA)
Excelsior Coll (NY)
Ferris State U (MI)
Fitchburg State U (MA)
Iowa State U of Science and Technology (IA)
James Madison U (VA)
Juniata Coll (PA)
King U (TN)
Kutztown U of Pennsylvania (PA)
Lubbock Christian U (TX)
Madonna U (MI)
Maryville Coll (TN)
Massachusetts Coll of Liberal Arts (MA)
Miami U (OH)
Michigan State U (MI)
Missouri State U (MO)
Missouri U of Science and Technology (MO)
Montana Tech of The U of Montana (MT)
Mount Mary U (WI)
New Jersey Inst of Technology (NJ)
New Mexico Inst of Mining and Technology (NM)
Ohio Northern U (OH)
Oregon Inst of Technology (OR)
Penn State Berks (PA)
Penn State Lehigh Valley (PA)
Purdue U (IN)
Saginaw Valley State U (MI)
Saint Leo U (FL)
St. Thomas U (FL)
San Francisco State U (CA)
Savannah Coll of Art and Design (GA)
Taylor U (IN)
Tennessee Technological U (TN)
Texas Tech U (TX)
U of Central Oklahoma (OK)
U of Hartford (CT)
U of Houston–Downtown (TX)
U of North Texas (TX)
U of Rhode Island (RI)
U of South Florida Sarasota-Manatee (FL)
U of Washington (WA)
U of Wisconsin–Stout (WI)
Valparaiso U (IN)
Walsh U (OH)
Weber State U (UT)
Winthrop U (SC)

Woodbury U (CA)
York Coll of Pennsylvania (PA)
Youngstown State U (OH)

PROJECT MANAGEMENT
Bryant U (RI)
Coll of Charleston (SC)
Davenport U, Grand Rapids (MI)
HEC Montreal (QC, Canada)
Malone U (OH)
Minnesota State U Moorhead (MN)
Northcentral U (CA)
Oakland U (MI)
U of the Incarnate Word (TX)
Wentworth Inst of Technology (MA)

PSYCHIATRIC/MENTAL HEALTH NURSING
Brandon U (MB, Canada)

PSYCHIATRIC/MENTAL HEALTH SERVICES TECHNOLOGY
Columbia Southern U (AL)

PSYCHOLOGY
Abilene Christian U (TX)
Acadia U (NS, Canada)
Adams State U (CO)
Adelphi U (NY)
Agnes Scott Coll (GA)
Alabama State U (AL)
Alaska Pacific U (AK)
Albion Coll (MI)
Albright Coll (PA)
Alcorn State U (MS)
Alfred U (NY)
Allegheny Coll (PA)
Alliant Intl U–San Diego (CA)
Alma Coll (MI)
Alverno Coll (WI)
American Intl Coll (MA)
American Public U System (WV)
American U (DC)
The American U in Cairo (Egypt)
American U of Beirut (Lebanon)
The American U of Paris (France)
Amherst Coll (MA)
Anderson U (IN)
Anderson U (SC)
Andrews U (MI)
Angelo State U (TX)
Antioch Coll, Yellow Springs (OH)
Appalachian State U (NC)
Aquinas Coll (MI)
Arcadia U (PA)
Arizona Christian U (AZ)
Arizona State U at the Polytechnic campus (AZ)
Arizona State U at the Tempe campus (AZ)
Arizona State U at the West campus (AZ)
Arkansas Tech U (AR)
Asbury U (KY)
Ashland U (OH)
Assumption Coll (MA)
Athabasca U (AB, Canada)
Athens State U (AL)
Auburn U (AL)
Auburn U at Montgomery (AL)
Augsburg U (MN)
Augustana Coll (IL)
Augustana U (SD)
Aurora U (IL)
Austin Coll (TX)
Austin Peay State U (TN)
Averett U (VA)
Avila U (MO)
Azusa Pacific U (CA)
Baker U (KS)
Baldwin Wallace U (OH)
Ball State U (IN)
The Baptist Coll of Florida (FL)
Barclay Coll (KS)
Bard Coll (NY)
Barnard Coll (NY)
Barry U (FL)
Barton Coll (NC)
Baruch Coll of the City U of New York (NY)
Bates Coll (ME)
Baylor U (TX)
Bay Path U (MA)
Beacon Coll (FL)
Becker Coll (MA)
Belhaven U (MS)
Bellarmine U (KY)

Belmont U (TN)
Beloit Coll (WI)
Bemidji State U (MN)
Benedictine Coll (KS)
Benedictine U (IL)
Bennett Coll (NC)
Bennington Coll (VT)
Berea Coll (KY)
Berry Coll (GA)
Bethany Lutheran Coll (MN)
Bethel Coll (IN)
Bethel Coll (KS)
Bethel U (MN)
Bethel U (TN)
Bethune-Cookman U (FL)
Binghamton U, State U of New York (NY)
Biola U (CA)
Birmingham-Southern Coll (AL)
Blackburn Coll (IL)
Black Hills State U (SD)
Bloomsburg U of Pennsylvania (PA)
Bluefield Coll (VA)
Blue Mountain Coll (MS)
Bluffton U (OH)
Boise State U (ID)
Boston Coll (MA)
Boston U (MA)
Bowie State U (MD)
Bowling Green State U (OH)
Bradley U (IL)
Brandeis U (MA)
Brandman U (CA)
Brandon U (MB, Canada)
Brescia U (KY)
Brewton-Parker Coll (GA)
Bridgewater Coll (VA)
Bridgewater State U (MA)
Brigham Young U–Idaho (ID)
Brock U (ON, Canada)
Bryan Coll (TN)
Bryant U (RI)
Bryn Athyn Coll of the New Church (PA)
Bryn Mawr Coll (PA)
Bucknell U (PA)
Buena Vista U (IA)
Buffalo State Coll, State U of New York (NY)
Butler U (IN)
Cairn U (PA)
Caldwell U (NJ)
California Baptist U (CA)
California Lutheran U (CA)
California Polytechnic State U, San Luis Obispo (CA)
California State Polytechnic U, Pomona (CA)
California State U, Dominguez Hills (CA)
California State U, East Bay (CA)
California State U, Fullerton (CA)
California State U, Long Beach (CA)
California State U, Los Angeles (CA)
California State U, Monterey Bay (CA)
California State U, Northridge (CA)
California State U, Sacramento (CA)
California State U, San Bernardino (CA)
California State U, San Marcos (CA)
California State U, Stanislaus (CA)
California U of Pennsylvania (PA)
Calumet Coll of Saint Joseph (IN)
Calvin Coll (MI)
Cameron U (OK)
Campbellsville U (KY)
Canisius Coll (NY)
Capital U (OH)
Cardinal Stritch U (WI)
Carleton Coll (MN)
Carlos Albizu U (PR)
Carlow U (PA)
Carnegie Mellon U (PA)
Carroll Coll (MT)
Carroll U (WI)
Carson-Newman U (TN)
Carthage Coll (WI)
Case Western Reserve U (OH)
Catawba Coll (NC)
The Catholic U of America (DC)
Cazenovia Coll (NY)
Cedar Crest Coll (PA)

Cedarville U (OH)
Centenary Coll of Louisiana (LA)
Central Connecticut State U (CT)
Central Methodist U (MO)
Central Michigan U (MI)
Central State U (OH)
Centre Coll (KY)
Chaminade U of Honolulu (HI)
Champlain Coll (VT)
Chapman U (CA)
Charleston Southern U (SC)
Charter Oak State Coll (CT)
Chatham U (PA)
Chestnut Hill Coll (PA)
Chowan U (NC)
Christian Brothers U (TN)
Christopher Newport U (VA)
The Citadel, The Military Coll of South Carolina (SC)
City Coll of the City U of New York (NY)
Claremont McKenna Coll (CA)
Clarion U of Pennsylvania (PA)
Clark Atlanta U (GA)
Clarke U (IA)
Clarkson U (NY)
Clark U (MA)
Clemson U (SC)
Cleveland State U (OH)
Coastal Carolina U (SC)
Coe Coll (IA)
Coker Coll (SC)
Colby Coll (ME)
Colgate U (NY)
The Coll at Brockport, State U of New York (NY)
Coll of Charleston (SC)
Coll of Coastal Georgia (GA)
The Coll of Idaho (ID)
Coll of Mount Saint Vincent (NY)
The Coll of New Jersey (NJ)
The Coll of New Rochelle (NY)
Coll of Saint Benedict (MN)
Coll of Saint Elizabeth (NJ)
Coll of Saint Mary (NE)
The Coll of Saint Rose (NY)
The Coll of St. Scholastica (MN)
Coll of Staten Island of the City U of New York (NY)
Coll of the Atlantic (ME)
Coll of the Holy Cross (MA)
Coll of the Ozarks (MO)
The Coll of William and Mary (VA)
The Coll of Wooster (OH)
Colorado Christian U (CO)
The Colorado Coll (CO)
Colorado Mesa U (CO)
Colorado State U (CO)
Colorado State U–Pueblo (CO)
Columbia Coll (MO)
Columbia Coll (SC)
Columbia U (NY)
Columbus State U (GA)
Concordia Coll–New York (NY)
Concordia U (QC, Canada)
Concordia U Chicago (IL)
Concordia U Irvine (CA)
Concordia U, Nebraska (NE)
Concordia U of Edmonton (AB, Canada)
Concordia U, St. Paul (MN)
Concordia U Wisconsin (WI)
Concord U (WV)
Connecticut Coll (CT)
Converse Coll (SC)
Corban U (OR)
Cornell Coll (IA)
Cornell U (NY)
Cornerstone U (MI)
Cottey Coll (MO)
Covenant Coll (GA)
Creighton U (NE)
Criswell Coll (TX)
Culver-Stockton Coll (MO)
Curry Coll (MA)
Daemen Coll (NY)
Dallas Baptist U (TX)
Dartmouth Coll (NH)
Davidson Coll (NC)
Dean Coll (MA)
Defiance Coll (OH)
Delaware State U (DE)
Denison U (OH)
DePaul U (IL)
DePauw U (IN)
DEREE - The American Coll of Greece (Greece)

DeSales U (PA)
Dickinson Coll (PA)
Dickinson State U (ND)
Doane U (NE)
Dominican Coll (NY)
Dominican U (IL)
Dominican U of California (CA)
Drake U (IA)
Drew U (NJ)
Drexel U (PA)
Duquesne U (PA)
D'Youville Coll (NY)
Earlham Coll (IN)
East Carolina U (NC)
East Central U (OK)
Eastern Mennonite U (VA)
Eastern Michigan U (MI)
Eastern Nazarene Coll (MA)
Eastern New Mexico U (NM)
Eastern Oregon U (OR)
Eastern U (PA)
Eastern Washington U (WA)
East Stroudsburg U of Pennsylvania (PA)
East Tennessee State U (TN)
East Texas Baptist U (TX)
Eckerd Coll (FL)
Edgewood Coll (WI)
Elizabethtown Coll (PA)
Elmhurst Coll (IL)
Elms Coll (MA)
Elon U (NC)
Emmanuel Coll (GA)
Emmanuel Coll (MA)
Emory & Henry Coll (VA)
Emory U (GA)
Emporia State U (KS)
Endicott Coll (MA)
Eugene Lang Coll of Liberal Arts (NY)
Evangel U (MO)
The Evergreen State Coll (WA)
Excelsior Coll (NY)
Fairfield U (CT)
Fairleigh Dickinson U, Florham Campus (NJ)
Fairleigh Dickinson U, Metropolitan Campus (NJ)
Fayetteville State U (NC)
Felician U (NJ)
Ferris State U (MI)
Fisher Coll (MA)
Fitchburg State U (MA)
Flagler Coll (FL)
Florida Ag and Mech U (FL)
Florida Atlantic U (FL)
Florida Gulf Coast U (FL)
Florida Inst of Technology (FL)
Florida Intl U (FL)
Florida National U (FL)
Florida Southern Coll (FL)
Florida State U (FL)
Fordham U (NY)
Fort Lewis Coll (CO)
Framingham State U (MA)
Francis Marion U (SC)
Franklin & Marshall Coll (PA)
Franklin Coll (IN)
Franklin Pierce U (NH)
Franklin U Switzerland (Switzerland)
Friends U (KS)
Frostburg State U (MD)
Furman U (SC)
Gannon U (PA)
Geneva Coll (PA)
George Mason U (VA)
Georgetown Coll (KY)
Georgetown U (DC)
The George Washington U (DC)
Georgia Gwinnett Coll (GA)
Georgian Court U (NJ)
Georgia Southern U (GA)
Georgia Southern U–Armstrong Campus (GA)
Georgia Southwestern State U (GA)
Georgia State U (GA)
Gettysburg Coll (PA)
Gonzaga U (WA)
Gordon Coll (MA)
Goshen Coll (IN)
Governors State U (IL)
Graceland U (IA)
Grambling State U (LA)
Grand Valley State U (MI)
Grand View U (IA)

Granite State Coll (NH)
Green Mountain Coll (VT)
Greensboro Coll (NC)
Greenville U (IL)
Grinnell Coll (IA)
Grove City Coll (PA)
Guilford Coll (NC)
Gustavus Adolphus Coll (MN)
Gwynedd Mercy U (PA)
Hamilton Coll (NY)
Hamline U (MN)
Hampden-Sydney Coll (VA)
Hampshire Coll (MA)
Hampton U (VA)
Hannibal-LaGrange U (MO)
Harding U (AR)
Hardin-Simmons U (TX)
Hartwick Coll (NY)
Harvard U (MA)
Haverford Coll (PA)
Hawai'i Pacific U (HI)
Heidelberg U (OH)
Hendrix Coll (AR)
High Point U (NC)
Hilbert Coll (NY)
Hillsdale Coll (MI)
Hiram Coll (OH)
Hobart and William Smith Colls (NY)
Hofstra U (NY)
Hollins U (VA)
Holy Family U (PA)
Holy Names U (CA)
Hood Coll (MD)
Hope Coll (MI)
Hope Intl U (CA)
Houston Baptist U (TX)
Howard Payne U (TX)
Humboldt State U (CA)
Hunter Coll of the City U of New York (NY)
Husson U (ME)
Huston-Tillotson U (TX)
Idaho State U (ID)
Illinois Coll (IL)
Illinois State U (IL)
Illinois Wesleyan U (IL)
Immaculata U (PA)
Indiana State U (IN)
Indiana Tech (IN)
Indiana U East (IN)
Indiana U Kokomo (IN)
Indiana U Northwest (IN)
Indiana U of Pennsylvania (PA)
Indiana U–Purdue U Indianapolis (IN)
Indiana U South Bend (IN)
Indiana U Southeast (IN)
Indiana Wesleyan U (IN)
Inter American U of Puerto Rico, Aguadilla Campus (PR)
Inter American U of Puerto Rico, Fajardo Campus (PR)
Inter American U of Puerto Rico, Metropolitan Campus (PR)
Inter American U of Puerto Rico, San Germán Campus (PR)
Iona Coll (NY)
Iowa State U of Science and Technology (IA)
Ithaca Coll (NY)
Jackson State U (MS)
Jacksonville U (FL)
James Madison U (VA)
John Brown U (AR)
John Carroll U (OH)
Johns Hopkins U (MD)
Johnson C. Smith U (NC)
John Wesley U (NC)
Judson U (IL)
Juniata Coll (PA)
Kalamazoo Coll (MI)
Kansas State U (KS)
Kansas Wesleyan U (KS)
Kean U (NJ)
Keene State Coll (NH)
Keiser U, Fort Lauderdale (FL)
Kennesaw State U (GA)
Kent State U (OH)
Kent State U at Ashtabula (OH)
Kent State U at East Liverpool (OH)
Kent State U at Geauga (OH)
Kent State U at Salem (OH)
Kent State U at Stark (OH)
Kent State U at Trumbull (OH)
Kent State U at Tuscarawas (OH)

Kentucky State U (KY)
Kenyon Coll (OH)
King's Coll (PA)
King U (TN)
Knox Coll (IL)
Kutztown U of Pennsylvania (PA)
Lafayette Coll (PA)
LaGrange Coll (GA)
Lamar U (TX)
Langston U (OK)
La Roche Coll (PA)
La Salle U (PA)
Lasell Coll (MA)
La Sierra U (CA)
Lawrence Technological U (MI)
Lawrence U (WI)
Lebanese American U (Lebanon)
Lebanon Valley Coll (PA)
Lee U (TN)
Lehigh U (PA)
Lehman Coll of the City U of New York (NY)
Le Moyne Coll (NY)
Lenoir-Rhyne U (NC)
LeTourneau U (TX)
Lewis U (IL)
Liberty U (VA)
Life U (GA)
Limestone Coll (SC)
Lincoln Christian U (IL)
Lincoln Memorial U (TN)
Lincoln U (MO)
Lincoln U (PA)
Lindenwood U (MO)
Lindsey Wilson Coll (KY)
Linfield Coll (OR)
Lipscomb U (TN)
Lock Haven U of Pennsylvania (PA)
Long Island U–LIU Brooklyn (NY)
Long Island U–LIU Post (NY)
Longwood U (VA)
Loras Coll (IA)
Louisiana Coll (LA)
Louisiana State U and A&M Coll (LA)
Loyola Marymount U (CA)
Loyola U Chicago (IL)
Lubbock Christian U (TX)
Luther Coll (IA)
Lycoming Coll (PA)
Lynchburg Coll (VA)
Lynn U (FL)
Lyon Coll (AR)
Macalester Coll (MN)
Madonna U (MI)
Malone U (OH)
Manchester U (IN)
Manhattan Coll (NY)
Manhattanville Coll (NY)
Mansfield U of Pennsylvania (PA)
Maria Coll (NY)
Marian U (IN)
Marian U (WI)
Marietta Coll (OH)
Marist Coll (NY)
Marlboro Coll (VT)
Marquette U (WI)
Marshall U (WV)
Mary Baldwin U (VA)
Marylhurst U (OR)
Marymount California U (CA)
Marymount Manhattan Coll (NY)
Marymount U (VA)
Maryville Coll (TN)
Maryville U of Saint Louis (MO)
Marywood U (PA)
Massachusetts Coll of Liberal Arts (MA)
McDaniel Coll (MD)
McKendree U (IL)
McMurry U (TX)
McNeese State U (LA)
McPherson Coll (KS)
Medgar Evers Coll of the City U of New York (NY)
Mercer U, Macon (GA)
Mercy Coll (NY)
Mercyhurst U (PA)
Meredith Coll (NC)
Merrimack Coll (MA)
Messiah Coll (PA)
Metropolitan State U of Denver (CO)
Miami U (OH)
Michigan State U (MI)
Michigan Technological U (MI)
Mid-America Christian U (OK)

MidAmerica Nazarene U (KS)
Middlebury Coll (VT)
Middle Georgia State U (GA)
Middle Tennessee State U (TN)
Millersville U of Pennsylvania (PA)
Milligan Coll (TN)
Millikin U (IL)
Millsaps Coll (MS)
Mills Coll (CA)
Minnesota State U Moorhead (MN)
Minot State U (ND)
Misericordia U (PA)
Mississippi State U (MS)
Missouri Baptist U (MO)
Missouri State U (MO)
Missouri U of Science and Technology (MO)
Missouri Valley Coll (MO)
Missouri Western State U (MO)
Molloy Coll (NY)
Monmouth Coll (IL)
Montclair State U (NJ)
Moravian Coll (PA)
Morehead State U (KY)
Morehouse Coll (GA)
Morningside Coll (IA)
Mount Aloysius Coll (PA)
Mount Holyoke Coll (MA)
Mount Marty Coll (SD)
Mount Mary U (WI)
Mount Mercy U (IA)
Mount St. Joseph U (OH)
Mount Saint Mary Coll (NY)
Mount Saint Mary's U (CA)
Mount St. Mary's U (MD)
Mount Vernon Nazarene U (OH)
Muhlenberg Coll (PA)
Multnomah U (OR)
Muskingum U (KS)
Naropa U (CO)
National Louis U (IL)
National U (CA)
Nazareth Coll of Rochester (NY)
Neumann U (PA)
Newberry Coll (SC)
New Coll of Florida (FL)
New Jersey City U (NJ)
Newman U (KS)
New Mexico Highlands U (NM)
New Mexico Inst of Mining and Technology (NM)
New Mexico State U (NM)
The New School for Public Engagement (NY)
New York Inst of Technology (NY)
New York U (NY)
Nichols Coll (MA)
North Carolina Central U (NC)
North Carolina State U (NC)
North Carolina Wesleyan Coll (NC)
North Central Coll (IL)
Northcentral U (CA)
North Dakota State U (ND)
Northeastern U (MA)
Northern Arizona U (AZ)
Northern Illinois U (IL)
Northern Kentucky U (KY)
Northern Michigan U (MI)
Northern State U (SD)
Northern Vermont U–Lyndon (VT)
North Greenville U (SC)
Northland Coll (WI)
Northwest Christian U (OR)
Northwestern Coll (IA)
Northwestern Oklahoma State U (OK)
Northwestern State U of Louisiana (LA)
Northwestern U (IL)
Northwest Missouri State U (MO)
Northwest Nazarene U (ID)
Northwest U (WA)
Notre Dame de Namur U (CA)
Nova Southeastern U (FL)
Nyack Coll (NY)
Oakland City U (IN)
Oakland U (MI)
Oberlin Coll (OH)
Occidental Coll (CA)
Oglethorpe U (GA)
Ohio Christian U (OH)
Ohio Dominican U (OH)
Ohio Northern U (OH)
The Ohio State U (OH)
The Ohio State U at Lima (OH)
The Ohio State U at Mansfield (OH)
The Ohio State U at Marion (OH)

The Ohio State U at Newark (OH)
Ohio U (OH)
Ohio Wesleyan U (OH)
Oklahoma Baptist U (OK)
Oklahoma Christian U (OK)
Oklahoma City U (OK)
Oklahoma State U (OK)
Old Dominion U (VA)
Olivet Nazarene U (IL)
Oral Roberts U (OK)
Oregon State U (OR)
Ottawa U (KS)
Otterbein U (OH)
Ouachita Baptist U (AR)
Our Lady of the Lake U (TX)
Pace U (NY)
Pace U, Pleasantville Campus (NY)
Pacific Lutheran U (WA)
Palm Beach Atlantic U (FL)
Palo Alto U (CA)
Penn State Abington (PA)
Penn State Altoona (PA)
Penn State Beaver (PA)
Penn State Berks (PA)
Penn State Brandywine (PA)
Penn State DuBois (PA)
Penn State Erie, The Behrend Coll (PA)
Penn State Fayette, The Eberly Campus (PA)
Penn State Greater Allegheny (PA)
Penn State Harrisburg (PA)
Penn State Hazleton (PA)
Penn State Lehigh Valley (PA)
Penn State Mont Alto (PA)
Penn State New Kensington (PA)
Penn State Schuylkill (PA)
Penn State Shenango (PA)
Penn State U Park (PA)
Penn State Wilkes-Barre (PA)
Penn State Worthington Scranton (PA)
Penn State York (PA)
Pepperdine U, Malibu (CA)
Pfeiffer U (NC)
Piedmont Coll (GA)
Pine Manor Coll (MA)
Pittsburg State U (KS)
Pitzer Coll (CA)
Point Loma Nazarene U (CA)
Point Park U (PA)
Point U (GA)
Pomona Coll (CA)
Portland State U (OR)
Post U (CT)
Prairie View A&M U (TX)
Presbyterian Coll (SC)
Princeton U (NJ)
Providence Coll (RI)
Purchase Coll, State U of New York (NY)
Purdue U (IN)
Purdue U Northwest (IN)
Queens Coll of the City U of New York (NY)
Quinnipiac U (CT)
Radford U (VA)
Ramapo Coll of New Jersey (NJ)
Randolph Coll (VA)
Randolph-Macon Coll (VA)
Redeemer U Coll (ON, Canada)
Reed Coll (OR)
Regent U (VA)
Rensselaer Polytechnic Inst (NY)
Rhode Island Coll (RI)
Rhodes Coll (TN)
Rice U (TX)
Rider U (NJ)
Ripon Coll (WI)
Rivier U (NH)
Roanoke Coll (VA)
Robert Morris U (PA)
Robert Morris U Illinois (IL)
Roberts Wesleyan Coll (NY)
Rochester Inst of Technology (NY)
Rockford U (IL)
Rockhurst U (MO)
Rocky Mountain Coll (MT)
Roger Williams U (RI)
Rollins Coll (FL)
Roosevelt U (IL)
Rosemont Coll (PA)
Rowan U (NJ)
Rutgers U–Camden (NJ)
Rutgers U–Newark (NJ)
Rutgers U–New Brunswick (NJ)
Sacred Heart U (CT)

The Sage Colls (NY)
Saginaw Valley State U (MI)
St. Ambrose U (IA)
St. Andrews U (NC)
Saint Anselm Coll (NH)
Saint Augustine's U (NC)
St. Bonaventure U (NY)
St. Catherine U (MN)
Saint Francis U (PA)
St. John Fisher Coll (NY)
Saint John's U (MN)
St. John's U (NY)
St. Joseph's Coll, Long Island Campus (NY)
St. Joseph's Coll, New York (NY)
Saint Joseph's U (PA)
St. Lawrence U (NY)
Saint Leo U (FL)
Saint Louis U (MO)
Saint Louis U–Madrid Campus (Spain)
Saint Martin's U (WA)
Saint Mary-of-the-Woods Coll (IN)
Saint Mary's Coll of California (CA)
St. Mary's Coll of Maryland (MD)
St. Mary's U (TX)
Saint Mary's U of Minnesota (MN)
Saint Michael's Coll (VT)
St. Norbert Coll (WI)
St. Olaf Coll (MN)
Saint Peter's U (NJ)
St. Thomas Aquinas Coll (NY)
St. Thomas U (FL)
St. Thomas U (NB, Canada)
Saint Vincent Coll (PA)
Salisbury U (MD)
Salve Regina U (RI)
Samford U (AL)
Sam Houston State U (TX)
San Diego State U (CA)
San Francisco State U (CA)
Santa Clara U (CA)
Sarah Lawrence Coll (NY)
Schreiner U (TX)
Scripps Coll (CA)
Seattle Pacific U (WA)
Seattle U (WA)
Seton Hill U (PA)
Sewanee: The U of the South (TN)
Shawnee State U (OH)
Shaw U (NC)
Shenandoah U (VA)
Shepherd U (WV)
Shippensburg U of Pennsylvania (PA)
Shorter U (GA)
Siena Coll (NY)
Sierra Nevada Coll (NV)
Silver Lake Coll of the Holy Family (WI)
Simmons Coll (MA)
Simon Fraser U (BC, Canada)
Simpson Coll (IA)
Skidmore Coll (NY)
Slippery Rock U of Pennsylvania (PA)
Smith Coll (MA)
Sonoma State U (CA)
Southeastern Louisiana U (LA)
Southeastern Oklahoma State U (OK)
Southeastern U (FL)
Southeast Missouri State U (MO)
Southern Adventist U (TN)
Southern Arkansas U–Magnolia (AR)
Southern Illinois U Carbondale (IL)
Southern Illinois U Edwardsville (IL)
Southern Methodist U (TX)
Southern Utah U (UT)
Southern Vermont Coll (VT)
Southwest Baptist U (MO)
Southwestern Adventist U (TX)
Southwestern Assemblies of God U (TX)
Southwestern Coll (KS)
Southwestern U (TX)
Spelman Coll (GA)
Spring Hill Coll (AL)
Stanford U (CA)
State U of New York at Fredonia (NY)
State U of New York at New Paltz (NY)
State U of New York at Oswego (NY)

State U of New York at Plattsburgh (NY)
State U of New York Coll at Cortland (NY)
State U of New York Coll at Geneseo (NY)
State U of New York Coll at Old Westbury (NY)
State U of New York Coll at Oneonta (NY)
State U of New York Coll at Potsdam (NY)
State U of New York Empire State Coll (NY)
State U of New York Polytechnic Inst (NY)
Stephen F. Austin State U (TX)
Stetson U (FL)
Stevenson U (MD)
Stockton U (NJ)
Stonehill Coll (MA)
Stony Brook U, State U of New York (NY)
Suffolk U (MA)
Susquehanna U (PA)
Sweet Briar Coll (VA)
Syracuse U (NY)
Tabor Coll (KS)
Tarleton State U (TX)
Taylor U (IN)
Temple U (PA)
Tennessee Technological U (TN)
Tennessee Wesleyan U (TN)
Texas A&M Intl U (TX)
Texas A&M U (TX)
Texas A&M U–Central Texas (TX)
Texas A&M U–Commerce (TX)
Texas A&M U–Corpus Christi (TX)
Texas A&M U–Kingsville (TX)
Texas A&M U–Texarkana (TX)
Texas Christian U (TX)
Texas Lutheran U (TX)
Texas State U (TX)
Texas Tech U (TX)
Texas Woman's U (TX)
Thomas Coll (ME)
Tiffin U (OH)
Touro Coll Los Angeles (CA)
Touro U Worldwide (CA)
Towson U (MD)
Transylvania U (KY)
Trent U (ON, Canada)
Trevecca Nazarene U (TN)
Trine U (IN)
Trinity Christian Coll (IL)
Trinity Coll of Florida (FL)
Trinity U (TX)
Troy U (AL)
Truett McConnell U (GA)
Tufts U (MA)
Tulane U (LA)
Tusculum Coll (TN)
Union Coll (NE)
Union Coll (NY)
Union U (TN)
Université de Sherbrooke (QC, Canada)
U at Albany, State U of New York (NY)
U at Buffalo, the State U of New York (NY)
The U of Akron (OH)
The U of Alabama (AL)
The U of Alabama at Birmingham (AL)
U of Alaska Fairbanks (AK)
The U of Arizona (AZ)
U of Arkansas (AR)
U of Bridgeport (CT)
U of California, Davis (CA)
U of California, Irvine (CA)
U of California, Los Angeles (CA)
U of California, Riverside (CA)
U of California, San Diego (CA)
U of California, Santa Barbara (CA)
U of California, Santa Cruz (CA)
U of Central Arkansas (AR)
U of Central Florida (FL)
U of Central Missouri (MO)
U of Central Oklahoma (OK)
U of Charleston (WV)
U of Cincinnati (OH)
U of Colorado Boulder (CO)
U of Colorado Colorado Springs (CO)
U of Colorado Denver (CO)
U of Dallas (TX)

U of Dayton (OH)
U of Denver (CO)
U of Dubuque (IA)
U of Evansville (IN)
The U of Findlay (OH)
U of Florida (FL)
U of Georgia (GA)
U of Guam (GU)
U of Guelph (ON, Canada)
U of Hartford (CT)
U of Hawaii at Manoa (HI)
U of Houston (TX)
U of Houston–Clear Lake (TX)
U of Houston–Downtown (TX)
U of Idaho (ID)
U of Illinois at Chicago (IL)
U of Illinois at Springfield (IL)
U of Jamestown (ND)
The U of Kansas (KS)
U of Kentucky (KY)
U of King's Coll (NS, Canada)
U of La Verne (CA)
U of Louisiana at Monroe (LA)
U of Louisville (KY)
U of Maine (ME)
U of Maine at Farmington (ME)
U of Maine at Machias (ME)
U of Maine at Presque Isle (ME)
U of Mary Hardin-Baylor (TX)
U of Maryland, Baltimore County (MD)
U of Maryland, Coll Park (MD)
U of Maryland U Coll (MD)
U of Mary Washington (VA)
U of Massachusetts Amherst (MA)
U of Massachusetts Boston (MA)
U of Massachusetts Dartmouth (MA)
U of Massachusetts Lowell (MA)
U of Memphis (TN)
U of Miami (FL)
U of Michigan–Dearborn (MI)
U of Michigan–Flint (MI)
U of Minnesota, Duluth (MN)
U of Minnesota, Morris (MN)
U of Minnesota, Twin Cities Campus (MN)
U of Missouri (MO)
U of Missouri–St. Louis (MO)
U of Mobile (AL)
U of Montana (MT)
U of Montevallo (AL)
U of Mount Union (OH)
U of Nebraska at Kearney (NE)
U of Nebraska–Lincoln (NE)
U of Nevada, Las Vegas (NV)
U of Nevada, Reno (NV)
U of New England (ME)
U of New Hampshire (NH)
U of New Haven (CT)
U of New Mexico (NM)
U of New Orleans (LA)
U of North Alabama (AL)
U of North Carolina at Asheville (NC)
The U of North Carolina at Chapel Hill (NC)
The U of North Carolina at Charlotte (NC)
The U of North Carolina at Greensboro (NC)
The U of North Carolina at Pembroke (NC)
The U of North Carolina Wilmington (NC)
U of North Dakota (ND)
U of Northern Colorado (CO)
U of Northern Iowa (IA)
U of North Florida (FL)
U of North Georgia (GA)
U of North Texas (TX)
U of Notre Dame (IN)
U of Oklahoma (OK)
U of Oregon (OR)
U of Pennsylvania (PA)
U of Pikeville (KY)
U of Pittsburgh (PA)
U of Pittsburgh at Bradford (PA)
U of Pittsburgh at Greensburg (PA)
U of Providence (MT)
U of Puget Sound (WA)
U of Regina (SK, Canada)
U of Rhode Island (RI)
U of Richmond (VA)
U of Rochester (NY)
U of St. Francis (IL)
U of Saint Joseph (CT)

U of Saint Mary (KS)
U of St. Thomas (MN)
U of St. Thomas (TX)
U of San Diego (CA)
U of San Francisco (CA)
U of Saskatchewan (SK, Canada)
U of Science and Arts of Oklahoma (OK)
The U of Scranton (PA)
U of Sioux Falls (SD)
U of South Alabama (AL)
U of South Carolina Aiken (SC)
U of South Dakota (SD)
U of Southern California (CA)
U of Southern Indiana (IN)
U of Southern Maine (ME)
U of Southern Mississippi (MS)
U of South Florida, St. Petersburg (FL)
U of South Florida Sarasota-Manatee (FL)
The U of Tampa (FL)
The U of Tennessee (TN)
The U of Tennessee at Chattanooga (TN)
The U of Tennessee at Martin (TN)
The U of Texas at Austin (TX)
The U of Texas at Dallas (TX)
The U of Texas at El Paso (TX)
The U of Texas at San Antonio (TX)
The U of Texas of the Permian Basin (TX)
The U of Texas Rio Grande Valley (TX)
U of the Fraser Valley (BC, Canada)
U of the Incarnate Word (TX)
U of the Pacific (CA)
U of the Virgin Islands (VI)
The U of Toledo (OH)
The U of Tulsa (OK)
U of Utah (UT)
U of Valley Forge (PA)
U of Vermont (VT)
U of Virginia (VA)
The U of Virginia's Coll at Wise (VA)
U of Washington (WA)
U of Washington, Tacoma (WA)
U of Waterloo (ON, Canada)
The U of West Alabama (AL)
U of Wisconsin–Eau Claire (WI)
U of Wisconsin–La Crosse (WI)
U of Wisconsin–Madison (WI)
U of Wisconsin–Milwaukee (WI)
U of Wisconsin–Parkside (WI)
U of Wisconsin–Platteville (WI)
U of Wisconsin–River Falls (WI)
U of Wisconsin–Stevens Point (WI)
U of Wisconsin–Stout (WI)
U of Wisconsin–Superior (WI)
U of Wisconsin–Whitewater (WI)
U of Wyoming (WY)
Upper Iowa U (IA)
Ursinus Coll (PA)
Ursuline Coll (OH)
Utah State U (UT)
Utah Valley U (UT)
Utica Coll (NY)
Valdosta State U (GA)
Valley City State U (ND)
Valparaiso U (IN)
Vanderbilt U (TN)
Vanguard U of Southern California (CA)
Villa Maria Coll (NY)
Villanova U (PA)
Virginia Commonwealth U (VA)
Virginia Military Inst (VA)
Virginia Polytechnic Inst and State U (VA)
Virginia Wesleyan U (VA)
Wabash Coll (IN)
Wagner Coll (NY)
Wake Forest U (NC)
Waldorf U (IA)
Walsh U (OH)
Warner Pacific Coll (OR)
Wartburg Coll (IA)
Washington & Jefferson Coll (PA)
Washington Coll (MD)
Washington State U (WA)
Washington State U–Global Campus (WA)
Washington State U–Tri-Cities (WA)

Washington State U–Vancouver (WA)
Washington U in St. Louis (MO)
Wayland Baptist U (TX)
Waynesburg U (PA)
Wayne State Coll (NE)
Wayne State U (MI)
Weber State U (UT)
Webster U (MO)
Wellesley Coll (MA)
Wells Coll (NY)
Wesleyan U (CT)
West Chester U of Pennsylvania (PA)
Western Connecticut State U (CT)
Western Illinois U (IL)
Western Kentucky U (KY)
Western Michigan U (MI)
Western New England U (MA)
Western Oregon U (OR)
Western State Colorado U (CO)
Western Washington U (WA)
Westfield State U (MA)
Westminster Coll (PA)
Westminster Coll (UT)
Westmont Coll (CA)
West Texas A&M U (TX)
West Virginia State U (WV)
West Virginia U (WV)
West Virginia U Inst of Technology (WV)
West Virginia Wesleyan Coll (WV)
Wheaton Coll (IL)
Wheaton Coll (MA)
Whitman Coll (WA)
Whittier Coll (CA)
Whitworth U (WA)
Wichita State U (KS)
Widener U (PA)
Wilkes U (PA)
Willamette U (OR)
William Jewell Coll (MO)
William Paterson U of New Jersey (NJ)
William Peace U (NC)
William Penn U (IA)
Williams Coll (MA)
William Woods U (MO)
Wilmington U (DE)
Winona State U (MN)
Winthrop U (SC)
Wisconsin Lutheran Coll (WI)
Wittenberg U (OH)
Wofford Coll (SC)
Woodbury U (CA)
Worcester Polytechnic Inst (MA)
Worcester State U (MA)
Wright State U (OH)
Wright State U–Lake Campus (OH)
Xavier U of Louisiana (LA)
York Coll of Pennsylvania (PA)
Youngstown State U (OH)

PSYCHOLOGY RELATED
Adams State U (CO)
Arcadia U (PA)
Augsburg U (MN)
Becker Coll (MA)
Buena Vista U (IA)
Butler U (IN)
Canisius Coll (NY)
Eastern Nazarene Coll (MA)
Kansas Wesleyan U (KS)
Kean U (NJ)
Marist Coll (NY)
Marlboro Coll (VT)
National U (CA)
Ohio Northern U (OH)
Palm Beach Atlantic U (FL)
Saint Mary's Coll of California (CA)
State U of New York at Oswego (NY)
Tiffin U (OH)
The U of North Carolina at Greensboro (NC)
Washington U in St. Louis (MO)
Western State Colorado U (CO)
Whitworth U (WA)

PSYCHOLOGY TEACHER EDUCATION
Albion Coll (MI)
Boise State U (ID)
Brigham Young U (UT)
California Lutheran U (CA)
Campbellsville U (KY)
Carroll U (WI)
Lee U (TN)

Ohio Wesleyan U (OH)
Pittsburg State U (KS)
Rocky Mountain Coll (MT)
U of Michigan–Flint (MI)
U of Wisconsin–Whitewater (WI)
Valparaiso U (IN)
Wayne State Coll (NE)
Weber State U (UT)
Widener U (PA)

PUBLIC ADMINISTRATION
Alfred U (NY)
American U of Beirut (Lebanon)
Athabasca U (AB, Canada)
Auburn U (AL)
Baldwin Wallace U (OH)
Baruch Coll of the City U of New York (NY)
Baylor U (TX)
Biola U (CA)
Blackburn Coll (IL)
Bowling Green State U (OH)
Brock U (ON, Canada)
Buena Vista U (IA)
California Baptist U (CA)
California Lutheran U (CA)
California State U, Dominguez Hills (CA)
California State U, Fullerton (CA)
Calvin Coll (MI)
Capital U (OH)
Catawba Coll (NC)
Central Methodist U (MO)
Cleveland State U (OH)
Colorado Mesa U (CO)
Columbia Coll (MO)
Concordia U (QC, Canada)
Doane U (NE)
Eastern Michigan U (MI)
Eastern Washington U (WA)
Elon U (NC)
Evangel U (MO)
The Evergreen State Coll (WA)
Flagler Coll (FL)
Florida Atlantic U (FL)
Florida Intl U (FL)
George Mason U (VA)
Grand Valley State U (MI)
Harding U (AR)
Indiana U Bloomington (IN)
Indiana U Kokomo (IN)
Indiana U Northwest (IN)
Indiana U–Purdue U Indianapolis (IN)
Iowa State U of Science and Technology (IA)
Jacksonville U (FL)
James Madison U (VA)
John Carroll U (OH)
John Jay Coll of Criminal Justice of the City U of New York (NY)
Johns Hopkins U (MD)
Kean U (NJ)
Keiser U, Fort Lauderdale (FL)
Kentucky State U (KY)
Kutztown U of Pennsylvania (PA)
La Salle U (PA)
Lee U (TN)
Lewis U (IL)
Lincoln U (MO)
Lindenwood U (MO)
Lipscomb U (TN)
Long Island U–LIU Post (NY)
Louisiana Coll (LA)
Metropolitan Coll of New York (NY)
Miami U (OH)
MidAmerica Nazarene U (KS)
Millsaps Coll (MS)
Missouri State U (MO)
Missouri Valley Coll (MO)
Muskingum U (OH)
National U (CA)
New York U (NY)
Northern Arizona U (AZ)
Northern Michigan U (MI)
Nova Southeastern U (FL)
Oakland U (MI)
The Ohio State U (OH)
Ohio Wesleyan U (OH)
Point Park U (PA)
Regent U (VA)
Rhode Island Coll (RI)
Rogers State U (OK)
Roger Williams U (RI)
Roosevelt U (IL)
Saginaw Valley State U (MI)
Saint Francis U (PA)

St. John's U (NY)
Samford U (AL)
Sam Houston State U (TX)
San Diego State U (CA)
Seattle U (WA)
Shaw U (NC)
Shippensburg U of Pennsylvania (PA)
Stephen F. Austin State U (TX)
Syracuse U (NY)
Tarleton State U (TX)
Texas State U (TX)
U at Albany, State U of New York (NY)
The U of Arizona (AZ)
U of Central Arkansas (AR)
U of Central Florida (FL)
U of Central Oklahoma (OK)
U of Guam (GU)
U of Guelph (ON, Canada)
U of Houston–Clear Lake (TX)
U of Illinois at Springfield (IL)
The U of Kansas (KS)
U of La Verne (CA)
U of Maine at Fort Kent (ME)
U of Maine at Machias (ME)
U of Maryland U Coll (MD)
U of Michigan–Flint (MI)
U of Missouri–St. Louis (MO)
U of Nevada, Las Vegas (NV)
The U of North Carolina at Pembroke (NC)
U of North Dakota (ND)
U of Northern Iowa (IA)
U of Oklahoma (OK)
U of Oregon (OR)
U of Pittsburgh (PA)
U of San Francisco (CA)
U of Saskatchewan (SK, Canada)
The U of Tennessee (TN)
The U of Tennessee at Martin (TN)
The U of Texas at Dallas (TX)
The U of Texas at San Antonio (TX)
U of Toronto (ON, Canada)
U of Wisconsin–La Crosse (WI)
U of Wisconsin–Stevens Point (WI)
U of Wisconsin–Whitewater (WI)
Upper Iowa U (IA)
Wagner Coll (NY)
Wayne State U (MI)
Western Oregon U (OR)
West Texas A&M U (TX)
Wilkes U (PA)
Willamette U (OR)
Winona State U (MN)

PUBLIC ADMINISTRATION AND SOCIAL SERVICE PROFESSIONS RELATED
Coll of Coastal Georgia (GA)
Delaware State U (DE)
Emory & Henry Coll (VA)
The Evergreen State Coll (WA)
Milligan Coll (TN)
National Louis U (IL)
New York U (NY)
Rutgers U–Newark (NJ)
San Diego State U (CA)
State U of New York Empire State Coll (NY)
Trevecca Nazarene U (TN)
Troy U (AL)
U of Colorado Denver (CO)
U of San Francisco (CA)

PUBLIC/APPLIED HISTORY
Arkansas Tech U (AR)
Baldwin Wallace U (OH)
Bryant U (RI)
Cairn U (PA)
Central Michigan U (MI)
Concordia U (QC, Canada)
Emory & Henry Coll (VA)
Flagler Coll (FL)
Goshen Coll (IN)
North Dakota State U (ND)
Rhode Island Coll (RI)
Western Michigan U (MI)

PUBLIC FINANCE
Husson U (ME)
Niagara U (NY)

PUBLIC HEALTH
Agnes Scott Coll (GA)
Albright Coll (PA)
Allen Coll (IA)
American Intl Coll (MA)

American Public U System (WV)
American U (DC)
Appalachian State U (NC)
Arcadia U (PA)
Arizona State U at the Downtown Phoenix campus (AZ)
Augustana Coll (IL)
Austin Coll (TX)
Baker U (KS)
Baldwin Wallace U (OH)
Belmont U (TN)
Bluffton U (OH)
Boise State U (ID)
Bowling Green State U (OH)
Brock U (ON, Canada)
Caldwell U (NJ)
California State U, Long Beach (CA)
Calvin Coll (MI)
Carroll U (WI)
The Coll of New Jersey (NJ)
The Coll of Saint Rose (NY)
Columbia Coll (SC)
Concordia U, Nebraska (NE)
Curry Coll (MA)
Delaware State U (DE)
Dominican U of California (CA)
Drexel U (PA)
D'Youville Coll (NY)
East Stroudsburg U of Pennsylvania (PA)
East Tennessee State U (TN)
Elon U (NC)
Excelsior Coll (NY)
Fairfield U (CT)
Ferris State U (MI)
Florida Gulf Coast U (FL)
Fort Lewis Coll (CO)
Franklin Pierce U (NH)
Gannon U (PA)
Guilford Coll (NC)
Hartwick Coll (NY)
Hawai'i Pacific U (HI)
Hunter Coll of the City U of New York (NY)
Indiana U of Pennsylvania (PA)
Indiana U–Purdue U Indianapolis (IN)
Ithaca Coll (NY)
Johns Hopkins U (MD)
Kent State U (OH)
Kent State U at Trumbull (OH)
Langston U (OK)
La Salle U (PA)
Long Island U–LIU Brooklyn (NY)
Marian U (IN)
Marshall U (WV)
Marymount Manhattan Coll (NY)
Mercer U, Macon (GA)
Mercyhurst U (PA)
Meredith Coll (NC)
Merrimack Coll (MA)
Miami U (OH)
Missouri Western State U (MO)
Montclair State U (NJ)
Muhlenberg Coll (PA)
Muskingum U (OH)
New York U (NY)
Northern Arizona U (AZ)
Ohio Northern U (OH)
The Ohio State U (OH)
Ohio U (OH)
Oregon State U (OR)
Portland State U (OR)
Roanoke Coll (VA)
Roger Williams U (RI)
Rutgers U–New Brunswick (NJ)
Saint Francis U (PA)
Saint Louis U (MO)
Saint Louis U–Madrid Campus (Spain)
Samford U (AL)
Sam Houston State U (TX)
San Diego State U (CA)
Santa Clara U (CA)
Slippery Rock U of Pennsylvania (PA)
State U of New York Coll at Old Westbury (NY)
Syracuse U (NY)
Tarleton State U (TX)
Texas A&M U (TX)
Texas A&M U–Commerce (TX)
Tufts U (MA)
U at Albany, State U of New York (NY)

U at Buffalo, the State U of New York (NY)
The U of Arizona (AZ)
U of Arkansas (AR)
U of Colorado Denver (CO)
U of Evansville (IN)
U of Florida (FL)
U of Hawaii at Manoa (HI)
U of Kentucky (KY)
U of Louisville (KY)
U of Massachusetts Amherst (MA)
U of Massachusetts Lowell (MA)
U of Miami (FL)
U of Nevada, Las Vegas (NV)
U of New England (ME)
The U of North Carolina at Charlotte (NC)
U of North Texas (TX)
U of Rochester (NY)
U of Saint Joseph (CT)
U of Southern Mississippi (MS)
The U of Tampa (FL)
The U of Texas at Austin (TX)
The U of Texas at San Antonio (TX)
U of Washington (WA)
Valparaiso U (IN)
Wartburg Coll (IA)
Wayne State U (MI)
Weber State U (UT)
Western Michigan U (MI)
Westminster Coll (UT)
West Virginia U (WV)
Wichita State U (KS)
William Paterson U of New Jersey (NJ)
Youngstown State U (OH)

PUBLIC HEALTH/COMMUNITY NURSING
Capital U (OH)
Northern Illinois U (IL)
U of Miami (FL)

PUBLIC HEALTH EDUCATION AND PROMOTION
American U (DC)
Appalachian State U (NC)
Arizona State U at the Downtown Phoenix campus (AZ)
Barton Coll (NC)
Baylor U (TX)
California Baptist U (CA)
California State U, Long Beach (CA)
Central Michigan U (MI)
Coastal Carolina U (SC)
Coll of Charleston (SC)
Columbia Coll (SC)
East Carolina U (NC)
Eastern Washington U (WA)
Excelsior Coll (NY)
Georgia Southern U (GA)
Iowa State U of Science and Technology (IA)
Ithaca Coll (NY)
Kennesaw State U (GA)
Liberty U (VA)
Lynchburg Coll (VA)
Malone U (OH)
New Mexico State U (NM)
North Carolina Central U (NC)
Oklahoma State U (OK)
Purdue U (IN)
Queens Coll of the City U of New York (NY)
Rhode Island Coll (RI)
Simmons Coll (MA)
Southeastern Louisiana U (LA)
Southern Illinois U Edwardsville (IL)
State U of New York Coll of Technology at Canton (NY)
Temple U (PA)
Texas State U (TX)
U of Arkansas (AR)
U of Central Oklahoma (OK)
U of Georgia (GA)
U of Michigan–Dearborn (MI)
U of Minnesota, Duluth (MN)
U of Mount Union (OH)
U of North Carolina at Asheville (NC)
The U of North Carolina at Greensboro (NC)
The U of North Carolina Wilmington (NC)
U of North Dakota (ND)
U of North Texas (TX)

U of St. Thomas (MN)
The U of Scranton (PA)
The U of Texas at Austin (TX)
The U of Toledo (OH)
Weber State U (UT)
West Chester U of Pennsylvania (PA)
Western Illinois U (IL)
Winona State U (MN)

PUBLIC HEALTH RELATED
Baptist Coll of Health Sciences (TN)
Concordia U of Edmonton (AB, Canada)
Franklin & Marshall Coll (PA)
Hampshire Coll (MA)
Indiana U Bloomington (IN)
Iowa State U of Science and Technology (IA)
Lehigh U (PA)
Rowan U (NJ)
Shenandoah U (VA)
Stockton U (NJ)
U of California, Irvine (CA)
U of Maryland, Coll Park (MD)
U of Michigan (MI)
U of Michigan–Flint (MI)
U of South Carolina (SC)
Utah State U (UT)

PUBLIC POLICY ANALYSIS
Albion Coll (MI)
Arizona State U at the Downtown Phoenix campus (AZ)
Bennington Coll (VT)
Bentley U (MA)
Brigham Young U (UT)
Bryant U (RI)
Carnegie Mellon U (PA)
Chatham U (PA)
Coll of the Atlantic (ME)
The Coll of William and Mary (VA)
Concordia U, St. Paul (MN)
Cornell U (NY)
Dallas Baptist U (TX)
DePaul U (IL)
Dickinson Coll (PA)
Elon U (NC)
The George Washington U (DC)
Georgia Inst of Technology (GA)
Georgia State U (GA)
Hamilton Coll (NY)
Hampshire Coll (MA)
Hobart and William Smith Colls (NY)
Hofstra U (NY)
Howard Payne U (TX)
Indiana Wesleyan U (IN)
Jacksonville U (FL)
Johns Hopkins U (MD)
Massachusetts Coll of Liberal Arts (MA)
Michigan State U (MI)
Mills Coll (CA)
Muskingum U (OH)
New Coll of Florida (FL)
Northwestern U (IL)
The Ohio State U (OH)
Olivet Nazarene U (IL)
Penn State Harrisburg (PA)
Pomona Coll (CA)
Princeton U (NJ)
Rice U (TX)
Rochester Inst of Technology (NY)
Rutgers U–New Brunswick (NJ)
St. Mary's Coll of Maryland (MD)
Saint Peter's U (NJ)
Saint Vincent Coll (PA)
Sarah Lawrence Coll (NY)
Scripps Coll (CA)
Southern Methodist U (TX)
Stanford U (CA)
State U of New York Empire State Coll (NY)
Suffolk U (MA)
Susquehanna U (PA)
Trevecca Nazarene U (TN)
U at Albany, State U of New York (NY)
U of California, Riverside (CA)
U of California, San Diego (CA)
U of Chicago (IL)
U of Denver (CO)
U of Illinois at Springfield (IL)
U of Michigan (MI)

The U of North Carolina at Chapel Hill (NC)
U of Pennsylvania (PA)
U of Pittsburgh at Greensburg (PA)
U of Rhode Island (RI)
U of Saint Joseph (CT)
The U of Texas at Austin (TX)
The U of Texas at Dallas (TX)
U of Virginia (VA)
Vanderbilt U (TN)
Virginia Polytechnic Inst and State U (VA)
Wagner Coll (NY)
Washington & Jefferson Coll (PA)
Washington State U (WA)
Washington State U–Vancouver (WA)
Wittenberg U (OH)

PUBLIC RELATIONS, ADVERTISING, AND APPLIED COMMUNICATION
Albright Coll (PA)
Anderson U (IN)
Anderson U (SC)
Ball State U (IN)
Belmont U (TN)
Biola U (CA)
Bluffton U (OH)
Bradley U (IL)
Butler U (IN)
California Baptist U (CA)
California State U, Dominguez Hills (CA)
Cardinal Stritch U (WI)
Carthage Coll (WI)
Central Connecticut State U (CT)
Coll of the Ozarks (MO)
Dallas Baptist U (TX)
Endicott Coll (MA)
Flagler Coll (FL)
Florida Inst of Technology (FL)
Florida Southern Coll (FL)
Florida State U (FL)
Franklin Coll (IN)
Goshen Coll (IN)
Howard Payne U (TX)
Kansas Wesleyan U (KS)
Kennesaw State U (GA)
Louisiana Coll (LA)
Loyola U New Orleans (LA)
Lynn U (FL)
Marymount Manhattan Coll (NY)
Massachusetts Coll of Liberal Arts (MA)
Meredith Coll (NC)
Messiah Coll (PA)
Minnesota State U Moorhead (MN)
Muskingum U (OH)
National U (CA)
New York Inst of Technology (NY)
Oakland U (MI)
Ohio Dominican U (OH)
Oklahoma City U (OK)
Pepperdine U, Malibu (CA)
Point Park U (PA)
Rhode Island Coll (RI)
Seattle U (WA)
Simpson Coll (IA)
Southeastern U (FL)
Taylor U (IN)
Texas Christian U (TX)
U of Central Oklahoma (OK)
U of Colorado Boulder (CO)
The U of Findlay (OH)
U of Kentucky (KY)
U of Mount Union (OH)
U of Nebraska–Lincoln (NE)
The U of Scranton (PA)
The U of Tampa (FL)
U of Wisconsin–River Falls (WI)
Wartburg Coll (IA)
Washington State U (WA)
Washington State U–Global Campus (WA)
Washington State U–Vancouver (WA)
Washington U in St. Louis (MO)
Webber Intl U (FL)
West Texas A&M U (TX)
William Jewell Coll (MO)

PUBLIC RELATIONS, ADVERTISING, AND APPLIED COMMUNICATION RELATED
Abilene Christian U (TX)
Alma Coll (MI)
Brigham Young U (UT)

Buena Vista U (IA)
Butler U (IN)
California Lutheran U (CA)
Carroll U (WI)
The Coll of St. Scholastica (MN)
Columbia Coll (MO)
DePaul U (IL)
Duquesne U (PA)
Fairfield U (CT)
La Sierra U (CA)
Lipscomb U (TN)
Loyola U Chicago (IL)
Marietta Coll (OH)
Marywood U (PA)
Metropolitan State U of Denver (CO)
Missouri Western State U (MO)
Muskingum U (OH)
Northern Arizona U (AZ)
Northern Michigan U (MI)
Ohio Northern U (OH)
Oklahoma City U (OK)
Oklahoma State U (OK)
Pepperdine U, Malibu (CA)
Rochester Inst of Technology (NY)
St. John's U (NY)
Saint Mary's U of Minnesota (MN)
Spring Hill Coll (AL)
Tulane U (LA)
U of Central Arkansas (AR)
U of Evansville (IN)
The U of Tampa (FL)
U of Vermont (VT)
Virginia Polytechnic Inst and State U (VA)
Weber State U (UT)
Western Michigan U (MI)

PUBLIC RELATIONS/IMAGE MANAGEMENT
Andrews U (MI)
Appalachian State U (NC)
Auburn U (AL)
Avila U (MO)
Baldwin Wallace U (OH)
Barry U (FL)
Belmont U (TN)
Biola U (CA)
Bowie State U (MD)
Bowling Green State U (OH)
Bradley U (IL)
Buena Vista U (IA)
Buffalo State Coll, State U of New York (NY)
California Lutheran U (CA)
California State U, Dominguez Hills (CA)
California State U, Fullerton (CA)
California State U, Long Beach (CA)
Capital U (OH)
Carroll Coll (MT)
Carroll U (WI)
Central Michigan U (MI)
Champlain Coll (VT)
Chapman U (CA)
Chatham U (PA)
Cleveland State U (OH)
Coe Coll (IA)
Columbia Coll Chicago (IL)
Delaware State U (DE)
Dominican U (IL)
Drake U (IA)
Eastern Michigan U (MI)
Emerson Coll (MA)
Ferris State U (MI)
Florida Ag and Mech U (FL)
Georgia Southern U (GA)
Gonzaga U (WA)
Greenville U (IL)
Hampton U (VA)
Harding U (AR)
Hofstra U (NY)
Hood Coll (MD)
Illinois State U (IL)
Indiana Wesleyan U (IN)
Iona Coll (NY)
Iowa State U of Science and Technology (IA)
Ithaca Coll (NY)
Keene State Coll (NH)
Kent State U (OH)
La Salle U (PA)
Lee U (TN)
Lewis U (IL)
Lipscomb U (TN)
Long Island U–LIU Post (NY)

Loras Coll (IA)
Manchester U (IN)
Mansfield U of Pennsylvania (PA)
Marquette U (WI)
The Master's U (CA)
McPherson Coll (KS)
Miami U (OH)
Minnesota State U Moorhead (MN)
Missouri Baptist U (MO)
Missouri Valley Coll (MO)
Monmouth Coll (IL)
Mount Mercy U (IA)
Mount Saint Mary Coll (NY)
Mount Vernon Nazarene U (OH)
Murray State U (KY)
North Dakota State U (ND)
Northern Kentucky U (KY)
Northern Michigan U (MI)
Northwestern Coll (IA)
Ohio U–Zanesville (OH)
Oklahoma Christian U (OK)
Olivet Nazarene U (IL)
Palm Beach Atlantic U (FL)
Pfeiffer U (NC)
Point Park U (PA)
Quinnipiac U (CT)
Rider U (NJ)
Rochester Inst of Technology (NY)
Rowan U (NJ)
St. Ambrose U (IA)
Saint Francis U (PA)
San Diego State U (CA)
Southern Adventist U (TN)
Southern Methodist U (TX)
State U of New York at Oswego (NY)
Suffolk U (MA)
Syracuse U (NY)
Taylor U (IN)
Texas Christian U (TX)
Texas State U (TX)
Texas Tech U (TX)
Tiffin U (OH)
Union U (TN)
The U of Akron (OH)
The U of Alabama (AL)
U of Central Missouri (MO)
U of Florida (FL)
U of Georgia (GA)
U of Houston (TX)
U of Idaho (ID)
U of Miami (FL)
U of Northern Iowa (IA)
U of Oregon (OR)
U of Pittsburgh at Bradford (PA)
U of Rhode Island (RI)
U of South Carolina (SC)
U of Southern California (CA)
The U of Tennessee (TN)
The U of Texas at Austin (TX)
U of Toronto (ON, Canada)
Ursuline Coll (OH)
Utica Coll (NY)
Wartburg Coll (IA)
Washington and Lee U (VA)
Washington State U (WA)
Wayne State U (MI)
Weber State U (UT)
Webster U (MO)
Western Kentucky U (KY)
Western New England U (MA)
Westminster Coll (PA)
West Virginia Wesleyan Coll (WV)
William Penn U (IA)
York Coll of Pennsylvania (PA)

PUBLISHING
Belmont U (TN)
Cornerstone U (MI)
Emerson Coll (MA)
Rochester Inst of Technology (NY)
U of Missouri (MO)

PURCHASING, PROCUREMENT/ ACQUISITIONS AND CONTRACTS MANAGEMENT
Arizona State U at the Tempe campus (AZ)
Athens State U (AL)
Central Michigan U (MI)
U of Houston–Downtown (TX)
U of the Potomac (DC)

QUALITY CONTROL AND SAFETY TECHNOLOGIES RELATED
Madonna U (MI)

QUALITY CONTROL TECHNOLOGY
Bowling Green State U (OH)
California State U, Long Beach (CA)

RABBINICAL STUDIES
Ohr Somayach/Joseph Tanenbaum Educational Center (NY)

RADIATION BIOLOGY
Suffolk U (MA)

RADIATION PROTECTION/ HEALTH PHYSICS TECHNOLOGY
Indiana U–Purdue U Indianapolis (IN)
Lewis U (IL)
Thomas Edison State U (NJ)

RADIO AND TELEVISION
Appalachian State U (NC)
Ashland U (OH)
Auburn U (AL)
Barry U (FL)
Bemidji State U (MN)
Biola U (CA)
Boston U (MA)
Bowling Green State U (OH)
Bradley U (IL)
Buffalo State Coll, State U of New York (NY)
Butler U (IN)
California State U, Fullerton (CA)
California State U, Long Beach (CA)
California State U, Los Angeles (CA)
California State U, Monterey Bay (CA)
Columbia Coll Chicago (IL)
Cornerstone U (MI)
Delaware State U (DE)
Drake U (IA)
Elon U (NC)
Emerson Coll (MA)
Evangel U (MO)
Franklin Pierce U (NH)
The George Washington U (DC)
Gonzaga U (WA)
Grand Valley State U (MI)
Hofstra U (NY)
Iona Coll (NY)
Ithaca Coll (NY)
La Sierra U (CA)
Lebanese American U (Lebanon)
Lewis U (IL)
Marietta Coll (OH)
Marist Coll (NY)
The Master's U (CA)
Minot State U (ND)
Missouri Baptist U (MO)
Montclair State U (NJ)
Murray State U (KY)
North Central Coll (IL)
Northern Arizona U (AZ)
Northwestern U (IL)
Ohio Northern U (OH)
Ohio U (OH)
Oklahoma Christian U (OK)
Palm Beach Atlantic U (FL)
Pepperdine U, Malibu (CA)
Point Park U (PA)
Rider U (NJ)
Rowan U (NJ)
St. Ambrose U (IA)
Sam Houston State U (TX)
San Diego State U (CA)
San Francisco State U (CA)
Savannah Coll of Art and Design (GA)
Southeastern U (FL)
Southern Illinois U Carbondale (IL)
Southwestern Coll (KS)
State U of New York at Fredonia (NY)
Suffolk U (MA)
Syracuse U (NY)
Temple U (PA)
Texas A&M U–Commerce (TX)
Texas State U (TX)
Texas Tech U (TX)
Troy U (AL)
Union U (TN)
The U of Akron (OH)
U of Central Florida (FL)
U of Central Missouri (MO)
U of Cincinnati (OH)

U of Dayton (OH)
U of Florida (FL)
U of Houston (TX)
U of Kentucky (KY)
U of La Verne (CA)
U of Missouri (MO)
U of Montevallo (AL)
U of North Texas (TX)
U of Pittsburgh at Bradford (PA)
U of Southern Indiana (IN)
The U of Texas at Austin (TX)
U of the Incarnate Word (TX)
Vanguard U of Southern California (CA)
Wartburg Coll (IA)
Waynesburg U (PA)
Wayne State U (MI)
Weber State U (UT)
Western Illinois U (IL)
Western Kentucky U (KY)
Westminster Coll (PA)
William Penn U (IA)
Youngstown State U (OH)

RADIO AND TELEVISION BROADCASTING TECHNOLOGY
Coll of the Ozarks (MO)
Emerson Coll (MA)
Ferris State U (MI)
Gannon U (PA)
La Salle U (PA)
Lincoln Coll (IL)
Long Island U–LIU Post (NY)
New England Inst of Technology (RI)
New York Inst of Technology (NY)
New York U (NY)
Northwest Nazarene U (ID)
Suffolk U (MA)
Wilmington U (DE)

RADIOLOGIC TECHNOLOGY/ SCIENCE
Adventist U of Health Sciences (FL)
Austin Peay State U (TN)
Baptist Coll of Health Sciences (TN)
Boise State U (ID)
Central Penn Coll (PA)
Charles R. Drew U of Medicine and Science (CA)
Colorado Mesa U (CO)
ECPI U, Virginia Beach (VA)
Fairleigh Dickinson U, Metropolitan Campus (NJ)
Friends U (KS)
The George Washington U (DC)
Gwynedd Mercy U (PA)
Holy Family U (PA)
Indiana U Northwest (IN)
Inter American U of Puerto Rico, Aguadilla Campus (PR)
Inter American U of Puerto Rico, Barranquitas Campus (PR)
Inter American U of Puerto Rico, San Germán Campus (PR)
Lewis U (IL)
Manhattan Coll (NY)
Marian U (WI)
Marshall U (WV)
McNeese State U (LA)
MCPHS U (MA)
Missouri State U (MO)
Nebraska Methodist Coll (NE)
North Dakota State U (ND)
Northern Kentucky U (KY)
Northern Michigan U (MI)
Northwestern State U of Louisiana (LA)
Northwest Missouri State U (MO)
Oakland U (MI)
Oregon Inst of Technology (OR)
Pennsylvania Coll of Technology (PA)
Quinnipiac U (CT)
Resurrection U (IL)
Rhode Island Coll (RI)
Sacred Heart U (CT)
St. John's U (NY)
Southern Vermont Coll (VT)
U of Charleston (WV)
U of Jamestown (ND)
U of Louisiana at Monroe (LA)
U of Missouri (MO)
U of Oklahoma Health Sciences Center (OK)

U of Pittsburgh at Bradford (PA)
U of St. Francis (IL)
U of South Alabama (AL)
U of Southern Indiana (IN)
U of Toronto (ON, Canada)
Virginia Commonwealth U (VA)
Weber State U (UT)
Widener U (PA)
York Coll of Pennsylvania (PA)

RADIOLOGIST ASSISTANT
Weber State U (UT)

RADIO, TELEVISION, AND DIGITAL COMMUNICATION RELATED
Asbury U (KY)
Ashland U (OH)
Brigham Young U (UT)
Central Michigan U (MI)
Clark Atlanta U (GA)
Dallas Baptist U (TX)
Drake U (IA)
Emerson Coll (MA)
Hofstra U (NY)
Lincoln Coll (IL)
Louisiana Coll (LA)
Madonna U (MI)
Marquette U (WI)
North Dakota State U (ND)
Rogers State U (OK)
San Francisco State U (CA)
Spring Hill Coll (AL)
Texas Christian U (TX)
Towson U (MD)
The U of Akron (OH)
Washington State U (WA)
William Penn U (IA)

RANGE SCIENCE AND MANAGEMENT
Colorado State U (CO)
Humboldt State U (CA)
New Mexico State U (NM)
North Dakota State U (ND)
Oregon State U (OR)
Texas A&M U (TX)
U of Idaho (ID)
U of Nebraska–Lincoln (NE)
U of Nevada, Reno (NV)
U of Wyoming (WY)
Utah State U (UT)
Washington State U (WA)

READING TEACHER EDUCATION
Aquinas Coll (MI)
Baylor U (TX)
Canisius Coll (NY)
Concordia U Chicago (IL)
Eastern Michigan U (MI)
Eastern Washington U (WA)
Grand Valley State U (MI)
Harding U (AR)
Michigan State U (MI)
Queens Coll of the City U of New York (NY)
Sam Houston State U (TX)
State U of New York Coll at Cortland (NY)
State U of New York Coll at Oneonta (NY)
The U of Arizona (AZ)
U of Central Missouri (MO)
U of Michigan–Dearborn (MI)
U of Providence (MT)
Upper Iowa U (IA)
William Penn U (IA)

REAL ESTATE
Ball State U (IN)
Baruch Coll of the City U of New York (NY)
Baylor U (TX)
Bowling Green State U (OH)
California State U, Dominguez Hills (CA)
Central Michigan U (MI)
Clarion U of Pennsylvania (PA)
Coll of Charleston (SC)
DePaul U (IL)
Drexel U (PA)
Florida Atlantic U (FL)
Florida Intl U (FL)
Florida State U (FL)
Georgia State U (GA)
Inter American U of Puerto Rico, Metropolitan Campus (PR)
Marquette U (WI)

Mississippi State U (MS)
New York U (NY)
The Ohio State U (OH)
Portland State U (OR)
San Diego State U (CA)
Southern Methodist U (TX)
Syracuse U (NY)
Temple U (PA)
Texas Christian U (TX)
The U of Akron (OH)
U of Central Florida (FL)
U of Cincinnati (OH)
U of Denver (CO)
U of Florida (FL)
U of Georgia (GA)
U of Guelph (ON, Canada)
U of Miami (FL)
U of Missouri (MO)
U of Nevada, Las Vegas (NV)
U of Northern Iowa (IA)
U of North Texas (TX)
U of Pennsylvania (PA)
U of St. Thomas (MN)
U of San Diego (CA)
U of South Carolina (SC)
U of Southern California (CA)
The U of Texas at San Antonio (TX)
U of West Georgia (GA)
U of Wisconsin–Madison (WI)
U of Wisconsin–Milwaukee (WI)
U of Wisconsin–Stout (WI)
Villanova U (PA)
Virginia Commonwealth U (VA)
Virginia Polytechnic Inst and State U (VA)
Washington State U (WA)

RECORDING ARTS TECHNOLOGY
Academy of Art U (CA)
American U (DC)
Belmont U (TN)
Butler U (IN)
Columbia Coll Chicago (IL)
Elon U (NC)
Greenville U (IL)
Husson U (ME)
Indiana U Bloomington (IN)
Ithaca Coll (NY)
Loyola Marymount U (CA)
Malone U (OH)
Michigan Technological U (MI)
Minnesota State U Moorhead (MN)
New England Inst of Technology (RI)
Northwest U (WA)
Savannah Coll of Art and Design (GA)
State U of New York at Fredonia (NY)
Texas State U (TX)
York Coll of Pennsylvania (PA)

REGIONAL STUDIES
The Colorado Coll (CO)
Mercer U, Macon (GA)
U of Regina (SK, Canada)
U of Saskatchewan (SK, Canada)
Washington U in St. Louis (MO)

REGISTERED NURSING, NURSING ADMINISTRATION, NURSING RESEARCH AND CLINICAL NURSING RELATED
Bethel Coll (IN)
Cardinal Stritch U (WI)
Cleveland State U (OH)
Columbia Central U, Caguas (PR)
Jacksonville U (FL)
Molloy Coll (NY)
Moravian Coll (PA)
Neumann U (PA)
Northwest U (WA)
Rowan U (NJ)
Tabor Coll (KS)
U of California, Los Angeles (CA)
U of Massachusetts Dartmouth (MA)
U of Pikeville (KY)
U of Saint Mary (KS)
The U of Texas at Austin (TX)
Wheaton Coll (IL)

REGISTERED NURSING/ REGISTERED NURSE
Abilene Christian U (TX)
Adams State U (CO)
Adelphi U (NY)

Adventist U of Health Sciences (FL)
Alcorn State U (MS)
Allen Coll (IA)
Alma Coll (MI)
Alverno Coll (WI)
American Intl Coll (MA)
American U of Beirut (Lebanon)
Anderson U (IN)
Anderson U (SC)
Andrews U (MI)
Angelo State U (TX)
Appalachian State U (NC)
Arizona State U at the Downtown Phoenix campus (AZ)
Arkansas Tech U (AR)
Athabasca U (AB, Canada)
Auburn U (AL)
Auburn U at Montgomery (AL)
Augustana U (SD)
Aultman Coll of Nursing and Health Sciences (OH)
Aurora U (IL)
Austin Peay State U (TN)
Avila U (MO)
Azusa Pacific U (CA)
Baker U (KS)
Baldwin Wallace U (OH)
Ball State U (IN)
Baptist Coll of Health Sciences (TN)
Barry U (FL)
Barton Coll (NC)
Baylor U (TX)
Becker Coll (MA)
Belhaven U (MS)
Bellarmine U (KY)
Belmont U (TN)
Bemidji State U (MN)
Benedictine U (IL)
Berea Coll (KY)
Berry Coll (GA)
Bethany Lutheran Coll (MN)
Bethel Coll (IN)
Bethel Coll (KS)
Bethel Coll (MN)
Bethel U (TN)
Bethune-Cookman U (FL)
Binghamton U, State U of New York (NY)
Biola U (CA)
Bloomsburg U of Pennsylvania (PA)
Bluffton U (OH)
Bob Jones U (SC)
Boise State U (ID)
Boston Coll (MA)
Bowie State U (MD)
Bowling Green State U (OH)
Bowling Green State U–Firelands Coll (OH)
Bradley U (IL)
Brandman U (CA)
Brigham Young U–Idaho (ID)
Caldwell U (NJ)
California Baptist U (CA)
California State U, Dominguez Hills (CA)
California State U, Long Beach (CA)
California State U, Los Angeles (CA)
California State U, Monterey Bay (CA)
California State U, Northridge (CA)
California State U, Sacramento (CA)
California State U, San Bernardino (CA)
California State U, San Marcos (CA)
California State U, Stanislaus (CA)
California U of Pennsylvania (PA)
Calvin Coll (MI)
Campbellsville U (KY)
Capital U (OH)
Cardinal Stritch U (WI)
Carlow U (PA)
Carroll Coll (MT)
Carson-Newman U (TN)
Case Western Reserve U (OH)
The Catholic U of America (DC)
Cedar Crest Coll (PA)
Cedarville U (OH)
Central Connecticut State U (CT)
Central Methodist U (MO)
Central Penn Coll (PA)
Chaminade U of Honolulu (HI)

Charleston Southern U (SC)
Chatham U (PA)
Chipola Coll (FL)
The Citadel, The Military Coll of South Carolina (SC)
Clarion U of Pennsylvania (PA)
Clarke U (IA)
Clayton State U (GA)
Clemson U (SC)
Cleveland State U (OH)
Coastal Carolina U (SC)
Coe Coll (IA)
Colegio Universitario de San Juan, San Juan (PR)
The Coll at Brockport, State U of New York (NY)
Coll of Central Florida (FL)
Coll of Coastal Georgia (GA)
Coll of Mount Saint Vincent (NY)
The Coll of New Jersey (NJ)
The Coll of New Rochelle (NY)
Coll of Saint Benedict (MN)
Coll of Saint Elizabeth (NJ)
Coll of Saint Mary (NE)
The Coll of St. Scholastica (MN)
Coll of Staten Island of the City U of New York (NY)
Coll of the Ozarks (MO)
Colorado Mesa U (CO)
Colorado State U–Pueblo (CO)
Columbia Coll (SC)
Columbus State U (GA)
Concordia U Irvine (CA)
Concordia U Wisconsin (WI)
Creighton U (NE)
Culver-Stockton Coll (MO)
Curry Coll (MA)
Daemen Coll (NY)
Davenport U, Grand Rapids (MI)
Daytona State Coll (FL)
Defiance Coll (OH)
Delaware State U (DE)
DeSales U (PA)
Dickinson State U (ND)
Dominican Coll (NY)
Dominican U (IL)
Dominican U of California (CA)
Drexel U (PA)
Duquesne U (PA)
D'Youville Coll (NY)
East Carolina U (NC)
East Central U (OK)
Eastern Mennonite U (VA)
Eastern Michigan U (MI)
Eastern New Mexico U (NM)
Eastern U (PA)
Eastern Washington U (WA)
East Stroudsburg U of Pennsylvania (PA)
East Tennessee State U (TN)
East Texas Baptist U (TX)
ECPI U, Virginia Beach (VA)
Edgewood Coll (WI)
Elmhurst Coll (IL)
Elms Coll (MA)
Emory U (GA)
Emporia State U (KS)
Endicott Coll (MA)
Excelsior Coll (NY)
Fairfield U (CT)
Fairleigh Dickinson U, Florham Campus (NJ)
Fairleigh Dickinson U, Metropolitan Campus (NJ)
Farmingdale State Coll (NY)
Fayetteville State U (NC)
Felician U (NJ)
Ferris State U (MI)
Fisher Coll (MA)
Fitchburg State U (MA)
Florida Ag and Mech U (FL)
Florida Atlantic U (FL)
Florida Gulf Coast U (FL)
Florida Intl U (FL)
Florida National U (FL)
Florida Southern Coll (FL)
Framingham State U (MA)
Franciscan Missionaries of Our Lady U (LA)
Francis Marion U (SC)
Frostburg State U (MD)
Gannon U (PA)
George Mason U (VA)
Georgetown U (DC)
Georgia Coll & State U (GA)
Georgia Gwinnett Coll (GA)
Georgia Highlands Coll (GA)

Georgian Court U (NJ)
Georgia Southern U (GA)
Georgia Southern U–Armstrong Campus (GA)
Georgia Southwestern State U (GA)
Georgia State U (GA)
Goldfarb School of Nursing at Barnes-Jewish Coll (MO)
Gonzaga U (WA)
Gordon State Coll (GA)
Goshen Coll (IN)
Governors State U (IL)
Graceland U (IA)
Grand View U (IA)
Granite State Coll (NH)
Gustavus Adolphus Coll (MN)
Gwynedd Mercy U (PA)
Hallmark U (TX)
Hampton U (VA)
Hannibal-LaGrange U (MO)
Harding U (AR)
Hardin-Simmons U (TX)
Hartwick Coll (NY)
Hawai'i Pacific U (HI)
Hesston Coll (KS)
Holy Family U (PA)
Holy Names U (CA)
Hood Coll (MD)
Hope Coll (MI)
Houston Baptist U (TX)
Howard Payne U (TX)
Hunter Coll of the City U of New York (NY)
Husson U (ME)
Idaho State U (ID)
Illinois State U (IL)
Illinois Wesleyan U (IL)
Immaculata U (PA)
Indiana State U (IN)
Indiana U Bloomington (IN)
Indiana U East (IN)
Indiana U Kokomo (IN)
Indiana U Northwest (IN)
Indiana U of Pennsylvania (PA)
Indiana U–Purdue U Indianapolis (IN)
Indiana U South Bend (IN)
Indiana U Southeast (IN)
Indiana Wesleyan U (IN)
Inter American U of Puerto Rico, Aguadilla Campus (PR)
Inter American U of Puerto Rico, Bayamón Campus (PR)
Inter American U of Puerto Rico, Metropolitan Campus (PR)
Inter American U of Puerto Rico, San Germán Campus (PR)
Iowa State U of Science and Technology (IA)
Jacksonville U (FL)
James Madison U (VA)
Jefferson Coll of Health Sciences (VA)
John Brown U (AR)
Johns Hopkins U (MD)
Kansas Wesleyan U (KS)
Keene State Coll (NH)
Keiser U, Fort Lauderdale (FL)
Kennesaw State U (GA)
Kent State U (OH)
Kent State U at Ashtabula (OH)
Kent State U at East Liverpool (OH)
Kent State U at Geauga (OH)
Kent State U at Salem (OH)
Kent State U at Stark (OH)
Kent State U at Trumbull (OH)
Kent State U at Tuscarawas (OH)
Kentucky State U (KY)
King's Coll (PA)
King U (TN)
LaGrange Coll (GA)
Lamar U (TX)
Langston U (OK)
La Roche Coll (PA)
La Salle U (PA)
Lawrence Technological U (MI)
Lee U (TN)
Lehman Coll of the City U of New York (NY)
Le Moyne Coll (NY)
Lenoir-Rhyne U (NC)
Lewis U (IL)
Liberty U (VA)
Lincoln Coll of New England, Southington (CT)
Lincoln Memorial U (TN)

Lincoln U (MO)
Lincoln U (PA)
Lindsey Wilson Coll (KY)
Linfield Coll (OR)
Lipscomb U (TN)
Lock Haven U of Pennsylvania (PA)
Long Island U–LIU Brooklyn (NY)
Long Island U–LIU Post (NY)
Longwood U (VA)
Louisiana Coll (LA)
Louisiana State U Health Sciences Center (LA)
Loyola U Chicago (IL)
Loyola U New Orleans (LA)
Lubbock Christian U (TX)
Luther Coll (IA)
Lynchburg Coll (VA)
Madonna U (MI)
Maine Coll of Health Professions (ME)
Malone U (OH)
Mansfield U of Pennsylvania (PA)
Maranatha Baptist U (WI)
Maria Coll (NY)
Marian U (IN)
Marian U (WI)
Marquette U (WI)
Marshall U (WV)
Marymount U (VA)
Maryville U of Saint Louis (MO)
Marywood U (PA)
McKendree U (IL)
McMurry U (TX)
McNeese State U (LA)
MCPHS U (MA)
Medgar Evers Coll of the City U of New York (NY)
Mercer U, Macon (GA)
Mercy Coll (NY)
Mercy Coll of Ohio (OH)
Mercyhurst U (PA)
Messiah Coll (PA)
Metropolitan State U of Denver (CO)
Miami Dade Coll (FL)
Michigan State U (MI)
MidAmerica Nazarene U (KS)
Middle Georgia State U (GA)
Middle Tennessee State U (TN)
Milligan Coll (TN)
Millikin U (IL)
Milwaukee School of Eng (WI)
Minnesota State U Moorhead (MN)
Minot State U (ND)
Misericordia U (PA)
Missouri Baptist U (MO)
Missouri State U (MO)
Missouri Valley Coll (MO)
Missouri Western State U (MO)
Molloy Coll (NY)
Montana Tech of The U of Montana (MT)
Montclair State U (NJ)
Moravian Coll (PA)
Morehead State U (KY)
Morningside Coll (IA)
Mount Aloysius Coll (PA)
Mount Carmel Coll of Nursing (OH)
Mount Marty Coll (SD)
Mount Mary U (WI)
Mount Mercy U (IA)
Mount St. Joseph U (OH)
Mount Saint Mary Coll (NY)
Mount Saint Mary's U (CA)
Mount Vernon Nazarene U (OH)
Murray State U (KY)
Muskingum U (OH)
National U (CA)
Nazareth Coll of Rochester (NY)
Nebraska Methodist Coll (NE)
Newberry Coll (SC)
New England Inst of Technology (RI)
Newman U (KS)
New Mexico Highlands U (NM)
New Mexico State U (NM)
New York Inst of Technology (NY)
New York U (NY)
Niagara U (NY)
North Carolina Central U (NC)
North Dakota State U (ND)
Northeastern State U (OK)
Northeastern U (MA)
Northern Arizona U (AZ)
Northern Illinois U (IL)
Northern Kentucky U (KY)
Northern Michigan U (MI)

Northwestern Coll (IA)
Northwestern Oklahoma State U (OK)
Northwestern State U of Louisiana (LA)
Northwest Nazarene U (ID)
Northwest U (WA)
Nova Southeastern U (FL)
Nyack Coll (NY)
Oakland U (MI)
The Ohio State U (OH)
The Ohio State U at Mansfield (OH)
The Ohio State U at Marion (OH)
The Ohio State U at Newark (OH)
Ohio U (OH)
Oklahoma Baptist U (OK)
Oklahoma Christian U (OK)
Oklahoma State U (OK)
Old Dominion U (VA)
Olivet Nazarene U (IL)
Oral Roberts U (OK)
Otterbein U (OH)
Pace U (NY)
Pace U, Pleasantville Campus (NY)
Pacific Lutheran U (WA)
Palm Beach Atlantic U (FL)
Penn State Abington (PA)
Penn State Altoona (PA)
Penn State Beaver (PA)
Penn State Berks (PA)
Penn State Brandywine (PA)
Penn State DuBois (PA)
Penn State Erie, The Behrend Coll (PA)
Penn State Fayette, The Eberly Campus (PA)
Penn State Greater Allegheny (PA)
Penn State Harrisburg (PA)
Penn State Hazleton (PA)
Penn State Lehigh Valley (PA)
Penn State Mont Alto (PA)
Penn State New Kensington (PA)
Penn State Schuylkill (PA)
Penn State Shenango (PA)
Penn State U Park (PA)
Penn State Wilkes-Barre (PA)
Penn State Worthington Scranton (PA)
Penn State York (PA)
Pennsylvania Coll of Health Sciences (PA)
Pennsylvania Coll of Technology (PA)
Pensacola State Coll (FL)
Piedmont Coll (GA)
Pittsburg State U (KS)
Point Loma Nazarene U (CA)
Polk State Coll (FL)
Post U (CT)
Prairie View A&M U (TX)
Purdue U (IN)
Purdue U Northwest (IN)
Quinnipiac U (CT)
Radford U (VA)
Ramapo Coll of New Jersey (NJ)
Rasmussen Coll New Port Richey (FL)
Regent U (VA)
Regis U (CO)
Research Coll of Nursing (MO)
Resurrection U (IL)
Rhode Island Coll (RI)
Rider U (NJ)
Rivier U (NH)
Robert Morris U (PA)
Robert Morris U Illinois (IL)
Roberts Wesleyan Coll (NY)
Rockford U (IL)
Rockhurst U (MO)
Rogers State U (OK)
Rowan U (NJ)
Rutgers U–Camden (NJ)
Rutgers U–Newark (NJ)
Rutgers U–New Brunswick (NJ)
Sacred Heart U (CT)
The Sage Colls (NY)
Saginaw Valley State U (MI)
St. Ambrose U (IA)
St. Catherine U (MN)
Saint Francis Medical Center Coll of Nursing (IL)
Saint Francis U (PA)
St. John Fisher Coll (NY)
Saint John's U (MN)
St. Joseph's Coll, Long Island Campus (NY)
St. Joseph's Coll, New York (NY)

Saint Louis U (MO)
St. Luke's Coll (IA)
Saint Martin's U (WA)
St. Olaf Coll (MN)
St. Thomas U (FL)
Salisbury U (MD)
Salve Regina U (RI)
Samford U (AL)
Sam Houston State U (TX)
Samuel Merritt U (CA)
San Diego State U (CA)
San Francisco State U (CA)
Seattle Pacific U (WA)
Seattle U (WA)
Sentara Coll of Health Sciences (VA)
Shawnee State U (OH)
Shenandoah U (VA)
Shepherd U (WV)
Shorter U (GA)
Silver Lake Coll of the Holy Family (WI)
Simmons Coll (MA)
Slippery Rock U of Pennsylvania (PA)
Sonoma State U (CA)
Southeastern U (FL)
Southeast Missouri State U (MO)
Southern Adventist U (TN)
Southern Arkansas U–Magnolia (AR)
Southern Illinois U Edwardsville (IL)
Southern Utah U (UT)
Southern Vermont Coll (VT)
South Florida State Coll (FL)
Southwest Baptist U (MO)
Southwestern Adventist U (TX)
Southwestern Coll (KS)
Spring Hill Coll (AL)
State U of New York at Plattsburgh (NY)
State U of New York Coll of Technology at Alfred (NY)
State U of New York Coll of Technology at Canton (NY)
State U of New York Coll of Technology at Delhi (NY)
State U of New York Empire State Coll (NY)
State U of New York Polytechnic Inst (NY)
Stephen F. Austin State U (TX)
Stevenson U (MD)
Stockton U (NJ)
Stony Brook U, State U of New York (NY)
Sullivan U (KY)
Tarleton State U (TX)
Temple U (PA)
Tennessee Technological U (TN)
Tennessee Wesleyan U (TN)
Texas A&M Intl U (TX)
Texas A&M U–Commerce (TX)
Texas A&M U–Corpus Christi (TX)
Texas A&M U–Texarkana (TX)
Texas Christian U (TX)
Texas Lutheran U (TX)
Texas State U (TX)
Texas Woman's U (TX)
Thomas Edison State U (NJ)
Thomas Jefferson U (PA)
Thomas U (GA)
Toccoa Falls Coll (GA)
Towson U (MD)
Trent U (ON, Canada)
Trevecca Nazarene U (TN)
Trinity Christian Coll (IL)
Troy U (AL)
Truett McConnell U (GA)
Truman State U (MO)
Tusculum Coll (TN)
Union Coll (NE)
Union U (TN)
Université de Sherbrooke (QC, Canada)
U at Buffalo, the State U of New York (NY)
The U of Akron (OH)
The U of Alabama (AL)
The U of Alabama at Birmingham (AL)
The U of Arizona (AZ)
U of Arkansas (AR)
U of Bridgeport (CT)
U of Central Arkansas (AR)
U of Central Florida (FL)

U of Central Missouri (MO)
U of Central Oklahoma (OK)
U of Charleston (WV)
U of Cincinnati (OH)
U of Colorado Colorado Springs (CO)
U of Colorado Denver (CO)
U of Dubuque (IA)
U of Evansville (IN)
The U of Findlay (OH)
U of Florida (FL)
U of Guam (GU)
U of Hartford (CT)
U of Hawaii at Manoa (HI)
U of Houston (TX)
U of Houston–Clear Lake (TX)
U of Illinois at Chicago (IL)
U of Jamestown (ND)
The U of Kansas (KS)
U of Kentucky (KY)
U of Louisiana at Monroe (LA)
U of Louisville (KY)
U of Maine (ME)
U of Maine at Fort Kent (ME)
U of Mary Hardin-Baylor (TX)
U of Maryland U Coll (MD)
U of Mary Washington (VA)
U of Massachusetts Amherst (MA)
U of Massachusetts Boston (MA)
U of Massachusetts Lowell (MA)
U of Memphis (TN)
U of Miami (FL)
U of Michigan (MI)
U of Michigan–Flint (MI)
U of Minnesota, Twin Cities Campus (MN)
U of Missouri (MO)
U of Missouri–St. Louis (MO)
U of Mobile (AL)
U of Mount Union (OH)
U of Nevada, Las Vegas (NV)
U of Nevada, Reno (NV)
U of New England (ME)
U of New Hampshire (NH)
U of New Mexico (NM)
U of North Alabama (AL)
The U of North Carolina at Chapel Hill (NC)
The U of North Carolina at Charlotte (NC)
The U of North Carolina at Greensboro (NC)
The U of North Carolina at Pembroke (NC)
The U of North Carolina Wilmington (NC)
U of North Dakota (ND)
U of Northern Colorado (CO)
U of North Florida (FL)
U of North Georgia (GA)
U of Oklahoma Health Sciences Center (OK)
U of Pennsylvania (PA)
U of Pittsburgh (PA)
U of Pittsburgh at Bradford (PA)
U of Puerto Rico–Humacao (PR)
U of Regina (SK, Canada)
U of Rhode Island (RI)
U of Rochester (NY)
U of St. Francis (IL)
U of Saint Francis (IN)
U of Saint Joseph (CT)
U of Saint Mary (KS)
U of San Francisco (CA)
U of Saskatchewan (SK, Canada)
The U of Scranton (PA)
U of Sioux Falls (SD)
U of South Alabama (AL)
U of South Carolina (SC)
U of South Carolina Aiken (SC)
U of South Dakota (SD)
U of Southern Indiana (IN)
U of Southern Maine (ME)
U of Southern Mississippi (MS)
The U of Tampa (FL)
The U of Tennessee (TN)
The U of Tennessee at Chattanooga (TN)
The U of Tennessee at Martin (TN)
The U of Texas at Austin (TX)
The U of Texas of the Permian Basin (TX)
The U of Texas Rio Grande Valley (TX)
U of the Fraser Valley (BC, Canada)
U of the Incarnate Word (TX)

U of the Virgin Islands (VI)
The U of Toledo (OH)
U of Toronto (ON, Canada)
U of Tulsa (OK)
U of Vermont (VT)
U of Virginia (VA)
U of Washington (WA)
U of Washington, Bothell (WA)
U of Washington, Tacoma (WA)
U of West Georgia (GA)
U of Wisconsin–Madison (WI)
U of Wisconsin–Milwaukee (WI)
U of Wisconsin–Parkside (WI)
U of Wisconsin–Stevens Point (WI)
U of Wyoming (WY)
Ursuline Coll (OH)
Utah Valley U (UT)
Utica Coll (NY)
Valdosta State U (GA)
Valparaiso U (IN)
Vanguard U of Southern California (CA)
Villanova U (PA)
Vincennes U (IN)
Virginia Commonwealth U (VA)
Wagner Coll (NY)
Walsh U (OH)
Washington State U (WA)
Washington State U–Spokane (WA)
Washington State U–Tri-Cities (WA)
Washington State U–Vancouver (WA)
Wayland Baptist U (TX)
Waynesburg U (PA)
Weber State U (UT)
Webster U (MO)
West Chester U of Pennsylvania (PA)
Western Connecticut State U (CT)
Western Illinois U (IL)
Western Kentucky U (KY)
Western Michigan U (MI)
Western Washington U (WA)
Westfield State U (MA)
Westminster Coll (PA)
Westminster Coll (UT)
West Texas A&M U (TX)
West Virginia U (WV)
West Virginia U Inst of Technology (WV)
West Virginia Wesleyan Coll (WV)
Whitworth U (WA)
Wichita State U (KS)
Widener U (PA)
Wilkes U (PA)
William Jewell Coll (MO)
William Paterson U of New Jersey (NJ)
Wilmington U (DE)
Winona State U (MN)
Wisconsin Lutheran Coll (WI)
Wittenberg U (OH)
Worcester State U (MA)
Wright State U (OH)
Wright State U–Lake Campus (OH)
York Coll of Pennsylvania (PA)
Youngstown State U (OH)

REHABILITATION AND THERAPEUTIC PROFESSIONS RELATED
Alabama State U (AL)
Assumption Coll (MA)
Boston U (MA)
California State U, Los Angeles (CA)
Coll of Saint Mary (NE)
East Stroudsburg U of Pennsylvania (PA)
Georgian Court U (NJ)
Indiana U of Pennsylvania (PA)
Ithaca Coll (NY)
Lock Haven U of Pennsylvania (PA)
Penn State Abington (PA)
Penn State Altoona (PA)
Penn State Beaver (PA)
Penn State Berks (PA)
Penn State Brandywine (PA)
Penn State DuBois (PA)
Penn State Erie, The Behrend Coll (PA)
Penn State Fayette, The Eberly Campus (PA)
Penn State Greater Allegheny (PA)
Penn State Hazleton (PA)

Penn State Lehigh Valley (PA)
Penn State Mont Alto (PA)
Penn State New Kensington (PA)
Penn State Schuylkill (PA)
Penn State Shenango (PA)
Penn State U Park (PA)
Penn State Wilkes-Barre (PA)
Penn State Worthington Scranton (PA)
Penn State York (PA)
Rutgers U–Newark (NJ)
Rutgers U–New Brunswick (NJ)
Southern Illinois U Carbondale (IL)
Thomas U (GA)
Troy U (AL)
U of Maryland Eastern Shore (MD)
U of Massachusetts Lowell (MA)
U of Waterloo (ON, Canada)

REHABILITATION SCIENCE
Arkansas Tech U (AR)
Boston U (MA)
George Mason U (VA)
Marshall U (WV)
New England Inst of Technology (RI)
Stephen F. Austin State U (TX)
U of Maine at Farmington (ME)
U of North Dakota (ND)
U of North Texas (TX)
U of Pittsburgh (PA)
The U of Texas Rio Grande Valley (TX)
U of the Incarnate Word (TX)

RELIGIOUS EDUCATION
Andrews U (MI)
Asbury U (KY)
Ashland U (OH)
Azusa Pacific U (CA)
The Baptist Coll of Florida (FL)
Barclay Coll (KS)
Benedictine Coll (KS)
Biola U (CA)
Bryan Coll (TN)
Campbellsville U (KY)
Cedarville U (OH)
Concordia Coll–New York (NY)
Concordia U Chicago (IL)
Concordia U Irvine (CA)
Concordia U, Nebraska (NE)
Concordia U, St. Paul (MN)
Corban U (OR)
Dallas Baptist U (TX)
Defiance Coll (OH)
Eastern Nazarene Coll (MA)
Edgewood Coll (WI)
Elms Coll (MA)
Florida Coll (FL)
Hannibal-LaGrange U (MO)
Harding U (AR)
Howard Payne U (TX)
Indiana Wesleyan U (IN)
Inter American U of Puerto Rico, Fajardo Campus (PR)
John Carroll U (OH)
Kentucky Mountain Bible Coll (KY)
Lee U (TN)
Lindsey Wilson Coll (KY)
Louisiana Coll (LA)
Loyola U Chicago (IL)
Loyola U New Orleans (LA)
Malone U (OH)
Marian U (IN)
Master's Coll and Sem (ON, Canada)
The Master's U (CA)
Messiah Coll (PA)
Morris Coll (SC)
Mount Vernon Nazarene U (OH)
Multnomah U (OR)
Muskingum U (OH)
Northwestern Coll (IA)
Northwest Nazarene U (ID)
Northwest U (WA)
Ohio Northern U (OH)
Oklahoma Christian U (OK)
Olivet Nazarene U (IL)
Oral Roberts U (OK)
Pfeiffer U (NC)
Presbyterian Coll (SC)
Saint Mary's U of Minnesota (MN)
Seattle Pacific U (WA)
Southern Adventist U (TN)
Southwest Baptist U (MO)
Taylor U (IN)

Theological U of the Caribbean (PR)
Toccoa Falls Coll (GA)
U of Dayton (OH)
The U of Findlay (OH)
U of Valley Forge (PA)
Vanguard U of Southern California (CA)
Wayland Baptist U (TX)
Welch Coll (TN)
Wheaton Coll (IL)

RELIGIOUS/SACRED MUSIC
Anderson U (IN)
Aquinas Coll (MI)
Arizona Christian U (AZ)
Asbury U (KY)
The Baptist Coll of Florida (FL)
Barclay Coll (KS)
Baylor U (TX)
Bethany Lutheran Coll (MN)
Bethel U (TN)
Bluefield Coll (VA)
Blue Mountain Coll (MS)
Bowling Green State U (OH)
Brewton-Parker Coll (GA)
Calvary U (MO)
Calvin Coll (MI)
Campbellsville U (KY)
Carson-Newman U (TN)
Charleston Southern U (SC)
Coll of the Ozarks (MO)
Concordia Coll–New York (NY)
Concordia U Chicago (IL)
Concordia U, Nebraska (NE)
Concordia U, St. Paul (MN)
Concordia U Wisconsin (WI)
Drake U (IA)
East Central U (OK)
East Texas Baptist U (TX)
Emmanuel Coll (GA)
Evangel U (MO)
Greenville U (IL)
Gustavus Adolphus Coll (MN)
Hardin-Simmons U (TX)
Hope Intl U (CA)
Howard Payne U (TX)
Indiana Wesleyan U (IN)
John Brown U (AR)
Johnson U (TN)
Johnson U Florida (FL)
Judson U (IL)
Kentucky Mountain Bible Coll (KY)
Lee U (TN)
Lenoir-Rhyne U (NC)
Liberty U (VA)
Madonna U (MI)
Malone U (OH)
Maranatha Baptist U (WI)
Marian U (IN)
The Master's U (CA)
Mid-America Christian U (OK)
MidAmerica Nazarene U (KS)
Missouri Baptist U (MO)
Mount Vernon Nazarene U (OH)
Multnomah U (OR)
Nebraska Christian Coll of Hope Intl U (NE)
North Greenville U (SC)
Northwest Christian U (OR)
Northwest Nazarene U (ID)
Northwest U (WA)
Nyack Coll (NY)
Oakland City U (IN)
Ohio Christian U (OH)
Oklahoma Baptist U (OK)
Oklahoma City U (OK)
Olivet Nazarene U (IL)
Oral Roberts U (OK)
Ouachita Baptist U (AR)
Pfeiffer U (NC)
Point Loma Nazarene U (CA)
Rider U (NJ)
St. Olaf Coll (MN)
Samford U (AL)
Seton Hill U (PA)
Shenandoah U (VA)
Shorter U (GA)
Southeastern U (FL)
Southwestern Assemblies of God U (TX)
Texas Christian U (TX)
Trevecca Nazarene U (TN)
Truett McConnell U (GA)
Union U (TN)
U of Mary Hardin-Baylor (TX)
U of Mobile (AL)

U of Sioux Falls (SD)
U of Valley Forge (PA)
Wartburg Coll (IA)
Wayland Baptist U (TX)
Welch Coll (TN)

RELIGIOUS STUDIES
Agnes Scott Coll (GA)
Albion Coll (MI)
Albright Coll (PA)
Allegheny Coll (PA)
Alma Coll (MI)
Alverno Coll (WI)
Amherst Coll (MA)
Anderson U (IN)
Andrews U (MI)
Appalachian State U (NC)
Aquinas Coll (MI)
Arizona State U at the Tempe campus (AZ)
Arlington Baptist U (TX)
Ashland U (OH)
Athens State U (AL)
Augsburg U (MN)
Augustana Coll (IL)
Augustana U (SD)
Aurora U (IL)
Austin Coll (TX)
Averett U (VA)
Avila U (MO)
Azusa Pacific U (CA)
Baker U (KS)
Baldwin Wallace U (OH)
Ball State U (IN)
Baptist U of the Americas (TX)
Bard Coll (NY)
Barnard Coll (NY)
Baruch Coll of the City U of New York (NY)
Bates Coll (ME)
Baylor U (TX)
Belmont U (TN)
Beloit Coll (WI)
Bemidji State U (MN)
Berea Coll (KY)
Bethany Lutheran Coll (MN)
Bethel Coll (KS)
Bethune-Cookman U (FL)
Biola U (CA)
Birmingham-Southern Coll (AL)
Bluefield Coll (VA)
Boston U (MA)
Bowdoin Coll (ME)
Bradley U (IL)
Brandon U (MB, Canada)
Brewton-Parker Coll (GA)
Bryn Athyn Coll of the New Church (PA)
Bryn Mawr Coll (PA)
Bucknell U (PA)
Butler U (IN)
Cairn U (PA)
California Lutheran U (CA)
California State U, Fullerton (CA)
California State U, Long Beach (CA)
California State U, Northridge (CA)
California State U, Sacramento (CA)
Calumet Coll of Saint Joseph (IN)
Calvin Coll (MI)
Campbellsville U (KY)
Canisius Coll (NY)
Capital U (OH)
Cardinal Stritch U (WI)
Carleton Coll (MN)
Carroll U (WI)
Carson-Newman U (TN)
Carthage Coll (WI)
Case Western Reserve U (OH)
Catawba Coll (NC)
The Catholic U of America (DC)
Centenary Coll of Louisiana (LA)
Central Methodist U (MO)
Central Michigan U (MI)
Centre Coll (KY)
Chaminade U of Honolulu (HI)
Chapman U (CA)
Charleston Southern U (SC)
Chowan U (NC)
Claremont McKenna Coll (CA)
Clark Atlanta U (GA)
Clarke U (IA)
Cleveland State U (OH)
Coe Coll (IA)
Colby Coll (ME)

Colgate U (NY)
Coll of Charleston (SC)
The Coll of Idaho (ID)
Coll of Mount Saint Vincent (NY)
The Coll of New Rochelle (NY)
The Coll of St. Scholastica (MN)
Coll of the Holy Cross (MA)
The Coll of William and Mary (VA)
The Coll of Wooster (OH)
Colorado Christian U (CO)
The Colorado Coll (CO)
Columbia U (NY)
Concordia Coll–New York (NY)
Concordia U (QC, Canada)
Concordia U Chicago (IL)
Concordia U Irvine (CA)
Concordia U of Edmonton (AB, Canada)
Concordia U Wisconsin (WI)
Connecticut Coll (CT)
Converse Coll (SC)
Corban U (OR)
Cornell Coll (IA)
Cornell U (NY)
Culver-Stockton Coll (MO)
Daemen Coll (NY)
Dartmouth Coll (NH)
Davidson Coll (NC)
Defiance Coll (OH)
Denison U (OH)
DePaul U (IL)
DePauw U (IN)
Dickinson Coll (PA)
Doane U (NE)
Dominican U of California (CA)
Drake U (IA)
Drew U (NJ)
Drury U (MO)
D'Youville Coll (NY)
Earlham Coll (IN)
Eastern Nazarene Coll (MA)
Eastern New Mexico U (NM)
East Texas Baptist U (TX)
Eckerd Coll (FL)
Edgewood Coll (WI)
Elizabethtown Coll (PA)
Elms Coll (MA)
Elon U (NC)
Emmanuel Coll (MA)
Emory & Henry Coll (VA)
Emory U (GA)
The Evergreen State Coll (WA)
Fairfield U (CT)
Felician U (NJ)
Florida Intl U (FL)
Florida Southern Coll (FL)
Fordham U (NY)
Franklin & Marshall Coll (PA)
Franklin Coll (IN)
Furman U (SC)
George Mason U (VA)
Georgetown Coll (KY)
The George Washington U (DC)
Georgian Court U (NJ)
Georgia State U (GA)
Gettysburg Coll (PA)
Gonzaga U (WA)
Goshen Coll (IN)
Graceland U (IA)
Grand View U (IA)
Greensboro Coll (NC)
Greenville U (IL)
Grinnell Coll (IA)
Grove City Coll (PA)
Guilford Coll (NC)
Gustavus Adolphus Coll (MN)
Hamilton Coll (NY)
Hamline U (MN)
Hampden-Sydney Coll (VA)
Hampshire Coll (MA)
Hampton U (VA)
Hartwick Coll (NY)
Harvard U (MA)
Haverford Coll (PA)
Heidelberg U (OH)
Hendrix Coll (AR)
High Point U (NC)
Hillsdale Coll (MI)
Hiram Coll (OH)
Hobart and William Smith Colls (NY)
Hofstra U (NY)
Hollins U (VA)
Holy Family U (PA)
Hood Coll (MD)
Hope Coll (MI)
Hope Intl U (CA)

Humboldt State U (CA)
Hunter Coll of the City U of New York (NY)
Huntingdon Coll (AL)
Illinois Coll (IL)
Illinois Wesleyan U (IL)
Indiana U Bloomington (IN)
Indiana U of Pennsylvania (PA)
Indiana U–Purdue U Indianapolis (IN)
Inter American U of Puerto Rico, Metropolitan Campus (PR)
Iona Coll (NY)
Iowa State U of Science and Technology (IA)
John Carroll U (OH)
Johnson U (TN)
Johnson U Florida (FL)
Juniata Coll (PA)
Kalamazoo Coll (MI)
Kenyon Coll (OH)
The King's Coll (NY)
King U (TN)
Lafayette Coll (PA)
LaGrange Coll (GA)
La Roche Coll (PA)
La Salle U (PA)
La Sierra U (CA)
Lawrence U (WI)
Lebanon Valley Coll (PA)
Lehigh U (PA)
Le Moyne Coll (NY)
Lenoir-Rhyne U (NC)
Lewis U (IL)
Liberty U (VA)
Lincoln U (PA)
Linfield Coll (OR)
Loras Coll (IA)
Loyola U New Orleans (LA)
Luther Coll (IA)
Lycoming Coll (PA)
Lynchburg Coll (VA)
Macalester Coll (MN)
Madonna U (MI)
Manchester U (IN)
Manhattan Coll (NY)
Manhattanville Coll (NY)
Marist Coll (NY)
Marlboro Coll (VT)
Marymount U (VA)
Maryville U (TN)
Marywood U (PA)
The Master's U (CA)
McDaniel Coll (MD)
McKendree U (IL)
Medgar Evers Coll of the City U of New York (NY)
Mercer U, Macon (GA)
Mercyhurst U (PA)
Meredith Coll (NC)
Merrimack Coll (MA)
Miami U (OH)
Michigan State U (MI)
MidAmerica Nazarene U (KS)
Middlebury Coll (VT)
Millsaps Coll (MS)
Missouri State U (MO)
Missouri Valley Coll (MO)
Molloy Coll (NY)
Monmouth Coll (IL)
Montclair State U (NJ)
Moravian Coll (PA)
Morehouse Coll (GA)
Morningside Coll (IA)
Mount Holyoke Coll (MA)
Mount Marty Coll (SD)
Mount Mercy U (IA)
Mount St. Joseph U (OH)
Mount Saint Mary's U (CA)
Mount Vernon Nazarene U (OH)
Muhlenberg Coll (PA)
Muskingum U (OH)
Naropa U (CO)
Nazareth Coll of Rochester (NY)
Nebraska Christian Coll of Hope Intl U (NE)
New Coll of Florida (FL)
New York U (NY)
Niagara U (NY)
North Carolina State U (NC)
North Carolina Wesleyan Coll (NC)
North Central Coll (IL)
Northeastern U (MA)
Northland Coll (WI)
Northwestern Coll (IA)
Northwestern U (IL)
Northwest Nazarene U (ID)

Northwest U (WA)
Nyack Coll (NY)
Oakland City U (IN)
Oberlin Coll (OH)
Occidental Coll (CA)
Ohio Northern U (OH)
The Ohio State U (OH)
Ohio U (OH)
Ohio Wesleyan U (OH)
Oklahoma Baptist U (OK)
Oklahoma Christian U (OK)
Oklahoma City U (OK)
Olivet Nazarene U (IL)
Oregon State U (OR)
Ottawa U (KS)
Otterbein U (OH)
Our Lady of the Lake U (TX)
Pacific Lutheran U (WA)
Penn State Abington (PA)
Penn State Altoona (PA)
Penn State Beaver (PA)
Penn State Berks (PA)
Penn State Brandywine (PA)
Penn State DuBois (PA)
Penn State Erie, The Behrend Coll (PA)
Penn State Fayette, The Eberly Campus (PA)
Penn State Greater Allegheny (PA)
Penn State Hazleton (PA)
Penn State Lehigh Valley (PA)
Penn State Mont Alto (PA)
Penn State New Kensington (PA)
Penn State Schuylkill (PA)
Penn State Shenango (PA)
Penn State Wilkes-Barre (PA)
Penn State Worthington Scranton (PA)
Penn State York (PA)
Pepperdine U, Malibu (CA)
Pfeiffer U (NC)
Piedmont Coll (GA)
Pitzer Coll (CA)
Pomona Coll (CA)
Portland State U (OR)
Presbyterian Coll (SC)
Princeton U (NJ)
Principia Coll (IL)
Providence Coll (RI)
Purdue U (IN)
Queens Coll of the City U of New York (NY)
Randolph Coll (VA)
Randolph-Macon Coll (VA)
Redeemer U Coll (ON, Canada)
Reed Coll (OR)
Regis U (CO)
Rhodes Coll (TN)
Rice U (TX)
Ripon Coll (WI)
Roanoke Coll (VA)
Roberts Wesleyan Coll (NY)
Rollins Coll (FL)
Rosemont Coll (PA)
Rutgers U–Camden (NJ)
Rutgers U–New Brunswick (NJ)
Sacred Heart U (CT)
Saint Francis U (PA)
St. John Fisher Coll (NY)
Saint Joseph's U (PA)
St. Lawrence U (NY)
Saint Leo U (FL)
Saint Martin's U (WA)
Saint Mary's Coll of California (CA)
St. Mary's Coll of Maryland (MD)
Saint Michael's Coll (VT)
St. Norbert Coll (WI)
St. Olaf Coll (MN)
Saint Peter's U (NJ)
St. Thomas Aquinas Coll (NY)
St. Thomas U (NB, Canada)
Salve Regina U (RI)
Samford U (AL)
San Diego State U (CA)
Santa Clara U (CA)
Sarah Lawrence Coll (NY)
Schreiner U (TX)
Scripps Coll (CA)
Seattle U (WA)
Seton Hill U (PA)
Sewanee: The U of the South (TN)
Shenandoah U (VA)
Shorter U (GA)
Siena Coll (NY)
Simpson Coll (IA)
Skidmore Coll (NY)
Smith Coll (MA)

Southern Adventist U (TN)
Southern Methodist U (TX)
Southwest Baptist U (MO)
Southwestern Adventist U (TX)
Southwestern U (TX)
Spelman Coll (GA)
Spring Hill Coll (AL)
Stanford U (CA)
State U of New York Coll at Old Westbury (NY)
Stetson U (FL)
Stonehill Coll (MA)
Stony Brook U, State U of New York (NY)
Susquehanna U (PA)
Sweet Briar Coll (VA)
Syracuse U (NY)
Temple U (PA)
Tennessee Wesleyan U (TN)
Texas Christian U (TX)
Towson U (MD)
Transylvania U (KY)
Trevecca Nazarene U (TN)
Trinity U (TX)
Tufts U (MA)
Tulane U (LA)
Union Coll (NY)
Union U (TN)
U at Albany, State U of New York (NY)
The U of Alabama (AL)
The U of Arizona (AZ)
U of Bridgeport (CT)
U of California, Davis (CA)
U of California, Irvine (CA)
U of California, Los Angeles (CA)
U of California, Riverside (CA)
U of California, San Diego (CA)
U of California, Santa Barbara (CA)
U of Central Arkansas (AR)
U of Central Florida (FL)
U of Colorado Boulder (CO)
U of Dayton (OH)
U of Denver (CO)
U of Dubuque (IA)
U of Evansville (IN)
U of Florida (FL)
U of Georgia (GA)
U of Hawaii at Manoa (HI)
U of Houston (TX)
U of Jamestown (ND)
The U of Kansas (KS)
U of King's Coll (NS, Canada)
U of La Verne (CA)
U of Miami (FL)
U of Michigan (MI)
U of Minnesota, Twin Cities Campus (MN)
U of Missouri (MO)
U of Mobile (AL)
U of Mount Union (OH)
U of New Mexico (NM)
U of North Carolina at Asheville (NC)
The U of North Carolina at Chapel Hill (NC)
The U of North Carolina at Charlotte (NC)
The U of North Carolina at Greensboro (NC)
U of North Dakota (ND)
U of Northern Iowa (IA)
U of North Florida (FL)
U of North Texas (TX)
U of Oklahoma (OK)
U of Oregon (OR)
U of Pennsylvania (PA)
U of Pikeville (KY)
U of Pittsburgh (PA)
U of Providence (MT)
U of Puget Sound (WA)
U of Regina (SK, Canada)
U of Richmond (VA)
U of Rochester (NY)
U of Saint Joseph (CT)
U of St. Thomas (MN)
U of San Diego (CA)
U of San Francisco (CA)
U of Saskatchewan (SK, Canada)
The U of Scranton (PA)
U of South Carolina (SC)
U of Southern California (CA)
U of Southern Mississippi (MS)
The U of Tennessee (TN)
The U of Texas at Austin (TX)
U of the Incarnate Word (TX)
U of the Pacific (CA)

The U of Toledo (OH)
The U of Tulsa (OK)
U of Utah (UT)
U of Vermont (VT)
U of Virginia (VA)
U of Washington (WA)
U of Waterloo (ON, Canada)
U of Wisconsin–Eau Claire (WI)
U of Wisconsin–Madison (WI)
U of Wisconsin–Milwaukee (WI)
U of Wyoming (WY)
Ursinus Coll (PA)
Vanderbilt U (TN)
Vanguard U of Southern California (CA)
Vassar Coll (NY)
Villanova U (PA)
Virginia Commonwealth U (VA)
Virginia Wesleyan U (VA)
Wabash Coll (IN)
Wake Forest U (NC)
Warner Pacific Coll (OR)
Wartburg Coll (IA)
Washington and Lee U (VA)
Washington State U (WA)
Washington U in St. Louis (MO)
Webster U (MO)
Wellesley Coll (MA)
Wesleyan U (CT)
Western Kentucky U (KY)
Western Michigan U (MI)
Westminster Coll (PA)
Westmont Coll (CA)
West Virginia Wesleyan Coll (WV)
Wheaton Coll (MA)
Whitman Coll (WA)
Whittier Coll (CA)
Whitworth U (WA)
Willamette U (OR)
Williams Coll (MA)
Wisconsin Lutheran Coll (WI)
Wittenberg U (OH)
Wofford Coll (SC)
Wright State U (OH)
Wright State U–Lake Campus (OH)
Youngstown State U (OH)

RELIGIOUS STUDIES RELATED
Agnes Scott Coll (GA)
Belmont U (TN)
Bryn Athyn Coll of the New Church (PA)
Colorado Christian U (CO)
Florida State U (FL)
Grand Valley State U (MI)
Louisiana Coll (LA)
Marlboro Coll (VT)
Newberry Coll (SC)
Ohio Northern U (OH)
U of San Francisco (CA)
Ursuline Coll (OH)
Webster U (MO)

RESEARCH AND DEVELOPMENT MANAGEMENT
Oregon State U (OR)

RESEARCH AND EXPERIMENTAL PSYCHOLOGY RELATED
Bowdoin Coll (ME)
Gannon U (PA)
Georgia Coll & State U (GA)
Georgia Inst of Technology (GA)
Indiana U Bloomington (IN)
Loyola U New Orleans (LA)
Mount Saint Mary's U (CA)
Murray State U (KY)
Niagara U (NY)
Northeastern State U (OK)
Truman State U (MO)
U of North Georgia (GA)
Vassar Coll (NY)
Washington and Lee U (VA)

RESEARCH METHODOLOGY AND QUANTITATIVE METHODS
Bryant U (RI)
Walsh U (OH)

RESORT MANAGEMENT
Coastal Carolina U (SC)
Florida Gulf Coast U (FL)
Green Mountain Coll (VT)
Lasell Coll (MA)
Rochester Inst of Technology (NY)
Sierra Nevada Coll (NV)

RESPIRATORY CARE THERAPY
Ball State U (IN)
Baptist Coll of Health Sciences (TN)
Bellarmine U (KY)
Boise State U (ID)
Bowling Green State U (OH)
Bowling Green State U–Firelands Coll (OH)
Canisius Coll (NY)
Cardinal Stritch U (WI)
Clarion U of Pennsylvania (PA)
Columbia Coll (SC)
Concordia U, St. Paul (MN)
Dakota State U (SD)
Fairleigh Dickinson U, Florham Campus (NJ)
Ferris State U (MI)
Florida Ag and Mech U (FL)
Florida National U (FL)
Gannon U (PA)
Georgia Southern U–Armstrong Campus (GA)
Georgia State U (GA)
Gwynedd Mercy U (PA)
Indiana U of Pennsylvania (PA)
Indiana U–Purdue U Indianapolis (IN)
Jefferson Coll of Health Sciences (VA)
Long Island U–LIU Brooklyn (NY)
Marshall U (WV)
Missouri State U (MO)
Nebraska Methodist Coll (NE)
North Dakota State U (ND)
Northern Kentucky U (KY)
Northern Michigan U (MI)
Nova Southeastern U (FL)
The Ohio State U (OH)
Oregon Inst of Technology (OR)
Rutgers U–Newark (NJ)
St. Catherine U (MN)
Salisbury U (MD)
Samford U (AL)
Shenandoah U (VA)
Stony Brook U, State U of New York (NY)
Texas State U (TX)
The U of Akron (OH)
The U of Alabama at Birmingham (AL)
U of Cincinnati (OH)
U of Hartford (CT)
The U of Kansas (KS)
U of Michigan–Flint (MI)
U of Missouri (MO)
The U of North Carolina at Charlotte (NC)
U of South Alabama (AL)
U of Southern Indiana (IN)
The U of Toledo (OH)
U of Waterloo (ON, Canada)
Valencia Coll (FL)
Weber State U (UT)
York Coll of Pennsylvania (PA)
Youngstown State U (OH)

RESPIRATORY THERAPY TECHNICIAN
Florida National U (FL)
Middle Georgia State U (GA)
Rhode Island Coll (RI)

RESTAURANT, CULINARY, AND CATERING MANAGEMENT
Bowling Green State U (OH)
Delaware Valley U (PA)
Pennsylvania Coll of Technology (PA)

RESTAURANT/FOOD SERVICES MANAGEMENT
Colorado State U (CO)
The Culinary Inst of America (NY)
ECPI U, Virginia Beach (VA)
Kennesaw State U (GA)
Metropolitan State U of Denver (CO)
Rochester Inst of Technology (NY)
U of Central Florida (FL)
U of Missouri (MO)
U of Nevada, Las Vegas (NV)

RETAILING
American Public U System (WV)
Bowling Green State U (OH)
Fisher Coll (MA)
Lamar U (TX)

Stevens–The Inst of Business & Arts (MO)
U of Minnesota, Twin Cities Campus (MN)
U of South Carolina (SC)
U of Wisconsin–Madison (WI)

RETAIL MANAGEMENT
Florida State U (FL)
Nichols Coll (MA)
The U of Arizona (AZ)
U of Arkansas (AR)
U of North Texas (TX)

RHETORIC AND COMPOSITION
Ashland U (OH)
Auburn U (AL)
Bates Coll (ME)
Bemidji State U (MN)
Black Hills State U (SD)
Bowling Green State U (OH)
Brigham Young U (UT)
California State U, Fullerton (CA)
California State U, Long Beach (CA)
California State U, Los Angeles (CA)
Calvin Coll (MI)
Carson-Newman U (TN)
Carthage Coll (WI)
Clark Atlanta U (GA)
Clemson U (SC)
Coe Coll (IA)
Coll of Saint Benedict (MN)
Columbus State U (GA)
Cornell Coll (IA)
Denison U (OH)
DePaul U (IL)
Drake U (IA)
Duquesne U (PA)
East Central U (OK)
East Tennessee State U (TN)
East Texas Baptist U (TX)
Emerson Coll (MA)
Evangel U (MO)
Ferris State U (MI)
George Mason U (VA)
The George Washington U (DC)
Georgia Coll & State U (GA)
Georgia Southern U (GA)
Gonzaga U (WA)
Graceland U (IA)
Gustavus Adolphus Coll (MN)
Humboldt State U (CA)
Illinois Coll (IL)
Ithaca Coll (NY)
Jackson State U (MS)
Lehman Coll of the City U of New York (NY)
Lipscomb U (TN)
Manchester U (IN)
Marietta Coll (OH)
Marshall U (WV)
The Master's U (CA)
McKendree U (IL)
Metropolitan State U of Denver (CO)
Missouri Valley Coll (MO)
North Central Coll (IL)
Northern State U (SD)
Northwestern Coll (IA)
Northwestern Oklahoma State U (OK)
Northwestern U (IL)
Oglethorpe U (GA)
Ohio U (OH)
Oklahoma Baptist U (OK)
Oklahoma Christian U (OK)
Old Dominion U (VA)
Ouachita Baptist U (AR)
Portland State U (OR)
Rider U (NJ)
St. Catherine U (MN)
Saint John's U (MN)
St. John's U (NY)
St. Joseph's Coll, Long Island Campus (NY)
St. Joseph's Coll, New York (NY)
Shippensburg U of Pennsylvania (PA)
State U of New York Coll at Cortland (NY)
State U of New York Coll at Oneonta (NY)
Stephen F. Austin State U (TX)
Texas A&M U–Commerce (TX)
Texas State U (TX)

Texas Tech U (TX)
Trinity U (TX)
Union U (TN)
U at Albany, State U of New York (NY)
U of Central Florida (FL)
U of Central Missouri (MO)
U of Cincinnati (OH)
U of Kentucky (KY)
U of Minnesota, Morris (MN)
U of Minnesota, Twin Cities Campus (MN)
U of Montevallo (AL)
U of Nebraska at Kearney (NE)
U of New Mexico (NM)
U of North Texas (TX)
U of Pittsburgh (PA)
U of Puget Sound (WA)
U of Rhode Island (RI)
U of Richmond (VA)
U of Sioux Falls (SD)
U of South Dakota (SD)
The U of Texas at Austin (TX)
U of Utah (UT)
U of Waterloo (ON, Canada)
Utah State U (UT)
Wabash Coll (IN)
West Chester U of Pennsylvania (PA)
West Virginia Wesleyan Coll (WV)
Whitworth U (WA)
Willamette U (OR)
Youngstown State U (OH)

RHETORIC AND COMPOSITION/WRITING RELATED
Augsburg U (MN)
Pepperdine U, Malibu (CA)
Syracuse U (NY)

ROBOTICS TECHNOLOGY
Alcorn State U (MS)
Central Connecticut State U (CT)
Idaho State U (ID)
Indiana State U (IN)

ROMANCE LANGUAGES
Beloit Coll (WI)
Bowdoin Coll (ME)
Bryn Mawr Coll (PA)
Carleton Coll (MN)
City Coll of the City U of New York (NY)
Colgate U (NY)
Dartmouth Coll (NH)
DePauw U (IN)
Emory U (GA)
Franklin U Switzerland (Switzerland)
Gettysburg Coll (PA)
Harvard U (MA)
Haverford Coll (PA)
Hunter Coll of the City U of New York (NY)
Iowa State U of Science and Technology (IA)
Johns Hopkins U (MD)
Loyola Marymount U (CA)
Merrimack Coll (MA)
Mount Holyoke Coll (MA)
Oberlin Coll (OH)
Pomona Coll (CA)
Rockford U (IL)
St. Thomas Aquinas Coll (NY)
Truman State U (MO)
Tufts U (MA)
U of Georgia (GA)
U of Illinois at Chicago (IL)
U of Maryland, Coll Park (MD)
U of Michigan (MI)
U of Notre Dame (IN)
U of Oregon (OR)
U of Toronto (ON, Canada)
U of Washington (WA)
Vanderbilt U (TN)
Washington and Lee U (VA)
Washington U in St. Louis (MO)
Wesleyan U (CT)

ROMANCE LANGUAGES RELATED
Boston U (MA)
Bryn Mawr Coll (PA)
The Ohio State U (OH)
U of Chicago (IL)
U of Maine (ME)
U of Michigan–Flint (MI)

U of Nevada, Las Vegas (NV)
The U of North Carolina at Chapel Hill (NC)
U of Pennsylvania (PA)

RURAL SOCIOLOGY
U of Wisconsin–Madison (WI)

RUSSIAN
American U (DC)
Amherst Coll (MA)
Arizona State U at the Tempe campus (AZ)
Bard Coll (NY)
Barnard Coll (NY)
Baylor U (TX)
Beloit Coll (WI)
Boston Coll (MA)
Boston U (MA)
Bowdoin Coll (ME)
Bowling Green State U (OH)
Bryn Mawr Coll (PA)
Bucknell U (PA)
Carleton Coll (MN)
Carnegie Mellon U (PA)
Colgate U (NY)
Coll of the Holy Cross (MA)
Columbia U (NY)
Cornell Coll (IA)
Cornell U (NY)
Dartmouth Coll (NH)
Dickinson Coll (PA)
Emory U (GA)
Florida State U (FL)
Georgetown U (DC)
The George Washington U (DC)
Grinnell Coll (IA)
Gustavus Adolphus Coll (MN)
Haverford Coll (PA)
Hofstra U (NY)
Hunter Coll of the City U of New York (NY)
Juniata Coll (PA)
Kent State U (OH)
Lawrence U (WI)
Lehman Coll of the City U of New York (NY)
Luther Coll (IA)
Macalester Coll (MN)
Michigan State U (MI)
Middlebury Coll (VT)
New Coll of Florida (FL)
New York U (NY)
Oberlin Coll (OH)
The Ohio State U (OH)
Ohio U (OH)
Penn State Abington (PA)
Penn State Altoona (PA)
Penn State Beaver (PA)
Penn State Berks (PA)
Penn State Brandywine (PA)
Penn State DuBois (PA)
Penn State Erie, The Behrend Coll (PA)
Penn State Fayette, The Eberly Campus (PA)
Penn State Greater Allegheny (PA)
Penn State Hazleton (PA)
Penn State Lehigh Valley (PA)
Penn State Mont Alto (PA)
Penn State New Kensington (PA)
Penn State Schuylkill (PA)
Penn State Shenango (PA)
Penn State U Park (PA)
Penn State Wilkes-Barre (PA)
Penn State Worthington Scranton (PA)
Penn State York (PA)
Pomona Coll (CA)
Portland State U (OR)
Purdue U (IN)
Queens Coll of the City U of New York (NY)
Reed Coll (OR)
Rutgers U–New Brunswick (NJ)
Saint Louis U (MO)
St. Olaf Coll (MN)
San Diego State U (CA)
Sarah Lawrence Coll (NY)
Scripps Coll (CA)
Seattle Pacific U (WA)
Sewanee: The U of the South (TN)
Smith Coll (MA)
Syracuse U (NY)
Texas A&M U (TX)
Trinity U (TX)
Tufts U (MA)

Tulane U (LA)
United States Military Acad (NY)
The U of Arizona (AZ)
U of California, Davis (CA)
U of California, Los Angeles (CA)
U of California, San Diego (CA)
U of Denver (CO)
U of Florida (FL)
U of Georgia (GA)
U of Hawaii at Manoa (HI)
U of Illinois at Chicago (IL)
U of Kentucky (KY)
U of King's Coll (NS, Canada)
U of Maryland, Coll Park (MD)
U of Michigan (MI)
U of Minnesota, Twin Cities Campus (MN)
U of Missouri (MO)
U of Montana (MT)
U of Nebraska–Lincoln (NE)
U of New Hampshire (NH)
U of Notre Dame (IN)
U of Oklahoma (OK)
U of Pennsylvania (PA)
U of Pittsburgh (PA)
U of Rochester (NY)
U of Saskatchewan (SK, Canada)
U of South Carolina (SC)
U of Southern California (CA)
The U of Tennessee (TN)
The U of Texas at Austin (TX)
U of Toronto (ON, Canada)
U of Utah (UT)
U of Vermont (VT)
U of Washington (WA)
U of Waterloo (ON, Canada)
U of Wisconsin–Madison (WI)
U of Wisconsin–Milwaukee (WI)
U of Wyoming (WY)
Vanderbilt U (TN)
Vassar Coll (NY)
Virginia Polytechnic Inst and State U (VA)
Wake Forest U (NC)
Washington State U (WA)
Wellesley Coll (MA)
West Chester U of Pennsylvania (PA)
Wheaton Coll (MA)
Willamette U (OR)
Williams Coll (MA)

RUSSIAN, CENTRAL EUROPEAN, EAST EUROPEAN AND EURASIAN STUDIES
Bowdoin Coll (ME)
Florida State U (FL)
Marlboro Coll (VT)
Pomona Coll (CA)
Portland State U (OR)
San Diego State U (CA)
Tufts U (MA)
U of California, San Diego (CA)
U of Missouri (MO)
U of Toronto (ON, Canada)
Washington U in St. Louis (MO)
Wayne State U (MI)
Wesleyan U (CT)
Wittenberg U (OH)

RUSSIAN STUDIES
American U (DC)
Bard Coll (NY)
Boston Coll (MA)
Bowling Green State U (OH)
Brandeis U (MA)
Carleton Coll (MN)
Colby Coll (ME)
Colgate U (NY)
The Coll of Wooster (OH)
The Colorado Coll (CO)
Columbia U (NY)
Cornell Coll (IA)
Dartmouth Coll (NH)
DePauw U (IN)
Emory U (GA)
George Mason U (VA)
The George Washington U (DC)
Grand Valley State U (MI)
Gustavus Adolphus Coll (MN)
Hamilton Coll (NY)
Hobart and William Smith Colls (NY)
Iowa State U of Science and Technology (IA)
Lafayette Coll (PA)
Lawrence U (WI)
Middlebury Coll (VT)

Mount Holyoke Coll (MA)
Muhlenberg Coll (PA)
Oberlin Coll (OH)
Rhodes Coll (TN)
Rutgers U–New Brunswick (NJ)
St. Olaf Coll (MN)
Smith Coll (MA)
Stetson U (FL)
Syracuse U (NY)
Texas Tech U (TX)
Tufts U (MA)
Tulane U (LA)
United States Military Acad (NY)
U of Alaska Fairbanks (AK)
U of California, Los Angeles (CA)
U of California, Riverside (CA)
U of California, San Diego (CA)
U of Colorado Boulder (CO)
The U of Kansas (KS)
U of Maryland, Coll Park (MD)
U of Massachusetts Amherst (MA)
U of Michigan (MI)
U of Missouri (MO)
U of New Mexico (NM)
U of Oregon (OR)
U of Richmond (VA)
U of Rochester (NY)
The U of Texas at Austin (TX)
U of Toronto (ON, Canada)
The U of Tulsa (OK)
U of Vermont (VT)
U of Waterloo (ON, Canada)
Washington and Lee U (VA)
Washington U in St. Louis (MO)
Wellesley Coll (MA)
Wheaton Coll (MA)

SALES AND MARKETING/ MARKETING AND DISTRIBUTION TEACHER EDUCATION
Bowling Green State U (OH)
Eastern Michigan U (MI)
Eastern New Mexico U (NM)
Fayetteville State U (NC)
North Carolina State U (NC)
State U of New York at Oswego (NY)
U of Wisconsin–Stout (WI)
Utah State U (UT)
Western Michigan U (MI)

SALES, DISTRIBUTION, AND MARKETING OPERATIONS
Avila U (MO)
Babson Coll (MA)
Baylor U (TX)
Bentley U (MA)
Black Hills State U (SD)
Bowling Green State U (OH)
Brock U (ON, Canada)
Florida State U (FL)
Hampton U (VA)
Harding U (AR)
HEC Montreal (QC, Canada)
Husson U (ME)
Kennesaw State U (GA)
Long Island U–LIU Brooklyn (NY)
Missouri Valley Coll (MO)
New York U (NY)
Quinnipiac U (CT)
St. Catherine U (MN)
Sam Houston State U (TX)
Seton Hill U (PA)
Southern Adventist U (TN)
Texas A&M U (TX)
The U of Akron (OH)
U of Houston (TX)
U of Memphis (TN)
U of Minnesota, Twin Cities Campus (MN)
U of Pennsylvania (PA)
The U of Toledo (OH)
U of Wisconsin–Stout (WI)
West Chester U of Pennsylvania (PA)

SANSKRIT AND CLASSICAL INDIAN LANGUAGES
Harvard U (MA)

SCANDINAVIAN LANGUAGES
Augustana Coll (IL)
Gustavus Adolphus Coll (MN)
Luther Coll (IA)
The U of Texas at Austin (TX)

SCANDINAVIAN STUDIES
American U (DC)

Gustavus Adolphus Coll (MN)
Pacific Lutheran U (WA)
U of California, Los Angeles (CA)
U of Washington (WA)
U of Wisconsin–Madison (WI)

SCHOOL LIBRARIAN/SCHOOL LIBRARY MEDIA
The Coll of St. Scholastica (MN)
East Central U (OK)
U of Providence (MT)

SCHOOL PSYCHOLOGY
Eastern Washington U (WA)
Kansas Wesleyan U (KS)
Northwest U (WA)
Sam Houston State U (TX)
Texas A&M U–Central Texas (TX)

SCIENCE TEACHER EDUCATION
Abilene Christian U (TX)
Adams State U (CO)
Albion Coll (MI)
Alice Lloyd Coll (KY)
Alverno Coll (WI)
Andrews U (MI)
Aquinas Coll (MI)
Arizona Christian U (AZ)
Arkansas Tech U (AR)
Ashland U (OH)
Auburn U (AL)
Ball State U (IN)
Baylor U (TX)
Bemidji State U (MN)
Biola U (CA)
Blackburn Coll (IL)
Black Hills State U (SD)
Bluefield Coll (VA)
Bob Jones U (SC)
Boston U (MA)
Bowie State U (MD)
Bowling Green State U (OH)
Bradley U (IL)
Brigham Young U (UT)
Brock U (ON, Canada)
Buena Vista U (IA)
Buffalo State Coll, State U of New York (NY)
California Lutheran U (CA)
Calvin Coll (MI)
Campbellsville U (KY)
Canisius Coll (NY)
Capital U (OH)
Carroll U (WI)
Catawba Coll (NC)
Cedarville U (OH)
Central Methodist U (MO)
Central Michigan U (MI)
Charleston Southern U (SC)
Chipola Coll (FL)
Christian Brothers U (TN)
City Coll of the City U of New York (NY)
Clemson U (SC)
Coe Coll (IA)
Coll of Saint Mary (NE)
Coll of the Atlantic (ME)
Columbus State U (GA)
Concordia Coll–New York (NY)
Concordia U Chicago (IL)
Concordia U Wisconsin (WI)
Cornerstone U (MI)
Covenant Coll (GA)
Daytona State Coll (FL)
Defiance Coll (OH)
Delaware State U (DE)
Dickinson State U (ND)
Doane U (NE)
East Carolina U (NC)
East Central U (OK)
Eastern Michigan U (MI)
Eastern Nazarene Coll (MA)
Eastern Washington U (WA)
Edgewood Coll (WI)
Elizabethtown Coll (PA)
Elon U (NC)
Evangel U (MO)
Florida Ag and Mech U (FL)
Florida Atlantic U (FL)
Florida Inst of Technology (FL)
Georgia Southern U–Armstrong Campus (GA)
Gettysburg Coll (PA)
Goshen Coll (IN)
Graceland U (IA)
Grand Valley State U (MI)
Greensboro Coll (NC)

Hannibal-LaGrange U (MO)
Harding U (AR)
Hardin-Simmons U (TX)
Heidelberg U (OH)
Hobe Sound Bible Coll (FL)
Hofstra U (NY)
Hope Coll (MI)
Houston Baptist U (TX)
Hunter Coll of the City U of New York (NY)
Huntingdon Coll (AL)
Immaculata U (PA)
Indiana State U (IN)
Indiana U South Bend (IN)
Indiana Wesleyan U (IN)
Inter American U of Puerto Rico, Metropolitan Campus (PR)
Inter American U of Puerto Rico, San Germán Campus (PR)
Ithaca Coll (NY)
Juniata Coll (PA)
Keene State Coll (NH)
Kent State U (OH)
Le Moyne Coll (NY)
LeTourneau U (TX)
Lincoln Memorial U (TN)
Lindenwood U (MO)
Loyola U Chicago (IL)
Madonna U (MI)
Malone U (OH)
Manchester U (IN)
Maranatha Baptist U (WI)
Marian U (IN)
Marquette U (WI)
Martin Luther Coll (MN)
Marywood U (PA)
The Master's U (CA)
McKendree U (IL)
Mercyhurst U (PA)
Merrimack Coll (MA)
Miami Dade Coll (FL)
Miami U (OH)
Michigan State U (MI)
Mid-Atlantic Christian U (NC)
Minot State U (ND)
Missouri Baptist U (MO)
Missouri State U (MO)
Missouri Valley Coll (MO)
Morningside Coll (IA)
Mount Mary U (WI)
Mount Mercy U (IA)
Mount Vernon Nazarene U (OH)
New Mexico Highlands U (NM)
New York U (NY)
North Carolina State U (NC)
North Dakota State U (ND)
Northeastern State U (OK)
Northern Michigan U (MI)
Northland Coll (WI)
Northwestern Oklahoma State U (OK)
Northwest Missouri State U (MO)
Ohio Dominican U (OH)
Ohio Northern U (OH)
Oklahoma Baptist U (OK)
Oklahoma Christian U (OK)
Olivet Nazarene U (IL)
Oral Roberts U (OK)
Otterbein U (OH)
Ouachita Baptist U (AR)
Pfeiffer U (NC)
Piedmont Coll (GA)
Queens Coll of the City U of New York (NY)
Rhode Island Coll (RI)
Rider U (NJ)
Rocky Mountain Coll (MT)
Saginaw Valley State U (MI)
Saint Francis U (PA)
Shawnee State U (OH)
Southeast Missouri State U (MO)
Southern Illinois U Edwardsville (IL)
Southern Utah U (UT)
Southwest Baptist U (MO)
State U of New York at Fredonia (NY)
State U of New York at New Paltz (NY)
State U of New York at Oswego (NY)
State U of New York Coll at Cortland (NY)
State U of New York Coll at Old Westbury (NY)
State U of New York Coll at Oneonta (NY)

Temple U (PA)
Texas Christian U (TX)
Tiffin U (OH)
Trine U (IN)
Union Coll (NE)
Union U (TN)
The U of Akron (OH)
The U of Arizona (AZ)
U of Central Arkansas (AR)
U of Central Oklahoma (OK)
U of Dayton (OH)
U of Dubuque (IA)
The U of Findlay (OH)
U of Georgia (GA)
U of Kentucky (KY)
U of Maine (ME)
U of Maine at Machias (ME)
U of Mary Hardin-Baylor (TX)
U of Michigan–Dearborn (MI)
U of Michigan–Flint (MI)
U of Minnesota, Duluth (MN)
U of Missouri (MO)
U of Nebraska–Lincoln (NE)
U of Nevada, Las Vegas (NV)
The U of North Carolina at Greensboro (NC)
The U of North Carolina at Pembroke (NC)
U of North Dakota (ND)
U of North Florida (FL)
U of Notre Dame (IN)
U of Oklahoma (OK)
U of Providence (MT)
U of Regina (SK, Canada)
U of St. Francis (IL)
U of St. Thomas (MN)
U of South Dakota (SD)
The U of Tennessee at Martin (TN)
U of Toronto (ON, Canada)
U of Vermont (VT)
U of Wisconsin–Eau Claire (WI)
U of Wisconsin–La Crosse (WI)
U of Wisconsin–Milwaukee (WI)
U of Wisconsin–Stevens Point (WI)
U of Wisconsin–Stout (WI)
U of Wisconsin–Superior (WI)
Upper Iowa U (IA)
Ursuline Coll (OH)
Utah State U (UT)
Utah Valley U (UT)
Valparaiso U (IN)
Vincennes U (IN)
Walsh U (OH)
Warner Pacific Coll (OR)
Washington U in St. Louis (MO)
Wayland Baptist U (TX)
Waynesburg U (PA)
Wayne State Coll (NE)
Weber State U (UT)
Webster U (MO)
Western Michigan U (MI)
Western State Colorado U (CO)
Western Washington U (WA)
Westfield State U (MA)
Widener U (PA)
William Penn U (IA)
Wilmington U (DE)
Winona State U (MN)
Wisconsin Lutheran Coll (WI)
Wright State U (OH)
Wright State U–Lake Campus (OH)
Xavier U of Louisiana (LA)
York Coll of Pennsylvania (PA)
Youngstown State U (OH)

SCIENCE TECHNOLOGIES
Baylor U (TX)
Embry-Riddle Aeronautical U–Daytona (FL)
Excelsior Coll (NY)

SCIENCE TECHNOLOGIES RELATED
Arizona State U at the Downtown Phoenix campus (AZ)
Arizona State U at the Polytechnic campus (AZ)
Arizona State U at the West campus (AZ)
Bridgewater State U (MA)
Kean U (NJ)
Madonna U (MI)
North Carolina State U (NC)
The U of Arizona (AZ)
U of Wisconsin–Stout (WI)
Willamette U (OR)

SCIENCE, TECHNOLOGY AND SOCIETY
Arizona State U at the Polytechnic campus (AZ)
Arizona State U at the Tempe campus (AZ)
Butler U (IN)
California State Polytechnic U, Pomona (CA)
Claremont McKenna Coll (CA)
Colby Coll (ME)
Cornell U (NY)
Eastern Michigan U (MI)
Farmingdale State Coll (NY)
Georgetown U (DC)
Georgia Inst of Technology (GA)
Iowa State U of Science and Technology (IA)
James Madison U (VA)
Lehigh U (PA)
Le Moyne Coll (NY)
Massachusetts Inst of Technology (MA)
New Jersey Inst of Technology (NJ)
North Carolina State U (NC)
Northwestern U (IL)
Penn State U Park (PA)
Pitzer Coll (CA)
Pomona Coll (CA)
Rensselaer Polytechnic Inst (NY)
Rutgers U–Newark (NJ)
St. Thomas U (NB, Canada)
Scripps Coll (CA)
Stanford U (CA)
Texas Tech U (TX)
Tufts U (MA)
U of King's Coll (NS, Canada)
U of Puget Sound (WA)
U of San Francisco (CA)
U of Washington, Bothell (WA)
Vanderbilt U (TN)
Vassar Coll (NY)
Washington U in St. Louis (MO)
Wesleyan U (CT)
Worcester Polytechnic Inst (MA)

SCULPTURE
Alberta Coll of Art & Design (AB, Canada)
Aquinas Coll (MI)
Bennington Coll (VT)
Binghamton U, State U of New York (NY)
Biola U (CA)
Birmingham-Southern Coll (AL)
Boston U (MA)
Bowling Green State U (OH)
Bradley U (IL)
Brigham Young U (UT)
Buffalo State Coll, State U of New York (NY)
California Coll of the Arts (CA)
California State U, Long Beach (CA)
Concordia U (QC, Canada)
Dominican U (IL)
Drake U (IA)
Escuela de Artes Plasticas y Diseño de Puerto Rico (PR)
Ferris State U (MI)
Inter American U of Puerto Rico, San Germán Campus (PR)
Kansas City Art Inst (MO)
Laguna Coll of Art & Design (CA)
Marlboro Coll (VT)
Maryland Inst Coll of Art (MD)
Marywood U (PA)
Massachusetts Coll of Art and Design (MA)
Minneapolis Coll of Art and Design (MN)
Northern Michigan U (MI)
Northwest Nazarene U (ID)
Ohio Northern U (OH)
Pacific Northwest Coll of Art (OR)
Portland State U (OR)
Pratt Inst (NY)
Providence Coll (RI)
Rhode Island Coll (RI)
Rhode Island School of Design (RI)
Rochester Inst of Technology (NY)
Rutgers U–New Brunswick (NJ)
San Francisco Art Inst (CA)
Savannah Coll of Art and Design (GA)
School of Visual Arts (NY)
Seton Hill U (PA)

Sonoma State U (CA)
State U of New York at New Paltz (NY)
Syracuse U (NY)
Temple U (PA)
Texas Christian U (TX)
The U of Akron (OH)
U of Dallas (TX)
U of Hartford (CT)
U of Houston (TX)
The U of Kansas (KS)
U of Massachusetts Dartmouth (MA)
U of Miami (FL)
U of Michigan (MI)
U of New Haven (CT)
U of Oregon (OR)
U of Puget Sound (WA)
U of Regina (SK, Canada)
U of Washington (WA)
Virginia Commonwealth U (VA)
Washington U in St. Louis (MO)
Western State Colorado U (CO)

SECONDARY EDUCATION
Abilene Christian U (TX)
Acadia U (NS, Canada)
Alabama State U (AL)
Alice Lloyd Coll (KY)
Alma Coll (MI)
Alverno Coll (WI)
American U (DC)
Andrews U (MI)
Aquinas Coll (MI)
Arcadia U (PA)
Arizona Christian U (AZ)
Arizona State U at the Polytechnic campus (AZ)
Arizona State U at the Tempe campus (AZ)
Arizona State U at the West campus (AZ)
Ashland U (OH)
Auburn U (AL)
Auburn U at Montgomery (AL)
Augsburg U (MN)
Augustana U (SD)
Aurora U (IL)
Austin Coll (TX)
Baker U (KS)
Baylor U (TX)
Bellarmine U (KY)
Belmont U (TN)
Beloit Coll (WI)
Bemidji State U (MN)
Benedictine Coll (KS)
Berry Coll (GA)
Biola U (CA)
Birmingham-Southern Coll (AL)
Blackburn Coll (IL)
Black Hills State U (SD)
Bluefield Coll (VA)
Boston Coll (MA)
Bowdoin Coll (ME)
Bowie State U (MD)
Bradley U (IL)
Bridgewater State U (MA)
Brock U (ON, Canada)
Bucknell U (PA)
Buffalo State Coll, State U of New York (NY)
Butler U (IN)
Caldwell U (NJ)
Calvary U (MO)
Calvin Coll (MI)
Campbellsville U (KY)
Canisius Coll (NY)
Cardinal Stritch U (WI)
Caribbean U (PR)
Carroll Coll (MT)
Carson-Newman U (TN)
Carthage Coll (WI)
The Catholic U of America (DC)
Cedar Crest Coll (PA)
Central Methodist U (MO)
Central State U (OH)
Chaminade U of Honolulu (HI)
Champlain Coll (VT)
Charleston Southern U (SC)
Chipola Coll (FL)
The Citadel, The Military Coll of South Carolina (SC)
City Coll of the City U of New York (NY)
Clarke U (IA)
Clark U (MA)
Clemson U (SC)

Coe Coll (IA)
Coll of Charleston (SC)
The Coll of New Jersey (NJ)
Coll of Saint Benedict (MN)
Coll of Saint Mary (NE)
The Coll of Saint Rose (NY)
Coll of the Atlantic (ME)
Concordia U Chicago (IL)
Concordia U, Nebraska (NE)
Concordia U, St. Paul (MN)
Concordia U Wisconsin (WI)
Concord U (WV)
Converse Coll (SC)
Corban U (OR)
Cornell Coll (IA)
Cottey Coll (MO)
Defiance Coll (OH)
Delaware State U (DE)
Delaware Valley U (PA)
DePaul U (IL)
DeSales U (PA)
Dominican Coll (NY)
Dominican U (IL)
Drake U (IA)
Drexel U (PA)
D'Youville Coll (NY)
Eastern Nazarene Coll (MA)
Elmhurst Coll (IL)
Elms Coll (MA)
Elon U (NC)
Emmanuel Coll (MA)
Emmaus Bible Coll (IA)
Emporia State U (KS)
Endicott Coll (MA)
Evangel U (MO)
Felician U (NJ)
Fitchburg State U (MA)
Florida Gulf Coast U (FL)
Fordham U (NY)
Fort Lewis Coll (CO)
Franklin Pierce U (NH)
Furman U (SC)
Gettysburg Coll (PA)
Gonzaga U (WA)
Gordon Coll (MA)
Goshen Coll (IN)
Graceland U (IA)
Grambling State U (LA)
Grand Valley State U (MI)
Grand View U (IA)
Granite State Coll (NH)
Greensboro Coll (NC)
Guilford Coll (NC)
Gustavus Adolphus Coll (MN)
Hamline U (MN)
Hampton U (VA)
Hannibal-LaGrange U (MO)
Harding U (AR)
Harris-Stowe State U (MO)
Heidelberg U (OH)
High Point U (NC)
Hofstra U (NY)
Hunter Coll of the City U of New York (NY)
Husson U (ME)
Huston-Tillotson U (TX)
Idaho State U (ID)
Illinois Coll (IL)
Indiana U Bloomington (IN)
Indiana U East (IN)
Indiana U Kokomo (IN)
Indiana U Northwest (IN)
Indiana U South Bend (IN)
Indiana U Southeast (IN)
Indiana Wesleyan U (IN)
Inter American U of Puerto Rico, Barranquitas Campus (PR)
Inter American U of Puerto Rico, San Germán Campus (PR)
Iona Coll (NY)
Iowa State U of Science and Technology (IA)
Ithaca Coll (NY)
John Carroll U (OH)
Judson U (IL)
Kansas State U (KS)
Kansas Wesleyan U (KS)
Keene State Coll (NH)
King U (TN)
Knox Coll (IL)
Kutztown U of Pennsylvania (PA)
Langston U (OK)
La Salle U (PA)
Lasell Coll (MA)
Le Moyne Coll (NY)
Lesley U (MA)
LeTourneau U (TX)

Lewis U (IL)
Lincoln Memorial U (TN)
Lindsey Wilson Coll (KY)
Lock Haven U of Pennsylvania (PA)
Loyola U Chicago (IL)
Lubbock Christian U (TX)
Maharishi U of Management (IA)
Manchester U (IN)
Manhattanville Coll (NY)
Mansfield U of Pennsylvania (PA)
Marian U (IN)
Marian U (WI)
Marietta Coll (OH)
Marquette U (WI)
Marshall U (WV)
The Master's U (CA)
McMurry U (TX)
Mercyhurst U (PA)
Merrimack Coll (MA)
Michigan State U (MI)
Mid-America Christian U (OK)
MidAmerica Nazarene U (KS)
Middle Georgia State U (GA)
Mississippi State U (MS)
Missouri Baptist U (MO)
Missouri State U (MO)
Missouri U of Science and Technology (MO)
Missouri Valley Coll (MO)
Molloy Coll (NY)
Mount Aloysius Coll (PA)
Mount Marty Coll (SD)
Mount Mercy U (IA)
Mount Saint Mary Coll (NY)
Mount Saint Mary's U (CA)
National U (CA)
Nazareth Coll of Rochester (NY)
Newman U (KS)
New Mexico State U (NM)
North Central Coll (IL)
Northcentral U (CA)
Northern Kentucky U (KY)
Northern Michigan U (MI)
Northland Coll (WI)
Northwest Christian U (OR)
Northwestern Coll (IA)
Northwestern Oklahoma State U (OK)
Northwestern State U of Louisiana (LA)
Northwestern U (IL)
Northwest Nazarene U (ID)
Northwest U (WA)
Nova Southeastern U (FL)
Ohio U (OH)
Ohio Wesleyan U (OH)
Oklahoma Christian U (OK)
Oklahoma City U (OK)
Oklahoma State U (OK)
Otterbein U (OH)
Ouachita Baptist U (AR)
Penn State Abington (PA)
Penn State Altoona (PA)
Penn State Beaver (PA)
Penn State Berks (PA)
Penn State Brandywine (PA)
Penn State DuBois (PA)
Penn State Erie, The Behrend Coll (PA)
Penn State Fayette, The Eberly Campus (PA)
Penn State Greater Allegheny (PA)
Penn State Hazleton (PA)
Penn State Lehigh Valley (PA)
Penn State Mont Alto (PA)
Penn State New Kensington (PA)
Penn State Schuylkill (PA)
Penn State Shenango (PA)
Penn State U Park (PA)
Penn State Wilkes-Barre (PA)
Penn State Worthington Scranton (PA)
Penn State York (PA)
Piedmont Coll (GA)
Point U (GA)
Polytechnic U of Puerto Rico (PR)
Providence Coll (RI)
Purdue U Northwest (IN)
Rhode Island Coll (RI)
Rider U (NJ)
Ripon Coll (WI)
Rivier U (NH)
Rockford U (IL)
Rockhurst U (MO)
Rocky Mountain Coll (MT)
Roger Williams U (RI)
St. Ambrose U (IA)

Saint Anselm Coll (NH)
St. Catherine U (MN)
Saint Francis U (PA)
Saint John's U (MN)
Saint Joseph's U (PA)
Saint Leo U (FL)
Saint Michael's Coll (VT)
St. Thomas Aquinas Coll (NY)
Salve Regina U (RI)
Samford U (AL)
Sam Houston State U (TX)
Shepherd U (WV)
Simmons Coll (MA)
Simpson Coll (IA)
Southwestern Assemblies of God U (TX)
Spring Hill Coll (AL)
State U of New York at Fredonia (NY)
State U of New York at Oswego (NY)
State U of New York Coll at Cortland (NY)
State U of New York Coll at Old Westbury (NY)
State U of New York Coll at Oneonta (NY)
Stonehill Coll (MA)
Susquehanna U (PA)
Tabor Coll (KS)
Taylor U (IN)
Temple U (PA)
Tennessee Technological U (TN)
Tennessee Wesleyan U (TN)
Texas Christian U (TX)
Thomas U (GA)
Toccoa Falls Coll (GA)
Trent U (ON, Canada)
Trine U (IN)
Troy U (AL)
Union U (TN)
Unity Coll (ME)
Université de Sherbrooke (QC, Canada)
Université Sainte-Anne (NS, Canada)
The U of Alabama (AL)
The U of Alabama at Birmingham (AL)
U of Alaska Fairbanks (AK)
U of Central Florida (FL)
U of Central Missouri (MO)
U of Cincinnati (OH)
U of Dallas (TX)
U of Dayton (OH)
U of Dubuque (IA)
U of Guam (GU)
U of Hartford (CT)
U of Hawaii at Manoa (HI)
U of Idaho (ID)
The U of Kansas (KS)
U of Louisiana at Monroe (LA)
U of Maine (ME)
U of Maine at Farmington (ME)
U of Maine at Presque Isle (ME)
U of Maryland, Coll Park (MD)
U of Michigan (MI)
U of Michigan–Dearborn (MI)
U of Minnesota, Morris (MN)
U of Missouri (MO)
U of Missouri–St. Louis (MO)
U of Nevada, Las Vegas (NV)
U of New England (ME)
U of New Mexico (NM)
U of New Orleans (LA)
U of North Alabama (AL)
The U of North Carolina at Greensboro (NC)
U of North Dakota (ND)
U of North Florida (FL)
U of North Georgia (GA)
U of Pittsburgh at Bradford (PA)
U of Providence (MT)
U of Regina (SK, Canada)
U of Rhode Island (RI)
U of St. Thomas (TX)
U of Saskatchewan (SK, Canada)
The U of Scranton (PA)
U of Sioux Falls (SD)
U of South Alabama (AL)
U of South Carolina Aiken (SC)
U of South Dakota (SD)
The U of Tampa (FL)
The U of Tennessee at Chattanooga (TN)
The U of Toledo (OH)
U of Valley Forge (PA)

U of Vermont (VT)
U of Wisconsin–Parkside (WI)
U of Wisconsin–Stevens Point (WI)
U of Wyoming (WY)
Utah State U (UT)
Utica Coll (NY)
Valparaiso U (IN)
Vanderbilt U (TN)
Vanguard U of Southern California (CA)
Villanova U (PA)
Virginia Polytechnic Inst and State U (VA)
Virginia Wesleyan U (VA)
Wagner Coll (NY)
Waldorf U (IA)
Walsh U (OH)
Warner Pacific Coll (OR)
Wartburg Coll (IA)
Washington U in St. Louis (MO)
Waynesburg U (PA)
Wayne State U (MI)
Webster U (MO)
Welch Coll (TN)
Wells Coll (NY)
Western Connecticut State U (CT)
Western New England U (MA)
Western Oregon U (OR)
Westmont Coll (CA)
West Virginia State U (WV)
West Virginia Wesleyan Coll (WV)
Wheaton Coll (IL)
Wheaton Coll (MA)
Whitworth U (WA)
Wichita State U (KS)
William Jewell Coll (MO)
William Paterson U of New Jersey (NJ)
William Penn U (IA)
William Woods U (MO)
Wisconsin Lutheran Coll (WI)
Xavier U of Louisiana (LA)
Youngstown State U (OH)

SECONDARY SCHOOL ADMINISTRATION/ PRINCIPALSHIP
Charleston Southern U (SC)

SECURITIES SERVICES ADMINISTRATION
American Public U System (WV)
Dean Coll (MA)
John Jay Coll of Criminal Justice of the City U of New York (NY)
St. John's U (NY)
Saint Louis U (MO)
Slippery Rock U of Pennsylvania (PA)
Southwestern Coll (KS)

SECURITY AND LOSS PREVENTION
Northern Michigan U (MI)

SELLING SKILLS AND SALES
Ball State U (IN)
Bradley U (IL)
High Point U (NC)
Manchester U (IN)
Purdue U (IN)
St. Catherine U (MN)
Stetson U (FL)
U of Central Oklahoma (OK)
U of Memphis (TN)
Weber State U (UT)
William Paterson U of New Jersey (NJ)

SIGN LANGUAGE INTERPRETATION AND TRANSLATION
Augustana U (SD)
Bethel Coll (IN)
Bloomsburg U of Pennsylvania (PA)
Columbia Coll Chicago (IL)
Framingham State U (MA)
Goshen Coll (IN)
Idaho State U (ID)
Indiana U–Purdue U Indianapolis (IN)
Kent State U (OH)
Madonna U (MI)
Maryville Coll (TN)
Mount Aloysius Coll (PA)
Nebraska Christian Coll of Hope Intl U (NE)
Rochester Inst of Technology (NY)
Troy U (AL)

U of Cincinnati (OH)
U of Louisville (KY)
U of New Mexico (NM)
U of Northern Colorado (CO)
U of North Florida (FL)
U of Wisconsin–Milwaukee (WI)
Valdosta State U (GA)
Western Oregon U (OR)
William Woods U (MO)

SLAVIC, BALTIC, AND ALBANIAN LANGUAGES RELATED
Rutgers U–Newark (NJ)

SLAVIC LANGUAGES
Boston Coll (MA)
Columbia U (NY)
Harvard U (MA)
Indiana U Bloomington (IN)
Northwestern U (IL)
Princeton U (NJ)
Stanford U (CA)
U of California, Los Angeles (CA)
U of California, Santa Barbara (CA)
U of Chicago (IL)
U of Illinois at Chicago (IL)
The U of Kansas (KS)
U of Pittsburgh (PA)
U of Toronto (ON, Canada)
U of Virginia (VA)
U of Washington (WA)
Wayne State U (MI)

SLAVIC STUDIES
Barnard Coll (NY)
Baylor U (TX)
Columbia U (NY)
Connecticut Coll (CT)
Northwestern U (IL)
U of Waterloo (ON, Canada)

SMALL BUSINESS ADMINISTRATION
Adams State U (CO)
Avila U (MO)
Babson Coll (MA)
Bradley U (IL)
Carroll U (WI)
Carson-Newman U (TN)
Chowan U (NC)
Florida Inst of Technology (FL)
Florida Southern Coll (FL)
Hilbert Coll (NY)
Husson U (ME)
North Central Coll (IL)
Northern Michigan U (MI)
Ohio Wesleyan U (OH)
Rocky Mountain Coll (MT)
Saint Joseph's U (PA)
U of Michigan–Dearborn (MI)
The U of Scranton (PA)

SOCIAL AND PHILOSOPHICAL FOUNDATIONS OF EDUCATION
Dickinson Coll (PA)
Eastern Washington U (WA)
High Point U (NC)
Hope Intl U (CA)
Northwestern U (IL)
Transylvania U (KY)
U of Wisconsin–Madison (WI)
Washington U in St. Louis (MO)

SOCIAL PSYCHOLOGY
Augsburg U (MN)
Bennington Coll (VT)
Brigham Young U (UT)
Clarion U of Pennsylvania (PA)
Eastern Nazarene Coll (MA)
Florida Atlantic U (FL)
Grand Valley State U (MI)
Maryville U of Saint Louis (MO)
Northwest Missouri State U (MO)
Palo Alto U (CA)
Penn State Abington (PA)
U of California, Irvine (CA)
U of California, San Diego (CA)
Western Michigan U (MI)

SOCIAL SCIENCES
Adelphi U (NY)
American Intl Coll (MA)
American U (DC)
Andrews U (MI)
Aquinas Coll (MI)
Arizona State U at the West campus (AZ)
Asbury U (KY)

Ashland U (OH)
Athens State U (AL)
Azusa Pacific U (CA)
Ball State U (IN)
Belhaven U (MS)
Bemidji State U (MN)
Benedictine Coll (KS)
Benedictine U (IL)
Bennington Coll (VT)
Berry Coll (GA)
Bethany Lutheran Coll (MN)
Bethel U (MN)
Binghamton U, State U of New York (NY)
Biola U (CA)
Black Hills State U (SD)
Bluffton U (OH)
Boise State U (ID)
Bowling Green State U (OH)
Brandman U (CA)
Brescia U (KY)
Brock U (ON, Canada)
Caldwell U (NJ)
California Lutheran U (CA)
California State U, Los Angeles (CA)
California State U, Monterey Bay (CA)
California State U, Sacramento (CA)
California State U, San Bernardino (CA)
California State U, San Marcos (CA)
California State U, Stanislaus (CA)
California U of Pennsylvania (PA)
Calvin Coll (MI)
Campbellsville U (KY)
Canisius Coll (NY)
Carthage Coll (WI)
Cazenovia Coll (NY)
Central Connecticut State U (CT)
Central Michigan U (MI)
Chaminade U of Honolulu (HI)
Charleston Southern U (SC)
Clarkson U (NY)
Cleveland State U (OH)
Colgate U (NY)
Coll of Mount Saint Vincent (NY)
The Coll of St. Scholastica (MN)
Colorado Christian U (CO)
Colorado Mesa U (CO)
Colorado State U–Pueblo (CO)
Concordia Coll–New York (NY)
Concordia U of Edmonton (AB, Canada)
Daemen Coll (NY)
Defiance Coll (OH)
Dickinson State U (ND)
Doane U (NE)
Dominican Coll (NY)
Eastern Mennonite U (VA)
Eastern Michigan U (MI)
Eastern New Mexico U (NM)
Edgewood Coll (WI)
Emporia State U (KS)
Excelsior Coll (NY)
Florida Atlantic U (FL)
Florida Southern Coll (FL)
Frostburg State U (MD)
Gettysburg Coll (PA)
Governors State U (IL)
Granite State Coll (NH)
Gustavus Adolphus Coll (MN)
Hampton U (VA)
Harding U (AR)
Harvard U (MA)
Hope Intl U (CA)
Howard Payne U (TX)
Humboldt State U (CA)
Inter American U of Puerto Rico, Metropolitan Campus (PR)
Ithaca Coll (NY)
Jacksonville U (FL)
Johns Hopkins U (MD)
Kansas State U (KS)
Kentucky State U (KY)
La Salle U (PA)
Lesley U (MA)
Liberty U (VA)
Lock Haven U of Pennsylvania (PA)
Long Island U–LIU Brooklyn (NY)
Louisiana Coll (LA)
Loyola U New Orleans (LA)
Manchester U (IN)
Manhattanville Coll (NY)
Mansfield U of Pennsylvania (PA)

Marlboro Coll (VT)
Marywood U (PA)
McKendree U (IL)
Mercy Coll (NY)
Mercyhurst U (PA)
Michigan State U (MI)
Michigan Technological U (MI)
MidAmerica Nazarene U (KS)
Minot State U (ND)
Missouri Baptist U (MO)
Morehead State U (KY)
Mount Mary U (WI)
Mount Saint Mary Coll (NY)
Mount Saint Mary's U (CA)
Muhlenberg Coll (PA)
National Louis U (IL)
National U (CA)
Nazareth Coll of Rochester (NY)
New Coll of Florida (FL)
New York U (NY)
Niagara U (NY)
North Central Coll (IL)
Northern Kentucky U (KY)
Northern State U (SD)
Northwestern Oklahoma State U (OK)
Oklahoma Baptist U (OK)
Olivet Nazarene U (IL)
Oregon State U (OR)
Our Lady of the Lake U (TX)
Pace U (NY)
Pace U, Pleasantville Campus (NY)
Palm Beach Atlantic U (FL)
Pfeiffer U (NC)
Piedmont Coll (GA)
Point U (GA)
Portland State U (OR)
Providence Coll (RI)
Queens Coll of the City U of New York (NY)
Quinnipiac U (CT)
Radford U (VA)
Ramapo Coll of New Jersey (NJ)
Robert Morris U (PA)
Rockford U (IL)
Rogers State U (OK)
Roger Williams U (RI)
Roosevelt U (IL)
Rust Coll (MS)
The Sage Colls (NY)
St. Andrews U (NC)
St. Catherine U (MN)
St. John's U (NY)
St. Joseph's Coll, Long Island Campus (NY)
St. Joseph's Coll, New York (NY)
Saint Mary's Coll of California (CA)
Saint Peter's U (NJ)
St. Thomas Aquinas Coll (NY)
Salisbury U (MD)
San Diego State U (CA)
Shawnee State U (OH)
Shorter U (GA)
Southeast Missouri State U (MO)
Southern Arkansas U–Magnolia (AR)
Southern Illinois U Carbondale (IL)
Southwestern Adventist U (TX)
Spring Hill Coll (AL)
State U of New York Coll at Old Westbury (NY)
State U of New York Empire State Coll (NY)
Stetson U (FL)
Stevens Inst of Technology (NJ)
Thomas Edison State U (NJ)
Thomas U (GA)
Towson U (MD)
Trent U (ON, Canada)
Trine U (IN)
Troy U (AL)
Tulane U (LA)
Union Coll (NY)
U at Buffalo, the State U of New York (NY)
The U of Akron (OH)
U of Bridgeport (CT)
U of California, Irvine (CA)
U of Central Florida (FL)
U of Chicago (IL)
U of Cincinnati (OH)
U of Dallas (TX)
U of Denver (CO)
U of Houston–Downtown (TX)
U of La Verne (CA)
U of Maine at Fort Kent (ME)
U of Maryland Eastern Shore (MD)

U of Maryland U Coll (MD)
U of Massachusetts Boston (MA)
U of Michigan (MI)
U of Michigan–Dearborn (MI)
U of Michigan–Flint (MI)
U of Minnesota, Morris (MN)
U of Mobile (AL)
U of Montevallo (AL)
U of Nevada, Las Vegas (NV)
U of North Alabama (AL)
U of North Dakota (ND)
U of North Texas (TX)
U of Oregon (OR)
U of Pennsylvania (PA)
U of Pittsburgh (PA)
U of Pittsburgh at Bradford (PA)
U of Pittsburgh at Greensburg (PA)
U of Providence (MT)
U of Puerto Rico–Humacao (PR)
U of Regina (SK, Canada)
U of St. Thomas (MN)
U of Sioux Falls (SD)
U of Southern California (CA)
U of South Florida, St. Petersburg (FL)
U of South Florida Sarasota-Manatee (FL)
The U of Texas Rio Grande Valley (TX)
U of the Pacific (CA)
U of the Virgin Islands (VI)
U of Utah (UT)
U of Washington (WA)
U of Wisconsin–Platteville (WI)
U of Wisconsin–River Falls (WI)
U of Wisconsin–Stevens Point (WI)
U of Wisconsin–Stout (WI)
U of Wisconsin–Superior (WI)
U of Wisconsin–Whitewater (WI)
U of Wyoming (WY)
Upper Iowa U (IA)
Utica Coll (NY)
Valley City State U (ND)
Valparaiso U (IN)
Vanderbilt U (TN)
Virginia Wesleyan U (VA)
Warner Pacific Coll (OR)
Wartburg Coll (IA)
Washington State U (WA)
Washington State U–Global Campus (WA)
Washington State U–Tri-Cities (WA)
Washington State U–Vancouver (WA)
Washington U in St. Louis (MO)
Wayland Baptist U (TX)
Wayne State Coll (NE)
Wesleyan U (CT)
Western Connecticut State U (CT)
Western Kentucky U (KY)
Western Oregon U (OR)
Westmont Coll (CA)
West Texas A&M U (TX)
Whittier Coll (CA)
Widener U (PA)
Wisconsin Lutheran Coll (WI)

SOCIAL SCIENCES RELATED
Bloomsburg U of Pennsylvania (PA)
Boston U (MA)
Bowling Green State U (OH)
California Polytechnic State U, San Luis Obispo (CA)
California U of Pennsylvania (PA)
Central Michigan U (MI)
Clarion U of Pennsylvania (PA)
Cleveland State U (OH)
The Coll of Idaho (ID)
Coll of Staten Island of the City U of New York (NY)
Concordia U (QC, Canada)
Covenant Coll (GA)
Curry Coll (MA)
Eastern Oregon U (OR)
The Evergreen State Coll (WA)
Georgetown U (DC)
Gettysburg Coll (PA)
Hamline U (MN)
Hilbert Coll (NY)
Indiana U of Pennsylvania (PA)
John Jay Coll of Criminal Justice of the City U of New York (NY)
Kalamazoo Coll (MI)
Marlboro Coll (VT)
Marywood U (PA)

Millersville U of Pennsylvania (PA)
Mount Aloysius Coll (PA)
Mount Holyoke Coll (MA)
Mount Mary U (WI)
New Mexico Highlands U (NM)
New York U (NY)
North Central Coll (IL)
Northern Vermont U–Lyndon (VT)
Northwestern U (IL)
Pace U (NY)
Pitzer Coll (CA)
Purchase Coll, State U of New York (NY)
Queens Coll of the City U of New York (NY)
Rutgers U–New Brunswick (NJ)
St. Lawrence U (NY)
Saint Mary's Coll of California (CA)
Simon Fraser U (BC, Canada)
Skidmore Coll (NY)
State U of New York Polytechnic Inst (NY)
Towson U (MD)
Union Coll (NE)
The U of Alabama at Birmingham (AL)
U of Denver (CO)
U of La Verne (CA)
U of Maine at Presque Isle (ME)
U of Massachusetts Amherst (MA)
U of New England (ME)
U of Pittsburgh (PA)
U of Puerto Rico–Humacao (PR)
U of Regina (SK, Canada)
U of Rhode Island (RI)
U of Rochester (NY)
U of Southern Maine (ME)
The U of Tennessee at Chattanooga (TN)
The U of Texas at San Antonio (TX)
U of Washington, Tacoma (WA)
U of Waterloo (ON, Canada)
Washington U in St. Louis (MO)
Whitman Coll (WA)
Williams Coll (MA)

SOCIAL SCIENCE TEACHER EDUCATION
Auburn U (AL)
Baylor U (TX)
Biola U (CA)
Blackburn Coll (IL)
Blue Mountain Coll (MS)
Boise State U (ID)
Bowling Green State U (OH)
Brigham Young U (UT)
Buena Vista U (IA)
California Lutheran U (CA)
Campbellsville U (KY)
Carroll Coll (MT)
Carroll U (WI)
Central Methodist U (MO)
Chowan U (NC)
Coll of Saint Mary (NE)
Concordia U Chicago (IL)
Corban U (OR)
Dickinson State U (ND)
Dominican Coll (NY)
Eastern Michigan U (MI)
Eastern Washington U (WA)
Emmanuel Coll (GA)
Emporia State U (KS)
Fayetteville State U (NC)
Ferris State U (MI)
Flagler Coll (FL)
Florida Ag and Mech U (FL)
Florida Atlantic U (FL)
Florida Southern Coll (FL)
Holy Family U (PA)
Jackson State U (MS)
Knox Coll (IL)
Lincoln U (MO)
Lindenwood U (MO)
Lindsey Wilson Coll (KY)
Manchester U (IN)
Mansfield U of Pennsylvania (PA)
Marywood U (PA)
Mercyhurst U (PA)
Michigan State U (MI)
Millikin U (IL)
Minot State U (ND)
Missouri Valley Coll (MO)
Mount St. Mary's U (MD)
Northern Michigan U (MI)
Northwest Missouri State U (MO)
Ohio Dominican U (OH)
Olivet Nazarene U (IL)

Rhode Island Coll (RI)
Rust Coll (MS)
Saginaw Valley State U (MI)
St. Ambrose U (IA)
Saint Mary's U of Minnesota (MN)
Shawnee State U (OH)
Southeastern U (FL)
Southern Utah U (UT)
Southwest Baptist U (MO)
State U of New York Coll at Oneonta (NY)
Union Coll (NE)
U of Maine at Farmington (ME)
U of Maine at Machias (ME)
U of Mobile (AL)
U of Nebraska–Lincoln (NE)
The U of North Carolina at Greensboro (NC)
U of North Dakota (ND)
U of Northern Iowa (IA)
U of Providence (MT)
U of South Dakota (SD)
U of Utah (UT)
U of Wisconsin–Whitewater (WI)
Upper Iowa U (IA)
Utica Coll (NY)
Valley City State U (ND)
Valparaiso U (IN)
Wartburg Coll (IA)
Washington U in St. Louis (MO)
Wayne State Coll (NE)
Weber State U (UT)
Western Michigan U (MI)
Western State Colorado U (CO)
Western Washington U (WA)
Westmont Coll (CA)
William Penn U (IA)
Wilmington U (DE)
Winona State U (MN)
Youngstown State U (OH)

SOCIAL STUDIES TEACHER EDUCATION

Abilene Christian U (TX)
Adams State U (CO)
Alice Lloyd Coll (KY)
Alverno Coll (WI)
Anderson U (IN)
Anderson U (SC)
Aquinas Coll (MI)
Arizona Christian U (AZ)
Arkansas Tech U (AR)
Augustana U (SD)
Averett U (VA)
Ball State U (IN)
The Baptist Coll of Florida (FL)
Barton Coll (NC)
Baylor U (TX)
Bethany Lutheran Coll (MN)
Bethel Coll (IN)
Bethel U (MN)
Bethune-Cookman U (FL)
Biola U (CA)
Blackburn Coll (IL)
Bluefield Coll (VA)
Bob Jones U (SC)
Boston U (MA)
Bowling Green State U (OH)
Bradley U (IL)
Brigham Young U–Idaho (ID)
Buffalo State Coll, State U of New York (NY)
Cairn U (PA)
Calvin Coll (MI)
Cameron U (OK)
Campbellsville U (KY)
Canisius Coll (NY)
Capital U (OH)
Carroll Coll (MT)
Carroll U (WI)
Cedarville U (OH)
Central Michigan U (MI)
Charleston Southern U (SC)
City Coll of the City U of New York (NY)
Cleveland State U (OH)
The Coll of Saint Rose (NY)
Columbus State U (GA)
Concordia U, St. Paul (MN)
Corban U (OR)
Cornerstone U (MI)
Daemen Coll (NY)
Duquesne U (PA)
East Carolina U (NC)
Eastern Michigan U (MI)
Eastern Washington U (WA)
East Texas Baptist U (TX)

Ferris State U (MI)
Florida State U (FL)
Franklin Coll (IN)
Gannon U (PA)
Geneva Coll (PA)
Goshen Coll (IN)
Grambling State U (LA)
Grand Valley State U (MI)
Granite State Coll (NH)
Green Mountain Coll (VT)
Greensboro Coll (NC)
Grove City Coll (PA)
Gustavus Adolphus Coll (MN)
Harding U (AR)
Hardin-Simmons U (TX)
Hiram Coll (OH)
Hofstra U (NY)
Holy Family U (PA)
Hope Coll (MI)
Houston Baptist U (TX)
Howard Payne U (TX)
Huntingdon Coll (AL)
Huston-Tillotson U (TX)
Immaculata U (PA)
Indiana State U (IN)
Indiana U Bloomington (IN)
Indiana U Northwest (IN)
Indiana–Purdue U Indianapolis (IN)
Indiana U South Bend (IN)
Indiana U Southeast (IN)
Indiana Wesleyan U (IN)
Inter American U of Puerto Rico, Barranquitas Campus (PR)
Inter American U of Puerto Rico, Metropolitan Campus (PR)
Inter American U of Puerto Rico, San Germán Campus (PR)
Iona Coll (NY)
Ithaca Coll (NY)
Juniata Coll (PA)
Kennesaw State U (GA)
Kent State U (OH)
LaGrange Coll (GA)
Le Moyne Coll (NY)
LeTourneau U (TX)
Long Island U–LIU Brooklyn (NY)
Long Island U–LIU Post (NY)
Louisiana Coll (LA)
Madonna U (MI)
Malone U (OH)
Manchester U (IN)
Manhattanville Coll (NY)
Mansfield U of Pennsylvania (PA)
Maranatha Baptist U (WI)
Marian U (WI)
Marist Coll (NY)
Martin Luther Coll (MN)
Maryville Coll (TN)
Merrimack Coll (MA)
Messiah Coll (PA)
Miami U (OH)
Michigan State U (MI)
MidAmerica Nazarene U (KS)
Minnesota State U Moorhead (MN)
Misericordia U (PA)
Morris Coll (SC)
Mount Mary U (WI)
Mount Vernon Nazarene U (OH)
Nazareth Coll of Rochester (NY)
New York U (NY)
Niagara U (NY)
North Dakota State U (ND)
Northeastern State U (OK)
Northern Michigan U (MI)
North Greenville U (SC)
Northland Coll (WI)
Northwest U (WA)
Nova Southeastern U (FL)
Nyack Coll (NY)
Ohio Northern U (OH)
Ohio Wesleyan U (OH)
Oklahoma Baptist U (OK)
Oklahoma Christian U (OK)
Oral Roberts U (OK)
Ouachita Baptist U (AR)
Pace U (NY)
Pace U, Pleasantville Campus (NY)
Penn State Harrisburg (PA)
Pfeiffer U (NC)
Point Park U (PA)
Purdue U (IN)
Queens Coll of the City U of New York (NY)
Rivier U (NH)
Roberts Wesleyan Coll (NY)
Rocky Mountain Coll (MT)

St. Catherine U (MN)
Saint Francis U (PA)
St. John Fisher Coll (NY)
St. John's U (NY)
St. Joseph's Coll, Long Island Campus (NY)
St. Joseph's Coll, New York (NY)
Saint Mary-of-the-Woods Coll (IN)
St. Olaf Coll (MN)
Simmons Coll (MA)
Southeastern Louisiana U (LA)
Southeastern Oklahoma State U (OK)
Southeast Missouri State U (MO)
Southwestern Adventist U (TX)
Southwestern Assemblies of God U (TX)
Spring Hill Coll (AL)
State U of New York at New Paltz (NY)
State U of New York Coll at Cortland (NY)
State U of New York Coll at Old Westbury (NY)
State U of New York Coll at Potsdam (NY)
Syracuse U (NY)
Taylor U (IN)
Temple U (PA)
Texas Christian U (TX)
Texas Lutheran U (TX)
Trine U (IN)
The U of Akron (OH)
U of Central Arkansas (AR)
U of Evansville (IN)
The U of Findlay (OH)
U of Georgia (GA)
U of Kentucky (KY)
U of Louisiana at Monroe (LA)
U of Maine (ME)
U of Michigan–Dearborn (MI)
U of Michigan–Flint (MI)
U of Minnesota, Duluth (MN)
U of Missouri (MO)
The U of North Carolina at Greensboro (NC)
The U of North Carolina at Pembroke (NC)
U of North Dakota (ND)
U of Northern Colorado (CO)
U of Oklahoma (OK)
U of Providence (MT)
U of Regina (SK, Canada)
U of St. Francis (IL)
U of St. Thomas (MN)
U of Vermont (VT)
U of Wisconsin–Eau Claire (WI)
U of Wisconsin–La Crosse (WI)
U of Wisconsin–Milwaukee (WI)
U of Wisconsin–Superior (WI)
U of Wisconsin–Whitewater (WI)
Ursuline Coll (OH)
Utah State U (UT)
Utica Coll (NY)
Virginia Wesleyan U (VA)
Warner Pacific Coll (OR)
Washington U in St. Louis (MO)
Wayland Baptist U (TX)
Waynesburg U (PA)
Weber State U (UT)
Western Michigan U (MI)
Western Washington U (WA)
Widener U (PA)
Xavier U of Louisiana (LA)
York Coll of Pennsylvania (PA)
Youngstown State U (OH)

SOCIAL WORK

Abilene Christian U (TX)
Adams State U (CO)
Adelphi U (NY)
Alabama State U (AL)
Alcorn State U (MS)
Alverno Coll (WI)
Anderson U (IN)
Andrews U (MI)
Angelo State U (TX)
Appalachian State U (NC)
Arizona State U at the Downtown Phoenix campus (AZ)
Arizona State U at the West campus (AZ)
Asbury U (KY)
Ashland U (OH)
Auburn U (AL)
Augsburg U (MN)

Aultman Coll of Nursing and Health Sciences (OH)
Aurora U (IL)
Austin Peay State U (TN)
Avila U (MO)
Azusa Pacific U (CA)
Ball State U (IN)
Barton Coll (NC)
Baylor U (TX)
Belhaven U (MS)
Belmont U (TN)
Bemidji State U (MN)
Bennett Coll (NC)
Bethel Coll (KS)
Bethel U (MN)
Biola U (CA)
Bloomsburg U of Pennsylvania (PA)
Bluffton U (OH)
Boise State U (ID)
Bowie State U (MD)
Bowling Green State U (OH)
Bowling Green State U–Firelands Coll (OH)
Bradley U (IL)
Brandman U (CA)
Brescia U (KY)
Bridgewater State U (MA)
Brigham Young U–Idaho (ID)
Buena Vista U (IA)
Buffalo State Coll, State U of New York (NY)
Cairn U (PA)
California State U, Long Beach (CA)
California State U, Los Angeles (CA)
California State U, Sacramento (CA)
California State U, San Bernardino (CA)
California U of Pennsylvania (PA)
Calvin Coll (MI)
Campbellsville U (KY)
Capital U (OH)
Caribbean U (PR)
Carlow U (PA)
Carthage Coll (WI)
The Catholic U of America (DC)
Cedar Crest Coll (PA)
Cedarville U (OH)
Central Connecticut State U (CT)
Central Michigan U (MI)
Central State U (OH)
Champlain Coll (VT)
Chapman U (CA)
Chatham U (PA)
Christopher Newport U (VA)
Clark Atlanta U (GA)
Clarke U (IA)
Cleveland State U (OH)
The Coll at Brockport, State U of New York (NY)
The Coll of New Rochelle (NY)
Coll of Saint Elizabeth (NJ)
The Coll of Saint Rose (NY)
The Coll of St. Scholastica (MN)
Coll of Staten Island of the City U of New York (NY)
Coll of the Ozarks (MO)
Colorado Mesa U (CO)
Colorado State U (CO)
Colorado State U–Pueblo (CO)
Columbia Coll (SC)
Concordia Coll–New York (NY)
Concordia U Chicago (IL)
Concordia U Wisconsin (WI)
Concord U (WV)
Cornerstone U (MI)
Creighton U (NE)
Daemen Coll (NY)
Defiance Coll (OH)
Delaware State U (DE)
Dominican Coll (NY)
East Carolina U (NC)
East Central U (OK)
Eastern Mennonite U (VA)
Eastern Michigan U (MI)
Eastern Nazarene Coll (MA)
Eastern U (PA)
Eastern Washington U (WA)
East Stroudsburg U of Pennsylvania (PA)
East Tennessee State U (TN)
Elizabethtown Coll (PA)
Elms Coll (MA)
Evangel U (MO)
Fayetteville State U (NC)

Ferris State U (MI)
Florida Ag and Mech U (FL)
Florida Atlantic U (FL)
Florida Gulf Coast U (FL)
Florida Intl U (FL)
Florida State U (FL)
Fordham U (NY)
Franklin Pierce U (NH)
Frostburg State U (MD)
Gannon U (PA)
George Mason U (VA)
Georgian Court U (NJ)
Georgia State U (GA)
Gordon Coll (MA)
Goshen Coll (IN)
Governors State U (IL)
Grambling State U (LA)
Grand Valley State U (MI)
Grand View U (IA)
Greenville U (IL)
Grove City Coll (PA)
Gwynedd Mercy U (PA)
Hampton U (VA)
Hannibal-LaGrange U (MO)
Harding U (AR)
Hardin-Simmons U (TX)
Hawai'i Pacific U (HI)
Hood Coll (MD)
Hope Coll (MI)
Howard Payne U (TX)
Humboldt State U (CA)
Idaho State U (ID)
Illinois State U (IL)
Immaculata U (PA)
Indiana State U (IN)
Indiana U Bloomington (IN)
Indiana U East (IN)
Indiana U Northwest (IN)
Indiana U–Purdue U Indianapolis (IN)
Indiana U South Bend (IN)
Indiana Wesleyan U (IN)
Inter American U of Puerto Rico, Aguadilla Campus (PR)
Inter American U of Puerto Rico, Fajardo Campus (PR)
Inter American U of Puerto Rico, Metropolitan Campus (PR)
Iona Coll (NY)
Jackson State U (MS)
James Madison U (VA)
Johnson C. Smith U (NC)
Juniata Coll (PA)
Kansas State U (KS)
Kentucky State U (KY)
Kutztown U of Pennsylvania (PA)
Lamar U (TX)
La Salle U (PA)
La Sierra U (CA)
Lebanese American U (Lebanon)
Lehman Coll of the City U of New York (NY)
Lewis U (IL)
Liberty U (VA)
Limestone Coll (SC)
Lincoln Memorial U (TN)
Lincoln U (MO)
Lindenwood U (MO)
Lipscomb U (TN)
Lock Haven U of Pennsylvania (PA)
Long Island U–LIU Brooklyn (NY)
Long Island U–LIU Post (NY)
Longwood U (VA)
Loras Coll (IA)
Louisiana Coll (LA)
Louisiana State U and A&M Coll (LA)
Loyola U Chicago (IL)
Lubbock Christian U (TX)
Luther Coll (IA)
Madonna U (MI)
Malone U (OH)
Manchester U (IN)
Mansfield U of Pennsylvania (PA)
Marian U (WI)
Marist Coll (NY)
Marshall U (WV)
Mary Baldwin U (VA)
Marywood U (PA)
McDaniel Coll (MD)
Medgar Evers Coll of the City U of New York (NY)
Mercy Coll (NY)
Mercyhurst U (PA)
Meredith Coll (NC)
Messiah Coll (PA)

Metropolitan State U of Denver (CO)
Miami U (OH)
Michigan State U (MI)
Middle Tennessee State U (TN)
Millersville U of Pennsylvania (PA)
Milligan Coll (TN)
Millikin U (IL)
Minnesota State U Moorhead (MN)
Minot State U (ND)
Misericordia U (PA)
Mississippi State U (MS)
Missouri State U (MO)
Missouri Western State U (MO)
Molloy Coll (NY)
Montclair State U (NJ)
Morehead State U (KY)
Mount Mary U (WI)
Mount Mercy U (IA)
Mount St. Joseph U (OH)
Mount Saint Mary Coll (NY)
Mount Saint Mary's U (CA)
Mount Vernon Nazarene U (OH)
Murray State U (KY)
National Louis U (IL)
Nazareth Coll of Rochester (NY)
Neumann U (PA)
New Mexico State U (NM)
New York U (NY)
Niagara U (NY)
North Carolina Central U (NC)
North Carolina State U (NC)
Northeastern State U (OK)
Northern Arizona U (AZ)
Northern Kentucky U (KY)
Northern Michigan U (MI)
Northwestern Coll (IA)
Northwestern Oklahoma State U (OK)
Northwestern State U of Louisiana (LA)
Northwest Nazarene U (ID)
Nyack Coll (NY)
Oakland U (MI)
Oglethorpe U (GA)
Ohio Dominican U (OH)
The Ohio State U (OH)
The Ohio State U at Lima (OH)
The Ohio State U at Mansfield (OH)
The Ohio State U at Marion (OH)
The Ohio State U at Newark (OH)
Ohio U (OH)
Olivet Nazarene U (IL)
Oral Roberts U (OK)
Our Lady of the Lake U (TX)
Pacific Lutheran U (WA)
Pittsburg State U (KS)
Point Loma Nazarene U (CA)
Portland State U (OR)
Prairie View A&M U (TX)
Providence Coll (RI)
Purdue U Northwest (IN)
Radford U (VA)
Ramapo Coll of New Jersey (NJ)
Redeemer U Coll (ON, Canada)
Rhode Island Coll (RI)
Roberts Wesleyan Coll (NY)
Rust Coll (MS)
Rutgers U–Camden (NJ)
Rutgers U–Newark (NJ)
Rutgers U–New Brunswick (NJ)
Sacred Heart U (CT)
Saginaw Valley State U (MI)
St. Ambrose U (IA)
Saint Anselm Coll (NH)
St. Catherine U (MN)
Saint Francis U (PA)
Saint Leo U (FL)
Saint Louis U (MO)
Saint Martin's U (WA)
St. Olaf Coll (MN)
St. Thomas U (NB, Canada)
Salisbury U (MD)
Salve Regina U (RI)
San Diego State U (CA)
San Francisco State U (CA)
Seattle U (WA)
Seton Hill U (PA)
Shaw U (NC)
Shepherd U (WV)
Shippensburg U of Pennsylvania (PA)
Siena Coll (NY)
Simmons Coll (MA)
Skidmore Coll (NY)
Slippery Rock U of Pennsylvania (PA)

Southeastern Louisiana U (LA)
Southeastern U (FL)
Southeast Missouri State U (MO)
Southern Adventist U (TN)
Southern Arkansas U–Magnolia (AR)
Southern Illinois U Carbondale (IL)
Southern Illinois U Edwardsville (IL)
Southwest Baptist U (MO)
Southwestern Assemblies of God U (TX)
State U of New York at Fredonia (NY)
State U of New York at Plattsburgh (NY)
State U of New York Coll at Cortland (NY)
Stephen F. Austin State U (TX)
Stockton U (NJ)
Stony Brook U, State U of New York (NY)
Syracuse U (NY)
Tabor Coll (KS)
Tarleton State U (TX)
Taylor U (IN)
Temple U (PA)
Tennessee Technological U (TN)
Texas A&M U–Central Texas (TX)
Texas A&M U–Commerce (TX)
Texas A&M U–Kingsville (TX)
Texas Christian U (TX)
Texas State U (TX)
Texas Tech U (TX)
Texas Woman's U (TX)
Thomas U (GA)
Touro U Worldwide (CA)
Trent U (ON, Canada)
Trevecca Nazarene U (TN)
Trinity Christian Coll (IL)
Troy U (AL)
Union Coll (NE)
Union U (TN)
Université de Sherbrooke (QC, Canada)
U at Albany, State U of New York (NY)
The U of Akron (OH)
The U of Alabama (AL)
The U of Alabama at Birmingham (AL)
U of Alaska Fairbanks (AK)
U of Arkansas (AR)
U of Central Florida (FL)
U of Central Missouri (MO)
U of Cincinnati (OH)
The U of Findlay (OH)
U of Georgia (GA)
U of Guam (GU)
U of Hawaii at Manoa (HI)
U of Houston–Clear Lake (TX)
U of Houston–Downtown (TX)
U of Illinois at Chicago (IL)
U of Illinois at Springfield (IL)
The U of Kansas (KS)
U of Kentucky (KY)
U of Louisiana at Monroe (LA)
U of Louisville (KY)
U of Maine (ME)
U of Maine at Presque Isle (ME)
U of Mary Hardin-Baylor (TX)
U of Maryland, Baltimore County (MD)
U of Maryland Eastern Shore (MD)
U of Memphis (TN)
U of Michigan–Flint (MI)
U of Minnesota, Duluth (MN)
U of Missouri (MO)
U of Missouri–St. Louis (MO)
U of Montana (MT)
U of Montevallo (AL)
U of Nebraska at Kearney (NE)
U of Nevada, Las Vegas (NV)
U of Nevada, Reno (NV)
U of New England (ME)
U of New Hampshire (NH)
U of North Alabama (AL)
The U of North Carolina at Charlotte (NC)
The U of North Carolina at Greensboro (NC)
The U of North Carolina at Pembroke (NC)
The U of North Carolina Wilmington (NC)
U of North Dakota (ND)
U of Northern Iowa (IA)

U of North Florida (FL)
U of North Texas (TX)
U of Oklahoma (OK)
U of Pikeville (KY)
U of Pittsburgh (PA)
U of Puerto Rico–Humacao (PR)
U of Regina (SK, Canada)
U of St. Francis (IL)
U of Saint Francis (IN)
U of Saint Joseph (CT)
U of St. Thomas (MN)
U of Sioux Falls (SD)
U of South Alabama (AL)
U of South Carolina (SC)
U of South Dakota (SD)
U of Southern Indiana (IN)
U of Southern Maine (ME)
U of Southern Mississippi (MS)
The U of Tennessee (TN)
The U of Tennessee at Chattanooga (TN)
The U of Tennessee at Martin (TN)
The U of Texas at Austin (TX)
The U of Texas at El Paso (TX)
The U of Texas of the Permian Basin (TX)
The U of Texas Rio Grande Valley (TX)
U of the Fraser Valley (BC, Canada)
U of the Virgin Islands (VI)
The U of Toledo (OH)
U of Utah (UT)
U of Valley Forge (PA)
U of Vermont (VT)
U of Washington (WA)
U of Washington, Tacoma (WA)
U of Waterloo (ON, Canada)
U of Wisconsin–Eau Claire (WI)
U of Wisconsin–Madison (WI)
U of Wisconsin–Milwaukee (WI)
U of Wisconsin–River Falls (WI)
U of Wisconsin–Stevens Point (WI)
U of Wisconsin–Superior (WI)
U of Wisconsin–Whitewater (WI)
U of Wyoming (WY)
Ursuline Coll (OH)
Utah State U (UT)
Utah Valley U (UT)
Valparaiso U (IN)
Virginia Commonwealth U (VA)
Virginia Wesleyan U (VA)
Warner Pacific Coll (OR)
Wartburg Coll (IA)
Washington State U (WA)
Wayne State U (MI)
Weber State U (UT)
West Chester U of Pennsylvania (PA)
Western Connecticut State U (CT)
Western Illinois U (IL)
Western Kentucky U (KY)
Western Michigan U (MI)
Western New England U (MA)
Westfield State U (MA)
West Texas A&M U (TX)
West Virginia State U (WV)
West Virginia U (WV)
Whittier Coll (CA)
Whitworth U (WA)
Wichita State U (KS)
Widener U (PA)
William Woods U (MO)
Winona State U (MN)
Winthrop U (SC)
Wright State U (OH)
Wright State U–Lake Campus (OH)
Youngstown State U (OH)

SOCIAL WORK RELATED
Davenport U, Grand Rapids (MI)
Eastern Washington U (WA)
King U (TN)
Marquette U (WI)
Southeastern U (FL)

SOCIOLOGY
Abilene Christian U (TX)
Acadia U (NS, Canada)
Adelphi U (NY)
Agnes Scott Coll (GA)
Albion Coll (MI)
Albright Coll (PA)
Alcorn State U (MS)
Alfred U (NY)
Alma Coll (MI)
Alverno Coll (WI)

American Intl Coll (MA)
American Public U System (WV)
American U (DC)
The American U in Cairo (Egypt)
Amherst Coll (MA)
Andrews U (MI)
Angelo State U (TX)
Appalachian State U (NC)
Aquinas Coll (MI)
Arcadia U (PA)
Arizona State U at the Tempe campus (AZ)
Arizona State U at the West campus (AZ)
Arkansas Tech U (AR)
Asbury U (KY)
Ashland U (OH)
Assumption Coll (MA)
Athabasca U (AB, Canada)
Athens State U (AL)
Auburn U (AL)
Auburn U at Montgomery (AL)
Augsburg U (MN)
Augustana Coll (IL)
Augustana U (SD)
Aurora U (IL)
Austin Coll (TX)
Austin Peay State U (TN)
Averett U (VA)
Avila U (MO)
Azusa Pacific U (CA)
Baker U (KS)
Baldwin Wallace U (OH)
Ball State U (IN)
Bard Coll (NY)
Barnard Coll (NY)
Barry U (FL)
Baruch Coll of the City U of New York (NY)
Bates Coll (ME)
Baylor U (TX)
Bellarmine U (KY)
Belmont U (TN)
Beloit Coll (WI)
Bemidji State U (MN)
Benedictine Coll (KS)
Benedictine U (IL)
Bennington Coll (VT)
Berea Coll (KY)
Bethany Lutheran Coll (MN)
Bethel Coll (IN)
Bethel U (TN)
Bethune-Cookman U (FL)
Binghamton U, State U of New York (NY)
Biola U (CA)
Birmingham-Southern Coll (AL)
Black Hills State U (SD)
Bloomsburg U of Pennsylvania (PA)
Bluffton U (OH)
Boise State U (ID)
Boston Coll (MA)
Boston U (MA)
Bowdoin Coll (ME)
Bowie State U (MD)
Bowling Green State U (OH)
Bradley U (IL)
Brandeis U (MA)
Brandman U (CA)
Brandon U (MB, Canada)
Brewton-Parker Coll (GA)
Bridgewater Coll (VA)
Bridgewater State U (MA)
Brigham Young U–Idaho (ID)
Brock U (ON, Canada)
Bryant U (RI)
Bryn Mawr Coll (PA)
Bucknell U (PA)
Buena Vista U (IA)
Buffalo State Coll, State U of New York (NY)
Butler U (IN)
Caldwell U (NJ)
California Baptist U (CA)
California Lutheran U (CA)
California Polytechnic State U, San Luis Obispo (CA)
California State Polytechnic U, Pomona (CA)
California State U, Dominguez Hills (CA)
California State U, East Bay (CA)
California State U, Fullerton (CA)
California State U, Long Beach (CA)
California State U, Los Angeles (CA)

California State U, Northridge (CA)
California State U, Sacramento (CA)
California State U, San Bernardino (CA)
California State U, San Marcos (CA)
California State U, Stanislaus (CA)
Calvin Coll (MI)
Cameron U (OK)
Campbellsville U (KY)
Canisius Coll (NY)
Capital U (OH)
Cardinal Stritch U (WI)
Carleton Coll (MN)
Carlow U (PA)
Carroll Coll (MT)
Carroll U (WI)
Carson-Newman U (TN)
Carthage Coll (WI)
Case Western Reserve U (OH)
Catawba Coll (NC)
The Catholic U of America (DC)
Centenary Coll of Louisiana (LA)
Central Connecticut State U (CT)
Central Methodist U (MO)
Central Michigan U (MI)
Central State U (OH)
Chapman U (CA)
Charleston Southern U (SC)
Charter Oak State Coll (CT)
Chestnut Hill Coll (PA)
Christopher Newport U (VA)
City Coll of the City U of New York (NY)
Clarion U of Pennsylvania (PA)
Clark Atlanta U (GA)
Clarkson U (NY)
Clark U (MA)
Clayton State U (GA)
Clemson U (SC)
Cleveland State U (OH)
Coastal Carolina U (SC)
Coe Coll (IA)
Coker Coll (SC)
Colby Coll (ME)
Colgate U (NY)
The Coll at Brockport, State U of New York (NY)
Coll of Charleston (SC)
Coll of Mount Saint Vincent (NY)
The Coll of New Jersey (NJ)
The Coll of New Rochelle (NY)
Coll of Saint Benedict (MN)
Coll of Saint Elizabeth (NJ)
Coll of the Holy Cross (MA)
Coll of the Ozarks (MO)
The Coll of William and Mary (VA)
The Coll of Wooster (OH)
The Colorado Coll (CO)
Colorado Mesa U (CO)
Colorado State U (CO)
Colorado State U–Pueblo (CO)
Columbia Coll (MO)
Columbia U (NY)
Columbus State U (GA)
Concordia Coll–New York (NY)
Concordia U (QC, Canada)
Concordia U Chicago (IL)
Concordia U of Edmonton (AB, Canada)
Concordia U, St. Paul (MN)
Concord U (WV)
Connecticut Coll (CT)
Converse Coll (SC)
Cornell Coll (IA)
Cornell U (NY)
Covenant Coll (GA)
Creighton U (NE)
Curry Coll (MA)
Dallas Baptist U (TX)
Dartmouth Coll (NH)
Davidson Coll (NC)
Dean Coll (MA)
Delaware State U (DE)
Denison U (OH)
DePaul U (IL)
DePauw U (IN)
DEREE - The American Coll of Greece (Greece)
Dickinson Coll (PA)
Doane U (NE)
Dominican U (IL)
Drake U (IA)
Drew U (NJ)
Drexel U (PA)
Duquesne U (PA)

D'Youville Coll (NY)
Earlham Coll (IN)
East Carolina U (NC)
East Central U (OK)
Eastern Michigan U (MI)
Eastern Nazarene Coll (MA)
Eastern New Mexico U (NM)
Eastern U (PA)
Eastern Washington U (WA)
East Stroudsburg U of
    Pennsylvania (PA)
East Tennessee State U (TN)
East Texas Baptist U (TX)
Eckerd Coll (FL)
Edgewood Coll (WI)
Elizabethtown Coll (PA)
Elmhurst Coll (IL)
Elms Coll (MA)
Elon U (NC)
Emmanuel Coll (MA)
Emory & Henry Coll (VA)
Emory U (GA)
Emporia State U (KS)
Eugene Lang Coll of Liberal Arts
    (NY)
Evangel U (MO)
The Evergreen State Coll (WA)
Excelsior Coll (NY)
Fairfield U (CT)
Fairleigh Dickinson U, Florham
    Campus (NJ)
Fairleigh Dickinson U, Metropolitan
    Campus (NJ)
Fayetteville State U (NC)
Ferris State U (MI)
Fitchburg State U (MA)
Flagler Coll (FL)
Florida Ag and Mech U (FL)
Florida Atlantic U (FL)
Florida Gulf Coast U (FL)
Florida Intl U (FL)
Florida State U (FL)
Fordham U (NY)
Fort Lewis Coll (CO)
Framingham State U (MA)
Francis Marion U (SC)
Franklin & Marshall Coll (PA)
Franklin Coll (IN)
Franklin Pierce U (NH)
Friends U (KS)
Frostburg State U (MD)
Furman U (SC)
Geneva Coll (PA)
George Mason U (VA)
Georgetown Coll (KY)
Georgetown U (DC)
The George Washington U (DC)
Georgia Coll & State U (GA)
Georgia Southern U (GA)
Georgia Southwestern State U
    (GA)
Georgia State U (GA)
Gettysburg Coll (PA)
Gonzaga U (WA)
Gordon Coll (MA)
Goshen Coll (IN)
Graceland U (IA)
Grambling State U (LA)
Grand Valley State U (MI)
Greensboro Coll (NC)
Greenville U (IL)
Grinnell Coll (IA)
Grove City Coll (PA)
Guilford Coll (NC)
Gustavus Adolphus Coll (MN)
Hamilton Coll (NY)
Hamline U (MN)
Hampshire Coll (MA)
Hampton U (VA)
Hannibal-LaGrange U (MO)
Hardin-Simmons U (TX)
Harris-Stowe State U (MO)
Hartwick Coll (NY)
Harvard U (MA)
Haverford Coll (PA)
Hawai`i Pacific U (HI)
Hendrix Coll (AR)
Hillsdale Coll (MI)
Hiram Coll (OH)
Hobart and William Smith Colls
    (NY)
Hofstra U (NY)
Hollins U (VA)
Holy Family U (PA)
Holy Names U (CA)
Hood Coll (MD)
Hope Coll (MI)

Howard Payne U (TX)
Humboldt State U (CA)
Hunter Coll of the City U of New
    York (NY)
Huston-Tillotson U (TX)
Idaho State U (ID)
Illinois Coll (IL)
Illinois State U (IL)
Illinois Wesleyan U (IL)
Immaculata U (PA)
Indiana U Bloomington (IN)
Indiana U East (IN)
Indiana U Kokomo (IN)
Indiana U Northwest (IN)
Indiana U of Pennsylvania (PA)
Indiana U–Purdue U Indianapolis
    (IN)
Indiana U South Bend (IN)
Indiana U Southeast (IN)
Indiana Wesleyan U (IN)
Inter American U of Puerto Rico,
    Metropolitan Campus (PR)
Inter American U of Puerto Rico,
    San Germán Campus (PR)
Iona Coll (NY)
Iowa State U of Science and
    Technology (IA)
Ithaca Coll (NY)
Jackson State U (MS)
Jacksonville U (FL)
James Madison U (VA)
John Carroll U (OH)
John Jay Coll of Criminal Justice of
    the City U of New York (NY)
Johns Hopkins U (MD)
Juniata Coll (PA)
Kansas State U (KS)
Kansas Wesleyan U (KS)
Kean U (NJ)
Keene State Coll (NH)
Kennesaw State U (GA)
Kent State U (OH)
Kent State U at Stark (OH)
Kenyon Coll (OH)
King's Coll (PA)
Knox Coll (IL)
Kutztown U of Pennsylvania (PA)
Lafayette Coll (PA)
LaGrange Coll (GA)
Lamar U (TX)
Langston U (OK)
La Roche Coll (PA)
La Salle U (PA)
Lasell Coll (MA)
Lebanon Valley Coll (PA)
Lee U (TN)
Lehigh U (PA)
Lehman Coll of the City U of New
    York (NY)
Le Moyne Coll (NY)
Lenoir-Rhyne U (NC)
Lewis U (IL)
Lincoln U (MO)
Lincoln U (PA)
Lindenwood U (MO)
Linfield Coll (OR)
Lock Haven U of Pennsylvania (PA)
Long Island U–LIU Brooklyn (NY)
Long Island U–LIU Post (NY)
Longwood U (VA)
Loras Coll (IA)
Louisiana State U and A&M Coll
    (LA)
Loyola Marymount U (CA)
Loyola U Chicago (IL)
Loyola U New Orleans (LA)
Luther Coll (IA)
Lycoming Coll (PA)
Lynchburg Coll (VA)
Macalester Coll (MN)
Madonna U (MI)
Manchester U (IN)
Manhattan Coll (NY)
Manhattanville Coll (NY)
Marian U (IN)
Marlboro Coll (VT)
Marquette U (WI)
Marshall U (WV)
Mary Baldwin U (VA)
Marymount Manhattan Coll (NY)
Marymount U (VA)
Maryville Coll (TN)
Maryville U of Saint Louis (MO)
Marywood U (PA)
Massachusetts Coll of Liberal Arts
    (MA)
McDaniel Coll (MD)

McKendree U (IL)
McMurry U (TX)
McNeese State U (LA)
McPherson Coll (KS)
Mercer U, Macon (GA)
Mercy Coll (NY)
Mercyhurst U (PA)
Meredith Coll (NC)
Merrimack Coll (MA)
Messiah Coll (PA)
Metropolitan State U of Denver
    (CO)
Miami U (OH)
Michigan State U (MI)
MidAmerica Nazarene U (KS)
Middlebury Coll (VT)
Middle Tennessee State U (TN)
Millersville U of Pennsylvania (PA)
Milligan Coll (TN)
Millikin U (IL)
Mills Coll (CA)
Minnesota State U Moorhead (MN)
Minot State U (ND)
Mississippi State U (MS)
Missouri State U (MO)
Missouri Valley Coll (MO)
Missouri Western State U (MO)
Molloy Coll (NY)
Monmouth Coll (IL)
Montclair State U (NJ)
Moravian Coll (PA)
Morehead State U (KY)
Morehouse Coll (GA)
Morris Coll (SC)
Mount Holyoke Coll (MA)
Mount Mercy U (IA)
Mount St. Joseph U (OH)
Mount Saint Mary Coll (NY)
Mount Saint Mary's U (CA)
Mount St. Mary's U (MD)
Muhlenberg Coll (PA)
Murray State U (KY)
Muskingum U (OH)
National U (CA)
Nazareth Coll of Rochester (NY)
Newberry Coll (SC)
New Coll of Florida (FL)
New Jersey City U (NJ)
Newman U (KS)
New Mexico State U (NM)
New York Inst of Technology (NY)
New York U (NY)
Niagara U (NY)
North Carolina State U (NC)
North Carolina Wesleyan Coll (NC)
North Central Coll (IL)
North Dakota State U (ND)
Northeastern State U (OK)
Northeastern U (MA)
Northern Arizona U (AZ)
Northern Illinois U (IL)
Northern Kentucky U (KY)
Northern Michigan U (MI)
Northern State U (SD)
Northland Coll (WI)
Northwestern Coll (IA)
Northwestern Oklahoma State U
    (OK)
Northwestern U (IL)
Notre Dame de Namur U (CA)
Nova Southeastern U (FL)
Nyack Coll (NY)
Oakland U (MI)
Oberlin Coll (OH)
Occidental Coll (CA)
Oglethorpe U (GA)
Ohio Dominican U (OH)
Ohio Northern U (OH)
The Ohio State U (OH)
The Ohio State U at Mansfield (OH)
The Ohio State U at Marion (OH)
Ohio U (OH)
Ohio Wesleyan U (OH)
Oklahoma Baptist U (OK)
Oklahoma City U (OK)
Oklahoma State U (OK)
Old Dominion U (VA)
Olivet Nazarene U (IL)
Oregon State U (OR)
Ottawa U (KS)
Otterbein U (OH)
Ouachita Baptist U (AR)
Our Lady of the Lake U (TX)
Pacific Lutheran U (WA)
Penn State Abington (PA)
Penn State Altoona (PA)
Penn State Beaver (PA)

Penn State Berks (PA)
Penn State Brandywine (PA)
Penn State DuBois (PA)
Penn State Erie, The Behrend Coll
    (PA)
Penn State Fayette, The Eberly
    Campus (PA)
Penn State Greater Allegheny (PA)
Penn State Harrisburg (PA)
Penn State Hazleton (PA)
Penn State Lehigh Valley (PA)
Penn State Mont Alto (PA)
Penn State New Kensington (PA)
Penn State Schuylkill (PA)
Penn State Shenango (PA)
Penn State U Park (PA)
Penn State Wilkes-Barre (PA)
Penn State Worthington Scranton
    (PA)
Penn State York (PA)
Pepperdine U, Malibu (CA)
Pfeiffer U (NC)
Piedmont Coll (GA)
Pittsburg State U (KS)
Pitzer Coll (CA)
Point Loma Nazarene U (CA)
Point U (GA)
Pomona Coll (CA)
Portland State U (OR)
Post U (CT)
Prairie View A&M U (TX)
Presbyterian Coll (SC)
Princeton U (NJ)
Providence Coll (RI)
Purchase Coll, State U of New York
    (NY)
Purdue U (IN)
Purdue U Northwest (IN)
Queens Coll of the City U of New
    York (NY)
Quinnipiac U (CT)
Radford U (VA)
Ramapo Coll of New Jersey (NJ)
Randolph Coll (VA)
Randolph-Macon Coll (VA)
Redeemer U Coll (ON, Canada)
Reed Coll (OR)
Regis U (CO)
Rhode Island Coll (RI)
Rice U (TX)
Rider U (NJ)
Ripon Coll (WI)
Rivier U (NH)
Roanoke Coll (VA)
Rockford U (IL)
Rocky Mountain Coll (MT)
Rollins Coll (FL)
Roosevelt U (IL)
Rosemont Coll (PA)
Rust Coll (MS)
Rutgers U–Camden (NJ)
Rutgers U–Newark (NJ)
Rutgers U–New Brunswick (NJ)
Sacred Heart U (CT)
The Sage Colls (NY)
Saginaw Valley State U (MI)
St. Ambrose U (IA)
Saint Anselm Coll (NH)
Saint Augustine's U (NC)
St. Bonaventure U (NY)
St. Catherine U (MN)
Saint Francis U (PA)
St. John Fisher Coll (NY)
Saint John's U (MN)
St. John's U (NY)
St. Joseph's Coll, Long Island
    Campus (NY)
St. Joseph's Coll, New York (NY)
Saint Joseph's U (PA)
St. Lawrence U (NY)
Saint Leo U (FL)
Saint Louis U (MO)
Saint Louis U–Madrid Campus
    (Spain)
Saint Mary's Coll of California (CA)
St. Mary's Coll of Maryland (MD)
St. Mary's U (TX)
Saint Mary's U of Minnesota (MN)
Saint Michael's Coll (VT)
St. Norbert Coll (WI)
Saint Peter's U (NJ)
St. Thomas U (NB, Canada)
Saint Vincent Coll (PA)
Salisbury U (MD)
Salve Regina U (RI)
Samford U (AL)
Sam Houston State U (TX)

San Diego State U (CA)
San Francisco State U (CA)
Santa Clara U (CA)
Sarah Lawrence Coll (NY)
Scripps Coll (CA)
Seattle Pacific U (WA)
Seattle U (WA)
Seton Hill U (PA)
Shawnee State U (OH)
Shaw U (NC)
Shenandoah U (VA)
Shepherd U (WV)
Shippensburg U of Pennsylvania
    (PA)
Shorter U (GA)
Siena Coll (NY)
Simmons Coll (MA)
Simon Fraser U (BC, Canada)
Simpson Coll (IA)
Skidmore Coll (NY)
Smith Coll (MA)
Sonoma State U (CA)
Southeastern Louisiana U (LA)
Southeastern Oklahoma State U
    (OK)
Southern Illinois U Carbondale (IL)
Southern Illinois U Edwardsville
    (IL)
Southern Methodist U (TX)
Southern Utah U (UT)
Southwest Baptist U (MO)
Southwestern U (TX)
Spelman Coll (GA)
Spring Hill Coll (AL)
Stanford U (CA)
State U of New York at Fredonia
    (NY)
State U of New York at New Paltz
    (NY)
State U of New York at Oswego
    (NY)
State U of New York at Plattsburgh
    (NY)
State U of New York Coll at
    Cortland (NY)
State U of New York Coll at
    Geneseo (NY)
State U of New York Coll at Old
    Westbury (NY)
State U of New York Coll at
    Oneonta (NY)
State U of New York Coll at
    Potsdam (NY)
State U of New York Polytechnic
    Inst (NY)
Stephen F. Austin State U (TX)
Stetson U (FL)
Stockton U (NJ)
Stonehill Coll (MA)
Stony Brook U, State U of New York
    (NY)
Suffolk U (MA)
Susquehanna U (PA)
Sweet Briar Coll (VA)
Syracuse U (NY)
Tarleton State U (TX)
Taylor U (IN)
Temple U (PA)
Tennessee Technological U (TN)
Tennessee Wesleyan U (TN)
Texas A&M Intl U (TX)
Texas A&M U (TX)
Texas A&M U–Central Texas (TX)
Texas A&M U–Commerce (TX)
Texas A&M U–Corpus Christi (TX)
Texas A&M U–Kingsville (TX)
Texas Christian U (TX)
Texas Lutheran U (TX)
Texas State U (TX)
Texas Tech U (TX)
Texas Woman's U (TX)
Thomas U (GA)
Transylvania U (KY)
Trent U (ON, Canada)
Trevecca Nazarene U (TN)
Trinity U (TX)
Troy U (AL)
Truman State U (MO)
Tufts U (MA)
Tulane U (LA)
Union Coll (NY)
Union U (TN)
United States Military Acad (NY)
U at Albany, State U of New York
    (NY)
U at Buffalo, the State U of New
    York (NY)

The U of Akron (OH)
The U of Alabama at Birmingham (AL)
U of Alaska Fairbanks (AK)
The U of Arizona (AZ)
U of Arkansas (AR)
U of California, Davis (CA)
U of California, Irvine (CA)
U of California, Los Angeles (CA)
U of California, Riverside (CA)
U of California, San Diego (CA)
U of California, Santa Barbara (CA)
U of California, Santa Cruz (CA)
U of Central Arkansas (AR)
U of Central Florida (FL)
U of Central Missouri (MO)
U of Central Oklahoma (OK)
U of Chicago (IL)
U of Cincinnati (OH)
U of Colorado Boulder (CO)
U of Colorado Colorado Springs (CO)
U of Colorado Denver (CO)
U of Dayton (OH)
U of Denver (CO)
U of Dubuque (IA)
U of Evansville (IN)
U of Florida (FL)
U of Georgia (GA)
U of Guam (GU)
U of Guelph (ON, Canada)
U of Hartford (CT)
U of Hawaii at Manoa (HI)
U of Houston (TX)
U of Houston–Clear Lake (TX)
U of Houston–Downtown (TX)
U of Idaho (ID)
U of Illinois at Chicago (IL)
The U of Kansas (KS)
U of Kentucky (KY)
U of King's Coll (NS, Canada)
U of La Verne (CA)
U of Louisiana at Monroe (LA)
U of Louisville (KY)
U of Maine (ME)
U of Mary Hardin-Baylor (TX)
U of Maryland, Baltimore County (MD)
U of Maryland, Coll Park (MD)
U of Maryland Eastern Shore (MD)
U of Mary Washington (VA)
U of Massachusetts Amherst (MA)
U of Massachusetts Boston (MA)
U of Massachusetts Dartmouth (MA)
U of Massachusetts Lowell (MA)
U of Memphis (TN)
U of Miami (FL)
U of Michigan (MI)
U of Michigan–Dearborn (MI)
U of Michigan–Flint (MI)
U of Minnesota, Duluth (MN)
U of Minnesota, Morris (MN)
U of Minnesota, Twin Cities Campus (MN)
U of Missouri (MO)
U of Missouri–St. Louis (MO)
U of Mobile (AL)
U of Montana (MT)
U of Montevallo (AL)
U of Mount Union (OH)
U of Nebraska at Kearney (NE)
U of Nebraska–Lincoln (NE)
U of Nevada, Las Vegas (NV)
U of Nevada, Reno (NV)
U of New England (ME)
U of New Hampshire (NH)
U of New Mexico (NM)
U of New Orleans (LA)
U of North Alabama (AL)
U of North Carolina at Asheville (NC)
The U of North Carolina at Chapel Hill (NC)
The U of North Carolina at Charlotte (NC)
The U of North Carolina at Greensboro (NC)
The U of North Carolina at Pembroke (NC)
The U of North Carolina Wilmington (NC)
U of North Dakota (ND)
U of Northern Colorado (CO)
U of Northern Iowa (IA)
U of North Florida (FL)
U of North Georgia (GA)

U of North Texas (TX)
U of Notre Dame (IN)
U of Oklahoma (OK)
U of Oregon (OR)
U of Pennsylvania (PA)
U of Pikeville (KY)
U of Pittsburgh (PA)
U of Pittsburgh at Bradford (PA)
U of Providence (MT)
U of Puget Sound (WA)
U of Regina (SK, Canada)
U of Rhode Island (RI)
U of Richmond (VA)
U of Saint Francis (IN)
U of St. Thomas (MN)
U of San Diego (CA)
U of San Francisco (CA)
U of Saskatchewan (SK, Canada)
U of Science and Arts of Oklahoma (OK)
The U of Scranton (PA)
U of Sioux Falls (SD)
U of South Alabama (AL)
U of South Carolina (SC)
U of South Carolina Aiken (SC)
U of South Dakota (SD)
U of Southern California (CA)
U of Southern Indiana (IN)
U of Southern Maine (ME)
U of Southern Mississippi (MS)
The U of Tampa (FL)
The U of Tennessee (TN)
The U of Tennessee at Martin (TN)
The U of Texas at Austin (TX)
The U of Texas at Dallas (TX)
The U of Texas at El Paso (TX)
The U of Texas at San Antonio (TX)
The U of Texas of the Permian Basin (TX)
The U of Texas Rio Grande Valley (TX)
U of the Fraser Valley (BC, Canada)
U of the Incarnate Word (TX)
U of the Pacific (CA)
The U of Toledo (OH)
U of Toronto (ON, Canada)
The U of Tulsa (OK)
U of Utah (UT)
U of Vermont (VT)
U of Virginia (VA)
The U of Virginia's Coll at Wise (VA)
U of Washington (WA)
U of Waterloo (ON, Canada)
The U of West Alabama (AL)
U of West Georgia (GA)
U of Wisconsin–Eau Claire (WI)
U of Wisconsin–La Crosse (WI)
U of Wisconsin–Madison (WI)
U of Wisconsin–Milwaukee (WI)
U of Wisconsin–Parkside (WI)
U of Wisconsin–River Falls (WI)
U of Wisconsin–Stevens Point (WI)
U of Wisconsin–Whitewater (WI)
U of Wyoming (WY)
Upper Iowa U (IA)
Ursuline Coll (OH)
Utah State U (UT)
Utica Coll (NY)
Valparaiso U (IN)
Vanderbilt U (TN)
Vanguard U of Southern California (CA)
Vassar Coll (NY)
Villanova U (PA)
Virginia Commonwealth U (VA)
Virginia Polytechnic Inst and State U (VA)
Virginia Wesleyan U (VA)
Wagner Coll (NY)
Wake Forest U (NC)
Walsh U (OH)
Wartburg Coll (IA)
Washington & Jefferson Coll (PA)
Washington Coll (MD)
Washington State U (WA)
Washington State U–Vancouver (WA)
Washington U in St. Louis (MO)
Wayland Baptist U (TX)
Waynesburg U (PA)
Wayne State Coll (NE)
Wayne State U (MI)
Weber State U (UT)
Webster U (MO)
Wellesley Coll (MA)

Wells Coll (NY)
Wesleyan U (CT)
West Chester U of Pennsylvania (PA)
Western Connecticut State U (CT)
Western Illinois U (IL)
Western Kentucky U (KY)
Western Michigan U (MI)
Western New England U (MA)
Western Oregon U (OR)
Western State Colorado U (CO)
Western Washington U (WA)
Westfield State U (MA)
Westminster Coll (PA)
Westminster Coll (UT)
Westmont Coll (CA)
West Texas A&M U (TX)
West Virginia State U (WV)
West Virginia U (WV)
West Virginia Wesleyan Coll (WV)
Wheaton Coll (IL)
Wheaton Coll (MA)
Whitman Coll (WA)
Whittier Coll (CA)
Whitworth U (WA)
Wichita State U (KS)
Widener U (PA)
Wilkes U (PA)
Willamette U (OR)
William Paterson U of New Jersey (NJ)
William Penn U (IA)
Williams Coll (MA)
Winona State U (MN)
Winthrop U (SC)
Wittenberg U (OH)
Wofford Coll (SC)
Worcester State U (MA)
Wright State U (OH)
Wright State U–Lake Campus (OH)
Xavier U of Louisiana (LA)
York Coll of Pennsylvania (PA)
Youngstown State U (OH)

SOCIOLOGY AND ANTHROPOLOGY
Albion Coll (MI)
American U of Beirut (Lebanon)
Centre Coll (KY)
Coll of Staten Island of the City U of New York (NY)
Fairfield U (CT)
Governors State U (IL)
Guilford Coll (NC)
High Point U (NC)
Keene State Coll (NH)
Lycoming Coll (PA)
Marlboro Coll (VT)
Millsaps Coll (MS)
Oakland U (MI)
Pace U (NY)
Rochester Inst of Technology (NY)
Roger Williams U (RI)
St. Olaf Coll (MN)
Spelman Coll (GA)
Transylvania U (KY)
U of Illinois at Springfield (IL)
U of Maine at Farmington (ME)
U of Massachusetts Dartmouth (MA)
U of Puget Sound (WA)
Ursinus Coll (PA)
Valdosta State U (GA)
Washington and Lee U (VA)
Wofford Coll (SC)

SOIL CHEMISTRY AND PHYSICS
The U of Tennessee (TN)

SOIL SCIENCE AND AGRONOMY
California Polytechnic State U, San Luis Obispo (CA)
Colorado State U (CO)
Michigan State U (MI)
New Mexico State U (NM)
North Dakota State U (ND)
Oklahoma State U (OK)
Penn State Abington (PA)
Penn State Altoona (PA)
Penn State Beaver (PA)
Penn State Berks (PA)
Penn State Brandywine (PA)
Penn State DuBois (PA)
Penn State Erie, The Behrend Coll (PA)

Penn State Fayette, The Eberly Campus (PA)
Penn State Greater Allegheny (PA)
Penn State Hazleton (PA)
Penn State Lehigh Valley (PA)
Penn State Mont Alto (PA)
Penn State New Kensington (PA)
Penn State Schuylkill (PA)
Penn State Shenango (PA)
Penn State Wilkes-Barre (PA)
Penn State Worthington Scranton (PA)
Penn State York (PA)
Purdue U (IN)
U of California, Davis (CA)
U of Florida (FL)
U of Georgia (GA)
U of Nebraska–Lincoln (NE)
U of Saskatchewan (SK, Canada)
The U of Tennessee at Martin (TN)
U of Wisconsin–Madison (WI)
U of Wisconsin–Stevens Point (WI)
Utah State U (UT)
Washington State U (WA)

SOIL SCIENCES RELATED
Brigham Young U (UT)
Clemson U (SC)
North Carolina State U (NC)
U of Hawaii at Manoa (HI)

SOUTH ASIAN LANGUAGES
Northwestern U (IL)
U of Chicago (IL)
U of Washington (WA)

SOUTHEAST ASIAN LANGUAGES
Harvard U (MA)

SPANISH
Abilene Christian U (TX)
Adams State U (CO)
Adelphi U (NY)
Agnes Scott Coll (GA)
Albion Coll (MI)
Albright Coll (PA)
Alfred U (NY)
Allegheny Coll (PA)
Alma Coll (MI)
American U (DC)
Amherst Coll (MA)
Anderson U (IN)
Anderson U (SC)
Andrews U (MI)
Angelo State U (TX)
Aquinas Coll (MI)
Arcadia U (PA)
Arizona State U at the Tempe campus (AZ)
Arizona State U at the West campus (AZ)
Asbury U (KY)
Ashland U (OH)
Assumption Coll (MA)
Auburn U (AL)
Auburn U at Montgomery (AL)
Augsburg U (MN)
Augustana Coll (IL)
Augustana U (SD)
Aurora U (IL)
Austin Coll (TX)
Azusa Pacific U (CA)
Baker U (KS)
Baldwin Wallace U (OH)
Ball State U (IN)
Baptist U of the Americas (TX)
Bard Coll (NY)
Barnard Coll (NY)
Barry U (FL)
Barton Coll (NC)
Baruch Coll of the City U of New York (NY)
Bates Coll (ME)
Baylor U (TX)
Bellarmine U (KY)
Belmont U (TN)
Beloit Coll (WI)
Bemidji State U (MN)
Benedictine Coll (KS)
Benedictine U (IL)
Bennington Coll (VT)
Bentley U (MA)
Berea Coll (KY)
Berry Coll (GA)
Bethel U (MN)
Binghamton U, State U of New York (NY)

Biola U (CA)
Birmingham-Southern Coll (AL)
Blackburn Coll (IL)
Black Hills State U (SD)
Blue Mountain Coll (MS)
Bluffton U (OH)
Bob Jones U (SC)
Boise State U (ID)
Boston Coll (MA)
Boston U (MA)
Bowling Green State U (OH)
Bradley U (IL)
Brescia U (KY)
Bridgewater Coll (VA)
Bridgewater State U (MA)
Brock U (ON, Canada)
Bryan Coll (TN)
Bryant U (RI)
Bryn Mawr Coll (PA)
Bucknell U (PA)
Buena Vista U (IA)
Buffalo State Coll, State U of New York (NY)
Butler U (IN)
Caldwell U (NJ)
California Baptist U (CA)
California Lutheran U (CA)
California State Polytechnic U, Pomona (CA)
California State U, Dominguez Hills (CA)
California State U, East Bay (CA)
California State U, Fullerton (CA)
California State U, Long Beach (CA)
California State U, Los Angeles (CA)
California State U, Monterey Bay (CA)
California State U, Northridge (CA)
California State U, Sacramento (CA)
California State U, San Bernardino (CA)
California State U, San Marcos (CA)
California State U, Stanislaus (CA)
California U of Pennsylvania (PA)
Calvin Coll (MI)
Canisius Coll (NY)
Capital U (OH)
Cardinal Stritch U (WI)
Carleton Coll (MN)
Carnegie Mellon U (PA)
Carroll Coll (MT)
Carroll U (WI)
Carson-Newman U (TN)
Carthage Coll (WI)
Case Western Reserve U (OH)
Catawba Coll (NC)
The Catholic U of America (DC)
Cedarville U (OH)
Central Connecticut State U (CT)
Central Michigan U (MI)
Centre Coll (KY)
Chapman U (CA)
Charleston Southern U (SC)
Chestnut Hill Coll (PA)
Christopher Newport U (VA)
City Coll of the City U of New York (NY)
Claremont McKenna Coll (CA)
Clarion U of Pennsylvania (PA)
Clark Atlanta U (GA)
Clarke U (IA)
Clark U (MA)
Clayton State U (GA)
Clemson U (SC)
Cleveland State U (OH)
Coe Coll (IA)
Colby Coll (ME)
Colgate U (NY)
The Coll at Brockport, State U of New York (NY)
Coll of Charleston (SC)
Coll of Coastal Georgia (GA)
The Coll of Idaho (ID)
Coll of Mount Saint Vincent (NY)
The Coll of New Jersey (NJ)
The Coll of New Rochelle (NY)
Coll of Saint Benedict (MN)
The Coll of St. Scholastica (MN)
Coll of Staten Island of the City U of New York (NY)
Coll of the Holy Cross (MA)
Coll of the Ozarks (MO)
The Coll of Wooster (OH)

The Colorado Coll (CO)
Colorado Mesa U (CO)
Columbia U (NY)
Columbus State U (GA)
Concordia U (QC, Canada)
Concordia U Chicago (IL)
Concordia U, Nebraska (NE)
Concordia U Wisconsin (WI)
Connecticut Coll (CT)
Converse Coll (SC)
Cornell Coll (IA)
Cornell U (NY)
Cornerstone U (MI)
Creighton U (NE)
Daemen Coll (NY)
Dartmouth Coll (NH)
Davidson Coll (NC)
Delaware State U (DE)
Denison U (OH)
DePaul U (IL)
DePauw U (IN)
DeSales U (PA)
Dickinson Coll (PA)
Dickinson State U (ND)
Doane U (NE)
Dominican U (IL)
Drew U (NJ)
Drury U (MO)
Duquesne U (PA)
Earlham Coll (IN)
Eastern Mennonite U (VA)
Eastern Michigan U (MI)
Eastern New Mexico U (NM)
Eastern U (PA)
Eastern Washington U (WA)
East Stroudsburg U of
  Pennsylvania (PA)
Eckerd Coll (FL)
Edgewood Coll (WI)
Elizabethtown Coll (PA)
Elmhurst Coll (IL)
Elms Coll (MA)
Elon U (NC)
Emmanuel Coll (MA)
Emory & Henry Coll (VA)
Emory U (GA)
Evangel U (MO)
Fairfield U (CT)
Fairleigh Dickinson U, Florham
  Campus (NJ)
Fairleigh Dickinson U, Metropolitan
  Campus (NJ)
Fayetteville State U (NC)
Ferris State U (MI)
Flagler Coll (FL)
Florida Atlantic U (FL)
Florida Intl U (FL)
Florida Southern Coll (FL)
Florida State U (FL)
Fordham U (NY)
Fort Lewis Coll (CO)
Framingham State U (MA)
Franklin & Marshall Coll (PA)
Franklin Coll (IN)
Friends U (KS)
Furman U (SC)
Georgetown Coll (KY)
Georgetown U (DC)
The George Washington U (DC)
Georgian Court U (NJ)
Georgia Southern U–Armstrong
  Campus (GA)
Georgia State U (GA)
Gettysburg Coll (PA)
Gonzaga U (WA)
Gordon Coll (MA)
Goshen Coll (IN)
Grand Valley State U (MI)
Grand View U (IA)
Greensboro Coll (NC)
Greenville U (IL)
Grinnell Coll (IA)
Grove City Coll (PA)
Guilford Coll (NC)
Gustavus Adolphus Coll (MN)
Hamline U (MN)
Hampden-Sydney Coll (VA)
Harding U (AR)
Hardin-Simmons U (TX)
Hartwick Coll (NY)
Haverford Coll (PA)
Heidelberg U (OH)
Hendrix Coll (AR)
High Point U (NC)
Hillsdale Coll (MI)
Hiram Coll (OH)

Hobart and William Smith Colls
  (NY)
Hofstra U (NY)
Hollins U (VA)
Holy Names U (CA)
Hood Coll (MD)
Hope Coll (MI)
Houston Baptist U (TX)
Howard Payne U (TX)
Humboldt State U (CA)
Hunter Coll of the City U of New
  York (NY)
Idaho State U (ID)
Illinois Coll (IL)
Illinois State U (IL)
Illinois Wesleyan U (IL)
Immaculata U (PA)
Indiana U Bloomington (IN)
Indiana U East (IN)
Indiana U Northwest (IN)
Indiana U of Pennsylvania (PA)
Indiana U–Purdue U Indianapolis
  (IN)
Indiana U South Bend (IN)
Indiana U Southeast (IN)
Indiana Wesleyan U (IN)
Inter American U of Puerto Rico,
  Metropolitan Campus (PR)
Iona Coll (NY)
Iowa State U of Science and
  Technology (IA)
Ithaca Coll (NY)
Jacksonville U (FL)
John Carroll U (OH)
John Jay Coll of Criminal Justice of
  the City U of New York (NY)
Johns Hopkins U (MD)
Johnson C. Smith U (NC)
Juniata Coll (PA)
Kalamazoo Coll (MI)
Kean U (NJ)
Keene State Coll (NH)
Kent State U (OH)
Kentucky State U (KY)
Kenyon Coll (OH)
King's Coll (PA)
King U (TN)
Knox Coll (IL)
Kutztown U of Pennsylvania (PA)
Lafayette Coll (PA)
LaGrange Coll (GA)
La Salle U (PA)
La Sierra U (CA)
Lawrence U (WI)
Lebanon Valley Coll (PA)
Lee U (TN)
Lehigh U (PA)
Lehman Coll of the City U of New
  York (NY)
Le Moyne Coll (NY)
Lenoir-Rhyne U (NC)
Lewis U (IL)
Liberty U (VA)
Lincoln U (PA)
Lindenwood U (MO)
Linfield Coll (OR)
Lipscomb U (TN)
Lock Haven U of Pennsylvania (PA)
Long Island U–LIU Post (NY)
Loras Coll (IA)
Louisiana State U and A&M Coll
  (LA)
Loyola Marymount U (CA)
Loyola U Chicago (IL)
Loyola U New Orleans (LA)
Luther Coll (IA)
Lycoming Coll (PA)
Lynchburg Coll (VA)
Lyon Coll (AR)
Macalester Coll (MN)
Madonna U (MI)
Manchester U (IN)
Manhattan Coll (NY)
Manhattanville Coll (NY)
Marian U (IN)
Marian U (WI)
Marietta Coll (OH)
Marist Coll (NY)
Marlboro Coll (VT)
Marquette U (WI)
Maryville Coll (TN)
Marywood U (PA)
McDaniel Coll (MD)
McKendree U (IL)
McMurry U (TX)
McPherson Coll (KS)
Mercer U, Macon (GA)

Mercy Coll (NY)
Meredith Coll (NC)
Merrimack Coll (MA)
Messiah Coll (PA)
Miami U (OH)
Michigan State U (MI)
Middlebury Coll (VT)
Millersville U of Pennsylvania (PA)
Milligan Coll (TN)
Millikin U (IL)
Millsaps Coll (MS)
Mills Coll (CA)
Minnesota State U Moorhead (MN)
Minot State U (ND)
Missouri State U (MO)
Monmouth Coll (IL)
Montclair State U (NJ)
Moravian Coll (PA)
Morehead State U (KY)
Morehouse Coll (GA)
Morningside Coll (IA)
Mount Holyoke Coll (MA)
Mount Mary U (WI)
Mount Saint Mary Coll (NY)
Mount Saint Mary's U (CA)
Mount St. Mary's U (MD)
Mount Vernon Nazarene U (OH)
Muhlenberg Coll (PA)
Murray State U (KY)
Muskingum U (OH)
National U (CA)
Nazareth Coll of Rochester (NY)
Newberry Coll (SC)
New Coll of Florida (FL)
New Jersey City U (NJ)
New Mexico Highlands U (NM)
New York U (NY)
Niagara U (NY)
North Carolina Central U (NC)
North Carolina State U (NC)
North Central Coll (IL)
North Dakota State U (ND)
Northeastern State U (OK)
Northeastern U (MA)
Northern Arizona U (AZ)
Northern Illinois U (IL)
Northern Kentucky U (KY)
Northern Michigan U (MI)
Northern State U (SD)
North Greenville U (SC)
Northwestern Coll (IA)
Northwestern U (IL)
Northwest Missouri State U (MO)
Northwest Nazarene U (ID)
Oakland U (MI)
Oberlin Coll (OH)
Occidental Coll (CA)
Oglethorpe U (GA)
Ohio Northern U (OH)
The Ohio State U (OH)
Ohio U (OH)
Ohio Wesleyan U (OH)
Oklahoma Baptist U (OK)
Oklahoma Christian U (OK)
Oklahoma City U (OK)
Oklahoma State U (OK)
Olivet Nazarene U (IL)
Oral Roberts U (OK)
Oregon State U (OR)
Otterbein U (OH)
Ouachita Baptist U (AR)
Our Lady of the Lake U (TX)
Pace U (NY)
Pace U, Pleasantville Campus (NY)
Penn State Abington (PA)
Penn State Altoona (PA)
Penn State Beaver (PA)
Penn State Berks (PA)
Penn State Brandywine (PA)
Penn State DuBois (PA)
Penn State Erie, The Behrend Coll
  (PA)
Penn State Fayette, The Eberly
  Campus (PA)
Penn State Greater Allegheny (PA)
Penn State Hazleton (PA)
Penn State Lehigh Valley (PA)
Penn State Mont Alto (PA)
Penn State New Kensington (PA)
Penn State Schuylkill (PA)
Penn State Shenango (PA)
Penn State U Park (PA)
Penn State Wilkes-Barre (PA)
Penn State Worthington Scranton
  (PA)
Penn State York (PA)
Pepperdine U, Malibu (CA)

Piedmont Coll (GA)
Pittsburg State U (KS)
Pitzer Coll (CA)
Point Loma Nazarene U (CA)
Pomona Coll (CA)
Portland State U (OR)
Presbyterian Coll (SC)
Princeton U (NJ)
Principia Coll (IL)
Providence Coll (RI)
Purchase Coll, State U of New York
  (NY)
Queens Coll of the City U of New
  York (NY)
Quinnipiac U (CT)
Ramapo Coll of New Jersey (NJ)
Randolph Coll (VA)
Randolph-Macon Coll (VA)
Reed Coll (OR)
Regis U (CO)
Rhode Island Coll (RI)
Rhodes Coll (TN)
Rice U (TX)
Rider U (NJ)
Ripon Coll (WI)
Rivier U (NH)
Roanoke Coll (VA)
Roberts Wesleyan Coll (NY)
Rockford U (IL)
Rockhurst U (MO)
Rollins Coll (FL)
Rosemont Coll (PA)
Rutgers U–Camden (NJ)
Rutgers U–Newark (NJ)
Rutgers U–New Brunswick (NJ)
Sacred Heart U (CT)
Saginaw Valley State U (MI)
St. Ambrose U (IA)
Saint Anselm Coll (NH)
St. Bonaventure U (NY)
St. Catherine U (MN)
Saint Francis U (PA)
St. John Fisher Coll (NY)
Saint John's U (MN)
St. John's U (NY)
St. Joseph's Coll, Long Island
  Campus (NY)
St. Joseph's Coll, New York (NY)
Saint Joseph's U (PA)
St. Lawrence U (NY)
Saint Louis U (MO)
Saint Louis U–Madrid Campus
  (Spain)
Saint Mary's Coll of California (CA)
St. Mary's U (TX)
Saint Mary's U of Minnesota (MN)
Saint Michael's Coll (VT)
St. Norbert Coll (WI)
St. Olaf Coll (MN)
Saint Peter's U (NJ)
St. Thomas Aquinas Coll (NY)
St. Thomas U (NB, Canada)
Saint Vincent Coll (PA)
Salisbury U (MD)
Salve Regina U (RI)
Samford U (AL)
Sam Houston State U (TX)
San Diego State U (CA)
San Francisco State U (CA)
Santa Clara U (CA)
Sarah Lawrence Coll (NY)
Scripps Coll (CA)
Seattle U (WA)
Seton Hill U (PA)
Sewanee: The U of the South (TN)
Shenandoah U (VA)
Shepherd U (WV)
Shippensburg U of Pennsylvania
  (PA)
Shorter U (GA)
Siena Coll (NY)
Simmons Coll (MA)
Simpson Coll (IA)
Skidmore Coll (NY)
Slippery Rock U of Pennsylvania
  (PA)
Smith Coll (MA)
Sonoma State U (CA)
Southeastern Louisiana U (LA)
Southeastern Oklahoma State U
  (OK)
Southern Adventist U (TN)
Southern Arkansas U–Magnolia
  (AR)
Southern Methodist U (TX)
Southern Utah U (UT)
Southwest Baptist U (MO)

Southwestern U (TX)
Spelman Coll (GA)
Spring Hill Coll (AL)
Stanford U (CA)
State U of New York at Fredonia
  (NY)
State U of New York at New Paltz
  (NY)
State U of New York at Oswego
  (NY)
State U of New York at Plattsburgh
  (NY)
State U of New York Coll at
  Cortland (NY)
State U of New York Coll at
  Geneseo (NY)
State U of New York Coll at Old
  Westbury (NY)
State U of New York Coll at
  Oneonta (NY)
State U of New York Coll at
  Potsdam (NY)
Stetson U (FL)
Stonehill Coll (MA)
Stony Brook U, State U of New York
  (NY)
Suffolk U (MA)
Susquehanna U (PA)
Sweet Briar Coll (VA)
Syracuse U (NY)
Tarleton State U (TX)
Taylor U (IN)
Temple U (PA)
Tennessee Technological U (TN)
Tennessee Wesleyan U (TN)
Texas A&M Intl U (TX)
Texas A&M U (TX)
Texas A&M U–Commerce (TX)
Texas A&M U–Corpus Christi (TX)
Texas A&M U–Kingsville (TX)
Texas Christian U (TX)
Texas Lutheran U (TX)
Texas State U (TX)
Texas Tech U (TX)
Transylvania U (KY)
Trinity Christian Coll (IL)
Trinity U (TX)
Troy U (AL)
Truman State U (MO)
Tufts U (MA)
Tulane U (LA)
Union Coll (NY)
Union U (TN)
United States Military Acad (NY)
U at Albany, State U of New York
  (NY)
U at Buffalo, the State U of New
  York (NY)
The U of Akron (OH)
The U of Alabama (AL)
The U of Arizona (AZ)
U of Arkansas (AR)
U of California, Davis (CA)
U of California, Irvine (CA)
U of California, Los Angeles (CA)
U of California, Riverside (CA)
U of California, San Diego (CA)
U of California, Santa Barbara (CA)
U of California, Santa Cruz (CA)
U of Central Arkansas (AR)
U of Central Florida (FL)
U of Central Missouri (MO)
U of Central Oklahoma (OK)
U of Cincinnati (OH)
U of Colorado Boulder (CO)
U of Colorado Colorado Springs
  (CO)
U of Colorado Denver (CO)
U of Dallas (TX)
U of Dayton (OH)
U of Denver (CO)
U of Evansville (IN)
The U of Findlay (OH)
U of Florida (FL)
U of Georgia (GA)
U of Guelph (ON, Canada)
U of Hawaii at Manoa (HI)
U of Houston (TX)
U of Houston–Downtown (TX)
U of Idaho (ID)
U of Illinois at Chicago (IL)
U of Jamestown (ND)
The U of Kansas (KS)
U of Kentucky (KY)
U of King's Coll (NS, Canada)
U of La Verne (CA)
U of Louisville (KY)

U of Maine (ME)
U of Mary Hardin-Baylor (TX)
U of Maryland, Coll Park (MD)
U of Massachusetts Amherst (MA)
U of Massachusetts Boston (MA)
U of Massachusetts Dartmouth (MA)
U of Miami (FL)
U of Michigan (MI)
U of Michigan–Dearborn (MI)
U of Michigan–Flint (MI)
U of Minnesota, Duluth (MN)
U of Minnesota, Morris (MN)
U of Minnesota, Twin Cities Campus (MN)
U of Missouri (MO)
U of Montana (MT)
U of Mount Union (OH)
U of Nebraska at Kearney (NE)
U of Nebraska–Lincoln (NE)
U of Nevada, Las Vegas (NV)
U of Nevada, Reno (NV)
U of New Hampshire (NH)
U of New Mexico (NM)
U of North Alabama (AL)
U of North Carolina at Asheville (NC)
The U of North Carolina at Charlotte (NC)
The U of North Carolina at Greensboro (NC)
The U of North Carolina at Pembroke (NC)
The U of North Carolina Wilmington (NC)
U of North Dakota (ND)
U of Northern Colorado (CO)
U of Northern Iowa (IA)
U of North Florida (FL)
U of North Texas (TX)
U of Notre Dame (IN)
U of Oklahoma (OK)
U of Oregon (OR)
U of Pennsylvania (PA)
U of Pikeville (KY)
U of Pittsburgh (PA)
U of Pittsburgh at Greensburg (PA)
U of Puget Sound (WA)
U of Regina (SK, Canada)
U of Rhode Island (RI)
U of Richmond (VA)
U of Rochester (NY)
U of Saint Joseph (CT)
U of St. Thomas (MN)
U of St. Thomas (TX)
U of San Diego (CA)
U of San Francisco (CA)
U of Saskatchewan (SK, Canada)
The U of Scranton (PA)
U of Sioux Falls (SD)
U of South Carolina (SC)
U of South Dakota (SD)
U of Southern California (CA)
U of Southern Indiana (IN)
The U of Tampa (FL)
The U of Tennessee (TN)
The U of Tennessee at Martin (TN)
The U of Texas at Austin (TX)
The U of Texas at El Paso (TX)
The U of Texas at San Antonio (TX)
The U of Texas of the Permian Basin (TX)
The U of Texas Rio Grande Valley (TX)
U of the Incarnate Word (TX)
U of the Pacific (CA)
The U of Toledo (OH)
U of Toronto (ON, Canada)
The U of Tulsa (OK)
U of Utah (UT)
U of Vermont (VT)
U of Virginia (VA)
The U of Virginia's Coll at Wise (VA)
U of Washington (WA)
U of Waterloo (ON, Canada)
U of Wisconsin–Eau Claire (WI)
U of Wisconsin–La Crosse (WI)
U of Wisconsin–Madison (WI)
U of Wisconsin–Milwaukee (WI)
U of Wisconsin–Parkside (WI)
U of Wisconsin–Stevens Point (WI)
U of Wisconsin–Whitewater (WI)
U of Wyoming (WY)
Ursinus Coll (PA)
Utah State U (UT)
Utah Valley U (UT)

Valdosta State U (GA)
Valley City State U (ND)
Valparaiso U (IN)
Vanderbilt U (TN)
Vassar Coll (NY)
Villanova U (PA)
Virginia Polytechnic Inst and State U (VA)
Virginia Wesleyan U (VA)
Wabash Coll (IN)
Wagner Coll (NY)
Wake Forest U (NC)
Walsh U (OH)
Wartburg Coll (IA)
Washington & Jefferson Coll (PA)
Washington and Lee U (VA)
Washington Coll (MD)
Washington State U (WA)
Washington U in St. Louis (MO)
Wayland Baptist U (TX)
Wayne State Coll (NE)
Weber State U (UT)
Webster U (MO)
Wellesley Coll (MA)
Wells Coll (NY)
West Chester U of Pennsylvania (PA)
Western Connecticut State U (CT)
Western Kentucky U (KY)
Western Michigan U (MI)
Western Oregon U (OR)
Western State Colorado U (CO)
Western Washington U (WA)
Westfield State U (MA)
Westminster Coll (PA)
Westmont Coll (CA)
West Texas A&M U (TX)
Wheaton Coll (IL)
Whitman Coll (WA)
Whittier Coll (CA)
Whitworth U (WA)
Widener U (PA)
Wilkes U (PA)
Willamette U (OR)
William Jewell Coll (MO)
William Paterson U of New Jersey (NJ)
Williams Coll (MA)
Winona State U (MN)
Wisconsin Lutheran Coll (WI)
Wittenberg U (OH)
Wofford Coll (SC)
Worcester State U (MA)
Wright State U (OH)
Xavier U of Louisiana (LA)
York Coll of Pennsylvania (PA)
Youngstown State U (OH)

SPANISH AND IBERIAN STUDIES
Arcadia U (PA)
Austin Coll (TX)
Bard Coll (NY)
Bowdoin Coll (ME)
Brandeis U (MA)
Coe Coll (IA)
Columbia U (NY)
Emory & Henry Coll (VA)
Fordham U (NY)
New York U (NY)
Saint Louis U–Madrid Campus (Spain)
Wabash Coll (IN)
Wesleyan U (CT)

SPANISH LANGUAGE TEACHER EDUCATION
Abilene Christian U (TX)
Adams State U (CO)
Albion Coll (MI)
Anderson U (IN)
Ashland U (OH)
Auburn U (AL)
Augustana Coll (IL)
Aurora U (IL)
Ball State U (IN)
Baylor U (TX)
Bethel U (MN)
Blackburn Coll (IL)
Blue Mountain Coll (MS)
Bob Jones U (SC)
Boise State U (ID)
Brigham Young U–Idaho (ID)
Bryan Coll (TN)
Buena Vista U (IA)
California Lutheran U (CA)
Calvin Coll (MI)
Canisius Coll (NY)

Carroll Coll (MT)
Carroll U (WI)
The Catholic U of America (DC)
Cedarville U (OH)
Central Michigan U (MI)
Charleston Southern U (SC)
Coll of Saint Mary (NE)
Coll of Staten Island of the City U of New York (NY)
Coll of the Ozarks (MO)
Concordia U Wisconsin (WI)
Cornerstone U (MI)
Daemen Coll (NY)
Delaware State U (DE)
Eastern Michigan U (MI)
Eastern Washington U (WA)
Edgewood Coll (WI)
Elmhurst Coll (IL)
Evangel U (MO)
Franklin Coll (IN)
Friends U (KS)
Goshen Coll (IN)
Grand Valley State U (MI)
Greensboro Coll (NC)
Greenville U (IL)
Grove City Coll (PA)
Harding U (AR)
Hardin-Simmons U (TX)
Hofstra U (NY)
Holy Family U (PA)
Hope Coll (MI)
Houston Baptist U (TX)
Howard Payne U (TX)
Immaculata U (PA)
Indiana U–Purdue U Indianapolis (IN)
Indiana U South Bend (IN)
Indiana Wesleyan U (IN)
Inter American U of Puerto Rico, Aguadilla Campus (PR)
Inter American U of Puerto Rico, Barranquitas Campus (PR)
Inter American U of Puerto Rico, Metropolitan Campus (PR)
Inter American U of Puerto Rico, San Germán Campus (PR)
Iona Coll (NY)
Ithaca Coll (NY)
Lee U (TN)
Le Moyne Coll (NY)
Lewis U (IL)
Lindenwood U (MO)
Lipscomb U (TN)
Long Island U–LIU Brooklyn (NY)
Long Island U–LIU Post (NY)
Louisiana Coll (LA)
Lubbock Christian U (TX)
Manchester U (IN)
Manhattanville Coll (NY)
Marian U (WI)
Marist Coll (NY)
Martin Luther Coll (MN)
Maryville Coll (TN)
Marywood U (PA)
McMurry U (TX)
Merrimack Coll (MA)
Messiah Coll (PA)
Miami U (OH)
Michigan State U (MI)
Minnesota State U Moorhead (MN)
Minot State U (ND)
Missouri Western State U (MO)
Morningside Coll (IA)
Mount Mary U (WI)
Mount Vernon Nazarene U (OH)
New York U (NY)
Niagara U (NY)
North Dakota State U (ND)
Northeastern State U (OK)
Northern Michigan U (MI)
Northern State U (SD)
North Greenville U (SC)
Northwest Missouri State U (MO)
Northwest Nazarene U (ID)
Ohio Northern U (OH)
Ohio U (OH)
Ohio Wesleyan U (OH)
Oklahoma Baptist U (OK)
Olivet Nazarene U (IL)
Oral Roberts U (OK)
Our Lady of the Lake U (TX)
Pace U (NY)
Piedmont Coll (GA)
Pittsburg State U (KS)
Providence Coll (RI)
Queens Coll of the City U of New York (NY)

Rhode Island Coll (RI)
Roberts Wesleyan Coll (NY)
Saginaw Valley State U (MI)
St. Ambrose U (IA)
St. Catherine U (MN)
St. John Fisher Coll (NY)
St. John's U (NY)
St. Joseph's Coll, Long Island Campus (NY)
St. Joseph's Coll, New York (NY)
Saint Joseph's U (PA)
Saint Mary's U of Minnesota (MN)
Salve Regina U (RI)
Southern Utah U (UT)
Spring Hill Coll (AL)
State U of New York at New Paltz (NY)
State U of New York Coll at Cortland (NY)
State U of New York Coll at Old Westbury (NY)
State U of New York Coll at Oneonta (NY)
State U of New York Coll at Potsdam (NY)
Syracuse U (NY)
Taylor U (IN)
Trinity Christian Coll (IL)
The U of Akron (OH)
U of Central Oklahoma (OK)
U of Evansville (IN)
The U of Findlay (OH)
U of Illinois at Chicago (IL)
U of Maine (ME)
U of Mary Hardin-Baylor (TX)
U of Michigan–Flint (MI)
U of Nebraska–Lincoln (NE)
U of Nevada, Las Vegas (NV)
The U of North Carolina at Greensboro (NC)
U of St. Thomas (MN)
U of Sioux Falls (SD)
U of South Dakota (SD)
The U of Tennessee at Martin (TN)
U of Wisconsin–Milwaukee (WI)
U of Wisconsin–Stevens Point (WI)
U of Wisconsin–Whitewater (WI)
Utah Valley U (UT)
Valley City State U (ND)
Valparaiso U (IN)
Washington U in St. Louis (MO)
Weber State U (UT)
Western Illinois U (IL)
Western Michigan U (MI)
Western State Colorado U (CO)
Western Washington U (WA)
Whitworth U (WA)
Widener U (PA)
Winona State U (MN)
Xavier U of Louisiana (LA)
York Coll of Pennsylvania (PA)
Youngstown State U (OH)

SPECIAL EDUCATION
Adams State U (CO)
Alabama State U (AL)
Alma Coll (MI)
Anderson U (SC)
Arizona State U at the Polytechnic campus (AZ)
Arizona State U at the Tempe campus (AZ)
Arizona State U at the West campus (AZ)
Asbury U (KY)
Ashland U (OH)
Athens State U (AL)
Auburn U (AL)
Auburn U at Montgomery (AL)
Augsburg U (MN)
Augustana U (SD)
Aurora U (IL)
Austin Peay State U (TN)
Avila U (MO)
Barry U (FL)
Barton Coll (NC)
Baylor U (TX)
Bellarmine U (KY)
Benedictine Coll (KS)
Benedictine U (IL)
Bennett Coll (NC)
Bethany Lutheran Coll (MN)
Bethel Coll (IN)
Bethel U (TN)
Black Hills State U (SD)
Bloomsburg U of Pennsylvania (PA)
Bluffton U (OH)

Boise State U (ID)
Boston U (MA)
Bowie State U (MD)
Bowling Green State U (OH)
Brescia U (KY)
Bridgewater State U (MA)
Brigham Young U (UT)
Buena Vista U (IA)
Buffalo State Coll, State U of New York (NY)
California U of Pennsylvania (PA)
Calvin Coll (MI)
Capital U (OH)
Caribbean U (PR)
Carson-Newman U (TN)
Carthage Coll (WI)
Cedarville U (OH)
Central State U (OH)
Christian Brothers U (TN)
Clarion U of Pennsylvania (PA)
Clemson U (SC)
Cleveland State U (OH)
Coastal Carolina U (SC)
The Coll at Brockport, State U of New York (NY)
Coll of Charleston (SC)
The Coll of New Jersey (NJ)
The Coll of New Rochelle (NY)
The Coll of Saint Rose (NY)
Colorado Christian U (CO)
Columbia Coll (SC)
Columbus State U (GA)
Concordia U Chicago (IL)
Concordia U, Nebraska (NE)
Concord U (WV)
Converse Coll (SC)
Curry Coll (MA)
Daemen Coll (NY)
Daytona State Coll (FL)
Delaware State U (DE)
DePaul U (IL)
Doane U (NE)
Dominican Coll (NY)
East Carolina U (NC)
East Central U (OK)
Eastern Nazarene Coll (MA)
Eastern New Mexico U (NM)
Eastern Washington U (WA)
East Tennessee State U (TN)
Elmhurst Coll (IL)
Elms Coll (MA)
Elon U (NC)
Evangel U (MO)
Felician U (NJ)
Fitchburg State U (MA)
Flagler Coll (FL)
Florida Atlantic U (FL)
Florida Gulf Coast U (FL)
Florida Intl U (FL)
Florida State U (FL)
Geneva Coll (PA)
Georgia Coll & State U (GA)
Georgia Gwinnett Coll (GA)
Georgia Southern U (GA)
Georgia Southern U–Armstrong Campus (GA)
Georgia Southwestern State U (GA)
Gonzaga U (WA)
Goshen Coll (IN)
Graceland U (IA)
Grand Valley State U (MI)
Granite State Coll (NH)
Greensboro Coll (NC)
Greenville U (IL)
Grove City Coll (PA)
Hampton U (VA)
Heidelberg U (OH)
High Point U (NC)
Holy Family U (PA)
Houston Baptist U (TX)
Idaho State U (ID)
Illinois State U (IL)
Indiana State U (IN)
Indiana U Bloomington (IN)
Indiana U of Pennsylvania (PA)
Indiana U South Bend (IN)
Indiana U Southeast (IN)
Indiana Wesleyan U (IN)
Inter American U of Puerto Rico, Barranquitas Campus (PR)
Inter American U of Puerto Rico, Fajardo Campus (PR)
Inter American U of Puerto Rico, Metropolitan Campus (PR)
Inter American U of Puerto Rico, San Germán Campus (PR)

Jackson State U (MS)
Jacksonville U (FL)
John Carroll U (OH)
Kean U (NJ)
Kent State U (OH)
Kutztown U of Pennsylvania (PA)
Langston U (OK)
Lebanon Valley Coll (PA)
Lee U (TN)
Le Moyne Coll (NY)
Lesley U (MA)
Lewis U (IL)
Liberty U (VA)
Lindenwood U (MO)
Lipscomb U (TN)
Loyola U Chicago (IL)
Manchester U (IN)
Manhattan Coll (NY)
Mansfield U of Pennsylvania (PA)
Marian U (IN)
Martin Luther Coll (MN)
Marymount U (VA)
Marywood U (PA)
McPherson Coll (KS)
Medgar Evers Coll of the City U of New York (NY)
Mercyhurst U (PA)
Merrimack Coll (MA)
Metropolitan State U of Denver (CO)
Miami Dade Coll (FL)
Miami U (OH)
Michigan State U (MI)
Middle Tennessee State U (TN)
Millersville U of Pennsylvania (PA)
Minnesota State U Moorhead (MN)
Mississippi State U (MS)
Missouri State U (MO)
Missouri Valley Coll (MO)
Morehead State U (KY)
Morningside Coll (IA)
Mount Marty Coll (SD)
Mount St. Joseph (OH)
Mount Vernon Nazarene U (OH)
Murray State U (KY)
Muskingum U (OH)
National Louis U (IL)
National U (CA)
Nazareth Coll of Rochester (NY)
New Jersey City U (NJ)
New Mexico Highlands U (NM)
New Mexico State U (NM)
New York U (NY)
Niagara U (NY)
North Carolina Wesleyan Coll (NC)
Northern Arizona U (AZ)
Northern Kentucky U (KY)
Northern Michigan U (MI)
Northern State U (SD)
Northern Vermont U–Lyndon (VT)
Northwestern Oklahoma State U (OK)
Oakland City U (IN)
Ohio Dominican U (OH)
The Ohio State U (OH)
Ohio U (OH)
Oklahoma Baptist U (OK)
Oklahoma City U (OK)
Olivet Nazarene U (IL)
Oral Roberts U (OK)
Our Lady of the Lake U (TX)
Pace U (NY)
Pace U, Pleasantville Campus (NY)
Penn State Abington (PA)
Penn State Altoona (PA)
Penn State Beaver (PA)
Penn State Berks (PA)
Penn State Brandywine (PA)
Penn State DuBois (PA)
Penn State Erie, The Behrend Coll (PA)
Penn State Fayette, The Eberly Campus (PA)
Penn State Greater Allegheny (PA)
Penn State Hazleton (PA)
Penn State Lehigh Valley (PA)
Penn State Mont Alto (PA)
Penn State New Kensington (PA)
Penn State Schuylkill (PA)
Penn State Shenango (PA)
Penn State York Park (PA)
Penn State Wilkes-Barre (PA)
Penn State Worthington Scranton (PA)
Penn State York (PA)
Pfeiffer U (NC)
Providence Coll (RI)

Rhode Island Coll (RI)
Rivier U (NH)
Roberts Wesleyan Coll (NY)
Rockford U (IL)
Roosevelt U (IL)
Rowan U (NJ)
Saginaw Valley State U (MI)
St. Bonaventure U (NY)
Saint Francis U (PA)
St. John Fisher Coll (NY)
St. John's U (NY)
St. Joseph's Coll, Long Island Campus (NY)
St. Joseph's Coll, New York (NY)
Saint Joseph's U (PA)
Saint Martin's U (WA)
Saint Mary-of-the-Woods Coll (IN)
St. Thomas Aquinas Coll (NY)
Salve Regina U (RI)
Sam Houston State U (TX)
Seattle Pacific U (WA)
Shawnee State U (OH)
Simmons Coll (MA)
Slippery Rock U of Pennsylvania (PA)
Southeastern U (FL)
Southeast Missouri State U (MO)
Southern Illinois U Carbondale (IL)
Southern Illinois U Edwardsville (IL)
State U of New York at Plattsburgh (NY)
State U of New York Coll at Geneseo (NY)
State U of New York Coll at Old Westbury (NY)
Stonehill Coll (MA)
Tennessee Technological U (TN)
Texas A&M Intl U (TX)
Texas A&M U–Commerce (TX)
Texas Christian U (TX)
Towson U (MD)
Trevecca Nazarene U (TN)
Trinity Christian Coll (IL)
Tusculum Coll (TN)
Union U (TN)
Université de Sherbrooke (QC, Canada)
The U of Akron (OH)
The U of Alabama (AL)
The U of Arizona (AZ)
U of Arkansas (AR)
U of Central Florida (FL)
U of Central Missouri (MO)
U of Central Oklahoma (OK)
U of Cincinnati (OH)
U of Dayton (OH)
U of Evansville (IN)
The U of Findlay (OH)
U of Florida (FL)
U of Georgia (GA)
U of Guam (GU)
U of Hartford (CT)
U of Hawaii at Manoa (HI)
U of Kentucky (KY)
U of Maine at Farmington (ME)
U of Maryland, Coll Park (MD)
U of Maryland Eastern Shore (MD)
U of Memphis (TN)
U of Michigan–Dearborn (MI)
U of Minnesota, Twin Cities Campus (MN)
U of Mount Union (OH)
U of Nebraska at Kearney (NE)
U of Nevada, Las Vegas (NV)
U of New Mexico (NM)
The U of North Carolina at Charlotte (NC)
The U of North Carolina at Greensboro (NC)
The U of North Carolina at Pembroke (NC)
The U of North Carolina Wilmington (NC)
U of Northern Colorado (CO)
U of North Florida (FL)
U of North Georgia (GA)
U of Oklahoma (OK)
U of Providence (MT)
U of St. Francis (IL)
U of Saint Francis (IN)
U of Saint Joseph (CT)
U of South Alabama (AL)
U of South Carolina Aiken (SC)
U of South Dakota (SD)
U of Southern Mississippi (MS)
The U of Tennessee (TN)

The U of Tennessee at Chattanooga (TN)
The U of Tennessee at Martin (TN)
The U of Texas at Austin (TX)
The U of Texas at San Antonio (TX)
U of the Pacific (CA)
The U of Toledo (OH)
U of Utah (UT)
The U of West Alabama (AL)
U of West Georgia (GA)
U of Wisconsin–Eau Claire (WI)
U of Wisconsin–Madison (WI)
U of Wisconsin–Milwaukee (WI)
U of Wisconsin–Parkside (WI)
U of Wisconsin–Stevens Point (WI)
U of Wisconsin–Stout (WI)
U of Wisconsin–Whitewater (WI)
U of Wyoming (WY)
Ursuline Coll (OH)
Utah State U (UT)
Valdosta State U (GA)
Vanderbilt U (TN)
Vincennes U (IN)
Virginia Wesleyan U (VA)
Walsh U (OH)
Waynesburg U (PA)
Wayne State Coll (NE)
Wayne State U (MI)
Weber State U (UT)
Webster U (MO)
West Chester U of Pennsylvania (PA)
Western Illinois U (IL)
Western Kentucky U (KY)
Western Washington U (WA)
Westfield State U (MA)
Westminster Coll (UT)
West Virginia Wesleyan Coll (WV)
Whitworth U (WA)
Widener U (PA)
William Paterson U of New Jersey (NJ)
William Penn U (IA)
William Woods U (MO)
Winona State U (MN)
Winthrop U (SC)
Wisconsin Lutheran Coll (WI)
Youngstown State U (OH)

SPECIAL EDUCATION–EARLY CHILDHOOD
Aurora U (IL)
Bowling Green State U (OH)
Canisius Coll (NY)
Cazenovia Coll (NY)
Clarion U of Pennsylvania (PA)
Daemen Coll (NY)
Daytona State Coll (FL)
Delaware State U (DE)
Eastern Washington U (WA)
East Stroudsburg U of Pennsylvania (PA)
Edgewood Coll (WI)
Harding U (AR)
Hope Coll (MI)
Indiana U of Pennsylvania (PA)
Inter American U of Puerto Rico, Aguadilla Campus (PR)
Judson U (IL)
Juniata Coll (PA)
Lee U (TN)
Lewis U (IL)
Lindenwood U (MO)
Lock Haven U of Pennsylvania (PA)
Missouri Baptist U (MO)
Roberts Wesleyan Coll (NY)
Shippensburg U of Pennsylvania (PA)
Silver Lake Coll of the Holy Family (WI)
State U of New York Coll at Geneseo (NY)
Syracuse U (NY)
The U of Akron (OH)
U of Maine at Farmington (ME)
U of Mount Union (OH)
U of Vermont (VT)
U of Wisconsin–Milwaukee (WI)
Western Washington U (WA)
Winona State U (MN)
York Coll of Pennsylvania (PA)
Youngstown State U (OH)

SPECIAL EDUCATION–ELEMENTARY SCHOOL
Abilene Christian U (TX)
Ball State U (IN)
Canisius Coll (NY)

Daemen Coll (NY)
Granite State Coll (NH)
La Salle U (PA)
Lee U (TN)
Molloy Coll (NY)
Neumann U (PA)
Niagara U (NY)
Northcentral U (CA)
Rhode Island Coll (RI)
Shawnee State U (OH)
Syracuse U (NY)
Towson U (OH)
U of Massachusetts Lowell (MA)
U of Mount Union (OH)
U of Wisconsin–Milwaukee (WI)
U of Wyoming (WY)
Weber State U (UT)

SPECIAL EDUCATION–GIFTED AND TALENTED
Canisius Coll (NY)
Delaware State U (DE)
Grand Valley State U (MI)
U of Providence (MT)

SPECIAL EDUCATION–INDIVIDUALS WHO ARE DEVELOPMENTALLY DELAYED
Millikin U (IL)
Saint Mary-of-the-Woods Coll (IN)

SPECIAL EDUCATION–INDIVIDUALS WITH EMOTIONAL DISTURBANCES
Central Michigan U (MI)
Eastern Michigan U (MI)
Grand Valley State U (MI)
Greensboro Coll (NC)
Hope Coll (MI)
Morningside Coll (IA)
Northern Michigan U (MI)
Western Michigan U (MI)

SPECIAL EDUCATION–INDIVIDUALS WITH HEARING IMPAIRMENTS
Barton Coll (NC)
Bowling Green State U (OH)
Canisius Coll (NY)
The Coll of New Jersey (NJ)
Converse Coll (SC)
Eastern Michigan U (MI)
Flagler Coll (FL)
Grand Valley State U (MI)
Michigan State U (MI)
Minot State U (ND)
Texas Christian U (TX)
The U of North Carolina at Greensboro (NC)
U of North Florida (FL)
U of Science and Arts of Oklahoma (OK)
U of Southern Mississippi (MS)
The U of Tulsa (OK)
Utah Valley U (UT)

SPECIAL EDUCATION–INDIVIDUALS WITH INTELLECTUAL DISABILITIES
Bowling Green State U (OH)
Brenau U (GA)
Central Michigan U (MI)
Eastern Michigan U (MI)
Grand Valley State U (MI)
Greensboro Coll (NC)
Manchester U (IN)
Minot State U (ND)
Morningside Coll (IA)
Northern Michigan U (MI)
Silver Lake Coll of the Holy Family (WI)
Walsh U (OH)

SPECIAL EDUCATION–INDIVIDUALS WITH MULTIPLE DISABILITIES
Adventist U of Health Sciences (FL)
Ball State U (IN)
Bowling Green State U (OH)
Bradley U (IL)
Daemen Coll (NY)
Dominican Coll (NY)
Grand Valley State U (MI)
Lee U (TN)
Missouri Baptist U (MO)
Northwest Missouri State U (MO)
The U of Akron (OH)

The U of North Carolina Wilmington (NC)
Walsh U (OH)
Wright State U (OH)
Wright State U–Lake Campus (OH)

SPECIAL EDUCATION–INDIVIDUALS WITH ORTHOPEDIC AND OTHER PHYSICAL HEALTH IMPAIRMENTS
Eastern Michigan U (MI)
Grand Valley State U (MI)

SPECIAL EDUCATION–INDIVIDUALS WITH SPECIFIC LEARNING DISABILITIES
Appalachian State U (NC)
Aquinas Coll (MI)
Baldwin Wallace U (OH)
Bethune-Cookman U (FL)
Bowling Green State U (OH)
Bradley U (IL)
Canisius Coll (NY)
Cornerstone U (MI)
Greensboro Coll (NC)
Hope Coll (MI)
Judson U (IL)
Malone U (OH)
Michigan State U (MI)
Northeastern State U (OK)
Northern Michigan U (MI)
Northwestern U (IL)
Silver Lake Coll of the Holy Family (WI)
State U of New York at Plattsburgh (NY)
Western Michigan U (MI)
West Virginia Wesleyan Coll (WV)

SPECIAL EDUCATION–INDIVIDUALS WITH SPEECH/LANGUAGE IMPAIRMENTS
Baylor U (TX)
Buffalo State Coll, State U of New York (NY)
Eastern Michigan U (MI)
Emerson Coll (MA)
Georgia Southern U–Armstrong Campus (GA)
Ithaca Coll (NY)
Minot State U (ND)
New Mexico State U (NM)
Pace U (NY)
State U of New York Coll at Cortland (NY)
The U of North Carolina at Greensboro (NC)

SPECIAL EDUCATION–INDIVIDUALS WITH VISION IMPAIRMENTS
Eastern Michigan U (MI)

SPECIAL EDUCATION–JUNIOR HIGH/MIDDLE SCHOOL
East Stroudsburg U of Pennsylvania (PA)
La Salle U (PA)
U of Wisconsin–Milwaukee (WI)

SPECIAL EDUCATION RELATED
Auburn U (AL)
Bowling Green State U (OH)
Canisius Coll (NY)
Catawba Coll (NC)
Clarion U of Pennsylvania (PA)
Dakota State U (SD)
Delaware State U (DE)
East Carolina U (NC)
Eastern Nazarene Coll (MA)
Hood Coll (MD)
Kean U (NJ)
Lee U (TN)
Lincoln U (MO)
Minot State U (ND)
Purdue U (IN)
Saint Mary-of-the-Woods Coll (IN)
Southeastern Oklahoma State U (OK)
Talladega Coll (AL)
U of Missouri (MO)
U of Nebraska–Lincoln (NE)
The U of North Carolina at Charlotte (NC)
U of Southern Indiana (IN)

SPECIAL EDUCATION–SECONDARY SCHOOL
Abilene Christian U (TX)

Canisius Coll (NY)
Lee U (TN)
Molloy Coll (NY)
Niagara U (NY)
Oklahoma City U (OK)
Rhode Island Coll (RI)
U of Wisconsin–Milwaukee (WI)

SPECIAL PRODUCTS MARKETING
Buffalo State Coll, State U of New York (NY)
Dominican U (IL)
Fashion Inst of Technology (NY)
Rochester Inst of Technology (NY)
Saint Joseph's U (PA)
Stephen F. Austin State U (TX)
U of Maryland Eastern Shore (MD)
U of North Texas (TX)

SPEECH COMMUNICATION AND RHETORIC
Abilene Christian U (TX)
Alabama State U (AL)
Albright Coll (PA)
Alfred U (NY)
Allegheny Coll (PA)
Alma Coll (MI)
Alverno Coll (WI)
American U (DC)
Appalachian State U (NC)
Aquinas Coll (MI)
Arizona State U at the Downtown Phoenix campus (AZ)
Arizona State U at the Polytechnic campus (AZ)
Arizona State U at the Tempe campus (AZ)
Arizona State U at the West campus (AZ)
Arkansas Tech U (AR)
Ashland U (OH)
Auburn U at Montgomery (AL)
Augsburg U (MN)
Augustana U (SD)
Austin Coll (TX)
Avila U (MO)
Azusa Pacific U (CA)
Baldwin Wallace U (OH)
Ball State U (IN)
Barry U (FL)
Baylor U (TX)
Belhaven U (MS)
Bellarmine U (KY)
Belmont U (TN)
Benedictine U (IL)
Bethany Lutheran Coll (MN)
Bethel Coll (IN)
Bethune-Cookman U (FL)
Biola U (CA)
Blackburn Coll (IL)
Bluffton U (OH)
Bowling Green State U (OH)
Brewton-Parker Coll (GA)
Bridgewater State U (MA)
Brock U (ON, Canada)
Bryan Coll (TN)
Bryant U (RI)
Buena Vista U (IA)
Buffalo State Coll, State U of New York (NY)
Caldwell U (NJ)
California Baptist U (CA)
California Polytechnic State U, San Luis Obispo (CA)
California State Polytechnic U, Pomona (CA)
California State U, Dominguez Hills (CA)
California State U, East Bay (CA)
California State U, Fullerton (CA)
California State U, Los Angeles (CA)
California State U, Sacramento (CA)
California State U, San Marcos (CA)
California State U, Stanislaus (CA)
California U of Pennsylvania (PA)
Calvin Coll (MI)
Capital U (OH)
Cardinal Stritch U (WI)
Carlos Albizu U (PR)
Carroll U (WI)
Carthage Coll (WI)
Catawba Coll (NC)
The Catholic U of America (DC)
Cedar Crest Coll (PA)

Cedarville U (OH)
Central Methodist U (MO)
Central Michigan U (MI)
Chaminade U of Honolulu (HI)
Champlain Coll (VT)
Chapman U (CA)
Chatham U (PA)
Christopher Newport U (VA)
Clarkson U (NY)
Clayton State U (GA)
Cleveland State U (OH)
Coastal Carolina U (SC)
Coe Coll (IA)
Coker Coll (SC)
The Coll at Brockport, State U of New York (NY)
Coll of Charleston (SC)
Coll of Saint Elizabeth (NJ)
The Coll of St. Scholastica (MN)
Coll of Staten Island of the City U of New York (NY)
The Coll of Wooster (OH)
Colorado State U (CO)
Columbia Coll (MO)
Columbia Coll (SC)
Concordia U Chicago (IL)
Corban U (OR)
Cornerstone U (MI)
Creighton U (NE)
Culver-Stockton Coll (MO)
Dallas Baptist U (TX)
DePaul U (IL)
Dickinson State U (ND)
Dominican U (IL)
Duquesne U (PA)
East Carolina U (NC)
East Central U (OK)
Eastern Michigan U (MI)
Eastern New Mexico U (NM)
Eastern Oregon U (OR)
Eastern U (PA)
Eastern Washington U (WA)
Eckerd Coll (FL)
Elmhurst Coll (IL)
Elon U (NC)
Embry-Riddle Aeronautical U–Daytona (FL)
Emerson Coll (MA)
Emmanuel Coll (MA)
Emporia State U (KS)
Excelsior Coll (NY)
Fairfield U (CT)
Fairleigh Dickinson U, Florham Campus (NJ)
Fairleigh Dickinson U, Metropolitan Campus (NJ)
Fayetteville State U (NC)
Felician U (NJ)
Fitchburg State U (MA)
Florida Atlantic U (FL)
Florida Gulf Coast U (FL)
Florida Intl U (FL)
Furman U (SC)
Georgia State U (GA)
Gonzaga U (WA)
Gordon Coll (MA)
Governors State U (IL)
Graceland U (IA)
Greensboro Coll (NC)
Greenville U (IL)
Grove City Coll (PA)
Gwynedd Mercy U (PA)
Hamline U (MN)
Hampshire Coll (MA)
Hannibal-LaGrange U (MO)
Harding U (AR)
Hardin-Simmons U (TX)
Hillsdale Coll (MI)
Hofstra U (NY)
Hope Coll (MI)
Howard Payne U (TX)
Illinois State U (IL)
Indiana State U (IN)
Indiana Tech (IN)
Indiana U Bloomington (IN)
Indiana U East (IN)
Indiana U Kokomo (IN)
Indiana U Northwest (IN)
Indiana U of Pennsylvania (PA)
Indiana U–Purdue U Indianapolis (IN)
Indiana U South Bend (IN)
Indiana U Southeast (IN)
Indiana Wesleyan U (IN)
Iona Coll (NY)
Iowa State U of Science and Technology (IA)

James Madison U (VA)
Judson U (IL)
Juniata Coll (PA)
Kansas State U (KS)
Kansas Wesleyan U (KS)
Kean U (NJ)
Keene State Coll (NH)
Kennesaw State U (GA)
Kent State U (OH)
Kent State U at Ashtabula (OH)
Kent State U at East Liverpool (OH)
Kent State U at Salem (OH)
Kent State U at Stark (OH)
Kent State U at Trumbull (OH)
Kent State U at Tuscarawas (OH)
La Sierra U (CA)
Lawrence Technological U (MI)
Lee U (TN)
Liberty U (VA)
Linfield Coll (OR)
Long Island U–LIU Brooklyn (NY)
Longwood U (VA)
Louisiana Coll (LA)
Louisiana State U and A&M Coll (LA)
Loyola Marymount U (CA)
Loyola U Chicago (IL)
Luther Coll (IA)
Lycoming Coll (PA)
Lynchburg Coll (VA)
Manchester U (IN)
Manhattanville Coll (NY)
Mansfield U of Pennsylvania (PA)
Marian U (IN)
Marian U (WI)
Marietta Coll (OH)
Marylhurst U (OR)
Marymount Manhattan Coll (NY)
McDaniel Coll (MD)
McKendree U (IL)
McPherson Coll (KS)
Mercer U, Macon (GA)
Mercyhurst U (PA)
Meredith Coll (NC)
Messiah Coll (PA)
Michigan State U (MI)
Millersville U of Pennsylvania (PA)
Millikin U (IL)
Millsaps Coll (MS)
Minnesota State U Moorhead (MN)
Mississippi State U (MS)
Missouri State U (MO)
Missouri Valley Coll (MO)
Missouri Western State U (MO)
Molloy Coll (NY)
Monmouth Coll (IL)
Montclair State U (NJ)
Mount Mary U (WI)
Mount Mercy U (IA)
Mount St. Joseph U (OH)
Mount St. Mary's U (MD)
Mount Vernon Nazarene U (OH)
Muskingum U (OH)
Nazareth Coll of Rochester (NY)
New Mexico Highlands U (NM)
New York U (NY)
North Carolina State U (NC)
North Carolina Wesleyan Coll (NC)
North Central Coll (IL)
Northeastern State U (OK)
Northeastern U (MA)
Northern Arizona U (AZ)
Northern Illinois U (IL)
Northern Kentucky U (KY)
Northern Michigan U (MI)
Northwest Christian U (OR)
Northwestern State U of Louisiana (LA)
Northwestern U (IL)
Northwest Missouri State U (MO)
Northwest Nazarene U (ID)
Notre Dame de Namur U (CA)
Nova Southeastern U (FL)
Oglethorpe U (GA)
Ohio Northern U (OH)
The Ohio State U (OH)
Ohio U (OH)
Oklahoma Baptist U (OK)
Olivet Nazarene U (IL)
Oral Roberts U (OK)
Oregon State U (OR)
Ottawa U (KS)
Ouachita Baptist U (AR)
Pace U, Pleasantville Campus (NY)
Pacific Lutheran U (WA)
Palm Beach Atlantic U (FL)
Penn State Abington (PA)

Penn State Altoona (PA)
Penn State Beaver (PA)
Penn State Berks (PA)
Penn State Brandywine (PA)
Penn State DuBois (PA)
Penn State Erie, The Behrend Coll (PA)
Penn State Fayette, The Eberly Campus (PA)
Penn State Greater Allegheny (PA)
Penn State Harrisburg (PA)
Penn State Hazleton (PA)
Penn State Lehigh Valley (PA)
Penn State Mont Alto (PA)
Penn State New Kensington (PA)
Penn State Schuylkill (PA)
Penn State Shenango (PA)
Penn State U Park (PA)
Penn State Wilkes-Barre (PA)
Penn State Worthington Scranton (PA)
Penn State York (PA)
Pepperdine U, Malibu (CA)
Pfeiffer U (NC)
Pine Manor Coll (MA)
Pittsburg State U (KS)
Point Loma Nazarene U (CA)
Prairie View A&M U (TX)
Purchase Coll, State U of New York (NY)
Purdue U Northwest (IN)
Radford U (VA)
Ramapo Coll of New Jersey (NJ)
Randolph Coll (VA)
Regis U (CO)
Rensselaer Polytechnic Inst (NY)
Rhode Island Coll (RI)
Rider U (NJ)
Ripon Coll (WI)
Robert Morris U (PA)
Roberts Wesleyan Coll (NY)
Rochester Inst of Technology (NY)
Rockhurst U (MO)
Rocky Mountain Coll (MT)
Roosevelt U (IL)
Rosemont Coll (PA)
Rowan U (NJ)
Rutgers U–New Brunswick (NJ)
Sacred Heart U (CT)
Saginaw Valley State U (MI)
Saint Anselm Coll (NH)
St. John's U (NY)
Saint Joseph's U (PA)
St. Lawrence U (NY)
Saint Mary's Coll of California (CA)
St. Mary's U (TX)
St. Norbert Coll (WI)
Saint Peter's U (NJ)
Saint Vincent Coll (PA)
Salisbury U (MD)
Samford U (AL)
Sam Houston State U (TX)
San Diego State U (CA)
San Francisco State U (CA)
Santa Clara U (CA)
Schreiner U (TX)
Seattle Pacific U (WA)
Seattle U (WA)
Seton Hill U (PA)
Shenandoah U (VA)
Shepherd U (WV)
Simmons Coll (MA)
Simon Fraser U (BC, Canada)
Slippery Rock U of Pennsylvania (PA)
Sonoma State U (CA)
Southeastern Louisiana U (LA)
Southeastern Oklahoma State U (OK)
Southeast Missouri State U (MO)
Southern Illinois U Edwardsville (IL)
Southern Utah U (UT)
Southwest Baptist U (MO)
Southwestern Coll (KS)
Southwestern U (TX)
State U of New York at New Paltz (NY)
State U of New York at Plattsburgh (NY)
State U of New York Coll at Cortland (NY)
State U of New York Coll at Old Westbury (NY)
Stockton U (NJ)
Stonehill Coll (MA)
Suffolk U (MA)

Susquehanna U (PA)
Syracuse U (NY)
Tabor Coll (KS)
Taylor U (IN)
Texas Christian U (TX)
Texas Lutheran U (TX)
Thomas U (GA)
Tiffin U (OH)
Trevecca Nazarene U (TN)
Trine U (IN)
Trinity Christian Coll (IL)
Trinity U (TX)
Troy U (AL)
Truman State U (MO)
U at Albany, State U of New York (NY)
U at Buffalo, the State U of New York (NY)
The U of Akron (OH)
The U of Alabama (AL)
The U of Alabama at Birmingham (AL)
U of Alaska Fairbanks (AK)
The U of Arizona (AZ)
U of Arkansas (AR)
U of California, Davis (CA)
U of Central Florida (FL)
U of Cincinnati (OH)
U of Colorado Boulder (CO)
U of Colorado Denver (CO)
U of Dayton (OH)
U of Denver (CO)
U of Georgia (GA)
U of Hartford (CT)
U of Hawaii at Manoa (HI)
U of Houston (TX)
U of Illinois at Chicago (IL)
U of Jamestown (ND)
The U of Kansas (KS)
U of Kentucky (KY)
U of La Verne (CA)
U of Louisville (KY)
U of Mary Hardin-Baylor (TX)
U of Maryland, Coll Park (MD)
U of Maryland U Coll (MD)
U of Memphis (TN)
U of Miami (FL)
U of Michigan (MI)
U of Michigan–Dearborn (MI)
U of Minnesota, Duluth (MN)
U of Missouri (MO)
U of Missouri–St. Louis (MO)
U of Montana (MT)
U of Nebraska–Lincoln (NE)
U of Nevada, Las Vegas (NV)
U of Nevada, Reno (NV)
U of New Hampshire (NH)
U of New Haven (CT)
U of North Alabama (AL)
The U of North Carolina at Chapel Hill (NC)
The U of North Carolina at Charlotte (NC)
The U of North Carolina at Greensboro (NC)
The U of North Carolina Wilmington (NC)
U of Northern Colorado (CO)
U of Northern Iowa (IA)
U of Oklahoma (OK)
U of Pennsylvania (PA)
U of Pikeville (KY)
U of Puget Sound (WA)
U of Rhode Island (RI)
U of St. Thomas (TX)
U of San Francisco (CA)
U of Science and Arts of Oklahoma (OK)
U of Sioux Falls (SD)
U of South Alabama (AL)
U of South Carolina Aiken (SC)
U of Southern California (CA)
U of Southern Maine (ME)
U of Southern Mississippi (MS)
The U of Tennessee (TN)
The U of Texas at Austin (TX)
The U of Texas Rio Grande Valley (TX)
U of the Incarnate Word (TX)
U of the Pacific (CA)
U of the Virgin Islands (VI)
The U of Tulsa (OK)
The U of Virginia's Coll at Wise (VA)
U of Washington (WA)
U of Waterloo (ON, Canada)
U of Wisconsin–La Crosse (WI)

U of Wisconsin–Madison (WI)
U of Wisconsin–Milwaukee (WI)
U of Wisconsin–Platteville (WI)
U of Wisconsin–River Falls (WI)
U of Wisconsin–Stevens Point (WI)
U of Wisconsin–Superior (WI)
U of Wisconsin–Whitewater (WI)
U of Wyoming (WY)
Utica Coll (NY)
Valdosta State U (GA)
Valley City State U (ND)
Valparaiso U (IN)
Vanderbilt U (TN)
Vanguard U of Southern California (CA)
Virginia Polytechnic Inst and State U (VA)
Wake Forest U (NC)
Waldorf U (IA)
Washington U in St. Louis (MO)
Wayland Baptist U (TX)
Waynesburg U (PA)
Wayne State Coll (NE)
Wayne State U (MI)
Webber Intl U (FL)
Weber State U (UT)
Webster U (MO)
Western Connecticut State U (CT)
Western Illinois U (IL)
Western Kentucky U (KY)
Western Michigan U (MI)
Western New England U (MA)
Western Washington U (WA)
Westfield State U (MA)
Westminster Coll (UT)
Westmont Coll (CA)
West Texas A&M U (TX)
West Virginia State U (WV)
West Virginia Wesleyan Coll (WV)
Wheaton Coll (IL)
Whitman Coll (WA)
Whitworth U (WA)
Wilkes U (PA)
Willamette U (OR)
William Jewell Coll (MO)
William Paterson U of New Jersey (NJ)
William Peace U (NC)
William Woods U (MO)
Winona State U (MN)
Wisconsin Lutheran Coll (WI)
Wittenberg U (OH)
Worcester State U (MA)
Wright State U (OH)
Wright State U–Lake Campus (OH)
York Coll of Pennsylvania (PA)
Youngstown State U (OH)

SPEECH-LANGUAGE PATHOLOGY
Abilene Christian U (TX)
Ball State U (IN)
Biola U (CA)
Clarion U of Pennsylvania (PA)
Cleveland State U (OH)
Columbia Coll (SC)
Duquesne U (PA)
Eastern Michigan U (MI)
Eastern Washington U (WA)
East Stroudsburg U of Pennsylvania (PA)
Elms Coll (MA)
Emerson Coll (MA)
Geneva Coll (PA)
Harding U (AR)
Inter American U of Puerto Rico, Aguadilla Campus (PR)
Inter American U of Puerto Rico, Fajardo Campus (PR)
Jackson State U (MS)
James Madison U (VA)
Lebanon Valley Coll (PA)
Lehman Coll of the City U of New York (NY)
Marshall U (WV)
Marymount Manhattan Coll (NY)
Maryville U of Saint Louis (MO)
Molloy Coll (NY)
Nazareth Coll of Rochester (NY)
Northern Michigan U (MI)
Northwestern U (IL)
Nova Southeastern U (FL)
Oklahoma State U (OK)
Rockhurst U (MO)
San Diego State U (CA)
Texas Christian U (TX)
Trinity Christian Coll (IL)

U of Central Missouri (MO)
U of Central Oklahoma (OK)
U of Montevallo (AL)
U of Nebraska–Lincoln (NE)
U of Nevada, Reno (NV)
U of Northern Iowa (IA)
U of Oklahoma Health Sciences Center (OK)
U of Science and Arts of Oklahoma (OK)
U of West Georgia (GA)
Valdosta State U (GA)
Xavier U of Louisiana (LA)

SPEECH-LANGUAGE PATHOLOGY ASSISTANT
Caribbean U (PR)

SPEECH TEACHER EDUCATION
Albion Coll (MI)
Anderson U (IN)
Arkansas Tech U (AR)
Augustana U (SD)
Austin Coll (TX)
Bemidji State U (MN)
Boise State U (ID)
Bowling Green State U (OH)
Brigham Young U (UT)
Buena Vista U (IA)
Capital U (OH)
Carroll Coll (MT)
Central Michigan U (MI)
Cornerstone U (MI)
Culver-Stockton Coll (MO)
Dallas Baptist U (TX)
East Texas Baptist U (TX)
Evangel U (MO)
Friends U (KS)
Harding U (AR)
Houston Baptist U (TX)
Howard Payne U (TX)
Kansas Wesleyan U (KS)
Lee U (TN)
Northwestern Coll (IA)
Northwest U (WA)
Oklahoma City U (OK)
Saginaw Valley State U (MI)
St. Ambrose U (IA)
St. Catherine U (MN)
Southwest Baptist U (MO)
Southwestern Coll (KS)
Trevecca Nazarene U (TN)
U of Mary Hardin-Baylor (TX)
U of Michigan–Flint (MI)
The U of North Carolina at Greensboro (NC)
U of Sioux Falls (SD)
U of South Dakota (SD)
Wayne State Coll (NE)
William Jewell Coll (MO)

SPORT AND FITNESS ADMINISTRATION/ MANAGEMENT
Abilene Christian U (TX)
Adelphi U (NY)
Alcorn State U (MS)
Alice Lloyd Coll (KY)
American Intl Coll (MA)
American Public U System (WV)
Anderson U (IN)
Arcadia U (PA)
Arizona State U at the Downtown Phoenix campus (AZ)
Asbury U (KY)
Athens State U (AL)
Augustana U (SD)
Aurora U (IL)
Averett U (VA)
Baker U (KS)
Baldwin Wallace U (OH)
Ball State U (IN)
Barclay Coll (KS)
Barry U (FL)
Barton Coll (NC)
Becker Coll (MA)
Belhaven U (MS)
Bellarmine U (KY)
Belmont U (TN)
Bemidji State U (MN)
Berry Coll (GA)
Bethel Coll (IN)
Blackburn Coll (IL)
Black Hills State U (SD)
Bluffton U (OH)
Bob Jones U (SC)
Bowling Green State U (OH)

Bridgewater State U (MA)
Brock U (ON, Canada)
Buena Vista U (IA)
Caldwell U (NJ)
California U of Pennsylvania (PA)
Calvin Coll (MI)
Canisius Coll (NY)
Cardinal Stritch U (WI)
Carthage Coll (WI)
Catawba Coll (NC)
Cazenovia Coll (NY)
Cedarville U (OH)
Central Methodist U (MO)
Central Michigan U (MI)
Chowan U (NC)
The Citadel, The Military Coll of South Carolina (SC)
Clarion U of Pennsylvania (PA)
Clarke U (IA)
Clayton State U (GA)
Cleveland State U (OH)
Coastal Carolina U (SC)
Coker Coll (SC)
The Coll at Brockport, State U of New York (NY)
The Coll of Idaho (ID)
Coll of Saint Elizabeth (NJ)
Colorado Mesa U (CO)
Columbia Coll (MO)
Columbia Coll Chicago (IL)
Concordia Coll–New York (NY)
Concordia U Chicago (IL)
Concordia U, St. Paul (MN)
Concordia U Wisconsin (WI)
Corban U (OR)
Cornerstone U (MI)
Culver-Stockton Coll (MO)
Dallas Baptist U (TX)
Davenport U, Grand Rapids (MI)
Dean Coll (MA)
Defiance Coll (OH)
Delaware State U (DE)
DEREE - The American Coll of Greece (Greece)
DeSales U (PA)
Drexel U (PA)
Eastern Mennonite U (VA)
Eastern Michigan U (MI)
Eastern Nazarene Coll (MA)
East Stroudsburg U of Pennsylvania (PA)
East Tennessee State U (TN)
East Texas Baptist U (TX)
Elmhurst Coll (IL)
Elon U (NC)
Emmanuel Coll (GA)
Emmanuel Coll (MA)
Emory & Henry Coll (VA)
Endicott Coll (MA)
Fairleigh Dickinson U, Florham Campus (NJ)
Fairleigh Dickinson U, Metropolitan Campus (NJ)
Farmingdale State Coll (NY)
Fisher Coll (MA)
Fitchburg State U (MA)
Flagler Coll (FL)
Florida Inst of Technology (FL)
Florida Southern Coll (FL)
Florida State U (FL)
Fort Lewis Coll (CO)
Franklin Pierce U (NH)
Friends U (KS)
Gannon U (PA)
Geneva Coll (PA)
Georgetown Coll (KY)
Georgia Southern U (GA)
Gonzaga U (WA)
Graceland U (IA)
Grand Valley State U (MI)
Grand View U (IA)
Greensboro Coll (NC)
Greenville U (IL)
Guilford Coll (NC)
Hampton U (VA)
Harding U (AR)
Hardin-Simmons U (TX)
Heidelberg U (OH)
Hilbert Coll (NY)
Hillsdale Coll (MI)
Holy Family U (PA)
Houston Baptist U (TX)
Howard Payne U (TX)
Huntingdon Coll (AL)
Husson U (ME)
Indiana Tech (IN)
Indiana U Kokomo (IN)

Indiana Wesleyan U (IN)
Inter American U of Puerto Rico, Metropolitan Campus (PR)
Iowa State U of Science and Technology (IA)
Ithaca Coll (NY)
Jacksonville U (FL)
Johnson C. Smith U (NC)
Judson U (IL)
Kansas Wesleyan U (KS)
Kennesaw State U (GA)
Kent State U (OH)
King U (TN)
Lamar U (TX)
Lasell Coll (MA)
La Sierra U (CA)
Lee U (TN)
Lenoir-Rhyne U (NC)
LeTourneau U (TX)
Lewis U (IL)
Liberty U (VA)
Limestone Coll (SC)
Lindenwood U (MO)
Lipscomb U (TN)
Lock Haven U of Pennsylvania (PA)
Long Island U–LIU Brooklyn (NY)
Long Island U–LIU Post (NY)
Loras Coll (IA)
Louisiana State U and A&M Coll (LA)
Lubbock Christian U (TX)
Lynchburg Coll (VA)
Lynn U (FL)
Madonna U (MI)
Malone U (OH)
Manchester U (IN)
Maranatha Baptist U (WI)
Marian U (WI)
Marietta Coll (OH)
Maryville U of Saint Louis (MO)
McKendree U (IL)
Merrimack Coll (MA)
Messiah Coll (PA)
Miami U (OH)
Michigan Technological U (MI)
MidAmerica Nazarene U (KS)
Millikin U (IL)
Minot State U (ND)
Misericordia U (PA)
Missouri Baptist U (MO)
Missouri Valley Coll (MO)
Morehead State U (KY)
Mount St. Joseph U (OH)
Mount St. Mary's U (MD)
Mount Vernon Nazarene U (OH)
Muskingum U (OH)
Neumann U (PA)
Newberry Coll (SC)
Niagara U (NY)
Nichols Coll (MA)
North Carolina State U (NC)
North Central Coll (IL)
North Dakota State U (ND)
Northern Kentucky U (KY)
Northern Michigan U (MI)
Northern State U (SD)
Northern Vermont U–Lyndon (VT)
North Greenville U (SC)
Northwestern Coll (IA)
Nova Southeastern U (FL)
Ohio Dominican U (OH)
Ohio Northern U (OH)
The Ohio State U (OH)
Oklahoma Baptist U (OK)
Oklahoma Christian U (OK)
Oklahoma State U (OK)
Old Dominion U (VA)
Olivet Nazarene U (IL)
Otterbein U (OH)
Pennsylvania Coll of Technology (PA)
Pepperdine U, Malibu (CA)
Pfeiffer U (NC)
Piedmont Coll (GA)
Post U (CT)
Purdue U Northwest (IN)
Rice U (TX)
Rider U (NJ)
Roanoke Coll (VA)
Robert Morris U (PA)
Rockford U (IL)
Rockhurst U (MO)
Rocky Mountain Coll (MT)
Rogers State U (OK)
Saginaw Valley State U (MI)
St. Ambrose U (IA)
St. Bonaventure U (NY)

St. John Fisher Coll (NY)
St. John's U (NY)
Saint Leo U (FL)
Saint Louis U (MO)
Saint Louis U–Madrid Campus (Spain)
Saint Mary's Coll of California (CA)
St. Thomas Aquinas Coll (NY)
St. Thomas U (FL)
Samford U (AL)
Schreiner U (TX)
Seattle Pacific U (WA)
Seton Hill U (PA)
Shawnee State U (OH)
Shenandoah U (VA)
Simpson Coll (IA)
Southeastern Louisiana U (LA)
Southeastern U (FL)
Southeast Missouri State U (MO)
Southern Adventist U (TN)
Southern Illinois U Carbondale (IL)
Southern Methodist U (TX)
Southern Vermont Coll (VT)
Southwest Baptist U (MO)
Southwestern Adventist U (TX)
Southwestern Assemblies of God U (TX)
Southwestern Coll (KS)
State U of New York at Oswego (NY)
Stetson U (FL)
Syracuse U (NY)
Taylor U (IN)
Temple U (PA)
Tennessee Wesleyan U (TN)
Texas A&M U (TX)
Texas A&M U–Commerce (TX)
Texas Lutheran U (TX)
Texas State U (TX)
Texas Tech U (TX)
Tiffin U (OH)
Toccoa Falls Coll (GA)
Towson U (MD)
Trevecca Nazarene U (TN)
Trine U (IN)
Troy U (AL)
Tusculum Coll (TN)
Union Coll (NE)
Union U (TN)
United States Sports Acad (AL)
The U of Akron (OH)
U of Charleston (WV)
U of Cincinnati (OH)
U of Dayton (OH)
U of Dubuque (IA)
The U of Findlay (OH)
U of Florida (FL)
U of Georgia (GA)
U of Houston (TX)
U of Jamestown (ND)
The U of Kansas (KS)
U of Louisville (KY)
U of Mary Hardin-Baylor (TX)
U of Massachusetts Amherst (MA)
U of Memphis (TN)
U of Miami (FL)
U of Michigan (MI)
U of Minnesota, Crookston (MN)
U of Minnesota, Twin Cities Campus (MN)
U of Mount Union (OH)
U of Nebraska at Kearney (NE)
U of Nevada, Las Vegas (NV)
U of New Haven (CT)
U of North Florida (FL)
U of Pittsburgh at Bradford (PA)
U of Regina (SK, Canada)
U of Saint Mary (KS)
U of San Francisco (CA)
U of Sioux Falls (SD)
U of South Carolina (SC)
U of Southern Indiana (IN)
U of Southern Mississippi (MS)
The U of Tampa (FL)
The U of Tennessee (TN)
The U of Texas at Austin (TX)
U of the Incarnate Word (TX)
The U of Tulsa (OK)
U of Valley Forge (PA)
The U of West Alabama (AL)
U of Wisconsin–Parkside (WI)
Valparaiso U (IN)
Waldorf U (IA)
Warner Pacific Coll (OR)
Wartburg Coll (IA)
Washington State U (WA)
Wayland Baptist U (TX)

Wayne State Coll (NE)
Wayne State U (MI)
Webber Intl U (FL)
Western Michigan U (MI)
Western New England U (MA)
Western State Colorado U (CO)
Westminster Coll (PA)
West Virginia Wesleyan Coll (WV)
Wichita State U (KS)
Widener U (PA)
William Paterson U of New Jersey (NJ)
William Penn U (IA)
William Woods U (MO)
Wilmington U (DE)
Winthrop U (SC)
Wittenberg U (OH)
York Coll of Pennsylvania (PA)

SPORTS COMMUNICATION
Arizona State U at the Downtown Phoenix campus (AZ)
Ashland U (OH)
Belhaven U (MS)
Bluffton U (OH)
Bradley U (IL)
Bryant U (RI)
Butler U (IN)
Clemson U (SC)
Culver-Stockton Coll (MO)
Ferris State U (MI)
Florida Southern Coll (FL)
Grand View U (IA)
LeTourneau U (TX)
Marist Coll (NY)
Oklahoma State U (OK)
Simpson Coll (IA)
U of Evansville (IN)
U of Nebraska–Lincoln (NE)
Youngstown State U (OH)

SPORTS STUDIES
Bethel Coll (IN)
Bryant U (RI)
Canisius Coll (NY)
Central Michigan U (MI)
Concordia U, St. Paul (MN)
Hillsdale Coll (MI)
Inter American U of Puerto Rico, San Germán Campus (PR)
Lubbock Christian U (TX)
Manhattanville Coll (NY)
National U (CA)
Northern Vermont U–Lyndon (VT)
Southwestern Coll (KS)
Texas Christian U (TX)
United States Sports Acad (AL)
U of Dubuque (IA)
U of Saint Mary (KS)
Western Kentucky U (KY)
Whitworth U (WA)

STATISTICS
American U (DC)
American U of Beirut (Lebanon)
Amherst Coll (MA)
Arizona State U at the Polytechnic campus (AZ)
Arizona State U at the West campus (AZ)
Barnard Coll (NY)
Baruch Coll of the City U of New York (NY)
Baylor U (TX)
Bowling Green State U (OH)
Brock U (ON, Canada)
California Baptist U (CA)
California Polytechnic State U, San Luis Obispo (CA)
California State U, East Bay (CA)
California State U, Fullerton (CA)
California State U, Long Beach (CA)
Carnegie Mellon U (PA)
Case Western Reserve U (OH)
Central Michigan U (MI)
Columbia U (NY)
Concordia U (QC, Canada)
Cornell U (NY)
Eastern Michigan U (MI)
Elon U (NC)
Emory U (GA)
Florida Intl U (FL)
Florida State U (FL)
George Mason U (VA)
The George Washington U (DC)
Grand Valley State U (MI)
Harvard U (MA)

Hunter Coll of the City U of New York (NY)
Idaho State U (ID)
Indiana U Bloomington (IN)
Iowa State U of Science and Technology (IA)
Jackson State U (MS)
Kansas State U (KS)
Lehigh U (PA)
LeTourneau U (TX)
Loyola U Chicago (IL)
Marlboro Coll (VT)
Miami U (OH)
Michigan State U (MI)
Michigan Technological U (MI)
Misericordia U (PA)
Montana Tech of The U of Montana (MT)
Mount Holyoke Coll (MA)
North Carolina State U (NC)
North Dakota State U (ND)
Northern Kentucky U (KY)
Northwestern U (IL)
Oakland U (MI)
Ohio Northern U (OH)
Ohio Wesleyan U (OH)
Oklahoma State U (OK)
Penn State Abington (PA)
Penn State Altoona (PA)
Penn State Beaver (PA)
Penn State Berks (PA)
Penn State Brandywine (PA)
Penn State DuBois (PA)
Penn State Erie, The Behrend Coll (PA)
Penn State Fayette, The Eberly Campus (PA)
Penn State Greater Allegheny (PA)
Penn State Hazleton (PA)
Penn State Lehigh Valley (PA)
Penn State Mont Alto (PA)
Penn State New Kensington (PA)
Penn State Schuylkill (PA)
Penn State Shenango (PA)
Penn State U Park (PA)
Penn State Wilkes-Barre (PA)
Penn State Worthington Scranton (PA)
Penn State York (PA)
Reed Coll (OR)
Rice U (TX)
Rochester Inst of Technology (NY)
Rutgers U–New Brunswick (NJ)
St. John Fisher Coll (NY)
St. Lawrence U (NY)
San Diego State U (CA)
San Francisco State U (CA)
Simon Fraser U (BC, Canada)
Sonoma State U (CA)
Southern Methodist U (TX)
State U of New York Coll at Oneonta (NY)
Temple U (PA)
Truman State U (MO)
U at Buffalo, the State U of New York (NY)
The U of Akron (OH)
U of California, Davis (CA)
U of California, Los Angeles (CA)
U of California, Riverside (CA)
U of California, Santa Barbara (CA)
U of Central Florida (FL)
U of Chicago (IL)
U of Florida (FL)
U of Georgia (GA)
U of Illinois at Chicago (IL)
U of King's Coll (NS, Canada)
U of Maine (ME)
U of Maryland, Baltimore County (MD)
U of Michigan (MI)
U of Michigan–Dearborn (MI)
U of Minnesota, Duluth (MN)
U of Minnesota, Morris (MN)
U of Minnesota, Twin Cities Campus (MN)
U of Missouri (MO)
U of New Mexico (NM)
The U of North Carolina Wilmington (NC)
U of North Florida (FL)
U of Pennsylvania (PA)
U of Pittsburgh (PA)
U of Regina (SK, Canada)
U of Rochester (NY)
U of St. Thomas (MN)
U of Saskatchewan (SK, Canada)

U of South Carolina (SC)
The U of Tennessee (TN)
The U of Tennessee at Martin (TN)
The U of Texas at Austin (TX)
The U of Texas at San Antonio (TX)
U of Vermont (VT)
U of Washington (WA)
U of Waterloo (ON, Canada)
U of Wisconsin–La Crosse (WI)
U of Wisconsin–Madison (WI)
U of Wyoming (WY)
Utah State U (UT)
Valparaiso U (IN)
Virginia Polytechnic Inst and State U (VA)
Washington U in St. Louis (MO)
Western Michigan U (MI)
Williams Coll (MA)
Winona State U (MN)
Wright State U (OH)
Wright State U–Lake Campus (OH)
Xavier U of Louisiana (LA)

STATISTICS RELATED
California Baptist U (CA)
Carnegie Mellon U (PA)
Ohio Northern U (OH)
U of Central Oklahoma (OK)
U of Evansville (IN)
U of New Hampshire (NH)
U of Northern Iowa (IA)

STRATEGIC INTELLIGENCE
Florida Inst of Technology (FL)

STRINGED INSTRUMENTS
Acadia U (NS, Canada)
Boston U (MA)
Brigham Young U (UT)
Carnegie Mellon U (PA)
Conservatorio de Musica de Puerto Rico (PR)
Converse Coll (SC)
Cornish Coll of the Arts (WA)
Heidelberg U (OH)
Hope Coll (MI)
Liberty U (VA)
The New School Coll of Performing Arts (NY)
Northwestern U (IL)
Oberlin Coll (OH)
Oklahoma City U (OK)
Roosevelt U (IL)
San Francisco Conservatory of Music (CA)
Seattle U (WA)
State U of New York at Fredonia (NY)
Stetson U (FL)
Syracuse U (NY)
Texas Christian U (TX)
The U of Akron (OH)
U of Central Oklahoma (OK)
The U of Kansas (KS)
U of Southern California (CA)
U of Washington (WA)
Vanderbilt U (TN)
Willamette U (OR)
Xavier U of Louisiana (LA)
Youngstown State U (OH)

STRUCTURAL BIOLOGY
Indiana U Bloomington (IN)

STRUCTURAL ENGINEERING
Penn State Harrisburg (PA)
U of California, San Diego (CA)
U of Central Florida (FL)
U of Southern California (CA)
Western Michigan U (MI)

SUBSTANCE ABUSE/ ADDICTION COUNSELING
Bay Path U (MA)
The Coll at Brockport, State U of New York (NY)
Drexel U (PA)
Indiana Wesleyan U (IN)
Kansas Wesleyan U (KS)
Keene State Coll (NH)
Minot State U (ND)
Newman U (KS)
Northwestern State U of Louisiana (LA)
Ohio Christian U (OH)
Rhode Island Coll (RI)
Tiffin U (OH)
U of Central Arkansas (AR)
U of Cincinnati (OH)

U of Michigan–Flint (MI)
U of Providence (MT)
U of St. Francis (IL)
U of South Dakota (SD)

SURGICAL TECHNOLOGY
Pennsylvania Coll of Technology (PA)
Weber State U (UT)

SURVEYING ENGINEERING
Ferris State U (MI)
Florida Atlantic U (FL)
Michigan Technological U (MI)

SURVEYING TECHNOLOGY
East Tennessee State U (TN)
Idaho State U (ID)
Kennesaw State U (GA)
New Mexico State U (NM)
Oregon Inst of Technology (OR)
Penn State Wilkes-Barre (PA)
Polytechnic U of Puerto Rico (PR)
State U of New York Coll of Technology at Alfred (NY)
Texas A&M U–Corpus Christi (TX)
Troy U (AL)
The U of Akron (OH)
U of Florida (FL)
U of Maine (ME)
Utah Valley U (UT)

SUSTAINABILITY STUDIES
Alaska Pacific U (AK)
Albion Coll (MI)
Aquinas Coll (MI)
Aurora U (IL)
Bentley U (MA)
Berry Coll (GA)
California Baptist U (CA)
Chatham U (PA)
Columbia U (NY)
Creighton U (NE)
Daemen Coll (NY)
The Evergreen State Coll (WA)
Florida Inst of Technology (FL)
Furman U (SC)
George Mason U (VA)
Goshen Coll (IN)
Guilford Coll (NC)
Harris-Stowe State U (MO)
Hartwick Coll (NY)
HEC Montreal (QC, Canada)
Hofstra U (NY)
Iowa State U of Science and Technology (IA)
Jacksonville U (FL)
Kean U (NJ)
Lipscomb U (TN)
Maryville U of Saint Louis (MO)
Messiah Coll (PA)
Miami U (OH)
Montclair State U (NJ)
Northern Vermont U–Lyndon (VT)
Oregon State U (OR)
Rensselaer Polytechnic Inst (NY)
Roosevelt U (IL)
Sewanee: The U of the South (TN)
Shippensburg U of Pennsylvania (PA)
Sierra Nevada Coll (NV)
Stephen F. Austin State U (TX)
Stockton U (NJ)
Stony Brook U, State U of New York (NY)
Taylor U (IN)
Toccoa Falls Coll (GA)
Trent U (ON, Canada)
U of Florida (FL)
U of Louisville (KY)
U of New Hampshire (NH)
U of New Haven (CT)
U of North Alabama (AL)
U of Northern Colorado (CO)
U of South Dakota (SD)
The U of Texas at Austin (TX)
U of Wisconsin–Parkside (WI)
U of Wisconsin–Platteville (WI)
U of Wisconsin–River Falls (WI)
U of Wisconsin–Stout (WI)
Virginia Wesleyan U (VA)
Western Washington U (WA)
Worcester Polytechnic Inst (MA)

SWEDISH
Brigham Young U (UT)
U of Washington (WA)

SYSTEM, NETWORKING, AND LAN/WAN MANAGEMENT
Alcorn State U (MS)
Dakota State U (SD)
Hallmark U (TX)
Northern Michigan U (MI)
Rochester Inst of Technology (NY)
State U of New York Coll of Technology at Alfred (NY)
Texas A&M U (TX)
U of Providence (MT)

SYSTEMS ENGINEERING
Case Western Reserve U (OH)
Delaware State U (DE)
Eastern Nazarene Coll (MA)
Ferris State U (MI)
George Mason U (VA)
The George Washington U (DC)
Kennesaw State U (GA)
Massachusetts Maritime Acad (MA)
Otterbein U (OH)
Providence Coll (RI)
Rochester Inst of Technology (NY)
Stanford U (CA)
Stevens Inst of Technology (NJ)
Taylor U (IN)
Texas A&M Intl U (TX)
United States Merchant Marine Acad (NY)
United States Military Acad (NY)
The U of Arizona (AZ)
U of California, Santa Cruz (CA)
U of Colorado Colorado Springs (CO)
U of Florida (FL)
The U of North Carolina at Charlotte (NC)
U of Pennsylvania (PA)
U of Virginia (VA)
U of Waterloo (ON, Canada)
U of Wyoming (WY)
Washington U in St. Louis (MO)

SYSTEMS SCIENCE AND THEORY
Boston U (MA)
Carnegie Mellon U (PA)
James Madison U (VA)
Marshall U (WV)
Pitzer Coll (CA)
Purdue U (IN)
Stanford U (CA)
Syracuse U (NY)
United States Military Acad (NY)
U of Wyoming (WY)
Washington U in St. Louis (MO)

TAXATION
Grand Valley State U (MI)

TEACHER ASSISTANT/AIDE
Blackburn Coll (IL)
East Central U (OK)
Waldorf U (IA)

TECHNICAL AND SCIENTIFIC COMMUNICATION
Indiana U–Purdue U Indianapolis (IN)
Iowa State U of Science and Technology (IA)
Lehigh U (PA)
Michigan Technological U (MI)
Missouri U of Science and Technology (MO)
Washington State U (WA)
Worcester Polytechnic Inst (MA)

TECHNICAL TEACHER EDUCATION
Athens State U (AL)
Auburn U (AL)
Ball State U (IN)
Bowling Green State U (OH)
Coll of the Ozarks (MO)
Ferris State U (MI)
The Ohio State U (OH)
Oklahoma State U (OK)
The U of Akron (OH)
U of Arkansas (AR)
U of Idaho (ID)
U of Kentucky (KY)
U of Missouri (MO)
U of Saskatchewan (SK, Canada)
U of Wisconsin–Stout (WI)
Utah State U (UT)
Valley City State U (ND)

Washington State U (WA)
West Virginia U Inst of Technology (WV)
Wright State U (OH)
Wright State U–Lake Campus (OH)

TECHNOLOGY/INDUSTRIAL ARTS TEACHER EDUCATION
Ball State U (IN)
Bemidji State U (MN)
Berea Coll (KY)
Bowling Green State U (OH)
Buffalo State Coll, State U of New York (NY)
Central Connecticut State U (CT)
The Coll of New Jersey (NJ)
Dickinson State U (ND)
Eastern Michigan U (MI)
Fitchburg State U (MA)
Illinois State U (IL)
Indiana State U (IN)
Jackson State U (MS)
Lindenwood U (MO)
Middle Tennessee State U (TN)
New Mexico Highlands U (NM)
North Carolina State U (NC)
Ohio Northern U (OH)
Pittsburg State U (KS)
Purdue U (IN)
Rhode Island Coll (RI)
Southeast Missouri State U (MO)
Southern Utah U (UT)
State U of New York at Oswego (NY)
Union Coll (NE)
U of New Mexico (NM)
U of Northern Iowa (IA)
U of Wisconsin–Platteville (WI)
U of Wisconsin–Stout (WI)
U of Wyoming (WY)
Utah State U (UT)
Valley City State U (ND)
Wayland Baptist U (TX)
Wayne State Coll (NE)
Western Michigan U (MI)
Westfield State U (MA)

TELECOMMUNICATIONS MANAGEMENT
St. Thomas U (FL)

TELECOMMUNICATIONS TECHNOLOGY
Canisius Coll (NY)
Farmingdale State Coll (NY)
Ferris State U (MI)
Kennesaw State U (GA)
Lawrence Technological U (MI)
Pace U (NY)
Pace U, Pleasantville Campus (NY)
Rochester Inst of Technology (NY)
St. John's U (NY)

TEXTILE SCIENCE
Iowa State U of Science and Technology (IA)
Michigan State U (MI)

TEXTILE SCIENCES AND ENGINEERING
Auburn U (AL)
North Carolina State U (NC)

THEATER DESIGN AND TECHNOLOGY
Ashland U (OH)
Baldwin Wallace U (OH)
Baylor U (TX)
Belmont U (TN)
Bennington Coll (VT)
Binghamton U, State U of New York (NY)
Biola U (CA)
Boston U (MA)
Brenau U (GA)
Brigham Young U (UT)
Coe Coll (IA)
Coker Coll (SC)
Columbia Coll Chicago (IL)
Concordia U (QC, Canada)
Cornish Coll of the Arts (WA)
DePaul U (IL)
Doane U (NE)
Elon U (NC)
Emerson Coll (MA)
Fitchburg State U (MA)
Florida Southern Coll (FL)
Gannon U (PA)
Greensboro Coll (NC)

Husson U (ME)
Illinois Wesleyan U (IL)
Ithaca Coll (NY)
Kean U (NJ)
Keene State Coll (NH)
Lindenwood U (MO)
Lipscomb U (TN)
Marymount Manhattan Coll (NY)
Michigan Technological U (MI)
Millikin U (IL)
Nazareth Coll of Rochester (NY)
New Jersey Inst of Technology (NJ)
North Central Coll (IL)
Oakland U (MI)
Ohio Northern U (OH)
Oklahoma City U (OK)
Oral Roberts U (OK)
Penn State Abington (PA)
Penn State Altoona (PA)
Penn State Beaver (PA)
Penn State Berks (PA)
Penn State Brandywine (PA)
Penn State DuBois (PA)
Penn State Erie, The Behrend Coll (PA)
Penn State Fayette, The Eberly Campus (PA)
Penn State Greater Allegheny (PA)
Penn State Hazleton (PA)
Penn State Lehigh Valley (PA)
Penn State Mont Alto (PA)
Penn State New Kensington (PA)
Penn State Schuylkill (PA)
Penn State Shenango (PA)
Penn State U Park (PA)
Penn State Wilkes-Barre (PA)
Penn State Worthington Scranton (PA)
Penn State York (PA)
Pepperdine U, Malibu (CA)
Piedmont Coll (GA)
Purchase Coll, State U of New York (NY)
Purdue U (IN)
Rhode Island Coll (RI)
Rocky Mountain Coll (MT)
Savannah Coll of Art and Design (GA)
Seton Hill U (PA)
Shenandoah U (VA)
Southwestern Coll (KS)
Syracuse U (NY)
Texas Christian U (TX)
Trinity U (TX)
U of Alaska Fairbanks (AK)
The U of Arizona (AZ)
U of Central Oklahoma (OK)
U of Cincinnati (OH)
The U of Kansas (KS)
U of Michigan (MI)
U of Michigan–Flint (MI)
U of Nevada, Las Vegas (NV)
U of New Mexico (NM)
U of North Carolina School of the Arts (NC)
U of Northern Iowa (IA)
U of North Georgia (GA)
U of Regina (SK, Canada)
U of San Francisco (CA)
U of Southern California (CA)
The U of the Arts (PA)
Vanguard U of Southern California (CA)
Western Michigan U (MI)
Western State Colorado U (CO)
Wilkes U (PA)
Wright State U (OH)
Wright State U–Lake Campus (OH)

THEATER LITERATURE, HISTORY AND CRITICISM
The American U in Cairo (Egypt)
Averett U (VA)
Bennington Coll (VT)
Bowdoin Coll (ME)
Buena Vista U (IA)
Clark Atlanta U (GA)
DePaul U (IL)
Hiram Coll (OH)
Marlboro Coll (VT)
Marymount Manhattan Coll (NY)
Northwestern U (IL)
Saint Mary's Coll of California (CA)
Sarah Lawrence Coll (NY)
Tufts U (MA)
U of Washington (WA)
Washington U in St. Louis (MO)

Western Michigan U (MI)
West Virginia U (WV)

THEATER/THEATER ARTS MANAGEMENT
Albright Coll (PA)
Berry Coll (GA)
Biola U (CA)
Buena Vista U (IA)
Catawba Coll (NC)
Columbia Coll Chicago (IL)
DEREE - The American Coll of Greece (Greece)
Florida State U (FL)
Graceland U (IA)
Ithaca Coll (NY)
Marymount Manhattan Coll (NY)
Massachusetts Coll of Liberal Arts (MA)
Messiah Coll (PA)
Michigan State U (MI)
MidAmerica Nazarene U (KS)
Nazareth Coll of Rochester (NY)
Oglethorpe U (GA)
Ohio Northern U (OH)
Ohio U (OH)
Oklahoma City U (OK)
Pace U (NY)
Quinnipiac U (CT)
Regent U (VA)
Rockford U (IL)
Seton Hill U (PA)
U of Evansville (IN)
U of New Haven (CT)
U of Regina (SK, Canada)
William Peace U (NC)

THEOLOGICAL AND MINISTERIAL STUDIES RELATED
Bob Jones U (SC)
California Christian Coll (CA)
Concordia U (QC, Canada)
Concordia U, St. Paul (MN)
Criswell Coll (TX)
Grove City Coll (PA)
Hardin-Simmons U (TX)
Hope Intl U (CA)
Howard Payne U (TX)
Lincoln Christian U (IL)
Lubbock Christian U (TX)
Malone U (OH)
Marquette U (WI)
Mid-America Christian U (OK)
Northwest U (WA)
Providence Coll (RI)
Saint Mary-of-the-Woods Coll (IN)
Southeastern U (FL)
Trinity Coll of Florida (FL)
Union Coll (NE)
Whitworth U (WA)

THEOLOGY
Ambrose U (AB, Canada)
American Baptist Coll (TN)
Anderson U (IN)
Anderson U (SC)
Andrews U (MI)
Appalachian Bible Coll (WV)
Assumption Coll (MA)
Azusa Pacific U (CA)
Bard Coll (NY)
Barry U (FL)
Bellarmine U (KY)
Benedictine Coll (KS)
Benedictine U (IL)
Bethel Coll (IN)
Biola U (CA)
Bluefield Coll (VA)
Boston Coll (MA)
Brescia U (KY)
Brewton-Parker Coll (GA)
Caldwell U (NJ)
California Lutheran U (CA)
Calvary U (MO)
Calvin Coll (MI)
Carlow U (PA)
Carroll Coll (MT)
Christendom Coll (VA)
Coll of Saint Benedict (MN)
Coll of Saint Elizabeth (NJ)
Coll of Saint Mary (NE)
Colorado Christian U (CO)
Concordia U (QC, Canada)
Concordia U Chicago (IL)
Concordia U Irvine (CA)
Concordia U, Nebraska (NE)
Concordia U, St. Paul (MN)

Concordia U Wisconsin (WI)
Corban U (OR)
Creighton U (NE)
DeSales U (PA)
Dominican U (IL)
Duquesne U (PA)
Eastern Mennonite U (VA)
Eastern Nazarene Coll (MA)
Eastern U (PA)
Elmhurst Coll (IL)
Fordham U (NY)
Gannon U (PA)
Georgetown U (DC)
Hardin-Simmons U (TX)
Holy Trinity Orthodox Sem (NY)
Houston Baptist U (TX)
Howard Payne U (TX)
Immaculata U (PA)
Indiana Wesleyan U (IN)
Johnson U (TN)
Johnson U Florida (FL)
John Wesley U (NC)
Kentucky Mountain Bible Coll (KY)
King's Coll (PA)
Lee U (TN)
LeTourneau U (TX)
Liberty U (VA)
Louisiana Coll (LA)
Loyola Marymount U (CA)
Loyola U Chicago (IL)
Marian U (IN)
Marian U (WI)
Marquette U (WI)
Master's Coll and Sem (ON, Canada)
The Master's U (CA)
MidAmerica Nazarene U (KS)
Morris Coll (SC)
Mount Mary U (WI)
Mount St. Mary's U (MD)
Mount Vernon Nazarene U (OH)
Multnomah U (OR)
Nebraska Christian Coll of Hope Intl U (NE)
Newman U (KS)
Northwest Nazarene U (ID)
Ohio Dominican U (OH)
Olivet Nazarene U (IL)
Oral Roberts U (OK)
Ouachita Baptist U (AR)
Pacific Lutheran U (WA)
Palm Beach Atlantic U (FL)
Point Loma Nazarene U (CA)
Providence Coll (RI)
Redeemer U Coll (ON, Canada)
Rockhurst U (MO)
St. Ambrose U (IA)
Saint Anselm Coll (NH)
St. Bonaventure U (NY)
St. Catherine U (MN)
Saint John's U (MN)
St. John's U (NY)
Saint Louis U (MO)
Saint Louis U–Madrid Campus (Spain)
Saint Mary's Coll of California (CA)
St. Mary's U (TX)
Saint Mary's U of Minnesota (MN)
Saint Peter's U (NJ)
St. Thomas U (FL)
Saint Vincent Coll (PA)
Seattle Pacific U (WA)
Silver Lake Coll of the Holy Family (WI)
Southern Adventist U (TN)
Southwest Baptist U (MO)
Southwestern Adventist U (TX)
Southwestern Assemblies of God U (TX)
Texas Lutheran U (TX)
Trinity Christian Coll (IL)
Trinity Coll of Florida (FL)
Union Coll (NE)
Union U (TN)
U of Chicago (IL)
U of Dallas (TX)
U of Notre Dame (IN)
U of Providence (MT)
U of St. Francis (IL)
U of Saint Francis (IN)
U of Saint Mary (KS)
U of St. Thomas (TX)
U of San Francisco (CA)
U of Sioux Falls (SD)
U of Valley Forge (PA)
Valparaiso U (IN)

Vanguard U of Southern California (CA)
Walsh U (OH)
Warner Pacific Coll (OR)
Whitworth U (WA)
Xavier U of Louisiana (LA)

THEOLOGY AND RELIGIOUS VOCATIONS RELATED
Abilene Christian U (TX)
American Baptist Coll (TN)
Arlington Baptist U (TX)
Belmont U (TN)
Cedarville U (OH)
Concordia Coll–New York (NY)
Concordia U of Edmonton (AB, Canada)
Dallas Baptist U (TX)
Eastern Nazarene Coll (MA)
Hobe Sound Bible Coll (FL)
Kentucky Mountain Bible Coll (KY)
Lee U (TN)
LeTourneau U (TX)
Martin Luther Coll (MN)
Master's Coll and Sem (ON, Canada)
Missouri Baptist U (MO)
Newman U (KS)
Northwest U (WA)
Ouachita Baptist U (AR)
Trevecca Nazarene U (TN)
Trinity Christian Coll (IL)
Union U (TN)
U of St. Thomas (TX)
U of Valley Forge (PA)

THEORETICAL AND MATHEMATICAL PHYSICS
Carnegie Mellon U (PA)
Chapman U (CA)
U at Buffalo, the State U of New York (NY)
U of Guelph (ON, Canada)

THERAPEUTIC RECREATION
Aurora U (IL)
Brigham Young U (UT)
Calvin Coll (MI)
Catawba Coll (NC)
Central Michigan U (MI)
Concordia U (QC, Canada)
East Carolina U (NC)
Eastern Michigan U (MI)
Eastern Washington U (WA)
Grand Valley State U (MI)
Hampton U (VA)
Indiana Tech (IN)
Ithaca Coll (NY)
Longwood U (VA)
St. Andrews U (NC)
St. Thomas Aquinas Coll (NY)
Slippery Rock U of Pennsylvania (PA)
State U of New York Coll at Cortland (NY)
Temple U (PA)
Unity Coll (ME)
The U of North Carolina Wilmington (NC)
U of Southern Maine (ME)
The U of Toledo (OH)
U of Waterloo (ON, Canada)
U of Wisconsin–La Crosse (WI)
U of Wisconsin–Milwaukee (WI)
Utica Coll (NY)

TOOL AND DIE TECHNOLOGY
Utah State U (UT)

TOURISM AND TRAVEL SERVICES MANAGEMENT
Arizona State U at the Downtown Phoenix campus (AZ)
Black Hills State U (SD)
Bowling Green State U (OH)
Brock U (ON, Canada)
Concord U (WV)
Delaware State U (DE)
Fisher Coll (MA)
Fort Lewis Coll (CO)
George Mason U (VA)
Indiana U–Purdue U Indianapolis (IN)
Niagara U (NY)
Northeastern State U (OK)
Texas A&M U (TX)
U of Guelph (ON, Canada)
U of Hawaii at Manoa (HI)
U of Maine at Machias (ME)

U of South Carolina (SC)
The U of Texas at San Antonio (TX)

TOURISM AND TRAVEL SERVICES MARKETING
Rochester Inst of Technology (NY)
U of Central Missouri (MO)
Western Michigan U (MI)

TOURISM PROMOTION
Bowling Green State U (OH)

TOXICOLOGY
Ashland U (OH)
Eastern Michigan U (MI)
John Jay Coll of Criminal Justice of the City U of New York (NY)
Nazareth Coll of Rochester (NY)
Penn State Beaver (PA)
Penn State Berks (PA)
Penn State DuBois (PA)
Penn State Fayette, The Eberly Campus (PA)
Penn State Greater Allegheny (PA)
Penn State Hazleton (PA)
Penn State Mont Alto (PA)
Penn State New Kensington (PA)
Penn State Shenango (PA)
Penn State U Park (PA)
Penn State Wilkes-Barre (PA)
Penn State York (PA)
St. John's U (NY)
U of Guelph (ON, Canada)
U of Louisiana at Monroe (LA)
U of Saskatchewan (SK, Canada)
U of Toronto (ON, Canada)

TRADE AND INDUSTRIAL TEACHER EDUCATION
Auburn U (AL)
Bemidji State U (MN)
Bowling Green State U (OH)
Buffalo State Coll, State U of New York (NY)
California State U, Long Beach (CA)
California State U, San Bernardino (CA)
Delaware State U (DE)
Fitchburg State U (MA)
Florida Ag and Mech U (FL)
Indiana State U (IN)
Indiana U of Pennsylvania (PA)
Kent State U (OH)
Lindenwood U (MO)
Southern Illinois U Carbondale (IL)
State U of New York at Oswego (NY)
Temple U (PA)
U of Central Florida (FL)
U of Central Oklahoma (OK)
U of Louisville (KY)
U of Nebraska–Lincoln (NE)
U of Saskatchewan (SK, Canada)
U of Southern Maine (ME)
U of Wyoming (WY)
Upper Iowa U (IA)
Valdosta State U (GA)
Wayland Baptist U (TX)
Western Kentucky U (KY)
Western Michigan U (MI)

TRANSPORTATION AND HIGHWAY ENGINEERING
U of Toronto (ON, Canada)

TRANSPORTATION AND MATERIALS MOVING RELATED
Lewis U (IL)
Niagara U (NY)
United States Merchant Marine Acad (NY)
U of Wisconsin–Superior (WI)

TRANSPORTATION/MOBILITY MANAGEMENT
Bridgewater State U (MA)
Bryant U (RI)
Texas A&M U (TX)
U of North Florida (FL)
U of Pennsylvania (PA)

TURF AND TURFGRASS MANAGEMENT
Clemson U (SC)
Delaware Valley U (PA)
New Mexico State U (NM)
North Carolina State U (NC)
Penn State Abington (PA)

Penn State Altoona (PA)
Penn State Beaver (PA)
Penn State Berks (PA)
Penn State Brandywine (PA)
Penn State DuBois (PA)
Penn State Erie, The Behrend Coll (PA)
Penn State Fayette, The Eberly Campus (PA)
Penn State Greater Allegheny (PA)
Penn State Hazleton (PA)
Penn State Lehigh Valley (PA)
Penn State Mont Alto (PA)
Penn State New Kensington (PA)
Penn State Schuylkill (PA)
Penn State Shenango (PA)
Penn State U Park (PA)
Penn State Wilkes-Barre (PA)
Penn State Worthington Scranton (PA)
Penn State York (PA)
Purdue U (IN)
Rutgers U–New Brunswick (NJ)
Tennessee Technological U (TN)
Texas A&M U (TX)
U of Georgia (GA)
U of Massachusetts Amherst (MA)
U of Minnesota, Crookston (MN)
U of Nebraska–Lincoln (NE)
Washington State U (WA)

TURKISH
The U of Texas at Austin (TX)

UKRAINIAN
U of Saskatchewan (SK, Canada)

URALIC LANGUAGES
U of Washington (WA)

URBAN EDUCATION AND LEADERSHIP
Belmont U (TN)
The Coll of New Jersey (NJ)
U of Wisconsin–Milwaukee (WI)

URBAN FORESTRY
U of California, Davis (CA)
U of Minnesota, Crookston (MN)
U of Wisconsin–Stevens Point (WI)

URBAN MINISTRY
Charlotte Christian Coll and Theological Sem (NC)
Greenville U (IL)
Tabor Coll (KS)

URBAN STUDIES/AFFAIRS
Albright Coll (PA)
Antioch U Los Angeles (CA)
Aquinas Coll (MI)
Arizona State U at the Downtown Phoenix campus (AZ)
Augsburg U (MN)
Barnard Coll (NY)
Boise State U (ID)
Boston U (MA)
Bryn Mawr Coll (PA)
Buffalo State Coll, State U of New York (NY)
California State U, Dominguez Hills (CA)
California State U, Northridge (CA)
California State U, Stanislaus (CA)
Canisius Coll (NY)
Cleveland State U (OH)
Coll of Charleston (SC)
Coll of Mount Saint Vincent (NY)
The Coll of Wooster (OH)
Columbia U (NY)
Concordia U (QC, Canada)
Delaware State U (DE)
Elmhurst Coll (IL)
Eugene Lang Coll of Liberal Arts (NY)
Fordham U (NY)
Furman U (SC)
Hampshire Coll (MA)
Harris-Stowe State U (MO)
Haverford Coll (PA)
Hobart and William Smith Colls (NY)
Hunter Coll of the City U of New York (NY)
Iowa State U of Science and Technology (IA)
Jackson State U (MS)
Lipscomb U (TN)
Loyola Marymount U (CA)

Loyola U Chicago (IL)
Manhattan Coll (NY)
Metropolitan Coll of New York (NY)
Morehouse Coll (GA)
New Coll of Florida (FL)
New Jersey City U (NJ)
New York Inst of Technology (NY)
New York U (NY)
Northwestern U (IL)
Oglethorpe U (GA)
Ohio U (OH)
Ohio Wesleyan U (OH)
Portland State U (OR)
Purchase Coll, State U of New York (NY)
Queens Coll of the City U of New York (NY)
Rhodes Coll (TN)
Rutgers U–Camden (NJ)
Rutgers U–New Brunswick (NJ)
Saint Peter's U (NJ)
San Diego State U (CA)
San Francisco State U (CA)
Sarah Lawrence Coll (NY)
Stanford U (CA)
Towson U (MD)
Trinity U (TX)
Tufts U (MA)
U at Albany, State U of New York (NY)
U of California, Irvine (CA)
U of California, San Diego (CA)
U of Cincinnati (OH)
U of Illinois at Chicago (IL)
U of Michigan–Dearborn (MI)
U of Minnesota, Duluth (MN)
U of Minnesota, Twin Cities Campus (MN)
U of New Orleans (LA)
U of Pennsylvania (PA)
U of Pittsburgh (PA)
U of San Francisco (CA)
The U of Texas at Austin (TX)
The U of Toledo (OH)
U of Utah (UT)
U of Washington, Tacoma (WA)
Vassar Coll (NY)
Virginia Commonwealth U (VA)
Virginia Polytechnic Inst and State U (VA)
Washington U in St. Louis (MO)
Wayne State U (MI)
Wheaton Coll (IL)
Worcester State U (MA)
Wright State U (OH)
Wright State U–Lake Campus (OH)

VEHICLE MAINTENANCE AND REPAIR TECHNOLOGIES RELATED
McPherson Coll (KS)

VETERINARY/ANIMAL HEALTH TECHNOLOGY
Becker Coll (MA)
Brigham Young U (UT)
Michigan State U (MI)
Mississippi State U (MS)
Morehead State U (KY)
Murray State U (KY)
North Dakota State U (ND)
Purdue U (IN)
State U of New York Coll of Technology at Canton (NY)
Tarleton State U (TX)
Texas A&M U–Kingsville (TX)
U of Nebraska–Lincoln (NE)

VETERINARY MICROBIOLOGY AND IMMUNOBIOLOGY
Penn State U Park (PA)

VISION SCIENCE/ PHYSIOLOGICAL OPTICS
Indiana U Bloomington (IN)
Providence Coll (RI)
U of the Incarnate Word (TX)

VISUAL AND PERFORMING ARTS
Antioch Coll, Yellow Springs (OH)
Arizona State U at the Tempe campus (AZ)
Arizona State U at the West campus (AZ)
Austin Coll (TX)
Azusa Pacific U (CA)

Barnard Coll (NY)
Bennett Coll (NC)
Bennington Coll (VT)
Blackburn Coll (IL)
Blue Mountain Coll (MS)
Boston U (MA)
Bowdoin Coll (ME)
Bucknell U (PA)
California Baptist U (CA)
California State U, San Marcos (CA)
Cardinal Stritch U (WI)
Cazenovia Coll (NY)
Centenary Coll of Louisiana (LA)
Champlain Coll (VT)
Chowan U (NC)
Clayton State U (GA)
Columbia U (NY)
Concordia U (QC, Canada)
Concordia U of Edmonton (AB, Canada)
DEREE - The American Coll of Greece (Greece)
Drexel U (PA)
Eckerd Coll (FL)
Emerson Coll (MA)
Emory U (GA)
The Evergreen State Coll (WA)
Fairleigh Dickinson U, Florham Campus (NJ)
Fairleigh Dickinson U, Metropolitan Campus (NJ)
Fayetteville State U (NC)
Fordham U (NY)
Gannon U (PA)
George Mason U (VA)
Gettysburg Coll (PA)
Harvard U (MA)
Indiana U of Pennsylvania (PA)
Inter American U of Puerto Rico, San Germán Campus (PR)
Iowa State U of Science and Technology (IA)
Ithaca Coll (NY)
Jackson State U (MS)
Jacksonville U (FL)
Johnson C. Smith U (NC)
Kansas Wesleyan U (KS)
Kennesaw State U (GA)
Kent State U (OH)
Kent State U at Stark (OH)
LaGrange Coll (GA)
Lebanese American U (Lebanon)
Longwood U (VA)
Louisiana Coll (LA)
Manhattanville Coll (NY)
Marlboro Coll (VT)
Marshall U (WV)
Mary Baldwin U (VA)
Massachusetts Coll of Liberal Arts (MA)
Michigan Technological U (MI)
MidAmerica Nazarene U (KS)
Mississippi State U (MS)
Missouri State U (MO)
Mount St. Mary's U (MD)
Naropa U (CO)
Neumann U (PA)
New Mexico Highlands U (NM)
New Mexico State U (NM)
Northwestern U (IL)
Occidental Coll (CA)
Ohio Northern U (OH)
Oregon State U (OR)
Penn State Abington (PA)
Penn State Altoona (PA)
Penn State Beaver (PA)
Penn State Berks (PA)
Penn State Brandywine (PA)
Penn State DuBois (PA)
Penn State Erie, The Behrend Coll (PA)
Penn State Fayette, The Eberly Campus (PA)
Penn State Greater Allegheny (PA)
Penn State Hazleton (PA)
Penn State Lehigh Valley (PA)
Penn State Mont Alto (PA)
Penn State New Kensington (PA)
Penn State Schuylkill (PA)
Penn State Shenango (PA)
Penn State U Park (PA)
Penn State Wilkes-Barre (PA)
Penn State Worthington Scranton (PA)
Penn State York (PA)
Pine Manor Coll (MA)

Point Loma Nazarene U (CA)
Purchase Coll, State U of New York (NY)
Ramapo Coll of New Jersey (NJ)
Rensselaer Polytechnic Inst (NY)
Rogers State U (OK)
Rutgers U–New Brunswick (NJ)
Saint Augustine's U (NC)
St. Bonaventure U (NY)
Saint Joseph's U (PA)
Saint Peter's U (NJ)
Southeastern U (FL)
Southeast Missouri State U (MO)
State U of New York at New Paltz (NY)
State U of New York Coll at Old Westbury (NY)
Stockton U (NJ)
Stonehill Coll (MA)
Suffolk U (MA)
Temple U (PA)
Tennessee Wesleyan U (TN)
Tusculum Coll (TN)
The U of Arizona (AZ)
U of California, Irvine (CA)
U of California, San Diego (CA)
U of Colorado Colorado Springs (CO)
U of Dayton (OH)
U of Dubuque (IA)
U of Houston–Downtown (TX)
U of Maine at Farmington (ME)
U of Maine at Machias (ME)
U of Mary Washington (VA)
U of Pennsylvania (PA)
U of Pittsburgh at Greensburg (PA)
U of Puget Sound (WA)
U of Regina (SK, Canada)
U of St. Francis (IL)
U of Saint Mary (KS)
U of San Francisco (CA)
U of Saskatchewan (SK, Canada)
U of South Dakota (SD)
U of Southern California (CA)
U of Southern Mississippi (MS)
U of South Florida, St. Petersburg (FL)
The U of Tennessee at Martin (TN)
The U of Texas at Austin (TX)
The U of Texas at Dallas (TX)
U of Toronto (ON, Canada)
U of Utah (UT)
Vassar Coll (NY)
Western Washington U (WA)
Wichita State U (KS)
Wittenberg U (OH)
Worcester State U (MA)
Youngstown State U (OH)

VISUAL AND PERFORMING ARTS RELATED
Adelphi U (NY)
Baldwin Wallace U (OH)
The Baptist Coll of Florida (FL)
Bluffton U (OH)
Brigham Young U (UT)
Cameron U (OK)
Clemson U (SC)
Cornell U (NY)
Endicott Coll (MA)
Grambling State U (LA)
Illinois State U (IL)
Illinois Wesleyan U (IL)
Long Island U–LIU Brooklyn (NY)
Marlboro Coll (VT)
Millikin U (IL)
New York U (NY)
Northwestern Coll (IA)
Ohio Northern U (OH)
Oklahoma City U (OK)
Penn State Altoona (PA)
Purchase Coll, State U of New York (NY)
Rice U (TX)
Saint Mary's Coll of California (CA)
Samford U (AL)
San Francisco Art Inst (CA)
Seton Hill U (PA)
Simon Fraser U (BC, Canada)
State U of New York Coll at Geneseo (NY)
U of California, Davis (CA)
U of California, Los Angeles (CA)
U of Chicago (IL)
U of Cincinnati (OH)
U of Michigan (MI)
U of Washington (WA)

U of Washington, Bothell (WA)
Virginia Wesleyan U (VA)
Western State Colorado U (CO)

VITICULTURE AND ENOLOGY
California Polytechnic State U, San Luis Obispo (CA)
Cornell U (NY)
Washington State U (WA)
Washington State U–Tri-Cities (WA)

VOCATIONAL REHABILITATION COUNSELING
Bowling Green State U (OH)
East Carolina U (NC)
East Central U (OK)
Emporia State U (KS)
Maryville U of Saint Louis (MO)
U of Wisconsin–Madison (WI)
U of Wisconsin–Stout (WI)
Wright State U (OH)
Wright State U–Lake Campus (OH)

VOICE AND OPERA
Abilene Christian U (TX)
Acadia U (NS, Canada)
Anderson U (IN)
Anderson U (SC)
Andrews U (MI)
Arizona Christian U (AZ)
Baldwin Wallace U (OH)
Barry U (FL)
Bennington Coll (VT)
Biola U (CA)
Birmingham-Southern Coll (AL)
Black Hills State U (SD)
Bob Jones U (SC)
Brandon U (MB, Canada)
Brigham Young U (UT)
Bucknell U (PA)
California Baptist U (CA)
California State U, Long Beach (CA)
Calvary U (MO)
Calvin Coll (MI)
Campbellsville U (KY)
Capital U (OH)
Carnegie Mellon U (PA)
Carson-Newman U (TN)
The Catholic U of America (DC)
Chapman U (CA)
Coker Coll (SC)
Conservatorio de Musica de Puerto Rico (PR)
Converse Coll (SC)
Cornish Coll of the Arts (WA)
Delaware State U (DE)
Drake U (IA)
East Central U (OK)
Furman U (SC)
Heidelberg U (OH)
Hope Coll (MI)
Houston Baptist U (TX)
Howard Payne U (TX)
Illinois Wesleyan U (IL)
Ithaca Coll (NY)
Jacksonville U (FL)
Liberty U (VA)
Lincoln Coll (IL)
Lipscomb U (TN)
Long Island U–LIU Post (NY)
Loyola U Chicago (IL)
Loyola U New Orleans (LA)
Madonna U (MI)
The Master's U (CA)
The New School Coll of Performing Arts (NY)
Northwestern U (IL)
Notre Dame de Namur U (CA)
Nyack Coll (NY)
Oakland U (MI)
Oberlin Coll (OH)
Ohio U (OH)
Oklahoma Baptist U (OK)
Oklahoma Christian U (OK)
Oklahoma City U (OK)
Oral Roberts U (OK)
Ouachita Baptist U (AR)
Palm Beach Atlantic U (FL)
Point Loma Nazarene U (CA)
Rider U (NJ)
Roberts Wesleyan Coll (NY)
Roosevelt U (IL)
Samford U (AL)
San Francisco Conservatory of Music (CA)

Shorter U (GA)
Southeastern U (FL)
Southern Methodist U (TX)
State U of New York at Fredonia (NY)
Stetson U (FL)
Syracuse U (NY)
Texas Christian U (TX)
Trinity U (TX)
Union U (TN)
The U of Akron (OH)
The U of Arizona (AZ)
U of Cincinnati (OH)
U of Idaho (ID)
The U of Kansas (KS)
U of Miami (FL)
U of Mobile (AL)
U of Southern California (CA)
The U of Tennessee at Martin (TN)
U of the Pacific (CA)
The U of Tulsa (OK)
U of Washington (WA)
U of Wisconsin–Superior (WI)
Valparaiso U (IN)
Vanderbilt U (TN)
Washington U in St. Louis (MO)
Weber State U (UT)
Western Michigan U (MI)
Whitworth U (WA)
Willamette U (OR)
Youngstown State U (OH)

WATER QUALITY AND WASTEWATER TREATMENT MANAGEMENT AND RECYCLING TECHNOLOGY
Virginia Polytechnic Inst and State U (VA)

WATER RESOURCES ENGINEERING
Central State U (OH)
U of Guelph (ON, Canada)
U of Nevada, Reno (NV)

WATER, WETLANDS, AND MARINE RESOURCES MANAGEMENT
Colorado State U (CO)
Florida Gulf Coast U (FL)
Florida Inst of Technology (FL)
Texas A&M U (TX)
Texas State U (TX)
U of Minnesota, Crookston (MN)
U of Wisconsin–Stevens Point (WI)
Western State Colorado U (CO)

WEB/MULTIMEDIA MANAGEMENT AND WEBMASTER
Georgia Coll & State U (GA)
Indiana Tech (IN)
Limestone Coll (SC)
Northern Michigan U (MI)
Pepperdine U, Malibu (CA)
Rochester Inst of Technology (NY)
Saint Leo U (FL)
State U of New York Coll of Technology at Alfred (NY)
Trevecca Nazarene U (TN)
U of Providence (MT)
U of St. Francis (IL)

WEB PAGE, DIGITAL/MULTIMEDIA AND INFORMATION RESOURCES DESIGN
Academy of Art U (CA)
Albright Coll (PA)
American Acad of Art (IL)
Azusa Pacific U (CA)
Beacon Coll (FL)
Belmont U (TN)
Cedarville U (OH)
Central Connecticut State U (CT)
Concordia U (QC, Canada)
Davenport U, Grand Rapids (MI)
Drexel U (PA)
Duquesne U (PA)
Eugene Lang Coll of Liberal Arts (NY)
Graceland U (IA)
Gwynedd Mercy U (PA)
Hampshire Coll (MA)
Harding U (AR)
Immaculata U (PA)
Indiana Wesleyan U (IN)
Iona Coll (NY)
Juniata Coll (PA)
Limestone Coll (SC)

Lindenwood U (MO)
Lipscomb U (TN)
Mount St. Joseph U (OH)
New England Inst of Technology (RI)
Northwest Missouri State U (MO)
Parsons School of Design (NY)
Pennsylvania Coll of Technology (PA)
Quinnipiac U (CT)
Rasmussen Coll Bloomington (MN)
Rasmussen Coll Brooklyn Park (MN)
Rasmussen Coll Eagan (MN)
Rasmussen Coll Mankato (MN)
Rasmussen Coll New Port Richey (FL)
Rasmussen Coll Ocala (FL)
Rasmussen Coll Rockford (IL)
Rasmussen Coll St. Cloud (MN)
Rochester Inst of Technology (NY)
Santa Clara U (CA)
Seattle U (WA)
Simmons Coll (MA)
Tennessee Technological U (TN)
Trevecca Nazarene U (TN)
Tulane U (LA)
The U of Arizona (AZ)
The U of Findlay (OH)
U of Mount Union (OH)
U of Providence (MT)
The U of the Arts (PA)
U of Washington, Bothell (WA)
U of Wisconsin–Stevens Point (WI)
Utah Valley U (UT)
Weber State U (UT)

WELDING ENGINEERING TECHNOLOGY
LeTourneau U (TX)
Weber State U (UT)

WELDING TECHNOLOGY
Brigham Young U–Idaho (ID)
Idaho State U (ID)
Pennsylvania Coll of Technology (PA)

WILDLIFE BIOLOGY
Adams State U (CO)
Coll of the Atlantic (ME)
Colorado State U (CO)
Friends U (KS)
Frostburg State U (MD)
Kansas State U (KS)
Liberty U (VA)
Ohio U (OH)
State U of New York Coll of Environmental Science and Forestry (NY)
Texas State U (TX)
Unity Coll (ME)
U of Guelph (ON, Canada)
U of Michigan–Flint (MI)
U of Vermont (VT)
U of Wyoming (WY)
West Texas A&M U (TX)

WILDLIFE, FISH AND WILDLANDS SCIENCE AND MANAGEMENT
Arkansas Tech U (AR)
Auburn U (AL)
Coll of the Ozarks (MO)
Delaware State U (DE)
Delaware Valley U (PA)
Eastern New Mexico U (NM)
Frostburg State U (MD)
Humboldt State U (CA)
Lincoln Memorial U (TN)
McNeese State U (LA)
Michigan State U (MI)
Michigan Technological U (MI)
Mississippi State U (MS)
Missouri State U (MO)
Missouri Western State U (MO)
Murray State U (KY)
New Mexico State U (NM)
Northwest Missouri State U (MO)
Oregon State U (OR)
State U of New York Coll of Environmental Science and Forestry (NY)
Stephen F. Austin State U (TX)
Tarleton State U (TX)
Tennessee Technological U (TN)
Texas A&M U (TX)
Texas A&M U–Commerce (TX)

Texas A&M U–Kingsville (TX)
Unity Coll (ME)
U of Alaska Fairbanks (AK)
U of Florida (FL)
U of Georgia (GA)
U of Idaho (ID)
U of Maine (ME)
U of Missouri (MO)
U of Montana (MT)
U of Nevada, Reno (NV)
U of New Hampshire (NH)
U of Puerto Rico–Humacao (PR)
U of Rhode Island (RI)
The U of Tennessee (TN)
The U of Tennessee at Martin (TN)
U of Wisconsin–Madison (WI)
U of Wisconsin–Stevens Point (WI)
Utah State U (UT)
Valley City State U (ND)
Washington State U (WA)
West Virginia U (WV)

WOMEN'S MINISTRY
Coll of Biblical Studies–Houston (TX)

WOMEN'S STUDIES
Agnes Scott Coll (GA)
Albion Coll (MI)
Albright Coll (PA)
Alverno Coll (WI)
American U (DC)
Amherst Coll (MA)
Appalachian State U (NC)
Arizona State U at the Tempe campus (AZ)
Arizona State U at the West campus (AZ)
Athabasca U (AB, Canada)
Augsburg U (MN)
Augustana Coll (IL)
Austin Coll (TX)
Ball State U (IN)
Barnard Coll (NY)
Bates Coll (ME)
Bennington Coll (VT)
Berea Coll (KY)
Bowling Green State U (OH)
Brandeis U (MA)
Brock U (ON, Canada)
Bryant U (RI)
Bucknell U (PA)
Butler U (IN)
California State U, Fullerton (CA)
California State U, Long Beach (CA)
California State U, Northridge (CA)
California State U, San Marcos (CA)
Canisius Coll (NY)
Carleton Coll (MN)
Case Western Reserve U (OH)
Central Michigan U (MI)
Chatham U (PA)
City Coll of the City U of New York (NY)
Clark U (MA)
Clemson U (SC)
Cleveland State U (OH)
Coe Coll (IA)
Colby Coll (ME)
Colgate U (NY)
The Coll at Brockport, State U of New York (NY)
Coll of Charleston (SC)
The Coll of New Jersey (NJ)
The Coll of New Rochelle (NY)
Coll of Saint Benedict (MN)
The Coll of William and Mary (VA)
The Coll of Wooster (OH)
The Colorado Coll (CO)
Colorado State U (CO)
Columbia U (NY)
Concordia U (QC, Canada)
Concordia U Chicago (IL)
Connecticut Coll (CT)
Cornell U (NY)
Dartmouth Coll (NH)
Denison U (OH)
DePaul U (IL)
DePauw U (IN)
Dickinson Coll (PA)
Dominican U (IL)
Dominican U of California (CA)
Drew U (NJ)
Duquesne U (PA)
Earlham Coll (IN)

Eastern Michigan U (MI)
Eastern Washington U (WA)
East Tennessee State U (TN)
Eckerd Coll (FL)
Emory U (GA)
Florida Intl U (FL)
Florida State U (FL)
Fordham U (NY)
Fort Lewis Coll (CO)
Georgetown U (DC)
Georgia Southern U–Armstrong Campus (GA)
Georgia State U (GA)
Gettysburg Coll (PA)
Grand Valley State U (MI)
Guilford Coll (NC)
Gustavus Adolphus Coll (MN)
Hamilton Coll (NY)
Hamline U (MN)
Hampshire Coll (MA)
Harvard U (MA)
Hobart and William Smith Colls (NY)
Hofstra U (NY)
Hollins U (VA)
Hope Coll (MI)
Hunter Coll of the City U of New York (NY)
Illinois Wesleyan U (IL)
Iowa State U of Science and Technology (IA)
Kalamazoo Coll (MI)
Kansas State U (KS)
Keene State Coll (NH)
Kenyon Coll (OH)
Knox Coll (IL)
Lafayette Coll (PA)
Lehigh U (PA)
Loyola Marymount U (CA)
Loyola U Chicago (IL)
Luther Coll (IA)
Macalester Coll (MN)
Manchester U (IN)
Marlboro Coll (VT)
Marquette U (WI)
Mercer U, Macon (GA)
Merrimack Coll (MA)
Metropolitan State U of Denver (CO)
Miami U (OH)
Michigan State U (MI)
Middlebury Coll (VT)
Minnesota State U Moorhead (MN)
Montclair State U (NJ)
Nazareth Coll of Rochester (NY)
New Jersey City U (NJ)
New Mexico State U (NM)
North Carolina State U (NC)
North Dakota State U (ND)
Northern Arizona U (AZ)
Northland Coll (WI)
Northwestern U (IL)
Oakland U (MI)
Oberlin Coll (OH)
The Ohio State U (OH)
Ohio U (OH)
Ohio Wesleyan U (OH)
Old Dominion U (VA)
Oregon State U (OR)
Otterbein U (OH)
Pace U (NY)
Pacific Lutheran U (WA)
Penn State Abington (PA)
Penn State Altoona (PA)
Penn State Beaver (PA)
Penn State Berks (PA)
Penn State Brandywine (PA)
Penn State DuBois (PA)
Penn State Erie, The Behrend Coll (PA)
Penn State Fayette, The Eberly Campus (PA)
Penn State Greater Allegheny (PA)
Penn State Hazleton (PA)
Penn State Lehigh Valley (PA)
Penn State Mont Alto (PA)
Penn State New Kensington (PA)
Penn State Schuylkill (PA)
Penn State Shenango (PA)
Penn State U Park (PA)
Penn State Wilkes-Barre (PA)
Penn State Worthington Scranton (PA)
Penn State York (PA)
Pitzer Coll (CA)
Pomona Coll (CA)
Portland State U (OR)

Providence Coll (RI)
Purchase Coll, State U of New York (NY)
Purdue U (IN)
Queens Coll of the City U of New York (NY)
Randolph-Macon Coll (VA)
Regis U (CO)
Rhode Island Coll (RI)
Rice U (TX)
Rutgers U–Newark (NJ)
Rutgers U–New Brunswick (NJ)
Sacred Heart U (CT)
St. Bonaventure U (NY)
St. Catherine U (MN)
Saint John's U (MN)
Saint Louis U (MO)
Saint Louis U–Madrid Campus (Spain)
Saint Mary's Coll of California (CA)
St. Olaf Coll (MN)
St. Thomas U (NB, Canada)
San Diego State U (CA)
San Francisco State U (CA)
Santa Clara U (CA)
Scripps Coll (CA)
Seattle U (WA)
Sewanee: The U of the South (TN)
Simmons Coll (MA)
Simon Fraser U (BC, Canada)
Smith Coll (MA)
Sonoma State U (CA)
Southwestern U (TX)
Spelman Coll (GA)
Stanford U (CA)
State U of New York at Fredonia (NY)
State U of New York at New Paltz (NY)
State U of New York at Oswego (NY)
State U of New York at Plattsburgh (NY)
State U of New York Coll at Geneseo (NY)
State U of New York Coll at Potsdam (NY)
Stony Brook U, State U of New York (NY)
Syracuse U (NY)
Temple U (PA)
Texas A&M U (TX)
Towson U (MD)
Trent U (ON, Canada)
Tufts U (MA)
Tulane U (LA)
U at Albany, State U of New York (NY)
The U of Arizona (AZ)
U of California, Davis (CA)
U of California, Riverside (CA)
U of California, San Diego (CA)
U of California, Santa Barbara (CA)
U of California, Santa Cruz (CA)
U of Cincinnati (OH)
U of Colorado Boulder (CO)
U of Dayton (OH)
U of Florida (FL)
U of Georgia (GA)
U of Hartford (CT)
U of Hawaii at Manoa (HI)
U of Houston–Clear Lake (TX)
U of Illinois at Chicago (IL)
The U of Kansas (KS)
U of King's Coll (NS, Canada)
U of Louisville (KY)
U of Maine (ME)

U of Maryland, Baltimore County (MD)
U of Maryland, Coll Park (MD)
U of Massachusetts Amherst (MA)
U of Massachusetts Boston (MA)
U of Massachusetts Dartmouth (MA)
U of Miami (FL)
U of Michigan (MI)
U of Michigan–Dearborn (MI)
U of Minnesota, Duluth (MN)
U of Minnesota, Morris (MN)
U of Minnesota, Twin Cities Campus (MN)
U of Montana (MT)
U of Nebraska–Lincoln (NE)
U of Nevada, Las Vegas (NV)
U of Nevada, Reno (NV)
U of New Hampshire (NH)
U of New Mexico (NM)
U of North Carolina at Asheville (NC)
The U of North Carolina at Chapel Hill (NC)
The U of North Carolina at Greensboro (NC)
U of Notre Dame (IN)
U of Oklahoma (OK)
U of Oregon (OR)
U of Pennsylvania (PA)
U of Pittsburgh (PA)
U of Regina (SK, Canada)
U of Rhode Island (RI)
U of Richmond (VA)
U of Rochester (NY)
U of Saint Joseph (CT)
U of St. Thomas (MN)
U of Saskatchewan (SK, Canada)
The U of Scranton (PA)
U of South Carolina (SC)
U of Southern Maine (ME)
The U of Texas at Austin (TX)
The U of Texas at San Antonio (TX)
The U of Toledo (OH)
U of Toronto (ON, Canada)
The U of Tulsa (OK)
U of Utah (UT)
U of Vermont (VT)
U of Washington (WA)
U of Waterloo (ON, Canada)
U of Wisconsin–Eau Claire (WI)
U of Wisconsin–La Crosse (WI)
U of Wisconsin–Madison (WI)
U of Wisconsin–Milwaukee (WI)
U of Wisconsin–Whitewater (WI)
U of Wyoming (WY)
Vanderbilt U (TN)
Vassar Coll (NY)
Villanova U (PA)
Virginia Commonwealth U (VA)
Virginia Wesleyan U (VA)
Washington & Jefferson Coll (PA)
Washington State U (WA)
Washington U in St. Louis (MO)
Webster U (MO)
Wellesley Coll (MA)
Wells Coll (NY)
West Chester U of Pennsylvania (PA)
Western Michigan U (MI)
Wheaton Coll (MA)
Wichita State U (KS)
Willamette U (OR)
William Paterson U of New Jersey (NJ)
Williams Coll (MA)

WOOD SCIENCE AND WOOD PRODUCTS/PULP AND PAPER TECHNOLOGY
North Carolina State U (NC)
Oregon State U (OR)
Purdue U (IN)
State U of New York Coll of Environmental Science and Forestry (NY)
U of Idaho (ID)
U of Toronto (ON, Canada)
West Virginia U (WV)

WOODWIND INSTRUMENTS
Acadia U (NS, Canada)
Conservatorio de Musica de Puerto Rico (PR)
Northwestern U (IL)
Oberlin Coll (OH)
Oklahoma Christian U (OK)
San Francisco Conservatory of Music (CA)
State U of New York at Fredonia (NY)
The U of Kansas (KS)
U of Michigan (MI)
U of Southern California (CA)
Vanderbilt U (TN)
Xavier U of Louisiana (LA)
Youngstown State U (OH)

WOODWORKING
Rochester Inst of Technology (NY)

WORK AND FAMILY STUDIES
Brigham Young U (UT)
Washington State U (WA)

WRITING
Augustana Coll (IL)
Aurora U (IL)
Baylor U (TX)
Bennington Coll (VT)
Bethel Coll (IN)
Biola U (CA)
Bluffton U (OH)
Brigham Young U (UT)
Calvin Coll (MI)
Canisius Coll (NY)
Cardinal Stritch U (WI)
Carroll Coll (MT)
Carroll U (WI)
Champlain Coll (VT)
DePauw U (IN)
Eastern Michigan U (MI)
Ferris State U (MI)
Geneva Coll (PA)
Georgia Southern U (GA)
Gettysburg Coll (PA)
Goshen Coll (IN)
Grand Valley State U (MI)
High Point U (NC)
Houston Baptist U (TX)
Indiana Wesleyan U (IN)
Kansas Wesleyan U (KS)
La Roche Coll (PA)
Lipscomb U (TN)
Lubbock Christian U (TX)
Madonna U (MI)
Marian U (MI)
Marlboro Coll (VT)
Marquette U (WI)
Massachusetts Coll of Liberal Arts (MA)
Northern Vermont U–Lyndon (VT)
Northwest Missouri State U (MO)
Northwest U (WA)
Oakland U (MI)
Oral Roberts U (OK)

Pacific Northwest Coll of Art (OR)
Pitzer Coll (CA)
Point Loma Nazarene U (CA)
San Diego State U (CA)
Sarah Lawrence Coll (NY)
Spring Hill Coll (AL)
U of California, San Diego (CA)
U of Central Arkansas (AR)
U of Colorado Denver (CO)
U of Evansville (IN)
The U of Findlay (OH)
U of Jamestown (ND)
U of Michigan–Flint (MI)
U of Mount Union (OH)
U of Providence (MT)
The U of Tampa (FL)
The U of Texas at Austin (TX)
U of Washington, Tacoma (WA)
U of Wisconsin–Superior (WI)
Western Michigan U (MI)
Whitworth U (WA)
William Peace U (NC)

YOUTH MINISTRY
Anderson U (IN)
Anderson U (SC)
Andrews U (MI)
Arizona Christian U (AZ)
Asbury U (KY)
Augsburg U (MN)
Bluffton U (OH)
Cairn U (PA)
Calvary U (MO)
Carson-Newman U (TN)
Cedarville U (OH)
Charleston Southern U (SC)
Colorado Christian U (CO)
Concordia U Wisconsin (WI)
Cornerstone U (MI)
Eastern Nazarene Coll (MA)
Eastern U (PA)
East Texas Baptist U (TX)
Emmaus Bible Coll (IA)
Florida Southern Coll (FL)
Geneva Coll (PA)
Gordon Coll (MA)
Greenville U (IL)
Harding U (AR)
Hope Intl U (CA)
Howard Payne U (TX)
Indiana Wesleyan U (IN)
Judson U (IL)
Kentucky Mountain Bible Coll (KY)
King U (TN)
Lee U (TN)
Liberty U (VA)
Lincoln Christian U (IL)
Lipscomb U (TN)
Malone U (OH)
Maranatha Baptist U (WI)
Master's Coll and Sem (ON, Canada)
MidAmerica Nazarene U (KS)
Mid-Atlantic Christian U (NC)
Mount Vernon Nazarene U (OH)
Multnomah U (OR)
North Greenville U (SC)
Northwest Christian U (OR)
Northwest U (WA)
Nyack Coll (NY)
Ohio Christian U (OH)
Ohio Northern U (OH)
Olivet Nazarene U (IL)
Pfeiffer U (NC)
Point Loma Nazarene U (CA)
Redeemer U Coll (ON, Canada)
Southeastern U (FL)

Southwestern Assemblies of God U (TX)
Taylor U (IN)
Toccoa Falls Coll (GA)
Trevecca Nazarene U (TN)
Trinity Christian Coll (IL)
Trinity Coll of Florida (FL)
U of Sioux Falls (SD)
U of Valley Forge (PA)
Vanguard U of Southern California (CA)

YOUTH SERVICES
Montclair State U (NJ)
Murray State U (KY)
Rhode Island Coll (RI)
Samford U (AL)

ZOOLOGY/ANIMAL BIOLOGY
Andrews U (MI)
Auburn U (AL)
Bennington Coll (VT)
Berry Coll (GA)
Brandon U (MB, Canada)
California State U, Long Beach (CA)
Canisius Coll (NY)
Coll of the Atlantic (ME)
Colorado State U (CO)
Delaware Valley U (PA)
The Evergreen State Coll (WA)
Humboldt State U (CA)
Kent State U (OH)
Liberty U (VA)
Malone U (OH)
Miami U (OH)
Michigan State U (MI)
Muskingum U (OH)
North Carolina State U (NC)
Northern Michigan U (MI)
The Ohio State U (OH)
Ohio U (OH)
Ohio Wesleyan U (OH)
Oklahoma State U (OK)
Olivet Nazarene U (IL)
Oregon State U (OR)
Otterbein U (OH)
Rutgers U–Newark (NJ)
San Diego State U (CA)
San Francisco State U (CA)
Sonoma State U (CA)
Southern Illinois U Carbondale (IL)
State U of New York at Oswego (NY)
Tarleton State U (TX)
Texas A&M U (TX)
Texas Tech U (TX)
The U of Akron (OH)
U of California, Davis (CA)
U of California, Santa Barbara (CA)
U of Florida (FL)
U of Guelph (ON, Canada)
U of Hawaii at Manoa (HI)
U of Maine (ME)
U of New Hampshire (NH)
U of Oklahoma (OK)
U of Toronto (ON, Canada)
U of Vermont (VT)
U of Wisconsin–Madison (WI)
U of Wyoming (WY)
Utah State U (UT)
Washington State U (WA)
Weber State U (UT)

ZOOLOGY/ANIMAL BIOLOGY RELATED
Beacon Coll (FL)

Entrance Difficulty

This index groups colleges by their own assessment of their entrance difficulty level. The colleges were asked to select the level that most closely corresponds to their entrance difficulty, according to the guidelines below. Institutions for which high school class rank and/or standardized test scores do not apply as admission criteria were asked to select the level that best indicates their entrance difficulty as compared to other institutions.

MOST DIFFICULT

More than 75 percent of the freshmen were in the top 10 percent of their high school class and scored over 1310 on the SAT (critical reading and mathematical combined) or over 29 on the ACT (composite); about 30 percent or fewer of the applicants were accepted.

Amherst Coll (MA)
Barnard Coll (NY)
Bowdoin Coll (ME)
Brandeis U (MA)
Bryn Mawr Coll (PA)
Bucknell U (PA)
California Inst of Technology (CA)
Carnegie Mellon U (PA)
Claremont McKenna Coll (CA)
Colby Coll (ME)
Colgate U (NY)
The Coll of William and Mary (VA)
Columbia U (NY)
Cornell U (NY)
Dartmouth Coll (NH)
Emory U (GA)
Franklin W. Olin Coll of Eng (MA)
Georgetown U (DC)
The George Washington U (DC)
Gettysburg Coll (PA)
Harvard U (MA)
Harvey Mudd Coll (CA)
Haverford Coll (PA)
The Juilliard School (NY)
Kenyon Coll (OH)
Lehigh U (PA)
Massachusetts Inst of Technology (MA)
Middlebury Coll (VT)
Northwestern U (IL)
Pomona Coll (CA)
Princeton U (NJ)
Rice U (TX)
Soka U of America (CA)
Stanford U (CA)
Tufts U (MA)
U of Chicago (IL)
U of Notre Dame (IN)
U of Pennsylvania (PA)
U of Southern California (CA)
Vanderbilt U (TN)
Washington and Lee U (VA)
Washington U in St. Louis (MO)
Webb Inst (NY)
Wellesley Coll (MA)
Wesleyan U (CT)
Williams Coll (MA)

VERY DIFFICULT

More than 50 percent of the freshmen were in the top 10 percent of their high school class and scored over 1230 on the SAT or over 26 on the ACT; about 60 percent or fewer applicants were accepted.

Allegheny Coll (PA)
American U (DC)
American U in Bulgaria (Bulgaria)
The American U in Cairo (Egypt)
ArtCenter Coll of Design (CA)
Austin Coll (TX)
Babson Coll (MA)

Baruch Coll of the City U of New York (NY)
Bates Coll (ME)
Bennington Coll (VT)
Bentley U (MA)
Binghamton U, State U of New York (NY)
Boston Coll (MA)
Boston U (MA)
Carleton Coll (MN)
Case Western Reserve U (OH)
Centre Coll (KY)
Chapman U (CA)
Clarkson U (NY)
Clemson U (SC)
The Coll of New Jersey (NJ)
Coll of the Atlantic (ME)
Coll of the Holy Cross (MA)
The Colorado Coll (CO)
Connecticut Coll (CT)
Davidson Coll (NC)
Denison U (OH)
Dickinson Coll (PA)
Earlham Coll (IN)
Emerson Coll (MA)
Fairfield U (CT)
Florida State U (FL)
Fordham U (NY)
Franklin & Marshall Coll (PA)
Grinnell Coll (IA)
Gustavus Adolphus Coll (MN)
Hamilton Coll (NY)
Hendrix Coll (AR)
Hillsdale Coll (MI)
Hobart and William Smith Colls (NY)
Illinois Wesleyan U (IL)
James Madison U (VA)
Kalamazoo Coll (MI)
Kettering U (MI)
Knox Coll (IL)
Laguna Coll of Art & Design (CA)
Lawrence U (WI)
Macalester Coll (MN)
Marist Coll (NY)
Maryland Inst Coll of Art (MD)
Missouri U of Science and Technology (MO)
Mount Holyoke Coll (MA)
Muhlenberg Coll (PA)
New Coll of Florida (FL)
New York U (NY)
North Carolina State U (NC)
Northeastern U (MA)
Oberlin Coll (OH)
Occidental Coll (CA)
Oglethorpe U (GA)
The Ohio State U (OH)
Ohio Wesleyan U (OH)
Penn State Abington (PA)
Penn State Altoona (PA)
Penn State Berks (PA)
Penn State Erie, The Behrend Coll (PA)
Penn State Harrisburg (PA)
Penn State U Park (PA)
Pepperdine U, Malibu (CA)
Pitzer Coll (CA)
Pratt Inst (NY)
Presbyterian Coll (SC)
Queens Coll of the City U of New York (NY)
Reed Coll (OR)
Rensselaer Polytechnic Inst (NY)
Rhodes Coll (TN)
Rose-Hulman Inst of Technology (IN)
Saint Louis U (MO)
St. Olaf Coll (MN)
Santa Clara U (CA)
Sarah Lawrence Coll (NY)
Scripps Coll (CA)
Sewanee: The U of the South (TN)
Skidmore Coll (NY)
Smith Coll (MA)
Southwestern U (TX)

Spelman Coll (GA)
State U of New York at New Paltz (NY)
State U of New York Coll at Oneonta (NY)
State U of New York Coll of Environmental Science and Forestry (NY)
State U of New York Maritime Coll (NY)
Stevens Inst of Technology (NJ)
Stockton U (NJ)
Stonehill Coll (MA)
Stony Brook U, State U of New York (NY)
Syracuse U (NY)
Texas Christian U (TX)
Thomas Aquinas Coll (CA)
Transylvania U (KY)
Trinity U (TX)
Tulane U (LA)
Union Coll (NY)
United States Coast Guard Acad (CT)
United States Merchant Marine Acad (NY)
U at Albany, State U of New York (NY)
U of California, Davis (CA)
U of California, Irvine (CA)
U of California, Los Angeles (CA)
U of California, Riverside (CA)
U of California, San Diego (CA)
U of California, Santa Barbara (CA)
U of California, Santa Cruz (CA)
U of Florida (FL)
U of Mary Washington (VA)
U of Miami (FL)
U of Michigan (MI)
The U of North Carolina at Chapel Hill (NC)
U of Pittsburgh (PA)
U of Richmond (VA)
U of Rochester (NY)
U of San Diego (CA)
The U of Texas at Dallas (TX)
U of Toronto (ON, Canada)
The U of Tulsa (OK)
U of Virginia (VA)
U of Washington (WA)
U of Wisconsin–Madison (WI)
Vassar Coll (NY)
Villanova U (PA)
Wake Forest U (NC)
Washington & Jefferson Coll (PA)
Wheaton Coll (IL)
Wheaton Coll (MA)
Whitman Coll (WA)
Willamette U (OR)
Wofford Coll (SC)
Worcester Polytechnic Inst (MA)

MODERATELY DIFFICULT

More than 75 percent of the freshmen were in the top half of their high school class and scored over 1010 on the SAT or over 18 on the ACT; about 85 percent or fewer of the applicants were accepted.

Abilene Christian U (TX)
Acadia U (NS, Canada)
Adams State U (CO)
Adelphi U (NY)
Agnes Scott Coll (GA)
Alberta Coll of Art & Design (AB, Canada)
Albion Coll (MI)
Albright Coll (PA)
Alcorn State U (MS)
Alfred U (NY)
Allen Coll (IA)
Alma Coll (MI)
Alverno Coll (WI)
American Acad of Art (IL)
American U of Health Sciences (CA)
The American U of Paris (France)
Anderson U (IN)
Andrews U (MI)

Angelo State U (TX)
Antioch U Los Angeles (CA)
Antioch U Santa Barbara (CA)
Appalachian State U (NC)
Aquinas Coll (MI)
Arcadia U (PA)
Arizona State U at the Downtown Phoenix campus (AZ)
Arizona State U at the Polytechnic campus (AZ)
Arizona State U at the Tempe campus (AZ)
Arizona State U at the West campus (AZ)
Arkansas Tech U (AR)
Asbury U (KY)
Ashland U (OH)
Assumption Coll (MA)
Auburn U (AL)
Auburn U at Montgomery (AL)
Augsburg U (MN)
Augustana Coll (IL)
Augustana U (SD)
Aultman Coll of Nursing and Health Sciences (OH)
Aurora U (IL)
Austin Peay State U (TN)
Averett U (VA)
Azusa Pacific U (CA)
Baker U (KS)
Baldwin Wallace U (OH)
Baptist Coll of Health Sciences (TN)
Bard Coll (NY)
Barry U (FL)
Baylor U (TX)
Bay Path U (MA)
Beacon Coll (FL)
Becker Coll (MA)
Belhaven U (MS)
Bellarmine U (KY)
Belmont U (TN)
Bemidji State U (MN)
Benedictine U (IL)
Berea Coll (KY)
Berry Coll (GA)
Bethany Lutheran Coll (MN)
Bethel Coll (KS)
Bethel U (MN)
Biola U (CA)
Birmingham-Southern Coll (AL)
Blackburn Coll (IL)
Blue Mountain Coll (MS)
Bluffton U (OH)
Boise State U (ID)
Bowling Green State U (OH)
Bradley U (IL)
Brenau U (GA)
Brescia U (KY)
Bridgewater Coll (VA)
Bridgewater State U (MA)
Brigham Young U (UT)
Brigham Young U–Idaho (ID)
Bryan Coll (TN)
Bryant U (RI)
Buena Vista U (IA)
Buffalo State Coll, State U of New York (NY)
Butler U (IN)
Cairn U (PA)
Caldwell U (NJ)
California Baptist U (CA)
California Lutheran U (CA)
California Polytechnic State U, San Luis Obispo (CA)
California State Polytechnic U, Pomona (CA)
California State U, Dominguez Hills (CA)
California State U, Fullerton (CA)
California State U, Long Beach (CA)
California State U, Los Angeles (CA)
California State U Maritime Acad (CA)
California State U, Monterey Bay (CA)
California State U, Northridge (CA)
California State U, Sacramento (CA)
California State U, San Bernardino (CA)
California State U, San Marcos (CA)
California State U, Stanislaus (CA)
California U of Pennsylvania (PA)
Calvin Coll (MI)
Campbellsville U (KY)
Canisius Coll (NY)
Capital U (OH)
Cardinal Stritch U (WI)

Carroll Coll (MT)
Carroll U (WI)
Carson-Newman U (TN)
Carthage Coll (WI)
Catawba Coll (NC)
Cedar Crest Coll (PA)
Cedarville U (OH)
Centenary Coll of Louisiana (LA)
Central Connecticut State U (CT)
Central Methodist U (MO)
Central Michigan U (MI)
Chaminade U of Honolulu (HI)
Champlain Coll (VT)
Charles R. Drew U of Medicine and Science (CA)
Charleston Southern U (SC)
Chatham U (PA)
Chestnut Hill Coll (PA)
Christendom Coll (VA)
Christian Brothers U (TN)
Christopher Newport U (VA)
The Citadel, The Military Coll of South Carolina (SC)
City Coll of the City U of New York (NY)
Clark Atlanta U (GA)
Clarke U (IA)
Clark U (MA)
Cleveland State U (OH)
Coastal Carolina U (SC)
Coe Coll (IA)
Cogswell Polytechnical Coll (CA)
Coker Coll (SC)
The Coll at Brockport, State U of New York (NY)
Coll of Charleston (SC)
The Coll of Idaho (ID)
Coll of Mount Saint Vincent (NY)
The Coll of New Rochelle (NY)
Coll of Saint Benedict (MN)
The Coll of Saint Rose (NY)
The Coll of St. Scholastica (MN)
Coll of the Ozarks (MO)
The Coll of Wooster (OH)
Colorado Christian U (CO)
Colorado State U (CO)
Columbia Coll (SC)
Concordia Coll–New York (NY)
Concordia U (QC, Canada)
Concordia U Chicago (IL)
Concordia U Irvine (CA)
Concordia U, Nebraska (NE)
Concordia U of Edmonton (AB, Canada)
Concordia U Wisconsin (WI)
Conservatorio de Musica de Puerto Rico (PR)
Converse Coll (SC)
Corban U (OR)
Cornell Coll (IA)
Cornish Coll of the Arts (WA)
Cottey Coll (MO)
Covenant Coll (GA)
Creighton U (NE)
The Culinary Inst of America (NY)
Culver-Stockton Coll (MO)
Curry Coll (MA)
Daemen Coll (NY)
Dakota State U (SD)
Dallas Baptist U (TX)
Dean Coll (MA)
Defiance Coll (OH)
Delaware State U (DE)
DePaul U (IL)
DePauw U (IN)
DEREE - The American Coll of Greece (Greece)
DeSales U (PA)
Dominican U (IL)
Dominican U of California (CA)
Drake U (IA)
Drew U (NJ)
Drexel U (PA)
Drury U (MO)
Duquesne U (PA)
D'Youville Coll (NY)
East Carolina U (NC)
Eastern Mennonite U (VA)
Eastern Michigan U (MI)
Eastern Nazarene Coll (MA)
Eastern U (PA)
East Stroudsburg U of Pennsylvania (PA)

East Tennessee State U (TN)
East Texas Baptist U (TX)
Eckerd Coll (FL)
ECPI U, Virginia Beach (VA)
Edgewood Coll (WI)
Elizabethtown Coll (PA)
Elmhurst Coll (IL)
Elms Coll (MA)
Elon U (NC)
Embry-Riddle Aeronautical U–Daytona (FL)
Endicott Coll (MA)
Escuela de Artes Plasticas y Dise&nno de Puerto Rico (PR)
Evangel U (MO)
The Evergreen State Coll (WA)
Fairleigh Dickinson U, Florham Campus (NJ)
Fairleigh Dickinson U, Metropolitan Campus (NJ)
Farmingdale State Coll (NY)
Fashion Inst of Technology (NY)
Felician U (NJ)
FIDM/Fashion Inst of Design & Merchandising, Los
  Angeles Campus (CA)
FIDM/Fashion Inst of Design & Merchandising, San
  Francisco Campus (CA)
Fitchburg State U (MA)
Florida Ag and Mech U (FL)
Florida Atlantic U (FL)
Florida Coll (FL)
Florida Gulf Coast U (FL)
Florida Inst of Technology (FL)
Florida Intl U (FL)
Florida National U (FL)
Florida Southern Coll (FL)
Fort Lewis Coll (CO)
Framingham State U (MA)
Francis Marion U (SC)
Franklin Coll (IN)
Franklin U Switzerland (Switzerland)
Friends U (KS)
Frostburg State U (MD)
Furman U (SC)
Gannon U (PA)
Geneva Coll (PA)
Georgetown Coll (KY)
Georgia Coll & State U (GA)
Georgian Court U (NJ)
Georgia Southern U (GA)
Georgia Southwestern State U (GA)
Georgia State U (GA)
Golden Gate U (CA)
Goldfarb School of Nursing at Barnes-Jewish Coll (MO)
Gonzaga U (WA)
Gordon Coll (MA)
Goshen Coll (IN)
Governors State U (IL)
Graceland U (IA)
Grand Valley State U (MI)
Green Mountain Coll (VT)
Greenville U (IL)
Grove City Coll (PA)
Guilford Coll (NC)
Gutenberg Coll (OR)
Gwynedd Mercy U (PA)
Hallmark U (TX)
Hamline U (MN)
Hampden-Sydney Coll (VA)
Hampshire Coll (MA)
Hampton U (VA)
Harding U (AR)
Hardin-Simmons U (TX)
Hartwick Coll (NY)
Hawai`i Pacific U (HI)
HEC Montreal (QC, Canada)
Heidelberg U (OH)
High Point U (NC)
Hiram Coll (OH)
Hofstra U (NY)
Hollins U (VA)
Holy Names U (CA)
Hood Coll (MD)
Hope Coll (MI)
Hope Intl U (CA)
Houston Baptist U (TX)
Howard Payne U (TX)
Hunter Coll of the City U of New York (NY)
Husson U (ME)

Huston-Tillotson U (TX)
Illinois Coll (IL)
Immaculata U (PA)
Indiana State U (IN)
Indiana Tech (IN)
Indiana U Bloomington (IN)
Indiana U East (IN)
Indiana U–Purdue U Indianapolis (IN)
Indiana U South Bend (IN)
Indiana Wesleyan U (IN)
Inter American U of Puerto Rico, Aguadilla Campus (PR)
Inter American U of Puerto Rico, Fajardo Campus (PR)
Inter American U of Puerto Rico, Metropolitan Campus (PR)
Inter American U of Puerto Rico, San Germán Campus (PR)
Iona Coll (NY)
Iowa State U of Science and Technology (IA)
Ithaca Coll (NY)
Jacksonville U (FL)
Jefferson Coll of Health Sciences (VA)
John Brown U (AR)
John Carroll U (OH)
John Jay Coll of Criminal Justice of the City U of New York (NY)
John Paul the Great Catholic U (CA)
Johnson C. Smith U (NC)
Johnson U (TN)
John Wesley U (NC)
Judson U (IL)
Juniata Coll (PA)
Kansas City Art Inst (MO)
Kansas Wesleyan U (KS)
Kean U (NJ)
Keene State Coll (NH)
Kennesaw State U (GA)
Kent State U (OH)
The King's Coll (NY)
King's Coll (PA)
King U (TN)
Kutztown U of Pennsylvania (PA)
LaGrange Coll (GA)
Langston U (OK)
La Salle U (PA)
Lasell Coll (MA)
Lawrence Technological U (MI)
Lebanese American U (Lebanon)
Lebanon Valley Coll (PA)
Lehman Coll of the City U of New York (NY)
Le Moyne Coll (NY)
Lenoir-Rhyne U (NC)
LeTourneau U (TX)
Lewis U (IL)
Lincoln Christian U (IL)
Lincoln Memorial U (TN)
Lindenwood U (MO)
Linfield Coll (OR)
Lipscomb U (TN)
Lock Haven U of Pennsylvania (PA)
Longwood U (VA)
Loras Coll (IA)
Louisiana Coll (LA)
Louisiana State U and A&M Coll (LA)
Loyola U Chicago (IL)
Loyola U New Orleans (LA)
Lubbock Christian U (TX)
Luther Coll (IA)
Lycoming Coll (PA)
Lynchburg Coll (VA)
Lynn U (FL)
Lyon Coll (AR)
Madonna U (MI)
Maharishi U of Management (IA)
Maine Coll of Health Professions (ME)
Malone U (OH)
Manchester U (IN)
Manhattan Coll (NY)
Manhattanville Coll (NY)
Mansfield U of Pennsylvania (PA)
Marian U (IN)
Marian U (WI)
Marietta Coll (OH)
Marlboro Coll (VT)
Marquette U (WI)
Marshall U (WV)
Martin Luther Coll (MN)
Mary Baldwin U (VA)
Marymount Manhattan Coll (NY)

Marymount U (VA)
Maryville Coll (TN)
Maryville U of Saint Louis (MO)
Marywood U (PA)
Massachusetts Coll of Art and Design (MA)
Massachusetts Coll of Liberal Arts (MA)
Massachusetts Maritime Acad (MA)
The Master's U (CA)
McDaniel Coll (MD)
McKendree U (IL)
McMurry U (TX)
McNeese State U (LA)
McPherson Coll (KS)
Mercer U, Macon (GA)
Mercy Coll (NY)
Mercy Coll of Ohio (OH)
Mercyhurst U (PA)
Meredith Coll (NC)
Merrimack Coll (MA)
Messenger Coll (TX)
Messiah Coll (PA)
Metropolitan Coll of New York (NY)
Miami U (OH)
Michigan State U (MI)
Michigan Technological U (MI)
Middle Tennessee State U (TN)
Millersville U of Pennsylvania (PA)
Milligan Coll (TN)
Millikin U (IL)
Millsaps Coll (MS)
Mills Coll (CA)
Milwaukee School of Eng (WI)
Minneapolis Coll of Art and Design (MN)
Minnesota State U Moorhead (MN)
Minot State U (ND)
Misericordia U (PA)
Mississippi State U (MS)
Missouri Baptist U (MO)
Missouri State U (MO)
Molloy Coll (NY)
Monmouth Coll (IL)
Montana Tech of The U of Montana (MT)
Montclair State U (NJ)
Moravian Coll (PA)
Morehouse Coll (GA)
Morningside Coll (IA)
Mount Carmel Coll of Nursing (OH)
Mount Mary U (WI)
Mount Mercy U (IA)
Mount Saint Mary Coll (NY)
Mount St. Mary's U (MD)
Mount Vernon Nazarene U (OH)
Multnomah U (OR)
Murray State U (KY)
Muskingum U (OH)
Naropa U (CO)
National Louis U (IL)
Nazareth Coll of Rochester (NY)
Nebraska Methodist Coll (NE)
Neumont Coll of Computer Science (UT)
Newberry Coll (SC)
New Hampshire Inst of Art (NH)
New Jersey City U (NJ)
New Jersey Inst of Technology (NJ)
New Mexico Inst of Mining and Technology (NM)
New Mexico State U (NM)
New Saint Andrews Coll (ID)
The New School Coll of Performing Arts (NY)
The New School–Parsons Paris (France)
New York Inst of Technology (NY)
Niagara U (NY)
North Carolina Wesleyan Coll (NC)
North Central Coll (IL)
North Dakota State U (ND)
Northeastern State U (OK)
Northern Arizona U (AZ)
Northern Illinois U (IL)
Northern Vermont U–Lyndon (VT)
Northland Coll (WI)
Northwestern Coll (IA)
Northwestern Oklahoma State U (OK)
Northwestern State U of Louisiana (LA)
Northwest Missouri State U (MO)
Northwest Nazarene U (ID)
Northwest U (WA)
Notre Dame de Namur U (CA)

Nova Southeastern U (FL)
Oakland U (MI)
Ohio Dominican U (OH)
Ohio Northern U (OH)
Ohio U (OH)
Ohr Somayach/Joseph Tanenbaum Educational Center (NY)
Oklahoma Baptist U (OK)
Oklahoma Christian U (OK)
Oklahoma State U (OK)
Old Dominion U (VA)
Olivet Nazarene U (IL)
O'More Coll of Design (TN)
Oral Roberts U (OK)
Oregon Inst of Technology (OR)
Oregon State U (OR)
Ottawa U (KS)
Otterbein U (OH)
Ouachita Baptist U (AR)
Pace U (NY)
Pace U, Pleasantville Campus (NY)
Pacific Lutheran U (WA)
Palm Beach Atlantic U (FL)
Penn State Beaver (PA)
Penn State Brandywine (PA)
Penn State DuBois (PA)
Penn State Fayette, The Eberly Campus (PA)
Penn State Greater Allegheny (PA)
Penn State Hazleton (PA)
Penn State Lehigh Valley (PA)
Penn State Mont Alto (PA)
Penn State New Kensington (PA)
Penn State Schuylkill (PA)
Penn State Shenango (PA)
Penn State Wilkes-Barre (PA)
Penn State Worthington Scranton (PA)
Penn State York (PA)
Pennsylvania Coll of Art & Design (PA)
Pennsylvania Coll of Health Sciences (PA)
Pfeiffer U (NC)
Piedmont Coll (GA)
Pine Manor Coll (MA)
Point Loma Nazarene U (CA)
Point Park U (PA)
Point U (GA)
Portland State U (OR)
Post U (CT)
Prairie View A&M U (TX)
Principia Coll (IL)
Purchase Coll, State U of New York (NY)
Purdue U (IN)
Purdue U Northwest (IN)
Quinnipiac U (CT)
Ramapo Coll of New Jersey (NJ)
Randolph Coll (VA)
Randolph-Macon Coll (VA)
Regis U (CO)
Research Coll of Nursing (MO)
Resurrection U (IL)
Rhode Island Coll (RI)
Rider U (NJ)
Ringling Coll of Art and Design (FL)
Ripon Coll (WI)
Rivier U (NH)
Roanoke Coll (VA)
Roberts Wesleyan Coll (NY)
Rochester Inst of Technology (NY)
Rockhurst U (MO)
Rocky Mountain Coll (MT)
Rollins Coll (FL)
Roosevelt U (IL)
Rosemont Coll (PA)
Rowan U (NJ)
Rutgers U–Camden (NJ)
Rutgers U–Newark (NJ)
Rutgers U–New Brunswick (NJ)
Sacred Heart U (CT)
The Sage Colls (NY)
Saginaw Valley State U (MI)
St. Ambrose U (IA)
St. Andrews U (NC)
Saint Anselm Coll (NH)
Saint Augustine's U (NC)
St. Bonaventure U (NY)
St. Catherine U (MN)
Saint Charles Borromeo Sem, Overbrook (PA)
Saint Francis U (PA)

St. John Fisher Coll (NY)
St. John's Coll (MD)
St. John's Coll (NM)
Saint John's U (MN)
St. John's U (NY)
St. Joseph's Coll, Long Island Campus (NY)
St. Joseph's Coll, New York (NY)
Saint Joseph's U (PA)
St. Lawrence U (NY)
Saint Leo U (FL)
St. Louis Coll of Pharmacy (MO)
Saint Louis U–Madrid Campus (Spain)
Saint Martin's U (WA)
Saint Mary's Coll of California (CA)
St. Mary's Coll of Maryland (MD)
St. Mary's U (TX)
Saint Mary's U of Minnesota (MN)
Saint Michael's Coll (VT)
St. Norbert Coll (WI)
Saint Peter's U (NJ)
St. Thomas Aquinas Coll (NY)
St. Thomas U (NB, Canada)
Saint Vincent Coll (PA)
Salisbury U (MD)
Samford U (AL)
Sam Houston State U (TX)
San Diego State U (CA)
San Francisco Art Inst (CA)
San Francisco State U (CA)
Savannah Coll of Art and Design (GA)
School of Visual Arts (NY)
Schreiner U (TX)
Seattle Pacific U (WA)
Seattle U (WA)
Seton Hill U (PA)
Shepherd U (WV)
Shorter U (GA)
Siena Coll (NY)
Sierra Nevada Coll (NV)
Simmons Coll (MA)
Simon Fraser U (BC, Canada)
Simpson Coll (IA)
Slippery Rock U of Pennsylvania (PA)
Sonoma State U (CA)
Southeastern Louisiana U (LA)
Southeastern Oklahoma State U (OK)
Southeast Missouri State U (MO)
Southern Adventist U (TN)
Southern Arkansas U–Magnolia (AR)
Southern Illinois U Carbondale (IL)
Southern Illinois U Edwardsville (IL)
Southern Methodist U (TX)
Southern Utah U (UT)
Southwest Baptist U (MO)
Spring Hill Coll (AL)
State U of New York at Fredonia (NY)
State U of New York at Oswego (NY)
State U of New York at Plattsburgh (NY)
State U of New York Coll at Cortland (NY)
State U of New York Coll at Geneseo (NY)
State U of New York Coll at Old Westbury (NY)
State U of New York Coll at Potsdam (NY)
State U of New York Coll of Technology at Alfred (NY)
State U of New York Coll of Technology at Delhi (NY)
State U of New York Polytechnic Inst (NY)
Stephen F. Austin State U (TX)
Stetson U (FL)
Stevenson U (MD)
Stevens–The Inst of Business & Arts (MO)
Suffolk U (MA)
Susquehanna U (PA)
Tabor Coll (KS)
Talladega Coll (AL)
Tarleton State U (TX)
Taylor U (IN)
Temple U (PA)
Tennessee Technological U (TN)
Texas A&M Intl U (TX)
Texas A&M U (TX)
Texas A&M U–Commerce (TX)
Texas A&M U–Corpus Christi (TX)
Texas A&M U–Kingsville (TX)
Texas State U (TX)
Texas Tech U (TX)
Thomas Jefferson U (PA)

Thomas More Coll of Liberal Arts (NH)
Tiffin U (OH)
Toccoa Falls Coll (GA)
Towson U (MD)
Trent U (ON, Canada)
Trevecca Nazarene U (TN)
Trine U (IN)
Trinity Christian Coll (IL)
Truman State U (MO)
Tusculum Coll (TN)
Union Coll (NE)
Union U (TN)
Unity Coll (ME)
Université de Sherbrooke (QC, Canada)
U at Buffalo, the State U of New York (NY)
The U of Akron (OH)
The U of Alabama (AL)
The U of Alabama at Birmingham (AL)
The U of Arizona (AZ)
U of Arkansas (AR)
U of Bridgeport (CT)
U of Central Arkansas (AR)
U of Central Florida (FL)
U of Central Missouri (MO)
U of Charleston (WV)
U of Cincinnati (OH)
U of Colorado Boulder (CO)
U of Colorado Colorado Springs (CO)
U of Colorado Denver (CO)
U of Dallas (TX)
U of Dayton (OH)
U of Denver (CO)
U of Dubuque (IA)
U of Evansville (IN)
The U of Findlay (OH)
U of Georgia (GA)
U of Guelph (ON, Canada)
U of Hartford (CT)
U of Hawaii at Manoa (HI)
U of Houston (TX)
U of Idaho (ID)
U of Illinois at Chicago (IL)
U of Illinois at Springfield (IL)
The U of Kansas (KS)
U of Kentucky (KY)
U of King's Coll (NS, Canada)
U of La Verne (CA)
U of Louisiana at Monroe (LA)
U of Louisville (KY)
U of Maine (ME)
U of Maine at Machias (ME)
U of Mary Hardin-Baylor (TX)
U of Maryland, Baltimore County (MD)
U of Maryland, Coll Park (MD)
U of Maryland Eastern Shore (MD)
U of Massachusetts Amherst (MA)
U of Massachusetts Boston (MA)
U of Massachusetts Dartmouth (MA)
U of Massachusetts Lowell (MA)
U of Memphis (TN)
U of Michigan–Dearborn (MI)
U of Michigan–Flint (MI)
U of Minnesota, Duluth (MN)
U of Minnesota, Morris (MN)
U of Minnesota, Twin Cities Campus (MN)
U of Missouri (MO)
U of Missouri–St. Louis (MO)
U of Mobile (AL)
U of Montana (MT)
U of Montevallo (AL)
U of Mount Union (OH)
U of Nebraska at Kearney (NE)
U of Nebraska–Lincoln (NE)
U of Nevada, Las Vegas (NV)
U of Nevada, Reno (NV)
U of New England (ME)
U of New Hampshire (NH)
U of New Haven (CT)
U of New Mexico (NM)
U of North Carolina at Asheville (NC)
The U of North Carolina at Charlotte (NC)
The U of North Carolina at Greensboro (NC)
The U of North Carolina at Pembroke (NC)
The U of North Carolina Wilmington (NC)
U of Northern Colorado (CO)

U of Northern Iowa (IA)
U of North Florida (FL)
U of North Georgia (GA)
U of North Texas (TX)
U of Oklahoma (OK)
U of Oregon (OR)
U of Pittsburgh at Greensburg (PA)
U of Puerto Rico–Humacao (PR)
U of Puget Sound (WA)
U of Rhode Island (RI)
U of St. Francis (IL)
U of Saint Joseph (CT)
U of Saint Mary (KS)
U of St. Thomas (MN)
U of St. Thomas (TX)
U of San Francisco (CA)
U of Science and Arts of Oklahoma (OK)
The U of Scranton (PA)
U of Sioux Falls (SD)
U of South Alabama (AL)
U of South Carolina (SC)
U of South Carolina Aiken (SC)
U of Southern Indiana (IN)
U of Southern Maine (ME)
U of Southern Mississippi (MS)
The U of Tampa (FL)
The U of Tennessee (TN)
The U of Tennessee at Chattanooga (TN)
The U of Tennessee at Martin (TN)
The U of Texas at Austin (TX)
The U of Texas at San Antonio (TX)
The U of Texas of the Permian Basin (TX)
The U of the Arts (PA)
U of the Pacific (CA)
U of Utah (UT)
U of Vermont (VT)
The U of Virginia's Coll at Wise (VA)
U of Washington, Bothell (WA)
U of Washington, Tacoma (WA)
U of Waterloo (ON, Canada)
U of West Georgia (GA)
U of Wisconsin–Eau Claire (WI)
U of Wisconsin–La Crosse (WI)
U of Wisconsin–Milwaukee (WI)
U of Wisconsin–Parkside (WI)
U of Wisconsin–River Falls (WI)
U of Wisconsin–Stevens Point (WI)
U of Wisconsin–Stout (WI)
U of Wisconsin–Whitewater (WI)
U of Wyoming (WY)
Upper Iowa U (IA)
Ursinus Coll (PA)
Utah State U (UT)
Utica Coll (NY)
Valdosta State U (GA)
Valparaiso U (IN)
Vanguard U of Southern California (CA)
Vaughn Coll of Aeronautics and Technology (NY)
Vermont Tech Coll (VT)
Virginia Military Inst (VA)
Virginia Polytechnic Inst and State U (VA)
Virginia Wesleyan U (VA)
Wabash Coll (IN)
Waldorf U (IA)
Walsh U (OH)
Warner Pacific Coll (OR)
Wartburg Coll (IA)
Washington Coll (MD)
Washington State U (WA)
Washington State U–Global Campus (WA)
Washington State U–Spokane (WA)
Washington State U–Tri-Cities (WA)
Washington State U–Vancouver (WA)
Waynesburg U (PA)
Wayne State U (MI)
Webber Intl U (FL)
Webster U (MO)
Wells Coll (NY)
Wentworth Inst of Technology (MA)
West Chester U of Pennsylvania (PA)
Western Connecticut State U (CT)
Western Illinois U (IL)
Western Michigan U (MI)
Western New England U (MA)
Western Oregon U (OR)

Western State Colorado U (CO)
Western Washington U (WA)
Westfield State U (MA)
Westminster Coll (PA)
Westminster Coll (UT)
Westmont Coll (CA)
West Texas A&M U (TX)
West Virginia U (WV)
West Virginia Wesleyan Coll (WV)
Whittier Coll (CA)
Whitworth U (WA)
Widener U (PA)
Wilkes U (PA)
William Jewell Coll (MO)
William Paterson U of New Jersey (NJ)
William Peace U (NC)
William Penn U (IA)
William Woods U (MO)
Winona State U (MN)
Winthrop U (SC)
Wisconsin Lutheran Coll (WI)
Wittenberg U (OH)
Woodbury U (CA)
Worcester State U (MA)
Xavier U of Louisiana (LA)
York Coll of Pennsylvania (PA)

MINIMALLY DIFFICULT

Most freshmen were not in the top half of their high school class and scored somewhat below 1010 on the SAT or below 19 on the ACT; up to 95 percent of the applicants were accepted.

Adventist U of Health Sciences (FL)
Alabama State U (AL)
Alaska Bible Coll (AK)
Alaska Pacific U (AK)
Alliant Intl U–San Diego (CA)
American Coll of Thessaloniki (Greece)
American Intl Coll (MA)
Amridge U (AL)
Anderson U (SC)
Austin Graduate School of Theology (TX)
Avila U (MO)
Barclay Coll (KS)
Barton Coll (NC)
Benedictine Coll (KS)
Bennett Coll (NC)
Bethel Coll (IN)
Bethel U (TN)
Bethune-Cookman U (FL)
Bloomsburg U of Pennsylvania (PA)
Bob Jones U (SC)
Bowie State U (MD)
Brewton-Parker Coll (GA)
Bryn Athyn Coll of the New Church (PA)
California Inst of Integral Studies (CA)
California State U, East Bay (CA)
Caribbean U (PR)
Carlow U (PA)
Cazenovia Coll (NY)
Central Penn Coll (PA)
Central State U (OH)
Chowan U (NC)
Clayton State U (GA)
Coleman U, San Diego (CA)
Coll of Business and Technology–Main Campus (FL)
Coll of Business and Technology–Miami Gardens (FL)
Coll of Coastal Georgia (GA)
Coll of Saint Mary (NE)
The Coll of Westchester (NY)
Colorado Mesa U (CO)
Colorado State U–Pueblo (CO)
Columbia Central U, Yauco (PR)
Columbia Coll (MO)
Columbia Coll Chicago (IL)
Columbus State U (GA)
Compass Coll of Cinematic Arts (MI)
Concordia U, St. Paul (MN)
Concord U (WV)
Cornerstone U (MI)
Criswell Coll (TX)
Delaware Valley U (PA)
Dickinson State U (ND)
DigiPen Inst of Technology (WA)

Dunwoody Coll of Technology (MN)
East Central U (OK)
Eastern Oregon U (OR)
EDP U of Puerto Rico–San Sebastian (PR)
Emmanuel Coll (GA)
Fayetteville State U (NC)
Ferris State U (MI)
Franciscan Missionaries of Our Lady U (LA)
Franklin Pierce U (NH)
Grand View U (IA)
Greensboro Coll (NC)
Hannibal-LaGrange U (MO)
Harrisburg U of Science and Technology (PA)
Hilbert Coll (NY)
Holy Family U (PA)
Humboldt State U (CA)
Idaho State U (ID)
Illinois State U (IL)
Indiana U Kokomo (IN)
Indiana U Northwest (IN)
Indiana U of Pennsylvania (PA)
Indiana U Southeast (IN)
Jackson State U (MS)
Johnson U Florida (FL)
Kansas State U (KS)
Kentucky Mountain Bible Coll (KY)
Lamar U (TX)
La Roche Coll (PA)
La Sierra U (CA)
Liberty U (VA)
Life U (GA)
Limestone Coll (SC)
Lincoln Coll (IL)
Lincoln Coll of New England, Southington (CT)
Lincoln U (CA)
Lincoln U (PA)
Lindsey Wilson Coll (KY)
Maria Coll (NY)
Marymount California U (CA)
Metropolitan State U of Denver (CO)
MidAmerica Nazarene U (KS)
Mid-Atlantic Christian U (NC)
Middle Georgia State U (GA)
Missouri Valley Coll (MO)
Morehead State U (KY)
Mount Aloysius Coll (PA)
Mount Marty Coll (SD)
Mount St. Joseph U (OH)
Neumann U (PA)
New England Inst of Technology (RI)
Newman U (KS)
New Mexico Highlands U (NM)
North American U (TX)
North Carolina Central U (NC)
Northcentral U (CA)
Northern State U (SD)
North Greenville U (SC)
Northwest Christian U (OR)
Nyack Coll (NY)
Oakland City U (IN)
Ohio Christian U (OH)
Pittsburg State U (KS)
Polytechnic U of Puerto Rico (PR)
Radford U (VA)
Rasmussen Coll Bloomington (MN)
Rasmussen Coll Brooklyn Park (MN)
Rasmussen Coll Eagan (MN)
Rasmussen Coll Fargo (ND)
Rasmussen Coll Mankato (MN)
Rasmussen Coll New Port Richey (FL)
Rasmussen Coll Ocala (FL)
Rasmussen Coll Rockford (IL)
Rasmussen Coll St. Cloud (MN)
Regent U (VA)
Robert Morris U (PA)
Robert Morris U Illinois (IL)
Rust Coll (MS)
St. Luke's Coll (IA)
Saint Mary-of-the-Woods Coll (IN)
Shaw U (NC)
Silver Lake Coll of the Holy Family (WI)
Southeastern U (FL)
Southwestern Adventist U (TX)
Southwestern Coll (KS)
Spencerian Coll (KY)
State U of New York Coll of Technology at Canton (NY)

Sullivan U (KY)
Sweet Briar Coll (VA)
Tennessee Wesleyan U (TN)
Texas Woman's U (TX)
Thomas U (GA)
Truett McConnell U (GA)
U of Alaska Fairbanks (AK)
U of Central Oklahoma (OK)
U of Houston–Clear Lake (TX)
U of Jamestown (ND)
U of Maine at Fort Kent (ME)
U of Maine at Presque Isle (ME)
U of Minnesota, Crookston (MN)
U of North Alabama (AL)
U of North Dakota (ND)
U of Pittsburgh at Bradford (PA)
U of South Carolina Union (SC)
U of South Dakota (SD)
The U of Texas at El Paso (TX)
U of the Incarnate Word (TX)
U of Valley Forge (PA)
The U of West Alabama (AL)
U of Wisconsin–Superior (WI)
Ursuline Coll (OH)
Wade Coll (TX)
Wayland Baptist U (TX)
Western Kentucky U (KY)
West Virginia State U (WV)
West Virginia U Inst of Technology (WV)
Wichita State U (KS)
Wright State U (OH)
Wright State U–Lake Campus (OH)
Youngstown State U (OH)

NONCOMPETITIVE

Virtually all applicants were accepted regardless of high school rank or test scores.

Academy Coll (MN)
Academy of Art U (CA)
AIC Coll of Design (OH)
American Baptist Coll (TN)
American Public U System (WV)
American Samoa Comm Coll (AS)
Antelope Valley Coll (CA)
Antioch U Midwest (OH)
Appalachian Bible Coll (WV)
Arlington Baptist U (TX)
Athabasca U (AB, Canada)
Athens State U (AL)
The Baptist Coll of Florida (FL)
Beulah Heights U (GA)
Boston Architectural Coll (MA)
Bowling Green State U–Firelands Coll (OH)
Brandon U (MB, Canada)
California Christian Coll (CA)
Calumet Coll of Saint Joseph (IN)
Calvary U (MO)
Cameron U (OK)
Capilano U (BC, Canada)
Carlos Albizu U (PR)
Carolina Christian Coll (NC)
Cecil Coll (MD)
Charter Oak State Coll (CT)
Chipola Coll (FL)
Colegio Universitario de San Juan, San Juan (PR)
Coll of Biblical Studies–Houston (TX)
Coll of Central Florida (FL)
Columbia Central U, Caguas (PR)
Columbia Southern U (AL)
Conception Sem Coll (MO)
Crowley's Ridge Coll (AR)
Davenport U, Grand Rapids (MI)
Daytona State Coll (FL)
Dominican Coll (NY)
Donnelly Coll (KS)
Eastern New Mexico U (NM)
EDP U of Puerto Rico (PR)
Emmaus Bible Coll (IA)
Emporia State U (KS)
Feather River Coll (CA)
Florida Keys Comm Coll (FL)
Georgia Gwinnett Coll (GA)
Georgia Highlands Coll (GA)
Georgia Military Coll (GA)

INDEXES

Grambling State U (LA)
Granite State Coll (NH)
Harris-Stowe State U (MO)
Hesston Coll (KS)
Hobe Sound Bible Coll (FL)
Holy Trinity Orthodox Sem (NY)
Horizon U (IN)
Huntington Coll of Health Sciences (TN)
Kent State U at Ashtabula (OH)
Kent State U at East Liverpool (OH)
Kent State U at Geauga (OH)
Kent State U at Salem (OH)
Kent State U at Stark (OH)
Kent State U at Trumbull (OH)
Kent State U at Tuscarawas (OH)
Lincoln U (MO)
Luther Rice Coll & Sem (GA)
Maranatha Baptist U (WI)
Marylhurst U (OR)
Master's Coll and Sem (ON, Canada)
Medgar Evers Coll of the City U of New York (NY)
Miami Dade Coll (FL)
Mid-America Baptist Theological Sem (TN)
Mid-America Christian U (OK)
Midland Coll (TX)
Missouri Western State U (MO)
Morris Coll (SC)

National U (CA)
New World School of the Arts (FL)
The Ohio State U at Lima (OH)
The Ohio State U at Mansfield (OH)
The Ohio State U at Marion (OH)
The Ohio State U at Newark (OH)
Ohio U–Zanesville (OH)
Oklahoma State U Inst of Technology (OK)
Oklahoma State U–Oklahoma City (OK)
Pacific Northwest Coll of Art (OR)
Palm Beach State Coll (FL)
Peirce Coll (PA)
Pennsylvania Coll of Technology (PA)
Pensacola State Coll (FL)
Polk State Coll (FL)
Potomac State Coll of West Virginia U (WV)
Pueblo Comm Coll (CO)
Renton Tech Coll (WA)
Rogers State U (OK)
Schoolcraft Coll (MI)
Seminole State Coll of Florida (FL)
Shawnee State U (OH)
Shiloh U (IA)
Southern Vermont Coll (VT)
South Florida State Coll (FL)
Southwestern Assemblies of God U (TX)
State U of New York Empire State Coll (NY)

Tallahassee Comm Coll (FL)
Texas A&M U–Texarkana (TX)
Thomas Edison State U (NJ)
Trinity Coll of Florida (FL)
Truckee Meadows Comm Coll (NV)
Tyler Jr Coll (TX)
U of Guam (GU)
U of Houston–Downtown (TX)
U of Maryland U Coll (MD)
U of Pikeville (KY)
U of Providence (MT)
U of Saint Francis (IN)
The U of Texas Rio Grande Valley (TX)
U of the Potomac (DC)
U of the Virgin Islands (VI)
The U of Toledo (OH)
Utah Valley U (UT)
Valley City State U (ND)
Vincennes U (IN)
Walsh Coll of Accountancy and Business Administration (MI)
Wayne State Coll (NE)
Weber State U (UT)
Welch Coll (TN)
Wilmington U (DE)

Cost Ranges

LESS THAN $2000

Colleges with Room and Board
United States Military Acad (NY)

$2000–$3999

Colleges with No Room and Board or with Room Only
American Samoa Comm Coll (AS)
Capilano U (BC, Canada)
Colegio Universitario de San Juan, San Juan (PR)
Conservatorio de Musica de Puerto Rico (PR)
Daytona State Coll (FL)
Escuela de Artes Plasticas y Dise&nno de Puerto Rico (PR)
Georgia Highlands Coll (GA)
Palm Beach State Coll (FL)
Pensacola State Coll (FL)
Seminole State Coll of Florida (FL)
Tallahassee Comm Coll (FL)
Valencia Coll (FL)

$4000–$5999

Colleges with No Room and Board or with Room Only
Bowling Green State U–Firelands Coll (OH)
Cecil Coll (MD)
Columbia Southern U (AL)
Inter American U of Puerto Rico, Aguadilla Campus (PR)
Inter American U of Puerto Rico, Fajardo Campus (PR)
Kent State U at Ashtabula (OH)
Kent State U at East Liverpool (OH)
Midwives Coll of Utah (UT)
Renton Tech Coll (WA)

$6000–$7999

Colleges with No Room and Board or with Room Only
Baruch Coll of the City U of New York (NY)
Coll of Biblical Studies–Houston (TX)
EDP U of Puerto Rico (PR)
EDP U of Puerto Rico–San Sebastian (PR)
Huntington Coll of Health Sciences (TN)
Indiana U East (IN)
Indiana U Kokomo (IN)
Indiana U Northwest (IN)
Indiana U South Bend (IN)
Indiana U Southeast (IN)
Inter American U of Puerto Rico, Barranquitas Campus (PR)
Medgar Evers Coll of the City U of New York (NY)
National Paralegal Coll (AZ)
State U of New York Empire State Coll (NY)
U of Houston–Downtown (TX)
U of Maryland U Coll (MD)
U of Oklahoma Health Sciences Center (OK)

Colleges with Room and Board
Coll of the Ozarks (MO)
Theological U of the Caribbean (PR)

$8000–$9999

Colleges with No Room and Board or with Room Only
American Coll of Thessaloniki (Greece)
Columbia Central U, Caguas (PR)
Columbia Central U, Yauco (PR)
Horizon U (IN)
Indiana U–Purdue U Indianapolis (IN)
Pueblo Comm Coll (CO)
Youngstown State U (OH)

Colleges with Room and Board
Alice Lloyd Coll (KY)
South Florida State Coll (FL)

$10,000–$11,999

Colleges with No Room and Board or with Room Only
Charlotte Christian Coll and Theological Sem (NC)
Criswell Coll (TX)
Indiana U Bloomington (IN)
Touro U Worldwide (CA)

Colleges with Room and Board
Inter American U of Puerto Rico, Bayamón Campus (PR)
Northwestern Oklahoma State U (OK)
Oklahoma State U Inst of Technology (OK)

$12,000–$13,999

Colleges with No Room and Board or with Room Only
Carolina Christian Coll (NC)
Charles R. Drew U of Medicine and Science (CA)
Coll of Business and Technology–Main Campus (FL)
Coll of Business and Technology–Miami Gardens (FL)
Florida National U (FL)
Franciscan Missionaries of Our Lady U (LA)
Louisiana State U Health Sciences Center (LA) **(room only)**
National U (CA)
Stevens–The Inst of Business & Arts (MO)

Colleges with Room and Board
American Baptist Coll (TN)
American U in Bulgaria (Bulgaria)
Arizona Christian U (AZ)
Brigham Young U (UT)
Coll of Coastal Georgia (GA)
Dickinson State U (ND)
Georgia Military Coll (GA)
Gordon State Coll (GA)
Hobe Sound Bible Coll (FL)
Kentucky Mountain Bible Coll (KY)
Middle Georgia State U (GA)
U of the Fraser Valley (BC, Canada)

$14,000–$15,999

Colleges with No Room and Board or with Room Only
Baptist Coll of Health Sciences (TN) **(room only)**
ECPI U, Virginia Beach (VA)
Maine Coll of Health Professions (ME) **(room only)**
United States Sports Acad (AL)

Colleges with Room and Board
Alaska Bible Coll (AK)
Auburn U at Montgomery (AL)
Black Hills State U (SD)
Brock U (ON, Canada)
Concordia U (QC, Canada)
Florida Gulf Coast U (FL)
Kentucky State U (KY)
Master's Coll and Sem (ON, Canada)
North Carolina Central U (NC)
Rust Coll (MS)
The U of North Carolina at Greensboro (NC)
The U of North Carolina at Pembroke (NC)

U of the Virgin Islands (VI)
U of Wisconsin–Parkside (WI)
U of Wisconsin–Superior (WI)
U of Wyoming (WY)
Valdosta State U (GA)

$16,000–$17,999

Colleges with No Room and Board or with Room Only
Nossi Coll of Art (TN)
Paier Coll of Art, Inc. (CT)

Colleges with Room and Board
Alabama State U (AL)
Austin Peay State U (TN)
Crowley's Ridge Coll (AR)
Florida Ag and Mech U (FL)
Florida Atlantic U (FL)
Florida State U (FL)
Grambling State U (LA)
Jackson State U (MS)
Messenger Coll (TX)
Minnesota State U Moorhead (MN)
Montana Tech of The U of Montana (MT)
Northern State U (SD)
Texas A&M U–Commerce (TX)
Texas Woman's U (TX)
U of Alaska Fairbanks (AK)
U of Maine at Fort Kent (ME)
U of Maine at Presque Isle (ME)
U of Montana (MT)
U of North Carolina at Asheville (NC)
U of North Texas at Dallas (TX)
U of West Georgia (GA)
U of Wisconsin–Stevens Point (WI)

$18,000–$19,999

Colleges with No Room and Board or with Room Only
Adventist U of Health Sciences (FL) **(room only)**
Aultman Coll of Nursing and Health Sciences (OH)
Calumet Coll of Saint Joseph (IN)

Colleges with Room and Board
Ambrose U (AB, Canada)
California State U, Long Beach (CA)
California State U, San Bernardino (CA)
Calvary U (MO)
Frostburg State U (MD)
Georgia Gwinnett Coll (GA)
Gutenberg Coll (OR)
Missouri U of Science and Technology (MO)
North American U (TX)
Prairie View A&M U (TX)
Shawnee State U (OH)
Shepherd U (WV)
Tarleton State U (TX)
U of Nevada, Las Vegas (NV)
U of Nevada, Reno (NV)
U of North Georgia (GA)
U of Southern Mississippi (MS)
The U of Texas of the Permian Basin (TX)

$20,000–$24,999

Colleges with No Room and Board or with Room Only
California Inst of Integral Studies (CA)
Columbia Coll (MO)
Design Inst of San Diego (CA)
Goldfarb School of Nursing at Barnes-Jewish Coll (MO)

Marylhurst U (OR)
Nebraska Methodist Coll (NE) **(room only)**
Palo Alto U (CA)
Saint Francis Medical Center Coll of Nursing (IL)
  (room only)
St. Luke's Coll (IA)

Colleges with Room and Board

Appalachian Bible Coll (WV)
Arlington Baptist U (TX)
Bethune-Cookman U (FL)
Bridgewater State U (MA)
California State Polytechnic U, Pomona (CA)
California State U, Dominguez Hills (CA)
California State U, Sacramento (CA)
The Coll at Brockport, State U of New York (NY)
Colorado State U–Pueblo (CO)
Framingham State U (MA)
Governors State U (IL)
Humboldt State U (CA)
Illinois State U (IL)
Johnson U (TN)
Johnson U Florida (FL)
Kent State U (OH)
Lincoln Christian U (IL)
Lincoln U (PA)
Longwood U (VA)
Louisiana Coll (LA)
Maranatha Baptist U (WI)
Mid-Atlantic Christian U (NC)
North Carolina State U (NC)
Northern Michigan U (MI)
Polytechnic U of Puerto Rico (PR)
Purchase Coll, State U of New York (NY)
Purdue U (IN)
Southern Illinois U Edwardsville (IL)
State U of New York at Fredonia (NY)
State U of New York at New Paltz (NY)
State U of New York at Plattsburgh (NY)
State U of New York Coll at Oneonta (NY)
State U of New York Coll of Environmental Science and
  Forestry (NY)
State U of New York Coll of Technology at Alfred (NY)
Texas A&M U (TX)
Thomas U (GA)
Trinity Coll of Florida (FL)
U at Albany, State U of New York (NY)
The U of Akron (OH)
U of Cincinnati (OH)
U of Illinois at Chicago (IL)
U of Mary Washington (VA)
The U of North Carolina at Chapel Hill (NC)
U of Northern Colorado (CO)
U of North Texas (TX)
U of Wisconsin–Milwaukee (WI)
West Virginia State U (WV)

$25,000–$29,999

Colleges with No Room and Board or with Room Only

Creative Center (NE)
Evangel U (MO) **(room only)**
LIM Coll (NY)
Paris Coll of Art (France)
Pennsylvania Coll of Art & Design (PA)
Robert Morris U Illinois (IL)
St. Andrews U (NC)
VanderCook Coll of Music (IL)

Colleges with Room and Board

Alaska Pacific U (AK)
Avila U (MO)
Bethel U (TN)
Birmingham-Southern Coll (AL)
Bob Jones U (SC)
Brewton-Parker Coll (GA)
California State U, San Marcos (CA)
Central Penn Coll (PA)
Coll of Saint Mary (NE)
Columbia Coll (SC)
Converse Coll (SC)
Cottey Coll (MO)

Emmaus Bible Coll (IA)
Husson U (ME)
Lee U (TN)
Lincoln Coll (IL)
Lincoln Coll of New England, Southington (CT)
Massachusetts Coll of Art and Design (MA)
Missouri Valley Coll (MO)
Pittsburgh Tech Coll (PA)
Saint Louis U–Madrid Campus (Spain)
St. Mary's Coll of Maryland (MD)
Southern Adventist U (TN)
Southwestern Assemblies of God U (TX)
U of Hawaii at Manoa (HI)
U of Jamestown (ND)
U of Pikeville (KY)
U of Sioux Falls (SD)
Vermont Tech Coll (VT)
Waldorf U (IA)
Welch Coll (TN)

$30,000 AND OVER

Colleges with No Room and Board or with Room Only

The American U of Paris (France)
Azusa Pacific U (CA) **(room only)**
California Coll of the Arts (CA) **(room only)**
DigiPen Inst of Technology (WA)
Emerson Coll (MA)
FIDM/Fashion Inst of Design & Merchandising, Los
  Angeles Campus (CA)
FIDM/Fashion Inst of Design & Merchandising, San
  Francisco Campus (CA)
Hallmark U (TX)
Harrisburg U of Science and Technology (PA) **(room only)**
John Paul the Great Catholic U (CA) **(room only)**
The King's Coll (NY) **(room only)**
Laguna Coll of Art & Design (CA) **(room only)**
Loyola U Chicago (IL)
Minneapolis Coll of Art and Design (MN) **(room only)**
Neumont Coll of Computer Science (UT) **(room only)**
Otterbein U (OH)
Resurrection U (IL)
Suffolk U (MA)
U of St. Francis (IL)
U of St. Thomas (TX)
Vanguard U of Southern California (CA)

Colleges with Room and Board

Academy of Art U (CA)
Agnes Scott Coll (GA)
Albion Coll (MI)
Albright Coll (PA)
Alfred U (NY)
Allegheny Coll (PA)
American Intl Coll (MA)
American U (DC)
Antioch Coll, Yellow Springs (OH)
Aquinas Coll (MI)
Assumption Coll (MA)
Augsburg U (MN)
Augustana Coll (IL)
Augustana U (SD)
Aurora U (IL)
Babson Coll (MA)
Baldwin Wallace U (OH)
Barry U (FL)
Barton Coll (NC)
Baylor U (TX)
Becker Coll (MA)
Belhaven U (MS)
Bellarmine U (KY)
Beloit Coll (WI)
Benedictine U (IL)
Bennington Coll (VT)
Bentley U (MA)
Bethany Lutheran Coll (MN)
Bethel Coll (IN)
Bethel Coll (KS)
Bethel U (MN)
Bluefield Coll (VA)
Bluffton U (OH)
Brenau U (GA)

Brescia U (KY)
Bridgewater Coll (VA)
Bryant U (RI)
Butler U (IN)
Cairn U (PA)
Caldwell U (NJ)
California Baptist U (CA)
Canisius Coll (NY)
Capital U (OH)
Carnegie Mellon U (PA)
Carroll U (WI)
Carthage Coll (WI)
Catawba Coll (NC)
Cedar Crest Coll (PA)
Cedarville U (OH)
Centenary Coll of Louisiana (LA)
Central Methodist U (MO)
Centre Coll (KY)
Chaminade U of Honolulu (HI)
Chapman U (CA)
Chatham U (PA)
Chestnut Hill Coll (PA)
Chowan U (NC)
Christendom Coll (VA)
Christian Brothers U (TN)
Clarke U (IA)
Clarkson U (NY)
Clark U (MA)
Coe Coll (IA)
The Coll of Idaho (ID)
The Coll of New Rochelle (NY)
Coll of Saint Elizabeth (NJ)
The Coll of Saint Rose (NY)
The Coll of St. Scholastica (MN)
Coll of the Atlantic (ME)
Colorado Christian U (CO)
Columbia Coll Chicago (IL)
Conception Sem Coll (MO)
Concordia Coll–New York (NY)
Concordia U Chicago (IL)
Concordia U Irvine (CA)
Concordia U, Nebraska (NE)
Concordia U, St. Paul (MN)
Corban U (OR)
Cornell Coll (IA)
Cornerstone U (MI)
Cornish Coll of the Arts (WA)
Covenant Coll (GA)
Creighton U (NE)
Culver-Stockton Coll (MO)
Curry Coll (MA)
Dallas Baptist U (TX)
Dean Coll (MA)
Defiance Coll (OH)
Dominican Coll (NY)
Dominican U (IL)
Dominican U of California (CA)
Drake U (IA)
Drew U (NJ)
Drexel U (PA)
Drury U (MO)
Earlham Coll (IN)
Eastern Mennonite U (VA)
Eastern Nazarene Coll (MA)
Eastern U (PA)
Eckerd Coll (FL)
Edgewood Coll (WI)
Elizabethtown Coll (PA)
Elmhurst Coll (IL)
Elms Coll (MA)
Elon U (NC)
Embry-Riddle Aeronautical U–Daytona (FL)
Emmanuel Coll (MA)
Emory U (GA)
Endicott Coll (MA)
Felician U (NJ)
Fisher Coll (MA)
Flagler Coll (FL)
Florida Inst of Technology (FL)
Franklin U Switzerland (Switzerland)
Franklin W. Olin Coll of Eng (MA)
Friends U (KS)
Geneva Coll (PA)
Georgetown Coll (KY)
Gordon Coll (MA)

Goshen Coll (IN)
Graceland U (IA)
Grand View U (IA)
Green Mountain Coll (VT)
Greensboro Coll (NC)
Greenville U (IL)
Grinnell Coll (IA)
Gustavus Adolphus Coll (MN)
Gwynedd Mercy U (PA)
Hamline U (MN)
Hampden-Sydney Coll (VA)
Hampshire Coll (MA)
Hardin-Simmons U (TX)
Hartwick Coll (NY)
Hawai`i Pacific U (HI)
Heidelberg U (OH)
Hendrix Coll (AR)
Hesston Coll (KS)
High Point U (NC)
Hilbert Coll (NY)
Hobart and William Smith Colls (NY)
Hollins U (VA)
Holy Family U (PA)
Holy Names U (CA)
Hood Coll (MD)
Hope Coll (MI)
Houston Baptist U (TX)
Howard Payne U (TX)
Illinois Coll (IL)
Illinois Wesleyan U (IL)
Immaculata U (PA)
Indiana Wesleyan U (IN)
Ithaca Coll (NY)
Jefferson Coll of Health Sciences (VA)
John Brown U (AR)
Judson U (IL)
Juniata Coll (PA)
Kalamazoo Coll (MI)
Kansas Wesleyan U (KS)
Kenyon Coll (OH)
King U (TN)
Knox Coll (IL)
La Roche Coll (PA)
La Salle U (PA)
Lasell Coll (MA)
La Sierra U (CA)
Lebanon Valley Coll (PA)
Le Moyne Coll (NY)
Lesley U (MA)
LeTourneau U (TX)
Lewis U (IL)
Limestone Coll (SC)
Lindsey Wilson Coll (KY)
Lipscomb U (TN)
Loras Coll (IA)
Loyola U New Orleans (LA)
Luther Coll (IA)
Lycoming Coll (PA)
Lynchburg Coll (VA)
Lynn U (FL)
Macalester Coll (MN)
Malone U (OH)
Manchester U (IN)
Manhattanville Coll (NY)
Marian U (IN)
Marietta Coll (OH)
Marlboro Coll (VT)
Mary Baldwin U (VA)
Maryland Inst Coll of Art (MD)
Marymount California U (CA)
Marymount Manhattan Coll (NY)
Maryville Coll (TN)
Maryville U of Saint Louis (MO)
Marywood U (PA)
Massachusetts Inst of Technology (MA)
The Master's U (CA)
McKendree U (IL)
McPherson Coll (KS)
MCPHS U (MA)
Messiah Coll (PA)
MidAmerica Nazarene U (KS)
Milligan Coll (TN)
Millsaps Coll (MS)
Mills Coll (CA)

Milwaukee School of Eng (WI)
Misericordia U (PA)
Monmouth Coll (IL)
Moravian Coll (PA)
Morehouse Coll (GA)
Mount Holyoke Coll (MA)
Mount Mary U (WI)
Mount Mercy U (IA)
Mount St. Joseph U (OH)
Mount Saint Mary Coll (NY)
Mount Saint Mary's U (CA)
Mount Vernon Nazarene U (OH)
Muskingum U (OH)
Nazareth Coll of Rochester (NY)
Newberry Coll (SC)
New England Inst of Technology (RI)
New Hampshire Inst of Art (NH)
Newman U (KS)
New York Inst of Technology (NY)
Niagara U (NY)
Nichols Coll (MA)
North Carolina Wesleyan Coll (NC)
Northland Coll (WI)
Northwestern Coll (IA)
Northwest Nazarene U (ID)
Northwest U (WA)
Notre Dame de Namur U (CA)
Nyack Coll (NY)
Oakland City U (IN)
Ohio Dominican U (OH)
Ohio Northern U (OH)
Ohio Wesleyan U (OH)
Oklahoma Baptist U (OK)
Oklahoma Christian U (OK)
Oklahoma City U (OK)
Oral Roberts U (OK)
Ottawa U (KS)
Ouachita Baptist U (AR)
Our Lady of the Lake U (TX)
Pace U (NY)
Pace U, Pleasantville Campus (NY)
Palm Beach Atlantic U (FL)
Pennsylvania Coll of Technology (PA)
Pepperdine U, Malibu (CA)
Point Loma Nazarene U (CA)
Pomona Coll (CA)
Post U (CT)
Pratt Inst (NY)
Princeton U (NJ)
Principia Coll (IL)
Quinnipiac U (CT)
Randolph Coll (VA)
Randolph-Macon Coll (VA)
Regis U (CO)
Rensselaer Polytechnic Inst (NY)
Rhodes Coll (TN)
Rider U (NJ)
Ringling Coll of Art and Design (FL)
Ripon Coll (WI)
Roanoke Coll (VA)
Roberts Wesleyan Coll (NY)
Rockford U (IL)
Rocky Mountain Coll (MT)
Roger Williams U (RI)
Rollins Coll (FL)
Roosevelt U (IL)
The Sage Colls (NY)
St. Ambrose U (IA)
Saint Anselm Coll (NH)
St. John's Coll (NM)
St. Lawrence U (NY)
St. Louis Coll of Pharmacy (MO)
Saint Martin's U (WA)
Saint Mary-of-the-Woods Coll (IN)
Saint Mary's Coll of California (CA)
St. Mary's U (TX)
Saint Mary's U of Minnesota (MN)
Saint Michael's Coll (VT)
St. Norbert Coll (WI)
St. Olaf Coll (MN)
St. Thomas U (FL)
Samford U (AL)
San Francisco Art Inst (CA)
Savannah Coll of Art and Design (GA)

School of Visual Arts (NY)
Sewanee: The U of the South (TN)
Shenandoah U (VA)
Siena Coll (NY)
Simmons Coll (MA)
Simpson Coll (IA)
Soka U of America (CA)
Southeastern U (FL)
Southern Methodist U (TX)
Southern Vermont Coll (VT)
Southwest Baptist U (MO)
Southwestern Coll (KS)
Southwestern U (TX)
Stetson U (FL)
Stevens Inst of Technology (NJ)
Stevenson U (MD)
Sweet Briar Coll (VA)
Tabor Coll (KS)
Texas Lutheran U (TX)
Thomas More Coll of Liberal Arts (NH)
Tiffin U (OH)
Toccoa Falls Coll (GA)
Transylvania U (KY)
Trevecca Nazarene U (TN)
Trinity Christian Coll (IL)
Trinity U (TX)
Tusculum Coll (TN)
Union Coll (NE)
Union U (TN)
U of California, Davis (CA)
U of California, Santa Barbara (CA)
U of Charleston (WV)
U of Denver (CO)
U of Evansville (IN)
U of Guelph (ON, Canada)
U of Hartford (CT)
U of Mary Hardin-Baylor (TX)
U of Mount Union (OH)
U of New Hampshire (NH)
U of Notre Dame (IN)
U of Pennsylvania (PA)
U of Providence (MT)
U of Puget Sound (WA)
U of Richmond (VA)
U of Rochester (NY)
U of Saint Francis (IN)
U of Saint Joseph (CT)
U of Saint Mary (KS)
U of San Diego (CA)
U of San Francisco (CA)
U of Southern California (CA)
The U of the Arts (PA)
The U of Tulsa (OK)
U of Valley Forge (PA)
Upper Iowa U (IA)
Ursinus Coll (PA)
Ursuline Coll (OH)
Valparaiso U (IN)
Virginia Wesleyan U (VA)
Wabash Coll (IN)
Wake Forest U (NC)
Wartburg Coll (IA)
Washington Coll (MD)
Washington U in St. Louis (MO)
Webber Intl U (FL)
Webb Inst (NY)
Wells Coll (NY)
Westminster Coll (UT)
West Virginia Wesleyan Coll (WV)
Wheaton Coll (IL)
Wheaton Coll (MA)
Whitman Coll (WA)
Whitworth U (WA)
Willamette U (OR)
William Jewell Coll (MO)
William Penn U (IA)
William Woods U (MO)
Wisconsin Lutheran Coll (WI)
Wittenberg U (OH)
Wofford Coll (SC)
Woodbury U (CA)
York Coll of Pennsylvania (PA)

Advertisers Index

Academy of Art University	92
Allegheny College	869
Aquinas College	506
Assumption College	458
Babson College	458
Baldwin Wallace University	788
Barnard College	648
Barry University	204
Bentley University	462
Bethel College	332
Boston University	464
Bryn Mawr College	873
California University of Pennsylvania	876
Castleton University	1077
The Catholic University of America	198
Clemson University	970
College for Creative Studies	509
The College of New Jersey	619
College of Staten Island of the City University of New York	660
Columbia University	662
Columbia University School of General Studies	663
Dean College	470
Drexel University	885
Earlham College	336
Elizabethtown College	889
Elmhurst College	299
Embry-Riddle Aeronautical University–Daytona	211
Embry-Riddle Aeronautical University–Prescott	77
Emerson College	472
Erskine College	975
The Evergreen State College	1123
Fashion Institute of Technology	671
Florida Southern College	219
Gannon University	891
Georgian Court University	625
Grand View University	368
Gwynedd Mercy University	895
Harding University	84
High Point University	760
Hillsdale College	513
Hofstra University	676
Holy Names University	122
John Cabot University	1218
Johns Hopkins University	443
Kettering University	516
King's College	900
Kutztown University of Pennsylvania	901
Le Moyne College	684
Lincoln University	906
Linfield College	857
Loyola University Maryland	444
Luther College	372
Lynchburg College	1100
Manhattan College	687
Marlboro College	1080
Marywood University	910
Millersville University of Pennsylvania	913
Mills College	130
Misericordia University	914
Molloy College	694
Monmouth University	626
Mount Aloysius College	916
Mt. Sierra College	132
Muhlenberg College	917
Neumann University	918
Neumont College of Computer Science	1071
New College of Florida	226
Niagara University	700
Northeastern University	486
Northern Arizona University	79
Northern Kentucky University	410
Northern Vermont University–Lyndon	1082
Ohio Northern University	817
Ohio Wesleyan University	823
Olivet Nazarene University	315
Pace University	702
Pacific University	863
Pepperdine University	136
Platt College San Diego	138
Pratt Institute	705
Quinnipiac University	186
Reed College	864
Regis College	488
Rider University	631
Ripon College	1159
Rivier University	612
Robert Morris University	934
Rochester Institute of Technology	710
Saint Anselm College	613
Saint Francis University	937
Saint Joseph's University	938
St. Lawrence University	716
Saint Mary's College	353
St. Norbert College	1161
St. Thomas Aquinas College	716
Saint Vincent College	939
Seton Hall University	636
Simpson College	378
Skidmore College	720
Southern Illinois University Carbondale	322
Southern Methodist University	1039
Southern New Hampshire University	615
Springfield College	490
State University of New York at Oswego	723
State University of New York College of Environmental Science and Forestry	729
Sterling College	1084
Stockton University	637
Temple University	944
Thomas Jefferson University	946
Trine University	354
University of Alaska Fairbanks	71
University of Calgary	1207
University of California, San Diego	153
University of Central Florida	242
University of Colorado Boulder	176
University of Denver	179
University of Dubuque	379
University of Evansville	356
University of Maine	434
University of New England	438
University of New Haven	191
The University of North Carolina Wilmington	777
University of Pittsburgh at Bradford	948
University of Redlands	157
University of San Francisco	158
University of Science and Arts of Oklahoma	851
The University of Tulsa	852
Utica College	742
Wayne State University	527
Webb Institute	745
Wentworth Institute of Technology	497
Western Connecticut State University	194
Westmont College	162
West Virginia Wesleyan College	1146
Wheaton College	330
Whittier College	164
Wilkes University	958
Worcester Polytechnic Institute	501

Alphabetical Listing of Colleges and Universities

Abilene Christian University	1018	Angelo State University	1019
Abraham Baldwin Agricultural College	250	Anna Maria College	457
Academy College	530	Antelope Valley College	94
Academy of Art University	92, 1228	Antioch College	786
Acadia University	1191	Antioch University Los Angeles	95
Adams State University	166	Antioch University Midwest	787
Adelphi University	646	Antioch University Santa Barbara	95
Adrian College	503	Antioch University Seattle	1120
Adventist University of Health Sciences	202	Apex School of Theology	749
Agnes Scott College	250	Appalachian Bible College	1139
AIC College of Design	786	Appalachian State University	749
Alabama Agricultural and Mechanical University	55	Aquinas College	506, 1232, 992
Alabama State University	55	Arcadia University	871
Alaska Bible College	70	Argosy University, Atlanta	251
Alaska Pacific University	70	Argosy University, Chicago	290
Albany College of Pharmacy and Health Sciences	647	Argosy University, Dallas	1019
Albany State University	250	Argosy University, Denver	166
Alberta College of Art & Design	1192	Argosy University, Hawai`i	282
Albertus Magnus College	181	Argosy University, Inland Empire	95
Albion College	503	Argosy University, Los Angeles	95
Albright College	869	Argosy University, Nashville	992
Alcorn State University	552	Argosy University, Northern Virginia	1087
Alderson Broaddus University	1138	Argosy University, Orange County	95
Alfred University	647	Argosy University, Phoenix	73
Alice Lloyd College	400	Argosy University, Salt Lake City	1069
Allegheny College	869, 1230	Argosy University, San Diego	96
Allegheny Wesleyan College	786	Argosy University, San Francisco Bay Area	96
Allen College	361	Argosy University, Sarasota	203
Allen University	967	Argosy University, Schaumburg	291
Alliant International University–San Diego	93	Argosy University, Seattle	1120
Alma College	504	Argosy University, Tampa	203
Altierus Career College	203	Argosy University, Twin Cities	530
Alvernia University	871	Arizona Christian University	73
Alverno College	1148	Arizona College–Las Vegas	603
Amberton University	1018	Arizona College–Mesa	73
Ambria College of Nursing	290	Arizona State University at the Downtown Phoenix campus	73
Ambrose University	1192	Arizona State University at the Polytechnic campus	74
American Academy of Art	290	Arizona State University at the Tempe campus	75
American Baptist College	991	Arizona State University at the West campus	76
American Business & Technology University	559	Arkansas Baptist College	82
American College Dublin	1218	Arkansas State University	82
American College for Medical Careers	203	Arkansas Tech University	82
American College of Healthcare Sciences	854	Arlington Baptist University	1019
American College of Thessaloniki	1217	Art Academy of Cincinnati	787
American InterContinental University Atlanta	251	ArtCenter College of Design	96
American InterContinental University Houston	1018	The Art Institute of Atlanta	251
American InterContinental University Online	290	The Art Institute of Austin, a branch of The Art Institute of Houston	1020
American International College	456	The Art Institute of California–Hollywood, a campus of Argosy University	96
American Jewish University	94		
American Musical and Dramatic Academy, Los Angeles	94	The Art Institute of California–Inland Empire, a campus of Argosy University	96
American National University	401, 1086, 1087		
American Public University System	1138	The Art Institute of California–Orange County, a campus of Argosy University	96
American Samoa Community College	1175		
American Sentinel University	166	The Art Institute of California–Sacramento, a campus of Argosy University	96
American University	197		
American University in Bulgaria	1214	The Art Institute of California–San Diego, a campus of Argosy University	96
The American University in Cairo	1215		
The American University in Dubai	1225	The Art Institute of California–San Francisco, a campus of Argosy University	97
American University of Beirut	1220		
American University of Health Sciences	94	The Art Institute of Charleston, a branch of The Art Institute of Atlanta	967
The American University of Paris	1215		
American University of Puerto Rico	1176	The Art Institute of Charlotte, a branch of Miami International University of Art & Design	750
The American University of Rome	1218		
American University of Sharjah	1226	The Art Institute of Colorado	167
Ameritech College of Healthcare	1069	The Art Institute of Dallas, a branch of Miami International University of Art & Design	1020
Amherst College	457		
Amridge University	55	The Art Institute of Fort Lauderdale	203
Anderson University	331, 967	The Art Institute of Houston	1020
Andrews University	505	The Art Institute of Indianapolis	332
Angeles College	94	The Art Institute of Las Vegas	603

The Art Institute of Michigan	507
The Art Institute of Philadelphia	872
The Art Institute of Phoenix	76
The Art Institute of Pittsburgh	872
The Art Institute of Portland	854
The Art Institute of Raleigh-Durham, a branch of Miami International University of Art & Design	750
The Art Institute of San Antonio, a branch of The Art Institute of Houston	1020
The Art Institute of Seattle	1120
The Art Institute of Tampa, a branch of Miami International University of Art & Design	203
The Art Institute of Tennessee–Nashville, a branch of The Art Institute of Atlanta	992
The Art Institute of Virginia Beach, a branch of The Art Institute of Atlanta	1087
The Art Institute of Washington, a branch of The Art Institute of Atlanta	1087
Asbury University	401
Ashford University	97
Ashland University	787
Ashworth College	251
Aspen University	167
Assumption College	458, 1234
Atenas College	1176
Athabasca University	1193
Athens State University	56
Atlantic University College	1177
Atlantis University	203
Auburn University	56
Auburn University at Montgomery	57
Augsburg University	530
Augustana College	291
Augustana University	985
Augusta University	251
Aultman College of Nursing and Health Sciences	788
Aurora University	291
Austin College	1020
Austin Graduate School of Theology	1021
Austin Peay State University	992
Ave Maria University	203
Averett University	1087
Avila University	559
Azusa Pacific University	97
Babson College	458, 1236
Bacone College	838
Bais Binyomin Academy	182
Bais HaMedrash and Mesivta of Baltimore	440
Bais Medrash Toras Chesed	617
Baker College	507
Baker University	384
Baldwin Wallace University	788, 1238
Ball State University	332
Baptist Bible College	560
The Baptist College of Florida	203
Baptist College of Health Sciences	993
Baptist Health System School of Health Professions	1021
Baptist Missionary Association Theological Seminary	1021
Baptist University of the Americas	1021
Barclay College	385
Bard College	648
Bard College at Simon's Rock	460
Barnard College	648, 1240
Barry University	204, 1242
Barton College	750
Baruch College of the City University of New York	650
Bastyr University	1120
Bates College	429
Bayamón Central University	1177
Baylor University	1022
Bay Path University	460
Bay State College	461
Beacon College	205
Becker College	461
Beckfield College	402
Be'er Yaakov Talmudic Seminary	650
Beis Medrash Heichal Dovid	650
Belhaven University	206, 553, 993
Bellarmine University	402
Bellevue College	1120
Bellevue University	595
Bellin College	1149
Belmont Abbey College	750
Belmont University	993
Beloit College	1149
Bemidji State University	531
Benedict College	967
Benedictine College	385
Benedictine University	292
Benjamin Franklin Institute of Technology	462
Bennett College	751
Bennington College	1076
Bentley University	462, 1244
Berea College	402
Bergin University of Canine Studies	97
Berkeley College–New York City Campus	650
Berkeley College–White Plains Campus	651
Berkeley College–Woodland Park Campus	617
Berklee College of Music	462
Berry College	251
Bethany College	386, 1139
Bethany Global University	531
Bethany Lutheran College	531
Bethel College	332, 1246, 386, 1088
Bethel University	532, 994
Bethesda University	97
Beth HaMedrash Shaarei Yosher Institute	651
Beth Hatalmud Rabbinical College	651
Bethlehem College & Seminary	533
Beth Medrash Govoha	617
Beth Medrash Meor Yitzchok	651
Bethune-Cookman University	206
Bet Medrash Gadol Ateret Torah	651
Beulah Heights University	252
Beverly Hills Design Institute	97
Binghamton University, State University of New York	651
Biola University	98
Birmingham-Southern College	58
Birthingway College of Midwifery	854
Bishop's University	1193
Bismarck State College	780
Blackburn College	293
Black Hills State University	986
Blessing-Rieman College of Nursing & Health Sciences	293
Bloomfield College	618
Bloomsburg University of Pennsylvania	872
Bluefield College	1088
Bluefield State College	1140
Blue Mountain College	554
Bluffton University	790
Bob Jones University	968
Boise Bible College	285
Boise State University	285
Bon Secours Memorial College of Nursing	1088
Booth University College	1193
Boricua College	652
Boston Architectural College	463
Boston Baptist College	464
Boston College	464, 1248
Boston University	464, 1250
Bowdoin College	430
Bowie State University	440
Bowling Green State University	790
Bowling Green State University–Firelands College	791
Bradley University	294
Brandeis University	466
Brandman University	98
Brandon University	1193
Brazosport College	1023
Brenau University	253
Brescia University	403
Brevard College	751
Brewton-Parker College	253
Briar Cliff University	362
Bridgewater College	1088
Bridgewater State University	466
Briercrest College	1194
Brigham Young University	1069
Brigham Young University–Hawaii	282
Brigham Young University–Idaho	286
British Columbia Institute of Technology	1194
Broadview Entertainment Arts University	1069
Broadview University–Madison	1150
Broadview University–West Jordan	1069

Brock University	1194
Brookline College	76, 77, 640
Brooklyn College of the City University of New York	652
Broward College	206
Brown University	960
Bryan College	995
Bryan College of Health Sciences	595
Bryant & Stratton College–Akron Campus	792
Bryant & Stratton College–Amherst Campus	653
Bryant & Stratton College–Bayshore Campus	1150
Bryant & Stratton College–Buffalo Campus	653
Bryant & Stratton College–Cleveland Campus	792
Bryant & Stratton College–Eastlake Campus	792
Bryant & Stratton College–Hampton Campus	1089
Bryant & Stratton College–Milwaukee Campus	1150
Bryant & Stratton College–Orchard Park Campus	653
Bryant & Stratton College–Parma Campus	792
Bryant & Stratton College–Richmond Campus	1089
Bryant & Stratton College–Virginia Beach Campus	1089
Bryant & Stratton College–Wauwatosa Campus	1150
Bryant University	961
Bryan University	560
Bryn Athyn College of the New Church	873
Bryn Mawr College	873, 1252
Bucknell University	875
Buena Vista University	362
Buffalo State College, State University of New York	653
Butler University	334
Cabarrus College of Health Sciences	751
Cabrini University	875
Cairn University	876
Caldwell University	618
California Baptist University	99
California Christian College	99
California Coast University	100
California College of the Arts	100
California College San Diego	100, 101
California Institute of Integral Studies	101
California Institute of Technology	101
California Institute of the Arts	102
California Intercontinental University	102
California Lutheran University	102
California Miramar University	103
California Polytechnic State University, San Luis Obispo	103
California State Polytechnic University, Pomona	103
California State University, Bakersfield	104
California State University Channel Islands	104
California State University, Chico	105
California State University, Dominguez Hills	105
California State University, East Bay	106
California State University, Fresno	106
California State University, Fullerton	107
California State University, Long Beach	108
California State University, Los Angeles	108
California State University Maritime Academy	109
California State University, Monterey Bay	110
California State University, Northridge	110
California State University, Sacramento	111
California State University, San Bernardino	111
California State University, San Marcos	112
California State University, Stanislaus	113
California University of Management and Sciences	113
California University of Pennsylvania	876, 1254
Calumet College of Saint Joseph	334
Calvary University	560
Calvin College	507
Cambridge College	467
Cameron University	838
Campbellsville University	404
Campbell University	752
Canisius College	654
Cape Breton University	1195
Capella University	533
Capilano University	1195
Capital University	792
Capitol Technology University	441
Cardinal Stritch University	1150
Careers Unlimited	1070
Caribbean University	1177
Caribbean University–Carolina	1177
Caribbean University–Ponce	1177
Caribbean University–Vega Baja	1177
Carleton College	533
Carleton University	1196
Carlos Albizu University	1178
Carlos Albizu University, Miami Campus	206
Carlow University	878
Carnegie Mellon University	878
Carolina Christian College	752
Carolina College of Biblical Studies	752
Carroll College	589
Carroll University	1151
Carson-Newman University	995
Carthage College	1151
Carver College	254
Cascadia College	1120
Case Western Reserve University	793
Castleton University	1077, 1256
Catawba College	752
The Catholic University of America	198, 1258
Cazenovia College	654
Cecil College	441
Cedar Crest College	879
Cedarville University	793
Centenary College of Louisiana	418
Centenary University	619
Centennial College	1196
Central Baptist College	83
Central Christian College of Kansas	387
Central Christian College of the Bible	561
Central College	363
Central Connecticut State University	182
Central Methodist University	561
Central Michigan University	508
Central Penn College	880
Central State University	794
Central Washington University	1120
Central Yeshiva Beth Joseph	655
Central Yeshiva Tomchei Tmimim-Lubavitch	655
Centre College	404
Centro de Estudios Multidisciplinarios	1178
Centura College	1089
Chadron State College	595
Chamberlain College of Nursing	77, 113, 207, 254, 294, 295, 335, 508, 561, 603, 619, 753, 795, 1023, 1089
Chaminade University of Honolulu	282
Champlain College	1077
Chapman University	114
Charles R. Drew University of Medicine and Science	114
Charleston Southern University	968
Charlotte Christian College and Theological Seminary	753
Charter College	71, 1121
Charter Oak State College	183
Chatham University	880
Chestnut Hill College	881
Cheyney University of Pennsylvania	882
Chicago State University	295
Chipola College	207
Chowan University	754
Christendom College	1090
Christian Brothers University	996
Christopher Newport University	1090
Christ's College	1225
Cincinnati Christian University	795
Cincinnati College of Mortuary Science	795
The Citadel, The Military College of South Carolina	969
City College	207, 208
City College of the City University of New York	655
City University of Seattle	1121
City Vision University	562
Claflin University	970
Claremont McKenna College	115
Clarion University of Pennsylvania	882
Clark Atlanta University	255
Clark College	1121
Clarke University	363
Clarkson College	595
Clarkson University	656
Clarks Summit University	883
Clark University	467
Clayton State University	255
Clear Creek Baptist Bible College	405
Cleary University	509
Clemson University	970, 1260

INDEXES

Cleveland Institute of Art	795
Cleveland Institute of Music	796
Cleveland State University	796
Cleveland University–Kansas City	387
Coastal Carolina University	971
Coe College	364
Cogswell Polytechnical College	115
Coker College	972
The Colburn School Conservatory of Music	116
Colby College	430
Colby-Sawyer College	608
Colegio Universitario de San Juan	1178
Coleman University	116
Colgate University	657
CollegeAmerica–Colorado Springs	167
CollegeAmerica–Flagstaff	77
CollegeAmerica–Fort Collins	167
CollegeAmerica–Phoenix	77
The College at Brockport, State University of New York	657
College for Creative Studies	509, 1262
College of Biblical Studies–Houston	1023
College of Business and Technology–Main Campus	208
College of Business and Technology–Miami Gardens	208
College of Central Florida	208
College of Charleston	972
College of Coastal Georgia	256
The College of Idaho	286
College of Mount Saint Vincent	658
The College of New Jersey	619, 1264
The College of New Rochelle	659
College of Saint Benedict	534
College of Saint Elizabeth	621
College of St. Joseph	1078
College of Saint Mary	595
The College of Saint Rose	659
The College of St. Scholastica	534
College of Southern Nevada	604
College of Staten Island of the City University of New York	660, 1266
College of the Atlantic	431
College of the Holy Cross	468
College of the Ozarks	562
The College of Westchester	661
The College of William and Mary	1091
The College of Wooster	796
Colorado Christian University	167
The Colorado College	167
Colorado Mesa University	168
Colorado Mountain College	169
Colorado School of Mines	169
Colorado State University	170
Colorado State University–Global Campus	170
Colorado State University–Pueblo	171
Colorado Technical University Aurora	171
Colorado Technical University Colorado Springs	171
Colorado Technical University Online	171
Columbia Bible College	1196
Columbia Central University	1179
Columbia College	562, 973
Columbia College Chicago	295
Columbia College Hollywood	116
Columbia College of Nursing	1152
Columbia International University	974
Columbia Southern University	58
Columbia University	662, 1268
Columbia University School of General Studies	663, 1270
Columbus College of Art & Design	797
Columbus State University	257
Compass College of Cinematic Arts	509
Conception Seminary College	563
Concordia College	535
Concordia College–New York	663
Concordia University	1196, 854
Concordia University Ann Arbor	509
Concordia University Chicago	296
Concordia University Irvine	116
Concordia University, Nebraska	596
Concordia University of Edmonton	1197
Concordia University, St. Paul	535
Concordia University Texas	1024
Concordia University Wisconsin	1152
Concord University	1140
Connecticut College	183
Conservatorio de Musica de Puerto Rico	1180
Converse College	974
Cooper Union for the Advancement of Science and Art	665
Coppin State University	441
Corban University	854
Cornell College	365
Cornell University	665
Cornerstone University	510
Cornish College of the Arts	1121
Cottey College	564
Covenant College	257
Cox College	564
Crandall University	1197
Creative Center	597
Creighton University	597
Criswell College	1024
Crossroads Bible College	335
Crowley's Ridge College	83
Crown College	536
The Culinary Institute of America	666
Culinary Institute of Virginia	1092
Culver-Stockton College	565
Cumberland University	997
Curry College	469
Curtis Institute of Music	883
Daemen College	667
Dakota State University	986
Dakota Wesleyan University	987
Dalhousie University	1198
Dallas Baptist University	1024
Dallas Christian College	1025
Dallas Nursing Institute	1025
Dalton State College	258
Dartmouth College	608
Davenport University	510
Davidson College	754
Davis & Elkins College	1141
Davis College	667
Daymar College	997
Daytona State College	209
Dean College	470, 1272
Defiance College	798
Delaware State University	196
Delaware Valley University	883
Delta State University	554
Denison University	798
Denver College of Nursing	172
DePaul University	296
DePauw University	335
DEREE - The American College of Greece	1217
DeSales University	884
Design Institute of San Diego	117
DeVry College of New York–Midtown Manhattan Campus	668
DeVry University–Addison Campus	297
DeVry University–Alpharetta Campus	258
DeVry University–Arlington Campus	1092
DeVry University–Charlotte Campus	755
DeVry University–Chesapeake Campus	1092
DeVry University–Chicago Campus	297
DeVry University–Columbus Campus	799
DeVry University–Decatur Campus	258
DeVry University–Folsom Campus	118
DeVry University–Fremont Campus	118
DeVry University–Ft. Washington Campus	884
DeVry University–Henderson Campus	604
DeVry University–Irving Campus	1025
DeVry University–Jacksonville Campus	209
DeVry University–Kansas City Campus	565
DeVry University–Long Beach Campus	118
DeVry University–Miramar Campus	210
DeVry University–Nashville Campus	997
DeVry University–North Brunswick Campus	621
DeVry University–Oklahoma City Campus	839
DeVry University Online	297
DeVry University–Orlando Campus	210
DeVry University–Phoenix Campus	77
DeVry University–Pomona Campus	118
DeVry University–San Diego Campus	118
DeVry University–Seven Hills Campus	799
DeVry University–Sherman Oaks Campus	118
DeVry University–Tinley Park Campus	298
DeVry University–Westminster Campus	172

Dewey University–Carolina	1180
Dewey University–Hato Rey	1180
Dewey University–Manati	1180
Dickinson College	884
Dickinson State University	781
DigiPen Institute of Technology	1122
Dillard University	418
Divine Word College	365
Dixie State University	1070
Doane University	598
Dominican College	668
Dominican University	298
Dominican University of California	118
Donnelly College	387
Dordt College	365
Drake University	365
Drew University	621
Drexel University	885, 1274
Drury University	566
Duke University	755
Dunlap-Stone University	77
Dunwoody College of Technology	536
Duquesne University	886
D'Youville College	669
Eagle Gate College	1070
Earlham College	336, 1276
East Carolina University	755
East Central University	839
Eastern Connecticut State University	184
Eastern Florida State College	210
Eastern Illinois University	298
Eastern International College	622
Eastern Kentucky University	405
Eastern Mennonite University	1092
Eastern Michigan University	511
Eastern Nazarene College	471
Eastern New Mexico University	640
Eastern Oregon University	855
Eastern University	887
Eastern Washington University	1122
East Georgia State College	259
East Stroudsburg University of Pennsylvania	888
East Tennessee State University	997
East Texas Baptist University	1026
East-West University	299
Eastwick College	622
Ecclesia College	84
EC-Council University	641
Eckerd College	210
Ecole Hôtelière de Lausanne	1224
École Polytechnique de Montréal	1198
Ecotech Institute	172
ECPI University	1093
Edgewood College	1153
EDIC College	1180
Edinboro University of Pennsylvania	889
EDP University of Puerto Rico	1180
EDP University of Puerto Rico–San Sebastian	1181
Edward Waters College	211
Elizabeth City State University	756
Elizabethtown College	889, 1278
Elizabethtown College School of Continuing and Professional Studies	890
Elmhurst College	299, 1280
Elmira College	669
Elms College	471
Elon University	757
Embry-Riddle Aeronautical University–Daytona	211, 1282
Embry-Riddle Aeronautical University–Prescott	77, 1284
Embry-Riddle Aeronautical University–Worldwide	212
Emerson College	472, 473, 1286
Emily Carr University of Art + Design	1198
Emmanuel Bible College	1198
Emmanuel College	259, 473
Emmaus Bible College	366
Emory & Henry College	1093
Emory University	260
Emporia State University	388
Endicott College	474
Epic Bible College	119
Erskine College	975, 1288
Escuela de Artes Plasticas y Diseño de Puerto Rico	1181
Eston College	1198
Eugene Lang College of Liberal Arts	670
Eureka College	300
Evangel University	566
Everglades University	212, 213
The Evergreen State College	1123, 1290
Excelsior College	670
Fairfield University	184
Fairleigh Dickinson University, Florham Campus	622
Fairleigh Dickinson University, Metropolitan Campus	623
Fairmont State University	1141
Faith Baptist Bible College and Theological Seminary	367
Faith Theological Seminary	441
Family of Faith Christian University	839
Farmingdale State College	671
Fashion Institute of Technology	671, 1292
Faulkner University	59
Fayetteville State University	758
Feather River College	119
Felician University	624
Ferris State University	512
Ferrum College	1094
FIDM/Fashion Institute of Design & Merchandising, Los Angeles Campus	120
FIDM/Fashion Institute of Design & Merchandising, San Francisco Campus	120
Finlandia University	512
Fisher College	475
Fisk University	998
Fitchburg State University	475
Five Towns College	672
Flagler College	213
Flagler College–Tallahassee	213
Florida Agricultural and Mechanical University	213
Florida Atlantic University	214
Florida College	215
Florida Gateway College	216
Florida Gulf Coast University	216
Florida Institute of Technology	216
Florida International University	217
Florida Keys Community College	218
Florida Memorial University	218
Florida National University	218
Florida Southern College	219, 1294
Florida SouthWestern State College	220
Florida State College at Jacksonville	221
Florida State University	221
Fontbonne University	567
Fordham University	673
Fort Hays State University	388
Fortis College	221
Fort Lewis College	172
Fort Valley State University	260
Fountainhead College of Technology	998
Framingham State University	476
Franciscan Missionaries of Our Lady University	418
Franciscan University of Steubenville	799
Francis Marion University	975
Franklin & Marshall College	890
Franklin College	337
Franklin Pierce University	609
Franklin University	800
Franklin University Switzerland	1224
Franklin W. Olin College of Engineering	477
Freed-Hardeman University	998
Fremont College	121
Fresno Pacific University	121
Friends University	388
Frostburg State University	441
Full Sail University	221
Furman University	976
Galen College of Nursing	405, 800
Gallaudet University	199
Gannon University	891, 1296
Gardner-Webb University	758
Geneva College	892
George Fox University	856
George Mason University	1094
Georgetown College	405
Georgetown University	200
The George Washington University	201
Georgia College & State University	260

Georgia Gwinnett College	261
Georgia Highlands College	262
Georgia Institute of Technology	262
Georgia Military College	263
Georgian Court University	625, 1298
Georgia Southern University	264
Georgia Southern University–Armstrong Campus	265
Georgia Southwestern State University	265
Georgia State University	266
Gettysburg College	893
Glenville State College	1141
Glion Institute of Higher Education	1225
Global University	567
Goddard College	1078
God's Bible School and College	800
Golden Gate University	121
Goldey-Beacom College	196
Goldfarb School of Nursing at Barnes-Jewish College	567
Gonzaga University	1124
Good Samaritan College of Nursing and Health Science	800
Goodwin College	185
Gordon College	477
Gordon State College	267
Goshen College	338
Goucher College	442
Governors State University	301
Grace Bible College	512
Grace College	339
Grace College of Divinity	759
Graceland University	367, 568
Grace Mission University	122
Grace School of Theology	1026
Grambling State University	419
Grand Canyon University	78
Grand Valley State University	512
Grand View University	368, 1300
Granite State College	609
Grantham University	389
Great Basin College	604
Great Lakes Christian College	513
Green Mountain College	1079
Greensboro College	759
Greenville University	301
Grinnell College	369
Grove City College	894
Guilford College	759
Gulf Coast State College	222
Gurnick Academy of Medical Arts	122
Gustavus Adolphus College	537
Gutenberg College	856
Gwynedd Mercy University	895, 1302
Hallmark University	1026
Hamilton College	673
Hamilton Technical College	370
Hamline University	537
Hampden-Sydney College	1095
Hampshire College	478
Hampton University	1096
Hannibal-LaGrange University	568
Hanover College	339
Harding University	84, 1304
Hardin-Simmons University	1027
Harrisburg University of Science and Technology	896
Harrison College	339, 800
Harrison Middleton University	78
Harris-Stowe State University	568
Hartwick College	674
Harvard University	479
Harvey Mudd College	122
Haskell Indian Nations University	389
Hastings College	598
Haverford College	896
Hawai`i Pacific University	283
Hebrew Theological College	302
HEC Montreal	1198
Heidelberg University	800
Helene Fuld College of Nursing	675
Hellenic American University	610
Hellenic College	479
Henderson State University	85
Hendrix College	86
Henley-Putnam University	122
Heritage Bible College	760
Heritage Christian University	59
Heritage College and Seminary	1199
Heritage University	1125
Herzing University	59, 222, 267, 420, 538, 801, 1153, 1154
Herzing University Online	1154
Hesston College	389
High Point University	760, 1306
Hilbert College	675
Hillsdale College	513, 1308
Hiram College	801
Hobart and William Smith Colleges	676
Hobe Sound Bible College	222
Hodges University	222
Hofstra University	676, 1310
Hollins University	1097
Holy Apostles College and Seminary	185
Holy Cross College	339
Holy Family University	897
Holy Names University	122, 1312
Holy Trinity Orthodox Seminary	678
Hood College	442
Hope College	515
Hope International University	124
Horizon College & Seminary	1199
Horizon University	340
Houghton College	678
Houston Baptist University	1028
Howard Payne University	1028
Howard University	201
Hult International Business School	1226, 479
Humacao Community College	1182
Humboldt State University	124
Humphreys University	125
Hunter College of the City University of New York	679
Huntingdon College	59
Huntington College of Health Sciences	998
Huntington University	340
Huntsville Bible College	60
Hussian College, School of Art	898
Husson University	432
Huston-Tillotson University	1029
Idaho State University	287
IGlobal University	1097
Illinois College	302
The Illinois Institute of Art–Chicago	302
The Illinois Institute of Art–Schaumburg	303
Illinois Institute of Technology	303
Illinois State University	303
Illinois Wesleyan University	303
Immaculata University	898
Independence University	1070
Indiana State University	340
Indiana Tech	341
Indiana University Bloomington	342
Indiana University East	343
Indiana University Kokomo	343
Indiana University Northwest	344
Indiana University of Pennsylvania	898
Indiana University–Purdue University Fort Wayne	345
Indiana University–Purdue University Indianapolis	345
Indiana University South Bend	346
Indiana University Southeast	346
Indiana Wesleyan University	347
Indian River State College	222
INSTE Bible College	370
Institute of American Indian Arts	641
Institute of Public Administration	1218
Instituto Tecnológico y de Estudios Superiores de Monterrey, Campus Central de Veracruz	1221
Instituto Tecnológico y de Estudios Superiores de Monterrey, Campus Chiapas	1221
Instituto Tecnológico y de Estudios Superiores de Monterrey, Campus Chihuahua	1221
Instituto Tecnológico y de Estudios Superiores de Monterrey, Campus Ciudad de México	1221
Instituto Tecnológico y de Estudios Superiores de Monterrey, Campus Ciudad Juárez	1221
Instituto Tecnológico y de Estudios Superiores de Monterrey, Campus Ciudad Obregón	1222
Instituto Tecnológico y de Estudios Superiores de Monterrey, Campus Colima	1222

INDEXES

Instituto Tecnológico y de Estudios Superiores de Monterrey, Campus Cuernavaca	1222
Instituto Tecnológico y de Estudios Superiores de Monterrey, Campus Estado de México	1222
Instituto Tecnológico y de Estudios Superiores de Monterrey, Campus Guadalajara	1222
Instituto Tecnológico y de Estudios Superiores de Monterrey, Campus Hidalgo	1222
Instituto Tecnológico y de Estudios Superiores de Monterrey, Campus Irapuato	1222
Instituto Tecnológico y de Estudios Superiores de Monterrey, Campus Laguna	1222
Instituto Tecnológico y de Estudios Superiores de Monterrey, Campus León	1222
Instituto Tecnológico y de Estudios Superiores de Monterrey, Campus Monterrey	1222
Instituto Tecnológico y de Estudios Superiores de Monterrey, Campus Querétaro	1223
Instituto Tecnológico y de Estudios Superiores de Monterrey, Campus Saltillo	1223
Instituto Tecnológico y de Estudios Superiores de Monterrey, Campus San Luis Potosí	1223
Instituto Tecnológico y de Estudios Superiores de Monterrey, Campus Sinaloa	1223
Instituto Tecnológico y de Estudios Superiores de Monterrey, Campus Sonora Norte	1223
Instituto Tecnológico y de Estudios Superiores de Monterrey, Campus Tampico	1223
Instituto Tecnológico y de Estudios Superiores de Monterrey, Campus Toluca	1223
Instituto Tecnológico y de Estudios Superiores de Monterrey, Campus Zacatecas	1223
Inter American University of Puerto Rico, Aguadilla Campus	1182
Inter American University of Puerto Rico, Arecibo Campus	1183
Inter American University of Puerto Rico, Barranquitas Campus	1183
Inter American University of Puerto Rico, Bayamón Campus	1183
Inter American University of Puerto Rico, Fajardo Campus	1184
Inter American University of Puerto Rico, Guayama Campus	1184
Inter American University of Puerto Rico, Metropolitan Campus	1185
Inter American University of Puerto Rico, Ponce Campus	1185
Inter American University of Puerto Rico, San Germán Campus	1186
Interior Designers Institute	125
International Baptist College and Seminary	78
International Business College	348
International University in Geneva	1225
The International University of Monaco	1224
Iona College	679
Iowa State University of Science and Technology	370
Iowa Wesleyan University	371
Ithaca College	680
Jackson State University	555
Jacksonville State University	60
Jacksonville University	222
James Madison University	1097
Jamestown Business College	681
Jarvis Christian College	1029
Jefferson College of Health Sciences	1098
John Brown University	86
John Cabot University	1218, 1314
John Carroll University	802
John F. Kennedy University	125
John Jay College of Criminal Justice of the City University of New York	681
John Paul the Great Catholic University	125
Johns Hopkins University	443, 1316
Johnson & Wales University	173, 223, 762, 962
Johnson C. Smith University	762
Johnson University	999
Johnson University Florida	223
John Wesley University	762
Jose Maria Vargas University	224
Judson College	61
Judson University	304
The Juilliard School	682
Juniata College	899
Kalamazoo College	515
Kansas City Art Institute	569
Kansas State University	390
Kansas State University Polytechnic Campus	391
Kansas Wesleyan University	391
Kaplan University, Augusta	433
Kaplan University, Cedar Falls	371
Kaplan University, Cedar Rapids	371
Kaplan University, Davenport	371
Kaplan University, Des Moines	371
Kaplan University, Hagerstown	444
Kaplan University, Lincoln	598
Kaplan University, Mason City	371
Kaplan University, Omaha	599
Kean University	626
Keene State College	610
Kehilath Yakov Rabbinical Seminary	682
Keiser University	224
Kendall College	305
Kennesaw State University	267
Kent State University	802
Kent State University at Ashtabula	803
Kent State University at East Liverpool	804
Kent State University at Geauga	804
Kent State University at Salem	805
Kent State University at Stark	805
Kent State University at Trumbull	806
Kent State University at Tuscarawas	807
Kentucky Christian University	406
Kentucky Mountain Bible College	406
Kentucky State University	407
Kentucky Wesleyan College	407
Kenyon College	807
Kettering College	808
Kettering University	516, 1318
Keuka College	682
Keystone College	900
The King's College	683
King's College	900
Kings College	1320
The King's University	1199, 1029
Kingswood University	1199
King University	999
Knox College	305
Kutztown University of Pennsylvania	901, 1322
Kuyper College	517
Lafayette College	903
LaGrange College	268
Laguna College of Art & Design	126
Lake Erie College	808
Lake Forest College	306
Lakehead University	1200
Lakeland University	1154
Lake Superior State University	517
Lakeview College of Nursing	306
Lamar University	1030
Lancaster Bible College	903
Lander University	977
Landmark College	1079
Lane College	1000
Langston University	839
La Roche College	903
La Salle University	904
Lasell College	479
La Sierra University	126
Laurentian University	1200
Lawrence Technological University	518
Lawrence University	1154
Lebanese American University	1220
Lebanon Valley College	905
Lees-McRae College	763
Lee University	1000
Lehigh University	906
Lehman College of the City University of New York	683
Le Moyne College	684, 1324
LeMoyne-Owen College	1001
Lenoir-Rhyne University	763
Lesley University	480
Les Roches International School of Hotel Management	1225
LeTourneau University	1030
Lewis & Clark College	856
Lewis-Clark State College	288
Lewis University	307
Liberty University	1099
Life Pacific College	127
Life University	269
LIM College	685
Limestone College	977
Lincoln Christian University	307

INDEXES

Lincoln College	308	The Master's University	129
Lincoln College of New England	185	Mayville State University	781
Lincoln Memorial University	1001	McDaniel College	446
Lincoln University	127, 569, 906, 1326	McGill University	1200
Lindenwood University	570	McKendree University	310
Lindsey Wilson College	408	McMaster University	1200
Linfield College	857, 1328	McMurry University	1032
Lipscomb University	1002	McNeese State University	423
The Jewish Theological Seminary	681	McPherson College	391
Living Arts College	764	MCPHS University	483
Livingstone College	764	Medaille College	691
Lock Haven University of Pennsylvania	908	Medgar Evers College of the City University of New York	691
Logan University	571	Medical University of South Carolina	978
Loma Linda University	128	Memorial University of Newfoundland	1201
London Metropolitan University	1226	Menlo College	130
Long Island University–LIU Brooklyn	686	Mercer University	270
Long Island University–LIU Post	686	Mercy College	692
Longwood University	1099	Mercy College of Health Sciences	374
Loras College	371	Mercy College of Ohio	810
Los Angeles Film School	128	Mercyhurst North East	911
Louisiana College	420	Mercyhurst University	911
Louisiana Culinary Institute	420	Meredith College	764
Louisiana State University and Agricultural & Mechanical College	420	Merrimack College	484
Louisiana State University at Alexandria	421	Mesivta of Eastern Parkway–Yeshiva Zichron Meilech	693
Louisiana State University Health Sciences Center	422	Mesivta Torah Vodaath Rabbinical Seminary	693
Louisiana State University in Shreveport	422	Mesivtha Tifereth Jerusalem of America	693
Louisiana Tech University	422	Messenger College	1032
Lourdes University	808	Messiah College	912
Loyola Marymount University	128	Methodist College	311
Loyola University Chicago	309	Methodist University	765
Loyola University Maryland	444, 1330	Metro Business College	572
Loyola University New Orleans	423	Metropolitan College of New York	693
Lubbock Christian University	1031	Metropolitan State University	539
Luther College	372, 1332	Metropolitan State University of Denver	173
Luther Rice College & Seminary	269	Miami Dade College	225
Lycoming College	908	Miami International University of Art & Design	226
Lynchburg College	1100, 1334	Miami Regional University	226
Lynn University	225	Miami University	811
Lyon College	87	Miami University Hamilton	812
Macalester College	538	Miami University Middletown	812
Machzikei Hadath Rabbinical College	687	Michigan State University	519
MacMurray College	309	Michigan Technological University	520
Madonna University	518	Mid-America Baptist Theological Seminary	1003
Maharishi University of Management	373	Mid-America Christian University	840
Maine College of Art	433	Mid-America College of Funeral Service	349
Maine College of Health Professions	433	MidAmerica Nazarene University	392
Maine Maritime Academy	433	Mid-Atlantic Christian University	765
Malone University	809	Middlebury College	1081
Manchester University	348	Middle Georgia State University	271
Manhattan Christian College	391	Middle Tennessee State University	1004
Manhattan College	687, 1336	Midland College	1033
Manhattan School of Music	689	Midland University	599
Manhattanville College	689	Mid-South Christian College	1004
Mansfield University of Pennsylvania	909	Midstate College	311
Maple Springs Baptist Bible College and Seminary	445	Midway University	408
Maranatha Baptist University	1155	Midwestern State University	1033
Marconi International University	225	Midwest University	572
Maria College	689	Midwives College of Utah	1070
Marian University	348, 1155	Miles College	61
Marietta College	810	Millennia Atlantic University	226
Marist College	690	Millersville University of Pennsylvania	913, 1342
Marlboro College	1080, 1338	Milligan College	1004
Marquette University	1156	Millikin University	311
Marshall University	1141	Millsaps College	555
Mars Hill University	764	Mills College	130, 1344
Martin Luther College	539	Milwaukee Institute of Art and Design	1157
Martin Methodist College	1003	Milwaukee School of Engineering	1157
Martin University	349	Minneapolis College of Art and Design	540
Mary Baldwin University	1101	Minnesota State University Mankato	540
Maryland Institute College of Art	445	Minnesota State University Moorhead	541
Marylhurst University	858	Minot State University	781
Marymount California University	129	Mirrer Yeshiva Central Institute	693
Marymount Manhattan College	691	Misericordia University	914, 1346
Marymount University	1102	Mississippi College	556
Maryville College	1003	Mississippi State University	556
Maryville University of Saint Louis	571	Mississippi University for Women	557
Marywood University	910, 1340	Mississippi Valley State University	557
Massachusetts College of Art and Design	481	Missouri Baptist University	572
Massachusetts College of Liberal Arts	481	Missouri Southern State University	573
Massachusetts Institute of Technology	482	Missouri State University	573
Massachusetts Maritime Academy	483	Missouri University of Science and Technology	574
Master's College and Seminary	1200	Missouri Valley College	575

Missouri Western State University	575
Mitchell College	185
Molloy College	694, 1348
Monmouth College	311
Monmouth University	626, 1350
Monroe College	695
Montana Bible College	590
Montana State University	590
Montana State University Billings	591
Montana State University–Northern	591
Montana Tech of The University of Montana	592
Montclair State University	627
Montreat College	766
Montserrat College of Art	485
Moody Bible Institute	312
Moore College of Art & Design	915
Moravian College	915
Morehead State University	408
Morehouse College	271
Morgan State University	447
Morningside College	374
Morris College	978
Morrisville State College	695
Morthland College	312
Mount Allison University	1201
Mount Aloysius College	916, 1352
Mount Angel Seminary	859
Mount Carmel College of Nursing	812
Mount Holyoke College	485
Mount Marty College	987
Mount Mary University	1158
Mount Mercy University	375
Mount Royal University	1201
Mount St. Joseph University	812
Mount Saint Mary College	695
Mount Saint Mary's University	131
Mount St. Mary's University	447
Mount Saint Vincent University	1201
Mt. Sierra College	132, 1354
Mount Vernon Nazarene University	813
Muhlenberg College	917, 1356
Multnomah University	859
Murray State University	409
Musicians Institute	132
Muskingum University	814
Naropa University	173
National American University	174, 349, 393, 541, 576, 599, 642, 841, 988, 1033, 1034
National College	1005
National College of Midwifery	642
National Intelligence University	201
National Louis University	312
National Paralegal College	78
National University	132
National University College	1186
Navajo Technical University	642
Nazarene Bible College	393
Nazareth College of Rochester	696
Nebraska Christian College of Hope International University	599
Nebraska Methodist College	599
Nebraska Wesleyan University	600
Ner Israel Rabbinical College	448
Ner Israel Yeshiva College of Toronto	1201
Neumann University	918, 1358
Neumont College of Computer Science	1071, 1360
Nevada State College	604
Newberry College	978
Newbury College	485
New Charter University	1072
New College of Florida	226, 1362
New England College	611
New England College of Business and Finance	486
New England Conservatory of Music	486
New England Culinary Institute	1081
New England Institute of Technology	962
New Hampshire Institute of Art	611
New Hope Christian College	859
New Jersey City University	628
New Jersey Institute of Technology	629
Newman University	393
New Mexico Highlands University	642
New Mexico Institute of Mining and Technology	643
New Mexico State University	643
New Orleans Baptist Theological Seminary	424
New Saint Andrews College	288
The New School College of Performing Arts	697
The New School for Public Engagement	697
NewSchool of Architecture and Design	133
The New School–Parsons Paris	1216
New World School of the Arts	227
New York City College of Technology of the City University of New York	698
New York College of Health Professions	698
New York Film Academy	133
New York Institute of Technology	699
New York School of Interior Design	699
New York University	699
Niagara University	700, 1364
Nicholls State University	424
Nichols College	486
Nightingale College	1072
Nipissing University	1201
Norfolk State University	1103
North American University	1034
North Carolina Agricultural and Technical State University	766
North Carolina Central University	766
North Carolina State University	767
North Carolina Wesleyan College	767
North Central College	313
Northcentral University	133
North Central University	542
North Dakota State University	782
Northeast Catholic College	612
Northeastern Illinois University	314
Northeastern State University	841
Northeastern University	486, 1366
Northern Arizona University	79, 1368
Northern Illinois University	314
Northern Kentucky University	410, 1370
Northern Marianas College	1176
Northern Michigan University	521
Northern New Mexico College	644
Northern State University	988
Northern Vermont University–Johnson	1082
Northern Vermont University–Lyndon	1082, 1372
North Greenville University	979
Northland College	1158
North Park University	315
Northpoint Bible College	487
Northwest Christian University	859
Northwest College of Art & Design	1125
Northwestern College	376
Northwestern Michigan College	521
Northwestern Oklahoma State University	841
Northwestern Polytechnic University	134
Northwestern State University of Louisiana	424
Northwestern University	315
Northwest Florida State College	228
Northwest Indian College	1125
Northwest Missouri State University	576
Northwest Nazarene University	288
Northwest University	1125
Northwood University, Michigan Campus	521
Norwich University	1083
Nossi College of Art	1005
Notre Dame College	815
Notre Dame de Namur University	134
Notre Dame of Maryland University	448
Nova Southeastern University	228
NSCAD University	1201
Nyack College	701
Oak Hills Christian College	542
Oakland City University	349
Oakland University	522
Oakwood University	61
Oberlin College	815
Occidental College	134
Oglala Lakota College	988
Oglethorpe University	272
Ohio Christian University	815
Ohio Dominican University	816
Ohio Northern University	817, 1374
The Ohio State University	818
The Ohio State University at Lima	819

INDEXES

The Ohio State University at Mansfield 820
The Ohio State University at Marion 820
The Ohio State University at Newark 821
Ohio University 821
Ohio University–Chillicothe 822
Ohio University–Eastern 822
Ohio University–Lancaster 823
Ohio University–Southern Campus 823
Ohio University–Zanesville 823
Ohio Valley University 1142
Ohio Wesleyan University 823, 1376
Ohr Hameir Theological Seminary 702
Ohr Somayach/Joseph Tanenbaum Educational Center 702
Okanagan College 1201
Oklahoma Baptist University 842
Oklahoma Christian University 843
Oklahoma City University 843
Oklahoma Panhandle State University 844
Oklahoma State University 844
Oklahoma State University Institute of Technology 845
Oklahoma State University–Oklahoma City 846
Oklahoma Wesleyan University 846
Old Dominion University 1103
Olivet College 522
Olivet Nazarene University 315, 1378
Olympic College 1126
O'More College of Design 1006
Open University 1226
Oral Roberts University 846
Oregon College of Art and Craft 860
Oregon Health & Science University 860
Oregon Institute of Technology 861
Oregon State University 861
Oregon State University–Cascades 862
Otis College of Art and Design 135
Ottawa University 394
Otterbein University 824
Ouachita Baptist University 88
Our Lady of the Lake University 1034
Ozark Christian College 577
Pace University 702, 1380
Pace University, Pleasantville Campus 704
Pacific College 135
Pacific Islands University 1176
Pacific Lutheran University 1126
Pacific Northwest College of Art 862
Pacific Oaks College 135
Pacific Rim Christian University 284
Pacific States University 135
Pacific Union College 136
Pacific University 863, 1382
Paier College of Art, Inc. 185
Paine College 273
Palm Beach Atlantic University 229
Palm Beach State College 229
Palmer College of Chiropractic 376
Palo Alto University 136
Paris College of Art 1216
Park University 577
Parsons School of Design 704
Pasco-Hernando State College 230
Patrick Henry College 1104
Patten University 136
Paul Quinn College 1035
Paul Smith's College 705
Peabody Conservatory of The Johns Hopkins University 448
Peirce College 920
Peninsula College 1127
Penn Foster College 80
Penn State Abington 920
Penn State Altoona 921
Penn State Beaver 921
Penn State Berks 922
Penn State Brandywine 922
Penn State DuBois 923
Penn State Erie, The Behrend College 923
Penn State Fayette, The Eberly Campus 924
Penn State Greater Allegheny 925
Penn State Harrisburg 925
Penn State Hazleton 926
Penn State Lehigh Valley 926
Penn State Mont Alto 927

Penn State New Kensington 927
Penn State Schuylkill 928
Penn State Shenango 928
Penn State University Park 929
Penn State Wilkes-Barre 930
Penn State Worthington Scranton 930
Penn State York 931
Pennsylvania Academy of the Fine Arts 931
Pennsylvania College of Art & Design 931
Pennsylvania College of Health Sciences 932
Pennsylvania College of Technology 932
Pensacola Christian College 230
Pensacola State College 230
Pepperdine University 136, 1384
Peru State College 600
Pfeiffer University 768
Philander Smith College 88
Phillips Beth Israel School of Nursing 705
Piedmont College 273
Piedmont International University 769
Pillar College 630
Pima Medical Institute 80, 137, 174, 604, 644, 1127
Pine Manor College 488
Pioneer Pacific College 863
Pittsburgh Technical College 933
Pittsburg State University 395
Pitzer College 137
Platt College 138, 174
Platt College San Diego 138, 1386
Plaza College 705
Plymouth State University 612
Point Loma Nazarene University 138
Point Park University 933
Point University 274
Polk State College 231
Polytechnic University of Puerto Rico 1187
Polytechnic University of Puerto Rico, Miami Campus 231
Polytechnic University of Puerto Rico, Orlando Campus 231
Pomona College 140
Pontifical Catholic University of Puerto Rico 1187
Pontifical Catholic University of Puerto Rico–Arecibo Campus 1187
Pontifical Catholic University of Puerto Rico–Mayaguez Campus 1187
Pontifical College Josephinum 825
Portland State University 863
Post University 186
Potomac State College of West Virginia University 1142
Prairie Bible Institute 1201
Prairie View A&M University 1035
Pratt Institute 705, 1388
Presbyterian College 980
Prescott College 81
Presentation College 989
Princeton University 630
Principia College 317
Providence Christian College 140
Providence College 962
Providence University College & Theological Seminary 1201
Pueblo Community College 174
Purchase College, State University of New York 706
Purdue University 350
Purdue University Northwest 351
Queens College of the City University of New York 707
Queen's University at Kingston 1201
Queens University of Charlotte 769
Quincy University 317
Quinnipiac University 186, 1390
Rabbi Jacob Joseph School 630
Rabbinical Academy Mesivta Rabbi Chaim Berlin 708
Rabbinical College Beth Shraga 708
Rabbinical College Bobover Yeshiva B'nei Zion 708
Rabbinical College of America 630
Rabbinical College of Long Island 708
Rabbinical College of Ohr Shimon Yisroel 708
Rabbinical College of Telshe 825
Rabbinical College Ohr Yisroel 708
Rabbinical Seminary of America 708
Radford University 1104
Ramapo College of New Jersey 630
Randall University 847
Randolph College 1105
Randolph-Macon College 1105
Ranken Technical College 577

Rasmussen College Aurora	317
Rasmussen College Blaine	542
Rasmussen College Bloomington	542
Rasmussen College Brooklyn Park	542
Rasmussen College Eagan	543
Rasmussen College Fargo	783
Rasmussen College Fort Myers	231
Rasmussen College Green Bay	1159
Rasmussen College Kansas City/Overland Park	395
Rasmussen College Lake Elmo/Woodbury	543
Rasmussen College Land O' Lakes	232
Rasmussen College Mankato	543
Rasmussen College Mokena/Tinley Park	318
Rasmussen College Moorhead	544
Rasmussen College New Port Richey	232
Rasmussen College Ocala	232
Rasmussen College Ocala School of Nursing	233
Rasmussen College Rockford	318
Rasmussen College Romeoville/Joliet	318
Rasmussen College St. Cloud	544
Rasmussen College Tampa/Brandon	233
Rasmussen College Topeka	395
Rasmussen College Wausau	1159
Redeemer University College	1202
Reed College	864, 1392
Regent's University London	1226
Regent University	1106
Regis College	488, 1394
Regis University	175
Reinhardt University	274
Remington College–Honolulu Campus	284
Remington College–Memphis Campus	1006
Remington College–Mobile Campus	61
Rensselaer Polytechnic Institute	708
Renton Technical College	1127
Research College of Nursing	577
The Restaurant School at Walnut Hill College	934
Resurrection University	319
Rhode Island College	963
Rhode Island School of Design	964
Rhodes College	1006
Rice University	1036
Richmond, The American International University in London	1226
Rider University	631, 1396
Ringling College of Art and Design	233
Rio Grande Bible Institute	1036
Ripon College	1159, 1398
Rivier University	612, 1400
Roanoke College	1107
Robert Morris University	934, 1402
Robert Morris University Illinois	319
Roberts Wesleyan College	709
Rochester College	523
Rochester Community and Technical College	544
Rochester Institute of Technology	710, 1404
Rockford University	320
Rockhurst University	578
Rocky Mountain College	1202, 592
Rocky Mountain College of Art + Design	175
Rogers State University	847
Roger Williams University	964
Rollins College	234
Roosevelt University	320
Rose-Hulman Institute of Technology	351
Rosemont College	936
Ross College	825
Rowan University	632
Royal Military College of Canada	1202
Royal Roads University	1202
Rush University	321
Rust College	557
Rutgers University–Camden	633
Rutgers University–Newark	634
Rutgers University–New Brunswick	635
Ryerson University	1203
Sacred Heart Major Seminary	523
Sacred Heart University	188
SAE Expression College	140
The Sage Colleges	711
Saginaw Valley State University	523
St. Ambrose University	376
St. Andrews University	769
Saint Anselm College	613, 1406
Saint Anthony College of Nursing	321
St. Augustine College	321
Saint Augustine's University	770
St. Bonaventure University	712
St. Catherine University	545
Saint Charles Borromeo Seminary, Overbrook	936
St. Cloud State University	545
St. Edward's University	1036
St. Francis College	713
Saint Francis Medical Center College of Nursing	321
Saint Francis University	937, 1408
St. Francis Xavier University	1203
St. Gregory the Great Seminary	600
St. John Fisher College	713
St. John's College	322, 448, 644
Saint John's University	546
St. John's University	713
St. John Vianney College Seminary	235
St. Joseph's College, Long Island Campus	714
St. Joseph's College, New York	715
Saint Joseph's College of Maine	433
Saint Joseph Seminary College	425
Saint Joseph's University	938
Saint Josephs University	1410
St. Lawrence University	716, 1412
Saint Leo University	235
Saint Louis Christian College	578
St. Louis College of Health Careers	579
St. Louis College of Pharmacy	579
Saint Louis University	580
Saint Louis University–Madrid Campus	1224
St. Luke's College	377
Saint Luke's College of Health Sciences	580
Saint Martin's University	1128
Saint Mary-of-the-Woods College	352
Saint Mary's College	353
Saint Marys College	1414
Saint Mary's College of California	140
St. Mary's College of Maryland	449
Saint Mary's University	1203
St. Mary's University	1037
Saint Mary's University of Minnesota	546
Saint Michael's College	1083
St. Norbert College	1161, 1416
St. Olaf College	547
Saint Paul University	1203
St. Petersburg College	235
Saint Peter's University	635
St. Thomas Aquinas College	716, 1418
St. Thomas University	1203, 236
Saint Vincent College	939, 1420
St. Vincent's College	188
Saint Xavier University	322
Salem College	770
Salem International University	1143
Salem State University	489
Salisbury University	449
Salish Kootenai College	593
Salve Regina University	965
Samford University	61
Sam Houston State University	1038
Samuel Merritt University	141
San Diego Christian College	142
San Diego State University	142
San Diego State University–Imperial Valley Campus	142
San Francisco Art Institute	142
San Francisco Conservatory of Music	143
San Francisco State University	144
San Ignacio University	236
San Jose State University	144
Santa Barbara Business College	144
Santa Clara University	145
Santa Fe College	236
Sarah Lawrence College	718
Savannah College of Art and Design	274
Savannah State University	275
Schiller International University	1217, 1224, 236
Schoolcraft College	524
School of the Art Institute of Chicago	322
School of Visual Arts	719
Schreiner University	1038

INDEXES

Scripps College	145
Seattle Pacific University	1128
Seattle University	1129
Selma University	62
Seminole State College of Florida	237
Sentara College of Health Sciences	1108
Seton Hall University	636, 1422
Seton Hill University	940
Sewanee	
The University of the South	1007
Shasta Bible College	146
Shawnee State University	825
Shaw University	770
Shenandoah University	1108
Shepherd University	1143
Shiloh University	378
Shippensburg University of Pennsylvania	941
Shorter University	275
Sh'or Yoshuv Rabbinical College	719
Siena College	719
Siena Heights University	524
Sierra Nevada College	604
Silver Lake College of the Holy Family	1162
Simmons College	489
Simmons College of Kentucky	411
Simon Fraser University	1204
Simpson College	378, 1424
Simpson University	146
Sinte Gleska University	989
Sitting Bull College	783
Skidmore College	720, 1426
Slippery Rock University of Pennsylvania	942
Smith College	490
Soka University of America	147
Sonoma State University	147
South Carolina State University	980
South College	1008
South Dakota School of Mines and Technology	989
South Dakota State University	989
Southeastern Baptist College	558
Southeastern Baptist Theological Seminary	771
Southeastern Louisiana University	425
Southeastern Oklahoma State University	848
Southeastern University	237
Southeast Missouri State University	580
Southern Adventist University	1008
Southern Alberta Institute of Technology	1204
Southern Arkansas University–Magnolia	89
The Southern Baptist Theological Seminary	411
Southern California Institute of Architecture	148
Southern California Institute of Technology	148
Southern California Seminary	148
Southern Connecticut State University	189
Southern Illinois University Carbondale	322, 1428
Southern Illinois University Edwardsville	324
Southern Methodist University	1039, 1430
Southern Nazarene University	848
Southern New Hampshire University	615, 1432
Southern Oregon University	865
Southern Technical College	238
Southern University and Agricultural and Mechanical College	426
Southern University at New Orleans	426
Southern Utah University	1072
Southern Vermont College	1084
Southern Virginia University	1109
Southern Wesleyan University	981
South Florida Bible College and Theological Seminary	238
South Florida State College	238
South Georgia State College	276
South Texas College	1040
South University	62, 239, 276, 524, 771, 826, 981, 1040, 1109
Southwest Baptist University	581
Southwestern Adventist University	1040
Southwestern Assemblies of God University	1041
Southwestern Christian College	1042
Southwestern Christian University	848
Southwestern College	396
Southwestern Oklahoma State University	848
Southwestern University	1042
Southwest Minnesota State University	548
Southwest University	426
Southwest University at El Paso	1043
Southwest University of Visual Arts	81
Spalding University	411
Spartan College of Aeronautics and Technology	849
Spelman College	276
Spencerian College	412
Spring Arbor University	524
Springfield College	490, 1434
Spring Hill College	62
Stanbridge University	148
Stanford University	148
State College of Florida Manatee-Sarasota	239
State University of New York at Fredonia	721
State University of New York at New Paltz	722
State University of New York at Oswego	723, 1436
State University of New York at Plattsburgh	724
State University of New York College at Cortland	725
State University of New York College at Geneseo	726
State University of New York College at Old Westbury	727
State University of New York College at Oneonta	727
State University of New York College at Potsdam	728
State University of New York College of Agriculture and Technology at Cobleskill	729
State University of New York College of Environmental Science and Forestry	729, 1438
State University of New York College of Technology at Alfred	731
State University of New York College of Technology at Canton	732
State University of New York College of Technology at Delhi	732
State University of New York Downstate Medical Center	733
State University of New York Empire State College	733
State University of New York Maritime College	734
State University of New York Polytechnic Institute	734
State University of New York Upstate Medical University	735
Steinbach Bible College	1204
Stephen F. Austin State University	1043
Stephens College	582
Sterling College	396, 1084, 1440
Stetson University	239
Stevens-Henager College	289, 1072, 1073
Stevens Institute of Technology	637
Stevenson University	450
Stevens–The Institute of Business & Arts	582
Stillman College	62
Stockton University	637, 1442
Stonehill College	490
Stony Brook University, State University of New York	735
Stratford University	451, 1109, 1110
Strayer University–Alexandria Campus	1110
Strayer University–Allentown Campus	943
Strayer University–Anne Arundel Campus	451
Strayer University–Arlington Campus	1110
Strayer University–Augusta Campus	277
Strayer University–Baymeadows Campus	240
Strayer University–Birmingham Campus	62
Strayer University–Cedar Hill Campus	1043
Strayer University–Center City Campus	943
Strayer University–Chamblee Campus	277
Strayer University–Charleston Campus	981
Strayer University–Cherry Hill Campus	639
Strayer University–Chesapeake Campus	1110
Strayer University–Chesterfield Campus	1110
Strayer University–Christiana Campus	196
Strayer University–Cobb County Campus	277
Strayer University–Columbia Campus	981
Strayer University–Columbus Campus	277
Strayer University–Delaware County Campus	943
Strayer University–Douglasville Campus	277
Strayer University–Fort Lauderdale Campus	240
Strayer University–Fredericksburg Campus	1111
Strayer University–Greensboro Campus	772
Strayer University–Greenville Campus	981
Strayer University–Henrico Campus	1111
Strayer University–Huntersville Campus	772
Strayer University–Huntsville Campus	62
Strayer University–Irving Campus	1043
Strayer University–Jackson Campus	558
Strayer University–Katy Campus	1043
Strayer University–Knoxville Campus	1009
Strayer University–Lithonia Campus	277
Strayer University–Little Rock Campus	89
Strayer University–Loudoun Campus	1111
Strayer University–Lower Bucks County Campus	943
Strayer University–Maitland Campus	240